Dat   ue

WHO'S WHO *of* CANADIAN WOMEN

Published by Who's Who Publications

SEVENTH EDITION

WHO'S WHO OF CANADIAN WOMEN

Co-Publisher
  Ted Hart, Who's Who Publications
Co-Publisher
  Lee Simpson, *Chatelaine*
General Manager
  Gillian Holmes

WHO'S WHO OF CANADIAN WOMEN is published by Who's Who Publications, a division of Canadian Business Media Ltd. Canadian Business Media Ltd. also publishes *Canadian Business* magazine and *PROFIT, The Magazine for Canadian Entrepreneurs.*

Chairman
  William Dimma
President and Chief Executive Officer
  James K. Warrillow
Executive Vice-President and Publisher
  Paul C. Jones

Who's Who Publications
  777 Bay Street, 5th Fl.
  Toronto, Ontario, M5W1A7
  (416) 596-5156
  FAX 596-5235

CONTENTS

WHO'S WHO PUBLICATIONS 1996

WHO'S WHO OF CANADIAN WOMEN
1997 — Seventh Edition

ISBN 0-920966-51-9
ISSN 0227-3411

Printed and bound in the US by Royal Book Manufacturing Inc.

INTRODUCTION

Chatelaine Magazine is pleased to continue its role as a co-publisher of *Who's Who of Canadian Women.*

A walk through this volume will inspire, inform and enlighten you as to the wealth of talent Canadian women share. Any page will inspire even the most casual observer.

As a resource book, this edition will put women on corporate boards of directors, see their talents used in charitable foundations, and help promote women in business management, the arts, and sciences.

I would like to gratefully acknowledge the contribution of our patron, Chrysler Canada, for their ongoing championing of this cause.

Who's Who of Canadian Women provides a unique opportunity to recognize and continue to celebrate the life and work of thousands of notable women from all walks of life. Read and enjoy.

Lee Simpson
Co-Publisher

PREFACE

Welcome to the new edition of *Who's Who of Canadian Women*. This volume is not quite like any other reference book in Canada. It focuses on women, but does not restrict itself to a single field of endeavour. Input has been sought, not just from the editorial staff but from business colleagues and from the general public.

Last year's edition was a great success and sold out within six months. With more than a thousand changes and over five hundred additions, this volume is the most comprehensive yet. You are invited to contribute to future editions by nominating notable women. Please see the nomination page at the back of the book for more details.

Readers who prefer to access information electronically will be interested to learn of the first time availablity of this volume in CD-ROM format. We are also pleased to announce the formation of the Editorial Advisory Committee, who in addition to the Advisory Board of Who's Who Publications, will provide invaluable input for future editions.

This book shows the breadth and depth of women's activities and achievements in Canada. We know you will find it a fascinating and useful reference tool.

Ted Hart
Publisher
Who's Who Publications

CHRYSLER CANADA
PATRON

G. Yves Landry
Chairman, President and Chief Executive Officer
Chrysler Canada Ltd.

On behalf of Chrysler Canada, I offer congratulations to the thousands of remarkable individuals who have been nominated and selected for inclusion in the seventh edition of *Who's Who of Canadian Women*. We are proud to be a Patron of this publication, since it celebrates the accomplishments of individual Canadians who are helping to define, and refine, our unique way of life in this country. They are, without doubt, people whose achievements provide inspiration to others.

At Chrysler, we have reason to be proud that in 1996, our assembly plants in this country will build nearly 700,000 vehicles, a new record. Of these, more than 90% will be exported...providing a significant positive contribution to Canada's balance of trade.

We are also proud of our enhanced commitment to Canadian-based Research & Development. The University of Windsor/Chrysler Canada Automotive Research & Design Centre has forged a vital link with educators in helping to prepare young people from all over Canada for high technology jobs in the next century.

At Chrysler Canada we are deeply aware of our responsibility to continue to strengthen the economy, our standard and quality of living and to maintain our competitive edge as we all prepare for an exciting journey into the next century.

Our support of this publication is a natural extension to our corporate philosophy, "We're not just building cars, we're building Canada."

A NOTE ABOUT MOTHERS

Once again *Who's Who of Canadian Women* invited nominations of remarkable women and again a substantial number came from loving children–daughters and sons–nominating their mothers "for always being there." Among the hundreds of such nominations, the following letter, to us, said it the best.

My recommendation for the most remarkable and notable woman would be Betty Wren. No, she does not work for, or manage, or own a large corporation. She has no use for a daytimer, fax or cellular phone. She has never had to "do lunch," run a board meeting or hire or terminate anyone. What she does do, and remarkably well, is be a mother, my mother.

For all of my life and the lives of my three older sisters, she has given us her unconditional love, support and friendship. She has sacrificed through the years for her family and never thought twice about it. I feel society should stand up and start applauding these women who have been the quiet heroes of our country.

The dictionary defines remarkable as, "worthy of being noticed or commented on; extraordinary; uncommon." Through all of my mother's acts of kindess towards her family and community, I feel she is the epitome of remarkable.

P.J. Wren

This book will never be big enough to include all the remarkable mothers but we wish to acknowledge these women, nominated or not, who have contributed so much to our community.

ACKNOWLEDGEMENTS

The Who's Who of Canadian Women is a sizable undertaking. It has been compiled once again through the efforts of the thousands of remarkable individuals listed herein. For their assistance, we extend our sincere thanks.

Our aim is to be as up-to-date and accurate as possible to make this the most useful reference work of its type available. To that effect we have tried to stay on top of changes as they take place. Any changes that occured after October 15, 1996, will not have been incorporated into this edition.

We would like to thank Donna Braggins, Sattie Cheddie, Kerry Holmes, Kathy Moore, June Yee for their help in completeing this volume.

Special thanks are owed to Kim Biggar for her outstanding and tireless work as copy editor and to Kirsten Stevenson, who graciously volunteered her time and expertise.

And special mention should go to my editorial associate, David Keyes, for his tremendous help through all phases of this book.

Gillian Holmes
General Manager

ABBREVIATIONS AND ICONS

Standard Abbreviations

Account - Acct
Accountant - Acctnt
Accounting - Acctg
Administration - Admin.
Advertising - Advtg
Anthropology - Anthro.
appointment - appt.
Assistant - Asst.
Advisory - Advisory
Analyst - Analyst
Associate - Assoc.
Association - Association
Banking - Bnkg
Biology - Biol.
Board - Bd. (Bd. of Dir./Bd. of Gov. - no 's')
Building - Bldg
Business - Bus.
Business Administration - Bus. Admin.
Canadian - Cdn
Chairman - Chrm
Chairperson - Chair
Chemistry - Chem.
Chief Accountant - Chief Acctnt
Chief Administrative Officer - CAO
Chief Executive Officer - CEO
Chief Financial Officer - CFO
Chief Operating Officer - COO
College - Coll.
Commercial - Commercial
Committee - Committee
Communications - Comm.
Comptroller - Compt.
Computer Science - Comp. Sci.
Controller - Cont.
Coordinator - Coord.
Corporate - Corp.

Council - Council
Counsel - Cnsl
Department - Dept.
Deputy - Deputy
Development - Dev.
Director - Dir.
Division - Div.
Divisional - Div'l
Economics - Econ.
Economist - Economist
Editor - Ed.
Education - Educ.
Engineering - Eng.
established - est.
Executive - Exec.
Faculty - Fac.
Federal - Fed.
Finance/Financial - Fin.
Floor - Fl.
Former - Former
Founding - Founding
General - Gen.
General Manager - Gen. Mgr
Geology - Geol.
Government - Gov't
Governor - Gov.
Graduate - Grad.
History - Hist.
Honorary - Hon.
Honours - Hons.
Human Resources - Hum. Res.
including - incl.
Individual - Indiv.
Information - Info.
Insurance - Insur.
International - Int'l
Introduction - Intro.
Management - Mgmt
Manager - Mgr
Managing - Mng
Market - Mkt
Marketing - Mktg
Mathematics - Math.
Mechanical - Mech.
Member - Mbr.
Minister - Min.
Ministry - Ministry
Municipal - Mun.
National - Nat'l
Network - Ntwk
Officer - Officer
Operations - Oper.
Partner - Ptnr
Physical - Phys.
Political Science - Pol. Sci.
President - Pres.
Producer - Prod.
Professor - Prof.
Programme - Program
Project - Proj.

Promotion - Promo.
Province/Provincial - Prov.
Psychology - Psych.
Region - Reg.
Regional - Reg'l
Relations - Rel'ns
Representative - Rep.
Room - Rm.
School - Sch.
Science - Sci.
Secretary - Sec.
Secretary-Treasurer - Sec.-Treas.
Senator - Senator
Senior - Sr.
Senior Vice-President - Sr. VP
Service - Svc
Services - Svcs
Sociology - Soc.
Technical - Tech.
television - TV
Treasurer - Treas.
Treasury - Treasury
Trustee - Trustee
University/Université - Univ.
Vice-Chairman - V-Chrm
Vice-President - VP
years - yrs.

marital status as follows:
d.   divorced
dec.   deceased
s.   single
sep.   separated
cl.   common law
w.   widowed

children as follows:
ch.   child
grch.   grandchild
stpch. stepchild
fch.   foster child

■■   New biography
■   Biography changed in one of the
     following ways: title, company, address,
     phone/FAX/EMAIL
*   Biography compiled by the editors

THE ARTS
Visual arts including photography and design. Music. Performing arts including theatre and dance. Art galleries and art museums. Artists, curators, and arts educators. Related organizations, government agencies and officials.

ACTIVISM & ASSOCIATIONS
Labour. Associations formed around causes, interests, social or professional activities. Includes elected officials and hired administrators. Related organizations, government agencies and officials.

AGRICULTURE
Farming and related industries. Fisheries. Related organizations, government agencies and officials.

ARTS AND LETTERS
Written arts. Drama, poetry, prose. History. Arts History. Museums, especially historical museums. Languages and linguistics. Translation. Commentators and educators. Related organizations, government agencies and officials.

BUSINESS/INDUSTRY/FINANCE
Big business, small business, entrepreneurs, industry and finance. Consultants. Management in business and other fields. Commentators and educators. Related organizations, government agencies and officials.

CHARITY/NOT FOR PROFIT
Charitable, not-for-profit, or NGO organizations. Arts, educations, medicine or policy related. Elected officials and paid administrators. Volunteer workers. Some associations and their personnel. Related government agencies and officials.

ENTERTAINMENT
Popular music, film, television, and fiction. Related organizations, government agencies and officials.

EDUCATION
Educators and administrators at the primary, secondary, college and university levels. Private teachers. Vocational training and retraining. Education in the arts. Related organizations, government agencies and officials.

GOVERNMENT AND POLITICS
Federal, provincial, and municipal government officials. Members of the public service. Political groups and parties. Politics or policy as a field of endeavour. Commentators and educators. Related organizations, agencies and officials.

JOURNALISM
Publication of newspapers, magazines or journals. Reporting in print or broadcast media. Related organizations, government agencies and officials.

LAW
Lawyers, judges, police. Corrections officials, inmates, and related charitable groups. Commentators and educators. Related organizations, government agencies and officials.

MEDIA CULTURE
Broadcast, narrowcast and cablecast television and radio, film and other electronic formats. Individuals in various capacities including production and performance; applied to corporate entities involved in production or distribution; also encompasses agents, advertising and some fashion-related activities. Related organizations, government agencies and officials.

MEDICAL/HEALTH
Medicine and allied professions such as nursing, dentistry, and nutrition, both mainstream and alternative. Psychology and social work. Health practitioners and educators. Related organizations, government agencies and officials.

SPIRITUALITY/RELIGION
Aspects of spirituality and religion. Movements and churches. Members of clergy or religious orders, administrators, lay workers and volunteers. Related organizations, government agencies and officials.

SPORTS
Athletes. Team and individual sports. Includes fitness and physical education. Commentators, coaches, and educators. Related organizations, government agencies and officials.

TECHNOLOGY AND SCIENCE
Physical sciences such as geology, biology, and physics. Engineering and computer science. Forestry. Most social sciences. Anthropology and archaeology. Economics and planning. Includes science and technology educators. Related organizations, government agencies and officials.

TEXT CULTURE
Includes publishers, writers, editors, librarians and archivists. Libraries and archives. Related organizations, government agencies and officials.

MILITARY
Members of the military and of military organizations. Related organizations, governments and officials

BIOGRAPHIES

A

aron, Gladys ■ ■ ⊗ ⊕

125 Neptune Dr., Ste. 1404, North York, ON M6A 1X3 (416) 781-8297. Born Poltava, Russia 1919. sep. Joseph. 2 ch. Raymond, Susan. **EDUC:** Peretz Shule, Certificate (Educ.) 1936; Seneca Coll., Certificate (Phys. Ed.) 1984. **CAREER:** Saleswoman, Cdn art, 1942-44; Artists' Model, 1944-50; Model Coord. for visual arts, Sheridan Coll., 1950-61; Seniors' Fitness Instructor, 1984 to date; Poetry Reader, 1992 to date. **SELECTED CREDITS:** 15-min. documentary made on her life, aired across Canada on WTN, 1995; delivered lectures & demonstrations on TV on vegetarian cooking & food combining. **SELECTED PUBLICATIONS:** author, *The Food Combining Chart* (1978); co-author, *The Vegetarian Persuasion* (1988); ed., *The CNHS Monthly Newsletter* (1973-93). **EXHIBITIONS:** exhibition of pottery, Brampton Museum, 1976. **AFFIL:** Canadian Natural Hygiene Society (mbr. 1960 to date; life mbr.; VP 1968-74; Co-Pres. 1975-84; Pres. 1985-93). **HONS:** Merit Plaque, Canadian Natural Hygiene Society, 1986; Merit Plaque, American Natural Hygiene Society, 1985. **INTERESTS:** dancing; theatre; pottery; sculpture; poetry; reading; fitness; cooking; vegetarianism; films; travel; lecturing. **COMMENT:** *"Coming from a talented musical family, I enjoyed the different stages of my life of dancing, modelling, pottery, theatre, poetry reading. Also, through my interest in health, I've loved teaching, vegetarianism and fitness."*

Abbott, Marni ■ ■ ⊘

Paralympic Athlete. Enderby, BC. **CAREER:** Level 2 coach. **SPORTS CAREER:** mbr., Nat'l Swim Team, 3 yrs.; mbr., Nat'l Wheelchair Basketball Team. Paralympic Games: Gold, 1996; Gold, 1992. Canadian Wheelchair Basketball League (CWBL): 2nd, Finals, 1995; 3rd, Women's Finals, 1995; 2nd, Women's Finals, 1994. World Championships: 1st, 1994. Pan American Games: 4 Gold & 1 Silver, swimming, 1986. HONS: All-Star, CWBL Women's Finals, 1995. MISC: became physically disabled in a downhill skiing accident in 1982; motivational speaker; coached B.C. wheelchair basketball team to Canada Games Silver medal.

Abbott, Patricia A., D.E.C.,B.A. ⊗ 🗎
Executive Director, ASSOCIATION OF CANADIAN CHORAL CONDUCTORS (ACCC), 49 de Tracy, Blainville, QC J7C 3B7 (514) 430-5573, FAX 430-4999. Born Montreal 1957. cl. Michel Hansé. EDUC: Vanier Coll., D.E.C. 1975; Carleton Univ., B.A.(Hist.) 1977; Concordia Univ., B.A.(Journalism) 1981; Goethe Institute, 1st-level certificate (German) 1985. CAREER: Journalism: Researcher, "Star Action Column," *The Montreal Star*, 1977-79; Researcher, "Gazette Probe Column," *The Gazette*, Montreal, 1979-81; Asst. Ed., *Protect Yourself Magazine*, Montreal, 1981-91; guest lecturer, & radio & TV commentator on consumer issues, 1984-92; Asst. Ed., *Protégez-Vous Magazine*, Montreal, 1991-93; Freelance ed., translator, 1993 to date. Music: Conductor, Chorale du Gesù, Montreal, 1982 to date; freelance clinician, workshop leader, & singer, 1987 to date; Asst. Conductor, Ensemble vocal Musical Viva, 1987 to date; Conductor, Protestant Sch. Bd. of Greater Montreal Sr. Chorale, 1990 to date; Exec. Dir., ACCC, 1993 to date; Conductor, The Study Senior Choir, 1995 to date; Artist in Residence, FACE Sch., 1996 to date. SELECTED PUBLICATIONS: articles published in *Chanter* (formerly *A L'Écoute*), *Anacrusis* & *International Choral Bulletin* on the choral music of French Canada. AFFIL: Alliance des chorales du Québec (Bd. Mbr. representing Montreal); Alliance régionale des chorales de L'Ile de Montréal (Pres.); American Choral Directors' Association; Canadian Association of Journalists; Corporation Tout en musique (Artistic Dir.); Editors' Association of Canada; Ensemble vocal Musica Viva; International Federation for Choral Music; Montreal Council of Women; Ontario Choral Federation. HONS: Award for Outstanding Contribution to Volleyball, Carleton Univ., 1977; Journalism Book Prize, Concordia Univ., 1981; Certificate of Merit for Outstanding Contribution to the Field of Choral Music, Montreal Council of Women, 1993. INTERESTS: choral music; arts admin.; arts educ.; travel; consumer issues; communication. MISC: private music studies (organ, theory, voice) with Henriette Tardif,

Gail Desmarais, Alliance des Chorales du Québec (conducting); Instructor for CAMMAC (choral ensembles) & for the Atelier lyrique de l'Opera de Montréal (English diction). COMMENT: *"Having been raised in both English and French, I feel equally at home in all parts of the country. Over the years, my hobby –choral music–has become my main career."*

Abdurahman, Muriel Ross, R.F.N. ✦
Member of Legislative Assembly, GOVERNMENT OF ALBERTA, Rm. 323, Edmonton, AB T5K 1E4 (403) 427-2293, FAX 427-3697. Born Lochmaben, Scotland 1938. m. Dr. Abdul Abdurahman. 4 ch. EDUC: Belvedere Hospital, Glasgow, UK, R.F.N. (Registered Fevers Nurse) 1957. CAREER: Alderman, Town of Fort Saskatchewan, 1978-81; Mayor, City of Fort Saskatchewan, 1981-86; Chair, Health Unit Association Alberta, 1981-84; V-Chrm/Mbr., Alberta Public Health Advisory Appeal Bd., 1987-92; Chair, Alberta Hospital, Edmonton, 1988-92. AFFIL: Alberta Hospital Foundation (Chair 1987-92; Gov.); Alberta Hospitals Auxiliary Association (Treas./Parliamentarian 1975-80); Dow Canada Community Advisory Panel, Western Canada Div. (Mbr. 1991-93); Pineview Sunday Sch., 1st United Church, Fort Saskatchewan (Superintendent). HONS: Communication Achievement, Toastmasters International, 1986; Outstanding Service Award-Outstanding Contribution to the Advancement of Community Health throughout Alberta, Health Unit Association of Alberta, 1986. COMMENT: *"I would prefer to let my community involvement speak for itself. Proud that I achieved rail relocation while I was Mayor of the City of Fort Saskatchewan."*

Abe, Kyoko (Suisei) ■ ■ ⊗ 🎐
Director, Toronto East Branch, SOGETSU IKEBANA (non-profit organization), 86 Mosedale Cres., Willowdale, ON M2J 3A4 (416) 491-7705. Born Japan. m. Yasuhiko. 2 ch. Naomi & Kevin Takahiko. EDUC: Tohoku Gaigo Gakuin, English 2 yrs.; Tokiwagi High Sch., Gen. 3 yrs.; Sogetsu Ikebana, Jonin Somu (degree); Tea Ceremony 1 yr.; Ikebana headquarters, Japan, workshop July-Aug. 1996. CAREER: teacher/volunteer, Japanese Canadian Cultural Centre, 33 yrs.; evening course, Centennial Coll., 6 yrs.; evening course, North York Bd. of Educ., 1 yr. AFFIL: Japanese Canadian Cultural Centre (volunteer-demonstrations, supervises booth for annual Spring Festival & annual Toronto Metro Caravan; teacher; Dir., 20th Annual Ikebana Show May 1996; participant, annual Ikebana Show, 20 yrs.). HONS: Merit Award, Head Master, Sogets Sch., 1970; Ont. Volunteer Service Award for

over 15 yrs. svc., Gov't of Ont.; Merit Award for outstanding & dedicated svc., Japanese Toronto Garden Club, 1968, & Japanese Cultural Centre, 1994. INTERESTS: photography; sewing; travel; Ikebana; meeting new friends. MISC: demonstration & workshop, African Violet Society, Oshawa Community Centre, Toronto Garden Club, Toronto Japanese Garden Club, Toronto Vocational Sch., Girl Guides, & many other groups; has appeared occasionally on TV. COMMENT: *"There have been flower arrangements decorating the altars of Shinto and Buddhist temples in ancient times. The flower arrangements as they were cannot be called Ikebana. In short, we may set the point of departure of Ikebana at the time when there arose a clear intention to decorate the living environment with flowers and to appreciate them by adding various ideas.*
The spirit under which the Soghetsu School was born was to create Ikebana that matches actual life, something that deserves the name of art. It is to be fresh, vital, and dynamic. Various poses of flowers and trees in their infinite beauty, variable according to the seasons; abundant creative ideas; and the beauty of the vessels in their environment–these three elements combined to make the Ikebana of the Sogetsu School
Arriving in Toronto from Japan in 1962, I soon discovered that the cohesiveness of the community could be achieved by the expression and teaching of Ikebana."

Abells, Susan, B.A. ⊜ ⊗

Executive Director, ALBERTA CRAFT COUNCIL, 10106 - 124 St., Edmonton, AB T5N 1P6 (403) 488-6611, FAX 488-8855. Born Edmonton 1954. d. 2 ch. Daniel Fridman, Joel Fridman. EDUC: Univ. of British Columbia, B.A.(Art Hist.) 1977. CAREER: Co-curator/Project Mgr, "Crafts of the World" exhibition, World Univ. Games, Universiade '83, 1983; Prod., Visual Arts component, Summerfest (festival), 1982-84; Coll. Instructor, 1983-85; Ptnr, Wedman Fridman Art Consultants, 1983-89; Co-Artistic Dir./Prod., The Works: A Visual Arts Celebration (festival), 1985-89; Exec. Dir., Alberta Craft Council, 1990 to date. SELECTED PUBLICATIONS: *Defining and Developing the Craft Industry in Alberta*, Summary Report (1995). AFFIL: Edmonton Professional Arts Council (Pres. 1992-94). INTERESTS: pottery; clay sculpture. MISC: participated in various int'l conferences; bilingual (English & Spanish). COMMENT: *"I have been involved in the design, production, marketing and management of visual arts and crafts projects, exhibitions, festivals and organisations in Alberta since 1979. I am currently implementing the Alberta Craft Council's craft industry development*

strategy, which includes marketing and training programs and services designed to develop, promote and market Alberta-made crafts and the Alberta craft industry."

Ablonczy, Diane, M.P. ■■ ✦

Member of Parliament, Calgary North, GOVERNMENT OF CANADA, Room 756, Confederation Bldg., House of Commons, Ottawa, ON K1A 0A6 (613) 996-2756, FAX 992-2537, Constituency Office, 1107 - 17th Ave. N.W., Calgary, AB T2M 0P7. Born 1949. m. Ron Sauer. 1 ch. Tanya. EDUC: Univ. of Calgary, B.Ed. 1973, LL.B. 1980. CAREER: jr. & elementary sch. teacher, 1969-74; grain farmer, 1973-86; law sch., 1977-80; lawyer in private practice, 1981-91; Chrm, Exec. Council, & Mgmt & Planning Committee, Reform Party, 1987-91; Asst. to Reform Party leader Preston Manning, 1991; Caucus Coordinator & mbr., Reform Party Expansion Committee & Immigration Committee of Caucus, 1993; Reform Critic for Hum. Res. Dev., 1994; special assignment, RRSP concept dev., 1995; Reform Deputy Critic for Justice & Atlantic Reg'l Critic, 1995; M.P. for Calgary North, 1993 to date. INTERESTS: current affairs; mechanisms for participatory democracy; conflict resolution; personal dev.; reading; travel; music; volunteer work.

Abrams, Gayle, B.A. ⊗ ⱳ

Co-owner, OSCARS AND ABRAMS ASSOCIATES INC., 59 Berkeley St., Toronto, ON M5A 2W5 (416) 860-1790, FAX 860-0236. Born Montreal 1954. m. Norbert. 2 ch. Daniel, Jesse. EDUC: Vanier Coll., Diplôme des Études Collégiales(Art Hist. & Psych.) 1973; McGill Univ., B.A.(Hons., English & Film) 1976. CAREER: Co-owner, Oscars and Abrams Associates Inc.; Pres., Danjess Productions. DIRECTOR: Danjess Productions; Oscars and Abrams Associates Inc. AFFIL: Toronto Women in Film & Television; T.A.M.A.C.; U.J.A.; New Israel Fund; F.H.P.S. (Staffing Committee). INTERESTS: environment; travelling; reading; sports; music; theatre; film. COMMENT: *"Happily married. I have achieved a noncompromise balance between office and home. I have never compromised moral or ethical standards to achieve success. My personal goal is to help broaden the directorial perceptions of the contribution of women to film beyond primal aesthetics."*

Abron Drache, Sharon, B.A.,Dip.C.S. ⌕

Writer. c/o The Writers' Union, 24 Ryerson Ave., Toronto, ON M5T 2P3. Born Toronto 1943. d. partner David Gurr. 4 ch. Deborah, Ruth, Joshua, Mordecai. EDUC: Univ. of

Toronto, B.A.(Psych.) 1965, Dip.C.S.(Child Study) 1966; Carleton Univ., special student (Religion) 1974-78. CAREER: freelance writer & journalist, 1976 to date; Trustee, Ottawa Public Library, 1985-88; Writer-in-Residence, Port Hope Public Library, 1987; Literary Consultant, Jewish Community Centre of Ottawa, 1990; Book Review Ed., *The Ottawa Jewish Bulletin and Review*, 1980-90; Ed. Bd., *Viewpoints Magazine* (Canadian Jewish Congress), 1981-82. SELECTED PUBLICATIONS: *The Mikveh Man and Other Stories* (Toronto: Aya Press, 1984); *Ritual Slaughter* (Kingston: Quarry Press, 1989); *The Golden Ghetto* (Victoria, BC: Beach Holme Books, 1993); several stories in anthologies incl. "Jeremiah Proosky" in *The Dancing Sun*, edited by Jan Andrews (Press Procepic, 1982) & "The Scribe" in *Canadian Jewish Stories*, ed. by Miriam Waddington (Oxford University Press, 1990); Book columnist, monthly, *The Glebe Report*, Ottawa, 1981 to date; Contributor, *Canadian Encyclopedia* (1985, 1988); numerous book reviews & articles for various newspapers incl. *The Ottawa Citizen, The Edmonton Journal, The Globe and Mail, Canadian Jewish News, The Jerusalem Post.* AFFIL: The Writers' Union of Canada; PEN. INTERESTS: passionately interested in my work, my loved ones & my religion. MISC: recipient of various Canada Council & Ontario Arts Council Grants; listed in *Contemporary Authors* (1986 to date), *Who's Who in Canadian Jewish Women* (1983); *Who's Who in Canada* (1987 to date); *Who's Who in Canadian Jewry* (1983); literary papers with the Public Archives of Canada, Manuscript Div., Ottawa, first deposit, 1983, second deposit, 1994; writing credits between 1976 & 1993 under name of Sharon Drache; since 1993, Sharon Abron Drache. COMMENT: *"I have been described as an energetic Jewish Feminist whose writing places me on a literary map bounded by Isaac Bashevis Singer and Madonna. As I discover and reread all of Erica Jong's superb novels, poetry and creative documentary, I believe the boundaries of this map have been extended."*

Ackerman, Nancy W., B.Sc. ∎ ⊗ ⊿ ∕

Freelance Documentary Photographer. R.R. #3, Bridgetown, NS B0S 1C0 (902) 665-4041. Born 1961. 2 ch. Hannah Wakerenhawi Watters Schell, Jonathan Graeme Ackerman Schell. EDUC: Univ. of Western Ontario, B.Sc.(Geol.) 1982. CAREER: Freelance Photographer, *The Globe and Mail*, Toronto, 1983-85; Freelance Photographer, *The Toronto Star*, 1985-87; Staff Photographer, *The Hamilton Spectator*, 1987-89; Staff Photographer, *The Montreal Gazette*, 1989-95; Freelance Documentary Pho-

tographer, 1995 to date. SELECTED PUBLICATIONS: *Circle of Nations* (Hillsboro, Ore.: Beyond Words Publishing, 1993); *Come Look with Me - Discovering Photographs with Children* by Jean Tucker (Charlottesville, VA: Thomasson-Grant Publishing, 1994). EXHIBITIONS: *Portraits*, World Trade Center, Centre des Femmes, Montreal (1994); *Woman of the Earth*, N.I.I.P.A. Gallery, Hamilton, Ont. (1994); *Traditions of Looking*, Institute of American Indian Arts Museum, Santa Fe, New Mexico (1994); *A Celebration of Women and Song*, Ogilvy's, Montreal (1995); *Wathahine: Photographs of Aboriginal Women*, McCord Museum, Montreal (1995; re-opened as a traveling exhibit, 1996-97); *Women Kind*, Edgemere Gallery, Kentville, N.S. (1996). AFFIL: Chrysalis House, women's shelter (Bd. of Dir.); Commonwealth Journalists' Association; Native Indian / Inuit Photographers' Associations. INTERESTS: small-scale farming; wilderness canoeing; hiking; tennis; piano. MISC: Freelance work done for *New York Times*, Gamma Liaison Network, *London Times*, *Maclean's* magazine, *Financial Post*, Reuters, *Native Peoples Magazine* & *International Herald Tribune*. COMMENT: *"Nancy Ackerman has been taking pictures professionally for over a decade. Her strength is in her powerful portraiture and 'photo documentary' work. Her work has appeared in many exhibits, several books and in such publications as the* Montreal Gazette, Maclean's, New York Times *and the* International Herald Tribune.*"*

Adam, Dyane, B.A.,B.Ps.,M.A., Ph.D. ⬦ ⊕ ⬤

Principal, GLENDON COLLEGE, York University, 2275 Bayview Ave., Toronto, ON M4N 3M6 (416) 487-6727, FAX (416) 487-6786, EMAIL adam@delphi.glendon.yorku.ca. Born Casselman, Ont. 1953. m. Jacques Carrière. EDUC: Univ. of Ottawa, B.A.(Concentration in Psych.) 1974, B.Ps.(Psych.) 1975, M.A.(Clinical Psych.) 1977, Ph.D.(Clinical Psych.) 1980; Univ. of Manitoba, Univ. Mgmt. Course 1989. CAREER: Lecturer, part-time, Univ. of Ottawa, 1977-80; Prof., 1980-81; Prof., Commission Scolaire Manicouagan, 1981; Prof., CEGEP de Hauterive, 1982; Clinical Psychologist, Centre Hospitalier Rouyn-Noranda, 1982-84; Clinical/Community Psychologist, Cornwall General Hospital, 1984-87; Psychologist, private practice, 1982-93; Asst. Prof., Laurentian Univ., 1987-80; Assoc. Prof., 1990-93; Asst. VP, 1988-93; Chair, part-time, Advisory Committee on Francophone Affairs, Ministry of Educ. & Training, Gov't of Ont., 1991-94; Principal, Glendon Coll., 1994 to date. SELECTED PUBLICATIONS: numerous articles in both scientific & professional journals as well as research reports, book chapters & reviews. **EDIT:** Ed. Bd., *Reflets*, Revue Ontaroise d'intervention sociale et communautaire; Ed. Bd., for Resources for feminist research, *Canadian Journal of Community Mental Health*; Co-Ed., *Proceedings of the Third Colloquium of the Réseau des chercheures féministes de l'Ontario français*. **AFFIL:** Canadian Directory of Psychologists in Clinical Practice; Ontario Board of Examiners in Psychology; Corporation professionnelle des psychologues du Québec; Canadian Psychological Association; Canadian Research Institute for the Advancement of Women; Réseau des chercheures féministes de l'Ontario français (Founding Mbr. & Treas.); Réseau des intervenantes et intervenants en santé et services sociaux; Consortium des Universités de la francophonie ontarienne; Centre de santé médico-social francophone de Toronto (Bd. Mbr.); RIFSSSO (Nominating Committee); Table féministe francophone de concertation provinciale (Exec. Mbr.); Collectif des femmes francophones du Nord-est ontarien (Hon. Mbr.). **HONS:** Ontario Grad. Scholar, 1971; Dean of Arts Award, 1973-74; Knights of Columbus Award, 1971-75; Summer Research Award, P.R.A.D., 1975; Coopératives Desjardins Award, 1975-76; Ontario Graduate Scholarship, 1976-78; Arts Council Doctoral Fellowship, 1978-89; President's Award for Exceptional Achievement, Laurentian Univ., 1993; Women of Change, special recognition given to 58 Ontario women, Ontario Women's Directorate, 1994. **MISC:** recipient of numerous research & community project grants. **COMMENT:** *"Dyane Adam is currently principal of Glendon College of York University. Previously, she was Assistant VP at Laurentian University and Chair of the Advisory Committee on Francophone Affairs for the Minister of Education of Ontario. She has a Ph.D. in Clinical Psychology and is the author of numerous articles concerning women and health, francophone university education and minority issues. Adam has been instrumental in launching numerous provincial and regional organizations and projects for francophones and women in Ontario and Canada."*

Adamec, Lila ■■ $ ⚛

President, LAMAR COMMUNICATIONS (high-tech. mktg & public rel'ns), 3219 Yonge St., Ste. 345, Toronto, ON M4N 2L3 (416) 444-9962, FAX 510-2323, EMAIL adamec@total.net. Born Toronto. **EDUC:** Ryerson Polytechnical Institute, studies in Extractive Metallurgy; York Univ., studies in Bus., Mktg & Advertising; Royal Conservatory of Music, violin. **CAREER:** mktg, U.S. mining co., 1979-82; Legislative Assembly, 1982-85; Mktg Mgr, high-tech. scientific co., 1985-92; Pres., Lamar Communications, 1992 to date; consulted on & developed a broad range of mktg & sales programs for firms worldwide in scientific, medical, aerospace & high-tech. industries. **SELECTED PUBLICATIONS:** developed & wrote course curriculum for Tradeshow Expo. **AFFIL:** Ontario Aerospace Council; Information Technology Association of Canada; St. Vladimir's Greek Orthodox Cathedral (Exec. Bd.). **INTERESTS:** travel—has been almost all the way around the world; fishing; reading; arts; entertainment. **MISC:** speaker, various conferences throughout N.Am.; frequently invited as guest speaker on a wide variety of topics; plans & implements mgmt conferences, retreats & awards nights for major Cdn & U.S. corporations; involvement with Royal/Presidential visits.

Adams, Patricia, B.A.,M.A. ■■ ☺ ⚛

Executive Director, PROBE INTERNATIONAL (non-governmental organization), 225 Brunswick Ave., Toronto, ON M5S 2M6 (416) 964-9223, FAX 964-8239, EMAIL eprobe@web.net, INTERNET: http://www.nextcity.com/ProbeInternational. President, ENERGY PROBE RESEARCH FOUNDATION. **EDUC:** Carleton Univ., B.A.(Econ. & Pol. Sci.) 1975; Univ. of Sussex, U.K., M.A.(Dev. Econ.) 1979. **CAREER:** Teacher, London & Cambridge Univ. Advanced & Ordinary Level Econ. & Commerce, Jamaican Ministry of Educ., 1975-77; Researcher, Science Council of Canada, Ottawa, 1978; Organizer, Charcoal Cooking Stove Proj., Kenyan Nat'l Council for Science & Technology, 1979-80; Econ. Consultant, Gov't of Kenya, 1979-80; Research Contributor to *Rural Energy and the Third World: A Review of Social Science Research and Technology Policy Problems* (Pergamon Press, 1982), Science Policy Research Unit, Univ. of Sussex, U.K., 1980; Economist on Ghana irrigation proj. & Sri Lanka Mahaveli Proj., Acres International, Toronto, 1980; Rapporteur & co-author, *Report on the Meeting of Energy Research Donors*, & Consultant to establish energy research program, International Development Research Centre, Ottawa, 1982; Exec. Dir., Probe International, Toronto, 1980 to date; Pres., Energy Probe Research Foundation, 1991 to date. **SELECTED PUBLICATIONS:** numerous scholarly/technical and popular books & articles, papers & presentations, & testimony to Cdn parliamentary committees & U.S. congressional committees. **EDIT:** Assoc. Editor, *The Ecologist*, U.K., 1990 to date; Contributing Editor, *World Rivers Review*, San Francisco, 1985 to date. **AFFIL:** Rainforest

Action Network, San Francisco (Bd. of Dir. 1991 to date).

Adamson, Nancy, B.A.,M.A.,Ph.D., B.Sc.N.,RN ■ ⬧

Director of Equity Services, CARLETON UNIVERSITY, 1125 Colonel By Dr., Ottawa, ON K1S 5B6 (613) 520-5622, FAX 520-4037. Born Atlanta, Ga. 1951. EDUC: Mount Holyoke Coll., B.A.(Hist.) 1973; Emory Univ., M.A.(Hist.) 1974; Univ. of Toronto, Ph.D. (Hist.) 1983, B.Sc.N.(Nursing) 1987. CAREER: Teaching Asst., Dept. of Hist., Univ. of Toronto, 1975-80; Instructor, Women's Studies Program, Univ. of Toronto, 1979-86, Summer 1987, 1990; Registered Nurse, Clarke Institute of Psychiatry, 1987-88; Sexual Harassment Officer, Univ. of Toronto, 1988-90; Writer (on grant from Canada Council), working on popular book on sexual harassment, 1990-91; Coord. for the Status of Women, Carleton Univ., 199-95; Dir. of Equity Svcs, 1996 to date. SELECTED PUBLICATIONS: *Feminist Organizing for Change: A Study of the Contemporary Women's Movement in Canada* (Toronto; Oxford University Press, 1988), with Linda Briskin & Margaret McPhail; "Artificial Insemination" (*Healthsharing: A Canadian Women's Health Quarterly* 6(4) 1985); "Sexual Harassment at the University: A Problem" (*The Bulletin* October 24, 1988); various book reviews; numerous conference papers & presentations. AFFIL: Canadian Women's Studies Association (Pres. 1993-94); National Action Committee on the Status of Women. INTERESTS: feminism; cooking; mystery novels. MISC: Mbr., Bd. of Dir., Canadian Women's Movement Archives/Archives canadiennes du mouvement des femmes, 1980-92; Mbr., March 8th Coalition, Toronto, 1978-83; Registered Nurse, Prov. of Ont.; trained Mediator (Conflict Resolution).

Addie, Barbara, B.Math.,F.C.A.S., F.C.I.A. ■ Ⓢ

Executive Vice President, AGF NAFTA LTD., 2200 Yonge St., Ste. 1200, Toronto, ON M4S 2C6 (416) 440-7757, FAX 487-9365, EMAIL addieb@cscw.com. Born Toronto 1956. m. Neil Witchlow. 2 ch. Alison Witchlow, Ian Witchlow. EDUC: Univ. of Waterloo, B.Math. 1979. CAREER: Mgr, Actuarial Svc, Ætna Canada, 1980-84; Sr. VP, Guardian Insurance Company of Canada, 1984-93; Exec. VP, The Canadian Surety Company, 1993 to date. AFFIL: The McGill Club (Past Pres.); Ontario Conference of Casualty Actuaries (Past Pres. 1993); Canadian Institute of Actuaries (Fellow 1983); Casualty Actuarial Society (Fellow 1983).

Adey, Elizabeth, B.N.,M.Ed.(Admin.) ⬧ ⊕

Executive Director, ASSOCIATION OF REGISTERED NURSES OF NEWFOUNDLAND, Box 6116, St. John's, NF A1C 5X8 (709) 753-6040, FAX 753-4940. Born St. John's. m. David Adey. 2 ch. EDUC: Memorial Univ., B.N. 1972, M.Ed.(Admin.) 1986; Dalhousie Univ., Diploma(Teaching in Schools of Nursing) 1965; Canadian Hospital Association, Diploma(Health Svcs Admin.1984. CAREER: Association of Registered Nurses of Newfoundland; Council Mbr., 1968-72 & 1976-80; Exec. Committee Mbr., 1981-86; Pres.-Elect, 1986-88; Pres., 1988-89; Exec. Dir., 1989 to date. SELECTED PUBLICATIONS: various articles on primary health care for the *Canadian Health Care Management Journal* & *Journal of Canadian Nursing Management*. AFFIL: Canadian Nurses' Association. HONS: award for publication on preceptorship programs in nursing, Newfoundland Hospital Association; recipient of the Collingwood Award for her contribution to her work organization.

Adey, Isobel Marion Moffat (née Peterkin) ⬧

Founder, THE INTERNATIONAL CLUB OF OTTAWA, 63 Avenue Rd., Ottawa, ON K1S 0N7 (613) 233-9171. Born Ottawa 1919. w. 1 ch. CAREER: British Security Co-ordination, Washington, DC, 1942-44; Sr. Admin. Officer, British Army Staff, Ottawa, 1944-46; Defence Research Bd., 1952-60. AFFIL: The International Club of Ottawa (Founder 1970); Beta Sigma Phi (Life Mbr.); Historical Society of Ottawa (Life Mbr.); Kingsway United Church (Founding Mbr.); Heritage Ottawa (Patron); Welcome to Washington International Club (Hon. Mbr.). HONS: Woman of the Year Award, Ottawa Beta Sigma Phi, 1992; Nominee for Outstanding Woman Award, YWCA. INTERESTS: photography; music; antiques; Canadian history; gardening; travel. COMMENT: *"Throughout my life I have been active in church and community events. I enjoy people and have always tried to help others. In 1970, I returned to Canada after living in Washington, DC for three years. I had learned what it is like to live in another country, and this inspired me to establish a club for international women."*

Adrian, Donna J., B.A.,B.L.S.,M.L.S. ▯ ⬧

Library Coordinator, LAURENVAL SCHOOL BOARD, 530 Northcote Rd., Rosemere, QC J7A 1Y2 (514) 621-5900, FAX 621-8043. Born Morden, Man. 1940. m. James Ross Adrian. EDUC: Brandon Coll., B.A. 1962; McGill Univ., B.L.S. 1963, M.L.S. 1969. CAREER: Librarian, Laurenvale Sch. Bd., 1963-66; Librarian, then Lib. Coord., Rosemere High Sch., 1966-

74; Lib. Coord., North Island Reg'l Sch. Bd.; Lib. Coord., Laurenval Sch. Bd., 1979 to date. SELECTED PUBLICATIONS: Ed. Bd., *Canadian Materials Reviewer*; Ed. Bd., *Emergency Librarian*. AFFIL: Canadian Library Association; Pres., Canadian School Library Association; Quebec School Library Association; International Association of School Librarians; Corporation of Professional Librarians of Quebec; Association for Teacher Librarianship in Canada. HONS: Governor General's Medalist, Brandon Collegiate Institute. INTERESTS: scuba diving; bridge; reading; swimming. MISC: Master Tutor Certificate, Laubach Literacy, 1984; Literacy teacher; serves on the Quebec Ministry of Educ. Copyright Committee. COMMENT: *"I take pride in my work. I enjoy challenges and working with people, encouraging them to look beyond the problem to see possible solutions."*

Adrian, Kathryn $

President, ELIA FASHIONS LTD., 1121 William St., Vancouver, BC V6A 2J1 (604) 254-1998, FAX 254-0831. Born Vancouver 1951. d. EDUC: British Columbia Institute of Technology, Mktg Mgmt 1971. CAREER: Sales Mgr, Eaton's; Western Reg'l Oper. Mgr, Dalmys Canada Ltd.; Pres., Elia Fashions Ltd. AFFIL: Young Presidents' Organization; Big Sisters (Fund Raising Committee); Vancouver Board of Trade. HONS: Women of Distinction Award, YWCA; Canadian Woman Entrepreneur, 1992; one of the Fastest Growing Companies, *Profit, The Magazine for Canadian Entrepreneurs*, four years in a row.

Agnew, Ella M., B.Sc.,LL.B. ⚖ ✕ $

Partner, MILRAD & AGNEW, 215 Carlton St., Toronto, ON M5A 2K9 (416) 964-0021, FAX 964-0744. Born London, UK 1948. m. Christopher Birt. 2 ch. EDUC: Univ. of Waterloo, B.Sc. 1975; Univ. of Toronto Law Sch., LL.B. 1973. BAR: Ont. 1975. CAREER: Lawyer, Aaron M. Milrad, 1975-79; Ptnr, Milrad & Agnew, 1979 to date. SELECTED PUBLICATIONS: *The Art World–Law, Business and Practice in Canada*, with Aaron Milrad (Merritt Publishing Company, 1980); *Legaleasy: A Step-by-step Guide to Collecting for Canadian Art Galleries and Museums* (Ontario Association of Art Galleries & Canadian Museums Association, 1991); various other articles & conference presentations. AFFIL: Law Society of Upper Canada; Univ. of Waterloo (Bd. of Gov. 1989-95); Univ. of Waterloo Foundation (Trustee 1993-96); Royal Ontario Museum (Public Programs Committee). INTERESTS: alpine skiing; home restoration & reinterpretation to Victorian style; reading; antiques; con-

temporary arts & crafts; family. MISC: frequent speaker; Mbr., Planning Committee for the Legal Affairs Symposium of the Canadian Museums Association/Canadian Bar Association, 1989 to date. COMMENT: *"Enjoy a general solicitor's practice with emphasis on copyright and cultural property issues. Clients include foreign and domestic corporations, manufacturers, distributors, agents, publishers, artists, charities, professional associations, partnerships and individuals."*

Ainley, Marianne Gosztonyi, B.A.,M.Sc., Ph.D. 🎓 ✑ 🏵

Professor and Chair, Women's Studies Programs, UNIVERSITY OF NORTHERN BRITISH COLUMBIA, 3333 University Way, Prince George, BC V2N 4Z9 (604) 960-6681, FAX (604) 960-5545, EMAIL ainley@ubc.edu.ca. Born Budapest 1937. m. David Ainley. 2 ch. EDUC: Sir George Williams Univ., B.A.(Humanities) 1964; Cornell Univ., Certificate in Ornithology 1979; Univ. de Montréal, M.Sc.(Hist. of Sci.) 1980; McGill Univ., Ph.D.(Hist. of Sci.) 1985. CAREER: Independent Scholar, Social Sciences & Humanities Research Council of Canada Strategic Grants Div., 1986-87, 1989-91; Visiting Scholar, Women's Studies, Carleton Univ., 1990; Principal, Simone de Beauvoir Institute & Dir. of Women's Studies Program, Concordia Univ., 1991-95; Prof. & Chair, Women's Studies Program, Univ. of Northern British Columbia, 1995 to date. SELECTED PUBLICATIONS: *Restless Energy–A Biography of William Rowan 1891-1957*; *Despite the Odds, Essays on Canadian Women and Science*; "The Emergence of Canadian Ornithology–An Historical Overview to 1950," *Contributions to the History of North American Ornithology*, eds. W.E. Davis & Jerome A. Jackson (1995); "Field Work and Family: North American Women Ornithologists, 1900-1950," *Uneasy Careers and Intimate Lives: Women in Science 1798-1979*, eds. Pnina Abir-Am & Dorinda Outram (1987); "Louise de Kiriline Lawrence (1984-1992) & the World of Nature: A Tribute," *The Canadian Field-Naturalist* (1994); "Canadian Women's Contributions to Chemistry, 1900-1970," *Canadian Chemical News* (1994); "A Woman of Integrity: Kathleen Gough's 'Career' in Canada," *Anthropoligical* (1993); "'Women's Work' in Canadian Chemistry," *Canadian Woman Studies* (1993); "A Select Few: Women and the National Research Council of Canada, 1916-1991," *Scientia Canadensis* (1991). AFFIL: McGill Centre for Research and Teaching on Women; Society of Canadian Ornithologists; Delta Kappa Gamma International; Canadian History of Education Society;

Canadian Women Studies Association; Canadian Science & Technology Historical Association; Canadian Research Institute for the Advancement of Women; History of Science Society of America; American Ornithologists' Union. **INTERESTS:** classical music; reading; birdwatching; camping. **MISC:** two forthcoming books on Canadian women & science; featured in *Herstory Calender* 1995; Consultant, National Film Board "Women and Science" Project. **COMMENT:** *"Research scholar: history of Canadian science, history of women and science. Avid birder and involved in environmental issues."*

Aitken, Mary S. $

President, RENAISSANCE SECURITIES INC., Standard Life Centre, 121 King St. W., Ste. 1740, Toronto, ON M5H 3T9 (416) 367-8000, FAX 367-5471. Born St. Thomas, Ont. 1948. m. Peter V. Gundy. 6 ch. Jason Aitken, James Aitken, Max Gundy, Harry Gundy, Ben Gundy, Sam Gundy. **CAREER:** Stockbroker, Thomas Clarke & Co., London, UK; Founder, Pronto Toronto Inc., 1977-81; Pres., Mary S. Aitken & Associates, 1981-87; Pres., Renaissance Securities Inc., 1987 to date. **DIRECTOR:** Advanced Material Resources Ltd.; Asia Media Group.

Albright, Penny S., B.A.,M.Sc., Ph.D. ■ $ ⊕

Vice-President, Government and Health Economics, JANSSEN-ORTHO INC., 19 Greenbelt Dr., Don Mills, ON M3C 1L9 (416) 382-4810, FAX 382-5171. Born Ont. 1950. m. Dr. Michael Herrington. 2 ch. **EDUC:** Sir George Williams Univ., B.A.(Psych.) 1971; McGill Univ., M.Sc.(Psych.) 1974; Univ. of Toronto, Ph.D.(Pharmacology) 1981. **CAREER:** Mgr, Product Dev., Parke Davis, 1984-88; Mgr, Medical Research, 1988-90; Mgr, Prov. Govt. Affairs, 1990-92; Dir., Regulatory & Gov't Affairs, Janssen Pharmaceutica Inc., 1992-94; Dir., Prov. & Professional Rel'ns, 1994-96; VP, Gov't & Health Econ., 1996 to date. **SELECTED PUBLICATIONS:** "The Effect of Taurine on Kindled Seizures in the Rat," with others (*Canadian Journal of Physiology and Pharmacology* 56, 1978); "Centrencephalic Mechanisms in the Kindling Model," with others, in *Kindling Two*, ed. by J.A. Wada (New York: Raven Press, 1981); "Reduction of Polypharmacy in Epileptic Patients," with J. Bruni (*Archives of Neurology* 42, 1984); "Reduction of Hospital Days in Chronic Schizophrenia Patients Treated with Risperidone: A Retrospective Study," with others (*Clinical Therapeutics* 15, 1993); various published abstracts. **DIRECTOR:** Janssen Pharmaceutica Inc. **AFFIL:** Canadian Pharmaceutical Association; Pharmaceutical Manufacturers' Association of Canada. **HONS:** Ont. Grad. Scholarship, 1976-80; Univ. of Toronto Fellowship, 1977-80; Medical Research Council Fellowship, 1981-84; Wellesley Hospital Research Grant, 1981-84. **INTERESTS:** photography; art; music. **COMMENT:** *"I have endeavoured to contribute significantly to the scientific community and to bring credibility and scientific expertise to the area of government relations."*

Aldana, Patricia 📖

Publisher, GROUNDWOOD BOOKS LTD., 585 Bloor St. W., 2nd Fl., Toronto, ON M6G 1K5 (416) 537-2501, FAX 537-4647. Born Guatemala 1946 4 ch. Carlota McAllister, Seth McAllister, Daniel Cohen, Madeline Cohen. **EDUC:** Stanford Univ., 1968; Bryn Mawr Coll., 1969. **CAREER:** Instructor in Art Hist., York Univ., 1971-72; Distribution & Sales Mgr, The Women's Press, 1975-78; Gov't Rel'ns & Policy Dir., The Association of Canadian Publishers (Paid Pres.), 1978-80; Publisher, Groundwood Books Ltd., 1978 to date; Fiction Publisher & Ptnr, Douglas and McIntyre, 1981 to date. **AFFIL:** Book & Periodical Development Council (Bd. Mbr. 1981-84); Children's Book Centre (Founding Bd. Mbr. 1981-85); Dept. of Communications Advisory Bd. (Advisor 1983-86); Canadian Telebook Agency (Chrm 1984-86); Organization of Book Publishers of Ontario (Pres. 1987-91); PEN Canada (Bd. 1988-90); Universidad del Valle de Guatemala (Bd.); Association for the Export of Canadian Books (Bd. 1990-92); Circular 14 Committee Organization of Book Publishers of Ontario (Chair 1993-95). **MISC:** Juror, Bologna Children's Book Fair Illustrators' Exhibition, 1989.

Alexander, Lisa ■■ ⚾

Olympic Athlete. c/o Canadian Olympic Association. Born Toronto 1968. **EDUC:** currently working on Cdn Securities Course. **SPORTS CAREER:** mbr., Cdn Nat'l Synchronized Swimming Team, 1985 to date. Olympic Games: Silver, team, 1996. World championships: 2nd, team, 3rd, solo, & 3rd, duet, 1994; 2nd, team, & 3rd, duet, 1991. Commonwealth Games: 1st, solo, & 1st, duet, 1994. Canadian championships: 1st, solo, 1st, duet, & 3rd, team, 1995; 1st, solo, 1st, duet, & 2nd, team, 1994. **AFFIL:** Female Athletes Motivating Excellence (FAME). **HONS:** Helen Vanderburg Trophy for top overall swimmer in Canada, 1991, 1993-95. **MISC:** started synchro after completing highest possible level of Red Cross program for a 12-yr.-old.

Alexander-Smith, Joann ■ ■ ⊗ ♂
General Director, MANITOBA OPERA (not-for-profit performing arts opera company), Portage Place, 393 Portage Ave., P.O. Box 31027, Winnipeg, MB R3B 3K9 (204) 942-7479, FAX 949-0377. Born Winnipeg 1941. m. Hershel (Harry) Smith. CAREER: Life Underwriter, Continental Assurance, Chicago, 1961-68; owner & Mng Ptnr, The Kensington Dependable Group, Winnipeg, 1982-92; Exec. Dir., Manitoba Opera, 1992-94; Gen. Dir., 1994 to date. AFFIL: Manitoba Cultural Coalition; Winnipeg Performing Arts Consortium; Women's Canadian Ort (mbr.; former Nat'l Pres.); World Ort Union, London, U.K. (former Bd. mbr.); Winnipeg Symphony Orchestra (former Pres., Women's Committee); Winnipeg Chamber of Commerce. INTERESTS: music; theatre; study of modern & ancient religions; technical educ. for young people. MISC: District Dir., Man. & E. Sask., Upper Midwest Council, Metropolitan Opera Nat'l Council Auditions. COMMENT: *"Possesses a strong business and arts background coupled with extensive volunteer experience. The first woman to manage and the only woman named General Director of a major Canadian opera company."*

Alford, Christine, B.Sc. ⓢ ☸
General Manager, Systems Integration, IBM CANADA LTD., 3600 Steeles Ave. E., Markham, ON L3R 2Z1 (905) 316-5726, FAX 316-5090. Born Sault Ste. Marie, Ont. 1957. m. Gregory Alford. 1 ch. EDUC: Univ. of Guelph, B.Sc.(Hons.) 1980. CAREER: Mgr, Token Ring Network Microcode Dev., IBM Canada Laboratory, 1985-88; Mgr, C Computer Language Dev., 1988-90; Mgr, Quality, 1991-93; Dir., Info. Technology, IBM Canada Ltd., 1994-96; Gen. Mgr, Systems Integration, 1996 to date. HONS: IBM Canada Excellence Award, 1992. INTERESTS: running; skiing; golfing.

Alford, Edna 📖 🕮
Writer. 4515 - 29 St., Lloydminster, SK S9V 1E7 (306) 825-2055. Born Turtleford, Sask. 1947. m. Don. 1 ch. Michael. CAREER: Co-founder & Co-ed., *Dandelion Magazine*, 1975-80; teaching & editorial, Mount Royal Coll., 1979-80; Okanagan Summer Sch. of the Arts, 1982; Saskatchewan Summer Sch. of the Arts, 1983, 1984, 1985; Writer-in-Residence, Regina Public Library, 1985-86; Canada Council Short Term Residency, Malaspina Coll., 1989; Sage Hill Writing Experience, 1990, 1992, 1993; Ed., *Grain* Magazine, 1990-95; Faculty, Writing Program, Banff Centre for the Arts, 1992, 1993, 1994; Assoc. Dir., Writing Studio Program, Banff Centre for the Arts, 1995.

SELECTED PUBLICATIONS: *A Sleep Full of Dreams*–short fiction collection (Oolichan Books); *The Garden of Eloise Loon* –short fiction collection (Oolichan Books); work appears in many anthologies incl. *The Oxford Collection of Canadian Short Stories, Saskatchewn Gold, Stories by Canadian Women* & *Liberté*. AFFIL: Writers' Union of Canada; Saskatchewan Writers' Guild; ACTRA. HONS: Marian Engel Award, 1988; Gerald Lampert Award, 1981. INTERESTS: social issues; writing; reading. MISC: served on various literary juries incl. Canada Council, Saskatchewan Arts Bd., & CBC Annual Short Fiction Competition; freelance ed., has edited short fiction collections by various authors incl. Bonnie Burnard & Fred Stenson; served on edit. bd. of Coteau Books. COMMENT: *"I am tempted to say that I am a rather ordinary woman who lives and works in extraordinary times in terms of the history of women participating in my field, particularly in my country. I endeavour to be worthy of their company."*

Alia, Valerie, B.A.,M.A.,Ph.D. ■ ☖ / 🕮
Distinguished Professor of Canadian Culture and Visiting Professor of Journalism, Center for Canadian-American Studies, WESTERN WASHINGTON UNIVERSITY, Bellingham, WA 98225-9110 (360) 650-7509, FAX 650-3995, EMAIL alia@cc.wwu.edu. Born N.Y. 1942. d. 2 ch. David Restivo, Dan Restivo. EDUC: Univ. of Cincinnati, B.A.(English Lit.) 1965; Michigan State Univ., M.A.(Comparative Lit.) 1967; York Univ., Ph.D.(Social & Pol. Thought) 1989. CAREER: Music & Dance Critic, Capital Newspapers, Albany, NY; Reporter, UPI, *Rutland (Vermont) Herald* & others; TV Production, WMHT (arts programming); Asst. Prof., Grad. Sch. of Journalism, Univ. of Western Ontario, 1989-96; Sessional Lecturer, Soc., Univ. of Toronto, 1989; Prof. of Ethics, Art Criticism, Broadcast Coord., Women in Media, Arctic Anthropology, Hist. of Print Journalism, Politics of Naming, Canada as a Northern Nation, 1989 to date. SELECTED CREDITS: photographs, Baffin Island, *Canadian Woman Studies* (Fall 1994); various broadcast credits, 1982 to date. SELECTED PUBLICATIONS: *Covering the North: News, Media and Northern People* (UBC Press, in progress); *Deadlines and Diversity: Journalism Ethics in a Changing World* (Halifax: Fernwood Books, 1996); *Names, Numbers and Northern Policy: Inuit, Project Surname and the Politics of Identity* (Halifax: Fernwood Books, 1994); various contributions to books, incl. "New Naming" in *Amazons, Bluestockings & Crones: A Feminist Dictionary*, C. Kramarae & P. Treichler (London: Pandora, 1992); "The Politics of

Eponymy: Power, Protection, Classification, Commemoration" (*Onomastica Canadiana* 73 1991) & other refereed articles; various book reviews & other articles. EDIT: Ed., occasional papers, Canadian Federation for the Humanities, 1992 to date. EXHIBITIONS: *Baffin Island: 1984-1994*, solo exhibition, Blackfriars Cafe, London, Ont. (April 1994) & Arctic Ventures, Iqaluit, NWT (1994-95); "The Land is Our Life," *Arctic Landscapes*, Performing Arts Center, Western Washington Univ., Bellingham, Wash. (1996); other photography exhibits. AFFIL: Westminster Institute for Ethics & Human Values (Fellow); American Association of University Women (Fellow); American Name Society; Arctic Institute of North America; Association for Practical & Professional Ethics; Canadian Communication Association; Canadian Federation for the Humanities (Nat'l Co-Chair, Women's Caucus 1993-95); Canadian Society for the Study of Names; Canadian Studies Association; Canadian Women in Communications; International Arctic Social Science Association; ACTRA; Canadian Association of Journalists; International Council on Onomastic Sciences; London Regional Art & Historical Museums (First Nations Circle); The Writers' Union of Canada; Canadian Arctic Resources Committee; International Gender Advisory Group, WETV; Native News Network of Canada (Bd. of Dir. 1991-92, Advisory Bd.); "Smoke Signals" (First Nations radio), London Ont. (Advisor). HONS: Poetry Finalist, Tilden/CBC/*Saturday Night* National Literary Awards, 1995; Strauss & Elliston Poetry Prizes, Univ. of Cincinnati; Cincinnati Literary Club Essay Award, Univ. of Cincinnati; National Endowment of the Arts (US), Fellowship in dance criticism; *Canadian Woman Studies* writing award, 1983; Elliston Poetry Fellow, Univ. of Cincinnati; AAUW American Fellowship, Ph.D., 1986-87; Ont. Grad. Scholarship, Ph.D., 1986-87; McCracken Prize for Journalism Research (first recipient), 1992 & 1995; Poynter Teaching Fellowship (Ethics) for Outstanding Teaching in Journalism, 1992. INTERESTS: travel; the North; my incredibly brilliant, delightful & talented sons. MISC: 1st person to hold endowed chair: Distinguished Professorship in Cdn Culture, Western Wash. Univ., 1996 to date; recipient of numerous grants; Juror for numerous grant panels, incl. OGS; Judge for various awards competitions; listed in *Canadian Who's Who* & *Who's Who in Toronto*; organized various conferences & symposia. COMMENT: "*I have a peculiar combination of passions and skills, as journalist, artist and academic...I'm a coalition-builder by belief and temperament, committed to finding ways we humans can assert,*

and share, our genders and ethnicities to benefit us all."

Allan, Elyse M., B.A.,M.B.A. ■ ☺ Ⓢ
Chief Executive Officer, THE BOARD OF TRADE OF METROPOLITAN TORONTO, 1 First Canadian Place, Box 60, Toronto, ON M5X 1C1 (416) 862-4536, FAX 366-6460. Born Mineola, N.Y. 1957. m. Donald. 1 ch. Stuart. EDUC: Dartmouth Coll., B.A.(Biol. & Environmental Studies) 1979; Amos Tuck Bus. Sch., M.B.A.(Gen. Mgmt) 1984. CAREER: Mng Consultant, Corp. Mktg, G.E. Company, 1984-87; Dir., Planning & Dev., GAF Corporation, 1987-88; Mgr, Customer Svc. Programs, G.E. Canada, 1988-92; Mktg Mgr, Commercial & Ind. Mkts, G.E. Lighting, 1990-92; Dir., Energy Svcs Mktg, Ontario Hydro, 1992-94; CEO, Board of Trade of Metropolitan Toronto, 1995 to date. AFFIL: Humber Coll. (Chair, Mktg Advisory Bd.); Arthritis Society, Ontario Div. (Bd. of Dir.).

Allan, Marion, B.A.,M.A.,LL.B. ⚖
Judge, BRITISH COLUMBIA SUPREME COURT, Law Courts, 800 Smithe St., Vancouver, BC V6Z 2E1 (604) 660-8049. Born Torpoint, Cornwall, UK 1946. d. 1 ch. EDUC: Univ. of British Columbia, B.A.(Int'l Rel'ns & Pol. Sci.) 1967, LL.B. 1977; Univ. of Alberta, M.A.(Int'l Rel'ns & Pol. Sci.) 1970. CAREER: Lawyer, Russell and DuMoulin, Vancouver, 1978-88; Adjunct Prof. of Law, Univ. of British Columbia, 1984-88; Judge, Vancouver County Court, 1988-90; Judge, British Columbia Supreme Court, 1990 to date. AFFIL: Attorney-General's Rules Revision Committee (Chair); Continuing Legal Education (Dir.).

Allan, Robyn, B.A.,M.A. ■■ Ⓢ ⊗
President, CYF CONSULTING LTD. (bus. dev. & econ. consulting), 1970 Haro St., Ste. 502, Vancouver, BC V6G 1H6 (604) 685-4160, FAX 689-4118. Born Vancouver. EDUC: Univ. of British Columbia, B.A.(Arts) 1976, M.A.(Econ.) 1978. CAREER: Exec. Dir., VanCity Community Foundation; Sr. Economist, B.C. Central Credit Union; Pres. & CEO, Insurance Corporation of British Columbia, 1992-93; VP, Fin., ParkLane Ventures Ltd.; Pres., CYF Consulting Ltd. SELECTED PUBLICATIONS: articles on sustainable dev., fin. institution mgmt, strategic planning, econ., social investment & the envir., *Enterprise Magazine*, *Credit Union Way*, *World Reporter*, *The Globe and Mail*, *The Financial Post*, *Business in Vancouver*; *Quest For Prosperity: The Dance of Success* (June 1995). DIRECTOR: Samoth Capital Corporation. HONS: named one of the top 200 CEOs

in Canada, *The Financial Post*, 1992; chosen as one of the 40 under 40 top business performers, *Business in Vancouver*; nominee, YWCA Women of Distinction Awards. **MISC:** 2nd career in acting, singing, dance - producing, choreographing & performing throughout Canada; founding mbr., Saskatchewan Theatre Ballet.

Allan-Davis, Lori, B.Math. ■ $

General Manager, AS/400 Division, **IBM CANADA LTD.**, 3600 Steeles Ave. E., Markham, ON L3R 9Z7 (905) 316-6189, FAX 316-2535. Born Brantford, Ont. 1955. m. William Davis. 2 ch. Lauren, Kyle. **EDUC:** Univ. of Waterloo, B.Math. 1978. **CAREER:** various positions incl.: Systems Eng.; Mktg Mgr; Retail Industry Strategies Mgr; Personal Computing Mktg; Programs Mgr; Bus. Process Re-eng. Mgr; Dir., Bus. Process Re-eng.; Gen. Mgr, AS/400 Div., IBM Canada, 1978 to date. **AFFIL:** Junior Achievement (1980-81). **HONS:** Mktg Excellence Award, IBM, 1979, 1980, 1981; 100% Sales Mktg Award, IBM, six times over 1981-90; Mktg Mgr of the Year, IBM, 1989. **INTERESTS:** golf; boating; cottaging; travelling; family. **COMMENT:** *"During an 18-year career at IBM, I have had increasing areas of responsibility in sales and marketing with a strong desire to dramatically impact/lead major change. I then moved to the area of re-engineering and change management where I lead the re-engineering initiative for IBM Canada. I am currently responsible for the AS/400 Division results in Canada. I spend all my leisure time with my family at our island cottage in Muskoka."*

Allen, Charlotte Vale 📖 📜 ☝

Author. Born Toronto 1941. d. 1 ch. **EDUC:** Harbord Collegiate; Northview Heights Collegiate Institute. **CAREER:** actor, singer, London, UK, 1961-64; actor, singer, cabaret performer, Toronto, 1964-66; nightclub singer, U.S., 1966-70; full-time writer, 1975 to date. **SELECTED PUBLICATIONS:** *Love Life* (1976); *Hidden Meanings* (1976); *Sweeter Music* (1976); *Gentle Stranger* (1977); *Another Kind of Magic* (1977); *Mixed Emotions* (1977); *Running Away* (1977); *Meet Me in Time* (1978); *Julia's Sister* (1978); *Becoming* (1978); *Believing in Giants* (1978); *Gifts of Love* (1978); *Acts of Kindness* (1979); *Moments of Meaning* (1979); *Time of Triumph* (1979); *Promises* (1980); *Daddy's Girl*, autobiography (1980); *Marmalade Man* (1981; pbk. title *Destinies*); *Perfect Fools* (1981); *Intimate Friends* (1983); *Pieces of Dreams* (1984); *Matters of the Heart* (1985); *Time/Steps* (1986); *Illusions* (1987); *Dream Train* (1988); *Night Magic* (1989); *Painted Lives* (1990); *Leftover Dreams* (1992); *Dreaming in Color* (1993); *Somebody's Baby* (1995); *Claudia's Shadow* (1996); writing as Katharine Marlowe: *Heart's Desires* (1991); *Secrets* (1992); *Nightfall* (1993). **AFFIL:** Authors' Guild, N.Y. **INTERESTS:** photography; travel; needlework; bicycling; cooking. **MISC:** part-time lecturer, seminars, workshops about incest/child abuse. **COMMENT:** *"Author of the groundbreaking autobiography* Daddy's Girl, *the first book on incest published in North America (and never out of print since publication in 1980)."*

Allen, Esther Ruth ■■ $ 🍁

Captain (Relief), **BRITISH COLUMBIA FERRY CORPORATION** (transportation—car/passenger ferries), 1112 Fort St., Victoria, BC V8V 4V2 (604) 381-1401. Mate, Minor Vessel. Born Portland, Ore. 1959. sep. **EDUC:** Pacific Marine Training Centre, Watch Keeping Mate 1986; Camosun Coll., Ferry Master 1991. **CAREER:** Relief Ship's Cook, Canadian Brotherhood Railway Transport & GW Loc. 400, 1977-78; Ship's Cook, Seaspan International, 1978-80; Deckhand & Mate, Dept. of Highways & B.C. Ferry Corporation, 1980-93; Relief Capt., minor vessels, B.C. Ferry, 1993 to date. **AFFIL:** Canadian Merchant Service Guild; B.C. Ferries and Marine Workers' Union. **INTERESTS:** horseback riding; skiing; motor cycling; woodworking; boating; water colour painting. **MISC:** featured in numerous magazine articles and in *Saltwater Women at Work* (book by Vicki Jensen); featured in *A Good Job for a Woman*, Knowledge Network, video.

Allen, Marion, B.N.,M.Sc.N.,M.N., Ph.D.,R.N. 🎓 ⊕

Professor, Faculty of Nursing, **UNIVERSITY OF ALBERTA**, Edmonton, AB T6G 2G3 (403) 492-6411, EMAIL mallen@ua-nursing.ualberta.ca. Born Jemseg, N.B. 1944. m. Greg Woytkiw. 3 stpch. Darryl, Dean, Marina. **EDUC:** Univ. of New Brunswick, B.N. 1966; Univ. of Western Ontario, M.Sc.N.(Nursing Educ.) 1974; Case Western Reserve Univ., MN 1983, Ph.D.(Nursing) 1985. **CAREER:** Staff Nurse, Moncton Hospital, 1966-67; Instructor, Sch. of Nursing, Moncton Hospital, 1967-68; Instructor, Sch. of Nursing, Halifax Infirmary, 1968-73; Lecturer, Sch. of Nursing, Dalhousie Univ., 1974-75; Asst. Prof., Sch. of Nursing, Dalhousie Univ., 1975-81; Staff Nurse, Univ. Health Svc., Case Western Reserve Univ., 1981-84; Teaching Asst., Masters Program, Sch. of Nursing, Case Western Reserve Univ., 1983-84; Assoc. in Nursing, Victorian Order of Nurses, Edmonton, 1986-89; Assoc. in Nursing, Charles Camsell General Hospital, Edmonton, 1986-95; Assoc. in Nursing, Royal Alexandra Hospital, Edmonton, 1992 to date; Assoc. Prof., Fac. of Nursing, Univ. of Alberta, 1985-91; Prof., 1991 to date. SELECTED PUBLICATIONS: "Perspectives: A Practical Goal for the 80's," with M. Slater (*Canadian Nurse* 76 1980); "Visual Impairment" (*Nursing Times* 85(42) 1989; "Breast Augmentation Surgery: A Women's Health Issue," with K. Oberle (*Journal of Advanced Nursing* 20 1994); "Assessment of the Visual System" in *Medical Surgical Nursing: Concepts and Clinical Practice*, 5th ed., edited by W. Phipp & others (St. Louis: Mosby, 1995); numerous other book reviews, articles, chapters in books & proceedings; numerous papers presented to conferences. AFFIL: Canadian Nursing Research Group; Council on Nursing & Anthropology; Canadian Society of Ophthalmic Registered Nurses; American Society of Ophthalmic Registered Nurses; Canadian Nurses Foundation; Canadian Association of University Schools of Nursing (W. Reg.); Alberta Association of Registered Nurses; Victorian Order of Nurses Edmonton; Victorian Order of Nurses Alberta (Past Pres., Bd. of Dir.); Victorian Order of Nurses Canada (Chair-Elect, Bd. of Dir. 1994-96; Chair 1996 to date); Sigma Theta Tau International. HONS: Entrance Scholarship, Univ. of New Brunswick, 1962; Life Saving Award, Royal Humane Society, 1963; Muriel Archibald Scholarship, Univ. of New Brunswick, 1963; Dr. Katherine MacLaggan Fellowship, Canadian Nurses Foundation, 1982; National Health & Welfare Ph.D. Fellowship, 1982-84; Nursing Grad. Students' Association Teaching Award, 1993-94; President's Award, Canadian Association of Enterostomal Therapy, 1994. INTERESTS: reading; jogging; skiing; community involvement. MISC: professional interests in the area of primary health care, health promotion & visual impairment. COMMENT: *"I would describe myself as: nurse, educator, researcher, writer, board member and wife. Achievements include association with the Victorian Order of Nurses and the Excellence in Teaching Award bestowed by graduate students."*

Almond, Alice ■ ✤ ✪

Manager, Human Resource Development Canada, Employment and Immigration, GOVERNMENT OF CANADA, 105 King St., North Sydney, NS B2A 3S1 (902) 794-5877, FAX 794-5724. Born Reserve Mines, N.S. 1938. m. Michael. 5 ch. Charlene, Natalie, Allison, Deanna, Michael. EDUC: St. Joseph's Sch. CAREER: 21 yrs. in the private sector as well as 21 yrs. as a public servant, 1975 to date;

Receptionist Interview Clerk, Manpower & Immigration Canada, 1975-81; PM 2 Counselor, 1981-85; Supervisor, Employment Svcs, Glace Bay, 1985-88; Mgr, North Sydney Canada Employment Centre, 1988 to date. AFFIL: Junior Achievement of Cape Breton (Bd. of Dir.); Isaac Walton Killam Hospital; Arleen MacNeil Trust Fund Foundation. HONS: First Lady of the Year, Beta Sigma Phi International, 1995; Commemorative Medal for the 125th Anniversary of Canadian Confederation; Merit Award for Public Service Entrepreneurship; Award for Outstanding Commitment to Community Service, N.S. Director General. INTERESTS: travel; reading; theatre; community; dancing. MISC: was instrumental in organizing the communities in Cape Breton in support of the surviving victim of the McDonald's tragedy & organized the Friends of Arleen MacNeil, which successfully raised $125,000. COMMENT: *"As a wife, mother and grandmother, I have faced many challenges and opportunities. I am a very logical, organized person who likes to take risks and I have a deep concern and interest in community work. I know who I am! I'm proud of who I am! I know where I'm going and I am true to myself."*

Aloi, Santa, B.A.,M.A. ✖ ✑ ✪

Professor, School for the Contemporary Arts and Associate Dean, Faculty of Arts, SIMON FRASER UNIVERSITY, Burnaby, BC V5A 1S6 (604) 291-3911, FAX 291-3033, EMAIL santa_aloi@sfu.ca. Born Syracuse, N.Y. 1943. m. Michael Fellman. EDUC: Cornell Univ., B.A.(Biol., English) 1965; Columbia Univ. Teachers' Coll., M.A.(English) 1967. CAREER: Teacher, Haaren High Sch., N.Y., 1967-70; Dancer, the Gus Solomons Dance Company, N.Y., 1970-76; Teacher, Placement & Ballet, Zena Rommett Studio, N.Y., 1971-73; Teacher, Modern Technique, The Solomons Company Studio, N.Y., 1972-76; Prof. of Dance, Simon Fraser Univ., 1976 to date. SELECTED CREDITS: company repertory with performances throughout the US & Canada, Gus Solomons Jr., 1971-76; Soloist, *Passage*, Karen Jamieson (Vancouver 1978); Soloist, *Woman Song*, Cliff Keuter (Vancouver 1980); Clytmenestra, *The Electra Project*, Grant Strate & Andrew McIlroy (Vancouver 1991); Choreographer for two solo concerts performed internationally, three evening length dance-theatre works & 50 dances, including *Postscript to Footnote to an Appendix*, solo, with Gus Solomons Jr. (1976); *Tangents and Truth Functions*, duet (1981); *Yeats, the Moon and Tower, Re:Visions*, full evening multidisciplinary work, with others (1987); *That Light and Dark That Did Not Clash*, full evening dance/theatre work, with others (1990); *My Life In Art*, solo dance/theatre work (1995). **EDIT:** Founding Ed., *Newsletter of the Association for Dance in Universities & Colleges in Canada*, 1988-94. **AFFIL:** Vancouver Dance Centre Society (Chair); Association for Dance in Universities & Colleges in Canada (Founding Bd. Mbr. 1988-92). **INTERESTS:** interdisciplinary approaches to the arts; Jungian psych.; writing. **MISC:** recipient of grants from Simon Fraser Univ., Koerner Foundation & the Canada Council; frequent guest teacher & artist-in-residence in North America & Europe; various master classes, lecture demonstrations & invited sessions, incl. the Taipei Festival of International Dance Academies, Taiwan, 1986, 1988, the Sichuan Dancers' Association, Chengdu, China, May 1989 & Hong Kong Academy of Performing Arts, Hong Kong, May 1989. **COMMENT:** *"International choreographer, dancer and teacher, and since 1976 a Professor of Dance at Simon Fraser University, she co-founded the Dance Major Program, chairs the Vancouver Dance Centre Board, and continues to choreograph and perform."*

Alonzo, Anne-Marie, B.A.,M.A., Ph.D. ■ 🗂 ⊗

Co-Founder and Director, ÉDITIONS TROIS, 2033 ave. Jessop, Laval, QC H7S 1X3 (514) 663-4028, FAX (514). Born Alexandria, Egypt 1951. s. **EDUC:** Univ. de Montréal, Baccalauréat ès Arts(Études françaises) 1976, Maîtrise ès Arts(Études françaises) 1978, Doctorat ès Arts(Études françaises) 1986. **CAREER:** Chargée de cours, Dépt. d'Études françaises, Univ. de Montréal, 1980, 1985; Correspondante québécoise, Des femmes en mouvements, 1980-84; Dir. de la collection Fiction, Éditions Nouvelle Optique, 1982-83; Co-fondatrice et dir., Éditions TROIS, 1985 to date; Fondatrice/directrice artistique, Production AMA, 1987 to date; Fondatrice/Coordonnatrice générale, Festival de TROIS, Laval, 1989-96. **SELECTED CREDITS:** *La rose et l'anneau*, film d'animation, prod. Gordon Martin, 1980; Écrivaine, *Veille*, radiodiffusée à Éscales, Radio-Canada, 1981; *Veille*, en tournée, 1981-82; Productrice, *Germaine Dugas*, Maison des Arts de Laval, 1991; Écrivaine, *Galia qu'elle nommait amour*, Maison des Arts de Laval, 1992; divers textes, Radio-Canada, 1977 to date. **SELECTED PUBLICATIONS:** numerous articles, interviews, critical pieces & reviews; *Geste* (Paris: Des Femmes, 1979); *Veille* (Paris: Des Femmes, 1982); *L'Immobile* (Montreal: L'Hexagone, 1990); *Une lettre rouge orange et ocre* (Montréal: La Pleine Lune, 1984); *Bleus de mine* (Saint-Lambert: Le Noroît, 1985); *Écoute, Sultane* (Montréal: l'Hexagone, 1987); *Seul le desir* (Montréal: NBJ, 1987); various books have been translated. **HONS:** Prix B'nai Brith de journalisme (*La Vie en Rose*), 1985; Prix Emile-Nelligan, 1985; Prix d'Excellence de Laval (*Galia qu'elle nommait amour*), section littéraire, 1993. **MISC:** mbr. of several literary juries; recipient of various grants. **COMMENT:** *"Anne-Marie Alonzo is a poet, fiction-writer, playwright, editor/publisher and literary critic. Co-founder and Director of TROIS, a review and publishing house. In 1987 she also launched AMA Productions, a company that produces books on cassette."*

Amiel, Barbara, B.A. ■ ■ 🗂

Vice-President, Editorial, HOLLINGER INC. (newspaper publishing), 10 Toronto St., Toronto, ON M5C 2B7 (416) 363-8721, FAX 367-0124. Born Herts., UK. m. The Hon. Conrad M. Black. **EDUC:** Univ. of Toronto, B.A.(Phil. & English). **CAREER:** Editor, *The Toronto Sun*, 1983-85; Columnist, *Maclean's*, 1976 to date; Columnist, *The Times*, London, England, 1986-90; Sr. Pol. Columnist, *The Sunday Times*, 1991-94; Columnist, *The Daily Telegraph*, 1996 to date; VP, Editorial, Hollinger Inc., 1995 to date. **SELECTED PUBLICATIONS:** *By Persons Unknown* (co-author, 1977); *Confessions* (author, 1980). **DIRECTOR:** Hollinger Inc.; Hollinger International Inc. **HONS:** Canadian Council grant, 1974; Media Club of Canada Award, 1976; Periodical Publishers Association Award, 1977; Edgar Allan Poe Award, Mystery Writers of America, 1978; British Press Award, 1987; Women of Distinction award, Britain, 1989.

Amirali-Hadjinicolaou, Evangelia-Lila, M.D. ⊕ ☆ ▩

Medical Doctor. 2875 Douglas Ave., Montreal, QC H3R 2C7 (514) 738-4018, FAX 738-4718. Born Iraklion, Crete 1962. m. Dr. John Hadjinicolaou. 3 ch. Aristides, George, Romanos. **EDUC:** Univ. of Athens, M.D. 1986; McGill Univ., M.Sc.(Psychiatry) in progress. **CAREER:** Research Fellow, Cardiology, McGill Univ., 1988-90; Clinical Fellow, Internal Medicine, 1990-92; Medical Resident, Psychiatry, McGill Univ. **AFFIL:** Shield of Athena (Bd. of Dir.); Doctors of the World (Greek association) (Founding Mbr.); Canadian Medical Association; Orthodox Christian Women of Montreal; Mental Health Team of the Sir Mortimer B. Davis Jewish General Hospital; Greek Community of Montreal. **HONS:** Bertha Mizne Fellowship on Liver & Vascular Diseases, S.M.B.D. Jewish General Hospital, 1988-89, 1989-90; "Alexander Onassis" Scholarship for Grad. Medical Students, 1990-92; various other scholarships. **INTERESTS:** transcultural studies; religion; women's issues; the problem of pain, suffering & death in our lives. **MISC:** has given various presentations. **COMMENT:** *"Medical Doctor from Greece. Came to Canada as a research fellow and then clinical fellow at McGill University, Montreal. Currently working on a Master's degree on Transcultural Psychiatry at McGill University, on the problem of pain in the Greek tradition. Member of the Mental Health Team of the Sir Mortimer B. Davis Jewish General Hospital and a Medical Resident,Psychiatry, McGill University. On the Board of Directors of the organization Shield of Athena, which is specializing in the provision of services to victims of family violence coming from the Greek and other ethnocultural groups in Quebec. Married to Dr. John Hadjinicolaou; they have three sons. With significant involvement in community work and particular interest in cultural, religious and women's issues."*

Amonson, Johanne Leslie, Q.C., B.A.,LL.B. 🔁

Partner, McLENNAN ROSS, Barristers and Solicitors, 600 W. Chambers, 12220 Stony Plain Rd., Box 12040, Edmonton, AB T5J 2L2 (403) 482-9200, FAX 482-9100, EMAIL mross@ supernet.ab.ca. Born Edmonton 1949. **EDUC:** Univ. of Oregon, B.A. 1970, Teaching Certificate 1971; Univ. of Alberta, LL.B. 1977. **BAR:** Alberta, 1978; Queen's Counsel, Alberta 1992. **CAREER:** Teacher, Staatliche Realschule Nurnberg, Nuremberg, Bavaria, 1972-73; Exhibitions Registrar, Glenbow Museum, Calgary, 1973-74; Researcher, Institute of Law Research & Reform, Summer 1976; Assoc., Weeks Joyce, Edmonton, 1978-85; Ptnr, Peterson Ross, Edmonton, 1985-89; Sessional Lecturer, Univ. of Alberta Law Sch., 1987, 1988; Ptnr, McLennan Ross, 1989 to date. **SELECTED PUBLICATIONS:** co-author of various materials for legal educ. seminars. **EDIT:** *Law Review*, Univ. of Alberta, 1975-77. **AFFIL:** Law Society of Alberta; Canadian Bar Association; International Commission of Jurists (Cdn Section); Canadian Tax Foundation; St. Thomas More Lawyers' Guild; Edmonton Bar Association; American College of Estate & Trust Counsel (Fellow). **HONS:** Queen Elizabeth Scholarship, 1966; Foreign Student Tuition Scholarship, Univ. of Oregon, 1967-68, 1969-70; Dean's List, Univ. of Oregon, 1967/68, 1969/70. **INTERESTS:** reading; sports; music; travel; gourmet cooking; gardening; camping. **MISC:** Designated Mentor for the Law Society of Alberta; appointed by Min. of Justice & Attorney Gen. of Canada to the Advisory Committee on Federal Judicial Appointments for the Prov. of Alberta, for the period September 23, 1991

to June 30, 1993; listed in *The World Who's Who of Women, Biography International, Who's Who of American Women, 2,000 Notable American Women, Dictionary of International Biography, Who's Who in American Law, Who's Who of Emerging Leaders in America, International Who's Who of Professional and Business Women* (1993), *Who's Who of America.*

Amos, Janet, B.A.,B.Ed. 🚫 ▯

Artistic Director, BLYTH FESTIVAL, Box 10, Blyth, ON N0M 1H0 (519) 523-4345, FAX 523-9804. Born Toronto 1944. m. Robert E. Johns. 2 ch. **EDUC:** Univ. of Toronto, B.A. (East Asian Studies) 1967, B.Ed. 1991. **CAREER:** freelance actor & dir., 1968-93; worked for Young People's Theatre, Theatre Toronto, Theatre Aquarius, Toronto Workshop Productions, The Red Barn & the Calgary Allied Arts Centre; worked extensively with Theatre Passe Muraille & Paul Thompson, Toronto, 1972-77; Artistic Dir., Blyth Festival, 1979-84; Artistic Dir., Theatre New Brunswick, 1984-88; Artistic Dir., Blyth Festival, 1993 to date. **SELECTED CREDITS:** Actor/Writer, *The Farm Show* (theatre), Theatre Passe Muraille; Dir./Writer, *Alligator Pie* (theatre), Theatre Passe Muraille, 1973; Dir., *John and the Missus* (theatre), Blyth Festival, 1980; Dir., *A Taste of Honey* (theatre), Theatre New Brunswick, 1984; Dir., *Steel Magnolias* (theatre), Stage West, Edmonton, 1987; Dir., *Bethune* (theatre), The Globe Theatre, Regina & 25th St. Theatre, Saskatoon, 1989; Dir., *Les Femmes Savantes* (theatre), George Brown Coll. Theatre Sch., 1991; Denise, *Bonjour la, Bonjour* (theatre), Tarragon Theatre, 1976; Barbara, *Major Barbara* (theatre), Shaw Festival, 1978; Rose, *My Wild Irish Rose* (theatre), Blyth Festival, 1983; Mrs. Fisher, *The Showoff* (theatre), Canadian Stage, 1990; Shirley Valentine, *Shirley Valentine* (theatre) Rainbow Stage, Parry Sound, 1993; Maria, *Taking Care* (feature); Eliza Massey, *The Masseys* (series), CBC; Clara Sturgess, *A Gift To Last* (series), CBC. **SELECTED PUBLICATIONS:** "Rural Roots, A Theatre Memoir" (*Canadian Theatre Review*, Summer/Fall, 1995). **AFFIL:** Canadian Actors' Equity Association ; Association of Canadian Television & Radio Artists, ACTRA (Council 1976-79). **INTERESTS:** theatre; educ.; politics; Canada. **MISC:** Mbr., Advisory Arts Panel of the Canada Council for 1979-81; Mbr., Assessment Task Force for Theatre for the Ontario Arts Council, 1988-91. **COMMENT:** *"I had the good fortune, after a fascinating four years at university studying, doing theatre and making two films, to participate as an actress and writer on* The Farm Show *at Theatre Passe*

Muraille. This led to many opportunities in television and directing and ultimately to the Blyth Festival as an Artistic Director. I love developing new work and I love directing theatre students at George Brown College."

Anawak, Caroline ■ ■ 3 ☼ /
President, KIVALLIQ CONSULTING MANAGEMENT & TRAINING SERVICES LTD. (consulting, research, training, tourism), P.O. Box 155, Rankin Inlet, NW X0C 0G0 (819) 645-2731, FAX 645-2419. Born Toronto 1948. m. Jack Anawak. 12 ch. Jason, Gloria, Sky, Annie, Darcy, Andrea, Stacy, Amanda, Robin, Haley, Abraham, Tommy. EDUC: Algonquin Coll., Diploma (Alcohol & Drug Intervention Counselling) 1992, Diploma (Teacher/Trainer of Adults) 1992, Diploma (Ont. Mgmt Dev. Program) 1993. CAREER: Exec. Officer, Keewatin Reg'l Council, 1982, 1985; Exec. Officer, Keewatin Inuit Association, 1983-84; Hamlet Councillor, Rankin Inlet Hamlet Council, 1983-85; Trustee, Keewatin Health Bd., 1987-96 (3 terms); Trustee, Keewatin Div'l Bd. of Educ., 1988 (1 term); Pres., Kivalliq Consulting, 1989 to date; Training Facilitator, Cross-Cultural Suicide Prevention, Peer Counselling, 1990-96. SELECTED CREDITS: *Cross-Cultural Video on Inuit* (2 videos, 1991). SELECTED PUBLICATIONS: *This Great Heart* (poetry, 1994); *Youth Peer Counselling Manual* (1994); *Caring for Aboriginal Children Manual* (Odawa Native Friendship Centre, 1994); *N.W.T. Suicide Prevention Training Manual* (1991); *Frontec Cross-Cultural Northern Orientation Program Manual* (1991); *The Keewatin Region* (for Gov't of N.W.T., 1987). AFFIL: Non-Partisan Parliamentary Association (VP); Canadian Association for Suicide Prevention (founding mbr.); American Association for Suicidology; Canadian Institute for Child Health (Volunteer Rep.); Keewatin Regional Health Bd. (Trustee); N.W.T. Status of Women Committee (co-founder); Kataujaq Society, women's shelter & day care centre (co-founder). HONS: Operator of the Year, N.W.T. Tourism, 1986. INTERESTS: psychology; facilitating workshops; music; poetry; archaeology; reading; singing; drawing; hand sewing. MISC: participated in the founding of many Aboriginal organizations; foster parent, 14 yrs. (8 children); spouse of M.P. for Nunatsiaq; mbr., 43-mbr. official Cdn delegation to World Women's Conference, Beijing, 1995; licenced N.W.T. Tourism Outfitter. COMMENT: *"Motivator, community activist, speaker, counsellor, speech writer, instructor, youth worker, former N.W.T. Justice of the Peace and Coroner. Originally volunteer, Company of Young Canadians, 1966."*

Andersen, Marguerite, Ph.D. ▯ ⬧ ▤
Writer, Editor, Academic. 110 The Esplanade, Ste. 605, Toronto, ON M5E 1X9 (416) 361-5070, FAX 361-5070. Born Magdeburg, Germany. 3 ch. Christian Nouvet, Marcel Nouvet, Tinnish Andersen. EDUC: La Sorbonne, DES 1953; Freie Universität Berlin, Staatsexamen 1958; Univ. de Montréal, Ph.D. 1964. CAREER: teaching of languages & literatures in Tunisia, Ethiopia, Germany, France, US & Canada, primary & secondary sch. levels & univ.; simultaneous translation in former W. Germany & France; freelance translation in Germany, France & Canada; numerous televised lectures & courses, Univ. of the Air, Canada; Prof., French Studies, Univ. of Guelph, 1973-89; Dept. Chair, French Studies, 1973-80; creative writing seminars in French, in Ontario schools & with writers' groups, 1980 to date; Distinguished Chair in Women's Studies, Mount Saint Vincent Univ., 1986-88; Summer Session Instructor, Women's Studies, Mount Saint Vincent Univ., 1990-93. SELECTED PUBLICATIONS: Ed., *Mother Was Not a Person* (Montreal: Content Publishing and Black Rose, 1972); *De mémoire de femme* (Montréal: Éditions Quinze, 1983); *L'Autrement pareille* (Sudbury: Prise de Parole, 1984); *Courts métrages et instantanés* (Sudbury: Prise de Parole, 1991); Ed., with Christine Klein-Lataud, *Paroles rebelles* (Montréal: Éditions du remue-ménage, 1992); *L'Homme-papier* (Montréal: Éditions du remue-ménage, 1992); *La chambre noire du bonheur* (Montréal: Hurtubise, 1993); *Conversations dans l'interzone*, with Paul Savoie (Sudbury: Prise de Parole, 1994); *La Soupe* (Sudbury: Prise de Parole and Montréal: Triptyque, 1995); chapters in several scholarly books; about 300 articles, book reviews, short stories & poems in scholarly & literary journals in Canada, US, France & Germany. EDIT: Ed. Bd., *Resources for Feminist Research/Documentation sur la recherche féminine* (OISE), 1975 to date. AFFIL: The Writers' Union of Canada; L'union des écrivaines et écrivains québécois; Association des auteures et auteurs de l'Ontario français; Société des écrivains de Toronto; Association des professeurs de français dans les universités et collèges canadiens; PEN International. HONS: Canada France Exchange Fellowship; Prix du *Journal de Montréal*, 1983, for *De mémoire de femme* (novel). INTERESTS: theatre; cinema; social justice; gender equality; art. MISC: Founder of East Word, creative writing workshop for women, 1989; recipient of Canada Council & Ontario Arts Council grants; has served on numerous literary award juries; Gestalt therapist; her play about the German-Canadian painter Christiane Pflug,

Christiane: Stations in a Painters Life, was part of the 1996 gathering, *A Woman's Plays Festival*, in Toronto. COMMENT: *"Marguerite Andersen is a writer who has fed herself and her children by teaching French at all levels, from kindergarten to university and by translating. She writes mostly in French. She is also a teacher of creative writing and has worked with groups of all ages."*

Anderson, Dianne E., M.H.Sc.,C.H.E. ⊕
Vice-President, NORTH YORK GENERAL HOSPITAL, 4001 Leslie St., North York, ON M2K 1E1 (416) 756-1040, ext. 8005, FAX 756-1844. President, ONTARIO NURSING HOME ASSOCIATION. Born Brantford, Ont. 1947. d. 2 ch. Joy C., Jill K. EDUC: Univ. of Guelph, B.H.Sc.(Foods & Nutrition) 1970; St. Michael's Hospital, Registered Professional Dietitian 1971; Univ. of Toronto, M.H.Sc.(Health Admin.) 1984. CAREER: Admin., Bestview Health Care Centre, 1984-87; Admin., Seniors Health Centre, North York General Hospital, 1987-89; VP, 1989 to date. AFFIL: Canadian Coll. of Health Service Executives (C.H.E.); Ontario Nursing Home Association (Pres.); Metropolitan Toronto District Health Council (Long Term Care Steering Committee; Wellness for Seniors Task Force; Coord. of Psychogeriatric Svcs: Mental Health & Long Term Care Interface 1996); Multicultural Alliance for Seniors & Aging (Dir. 1991-93); The Laughlen Centre (Dir. 1991-93; Nomination Committee 1993-95; V-Chair 1993-95; Chair, Building Committee 1994-95). HONS: Garland Commercial Ranges Scholarship, 1970; The Harshmann Foundation Scholarship, 1982; The W.D. College Award, 1982. MISC: guest speaker & panelist. COMMENT: *"I am committed to promoting a positive living environment for residents (patients) and working environment for staff through management excellence. This year, as President of the Ontario Nursing Home Association and in my other volunteer positions, I have the opportunity to advocate on behalf of seniors living in the community and institutional settings."*

Anderson, Doris H., B.A.,LL.D. 🕮 ▢ ⟨⟨
Chancellor, UNIVERSITY OF PRINCE EDWARD ISLAND. Born Calgary 1921. w. David A. Anderson. 3 ch. Peter, Stephen, Mitchell. EDUC: Univ. of Alberta, B.A. 1945. CAREER: Ed. Asst., *Star Weekly*, 1945; Advtg Dept., Eaton's. 1946-49; Asst. Ed., *Chatelaine*, Maclean-Hunter Limited, 1951-54; Assoc. Ed., 1954-55; Mng Ed., 1955-58; Ed., 1958-77; Pres., Advisory Council on the Status of Women, 1978-81; Pres., National Action Committee on Status of Women, 1982-84; Colum-

nist, *The Toronto Star*, 1982-92; Chancellor, Univ. of Prince Edward Island, 1992-96. SELECTED PUBLICATIONS: *Two Women* (1978); *Rough Layout* (1981); *Affairs of State* (1988); *The Unfinished Revolution*, nonfiction (1991); *Rebel Daughter* (1996). AFFIL: Harbourfront, Toronto (Bd.); National Action Committee on Status of Women (Trust Foundation Bd.); Women's Foundation of Canada (Trustee); Asean Group, CIDA (Advisor). HONS: B'nai Brith Scholarship, 1942; Centennial Medal, 1967; Officer, Order of Canada, 1974; News Hall of Fame, Press Club, 1981; City of Toronto Award, 1981; Woman of Distinction, YWCA, 1982; Mediawatch Award, 1990; Person's Award, 1991; Hall of Fame, Univ. of Alberta, 1993; Distinguished Alumni Award, Univ. of Alberta, 1994; Order of Ontario, 1995; LL.D.(Hon.), Univ. of Alberta, 1974; LL.D.(Hon.), Conestoga Univ., 1981; LL.D.(Hon.), Univ. of Dalhousie, 1984; LL.D. (Hon.), Ryerson Polytechnic Univ., 1987; LL.D.(Hon.), Concordia Univ., 1990; LL.D.(Hon.), Univ. of Waterloo, 1992; LL.D. (Hon.), Mount St. Vincent Univ., 1992. INTERESTS: literature; theatre; ballet; Cdn unity; the environment. MISC: Drummond Lecture, Queen's Univ., 1975; Newlove Lecture, Univ. of Windsor, 1981; Eminent Scholar, Grad. Sch. of Journalism, Univ. of Western Ontario, 1985; Lecturer, Goethe Institute, Montreal, 1990. COMMENT: *"My main work has been to advance the career of women, first through* Chatelaine, *then as president of the government's advisory council on women. Then as president of the volunteer lobby group–The National Action Committee on the Status of Women. As well, in my three novels and one non-fiction book, I have endeavoured to advance women. In my other writing I've tackled national unity, politics, the environment, etc."*

Anderson, Gail S., B.Sc.,M.P.M., Ph.D. ❀ ⟨⟨ 🜛 ♂
Assistant Professor, Department of Biological Sciences, SIMON FRASER UNIVERSITY, Burnaby, BC V5A 1S6 (604) 291-3512, FAX (604) 291-3496, EMAIL ganderso@sfu.ca. Born Yorkshire, UK 1961. m. Greg St. Hilaire. EDUC: Manchester Univ., B.Sc.(Zoology) 1983; Simon Fraser Univ., Master of Pest Mgmt 1986, Ph.D.(Medical & Veterinary Entomology) 1992. CAREER: Teaching Asst., Animal Physiology, Simon Fraser Univ., 1986-90; Research Asst., determining causal allergen in *Culicoides* spp. responsible for *Culicoides* Hypersensitivity, for Dr. Norbert Haunerland, Simon Fraser Univ., 1991; Forensic Entomology Consultant, 1988 to date; Asst. Prof., Forensic Entomology, Simon Fraser Univ., 1992 to date. SELECTED

PUBLICATIONS: "A Population Study of *Culicoides obsoletus Meigen* (Diptera: Ceratopogonidae) & other *Culicoides* species in the Fraser Valley of British Columbia," with P. Belton (*Canadian Entomologist* 125 1993); "The use of insects in death investigations: an analysis of forensic entomology cases in British Columbia over a five year period," (*Canadian Society of Forensic Science Journal*, 28(4): 277-292 1995); "Initial observations on insect succession on carrion in British Columbia," (with S.L. VanLaerhoven, *Journal of Forensic Science*, 41(4) 613-621 1996); "Hyposensitization of horses in British Columbia affected by *Culicoides* Hypersensitivity ("sweet itch")," (with P. Belton, E. Jahren, H. Lang and N. Kleider, *Medical Entomologist*, 33(3) 458-466 1996); a series of more than 80 consultant reports entitled, "The Rearing, Development and Identification of Insects Associated with Human Remains and Estimation of Elapsed Time Since Death," for B.C. Coroner's Service & for other provinces in cases of homicide, suicide & accidental death, 1988 to date; numerous addresses to scientific & professional societies. **AFFIL:** B.C. Entomological Society (Pres.-Elect); American Academy of Forensic Sciences; American Board of Forensic Entomologists (Dir.); Canadian Society of Forensic Sciences; Entomological Society of America; Canadian Identification Society; Society of Vector Ecologists; Pacific Northwest Forensic Study Group. **HONS:** Outstanding Alumni Award for Academic Achievement, Simon Fraser Univ., 1995; Canadian Wild Horse Society Award, 1985. **INTERESTS:** horseback riding; wine making; animals; wildlife. **MISC:** featured in *The Nature of Things* "Postmortem" (1991), *Forbidden Places*, Discovery Channel, 1995, *WWF*, Spring 1995; numerous presentations, speeches & workshops given; invited to instruct on an ongoing basis for Police Academy, Justice Institute of B.C., for Canadian Police Coll., & for others; Bd. Mbr. for establishing a forensic entomology certificate program, American Board of Forensic Entomology, through AAFS; listed in *Canadian Who's Who*; numerous TV & radio interviews; expert witness in homicide cases. **COMMENT:** *"I am Canada's first full-time forensic entomologist. I am jointly funded by the B.C. Coroner's Service, R.C.M.P. and SFU. I handle forensic cases, supervise graduate students and teach at the graduate and undergraduate level."*

Anderson, Isabel B., B.A.,M.A. ■ $ ✎ 🎓
President and Chief Executive Officer, AAL INFOSERVE, 1212 Colony St., Saskatoon, SK S7N 0S6 (306) 653-5352, FAX 975-1392. Born Unity, Sask. 1939. m. Frederick F. Langford. 3 ch. **EDUC:** Univ. of Saskatchewan, B.A.(Math.) 1960, B.A.(Econ.) 1961, M.A.(Econ.) 1963; Queen's Univ., Doctoral Studies (abd), Econ., 1963-72; Troisième Niveau, Centre Universitaire d'Études Françaises, Univ. de Domaine, Grenoble, France, 1981. **CAREER:** Researcher, Economic Council of Canada, 1964-66; Visiting Asst. Prof. of Econ., Univ. of Victoria, 1972-73; Cdn NGO Delegation, United Nations Conference on Trade & Dev., Nairobi, Kenya, 1976; Cdn Delegation, U.N. Conference on Science & Technology, Vienna, Austria, 1979; Trade Commissioner, Panel to conduct public hearings on the Canada-U.S. bilateral trade negotiations, Prov. of Sask., 1986; Commentator, Editorialist, Freelance Writer, radio & TV, on econ. policy & change for more than 25 yrs.; Prof., Econ., Univ. of Saskatchewan, 1968-93; Chair & Co-Chair, Int'l Studies Program, Coll. of Arts & Sciences, Univ. of Saskatchewan, 1989-93; Pres. & Research Dir., AAL Infoserve, Info. Broker, 1993 to date. **SELECTED PUBLICATIONS:** "Policy Coordination and Wider Powers for the Federal Government on Matters of Economic Policy," in *Economic Union and Constitutional Change* (Calgary; Canada West Foundation, 1992); "An Overview of Canada's Economy" (*Current History* March 1988); various discussion papers; numerous presentations to conferences. **DIRECTOR:** Potash Corporation of Saskatchewan, Inc. **AFFIL:** Western Economic Association; Canadian Economics Association; International Association for Research on Income & Wealth; Association of Canadian Studies of Australia & New Zealand; International Association of Canadian Studies; American Economic Association (Committee on the Status of Women in the Economics Profession); Canadian Association on the Status of Women in the Economics Profession; Association of Feminist Economics; Saskatoon Nutana Rotary (Pres. 1996-97); Saskatoon Free-Net Association Inc. (Dir.); 25th Street Theatre, Saskatoon (Dir). **INTERESTS:** skiing; sailing; reading; writing; lively discussion on a wide range of issues. **MISC:** listed in *Canadian Who's Who*, *Who's Who in Canadian Business*, *The Dictionary of International Biography*, *The International Who's Who of Contemporary Achievement*, *The International Who's Who of Professional and Business Women*, & *The World Who's Who of Women*. **COMMENT:** *"Endeavours: to participate honestly and to the best of my ability and education in making our democratic society alive and well. Achievements: a bit of success."*

Anderson, Janice P., B.A.,M.B.A.,C.M.A. $
Strategy and Business Development Vice-Presi-

dent. 211 Mt. Airy Rd., Basking Ridge, NJ 07920 (908) 953-2700, FAX 953-4001. Born Toronto. **EDUC:** Univ. of Toronto, B.A.(Commerce) 1984; York Univ., M.B.A.(Fin. & Strategy) 1988. **CAREER:** Product Mgr, Nat'l Mktg Rep. & Sales Support Analyst, Mohawk Data Sciences Canada Ltd., 1982-86; Mgr, Computer Product Mktg, AT&T Canada Inc., 1986-87; Dir./Mgr, Corp. Planning & Dev., 1987-90; VP, Hum. Res. & Corp. Dev., 1990-91; VP & Gen. Mgr, 1991-94; VP, Corp. Dev., AT&T Corp., 1994 to date. **AFFIL:** Society of Management Accountants (Certified Management Accountant); National Ballet Sch. (Patron); The Planning Forum; Young Presidents' Organization; Canadian Opera Company (Dir.); Information Technology Association of Canada (Dir.); Ryerson Polytechnic Univ. (V-Chair, Bd. of Gov.). **HONS:** Entrance Award, Univ. of Toronto, 1981; W. Mercer Scholarship, York Univ., 1988; Alumni Award for Outstanding Progress & Achievement, York Univ. Fac. of Admin. Studies, 1993; Cdn Recipient, 'Personalities of the Future' worldwide program, Gov't of France, 1994. **INTERESTS:** cycling; running; music; skiing; reading; French.

Anderson, Joan, B.A. ■■ ⌐ ○

Executive Director, University Relations, UNIVERSITY OF WINNIPEG, 515 Portage Ave., Winnipeg, MB R3B 2E9 (604) 786-9266, FAX 783-8983, EMAIL anderson@wesley.uwinnipeg.ca. Born Winnipeg 1944. m. Robert C. 2 ch. Robynne, Christopher. **EDUC:** Manitoba Teachers' Coll., Permanent Certificate 1962; Univ. of Winnipeg, B.A.(Pol. Sci./Admin. Studies) 1983. **CAREER:** Teacher, Man. public schools, 1962-68; Coord., Events & Conferences, Univ. of Winnipeg, 1983-87; Dir., Public Rel'ns, 1987-91; Exec. Dir., Univ. Rel'ns, 1991 to date. **VOLUNTEER CAREER:** Canadian Cancer Society, Nat'l: Co-Chair, Planning Committee, Nat'l Forum on Prostate Cancer, 1995-96; Bd. of Dir., 1985-93; Nat'l VP, 1988-92; Co-Chair, Women & Cancer Task Force, 1993; Chair, Joint Task Force on Int'l Affairs, 1993; Chair, Joint Committee on Int'l Affairs, 1992-93; Chair, Joint Working Group on Nat'l Archives, 1992-93; mbr., Exec. Committee, 1985-92. Canadian Cancer Society, Man. Div.: Chair, Volunteer Dev. Committee, 1993 to date; mbr., Bd. of Dir., 1977-84. **AFFIL:** Canadian Council for the Advancement and Support of Education (mbr. 1987 to date; Bd. of Dir. 1991-93); Winnipeg Chamber of Commerce (Committee on Educ. 1996 to date); Univ. of Winnipeg (Alumni Association 1983 to date); Winnipeg Real Estate Board (Citizen of the Year Selection Committee 1996 to date); Premier's Volunteer Award Selection Committee

(mbr. 1994-95); Public Affairs Council on Education (mbr. 1987-92; Pres. 1991-92; Exec. Committee 1987-92); Manitoba Cancer Research and Treatment Foundation (Bd. of Dir. 1988-91); Prairie Theatre Exchange (Bd. of Dir. 1987-89). **HONS:** Special Award for Volunteers, Canadian Cancer Society; Atchison Award for community svc., Univ. of Winnipeg; Canada Volunteer Award (Certificate of Honour), Gov't of Canada; Canada 125 Medal. **INTERESTS:** reading, esp. mysteries & cookbooks; cooking; travel; theatre. **COMMENT:** *"My professional and volunteer interests are focused on education and health with a particular interest in governance, volunteer development and advocacy."*

Anderson, Margaret Seguin, B.A.,M.A., Ph.D. ⌐ 📚 🗋

Northwest Regional Coordinator, UNIVERSITY OF NORTHERN BRITISH COLUMBIA, 100 McBride St., Prince Rupert, BC V8J 3E8 (604) 624-2862, FAX 624-9703. Born St. Clair, Mich. 1945. m. Clarence Anderson. 3 ch. Ralph Seguin, Michael Seguin, Tammy Blumhagen. **EDUC:** Univ. of Michigan, B.A.(Anthropology) 1967, M.A.(Linguistics) 1968, Ph.D.(Linguistics) 1977. **CAREER:** Lecturer, Asst. Prof., Assoc. Prof., Chair, Dept. of Anthropology, Univ. of Western Ontario, 1973-92; Prof., Coord. (First Nations Studies), Chair (First Nations Studies), Univ. of Northern British Columbia, 1992 to date; Dir. of First Nations Program, 1993-94; N.W. Reg'l Coord., 1994 to date. **SELECTED PUBLICATIONS:** *Interpretive Contexts for Traditional and Modern Coast Tsimshian Feasts* (Ottawa: Mercury Series, National Museum of Man, 1985); *The Tsimshian: Images of the Past, Views of the Present* (UBC Press, 1984; pbk. 1993); "The Tsimshian," *Handbook of North American Indians: Northwest Coast Volume,* with Marjorie Halpin, Ed. W. Suttles (Washington, D.C.: Smithsonian Institute, 1990); "Memories and Moments: Conversations and Re-collections with Tammy Blumhagen" (*BC Studies,* No. 104, Winter 1994). **EDIT:** *Culture,* Journal of Canadian Anthropology Society/Société Canadienne d'anthropologie, 1990-94; Ed. Bd., *B.C. Studies.* **AFFIL:** Open Learning Agency of British Columbia (External Mbr., Academic Council); Wilp Wilxo'oskwhl Nisga'a (Community Advisory Bd.); Canadian Anthropology Society; Society for the Study of Indigenous Languages of the Americas; Society for Applied Anthropology. **HONS:** Canada 125 Medal. **COMMENT:** *"The opportunity to participate in shaping a new university in the region in which I have done research for two decades has been exciting. Facilitating development of*

UNBC's courses in the languages and cultures of the Nisga'a, Tsimshian and Haisla through partnership with the First Nations groups and dedicated scholars has been the most satisfying achievement of my career."

Andreachuk, Lori, QC,B.A., LL.B. ■ ⚖
Partner, ANDREACHUK HARVIE MACLENNAN, Lethbridge, AB T1J 4J7 (403) 380-4000, FAX 320-6320. Born Lethbridge, Alta. 1953. s. EDUC: Univ. of Lethbridge, B.A. 1974; Univ. of Alberta, LL.B. 1977; Canadian Family Mediation Society & Alberta Family Mediation Society, Certified Family & Divorce Mediator, 1987; Haynes Mediation Training Institute, N.Y., Certified Mediator 1987. BAR: Alberta, 1979; Queen's Counsel, Alberta 1992. CAREER: Part-time Receptionist, Dr. W.N. Myers, Orthopedic Surgeon, Lethbridge, 1969-71; Store-Front Lawyer, Lethbridge Legal Guidance Services, Alberta Law Foundation, 1974-77; Articled Student, Paterson North, Lethbridge, 1977-78; Assoc. Lawyer, 1978-80; Ptnr, 1980-91; Ptnr, North Petersen Lint Andreachuk, Lethbridge (now Andreachuk Harvie MacLennan), 1991 to date. SELECTED PUBLICATIONS: co-authored recommendations on behalf of the Advisory Council on Women's Issues to the Gov't of Alberta on daycare, midwifery, abortion, constitutional issues & many other topics of importance to Alberta women; authored recommendations to the Alberta Gov't on the Maintenance Enforcement Program. DIRECTOR: Fiorino Homes Ltd.; Bolero Investments Ltd. AFFIL: Canadian Bar Association; Alberta Bar Association; Lethbridge Bar Association; Family Law Subsection, Canadian Bar Association; Canadian Family Mediation Society; Alberta Family Mediation Society; American Academy of Family Mediators; Business & Professional Women's Club; Univ. of Lethbridge Foundation; United Way (Bd. Mbr.); Society for the Prevention of Child Abuse & Neglect; Univ. of Lethbridge (President's Advisory Council, Bd. of Trustees); Southern Alberta Ethnic Association. HONS: numerous scholarships & academic awards; Best All-Around Student, Lethbridge Collegiate Institute, 1971; Chief Justice Louis Sherman Turcotte Award, Pre-Law, Univ. of Lethbridge, 1973; YWCA Woman of the Year, 1991. INTERESTS: reading; cooking; golf; women's issues; sports. MISC: Commissioner, Alberta Human Rights Commission, 1995 to date; numerous keynote speaker engagements in Alberta & Canada, primarily in family law, women's rights, & women's issues. COMMENT: *"Practice of law in the areas of family law, mediation, arbitration, civil litigation."*

Andrew, Caroline, B.A.,M.A.,Ph.D. ⚲
Chair, Department of Political Science, UNIVERSITY OF OTTAWA, 75 Laurier Ave. E., Ottawa, ON K1N 6N5 (613) 562-5865, FAX 562-5106. Born Toronto 1942. m. Jean-Paul St.-Amand. 2 ch. Anne-Bridget, Louise. EDUC: Univ. of British Columbia, B.A.(Pol. Sci.) 1964; Univ. Laval, M.A.(Pol. Sci.) 1966; Univ. of Toronto, Ph.D.(Pol. Sci.) 1975. CAREER: Lecturer, Dept. of Pol. Sci., Univ. of Ottawa, 1971-75; Asst. Prof., 1975-78; Assoc. Prof., 1978-89; Prof., 1989 to date. SELECTED PUBLICATIONS: "Canada Infrastructure Works: Between 'Picks and Shovels' and the Infrastructure Highway," with Jeff Morrison, *How Ottawa Spends 1995-96* (Carleton University Press, 1995); "Getting Women's Issues on the Municipal Agenda: Violence Against Women," *Gender in Urban Research* by Judith A. Garber & Robyne S. Turner (Sage Publications, 1995); "Recasting Political Analysis for Canadian Cities," *Urban Lives* by Vered Amit-Talai & Henri Lustiger-Thaler (McClelland & Stewart, 1994); "The Feminist City," *Political Arrangements: Power and the City*, ed. Henri Lustiger-Thaler (Black Rose Books, 1992); numerous other publications. AFFIL: Women's Action Centre Against Violence (Ottawa-Carleton) (Pres., Bd. of Dir.); Lowertown Resource Centre (Bd. of Dir.); Canadian Research Institute for the Advancement of Women (CRIAW) (Past Pres.). HONS: Médaille du Lieutenant-Gouverneur, Fac. des Sciences sociales, Univ. Laval, 1966; Bourse de la banque de la Nouvelle-écosse, 1965-66. COMMENT: *"Professor of political science specializing in the study of urban politics, and women and politics. Active in community activities, particularly relating to women's issues and local development in Ottawa-Carleton."*

Andrew, Judith, B.Comm.,M.B.A. ⚘ Ⓢ ♦
Director, Provincial Policy, CANADIAN FEDERATION OF INDEPENDENT BUSINESS. m. David Andrew. 3 ch. Matthew, Jocelyn, Melissa. EDUC: Univ. of Toronto, B.Comm. 1979; York Univ./Laval Univ., M.B.A. 1982; Canadian Securities Course 1984. CAREER: Admin. Officer, Toronto-Dominion Bank, 1979-80; Asst. Dir. of Research/Assoc. Dir. of Research, Canadian Federation of Independent Business, 1982-84; Dir. of Prov. Affairs, 1985-89; Dir. of Prov. Policy, 1989 to date. AFFIL: Employers' Council on Workers' Compensation (V-Chair); Ontario Workplace Health & Safety Agency (Employer Mbr., Bd. of Dir. 1990-92); Workplace Health & Safety Review Panel; Toronto-Eglinton Rotary Club (first female mbr.); Toronto Alumnae Chapter of Delta Delta Delta (Past Pres.); House Corporation (Past Pres.).

MISC: served on Attorney Gen. Ian Scott's advisory committee on class actions, 1989-90; various advisory committees to successive Ont. Ministers of Consumer & Commercial Relations concerning revisions to consumer protection legislation, 1987-92; appointed to the Ont. Task Force on Hours of Work & Overtime by the Hon. William Wyre, Min. of Labour, 1986-87.

Andrew, Maureen, M.D. ☞ ⊕
Professor of Pediatrics, CHILDREN'S HOSPITAL AT CHEDOKE-MCMASTER, Hamilton Civic Hospitals Research Centre, Henderson General Division, 711 Concession St., Hamilton, ON L8V 1C3 (905) 527-2299, ext. 3770, FAX 575-2646. Prof. of Pediatrics (part-time), HOSPITAL FOR SICK CHILDREN. Born Arvida, Que. 1952. m. Dr. Hugh O'Brodovich. 2 ch. EDUC: Univ. of Manitoba, M.D. 1976. CAREER: Pediatric Intern, Children's Hospital, Univ. of Manitoba, 1976-77; Pediatric Resident, 1977-78; Pediatric Hematology Fellow, New York Univ. Medical Center, 1978-80; Pediatric Hematology Lecturer, 1981; Asst. Prof. of Pediatrics, McMaster Univ., 1981-86; Dir. of the Coagulation Lab., McMaster Univ. Medical Centre, 1985-95; cross-appointment to Lab. Medicine, McMaster Univ., 1985-95; Assoc. Prof. of Pediatrics, 1986-91; part-time appointment to The Hospital for Sick Children, Toronto, 1990 to date; Prof. of Pediatrics, McMaster Univ., 1991 to date. SELECTED PUBLICATIONS: "The Development of the Human Coagulation System in the Fullterm Infant" (*Blood* 70 1987) with others; "Development of the Coagulation System in the Healthy Premature Infant" (*Blood* 72 1988) with others; "An Anticoagulant Dermatan Sulphate Proteoglycan Circulates in the Pregnant Woman and Her Fetus" (*Journal of Clinical Investigation* 89(1) 1992) with others; "Report of Scientific and Standardization Subcommittee on Neonatal Hemostasis Diagnosis and Treatment of Neonatal Thrombosis" (*Thrombosis and Haemostasis* 67(3) 1992) with B. Schmidt; "Maturation of the Hemostatic System During Childhood" (*Blood* 80(8) 1992) with others; various book chapters & review articles. AFFIL: Canadian Children's Thrombophilia Program (Dir.); Canadian Children's Thrombophilia Society (Pres.); International Society for Thrombosis & Haemostasis (Chair, Perinatal Hemostasis Subcommittee); Society for Pediatric Research (Sec.-Treas.); Heart & Stroke Foundation of Canada (Health Sciences Policy Council); American Heart Association; Canadian Pediatric Society; Canadian Society for Clinical Investigation; American Society of Hematology; American Academy of Pediatrics; American Federation for Clinical Research; Royal Coll. of Physicians & Surgeons of Canada. HONS: Canadian Heart Foundation Scholarship, 1983-89; Young Investigator Award, American Academy of Pediatrics, 1985; Heart & Stroke Foundation of Ontario–Career Investigator, 1989 to date; Medical Research Council–Scientist Award, 1989 (awarded & declined); PAIRO Excellence in Clinical Teaching Award, 1991. MISC: numerous invited presentations at int'l meetings; Program Reviewer, Moderator & Session Chair at various int'l meetings; recipient of numerous grants from MRC, Heart & Stroke Foundation, Canadian Red Cross Society & others.

Andrews, Ann, C.A.E. ✆ ○ ⊕
Executive Director, CANADIAN ANAESTHETISTS' SOCIETY, 1 Eglinton Ave. E., Ste. 208, Toronto, ON M4P 3A1 (416) 480-0602, FAX 480-0320. Born Bangor, Wales. s. EDUC: Canadian Society of Association Executives, C.A.E. (Certified Association Exec.) 1993. CAREER: customer svc., K.L.M. Royal Dutch Airlines, 1974-82; corp. sales, Four Seasons Hotels, 1982-84; Meeting Planner, Canadian Real Estate Association, 1985-86; Exec. Dir., Canadian Anaesthetists' Society, 1987 to date. INTERESTS: creating in the kitchen. COMMENT: *"A challenge-oriented, self-motivating individual with a great sense of humour. A leader who understands teamwork. A proven success in the non-profit world."*

Andrews, Jan, B.A.,M.A. $ ✿ ♥
Partner, ANDREWS-CAYLEY ENTERPRISES, 501 Edison Ave., Ottawa, ON K2A 1V3 (613) 725-9119, FAX 728-3872. Born Shoreham-By-Sea ,Sussex ,UK 1942. d. 2 ch. Miriam Andrews, Kieran Andrews. EDUC: Univ. of Reading, B.A.(English & Latin) 1963; Univ. of Saskatchewan, M.A.(English) 1969. CAREER: Dept. of Sec. of State, Gov't of Canada, 1972-76; children's writer, readings across the country, 1973 to date; Arts Administrator, various exhibitions & festivals, 1985-90; Ptnr, Andrews-Cayley Enterprises, 1987 to date; Storyteller, appeared at festivals in Ottawa, Toronto, Fredericton, Whitehorse, Winnipeg, Saskatoon, Edmonton, 1990 to date. SELECTED CREDITS: *Tales of Courage and Kindness* (tape) (1992); Script, *Coming of Age*, Sec. of State (Multiculturalism) dramatic montage (1985); *Heart/Bones* (storytelling & dance), 1996; Inanna, *Queen of Heaven & Earth* (storytelling), 1996. SELECTED PUBLICATIONS: *Fresh Fish...And Chips* (Women's Press, 1973); *Ella, An Elephant, Un Elephant* (Tundra Books, 1976); *Very Last First Time* (Groundwood Books, 1985); *The Auction*

(Groundwood Books, 1990); *Pumpkin Time* (Groundwood Books, 1990); Ed., *The Dancing Sun*, multicultural children's anthology (Press Porcepic, 1981); Contributor, *Canadian Family Tree* (Ottawa: Sec. of State (Multiculturalism), 1979); various papers for the Sec. of State (Multiculturalism); children's stories in major language arts publications by Gage, Ginn and Nelson; children's stories in various annuals & magazines. **AFFIL:** MASC-Multicultural Arts for Schools & Communities (Co-founder 1989; Bd. of Dir.); Storytellers of Canada/Raconteurs du Canada (Founding Mbr.); CANSCAIP; Writers' Union of Canada; Ottawa Storytellers; Toronto Sch. of Storytellers. **HONS:** Shortlist, Ruth Schwartz Award (*Very Last First Time*), 1986; Shortlist, Washington State Children's Picture Book Award (*Very Last First Time*), 1985; Shortlist, Gov. General's Award for Children's Literature (*The Auction*), 1990. **INTERESTS:** cross-country skiing; canoeing; wilderness. **MISC:** Jury mbr. for Canada Council; recipient of various grants from Canada Council, Ontario Arts Council & others; leads wilderness canoe trips; leads adult workshops in spiritual development through finding voice as teller & writer. **COMMENT:** *"My passion lies in stories of depth and power. I am concerned with the way oral tradition and literature nourish and foster growth. Everything I do is focused in this direction."*

Andrews, Maxine $

Project Manager, Residential Construction, V.V. DE MARCO PROPERTIES LIMITED, 7300 Warden Ave., Ste. 501, Markham, ON L3R 9Z6. Born Toronto 1957. m. Danny Alushi. **EDUC:** Toronto Construction Association, Advanced Estimation & Blue Print Reading 1984; Ministry of Housing, 'Part 9' Educational Program for Mun. Building Inspectors 1993. **CAREER:** Administrator, Pool World Accessories Ltd., 1975-79; Contracts Mgr, V.V. DeMarco Properties Ltd., 1979-85; Proj. Coord., Wycliffe Homes, 1986-87; Proj. Mgr, Packard Homes, 1985-86; Proj. Coord., Tridel, 1989-91; Proj. Mgr, Residential Construction, V.V. DeMarco Properties Ltd., 1992 to date. **INTERESTS:** downhill skiing; renovating; horseback riding. **COMMENT:** *"Commenced career in construction directly from high school. On-job training through dedication and interest in field provided pathway to present position. Have built industrial/commercial buildings, high-rise condominiums and low-rise residential projects."*

Ang, Roxanne S.L. (A)CTC,ITC,DMATP, M.Ed. ■■ $

National President, CANADIAN INSTITUTES OF TRAVEL COUNSELLORS, 50 Burnhamthorpe Rd. W., Ste. 401, Mississauga, ON L5B 3C2 (905) 281-1221, FAX 281-1254. Managing Director, GLOBAL EDUCATION IN TOURISM LTD. (DBA TOURISM TRAINING INSTITUTE). Born Philippines. 2 ch. Nathan, Cassandra. **EDUC:** Univ. of California, Los Angeles, B.A.(Communication Studies, cum laude) 1974; Ministry of Educ., Prov. of B.C., Prov. Instructor's Diploma 1986; Univ. of British Columbia, M.Ed.(Adult Educ.) 1991; Canadian Institute of Travel Counsellors, Certified Travel Counsellor (highest mark in W. Canada) 1983; International Air Transport Association, Int'l Travel Consultant 1991; ACTA-CITC Canadian Educational Standards System, ACCESS Certified Travel Consultant 1992; Association of Tourism Professionals, Distinguished Mbr. designation 1992. **CAREER:** Jr. travel agent to Mgr, Traders Travel Ltd., 1975-82; Mgr, Asian Express Ltd., 1979-82; Instructor to Educ. Mgr, Canadian Travel Sch., 1982-89; Pavilion Guide, Telecom Canada, Expo 86; Customer Sales & Svc. Rep., Air Canada, 1987; Outside Sales Rep., Amica Travel, 1989 to date; contract work, Marlin Travel/Uniglobe Travel/Canadian Airlines, 1989 to date; Tourism Training Institute, 1989 to date; Global Education in Tourism Ltd., 1989 to date. **SELECTED PUBLICATIONS:** *Airline Tariff and Ticketing*, Domestic & Int'l Volumes (Canadian Institute of Travel Counsellors - Ont., 1st printing 1992, currently on 3rd printing). **DIRECTOR:** Maple Vines Corp. **AFFIL:** Pacific Rim Institute of Tourism (Bd. mbr.-Ministerial appt.); ACTA-CITC Canadian Educational Standards System (Pres., Bd. of Dir.); Association of Tourism Professionals (founding mbr.); Canadian Tour Guide Association of B.C. (founding mbr.); St. Anthony's Youth Choir (Dir.); National Association of Career Colleges; Alliance of Canadian Travel Associations; Private Career Training Association. **INTERESTS:** playing the organ/keyboard; live theatre; watersports. **MISC:** guest speaker, seminar presenter, various nat'l & int'l industry conferences. **COMMENT:** *"I have always embraced the philosophy of striving to be the best and encouraging others to do the same and my vehicle to achieving this is through education. Through Tourism Training Institute, I am able to combine my two passions—travel and education. The achievement that I prize the most is being able to nurture the musical talents of my children. Nathan is an accomplished organist and has won numerous prizes in interprovincial competitions. Cassandra is also talented as a harpist and has been a guest artist of the Vancouver Symphony Orchestra's Kids Concert series. In all that I do, whether with family or students, I* *try to share my values of family, faith, self-discipline and a desire to succeed."*

Angelico, Irene, B.A. ■ 📺 🎭 📖

Chief Executive Officer, DLI PRODUCTIONS, 4879 Ave. DuParc, Montreal, QC H2V 4E7 (514) 227-2220, FAX 272-6837. Born Munich, Germany 1946. m. Abbey Neidik. 1 ch. Toben Neidik. EDUC: Concordia Univ., B.A.(Hons., Humanities of Sci.) 1974. CAREER: CEO, DLI Productions. SELECTED CREDITS: Co-Prod./Co-Dir., *Dark Lullabies*; Prod., *Entre Solitudes*; Prod., *Mile Zero: The Sage Tour*; Prod., *Snowcat.*; Dir., *The Big Fizz*; Prod., *The Endtime*. SELECTED PUBLICATIONS: Ed. & Co-Publisher, *The Aftermath*. AFFIL: Canadian Independent Film Caucus (Founding Chair); Academy of Canadian Cinema & Television; Holocaust Memorial Committee. HONS: First Prize, Most Socially-Politically Engaging Film, Mannheim; First Prize, Most Memorable Film, Tokyo; First Prize, Ecumenical Award, Mannheim; Blue Ribbon, American Film Festival; numerous other int'l film awards. INTERESTS: family & friends; travel; art; dance; reading; film. COMMENT: *"I value first my relationships with family and friends, which I constantly struggle to keep in some balance with my work. I hope to make the world a little better with my films, touch the hearts and minds of those who see them, and have some fun in the process."*

Angus, Elisabeth, B.A.,M.,A., M.B.A. $ ⚛ 📺

Executive Vice-President, ANGUS TELEMANAGEMENT GROUP INC., 8 Old Kingston Rd., Ajax, ON L1T 2Z4 (905) 686-5050, ext. 221, FAX 686-2655, EMAIL lisangus@angustel.ca. Vice-President, ANGUS DORTMANS ASSOCIATES, 20 Bay St., Ste. 1205,Toronto, ON M5J 2N8. Co-Editor, *TELEMANAGEMENT* MAGAZINE. Born Rimbey, Alta. 1946. m. Ian Cole Angus. 2 ch. Jessica Margaret, Amanda Katherine. EDUC: Carleton Univ., B.A.(Soc.) 1968; York Univ., M.A.(Psych.) 1978, M.B.A.(Mktg Analysis) 1988. CAREER: Royal Ottawa Hospital, 1968-70; Dellcrest Children's Centre, 1970-71; Child & Adolescent Unit, Lakeshore Psychiatric Hospital, 1971-75; CM Hincks Treatment Centre, 1977-78; Co-Founder, Co-Owner & Exec. VP, Angus TeleManagement Group Inc., 1980 to date; Co-Ed., *TELEMANAGEMENT*. SELECTED PUBLICATIONS: *Feasibility of a Metropolitan Toronto Telecom Network: Examining Metro Toronto's Network Needs and Options* (study for Metropolitan Toronto, 1993); *Telecommunications and Business Competitiveness in Canada and the U.S.* (study for Industry Canada, 1992); *A Comparison of Interexchange Services in Canada and the U.S.* (study for Unitel, 1991); *The Cost of Business Telephone Service in Canada and the USA* (study for Unitel, 1991); "The Connected Municipality: Telecom Infrastructure for Economic Development" (*Economic Development Journal of Ontario*, 1994); *Canada's Information Highway: Services, Access and Affordability* (a policy study conducted jointly with Decima Research for Industry Canada, 1994) ; "Long Distance Alternatives in Canada," with Ian Angus (Telemanagement Press, 1994); *Access, Affordability and Universal Service on the Canadian Information Highway*, co-author (a discussion paper issued by the Fed. Info. Highway Advisory Council, Jan. 1995); *Canadian Telecom in Transition*, co-author (1995); "Beyond the Copper Monopoly: Alternatives for Local Telecom Networks," *The Future of Telecommunications Policy in Canada*, ed. G. Globerman, W. Stanbury & T. Wilson (1995); "Canadian Telecom in Transition - And More to Come," *Perspectives on the New Economics and Regulation of Telecommunications*, ed. W.T. Stanbury (1996). DIRECTOR: Angus TeleManagement Group Inc.; Angus Dortmans Associates Inc. AFFIL: Canadian Telecommunications Consultants Association (Past Pres.); International Society of Telecommunications Consultants: Canadian Women in Communications; Ryerson Polytechnic Univ. (Advisory Bd., Admin. & Info. Mgmt program); Sheridan Coll. (Chair, Program Advisory Council). HONS: Co-recipient with Ian Angus, Hon. Award in recognition of their leadership & significant influence on the Canadian telecommunications environment, Canadian Business Telecommunications Alliance, 1990. INTERESTS: public policy; telecommunications industry; educ.; writing; gardening; reading; family. MISC: expert witness in front of the CRTC in the 1991 public hearings on long distance competition in Canada.

Angus, Margaret Sharp, C.M.,B.A., LL.D. 📜 📖

Historical Consultant, Author, and Lecturer. 22 Brock St., Ste. 1201, Kingston, ON K7L 1S9 (613) 546-9855. Born Chinook, Mont. 1908. m. Professor William Angus. 2 ch. EDUC: Univ. of Montana, B.A.(Hist.) 1930. CAREER: Supervisor, Publications Office, Cornell Univ., 1933-35; Asst. in Drama, Queen's Univ., 1941-57; Dir. of Radio, 1957-68; Curator, Costume Collection, 1968-85. SELECTED CREDITS: CBC Radio Series, *Had You Lived Then* & *In Those Days* (1948-50, rebroadcast 1951-52); numerous other works for radio; series of eight talks on Kingston Radio for CKWS TV. SELECTED PUBLICATIONS: *The*

Old Stones of Kingston (Toronto: University of Toronto Press, 1966); *The Story of Bellevue House* (The Queen's Printer, 1967); *History of the Kingston General Hospital* (McGill-Queen's Press, Vol. 1, 1973; Vol. 2, 1995); *John A. Lived Here* (Frontenac Press, 1984); *Kingston City Hall* (Kingston: City of Kingston, 1974); *A Biography of Dr. Alexander Sharp, Major and Paymaster; His Antecedents and Descendants* (privately printed, 1988); *Queen's History in Names* (Kingston: Queen's University, 1991); Essay in *Oliver Mowat's Ontario* (Macmillan, 1972); numerous papers in *Historic Kingston*, annual publication of the Kingston Historical Society; numerous biographies for *The Dictionary of Canadian Biography*; feature articles for *The Kingston Whig-Standard*; major studies & reports for the fed. gov't, the St. Lawrence Parks Commission, the Ontario Heritage Foundation, & the Royal Military Coll.; book reviews for publishers & *Queen's Quarterly*; four one-act stage plays. EDIT: Ed., *Buildings of Architectural and Historic Significance in Kingston*, volumes I-VII, 1971 to date. AFFIL: Ontario Historical Society (Life Mbr.); Ontario Genealogical Society (Life Mbr.); Kingston Historical Society (Life Mbr.); Architectural Conservancy of Ontario (Life Mbr.); Frontenac Historical Foundation (Life Mbr.); Heritage Canada (Life Mbr.); National Trust of Scotland (Life Mbr.); Local Architectural Conservancy Advisory Committee (Advisor); Kingston General Hospital (Gov.); Kingston General Hospital (Archives & History Committee). HONS: Jaycees' Citizen of the Year, 1967; Alumni Award, Queen's Univ. (Kingston), 1968; Cruikshank Gold Medal, Ontario Historical Society , 1974; Travel Award, Heritage Canada, 1974; Queen's Alumni Montreal Award, 1975; Her Majesty's Silver Jubilee Medal, 1977; Heritage Award, Parks Canada, 1985; Allied Award, Ontario Architects' Association, 1989; Paul Harris Fellow, Rotary Foundation, 1990; Order of Canada, 1992; Canada 125 Medal, 1992; Special Recognition Award, Kingston General Hospital, 1995; LL.D.(Hon.), Queen's Univ., 1973. MISC: Chrm, Advisory Committee to the Min. on the proposed Heritage Act, 1973; Mbr., Heritage Policy Review Committee, 1970; numerous lectures to societies, svc clubs, local councils, sch. classes & conferences, throughout Ont. & across Canada.

Annis, Helen M., B.A.,M.A., Ph.D. ⊕ ⊛

Chief, Behaviour Change Unit, ADDICTION RESEARCH FOUNDATION, 33 Russell St., Toronto, ON M5S 2S1 (416) 595-6802, FAX 595-5017. Professor, Faculty of Medicine, UNIVERSITY OF TORONTO. Born 1942. EDUC: Univ. of Toronto, B.A. 1964; York Univ., M.A. 1967, Ph.D. 1970. CAREER: Child Assessment, East York Leaside Clinic, Toronto, 1964-65; various clinical responsibilities, Whitby Psychiatric Hospital, 1965-69; Lecturer, Dept. of Psych., York Univ., 1967-73; Sr. Scientist, Research Div., Addiction Research Foundation, 1970-78; various clinical & supervisory responsibilities, Clinical Institute, 1976 to date; Assoc. Prof., Dept. of Health Admin., Fac. of Medicine, Univ. of Toronto, 1978-89; Sr. Scientist, Addiction Research Foundation, 1984 to date; Head of Psych., 1985-92; Prof., Dept. of Behavioural Sciences, Fac. of Medicine, Univ. of Toronto, 1989 to date; Adjunct Prof., Dept. of Psych., York Univ., 1990 to date. SELECTED PUBLICATIONS: *The Ontario Detoxication System*, with others (Toronto: Addiction Research Foundation Books, 1976); *Research Advances in Alcohol and Drug Problems*, Vol. 10, Ed. with others (New York: Plenum Press, 1990); *Drug Use By Adolescents: Identification, Assessment and Intervention*, Ed. with C.S. Davis (Toronto: Addiction Research Foundation Books, 1991); "Directions in Treatment Research" (*Addictions* 20 1973); "Treatment in Corrections: Hoax or Salvation?" (*Canadian Psychology* 22(4) 1981); "Relapse to Substance Abuse: Empirical Findings Within a Cognitive-Social Learning Approach" (*Journal of Psychoactive Drugs* 22 1990); numerous other articles & chapters in books, four assessment instruments; various unpublished reports. EDIT: Ed., *Canadian Psychology/Psychologies Canadienne*, 1983-87, 1988 to date; Ed., *The American Journal of Drug and Alcohol Abuse*, 1991 to date. AFFIL: Canadian Psychological Association (Fellow); Ontario Psychological Association; American Psychological Association (Div. on Addictions); Donwood Institute (Bd. of Dir. & Exec. Committee); Committee of Heads of Psychology, Univ. of Toronto Teaching Hospitals; Jellinek Memorial Award (Bd. of Dir.). HONS: Prov. of Ont. Scholarship, 1961; The Prince of Wales Award, 1964; Prov. of Ont. Grad. Fellowship, 1965, 1966, 1967. MISC: Registered Psychologist, Prov. of Ont.; consultant to numerous bodies, incl. the Social Science Federation of Canada, the National Institute on Alcohol Abuse & Alcoholism in the US, & the World Health Organization; External Reviewer for various granting agencies, incl. The Hospital for Sick Children Foundation, Medical Research Council, & Alberta Mental Health Advisory Council; External Reviewer for various publications, incl. *Canadian Psychological Review, British Journal of Addictions*, & *The American Journal of Drug and Alcohol Abuse*; numerous conference presentations & invited speeches & workshops. COMMENT: *"Dr. Annis has been conducting research on the treatment of alcoholics and other drug abusers since 1970. Her work in developing a relapse prevention model for alcoholics and other drug abusers has received international recognition."*

Annis, Susan, B.A.,M.A. ■ ⊗
Arts Consultant. 20 Monkland Ave., Ottawa, ON K1S 14B (613) 234-2742, FAX 234-7556, EMAIL susan_annis@mail.culturenet.ca. Born Edmonton 1948. m. Peter B. Annis. 3 ch. EDUC: L'Univ. d'Aix-Marseilles, Diplôme d'études françaises(degré supérieur) 1969; Queen's Univ., B.A.(Hons., English & French) 1970, M.A.(Cdn Lit.) 1971. CAREER: Legislative Asst., Ministry of Transport, Revenue Canada, Ministry of Employment & Immigration, 1975-77; Assoc. Dir., Canadian Conference of the Arts, 1989-93; Dir., Nat'l Sectoral Council for Culture/Cultural Hum. Res. Council, 1993-94; independent arts consultant, Assoc. Dir. of the Canadian Conference of the Arts, 1995 to date. AFFIL: Ottawa School of Speech & Drama (Bd. 1995 to date); Council for the Arts in Ottawa (Chair 1983-88); Arts Court, Ottawa Arts Centre Foundation (Chair 1988-90); Pierrot Ensemble (Chair 1993-96); Ottawa Symphony (Bd. Mbr. 1994 to date); Ottawa Bd. of Educ. (Arts Advisory Committee 1994 to date). HONS: McTavish Entrance Scholarship; Ont. Scholarship; Ont. Grad. Fellowship. COMMENT: *"My career has been devoted to safeguarding and promoting culture and the arts in English and French Canada at all levels of government and in the school system. This has included playing an integral part in building three major cultural organizations: the Council for the Arts in Ottawa, Arts Court (Ottawa's Municipal Arts Centre), and the Cultural Human Resources Council."*

Anthony, Geraldine, S.C.,Ph.D., LL.D. ⌘ 📕 ☼
Professor Emeritus, Department of English, MOUNT SAINT VINCENT UNIVERSITY, Halifax, NS. (902) 457-3500, ext. 399, FAX 457-3506. Biographer and Historian for the Congregation of Sisters of Charity of Halifax, Sisters of Charity of Saint Vincent de Paul, MOUNT SAINT VINCENT MOTHERHOUSE, 150 Bedford Hwy., Halifax, NS, B3M 3J5. Born Brooklyn, N.Y. 1919. EDUC: Mount Saint Vincent Univ., B.A. 1951; Saint John's Univ., M.A.(Phil.) 1956, Ph.D. (English) 1963. CAREER: Teacher, St. Margaret's Sch., Dorchester, Mass., 1942-48; Teacher, St. Peter's Sch., Lowell, Mass., 1948-51; Teacher, St. Barnabas Sch., Bellmore, N.Y., 1951-62; Instructor of Phil., Mount Saint Vin-

cent Univ., Extension Sch., N.Y., 1956-58; Instructor of Phil., Mount Saint Vincent, Wellesley Hills, Mass., Summer 1957; Teacher, Mount Saint Vincent Academy, Halifax, 1963-65; Asst. Prof. of English, Mount Saint Vincent Univ., 1965-71; Assoc. Prof. of English, Hofstra Univ., Summer Sessions, 1970-74; Assoc. Prof. of English, Mount Saint Vincent Univ., 1971-77; Prof., 1977-87; Chair, Dept. of English, 1983-86; Prof. Emeritus of English, 1987 to date. EDIT: Series Ed., *Profiles in Canadian Drama*, Gage Educational Publishers, 1977; Advisory Bd., *Canadian Drama/L'Art Dramatique Canadien*, Univ. of Waterloo, 1978-91; edited articles, *Canadian Theatre History*, Univ. of Toronto, 1980; Bd. of Ed., *Canadian Theatre and Drama*, Univ. of Calgary, 1990-92. AFFIL: Association for Canadian Theatre Research; History of Women Religious; The Canadian Catholic Historical Association. HONS: Fellowship in Journalism granted by *Wall Street Journal*, Univ. of Minnesota, Summer 1965; Post-doctoral Fellow, Modern Drama, Columbia Univ., Summer 1969; Canada 125 Medal, 1992; LL.D.(Hon.), St. Thomas Univ., 1993. INTERESTS: theatre; art; dance; music. MISC: recipient of various grants; Assessor for Canada Council; listed in *Men and Women of Distinction 1983-84*, *The World Who's Who of Women in Education*, *Contemporary Authors*, *A Bio-Bibliographical Guide to Current Authors and Their Works*, *Who's Who of American Women*, *Who's Who of World Professors*, *Who's Who in America*, *International Who's Who of Contemporary Achievement*, *Community Leaders of America*, *International Who's Who of Professional and Business Women* (1993), *Who's Who in the World*. COMMENT: *"The main thrust of my life in Canada has been devoted to serious and extended research on Canadian dramatists and their plays. My present work is focused on contemporary Canadian religious women and their contributions to the people of Canada. Presently, The Biography of Sister Irene Farmer, a history of the Federation of Sisters of Charity is ready for publication by the University of Calgary Press, October 1996. The Sisters of Charity Federation in the Vincentian - Setonian Tradition will be published by Sheed & Ward in 1997."*

Antler, Susan P., B.A.,M.B.A. Ⓢ ⓜ Ⓞ
President, ENVIROBUSINESS DIRECTIONS, 16 Northumberland St., Toronto, ON M6H 1P7 (416) 535-6710, FAX 536-9892. EDUC: Univ. of Toronto, Trinity Coll., B.A. 1979; Queen's Univ., M.B.A. 1981. CAREER: Product Supervisor (Schick, Efferdent, Listerine), Warner-Lambert Canada Ltd., 1981-83; Product Mgr

(Benylin, Sinutab, Listerine, Efferdent, Schick), 1983-86; Group Product Mgr, OTC Healthcare, 1986-88; Group Product Mgr, New Products, OTC Healthcare, 1989-90; Proj. Leader, Environmental Strategy & Action Plan, 1991; Pres., EnviroBusiness Directions Inc., 1992 to date. AFFIL: Canadian Household Battery Association (Exec. Dir.); The Composting Council of Canada (Exec. Dir.); Grocery Products Manufacturers of Canada (Environmental Issues Council); Rechargeable Battery Recycling Corporation (Cdn Rep.); Recycling Council of Ontario (Bd. of Dir. 1994-96). MISC: while proj. leader of the Environmental Strategy & Action Plan at Warner-Lambert, the company became the recipient of the Recycling Council of Ontario's National Office Recycling Award.

Aponiuk, Natalia, B.A.(Hons.),M.A., Ph.D. 🐿 🗐
Director and Associate Professor, Centre for Ukrainian Canadian Studies and Department of German and Slavic Studies, UNIVERSITY OF MANITOBA, Winnipeg, MB R3T 2N2 (204) 474-8906, FAX 275-0803. Born Gronlid, Sask. 1940. s. EDUC: Univ. of Saskatchewan, B.A.(Hons., Slavic Studies & English) 1962; Univ. of Toronto, M.A.(Slavic Languages & Lits.) 1963, Ph.D.(Slavic Languages & Lits.) 1974; Moscow State Univ., Exchange Student (Russian Lit.) 1965-66. CAREER: Instructor, Univ. of Saskatchewan, Summer 1962; Teaching Asst., Dept. of Slavic Language & Lit., Univ. of Toronto, 1963-65, 1966-67, 1973-74; Asst. Prof., Reed Coll., 1967-72; Sessional Lecturer, Dept. of Slavic Languages, Univ. of Alberta, 1974-75; Instructor, English as a Second Language, 1975-77; Coord., English as a Second Language, Grant MacEwan Community Coll., 1976-77; Asst. Prof., Dept. of Slavic Studies, Univ. of Manitoba, 1977-86; Coord., Soviet & East European Studies, 1979-83; Dir., Centre for Ukrainian Cdn Studies, 1982-93, 1994 to date; Assoc. Prof., Dept. of German & Slavic Studies, 1986 to date. SELECTED PUBLICATIONS: "Perspectives on an Ethnic Bestseller: *All of Baba's Children*" (*Canadian Ethnic Studies* 10(1) 1978); "Iordan-Vodokhreshcha na til ukrains'koho mynuloho– The Feast of Jordan–The Epiphany in Light of the Ukrainian Past" (*Promin'* 22(3) 1981); "Some Images of Ukrainian Women in Canadian Literature" (*Journal of Ukrainian Studies* 8(1) 1983); "Ukrainian Canadian Heritage Studies" (*Horizons* I. 2 1992); special issue, "Ethnic Themes in Canadian Literature" (*Canadian Ethnic Studies*); various reviews & book chapters; numerous presentations to various academic conferences. EDIT: Co-Ed.,

CESA Bulletin de la SCEE, 1991-93, Ed., 1993-95; Ed. Bd., *Visnyk/The Herald*. AFFIL: Conference on Ukrainian Studies; Ukrainian Cultural & Educational Centre (Advisory Bd.); Canadian Association of Slavists; Ukrainian Academy of Arts & Sciences; St. Andrew's Coll. (Senate); Council of Associates, Canadian Institute for Ukrainian Studies, Univ. of Alberta; Ukrainian Canadian Committee (Nat'l); Canadian Ethnic Studies Association (Pres. 1991-95); Ukrainian National Home Association (VP); Ukrainian Self-Reliance League of Canada (Educ. & Publications Committees); Association for Canadian Studies in the US; Senior Women Academic Administrators of Canada; Ukrainian Orthodox Church of Canada (Presidium & Consistory); American Association for the Advancement of Slavic Studies; Ukrainian Professional & Business Club; Alpha Omega Women's Alumnae; Association for Women in Slavic Studies; Canadian Society for the Study of Names; Canadian Women's Studies Association. HONS: Canada Council Pre-Master's Scholarship, 1962-63; Hantelman Postgrad. Fellowship, Univ. of Saskatchewan, 1962-63; Prov. of Ont. Gov't Fellowship, 1963-67; Taras Schevchenko Memorial Scholarship, 1964-65; Centre for Russian & East European Studies Exchange Fellowship, Univ. of Toronto, 1965-66; Canada Council Pre-Doctoral Fellowship, 1970-71; Finnish Ministry of Educ. Research Fellowship, 1979; Ukrainian Woman of the Year, Winnipeg, 1987; Univ. of Manitoba Outreach Award, 1992; Univ. of Manitoba Award for Service, 1993. MISC: recipient of numerous grants from the Canada Council, SSHRC, Ukrainian Canadian Foundation, & others; negotiated academic exchange agreements between the Univ. of Manitoba & Kyiv-Mohla Academy Univ. & L'viv State Univ.; organized nat'l conferences of the Canadian Ethnic Studies Association, 1991 & 1995; est. endowment funds for the Centre for Ukrainian Canadian Studies.

Appel, Bluma, C.M. ⊗ ✒ ⌣
Chairman, APPEL CONSULTANTS INC., 18A Hazelton Lanes, Toronto, ON M5R 2E2. Born Montreal. m. A. Bram Appel. 2 ch. David, Mark. CAREER: Fashion Designer, Town Hall Clothes Inc. 1948-51; journalist, specializing in politics & travel; broadcaster; Chargée de Mission to the Hon. Gerard Pelletier, Sec. of State, 1970-72; Founder, "The American Friends of Canada," 1972; Special Asst. to the Hon. Marc Lalonde, Fed. Min. Responsible for the Status of Women, 1975-79; stood for M.P. (Nepean-Carleton), 1979. SELECTED CREDITS: Host, *Let's Find Out*, Montreal; Guest Host, *The*

Shulman Show, Toronto; Rogers Cable Political Panel, Toronto; *Bluma Appel Interviews* (Ottawa); Off Broadway, *The Opening of a Window* (1962); Broadway, *One for the Dame* (1970), Exec. Co-Prod., *Lorne Greene's New Wilderness*; various other theatricals & feature films. SELECTED PUBLICATIONS: published in numerous magazines & newspapers. DIRECTOR: Appel Consultants Inc.; Canmont Investment Corp. Ltd.; Electroline Equipment Inc.; Canmont Reality Corp.; Radam Inc. AFFIL: American Friends of Canada (Dir. & Founder); Couchiching Institute of Public Affairs; Metropolitan Toronto Community Foundation; Prime Mentors; Ontario Crafts Council; Committee of Senior Executives to Clean Up Lake Ontario (Founder); Brock Univ.; Partners in Research (Founder); The Shakespeare Globe Centre of Canada; CANFAR-Canadian Foundation for AIDS Research (Chair); Royal Ontario Museum; Second Harvest; National Symphony, Washington; Niagara Symphony. HONS: renovated theatre in the St. Lawrence Centre named the "Bluma Appel Theatre," 1983; Soroptomist Award for Volunteerism, 1986; National Community Leadership Award, National Council of Jewish Women, 1987; Order of Canada; "Women Who Make a Difference," *Toronto Life*, 1992; Award of Merit, City of Toronto, 1992; "Hero Award," Metropolitan Community Church of Toronto, 1993; Variety Club of Canada, 1993; Arbour Award, Univ. of Toronto. MISC: frequent speaker.

Apple, Heather, B.Sc. 🖊
Editor, Past President, and Executive Director, HERITAGE SEED PROGRAM, R.R. 3, Uxbridge, ON L9P 1R3 (905) 852-7965, FAX (905) 852-5635. Born Toronto 1948. s. EDUC: Univ. of Toronto, B.Sc.(Biol.) 1972. CAREER: Horticulturist; Ed., Past Pres. & Exec. Dir., Heritage Seed Program. SELECTED PUBLICATIONS: *How to Save Your Own Vegetable Seeds*; various gardening articles for nat'l gardening magazines. AFFIL: Seed Savers Exchange; Garden Club of Toronto; North American Fruit Explorers; Henry Doubleday Research Association; Flower & Herb Exchange. HONS: Commemorative Medal for the 125th Anniversary of the Confederation of Canada. INTERESTS: reading; gardening; research; crafts. MISC: writer, teacher & speaker on biodiversity & organic growing; subject & consultant for videos & TV programs on these subjects. COMMENT: *"Dedicated to working for the preservation of biodiversity and sustainable agriculture."*

Applin, Anne-Marie H., B.A. Ⓢ
President, APPLIN MARKETING & COMMUNICA-TIONS, 512 Briar Hill Ave., Toronto, ON M5N 1M9 (416) 485-7804. Born Toronto 1952. m. Michael. 2 ch. EDUC: Univ. of Toronto, B.A. CAREER: Nat'l Training Dir., Clinique Laboratories (Estée Lauder); Lecturer, George Brown Coll.; Pres., Applin Marketing & Communications. AFFIL: Fashion Group International, Toronto; Stratford Festival; Royal Ontario Museum; Univ. of Toronto Coll. of Electors; Toronto Symphony; Oolagen (a children's mental health agency); Parkinson Foundation of Canada. MISC: various public speaking engagements as well as TV & radio guest appearances; expert on the topic of "Fundraising & Friendraising"–the interplay of volunteerism & dev. of funding.

Arai, Mary Needler, B.Sc.,M.A., Ph.D. ■ 🖰 🏵
Professor Emeritus, Department of Biological Sciences, UNIVERSITY OF CALGARY, 2500 University Dr. N.W., Calgary, AB T2N 1N4 (403) 220-5261, EMAIL arai@acs.ycalgary.ca. Senior Volunteer Investigator, PACIFIC BIOLOGICAL STATION, Nanaimo, BC V9R 5K6 (250) 756-7000. Born Summerside, P.E.I. 1932. m. Hisao P. Arai. 3 ch. EDUC: Univ. of New Brunswick, B.Sc.(Biol.) 1952; Univ. of Toronto, M.A. 1956; Univ. of California, Ph.D. 1962. CAREER: Asst. Prof., Dept. of Biological Sci., Illinois State Univ., 1961-62; Visiting Instructor, Dept. of Physiology & Biophysics, Univ. of Illinois, 1962; Sessional Instructor, Dept. of Biol., Univ. of Calgary, 1963-64; Special Instructor, 1964-68; Visiting Asst. Prof., Dept. of Biol., Rice Univ., Houston, 1968-69; Asst. Prof., part-time, Dept. of Biol., Univ. of Calgary, 1969-73; Assoc. Prof., part-time, 1973-74; half-time Assoc. Prof., 1974-83; half-time Prof., 1983-96. SELECTED PUBLICATIONS: *Functional Biology of Scyphozoa* (London: Chapman and Hall, in press); numerous articles in refereed journals; numerous lectures & addresses. AFFIL: American Association for the Advancement of Science; Marine Biological Association of the U.K.; The Society of Sigma Xi; Canadian Society of Zoologists (numerous positions incl. Interim VP 1992-93; Past Pres. 1993-94); American Society of Zoologists; American Society of Limnology & Oceanography. HONS: Gilbert W. Ganong Entrance Scholarship, Univ. of New Brunswick, 1948-49; Noel Stone Memorial Scholarship, Univ. of New Brunswick, 1951-52; National Research Council Bursary, Univ. of Toronto, 1952-53; Research Council of Ontario Scholarship, Univ. of Toronto, 1953-54; Killam Resident Fellowship, Univ. of Calgary, 1993. MISC: recipient of numerous grants; referee on various journals.

Archer, Violet Balestreri, B.Mus.,M.Mus., D.Mus.,LL.D.,O.C. ⊗ ⟡

Composer, Professor of Music Emerita, UNIVERSITY OF ALBERTA, Edmonton, AB T6C 2C9. Born Montreal 1913. EDUC: McGill Univ., Teacher's Licentiate in piano 1934, B.Mus.(Composition) 1936; Royal Canadian Coll. of Organists, Assoc. Diploma 1938; Yale Univ., B.Mus.(Composition) 1948, M.Mus. (Composition) 1949; composition teachers at McGill Univ. were Claude Champagne & Douglas Clarke; studies in composition with Bela Bartok, N.Y., summer of 1942, & with Richard Donovan & Paul Hindemith at Yale Univ., 1947-49; studies in electronic music, Summer 1968 at the Royal Conservatory of Music, Toronto & in 1973 at Goldsmith Coll. in London, UK. CAREER: Music Instructor, McGill Univ., 1948-49; Visiting Music Instructor, Summers of 1948-49; Resident Composer, North Texas State Coll., 1950-53; Visiting Music Instructor, Cornell Univ., Summer 1952; Asst. Prof. of Music, Univ. of Oklahoma, 1953-61; Assoc. Prof. of Music, Univ. of Alberta, 1962-70; Chair of Theory & Composition, 1962-78; Prof., 1970-78; Visiting Lecturer in Music, Univ. of Saskatchewan, Nov. 1978 & Mar. 1990; Resident Composer, Banff Sch. of Fine Arts, Summers of 1978 & 1979, part-time Lecturer, Univ. of Alberta, 1982-83, 1988-89, 1989-90; Visiting Lecturer in Music, Univ. of Calgary, Feb. 1986; Visiting Lecturer in Music, Grande Prairie Regional Coll., Sept. 1987; Visiting Lecturer in Music, Univ. of Alaska, Apr. 1988 & 1992; Prof. of Music Emerita, Univ. of Alberta & Prof. of Composition. SELECTED CREDITS: Three Scenes for Piano (Habitant Sketches) (Mercury Music Corp., 1946); Cradle Song for medium voice & piano (Frederick Harris, 1954); Fanfare and Passacaglia for Orchestra (Berandol Music Ltd., 1964); Shout With Joy, an anthem for mixed chorus & organ (Waterloo Music Co. Ltd., 1977); Six Miniatures for String Bass and Piano (Waterloo Music Co. Ltd., 1987); Three Christmas Carols of Canada (CMC, 1994); Four Moods for Solo Oboe (1995); Four Short Pieces for Solo B-flat Clarinet (1995); Three Moods for Bassoon (1995); total of 90 published compositions. AFFIL: Royal Canadian Coll. of Organists Association (Fellow); Accademia Tiberina of Rome (lifetime Academic Mbr.); Pi Kappa Lambda; Canadian Music Centres (Assoc. Composer Mbr.); Canadian League of Composers; Canadian Federation of Music Teachers (Hon. Life Mbr.); Alberta Registered Music Teachers' Association (Hon. Life Mbr.); Music Educators' National Conference, U.S.; Canadian Music Educators' Association; Canadian Folk Music Society; Canadian Association of University Schools; Coll. Music Society; Edmonton Musicians' Association Local 390 AFM; Unione Della Legion D'Oro (learned society in Rome, Italy); Canadian Federation of University Women; American Women Composers Inc. (Assoc. Mbr.); Canadian Music Centre, Prairie Reg. (Council Mbr.); Association of Canadian Women Composers (Composer Mbr.); Edmonton Composers' Concert Society (Founder 1984; VP 1986; Hon. Pres. 1995); International Biographical Association of Cambridge (Fellow); American Biographical Institute Research Association (Deputy Gov.). HONS: Composition Trophy, Quebec Music Festival, 1938; Bradley Keeler Memorial Scholarship, Yale Univ., 1947; Charles Ditson Fellowship, Yale Univ., 1948; various other academic awards & scholarships; Queen's Silver Jubilee Medal, 1978; Award for Outstanding Success in Concert Music, Performing Rights Organization of Canada Ltd., 1981; Order of Canada, 1983; Composer of the Year, The Canadian Music Council, 1984; Award, Women in the Arts, YWCA, 1985; inducted into the Cultural Hall of Fame, Edmonton, 1987; Sir. Frederick Haultain Prize, the Gov't of Alberta, 1987; Lifetime Achievement Award, Prov. of Alberta & the CBC, 1990; President's Certificate of Merit, Canadian Federation of Music Teachers' Association, 1990; Great Canadian Award, 1992; D.Mus.(Hon.), McGill Univ., 1971; D.Mus.(Hon.), Univ. of Windsor, 1986; LL.D.(Hon.), Univ. of Calgary, 1989; D.Mus.(Hon.), Mount Allison Univ., 1992; LL.D.(Hon.), Univ. of Alberta, 1993; an ornamental park has been named in her honour in Edmonton; a festival of her music "The Violet Archer Music Festival" took place Oct. 18-20, 1985; the Canadian Music Centre, Prairie Reg. Library in Calgary has been given her name; the composition scholarship at the Univ. of Alberta is named the Violet Archer Scholarship; the Dept. of Music, Univ. of Alberta has named a fellowship, "The Violet Archer Fellowship," 1992; Canada 125 Medal, 1992; Int'l Woman of the Year, International Biographical Centre of Cambridge, UK, 1993; elected Most Admired Woman of the Decade, American Biographical Institute Inc., 1993 as well as Mbr., Women's Inner Circle of Achievement; various other honours & awards. INTERESTS: great literature, sculpture & art of the past & present; travel; the great out-of-doors; nature. MISC: compositions performed in Canada, US, UK, France, Belgium, Switzerland, Russia, Japan, Thailand, Hong Kong & numerous other countries; listed in numerous biographical sources & encyclopedias including The American Women's Who's Who, The Canadian Who's Who, International Who's Who of Intel-

lectuals & *Who's Who in the World.* **COMMENT:** *"My goal in life is to create music in the present and future that will reach both children and adults, bringing them a message of positive and contrasting moods."*

Archibald, Isabel
Past President, WOMEN'S INSTITUTES OF NOVA SCOTIA, Box 550, Truro, NS B2N 5E3 (902) 893-6520, FAX 893-6393. Born New Glasgow, N.S. 1934. m. Robert. 6 ch. **EDUC:** Nova Scotia Agricultural Coll., Sci. 1952. **VOLUNTEER CAREER:** 4-H Leader, 1974-82; Sec.-Treas., New Town-Denver Women's Institute; Pres., United Church Women of local congregation, 1990 to date; Pres., Women's Institutes of Nova Scotia, 1993 to date. **HONS:** 4-H Friend, 1979; Volunteer chosen for St. Mary's Municipality, 1985; Award for Leadership, Guysborough District Women's Institute, 1994; Commemorative Medal for the 125th Anniversary of Canadian Confederation. **MISC:** represented Women's Institutes of N.S. at World Conference in Holland in 1992 & New Zealand in 1995; Co-Chair of Triennial Conference of Women's Institutes of Canada in Truro, 1994. **COMMENT:** *"Involvement in 4-H and general day-to-day operations of a dairy family farm have been both interesting and challenging. Many technical changes require much reading to better our situations in an ever-changing society. I am fortunate to have had so many opportunities to see life beyond my own area; I have a responsibility to give back to others in any manner that I can."*

Ardiel, June Victoria, M.A. $
President, JUNE ARDIEL LTD., 33 Harbour Square, Ste. 410, Toronto, ON M5J 2G2 (416) 363-8326, FAX 363-8376. Born London, Ont. 1921. **EDUC:** Univ. of Toronto, M.A.(Art Hist.). **CAREER:** VP & Creative Dir., The Ardiel Advertising Agency Ltd. **DIRECTOR:** Toronto Mutual Life; Leidra Lands Ltd.

Armann, Donna Marie, B.Sc.N.,R.N., M.Ed.,CHE ■
Director of Nursing, CROSS CANCER INSTITUTE, 11560 University Ave., Edmonton, AB T6G 1Z2 (403) 432-8543, FAX 432-8886. Born Edmonton 1950. 2 ch. Barret, Michael. **EDUC:** Univ. of Alberta, B.ScN.,R.N. 1972, M.Ed.(Admin.) 1981; Canadian Coll. of Health Service Executives, CHE 1992; American Coll. of Health Executives, 1995. **CAREER:** Staff Nurse, Orthopedics, Charles Camsel Hospital, 1972-73; Staff Nurse, Intensive Care Unit, Univ. of Alberta Hospitals, 1973-74; Nursing Instructor, Sch. of Nursing, Univ. of Alberta Hospitals, 1974-78; Staff Nurse, 1978-81; Evening/Night Supervisor, 1981-84; Asst. Dir. of Nursing, 1985-87; Dir. of Nursing, 1987-88; Assoc. Fac., Fac. of Nursing, Univ. of Alberta, 1988 to date; Dir. of Nursing, Cross Cancer Institute, 1988 to date. **AFFIL:** Alberta Breast Cancer Foundation (Bd. of Dir.); Alberta Association of Registered Nurses (Planning & Priorities Committee); Oncology Nurses Society, Oncology Nurses Interest Group of Alberta; International Society of Nurses in Cancer Care; Sigma Theta Tau Nursing Honor Society; Canadian Coll. of Health Service Executives; Canadian Association of Nurses in Oncology. **MISC:** Rep., Prov. Nursing Action Plan, 1990-93; Surveyor, Canadian Council of Healthcare Facilities Accreditation, 1992 to date; in 1983 founded Western Canada's first Allergy Information Association. **COMMENT:** *"I have been very fortunate in my personal and professional career to have had the opportunity to work with a variety of patients and healthcare providers. In my attempts to address identified needs, I have taken the initiative to organize patient support groups, be involved in my professional association and promote and implement programs for my colleagues' professional development. I am continuously impressed with the opportunities that are available and the excitement that is generated by fully participating in life on a day-to-day basis. I am very grateful for the support and participation of everyone with whom I have had the opportunity to work and am hopeful that the benefits of my endeavours will continue to be of assistance to others on an ongoing basis."*

Armour, Margaret-Ann, B.Sc.,M.Sc., Ph.D.
Assistant Chair, Department of Chemistry, UNIVERSITY OF ALBERTA, Edmonton, AB T6G 2G2 (403) 492-4969, FAX 492-8231, EMAIL margaret-ann.armour@ualberta.ca. Born Newton Mearns, Scotland 1939. s. **EDUC:** Univ. of Edinburgh, B.Sc.(Chem.) 1961, M.Sc.(Phys. Organic Chem.) 1966, Postdoctoral Fellow (Phys. Organic Chem.) 1970-71; Univ. of Alberta, Ph.D.(Phys. Organic Chem.) 1970, Postdoctoral Fellow (Biochem.) 1971-73. **CAREER:** Research Chemist, Alex Cowan & Sons, Papermakers, Penicuik, Scotland, 1961-66; Lab. Supervisor, Dept. of Chem., Univ. of Alberta, 1973-89; Asst. Chair, Dept. of Chem., 1989 to date. **SELECTED PUBLICATIONS:** numerous books, articles & conference papers, incl. *Potentially Carcinogenic Chemicals Information and Disposal Guide*, with others (Univ. of Alberta, 1986); "Tested Disposal Methods for Some Potentially Carcinogenic Chemicals Including Hazardous Pharmaceuticals" (*Proceedings of Institute for International Research*

Conference on the Handling and Disposal of Toxic Industrial Waste, Jakarta & Singapore, Mar. 12 & Mar.14-15, 1990); *Hazardous Laboratory Chemicals Disposal Guide* (Boca Raton, Fla.: CRC Press, 1991, 2nd edition 1996); "Getting and Keeping Girls Interested in Science" (*Alberta Science Education Journal* 24(1) 1991); "Controversial Chemicals in the Environment" (*Alberta Science Education Journal* 24(2) 1991); "WISEST–An Initiative at the University of Alberta to Encourage Women into the Sciences and Engineering", chapter in *Standing on New Ground*, ed. C.A. Cavanaugh & R.R. Warne (University of Alberta Press, 1993). **AFFIL:** Chemical Institute of Canada (Mbr. 1980-89, Fellow); American Chemical Society; New York Academy of Science; Edmonton Glenora Rotary Club (Pres. 1992-93); Women In Scholarship, Engineering, Science & Technology (V-Chair & Convenor). **HONS:** National Research Council of Canada Scholarship, 1968-70; National Research Council of Britain Fellowship, 1970-71; Medical Research Council of Canada Fellowship, 1971-72; Fellow, Chemical Institute of Canada, 1989; Alberta Environment Award, 1989; Edmonton YWCA Tribute to Women Award for Business, Labour, Professions & Technology, 1990; "Woman of the Year", Edmonton Business & Professional Women's Club & the *Edmonton Sun*, 1991; Distinguished Service Citation, Science Council of Alberta Teachers' Association, 1992; 125th Anniversary of the Confederation of Canada Medal, 1992; McNeil Medal, Royal Society of Canada, 1994; 3M Teaching Fellowship, 1996. **INTERESTS:** talking to young children & to the public in general about science; gardening; classical music; theatre. **COMMENT:** *"I have published books with tested disposal procedures for hazardous chemicals, which have proved useful to generators of small quantities of these materials. I share my love of science with school children and encourage young women to pursue careers in the sciences and engineering."*

Armstrong, Cathryne Hildriethe, C.M., B.A., ○ ◉
Volunteer. 8020 Arthur Dr., Saanichton, BC V8M 1V4. Born Emsdale, Ont. 1922. m. Gordon. 4 ch. Rosalind, Barton, Michael, Patricia. **EDUC:** Teresa Sch. of Design, 1940-42; École des Beaux Arts, Paris, 1945; Univ. of Toronto, B.A. 1965. **CAREER:** Canadian Women's Army Corps, 1940-46. **VOLUNTEER CAREER:** Pres., Royal Canadian Army Medical Corps (Women's Auxiliary), 1959-63; Pres., Swansea Home & School Association, 1963-65; Charter Mbr., Ontario Food Council, Ont. Dept. of Agriculture, 1965-67; Pres., Inter Club Council

for Women in Political Affairs, 1965-67; Pres., Toronto Consumers' Association of Canada, 1965-67; Dir., Health League of Canada, Ont., 1969-73; Pres., Provincial Council of Women of Ontario, 1969-71; Pres., National Council of Women of Canada, 1973-76; Dir. Council for Canadian Unity, B.C., 1975-81; Founding Mbr., Dir. & VP, Match International, Ottawa, 1976-80; Chair, Laws & Suffrage, International Council of Women, 1976-79; VP, International Council of Women, 1976-79; Pres., American Regional Council of Women (North, South, Central America & Caribbean Reg.), 1981-86; Cdn Delegate, A.P.E.C. Conference, Halifax, 1992; Project Literacy, Saanich Peninsula, 1992; Hon. Patron & Founding Mbr., Canadian Women's History Month, 1992-94; Pres. of the Foundation Fund, Saanich Peninsula Hospital, 1994 to date; presiding officer at citizenship ceremonies, Victoria & Nanaimo, 1995. **HONS:** Star, France-Germany Star, Victory Medal, Defence Medal CVSM & Clasp, 1939-45; Queen's Silver Jubilee Medal, 1977; Commendation, City of Los Angeles, US, 1977; *International Who's Who in Community Service*, UK, 1979; Woman of the Year, Victoria BC, 1982; Member of Order of Canada, 1982; Ventures Award, Victoria Business & Professional Women, 1988; Persons Award, Government of Canada, 1989; Canada 125 Medal, 1992. **INTERESTS:** travel; gardening; music. **MISC:** participated in numerous local & int'l conferences & organizations; presented numerous papers & briefs to int'l conferences & prov. & fed. commissions. **COMMENT:** *"Whatever my achievements may be, they have been a result of my endeavours over the years to help others, and in particular those who needed someone to go that additional distance on their behalf. A description of myself I leave to others."*

Armstrong, Jane, B.Sc.,M.Sc. ■■ ⌧ 💆 /
President, CINENOVA PRODUCTIONS INC. (documentary films), 87 Front St. E., Toronto, ON M5E 1B8 (416) 363-2600, FAX 363-3348, EMAIL 103006.245@compuserve.com. Born London, UK 1953. m. David Lint. **CAREER:** TV Researcher/Writer, UK, 1982-85; freelance TV Writer/Prod./Dir., Canada, 1985-90; Pres., CineNova Productions, Toronto, 1991 to date. **SELECTED CREDITS:** Prod./Series Ed., *Shipwrecks* (current production); Prod./Series Ed./Ep. Dir., "Klondike," *Great Adventures of the 20th Century* (1996); Prod./Dir./Writer, *Ultimate Guide to T. Rex* (1996); Prod./Dir./Writer, *In Search of Lost Worlds* (1995); Prod./Writer, *Shipwreck: The Mystery of the Edmund Fitzgerald* (1995); Prod./Writer, *T. Rex: Journey to its Lost World* (1994);

Prod., *Mission: Northwest Passage* (1993); Assoc. Prod., *Dinosaur* (1991); Assoc. Prod., *Floating Over Canada* (1990); *Born Talking* (1989); Head of Research/Writer, *The Life Revolution* (1988). **DIRECTOR:** CineNova Productions Inc. **AFFIL:** Canadian Film & Telvision Production Association; Association of Computing Machinery (Siggraph chpt.); Friends of the Thomas Fisher Rare Book Library, Univ. of Toronto. **HONS:** Cable Ace nomination for Best Documentary (*Ultimate Guide to T. Rex*), 1996; Bronze Plaque (*Shipwreck: The Mystery of the Edmund Fitzgerald*), Columbus Int'l Film & Video Festival, 1996; Silver Award (*Shipwreck: The Mystery of the Edmund Fitzgerald*), Worldfest Houston, 1996; Gold Camera Award (*Shipwreck: The Mystery of the Edmund Fitzgerald*), Int'l Film & Video Festival, 1996; Bronze Award (*Mission: Northwest Passage*), Worldfest Houston, 1995; Bronze Plaque (*Mission: Northwest Passage*), Columbus Int'l Film & Video Festival, 1994; Irene Marshal Fellowship, London, UK, 1982. **INTERESTS:** science; gardening. **COMMENT:** *"Jane Armstrong is a film and television director, producer and writer. She is President of CineNova Productions, a multimedia film company dedicated to productions that are entertaining, enlightening and authoritative. Jane's productions are seen by millions of people around the world."*

Armstrong, Pam Bovey $

President, MILLENITEX INC., 20 Maud St., 5th Fl., Toronto, ON M5V 2M5 (416) 504-6043, FAX 504-4788. **HONS:** Finalist, Entrepreneur of the Year Awards, 1994.

Armstrong, Pat, B.A.,M.A., Ph.D. ■■ 🎓 📜 📖

Director and Professor, School of Canadian Studies, CARLETON UNIVERSITY, 1207 Dunton Tower, 1125 Colonel By Dr., Ottawa, ON K1S 5B6 (613) 520-2366, FAX 520-3903, EMAIL patarms@superior.carleton.ca. Born Ont. 1945. m. Hugh Armstrong. 2 ch. Jillian, Sarah. **EDUC:** Univ. of Toronto, B.A.(Sociology) 1966; Carleton Univ., M.A.(Cdn Studies) 1975, Ph.D. (Sociology) 1984. **CAREER:** Coord., Women's Studies Program, Vanier Coll., Montreal, 1975-76 & 1986-87; Coord., Social Sci. Dept., 1979-81; Prof. & Chair, Dept. of Sociology, York Univ., 1989-92; Dir. & Prof., Sch. of Cdn Studies, Carleton Univ., 1994 to date. **SELECTED PUBLICATIONS:** author/co-author, 10 books (& one French translation) incl.: *Wasting Away: The Undermining of Canadian Health Care* (Toronto: Oxford Univ. Press, 1996); *The Double Ghetto: Canadian Women and Their Segregated Work*, 3rd revised ed. (Toronto: McClelland and Stewart, 1993); *Labour Pains: Women's Work in Crisis* (Toronto: The Women's Press, 1984); 31 chapters in edited books; 16 articles in refereed journals; 9 published technical reports; 40 other publications.

Armstrong, Ruth R., B.A., M.B.A. ■ $ 🎓 ♡

President, VISION MANAGEMENT SERVICES, 66 Glen Davis Cres., Toronto, ON M4E 1X5 (416) 691-7302, FAX (416) 691-9499, EMAIL rutharm@web.net. Born Montreal 1950. m. Michael L. Armstrong. **EDUC:** McGill Univ., B.A.(Psych.) 1971; Univ. of Toronto, M.B.A. 1981. **CAREER:** Social Svcs, Browndale, Toronto General Hospital, Metro Toronto Children's Aid Society, 1971-79; Mktg & Sales, Drake International; Mgmt Consultant & Strategic Planning, Public Health Branch, Ont. Ministry of Health, 1981-86; Teaching Fac., Nonprofit Management and Leadership Program, York Univ., 1986 to date; Mgmt Consultant, Vision Management Services, 1986 to date. **SELECTED PUBLICATIONS:** *Making a Difference: A Guide to Effective VON Board Membership*, with Jacquelyn Scott (Toronto: 1991); "A Rose By Any Other Name: Using Board Development to Achieve Board Reform" (*The Philanthropist* Spring 1992); *Remembering the Future: Creating Change-ability at Linda Lundström Ltd.*, with Brenda Zimmerman (Toronto: York Univ., 1994). **DIRECTOR:** Armstrong and Armstrong Enterprises Inc.; FutureShift Group Inc.; Ontario Prevention Clearinghouse (Past Pres.). **AFFIL:** Greenhouse Group (Learning Circle); Stewardship of Urban Land–S.O.U.L. **INTERESTS:** gardening; travel; scuba-diving; cycling; reading; citizen participation; democratic processes; community & organizational development. **COMMENT:** *"From an early age I have had an insatiable curiosity about people (psychology, culture, language, dynamics, etc.). This curiosity led me to my love of travel and to my work in organizational change and community development. My achievements have focused on facilitating organizations and groups to achieve their goals."*

Armstrong, Sally, B.Ed. ✏ 📖

Editor-in-Chief, *HOMEMAKER'S* MAGAZINE, 25 Sheppard Ave. W., Ste. 100, North York, ON M2N 6S7 (416) 218-3598, FAX 733-8683. Born Montreal 1943. m. Ross. 3 ch. **EDUC:** McGill Univ., B.Ed.(Phys. Educ.) 1966. **CAREER:** Teacher, Phys. Educ. & English, 1966-70; *Canadian Living Magazine*, 1975-88; Editor-in-chief, *Homemaker's* Magazine, 1988 to date. **SELECTED PUBLICATIONS:** *Mila*. A biography of Mila Mulroney (Macmillan,

1992). **AFFIL:** National Magazine Awards Foundation (Pres. 1991-93); Canadian Society of Magazine Editors (Founder; Program Dir. 1990-92); Canadian Association of Community Living (Chairperson, Comm.); Canadian Journalism Foundation (Gov.). **HONS:** Breakthrough Award, Canadian Association for the Advancement of Women in Sports, 1988; Finalist, Yorkton Short Film & Video Festival, 1987 for "Human Rights and Human Wrongs"; Finalist, American Film & Video Festival, 1988 for "Broken Trust"; Author's Award First Place, Foundation for the Advancement of Canadian Letters, 1993 for "Eva: Witness for Women"; Gold Award, Public Issues Category, National Magazine Award, 1994 for "Eva: Witness for Women"; Author's Award First Place, 1995 for "Physician on a Mission"; Golden Maple Award, Video Festival of Canada, 1994 for "Keys of Our Own"; Woman of Distinction, YWCA, 1995. **INTERESTS:** middle distance-running; skiing; hiking; white-water kayak & canoe expeditions; work with the women's movement. **COMMENT:** *"I have endeavoured, since my university days, to work on improving the status of women in Canada and in countries around the world. Using magazine articles, speeches and documentaries I feel that, along with the hundreds of women I have worked with, we have indeed seen some improvement."*

Armstrong, Susan, B.Com.,C.A. ⑤

Vice-President and Chief Financial Officer, THE DOMINION OF CANADA GENERAL INSURANCE COMPANY, 165 University Ave., Toronto, ON M8Z 4T8 (416) 947-2516, FAX 362-0990. Born Brockville, Ont. 1954. s. **EDUC:** Univ. of Toronto, B.Com. 1976; Canadian Institute of Chartered Accountants, C.A. 1980. **CAREER:** Asst. Corp. Cont., Bow Valley Resource Services, 1983-86; Corp. Cont., Western Star Trucks Inc., 1986-88; Sr. Mgr, Price Waterhouse, 1976-81, 1988-92; VP & CFO, The Dominion of Canada General Insurance Company, 1992 to date. **DIRECTOR:** The Dominion Group Foundation. **AFFIL:** Financial Executives Institute; Insurance Bureau of Canada (Fin. Affairs Committee); The National Club; Islington Golf Club; Association of Canadian Insurers (Chrm, Fin. Committee). **INTERESTS:** opera; classical music; reading; golf; tennis; skiing.

Arsenault, Francine H. ■■ ⓐ ♡ ⊕

President, INTERNATIONAL CENTRE FOR THE ADVANCEMENT OF COMMUNITY-BASED REHABILITATION (ICACBR), Queen's University, Kingston, ON K7L 3N6 (613) 353-2773, FAX 353-1859, EMAIL fa2@post.queensu.ca. Past

Chairperson, COUNCIL OF CANADIANS WITH DISABILITIES (CCD), 294 Portage Ave., Ste. 926, Winnipeg, MB R3C 0B9. Born Kingston, Ont. 1942. m. Richard J. Arsenault. 3 ch. David, Kathleen, Jamie. **EDUC:** Notre Dame Business Coll., Sr. Sec.(Acctg) 1962; U.N. Leadership Training course, Jamaica 1987; Cdn Hum. Rights Commission, courses on Hum. Rights 1989; Queen's Univ., research techniques 1991; Solo Centre for Community-Based Rehabilitation (CBR), Indonesia, Eval. & Design of Programs & Instruments 1992; U.N. Report for Disabled Women 1994; Sustainability of ICACBR 1995; Hum. Res. Dev. in CBR, Indonesia, 1996. **CAREER:** served as Proj. Dir., CUSO, Caribbean, Africa, Asia; Int'l Consultant, CIDA, 1988; Lecturer, Queen's Univ., 1991; presenter, numerous nat'l & int'l conferences & training seminars, parliamentary committees, embassies & Royal Commissions, 1981-94. **SELECTED PUBLICATIONS:** contributor, *Anthology of Disabled Women*; contributor, *Across Borders*; numerous papers for int'l forums; columnist on sr. citizens, *Kingston Whig-Standard* & *Heritage* (1980-86); gen. issues columnist, *The Triangle* (1980-86). **AFFIL:** ICACBR (Dir.); CCD (Dir.); District Health Council, Kingston (Dir.); Independent Living Resource Centre (Dir.); Canadian Associations of Independent Living Centres; Disabled Women's Network; PUSH (Persons United for Self-Help) Ontario (Pres. 1987-92); Disabled Peoples International, N.Am.-Caribbean Reg. (Exec. Sec. 1987); Access Place Canada (Community Consultant on Disability 1992). **HONS:** Award for most valuable Ont. delegate, CCD, 1992; ARCH Consumer of the Year Award; PUSH Ontario Award from Premier Peterson for contribution to disabled persons movement. **INTERESTS:** int'l affairs; writing; reading; sewing; swimming. **MISC:** mbr., Advisory Council on Assistance Devices, Ont. Ministry of Health, 1985; Chairperson, Nat'l Access Awareness Week, 1989; Advisor on Disability, Beijing Women's Conference, 1994. **COMMENT:** *"Since I had polio at 8 months and rheumatic fever at 8 years, my life moved forward as anyone else's except I had 30 operations to work around (8-20). My husband, children and home took priority until 1981 when I joined the movement to eliminate barriers for persons with disabilities. Much has been done; there is still much more to achieve."*

Arsenault, Shiela, R.P.N. ⓐ ⊕

Secretary to Board of Directors, REGISTERED PRACTICAL NURSES ASSOCIATION OF ONTARIO, Bldg. 4, 5025 Orbitor Dr., Ste. 200, Mississauga, ON L4W 4Y5 (905) 602-4664, FAX 602-4666. Born Belleville, Ont. 1943. m.

Cedric Arsenault. 2 ch. Kimberley, Shawn. **EDUC:** Napanee & District Collegiate Institute, 1960; Belleville General Hospital, Operating Room Tech.(Nursing) 1965; Durham Coll., R.P.N.(Nursing) 1979. **CAREER:** full-time Registered Practical Nurse. **AFFIL:** Registered Practical Nurses Association of Ontario (mbr.; VP 1988; Pres. 1992-94; Sec.; Dir.; Chair, Lakeview chpt. 1989-95); Canadian Association of Practical Nurses/Nursing Assistants (Dir. 1991; Pres.); Cardiac Rehabilitation Organization; Royal Canadian Legion Ladies Auxiliary Br. 384; Durham Coll. (Nursing Advisory Council). **INTERESTS:** cooking; reading. **COMMENT:** *"Self-motivated, caring - endeavour to do my best for those I work with and will honour any commitment. Dedicated to promoting R.P.N.'s and the R.P.N. profession as an individual and a leader within the profession."*

Arsie, Laura ⊗

Owner, LAURA ARSIE PHOTOGRAPHY, 110 Spadina Ave, Ste. 607, Toronto, ON M5V 2K4 (416) 504-8601, FAX 504-8603. Born Windsor, Ont. 1955. m. Ivan Tramontin. 1 ch. Giulia Francesca Tramontin. **EDUC:** Ryerson Polytechnic Univ., B.A.A.(Photography), 1988; Univ. of Padua, Italy, Languages (not completed), 1974-76; Royal Conservatory of Music, Grade 8 Piano. **CAREER:** after studying in Italy, worked in the freight forwarding/import-export field, using her knowledge of languages; upon returning to Canada, studied photography, asst. for two years; self-employed photographer, 1991 to date. **SELECTED PUBLICATIONS:** work has been published *in Canadian Living, Canadian Business, Chatelaine, Financial Post Magazine, Report on Business, Toronto Life, Imperial Oil Review, The Next City.* **EXHIBITIONS:** group show, St. Lawrence Market Gallery, Toronto (1988). **HONS:** nominated, National Magazine Award, 1994. **INTERESTS:** tennis; cooking; film; history; gardening; travel. **COMMENT:** *"I am a self-motivated adventurous person. I traveled to Europe when I was 19, decided to learn Italian by studying and living in Italy for nine years. I returned to Canada and pursued photography as a profession. My work provides the challenges and satisfactions I need daily in my life."*

Arvo, Paula H. ■ ■ ⊛ ⌀

Environmental Technician, TROW CONSULTING ENGINEERS, 807 Harold Cres., Thunder Bay, ON P7C 5H8 (807) 623-9495, FAX 623-8070. s. **EDUC:** Lakehead Univ., Diploma in Chem. Eng. Technology 1994; Confederation Coll., Diploma in Envir. Eng. Technology 1996. **CAREER:** Environmental Technician, Ont. Ministry of Envir. & Energy, May-July 1995; Pol-

lution Prevention Coord., July 1995-Apr. 1996; Environmental Technician, Trow Consulting Engineers, 1996 to date; joined Infantry reserves, Dept. of Nat'l Defence, 1990; Sergeant, 1996 to date. **AFFIL:** Alzheimer Society of Thunder Bay (volunteer). **HONS:** Canada Scholar, 1990. **INTERESTS:** running; cross-country skiing; bowling; camping; music; gardening. **MISC:** promoted as 1st female infantry sergeant; completed 1st marathon, Twin Cities Marathon, Oct. 1995; fluent in Finnish, good knowledge of French. **COMMENT:** *"I am currently beginning a career in environmental consulting and hope to continue my military career as well. I hope to, one day, operate my own consulting firm and complete the Boston Marathon."*

Ashford, Mary-Wynne, B.Sc.,B.Ed., M.D.,Ph.D. ■ ⊕ ⌀ ⊚

Physician, Educator, Disarmament Activist. Assistant Professor, Department of Social and Natural Sciences, UNIVERSITY OF VICTORIA, P.O. Box 310, Victoria, BC V8W 3N4 (604) 721-7779, FAX 721-7767, EMAIL mash@web.apc.org. Born Indian Head, Sask. 1939. cl. 3 ch. Karen A., Graham A.R., Patrick R. **EDUC:** Univ. of Alberta, B.Sc.(H.Ec.) 1960, B.Ed. 1961; Univ. of Calgary M.D. 1981; Hospice Victoria, Certificate in Palliative Care, 1992; Simon Fraser Univ., Ph.D. 1996. **CAREER:** Teacher, Bonnie Doon High Sch., Edmonton, 1960-65; Intern, Victoria General Hospital, 1981-82; Physician in family practice, Victoria, 1982-92; Hospice Assoc. Physician, 1982-92; Coord. of R.&D. in Global Studies (SFU, UBC, UVic, & MUC), 1993-95; Exec., BC Teachers' Federation Global Educ. Proj., 1993 to date; writer, speaker. **DISARMAMENT CAREER:** Speaker or Moderator at World Congresses of International Physicians for Prevention of Nuclear War, 1985 to date; Pres., Canadian Physicians for Prevention of Nuclear War, 1988-90; Special Advisor to Cdn Dept. of External Affairs at UN Special Session on Disarmament, 1988; Mbr. of Consultative Group to Cdn Ambassador for Disarmament, 1988 to date; Nobel Emissary for International Physicians for Prevention of Nuclear War, working in France for three months with French physicians, 1988; Pres., International Physicians for Prevention of Nuclear War World Congress, Montreal, 1988; VP, International Physicians for Prevention of Nuclear War, 1991-93; Advisory Panel, Physicians for Social Responsibility, USA, 1993-95; Bd., Science for Peace, 1994; Fd. Bd., *Peace* Magazine 1994 to date; Canadian Pugwash Group, 1994 to date; Mbr., Organizing Committee & Moderator of Plenary Sessions of First & Second International

Conference on Health & Human Rights, Harvard Univ., 1994; three week lecture tour of India & Pakistan on the role of the physician in preventing nuclear war, 1994; Ed. Advisory Bd., *Public Health and War*, V. Sidel & B. Levy, eds. (American Public Health Association, in press) 1995. SELECTED PUBLICATIONS: *Proposal for a New Canadian Security Corps* (CPPNW, 1989); "We Were the World" (*Medical Post* Nov. 20, 1990); "Anger, Boredom and the Search for Meaning" in *Anger in Our City; Youth Seeking Meaning*, H. Coward, ed. (Victoria: Centre for Studies in Religion & Society, Univ. of Victoria, 1994); "Boredom as a neglected issue in violence prevention programs in public schools," dissertation; book reviews & other articles; numerous special lectures incl. "Gender and the Peace Movement," Women & Sustainable Development Conference, UBC, May 26-31, 1994. AFFIL: Child Abuse Research Education Association (Advisory Bd.); Victoria Family Violence Prevention Society (Bd.); Victoria Centre for Studies in Religion & Society (Program Committee); Univ. of Victoria (Bd. of Gov. 1993-95); Foundation for the Univ. of Victoria (Dir. 1993-95); B.C. Medical Association (Committee on Violence); Victoria YM/YWCA; YWCA of/du Canada; Gov't of B.C. Peace Advisory Council. HONS: Univ. of Alberta Honour Prize, 1960; Mamie Shaw Simpson Award for Most Outstanding Woman Student on Campus, 1960; YMCA Peace Medal, 1989; Simons Foundation Doctoral Fellowship Award, 1992; Ancie & Arthur Fouks Scholarship for Public Service, 1992; Tom Perry Peace Award, Canadian Physicians for Prevention of Nuclear War, 1993; Canada 125 Medal, 1993; Gender Equity in Educ. Bursary, 1995; Rotary Club of Burnaby-Kingsway Fellowship, 1995; Grad. Fellowship, Simon Fraser Univ., 1995. MISC: Rep., YWCA of/du Canada at U.N. meeting for End of Decade for Women, Nairobi, 1985. COMMENT: *"I am a physician and educator writing and speaking on violence and disarmament. My research is on adolescent violence prevention."*

Ashton, Toni Polson, B.A.,LL.B. ⚖
Partner, SIM HUGHES ASHTON & MCKAY and SIM & MCBURNEY, 330 University Ave., 6th Fl., Toronto, ON M5G 1R7 (416) 595-1155, FAX 595-1163. Born Port Arthur, Ont. 1948. m. Hugh E. Ashton. 2 ch. Meridith Katherine, Courtney Elizabeth. EDUC: Univ. of Toronto, B.A. 1970; Queen's Univ. & Osgoode Hall, LL.B. 1973. BAR: Ont., 1975. CAREER: Ptnr, Sim, Hughes, Ashton & McKay; Ptnr, Sim & McBurney. SELECTED PUBLICATIONS: *Hughes on Trade Marks*, co-author (Butter-

worths, Canada); "Trademarks," an entry in *Canadian Forms and Precedents* co-author (Butterworths, Canada). AFFIL: The Canadian Bar Association (Chair, Nat'l Intellectual Property Section 1992-93); International Trademark Association (Mbr, Bd. of Dir. 1995-97; Exec. Committee of the Bd. of Dir. 1996-97; Legislative Analysis Committee; Meetings Committee); Patent & Trademark Institute of Canada (Fellow); Marques; County of York Law Association; Granite Club; Phi Delta Phi. INTERESTS: waterskiing; swimming; travel.

Asper, Gail, B.A.,LL.B. ⚖ ❀ ☺
General Counsel, Corporate Secretary, CANWEST GLOBAL COMMUNICATIONS CORP., T.D. Centre, 201 Portage Ave., Ste. 3201, Winnipeg, MB R3B 3X7 (204) 956-2025, FAX 947-9841. Born Winnipeg 1960. m. Dr. Michael Paterson. 2 ch. Stephen Paterson, Jonathan Paterson. EDUC: Univ. of Manitoba, B.A.(French Lit.) 1981, LL.B. 1984. BAR: Nova Scotia; Manitoba. CAREER: Assoc. Lawyer, Goldberg Thompson, Halifax, 1984-89; Gen. Cnsl, CanWest Global Communications Corp., 1989 to date. AFFIL: Manitoba Theatre Centre (Pres., Treas.); St. Boniface General Hospital Research Foundation (Dir.); Jewish Child & Family Services (Dir. 1994-96); Canadian Friends of the Hebrew Univ. (Co-Chair, Professional & Bus. Div. 1989-93); Winnipeg Chamber of Commerce (Council Mbr. 1992-93); The Manitoba Club; Canadian Women in Communications; National Association of Women & the Law; Canadian Bar Association; Manitoba Bar Association; Nova Scotia Bar Association. INTERESTS: singing; theatre; travel; skiing.

Aston-McCrimmon, Edith Pauline, B.Sc., M.Sc. ■ ☜ ⊕
Associate Professor, Physical Therapy Program, MCGILL UNIVERSITY, 3654 Drummond St., Montreal, QC H3G 1Y5 (514) 398-4500, ext. 4523, FAX 393-6360. Born Verdun, Que. 1929. m. Mungo Donald McCrimmon. EDUC: McGill Univ., Physiotherapy Diploma 1950, Physiotherapy Educ. Diploma 1956, B.Sc.(P.+O.T.) 1960, M.Sc.(A) 1980. CAREER: Sole Charge Physiotherapist, Belleville General Hospital, 1950-52; Staff Physiotherapist, California Rehabilitation Centre, Vallejo, Calif., 1952; Demonstrator, Staff, Sch. of Physical & Occupational Therapy, McGill Univ., 1952-57; in charge of physiotherapy svcs at the Camp for Crippled Children (Summers), McKay Centre for Deaf & Crippled Children, Ayers Cliff, Que., 1953-63; Lecturer, Sch. of Phys. & Occupational Therapy, McGill Univ., 1957-62; Asst. Prof., Sch. of Phys. & Occupational Therapy, 1962-86; Demonstrator in Anatomy, 1966-74;

Coord., Phys. Therapy Program, 1974-79; Assoc. Prof., Sch. of Phys. & Occupational Therapy, 1986 to date; Assoc. Dir., Phys. Therapy Program, 1988-89, 1991 to date. SELECTED PUBLICATIONS: various articles, reports & abstracts; "Stretch Workshop" (*Journal of the Canadian Physiotherapy Association* Sept. 1961); "Trends in Clinical Practice: An Analysis of Competence" (*Physiotherapy Canada* July/Aug. 1984); "An Analysis of the Ratings of Competencies Used in Physical Therapy Practice" (*Physical Therapy*, Journal of the American Physical Therapy Association Nov. 1984). EDIT: Chair, Ed. Bd., *Physiotherapy Canada*, Canadian Physiotherapy Association, 1982-85. AFFIL: Canadian Association of University Schools of Rehabilitation (Sec.-Treas.); Canadian Physiotherapy Association; Corporation Professionnelle des Physiothérapeutes du Québec (Pres., Comité d'admission 1985 to date); Physiotherapy Foundation of Canada (Founding Mbr.); McGill Univ. (Senate 1993-96); Sigma Xi. HONS: Distinguished Service Award, Graduates' Society, McGill Univ., 1984; Gouverneur, Corporation Professionnelle des Physiothérapeutes du Québec, 1987; Mérite du Conseil Interprofessionnel du Québec, 1993-94. MISC: numerous invited presentations; active on committees & executives of professional organizations; Reviewer for research grant applications for the Physiotherapy Foundation of Canada, 1985 to date; Mbr., Exec. Organizing Committee of the World Confederation for Physical Therapy for the 7th Int'l Meeting, Montreal, 1970-74. COMMENT: *"To promote the recognition and expansion of the profession of physical therapy through EDUCATION, RESEARCH, PRACTICE and GOVERNANCE at provincial, federal and international levels."*

Atkinson, The Hon. Pat, B.A.(Hon.), B.Ed. ■ ✦ ⊗

Minister of Education, GOVERNMENT OF SASKATCHEWAN, Legislative Building, Rm. 302, Regina, SK S4S 0B3 (306) 787-1684, FAX 787-0237. Born Biggar, Sask. 1952. s. EDUC: Univ. of Saskatchewan, B.A.(Hons.), B.Ed. CAREER: Office of the Rentalsman; Principal, Radius Tutoring Proj., Saskatoon; elected M.L.A. (Saskatoon Nutana), Gov't of Sask., 1986; in Opposition served as critic for Health, Educ. & Privatization; re-elected M.L.A. (Saskatoon Broadway), 1991; Min. of Social Svcs, Min. Responsible for Seniors, 1992-93; Min. of Educ., Training & Employment, Min. Responsible for Sask. Comm. Network & New Careers Corp.,1993-95; Min. of Educ. & V-Chair, SGI, 1995 to date. AFFIL: Canadian Day Care Advocacy Association (Past Sask.

Rep.); Saskatoon Community Clinic (Past V-Chair); Saskatchewan Cooperative Housing Association (Past Dir.); Big Sisters (Public Rel'ns Committee). INTERESTS: hiking; Irish music; restoration of antique furniture & early 1900s home.

Atwood, Margaret, A.M.,D.Litt., LL.D. ■ 📖 📚

Author and Poet. c/o McClelland & Stewart, 481 University Ave., Ste. 900, Toronto, ON M5G 2E9. Born Ottawa 1939. EDUC: Victoria Coll., Univ. of Toronto, B.A. 1961; Radcliffe Coll., A.M. 1962. CAREER: Lecturer in English, Univ. of British Columbia, 1964-65; Instructor in English, Sir George Williams Univ., Montreal, 1967-68; Instructor in English, Univ. of Alberta, 1969-70; Asst. Prof. of English, York Univ., 1971-72; Writer-In-Residence, Univ. of Toronto, 1972-73; M.F.A. Hon. Chair, Univ. of Alabama, 1985; Berg Chair, New York Univ., 1986; Writer-In-Residence, Macquarie Univ., Australia, 1987; Writer-In-Residence, Trinity Univ., San Antonio, Tex., 1989. SELECTED CREDITS: *The Poetry and Voice of Margaret Atwood* (1977); *Margaret Atwood Reads from A Handmaid's Tale; Margaret Atwood Reads Unearthing Suite* (1985). SELECTED PUBLICATIONS: *The Edible Woman* (Toronto: McClelland & Stewart, 1969); *Surfacing* (Toronto: McClelland & Stewart, 1972); *Lady Oracle* (Toronto: McClelland & Stewart, 1976); *Life Before Man* (Toronto: McClelland & Stewart, 1979); *Bodily Harm* (Toronto: McClelland & Stewart, 1981); *The Handmaid's Tale* (Toronto: McClelland & Stewart, 1985); *Cat's Eye* (Toronto: McClelland & Stewart, 1988); *The Robber Bride* (Toronto: McClelland & Stewart, 1993); *Alias Grace* (Toronto: McClelland & Stewart, 1996); five collections of short fiction, incl. *Bluebeard's Egg* (Toronto: McClelland & Stewart, 1983) & *Wilderness Tips* (Toronto: McClelland & Stewart, 1991); 14 collections of poetry, incl. *The Circle Game* (Cranbrook Academy of Art, 1964) & *Interlunar* (Oxford, 1984); *Up in the Tree*, children's book (Toronto: McClelland & Stewart, 1978); *Anna's Pet*, children's book (James Lorimer & Co., 1980); *For the Birds*, children's book (Douglas McIntyre, 1990); poetry published in many magazines, incl. *Tamarack Review, The New Yorker, The Atlantic Monthly & Quarry,* & many anthologies in Canada & the US; short stories have appeared in many magazines, incl. *Harper's, Ms., & Saturday Night*; anthology ed.; three nonfiction works, incl. *Survival: A Thematic Guide to Canadian Literature* (Anansi, 1972); reviews & critical articles have appeared in numerous magazines & journals, incl. *Maclean's, Books in Canada* & *The Globe and Mail*. **AFFIL:** The Writers' Union of Canada (Pres. 1981-82); PEN. **HONS:** Governor General's Award, *Circle Game*, 1966; Guggenheim Fellowship, 1981; Companion of the Order of Canada, 1981; Governor General's Award, *The Handmaid's Tale*, 1986; Commonwealth Literary Prize, Reg'l winner, 1987; Order of Ontario, 1990; Trillium Award for Excellence in Ontario Writing, *Wilderness Tips*, 1992; Canada 125 Medal, 1992; Trillium Award for Excellence in Ontario Writing, *The Robber Bride*, 1994; Commonwealth Writers' Prize for Canadian & Caribbean Region, *The Robber Bride*, 1994; Chevalier dans l'Ordre des Arts et des Lettres, Gov't of France, 1994; *Sunday Times* Award for Literary Excellence (London, UK), *The Robber Bride*, 1994; numerous other awards; D.Litt.(Hon.), Trent Univ., 1973; D.Litt.(Hon.), Queen's Univ., 1974; D.Litt.(Hon.), Concordia Univ., 1980; D.Litt.(Hon.), Smith Coll., Northampton, Mass., 1982; D.Litt.(Hon.), Univ. of Toronto, 1983; D.Litt.(Hon.), Univ. of Waterloo, 1985; D.Litt.(Hon.), Univ. of Guelph, 1985; D.Litt.(Hon.), Mount Holyoke Coll., 1985; D.Litt.(Hon.), Univ. of Toronto, 1987; D.Litt.(Hon.), Univ. de Montréal, 1991; D.Litt.(Hon.), Univ. of Leeds, 1994.

Auch, Susan ⓪
Athlete, Speed Skater. c/o Canadian Amateur Speed Skating Association, 1600 James Naismith Dr., Gloucester, ON K1B 5N4. Born Winnipeg 1966. **EDUC:** Univ. of Calgary, Journalism/Broadcasting. **SPORTS CAREER:** Mbr. of bronze-medal winning Cdn women's relay team, 1988 Olympics; First Overall, Cdn Sprint Championship, 1989, 1990, 1991; Fourth, women's 500m, World Cup, The Hague, 1991; Fourth, women's 500m, World Cup, Warsaw, 1991; Fourth, women's 500m, World Cup, Karuizawa, 1992; Third, women's 500m, World Cup, Seoul, 1992; Fourth, women's 500m, World Cup, Nagano, 1992; Third, women's 500m, World Cup, Seoul, 1992; Second, women's 500m, World Cup, Davos, 1993; Third overall, women's 500m, Final World Cup Standings–Sprint, 1993; Fourth, women's 500m World Cup, Hamar, 1993; First Overall, Cdn Sprint Championship, 1993; Fourth, women's 500m, World Cup, West Allis, 1994; Second, women's 500m, World Sprint Championships, Calgary, 1994; Silver Medal, women's 500m, Winter Olympics, Lillehammer, 1994. **AFFIL:** Canadian Amateur Speed Skating Association. **HONS:** Athlete of the year in long track, Canadian Amateur Speed Skating Association, 1990, 1991, 1992, 1994. **INTERESTS:** dogs; horses. **MISC:** best time in the women's

500m, 39.51, is a Cdn record; second Cdn woman to win an Olympic longtrack speed skating medal.

Augustine, Jean, B.A.,M.Ed.,LL.D. ✦ 𝕊
Member of Parliament (Etobicoke-Lakeshore), GOVERNMENT OF CANADA, House of Commons, 433 West Block, Parliament Buildings, Ottawa, ON K1A 0A6 (613) 995-9364, FAX 992-5880. Toronto Constituency Office (416) 251-5510, FAX 251-2845. Born Grenada, WI 1937. d. 2 ch. Cheryl, Valerie. **EDUC:** Univ. of Toronto, B.A., M.A.; Ontario Supervisory Officer's Certificate. **CAREER:** Chair of the Bd., Metropolitan Toronto Housing Authority; Elementary Sch. Principal, Metropolitan Toronto Separate Sch. Bd.; M.P. (Etobicoke-Lakeshore), 1993 to date; former Parliamentary Sec. to the Prime Minister; Mbr., House of Commons Standing Committee on Hum. Res. Dev.; V-Chair, Ministerial Task Force on Social Security Reform; Mbr., Standing Committee on Hum. Rights & Status of Disabled Persons. **AFFIL:** Harbourfront (Bd. Mbr.); Catholic Children's Aid Society; Canadian Advisory Council on the Status of Women; Ontario Judicial Council; Urban Alliance on Race Relations; Grenada Association; Metro Action Committee on Public Violence Against Women & Children; Hospital for Sick Children (Trustee); Etobicoke Social Development Council; York Univ. (Bd. of Gov.); Congress of Black Women of Canada (Pres.); Toronto Mayor's Task Force on Drugs; Metro Toronto Drug Abuse Prevention Task Force. **HONS:** Ontario Volunteer Award & Pin; Caribana Achievement Award; Bob Marley Award; Kay Livingstone Award; YWCA Women of Distinction Award (Community Svc.); Women On The Move Award, *The Toronto Sun*; 1994 Canadian Black Achievement Award; Ontario Award & Pin for Community Service; LL.D.(Hon.), Univ. of Toronto. **MISC:** Mbr., Toronto Crime Enquiry, 1991. **COMMENT:** *"Throughout my life, I have struggled to fulfill many roles. I strive for excellence and commit myself through hard work to being and doing the best I can each day. I work to ensure that equity and diversity issues are addressed in all aspects of Canadian society. I believe, with dedication, nothing is impossible to achieve."*

Austen-Leigh, Joan H., B.A., M.F.A. ■■ ⊗ 🗍
Writer. FAX (604) 598-8458. Born Victoria, B.C. 1920. w. Denis Mason Hurley. 4 ch. Freydis, Robert, Tibbie, Damaris. **EDUC:** Univ. of Victoria, B.A.(English) 1973; Univ. of British Columbia, M.F.A.(Playwriting) 1976. **SELECTED CREDITS:** several plays on CBC

Radio & on Australian radio; plays performed in high schools throughout North America. SELECTED PUBLICATIONS: novels: *Stephanie* (1979); *Stephanie at War* (1986); *A Visit to Highbury* (1995); *Later Days at Highbury* (1996); plays (under name Joan Mason Hurley): *Our Own Particular Jane* (1975); *Women's Work* (1979); *Women & Love* (1983); *Four Canadian One Act Plays* (1990); plays printed in anthologies by various publishers. AFFIL: Jane Austen Society of North America, JASNA (co-founder; Bd. mbr.; founding editor & 1 of 3 current editors, *Persuasions*-journal of JASNA). HONS: 1st prize, Canadian Playwriting Competition, Ottawa, 1985; numerous other awards for plays. INTERESTS: sailing; opera; painting; playing the cello. COMMENT: *"Joan Austen-Leigh is the great, great, great niece of Jane Austen."*

Auster, Ellen R., B.A.,M.A.,Ph.D. ✿ $
Associate Professor, Strategic Management and Organization Behaviour, Faculty of Administrative Studies, YORK UNIVERSITY, 4700 Keele St., North York, ON M3J 1P3 (416) 736-5088, FAX 736-5687. Born Jeffersonville, Ind. 1957. m. Steven E. Weiss. 2 ch. Lindsay Amundson Auster-Weiss, Shannon Ross Auster-Weiss. EDUC: Colgate Univ., B.A.(Soc.) 1979; Cornell Univ., M.A.(Organizational Soc.) 1981, Ph.D.(Organizational Soc.) 1983. CAREER: Asst. Warehouse Employment Mgr, Industrial Rel'ns Dept., Twin County Grocers, Inc., Edison, N.J., 1978; Employee Rel'ns Advisory Bd., Clement Communications, Inc., Concordville, Pa 1983 to date; Asst. Prof. of Mgmt, Grad. Sch. of Bus., Columbia Univ., 1983-87; Case Leader, Exec. Program in Bus. Admin., Arden House Campus, 1984-91; Assoc. Prof. of Mgmt, Grad. Sch. of Bus., 1987-90; Visiting Assoc. Prof., Amos Tuck Sch. of Bus., Dartmouth Coll., 1990-91; Assoc. Prof. of Strategic Mgmt & Organization Behaviour, Fac. of Admin. Studies, York Univ., 1991 to date. SELECTED PUBLICATIONS: "Behind Closed Doors: Sex Bias at Professional and Managerial Levels" (*Employee Responsibilities and Rights Journal*, Vol. 1(2) 1988); "Sex and Equality at Higher Levels in the Hierarchy: An Interorganizational Perspective" (*Sociological Inquiry*, Vol. 58, 1988); "The Impact of Owner and Organizational Characteristics of Black and White Owned Businesses on Firm Profitability and Survival" (*American Journal of Economics and Sociology*, Vol. 47, 1988); "International Corporate Linkages: Dynamic Forms in Changing Environments" (*The Columbia Journal of World Business*, Vol. 22(2) 1987); "Task Characteristics as a Bridge Between Macro and Micro Research on Salary and Equality

Between Men and Women" (*Academy of Management Review*, Vol. 14, 1989); "The Relationship of Industry Evolution to Patterns of Technological Linkages, Joint Ventures, and Direct Investment Between the U.S. and Japan" (*Management Science*, Vol. 38(6) 1992); "Demystifying the Glass Ceiling: The Organizational and Interpersonal Dynamics of Gender Bias" (*Business in the Contemporary World*, Vol. 5(3) 1993); "Macro Perspectives on Interorganizational Linkages: A Comparative Analysis and Review With Suggestions For Reorientation" (*Advances in Strategic Management*, Vol. 10, 1994); "Exploring Multiple Forms of Japanese Resource Investment in the U.S. and Organization Theory and Network Approach" (*Journal of International Management*, Vol. 1, 1995); various book reviews; numerous conference presentations. EDIT: Ed. Bd., *The Columbia Journal of World Business*; Manuscript Reviewer, various journals incl. *Administrative Science Quarterly*, *Sociological Forum* & *Sex Roles*. AFFIL: Academy of Management (Exec. Committee, Women in Mgmt Div. 1990-92); Strategic Management Society; American Sociological Association; National Science Foundation (Grant Proposal Review Bd.). HONS: Outstanding Educator of the Year Award, Fac. of Admin. Studies, York Univ., 1993; Recognition Award: Outstanding Service to the Exec. Committee of the Women in Mgmt Div. of the Academy of Management, 1993; Recognition Award: Outstanding Service to the Academy of Management's Women in Mgmt Div., 1991; Best Paper Award, Int'l Mgmt Div., National Academy of Management, 1990. COMMENT: *"Researches, teaches and consults in the areas of strategic organizational design and human resource management."*

Austin, Barbara, B.A.,M.A.,M.B.A., Ph.D. ✿ $
Professor, Faculty of Business, BROCK UNIVERSITY, St. Catharines, ON L2S 3A1 (905), FAX 984-4188, EMAIL baustin@spartan.ac. brocku.ca. Born Thunder Bay, Ont. 1943. EDUC: McMaster Univ., B.A.(Hist.) 1966; Bishop's Univ., M.A.(Hist.) 1970; Concordia Univ., M.B.A. 1980, Ph.D.(Admin.-Strategy) 1985. CAREER: Prof. of Bus. Strategy & Cdn Bus. Hist., Brock Univ. SELECTED PUBLICATIONS: numerous journal articles & chapters in books on Cdn bus. hist. & bus. strategy; Ed. Bd., *Journal of Management History*, *Brock Review*. AFFIL: Administrative Sciences Association of Canada; Academy of Management; Business History Conference; Economic & Business History Society; Society of Socio-Economists. HONS: Best Paper Awards,

Administrative Sciences Association of Canada, Academy of Management. **INTERESTS:** curling; skating.

Autio, Karen, B.Math. ⚛ 🎓 $
President, KEA MEDIA, 2282 Meadows St., Abbotsford, BC V2T 3A7 (604) 859-6522. Born Thunder Bay, Ont. 1958. m. Will Autio. 2 ch. **EDUC:** Univ. of Waterloo, B.Math.(Comp. Sci.) 1981; Regent Coll., Diploma in Christian Studies(Theology) 1986. **CAREER:** Programmer, Co-op Work terms, Shell Canada, 1977-78, 1979; Programmer/Analyst & System Mgr, 1981-84; Programmer/Analyst, MacDonald Dettwiler & Associates, 1985-87; self-employed, educational software dev. & children's computer educ., 1994 to date. **AFFIL:** Spina Bifida Association of Canada (Dir.; Educ. Dev. & Research Committees 1991-92, 1994 to date); Spina Bifida Association of B.C. (Dir.; Educ. Dev.); Girl Guides of Canada (Guider 1993-95). **INTERESTS:** creative arts (drawing, singing, writing); "edutainment" software. **MISC:** working on a committee to establish a local community children's museum; key communicator for neighbourhood elementary sch. (liaise with sch. District Superintendent). **COMMENT:** *"I am seeking to combine my computer knowledge and creative skills with my experience with children to design and evaluate educational software."*

B

abe, Jennifer E., LL.M, LL.B, B.A. ⚖

Partner, MILLER THOMSON, Barristers and Solicitors, 20 Queen St. W., Ste. 2700, Toronto, ON M5H 3S1 (416) 595-8500, FAX 595-8695. Born Thunder Bay, Ont. 1953. s. **EDUC:** Univ. of Toronto, B.A. 1976; Osgoode Hall, LL.B. 1979; London Sch. of Econ., LL.M. 1981. **BAR:** Ont., 1982. **SELECTED PUBLICATIONS:** *Sale of a Business* (Butterworths, 1992); *Creditors' Remedies in Ontario* (Butterworths, 1994); numerous articles & papers for Canadian Bar Association, Law Society of Upper Canada & others. **EDIT:** Ed., *Imperfections*, Canadian Bar Association newletter on secured transactions & Personal Property Security Act developments. **AFFIL:** Canadian Bar Association (Past Chair, Bus. Section); Law Society of Upper Canada. **INTERESTS:** hiking & being outdoors; desperate & failed gardener. **MISC:** lecturer for the Canadian Bar Association, the Law Society of Upper Canada, Insight, & the Canadian Institute on various bus. subjects; Sr. Lecturer in Insolvency, Bar Admission Course, LS of UC. **COMMENT:** *"Ms. Babe practises corporate-commercial law, with an emphasis on secured transactions and insolvency. She also frequently writes and teaches in the area. When she can, Ms Babe tries to spend time where there are no phones."*

Bacon, The Hon. Lise ✢

Senator (De la Durantaye), THE SENATE OF CANADA, 303 Victoria Building, Ottawa, ON K1A 0A4 (613) 995-6194, FAX 992-7380. Born Valleyfield, Qué. 1934. **CAREER:** Gérante de service, La Prudentielle d'Amérique, 1951-71; Députée (Bourassa), Assemblée Nationale, Prov. du Qué., 1973-76; Min. d'État aux

Affaires sociales, 1973-75; Min. des Consommateurs, Coopératives et Institutions financières, 1975-76; Min. de l'Immigration, 1976; Juge, Cour de la citoyenneté canadienne, 1977-79; VP (Qué.), Association canadienne des compagnies d'assurances de personnes inc., 1979-81; Députée (Chomedey), Assemblée Nationale, Prov. du Qué., 1981-94; VP, Commission de l'aménagement et des équipements, Prov. du Qué., 1984-85; Vice-première min./Min. des Affaires culturelles/Responsable de l'Office des ressources humaines, de la Commission de la fonction publique et de l'application de la Charte de la langue française, 1985-88; Min. de l'Environnement/Vice-première min./Min. des Affaires culturelles, 1988-89; Min. de l'Énergie et des Ressources/Prés. du Comité ministériel permanent pour l'aménagement du développement régional et de l'environnement, 1989-94; Min. responsable du Développement régional, 1989-90; Sénateur (De la Durantaye), Le Sénat du Canada, 1994 to date. **AFFIL:** Fédération des jeunes libéraux du Québec (Directrice exéc. 1954-56); Parti libéral du Québec (Sec. 1968; Prés. 1970-73; Membre du Secrétariat permanent 1971); Fédération des femmes libérales du Québec (Prés. 1967-70); Fédération des femmes libérales du Canada (1967); Théâtre Espace GO (Prés. de la campagne de financement; Conseil d'admin. 1994-95); Coll. Marie-de-l'Incarnation de Trois-Rivières (Conseil du consulteurs 1994-95); OXFAM-Québec (Conseil d'admin. 1994-95); Institut de formation de la Société canadienne des postes (Conseil d'admin. 1994); Table ronde nationale de l'environnement et de l'économie (1994).

Bacon, Marilyn, R.N.,B.A.,M.Ed. ■ ⊕

Vice-President, Nursing, IWK GRACE HEALTH CENTRE FOR CHILDREN AND FAMILIES, 5850 University Ave., Halifax, NS B3H 4N1 (902) 428-8183, FAX 428-3206. Born St. John's 1943. m. Eric. 2 ch. **EDUC:** Windsor Grace Sch. of Nursing, R.N. 1964; York Univ., B.A.(Psych.) 1987; Ontario Institute for Studies in Education, M.Ed.(Adult Educ.) 1992. **CAREER:** Supervisor, Obstetrics/Gynecology, Etobicoke General Hospital, 1974-85; Dir. of Nursing, Scarborough Grace Hospital, Scarborough, Ont., 1985-91; VP, Nursing, Grace Maternity Hospital, Halifax, 1991-95. **AFFIL:** Canadian Association for Quality in Health Care (Pres. 1985-86); Registered Nurses' Association, N.S. & Ont.; Salvation Army Victim Witness Assistance Program; Outreach Committee, United Church, Halifax (past Chair); Dalhousie Univ. Childcare Centre (past Bd. Mbr.). **INTERESTS:** facilitating adult educ. in community & church settings. **COMMENT:** *"Active over 30 years in advancing innovative and empowering programs around women's health, especially in maternity and gynecological care. Also very active in church life in area of women's spirituality and community outreach."*

Baday, Lida ✂ $

President, LIDA BADAY LTD., 70 Claremont St., Studio 200, Toronto, ON M6J 2M5 (416) 603-7661, FAX 603-3245. Born Hamilton, Ont. 1957. m. Mario Zuliani. **EDUC:** Ryerson Polytechnic Univ., 3-yr. Program 1979. **CAREER:** Pattern Maker, Becker Fashion; Designer, Kira Fashion; Designer, Miller Group; Owner, Designer & Pres., Lida Baday Ltd., 1987 to date. **HONS:** Fil D'Argent (for Canada), given by Maison du Lin, Paris; Designer of the Year, City of Toronto, 1992; "Buyer's Designer of the Year Award," in recognition of Excellence in Canadian Fashion, Vidal Sassoon Int'l, 1996. **COMMENT:** *A fashion minimalist who creates ageless, urban clothes, Lida Baday literally grew up in the fashion business, the daughter of a custom dress maker. In 1987 she launched her own Toronto-based company under the LIDA BADAY label and has established herself as one of Canada's preeminent designers. Her collection is now sold in more than 200 stores across Canada and Europe.*

Bagnall, Janet, B.A.,B.Ed.,M.A. ✎

Senior Feature Writer, *THE GAZETTE*, 250 ouest rue St. Antoine, Montreal, QC H2Y 3R7 (514) 987-2483, FAX 987-2933. Born Charlottetown 1948. m. William J. Marsden. 2 ch. Caroline, Katharine. **EDUC:** Univ. of Toronto, B.A.(Modern Languages & Lit.) 1971, B.Ed. (French & Spanish) 1972, M.A.(Latin Am. Lit.); Univ. of Western Ontario, M.A.(Journalism) 1976. **CAREER:** Reporter, *The St. Catharines Standard*, 1976-78; Reporter, Ed., Feature Writer, *The Gazette*, 1978 to date; Guest Lecturer, Concordia Univ. **AFFIL:** Fédération professionnelle des journalistes du Québec; Cascade Golf & Tennis Club, Métis, Qué.

Bailey, Madonna, B.Comm.,M.B.A., C.F.A. ■ $

Vice-President, Foreign Exchange and Money Market, LAURENTIAN BANK OF CANADA, 1981 McGill College Ave., Ste. 1975, Montreal, QC H3A 3K3. Born St. John's. **EDUC:** Memorial Univ. of Newfoundland, B.Comm. 1975; Queen's Univ., M.B.A. 1977; Association for Investment Management Research, C.F.A. 1986.

Bailey, Norma 🎭

President, FLAT CITY FILMS INC., 336 Queenston St., Winnipeg, MB R3N 0W8 (204) 489-6181, FAX 488-3041. Born Winnipeg 1949. m. Ian Elkin. 2 ch. EDUC: Univ. of Manitoba, Architecture 1971. SELECTED CREDITS: Assoc. Prod./Prod. Mgr, *The Rubber Gun* (feature), with Allan Moyle & Steven Lack, 1976; Dir.,*The Performer* (short film), 1978; Dir., *Chasing an Eclipse* (documentary), 1979; director, *Bush Pilot* (documentary); Dir., *It's Hard to Get It Here* (documentary); Dir., *Nose & Tina* (documentary), 1981; Prod./Dir.("Ikwe" & "The Wake"), *Daughters of the Country* (series), 1984; Prod./Dir., *Bordertown Cafe* (feature), 1989; Dir., *Martha, Ruth & Edie*, Sunrise Films; dir. various segments, *Heartland*, IMAX; Dir., *Women in the Shadows* (documentary), Direction Films, 1991; Dir., *The True Story of Linda M.* (documentary), 1995; Dir., segments of *My Life As A Dog*; Dir., *For Those Who Hunt The Wounded Down*, CBC movie, 1996. HONS: Best Documentary Film (*Chasing an Eclipse*), Yorkton, 1979; Bijou Award, Best Documentary (*Nose & Tina*), 1981; Best Documentary (*Women in the Shadows*), Vancouver Film Festival, 1992; nominated, Donald Brittain Award for Best Documentary (*Women in the Shadows*), Gemini Awards, 1993. MISC: *Daughters of the Country* has won numerous awards incl.: Blue Ribbon, American Film & Video Festival (N.Y.); Best TV Series, Women in Film Festival, L.A.; Best Film, American Indian Film Festival, San Francisco; three Gemini Awards.

Bailey, Sheila ☼
World President, CHRISTIAN WOMEN'S FELLOW-SHIP (DISCIPLES OF CHRIST), c/o 1205 Jubilee Ave., Regina, SK S4S 3S7. m. Mervin Bailey. 4 ch. Glenn Edward, David Forrest, Brian James, Coralie Sheila. VOLUNTEER CAREER: Women's Inter-Church Council of Canada, 1 term; Cdn Pres., Christian Women's Fellowship (Disciples of Christ), 1990-92; World Pres., 1992-96. AFFIL: Women's Aglow Fellowship (Recording Sec. 1 term). INTERESTS: travel. MISC: has served as an elder in her congregation since 1978; was Bd. Chair, 1991-93, as well as most other committee Chairs; speaker at several Women's Aglow Fellowship meetings & has spoken at World Day of Prayer services.

Baird, Maeve, B.A.,LL.B. ⚖
Lawyer, FRENCH BROWNE, 329 Duckworth St., St. John's, NF A1C 5P5 (709) 754-1628, FAX 754-2701, EMAIL randyp@public.compusult.nf.ca. Born St. John's 1965. m. Randy Pelletier. EDUC: Memorial Univ. of Newfoundland, B.A.(Pol. Sci.); Dalhousie Univ. Law Sch., LL.B. 1990. BAR: Newfoundland 1991.

CAREER: Mbr. of Adjudicative Panel, Newfoundland Human Rights Commission; Articling Student, Newfoundland Legal Aid Commission; private practice of law, 1990 to date. SELECTED PUBLICATIONS: *A Family Law Guide for Women in Newfoundland*, Contributor & Ed.; *Pursuing Equality*, Contributor (Institute of Social & Economic Research). AFFIL: National Association of Women & the Law (Mbr., Nat'l Steering Committee 1991-95; Mbr., Organizing Committee, Nat'l Conference 1995); Canadian Bar Association. INTERESTS: equality & human rights law. MISC: presently doing a critical evaluation of the Newfoundland Human Rights Code for the Newfoundland & Labrador Human Rights Association, to be presented to prov. gov't. COMMENT: *"I have been involved with the National Association of Women and the Law since I was a student at Dalhousie in 1987. This was my first real involvement in the women's movement, and through this organization, I had the opportunity to participate in a number of national initiatives for women. Through my involvement with women's organizations on both a national and a provincial level, I have been incredibly fortunate to have had the opportunity to meet a number of the women who have been in the forefront of the struggle for women's equality in this country."*

Baird, Patricia, B.Sc.,M.D.,C.M., F.R.C.P.(C).,F.C.C.M.G. ⚗ ⊕ ⚱
University Professor, UNIVERSITY OF BRITISH COLUMBIA, Department of Medical Genetics, 6174 University Blvd., Ste. 222, Vancouver, BC V6T 1Z3 (604) 822-6115, FAX 822-3565, EMAIL pbaird@unixg.ubc.ca. Born Rochdale, UK. m. Robert M. Baird. 3 ch. EDUC: McGill Univ., B.Sc.(Hons., Biol.) 1959, M.D.,C.M. (Medicine) 1963. CAREER: Head, Dept. of Medical Genetics, Univ. of British Columbia, 1979-89; Head, Dept. of Medical Genetics, Children's, Grace, & University Hospitals, 1981-89; Nat'l Advisory Bd. on Science & Technology, 1987-91; Medical Research Council of Canada, 1987-90; Chair, Royal Commission on New Reproductive Technologies, 1989-93; VP, Canadian Institute for Advanced Research, 1991 to date. SELECTED PUBLICATIONS: more than 350 papers & abstracts focusing on the distribution & natural hist. of birth defects & genetic disorders in the population, & the analysis of ethical & social implications of genetic knowledge & reproductive technologies. AFFIL: Science & Technology Council (Co-Chair, Nat'l Forum 1991); International Pediatric Association (Ethics Panel 1991-95); Canadian Bioethics Society; FIGO Committee for Study of Ethical Aspects of

Human Reproduction; Population Health Group of CIAR; American Society of Human Genetics. **HONS:** Order of British Columbia, 1992; Osler Lecturer, Vancouver Medical Association, 1991; Women of Distinction Award, YWCA, 1988; D.S.(Hon.), McMaster Univ., 1991; D.Univ.(Hon.), Univ. of Ottawa, 1991. **INTERESTS:** skiing; bicycling; reading. **MISC:** Chrm, Genetics Grants Committee, Medical Research Council of Canada, 1982-87; Bd. of Gov., Univ. of British Columbia, 1984-90; has served on many boards incl. B.C. Cancer Research Centre, B.C. Medical Services Foundation, & the Vancouver Institute; first woman to receive title of Univ. Prof. in history of Univ. of BC.

Bairstow, Frances, B.S. $ ✎

Arbitrator/Mediator. 1430 Gulf Blvd., Ste. 507, Clearwater, FL 34630 (813) 595-0198. Born Racine, Wisc. 1920. m. David Bairstow. 2 ch. Dale Owen, David Anthony. **EDUC:** Univ. of Wisconsin, B.S. 1942. **CAREER:** Labour Educ. Specialist, Univ. of Puerto Rico, 1950-51; Research Economist, US Senate Labor Committee, Washington, DC, 1949-50; Chief, Wage Data Unit, Wage Stabilization Bd., Washington, DC, 1951-53; Research Economist, Canadian Pacific Railway, 1956-58; Consultant, labour-mgmt films, National Film Board of Canada, 1955-75; Dir., Industrial Rel'ns Centre & Prof. of Labour Rel'ns, McGill Univ., 1964-85; Arbitrator, ad hoc labour disputes, 1964 to date; Consultant, labour mgmt films, Australian Film Unit, 1969-70; Mediator, Public Svc. Staff Rel'ns Bd., Gov't of Canada, 1970-78; Chrm, Fed. Inquiry Commission (on the structure of bargaining in airlines, airports, grain handling), Gov't of Canada, 1978; Essential Svcs Commissioner, Prov. of Que., 1978; Consultant, Organization for Economic Cooperation & Development, France, 1979; Mediator & Labour Disputes Facilitator, Air Canada & Association of Flight Attendants for Canada, 1980-85; Visiting Prof., Univ. of New South Wales, 1983; Special Master, Florida Public Employees' Rel'ns Commission, 1985-97; Mediator, Southern Bell Telephone & Communications Workers of America, 1985 to date; Mediator, American Telephone & Telegraph Co., 1989 to date; Arbitrator, United Airlines & Association of Flight Attendants, 1989 to date; Arbitrator, State Univ. System of Florida, 1990 to date; Arbitrator, US Treasury Employees, 1995. **SELECTED PUBLICATIONS:** "Grievance Arbitration in U.S. & Canada" (*Labour Arbitration Yearbook*, Canada, 1993); "The Trend Toward Centralized Bargaining: A Patchwork Quilt of International Diversity" (*Columbia Journal of World Business* 1985); *Bargaining over Work Standards by Professional Unions* with Prof. L.B. Sayles (1975); *Employment Security in Civil Aviation* (1977); "Labour Relations in Quebec" (*Financial Times of London* 1978); "Rethinking Bargaining Structures" (*Labour Law Journal* 1980); *Avoiding Confrontation in Labour-Management Relations* (1982); contributor of columns on labour matters, *Montreal Gazette*. **AFFIL:** National Academy of Arbitrators. **HONS:** Fulbright Scholar, Oxford Univ., 1953-54. **INTERESTS:** travel; swimming; reading. **MISC:** frequent speaker on labour rel'ns issues to local & nat'l radio & TV; mentioned in *Who's Who in the World*; *World Who's Who of Women*; *Who's Who of American Women*; *Canadian Who's Who; Most Admired Women of the Decade*; *International Who's Who in American Education*; *Who's Who in the South and Southwest*.

Baker, Carroll ■■ 🎭 $ ☝

Singer, CARROLL BAKER ENT. INC. (music publishing & artist mgmt), 210 Dimson Ave., Guelph, ON N1G 3C8 (519) 822-2732, FAX 822-2732. Born N.S. 1949. m. John Beaulieu. 1 ch. Candace Carroll Beaulieu. **EDUC:** high school. **CAREER:** country music star–singer, songwriter, TV & radio performer. **SELECTED CREDITS:** several CBC super specials; CBC mini-series; many guest performances on TV; BBS TV special; 1st Cdn to host a TV special from the Grand Ol' Opry, Nashville; 1st Cdn country music performer to perform at The London Palladium, London, U.K. **HONS:** has received every major country music award in Canada; 5 gold singles, 4 gold albums incl. 1 in Australia, 3 platinum albums; humanitarian award for work with charities; youngest performer to be inducted into the Canadian Country Music Hall of Honour; best-selling album of the year, *Hymns of Gold* album. **INTERESTS:** being with family, friends; bridge; visiting Nova Scotia; hopes to open a seafood restaurant in home town of Port Medway, N.S. **MISC:** recorded a duet with balladeer, Roger Whittacker; original host, Easter Seals Superthon, CBC TV; Sick Kids Telethon, BBS. **COMMENT:** *"I have always been an independent person who believed I could accomplish anything if I worked hard and maintained my integrity and honesty. I love my family more than life itself, cherish my friends and fans and I have an abounding faith in God and humanity."*

Baker, Nancy, B.A. 📕 📜 🎭

Author. c/o Penguin Books Canada Ltd., 10 Alcorn Ave., Ste 300, Toronto, ON M4V 3B2 (416) 925-2249. Born Kitchener, Ont. 1959.

m. Richard Shallhorn. **EDUC:** Univ. of Toronto, B.A. 1982. **SELECTED PUBLICATIONS:** "The Party Over There" (*Rod Serling's The Twilight Zone Magazine* June 1988); "Exodus 22:18" (*Rod Serling's The Twilight Zone Magazine* June 1989); "Cold Sleep" (*Northern Frights*, Mosaic Press, 1992); "Consent" (*Deathport*, Pocket Books, 1993); *The Night Inside* (Viking Penguin, 1993); *Blood and Chrysanthemums* (Viking Penguin, 1994); *A Terrible Beauty* (Viking Penguin, 1996). **HONS:** Finalist for the City of Toronto Book Award, 1994. **INTERESTS:** literature; film; art. **COMMENT:** *"Spent nine years in the magazine publishing business prior to embarking on career as full-time writer."*

Bales, Laura $

President and Chief Executive Officer, **ALBERTA RE-TECH LTD.**, P.O. Box 510, Vulcan, AB T0L 2B0 (403) 485-6076, FAX 288-4348. President and Chief Executive Officer, **EVERGREEN RECYCLING TECHNOLOGIES LTD.** Born Edmonton 1959. m. Jim Bales. 2 ch. Benjamin, Matthew. **EDUC:** Westlock Sr. High Sch., Matriculation, 1976; Univ. of Alberta. **CAREER:** VP, Oper., Institute for Executive Development, 1984-87; Pres., KYL International Ltd., 1987-89; Compt., 3435 Investments Ltd., 1989-92; Pres. & CEO, Evergreen Recycling Technologies Ltd., 1992 to date; Pres. & CEO, Alberta Re-Tech Ltd., 1993 to date. **DIRECTOR:** Evergreen Recycling Technologies; Alberta Re-Tech Ltd. **AFFIL:** Westlock Day Care Society (Bd.). **HONS:** Emerald Award Finalist for Environmental Excellence, Alberta 1995. **INTERESTS:** collecting books; antiques; decorating; attending courses. **MISC:** numerous professional dev. courses. **COMMENT:** *"Being the only woman in the tire recycling industry has helped me to be an ambassador for recycling. My marketing background has helped to formulate a clear message about cleaning up the environment and using our tire waste in productive ways. I am carrying this message not only to the different levels of government, but also to prospective recyclers in other countries."*

Balke, Noël M., B.A. 📖 ✏

Retired Librarian. Sea Dog, RR 1, Box 27, Nanoose Bay, BC V0R 2R0. Born Londonderry, N. Ireland 1918. m. Nicholas Balke. 2 ch. William Greer, Jennifer Mary Eileen. **EDUC:** Univ. of Sheffield, B.A.(Math. & Modern Languages) 1939; Library Association, UK, A.L.A.(Library Sci.) 1942. **CAREER:** Chief Librarian & Info. Officer, Ministry of Supply Signals Research & Development Establishment, Christchurch, UK, 1942-45; freelance writing & broadcasting (CBC, *The Globe & Mail, Manchester Guardian*), 1949-59; Librarian, Ottawa Public Library, 1959-64; Chief Librarian, National Gallery of Canada, 1964-79. **SELECTED PUBLICATIONS:** radio scripts; book reviews; newspaper articles; papers in professional library journals. **AFFIL:** Library Association, UK (Life Mbr.); Coastal Tai Chi Club (Founding Mbr. 1985-95). **HONS:** Memorial Award, Canadian Women's Press Club, 1956; Canada 125 Medal, 1992. **INTERESTS:** theatre; ballet; politics; environment; Tai Chi; art; libraries; literature. **MISC:** Chair, Art Libraries Committee, Canadian Library Association, 1967-69; Chair, Museums Div., Special Libraries Association, 1974-75.

Ball, Elizabeth ✪ 🎓 ☝

Founder and Managing Artistic Director, **CAROUSEL THEATRE COMPANY AND SCHOOL**, 1405 Anderson St., Vancouver, BC V6H 3M8. General Manager, **THE WATERFRONT THEATRE**, Granville Island, Vancouver, BC. **CAREER:** Mgr, Ticket Bureau, Yale Co-op, 1967-70; Dir., Inner City Drama Program, New Haven, Conn., 1967; Exec. Ed., *Yale Graduate* (professional newspaper), New Haven, Conn., 1969-70; Literary Consultant, Arts Club Theatre, 1972-78; Dir., Arts Club Theatre Sch., 1973-78; Fac., Developmental Drama, Theatre/Educ. Dept., Univ. of British Columbia, 1973-78; Founding Mng Artistic Dir., Carousel Theatre, 1974 to date; Asst. to Assoc. Dir., Actors Theater of Louisville, 1981-82; Asst. Prod. & Dir., Nederlander Organization, N.Y. City, 1982-83; Gen. Mgr, The Waterfront Theatre, 1992 to date. **SELECTED CREDITS:** Dir., *The Miracle Worker*; Dir., *The Secret Garden*; Dir., *The Diary of Anne Frank*; Dir., *Billy Bishop Goes To War*; Dir., *Mavor Moore's A Christmas Carol–The Musical*; Dir., *Chatauqua Girl*; Dir., *Dying To Be Thin*; Dir., *Goodbye Marianne*; Prod., *Amelia!*. **AFFIL:** Canadian Actors Equity Association; Vancouver Professional Theatre Alliance; Professional Association of Canadian Theatres; Vancouver Civic Theatres Board; Vancouver Arts Initiative; Studio 58 Theatre Sch., Vancouver Community Coll. (Bd.). **HONS:** Canadian Institute of the Arts Award, Outstanding Contribution, 1994. **INTERESTS:** politics; motivating youth. **MISC:** recipient of various grants; guest lecturer at various academic institutions; Dir., int'l UNESCO tour of *Ice Wolf*, Paris & London, 1979; Mbr., Nat'l Negotiating Team, P.A.C.T./Equity Canadian Theatre Agreement, 1985-86; first professional artist to enter Vancouver civic politics; first Artistic Dir. in Canada to provide signed performances for the deaf; guest dir. & artist for a number of distinguished US theatres. **COM-**

MENT: *"Has devoted her life to the study and practice of professional theatre, and to the training and encouragement of theatre artists in British Columbia. A professional artist passionately concerned about the cultural life of her community and her country."*

Ball, Tracey, B.Comm.,C.A. ⑤

Vice President, Finance and Chief Accountant, CANADIAN WESTERN BANK, 10303 Jasper Ave, Ste. 2300, Edmonton, AB T5J 3X6. Born Calgary 1957. m. Gary Reynolds. 2 ch. EDUC: Simon Fraser Univ., B.Comm. 1980; Institute of Chartered Accountants, C.A. 1982. CAREER: various positions from student to Audit Supervisor/Mgr, Thorne Riddell, Chartered Accountants, Vancouver, 1980-86; Consultant for resource companies & aquaculture/seafood companies, 1986-87; Consultant, Western & Pacific Bank, 1987; Mgr, Fin. & Chief Acctnt, Canadian Western Bank, 1987; Asst. VP & Chief Acctnt, 1988; VP & Chief Acctnt, 1990 to date; also Asst. Corp. Sec., 1991. AFFIL: Junior Achievement of Northern Alberta & Northwest Territories (Dir.); Financial Executives Institute of Canada–Edmonton Chapter (Dir. & Pres.); Edmonton Community Foundation (Mbr. of Audit Committee); Financial Executives Institute of Canada (Dir.). INTERESTS: skiing; fine wine; travel; family. COMMENT: *"Being the CFO of Canada's only western-based Schedule I bank, together with being the mother of two children in elementary school and the wife of a working professional (also a C.A.), has created a very challenging environment. The fact that I can contribute meaningfully to other organizations sometimes surprises me."*

Bandeen, Mona H., B.A.,M.A., M.B.A. ⑤ ⑤ ⑨

Director, Women's Entrepreneurship Program and Family Business Management Program, UNIVERSITY OF TORONTO, Faculty of Management, 105 St. George St., Toronto, ON M5S 3E6 (416) 978-3831, FAX 978-5433. Born UK. m. Dr. Robert A. 4 ch. EDUC: Univ. of Toronto, B.A.(Sci.) 1953, M.A.(Bio. Sci.) 1955, M.B.A. 1983. AFFIL: Canadian Institute for Advanced Research (Dir.); Robarts Research Institute at the Univ. of Western Ont.; (Dir.); Institute of Corporate Directors; Canadian Woman Entrepreneur of the Year Awards (Founding &Present Chair); Exec. Corp. of Bishop's Univ. (Dir. & Mbr.); The National Theatre Sch. (Dir. & Mbr.); Fashion Group Int'l (Mbr. Advisory Bd.); S.M. Blair Foundation (Pres.). INTERESTS: developing opportunities for women entrepreneurs across Canada; sports; skiing; golf; tennis.

Banks, Catherine Ann, B.A.,B.Ed. ✎ ⊗

Playwright. 21 Hampstead Court, Truro, NS B2N 3E5 (902) 897-7314. Born Middleton, N.S. 1957. m. Peter Martin Rogers. 2 ch. Rilla Banks, Simon Rogers. EDUC: Acadia Univ., B.A.(English) 1978, B.Ed. 1979. CAREER: Teacher, 1980-85. SELECTED CREDITS: *The Summer of the Piping Plover*, Upstart Theatre, Halifax, 1991. AFFIL: Playwrights' Union of Canada (Atlantic Rep. 1993-94); Playwrights' Atlantic Resource Centre (Founding Bd. Mbr. 1990; Co-Chair 1993-94; Bd. Mbr. & Interim Exec. Dir. 1995); N.S. Dramatists' Co-op; N.S. Writers' Federation; Cobequid Arts Council (Bd.); Upper Stewiacke Community Sch. (Bd.). HONS: Honourable Mention, Ottawa Little Theatre Competition, 1984, for *Eula's Offer* (one act); Second, Kings Theatre Competition, 1989, for *Eula's Offer*; MacLennan Foundation Grant, 1992; Silver Medalist (*Three Storey, Ocean View*), du Maurier/Vancouver's Playwright Theatre Centre Competition, 1996. INTERESTS: poetry; walking; reading; rug hooking. MISC: Canada Council Grant, 1991, 1993, 1996. COMMENT: *"I am a mother and a playwright. I strive to put women's lives, particularly the lives of rural women, front and centre on the stage."*

Barber, Joy P., LL.B. ■ ⚖ ⑤

Barrister, Solicitor, Notary, Commissioner for Oaths. 500 Rossland Rd. W., P.O. Box 58013, Oshawa, ON L1J 8L6 (905) 436-3939, FAX 436-5885. Born UK 1947. m. Jerry. EDUC: Osgoode Hall Law Sch., LL.B. 1987; Osgoode Hall, Bar Admission Course 1988. BAR: Ontario, 1988. CAREER: Sch. Teacher, 1967-70; Legal Sec., 1971-74; Law Clerk, 1974-84; Law Student, Swartz & Swartz, 1984-88; Lawyer, 1988 to date; Part-time Teacher, Durham Coll. of Applied Arts & Technology, 1995-96. AFFIL: Law Society of Upper Canada; Durham Coll.; Oshawa General Hospital Auxiliary (Bd. of Dir. 1993-96); Oshawa General Hospital Task Force on Advocacy (1994-95); City of Oshawa (Chair, Property Standards Committee); Oshawa Senior Citizens' Centre (Bd. of Dir. 1994-95); Canadian Mental Health Association (Mbr., Forum Committee Durham). HONS: Charles M. Ewing Award for outstanding achievement in Latin & Greek, 1965; Alger Press Ltd. Award for outstanding achievement in French; Ont. Scholarship (O'Neill C.V.I.), 1966; Osler, Hoskin & Harcourt Prize for highest grades in Labour Rel'ns Law at Osgoode Hall Law Sch., 1987. INTERESTS: piano; contract bridge; travelling; live theatre; attending courses & seminars; public speaking; legal writing. MISC: conducts seminars & workshops on wills, powers of attorney, elder abuse, advocacy legislation. COM-MENT: *"I obtained my law degree at age 40. In addition to practising law, I speak publicly on various legal topics, volunteer in the community and teach part-time at the local community college. I have enjoyed a 28-year marriage and hope to continue to grow personally, academically and professionally."*

Barber, Katherine, B.A.,M.A. 📖 📚
Editor-In-Chief, Canadian Dictionaries, OXFORD UNIVERSITY PRESS CANADA, 70 Wynford Dr., Don Mills, ON M3C 1J9 (416) 441-2941, FAX 441-0345, EMAIL kbarber@oupcan.mail.net. Born Ely, Cambridgeshire, UK 1959. EDUC: Univ. of Winnipeg, B.A.(Hons.) 1986; Univ. of Ottawa, M.A.(Lettres françaises) 1990. CAREER: Lecturer, Sch. of Translators & Interpreters, Univ. of Ottawa, 1984-91; Research Assoc., Bilingual Cdn Dictionary, Univ. of Ottawa, 1989-91; Ed.-in-Chief, Cdn Dictionaries, Oxford University Press Canada, 1991 to date. AFFIL: European Association for Lexicography; Dictionary Society of North America; American Dialect Society; St. Thomas Anglican Church (Toronto) Choir. INTERESTS: choral music, ballet, reading. COMMENT: *"I am a lexicographer in charge of a major study of Canadian English, which will be published as the* Canadian Oxford Dictionary.*"*

Barber, Susan B., B.A.,LL.B. ⚖️
Partner, MCDOUGALL, READY, 700 Royal Bank Building, 2010 - 11th Ave., Regina, SK S4P 0J3 (306) 757-1641, FAX 359-0785. Born Seattle, Wash. 1962. s. EDUC: Luther Coll., 1980; Univ. of Regina, B.A.(English) 1984; Univ. of Saskatchewan, Coll. of Law, LL.B. 1987. BAR: Saskatchewan, 1988. CAREER: served articles of clerkship, Gordon J. Kuski, Q.C., McDougall, Ready, 1987; lawyer, 1988-94; Ptnr, 1994 to date. AFFIL: Canadian Bar Association (Alternate, Nat'l Council; Sask. Branch Nominating Committee; Annual Meeting Planning Committee); Regina Bar Association (Pres. 1996, Annual Meeting Planning Committee); Law Society of Saskatchewan; Provincial Court Bar Judicial Council; Family Mediation Canada; Univ. of Regina Alumni Association (Dir.); 1995 Grey Cup Organizing Committee (VP, Legal; Mgmt Committee); Canada Day Committee, Saskatchewan (VP); Univ. of Regina Planned Giving Committee. HONS: Dorthea Sauer Memorial Scholarship, Luther Coll.; D.C. Kyle Prize, Univ. of Saskatchewan, 1987; Presidents' Gold Medal, Luther Coll. INTERESTS: golfing; swimming; reading; singing; snow skiing; painting. MISC: recipient of numerous scholarships; was the second female president in the history of the Law Stu-dents' Association of the Coll. of Law, Univ. of Saskatchewan; Sessional Lecturer ("The Law & Bus. Admin."), Fac. of Bus. Admin., Univ. of Regina. COMMENT: *"I have always been actively involved as a volunteer in the legal community as well as in my local community and the province as a whole. At the same time I maintain a busy practice as a partner with a large Saskatchewan law firm. Add to the mix, five siblings and 18 nieces and nephews and my life is never dull! The challenges which I face in my career and volunteer pursuits keep me very busy but are always balanced by the wonderful experiences and the satisfaction I receive from all of my endeavours and the support I always have from my family."*

Barclay, Byrna Robin, B.A. 📚 ⭕ ✖️
President, SASKATCHEWAN WRITERS GUILD, 6 Hogarth Place, Regina, SK S4S 4J8 (306) 586-2080. Born Saskatoon, Sask. 1940. m. 2 ch. Julianna, Bruce. EDUC: Univ. of Saskatchewan, B.A. 1961. CAREER: Social Worker; Children's Librarian; Puppeteer; Researcher & Writer, Council on Indian Rights & Treaties, Federation of Saskatchewan Indians, 1970-72; Instructor, Indian Studies, Wascana Institute of Applied Arts & Sciences, 1975-80; Instructor, "The Art of Interpretation," Gov't of NWT, 1981; Creative Writing Instructor, Univ. of Regina, Extension, 1980-82. SELECTED CREDITS: Poets Combine, *Tabloid Love* (performance). SELECTED PUBLICATIONS: *Summer of the Hungry Pup* (Edmonton: NeWest Publishers, 1981); *The Last Echo* (Edmonton: NeWest Publishers, 1985); *Winter of the White Wolf* (Edmonton: NeWest Publishers, 1989); *From the Belly of a Flying Whale* (Vancouver: Douglas & McIntyre); *Crosswinds* (Coteau Books, 1995); *Searching for the Nude in the Landscape* (Thistledown Press, Saskatoon, 1996); short stories published in various anthologies & literary magazines; Ed., two books of poetry, Thistledown Press. EDIT: Fiction Ed., *Grain* Magazine, 1988-90; Ed.-in-Chief, *Transition*, 1988-94; Ed., *FreeLance*, 1977-79. AFFIL: Saskatchewan Writers' Guild (Pres. 1980-81, 1993-95); Writers' Union of Canada; Poets Combine; Saskatchewan Arts Bd. (V-Chair 1982-89); CMHA (Dir., Prov. Bd. 1984-94; Pres. 1991-93). HONS: Saskatchewan Culture & Youth First Novel Award, *Summer of the Hungry Pup*, 1977; YWCA Woman of the Year, Community & Humanitarian Svc., 1989; CMHA Nat'l Distinguished Svc. Award, 1992; SWG Member Achievement Award, 1992; Canada 125 Medal, 1992; 1st Prize, *Room of One's Own* first annual fiction contest, "Where My Mother Goes," 1994; "Crosswinds," winner of Best Fiction Award,

Saskatchewan Book Awards 1995. INTER-ESTS: advocating for status of the artist; advocating for the mentally ill. MISC: workshops on creative writing sponsored by Saskatchewan Writers Guild, 1980 to date; Dir./Coord., Submissions to Saskatchewan on Directions in Health Care, 1989-90; First Chrm, Saskatchewan Advisory Council on Mental Health, 1990-93; "Speak Under Covers," first published in event, listed as one of the most distinguished short stories of 1988, *Best American Short Stories* (Houghton Miflin). COMMENT: *"Daughter, wife, mother, writer, editor, teacher–and advocate. In all these roles I dare to dream, and the endeavour is everything. One hundred years from now will be the time to determine what is lasting, and what was accomplished."*

Barclay, Marion H. ⊗
Chief Conservator, NATIONAL GALLERY OF CANADA, 380 Sussex Dr., Ottawa, ON K1N 9N4 (613) 990-1941, FAX 991-2680. Born Glasgow, Scotland 1939. d. 1 ch. EDUC: Ontario Coll. of Art, Fine Arts 1969. CAREER: National Gallery of Canada, 1971 to date; Tate Gallery, London, UK, 1984-85. SELECTED PUBLICATIONS: *Aspects of Varnishing* (Archtype Books, 1995); "A Conservator's Thoughts Regarding Policy and Travelling Exhibitions at the National Gallery of Canada" (*Journal IIC-Canadian Group*, Vol. 18, 1994); "Materials Used in Certain Canadian Paintings from the 1950s," technical essay in catalogue for the exhibition, *The Crisis of Abstraction in Canada: The 1950s* (National Gallery of Canada, 1992). AFFIL: International Institute for the Conservation of Historic & Artistic Works, UK (Fellow). HONS: Forsyth Travel Scholarship, Ontario Coll. of Art, 1969. INTERESTS: drawing with a variety of materials; biking; hiking; swimming. COMMENT: *"Born in Glasgow, Scotland, I attended boarding school in Edinburgh, married at 21 in Winnipeg, and went to Povungnetuk, Northern Quebec, where I spent five years with my then husband who was employed by the Hudson's Bay Company. We divorced and I went on to OCA, coming to the National Gallery of Canada in Ottawa in 1971 where I apprenticed in painting conservation."*

Bard, Margaret, B.F.A. ⊗ 👁 📁
Co-founder and Associate Director, LUNCHBOX THEATRE, Bow Valley Square, 205 - 5th Ave. S.W., 2nd Flr., Calgary, AB T2P 2V7 (403) 265-4297, FAX 264-5461. Producer, PACIFIC VICTORY PICTURES. Born Auburn, N.Y. 1950. m. Bartley Bard. EDUC: Univ. of Texas, B.F.A.(Drama/English); National Theatre Sch.,

Montreal, Acting; UCLA Extension, Writer's Program, Screenwriting. CAREER: dir., writer, actor; Co-founder &Assoc. Dir., Lunchbox Theatre; Dir., Stage One, the Petro-Canada Plays (dev. wing of Lunchbox). SELECTED CREDITS: has directed numerous plays incl.: *The Wild Guys* & *The Sisters Rosensweig*, Vancouver Arts Club; *Small Family Business* (Cdn premiere), A.T.P.; *Man of the Moment*, A.T.P.; Cdn premiere of *Season's Greetings*, Vancouver Playhouse & A.T.P.; *Cloud 9*, Theatre Calgary; *I'm Not Rappaport*, Stage West; Cdn premiere of *As Is*, Toronto Free Theatre & the N.A.C.; *Dads in Bondage*; Cdn premiere of *The Cemetery Club*; has dir. numerous prods. for Lunchbox; as an actor, has performed in major theatres across Canada, the US & UK incl.: the Shaw Festival, National Arts Centre, M.T.C., Canadian Stage, Theatre Calgary, the Citadel, the Centaur & Alley Theatre in Houston; more than 50 radio dramas; various commercials; feature film credits incl.: *The Good Mother, Bye Bye Blues, Primo Baby, As Is, Superman III* & *Friends, Lovers and Lunatics*. SELECTED PUBLICATIONS: *Coasting: The Women's Club* (also known as *37 Middlesex*); *Show and Tell*. AFFIL: AEA; CAEA; ACTRA; SAG. HONS: nominated, Women of Distinction Award, YWCA, 1987; co-recipient (with Bartley Bard), Harry & Martha Cohen Award for outstanding & sustained contribution to theatre in Alberta, 1988. MISC: *Dads in Bondage*, winner of the Fringe First Edinburgh Festival, 1990; trained with dir. Alan Ayckbourn, UK, 1981; served as Asst. Dir. to Marshall W. Mason on the Broadway prod. of *As Is*. COMMENT: *"Graduate of the National Theatre School. Co-founder of Lunchbox Theatre. Producer, Pacific Victory Pictures. Freelance director. Bestselling novelist–popular women's fiction. Screenplay writer for Columbia/Tri Star Television."*

Barde, Barbara, M.A.,B.A. ■ 👁 ⊗ 👄
President, UP FRONT ENTERTAINMENT INC., P.O. Box 980, Stn. A, Toronto, ON M5W 1G5 (416) 366-6855, FAX 366-5711, EMAIL barbara_barde.local@tor.wtn.ca. Born St. Paul, Minn. s. EDUC: Syracuse Univ., B.A. 1968, M.A. 1969. CAREER: Freelance Researcher, Story Ed., Prod., Dir., 1973-78; Prod./Dir., TVOntario, 1978-85; Pres. & Owner, Why Not Productions Inc., 1985-94; VP, Programming, WTN (Women's Television Network) 1994-95. AFFIL: Canadian Film Centre (Chair, Bd. of Dir.); Toronto Women in Film & Television; Canadian Film & Television Producers Association; Academy of Canadian Cinema & Television; Canadian Women in Radio & Television. HONS: Dodi Robb Award, Media

Watch, 1994; honoured as outstanding film-maker by Toronto Women in Film & Television, 1989; numerous other awards from int'l festivals & competitions incl. a 1993 Gemini nomination. INTERESTS: travel; reading; the role of women in the media; the roles of educ. & communication in int'l dev. MISC: recipient of several travel & study awards; int'l communications consultant; Prod. of more than 250 TV programs incl. 16 major series shot on location around the world; research & strategic planning for CRTC application culminating in the licensing of WTN; numerous papers presented at conferences, associations & festivals; presented numerous briefs to gov't on the role of women in the film & TV industry. COMMENT: *"For more than 20 years Barbara Barde has been committed to issue-based thought-provoking programming that forces the audience to think about the world they live in."*

Bardos, Julia, B.A. Ⓢ
Vice-President, Human Resources, B.C. FERRY CORPORATION, 1112 Fort St., Victoria, BC V8V 4V2 (604) 381-1401, FAX 389-2803. Born Budapest. EDUC: Univ. of Calgary, B.A.(Pol. Sci.) 1972.

Barfoot, Joan, B.A. 🗔 / 🕮
Writer. 286 Cheapside St., London, ON N6A 2A2. EDUC: Univ. of Western Ontario, B.A.(English) 1969. CAREER: journalist, *Owen Sound Sun-Times* & *The London Free Press*, 1965-67; news editor & co-editor, Univ. of Western Ontario student *Gazette*, 1966-67; journalist, *Windsor Star*, 1967-69; journalist, Mirror Publications Toronto, 1969-73; journalist, *The Toronto Sunday Sun*, 1973-75; journalist, *The London Free Press*, 1976-79, 1980-94; lecturer, Sch. of Journalism, Univ. of Western Ontario, 1987-94. SELECTED CREDITS: *Dancing in the Dark* (1986) based on novel of the same name. SELECTED PUBLICATIONS: *Abra* (McGraw-Hill Ryerson, 1978); *Dancing in the Dark* (Macmillan of Canada, 1982); *Duet for Three* (Macmillan of Canada, 1985); *Family News* (Macmillan of Canada, 1989); *Plain Jane* (Macmillan of Canada, 1992); *Charlotte and Claudia Keeping in Touch* (Key Porter, 1994); translations incl. French, Italian, German & Scandinavian; published in various countries, incl. UK & US. AFFIL: Writers' Union of Canada; Women & Words; PEN International. HONS: Marian Engel Award, 1992; *Books in Canada* First Novel Award, 1978; Women of Distinction Award, London YM-YWCA, 1985. MISC: Cdn delegate to the First Int'l Feminist Book Fair & Festival, UK, 1983.

Barlow, Elizabeth, B.Sc.,B.L.S. 🗔 ✆ ✤
Manager, Collections and Electronic Resources, CALGARY PUBLIC LIBRARY, 616 Macleod Trail S.W., Calgary, AB T2G 2M2 403) 260-2607, FAX 234-8763. Born Drumheller, Alta. 1950. EDUC: Univ. of Alberta, B.Sc. 1971, B.L.S. 1972. CAREER: Cataloguer, Univ. of Manitoba Library, 1972-74; Health Sciences Ref. Librarian, Univ. of Saskatchewan, 1974-78; Gov't Publications Dept. Head, Univ. of Saskatchewan Library, 1978-81; Head of Info. Svcs, Saskatoon Public Library, 1981-89; Mgr, Humanities Dept., Calgary Public Library, 1989-91; Head, Public Svcs, Calgary Public Library, 1991-95. AFFIL: Canadian Library Association; Canadian Association of Special Libraries & Information Services; Canadian Association of Public Libraries; Foothills Library Association; Library Association of Alberta; Public Legal Association of Saskatchewan. INTERESTS: reading; cross-country skiing; hiking; cooking. COMMENT: *"Dedicated to the library profession and to excellent service to library customers. Have been actively involved in many areas of the profession."*

Barlow, Maude, B.A.,LL.D. ✆
Chairperson, THE COUNCIL OF CANADIANS, 251 Laurier Ave. W., Ste. 904, Ottawa, ON K1P 5J6 (613) 233-2773, FAX 233-6776, EMAIL coc@web.apc.org. Born Toronto 1947. m. Andrew Davis. 2 ch. EDUC: Carleton Univ., B.A. 1976. CAREER: Sr. Advisor on Women's Issues, to then Prime Minister Pierre Trudeau; Visiting Scholar in residence, Queen's Univ., 1986; Dir., Office of Equal Opportunity for Women in the City of Ottawa; VP, Women Associates Consulting Inc., a mgmt consulting firm specializing in the design & implementation of Affirmative Action programs; Nat'l Voluntary Chair for the Council of Canadians. SELECTED PUBLICATIONS: *Parcel of Rogues: How Free Trade is Failing Canada* (Toronto: Key Porter Books, 1990); *Take Back the Nation*, with Bruce Campbell (Toronto: Key Porter Books, 1992); *Class Warfare: The Assault on Canada's Schools*, with Heather-Jane Robertson (Toronto: Key Porter Books, 1994); *Straight Through The Heart: How the Liberals Abandoned the Just Society* (Harper Collins 1995); numerous publications in journals, periodicals & magazines. AFFIL: Canadian Coalition for Arms Control & Disarmament (Council of Advisors); Canadian Coalition Against Media Pornography (Founder & Past Pres.); Association for Women's Equity in the Canadian Forces (Founding Mbr.); Women for Justice (Founding Mbr.); Council of Canadians (Nat'l Bd.); Annual Council of Canadi-

ans' Conference–Toward a Canadian Alternative (Chair); Media Watch Canada (former Bd. Dir.); Ottawa Task Force on Wife Assault (Past Chair); Amethyst Women's Drug & Alcohol Abuse Centre (Past Pres.); Committee of '94 (Founding Mbr.). HONS: Ontario Teachers' Federation award for outstanding contribution to educ. & equality in Cdn schools; Meritorious Award, The Ontario Teachers' Federation, 1996; LL.D. (Hon.), Memorial Univ. of Newfoundland. MISC: only Canadian on an international women's peace mission to Iraq on the eve of the Gulf War, 1991. COMMENT: *"Maude Barlow is an internationally known keynote speaker, author, political activist and outspoken crusader for Canada. She has spoken to hundreds of conferences on the connection between human rights, social structures and the erosion of equality in the face of growing corporate control of our social, environmental and political lives."*

Barman, Jean, B.A.,M.A.,M.L.S.,Ed.D. 🕱
Professor, Department of Educational Studies, UNIVERSITY OF BRITISH COLUMBIA, Vancouver, BC V6T 1Z4 (604) 822-5331, FAX (604) 822-4244, EMAIL jbarman@unixg.ubc.ca. 2 ch. Roderick A., Emily. EDUC: Macalester Coll., B.A.(Hist. & Int'l Rel'ns) 1961; Harvard Univ., M.A.(Russian Studies) 1963; Univ. of California at Berkeley, M.L.S. 1970; Univ. of British Columbia, Ed.D.(Hist. of Educ.) 1982. CAREER: Researcher & writer, *Mizan* (scholarly journal), London, 1963-64; Portuguese-language Original Cataloguer, State Univ. of N.Y. at Albany, 1970-71; Extra-sessional Lecturer, Dept. of Educ. Studies, Univ. of British Columbia, 1983-85; Sessional Lecturer, 1985-87; Asst. Prof., 1987-91; Assoc. Prof., 1991-94; Prof., 1994 to date. SELECTED PUBLICATIONS: *The West Beyond the West: A History of British Columbia* (Toronto: University of Toronto Press, 1991, rev. ed., 1991); *Growing Up British in British Columbia: Boys in Private School* (Vancouver: UBC Press, 1984); *Children, Teachers and Schools in the History of British Columbia,* ed. with N. Sutherland & J.D. Wilson (Calgary: Detselig, 1995); other books; "'Oh, no, it would not be proper to discuss that with you.' Reflections on Gender and the Experience of Childhood" (*Curriculum Inquiry* Spring 1994); "Birds of Passage or Early Professionals? Teachers in Nineteenth-century British Columbia" (*Historical Studies in Education* Spring 1990); "The Role of the Law Graduate in the Political Elite of Imperial Brazil" with R.J. Barman (*Journal of Inter-American Studies and World Affairs* 1974); various other refereed articles; "Lost Opportunity: All Hallows School for Indian and White

Girls, 1884-1920" (*British Columbia Historical News* Spring 1989); numerous other articles, chapters in books, & book reviews. EDIT: Co-Ed., *BC Studies,* 1995 to date; Gen. Ed., *Pioneers of British Columbia* monograph series UBC Press, 1992 to date; Ed. Bd., *Journal of the Canadian Church History Society,* 1991 to date; Ed. Bd., *History of Education Quarterly,* 1991-93. AFFIL: Heritage Trust BC (1st V-Chair & Dir.); Pacific BookWorld News Society (Dir.); B.C. Central Credit Union History Project (Advisory Committee); Canadian History of Education Association; Canadian Historical Association (Council); American Historical Association; Canadian Church Historical Society; B.C. Historical Federation; Vancouver Historical Society; Okanagan Historical Society; Nicola Valley Archives Association; Campbell River Museum & Archives Association; Nuyumbalees Society, Cape Mudge Village. HONS: Merit Scholarship Finalist, 1957; various undergrad. scholarships, 1957-61; Grad. Fellowship, Harvard Univ., 1961-62; Wallace Fellowship, Harvard Univ., 1961-62; Conference of Latin Am. Hist. Award, 1977; Killam Doctoral Fellow, Univ. of British Columbia, 1979-81; Founders' Prize, Canadian History of Education Association, 1988-89, 1992-94; Canadian Historical Association Reg'l History Prize for B.C. & the Yukon, 1992; Univ. of British Columbia Alumni Prize in the Social Sciences, 1992; Killam Research Fellow, 1992-93. MISC: numerous public lectures; numerous press & broadcast interviews; various consultancies; recipient of numerous grants from various agencies; numerous conference papers; reviewer for various journals & granting agencies

Barnabe, Claire M. ■ ✥ 🕮
Administration Assistant, THE NATIONAL GALLERY OF CANADA. Born Eastview, Ont. (now Vanier) 1940. s. EDUC: Ottawa Teachers' Coll.; Carleton Univ., Grad. Diploma in Public Admin. 1979. CAREER: Teacher, Ont. & Que.; Teacher, N.W.T., 1965-69; worked in hotel bus. at Mackenzie Mountain Lodge, Norman Wells, N.W.T. & Arychuk's, Fort Providence, N.W.T., 1969-70; Candidate in Territorial council elections, Lower Mackenzie constituency, Dec. 1970; Settlement Mgr, Port Burwell, N.W.T., 1971-73; Settlement Mgr-at-Large, Baffin Reg., 1973; Settlement Mgr, Repulse Bay, 1973-74; Settlement Mgr, Norman Wells, 1974-76; Policy Analyst for the Hon. C.N. Drury, the Prime Minister's Special Rep. for Constitutional Dev. in the N.W.T., 1978-80; Policy Advisor, Exec. Committee Secretariat, Gov't of N.W.T., 1980; Sr. Advisor in Intergovernmental Affairs, 1980-86; seconded

to Constitutional Dev. & Strategic Planning Branch, Dept. of Indian Affairs & Northern Dev., Gov't of Canada, 1986-89; Dir., Policy Planning & Evaluation, Dept. of Personnel, Gov't of N.W.T., 1989-90; seconded, Sr. Claims Implementation Analyst (Dene/Métis), Constitutional Dev. & Strategic Planning Branch, Northern Affairs Branch, Gov't of Canada, 1990-96. SELECTED PUBLICATIONS: freelance writer & historical researcher. MISC: Justice of the Peace, N.W.T., 1973; member, N.W.T. Historical Advisory Bd., 1973; travelled extensively throughout the North.

Barnard, Dorothy, B.Sc.,M.D.,F.A.A.P., F.R.C.P.C. ⊕ ⌇
Pediatric Hematologist, Oncologist, Hematopathologist, IWK-GRACE HEALTH CENTRE FOR CHILDREN, WOMEN & FAMILIES, 5850 University Ave., Halifax, NS B3J 3G9 (902) 428-8291, FAX 428-3215, EMAIL dbarnard@ iwkhosp.ns.ca. Associate Professor, DALHOUSIE UNIVERSITY. Born Halifax 1946. s. EDUC: Dalhousie Univ., B.Sc. 1966, M.D. 1971; Master of Health Svcs Admin. 1994. CAREER: Residency, Dept. of Pediatrics, IWK Children's Hospital, Halifax, 1971-72; Residency, Pediatric Hematology, 1972-73; Residency, Dept. of Pediatrics, McMaster Univ., 1973-76; Residency, Dept. of Perinatology, Univ. of Colorado, 1976-78; Lecturer, Dept. of Pediatrics, Dalhousie Univ., 1978-79; Asst. Medical Dir., Red Cross, Transfusion Svcs, Halifax, 1978 to date; Asst. Prof., Dept. of Pediatrics, Dalhousie Univ., 1979-94; Consultant to Immunohematology Lab, IWK Children's Hospital, 1983-86; Lecturer, Dept. of Pathology, Dalhousie Univ., 1986-87; Emergency Dept. Physician, IWK Children's Hospital, 1986-91; Asst. Prof., Dept. of Pathology, Dalhousie Univ., 1987 to date; Dir., Immunohematology Labs, IWK-Grace Health Centre for Children, Women & Families, 1987 to date; Pediatric Medical Dir., Comprehensive Care Clinic, Congenital Hemostatic Disorders, 1987 to date; Lecturer, Dept. of Medicine (Medical Oncology), Dalhousie Univ., 1990 to date; Pediatric Tumour Site Coord., N.S. Cancer Centre, Halifax, 1992 to date; Oncologist, Dept. of Medical Oncology, Cancer Treatment & Research Foundation of N.S., Halifax, 1992 to date; Assoc. Prof., Dept. of Pediatrics, Dalhousie Univ., 1994 to date; Clinical Head, Pediatric Hematology/Oncology, IWK Children's Hospital, 1994 to date; Residency Program Dir., Hematopathology, Dalhousie Univ., 1994 to date; Pediatric Medical Dir., Comprehensive Care Clinic, Thrombophilia, Halifax, 1995 to date. SELECTED PUBLICATIONS: "GATA-1 is Expressed in Acute Erythroid Leukemias," with H. Ekert *et* *al* (*British Journal of Haematology* 86 1994); "Randomized Trial of Intravenous Immunoglobulin G, Intravenous Anti-D, and Oral Prednisone in Childhood Acute Immune Thrombocytopenic Purpura," with V. Blanchette *et al* (*Lancet* 344 1994); "Venous Thromboembolic Complications (VTE) in Children: First Analyses of the Canadian Registry of VTE," with M. Andrew *et al* (*Blood* 83 1994); various other publications. AFFIL: Royal Coll. of Physicians & Surgeons of Canada; American Academy of Pediatrics (Fellow); Atlantic Provinces Pediatric Association; The Histiocyte Society; Atlantic Society of Obstetricians & Gynecologists; International Society of Hemostasis/Thrombosis; Canadian Coll. of Health Service Executives; American Coll. of Health Service Executives; Alpha Omega Alpha Honour Medical Association; Canadian Medical Association; Canadian Society of Palliative Care Physicians; International Association of Pediatric Laboratory Medicine; Canadian Palliative Care Association; Canadian Health Economics Research Association; Canadian Home Care Association; N.S. Medical Society, Pediatric Section (Chair); Association of Hemophilia Directors of Canada (Pediatric N.S. Rep.); Atlantic Provinces Pediatric Hematology Oncology Network (Chair); Children's Cancer Study Group (Principal Investigator, N.S.); Metropolitan Halifax Working Group for Palliative Care; N.S. Institute of Technology (Advisory Committee); First United Church, Musquodoboit Harbour, N.S. (Bd. of Trustees). MISC: numerous conference presentations. COMMENT: *"Continually striving, with the help of many other dedicated health team members, to improve the system of healthcare delivery for Maritime province children and adolescents with cancer and serious hematology diseases."*

Barnes, Susan Carol, B.A.,LL.B., M.P. ✦ ⌇ ⌂
Member of Parliament (London West), GOVERNMENT OF CANADA, House of Commons, 260 West Block, Ottawa, ON K1A 0A6 (613) 996-6674, FAX 996-6772. Constituency Office, 187 Wharncliffe Rd. N., London, ON N6H 2B1 (519) 679-6361, FAX 679-6613. Born 1952. m. 3 ch. EDUC: Univ. of Western Ontario, B.A.(English Lit.) 1974, LL.B. 1977. BAR: Ontario, 1979. CAREER: Lawyer, Past Legal Mbr., Ont. Criminal Code Review Bd. (Lieutenant-Governor's Bd. of Review); Mbr. of Parliament 1993 to date; Gov't V-Chair, Standing Committee on Justice & Legal Affairs, Gov't of Canada 1994-96; Chair, Fed. Ont. Liberal Caucus, 1995-96; Parliamentary Sec. to the Min. of Nat'l Revenue, 1996 to date.

SELECTED PUBLICATIONS: report, "Access to Capital by Small Business." AFFIL: Ontario Caucus Task Force (Mbr.); Canadian National Institute for the Blind, London - St. Thomas (former Mbr. Advisory Bd.); Brain Tumour Foundation of Canada; Maltese Canadian Club of Canada; London West Liberal Association (Exec. Dir., Pres. 1987-89).

Barnhill, Joan Elizabeth Meadows 🍁 ○
Publicity and Promotions Manager, BLOCK PARENT PROGRAM OF CANADA INC., R.R. 1, 1160 Wittenburg Rd., Stewiacke, NS B0N 2J0 (902) 639-2074, FAX 639-9969. Born Amherst, N.S. 1934. d. 1 ch. EDUC: Certificates in Advertising & Copywriting, Classroom Instruction, Public Speaking. CAREER: Operator, Maritime Telegraph and Telephone, 1952-53; Classified Advtg, Halifax Herald Ltd., 1953-54; Advtg Artist/Copywriter, Kline's Department Store, 1961-64; drafting & graphic arts, Federation Civil Svc., 1964-82. VOLUNTEER CAREER: Prov. Block Parent Bd., 1990 to date; Past Prov. Chair. SELECTED PUBLICATIONS: assorted articles in local newsletters; drawings & charts published in Naval hardcover STANAVFORLANT Review. AFFIL: Colchester/Pictou Association of Baptist Churches (Clerk); Canadian Diabetes Association (Charter Mbr.); Canadian Kennel Club. INTERESTS: crime prevention; purebred dog breeding & exhibiting; genealogy; church work; art; music; outdoor activities; gardening; reading; family (daughter & grandson). COMMENT: "Coming from a clergy and military background, it is my belief that we are obligated to return to the community in which we live what we have taken from it, which is why I am involved in so many pursuits on a voluntary basis."

Barra, Gemma ⊗ 🔆 📖 ⚬
c/o Les Éditions Vient de la Mer, 400 boul. Père Lelièvre, Vanier, QC G1M 1N1 (418) 527-5167, FAX 527-5167. Auteur, Compositeur, Interprète, Scénariste, Écrivaine. Born Que. 1936. EDUC: Congrégation St-Louis de France et Ursulines de Québec; école dramatique; Sir George William Univ., études en cinéma. CAREER: est découverte au concours d'amateurs de la radio CKCV, 1950; participe à des tournées avec la troupe de Roland S. Chevrier, 1951; sous le pseudonyme Claude Romance, participe à l'émission Chansonniers Canadiens, CKVL, Verdun, 1952; comédienne, Radio-Canada, 1953; animatrice, Mes Chansons, CHRC, 1956; narratrice, Mon Pays, mes chansons, télévision de Radio-Canada, 1967; animatrice à la radio puis à la télé, comédienne, chanteuse, écrivaine et scénariste, 1970 à ce

jour. SELECTED CREDITS: enregistrement, Jacques, 1961; Auteur et Recherchiste, L'assurance-maladie (documentaire), 1970; Auteur et Scénariste, Hirsy la fabuleuse, 1992; Co-scénariste, La Maîtresse, 1972; Auteur-Compositeur, Scénariste, Une grande fille toute simple, 1991; plusieurs autres films; Retour des chansons de Gemma Barra, CD et cassette, Topaz, 1995 (Vox 7894-2); CD, Fonovox, 1996; spectacle La Rentrée, 1996; divers autres. SELECTED PUBLICATIONS: Mon Cahier de chansons... Sous le ciel du Québec (Éds. Vient de la Mer 1987); Père Noël te raconte ses histoires (Éds. Québec Agenda, 1988); Chant choral Gemma Barra, vol. 1 & 2 (Éds. Vient de la Mer, 1995); 300 chansons (paroles et musique) publiées par Éds. Vient de la Mer et Éds. Boul de Neige (1949-1995); autres publications diverses. DIRECTOR: Les Editions Vient de la Mer. AFFIL: Fonovox; SARDEC; L'UNEC (Union des écrivaines et écrivains québécois); SOCAN. HONS: trophée Mérite, 1960; trophée, Talent, 1961; Trophée Ass. Malaedie; nomination Festival d'Allemagne, 1971; Trophée, Léonard culture, 1988; exposition, Musée de la civilisation, 1995; Marraine d'un centre culturel, 1991. MISC: première auteure-compositeure-interprète à posséder une émission régulière à la radio du Québec, 1956; Ma mère...une auteur-compositeure très convenable, par son fils Cyrus Olivier (1993). COMMENT: "Je suis une personne active qui croit en l'avenir et chacune de mes oeuvres tend à démontrer mon attachement envers l'humain et veut semer l'espoir là où détresse s'installe. Mon oeuvre est réaliste mais conserve l'équilibre de l'être."

Barrat, Olga, Ph.D. 🔬
Research Scientist, BARRAT AND ASSOCIATES INC., 5646 Honeysuckle Place, North Vancouver, BC V7R 4S4 (604) 922-4061, FAX 987-3394. 1 ch. Sasha. EDUC: Ph.D. CAREER: Post-Doctoral Fellow, Dept. of Biochem., Univ. of Alberta, 1966; Prof.'s Asst., 1971; Visiting Scientist, Dept. of Biochem., Univ. of Oxford, 1974; Research Scientist, Kinsmen Lab., Univ. of British Columbia, 1975; Research Scientist, Biophysics Group, Dept. of Physics, Simon Fraser Univ., 1978; Research Assoc. for Acting Dean of Science, Dept. of Chem., Univ. of British Columbia, 1982 to date. SELECTED PUBLICATIONS: co-ed of a series of scientific books under the title: "Coenzymes and Cofactors" (New York: John Wiley & Sons); "Biochemical Effects of Environmental Pollutants and Mechanism of Action," Chemicals in the Environment (manuscript in preparation for book); research results published in reputable scientific journals &presented at nat'l & int'l biochemical conferences. EDIT: newsletter, Sav-

ing the Environment, Canadian Federation of University Women, 1990 to date. **AFFIL:** Canadian Society for Biochemistry & Molecular Biology; New York Academy of Science; American Association for Clinical Chemists; Canadian Institute of Energy; Air & Waste Management Association; International Society for Air Quality & Climate; International Society for Ecosystem Health & Medicine; Canadian Federation of University Women; American Association for Advancement of Science. **MISC:** mbr., B.C. Environment Appeal Board, 1989-94.

Barrett, Becky, B.A.,B.S.W.,M.S.W. 🍁
Member of the Legislative Assembly, GOVERNMENT OF MANITOBA, Legislative Building, Rm. 234, Winnipeg, MB R3C 0V8 (204) 945-2698, FAX 945-0535. Born Pensacola, Fla. **EDUC:** Univ. of Chicago, B.A.(English) 1963; Univ. of Manitoba, B.S.W.(Social Work) 1978, M.S.W. 1979. **CAREER:** Asst. Prov. Sec., Dir. of Organization, New Democratic Party of Manitoba, 1979-86; Policy Analyst, Gov't of Manitoba, 1986-88; Exec. Dir., Women in Second Stage Housing, 1989-90; Member of Legislative Assembly, Prov. of Manitoba, New Democratic Party Caucus, 1990 to date; Critic Areas have included: Family Services, Status of Women, Justice, Civil Service & Urban Affairs. **AFFIL:** New Democratic Party of Manitoba.

Barrie, Mary C., B.A.,M.A.T.,M.A., Ph.D. 🎓 $
Director, School of Continuing Studies, UNIVERSITY OF TORONTO, 158 St. George St., Toronto, ON M5S 2V8 (416) 978-2417, FAX 978-4846. **EDUC:** Sarah Lawrence Coll., B.A.; Brown Univ., M.A.T.(Educ. Psych.); Univ. of Toronto, M.A.(Educ. Theory/Adult Educ.), Ph.D.(Educ. Theory/Adult Educ.). **CAREER:** Mgr, Educ. Svcs of the Nat'l Tech. Centre, Deloitte & Touche, 1981-86; Assoc., Nat'l Office/Professional & Mgmt Dev., Clarkson Gordon/Woods Gordon, 1986; Ptnr, Organizational Learning, 1986-88; Dir., Educ. & Hum. Res. Planning & Dev., Sunnybrook Health Science Centre, 1988-94; Dir., Sch. of Continuing Studies, Univ. of Toronto, 1994 to date. **AFFIL:** The Conference Board of Canada (Cdn Training Directors Forum); The Board of Trade of Metropolitan Toronto. **MISC:** numerous presentations to conferences, societies, associations & corporations. **COMMENT:** *"An adult educator with experience in strategic planning of workplace education and the direction of programming in the corporate, academic, healthcare and government sectors."*

Barris, Kate, B.A.A. 🎭 📺
Writer & President, KATE'S WORD INC., 192 Gillard Ave., Toronto, ON M4J 4N8 (416) 778-0241, FAX 778-8476. Born Toronto 1953. d. **EDUC:** Ryerson Polytechnic Univ., B.A.A.(Radio & TV Arts) 1974. **CAREER:** Jr. Copywriter, MacLaren Advertising, 1974-75; Copywriter, Leo Burnett Advertising, 1975-76; Copywriter, McKim Advertising, 1976-79; Sr. Writer, Hayhurst Advertising, 1979-80; freelance writer, working primarily for Bowen & Binstock, 1980-85; Creative Dir., Bowen & Binstock Advertising, 1985-90; Teacher, Ryerson Polytechnic Univ., 1987 to date. **SELECTED CREDITS:** Co-Writer, sketch material, 18 specials, *The Wayne & Shuster Comedy Hour*, 1977-83; Writer, 20 eps., *Today's Special* (series), 1981-86; Writer, 30+ eps., *Mr. Dressup* (series), 1983-87; Writer, numerous insertion sketches, Cdn version, *Sesame Street* (series), 1988-95; Writer, *The Big Comfy Couch* (series), 1993-95; Writer, several eps., *Kratts Creatures* (series), 1994-95; Writer, *Top Cops* (series), 1991-93; Story Ed., *The Composers Series*, 1992-94; Writer, hosts' commentary, *The Santa Claus Parade*, 1985-95; Co-writer, *Easter Seals Telethon*, 1994-95; numerous other television credits; numerous video credits; Co-writer & co-prod., *Beyond Hope*, a comedy/clown/musical stage show, performed as part of Toronto's SummerWorks Festival, 1994; Writer, *Stickin' Around* (animated series), YTV, 1995-96; Writer & Story Ed., *Flash Forward* (TV series), Atlantis/Disney, 1996. **HONS:** Creativity in Writing Award, sponsored by CFRB Radio, 1972; Creativity in Advertising Award, sponsored by Foster Advertising, 1974; Peabody Award, 1980; US TV Commercials Festival Award, 1981; Art Directors' Merit Award, 1982; Billi Award, 1983; ACTRA Award, Best TV Variety Writing, 1983; Mobius Award, 1985; Silver Bessie, 1987; AMPIA Award, 1990; Art Directors' Merit Award, 1993; National Golden Maples Award, Info. Category, 1991; Regional Gold EVA, Info. Category, 1991; Golden Reel Award, Comm. category, 1991; Birmingham Festival & Ohio State Award, 1992. **INTERESTS:** all. **MISC:** volunteer work, as writer, for Alzheimer Canada, The Hospital for Sick Children, The Muscular Dystrophy Association of Canada, & others; guest lecturer to high sch. & univ. students on advtg & broadcast writing, 1978 to date. **COMMENT:** *"I'm a versatile writer, with a long, interesting line of credits behind me, and, being an optimist, quite convinced there are at least as many ahead."*

Barry, The Honourable Jane, B.Sc. 🍁
Solicitor General, GOVERNMENT OF NEW BRUNSWICK, Box 6000, Fredericton, NB E3B 5H1. Born Halifax. m. Dave Barry. 5 ch.

Patrick Gerard, Jonathan David, Colin Andre, Ryan Edward, Gregory Baird. **EDUC:** St. Francis Xavier Univ., B.Sc.(Chem.). **CAREER:** Chemist, Lantic Sugar; Research Asst., Fac. of Pharmacy, Univ. of Alberta; MLA, Saint John West, Gov't of N.B., 1987; Min. of State for Childhood Svcs, 1989; re-elected, 1991; Min. of the Environment, 1991-94; Solicitor Gen., 1994 to date. **AFFIL:** Saint John Co-Op Supply Depot (former Pres.); District 20 School Board (former Bd. mbr.); West Saint John Co-Op Preschool (Past Pres.); Saint John Univ. Women's Club (Past Pres.) Salvation Army Red Shield Appeal, Saint John (Chair 1991-92); St. Francis Xavier Alumni Association. **HONS:** Commemorative Medal for the 125th Anniversary of the Confederation of Canada. **MISC:** Co-Chair, Select Committee on the 1987 Constitutional Accord, 1987; Chair, Gulf of Maine Council on the Marine Environment, 1991-92; Chair, Atlantic Environment Ministers Committee, 1992; Chair, Canadian Council of Ministers of Environment, 1993-94; first woman in the Gov't of N.B. to hold the post of Min. of the Environment & Solicitor Gen.; mbr., Premier's Round Table on the Environment & the Economy, & the Cabinet Committee on Policy & Priorities.

Barsoski, Diane, B.Sc.,B.Ed.,M.Ed. ■ $ ✎
Vice-President and Director, Human Resources, THE CANADIAN LIFE ASSURANCE COMPANY, 330 University Ave., Toronto, ON M5G 1R8 (416) 597-1456, FAX 204-2374. Born Washington, D.C. 1944. s. **EDUC:** Univ. of Toronto, B.Sc. (Chem.), B.Ed.(Chem. & Comp. Sci.); Ontario Institute for Studies in Education, M.Ed.(Educ. Admin.). **CAREER:** Dir., Employee & Labour Rel'ns, The Bank of Nova Scotia, 1986; Dir., Hum. Res., The Globe and Mail, 1986-91; VP, Hum. Res., 1991-93; VP, Hum. Res., Thomson Newspapers Canada, 1993-96; VP & Dir., Hum. Res., The Canadian Life Assurance Co., 1996 to date. **AFFIL:** Canadian Daily Newspapers Association (Chair, Hum. Res. Committee). **INTERESTS:** books; birds; travel.

Bartle, Jean Ashworth, ARCT,B.A. ✪ 🎓
Founder and Music Director, TORONTO CHILDREN'S CHORUS, 156 Front St. W., Ste. 303, Toronto, ON M5J 2L6 (416) 979-7621, FAX 971-4841. Born Lancashire, UK 1947. m. Donald Ernest Bartle. 3 stpch. **EDUC:** Lakeshore Teachers Coll., 1966; Royal Conservatory of Music, ARCT(Singing/Performance) 1970, ARCT(Teachers) 1973; Univ. of Toronto, B.A. 1977. **CAREER:** Primary Sch. Teacher, 1966-70; Music Teacher, Howard Public Sch., 1970-89; Soloist & Dir., Jr. & Youth Choirs, Kingsway Lambton United Church, 1970-87; Soprano, Toronto Mendelssohn Choir, 1975-91; Music Teacher, Blythwood Sch., 1989 to date; Founder & Music Dir., Toronto Children's Chorus, 1978 to date. **SELECTED CREDITS:** numerous recordings as conductor of the Toronto Children's Chorus, incl. Adeste Fideles with Louis & Gino Quilico & members of the Toronto Symphony. **SELECTED PUBLICATIONS:** *Toronto Children's Chorus Series*, Ed. (Gordon V. Thomson Music); *Jean Ashworth Bartle Series for Treble Voices*, Ed. (Hinshaw Music); author of numerous articles. **AFFIL:** Association of Canadian Choral Directors (Dir., Children's Chorus); Canadian Music Educators' Association; Lifeline for Children's Choir Directors (1987). **HONS:** Leslie Bell Conducting Scholarship, 1977; Sir Ernest MacMillan Conducting Scholarship, 1982; Roy Thomson Hall Award for Outstanding Contribution to the Musical Life of Toronto, 1986. **INTERESTS:** traveling; reading; gardening; bridge; swimming; aerobics. **MISC:** has premiered new works by Glenn Buhr, Jean Coulthard, Malcolm Forsyth, Harry Freedman, Srul Irving Glick, William Mathias, Stephen Hatfield & John Greer; conducted the world premiere of R. Murray Schafer's *Star Princess and the Waterlilies*, featuring Maureen Forrester, at Expo '86; guest lecturer, choral clinician, adjudicator, conductor throughout the world; The Toronto Children's Chorus has won many prizes incl.: First Prize, International Eisteddfod, Wales (1982); First Prize, International Choral Kathaumixw, BC; First Prize, CBC Radio Amateur Choral Competition (1982, 1984, 1986, 1990, 1994); Healey Willan Prize, Canada Council, 1983. **COMMENT:** *"I have developed the concept of the children's choir to an art form, which is now treated with the same respect as an adult choir or instrumental ensemble or orchestra. The Children's Choir is an instrument of artistic excellence."*

Bartlette, Deborah, Dip.Bus.Admin., B.A. $ ♡ ✲
Founder, GROUPSKILLS SEMINARS, 6573 Knight Dr., Delta, BC V4E 1S6 (604) 594-6393, FAX 594-0373. Born Winnipeg 1958. m. Eric Hueber. 2 ch. Kari Hueber, Rob Heuber. **EDUC:** Red River Community Coll., Diploma (Bus. Admin.) 1979; Open Univ., B.A.(Admin. Studies) 1995; currently working on Master's in Theology, Vancouver Sch. of Theology; currently working on Master's in Distance Educ., Athabasca Univ. **CAREER:** Pharmaceutical Sales Rep., Burroughs-Wellcome Inc., 1979-81; Oncology Specialty Rep., ICI Pharma, 1981-84; Sales Rep., Office Assistance Ltd. 1985-89; Consultant & trainer to non-profit groups,

GroupSkills Seminars (self-employed), 1994 to date. SELECTED PUBLICATIONS: "A Christian Feminist" (*Canada Lutheran* 9(7)1994); "Painting the Sky" (*Canada Lutheran* 10(1)1995); "A New Way of Doing Things" (*Canada Lutheran* 10(2)1995). AFFIL: Transition Management Team, ELCIC; National Church Council of the Evangelical Lutheran Church in Canada (BC Rep.); Council of Parent Participation Preschools in B.C. (Past Chair); LutherPlace Care Society (Sec.); Sunshine Hills Parent Group (VP); Lutheran World Federation "Women in Church & Society" program (Liaison for Canada); Gifted Children's Association, Delta Chapter. HONS: Distinguished Sales Award, Sales & Marketing Executives of Vancouver, 1989; District Award, Parent Cooperative Preschools International, 1994; Cdn Delegate, Lutheran World Federation Conference on Women, Geneva, 1995. INTERESTS: active in a proj. to develop seniors' housing; running; reading (esp. CanLit); music; being an involved & supportive parent. MISC: extensive experience in public speaking & presentation; involved in a major renewal proj. for the evangelical Lutheran Church in Canada. COMMENT: *"My achievement lies in my ongoing growth as a person through education, self-awareness and service to others. Raising well-adjusted children is my most important endeavour. I hope that people will say of me, 'She makes a difference.'"*

Bassett, Isabel, M.P.P., B.A.,M.A. ❦

Politician. Author and Broadcaster. Member of the Provincial Parliament (St. Andrews-St. Patrick), GOVERNMENT OF ONTARIO, Ministry of Treasury, Frost Building, 7 Queen's Park Cres. S., 7th Fl., Toronto, ON M7A 1Y7 (416) 325-0367, FAX 325-1584. Born Halifax 1939. m. The Hon. John W. H. Bassett, P.C., C.C., O.Ont. 3 ch. Avery, Sarah, Matthew. EDUC: Queen's Univ., B.A. 1960; Ontario Coll. of Educ., Teacher's Certificate in English & French 1967; York Univ., M.A.(English) 1973. CAREER: research officer, Proj. on the Interaction between the Inuit & White Communities in Frobisher Bay, Association of Indian & Eskimo Affairs, 1960; teacher, Humberside Collegiate Institute, Toronto, 1961-64; reporter, *The Toronto Telegram*, 1965-67; teacher, Calabar High Sch., Kingston, Jamaica, 1967; guest lecturer, York Univ., 1975; reporter on *W5*, CTV, 1976-77; host & reporter on *Hourlong*, CFTO-TV, 1977-84; prod. & reporter, CFTO-TV, 1984-93. SELECTED CREDITS: Prod. & Reporter, CFTO-TV, *Dark Society*; *Beyond the Blues*; *Nightmare in the Neighbourhood*; *Teen Gangs*; *No Place to Hide*; *Children Take Care*. SELECTED PUBLI-

CATIONS: scholarly intro., *Janey Canuck in the West* by Emily Murphy (reprint Toronto: McClelland & Stewart, 1975); *The Parlour Rebellion* (Toronto: McClelland & Stewart, 1975); *The Bassett Report: Career Success and Canadian Women* (Toronto: Collins, 1985). PAST AFFIL: Women's Coll. Hospital Foundation (Hon. Chair); Ryerson Polytechnic Univ. Foundation (Dir.); Canadian Centre for Social Justice (Bd. of Councillors); Canadian Foundation for AIDS Research (Bd. of Advisors); Harbourfront Centre (Chrm's Advisory Council); Toronto Women In Film & Television (Dir.); Scarborough Women's Centre (Patron); Outward Bound Canada (Patron); Canadian Association for Community Living (Hon. Advisory Bd.); Ryerson Polytechnic Univ. (Gov.; former Chair). HONS: Outstanding Woman of the Community Award, Variety Club of Ontario, 1994; Alumni Award for Outstanding Achievement, Queen's Univ., 1991; Metropolitan Toronto Police Association 36th Annual News Award for documentary *Dark Society*; National Media Award, Canadian Mental Health Association Award for documentary *Beyond the Blues*; medalist at Cdn & int'l film & TV festivals for documentaries *Nightmare in the Neighbourhood*, *Teen Gangs*, *No Place to Hide*, *Children Take Care*.; LL.D.(Hon.), Dalhousie Univ., 1995.

Bassett, Sandra, C.H.E. ■■ ⊕

Program Director, Surgical Services, NORTH YORK GENERAL HOSPITAL. 2 ch. Kyle Bassett, Jeff Bassett. EDUC: George Brown Coll., R.N. 1975; Univ. of Western Ontario, B.Sc.(Nursing) 1983 (Dean's Hon. List; Gold Medalist, Post-R.N. Program), 1st yr. of M.D. programme 1983-84; Univ. of Toronto, part-time studies 1988-89, M.H.Sc.(Health Admin.) 1995; Canadian Coll. of Health Service Executives, C.H.E. 1992. CAREER: Staff Nurse, Orthopedic Fl., Toronto General Hospital, 1975-76; Charge Nurse, Orthopedic & Oncology Fl., Victoria Hospital, Miami, 1976-77; Staff Nurse, Recovery Rm. & the I.C.U., Toronto General Hospital, 1977-80; Staff Nurse, part-time, 1980-83; Sessional Teacher, Nursing, Humber Coll., Sept.-Dec. 1984; Acting Dir. of Nursing, Dept. of Surgical Nursing Svcs, The Wellesley Hospital, Jan.-Feb. 1989; Acting Nurse Unit Administrator-Obstetrics, May-Nov. 1989; Nursing Unit Administrator-Post Anaesthetic Care Unit, 1985-90; Dir. of Nursing, Surgical Nursing Svcs, North York General Hospital, 1990-94; Program Dir., Surgical Svcs, 1994 to date. SELECTED PUBLICATIONS: co-author with P. Berger, K. Croteau *et al*, "The Development of a Role Charter for Nursing Unit Administrators" (*Canadian Jour-*

nal of Nursing Administration, 1 (4), 21-24, 1988); co-author with S. Rodgers & M. Javidji, "An Analysis of the Cost Savings Associated with Closure of an Orthopaedic Service within an Acute Care Hospital" (*Health Services Accounting Course Notes*, M.H.Sc. program, 1992). **AFFIL:** Canadian Nurses' Association; International Council of Nurses; Registered Nurses' Association of Ontario; Provincial Nurse Administrators' Interest Group; Ontario Nursing Informatics Group; Sigma Theta Tau, Int'l Honour Society in Nursing; Canadian Council of Health Services Executives; Canadian Cancer Society, Metro Toronto Reg. (Co-Chair, Health Promo. Committee 1993-95); Scouts Canada, 1st Ballantrae Colony (Beaver Leader 1995-96); Parent Council, St. Mark Sch., Stouffville, Ont. (elected mbr. 1996 to date). **HONS:** Charter mbr., Sigma Theta Tau, Int'l Honour Society of Nursing, 1988.

Bastness, Joy ■ 🐾 ⚪ 🌿
Executive Director, SASKATCHEWAN ASSOCIA-TION OF SCHOOL COUNCILS, 221 Cumberland Ave. N., Saskatoon, SK S7N 1M3 (306) 955-5723. Born Birch Hills, Sask. 1938. m. Harry Bastness. 2 ch. Lori, Bev. **EDUC:** Univ. of Saskatchewan, Commerce 1986-90. **CAREER:** Bank of Commerce, 1956-59; Farmer, Hagen, Sask., 1964 to date; positions with the Saskatchewan School Trustees' Association: Local Bd. of Trustees, Birch Hills, 1975-85; Bd. of Educ., Kinistino Sch. Div., 1985 to date; V-Chair, 1991-95; English Language Arts Curriculum Advisory Committee, 1989-93; positions with the Birch Hills Home & School Association: Treas., 1970-73; Pres., 1975-78; Constitution Committee; positions with the Saskatchewan Federation of Home & School Associations: Fin. Chair, 1976-79; Pres., 1979-83; Constitution, Resolutions & Policy Chair, 1986-90; VP, 1990-94; Min.'s Advisory Committee on Student Retention, 1990-92; Exec. Dir., 1994 to date; positions with the Canadian Home & School & Parent-Teacher Federation: Western VP, 1983-84; Pres., 1984-86, 1990-91; Fin. Chair, 1987-89, 1990-93, 1995 to date; Treas., 1995 to date. **AFFIL:** The Canadian Home & School & Parent-Teacher Federation (Life Mbr.); Saskatchewan Federation of Home & School Associations (Life Mbr.); Active Living Alliance for Children & Youth (Fitness Canada); Canadian Education Association; Saron Lutheran Church (Pres.); Saron Evangelical Lutheran Church Women. **HONS:** Woman of the Year, YWCA, 1990. **MISC:** President's Advisory Committee, Canadian Education Association, 1991-92; Min. of Education's Advisory Educational Council, 1984-89.

Bata, Sonja, D.Hum.L.,L.L.D. Ⓢ 📖 🕐
Director, BATA LIMITED, 59 Wynford Dr., Don Mills, ON M3C 1K3 (416) 446-2206, FAX 446-2187. Chairman, BATA SHOE MUSEUM FOUNDATION. m. Thomas J. Bata. 4 ch. **EDUC:** studied architecture at the Swiss Federal Institute of Technology, Zurich. **DIRECTOR:** Bata Limited; Alcan Aluminium Limited; Canada Trustco. **AFFIL:** Bata Shoe Museum Foundation (Chair); North York General Hospital Governors' Council (Chair); Junior Achievement of Canada; World Wildlife Fund (Canada) (Hon. Chair); The Council for Canadian Unity; Community Foundation of Greater Toronto; The Council for Business and the Arts in Canada; Shastri Indo-Canadian Institute (Cdn Avdisory Council); Toronto French Sch. (Hon. Mbr., Bd. of Advisors). **HONS:** Silver Medal of the United Nations Environmental Program. 1982; Officer of the Order of Canada, 1983; Paul Harris Fellow Recognition, Rotary Internationa,l 1983; B'Nai B'rith Humanitarian Award, 1984; Shoe Person of the Year Award, 1985; Hon. Captain(N), Fifth Canadian Destroyer Squadron, 1989; Award for International Development,CESO, 1990; named to Canadian Business Hall of Fame, 1991; McClure International Service Award, 1991; Woman of the Year Award, North York Chamber of Commerce, 1992; Prime Mentors of Canada Award, 1995; Hon. Associate Award, Conference Board of Canada, 1995; Doctor of Humane Letters (Hon.), Mount Saint Vincent Univ., 1989; LL.D.(Hon.), Willson Coll.; hon. Diploma for Applied Arts & Technology, Loyalist Coll.; LL.D.(Hon.), York Univ., 1992; LL.D.(Hon.), Dalhouse Univ.

Battson, Jill ■ 📿 Ⓢ ⊗
Executive Producer, TALKING PICTURES, 17 Penrose Rd., Number 12, Toronto, ON M4S 1P2 (416) 410-8300, FAX 488-9883. Born UK 1958. **EDUC:** Ware Coll. of Art & Design, UK, Graphic Design 1974-76; Ryerson Sch. of Media Studies, Film 1987-89, Intensive TV Production 1990. **CAREER:** Advtg Agency Art Dir., 1976-83; Journalist, 1986 to date; corp. & industrial video prod., 1983 to date. **SELECTED CREDITS:** *Thirty* (film), 1988; *Going Home* (film), 1992; *Wanted* (film), 1994; Prod., *Word Up* (recording), 1995; Prod., *On the Arts* (series), CBC Newsworld, 1994; Prod., *Word Up*, MuchMusic, 1994; Prod., *Poetry Express*, Fringe Theatre Festival, Toronto, 1994-95; Coord., *Wordapalooza*, Lollapalooza, Toronto, 1994. **SELECTED PUBLICATIONS:** *Word Up*, spoken word poetry in print, ed. with Ken Norris (Key Porter, 1995); *Playing in the Asphalt Garden*, poetry (Insomniac Press, 1994); *Fifteen LA Poems, Fifteen*

Sensual Poems, Fifteen Toronto Poems, Conchinilla Dreams, Elvis Is Everywhere (1992-93); work appears in literary magazines throughout North America & UK. **EDIT:** Ed., *Silver Screen*, 1992-93. **AFFIL:** League of Canadian Poets; AIDS Committee of Toronto. **HONS:** Bronze AMI, "Careers 2001," 1985; Silver AMI, "Purolator Courier," 1987; Silver AMI, "Bramalea," 1988; People's Choice Award & National Poetry Video Slam Champ, *Word Up* segment, Chicago National Poetry Video Festival, 1995. **COMMENT:** *"Jill Battson is an internationally published action poet and spoken word organizer whose career is producing independent film as well as television."*

Batty, Helen P., M.D.,C.C.F.P, F.C.F.P. ⊕ ⌂
Associate Chair, Department of Family and Community Medicine, Faculty of Medicine, UNIVERSITY OF TORONTO, 620 University Ave., Ste. 801, Toronto, ON M5G 2C1 (416) 978-8530, FAX 978-3912, EMAIL hpb@dfcm. utoronto.ca. Born London, UK 1949. m. J. David Beattie. 2 ch. **EDUC:** Univ. of Toronto, M.D. 1973; O.I.S.E., Univ. of Toronto, M.Ed. 1982. **CAREER:** Demonstrator, Dept. of Family Medicine, Fac. of Medicine, Univ. of Toronto, 1975-76; Lecturer, 1976-79; Asst. Prof., 1979-90; Sessional Physician, Bay Centre for Birth Control, Women's Coll. Hospital, 1980-81; Sessional Physician, Cancer Detection Centre, Women's Coll. Hospital, 1985-86; Family Physician, Family Practice Health Centre, Woman's Coll. Hospital, 1978 to date; Centre for Studies in Medical Educ., Fac. of Medicine, Univ. of Toronto, 1984 to date; Assoc. Prof., Dept. of Family Medicine, Fac. of Medicine, Univ. of Toronto, 1990 to date. **SELECTED PUBLICATIONS:** "Corynebacterium Vaginale: A Neglected Pathogen in Family Practice" (*Canadian Family Physician* Jan. 1981); "The Family Physician and Smoking in Pregnancy," with H.F. King (*Journal of Family Practice* 30(3) 1990). **AFFIL:** Coll. of Family Physicians of Canada (Fellow; Dir., Ont. Chapter). **INTERESTS:** watercolour painting; gardening; reading; walking. **MISC:** recipient, various grants. **COMMENT:** *"Special interests are education, adult development and women's health. Founding Director, Woman's Health Scholars Program for Health Professionals, Women's College Hospital, and Academic Fellowship and Master's Program, Department of Family and Community Medicine."*

Batty, Michelle, B.A. ◐ ⊜
Executive Director, SEXUAL ASSAULT SURVIVORS' CENTRE SARNIA-LAMBTON, 118 Victoria St. N.,

Sarnia, ON N7T 5W9 (519) 337-3154, FAX 337-0819. Born Woodstock, Ont. 1956. m. Edward. 2 ch. Jonathan, Alexander. **EDUC:** Univ. of Western Ontario, B.A.(French) 1977; Univ. of Waterloo, B.A.(Psych.) 1983; Renison Coll., Certificate of Study (Social Work) 1987. **CAREER:** Micro-Fiche Technician, Lambton County Library, 1978-80; Social Worker, Sarnia-Lambton Children's Aid Society, 1980-90; Social Worker, Sarnia General Hospital, 1990-91; Exec. Dir., Sexual Assault Survivors' Centre, 1992 to date. **AFFIL:** Sarnia-Lambton Co-ordinating Committee on Violence Against Women; Ontario Coalition of Rape Crisis Centres (VP 1993-94); Volunteer Co-ordinators Association, Lambton Outreach Community Services (Exec. Mbr. 1994 to date); Sexual Assault Treatment Centre; Advisory Committee, Sexual Assault Network Committee; Sexual Assault Outreach Advisory Committee. **INTERESTS:** reading; travelling; swimming; snowmobiling. **COMMENT:** *"I am a feminist, mother of two sons, and have worked with survivors of sexual abuse/assault for 15 years in various capacities. Through hard work, determination and strong organizational skills, I have persevered in my beliefs and endeavours toward preventing violence against women and children. Thus, in the past years, the Sexual Assault Survivors' Centre has flourished and grown to offer a viable service for survivors of sexual assault/abuse."*

Bauer, Nancy, B.A. ⌂ ⊗ ☼
Writer. 252 Stanley St., Fredericton, NB E3B 3A3 (506) 455-8169, EMAIL wbauer@unb.ca. 3 ch. Ernest, Grace, John. **EDUC:** Mount Holyoke College, B.A.(English) 1956. **CAREER:** Ed./Publ., New Brunswick Chapbooks, 1967-82; Teacher, various part-time for universities & writers' workshops; Writer-in-Residence, Bemidji State Univ., 1987; Writer-in-Residence, Univ. of New Brunswick, 1989-90. **SELECTED PUBLICATIONS:** *Flora, Write This Down* (Goose Lane Editions, 1982); *Wise-Ears* (Oberon Press, 1985); *The Opening Eye* (Oberon Press, 1988); *Samara the Wholehearted* (Goose Lane Editions, 1991); *The Irrational Doorways of Mr. Gerard* (Goose Lane Editions, 1994); "Prologue" (*Canadian Fiction Magazine* 1983); "Like A Green Olive Tree in the House of God" (*Abba*, 1976); "Dance, Dance, Wherever You May Be" (*Canadian Fiction Magazine* 1976; anthologized in *Stubborn Strength*, 1983); *Here We Are*, Ed. (1984); weekly column on arts & crafts in *The New Brunswick Reader* & *The Telegraph Journal*; numerous articles & reviews. **AFFIL:** Writers Federation of N.B. (Founding Committee Mbr.); Gallery Connexion Coop (Charter

Mbr.; Vice-Chair 1985-94); McCord Hall Writers Group (Advisor 1967-83); Wilmot United Church (Comm. Committee, Min. Search Committee); N.B. Arts Bd. HONS: winner, CBC Literary Competition, fiction, 1982; Certificate of Recognition, N.B. Arts Bd., 1994; Chelmsford High Sch. Hall of Fame, 1995. MISC: Canada Council Explorations Jury, 1984-85; Canada Council Short-Term Writing Grant Jury 1992; readings at Milton Acorn Festival; Atlantic Reading Circuit; Harbourfront; Writers in Schools; Assoc. Prod., "The Art in Wilmot United Church," Vision TV, 1993. COMMENT: *"Bauer has participated in the arts of the Maritimes as writer, organizer, editor and teacher. She has published five novels and many articles on writers and artists."*

Baulu-MacWillie, Mireille, B.A.,L.PH., D.E.N.S.,M.A.,Ph.D. ■ ⬤
Professor, Department of Education, UNIVERSITÉ SAINTE-ANNE, Pointe-de-l'Église, NS B0W 1M0 (902) 769-2114, FAX 769-2930. Born Montreal 1940. m. Gordon J. MacWillie. 4 ch. EDUC: Univ. de Montréal, B.A.(Lib. Arts) 1961, L.PH.(Phil.) 1965, D.E.N.S.(Educ.) 1971, M.A.(Psych. of Educ.) 1975, Ph.D.(Foundations of Educ.) 1982. CAREER: Teacher, Coll. Marguerite Bourgeoys, Coll. Regina Assumpta, École Secondaire Villa Maria, Montréal, 1962-68; Assoc. Prof., Dept. of Phil., Coll. Jean-de-Brébeuf, 1968-78; Lecturer, Coll. Bois-de-Boulogne, 1971-72; Lecturer, Univ. de Montréal, 1972-78; V-Principal, École Alexandra, London Bd. of Educ., 1978-81; Principal, 1981-85; Prof., Dept. of Educ., Univ. Sainte-Anne, 1985 to date; Dir., Dept. of Educ., 1991-96; Chair, Inter-Univ. Council on Teacher Educ., N.S., 1995-97. SELECTED PUBLICATIONS: *Apprendre. c'est un beau jeu* with R. Samson (Montréal: Les Éditions de la Chenelière, 1990); "La découverte magique de nos racines: une trousse d'animation et d'apprentissage" (*Les cahiers,* La société historique acadienne July-Dec. 1992); "La maternelle, premier jalon du système éducatif français" (*Le Phare de la Pointe,* Univ. Sainte-Anne, Sept. 1992). EDIT: Guest Ed., special edition, Éducation et francophonie, *Le préscolaire au Canada Francophone,* Vol. XXII, no. 3, Dec. 1995. AFFIL: Association canadienne d'éducation de langue française; Canadian Society for the Study of Education; Canadian Association for Young Children; Le Centre préscolaire de la Baie Ste-Marie (Dir.). HONS: Bursary for two-month study leave in France, Gov't of France & Société nationale des Acadiens; Bursary, Canada Council, 1976-78; Bursary, Min. de l'éduc. du Qué., 1976-78; Bursary, Coll. Jean-de-Brébeuf, 1974-75. INTERESTS: teaching/

learning environments; educational psych.; early childhood educ.; playing the flute; reading good books; enjoying the wildlife around my seaside home. COMMENT: *"In my career, I have tried to discover what makes a rich and positive teaching/learning environment by developing my own personal resources, by studying the relevant research literature, by working with my peers, and by developing models that might make some modest contribution to our present knowledge. I feel privileged to be involved in the education of the next generation of teachers because it represents an enormous challenge and a rewarding pursuit."*

Baum, Nehama T., Ph.D.,C.Psych. ■■ ⊕
Executive Director, Clinical Psychologist, MUKI BAUM ASSOCIATION FOR THE REHABILITATION OF MULTI HANDICAPPED INC. (day treatment centres for children & adults, & high-support residential program with 3 group homes; intensive psycho-educational psycho-therapeutic program), 265 Rimrock Rd., Ste. 209, Downsview, ON M3J 3C6 (416) 630-2222, FAX 630-2236. 4 ch. (2 adopted & 1 with special needs). Muki, Karnie, Michael, Mark. EDUC: Univ. of Tel Aviv, Sch. of Social Work, Diploma of Social Work 1958; Hebrew Univ., Jerusalem, B.A.(Art Hist.) 1970, B.A.(Special Educ. & Counselling) 1970, M.A.(Special Educ. & Counselling) 1975; Bezalel Academy of Art, Jerusalem, grad. study in clay modeling & sculpture 2 yrs.; Ontario Institute for Studies in Education, Univ. of Toronto, Ph.D.(Applied Psych.) 1980; ongoing therapy training. CAREER: actress, theatre, Israel, 1948-56; various positions in social work, group therapy, sex educ., univ. lecturing, research, 1959-76; private practice, family therapy with families of physically & mentally handicapped children, 1959-76; left Israel for Canada, 1976 (to find educational rehab. program for son, born with cerebral palsy & severe hearing impairment); private practice, 1976 to date; Supervisor, Learning Potential Proj., Ontario Institute for Studies in Education, 1978-79; founder & Exec. Dir., Muki Baum Association for the Rehabilitation of Multi Handicapped Inc., 1979 to date. SELECTED PUBLICATIONS: conference proceedings & articles incl.: "The Phenomena of Playing within the Process of Sandplay Therapy" (chpt., *Mental Health in Mental Retardation: Recent advances and practices,* Nick Bouras (ed.), London: Cambridge Univ. Press, 1994); "Attending to the Mental Health Needs of People with Developmental Handicaps: The Prevention of Emotional and Behavioral Disorders" (*BrOADD Perspectives,* OADD Press, Fall/Winter 1990); "Therapy for People with

Dual Diagnosis: Treating the Behaviors or the Whole Person?" (chpt., *Treatment of Mental Illness and Behavioral Disorder in the Mentally Retarded*, Proceedings of the Int'l Congress, May 1990. Amsterdam: Logon Publications, 1990); "An Analysis of a Sample of Picasso Bull Drawings According to Various Creativity Theories" (*The Hebrew University Bi-Monthly*, Hebrew Univ. of Jerusalem, 1972). AFFIL: Canadian Register of Health Service Providers in Psychology; Ontario Psychological Association; International Society for Sandplay Therapy; Sandplay Therapists of America; Canadian Association for Sandplay Therapy (Pres.); National Association for the Dually Diagnosed; European Association for Mental Health in Mental Retardation; Fragile X Foundation; North York Inter-Agency & Community Council (Children's Svcs Committee); ORTHO. HONS: Confederation Medal, Gov. Gen. of Canada, 1992; Woman of the Year, B'nai Brith Women's Council of Toronto, 1990. MISC: numerous int'l & reg'l conferences/workshops incl.: "On Becoming an Artist: The Reduction of Aggressive Behavior as a Result of Art Education," 10th World Congress of International Association for the Scientific Study of Intellectual Disabilities, Helsinki, 1996; "In-Depth Psycho-Dynamic Psychotherapy for People with Dual Diagnosis: Reality or Fiction?," First Congress, European Association for Mental Health in Mental Retardation, Amsterdam, Sept. 1995; "Innovative Psychotherapeutic Approaches with People with Fragile X Syndrome," Third Int'l Fragile X Conference, Snowmass, Colorado, June 1992; listed in *Who's Who of American Women*, 1983-84 & 1984-85.

Baxter, Moyra ■ ◉ ◐ ⬿
Consultant, BAXTER, PHILLIPS & ASSOCIATES, R.R. 2, S-29B, C-F1, Peachland, BC V0H 1X0 (250) 767-6153, FAX 767-6193. Born Belfast, N. Ireland 1943. s. 3 ch. EDUC: State Registered Nurse, UK, 1965. VOLUNTEER CAREER: Pres., Raymer Elementary Parent Auxiliary, Kelowna, B.C., 1985-87; Pres., KLO Secondary Parent Advisory Council, Kelowna, 1987-90; Exec. Mbr., Central Okanagan Parent Advisory Council, 1987-96; Mbr., Bd. of Dir., BC Confederation of Parent Advisory Councils, 1989-96; Prov. Coord., CHSPTF/Health & Welfare Canada Proj., "Talking With Your Children About AIDS," 1990; Pres., Central Okanagan Parent Advisory Council, 1990-92; Exec. Mbr., Canadian Home & School Parent-Teacher Federation, 1990 to date; Mbr., The Educ. Advisory Committee, Ministry of Educ., 1991-94; Pres., BC Confederation of Parent Advisory Councils, 1991-94; Mbr., Educ.

Change Committee, Ministry of Educ., 1992-94; Mbr., Educ. Fin. & Facilities Advisory Committee, Ministry of Educ., 1995-96; Mbr., Partners in Science Awareness Committee, Ministry of Employment & Investment, 1994-96. SELECTED PUBLICATIONS: Co-author, *Building Partnerships Manual* (BC Ministry of Educ.); Coord. & Author, "BCCPAC Secondary School Project Report" (BC Ministry of Educ.); Writer & Ed., *BCCPAC Leadership Manual*. AFFIL: Guy's Hospital Nurses' League (UK); Central Okanagan Child & Family Resources Society (Pres.). MISC: workshop presenter & speaker at various conferences; frequent radio & TV guest; past member, various Ministry of Educ. Advisory Committees. COMMENT: *"For 22 years I have been involved in promoting parent involvement in the public school system and truly believe in public input into education decision-making."*

Bayefsky, Anne F., B.A.,M.A.,LL.B., M.Litt. ■ ⬿ ⚖
Director, Centre for Refugee Studies, YORK UNIVERSITY, York Lanes, 4700 Keele St., 3rd Fl., North York, ON M3J 1P3 (416) 736-5663. Born Toronto 1953. m. Raj Anand. 3 ch. EDUC: Univ. of Toronto, B.A. 1975, M.A. 1976, LL.B 1979; Oxford Univ., M.Litt. 1982; Strasbourg, Certificate of Attendance 1980. BAR: Ontario 1983. CAREER: Univ. of Ottawa, Fac. of Law, 1981-96; Special Observer to the Cdn Delegation to the 39th & 44th Regular Sessions of the U.N. Gen. Assembly, 1984 & 1989; Fellow, Centre for the Study of Human Rights, Columbia Univ., 1985; Bd. of Inquiry under Ont. Human Rights Code, 1986 to date; Mbr., six-mbr. Nat'l Task Force of the Canadian Bar Association on Constitutional Amendment, 1991; Academic Advisor to the Cdn Delegation to the World Conference on Human Rights, 1993; Academic Observer to Cdn Delegation to the 40th, 50th, 51st & 52nd sessions of the U.N. Commission on Human Rights, 1993-96; Dir., Centre for Refugee Studies, York Univ., 1996 to date. SELECTED PUBLICATIONS: *International Human Rights Law: Use in Canadian Charter of Rights and Freedoms Litigation* (Butterworths, 1992); *Canada's Constitution Act 1982 and Amendments: A Documentary History* (McGraw-Hill Ryerson, 1989); *Legal Theory Meets Legal Practice* (Academic Printing and Publishing, 1988); *Equality Rights and the Canadian Charter of Rights and Freedoms* (Carswell Co. Ltd., 1985); numerous articles in the field of int'l protection of human rights, civil liberties, constitutional law, int'l law, equality rights theory & women's rights. EDIT: Ed. Bd., *The National Journal of Constitutional Law*, 1990

to date; Consulting Ed., *Canadian Journal of Law and Jurisprudence*, 1992 to date; Ed. Bd., *Canadian Journal of Women and the Law*, 1985-8; Advisory Bd., 1987-92. AFFIL: The International Centre for the Legal Protection of Human Rights (Advisory Council, Interights); International Law Association (Committee on Int'l Law in Municipal Courts; Committee on Enforcement of Human Rights Law); American Society of International Law (Exec. Council); International Association for Philosophy of Law & Social Philosophy (Cdn Section); Canadian Council on International Law (Exec. Bd.). HONS: Commonwealth Scholarship, 1980-81; Fellowship, Columbia Univ. Center for the Study of Human Rights, 1984-85; Bora Laskin Nat'l Fellowship in Human Rights Research, 1992; Grant for Research & Writing, The John D. & Catherine T. MacArthur Foundation Program on Peace & Int'l Cooperation, 1995.

Bayer, Fern, B.A.,M.A. ■ 📖 ⊗ ✿
Independent Curator. 131 Bloor St. W., Ste. 1017, Toronto, ON M5S 1S3 (416) 921-6602, FAX 921-9239. EDUC: McGill Univ., B.A. 1971; Università Internazionale dell'Arte, Diploma(Museum Sci. & Restoration of Works of Art) 1972; Univ. of Toronto, M.A. 1975, doctoral studies 1976. CAREER: Freelance Art Consultant, 1975-77; Chief Curator, Gov't of Ont. Art Collection, 1977-95. SELECTED PUB-LICATIONS: *The Ontario Collection* (Markham: Fitzhenry & Whiteside, 1984); "Travelling Theory Introduction," with Jamelle Hassan (*Harbour Magazine of Art and Everyday Life* Fall 1992); "Lost and Found: The Extraordinary Story of the Ontario Collection" (*Canadian Parliamentary Review* Summer 1986); "A New Look For Ontario's Vice Regal Suite," with Judith Margles (*Canadian Collector* Nov./Dec. 1980). AFFIL: Art Metropole, Toronto (Bd.). MISC: involved in the organization of various int'l projects incl. *David Cronenberg in Tokyo: A Retrospective and Exhibition*; Curatorial Consultant, The Ontario Heritage Foundation, 1983-86.

Bayless, Betty, B.A. ■ ■ ⚅ ⛌
President, CANADIAN FEDERATION OF UNIVERSITY WOMEN (supports educ. & nurtures women in Canada; participates in public affairs), 297 Dupuis St., Ste. 308, Ottawa, ON K1L 7H8 (613) 747-7339, FAX 747-8358, EMAIL 76501.1352@compuserve.com. Born St. Paul, Minn. 1938. m. Thomas. EDUC: Coll. of St. Catherine, B.A.(Math.) 1960. CAREER: Scientific Computer Programmer/Supervisor, Sperry Univac, 1960-75; Exec. Dir., Common Cause, Minn., 1975-78; Teaching Asst., McGill Univ., 1992-94. SELECTED PUBLICATIONS:

Nuts and Bolts of Influencing Public Policy (with Susan Russell, 1995, 1996); *An Introduction to Pascal Programming* (with Leo Kerulaan, 1992). AFFIL: Canadian Federation of University Women (Pres. 1996-98; Nat'l Legislation Chair 1994-96; Pres., UWC Montreal Inc. 1992-94; prov. (Que.) & local positions 1984-94); League of Women Voters of Minnesota (Action/Citizen Info. Chair 1978-84; local & reg'l positions 1965-78); Saint John, N.B. Special Olympics (Public Rel'ns Dir. 1987-90). HONS: Phi Beta Kappa (Liberal Arts); Pi Gamma Mu (Math.). INTERESTS: golf; counted X-stitch; computers; travel; issues. COMMENT: *"Involvement in missile guidance programming in the 1960s was unique and special for women. My volunteer life has and will always include support for people and issues. I am proud to serve as CFUW President, representing more than 10,000 members."*

Bazarkewich, P. Jane, B.A.,M.A. ■ Ⓢ
Senior Vice President, CIBC, Commerce Court (W4), Toronto, ON M5L 1A2. EDUC: Univ. of Toronto, B.A, M.A. CAREER: various positions, CIBC, 1969-82; VP, Consumer Div., 1982-86; VP, Private Bnkg, 1986-90; Pres., CIBC Trust Corporation, 1990-96; Sr. VP, CIBC, 1996 to date. AFFIL: Dellcrest Children's Centre (Bd.); Centennial Road Home & School Association (Bd.); Parent Advisory Bd.

Bear, Merryl Jean, B.A., M.Ed.(Psych) ■ ⊕ ⓞ
Program Coordinator, NATIONAL EATING DIS-ORDER INFORMATION CENTRE, 200 Elizabeth St., College Wing, 1-211, Toronto, ON M5G 2C4 (416) 340-4156, FAX 340-4736. Born Dundee, South Africa 1961. EDUC: Univ. of Natal, S.Africa, B.A.(English), Psych.(Hons.) 1983, Higher Diploma in Educ. 1984, M.Ed.(Psych.) 1990. CAREER: Typist & Receptionist, Hart Plastics and Aluminium Factory, Durban, 1982; Grad. Asst., Psych. Dept., Univ. of Natal, 1983-84; Teacher-Counsellor, Northlands Boys' High Sch., 1985-87; Grad. Asst., Dept. of Educ. Psych., Univ. of Natal, 1988; Psychologist, Pietermaritzburg Schools' Psychological Clinic, 1989-90; Lecturer, Dept. of Educ. Psych., Univ. of Natal (Pietermaritzburg), 1991; Psychometrist (Locum), North York Bd. of Educ., 1992; Program Dir., National Eating Disorder Information Centre, 1992 to date; Instructor, Assaulted Women & Children Counsellor/Advocate Program, George Brown Community Coll., 1994 to date. SELECTED PUBLICATIONS: "The National Eating Disorder Information Centre: A Profile" with A. Gayle in *Consuming Passions: Feminist Approaches to Weight Preoccupation and Eat-*

ing Disorders ed. C. Brown & K. Jasper (Toronto: Second Story Press, 1993); "Prevention of Eating Disorders" with N. Piran & K. Jasper *in University of Toronto Handbook on Eating Disorders* ed. S.H. Kennedy (1993); "The Healing Process" (*Bulletin of the National Eating Disorder Information Centre* Sept. 1994); "Finding Help in Overcoming Eating Problems: Looking For A Therapist" (*Bulletin of the National Eating Disorder Information Centre* July 1994); "Foxy Fables and Facts: A Journal to Healthy Lifestyles" (co-author). HONS: Int'l Exchange Scholarship to US, Rotary Club, 1979; Academic Scholarship, Human Sciences Research Council, 1987; Genesis Foundation Grant, 1993, 1994, 1995; Women on the Move, *The Toronto Sun*, 1995. INTERESTS: social justice issues; reading; travel. MISC: speaker & organizer at various conferences & professional dev. workshops; supportive of social justice movements & issues, incl. anti-apartheid movements. COMMENT: "*A life lived with a philosophy of respect and justice for all, beginning with my own treatment of each individual with whom I have dealings. Accomplishments include public awareness and education projects around race-relations, sexual abuse and eating problems aimed to increase social justice for women in particular.*"

Beare-Rogers, Joyce, B.A.,M.A., Ph.D. ⊕ 🏵 🐟
Consultant, lipid nutrition. 41 Okanagan Dr., Nepean, ON K2H 7E9 (613) 828-1791, FAX 828-1791. Born Pickering Township, Ont. 1927. m. Dr. Charles G. Rogers. EDUC: Univ. of Toronto, B.A.(Sci.) 1951, M.A.(Nutrition) 1952; Carleton Univ., Ph.D.(Biochem.) 1966. CAREER: Research Assoc., Univ. of Toronto, 1952-54; Instructor in Physiology, Vassar Coll., Poughkeepsie, NY, 1954-56; Chemist, Food & Drug Directorate (now the Health Protection Branch), Ottawa, 1956-65; Research Scientist, 1965-75; Chief, Nutrition Research Div., Bureau of Nutritional Sciences, Health & Welfare Canada, 1975-91; Adjunct Prof., Dept. of Biochem., Univ. of Ottawa, 1980-92; Consultant, Food & Agriculture Organization of the United Nations, 1992-95. SELECTED PUBLICATIONS: 109 scientific articles on nutrition; editor of two books on lipid nutrition. AFFIL: International Union of Nutritional Sciences (Chair, Committee on Biological Evaluation of Fat 1986 to date); International Union of Pure & Applied Chemistry, Commission of Oils, Fats & Derivatives (Chair 1987-89; titular mbr. of Applied Chemistry Div. 1989-93; co-opted mbr. 1993-95); Canadian Society for Nutritional Sciences (Pres. 1984-85); Canadian Biochemical Society; American Insti-

tute of Nutrition (Fellow 1994); Canadian Institute of Food Science & Technology; American Oil Chemists' Society (Pres. 1985-86); International Society for Fat Research (Pres. 1991-92); Royal Society of Canada (Fellow 1989). HONS: Canadian Borden Award, 1972; Queen's Silver Jubilee Medal, 1977; Médaille Chevreul, Association française pour l'étude des corps gras, 1984; Ottawa Biological & Biochemical Society Award, 1985; Crampton Award, McGill Univ., 1986; Normann Award, Deutsche Gesellschaft für Fettwissenschaft, Hamburg, Germany, 1987; Fellow of the Royal Society of Canada, 1989; Member of the Order of Canada, 1992; Commemorative Medal for the 125th Anniversary of the Confederation of Canada; McHenry Award, Canadian Society for Nutritional Sciences, 1993; D.Sc.(Hon.), Univ. of Manitoba, 1985; D.Sc.(Hon.), Univ. of Guelph, 1993. INTERESTS: lipid nutrition; science & health in general. MISC: Mbr. of FAO/WHO Expert Consultation on the Role of Dietary Fats & Oils in Human Nutrition; Visiting Prof., Technical Univ. of Denmark, 1983; C-I-L Distinguished Visiting Lectureship in the Sciences, Mount St. Vincent Univ., 1985; Hilditch Lecturer, British Society of Chemical Industry, Liverpool, 1994. COMMENT: "*I pursued an education in food chemistry and biochemistry and worked in the Canadian government for 35 years, as a chemist, research scientist and research manager.*"

Beaton, Brenda ⊘ 🎨 ○
President, RINGETTE PEI, 12 Woodbine St., Charlottetown, PE C1A 2X9 (902) 894-8026, FAX 892-0383. President, GATT INC. Born Charlottetown 1953. m. Wayne. 3 ch. EDUC: Colonel Gray Sr. High Sch., Grade 12 1971. CAREER: wife & mother, 1972 to date; community volunteer, 1972 to date; Mgr, bookstore, 1973-75; Pres., Gatt Inc. (mgmt company), 1987 to date; working with East Isle Restaurants. AFFIL: Ringette Canada (Dir.); Ringette PEI (Pres.); Ringette Charlottetown (Coaching Dir.); 1997 PEI Women's Soccer Team (Mgr); Canadian Coaches' Association; PEI Coaches' Association (Dir.); IODE (Exec. Sec.); QEH Auxiliary (Assoc. Mbr.); Home & School Association; Spring Park Church; Spring Park UCW (Assoc. Mbr.); Sport PEI (Dir.). HONS: Award for 1,000 volunteer hours to the Queen Elizabeth Hospital. INTERESTS: family; reading; young people & their dev.; ringette; friends; travelling; soccer; basketball; hockey; quiet time. MISC: Full level 3 coaching certification in ringette; Community level 1 referee's certification for ringette; attended two nat'l ringette championships as mgr & two as coach; on PEI Prov. Fair Play Committee; coached at

the 1995 CWG. COMMENT: *"In my role as mother and coach of youth, I try to teach the lifeskills of hard work, honesty, fair play. If I help these young people, that is my achievement."*

Beaton, Carol Ann, B.Sc.,B.Ed. ■ ⌇ ○
Children's Centre Coordinator, Extension and Community Affairs, UNIVERSITY COLLEGE OF CAPE BRETON, Box 5300, Sydney, NS B1P 6L2 (902) 539-5300, ext 647, FAX 563-1449, EMAIL cbeaton@caper2.uccb.ns.ca. Born Dartmouth, N.S. 1948. m. G. Wayne Beaton. 2 ch. EDUC: Acadia Univ., B.Sc.(Psych.) 1968, B.Ed.(Elementary Educ.) 1969. CAREER: Clerk, Water Dept., City of Dartmouth, Summer 1966; Research Asst., Univ. of Calgary, Summer 1968; Teacher, Dartmouth City Schools, 1969-72; Substitute Teacher, City of Sydney Schools, 1972-73; Resource Teacher, Dartmouth Public Schools, 1973-74; CA student, H.R. Doane Co., 1975-76; Ptnr, Tinker Tailor (craft bus.) 1977 to date; Ptnr, Bluebell Silk & Design, 1994 to date; Substitute Teacher, Cape Breton District Sch. Bd., 1987 to date; Program Coord. of Children's Centre, University Coll. of Cape Breton, 1994 to date. AFFIL: Women's World Finance/Cape Breton Association (Bd.); IWK Children's Hospital (Bd. of Gov.); IWK Children's Hospital Foundation (Bd.); IWK Children's Miracle Network Telethon, Cape Breton Div. (Co-Chair, 1986-87; Chair, 1987-88; Committee Mbr., 1988 to date); Coord., Cape Breton IWK Children's Miracle Telethon, 1989-1993. HONS: Birk's Medal, Dartmouth High Sch., 1965; Entrance Scholarship, Acadia Univ., 1965-66; Dean's List, Acadia Univ., 1966-67; Silver A, Extracurricular Activities, Acadia Univ., 1969; S.C. Gordon Prize in Educ., 1969. MISC: Mbr., Craft Development Advisory Bd., Enterprise Cape Breton, 1987 to date.

Beattie, Judith Hudson, B.A.,M.A. ▯ ✤
Keeper, Hudson's Bay Company Archives, PROVINCIAL ARCHIVES OF MANITOBA, 200 Vaughn St., Winnipeg, MB R3C 1T5 (204) 945-2626, FAX 948-3236, EMAIL jbeattie@chc.gov.mb.ca. Born Sydney, N.S. 1944. m. Francisco Valenzuela. 1 ch. Janet Beattie. 2 stpch. Marcia Boey, Hector Leon Valenzuela. EDUC: Carleton Univ., B.A.(Cdn Hist.) 1967; Univ. of Toronto, M.A.(Cdn Hist.) 1968. CAREER: Archivist, Ont. Archives, 1969-73; Archiviste, Centre de recherche en civilisation canadienne-française, Univ. d'Ottawa, 1977-81; Sr. Archivist, Hudson's Bay Company Archives, 1981-90; Keeper, 1990 to date. SELECTED PUBLICATIONS: "My Best Friend: Evidence of the Fur Trade Libraries" (*Epilogue*

(8) 12, 1993); "The Company and the Cross" (*Western Oblate Studies* (3) May 1993); various other journal articles. AFFIL: Association of Canadian Archivists; Association for Manitoba Archives; Westworth United Church (Volunteer Archivist). MISC: various presentations; numerous lectures & papers.

Beattie, Laurie A.E., B.A.,M.B.A.,C.A. Ⓢ
Vice-President, Financial Reporting and Budgets, THE CONSUMERS' GAS COMPANY LTD., Box 650, Scarborough, ON M1K 5E3 (416) 495-6041, FAX 495-6451. Born Windsor, Ont. 1955. m. James S. Saloman. 1 ch. EDUC: Queens Univ., B.A.(Hons., Econ.) 1978; Univ. of Alberta, M.B.A.(Fin.) 1986. CAREER: Sr. Computer Audit, Coopers and Lybrand, 1979-81; Articling Student, Clarkson Gordon, 1977-79; Audit Mgr, 1981-84; Univ. of Alberta, Sch. of Bus., & the Centre for the Advancement of Professional Acctg Educ., 1984-86; Sr. Mgr, Audit & Acctg, Thorne Ernst and Whinney, 1986-89; Dir., Fin. Reporting, Consumers' Gas Company Ltd., 1989-94; VP, Fin. Reporting & Budgets, 1994 to date. AFFIL: Chartered Accountant; YMCA Canada (Audit Committee); Gas Technology Canada (Treas.); Ontario Natural Gas Association (Dir.). INTERESTS: travel; hiking; skiing; theatre.

Beattie, Margaret Ann, B.Sc.,M.Sc., Ph.D. ■ ⌇ ✿
Professor, MOUNT ALLISON UNIVERSITY, Sackville, NB E0A 3C0 (506) 364-2533, EMAIL mbeattie@mta.ca. EDUC: McMaster Univ., B.Sc. 1968; Queen's Univ., M.Sc. 1971, Ph.D. 1977. CAREER: Teaching Asst., Queen's Univ., 1969-74; Wissenschaftlich Hilfskraft, Universitat Mannheim, 1974-78; Prof., Mount Allison Univ., 1993 to date; Head, Dept. of Math & Comp. Sci., 1994-96. SELECTED PUBLICATIONS: "A cohomological approach to the Brauer-Long group and the groups of Galois extensions and strongly graded rings" (*Transactions of the American Mathematics Society* 1991); "Prime ideals and finiteness conditions for Gabriel topologies over commutative rings," with S. Caenepeel (*Rocky Mountain Journal of Math* 1992); "A right crossed product and duality" (*Communications in Algebra* 1994); other articles in journals & conference proceedings. AFFIL: Canadian Mathematical Society; American Mathematical Society; Association for Women in Mathematics; Mathematical Association of America; Canadian Math Society (Bd. of Dir.).

Beauchamp, Hélène, B.A.,L.Lett., Ph.D. ⌇ ⊗ ▯
Professor and Graduate Studies Coordinator,

Theatre Department, UNIVERSITÉ DU QUÉBEC À MONTRÉAL, CP 8888, Succ. Centre-Ville, Montréal, QC H3C 3P8 (514) 987-8437, FAX 987-7881, EMAIL beauchamp.helene@uqam.ca. Born Ottawa 1943. s. 1 ch. Manouane Couillard. EDUC: Univ. d'Ottawa, B.A. 1964, Diplôme d'Études Supérieures 1970; Univ. de Paris, L.Lett. 1966; Univ. de Sherbrooke, Ph.D. 1982. CAREER: Prof., Dépt. des Lettres françaises, Univ. d'Ottawa, 1966-70; Prof., Dépt. de Théâtre, 1970-75; Prof., Dépt. de Théâtre, Univ. du Québec à Montréal, 1975 to date; Assoc. Researcher, Institut de Sociologie, Univ. Libre de Bruxelles, 1983 to date; Chair, Dépt. de Théâtre, Univ. du Québec à Montréal, 1984-89; Coord., Grad. Studies, Dépt. de Théâtre, 1995 to date. SELECTED PUBLICATIONS: *Le Théâtre canadien-français* (Fides, 1976); *Les Enfants et le jeu dramatique* (de Boeck, 1984); *Le Théâtre pour enfants au Québec: 1950-1980* (Hurtubise HMH, 1985); *Théâtre et Adolescence* (UQAM, 1988); *Travail théâtral en cours* (Presses collégiales du Québec, 1992); *Le Théâtre dans l'école* (Presses collégiales du Québec, 1992); "Montreal's Maison Théâtre–Dreams With An Impact" (*Canadian Theatre Review* 1990); "Le théâtre à l'intention des étudiants: Du Théâtre-Club à la Nouvelle Compagnie Théâtrale" (*L'Annuaire Théâtral* 1991); "Forms and Functions of Scenography in Theatre Productions for Young Audiences in Quebec" (*Canadian Theatre Review* Spring 1992); "Artistes et inventeurs de territoires–Jeune théâtre, Jeune Public" (*Théâtre/Public* (Paris) 1994); other articles in journals & anthologies; various entries in reference works; various conference papers. EDIT: *Art dramatique/Repères pédagogiques*, by André Maréchal (PCQ, 1993); *Jeunes Publics*, play collection (Éditions Québec/Amérique); Ed. Bd., *Theatre Research in Canada/ Recherches théâtrales au Canada*; Advisory Bd., *Essays in Theatre/Études théâtrales*; former mbr., Ed. Bd., *Jeu, Cahiers de théâtre*; former mbr., Ed. Bd., *Veilleurs de nuit*; former mbr., Ed. Bd., *L'Annuaire Théâtral*. AFFIL: Association for Theatre Research in Canada (Exec. Committee); Nouvelle Compagnie Théâtrale (Bd. of Admin. 1993); L'Association québécoise des professeurs d'art dramatique (VP 1992-93); Canadian Child & Youth Drama Association; Association Québécoise du Jeune Théâtre; Association for Canadian Theatre History. HONS: First Laureate, Concours provincial de langue et de littérature françaises de l'Ontario, 1960; Literature Prize, Univ. d'Ottawa, 1964; Award for best article, Association for Theatre Research in Canada, "Le théâtre à l'intention des étudiants: Du Théâtre-Club à la Nouvelle Compagnie Théâtrale," 1991. MISC: recipient of grants & fin. awards from various agencies; Chair, Ann Saddlemyer book prize committee, Association for Theatre Research in Canada, 1989, 1990, 1993; Co-founder, Theatre Dept., Univ. of Ottawa, 1970; Co-founder, Maison Québécoise du Théâtre pour l'Enfance et la Jeunesse, Montréal, 1980. COMMENT: *"Does research in the fields of theatre pedagogy and professional training, theatre for young audiences, and is particularly interested in the evolution of professional theatre in Québec since 1940 especially focusing her research on mise en scène, scenography and the material conditions of production."*

Beauchemin, Micheline, R.C.A. ⊗
Artist, Sculptor and Weaver. 22 chemin du Roy, Les Grondines, QC G0A 1W0 (418) 268-8368, FAX 268-8368. Born Longueuil, Que. EDUC: École des Beaux-Arts, Paris. CAREER: Dessinateur naval, Marine Industries, Sorel, Que., 1952-53; Dessine des costumes pour la télévision de Radio-Canada, 1958-59. SELECTED CREDITS: Actor, *Les Têtes*, dir. Alexandor Jodorowsky. COMMISSIONS: Costumes pour *Magie Rouge*, Théâtre de l'Egrégore, Montréal, 1961; costumes pour *Entrailles de Claude Gauvreau*, 1961; tapisserie pour la Salle Wilfrid Pelletier, Place des Arts de Montréal, 1963; tapisserie pour l'Église St.-Jean Vianney, Rosemont, 1964; tapisserie pour l'Aéroport International de Toronto; rideau d'Opéra du Centre National des Arts, Ottawa, 1968; tapisserie pour Statistique Canada, 1969; tapisserie pour l'Univ. York, 1970; tapisserie pour le Pavillon du Canada, Exposition Mondiale d'Osaka, Japan, 1970; tapisseries pour le film *Réjeanne Padovani* de Denys Arcand, 1971; tapisserie pour l'édifice de la Défense Nationale, 1972; tapisserie pour l'édifice du ministère du Revenu, Sainte-Foy, Que., 1979; sculpture spatiale, édifice Nova, Alberta Corporation, Calgary, 1983; sculpture spatiale en cuivre, hall de l'édifice Lavalin, Montréal, 1985; sculpture spatiale pour le hall du nouvel Hôtel de Ville d'Ottawa, 1994. EXHIBITIONS: Palais des Beaux-Arts, Paris (1956); Musée d'Art Moderne, Paris (1956); Galerie Denyse Delrue, Montréal (1959); Galerie Nationale du Canada (1960); Nihon Bashi Gallery, Tokyo (1969); Centre Culturel Canadien, Paris (1971); Galerie Susy Langlois, Paris (1972); *Microcosma*, Barbican Centre, London, UK (1982); Galerie Artcurial, Paris (1982); *Objet de Magie*, Musée de la Civilisation (1989); *Hommage au Fleuve St.-Laurent*, Place des Arts de Montréal (1990); Domaine Forget, Charlevoix (1994); Maison Hamel-Bruneau, Sainte-Foy (1995). COLLECTIONS: well-represented in collections in Canada & abroad. AFFIL:

Québec Sculptors' Association; Québec Textile Art Association; Royal Canadian Academy of Arts. **HONS:** Prix de la Prov. de Qué., 1959; Officer, Order of Canada, 1974; Médaille, Institut Royal d'architecture du Canada, 1976; Prix d'excellence Saidye Bronfman, 1982; Prix "Philippe Hébert," Société Saint-Jean-Baptiste, 1983; Prix d'excellence, Lucien Desmarais "La navette d'or," 1988; Prix d'excellence, Institut Canadien du Québec, 1988; Chevalier, Ordre National du Québec, 1991; Doctorat ès arts (Hon.), Univ. Laval, 1983. **INTERESTS:** arts; poetry; travel. **MISC:** recipient of various grants; speaker & presenter at various conferences. **COMMENT:** *"Toute petite fille, avant même de savoir écrire, déja je brodais. Depuis, j'ai installé mes ateliers de tapisseries sur les falaises qui surplombent le Fleuve St.-Laurent, aux Grondines."*

Beaudoin, Patricia, M.B.A. $

Vice-President, Human Resources, SEARS CANADA INC., 222 Jarvis St., Toronto, ON M5B 2B8 (416) 941-4568. **EDUC:** McMaster Univ., M.B.A. 1972. **CAREER:** VP, Hum. Res., Aikenhead's H.I.W., 1992-94; Sr. VP, Hum. Res., Ætna Canada, 1988-92; VP, Hum. Res., CIBC, 1972-88. **AFFIL:** Seneca Coll. of Applied Arts & Technology (Gov. 1994-96); Human Resource Professionals Association of Ontario (Pres. 1981-82); Univ. of Toronto (Hum. Res. Advisory Council 1982 to date); Conference Board of Canada (Hum. Res. Exec. Committee); Board of Trade (Hum. Res. Committee).

Beaudoin, Louise ■■ 🍁 📜

Member of the National Assembly for Chambly, Minister of Culture and Communications, and Minister responsible for the application of the Charter of the French Language, GOVERNMENT OF QUEBEC/GOUVERNEMENT DU QUÉBEC, 225, Grande-Allée E., Bloc A, 1er étage, Québec, QC G1R 5G5 (418) 643-2110, FAX 643-9164. Born Quebec City 1945. **EDUC:** Univ. Laval, licence (hons. degree) & Master's degree (Hist.); Sorbonne, Paris, licence (Sociology). **CAREER:** in charge of cooperation, École nationale d'administration publique du Québec; Exec. Asst. to Min. of Intergovernmental Affairs, 1976; Dir. of Rel'ns with France, Ministère des relations internationales du Québec, 1981;Que.'s Delegate-Gen. in Paris, 1983; Min. of Int'l Affairs, 1985; Proj. Leader in Europe, Canadair, 1986; Dir. of Distribution, Mktg & Int'l Affairs, Telefilm Canada, 1987; Dir. Gen., Société du Palais de la civilisation, 1990; VP, Mkt Dev., Raymond, Chabot International, 1992; elected MNA for Chambly, 1994; joined Cabinet as Min. responsible for Cdn Intergovernmental Affairs, 1994; Min. of Culture & Communications, 1995 to date; Min. responsible for the application of the Charter of the French Language, 1996 to date; Min. resp. for the Info. Highway. **AFFIL:** Théâtre Espace Go (Chairwoman of the Bd. 1988-94); Domaine Forget, Charlevoix (Bd. of Dir. 1990-94). **HONS:** Officer, Legion of Honour, Gov't of France.

Beaumont, Anne, B.A.,M.Sc. 🍁 $

Assistant Deputy Minister, Housing Policy and Programs, ONTARIO MINISTRY OF MUNICIPAL AFFAIRS AND HOUSING, 777 Bay St., 10th Fl., Toronto, ON M5G 2E5 (416) 585-7482, FAX 585-7233. Born Holywell, UK 1940. m. Dane. **EDUC:** Univ. of Wales, B.A.(Geography & Int'l Pol.) 1962; Univ. of Toronto, M.Sc.(Urban & Reg'l Planning) 1971. **CAREER:** Exec. Dir., Community Planning Programs, Ministry of Mun. Affairs & Housing, 1982-85; Exec. Dir., Hum. Res. Svcs, Ministry of Gov't Svcs, 1985-87; Asst. Deputy Min., Supply & Svcs, 1987-89; Asst. Deputy Min., Housing Planning, & Policy, Ont. Ministry of Housing, 1989-96. **AFFIL:** Canadian Institute of Planners (Nat'l Pres. 1979-80); Institute of Public Administration of Canada (Dir., Toronto Reg'l Group 1986-88); Ryerson Polytechnic Univ. (Advisory Committee, Planning Program); The McGill Club (Dir. 1990-91, 1993-94).

Beck, Eve, B.A. $

Agent, STATE FARM INSURANCE COMPANIES, 1556 Dundas St. W., Mississauga, ON L5C 1E4 (905) 279-691, FAX 949-8643. Born Montreal 1940. w. 4 ch. **EDUC:** State Univ. of New York, 1983. **CAREER:** Elementary Sch. Teacher, Montreal; Radio & TV Broadcaster, CBC, St. John's; Chair & CEO, Alcohol & Drug Commission, Newfoundland & Labrador; Bus. Consultant, Mississauga, Ont.; Agent, State Farm Insurance. **DIRECTOR:** 1556 Dundas St. West, Ltd.; Eve Beck Insurance Agency, Ltd. **AFFIL:** City Centre Rotary Club of Mississauga (Past Pres. & Charter Mbr.). **HONS:** Small Business Award of Excellence, Mississauga, 1992; Life-Time President's Club, State Farm Insurance Companies. **INTERESTS:** painting. **MISC:** Reg'l VP Council, State Farm Insurance Canada; background in Child Play Therapy; numerous presentations to State Farm agents & managers across North America; videotape training productions. **COMMENT:** *"Deeply interested in enriching the lives of others, especially young people, in helping them in goal determination, skills development and personal motivation. My personal skills in communication and motivation through a positive outlook in life have given me personal and business success and recognition."*

Beck, Nuala M., B.A. $

President, NUALA BECK & ASSOCIATES INC., BCE Place, 161 Bay St., Ste. 1300, Box 531, Toronto, ON M5J 2S1 (416) 364-8517, FAX 364-7695. Born Montreal 1951. m. Frank J. Beck. EDUC: Le Couvent Anglais, Bruges, Belgium, 1967; Carleton Univ., B.A.(Econ.) 1974. CAREER: Economist, Bank Credit Analyst, 1974-77; VP & Sr. Economist, McLeod Young Weir Limited, 1977-81; VP & Dir., Pitfield Mackay Ross Limited, 1981-84; Pres., Nuala Beck & Associates Inc., 1984 to date. SELECTED PUBLICATIONS: *Collision* (1985); *Free Trade* (1985); *Who Owns America?* (1987); *Financial Disinflation* (1988); *Sunrise Statistics* (1989); *Shifting Gears: Thriving in the New Economy* (1992); *Excelerate: Growing in the New Economy* (1995); numerous other publications. DIRECTOR: Ontario Hydro. AFFIL: National Research Council Institute for Marine Dynamics (Dir.); Institute for Research on Public Policy (Chair, Investment Committee); Roy Thomson Hall (Bd. of Gov.); Toronto Hospital (Cardiac Centre Campaign Committee); Board of Trade of Metro Toronto (Mbr. of Council; Chair, New Economy Task Force). INTERESTS: travel; theatre; symphony; reading. MISC: frequent speaker & guest lecturer; mbr., Int'l Trade Advisory Committee, Investment Canada, 1994 to date. COMMENT: *"Pioneered a new framework for contemporary economic and financial analysis, developed 25 new financial ratios and 160 new economic indicators, best known for her ground-breaking work on 'The New Economy'."*

Beck, Pat, B.A. ♣ ⊙

Regional Representative, Manitoba/Saskatchewan National Women's Liberal Commission, LIBERAL PARTY OF CANADA, 200 Laurier Ave. W., Ottawa, ON K1P 6M8. Born Man. EDUC: Univ. of Manitoba, B.A. 1962. CAREER: Child Welfare Worker, 1962-66; Co-Owner/Mgr, Lawtek Computer Systems, 1980-93; researcher, Health Services Utilization & Research Commission, 1996. AFFIL: International Council of Women (Convener of Laws & Status of Women 1994-96); Canadian Commission of UNESCO (Chair of Subcommission on Status of Women 1994-96); Canadian Beijing Facilitating Committee (elected member 1994-95); Consumers Association of Canada; National Council of Women; Centennial Auditorium & Convention Centre (V-Chair 1995-97). INTERESTS: gardening; walking; theatre; music; reading; politics at all levels. MISC: mbr., Cdn Delegation, UN Fourth World Conference on Women, 1995. COMMENT: *"I have been very interested in the involvement of women at all levels of politics, both as a mem-* ber of a party and member of organizations that lobby for better conditions for women in society. I believe in women's equality in all spheres of life."*

Beckman, Margaret, B.A.,B.L.S., M.L.S.,LL.D. 📖 ⊛ 📚

President, BECKMAN ASSOCIATES LIBRARY CONSULTANTS INC., 168 John Blvd., Waterloo, ON N2L 1C5 (519) 742-7064, FAX 579-2052. Born Hartford, Conn. 1925. m. Arthur K. Beckman. 3 ch. Kip, Susan, David. EDUC: Univ. of Western Ontario, B.A. 1946; Univ. of Toronto, B.L.S. 1949, M.L.S. 1969. CAREER: Children's Librarian, Galt Public Library, 1949-50; Cataloguer, Univ. of Western Ontario, 1950-51; Dir. of Tech. Svcs, Univ. of Waterloo, 1958-66; Systems Librarian, Univ. of Guelph, 1966-71; Chief Librarian, 1971-84; Exec. Dir., Info. Tech., 1984-88; Pres., Beckman Associates Library Consultants Inc., 1988 to date. SELECTED PUBLICATIONS: *New Library Design*, with Stephen Langmead (Wiley, 1971); *The Best Gift; a record of the Carnegie libraries of Ontario*, with John Black & Stephen Langmead (1984); *Building Libraries: guidelines for the planning and design of Ontario public libraries*, with Stephen Langmead & others (1986); contributor to more than 120 other publications. AFFIL: Canadian Association of College & University Libraries (CACUL); American Library Association. HONS: Outstanding Woman Award, Prov. of Ont., 1975; Award of Merit, Ontario College & University Library Association, 1986; Academic Librarian of the Year, American Library Association, 1986; Distinguished Grad. Award, Fac. of Library & Info. Sci., Univ. of Toronto, 1989; Distinguished Academic Librarian Award, CACUL, 1989; Distinguished Award Recipient, 13th Symposium on Info. Technology, Univ. of Essen, 1990; LL.D.(Hon.), Univ. of Western Ontario, 1987; Doctor of Letters (Hon.), Laurentian Univ., 1990. INTERESTS: library consulting; music; theatre; gardening; skiing; swimming; sewing; reading; children/grandchildren. MISC: Chair, Nat'l Research Council, Advisory Board for Scientific & Technical Info. COMMENT: *"I have been fortunate in being in library and information science at a time when new developments and technologies were being invented and encouraged."*

Bédard, Myriam, M.A.C.,LL.D. ⊘ ♦

Athlete. 4925 du Golf, Québec, QC G2A 4E3 (418) 847-4490, FAX 847-4380. Born Quebec City 1969. m. Jean Paquet. 1 ch. Maude. SPORTS CAREER: began rifle shooting with the Army Cadets, Valcartier, Que., 1984; first biathlon competition, 1985; two Gold Medals, biathlon World Cup, 1991; ranked number two in the world, 1991; Bronze Medal, Women's 15 km Biathlon, Winter Olympics, Albertville, 1992; two Gold Medals, Winter Olympics, Lillehammer, 1994. HONS: Meritorious Service Cross, 1994; Bobbie Rosenfeld Award, 1994; Canadian Female Athlete of the Year, 1994; Lou Marsh Award as Canada's Top Athlete of 1994; LL.D.(Hon.), Royal Military Coll., 1995. MISC: first Cdn to win gold in biathlon World Cup events, 1991; first North American to win an Olympic medal for biathlon, 1992.

Bedell, Graysanne, B.A.,LL. B. ■ ⬗ Ⓢ
Vice-President, Law, SCOTT'S RESTAURANTS INC., 500 Hood Rd., Markham, ON L3R 0P6 (905) 946-7100, FAX 946-7104. Born Toronto. m. 1 ch. Emma. EDUC: Trent Univ., B.A. 1976; Osgoode Hall Law Sch., LL.B. 1979. CAREER: Lawyer, Kingsmill, Jennings, 1981-88; Ptnr, 1986-88; Assoc. Gen. Cnsl & Sec., Scott's Hospitality Inc., 1988-91; VP, Law, Food Svcs Div., 1991 to date. AFFIL: Streethaven at the Crossroads (Dir. & former VP); Law Society of Upper Canada; Canadian Bar Association; Canadian Corporate Counsel Association. INTERESTS: businesswomen's issues; writing fiction; nordic skiing. MISC: involved through an informal corp. bus. women's forum in panel presentations to North York Bd. of Educ. teachers & students through their "Learning is for Life" program. COMMENT: *"I value the opportunities for growth and balance through all my career, personal, and community interest relationships."*

Bedford, Hazel, B.Math. ■ ⑨ ⊕
Past President, SLEEP/WAKE DISORDERS CANADA, 3080 Yonge St., Ste. 5055, Toronto, ON M4N 3N1 (416) 483-9654, FAX 483-7081. Born Wawa, Ont. 1952. EDUC: Univ. of Waterloo, B.Math. 1972. CAREER: Mgmt Trainee & Asst. Mgr, Bank of Montreal, 1972-84. VOLUNTEER CAREER: Sleep/Wake Disorders Canada, 1986 to date. SELECTED PUBLICATIONS: "Sleep Disorders: A Patient's Perspective" (special journal for the Canadian Gynecological Physicians, Sept. 1993). AFFIL: Housing Alternatives Inc. (Treas. 1990-95); Self-Help Link; Coverdale Centre. INTERESTS: ocean kayaking; hiking. COMMENT: *"S.W.D.C. is a relatively new national network of people affected by any of more than 70 various sleep disorders. Most common are narcolepsy, sleep apnea, restless legs and insomnia, chronic fatigue and fibromyalgia. Shortly after being diagnosed with narcolepsy in 1984, I moved from Toronto to N.B. At that time there was no professional or self-help support for sleep disorders east of Montreal. I initiated self-help*

groups in N.B., N.S., Prince Edward Island and Newfoundland. In 1989, I joined the national board and became President in 1992."

Bedingfield, E. Wendy, B.P.E.,M.Sc., Ph.D. ⬗ Ⓢ
Faculty of Management and Education, ACADIA UNIVERSITY, Wolfville, NS B0P 1X0 (902) 542-2200, FAX 542-4029, EMAIL WBedingf@admin.acadiau.ca. Born Cornerbrook, Nfld. 1947. d. 1 ch. EDUC: Memorial Univ. of Newfoundland, B.P.E. 1967; Univ. of Oregon, M.Sc. 1970; Indiana Univ., Ph.D.(Biomechanics) 1978. CAREER: Asst./Assoc. Prof., Univ. of Alberta, 1976-86; Dir., Sch. of Recreation & Phys. Educ., Acadia Univ., 1986-92; Prof. & Dean, Fac. of Mgmt & Educ., Acadia Univ., 1992 to date. AFFIL: Canadian Association for the Advancement of Women & Sport (CAAWS); Acadia Centre for Small Business & Entrepreneurship (Bd.); Senior Women Academic Administrators of Canada (Exec. 1994-95); Recreation Resource Centre of N.S. (Chair, Mgmt Bd.). INTERESTS: children's sports; women's sports; management of change. MISC: Founding Mbr., CAAWS. COMMENT: *"Successful in changing organizations and groups to future-oriented and people-centred approaches."*

Beecroft, Norma ⊗ ⛏
Composer, Producer, Arts Administrator, Broadcaster. 1866 Glendale Dr., Pickering, ON L1V 1V5 (905) 837-0957, FAX 837-0957. Born Oshawa, Ont. 1934. m. Dr. Ronald G. Turner. EDUC: Royal Conservatory of Music, Composition 1957; Berkshire Music Center, Tanglewood, Mass., Composition 1958; Accademia di Santa Cecilia, Rome, Composition 1959-62; studied piano with Aladar Escedy, Gordon Hallett & Weldon Kilburn; composition with John Weinzweig, Lukas Foss, Aaron Copland, Goffredo Petrassi & Burno Maderna; flute with Keith Girard & Severino Gazzelloni. CAREER: various positions with CBC Television & Radio, 1954-58, 1962-69; freelance Prod., 1969 to date; Pres. & Gen. Mgr, New Music Concerts; formed N. Beecroft Sound Inc., 1982; Interim Music Dir., CJRT-FM, 1993. SELECTED CREDITS: orchestra with soloists, *From Dreams of Brass* (1963-64); choral, *The Living Flame of Love*, Waterloo Lutheran Choir (1967); chamber, *Collage '76*, New Music Concerts (1976); ballet score, *Hedda*, National Ballet of Canada (1983); orchestra, *Jeu de Bach*, Bach 300 Festival (1985); with Harry Somers, music for *Macbeth* and *A Midsummer Night's Dream*, Stratford Festival; incidental music, *Fish On*, TVOntario; electroacoustic, *The Dissipation of Purely*

Sound, CKLN Radio (1988); digital composition, *Evocations: Images of Canada*, CBC Radio (1991); numerous other compositions; Prod., *R.S.V.P.*, CBC Radio; Prod., *Music of Today*, CBC Radio; Exec. Prod., Canadian Composer Retrospective Week, CJRT-FM (1992, 1993-94); Prod., weekly series *Passage of the 20th Century*, CJRT-FM (1992 to date); numerous other broadcast credits. AFFIL: SOCAN; American Federation of Music; Canadian League of Composers; Canadian Electroacoustic Community. HONS: numerous awards & grants in composition, incl. the Victor Martyn Lynch-Staunton Award, Canada Council, twice; Doctor of Letters, honoris causa, York Univ., 1996. COMMENT: *"While her musical style has evolved from neo-classic pieces in her student years, to serial works, improvisation, collage, and other contemporary techniques, Beecroft's one constant interest has been electroacoustic music since her first exposure to this medium in the early 1950s. More than 20 of her compositions use technology in some manner, most of them in combination with instruments."*

Befus, Mariann, B.Sc.,M.H.Sc. ⊕
Supervisor, Rehabilitation Services Unit, MEDI-CAL TECHNICAL SUPPORT SERVICES, Dhahran Health Centre, Rm. 0.062, Box 76, Dhahran, Saudi Arabia 31311 (011) 966-3-877-9987, FAX 966-3-877-3775. Born Drumheller, Alta. 1953. s. EDUC: Univ. of Strasbourg, France, Humanities (Program for foreign students) 1972-73; Univ. of Alberta, Diploma (Occupational Therapy) 1976, B.Sc.(Occupational Therapy) 1982; McMaster Univ., M.H.Sc. 1986. CAREER: Occupational Therapist, Victoria General Hospital, Halifax, Summer 1976; Occupational Therapist, Abbie J. Lane Memorial Hospital, Halifax, 1976-78; Alberta Social Svcs & Community Health, Alberta Hospital, Edmonton, 1978-79; Alberta Social Svcs & Community Health, Mental Health Svcs, Edmonton Reg., 1980-84; Community Occupational Therapy Associates, Toronto, Summer 1985; Mgr, Div. of Occupational/Recreation Therapy, Dept. of Psychiatry, Calgary General Hospital, 1986-91; Asst. Prof., Dept. of Occupational Therapy, Fac. of Rehabilitation Medicine, Univ. of Alberta, 1990-95; Dir., Dept. of Rehabilitation, Calgary General Hospital, 1991-95. AFFIL: Canadian Association of Occupational Therapy; World Federation of Occupational Therapy; Alberta Association of Registered Occupational Therapists (Chair, Practice Review Bd.); Canadian Society of International Health; Alberta Association of Registered Occupational Therapists. HONS: President's Award, Alberta Association of Registered

Occupational Therapists, 1992; Labe Schienberg Award, Multiple Sclerosis Consortium, 1993. MISC: Multiple Sclerosis Program, Dept. of Rehabilitation, Calgary General Hospital won the MS Society (Alta. Chapter) Professional Care Award, 1994; numerous conference presentations & workshops.

Begg, Fiona, M.A.,LL.B. ■ ⚖
Lawyer. 207 W. Hastings St., Ste. 601, Vancouver, BC V6B 1H7 (604) 683-2206, FAX 683-0950. 1 ch. Caitlin Fung. EDUC: St. Andrews Univ., M.A. 1981; McGill Univ., LL.B. 1986. BAR: B.C., 1987. CAREER: articling, Baigent, Jackson, Blair, Vancouver, 1986-87; sole practitioner, 1988-95. SELECTED PUBLICATIONS: *Getting Started in Vancouver* (Vancouver: Legal Services Society). AFFIL: Immigration Section, Canadian Bar Association; Association of Legal Aid Lawyers, Vancouver (Immigration Chair 1992-95); MOSAIC, Vancouver (Pres., Bd. of Dir. 1992-95). HONS: Lord Reading Society Prize, 1984; H.Y. Reid Scholarship, 1984; Wainwright Scholar, 1984; Fac. Scholar, 1984; Carswell Prize, 1985, 1986; Univ. Scholar, 1986. MISC: appears regularly in Provincial Court of BC, Supreme Court of BC, Federal Court of Canada, & before the Immigration & Refugee Board. COMMENT: *"Specializes in refugee, criminal and human rights matters. Working with refugees, providing legal counsel on pro bono basis since October 1987."*

Bégin, The Honorable Monique, P.C.,M.A., Ph.D.,LL.D.,D.Hum.L.,D.Sc. ⚜ ✚ ⌂
Dean, Faculty of Health Sciences, UNIVERSITY OF OTTAWA, 451 Smyth Rd., Ottawa, ON K1H 8M5 (613) 562-5432, FAX 562-5437. Born Rome 1936. EDUC: Teachers' Coll., Rigaud; Univ. de Montréal, B.A., M.A.; La Sorbonne, Paris, France, Doctoral Studies. CAREER: Teacher, 1955-61; Sociologist Consultant, Montreal, 1963-67; Exec. Dir., Royal Commission on the Status of Women in Canada, 1967-70; Asst. Dir., Research, Canadian Radio-television & TelecommunicationsCommission, 1970-72; M.P., Montréal-St-Michel (later Saint-Léonard-Anjou), gen. election, 1972, re-elected 1974, 1979, 1980; Parliamentary Sec. to Sec. of State for External Affairs, 1975-76; Min. of Nat'l Revenue & Sworn to Privy Council, 1976-77; Min. of Nat'l Health & Welfare, 1977-79, 1980-84; Visiting Gilbert Schaefer Prof., Dept. of Econ., Univ. of Notre Dame, Indiana, 1984-85; Visiting Lecturer, Dept. of Sociology, McGill Univ., 1985-86; Joint Chair in Women's Studies, Univ. of Ottawa & Carleton Univ., 1986-90; Co-chair, Royal Commission on Learning (Ontario), 1993-94.

SELECTED PUBLICATIONS: publishes on healthcare system, women's issues & women's health. **AFFIL:** International Independent Commission for Population & Quality of Life. **HONS:** Distinguished Service Award, Canadian Society for Clinical Investigations, 1979; LL.D.(Hon.), Queen'sUniv.; Ph.D. (Laws) (Hon.), Dalhousie Univ.; D.Hum.L.(Hon.), Saint Thomas Univ.; D.Sc.(Hon.), Mount Saint Vincent Univ.; Ph.D.(Laws) (Hon.), Laurentian Univ.; Ph.D.(Laws)(Hon.), Univ. of Toronto; Ph.D.(Laws)(Hon.),Univ. of Alberta; Ph.D.(Sci.)(Hon.),McGillUniv.; Ph.D.(Laws)(Hon.), McMaster Univ.; Ph.D.(Letters)(Hon.), York Univ. **MISC:** 1st Que. woman elected to fed. Parliament; re-elected 1979 & 1980 with the biggest majority in Cdn history.

Beker, Jeanne 📺 ✏

Host/Segment Producer, *FASHION TELEVISION*, Citytv, 299 Queen St. W., Toronto, ON M5V 2Z5 (416) 591-5757, FAX 591-3545. Contributor, *MOVIE TELEVISION*. Style Correspondent, *REAL LIFE*, NBC. Born Toronto 1952. m. Denis O'Neil. 2 ch. **EDUC:** Humber Coll., Media Arts 1971; Herbert Berghoff Studio, NY, Acting 1972; York Univ., Theatre Performance 1975. **CAREER:** Writer/Performer/Interviewer, CBC Radio, St. John's, 1975-78; Prod./Host, CHUM Radio, Toronto, 1978-81; Host/Segment Prod., Citytv, 1979 to date. **SELECTED CREDITS:** Co-Host, *The New Music* (ground-breaking rock magazine show), 6 yrs. **SELECTED PUBLICATIONS:** contributions to *Chatelaine*, *Mirabella*, *Modern Woman*, *Flare*, *Marquee*; currently writing a monthly column for *Flare*. **AFFIL:** ACTRA; AIDS Committee of Toronto (Hon. Chair for "Fashion Cares" Fundraiser); ASTRA US. **HONS:** Diamond Award, Variety Club, 1996; Award, Fashion Group International, 1996. **INTERESTS:** hosting a multitude of charitable fund-raising events for a number of organizations. **MISC:** studied mime in Paris under Étienne Decroux, 1974-75; Ed. Dir. of *@fashion*–a fashion magazine designed especially for the Internet for MCI (the US telecommunications giant), launched April 1995; helped to dev. *Fashion TV* (a magazine show now seen in over 120 countries).

Bélanger, Francine, B.A.,C.F.A. ■■ $

First Vice-President, T.A.L. INVESTMENT COUNSEL LTD., The Exchange Tower, 2 First Canadian Place, Ste. 2200, Toronto, ON M5X 1B1 (416) 364-5620, FAX 364-4472. Born Lévis, Que. 1956. m. Sylvain Goulet. **EDUC:** Laval Univ., B.A.(Actuarial Sci.) 1979; Institute of Chartered Financial Analysts, C.F.A. 1983. **CAREER:** Investment Analyst, Continental Bank of Canada, 1980-83; Asst. Mgr, Equities, CIBC, 1983-85; Acct. Exec., McLean McCarthy Ltd., 1985-88; VP, Prudential-Bache Securities Canada Ltd., 1988-89; VP, Nesbitt Thomson Inc. (now Nesbitt Burns Inc.), 1989-91. **AFFIL:** Canadian Council of Financial Analysts (former Chrm); Toronto Society of Financial Analysts (former Pres.); Association for Investment Management & Research. **INTERESTS:** photography; reading; wine tasting.

Belicki, Kathryn, B.A.,Ph.D. 🎓 ⊕ ✊

Associate Professor of Psychology, BROCK UNIVERSITY, St. Catharines, ON L2S 3A1 (905) 688-5550, FAX 688-6922, EMAIL kbelicki@spartan.ac.brocku.ca. Partner, BELICKI AND BELICKI. Psychology private practice. Born London, UK 1955. m. Denis A. Belicki. **EDUC:** Brock Univ., B.A.(Psych.) 1976; Univ. of Waterloo, Ph.D.(Clinical Psych.) 1984. **CAREER:** Lecturer, Dept. of Psych., York Univ., 1983-84; Asst. Prof., 1984-86, 1986-88; Assoc. Prof., 1988 to date. **SELECTED CREDITS:** appeared in documentary, *Donuts, People and Their Dreams*. **SELECTED PUBLICATIONS:** "The Role of Hypnotic Ability and Demand Characteristics in Dream Change Following a Presleep Instruction," with P. Bowers (*Journal of Abnormal Psychology* 1982); "Predisposition for Nightmares: A Study of Hypnotic Ability, Vividness of Imagery, and Absorption," with D. Belicki (*Journal of Clinical Psychology* 1986); "The Relationship of Nightmare Frequency to Nightmare Suffering with Implications for Treatment and Research" (*Dreaming* 1992); "Nightmare Frequency and Nightmare Distress: Relationship to Psychopathology and Cognitive Style" (*Journal of Abnormal Psychology* 1992); "Nightmare Frequency, Night Terrors and Related Sleep Disturbance as Indicators of a History of Sexual Abuse," with M. Cuddy (*Dreaming* 1992); various other articles. **EDIT:** Consulting Ed., *Dreaming*, 1990-95; Sr Ed., *Dreaming*, 1995 to date. **AFFIL:** Association for the Study of Dreams; Sleep Research Society; Canadian Psychological Association; American Psychological Association; American Psychological Society. **HONS:** Vice Chancellor's Medal, Brock Univ., 1976. **INTERESTS:** travel; rehabilitating injured wildlife; finding homes for strays; reading; developing home renovation skills. **MISC:** Registered Psychologist, Prov. of Ont.; mbr., Special Advisory Bd. of Directors, Newport Treatment Centre Women's Program, 1994-96; Grievance Officer, Brock Univ., 1995; frequent radio & TV guest; advocacy work on behalf of survivors of childhood abuse. **COMMENT:** *"A researcher and practising psychologist, I am deeply interested in 1) dreams and nightmares; 2) the* *sequels of childhood abuse; and 3) psychological factors in physical health."*

Bell, Lesley, B.Sc.N.,R.N. ✊ ⊕
Chief Executive Officer, ONTARIO NURSES' ASSOCIATION, 85 Grenville St., Ste. 400, Toronto, ON M5S 3A2 (416) 964-8833, FAX 964-5659. Born Darlington, UK 1952. **EDUC:** Salvation Army Grace Hospital, Ottawa, R.N.A. 1974; Algonquin Coll., Upper Ottawa Valley Campus, R.N. 1977; Univ. of Ottawa, B.Sc.N.(cum laude, Nursing) 1982. **CAREER:** Asst. Dir., Gov't Rel'ns, Ontario Nurses' Association, 1991; Assoc. Dir., Gov't Rel'ns, 1993; CEO, 1993 to date. **SELECTED PUBLICATIONS:** monthly column in *O.N.A. News*, Provincial Nurse Educators Interest Group Newsletter. **AFFIL:** Ontario Workers Health & Safety Centre (Dir. 1990); H.R.H. the Duke of Edinburgh's Seventh Commonwealth Study Conference, Oxford, UK (1992). **HONS:** Class Pres. & Valedictorian, Registered Nursing Asst. Program, 1974; Class Pres. & Valedictorian, Registered Nursing Program, 1977; Class Pres., Univ. of Ottawa B.Sc.N. Program, 1982. **INTERESTS:** travelling; skiing; bridge; sewing. **COMMENT:** *"Lesley is an open and frank individual, who strives to improve working conditions for staff nurses recognizing the inter-relationship among professional, union and women's issues."*

Bell, The Hon. Judith Miriam, B.A., LL.B. ⚖
Judge, ONTARIO COURT OF JUSTICE (GENERAL DIVISION), 161 Elgin St., Ste. 6031, Ottawa, ON K2P 2K1 (613) 239-1400, FAX 239-1507. Born Ottawa 1940. **EDUC:** Dalhousie Univ., B.A.(Pol. Sci.) 1960, LL.B. 1962. **BAR:** Ontario, 1964. **CAREER:** Jr. Lawyer, Fraser & Beatty, 1964-65; Assoc. & Ptnr, Bell, Baker, 1965-86; Lecturer, Community Planning & Land Use, Ottawa Univ. Law Sch., 1976-83; Lecturer, Mun. Law, Algonquin Coll., 1986; appointed to the Bench, 1986. **AFFIL:** Law Society of Upper Canada (Bencher 1983-86). **HONS:** Queen's Counsel, 1975.

Bellamy, Denise, B.A.,LL.B. ■ 🍁 ⚖ ✊
Director, Legal Services Branch, MANAGEMENT BOARD SECRETARIAT, 7 Queens Park Cres. E., Rm. 228, Toronto, ON M7A 1Z5 (416) 325-9391, FAX 325-9404. Born Saskatoon, Sask. 1949. **EDUC:** Willis Bus. Coll., Ottawa, Secretarial Diploma (with Hons.) 1969; Carleton Univ., B.A.(with distinction, Pol. Sci.) 1975; Osgoode Hall Law Sch., LL.B. 1978. **BAR:** Ontario, 1980. **CAREER:** Lab. Technician, Noranda Mines Limited, 1966-69; Sec., House of Commons, Ottawa, 1969-72; Asst. Crown Attorney, Ministry of the Attorney Gen., Toronto & Newmarket, 1980-84; Sr. Policy Advisor for Justice Issues, Policy & Research Branch, Ontario Women's Directorate, Toronto, 1984-86; Crown Cnsl, Criminal Law Policy, Ministry of the Attorney Gen., 1986-88; Mbr., Court Reform Task Force, & Coord., Delay Reduction Proj., 1988-90; Dir., Legal Svcs Branch, Ministry of the Solicitor Gen. & Correctional Svcs, 1990-95; Dir., Legal Svcs Br., Management Bd. Secretariat, 1995 to date. **AFFIL:** Law Society of Upper Canada (Bencher); Federation of Law Societies (Pres.); The Centre for Advocacy Training (VP); Canadian Bar Association; l'Association des juristes d'expression française de l'Ontario. **HONS:** Canadian Club Women's Memorial Scholarship, 1974; Francophone of the Month, Centre Francophone de l'Ontario, 1984. **INTERESTS:** wine tasting; travel; gardening; bicycling. **MISC:** mbr. of the Cdn delegation & rep. of Ont. in Vienna, Austria, at the U.N. Committee on the Convention of the Elimination of All Forms of Discrimination against Women.

Bellan, Susan, B.A. ■ $
President and General Manager, FRIDA CRAFT STORES, 39 Front St. E., Toronto, ON M5E 1B3 (416) 366-3169, FAX 366-3321. Born Winnipeg 1952. 3 ch. Adam, Melissa, Monica. **EDUC:** Univ. of Manitoba, B.A.(Pol. Sci.) 1973; McGill Univ., B.A.(Econ.) 1974. **CAREER:** Pres. & Gen. Mgr, Frida Craft Stores; Econ. Consultant. **SELECTED PUBLICATIONS:** "Bankrupt" (*Canadian Forum* March 1993); *Small Business and the Big Banks* (Lorimer Press, 1995). **AFFIL:** Canadian Organization of Small Business (Chair, Bnkg Issues 1992 to date); St. Lawrence Business Association; Committee on Monetary & Economic Reform; Cabbagetown Women's Reading Club; Fort York Business Association; C.D. Howe Institute; Bank of Canada for Canadians Committee. **HONS:** Trophy, Junior Musical Club, 1970. **INTERESTS:** reading; gardening; history; monetary reform. **COMMENT:** *"My business has employed hundreds in developing countries since 1979. I made the poor treatment of small business by banks a national issue and advised governments on bank reform."*

Bellegris, Agnes, B.A. ✎ $ ✪
Managing Editor, *BUSINESS QUARTERLY*, The University of Western Ontario, London, ON N6A 3K7 (519) 661-4115, FAX 661-3838. Born Toronto 1970. s. **EDUC:** Univ. of Toronto, B.A.(Criminology/Pol. Sci.); Ryerson Polytechnic Univ., Certificate (Magazine Journalism) 1993. **CAREER:** Ed. Asst., Style Communications, Toronto, 1992-93; Media & Pub-

lic Rel'ns Coord., Fruitman Communications Group, Toronto, 1993-95; Mng Ed., *Business Quarterly*, 1995 to date. INTERESTS: painting; sketching; writing; poetry; canoeing; in-line skating. COMMENT: *"I am a hardworking, motivated person always seeking to improve myself both professionally and personally. As a woman dedicated to my career, I hope I can be as ground-breaking as the women in whose footsteps I follow."*

Bellward, Gail D., B.S.P.,M.Sc., Ph.D. ⌾ ⊕ ♂
Professor of Pharmacology and Toxicology, Faculty of Pharmaceutical Sciences, UNIVERSITY OF BRITISH COLUMBIA, 2146 East Mall, Vancouver, BC V6T 1Z3 (604) 822-4103, FAX 822-3035, EMAIL gailbe@unixg.ubc.ca. Born Brock, Sask. 1939. d. EDUC: Univ. of British Columbia, B.S.P. 1960, M.Sc. 1963, Ph.D. 1966; Emory Univ., Post-Doctoral Fellow 1968-69. CAREER: Prof. of Pharmacology & Toxicology, Fac. of Pharmaceutical Sciences, Univ. of British Columbia, 1967 to date; Visiting Prof., Royal Postgrad. Medical Sch., London, UK, 1975; Chair, Div. of Pharmacology & Toxicology, Fac. of Pharmaceutical Sciences, 1981-85; Asst. Dean, Research & Grad. Studies, Fac. of Pharmaceutical Sciences, 1985-88; Visiting Prof., Hoffmann-La Roche Incorporated, 1989. SELECTED PUBLICATIONS: "Comparison of Polychlorinated Dibenzodioxin Levels with Mixed Function Oxidase Induction in Great Blue Herons," with others (*Journal of Toxicology and Environmental Health* 1990); "Monitoring Biological Effects of Polychlorinated Dibenzo-p-dioxins, Dibenzofurans and Biphenyls in Great Blue Herons in British Columbia," with others (*Journal of Toxicology and Environmental Health* 1994); "Effects of cimetidine on hepatic cytochrome, P450 evidence for formation of a metabolite-intermediate complex" with M. Levine (*Drug Metabolism and Distribution*, 23:1407-1411 1995); "Impact of tamoxifen on peripubertal androgen imprinting of rat hepatic cytochrome P450 2C11, Cytochrome P450 3A2, and steroid 5a-reductase," with T.K.H. Chang, M.M.Y. Chan, S.L. Holsmer, & S.M. Bandiera (*Biochemical Pharmacology*, 51:357-368 1996). AFFIL: Pharmacological Society of Canada; Society of Toxicology of Canada; American Society for Pharmacology & Experimental Therapeutics; Association of Faculties of Pharmacy of Canada; Society of Toxicology (U.S.). HONS: Award of Merit, Lambda Kappa Sigma Pharmacy Fraternity, 1980; Izaac Walton Killam Sr. Fellowship, 1988-89. INTERESTS: music; gardening; walking; travel. MISC: expert advisor to various levels of gov't & scientific organizations, incl. mbr., Expert Advisory Committee, Canadian Network of Toxicology Centres, 1992 to date; Chair, 10th Int'l Symposium on Microsomes & Drug Oxidations, Toronto, 1994; 1st woman full prof. in a Cdn fac. of pharmacy; 1st woman pres. of the Pharmacological Society of Canada & of the Society of Toxicology of Canada. COMMENT: *"Goals: To better understand drug toxicities and interactions in order to avoid or successfully treat them in patients. To train highly competent health professionals and young researchers."*

Belisle, Carol-Ann Elizabeth, B.A.,B.Ed., M.L.S.,M.A. ■■ ⌾ ▯
Coordinator, School Libraries, Department of Education and Culture, GOVERNMENT OF NOVA SCOTIA, 3770 Kempt Rd., Halifax, NS B3K 4X8 (902) 424-2453, FAX 424-0633, EMAIL cbelisle@nshol.library.ns.ca. m. John Belisle. 2 ch. André Joseph, Jacqueline Rose. EDUC: Dalhousie Univ., B.A. 1973, B.Ed. 1975, M.L.S. (Librarianship) 1977; Saint Mary's Univ., M.A.(Educational Admin.) 1984. CAREER: Commissioned Officer, Full Lt., Cdn Armed Forces, 1975; Teacher, high sch. French, German, English, Hist.; Teacher/Librarian, high sch., jr. high & elementary schools; Prof., Educ. Fac., Univ. of Prince Edward Island. AFFIL: N.S. School Library Association (former Pres.); Association for Teacher-Librarianship in Canada (former Dir.); Canadian School Library Association. HONS: Teacher-Librarian of the Year, Canadian School Library Association, 1995; Susanna Almon Scholarship, King's Coll.; Valedictorian, Prince Andrew High Sch., Dartmouth, 1970. INTERESTS: music (esp. guitar); recycling; organic gardening; hiking. MISC: extensive in-servicing & training of teachers in the educational application of technology - CD-ROM, Internet, multimedia. COMMENT: *"My credibility lies in my work as a grassroots educator. Advocacy of literacy and school libraries at the provincial and national levels is a key thrust of my committee work."*

Beltzner, Eileen ■ ⌾ ⊕ ▯
Executive Director (currently on sabbatical), PASS-CAN (Postpartum Adjustment Support Services - Canada), Box 7282, Oakville, ON (905) 844-9009, FAX (905) 844-5973. Born Winnipeg 1950. m. Rainer. 2 ch. Stephen, Carrie Anne. EDUC: Vanier Coll., Special Care Counsellor 1976; Univ. of Waterloo, B.A. 1996; Wilfrid Laurier Univ., M.S.W. in progress. CAREER: work experience in the past 20 yrs. includes Parent Infant Therapist in the first infant stimulation program in Canada; Parent Infant Educator & Parent Infant Psy-

chotherapist, Halton Community Health Dept.; volunteer, PASS-CAN, 1983-86; Exec. Dir., 1987 to date. **SELECTED PUBLICATIONS:** numerous publications incl., *The Handbook for First Time Parents & Ups and Downs: A New Mother's Guide*; *Reducing Stress in First Time Mothers*, report, researcher & co-author (Halton Family Services). **AFFIL:** Postpartum Support International (Past Pres.); Ontario Association of Child & Youth Counsellors; Ontario Association for Infant Development (former Bd. Mbr.). **HONS:** Mary Neville Award for work in the areas of prevention & early intervention in children's mental health svcs, 1989. **INTERESTS:** community service; badminton; family. **MISC:** organizer & Chair, 8th Postpartum Support Int'l Conference, Toronto, 1994.

Bendaly, Leslie, B.A. $ 📖
President, OTRAN ASSOCIATES INC., 277 Oriole Pkwy, Toronto, ON M5P 2H4 (416) 440-0532, FAX 489-1173. Born Mitchell, Ont. 1945. m. Elie Bendaly. 2 ch. Nicole, Charles. **EDUC:** Univ. of Western Ontario, B.A. 1967; Althouse Coll. of Educ., Certificate of Educ. 1969. **CAREER:** Teacher, Canadian University Services Overseas; Reporter, *The Stratford Beacon Herald*; Teacher, The London Bd. of Educ.; personnel, The Bank of Nova Scotia; mgmt, Statistics Canada; consulting & mgmt, Humber Coll.; Hum. Res. Mgmt Consultant, ARA Consultants; Pres. & teamwork consultant, Otran Associates Inc., 1985 to date. **SELECTED PUBLICATIONS:** *Strength in Numbers*, *Turning Work Groups Into Teams* (McGraw-Hill Ryerson, 1990); *Games Teams Play* (McGraw-Hill Ryerson, 1996); *Organization 2000* (HarperCollins, 1996). **EDIT:** Pub. & Ed., *Teamwork Essentials*. **INTERESTS:** hiking; fitness; writing; lifelong learning. **COMMENT:** *"Committed to supporting organizations and individuals in tapping their success potential in the new economy."*

Bendeth, Marian ■■ $ ⚛ ✪
Fragrance Specialist, SIXTH SCENTS (consulting with & on behalf of 29 fragrance companies-prestige lines only), 3555 Don Mills Rd., Ste. 6, Willowdale, ON M2H 3N3 (416) 494-3191. Born London, UK 1958. s. **EDUC:** Seneca Coll., Public Rel'ns (with Hons.) 1985. **CAREER:** advertising consulting, London, England, 1978-80; publicity/promotion/freelance critic, music industry with CRIA/CARAS/*Music Express*, 1980-84; fragrance industry, 1984-89; est. Sixth Scents, 1989. **SELECTED CREDITS:** Publicist, TV/radio, *Rock Express Awards Show*, 1983-84; Publicist for opening of Gallery Five Hundred, 1990; endorsed & presented to the press on behalf of numerous perfume manufacturers. **SELECTED PUBLICATIONS:** contributed to book, *A collector's handbook of miniature perfume bottles, minis, mates and more* (by Jeri Lyn Ringblum, Schiffer Publishing Co., USA, 1996); "Chic to Cheek" (*Canadian Living* magazine, 1992). **AFFIL:** Toronto Wildlife Centre. **HONS:** invited by Fragrance Foundation to be featured at Trump Tower, Manhattan, for Fragrance Week, 1993. **INTERESTS:** travelling & collecting rare & sophisticated fragrances; dog shows; collecting Brazilian bossa nova & jazz music; gardening; visiting the library. **MISC:** featured in numerous articles, as well as in interviews on radio & TV; lectures in colleges; is featured in dept. stores; trains personnel; creates special events; has become one of Canada's leading authorities on scents for men & women. **COMMENT:** *"Helping people through fragrance enhancement has been very rewarding. It has been a challenge to break new ground with my concept; and through perseverance, I feel I have succeeded."*

Benn, Denna M., B.Sc.,D.V.M., Dip.Vet.Med.,M.Sc. ■■ 🎓 ⚛ ⊕
Director, Animal Care Services, UNIVERSITY OF GUELPH, Guelph, ON N1G 2W1 (519) 824-4120, ext. 4305, FAX 837-2341. **EDUC:** Univ. of Guelph, B.Sc. 1973; Ontario Veterinary Coll., Univ. of Guelph, D.V.M. 1976, Dip.Vet.Med. 1977, M.Sc. 1983; 14 mgmt courses 1990 to date; has attended numerous educ. conferences for professional dev. **CAREER:** Internship, Dept. of Clinical Studies, Ont. Veterinary Coll., 1976-77; Teaching Master, Seneca Coll., King City, Ont., 1977-81 & Apr.-May 1983; Grad. Teaching Asst., Dept. of Clinical Studies, Ont. Veterinary Coll., 1978-80; Research Assoc., 1979-81; Staff Vet., Animal Care Svcs, Univ. of Guelph, 1980-87; Acting Dir., Animal Care Svcs, 1984, 1987, 1988; Dir., Animal Care Svcs, & Sec., Animal Care Committee, 1988 to date; Special Grad. Fac., Ont. Veterinary Coll., 1988 to date; Adjunct Prof., Dept. of Pathology, 1989 to date. **AFFIL:** Canadian Association of Laboratory Animal Medicine (VP 1987-88; Pres. 1988-90; Rep., CCAC 1990-93; mbr., OMAF-Research Community Liaison Committee 1991-95); American Society of Laboratory Animal Practitioners; Canadian Association for Laboratory Animal Science (Bd. of Dir. 1994 to date); Canadian Veterinary Medical Association; Scientist Centre for Animal Welfare; Centre for the Study of Animal Welfare (Steering Committee 1989 to date); American Association for Laboratory Animal Science; International Society for Applied Ethology; Atomic Energy Board of Canada (Consultant 1993 to date); Wellington Board of Educ. (Advisory Committee re use

of animals in elementary & secondary schools 1995-96); Seneca Coll. (Veterinary Technician Advisory Committee 1983 to date; Chair 1992-95). **HONS:** 3 vet. student prizes; nominated for Univ. of Guelph Fac. Association Award for Teaching Excellence, 1985; Frederic A. McGrand Award for "outstanding contributions to animal welfare in Canada," 1993; The C.V.M.A. Humane Award, for "continuous work in the care & well-being of lab. animals," 1993; Charles River Award for "outstanding accomplishments in the improvement of the care & quality of animals used in research," 1995. **MISC:** numerous speaking engagements re care & use of animals, media rel'ns, training programs, women in the profession, etc.

Benn-Ireland, Tessa Judith, B.A.(Hons.) 🍁 📖 ✏

Librarian, MARKHAM PUBLIC LIBRARIES, 7600 Kennedy Rd., Unit 1, Unionville, ON L3R 9S5 (905) 940-8323, FAX 940-8326. Born Guyana, S. America. m. Opeton. 2 ch. **EDUC:** Ryerson Polytechnic Univ., Dipl. in Library Arts 1972; Univ. of Toronto, B.A.(Hons.) 1982; M.L.S. (in progress). **CAREER:** Head, Children's Svcs & Programs, Milliken Mills Branch, Markham Public Libraries. **SELECTED PUBLICATIONS:** *Black Business and Professional Women's Calendar* (1984, 1986); *Some Black Women*, co-author; Book Review Ed., *Women in Business*. **AFFIL:** Markham Hope Foundation (Founding Bd. Mbr.); Canadian Library Association; Association of African-Caribbean Canadian Information Specialists; York Region District Health Council (Bd. of Dir.); Harry Jerome Scholarship (Bd. of Trustees 1993-95); Markham Historical Museum (Bd. of Mgmt 1991-93). **HONS:** Gov. Gen.'s Commemorative Medal Winner, Author, Librarian. **INTERESTS:** business (small); entrepreneurship; writing; politics; youth & education. **MISC:** newspaper columnist.

Bennet, Laura, APR $ ♡ ✋

President and Chief Executive Officer, BENNET COMMUNICATIONS LIMITED, Xerox Building, 1949 Upper Water Street, Ste. 308, Halifax, NS B3J 3N3 (902) 422-5999, FAX 422-1690. Born Montreal 1935. m. James Lawrence Bennet. 4 ch. Christine Louise Hammel, Victoria Jane Maltzan, Neale Sandford, Amy Brook Morrow. **EDUC:** Hochelaga Convent, Montreal; Accredited Public Rel'ns Practitioner. **CAREER:** Public Rel'ns Dir., Dalhousie Arts Centre, Dalhousie Univ., 1974-76; Reg'l Promo. Mgr, CBC Maritimes Reg., 1977-78; Assoc., Corporate Communications Limited, 1978-80; Sr. VP & Dir. of Creative Svcs, 1980-86; Pres., CEO & Principal, Sight and Sound Productions Limited, 1982-88; Pres., CEO & Principal, Bennet Communications Limited, 1988 to date. **DIRECTOR:** Chrysler Canada Ltd. **AFFIL:** Canadian Public Relations Society; Canadian Public Relations Exchange; American Management Association (Gen. Mgmt Advisory Council on Growing Organizations 1995 to date). **HONS:** Recognition of Women, YWCA, 1985; Honorary Life Member, Izaak Walton Killam Hospital for Children Corporation, 1988; Volunteer of the Year, Canadian Society of Fundraising Executives, 1990; Shield of Public Service, Canadian Public Relations Society, 1990; Women of Distinction Award, Corp. Mgmt Category, The Canadian Progress Club, 1991; Canada Volunteer Award Medal, Gov't of Canada, 1991. **INTERESTS:** genealogy; golf; sailing. **COMMENT:** *"Ms Bennet is highly regarded in the region as a business leader and active participant in a number of business and community organizations. Her professional and volunteer work has earned her a number of prestigious awards."*

Bennett, Alison, M.D.,C.C.F.P. ■■ ✋ ⊕

President, FEDERATION OF MEDICAL WOMEN OF CANADA (not-for-profit organization committed to the dev. of women physicians & the well-being of all women), 1815 Alta Vista Dr., Ste. 107, Ottawa, ON K1G 3Y6 (613) 731-1026, FAX 731-8748. Born Red Deer, Alta. 1961. m. Geoff Bennett. 2 ch. Marla, Rory. **EDUC:** Univ. of Alberta, B.Sc.(with distinction) 1981; Univ. of Calgary, M.D. 1984; Coll. of Family Physicians of Canada, C.C.F.P. 1986. **CAREER:** practice of family medicine, Calgary, 1986-95; active staff, Foothills Hospital; Contract Physician, Calgary Health Services' Family Planning Clinics, 1992 to date; Medical Advisor to Family Planning Clinics, 1993 to date; svc. provider, Foothills Hospital N.W. Clinic, 1992-95. **AFFIL:** Alberta Medical Association; Canadian Medical Association; Federation of Medical Women of Canada (mbr., Calgary chpt. 1981 to date; Pres., Calgary chpt. 1990-91; Reg'l Rep. for Prairies then Alta./NWT 1991-93; Pres.-elect 1996; Pres. 1996-97); Foothills Hospital Therapeutic Abortion Review Committee (1987-88); St. David's United Church Foundation Bd. (1992-93). **INTERESTS:** sexual health, i.e.: family planning, contraception, STD prevention & treatment, adolescent sexuality & sexuality education; skiing; camping; music; theatre; cycling; golf; travel. **MISC:** numerous invited addresses on topics of contraception, STD mgmt, adolescent sexuality, 1993 to date. **COMMENT:** *"I had a very rewarding career as a busy family physician from 1986 to 1995. I delivered close to 500 babies in that time. I made the decision in 1995 to restrict my pro-*

fessional activities to family planning clinics, giving me more time to spend with my young children and to devote to the Federation of Medical Women."

Bennett, Gale Diana, B.A.,M.A. 📺 ✪
Managing Director, TVONTARIO, 2190 Yonge St., Toronto, ON M4T 2T1 (416) 484-2653, FAX 484-7205. Born Toronto 1943. m. Garry Gordon Gale. 4 ch. Cameron, Matthew, Jay, Loron. **EDUC:** Univ. of Toronto, B.A.(Fine Arts) 1965, M.A.(Art Hist.) 1968; Interim Secondary Sch. Principal's Certificate 1977. **CAREER:** Dept. Head, Visual Arts Dept., North York Bd. of Educ., 1965-80; Adjunct Prof., York Univ., 1975-76; Teaching Assoc., Fac. of Educ., Univ. of Toronto, 1976-79; Mgr, Bus. Rel'ns, TVOntario, 1980-81; Dir., Revenue Dev., 1981-87; Exec. Dir., Zoological Society of Metropolitan Toronto, 1987-91; Mng Dir., Corp. Affairs, TVOntario, 1991-95; Mng Dir., Mktg & Dev., 1995 to date. **EXHIBITIONS:** Gallery 0, Toronto, 1978; Factory 77, Toronto, 1979; Baas Gallery, Toronto, 1988. **DIRECTOR:** Toronto Stock Exchange (Public Gov.); Canadian Publishing. **AFFIL:** United Way (Leading Women Advisory Council); Women's Executive Forum; Art Gallery of Ontario; Guild of Crafts, Ontario. **HONS:** various awards in curriculum design, mktg & dev., 1970-93. **MISC:** guest speaker, conference facilitator & writer for various organizations; consultant to numerous voluntary & professional organizations.

Bennett, Jalynn H., B.A. $ 🍁 ✏
President, JALYNN H. BENNETT AND ASSOCIATES LTD., 247 Davenport Rd., Ste. 303, Toronto, ON M5R 1J9 (416) 975-3958, FAX 975-3960. Born Toronto 1943. d. 3 ch. **EDUC:** Univ. of Toronto, B.A.(Econ.) 1965. **CAREER:** Manufacturers Life Insurance Company, 1965-70, 1972-89 (latterly VP, Corp. Dev.); Pres., Jalynn H. Bennett and Associates Ltd. (consulting), 1989 to date. **AFFIL:** Canadian Association of Business Economists; Institute of Corporate Directors; Toronto Society of Financial Analysts; Trent Univ. (Chair, Bd. of Gov.); Wellesley Central Hospital (Dir.). **DIRECTOR:** St. Mary's Cement Corp., Sears Canada Inc., CIBC, Westburne Inc., Mediacom Inc. **HONS:** Women of Distinction Award, YWCA Metro Toronto, 1988; Fac. of Mgmt Award, McGill Univ., 1994. **INTERESTS:** macro economic & monetary policy; human resources policy; trade policy; post-secondary & health care policy.

Bennett, Susan, B.A.,M.A., Ph.D. ■■ 🎓 ✪ 📜
Associate Professor, Department of English, UNIVERSITY OF CALGARY, 2500 University Dr. N.W., Calgary, AB T2N 1N4 (403) 220-6450, FAX 289-1123, EMAIL sbennett@acs.ucalgary.ca. Born London, UK 3 ch. **EDUC:** Univ. of Kent, B.A.(Hons., English & Drama) 1981; McMaster Univ., M.A.(English) 1983, Ph.D.(English) 1988. **SELECTED PUBLICATIONS:** *Performing Nostalgia: Shifting Shakespeare and the Contemporary Past* (London: Routledge, 1996); *Theatre Audiences* (London: Routledge, 1990). **AFFIL:** Maenad Theatre, Calgary (VP); *Theatre Research in Canada* (Edit. Bd.); Broadview Press (Edit. Bd.). **INTERESTS:** women & performance; Shakespeare on the contemporary stage.

Benoit, Bonnie E. ■ 📖 ✏ 🎓
Applied Arts and Science Instructor, SOUTHERN ALBERTA INSTITUTE OF TECHNOLOGY, 1301 - 16 Ave. N.W., Calgary, AB T2M 0L4 (403) 284-8590. Owner, BONNIE BENOIT & ASSOCIATES, 2831 - 39 St. S.W., Calgary, AB T3E 3G8 (403) 242-6730. m. Edgar Benoit. 3 ch. **EDUC:** Herzing Institute, Legal Asst./Secretarial Program, 1979; Calgary Real Estate Bd., Introductory Course 1981; Mount Royal Coll., Adult Educator Seminar Series; Athabasca Univ., B.A.(Psych.) in progress. **CAREER:** Legal Sec., Pitblado & Hoskin, Winnipeg, 1979-80; Legal Sec., Monk, Goodwin & Company, Winnipeg, 1980-81; Legal Sec., MacKimmie Mathews, Calgary, 1981-85; Paralegal, Williams, Harris, Roebothan & McKay, St. John's, 1988-91; Applied Arts & Sci. Instructor, Southern Alberta Institute of Technology, 1991 to date; Owner, Bonnie Benoit & Associates Ltd., 1994 to date; Mng Ed.,*Dandelion* Magazine, 1994-96; Volunteer, *Dandelion*, 1996 to date. **SELECTED PUBLICATIONS:** modules & courses for distance educ. **AFFIL:** SAIT Teachers, Toastmasters; Ch.A.D.D. (Children & Adults with Attention Deficit Disorder), Calgary Chapter (Founding Mbr. & Sec. 1993-94). **MISC:** provides editorial assistance for manuscripts currently under consideration; conducted editorial review for *Style Guide* for the Southern Alberta Institute of Technology & Nelson Canada **COMMENT:** *"I wish to increase the profile of* Dandelion *Magazine, build my business into a successful literary agency, further my education and assist students with learning disabilities. My success and achievements are due not only to my hard work and abilities, but also to my strong network of friends and family."*

Benoit, Chantal ■■ 🏀
Paralympic Athlete. Mt. St.-Hilaire, QC. **EDUC:** Soc. grad. **SPORTS CAREER:** mbr., Nat'l Wheelchair Basketball Team. Paralympic

Games: Gold, 1996; Gold, 1992; 4th, 1988. Canadian Wheelchair Basketball League (CWBL): 3rd, Women's Finals, 1996; 1st, Women's Finals, 1995. World Championships: 1st, 1994. Stoke Mandeville Games, 1st, 1991. Pan American Games: 2nd, 1986. HONS: Québec Sport Merit Award, 1994; MVP, CWBL Women's Finals, 1995. MISC: former local, reg'l, prov. & nat'l diver. COMMENT: *"Known as the Michael Jordan of women's basketball because of the intensity of her offensive play and ability to motivate."*

Benoit, Claude 🏛
Executive Director, McCORD MUSEUM OF CANADIAN HISTORY, 690 Sherbrooke St. W., Montréal, QC H3A 1E9 (514) 398-7100, FAX 398-5045., EMAIL christine@mccord. lan.mcgill.ca. Born Montréal 1952. s. EDUC: Univ. de Montréal, Baccalauréat en Biologie (Physiologie) 1975; Univ. du Québec à Montréal, Certificat (Sciences de l'éduc.) 1980. CAREER: Prof. en biologie et physique, Commission scolaire régionale Harricana, Amos, Abitibi, 1975-78; Chargée de projet responsable des programmes publics, Conseil de développement du loisir scientifique, 1979-83; Dir. de la programmation des expositions scientifiques et techniques, Corporation des Fêtes du Québec 1534-1984, 1983-84; Chargée de projets et muséologue responsable de l'élaboration du concept et de la programmation, Musée de la civilisation de Québec, 1986-87; Consultante, muséologue et gestionnaire de projet, 1987-89; VP, loisir et culture, Lavalin Inc., 1989-90; Prés., muséologue et gestionnaire des projets, Les Productions Métamorphoses inc., 1990 to date; Dir. gén., McCord Museum of Canadian History, 1994 to date. SELECTED PUBLICATIONS: numerous conference papers; "Les musées et les centres de sciences dans le monde, portrait d'une situation" (*Revue du Dept. de l'histoire de l'art*, UQAM Dec. 1906), "Passer à l'action" (*Musées* Fall 1987). AFFIL: Société des musées québécois; Association des musées canadiens; American Association of Museums; ICOM-International; Association canadienne française pour l'avancement des sciences. MISC: mbr. of numerous juries for granting agencies & prizes. COMMENT: *"Éducatrice et organisatrice, Claude Benoit a toujours voulu allier ses deux passions à travers son intervention de muséologue et de gestionnaire. Madame Benoit dirige maintenant l'équipe du Musée McCord."*

Benson, Leslie Jane, B.Sc.(Eng.), P.Eng. ■ ❁ ♣ ♂
Director of Public Works, AUTHORITY OF SIDNEY TOWNSHIP, Tucker's Corners, RR #5, Belleville, ON K8N 4Z5 (613) 966-8330. Born 1955. EDUC: St. Clement's Sch., Toronto; Coll. of Applied Arts & Technology, Certificate Program in Real Estate 1976; Univ. of Guelph, B.Sc.(Eng.) 1981. CAREER: survey & designer of drainage systems, Dockart Brick & Tile, Arnprior, Ont., 1978; Gas Pipeline Inspector, Consumers' Gas Company, Toronto, 1980; Design Eng., Totten Sims Hubicki, Cobourg, Ont., 1981-82; Quality Control Inspector, during construction of Eldorado Resources Limited UF6 Plant, Port Hope, Ont., Lummus Canada Inc., 1982-83; Proj. Mgr, Port Hope Flood Control Proj., Ganaraska Conservation Authority, 1983-85; Water Resources Eng., Ont. Ministry of Natural Res., Head Office, Central Reg., Richmond Hill, Ont., 1985-86; Water Res. Eng., Central Lake Ontario Conservation Authority (Oshawa), Ganaraska Reg. Conservation Authority (Port Hope), Kawartha Reg. Conservation Authority (Lindsay), & Otonabee Reg. Conservation Authority (Peterborough), 1987-96; Dir. of Public Works, Sidney Township, 1996 to date. AFFIL: Professional Engineers Ontario; Canadian Dam Safety Association; Canadian Coastal Science & Engineering Association; St. Clement's Sch. Alumnae Association (Life Mbr.); Univ. of Guelph Engineering Alumni Association; Mensa Canada; Architectural Conservancy of Ontario; Capitol Theatre Foundation (Dir.). MISC: first-ever woman gas pipeline inspector, Consumers' Gas Company, Toronto, 1980.

Benson, Renate, L.èsL.,Ph.D. ■ ◈ 🏛 ♂
Professor, German Studies, UNIVERSITY OF GUELPH, Guelph, ON N1G 2W1 (519) 824-4120, ext 3182, FAX 763-9572., EMAIL rbenson@langlit.arts.uoguelph.ca. Born Germany 1938. m. Eugene. 2 ch. EDUC: Univ. of Cologne, German/French 1956-61; Univ. of Nancy, France, French 1961-62; Univ. of Montreal, L.èsL.(French/Fine Art) 1965; McGill Univ., Ph.D.(German) 1970. CAREER: Lecturer, Asst. Prof., Assoc. Prof., Full Prof., Univ. of Guelph, 1967 to date. SELECTED PUBLICATIONS: *Erich Kästner, Studien zu seinem Werk* (Bonn: Bouvier, 1973); *German Expressionist Drama: Ernst Toller and Georg Kaiser* (London: Macmillan, 1984); "Aspects of Love in Anne Hébert's Short Stories" (*Journal of Canadian Fiction* 1979); "Character and Symbol in Anne Hébert's *Les invités au procès*" (*Canadian Drama/L'Art dramatique canadien* 6(1) 1980); various translations, to German from French, & to English from German & French; various book reviews, reports, & entries in reference works. AFFIL: MLA; CAUTG; OATG; Humanities Association. HONS: Distinguished Prof. Award, Coll. of Arts, 1990. MISC: recipi-

ent of grants from various agencies; mbr., SSHRCC Adjudication Committee IV, Ottawa, 1981-86; involved in the creation & dev. of an Hons. B.A. European Studies Program, the first of its kind in Canada. **COMMENT:** *"Feminist, dedicated teacher and active member of the university and town community, involved in the development of new, international programs, notably European studies."*

Benson, Susan ■■ 🎞 🎭 📺

Theatre Designer. Born Kent, UK 1942. m. Michael Whitfield. **EDUC:** West of England Coll. of Art, Bristol, A.T.D. 1963. **CAREER:** theatre designer, sets & costumes, Canada, 1966 to date; designer for Stratford Festival Theatre, Royal Winnipeg Ballet, National Ballet of Canada, Canadian Opera Company, The Australian Opera, New York City Opera, among many companies across Canada & abroad; Head of Design, Stratford Festival, 3 seasons; Assoc. Dir., 1995. **SELECTED CREDITS:** designer, *Madama Butterfly*, Canadian Opera Company; *The Marriage of Figaro* & *Cosi Fan Tutte*, Banff Centre; *The Taming of the Shrew* & *Romeo and Juliet*, National Ballet of Canada; over 20 productions, Stratford Festival incl. *The Mikado*, which toured to The Old Vic, London, & on Broadway, & appeared on Arts & Entertainment ntwk. **EXHIBITIONS:** "Susan Benson Artist/Designer," The Gallery, Stratford, 1988. **COLLECTIONS:** theatre designs in collections in U.S. & Canada incl. The Bronfman Collection, Montreal, & The Gallery, Stratford permanent collection. **AFFIL:** Royal Canadian Academy; United Scenic Artists; Associated Designers of Canada; U.S. Institute of Theatre Technology. **HONS:** 7 Dora Mavor Moore awards; 1 Jessie; 1 Academy of Cable Television ACE Award; Sr. Canada Council Award, 1992. **MISC:** represented Canada at Prague Quadrennials, 1979, 1983, 1987, 1991; teaching exper. includes: Asst. Prof., Univ. of Illinois, Champaign/Urbana; Resource Fac., Banff Sch. of Fine Arts; Guest Lecturer, York Univ. Theatre Dept. & National Theatre Sch., Montreal, Univ. of Michigan.

Bentley, Myrna J. $

Vice-President, Business Development, CO-OPERATIVE TRUST COMPANY OF CANADA, 333 - 3rd Ave. N., Saskatoon, SK S7K 2M2 (306) 956-1993, FAX 652-7614, EMAIL bentb@sk.sympatico.ca. Born Humboldt, Sask. 1954. m. Brian. 1 ch. **EDUC:** Univ. of Saskatchewan, Bus. Admin. Cert., Exec. Mgmt Program; Trust Companies Institute, Educ. Cert.; Canadian Securities Institute, Certificate; American Management Development Cert. **CAREER:** various positions, Co-operative Trust Company of Canada, 1974-81; Mgr, Mortgage Svcs, 1981-85; Exec. Asst., Mortgage Svcs, 1985-86; VP, Mortgage Svcs, 1986-90; VP, Products & Svcs, 1990-94; VP, Bus. Dev., 1995 to date. **INTERESTS:** family; reading; change in business environment. **COMMENT:** *"The means of business development, delivery and practice is changing rapidly and provides constant and welcome challenges."*

Bentley, Susan 📖 ✏

General Manager, CANADIAN POETRY PRESS, Department of English, University of Western Ontario, London, ON N6A 3K7 (519) 673-1164. Born London, UK 1948. m. David. 3 ch. **EDUC:** Froebel Institute Coll. of Educ., London, UK, 1969. **CAREER:** Primary Sch. Teacher, Rotherhithe Jr. Sch., UK, 1969-71; Preschool Teacher, Calvary United Church, 1976-77; Storyteller, Univ. Pre-Sch., Univ. of Western Ontario, 1991-92; Teacher, Univ. Pre-Sch., 1992-93. **SELECTED PUBLICATIONS:** Preface to 2nd edition of *Broughdale: Looking for its Past* by J. Shawyer, index by Elizabeth Spicer. **AFFIL:** Broughdale Community Association (Sec. 1976-77; Pres. 1979-81, 1993 to date); Matthews Hall independent school (Gov.); St. Luke's Anglican Church (Superintendent of Sunday Sch. 1992 to date); UWO Madrigalers. **INTERESTS:** education; music; gardening; reading–social history; local politics/community concerns. **MISC:** garden selected for the 1994 I.O.D.E. Garden Tour in London, Ont. **COMMENT:** *"Primarily a wife and mother, I helped to found and sustain* Canadian Poetry *in 1977 (38 issues published) and Canadian Poetry Press in 1986 (18 books published). Education, neighbourhood and urban planning issues take up much of my time."*

Benyk, Pearl, B.A. ■ ⚛ ✊

Study Assistant (Communications), WEST KITIKMEOT SLAVE STUDY SOCIETY, 4920 - 52nd St., Yellowknife, NT X1A 2N3 (403) 669-6235, EMAIL wkssb@internorth.com. Born Flin Flon, Man. 1949. s. **EDUC:** Univ. of Manitoba, B.A.(English/Soc.) 1971; Red River Community Coll., Winnipeg, Creative Comm. 1973. **CAREER:** Reporter, Northern News Services, Yellowknife, 1979-81; Comm. Officer, Kitikmeot Inuit Association, Cambridge Bay, 1981-85; Instructor, Arctic Coll., Tuktoyaktuk, 1985; Owner/Operator, Acme, Etc., Yellowknife, 1985-91; Exec. Dir., Arctic Public Legal Educ. & Info. Society, 1991-96; Study Asst. (Comm.), West Kitikmeot Slave Study Society, 1996 to date. **SELECTED PUBLICATIONS:** numerous pieces in newspapers, magazines & newsletters.

AFFIL: Northlands Mobile Home Association (Founding Bd. Mbr.); direct charge co-operatives in Yellowknife & Winnipeg; Yellowknife Food Bank; Katimavik Alcohol & Drug Committee, Cambridge Bay (Dir.); Canadian Crossroads International & other developing world volunteer work, incl. 10 months in St. Vincent & the Grenadines; City of Winnipeg (Resident Advisory Group; Research/Facilitating); Public Legal Education Association of Canada (Sec. 1993 to date). INTERESTS: Third World development (both overseas & in Canada); crafts; creative writing; photography; non-North American music; travel; NWT political dev.; home maintenance/carpentry; oral histories. COMMENT: *"I'm fortunate in many ways, including being a Northerner. I feel I should help those less fortunate than myself, but enjoy life at the same time."*

Beresford-Howe, Constance, B.A.,M.A., Ph.D. 🗂

Writer. 225 Moore Ave., Toronto, ON M4G 1C6. Born Montreal 1922. m. C.W. Pressnell. 1 ch. Jeremy. EDUC: McGill Univ., B.A. (English) 1945, M.A.(English) 1946; Brown Univ., Ph.D.(English) 1950. CAREER: Lecturer, Asst. Prof., Assoc. Prof., McGill Univ., 1950-70; Prof., Ryerson Polytechnic Univ., 1973-87; Writer in Library, North York Public Library, 1988-89. SELECTED PUBLICATIONS: *The Unreasoning Heart* (1946); *Of This Day's Journey* (1948); *The Invisible Gate* (1949); *My Lady Greensleeves* (1953); *The Book of Eve* (1973); *A Population of One* (1976); *The Marriage Bed* (1980); *Night Studies* (1984); *Prospero's Daughter* (1989); *A Serious Widow* (1992). AFFIL: International PEN, Canadian Branch; International PEN, Montreal Branch (former Pres.). HONS: Dodd, Mead Intercollegiate Literary Fellowship, 1945; Canadian Booksellers Award, 1973. INTERESTS: being alive; cooking; music; cats; wine; summers in Suffolk; reading; writing; gardens; laughing.

Bergman, June S., M.D.,L.M.C.C., C.C.F.P. ⊕

Clinical Director, Family Medicine Centre, PETER LOUGHEED CENTRE, 3500 - 26 Ave. N.E., Calgary, AB T1Y 6J4. Born Alta. 1947. m. 3 ch. Joseph, Robert, Edward. EDUC: Univ. of Toronto, M.D. 1970. CAREER: Family Practice Residency, Sunnybrook Medical Centre, 1970-71; Emergency Dept., Belleville General Hospital, 1971-73; part-time solo family practice in Northern Ontario, 1973-74; part-time family medicine (in association with Dr. A. Lam) & Medical Clearance Officer, airport, 1975-86; Physician svcs, SAIT, 1982 to date; full-time family practice (in association with Dr.

S. Leung), 1986 to date; Founding Mbr. & Clinical Dir., Family Medicine Centre, Peter Lougheed Centre, 1992 to date; Specialty Coord., Women's Health, Dept. of Family Medicine, Univ. of Calgary, 1992; Asst. Clinical Prof., Dept. of Family Medicine, 1992. AFFIL: Coll. of Physicians & Surgeons of Alberta; Coll. of Family Physicians of Canada (Teachers Section 1991); Women's Medical Federation, Calgary & Canada; Calgary General Hospital (active staff); Grace Hospital (active staff); CCFP Convention (Mbr., Organizing Committee for the scientific program, Alta. Chapter 1993); FM - CGH (Dir. 1994-96); FM - CRHA (Clinical Dir. 1996 to date); various community & medical related organizations & events. MISC: Olympic Volunteer, Athletes' Physician, 1988; Community Preceptor, 1990 to date.

Berkeley, Vivian ■ ■ ⊗

Paralympic Athlete. Glace Bay, NS. CAREER: volunteer. SPORTS CAREER: mbr., Nat'l Team, Lawn Bowls, 1994 to date. Paralympic Games: Silver, singles, 1996. Canadian Championship: 1st, singles, 1995. IPC World Lawn Bowls Championship: 5th, singles, 1995

Berkhold, Beverly F., B.Ed. ◐

Trustee, ALBERTA CANCER FOUNDATION, ALBERTA CANCER BOARD. President, FLYING "G" INVESTMENTS LTD. Born Medicine Hat, Alta. 1938. m. Gerald Berkhold. 2 ch. EDUC: Univ. of Alberta, B.Ed. 1961. CAREER: taught jr. high sch. several yrs. prior to marriage. VOLUNTEER CAREER: Chair, Calgary Daffodil Days, & Pres., Calgary Unit, Canadian Cancer Society; Trustee, Alberta Cancer Foundation; Protocol Chair, YONEX Canadian Open Badminton Championships; Mktg Volunteer, three venues, Calgary Olympics. AFFIL: Alberta Cancer Foundation (Trustee); Canadian Cancer Society; Kappa Alpha Theta Alumni Club (Pres.). HONS: Award of Merit, Canadian Cancer Society, 1988; Commemorative Medal for the 125th Anniversary of Canadian Confederation, 1992. INTERESTS: tennis; yoga; gardening; reading; music; hiking. MISC: was the Co-Chair on a committee to organize & operate a gift shop for the Alberta Theatre Projects. COMMENT: *"For more than 20 years I have been a community volunteer contributing to the growth and fundraising development of several organizations. I am proud of my affiliation with the Canadian Cancer Society and the dollars raised during my three-year term as president."*

Berman, Brigitte, B.A.,B.Ed. 🐦

Director, Writer and Producer, BRIDGE FILM PRODUCTIONS INC., 44 Charles St. W., Ste.

2518, Toronto, ON M4Y 1R7. Born Frankfurt, Germany. EDUC: Queen's Univ., B.A.(English/Film Studies) 1974; MacArthur Coll., B.Ed.(Drama & English) 1975. CAREER: Researcher, Current Affairs Dept., CBC-TV, Toronto; Prod., Dir. & Writer of more than 100 documentaries, CBC, 9 yrs.; Dir., Prod. & Writer, Bridge Film Productions Inc. SELECTED CREDITS: Prod./Dir./Writer, *The Many Faces of Black* (documentary), CBC; Prod./Dir./Writer, *How Music Came to the Garden City* (documentary), CBC; Prod./Dir./ Writer, *The Osbornes: A Very Special Family* (documentary), CBC; Prod./Dir./Writer, *Elmira: A Look at the Mennonites* (documentary), CBC; Co-Writer/Prod./Dir./Ed., *BIX: Ain't None of Them Play Like Him Yet* (feature documentary), 1981; Writer/Prod./Dir./Ed., *ARTIE SHAW; Time Is All You've Got* (feature documentary), 1986; Writer/Dir./Co-Prod., *The Circle Game* (feature), 1994; Dir./Co-Writer, *The Door is Closed Backwards* (theatrical play). DIRECTOR: Bridge Film Productions Inc.; Shadowlife Film Inc. AFFIL: Academy of Motion Picture Arts & Sciences, U.S.; Directors' Guild of Canada; Academy of Canadian Cinema & Television. HONS: recipient, Academy Award (Oscar) for Best 1986 Documentary Feature (*ARTIE SHAW: Time Is All You've Got*), 1987; Bronze Hugo (*BIX: Ain't None of Them Play Like Him Yet*), Chicago International Film Festival, 1981; First Prize (*ARTIE SHAW: Time Is All You've Got*), Valladolid International Film Festival; Chris Plaque Award, Columbus International Film Festival; Merit Award, Athens International Film Festival; various Genie nominations; Canada 125 Medal. INTERESTS: film; drama; music; arts; gardening. MISC: was chosen as one of the first 12 residents at the prestigious Canadian Film Centre, 1988; Bridge Films Productions Inc. is the prod. co. for *ARTIE SHAW: Time Is All You've Got* & *BIX: Ain't None of Them Play Like Him Yet.*

Bertell, H Rosalie, Ph.D.,G.N.S.H. ✛ ✿ ✩
President, INTERNATIONAL INSTITUTE OF CONCERN FOR PUBLIC HEALTH, 264 Queen's Quay W., Ste. 710, Toronto, ON M5J 1B5 (416) 260-0575, FAX 260-3404. Born Buffalo, N.Y. 1929. EDUC: D'Youville Coll., B.A.(Math.) 1951; Catholic Univ. of America, M.A.(Math.) 1959, Ph.D.(Math.) 1966;. CAREER: Registrar & Assoc. Prof., Math. Dept., Sacred Heart Jr. Coll., Pa., 1958-68; Coord., High Sch. Math. Teachers, Diocese of Atlanta, 1968-69; Assoc. Prof., Math. Dept., D'Youville Coll., Buffalo, 1969-72; Sr. Cancer Research Scientist, Roswell Park Memorial Institute, Buffalo, 1970-78; Coord. of Institutional Research, D'Youville

Coll., Buffalo, 1971-72; Visiting Prof., State Univ. of New York, Buffalo, 1972-73; Assoc. Research Prof., Grad. Sch., State Univ. of New York, Buffalo, 1974-78; Dir. of Research & Biostatistical & Radiation Health Consultant, Ministry for Public Health, Buffalo, 1978-80; Energy & Public Health Specialist, Jesuit Centre for Social Faith & Justice, Toronto, 1980-84; Dir. of Research, Pres., Bd., International Institute of Concern for Public Health, 1984-87; Founding Mbr., International Commission of Health Professionals, 1985-95; Pres., International Institute of Concern for Public Health, 1987 to date; Mbr., Exec. Committee, International Commission of Health Professionals, 1988-95; Sec. Gen., International Commission of Health Professionals, 1991-95. SELECTED CREDITS: "Speaking Our Peace," and "Nuclear Addiction," NFB Canada. SELECTED PUBLICATIONS: *Handbook for Estimating Health Effects from Exposure to Ionizing Radiation*, compiler (Buffalo: International Institute of Concern for Public Health, 1984); *No Immediate Danger - Prognosis for a Radioactive Earth* (London, UK: Women's Press, 1985); "Destruction of the Environment," in *Horrendous Death, Health and Well Being*, Dr. Dan Leviton, editor (Washington, DC: Hemisphere Publishing Corporation, 1990); "Ethics of the Nuclear Option in the 1990's," in *Nuclear Energy and Ethics*, Kristen Schrader-Frechette, editor (Geneva: World Council of Churches, 1991); "Chernobyl - April 1991" (*Environmental Health Review* Fall 1991); "Breast Cancer and Mammography" (*Mothering* Summer 1992); numerous other articles, book chapters & other publications. EDIT: Ed.-in-Chief, *International Perspectives in Public Health*, 1984 to date. AFFIL: International Institute of Concern for Public Health (Dir.); Global Education Association (Dir.); The Greater Toronto Clearing House (Dir.); American Academy of Political & Social Sciences; American Association of University Women; American Public Health Association; Grey Nuns of the Sacred Heart; Institute of Society, Ethics & Life Sciences; International League of Women for Peace & Freedom; International Medical Commission, Bhopal (Dir. 1994); International Medical Commission, Chernobyl (Dir. 1996); Kappa Gamma Pi; Nuclear Task Force, International Joint Commission US-Canada; New York Academy of Science; Sigma Xi; Health Physics Society (Plenary Mbr.); Lawyers for Social Responsibility, Canada (Advisory Bd.); Food & Water, Inc., Denville, N.J. (Dir.); Food Irradiation Alert, Burnaby, B.C. (Bd. of Advisors); Great Lakes Health Effects Program, Health Canada (Advisory Bd.); Rotary. HONS: Outstanding Civic Leader of America Award,

1970; Outstanding Educators of America, 1973; Award, National Organization of Women, WNY Chapter, 1981; Award, New York Public Interest Group, 1981; Hans Adalbert Schweigart Medal, World League for the Protection of Life, 1983; Fellow of the Indian Society of Naturalists, Baroda, India, 1985; Right Livelihood Award, 1986; Distinguished Alumnae Award, Mount St. Joseph Academy, 1987; Women of Distinction Award, YWCA, Toronto, 1987; World Peace Award, World Federalists of Canada, 1988; UNEP Global 500; Ryerson Fellowship, Ryerson Polytechnical Institute, 1988; Distinguished Educator, OISE, 1990; Health Innovator Award, Ontario Premier's Council on Health, 1993; D.Hum.L.(Hon.), Mount St. Vincent Univ., 1985; Doctor of Laws(Hon.), Laurentian Univ., 1988; D.Sc.(Hon.), Univ. of Windsor, 1988; D.Sc.(Hon.), D'Youville Coll., 1988. **MISC:** numerous consultancies, incl. President's Commission on the Accident at Three Mile Island, Citizen's Advisory Committee, USA; Science Advisory Bd., Int'l Joint Commission of the US & Canada; & Int'l Policy Action Committee - Women's Preparatory Committee for UNCED; elected Delegate, Grey Nuns' Legislative Chapter, 1971, 1974, 1975; House of Delegates, Nat'l Assembly of Women Religious, 1973-76; Nat'l Exec. Bd., Nat'l Assembly of Women Religious, 1977-80; listed in numerous biographical directories, incl. *American Catholic Who's Who*, 1977, 1978, 1979, 1980, 1981; *Canadian Who's Who*, 1992, 1993; *International Directory of Distinguished Leadership*, 1992; *Who's Who in Health Care*, 1977 and *The World Who's Who of Women*, 1976, 1977, 1981; No *Immediate Danger* translated into Swedish, German, French & Finnish; various conference papers & speeches to associations.

Berton, Janet ■ ■ / 📖 ○

Community Volunteer. Kleinburg, ON. Born Fernie, B.C. 1920. m. Pierre Berton. 8 ch. Penny, Pamela, Patsy, Peter, Paul, Peggy Anne, Perri, Eric Basciano. **EDUC:** Univ. of British Columbia, English & Hist. 1941. **CAREER:** Reporter, *Vancouver Province*, 1941-46; 4 columns every day for children, Tillicum Club, 1942-44; after marriage, moved to Church Editor (to eliminate rivalry for scoops—Pierre worked for rival paper, *The Vancouver Sun*); public rel'ns for 1st free Red Cross Blood Transfusion svc. in the world, B.C., 1946; publicity, Canadian Opera Company (Royal Conservatory), 1947-48; public rel'ns for Canadian Arthritis & Rheumatism Society for all of Canada, 1951; Food Writer (3 pages an issue), *York Magazine*, 3 yrs., late 1980s. **SELECTED**

PUBLICATIONS: co-editor, *CFUW Calendar/History, 1919-1980*; *Seventy-Five Years of CFUW History/Soixante-quinze ans de FCFDU* (1994); co-author, *Canadian Centennial Food Guide, Pierre & Janet Berton's Canadian Food Guide*, & *Berton Family Cookbook*. **AFFIL:** Canadian Federation of University Women (former Pres., North York &Vaughan chpt.; Publications Chair 1973-76); Vaughan Community Information (co-founder, Exec. mbr.); Kleinburg Binder Twine (Exec. 1967-96; Ed., 16 Kleinburg history booklets); Dellcrest Children's Centre (former Bd. mbr.; former Pres., Women's Committee); *United Church Observer* (former Bd. mbr.); Heritage Vaughan; Humber Heritage; Community Heritage Ontario; Committee for the Adoption of Coloured Youngsters, Social Planning Council of Toronto (former mbr.); Kleinburg Home & School (co-founder & Pres. 1955). **HONS:** 5 & 10 Yr. Awards for Voluntarism, Ont. Ministry of Culture & Communications, & Citizenship; 35 Yr. Award, Canadian Cancer Society, Woodbridge; Heart of Gold Award, Air Canada & local newspapers; City of Vaughan Heritage Award, 1995. **MISC:** Explorer leader (9-11 yr.-old girls), 20 yrs. **COMMENT:** *"I am interested in the "community" and its history and I am seriously concerned about the wanton destruction of Canada's built and natural heritage."*

Bertrand, Marie-Andrée, M.S.W., M.Sc.,Ph.D. 🔱 🕐 🦅

Professor, School of Criminology, UNIVERSITY OF MONTREAL, Box 6128, Montreal, QC H3C 3J7 (514) 343-5864, FAX 343-5650. Born Montreal 1925. **EDUC:** Univ. of Ottawa, B.A.; École Vincent d'Indy d'Outrement, B.M., M.M.; Univ. of Montreal, M.S.W. 1951, M.A. (Crim.) 1963; Univ. of California, D.Crim. 1967. **CAREER:** Asst. Prof. of Criminology, Univ. of Montreal, 1967-70; Assoc. Prof. of Criminology, 1970-72; Visiting Prof., Sch. of Criminology, Univ. of California, Berkeley, 1973-77; Full Prof. of Criminology, Univ. of Montreal, 1977 to date. **SELECTED PUBLICATIONS:** *La femme et le crime* (Montreal: L'Aurore, 1979); "The Deconstruction of Truth Epistemologies" in *Proceedings of the International Feminist Conference on Women, Law and Social Control*, ed. by M.A. Bertrand, K. Daly & D. Klein (Vancouver: The International Centre for Comparative Law Reform, UBC, 1992); "The place and status of feminist criminology in Germany, Denmark, Norway and Finland," *International Feminist Perspectives in Criminology: Engineering a Discipline*, eds. Nicole Hahn Rafter & Frances Heidensohn (Buckingham, UK: Open University Press,

1995); "Les effets de l'analyse de genre sur les théories du contrôle social," *Perspectives actuelles en criminologie*, dir. S. Brochu (Centre internationale de criminologie, Univ. de Montréal, 1996); "Constructivism and postmoderism seen from feminism," *Politischer Wandel, Gesellschaft und Kriminalotatsdiskurse. Feststricht in Honour of Fritz Sack*, ed. Trutz von Trotha (Baden-Baden: Nomos Publishing Co., 1996); numerous articles & chapters in books. **AFFIL:** International Antiprohibitions League (Pres.); Canadian Bar Association (Committee on Imprisonment & Release); Centre de recherche et d'aide pour narcomanes, Montréal (Bd.).

Bertrand de Muñoz, Maryse, L.Ls.M.A., D.U.P.
Professeure titulaire et Directrice du Département littératures et langues modernes, UNIVERSITÉ DE MONTRÉAL, 3150 Jean-Brillant, Montréal, QC H3C 3J7 (514) 343-7050, FAX 343-2255. Born Montréal. m. J. Pedro Muñoz Robles. 3 ch. Cristina, Maria Josém Elena. **EDUC:** Univ. de Montréal, L.Ls.(Mod. Lang.) 1959, M.A.(Spanish Lit.) 1959; Univ. de Paris, Doctorat(Comparative Lit.) 1962. **CAREER:** Conseillière de l'enseignement de l'espagnol, Fac. des Arts, Univ. de Montréal, 1963-67; Prof. de langue et littératures espagnole et étrangère, 1966 to date; Prof. agrégée et Chef de la section d'Études hispaniques, 1972-78; Lectrice du Gouvernement espagnol, 1972-78; Prof. titulaire, 1978 to date; Dir. du Dépt. de littératures et langues modernes, 1989 to date; Mbr. du Comité ececutif de la Fac. des Arts et des Sciences, 1992-96. **SELECTED PUBLICATIONS:** *La guerre civile espagnole et la littérature française* (Paris, Bruxelles, Montréal: Didier, 1972); "La pluma y la espada. La literatura del conflicto (1936-39)" (*La guerra civil espanola* ed. Hugh Thomas, Madrid: Urbión, Fascículos 77-78, Vol. VI, 1980); *La guerra civil española en la novela. Bibliografía comentada* (Madrid: José Porrúa Turanzas, 1982); "The Civil War in the Recent Spanish Novel, 1966-76" (*Red Flags, Black Flags. Critical Essays on the Literature of the Spanish War*, Madrid: José Porrúa Turanzas, 1983); *La guerra civil española en la novela. Los años de la democracia* (Madrid: José Porrúa Turanzas, 1986); "Bibliografía de la creación literaria de la guerra civil española" (*Anales de Literatura Española Contemporánea*, Vol. 1/Vol. II, issue 3, 1986-87); *La novela europea y americana y la guerra civil española* (Gijón-Madrid: Júcar, 1994); *La guerra civil española y la literatura francesa* (Seville: Alfar, 1995. **AFFIL:** Association Canadienne des Hispanistes (Pres.); Modern Language Association of America; American Association of Teachers of Spanish & Portuguese; Association Canadienne de Littérature Comparée; Asociación Internacional de Hispanistas; Association Internationale de Littérature Comparée; Association canadienne-française pour l'avancement des sciences (Fondatrice de la section des Études hispaniques); Asociación Española de Semiótica; Asociación Vasca de Semiótica; Association Internationale de Sémiotique; Asociación de Profesores de Español de Québec; Association des docteurs de l'Univ. de Paris; Association des Diplômés de l'Univ. de Montréal; Fédération Internationale des Langues et Littératures Modernes.

Besen, Ellen
135 Aldwych Ave., Toronto, ON M4J 1X8 (416) 463-9705, FAX 463-7498. Born Chicago 1953. m. Arnie Lipsey. 1 ch. **EDUC:** Sheridan Coll., Sch. of Animation, 1971-73. **CAREER:** Prod., Dir., Prod. Mgr, RRED Studio Ltd., 1973-76; freelance Animation Dir., National Film Board,& independent animation filmmaker/prod., 1977 to date; Animator, Ein Gedi Studios, Israel, 1983; Curator, various animation programs, 1987 to date; Radio Journalist, Infotape & Basic Black, CBC Radio, 1994-96; Instructor, Sheridan Coll. Sch. of Animation, 1987-88, 1994-97. **SELECTED CREDITS:** Dir./Writer,*To Spring*, 1973; Writer/Dir./Prod., *Metric-Métrique*, 1976; Dir., *Sea Dream*, 1979; Animator, *Lights*, 1983; Co-Prod./Co-Dir., *Slow Dance World*, 1986; Co-Prod., *The Crow and the Canary*, 1988; Animation Coord., *Comic Book Confidential*, 1988; Dir., *Illuminated Lives: A Brief History of Women's Work in the Middle Ages*, 1989; contributed films or artwork to numerous shows & festivals, incl. Zagreb Animation Festival (1980), Expo '86 Amiga Studio Theatre, Canada Pavilion (1986), & National Gallery Opening, Ottawa (1988); organized animation screenings & events in association with Toronto Animated Image Society & ASIFA Canada, incl. Soviet Animation Event (1987). **SELECTED PUBLICATIONS:** co-writer with Barbara Sternberg & Keith Lock, *Through a Filmmaker's Eyes: A Guide to Teaching Film in Media Literacy* (CFMDC, 1992); co-writer with Marc Glassman, "3 Men and a Bear: Nelvana at 25" (*Take One*). **AFFIL:** Toronto Animated Image Society; ASIFA; Canadian Filmmakers Distribution Centre; Sheridan Coll. (Animation Advisory Committee); Ottawa International Animation Festival (Advisory Bd.). **HONS:** Award of Merit, New York Animation Festival, *To Spring*, 1974; Third Prize, Berlin Educational Film Festival, *Metric-Métrique*, 1976; Second Prize for children's films, Ottawa Animation Festival, *Sea Dream*,

1980; First Prize, American Film Festival, *Sea Dream*, 1980. **INTERESTS:** film; animation; storytelling; art education; children's literature. **MISC:** recipient of various grants from the Canada Council & the Ontario Arts Council; Juror, several Ontario Arts Council film juries; Coord. & Speaker; Film Programmer, 1992-96; Storytelling Workshop, Canadian International Animation Festival, Ottawa; has given lectures & demonstrations at Canada House, London, UK; Concordia Univ.; Montreal Museum of Fine Arts; York Univ. **COMMENT:** *"Ellen Besen has worked in animation for 25 years, as an NFB director, independent filmmaker, teacher, curator and commentator/broadcaster. Her goal, always, has been to encourage excellence in this field."*

Besen, Joan 🎭 ⊛ 📖
Songwriter/Musician/Limerick Laureate, Keyboard player with Prairie Oyster. 156 Hiawatha Rd., Toronto, ON (416) 466-1556 or (615) 298-4802, EMAIL 76326.3270@compuserve.com. Born Chicago 1951. 1 ch. **EDUC:** Toronto Teachers' Coll., 1970. **CAREER:** Teacher, East & North York, 1970-74; played piano with Sylvia Tyson, 1978-84; has played piano & written with Prairie Oyster, 1982 to date. **SELECTED PUBLICATIONS:** *Morningside Papers* (Limerick Chapter). **AFFIL:** TMA; SOCAN; CCMA; Songwriters' Association of Canada (Bd. of Dir.); CARAS (head of SOCAN Juno for 'Composer of the Year" committee); CMA (U.S.). **HONS:** Juno, Country Group of the Year (with Prairie Oyster) 1985-86, 1986-87, 1990, 1991; CCMA Group of the Year, 1990, 1991, 1992, 1994, 1996; RPM Big Country Group of the Year, 1991, 1992, 1994, 1996; Entertainer of the Year, 1992; Album of the Year, 1992; CCMA Entertainer of the Year, 1994; CCMA Keyboardist of the Year, 1996, & many others. **INTERESTS:** music; writing; cryptic crosswords; all arts; sailing; downhill skiing; literacy; environmental concerns. **COMMENT:** *"I love to play, write, perform and record music. I have been very fortunate to be able to spend my whole life doing this. My favourite endeavour, however, has been the care and feeding of my son, Sunny Besen Thrasher, now 21 years old, who works in various capacities in film and theatre."*

Besse, Irene ■■ $ 🎓 ⊛
President and owner, IRENE BESSE KEYBOARDS LTD. (retail pianos, digital keyboards, organs; music academy with 500 students; complete svc. dept.), 6999 - 11 St. S.E., Unit 152, Calgary, AB T2H 2S1 (403) 252-7770, FAX 252-9047, INTERNET http://www.cwave.com/ibk. Born Edmonton 1941. m. Thomas. 2 ch. Michael, Nicole. **EDUC:** Royal Conservatory of Music, Performance Music 1963. **CAREER:** sports organist, various organizations incl. Stampeder Football Club, Calgary 88s basketball league, Calgary Cannons Baseball Club, Calgary Boomers Soccer Club, many yrs.; Organist, Calgary Flames, National Hockey League, 7 yrs.; 1st organist to provide live organ music at Olympic Games, figure skating & hockey games, 1988 Olympics. **AFFIL:** Better Business Bureau of Southern Alberta (Dir. 1992 to date); Friends of the Esther Honens Int'l Piano Competition (Dir. 1992 to date); Calgary Association of Piano Dealers; Alberta Piano Teachers' Association; Alberta Registered Music Teachers' Association; Calgary Musicians' Association; Rotary Club of Calgary (active mbr., downtown chpt. 1994 to date); National American Music Merchants. **HONS:** Milner Fennerty Pinnacle Award, 1990; Reg'l Winner, Female Entrepreneur of the Year, 1996; Best Business Award, 2 consecutive yrs., 1987/88 & 1988/89. **MISC:** supports/helps Calgary Philharmonic Orchestra (fundraising), Mount Royal Coll. Conservatory of Music, Canadian Music Competitions, Calgary Concerto Competition through donations of pianos or avenue for performances; featured in Apr./May 1996 issue of *Canadian Music Trade* magazine. **COMMENT:** *"Vision to see needs for my customers, always looking to improve and streamline business, education and personal needs for a more educated customer. Setting goals and dreams, always having a fresh positive attitude, which of course helps make things happen. Biggest goal was the present dream of putting all services under one roof to include the jewel, our own concert hall."*

Best, Lynette, B.Sc.,M.Sc.,R.N., C.H.E. ■ ⊕ 🎓 ♥
Chief Operating Officer, LIONS GATE HOSPITAL, 231 E. 15th St., North Vancouver, BC V7L 2L7 (604) 984-5772, FAX 984-5788. Born Man. 1946. m. Robert L. Best. 2 ch. Janet, Michael. **EDUC:** Winnipeg General Hospital, Grad. Nurse 1968; Univ. of British Columbia, B.Sc.(Nursing) 1972, M.Sc.(Nursing) 1982. **CAREER:** Staff Nurse, Surgery, Winnipeg General Hospital, 1968; Staff Nurse, Casual, Burnaby General Hospital, 1969-72, 1978-82; Head Nurse, Extended Care, 1972-74; Inservice Educator, 1974-75; Nursing Coord., Surgery/ICU, 1975-78; Summer Lecturer/Clinical Instructor, Univ. of British Columbia Sch. of Nursing, 1979; Nursing Coord., Medicine/ICU, Univ. of British Columbia Acute Care Hospital, 1980-82; Assoc. Dir. of Nursing, Lions Gate Hospital, 1982-86; VP, Nursing/Patient Care Svcs,

1986-96. **AFFIL:** Registered Nurses' Association of B.C. (various exec. positions, Vancouver District & Continuing Nursing Educ. Interest Group 1973-76; Dir., Elected District Mbr. 1979-81); B.C. Institute of Technology (Advisory Committee, R.N. Program 1977-79); Nurse Administrators' Association of B.C. (VP 1984-86); B.C. Health Association (Health Care Hum. Res. Policy Advisory Committee); Provincial Pediatric Hospital (Utilization Review Committee); Univ. of British Columbia, Sch. of Nursing (President's Advisory Committee 1992-93); Registered Nurses Foundation of B.C. (Bd. 1993-96); B.C. Health Care Risk Management Society (Bd.); Vancouver Community Coll. (Prov. Advisory Committee, R.N. Program); Canadian Coll. of Health Service Executives; Sigma Theta Tau–Xi Eta Chapter; North Shore Home Support Society (Bd. of Dir. 1990-96; Chair 1993-95). **HONS:** various scholarships & medals; Award of Excellence in Nursing Administration, R.N.A.B.C., 1992. **INTERESTS:** sailing; skiing; walking; reading. **MISC:** frequent speaker at various health care groups; participant in numerous ad hoc groups/advisory programs concerning patient care issues; Certified Instructor for Zenger Miller FrontLine Leadership Training System; Certified Trainer for William Bridges and Associates Transition Management. **COMMENT:** *"People who work in health-care started their careers with the belief that they would help others and make a difference. As a nurse, a teacher, and health care administrator, my work focuses on keeping that belief alive for, and with, others, toward the goal of helping people achieve health for themselves."*

Bethel, Judy, M.P.,B.A. ■■ ✦

Member of Parliament, Edmonton East, GOVERNMENT OF CANADA, 9111 - 118th Ave., Edmonton, AB T5G 0T9 (403) 495-3278, FAX 495-7175, 403 W. Block, House of Commons, Ottawa, ON K1A 0A6 (613) 992-3821, FAX 992-6898. Born Winnipeg. m. Bruzz. 2 ch. Marnie, John. **EDUC:** Univ. of North Dakota, B.A.(Educ.) 1965. **CAREER:** Teacher, U.S. & Canada, 1965-80; Investment Broker, Richardson Greenshields, 4 yrs.; Alderman, Ward 3, City of Edmonton, 1985-93; elected Liberal M.P. for Edmonton E., 1993; Chair, Northern & Western Caucus; mbr., Standing Committee on Citizenship & Immigration; served on Industry Committee & Justice & Legal Affairs Committee; served as Chair, Standing Committee on Citizenship & Immigration. **AFFIL:** Edmonton Police Commission (former mbr.); Royal Alexandra Hospital (former mbr. of Bd.); Kilkenny Community League (former Pres.); Area Council 17 (former Pres.).

Betteridge, Lois Ethrington, B.F.A.,M.F.A., R.C.A. ⊗

Silversmith. 9 Kirkland St., Guelph, ON N1H 4X7 (519) 763-2231. Born Drummondville, Que. 1928. m. Keith James Betteridge. 2 ch. Eric Beasley, Lise Miranda. **EDUC:** Ontario Coll. of Art, 1st yr. 1948; Univ. of Kansas, B.F.A.(Silversmithing & Design) 1951; Cranbrook Academy of Art, M.F.A.(Silversmithing) 1957. **CAREER:** studio artist since 1952, in Canada & the UK; Teacher, Ryerson Institute of Technology, 1952-54; Lecturer of Design, Macdonald Institute, 1957-60; Visiting Artist, Nova Scotia Coll. of Art & Design, Summer 1983. **COMMISSIONS:** Royal Scottish Museum; IBM Canada; National Museum of Natural Sciences, Ottawa; Canadian Crafts Council, Ottawa; Ontario Crafts Council, Toronto; Cranbrook Art Gallery, Michigan; National Museum of Civilization, Ottawa. **EXHIBITIONS:** more than 120 various juried, invitational & group exhibitions in Canada, US, UK, France, Belgium & Japan incl. *Canadian Abstract Art–Centennial Exhibition*, England & Scotland (1967); *Contemporary Ontario Crafts*, Kingston, Ont. (1977); *Grand Prix des Metiers d'art*, Paris, Brussels, London (1985); *Masters of American Metalsmithing*, U.S. (1988); *Master of the Crafts*, Canada, touring show (1989-94); *Silver: New Forms and Expressions*, U.S. (1990); *R.C.A. exhibition*, Budapest (1995); *Second Skin*, McDonald Stewart Art Gallery, Guelph (1996); *Heritage & Diversity*, Rockville, Maryland (1996); 21 solo exhibitions incl. *Reflections in Silver and Gold*, toured eight major Cdn art centres (1981-83); Harbinger Gallery, Waterloo, Ont. 1986; *Recent Works*, Art Gallery of Hamilton, Ont., toured nine major public galleries across Canada (1988-90). **AFFIL:** Society of North American Goldsmiths (Distinguished Mbr.); Royal Canadian Academy of Arts. **HONS:** The Helen Scripps Booth Scholarship, Cranbrook Academy of Art, 1955; Citation for Distinguished Professional Achievement, Univ. of Kansas, 1975; Saidye Bronfman Award for Excellence in Crafts, 1978; Fellow, N.B. Craft Sch., 1988; Fellow, Ontario Coll. of Art, 1992. **MISC:** has conducted numerous workshops to colleges & guilds across Canada & the U.S. since 1971; occasionally trains apprentices in her studio.

Bey, Salome ■■ ♥ ⊗

Singer, Actress, Composer, Recording Artist. c/o Howard Matthews, Canadian Artists Network/Black Artists in Action, 54 Wolseley St., 2nd Fl., Toronto, ON M5T 1A5 (416) 703-9040, FAX 703-0059, EMAIL can.baia@sympatico.ca. Born Newark, N.J. **CAREER:** left

2nd-yr. law studies, Rutger's Law Sch., to become full-time entertainer; formed vocal group, "Andy and the Bey Sisters," with brother & sister; toured throughout N.Am. & Europe; came to Toronto, 1964; played jazz club circuit; acting, Toronto, on Broadway; TV, theatre & festival performances; recording projects. **SELECTED CREDITS:** blues & jazz cabaret show, *Indigo*, extended runs, taped for TV specials on CBC & sold to A&E ntwk in U.S. & European ntwks; TV credits include CBC Super Specials with Anne Murray, Paul Williams & Toller Cranston, & her own specials, *Salome Bey's Christmas Soul & Special Moments*; several albums; participated in recording of "Tears Are Not Enough" (single & video); concerts, National Arts Centre, Massey Hall, Roy Thomson Hall (with Toronto Symphony), CNE Grandstand (with Bill Cosby). **HONS:** OBIE Award for Best *Actress (Love Me, Love My Children)*, 1972; nominated for Grammy award (for performance on cast album, *Your Arm's Too Short to Box with God*); Dora Mavor Moore awards for *Indigo* (one for show & one for her performance); Toronto Arts Award; 3 Black Music Awards; Martin Luther King, Jr. Award; performed twice for Queen Elizabeth, Toronto & Ottawa; performed for Cdn Gov't at Nelson Mandela's visit to Toronto when he was released from prison; Cdn musical ambassador, Expo '92, Seville, Spain. **COMMENT:** *"'Canada's First Lady of the Blues,' Salome Bey has never been satisfied to rest on the laurels of her distinguished career. Having performed in virtually every type of musical venue from children's theatre to Royal Command performances, from Broadway shows to jazz festivals, in television specials, radio programs and recording projects, Salome Bey continues to expand her musical dossier in Canada and abroad."*

Beyea, Marion, B.A. 🔲 ⊗ ✤
Provincial Archivist, PROVINCIAL ARCHIVES OF NEW BRUNSWICK, Box 6000, Fredericton, NB E3B 5H1 (506) 453-3811, FAX 453-3288, EMAIL marionb@gov.nb.ca. Born Saint John 1945. d. 4 ch. Martin, Kari, Robin, Sarah. **EDUC:** Univ. of New Brunswick, B.A. 1967. **CAREER:** Manuscript Archivist, Archives of Ont., 1967-75; Archivist, Anglican Church of Canada, 1975-78; Prov. Archivist, Provincial Archives of N.B., 1978 to date. **SELECTED PUBLICATIONS:** "The Professional Associations and the Formation of the Canadian Archival System" (*Janus* 1987); "Technology, Industry and the Archival Heritage, Possibilities and Needs" (*Janus* 1992); various other journal publications; book reviews. **EDIT:** Co-Ed.,

Archives Bulletin, 1973-75; Guest Ed., Maritime Issue, *Journal of the Canadian Church Historical Society*, Oct. 1983; Ed. Bd., *Acadiensis*, 1986 to date; Ed. Bd., *Janus*, 1992 to date; Assoc. Ed., *Canadian Archives in 1992*, 1992. **AFFIL:** Anglican Diocese of Fredericton (Archives Committee); Provincial Conservation Program Committee (Chair & Admin.); Canadian Council of Archives (Chair, Standards Committee); Association of Canadian Archivists; Council of Archives N.B.; Historic Sites & Monuments Board of Canada; Anglican Diocese of Fredericton, Sesquicentennial Committee; Fredericton Heritage Trust. **INTERESTS:** built heritage, drama, athletics.

Biedermann, Mary Margaret, B.Comm. ■■ 💲 ❀ ∅ ♻
President, MB & ASSOCIATES INC. (Contract Executives, Business Turnaround, Business Plans, High Tech, Marketing), 27 Willow Ave., Toronto, ON M4E 3K1 (416) 690-1176, FAX 690-5919. Born Burlington, Vt. 1939. s. 2 ch. **EDUC:** McGill Univ., Sch. of Mgmt, B.Comm. 1960; Harvard Bus. Sch., Presidents' Class; qualified as Therapeutic Touch practitioner. **CAREER:** Mgr of Host Software/Mktg Mgr P.O.S. & Retail/Mgr of Open Systems for Fin. Industry, IBM Canada; Pres., MB & Associates Inc., 1992 to date. **DIRECTOR:** The Omega Centre Book Store and Conference Centre (Acting Chair & CEO). **AFFIL:** Canadian Venture Capital Association; MIT/York Enterprise Forum; Toronto Venture Group; Business Centurions; Therapeutic Touch Network of Ontario (Treas. & Dir.); Mensa. **HONS:** several IBM Mktg Excellence Awards; 12 One Hundred Percent Clubs, IBM Canada. **INTERESTS:** metaphysics; business; sports; languages; Tai Chi; meditation; family; friendships; reading; the outdoors; renovating. **COMMENT:** *"Grew up and educated in Montreal with a year at the International School in Geneva, Switzerland. A home and a corner of my heart in the Laurentian mountains. Always at the forefront of change. As a female, this provided many opportunities for personal growth as I encountered social barriers and disfavour in my path. First woman to be presented with IBM Canada's 100% Club Award for Sales. Owned and drove a 4-wheel drive 10 years before they were in vogue. Canoed through the wilderness of La Verendrye Park for many days at a time. One of the first female Marketing Managers at IBM Canada. Graduated a Business Degree as a female minority. Early entrant in the computer field. Pursued a deep interest in metaphysics before it became popular. A lateral thinker with a sense of humour and a people person."*

Bielby, Myra B., B.A., LL.B. ■■ ⚖
Judge, COURT OF QUEEN'S BENCH OF ALBERTA, Law Courts Building, 1A Sir Winston Churchill Square, Edmonton, AB T5J 0R2 (403) 422-2200, FAX 427-0334. Born Port Colborne, Ont. 1951. m. Dr. Gordon Thomas. 2 ch. Jennifer, Sandra. EDUC: Univ. of Alberta, B.A. 1974, LL.B. 1974. CAREER: Ptnr, Field & Field Perradon, 1974-90; Bencher, Law Society of Alberta, 1990 to date. AFFIL: Edmonton Bar Association (Pres. 1986).

Bienstock, Ric Esther ✇ ✒ ⚰
Producer/Director, GOOD SOUP PRODUCTIONS INC., 44 Browning Ave., Toronto, ON M4K 1V7 (416) 413-1303, FAX 461-1144. Born Montreal 1959. m. Richard Mortimer. SELECTED CREDITS: prod./dir. Ebola: Inside an Outbreak/The Plague Fighters (documentary), 1996; prod./dir., Ms. Conceptions (documentary), Good Soup Productions, 1995; location dir., The Plague Monkeys (documentary), Reunion Film Ltd., 1994; prod., Deadly Currents (feature documentary), Reunion Film Ltd., 1991; prod., Burden on the Land (documentary), Roger Pyke Productions, 1990; prod./PM, AIDS in Africa (documentary), Roger Pyke Productions Ltd., 1990; prod./PM, "Meeting the Challenge" (Man Alive), Roger Pyke Productions, 1989. AFFIL: Canadian Independent Film Caucus (Exec. Bd. 1995-96); Academy of Canadian Film and Television; Toronto Women in Film & Television. HONS: Best Feature Documentary (Deadly Currents), Genie Awards, 1992; Best International Documentary Special (Deadly Currents), Cable Ace Awards, 1994; Gold Hugo (Deadly Currents), Chicago International Film Festival, 1992; Gold Award (Deadly Currents), Houston International Film Festival, 1992; Grand Prix (Deadly Currents), Nyon International Documentary Festival, 1991; Best Documentary, Donald Brittain Award (Ms.Conceptions); Best International Documentary, Gemini Awards 1996; Cable Ace Awards Special (The Plague Monkeys), 1995.

Biesenthal, Laryssa ■■ ⊘
Olympic Athlete. c/o Canadian Olympic Association. Born Walkerton, Ont. 1971. EDUC: currently studying Landscape Architecture. SPORTS CAREER: mbr. Cdn Nat'l Rowing Team, 1995 to date. Olympic Games: Bronze, 4x, 1996. World championships: 2nd, 4x, 1995. Int'l regattas: 8th, 2- (Switzerland), 1995; 2nd, 4- (Ont.), 1994. Canadian championships: 1st, 4x, & 1st, 2x, 1993; 1st, 4-, 1st, 8+, & 1st, 4+, 1992. US championships: 4th, 2x, & 1st, 4x, 1995; 1st, 8+, & 4th, 2-, 1994.

Bigelow, Ann, B.A.,M.A.,Ph.D. ⚕ ✿ ⊕
Professor, Department of Psychology, ST. FRANCIS XAVIER UNIVERSITY, Box 5000, Antigonish, NS B2G 2W5 (902) 867-3900, FAX 867-2448, EMAIL abigelow@juliet.stfx.ca. Born Bluffton, Ohio 1946. m. Chris Tragakis. 1 ch. Adam. EDUC: Coll. of Wooster, Ohio, B.A.(Psych./Hist.) 1968; Univ. of Iowa, M.A.(Child Behaviour & Dev.) 1970; Simon Fraser Univ., Ph.D.(Psych.) 1975. CAREER: Asst. Prof., Dept. of Psych., St. Francis Xavier Univ., 1975-80; Assoc. Prof., 1980-90; Prof., 1990 to date. SELECTED PUBLICATIONS: "The Correspondence between Self and Image Movement as a Cue to Self Recognition in Young Children" (Journal of Genetic Psychology 1981); "Early Words of Blind Children" (Journal of Child Language 1987); "Blind Children's Concepts of How People See" (Journal of Visual Impairment and Blindness 1988); "Infants' Responses to Child and Adult Strangers: An Investigation of Height and Facial Configuration Variables," with J. MacLean et al (Infant Behavior & Development 1990); "Hiding in Blind and Sighted Children" (Development and Psychopathology 1991); "The Development of Blind Children's Ability to Predict What Another Sees" (Journal of Visual Impairment and Blindness 1992); "Blind and sighted children's spatial knowledge of their home environment" (International Journal of Behavioral Development, in press); "The effects of blindness on the early development of the self," The self in early infancy: Theory and research, ed. P. Rochat (Advances in Psychology Book Series. Amsterdam: North-Holland-Elsevier Science Publishers, in press); "The development of infants' search for their mothers, unfamiliar people and objects," with D. MacDonald & M. MacDonald (Merrill-Palmer Quarterly, 41(2), 1995); "Infant's response to live and replay interactions with self and mother," with B.K. MacLean & D. MacDonald (Merrill-Palmer Quarterly 42(4) 1996); numerous other articles & abstracts. EDIT: Ed. Bd., Journal of Genetic Psychology, 1985 to date. AFFIL: Canadian Psychological Association (Fellow); Canadian Psychological Association, Section on Developmental Psychology (Chair 1992-93); Canadian Psychological Association, Section on Women; Society for Research in Child Development; International Society for Infant Studies. MISC: Registered Psychologist, N.S.; recipient of numerous grants; various invited lectures; reviewer for various journals & granting agencies; numerous conference presentations. COMMENT: "Teacher. Researcher of cognitive development in blind children and the interrelationship of perceptual, motor, cognitive, social and emotional development in infancy. Mother."

Bignucolo, Amy Amneris DeMonte, C.H.A. $ ✚ ♡ ♢
Vice-President, QUALITY INN FALLSVIEW, 6663 Stanley Ave., Niagara Falls, ON L2G 3Y9 (905) 354-2322, FAX 354-4955. Born Italy 1945. m. Oscar A. Bignucolo. 3 ch. Robert, Donald, Raquel. EDUC: North Bay Teachers' Coll., 1964; Univ. of Michigan, Certified Hotel Administrator 1989. CAREER: Elementary Sch. Teacher, 1964-72; sales/mktg, Quality Inn, 1973-77; Gen. Mgr, 1978-87; VP, 1988 to date. AFFIL: Niagara Falls Canada Visitor & Convention Bureau (Pres. 1978, 1991-94; Dir. 1995); Project Share (Pres. 1994-95); Social Planning Council (Pres. 1989); Winter Festival of Lights (Dir. 1993-94, 1996); Niagara Falls Economic Development Agency (Dir. 1991-93); Niagara Falls United Way (1988-89); U.S./Canadian Business Relations Committee; Quality Service Steering Committee; Greater Niagara General Hospital (Corp. Fund Raising Committee for Cat Scan); Our Lady of Peace Shrine, Niagara Falls (Fundraising Committee); Niagara Falls Chamber of Commerce (Dir. 1996); Gateway Steering Committee (1995-96); Niagara Coll. (Bd. of Gov.). HONS: Progressive Development Award in Tourism, 1976; Hospitality Award in Tourism; Grand Misty Award, Overall Achievement in Tourism, Visitor & Convention Bureau, 1990; Misty Awards Service to the Bureau Award, Niagara Falls Visitor & Convention Bureau, 1994. INTERESTS: reading; sightseeing; theatre; design & sewing; walking; badminton. MISC: pilot teacher for open-class concept of teaching, Niagara Separate Sch. Bd.; first woman Pres., Visitor & Convention Bureau, & first woman to receive Grand Misty Award; future endeavours to publish & illustrate children's books. COMMENT: *"My self-motivated, goal-oriented nature, coupled with planning, organizational and executing skills have assisted in balancing being a mother, teacher, businesswoman and, in future, a publisher."*

Bigras, Sylvie, B.A.,M.A. ☺ ⊘
Director General, VOLLEYBALL CANADA, 1600 James Naismith Dr., Gloucester, ON K1B 5N4 (613) 748-5681, FAX 748-5727, EMAIL sylvie.bigras@cdnsport.ca. Born Ottawa 1957. m. André Pajot. 2 ch. EDUC: Univ. of Ottawa, B.A.(Phys. Educ.) 1980, M.A.(Sport Admin.) 1981. CAREER: Nat'l programs Coord., Canadian Volleyball Association, 1982-85; Exec. Dir., Shooting Federation of Canada, 1985-89; Dir. Gen., Volleyball Canada, 1989 to date. AFFIL: Canadian Sport Council (Dir. 1993-94); Sports Federation of Canada (Dir. & VP 1992-93); Canadian Sport & Fitness Administration Centre (Dir. 1986-90). HONS: Canadian Sport

Administrator of the Year, 1991. MISC: Master of Ceremonies, Canada Sport Awards, 1992-93; appointed to the Special Task Force on Nat'l Sport Policy by the Min. of State for Fitness & Amateur Sport, 1987-88; Press Attaché, 1988 Seoul Olympic Games & 1990 Commonwealth Games; Asst. Chef de Mission, 1992 Barcelona Olympic Games.

Bigue, Ann M., B.A.,LL.L.,LL.B.,LL.M. ⊿卬
Partner, MCCARTHY TÉTRAULT, 1170 Peel St., Montreal, QC H3B 4S8 (514) 397-4127, FAX 397-4187, EMAIL ambigue@mccarthy.ca. Born Amos, Que. 1951. EDUC: Coll. Jean-de-Brébeuf, B.A. 1971; Univ. of Montreal, LL.L. 1974; Dalhousie Univ., LL.B. 1979; Univ. of Ottawa, LL.M. 1980. CAREER: Articling Student, Dept. of Justice, Gov't of Canada, 1975; Cnsl, National Energy Bd., 1976-82; Assoc., McCarthy Tétrault, 1982-85; Ptnr, 1985 to date. AFFIL: Quebec Bar; Canadian Bar Association (Bd. & Exec., Que. Branch; Pres., Que. Admin. Law Section); U.S. Federal Energy Bar Association; Quebec Electricity Club; Quebec Environmental Impact Assessment Association; several other associations pertaining to energy & environmental concerns. HONS: Award, Commercial Law, Barreau de Montréal, 1974; Award, Administrative Law, Ambassade de France, 1981. COMMENT: *"Mtre. Bigué advises a variety of Canadian and US clients with respect to the planning, development, construction and implementation of energy, natural resources, transportation and industrial projects in Quebec and elsewhere in Canada, with specific support pertaining to contractual matters as well as federal and provincial regulatory matters, including public hearings and environmental assessments and reviews. She first developed this area of expertise as Counsel to the National Energy Board, a position she held for six years before joining McCarthy Tétrault in 1982. She also provides legal services to aboriginal and nonaboriginal clients involved in transactions that require expertise regarding aboriginal law issues and environmental assessment and review processes in territories subject to aboriginal and treaty rights."*

Billes, Martha, B.Sc. $
President, ALBIKIN MANAGEMENT INC., 2929 Wolfe St. S.W., Calgary, AB T2T 3S1 (403) 244-2610, FAX 244-2684. Born Toronto. d. 1 ch. EDUC: Univ. of Toronto, B.Sc. 1963. DIRECTOR: Canadian Tire Corporation; Saxon Petroleum. AFFIL: Ranchmen's Club, Calgary. COMMENT: *"Corporate governance has been my major focus since the late '70s. I have helped structure our corporation's Board of Directors (Canadian Tire) and currently chair*

its Governance Committee and the Audit Committee of Saxon."

Bindon, Kathryn, B.A.,M.A.,Ph.D. ✍ 📖
Principal, Sir Wilfred Grenfell College, MEMO-
RIAL UNIVERSITY OF NEWFOUNDLAND, Corner
Brook, NF A2H 2P9 (709) 637-6263, FAX
637-6390, EMAIL kbindon@beothuk.swgc.
mun.ca. Born Toronto 1949. d. 1 ch. EDUC:
Sir George Williams Univ., B.A.(Hist.) 1971;
Queen's Univ., M.A.(Hist.) 1973; Ph.D.(Hist.)
1979. CAREER: Lecturer in Hist., Concordia
Univ., 1978-80; Asst. Prof. in Hist., 1980-83;
Principal, Sch. of Community & Public
Affairs/École des Affaires Publiques et Commu-
nautaires, Concordia Univ., 1981-84; Assoc.
Prof., 1983; Exec. Asst. to the Rector, 1984-87;
VP, Academic & Assoc. Prof. of Hist., Mount
Saint Vincent Univ., 1987-91; Principal & Prof.
of Hist., Sir Wilfred Grenfell Coll., 1991 to
date. SELECTED PUBLICATIONS: *More Than
Patriotism: Canada at War, 1914-1918*
(Toronto: Nelson and Personal Library Pub-
lisher, 1979); "Hudson's Bay Company Law:
Adam Thom and the Institution of Order in
Rupert's Land, 1839-1854," *Essays in the His-
tory of Canadian Law*, Vol. 1, ed. by David H.
Flaherty (Univ. of Toronto Press for the
Osgoode Society, 1981); co-author with Paul
Wilson, "Newfoundland: More Canadian Than
British, But Longer Getting There," *Higher
Education in Canada: Different Systems, Dif-
ferent Perspectives*, ed. Glenn Jones (Garland
Press); various scholarly publications. AFFIL:
Canadian Historical Association; Champlain
Society; Institute of Public Administration of
Canada; World University Service of Canada
(Treas. 1988-92; VP 1992-93); Minister's Advi-
sory Bd. on Gender Integration in the Cana-
dian Forces (Chair 1993-95); Red Bay,
Labrador (Advisory Committee 1996 to date);
Advisory Committee on Tourism & Culture,
Prov. of Newfoundland & Labrador (Chair
1994-96); Rotary International, Corner Brook
Club (Mbr. of the Bd.); Nova Scotia Council on
Higher Learning (Mbr. 1989-91); Maritime
Provinces Higher Education Commission (Mbr.
1989-91); Governor General's Canadian Study
Conference (May-June 1983); National Defence
Coll. of Canada (Course XL 1986-87). HONS:
Woodrow Wilson Fellowship, 1971-72; R.
Samuel McLaughlin Scholarship, Queen's
Univ., 1971-72; Sir John A. Macdonald Grad.
Fellowship in Cdn Hist., 1972-74; Canada
Council Doctoral Fellowship, 1972-76. INTER-
ESTS: music; scuba diving; skiing; printmaking;
reading. MISC: Mbr., Minister's Advisory Bd.
on Women in the Cdn Forces, 1990-93; Mbr.,
Minister's Advisory Group on Defence Infrastructure, 1991-92; Mbr., Consultative Committee for Social Change in the Cdn Forces, 1991-
94. COMMENT: *"The discipline of history has
led me to an applied interest in public policy
and process. My various involvements have cut
across many sectors, with a view to maximizing
opportunities and results in the application of
fair procedural considerations and principles of
education in the knowledge that we must constantly seek new and better ways of doing
things to the benefit of all members of society."*

Birdsell, Judith, B.Sc.N.,M.Sc. 🖋 ⊕
President, CANADIAN CANCER SOCIETY, c/o
Management of Organizations and Human
Resources, Faculty of Management, University
of Calgary, Calgary, AB T2N 1N4 (403) 229-
9370, FAX 229-9370, EMAIL birdsell@acs.
ucalgary.ca. Born Stettler, Alta. 1950. m. Terry
Brooker. 2 ch. Sarah, Rhys. EDUC: Edmonton
General Hospital Sch. of Nursing, Coll. St.
Jean, Registered Nurse Diploma 1971; Univ. of
Alberta, Fac. of Nursing, B.Sc.N. 1976; Univ.
of Calgary, Fac. of Medicine, M.Sc. 1987, Fac.
of Mgmt, Ph.D. candidate 1992 to date.
CAREER: gen. duty hospital & public health
nursing, 1971-75; Nursing Instructor, Royal
Alexandra Hospital Sch. of Nursing, Edmon-
ton, 1976-77; Sessional Instructor, Fac. of
Nursing, Univ. of Calgary, 1977; Asst. Dir.,
Dept. of Epidemiology, Alberta Cancer Bd.,
1977-81; Special Projects, Dept. of Nursing,
Tom Baker Cancer Centre, Calgary, 1982-83;
Coord. (Prevention), Dept. of Epidemiology &
Preventive Oncology, Alberta Cancer Bd.,
1983-84; Proj. Dir., Steve Fonyo Cancer Pre-
vention Program, 1986-91; Consultant, 1991-
92. SELECTED PUBLICATIONS: "Ocular
Melanoma–A Population Based Study" (*Cana-
dian Journal of Opthalmology*, Jan. 9-12) with
BK Gunther *et al*; "Coping With the Cancer
Crisis" (*Health*, 1983) with Henry Davis *et al*;
"Steve Fonyo Cancer Prevention Program:
Description of an Innovative Program" (*Cana-
dian Journal of Public Health*, 83(3), 1992)
with Sharon Campbell *et al*; "Knowledge,
Beliefs and Sun Protection Behaviours of
Alberta Adults" (*Preventive Medicine*, 23,
1994) with H. Sharon Campbell; various other
scholarly papers, abstracts & gen. articles.
AFFIL: Canadian Cancer Society (Dir.,
AB/NWT Div. 1986-90; V-Chair, Long-Range
Planning Task Force, Nat'l Public Educ. Com-
mittee 1988-90; Chair, Nat'l Public Educ.
Committee 1990-92; Dir. 1990-92; Joint Nat'l
Cancer Institute/Canadian Cancer Society Task-
force on Behavioural Research 1990-91; Joint
Nat'l Cancer Institute/Canadian Cancer Soci-
ety Committee on Int'l Affairs 1991-94; Chair,
Program Delivery Proj. Team, Nat'l Public
Educ. Committee 1992-94; Dir., AB/NWT Div.

1993 to date; Pres. Elect 1995-96); National Health Research Development Program (NHRDP) Review Committee; Alberta Heart Health Project (coord. committee); National Cancer Institute (Tobacco Control Research Task Force 1992-93); Canadian Evaluation Society; Academy of Management; Association for Research on Nonprofit Organizations & Voluntary Action; The International Society for Strategic Management & Planning; Association for Health Services Research. INTERESTS: travelling with family; hiking. MISC: recipient of numerous grants; numerous presentations to conferences and associations. COMMENT: *"A committed health professional and community member who loves the challenge of working with a diverse group of individuals to accomplish a common goal."*

Birdsell-Smith, Patricia Mae (Trish), B.A., B.Sc. ⃝ ⃝ ⃝
President, Owner-Operator, HERIZEN™ SAILING FOR WOMEN INC., 36 Cutlass Lookout, Nanaimo, BC V9R 6R1 (604) 741-1753, FAX 754-4778. Born Brantford, Ont. 1953. m. William R. (Bill) Birdsell-Smith. EDUC: Univ. of Windsor, B.A.(Psych. & Soc. Work) 1974; Univ. of Ottawa, B.Sc.(Dietetics) 1977; Kingston General Hospital, Dietetic Intership, R.P.Dt. 1978; Canadian Power Squadron, Boating Course 1983-84, Seamanship 1984-85, Advanced Piloting 1984-85, Celestial Navigation 1985-86; US Coast Guard, Captain's Licence 1987; Canadian Yachting Association, Coastal Cruising Instructor Certification 1988, Intermediate Instructor Certification 1991. CAREER: Prov. Nutritionist, West Sepik Prov., Papua New Guinea, 1978-79; Officer-In-Charge, Nutrition Diploma Course, Dept. of Health, Papua New Guinea, 1979-82; Dir. of Food Svcs, Langley Lodge, Langley, BC, 1983-86; Captain, First Mate & Delivery Crew aboard a variety of private & charter sailing vessels in the Caribbean & the eastern US, 1987; Instructor, Womanship, Annapolis, Md., 1987; Dietetic Consultant, Broadway Pentecostal Lodge, Vancouver, 1988; Proprietor & Instructor, Herizen™: Sailing for Women Inc., Vancouver, 1988-91; Nanaimo, BC, 1992 to date; Instructor, Community Educ., Malaspina Coll., 1993 to date. SELECTED PUBLICATIONS: nutrition & health educ. booklet written in Pidgin for locals, Papua New Guinea; policy & procedures manual for nutrition educators, Papua New Guinea; manuals for use in Herizen™ sailing courses; working on a book on sailing & self-awareness for women. AFFIL: Canadian Yachting Association; Vancouver Women's Sailing Association, Vancouver (Founder); Herizen Sailing Association,

Nanaimo (Founder). HONS: various Excellence Awards, Junior Achievement, 1967-72; President's Roll of Scholars, Univ. of Windsor; President's Roll of Scholars, Univ. of Ottawa, 1975; Founder's Trophy, Centennial Sailing Club, 1985. INTERESTS: travelling; bicycling; swimming; dancing; writing; yoga. MISC: first woman to directly address the issue of the differences between male & female realities in the sailing world; first sailing school to teach sailing &self-awareness. COMMENT: *"Taking many aspects of my varied background, I created a unique, successful business, which supports me and my clients in reaching our potential as sailors and human beings."*

Birnie-Danzker, Jo-Anne, B.A.,Dip.Ed., B.Ed. ■ ⃝
Director, MUSEUM VILLA STUCK, Von-der-Tann-Str. 3, D-80539, Munich, Germany (49) 89-28 19 07, FAX 89-28 19 67. Born Brisbane, Australia 1945. m. Otfried Zimmerman. 3 ch. EDUC: Univ. of Queensland, B.A. 1966, Dip.Ed. 1967, B.Ed. 1971. CAREER: Teaching Asst., Dept. of Fine Arts, York Univ., 1973-74; Curator, The Electric Gallery, Toronto, 1973-74; Visual Arts Consultant, Dept. of Cultural Affairs, Canada House, London, UK, 1974; Exhibition Programer, Galleria Arte Borgogna, Milan, 1975-76; Mng Ed., *Flash Art*, Milan, 1975-76; Organizer, First National Conference of Canadian Art Magazines, Toronto, 1977; Curator, Vancouver Art Gallery, 1977-84; Acting Dir., 1984; Dir., 1985-87; independent curator & critic, 1987-90; Head Moderator for B.C., Citizen's Forum on Canada's Future Royal Commission, 1991; Dir., Museum Villa Stuck, 1992 to date. SELECTED PUBLICATIONS: numerous catalogues incl. *Edvard Munch* (May-Aug. 1986); *The Avantgarde and the Ukraine*, ed. & author (Klinkhardt & Biermann, 1993); *Max Beckmann World Theatre: The Graphic Works*, ed. & author (Cantz, 1993); *Dreamtime–Tjukurrpa: Aboriginal Art of the Western Desert*, ed. & author (Prestel, 1994); *Loie Fuller: Jugendstil as Dance*, ed. & author (Prestel, 1995); *Marina Abramovic* (Museum Villa Stuck 1996); *Franz von Stuck and Photography: The staged and documentary image* (Prestel 1996); articles in numerous other publications incl. "Museum and Guerrilla Television" (*Video-Art, Eine Dokumentation*, Berlin, 1981); "West Coast Performance: Praxis Without Ideology?" (*Living Art*, Vancouver, 1980). AFFIL: Association International des Critiques d'Art; International Council of Museums; Canadian Museums Association, I.K.T.; The City of Munich Public Art Commission (Mbr. 1996-1999); Awards Committee for the Applied Arts, City of Munich (Mbr. 1996).

Birt, Nancy E., B.B.A.,LL.B. ⚖
Partner, BIRT AND MCNEILL, Barristers and
Solicitors, 12 Brackley Point Rd., Box 20063,
Charlottetown, PEI C1A 9E3 (902) 566-3030,
FAX 628-8820. Born Charlottetown. m. Gre-
gory A. Cann. 2 ch. William, Emily. EDUC:
Univ. of Ottawa, LL.B. 1988; Univ. of Prince
Edward Island, B.B.A. 1990. BAR: PEI, 1989.
CAREER: Assoc. Lawyer, Ross Hooley Douglas
Murphy, 1989-93; Sessional Lecturer in Bus.
Law, Univ. of Prince Edward Island, 1990-94;
Ptnr in own law firm, 1993 to date. AFFIL:
Canadian Bar Association (PEI Branch
Chair–Environmental Law Section); Gender
Equality Joint Committee of PEI Law Society
& PEI Canadian Bar Association; Law Society
of PEI; Atlantic Association of Women Busi-
ness Owners; Friends of Confederation (Dir.;
Sec. 1993 to date); 1994 National Gymnastics
Championships (VP 1992-94). INTERESTS:
travel; reading; gymnastics; karate; ballet.
MISC: delegate to 1st Cdn Jeanne Sauvé Foun-
dation Conference for Young Leaders, May
1991; delegate to 1st Int'l Conference for
Young Leaders, May 1992; V-Chair, Mental
Health Review Bd., 1993-94; Chair, Mental
Health Review Bd., 1994 to date; V-Chair, PEI
Workers' Compensation Bd. Appeals Tribunal,
1995 to date.

Bishop, Gloria, B.Sc. 🖌
Executive Producer, *Morningside*, CBC RADIO,
Box 500, Stn A,, Toronto, ON M5W 1E6
(416) 205-6151. d. 2 ch. EDUC: McGill Univ.,
B.Sc.; Univ. of Washington, grad. work.
CAREER: Exec. Prod., Radio Current Affairs,
CBC Montreal; Host & Prod., daily radio pro-
gram; consumer commentator on radio & TV;
Head of Training, CBC Radio; Asst. Prof.,
Comm. & Journalism Depts., Concordia Univ.;
Prog. Dir., Radio Networks, CBC, Toronto;
Dir. of Radio, Toronto; Deputy Head, Radio
Current Affairs; Exec. Prod., *Morningside*, CBC
Radio, 1995 to date.

Bishop, Janet, B.A. 💲
Manager, Customer Service Development, CEN-
TRA GAS MANITOBA INC., 35 Sutherland Ave.,
Winnipeg, MB R3C 3T7 (204) 925-0522, FAX
949-0855. Born Winnipeg 1958. m. Gregory.
2 ch. Stephen J., Christa M. EDUC: Univ. of
Winnipeg, B.A.(Econ.). CAREER: various positions, Centra Gas, 1976-90; Supervisor, Customer Svc., 1990-93; Mgr, CIS, Planning &
Dispatch, 1993-96; Mgr, Cust. Svc. Dev. 1996
to date. AFFIL: Winnipeg Chamber of Commerce; MHDA; Sons of Scotland. INTERESTS:
skiing; travel. COMMENT: *"I am currently
pursuing my MBA in evenings at the University
of Manitoba."*

**Bishop, Olga, B.A.,B.Pub.Admin.,M.A.,
A.M.L.S.,Ph.D.,LL.D.** 🎗📖
Professor Emeritus, UNIVERSITY OF TORONTO,
Toronto, ON. Born Dover, N.B. 1911. s.
EDUC: Mount Allison Univ., B.A. 1938, M.A.
(Hist.) 1951; Carleton Univ., B.Pub.
Admin. 1946; Michigan Univ., A.M.L.S. 1952,
Ph.D.(Library Sci.) 1962. CAREER: Sr. Admin.
Officer, RCAF Record of Svc., Cdn Civil Svc.,
1940-46; Asst. Librarian, Mount Allison Univ.,
1946-53; Gen. Librarian, Univ. of Western
Ontario, 1953-54; Medical Librarian, 1954-65;
part-time Lecturer, 1953-60; Assoc. Prof., Univ.
of Toronto, 1965-70; Prof., 1970-76; Prof.,
part-time, 1976-77; Prof. Emeritus, 1977 to
date. SELECTED PUBLICATIONS: *Canadian
Association of Special Libraries and Information Services Handbook* 2nd edition, editor
(1976); various books on librarianship & bibliography; book chapters; reviews & articles in
monographs and periodicals; editor of historical
monographs. EDIT: Ed., *Agora*, the Bulletin of
the Research and Special Libraries Section of
the Canadian Library Association, 1968.
AFFIL: Canadian Library Association; Canadian
Association of College & University Libraries;
Canadian Association of Special Libraries &
Information Services; Ontario Library Association; Ontario Association of College & University Libraries; Maritime Library Association;
Special Libraries Association; Institute of Pro-
fessional Librarians of Ontario; Bibliographi-
cal Society of Canada; Canadian Association
of Library Schools; Canadian Association of
University Teachers; Univ. of Toronto Fac.
Association; Ontario Historical Society; Associ-
ation for Canadian Studies; Beta Phi Mu.
HONS: Highest Average Scholarship, Mount
Allison Ladies' Coll., 1927-28; Birks Gold
Medal, Mount Allison Ladies Coll., 1928; The
Marie Tremaine Medal in Canadian Bibliogra-
phy, 1981; Award for Special Librarianship in
Canada, Canadian Association of Special
Libraries & Information Services, 1981;
Alumni Recognition Award, Sch. of Library &
Info. Sci. & the Library Sci. Alumni Society,
Univ. of Michigan, 1985; Plaque from the
Metropolitan United Church mbrs. for volun-
teer work in the Library, Archives & United
Church Women (1981-92), 1993; LL.D.(Hon.),
Mt. Allison Univ., 1971.

Bishton-Fox, Lesley ■■ ⊕ 🎗 ◉
District Administrator, 511670 ALBERTA LTD.
(o/a Coram Construction - gen. commercial
construction), 8611 - 63rd Ave., Edmonton, AB
T6E 0E8 (403) 466-1262/466-1508. Born Bad
Oeynhausen, Germany 1948. m. Robert Fox.
EDUC: in Europe, with continuing updates in
Alta.; Nursing Diploma; Occupational Health

& Safety, U.K.; Rehab. Practitioner Certificate, Alta.; Certified Safety Officer, Alta. **CAREER:** worked in hospitals in U.K.; Area Coord., St. John Ambulance, Calgary, 1980; Safety Supervisor, Partec Lavalin Inc., 1981; Sr. First Aid Trainer/Industrial Nurse, Safety Dept., Dreco Ltd., Edmonton, 1982; Construction Site Nurse & Safety Inspector, Cana Construction Ltd., 1982; Industrial Nurse/Safety for Construction Night Shift, Associated Kellogg Ltd., 1982; Occupational Health & Safety Coord., Central Svc. Facility - North, Alberta Transportation & Utilities, 1983-89; Occupational Health & Safety Coord., City Centre Worksite, Ellis Don Management Services Ltd., 1989-90; field placements (Rehab. Practitioner Program), Jan.-June 1991; Occupational Health & Safety Coord., Ellis Don Management Services Ltd., July-Dec. 1991; Job Club Facilitator, Niehaus & Associates, 1992; Occupational Health & Safety Coord., Aman Building Corporation, Sherwood Park, Alta., 1993. **AFFIL:** National Association of Women in Construction (Pres., Edmonton chpt. 1995-97); Nursing Sisters' Association of Canada (VP, Edmonton chpt. 1995-97); St. John Ambulance, Brigade & Fellowship. **HONS:** Provincial & Priory Votes of Thanks, St. John Ambulance; Long Service Medal, Serving Sister Medal; the guys from the field bring cookies & flowers (which actually mean more than the medals). **COMMENT:** *"I'm a people person who endeavours to make life a little better for those around me. I prefer to work as part of a team. I tend to sit on the sidelines until I make up my mind that I can endorse a group totally. I then commit and give 110%. We can achieve anything we choose to, provided we are prepared to attain the education and updates required. Our current endeavour is to rebuild the Edmonton NAWIC chapter with a broad representation of professions, trades and services related to construction."*

Bismanis, Maija R., B.A.,M.A., Ph.D. ■ 🐟 📚 ⊗

Associate Professor of Art History, UNIVERSITY OF REGINA, 3737 Wascana Parkway Dr., Regina, SK (306) 779-5715, FAX 779-7474. Born Riga, Latvia 1945. s. **EDUC:** Univ. of British Columbia, B.A.(Art Hist./Hist.), M.A.(Art Hist.) 1968; Univ. of Nottingham, Ph.D.(Art Hist./Archaeology) 1974; Oriel Coll. Oxford, post-doctoral research (Art Hist.) 1974-76. **CAREER:** Educ. & Research Curator, Vancouver Art Gallery, 1968-70; Prof., Univ. of Regina, 1970 to date. **SELECTED PUBLICA-TIONS:** *Canada Collects: the Middle Ages; The English Medieval Timber Roof: A Handbook of Types; Medieval Sculpture in Canadian Collections;* numerous articles & conference papers. **AFFIL:** University Art Association of Canada (Pres. 1992-94); International Center for Medieval Art (Foreign Advisor 1989-96; Publications Bd. 1992-95); Medieval Academy of America; Society of Architectural Historians; International Corpus of Stained Glass (Sec.); Mackenzie Art Gallery, Regina (Adjunct Curator). **HONS:** Heritage Award, City of Regina, 1982; Provincial/Municipal Heritage Award, 1988. **INTERESTS:** naturalist, esp. in life in inter-tidal areas of West Coast; drawing; photography. **COMMENT:** *"Generally cheerful but can be difficult. In spite of straight university academic activity feel that best achievement is in the area of public education about the visual arts/architecture. Currently working with museums and artist in Latvia in post-USSR reconstruction of the art infrastructure."*

Bismilla, Vicki H., B.A., M.Ed. ■ ■ 🖐 🐟 ○

Principal, HIGHLAND HEIGHTS JUNIOR PUBLIC SCHOOL, 35 Glendower Circuit, Agincourt, ON M1T 2Z3 (416) 396-6335, FAX 396-6337. President, SCARBOROUGH WOMEN'S CENTRE, 2100 Ellesmere Rd., #245, Scarborough, ON M1H 3B7. Born South Africa. m. Yusuf Bismilla. 2 ch. Zia, Zeyd. **EDUC:** Univ. of South Africa, B.A.(Hons., English & Drama) 1969 & Univ. of Toronto, 1976; Ontario Institute for Studies in Education, M.Ed.(Admin.) 1991; numerous certificates. **CAREER:** seconded as Educ. Officer, Teacher Educ. Policy Unit, Ministry of Educ. & Training, 1994. **AFFIL:** Scarborough Women Teachers' Association (Exec. mbr. 1996-97; Equal Opportunity Rep. to Scarborough Bd. of Educ.; Chair, Race Rel'ns Committee & Ntwk); Federation of Women Teachers of Ontario (Chair, Race Rel'ns Committee & Ntwk, Reg. 3); Scarborough Board of Education (Promotion Policy (Employees) Review Team; Program-Assisted (Inner-city) Schools Steering Committee; Principals' Conference Organization Committee 1989-95; Hiring Team 1989-95; Focused Interview Steering Committee 1990-92); Canadian Association of Principals (Co-Chair, 1990 Conference, Toronto); Riverdale Immigrant Women's Centre (Bd. of Dir. 1992-93); U.N. Organization for Women in Developing Countries (mbr., Toronto 1994-95). **HONS:** Carol Harrison Memorial Award for leadership, Scarborough Women Teachers' Association; Highland Heights Jr. P.S. won exemplary sch. award for antiracism, 1996. **INTERESTS:** reading; family; ocean-front vacations. **MISC:** guest, TVOntario's "Principal's Report," & on racism panel, 1992-93; unpublished manuscript, novel re apartheid in South Africa. **COMMENT:** *"I was born and raised a woman of colour in a white*

South Africa where I witnessed first-hand the heinous apartheid system for 22 years. My earliest memories of childhood are of the apartheid regime's secret police raiding our home in the middle of the night. Now, as a Canadian for 26 years, my work, endeavours and commitment are to advocate for the oppressed."

Bjornson, Michelle 👁📖⊗
President, POINT OF VIEW FILM INC., 3216 W. 2nd Ave., Vancouver, BC V6K 1K8 (604) 734-5035, FAX 737-0123. Born Toronto 1945. m. Michael Bjornson. 2 ch. EDUC: Univ. of Toronto, B.A.(Hist.) 1966; Univ. of British Columbia, M.A.(Theatre) 1971, Diploma (Film & TV Arts) 1987. CAREER: Freelance Stage Designer, 1970-76; independent Filmmaker, 1987 to date. SELECTED CREDITS: *It Will Not Last the Night; The Mailboat Doesn't Stop Here Anymor; End of the Game*. AFFIL: Vancouver Women in Film & Video (Dir. 1992-95; Pres. 1994-95); Moving Images Distribution (Dir. 1989 to present; VP 1995); Cineworks Independent Filmmakers Society (Dir. 1989-91); Pink Ink Theatre (Dir. 1995). HONS: Award for Film Production & Screenwriting, Arts Council; Silver Plaque, Chicago International Film Festival; Bronze Apple, National Educational Film & Video Festival. INTERESTS: theatre; Cdn literature; historical readings; fine arts. MISC: various screenings, broadcasts, nominations & invitations. COMMENT: *"Producer/director of film and TV projects (drama and documentary); also freelance drama editor and freelance scriptwriter."*

Bjornson, Pam, B.A.,B.F.A. 📖📚🦅
Executive Director, CANADIAN INSTITUTE FOR HISTORICAL MICROREPRODUCTIONS, Box 2428, Stn D, Ottawa, ON K1P 5W5 (613) 235-2628, FAX (613) 235-9752, EMAIL pmb@nlo.nlc-bnc.ca. Born Sask. 1953. m. Brian E. Spurling. EDUC: Univ. of Regina, B.A.(Art Hist.), B.F.A.(Visual Arts); currently pursuing grad. studies in Bus. Admin.; Univ. of Ottawa, M.B.A. (in progress). CAREER: Arts Consultant, & Mgr, Arts & Cultural Industries, Gov't of Sask., 1981-88; Exec. Dir., Canadian Institute for Historical Microreproductions, 1992 to date; Exec. Dir., Saskatchewan Writers' Guild, 1988-91. AFFIL: Bibliographical Society of Canada (Nat'l Council); Saskatchewan Arts Alliance (Pres.); Regina Arts Commission (Advisory Group). INTERESTS: books; cross-country skiing; travel. COMMENT: *"Has managed provincial and national nonprofit cultural organizations, as well as a provincial government arts branch. Special focus on organizational development and the marketing function."*

Bjornson, Rosella, B.Sc. ■ 💲♐
Captain, CANADIAN AIRLINES INTERNATIONAL LTD., Edmonton International Airport, P.O. Box 9815, Edmonton, AB T5J 2T2 (403) 890-4163, FAX 890-4175. Born Lethbridge, Alta. 1947. m. Bill Pratt. 2 ch. Ken, Valerie. EDUC: Univ. of Calgary, B.Sc.(Geography) 1969. CAREER: private pilot's licence, 1964; commercial pilot's licence, 1968; Air Transport Rating, 1972; Pilot, Transair, 1973-79; First Officer, F-28; First Officer, B737, Pacific Western Airlines, 1980-87; First Officer, Canadian Airlines International, 1987-90; Captain, B737, 1990 to date. AFFIL: Ninety-Nines–International Organization of Women Pilots; International Society of Women Airline Pilots; Canadian Owners' & Pilots' Association; Western Canada Aviation Museum. HONS: Amelia Earhart Award, 1987; Pioneer Award, Western Canada Aviation Museum, 1988; Forest of Friendship Award, 1988; Award of Achievement, National Transport Week, 1991. INTERESTS: my home & my children. MISC: first woman to be hired as a First Officer flying a jet for a scheduled airline in North America; first woman Captain with a major airline in Canada. COMMENT: *"As a Captain of a Boeing 737 with Canadian Airlines, I feel that I have reached the goal that I set for myself when I was a young girl flying with my father in his light aircraft."*

Black, Elizabeth M. (Betty) 💲☺
Director, Human Resources, NORTH AMERICAN LIFE ASSURANCE COMPANY, 333 Broadway, Winnipeg, MB R3C 0S9 (204) 944-3235, FAX 947-0150. Chair, YMCA CANADA. Born Winnipeg 1946. m. Gary Black. 2 ch. Denny, Jennifer. EDUC: Univ. of Manitoba, Diploma in Hum. Res. Mgmt 1978. CAREER: Dir. of Hum. Res., Westin Hotels, 1970-74; Hum. Res. Officer, Royal Canadian Mint, 1974-76; Mgr, Hum. Res., Turnbull & Turnbull, 1976-80; Dir., Hum. Res., Jostens Canada, 1980-85; Sr. Consultant, Deloitte & Touche, 1986-91; Dir., Hum. Res., North American Life Assurance Company, 1991 to date. AFFIL: YMCA Canada (Chair); World YMCA (Exec. Committee & Chair, Women's Task Force); Human Resource Management Association of Manitoba (Past Pres.); Manitoba Labour Board (Employer Rep.); YM-YWCA of Winnipeg (Pres. 1986-88); St. John Ambulance (Chair, Personnel Committee 1989-92); Manitoba Museum of Man & Nature (Personnel Committee); United Way of Winnipeg (Campaign Cabinet & Chair, Loaned Rep. Committee); Univ. of Manitoba Management Development Program for Women (Steering Committee); Royal Winnipeg Ballet (Sch. Committee; Special

Events Committee). **HONS:** Canada 125 Medal; Serving Sister, Order of St. John. **INTERESTS:** volunteer work; family. **COMMENT:** *"Second woman to become chair of the Canadian YMCA and chaired a committee that made recommendations to ensure equal participation of women in YMCAs around the world."*

Black, Elizabeth Stewart ♥ ⊛

Past President and Member, CANADIAN OPERA WOMEN'S COMMITTEE, 227 Front St. E., Ste. 101, Toronto, ON M5A 1E8. Born Toronto 1931. m. James A. Black. 3 ch. Nancy Foley, Dave Black, Bruce Black. **EDUC:** Victoria Coll., Univ. of Toronto, Arts 1953. **CAREER:** travelled extensively on husband's bus./social events for Wood Gundy Inc., in Europe & Japan, 1972-85, assisted him during his Presidency of the National Club, 1993-94. **VOLUNTEER CAREER:** Mbr., Canadian Opera Women's Committee (C.O.W.C.) 1978 to date; Chair of various committees, C.O.W.C.; Ed., *ARIAS* Magazine, 1984; art sale at O'Keefe Centre, 1986-87; Chair, Performance Fund, 1990; VP, 1991-92; Pres.-Elect, 1992-93; Pres., 1993-94; Chair, *Sunset Boulevard* gala, C.O.W.C. fundraiser, 1995; Chair, *Ragtime* gala, C.O.W.C. fundraiser, 1996. **AFFIL:** Granite Club; National Club.

Black, F. Marjorie ■■ $ ☼ ☝

President, MCGINNIS BUILDING BLOCK CO. LTD. (concrete mfg., underground svcs–pipe, catchbasins, manholes), 6 Forest St., Guelph, ON N1G 1H6. Born Canada 1923. m. Donald. 2 ch. Barba Munro, Drew Black. **EDUC:** Conestoga Coll., Volunteer Mgmt (Dean's Hon. Roll) 1986. **AFFIL:** Canadian Red Cross (Exec. mbr., Guelph branch 1965-96; Pres. 1981-82); World Convention of Churches of Christ (Pres. (1st woman) 1992-96); Kinzie/Bean Pioneer Cemetery (Sec.-Treas. 1978-96); Guelph Mental Health Association (Exec. mbr. 1948-55); Guelph Services for Physically Disabled (Exec. mbr. 1974-82); Women's Inter-Church Council of Canada (Exec. mbr. 1964-80); World Christian Women's Fellowship (Pres. 1974-80); Canadian Council of Churches (former Exec. mbr., Int'l Dev. Committee); Council on Christian Unity (mbr. 1979). **HONS:** award for citizenship & public svc., 1982. **INTERESTS:** freighter travel (has sailed all oceans & been around the world 3 times as well as separate trips to S. America, Asia & India); cross-country skiing; reading. **MISC:** had to leave sch. during Depression, took office training at night sch. & continues to take short courses at univ./coll.; gave blood more than 200 times (had to stop at age 71); mbr., Seminar on Hum. Rights, U.N., N.Y., 1968; Cdn Rep. to Asian Church Women's Conference, Bangkok, 1974; invited by Chinese Friendship Society to visit China, 1984. **COMMENT:** *"Grew up in village of Blair (Langdon Hall location)—population perhaps 300—still return because it's hard to believe I'm privileged to have friends on every continent in the world after coming from such humble roots. Wow! have I ever been blessed."*

Black, Mary Elizabeth, B.A. $ 🎓 ☝

President, COLOUR TECHNOLOGIES, 450 Front St. W., Ste. 300, Toronto, ON M5V 1B6 (416) 340-0654, FAX 340-0659. Chair, RYERSON POLYTECHNIC UNIVERSITY, School of Graphic Communications Management (416) 979-5000, ext. 6067, FAX 979-5090. Born Montreal 1939. d. 2 ch. **EDUC:** Atkinson Coll., York Univ., B.A.(Psych.). **CAREER:** Tracer/Draftsman, Atomic Energy of Canada Ltd., Chalk River, 1959-63; Draftsman, Ian Martin Consulting Engineers, 1967-69; Creative Dir., Ginn & Co. Publishing, Toronto, 1969-76; Sales Rep., Graphic Litho Plate, 1976-83; Pres., Colour Technologies (incorporated as Mary Black Graphics), 1984 to date. **AFFIL:** Canadian Printing Industries Association (Dir. 1990-92; Pres. 1993-94; Past Pres. 1994-95); Ontario Pre Press Association (Founding Dir. 1992-95); Jessie's Centre for Teenagers (Pres. 1986); Windfall (Dir.; First VP 1994-95). **HONS:** Woman on the Move, *The Toronto Sun*, 1992; YWCA Woman of Distinction, 1993.

Black, Naomi, A.B.,M.A.,Ph.D. 🎓 📖

Professor Emerita, Political Science, YORK UNIVERSITY, 4700 Keele St., North York, ON M3J 1P3. Born Newcastle-upon-Tyne, UK 1935. m. S.P. Rosenbaum. 2 ch. **EDUC:** Cornell Univ., A.B.(Gov't) 1955; Yale Univ., M.A.(Pol. Sci.) 1957, Ph.D.(Pol. Sci.) 1964. **CAREER:** Instructor in Pol. Sci., Brown Univ., Providence, RI, 1963-64; Instructor in Gov't, Indiana Univ., 1964-65; Asst. Prof., Dept. of Pol. Sci., York Univ., 1965-71; Assoc. Prof., 1971-84; Prof., 1985 to date; V-Chair, Univ. Senate, 1988-89; Chair, Univ. Senate, 1989-90. **SELECTED PUBLICATIONS:** *Social Feminism* (Ithaca, NY; Cornell University Press, 1989); *Canadian Women: A History* with Alison Prentice *et al* (Toronto; Harcourt Brace Jovanovich, 1988; revised ed. 1996); articles on int'l rel'ns, women & politics, & feminism. **AFFIL:** Canadian Political Science Association; Council of Ontario Universities (Committee on the Status of Women; Committee on Enrollment Statistics & Projections; Committee on Educational & Employment Equity; Academic Colleague for York Univ.); Ontario Council on Graduate Studies (Chair, Appraisal Committee); Ontario Advisory Council on the Status of Women; Toronto Business & Professional Women's Club; Ontario Committee on the Status of Women; Metro Toronto Committee on Public Violence Against Women & Children (Dir.); Panel Member, Bd. of Enquiry, under the Metropolitan Toronto Police Force Complaints Act; National Film Board (Ontario Centre Women's Program Advisory Committee). MISC: grant recipient incl.: research grants, Social Sciences & Humanities Research Council, 1985-88 & 1991-95. COMMENT: *"Feminist activist, researcher and university instructor."*

Black, The Hon. Patricia L., B.Comm. ✦ ❀
Minister of Energy and Deputy Government House Leader, Legislative Assembly, GOVERNMENT OF ALBERTA, Legislature Building, Rm. 408, Edmonton, AB T5K 2B6 (403) 427-3740, FAX 422-0195. Born Calgary. EDUC: Univ. of Calgary, B.Comm. CAREER: Cont. & Mgr of Acctg & Admin., Sabre Energy Ltd.; Cont., Petroleum Natural Resources Ltd.; Mgr of Fin. Control, Suncor; M.L.A. (Calgary Foothills), Gov't of Alta., 1989 to date; Min. of Energy, 1992 to date; Deputy Gov't House Leader, 1993 to date; also Mbr., Agenda & Priorities; Treasury Bd.; Standing Policy Committee on Natural Resources & Sustainable Dev.; Standing Policy Committee on Fin. Planning. AFFIL: Calgary Winter Club. MISC: 15 yrs. of experience in the oil & gas industry.

Blackburn, Jeanne L., M.N.A. ■ ✦
Députée du comté de Chicoutimi and Présidente de la Commission de l'Éducation, GOUVERNEMENT DU QUÉBEC, Hôtel du Parlement, Bur. R.C.79, Québec, QC G1A 1A4 (418) 646-6362, FAX 646-0702. Born Saint-Elzéar-de-Bonaventure, Qué. 1934. m. Gilles Blackburn. 2 ch. CAREER: Enseignante, Commission scolaire Sainte-Anne de Chicoutimi; Secrétaire régionale et agente de dév., Radio-Québec, Saguenay-Lac-Saint-Jean, 1977-80; Prés., Conseil des collèges du Québec, 1979-85; Députée (Chicoutimi), Assemblée Nationale, 1985 à ce date; Commission du budget et de l'admin., 1986-89; Porte-parole de l'Opposition officielle en matière d'enseignement supérieur, de sciences et de technologie, d'éduc., de santé et de services sociaux, des corporations professionelles, 1986-89; Commission de l'éduc., 1989-91, 1993-94; Commission de l'écon. et du travail, 1989-93; Porte-parole de l'Opposition officielle en matière de recherche et de dév., de sciences et de technologie, 1989-91, 1993-94; Porte-parole de l'Opposition officielle en matière de la Charte de la langue française, 1990-94; Porte-parole de l'Opposition officielle en matière de travail et de CSST, 1991-93;

Commission sur l'avenir politique et constitutionnel du Québec, 1990-91; Conseil exécutif national, Parti Québécois, 1991 to date; Commission de la culture, Assemblée Nationale, 1993-94; Prés. de la Commission du l'Education, 1996 à ce date.

Blackstone, Mary A., B.A.,M.A., Ph.D. ■ ⊗ ⊲
Faculty of Theatre Arts (on leave), UNIVERSITY OF REGINA, Regina, SK S4S 0A2 (306) 585-5860, FAX 585-5744, EMAIL mblackst@max.cc.uregina.ca. Born Ellsworth, Me. 1949. m. Cameron Louis. EDUC: Univ. of Maine at Orono, B.A.(English/Drama) 1971; Univ. of New Brunswick, M.A.(English) 1973; Univ. of New Brunswick, Ph.D.(English) 1978. CAREER: Postdoctoral Fellow & Researcher, Records of Early English Drama, 1978-81; Lecturer, English, Erindale Coll., Univ. of Toronto, 1979-81; Asst. Prof., English, Washington & Jefferson Coll., 1981-82; Univ. of Regina, 1982-87; Coord., Grad. Studies in Drama, Univ. of Alberta, 1987-90; Assoc. Prof., Theatre, Univ. of Regina, 1990 to date; Dean, Fac. of Fine Arts, 1990 to date. SELECTED PUBLICATIONS: *Robin Hood and the Friar*, 1981, one book chapter, numerous reviews & articles; Dramaturg: *Dancing in Poppies*, 1993, *Beauty and the Beast*, 1993, *The Tree*, 1994. AFFIL: Saskatchewan Arts Education Conference, '94 Planning Committee (Chair); Sask. Film/Video Professional Dev. Co-ord. Committee; Canadian Association of Fine Arts Deans (Chair); International Council of Fine Arts Deans (Exec. Bd.); MacKenzie Art Gallery (Bd. of Trustees); Regina Symphony Orchestra (Sec., Bd. of Trustees & Exec. Committee; Chair, Program Committee); American Society for Theater Research; Shakespeare Association of America; International Shakespeare Association; Poculi Ludique Societas; Malone Society; Société Internationale pour l'Étude du Théâtre Medieval; Alberta Conference on Theatre; Canadian Conference on the Arts; Saskatchewan Writers Guild; Saskatchewan Playwrights Centre; Association of Cultural Executives; Literary Managers and Dramaturgs of America; International Federation for Theatre Research. HONS: Maine/NB Exchange Scholarship, 1969-70; Canada Council Doctoral Fellowships, 1974-76; REED Postdoctoral Fellowship, Univ. of Toronto, 1978-79; holder of SSHRCC & NEH grants. INTERESTS: vocal soloist; tennis; gardening; piano. COMMENT: *"I am a university-based educator, researcher and administrator specializing in Shakespeare, theatre history and cultural studies relating to early England. I am also a professional dramaturg involved in the development of new plays."*

Blackstone, Renee A., B.A. /
Lifestyles Editor, THE PROVINCE, 2250 Granville St., Vancouver, BC V6H 3G2 (604) 732-2049, FAX 732-2720. Born Surakarta, Indonesia 1946. d. 3 ch. EDUC: Kalamazoo Coll., B.A.(German/Pol. Sci.). CAREER: Ed., The White Rock Sun, 1973-75; Reporter, The Columbian, 1976-80; Publisher, Burnaby Today, 1980-83; Ed., Burnaby and New Westminster News, 1983-88; Food Ed., The Province, 1988-89; Lifestyles Ed., 1989 to date. SELECTED PUBLICATIONS: currently writes occasional freelance food & travel features for The Province & other Southam newspapers; various articles & columns in local magazines & newspapers. DIRECTOR: Now Newspapers (Founder; Sec. 1983-88). HONS: full four-yr. scholarship, Kalamazoo Coll., Kalamazoo, Mich., 1964-68; several awards while editor of The White Rock Sun. INTERESTS: gardening; collecting antiques; travel; hiking; camping; wild mushroom hunting; reading. COMMENT: *"When I was in my mid-20s, someone described me as solid and steady. It was not until I was much older that I recognized it for the fine compliment it is. This has helped me deal with much pain and stress throughout a sometimes hectic life. My children are my pride."*

Blackwell, Bonnie, B.A.,M.Sc.,Ph.D., F.G.A.C.,F.G.S.A. 🐟 🏵
Professor, Department of Geology, Queens College, CITY UNIVERSITY OF NEW YORK, Flushing, NY 11367-1597 (718) 997-3332, FAX 997-3349, EMAIL bonn@qcvaxa.acc.qc.edu. Born Hamilton, Ont. EDUC: McMaster Univ., B.A.(Anthropology) 1978, M.Sc.(Geology) 1980; Univ. of Alberta, Ph.D. 1987. CAREER: Geological Tech., Alberta Research Council, 1981-84; Instructor Trainer for Instructor Schools, Canadian Red Cross Society, 1981 to date; Tech. Dir., Royal Life Saving Society, Canada, 1986-87; Visiting Scholar, Dept. of Geography, Monash Univ., 1987; Post-doctoral Fellow, GEOTOP, Univ. du Québec à Montréal, 1987-89; Post-doctoral Fellow, Dept. of Geology, McMaster Univ., 1989-91; Visiting Asst. Prof., Dept. of Earth & Atmospheric Sciences, Purdue Univ., 1991-92; Visiting Asst. Prof., Dept. of Physics, 1992; Section Chief, Geoscience Labs, Ministry of Northern Dev. & Mines, Ont. Geological Survey, 1992-93; Lecturer, Arts & Sci. Fac., Nipissing Univ., 1993; Asst. Prof., Dept. of Geology, Univ. of Windsor, 1993-94; Asst. Prof., Dept. of Geology, Queens Coll., & Dept. of Earth & Environmental Sciences, City Univ. of N.Y., 1994 to date. SELECTED PUBLICATIONS: "Uranium series dating of travertines from archaeological sites, Nahal Zin, Israel" (*Nature* 277: 558-560); "Absolute dating of hominids and palaeolithic artifacts from the cave of La Chaise-de-Vouthon (Charente), France" (*Journal of Archaeological Science* 10:493-513); "Uranium Series dating of archaeological sites," *Uranium Series Disequilibrium: Application to Environmental Problems*, eds. M. Ivanovich, R.S. Harmon (Oxford: Clarendon, 1992); "Summary of Field Work and Other Activities" *Ontario Geological Survey Miscellaneous Paper 160*, ed. with B.O. Dressler & C.L. Baker (1992); "Annealing and etching of corals of ESR dating" (*Applied Radiation and Isotopes* 44: 153-156); "Problems associated with reworked teeth in electron spin resonance (ESR) dating" Quaternary Geochronology (*Quaternary Science Review* 13: 651-660); numerous other articles & chapters in books; numerous abstracts & other publications. AFFIL: Geological Society of America; Geological Association of Canada; Sigma Xi, The Scientific Research Society; CANQUA, Canadian Quarternary Association; AMQUA American Quarternary Association (Councillor 1994-98); Hamilton-Wentworth Archaeological Foundation; International EPR (ESR) Society; Society for Archaeological Sciences; Great Lakes Institute for Environmental Research; Canadian Geoscience Education Board; Canadian Geoscience Council. HONS: Chancellor's Scholarship, McMaster Univ., 1974-75; Hon. Assoc., Royal Life Saving Society Canada, 1983; Jack Boddington Award, Royal Life Saving Society Canada, 1984; Certificate of Thanks, Royal Life Saving Society Canada, 1985; Recognition Badge, Royal Life Saving Society Canada, 1986; Service Award, Canadian Red Cross Society, 1991. INTERESTS: swimming; training for life saving; skin diving; scuba diving; sailing; hiking; caving; canoeing; windsurfing; camping; macramé; furniture refinishing; photography; jewelry design. MISC: recipient of various grants & fellowships; numerous conference presentations; field work in Canada, US, Hungary, France & Tobago.

Blackwell, Judith, B.A.,M.A., Ph.D. 🐟
Associate Professor, Sociology, BROCK UNIVERSITY, St. Catharines, ON L2S 3A1 (905) 688-5550, FAX 688-8337, EMAIL blackwel@spartan.ac.brocku.ca. Born Ottawa 1944. EDUC: Carleton Univ., B.A.(Soc.) 1965; The New Sch. for Social Research, N.Y., M.A.(Soc.) 1967; London Sch. of Econ. & Pol. Sci., Ph.D.(Econ.) 1986. CAREER: Research Asst., Mount Sinai Hospital Sch. of Nursing, N.Y. City, 1968-69; Sr. Research Asst., Commission of Inquiry into the Non-Medical Use of Drugs (The Le Dain

Commission), Ottawa, 1970-73; doctoral research, London Sch. of Econ., UK, 1973-78; Policy Advisor, Health & Welfare Canada, 1978-80; Scientist, Addiction Research Foundation, Social & Biological Studies, 1980-87; Asst. Prof. of Soc., Brock Univ., 1987-92; Chair of Soc., 1989-94; Assoc. Prof. of Soc., 1992 to date. **SELECTED PUBLICATIONS:** *Ilicit Drug Use in Canada: A Risky Business*, ed. with P. Erickson (Toronto: Nelson, 1988); "Drifting, Controlling & Overcoming: Opiate Users Who Avoid Becoming Chronically Dependent" (*Journal of Drug Issues* 13 1983); "Opiate Dependence as a Psychophysical Event: Users' Reports of Subjective Experiences" (*Contemporary Drug Problems* 12(3) 1985); "Cannabis Self-Medication and Adverse Reactions in Psychiatric Patients," with J. Beresford & S. Lambert (*Social Pharmacology* 1(4) 1987); "Patterns of Alcohol Use and Psychiatric Inpatient Admissions," with J. Beresford & S. Lambert (*Journal of Substance Abuse Treatment* 5(1) 1988); "The Saboteurs of Britain's Opiate Policy: Overprescribing Physicians or American-Style Junkies?" (*International Journal of the Addictions* 23(5) 1988); "Discourses on Drug Use: The Social Construction of a Steroid Scandal" (*Journal of Drug Issues* 21(1) 1991); various book chapters; book reviews; various Cdn fed. gov't reports. **AFFIL:** Canadian Sociology & Anthropology Association; Canadian Women's Studies Association; Project S.H.A.R.E., Niagara Falls, Ont. (Bd. of Dir.). **MISC:** recipient of various grants; numerous conference presentations; assessor, various journals, publishers & granting agencies; various radio & press interviews. **COMMENT:** *"Judith Blackwell has served as an advisor on alcohol and other drug policy in Canada and the UK. Research and teaching interests include: social inequality in psychiatry, education and Canadian law; policy issues on the use of performance-enhancing drugs in sports, in drug testing in the workplace and in women's use of alcohol and other drugs; feminist theory and research methodology."*

Blades, Ann 📖 ⊗

Author, Illustrator. Surrey, BC. Born Vancouver 1947. d. 2 ch. Jack Morrison, Angus Morrison. **EDUC:** Univ. of British Columbia, Standard Teaching Certificate 1967; B.C. Institute of Technology, R.N. 1974. **CAREER:** elementary sch. teacher, 1967-71; writer & illustrator of children's books, 1968 to date; Registered Nurse (part time), 1974-80; artist, 1982. **SELECTED PUBLICATIONS:** *Mary of Mile 18*, author & illustrator (Montreal: Tundra Books, 1971); *A Boy of Taché*, author & illustrator (Montreal: Tundra Books, 1973); *The Cottage*

at Crescent Beach, author & illustrator (Toronto: Magook Publishers, 1977); *Jacques the Woodcutter*, by Michael Macklem, illustrator (Ottawa: Oberon Press, 1977); *A Salmon for Simon*, by Betty Waterton, illustrator (Vancouver: Douglas McIntyre, 1978); *Six Darn Cows*, by Margaret Laurence, illustrator (Toronto: James Lorimer & Co., 1979); *Anna's Pet*, by Margaret Atwood & Joyce Barkhouse, illustrator (Toronto: James Lorimer & Co., 1979); *Pettranella*, Betty Waterton, illustrator (Vancouver: Douglas McIntyre, 1980); *By the Sea: An Alphabet Book*, author & illustrator (Toronto: Kids Can Press, 1985); *A Candle for Christmas*, by Jean Speare, illustrator (Toronto: Douglas McIntyre, 1986); *Ida and the Wool Smugglers*, by Sue Ann Alderson, illustrator (Toronto: Douglas McIntyre, 1987); *Seasons Board Books*, author & illustrator (Toronto: Douglas McIntyre, 1989); *The Singing Basket*, by Kit Pearson, illustrator (Toronto: Douglas McIntyre, 1990); *A Dog Came, Too*, by Ainslie Manson, illustrator (Toronto: Douglas McIntyre, 1992); *A Ride for Martha*, by Sue Ann Alderson, illustrator (Toronto: Douglas McIntyre, 1993); *Back to the Cabin*, author & illustrator (Victoria: Orca Book Publishers, 1996); cover illustration, *Canadian Books for Children & A Guide to Authors and Illustrators* (Toronto: Harcourt, Brace Jovanovich, 1988). **EXHIBITIONS:** various exhibitions of book illustrations, incl. *Mary of Mile 18*, Vancouver Art Gallery (1971), *A Salmon for Simon*, Master Eagle Gallery, N.Y. City (1980), & *Ida and the Wool Smugglers*, Canada at Bologna (1990); various group & solo exhibitions of paintings, incl. Dunlop Art Gallery, Regina Public Library (1982) & multiple shows at Bau Xi Gallery, Vancouver & Toronto. **HONS:** Book of the Year Award, *Mary of Mile 18*, 1972; Canada Council Children's Literature Award for Illustration, *A Salmon for Simon*, 1979; Amelia Frances Howard-Gibbon Award, CACL, *A Salmon for Simon*, 1979; Honourable Mention, Canada Council Children's Literature Award for Illustration, *Pettranella*, 1981; Elizabeth Mrazik-Cleaver Canadian Picture Book Award, *By the Sea: An Alphabet Book*, 1986. **INTERESTS:** gardening; refinishing furniture; garage sales. **MISC:** manuscripts & illustrations for *Mary of Mile 18*, *A Boy of Taché* & *By the Sea: An Alphabet Book* owned by National Library, Ottawa. **COMMENT:** *"Ann began painting watercolours at a school in the UK when she was 11. She wrote and illustrated her first two books for children in 1968 because of the isolation she experienced teaching in a two-room school at Mile 18 in the Peace River Country of BC. She now works as an illustrator of children's books and as an artist."*

Blainey, Justine, B.Sc. ⚾
Athlete. 83 Pickering St., Toronto, ON M4E 3J5 (416) 698-0297, FAX 698-0297. Born Canada 1973. **EDUC:** Univ. of Toronto, B.Sc. (Psych.) 1995; Canadian Memorial Chiropractic Coll., current. **CAREER:** championed five court cases to promote equality in sport, 1985-88; public speaking with regard to equality in sport & motivating youth, 1985 to date; hockey player, Senior "AA" Scarboro Sting, 1989-92; promoted, developed & coached two new female sports teams (field hockey & ice hockey), East York Collegiate Institute, 1990-92; player, Varsity Blues Ice Hockey Team, 1992-94; agitated & raised funds to prevent cancellation of Univ. of Toronto Lady Blues hockey team, 1993; Ptnr in starting & running Canada's Nat'l Summer Sports Camp, 1993; hockey player, Senior "AA" Toronto Aeros, 1993-94. **SELECTED PUBLICATIONS:** short pieces in several feminist writings & sch. textbooks. **AFFIL:** FAME (Female Athletes Motivating Excellence). **HONS:** Legal & Education Action Fund (LEAF) National "Breakthrough" Award, 1987; Canadian Youth Award, 1991; Hager Hugh Miller Award, 1992; 1992 Canada's Birthday Achievement Awards, 1992; Univ. of Toronto National Scholarship, 1992 to date; Provincial Members Award, 1992; Ont. Scholar, 1992; Canada Scholarship, 1992; Varsity Blues Ice Hockey Team, League Champions, 1992-94; Most Academic Player Award, Varsity Blues Ice Hockey Team, 1994; Senior "AA" Toronto Aeros, Ont. Champions 1994, Silver Canada 1994. **INTERESTS:** studies; hockey; weightlifting; public speaking. **MISC:** with the help of lawyer J. Anna Fraser, changed the Ont. Human Rights Code to ensure equal access for capable female athletes to elite male sports through five court cases, incl. the Supreme Court of Canada, with one case setting a legal precedent to ensure human rights cases are heard in public as opposed to behind closed doors. **COMMENT:** *"Justine's 'I can and I shall' bugle call has been changed to 'you can and you will' as she encourages young Canadians to aim high, work hard and NEVER give up."*

Blais, Diane, B.A. $ 📜 ☝
Partner and First Partner in Communications, Accounting and Management Consulting Firms, ERNST & YOUNG, 1 Place Ville Marie, Ste. 2400, Montreal, QC H3B 3M9 (514) 874-4312, FAX 871-8713. **EDUC:** Univ. de Montréal, B.A.(Psych.) 1969, B.A. in translation 1973; Canadian Institute of Chartered Accountants, computer & office automation courses; Ordre des traducteurs et interprètes agréés du Québec, compulsory course on the new Civil Code 1993. **CAREER:** Translator, Clarkson Gordon, 1973-76; Head of Translation Svcs, Canadian Bankers' Association, 1976; various positions, Caron Bélanger Ernst & Young, 1976-82; Gen. Mgr, Montreal office, Hum. Res. Mgr & Office Automation Consultant, 1982-87; Ptnr, 1987 to date. **SELECTED PUBLICATIONS:** co-authoured a book on taxation & budget anlysis; numerous newspaper articles. **AFFIL:** Canadian Translators & Interpreters Council (Chair); Ordre des traducteurs et interprètes agréés du Québec (Founding Pres. 1992-93; Mbr.-Ambassador & Spokesperson); Quebec Translators Society (Dir.; Head, Computer Committee 1988-89; VP & Head, Comm. 1990-91); Refuge des jeunes de Montréal (Mbr, Fin. Committee 1995 to date). **MISC:** Mbr., Cdn delegation to the Int'l Federation of Translators Conference, Brighton, UK, 1993 & Melbourne, Australia, 1996; jury mbr., *Mérites du français au travail* contest, 1992-93; delegate, Que. Interprofessional Council, 1992-94; inaugurated the 1st Nat'l & Int'l Translation Day at the official ceremony at Parliament, Ottawa, 1992; speaker on various topics in numerous countries; teaches many courses and seminars. **COMMENT:** *"Bright, swift, good judgment and sense of humour, hardworking, very active, client-oriented, business-oriented. Partner at Ernst & Young."*

Blais, Marie-Claire C.M. 📖 📜
Writer, Novelist, Poet, Playwright. c/o Agence Goodwin Nathalie Goodwin, 839 Sherbrooke est., Ste. 2, Montréal, QC (514) 598-5252, FAX 598-1878. Born Que. 1939. **EDUC:** Univ. Laval. **SELECTED PUBLICATIONS:** romans: *La Belle Bête* (1959); *Tête blanche* (1960); *Le Jour est noir* (1962); *Une saison dans la vie d'Emmanuel* (1965); *L'Insoumise* (1966); *David Sterne* (1967); *Manuscrits de Pauline Archange* (1968); *Vivre! Vivre!* (1969); *Les Apparences* (1971); *Le Loup* (1972); *Un joualonais, sa Joualonie* (1973); *Une Liaison parisienne* (1975); *Les Nuits de l'Underground* (1978); *Le Sourd dans la ville* (1979); *Visions d'Anna* (1982); *Pierre* (1986); *L'Ange de la solitude* (1989); *Un jardin dans la tempête* (1990); *L'Exilé*, nouvelles (1993); théâtre: *L'Exécution* (1968); *Fièvre et autres textes dramatiques* (1974); *L'Océan suivi de Murmures* (1977); *Sommeil d'hiver* (1986); *La Nef des sorcières* (1977); *L'Île* (1988); poèsie: *Pays violés* (1964); *Existences* (1964); *Pays violés et Existences* (1967); récit; carnets (autobiographiques); ouevres traduites. **AFFIL:** Royal Society of Canada (Fellow). **HONS:** Prix de la Langue française (*La Belle Bête*), 1961; Bourse Guggenheim (US), 1963; Prix France-Québec, Paris (*Une saison dans la vie d'Emmanuel*),

1966; Prix Médicis, Paris (*Une saison dans la vie d'Emmanuel*), 1966; Prix du Gouverneur Général du Canada (*Les Manuscrits de Pauline Archange*), 1969; Member of the Order of Canada, 1975; Prix Belgique-Canada, Brussels, pour l'ensemble de l'oeuvre, 1976; Prof. honoraire à la Fac. des Humanités de l'Univ. de Calgary, 1978; Prix du Gouverneur Général du Canada (*Le Sourd dans la ville*), 1979; Prix Athanase-David, Qué., pour l'ensemble de l'oeuvre, 1982; Prix de l'Académie Française, Paris (*Visions d'Anna*), 1983; Prix Wessim Habif de l'Académie Royale de langue et de littérature françaises de Belgique pour l'ensemble de l'oeuvre, 1990; Canada 125 Medal, 1992; élue a l'Académie Royale de langue et de littérature francaises de Belgique, 1993; Élue à l'Academié des Lettres du Quihe; Ordre du Québec, 1995; Hon. Doctorate,York Univ., 1975; D.Litt.(Hon.), Victoria Univ., B.C., 1990. **INTERESTS:** arts; painting. **COMMENT:** *"Author of many books, published and translated in many countries."*

Blais-Ramsay, Michelle ■ $ ♡

President, MICHELLE RAMSAY & COMPANY INC., 10 Price St., Toronto, ON M4W 1Z4 (416) 515-8571, FAX (416) 515-8929, EMAIL michelle.ramsay@sympatico.ca. Vice-President, Corporate Identity, KARO (TORONTO) INC. Born Ottawa 1949. s. 2 ch. Derek, Suzanne. **EDUC:** Nepean High Sch., 5-yr. Arts & Science Diploma 1967; Laurentian Univ., Pol. Sci. 1979-81. **CAREER:** Special Asst. to Hon. J.J. Blais, Min. of Supply & Svcs Canada, 1980-81; Acct Mgr, The Houston Group Communications Limited, 1981-84; Mktg Programs Mgr, IBM Canada Ltd., 1985-87; Brand Mgr, ROLM Telecommunications, 1987-88; Mktg & Public Affairs Mgr, IBM Canada Ltd., 1989-92; Mktg Mgr, Celestica Inc., 1992-94; Pres., Michelle Ramsay & Company Inc., 1994 to date; VP, Corp. Identity, KARO (Toronto) Inc., 1996 to date. **AFFIL:** Scarborough General Hospital (Chair, Bd. of Gov. & Trustee); Scarborough Hospitals Group (Dir.); Toronto Sunrise Rotary Club; Ontario Hospital Association (Chair, GTA Planning Committee 1993-96); Ontario Medal for Good Citizenship Award Committee (Chair 1992-96); Ontario Liberal Party (Co-founder, Ont. Liberal Women's Advisory Committee 1983-86; VP 1985-86; Conference Co-Chair, Bi-Annual Meeting 1986); Toronto-Ontario Olympic Bid Committee (1990).

Blak, Groovella ■ ■ $ 🎨

Owner, SIREN (alternative clothing & accessory store for men & women), 463 Queen St. W., Toronto, ON M5V 2A9 (416) 504-9288, FAX 504-5145. Born Toronto. m. Morpheus Blak. **EDUC:** York Univ., Fine Arts (Dance); Univ. of Toronto, Hist.(Music/Theatre); George Brown Coll., Fashion Design; dance study, Toronto Dance Theatre, Russian Academy of Classical Ballet. **CAREER:** ballet, modern & baroque dance, studying & performing (ongoing); opened Siren, 1988. **MISC:** she & husband are co-founders & co-presidents of the Gothic Society of Canada, which holds many events such as fancy dress picnics, high teas, masquerade balls & soirees in Victorian rooms. **COMMENT:** *"We carry our own exclusive clothing designs at Siren, of which I have been designing and developing for both men and women over the past few years. Due to my personal love of fashion and working in the fashion industry, I have developed a good eye for the styles that please both our customers and myself. A challenging yet rewarding enterprise! I am an extremely hard worker and set high standards for myself and my business. My goal and vision is to combine my dance and fashion training by one day presenting a very theatrical fashion show."*

Blake, Laura Denise ■ ♡ 🏳️

Transgender Activist. 165 Ontario St., Ste. 609, St. Catherines, ON L2R 5K4 (905) 688-0276, EMAIL ldblake@iaw.on.ca. Born 1952. s. **CAREER:** Founder, TransEqual, transgenderist lobby group; negotiated human rights enforcement packages for transsexuals, transgenderists & transvestites with both the Ont. & Cdn Human Rights Commissions; available for no-fee consultation with legal and caring professionals who are involved with the transgender community. **SELECTED PUBLICATIONS:** self published essays, using nom-de plume "Laura Masters" and dealing with transgender identity and surrounding legal issues. **MISC:** essays being translated into German & Romanian for use by emerging transgender rights movement in formerly Communist countries in Europe. **COMMENT:** *"Like most womanmales my life has been a series of upheavals and reformations. My peers and I are often denied even the simplest of inclusions in life and for the past 8 years it has been my purpose to raise professional awareness of the injustices we suffer."*

Bland, Ruby M. $

Presentation Specialist - Visits, Switching Networks, NORTEL CANADA LIMITED, 8200 Dixie Rd., Brampton, ON L6V 2M8 (416) 452-2540, FAX 452-2206. m. Billy. 2 ch. Randy, Greg. **EDUC:** Bus. Coll. **CAREER:** various positions, quality control to relief operator, Benson & Hedges, 1961-74; law office secretarial, 1974-

79; Presentation Specialist, Nortel Canada Limited, 1979 to date. **INTERESTS:** family; travel; driving; cottage. **MISC:** also involved in small bus.: jewelry, special events, health food. **COMMENT:** *"I have been employed as a Visit Presentation Specialist with Northern Telecom for more than 15 years. I handle all the VIP/International/CALATours that come into our building in Bramalea.. I guess my motto is do whatever it takes to get the job done."*

Blaney, E. Sharon, R.N. ⊕ $
Manager of Corporate Health, BC TEL, 3777 Kingsway, Ste. 5, Burnaby, BC V5H 3Z7 (604) 432-4012, FAX 432-9456. Born Vancouver 1943. m. Michael Blaney. 2 ch. **EDUC:** St. Paul's Hospital Sch. of Nursing, R.N. 1965; Douglas Coll., Certificate (Occupational Health Nursing) 1982; B.C. Institute of Technology, Advanced Diploma in Health Sci. 1990; Open Learning Univ., Bachelor of Health Science, in progress; Canadian Occupational Health Nurse (COHN(C)); American Certified Occupational Health Nurse Specialist (COHN-S). **CAREER:** Gen. Staff Nurse, St. Mary's Hospital, Sechelt, B.C., 1965-67; Head Nurse, 1967-70; Office Mgr, Blaney Antique Mirror and Tile, Gibson's, B.C., 1970-74; Occupational Health Nurse, B.C. Telephone Company, Kamloops, B.C., 1974-76; Health Counsellor, Vancouver, 1976-80; Asst. Mgr, Health Svcs Dept., B.C. Telephone Company, Burnaby, B.C., 1980-90; Mgr of Corp. Health, BC TEL, 1990 to date. **SELECTED PUBLICATIONS:** "Healthtrac Implementation BC TEL" (*Computer in Nursing Newsletter* Fall 1990); modules for BCIT Occupational Health Nursing Program. **AFFIL:** Canadian Occupational Health Nurses' Association (Pres. 1993 to date; VP 1991-93); American Occupational Health Nurses' Association; Registered Nurses' Association of B.C.; B.C. Occupational Health Nurses Group. **HONS:** Award of Excellence in Nursing Admin., RNABC, 1995. **INTERESTS:** reading; gardening. **MISC:** Chrm, Post-Basic Occupational Health Nursing Advisory Committee, BCIT, 1986-94; Mbr., Exec. Committee, 1987 Health Conference "For the Health of It," Vancouver, co-sponsored by RNABC & BCHA. **COMMENT:** *"Career-oriented and professionally goal-oriented, I have played an active part in shaping the direction of occupational health Nursing at the provincial and federal levels. Have been instrumental in establishing a Canadian recognized occupational health service at BC Telecom Inc."*

Blankinship, Jennie, B.A. ■■ ✋
President, INDIAN HOMEMAKERS' ASSOCIATION OF BRITISH COLUMBIA, 175 E. Broadway St., Ste. 208, Vancouver, BC V5T 1W2 (604) 876-0944, FAX 876-1448. Born Port Angeles, Wash. 1958. m. Lloyd Attig. 2 ch. Robbyn, Jaime. **EDUC:** Simon Fraser Univ., B.A.(Criminology) 1995. **CAREER:** Research Asst., Northern Justice Resource Centre, Simon Fraser Univ., 1992-94; Pres., Indian Homemakers' Association of B.C., 1994 to date; Educ. Policy Coord., Union of B.C. Indian Chiefs, 1995 to date. **AFFIL:** Vancouver Aboriginal Friendship Society; Conayt Indian Friendship Centre; First Nations Breast Cancer Society (VP); Union of B.C. Indian Chiefs (Chiefs' Council representing First Nations women & children on/off reserve); Institute of Indigenous Government (V-Chair, Bd. of Gov.); Institute of Indigenous Government (V-Chair). **INTERESTS:** traditional First Nations dance, art, poetry, sewing; cooking new dishes; meeting people from around the world; advocacy for women's & children's rights. **COMMENT:** *"First Nations woman from the Nlaka'pamux Nation (Interior B.C.). Mother of two daughters. Career is dedicated to empowering indigenous peoples to exercise their right of self-determination, which reflects indigenous philosophy, values and experience throughout the world."*

Blankstein, Marjorie, C.M.,B.A., M.S.W. ■■ ♡ ✋ 📜
Volunteer. Born Winnipeg. m. Morley Blankstein. 5 ch., 5 grch. **EDUC:** Univ. of Manitoba, B.A. 1950; Univ. of Minnesota, M.S.W. 1952. **VOLUNTEER CAREER:** Pres., Jewish Child & Family Service, 1963-65; Pres., Winnipeg Section, National Council of Jewish Women of Canada (NCJW), 1965-67; mbr., Man. Study Committee for Children with Emotional & Learning Disorders, 1968-69; Dir., Community Welfare Planning Council of Winnipeg, 1969-72; Rep., Int'l Council of Jewish Women seminar, Israel, 1970; founding mbr., MATCH International; Pres., Age & Opportunity Centre Inc., 1972-74; Hon. Sec., Winnipeg Symphony Orchestra, 1974-78; Membership Chrm, Winnipeg chpt., Canadian Friends of the Hebrew Univ., 1976-77; Nat'l Pres., National Council of Jewish Women, 1977-79; Pres., Winnipeg Jewish Community Council, 1979-81, 1986; VP, Man./Sask. Reg., Canadian Jewish Congress, 1982-85; mbr., The Mayor's Arts Policy Advisory Committee, 1982; founding Bd. mbr., Women's Health Research Foundation of Canada, 1983-86; Sec. & Chair, Distribution Committee, Jewish Foundation, Man., 1980-90; Nat'l Sec., Canadian Jewish Congress, 1989-92; Exec. mbr., LEAF Foundation, 1990-93; Bd. of Trustees, United Way of Greater Winnipeg, 1990-96; Chair, 1994. **AFFIL:** Jewish Community Campus of Winnipeg (Chair,

Capital Fund Drive 1992 to date; VP 1993 to date); United Way of Greater Winnipeg (Leadership Giving Committee-Major Gifts; Recognition Advisory Committee); Jewish National Fund of Canada (Winnipeg Advisory Bd.); Ben Gurion Univ. of the Negev (Winnipeg Associates Advisory Bd.). HONS: Hon. Life Mbr., Jewish Child & Family Svc., 1966; Queen's Silver Jubilee Medal, 1977; Woman of the Year, Community Svc., YWCA, 1978; Honoree, Jewish National Fund, Negev Dinner, 1980; Member of the Order of Canada, 1982; Sam N. Filer Award for Distinguished Svc. (1st recipient), Canadian Jewish Congress, 1989; Commemorative Medal for 125th Anniversary of Cdn Confederation, 1992; Sol Kanee Distinguished Community Svc. Medal (1st recipient), Winnipeg Jewish Community Council, 1995. MISC: 1st woman Pres., Winnipeg Jewish Community Council.

Blaszczyk, Yvonne, C.H.R.P. ■■ ☺ ⑤
President, HUMAN RESOURCES PROFESSIONAL ASSOCIATION OF ONTARIO (education & dev. of human resources practitioners; more than 7,000 members), 61 Neilson Dr., Etobicoke, ON M9C 1V9 (416) 622-1265, FAX 622-0807. President, CANADIAN PAY & BENEFITS CONSULTING GROUP INC. Publisher, *COMPENSATION NEWS*. Born 1953. CAREER: The Toronto Hospital; Royal LePage; The Permanent Trust; The Anti-Inflation Bd.; Dir., CIBC, 1992. AFFIL: HRPAO (Bd. of Dir. 1989, 1992 to date; VP 1994-95); Ontario Hospital Association (Advisory on Pay Equity); RCMP (Pay Council); Human Resources Board (committees); Epilepsy Foundation; Girl Guides of Canada; American Compensation Association. INTERESTS: wine; public speaking; global business strategies. MISC: seminar leader; conference speaker.

Blatt, Rena, B.A. ⑤ ♣ ⑳
Senior Consultant, Ministry of Economic Development, Trade and Tourism, GOVERNMENT OF ONTARIO, Hearst Block, 900 Bay St., Toronto, ON M7A 2E1 (416) 325-6495, FAX 3256538. Born N.Y. 1945. d. EDUC: City Univ. of New York, B.A.(Soc./Town Planning) 1966. CAREER: Owner, RWB Consulting Services, 1972-76; Sr. Policy Advisor, Ont. Ministry of Housing; Dir., Econ. Intelligence, Small Business Secretariat, Industry Science Technology Canada; Owner, Integrity Research. SELECTED PUBLICATIONS: "Survey of Small Business Registrants" (*Journal of Small Business and Entrepreneurship* 3(2) Fall 1985); "The Culture of the Entrepreneur: Fact or Fiction," with J.D. Kyle, R.A. Blais & A.J. Szonyi (*Journal of Small Business & Entrepreneurship*

8(1) Oct.-Dec. 1990); "Les entrepreneurs franco-ontariens" (*Revue du nouvel-Ontario* 13-14, mai 1993); "The Effect of Aspirations Upon the Business Achievements of Women Entrepreneurs" (*Canadian Woman Studies* 15(1) Winter 1994). AFFIL: Academy of Management; International Council for Small Business; Step Ahead; Wellesley Hospital Auxiliary. INTERESTS: business research; the relationship between the individual & the corporation. MISC: various conference presentations. COMMENT: *"For more than ten years, I have been working to increase the quality of business research in Canada. At the same time, I have been assisting businesses to meet their potential."*

Block, Sheila R. ⚑
Partner, TORY TORY DESLAURIERS & BINNINGTON, Aetna Tower, Toronto Dominion Centre, Ste. 3000, Toronto, ON M5K 1N2 (416) 865-7319, FAX 865-7380. Born Toronto 1947. m. Prof. James Seckinger. 3 ch., 4 stepch. EDUC: Univ. of Toronto, 1965-68; Carleton Univ., B.A.(Hist.) 1969; Univ. of Ottawa, LL.B. 1972. BAR: Ont., 1974. CAREER: Ptnr, Tory Tory DesLauriers & Binnington. AFFIL: American Coll. of Trial Lawyers (Fellow); International Society of Barristers. HONS: Gold Medalist, LL.B., Univ. of Ottawa.

Blois, Ruby, R.N.,B.sc.N.,CHE ⊕ ⑤
Director, Partnership Development, IWK-GRACE HEALTH CENTRE FOR CHILDREN, WOMEN & FAMILIES, 5850 University Ave., Halifax, NS B3J 3G9 (902) 420-3071, FAX 492-1446. Born Halifax 1942. m. Eugene Harrison Blois. 1 ch. EDUC: Children's Hospital Sch. of Nursing, Diploma in Nursing 1962; Dalhousie Univ., Diploma (Nursing Unit Admin.) 1965; Mount Saint Vincent Univ., B.Sc.(Nursing) 1973; Canadian Hospital Association, Certificate (Nursing Unit Admin.) 1975; Univ. of Saskatoon, Certificate (Health Care Organization & Mgmt) 1979; Canadian Coll. of Health Service Executives, Exec. Certification 1986. CAREER: Staff Nurse, Gen. Surgery Unit, IWK-Grace Health Centre for Children, Women & Families (formerly Izaak Walton Killam Hospital for Children), 1962-66; Head Nurse, Gen. Surgery Unit, 1967-69; Nursing Supervisor, hospital wide, 1969-77; Assoc. Dir., Nursing Svcs, 1977-82; Dir., Nursing Svcs, 1982-85; Consultant, Nursing Unit Admin. Program, Canadian Hospital Association, 1982-84; VP, Nursing & Special Svcs, 1985-95; Dir., Partnership Dev., 1995 to date; joint appointment, Sch. of Nursing, Dalhousie Univ., 1993 to date. SELECTED PUBLICATIONS: Research Study, "Effect of Care Deliv-

ery Systems on Nurses and the Quality of Care," with Judi Ritchie & Sonya Franklin; articles in Canadian Association of Pediatric Hospitals Newsletter & RNANS Newsletter. **DIRECTOR:** IWK/Grace Hospital. **AFFIL:** Registered Nurses' Association of N.S. (Dir.); Canadian Nurses' Association; Pediatric Nurses Interest Group of N.S. (Charter Mbr.); Academy of Chief Nursing Executive Officers of Canada; Association of Senior Nursing Administrators of N.S. (Past Pres.); Canadian Association of Pediatric Hospitals (Past Dir.); Association for the Care of Children's Health (Life Mbr.); N.S. Provincial Health Council (Counsellor); Canadian Coll. of Health Service Executives (Exec. Category); United Way; Ronald McDonald House (Bd.); Dartmouth Citizens Against Incineration; Alumnae Association, Dalhousie Univ., Mount Saint Vincent Univ., Children's Hospital Sch. of Nursing; IWK/Grace Hospital (Auxiliary; Standards Committee). **HONS:** Hon. Life Membership with the Corporation, I.W.K. Hospital for Children, 1993; Long Svc. Award, I.W.K. Hospital for Children, 1987 & 1992; Staff Recognition Award, I.W.K. Hospital for Children, 1983. **MISC:** various workshops & presentations focusing on the changing role of the nurse manager. **COMMENT:** *"Successful nursing leader with a strategic focus on pediatric health care; significant focus on evolving improvements in pediatric health care and the nursing profession."*

Blondin-Andrew, Ethel, P.C.,M.P. ■ 🍁 🎓
Secretary of State, Training and Youth and Member of Parliament (Western Arctic), GOVERNMENT OF CANADA, Ottawa, Canada K1A 0J9 (819) 953-0927, FAX 953-0944. Born Fort Norman, N.W.T. 1951. m. Leon Andrew. 3 ch. **EDUC:** Univ. of Alberta, B.A. **CAREER:** teacher; Aboriginal language specialist; Acting Dir., Public Svc. Commission; Nat'l Mgr, Deputy Min. of Culture & Comm., Gov't of the NWT; Teaching Instructor, Univ. of Calgary & Arctic Coll.; elected MP (Western Arctic), 1988, re-elected, 1993; Parliamentary Committee on Aboriginal Affairs; Parliamentary Committee on Electoral Reform; Parliamentary Committee on Literacy; Parliamentary Committee on the Constitution; Opposition Critic for Aboriginal Affairs; Sec. of State for Training & Youth, 1993 to date. **AFFIL:** Liberal Party of Canada; actively involved with several communities. **HONS:** numerous awards.

Blue, Mary $ ✪
Senior Vice-President, Land and Administration, JORDAN PETROLEUM LTD., 255-5 Ave. S.W., Ste. 850, Calgary, AB T2P 3G6 (403) 266-1024, FAX 266-4325. **CAREER:** Sr. VP, Land & Admin., Jordan Petroleum Ltd. **DIRECTOR:** Jordan Petroleum Ltd.; American Lariat Inc. **AFFIL:** Blue Collar Dance Company; Live Arts Theatre Alberta (Founding Pres.).

Boake-Wuthrich, Kathy (K. Boake W.) ✪
Illustrator. 1061 Habgood St., White Rock, BC V4B 4W7 (604) 538-5186, FAX (604) 538-0985. m. Bruno Wuthrich. 2 ch. Beau Wuthrich, Annabelle Wuthrich. **EDUC:** Central Technical Sch., Toronto, 3-yr. special art 1972-75. **CAREER:** before being encouraged to pursue illustration, I worked at many other types of lousy jobs. **SELECTED PUBLICATIONS:** *Toronto Life*, *Owl Magazine*, *Flare*, *Saturday Night*, *Vancouver Magazine*, *Western Living*, *Ottawa Magazine*, *Outside*, *L.A. Magazine*, *Ryerson Review of Journalism*, *Seventeen*, *In Style*, etc.. **HONS:** numerous golds, silvers & honorable mentions, National Magazine Awards; gold & honorable mentions, Toronto Art Directors' Club; Lotus Awards; Western Magazine Awards; Applied Arts Awards Annual. **INTERESTS:** family; garden; creative problem solving. **COMMENT:** *" For about 15 years I have worked as a very happy freelance illustrator with my husband Bruno's support. Our family has created dimension in my work and life."*

Bobrow-Zuckert, Ella 📖 ✏
Writer. Toronto, ON M6S 2N8. Born Nikolaiev, Russia. w. 1st m. Nikolai Bobrow, 1935-65; 2nd m. Léon. Zuckert, 1969-92. 2 ch. **EDUC:** Institute of Trade & Commerce, Fin. & Acctg 1929; various writing courses in Canada & U.S. **CAREER:** various offices, industrial & educational, Lugansk & Voroshilovgrad, Ukraine, 1930-42; Atlanta Import and Export Co., Bavaria, Germany, 1945-48; Office work/literary activities, Toronto, 1950-74; Co-Ed., *Sovremennik*, Toronto, 1963-76; Freelance Reporter, Russian Section, Radio Canada International, 1971-79. **SELECTED PUBLICATIONS:** *Irina Istomina* (Russian 1967, English 1980, German 1983); *I Wait for a Miracle* (1970); *Amber Elixir* (1977); *Autumnal Cadenza* (1985); *The Three Brave Snowflakes* (Russian 1961, English 1982, German 1986); *A King in Space* (Russian 1992, Literaturny Kyrgyzstan; German 1993, Kazakhstan); *Irina Odoevtseva – A Literary Portrait* (Russian and English 1995); included in various anthologies worldwide. **AFFIL:** League of Canadian Poets; Writers' Union of Canada; CANSCAIP; Children's Book Centre; Regensburger Schriftstellergesellschaft International (Germany); Friends

of the Globe Poetry Library; International PEN. **HONS:** Order of Pegasus, Barcelona, 1992; Cultural Doctor in Poetic Literature, World Literature Round Table, 1993. **INTERESTS:** music (piano); gardening; theatre. **MISC:** read poetry on a Canada Council public reading grant. **COMMENT:** *"E.B. writes in Russian, English, and German: poems, short stories, essays, literary criticism, and song lyrics. She lectured on poetry in Canada and the United States."*

Boddy, Janice, B.A.,M.A.,Ph.D. 🎓 ⚛
Associate Professor, Anthropology Department, Social Sciences Division, UNIVERSITY OF TORONTO, Scarborough Campus, 1265 Military Trail, Scarborough, ON M1C 1A4 (416) 287-7821. **EDUC:** McGill Univ., B.A.(Anthropology) 1972; Univ. of Calgary, M.A.(Anthropology) 1974; Univ. of British Columbia, Ph.D.(Anthropology) 1982. **CAREER:** Instructor, Dept. of Anthropology, Univ. of Alberta, Summer, 1975; Lecturer, Dept. of Anthropology, Univ. of Toronto, Erindale Campus, 1978-79; Lecturer, Dept. of Anthropology, Univ. of Manitoba, 1979-80; Lecturer, Dept. of Anthropology, Lakehead Univ., 1980-81; Lecturer, Dept. of Anthropology, Univ. of Toronto, Scarborough Campus, 1981-82; Asst. Prof., 1982-90; Instructor, Liberal Arts Dept., Ontario Coll. of Art, 1985; Assoc. Prof., Dept. of Anthropology, Univ. of Toronto, Scarborough Campus, 1990 to date. **SELECTED PUBLICATIONS:** *Wombs and Alien Spirits: Women, Men and the Zar Cult in Northern Sudan* (Madison, Wis.: University of Wisconsin Press, 1989); *Aman: The Story of a Somali Girl*, with Virginia Lee Barnes (Toronto: Knopf, 1994); "Purity and Enclosed Space Among Sudanese Ja'ali and Jawabra Arabs" (*Canadian Newsletter for Research on Women* 7(3) 1978); "Womb as Oasis: The Symbolic Context of Pharaonic Circumcision in Rural Northern Sudan" (*American Ethnologist* 9(4) 1982); "Anthropology, Feminism, and the Postmodern Context" (*Culture* 11(1-2) 1991); "The Body Nearer the Self" (*American Anthropologist* 96(1) 1995); numerous book reviews; numerous papers presented at meetings, symposia, and invitational colloquia. **EDIT:** Ed. Bd., *Anthropological Horizons*, University of Toronto Press, 1991 to date; Assoc. Ed., *American Ethnologist*, 1995-98; Co-Ed., *Social Analysis*, 1995 to date. **AFFIL:** Canadian Anthropology Society; Royal Anthropological Society; American Anthropological Association; American Ethnological Association; Society for Medical Anthropology; Society for Cultural Anthropology; Sudan Studies Association; Association for Feminist Anthropology; Association of Africanist Anthropologists; H.F. Guggenheim Foundation (Int'l Cross-Disciplinary Working Group on Violence Against Women). **HONS:** Connaught Fellowship, 1994. **MISC:** recipient of various grants; numerous invited scholarly lectures; Bd. Horizons of Friends Development Agency, 1990-94; external reviewer for numerous journals, granting agencies and publishers.

Bodkin, M.A. (Jill), B.A. ■ $
Chairman, GOLDEN HERON ENTERPRISES, 800 W. Pender St., 3rd Fl., Vancouver, BC V6C 2V6 (604) 691-8805. Born Belleville, Ont. 1943 1 ch. Alicyn. **EDUC:** Univ. of Alberta, B.A. 1963; Maxwell Sch. of Public Affairs, Syracuse Univ., M.A. course work completed in Public Admin. 1979. **CAREER:** Secretariat to Cabinet Committee on Econ. Dev., Gov't of Canada, 1965-81; Deputy Min. of Consumer & Corp. Affairs, Gov't of B.C., 1981-86; Founding Chrm & CEO, Securities Commission, 1986-87; Exec.-in-Residence, Univ. of B.C., 1987; Ptnr, Dir. of Fin. Svcs, Ernst & Young (formerly Clarkson Gordon), 1988-96. **SELECTED PUBLICATIONS:** *Deregulation of Canada's Financial Sector* (Canada/U.K. Colloquium, 1987); *Export of Canadian Financial Services* (Institute for Research in Public Policy, 1987); *Independence and Accountability of Courts and Tribunals* (Canadian Institute for the Administration of Justice (the judiciary), 1986); *Liability Insurance: The Business Perspective* (CIAJ, 1987). **AFFIL:** Canadian Institute of Chartered Accountants (Communications & Gov't Affairs Committee 1994 to date); Thailand Development Research Institute Foundation (Trustee 1993 to date); Vancouver Board of Trade (Gov.; Chair 1994-95; Dir. 1989-96); Sectoral Advisory Group on International Trade (Fin. Svcs Section); Conference Board of Canada (former Dir., Fin. Svcs Research Program); B.C. Science Council (Committee on Financing Technology Companies); Canada West Foundation (Dir.); National Forum on Post-Secondary Education (Organizing Committee); Institute for Research in Public Policy (Dir.); Swiss Canadian Chamber of Commerce; Hong Kong Canada Business Association; World Wildlife Fund (former Dir.); Canadian Club (former Dir.). **HONS:** Cdn rep., International Services Coalition, Geneva, 1989; U.S. gov't visitor examining domestic & int'l bnkg issues, 1984; member, Selection Committee, Lt.-Gov.'s Award of Merit, 1990-93; Canada 125 Medal. **INTERESTS:** sailing; gardening. **MISC:** Chrm, Celgar Expansion Review Bd., Environmental Assessment Review Process/Major Projects Review Process, 1991; Pres., B.C. Primorye Market Integration Consortium (Primorye is a region in Russia); Pres., Tianjin Harbour Coal Terminal.

Bodogh, Marilyn C. ⓓ 🦅 ♠

Manager, F.L. BODOGH LUMBER CO. LTD., Box 686, St. Catharines, ON L2R 6W8 (905) 688-3533, FAX 688-1469. Born Toronto 1955. d. 2 ch. Gregory Bodogh-Darte, Christopher Bodogh-Darte. EDUC: Denis Morris High Sch., Grade 12 Diploma 1973. CAREER: Owner/ Operator, Darte Flowers, 1977-82; Owner/ Operator, Darte Funeral Home, 1977-92; Mgr, F.L. Bodogh Lumber Co. Ltd., 1994 to date. SELECTED PUBLICATIONS: *Curl to Win with Ed Lukowkich* (1986). AFFIL: St. Catharines Curling Club; St. Catharines Golf & Country Club. HONS: Team of the Year, 1986; Canadian & World Curling Champion, 1986. INTERESTS: reading; writing letters; tasting great wines; travelling; chatting with good friends; working hard; golfing 37 games a year. MISC: public speaker, 1992 to date. COMMENT: *"Winning the Canadian and World Titles were real goals achieved in my life. But the true victory was building the championship team with both wins and losses along the way. My biggest achievements in my life are my two sons—Greg and Chris. My motto is, 'Live, love and laugh and have fun doing it!'"*

Boehm, Beverley ■ ☺

Executive Director, SASKATCHEWAN VOICE OF PEOPLE WITH DISABILITIES, 1024 Winnipeg St., Regina, SK S4R 8P8 (306) 569-3111. Born 1945. d. 2 ch. EDUC: Secretarial & Bookkeeping diploma; Real Estate & Gen. Insur. Diplomas. CAREER: office worker, T. Eaton Company, 1965-67; Confidential Clerk (trained as Credit Mgr), Hudson's Bay Company, 1972-73; Bookkeeper, P.A. Mobile Homes, 1973-74; self-employed, Yorkton Mobile Homes, 1974-79; self-employed, real estate, 1976-82; Saskatchewan Voice of the Handicapped, 1986 to date. AFFIL: Saskatchewan Special Interest Co-op (Sec.-Treas.); North Saskatchewan Independent Living Centre (Dir. & Treas.); Provincial Partnership on Family Violence; Provincial National Access Awareness Committee; Saskatchewan Library Print Handicap Committee. HONS: awards from National Access Awareness Week, & Saskatoon Indian & Métis Federation.

Bogo, Marion, B.A.,M.S.W. ☜

Acting Dean, Faculty of Social Work, UNIVERSITY OF TORONTO, 246 Bloor St. W., Toronto, ON M5S 1A1 (416) 978-3263, FAX 978-7072, EMAIL marion@fsw.utoronto.ca. Born Montreal 1942. m. Dr. Norman Bogo. 2 ch. Geoffrey, Jonathan. EDUC: McGill Univ., B.A. 1963, M.S.W. 1965; Univ. of Toronto, Advanced Diploma in Social Work 1976. CAREER: Caseworker, Baron de Hirsch Insti-

tute, 1965-67; Social Worker, Veteran's Admin. Hospital, 1967-69; Sr. Social Worker, Mental Hygiene Institute, Montreal, 1969-72; social work practice, Prof. & Practicum Coord., Univ. of Toronto, 1979-92; Assoc. Prof./Assoc. Dean/Acting Dean, 1993-95. SELECTED PUBLICATIONS: *The Practice of Field Instruction in Social Work; Theory and Process with An Annotated Bibliography,* with E. Vayda (Toronto: University of Toronto Press, 1987); *Training Program: Practice Skills for Social Work Students* (Univ. of Toronto: Fac. of Social Work, 1982); *The Practice of Field Instruction in Social Work: A Teaching Guide,* with E. Vayda (Toronto: Univ. of Toronto, 1993); "Educating Students for Social Work Practice in the Health Field" in *Social Work Administrative Practice in Health Care,* ed. by P. Taylor & J. Devereaux (Toronto: Canadian Scholars Press, 1991); "An educationally focused faculty/field program for first-time field instructors" (*Journal of Education for Social Work* 1981); "Social work practice with family systems in admission to homes for the aged" (*Journal of Gerontological Social Work* 1987); "A teaching model to unite classroom and field," with E. Vayda (*Journal of Social Work Education* 1991); "The student/field instructor relationship: the critical factor in field education" (*The Clinical Supervisor* 1993); numerous other publications. AFFIL: American Association for Marriage & Family Therapy (Clinical Mbr. & Approved Supervisor); Ontario Association of Professional Social Workers; Council on Social Work Education; Ontario Coll. of Certified Social Workers; Canadian Association of Schools of Social Work; International Association of Schools of Social Work; Baycrest Centre for Geriatric Care (Dir.). HONS: Teaching Excellence Award, Fac. of Social Work, Univ. of Toronto, 1990, 1991, 1992, 1995. INTERESTS: social work clinical practice; social work educ. in nat'l & int'l context. COMMENT: *"I am a clinical social worker, educator and researcher and have developed models for educating professional social workers. I have authored numerous articles, books, and manuals on social work education and have been an international consultant to schools of social work, especially in Japan."*

Bohac-Konrad, Lucie M., B.A.,M.A. ♡ ☺

Executive Director, CANADIAN YOUTH FOUNDATION, 215 Cooper St., 3rd Fl., Ottawa, ON K2P 0G2 (613) 231-6474, FAX 231-6497, EMAIL lbk@cyberplus.ca. Born Litomerice, Czech Republic 1962. m. Victor A. Konrad. EDUC: Univ. of Lethbridge, B.A.(Modern Languages & Pol. Sci.) 1984; Carleton Univ., M.A.(Public Admin.) 1989. CAREER: Consultant, Canadian International Development Agency, 1987; Program Officer, Canadian Studies Awards Program, International Council for Canadian Studies, 1987-88; Dir. of Youth Initiatives Program, Canadian International Development Agency, 1988-91; Exec. Dir., Canadian Youth Foundation, 1991 to date. SELECTED PUBLICATIONS: *More Than Words: Meeting the Needs of Youth Literacy Learners*, ed.; *Youth Action: A Report of the Canada 125 Youth Community Workshops*, ed.; *Youth Unemployment: Canada's Rite of Passage*, ed.; *Youth Unemployment: Canada's Hidden Deficit*, ed. AFFIL: National Youth-Serving Agencies Executives; Canadian Society of Association Executives; Canadian Commission to UNESCO, The Canadian Youth Business Foundation (Dir. of the Bd.); AIESEC (Dir. of the Bd.); Social Sciences & Humanities Subcommission; World University Service of Canada (Alumnus). INTERESTS: music of the Renaissance; writing; poetry; travel; debating; theatre (acting & directing); showing & training dogs; cycling; swimming. COMMENT: *"As one of the key forces behind the conception and development of the Canadian Youth Business Foundation, Ms. Bohac Konrad has not only been instrumental in putting the issue of youth unemployment on the public agenda, but also taking the issue one step further, in creating an innovative solution to the employment challenges facing young Canadians."*

Bol, Nancy Ann, B.Sc.N.,M.Sc.N. ⊕
Clinical Nurse Specialist - Gerontology, PARKWOOD HOSPITAL, 801 Commissioners Rd. E., London, ON N6C 5J1 (519) 685-4292, ext 2016, FAX 685-4052. Born Chatham, Ont. 1949. d. 1 ch. EDUC: Univ. of Western Ontario, B.Sc.N. 1972, M.Sc.N.(Educ.) 1989. CAREER: Staff Nurse, Victoria Hospital, 1972; Staff Nurse, Middlesex-London Health Unit, 1972-80; Coord., Pyschogeriatric Clinic, Victoria Hospital, 1980-87; Clinical Nurse Specialist-Gerontology, St. Joseph's Health Centre, 1987-90; Clinical Nurse Specialist–Gerontology, Parkwood Hospital, 1987 to date. SELECTED PUBLICATIONS: "The Gerontological Nursing Standards: A Survey Report", with G. Molloy (*Perspectives* 17(1) 1993); "Extra, Extra Read All About It!," book review (*The Canadian Gerontological Nurse* 10(3) 1993); "Behaviour Therapy in Long-Term Care," with M. Gibson (*Canadian Nursing Home*, 7 (1), 16-20); "Residents' perspectives of their first two weeks in a long-term care facility," with C. Iwasiw, D. Goldenberg, E. MacMaster & S. McCutcheon (*Journal of Clinical Nursing*, in press). AFFIL: Committee on Abuse & Neglect of the Elderly, Inc. (Chair 1994-96); Univ. of

Western Ontario/Fanshawe Coll. (Collaborative Curriculum Committee); Canadian Gerontological Nursing Association (Pres. 1993-95); Canadian Clinical Nurse Specialist Interest Group; Registered Nursing Association of Ontario; Gerontological Nursing Association of Ontario; Alzheimer Society for London & Middlesex. HONS: Mbr., Sigma Theta Tau, International Honour Society of Nursing; Being the Best You Can Be tribute, for "Exemplary Professional Commitment to patient care, her profession & her community," Parkwood Hospital, 1993. INTERESTS: promotion of women's health issues. MISC: numerous community presentations; various conference presentations; enrolled part-time in the Primary Care Nurse Practitioner Program. COMMENT: *"My achievements are reflections of colleagues and mentors who, over the years, encouraged and supported my endeavours."*

Boland, The Hon. Janet Lang, B.A.,Q.C., D.C.L.,LL.D. ⚖
Judge, Trial Division, SUPREME COURT OF ONTARIO, Osgoode Hall, Toronto, ON M5H 2N5. Born Kitchener, Ont. 1928. m. 3 ch. EDUC: Univ. of Western Ontario, B.A.; Osgoode Hall Law Sch. BAR: Ont., 1950. CAREER: private law practice, 1950-58; Lawyer, White, Bristol, Beck & Phipps, Toronto, 1958-68; Ptnr, Lang, Michener, Farquharson, Cranston & Wright, Toronto, 1968-72; Judge, County of York, 1972-76; Judge, Trial Div., Supreme Court of Ontario, 1976 to date. HONS: D.C.L.(Hon.) 1974 & LL.D. (Hon.) 1976, Wilfrid Laurier Univ. INTERESTS: skiing; tennis; travel.

Bolley, Andrea, B.F.A. ⊗
Artist. 3 Riverdale Ave., Toronto, ON M4K 1C2 (416) 466-0742. Born Guelph, Ont. 1949. EDUC: Univ. of Windsor, B.F.A. 1975. EXHIBITIONS: numerous group exhibitions incl. *49th Annual Canadian Painters in Watercolour*, Toronto (1974), Gallery One, Toronto (1984, 1985, 1987), & Triangle, N.Y. City (1985, 1991, 1992, 1993); solo exhibitions: IDA Gallery, York Univ. (1976), Pollock Gallery, Toronto (1977, 1978, 1980), the Art Gallery of Brant, Brantford, Ont. (1977), Agnes Etherington Art Centre, Kingston, Ont. (1981), Gallery One, Toronto (1984, 1985, 1986), Klonardis Gallery, Toronto (1989, 1990, 1991), & Upper Canada Brewing Co. (1993); Studio Show, Toronto (1994, 1995, 1996). COLLECTIONS: Canada Council Art Bank; Art Gallery of Windsor; American Express; Triangle, NY, The Elmwood Club; numerous other corp. collections; private collections in Canada, US & Europe. HONS: OSA Purchase Award,

1976; Labatt's Ltd. Purchase Award, 1976; Canadian Imperial Bank of Commerce Purchase Award, 1977; First Prize, painting, Annual Aviva Show, 1979; OSA Purchase Award, J.E. Seagram and Son Ltd., 1980. MISC: recipient of various grants; subject of articles in various periodicals.

Bondar, Roberta Lynn, O.C.,O.Ont.,M.D., Ph.D.,F.R.C.P.(C),CIBC Disting. ❀ ⊕ ♂
CIBC Distinguished Professor, Faculty of Kinesiology, THE UNIVERSITY OF WESTERN ONTARIO, Thames Hall, London, ON N6A 3K7 (519) 661-4091, FAX 661-3774. Born Sault Ste. Marie, Ont. EDUC: Univ. of Guelph, B.Sc. 1968; Univ. of Western Ontario, M.Sc. 1971, F.R.C.P.(C) 1981; Univ. of Toronto, Ph.D. 1974; McMaster Univ., M.D. 1977. CAREER: Research Asst. (Genetics), Fed. Dept. of Fisheries & Forestry, 1963-68; Lecturer, Dept. of Phys. Educ., Univ. of Guelph, 1966-67; Coach, Univ. Archery Team, 1966-67; Histology Tech. (part-time), Dept. of Zoology, 1967-68; Teaching Asst., Dept. of Zoology, Univ. of Toronto, 1970-74; Intern, Internal Medicine, Toronto General Hospital, 1977-78; Resident, Neurology, Dept. of Clinical Neurosciences, Univ. of Western Ontario, 1978-80; Resident, Neuropathology, 1980; Neuroopthamology Fellow, MOH Fellowship, Dept. of Opthamology, Tuft's New England Medical Center, 1981; Neuro-opthamology Fellow, MRC Fellowship, Playfair Neuroscience Unit, Toronto Western Hospital, 1981-82; Asst. Prof., Dept. of Medicine, Div. of Neurology, McMaster Univ., 1982-84; Dir., Multiple Sclerosis Clinic, Hamilton Wentworth Reg., 1982-84; Cdn Astronaut, Cdn Astronaut Program, Canadian Space Agency, 1984-92; Lecturer, Dept. of Nursing, Univ. of Ottawa, 1985-88; Chair, Cdn Life Sciences Committee for Space Station, Nat'l Research Council of Canada, 1985-89; Civil Aviation Medical Examiner, Health & Welfare Canada, 1986-93; Research Fellow, Playfair Institute Oculomotor Laboratory, 1989; Mbr. of Premier of Ontario's Council on Science & Technology, 1986-90; Life Sciences Rep., Canadian Advisory Council on the Scientific Utilization of Space Station, 1986-88; Lecturer, Dept. of National Defence Flight Surgeon course, 1986-92; Payload Specialist Candidate for the First Int'l Microgravity Lab. Shuttle Flight, 1989-90; Prime Payload Specialist for the First Int'l Microgravity Lab. Shuttle Flight, 1990-92; Adjunct Prof., Dept. of Biol., Univ. of New Mexico, 1991-93; Crew Mbr., PS1, STS-42, First Int'l Microgravity Lab., 1992; Mbr., Public Advisory Commission on State of the Environment Reporting, 1992-95; Visiting Distinguished Fellow, Fac. of Health

Sciences, McMaster Univ., 1993-94; Sr. Advisor, Royal Commission on Learning, Prov. of Que., 1993-95; Chair, Friends of the Environment Foundation, Canada Trust, 1993-96; Mbr., Advisory Bd., Order of Canada, 1993-94; Visiting Distinguished Prof., Fac. of Kinesiology, Univ. of Western Ontario, 1994-96; CIBC Distinguished Prof., 1996-97; Consultant, Nominations to the Order of Canada, 1995. SELECTED PUBLICATIONS: *Touching The Earth* (Toronto: Key Porter, 1994); *On The Shuttle*, with B.C. Bondar (Toronto: Greey de Pencier, 1993); "Neurofilamentous Changes in Goldfish (*Carassius auratus*, L.) Brain in Relation to Environmental Temperature" (*Journal of Neuropathology and Neurology* 36 1977); "Development of Gila" In E. Schoffeniels, G. Franck, L. Hertz, D.B. Tower (Eds.), *Dynamic Properties of Gila Cells* (Pergamon Press 1978); "Medical Technology in Space" (*Ontario Medical Technology* 1984); "Canadian Medical Experiments on Shuttle Flight 41-G" (*Canadian Aeronautics and Space Journal* 31 1985); "Flow Velocities by Transcranial Doppler during Parabolic Flight" (*Journal of Clinical Pharmacology* 31 1991); "Space Qualified Humans: The High Five" (*Aviation, Space and Environmental Medicine* 65(2) 1994); "Spacelog STS-42–Discovery," in *If You Love This Country* (Penguin Books Canada Limited, 1995); "Simultaneous Cerebrovascular and Cardiovascular Responses During Presyncope," with M.S. Kassam, F. Stein *et al* (*Stroke* 26 1995); "Subnormal Norepinephrine release relates to presyncope in astronauts after spaceflight," with J.M. Fritsch-Yelle *et al* (*Journal of Applied Physiology*, in press); "Coarse Graining Spectral Analysis of Heart Rate and Blood Pressure Variability in Patients with Automatic Failure," with A.P. Blaber & R. Freeman (*American Journal of Physiology*, in press); numerous other refereed & unrefereed publications; 30+ abstracts. AFFIL: Aerospace Medical Association; American Academy of Neurology; Association of Space Explorers; Canadian Aeronautics & Space Institute; Canadian Association of Sports Medicine; Canadian Federation of University Women; Canadian Medical Protective Association; Canadian Society of Aerospace Medicine; Coll. of Physicians & Surgeons of Ont.; Federation of Medical Women of Canada; Greater Albuquerque Medical Association; Royal Coll. of Physicians & Surgeons of Canada. HONS: Reg'l Winner, Rotary Science Fair, 1963; Sports Woman of the Year, Sir James Dunn Collegiate & Vocational Sch., 1963; G.A.A. Leadership Award, Sir James Dunn Collegiate & Vocational Sch., 1964; William A. Vanderburgh, Sr. Travel Award, 1976; Career Scientist Award, Prov. Ministry of

Health, 1982-83; Special Achievement Award, Hamilton Status of Women Committee, Women of the Year Awards, 1984; Co-recipient, F.W. (Casey) Baldwin Award, Canadian Aeronautics & Space Institute, 1985; Vanier Award, Outstanding Young Canadian, Jaycees of Canada, 1985; Excellence in Public Educ. Awards, Ont. Secondary Sch. Teachers' Federation, 1990; Presidential Citation of Honor, Alabama Agricultural & Mechanical Univ., 1990; William R. Franks M.D. Award, Canadian Society of Aerospace Medicine, 1990; Sault Ste. Marie Medal of Merit, 1991; Alumnus of the Year, Univ. of Western Ontario, 1992; Award of Merit, Univ. of Western Ontario Alumni, 1992; Canada 125 Medal, 1992; Hubertus Strughold Award, Space Medicine Branch - Aerospace Medicine Association, 1992; La Personalité de L'Année 1992, *La Presse*; Médaille de L'Excellence, L'Association des Médecins de Langue Française du Canada, 1992; NASA Space Medal, 1992; President's Award, The Coll. of Physicians & Surgeons of Ont., 1992; Presidential Citation, American Academy of Neurology; Proud to be Canadian Medal, Canada 125, MacLachlan Coll. & Preparatory Sch., Oakville, Ont., 1992; Officer of the Order of Canada, 1992; Paul Harris Recognition Award, 1992; Order of Ontario, 1993; Alumnus of the Year, Univ. of Guelph, 1993; *Eaton's Salutes Canadian Women: A Premiere in Canada*, in collaboration with the Status of Women Canada & the Sec. of State, 1993; Inductee, Hamilton Gallery of Distinction, 1993; Kurt Hahn Award, Outward Bound, 1993; Outstanding Canadian, Armenian Community Centre of Toronto, 1993; YWCA Woman of Distinction Award, 1993; Communication & Leadership Award, Toastmasters District 60, 1994; Int'l Women's Day Award, Women's Intercultural Ntwk, 1995; Canadian Unity Award, Thornhill Secondary Sch., Thornhill, Ont., 1995; D.Sc.(Hon.), McMaster Univ., 1992; D.Sc.(Hon.), Mount Allison Univ., 1989; D.Hum.L.(Hon.), Mount Saint Vincent Univ., 1990; Fellow, Ryerson Polytechnic Institute, 1990; D.Sc.(Hon.), Univ. of Guelph, 1990; D.Sc.(Hon.), Lakehead Univ., 1991; D.Sc. (Hon.), Algoma Coll., Laurentian Univ., 1991; D.Sc.(Hon.), Saint Mary's Univ., 1992; LL.D.(Hon.), Univ. of Regina, 1992; D.Sc. (Hon.), Univ. of Toronto, 1992; LL.D.(Hon.), Univ. of Calgary, 1992; D.U.(Hon.), Univ. of Ottawa, 1992; D.Sc.(Hon.), McGill Univ., 1992; D.Sc.(Hon.), York Univ., 1992; D.S.L.(Hon.), Wycliffe Coll., Univ. of Toronto, 1993; D.Sc.(Hon.), Royal Roads Military Coll., 1993; D.Sc.(Hon.), Laval Univ., 1993; D.Sc.(Hon.), Carleton Univ., 1993; D.Sc.

(Hon.), Univ. of Prince Edward Island, 1994; D.Sc.(Hon.), Univ. of Montréal, 1994; D.Sc. (Hon.), Univ. of Western Ontario, 1995. **HONORARY APPOINTMENTS:** Hon. Life Mbr., Canadian Federation of University Women, 1985; Hon. Life Mbr., Girl Guides of Canada, 1986; Hon. Patron, Young Scientists of Canada, 1987; Hon. Event Dir., Echo Valley '88, International Camp, Girl Guides for Canada, 1987; Hon. Life Mbr., Federation of Medical Women in Canada, 1991; Mbr. Hon., L'Association des Médecins de Langue Française du Canada, 1992; Hon. Patron, Mission Air Transport Network, 1992; Hon. Patron, Canadian Federation of Business & Professional Women's Clubs, 1992; Hon. Mbr., Algoma West Academy of Medicine, 1992; Hon. Mbr., The Dominion of Canada Rifle Association, 1992; Hon. Life Mbr., Science North, 1992; Hon. Chair, Parkinson Foundation of Canada, 1993; Hon. Life Mbr., Zonta International, 1993; Hon. Patron, The Aphasia Centre, 1993; Hon. Patron, Ontario Bushplane Heritage Centre, 1993; Hon. Patron, Ontario Parks Association, 1993; Hon. Mbr., Bootmakers of Canada (Sherlock Holmes Society), 1993; Hon. Event Dir., Guelph '93, International Camp, Girl Guides of Canada, 1993; Hon. Dir., Canadian Space & Technology Centre, London, 1993; Hon. Dir., Save our North Atlantic Resources, 1993; Hon. Col., 22 Wing, Cdn Armed Forces, 1993-96; Hon. Chair, 24-Hour Relay For Health, Chedoke-McMaster Hospital Foundation, 1993; Hon. Chair, Women's Soccer Competition, World Student Games, 1993; Hon. Chair, Cdn Coalition for Quality Daily Phys. Educ., 1993; Hon. Patron, Youth Science Foundation, 1994; Hon. Patron, Trinity Coll. Sch., 1994; Hon. Patron, Earth Observation Theatre, Fort Whyte Centre, Winnipeg, 1994; Hon. Chair, Canadian National Marsville Program, Ontario Science Centre, 1995; Hon. Patron, 1995 International Math Olympiad; Hon. Dir., The Klondike "All Canadian" Centennial Expedition, 1995; Hon. Life Mbr., Hamilton Academy of Music, 1995; Hon. Chair, Breast Cancer Awareness Month, Canadian Breast Cancer Foundation, 1996. **HONOURS IN THE NAME OF ROBERTA LYNN BONDAR:** Alex Muir Public Sch. Res. Centre, 1992; Place Roberta Bondar Place - Prov. of Ont., 1992; Bawating Collegiate & Vocational Sch. Scholarship, 1992; Girl Guides of Canada Scholarship, 1992; Prov. of Ont. Science & Technology Awards, 1992; Queen Elizabeth Public Sch. Res. Centre, 1992; Roberta Bondar Earth & Space Centre, Seneca Coll., 1992; Roberta Bondar Gymnasium, Sir James Dunn Collegiate & Vocational Sch., 1992; Sir James Dunn Collegiate & Vocational Sch.

Scholarship, 1992; Soo Coll. Scholarship, 1992; Trophies for Outstanding Male & Female Athletes of the Year, Sir James Dunn Collegiate & Vocational Sch., 1992; USS Bondar, The Guelph Trek Club, 1992; Roberta Bondar Science & Technology Awards, Toronto, 1993; Roberta Bondar Rose, Hortico Nurseries, 1993; YWCA Scholarship, Prince Albert, 1993; Roberta Bondar Science & Technology Awards, Toronto, 1994; Roberta Bondar Park & Tent Pavilion, Sault Ste. Marie, 1994; Roberta Bondar Marina, Sault Ste. Marie; Roberta Bondar Sch., Ottawa, 1995; Roberta Bondar Science & Technology Awards, 1995; Dr. Roberta Bondar Public Sch., Ajax, Ont., 1996. **INTERESTS:** flying; photography; biking; hot air ballooning; roller blading. **MISC:** first Cdn woman in space; numerous invited professional & public presentations; Space Flight Surgeon's Training Course, Johnson Space Centre, 1992; Private Pilot's Licence, U.S.; Private Pilot's Licence, Canada; Mbr., Exec., Space Medicine Branch, Aerospace Medical Association, 1992; Co-Chrm, Life Sciences Symposium, Canadian Aeronautics & Space Institute, 1988; Mbr., Gov't of Canada Space Delegation to Moscow, 1988-87; Chair, Biomedicine in Space, 1986; many distinguished lectures, incl. Royal Coll. Lecture, Royal Coll. of Physicians & Surgeons of Canada, 1993 & Lynda Shaw Memorial Lecture, Univ. of Western Ontario, 1994; recipient of various grants; featured, IMAX Film, *Destiny in Space* (1994). **COMMENT:** *"Dr. Roberta L. Bondar, O.C.,O.Ont., Canadian astronaut, medical doctor and scientist, flew aboard the Space Shuttle Discovery on the First International Microgravity Mission, January 22-30, 1992."*

Bonetta, Laura, B.Sc.,Ph.D. ■■ ⚛ 📖 ✊

Assistant Professor, THE PICOWER INSTITUTE FOR MEDICAL RESEARCH (not-for-profit medical research & educ.), 350 Community Dr., Manhasset, NY 11030 (516) 562-9415, FAX 868-8428, EMAIL lbonetta@picower.edu. Born Cremona, Italy 1963. s. **EDUC:** Univ. of Toronto, B.Sc.(Hons., Genetics & English Lit.) 1987, Ph.D.(Human Genetics) 1992. **CAREER:** Post Doctoral Fellow, Imperial Cancer Research Fund, London, U.K., 1992-93 (research topic: genetics of breast cancer); Asst. Editor, *Nature* magazine, McMillan, London, 1993-94; Asst. Prof. & Mng Editor, *Molecular Medicine*, The Picower Institute for Medical Research, 1994 to date. **SELECTED PUBLICATIONS:** numerous incl.: co-author with S. Kuehn *et al*, "Wilms tumor locus of 11p13 defined by multiple CpG island-associated transcripts" (*Science*, 1990); co-author with A. Huang *et al*, "Tissue developmental and tumor-specific expression of divergent transcripts implicated in Wilms tumor locus" (*Science*, 1990); author, "Open questions on p16" (*Nature*, 1994). **AFFIL:** Molecular Medicine Society; Long Island AIDS Association (volunteer). **HONS:** McPherson Award in recognition of Ph.D. thesis, 1990; Postdoctoral research scholarship from Medical Research Council of Canada, 1992-93. **INTERESTS:** films; theatre; travel; literature. **MISC:** fluent in Italian (family moved to Canada, 1975); research carried out for Ph.D. thesis resulted in discovery of a gene that predisposes to kidney cancer in children (Wilms tumour). **COMMENT:** *"I have been drawn to scientific research by my curiosity. The sense of personal achievement and the freedom of being creative are two very rewarding aspects of this work. The added bonus is the opportunity to travel."*

Bonney, Lynda D., B.Math.,C.A.,C.M.A. $

Vice-President, Pension Adminstration and Finance, CROWN LIFE INSURANCE COMPANY (financial svcs), 1901 Scarth St., Regina, SK S4S 6L2 (306) 751-7255, FAX 751-7250. Born Toronto 1958. s. **EDUC:** Univ. of Waterloo, B.Math.(co-op, Acctg) 1982. **CAREER:** Acctnt, Thorne Riddell (now Peat Marwick Thorne), 1982-86; Mgr, Crownx (now Extendicare Inc.), 1986-88; Asst. VP, Corp. Planning, Crown Life Insurance Company, 1988-91; Asst. VP, Pension Admin. & Cont., 1991-94; VP, Pension Admin. & Fin., 1994 to date. **AFFIL:** Association of Chartered Accountants of Ontario; Association of Chartered Accountants of Saskatchewan; Certified Management Accountants' Association.

Boone, Lois, M.L.A. ■ 🍁

Member of Legislative Assembly (Prince George-Mount Robson), GOVERNMENT OF BRITISH COLUMBIA, Legislative Buildings, Victoria, BC V8V 1X4 (604) 387-1978, FAX 356-2290. Born Vancouver 1947. sep. 2 ch. Sonia, Tanis. **EDUC:** Simon Fraser Univ., Teaching Certificate (Hist./English Major) 1969. **CAREER:** elected Member of Sch. Bd., V-Chair & Chair, Fin. & Educ. Committees, Sch. District 57, 1981-85; elected M.L.A., Prov. of B.C., 1986; Min. of Gov't Svcs, 1991-94; Min. Responsible for three Crown Corporations (B.C. Systems, B.C.B.C., B.C. Lottery Group), 1991-93; Min. of Municipal Affairs, 1996; Min. of Trans. & Highways, 1996. **AFFIL:** NDP. **COMMENT:** *"I like to think of myself as a strong voice for the northern interior who has fought for a 'fair share' for that region."*

Boot, Sunni ■■ $ 📺

Senior Vice-President and Executive Director,

OPTIMEDIA CANADA (media mgmt), 245 Eglinton Ave. E., Toronto, ON M4P 3C2 (416) 483-4728, FAX 483-4493. Born Germany. m. J. Gurd Agnew. 2 ch. **AFFIL:** Concerned Children's Advertisers (Pres.); Broadcast Executives' Society (VP); Canadian Film Centre (Dir.); Bureau of Broadcast Measurement (former Bd. mbr.); Canadian Media Directors' Council (Dir.). **HONS:** Media Dir. of the Year, 1992 & 1994. **INTERESTS:** interior design; dogs. **COMMENT:** *"Started Optimedia in July, 1992, and moved it to one of the top five media management companies."*

Booth, Kathleen H.V., B.Sc.,Ph.D. 🏵 🐟

Chief Executive Officer, AUTONETICS RESEARCH ASSOCIATES INCORPORATED, Box 581, Sooke, BC V0S 1N0 (604) 642-5352. Born Warwickshire, UK. m. Dr. Andrew D. Booth. 2 ch. Dr. Ian J. M. Booth, Dr. Amanda J. Booth. **EDUC:** Royal Holloway Coll., B.Sc. 1944; Kings Coll., Univ. of London, Ph.D. 1950. **CAREER:** Jr. Scientific Officer, Royal Aircraft Establishment, 1944-46; Research Scientist, British Rubber Producers' Research Association, 1946-52; Asst., Sch. of Math., Institute for Advanced Study, Princeton, 1947; Research Fellow & Lecturer, Birkbeck Coll., Univ. of London, 1952-62; Research Fellow & Lecturer, Univ. of Saskatchewan, 1962-68; Assoc. Prof. of Math., 1968-72; Hon. Full Prof. of Math., Lakehead Univ., 1972-78; Dir., N.R.C. Proj. on Machine Translation of Language, 1965-73; Mbr., N.R.C. Assoc. Committee on Instructional Technology, 1975-78; CEO, Autonetics Research Associates, 1978 to date. **SELECTED PUBLICATIONS:** *Automatic Digital Calculators*, with A.D. Booth (Academic Press, 1953); *Programming for an Automatic Digital Calculator* (Academic Press, 1958); various conference papers; numerous reviews in *Mathematical Reviews* & *Computing Reviews*. **DIRECTOR:** Autonetics Research Associates Inc.; Wharf Engineering Labs, UK. **INTERESTS:** gardening; travel. **COMMENT:** *"Co-designer of one of the world's first three operational computers, author of two of the earliest books on computer design and programming."*

Borenstein, Joyce, B.A.,M.F.A. 😃 ⊗

Freelance Filmmaker, ILLUMINATION MAGIQUE INC., 2168 Sherbrooke St. W., Ste. 2, Montréal, QC H3H 1G7. **EDUC:** McGill Univ., B.A. 1971; California Institute of the Arts, M.F.A.(Film Animation) 1974. **CAREER:** Animation Lecturer, Fine Arts Coll., Banff, 1973; Animation Lecturer, Montreal Museum Sch. of Fine Arts, 1975-76; Part-time Prof. of Animation, Cinema, Fac. of Fine Arts, Concordia Univ., 1980 to date. **SELECTED CREDITS:**

Opus 1 (1972); *Revisited* (1974); *Traveller's Palm* (1976); *Onions and Garlic* (1977); *Five Billion Years* (1981); *La Plante* (1983); *The Man Who Stole Dreams* (1987); *Colours of My Father, a Portrait of Sam Borenstein* (1991). **HONS:** Second Prize Animation, Cdn Student Film Festival, 1973; First Prize, Cdn Student Film Festival, 1974; Silver Award, Children's Films, Houston Int'l Film Festival, 1983; Second Prize, Cracow Int'l Film Festival, 1983; First Prize, World Film Festival, Montreal, 1983; First Prize, Nat'l Educational Film Festival, 1985; Special Jury Prize, Banff Int'l TV Festival, 1991; Best Short Documentary, Yorkton Film Festival, 1991; Quebec-Alberta Prize for Innovation in Cinema, 1991; Prime de la Qualité, SOGIC, 1991; Best Short Documentary, Genie Awards, 1991; Special Jury Prize, Nat'l Educational Film & Video Festival, Oakland, Calif., 1992; Blue Ribbon, American Film & Video Festival, Chicago, 1992; FIFART Prize, Festival of Films on Art, Lauzanne, Switzerland, 1992. **COMMENT:** *"Filmmaker of animation/documentary films; teacher of animation; writer/illustrator of children's books."*

Borenstein, L'Honorable Sylviane, LL.B., Q.C. ⚖️

Justice, SUPERIOR COURT OF QUEBEC, Courthouse, 1 Notre-Dame St. E., Rm. 11.96, Montreal, QC H2Y 1B6 (514) 393-6683. Born 1943. 4 ch. Richard, Lorna, Marianne, Marc. **EDUC:** graduated Sir George Williams Univ. (now Concordia), 1963; graduated McGill Univ., 1966. **BAR:** Que., 1967. **CAREER:** Assoc., Amaron & Stead, Dorval, 1967-73; Dir., Legal Aid Office, Outremont/Parc Extension, 1973-94; Justice, Superior Court of Que., 1994 to date. **SELECTED PUBLICATIONS:** numerous newspaper, magazine & other articles. **AFFIL:** mbr. until appointment as Justice: Que. Bar (Pres. 1990-91); Canadian Bar Association (Task Force on Racism; Council; Int'l & Nat'l Committee consulting committees of the Ministry of Justice on legal aid for francophone women in Africa 1992-93; Advisory Committee for the prep. of the Nat'l Seminar on Women, Law & Justice 1991); Canadian Foundation for Human Rights (First VP); l'Auberge Transition (shelter for battered women) (Hon. Pres.); Canadian Jewish Congress (Nat'l Exec.; Dir., Que. Div.; Co-Pres., Law & Social Action Committee; Constitution & Charter Revision Committee; Status of Women Committee, Que. Branch); Baron de Hirsch Institute (Exec., Jewish Family Svcs); Federation of Jewish Women's Career Network; Association of Women University Graduates; F.R.A.P.P.E. (Femmes regroupées pour l'accessibilité au Pouvoir Politique et Economique). **HONS:** Queen's Counsel, Q.C., 1992; Canada 125 Medal. **MISC:** speaker at many seminars & conventions; guest on radio & TV shows; chair of many workshops & panels.

Boreskie, Suzanne Louise (Rocan), B.Phys.Ed.,M.Phys.Ed. ⊕ Ⓢ ⑪
Executive Director, THE WELLNESS INSTITUTE AT SEVEN OAKS GENERAL HOSPITAL, 2300 McPhilips St., Winnipeg, MB R2Y 3M3 (203) 632-3441, FAX 697-2106. Born Winnipeg 1958. m. Mark. 2 ch. **EDUC:** Univ. of Manitoba, B.Phys.Ed. 1980, M.Phys.Ed. 1982. **CAREER:** Fitness & Lifestyle Instructor, Kinsmen Reh-Fit Centre, Winnipeg, 1981-84; Cardiac Tech., Cardiology Dept., Health Sciences Centre, 1984-85; Dir., Target Fitness Centre, Fac. of Phys. Educ. & Recreation Studies, Univ. of Manitoba, 1985-93; Dir. of Recreation Svcs, 1993-94; Research Assoc., Health, Leisure & Human Performance Research Institute, Univ. of Manitoba, 1993 to date; Asst. Prof., Univ. of Manitoba, 1994 to date; Exec. Dir., The Wellness Institute at Seven Oaks General Hospital, 1994 to date. **SELECTED PUBLICATIONS:** *For Nine Months and More: a Guide for Physical Activity During Pregnancy* (1994); "Heart Rate Response and Time Motion Analysis of Rhythmic Sportive Gymnastics," with M.J.L. Alexander & S.A. Law (*Journal of Human Movement Studies* 1987); "Exercise, Obesity & Type II Diabetes," with A.E. Ready (*Diabetes Dialogue* 40(2) 1993); various refereed articles & abstracts, unrefereed articles & confidential reports to gov'ts & granting agencies. **AFFIL:** Canadian Society of Exercise Physiology; American Coll. of Sport Medicine; Canadian Association for Health, Physical Education & Recreation; Association for Worksite Health Promotion; Canadian Aerobic Instructors' Network (CAIN) Inc.; International Dance & Exercise Association (IDEA); International Committee for Athletes with Mental Handicaps (Tech. Committee); Commonwealth Games Association of Canada (Mbr. at large); Canadian Association for Athletes with a Mental Handicap (Pres.); Canadian Olympic Association ("B" Mbr.); Manitoba Fitness Appraisal Certification & Accreditation (Dir.). **HONS:** YM-YWCA Women of the Year Award, Fitness, Recreation & Sport Category, 1990; Syd B. Glenesk Award of Merit, Manitoba Parks & Recreation Association, 1990; Young Professional Award, Canadian Association of Health, Physical Education & Recreation, 1991; Dr. & Mrs. D.R. Campbell Outreach Award, Univ. of Manitoba, 1993; Hon. Life Mbr., Manitoba Sports Federation, 1996. **INTERESTS:** gourmet club; physical activity; gardening. **MISC:** recipient of various grants; numerous presentations

& workshops; Olympic Youth Camp Cdn Delegation Leader, Seoul Olympics, chosen by the Canadian Olympic Association, 1988. **COMMENT:** *"Executive Director of the Wellness Institute, first of its kind in Canada, Sue Boreskie has focused on women's health issues, sport and wellness, and seeks to advance health promotion programs Canada-wide."*

Borgese, Elisabeth Mann, B.A. ⊗ ❀
Founder and Honorary President, INTERNATIONAL OCEAN INSTITUTE, MALTA, 1226 Le Marchant St., Halifax, NS B3H 3P7 (902) 494-1737, FAX 494-2034, EMAIL ioihfx@ ac.dal.ca. Professor, Political Science, DALHOUSIE UNIVERSITY. Born Munich, Germany 1918. w. 2 ch. Angelica, Dominica. **EDUC:** Freies Gymnasium, Zurich, B.A.(Classical Studies) 1935; Conservatory of Music, Zurich, Diploma (Piano) 1937. **CAREER:** Research Assoc., Univ. of Chicago, 1939; Ed., *Common Cause*, Univ. of Chicago Press, 1948-52; Ed., *Diogenes* (UNESCO) Perspectives USA (Intercultural Publications), 1953-63; Exec. Sec., Bd. of Ed., Encyclopedia Britannica, 1964-66; Sr. Fellow, Center for the Study of Democratic Institutions, 1964-79; Chrm, Int'l Centre for Ocean Dev., 1987-92; Prof., Pol. Sci., Dalhousie Univ., 1979 to date. **SELECTED PUBLICATIONS:** *To Whom it May Concern* (1962); *Ascent of Woman* (1962); *The White Snake* (1964); *The Ocean Regime* (1968); *The Drama of the Oceans* (1976); *Seafarm* (1981); *The Mines of Neptune* (1985); *The Future of the Oceans* (1987); *Chairworm and Supershark* (1992), a book for children; *Ocean Governance and the United Nations* (1995); *Pacem in Maribus* (Ed., 1972); *Tides of Change* (Ed., 1976); *Ocean Frontiers* (Ed., 1992); *Ocean Yearbook* (Ed., Vols. 1-10, 1982 to date); *Only the Pyre* a play performed at Pirandello festival in Italy, with music by Franco Mannino); numerous monographs in ocean affairs & papers in int'l law & pol. sci. journals. **AFFIL:** Club of Rome; World Academy of Arts and Sciences; Third World Academy of Science Club of Rome; World Academy of Arts & Sciences. **HONS:** Medal of High Merit, Gov't of Austria; Gold Medal, Gov't of Malta; Order of Canada; Sasakawa United Nations Environment Prize; Order of Columbia; Friendship Award, Gov't of China; St. Francis of Assisi Int'l Environment Prize; Doctor in Humanities (Hon.), Mount St. Vincent Univ. **INTERESTS:** int'l rel'ns; int'l law; law of the sea; environment; development; disarmament; music; literature; animal intelligence. **COMMENT:** *"Founded International Ocean Institute 25 years ago, remained very active throughout as Chairman of the Planning Council in the devel-*

opment, expansion (worldwide) and intellectual leadership."

Borghesi, Carol ■ $ ☝

Assistant Vice-President, Business and Corporate Accounts, **BC TEL**, 768 Seymour, Ste. 2A, Vancouver, BC V6B 3K9 (604) 663-6286, FAX 685-6903. Born Vancouver 1957. m. George. 1 ch. **EDUC:** B.C. Institute of Technology, Diploma of Technology (Int'l Mktg, magna cum laude) 1981. **CAREER:** Product Analyst, Prod. Mktg Dept., BC Tel, 1981; Sales Merchandising Coord., Bus. Telecom Equip. Div., 1982; Sales Admin. Mgr, B.T.E. Div., 1986; Account Mgr, BC Tel Mobility Cellular, 1987; Major Acct. Sales Mgr, Bus. Div., 1989; Gen. Sales Mgr, Small Bus. & Consumer Div., 1991; Dir., Residential Sales, 1993-95; Asst. VP, Bus. & Corp. Accts, 1995 to date. **AFFIL:** Board of Trade; Technical Sales Advisory Committee; Telephone Pioneers of America General Assembly (Chair, Host/Hostess Sub-Committee); B.C./Yukon Heart & Stroke Foundation. **HONS:** Outstanding Achievement Award, Int'l Mktg Program, BCIT, 1981; Mktg Executive of the Year, B.C. Sales & Mktg Executives, 1996. **INTERESTS:** theatre; movies; horseback riding; walking; reading; cooking; sales & mktg; strategy dev. & implementation; public speaking. **MISC:** 1st woman to be appointed sales mgr, BC Tel Bus. Div.; mbr., Stentor National Telemarketing User Group & Stentor Consumer Long Distance Strategy Team; mbr., Total People Strategy Team, 1992 to 1994. **COMMENT:** *"Joined BC Tel "pre-competition," enjoying a variety of increasingly challenging, responsible roles in the rapidly changing telecommunications environment. Have had the opportunity to work in senior positions in strategically important areas of this business. Spare time these days is spent enjoying my finest achievement, my daughter Julia."*

Bornemann, Rebeccah ■■ ⚾

Paralympic Athlete. Vancouver, BC. **EDUC:** Univ. of Alberta, grad. student in sports studies. **SPORTS CAREER:** mbr., Nat'l Swim Team, 1989 to date. Paralympic Games: Gold, 400m freestyle, 1996; Bronze, 100m & 400m freestyle, 4th 50m freestyle, 1992. Int'l Paralympic Swim Trials: 1st, 100m & 400m freestyle, 2nd 50m freestyle. IPC World Championships: 4th, 400m freestyle, 5th, 50m & 100m, freestyle, 100m butterfly, 1994. Commonwealth Games: 6th, 100m freestyle, 1994.

Borson, Roo, B.A.,M.F.A. 📜 ✲ 🎓

Writer. c/o The Writers' Union of Canada, 24 Ryerson Ave., Toronto, ON M5T 2P3. Born Berkeley, Calif. 1952. **EDUC:** Goddard Coll., B.A.(Poetry) 1973; Univ. of British Columbia, M.F.A.(Creative Writing) 1977. **SELECTED PUBLICATIONS:** *Landfall* (Fiddlehead, 1977); *In the Smoky Light of the Fields* (Three Trees, 1980); *Rain* (Penumbra Press, 1980); *A Sad Device* (Quadrant Editions, 1981); *The Whole Night, Coming Home* (McClelland & Stewart, 1984); *The Transparence of November/Snow*, with Kim Maltman (Quarry Press, 1985); *Intent, or the Weight of the World* (McClelland & Stewart, 1989); *Night Walk: Selected Poems* (Oxford University Press, 1994); *Water Memory* (McClelland & Stewart, 1996). **AFFIL:** The Writers' Union of Canada; PEN Canada; League of Canadian Poets; PMB (collaborative poetry group consisting of Roo Borson, Kim Maltman, Andy Patton). **HONS:** MacMillan Prize for Poetry, 1977; 1st Prize for Poetry, CBC Literary Competition, 1982; CBC Literary Awards, 2nd Prize for Poetry, 1989 & 3rd Prize for Essay, 1991; nominated for Gov. Gen.'s Award, 1984, 1994. **INTERESTS:** math; Mandarin Chinese. **MISC:** Writer In Residence, Univ. of Western Ontario, 1987-88 & Concordia Univ., 1993. **COMMENT:** *"Poet and essayist."*

Borwein, Bessie, Ph.D. ■■ ⊕ ♡ ☺

Assistant Dean - Research, Faculty of Medicine, **UNIVERSITY OF WESTERN ONTARIO**, Medical Science Bldg., London, ON N6A 5C1 (519) 661-4097, FAX 661-4043, EMAIL bborwein@do.med.uwo.ca. Born Johannesburg, S. Africa 1927. m. David Borwein. 3 ch. Jonathan, Peter, Sarah. **EDUC:** Univ. of the Witwatersrand, B.Sc.(Botany & Zoology) 1947, B.Sc.(Hons., Botany) 1948; Univ. of Western Ontario, Ph.D. (Anatomy) 1973. **CAREER:** High Sch. Biol. Teacher, St. Leonard's Sch. for Girls, St. Andrew's, Scotland, 1955-59; Assoc. Prof., Anatomy, Univ. of Western Ontario, 1984 to date; Assoc. Dean-Research, Fac. of Medicine, 1987-92; Asst. Dean-Research, Fac. of Medicine, 1992 to date; Chrm, Review Bd. for Health Sciences Research Involving Human Subjects, 1986 to date. **SELECTED PUBLICATIONS:** 15 articles on ultra-structure of retina in scientific journals; 1 book chpt. **AFFIL:** Partners in Research (founding Bd. mbr. 1988); Foundation for Gene & Cell Therapy (Bd. Mbr. 1994 to date); Youth Science Foundation (Team Canada Judge 1994, 1995); Ontario Breast Screening Program (Chair, Community Advisory Committee, London 1994; Research Advisory Panel, Ont. 1994); Alzheimer Society of London (Research Committee); Professional Women of London; National Council of Jewish Women; Canadian Bioethics Society. **HONS:** Gordin Kaplan Award for public awareness of science, Canadian Federation of Biological Societies, 1992; Commemorative Medal for 125th Anniversary of Cdn Confederation, 1993; Women of Distinction Award, YM-YWCA, 1984. **COMMENT:** *"My activities, occupations and interests have included: high school biology teacher (Scotland); researcher; public awareness and knowledge of science—many talks, radio, TV, articles; being a mother; grandmother of 9; friends; attracting the young into science; Jewish affairs; community activities; walking; travel; bridge; film; theatre; public issues and affairs."*

Bosley, Nicole, B.A. ■■ $ ♡
Executive Director, WATERCAN/EAU VIVE (int'l dev.-water), 323 Chapel St., Ottawa, ON K1N 7Z2 (613) 230-5182, FAX 230-5934 or 237-5969, EMAIL ag995@freenet.carleton.ca. Born Rougemont, Que. 1941. m. The Hon. John W. Bosley. 1 ch. Stephane Novak. **EDUC:** Coll. Édouard Montpetit, Humanities 1974; Concordia Univ., B.A.(Communications) 1976. **CAREER:** Exec. Dir., Parliament Hill TV Bureau, Rogers Cable, 1981-83; Communications Consultant to MPs & sr. executives, 1983-84; (as wife of Speaker of the House of Commons) managed 100+ diplomatic dinners & decorated the official residence of the Speaker, the Farms at Kingsmere, 1984-87. **SELECTED CREDITS:** *Hommage à Ozias Leduc* (TV production, 1977). **SELECTED PUBLICATIONS:** *Les Grandes Recettes d'Ambassades* (Art Global, 1991–award winning). **AFFIL:** Nectar et Ambroisie. **INTERESTS:** travel; reading; music; theatre; entertaining. **COMMENT:** *"I have done volunteer work for several organizations, including Canfar, the World Monument Fund, the National Ballet of Canada, Alliance Française, and the Parliamentary Spouses' Association. I have also been a television producer and program analyst."*

Bottone, Kelly F., B.Comm., M.B.A. ■ $
Director, Planning and Research, and Secretariat for Full Service Credit Unions, CREDIT UNION CENTRAL OF ONTARIO, 2810 Matheson Blvd. E., Mississauga, ON L4W 4X7 (905) 629-5507, FAX 238-8691. Born Toronto. m. Gary D. Eisen. 1 ch. Caroline Siobhan Eisen. **EDUC:** Univ. of Toronto, B.Comm. 1983; Univ. of British Columbia, M.B.A. 1985. **CAREER:** Coord., Lease Control Group, Husky Oil Operations Ltd., 1985-87; Sr. Consultant, Ernst & Young, 1987-91; Mgr, Planning, Central Guaranty Trust, 1991-92. **AFFIL:** Certified Management Consultant (CMC).

Bouchard, Linda, D.E.C.,B.A.,M.M. ■ ⊛
Composer/Conductor. P.O. Box 530, Stn C, Montreal, QC H2V 3Z9 (514) 276-2694, FAX 276-2696. Born Val d'Or, Que. 1957. **EDUC:** Vanier Coll., D.E.C.(Music) 1976; Bennington Coll., Vermont, B.A.(Music) 1979; Manhattan Sch. of Music, M.M.(Composition) 1982. **CAREER:** Teacher, Bronx Music Sch., 1982-85; Teacher, Schumiatcher Sch., 1982-83; Asst. to the Music Dir., St. Luke's Performing Arts Ensemble, 1984-86; Asst. Conductor, Children's Free Opera of N.Y., 1985-88; Artistic Dir., Abandon, 1987 to date; Principal Conductor, Putnam Symphony, 1988-90; Principal Conductor, Essential Music, 1988-91; Artistic Coord., GRIMVS, Univ. of Montreal, 1991; Guest Conductor, Atelier de Musique Contemporaine, Univ. of Montreal, 1990-92; Music Dir., Banff Centre for the Performing Arts, 1994; Composer-in-residence, National Arts Centre Orchestra, 1992-95. **SELECTED CREDITS:** *Pourtinade*, with Kim Kashkashian (Germany: ECM, 1990); *Élan* with l'Orchestre Métropolitain conducted by Walter Boudreau (Canada: SRC/CBC, 1991); *Black Burned Wood* with Dora Ohrenstein (US: CRI, 1993); *Lung Ta* with Bang on a Can (US: CRI, 1994); has conducted for numerous bodies incl. the Oregon Bach Festival, the San Francisco Contemporary Music Players, the National Arts Centre Orchestra, the American Dance Festival, N.Y. New Music Ensemble, New Music Consort; organized & produced new music concerts incl. "New Music for Violas," N.Y., 1979, "Spatial Music," N.Y., 1983, & "Precious Metals," N.Y., 1986; provided reductions, arrangements & orchestrations for various bodies incl. Washington Ballet, the Rutgers Musikfest & various churches; numerous commissions incl. Musée d'Arts Contemporain de Montréal, 1990, & Bang-on-a-Can Festival, N.Y., 1992. **AFFIL:** Canadian Music Centre (Assoc. Composer 1991); MacDowell Colony (Alpha Chi Omega Fellow); Guilde des Musiciens; Performing Rights Organization of Canada-SOCAN; American Music Center; N.Y. Women Composers; Minnesota Composers' Forum; N.Y. Composers' Forum. **HONS:** Presser Scholar Foundation Award, 1978; First Prize, National Association of Composers USA Contest, *Ma Lune Maligne*, 1981; First Prize, PROCAN Composition Contest in Vocal Music, *Triskelion*, 1983; First Prize, PROCAN Composition Contest in Chamber Music, *Revelling of Men*, 1984; First Prize, Indiana State Univ. Contest, Fanorev, 1986; First Prize, PROCAN Composition Contest in Chamber Music, *Icy Cruise*, 1986; First Prize, PROCAN (BMI) Composition Contest in Orchestral Music, *Fanorev*, 1986; First Prize, Princeton Orchestral Composition Contest, *Élan*, 1992. **MISC:** various lectures incl. "Cana-

dian Women Composers" at Conference on Women in Music, N.Y. Univ., 1982; Composer-in-residence at various events incl. Chamber Music Conference, Vermont, 1982 & Festival of the Americas, Indiana State Univ., 1986; numerous fellowships incl. Millay Colony for the Arts, N.Y., 1980, Wurlitzer Foundation, New Mex., 1985, & Camargo Foundation, France, 1991; MacDowell Colony, 1982, 1985, 1992; the Rockefeller Foundation in Italy, 1995; various grants & commission awards.

Bouchard, Micheline, B.Appl.Sc., M.Appl.Sc. ■ Ⓢ ❀
Vice-President, Quebec Operations, HEWLETT-PACKARD (CANADA) LTD., 17500 Trans-Canada Hwy, Kirkland, QC H9J 2X8 (514) 428-4726, FAX 428-4730. Born Montreal 1947. m. Jean-Paul Sardin. 2 ch. EDUC: École Polytechnique, B.Sc. 1969, M.Sc. 1978. CAREER: Engineer, Hydro-Québec, 1969-87; Asst. VP, Info., 1980-81; Asst. to the Pres. & CEO, 1981-83; Dir., Large Accts, 1983-87; VP, Mgmt Consulting Svcs, CGI Group Inc., 1987-88; VP, Mktg, DMR Group Inc., 1988-94; VP, Bus. Dev., 1995-96; VP, Que. Oper., Hewlett-Packard (Canada) Ltd., 1996 to date. DIRECTOR: Ford Motor Company of Canada Limited; Gaz Métropolitain Inc.; Corby Distilleries Limited; London Life Insurance Company. AFFIL: Advisory Council on Public Service Renewal (Privy Council); Canadian Council of Professional Engineers (Past Pres.); Canadian Academy of Engineering (Exec. Committee); Public Policy Forum (Founding Mbr.); Order of Engineers of Quebec (Pres. 1978-80). HONS: Woman of the Year–Bus., 1981; Woman of the Year–Merit Award, YWCA, 1994; Order of Canada, 1995. INTERESTS: sailing. COMMENT: *"Have more than 20 years of experience in the information technology, power utility and engineering fields. Actively involved in the business, engineering, governmental and educational communities. Have lead many initiatives to promote women in engineering."*

Bourgonje, Colette ■■ Ⓥ ♙
Paralympic Athlete. Saskatoon, SK. CAREER: teacher. SPORTS CAREER: mbr., Nat'l Track Team. Paralympic Games: Bronze, 100m shotput & 200m, 1996; Bronze, 800m & 100m, 1992. Black Top Invitational: 1st, 100m & 200m, 2nd, 500m & 800m, 1996. Stoke Games: 2nd, 100m & 400m, 3rd, 200m & 800m, 1995. IPC World Athletic Championships: 2nd, 200m, 800m & 400m, 4th, 100m, 1994. Francophone Games: 3rd, 800m, 1994. Nat'l Marathon Championships: 2nd, 1993. HONS: winner, Breakthrough Individual Award, 1995. MISC: has held many Cdn records; winner of 1st 800m wheelchair demonstration race, Commonwealth Games, 1990.

Bouma-Pyper, Marilyn, B.PE. ⊗ 🐾 ❤
Graphic Designer, Creative Services, ART GALLERY OF ONTARIO, 317 Dundas St. W., Toronto, ON M5G 1T4 (416) 979-6660, ext. 222, FAX 977-8547. Born Meaford, Ont. 1955. EDUC: McMaster Univ., B.PE. 1976; York Univ., Fine Arts 1977. CAREER: Graphic Designer, Art Gallery of Ontario. AFFIL: Art Directors & Design Club of Canada; Graphic Design Society of Canada; American Institute of Graphic Design. HONS: various design awards from *Applied Arts Magazine*, *Studio Magazine*, Ontario Association of Art Galleries, & the Alcuin Society; Senate Award (hons. student), McMaster Univ. INTERESTS: athletics; running; swimming; biking. COMMENT: *"I love all the art forms: literature, dance, painting, drawing, drama. I also enjoy athletic endeavours and challenges. I believe in the ancient Graeco-Roman ideal of healthy mind/healthy body. I'm also a believer in spirituality and humour; the sublime and the ridiculous."*

Bourassa, Louise, B.Comm.,C.A. Ⓢ
Vice-President and Chief Accountant, LAURENTIAN BANK OF CANADA, 1981 McGill College Ave., Rm. 1960, Montreal, QC H3A 3K3 (514) 284-7914, FAX 284-3959. Born Cowansville, Que. 1955. s. EDUC: Sherbrooke Univ., B.Comm.(Acctg) 1977. CAREER: Auditor, Mallette Benoit, 1977-81; Mgr, Fin., Société Québécoise d'assainissement des eaux, 1981-86; Mgr, Acctg, Laurentian Bank of Canada, 1986-89; Asst. VP, Acctg, 1989-93; VP & Chief Acctnt, 1993 to date. AFFIL: Chartered Accountant; Canadian Bankers' Association (Chief Acctnt Committee). COMMENT: *"I am dynamic and have become, after nine acquisitions, an expert at understanding systems of other companies in order to integrate them into the bank's system."*

Bourne, Lesley-Anne, B.A., M.F.A. 🐾 ✑ 📗
Lecturer, UNIVERSITY OF PRINCE EDWARD ISLAND, 550 University Ave., Charlottetown, PE C1A 4P3 (902) 628-4349, FAX 566-0420, EMAIL lbourne@upei.ca. EDUC: York Univ., B.A.(English & Creative Writing); Univ. of British Columbia, M.F.A.(Creative Writing) 1989. CAREER: Coord., Teaching Centre, Senate Committee on the Enhancement of Teaching, Univ. of Prince Edward Island, 1990-92; Lecturer, Creative Writing & Univ. 100, 1991 to date; Acting Dir., Univ. 100 Program, 1995.

SELECTED PUBLICATIONS: *The Story of Pears* (Penumbra Press, 1990); *Skinny Girls* (Penumbra Press, 1993); *Field Day* (Penumbra Press, 1996). **AFFIL:** League of Canadian Poets (Atlantic Canada rep.; Nat'l Council 1992 to date). **HONS:** Bliss Carman Poetry Award, Banff Centre for the Arts, 1986; Air Canada Award, Canadian Authors' Association, 1994.

Bourque, Diane, B.Mus.,LL.B. ⚖ ✈
Executive Director, FEDERATION OF LAW SOCIETIES OF CANADA, 480-445 boul. Saint-Laurent, Montreal, QC H2Y 2Y7 (514) 875-6351, FAX 875-6115, EMAIL dbourque@flsc.ca. Born Bouctouche, N.B. 1959. s. **EDUC:** Univ. of Moncton, B.Mus. 1981, LL.B. 1986; Univ. of Montreal, Music 1982; Intensa Institute, Costa Rica, Certificate (Spanish Studies) 1992; École internationale de Bordeaux, France, Certificate (Int'l Commercial Arbitration) 1992. **BAR:** N.B., 1987. **CAREER:** Admin. Sec., Coopers & Lybrand, Montreal, 1982-83; Legal Asst., Dept. of Fisheries, Memramcook, N.B., 1984; Research Asst., N.B. Court of Queen's Bench, 1985; Research Asst. to Andréa Ouellet, Prof., Law Sch., Moncton, N.B., 1985; Research Asst. to James Lockyer, Dean, Law Sch., 1986; Research Asst., N.B. Court of Appeal, 1986; Solicitor, Canadian Union of Public Employees, 1986-92; Asst. to the Dir., Centre international de la common law en français, Univ. of Moncton, 1993-94; Exec. Dir., Federation of Law Societies of Canada, 1994 to date. **AFFIL:** New Brunswick Law Society (Council 1988-92); Canadian Bar Association; Association des juristes d'expression française du Nouveau-Brunswick (Council 1988-92). **HONS:** Bursaries, N.B. Law Foundation, 1984, 1985, 1986; Landry Trophy for Best Student Advocate, Moot Court Competition, 1986. **MISC:** several speaking engagements; N.B. Rep. in China, Cdn Educational Travel Association (CETA), 1977; participant in "Gale Cup Moot Court Competition" in Advocacy, Osgoode Hall, Toronto, 1986.

Bourque, Pauline, B.Sc.,LL.B. ■■ ⚖ ✐ ⚫
Associate, LEBLANC BOUCHER RODGER BOURQUE (law firm), 740 Main, Moncton, NB E1C 1E6 (506) 858-0110, FAX 858-9497 and 15 boul. Irving, Bouctouche, NB E0A 1G0 (506) 743-5778. **EDUC:** Univ. de Moncton, Teacher's Licence 1973, B.Sc.(Nutrition & Family Studies) 1977; Univ. of Montreal, Certificate in Civil Law 1992; Univ. de Moncton, LL.B. 1994. **BAR:** N.B., 1995. **CAREER:** Teacher, 1969-75; mktg, Catelli Inc., 1977-89; consultant, mktg communications, Montreal, 1989-91; Assoc., LeBlanc Boucher Rodger Bourque, 1995 to date. **SELECTED PUBLICA-**

TIONS: writes monthly article focusing on different aspects of law for local paper. **AFFIL:** Univ. de Moncton (former mbr., committee that studied recommendations of *Report on Gender Equality in the Legal Profession*); N.B. Bar Association (former mbr., committee that studied recommendations of *Report on Gender Equality in the Legal Profession*); *Ven d'Est, Acadian* magazine (Bd. of Dir.); Film Zone Inc./Le Festival international du cinéma francophones en Acadie (Bd. of Dir.); Committee studying "Le droit des artistes au Nouveau-Brunswick." **MISC:** in law sch., responsible for "Caucus de la femme et le droit."

Bouw, Joanne, B.Sc.Phm. ■■ ⚪ ⊕
Pharmacist, NIAGARA FALLS CENTRE PHARMACY, 6453 Morrison St., Niagara Falls, ON L2E 7H1 (905) 374-2050, FAX 374-1232. Born St. Catharines, Ont. 1963. s. **EDUC:** Univ. of Toronto, B.Sc.Phm.(Pharmacy) 1986. **CAREER:** staff pharmacist. **SPORTS CAREER:** mbr., Sport By Ability Club, St. Catharines; competes in field events for athletes with cerebral palsy (class 7); currently competes in discus & shotput; world record holder in discus, shotput & javelin for C.P. class 7; undefeated in discus, shotput & javelin, 1984-92; triple gold medalist, Paralympics, Seoul, 1988 & Barcelona, 1992; competed in Atlanta Paralympics, 1996. **AFFIL:** Martindale Place, Christian retirement community (Bd. of Dir.); Canadian Cerebral Palsy Sports Association (committee mbr. 1992-95); Sport by Ability-Niagara (committee mbr. 1989-93). **HONS:** Terry Fox Humanitarian Award, 1982-86; finalist, Velma Springsteed Award for Cdn Female Athlete of the Year, Canadian Sports Federation, 1989; Edna Peace Memorial Award for Female Athlete of the Year, presented by Ontario Cerebral Palsy Sports Association, 1986, 1989, 1993; Athlete of the Decade, 1980-90, OCPSA; St. Catharines Athlete of the Year, 1989; Jim Vipond Award for Disabled Athlete of the Year, Ontario Sportscasters & Sportswriters Association, 1986, 1989; Robert Jackson Award for Ontario Disabled Athlete of the Year, 1986, 1989; Ontario Pharmacist of the Year, Ontario Pharmacist Association, 1992; King Clancy Award, Canadian Foundation for Physically Disabled Persons, 1994. **MISC:** speaker for F.A.M.E. (Female Athletes Motivating Excellence); guest editor, "Women and Girls in Sport and Physical Activity," *Canadian Women Studies Journal*, Fall 1995. **COMMENT:** *"Although a pharmacist by profession, my second career is in sports, particularly athletics. In the world of sport for the disabled, I have been actively involved for 16 years. I have been richly rewarded competitively (3 world*

records and 3 gold medals in Barcelona). But I have also been involved as a role model and in public speaking about the benefits of sports in your life. The Xth Paralympic Games in Atlanta are my last world competition and, although I look forward to retiring, I know I will still be actively involved in a volunteer role."

Bowen, Gail Dianne, B.A., M.A. ■ ◁ 🕮 🗋

Assistant Professor of English, SASKATCHEWAN INDIAN FEDERATED COLLEGE, University of Regina, Regina Campus, Room 118, College West Bldg., Regina, SK S4S 0A2 (306) 779-6202, FAX 584-0955. Born Toronto 1942. m. Ted. 3 ch. Hildy Wren, Max, Nathaniel. EDUC: Univ. of Toronto, B.A.(English) 1964; Univ. of Waterloo, M.A.(English) 1975; Univ. of Saskatchewan, Post-Grad. Studies in Cdn Lit. 1976-79. CAREER: Author, 1985 to date; Asst. Prof., Saskatchewan Indian Federated Coll., 1986 to date; Arts Columnist, CBC Radio, Regina, 1991 to date. SELECTED CREDITS: *Dancing in Poppies*, Globe Theatre, 1993; *Beauty and the Beast*, Globe Theatre, 1993; *The Tree*, Globe Theatre, 1994; *The Wandering Soul Murders* performed on *Between the Covers*, CBC Radio, May-June 1994. SELECTED PUBLICATIONS: *1919: The Love Letters of George and Adelaide*, with Ron Marken (Saskatoon: Western Producer Press, 1987); *Deadly Appearances* (Vancouver: Douglas & McIntyre, 1990); *Murder at the Mendel* (Vancouver: Douglas & McIntyre, 1991); *The Wandering Soul Murders* (Vancouver: Douglas & McIntyre, 1992); *A Colder Kind of Death* (Toronto: McClelland & Stewart, 1994); "A Killing Spring" (Toronto, McClelland & Stewart, 1996); "Guides to the Treasure of Self: The Function of Women in the Fiction of Robertson Davies" (*Waves* Fall 1976); "The Fiction of Sinclair Ross" (*Canadian Literature* Spring 1979). AFFIL: Saskatchewan Writers' Guild; Playwrights' Union of Canada; All Saints Church Sch. Program; URFA; Writers' Union of Canada, PEN Int'l. HONS: nominated, best first novel award, W.H. Smith-*Books in Canada*, 1990; nominated, best crime book, Crime Writers of Canada, 1992.; Winner, Best Crime Novel, Crime Writers of Canada, 1995. INTERESTS: contemporary fiction (esp. mysteries); children's lit.; popular culture; walking, aerobics. MISC: popular culture columnist, CBC, Sask.; frequent guest lecturer; periodic contributor, nat'l CBC Radio; listed in *Canadian Who's Who* since 1992; novels have been pub. in the US. & the UK. COMMENT: *"I'm a wife, a mother, a teacher, a writer and a church school teacher (probably in that order). I'm*

fifty-two years old, and I think, like many women my age, my passage has been interesting and my life has turned out better than I could have imagined."

Bowen, Lynne Elizabeth (Crossley), B.Sc., M.A. 🗋 🕮

Freelance Writer and Lecturer. 4982 Fillinger Cres., Nanaimo, BC V9V 1J1 (604) 758-0725, FAX 753-5422. Maclean Hunter Lecturer in Creative Non-Fiction, UNIVERSITY OF BRITISH COLUMBIA. Born Indian Head, Sask. 1940. m. Richard A. Bowen. 3 ch. Michael, Andrew, Elizabeth. EDUC: Univ. of Alberta, R.N. 1962, B.Sc.(Public Health Nursing) 1963; Univ. of Victoria, M.A.(W. Cdn Hist.) 1980. CAREER: Victorian Order of Nurses, 1963-64; freelance writer, 1980 to date; Sessional Lecturer, Malaspina Coll., 1987-90; Maclean Hunter Lecturer in Creative Non-Fiction, Univ. of British Columbia, 1992 to date. SELECTED CREDITS: Co-writer, *One Hundred Years Below* (video), 1987. SELECTED PUBLICATIONS: *Boss Whistle. The Coal Miners of Vancouver Island Remember* (Lantzville: Oolichan Books, 1982); *Three Dollar Dreams* (Lantzville: Oolichan Books, 1987); *The Dunsmuirs of Nanaimo* (Nanaimo: the Nanaimo Festival, 1989); *Muddling Through: The Remarkable Story of the Barr Colonists* (Vancouver: Douglas & McIntyre, 1992); *Those Lake People* (Vancouver: Douglas & McIntyre, 1995); "The Coal Miners of Vancouver Island Remember" (*Canadian Oral History Association Journal* 1983); "Shot Off the Solid: Technological Advances in Nineteenth Century Vancouver Island Coal Mining Fail to Prevent a Coal Dust Explosion" (*CIM Bulletin* Sept. 1992); various other articles. AFFIL: Canadian Historical Association; Canadian Oral History Association; Nanaimo Historical Society; Nanaimo Harbourfront Art Centre Society (Dir.); International PEN; The Writers' Union of Canada; BC Federation of Writers. HONS: Eaton's B.C. Book Award, 1983; Canadian Historical Association Reg'l Certificate of Merit, 1984, 1992; Lieutenant Governor's Medal for Writing B.C. History, 1987; B.C. Book Prizes–The Hubert Evans Non-Fiction Prize, 1992. INTERESTS: sailing; bicycling; travel; reading. MISC: recipient of Canada Council grants; guest lecturer at elementary & secondary schools, colleges & universities; various media appearances; various presentations to societies & associations. COMMENT: *"I'm a late bloomer whose writing career began at the age of 40 and who is making up for lost time as hard as I can go."*

Bowering, Marilyn, B.A.,M.A. 🕮 ⊗

Writer. 3007 Manzer Rd., R.R. 1, Sooke, BC

V0S 1N0 (604) 642-3793, FAX 642-3793. Born Winnipeg 1949. EDUC: Univ. of Victoria, B.A.(English) 1971, M.A.(English) 1973. CAREER: Radio Control Room Operator, CKDA, 1972-73; Writer in Residence, Aegean Sch. of Fine Arts, Paros, Greece, 1973-74; Secondary Sch. Teacher, G.M. Dawson, Masset, B.C., 1974-75; Instructor, Continuing Educ., Univ. of British Columbia, 1977; Lecturer, Dept. of Creative Writing, Univ. of Victoria, 1978-80, 1982-86, 1989, 1992-96; Ed. & Writer, gregson/graham, marketing and communications, 1978-80; Ed., Noel Collins and Blackwells (Edinburgh), 1980-82; Fac., The Banff Centre Writing Program, 1992; Visiting Assoc. Prof., Dept. of Creative Writing, Univ. of Victoria, 1993-94; Writer-in-Residence, Memorial Univ. of Newfoundland, 1995. SELECTED CREDITS: writer, *Grandfather Was a Soldier*, BBC Radio Scotland, 1983; writer, *Anyone Can See I Love You*, BBC Radio Scotland, 1986; writer, *Hajimari-No-Hajimari*, drama, Japan, 1986; writer, *Laika and Folchakov: A Journey in Time and Space*, CBC Radio, 1987; writer, *Anyone Can See I Love You*, Bastion Theatre Company, Victoria, 1988; writer, *A Cold Departure: The Liaison of Georges Sand and Frederic Chopin*, CBC Radio, 1989; writer, *Divine Fate*, animated, Nat'l Film Bd., 1993; writer, *Temple of the Stars* (drama), 1996. SELECTED PUBLICATIONS: *Grandfather Was A Soldier* (Press Porcepic, 1987); *Anyone Can See I Love You* (Porcupine's Quill, 1987); *To All Appearances a Lady* (Random House Canada, 1989); *Calling All the World: Laika and Folchakov 1957* (Press Porcepic, 1989); *Love As It Is* (Beach Holme/Press Porcepic, 1993); various other works of poetry & fiction. MISC: gives readings & workshops in Canada, Spain & the UK.

Bowker, Marjorie Montgomery, C.M., B.A.,LL.B.,LL.D. ■ ■ ⚖ ☻ ♟
Retired Judge, Family and Juvenile Courts of Alberta. 10925 - 85 Ave., Edmonton, AB T6G 0W3 (403) 439-9759. Born Bedeque, P.E.I. 1916. m. Wilbur F. Bowker, O.C.,Q.C. 3 ch. Blair, Lorna, Keith. EDUC: Univ. of Alberta, B.A., LL.B. 1939. BAR: Alta., 1940. CAREER: practised with Edmonton law firm; Judge, Family & Juvenile Courts, 1966-83; author, several best-selling books on public issues, 1988-92. SELECTED PUBLICATIONS: *On Guard for Thee: An Independent Analysis of the Canada-US Free Trade Agreement* (nat'l best seller, 1988); *The Meech Lake Accord: What it will mean to you and to Canada* (1990, on *The Globe and Mail* best seller list, 9 weeks, Apr.-June 1990); *Canada's Constitutional Crisis: Making Sense of it All* (1991, on *The Globe*

and Mail year-end best seller list for 1991); *Canada's National Referendum: What is it all about?* (40-pg. booklet for circulation & reproduction); major articles in legal journals. AFFIL: Alberta Legal Archives Society; Phi Delta Phi (int'l legal fraternity); Univ. of Alberta (Visiting Committee, Fac. of Nursing); Junior League of Edmonton (sustainer); Women's Canadian Club; United Church of Canada. HONS: numerous incl.: hon. LL.D., EWHA Women's Univ., Seoul, Korea, 1968; Queen Elizabeth Silver Jubilee Medal, 1977; Alberta Achievement Award for excellence in legal svcs, 1981; Life Mbr., YWCA of Edmonton, 1983; Distinguished Cdn Award, Council of Canadians, 1989; Order of Canada, 1990; hon. LL.D., Univ. of Alberta, 1991; hon. doctorate, Athabasca Univ., 1991; hon. mbr. (1st woman), Legal Archives Society of Alberta, 1994; honoured as Pioneer Woman Judge of Canada, Canadian Judicial Council, 1995. INTERESTS: family life (married 55 yrs., husband retired Dean of Law, Univ. of Alberta); 7 grandchildren; women's issues; domestic violence; child abuse; youth concerns; health & educ. restructuring in Alta.; penology; prison reform; legislation changes. MISC: numerous personal interviews (press, radio & TV), local & nat'l on public affairs & constitutional issues; public speaking major interest (4 volumes & booklets of speeches on file at Prov. Archives of Alberta). COMMENT: *"Concerned for disadvantaged in all aspects. Greatest personal achievement is founding first-in-Canada Court Conciliation Project, the recognized forerunner of mediation in divorce."*

Bowkun, Heléna, B.Mus. ⊗ ❏ ⊲
Concert Pianist, Writer and Teacher. 149 St. George St., Apt. 201, Toronto, ON M5R 2L9 (416) 964-2731. Born Toronto 1951. EDUC: Univ. of Toronto, B.Mus.(Performance-Piano) 1974. CAREER: debuted with the Toronto Symphony, performing the Rachmaninoff Second Piano Concerto; has performed extensively in recital, on TV, radio & with orchestras in Canada, the U.S. & Europe; mbr., Teaching Fac., Royal Conservatory of Music & the Fac. of Music, Univ. of Toronto. SELECTED CREDITS: has appeared with the Edmonton Symphony, Toronto Symphony, Hamilton Symphony, Thunder Bay Symphony, the CJRT Orchestra, the National Arts Centre Orchestra, the Toulouse Symphony; has performed with Philippe Entremont, Eugene List, Steven Staryk, Robert Aitken, Ofra Harnoy, Vladimir Orloff, Linda Maguire, William Aide & the Orford Quartet; performances frequently broadcast on the CBC, CJRT, WQXR (N.Y.) & Radio France; has recorded for Jubal, the CBC SM

series, & the Mastersound & RCA Red Seal labels. **SELECTED PUBLICATIONS:** regular contributor to *Classical Music Magazine*; articles on music for various publications incl. *The Toronto Star*. **MISC:** presents master classes on performance & pedagogy, & lectures on related subjects, incl. prevention of performance related injuries; active as an adjudicator for local & reg'l music competitions. **COMMENT:** *"It has always been my hope that I could communicate through music the universality of mankind. Although originally I endeavoured to do this through performance, writing about music has become an important medium to me and all other forms of communication as well. The initial dream still stands and I shall continue to lift it up."*

Bowles, Lynda, B.A.Sc.,M.Sc.,C.A. $

Partner, DELOITTE & TOUCHE, BCE Place, 181 Bay St., Ste. 1400, Toronto, ON M5J 2V1 (416) 601-6161, FAX 601-6151. Born Toronto 1949. 1 ch. Caitlin (Katie). **EDUC:** Univ. of Guelph, Coll. of Family & Consumer Studies, B.A.Sc. 1972, M.Sc. 1974; Ont. Institute of Chartered Accountants, C.A. 1981. **CAREER:** Lecturer, Univ. of Guelph, 1973-78; Audit Staff Mbr., Deloitte & Touche, 1979-85; Sr. Mgr, 1985-90; Ptnr, 1990 to date. **SELECTED PUBLICATIONS:** *Current Trends in Fundraising* (Deloitte & Touche, 1993); "Metric Conversion Requires Sensory Testing to Produce Equivalent Food Products," with P.K. Deiteh & T.A. Watts, Dept. of Consumer Studies, Univ. of Guelph (*Food Products Development*, Sept. 1979); "Colour Classification of Honey Using Reflectance Measurement," with E.A. Gullett, Dept. of Consumer Studies, Univ. of Guelph (*Canadian Institute of Food Science and Technology*, Vol. 9, No. 3, 1976). **AFFIL:** for Deloitte & Touche: Health-Care Sector Group, Women's Bus. Dev. Group (Sr. Advisor), Toronto Office Mktg Committee; Ontario Institute of Chartered Accountants; Zoological Society of Metropolitan Toronto (V-Chair & Treas.); Bloorview Children's Hospital (former Mbr.); Big Sisters' Association. **INTERESTS:** sailing; reading; walking the dog. **MISC:** Judge, *The Toronto Sun* "Women on the Move" contest, 1993. **COMMENT:** *"I am a successful partner at Deloitte & Touche. I have been active in promoting women at the firm by providing opportunities for them to demonstrate their skills. I have also been active in the community by volunteering my time to serve on the boards of various charities, and have used my university lecturing skills in my current career by giving presentations and by participating in the firm's professional development courses."*

Bowman, Marilyn, B.A.,M.Sc.App., Ph.D. ■■ 🎓 ⊕ ⚛

Associate Professor, Department of Psychology, SIMON FRASER UNIVERSITY, Burnaby, BC V6M 4H2 (604) 291-4777, FAX 291-3427, EMAIL Marilyn_Bowman@sfu.ca. Born McLennan, Alta. 1940. s. **EDUC:** Univ. of Alberta, B.A. (Psych.) 1961; McGill Univ., M.Sc.App. (Clinical Psych.) 1965, Ph.D.(Clinical Psych.) 1972. **CAREER:** Analyst, Pol. & Econ. Planning, London, U.K., 1962-63; Dir., Psychological Svcs, Lethbridge Rehab. Centre, Montreal, 1965-70; Asst. Prof., Queen's Univ., Kingston, Ont., 1972-76; Assoc. Prof., Dept. of Psych., Simon Fraser Univ., 1976 to date. **AFFIL:** B.C. Psychological Association (Bd. mbr. early 1980s); Canadian Psychological Association (Fellow); American Psychological Association; International Neuropsychology Society; National Academy of Neuropsychology. **HONS:** Best Ph.D. dissertation in Psychopharmacology, American Psychological Association, 1972. **COMMENT:** *"I am a clinical neuropsychologist with considerable administrative experience in universities and the non-profit sector. My interests in literature and human diversity have led me to travel extensively in around the world. My training and interests in music led to years of participation in the Vancouver Bach Choir."*

Boxall, Linda 🌾 $

President, SUNSHINE INTERNATIONAL INC. and SUNSHINE EGGS INC., Post Office Box 491, Regina, SK S4P 3A2 (306) 757-4848, FAX 757-4849. President, L.B.'S CAFE INC. Born Regina 1945. d. 3 ch. **EDUC:** Univ. of Regina, Study of French 1990. **AFFIL:** National Farm Products Marketing Council (Exec. Mbr.); Canadian Agricultural Employment Services Bd. (Chair); Western Canadian Agribition Egg Show Committee (Chair); Canadian Egg Producers' Council (VP); Saskatchewan Sch. Trustees Association (Exec. Mbr.); Farm Credit Corporation (Appeals Bd.); Grand Coulee Sch. Div. (Chair); Canadian Club of Saskatchewan (VP); Luther Coll. Alumni Association (Pres.). **HONS:** Canada 125 Medal. **MISC:** various activities with the Liberal Party; Hon. Mbr., Agricultural Services Advisory Bd. **COMMENT:** *"I am an active entrepreneur, having taken over the farm in 1966. We have celebrated sixty years in business. I have also expanded into the food service business. As well, I have diversified my interests with some real estate investments in Mexico."*

Boyanoski, Christine, B.A.,M.A., M.Phil. ■ 📜 ✪

Art Historian. c/o Birkbeck College, University

of London. Born Montreal 1955. s. **EDUC:** Univ. of Toronto, B.A.(Arts) 1978, M.A.(Hist. of Art) 1979; Courtauld Institute of Art, Univ. of London, UK, M.Phil.(Modern Art) 1981; Birkbeck Coll., Univ. of London, Ph.D. studies 1996 to date. **CAREER:** Asst. Curator of Cdn Historical Art, Art Gallery of Ontario, 1981-91; Assoc. Curator of Cdn Art, 1991-96. **SELECTED PUBLICATIONS:** numerous articles & exhibition catalogues, incl. *Towards a Lyrical Abstraction: The Art of L.A.C. Panton*, catalogue (Art Gallery of Ontario, 1990); "Milne and His Contemporaries," *David Milne*, ed. Ian M. Thom (Vancouver: The Vancouver Art Gallery & McMichael Canadian Art Collection in association with Douglas & McIntyre, 1991). **EXHIBITIONS:** curator of numerous exhibitions, incl. *Reading Pictures*, an innovative interpretation of the Cdn collection by bringing together art, literature & technology, Art Gallery of Ontario (1995-96); *The Artists' Mecca: Canadian Art and Mexico*, Art Gallery of Ontario & touring (1992); *Permeable Border: Art of Canada and the United States, 1920-1940*, Art Gallery of Ontario (1989-90); *Loring & Wyle: Sculpturers' Legacy*, Art Gallery of Ontario (1987). **AFFIL:** College Art Association of America; Canadian Museums Association; Universities Art Association of Canada (UAAC). **HONS:** Commonwealth Scholarship, 1979-81; Ont. Grad. Scholarship, 1978-79; Univ. of Toronto Master's Fellowship, 1978-79; S.H. Jaynes Silver Medal in Hist. of Art, Univ. of Toronto, 1978; ORS Award, CUCP, Great Britain, 1996; SSRHCC Doctoral Fellowship, 1996. **MISC:** has given many lectures. **COMMENT:** *"Professionally speaking, I am interested in all aspects of Canadian culture, particularly in comparison with those of other post-colonial nations–Australia, New Zealand, South Africa and India."*

Boyd, Jasna $

Vice-President, Facilities Management, NATIONAL TRUST COMPANY, 1 Adelaide St. E., Toronto, ON M5C 2W8 (416) 361-3711, FAX 361-4448. Born Karlovac, Croatia 1954. m. Andrew Boyd. **CAREER:** Proj. Coord., Continental Bank of Canada, 1977-86; Mgr, Premises, Lloyds Bank Canada, 1986-88; Asst. VP, Lloyds Bank Canada/Hong Kong Bank of Canada, 1988-91; Real Estate Consultant, Municipality of Metro Toronto, 1991-92; VP, Facilities Mgmt, National Trust Company, 1992 to date. **AFFIL:** International Facilities Management Association; St. Joseph's Health Centre (Dir.); McMichael Art Gallery. **COMMENT:** *"Ms. Boyd's career consists of progressively senior positions in real estate/facilities management and support services, primarily with financial institutions. She has travelled extensively across Canada in these various roles."*

Boyd, Liona, B.Mus.,C.M.,LL.D., D.Mus. ✪ 🎭 ☝

Musician, Composer and Classical Guitarist. Born London, UK. m. John Simon. **EDUC:** Univ. of Toronto, B.Mus. 1972; studied under Eli Kassner & Alexandre Lagoya (Paris). **SELECTED CREDITS:** *The Guitar* (1975); *The Guitar Artistry* (1976); *Miniatures for Guitar* (1977); *The First Lady of the Guitar* (1978); *Liona Boyd with Andrew Davis and the English Chamber Orchestra* (1979); *Liona Boyd and the First Nashville Guitar Quartet, Spanish Fantasy* (1980); *A Guitar For Christmas* (1981); *The Best of Liona Boyd* (1982); *Virtuoso* (1983); *Liona Live in Tokyo* (1984); *The Romantic Guitar* (1985); *Persona* (1986); *Encore* (1989); *Paddle to the Sea* (1990;, *Highlights* (1990); *Christmas Dreams* (1991); *Dancing on the Edge* (1992); *Classically Yours* (1995); appearances on major Cdn & US TV shows; concerts in N. Am., Europe, UK, S. & Central Am., the Far East & Caribbean; performed at Summit Conference & for many Heads of State; four Royal Command performances, Edinburgh, Ottawa, Glasgow, Windsor. **SELECTED PUBLICATIONS:** has composed numerous guitar works & has five music books released by Hal Leonard Publishing. **AFFIL:** American Federation of Musicians; SOCAN; AFTRA. **HONS:** LL.D.(Hon.), Lethbridge Univ., 1981; LL.D.(Hon.), Brock Univ., 1984; LL.D. (Hon.), Simon Fraser Univ., 1991; Doc.Mus.(Hon.), Univ. of Victoria, 1996; Vanier Award 1979; four Gold & Platinum recordings; Best Instrumental Artist, Juno Awards, 1979, 1982, 1983, 1984, 1995; inducted into Gallery of Guitar Greats by *Guitar Player Magazine,* 1994, after winning five years. **MISC:** first classical album to attain Gold status in Canada; played guitar on film score to "A Walk in the Clouds," which won 1996 Grammy.

Boyd, Marion, B.A.,M.P.P. 🍁 ☝

Member of Provincial Parliament (London Centre), GOVERNMENT OF ONTARIO, Queen's Park, Toronto, ON. Born Toronto 1946. m. Terry. 1 ch. **EDUC:** Glendon Coll., York Univ., B.A. 1968. **CAREER:** various capacities, incl. personal Asst. to the Pres., York Univ.; Sole Staff Person, York Univ. Fac. Association; Admin., Kaleidoscope Presch. Resource Centre, 1977-81; Exec. Dir., London Battered Women's Advocacy Clinic, 1984-90; elected M.P.P. (London Centre), 1990; Min. of Educ.; Min. Responsible for Women's Issues, 1991-

95; Min. of Community & Social Svcs; Attorney Gen., 1993-95; re-elected, 1995. SELECTED PUBLICATIONS: *The Final Report* (London: London Battered Women's Advocacy Clinic, 1985); *The Handbook for Advocates and Counsellors of Battered Women* (London: London Battered Women's Advocacy Clinic, 1985). AFFIL: NDP. HONS: Outstanding Young Londoner, Jr. Chamber of Commerce, 1985; John Robinson Award, London Co-ordinating Committee on Wife Abuse, 1990; Mary Campbell Community Service Award, Information London, 1990; Maureen Mayne Award, Cross Cultural Learner Centre, London, 1991. INTERESTS: gardening; mystery stories; family cottage. MISC: Ontario's 1st woman Attorney Gen.; organized 4th Nat'l Conference of Women in Colleges & Universities, 1974.

Boyd, Mary ⊕ ○

Executive Director, CENTRAL ALBERTA WOMEN'S EMERGENCY SHELTER, Box 561, Red Deer, AB T4N 5G1 (403) 346-5643, FAX 341-3510. Born Turner Valley, Alta 1940. 4 ch. EDUC: Red Deer Coll., Social Work Diploma 1975; Holy Cross Hospital, Certification in Group Psychotherapy. CAREER: part-time Instructor, Red Deer Coll., 1976-77; Social Worker, Alberta Social Svcs & Community Health, 1978-82; Child Welfare, 1982-83; Instructor, Basic Job Readiness Training Program, 1983-84; Exec. Dir., Central Alberta Women's Emergency Shelter, 1984 to date. SELECTED PUBLICATIONS: article in victims' advocate journal, *Children At Risk*, 1985. AFFIL: Alberta Association of Social Workers; Canadian Association of Social Workers; past affiliations include Alberta Council on Aging (Chair); The John Howard Society; Lacombe Family Dev. Council; Red Deer Sexual Assault Committee; Suicide Education Committee; Red Deer Victims Services Community Advisory Committee. HONS: Women of Distinction Award for Outstanding Achievement in the Area of Human Rights/Status of Women, Soroptomist International of Central Alberta, 1989. INTERESTS: Interested in acquiring knowledge about transition houses & programs for victims of violence in the UK & Australia. MISC: expert witness in the Battered Women's Syndrome, Court of Queen's Bench, 1990, 1992, 1994; administers the "Treatment Program for Men Who Batter Their Spouses," Central Alberta Women's Emergency Shelter; mbr., Canadian Mental Health Association Provincial Committee on Child Welfare Legislation (Alberta), 1983-84; presently co-facilitates a family violence treatment program for federal offenders at Bowden Penitentiary. COMMENT: *"I have been the Executive Director for 12 years in Red Deer. In 1984 there were four staff including myself. I now have 16 staff and nine programs to administer. There have been many dedicated people who have helped us grow."*

Boyd, Melanie, B.A. ⊜ $

Owner, METHODS CONSULTING, WITH PEOPLE IN MIND, 2105 - 8th St. E., Box 21054, Saskatoon, SK S7H 5N9 (306) 653-0545. Born Kindersley, Sask. 1954. EDUC: Univ. of Calgary, B.A. 1981. CAREER: Proj. Mgr, Boys & Girls Clubs of Saskatoon, 1978-79; Asst. Program Developer, Bilingual Educ. Centre, Saskatoon, 1980; Guide/Interpreter, Que. Fortifications, Quebec City, summer 1981; Community School Coord., Westmount Community Sch., Saskatoon, 1982-84; Curriculum Developer, Co-operative Coll. of Canada, 1984-85; Mgmt Educ. Consultant, Co-operative Housing Association of Saskatchewan, Saskatoon, 1985-87; Coord., Youth Volunteer Programs, Sherbrook Community Centre, Saskatoon, 1988-92; Officer, Visitor & Cultural Resources, Univ. of Saskatchewan, 1992-94; Exec. Dir., Saskatchewan 4-H Council, 1994-95; Owner, METHODS CONSULTING, With People in Mind, 1994 to date. SELECTED PUBLICATIONS: "Silver Threads Among the Gold: An Intergenerational Program with a Difference" (*Recreation Canada*, May 1985); four curriculum manuals for Saskatchewan Co-operative Youth Program, April 1985; curriculum writer/ed. for the Isolated Resort Operator Program, SIAST, June 1990. HONS: Dean's List & Francis F. Reeve Foundation Bursary of $500, 1973-74. MISC: participant in Canada World Youth, a crosscultural exchange program, which involved extensive travel & work experience in eastern Canada & Cameroon, Africa, 1971-72; extended travel & work in eastern Canada, UK & Greece, 1975-77; performs with Cornellya Joss in an acappella duo called *None of the Above*. COMMENT: *"I seek always new challenges, and ways to do things that improve upon quality–especially as it relates to human development and interaction. My path has been broad rather than narrow. I think it is the pursuit of 'breadth' that has provided me with limitless opportunities to contribute and grow; my goal is to consistently do both these things better."*

Boyle, Christine Lesley Maureen, LL.B., LL.M. ⊜ ⊕

Professor, Faculty of Law, UNIVERSITY OF BRITISH COLUMBIA, Vancouver, BC V6T 1Z1 (604) 822-3403, FAX 822-8108. Associate Counsel, SMART AND WILLIAMS, Vancouver. Born Lisburn, N. Ireland 1949. EDUC: Queen's

Univ., Belfast, N. Ireland, LL.B. 1971; Queen's Univ., Kingston, Ont., LL.M. 1972. **BAR:** N. Ireland, 1973; N.S., 1984-91; B.C., 1995. **CAREER:** Lecturer in Law, Queen's Univ., Belfast, 1971-72; Lecturer in Law, Univ. of the West Indies, Barbados, 1973-75; Asst. Prof., Univ. of Windsor, Ont., 1975-77; Visiting Lecturer, Queen's Univ., Belfast, 1978-79; Assoc. Prof., Univ. of Windsor, Ont., 1977-81; Visiting Prof., Sch. of Criminology, Simon Fraser Univ., 1989; Prof. of Law, Fac. of Law, Dalhousie Univ., 1981-92; Walter S. Owen Visiting Prof., Fac. of Law, Univ. of British Columbia, 1990-92; Prof. of Law, Fac. of Law, Univ. of British Columbia, 1992 to date. **SELECTED PUBLICATIONS:** *Sexual Assault* (Carswell, 1984); *A Feminist Review of Criminal Law*, with others (Status of Women Canada, 1986); *Charterwatch: Reflections on Equality*, ed. with others (Carswell, 1986); *Contracts, Cases and Commentaries*, fifth edition, ed. with Professor Percy (Carswell, 1994); "Confidentiality in Correctional Institutions" (*Canadian Journal of Criminology and Corrections* 1976); "A Forum on *Lavallee v. R.*: Women and Self-Defence," with others (*U.B.C. Law Review* 1991); "The Role of the Judiciary in the Work of Madame Justice Wilson" (*Dalhousie Law Journal* 1992); numerous other articles & book chapters; numerous case & legislation comments, book reviews & teaching materials. **EDIT:** Advisory Bd., *Queen's Law Journal.* **AFFIL:** Canadian Association of Law Teachers; Canadian Research Institute for the Advancement of Women; National Association of Women & the Law; Women's Legal Education & Action Fund; Supreme Court of Canada Historical Society. **HONS:** Canadian Assoc. of Law, Award for Academic Excellence, 1995. **MISC:** numerous public legal educ. lectures in Barbados & Canada; numerous conference presentations; delegate at int'l meeting of experts on domestic violence organized by the International Centre for Criminal Justice Policy Law Reform & Criminal Justice Policy, 1992; member of the Canadian Advisory Council on Firearms, 1990-93.

Braak, Geraldine ■ ■ 🎨 📧 ⊕
National President and Chief Executive Officer, CANADIAN COUNCIL OF THE BLIND. Born Netherlands. m. 2 ch., 1 grch. **CAREER:** became legally blind, 1971; instrumental in establishing Canadian Council of the Blind (CCB) White Cane Club, Powell River, 1976; 1st Pres., & except for 3-month period, has held this position since; elected delegate to CCB B.C.-Yukon Div., 1977; various positions incl. Div. 1st VP, Nat'l Dir. of Legislation, 1st Nat'l VP; Nat'l Pres., 1986 to date; operates Innova-

tive Skills Development Centre, an accredited post-secondary sch. that places students in training programs. **AFFIL:** World Blind Union (VP & Exec. mbr., & mbr., Women's Committee, N.Am./Caribbean Reg.; mbr., Cdn delegation, representing Canada at various world congresses & exec. meetings); Advisory Committee on Accessible Transportation; Joint Organizational Efforts Committee; Community Services Task Team, B.C. Premier's Advisory Committee (former mbr.); Canadian Braille Authority (Treas.; former Pres. & Exec. mbr.); Friends of Libraries for the Blind (Bd. mbr.); Powell River & District United Way (Dir.); Canadian National Institute for the Blind (Community Coord., Powell River District); Powell River Model Community for Persons with Disabilities (Dir.); Accessible Transit Buses, Vancouver & Victoria (Eval. Committee). **MISC:** presented various policy statements to numerous Royal Commission Hearings, & appeared as witness in front of Parliamentary Standing Committee on Human Rights & the Status of Disabled Persons; worked closely with Bank of Canada in developing & distributing audible banknote reader, with Consumer & Corp. Affairs Canada on identifying & labelling hazardous spray products in a more tactile manner, & with Revenue Canada in providing alternative formats; has organized & conducted numerous seminars & workshops. **COMMENT:** *"The many different levels and various aspects of Geraldine's involvement have afforded her the opportunity to gain extensive knowledge, most particularly in dealing with issues that affect blind and visually impaired people. However, Geraldine's interest is not exclusively with this group, as she is deeply involved in all issues affecting people with disabilities."*

Bradley, Elizabeth Anne,
B.F.A. ■ ⊗ 📧 📧 👘
General Manager, HUMMINGBIRD CENTRE FOR THE PERFORMING ARTS (formerly The O'Keefe Centre for the Performing Arts), 1 Front St. E., Toronto, ON M5E 1B2 (416) 393-7450, FAX 393-7454. Born Toronto 1954. m. Keith. 2 ch. **EDUC:** York Univ., B.F.A.(Concentration in Theatre Mgmt) 1976. **CAREER:** Dir. of Public Rel'ns & Mktg, Theatre Plus, Toronto, 1976-78; Production Apprentice/Exec. Asst., Transart Productions/Broadway Producers, NYC, 1978-79; Theatre Rep./Touring & Artist Mgr, Haber Artists, 1980-82; Dir. of Comm., Stratford Festival of Canada, 1982-85; Independent Commercial Prod./Gen. Mgr, 1986-89; Acting Gen. Mgr/Dir. of Planning, Canadian Stage Company, 1989-90; Mgr, Programming & Dev., O'Keefe Centre/Hummingbird Centre,

1991 to date; Gen. Mgr, 1994 to date; Guest Lecturer, Theatre Mgmt, York Univ. **AFFIL:** Equity Showcase Theatre (Bd.); Performing Arts Development Fund (Founder); First Night Toronto (Dir.); International Society for the Performing Arts Foundation (Dir.); League of New York Theaters & Producers; Canadian Arts Presenters' Association. **HONS:** Dean's List Grad., York Univ., 1976; Floyd S. Chalmers Scholarship; Dora Mavor Moore Award, twice, for Prod., Best Musical of the Year. **INTERESTS:** educ.; film; cuisine; the 19th century. **MISC:** conducted numerous seminars & workshops in theatre mgmt. **COMMENT:** *"Elizabeth Bradley is the first woman to head the Metro-owned, internationally recognized Hummingbird Centre for the Performing Arts. Her creative expertise, management savvy and willingness to mentor the next generation of administrators, producers and presenters have made a significant contribution to the arts in Canada during the past 20 years."*

Bradley, Judy L., B.Sc.,B.Ed.,M.L.A. ■ ✦
Member of the Legislative Assembly (Weyburn-Big Muddy), GOVERNMENT OF SASKATCHEWAN, 17 - 3rd St., Weyburn, SK S4H 0W1 (306) 842-5839, FAX 842-5454. Born Regina 1952. m. Gary. 3 ch. **EDUC:** Univ. of Saskatchewan, Regina, B.Sc.(Biol.) 1974; Univ. of Regina, B.Ed. (with great distinction) 1975. **CAREER:** Teacher, Sheldon Williams Collegiate, 1974-77; Teacher, Special & Elementary Educ., Milestone, 1978-91; elected M.L.A. (Bengough-Milestone), 1991; re-elected M.L.A. (Weyburn-Big Muddy), 1995; Chair, Caucus; Mbr., Admin., Planning & Priorities, Legislative Review & House Leader's Committees; Mbr., Legislative Standing Committees on Crown Corporations & Private Members' Bills, & The Special Committee on Rules. **AFFIL:** Saskatchewan Science Centre (Bd. Mbr.); Terry Fox Run (Coord.); Amnesty International. **INTERESTS:** skiing; ball; figure skating; curling; music; Saskatchewan Roughriders. **COMMENT:** *"I believe in the spirit of Saskatchewan, community, cooperation, compassion and a strong work ethic. This belief is part of my being, my endeavours and achievements."*

Bradley, Mary M., B.A.,LL.B. $ ✶ ⛏
Vice-President, Business Affairs, ALLEGRO FILMS INC., 2817 Larivière St., Montreal, QC H2K 1P5 (514) 529-0320, FAX 529-0328, EMAIL mary.bradley@allegrofilms.com. Born Kingston, Ont. 1964. s. **EDUC:** Queen's Univ., B.A.(English) 1986, LL.B. 1989. **BAR:** Ont., 1991. **CAREER:** Chair, Fine Arts & Public Lectures Senate Committee, Queen's Univ., 1984-86; Radio Host & Prod., CFRC Radio,

Kingston, Ont., 1985-87; Educ. Coord., Teleconference, Resource, Educational & Advocacy Centre for the Handicapped (REACH), 1987; Legal Educ. Dir., Queen's Legal Aid Clinic, 1987-88; Lawyer, Intellectual Property Section, McCarthy Tétrault, Barristers, Solicitors, Patent & Trade Mark Agents, 1991-93; Legal Columnist, *Newsletter of Canadian Copyright Institute*, 1991-95; Sec., Canadian Copyright Institute, 1991-94; Coord., Arts & Entertainment, Bus. Affairs, CBC, 1993-94; VP, Bus. Affairs, Allegro Films Inc., 1994 to date. **SELECTED PUBLICATIONS:** published in *Wordworks* (Federation of B.C. Writers). **DIRECTOR:** Canadian Retransmission Collective (Dir.). **AFFIL:** Law Society of Upper Canada; Toronto Women in Film & Television; International Literary & Artistic Association of Canada; Canadian Bar Association of Quebec (Bus., Media & Comm., Insolvency, & Int'l Sections); Association littéraire des artistes international. **INTERESTS:** skiing; sailing. **MISC:** has been a guest lecturer at Osgoode Hall Law Sch., Queen's Univ. & Humber Coll. **COMMENT:** *"As VP, Business Affairs, Bradley is responsible for the business and legal affairs of Allegro Films, a producer and distributor of feature films and television programs. Allegro is a subsidiary of Le Groupe Coscient Inc., a publicly traded entertainment company."*

Bradley, Susan, B.Sc.,M.D.,F.R.C.P.(C) ⊕
Psychiatrist-in-Chief, THE HOSPITAL FOR SICK CHILDREN, 555 University Ave., Toronto, ON M5G 1X8 (416) 813-7524, FAX 813-5326, EMAIL susan.bradley@mailhub.sickkids.on.ca. Head, Division of Child Psychiatry, UNIVERSITY OF TORONTO. Born Niagara Falls, Ont. 1940. m. James Michael Bradley. 2 ch. **EDUC:** Univ. of Toronto, B.Sc.(Physiology & Biochem.) 1962, M.D. 1966, Dipl. in Psychiatry 1971; F.R.C.P.(C) 1972; Dipl. in Child Psychiatry. **CAREER:** Consultant, Thistletown Regional Centre, 1972-73, 1975-82; Consultant, Child & Family Studies Centre, Clarke Institute of Psychiatry, 1972 to date; Consultant, Metro Toronto Children's Aid, Richardson Residence, 1980-82; Assoc. Prof., Univ. of Toronto, 1982; Dir., Adolescent Psychiatry, The Hospital for Sick Children, 1982-86; Clinical Dir., 1984-88; Psychiatrist-in-Chief, 1988 to date; Head, Div. of Child Psychiatry, Univ. of Toronto, 1988 to date. **SELECTED PUBLICATIONS:** "Female Transsexualism–A Child and Adolescent Perspective" (*Child Psychiatry and Human Development* (11), 1980); "The Borderline Diagnosis in Children and Adolescents" (*Child Psychiatry and Human Development*, 1981); " Patterns of Gender-Role Behaviour in Children Attending Traditional and Non-Traditional Day-Care

Centres," with H.J. Cole & K.J. Zucker (*Canadian Journal of Psychiatry* (27), 1982); "Childhood Female Masturbation" (*Canadian Medical Association Journal* (132), 1985); "Gender Identity and Psychosexual Problems in Children and Adolescents," with K.J. Zucker (*Canadian Journal of Psychiatry* (35), 1990); "Body Image and its Measurement in Children and Adolescents–an overview," with H. Offman (*Canadian Journal of Psychiatry*, special edition (32), 1992); "Behavioural Inhibition, Attachment and Anxiety in Children of Mothers with Anxiety Disorders," with K. Manassis, S. Goldberg, J. Hood & R. Swinson (*Canadian Journal of Psychiatry* (4), 1995); *Gender Identity Disorder and Psychosexual Problems in Children and Adolescents* with K.J. Zucker (New York: Guilford Publications, Inc., 1995); numerous articles in refereed journals, chapters in books; reports & book reviews. **AFFIL:** Infant Mental Health Promo. Proj. (Chair); Institute for the Study of Antisocial & Violent Behaviour in Youth (Advisory Bd.); Adolescent Psychosis Coordinating Committee (Chair); Ontario Psychiatric Association; Canadian Psychiatric Association; Ontario Medical Association; Canadian Medical Association; Canadian Academy of Child Psychiatry. **HONS:** Honours AOA Society, 1965. **MISC:** consultant to Chilean Ministry of Health re: children's mental health programs, Santiago, Oct. 1990; numerous presentations & invited addresses; guest on *Canada A.M.*, "State of the Canadian Family," June, 1994; "Troubled Youth" Panel, *Cross Currents*, Vision TV, 1993-94; Co-Chair, with Judge Grant Campbell, "Youth in Crisis" Conference, TVOntario, 1993-94; *The Trouble with Evan* (documentary), CBC, comments, July 1994.

Bradshaw, Claudette Arsenault ○ ⊕
Executive Director, MONCTON HEADSTART, 155 Hazen Dr., Moncton, NB E1C 8W8 (506) 384-2506, FAX 857-3170. Born Moncton 1949. m. Douglas Bradshaw. 2 ch. **EDUC:** Vanier High Sch., graduated 1968. **CAREER:** part-time Sales Clerk, Co-op Centre, 1964-68; Girls' Program Dir., Moncton Boy's & Girl's Club, 1968-74; Exec. Dir., Moncton Headstart, 1974 to date. **AFFIL:** National Health & Welfare Council (1985-87); Provincial Task Force on Early Childhood (1986-87); Nat'l Bd. of Directors on Child Health (1986-88); Provincial Task Force on Housing (1988-89); Moncton Housing Coalition (1988-90). **HONS:** Canadian Achiever, Fed. Gov't, 1982; Paul Harris Award, Rotary Club, 1987; Beta Sigma Phi Award, 1987; Person of the Year, N.B. Day Care, 1987; Ann Bell Award, N.B. Child Welfare Association, 1989; Muriel Fergusson

Award, Greater Moncton Chamber of Commerce, Business Woman of the Year, 1991; honoured by National Welfare Council & National Crime Prevention, 1994. **MISC:** Speakers' Bureau, United Way Moncton, 1990; presentation to Senate Committee on Child Poverty, 1990; presentation to House of Commons Standing Committee on Child Poverty, 1991; community awareness presentation on effects of poverty, "Poverty Game," 1990-91. **COMMENT:** *"The past 26 years have been challenging, but every year we see lives being changed. Every day we feed hungry children, every day we hug and see a smile on a child."*

Bradshaw, Leah, B.A.,M.A., Ph.D. ✎ ❀ 📖
Professor, Department of Politics, BROCK UNIVERSITY, St. Catharines, ON L2S 3A1 (905) 668-5550, ext. 3482, FAX 988-9388. Born Sherbrooke, Que. 1954. m. Charles Burton. 3 ch. Emma, Jacob, Lucy. **EDUC:** Bishop's Univ., B.A.(Pol. Studies) 1975; York Univ., M.A.(Pol. Sci.) 1978, Ph.D.(Pol. Sci.) 1984. **CAREER:** Prof., Bishop's Univ., 1982-84; Prof., Brock Univ., 1986 to date. **SELECTED PUBLICATIONS:** *Acting and Thinking: The Political Thought of Hannah Arendt* (Toronto: University of Toronto Press, 1989); *Love and Will in the Miracle of Birth*, ed. Arthur Davis; *George Grant and the Subversion of Modernity* (University of Toronto Press, 1997); scholarly articles on subjects of tyranny, & women in the hist. of pol. thought. **AFFIL:** Canadian Political Science Association (Chair, Political Theory Section 1993). **HONS:** *Choice Award* for one of the outstanding academic books of 1989; doctoral & post-doctoral awards, Social Sciences & Humanities Research Council of Canada. **INTERESTS:** pol. theory, ancient & modern. **MISC:** Juror for Lionel Gelber Prize, 1994. **COMMENT:** *"Primary goal is to combine a teaching and writing career with raising three small children."*

Braggins, Donna ⊗ ✎ 📖
Art Director, CANADIAN BUSINESS MEDIA LTD. (publishers of *Canadian Business, Profit, The Magazine for Canadian Entrepreneurs* & *Who's Who Publications*), 777 Bay St., 5th Fl., Toronto, ON M5W 1A7 (416) 596-6059, FAX 596-5155. Born Toronto 1954. m. Richard A. Braggins. **CAREER:** Designer, Canadian Business Media Ltd., 1978-87; Assoc. Art. Dir., 1987-91; Acting Art Dir., 1990-91; Art Dir., 1991 to date. **AFFIL:** National Magazine Awards Foundation (Dir.). **HONS:** National Magazine Awards; Author's Awards; Advertising & Design Club Awards; Kenneth R. Wilson Awards.

Bramwell, Vivien, B.Sc.,M.B.B.S.,Ph.D., F.R.C.P.,F.R.C.P.C. ⊕

Head of Medical Oncology, LONDON REGIONAL CANCER CENTRE OF ONTARIO CANCER TREATMENT AND RESEARCH FOUNDATION, 790 Commissioners Rd. E., London, ON N6A 4L6 (519) 685-8640, FAX 685-8624. Born Kent, UK 1948. m. Patrick Wesley. **EDUC:** St. Bartholomew's Hospital Medical Sch., B.Sc. (Medicine) 1969, M.B.B.S.(Medicine) 1972; Univ. of Manchester, Ph.D.(Oncology) 1981. **CAREER:** Research Fellow, Christie Hospital, Manchester, UK, 1975-80; Sr. Registrar, 1980-84; Consultant, London Regional Cancer Centre, London, Ont., 1984-87; Head of Medical Oncology, 1987 to date; Interim CEO, 1994-95. **SELECTED PUBLICATIONS:** "A pilot study of intensive cyclophosphamide, epirubicin and fluorouracil in patients with auxiliary node positive or locally advanced breast cancer" (*European Journal of Cancer and Clinical Oncology*, 29A, 1993); "Adjuvant CYVADIC chemotherapy for adult soft tissue sarcoma–reduced local recurrence but no improvement in survival" (*Journal of Clinical Oncology*, 12, 1994); "A comparison of two short intensive adjuvant chemotherapy regimens in operable osteosarcoma of limbs in children and young adults" (*Journal of Clinical Oncology*, 10, 1992); "Timing of surgery in relation to the menstrual cycle in premenopausal women with operable breast cancer" with others (*British Journal of Surgery*, 81, 1994). **AFFIL:** American Society of Clinical Oncology; Canadian Oncology Society; Canadian Association of Medical Oncology; Canadian Sarcoma Group (Founder & Chair); Royal Coll. of Physicians, UK (Fellow); Royal Coll. of Physicians, Canada (Fellow). **HONS:** Herbert Paterson Medal in Physiology, St. Bartholomew's Hospital, 1968; Knott Prize in Surgery, St. Bartholomew's Hospital, 1970; Brackenbury Scholarships in Medicine & Surgery, St. Bartholomew's Hospital, 1972; George Burrow's Prize in Medical Pathology, St. Bartholomew's Hospital. **INTERESTS:** skiing; riding; squash; theatre. **COMMENT:** *"Dr. Bramwell established and chairs the Canadian Sarcoma Group, which undertakes clinical trials in soft tissue and bone sarcomas and administers the database for a national soft tissue sarcoma tumour bank for molecular studies."*

Brandow, Judy [$] ✎ 🍁

President, SANIPOUCH PRODUCTS INC., 227 Lakeshore Dr., Toronto, ON M8V 2A7 (416) 255-2754, FAX 255-2273. Born Hamilton, Ont. **CAREER:** Gen. Reporter, *The St. Catharines Standard*, 1966-68; Reporter, then Asst. City Ed. (women's), *The Toronto Telegram*, 1968-71; Women's Ed., *The Hamilton Spectator*, 1971-72; Ed., *Yours Magazine*, 1972-73; Journalism Instructor, Ryerson Polytechnical Institute, 1973-74; Copy Ed., then Family Ed., *The Toronto Star*, 1974-77; Ed.-in-Chief, *Canadian Living* Magazine, 1977-88; Features Ed., *The Toronto Sun*, 1989-90; Special Projects Dir., Participaction, 1990-91; lifestyle column, *The Toronto Sun*, 1991-93; magazine consultant, 1988 to date; freelance writer, 1991 to date; Pres., Sani-Pouch Products Inc., 1992 to date. **AFFIL:** Metro Toronto Convention Centre (Chair 1991 to date). **INTERESTS:** skiing; sailing; antiques; swimming; gardening. **COMMENT:** *"As a journalist I have worked for both newspapers and magazines. I am presently working as a magazine consultant and freelance writer. I am president of Sani Pouch Products Inc. which, manufactures disposal bags for tampons."*

Brandt, Di (Diana Ruth), B.Th.,B.A.(Hons.), M.A.,Ph.D. ■ 📜 🎓 ☝

Writer and Research Fellow in English, UNIVERSITY OF ALBERTA, Edmonton, AB T6G 2E5 (403) 492-3258, FAX 492-8142. Born Winkler, Man. 1952. d. 2 ch. Lisa, Alison. **EDUC:** Canadian Mennonite Bible Coll., B.Th. 1972; Univ. of Manitoba, B.A.(Hons., English) 1975, Certificate in Educ. 1981, Ph.D.(English) 1993; Univ. of Toronto, M.A.(English) 1976. **CAREER:** Writer, 1983 to date; Lecturer, Asst. Prof. in English, Univ. of Winnipeg, 1986-95; Writer in Residence, Univ. of Alberta, 1995-96; Research Fellow, Univ. of Alberta, 1996 to date. **SELECTED PUBLICATIONS:** *questions i asked my mother* (Winnipeg: Turnstone Press, 1987); *Agnes in the sky* (Winnipeg: Turnstone Press, 1990); *mother, not mother* (Mercury Press 1992); *Wild Mother Dancing: Maternal Narrative in Canadian Literature* (Winnipeg: Univ. of Manitoba Press, 1993); *Jerusalem, beloved* (Winnipeg: Turnstone Press, 1995); *Dancing Naked: Narrative Strategies for Writing Across Centuries* (Stratford: Mercury Press, 1996); work in various anthologies, incl. *Section Lines: A Manitoba Anthology*, ed. by Mark Duncan (Winnipeg: Turnstone Press, 1992). **EDIT:** Poetry editor, *Prairie Fire*, 1989-93; guest editor, *SPARKS!* Special High School Edition, Winter 1992-93. **AFFIL:** Writers' Union of Canada (Floating Rep. 1995-96); PEN (Man. Rep. 1992-94); League of Canadian Poets (Man. Rep. 1988-90; 2nd VP 1990-91); Manitoba Writers' Guild; A.C.C.U.T.E. **HONS:** A.L. Wheeler Book Prize, Univ. of Manitoba, 1975; Gerald Lampert Award, 1987; nominated, Gov. General's Award for Poetry, 1987; nominated, Dillons Commonwealth Poetry Prize, 1988; Patrick Mary Plunkett Memorial Scholarship, Univ. of Manitoba,

1989; Drummond Scholarship in Cdn Studies, Univ. of Manitoba, 1990; McNally Robinson Award for Manitoba Book of the Year, 1990; Nat'l Poetry Award, Canadian Authors' Association, 1995; Silver, National Magazine Awards, 1995; nominated, Gov. General's Award for Poetry, 1995; nominated, McNally Robinson Award, Manitoba Book of the Year, 1993, 1995; nominated, Pat Lowther Award, 1992, 1995. **INTERESTS:** maternal narrative; poetry; feminism; women's cultural production. **MISC:** one of the first women in the Mennonite community to become a writer & break the public silence of women; recipient of various grants; juror, various contests & grants; poetry readings across Canada & internationally; teacher of writing workshops across Canada & in Germany. **COMMENT:** *"A writer of poetry, fiction and non-fiction, including literary criticism. An editor and teacher of creative writing and English Literature, currently Research Fellow at the University of Alberta."*

Braun, Liz ■■ ✏ 📺

Film Critic and Entertainment Writer, *THE TORONTO SUN*, 333 King St. E., Toronto, ON M5A 3X5. m. 3 ch.

Braverman, Doreen, B.Ed.,M.B.A. $

Managing Director and Secretary, J. BRAVERMAN INC., 1755 W. 4th Ave., Vancouver, BC V6J 1M2 (604) 732-7586, FAX 736-6439. Secretary, BRAVERMAN HOLDINGS LTD.; THE VANCOUVER FLAG SHOP INC.; ATLAS TEXTILE PRINT LTD.; THE FLAG SHOP INC. Born Vancouver 1932. m. Jack Braverman. 4 ch. William Turecki, Robert Turecki, Laura Hansen, Susan Braverman. **EDUC:** Univ. of British Columbia, B.Ed. 1964; Canadian Sch. of Mgmt, M.B.A. 1983. **CAREER:** Teacher, Vancouver Sch. Bd., 1962-65, 1966-68; Mng Dir., J. Braverman Inc., 1974 to date. **EDIT:** Ed., *The Flag* & Banner, 1988 to date. **DIRECTOR:** Business Development Bank of Canada. **AFFIL:** American Association of Textile Colorists & Chemists; Canadian Flag Association (Founder); CanAsian Businesswomen's Network; Canadian Mental Health Association (Vancouver-Burnaby); B.C. Liberal Party; Liberal Party of Canada, B.C.; Non-Partisan Association; Salvation Army Red Shield Appeal (Zone Captain); Alpha Gamma Delta Fraternity; Vancouver Lawn Tennis & Badminton Club. **HONS:** Businesswoman of the Year, Vancouver Jr. Board of Trade, 1987; Canada 125 Medal. **INTERESTS:** tennis; vexillology; my grandchildren; volunteer work. **MISC:** Political Commentator, *Early Edition*, CBC, 1992; Political Commentator, CBC-TV, 1992. **COMMENT:** *"My greatest achievement was balancing my career with high-profile community service and family–seven grandchildren. We created our business, The Flag Shop. We were first in North America (perhaps the world)."*

Bray, Tammy M., B.Sc.,M.Sc., Ph.D. ■ 🎓 ⊕

Professor and Chair, Department of Human Nutrition and Food Management, College of Human Ecology, THE OHIO STATE UNIVERSITY, Columbus, OH 43210-1295. Born China 1947. m. John. 3 ch. **EDUC:** Fu-Jen Univ., B.Sc. 1967; Washington State Univ., M.Sc. 1970, Ph.D. 1974. **CAREER:** Post-Doctoral Research Assoc., Washington State Univ., 1974-78; Asst. Prof., Nutritional Sciences, Univ. of Guelph, 1978-83; Assoc. Prof., 1983-89; Acting Chair, 1991-92; Acting Assoc. VP, Academic, 1992-94; Prof., Dept. of Nutritional Sciences, 1989-95; Prof. & Chair, Dept. of Human Nutrition & Food Mgmt, Coll. of Human Ecology, The Ohio State Univ., 1995 to date. **SELECTED PUBLICATIONS:** author/co-author of 76 papers published in refereed journals or books. **AFFIL:** American Institute of Nutrition; Canadian Society for Nutritional Science; The Oxygen Society; Society of Toxicology; Society of Experimental Biology & Medicine; Sigma Xi; The Scientific Research Society. **HONS:** Award of Merit, Society for Experimental Biology & Medicine, 1973; Career Award for Excellence in Research, Sigma Xi (Guelph) 1991; Certificate of Innovation Award, Univ. of Guelph, 1991; Award of Excellence for Teaching, Univ. of Guelph, 1992. **INTERESTS:** golf; art.

Breault, Ann, R.N.,M.L.A. 🍁

Member of the Legislative Assembly (St. Stephen-St. Andrews), Minister of Municipalities, Culture and Housing, GOVERNMENT OF NEW BRUNSWICK, Box 6000, Fredericton, NB E3B 5H1 (506) 453-3001, FAX 453-3283. Born Moncton 1938. m. Michel Breault. 6 ch. **EDUC:** N.B. Teachers' Coll.; Saint John Sch. of Nursing. **CAREER:** Teacher; Registered Nurse; Journalist; elected M.L.A. (St. Stephen-Milltown), 1987; re-elected, 1991; Min. of Income Assistance, 1991 to date; Min. of State for Literacy, 1991-95; re-elected 1995 to Min. of Municipalities, Culture & Housing. **AFFIL:** Centracare Saint John Inc. (Dir.); Charlotte County Women's Council; N.B. Div., Canadian Mental Health Association.

Bremner, Janice ■■ 🏐

Olympic Athlete. c/o Canadian Olympic Association. Born Burlington, Ont. 1974. **SPORTS CAREER:** started competing at age 9; mbr., Cdn Nat'l Synchronized Swimming Team, 1990 to date. Olympic Games: Silver, team, 1996.

World championships: 2nd, team, 1994. World jr. championships: 3rd, solo, & 4th, team, 1991. World Cup: 2nd, team, 1995; 2nd, team, 1993. Canadian championships: 1st, team, & 4th, solo, 1995; 3rd, duet, 3rd, team, & 4th, solo, 1994; 3rd, duet, 4th, team, & 5th, solo, 1993; 1st, solo, & 1st, team, 1991. **HONS:** Petro-Canada Olympic Torch Scholarship, 1994. **INTERESTS:** hockey (Vancouver Canucks).

Brent, Audrey S., B.A.,LL.B.,LL.M. ⚖

Managing Partner, BRENT & GREENHORN, 3501 - 8th St. E., Ste. 216, Saskatoon, SK S7H 0W5 (306) 955-9544, FAX 955-2656. Born Winnipeg. s. **EDUC:** Univ. of Saskatchewan, B.A.(Hist. & English) 1974, LL.B.(Law) 1974; Univ. of Illinois, LL.M.(Evidence) 1982. **BAR:** Sask., 1975; Alta., 1985; Man., 1985. **CAREER:** Dir., South East Legal Aid, 1976; Sr. Prosecutor, Fed. Dept. of Justice, 1977-79; Special Prosecutor, Sask. Dept. of Justice, 1979-84; Halyk Brent Dovell, 1984-89; Brent & Greenhorn, 1989 to date. **SELECTED PUBLICATIONS:** "Horsley v. MacLaren–A Case Comment," (*Saskatchewan Law Review* (37) 1972-73); "Legal Notes: Tendering Intercepted Communications as Evidence" (*R.C.M.P. Gazette* (44) 2, 1982); "Farmers' Legal Rights and Obligations," *Farm Crisis: Struggle For Hope* (Fifth House, 1987); various articles & chapters. **EDIT:** Sask. Ed., *Law Review*, Canadian Bar Association. **AFFIL:** Law Society of Saskatchewan; Law Society of Alberta; Law Society of Manitoba; Canadian Club of Saskatoon (Pres.); Saskatchewan Association of Trial Lawyers (Pres.); Association of Trial Lawyers (Gov. & State Delegate); Canadian Bar Association (Nat'l Exec.; Chair, Legislative & Law Reform); National Farmers' Union; Saskatoon Criminal Defence Association; Family Mediation, Canada; Family Mediation, Saskatoon.

Brewer, Hon. Jane 🍁

Regional Councillor and Mayor, CITY OF CAMBRIDGE, 73 Water St. N., Cambridge, ON N1R 5W8 (519) 740-4517, FAX 740-7512. Born Toronto 1924. d. 2 ch. **CAREER:** Acctnt, automotive retail store; Alderman, City of Cambridge, 1979-88; Reg'l Councillor, 1983 to date; Mayor, 1988 to date. **DIRECTOR:** Cambridge & North Dumfries Hydro Commission (ex officio); Cambridge Memorial Hospital Corporation (ex officio). **AFFIL:** Preston I.O.D.E.; St. Peter's Lutheran Church Women (Past Pres.); St. Peter's Lutheran Church (Past Constitution Committee Chrm); Evangelical Lutheran Church in Canada (Chair, Court of Adjudication; Past Chair, Office & Fin.; Past VP, Eastern Synod); Lutheran Church in America (Past Pres., Eastern Synod; Past Chrm, Stewardship Committee; Past Dir., Canada Section); Lutheran World Federation (Exec. Committee); Conestoga Coll. (Past Gov.); Cambridge United Way (Hon. Chair); Can Amera Games (Hon. Chair); Preston Figure Skating Club; Cambridge Employment Options; numerous committees, City of Cambridge Local Council & Reg'l Municipality of Waterloo Council. **HONS:** Woman of the Year (Politics), Kitchener-Waterloo Oktoberfest Women of the Year Committee, 1991; Paul Harris Award, Rotary Club, 1991; Woman of Distinction in the Political Field, YWCA, 1996. **COMMENT:** *"I am a grandmother with five grandchildren, and have been a politician for 17 years, six of them as mayor. I function at a world level for Lutheran World Federation, Geneva."*

Brewin, Gretchen, B.A.,M.L.A. 🍁 ☝

Member of Legislative Assembly (Victoria-Beacon Hill), GOVERNMENT OF BRITISH COLUMBIA, Parliament Building, Victoria, BC V8V 1X4 (604) 356-3031, FAX 356-6538. Born Ottawa. 4 ch. **EDUC:** Univ. of Victoria, B.A. 1976. **CAREER:** Councillor, City of Victoria, 1979; Mayor, 1985; M.L.A. (Victoria-Beacon Hill) & N.D.P. Caucus, Prov. of B.C., 1991 to date. **DIRECTOR:** B.C. Ferry Corporation. **AFFIL:** City of Victoria Police Board (Chair 1985); Cdn Nat'l Committee to Celebrate U.N. 50th Anniversary (Gov't of B.C. Rep. 1995-96); Team Canada, Commonwealth Games 1994 in Victoria (Attaché); Commonwealth Games Association of Canada (Bd. Mbr. 1994-98); Native Friendship Centre; Capital Project Committee; Silver Threads Service; Project Literacy; Capital Regional Housing Corporation; Prime Time Voice of Women; B.C. Transit Commission; New Democratic Party of B.C.; Arts & Cultural Festival Committee. **INTERESTS:** politics. **MISC:** first woman Mayor of Victoria; initiated Victoria First Social Planning Committee & position of Social Planner; est. City Task Force on Violence Against Women, Children & the Elderly; mbr., presentation team that brought Commonwealth Games to Victoria, 1994; first woman to be Dep. Speaker of BC Legislature.

Brien, Danielle Carle, B.A.,B.B.A., M.B.A. ■ $

Vice-President, Business Development, Confectionery Products, CULINAR INC., Grocery Division, 4945 East Ontario St., Montréal, QC H1V 1M2 (514) 255-2811, FAX 251-2184. Born Shawinigan, Que. 1949. m. Denis Brien. **EDUC:** Univ. Laval, B.A. 1969; Univ. du Québec, B.B.A. 1971; Univ. of Western Ontario, M.B.A. 1973. **CAREER:** Mktg Mgr,

Bank of Nova Scotia, 1980-89; Dir., Mktg & Sales, Coopérative Fédérée du Québec, 1989-93; VP, Larson and Company, 1993-94; VP, Mktg, Culinar Inc., 1994 to date. **AFFIL:** Réseau de Capital de Risque (Dir., Members' Bulletin 1994-95); YMCA Montréal (Mbr., Mktg Committee 1993-94); Centre des dirigeants d'entreprise (Pres.). **INTERESTS:** bus. dev. integrating problem solving, team building & creativity to improve company market position. **COMMENT:** *"Hands-on experience in marketing, sales and distribution coupled with a close link to production has resulted in successful development and implementation of company restructuring and repositioning programs throughout my career."*

Briskin, Linda, B.A.,M.A.,Ph.D. ⌐ ❀
Associate Professor, Social Science Division, YORK UNIVERSITY, 4700 Keele St., North York, ON M3J 1P3 (416) 736-5054, ext. 77824, FAX 736-5615, EMAIL lbriskin@yorku.ca. Born Montreal 1949. **EDUC:** McGill Univ., B.A. 1970, Class 1 Teaching Certificate (English & Hist.) 1971, Diploma in the Teaching of Reading 1974; York Univ., M.A.(Soc. & Pol. Thought) 1977, Ph.D.(Soc. & Pol. Thought) 1986. **CAREER:** High Sch. Teacher, Protestant Sch. Bd. of Greater Montreal, 1971-75; Teaching Master, Sch. of Applied Arts & Comm., Sheridan Coll., 1978-86; Dir., Centre for Women, Sheridan Coll., 1980-82; Asst. Prof., Soc. Sci. Div., York Univ., 1986-91; Assoc. Prof., 1991 to date. **SELECTED CREDITS:** *Rising Up Strong* (video documentary), 1981, updated 1992. **SELECTED PUBLICATIONS:** *The Day the Fairies Went On Strike*, children's book, with Maureen Fitzgerald (Vancouver: Press Gang Publishers, 1982); *Union Sisters: Women in the Labour Movement*, ed. with Lynda Yanz (Toronto: Women's Press, 1983); *Feminist Organizing for Change: A Study of the Contemporary Women's Movement in Canada*, with Nancy Adamson & Margaret McPhail (Toronto: Oxford University Press, 1988); *Feminist Pedagogy: Teaching and Learning Liberation* (Ottawa: CRIAW, 1990); *Women Challenging Unions: Feminism, Democracy and Militancy*, ed. with Patricia McDermott (Toronto: University of Toronto Press, 1993); *Gender Union Democracy: A Swedish-Canadian Comparison* (Centre for Research on Work and Society, York University, 1996); numerous journal articles, chapters in books, reviews & other publications; numerous conference papers. **EDIT:** Guest Ed., with Rebecca Coulter, special issue on feminist pedagogy, *Canadian Journal of Education*, Summer 1992. **AFFIL:** Canadian Women's Studies Association; Canadian Research Institute for

the Advancement of Women; Labour Studies Association; Critical Pedagogy Network; Society for Socialist Studies. **HONS:** Muriel V. Roscoe Scholarship, McGill Univ., 1969; MH Beatty Bursary, McGill Univ., 1971; Clara Capp Travel & Study Scholarship, 1971. **MISC:** recipient of numerous grants from various agencies; listed in *Canadian Who's Who*, 1989 to date; *Biography International*, 1990 to date; *Dictionary of International Biography*, 1992 to date; Guest Researcher, Arbetslivcentrum, Stockholm, Sweden, 1992, 1993, 1994; various workshops on feminist pedagogy; numerous keynote addresses public & invited lectures; peer reviewer for journals, grants, universities; numerous media appearances; participant, Invitational Round Table Discussion on Women & Unions, Ottawa, 1989; expert witness on women & unions & gendered teaching practices, for the Federation of Women's Teachers' Associations of Ontario in front of the Ont. Human Rights Commission, 1990-91. **COMMENT:** *"As a feminist scholar and activist, I am interested in change-making strategies for women–in the labour movement, the community-based women's movement, and in the classroom."*

Brister, Stephanie J., B.Sc.,M.D. ■ ⊕ ⌐
Cardiovascular Surgeon, HAMILTON CIVIC HOSPITALS, The Wellington Medical Centre, 293 Wellington N., Ste. 132, Hamilton, ON L8L 8E7 (905) 521-8795, FAX 523-4885. Associate Clinical Professor of Surgery, MCMASTER UNIVERSITY. Born Rivers, Man. 1953. **EDUC:** Univ. of Calgary, B.Sc.(Biol.) 1974, M.D. 1979. **CAREER:** Research Asst., Div. of Gen. Surgery, McGill Univ., 1983-86; Chief Resident, Gen. Surgery, Montreal General Hospital, McGill Univ., July-Oct. 1986; Chief Resident, Cardiovascular & Thoracic Surgery, Div. of Cardiovascular & Thoracic Surgery, Kingston General Hospital, Queen's Univ., 1986-88; Clinical Research Fellow, Div. of Cardiovascular Surgery, The Toronto General Hospital, Univ. of Toronto, 1988-89; Asst. Prof., Dept. of Surgery, McMaster Univ., 1989-94; Staff Surgeon, Div. of Cardiovascular Surgery, Hamilton Civic Hospitals, 1989 to date; Assoc. Mbr., Hamilton Civic Hospitals Research Centre, 1989 to date. **SELECTED PUBLICATIONS:** "Clinical Impact of Intravenous Hyperalimentation in Esophageal Carcinoma: Is It Worthwhile?" with others (*Annals of Thoracic Surgery* Dec. 1984); "Transforming Skeletal Muscle for Myocardial Assist: A Feasibility Study," with others (*Canadian Journal of Surgery* July 1985); "Is Heparin the Ideal Anticoagulant for Cardiopulmonary Bypass? Dermatan Sulfate May Be An Alternate Choice,"

with others (*Thrombosis and Haemostasis* 71(4) 1994); numerous articles in nonrefereed journals, chapters in books, & abstracts. **AFFIL:** Royal Coll. of Physicians & Surgeons; Ontario Medical Association; Quebec Medical Association; Canadian Medical Association; Canadian Cardiovascular Society; Canadian Society of Cardiovascular Surgery; American Heart Association; Medical Staff, Hamilton Civic Hospitals (Sec. 1992-93; VP 1993-94; Pres. 1994-95). **HONS:** Prov. of Alberta–Honours Award, 1971. **MISC:** recipient of grants from Ontario Heart & Stroke Foundation; various media interviews; numerous invited talks & lectures. **COMMENT:** *"Professional interests are cardiovascular surgery, research in the area of cardiovascular disease, specifically in adult cardiac surgery with particular interest in valvular heart surgery. In addition to clinical responsibilities, I participate in a number of research projects with other investigators at the university."*

Brodsky, Lynn M., B.Sc.,M.Sc.,Ph.D., B.Ed. ■ 🎓 ⚛

Biology Teacher, ASHBURY COLLEGE, 362 Mariposa Ave., Ottawa, ON K1M 0T3 (613) 749-5954, FAX 749-9727. Born Ottawa 1958. m. Michael R. Leslie. **EDUC:** Carleton Univ., B.Sc.(Hons., Biol.) 1980, M.Sc.(Biol.) 1983; Queen's Univ., Ph.D.(Biol.) 1986; Univ. of Western Ontario, B.Ed.(Biol. & Environmental Sci.) 1989. **CAREER:** N.S.E.R.C. Postdoctoral Fellow, Zoology Dept., Univ. of Western Ontario, 1986-88; Biol. Teacher, London Bd. of Educ., 1989-91; Biology Teacher & Boarding Housemaster, Upper Canada Coll., 1991-96; Biol. Teacher, Ashbury Coll., 1996 to date. **SELECTED PUBLICATIONS:** "Time and energy constraints on courtship in wintering black ducks: balancing energy supply and demand," with P.J. Weatherhead (*Canadian Journal of Zoology* 63 1985); "Escape responses of the pea aphid, Acyrthosiphon pisum (Harris) (*Homoptera: Aphididae*): Influence of predator type and temperature," with C.A. Barlow (*Canadian Journal of Zoology* 64 1986); "The influence of male dominance on pairing behaviour in black ducks and mallards," with C.D. Ankney & D.G. Dennis (*Animal Behaviour* 36 1988); "Ornament size influences mating success in male rock ptarmigan" (*Animal Behaviour* 36 1988). **AFFIL:** Science Teachers' Association of Ontario. **HONS:** R.H. Webster Fellowship, Delta Waterfowl Research Centre, 1983; N.S.E.R.C. Postgrad. Scholarship, Queen's Univ., 1984-86; various other scholarship & fellowships; Bishop Townshend Award for Excellence in Teaching, London Bd. of Educ., 1991. **INTERESTS:** travel; swimming; hiking; horticulture; natural history; environmental issues; biotechnology; birding; fitness.

Brodylo, Ellen M., B.A. ■ 🎬 🎭 $

President, BRODYLO/MORROW PHOTOGRAPHY, 822 - 11th Ave. S.W., Ste. 203, Calgary, AB T2R 0E5. Born Calgary 1960. s. **EDUC:** Univ. of Calgary, B.A.(English) 1985. **CAREER:** Pres., Co-owner, Photographer, Brodylo/Morrow Photography, 1986 to date; Film Dir., Red Motel Pictures Inc., 1994 to date. **COMMISSIONS:** commissioned work has appeared in numerous magazines incl. *Canadian Business* magazine, *Saturday Night*, *Rolling Stone*, *The Globe and Mail*, *Report on Business*, *Time* & *Outside*. **HONS:** National Magazine Awards; Art Directors' Club of Toronto Awards; Applied Art Award; Western Magazine Awards; various other industry awards. **INTERESTS:** travel; skiing; music. **MISC:** art photographs represented by Canadian Art Galleries; still photographs represented by Brodylo/Morrow Photography; film & video projects represented by Red Motel Pictures. **COMMENT:** *"I am a corporate, editorial, and advertising photographer, a film director and visual artist. Have photographed prime ministers, premiers, the corporate elite, celebrities, rock personalities. Have recently moved into the field of motion pictures."*

Brooks, Bonnie ■ $

Senior Vice-President, Marketing, HOLT, RENFREW & CO., LIMITED, 50 Bloor St. W., Toronto, ON M4A 1A1 (416) 960-2911, FAX 920-7284. Born Windsor, Ont. s. **EDUC:** Univ. of Toronto, Arts/English; York Univ., Soc./Psych.; Ryerson Polytechnic Univ., Mktg. **CAREER:** Nat'l Advtg Mgr, Fairweather/Big Steel/Braemar, Dylex Limited, 1978-81; Dir., Mktg & Sales Promo., Holt Renfrew & Co. Limited, 1981-82; VP, Mktg & Sales Promo., 1982-85; Exec. VP, 1985-90; Pres., Town & Country, 1990-91; Pres., Kert Advertising Ltd., 1992-94; Ed., *Flare* Magazine, Maclean Hunter Publishing Limited/Rogers Multimedia, 1994-96; Sr. VP, Mktg, Holt Renfrew & Co., Limited, 1996 to date. **DIRECTOR:** Household Financial Corporation; Fashion Group International Inc. **AFFIL:** Canadian Women's Opera Committee; Brazilian Ball Committee; Royal Ontario Museum; Canadian Women's Breast Cancer Foundation; Heart & Stroke Foundation. **HONS:** 12 Advertising Awards of Excellence, R.A.C., Chicago, 1978-88; Woman Who Makes a Difference Award, Toronto, 1989.

Brooks, Nan, LL.B.,M.H.S.A.,CHE ⚖ ✚

Consultant. Born Toronto 1961. m. Saverio Rinaldi. **EDUC:** Dalhousie Univ., LL.B. 1985,

Master's in Health Svcs Admin. 1988. **BAR:** Ont., 1990. **CAREER:** Consultant, Centenary Health Centre, 1990-92; Hospital Consultant, Ministry of Health, 1992-94; Consultant, Johnston, Smith, Franklin, 1994-95; Consultant, The Lyra Group, 1995-96. **DIRECTOR:** The Health Station. **AFFIL:** Law Society of Upper Canada; Canadian Coll. of Health Services Executives (Certified Health Exec. 1991 to date). **HONS:** Honour Award, Dalhousie Univ., 1988. **INTERESTS:** sailing; quilting; stained glass; volleyball; playing jazz trombone; running; knitting; skiing; cross-stitch; cooking; piano. **COMMENT:** *"Nan Brooks has a broad range of experience as a lawyer, administrator and consultant in health care reform. She has been critical in the Essex County Health Care Reform labour negotiations and the York Region Restructuring Project."*

Brooks, Patricia J., B.A.(Hons.), M.A. $ 📖 ⊛

Manager, National Communications, DELOITTE & TOUCHE, Chartered Accountants and Management Consultants, 95 Wellington St. W., Toronto, ON M5J 2P4 (416) 601-5920, FAX 601-5921. Born Montreal 1961. s. **EDUC:** Univ. of Windsor, B.A.(Gen.) 1982, B.A. (Hons.) 1983; Concordia Univ., M.A. 1984. **CAREER:** Customer Svc Rep., Cala Advertising, 1984-86; Prod. Coord. & Ed., ScotiaMcLeod Inc., 1986-88; Asst. Comm. Coord., ScotiaMcLeod Inc., 1988; Tech. Writer & Ed., Liquor Control Board of Ontario, 1988-89; Public Rel'ns & Proj. Coord., 1989-90; Public Consultation & Comm. Coord., Rouge Valley Project, Ministry of Natural Resources, 1991-92; Sr. Comm. Advisor, Price Waterhouse, 1992-93; Mgr, Nat'l Comm., Deloitte & Touche, 1993 to date. **EDIT:** Assoc. Ed., newsletter of Save the Rouge Valley System, 1991 to date. **EXHIBITIONS:** photographs published & on display incl. in the offices of the Crombie Commission, Toronto, & the Univ. of Toronto Fac. of Social Work. **AFFIL:** Canadian Women in Communications; International Association of Business Communicators; Society for Technical Communications; Professional Photographers of America; Professional Photographers of Ontario; Toronto Women's Marketing Professionals; United Way (Volunteer Coord.); Friends of the Altona Forest (Comm. Consultant); Fac. of Social Work, Univ. of Toronto (Volunteer Mgr of Comm.); Friends of Scarborough (Bd. of Dir.; Dir. of Comm.); Rouge Valley Community Trust Fund (Bd. of Dir.). **HONS:** President's Roll of Scholars, Univ. of Windsor, 1983; Finalist, Women Who Make a Difference, 1995. **INTERESTS:** consulting; volunteer work; mentoring women professionals. **MISC:** Trillium Cable, Host for *Roundtable* (public affairs program). **COMMENT:** *"I am fortunate that I can combine my skills in media/public relations, computer graphic arts and photography with both my paid and volunteer interests."*

Brossard, Nicole, B.A. ✒ 📖

Poet and Novelist. Born Montréal 1943. 1 ch. Julie. **EDUC:** Univ. de Montréal, Licence ès Lettres 1968; Univ. du Québec à Montréal, Baccalauréat (Spécialisé en Pédagogie) 1971. **SELECTED CREDITS:** Narrateur et personnages, dramatique d'une demi-heure, Radio-Canada, 1971; l'écrivaine, *La nef des sorcières*, 1976; Co-Dir., *Some American Feminists–1976*, National Film Board, 1976; *Une impression de fiction dans le retroviseur*, Radio-Canada, 1978; *La Falaise*, Radio-Canada, 1985; *Souvenirs d'enfance et de jeunesse*, Radio-Canada, 1987; *Correspondance*, with Michèle Causse, Radio-Canada, 1987. **SELECTED PUBLICATIONS:** numerous collections of poetry, incl. *Mordre sa chair* (Montréal: Esterel, 1966); *L'écho bouge beau* (Montréal: Esterel, 1968); *Suite logique* (Montréal: Hexagone, 1970); *Le centre blanc* (Montréal: Orphée, 1970); Mécanique jongleuse (Paris: Génération, 1973); *Mécanique jongleuse/Masculin grammaticale* (Montréal: Hexagone, 1974); *La partie pour le tout* (Montréal: L'aurore, 1975); *Double Impression* (Montréal: Hexagone, 1984); *L'Aviva* (Montréal: Nouvelle Barre du Jour, 1985); *Domaine d'écriture* (Montréal: Nouvelle Barre du Jour, 1985); *Mauve*, with Daphne Marlatt (Montréal: NBJ, 1985); *Character/Jeu de lettres*, with Daphne Marlatt (Montréal: NBJ, 1986); *A Tout Regard* (Montréal: NBJ/Bibliothèque Québécoise, 1989); *Installations* (Trois-Rivères: Écrits des Forges, 1989); *Typhon Dru*, with Christine Davies (Paris: Collectif Génération, 1990); *La subjectivité des lionnes* (Bruxelles: L'arbre à paroles, asbl identités, 1990); *Langues obscures* (Montréal: Hexagone, 1992); *La nuit verte du Parc Labyrinthe* (Montréal: Trois, 1992); numerous novels, including *Un Livre* (Montréal: Édition du Jour, 1970); *Sold-Out* (Montréal: Éditions du Jour, 1973); *French Kiss* (Montréal: Éditions du Jour, 1974); *L'amèr ou le chapitre effrité* (Montréal: Quinze, 1977); *Le sens apparent* (Paris: Flammarion/Collection Textes, 1980); *Picture Theory* (Montréal: Nouvelle Optique, 1982); *Journal intime* (Montréal: Les Herbes rouges, 1984); *Le désert mauve* (Montréal: Hexagone, 1987); *Baroque d'Aube* (Montréal: Hexagone, 1995); various novels have been translated; editor of two anthologies, *The Story So Far/Les Stratégies du Réel* (Toronto: Coach House Press, 1978); *Anthologie de la* *poésie des femmes au Québec 1677-1988,* with Lisette Girouard (Montréal: Éditions Remue-Ménage, 1991); essay *La lettre aérienne* (Éditions Remue-Ménage, 1985), translated. **AFFIL:** Union des écrivaines et écrivains du Québec; Académie des Lettres du Québec; Council of Arts of the Urban Community of Montréal (Bd.). **HONS:** Gov. General's Prize, 1974, 1984; Chapbook Award, Therafields Foundation, 1986; Grand Prix de Poésie, Fondation Les Forges, 1989; Prix Athanase-David, 1991; Prize, Harbourfront Festival, 1991; Hon. Doctorate, Univ. of Western Ontario, 1991. **INTERESTS:** feminism. **MISC:** Co-founder & Co-Dir., literary journal *La Barre du Jour,* 1965-75; Co-founder & Co-Dir., feminist newspaper *Les Têtes de Pioche,* 1976-79.

Brotchie, Doneta, B.Comm. $

Senior Vice-President, Central Prairie Region, CIBC, Box 814, Winnipeg, MB R3C 2P3 (204) 944-5324, FAX 956-1582. Born Winnipeg 1951. m. Henry "Harry" Brotchie. 2 ch. Harry, Annie. **EDUC:** Univ. of Manitoba, B.Comm. (Mktg & Organizational Behaviour) 1973. **CAREER:** Div. Merchandise Mgr, Fashion Accessories, 1981-87; Mgr, downtown store, The Bay, 1987-88; Softgoods Mktg Mgr, Prairie Reg., 1988-89; self-employed, fashion accessories retailer & mktg consultant, 1989-90; District Mgr, CIBC, 1990-91; Sr. VP, Central Prairie Reg., 1991 to date. **DIRECTOR:** Comcheq Services. **AFFIL:** 1999 PanAmerican Games (V-Chair, Mktg); 1999 PanAmerican Games Society (Winnipeg 1999); Brandon Univ. Foundation (Trustee); Health Sciences Centre Foundation; Univ. of Saskatchewan, Institute for Society & Humanities (Trustee); Canadian Club. **INTERESTS:** theatre; symphony; art; ballet; sports; travel.

Brown, Alice J., R.N. ■ 🌾 $

Secretary-Treasurer, BROWNHILL FARMS LTD., Box 21, Kathyrn, AB T0M 1E0 (403) 935-4992, FAX 935-4470. Born Oklahoma City 1938. m. Bert Brown. 1 ch. Angela. **EDUC:** Univ. of Oklahoma Sch. of Nursing, R.N. 1959. **CAREER:** Operating Room Supervisor, Central Supply Supervisor, Central State Hospital, Norman, Oklahoma, 1959-66; Shift Head Nurse, 1967-68; Dir., Federated Co-operatives Ltd., 1987-96. **AFFIL:** Calgary Co-operative Association Ltd. (Dir. 1982-94, 1995 to date); Canadian Co-operatives Association (Mbr., Task Force on Women & Co-operatives); Canada West Foundation (Sec.-Treas.); Olds Coll. (Bd. of Gov.); Unifarm; Women for the Survival of Agriculture. **HONS:** Calgary YWCA Women of Distinction Awards in Bus., Labour & Professions, & Award for Advancement of Women, 1994. **MISC:** Chair, First Alberta Farm Women's Conference, 1986. **COMMENT:** *"Active advocate for women's advancement in agriculture, cooperatives and business management. Working for equal opportunity for women in Canadian society at all levels."*

Brown, Betty ■ ✊ 🌾

President, NEW BRUNSWICK FARM WOMEN'S ORGANIZATION, R.R. 2 (Summerfield), Florenceville, NB E0J 1K0 (506) 278-5439, FAX 278-5290. Born Bath, N.B. 1947. m. Ronald. 3 ch. Kevin, Jane, Andrea. **CAREER:** Farmer, 1965 to date; Owner/Operator, small cow/calf beef oper., 1981 to date. **AFFIL:** Canadian Farm Women's Network (Alternate Dir. 1993); N.B. Federation of Agriculture (Dir., N.W. Reg. 1991-94); N.B. Farm Women (Pres.). **INTERESTS:** anything connected with agriculture & food esp. gov't involvement in agricultural policy & trade agreements & their effect on Cdn agriculture, Cdn farm families & safe, quality food for Cdn consumers; reading; sewing. **COMMENT:** *"Personally became involved in formation of N.B.F.W. to ensure education and awareness of the role of farm women. Have taken an active role in other boards and committees working to improve the agriculture industry and lives of farm families. Continuing to lobby on behalf of farm families to ensure a future industry for the next generation of food production."*

Brown, Caroline Margaret, B.A., B.Ed. ☼ ✊ ⊕

President, SOCIETY OF NOVA SCOTIANS FOR A CLEAN ENVIRONMENT, Yarmouth, NS B5A 4H6 (902) 742-0958. Born Newport, UK 1951. m. Gregory A. Brown. 2 ch. Christina Caroline, Gregory Ronald W. **EDUC:** Mount Allison Univ., B.A.(English) 1972, B.Ed.(Secondary Educ.) 1973. **CAREER:** Teacher, High Sch. English & Math., 1973-83. **VOLUNTEER CAREER:** Sec., N.S. Childbirth Educ. Association, 1984-90; Pres., Society of Nova Scotians for a Clean Environment, 1990 to date. **SELECTED PUBLICATIONS:** numerous position papers & press releases for the Society of Nova Scotians for a Clean Environment & the N.S. Childbirth Educ. Association. **AFFIL:** Arcadia Home & Sch. Association (VP 1991-93; Treas. 1993); St. Ambrose Cathedral Parish (Dir., Vacation Bible Sch.); Yarmouth Junior High Sch. Advisory Council (Chair 1996-97). **HONS:** honored at local volunteer night by the municipality. **INTERESTS:** Christianity; environment; childbirth reform; children. **MISC:** Teacher, Grade 6 Sunday Sch.; Advisor, Grade 6 Debating Club, Arcadia Sch. **COMMENT:**

"As a committed Christian, working to protect people, I have defeated a planned incinerator, prevented a tin mine pit from becoming a garbage dump, and had a study on childbirth done."

Brown, Fran ■ ■ ◑ ⊕
Vice-Chair of the Board of Trustees, BLOORVIEW MACMILLAN CENTRE. m. 4 ch. EDUC: Royal Victoria Hospital, Montreal, R.N. CAREER: Neonatal Research Unit, Sick Children's Hospital, 1963-71. VOLUNTEER CAREER: Bd. mbr., J.D. Griffin Adolescent Centre, 6 yrs.; Bd. mbr., Junior League of Toronto, 1979-81; Chair of the Bd., Extend-a-Family, Toronto, 1982-83; Chair of the Bd., POINT, 1987-88; Chrm of the Bd., Yonge Eglinton Health Centre, 1990-93; Chair, Community Advisory Council & mbr., Bd. of Trustees, Sunnybrook Health Science Centre, 1994 to date; mbr., Prov. Interministerial Advisory Committee on Child & Youth Health Policy, 1994-96; V-Chair & mbr., Bd. of Trustees, Bloorview Children's Hospital, 1990-96; V-Chair of the Bd. of Trustees, Bloorview MacMillan Centre, 1996 to date. AFFIL: Granite Club; Devil's Glen Ski Club; St. George's United Church; Junior League. HONS: awards in ward mgmt & metabolic nursing; Provincial Community Svc. Award, 1991; Fed. Canada 125 Medal for volunteerism, 1992; POINT Volunteer Award, 1992. INTERESTS: farming (Simmental cattle breeding); skiing; music; tennis; travel.

Brown, Jan, B.Ed.,M.C.S.,M.A.,M.P. ♣
Member of Parliament (Calgary Southeast), GOVERNMENT OF CANADA, House of Commons, Ottawa, ON K1A 0A6 (613) 996-2791. Calgary Office: Ste. 111, Willowpark Centre, 10325 Bonaventure Dr. S.E., Calgary, AB T2J 7E4 (403) 271-1127, FAX 271-5832. Born Nanaimo, B.C. 1947. m. Tony Brown. 2 ch. EDUC: Univ. of British Columbia, B.Ed. 1980; Univ. of Calgary, M.C.S.(Comm. Studies) 1986; Fielding Institute, California, M.A.(Organizational Dev.) 1991. CAREER: educator, 1980-87; entered agribusiness sector, 1987; owner of a consulting bus. focusing on proj. mgmt & organizational dev., started 1991; former Critic for Cdn Heritage & Culture; current Critic, Hum. Res. Dev. & Status of Women, Reform Party of Canada; MP, Calgary S.E., Gov't of Canada, 1993 to date; Alternate Mbr., Agriculture Standing Committee, Reform Party of Canada, 1993-96; resigned as Mbr. of Reform Party Caucus, 1996; currently sitting as Mbr. with Independent status in House of Commons. SELECTED PUBLICATIONS: "Changing the Gender Agenda of Poli-

tics" (*Canadian Parliamentary Review*, June 1993). AFFIL: Canada-Cyprus Parliamentary Association (VP). INTERESTS: political reform (people & policy); reading; writing; hiking; travel. MISC: many published works & keynote addresses. COMMENT: *"Jan is committed to the needs and expectations of her constituents in Calgary Southeast. Her personal, intellectual and professional background lend strong support to her efforts in building a new Canada."*

Brown, Janet L., B.A. ◑
Volunteer. 5650 Hampton Place, Ste. 3, Vancouver, BC V6T 2G5. Born N.Y. m. John. 4 ch. EDUC: Univ. of British Columbia; San José State Univ., B.A.(Educ.). CAREER: taught elementary & jr. high sch. VOLUNTEER CAREER: Dir., University Women's Club of Vancouver; Pres., 1982-84; currently, Chair, Constitution & By-Laws Committee; Bd. Mbr., Catholic Community Svcs; Pres.; Chair, Selection Committee (to select current Exec. Dir.); Consumer Advisory Bd., Hudson Bay Co., 1986-87; Volunteer Liaison Officer (worked with the organizing committee & the RCMP), Commonwealth Conference, Vancouver, 1987; Bd. of Dir., Vancouver College Ltd.; Pres., 1990-92. AFFIL: BC Health Association (Bd. 1995 to date); Vancouver Museum (Bd. of Trustees; Chair, Mbrship Committee); St. Paul's Hospital (Bd. of Trustees 1993 to date; Chair, Patient Care & Quality Assurance Committee); B.C. Transplant Society (Bd. 1994 to date); Caraim, Catholic Health Care Society of Vancouver; Shaughnessy Golf & Country Club (Bd. 1990-92).

Brown, Jennifer S.H., A.B.,A.M., Ph.D. ■ ⌂ ▨
Professor, Department of History, UNIVERSITY OF WINNIPEG, 151 Portage Ave., Winnipeg, MB R3B 2E9 (204) 786-9003, FAX 774-4134. Born Providence, R.I. 1940. m. Wilson B. Brown. 1 ch. EDUC: Brown Univ., A.B. (Ancient & Medievel Culture) 1962; Harvard Univ., A.M.(Classical Archaeology) 1963; Univ. of Chicago, Ph.D.(Anthro.) 1976. CAREER: Teacher, Colby Coll., Northern Illinois Univ., Indiana Univ., 1966-82; Assoc. Prof., Univ. of Winnipeg, 1982-88; Prof., 1988 to date. SELECTED PUBLICATIONS: *Strangers in Blood: Fur Trade Company Families in Indian Country* (1980); Co-ed., *The New Peoples: Being and Becoming Métis in North America* (1985); Co-author, *The Orders of the Dreamed: George Nelson on Cree and Northern Ojibwa Religion and Myths* (1988); Ed., *The Ojibwa of Berens River*, Manitoba: Ethnography into History by A. Irving Hallowell (1992); Co-ed.

Reading Beyond Words: Contexts for Native History (1996); author of more than 60 articles on the fur trade, Northern Algonquin & Métis history, culture, biography & interactions with Europeans. **AFFIL:** American Society for Ethnohistory (Councillor 1984-86; Pres. 1989-90); Champlain Society (Council 1986 to date); Manitoba Record Society (Dir. 1986 to date); Rupert's Land Record Society (Gen. Ed. 1986 to date). **HONS:** Hon. Mention (*Stranger in Blood*), Sir John A. Macdonald Prize, 1981; Erica & Arnold Rogers Award for Excellence in Research and Scholarship, Univ. of Winnipeg, 1992; SSHRC research grant, 1990-95. **INTERESTS:** issues & problems in the study of texts & their subtexts & contexts in historical research; Native & women's history & biography; countering stereotypes; advancing the knowledge & understanding of students–especially of those who will go on in these fields. **MISC:** presenter at numerous conferences & meetings; consultant on film, radio & popular-history publications. **COMMENT:** *"Deeply involved in research, writing, reading, teaching, I come from a professional family and enjoy books and texts, collaborative discussion and the sharing of knowledge and understanding, crossing boundaries whether disciplinary, territorial, temporal, or other."*

Brown, Joanne C., AIIC ■■ ⊛ Ⓢ
Executive Director, INSURANCE BROKERS' ASSOCIATION OF CANADA, 181 University Ave., Ste. 1902, Toronto, ON M5H 3M7 (416) 367-1831, FAX 367-3687. Born Chatham, Ont. s. **EDUC:** Insurance Institute of Canada, Assoc. **CAREER:** in property & casualty insur. industry, 1966 to date; VP, Marsh & McLennan Limited, to 1992; joined IBAC, 1992. **AFFIL:** Centre for the Studies of Insurance Operations (Bd. mbr.); Toronto Insurance Conference (Exec. Committee 1988; Pres. 1990; served on various committees); Insurance Institute of Canada (former Gov.); Insurance Bureau of Canada (former mbr., Task Force on Insur. Fraud); Ajax & Pickering General Hospital Auxiliary (volunteer); Ajax & Pickering General Hospital (fund raising).

Brown, Joy, B.E.,M.Sc. ⊛ ⋞
Geophysicist, CHEVRON CANADA RESOURCES, 500-5th Ave. S.W., Calgary, AB T2P 0L7 (403) 234-5331, FAX 234-5947. Born Saskatoon, Sask. 1964. s. **EDUC:** Univ. of Saskatchewan, B.E. 1986, M.Sc. (Geophysics) 1992. **CAREER:** Lab Instructor, Dept. of Geological Sciences, Univ. of Saskatchewan, 1988; Res. Asst., Dept. of Mining Geophysics, Delft Univ., Holland, 1989; Physics Tutor, Univ. of Calgary ("Women in Science & Engineering" tutorial),

1992; Geophysicist, Chevron Canada Resources, 1990 to date. **SELECTED PUBLICATIONS:** "A Crustal Refraction Survey over the Peace River Arch, Alberta, Canada" (*Society of Exploration Geophysicists Annual Meeting Expanded Technical Progam Abstracts with Biographies*, 1988). **AFFIL:** Alberta Women's Science Network (Chair); Association of Women in Engineering & Science (Past Pres.); Society of Exploration Geophysicists. **INTERESTS:** sports; travel. **COMMENT:** *"My love of math and science paved the path into engineering and a career in geophysics. The Association of Women in Engineering and Science and the Alberta Women's Science Network provide the opportunity to share this love and inspire young minds."*

Brown, Laurie ✧ ⊗ ⌂
Author, TV Journalist, CANADIAN BROADCASTING CORPORATION, 205 Wellington St. W., Toronto, ON M5V 3G7 (416) 205-7999, FAX 205-6759. Born Toronto 1957. m. 2 ch. **CAREER:** Co-host/Assoc. Prod., *The New Music*, Citytv; VJ, MuchMusic, 1986-90; Arts Journalist, *The Journal*, CBC, 1990-92; Arts Journalist, *Prime Time News*, CBC, 1992 to date. **SELECTED PUBLICATIONS:** *Success Without College: Days and Nights in Rock'n'Roll* (Penguin Books, 1994); "Songs from the Bush Garden" (*Cultural Studies* vol. 5, no. 3). **HONS:** Award for Excellence in Arts Journalism, Canadian Conference on the Arts, 1993. **MISC:** singer, *The Crowd in History*, 1981-86. **COMMENT:** *"My interests lie not only with the artists in this country but with the media that deliver them to us. Our complex, changing mediascape deserves more serious, critical reportage."*

Brown, Nancy J., A.B.,M.S.W.,C.S.W., N.A.S.W. ⊘ ⋞
Executive Director, HALTON FAMILY SERVICES, 235 Lakeshore Rd. E., Box 69523, Oakville, ON L6J 7R4 (905) 845-3811, FAX 845-3537. Born Pittsburgh, Penn. 1943. m. George. 2 ch. Rob, Jan. **EDUC:** Mount Holyoke Coll., Mass., A.B.(Psych.) 1965; Smith Coll. Sch. for Social Work, Northampton, MA, M.S.W. 1967; N.A.S.W. 1995. **CAREER:** field placement, V.A. Hospital, Brockton, Mass., 1965-66; field placement, Family & Children's Svcs, Washington, D.C., 1966-67; Caseworker I, Child & Family Svc., Norfolk, Virg., 1967-68; Sch. Social Worker, Special Svcs Proj., Middletown Sch. System, Middletown, R.I., 1969; Sr. Psychiatric Social Worker, Newport County Mental Health Clinic, Newport, R.I., 1969-72; Sch. Social Worker, Wayne-Westland Community Schools, Wayne, Mich., 1972-73; Consultant,

Comprehensive Mental Health Center, Newport, R.I., 1973; Staff Social Worker, Barnert Memorial Hospital Center, Paterson, N.J., 1974-75; Unit Supervisor, Catholic Children's Aid Society of Metropolitan Toronto, 1975-76; Exec. Dir., Halton Family Services, 1976 to date. **AFFIL:** Academy of Certified Social Workers; Ontario Coll. of Certified Social Workers. **INTERESTS:** reading; Christian service. **COMMENT:** *"My life has been devoted to serving God by helping people of all ages and types to overcome adversity through counselling."*

Brown, Ruth Louise, B.A.,M.S.W. ✆
Past President, NATIONAL COUNCIL OF WOMEN OF CANADA, 270 MacLaren St., Ottawa, ON K2P 0M3 (613) 232-5025, FAX 232-8419. Born Sunkist, Sask. 1922. m. Kenneth C. Brown. 4 ch. David, Deborah, Christopher, Andrew. **EDUC:** Univ. of Toronto, B.A.(Modern Languages) 1945; M.S.W. 1947. **CAREER:** many years on staff of Children's Aid Society of Ottawa-Carlton as worker, Supervisor & Volunteer Coord. **AFFIL:** National Council of Women of Canada (Past Pres.); N.E. Ottawa Senior Support Services (Past Chair & Mbr., Advisory Committee); Ontario Association of Professional Social Workers, E. Ont. Branch; Canadian Association of Social Workers; Mackay United Church; International Social Services (ISS Canada) (Bd. Mbr.). **HONS:** award recognizing work on social issues affecting women & children, Ontario Association of Professional Social Workers, Eastern Branch. **INTERESTS:** involvement with community organizations. **MISC:** accompanied husband on five foreign-service postings.

Brown, Sandra (Sandy), B.A. ✆ ♣
Director, Development and Alumni Affairs, Trinity College, UNIVERSITY OF TORONTO, 6 Hoskin Ave., Toronto, ON M5S 1H8 (416) 978-2651, FAX 978-2797. Born London, Ont. 1937. d. 3 ch. Meridith Jane, Michael Jeremy, Stephen Edward Julian. **EDUC:** Trinity Coll., Univ. of Toronto, B.A. 1959; Ont. Coll. of Educ., Ont. Secondary Sch. Teacher Certificate 1960; Canadian Centre for Philanthropy, Certificate Program (Fundraising Mgmt) 1992; Certificate, The Canadian Securities Institute; Certificates in Music, Royal Conservatory of Music; studies in Italy & Mexico. **CAREER:** Teacher, Mackenzie Collegiate, North York, 1959-62; Teacher, St. Hilda's Coll., Belize City, Belize, 1969; Teacher, St. Clement's Sch., Toronto, 1970-75; Teacher, Lakehead Bd. of Educ., 1975-79; Exec. Asst., Office of the Leader of the Opposition, Queen's Park, 1979-83; Dir., Dev. & Alumni Affairs, Trinity Coll.,

1984 to date. **SELECTED PUBLICATIONS:** "College Pursuits," *Sanctam Hildam Canimus* (Toronto: St. Hilda's Coll., Univ. of Toronto Press, 1988); wrote introductory section to *Harris Alumni Directory 1990, 1995.* **EDIT:** Ed., *TRINITY*, the Convocation Bulletin, Trinity Coll., Univ. of Toronto, 1984 to date. **AFFIL:** Liberal Party of Canada (Nat'l Exec.); National Women's Liberal Commission (Ont. Rep.); University Women's Club, Toronto (Dir. 1992-94); St. Thomas's Anglican Church. **INTERESTS:** languages, sewing, reading, cooking.

Brown, Stephanie, B.F.A.,M.A. ■ ✆ ♡ ✎
Owner, STEPHANIE BROWN JEWELLERY, 117 Cottingham St., Toronto, ON M4V 1B9 (416) 920-4984, FAX 923-3491, EMAIL brown@idirect.com. Born Mansfield, Ohio 1945. m. Kenneth R. Brown. 2 ch. Lia, Melanie. **EDUC:** Ohio Univ., B.F.A.(Graphic Design) 1967, M.A.(Art Educ.) 1969. **CAREER:** Owner, Stephanie Brown Jewellery. **SELECTED PUBLICATIONS:** *WhaleKind*, Ed.; *Caring for Animals*, Ed. **AFFIL:** Canadian Federation of Humane Societies (Pres. 1989-92); Toronto Humane Society (Pres. 1974-78); Canadian Council on Animal Care; Centre for the Study of Animal Welfare, Univ. of Guelph (Advisory Bd.; Chair 1992-96). **HONS:** Queen's Jubilee Medal; Canada 125 Medal, 1993. **INTERESTS:** antiques; cycling; gardening. **COMMENT:** *"My focus is the improvement of conditions for all animals, but with particular attention to laboratory animals and whales."*

Brubaker, Patricia, B.Sc.,Ph.D. ■ ✆ ❀ ⊕
Associate Professor, Department of Physiology, UNIVERSITY OF TORONTO, Medical Sciences Building, 1 King's College Circle, Rm. 3366, Toronto, ON M5S 1A8 (416) 978-2593, FAX 978-4940. Born Brandon, Man. 1957. m. Stephen Poulin. **EDUC:** McGill Univ., B.Sc.(with distinction, Biochem.) 1978, Ph.D.(Biochem.) 1982. **CAREER:** Postdoctoral Fellow, Univ. of Toronto, 1982-85; Asst. Prof., 1985-93; Assoc. Prof., 1993 to date. **SELECTED PUBLICATIONS:** "Alterations in proglucagon processing and inhibition of proglucagon gene expression in transgenic mice which contain a chimeric proglucagon-SV40 T antigen gene," with Y.C. Lee & D.J. Drucker (*Journal of Chemical Biology* (267) 1992); "Regulation of intestinal proglucagon-derived peptide secretion by glucose-dependent insulinotropic peptide in a novel enteroendocrine loop," with J.N. Roberge (*Endocrinology* (133) 1993); "Regulation of proglucagon gene transcription and biosynthesis in a novel mouse enteroendocrine cell line," with D.J.

Drucker, T. Jin, S.L. Asa & T.A. Young (*Molecular Endocrinology* (8) 1994); "Induction of intestinal epithelial proliferation by glucagon-like peptide -2," with D.J. Drucker, P. Ehrlich, S.L. Asa & P.L. Brubaker (*Proc. Nat'l Acad. Sci.* USA 93:7911-7916, 1996). **HONS:** Entrance Scholarship, McGill Univ., 1975-76; Conseil de la recherche en sante du Québec (Quebec MRC) Studentships, 1979-80 & 1980-81; Dean's Hon. List, McGill Univ., 1982; Int'l Fellowships, Juvenile Diabetes Foundation, 1982-84 & 1984-85; Int'l Career Dev. Award/Scholarship, Juvenile Diabetes Foundation, 1985-88; Diabetes Canada Scholarship, 1987-92; Award for Excellence in Teaching, Dept. of Physiology, Univ. of Toronto, 1989; Aikens Award for Excellence in Course Dev. (MNU111S), Fac. of Medicine, Univ. of Toronto, 1995. **COMMENT:** *"My research goals are to establish the factors regulating secretion of intestinal hormones that stimulate intestinal growth or insulin secretion after a meal. These hormones are currently being tested in clinical trials as treatments for intestinal disease or Type II diabetes."*

Bruce, Phyllis Louise, B.A.,M.A. 📖 $

Publisher, PHYLLIS BRUCE BOOKS, an imprint of HarperCollins, Hazelton Lanes, 55 Avenue Rd., Ste. 2900, Toronto, ON M5B 3L2 (416) 975-9334, FAX 975-9884. Born Ottawa 1939. s. **EDUC:** Carleton Univ., B.A.(English) 1961; Ont. Secondary Sch. Teaching Certificate 1964; Univ. of Toronto, M.A.(English) 1967. **CAREER:** Teacher, Glebe Collegiate Institute, 1961-64; Teacher, Lawrence Park Collegiate Institute, 1964-65; Ed., Nelson Canada, Copp Clark, Van Nostrand Reinhold, 1967-72, 1977-83; Teacher, Vancouver Community Coll., Langara Coll., 1974-77; VP, Ed.-in-Chief, Key Porter Books, 1983-92; Instructor, Ryerson Publishing Program; Instructor, Banff Editing Workshop, 1994; Publisher, Phyllis Bruce Books, HarperCollins, 1992 to date. **SELECTED PUBLICATIONS:** *15 Canadian Poets.*, co-ed. with Gary Geddes. **AFFIL:** Book Publishers' Professional Association (Pres. 1981-83); Canadian Reprography Collective (Bd., Co-Chair 1988-92). **INTERESTS:** yoga. **COMMENT:** *"I have spent more than 20 years in Canadian publishing and now develop my own line of books, reflecting my interest in Canadian fiction, politics, history, and social and women's issues."*

Bruneau, Laura 🎞 🎭 📺

Actor, DREAMQUEST ENTERTAINMENT PRODUCTIONS INC., c/o Lee Bonnell, The Characters, 1505 W. 2nd Ave., Ste. 200, Vancouver, BC V6H 3Y4 (604) 733-9800, FAX 733-6000. Born Calgary 1960. s. **EDUC:** American Academy of Dramatic Arts, Pasadena, Calif., Assoc. of Art degree (3 yrs. completed in 2), 1980; Ryerson Polytechnic Univ., Creative Writing 1989; Ontario Coll. of Art, Film for Artists 1991; Univ. of British Columbia, Creative Writing Dept. current. **SELECTED CREDITS:** guest star, various TV shows incl.: *Outer Limits, Matrix, Beyond Reality, Top Cops, Counterstrike, Street Legal, Hangin' In, Knightrider* & *The Beachcombers*; Lead, *Material World* (series), 4 seasons, CBC; Principal, *Love & Hate* (miniseries), CBC; Lead, *Coming & Going* (pilot), CBC; Regular, *P.M. Magazine* (series); Regular, *Bare Essence* (series), NBC; Charlene, *The Working Man*, Theatre Centre, Toronto; Agnes, *Agnes of God*, The Actor's Playhouse, LA; various, *Hot & Cold*, Back Alley Theater, L.A.; Melinda, *East West Game*, Call Board Theater, LA; Molly, *Jenny's Story*, New Play Theatre, Vancouver; Columbia, *The Rocky Horror Show*, Arts Club Theatre, Vancouver. **AFFIL:** ACTRA; CAEA; SAG; AAEA; UBCP. **HONS:** L.A. Emmy nominee (*P.M. Magazine*), comedy skits. **INTERESTS:** sports; music; Jungian psychology; art. **MISC:** currently enrolled in UBC Creative Writing Dept. **COMMENT:** *"I am a Canadian actress; had the lead in the series* Material World *on CBC for four years; have done numerous other jobs for television, etc."*

Brunel, Cindy ✏ 📖 $

Publisher, *THE FREE PRESS–FERNIE* (a division of Sterling Newspapers/Hollinger), 342 - 2nd Ave., Bag 5000, Fernie, BC V0B 1M0 (604) 423-4666, FAX 423-3110. Born Ste. Rose, Man. 1955. m. Alan. 2 ch. Renee, Beau. **EDUC:** Ste. Rose High Sch., Grade 12 1972. **CAREER:** Civil Servant, Gov't of Man., 1975-81; Public Affairs Rep., Crows Nest Resources Coal Mine, 1981-85; Owner, Creative Communications, 1985-91; Councillor, City of Fernie, 1985-90; Publisher, *The Free Press–Fernie*, 1991 to date. **SELECTED PUBLICATIONS:** produced newsletters for local area mines; numerous editorials. **AFFIL:** East Kootenay Community Coll. (Dir.); Knowledge Network, Vancouver (Dir.); Open Learning Agency, Vancouver (Dir.); Opimian Society; Toastmasters; Downtown Enhancement Committee; Fernie Rescue Competition Committee. **HONS:** Toastmaster of the Year, 1988. **INTERESTS:** family; fitness; interior decorating; gourmet cooking. **MISC:** Real Estate Licence, 1986; Securities Licence, 1986; *The Free Press* received several awards from BCYNA and CCNA, incl. a Gen. Excellence Award from Sterling Newspapers. **COMMENT:** *"An enthusiastic and ambitious, self-taught professional who is very involved in the* *community. I helped turn around a failing century-old newspaper that now makes a significant contribution to the community."*

Brunelle, Wendy A., B.A.,B.L.S., M.L.S. 📖 📺 $
Writer, Public Relations Consultant, Television Host, Facilitator, **W.W. WEST COMMUNICATIONS**, 360 Bloor St. E., Ste. 705, Toronto, ON M4W 3M3 (416) 922-5103, FAX 924-6681. Born Regina. m. 1 ch. Owen Brunelle. **EDUC:** Univ. of Saskatchewan, B.A.(English & Drama) 1964; Univ. of Ottawa, B.L.S. 1967; Univ. of Toronto, M.L.S. 1974. **CAREER:** Asst. Librarian & Lecturer, Sch. of Library Sci., Univ. of Ottawa, 1967-68; Chief Librarian, Imperial Oil Library, Toronto, 1971-73; Host/Prod., QCTV, Edmonton, 1975-77; Interviewer, CBC Radio, Edmonton, 1977; Host/Researcher, *Artists In Depth*, Access Alberta, Edmonton, 1978; Host/Researcher, *Only Yesterday*, CBC TV, Edmonton, 1978-79; Consulting Ed., *Interface: The West's View of Arts and Entertainment*, 1982; Host/Prod., CFRN-TV, Edmonton, 1979-83; Host, *Technology West*, Knowledge Ntwk, Vancouver, 1983-84; Administrator, Promo. Svcs, Canadian Cancer Society, BC & Yukon Div., Vancouver, 1983-85; Coord. of Public Rel'ns, Burnaby Hospital, 1985; Dir. of Public Rel'ns, Stage West Theatre Restaurant, Mississauga, 1986-88; freelance Columnist, 1993 to date; Media Rel'ns, The Travel & Leisure Show, Mississauga, 1994, 1995, 1996; Director of Training & Dev., Thomas International Management Systems Ltd., Toronto, 1994 to date. **SELECTED CREDITS:** Writer/Dir., *Sculptor in Paradise*, 1978; Writer/Dir., *A Contrast of Visions*, 1979; Exec. Prod., *New Light on Cancer*, 1984; Host/ Assoc. Prod., *Morning Magazine*, CFRN, Edmonton, 1979-83; Host/Assoc. Prod., *SPAA-CAATS* (Super Program About Art, Culture and All That Stuff), CFRN, Edmonton, 1979-83; Host/Prod., *People Coping With Cancer*, Knowledge Ntwk, BC, 1985; Prod./Dir./Host, *Expo '86*, 1986; Host/Assoc. Prod., *On the Scene* & *Dayscene*, CHCH-TV, Hamilton, 1989-93; Co-host, *Mother's Day Telethon: Chedoke-McMaster Children's Hospital*, CHCH-TV, Hamilton, 1993, 1994, 1995. **SELECTED PUBLICATIONS:** "Wendy Brunelle Talks to Jack Bush" in *Jack Bush* (Toronto: McClelland & Stewart, 1984). **EDIT:** Ed., *Pacific Report*, BC & Yukon Div. Newsletter, Canadian Cancer Society. **AFFIL:** Academy of Canadian Cinema & Television; National Yacht Club. **HONS:** Arts/Culture Entry, *A Contrast of Visions*, Banff Festival of Films for TV, 1981; Special Appreciation Award for Broadcasting, Alberta Psychic Society, 1981; Expo '86 Award of Achievement, 1986; Ont. Fire Prevention & Public Educ. Award, *Dayscene*, 1992. **INTERESTS:** family & friends; cooking; movies; restoring 200-yr.-old log house; sailing; gardening; writing. **MISC:** novel in progress, *Knock On Wood*. **COMMENT:** *"Flexible and persevering, I'm proud of my ability to work with people, creating positive situations (during six careers in seven cities). I cherish my friends and family."*

Brunet, Caroline ■■ ⚾
Olympic Athlete. c/o Canadian Olympic Association. Born Québec, Qué. 1969. **EDUC:** Laval Univ., studying Science. **SPORTS CAREER:** mbr., Cdn Nat'l Canoeing Team, 1988 to date. Olympic Games: Silver, K-1 500m, 1996; 6th, K-4 500m, & 7th, K-1 500m, 1992; 10th, K-4 500m, & 13th, K-1 500m, 1988. World championships: 1st, K-4 200m, 2nd, K-1 200m, & 2nd, K-1 500m, 1995; 3rd, K-1 200m, 3rd, K-4 200m, & 4th, K-1 500m, 1994; 3rd, K-1 500m, 4th, K-4 500m, 1993; 4th, K-1 500m, 1991; 7th, K-1 500m, & 8th, K-1 5000m, 1990; 6th, K-4 500m, & 7th, K-1 500m, 1989. Int'l regattas: 1st, K-1 500m (Belgium), 1996; 1st, K-1 200m (Hungary), & 1st, K-1 500m, 1st, K-1 200m (Germany), 1995; 1st, K-1 500m (Austria), 1st K-1 200m, 1st K-4 500m (Paris), 1st, K-1 500m, 1st, K-1 200m (Germany), & 3rd, K-1 200m, 4th, K-4 500m (Germany), 1994; 1st, K-4 500m, 3rd, K-1 500m (Hungary), & 1st, K-1 500m (Russia), 1991. Cdn championships: 1st, K-4 500m, 1995; 1st, K-4 500m, & 1st, K-2 500m, 1994; 1st, K-1 500m, 1st, K-2 1000m, 1st, K-4 500m, 1st, K-1 200m, & 1st, K-1 1000m, 1993; 1st, K-1 500m, 1st, K-4 500m, & 1st, K-1 1000m, 1992; 1st, K-1 500m, 1st, K-2 1000m, 1st, K-2 500m, & 1st, K-4 500m, 1991. **HONS:** Petro-Canada Olympic Torch Scholarship, 1993. **INTERESTS:** cross-country skiing.

Brunsek, Judy, B.A. 📖 📜 ✪
Vice-President, Marketing and Sales, **HARPERCOLLINS CANADA LTD.**, 55 Avenue Rd., Ste. 2900, Toronto, ON M5R 3L2 (416) 975-9334, FAX 975-5223. Born Toronto 1958. m. Mike De La Haye. **EDUC:** Univ. of Toronto, B.A. (French Lit.) 1981. **CAREER:** Publicity Coord., Prentice Hall Canada Ltd., 1981-85; Publicity Dir., McClelland and Stewart, 1985-88; Publisher, *Quill and Quire* magazine, 1988-91; VP, Mktg & Sales, HarperCollins Canada, 1991 to date. **DIRECTOR:** HarperCollins Canada Ltd. **AFFIL:** Book Publishers' Professional Association (Exec. 1987-92; Pres. 1988); Book Promoters' Association of Canada (Co-founder; Pres. 1987). **INTERESTS:** cooking; volleyball; skiing; herb gardening; travel. **COMMENT:** *"I*

am dedicated to my industry and the pursuit of reading, as well as personal development within my job. I maintain a wide network of friends in my many areas of interest to maintain balance in life."

Brushett, Dianne, B.A.,M.P. 🍁
Member of Parliament (Cumberland-Colchester), GOVERNMENT OF CANADA, 449-D, Centre Block, Ottawa, ON K1A 0A7 (613) 992-3366, EMAIL ar863 freenet.carlton.ca. Born Kilfoil, N.B. 1942. d. 2 ch. Samara, Sean. **EDUC:** St. Mary's Univ., B.A. 1989. **CAREER:** co-founder & Dir., Dominion Biologicals Ltd., 1972-87; Truro Town Councillor, Mun. Gov't, 1987-93; MP, Cumberland-Colchester, Gov't of Canada, 1993 to date; appointed by P.M., Party Whip, Atlantic Reg., 1993; reappointed, 1996; appointed by P.M., Co-Chair, Task Force on the Commercialization of Gov't Scientific Research; mbr., Standing Committee on Fin., 1995 to date. **HONS:** honoured by the Baha'i Society for efforts in promoting racial unity in Truro & area. **MISC:** currently enrolled part-time in Masters Program in Politics & Economy–Atlantic Canada Studies at St. Mary's Univ. **COMMENT:** *"In 1972, Sam Brushett and I built a successful scientific company in Truro which was able to compete worldwide, and employed young scientists in Atlantic Canada. When we separated our business and private lives, I turned to further education focusing on politics in Atlantic Canada and a political career, which I had always wanted to do, but never had the time. I am dedicated to hard work and achieving success. I see success as a journey in everything we do, not a single destination throughout life."*

Bryant, Carole Y., B.A., B.S.W., M.S.W. $
Executive Vice-President, Corporate & Business Services, SASKPOWER (Saskatchewan Power Corporation), 2025 Victoria Ave., Ste. 12C, Regina, SK S4P 0S1 (306) 566-3515, FAX 566-3523. Born Benito, Man. 1952. m. 2 ch. Timothy, Amanda. **EDUC:** Univ. of Saskatchewan, B.A.(Sociology) 1973; Univ. of Regina, B.S.W. 1978, M.S.W. 1988. **CAREER:** Medical Social Worker, Wascana Rehabilitation Centre, eight yrs.; sr. position, Crown Investments Corporation; Asst. Chief Electoral Officer & Chief Electoral Officer, Prov. of Sask.; Exec. VP, SaskPower. **AFFIL:** Canadian Electrical Association (Public Affairs Committee); Saskatchewan Association of Social Workers (Past Pres.); Regina Food Bank (Past Pres.); many volunteer-oriented & community-related activities.

Bryant, Heather, B.Sc.,M.D.,C.C.F.P., Ph.D.,F.R.C.P. ■ ⊕ 🎓
Director, Division of Epidemiology, Prevention and Screening, and Director, Alberta Program for the Early Detection of Breast Cancer, ALBERTA CANCER BOARD, 3330 Hospital Dr. N.W., Rm. 382, Calgary, AB T2N 4N1 (403) 220-4302, FAX 270-3898, EMAIL heatherb@cancerboard.ab.ca. Clinical Associate Professor, Department of Oncology and Department of Community Health Sciences, UNIVERSITY OF CALGARY. Born Winnipeg 1956. m. Richard. 2 ch. Meghan, Adam. **EDUC:** Univ. of Calgary, B.Sc.(Plant Biol.) 1976, M.D. 1979, Ph.D.(Epidemiology) 1986; Foothills Hospital, Calgary, Family Medicine Residency Training Program, C.C.F.P. 1981; Royal Coll. of Physicians & Surgeons of Canada, Community Medicine, F.R.C.P. 1986. **CAREER:** Medical Officer, Drumheller Health Unit, 1986-90; Physician, Int'l Travel & Immunization Clinic, Univ. of Calgary, 1986-90; Lecturer, Dept. of Community Health Sci., 1986-87; Asst. Prof., 1987-90; seconded on leave to Alberta Cancer Bd., 1990-92; Consulting Medical Staff, Dept. of Infectious Diseases & Microbiol., Foothills Hospital, 1989-93; Dir., Alberta Program for the Early Detection of Breast Cancer, Alberta Cancer Bd., 1990 to date; Consulting Medical Staff, Tom Baker Cancer Centre, 1990 to date; Clinical Assoc. Prof., Dept. of Community Health Sci., Univ. of Calgary, 1992 to date; Acting Dir., Div. of Epidemiology & Preventive Oncology, Alberta Cancer Bd., 1993-94; Dir., Div. of Epidemiology, Prevention & Screening, 1994 to date; Clinical Assoc. Prof., Dept. of Oncology, Univ. of Calgary, 1994 to date. **SELECTED PUBLICATIONS:** various articles in peer-reviewed journals; numerous book chapters, monographs, letters, book reviews; numerous technical research reports & proceedings papers; numerous abstracts. **AFFIL:** Royal Coll. of Physicians & Surgeons (Scientific Program Committee; Nucleus Committee on Community Medicine); Mulit-Centre Study of Fatal Asthma, National Health & Welfare (Advisory Committee); Alberta Heritage Foundation (Chair, Medical Research Studentship Applications Advisory Committee; Fellowship 1983-86); National Forum on Breast Cancer (Steering Committee; Chair, Prevention & Early Detection Sub Committee; Chair, Screening Working Group); Alberta Breast Screening Policy Council (1995); Health Canada (Chair, Nat'l Committee for the Cdn Breast Cancer Screening Initiative). **HONS:** Reg Prince Memorial Award (Botany), 1975; First Class (Distinction) Honours, B.Sc., 1976; Bristol Laboratories of Canada Bursary, 1976; Fellowship, National Health & Welfare R.&D. Program Canada

(declined), 1981; Ortho Literary Award, Best Review Article, Canadian Coll. of Physicians & Surgeons, 1986; Gold Star Award for Teaching Excellence, Medical Undergrad. Program, 1989, 1991, 1992, 1993. **MISC:** named to the *Directory of Women in Science & Technology in Alberta*, 1994. **COMMENT:** *"Dr. Bryant has done epidemiologic research on women's health, with a special interest in breast cancer and developed breast screening as a public health program in Alberta. She serves on several national committees on scientific research and cancer screening and control in Canada."*

Bryant Ballingall, Sally, B.Ed., LL.B. ■ ⚖ ✆
Lawyer, McCarthy Tétrault, 32 Browning Ave., Toronto, ON M4K 1V7 (416) 601-7909, FAX 868-0673. Born St. Helier, Jersey, Channel Islands 1946. m. Brian Ballingall. 2 ch. **EDUC:** Univ. of British Columbia, B.Ed.(Spec. Educ.) 1977; Univ. of Toronto, LL.B. 1994. **CAREER:** teacher; artist; Mgr, real estate dev. company; Articling Student, McCarthy Tétrault. **AFFIL:** Canadian Bar Association; YWCA of Canada (former Nat'l Pres.); Canadian Centre for Global Security (Nat'l Bd. Mbr.); Children's Heart Association for Support & Education (former Exec. Mbr.); Task Force on Churches & Corp. Responsibilities (former Bd. Mbr.); Advisory Committee, Canadian Panel on Violence Against Women (Mbr. 1991-93). **HONS:** Bertha Wright Award; Canada 125 Medal. **INTERESTS:** law; women's issues, particularly violence against women; global human rights; refugees; children with chronic illnesses. **MISC:** Delegate, U.N. Conference on Human Rights, Vienna, 1993. **COMMENT:** *"Broad interests in: healthy communities, empowerment of women, law and social change, leadership and group effectiveness, human rights and lifelong learning."*

Brydon, Diana, B.A.,M.A.,Ph.D. ✎ 📖
Professor, Department of English, University of Guelph, Guelph, ON N1G 2W1 (519) 824-4120, ext. 3252, FAX 766-0844, EMAIL dbrydon@uoguelph.ca. Born Hamilton, Ont. 1950. m. William. **EDUC:** Univ. of Toronto, B.A. 1972, M.A. 1973; Australian National Univ., Ph.D. 1977. **CAREER:** Asst. Prof., Univ. of British Columbia, 1979-87; Assoc. Prof., 1987-89; Assoc. Prof., Univ. of Guelph, 1989-92; Prof., 1992 to date. **SELECTED PUBLICATIONS:** Ed., *World Literature Written in English*, 1989-93; *Decolonising Fictions*, with Helen Tiffin (Dangaroo, 1993); *Christina Stead* (Macmillan and Barnes Noble, 1987); *Writing on Trial: Timothy Findley's 'Famous Last Words'* (ECW, 1995); Guest Ed., *Essays on*

Canadian Writing, 56, Fall 1995; various articles & book chapters. **AFFIL:** Canadian Association for Commonwealth Literature & Language Studies. **HONS:** Commonwealth Scholarship; George Drew Memorial Trust Fund Award; Distinguished Prof. Teaching Award, Fac. Association. **INTERESTS:** Australian, Canadian & Caribbean literature; feminist & postcolonial theories. **MISC:** recipient of SSHRC research grant. **COMMENT:** *"In my search for reading and teaching strategies appropriate to an inclusive learning environment, I have focused on the literatures of formerly colonized countries and on writings by women."*

Brydone, J. Eleanor, ARIDO,IDC,FASID, IIDA,FOCA ✖ $
President, Rice Brydone Limited, 553 Richmond St. W., Toronto, ON M5V 1Y6 (416) 504-9094, FAX 504-2007. Born Milverton, Ont. m. Robert Hagarty. **EDUC:** Ont. Coll. of Art, 1963. **CAREER:** Design Dir., A.D. Pollard & Associates, 1963-71; Pres., Rice Brydone Limited, 1971 to date. **SELECTED PUBLICATIONS:** *Organization and Design: The Double Discipline* (co-author, Toronto; McClelland & Stewart, 1983; US: Harper & Row). **AFFIL:** Association of Registered Interior Designers of Ontario (ARIDO); Interior Designers of Canada (IDC); International Interior Design Association (IIDA); American Society of Interior Designers (Fellow); Ontario College of Art (Fellow); Ontario Chamber of Commerce. **HONS:** various book-design awards for *Organization and Design* incl. The American Institute of Graphic Arts Certificate of Excellence for Book Design, 1983; National Presidential Citation, ASID, 1987, 1990, 1991, 1992; Presidential Citation, ARIDO, 1990; numerous ARIDO awards incl. Award for Gen. Office Design, Metro Hall for the Municipality of Metro Toronto, 1993; numerous ASID Chapter Awards; numerous other awards. **INTERESTS:** playing classical piano; opera; baseball fan; biking. **MISC:** subject of numerous articles in trade publications; listed in *Who's Who in Interior Design*. **COMMENT:** *"Our clients face uncertainty and constant change as they prepare for the 21st century. We are responding by creating new services that support them, because while we can't predict the future we can help them invent it."*

Buchner, Barbara, B.A.,M.A. ✎ ⊕
Virologist (retired) and Chair, Blood Services, Canadian Red Cross, 107 Concession St., Cambridge, ON N1R 2H2. s. **EDUC:** McMaster Univ., B.A.(Chem. & Physics); Univ. of Toronto, M.A.(Virology). **CAREER:** Bacteriol-

ogy Dept., Univ. of Toronto; Connaught Medical Research Laboratories; Canadian Red Cross. **AFFIL:** Canadian Red Cross (Chair, Blood Svcs); Canadian Cancer Society; Ontario Hearing Society; Cambridge Memorial Hospital Auxiliary (Immediate Past Pres.); Central Presbyterian Church (Chair, Congregational Dev.); Cambridge Seniors Duplicate (Treas.). **HONS:** inducted, McMaster Alumnae Gallery. **INTERESTS:** bridge; knitting; travel; cribbage. **COMMENT:** *"Worked in Elliot Lake–epidemiological study of the largest hepatitis outbreak in Canada. Seconded to West African Council Medical Research in Lagos, Nigeria, for hepatitis studies."*

Buckley, Helen, B.A.,B.A. 🍁 $

Retired Economist. Ottawa, ON. Born Winnipeg 1923. w. Ken Buckley. 3 ch. **EDUC:** Univ. of Manitoba, B.A. 1943; Univ. of Saskatchewan, B.A. 1948. **CAREER:** Centre for Community Studies, Univ. of Saskatchewan, 1956-67; Labour Mkt Analyst, Statistics Canada, 1967-72; Labour Mkt Analyst, Dept. of Manpower, Ottawa, 1972-77; Reg'l Policy Analyst, Dept. of Fin., Ottawa, 1977-82. **SELECTED PUBLICATIONS:** *Canadian Policies for Rural Adjustment*, with Eva Tihanyi (ECC, 1967); *From Wooden Ploughs to Welfare* (McGill-Queen's); *The Indian & Métis of Northern Saskatchewan* (Centre for Community Studies, 1965); *Brief to Royal Commission on Aboriginal People.* **AFFIL:** National Council of Women (Chair, Econ. Committee). **INTERESTS:** writing; gardening; family life. **MISC:** currently writing a book that explains how Canada built debt to present level. **COMMENT:** *"I've tried to show that the situation of Indian people is due entirely to bad policies and programs. Am using my firsthand knowledge of other government programs to show the waste over many years through inappropriate programs."*

Budd, Ruth ⊛

Musician (Bass). 407 St. Clair Ave. E., Toronto, ON M4T 1P6 (416) 488-9452. Born Winnipeg 1924. d. 2 ch. Gillian, Kevin. **EDUC:** B.C. Sch. of Pharmacy & Science; Toronto Conservatory of Music; Univ. of Toronto Fac. of Music. **CAREER:** Toronto Symphony Orchestra; Vancouver Symphony Orchestra, Halifax Symphony Orchestra; CBC Symphony Orchestra; Hart House Orchestra; Canadian Opera Company; National Ballet of Canada; Stratford Festival Orchestra; founder, Toronto Sr. Strings; numerous cross-country children's concerts in groups & as soloist. **AFFIL:** Toronto Musicians' Association; Canadian Civil Liberties Association; Toronto Sr. Strings (Founder); Vancouver Opera Company; Toronto Mandolin Orchestra (Shevchenko); Organization of Canadian Symphony Musicians (Founding Chair). **HONS:** YWCA Women of Distinction Award (Arts). **INTERESTS:** folk arts; films; music; theatre; music educ.; reading; politics; etc. **MISC:** Pan Accord Trio with son Kevin on pan flute, accordion and bass. **COMMENT:** *"I've also done hundreds of children's educational concerts from Vancouver to Fredericton, Western Arctic (Tuktoyaktuk) to Iqaluit and Igloolik, Rankin Inlet, etc."*

Budovitch, Judith Chernin, B.A.,B.Ed., LL.B. ■ 🍁 $ ⚖

Director of Consumer Affairs, GOVERNMENT OF NEW BRUNSWICK, Centennial Building, Box 6000, Fredericton, NB E3B 5H1 (506) 453-2682, FAX 444-4494, EMAIL judyb@gov.nb.ca. Born Sydney, N.S. 1947. m. Arnold Richard Budovitch. 2 ch. Eric Louis, Paul Ross. **EDUC:** Dalhousie Univ., B.A.(Hist.) 1969; Univ. of New Brunswick, B.Ed. 1970, LL.B. 1975. **CAREER:** practice of law, Hoyt, Mockler, Dixon, Fredericton, 1975-76; Lecturer, Univ. of New Brunswick Law Sch., 1977-81; Lawyer, Dept. of Justice, Prov. of N.B., 1983 to date; Dir. of Consumer Affairs & Tenancy Program, 1992 to date. **AFFIL:** Barristers' Society of N.B.; Canadian Bar Association; Legal Education Action Fund (LEAF); Univ. of New Brunswick (Gov.); Mount Saint Vincent Univ. (Gov.); Beaverbrook Art Gallery (Chair, Bd. of Gov.); United Israel Appeal of Canada (Dir.); Delta Theta Phi (Hon. Mbr.). **HONS:** Lescarbot Award, 1991. **COMMENT:** *"My life has been focused on my family and has been enriched by my career in law and the opportunities afforded me to serve the arts and education through volunteer initiatives."*

Budz, Denise, B.S.N. ■■ ⊕

General Manager, Palliative Care Service, SASKATOON DISTRICT HEALTH, Saskatoon, SK. Born Saskatoon, Sask. 1961. m. Mark. 2 ch. Breanne, Marlee. **EDUC:** Coll. of Nursing, Univ. of Saskatchewan, B.S.N. 1983. **CAREER:** Rural Relief R.N., Asquith, Home Care District #45, Saskatoon, 1985-93; Staff Nurse, Gen. Medicine/Respiratory, Royal University Hospital, 1983-86; Nursing Unit Coord., Medicine 6100 (Oncology/Hematology), 1986-89; Acting Nurse Unit Mgr, Medicine 6300 (Mixed Medical Unit), May-Nov. 1989; Clinical Coord., Palliative Care Svcs, St. Paul's Hospital, Saskatoon, Nov. 1989-Mar. 93 & Nov. 1993-Mar. 1996; Acting Nurse Mgr, Palliative Care Svcs, Mar.-Oct. 1993 & Apr.-June 1996; Gen. Mgr, Palliative Care Svc., Saskatoon District Health, June 1996 to date. **AFFIL:** Saskatchewan Palliative Care Association; Canadian Palliative Care Association; Saskatchewan Oncology Nurses Group (VP 1995 to date; Sec. 1992-95); Canadian Association of Nurses in Oncology; Saskatoon & District Oncology Nurses Group (Program Chairperson 1989-91); Saskatoon Cancer Centre (Quality of Life Committee 1996 to date); St. Paul's Hospital (Ethics Committee & Sub-committee on Advanced Health Care Directives 1995 to date); Palliative Care Working Group (mbr. 1994-96); Oncology Working Group (mbr. 1994-95); Asquith Housing Authority (Bd. of Dir. 1991-94); Asquith Rink (Bd. mbr. 1991-93); Meewasin Valley United Church. **HONS:** Excellence in Nursing Award, Nursing Practice, sponsored by SUN & SRNA, 1994. **INTERESTS:** curling; reading; gardening. **MISC:** numerous presentations to health care providers at local, nat'l & int'l level on topics related to palliative care, & to community organizations re palliative care, death & dying, grief & bereavement, & communication; CPR instructor, 1988 to date.

Buffie, Margaret, B.A. 📋
Writer. 165 Grandview St., Winnipeg, MB R2G 0L4 (204) 338-5971. Born Winnipeg 1945. m. James Macfarlane. 1 ch. Christine. **EDUC:** Univ. of Manitoba, B.A.(Fine Arts) 1967, Certificate of Educ. 1976. **CAREER:** illustrator, Hudson's Bay Co., 1968-70; drawing & painting instructor, Winnipeg Art Gallery, 1974-75; high sch. art instructor, River East Sch. Div., 1976-77; freelance illustrator & painter, to 1985; Cont. Ed. Instructor (Creative Writing), Univ. of Winnipeg, 1993-95. **SELECTED PUBLICATIONS:** *Who Is Frances Rain?* (Toronto: Kids Can Press 1987); *The Guardian Circle* (Toronto: Kids Can Press 1989); *My Mother's Ghost* (Toronto: Kids Can Press 1992); *The Dark Garden* (Toronto: Kids Can Press, 1995). **AFFIL:** Canadian Authors' Association; Manitoba Writers' Guild; Canadian Society of Authors, Illustrators & Performers; International Board on Books for Young People. **HONS:** Young Adult Canadian Book Award, 1988; First runner-up, The Canadian Library Association Book of the Year Award, 1988; nominated, Ruth Schwartz Children's Book Award, 1988/89, 1993/94, 1996; Notable Canadian Fiction List, 1989 & 1993; ALA Best Books of the Year List, 1990; International Youth Library Notable YA Book, 1991; nominated, Gov. General's Award, 1992; nominated, Manitoba Artist of the Year Award, 1992; nominated, Book of the Year, Canadian Library Association, 1993; nominated, Mr. Christie's Book Award, 1993, 1996;

Canada Council Grant, 1994; Ontario Arts Council Grants, 1987, 1989, 1990, 1993; Manitoba Arts Council Grant, 1996; nominated, Silver Birch Award, 1994; Canadian Children's Book Centre's "Our Choice List," 1989, 1990, 1993; Vicky Metcalf Award for Body of Work, 1996; McNeally Robinson Book for Young People Award, 1996. **INTERESTS:** cooking; canoeing; birding; cottage life.

Bujalski, Wanda ■ 🕐 🖘 📖
President, POLISH TEACHERS' ASSOCIATION IN CANADA, 288 Roncesvalles Ave., Toronto, ON M6R 2M4 (416) 532-2876. Born Warsaw 1925. w. 3 ch. Eva Gabrielle, Teresa Marie, Martha Barbara. **EDUC:** Warsaw Teachers' Coll., Teaching Certificate 1943. **CAREER:** Heritage Language Teacher, Germany, 1944-50; Heritage Language Teacher, Hamilton, Ont., 30 yrs. (Principal, 30 yrs.); Asst. Librarian, Mills Memorial Library, McMaster Univ., 1970-89; Secondary Sch. Teacher (Polish Language), 1971-85; Coord., Polish Language, Hamilton, 1987-96. **SELECTED PUBLICATIONS:** various editorials & articles in quarterly *Polish* magazine & *Toronto Polish* newspapers; *Poland Yesterday and Today* textbook (1989). **AFFIL:** Polish Teachers' Association in Canada (Pres. 16 yrs.; Mbr., Ed. & Publishing Committee); Canadian Polish Congress; S.P.K. (Polish Combatants' Association); McMaster Univ. Language Studies (Fundraiser 9 yrs.); The Polish Canadian Millennium Fund (Dir.). **HONS:** Gold Medal, Canadian Polish Congress, 1980; Gold Medal, Volunteer Svc., Ministry of Multiculturalism & Culture, 1986; Jesse Flis MP Award of Recognition, House of Commons, 1991; Gold Medal, Polish Alliance of Canada, 1992; Award of Recognition, Consul Gen. of Poland in Toronto, 1993; Medal of Recognition, Nat'l Educ. Ministry of the Republic of Poland, 1995; 25-yr. Volunteer Service Award for Ontario, 1996. **INTERESTS:** music; literature; fundraising; organizing children's concerts. **MISC:** fundraiser for publishing of Polish reader for grades 3 to 10; panelist at conference "Polonia 2000" in Toronto; presented wreath at grave of the Unknown Soldier, Washington, DC, Memorial Day, 1992. **COMMENT:** *"My vision in educating my children and those entrusted to my care is to impart an appreciation of Polish language/culture to enrich Canada's mosaic."*

Bujold, Geneviève · 💓 ⊗ 🏳
Actor. Born Montreal 1942. 1 ch. Matthew James. **EDUC:** Conservatory of Dramatic Arts, Montreal, 3 yrs. **SELECTED CREDITS:** numerous features incl. *Kamouraska; Anne of a Thousand Days; Act of the Heart; Murder by*

Decree; *Tightrope*; *The Moderns*; *Dead Ringers*; various TV appearances. **HONS:** numerous awards & nominations for film & TV.

Bulte, Sarmite ("Sam"), B.A., LL.B. ■■ ⚖ ○

Barrister and Solicitor, SARMITE D. BULTE BAR-RISTERS & SOLICITORS, 390 Bay St., Ste. 1200, Toronto, ON M5H 2Y2 (416) 860-0082, FAX 860-1188. Born Hamilton, Ont. 1953. m. Dr. Steven Treiber. 3 ch. **EDUC:** Univ. of Toronto, B.A.; Univ. of Windsor, LL.B. **BAR:** called to Bar of Upper Canada, 1980. **CAREER:** owner, Sarmite D. Bulte Barristers & Solicitors, law firm. **SECRETARY:** Latvian Credit Union. **AFFIL:** Canadian Stage Company (Dir. 1988 to date; Pres. & Chrm, Bd. of Dir.); Women Entrepreneurs of Canada (founding Mbr., Dir. & VP, Int'l); Judy LaMarsh Fund (Bd.); L.E.A.F. Endowment Committee (Bd.); Latvian National Federation in Canada (Gov. Council); Bell Canada Consumer Advisory Panel (1993 to date); Canada Council Task Force on Tax Reform (1995 to date); Canadian Association of Women Executives & Entrepreneurs (former Pres.). **MISC:** currently chairing the 1997 International Les Femmes Chefs d'Enterprises Mondiales (FCEM) Conference Committee.

Burak, Rita, B.A. ■■ ❀

Secretary of the Cabinet and Clerk of the Executive Council, GOVERNMENT OF ONTARIO, Whitney Block, 99 Wellesley St. W., Rm. 4340, Toronto, ON M7A 1A1 (416) 325-7641, FAX 314-8980. Born US 1946. m. Peter Barnes. **EDUC:** York Univ., B.A.(Pol. Sci.) 1977. **CAREER:** Mgmt Bd. Secretariat, Dir./Exec. Dir., Ministry of Labour; Asst. Deputy Min., Ministry of Agric., Food & Rural Affairs; Asst. Deputy Min., Ministry of Municipal Affairs & Housing; Deputy Min., Ministry of Agric., Food & Rural Affairs.

Burdsall, A. Margaret, B.H.Sc. ○ ⊕

Born St. Catharines, Ont. 1921. m. Bernard H. Burdsall. 5 ch. Kay, Elizabeth, Anne, Marian, Jane. **CAREER:** Dietitian, Toronto General Hospital, Toronto, 1943-44; Staff, YWCA Leave Centre, London, UK, 1945-46; Resource Staff, United Way of Kingston & District, 1975-87; Ed. Asst., *The Canadian Amateur Magazine*, 1992-93. **VOLUNTEER CAREER:** Sec., Kingston Historical Society, 1978-86; Pres., Memorial Society of Kingston & District, 1978-94; Ontario Dir., Huguenot Society of Canada, 1987-89; Nat'l Sec., Thyroid Foundation of Canada, 1987-91; VP Oper., 1992-95; Pres., Kingston Area Chapter, Thyroid Foundation of Canada, 1990-94. **HONS:** 10-Yr. Pin

for Volunteering, Ministry of Culture & Recreation. **INTERESTS:** genealogy; history; art; reading; volunteering. **COMMENT:** *"Two achievements–happily married 53 years; five daughters of whom I am extremely proud."*

Burgess, Ellen, M.D. ■ ⌖ ⊕

Associate Professor, Faculty of Medicine, UNIVERSITY OF CALGARY, 1403 - 29th St. N.W., Calgary, AB T2N 2T9 (403) 670-1598, FAX 283-2494. President, HEALTHWEST CONSULTANTS INC. Born Winnipeg 1953. m. Graham Larking. 2 ch. **EDUC:** Univ. of Manitoba, M.D. 1976, Post-Grad. 1979. **CAREER:** Fellow, Section of Nephrology, Dept. of Internal Medicine, Univ. of Washington, 1979-81; Chief Medical Resident, Dept. of Medicine, Univ. of Alberta Hospital, 1981-82; Asst. Prof., Univ. of Calgary, 1982-88; Assoc. Prof., 1988 to date. **SELECTED PUBLICATIONS:** "Serum Phenytoin Concentrations in Uremia," with others (*Annals of Internal Medicine* 1981); "The Kidney in Pregnancy" (*Current Problems in Obstetrics and Gynecology* 1983); "Hypertension in Women" (*Canadian Journal of Cardiology* 1993); numerous other articles & book chapters; 99 abstracts; more than 100 papers & presentations. **AFFIL:** Canadian Hypertension Society (Pres.); International Society of Hypertension; International Society of Nephrology; American Society of Law, Medicine & Ethics; Canadian Bioethics Society; Royal Coll. of Physicians & Surgeons of Canada (Fellow); American Coll. of Physicians (Fellow). **HONS:** "Gold Star Letters" for teaching by Univ. of Calgary medical students. **INTERESTS:** educ.; ethics; research. **MISC:** Chair, Conjoint Research Ethics Board, Univ. of Calgary. **COMMENT:** *"Primary interests in clinical medicine, teaching and research have led to new endeavours in patient education and research ethics. I have been involved in visiting junior high schools as a role model for women to follow non-traditional occupations."*

Burgess, Rachel Lillian, C.M.,B.S., Ph.D. ⊕ ○ ⌖

Psychologist, Teacher, Consultant, Counsellor, Hypnotist. Born Grand Falls, N.B. 1935. m. Lee A. Burgess. 5 ch. Jimmy, Leah, Donna, Carl, Alison. **EDUC:** Nursing Sch., Montreal, 1951-52; Univ. of Maine, B.A.(Psych.) 1971, M.A.(Emotionally Disturbed) 1974, B.S. 1975, Teacher's Licence 1976, M.A.(Counselling) 1979; Univ. of Maine at Orono, Certificate of Advanced Studies in degree, C.A.S. 1986. **CAREER:** Past Principal & Dir., Burgess Centre for Handicapped, founder of sch. & sheltered workshop, teacher & counsellor; private counselling practice, 1987. **AFFIL:** Mbr., literacy, mental, psychological, teachers', counsellors' & mentally retarded associations; Association Jeunesse-Education (Hon. Pres.). HONS: Record Achievement, Univ. of Maine, 1971; Vanier Award, 1971; Order of Canada, 1978; Model Educator, N.B., 1989; Mbr., Order of Souverain et Militaire de la Milice du Saint Sepulcre, 1989; Dame Commandeur, Confederation of Chivalry, Sydney, Australia; Mbr., Merit for Life, Sydney, Australia, 1989; Canada 125 Medal, 1993; Certificate Award, Grand Falls, N.B. 100th Centennial Yr., in acknowledgement of efforts to improve & develop educ. for Handicapped people in Grand Falls; Ph.D.(Hon.), Univ. of St. Thomas, 1980. INTERESTS: skiing; guitar; reading; meditation; philosophy; gardening; music; Bible reading; religious & spiritual reading & thinking. MISC: listed in *Community Leaders of the World*, *International Directory of Distinguished Leadership*. COMMENT: *"I am the type of person who likes to be helpful; a sensitive nature and hurt easily; very private and like to spend time with God; am a spiritual person who seeks to know God's will. I will help others outside my family if the need is there, but I do not quickly volunteer for anything."*

Burgess, Wendy, M.B.A. ■ Ⓢ ❀
Vice-President of Quality, Education and Communications, GANDALF TECHNOLOGIES INC., 130 Colonnade Rd. S., Nepean, ON K2E 7M4 (613) 274-6500, ext. 6550, FAX 274-6505. Born Longueuil, Que. 1956. 1 ch. EDUC: Algonquin Coll., Diploma (Electronics Technology) 1982; Univ. of Warwick, UK, M.B.A. 1989. CAREER: Mktg Mgr, Gandalf Technologies Inc., 1986-87; Exec. Asst. to the Chrm, 1989-91; Dir., Corp. Planning, 1991-92; VP, Quality & Comm., 1992-94, VP, Quality, Educ. & Comm., 1994 to date. AFFIL: Electronics Technology Program, Algonquin Coll. (Advisory Council). HONS: Des Cunningham Scholarship, Gandalf Technologies Inc., 1988.

Burka, Sylvia May ■ ■ Ⓢ ⑦
Financial Officer and Partner, CANCORE BUILDING SERVICES LTD., 1306 Queen St. E., Toronto, ON M4L 1C4 (416) 406-1900, FAX 406-1903. Born Winnipeg 1954. cl. W. David Hogg. EDUC: various univ. courses. SPORTS CAREER: speedskating career, 1965-80; broke every prov. & nat'l record & many track records in Europe; Canada's top female speedskater, 1969-80; competed in Winter Olympics, 1972, 1976, 1980; in World Overall & Sprint Championships, 1970-80; Jr. World Champion, Assen, Holland, 1973; Sr. Ladies World Champion, Gjovik, Norway, 1976; Sr. World Sprint Champion, Alkmaar, Holland, 1977;

Cdn Skater of the Year, 7 times; world records in speedskating, Davos, Switz., 1973, & Inzell, Germany, 1976; in cycling 1000m., Montreal, 1982; competed World Cycling Championships, 1980, 1981, 1982; Cdn championship medals & records in cycling; best performance in Olympic Games (4th in 1000m.), 1976. HONS: Female Athlete of the Year in Canada, 1977; inducted into Canada Sports Hall of Fame, 1977; various prov. awards; Order of Buffalo Hunt; Gov't House Award. INTERESTS: nordic skiing; water skiing; running; inline skating. COMMENT: *"'If it's worth doing, it's worth doing well' is the belief I follow with everything I do. I'm a perfectionist—and stubborn—a good combination for athletic and business success. I try to love everything I do—and do everything I love."*

Burke, Audrey N. (née MacLean) Ⓢ ╱
Director, Operations Planning and Control, TORONTO STAR NEWSPAPERS LIMITED, 1 Yonge St., 7th Fl., Toronto, ON M5E 1E6 (416) 869-4763, FAX 865-3586. Born N.S. 1939. m. Larry Burke. 2 ch. (from first marriage). CAREER: Teacher, 1956-57; Accts Clerk, Bell Canada, 1957-59; Air Hostess, Air Canada, 1962-63; various positions, Classified Advtg Dept., Toronto Star Newspapers Limited, 1963-70; various supervisory & asst. managerial positions, Sales & Svc., Classified Advtg Dept., 1970-75; Classified Ad. Mgr, 1975-78; Pres., StarGuide Limited (a wholly-owned subsidiary), 1981-82; Newspaper Dev. Mgr, Electronic Publishing, Toronto Star Newspapers Limited, 1980-83; Oper. Control Mgr, 1983-88; Dir., Oper. Planning & Control, 1988 to date. AFFIL: chairing & participating in large association conferences on various subjects incl. sales, employee rel'ns & technology. HONS: "Canadian Achievers" Award. INTERESTS: fitness; knitting. MISC: chaired the Oper. Transitions committee when production of Toronto Star Newspapers Limited was moved to the new press centre at Vaughan, 1992; numerous media interviews on newspaper policy issues, electronic systems & sales opportunities; past mbr., numerous newspaper technological task forces in Canada & the U.S.; Classified Chair, Newspaper Systems Development Group (NSDG) representing the Classified requirements of nine major dailies, 1974-75. COMMENT: *"I worked my way up through the organization to my present position through hard work, a caring for people, high energy level and a strong desire for increased productivity in the organization."*

Burke, Earla, B.A.,B.J.,C.F.P. Ⓢ
President, MONEYSTRATEGY INC., 1177 Yonge

St., Toronto, ON M4T 2Y4 (416) 968-1444, FAX 968-7808. Born Kirkland Lake, Ont. 1935. d. 5 ch. Clayton, Virginia, Stacy, Cindy, Jason. **EDUC:** Univ. of Toronto, Certificate in Bus.1970; York Univ., B.A.(Psych.) 1976; Carleton Univ., B.J.(Journalism) 1978; Coll. For Fin. Planning, Denver, Co., C.F.P.(Fin. Planning) 1987. **CAREER:** Bus. Admin. & Mgmt, 1969-71; Bus. Teacher, Seneca Coll., Ryerson Univ., York Univ., 1969-85; Fin. Svcs, 1981 to date. **AFFIL:** Canadian Institute of Management (Dir. 1984-86); Investment Funds Institute of Canada (Gov. 1986-92; Chair, Independent Dealers 1983-88); Independent Life Insurance Brokers of Canada; International Association for Financial Planning, Inc.; Institute of Certified Financial Planners, U.S.; International Board of Standards & Practices for Certified Financial Planners. **INTERESTS:** freelance writing; travel; flying; scuba diving; skiing; bridge; motorcycling; knitting; carpentry; reading. **MISC:** Private Pilot's Licence, 1972; Commercial Pilot's Course, 1973; NAUI Certification in Scuba Diving, 1972; conducts fin. planning seminars. **COMMENT:** *"I moved to Toronto from Northern Ontario at age 14 and began working. My education involved more than 20 years of evening classes. The process of increasing wealth and decreasing tax has always fascinated me, and I enjoy helping clients become, or remain, financially independent."*

Burke, Elaine ■ ⊛

Owner, RIVER 'B' DOWN HOME QUILTS INC., 6001 St. Margaret's Bay Rd., Head of St. Margaret's Bay, NS B0J 1R0 (902) 826-1991, FAX 826-7008. Born St. Laurent, Que. 1956. s. **EDUC:** high sch. **CAREER:** Mgr & Paralegal, Int'l Corp. Tax Law, Malcolm, 1979-90; designer & owner, River 'B' Quilts, 1990 to date; Founder, Peaceful Dreams Society, 1994-95. **COMMISSIONS:** original design, "Dancing Thistle" quilt commissioned for the World Scottish Festival in Montreal. **EXHIBITIONS:** more than 80 wool tartans, McCord Museum, Montreal. **AFFIL:** St. Margaret's Bay Business Association (Dir.); Halifax Optimist Club (Dir.). **HONS:** Canada Peace Medal, YMCA Halifax/Dartmouth, 1994. **INTERESTS:** fabric art; music; design; gourmet cooking; collecting good friends. **MISC:** raffle of original design, "Peaceful Dreams" quilt, raised money for women's shelters in N.S. & broke records across Canada & US by raising over $60,000; original quilt designs can be found in private homes, art collections & businesses around the world; has own line of patterns for quilts & clothing; teacher; numerous speaking engagements; River 'B' Quilts hosts the largest selection of hand-made quilts in Canada. **COMMENT:** *"Those who sleep beneath a quilt sleep under a blanket of love."*

Burke, Rebecca, B.A.,M.F.A. ■ ⊛ 🎓

Professor, Department of Fine Arts, MOUNT ALLISON UNIVERSITY, Sackville, NB E0A 3C0 (506) 364-2490, FAX 364-2595, EMAIL rburke@mta.ca. Born Kalamazoo, Mich. 1946. m. Robert Rosebrugh. 1 ch. Shawn P. Bruce. **EDUC:** Univ. of Guam, B.A.(English Lit.) 1969; Ohio State Univ., M.F.A.(Painting) 1972. **CAREER:** Teaching Asst., Drawing, Ohio State Univ., 1969-70; Instructor, Painting & Drawing, Dept. of Design Arts, Grant MacEwan Community Coll., Edmonton, 1976-80; Tenured Assoc. Prof., Mount Allison Univ., 1986-92; Head of Dept., 1990-93; Full Prof., 1992 to date. **EXHIBITIONS:** *Recent Work*, The Art Gallery, Univ. of Waterloo (1974); *Art-Painted Ladies*, Vehicule Gallery, Montreal (1976); *Musclemen*, Struts Gallery, Sackville, N.B. (1983); *Bodybuilders*, The Confederation Centre Art Gallery (1985); *Aller et Retour*, Struts Gallery (1988); *2 1/2*, Gallery Connexion, Fredericton (1992); *In Search of Medusa*, The Owens Art Gallery (1995); 55 Mercer Gallery, New York, N.Y. (1996); Confederation Centre Art Gallery (1996); various other solo & group exhibitions. **COLLECTIONS:** The Owens Art Gallery, Mount Allison Univ.; The Art Bank, The Canada Council; McIntosh Art Gallery, Univ. of Western Ontario; The New Brunswick Art Bank. **AFFIL:** Canadian Artists' Representation; Mount Allison Faculty Association (Sec. 1987); Struts Gallery (VP 1989-90); University Artists' Association of Canada. **HONS:** numerous grants, Ont. Arts Council, The Canada Council; Marjorie Young Bell Fac. Fund Award, 1985; Award, Social Sciences & Humanities Research Council of Canada, 1988; Arts Branch Award, N.B. Dept. of Tourism, Recreation & Heritage, 1991; Award, Marjorie Young Bell Fine Arts & Music Committee, 1993. **INTERESTS:** gardening; nordic skiing; music. **MISC:** subject of numerous articles; numerous public lectures.

Burkinshaw, Sylvia Mary, S.T.D.,D.N., B.N.,B.A.,M.P.A. ⊕ $ ♡

Hospital Administrator (retired). 100 Medley Ct., Ste. 16, Kingston, ON K7K 6X1 (613) 545-0913. Born Scarborough, Yorkshire, UK 1919. s. **EDUC:** London Univ., UK, S.T.D. (Teaching) 1946, D.N.(Admin.) & Certificate in Tropical Diseases 1947; Univ. of Toronto, Certificate in Advanced Nursing Educ. 1953; McGill Univ., B.N.(Nursing Admin.) 1956; Queen's Univ., B.A.(Phil.) 1988, M.P.A.(Public Admin.) 1992. **CAREER:** staff nurse; midwife;

Queen Alexandra's Royal Naval Nursing Svc., 1941-50; Asst. Dir., Sch. of Nursing, University Coll. Hospital, London, UK, 1950-52, 1953-55; Nursing Dept., Hospital For Sick Children, Toronto, 1955-60; Dir. of Nursing, Kingston General Hospital, 1961-70; Dir., Medical Support Svcs, 1971-78; Exec. Asst. to the Exec. Dir., 1978-84. **SELECTED PUBLICATIONS:** *Nurse Wastage in the Province of Ontario* (Univ. of Toronto, 1953); *Community Health Experience in the Nursing Curriculum* (McGill Univ., 1956); "Trends in Nursing Education" (*Nursing Times*, UK, Feb. 1954); *Development of Hospital Archives and Record Management: Canadian Hospitals* (1983); *Hospital Ombudsman* (Queen's Univ. Sch. of Public Admin., 1992). **AFFIL:** Salvation Army Advisory Bd., Kingston (Chair 1986-90); St. John Ambulance Association, Kingston (Chair 1977-79); Canadian Club of Kingston (Pres. 1993-95); Kingston General Hospital (Archives & Museum Committee; Membership Committee); Kingston General Hospital Auxiliary (Archivist); Kingston General Hospital Foundation (Founders' Advisory Council; Healthcare 2000 Fundraising Campaign; Pres. 1988-90); Frontenac Condominium Corporation No. 41 (Pres. 1992-95); Kingston & Area Condominium Association; Eastern Ontario Sch. of X-Ray Technology (Advisory Bd.); Agnes Etherington Art Centre, Kingston; Kingston Humane Society; World Wildlife Fund; Canadian Wildlife Federation; PETA (People's Ethical Treatment of Animals); Senior Citizens' Council of Kingston; Diocese of Ontario Synod (Delegate 1993-96); St. George's Cathedral, Kingston (Vestry Council 1973-84, 1990 to date; Churchwarden 1976-80); Prayer Book Society of Canada; Diocese of Ontario (Bishop's Matrimonial Commission); Queen's Sr. Alumni Association; Grad. Society of McGill; Angada Children's Foundation. **HONS:** Queen's Silver Jubilee Medal; Dame, Order of St. John of Jerusalem; Officer, Order of St. Lazarus of Jerusalem; Paul Harris Fellow, Rotary International; Life Gov., Kingston Hospital. **INTERESTS:** medical, moral & legal issues affecting patient care. **COMMENT:** *"I am an optimist with a friendly, cheerful disposition. I put my best efforts into everything that I try to accomplish. The war years (1939-45) inevitably changed my personal plans for my own future. I am uncertain what subject to study next. I have so many choices, but I want to continue to study."*

Burnham, M.E. (Libby), B.A.,LL.B., Q.C. ⚖ ☺ ✿
Counsel, BORDEN & ELLIOT, Scotia Plaza, 40 King St. W., Toronto, ON M5H 3Y4 (416)

367-6011, FAX 361-2773. Born Florenceville, N.B. 1938. m. Mr. Justice G. Gordon Sedgwick, Q.C. 3 ch. John Burnham Sedgwick, James Burnham Sedgwick, Anne Burnham Sedgwick. **EDUC:** Univ. of New Brunswick, 1956-57; Acadia Univ., B.A. 1960; Dalhousie Univ., LL.B. 1963. **BAR:** N.B., 1963; Ont., 1978. **CAREER:** gen. practice of law, Gilbert McGloan and Gillis, Saint John, 1963-67; Legal Cnsl, The T. Eaton Co., 1967-71; Sr. Advisor to the Premier of N.B., & Legal Cnsl to the N.B. P.C. Party, 1971-76; Dir., CBC, 1987-91; Cnsl, Borden & Elliot, 1991 to date. **SELECTED PUBLICATIONS:** *Let Women Play Too* (Toronto: Univ. of Toronto, 1988). **DIRECTOR:** Life Network (formerly YOU-YOUR Channel) (also Exec. Committee); Trillium Growth Capital Inc. (also Investment Committee); Ranbaxy Genpharm Inc. **AFFIL:** Wellesley Hospital (Dir.; Chair, Patient Svcs Committee); Queen Elizabeth Hospital Foundation (Dir.); Cornerstone Club, Ontario P.C. Fund (Dir.); WIN (Support Fund for P.C. Women) (Founder & Dir.); The Canadian Club of Toronto, premier platform for speakers in Canada (Pres. 1995-96); Committee for '94. **HONS:** appointed Fed. Queen's Counsel, 1992; honoured at a special Founder's tribute event of WIN (Women in Nomination), May 26, 1993; nominated, Women of Distinction Award, YWCA of Metropolitan Toronto, 1993; Women of Distinction Award for Public Affairs, Metropolitan Toronto YWCA, 1996. **MISC:** organized & participated in various conferences on women & politics in Canada; presented briefs to various royal commissions, incl. Royal Commission on New Reproductive Technologies, 1990; Commentator for the Royal Commission on Electoral Reform & Party Financing in Canada (symposium on the active participation of women in political life), Dec. 1990; Canada's Rep. at UN Expert Group Meeting on Women in Public Life, Vienna, Austria, May 1991; Sr. Advisor & Strategist to the 1993 leadership campaign of the Hon. Kim Campbell; Co-chair for the successful Barbara Hall Campaign for Mayor of Toronto, 1994; Advisor to Isabel Basset, MPP (St. Andrew-St. Patrick) & Bill Saunderson, MPP (Eglinton), 1995 prov. election; Chair, Ontario Gov't Review Panel on the Greater Toronto Area Task Force Report, 1996; Nat'l Campaign Committee, Acadia Advantage, 1996. **COMMENT:** *"Committed parent of three, participating in community, school and sports activities; an advocate for the advancement of women in professional and public life for more than three decades; has broad experience in law, business and politics, including strategic advisor to provincial premiers and three national leaders."*

Burton, Barbara, B.Admin. ■ ■ Ⓢ
Vice-President, Human Resources, EPCOR (electric utility), Capitol Square, 18th Fl., 10065 Jasper Ave., Edmonton, AB T5J 3B1 (403) 448-3597, FAX 448-3192, EMAIL bburton@edpower.com. Born Winnipeg 1952. m. Ken. 2 ch. Erin, Tyler. EDUC: Univ. of Regina, B.Admin.(Behavioural Sc.) 1975. CAREER: Labour Rel'ns, Personnel Dept., City of Edmonton, 1975-93. AFFIL: Skills Canada (Bd. mbr.); Strategic Leadership Forum; Canadian Mental Health Association (former Bd. mbr.); Edmonton Social Planning Council (former Bd. mbr.). INTERESTS: participation in health & fitness activities; golf; skiing.

Burton, Frances, B.A.,M.Sc., Ph.D. ☜ ☸ ⌂
Professor, UNIVERSITY OF TORONTO, Department of Anthropology, Scarborough Campus, 1265 Military Trail, Scarborough, ON M1C 1A4 (416) 287-7345, FAX 287-7823, EMAIL burton@lake.scar.utoronto.ca. Born Villecresnes, France 1939. m. Peter G. Silverman. 2 ch. Alexis Corinna Silverman, Leah Andrea Silverman. EDUC: New York Univ., B.A.(Liberal Arts) 1960, M.Sc.(Anthropology) 1962; City Univ. of N.Y., Ph.D.(Anthropology) 1969. CAREER: Prof., Dept. of Anthropology, Univ. of Toronto. HONS: Founders' Day Award, New York Univ., 1960. MISC: 1st person to discover that non-human primate females experience orgasm, 1972; 1st person in anthropology to produce a multimedia CD-ROM guide to the non-human primates.

Bury, Brenda, BFA ⊗
Portrait Painter. 96A Beverley St., Toronto, ON M5T 1Y2. Born UK. EDUC: Univ. of Reading, Berkshire, B.F.A. CAREER: freelance portrait painter, 1950 to date; first English royal portrait, Lord Mountbatten of Burma, 1965; came to Canada, 1983. COMMISSIONS: more than 150 portraits of individuals & groups, incl. the Rt. Hon. John Diefenbaker, the Hon. Maurice Duplessis, Her Majesty Queen Elizabeth II (1969), & Her Excellency Madame Jeanne Sauvé (1984). INTERESTS: reading; walking around cities; looking at pictures. MISC: supported herself as a freelance portrait painter since leaving university in the '50s. COMMENT: *"Brenda Bury was born and educated in the UK. She is now Canadian and lives in Toronto. She includes the Queen, Lady Thatcher, prime ministers, and many distinguished Canadians among her subjects."*

Busby, Ellen, B.A.,C.G.A. 2 7 3
Executive Director, CANADIAN ASSOCIATION OF PROFESSIONAL DANCE ORGANIZATIONS (CAPDO), RR 1, 3790 Farmview Rd., Kinburn, ON K0A 2H0 (613) 832-0397, FAX 832-1321, EMAIL capdo@magi.com. Born Ishpeming, Mich. 1953. m. Michael (Sandy) Twose. EDUC: Concordia Univ., B.A.(cum laude, Drama) 1975. CAREER: Theatre & Dance Technician & Stage Mgr, various companies, Montreal, Regina, Toronto, 1975-81; Asst. Gen. Mgr, Toronto Dance Theatre, 1981-83; Gen. Mgr, 1984-87; Fin. Office, Dance Section, Canada Council, 1988-93; Co-Acting Head, Dance Section, 1990-91; Exec. Asst., Arts Div., 1993-94; Exec. Dir., CAPDO, 1994 to date. EDIT: Working Committee Mbr., *Dance Manager's Handbook* (Dance in Canada Association, 1986). AFFIL: Certified General Accountant (C.G.A.). INTERESTS: weaving; photography; sports; renovating a 150-year-old farmhouse. COMMENT: *"Ellen Busby's early involvement in amateur theatre has resulted in a career built on fulfilling supportive roles, with the desire of 'making a difference' for artists."*

Bussières, Simone ■ ■ ☜ ▯ ▤
Écrivain/Writer. Born Québec City 1918. EDUC: Bureau Central, Dépt. de l'Instruction publique, Diplôme Supérieur d'enseignement 1935. CAREER: Animatrice à la radio et à la TV, 1948-60; Directrice de l'enseignement, la Commission des Écoles catholiques de Qué., 1955-68; P.-D.G., Les Presses Laurentiennes inc. (maison d'éditions), 1963-88. SELECTED PUBLICATIONS: *L'Héritier* (roman, 1951); *Je veux lire - Je sais lire - J'aime lire* (méthode d'apprentissage de la lecture); *Le Petit Lapin qui a poussé sur une étoile* (conte de Noël, 1972); *C'est ta fête* (poèmes pour enfants, 1981); *Les Joies de la lecture* (choix de lectures pour élèves de 4e-6e années, 1995). AFFIL: La Société des Écrivains canadiens (Prés., section Qué. 1980-81). HONS: Médaille (Children's Book of the Year) pour *Le Petit Lapin qui a poussé sur une étoile*, Canadian Library Association, 1972. INTERESTS: lecture; vitrail; peinture; jardinage.

Bustamante, Rosalina, B.Sc.,M.A., M.Ed. ■ ■ ☜ ✄ ♡
Multilingual Assessor, YORK REGION ROMAN CATHOLIC SEPARATE SCHOOL BOARD (905) 881-7363. Born Manila, Philippines. s. EDUC: Manuel L. Quezon Univ., Philippines, Elementary Teacher's Certificate (with highest honours) 1951, B.Sc.(Elementary Educ., magna cum laude) 1963, M.A.(Guidance & Counselling) 1970; Ontario Institute for Studies in Education, Univ. of Toronto, M.Ed.(Multicultural Studies) 1980. CAREER: Sec., Sch. of Educ. & Asst. Prof., M.L. Quezon Univ., Philippines, 1963-73; Supervisor, Student Resi-

dence, Willard Hall, WCTU, 1974-82; Elementary Sch. Teacher, Metropolitan Separate Sch. Bd., 1982-95 (retired 1995); Multilingual Assessor (part-time), York Reg. R.C. Separate Sch. Bd. **SELECTED PUBLICATIONS:** 6 articles re Filipino-Canadians in *Polyphony*, The Bulletin of the Multicultural Society of Ontario; short articles & features in Filipino ethnic newspapers; monthly column, "On Mainstreaming," *Filipino Life* magazine. **AFFIL:** Catholic Cross-Cultural Services (Bd. mbr. 1985-1991; 1995 to date; Sec. 1996 to date); Markham Federation of Filipino-Canadians (Bd. mbr. & Chrm, Educ. Committee 1989 to date); Pillars (Filipino-Canadian seniors' group); Prime Mentors of Canada (mbr. 1995 to date); Our Place, Community of Hope Centre (volunteer 1995 to date); Women's Christioan Temperance Union; Metropolitan Separate Sch. Bd. **HONS:** TOFCO Award, The Outstanding Filipino Canadians of Ontario, 1996; award for 10-yr. commitment to volunteerism, Prov. of Ont., 1992; award for outstanding contribution toward the promotion of racial harmony in Markham, Markham Multicultural Association, 1992; award for outstanding svcs as Bd. mbr., Catholic Immigration Bureau, 1991; Special Recognition for assistance, guidance & support of community dev. as Mentor, Ontario Young Leaders of Tomorrow Program, 1988. **INTERESTS:** reading; writing; community work; crafts (flower making). **MISC:** presenter to educators, "Understanding Filipino Children in Canadian Schools," 1986 to date; mbr., Ad Hoc Advisory Committee to the Mayor of Markham on racism, 1995-96; volunteer instructor, Filipino heritage classes, Markham Federation of Filipino Canadians, 1996 to date; volunteer tutor, Filipino-Cdn children experiencing difficulties in Cdn schools; mbr., Writing Team, Document on Multicultural & Anti-Racist Educ., Ont. Ministry of Educ., 1989-90. **COMMENT:** *"I am a Canadian of Filipino roots, proud of belonging to this country as well as of my original heritage. In appreciation of what Canada has done for me, I have committed much of my time to volunteer work in the community, especially with those promoting racial harmony."*

Bustard, Patricia R. ■ $

Vice-President, Administration, TRANSAMERICA LIFE INSURANCE COMPANY OF CANADA, 300 Consilium Place, Scarborough, ON M1H 3G2. Born Canada 1950. d. 1 ch. **CAREER:** various positions to VP, London Life Insurance Company, 1969-90; VP, Imperial Life, 1990-95; VP, Admin., Transamerica Life Insurance Company, 1995 to date. **INTERESTS:** family; reading.

Butala, Sharon Annette, B.Ed.,B.A. ✇

Author. Box 428, Eastend, SK S0N 0T0 (306) 295-3810, FAX 295-3810. Born Nipawin, Sask. 1940. m. Peter Butala. 1 ch. (previous marriage). **EDUC:** Univ. of Saskatchewan, B.Ed. 1962, B.A.(Art) 1963, Post-grad. Diploma (Special Educ.) 1973. **CAREER:** Teacher, 1963-72; Lecturer, Dept. for the Educ. of Exceptional Children &/or Institute for Child Guidance, Coll. of Educ., Univ. of Saskatchewan, 1973-76; Educ. Psychologist, Special Educ. Consultant, 1977-83; Writer, 1978 to date. **SELECTED CREDITS:** six plays performed, incl. *Natural Disasters* (two acts), Regina, 1985, *A Killing Frost*, Vancouver Fringe Festival, 1988, & *The Element of Fire* (three acts), Pink ink Theatre Productions, Vancouver, 1989; *Rodeo Life*, Twenty-Fifth Street Theatre, Saskatoon, 1993; numerous radio credits. **SELECTED PUBLICATIONS:** *Coming Attractions*, short story collection, co-authored (Ottawa: Oberon, 1983); *Country of the Heart* (Saskatoon: Fifth House, 1984); *Queen of the Headaches*, short story collection (Regina: Coteau, 1985); *The Gates of the Sun* (Saskatoon: Fifth House, 1986; HarperCollins, 1994); *Luna* (Saskatoon: Fifth House, 1988; HarperCollins, 1994); *Fever*, short story collection (Toronto: HarperCollins, 1990); *Upstream* (Saskatoon: Fifth House, 1991; HarperCollins, 1996); *The Fourth Archangel* (Toronto: HarperCollins, 1992); *The Perfection of the Morning: An Apprenticeship in Nature*, non-fiction (Toronto: HarperCollins, 1994); *Coyote's Morning Cry*, non-fiction (Toronto: HarperCollins, 1995); stories, essays, plays, poetry & reviews appear in numerous journals & anthologies. **AFFIL:** Saskatchewan Writers' Guild; The Writers' Union of Canada; PEN; ACTRA; Saskatchewan Heritage Foundation Bd.; Eastend Arts Council (Founding Mbr.). **HONS:** Univ. of Saskatchewan Grad. Fellowship; Saskatchewan Association for the Mentally Retarded Scholarship; Long Fiction Award, Saskatchewan Writers' Guild, *Shortgrass*, 1982; Major Drama Award, Saskatchewan Writers' Guild, *Natural Disasters*, 1985; Major Drama Award, Saskatchewan Writers' Guild, *The Element of Fire*, 1989; Silver Award for short fiction, National Magazine Awards, "Justice" (*Saturday Night* Magazine), 1991; Member Achievement Award, Saskatchewan Writers' Guild, 1991; First for Paperback Fiction, Canadian Author's Awards, *Fever*, 1992; Saskatchewan Gold Award, Western Magazine Awards, "A Change of Heart" (*Western Living*), 1993; Canada 125 Medal, 1993; Saskatchewan Gold Award, Western Magazine Awards, "Dances With Woodchucks" (*Western Living*), 1994;

"Spirit of Saskatchewan" Award, Saskatchewan Book Awards, *The Perfection of the Morning*, 1994; Non-fiction Award, Saskatchewan Book Awards, *The Perfection of the Morning*, 1994. INTERESTS: books; nature; the environment; spiritual matters. MISC: recipient of various grants; numerous readings & lectures; The *Perfection of the Morning* No. 1 on *The Globe and Mail* Bestseller List, July 1994. COMMENT: *"I was 44 when my first novel was published and I knew I had at last found my vocation. All my desire and energy goes into writing."*

Butler, Alison Scott, B.A.,LL.B.,LL.M. ■ ⚖
Barrister and Solicitor. 264 Canard St., RR#1, Port William, NS B0P 1T0 (902) 582-7588, FAX 582-7121, EMAIL butlag@istar.ca. 2 ch. Matthew, Rebecca. EDUC: Univ. of Western Ontario, B.A. 1970; Dalhousie Univ., LL.B. 1974, LL.M. 1992. BAR: N.S., 1974. CAREER: Clerk, Dalhousie Univ. Law Library, 1970-71; Researcher, Dalhousie Legal Aid, 1971-73; Articled Clerk, Daley, Black and Moreira, 1973-74; Staff Lawyer, N.S. Legal Aid, 1974-75; Lawyer, Dept. of Justice, Gov't of Canada, 1975-81; Assoc., Taylor MacLellan and Cochrane, 1981-86; Ptnr, 1986-88; sole practitioner of law, 1988 to date; part-time Fac., Dalhousie Univ., 1990-92. SELECTED PUBLICATIONS: "The GST: Practitioners Beware!" (*Nova Scotia Law News* 1990); "Making Charter Arguments in Civil Tax Cases: Can the Courts Help Taxpayers?" (*Canadian Tax Journal* 1994); various newspaper articles for nonlawyers on income tax topics & other legal issues. AFFIL: N.S. Human Rights Commission (Commissioner 1994); Canadian Bar Association (V-Chair, Tax Committee); Canadian Tax Foundation; Public Legal Education Society (Sec., Chair of Lawyer Referral Committee 1993-95); Continuing Legal Education Society of N.S. (Pres. 1993-95); Better Business Bureau (Consumer Arbitrator); Annapolis Valley Affiliated Boards of Trade; Aylescot Village Lot Owners' Association (Founding Dir.); Chrysalis House (Dir. 1993-95); Family & Children's Services (Dir.; VP 1992-95; Pres.); Kings County Historical Society; Women's Legal Education & Action Foundation; Univ. Women's Club; John Murphy Fed. Liberal Campaign (Co-chair, Policy Committee 1993). MISC: numerous presentations on legal matters to law students, governments & the public.

Butler, Edith, B.A.,M.Litt.,D.M.,D.Litt. ⊗
Singer-Songwriter. 86 Côte Ste-Catherine, Outremont, QC H2V 2A3 (514) 270-9556, FAX 270-4252. Born Paquetville, N.B. EDUC:

Univ. de Moncton, B.A. 1964; Univ. de Laval, M.Litt. 1969. SELECTED CREDITS: *Avant d'être dépaysée*, 1973; *L'Acadie s'marie*, 1974; *Chansons d'Acadie*, 1975; *Je vous aime ma vie recommence*, 1976; *La récréation*, 1977; *L'espoir*, 1978; *Asteur qu'on est là*, 1979; *Paquetville Live*, 1980; *Barbichon, Barbiché*, 1980; *Je M'appelle Edith*, 1981; *De Paquetville à Paris*, 1983; *un million de fois je t'aime*, 1984; *Le party d'Edith*, 1985; *Les grands succès d'Edith Butler*, 1985; *Et le party continue*, 1986; *Party pour danser*, 1987; *Edith Butler*, 1990; *Mon Folklore* (Vol. 1) (J. Lemay/E. Butler), 1991; *Ca Swingue!*, 1992; *Mon Folklore* (Vol. 2) (J. Lemay/E. Butler), 1993; *Mon Folklore* (Vol. 3) (J. Lemay/E. Butler), 1994; *Edith A l'Année Longue*, 1995. AFFIL: Canada Arts Council; Fondation Teleglobe (Admin & 'porte-parole' 1996). HONS: Officer of the Order of Canada; Chevalier de l'Ordre des francophones d'Amérique; Chevalier de l'Ordre de la Pléïade; Princess Abénakise; Prix International de la chanson, Paris, 1981; Grand Prix du Disque Académie Charles Cros, Paris, 1983; Félix du Meilleur spectacle sur scène, Montréal, 1985; Nellie Award for the Best Performance in Radio, Toronto, 1986; Félix de la Meilleure vente de disques de l'année, Montréal, 1986; Félix de l'Artiste s'étant le plus illustrée à l'étranger, Montréal, 1986; Cinq disques d'or et trois de platine; Prix Méritas, 1994; D.M. (Hon.), Univ. of Moncton, 1987; D.Litt.(Hon), Univ. of New Brunswick, 1989; D.Litt.(Hon.), Acadia Univ., 1994. COMMENT: *"Acadian singer and songwriter, I started my career on a TV show:* Sing Along Jubilee. *Toured the world from France to Japan and still going strong!*

Butler, Sheila M., B.F.A., M.A. ■ ■ ⊗ ⚜ 📖
Associate Professor, Department of Visual Arts, UNIVERSITY OF WESTERN ONTARIO, John Labatt Visual Art Centre, London, ON N6A 5B7 (519) 679-2111. Born McKeesport, Penn. 1938. m. 2 ch. EDUC: Carnegie Mellon Univ., Pittsburgh, B.F.A.(Hons., Painting & Printmaking) 1960; Univ. of Western Ontario, M.A.(Theory & Criticism) 1993. CAREER: Art Instructor, St. Johnsville Public Schools, N.Y., 1960-61; Art Instructor, J.W. Eater Jr. High Sch., Rantoul, Ill., 1961-62; Instructor in Drawing & Art Hist., Ivy Sch. of Professional Art, Pittsburgh, 1966-67; artist, Irene Pasinski Associates, Industrial Design Studio, 1967-69; Special Projects Officer (developed printmaking proj. with Eskimo artists), Gov't of N.W.T., Baker Lake, 1969-72; Dir., Baker Lake Sewing Shop, 1971-73; Fine Arts Consultant, Sanavik Eskimo Coop., 1973-76. SELECTED PUBLICA-

TIONS: 9 monographs incl.: *The First Passionate Collector: The Ian Lindsay Collection of Inuit Art* (Winnipeg Art Gallery, 1991); *Regionalism in Canadian Art* (The Tom Thomson Memorial Gallery, Owen Sound, 1990); *Baker Lake Prints and Print Drawings 1970-76* (Winnipeg Art Gallery, 1983; numerous articles incl.: "Sue-Ellen Gerritsen" (*Parachute*, 72, Oct. 1993); "We Need a New History" (*Meaning*, no. 13, Fall 1993); "Fortunate Heirs" (*Border Crossings*, vol. 8, Mar. 1989); "Baker Lake Wall Hangings" (*The Beaver Magazine*, 1972). EXHIBITIONS: Exhibition Curator, Art Gallery of Dalhousie Univ., 1986; Exhibition Curator, Ace Art, Inc., Winnipeg, 1985, 1989; Exhibition Curator, Univ. of Manitoba Gallery III, 1984, 1985. AFFIL: The Canada Council ("A" Grants Jury 1993; Visual Arts Grants Juries for Indiv. Projects; Purchasing Selection Juries, Art Bank 1985, 1986, 1989, 1991); Ontario Arts Council (Indiv. Grants Jury 1992); Canadian Tribute to Human Rights (Jury mbr., Nat'l Competition for Sculpture Commission, Ottawa 1985); Manitoba Arts Council (Visual Arts Grants Juries for Exhibition Funding 1982-83 & 1987-88; Teacher & Consultant, Artists in the Schools Program 1988-89). HONS: Artist-in-Residence in Printmaking, Univ. of Windsor Sch. of Visual Art, Windsor, Ont., 1988; Leon A. Brown Award as Artist of the Year, Winnipeg Art Gallery, 1984; edition of prints commissioned by Manitoba Association of Canadian Television & Radio Actors to be awarded to ACTRA award recipients, 1984; edition of prints commissioned by Volunteer Committee of Winnipeg Art Gallery, 1978; Pennsylvania Industrial Chemical Corporation Scholarship, 1956; Sarah Mellon Scaife Foundation Scholarship for Exceptionally Able Youth, 1956. MISC: numerous research grants.

Butt, Catherine (Kelly), B.Sc. ■ ■ Ⓢ
Senior Vice-President, Information Services, LONDON LIFE INSURANCE COMPANY, 255 Dufferin Ave., London, ON N6A 4K1 (519) 432-5281, FAX 432-3862, EMAIL kelly.butt@londonlife.com. Vice-President, LONDON INSURANCE GROUP INC. Born Liverpool 1949. m. Doug. 1 ch. Kathleen. EDUC: Brock Univ., B.Sc.(Hons., Math.) 1971. CAREER: VP, Data Processing, Manufacturers Life Insurance Company, 1979-84; VP, Oper., Commercial Bnkg Group, Bank of Montreal, 1984-88; VP/Sr. VP, Info. Svcs, London Life Insurance Company, 1988 to date; mbr., Sr. Mgmt Partnership, 1989 to date. AFFIL: Life Insurance Institute of Canada (Bd. mbr.); London Chamer of Commerce; London Health Science Centre (Bd. of Dir.); Victoria Hospital (Chair of the Bd. 1995

to date); London Acute Care Hospital Restructuring Committee.

Butt, Dorcas Susan, B.A.,M.A., Ph.D ◈ ⊕
Associate Professor, Department of Psychology, UNIVERSITY OF BRITISH COLUMBIA, 2136 West Mall, Vancouver, BC V6T 1Z4 (604) 822-3269, FAX 822-6923. Born Vancouver 1938. d. 2 ch. EDUC: Univ. of British Columbia, B.A. 1960, M.A. 1963; Univ. of Chicago, Ph.D. 1967. SELECTED PUBLICATIONS: *Psychology of Sport: The behavior, motivation, personality and performance of athletes* (New York: Van Nostrand Reinhold, 1987); *Mental health, cultural values and social development* (Dordrecht, Holland: Reidel Publishing, 1984); "Sex Role Adaptation, Socialization and Sport Participation in Women," with M.L. Shroeder (*International Journal of Sport Psychology* 1980); "The Sexual Response as Exercise: A Brief Review and Theoretical Proposal" (*Sports Medicine* 1990); numerous other publications.

Bye, Cristine ■ ／ ▯ ▨
Editor and Senior Writer, Communications and Development Department, THE BANFF CENTRE FOR CONTINUING EDUCATION, Box 1020, Stn 12, Banff, AB T0L 0C0 (403) 762-6159, FAX 762-6398. Born Coronation, Alta. 1954. d. 2 ch. Georgina Beaty, Lawson Beaty. EDUC: Ryerson Polytechnic Institute, Degree in Journalism 1976. CAREER: Writer, police beat, educ. beat, gen. reporting, *Calgary Herald*, 1976-78; Writer, entertainment dept. & Sunday magazine, *Calgary Albertan* (later, the *Calgary Sun*), 1979-81; Sr. Writer, "Saturday Spotlight," *Calgary Herald*, 1981-85; Sr. Writer, "Sunday Magazine," *Calgary Herald*, 1985-87; Instructor, Write On Target correspondence course, Lakeland Coll., 1987-94; Contributing Ed., *The United Church Observer*, 1988-96; Ed./Sr. Writer, Comm. & Dev. Dept., Banff Centre for Continuing Educ., 1992 to date; freelance writer/ed./consultant, 1979 to date; fiction writer, 1982 to date. SELECTED CREDITS: "Box Social" broadcast on CBC Radio's *Alberta Anthology*, 1986; "Tangible Things," broadcast on CBC radio's "The Home Stretch." SELECTED PUBLICATIONS: *The Banff Centre–Mountain Campus*, Ed. (Altitude Publishing, 1993); *Coyote Hunt* (*Grain* literary magazine, 1996); *The Banff Centre Style Guide* (1994); "Box Social," *Turning Points* anthology (Nelson Canada, 1993); "Coyote on the Road," *Eaten of Worms* anthology (Second Wednesday Press, 1991) & *Alberta Bound* anthology (NeWest Press, 1986); "Worth Saving," *Letters to You* anthology (Second Wednesday Press, 1990); "Embroidery" (*Other*

Voices literary magazine, Oct. 1989); "The Perfect Strawberry" (*Secrets From the Orange Couch* literary magazine, May 1989); "Love and Kindness," *The Real Eric Manx* anthology (Second Wednesday Press, 1989); contributor to: *The Toronto Star, Alberta Business Magazine, Health Savvy Magazine; Calgary Magazine, Banff Letters, Quest* magazine. **AFFIL:** Calgary Council of Professional Writers (Founder); Writers' Guild of Alberta. **HONS:** Alberta Farm Writers' Award for "A Deadly Occupation," *Calgary Herald* Saturday Spotlight story, 1980; Lamplighter Award, Calgary Volunteer Association for "The Gift of Giving," *Calgary Herald* Saturday Spotlight story, 1984; Monthly Excellence Awards, *Calgary Herald* for "Love is not Enough–Marriage in the '80s" and "Our Son Has Cancer," 1987; Honorable Mention, A.C. Forrest Award, Canadian Church Press Annual Awards, 1992, for "More Than a River," *United Church Observer* story that was part of an entry; various scholarships & grants. **MISC:** founder & mbr., Calgary fiction writers' group, Second Wednesday; various lectures on journalism & fiction writing; given numerous readings; designed *Eaten of Worms* for Second Wednesday Press, 1991.

Byers, Mary Gill, B.A., M.A. ■■ 🎋 ▢ ○
Author. Volunteer. 7 Thornwood Rd., Apt. 203, Toronto, ON M4W 2R8 (416) 968-7828. Born 1933 4 ch. Edward Gill Paterson Byers, Richard Clark Byers, Diana Leslie Byers Coen, Chistopher Leonard Byers. **EDUC:** Univ. of Toronto, B.A.(English Lit.) 1954, M.A.(English Lit.) 1976. **CAREER:** The Manufacturers Life Assurance Company, 1953-55. **SELECTED PUBLICATIONS:** author/co-author, 8 books and 2 in progress, non-fiction, historical works. **AFFIL:** Anglican Church of Canada (former Warden, Christ Church Deer Park; Exec. Committee, Diocese of Toronto); Trinity College Sch. (Hon. Life Gov.; former mbr. Exec. Committee); Junior League of Toronto (mbr. of Bd.; Ed., *The Key*); Empire Club of Canada (mbr. of Bd. 1988 to date; Ed., *Yearbook*, 1988-94); York County Historical Association; Lake Simcoe Historical Association; Architectural Conservancy of Ontario. **HONS:** Canada Council Grant, 1988; Jackman Foundation Grant, 1988; Ontario Arts Council Grant, 1989; Ontario Heritage Foundation Grant, 1989.

Byers, Sandra, M.D., B.A., M.A., Ph.D. 🐿 ⊕
Professor of Psychology and Acting Director of the Muriel McQueen Fergusson Center for Family Violence Research, UNIVERSITY OF NEW BRUNSWICK, Fredericton, NB E3B 6E4 (506) 453-4707, FAX 453-4505, EMAIL byers@unb.ca. Born Montreal 1951. m. Larry Heinlein, Ph.D. 2 ch. **EDUC:** Univ. of Rochester, B.A. 1973; West Virginia Univ., M.A. 1975, Ph.D. 1978. **CAREER:** Asst. Prof., Univ. of New Brunswick 1978-82; Assoc. Prof., 1982-87; Prof., 1987 to date. **SELECTED PUBLICATIONS:** "Sexual Coercion in Dating Relationships," with L. O'Sullivan (New York, Haworth Press 1996); "Sexual Satisfaction in Long-term Heterosexual Relationships: The Interpersonal Exchange Model of Sexual Satisfaction," with K. Lawrance (*Personal Relationships* 1995); "Ejaculation: A Review of Conceptual, Etiological and Treatment Issues," with G. Grenier (*Archives of Sexual Behavior* 1995); "How Well does the Traditional Sexual Script Explain Sexual Coercion: A Review of a Program of Research" (*Journal of Psychology and Human Sexuality* 1996); *Guidelines for the Elimination of Sexual Harassment* with D. Price (Ottawa: Canadian Psychological Association 1985); "Predicting Initiations and Refusals of Sexual Activities in Married and Cohabiting Couples," with L. Heinlein (*The Journal of Sex Research* 1989); "Eroding Stereotypes: College Women's Attempts to Influence Reluctant Male Sexual Partners," with L. O'Sullivan (*The Journal of Sexual Research* 1993); numerous other publications. **EDIT:** Assoc. Ed., *Journal of the New Brunswick Psychological Association*, 1979-82; Consulting Ed., *Journal of Sex Research*; 1992-94; Ed., *Journal of Psychology and Human Sexuality*; Assoc. Ed., *Canadian Journal of Human Sexuality*, 1995 to date; Ed. Committee, *Canadian Pyschology*, 1993-94. **AFFIL:** American Psychological Association; Association for the Advancement of Behavior Therapy; Canadian Psychological Association; Coll. of Psychologists of N.B.; Canadian Sex Research Forum; Sex Information & Education Council of Canada; Society for the Scientific Study of Sex (Fellow); International Academy of Sex Research; Canadian Research Institute for the Advancement of Women. **HONS:** Univ. Scholar, Univ. of Rochester, 1969-73; Doctoral Fellowship, The Canada Council, 1974-77; Merit Award, Univ. of New Brunswick, 1990, 1993. **MISC:** recipient of numerous grants from various agencies; numerous consultancies; numerous conference papers; licensed Psychologist, N.B., 1979; Chair, Victim Svcs Committee, Dept. of the Solicitor Gen., Prov. of N.B., 1992 to date. **COMMENT:** "*She is a prominent researcher, teacher and therapist in the field of human sexuality. She is also the Founding Director of the Muriel McQueen Furgusson Centre for Family Violence Research at the University of New Brunswick.*"

Byrne, Dorothy, B.A.,LL.B.,M.Sc. Ⓢ
Vice-President, Law and Regulatory Affairs, BC
TELECOM INC., 21-3666 Kingsway, Burnaby,
BC V5H 3Z7 (604) 432-4210, FAX 432-9681.
Vice-President, Law and Regulatory Affairs, BC
TEL. Born Kimberley, B.C. 1947. EDUC: Car-
leton Univ., B.A.(Pol. Sci.) 1971; Univ. of
British Columbia Law Sch., LL.B. 1977; Stan-
ford Grad. Sch. of Bus., M.Sc.(Mgmt) 1986.
BAR: B.C., 1978. CAREER: private practice of
law, 1978-79; VP, Law & Regulatory Affairs,
BC TEL, 1979 to date (with time away for edu-
cational leave). DIRECTOR: Export Develop-
ment Corporation. AFFIL: Law Society of B.C.;
Canadian Bar Association; Canadian Women
in Communications (Dir.)

C

abott, Laura I., B.Phys.Ed.,LL.B. ■ ⚖ ♣ ⊘
Lawyer, DAVIS AND CO., Barristers and Solicitors, 307 Jarvis St., Ste. 101, Whitehorse, YT Y1A 2H3 (403) 668-6444, FAX 667-2669. Born New Westminster, B.C. 1962. s. **EDUC:** Univ. of Alberta, B.Phys.Ed. 1985, LL.B. 1991. **BAR:** 1992. **CAREER:** Lawyer, 1992 to date. **DIRECTOR:** Town and Country Building Consultants. **AFFIL:** Yukon Liberal Party (Pres. 1992-93; Dir.); Yukon Coll. (Native Law Instructor); Yukon Mental Health Review Board; Canadian Bar Association (Sec.-Treas., Yukon Branch). **HONS:** Academic/Athletic Scholarship, Univ. of Alberta, 1983-85; Law Sch. Advocacy Scholarships, 1991. **INTERESTS:** skiing; canoeing; politics; hockey (women's); organizing & running political campaigns. **COMMENT:** *"I am a lawyer living in Whitehorse. I'm very active in the Yukon Liberal Party, my community and sports."*

Caceres, Penny, B.A.,M.A. ⚲ $
Dean, Developmental, Trade and Apprenticeship Studies, SENECA COLLEGE, 1750 Finch Ave. E., North York, ON M2J 2X5 (416) 491-5050, FAX 491-4606, EMAIL pcaceres@library. senecac.on.ca. Born Toronto 1948. m. Rod Rork. 1 ch. **EDUC:** McGill Univ., B.A.(French) 1969; California State Univ., M.A.(Counselling) 1980. **CAREER:** Teacher (ESL), International Institute, Toronto, 1970-71; Teacher, Counsellor & Coord., L.A. Unified Sch. District, 1971-80; Coord., Newmarket Campus, Seneca Coll., 1980-85; Academic Chair, King & Newmarket Campus, 1985-92; Chair/Principal, Newmarket & Richmond Hill Campus, 1992; Dean, Developmental, Trade & Apprenticeship Studies, 1992 to date. **AFFIL:** Strategic Planning Com-

mittee; West of Yonge Focus Group; Hay Committee; LINC Consultation Group–York Reg.; York Reg. (Local Bd. Steering Committee); Learning Centre Committee; Academic Chairs Committee; King Council; York Region Sch. (Basic Gen. Committee 3 yrs.); L.A. Sch. District (Chair, Reading Committee 5 yrs.). INTERESTS: travel (esp. S. America & the Caribbean); hiking; canoeing; sailing. COMMENT: *"I am first and foremost a teacher and educator and I have devoted my career to the development of training for the unemployed and the disenfranchised. Of equal importance to me is my role as a mother and a spouse. The challenge in my life has been and will continue to be maintaining a balance between the two."*

Cadbury, Barbara ⊘ ⊕
Family Planning Advocate. Churchill Place, 345 Church St., Ste. 308, Oakville, ON L6J 7G4. Founder, PLANNED PARENTHOOD TORONTO. Born London, UK 1910. w. George Cadbury. 2 ch. Lyndall Elizabeth Boal, Caroline Ann Woodroffe. EDUC: Central Foundation, Bishops Gate. CAREER: Staff, League of Nations, London, UK; Sec., Frank Wise, M.P., UK; Councillor, Borough of Stoke Newington, London, UK, 1934; moved to Canada, 1946; worked with Margaret Sanger, Planned Parenthood, NYC, 1951-54; Pres., Family Planning Association of Jamaica, 1955-60; Bd. Mbr., Jamaica Welfare, 1955-60; appointed, with husband, Special Reps., International Planned Parenthood Federation, travelling extensively through Asia, 1960; Founder, Planned Parenthood Toronto, 1961; helped found the Family Planning Federation of Canada, 1963; Mbr., Canadian Welfare Council, 1965; Mbr., Planned Parenthood Hamilton & Planned Parenthood Toronto. SELECTED PUBLICATIONS: has written extensively on family planning. HONS: Gov. General's Persons Award, 1981; Women of Distinction Award, Toronto YWCA, 1982; honoured by Population & Family Planning Section, American Public Health Association, 1982; Mbr. of the Order of Canada, 1990. INTERESTS: children; grandchildren; wildlife; politics. MISC: directed a campaign for amending the Canadian Criminal Code regarding contraception from 1961-69, which ended when the code was reformed in 1969; planned first Nat'l Conference on Family Planning in Canada, 1971.

Cadeau, Lally ■■ ⊗ ⩔ ⩗
Actor. c/o Oscars and Abrams, 59 Berkeley St., Toronto, ON M5A 2W5. Born Hamilton, Ont. 1948. 3 ch. Sara Brooke, Christopher Cadeau, Bennett Mitchell. EDUC: Loretto Academy, Hamilton; Stoneleigh-Prospect Hill

Sch., Greenfield, Mass.; Edenhall Convent of Sacred Heart, Philadelphia; Havergal Coll., Toronto. CAREER: professional actress, 1974 to date. SELECTED CREDITS: numerous credits incl,. Janet King, *Road to Avonlea*. AFFIL: Canadian Council (Disciplinary Advisory Committee, Theatre Dept. 1982-85). HONS: Du Maurier Award, Best Newcomer, Cdn TV (*Harvest*), ACTRA, 1981; Bijou Award, Best Actress (*You've Come A Long Way Katie*), 1981; Earle Grey Award, Best Acting Performance, TV Leading Role (*You've Come A Long Way Katie*), ACTRA, 1982; Dora Mavor Moore Award, Outstanding Performance by Female in Leading Role (*Saturday, Sunday, Monday*), 1986-87; Gemini Award, Best Actress (*Road to Avonlea*), 1995; various nominations, radio, film & TV. INTERESTS: swimming; walking; reading; cooking; decorating; gardening.

Cadieux, Louise, LL.L. ■ ⩗
Partner, LAFORTUNE LEDUC, Barristers and Solicitors, 329 De la Commune St. W., Ste. 200, Montreal, QC H2Y 2E1 (514) 287-7171, FAX 287-7588. 1 ch. Justine Cadieux. EDUC: Univ. of Montreal, LL.L. 1974. BAR: Quebec, 1975. CAREER: Lawyer, Robitaille, Trempe, Dansereau, 1975-77; Ptnr, Robert Dansereau Barré Marchessault & Lauzon, 1977-90; Ptnr., Langlois Robert, 1990-96; Ptnr, Lafortune Leduc, 1996 to date. SELECTED PUBLICATIONS: *Le droit québécois de l'eau*, co-author (Que. Dept. of Natural Resources); several conference papers on women & the law, & the protection of privacy. AFFIL: Transit 24 Inc. (Chair); Société internationale de droit du travail et de la sécurité sociale; Approvisionnement Montréal; Société du droit administratif; Association of Human Resource Professionals of the Province of Quebec; Canadian Bar Association. MISC: was Prof. of Labour Law at the Sch. of Professional Training, Que. Bar, 1983-85. COMMENT: *"For the past 20 years, Mrs. Cadieux has practised primarily in labour, administrative and health law. She was one of the lawyers for the Government of Canada (Keable and MacDonald Commissions) and has also represented the Federal Government in the matter of the Canadian Constitution Patriation Reference and in the matters of the Quebec Veto Reference."*

Cahoon, Margaret Cecelia, B.A.,B.Ed., M.Ed.,Ph.D. ⩔ ⊕
Professor Emeritus, Nursing, UNIVERSITY OF TORONTO, Toronto, ON M5A 1A1. Born Hallowell, Ont. 1916. EDUC: Women's Coll. Hospital Sch. for Nurses, Nursing 1943; Univ. of Toronto, Certificate in Public Health Nursing

1946, B.Ed. 1953, M.Ed. 1960; Queen's Univ., B.A. 1950; Univ. of Michigan, Ph.D. 1967; Univ. of Edinburgh, Post-doctoral Fellowship (Research) 1976. **CAREER:** various positions, Prince Edward County Hospital, 1943-44; Public Health Nurse, Town of Picton, 1944-45; Public Health Nurse, Ont. Cancer Treatment & Research Foundation, Kingston Clinic, & Instructor, Community Health Nursing, Kingston General Hospital Sch. of Nursing, 1946-49; Fellow, Public Health, Sch. of Hygiene, Univ. of Toronto, 1950-52; Assoc. in Public Health, 1952-64; Asst. Prof., 1964-68; Assoc. to Prof. of Nursing, 1961-83; with cross-appointment to Sch. of Hygiene, 1968-70; Community Health Svc., East York-Leaside Health Unit, 1950-68; Visiting Prof. of Nursing, Univ. of Manitoba, 1980; Rosenstadt Prof. of Healthcare Research, Sunnybrook-Univ. of Toronto; part-time fac., Dalhousie Univ., 1983-85. **SELECTED PUBLICATIONS:** author-consultant, Cdn edition, *Health Science Books* 4-8, 1968-71; author or co-author of various papers, articles & book chapters. **AFFIL:** Registered Nurses' Association of Ontario; Canadian Nurses' Association (Chrm, Committee on Research in Nursing 1971-72); Ontario Public Health Association (Pres. 1963-64); Canadian Public Health Association (Gov. Council 1961-64); American Public Health Association (Gov. Council 1979-81); Conference of Emeritus Members of APHA; Canadian Association of University Teachers; Association of University Schools of Nursing, Ont. Reg'l Council on Long Term Care (Chrm, Committee of Studies 1970-75; Council 1976-80); Pi Lambda Theta; Univ. of Toronto (Gov. Council; Councils of Faculties of Dentistry & Pharmacy (Mbr. from Gov. Council 1979-82); National Council of Jewish Women (Fellowship in Gerontology 1961); Ontario Cancer Treatment & Research Foundation (Hon. Clinical Fellow 1971-72). **HONS:** Yaffe Award, Canadian Cancer Society, 1947; Centennial Award, Ontario Education Association, 1960; World Health Organization Award, 1963; Ont. Ministry of Health Fellowship, 1975; Sesqui-centennial Award, Univ. of Toronto, 1975; Educ. Dev. Award, 1978. **INTERESTS:** senior's rights & issues; spinning; weaving; painting; travel. **COMMENT:** *"My major achievements have been the promotion of health education in community healthcare and the introduction of research in nursing in baccalaureate nursing education, the development of the research component in graduate studies in nursing, and my emphasis on research in chronic care."*

Cailhier, Diane, Bacc.A.,L.L.,M.A. 🖉📾 ☟
Scénariste, LINO PRODUCTIONS INC., 205 ch.

North-Hatley, Katevale, QC J0B 1W0 (819) 843-1944, FAX 843-2700. Born Valleyfield, Que. 1947. s. 1 ch. **EDUC:** École Vincent d'Indy, Lauréat (Piano) 1964; Coll. Jésus-Marie, Bacc. ès Arts (Cour Classiques) 1967; Univ. de Montréal, Licence ès Lettres (Lit.), Maîtris ès Arts (Lit.) 1975. **CAREER:** Scénariste de dramatiques, de séries télévisées et documentaries depuis 20 ans; Enseignement, Histoire de théâtre, CEGEP de Rosemount, 1970; Enseignement, Cinéma, Coll. Jean-de-Brébeuf, 1976-77; enseignement, cours divers, Coll. de Sherbrooke, 1978-86. **SELECTED CREDITS:** texte dramatique, "Et Perdue," *L'Atelier,* emission radio, Radio-Canada, 1970; texte dramatique, "Cantante décantée," *Studio d'essais,* emission radio, Radio Canada, 1971; recherche et adaptation de romans, *Lecture de chevet,* 39 émissions/an, Radio-Canada, 1970-72; recherche et entrevues, *Gens de mon pays,* radio séries, Radio-Canada, 1972-75; collaboration au scénario, *La Piastre,* fiction, ACPAV, 1975; collaboration au scénario, *L'Etau-bus,* fiction, ACPAV, 1982; recherche et scénario, *Images de l'Estrie,* documentaire, Radio-Québec, 1980; scénario et dialogue, *Des amis pour la vie,* fiction, Vision 4 Inc., 1988; scénario et commentaire, *Terre et mémoire,* documentaire, Radio-Québec, 1983; scénario et commentaire, *Un homme de parole,* documentaire, ONF, 1990; scénario et dialogue, *Une nuit à l'école,* fiction, Cléo inc., 1991; scénario et dialogue, *Le jardin d'Anna,* fiction, Videofilms, 1992; autres films divers; *Les enquêtes de chlorophylle,* séries télévisée, Espace Vert, Damned Prod. et Fr 3, 1992; *Les intrépides,* séries télévisée, 1991; *Les Belmine,* série télévisée, Les Productions B!bi et Geneviéve, 1993; *Zap,* série télévisée, Productions Verseau International Inc., 1993; Les grands procès: *L'affaire Durand,* télévisée, les Productions Sovimage et Sagittaire, 1995; recherche, scénario et réalization, *Une vie comm rivière,* documenatire, ONF, 1996. **SELECTED PUBLICATIONS:** *Le métier d'assistant réalisateur au cinéma,* avec Alain Chartrand (Ed. Lidec, 1990); collaboration à la rédaction, *Les Québecoies et le mouvement pacifiste de Simonne Monet Chartrand* (Ed. Ecosociété, 1993); collaboration à la rédaction, *Pionnières Québécoies et regroupement de femmes de Simonne Monet Chartrand* (Ed. Remue-Ménage, 1994). **AFFIL:** SARDEC (Conseil d'Administration 1992-95); SODEC (Conseil national du cinéma et de l'audiovisuel 1995); ACPAC; Académie Canadienne du cinéma et de la télévision. **HONS:** Prix Rocky, *Une nuit à l'école;* Prix Québec Alberta, *Une nuit à l'école;* Moniteur d'Or, Umbriafiction, Italie, *Une nuit à l'école;* Grand Prix, 11e Festival du cinéma international en Abitibi, *Le Jardin d'Anna.* **INTERESTS:** scénarios de film ou de série fiction. **COMMENT:** *"Scénariste de dramatiques, de séries télévisées e documentaires depuis 20 ans. Formation en littérature, arts plastiques et musique."*

Cairns, Penny A., B.A. ✊ ✪
Executive Director and Registrar, ALBERTA ASSOCIATION OF ARCHITECTS, Duggan House, 10515 Saskatchewan Dr., Edmonton, AB T6E 4S1 (403) 432-0224, FAX 439-1431. Born Calgary 1948. m. Dr. Don Starritt. **EDUC:** Univ. of British Columbia, B.A.(Psych.) 1969. **CAREER:** Educ. & Info. Officer, Canadian Mental Health Association, 1970-72; Proj. Officer, Opportunities for Youth, Gov't of Canada, 1972; Dir., Calgary Drug Advisory Society, 1972-76; Supervisor, Career Resources, Alta. Advanced Educ. & Manpower, 1976-77; Coord., Field Svcs, 1978-80; Asst. to the VP, Admin., Northern Alberta Institute of Technology, 1980-81; Exec. Asst. to the Exec. Dir., Committee to Establish a New Trades & Tech. Institute, 1981; Dir. of Admin., Westerra Institute of Technology, Stony Plain, Alta., 1982-87; Exec. Dir. & Registrar, Alberta Association of Architects, 1987 to date; Principal, CB Associates Inc. **AFFIL:** Alberta Mental Health Advisory Council (Crisis Care Task Force); Local Initiatives Program (Selection Committee for S. Alberta); Non-Medical Use of Drugs Directorate (Projects Approval Committee, Alta. & BC); Opportunities for Youth (Selection Committee, Calgary District, 2 yrs.); Alma Mater Society, Univ. of British Columbia (Exec. 1968). **HONS:** Vanier Award for the five Outstanding Young Canadians of the Year, nominated by Calgary Jaycettes, 1975.

Cairns-McVicar, Sue Mora $
President, 056534 N.B. INC. (operating as The Body Shop in Saint John and Moncton, NB and Charlottetown, PEI, 28 Mecklenburg St., Saint John, NB E21 1P6 (506) 652-2639, FAX 652-9283. Born Newcastle, N.B. 1959. m. Bob McVicar. 1 ch. MeiLing Morissa. **EDUC:** Saint Mary's Univ., Bus. 1978; Barbizon Modelling Sch., 1980; Humber Coll., Exec. Secretarial 1981; Ryerson, Retail Mgmt Diploma 1989. **CAREER:** English Teacher, Army Base Sch., Iranian Military, Rasht, Iran, 1978-79; Exec. Asst., Deloitte Haskins & Sells, 1981-84; Exec. Asst., Big Steel (Dylex Ltd.), 1984-86; Exec. Asst., Johnson & Higgins Willis Faber Ltd., 1986-87; Office Mgr, Sibson & Company, 1987-89; Pres., 056534 NB Inc., 1990 to date. **AFFIL:** Saint John Board of Trade; Rape Crisis Centre, Saint John; Support to Single Mothers, Moncton; Anderson House, Charlottetown; Inner City Youth Ministry, Saint John (Bd. Mbr.); Children's Wish Foundation (Dir. 1992-93). **HONS:** Best Picture, The Body Shop Canada, 1991; Small Bus. Achievement Award, Saint John Board of Trade, 1992; Spirit Award, The Body Shop Canada, 1993. **INTERESTS:** volunteer work; travel; interior decorating; swimming; boating. **MISC:** spent 2 weeks volunteering at a Body Shop-sponsored orphanage in Romania, Aug. 1993. **COMMENT:** *"I set a goal to own my own business by the age of 30. At 35, I'm the President and owner of 4 successful stores. I believe dreams are attainable and that determination is the key to success."*

Calahasen, Hon. Pearl, B.Ed.,M.A. ■■ 🍁 ☝
Minister Without Portfolio, Minister Responsible for Children's Services, within the portfolio of Family and Social Services, MLA Lesser Slave Lake, GOVERNMENT OF ALBERTA. Born Grouard, Alta. **EDUC:** Univ. of Alberta, B.Ed.; Univ. of Oregon, M.A. **CAREER:** taught in minimum-security prison; Continuing Educ. Coord., Alberta Vocational Coll.; private consultant developing & evaluating educ. materials; elected to Alta. Legislature as MLA for Lesser Slave Lake, 1989; re-elected, 1993; Chair, Standing Policy Committee on Natural Resources & Sustainable Dev.; Min. without Portfolio resp. for Children's Svcs, 1996 to date. **AFFIL:** Native Economic Development Program (former mbr.); Heart Fund (volunteer canvasser); Cancer Society (volunteer canvasser); Métis Nation of Alberta; World Congress on Education; High Prairie Native Friendship Centre; Alberta Teachers' Association; Métis Economic Development Board; Univ. of Alberta Native Student Club (founder). **MISC:** developed 1st Native Language Program in Alta. schools & Cree Language Program for adult students; principal advisor for dev. of Native Educ. Policy, Native curriculum materials & Native language programming; served as Alta. Human Rights Commissioner & as volunteer tutor for illiterate adults.

Calder, Eleanor, B.Sc.,R.N. ⊕
Manager, COOPERATIVE HEALTH CENTRE, 110-8th St. E., Prince Albert, SK S6V 2S9 (306) 953-6269, FAX 763-2101. Born Cupar, Sask. 1950. m. Dearle Calder. 2 ch. Norley, Brett. **EDUC:** Regina General Hospital, Diploma (Nursing) 1970; Univ. of Saskatchewan, B.Sc.(Nursing) 1989; California Coll. of Health Sciences, M.Sc.(Community Health Admin. & Health Promo.) in progress. **CAREER:** Registered Nurse, Pediatrics, Regina General Hospital, 1970-72; Registered Nurse, Intensive Care Unit, St. Paul's Hospital, 1972-73; Asst. Head

Nurse, Intensive Care Unit, & Coord., Staff Dev., Univ. Hospital, Saskatoon, 1974-80; Sessional Lecturer, Univ. of Saskatchewan, 1980-82; Salesperson, Mary Kay Cosmetics, 1980-89; Portamedic, Hooper Holmes Medical, Edmonton, 1980-89; Dir. of Care, Cooperative Health Centre, Prince Albert, 1989-93; Mgr, 1993 to date. **SELECTED PUBLICATIONS:** "Research and Practice" (*Concern*, Saskatchewan nursing journal, 1989); "Primary Health Care" (*Concern*, 1992). **AFFIL:** Saskatchewan Registered Nurses' Association (Bd. 1990-92; VP, Prince Albert Chapter 1989-90; Sec. 1994 to date); Heart & Stroke Foundation of Canada (Pres.; Bd. 1991-93); Women's Wellness Centre (Rotating Chair; Founding Mbr. 1993); Community Pregnancy Support Group (Rotating Chair; Founding Mbr. 1992); Child Mother's Future Project 1994 (Founding Ptnr); Prince Albert Palliative Care Association/Program (Treas. 1991 to date); Toastmasters International. **HONS:** Women of Distinction Award, Prince Albert YWCA, 1990; Volunteer Appreciation (CPR Instructor), Heart & Stroke Foundation, 1994. **INTERESTS:** golf; bridge; strategic planning. **MISC:** CPR Instructor, Instructor Trainer, 1977-96; assisted in bringing "911" to Saskatoon & Prince Albert; presentations on various topics ranging from wellness to holistic health care to various groups in Sask. communities. **COMMENT:** *"As a change agent, I have a management style that encourages an open workplace and supports wellness. 'It will always work out in the end'–my motto in which I never let myself get down or stressed out. This motivates others to get through difficult situations."*

Caldwell, Erin P., A.A. $ ☼ 📺
Director, Communications and Client Relations, BRITISH COLUMBIA FERRY CORPORATION, 1112 Fort St., Victoria, BC V8V 4Y2 (604) 381-1401, FAX 381-4569. Born Kindersley, Sask. 1950. d. 1 ch. Adam John Sawatsky. **EDUC:** Trinity Western Univ., Assoc. of Arts 1969; British Columbia Institute of Technology, Comm. 1971. **CAREER:** freelance writer (print & radio), 1972-73; Creative Dir., CKLG, Vancouver, 1973-75; Creative Dir., CFAX, Victoria, 1976-85; Info. Officer/Public Rel'ns Officer, B.C. Ferries, 1985-91; Mgr, Public Rel'ns & Advtg, 1991-92; Dir., Comm. & Client Rel'ns, 1992 to date. **SELECTED PUBLICATIONS:** *Angels & Oranges* (1995); *Close to Home* (1996). **AFFIL:** International Association of Business Communicators; Radio-Television News Directors' Association. **HONS:** Peace Arch Public Speaking Trophy; Soundcraft Award, Radio Bureau of Canada (four-time nat'l winner); First Place Trophy, Radio Bureau of Canada; Creative Achievement Award, Radio Bureau of Canada; Second Place Winner, S.A.M. Awards; Recognition & Appreciation Award, Pulse of Life Society of B.C.; Nat'l Winner, Canadian Radio Commercial Awards. **INTERESTS:** stretching my limits–body, mind & spirit; health/healing; communications/relationships; ecology; exploring the kinship of all life; liberated leadership/mgmt. **COMMENT:** *"I have expanded my understanding of what it means to be a communicator to embrace the possibility of transformation and the power of an open heart."*

Caldwell, Nanci, B.A. ■ $
Vice-President and General Manager, Computer Systems Organization, HEWLETT PACKARD (CANADA) LIMITED, 5150 Spectrum Way, Mississauga, ON L4W 5G1 (905) 206-3149, FAX 206-4163. Born Brockville, Ont. 1958. m. Larry Kwicinski. 1 ch. Adriana. **EDUC:** Queen's Univ., B.A.(Psych.) 1979. **CAREER:** Hewlett Packard, 1982 to date; District Sales Mgr responsible for Northern Telecom 1986-89; Global Acct Mgr, Northern Telecom, 1989-92; Regional Mktg Mgr, Computer Systems Organization, 1992-96; VP & Gen. Mgr, Computer Systems Organization, 1996 to date. **DIRECTOR:** Hewlett Packard (Canada) Ltd. **AFFIL:** Smart Toronto (Bd. of Dir.); Canadian Native Arts Foundation (Dir.).

Callbeck, The Hon. Catherine S., B.Comm., B.Ed. 🍁 ☝
Premier and President of the Executive Council, GOVERNMENT OF PRINCE EDWARD ISLAND, Box 2000, Charlottetown, PE C1A 7N8 (902) 368-4400, FAX 368-4416. Born Summerside, P.E.I. 1939. s. **EDUC:** Mount Allison Univ., B.Comm. 1960; Dalhousie Univ., B.Ed. 1963. **CAREER:** Mbr., Fourth District of Prince, P.E.I. Legislative Assembly, 1974-78; Min. of Health & Social Svcs & Min. Responsible for the Disabled, Gov't of P.E.I., 1974-78; Callbeck's Ltd., Central Bedeque, 1978-88; M.P., Malpeque, 1988; Official Opposition Critic for Consumer & Corp. Affairs; Energy, Mines & Resources; Fin. Institutions; Assoc. Critic for Privatization & Regulatory Affairs; V-Chair for the caucus committee on sustainable dev.; Leader, Liberal Party of P.E.I., 1993 -96; Premier & Pres. of the Exec. Council, Gov't of P.E.I., 1993-96; Mbr., First District of Queens, P.E.I. Legislative Assembly, 1993 to date. **AFFIL:** Prince Edward Island United Fund (Dir.); Canadian Heart Foundation (Dir., P.E.I. Div.); Committee for the International Year of the Disabled; Bedeque United Church; active involvement with charitable & public service groups & organizations

at all levels. MISC: first woman in Canada to be elected Premier; announced that she will be stepping down once Leadership Convention is held to select successor.

Calliste, Agnes, B.A.,M.A.,Ph.D. ■ ⌖ ❁
Associate Professor and Chair, Department of Sociology and Anthropology, ST. FRANCIS XAVIER UNIVERSITY, Box 5000, Antigonish, NS B2G 2W5 (902) 867-3990, FAX 867-2448, EMAIL acallist@stfx.ca. Born Grenada. EDUC: Mausica Teachers' Coll., Teacher's Diploma 1965; Univ. of West Indies, B.A. 1971; Univ. of Toronto, M.A. 1975, Ph.D. 1980. CAREER: Teacher (elementary level), Grenada, 1965-68; Instructor, Sch. of Nursing, Grenada, 1970; Teacher, Grenada Boys' Secondary Sch., 1971-73; Substitute Teacher, Metropolitan Separate Sch. Bd., 1973-80; Teaching Asst., Ontario Institute for Studies in Education, 1975-76; Instructor, OISE, 1977-80; Lead Instructor (Coord.), Black Cultural Heritage Program, 1980-81; Instructor, York Univ., 1980-81; Asst. Prof., Univ. of Manitoba, 1981-84; Assoc. Prof., Dept. of Soc./Anthropology, St. Francis Xavier Univ. 1984 to date; Chair, 1993-96. SELECTED PUBLICATIONS: "Influence of the Civil Rights and Black Power Movement in Canada" (*Race, Gender and Class*, 1995); "Struggle for Employment Equity by Blacks on American and Canadian Railroads" (*Journal of Black Studies* Jan. 1995); "Race, Gender and Canadian Immigration Policy: Blacks from the Caribbean, 1900-1932" (*Journal of Canadian Studies* Winter 1993/94); "Women of Exceptional Merit: Immigration of Caribbean Nurses to Canada" (*Canadian Journal of Women and the Law*, 1993); "Sleeping Car Porters in Canada: An Ethnically Submerged Split Labour Market" (*Canadian Ethnic Studies* 1987); "Educational and Occupational Expectations of High School Students" (*Multiculturalism* 1982). EDIT: Ed. Bd., *Interchange, a Journal of Educational Studies*, 1976-78; Ed. Bd., *International Journal of Intercultural Relations*, 1979; Assoc. Ed., *Race, Gender and Class: An Interdisciplinary Journal*, 1993 to date. AFFIL: Atlantic Association of Sociologists & Anthropologists; Black Educators' Association/National Council of Black Educators of Canada; Canadian Ethnic Studies Association (VP & Dir.); Canadian Sociology & Anthropology Association (Chair, Status of Women Committee 1996-97); American Sociological Association; James Robinson Johnson Chair in Black Canadian Studies (Exec. Mbr., Nat'l Advisory Bd.); St. Francis Xavier Univ. (Anti-racism Committee); Congress of Black Women of Canada (Antigonish-Guysborough Chapter); Delta Kappa Gamma International

Society. HONS: Ont. Grad. Scholarships, 1976-77; Social Sciences & Humanities Research Council of Canada, Post-Doctoral Fellowships. INTERESTS: anti-racist & feminism organizing. MISC: numerous invited papers, presentations at learned societies & invited lectures; Chair, Int'l Symposium on "Women: Voices from Our Communities," St. Francis Xavier Univ., 1993; Chair, Symposium on "Anti-Racist Educ.," St. Francis Xavier Univ., 1992; recipient of various grants. COMMENT: *"Dr. Agnes Calliste is an Associate Professor and Chair, Department of Sociology and Anthropology, St. F.X.U. She has published on race, gender and Canadian immigration policy; anti-racism organizing & resistance in Canada; black education; and blacks on Canadian and American railways. She is currently working on black families in Canada and racism, anti-racism organizing and resistance in nursing in Canada."*

Callwood, June 🗋 ⚅ ✎ ♟
Writer, Broadcaster. Born Chatham, Ont. 1924. m. Trent Frayne. 4 ch. (1 dec.) Jill, Brant, Jesse, Casey (dec. 1982). CAREER: Reporter, *Brantford Expositor*, 1941-42; Reporter, *The Globe and Mail*, 1942-45; freelance Writer, 1945-83; *Court of Opinions*, CBC Radio, 1959-67; *Human Sexuality*, CBC Radio, 1966; Host, *Generations*, CBC-TV, 1966; Columnist, *The Globe and Mail*, 1975-78; Host, *In Touch*, CBC-TV, 1975-78; Columnist, *The Globe and Mail*, 1983-89; Host, *Callwood's National Treasures*, VISION TV, 1991-95. SELECTED PUBLICATIONS: 26 books, incl. *Love, Hate, Fear & Anger* (Doubleday, 1964); *Canadian Women and the Law*, with Marvin Zuker (Copp Clark, 1973); *Emma* (Stoddart, 1984); *Twelve Weeks in Spring* (Lester & Orpen Dennys, 1986); *Jim: A Life With AIDS* (Lester & Orpen Dennys, 1988); *June Callwood's National Treasures* (Stoddart, 1994); *Trial Without End* (Knopf Canada, 1995); more than 400 articles in numerous magazines incl. *Maclean's*, *Chatelaine*, *Homemaker's* & *Canadian Living*. EDIT: Ed. Bd, *Humane Medicine Journal*, 1989-94. AFFIL: The Writers' Union of Canada (Chair 1979-80; Life Mbr.); Canadian Centre PEN International (Pres. 1989-90); Toronto Arts Council; Book & Periodical Council (V-Chair 1994-95; Chair 1995-96); Canadian Magazines Awards Foundation (Dir. 1981-83); The Writers' Development Trust (Author's Endowment Sub-Committee); Periodical Writers' Association of Canada; Toronto Arts Awards; Writers to Reform the Libel Law; Canadian Civil Liberties Association (VP 1964-88; Lifetime Hon. Dir.); Law Society of Upper Canada (Bencher 1987-91); Jessie's Centre for Teenagers (Pres. 1982-

83, 1987-89; Dir. 1982-85, 1986-89); Nellie's Hostel for Women (Pres. 1974-78; Dir. 1985-89, 1990-92); Casey House Hospice (Pres. 1987-88; Hon. Dir.); Casey House Foundation (Pres. 1992-93; Hon. Dir.); Justice for Children (Pres. 1979-80); Canadian Association for the Repeal of Abortion Laws (Hon. Dir.); Women for Political Action; Maggie's, Toronto Prostitutes Community Service Proj. (Pres. 1988-93); Partners in Research (Hon. Patron); Women's Health Care Advisory Committee, Women's College Hospital; Etobicoke General Hospital (Bd. of Gov.); Women's Television Network Foundation (Dir.);Willow Breast Cancer Support & Resource Centre (Dir. 1994-95); numerous other affiliations. **HONS:** B'nai Brith Woman of the Year, 1969; Mbr., Order of Canada, 1978; Order of the Buffalo Hunt, Manitoba, 1984; Canadian News Hall of Fame, 1984; Officer, Order of Canada, 1986; YWCA Toronto Woman of Distinction, 1986; Windsor Press Club Quill Award, 1987; Order of Ontario; Gardiner Award for Citizenship, Metro Toronto, 1988; Lifetime Achievement Award, Toronto Arts Foundation, 1990; Award of Merit, Print Journalism, MediaWatch, 1990; Bob Edwards Award, Alberta Theatre Projects, 1991; Hall of Fame, City of Etobicoke, 1992; Canada 125 Medal, 1992; Distinguished Canadian Award, Univ. of Regina, 1993; Muriel McQueen Fergusson Award, Fredericton, 1993; June Callwood Award for Palliative Care, Toronto PWA Foundation, 1994; numerous other honours & awards; Fellow (Hon.), Ryerson Polytechnical Institute, 1990; Diploma (Hon.), Argyle Alternative High Sch., 1993; D.Univ.(Hon.), Univ. of Ottawa, 1978; D.S.L.(Hon.), Trinity Coll., Univ. of Toronto, 1988; LL.D.(Hon.), Memorial Univ. of Newfoundland, 1988; LL.D. (Hon.), Univ. of Toronto, 1988; LL.D. (Hon.), Osgoode Hall, York Univ., 1988; D.Lit. (Hon.), Carleton Univ., 1988; D.L.(Hon.), Univ. of Alberta, 1988; D.L.(Hon.), Univ. of Guelph, 1989; D.L.(Hon.), Univ. of New Brunswick, 1990; LL.D.(Hon.), Univ. of Prince Edward Island, 1992; D.C.L.(Hon.), Acadia Univ., 1993; D.Hum.L.(Hon.), Mount Saint Vincent Univ., 1993; LL.D.(Hon.), Univ. of Western Ontario, 1993; LL.D.(Hon.), McMaster Univ., 1994. **MISC:** founding mbr. of numerous organizations, incl. the Writers' Union of Canada, Periodical Writers' Association of Canada, Canadian Civil Liberties Association, Canadian Association for the Repeal of Abortion Laws, & Feminists Against Censorship; founding director of various organizations, incl. Toronto Arts Awards, Ontario Film Development Corporation, & Willow Breast Cancer Support & Resource Centre; founder

or co-founder of various organizations, incl. Jessie's Centre for Teenagers, Nellie's Hostel for Women, & Casey House Hospice; Mbr., Writing & Publishing Advisory Committee, Canada Council, 1989-94; Mbr., Assistive Devices Advisory Committee, Ministry of Health, 1981-88; judge for numerous literary & media awards incl. National Newspaper Awards, 1976-83, Stephen Leacock Award, 1977-80, & Gov. General's Non-Fiction Award, 1984-86; numerous invited lectures, incl. the Atkinson Lecture, Ryerson Sch. of Journalism, 1988, the Duthie Lecture, Simon Fraser Univ., 1990, & the Margaret Laurence Lecture, Writers' Development Trust, 1993; first recipient, June Callwood Award for Palliative Care, Toronto PWA Foundation, 1994; Writer in Residence, North York Library, 1995-96.

Caloz, Danièle, M.A. 👤 💼 ⊗
President, MÉDIATIQUE INC., 62 Wellesley St. W., Ste. 606, Toronto, ON M5S 2X3 (416) 968-1683, FAX 968-7579. Born Switzerland 1942. m. Raymond. 2 ch. **EDUC:** Univ. of Fribourg, Licence (Hist.) 1964; Univ. of Toronto, M.A.(Hist.) 1973. **CAREER:** Educ. Ed., Copp Clark, Gage Publishing & D.C. Heath Canada, 1970-76; Prod., La Chaîne/TVOntario, 1976-91; Dir. of Adult Programming, 1992-94; Dir. of Independent Prod., Co-Prod. & Acquisitions, 1994; Pres., Médiatique Inc., 1994 to date. **SELECTED CREDITS:** Prod., *Panorama* (live daily public affairs magazine), TVOntario, 1992; Prod., *Les Ontariens* (series), TVOntario, 1988-92; Prod., *A Comme Artiste* (cultural magazine), TVOntario, 1988-92; Prod., *Maman et Eve* (*Mum's the Word*) (documentary), 1996; Prod., *25 ans de théâtre franco-ontarien* (documentary), multimedia kit, 1996. **AFFIL:** Toronto Historical Board (VP, Fin. & Mgmt); Société d'histoire de Toronto (Founder & Past. Pres.). **HONS:** Ten-Year Award, Ont. Ministry of Culture & Communications; nomination (*A Comme Artiste*), Les Prix Gémeaux; selection in Montreal & Toronto Film festivals (*Maman et Eve*). **INTERESTS:** skiing; night courses in various arts & media subjects.

Cameron, Barbara Jamie, B.A.,LL.B., LL.M. 🎓 ⚖
Associate Professor, OSGOODE HALL LAW SCHOOL, York University, 4700 Keele St., North York, ON M3J 1P3 (416) 736-5033, FAX 736-5546. **EDUC:** Univ. of British Columbia, B.A. 1975; McGill Univ., LL.B. 1978; Columbia Univ., LL.M. 1983. **BAR:** B.C., 1979 (inactive); Ont., 1987. **CAREER:** Assoc. in Law, Columbia Law Sch., 1981-82; Visiting Asst. Prof. of Law, Cornell Law Sch.,

1982-83 & Fall 1983; Asst. Prof., Osgoode Hall Law Sch., York Univ., 1984-87; Adjunct Prof., Pol. Sci. Dept., Assoc. Prof., 1987 to date; Adjunct Prof., Pol. Sci. Dept., Univ. of Toronto, 1987-88 & 1993-94; Visiting Scholar & Prof., SUNY at Buffalo, Fall 1989; Visiting Scholar & Prof., Cornell Law Sch., Winter 1989; Asst. Dean, Osgoode Hall Law Sch., 1991-93; Dir., Centre for Public Law & Public Policy, 1993-95. SELECTED PUBLICATIONS: various articles, reviews & chapters in books; various articles in *Canada Watch*. EDIT: *Media and Communications Law Review*, Ed., 1990-95; *Canada Watch*, Legal Ed., 1992-93 & Co-Ed., 1993-95; *Ontario Reports*, Bd. of Ed., 1990 to date; *Canadian Rights Reporter*, Asst. Ed., 1987 to date; *Annuals of Health Law*, Ed. Bd., 1993 to date. AFFIL: Canadian Civil Liberties Union (Dir. & VP); The Canada-U.S. Fulbright Committee (Adjunction Committee); Infertility Awareness Association of Canada (Dir. 1991-93); Social Science & Humanities Research Council (Selection Committee 1989-91). MISC: moderator, the Toronto session, Public Consultation on Immigration, June 1994; witness, the Standing Committee on Justice & Legal Affairs: Criminal Code amendments, June 1994 & Bill C-81, May 1992; brief, The Royal Commission on New Reproductive technologies, 1990; speaker on reproductive health care; speaker & panelist at numerous conferences, panel debates & public lectures in Canada & the U.S.; numerous invited media appearances incl. CBC *Morningside*, *Prime Time News* & *The National*; participation in constitutional reform initiatives, the Meech Lake & Charlottetown accords, incl.: adviser to the Hon. David Peterson, then Premier of Ont., First Minister's Conference, May-June 1990; speaker & participant, the Renewal of Canada Conferences, Toronto & Vancouver, Feb. 1992; appointed mbr., the national YES Committee, Charlottetown Accord, Sept.-Oct. 1992.

Cameron, Christina S., B.A.,M.A., Ph.D. ♦ 🐾
Director General, National Historic Sites, PARKS CANADA, Department of Canadian Heritage, Government of Canada, 25 Eddy St., Hull, QC K1A 0M5 (819) 994-1808, FAX 953-4909. Born Toronto 1946. m. Hugh Winsor. 3 stpch. EDUC: Univ. of Toronto, B.A. 1967; Brown Univ., M.A. 1970; Laval Univ., Ph.D. 1983. CAREER: summer student, Extension Svcs, National Gallery of Canada, 1966-67; Doctoral Fellow, Brown Univ., 1967-71; Research Asst., Parks Canada, Indian & Northern Affairs, 1970-74; Architectural Analyst, Canadian Inventory of Historic Building, Parks Canada,

Environment Canada, 1974-76; Guest Lecturer in Architectural Hist., Dept. of Fine Arts, Concordia Univ., 1975-78; Head, Architectural Analysis, Canadian Inventory of Historic Building, 1982-86; Dir. Gen., Nat'l Historic Sites, Parks Canada, Environment Canada/Dept. of Cdn Heritage, 1986 to date; Adjunct Prof., Art Hist., Carleton Univ., 1991 to date. SELECTED CREDITS: "Gothic Revival in Canadian Architecture," "The Second Empire Style in Canadian Architecture," slide kits in *Styles in Canadian Architecture* (Ottawa: National Film Board & Environment Canada, 1983); *François Baillairgé*, filmstrip in collaboration with National Film Board (1985). SELECTED PUBLICATIONS: *Québec au temps de James Patterson Cockburn*, with Jean Trudel (Québec: Garneau, 1976); *Index of Houses Featured in Canadian Homes and Gardens from 1925 to 1944* (Ottawa: Parks Canada, Environment Canada, 1980); "Selecting an Appropriate Vernacular Moulding" (*Bulletin for the Association of Preservation Technology* 4 1978); "Domestic Interiors: Parks Canada's Designated Houses in Quebec" (*Canadian Collector* May 1985); "Heritage Conservation: Managing Change in the 1990s" (*ICOMOS Canada Bulletin* 1 1994); numerous other books & articles; numerous reviews. EDIT: Ed. Bd., *Journal of Canadian Art History*, 1981 to date. AFFIL: Society for the Study of Architecture in Canada; World Heritage Committee; Ontario Association of Architects (Hon. Mbr.); Heritage Canada Foundation (Gov.); Canadian Commission of UNESCO (Sub-Commission on Culture); Royal Canadian Geographical Society (Dir.); Society of Architectural Historians; Heritage Interpretation International. HONS: Doctoral Fellowship, Brown Univ. INTERESTS: skiing; tennis; sailing; bicycling; theatre; opera; Scottish country dancing. MISC: speaker on heritage, environment, historic sites, cultural tourism, interpretation & conservation; Mbr. of Dir. Gen., UNESCO's Scientific Advisory Committee on Angkor World Heritage Site, 1993 to date. COMMENT: *"Architectural historian and career public servant, Christina Cameron leads a national program of heritage commemoration for national historic sites, railway stations and federal heritage buildings. She has written and lectured extensively on Canadian architecture, heritage management and world heritage issues."*

Cameron, Deborah M.D.,B.A. ■ ■ Ⓢ
General Manager, Education and Training, IBM CANADA LTD., 3600 Steeles Ave. E., A2/814, Markham, ON L3R 9Z7 (905) 316-3580, FAX 316-3101, EMAIL deborahc@vnet. ibm.com. Chairman, POLAR BEAR SOFTWARE

CORP. Born Pembroke, Ont. 1954. m. John Hilliard Cameron. 1 ch. Aaron Glenn Cameron. EDUC: Univ. of Guelph, B.A.(Econ. & Math.) 1977. CAREER: joined IBM, 1977; various SE & mktg mgmt positions; Admin. Asst. to Chrm & CEO, 1988; Branch Mgr for Transportation, Utilities & Communications, 1989; Asst. Gen. Mgr, Leasing, 1992; Dir., Bus. Strategies, 1994; Gen. Mgr, Educ. & Training, 1995 to date. AFFIL: Software Human Resources Council (Bd. of Dir.); Conference Board of Canada; The Planning Forum; Toronto Cricket, Skating & Curling Club. INTERESTS: squash doubles; figure skating.

Cameron, Elspeth MacGregor, B.A.,M.A., Ph.D. 🐋 📚
Professor, Canadian Studies (University College), English Department, UNIVERSITY OF TORONTO, University College, 15 King's College Circle, Rm. F-104, Toronto, ON M4S 1A1 (416) 978-8268. Born 1943. m. Paul E. Lovejoy. 3 ch. EDUC: Univ. of British Columbia, B.A.(English) 1964; Univ. of New Brunswick, M.A.(English) 1965; McGill Univ., Ph.D. (English) 1970. CAREER: Grad. Instructor, Special Summer Institute of English Studies, Sir George Williams Univ., 1974; Assoc. Prof., Concordia Univ., Loyola Campus, 1975-77; Acting Asst. Dean (Curriculum), 1976-77; Course Dir., English Dept., Atkinson Coll., York Univ., 1979-80; Tutor, Humanities Div., 1979-80; Tutor, Essay Workshop, University Coll., Univ. of Toronto, 1979-80; Tutor, cross-appointed at New Coll., University Coll., English Dept., Univ. of Toronto, 1980-81; Coord., Cdn Lit. & Lang. Option, New Coll., Univ. of Toronto, 1980-88; Sr. Tutor, cross-appointed at New Coll., University Coll., Univ. of Toronto, 1982-89; Hall Prof., Univ. of Kansas, Spring 1987; Prof., jointly appointed in Cdn Studies, University Coll. & in English Dept., Univ. of Toronto, 1990 to date; Dir., Cdn Studies Program, 1994 to date. SELECTED PUBLICATIONS: *Robertson Davies* (Toronto: Forum House Press, 1971); *Hugh MacLennan: A Writer's Life* (Toronto: Univ. of Toronto Press, 1981); *Irving Layton: A Portrait* (Toronto: Stoddart, 1984); *Earle Birney: A Life* (Toronto: Viking Press, 1994); "T.S. Eliot's 'Marina': An Exploration" *(Queen's Quarterly* June 1970); "Parody of Autonomy: Anorexia Nervosa and *The Edible Woman*" *(Journal of Canadian Studies* Summer 1985); "Sweet Sub/Versions: The Feminizing Effect of Postmodernism on Canadian Literature" *(Canadian Revue of Comparative Literature* Sept.-Dec. 1993); various other scholarly articles & chapters in books; "Adventures in the Book Trade: Jack McClelland" *(Saturday Night* Nov. 1983);

"Anne Murray's Double Life" *(Chatelaine* Sept. 1988); "Employment Equity at the Ontario College of Art" *(Chatelaine* Apr. 1991); various other articles in newspapers & magazines; numerous book reviews. EDIT: Ed. Bd., *Journal of Canadian Studies,* 1983 to date; Contributing Ed., *Saturday Night,* 1986 to date; Ed. Bd., *Studi e recerche di aglisticia,* Italy, 1989 to date. HONS: Canadian Biography Award, Univ. of British Columbia, 1981; Fiona Mee Award, 1982; Honourable Mention, Fiona Mee Award, 1983; Silver, The Brascan Awards for Writing on Culture, 1986; Silver, Univ. of Western Ontario President's Medal for Excellence in Magazine Writing, 1986; City of Vancouver Book Award, 1996. MISC: recipient of various grants; juror for various grants & awards; manuscript assessor, Univ. of Toronto Press, 1982 to date; numerous conference presentations; numerous invited lectures; Convenor, Hugh MacLennan Conference, University Coll., Univ. of Toronto, 1982; Contributor, *What She Taught Me,* a book auction celebrating women's lives & voices, Adrienne Rich, chairperson, Apr. 1995.

Cameron, Stevie (Stephanie Graham), B.A. ■ ✍ 🏠
Author. Editor-in-Chief, ELM STREET MAGA-ZINE, 655 Bay St., Ste. 1100, Toronto, ON M5G 2K4 (416) 595-9944, FAX 595-7217. Born Belleville, Ont. 1943. m. David Cameron. 2 ch. Tassie, Amy. EDUC: Univ. of British Columbia, B.A.(English Lit./Fine Arts) 1964; University Coll., Univ. of London, grad. studies in English Lit. 1966-68. CAREER: Comm. Officer, Nat'l Research Council of Canada, 1964-65; External Affairs Officer, Dept. of External Affairs Canada, 1965; Library Asst., Royal Anthropological Institute, London, UK, 1965-66; Lecturer, English Lit., Trent Univ., 1968-69; freelance magazine writer, 1975 to date; Food Ed., *The Toronto Star,* 1977-78; Lifestyles Ed., *The Ottawa Journal,* 1978-80; Lifestyles & Travel Ed., *The Citizen,* 1981-84; weekly Ottawa Commentator for *Newsday,* CBC television, 1984-86; weekly Ottawa Commentator for CBC morning radio in Prince Rupert, Fredericton & St. John's, 1984-86; Parliamentary Columnist & Reporter, *Ottawa Citizen,* 1984-86; Columnist & Reporter, *The Globe and Mail,* 1986-90; Host, CBC's *The Fifth Estate,* 1990-91; Contributing Ed., *Saturday Night;* weekly pol. columnist, *The Globe and Mail,* 1991-93; Contributing Ed., *Maclean's;* Columnist, *Equity Magazine;* frequent commentator, CBC. SELECTED CREDITS: frequent commentator on *Morningside, CBC Commentary, As It Happens.* SELECTED PUBLICATIONS: *Ottawa Inside Out* (Toronto:

Key Porter, 1989); *On the Take: Crime, Corruption and Greed in the Mulroney Years* (Macfarlane, Walter & Ross, 1994); contributor to *The Financial Post, Chatelaine, Toronto Life,* & other magazines. AFFIL: Out of the Cold program, St. Andrew's Presbyterian Church (Convenor); Photojournalism & Print Journalism program, Loyalist Coll., Belleville, Ont. (Chair, Advisory Committee). HONS: Robertine Barry Prize, Canadian Research Institute for the Advancement of Women, 1990; Author of the Year & Book of the Year (*On The Take*), Periodical Marketers' Awards, 1995. MISC: Certificate, Cordon Bleu, Paris, 1975.

Cameron, W. Sheila Johnston, R.S.C.N., R.S.N.,B.A.,M.A.,Ed.D. ■ ⊕ ⊰ ❀

Dean of Gaduate Studies and Research, Professor of Nursing, UNIVERSITY OF WINDSOR, 401 Sunset, Windsor, ON N9B 3P4 (519) 253-4232, FAX 973-7084, EMAIL camero2@ uwindsor.ca. Born York, UK 1940. m. Allen. 3 ch. Jainie, Steven, Andrew. EDUC: Royal Hospital for Sick Children, Edinburgh, Registered Sick Children's Nurse 1960; Royal Victoria Infirmary, Newcastle-on-Tyne, State Registered Nurse 1963; McMaster Univ., B.A.(Psych./Soc.) 1971; Univ. of Detroit, M.A.(Educ. for Nurses) 1975; Wayne State Univ., Detroit, Ed.D.(Curriculum/Admin.) 1983. CAREER: Staff Nurse, Royal Victoria Infirmary, Newcastle-on-Tyne, 1963-64; Staff Nurse, St. Joseph's Hospital, Hamilton, Ont., 1964-67; Staff Nurse, Hamilton Psychiatric Hospital, 1967-70; Supervisor/Asst. Dir. of Nursing, Deaconess Hospital, Detroit, 1970-75; Nursing Educ., St. Clair Coll., Windsor, 1976-96; Nursing Prof., Dir. of Sch. of Nursing, Univ. of Windsor, 1986-95. AFFIL: Coll. of Nurses of Ontario; Registered Nurses' Association of Ontario; Metropolitan General Hospital (Gov. 1990-95; Exec. 1993-95); Univ. of Windsor (Gov. 1993-95); Ontario Mental Health Foundation (Bd.); Sigma Theta Tau-Iota Omicron Chapter (int'l honour society of nursing). HONS: Scholar Award, Canadian Nurses' Foundation, 1982; Fellowship Award, American Association on Mental Retardation, 1993. INTERESTS: research interests–stress/coping in families experiencing chronic illness; seniors with breast cancer; quality of nursing worklife. MISC: Proj. Dir., collaborative program between Univ. of Windsor Sch. of Nursing & Jordan Univ. of Science & Technology, Fac. of Nursing, funded by the Assoc. of Univ. & Coll. and the Canadian International Development Agency, 1990-2000. COMMENT: *"As a nursing education administrator, provided guidance and leadership to faculty and students. Chair of local and provincial committees related to a range of health issues."*

Campbell, The Right Hon. A. Kim, P.C., Q.C.,LL.D. ■ ✦ ⅏ ♂

Former Prime Minister. Consul General for Canada in Los Angeles, GOVERNMENT OF CANADA, 550 South Hope, 9th Fl., Los Angeles, CA 90071-2627. Born Port Alberni, B.C. 1947. EDUC: Univ. of British Columbia, B.A.(Pol. Sci.) 1969, grad. work (Pol. Sci.) 1969-70, LL.B. 1983; Univ. of Oregon, grad. course (Pol. Sci.) Summer 1969; London Sch. of Econ. & Pol. Sci., doctoral work in Soviet Gov't, Canada Council Doctoral Fellow 1970-73. BAR: B.C., 1984; Ont., 1990. CAREER: Lecturer, Dept. of Pol. Sci., Univ. of British Columbia, 1975-78; Lecturer, Pol. Sci., Langara, 1978-81; articled student, Ladner Downs, Vancouver, 1983-84; Assoc., Gen. Litigation, 1984-85; Exec. Dir., Office of Wm. R. Bennett, Premier of B.C., 1985-86; M.L.A., Vancouver Point Grey, 1986-88 (resigned to contest fed. election); M.P., Vancouver Centre, Gov't of Canada, 1988-93; Min. of State, Indian Affairs & N. Dev., 1989-90; Min. of Justice & Attorney Gen., 1990-93; Min. of Nat'l Defence & Min of Veterans' Affairs, 1993; elected Leader, P.C. Party, 1993; Prime Minister, June-Nov. 1993; Fellow, Institute of Pol., John F. Kennedy Sch. of Gov't, Harvard Univ., Spring 1994; Fellow, Joan Shorenstein Barone Center on the Press, Politics & Public Policy, Fall 1994; Cdn Consul Gen., Calif., Utah, Nevada, Arizona, Hawaii & Guam, 1996 to date. SELECTED PUBLICATIONS: *Time and Chance*, memoir (Doubleday Canada, 1996). AFFIL: London Sch. of Econ. (Hon. Fellow); Vancouver Sch. Bd. (Trustee 1980-84; Chrm 1982-83; V-Chrm 1983-84); Centre for International Affairs, Harvard (Visting Committee 1995 to date); KPMG Centre for Government Foundation (Dir. 1995) Writers' Union of Canada. HONS: Queen's Counsel, Prov. of B.C., 1990; LL.D.(Hon.), Law Society of Upper Canada, 1992; Woman of the Year, *Chatelaine*, 1993; YWCA Woman of Distinction, Public Affairs & Comm., 1994. MISC: invited speaker & lecturer on issues relating to gov't & int'l politics, US & Europe; broadcaster, Canada & Britain; 1st woman Min of Justice & Attorney Gen. of Canada, Min. of Nat'l Defence & Veteran's Affairs, Leader of the PC Party & Prime Minister.

Campbell, Anne ⊗ ▯ ✦

Writer and Head of Community Relations, REGINA PUBLIC LIBRARY, 2311 - 12th Ave., Box 2311, Regina, SK S4P 3Z5 (306) 777-6036, FAX 352-5550. Born Paddockwood, Sask. d. 3 ch. Joseph, Jill, Jacqueline. EDUC: Regina Conservatory; Univ. of Regina; Saskatchewan Sch. of the Arts. CAREER: MacKenzie Art Gallery, Regina, 1975-78; Glenbow Museum,

Calgary, 1978-80; Heritage Park, Calgary, 1980-81; Regina Public Library, 1981 to date; Instructor, Creative Writing, Univ. of Regina Extension, 1989; Juror, Kalamalka New Writers' Society, 1989; Writer in Residence, Miller Collegiate, 1990. SELECTED PUBLICATIONS: *No Memory of a Move* (Longspoon Press 1983); *Death is an Anxious Mother* (Thistledown 1986); *Red Earth, Yellow Stone* (Thistledown 1989); *Angel Wings All Over* (Thistledown 1994); poetry published in various anthologies incl. *Writing Right: Poetry by Canadian Women* (Longspoon Press 1982); poetry published in journals & magazines incl. *Grain, Quarry* & *Prairie Fire*; prose published in various anthologies & magazines. AFFIL: The Writers' Union of Canada; The League of Canadian Poets; Saskatchewan Writers' Guild; Canadian Public Relations Society. HONS: City of Regina Writing Grant, 1982; Major Award, Saskatchewan Writers' Guild, 1984, 1989; Saskatchewan Arts Bd. Award, 1990. INTERESTS: ice skating, walking. MISC: numerous talks, readings & workshops; personal papers on deposit, Univ. of Regina Library Archives.

Campbell, Barbara 🌐 ⍥ ⃝

Executive Director, MULTICULTURAL ASSOCIATION OF NOVA SCOTIA, 1809 Barrington St., Ste. 901, Halifax, NS B3J 3K8 (902) 423-6534, FAX 422-0881. Born Germany 1935. 5 ch. Elizabeth, Cathy, Gregory, Susan, Michael. EDUC: high sch. grad., Germany, 1951; vocational sch., Commerce 1951-54; Dalhousie Univ., Social Anthropology 1983, Pol. Sci. 1984; Saint Mary's Univ., Multiculturalism 1985. CAREER: ladies' fashion industry, incl. modelling, 1969-74; hotel industry, Supervisor of hotel cashiers, 1974-75; Host of weekly German radio program, CHFX-FM, 1974-82; Exec. Dir., Multicultural Association of N.S. incl. serving on the following: N.S. Arts Advisory Committee, N.S. Dept. of Educ. Advisory Committee, Advisory Committee on Race Rel'ns, Cross-Cultural Understanding & Human Rights; Halifax County-Bedford District Sch. Bd., Race Rel'ns Advisory Committee on Policing, Dept. of the Solicitor Gen. AFFIL: German Canadian Association of N.S. (VP 1971-73); Halifax-Dartmouth Multicultural Council (Pres. 1974-75); Pier 21 Society (VP 1990-95). MISC: N.S. table tennis champion: Ladies Single 1969-71, Mixed Doubles 1970-71.

Campbell, Daphne, B.Sc.,M.S.W., B.Ed. ⍥ ⊕

Guidance Counsellor. Past President, PRINCE EDWARD ISLAND GUIDANCE AND COUNSELLING ASSOCIATION, 175 Spring Park Rd., Charlottetown, PE C1A 3Y8 (902) 368-1177, FAX 894-7887. Born Charlottetown 1952. m. Shane

Campbell. 3 ch. EDUC: Acadia Univ., B.Sc. (Psych.) 1973; Dalhousie Univ., M.S.W.(Social Work, Child/Family Specialization) 1985; Univ. of Prince Edward Island, B.Ed. 1993. CAREER: Psychometrician, P.E.I. Dept. of Health & Social Svcs, 1973-84, 1985-87; Guidance Counsellor, Queen Charlotte Jr. High Sch., 1987-94; Affiliate Counsellor, Warren Shepell Consultants Corp., 1990-93; Guidance Counsellor, Colonel Gray Sr. High Sch., 1994 to date. AFFIL: P.E.I. Association of Social Work (V-Chair, Registration Bd. 1992-95; Chair, Reg. Bd.); Canadian Guidance & Counselling Association (Certified Cdn Counsellor; P.E.I. Bd. Rep. & Treas.); P.E.I. Guidance & Counselling Association (Past Pres.); P.E.I. Council for the Family (V-Chair); Roman Catholic Diocesan Choir (Exec.; Gyro/Gyrette Club); Church Choir (Dir. 1981-91); Christmas House Tour Fundraiser (Coord.). INTERESTS: collecting unicorns, depression glass & Christmas wooden nutcrackers; cross-country skiing; snowmobiling; cottaging; helping her husband at the Water Prince Corner Shop; singing; stained glass. MISC: vocal coach for sch. musical; Sunday sch. teacher; mbr., church bldg committee: a multifunctional church for Roman Catholics was officially opened Aug. 15, 1989. COMMENT: *"I strive to be actively involved in my family, church, work, professional organizations, and community. Advocating for the needs and rights of youth and families continues to be a priority for me."*

Campbell, Diane O., B.A.,LL.B.,LL.M. ⚖ $

Sole Proprietor, DIANE CAMPBELL LAW OFFICES, 740 Water St. E., P.O. Box 1300, Summerside, PE C1N 4K2 (902) 436-2232, FAX 436-0318. Born Summerside, P.E.I. s. EDUC: Univ. of Prince Edward Island, B.A.(Soc./Psych.) 1972; Univ. of New Brunswick, LL.B. 1975; Harvard Law Sch., LL.M.(Contract Law) 1976. BAR: P.E.I. CAREER: Ptnr, Ramsay, Campbell and Riley, 1979-87; Ptnr, Ramsay, Campbell, Lyle, Riley and Shaw, 1987-89; Sole Ptnr, Law Offices of Diane Campbell, 1991 to date. AFFIL: Council for the Law Society of P.E.I.; Canadian Bar Association; Summerside Chamber of Commerce (Dir.); Summerside Regional Development Corporation (Dir.); East Prince Development Corporation (Dir.); Canadian Rights Tribunal (Mem.); Canadian Kennel Club. HONS: Lord Beaverbrook Law Scholarship; Scholarship, Harvard Univ.; Bursary, I.O.D.E.; Tuition Scholarship, Univ. of Prince Edward Island.

Campbell, H. Sharon, M.N.,Ph.D. ⊕ ⍥ ❀

Behavioural Research Scientist, ALBERTA CANCER BOARD, 1331 - 29th St. N.W., Calgary, AB

T2N 4N2. Born Edmonton. **EDUC:** Univ. of Alberta, M.N.(Nursing) 1980; Univ. of North Carolina at Chapel Hill, Ph.D.(Public Health) 1990. **CAREER:** Research Assoc., Center for Health Promotion & Disease Prevention, Univ. of North Carolina at Chapel Hill, 1985-90; Research Scientist, Cancer Prevention, Alberta Cancer Bd., 1990 to date. **SELECTED PUBLICATIONS:** "Teaching Medical Students Clinical Breast Examination Skills," with M. McBean, H. Mandin & H. Bryant (*Academic Medicine*, 69(12), 1994); "Knowledge, Beliefs and Sun Protection Behaviours of Alberta Adults," with J.M. Birdsell (*Preventive Medicine*, 23, 1994); "Skin Cancer Program in Alberta" (*Chronic Diseases in Canada*, 13(5), 1992); "Risk Factors for Cancer" (*Cancer Nursing*, 10(supp 1), 1987); various other scholarly publications. **AFFIL:** Alumni Association of the Univ. of Calgary (Bd. of Dir.); Canadian Cancer Society (Public Educ. 1995); Calgary Horticultural Society; Canadian Public Health Association; National Cancer Institute of Canada (Behavioural Research Ntwk). **HONS:** National Health R.&D. Program Fellowship, 1985-90. **INTERESTS:** gardening; bird-watching; health policy; travelling. **COMMENT:** "*Keen behavioural researcher to understand how and why people behave the way they do. Directed development of cancer prevention research program in Alberta.*"

Campbell, Karen, B.Ed.,LL.B. ■ ■ ⚖ Ⓢ
Lawyer, PATTERSON PALMER HUNT MURPHY (law firm), 20 Great George St., P.O. Box 486, Charlottetown, PE C1A 7L1 (902) 629-3911, FAX 566-2639, EMAIL pphmpei@peinet.pe.ca. Born Charlottetown 1960. m. Neil MacNair. 1 ch. Andrew Campbell MacNair. **EDUC:** Univ. of Prince Edward Island, B.Ed.(English) 1982; Dalhousie Law Sch., LL.B. 1986. **BAR:** N.S., 1987; P.E.I., 1988. **CAREER:** Lawyer, Patterson Palmer Hunt Murphy, 1987 to date; Ptnr, 1996 to date. **AFFIL:** N.S. Barristers' Society; Law Society of P.E.I. (mbr.; former mbr., Council; former Chair, Law Library Committee; former mbr., Law Day Committee); Canadian Bar Association (mbr.; former Prov. Rep., Administrative Law subsection); Canadian Institute for the Administration of Justice; P.E.I. Canada Games (Legal Consultant, Organizing Committee); yearly coaching liability seminars; nurses' liability seminars. **INTERESTS:** family; running; biking; skiing; tennis; writing fiction. **MISC:** volunteer fundraiser, various charities. **COMMENT:** "*Primary focus:wife; mother to young son, Andrew; lawyer and partner in newly merged Atlantic Canada law firm, PPHM. I practise full-time, mainly in the areas of labour, administrativ and litigation. Cur-*

rently, my interests, other than family and work, are in new marketing and operating strategies for merged firm and lawyers in general in the 1990s and beyond, and maintaining a reasonably high level of physical fitness."

Campbell, Leslie Ann ■ ■ ╱ ▯ Ⓢ
Editor and Publisher, CAMPBELL COMMUNICATIONS INC. (publishing - periodicals & books), 1218 Langley St., Ste. 3A, Victoria, BC V8W 1W2 (604) 388-7231, FAX 383-1140, EMAIL focus@octonet.com. Born Hamilton, Ont. 1952. m. David Broadland. **EDUC:** Univ. of Winnipeg, B.A.(Hons., Phil.) 1973; Univ. of Manitoba, M.A.(Phil.) 1974; non-credit courses in book publishing, journalism, TV production, filmmaking, mgmt, etc. **CAREER:** Sessional Instructor, Women's Studies, Phil., writing workshops, Univ. of Winnipeg, 1974-82; self-employed stained glass artist, Winnipeg, 1982-84; Office & Branch Mgr, Northwest Media Centre, Victoria, 1985-87; freelance writer/editor, 1985-88; Pres., Campbell Communications Inc., 1988 to date - Publisher/Editor of monthly & quarterly magazines & annual book, event organizer & sponsor. **SELECTED PUBLICATIONS:** editor & publisher, *Focus on Women* magazine (96 editions); *A Woman's Business* (7 editions); *West Coast Women* (7 editions); co-author with Hilary Lips, "Images of Power and Powerlessness" (in *Women, Men and the Psychology of Power*, by Hilary Lips, Prentice-Hall, 1981); *Career Planning and Job Search Techniques* (YWCA, Winnipeg, 1980); *Coping with Crises* (YWCA, Winnipeg, 1977). **AFFIL:** Women's Business Network; Canadian Federation of Independent Business; Victoria Status of Women Action Group; Women's Run for Shelter Committee; Winning Women (Steering Committee 1989-93); Manitoba Film Classification Board (mbr. 1981-84); Manitoba Action Committee on the Status of Women (Exec. mbr. 1979-82); Winnipeg YWCA (Exec. mbr., Bd. of Dir. 1976-79). **HONS:** Businesswoman of the Year, Victoria Business & Professional Women's Club, 1991/92; runner-up, Businessperson of the Year, C-FAX Community Awards, 1992; Woman of Distinction, Entrepreneurial category, YM-YWCA, Victoria, 1995. **INTERESTS:** human nature; communication; health; media; words & images. **MISC:** on-air broadcaster & tech. producer, Rogers Studio 11, Victoria, 1985-88. **COMMENT:** "*I like to use my communication skills to make a difference in the world-or at least in my own community of Victoria-and especially for women.*"

Campbell, Mona Louise, O.C.,LL.D. Ⓢ
President, DOVER INDUSTRIES LIMITED, 96

Avenue Rd., Toronto, ON M5R 2H3 (416) 928-9099, FAX 928-2396. Born Toronto 1919. w. 3 ch. EDUC: Dalhousie Univ., LL.D. 1982. CAREER: Pres., Dover Industries Limited. DIRECTOR: Movisa Securities Limited. AFFIL: Toronto General Hospital Auxiliary (Life Mbr.); Equine Research Centre, Guelph (Trustee); Metro Toronto Zoo; Royal Ontario Museum (Founder); National Ballet Sch. (Hon. Dir.); Canadian Medical Veterinary Association (Life Mbr.); Gardiner Museum (Acquisitions Committee). HONS: LL.D.(Hon.), Univ. of Guelph, 1994; Order of Canada.

Campbell, Paulette, B.Ed. ■ ⊲ ✦
Dean, Business and Community Services Division, Woodland Institute, SASKATCHEWAN INSTITUTE OF APPLIED SCIENCES AND TECHNOLOGY, Box 3003, Prince Albert, SK S6V 6G1 (306) 953-7154, FAX 953-7099, EMAIL campbellp@siast.sk.ca. Born Yorkton, Sask. 1949. m. Joe Campbell. 2 ch. EDUC: Univ. of Regina, B.Ed.(Bus.) 1971. CAREER: Bus. Educ. Instructor, Success Bus. Coll., 1971-73; Bus. Educ. Instructor, Natonum Community Coll., 1972-79; Rural Program Coord., 1979-84; Ind./Bus. Program Coord., Prince Albert Reg'l Community Coll., 1984-87; Training Consultant, SIAST, Woodland Campus, 1988-92; Dean, Tech. & Vocational Programs, 1992 to date; Acting Principal, 1994-95. AFFIL: PALS & SPRITES Swim Clubs (Exec. Mbr.). INTERESTS: Tai Chi Chuan; holistic health & lifestyles; cross-country, downhill & water skiing; gardening & landscaping; walking; reading. COMMENT: *"My major achievement would be the role I have played in my organization as a facilitator of healing, and supporting it through various phases of changes that have occurred, some being very dramatic. I have had acting positions, dealt with staff issues and initiated positive changes, all in very stressful environments. I would go as far as to say the effectiveness has been due to using what I would call a 'woman's approach.'"*

Campbell, Rita, B.Sc., M.L.S. ▯ ◫
University Librarian, ST. FRANCIS XAVIER UNIVERSITY, Angus L. Macdonald Library, Box 5000, Antigonish, NS B2G 2W5 (902) 867-2267, FAX 867-5153, EMAIL rcampbel@juliet.stfx.ca. Born Johnstown, N.S. s. EDUC: St. Francis Xavier Univ., B.Sc.(Hons., Math.) 1978; Univ. of Western Ontario, M.L.S. 1981. CAREER: Univ. Librarian, St. Francis Xavier Univ. AFFIL: Atlantic Provinces Library Association; Canadian Library Association; AAULC; CASUL; CONSUL; Grassroots Information Association.

Campbell, Sabine ⊠
Manager and Associate Editor, THE FIDDLEHEAD and STUDIES IN CANADIAN LITERATURE, University of New Brunswick, Campus House, Box 4400, Fredericton, NB E3B 5A3 (506) 453-3501, FAX 453-4599, EMAIL scl@unb.ca. Born Riga, Latvia. sep. 2 ch. Christopher, Pamela. EDUC: Victoria General Hospital, R.N. 1964; Univ. of New Brunswick, B.A. (English/Classics) in progress. CAREER: Office Mgr, local CUSO office; Asst. Head & Ward Nurse, Victoria General Hospital; Assoc. Ed. & Mgr, *The Fiddlehead* & *Studies in Canadian Literature*, 10 yrs. SELECTED PUBLICATIONS: *Fiddlehead Gold*, an anthology of selected works of 50 yrs. of *The Fiddlehead* magazine, Co-ed. (1995). AFFIL: N.B. Crafts Council (Awards & Acquisitions Committee); Fredericton Voice of Women for Peace; Fredericton Choral Society (former VP); N.B. Crafts Council (Dir., Curator for Craft Exhibits). INTERESTS: literature; music; the outdoors; gardening; travel; art; crafts. MISC: independent potter. COMMENT: *"I'm a peaceloving former nurse who drifted into craft as my children grew more independent, and from there into administration, curating and finally, the academic world."*

Campbell, Wanda, B.A.,M.A.,Ph.D. ⊠ ⊲
Author, Professor, Editor, UNIVERSITY OF WINDSOR, Windsor, ON N9B 3P4 (519) 253-4232, ext. 2300. Born Vuyyuru, South India 1963. m. Sandy Campbell. 2 ch. Piper, Tilly. EDUC: Univ. of New Brunswick, B.A.(English) 1985; Univ. of Windsor, M.A.(English & Creative Writing) 1987; Univ. of Western Ontario, Ph.D.(English) 1991. CAREER: Prof. of Cdn Lit. & Creative Writing, Univ. of Windsor, 1991 to date. SELECTED PUBLICATIONS: *The Poetry of John Strachan*; *Sky Fishing*; various articles on Cdn poets. INTERESTS: adventures with her husband & daughters; travel; films; books; int'l cuisine. MISC: current writing projects incl. *Down River Room* (fiction), *Haw/Thorn* (poetry) & *Herself at War* (anthology of early Cdn female poets). COMMENT: *"Without words we are lost; believing this, I seek to perfect my skills as a writer and teacher, but not at the expense of my family or faith."*

Cannell, Lynda, M.Sc. ■■ ♡ ⦰
Executive Director, SPORT MEDICINE COUNCIL OF BRITISH COLUMBIA (non-profit, involved in public educ. & athlete dev.), 6501 Sprott St., Ste. 3, Burnaby, BC V5B 3B8 (604) 473-4850, FAX 473-4860. Born Vancouver 1957. EDUC: Univ. of British Columbia, M.Sc.(Exercise Physiology) 1982. CAREER: Research Assoc., Allan McGavin Sport Medicine Centre,

1981-82; Exec. Dir., Sport Medicine Council of B.C., 1982 to date. SELECTED PUBLICATIONS: columnist, Sports Medicine, *Peace Arch News*; contributing author, Int'l Olympic Committee's *Book on Sport Medicine*, 1990. AFFIL: Canadian Centre for Ethics in Sport (V-Chair, Nat'l Advisory Council; Expert Advisory Committee on Doping Control); B.C. Injury Prevention Centre (Advisory Bd.); B.C. Medical Association (Sports Medicine Committee). HONS: Big Block Award, Univ. of B.C.; nominee, B.C. Women of Distinction Award; John Owen Scholarship, Univ. of B.C. INTERESTS: all sports, esp. fitness, golf, horseback riding. MISC: Med. Coord., Canada, 1988 Olympics, Seoul, Korea; Mission Staff, Cdn Team, 1996 Olympics, Atlanta; Med. Coord., Canada, World Univ. Games, Buffalo, 1993; Med. Advisor, Team B.C., Canada Games, Grande Prairie, Alta.; Consultant, Int'l Congress & Exposition on Sports Medicine & Human Performance, Vancouver, 1991. COMMENT: *"I have been involved in the areas of sport safety, injury prevention and elite athlete development for the past 15 years. As medical services coordinator for many provincial, national and international sports events, I have worked with a variety of different sports and have had the opportunity to participate in two Olympic Games."*

Cannon, Georgina, APR ■ $ ⌣

President, CANNON ASSOCIATES, 49 Fairfield Rd., Toronto, ON M4P 1S9 (416) 487-6168, FAX 484-8546, EMAIL geecee@astral. magic.ca. m. Tim Pervin. CAREER: Ed., various consumer & industry magazines; Pres., Cannon Associates, Inc.; VP/Creative Dir., Burson-Marsteller, 1984-89; Mng Dir., Cohn & Wolfe/Canada, 1989; Gen. Mgr, Toronto Office, Burson-Marsteller. AFFIL: Canada-US Business Association (Bd.); The National Club (Bd.); Music Toronto (Bd.); Second Harvest (Advisory Bd.). COMMENT: *"Responsible, through communication for strategic planning, facilitation and image change management."*

Cannon, L. Louise, B.A.,M.B.A. $

Senior Vice-President, Compliance, THE BANK OF NOVA SCOTIA, 44 King St. W., Toronto, ON M5H 1H1 (416) 866-7033, FAX 866-5011. Born Winnipeg. s. EDUC: Univ. of Manitoba, B.A.(Econ.) 1970; York Univ., M.B.A.(Fin.) 1972. CAREER: various positions in credit, investments & gov't rel'ns, The Bank of Nova Scotia, 1972-82; Gen. Mgr, Loan Policy & Admin., Cdn. Commercial Credit (CCC), 1982-86; Sr. VP, CCC, 1986-92; Sr. VP, Special Accts Mgmt, 1992-94; Sr. VP, Compliance, 1994 to date. AFFIL: The Canadian Bankers' Association (Chair, Task Force on Bankruptcy); Queen's Univ. (V-Chair, Invest. Committee, Bd. of Trustees); The Board of Trade of Metropolitan Toronto (Creditors' Rights Committee); The Canadian Club (Dir. 1992-93); Royal Canadian Yacht Club; Toronto Lawn Tennis Club. INTERESTS: sailing; skiing; tennis; riding; reading; travel. MISC: presently serve as a mbr. of the Fed. Gov't's Bankruptcy & Insolvency Advisory Committee. COMMENT: *"I am a career banker with a major Canadian chartered bank. My business endeavours have focused on credit granting, loan administration, problem loan workout and regulatory compliance. In the area of problem loan workout and insolvency matters, I have represented the banking industry as chair of the Canadian Bankers' Association Task Force on Bankruptcy on many occasions in a variety of forums."*

Cantin, Solange, M.A.,B.S.S. ⌣

Responsable, Bureau d'intervention en matière de harcèlement sexuel, UNIVERSITÉ DE MONTRÉAL, C.P. 6128, Succursale Centre-Ville, Montréal, QC H3C 3J7 (514) 343-7020, FAX 343-2146, EMAIL cantinso@ere.umontreal.ca. Born St.-Ulric, Que. 1944. m. Gilles Caron. 3 ch. EDUC: École normale de Matane, Brevet B (Pédagogie) 1962; Univ. de Montréal, B.S.S. (Svc. social) 1971, M.A.(Educ.) 1990. CAREER: Prof., École normale de Matane, 1962-65; Svc. social, Agence de svc. social du diocèse de Rimouski, 1965-67; divers travaux, svc. social et recherche, 1972-80; Agente de recherche et de planification socio-écon., Gouv. du Qué., 1980-85; Agente de recherche, surtout à l'Univ. de Montréal, et chargée de cours à l'Univ. de Montréal et à l'Univ. de Sherbrooke, 1985-91; Responsable, Bureau d'intervention en matière de harcèlement sexuel de l'Univ. de Montréal, depuis 1991; Coord., Centre de recherche interdisciplinaire sur la violence familiale et la violence faite aux femmes, depuis 1992. SELECTED PUBLICATIONS: differents articles, et volumes dont "La violence conjugal" (en co-edition publié chez Gaëtan Morin); "Le silence des victimes d'agression ou de harcèlement sexuel." AFFIL: Ordre professionnel des travailleurs sociaux du Québec; Association canadienne contre le harcèlement sexuel en milieu d'enseignement supérieur (Sec.); CLSC Longueuil-Ouest (VP, Conseil d'admin.); Fondation Carrefour pour elle; Amnesty International. INTERESTS: activités familiales; ski; équitation; bicyclette; peinture; lecture. MISC: plusieurs conférences. COMMENT: *"Je suis une femme qui a toujours cherché à maintenir l'enthousiasme, tant dans ma vie professionnelle que dans ma vie personnelle et familiale.*

Mes plus grandes réalisations: mes enfants, ma vie de couple et la confiance que je suscite dans mon milieu de travail."

Canty, Shirley, C.A.E. ✊ $

Executive Director, MANITOBA MOTOR DEALERS ASSOCIATION, 2281 Portage Ave., Ste. 203, Winnipeg, MB R3J 0M1 (204) 889-4924, FAX 885-6552. Born UK 1944. m. Richard. 2 ch. **EDUC:** Canadian Society of Association Executives, Association Mgmt Educ. Program; C.A.E. (Certified Association Exec.). **CAREER:** varied. **SELECTED PUBLICATIONS:** research, writes & produces a monthly newsletter. **AFFIL:** many through the years.; always held an exec. position. **HONS:** many small ones. **INTERESTS:** travel; family. **COMMENT:** *"I have been very fortunate to have a good family life and jobs that I have enjoyed. I seem to relate very well with people, both men and women of all ages."*

Caplan, Paula Joan, A.B.,M.A., Ph.D. ⊕ ✊ ⊛

Psychologist and Writer. c/o Addison Wesley Publishing, P.O. Box 580, Don Mills, ON M3C 2T8. Born 1947. **EDUC:** Radcliffe Coll., A.B.(English) 1969; Duke Univ., M.A.(Psych.) 1971, Ph.D.(Psych.) 1973. **CAREER:** Postdoctoral Fellow, Neuropsych. Div., Research Institute, The Hospital for Sick Chiildren, Toronto, 1974-76; Lecturer, Dept. of Psychiatry, Univ. of Toronto, 1978-79; Psychologist, Toronto Family Court Clinic, Clarke Institute of Psychiatry, 1977-80; Asst. Prof., Dept. of Applied Psych., Ont. Institute for Studies in Educ., 1980-81; Principal Investigator, Toronto Multi-agency Child Abuse Research Proj., 1979-84; Lecturer in Women's Studies, Univ. of Toronto, 1979 to date; Asst. Prof. of Psychiatry, 1979 to date; Assoc. Dir., Centre for Women's Studies in Educ., Ont. Institute for Studies in Educ., 1984-85; Head, 1985-71; Assoc. Prof., Dept. of Applied Psych., Ont. Institute for Studies in Educ., 1982-87; Full Prof., 1987 to date; Visiting Scholar, Pembroke Center, Brown Univ., 1993-94; affiliated Scholar, 1994-95; Visiting Prof., Erindale Coll., Univ. of Toronto, 1994-95. **SELECTED CREDITS:** more than 200 appearances on radio & TV to discuss psychological research, incl. *Donahue, Today Show, Canada A.M.* & *Speaking Out*; guest for regular psych. segments, *McLean At Large*, CBC-TV (1981-82); numerous newspaper interviews; four segments of *The Winning Woman* audiotape series (Chicago: Nightingale-Conant Corporation, 1991). **SELECTED PUBLICATIONS:** *The Myth of Women's Masochism* (New York: E.P. Dutton, 1985); *Lifting a Ton of Feathers: A Woman's Guide to Surviving in the Academic World* (Toronto: Univ. of Toronto Press, 1993); *You're Smarter Than They Make You Feel: How the Experts Intimidate Us and What We Can Do About It* (New York: The Free Press, 1994); *They Say You're Crazy: How the World's Most Powerful Psychiatrists Decide Who's Normal* (Reading, Mass: Addison Wesely, 1995); various other books & monographs; "Sex Differences in Response to School Failure," with Marcel Kinsbourne (*Journal of Learning Disabilities* 1974); "The Name Game: Psychiatry, Misogyny, and Taxonomy," in *Women, Power, and Therapy: Issues for Women*, ed. by Marjorie Braude (New York: Haworth, 1988); "Gender Issues in the Diagnosis of Mental Disorder" (*Women and Therapy* 1992); "Don't Blame Mother: Scapegoating and Myths Often Keep Natural Allies Apart" (*MS*, Sept./Oct. 1993); numerous other articles & book chapters; numerous conference papers. **EDIT:** Newsletter Ed., Canadian Psychological Association Interest Group on Women & Psych., 1979-80; Ed., *Resources for Feminist Research/Documentation sur la Recherche Feministe*, 1982-84, 1985-86, Advisory Bd. 1986-87; Consultant, special issue on the application of social psych. to social issues in Canada, *Canadian Journal of Behavioural Science*, Oct. 1984; Ed., four special issues on feminist psych., *International Journal of Women's Studies*, 1985; Founder & Co-Ed., Critical Papers Series, Ont. Institute for Studies in Educ., Centre for Women's Studies in Educ., 1985-87; Ed. Bd., *Canadian Journal of Community Mental Health*, 1990-93; Ed. Bd., *Women and Therapy*, 1992 to date; Int'l Advisory Bd., *Feminism and Psychology*, 1993 to date. **AFFIL:** Canadian Psychological Association (Fellow); American Psychological Association (Fellow); Division 35 (Women), American Psychological Association (Fellow); American Orthopsychiatric Association (Fellow); Toronto Area Women's Research Colloguium; Linden Sch. (Bd. Mbr.); Harvard-Radcliffe Club of Toronto. **HONS:** Award for Coll. & Univ. Teaching, Ont. Confederation of Univ. Fac. Associations, 1984; Woman of Distinction Award, YWCA, 1986; Woman of the Year Award, Canadian Association for Women in Science, 1991; Outstanding Young Grad., Greenwood High Sch., Springfield, Mo., 1994; Eminent Woman Psychologist, American Psychological Association, 1996. **MISC:** Registered Psychologist, Ont.; listed in *Canadian Who's Who*, *International Who's Who of Professional and Business Women*, & *American Men and Women of Science* (1976 to date); recipient of various grants & fellowships; grants juror for Hospital for Sick Children Foundation & SSHRC; reviewer for numerous journals; over 200 invited addresses & workshops; Coord.,

1st Cdn Women's Studies Conference, 1991; Mbr., National Film Bd. of Canada, Ont. Centre, Women's Film Program Advisory Committee, 1990-91; Mbr., Community Advisory Bd., Women & Body Image Program, Reg'l Women's Health Centre, Women's College Hospital, 1992-93; expert witness testimony in courts, in the Law Society of Upper Canada, for Women's Legal Education & Action Fund, & for the Ont. Bd. of Examiners in Psych.; consultant on application of recent & feminist research on educ. of females to the oper. of St. Clement's Sch., Toronto, 1991-92.

Caplan, The Hon. Elinor, MPP ❦ ⊕
Member of the Provincial Parliament (Oriole), Chief Opposition Whip and Critic for Health and Women's Issues for the Official Opposition, GOVERNMENT OF ONTARIO, Legislative Building, Queen's Park, Rm. 349, Toronto, ON M7A 1A (416) 325-3607, FAX (416) 325-3968. Oriole Community Office, 30 Esterbrooke Ave., Ste. 100, North York, ON M2J 2C4 (416) 494-6856. Born Toronto 1944. m. Wilf. 4 ch. David, Mark, Zane, Meredith. CAREER: Pres., Elinor Caplan and Associates, 1973-78; Alderman, Ward 13, City of North York, 1978-85; elected MPP (Oriole), Gov't of Ontario, 1987; re-elected, 1990 & 1995; Chair, Mgmt Bd. of Cabinet, Min. of Gov't Svcs, Cabinet Chair & Min. of Health, 1987-90; variety of critic roles incl. Revenue, Treasury Bd., Mgmt Bd. & Mun. Affairs, 1990-95; Deputy House Leader for the Official Opposition, Mbr., Standing Committee on Fin. & Econ. Affairs, & Chair, Standing Committee on Social Dev., 1990-95; Chief Opposition Whip & Critic for Health & Women's Issues for the Official Opposition, 1995 to date. MISC: as Chair of the North York Dev. & Econ. Growth Association, she founded the North York Bus. Association.

Carbis, Cheryl A. ❀ ⬠ ☺ ⬧
Journeyman Electrician. Born Weston, Ont. 1965. m. Geoffrey. 2 ch. Travis John, Logan Terry. EDUC: Central Peel Secondary Sch. (Electricity & Drafting); George Brown Coll., Sheridan Coll., Electrical Construction Maintenance Program Diploma 1987; Humber Coll., Electronics Tech. Diploma 1994; Sheridan Coll., CFAA Certification 1996. CAREER: Sound & Light Technician, Central Peel Auditorium, Peel Bd. of Educ., 1982-83; Apprentice Electrician, Comstock Canada, 1984; Apprentice Electrician, State Contractors, 1984-85; Apprentice then Journeyman Electrician on service truck, Canber Electric, 1985-89; Instructor, S.S.T.C. (Basic Electrical), George Brown Coll., 1987-88; Journeyman Electrician on service

truck, Robert Edwards Electrical Services, 1989-90; Shop Instructor, Pre-Apprenticeship Basic Electrical, Humber Coll., 1991-92; Electrical Trades Sch. Instructor, The Skills Training Centre, Sheridan Coll., 1994; Con-Ed. Instructor, Sheridan Coll., 1993-95; Elec. Trades Instructor, Humber Coll., 1995; Journeyman Electrician, The State Group, 1996 to date. AFFIL: National Association of Women in Construction (Dir. 1986-87); National Association of Women in Construction (Chair, Trades Women Committee); Women in Trades & Technologies, Toronto Chapter; International Brotherhood of Electrical Workers (IBEW); Block Parents. HONS: VIP Award, National Association of Women in Construction, 1988; Women on the Move Award, *The Toronto Sun*, 1989. INTERESTS: home decorating; family; outdoors. MISC: Delegate to the Canadian Federation of Labour Convention, 1987/88; Delegate to the Canadian Conference on "Women in Trades & Technologies," B.C., 1988/89; Guest Speaker, Coalition of Visible Minorities Conference, 1990; Alternate Delegate to the IBEW's 100th Anniversary Convention, 1991. COMMENT: *"As one of the few female Journeyman Electricians in the less than 2% category of women in the trades, I find my career rewarding, challenging and never dull. Being a role model has given me the opportunity to demonstrate and encourage women not to limit themselves in their endeavours, and that being a mother reinforces that yes, we (women) can do a lot–and then some."*

Cardiff, Janet, B.F.A.,M.V.A. ⊗ ⊰
Artist and Associate Professor, Department of Art, UNIVERSITY OF LETHBRIDGE, Lethbridge, AB T1K 3M4 (403) 329-2091, FAX 382-7127, EMAIL cardiff@hg.uleth.ca. Born Brussels, Ont. 1957. m. George Bures Miller. EDUC: Queen's Univ., B.F.A.(Fine Arts) 1980; Univ. of Alberta, M.V.A.(Printmaking) 1983. EXHIBITIONS: various solo exhibitions at The New Gallery, Calgary (1991); YYZ, Toronto (1992); Eye Level Gallery, Halifax (1992); The Edmonton Art Gallery (1993); La Chambre Blanche, Quebec City (1993); Randolph Street Gallery, Chicago (1994); The Southern Alberta Art Gallery, Lethbridge (1994); The Powerplant Art Gallery, Toronto (1994); The Walter Phillips Gallery, The Banff Centre (collaboration with George Bures Miller, 1995); Eastern Edge Gallery, St. John's (1995); Front Gallery, Vancouver (collaboration with George Bures Miller, 1995); *A Night at the Show*, Zurich (1995); Gallerie Optica, Montreal (1996); Louisiana Museum, Denmark (1996); *Alberta Biennial of Contemporary Art*, Edmonton Art Gallery (1996); Glenbow Museum of Art

(1996); *Sculpture Project 97*, Muenstar, Germany (1997); Barbara Weiss Gallery, Berlin (1997); Raum Artuelle Kunst, Vienna (1997). **AFFIL:** Southern Alberta Art Gallery (Univ. Rep. to the Bd.).

Cardinal, Tantoo ⊗ ♥ ⍩
Actor, c/o Talent Group, 401 Richmond St. W., Ste. 401, Toronto, ON M5V 3A8 (416) 408-3304. Born Ft. McMurray, Alta. 1950. m. John Lawlor. 3 ch. Cheyenne, Clifford, Riel. **EDUC:** Bonnie Doon Comprehensive High Sch., diploma 1968. **SELECTED CREDITS:** *Dances With Wolves* (feature); *Black Robe* (feature); *Where the Rivers Flow North*; *Legends of the Fall* (feature). **AFFIL:** ACTRA; SAG. **HONS:** Outstanding Achievement in Film, Women in Film (Toronto 1993 & Beverly Hills 1995); Best Actress, Eagle Spirit Awards, 1987 & 1994, San Francisco American Indian Film Festival; *Maclean's* Magazine Honour Roll, 1991; Hon. Doctorate, Rochester Univ., 1993. **INTERESTS:** to see the arts as a living force in our culture & society. **MISC:** speaking engagements to a wide range of groups. **COMMENT:** *"Tantoo Cardinal is a Métis woman, actor and mother. She is sustained in her life and work by drawing deeply from all her relations."*

Careless, Virginia A.S., B.A.,M.A. ■ ♣ 🗎
Research Officer, Recreation Branch, Small Business, Tourism and Culture, GOVERNMENT OF BRITISH COLUMBIA, 1019 Wharf St., Victoria, BC V8W 1X4 (604) 356-0405, FAX 387-4253, EMAIL virginia.careless@system3.lcs.gov.bc. Born Toronto 1946. **EDUC:** Univ. of Toronto, B.A.(Anthro.) 1968; Univ. of British Columbia, M.A.(Anthro./Hist.) 1974. **CAREER:** Archival Asst., Prov. Archives of Ont., Summers 1965-68; Teaching Asst., Anthro. Dept., Univ. of British Columbia, 1968-70; Asst. Historian, Vancouver Centennial Museum, 1969; Artifacts Researcher, National Museum of Man, Ottawa, 1973-74; Curator of Furnishings & Interior Design, B.C. Provincial Museum, 1974-75; freelance Historical Researcher, 1975-79; Social Hist. Collections Mgr, Royal British Columbia Museum, 1979-86; Curator of Hist., 1986-93. **SELECTED PUBLICATIONS:** *Impression of an Age*, co-author, exhibit catalogue (1969); *Bibliography for the Study of B.C.'s Domestic Material History* (1976); *Responding to Fashion: the Clothing of the O'Reilly Family* (1993); *Clue to a Culture: Food Preparation of the O'Reilly Family* (1993); various reviews; biography of L.M. Montgomery in *Pathfinders: Canadian Tributes* (Toronto: Heirloom Publishing, 1994); biography of Mazo de la Roche in *Wayfarers* (Toronto: Heirloom Publishing, 1996). **AFFIL:**

P.E.I. Museum & Heritage Association; Ontario Historical Society; Society for the Prevention of Cruelty to Animals; Friends of the UBC Library; Friends of Trinity Library; Vancouver Symphony Society; Victoria Symphony Society; Hallmark Society of Victoria; Endometriosis Association; Toronto Heritage Partner; B.C. Museums Association; Canada Museums Association; Association for Agriculture Museums. **HONS:** Ont. Scholarship, 1964; Trinity Scholarship, 1965, 1967; Ont. Grad. Fellowship, 1968; Trinity Fellowship, 1968; Univ. of British Columbia Scholarship, 1973; Royal Conservatory of Music of Toronto Scholarship, 1961, 1964. **INTERESTS:** replicating historical handicrafts & recipes; hiking; genealogy; music; writing; dance; photography; pets. **MISC:** Jury Mbr., Canada Council Explorations Program, 1982-85. **COMMENT:** *"I have long been interested in studying the everyday life of ordinary, and often forgotten, people. I have shaped my education and employment experience so that I could work in this field and it remains a fascinating and rewarding occupation."*

Carey, Elaine, B.A. ■ ╱ 🗎
Demographics Reporter, THE TORONTO STAR, 1 Yonge St., Toronto, ON M4T 1G8 (416) 864-4921, FAX 869-4328. Born Toronto 1948. m. John S. Kelly. 3 ch. Matthew Miller, Carey Miller, Adam Miller. **EDUC:** Univ. of Western Ontario, B.A.(Journalism) 1970. **CAREER:** Reporter–*Hamilton Spectator*, 1968-72; Reporter–Educ., Queen's Park, *The Toronto Star*, 1973-80; Sr. Writer, 1980-89; Southam Fellow, 1989-90; Deputy Saturday Ed., *The Toronto Star*, 1990-92; Asst. City Ed., *Beats*, 1992-95; Demographics Reporter 1995 to date. **HONS:** Southam Fellowship, 1989; Feature Writing Award, Canadian Nurses' Association, 1991; Feature Writing Award, Metro Toronto Police Association, 1991. **INTERESTS:** fitness; skiing; golf.

Carle Dagenais, Manon ㉙ ⊕
Directrice générale, SOCIÉTÉ QUÉBÉCOISE DE L'AUTISME, 2300, boul. René Lévesque ouest, Montréal, QC H3H 2R5 (514) 931-2215, FAX 931-2397. Born Val d'Or, Que. 1946. m. Philippe. 2 ch. **EDUC:** Univ. de Montréal, Physiothérapie 1967. **CAREER:** Physiothérapeute, 1967-72; Bénévolat, Société québécoise de l'autisme, 1979-88; Dir. gén., 1988 to date. **SELECTED PUBLICATIONS:** various newsletters & papers on autism. **AFFIL:** Corporation des Physiothérapeutes du Québec; Société québécoise de l'autisme. **INTERESTS:** général; lecture; cinéma; sports. **MISC:** various conference presentations. **COMMENT:** *"Mère de 2 enfants*

adoptés: 1 fille (25 ans), garçon "autiste" (21 ans). Curieuse de tout. J'ai toujours aimé travailler avec l'humain. De là, mon orientation en physiothérapie, puis en autisme."

Carlson, Debby, M.L.A. ✤

Member of the Legislative Assembly (Edmonton Ellerslie), GOVERNMENT OF ALBERTA, 301 Legislative Annex, 9718-107 St., Edmonton, AB T5K 1E4 (403) 427-2293, FAX 427-3697. Born Cereal, Alta. 1957. d. 2 ch. Melissa Zacoar, Michael Zacour. CAREER: Consultant for small bus., 1979-93; elected M.L.A., Prov. of Alta., 1991. AFFIL: prior to being elected, was a community activist & involved in many local & reg'l issues; Liberal Party of Canada. MISC: co-ordinated a pilot proj. (joint venture between the Federal Business Development Bank & Canada Employment & Immigration) for women in bus. (training & consulting in a 10-month program for 30 businesses); currently working on a TV magazine-format half-hour program for women in bus. called We Mean Business. COMMENT: *"I look forward to being a full participant in the changing political, economic and cultural climate we live and work within. We are working towards proactive, progressive change."*

Carmichael, Jo Ann, B.A.,L.L.B. ⚖

Partner, ALEXANDER, HOLBURN, BEAUDIN & LANG, Barristers & Solicitors, 700 W. Georgia St., Ste. 2700, Vancouver, BC V7Y 1B8 (604) 688-1351, FAX 669-7642. EDUC: Univ. of Ottawa, B.A.(Pol. Sci.) 1972; Dalhousie Univ., LL.B. 1976. CAREER: articled then lawyer, Owen Bird, Barristers & Solicitors, 1976-80; Ptnr, 1981-89; Ptnr, Alexander, Holburn, Beaudin & Lang, 1990 to date. SELECTED PUBLICATIONS: various papers. AFFIL: Canadian Bar Association (Insur., Civil Litigation & Family Law Sections); Vancouver Bar Association (former Exec.). MISC: frequent speaker at insur. industry meetings & Continuing Legal Educ. courses on insur. & family law. COMMENT: *"Practice restricted to family law and to life and health insurance issues, including disability claims, agency and contractual issues, human rights issues, with a particular interest in fraudulent life and disability insurance claims."*

Carney, Hon. Pat, P.C. ■ ✤ 🖎

Senator, SENATE OF CANADA, Ottawa, ON K1A 0A4 (613) 943-1433, FAX 943-1503. Born Shanghai 1935. 2 ch. EDUC: Univ. of British Columbia, B.A.(Econ. & Pol. Sci.) 1960, M.A. 1977. CAREER: Journalist, 1955-70; Econ. Consultant, Gemini North Limited, 1970-80; M.P. (Vancouver Centre), 1980-88; elected Feb. 1980, re-elected 1984; Opposition Critic for Sec. of State, 1980-84; Opposition Critic for Min. of State (Finance), 1981-83; Opposition Critic for Min. of Fin., 1983; Min. of Energy, Mines & Resources, 1984-86; Min. for Int'l Trade, responsible for the Canada/US Free Trade Agreement, 1986-88; Pres. of the Treasury Bd., 1988; Min. Responsible for Asia Pacific Initiative, 1984-88; summoned to the Senate, Aug. 30, 1990; served as Chair, Standing Senate Committee on Energy, the Environment & Natural Resources; Chair, Standing Senate Foreign Affairs Committee; Adjunct Prof., Sch. of Community & Reg'l Planning, Univ. of British Columbia. SELECTED PUBLICATIONS: "Foreword," *Beneath the Veneer* report of the Task Force on Barriers to Women in the Public Svc (1990). AFFIL: Association of Professional Economists of B.C.; Canadian Institute of Planners; Royal Architects' Institute of Canada (Hon. Fellow). HONS: Award for Outstanding Achievement in the Field of Int'l Law & Affairs, N.Y. Bar Association, 1988; Award for Distinguished Service, UBC Alumni, 1989; LL.D.(Hon.), Univ. of British Columbia, 1990; LL.D.(Hon.), British Columbia Open Univ., 1991. MISC: 1st woman appointed Fed. Min. of Energy, Mines & Resources, 1984; 1st woman appointed Fed. Min. of Int'l Trade, 1986; 1st woman appointed Pres., Treasury Bd., 1988.

Carpenter, Carole Henderson, B.Sc.,A.M., Ph.D. ⚲ 📖 🏛

Associate Professor, Division of Humanities, YORK UNIVERSITY, 4700 Keele St., North York, ON M3J 1P3. Born 1944. m. Kenneth E. Carpenter. 2 ch. Geoffrey, Carolyn. EDUC: Dalhousie Univ., B.Sc.(Psych.) 1966; Univ. of Pennsylvania, M.A.(Folklore-Folklife) 1968, Ph.D.(Folklore-Folklife) 1975. CAREER: Asst. to the Dean of Women, Univ. of Pennsylvania, 1966-69; Lecturer, York Univ., 1971-74; Visiting Summer Lecturer in Folklore, Memorial Univ. of Newfoundland, 1972; Asst. Prof., Div. of Humanities, York Univ., 1974-78; Assoc. Prof., 1978 to date; Dir. of Undergrad. Studies, 1988-90; J.P. Robarts Prof. of Cdn Studies, The Robarts Centre for Cdn Studies, York Univ., 1994-95. SELECTED PUBLICATIONS: *Many Voices: A Study of Folklore Activities and Their Role in Canadian Culture* (Ottawa: National Museums, 1979); *Bibliography of Canadian Folklore in English*, with Edith Fowke (Toronto: Univ. of Toronto Press, 1981); *Explorations in Canadian Folklore*, with Edith Fowke (Toronto: McClelland & Stewart, 1985); *In Our Own Image: The Child, Canadian Culture and Our Future* (North York: Robarts Centre, 1996); "Enlisting Children's Literature in the Goals of Multiculturalism"

(*Mosaic* 29(3) 1996); various other publications. **EDIT:** Founding Ed., *Bulletin of the Folklore Studies Association of Canada*, 1976-78; Founding Ed., *Canadian Folklore canadien*, 1978-84; Guest Ed., "Borders & Boundaries: Canadian/U.S.A. Interactions," vol. 13(1), 1989; Ed. Bd., *Newfoundland Studies*, 1994 to date. **AFFIL:** Ontario Folklife Centre (Pres.); Ontario Folklore-Folklife Archive (Dir.); Folklore Studies Association of Canada (Pres. 1988-89); Children's Folklore Section, American Folklore Society (Pres. 1993-94); Humanities and Social Sciences Federation of Canada (York Univ. Rep. 1995 to date); Robarts Centre (Dir. 1996-97). **HONS:** Award for Excellence in Teaching, Fac. of Arts, York Univ., 1987; Writing Award, Association for Canadian Studies, 1993. **MISC:** regular radio & TV appearances, 1972 to date; recipient of various grants & fellowships; juror for Aesop Prize (1993-96), Mr. Christie Prize for Children's Literature (1990 to date) & the 1995-96 H.A. Innis Prize (SSHRC); Robarts Chair in Cdn Studies Seminar Series on "Childhood in Canada: Cultural Images & Contemporary Issues," 1994-95. **COMMENT:** *"Dr. Carpenter helped establish the Folklore Studies Association of Canada (1975) and was founding editor of its bulletin and journal. She also organized the Ontario Folklore-Folklife Archive, of which she is the Director. In recent years, she has been active in public folklore activities within the Ontario heritage community."*

Carpenter, Helen M., B.S.,M.P.H., Ed.D. 🎓 ⊕
Professor Emeritus, Nursing, UNIVERSITY OF TORONTO. Born Montreal 1912. s. **EDUC:** Univ. of Toronto, Dip.(Nursing) 1933; Columbia Univ., B.S.(Nursing) 1943; Ed.D. 1965; Johns Hopkins Univ., M.P.H. 1945. **CAREER:** Red Cross Outpost Hospital, 1933-34; Victorian Order of Nurses, 1934-42; Consultant, B.C. Dept. of Health, 1943-44; Dir., Public Health Nursing, East York Health Dept., 1945-48; Asst. Prof., Nursing, Univ. of Toronto, 1948-61; Prof., 1962-77; Dean, 1962-72; Chrm, Grad. Dept., Nursing, 1970-76; Prof. Emeritus, 1976 to date. **SELECTED PUBLICATIONS:** *An Improved System of Nursing Education for New Zealand* (Wellington, N.Z.: Dept. of Health, 1971); *A Divine Discontent. Edith Kathleen Russell: A Reforming Educator* (Fac. of Nursing, Univ. of Toronto, 1982); "Appraisal of Student Work" (*The Canadian Nurse* Feb. 1940); "An Analysis of Home Visits to Newborn Infants Made by the Public Health Nurses in the East York-Leaside Health Unit, Ontario" (*The Canadian Nurse* Sept. 1959); "Services for Patients with Long-Term Illnesses: A Planned Approach" (*Canadian Journal of Public Health* July/Aug. 1976); various other publications. **AFFIL:** Registered Nurses Association, Ontario; International Council of Nurses (Educ. Committee); Canadian Red Cross Society (VP). **HONS:** Rockefeller Foundation Fellowship, 1944; Canadian Red Cross Scholarship, 1959. **INTERESTS:** health svcs; preventative medicine; educ.; the dev. of the nursing profession, provincially, nationally & internationally; travel; photography; sports. **COMMENT:** *"My years in nursing service and education provided opportunities for participation in the development of the profession in Canada and many other countries through the Canadian Nurses' Association, the International Council of Nurses and the World Health Organization."*

Carpenter, Lynn ✊ ✎
Executive Assistant, THE TORONTO SUN PUBLISHING COMPANY, 333 King St. E., Toronto, ON M5A 3X5. Director and Co-Founder, SHEENA'S PLACE. **CAREER:** Thc Toronto Sun Publishing Corporation, 1977 to date. **COMMENT:** *"Sheena's Place is a recently established charitable organization whose purpose is to develop and run a transition centre for people living with eating disorders, their families, caregivers and community service providers. Sheena's Place will offer its programs and services in a comfortable house, accessible by public transit and close to supportive services. It will be non-residential, warm, welcoming and supportive."*

Carr, Mary C., B.Mus.,C.F.P. ✪ ♡ $
Arts Management Consultant and General Manager, SOUNDSTREAMS/CHAMBER CONCERTS CANADA, MCC Associates, 653 Village Pkwy, Unit 62, Markham, ON L3R 2R2 (905) 940-4599, FAX 940-4599. Born New Liskeard, Ont. 1937. s. **EDUC:** Univ. of Toronto, B.Mus.(Educ.) 1958. **CAREER:** Secondary Sch. Teacher, David & Mary Thomson C.I., Scarborough, Ont., 1959-62; Performer (Vocalist), 1962-69; Administrator, Prologue to the Performing Arts, 1969-76; Gen. Mgr, Thunder Bay Symphony Orchestra, 1976-78; Arts Consultant, 1978-79; Dev./Special Projects Coord., Vancouver Symphony Orchestra, 1979-82; Dev. Dir., National Ballet of Canada, 1982-86; Consultant, 1986-89; Consultant/Fin. Planner, 1989-91; Consultant/Arts Mgr, 1991-94; Arts Mgmt Consultant/Gen. Mgr, Soundstreams/Chamber Concerts Canada, 1994 to date. **AFFIL:** Association of Cultural Executives; Canadian Institute of Financial Planning (Chartered Fin. Planner). **COMMENT:** *"As a consultant, manager and fundraiser, Mary Carr has*

been associated with many of Canada's performing arts organizations."

Carr, Shirley G.E., O.C.

Labour Activist. 6757 Buckingham Dr., Niagara Falls, ON L2H 2S2 (905) 358-3390, FAX 358-3390. Born Ont. m. **EDUC:** Stamford Collegiate Vocational Institute; Niagara Coll. of Applied Arts & Technology Sch. of Labour Studies. **CAREER:** Exec. VP, Canadian Labour Congress, 1974-84; Sec.-Treas., 1984-86; Pres., 1986-92. **AFFIL:** International Labour Organization (Governing Body 1980-85 & 1991-93; V-Chair 1991-93; Spokesperson, Workers' Group 1991-93; Chair, Workers' Group, Committee on Discrimination & Conference Committee on Apartheid); International Confederation of Free Trade Unions (former VP); Commonwealth Trade Union Council (Exec. Bd. 1980-93; Chair 1988-93); Queen's Univ. (Bd. of Trustees 1980-86); Mega Projects Task Force (Co-Chair 1973-83); Canadian Labour Market & Productivity Centre (Co-Chair 1983-92). **HONS:** Member of the Order of Canada, 1980; Centennial Medal for Exemplary Contribution to Vocational Training/Tech. Educ., Canadian Organization for Rehabilitation Through Training, 1980; Order of Diego de Losada, First Class, one of Venezuela's most prestigious honours for her "tireless battle for human rights around the world, & also for her fight against Apartheid," 1992; Commemorative Medal for the 125th Anniversary of the Confederation of Canada, 1992; Gov. Gen. Award in commemoration of the "Person's Case," 1994; Officer of the Order of Ontario, 1995; hon. doctorates from: McMaster Univ.; Univ. of Western Ontario; Univ. of Victoria; Brock Univ.; Acadia Univ.; York Univ.; Univ. of Northern British Columbia; Fellow, Ryerson Polytechnical Institute. **MISC:** 1st woman in the free world to be elected as leader of a nat'l labour congress.

Carrell, Nancy J., B.A.,M.L.S.,LL.B.,LL.M., B.C.L.,D.E.S.U. $

Deputy Secretary, CANADIAN NATIONAL RAILWAYS, 935 de la Gauchetiere St. W., 16th Fl., Montreal, QC H3B 2M9 (514) 399-4743, FAX 399-3779. Born Longview, Tex. m. 1 ch. **EDUC:** Texas Tech. Univ., B.A.(Pol. Sci.) 1966; North Texas State Univ., M.L.S. 1971; McGill Univ., LL.B.(Common Law) 1977, LL.M. (Comparative Law) 1979, B.C.L.(Civil Law) 1980; Univ. Aix-en-Provence, D.E.S.U.(Law) 1981. **BAR:** Que. **CAREER:** Lecturer, Legal Aspects of Mktg, Concordia Univ., 1978 to date; private practice of law, Clarkson, Tétrault, 1982-84; private practice, McMaster Meighen, 1984-87; Gen. Cnsl, Tee-Comm Electronics Inc., 1987-89; Legal Cnsl, Avon Canada Inc., 1990-92; Dir., Legal and Gov't Affairs, 1992 to date. **AFFIL:** Direct Sellers Association (Chair of the Bd.); Canadian Corp. Counsel Association (Dir.); Quebec Bar Association; Canadian Bar Association. **COMMENT:** *"Deputy Secretary for Canadian National Railways since August, 1995. Responsible for the Office of the Secretary, all Board of Directors Meetings, committee meetings and regulatory requirements as an issuer of securities with the Toronto and Montreal Stock Exchanges and the Securities and Exchange Commission in Washington, D.C. Has taught consumer and business law marketing at Concordia since 1978."*

Carrington, Margaret Elise, A.B.,M.A., Ph.D.

Assistant Professor, Physics Department, UNIVERSITY OF WINNIPEG, 515 Portage Ave., Winnipeg, MB R3B 2E9 (204) 786-9119, EMAIL meg@theory.uwinnipeg.ca. Born Washington, D.C. 1960. s. **EDUC:** Bryn Mawr Coll., Pa., A.B.(Physics) 1983; State Univ. of N.Y. at Stony Brook, M.A.(Physics) 1987, Ph.D. (Physics) 1989. **CAREER:** Visiting Scientist, Niels-Bohr Institute, 1987; Visiting Scientist, Dept. of Theoretical Physics, Oxford Univ., 1987; Postdoctoral Fellow, Theoretical Physics Institute, Univ. of Minnesota, 1989-92; Postdoctoral Fellow, Univ. of Winnipeg, 1992-94; Instructor, 1993-94; Asst. Prof., 1994 to date. **SELECTED PUBLICATIONS:** "Phonon Peaks in the Dynamic Structure of a Two-Dimensional Harmonic Crystal," with F. Weling & A. Griffin (*Physics Review* 1983); "Linear Response of Hot Gluons," with T.H. Hansson *et al* (*Annals of Physics* 1989); "Massless Scalar QED with Non-Minimal Chern-Simons Coupling," with G. Kunstatter (*Physics Review* 1994); other research papers. **HONS:** Alexander von Humboldt Fellowship, 1995; NSERC Women's Fac. Award, 1994. **INTERESTS:** rowing. **MISC:** various invited talks incl. "Ring Diagram Summations in the Finite Temperature Effective Potential," Canadian Association of Physicists, 1992, & "The Effective Potential at Finite Temperature in the Standard Model," Workshop on Phenomena at High Temperature and Density–Thermal Field Theory Approach, 1992.

Carroll, Esme, B.A. ■■ $

President and Chief Executive Officer, AMBROSE CARR LINTON CARROLL INC. (advertising), 939 Eglinton Ave. E., Ste. 203, Toronto, ON M4G 4E8 (416) 425-8200, FAX 425-5962, EMAIL esmec@aclc.on.ca. m. Dr. Earl Bogoch. 2 ch. Caitlin Raftis, Lindsay Raftis. **EDUC:** Carleton Univ., B.A.(English) 1970; Eurocentre, Switzerland, Alliance Fin. Certificate 1971. **CAREER:** Krohn Advertising, Montreal, 1972-76; Cockfield Brown, Toronto, 1976-78; Maclaren Advertising, which became Maclaren Lintas, then Maclaren McCann, 1978-95; Dir. of Client Svcs, 1984; shareholder & mbr., Bd. of Dir., 1985; Gen. Mgr, 1994. **AFFIL:** National Advertising Benevolent Society (Exec. VP; Chair, Exec. Committee; Bd. of Dir.); Institute of Canadian Advertising (Bd. of Dir.); Brazilian Ball (Committee mbr.). **HONS:** Gold Award, The Cassies (for most successful advtg campaign on generating sales results for Oh Henry! choc. bars), 1994. **INTERESTS:** sailing; reading historical novels; fitness. **COMMENT:** *"When I started in advertising 20 years ago, there were virtually no women in the business. Today women dominate the industry. I've had a wonderful career being at the forefront of that change."*

Carroll, Irene, B.A. ○ ⊛

Founder and Chair, PHOTOGRAPHERS & FRIENDS UNITED AGAINST AIDS, CANADIAN CHAPTER, 25 The Esplanade, Ste. 505, Toronto, ON M5E 1W5 (416) 594-1856, FAX 368-8594. Born Chatham, Ont. 1959. **EDUC:** Univ. of Western Ontario, B.A. 1980. **CAREER:** Founder & Chair, Photographers & Friends United Against AIDS, Cdn Chapter, 1993 to date. **SELECTED PUBLICATIONS:** *People Who Make a Difference* (Toronto: Penguin Books, 1995). **AFFIL:** Head Injury Association; MS Society. **INTERESTS:** health & wellbeing of her family & friends. **MISC:** *People Who Make a Difference* is a black & white study of more than 100 Canadians who have made a difference in their respective fields, photographed by Cdn photographers, with proceeds from sales supporting AIDS research in Canada. **COMMENT:** *"I consider myself to be not only a visionary, but a creator committed to the end result. In this particular circumstance, my power of enrolment has touched the lives of hundreds, all standing in the possibility of a Canada that is free of AIDS."*

Carron, Christine A., B.A.,M.A., B.C.L. ⚎

Partner, OGILVY RENAULT, S.E.N.C., 1981 McGill College Ave., Ste. 1100, Montreal, QC H3A 3C1 (514) 847-4404, FAX 286-5474. Born Mich. 1951. 1 ch. **EDUC:** Univ. of Michigan, B.A.(with highest distinction) 1972; McGill Univ., M.A.(Soc.) 1974, B.C.L.(Civil Law) 1977. **BAR:** Que., 1978. **CAREER:** practice of law, Ogilvy Renault, 1978 to date. **SELECTED PUBLICATIONS:** has given numerous conferences papers on the subject of banking, letters of credit & privacy legislation.

AFFIL: Canadian Bar Association; Quebec Bar Association; McGill Faculty of Graduate Studies and Research (Advisory Bd.); Bar of Montreal (Council 1990-92; various bar committees); University Club. **HONS:** Alexander Scholarship, 1975, 1976; Joseph Cohen, Q.C. Prize, 1976; University Scholar, 1976, 1977; Bar of Quebec Prize, 1977; Bar of Montreal Prize, 1977; J.W. Cook Prize, 1977; Elizabeth Torrance Gold Medal, 1977. **INTERESTS:** tennis; skiing. **COMMENT:** *"I have an active commercial litigation practice that often includes representation of financial institutions in various forms ranging from CCAA proceedings to participation, on behalf of a major Canadian bank, before the Estey Commission, which was mandated to investigate the causes of the insolvency of the CCB and Northland banks."*

Carse, Ruth, CM,LL.D.,ARAD(ATC) ⊛ ⚐

Founder and Executive Director, ALBERTA BALLET SCHOOL, 10210 - 108 St., Edmonton, AB T5H 1A8 (403) 428-7808, FAX 425-2152. Born Edmonton 1916. s. **EDUC:** Strathcona High Sch.; Royal Academy of Dancing, Advanced Teacher's Certificate 1954; studied dance with Madame Boucher at Boucher Sch. of Dance, with Boris Volkoff, with Gweneth Lloyd, with Berenice Holmes & Ruthanna Boris at Banff Sch. of Fine Arts, with Aubrey Hitchins, Martha Graham & Vitale Fokine at Sch. of American Ballet, & with Audrey de Vos, Maria Fay & Winnifred Edwards at Royal Academy of Dancing. **CAREER:** Soloist, Volkoff Canadian Ballet, 1942-49; Dancer, Radio City Music Hall, 1950-52; Founding Mbr., National Ballet of Canada; career as professional terminated due to injury, 1954; Ballet Dir., Muriel Taylor Sch., Edmonton, 1954-71; founded Dance Interlude, student dancer troupe, which became Edmonton Ballet, 1960, then Alberta Ballet, 1966; Dir., Alberta Ballet, 1966-75; appointed to first panel of Cdn Children's Examiner, RAD, 1966; Founder, Alberta Ballet Sch., 1971; Principal, 1971-83; Exec. Dir., 1983 to date; Choreographer, Alberta Ballet, Edmonton Light Opera, Edmonton Opera Association & Edmonton Civic Opera. **AFFIL:** Royal Academy of Dancing, London, UK (Life Mbr.); Alberta Dance Alliance (Hon. Mbr.); Alberta Dance Educators' Association (Hon. Mbr.); Alberta Ballet Sch. (Lifetime Bd. Mbr.). **HONS:** Creative Arts Award, City of Edmonton, 1968; Achievement Award, Gov't of Alberta, 1976; Queen's Silver Jubilee Medal, 1977; YWCA Tribute to Women, 1982; Sir Frederick Haultain Prize, Gov't of Alberta, 1983; Grace Bosustow Award, Royal Academy of Dancing, 1987; Dance in Canada Award, 1989; LL.D.(Hon.), Univ. of Alberta, 1991;

Order of Canada, 1992; other awards. INTER-ESTS: arts; music; sports; politics. MISC: performed in first & sixth Canadian Ballet Festivals, 1948, 1954; 1st Cdn Examiner, RAD, to do a US tour, 1972; Canada Council grant recipient. COMMENT: *"Dr. Ruth Carse has committed her love of dance to over six decades of development of professional ballet in Alberta. From performer to choreographer to instructor, Dr. Carse is often referred to as Alberta's First Lady of Dance as she is an example of dedication and excellence in the world of ballet, earning her the respect and love of Canada's dance community."*

Carstairs, Sharon, B.A.,M.A. ■■ ✦

Senator, THE SENATE OF CANADA, Victoria Building, Room 202, Ottawa, ON K1A 0A4. Born N.S. 1942. m. John Esdale Carstairs. 2 ch. Catherine, Jennifer. EDUC: Dalhousie Univ., B.A.(Pol. Sci. & Hist.) 1962; Smith Coll., Northampton, Mass., M.A.(Teaching of Hist.) 1963; Georgetown Univ., Foreign Svc. Sch., Washington, D.C., 1964; Univ. of Calgary, 1968. CAREER: teacher, Dana Hall Sch. for Girls, Wellesley, Mass., 1963-65; teacher, Calgary Separate Sch. Bd., 1965-71; scriptwriter & narrator, Calgary & Region Educational TV, 1967-69; Bd. of Referees, Unemployment & Insurance Commission, 1973-77; teacher, St. John's Ravenscourt Sch., Winnipeg, 1978-81; teacher, St. Norbert Collegiate, St. Norbert, Man., 1982-84. POLITICAL CAREER: N.S.: campaign worker, prov. elections, 1948, 1952, 1956, 1960; exec. positions, Dalhousie Univ. Liberal Club, 1958-62; Nat'l Exec., Univ. Liberals, 1960-62. Alberta: Poll Captain, fed. elections, 1965, 1968, 1972, 1974; Exec., Alberta Women's Liberal Association, 1965-68; Sec., Liberal Party in Alberta, 1968-70; Calgary Reg'l VP, 1970-72; VP, 1972-74; Pres., 1976-77; Fed. Campaign Committee, 1972, 1974; Prov. Liberal Candidate, 1975; Nat'l Exec., Liberal Party of Canada, 1976-77. Manitoba: poll worker, Ft. Rouge prov. constituency, 1977, & Fort Garry fed. constituency, 1979, 1980; Office Mgr, Tuxedo prov. constituency, 1981; Exec., River Heights prov. constituency, 1983 to date; Co-Chair, Donors' Dinner, 1983; Fed. Campaign Committee, 1983-93; elected Leader, Liberal Party in Manitoba, 1984; elected M.L.A. for River Heights, 1986; re-elected, 1988, 1990; elected Leader of Official Opposition, 1988 - served 1988-90; resigned as Leader, 1993; appointed to Senate of Canada, 1994. SELECTED PUBLICATIONS: *Not One of the Boys* (1993). AFFIL: West-end Cultural Centre (Deficit Reduction Committee); Knowles Centre (Hon. Bd. mbr.); Kids Swim, Friends of Sherbrooke Pool (Hon. Bd. mbr.);

Women's Post Treatment Centre Inc. (Hon. Bd. mbr.); Royal Winnipeg Ballet (Nat'l Council).

Carwell, Judy ◑ ⊕

Executive Director, Northern Alberta and The Territories Branch, THE KIDNEY FOUNDATION OF CANADA, 14121 - 128A Ave. N.W., Edmonton, AB T5L 4P5 (403) 451-6900, FAX 451-7592. Born Vancouver 1944. m. Robert Carwell. 3 ch. EDUC: post-secondary sch., grad. (Mktg & Bus. Admin.) 1962-65. CAREER: Exec. Dir., N. Alta. & The Territories Branch, The Kidney Foundation of Canada, 1981 to date; Chair, Kidney Foundation Cyclothon, 1981; Chair, Residential Campaign, 1982; Mbr., Patient Svcs Committee, 1981-82; Mbr., Edmonton Chapter Bd., 1981-82. DIRECTOR: Carwell Financial Corporation; Diamond R. Holdings (Officer). AFFIL: Alberta Association of Fundraising Executives; Univ. of Alberta Hospital Foundation (Volunteer Fundraiser, Festival of Trees); Douglas Coll., Vancouver (Day Care Exec. Committee; Social Committee). HONS: President's Award, The Kidney Foundation of Canada, 1982, 1983; Fund Raising Award, Kidney Foundation of Canada, 1984; A Tribute to Women Award, Health, Social Sciences & Social Svcs, YWCA, 1988; Supervisor Award, Kidney Foundation of Canada, 1990; Lawrence D. Bresinger Award, presented to a Kidney Foundation staff mbr. who merits special recognition for significant effort, 1990; Employee Appreciation Award, Kidney Foundation of Canada, 1989, 1990; Boss of the Year Award, Kidney Foundation of Canada, 1991. INTERESTS: golf; gardening; entertaining; decorating for special events; spending time with her grandson. MISC: Conference Registration Coord. for Association for Media & Technology in Educ. in Canada, Vancouver; was Community Sports Dir., Girl Guide leader, baseball coach for the girls' team, condo Bd. Mbr. & Figure Skating Coord. in Calgary & Edmonton. COMMENT: *"I'm a strong minded, determined, and persuasive person who believes hard work is a virtue. I took this charity from raising $117,000 to over $975,000. I believe that to achieve success, you need the drive to make it happen."*

Cass, Carol, B.Sc.,M.Sc.,Ph.D. ■ ⊲ ❀ ⊕

Professor, Biochemistry and Oncology, and Chair, Department of Oncology, UNIVERSITY OF ALBERTA, 474 Medical Sciences Bldg., Edmonton, AB T6G 2H7 (403) 492-2139, FAX 492-0886. Associate Director, Research, CROSS CANCER INSTITUTE, 11560 University Ave., Edmonton, AB T6G 1Z2 (403) 432-8320, FAX 432-8886. Born Lexington, Ky. 1942. m. David Cass. EDUC: Univ. of Oklahoma, B.Sc.(Zoology) 1963, M.Sc.(Zoology) 1965; Univ. of California at Berkeley, Ph.D. (Zoology) 1971. **CAREER:** Asst. Prof., Dept. of Biochem., Univ. of Alberta, 1976-80; Research Assoc., Dept. of Medicine, Cross Cancer Clinic, 1978 to date; Assoc. Prof., Dept. of Biochem., Univ. of Alberta, 1980-87; Sr. Research Scientist, National Cancer Institute of Canada, 1982-93; Prof., Dept. of Biochem., Univ. of Alberta, 1987 to date; Terry Fox Cancer Research Scientist, National Cancer Institute of Canada, 1993 to date. **SELECTED PUBLICATIONS:** "Density-dependent resistance to puromycin in cell cultures" (*Journal of Cell Physiology* (79) 1972); "Effect of lithium on the myelosuppressive and chemotherapeutic activity of vinblastine," with M. Selner *et al* (*Cancer Research* (41) 1981); "The Effect of verapamil on accumulation and antiproliferative activity of vincristine in cultured human leukemic cells with high and low levels of resistance," with A. Janowska-Weiczorek *et al* (*Cancer Research* (49) 1989); "Quantification of mitochondrial DNA in heteroplasmic fibroblasts with competitive PCR," with H. Wang *et al* (*Biotechniques* (17) 1994); numerous other refereed articles; active in various symposium proceedings, incl. "Membrane transport of anticancer drugs and drug resistance" (Proc., 12th Int'l Congress of Pharmacology, 1995); "Zidovudine and dideoxynucleosides deplete wild-type mitochondrial DNA levels and increase deleteed mitochondrial DNA levels in cultured Kearns-Sayre syndrome fibroblasts," with H. Wang, B.D. Lemire, J.H. Weiner, M. Michalak, A.M.W. Penn and L. Fliegel (*Biochem, Biophys. Acta*, 1316:51-59 1996); "Molecular cloning and functional expression of cDNAs encoding a human na+/nucleoside cotransporter (hCNTI)," with M.W.L. Ritzel, S.Y.M. Yao, M.-Y. Huang, J.F. Elliott & J.D. Young (*American Journal Physiol. Cell Physiol*, in press 1996); "Transport of adenosine by reencombinant N1/*cif* and N2/*cit* sodium/nucleoside cotransporters from rat jejunum expressed in *Xenopus oocytes*," with S.Y.M. Yao, A.M.L. Ng, M.W.L. Ritzel & J.D. Young (*Molecular Pharmacology*, in press 1996); numerous reviews, book chapters & abstracts. **EDIT:** Specialist Subject Ed., *The International Encyclopedia of Pharmacology and Therapeutics.* **AFFIL:** Canadian Cancer Society (Scientific Advisory to Edmonton Unit Bd. of Dir.); Canadian Society of Cellular & Molecular Biology (Pres. 1992-94; Past Pres. 1994-95); Canadian Federation of Biological Sciences (Bd. of Dir. 1992-94; Sci. Policy Commission 1994-95); Phi Beta Kappa; Phi Sigma; Sigma Xi; American Society for Cell Biology; American Association for Cancer Research; Canadian Society for Cell Biology; Tissue Culture Association; Cell Kinetic Society; Canadian Biochemical Society; Society for Analytical Cytology. **HONS:** Letseizer Gold Medal, Univ. of Oklahoma, 1963; Phi Sigma Award, Fac. of Sci., Univ. of Oklahoma, 1963; Predoctoral Fellowship, Bd. of Regents, Univ. of California, 1965-66; Predoctoral Fellowship, NSF (U.S.), 1966-70; Predoctoral Fellowship, MRC (Cda), 1970-73. **MISC:** grant recipient; reviewer for various journals.

Casselman, Barbie, B.A.A.,FnCFS ⊕ $ ✎
President, CASSELMAN & CO. INC., 150 York St., Ste. 1500, Toronto, ON M5H 3S5 (416) 862-5546, FAX 862-2474, President, BARBIE CASSELMAN INC. Born Toronto 1956. m. Brian Casselman. **EDUC:** Ryerson Polytechnical Institute, B.A.A.(Nutrition) 1979. **CAREER:** Dietary Aid, North York General Hospital, 1978; Supervisor & Counsellor, Weight Loss Clinic, 1979-85; Consultant, Texaco Canada, 1985; joint lipid program with Dr. Josephine Bird, 1985-88; Nutrition Consultant, The Elmwood, Cambridge & Adelaide health clubs, 1985-91; Nutritional Advisor, *The Financial Post*, "Inside Sports," 1989-91; Consultant, "Too Good to be True" products, Loblaw International Merchants, 1991-93; Assoc., Medcan (Inc.), 1985 to date; Pres., Barbie Casselman Inc., 1985 to date; Pres., Casselman & Co. Inc., 1990 to date. **SELECTED CREDITS:** writer/host, "Nutrition Tips," *Newsworld*, CBC. **SELECTED PUBLICATIONS:** *Barbie Casselman's Good-For-You Cooking; A Healthy Eating Guide* (1993); numerous magazine articles. **INTERESTS:** snow skiing; skating; cooking; aerobics; jogging; fiction. **MISC:** invited speaker, Empire Club of Canada, 1992 & Canadian Dental Association, 1993; created alternative cuisine menu & recipes for the King Edward Hotel, Toronto & the 'Nutrifit' menu for the Rothman's Corporation, 1986; lecturer to academic, corp. & charitable institutions; media spokesperson; listed in *Canadian Who's Who & Who's Who in Canadian Business.* **COMMENT:** *"In addition to personal nutrition counselling for individuals, through her companies, Barbie Casselman develops healthy products for food retailers, and consults to corporate clients, spas, health organizations, etc. on a variety of nutrition projects."*

Castonguay-Thibaudeau, Marie-France, D.P.H.,B.N.,M.Sc.N. ■■ ⊕ 🎓
Professor, Faculté des sciences infirmières, UNIVERSITÉ DE MONTRÉAL, C.P. 6128, Succursale Centre-ville, Montréal, QC H3C 3J7 (514) 343-6437, FAX 343-2306. Born Causapscal 1931. m. Louis Thibaudeau. 1 ch. Pierre. **EDUC:** Univ. de Montréal, D.P.H.(Public

Health) 1954; McGill Univ., B.N.(Public Health Nursing) 1963; Yale Univ., M.Sc.N.(Psychiatry & Mental Health) 1967. **CAREER:** Public Health Nurse, Hôpital Ste-Justine, Montréal, 1954-57; nursing in Europe, London & Paris, 1958-59; Public Health Nurse & Supervisor, Ministry of Health, Ont., 1960-65; Prof., Fac. des sciences infirmières, Univ. de Montréal, 1967 to date; Dean, Fac. des sciences infirmières, 1981-93. **SELECTED PUBLICATIONS:** "Status of Community Health Nursing Research in Canada" in M. Stewart (ed.), *Community Nursing* (W.B. Saunders, chpt. 26, 1995); "L'évolution de la recherche infirmière au Québec" in O. Goulet (ed.), *La profession infirmière: valeurs, enjeux, perspectives* (*Boucherville: Gaétan Morin* (ed.), chpt. 10, 1993); "A qualidade dos cuidados de saude: uma necessidade" (*Enfermagen Em Foco*, IV(15), 1994, 14-16). **AFFIL:** Cégep Bois-de-Boulogne, Montréal (Admin. Bd. 1994 to date); Hôpital Hôtel-Dieu de Montréal (Admin. Bd. 1996 to date); Centre hospitalier Côte-des-Neiges (Admin. Bd. 1982 to date); Foundation for Nursing Research in Quebec (Pres. 1995 to date). **HONS:** hon. doctorate, Univ. du Québec à Trois-Rivières, 1993; Officier, Ordre national du Québec, 1992; Ethel Johns Award, Canadian Association of University Schools of Nursing, 1993. **INTERESTS:** choral music (Gregorian chants); gardening. **COMMENT:** *"Has promoted community health, research and higher education in nursing for 30 years. Developed the joint McGill University/Université de Montréal doctorate program in nursing. WHO consultant."*

Castracane, Luba (S) ⌘
President and Chief Executive Officer, **A OK ROAD SAFETY SYSTEMS LIMITED** (o/a Sears Driver Training), 247 N. Service Rd., Ste. 301, Oakville, ON L6M 3E6 (416) 363-7483, FAX 842-4251. Born 1 ch. Nick. **EDUC:** Univ. of Buffalo, Gen. Arts Program 2 yrs.; B&S Bus. Institute, Data Processing; various driving/driver-related courses. **CAREER:** Undercover Investigator, Wackenhut of Canada, 1970-72; Private Investigator, Centurion Investigations, 1972-75; Pres., A ok Driving School Inc., 1975-92; Pres. & CEO, A ok Road Safety Systems, 1992 to date. **AFFIL:** Road Safety Educators' Association; Driving Sch. Association of Ontario (Cont.; Convention, Corp. Sponsorship; Staffing, Exec., Fin. & Ethics Committees; various exec. positions); Driving Sch. Association of the Americas (Dir.; various exec. positions); Ukrainian American Youth Association; Chamber of Commerce. **HONS:** Employee of the Year, Centurion Investigations, 1974; President's Award, Driving Sch. Associa-

tion of Ontario, 1984-85; Joe Dollinger Leadership Award, Driving Sch. Association of the Americas, 1985; President's Award, Driving Sch. Association of the Americas, 1988-89; President's Award, Driving Sch. Association of Ontario, 1989; Catherine Hensel Award, Driving Sch. Association of the Americas, 1989; nominated, Outstanding Entrepreneur Award, Chamber of Commerce, 1992; nominated, "Women on the Move," *The Toronto Sun*, 1994. **COMMENT:** *"A seasoned traveller, Luba's spirit of adventure allows her to be as at ease rafting down the Amazon River as pitching her vision in the boardrooms of corporate Canada. President and CEO of A ok Road Safety Systems Limited, master franchisor of Sears Driver Training Canada, responsible for the supervision of 11 corporate centres and five independent franchised centres. Although currently operating only in Ontario, Luba is gearing up to bring additional centres on line coast to coast and is uniquely poised to play a major role in how the delivery of road safety will unfold in the future."*

Caswell, Brenda ■ (S)
Vice-President and General Manager, **BROWN COMMUNICATIONS GROUP**, 2275 Albert St., Regina, SK S4V 2S (306) 352-6625, FAX 757-1980. Born Swift Current, Sask. 1954. m. Dwight Kayto. **EDUC:** Univ. of Saskatchewan, Teaching Certificate 1972. **CAREER:** Creative Dir., CHAB Radio, 1974-75; Creative Dir., CKRM-CFMQ, 1975-85; Copywriter, Acct Supervisor, Acct Dir., VP & Gen. Mgr, Brown Communication Group, 1976 to date. **DIRECTOR:** Brown Communication Group. **AFFIL:** International Association of Business Communicators (Comm. Chair 1990-92; Membership Chair 1992-94; Visual Identity Chair; Chair of Silver Leaf Awards Banquet for 1996 Nat'l Conference); Saskatchewan Nurses' Foundation (Dir. & Comm. Committee 1990-93); Saskatchewan Centre of the Arts (25th Anniversary Committee 1994-95). **HONS:** Silver Leaf Award, International Association of Business Communicators, 1994, 1995, 1996; Canadian Daily Newspapers Award. **INTERESTS:** collies; collecting & creating scale miniature dolls, houses & accessories; gardening; camping; quilting. **COMMENT:** *"Our fast-paced industry requires tremendous amounts of energy, enthusiasm and creativity. In this environment, I've learned a great deal about communications, management, people and survival!"*

Catley-Carlson, Margaret, B.A.,LL.D., Litt.D. ✿ ⊕ ✿ ⌂
President, **THE POPULATION COUNCIL**, One Dag Hammerskjold Plaza, New York, NY 10017

(212) 339-0500, FAX 755-6052. Born Sask. 1942. m. Stan Carlson. **EDUC:** Univ. of British Columbia, B.A. 1966. **CAREER:** Dept. of External Affairs, Gov't of Canada, 1966-77; posting to Sri Lanka, 1968; posting to London, 1975; VP, Multilateral, Canadian International Development Agency (CIDA), 1978; Sr. VP, 1979-80; Asst. Under-Sec., Dept. of External Affairs, 1981; Deputy Exec. Dir., Oper., UNICEF (with the rank of Asst. Sec.-Gen. of the U.N.), 1981-83; Pres., CIDA, 1983-89; Deputy Min., Health & Welfare, Gov't of Canada, 1989-92; Pres., The Population Council, 1993 to date. **AFFIL:** Water & Supply & Sanitation Collaborative Council (Chair); Institute of Medicine of the National Academy of Sciences (Bd. of Health); Appropriate Technology International (Bd. of Trustees); Women's World Banking (Bd. of Dir.); The Club of Rome; Overseas Development Council; World Health Organization's Global Program for Vaccines & Immunization (Scientific Advisory Group of Experts); InterAmerican Dialogue; Yale Sch. of Medicine (Dean's Council); The Centre for Agriculture and Bioscience Int'l (Gov. Bd.). **HONS:** LL.D.(Hon.), Univ. of British Columbia, 1994; LL.D.(Hon.), Univ. of Regina, 1985; Litt.D.(Hon), Saint Mary's Univ.; Fellow, Ryerson Polytechnic Univ., 1986; LL.D.(Hon.), Concordia Univ., 1989; LL.D.(Hon.), Mount Saint Vincent Univ., 1990; LL.D.(Hon.), Carleton Univ., 1994; LL.D. (Hon.), Univ. of Calgary, 1994. **MISC:** is the 6th Pres. of The Population Council, the 1st woman & the first non-American to hold the position. **COMMENT:** *"The Population Council, established in 1952, undertakes social and health science programs and research relevant to developing countries, and conducts biomedical research to develop and improve contraceptive technology."*

Cavan, Susan, B.A.,LL.B. $ 📺 🎭

Chairman and Chief Executive Officer, ACCENT ENTERTAINMENT CORPORATION, 207 Adelaide St. E., Ste. 300, Toronto, ON M5A 1M8 (416) 867-8700, FAX 867-1764. Born Toronto 1952. **EDUC:** Univ. of Toronto, B.A. 1973; Queen's Univ., LL.B. 1976. **BAR:** Ont., 1978. **CAREER:** Assoc. specializing in entertainment law, Roberts and Drabinsky, 1978-79; VP, Bus. & Legal Affairs, Cineplex Corporation, 1979-82; Prod., ICC International Cinema Corporation, 1982-85; VP, then Pres., Alliance Communications Corporation, 1985-89; Chair & CEO, Accent Entertainment Corporation, 1989 to date. **SELECTED CREDITS:** Exec. Prod., *The Bay Boy* (feature), ICC, 1984; Exec. Prod., *Bordertown* (series), CBN/Family Channel & CTV; Exec. Prod., *Wisecracks* (documentary), Gail Singer; Co-Prod., *Mesmer*; Prod., *Mrs. 'Arris Goes to Paris* (MOW), CBS & CTV, & Hearst Entertainment Productions; Prod., *Joe's So Mean to Josephine* (feature), 1995; Prod., *Saturday Night Live* (shorts) 1994; various other film & TV credits. **AFFIL:** CFTPA; Toronto Women in Film. **INTERESTS:** film; sports; travel; border collies; reading; theatre.

Cawker, Ruth, B.A.,B.Arch., D.E.A. ■■ $ ⚛ 🏃

RUTH CAWKER ARCHITECT, 110 Spadina Ave., Ste. 900, Toronto, ON M5V 2K4 (416) 504-7985. Born Edmonton 1953. m. Marc Baraness. 1 ch. Julien Edgar Francis Baraness. **EDUC:** Glendon Coll., York Univ., B.A.(Hons., English/French) 1974; Univ. of Toronto, B.Arch. 1980; Univ. de Paris, D.E.A.(Arch.) 1996. **CAREER:** Grad. Architect, Barton Myers Associates, 1980-84; Assoc., 1984-86; Chief Architect, CIBC, 1992-95; Ruth Cawker Architect, 1986 to date. **SELECTED PUBLICATIONS:** *Toronto Modern* (Toronto: Coach House Press, 1987); *Toronto: Le nouveau nouveau monde* (Toronto: Ministry of Gov't Svcs, 1988); *Viewpoints* (Toronto: Ontario Association of Architects, 1989). **AFFIL:** Ontario Association of Architects; Royal Architectural Institute of Canada. **HONS:** honorary doctorate, Glendon Coll., York Univ., 1996.

Cecil-Cockwell, Wendy Marion, B.A. $ ♡ 🎓

Chairman and President, BROOKMOOR ENTERPRISES LIMITED, 34 Whitney Ave., Toronto, ON M4W 2A8 (416) 606-4448. Born Stratford, Ont. 1948. 3 ch. Tess, Malcolm, Gareth. **EDUC:** Univ. of Toronto, B.A. 1971; Fac. of Exec. Dev., York Univ., Exec. Mgmt Program 1977. **CAREER:** Asst. Mgr, Public Rel'ns, The Toronto Stock Exchange, 1971-74; VP, Bus. Dev., Brascan Limited, 1975-85; Chair & Pres., Brookmoor Enterprises Limited, 1986 to date. **DIRECTOR:** Brookmoor Enterprises; Sanford Investment Corporation. **AFFIL:** Univ. of Toronto (V-Chair, Governing Council); St. Michael's Hospital Foundation (Chrm); Fraser Institute (Bd. of Trustees); Olympic Trust of Canada (Hon. Gov.); Dancer Transition Centre (Advisory Council); Branksome Hall (Annual Fund Committee). **HONS:** Ont. Scholar, 1967; Gold Medalist, Canadian Masters Cross Country Championship 10K, 1984; Silver Medalist, Ontario Masters Indoor Track & Field Championships 3,000m, 1985; Univ. of Toronto Arbor Award, 1992. **INTERESTS:** running; hiking; gardening; reading; visual arts; performing arts. **MISC:** winner of various nat'l & int'l distance races, incl. the Toronto Marathon, 1980, Sao Paulo, Brazil 10K, 1980, & the New

Orleans Marathon, 1981; mbr., Canadian Nat'l Team, World Masters Track & Field Championships, Rome, Italy, 1985 (10K & 5K track, & 10K cross country race).

Cederstrom, Lorelei Sajeck, B.A.,M.A., Ph.D. ■■ 📜 🎓 ✪

Professor of English, BRANDON UNIVERSITY, Brandon, MB R7A 6A9 (204) 727-9791. Born Milwaukee, Wisc. 1938. d. D.W. Barnes (partner). 2 ch. Christopher, Greta. **EDUC:** Valparaiso Univ., B.A.(English/Music) 1959; Carleton Univ., M.A.(English) 1968; Univ. of Manitoba, Ph.D.(English) 1978; grad. work, several universities & winter seminar at C.G. Jung Institute, Zurich, 1996. **CAREER:** Lecturer in English, Univ. of Manitoba, 1975-78; Asst. Prof. of English, Brandon Univ., 1979-86; Assoc. Prof. of English, 1987-94; Prof. of English, 1994 to date. **SELECTED PUBLICATIONS:** author, *Fine Tuning the Feminine Psyche: Jungian Patterns in the Novels of Doris Lessing* (Peter Lang: N.Y., Bern, Frankfurt am Main, Paris, 1990); "The Great Mother in *The Grapes of Wrath*" in *Steinbeck & The Environment*, S. Beegle & S. Shillinglaw (eds.) (Univ. of Alabama Press, 1996); "Walt Whitman and the Imagists" in *Walt Whitman of Mickle Street: A Centennial Collection*, G.M. Sill (ed.) (Univ. of Tennessee Press: Knoxville, 1994); several other contributions to books; numerous articles, critical reviews in scholarly journals; creative writing; many papers at academic conferences, public lectures & symposia; forthcoming: 3 contributions to *The Walt Whitman Encyclopedia*, J.R. LeMaster & D.D. Kummings (eds.) (Garland Publishing Company: N.Y., 1997). **EDIT:** Disciplinary Ed., Women & Lit., *Atlantis: A Women's Studies Journal*, Mount Saint Vincent Univ., 1989-94; Edit. Consultant, Univ. Textbook Div., HBJ Holt, Canada. **AFFIL:** Modern Language Association; Greenpeace; Canadian Association of University Teachers (Reg'l Rep., Status of Women Committee 1987-90); Brandon Univ. Fac. Association (Pres. 1986-87). **HONS:** numerous research grants incl. SSHRCC grant, 1992-95. **MISC:** daughter Greta Lauran is singer/songwriter of The Syrens. **COMMENT:** *"I am a professor, researcher, wilderness lover with a special interest in women's writing, Jungian literary criticism, Whitman, writings on the spiritual quest and the development of the feminine psyche."*

Cefis, Alberta G., B.A.,M.B.A. ■ $

Vice-President, Personal Credit Services, ROYAL BANK OF CANADA, 123 Front St. W., 7th Fl., Toronto, ON M5J 2M2 (416) 974-9783, FAX 974-9793. Born Italy 1953. m. Ilio Santilli. **EDUC:** McGill Univ., B.A.(Pol.Sci. & Lit.) 1975, M.B.A.(Mktg) 1979. **CAREER:** Teaching Asst. & Lecturer, McGill Univ., 1978-81; Mktg Mgr, Burroughs Business Machines, 1979-80; Mgr, Corp. Planning & Organization, Royal Bank of Canada, 1980-86; Mgr, Retail Bnkg, Mktg, 1986-90; Mgr, Oper. & Svc Delivery, 1990-92; VP, Strategic Dev., 1992-95; VP, Personal Credit Svcs., 1995 to date. **AFFIL:** Conference Board; American Management Association; Royal Bank Art Committee. **HONS:** Gold Medal, high sch., 1969; McGill Univ. Scholarship, 1973-74. **INTERESTS:** travel; sports; theatre; cultural events.

Cerilli, Marianne, B.Phys.Ed.,B.Ed., M.L.A. 🍁

Member of the Legislative Assembly (Radisson), GOVERNMENT OF MANITOBA, 450 Broadway, Rm. 234, Winnipeg, MB R3C 0V8 (204) 945-1567, FAX 945-0535. Born Toronto 1961. s. **EDUC:** Univ. of Manitoba, B.Phys.Ed. 1982, B.Ed. 1984. **CAREER:** Youth Program Consultant, Man. Gov't Employment Svcs, 1985-88; Counsellor, Tech./Vocational High Sch., Winnipeg Sch. Div., 1988-90; MLA (Radisson), Prov. of Man. **AFFIL:** Winnipeg Folk Festival (Dir.); Winnipeg Career Symposium; Athletics Manitoba; New Democratic Party of Manitoba.

Chabot, Diane ■ $ 🎭 📺

President, DCM ENTERPRISES, 15 Brule Gardens, Toronto, ON M6S 4J3 (416) 763-3711, FAX 767-6875. Born Montreal. **CAREER:** various positions, Bell Canada, Montreal, 1969-79; Div. Mgr, Customer Svc., Ottawa, 1979-81; Div. Mgr, Regulatory Matters, 1981-82; Div. Mgr, Cost & Performance, Toronto, 1982-83; Asst. VP, Cost & Performance, 1983-84; Pres., Info-Pro, 1984-87; Asst. VP, Public Affairs, 1987-88; Asst. VP, Public Rel'ns, Northern Telecom, 1988-90; VP, Logistics, Toronto, Bell Canada, 1990-93; Group VP, Logistics, 1993-95; Pres., DCM Ent., 1996 to date. **DIRECTOR:** Commemorative Services of Ontario; Bell Sygma System Management Inc. (1993-95); Ontario Film Development Corporation; Ontario/Rhône-Alps Committee. **AFFIL:** Arts Foundation of Greater Toronto (Dir. 1988-96); Premier's Council on Health, Well-being & Social Justice (Vice-Chair 1991-94); Advisory Committee on Cultural Industries Sectoral Strategy (1993-94); Conference of Independent Schools (Dir. 1993-95); Bishop Strachan Sch. (Chair); Canadian Olympic Association (Gala Committee mbr. 1994); INNET (Founder 1990). **MISC:** in Nov. 1994, profiled as part of "Acknowledgement of Accomplishments for Canadian Women in Radio and Television."

Chagnon, Françoise Pierrette, M.D. C.M. ☿ ✤

Otolaryngologist-in-Chief, Department of Otolaryngology, and Interim Director of Professional Services, MONTREAL GENERAL HOSPITAL, 1650 Cedar Ave., Ste. A2 141, Montreal, QC H3G 1A4 (514) 937-6011, ext. 2273, FAX 934-8238. Asstistant Professor, Otolaryngology, MCGILL UNIVERSITY. Born Montreal 1959. s. EDUC: Coll. Jean de Brébeuf, D.E.C.(Health Sci.) 1976; McGill Univ., M.D.C.M. 1981. CAREER: Internship, Montreal General Hospital, 1981-82; Residency, McGill Univ., 1982-86; Otolaryngologist, Centre Hospitalier Honore-Mercier, 1986-87; Attending Staff, Montreal General Hospital, 1986 to date; Asst. Prof., Otolaryngology, McGill Univ., 1987 to date; Consulting Otolaryngologist, Centre Medical Decelles, 1987-90; Otolaryngologist, Montreal General Hospital, 1987-90; Consulting Otolaryngologist, Clinique PriMedic, 1987-96; Consulting Otolaryngologist, Clinique Medi Club du Sanctuaire, 1988 to date; Consulting Otolaryngologist, Douglas Hospital, 1988 to date; Consulting Otolaryngologist, St. Anne's Veterans' Hospital, 1988 to date; Asst. Otolaryngologist, Royal Victoria Hospital, 1987 to date; Dir., Voice Lab., Montreal General Hospital, 1989 to date; Assoc. Otolaryngologist, Montreal Chest Institute, 1994 to date; Otolaryngologist-in-Chief, Dept. of Otolaryngology, Montreal General Hospital, 1990 to date. SELECTED PUBLICATIONS: "Dealing with Upper Airway Emergencies" (*Canadian Journal of Diagnosis* Aug. 1993); "Hoarseness: What's Wrong with Your Patient's Voice?" (*Canadian Journal of Diagnosis* Dec. 1994). EDIT: Ed. Bd. (Expert Analyst), *Otolaryngology: The Journal Club Journal*; Ed. Bd. (Referee), *Diagnostic and Therapeutic Endoscopy*. AFFIL: Royal Coll. of Surgeons of Canada (Fellow); American Board of Otolaryngology & Head & Neck Surgery (Fellow); American Coll. of Surgeons (Fellow); Canadian Association of Otolaryngology, Head & Neck Surgery; American Academy of Otolaryngology, Head & Neck Surgery; Quebec Association of Otolaryngology, Head & Neck Surgery; Canadian Medical Association; Quebec Medical Association; Federation des Médecins Spécialistes du Québec; American Society for Laser Medicine & Surgery; Laser Institute of America; Performing Artists' Medical Association; National Association of Teachers of Singing; The Voice Foundation; Montreal Med-Chi Society, Otolaryngology Section; Osler Library (Supporting Friend); La Guilde de L'Opéra de Montréal. HONS: H.S. Birkfant Memorial Prize in Otolaryngology, McGill Univ., 1981; Walter C. Mackenzie - Ethicon -

Johnson & Johnson Fellowship, Royal Coll. of Physicians & Surgeons of Canada, 1993. MISC: numerous lectures & presentations. COMMENT: *"Director of the Montreal General Hospital Voice Laboratory (research in voice and throat disorders), specializing in the care of the professional voice."*

Chalifoux, Thelma J. ⊗ ♙

Chairman, SENATE OF THE MÉTIS NATIONAL COUNCIL, 13140 St. Albert Trail, Edmonton, AB T5L 4R8 (403) 455-2200, ext. 247, FAX 452-8946. Born Calgary 1929. d. 7 ch. Robert, Scott, Clifford, Deborah, Orleane, Sharon, Paul. EDUC: Chicago Sch. of Interior Design; S.A.I.T., Construction Estimating; Lethbridge Community Coll., Sociology. CAREER: Métis Association of Alberta, 1969-71; Slave Lake Local Initiative Program, 1971; Slave Lake Native Friendship Centre, 1971; Company of Young Canadians, 1973-74; Alberta Housing Corporation, 1976-77; Northern Basic Economy Corporation, 1980-81; CKYL–Radio Peace River, 1981-84; Allarcom (ITV), 1984; Métis Urban Housing Corporation, 1984-85; Musqua Publishing and Advertising Ltd., 1985-86; Owner & Mgr, Secret Garden Originals, 1987 to date; Community Dev. Consultant, 1987-88; AISH Appeal Panel Mbr. (Relief), 1989-90; Employment Consultant, 1989 to date; Social Allowance Appeal Panel Mbr., 1989 to date; Co-Chair, Senate of the Métis Nation of Alberta, 1990 to date; Chrm, Senate of the Métis National Council; Child Welfare Appeal Panel Mbr, 1992-96. AFFIL: Child Welfare Appeal Panel, Prov. of Alberta; Salvation Army League of Mercy; Alberta Native Communications Society; Provincial Association of Friendship Centres (VP); Senate of the Univ. of Alberta; Métis Women's Council (Pres.); Aboriginal Women's Business Development Corporation (VP); Métis Local 1984 (Pres.); Métis Tenants' Association (Pres.); Métis Urban Housing Corporation (Bd. Mbr.); Apeetogosan Development Inc. Corporation (Trustee); Métis Association of Alberta (Elected Bd. Mbr. 1988-90); One Voice Seniors' Network (Treas.); Adrian Hope Youth Drop-In Centre (Pres.). HONS: Canada 125 Medal; National Aboriginal Achievement Award; Gold Medal, Métis National Council. INTERESTS: Métis history; floral design; writing. MISC: lecturer on Métis history, culture & value systems; 1st Métis woman, Senate of the Univ. of Alberta; Minister's Advisory Committee on Suicide Prevention.

Chamberlain, Brenda Kay, M.P. ✤

Member of Parliament (Guelph-Wellington), GOVERNMENT OF CANADA, House of Commons,

Confederation Building, Rm. 152, Ottawa, ON K1A 0A6 (613) 996-4758, FAX (613) 996-9922, Constituency Office, 40 Cork St. E., Guelph, ON N1H 2W8 (519) 837-8276. Born Toronto 1952. m. David Chamberlain. 3 ch. **CAREER:** home daycare owner & operator, 1979-83; Admin. Asst. to family-owned bus., 1984-87; Trustee, Wellington County Bd. of Educ., 1985-93, Chair, 1987-90; Exec. Dir., Wellington County Literacy Council, 1989-93; Exec. Dir., Guelph-Wellington Educ. Council, 1992-93; MP, Guelph-Wellington, 1993 to date; Mbr., Standing Committee on Gov't Oper., 1994 to date; Chair, Liberal Caucus Committee on Econ. Dev., 1994 to date; Assoc. Mbr., Standing Committee on Fin., 1996 to date.

Chambers, Gretta, B.A.,LL.D. ■ ○ ⌺ ♂
Chancellor, McGILL UNIVERSITY, James Administration Bldg., 845 Sherbrooke St. W., Montreal, QC H3A 2T5 (514) 398-8913, FAX 398-3370. Born Montreal 1927. m. Egan Chambers. 5 ch. **EDUC:** McGill Univ., B.A.(Pol. Sci.) 1947. **CAREER:** Sec., Red Cross Blood Transfusion Svc., 1947-51; freelance translator of books & pol. treatises from French to English, 1959-70; researcher, writer, host, *The Province In Print*, CBC Radio, 1966-78; weekly columnist, *Montreal Gazette*, 1976; host, *The Editors*, CFCF-12, Montreal & other stations, 1977-80; syndicated columnist, Southam News, 1978-83; Mbr., Ed. Bd., & contributor, *Report Magazine*, 1977-80; bi-monthly columnist, *Regina Leader Post*, 1985; bi-monthly columnist, *The London Free Press*, 1988; freelance journalist; Gov., McGill Univ., 1978-88; Gov. Emeritus, 1988 to date; Chancellor, 1991 to date. **SELECTED PUBLICATIONS:** regular contributions to *Language and Society*; occasional contributions to *The International Herald Tribune*, *Liberté*, *Content* & *Quill & Quire*. **EDIT:** Chair, Ed. Bd., *McGill News*. **DIRECTOR:** Boréal Assurances, Insurance Company Inc.; Capital International CDPQ Inc. **AFFIL:** Foundation of the YWCA of Montreal (Pres. of the First Bd. of Dir. 1996); Groupe de travail chargé d'examiner les pratiques en matière d'enquêtes criminelles au sein des corps de police du Québec; Groupe de travail sur l'entreprise et l'emploi–Le devenir social et économique du Québec (1996); Montreal Exchange (Public Gov.); McCord Museum (Bd. Mbr.); Passages (Bd. Mbr.); Geordie Productions (Bd. Mbr.); Portage (Bd. Mbr.); McGill Univ.-Montreal Children's Hospital Research Institute (Chair, Bd. of Gov.); Conseil de la magistrature du Québec (1992-95); Task Force on English Education in Quebec (Chair); Advisory Bd. on English Education (Chair); Institut

de Design (Dir.); Montreal Association for the Intellectually Handicapped (Hon. Patron). **HONS:** Officier de l'Ordre National du Québec, 1993; Order of Canada, 1994; named a "Great Montrealer," by the Board of Trade of Metropolitan Montreal, 1996; LL.D.(Hon.), Univ. of Victoria, 1994. **MISC:** regular contributions to CBC Newsworld & CBC Radio; occasional contributions to CJAD, CBF, CJMS, Radio Canada & Radio Québec.

Chan, Shirley, B.A.,M.A. ■ Ⓢ
Manager, Non-Market Housing, CITY OF VANCOUVER, 453 W. 12th Ave., Vancouver, BC V5Y 1V4 (604) 873-7437, FAX 873-7064. Past Chairman, VANCITY SAVINGS CREDIT UNION. Born Vancouver 1947. m. Stephen C. Hopkins. 2 ch. Heming Hopkins, Emma Hopkins. **EDUC:** Simon Fraser Univ., B.A.(English) 1971; York Univ., M.A.(Environmental Studies) 1978. **CAREER:** Environmental Planner, Dept. of Indian Affairs & Northern Dev., Ont. Reg., 1979-81; Exec. Asst. to Mayor, City of Vancouver, 1981-86; private consultant, 1987; Exec. Asst. to Pres., B.C. Institute of Technology, 1987-88; Mgr, Non-Mkt Housing Div., Community Svcs Group, City of Vancouver, 1988 to date. **DIRECTOR:** VanCity Savings Credit Union; Citizens Trust; VanCity Enterprises (V-Chair). **AFFIL:** Univ. of British Columbia (Chair, Bd. of Gov.); Granville Island Art Project (Advisor); Little Mountain Resort Care & Housing Society (Dir.); Scenarios for the Future (participant). **HONS:** Outstanding Alumni Award, Simon Fraser Univ., 1993. **INTERESTS:** visual & performing arts; educ.; environment & human settlement; housing & social svcs; health care; race rel'ns; multicultural issues; women's issues. **COMMENT:** *"Since organizing the Chinese community in 1968 to develop an alternative to the bulldozer approach to urban renewal, I have maintained an active interest in my community. I am moved to act by social-justice concerns."*

Chandler, Marsha, B.A.,Ph.D. ⌺ Ⓢ ♂
Dean, Faculty of Arts and Science, UNIVERSITY OF TORONTO, 100 St. George St., Rm. 2020, Toronto, ON M5S 1A1 (416) 978-3383, FAX 978-3887. Born Bristol, Va. m. William. 1 ch. Alice. **EDUC:** Coll. of the City of N.Y., B.A. 1965; Univ. of North Carolina, Ph.D. 1972. **CAREER:** Asst. Prof., Univ. of Toronto, Dept. of Pol. Sci. & Fac. of Law, 1977-82; Assoc. Prof., 1982-86; Full Prof., 1986-90; Dean, 1990 to date. **SELECTED PUBLICATIONS:** *Public Policy and Provincial Politics* (McGraw-Hill Ryerson, 1979); *The Politics of Canadian Public Policy* (Univ. of Toronto Press, 1983); *The Political Economy of Business Bailouts*

(Univ. of Toronto Press, 1986); *Trade and Transitions* (Routledge Publishers, 1990); "Interest Representation and the Canadian Administrative State" (*University of Toronto Law Journal* 1990); "The Problem of Indicator Formation in Comparative Research" (*Comparative Political Studies* Apr. 1974); various other publications. **EDIT:** Bd. of Ed., *Canadian Public Administration*, 1983-90. **AFFIL:** Art Gallery of Ontario (Bd. of Trustees); Judicial Appointments for Ontario (Advisory Committee); Canadian Institute for Advanced Research (Research Bd.); Hebrew Univ. (Int'l Advisory Committee for Cdn Studies); Mt. Sinai Hospital (Bd. of Gov.); Ontario Lightwave & Laser Research Centre (Bd. of Dir.); Huntsman Marine Science Centre (Bd. of Dir.); Univ. of Toronto. **HONS:** Fellow, Royal Society of Canada, 1995; Women of Distinction, YWCA 1994. **INTERESTS:** tennis; golf; orchid cultivation; cats; dogs. **MISC:** former Gov., Univ. of Toronto, 1992-94; recipient of various grants; reviewer for various journals, publishers & grant providers; first female to hold position of Dean of Arts and Science at Univ. of Toronto. **COMMENT:** *"Dean Chandler is a Professor of Political Economy and Law. Since 1990, she has held a senior academic management position as Dean of the Faculty of Arts and Science at the University of Toronto. Her term as Dean has been dedicated to enhancing the University's ability to deliver excellence in teaching and research."*

Chang, Patricia Lai-Yung, B.Sc., Ph.D. ⚛ 🎓

Professor, Department of Pediatrics, McMaster University, HSC-3N18, 1200 Main St. W., Hamilton, ON L8N 3Z5 (905) 521-2100 ext. 3716, FAX 521-2651, EMAIL changp@fhs.mcmaster.ca. Born Hong Kong 1943. m. 1 ch. **EDUC:** Univ. of Hong Kong, B.Sc. (Chem./Zoology) 1967; Univ. of Western Ontario, Ph.D.(Biochem.) 1971. **CAREER:** Asst. Prof., Dept. of Pediatrics, McMaster Univ., 1979-83; Assoc. Prof., 1984-90; Prof., 1990 to date; Assoc. Mbr., Dept. of Biomedical Sciences, 1990 to date; Assoc. Mbr., Dept. of Biol., 1991 to date. **SELECTED PUBLICATIONS:** "Nonautologous somatic gene therapy" in *Somatic Gene Therapy*, ed. (pp. 203-223 Boca Raton, Fla.: CRC Press Inc., 1995); "Non-selective isolation of human somatic cell hybrids by unit-gravity sedimentation," with G.I. Joubert & R.G. Davidson (*Nature*, 278, 1979); "Complementation of arylsulfatase A in somatic hybrids of metachromatic leukodystrophy and multiple sulfatase deficiency disorder fibroblasts," with R.G. Davidson (*Proc. National Academy of Science* USA 77(10), 1980); "Correction of the growth defect in dwarf mice with nonautologous microencapsulated myoblasts, an alternate approach to somatic gene therapy," with A. Al-Hendy *et al* (*Human Gene Therapy*, 6, 1995); "Delivery of human factor IX in mice encapsulated recombinant myoblasts: A novel approach towards allogenic gene therapy of hemophilia B.," with G. Hortelano *et al* (*Blood*, 87:5095-5103, 1996); various other journal articles & book chapters. **AFFIL:** Canadian Biochemical Society; American Society of Human Genetics; American Society of Cell Biology; Association for Women in Science; American Society for Biochemistry & Molecular Biology; Genetics Society of Canada; Society of Chinese Bioscientists in America. **HONS:** Grantham Scholarship, 1962-64; Velleman Scholarship, 1980-84; Ont. Mental Health Scholarship, 1984-89. **MISC:** referee for various journals; reviewer for various granting agencies; consultant to neurologists & geneticists on inborn errors of metabolism deficiencies of lysosomal enzymes in neurodegenerative diseases; member of Res. Grant Review Committee for the Ont. Mental Health Fdn; member of NIH site visit for GCRC Gene Therapy Unit, Children's Hosp. of LA, CA, Nov. 1993.

Chant, Diana, B.Sc.,C.A. $

Partner, Price Waterhouse, 1 First Canadian Place, Toronto, ON M4R 1Y3 (416) 365-8207, FAX 947-8956. Born Montreal 1952. m. Bill Mitchell. 3 ch. **EDUC:** McGill Univ., B.Sc. 1974; C.A., 1976. **CAREER:** Price Waterhouse, Montreal, 1974-85; Ptnr, Toronto, 1985 to date. **AFFIL:** National Ballet of Canada (Dir.; V-Chair, National Ballet of Canada Foundation); Empire Club of Canada (Dir. & Treas). **INTERESTS:** skiing; tennis.

Chaput-Rolland, Hon. Solange, O.C., O.N.Q. ■■ 🍁 📖 📜

Senator (Thousand Islands), The Senate of Canada, Ottawa, ON K1A 0A4 (613) 995-6194. Born Montreal 1919. w. André Rolland (deceased 1988). 2 ch. Suzanne Monange, Claude Rolland. **EDUC:** Couvent d'Outremont; the Sorbonne; Institut catholique de Paris. **CAREER:** political writer, radio & TV broadcaster, TV playwright; founded monthly publication, *Points de Vue*, 1956; Observer, United Nations, 1969; elected Member of National Assembly of Que., 1979 (defeated in 1981); freelance journalist, *Le Devoir*, *The Gazette*, *Windsor Star*, & *The Globe and Mail*, & host, public affairs series, *Télé-Métropole*, 1979; broadcaster, CFCF Radio, 1982; editorialist, *Dimanche Matin*, & correspondent, *Le Devoir*, 1985; appointed to the Senate, 1988.

SELECTED CREDITS: Writer with Michèle Bazin, *Monsieur le Ministre* (TV series, Radio Canada, 1981). SELECTED PUBLICATIONS: numerous incl.: *Et tournons la page* (Editions Libre Expression, 1989); *Le Tournons La Page*, Mémoires (Editions Libre Expression); *Le Tourment et L'Apaisement*, Mémoires (Editions Libre Expression); *Nous Deux*; *Les Saisons D'Isabelle* (Movel); *Ni Noir, Ni Blanc* (with Claude Charron, 1986); *Le Mystère Québec* (Editions Pierre Tisseyre, 1984); *De l'Unité à la Réalité* (Editions Pierre Tisseyre, 1977-81); *La Riviere du Temps* (in preparation for Oct 1996). AFFIL: Canada Arts Council (mbr. 1977); National Capital Commission (Commissioner 1974); Cercle des Femmes Journalistes (Chair 1974). HONS: Alcan Prix Liberté for "prestigious career in communications," 1987; named 1 of 50 most important women in communications, Int'l Association of Women Writers & Journalists, 1987; Ordre national du Québec, 1985; LL.D.(Hon.), Queen's Univ., 1984; Woman of the Year, B'nai Brith, 1977 & 1979; Dan McArthur Prize for "exceptional quality in a radio documentary," 1974; Officer of the Order of Canada, 1973; 3 medals for excellence, Media Club of Canada, 1972.

Charbonneau, Yvonne, B.A.A. ✖ $

Senior Design Partner and President, MCGREGOR CHARBONNEAU INC. DESIGN CONSULTANTS, 507 King St. E., Ste. 10, Toronto, ON M5A 1M3 (416) 359-0002, FAX 359-0005. Born Hong Kong. m. Pierre C. Charbonneau. EDUC: Ryerson Polytechnic Univ., B.A.A.(Interior Design) 1981. CAREER: Design Consultant, McGregor Charbonneau Inc., 1988 to date. DIRECTOR: McGregor Charbonneau Inc.; MaxCandy Investments Limited. AFFIL: Association of Registered Interior Designers; Interior Designers of Canada; American Society of Interior Designers. HONS: Interior Design Award, Association of Registered Interior Designers, 1990, 1993. MISC: featured in several trade & professional publications. COMMENT: *"In pursuit of my profession, the interior design consulting firm of McGregor Charbonneau Inc. was formed with my partner Lynn McGregor seven years ago; specializing in corporate commercial interiors. Our design philosophy embraces passion, vision, and relevance. We endeavour to form "business partnerships" with our clients; constantly reinforcing, educating and validating the positive value that good design brings to commercial enterprises. In an age where the office environment can often be the residue of bottom-line butchery, we are building long term relationships with clients who are inspired by creative and exciting spaces, that articulate their corporate message and stimulate their employees."*

Chard, Elizabeth, B.A.,M.A.,B.Ed., LL.D.(Hon.) ✇

Registrar, SAINT MARY'S UNIVERSITY, 923 Robie St., Halifax, NS B3H 3C3 (902) 420-5581, FAX 420-5151. Born Halifax 1939. d. EDUC: Dalhousie Univ., B.A.(Hist.) 1960, M.A.(Hist.) 1961, B.Ed. 1962. CAREER: Assoc. Prof. of Hist., Saint Mary's Univ., to 1973; Chair, Dept. of Hist., 1968-73; Dean of Residence (Women), 1970-73; Registrar, 1973 to date. AFFIL: The Abilities Foundation of N.S. (Chair); N.S. Special Olympics (Co-Pres.); Easter Seals/March of Dimes Nat'l Council (Dir.); Presbyterian Church of Saint David (Superintendent, Jr. Sunday Sch.; Ordained Elder). HONS: Doctor of Laws (Hon.), St. Thomas Univ., 1991.

Charest, Micheline ◼ 👄 🐝

Chairman and Chief Executive Officer, CINAR FILMS INC., 1055 René-Lévesque Blvd. E., Montreal, QC H2L 4S5 (514) 843-7070, FAX 843-9779. Born UK 1953. m. Ronald A Weinberg. 2 ch. Eric, Alex. EDUC: International London Film Sch., UK, 1972. CAREER: Prod., National Film Bd. of Canada, 1973-76; founded CINAR Films Inc. with partner, Ronald A. Weinberg (distributing foreign films to U.S. mkt), N.Y., 1976; relocated to Montreal & diversified to include post-production, 1984; broadened to include production & sales of 26 original TV series, 1986; company underwent a public share offering, 1993. SELECTED CREDITS: Exec. Prod., *The Busy World of Richard Scarry* (animated series), current; Exec. Prod., *Are You Afraid of the Dark?* (series), current; Exec. Prod., *Million Dollar Babies* (miniseries), 1994; Exec. Prod., *The Little Lulu Show* (animated series), current; Exec. Prod., *Arthur* (animated series), current; Exec. Prod., *Gift of Munsch* (special). DIRECTOR: Métro-Richelieu Inc.; Royal Bank Capital Corporation; YTV Canada, Inc. HONS: Cdn Entrepreneur of the Year, Association of Canadian Venture Capital Companies, 1993. MISC: CINAR Films Inc. won the Chetwynd Prize for Entrepreneurial Excellence, Canadian Film & Television Production Association, 1991; CINAR Films Inc. was awarded the prestigious Mercury Award for Bus. Excellence, Que. Chamber of Commerce, 1993.

Charest, Solange, B.A.,M.A.,M.N.A. ◼ ✦

Députée (Rimouski), Assemblée nationale, GOUVERNMENT DE QUÉBEC, Hôtel du Parlement, bur. 1.72, Québec, QC G1A 1A4 (418) 646-0999, FAX 643-5462. Born Amqui, Qué.

1950. m. Raymond Lemieux. EDUC: Univ. du Québec à Rimouski, Baccalauréat (Sociologie) 1982, Certificat (Animation) 1983; Univ. Laval, Maîtrise (Comm.) 1993. CAREER: Agente en planification et en programmation socio-sanitaire à l'Unité de santé publique du Centre hospitalier régional de Rimouski, 1982 to date; Chargée d'enseignement au Dépt. De médecine sociale et préventive de l'Univ. Laval, 1992 to date; Députée (Rimouski), Assemblée nationale, prov. de Qué. SELECTED PUBLICATIONS: numerous reports; "La force de l'expérience" (*Santé et Société* Fall 1986). AFFIL: Fondation québécoise pour la prévention des blessures (Cofondatrice; Conseil d'admin.); Maison des femmes de Rimouski (mbr. du conseil d'admin.); Parti Québécois (prés. du comté et Sec. du conseil exécutif régional, région Bas-du-Fleuve/Gaspésie/Îles-de-la-Madeleine); Centre hospitalier rég. de Rimouski (VP du conseil d'admin.); Association coopérative d'économie familiale (conseil d'admin.); Musée rég. de Rimouski (VP). COMMENT: *"Dans le cadre de mes fonctions comme députée, je me suis donné comme principal mandat la mise en place de structures favorisant le développement régional, tant au plan social, économique que culturel. Cet exercice se réalise et trouve sa place à l'intérieur du projet de souveraineté mis de l'avant par le Parti Québécois."*

Charlton, Margo, B.A. ■ ⊗ ☺ ➹

Cultural Consultant, Theatre Director and Facilitator. Owner, MARGOT CHARLTON CREATIVE SERVICES, 205 Walnut St., Winnipeg, MB R3G 1P4 (204) 775-5320, FAX 775-3664. Born Yorkshire, UK 1951. EDUC: Univ. of Manitoba, Assoc. Degree in Educ. 1971; Univ. of Winnipeg, B.A.(English/Drama) 1975; Univ. of Alberta, Drama & Dev. Credit Program 1983; various training workshops. CAREER: Dev. Educ. Officer, Manitoba Council for International Cooperation, 1980-84; Founder, Popular Theatre Alliance of Manitoba, 1980; Artistic Dir., 1985-94; Theatre/Touring Officer, Manitoba Arts Council. SELECTED CREDITS: Dir., *Bag Babies* (by Alan Stratton), Popular Theatre Alliance, 1994; Dir., *Short Shots* (various playwrights), Manitoba Association of Playwrights, 1993-94; Dir., *Hang Up* (Collective Creation), Testing Ground, 1993; Dir., *Heart Like a Donut* (Collective Creation), Queer Stages, 1995. SELECTED PUBLICATIONS: *Everybody's Business: A Community Manual.* AFFIL: Canadian Popular Theatre Alliance (Steering Committee 1983-94); Manitoba Association of Playwrights (Dir. 1995-96). HONS: nominated, YWCA Women of Distinction Award, 1994; Major Arts Grant (to conduct independent theatre research in the areas

of community play dev. in Canada & Cuba & contemporary Cdn gay & lesbian theatre), Manitoba Arts Council, 1995-96. MISC: grants from various associations incl. Manitoba Arts Council & the Canada Council; coordinated nat'l popular theatre festival, *Bread & Dreams*, 1984; drama instructor & lecturer; speaker & resource person for local, nat'l & int'l conferences & festivals focusing on the topic of popular theatre & popular educ. as a community organizing tool; Margot Charlton Creative Services is a mgmt & consulting co. for women performing artists. COMMENT: *"She is the founder of the Popular Theatre Alliance of Manitoba, a theatre company committed to creating theatre for social change. In addition to her work as a theatre director, Margo has developed a method of collectively creating plays with non-professionals to create theatre out of the participants' own lives and experiences. This work has addressed issues including: violence against women, unemployment, poverty, AIDS/HIV infections and the images of older women. She has worked with many organizations and community agencies to develop adult education methodology and training models. Her participatory creative techniques have been used by women's groups, literary agencies, disabled networks and international development coalitions."*

Charnetski, Joanne Louise, B.A., M.Sc. ■ Ⓢ ☺

President, JCI - GLOBAL STRATEGISTS, 15 Lakeside Ave., Ottawa, ON K1S 3H1 (613) 563-4932, FAX 563-4928. Vice-President, Market Development and Strategic Planning, CIC INTERNATIONAL TRADING (ASIA) LTD. Born Lethbridge, Alta. 1967. s. EDUC: Sarbonne Univ., Cert. (Med. Level French) 1986; Carleton Univ., B.A.(Econ.) 1990; Univ. of Rhode Island, M.Sc.(Industrial & Labor Rel'ns) 1992; George Washington Univ., Cert. (Cross Cultural Comm. & Diversity) 1992. CAREER: Jr. Assoc., Int'l Labour Office, Cdn Office, 1991-92; Sr. Proj. Assoc., Defence Industries Conversion Proj., Canadian Centre for Global Security, 1992-93; Pres., JCI - Global Strategists, 1993 to date; VP, CIC Int'l Trading (Asia) Ltd., 1996 to date. SELECTED PUBLICATIONS: "Canada, Ukraine and Nuclear Weapons: The Way Forward" with Tariq Rauf (*Ukraine-Canada Policy and Trade Monitor* 1993); "Energy Options for Ukraine to Replace the Chernobyl Nuclear Plant" with Tariq Rauf (*Ukraine-Canada Policy and Trade Monitor* 1994); "Swords into Ploughshares: Canada Could Play Key Role in Transforming Nuclear Arms Material into Electricity" with Tariq Rauf (*The Ottawa Citizen* Aug. 22, 1994); "Let

Canada Cremate Nuclear Swords" with Tariq Rauf (*Defence News* Oct. 1994); "Foreign Policy Challenges: Canada Can't Protect Sovereignty or Quality of Life in Isolation" with Tariq Rauf (*The Ottawa Citizen* Nov. 17, 1994). **DIRECTOR:** Canada-Russia Bus. Faciliation Corp.; The Power Card Team. **AFFIL:** Ukrainian Canadian Professional & Business Association (Promo. Dir.); Ukrainian Canadian Congress; Canadian Association of International Development Consultants; International Development & Research Society; Society for Intercultural Education, Training & Research; various embassies and high commision's around the world. **HONS:** Labor Rel'ns State Award for Recognition of Outstanding Efforts in the Area of Labor & Industrial Rel'ns, Providence, R.I., 1992; univ. letter for varsity rowing, Carleton Univ., 1989. **INTERESTS:** competitive varsity rowing; competitive figure skating (1974-85); world travel; goumet cooking; mountain biking; rock climbing; snow skiing. **COMMENT:** *"Finishing in the top five of her graduating class and believing in the importance of strategic planning and cross-cultural industrial relations at both the national and international levels, Joanne is a results-oriented professional with strong problem-solving, communicative and management skills. As founder of JCI and VP of CIC, she undertakes a synergistic approach to inform, and sustain Canadian involvement in global ventures."*

Charron, Louise, B.A.,LL.B. ◼ 🔲
Justice, COURT OF APPEAL FOR ONTARIO, 130 Queen St. W., Toronto, ON M5H 2N5 (416) 327-5000, FAX 327-6241. Born Sturgeon Falls, Ont. 1951. m. William Blake. 1 ch. 2 stepch. **EDUC:** Carleton Univ., B.A.(Psych.) 1972; Univ. of Ottawa, LL.B. 1975. **BAR:** Ont., 1977. **CAREER:** private practice of law, Lalonde, Chartrand, Charron and Gouin, 1977-80; Asst. Crown Attorney, 1980-85; Asst. Prof., Fac. of Law, Univ. of Ottawa, 1985-88; Judge, Ottawa District Court, 1988-90; Justice, Ont. Court of Justice (Gen. Div.), 1990-95; Justice, Court of Appeal for Ont., 1995 to date. **SELECTED PUBLICATIONS:** *The Canadian Criminal Jury*, with others (Carswell, 1985). **AFFIL:** National Judicial Institute (Assoc. Dir. 1994 to date).

Chaudaquock (Tahltan First Nation Name), Vera Asp ◼ 🔲🔲🔲
Vice-President, First Nations Programs and Services, YUKON COLLEGE, Box 2799, Whitehorse, YT Y1A 5K4 (403) 668-8715, FAX 668-8896. Born Good Hope Lake, B.C. 4 ch. Vernon Asp, Rosemary Asp, Reg McGinty, Rueben McGinty. **EDUC:** Trent Univ., Peterborough,

Native Studies Diploma Program 1975-76; various workshops & dev. projects. **CAREER:** Justice of the Peace III, Dept. of Justice, 1982 to date; Substitute Teacher, J.V. Clark Elementary & High Sch., 1986-90; Substitute Instructor, Yukon Coll., Mayo Campus, 1984-90; Asst. to VP, Instructional Svcs, 1990-92; VP, First Nations Programs & Svcs, 1992 to date. **VOLUNTEER CAREER:** Pres., Yukon Native Youth Association, 1973; Coord., Int'l Women's Year, Yukon Program, 1975; Coord. & Ed., Association of United Tahltans, May-Sept. 1976; est. community land claims offices & provided liaison support to community offices & head office, 1976-77; Coord., founding meeting, CYI Elders, Summer 1977; Coord., Yukon Association of Non-Status Indians Annual Assembly & the Native Council of Canada Nat'l Bd. Meeting, Mar.-June 1978; Nat'l Native Alcohol & Drug Counsellor with the Nacho Nyak Dun, 1985-87; Ministerial Advisory Committee on Substance Abuse, 1986-88; Coord., Circumpolar Youth Healing Conference, 1987; Coord., Mayo Campus Cultural Week, 1990-91. **SELECTED CREDITS:** Writer/Co-Prod., *Little Voice in the Dark* (short video), 1992. **SELECTED PUBLICATIONS:** journalist & photographer, *Yukon Indian News*, 1979; author, children's books (Northern Native theme); wrote & assisted in publication, 6 videos for CBC *Sesame Street* program; author, various Mayo Indian Band position papers. **AFFIL:** Yukon Education Council (Min. appointee); Women's Legal Education & Action Fund (LEAF) (Yukon Mbr. 1990-93); Yukon Coll. (Co-V-Chair, Bd. of Gov. 1990). **MISC:** only Yukon delegate in Cdn delegation to the 10th World Youth Festival, East Berlin, 1973; 1st First Nations Justice to sentence in "Circle" in Canada (Regina vs. Moses), 1988.

Chee Wah, Immee, B.A. ◼◼ / $
Publisher, *Maclean's* Chinese Edition, MACLEAN HUNTER PUBLISHING LIMITED (publishing), 777 Bay St., Toronto, ON M5W 1A7 (416) 596-5324, FAX 596-6001 email: 76504.2550@compuserve.ca Director of Business Operations, MACLEAN'S MAGAZINE Born Macao. s. **EDUC:** Univ. of Toronto, B.A. 1980; Western Exec. Program 1994. **CAREER:** Group Circulation Dir., *Maclean's*, *L'Actualité*, *Flare*, 1987-90; Bus. Mgr, *Maclean's*, 1990-92; Dir. of Bus. Oper., 1992 to date. **AFFIL:** Hong Kong Canada Business Association.

Cheechoo, Shirley 🔲🔲 ⊗
Artist, Writer and Performer. c/o The Talent Group Limited, 401 Richmond St. W., Ste. 401, Toronto, ON M5V 3A8 (416) 408-3304 or (705) 377-4141. **SELECTED CREDITS:**

Prod./Writer/Dir./Actor, *Silent Tears* (TV drama); Ma Crow, *The Rez* (series); Cindy, *Medicine River* (feature), Medicine River Productions; Host/Writer, *Full Circle: Native Way*, (series) TVOntario; Judy, "The Wake," *Daughters of the Country*, National Film Bd.; Doris, *Spirit Bay* (series), Spirit Bay Productions; *Spirits Speaking Through* (documentary), CBC; Narrator, *Mistaben* (radio), CBC Radio; Writer/Prod./Composer/Actor (Shirley), *Path With No Moccasins* (theatre); Sophie, *Magnificent Voice of Emily Carr* (theatre), Belfry Theatre, Victoria; Writer/Prod./Actor (Linda), *Tangled Sheets* (theatre), FOCUS & West Bay of the Arts; various, *Son of Ayash* (theatre), Native Earth Performing Arts; Annie Cook & Marie Adele, *The Rez Sisters* (theatre), various productions; Dir., *Toronto at Dreamers Rock* (theatre), The Globe Theatre, Regina; Co-Writer, *Nothing Personal* (theatre), De-Ba-Jeh-Mu-Jig Theatre; Dir., *Emergency* (theatre), West Bay Children's Theatre; performer at various nat'l & int'l festivals; opening act for Buffy Ste Marie (West Bay, Ont.) & Blue Rodeo (Wikwemikong, Ont.). **SELECTED PUBLICATIONS:** illustrations for various books & magazines. **COMMISSIONS:** numerous commissions incl.: 1992 UNICEF Christmas card; various posters; Amnesty International Christmas card; Hospital for Sick Children Christmas card, 1983. **EXHIBITIONS:** numerous exhibitions incl.: Homer Watson Gallery, Kitchener, 1986; Whetung's Native Gallery, Curve Lake, Ont., 1985; Kasheese Studios, West Bay, Ont., 1982-86; Contemporary Indian & Inuit Art of Canada Touring Exhibition, 1983-85; Buckhorn Wildlife Art Festival, Ont., 1983 & 1985. **COLLECTIONS:** numerous collections incl.: Dept. of Indian & Northern Dev., Ottawa; Dofasco, Inc.; Women Teachers' Federation; McMichael Canadian Collection; Royal Ontario Museum; Air Canada; Dr. Bernard Cinader; Roy McMurtry; Walter Engel; Eric & Rita Levitt. **AFFIL:** ACTRA; EQUITY; SOCAN. **HONS:** Eagle Spirit Award, San Francisco American Indian Festival; CTV Fellowship Award, Banff Film Festival; various Canada Council & Ont. Arts Council awards; D.L.(Hon), Laurentian Univ. **MISC:** has completed various writing & performing workshops; has assisted in casting native talent for various film & TV productions; Founder & Artistic Dir., De-Ba-Jeh-Mu-Jig Theatre.

Chellas, Merry, B.A.,M.A.,A.P.R., A.B.C. $ ✎

Principal, CHELLAS COMMUNICATION, 2755 Cannon Rd. N.W., Calgary, AB (403) 282-4923, FAX 282-4223, EMAIL chellasm@tcel.com. Born New York City 1940. m. Brian Farrell Chellas. 1 ch. Anne Morehouse. **EDUC:** Florida State Univ., B.A.(English/Phil.) 1962; Stanford Univ., M.A.(Comm./Journalism) 1968. **CAREER:** Lifestyle Reporter, *Palo Alto Times*, California, 1965-68; News Officer, Univ. of Pennsylvania, 1974-75; Ed., *Calgary Women's Newspaper*, 1976-78; various positions, Nova Corporation, 1979-84; Mgr, Corp. Comm., Nova Corporation, 1984-90; Exec. Dir., Petroleum Communication Foundation, 1991-93; VP, Canadian Association of Petroleum Producers, 1995. **AFFIL:** Canadian Public Relations Society (Pres., Calgary chapter 1988-89; Nat'l Bd.; Accredited Public Rel'ns); International Association of Business Communication (Accredited Bus. Communicator); Calgary Free-Net Association (Founding Bd. 1993-96); EECOM Environmental Education Network; Dissemination Adv. Committee; Alberta Heritage Fdn for Med. Research.

Chernecki, Vera, R.N. ■■ ✊ ⊕

President, MANITOBA NURSES' UNION (labour union), 275 Broadway, Ste. 502, Winnipeg, MB R3C 4M6 (204) 942-1320, FAX 942-0958. Born Ethelbert, Man. 1941. m. Raymond. 4 ch. Denise, Donna, Lisa, Leanne. **EDUC:** St. Boniface Sch. of Nursing, R.N. Diploma 1962. **CAREER:** Registered Nurse, St. Boniface Grace Hospital/Oakview Place Nursing Home; Pres., Manitoba Nurses' Union, 1981 to date. **AFFIL:** National Federation of Nurses' Unions, NFNU (Nat'l Officer, Bd. of Dir. 1981 to date); Univ. of Manitoba (Bd. of Continuing Educ.). **HONS:** Gov. Gen.'s Commemorative Award for contribution to community & Canada, 1992; Bread & Roses Award, NFNU, 1995.

Chilton, Meredith, B.A.(Hons.) ✪

Curator, THE GEORGE R. GARDINER MUSEUM OF CERAMIC ART, 111 Queen's Park, Toronto, ON M5S 2C7 (416) 586-8080, FAX 586-8085. Born UK 1953. m. David Chilton. 1 ch. Thomas. **EDUC:** Univ. of East Anglia, B.A. (Hons., Art Hist.) 1979; Manchester Univ., Post-Grad. Diploma in Museum Studies 1980. **CAREER:** Curator, Mildenhall Museum, Suffolk, UK, 1977-78; Curatorial Asst., Gibson House Museum, Toronto, 1981-83; Curator, Gardiner Museum, 1983 to date; Fac. Mbr., M.A. Program, Grad. Center for Studies in the Decorative Arts, Bard Coll., N.Y., 1994 to date. **SELECTED CREDITS:** involved in the dev. of the concept, provided the research, storyline, selection of objects & narration for 4 short films for CBC Arts Entertainment: *Scented Treasures*, 1994; *Soviet Porcelain*, 1994; *Amazing Glazing Gazing*, 1994; *The Commedia dell'arte*, 1994. **SELECTED PUBLICATIONS:** *A Taste of Elegance, 18th Century English Porce-*

lain from Private Collections in Ontario, exhibition catalogue, with J.P. Palmer (1986); "'Hausmaler' Decorated Porcelain" (*The International Ceramic Fair & Seminar Journal*, June 1987); *The Meissen Collection of Robert T. Anderson*, catalogue of collection, by Allen, Armin *et al*, ed. of all preliminary essays (Orlando Museum of Art, 1988); introduction, *Bottger Stoneware, Bottger Porcelain and Hausmalerei* (1988); section intro. "Technical Masterpieces: Creating Porcelain Figures," *Figures from Life: Porcelain Sculpture from the Metropolitan Museum of Art*, by Cynthia David (Jan. 1992); "Rooms of Porcelain" (*The International Ceramic Fair & Seminar Journal*, June 1992); "Chelsea Gold Anchor Period Rococo Vases," *Versailles: French Court Style and Its Influence*, ed. Howard C. Collinson (1992); "Perfume and Porcelain in the 18th Century Bedroom," *The Bedroom: From the Renaissance to Art Deco*, ed. of the publication of the lectures (Univ. of Toronto, Sch. of Continuing Studies, 1995); *Treasurers of the George R. Gardiner Museum of Ceramic Art*, with J.P. Palmer (the handbook of the Museum, 1984); "A Fugitive Pleasure: Perfume in the 18th Century," *Best Canadian Essays*, ed. Doug Featherling (Fifth House Publishers, 1990). **EXHIBITIONS:** curator, *White Gold: The Discovery of Meissen Porcelain* (Mar. 96-Jan. 97); on-site curator, *News from a Radiant Future*, Art Institute of Chicago (Spring 1994); on-site curator, *Figures from Life*, travelling exhibition (Fall 1992); curator, *Porcelain Boxes*, Gardiner Museum (Fall 1991); joint curator, *Ceramics of the French Revolution*, Gardiner Museum (July-Sept. 1989); curator & prod., *Painters and the Derby China Works*, Gardiner Museum (Oct. 1988-Jan. 1989); 8 other exhibits curated & produced at the Gardiner from 1984-88. **AFFIL:** American Ceramic Circle (Bd. 1985-93; Ed. 1987-93); English Ceramic Circle; Gesellschaft der Keramikfreunde; Keramic-Freunde der Schweiz; The French Porcelain Society. **HONS:** *Porcelain Boxes* exhibit judged The Most Exquisite Fine Arts Show in Canada, 1991, *Sunday Sun Fine Arts Best of '91 Review*. **INTERESTS:** hist. of porcelain & its social uses; hist. of dining.

Ching, Denise, B.Sc.,M.B.A.,C.F.A. $

Vice-President, Portfolio Manager, ROYAL BANK INVESTMENT MANAGEMENT INC., Royal Centre, 1055 W. Georgia St., Ste. 2100, Box 11105, Vancouver, BC V7S 3G5 (604) 665-0176, FAX 665-0180. Born Hong Kong 1952. m. Robert. 2 ch. Casey, Samantha. **EDUC:** Univ. of Toronto, B.Sc.(Food Sci.) 1975; Univ. of British Columbia, M.B.A.(Fin. & Int'l Bus.); Chart. Fin. Analyst 1982. **CAREER:** Fixed Income Analyst, Pemberton Securities, 1978-81; Portfolio Mgr, Pemberton Securities, RBC Dominion Securities, 1981-93; VP, Royal Bank Investment Management, 1993 to date. **AFFIL:** Univ. of British Columbia Portfolio Mgmt Society; BC Lions Foundation for Children with Disabilities (Dir.); Vancouver Society of Financial Analysts (Advocacy Committee); Association of Investment Management & Research; Chartered Financial Analyst. **INTERESTS:** knowing more about cultures & customs of other nations & their people. **MISC:** interviewed several times on TV & in magazines. **COMMENT:** *"I am an independent forward-thinking person who wants to use the best of my abilities for my profession, and maintain a balance between work and family."*

Ching, Hilda, B.A.,M.S., Ph.D. ⚛ $ 🎓

Consultant, HYDRA ENTERPRISES LTD., Box 2184, Vancouver, BC V6B 3V7 (604) 736-0757, FAX 687-4125. Born Honolulu 1934. m. Joe Quan. 3 ch. Walter, Thomas, Andrew. **EDUC:** Oregon State Univ., B.A.(Zoology) 1956, M.S.(Zoology) 1957; Univ. of Nebraska, Ph.D.(Zoology) 1959. **CAREER:** Asst. Parasitologist, Univ. of Hawaii, 1959-60; Research Assoc., Univ. of British Columbia, 1960-74; Lecturer, Simon Fraser Univ., Douglas Coll., 1974-79; Parasitologist, Envirocon Ltd., 1979-85; self-employed consultant, Hydra Enterprises, 1986-90; Ruth Wynn Woodward Endowed Prof., Women's Studies, Simon Fraser Univ., 1990-91; Advisor, Eastern Indonesia Universities Proj., 1995-96. **SELECTED PUBLICATIONS:** 45 on parasitology; 5 on women in science. **AFFIL:** Society for Canadian Women in Science & Technology (Founding Mbr.; Pres. 1984-86, 1994-95); American Society of Parasitologists; Helminthological Society of Washington; Association for Women in Science; Premier's Advisory Council on Science & Technology; Knowledge Network Planning Council; Green Coll. Community Fac. **HONS:** Women of Distinction Award, YWCA, 1991. **INTERESTS:** women in science; Chinese antiques; gardening.

Ching, Julia, B.A.,M.A.,Ph.D.,L.H.D 🎓 📜

University Professor, Victoria College, UNIVERSITY OF TORONTO, Toronto, ON M5S 1K7 (416) 585-4407, FAX 585-4584, EMAIL jching@chass.utoronto.ca. Born Shanghai 1934. m. Willard G. Oxtoby. 2 stepch.: David Oxtoby, Susan Oxtoby; 1 adopted ch.: John Ching. **EDUC:** Coll. of New Rochelle, N.Y., B.A.(Liberal Arts) 1958; Catholic Univ. of America, M.A.(European Hist.) 1961; Australian National Univ., Ph.D.(Asian Phil.) 1972;

St. Andrew's Coll., NC, L.H.D. 1993. **CAREER:** Lecturer, Australian National Univ., 1971-74; Assoc. Prof., Columbia Univ., 1974-75; Assoc. Prof., Yale Univ., 1975-78; Assoc. Prof., Univ. of Toronto, 1978-81; Full Prof., 1981-94; Univ. Prof., Victoria Coll., 1994 to date. **SELECTED PUBLICATIONS:** twelve books, incl. *Probing China's Soul* (Harper, 1990); *Chinese Religions* (London: Macmillan, 1993). **AFFIL:** Chinese Cultural Centre of Greater Toronto (Hon. Advisor); Royal Society of Canada (Fellow; Counsellor, Academy II); Canadian Pugwash Group; NGO Religious Consultation for Population, Reproductive Health & Ethics. **INTERESTS:** comparative phil. & religion; East Asian (esp. Chinese) culture. **COMMENT:** *"I see myself as interpreter of East Asia for the West, and attempt to make East Asian thought more relevant for problems such as environment, population, gender, etc."*

Chir-Stimpson, Susanne, B.A., M.A. ■ $ ✿ ⊕
President, STRATEGIC SOLUTIONS, 5508 Durie Rd., Mississauga, ON L5M 5R2 (905) 826-9493, FAX 819-1057. Born Montreal. **EDUC:** CEGEP Bourgchemin Saint-Hyacinthe, Textile Chem. Dip. 1974; Concordia Univ., B.A. (English) 1981; York Univ., M.A.(English) 1986. **CAREER:** Parenteral Worker, Schering Inc., 1971-72; Printing & Textile Technician, CIBA-Geigy Canada Ltd., 1972-76; *CHIMO* Ed., 1976-80; Mgr, Public Rel'ns, 1980-84; Dir., Corp. Rel'ns, 1984-90; VP, Decima Research, 1990; VP, Glaxo Canada Inc., 1990-95; Pres., Strategic Solutions, 1995 to date. **AFFIL:** Credit Valley Hospital Foundation (Bd. of Dir.); Canadian Public Relations Society; International Association of Business Communicators; Canadian Science Writers' Association; York Univ. Alumni; Concordia Univ. Alumni; Canadian Association of Textile Chemists & Colourists; Canadian Chamber of Commerce (Ottawa Liaison Committee). **MISC:** Creator of Issues Management Model, educational game, Three Hat Model.

Chisholm, Sharon, B.A. ⊕ ✤ ○
Executive Director, CANADIAN HOUSING AND RENEWAL ASSOCIATION, 251 Laurier Ave., Ste. 401, Ottawa, ON K1P 5J6 (613) 594-3007, FAX 594-9596, EMAIL chra@web.net. Born Sydney, N.S. 1951. d. 2 ch. Geneviève, Joshua. **EDUC:** Dalhousie Univ., B.A.(Soc.) 1973; Carleton Univ., Masters in Cdn Studies in progress. **CAREER:** Co-Mgr, Access Housing, 1982-88; Dir. of Housing, City of Dartmouth, N.S., 1985-88; Mgr, Proj. Planning, City of Ottawa, 1988-94; Exec. Dir., Canadian Housing & Renewal Association, 1994 to date.

Chislett, Anne, B.A. ⊕ 📖 🖊
Playwright. c/o Robert A. Freedman Dramatic Agency Inc., 1501 Broadway, Ste. 2310, New York, NY 10036. (416) 920-8231 or (519) 524-8651. Born St. John's 1942. sep. **EDUC:** Memorial Univ. of Newfoundland, B.A. (English) 1964; Univ. of British Columbia, grad. studies in theatre. **CAREER:** Co-Founder, Blyth Festival, 1975; Assoc. Dir., Blyth Festival, 1975-78. **SELECTED CREDITS:** *A Summer Burning*, adapted from the novel by Harry J. Boyle, Blyth Festival, 1977; *The Tomorrow Box*, Kawartha Theatre, 1980; *Quiet in the Land*, Blyth Festival, 1981; *Another Season's Promise*, with Keith Roulston, Blyth Festival, 1986; *Half a Chance*, Lighthouse Theatre, 1987; *The Gift*, for young audiences, Carousel Theatre, 1987; *Yankee Notions* (radio play), Morningside, CBC, 1989; *Rat Calculus* (radio play), Canadian Free Theatre, 1989; *Off the Deep End* (radio play), Morningside, CBC, 1990; *Venus Sucked In* (radioplay), Morningside, CBC, 1991; *Chandler's Mill* (feature), based on a story by Joan Henson, National Film Board, 1991; *Yankee Notions*, Blyth Festival, 1992; *Glengarry School Days*, with Janet Amos, based on the novels by Ralph Connor, Blyth Festival, 1994; *Flippin' In*, Young People's Theatre, 1995. **SELECTED PUBLICATIONS:** *The Tomorrow Box* (Toronto: Playwrights Press, 1980); *Quiet in the Land* (Toronto: Coach House Press, 1983); *Another Season's Promise*, with Keith Roulston (New York: Dramatists' Play Service, 1986); *The Tomorrow Box*, translated by Toyoshi Yoshihara (*Teatro Magazine*, Tokyo 1989); *Venus Sucked In*, in *Airborne* (Winnipeg: Blizzard, 1991); *Yankee Notions* (Toronto: Playwrights Press, 1993). **AFFIL:** Playwrights' Union of Canada; ACTRA. **HONS:** Chalmers, Canadian Play Award (*Quiet in the Land*), 1982; Gov. General's Award for Drama (*Quiet in the Land*), 1983; W.C. Good Award, Ont. Federation of Agriculture (*Another Season's Promise*), 1986; Best Production, Hiroshima (*The Tomorrow Box*), (Bunkaza Theatre); Chalmers Award Theatre Young-Audience (*Flippin' In*). **INTERESTS:** bridge; gardening. **MISC:** 'study' in *Playwriting Women* (1994); numerous professional productions; *The Tomorrow Box* translated into Japanese & French.

Chodan, Lucinda, B.Ed. 📖 🖊 ⌂
Entertainment Editor, THE GAZETTE, 250 Saint-Antoine W., Montreal, QC H2Y 3R7 (514) 987-2460, FAX 987-2638. Contributing Editor, COUNTRY MAGAZINE. Born Edmonton 1955. s. **EDUC:** Univ. of Alberta, B.Ed. 1979. **CAREER:** Entertainment Writer, *Edmonton Sun*, 1981-84; Entertainment Features Writer,

The Gazette, 1984-87; Asst. Entertainment Ed., 1987-88; Asst. Sunday Ed., 1989-90; Journalism Teacher, Concordia Univ., 1989-90; Sunday Ed., *The Gazette*, 1990-91; Sr. News Ed., 1991-93; TV Scriptwriter, *Urban Angel*, CBC-TV, 1991-92; Asst. Mng Ed., *The Gazette*, 1993-94; Entertainment Ed., 1994 to date; Contributing Ed., *Country Magazine*; Mgr/Songwriter, folk-country-bluegrass band Steel Rail. **SELECTED PUBLICATIONS:** published in *Country Magazine, The Toronto Star, Edmonton Magazine*, & *Great Canadian Character Anthology* (Eden Press); Ed., *Buntys and Pinkies: Chronicals of a New Canadian* (Robert Davies Publishing, 1996). **AFFIL:** Songwriters' Association of Canada; SOCAN. **HONS:** Bd. of Governors' Prize in Educ., Univ. of Alberta, 1976; National Newspaper Award for Feature Writing, 1987; National Newspaper Certificate of Merit, Enterprise Reporting, 1987. **INTERESTS:** songwriting; music generally; the arts; travel; literature. **COMMENT:** *"I believe I am a hard-working and innovative journalist and writer committed to the pursuit of excellence in all kinds of writing and to the passing on of a love of words and music to those who follow me."*

Chong, Vivian Yuen Fun, B.A. ■ /
News Editor, MING PAO NEWSPAPERS (CANADA) LTD., 1355 Huntingwood Dr., Scarborough, ON M1S 3J1 (416) 321-0088, ext. 258, FAX 321-3499. Born Hong Kong. s. **EDUC:** Hong Kong Shue Yan Coll., Diploma (Journalism) 1983; Concordia Univ., B.A.(Pol. Sci.) 1993. **CAREER:** Summer Intern, *South China Morning Post*, 1982; Chief Reporter, Educational & Cultural News Page, Express News Ltd., 1983-87; Sr. Reporter, *Hong Kong Ming Pao Daily News*, 1987-91; Asst. News Ed., Ming Pao Newspapers (Canada) Ltd., 1991-95; News Ed., 1995 to date. **SELECTED PUBLICATIONS:** numerous special reports in Hong Kong newspapers and in *Ming Pao* (Canada Edition). **INTERESTS:** travel; movies; writing; taking photographs; cultural & arts activities; listening to music; cooking & eating. **COMMENT:** *"My several years of experience in journalistic work have established for me an extensive knowledge of the political and social scene in Hong Kong and Canada. My sharp news sense, together with my keen and persistent interest in journalistic work, has often led to exclusive stories on issues untouched by others. I am dedicated to promoting journalism as a professional field and an independent one, which is so indispensable to a society."*

Chouinard, Josée ■ ■ ⊘ ⊗
Figure Skater. c/o International Management

Group, 1 St. Clair Ave. E., Ste. 700, Toronto, ON M4T 2V7 (416) 960-5312, FAX 960-0564. Born Rosemont, Que. 1969. **SPORTS CAREER:** Canadian Championships: 7th place finish, 1989; 3rd place finish, 1990; 2nd place finish, 1992; 1st place finish, 1991, 1993, 1994; int'l competitions: 1st, Vienna, 1989; 1st, Skate Canada, 1990; 9th, Olympics, 1992; 5th, World Championships, 1992; 9th, World Championships, 1993; 9th, Olympics, 1994; 3rd, Skate Canada, 1995; 1st, Trophée de France, 1995; as professional skater (from July-Dec. 1994 - reinstated as amateur, Apr. 1995): 1st, Toyota Canadian Professional Figure Skating Championships; 2nd, North American Open. **MISC:** named one of "Top 5 Best-Dressed Women in Canada," *The Globe & Mail*, 1994; commentated for TVA, Canadian Figure Skating Championships, Halifax, 1994. **COMMENT:** *"Josée won three Canadian Ladies' Championships and finished in the top ten at the two most recent Winter Olympic Games. Her best showing at the World Championships was a fifth place finish in 1992. In her first year as a professional, Josée won the 1994 Toyota Canadian Professional Figure Skating Championship."*

Christakos, Margaret, M.A., B.F.A. ■ ⊗ ▯ ▤
Editor, *MIX: THE MAGAZINE OF ARTIST-RUN CULTURE*, 401 Richmond St. W., Ste. 446, Toronto, ON M5V 3A8 (416) 506-1012, FAX 340-8458. Founding Publisher, PARALLÉLOGRAMME ARTIST-RUN CULTURE AND PUBLISHING, INC. Born Sudbury, Ont. 1962. cl. Bryan Gee. 1 ch. **EDUC:** York Univ., B.F.A.(Visual Arts) 1985; Univ. of Toronto, M.A.(Hist. & Phil. of Educ.) 1995. **CAREER:** Ed., *Fuse* Magazine, 1987-88; Poetry Ed., *Women's Education des femmes*, 1990-92; Ed. & Dir., *Fireweed* 1991-94; Co-Ed., *MIX: the magazine of artist-run culture*, 1994 to date; Instructor, Creative Writing, The Ontario Coll. of Art; writer, freelance editor & production coord. for feminist & art-based organizations. **SELECTED PUBLICATIONS:** *Other Words for Grace*, poetry (The Mercury Press, 1994); *Not Egypt*, poetry (Coach House Press, 1989); Contributor, *The Last Word*, ed. Michael Holmes (Insomniac Press, 1995); Contributor, *Plural Desires*, bisexual women's anthology (Sistervision Press, 1995); "Axioms to Grind" (*Room of One's Own*, Dec. 1989). **INTERESTS:** poetry; anti-censorship; children's rights; visual arts; cultural & critical ideas & writing; feminist practice & philosophy. **COMMENT:** *"For the past 12 years I have developed skills and experience working in the alternative arts and writing communities, challenging my comfort level by examining my own*

practices and the world outside through a feminist, inquiring, risk-taking lens interested in compassionate community and individual excellence."

Christensen, Ione J., A.A.,C.M. 🏃 📖
Photographer and Writer. 26 Takhini Ave., Whitehorse, YT Y1A 3N4 (403) 667-7390, FAX 667-7390. Born Dawson Creek, B.C. 1933. m. Art K. 2 ch. **EDUC:** Coll. of San Mateo, San Mateo, CA, Assoc.A. 1955. **CAREER:** various positions, Gov't of Yukon Territory, 1958-67; home with children & community volunteer, 1967-71; various positions, incl. Juvenile Court Judge (fed. appt.) & Justice of the Peace, Gov't of Yukon Territory, 1971-75; Mayor, City of Whitehorse, 1975-79; Commissioner of Yukon, Gov't of Canada, 1979; Pres., Hospitality North, 1981-86; Chair, Yukon Placer Mining Guidelines Review Committee, 1983-84; Chief, R.T.S., EMR Programs Office, Whitehorse, Energy, Mines & Resources Canada, 1984-89; Bd. Mbr, Yukon Squatter Appeal Bd., 1988; Exec. Dir., Yukon Foundation; Exec. Sec., Yukon Outfitters; Ptnr, Cameras North, 1985 to date. **SELECTED CREDITS:** *Outdoor Reporter*, weekly summer program, CBC Radio. **SELECTED PUBLICATIONS:** 3 books of photography, *Whitehorse the Wilderness City*, *Klane the Wilderness Park*, *Chilkoot the Goldrush Trail*; writings published in *Up Here Magazine*, *Canada Fiction Magazine*, *My Canada*, & the Yukon anthology *Writing North*. **AFFIL:** Yukon Outdoors Club; Northern Writers' Circle; Crossroads. **HONS:** appointed a Mbr. of the Order of Canada, 1995. **INTERESTS:** hiking; backpacking; skiing; bicycling; writing; gym workout. **MISC:** Chair, Advisory Committee on Waste Mgmt, Gov't of Yukon, 1989-92. **COMMENT:** *"A fourth-generation Yukoner who has had the good fortune to have opportunity knock many times. With good organizing skills, a gift for diplomacy and a supportive husband, Christensen has seized each opportunity and taken it to a conclusion."*

Christensen, Rosemary L., B.A.,B.C.L. $
President, SOMERVILLE HOUSE GROUP OF COMPANIES, 4333 Ste. Catherine St. W., Ste. 610, Montreal, QC H3Z 1P9 (514) 935-2445, FAX 935-8161. Secretary-Treasurer, O.T. MINING CORPORATION. Born Walton-on-Thames, Surrey, UK 1941. s. **EDUC:** McGill Univ., B.A. 1964, B.C.L. 1967. **BAR:** Que., 1968. **DIRECTOR:** Somerville House Group of Companies; O.T. Mining Corporation. **AFFIL:** The North Hatley Club Inc. **COMMENT:** *"Was a pioneer in Canadian movie tax shelter syndication. Was involved in the production and/or financing of some 16 motion pictures. Formed own specialized brokerage firm to market both tax shelters and mutual funds. Currently active in mineral exploration in both the U.S. and Canada."*

Christie, Dinah ■■ 🎭 $ ✊
President, DINAH CHRISTIE PRESENTS (entertainment), R.R. #1, Holstein, ON N0G 2A0 (519) 323-1380, FAX 323-3623. President, BADD SISTERS. Born London, UK 1942. m. Robert Warren. **EDUC:** North Toronto Collegiate, 1955-60. **SELECTED CREDITS:** born into theatrical family; started career at age 13 as call boy, Stratford Festival Theatre; soon on stage; resident mbr. of Company, 4 seasons; toured Holiday Inn circuit as singer, early 1960s; singing hostess, *This Hour Has Seven Days*; starred with Tom Kneebone in *Ding Dong at the Dell*, Theatre-in-the-Dell, Toronto, 1965; led to numerous other successful collaborations in following yrs. with Tom Kneebone, incl. show on Broadway; cabaret show, *D.C. and Friends*, 1979; became regular Mon. morning feature on *Morningside*, CBC Radio; TV appearances incl. mbr., *Party Game*, charade show, 10 yrs.; writes musicals, film scripts, children's TV show; performs with several symphony orchestras, & in revues; role in *Crazy For You*, 1995; film producer, *The Martello Tower Hamlet*, 1996. **HONS:** Best Variety Performer Award, *The Telegram*, 1965; nominated for Best Supporting Actress (CBC film *One Night Stand*), 1978; ACTRA Award for Best Variety Performer, 1980 & 1985; Gemini Award for Best Actress in Comedy Series (*Check It Out*), 1987; Nelly Awards for *Dinah Christie & Friends* (CBC TV) & *Tom & Dinah* (CBC Radio). **MISC:** inventor, shoe heel protector "Hot Heels"; formed Badd Sisters ("Blondes Against Drunk Drivers"), cottage industry to fabricate "Hot Heels" & other enviro-friendly natural cotton products incl. the Ultra-Visor.

Christie, Nancy P., Dip.P&OT,B.A., C.A.E. ■■ ✊ ♥ ⊕
President, NPC CONSULTING (rehab. & disability issues; association & proj. mgmt), 33 Alamosa Dr., Willowdale, ON M2J 2N6 (416) 222-6164, FAX 222-2570, EMAIL nancy.christie@utoronto.ca. Executive Director, INTERNATIONAL SOCIETY OF AUGMENTATIVE AND ALTERNATIVE COMMUNICATION. Born Toronto 1941. m. Edward A. 2 ch. **EDUC:** Univ. of Toronto, Dip.(Phys. & Occupational Therapy) 1962; Univ. of Western Ontario, B.A.(Pol. Sci.) 1967; Canadian Society of Association Executives, Certified Association Exec. 1985. **CAREER:** Phys. Therapist, CUSO, Nagpur, India, 1962-63; Phys. Therapist, St. Joseph's Hospital, Toronto, 1964-65; Asst. Supervisor, Physio-

therapy, St. Michael's Hospital, 1967-70; Exec. Dir., Canadian Physiotherapy Association, 1979-87; Nat'l Exec. Dir., Canadian Rehabilitation Council for the Disabled, 1987-92; Principal, NPC Consulting, 1992 to date; Exec. Dir., International Society of Augmentative & Alternative Communication, 1996 to date. **SELECTED PUBLICATIONS:** "Community-Based Rehabilitation in the Rupununi, Guyana" (*Rehabilitation Digest* 26:3, 1996); "Client Service Facilitator: A Contemporary Approach to Assisting Clients and their Families" (*Rehabilitation Digest* 26:4, 1996); editor, *Entry-Level Curriculum for Canadian Physical Therapy Programs* (Toronto: The Council of Directors of Physical Therapy Academic Programs/The Canadian Physiotherapy Association, 1995); papers for presentation at int'l conferences/workshops, etc. **AFFIL:** International Centre for the Advancement of Community-Based Rehabilitation, Queen's Univ. (Chair, Bd. of Dir. 1991-94; Convenor, Demonstration Projects 1994 to date; mbr., Bd. of Dir. 1991 to date); Univ. of Toronto (Coll. of Electors 1994 to date; Exec. Committee, Physical & Occupational Therapy Alumni Association 1994 to date); Georgian Bay Land Trust Foundation, Inc. (Bd. of Dir. 1995 to date); Sans Souci and Copperhead Association (Past Pres. 1992 to date); Georgian Bay Association (Bd. of Dir. 1994 to date). **HONS:** Honour Award, Award of Merit, Univ. of Toronto, 1962; Canada 125 Medal, 1992; Certificate of Appreciation, Rehabilitation International, 1993. **COMMENT:** *"Nancy Christie is active nationally and internationally promoting quality of life issues for persons with disabilities, and addressing health and environmental concerns as they affect ordinary Canadians."*

Christopher, Jeannette B., R.N. ⊕ ☜ ✿
Staff Education Co-ordinator, WESTERN MEMORIAL REGIONAL HOSPITAL, Brookfield Ave., Box 2005, Corner Brook, NF A2H 6J7 (709) 637-5360, FAX 632-5111. President, GREAT HUMBER JOINT COUNCIL. Born Corner Brook, Nfld. 1951. m. Eric. 2 ch. Leanne, Stephen. **EDUC:** Grace General Hospital Sch. of Nursing, R.N. 1972. **CAREER:** Staff Nurse, Western Memorial Reg'l Hospital, 1972-76; Nursing Unit Supervisor, 1976-78; City Councillor, City of Corner Brook, 1985 to date; Exec. Mbr., Civic Centre Association, 1986 to date; Mbr., Econ. Dev. Committee, City of Corner Brook, 1986 to date; Pres., Great Humber Joint Council, 1992-96; Staff Educ. Coord., Western Memorial Reg'l Hospital, 1980 to date. **AFFIL:** 1999 Canada Winter Games Host Society (VP, Strategic Planning & Community Rel'ns); Civic Centre Association (Exec. Mbr.); Corner Brook

Chamber of Commerce (Dir.); Corner Brook Winter Carnival, Inc. (Pres.); Roman Catholic Episcopal Corporation of St. George's (Bd. of Admin.); Bid to host 1999 Jeux du Canada Games (Co-Chair, Site Evaluation Committee); Humber Arm Environment Committee, Atlantic Canada Action Plan (ACAP) Program. **HONS:** Dedicated Service Award, Heart & Stroke Foundation of Canada, 1987; Outstanding Service Award, Humber Community YMCA, 1988; Dedicated Service Award, Great Humber Joint Council, 1992. **INTERESTS:** volunteer work; Alpine skiing; spending time at the cottage. **COMMENT:** *"I am committed to my family, my profession and my community. I believe it is a privilege to be able to serve my community as an elected municipal councillor and a volunteer. I have particularly enjoyed work with the Canada Games Committee in our successful bid to host the Jeux du Canada Games in the winter of 1999."*

Chrzanowski, Maria J., M.Sc.E. ☜
Senior Teaching Associate, UNIVERSITY OF NEW BRUNSWICK, Box 4400, Fredericton, NB E3B 5A3 (506) 453-4803, FAX 453-5055. Born Poland 1932. d. 1 ch. Peter. **EDUC:** Technical Univ. of Mining & Metallurgy, Cracow, Poland, M.Sc.E.(Geological Eng.) 1955. **CAREER:** Geologist, Poland, 1955-66; Consultant, Fredericton, N.B., 1968-71; Travelling Geologist, S. America, 1972-73; Research Asst., Dept. of Geol., Univ. of New Brunswick, 1979-81; Fac. Mbr., Dept. of Geol., 1981 to date. **SELECTED PUBLICATIONS:** "Manganese occurrences in Atlantic Canada," with W.E. Hale; "Barite occurrences in Atlantic Canada," with others (*Field School Guide Book*, N.B., 1994). **AFFIL:** Association of Professional Engineers of the Province of N.B.; Women in Science & Engineering; several departmental committees, incl. Ethics Committee, Univ. of New Brunswick; A.P.I.C.S./Power Utility Adjudication Committee (Mbr. 1990-93). **INTERESTS:** engineering; environmental geology. **MISC:** Commonwealth Scholarship Committee, 1994; "Science from the Hill," Fundy Cable Ltd., aired Dec. 1993. **COMMENT:** *"For the past 15 years, I have been teaching labs for Introductory Geology and Engineering Geology at the University of New Brunswick to large numbers of engineering students. Before I came to Canada, I worked as a field geologist in Poland."*

Chu, Alice I-Fang, B.F.A.,M.A., Dip.Ed. ■■ ☜ ⊗ ⌣
Professor, Faculty of Applied Arts, RYERSON POLYTECHNIC UNIVERSITY, 350 Victoria St., Toronto, ON M5B 2K3 (416) 979-5333, FAX

979-5227. President, **A. CHU ASSOCIATES.** Born Shanghai 1943. m. Dr. Vincent H. Chu. 1 ch. Eric K. Chu. **EDUC:** Taiwan Normal Univ., B.F.A.(Fine Art) 1966; Columbia Univ., M.A. (Art/Design) 1969; McGill Univ., Dip.Ed.(Art Educ.) 1972. **CAREER:** Graphic Designer, Gene Murray Advertising, N.Y. City, 1966-68; Designer, Ginn & Company, Publisher, Boston, 1968-70; Art Dir., Creative Marketing Inc., Montreal, 1970-72; Pres., A. Chu Associates, Design & Illustration, 1971 to date; Prof., Visual Arts, Dawson Coll., 1972-77; Chair, Graphic Design Dept., 1974-77; Prof., Fac. of Applied Arts, Ryerson Polytechnical Univ. (formerly Ryerson Polytechnical Institute), 1977 to date; Coord., Cultural Affairs, Ryerson Int'l Dev. Centre, 1987-90; Academic Supervisor, World University Service of Canada, Ottawa, 1986-91. **SELECTED CREDITS:** multimedia presentations, *Design Elements and Design Principles*, produced with the assistance of the Media Centre, Ryerson. **SELECTED PUBLICATIONS:** *Design and Colour for Fashion Communication* (Ryerson, 1992). **EXHIBITIONS:** group shows, 9th, 10th, 11th & 12th annual juried shows of Toronto Watercolour Society. **AFFIL:** Colour Marketing Group (Chair); Inter-Society Color Council of U.S. (delegate from CMG); Society of Graphic Designers of Canada (Registered Graphic Designer of Canada); Fashion Group International; Toronto Watercolour Society; Design Exchange. **HONS:** Grad. Study Scholarship, Columbia Univ., 1968; Merit Award for fac. direction of design students participating in Young Designers Competition, permanent pkg exhibit, NYC, 1979; Merit Award, Canadian Society for Colour, 1985; research & travel grant, Ontario Jiangsu Educational Exchange, 1988; Prof. of the Year, Ryerson, 1989; award for "Blue Poppy," 9th annual show, Toronto Watercolour Society, 1993; award for "Upon Closer Examination," Aquavision Show, 1994; award for "Temple of the Earth God," 11th annual show, Toronto Watercolour Society, 1995. **INTERESTS:** watercolour painting; travel. **COMMENT:** *"For the past 25 years, I have worked and taught in the area of colour and design and have thoroughly enjoyed the experience. Above all, I hope I have fostered students creativity, their powers of expression and their love of colour."*

Chyczij, Alexandra, B.A., LL.B. ✋ ⚏

Executive Director, **THE ADVOCATES' SOCIETY,** 160 Queen St. W., Toronto, ON M5H 3H3 (416) 597-0243, FAX 597-1588. Born Toronto 1956 1 ch. Kassandra. **EDUC:** Univ. of Toronto, B.A.(Pol. Sci.) 1978; Univ. of Windsor, LL.B. 1981. **BAR:** Ont. **CAREER:**

Articling Student, Raphael, Wheatley and MacPherson, 1981-83; litigation, Harris, Barr, 1983-85; litigation, Raphael, Wheatley and MacPherson, 1985-87; litigation, Sloan, Edmonds, Klaiman, 1987-90; litigation, Cunningham, Swan, Carty, Little and Bonham, 1991-93. **AFFIL:** The Advocates' Society (Exec. Dir.); Canadian Bar Association; Ukrainian Professional & Business Federation of Canada; Ukrainian Canadian Civil Liberties Association; Law Society of Upper Canada.

Cimicata, Carmi, B.A.A. ✋ ♡

Executive Director and Founder, **BACCHUS CANADA,** Box 312, Stn. D, Toronto, ON M6P 3J9 (416) 243-1338, FAX 243-2337. Born Toronto 1964. Engaged Paul Godin. **EDUC:** Ryerson Polytechnic Univ., B.A.A.(Fashion) 1986. **CAREER:** Exec. Dir. & Founder, BACCHUS Canada, 1986 to date. **AFFIL:** Task Force on Alcohol & Other Drug Issues; Association of Campus Beverage Mgmt (Comm. Coord.). **HONS:** 2 awards for extracurricular achievements; nominated, Women on the Move Award, *The Toronto Sun*, 1995. **INTERESTS:** collector of boxes, Napoleon memorabilia, Russian lacquer boxes, metallic pins, books on Catherine the Great. **COMMENT:** *"During her time with the student government, was asked to start an alcohol awareness campaign following the death of a young person during regular orientation programming. Carmi worked with her student government for three years before officially leaving campus politics to organize and operate BACCHUS Canada as a national non-profit. Since 1986, when BACCHUS Canada was officially incorporated, Carmi has worked to create a national movement among post-secondary student leaders in Canada. Getting alcohol awareness to the top of the campus agenda has kept her extremely busy. She is responsible for launching a number of high-profile awareness campaigns, which have been used throughout North America."*

Cinnamon, Shelley L., B.F.A. ▯ ⊗

Director, Art Services, **HARLEQUIN ENTERPRISES LIMITED,** 225 Duncan Mills Rd., Don Mills, ON M3B 3K9 (416) 391-7024, FAX 445-5860. Born New Castle, N.B. s. **EDUC:** Univ. of Alberta, B.F.A.(Painting) 1975. **CAREER:** Designer, City of Edmonton; Graphic Artist, City of Toronto; Dir., Art Svcs, Harlequin Enterprises. **INTERESTS:** painting; rollerblading; cycling; skiing; music; reading. **COMMENT:** *"Energetic and passionate about my work and my interests. Extensive travel throughout the Pacific Rim countries, Europe and North America has greatly influenced my life and my art."*

Cinq-Mars, Irène, B.A.,B.A.P., M.Sc.A. ⌘ ⊗
Vice-Rector, Academic, UNIVERSITÉ DE MONTRÉAL, Box 6128, Succ. Centre-Ville, Montréal, QC H3C 3J7 (514) 343-7922, FAX 343-5750. Born Montréal 1947. 2 ch. EDUC: Univ. de Montréal, B. ès Arts 1968, B.A.P.(Architecture de paysage) 1973, M.Sc.A.(Aménagement) 1976. CAREER: V-Dean, Environmental Studies Fac., Univ. de Montréal, 1985-89; Dir., Sch. of Landscape Arch., Univ. de Montréal, 1988-90; V.-Rector Academic, Univ. de Montréal, 1990 to date. SELECTED PUBLICATIONS: numerous scientific publications, incl. "Le paysage à redécouvrir de l'intérieur" with Geneviève Corfa & Sandra Barone (*Loisir et société* Vol. 8, 1985); "Femmes et espaces publics: l'appropriation et la maîtrise du temps" with C. Perraton (*Recherches féministes*, Vol. 2, 1989); numerous professional publications, incl. "Le rôle de l'architecte de paysage face à la crise de l'environnement" (*Revue architecture de paysage* Nov. 1977); "L'évolution de l'architecture de paysage au Québec," with P. Jacobs & P. Poullaouec-Gonidec (*Revue paysage et aménagement* Sept. 1986); various reports & conference papers. AFFIL: Canadian Association of Landscape Architects; Association des architectes paysagistes du Québec (Fellow); Environmental Design Research Association. INTERESTS: nature; painting; philosophy; children; peace & justice.

Cira, Anne A., B.Sc.,F.I.C.B. ■■ Ⓢ ⊕
Senior Vice-President, CIBC, 40 Dundas St. W., Ste. 221, Toronto, ON M5G 2C2 (416) 408-2923, FAX 408-3234. Executive Director, CANADIAN YOUTH BUSINESS FOUNDATION. Born Penrith, UK 1951. m. Joseph. EDUC: Univ. of Toronto, B.Sc.(Math. & Psych.) 1974; Institute of Canadian Bankers, Fellow 1981; Univ. of Michigan, Exec. Program 1988. AFFIL: Scarborough General Hospital Foundation (Dir.). HONS: Silver Medal, Institute of Canadian Bankers, 1981.

Clancy, Mary, B.A.,LL.B.,LL.M. ■■ ✤
Member of Parliament (Halifax) and Chair of Standing Committee on National Defence and Veterans' Affairs, GOVERNMENT OF CANADA, House of Commons, Ottawa, ON K1A 0A6 (613) 995-9368, FAX 995-0945, EMAIL clancm@parl.ca. Born Halifax 1948. s. EDUC: Mount St. Vincent Univ., B.A.(Hons., English) 1970; Dalhousie Univ., LL.B. 1974; Univ. of London, U.K., LL.M. 1975. CAREER: before entry into politics, worked as lawyer, broadcaster (CBC), lecturer at Univ. of B.C. & Mount Saint Vincent Univ., social worker, newspaper columnist & actress. POLITICAL

CAREER: elected M.P. for Halifax, 1988; re-elected, 1993; Parliamentary Sec. to Min. of Citizenship & Immigration, 1993-96; has served as official Opposition Critic for the Status of Women & Assoc. Critic for Communications; positions on numerous committees incl. Citizenship & Immigration, Health & Welfare, Social Affairs, Seniors, & the Status of Women; Chair, Standing Committee on Nat'l Defence & Veterans' Affairs, 1995 to date. AFFIL: YMCA (former mbr., Bd. of Dir.); Dalhousie Legal Aid Board (former mbr.); St. Joseph's Day Care Centre, Halifax (former mbr., Bd. of Mgmt). INTERESTS: theatre; travel; music; reading. MISC: mbr., Cdn delegation to U.N. 4th World Conference on Women, Beijing, 1995.

Clark, Brenda ⊗ ▯
Illustrator, BRENDA CLARK-ILLUSTRATOR INC., Port Perry, ON. Born Toronto 1955. m. 1 ch. Robin Courtice. EDUC: Sheridan Coll., Illustration 1977. CAREER: freelance illustrator for a number of educational publishers that were revising &/or developing schoolbooks for children; children's book illustrator associated with Kids Can Press. SELECTED CREDITS: *Sadie and the Snowman* by Allen Morgan (Toronto: Kids Can Press, 1985); *Franklin in the Dark* by Paulette Bourgeois (Toronto: Kids Can Press, 1986); *Puddleman* by Ted Staunton (Toronto: Kids Can Press, 1994); *Little Fingerling* by Monica Hughes (Toronto: Kids Can Press, 1989); *Franklin is Lost* by Paulette Bourgeois (Toronto: Kids Can Press, 1992); *My Dog: A Scrapbook of Drawings, Photos and Facts* by Marilyn Baillie (Toronto: Kids Can Press, 1993); *Franklin is Messy* by Paulette Bourgeois (Toronto: Kids Can Press, 1994); *Franklin Plays the Game* by Paulette Bourgeois (Toronto: Kids Can Press, 1995). HONS: IODE Book Award–Toronto Chapter, for *Little Fingerling*, written by Monica Hughes, 1989. INTERESTS: reading; camping; canoeing; hiking; travelling; squash. MISC: The Franklin turtle series continues with 4 new titles per year plus related activity books & CD-ROM's; Franklin is being animated by Nelvana, Toronto & should appear on the screen by fall 1997.

Clark, Carolyn J., B.A. Ⓢ ▯
Vice-President, Human Resources, CANADIAN PACIFIC HOTELS AND RESORTS, 1 University Ave., Ste. 1400, Toronto, ON M5J 2P1 (416) 367-7131, FAX 367-7291. EDUC: York Univ., B.A.(Soc.) 1971; Univ. of Toronto, Sch. of Continuing Studies, Compensation Mgmt 1976-77, Labour Rel'ns Mgmt 1978-79. CAREER: Exec. Search Consultant; Supervisor of Recruitment, Canadian Pacific Hotels & Resorts, 1974-75;

Mgr, Recruitment & Training, 1975-76; Corp. Dir., Personnel, 1976-82; Exec. Dir., Hum. Res., 1982-88; VP, Hum. Res., 1988 to date. **AFFIL:** Canadian Tourism Human Resources Council (Bus. Co-Chair); Canadian Hospitality Foundation (Bd. of Dir.); Canadian Restaurant & Foodservice Association; SmartRisk Foundation; Conference Board of Canada (Council of Hum. Res. Exec.); Hospitality & Tourism Mgmt Program Advisory Committee, Ryerson Polytechnical Univ.; Personnel Association of Ontario; Univ. of Guelph (Advisory Committee on Educ. & Training, Sch. of Hotel & Foodservice Mgmt); Ontario Hostelry Institute (Fellow). **COMMENT:** "*As a result of the progressive Human Resources initiatives that have been implemented within Canadian Pacific Hotels & Resorts, the company has been included in both editions of* The Financial Post's *The 100 Best Companies to Work For in Canada, and has also been included in the recently published* Canada's Best Employers for Women - A Guide for Job Hunters, Employees and Employers."

Clark, Eileen, B.Sc. ♡
Born Twechar, Scotland 1924. m. E. Ritchie Clark. 4 ch. Alison Vannah, Ritchie Rosemary Clark-Beattie, L'orna. **EDUC:** Radar Tech. Officer, Women's Auxiliary Air Force, Royal Air Force, 1943-46. **VOLUNTEER CAREER:** Pres., Canadian Federation of Univ. Women, 1979-82; Senator, Presbyterian Coll., 1982-89; VP, International Federation of Univ. Women, 1983-89; Pres., St. Andrew's Society of Montreal, 1984-85; V-Chair of Senate, Presbyterian Coll., 1986-89; Docent, McCord Museum of Canadian History, 1991-96; First VP, Virginia Gildersleeve Int'l Fund for Univ. Women, 1993 to date; Convenor of Grants 1992-96; Trustee, Mount Royal Cemetery Co., 1992 to date. **SELECTED PUBLICATIONS:** articles & reviews in *Journal of Canadian Federation of University Women*. **HONS:** Hon. Citizen, City of WInnipeg, 1982. **INTERESTS:** reading; history; travel; antique porcelain; gardening; 12 grandchildren. **COMMENT:** "*Coming to Canada as a war bride, I am basically a homemaker, but have always done voluntary work. I am active in N.G.O.'s that focus on education and the status of women worldwide.*"

Clark, Lillian, M.D.,F.R.C.P.(C),FAAP ⊕ 🎓
Physician. 7071 Brookfield Ave., Niagara Falls, ON L2G 5R7. Born Baltimore 1919. m. Dr. John W. Clark. 2 ch. Deborah Clark Allerton, James Richard Clark. **EDUC:** Univ. of Toronto, M.D. 1941. **CAREER:** Rotating General Internship, St. Joseph's Hospital, Toronto, 1941-42; Intern in Medicine, Hospital for Sick Children, Toronto,1942-43; Chief Medical Resident, 1943-44; Medical Officer, Royal Canadian Navy, 1944-46; Montreal Children's Hospital, 1946-49; Greater Niagara General Hospital, 1950-93; Chief of Paediatrics; retired, 1993; Hon. Mbr. of Staff. **AFFIL:** Greater Niagara Medical Society; Ontario Medical Association; Canadian Medical Association; Canadian Paediatric Society; American Academy of Paediatrics (Fellow); Coll. of Physicians & Surgeons of Ontario (Fellow); Royal Coll. of Physicians & Surgeons of Canada (Fellow); Greater Niagara Big Sister Association (former Hon. Pres.); Brock Univ. (Bd. of Gov.); Local Univ. Women's Club. **HONS:** Glenn Sawyer Award, Ontario Medical Association, 1989. **INTERESTS:** education; bridge; tennis; Nordic skiing; travel; river rafting; the Canadian outdoors. **MISC:** worked as paediatrician at Moose Factory Hospital on James Bay with the Crees in Fall of 1991.

Clark, Karen ■■ ⚾
Olympic Athlete. c/o Canadian Olympic Association. Born Montreal 1972. **EDUC:** currently studying Commerce. **SPORTS CAREER:** mbr., Cdn Nat'l Synchronized Swimming Team, 1988 to date. Olympic Games: Silver, team, 1996. World championships: 2nd, team, 1994; 2nd, team, 1991. World jr. championships: 2nd, solo, 2nd, duet, & 2nd, team, 1989. World Cup: 2nd, team, 1995; 2nd, team, 1993; 2nd, team, 1989. Pan American Games: 2nd, solo, & 2nd, team, 1995. Canadian championships: 2nd, solo, 1995; 1st, team, & 2nd, solo, 1994. **HONS:** Helen Vanderburg Award, 1987. **INTERESTS:** acting.

Clark, Lynne, B.Sc.,M.B.A.,C.A. $
Partner, DELOITTE & TOUCHE, BCE Place, 181 Bay St., Ste. 1400, Toronto, ON M5J 2V1 (416) 601-6169. Born Toronto 1952. **EDUC:** Univ. of Toronto, B.Sc. 1974; York Univ., M.B.A. 1978. **CAREER:** Public Acctnt, Deloitte & Touche, 1978-89; Ptnr, 1989 to date. **SELECTED PUBLICATIONS:** author of several articles, *Chartered Accountant* magazine. **AFFIL:** Junior Achievement Metro Toronto (Dir. & Treas.); E.D.P. Auditors' Association (former Dir.); Chartered Accountant. **INTERESTS:** running; avid reader of non-fiction; refinishing antique furniture; skiing; writer of "odes"; travel. **MISC:** foster parent of child in Sri Lanka since 1990.

Clark, Patricia, B.P.H.E. ■ ⚾ ✊ ♡
Executive Director, ONTARIO ASSOCIATION OF SPORT AND EXERCISE SCIENCES, 75 Broadway, Orangeville, ON L9W 1K1 (519) 942-2620, FAX 942-2285. Born Toronto 1956. m.

Daniel Clark. 2 ch. Daniel Alexander, Patrick James. **EDUC:** Univ. of Toronto, B.P.H.E. (Phys. Educ.) 1981; Seneca Coll., Bus. Certificate 1988. **CAREER:** Nat'l Sales Rep., Owl Instruments, 1982-83; Employee Fitness Coord., Texaco Canada, 1983-84; Program Dir., Ontario Fitness Council, 1984-89; Exec. Dir., Ontario Group Fitness Office, 1984-91; Exec. Dir., Ontario Association of Sport & Exercise Sciences, 1984 to date. **AFFIL:** Ontario Association of Sport & Exercise Sciences (Certified Fitness Appraiser); Ontario Fitness Council (Charter Mbr.; Chair, Committee for Dev. of Special Interest Groups); Humber Coll. (Fitness Leadership Advisory Committee); Seneca Coll. (Fitness Instructor Advisory Committee); Leaside High Sch. Alumni Association (Pres. 1984-90; Comm. Dir. 1990-94). **HONS:** Award for Leadership, Ontario Fitness Council, 1982; Award for Professional Work in the Fitness Field, Ontario Ministry of Culture, Tourism & Recreation; Ministry Award, Provincial Fitness Citation, 1994. **INTERESTS:** an active lifestyle; family; tennis; gardening. **MISC:** chaired 1990 Ontario Fitness Council conference; presenter, fitness & safety standards info. **COMMENT:** *"I have achieved a happy balance in my life with my family and work. My work as executive director for O.A.S.E.S. is challenging and rewarding, and I hope I have helped to better the fitness industry in Ontario."*

Clark, Susan ♥ ☖ ⊗

Actor and Vice-President, GEORGIAN BAY PRODUCTIONS, LTD., 3815 W. Olive Ave., Ste. 202, Burbank, CA 91505 (818) 843-7704, FAX 843-0528. Born Sarnia, Ont. 1943. m. Alex Karras. 1 ch. **EDUC:** Royal Academy of Dramatic Art, London, UK; Stella Adler Academy. **CAREER:** joined Toronto Children's Players, age 12; professional debut, *Silk Stockings*, with Don Ameche, summer theatre, Michigan, age 15; various roles in the English repertory system & London's West End; various roles, CBC; various roles (10-yr. exclusive contract), Universal Studios; actor, Prod. & VP, Georgian Bay Productions, Ltd. (in partnership with husband Alex Karras), 1980 to date. **SELECTED CREDITS:** Elizabeth, *Emily of New Moon* (series); Lila Young, *Butterbox Babies* (movie), Sullivan Entertainment; actor/Prod., *Meetins' on the Porch* (theatre); actor, *The Vortex*, Walnut Street Theatre, Philadelphia; Babe Didrickson Zaharias, *BABE* (movie), CBS; Amelia Earhart, *Amelia Earhart* (movie), NBC; actor, *Tell Them Willie Boy is Here* (feature), Universal; actor, *The Apple Dumpling Gang* (feature), Walt Disney; actor, *Murder By Decree* (feature), Avco-Embassy; actor/Prod., *Jimmy B and Andre*

(movie), Georgian Bay Productions, Ltd., CBS; actor/Co-Prod., *Webster* (series), Georgian Bay Productions, Ltd., ABC/Paramount; Heloise, *Heloise & Abelard* (movie), CBC; Eleanor, *Lion in Winter*, Walnut Street Theatre, Philadelphia; actor, *Poor Bitos*, Duke of York Theatre, West End, London; actor, *Man and Superman*, Shaw Festival. **HONS:** Emmy (*BABE*); nomination, Emmy (*Amelia Earhart*); Women of Achievement Award; Dove of Peace, B'nai B'rith; Ralph Bunche Peace Award, United Nations; honoured by Physicians for Social Responsibility for her work in protecting the environment; honoured by CARECEN for her work for social justice; nomination (*Butterbox Babies*), Gemini Awards, 1996. **MISC:** currently developing projects for Georgian Bay Productions.

Clark, Terri ■■ ♥

Country Music Artist. 1114 Seventeenth Ave. S., Ste. 202, Nashville, TN, USA 37212 (615) 327-9966, FAX 322-9177. Born Medicine Hat, Alta. 1968. s. **SELECTED CREDITS:** *Terri Clark* (debut album); *Just the Same* (2nd album); singles incl.: "Better Things to Do" (#1 Gavin Chart, #3 *Billboard* Chart, video #1 CMT); "When Boy Meets Girl" (#1 Gavin Chart, #3 *Billboard* Chart, video #3 both CMT & TNN); "If I Were You" (#4 R & R Chart, #6 Gavin chart, video #3 CMT, #5 TNN); "Suddenly Single" (#21 Gavin Chart, #28 R & R Chart, no video); "Poor Poor Pitiful Me" (released Sept. 23/96). **AFFIL:** Academy of Country Music; Country Music Association. **HONS:** Top New Female Country Artist, *Billboard* magazine, 1995; named Star of Tomorrow, *Music City News*, 1995; Golden Pick Award for Favorite Female Newcomer, *Country Weekly*, 1995; nominated for Best New Touring Artist, both *Pollstar* & *Performance* magazines, 1995; nominated for Best New Female Vocalist, Academy of Country Music, 1996; nominated for 7 Canadian Country Music Awards incl. Entertainer of the Year, 1996; nominated for Horizon Award, Country Music Association, 1996; named Rising Star, Canadian Country Music Association, 1996; Single of the Year ("Better Things to Do"), Canadian Country Music Association, 1996; Album of the Year (*Terri Clark*), Canadian Country Music Association, 1996; named one of top 10 new stars, *Country America*, 1996. **MISC:** during 1996 will have played before approx. 1.5 million people on tour.

Clark-Jones, Melissa, B.A.,M.A., Ph.D. ⊲ ▒

Full Professor and Chair, Sociology Department, BISHOP'S UNIVERSITY, Lennoxville, QC

J1M 1Z7 (819) 822-9600, FAX 822-9661. Born Bethlehem, Penn. 1947. m. Sean B. Jones. **EDUC:** Mount Holyoke Coll., Mass., B.A.(Soc.) 1969; American Univ. in Cairo, Egypt, TEFL 1973; McMaster Univ., M.A.(Soc.) 1975, Ph.D. 1980. **CAREER:** Media Researcher, Public Relations Aids & Oxbridge Publishing Companies, 1969-71; Teaching Fellow, TEFL Program, American Univ. in Cairo, 1971-73; Ed. & Conference Coord., 1973; part-time fac., Soc., Dawson Coll., Montreal, & Archambault Prison, 1977-78; full-time fac., Soc., Concordia Univ., 1978-80; Chair (7 out of 13 yrs.), Soc. Dept., Bishop's Univ., 1982-92 & 1995-97; Prof., 1981 to date. **SELECTED CREDITS:** created video "Sociological Analysis of Rape in Film: *Marnie*; *Gina*; *Thelma & Louise*", 1992. **SELECTED PUBLICATIONS:** *A Staple State: Canadian Industrial Resources in Cold War* (Univ. of Toronto Press, 1987); "Continental Capital Accumulation: The Canadian State and Industrial Resource Development" (*Contemporary Crises* Sept. 1984); "Through the Backdoor," with Pat Coyne (*Atlantis: A Women's Studies Journal* Spring 1990); "Labour and the Tools of Nostalgia" (*Studies in Political Economy* Summer 1990); "The Parachute Dress" with C. Gaskell (*Journal of Eastern Townships Research* Spring 1993); various other publications. **EDIT:** Contributing Ed., translator, reviewer, "Ma'ra", *Cineaste*, 1978-80. **AFFIL:** Popular Culture Association; Canadian Sociology & Anthropology Association; Film Studies Association of Canada; Canadian University Women's Association; Association of Professors at Bishop's Univ. **INTERESTS:** women's studies; industrial sociology & cultural studies; film analysis; riding horses; travel; opera; skiing. **MISC:** organized video/panel "The Montreal Massacre" presented at CSAA Learneds, 1990; in a commuter marriage since 1984 between NYC & Quebec; recipient of various grants & fellowships. **COMMENT:** *"My research and teaching, as an academic, have allowed me to involve myself with young Canadians and their search for change and for ways to improve society. I love the country and its culture."*

Clarke, Heather F., B.N.Sc.,M.N., Ph.D. ⊕ ○

Nursing Research Consultant, REGISTERED NURSES ASSOCIATION OF BRITISH COLUMBIA, 2855 Arbutus St., Vancouver, BC V6J 3Y8 (604) 736-7331, FAX 738-2272, EMAIL clarke@rnabc.bc.ca. Born Toronto 1943. s. **EDUC:** Wellesley Hospital, nursing diploma; Queen's Univ., B.N.Sc. 1966; Univ. of Washington, M.N. 1972, Ph.D.(Nursing) 1985. **CAREER:** Teacher, Pediatrics, Holy Cross Hos-

pital, Calgary, 1966-67; Pediatric Nurse, Mississauga Hospital, 1967-68; Teacher, Biological Sciences, Credit Valley Sch. of Nursing, Mississauga, Ont., 1968-70; Coord., Svc to Patients, Ont. Div., Canadian Cancer Society, 1970-71; Asst. Prof., Health Care & Epidemiology, Univ. of British Columbia, 1972-75; Nurse Practitioner, Univ. of British Columbia, 1972-75; Nurse Consultant, Dev. Group for Community Hum. Res. & Health Centres, 1975-77; Asst. Prof., Univ. of Victoria, Sch. of Nursing, 1978-85; Chief, Family & Child Health Unit, Health Promo. Directorate, Health & Welfare Canada, 1985-87; Nursing Research Consultant, Registered Nurses' Association of B.C., 1987 to date; Adjunct Prof., Sch. of Nursing, Univ. of British Columbia, 1988 to date; Fac. Assoc., UBC, Institute for Health Promotion Research. **SELECTED CREDITS:** Exec. Prod., *Nursing Research From Question to Funding*, film, Lena Productions; various other films, videos & slide presentations. **SELECTED PUBLICATIONS:** *Care of Children in Hospitals: A Review of Contemporary Issues*, with Dr. G. Robinson (New York: Oxford Press, 1980); *Nursing Research: From Question to Funding. A Workbook*, ed. (Vancouver: RNABC, 1990); "Developing Consensus on Canadian Family Health Needs: A Step Towards Policy Development" (*Canadian Journal of Nursing Research* 1989); "Vision for the Future of Public Health Nursing: A Case for Primary Health Care," with G. Beddome & N. Whyte (*Public Health Nursing* 1993); "Cervical Cancer Screening in Canadian Native Women," with others (*Acta Cytalogica* 1994); various other articles, chapters in books, unrefereed articles & monographs; various published conference proceedings, with special emphasis on research utilization and evidence-based healthcare. **EDIT:** Ed. Bd., *Health Care for Women International*, 1984. **AFFIL:** Canadian Public Health Association; Canadian Nurses' Foundation (Past Pres.); Western Institute of Continuing Higher Education in Nursing, USA; Canadian Nursing Research Group (Past Pres.); Nursing Research Interest Group–B.C.; International Council of Women's Health Issues; Transcultural Nursing Society; B.C. Council for the Family (Bd. Mbr.); Fetal Alcohol Syndrome Resource Society of B.C.; BC Council for the Family (Bd. Mbr.); Option Youth (Bd. Mbr.); Sigma Theta Tau (Pres., Xi Eta Chapter). **HONS:** WHO Fellowship, 1974; Canadian Nurses' Foundation Fellowship, 1980; RNABC Award, 1985; Recognition Award for Excellence in Nursing, Xi Eta Chapter, Sigma Theta Tau International Nursing Honour Society, 1994. **INTERESTS:** hiking; biking; opera. **MISC:** recipient of various grants & fellowships; reviewer for various journals &

granting agencies; Mbr., ad hoc committee of the Canadian Nurses' Foundation to est. the Canadian Institute of Nursing & Health, 1989 to date; numerous unpublished conference presentations, guest lectures & invited talks; consultant, World Health Organization, 1975-83. COMMENT: *"My career has centred primarily on community and family health, as a nurse practitioner, educator, manager and researcher. More recently I have focused on policy development and health of First Nations women."*

Clarke, Shirley ■ ■ Ⓢ ⊚
Executive Director, BUILDING OWNERS AND MANAGERS ASSOCIATION, ATLANTIC (comprehensive professional education in the real property industry), 1505 Barrington St., Halifax, NS B3J 3K5 (902) 425-3717, FAX 425-3746. Born Halifax Co. 1931. m. Arthur Clarke. 6 ch. EDUC: Miss Murphy's Business Coll., 1950. AFFIL: Society of Management Accountants, Atlantic Reg. (Exec. Asst. 1974-91); Boy Scouts of Canada (various positions 1976-79). HONS: public speaking awards. INTERESTS: reading; writing; needlepoint; bowling. COMMENT: *"Ambitious, resourceful wife, mother and grandmother. Main ambition: to educate and train my family to become mature, good community citizens. Endeavour: to continue to live the quiet, peaceful life my husband and I now enjoy."*

Clarkson, Adrienne, B.A.,M.A., LL.D. ⌘ 🗋 ✎
Executive Producer, Host and Writer, ADRIENNE CLARKSON PRESENTS, CBC Television, Box 500, Stn. A, Toronto, ON M5W 1E6. Born Hong Kong. EDUC: Trinity Coll., Univ. of Toronto, B.A.(English Lang. & Lit.) 1960; Univ. of Toronto, M.A.(English Lit.) 1962; Sorbonne, France, post-grad. work 1962-64. CAREER: freelance journalist, 1964-82; Monthly Book Reviewer, *Chatelaine* Magazine, 1965-67; Host, Writer, Interviewer, *Take Thirty*, CBC Television, 1965-75; Host, Writer, Interviewer, *Adrienne At Large*, CBC Television, 1975-76; Host, Writer, Interviewer, *the fifth estate*, CBC Television, 1976-82; Exec. Prod., Host & Writer, *Adrienne Clarkson's Summer Festival*, CBC Television, 1980-90; Pres. & Publisher, McClelland & Stewart, 1987-88; Agent Gen. for Ont. in France, 1987-88; Exec. Prod., Host & Writer, *Adrienne Clarkson Presents*, CBC Television, 1990 to date. SELECTED CREDITS: Dir./Writer, *Artemesia: A Woman's Story* (1992); Dir./Writer, *Borduas And Me* (1992); Dir./Writer, *The Lust of His Eye* (1992). SELECTED PUBLICATIONS: *A Lover More Condoling* (Toronto: McClelland & Stewart, 1968);

Hunger Trace (Toronto: McClelland & Stewart, 1970); *True to You in My Fashion* (New Press, 1972); contributed numerous articles to all major newspapers & magazines in Canada. AFFIL: Canadian Centre, International PEN (former Dir.); The Royal Conservatory of Music (Hon. Fellow; Bd. Mbr.); President's Committee, Univ. of Toronto; The Municipality of Metropolitan Toronto (Chrm's Committee for Mass Deacidification); Corporation of Trinity Coll.; Univ. of Toronto, St. Michael's Hospital (Hon. Patron, Bone & Mineral Group); Univ. of Toronto (Hon. Patron, Hepatitis "B" Proj.); Association canadienne-française de l'Ontario (Hon. Patron); Massey Coll., Univ. of Toronto (Cont. Fellow); Trinity Coll., Univ. of Toronto (Hon. Fellow). HONS: Best Public Affairs Journalist, ACTRA Award, 1974; Gordon Sinclair Award for Outspokenness & Integrity in Broadcasting, ACTRA, 1976; Best TV Documentary Writer, ACTRA Award, 1977; Best TV Journalist, ACTRA Award, 1982; Leonard Brockington Visitor, Queen's Univ., 1987; N.Y. Film & Video Gold Medal, 1991; Officer of the Order of Canada, 1992; Best Host on a Light Info., Variety, Performing Arts Program, Gemini Award, 1993; Best Drama, Short Subject - *The Lust of His Eye: Visions of James Wilson Morrice*, Columbus Int'l Film & Video Fest. 1995; Prix Gemeaux, Best Performing Arts Program, *Peau, Chair et Os*,1995; LL.D.(Hon.), Dalhousie Univ., 1988; D.Litt.(Hon.), Lakehead Univ., 1989; LL.D.(Hon.), Acadia Univ., 1991. INTERESTS: decorative arts; gardening; hunting for mushrooms; fishing; reading; opera. MISC: juror for various awards & festivals; numerous invited speeches & lectures; Mbr., International PEN, Canadian Centre Mission to Chile to investigate human rights status of writers, directors & actors, 1988; Mbr., francophone delegation of nongovernmental observers for plebiscite in Chile, organized by CISO & Développement et Paix, 1988.

Clarkson, Persis B., B.A.,M.A., Ph.D. ■ ⬕ ❀
Associate Professor, Department of Anthropology, UNIVERSITY OF WINNIPEG, 515 Portage Ave., Winnipeg, MB R3B 2E9 (204) 786-9718, FAX 774-4134. EDUC: Colgate Univ., B.A.(Precolumbian Studies) 1975; Univ. of Calgary, M.A.(Archaeology) 1979, Ph.D.(Archaeology) 1985. CAREER: Visiting Prof., Universidad del Norte, Chile, 1983; Sessional Instructor, Mount Royal Coll., 1985-86; Sessional Instructor, Univ. of Alberta, 1985-86; Instructor, Red Deer Coll., 1987-89; Sessional Instructor, Univ. of Calgary, 1988; Asst. Prof., Athabasca Univ., 1990-91; Asst. Prof., Univ. of

Winnipeg, 1992-95; Assoc. Prof., 1995 to date. SELECTED PUBLICATIONS: "The Archaeology of the Nazca Pampas, Peru: Environmental and Cultural Parameters" in *The Lines of Nazca* ed. by A.F. Aveni (Philadelphia: American Philosophical Society 1992); "New chronometric dates for the puquios of Nasca, Peru," with R. Dorn (*Latin American Antiquity* 1995); "Radiocarbon Dating Inclusions of Organic Matter in Rock Varnish, with Examples from Drylands," with R. Dorn (*Annals of the American Geographical Association* 1992); "The Cultural Insistence of Geoglyphs: The Andean and Southwestern Phenomena" in *Recent Research Along the Lower Colorado River* ed. by J.A. Ezzo (Tuscon: Statistical Research Technical Series, 1994); "New Chronometric Dates for the Puquios of Nasca, Peru," with R. Dorn (*Latin American Antiquity* 1995); various other writings. AFFIL: Society for American Archaeology; N.Y. Academy of Sciences; Institute of Andean Studies; American Anthropological Association; Sigma Xi. HONS: Chacmool Student Paper Prize, Univ. of Calgary, 1983. MISC: recipient of various grants; various invited papers.

Clayton, Nicola, B.A. $ / ⊗
Director, Marketing and Research, MACLEAN'S MAGAZINE, 777 Bay St., Toronto, ON M5W 1A7 (416) 596-6049, FAX 596-6001. Born Montreal 1959. EDUC: Univ. of Toronto, B.A. 1981; Banff, Magazine Publishing 1983; Univ. of Western Ontario, Western Bus. Sch., Exec. Program Spring 1995. CAREER: Accts Supervisor, Toronto & N.Y., *Maclean's*, 1985-93; Dir., Mktg & Research, 1993 to date. AFFIL: Esprit Orchestra Bd. (Dir.); AIDScare AIDSCare Sub-committee of CANFAR (Co-Chair 1992-94); 1996 Brazilian Ball (Magazine Committee); CCFTA Look Good Feel Better (Comm. Committee); Teaching to Promote Women's Health Conference (Chair, 1996). INTERESTS: producing special events for fundraising purposes; tennis; sailing; flying trapeze. COMMENT: *"I am committed to a variety of fundraising initiatives and enjoy playing tennis and attending cultural events."*

Clemenhagen, Carol, B.A., M.H.A. ■ ✿ ⊕
Secretary, MEDICAL RESEARCH COUNCIL OF CANADA, 1600 Scott St., 5th Fl., Ottawa K1A 0W9 (613) 941-2672, FAX 954-1802. Born Buckingham, Que. 1954. m. Jacques Labelle. EDUC: Carleton Univ., B.A.(Pol. Sci./Soc.); Univ. of Ottawa, Master of Health Admin. 1977. CAREER: Pres., Canadian Hospital Association, 1990-96; Sec., Medical Research Council of Canada, 1996 to date. HONS: Trudeau Award,

Univ. of Ottawa Alumni Association. COMMENT: *"Committed to enhancing the delivery of health services to Canadians."*

Clement, Hope E.A., B.A.,M.A.,B.L.S. ▯
Retired Librarian. 252 Daniel Ave., Ottawa, ON K1Y 0C8 (613) 722-8663. Born 1930. EDUC: Univ. of King's Coll., B.A.(French) 1951; Dalhousie Univ., M.A.(English) 1953; Univ. of Toronto, B.L.S. 1955. CAREER: various positions of increasing responsibility, at the National Library of Canada, 1955-77; Assoc. Nat'l Librarian of Canada, 1977-92. SELECTED PUBLICATIONS: numerous articles & papers on aspects of library planning, admin., svcs & automation. AFFIL: Canadian Library Association; International Federation of Library Associations (various officers' positions 1985-93). HONS: Gov.-General's Medals, Edgehill Sch., 1948, Univ. of King's Coll., 1951; Distinguished Grad. Award, Univ. of Toronto, Sch. of Library Sci., 1989; International Federation of Library Associations Medal, 1991; Distinguished Librarian Award, Canadian Library Association, 1992; Doctorate of Civil Law (Hon.), Univ. of King's Coll., 1992. INTERESTS: travel; music; literature. COMMENT: *"Instrumental in the development of the National Library and its services, including directing its automation."*

Clements, Mary Louise ■ ■ ○ $
Volunteer. 265 Inglewood Dr., Toronto, ON M4T 1J2 (416) 483-9255. CAREER: Dir., Ont., The Canadian Centre for Business in the Community/The Conference Board of Canada, 1982-95. VOLUNTEER CAREER: Pres., Junior League of Toronto, 1971-72; V-Chair, Ontario Advisory Council on Multiculturalism, 1972-79; mbr., Bd. of Dir., Social Planning Council of Metro Toronto, 1974-80; Bd. mbr., Children's Aid Society of Metro Toronto, 1977-84; Pres., 1982-83; Bd. mbr., CAA Toronto Club (formerly Ontario Motor League), 1974-84; Pres., 1982-83; Chair, CAA Insurance Company, 1982-83; Trustee, United Way of Greater Toronto, 1976-85; mbr., Exec. Committee, 1980-85; Chair, Dev. Funding, 1982-85; Bd. mbr., Urban Alliance on Race Relations, 1977-79; mbr., Bd. of Gov., Canadian Automobile Association (1st woman Gov.), 1980-82; mbr., Civic Award of Merit Committee, City of Toronto, 1983-89; mbr., Bd. of Gov., Branksome Hall Sch., 1984-88; Chair, Exec. Committee, Areawide United Way, 1986-94; mbr., Bd. of Dir., Canadian Centre for Philanthropy, 1987-90; mbr., Bd. of Trustees, Community Foundation for Toronto, 1990-92; Chair, Grants Committee, 1990-92. AFFIL: VISION/TV (Bd. of Dir.); Timothy Eaton

Memorial Church (Congregational Bd. Exec.); Community Foundation for Greater Toronto (Safe City Awards Committee); Canadian Cancer Society, Ont. Div. (Reach to Recovery Volunteer Visiting Program). HONS: Margaret Rolph Award, Junior League of Toronto, 1991.

Cloutier, Cécile, B.A.,L.ésl.C.,D.E.S.,M.A., M.PH.,M.TH.,D.Ps.,D.U.P. ■ ⌾ 🕮 ⬚
Writer. Professor Emerita, Department of French, UNIVERSITY OF TORONTO, 7 King's College Circle, Toronto, ON M5S 1A1 (416) 978-7165, FAX 978-3211. Born Quebec City 1930. m. Dr. Jerzy Wojciechowski. 2 ch. EDUC: Laval Univ., B.A. 1951, L.èsL. 1953, D.E.S. 1954; La Sorbonne, D.U.P.(Ph.D.) 1962; McMaster Univ., M.PH. 1981; Univ. of Toronto, M.TH. 1982; Univ. de Tours, D.Ps. 1983. CAREER: Prof., Univ. of Ottawa, 1958-64; Prof., Univ. of Toronto, 1964-95; Guest Prof., Laval Univ., Queen's Univ., Univ. di Napoli. SELECTED PUBLICATIONS: numerous books incl.: *Mains de sable* (Québec; Éditions de l'Arc, 1960); *Cuivre et soies* (Montréal; Éditions du Jour, 1964); *Paupières* (Montréal; Déom, 1970); *Chaleuils* (Montréal: Hexagone, 1979); *Springtime of Spoken Words*, poèmes traduits par Alexandre Amprimoz (Toronto; Hounslow Press, 1979); *Près* (Paris; Éditions Saint Germain-des-Prés, 1983); *´L'Écouté*, poèmes (1960-1983) (Montréal: Hexagone, 1986); *Périhélie* (Paris; Caractères, 1990); *Ostraka* (Montréal; Hexagone, 1994); *Bagues* (Chatel-Guyon, 1996). AFFIL: Pen Club, Paris; Pen Club, Montreal; Association des Écrivains de Langue française; La Société des Poètes de France; La Société des Gens de Lettres de France; Union des Écrivains; Société des Écrivains canadiens; International Society of Aesthetics; Association canadienne d'Esthétique; Association québécoise d'Esthétique; Association des Professeurs de français des Universités canadiennes; Association des Littératures canadiennes et québécoise; Association de Littérature Comparée; Société d'Études et de Conférences; Salon du Livre de Toronto (Pres.). HONS: Gov. Gen. Award for Poetry, *L'Écouté*, poèmes, 1986; Univ. of Peking Medal, 1993, Beijing, China; Médaille de la Société des Poètes français, Paris, 1994; research award, Univ. of Toronto, 1987. INTERESTS: writing; reading; travelling; ancient languages; psychosynthesis; bobbin lace; medieval cooking; studying modern languages; giving writing workshops. MISC: play, *Utinam*, performed in Quebec, Montreal, Paris & N.Y. COMMENT: *"Mother, writer, professor, married to a philosopher, proud of her two daughters, happy with her antique house in Neuville, enjoys seeing her friends, likes cats."*

Cochrane, Diane, B.Sc.N.,R.N. ◐ ⊕
President, Saskatchewan Branch, THE KIDNEY FOUNDATION OF CANADA, 2217 Hanselman Ct., Ste. 1, Saskatoon, SK S7L 6A8 (306) 664-8588, FAX 653-4883. Born Souris, Man. 1957. m. Duncan Grant. 1 ch. Chad Grant. EDUC: Brandon General Hospital, Diploma in Nursing 1977; Univ. of Saskatchewan, Certificate in Health Care Admin. 1984, B.Sc.N. 1989. CAREER: various positions incl.: Staff Nurse, Nursing Unit Coord., Nursing Mgr & Transplant Coord., Royal University Hospital, Saskatoon, 1981-95; Study Coord. for several clinical trials, Coll. of Medicine, Univ. of Saskatchewan, 1983-95. AFFIL: The Kidney Foundation of Canada (Pres. & Bd. Mbr., Sask. Branch; Dir., Nat'l Bd.); Saskatchewan Registered Nurses' Association (Pres., Saskatoon Chapter 1991-95). INTERESTS: sewing; camping; nephrology nursing. COMMENT: " *I consider myself fortunate to have worked with people affected by kidney disease through my employment and volunteer work and feel that I have made a difference in Saskatchewan.*"

Cockburn, Lyn, B.A. ✎ ⬚
Columnist and Features Writer, THE CALGARY SUN, 2615-12th St. N.E., Calgary, AB T2E 7W9 (403) 250-4201, FAX 250-4180. Born Victoria, B.C. s. 1 ch. EDUC: Univ. of British Columbia, B.A.(English) 1972. CAREER: High Sch. Teacher/Librarian; Journalist, *The Province*; Journalist, *The Calgary Sun*; Columnist, *The Toronto Sun* & *Ottawa Sun*. SELECTED PUBLICATIONS: regular columns in *Herizons* magazine; columns have been published in the *Hamilton Spectator, Montreal Gazette, The London Free Press,* & *Homemakers* magazine. AFFIL: Immigrant Aid Society in Calgary (volunteer E.S.L. teacher); Immigrant Services in Vancouver (volunteer E.S.L. teacher); Canadian Mental Health Association (Bd., Comm. Committee, Vancouver). HONS: Nominee, National Newspaper Award, 1989, 1990. INTERESTS: reading; issues of importance to women; African violets; sushi; volleyball; travel. MISC: active mbr. of the feminist community. COMMENT: *"My philosophy as a columnist is that the tongue in the cheek is often far more powerful than the sword."*

Cody-Rice, Edith, B.Sc.N.,B.A.,M.A., LL.B. ⚖ 🖇 🕮
Senior Legal Counsel, CANADIAN BROADCASTING CORPORATION, 1500 Bronson Ave., Ottawa, ON (613) 738-6619, FAX 738-6688. Born Regina, Sask. s. EDUC: Univ. of Toronto, B.Sc.N.(Nursing) 1966; Sorbonne, Diplome (Civilisation française) 1967; Univ. of Waterloo, B.A.(English Lit.) 1968, M.A.(English Lit.)

1973; Univ. of Toronto, LL.B. 1977. **BAR:** Ont., 1979. **CAREER:** Sessional Lecturer, Univ. of Waterloo, 1967-73; Administrator, Inter-Fac. Program Bd., 1972-73; private practice of matrimonial law, Toronto, 1979-82; Legal Cnsl, CBC, 1982-91; Instructor, Bar Admission Course, Law Society of Upper Canada, 1990 to date; Sr. Legal Cnsl, CBC, 1991 to date. **AFFIL:** Law Society of Upper Canada; Canadian Bar Association; The Writers' Development Trust (Dir.; former Nat'l Pres.); Ottawa Valley Book Festival (Charter Mbr.). **INTERESTS:** literature; history; visual & performing arts; archery.

Coghill, Joy, C.M.,M.F.A. 🎭 🎬 ⊕
Freelance Actor, Director and Theatre Consultant; Artistic Director, WESTERN GOLD THEATRE CO., 2020 E. Kent Ave. S., Ste. 311, Vancouver, BC V5P 4X1 (604) 324-1302, FAX 324-1302. Born Findlatter, Sask. 1926. m. John Thorne. 3 ch. Debra, Gordon, David. **EDUC:** Univ. of British Columbia, B.A. 1947; The Art Institute of Chicago, M.F.A. 1950. **CAREER:** Drama Teacher, private studio, 1943-48; Co-Prod., Everyman Theatre, 1950-52; Instructor, Goodman Theater, Chicago, 1952-53; Instructor, DePaul Univ., Chicago, 1952-53; Instructor, Univ. of British Columbia Extension Dept. & English Dept., 1952-62; Prod., Frederick Wood Theatre, UBC, 1953-54; Founder & Artistic Dir., Holiday Theatre, 1953-66; Prod. & Artistic Dir., Holiday Playhouse, 1966-67; Artistic Dir., Vancouver Playhouse Theatre Company, 1967-69; Artistic Dir., English Acting Section, National Theatre Sch. of Canada, 1970-73; Founder & Artistic Dir., Western Gold Theatre Society, 1994. **SELECTED CREDITS:** Prod., *The Ecstasy of Rita Joe*; Prod., *Grass and Wild Strawberries*; Playwright, *Yes*, radio play for CBC (1979); Playwright/Prod., *Song of This Place* (1987); Dir., *Month in the Country* (1965); Dir., *Noye's Fludde* (1960, 1967, 1995); Puck, *A Midsummer Night's Dream* (opera), 1961; Arkadine, *Seagull*, 1980; Sara Bernhardt, *Memoir*, 1981-92; Margaret Murray, *Ma!*, 1981; Helen, *Road to Mecca*, 1988-91; Lear in *Lear*, 1996; extensive radio, TV & film experience. **AFFIL:** Canadian Actors' Equity; ACTRA; Canadian Theatre History Society (Hon. Mbr.). **HONS:** Dominion Drama Festival Acting Award, 1946; Canadian Drama Award, 1963; Canada Centennial Medal, 1967; Canadian Silver Jubilee Medal, 1977; The Sam Payne Award, ACTRA-CBC, 1986; Woman of Distinction Award, YWCA, 1986; Lifetime of Service, Jessie Award, Vancouver Professional Theatre Alliance, 1989; Community Recognition (Curtains), Jessie Award, Vancouver Professional Theatre Alliance, 1990; Gascon-

Thomas Award, Lifetime of Service, National Theatre Sch., 1990; Outstanding Performance by an Actor, (*Province*) People's Choice Award, 1991; Best Actress (*Road to Mecca*), Jessie Award, 1991; Order of Canada, 1991; Canada 125 Medal, 1992; D.Litt.(Hon.), Univ. of British Columbia, 1995; LL.D.(Hon.), Simon Fraser Univ., 1994. **COMMENT:** *"Dr. Dorothy Somerset, an inspirational teacher in the Theatre Department at UBC in the 1950s, convinced me that a life in theatre is 'the pursuit of the good'. I have proceeded in that belief, exploring all avenues in order to enrich my life and those of colleagues and that of my country."*

Cohen, Annette, B.A. 🎬📖🎭✏️
President, ANNETTE COHEN PRODUCTIONS LIMITED, 25 Imperial St., Ste. 500, Toronto, ON M5P 1C1 (416) 483-8018, FAX 483-9763. Vice-President, VECTOR MANAGEMENT LIMITED. Born Toronto 1935. d. 2 ch. Richard B. Cohen, Jessica A. Cohen. **EDUC:** Univ. of Toronto, B.A.(English Lit.) 1956. **CAREER:** Educator/Literary Critic, 1958-65; Prod./Dir./Writer for film & TV, 1974 to date; Pres. & CEO, Primedia Pictures Inc., 1989-94; Pres., Annette Cohen Productions Limited, 1994 to date. **SELECTED CREDITS:** Prod./Writer, *The Burning Season* (feature), Primedia Pictures Inc., 1993; Prod., *April One* (feature), Primedia Pictures Inc., 1993; Prod., *Unfinished Business* (feature), Zebra Films Limited, 1983; Prod./Writer, *Romance* (feature), Genesis International, 1982; Dir., *Love* (feature), Velvet Productions, 1980; Prod./Dir./Writer, *The Doll Factory* (short drama), ABC Productions, 1978; Prod./Dir., *One People, One Destiny* (documentary), Hadassah-Wizo of Canada, 1977; Writer, *Nellie McClung* (drama), CBC, 1977; Prod./Dir., *The Visible Woman* (documentary), Federation of Women Teachers of Ontario, 1976; Writer, "Dentist to the Stars," *The King of Kensington* (series), CBC, 1976; Writer, *Report Metric* (series), TVOntario, 1975; Writer, *IBM* (industrial documentary), 1974. **SELECTED PUBLICATIONS:** numerous book reviews, short stories & poems. **AFFIL:** Canadian Film & Television Production Association; Toronto Women in Film & Television; Toronto International Film Festival; Canadian Women in Communications (formerly Canadian Women in Radio & Television). **MISC:** in 1980 she became one of the 1st women in Canada to direct for feature film when she directed four segments of *Love*. **COMMENT:** *"At 40, I chose to begin a career in film and television. The world I entered was not always hospitable to women, so while I was building my career I was also working politically to open up opportunities for women. In 20 years, I have achieved most*

of my professional goals and have had the satisfaction of seeing the workplace become more equitable. Against the odds of gender and age, it's been a great ride."

Cohen, Dian, B.A. $ 📺 📖

President, DIAN COHEN PRODUCTIONS LIMITED, 46 Wellington St. E., Aurora, ON L4G 1H5 (905) 841-0942, FAX 841-6417, EMAIL 70571.3702@compuserve.com. Born Winnipeg. **EDUC:** Univ. of Toronto, B.A.(Pol. Sci. & Econ. Hist.) 1956; McGill Univ., Postgrad. Studies (Econ.) 1956-63; Univ. of Miami, Independent Studies 1963. **CAREER:** syndicated newspaper & magazine columnist on personal money mgmt, econ. & bus. affairs, 10 magazines & 15 newspapers, 1968-88; Columnist, *Maclean's* Magazine, 1982-87; Columnist, *Benefits Canada*, Maclean Hunter, 1989 to date; Pres., Dian Cohen Productions Limited. **SELECTED CREDITS:** syndicated econ. & bus. commentator, CBC, 1964-85; money mgmt columnist, *Pulse News*, CFCF-TV, Montreal, 1979-82; Author & Host, *Microecon./Macroecon.*, CJRT-FM/Open Coll., credit course, Ryerson Polytechnic Univ., 1981 to date; Bus. & Econ. Ed., CTV TV Ntwk, 1985-91; Author & Host, *Growth Can be Green*, CJRT-FM/Open Coll., Ryerson Polytechnic Univ., 1989; Co-Host, *This Week in Business*, World Affairs/Baton Broadcasting System, 1994-96; Author & Host, *The Global Economy*, CJRT-FM/Open Coll., Ryerson Polytechnic Univ., 1994 to date. **SELECTED PUBLICATIONS:** *Your Money Matters*, dev. & prod. (Royal Bank's award-winning educ. kit., 1970); *The Next Canadian Economy*, co-author (1984); *To Save a Continent–Business Responds to North America's Environmental Needs*, co-ed. & conference organizer (Americas Society, 1990); *No Small Change-Success in Canada's New Economy*, co-author (Macmillan Canada, 1993); *Class Action–Making the Future Work Now* (*Quitte ou Double* en francais), co–author (Robert Davies Publishing, 1994). **DIRECTOR:** Noranda Forest Inc.; PanCanadian Petroleum; Royal Insurance; Canadian Pacific Limited; Monsanto Canada. **AFFIL:** Institute for Sustainable Development (Dir.); Colleges of Applied Arts & Technology Pension Fund (Trustee); Corporate Fund for Breast Cancer Research (Co-Chair); YMCA Employment Initiatives Programs (Advisor); Public Policy Forum; Canadian Merit Scholarship Foundation (Trustee); Junior Achievement (Dir.-at-Large); Ryerson Polytechnic Univ. (Fellow). **HONS:** Woman of Achievement, YWCA, Montreal, 1975; National Business Writing Award, 1978, 1983; *Money*, Literary Guild, 1988; *No Small Change*, Book of the Month, 1993; Order of Canada, 1993. **COMMENT:** *"Economic broadcaster, author and consultant, Dian Cohen advises governments, businesses, educators and the voluntary sector about their roles in the rapidly changing economic environment."*

Cohen, Esther Abigail ✪ $

President, CANADIAN POSTERS INTERNATIONAL INC., 1200 Castlefield Ave., Toronto, ON M6B 1G2 (416) 789-7156, FAX 789-7159. Born Toronto 1938. d. 3 ch. **EDUC:** Toronto Teachers' Coll., 1959. **CAREER:** Teacher, 1960-63; Publisher, 1978 to date; Pres., Canadian Posters International Inc., 1980 to date. **DIRECTOR:** Canadian Posters International Inc. **AFFIL:** Starlight Foundation; Israel Forum; Baycrest Home for the Aged; Art Gallery of Ontario; AIDS Committee of Toronto. **HONS:** Certificate of Recognition (volunteer teacher of English to Soviet immigrants in Israel), Israel Forum; Certificate for the preservation of Brazil's Atlantic Rainforest, The Nature Conservancy. **INTERESTS:** travel; reading; antique collecting; American contemporary art; scrabble; theatre; her dog. **MISC:** profiled in various newspapers incl. *The Toronto Star*, *The Globe and Mail*, *Decor Magazine* & *Canadian Collector*; interviewed on CTV Channel 9, Aug. 1995; listed in *Toronto Registry Who's Who* 1995; speaker at bus. seminar for City of York re: Free Trade with Mexico; participated in Free Trade Expo in Mexico City, 1994. **COMMENT:** *"I export Canadian artwork world wide and did an extensive sales trip to Asia in 1993 with the aid of the provincial and federal governments. Met with Trade Consuls in Hong Kong, Singapore, Taiwan, Thailand, Malaysia, Korea and Japan. We have donated artwork to Casey House, Ronald McDonald House, The Hospital for Sick Children, Baycrest Home for the Aged and Hospital, schools and many charitable organizations."*

Cohen, Judith R., B.A.,B.F.A.,M.A., Ph.D. 🎭 📺 🎓

President, CANADIAN SOCIETY FOR TRADITIONAL MUSIC/SOCIÉTÉ CANADIENNE POUR LES TRADITIONS MUSICALES, 751 Euclid Ave., Toronto, ON M6G 2V3 (416) 533-2666, FAX 533-2666, EMAIL jcohen@epas.utoronto.ca. Born Montreal 1949. s. 1 ch. **EDUC:** McGill Univ., B.A.(English Lit.) 1971; Concordia Univ., B.F.A.(Music) 1975; Univ. de Montréal, M.A. (Medieval Studies) 1980, Ph.D.(Ethnomusicology) 1989. **CAREER:** Instructor, Music Dept., Concordia Univ., 1977-81; Instructor, Royal Conservatory of Music, Toronto, 1983-88; Recorder Instructor, Toronto Educ., 1986-90; Tutor, Vanier Coll., York Univ., 1990-93; Visiting Lecturer, Hebrew Univ., Jerusalem, Dec. 1993; Instructor, Balkan Vocal Ensemble, Univ. of Toronto, 1988-95; Adjunct Grad. Fac., Music Dept., York Univ., 1993 to date; freelance consultant, performer, lecturer; Founding Mbr., *Gerineldo*, Moroccan Judeo-Spanish ensemble; Founder-Dir., *Nova Tradicija*, a capella Balkan singing ensemble. **SELECTED CREDITS:** *Con Viela y Mochila* (Madrid: Tecnosaga); *Primavera en Salonica* (Madrid: Tecnosaga, 1992); *Dized',¡ay! Trobadores: Medieval Monophonies* (Madrid: Tecnosaga, 1994). **SELECTED PUBLICATIONS:** "Judeo-Spanish Songs in Montreal and Toronto" (*Canadian Folk Music Journal* 1985); "Una mujer sefardita en una reserva indigena canadiense" (*Maguen*, Caracas 1991); various other articles, conference papers & chapters in books. **HONS:** Marcel Blouin Award, Best Music Program, Radio Canada, 1993-94. **MISC:** recipient of various grants; field work in Canada, Israel, Spain, Morocco, Istanbul, Thessaloniki, Paris, Brussels, US. **COMMENT:** *"Performer and ethnomusicologist specializing in Judeo-Spanish Sephardic songs, as well as in medieval and traditional music."*

Cohen, Marjorie Griffin, B.A.,M.A., Ph.D. ✊ 🎓 $

Professor, Political Science and Chair, Women's Studies, SIMON FRASER UNIVERSITY, Burnaby, BC V5A 1S6 (604) 291-5838, FAX 291-4786, EMAIL mcohen@sfu.ca. Born Franklin, N.J. 1944. m. Michael Goldrick. 2 ch. Sam, Sophie. **EDUC:** Iowa Wesleyan Coll., B.A.(Econ. & English) 1965; New York Univ., M.A.(Econ.) 1969; York Univ., Ph.D.(Soc. & Pol. Thought) 1985. **CAREER:** Sec. to the Dir., National Planning Association, Washington, D.C., 1965-66; Statistical Analyst & Computer Programmer, McKinsey and Co., N.Y., 1967-68; Lecturer, Social Science, York Univ., 1971-81; Prod. & Host, *Counterparts*, York Univ.'s Public Affairs TV series, 1980-81; Asst. Prof., Social Sci., York Univ., 1984-86; Assoc. Prof., Soc., Ont. Institute for Studies in Educ., 1986-89; Prof., 1989-91; Ruth Wynn Woodward Chair in Women's Studies, Simon Fraser Univ., 1989-90; Commissioner, B.C. Industrial Inquiry Commission on the Fisheries, 1990-91; Prof., Pol. Sci./Women's Studies, Simon Fraser Univ., 1991 to date. **SELECTED PUBLICATIONS:** *Canadian Women's Issues*, Vol. II, "Bold Visions," with Ruth Pierson (Halifax; Lorimer, 1995); *Canadian Women's Issues*, Vol. I, "Strong Voices," with Ruth Pierson, Paula Bourne, Philinda Masters (Halifax; Lorimer, 1993); *Women's Work, Markets, and Economic Development in Nineteenth Century Ontario* (Toronto; Univ. of Toronto Press, 1988); *Free Trade and the Future of Women's Work: Manufacturing and Service Industries* (Toronto: Garamond, 1987); numerous chapters in books & articles in scholarly journals. **DIRECTOR:** B.C. Hydro; B.C. Power Exchange. **AFFIL:** Canadian Centre for Policy Alternatives (Dir.); National Action Committee on the Status of Women (Treas. 1977-79; VP 1979-80, 1985-87 & 1988-89;Chair, Employment & Econ. Committee 1985-89); Pro-Canada Network (Spokesperson 1987-90); Coalition Against Free Trade (Co-Chair 1985-89). **HONS:** Laura Jamieson Prize for best book on women in Canada, Canadian Research Institute for the Advancement of Women, 1988; Marian Porter Prize for Feminist Research, Canadian Institute for the Advancement of Research on Women, 1985; Fac. of Grad. Studies Dissertation Prize, York Univ., 1985; appt. to Ruth Wynn Distinguished Chair in Women's Studies, 1989-90. **MISC:** recipient of numerous grants; numerous conference papers, seminars & panels.

Cohen, Martha Ruth, B.A.,LL.D., C.M. ♥ ✱ ☝

Volunteer. 318 - 26th Ave. S.W., Ste. 1701, Calgary, AB T2S 2T9 (403) 244-1098, FAX 245-1529. Born Calgary 1920. w. Harry Cohen. 4 ch. Philip, Cheryl, Faye Cohen-Hersh, David. **EDUC:** Univ. of Alberta, B.A. 1940; Univ. of Toronto, Social Work Diploma 1945. **CAREER:** Bookkeeper, Empire-Universal, 1940-43; Social Worker, Calgary Family Service Bureau, 1947-49. **AFFIL:** Calgary Jewish Family Service (Founder, former Exec. Dir., Hon. Bd. Mbr.); Calgary Folk Arts Council (Hon. Patron); Calgary Downtown Rotary Club (Mbr. 1993); Calgary Pro-Musica Society (Dir.); Jewish Community Commission on Aging; National Council of Jewish Women of Canada (Life Mbr.); Hadassah-Wizo Organization of Canada (Life Mbr.); Calgary Ort (Life Mbr.); Canadian Association of Social Workers; Canadian Numismatic Association; Canyon Meadows Golf & Country Club; Beth Tzedec Congregation & Sisterhood; Calgary Boy Scouts Foundation (Fellow 1983). **HONS:** Prime Minister's Medal, State of Israel, 1970; Order of Canada Medal, 1975; Alberta Achievement Award, Prov. of Alta., 1975; Citizen of the Age of Enlightenment, Transcendental Meditationists, 1976; Jubilee Medal, Queen Elizabeth, 1977; Sesquicentennial Year Award, Univ. of Toronto, 1977; Calgary Citizen of the Year, Calgary Jaycees, 1979; Canada 125 Medal; Mt. Scopus Award, Friends of Hebrew Univ., 1994; Hon. Chair, 35th Anniversary Fac. of Soc. Work, Univ. of Toronto, 1995; Ansel Award from Int'l Society for Performing Arts,

1995; Hon. Patron, Royal Cdn Sea Cadets "Undaunted," 1995; LL.D.(Hon.), Univ. of Calgary, 1982. MISC: 1st woman appointed chrm of an educational institution in Alta., Mount Royal Coll. Bd. of Gov., Chrm 1970-74; one of the two 1st women admitted to the formerly all-male Calgary Downtown Rotary Club, 1991; past mbr., Burgess Advisory Committee, prov. gov't appt. to plan for a Children's Medical Centre in Calgary; Past Chrm of Bd. (gov't appt.), William Roper Hull Home for Boys & Girls; Past V-Chrm, Old Sun Coll., Gleichen, Alta.; Founding Chrm, Calgary Centre for Performing Arts, 1975-85; former Mbr., Cdn Committee, U.N. Decade for Cultural Advancement; former Mbr., Council of the Alberta Order of Excellence (prov. appt.), 1980-85.

Cohen, The Hon. Erminie J. ✦
Senator, THE SENATE OF CANADA, Victoria Building, Rm. 806, Ottawa, ON K1A 0A4 (613) 947-3187. Born Saint John 1926. m. Edgar R. Cohen. 3 ch. EDUC: Mount Allison Univ., 1948. CAREER: VP, Hoffman's Limited; VP, Mitchell Apartments; Sec., National P.C. Women's Federation, 1985-88; VP, P.C. Party of Canada, 1989-91; Senator, The Senate of Canada, 1993 to date. AFFIL: Saint John-Fundy Fed. P.C. Women's Caucus (Founder & First Pres.); Hestia House (Founding Mbr. & Dir.); Women's Resource Centre (Dir.); Saint Joseph's Hospital & Family Services Saint John Inc. (Dir.); Saint Joseph's Hospital (Trustee); Shaarei Zedek Synagogue (Pres.); Saint John Free Public Library (Trustee); Muriel McQueen Ferguson Foundation Centre for the Study of Family Violence (Co-Chair of Fundraising); N.B. Advisory Council on the Status of Women (Mbr. of first Council); Canadian Advisory Council on the Status of Women; National Capital Commission (Past Dir., Bd. & Exec. Committee); Hadassah-Wizo Organization of Canada (Nat'l VP); Saint John United Way ("Leaders of the Way" Council); Royal Society of Canada (Advisory Bd.). HONS: Woman of the Year, the State of Israel Bond Organization.

Cohon, Susan Silver, B.Sc. ◑ ⊛
Volunteer. Born Buffalo, N.Y. 1938. m. George A. Cohon. 2 ch. Craig, Mark. EDUC: Northwestern Univ., Evanston, Ill., B.Sc. 1960. VOLUNTEER CAREER: Cabinet, United Way, 1987; Bd. Mbr., Ontario Coll. of Art, 1988-93; Chrm of the Bd., Variety Village Sport Training & Fitness Centre, 1990-92; Exec. Comm.; Founding Mbr., Oper. "Herbie"; Co-Chair, Chair of Neurosurgery, Univ. of Toronto; Bd. Mbr., Canadian Paraplegic Association; Bd. Mbr., Auxiliary of Mount Sinai Hospital; Bd.

Mbr., Jewish Family Service; Bd. Mbr., United Jewish Appeal; Bd. Mbr., Canadian Foundation for Ileitis & Colitis; Bd. Mbr., Hugh MacMillan Medical Centre; Bd. Mbr., Univ. of Toronto Crown Foundation; Bd. Mbr., Baycrest Centre for Geriatric Care; Mbr., Advisory Bd., Toronto Humane Society Building Fund; Co-Chair, first major fundraising event, Canadian Paraplegic Association; Fundraising Committee, Variety Village Swim; Hon. Co-Chair, The Mandarin Club Run for Mount Sinai Hospital; Chrm, Arrangements Committee, Tribute Dinner, Univ. of Haifa; Stratford Festival Fundraising Committee for *Much Ado About Nothing*; Chrm, Canadian Cancer Society Fashion Show, 2 yrs.; Arrangements Chrm, Confederation Dinner for the Prime Minister of Canada; Arrangements Chrm, Dinner Awarding Israel's Prime Minister's Medal to "Man of the Year"; Committee, Neurosciences Campaign, Toronto Hospital; Visiting Committee, Arts & Sciences Coll. at Northwestern Univ.; Patron, Toronto Garden Club; fundraising for various organizations incl. Ronald McDonald House, Toronto & Canada-Israel Cultural Foundation. HONS: Gardiner Award, 1991.

Colas, Réjane (née Laberge), B.A., LL.B. ■■ ⚖ ♟
Retired Justice of the Superior Court of Quebec. Born Montreal 1923. m. Émile J. Colas. 3 ch. Bernard, Hubert, François. EDUC: Univ. de Montréal, B.A.(cum laude), LL.B.(cum laude - first in Que. Bar exam.). BAR: Bar of Montreal, 1952-69; Canadian Bar Association, 1952 to date. CAREER: Aluminium Secretariat Limited, 1952-57; Assoc., Geoffrion & Prud'homme, 1957-69; appointed Justice of the Superior Court of Quebec (first woman in Canada), 1969; early retirement, 1994. AFFIL: Portage Program for Drug Dependencies Inc. (Gov. 1989 to date); Univ. de Montréal (Hon. mbr., Bd. of Dir. 1978 to date; mbr., Bd. of Dir. 1970-77); Canadian Bar Association (Chrm, Family Law Committee, Que. 1967-68); Judges of the Superior Court of Quebec (Treas., Gen. Committee 1978-82; Chrm, Gen. Committee 1982-84). HONS: 1st woman to be appointed Justice of a Superior Court in Canada; honorary Doctor of Civil Law, Bishop's Univ., 1971; Dame of Grace & Devotion, Order of Malta; Papal Decoration, "Pro Ecclesia e Pontifice"; Special Advisor, Selection Committee, Order of Canada, 1988-89; appointed to Extraordinary Challenge Committee, est. under Chpt. 19 of NAFTA, 1994; honorary diploma, Association des diplômés en droit, Univ. de Montréal, 1994. INTERESTS: singing; piano; tennis; golf; swimming. MISC: as contralto (soloist & choir mbr.), participated

in European tour of the Montreal Bach Choir, 1958; Cdn Delegate, Congrès international des Femmes des Carrières Juridiques, Bulgaria, for International Women's Year, 1975; invited to Rome for canonization of Sister Marguerite Bourgeoys, 1982.

Coldwell, Joan, B.A.,M.A.,Ph.D. ■ ⌲ 🝙 𝕆
Professor Emeritus, MCMASTER UNIVERSITY, Hamilton, ON L8S 4L9 (905) 525-9140, ext. 24715, FAX 845-7862, EMAIL coldwell@ mcmail.cis.mcmaster.ca. Born Huddersfield, UK 1936. EDUC: Univ. of London, B.A. (English) 1958, M.A.(with distinction, English) 1960; Harvard Univ., Ph.D. 1967. CAREER: Instructor & Asst. Prof., Univ. of Victoria, 1960-72; Book Page Ed., *Victoria Daily Times*, 1968-71; Assoc. Prof. & Prof., McMaster Univ., 1972-96; Dir., Women's Studies program, 1989-95; Prof. Emeritus, 1996 to date. SELECTED CREDITS: freelance Prod., *Ideas*, CBC Radio, 1971-72. SELECTED PUBLICATIONS: *Charles Lamb on Shakespeare* (1978); *The Collected Poems of Anne Wilkinson*, ed. (1990); *The Tightrope Walker: Autobiographical Writings of Anne Wilkinson* (1992); numerous articles on Wilkinson, women's lit. & Cdn writing in gen. AFFIL: Canadian Research Institute for the Advancement of Women; International Association for the Study of Anglo-Irish Literature; Women's Centre of Hamilton/Wentworth; McMaster Univ. (Bd. of Gov. 1988-91; Mbr. of Senate 1992-95). HONS: Teaching Award, McMaster Univ. Students' Union, 1981-82; Teaching Award, Ont. Confederation of Univ. Fac. Associations, 1989; Woman of the Year (Comm.), Hamilton City Council, 1989. INTERESTS: walking; swimming; theatre; art; feminism in all its aspects. COMMENT: *"I hope to be thought of as a fine feminist teacher and educational leader. The most important feature of my life is the company of a large circle of loving friends."*

Cole, Laura ■■ 𝕆
National Executive Director and Founder, THE CHILDREN'S WISH FOUNDATION OF CANADA (not-for-profit, grants wishes to children with high-risk, life-threatening illnesses), 1735 Bayly St., Ste. 8C, Pickering, ON L1W 3G7 (905) 420-4055, FAX 831-9733. Born Orillia, Ont. 1952. m. David. 2 ch. Sarah, Heather. EDUC: Sir John A. MacDonald High Sch., grad. 1970. CAREER: stay-at-home mother; founded the Foundation, 1984. HONS: Ontario Medal for Good Citizenship, 1987; Women on the Move Award, 1990; Woman of the Year, B'nai Brith Women's Council, 1991. INTERESTS: family of people & animals; work with the Foundation. COMMENT: *"My greatest achievements are my two daughters, next is the success of The Children's Wish Foundation over the past 12 years. We have succeeded in bringing happiness to over 4,500 children and their families. My work with the Foundation has been so very gratifying, having the opportunity to meet these special children and the wonderful people who support us across the country."*

Cole, Dianne M. ■■ 𝕆 ☼ 𝕆
President, REBEKAH ASSEMBLY OF ONTARIO (non-profit fraternal organization), P.O. Box 482, Marmora, ON K0K 2M0 (613) 472-2777. Born London, Ont. 1945. m. Howard Cole. 2 ch. Jennifer, Lisa. CAREER: Educ. Asst., 9 yrs. (after 5 yrs. of volunteer work in schools assisting with music programmes & children with special needs). AFFIL: Rebekah Lodge (initiated 1971; Musician 16 yrs.; Degree Capt. 19 yrs.; Noble Grand 1981-82; District Deputy Pres. 1985-86; Rebekah Assembly of Ontario (Musician 1982-83; Soloist 1989-90; Warden 1994-95; VP 1995-96; Pres. 1996-97); Order of the Eastern Star (initiated 1984; former Worthy Matron & Organist); St. Paul's Anglican Church (Choir Dir.; Lay Reader 12 yrs.); Red Cross Society (11-yr. mbr.; Chairperson, Emergency Svcs 7 yrs.); Canadian Cancer Society (Chairperson, annual campaign; driver for patients to Toronto & Kingston). HONS: Decoration of Chivalry for service to church, community & lodge, 1984; Community Award for volunteer work, 1987. INTERESTS: music; people. MISC: assists seniors with general errands, trips to doctors, etc.; has helped with several community "special days." COMMENT: *"I have tried to live out the principles of Rebekah—odd fellowship, friendship, love and truth. I try each day to lighten someone else's burden and to help whenever and wherever called upon. I enjoy people. My achievements are not of worldly fame or renown; they are my duty and I enjoy helping and doing for others."*

Cole, Holly ■■ 🝙 ⊗
International Singer. c/o Alert Music Inc., 41 Britain St., Ste. 305, Toronto, ON M5A 1R7 (416) 364-4200, FAX 364-8632. Born Halifax 1963. s. CAREER: forms Holly Cole Trio, 1988; signed to Manhattan Records, 1991; become a quintet in 1995 (the "trio" is dropped from their name). SELECTED CREDITS: *Christmas Blues*, self-produced commercial EP of 4 seasonal songs, 1989; *Girl Talk*, album, prod. Peter Moore, 1990; lead, *HUSH*, musical, Theatre Passe-Muraille, Nov. 1990; *Blame It On My Youth*, album, prod. Greg Cohen, 1991; *Don't Smoke in Bed*, prod. Dave Was, 1993; *Intimate & Interactive with the Holly Cole*

Trio, MuchMusic, Feb. 1995; *Temptation,* album, prod. Craig Street, 1995; *Temptation Live,* TV special, 1995; numerous sold-out shows in Canada, US, Europe & Japan. HONS: Grand Prix Gold Disc Award, Best Jazz Album, *Blame It On My Youth* & Best New Artist, Holly Cole Trio, Japan, 1993; Best Performance in A Performance Arts Program or Series (Holly Cole), Gemini Awards, 1993; Best Performing Arts Program or Series, *My Foolish Heart,* Gemini Awards, 1993; Best Performance in A Performing Arts Program or Series (Holly Cole Trio), *Intimate & Interactive with the Holly Cole Trio,* Gemini Awards, 1995. INTERESTS: film; theatre; horseback riding; flamenco; dance; hanging with my dog; the ocean; my wonderful family. MISC: *Girl Talk* certified Gold & is one of the Top 2 selling Cdn jazz recordings ever released; "Calling You," from *Blame It On My Youth,* #1 int'l recording in Japan for over 10 weeks; *Don't Smoke in Bed* achieved Platinum status in Canada; Holly Cole Trio subjects of 1-hr. documentary, *My Foolish Heart,* Jan. 1993; *Temptation* certified Gold. COMMENT: *"One of the most distinctive and alluring pop stylists in years"*–Chicago Sun Times.

Cole, Susan P.C., B.Sc.,Ph.D. ⊕ ⚙ ⪦
Professor of Oncology, Pathology, Pharmacology and Toxicology, Career Scientist of the Ontario Cancer Foundation, QUEEN'S UNIVERSITY, Cancer Research Laboratories, Kingston, ON K7L 3N6 (613) 545-6358, FAX 545-6830, EMAIL coles@qucdn.queensu.ca. Born Toronto 1954. m. Ralph Whitney. 3 ch. John Cameron Whitney, Anne France Cole Whitney, Ellen Patrice Cole Whitney. EDUC: Queen's Univ., B.Sc. 1976, Ph.D. 1981. CAREER: Research Technologist, Univ. of Alberta Cancer Research Unit, 1976-77; Postdoctoral Fellow, Lab. of Molecular Carcinogenesis, National Institute of Health, Bethesda, Md., 1981-82; Sr. Postdoctoral Fellow, Dept. of Microbiology & Immunology, Queen's Univ., 1982-85; Asst. Prof., Dept. of Oncology, 1985-89; Assoc. Prof., 1989-94; Asst. Prof., Dept. of Pathology, 1989-90, Assoc. Prof., 1990-95; Prof., 1994 to date; Assoc. Prof., Dept. of Pharmacology & Toxicology, 1989-94; Prof., 1994 to date; Career Scientist, Ontario Cancer Treatment & Research Foundation, 1985 to date; consultant to Eli Lilly Pharmaceutical Co., ISIS Pharmaceutical Co., Monsanta/Searle. SELECTED PUBLICATIONS: more than 175 papers, chapters in books & abstracts; "Multidrug resistance in human lung cancer and topoisomerase II" (*Lung Cancer: Principles and Practice,* pp.169-204, Lippincott-Raven 1996); "Multidrug resistance in a human small cell lung can-

cer cell line selected in adriamycin" (*Cancer Research* 47, 1989); "Overexpression of a transporter gene in multidrug resistant human lung cancer cell line" (*Science* 258, 1992); "Detection of the Mr 190,000 multidrug resistance protein, MRP, with monoclonal antibodies" (*Cancer Research* 54, 1994). EDIT: Int'l Advisory Bd., *Tumori,* 1993 to date. AFFIL: American Association for Cancer Research; Pharmacological Society of Canada; American Association for the Advancement of Science; American Association for Cancer Research (Bd. of Dir. 1996-2000). HONS: Annual Grad. Student Award, Pharmacological Society of Canada, 1979; Fogarty Int'l Fellow Award, 1981; Mihran & Mary Basmajian Award for Excellence in Biomedical Research, 1988; Merck-Frosst Award, Pharmacological Society of Canada, 1991; Queen's Univ. Prize for Excellence in Research, 1994; Monbusho Visiting Professorship at Kyushu Univ., Japan. MISC: recipient of numerous grants; US patent #5489519 for Multidrug Resistance Protein 1992; numerous invited talks; reviewer/referee for various journals & granting agencies. COMMENT: *"My laboratory-based investigations have resulted in the identification of several novel mechanisms by which human tumour cells can become resistant to anticancer drugs. Our goal is to use this information to develop new and effective therapies against drug-resistant tumours."*

Coleman, Anne Marguerite (Margo) (née Rudolf), B.A. ■■ ○
4 ch. Rob, Bill, Mary, Dave. EDUC: Univ. of Toronto, B.A. 1958; Ontario Coll. of Educ., Certificate 1959. CAREER: taught high sch. English & Phys. Ed., Oakville Trafalgar High Sch. & Forest Hill Collegiate, Toronto; Conference Coord., Centennial Coll. VOLUNTEER CAREER: Pres., C.M. Hincks Treatment Centre, 1986-88; Bd. Mbr., Volunteer Centre of Metro Toronto; Bd. Mbr., People and Organizations in North Toronto; Bd. Mbr., Cheshire Homes Foundation; Bd. mbr., J.D. Griffin Adolescent Centre; Red Cross Homemakers Advisory Committee for Ont.; Bd. Mbr., Extend-a-Family (Canada); Bd. Mbr., Ashby House–Rehabilitation for Head-Injured Adults; Bd. Mbr., Hincks Institute; Exec. Bd. Mbr., Ontario Association of Children's Mental Health Centres. AFFIL: Univ. of Toronto (Gov.; Bus. Bd.; Univ. Affairs Bd.; Exec. Committee, Academic Appeals Bd.; Chair, Elections Committee; Presidential Search Committee 1989; Alumni Gov. 1989-99); Downtown Church Workers' Association (Bd. mbr.); New Directions (Bd. mbr.); Muskoka Lakes Association (Bd. mbr.); Junior League of Toronto (4 terms Bd. mbr.; Sustain-

ing Mbr.). HONS: Arbor Award, Univ. of Toronto; Margaret Rolph Award & Margaret Whealy Award, Junior League of Toronto. COMMENT: *"When I was about to retire from teaching to raise a family of 4 children, I joined the Junior League of Toronto in 1964. Through its orientation, leadership training, community involvement, and four years on the board, I became involved with many non-profit agencies. Volunteerism is a stimulating and rewarding experience and lifestyle."*

Coles, Brenda, L.N.A. ⊕ ☻
President, PRINCE EDWARD ISLAND LICENSED NURSING ASSISTANTS ASSOCIATION, Box 1254, Charlottetown, PE C1A 7M8 (902) 566-1512, FAX 892-6315. Born Albery Plains, P.E.I. 1936. d. 5 ch. EDUC: Central Sch. for Nursing Assistants, Ont., Nursing 1962. CAREER: Licensed Nursing Asst., 1962 to date; Council Mbr., Pres., P.E.I. Licensed Nursing Assistants' Association, 1986 to date; VP, Dir., Canadian Association of Practical Nurses/Nursing Assistants, 1988-96; Lobbyist, Nursing Assistants Association, 1995-96. HONS: Life Saving Award, Red Cross, 1972; Hon. Mention for C.P.R.–Labour & Delivery. INTERESTS: cooking; quilting; decorating. MISC: participated in dev. of nat'l position papers, papers, & briefs made to fed. & prov. gov'ts. COMMENT: *"I am a 59-year-old lady who completes a job when it's started, looks for the best in anything and will work until I achieve the best."*

Collard, Elizabeth, C.M.,M.A.,LL.D. 📖 ⊗
Historian. Ottawa, ON K1N 6L2. Born Sawyerville, Que. 1917. m. Edgar Andrew Collard. EDUC: Mount Allison Univ., B.A. (English) 1939; Univ. of Maine, M.A.(English) 1940. CAREER: Educ. Ed., *The Gazette*, Montreal, 1942-47; Consultant on Ceramics, Canadian Museum of Civilization (formerly National Museum of Man), 1971 to date; Lecturer, Adult Educ. Dept., Univ. of Ottawa, 1984-89; McGill Univ., 1986, 1988; Hon. Curator, Ceramics, McCord Museum of Canadian History, 1984 to date; Mbr., Advisory Committee, Official Residences Collection, 1989-93. SELECTED PUBLICATIONS: *Nineteenth Century Pottery and Porcelain in Canada* (McGill Univ. Press, 1967; 2nd revised ed., McGill-Queen's Univ. Press, 1984); *The Potters' View of Canada: Canadian Scenes on Nineteenth Century Earthenware* (McGill-Queen's Univ. Press, 1983); *Victorian Pottery and Porcelain in the Canadian Home* (Canada's Visual History Series, National Museum of Man & NFB, Vol. 6, 1984); contributing author to: *Book of Canadian Antiques* (Toronto, 1974); *English Pottery and Porcelain*

(London, 1980); essay on ceramics, *The Earthly Paradise: William Morris in Canadian Collections*, exhibition catalogue (Art Gallery of Ontario, 1993); profiles of potters & Cdn furniture makers in various volumes of the *Dictionary of Canadian Biography*; *The Canadian Encyclopedia* (Hurtig); over 100 articles on the hist. of ceramics, furniture, etc. in both scholarly & popular publications. EXHIBITIONS: guest curator for exhibitions on ceramics & toys, McCord Museum of Canadian History, Montreal (1980s); Guest Curator, exhibition of 19th-century pottery & porcelain, Canadian Museum of Civilization (1994-97). AFFIL: English Ceramic Circle, UK; Wedgwood Society, UK; Northern Ceramic Society, UK; The Royal Society of Arts, UK (Life Fellow); Ottawa-Carleton Humane Society (Life Mbr.); has served over the years on many boards & committees. HONS: LL.D.(Hon.), Mount Allison Univ., 1971. INTERESTS: the hist. of ceramics, furniture & antiques in gen., Cdn in particular; animal welfare, herpetology in particular. MISC: has given scores of lectures to women's clubs, historical societies, etc. COMMENT: *"Historian with a special interest in 19th-century Canadian material history. Author, museum consultant, guest curator. Recipient of the Order of Canada in 1987 for contributions to the history of the decorative arts in Canada."*

Collenette, Penny (née Hossack), B.A., LL.B. ✦ ☻ ⚔
Director of Appointments, Office of the Prime Minister, GOVERNMENT OF CANADA, 406 Langevin Block, Ottawa, ON K1A 0A2 (613) 957-5540, FAX 957-5743. Born Oakville, Ont. 1950. m. Hon. David Collenette. 1 ch. Christopher. EDUC: Carleton Univ., B.A.(Law & Pol. Sci.) 1986; Univ. of Ottawa, LL.B. 1991. BAR: Ont., 1993. CAREER: Exec. Asst., Professional Association of Interns & Residents of Ontario, 1976-78; Nat'l Campaign Dir., Jean Chrétien Leadership Campaign, 1990; Acting Nat'l Dir. & Dir. of Legal Svcs, Liberal Party of Canada, 1993 Fed. Election Campaign; Dir. of Appts., Office of the Prime Minister, Gov't of Canada, 1993 to date. AFFIL: Liberal International Human Rights Committee (V-Chair); Parliamentary Spouses' Association (Past Founding Chair, Human Rights Committee & Society Jewry Committee); served on fundraising committees of LEAF, Great Canadian Theatre Company & the Famous People Players. MISC: invited participant, Campaign Reform Conference, Lortie Commission of Electoral Reform, JFK Sch. of Gov't, Harvard Univ., 1990; observer, 1989 U.N. Human Rights Commission, Geneva; participant, "Get-

ting to Yes" Negotiation Workshop, Toronto, 1995.

Colley-Urquhart, Diane, B.Sc. ♥ ⊕
Executive Director and Chief Executive Officer, Alberta/N.W.T. Division, CANADIAN CANCER SOCIETY, 2424 - 4th St. S.W., 2nd Fl., Calgary, AB T2S 2T4 (403) 228-4487, FAX 281-7411. Born Oyen, Alta. 1948. m. N. David Urquhart. 1 ch. EDUC: Univ. of Calgary/ Foothills Hospital, Nursing 1970; Columbia Univ., B.Sc.(Health & Human Svcs) 1994. CAREER: Dir. of Care & Svcs/Dir. of Educ./ Instructor, Foothills Hospital, 1967-82; Pres., Westhampton Management Ltd., 1982-89; Owner & Operator, country antique store, 1978-83; Corp. Dir. of Oper., Beverly Long Term Care Centre, 1985-89; Dir. of Mktg/Dir. of Comm./Dir. of Fund Dev., Heart & Stroke Foundation of Alberta/N.W.T., 1989-92; Exec. Dir. & CEO, Alberta/N.W.T. Div., Canadian Cancer Society, 1992 to date. SELECTED CREDITS: Host/Prod., *Sharing Canada's Future*, cable TV program. AFFIL: Calgary Police Commission (Commissioner 1994-97); Canadian Pension Tribunal (fed. appt. 1992-97); Community-Based Policing Advisory Committee; Calgary Chamber of Commerce (Unity Task Force); Coalition Against Racial & Religious Discrimination; Canadian Association of Executives; Alberta Association of Registered Nurses. HONS: Gov. General's Medal of Honour for Community Service. INTERESTS: sailing; cycling; fitness; community involvement. MISC: grad., 1994 Calgary Citizen's Police Academy; initiated the National People's Unity Fax Campaign during the Meech Lake Accord; founder of the Dini Petty Women's Invitational Golf Tournament for bringing attention to women re: heart disease; instrumental in the dev. & approval of an Alzheimer long-term care facility; completed the N.Y. City Marathon. COMMENT: *"An energetic, enthusiastic, resourceful, and innovative individual with a collaborative consensus-building leadership style, which is inclusive, and results in strong work teams with a high degree of organization effectiveness. An excellent public speaker with strong written and oral communication skills, creative problem-solving, excellent interpersonal skills and the ability to relate to senior levels of business, government agencies, the medical profession and community organizations and citizens."*

Collin, Emmanuelle $
Vice-President, Communications and Governmental Affairs, AVENOR INC., 1250 René-Lévesque Blvd. W., Montreal, QC H3B 4Y3 (514) 846-5072, FAX 846-5132. Born Montreal. m. Denis Rousseau. EDUC: École des Hautes Études Commerciales, Mgmt Course 1979; Univ. of Western Ontario, M.B.A. Mgmt Course 1982. CAREER: Dir., Public Rel'ns, COJO of Montréal (Olympic Games), 1974-76; Dir., Public Affairs, Johnson & Johnson, 1977-85; VP, Public Affairs, Focus Pharmaceuticals, 1986; Dir., Public Affairs & Office Svcs, Johnson and Johnson, 1986-89; VP, Nat'l Public Rel'ns, 1989-91; VP, Comm. & Governmental Affairs, Avenor Inc., 1991 to date. AFFIL: Canadian Public Relations Society; Publicity Club of Montreal; Montréal Chamber of Commerce; International Association of Business Communicators; Conference Board of Canada; Canadian Chamber of Commerce; The Canadian Council for International Business. HONS: Winner, Best Environmental, Annual Reports Contest, CMA-UQAM, 1992.

Collins, Anne, B.A. ✎ 📖
Managing Editor, *TORONTO LIFE* MAGAZINE, 59 Front St. E., Toronto, ON M5E 1B3 (416) 364-3333, FAX 861-1169. Born Whitby, Ont. 1952. m. Eric Rosser. 2 ch. EDUC: York Univ., B.A.(English) 1973. CAREER: various positions, *Chatelaine*, *The Canadian*; Arts Ed., *Maclean's* magazine, 1979-81; freelance writer & Consulting Ed., *City Woman*, *Canadian Business*, *Harrowsmith*, *The Globe and Mail*, *Saturday Night*, *Books in Canada*, 1981-90; Sr. Ed., *Saturday Night*, 1990-95; Mng Ed., *Toronto Life*, 1995 to date. SELECTED PUBLICATIONS: *The Big Evasion: Abortion, The Issue that Won't Go Away* (Lester & Orpen Denys, 1985); *In The Sleep Room: The Story of the CIA Brainwashing Experiments in Canada* (Lester & Orpen Dennys, 1988); "Trial by CSIS," *Best Canadian Essays*, 1990 (Fifth House, 1990); "The Battle over *The Valour and the Horror*," (*Saturday Night*, May 1993). EDIT: Ed. Bd., *This Magazine*. AFFIL: Toronto Arts Council (Pres.; VP 1992-94; Co-Chair, Lit. Committee 1991-94); P.E.N. Canada (Membership Chair 1989-90); Canadian Magazine Publishers' Association (committee work); National Magazine Awards Foundation (committee work); Writers' Union of Canada; Writers to Reform Libel Law. HONS: Southam Fellowship, Univ. of Toronto, 1994-95; Gold Author's Award ("The Battle Over *The Valour and the Horror*"), 1994; Gov. General's Literary Award for Nonfiction (*In The Sleep Room: The Story of the CIA Brainwashing Experiments in Canada*), 1988. INTERESTS: writing; reading; farming. MISC: served on juries & advisory bodies of the Canada Council & Ontario Arts Council; has taught magazine journalism at the Banff Centre & the Ryerson Sch. of Journalism. COMMENT: *"A writer and*

editor of books and magazines, with a bent for stories on complicated social and ethical issues."

Collins, Lisa M., B.Sc.,LL.B. ■ ⚖

Partner, THOMPSON DORFMAN SWEATMAN, Toronto Dominion Centre, 201 Portage Ave., Ste. 2200, Winnipeg, MB R3B 3L3 (204) 834-2581, FAX 943-6445. Born Pilot Mound, Man. 1958. m. A. Derek Clarke. 3 ch. **EDUC:** Univ. of Winnipeg, B.Sc.(Math.) 1979; Univ. of Manitoba, LL.B.(Law) 1982. **SELECTED PUBLICATIONS:** "The Terminated Employee: Minimizing the Tax Bite," *Report of the Proceedings of the Forty-Fifth Tax Conference*, 1993 Conference Report (Toronto: Canadian Tax Foundation, 1994); "Family Trusts: An Update," Prairie Provinces Tax Conference (1995). **AFFIL:** Law Society of Manitoba; Manitoba Bar Association; Canadian Tax Foundation. **INTERESTS:** family; travel. **MISC:** involved in Law Society of Manitoba educ. programs: Course Head, Bar Admission Tax Course, 1988-92 & 1996 to date, Lecturer, 1986-94 & 1996 to date; periodic presenter on tax topics to various associations. **COMMENT:** *"I have practised law for 13 years, primarily in the tax field, with particular emphasis on corporate and commercial related work. While doing so, I have held various volunteer board and committee positions."*

Collins, Marianne, B.Sc. ■ ⚔ ✿ ▢

Illustrator, Multimedia Computer Artist (905) 857-7207. Research Associate, ROYAL ONTARIO MUSEUM, Department of Palaeobiology, 100 Queen's Park, Toronto, ON M5S 2C6, FAX (416) 586-5863. Born Guelph, Ont. 1956. **EDUC:** Univ. of Guelph, B.Sc.(Hons.) 1980; Sheridan Coll., Computer Graphics Certificate 1996. **CAREER:** Biol. Tech., Ministry of Natural Resources, 1980-83; independent illustrator, 1983 to date; Staff Artist, Royal Ontario Museum, 1984-96; Multimedia Computer Artist, 1994 to date; Research Assoc., Royal Ontario Museum, 1996 to date. **SELECTED CREDITS:** *Seven Wonders of the World*, BBC-TV, London, UK, 1994; "The Burgess Shale," "Creatures of the Night," *The Nature of Things*, with Dr. David Suzuki, CBC. **SELECTED PUBLICATIONS:** *Life, The Science of Biology*, ed. Purves, Orians and Heller (Massachusetts: Sinauer Associates Inc./Utah: W.H. Freeman & Co., 4th edition, 1995); *The Fossils of the Burgess Shale* (Washington, DC: Smithsonian Institution Press, 1994); *The Book of Life* (General Edition), author Dr. Stephen Jay Gould (New York: W.W. Norton & Co. Ltd./London, UK; Random Century Group, 1993); *Wonderful Life: The Burgess Shale and*

the Nature of History, author Dr. Stephen Jay Gould (New York: W.W. Norton & Co. Ltd., 1989); illustrations for various books, scientific journals & bulletins. **EXHIBITIONS:** solo exhibition, Royal Ontario Museum (1994); Galerie de l'Évolution, Grande Galeries Musée National d'Histoire Naturelle (new gallery), Paris, France (1994); *L'âme au corps, Arts et Science 1793-1993*, Réunion des Musées Nationaux, Galerie Nationales du Grand Palais, Paris, France (1993); Preuter Collection of Canadian Art, 25th Anniversary Exhibition & Permanent Collection, Toronto (1990); *Art for the Birds*, ROM, Toronto (1986); Ducks Unlimited Fundraising Auction (1981, 1982); Canadian Nature Art Exhibition, Canadian Nature Federation & National Museum of Natural Sciences, touring exhibit (1981); *Impressions in Nature*, Art Exhibition & Auction (1981). **AFFIL:** Guild of Natural Science Illustrators; Ontario Underwater Council; Underwater Canada (Planning Committee); Etobicoke Underwater Club. **INTERESTS:** scuba diving; wildlife photography; Tai-Chi; travelling off the beaten path. **MISC:** guest speaker, "Images of the Burgess Shale," Brock Univ. 1990, & Univ. of Toronto Alumnus, 1990. **COMMENT:** *"Originally educated as a biologist, Marianne has since combined biology and artistic interests, illustrating the natural world in the service of science. She currently produces artwork for nature and science magazines and popular publications as well as for museums and other educational institutions. She has been commissioned and her illustrations reprinted by publishers worldwide. She has had the pleasure of collaborating with such notable authors as Dr. Stephen Jay Gould. From his international best-selling book* Wonderful Life, *several of her illustrations were displayed in a special exhibition celebrating the bicentennial of the Louvre and its associated Museums in Paris, France. During her tenure at the Royal Ontario Museum, she has reconstructed fossil animals, sculpted, modelled and illustrated Bat Caves, Maiasaurs and other natural history subjects for exhibit projects and for research purposes. Her artistic interpretations of the prehistoric wonders of the Burgess Shale and ongoing contributions to Palaeobiology research at the ROM have earned her the appointment of Research Associate. The addition of digital media to her repertoire of skills has greatly increased the scope of her work. As well as ink and paint, she also produces computer artwork for publication and multimedia presentations. She now has her sites set on the world of CD ROM development and 3D animation in order to educate and bring awareness of the natural world to a new audience."*

Collins-Nakai, Ruth L., M.D. ⊲ ⊕

Professor of Pediatrics and Associate Dean, Faculty of Medicine, UNIVERSITY OF ALBERTA, Walter C. Mackenzie Centre, 2J2.03, Edmonton, AB T6G 2R7 (403) 492-9727, FAX 492-7303, EMAIL ruth.collins-nakai@ualberta.ca. Born Pincher Creek, Alta. 1949. m. Dr. S.S. Nakai. 2 ch. Natasha Jasleen, Sunil Collins. **EDUC:** Univ. of Alberta, M.D. 1972. **CAREER:** Intern, Montreal General Hospital, 1972-73; Intern, Children's Hospital, McGill Univ., 1972-73; Jr./Sr. Resident in Pediatrics, Univ. of Alberta, 1973-74; Fellowship in Pediatric Cardiology & Clinical Teaching Fellow in Pediatrics, Harvard Univ., 1974-76; Co-Chief Resident in Pediatrics, Univ. of Alberta, 1976-77; Asst. Prof., Univ. of Alberta, 1977-80; Consulting Staff, Charles Camsell Hospital, 1977-93; Consulting Staff, Royal Alexandra Hospital, 1977 to date; Consulting Staff, Edmonton General Hospital/Grey Nuns' Hospital, 1977 to date; Consulting Staff, Misericordia Hospital, 1977 to date; Assoc. Prof., Univ. of Alberta, 1980-88; Consulting Staff, Fort McMurray Regional Hospital, 1982 to date; Consulting Staff, Queen Elizabeth II Hospital, 1982 to date; Consulting Staff, High Level Hospital, 1982 to date; Consulting Staff, Red Deer Regional Hospital, 1982 to date; Prof., Univ. of Alberta, 1988 to date; Dir., Alberta Heritage Pediatric Cardiology Program, 1979-80, 1982-84; Dir., Pediatric Cardiology Training Program, 1990-93; Assoc. Dean (Fac. Affairs), Fac. of Medicine, 1993 to date. **SELECTED PUBLICATIONS:** numerous articles, incl. "Interrupted Aortic Arch in Infancy," with M. Dick *et al* (*Journal Pediatrics* 1976); "Pharmacokinetics of Digoxin in Low-Birth-Weight Infants," with D. Schiff & P. Ng (*Developmental Pharmacology & Therapy* 1982); "Epinephrine Increases ATP Production in Hearts by Preferentially Increasing Glucose Metabolism," with D. Noseworthy & G.D. Lopaschuk (*American Journal of Physiology* 1994); over 50 abstracts. **EDIT:** Advisory Bd., *International Heart Health,* 1992 to date; Ed. Bd., *International Journal of Cardiology,* 1993 to date; Ed. Bd., Quebec Heart Health Demonstration Project, 1994 to date; Ed. Bd., *Canadian Journal Cardiac;* Ed.-in-Chief, *Pediatric & Adult Congenital Cardiac Self-Assessment Program* (CD-ROM, American Coll. of Cardiology, 1995 to pres. **AFFIL:** Canadian Society of Cardiology Technologists (Hon. Pres. 1994); Alpha Omega Alpha; Univ. of Alberta Medical Alumni Association; Royal Coll. of Physicians & Surgeons of Canada (Fellow, Pediatrics; Fellow, Pediatric Cardiology); American Coll. of Cardiology (Fellow; Chrm, Bd. of Gov. 1992-93; Bd. of Trustees 1995-99); American Academy of Pediatrics (Fellow); Alberta Car-

diovascular Society (Pres. 1986-87); Heart & Stroke Foundation of Alberta (Bd. of Dir); Alberta Medical Association (Pres. 1987-88); Alberta Pediatric Society (Sec.-Treas. 1984-87); Canadian Cardiovascular Society (Mbr., Council 1991 to date; Chrm, Ethics Committee); Canadian Medical Association; Canadian Pediatric Cardiology Association; Heart & Stroke Foundation of Canada; Canadian Pediatric Society; American Heart Association; Canadian Association for Medical Education; Canadian Society for International Health; The Muttart Foundation (Dir. 1989-95; VP 1994; Pres. 1995-96; Mbr. 1996 to date); Premier's Commission on Future Health Care for Albertans (Commissioner 1987-89); Alberta Science & Research Authority (Bd. of Mgmt 1994 to date). **HONS:** Queen Elizabeth II Scholarships for Academic Achievement, 1966-67, 1967-68; First Pediatric Resident Teacher of the Year Award, Univ. of Alberta Pediatric Resident Conference, 1988. **INTERESTS:** cardiac metabolism; preventive cardiology; encouraging science & research. **MISC:** Mbr., Transplant Candidate Review Committee, Univ. of Alberta Hospitals, 1990 to date; Chrm, Pediatric Cardiac Svcs Subcommittee, Prov. Advisory Committee on Cardiovascular Svcs , 1991-95; Chair, Task Force on Research Coordination in Alberta, Premier's Council on Science & Technology, Alta., 1993-94; recipient of numerous grants; numerous media appearances; frequent invited speaker. **COMMENT:** *"I am an academic pediatric cardiologist with interests in research and teaching in the area of improving the lives of children with heart disease and in producing healthy Albertans and Canadians in future preventative and research initiatives."*

Colwill, Nina Lee, B.A.,M.A., Ph.D. ■ ■ ⊲ ⑂

President, DECISION RESEARCH LTD., 463 - 13th St., Brandon, MB R7A 4P9 (204) 727-1800, FAX 729-0921, EMAIL nina@ccm.umanitoba.ca. Adjunct Professor, UNIVERSITY OF MANITOBA. Born Gaspé, Que. 1944. m. Dennis Anderson. 2 ch. Guy William Colwill Anderson, Erla Louise Colwill Anderson. **EDUC:** Univ. of Western Ontario, B.A.(Psych.) 1974; Univ. of Manitoba, M.A.(Psych.) 1976, Ph.D. (Psych.) 1981. **CAREER:** receptionist, later bookkeeper, Canada Law Book; bookkeeper, Con Bridge Ltd.; bookkeeper, Chagnon MacGillvray Accountants; Asst. Prof., Univ. of Manitoba; Assoc. Prof.; Full Prof.; Adjunct Prof.; Sec., Decision Research Ltd.; Pres. **SELECTED PUBLICATIONS:** *The Psychology of Sex Differences* (with H. Lips); *The New Partnership; The Essence of Women in Manage-*

ment (with S. Vinnicombe); numerous articles. **AFFIL:** Manitoba Psychological Association; PEO; CNIB (volunteer); Plan International. **HONS:** Touche Ross Award for Contribution to Women in Management. **INTERESTS:** reading; travel; writing.

Comeau, Mildred, B.A.,B.L.S., M.L.S. 🗋 🦅
University Librarian, UNIVERSITÉ SAINTE-ANNE, Box 40, Church Point, NS B0W 1M0 (902) 769-2114, FAX 769-0137, EMAIL mildred@cat.ustanne.ns.ca. Born Dartmouth, N.S. 1942. d. 2 ch. Stéphane, Nadine. **EDUC:** Univ. Sainte-Anne, B.A. 1965; Univ. of Ottawa, B.L.S. 1966; Dalhousie Univ., M.L.S. 1980. **CAREER:** Librarian, Univ. de Moncton, N.B., 1966-68, 1969-70, 1979-80; Research Asst., Queen's Univ., 1970-71; Univ. Librarian, Univ. Sainte-Anne, 1980 to date; Proprietor/Mgr, health food store, Saulnierville, N.S., 1993 to date. **SELECTED PUBLICATIONS:** Columnist on natural health in *Le Courrier de la Nouvelle-Écosse.* **AFFIL:** A.P.L.A.; A.A.U.L.C.; C.O.N.S.U.L.; A.B.C.D.E.F.; A.P.B.U.S.A. (Treas. 1987-94); Société historique acadienne de la Baie Sainte-Marie (Treas. 1986-93); Festin de musique de la Baie Sainte-Marie (Pres. 1984-85); Société Madeleine LeBlanc (Dir. 1991-93); Foyer École Joseph Dugas (Dir. 1984-88). **HONS:** Bursary: France-Acadie, Univ. de Paris, 1968-69. **INTERESTS:** piano; guitar; painting; parapsych.; natural health.

Compton, Jo Ann L., CMC Ⓢ
President, COMPTON GRAHAM INTERNATIONAL INC., 1177 Yonge St., Ste. 314, Toronto, ON M4T 2Y4 (416) 944-2000, FAX 944-2020, EMAIL 75051.1640@compuserve.com. **EDUC:** Secord Bus. Coll., Certificate (Bus. Admin.). **CAREER:** Personnel Mgr, TVOntario, 1973-75; Owner & Dir., Compton Consulting Limited, 1975-84; Principal, Exec. Search, Hickling-Johnston Limited, 1978-84; Ptnr-in-Charge, Exec. Search, Coopers & Lybrand, 1985-92; Pres., Compton Graham International Inc., 1992 to date. **SELECTED PUBLICATIONS:** "The New Deal" (*Executive Search Review* Dec. 1991); "Comparative Advantage in Canadian Leadership Styles" co-authored (1991); "Effective Hiring: The Entire Process" (*Society for Human Resources* 1989). **AFFIL:** International Association of Corporate & Professional Recruiters, Inc. (Cdn & Int'l Dir.; Officer; Founding Mbr., Cdn Chapter; Chair, 1993 Int'l Conference, Washington, DC); Metropolitan Toronto Board of Trade (Past Chair, Bus. Info. Committee); Institute of Certified Management Consultants of Canada (Certified Management Consultant); Human Resources Professional

Association of Ontario (Certified Hum. Res. Professional; Past Chair, Membership Meetings); The Institute of Corporate Directors; Canadian Association of Women Executives (Dir. 1979-80); Sales & Marketing Executives of Toronto (former Dir., VP & Chair); Badminton & Racquet Club of Toronto. **HONS:** Presidential Award for Service, Sales & Marketing Executives of Toronto; Distinguished Award for Service, International Association of Corporate & Professional Recruiters; Ursaki Award, Sales & Marketing Executives of Toronto. **INTERESTS:** tennis; theatre; computers; golf.

Comrie, Charlotte, R.N. ⭘ 🦅
Executive Director, HOLLAND COLLEGE FOUNDATION, 140 Weymouth St., Charlottetown, PE C1A 4Z1 (902) 566-9590, FAX 629-4268. Born Kentville, N.S. 1953. m. Jeff Davidson. 3 ch. Jessica Davidson, John Davidson, Alexander Davidson. **EDUC:** Saint Joseph's Sch. of Nursing, Diploma (Registered Nursing); Univ. of Prince Edward Island, Bus. (in progress). **CAREER:** Registered Nurse, 1974-81; Educ. Coord., P.E.I. Div., Canadian Heart Foundation, 1981-85; Exec. Dir., Heart & Stroke Foundation of P.E.I., 1986-96. **SELECTED PUBLICATIONS:** Ed., "Brainstorms" series of publications, booklet series used nationally explaining what a stroke is, how to respond & what to expect. **AFFIL:** Great St. George Art Gallery. **HONS:** Dedicated Service Award, Heart & Stroke Foundation of Canada. **INTERESTS:** skiing; travelling; swimming. **COMMENT:** *"I strive to provide and develop innovative leadership. Empowering people to make informed decisions and then respecting the consequences is vitally important."*

Comtois, Céline Ⓢ
Assistant Secretary and Shareholder Relations Director, AIR CANADA, Saint-Laurent, QC H4Y 1H4 (514) 422-5785, FAX 422-5789, INTERNET http://www.aircanada.ca. Born Quebec City. **EDUC:** McGill Univ., Transportation Mgmt Certificate, 1980; Institute for Balkan Studies, Thessaloniky, Greece, Certificate in Greek Studies 1983; Univ. de Montréal (Neo-Greek Studies, Modern Greek) 1985. **CAREER:** Passenger Agent, Air Canada, 1962-74; Supervisor, Reservations-Montreal, 1974-75; Administrative Asst. to the Gen. Mgr-Que., 1975-77; Customer Svc. Mgr, Mirabel Airport, 1977-79; Commercial Sales Mgr, Montreal District, 1979-81; Reservations Mgr, Quebec & Ottawa, 1981-88; Mgr, Shareholder Rel'ns, 1988-90; Asst. Sec. & Shareholder Rel'ns Dir., 1990 to date. **AFFIL:** Montreal Board of Trade; Canadian Corporate Shareholder Services Association (Dir.). **HONS:** Scholarship, Univ. of

Montreal in conjunction with the Min. of Culture & Science of Greece. INTERESTS: painting; skiing; golfing; travelling.

Comuzzi, Debbie, B.A.,B.Ed. ◐ ◉
National Executive Director, THE SUNSHINE FOUNDATION OF CANADA, 4026 Meadowbrook Dr., Ste. 141, London, ON N6L 1C9 (519) 652-2901, FAX 652-9605. Born Thunder Bay, Ont. s. EDUC: Univ. of Western Ontario, B.A. (English); Univ. of Windsor, B.Ed. CAREER: Reg'l Mgr, Canadian Red Cross, 1979-81; Prov. Mgr, First Aid, 1982-86; Health Planner, Metropolitan District Health Council, 1987; Dir., Planning, Volunteer Dev. & Field Oper., Canadian Cancer Society, 1987-93; Nat'l Exec. Dir., The Sunshine Foundation of Canada, 1993 to date. AFFIL: Ontario Association for Volunteer Administration (Past Pres.); Volunteer London (Bd. of Dir., Sec. 1994-96); London-Lambeth Rotary Club; Ontario Association for Volunteer Administration. HONS: President's Honour Roll, Univ. of Windsor; The Commonwealth Council Certificate of Thanks, Royal Life Saving Society; Service Award, The Canadian Red Cross Society; Certificate of Merit, The Canadian Red Cross Society; Certificate of Thanks, Canadian Red Cross Society; Certificate of Thanks, Ontario Association for Volunteer Administration. INTERESTS: sailing; cooking. MISC: involved with the writing of three organizations' strategic plans & one training plan. COMMENT: *"Giving to the community is her motto. Debbie is committed to the profession of volunteer administration. Her career spans 20 years of being both a volunteer and a manager of volunteers."*

Coniglio, Constance Barbara, B.A.,B.Ed., M.Ed.,Ed.D. ⊕ ⇎ ◉
Counsellor/Therapist, UNIVERSITY OF WESTERN ONTARIO, University Community Centre, Rm. 210, London ON N6A 3K7, EMAIL connie@sdc,uwo.ca. President, CANADIAN UNIVERSITY AND COLLEGE COUNSELLING ASSOCIATION. Born Hamilton, Ont. 1961. m. Leslie Richard Draisey. EDUC: Brock Univ., B.A. (Psych.) 1982; Univ. of Western Ontario, B.Ed. 1984, M.Ed. 1987; Ont. Institute for Studies in Educ., Ed.D.(Counselling Psych.) 1995; Reg. Psychologist, Prov. Of BC 1996. CAREER: Counsellor/Therapist, Student Dev. Centre, Univ. of Western Ontario, 1986-95; Researcher, Counselling & Career Dev., 1985-86; Researcher, Univ. & Coll. Placement Association, 1986; Counsellor II, Student Dev. Centre, Univ. of Western Ontario, 1986-95; Instructor, Dept. of Educ. Psych., 1986-93; Instructor, Dept. of Psych., 1988-95; Research Assoc., Student Dev. Centre, 1989-95; Instruc-

tor, Art Therapy Diploma Program, 1991-95; Counsellor/Therapist, King's Coll., Univ. of Western Ontario, 1992-93. SELECTED PUBLICATIONS: *Women in the Professions* (London, Ont.: Counselling and Career Development Services, 1988); *Women Adult Children of Alcoholics*, with C. Witherow (Halifax: N.S. Commission on Drug Dependency, 1989); "Making Connections: Eating Disorders and Addictions" (*National Eating Disorders Information Centre Bulletin* Feb. 1990); various other publications. AFFIL: Ontario Psychological Association; Ontario Association of Consultants, Counsellors, Psychometrists & Psychotherapists; Canadian Univ. & Coll. Counselling Association (Dir., Pres. 1994-96); Womanpower Inc., London, Ont. (Dir.; Pres. 1989-92); Sexual Assault Centre, London (Dir.; Pres. 1992-94); Women's Caucus at Western; London Status of Women Action Group; Hersize–A Weight Prejudice Action Group; Canadian Association of College & Univiversity Student Services (Sec./Treas.). INTERESTS: sailing; gardening; interior decorating. MISC: numerous conference presentations; numerous workshops given; Coord., Date & Acquaintance Rape Prevention Program, Univ. of Western Ontario, 1992-95. COMMENT: *"She has made numerous contributions through her teaching, facilitation, leadership, writing and counselling in the areas of women's issues, childhood maltreatment and adult adjustment, and counselling theory and practice."*

Conley, Corinne, B.A. ⚰ ♈ ⊗
Actor. c/o Ron Barry, The Characters, 150 Carlton St., Toronto, ON M5A 2K1 (416) 964-8522, FAX (416) 964-8206. Born Batavia, N.Y. m. Bonar Stuart. 2 ch. Anthony Stuart, Curtis Stuart. EDUC: Mary Washington Coll., Fredericksburg, Va., B.A.(Dramatic Art). CAREER: early performer on the CBC in such productions as *Flight into Danger*, Wayne & Shuster Premier, Harold Pinter's *The Lover* & Host, *CBC Open House*, 1955. SELECTED CREDITS: *Saltwater Moose* (feature) 1995; *Road to Avonlea*; *Butterbox Babies* (TV feature); *War of the Worlds* (series); Phyliss Anderson Curtis, *Days of Our Lives* (series), NBC-TV, 1973-81; *Hollywood Wives* (miniseries), ABC; *Dear Detective* (miniseries), CBS; various lead & starring roles in U.S. productions incl.: *Quincy, The Dean Martin Show, The Jonathan Winters Show, The New Dick Van Dyke Show, That Girl, Hogan's Heroes, Get Smart, Sanford & Son*; various lead & guest starring roles on Cdn productions incl., *Seeing Things, Red Serge, Check It Out, Snow Job*; Lead, *Love & Libel* (theatre), Martin Beck Theatre, Broadway, N.Y./Tyrone Guthrie Theatre Guild

Production; *Clap Hands*, London, West End, Prince Charles Theatre/Lyric Hammersmith; Julia, *Lend Me a Tenor* (theatre), Theatre Aquarius; Truvy, *Steel Magnolias* (theatre), Stage West Mississauga; Amanda, *The Glass Menagerie* (theatre), Theatre West, L.A.; Featured Artist, *Spring Thaw*, Star of Jubilee, Toronto; recurring role, *Wind at my Back* (CBC series); starring role, *The Dreamland* (Muskoka Theatre Festival); *The Care and Handling of Roses* (ABC TV movie); *Desparate Justice* (Lifetime TV movie); recurring role, *Flash Forward* (ABC/Disney TV series); *Goosebumps* (Disney TV series). **AFFIL:** AFTRA (Nat'l Council 1974-86); SAG (Bd.); EQUITY; ACTRA (Council 1987-93); British EQUITY. **HONS:** nominated (Phyliss Anderson Curtis, *Days of Our Lives*), Daytime EMMY; Award for Most Distinguished Contribution of Cdn Film, Canadian Council of Authors & Artists, 1956. **MISC:** served on the first Canadian Actors' Equity Committee, 1955; volunteer reader for Recording for the Blind, CNIB Toronto; naturalized Canadian citizen.

Conlinn, Carollyne B. Clark, B.A.,M.P.H., M.B.A.,C.H.E. ■ ⓢ ⊕
Vice-President, Health Care Business Development, VERSA SERVICES LTD., The Rogers Building, 476 Granville St., Vancouver, BC (604) 682-3436, FAX 681-0242. Born Quebec City 1946. m. Kurtis Conlinn. 2 ch. **EDUC:** Atlantic Union Coll., B.A.(French & Nutrition) 1968; Loma Linda Univ., M.P.H. 1976; Simon Fraser Univ., M.B.A. 1986; Canadian Coll. of Health Service, Certified Health Exec. 1994. **CAREER:** Chief Dietitian, Olympic Summer Games, Versa Services, 1974-76; Exec. Dietitian, 1976-79; Dir., Nutrition Svcs, Fraser Burrard Hospital Society, 1979-85; Dir., Materiel Mgmt, 1985-89; Sessional Lecturer, Sch. of Family & Nutritional Sciences, Univ. of British Columbia, 1989; B.C. Reg'l Mgr, Versa Services, 1989-94; VP, B.C. & Alta. Oper., 1994-96; VP, Health Care Bus. Dev., 1996 to date. **AFFIL:** Canadian Dietetic Association (Pres. 1994-95; Charter Fellow 1989); Public Education for Peace Society (Founding Bd. Mbr.); B.C. Dietitians' & Nutritionists' Association (1981-82); National Food Service Training Association (1995); on various Bds. of Dir. of prov. & nat'l organizations. **HONS:** Goodhost Award, Canadian Dietetic Association, 1986; Award of Merit, B.C. Dietitians' & Nutritionists' Association, 1986. **INTERESTS:** alternative medicine. **COMMENT:** *"My commitment is to create healthy work environments that enable people to succeed. Success means achieving results, which include both spiritual and financial goals for people and organizations."*

Connell, Meg, B.A.,M.B.A. ■ ■ ⌣ ☻
Executive Director, THE CANADIAN CLUB OF TORONTO (speakers' club featuring prominent speakers of nat'l & int'l importance), 100 Front St. W., Toronto, ON M5J 1E3 (416) 364-5591, FAX 364-5676. Born Toronto. **EDUC:** Univ. of Western Ontario, B.A.(Hons., Pol. Sci.) 1986; Univ. of Toronto, M.B.A. 1991. **AFFIL:** YWCA of Metropolitan Toronto (Steering Committee, Women of Distinction Awards).

Connelly, M. Patricia, B.A.,M.A.,Ph.D. ⌕ ⚘
Coordinator, International Development Studies Program, Department of Sociology, SAINT MARY'S UNIVERSITY, Halifax, NS B3H 3C3 (902) 420-5871, FAX 420-5561, EMAIL pconnelly@husky1.stmarys.ca. **EDUC:** Dalhousie Univ., Diploma in Educ. 1966, M.A. 1970; Saint Mary's Univ., B.A. 1968; Univ. of Toronto, Ph.D. 1976. **CAREER:** Lecturer, St. Mary's Univ., 1970-73; Asst. Prof., 1973-79; Assoc. Prof., 1979-86; Full Prof., 1986 to date; Chair, Soc. Dept., 1981-82, 1985-89, 1991-92; Co-Dir., Summer Institute on Gender & Dev., 1987-91; Coord., Int'l Dev. Studies Program, 1994 to date. **SELECTED PUBLICATIONS:** *Last Hired, First Fired: Canadian Women and the Labour Force* (Toronto: Women's Educational Press, 1978); "Feminism and Political Economy," ed. (with Intro.) with P. Armstrong (*Studies in Political Economy*, special issue (30), 1989); *Sharing Knowledge: South and North: The Summer Institute on Gender and Development*, with J. Fiske, *et al* (Vancouver: Commonwealth of Learning, 1992); "Gender Matters: Restructuring and Adjustment, South and North" (*Social Politics*, 1995); "Restructured Worlds/Restructured Debates: Globalization, Development and Gender," with T. Li, M. MacDonald & J. Parpart (*The Canadian Journal of Development Studies*, Special Beijing issue, Fall 1995); "Theoretical Perspectives in Feminism and Development," with T. Murray Li *et al* in *Theoretical Perspectives on Gender and Development* (Vancouver: Commonwealth of Learning, 1996); "Gender Matters: Restructuring and Adjustment, South and North" (*Social Politics* 3(1) Spring 1996); "The Labour Market, the State, and the Reorganizing of Work: Policy Impacts," with M. MacDonald in *Rethinking Restructuring: Gender and Change in Canada*, ed. I. Bakker (Toronto: Univ. of Toronto Press.); "Workers, Households, Community: A Case Study of Restructuring in the Nova Scotia Fishery," with M. MacDonald, *Social Research and Public Policy Formation in the Fisheries, Norwegian and Canadian Experiences*, ed. D. MacInnes, S. Jentoff & A. Davis (Ocean Institute of Canada, Halifax, 1991); numerous ed. books, mono-

graphs, special issues, articles in journals, ed. book collections; various contract research, consultations, workshops & research reports; numerous presentations; over 40 papers presented at conferences or workshops around the world. **EDIT:** Ed. Bd., *Studies in Political Economy: A Socialist Review*, 1982 to date; Assoc. Ed., *The Canadian Review of Sociology and Anthropology*, 1990-92; Ed. Bd., *Atlantis: Women's Studies Journal*, 1991-95. **AFFIL:** Canadian Commission for UNESCO (Advisory Committee on Social & Human Sci.; Advisory Committee on the Status of Women); N.S. Gaming Commission (Commissioner). **HONS:** Canada Council Doctoral Fellowship, 1975-76. **INTERESTS:** women in the Cdn economy; gender & dev.; feminist theory; Cdn pol. economy; social policy. **MISC:** numerous research & travel grants.

Connolly, Bea Broda, B.A. ⊗ ⊗ ⊔
Producer, Writer, Host, Narrator, Co-Founder, BC PICTURES, 245 Britannia Rd. E., Mississauga, ON L4Z 2Y7 (905) 890-3400, FAX 890-4507. m. Bob Connolly. **EDUC:** Univ. of Manitoba, B.A.(Psych.); variety of theatre & acting courses; grade 10 piano; Toronto Conservatory, grade 9 voice. **CAREER:** Host/Prod., *Manitoba Morning* & *CKND Magazine*, CKND TV, Winnipeg, 1981-85; Weathercaster, "The 6:00 Report," CKND, 1983-85; Host, *The Music Room*, 1982-85; various commercials, voice-overs, hosting & emcee positions incl.: Co-Host, Variety Club Telethon (Winnipeg); Contributing Host/Prod., *For Arts' Sake*, 1981-85; Co-Host/Assoc. Prod., *Discover Your World*, CHCH-TV, 1987-88; Co-Prod./Writer/Host/Narrator, *Passport to Adventure*, 1989-92; monthly feature, "The Global Traveller," *Global News at Noon*, 1991-92; Co-Writer/Co-Prod./Co-Narrator/co-computer programmer, *Timeless Places*, documentary TV series, 1991-96; Co-Writer/Co-Prod./Co-Narrator/co-computer programmer, *The Search for Ancient Wisdom*, CD-ROM distributed on Apple and Cambrix labels, debut 1995; Co-Founder (with husband Bob Connolly), BC Pictures, 1988 to date. **SELECTED CREDITS:** *Passport to Adventure* (series); *Timeless Places* (TV series); *The Search For Ancient Wisdom* (CD-ROM, TV documentary); *Play It Again Thor* (TV & video); *Aruba Bonbini* (travel video); *Costa Rica* (travel video); *Royal Denmark and Cycling Hans Christian Andersen's Denmark* (video); *The Search for Red Gold* (video). **MISC:** 3,000 of her photographs of the world have been assembled into several sets of photo CDs called *Photophile World Image Library* & distributed by Aztech New Media Inc.; many of the videos

and CD-ROMs can be found in libraries. **COMMENT:** *"My husband and I formed a production company called BC Pictures, in which we own all of the equipment necessary to produce broadcast quality television programs, videos and CD-ROMs. We have amassed an immense stock footage library of the world for the purpose of creating our productions whose main purpose is to further the cause of understanding the world's cultures and religions and to shed light on the archaeological mysteries that have baffled the world throughout time."*

Conrad, Margaret Rose, B.A.,M.A., Ph.D.,FRSC ■ ⊗ ⊗ ⊏
Nancy Rowell Jackman Chair in Women's Studies, MOUNT SAINT VINCENT UNIVERSITY, Halifax, NS B3M 2J6 (902) 457-6257, FAX 443-1352. Born Bridgewater, N.S. 1946. d. **EDUC:** Acadia Univ., B.A.(Hist.) 1967; Univ. of Toronto, M.A.(Hist.) 1968, Ph.D.(Hist.) 1979. **CAREER:** Ed., Clark, Irwin Publishing Company, 1968-69; Lecturer, Asst. Prof., then Assoc. Prof., Dept. of Hist., Acadia Univ., 1969-87; Prof., 1987 to date; Visiting Lecturer, Summer Sch., Univ. of Victoria, 1979; Visiting Scholar, Ont. Institute for Studies in Educ., 1981-82; Adjunct Prof., Dept. of Hist., Dalhousie Univ., 1991 to date; Head, Dept. of Hist., Acadia Univ., 1992-95. **SELECTED CREDITS:** Prod., *History of Atlantic Canada*, CTV University of the Air (1979); Prod., *Perspectives on Canada*, TV series (1984-85); Co-Prod., *Targeting Tomorrow*, video, Annapolis Valley Bd. of Trade, Acadia Institute & Atlantic Canada Opportunity Agency (1988-89). **SELECTED PUBLICATIONS:** *Twentieth Century Canada*, with John Ricker (Toronto: Clarke, Irwin, 1974); *Women at Acadia University: The First Fifty Years, 1884-1934*, with Elizabeth Rice & Patricia Townsend (Kentville: Acadia Univ., 1983); various other books & ed. works; *George Nowlan: Maritime Conservative in National Politics* (Toronto: Univ. of Toronto Press, 1986); *No Place Like Home: The Diaries and Letters of Nova Scotia Women, 1771-1938* with others (Halifax: Formac, 1988); *They Planted Well: New England Planters in Maritime Canada* (Fredericton: Acadiensis Press, 1988); *Making Adjustments: Change and Continuity in Planter Nova Scotia, 1759-1800*, ed. (Fredericton: Acadiensis Press, 1991); *History of the Canadian Peoples*, with others (Toronto: Copp Clark Pitman, 1993); various other articles & chapters in books; over 75 book reviews in various academic journals. **EDIT:** Co-ed., *Atlantis: A Women's Studies Journal*, 1975-85; Advisory Bd., 1985 to date; Advisory Bd., *Acadiensis: Journal of the His-*

tory of the Atlantic Region, 1980 to date; Ed. Bd., *Historical Papers*, Canadian Historical Association, 1988-91; Ed., *Planter Notes*, 1989-92; Advisory Bd., *Historie Sociale/Social History*, 1989 to date; Advisory Bd., *Newfoundland Studies*, 1993 to date; Ed. Bd., *Canadian Historical Review*, 1994-97. **AFFIL:** Association for Canadian Studies; Atlantic Association of Historians; Canadian Historical Association; Canadian Research Institute for the Advancement of Women; Canadian Women's Studies Association; Historic Sites & Monuments Bd. of Canada (N.S. Mbr.); Royal Society of Canada (Fellow). **HONS:** Lieutenant-Governor's Medal, Annapolis County, 1963; Math Congress Prize for Annapolis County, 1963; Woodrow Wilson Fellowship, 1967-68; Gov. General's Medal, Acadia Univ., 1967. **MISC:** various print & broadcast interviews; recipient of various grants & fellowships; juror for various awards; numerous papers & addresses. **COMMENT:** *"Member of Acadia University's History Department for 27 years, Dr. Conrad has written extensively on the history of Atlantic Canada and participated in a wide variety of professional organizations. She has a two year tenure from Acadia University (1996-98) to take up the position of Nancy Rowell Jackman Chair of Women's Studies, Mount Saint Vincent University."*

Conway, Susan Lucente, B.A.,B.Ed. ○
Executive Director, WOMEN IN CRISIS ALGOMA INC., 23 Oakland Ave., Sault Ste. Marie, ON P6A 2T2 (705) 759-1230, FAX 759-3239. Born Italy 1946. 4 ch. Lorne, Liane, Tim, Darcie. **EDUC:** Algoma Univ., B.A.(Psych./Hist.) 1977; Nipissing Univ., B.Ed. 1978; Mich. State Univ., M.S.W. (ABD). **CAREER:** Family Worker, Downtown Settlement House; Proj. Officer, Canada Employment & Immigration; Exec. Dir., Women in Crisis Algoma Inc. **AFFIL:** Algoma Women Sexual Assault Services (Treas. 1992-93; Chair 1994-95); Sexual Assault Coordinating Committee (Treas. 1993-94); Supervised Access Program (Chair 1993); Liuna Housing Corp.; John Howard Society (Pres.); Sault Ste. Marie Canadian Mental Health Association. **HONS:** Woman of the Week, Business & Professional Women's Club; Award In Recognition of Work on Behalf of Women in Our Community, Haddassah-Wizo (local). **INTERESTS:** reading; gardening; Eastern philosophies/spirituality; Goddess spirituality.

Cook, Eleanor, B.A.,Ph.D.,F.R.S.C. 📖 🐦
Professor, Department of English, UNIVERSITY OF TORONTO, Victoria College, 326 NF, Toronto, ON M5S 1K7 (416) 585-4444, FAX 585-4584. Born Toronto 1933. m. G. Ramsay. 2 ch. **EDUC:** Univ. of Toronto, B.A.(English) 1954, Ph.D.(English) 1967. **CAREER:** Lecturer, Univ. of British Columbia, 1958-59; Ed., Univ. of Toronto Press, 1960-63; Lecturer, Asst. Prof., Assoc. Prof., Victoria Coll., Univ. of Toronto, 1967-84; Prof., 1985 to date. **SELECTED PUBLICATIONS:** *Browning's Lyrics: An Exploration* (Toronto: Univ. of Toronto Press, 1974); *Centre and Labyrinth: Essays in Honour of Northrop Frye* Co-Ed. (Toronto: Univ. of Toronto Press, 1983); *Poetry, Word-Play and Word-War in Wallace Stevens* (Princeton, 1988); *University of Toronto Quarterly* Ed. Spring 1992 issue on allusion; *About the Size of Our Abidance: Essays on Poetry and History* (Stanford, forthcoming); various articles, notes, etc., 1955 to date. **AFFIL:** Royal Society of Canada (Fellow); Massey Coll. (Assoc.). **HONS:** numerous fellowships & grants, incl. Jr. Fellowship, Canadian Association of University Women, 1954; A.S.P. Woodhouse Thesis Prize, 1968; research grants, Social Sciences & Humanities Research Council; Connaught Fellow (Hon. 1994); Guggenheim Fellow, 1994; Killam Fellow, 1995. **COMMENT:** *"I am strongly drawn by the power of words, and so by their highest-organized form, poetry, which I can teach anyone to read (except liars)."*

Cook, Heather Maggs, B.A. 🎭 ✐
Director and Producer, *The Nature of Things*, CANADIAN BROADCASTING CORPORATION, Box 500, Stn. A, Toronto, ON M5W 1E6. Born Montreal 1935. d. 2 ch. Hilary Cook, Jesse Cook. **EDUC:** Bishop's Univ., B.A.(English) 1956. **CAREER:** Reporter, *Cornwall Daily Standard Freeholder*; Writer & Host, *Heather Here*, daily radio show, *Cornwall*; freelance journalist, London & Paris; Writer, Prod. & Dir., *The Nature of Things*, CBC, 1969 to date. **SELECTED CREDITS:** for *The Nature of Things*: "Newborn"; "Children's Hospital Skin, The Bare Necessity"; "One Two Three-Zero, Out of the Mouth of Babes"; "Twins—And Then There Were Two"; "Bring Back My Bonnie"; "The Children Who Learned to Listen"; "I Never Planned on This"; "The Familiar Face of Love"; "You Must Have Been a Bilingual Baby"; "Post Mortem"; "Memory–The Past Imperfect"; "Easy Targets"; "The Child Who Couldn't Play"; for *Planet for the Taking*: "Improving on Nature"; "At War With Death." **HONS:** various awards for documentaries from: The American Film Festival; Columbus Film Festival; American Psychological Association (Nat'l Media Award); Children's Broadcast Institute; Prix ANIK; Festival International de Films, Croix Rouge et de la

Santé; International Rehabilitation Film Festival. INTERESTS: France; photography; writing; architecture; food; antiques; travel; films. COMMENT: *"I have been lucky enough to have the opportunity to work on subjects that impassion and inspire me, which I hope is reflected in the resulting programs."*

Cook, Kathryn, B.A.,M.Ed. ✿
Chaplain, UNITARIAN CONGREGATION OF NORTHWEST TORONTO, 212 Briar Hill Ave., Toronto, ON M4R 1J2 (416) 483-1370. Born Meaford, Ont. m. Herbert Cook. 4 ch. Sheila, Heather, James, Kathryn. EDUC: Univ. of Toronto, Victoria Coll., B.A.(Psych.), O.I.S.E., M.Ed.(Adult Educ. & Counselling). CAREER: Unitarian Chaplain, 1973 to date. SELECTED PUBLICATIONS: *Create Your Wedding Ceremonies and Invitations* (Royce Publications, 1987). EXHIBITIONS: The Gallery at The Elmwood (Nov.-Dec. 1995; Nov.-Dec. 1996); First Unitarian Congregation (Mar. 1996). AFFIL: McGill Club; Canadian Association of Unitarian Chaplains. INTERESTS: paints in acrylics; sings in community choirs; plays classical & jazz piano; retreats to country home, which is a renovated church. COMMENT: *"A Unitarian chaplain since 1973, has achieved prominence and considerable media attention for conducting nontraditional rites of passage–services for births, marriages and deaths."*

Cook, Lyn, B.A.,B.L.Sc. 📖
Children's Author. Born Weston, Ont. 1918. w. 2 ch. Christopher Robb Waddell, Deborah Lynn Waddell. EDUC: Univ. of Toronto, B.A.(English Language & Lit.) 1940, B.L.Sc. (Library Sci.) 1941. CAREER: Librarian, Toronto Public Library, 1941-42; Meteorological Observer & Librarian, Royal Canadian Air Force (Women's Div.), 1942-46; Children's Librarian, Sudbury Public Library, 1946-47; Scriptwriter, Dir., Narrator, children's radio show *A Doorway in Fairyland*, CBC Toronto, transCanada & U.S. stations, 1947-52; Writer, *Sounds Fun*, CBC Radio series, 1954-55; Creative Drama Teacher, New Play Society Theatre Sch., 1956-65; Pre-sch. Story Hour, Monthly Festival (Drama), Scarborough Public Libraries, Bendale Branch, 1962-76; Writer, *Samantha's Secret Room*, children's series, CBC TV children's telecast *The Mystery Makers*, 1967; Speaker & Lecturer, libraries, schools, teacher associations. SELECTED PUBLICATIONS: *The Bells on Finland St.* (1950, 1951); *The Little Magic Fiddler* (1951); *Rebel on the Trail* (1953); *Jady and the General* (1955); *Pegeen and the Pilgrim* (1957); *The Road to Kip's Cove* (1961); *Samantha's Secret Room* (1963, 1991); *The Brownie Handbook* (1965); *The

Secret of Willow Castle (1966, 1984); *The Magical Miss Mittens* (1970); *Toys from the Sky* (1972); *Jolly Jean-Pierre/Voyage Extraordinaire de Jean-Pierre* (1973); *If I Were All These* (1974); *The Magic Pony* (1981); *Sea Dreams* (1981); *A Treasure for Tony* (1981); *A Canadian ABC* (1990); *The Hiding-Place* (1990, 1994); *Where Do Snowflakes Go?* (1994). AFFIL: CANSCAIP. HONS: Vicky Metcalf Award, 1978.

Cook, Rebecca, M.P.A.,J.D,LL.M., J.S.D. ✿ ⚖
Professor and Director, International Human Rights Program, Faculty of Law, UNIVERSITY OF TORONTO, 84 Queen's Park Cres., Toronto, ON M5S 2C5 (416) 978-4446, FAX 978-7899. m. Bernard M. Dickens. EDUC: Harvard Univ., Kennedy Sch. of Gov't, M.P.A. 1973; Georgetown Univ., J.D. 1982; Columbia Univ., LL.M. 1988, J.S.D 1994. BAR: Washington, D.C. CAREER: Research Assoc., Carnegie Endowment for International Peace, 1966; Research Assoc., Lester Pearson Commission, World Bank, 1969; Research Assoc., Woodrow Wilson Int'l Center, Smithsonian Institute, 1970-71; Research Assoc., Population Council, N.Y., 1972; Research Assoc., U.N. Population Fund, 1973; Research Officer, US Congress, 1978-81; Dir., Law Program, International Planned Parenthood Federation, London, UK, 1973-78; Lawyer, Beveridge, Fairbanks and Diamond, 1980; Adjunct Fac. Mbr., Univ. of Minnesota, 1986-90; Asst. Prof., Sch. of Health, Div. of Population & Family Health, Columbia Univ., 1983-87; Asst. Prof. (Research), Fac. of Law & Fac. of Medicine, Univ. of Toronto, 1987-90; Asst. Prof. (Research), Fac. of Law & Fac. of Medicine, 1990-95; Dir., Int'l Human Rights Law Program, 1987 to date. SELECTED PUBLICATIONS: *Women's Health and Human Rights* (Geneva: World Health Organization, 1993); *Human Rights of Women: National and International Perspectives* (Philadelphia: Univ. of Pennsylvania Press, 1994); "New Reproductive Technologies: International Legal Issues and Instruments" in *Overview of Legal Issues in Reproductive Technologies* (Ottawa: Royal Commission on New Reproductive Technologies, 1993); "Human Rights and Infant Survival: A Case for Priorities" (*Columbia Human Rights Review* 1986-87); "State Responsibility for Violations of Women's Human Rights" (*Harvard Human Rights Journal* 1994); various other publications. EDIT: Advisory Bd., *Family Planning Perspectives*, 1990 to date; Advisory Bd.,*Journal of Third World Legal Studies*, 1986 to date; Advisory Bd., *Human Rights Quarterly*, 1994 to date; Advisory Bd., *Reproduc-

tive Health Matters, 1993 to date. **AFFIL:** Alan Guttmacher Institute (Dir.); Human Rights Internet (Dir). **MISC:** numerous consultancies & appointments incl. Food Foundation; World Health Organization, Geneva, Special Program of Research, Dev. & Research Training in Human Reproduction, Scientific & Ethical Review Group, 1990 to date; Yale Law Sch., Schell Center for Int'l Human Rights, Advisory Bd. of the Direct Info. Access Ntwk, 1994 to date.

Cook, Tracey ■ ■ ♥ ⊗
Actor. c/o Oscars & Abrams Associates Inc., 59 Berkeley St., Toronto, ON M5A 2W5 (416) 860-1790, FAX 860-0236. **EDUC:** training with Sears & Switzer (TV, Film Technique), Theatre Works (Scene Study, On-Camera Audition Technique). **SELECTED CREDITS:** TV: Guest Star, *Due South*, CBS/CTV; Series Lead, Sarah, *North of 60* (5th season), CBC/Alliance; Guest Star, *Catwalk* (3 eps.), YTV/Catrun II Prods.; Guest Star, *Bermuda Grace*, NBC/MOW; Guest Star, *Forever Knight* (2 eps.), CBS/CTV/Paragon; Principal, *Police File*, CBS; Principal, *Top Cops* (several eps.), CBS/Grosso-Jacobson; Principal, *Counterstrike*, CTV/Cinegramme; Principal, *The Judge* (3 eps.), Variety Artists prod.; Presenter, *Fashion Cares* (benefit), The Diamond; Films: Lead, *Snake Eaters*, Feature; Principal, *Drop Dead Gorgeous*, Feature. **HONS:** nominated for Gemini Award for Best Performance in a leading role, 1995 & 1996. **INTERESTS:** downhill skiing; volleyball; swimming; tennis.

Cook-Bennett, Gail, B.A.,M.A.,Ph.D. Ⓢ
Vice-Chairman, BENNECON LIMITED, Commercial Union Tower, Toronto Dominion Centre, Ste. 1416, Box 59, Toronto, ON M5K 1E7 (416) 365-1418. Born Ottawa. m. Roy F. Bennett. 1 ch. **EDUC:** Carleton Univ., B.A.(Econ.) 1962; Univ. of Michigan, M.A.(Econ.) 1965, Ph.D.(Econ.) 1968. **CAREER:** Research Assoc., Centre for Urban & Community Studies, Univ. of Toronto, 1968-72; Research Assoc., Institute for the Quantitative Analysis of Social & Econ. Policy, Univ. of Toronto, 1968-72; Policy Analyst, Planning Branch, Treasury Bd., Gov't of Canada, Summer 1970; Asst. Prof., Econ., Univ. of Toronto, 1968-74; Dir. of Research, Canadian Economic Policy Committee, C.D. Howe Research Institute, 1974-76; Exec. VP, 1977-78; Freelance Econ. Consultant, 1979-82; Co-Chair, Bennecon Limited, 1982 to date. **SELECTED PUBLICATIONS:** articles & reports on econ. policy issues. **DIRECTOR:** The Consumers' Gas Company Ltd.; The Manufacturers Life Insurance Company; Ontario Teachers' Pension Plan; The Toronto-Dominion Bank;

Petro-Canada. **AFFIL:** Salvation Army (Chair, Metro Toronto Advisory Bd.); Institute for Research on Public Policy (member of Bd.). Former member: Sectoral Advisory Group on International Trade (SAGIT) for General Services (Chair); Canadian Group, The Trilateral Commission; Ontario Economic Council; Manning Awards Foundation (Selection Committee); Social Sciences and Humanities Research Council of Canada; IDEA Corporation (Bd. of Dir.); *Canadian Public/Analyse de Politiques* (Edit. Bd.); Premier of Ontario's Advisory Committee on Confederation; Canadian Opera Company (Bd. of Dir.); Multiple Sclerosis Society of Canada (Bd. member); Banff Centre Sch. of Mgmt (Advisory Committee); Niagara Institute (Advisory Committee.) **HONS:** Montreal YWCA Honour for Contribution to Working Women, 1977.

Cooke, Brenda, B.A.,M.Ed. ■ ■ ⊲
President, ASSINIBOINE COMMUNITY COLLEGE, 1430 Victoria Ave. E., Brandon, MB R7A 2A9 (204) 726-6610, FAX 726-6753, EMAIL cooke@adminnet.assiniboinec.mb.ca. 2 ch. Sarah Cooke, Fraser Cooke. **EDUC:** Queen's Univ., B.A.(English, Phil. & Art) 1967; Moray House, Edinburgh, Scotland, Teacher Training Certificate 1970; Univ. of Manitoba, Continuing Educ., Personnel Mgmt Program 1979-81; Red River Community Coll., Winnipeg, Certificate in Adult Educ. 1981; Univ. of Manitoba, M.Ed.(Curriculum & Humanities) 1990; numerous professional dev. seminars/conferences. **CAREER:** Instructor, Adult Basic Educ., Red River Community Coll., 1974-84; Coord., English in the Workplace, Adult & Continuing Educ. Branch, Man. Educ. & Training, 1984-86; Mgr, Community-Based Training Programs, Winnipeg Core Area Initiative, Employment & Training, Dept. of Educ. & Training, 1986-88; Exec. Dir., 1988-91; Dir., Workforce 2000, Dept. of Educ. & Training, Feb.-July 1991; Pres., Assiniboine Community Coll., 1991 to date. **AFFIL:** Canadian Bureau for International Education (Dir. 1996 to date); Civil Justice Review Task Force (mbr. 1996 to date); Economic Innovation & Technology Council (Dir. 1993 to date); College Presidents' Network (Sec. 1994-95; Treas. 1995-96; VP 1996 to date); Association of Canadian Community Colleges (Advisory Committee on Statistics 1995); Brandon Chamber of Commerce (Dir. 1991 to date); Civil Service Commission (Hum. Res. Planning Initiative Steering Committee 1994). **MISC:** Mgmt Audit, Jordan Vocational Training Corporation, Association of Canadian Community Colleges EDTS Proj. Assignment, Amman, Jordan, Aug.-Oct. 1995; Partners for Prosperity, Third Gen. Mtg on

Higher Educ., Research & Training Collaboration in N.Am., Guadalajara, Mexico, Apr. 1996.

Cools, The Hon. Anne Clare, B.A., OLJ ✦

Senator and Liberal Member of the Government, THE SENATE OF CANADA, Parliament Buildings, Rm. 178-F, Centre Block, Ottawa, ON K1A 0A4 (613) 992-2808, FAX 992-8513. Born Barbados, WI 1943. m. S. Rolf Calhoun. EDUC: McGill Univ., B.A. CAREER: Founder, Exec. Dir. & Special Projects Mgr, Women in Transition, Inc., 1974-90; Field Instructor, Fac. of Social Work, Univ. of Toronto, 1977-78; Seneca Coll., 1977-89; Ryerson Polytechnic Univ., 1978-80; candidate, fed. riding of Rosedale, fed. gen. elections, 1979, 1980; Mbr. (Temp.), Nat'l Parole Bd., 1980-84; Senator, Senate of Canada, 1984 to date; Senate Standing Committee of Social Affairs, Science & Technology; Senate Sub-Committee of Social Affairs, Science & Technology on Veterans' Affairs; Senate Library of Canada (Joint) Committee. AFFIL: Liberal Party of Canada (V-Chair, Greater Toronto Liberal Caucus 1993, 1994, 1995); Metro Toronto Justice Committee on Spousal Abuse (Founding V-Chair & Exec. Committee); Military & Hospitaller Order of St. Lazarus of Jerusalem; Prayer Book Society of Canada (Hon. Patron & Mbr., Ottawa Branch); St. Alban the Martyr Anglican Church (Parish Council); Codrington Coll. Restoration Appeal of Canada (Cdn Patron); Errol Barrow Memorial Trust (Bd. of Dir.); National Associations Active in Criminal Justice (Advisory Committee); National Development Foundation of Jamaica (Bd. of Dir.); Another Shakespeare Proj., Ottawa (Friend); Anglican Church of Canada; Black Educ. Proj. (former Mbr., Bd. of Dir.); Black Theatre Canada (former Mbr., Bd. of Dir.); The Pauline McGibbon Cultural Centre (former Mbr., Bd. of Dir.); Social Planning Council of Metro Toronto (former Mbr., Bd. of Dir.); Family Mediation-Canada (former Mbr., Advisory Bd.); Native Council of Canada (former Mbr., Advisory Bd., Health Committee). INTERESTS: classical music; history; antiquities. MISC: has served as mbr. of the Special Senate Committee on Bill C-21; the Senate Standing Committee on Bnkg, Trade & Commerce Committee for Bill C-62; Senate Task Force on the Meech Lake Accord; Nat'l Fin., Legal & Constitutional Affairs; Foreign Affairs; Foreign Affairs SubCommittee on Security & Nat'l Defence; Senate Committee Reviewing Canada's Foreign Policy (Special Joint). COMMENT: *"Leader and innovator in creating services to assist battered women, families in crises and families troubled by domestic violence. Was instrumental in developing social services and social policy on the issue of violence in families."*

Coombs, Ann ■ Ⓢ ♂

President, COOMBS CONSULTING LTD., Bentley Place, 1265 W. 11th Ave., Ste. 401, Vancouver, BC V6H 1K6 (604) 733-9104, FAX 736-6443, EMAIL ann@coombs.ca, INTERNET http://coombs.ca/futurist. Born Toronto 1945. s. EDUC: Havergal Coll., 1964. CAREER: Admin. Asst., Royal Ontario Museum, 1966-67; Dir., Travelmaster's Guild, Vancouver, 1968-70; Sr. Buyer, Eaton's of Canada, 1970-80; Pres., Coombs Consulting Ltd., 1980 to date. AFFIL: American Marketing Association; National Speakers' Association; B.C. Shopping Centre Association; Downtown Parking Corp. (Bd. of Dir.). INTERESTS: passionate gardener; AIDS advocate; photographer; jazz; hiking; kayaking; interior design; arts fundraising; forever observing consumer trends. MISC: sole Cdn woman to present at Carrier's World Business Conference, Spain, 1994, & sole Cdn woman chosen to present at Canada's First Disability Insurance Conference, Toronto, 1994; keynote speaker for The Breast Cancer Research Foundation - Gillette Tour, 1996; addressed 8th general assembly of the World Future Society, Wash. D.C., 1996. COMMENT: *"A futurist, facilitator, international speaker, whose work and personal life are committed to change and the ethics and integrity our upcoming working environment demands. A survivor of a life-threatening illness, and mentor to 15 women annually, she supports women in business, and addresses audiences internationally on change."*

Coombs, Diane, B.A. ■■ ⧼ ♡

President, LAUBACH LITERACY ONTARIO (literacy volunteer ntwk), 120 Main St., Vankleek Hill, ON K0B 1R0 (613) 678-3409, FAX 678-3409, EMAIL (in Ont.) Alpha Com ID: dcoombs. Reading Program Manager, PRESCOTT-RUSSELL COUNTY BOARD OF EDUCATION. Born Ottawa 1951. EDUC: McGill Univ., B.A.(Anthropology) 1973; Cambridge Univ., England, independent studies (Anthropology) 1976; Carleton Univ., working on M.A.(Linguistics & Applied Languages). CAREER: Editor/Publisher, Review Publishing Co. (VKH) Ltd., 1982-90; Reading Program Mgr, Prescott-Russell Co. Bd. of Educ., 1991 to date. SELECTED PUBLICATIONS: *Tartan Bonjour* (1996); *Road Apple Farm* (Winter 1994); numerous articles, Review Publishing Co. (VKH) Ltd., 1982-90. AFFIL: Laubach Literacy Ontario (Pres. 1995-96; VP 1994-95; Dir. 1992-94); Laubach Literacy Canada (Tutor-

Trainer 1994; Writer 1993); Literacy Fund of Ontario (Transition Team); National Literacy Secretariat (Mgmt Team, Ont. Tutor Training Proj.). HONS: Harold Newlin Hill Foundation Scholarship; Ont. Scholar; Reserve Champion High Point Rider on "Frosted Chex," Advanced Div., Vankleek Hill, 1991. INTERESTS: language & literacy; research & writing; horses; Newfoundland. MISC: conference presenter on literacy, Ont. & Atlantic provinces. COMMENT: *"Growing up in Quebec-my greatest heritage-has allowed bilingualism and biculturalism to define me. C'est à dire que je ne peux pas imaginer un monde sans le français et l'anglais ensemble. This has allowed insight into literacy and communication issues, has inspired good (I hope) research. Promoting literacy tutoring.that's the practical side. What is theory without practice?"*

Cooney, Jane, B.A.,B.L.S.,M.L.S. Ⓢ
President, BOOKS FOR BUSINESS, 120 Adelaide St. W., Toronto, ON M5H 1T1 (416) 362-7822, FAX 362-9775, EMAIL info@booksforbusiness.on.ca. President, CANADIAN BOOKSELLERS ASSOCIATION. Born Montreal 1943. d. EDUC: Marianopolis Coll., B.A. 1963; Univ. of Toronto, B.L.S. 1964, M.L.S. 1974. CAREER: various positions in public & academic libraries, 1964-69; Mgr, Info. Svcs, CIBC, 1969-83; Fac. Mbr., Fac. of Info. Studies, Univ. of Toronto, 1974-79, 1995-96; VP & Dir., Bank Mktg Association, Chicago, 1983-86; Exec. Dir., Canadian Library Association, 1986-89; Pres., Books for Business, 1990 to date. SELECTED PUBLICATIONS: numerous articles in professional publications. AFFIL: Canadian Booksellers' Association (Dir. 1993-97; Pres.); Ontario Retail Sector (Chair, Advisory Bd. 1996 to date); Special Libraries Association (Dir. 1981, 1984); Ontario Library Association; Canadian Library Association; American Booksellers' Association. HONS: Mbr. of the Year, Special Libraries Association, 1983; Jubilee Award, Univ. of Toronto Alumni, 1983.

Cooper, Angela, R.N.,M.N. ⊕
Director of Nursing, OSHAWA GENERAL HOSPITAL, 24 Alma St., Oshawa, ON L1G 2B9 (905) 576-8711, ext. 3590, FAX 433-4363. Born Trinidad, WI. s. EDUC: San Fernando General Hospital, Diploma in Nursing 1972; Sch. of Midwifery, San Fernando General Hospital, Diploma in Midwifery 1975; Open Bible Institute, Diploma in Christian Educ. & Theology 1975; Memorial Univ. of Newfoundland, B.N. 1979; Univ. of Manitoba, M.N. 1985. CAREER: Nurse, San Fernando General Hospital, Trinidad, 1972-74; Nurse Midwife, 1975;

Nurse Midwife, Grenfell Regional Health Services, St. Anthony, Nfld., 1975-77; Reg'l Nurse II, Roddickton Health Centre, Nfld., 1979-81; Gen. Duty Nurse, Victoria General Hospital, Winnipeg, 1981-85; Nursing Instructor, Red River Community Coll., Winnipeg, 1985-87; Clinical Nurse Specialist, Whitby Psychiatric Hospital, Ont., 1987-90; Gen. Duty Nurse, Ajax/Pickering Hospital, 1988-94; Angela E. Cooper Hum. Res. Consultant, 1989 to date; Dir. of Nursing, Oshawa General Hospital, 1990 to date. SELECTED PUBLICATIONS: "Community Hospital Advances Nurses Knowledge Through Research," with Janet Bidgood, Robin Anthony, Monica Lancaster & Marcy Saxe-Braithwaite (*Registered Nurse* 5(4) 1993); "Prevention and Management of Aggressive Behaviour" (*Canadian Nurse* 90(6) 1994); various other publications. AFFIL: Canadian Nurses' Association (Int'l Affairs Committee); Coll. of Nurses of Ontario; Registered Nurses' Association of Ontario; Registered Nurses' Association of Ontario, Northumberland Chapter (Pol. Action Committee); St. John Ambulance, Durham Region & District (Bd. Mbr. 1991-95); Federation of University Women, Oshawa & District; European Women's Health Club (Lifetime Mbr.). HONS: Challenge Trophy, Paediatric Nurse of the Year, San Fernando, WI, 1973; Dr. & Mrs. G.W. Thomas Scholarship, St. Anthony, Nfld., 1982; nominated Teacher of the Year by Grad. Nurses of Red River Community Coll., 1987; Bursary, Nursing Innovation Fund, Ont. Ministry of Health, 1991, 1992; Certificate of Appreciation, St. John's Ambulance, 1994. INTERESTS: poetry writing; floral arrangement; the arts; church choir. MISC: Cdn citizen; Registered Nurse, Ont.; licensed Midwife, Trinidad & Tobago; conducted seven research studies between 1984 & 1995, three of which investigated the quality of worklife for nurses; various conference presentations; reviewer for various journals. COMMENT: *"I am a highly motivated, self-directed person, who enjoys the arts. My life work has been helping others, through nursing and volunteer work. Some of my major accomplishments have been in education, research, lobbying the government on behalf of nurses and patient care."*

Cooper, Barbara J., B.A. ■ Ⓒ Ⓧ
Executive Director, NEW BRUNSWICK CHORAL FEDERATION, Old Soldiers Barracks, P.O. Box 6000, Fredericton, NB E3B 5H1 (506) 453-3731, FAX 457-4880. Owner/Founder, PUBLICATIONS PLUS. Born Ingersoll, Ont. 1956 3 ch. Philip, Daryl, Benjamin. EDUC: Univ. of Waterloo, B.A.(Psych.) 1992. CAREER: private piano teacher, 1972 to date; Owner/Founder,

Publications Plus, 1988 to date; Exec. Dir., New Brunswick Choral Federation, 1989 to date. EDIT: *Double Feature*, publication of Parents of Multiple Births Association of Canada. HONS: Dean's Honours List, Univ. of Waterloo; Student of the Year, Herzing Institute, Toronto. INTERESTS: music; softball; swimming.

Cooper, Barbara Acheson, B.A.,M.H.Sc., Ph.D. ■ ⬡ ⊕ ⊗
Associate Dean, Health Sciences (Rehabilitation) and Director, School of Rehabilitation Science, MCMASTER UNIVERSITY, Health Sciences Centre, 1200 Main St. W., Rm. 1J11, Hamilton, ON L8N 3Z5 (905) 525-9140, ext. 22867, FAX 522-6095, EMAIL cooperb@ fhs.mcmaster.ca. Born Havana 1935. m. William Cooper. 2 ch. Liane Louise Ormond, James Gill Cooper. EDUC: Univ. of Toronto, Dip. Phys. & Occupational Therapy 1956; McMaster Univ., B.A.(Art & Art Hist.) 1975, B.A.(Painting) 1977, M.H.Sc.(Health Care Practice) 1981; Univ. of Wisconsin, Milwaukee, Ph.D.(Architecture) 1995. CAREER: Staff Therapist, Henderson Hospital, 1956-58; Charge Therapist, Charlton Ave. Physiotherapy Clinic, Hamilton, Ont., 1958-60; Staff Therapist, McGregor Clinic, 1963-76; Assoc. Prof., McMaster Univ., 1981 to date; Assoc. Dean, 1991 to date. SELECTED PUBLICATIONS: *Proceedings of the Population Health Special Lecture Series*, with D. McCalla & F. Mustard (Hamilton: McMaster Univ. Press, 1984); *The Environment: A Critical Review of Person-Environment Relations and Environmental Assessment*, with others (Hamilton: McMaster Univ. Neurodevelopmental Clinical Research Unit, 1992); "A Model for Implementing Colour Contrast in the Environment of the Elderly" (*The American Journal of Occupational Therapy* 1985); "Exploring the Use of Colour Cueing on an Assistive Device in the Home: Six Case Studies" (*Physical and Occupational Therapy in Gerontology* 1993); various other publications. EXHIBITIONS: numerous solo, two-person and group art shows. AFFIL: Gerontological Society of America; Canadian Physiotherapy Association; Canadian Occupational Therapy Association; Society of Canadian Artists; Environmental Design & Research Association; Dundas Valley Sch. of Art (Chair 1980-82); McMaster Museum of Art. HONS: Delta Gamma Fraternity Academic Award (Pledge Class), Univ. of Toronto, 1954; Goldwyn Howland Scholarship, Canadian Occupational Therapy Foundation, 1989; Progressive Architecture Citation for Applied Research & Health Care Interior Design Symposium Award, *Holding on to Home: Design-*

ing Environments for People with Dementia, 1990; The American Institute of Architects Citation for Excellence, 1991; Citation for Excellence, Johns Hopkins Press, 1991; Gerontology Interdisciplinary Educ. Proj. Award, Educational Centre on Aging & Health Coalition, "The Evolution on Interdisciplinary Education in the New Bachelor of Health Science Programmes at McMaster University," 1992. INTERESTS: painting; music; gardening. MISC: numerous invited presentations & workshops; numerous peer-reviewed conference presentations; SSHRC Doctoral Fellowship, 1989-90, 1990-91.

Cooper, Helen, B.Sc.,M.Sc. ■ ✿ ⓐ ⬡
55 West St., Kingston, ON K7L 2S3 (613) 549-4823, EMAIL cooper@adan.kingston.net. Born Melbourne, Australia 1946. m. Jack Cooper. 2 ch. Ann Helen, Heather Jane. EDUC: Queen's Univ., B.Sc.(Chem./Math.) 1968; London Sch. of Econ., M.Sc. (Econometrics) 1973. CAREER: Product Dev. Supervisor, Procter & Gamble, Inc., Canada, 1968-69; Secondary Sch. Teacher, Canadian University Services Overseas, Moshi, Tanzania, 1969-71; Lecturer, Polytechnic of the South Bank, London, UK, 1973-74; Research Asst., Econ., Queen's Univ., 1974-75; part-time Instructor, St. Lawrence Community Coll., Kingston, 1975-80; City Councillor, City of Kingston, 1980-88; Mayor, 1988-93; Pres., Association of Municipalities of Ontario, 1991-92; Chair, Ontario Municipal Bd., 1993-96; Visiting Fac., Sch. of Urban & Reg'l Planning, Queen's Univ. AFFIL: Institute for Research on Environment & Economy, Univ. of Ottawa (Dir., "New Forms of Governance" Proj.); Alumni Association, Queen's Univ. (Bd. of Dir.); Laidlaw Foundation (Conservation Program Advisory Committee); The Order of St. John (Serving Sister); Univ. of Waterloo (Mbr., Pragma Council); HMCS Kingston (Patron). INTERESTS: old house restoration; skating; skiing; hiking. COMMENT: *"I have found the realm of municipal decision-making absolutely fascinating in terms of the human relationships and in terms of the immediate and direct effect on peoples' lives. I have worked to create environments in which people find solutions to their own problems."*

Cooper, Jennifer A., LL.B. ▱ ⬡
Lawyer, PITBLADO AND HOSKIN, 360 Main St., Ste. 1900, Winnipeg, MB R3C 3Z3 (204) 942-0391, FAX 957-1790. Born Burnaby, B.C. 1956. m. Robert Morrison. 2 ch. Christopher, Jessica. EDUC: Univ. of Manitoba, LL.B. 1980. BAR: Man. CAREER: Lawyer, 1980-86;

Exec. Dir., Women's Health Clinic, 1986-91; Ptnr, Pitblado and Hoskin, 1991 to date. **AFFIL:** Manitoba Bar Association (Treas.); Canadian Bar Association (Nat'l Family Law Sec., Exec.); Manitoba Community Notification Advisory Committee (Chair). **INTERESTS:** watercolours; piano; aerobics. **MISC:** frequent lecturer in community; 1st & only female partner of 30 current partners in Pitblado and Hoskin (est. 1903); chaired the Man. working group of lawyers & judges that looked at women's experiences in the legal profession, 1992-94. **COMMENT:** *"Active in the community and the profession in promoting the equality rights of women."*

Cooper, Joanne S. ○ ⊕

Executive Director, VOLUNTEER CENTRE OF METROPOLITAN TORONTO, 344 Bloor St. W., Ste. 207, Toronto, ON M5S 3A7 (416) 961-6888, FAX 961-6859. Born 1938. m. Gordon E. Cooper. 3 ch. **EDUC:** Ryerson Polytechnical Institute, Library Arts; York Univ., Studies in Mgmt, Organization & Dev.; Ont. Institute for Studies in Educ., Adult Educ. Program; Royal Ontario Museum, Tourers Training Course; Modern Art Institute, London, UK, Modern Art Studies. **CAREER:** Co-Founder & Dir., Institute for Non-Profit Organizations. **SELECTED CREDITS:** Co-Prod., *Women's Journal* (eight-part TV series); Co-Prod., *Rape Once Is Too Often* (three-part TV series). **SELECTED PUBLICATIONS:** numerous publications, incl. *Money Isn't Everything; Organizing Your Way to Dollars; On Your Own: A Directory for Young Women; On Your Own: A Directory for Young Men; Volunteers From the Multicultural Community & Youth Volunteer Program: A Classroom Guide.* **AFFIL:** Community Information Centre of Metropolitan Toronto (Dir.); Volunteer Ontario (Dir.); Community Foundation of Greater Toronto (Dir., Chair Grants Committee); Canadian Association of Volunteer Bureaux & Centres (Dir., Treas.); Serve Canada (Dir. & Pres.).

Cooper, Sherry S., B.A.,M.A.,Ph.D. 6

Senior Vice-President and Chief Economist, NESBITT BURNS INC., 1 First Canadian Place, 3rd Fl., Toronto, ON M5X 1H3 (416) 359-4112, FAX 359-4173. Born 1950. m. Peter Cooper. 1 ch. **EDUC:** Goucher Coll., Baltimore, B.A. 1972; Univ. of Pittsburgh, M.A. 1976, Ph.D. 1978; Univ. of Illinois, Bond Analysis & Portfolio Mgmt Certificate 1989. **CAREER:** Economist, Bd. of Gov., Fed. Reserve System, Washington, DC, 1977-82; Dir. of Fin. Econ., Fed. Nat'l Mortgage Association, Washington, DC, 1982-83; Chief Economist, Burns Fry Limited, 1983-94; Co-Head, Global Fixed

Income, 1989-93; V-Chrm, 1994; Sr. VP & Chief Economist, Nesbitt Burns Inc., 1994 to date. **SELECTED PUBLICATIONS:** *Introduction to International Trade and Finance*, with Dr. Norman C. Miller (1974); contributes to & oversees all of Nesbitt Burns' econ. publications; many articles in econ. journals, incl. *Journal of Money, Credit and Banking, Southern Economic Journal & American Economist.* **AFFIL:** INNET (Chrm); Phi Beta Kappa; Temple Sinai Congregation of Toronto (Exec.); Fraser Institute (Bd.). **HONS:** Eleanor Voss Prize, Goucher Coll., 1972; Provost's Grad. Scholarship, Univ. of Pittsburgh, 1974; Mellon Fellowship, Univ. of Pittsburgh, 1974; Merit Award, Bd. of Gov., Fed. Reserve System, 1978; has been on the Brendan Wood International All-Star Analyst team consistently, 1986 to date. **INTERESTS:** fitness & nutrition; aerobic weight training; travel; reading.

Copleston, Marion, B.A.,B.Ed. ✦ ⊕ ⱳ

Editorial Committee, COMMON GROUND, Box 233, Charlottetown, PE C1A 7K4 (902) 368-5040. Born Montreal 1950. m. Tony Reddin. 2 ch. Lindsey, Andy. **EDUC:** Univ. of Toronto, B.A.(French) 1972, B.Ed.(French & Indust. Arts) 1973. **CAREER:** Indust. Arts Teacher, École Secondaire Etienne Brulé, Toronto, 1973-79; French Teacher, Language Training Canada, Public Svc. Commission, Charlottetown, 1984-95; part-time, 1995 to date. **SELECTED PUBLICATIONS:** "How-To" column, *Common Ground*, 1995-96; *Wild Flowers of P.E.I.*, photo used (1992). **EXHIBITIONS:** *Great Garden of the Gulf*, juried (1994); *Women's Art*, U.P.E.I. (1994); *The Wild Side of the Isle* (1983); *12 Photographers*, Confederation Centre (1981); numerous contributions to *Island Images & Island Visual Artists*, Holland Coll., 1985-95; numerous slide presentations; shows on housebuilding presented in English & French (1985 to date). **COLLECTIONS:** *Art to Seniors* Collection (1984). **AFFIL:** PEI Scottish Country Dancers (Sec.; Treas.; Pres. 1985 to date); Girl Guides of Canada (1994 to date); Women's Network (Bd. Mbr.; Co-Chair 1989-91); Transition House Association (Bd.); PEI Natural History Society. **HONS:** Island Telephone Co. Award, *Great Garden of the Gulf*, annual juried exhibition, 1994. **INTERESTS:** photography; gardening; camping; cross-country skiing; Scottish country dancing; travel; building construction & repair; co-operative self-sufficiency; women's issues & spirituality; family. **MISC:** chosen as Cdn delegate to the NGO Forum on Women in Beijing, China, Sept. 1995; have many nontraditional skills such as using chainsaws, welding etc. **COMMENT:** *"Teaching industrial arts for* six years, using a problem-solving approach, provided me with the skills and confidence necessary to build a passive solar house in the woods of P.E.I. Teaching French to adults is both demanding and rewarding. I live a simple 'back-to-the-land' lifestyle, including cooking and heating with wood and sun, and I try to make time in my life to pursue my many interests."

Copp, Joan C., B.A.,LL.B. ■ ⚖ 🖉
Director, Professional Development, LEGAL EDUCATION SOCIETY OF ALBERTA, Canada Trust Tower, 10104 - 103 Ave., Ste. 2610, Edmonton, AB T5J 0H8 (403) 420-1987, FAX 425-0885. Born Cambridge, Ont. m. 2 ch. EDUC: Carleton Univ., B.A. 1973; Osgoode Hall Law Sch., York Univ., LL.B. 1976. BAR: Ont., 1978; Alta., 1981. CAREER: Ptnr, Lucas Bowker & White, 1986-93; Cnsl, 1994-96; Dir., Professional Dev., Legal Education Society of Alberta, 1996 to date. SELECTED PUBLICATIONS: author of numerous publications in the environmental law area. AFFIL: Law Society of Alberta; Canadian Bar Association (Chair, Environmental Law Section, N. Alberta; Exec. Committee, Nat'l Environmental Law Section); Edmonton Bar Association; Canadian Environmental Auditing Association; Canadian Institute of Chartered Accountants (Environmental Mgmt Interest Group); Alberta Environmental Advocates Society; Environmental Services Association of Alberta; Carleton Univ. (Reg'l Presidential Advisory Council). MISC: lecturer & participant at various seminars & conferences on environmental issues. COMMENT: "Responsible for a number of special projects encompassing both continuing legal education and the bar admission course within the province of Alberta."

Copps, The Hon. Sheila, P.C.,M.P. ■ ✤
Deputy Prime Minister and Minister of Canadian Heritage, Member of Parliament (Hamilton East), GOVERNMENT OF CANADA, House of Commons, Ottawa, ON K1A 0A6. Born Hamilton, Ont. 1952. EDUC: Univ. of Western Ontario, Hons. B.A.(French & English); Univ. of Rouen, France; McMaster Univ. CAREER: Journalist, The Ottawa Citizen, 1974-76; Journalist, The Hamilton Spectator, 1977; Constituency Asst. to former Ont. Liberal Party Leader, Dr. Stuart Smith, 1977-81; M.P.P. (Hamilton Centre), Gov't of Ont., 1981-84; Official Opposition Critic for Labour, 1981-82; candidate, Ont. Liberal Party Leadership, 1982; Official Opposition Critic for Health, Prov. of Ont., 1982-84; M.P. (Hamilton East), Gov't of Canada, 1984 to date; Official Opposition Critic for Housing & Labour, 1984-87;

Chrm, Liberal Caucus Social Policy Committee, 1985; V-Chair, Standing Committee on Human Rights, 1986-87; Official Opposition Critic for Nat'l Health & Welfare, & for Fitness & Amateur Sport, 1987-89; Official Opposition Critic for Environment, & Co-Critic for Social Policy, 1989-90; candidate for leadership of the Liberal Party of Canada, 1990; Official Opposition Critic for Industry, 1990-91; Deputy Leader, Liberal Party of Canada, 1991-93; Deputy P.M. & Min. of the Environment, 1993-96; Deputy P.M. & Min. of Cdn Heritage, 1996 to date. AFFIL: Liberal Party of Canada.

Corbeil, Johanne, B.Th. ⊛ 🖐
President, LE CENTRE DE RECHERCHES D'ANTÉCÉDENTS SOCIO-BIOLOGIQUES DU QUÉBEC, 203 rue Fullum, Montréal, QC H2K 3N7 (514) 385-3658. Born Montréal 1959. s. EDUC: Univ. of Montreal, Bachelor of Theology 1978. CAREER: Pres., Le Centre de Recherches d'antécédents Socio-Biologiques du Québec; VP then Pres., Caisse Populaire Notre-Dame de la Merci. INTERESTS: helping people who are suffering from discrimination. MISC: 1st woman to occupy VP & Pres. positions at the Caisse Populaire Notre-Dame de la Merci; 1st woman administrator of Caisse Populaire. COMMENT: "I provide services for people seeking help in finding their natural families for medical or humanitarian reasons. I put pressure on government bureaucracies that fail to provide adequate services in that field."

Corbella, Licia ■ 🖉
Associate Editor and Columnist, THE CALGARY SUN, 2615 - 12th St. N.E., Calgary, AB T2E 7W9 (403) 250-4129, FAX 250-4180. Born Montreal 1963. m. James Stephen Gardiner. EDUC: Vancouver Community Coll., 2-yr. Diploma (Arts & Sciences) 1985, 2-yr. Diploma (Journalism) 1987. CAREER: Gen. Assignment Reporter, The Province, Vancouver, 1986-88; Reporter & Columnist, Scarborough Mirror, 1988-89; Temp. Gen. Assignment Reporter, The Toronto Star, 1989; Feature Writer & Gen. Assignment Reporter, The Toronto Sun, 1989-93; Asst. City Ed. & Investigative Reporter, The Calgary Sun, 1993-94; Lifestyle & Travel Ed., 1994-95; Columnist, 1995 to date; Assoc. Ed., 1996 to date. SELECTED PUBLICATIONS: co-author, For Love and Money: The Tale of the Joudries (Toronto Sun Publishing, 1996). AFFIL: Calgary Educational Partnership Foundation (Bd.). HONS: Award for Feature Writing, Ont. Reporters' Association, 1992; Edward Dunlop Award of Excellence for Feature Writing, 1993. INTERESTS: literature; travel; swimming; skiing; nature; wildlife–all animals. MISC: former Cdn record

holder in swimming for 11-12 & 13-14-year-old girls. COMMENT: *"My goal is to live life laughing as much as possible."*

Corbett, Daphne E., B.A.,C.M.A. $
Vice-President and Chief Auditor, HONGKONG BANK OF CANADA, 885 W. Georgia St., Ste. 500, Vancouver, BC V6C 3E9 (604) 641-1997, FAX 641-3002. Born Vancouver 1948. EDUC: Univ. of Victoria, B.A.(Psych.) 1970. CAREER: various positions, Admin. & Credit, CIBC, 1972-81; various positions becoming Asst. VP & Branch Mgr, Hongkong Bank of Canada, 1981-94; VP & Chief Auditor, 1994 to date. AFFIL: Institute of Canadian Bankers (Fellow); Society of Management Accountants; Rotary Club of Vancouver; Community House Support Service Association; Judith Marcuse Dance Project Society (former Dir. & Treas.). HONS: Silver Medal, Institute of Canadian Bankers. INTERESTS: hiking; fishing; reading.

Corbett, Hon. Marie, B.A.,LL.B. ⚖ 👍
Justice, ONTARIO COURT OF JUSTICE, Court House, 361 University Ave., Toronto, ON M5G 1T3 (416) 327-5284. Born Nfld. 1943. m. C. Alexander Squires. 2 ch. EDUC: McGill Univ., B.A. 1964; Univ. of Toronto, LL.B. 1968. BAR: Ont., 1970. CAREER: articled to Richard Rohmer, Q.C., 1968-69; Lawyer, Legal Dept., The Corporation of the City of Toronto, 1970-72; private practice, 1972-74; Mbr., Ont. Municipal Bd., 1974-77; Cnsl, Royal Commission on the Status of Pensions in Ontario, 1977-80; Ptnr, Corbett and Barton, Toronto, 1980-86; Judge, District Court of Ont. at Toronto, 1986-90; Justice, Ontario Court of Justice, 1990 to date; Criminal law leader, 1993. SELECTED CREDITS: contributor & participant, *Family Property Law*, film produced for the Ministry of the Attorney Gen. (1974). SELECTED PUBLICATIONS: *Pension Benefits Legislation Reform* (Toronto: Law Society of Upper Canada, 1985); "Disclosure of Complainant's Records in Sexual Assault Trials," with Anne Sonnen (*Criminal Law Quarterly* 1994); various other publications. AFFIL: International Association of Women Judges (Founding Pres., Cdn Chapter; Int'l Dir.); Canadian Judges' Conference; Canadian Institute for the Administration of Justice; Ontario Superior Court Judges' Association; The Osgoode Society; Supreme Court of Canada Historical Society; Clara Brett Martin Centennial Committee (Convenor); Women's Law Association (Life Mbr.); Osler Bluff Ski Club; Cedarhurst Golf Club; Empire Club (Dir. 1985-86). HONS: Q.C., 1983; Women of Distinction Special Award, YWCA, 1993. MISC: Dir. & founder, proj. to produce biography of 1st woman judge, Helen Kinnear, & other commemorative acts, 1992 to date; successfully obtained printing of stamp of Judge Kinnear for 50th anniversary of her appt., 1993; 1st woman member of the Empire Club; frequent public speaker.

Corbiere, Alice A., B.A. ■■ 🍁 $
Co-ordinator, GARDEN RIVER DEVELOPMENT CORP. (4-lane highway construction), Box 46, Site 5, R.R. #4, Garden River, ON P6A 5K9 (705) 942-1825, FAX 942-3127. Born Sault Ste. Marie, Ont. 1937. d. 3 ch. Joe, Gary, Darlene. EDUC: Laurentian Univ., B.A.(Hons., Psych.) 1984; Lake Superior State Univ., Michigan, M.B.A. in progress. CAREER: Student Counsellor, Sault Ste. Marie Bd. of Educ., 1970s; Employment Counsellor, Canada Employment Centre, 1980s. INTERESTS: outdoor activities; enjoying 3 grandchildren; gardening. MISC: served 2-yr. elected term as Batchewana First Nation Council mbr. COMMENT: *"While raising my family, I worked to assist in the organization and development of the Rankin Reserve Community infrastructure, the indoor ice arena and hall. I have worked with First Nation high school students who boarded in the city. In 1994, I co-ordinated successful negotiations between Ontario-Canada and First Nations which resulted in acceptance by a community referendum on land issues and four-lane highway. I enjoy keeping active, productive and working in the First Nation community."*

Corder, Sharon, B.A. 🎞 🎭
Writer, Producer, Actor, BURNING PAST PRODUCTIONS, 10 Sackville Place, Toronto, ON M4X 1A4 (416) 923-3357, FAX 923-6854. Born Waco, Tex. m. Jack Blum. EDUC: Univ. of California, Davis, B.A.(Theatre). CAREER: writer, prod. & actor in film, TV & theatre. SELECTED CREDITS: Prod./Writer, *Babyface* (feature), Burning Past Prod.; Prod./Writer, *Traders* (series), Atlantis Films; Story Ed./Writer, *Catwalk* (series), Franklin/Waterman Prod.; Writer, "Deadly Fashion," *Kung Fu: The Legend Continues* (series), Warner Bros.; Writer, "The Matchmaker," *Max Glick* (series), CBC; Writer, 2 eps., *Top Cops*, CBS; Writer/Co-Prod./Exec. Story Ed., *On Our Own* (series); Writer, "My Girlfriend's Back.," *Dracula: The Series*, Cinexus Ltd.; Writer, "Otis the Amazing," *The Twilight Zone*, CBS/Atlantis; Writer, "Jack of Hearts," *Global Playhouse*, Atlantis Films/NFB; Writer, *A Child's Look at Mozart* (spoken word recording), Kids Records; Co-Prod., *Funny Girls* (13, 30-min. episodes), WTN, The Women's Television Network; Co-Prod., *Life, Liberty and Laughter* (seven, 60-min. comedy specials), WTN, The Women's

Television Network; Lead/Prod., *Getting Out* (theatre), Harbourfront Theatre; Featured Actor, *The Outside Chance of Maximilian Glick* (feature). SELECTED PUBLICATIONS: "Jack of Hearts," teleplay, *ON CUE II*, high sch. anthology (Harcourt, Brace, Jovanovich). AFFIL: Writers' Guild of Canada; Writers' Guild of America; ACTRA; Actors' Equity, Canada & U.S.; PEN; Academy of Canadian Cinema & Television; Artists in the Schools. HONS: Dora Mavor Moore Award for Artistic Excellence & Theatrical Innovation for *Getting Out*. MISC: has co-written & performed in numerous stage productions incl. *Waves* (Theatre Centre) & *Bob Gets A Job* (Genesis Company Theatre); Co-Artistic Dir., Genesis Company Theatre, Vancouver; juror for various film festivals & industry awards.

Corkin, Jane, B.A.(Hons.) ⊗
Owner and President, JANE CORKIN GALLERY INC., 179 John St., Ste. 302, Toronto, ON M5T 1X4 (416) 979-1980, FAX 979-7018. Born Boston 1949. EDUC: Queen's Univ., B.A. (Hons., Art Hist. & Pol. Sci.) 1971. CAREER: Asst., David Mirvish Gallery, 1972-78; est. Dept. of Photography, 1974; Owner & Pres., Jane Corkin Gallery, 1979 to date; Consultant, National Archives, Ottawa, 1985; Evaluation Team, National Gallery of Canada, 1986; Advisor, Soane Museum, London, UK, 1988. SELECTED PUBLICATIONS: *Twelve Canadians, Contemporary Canadian Photography*, ed. (Toronto: Jane Corkin Gallery, 1981; dist., McClelland & Stewart Ltd.); *André Kertész, A Lifetime of Perception*, ed. (Prentice Hall Canada Inc., 1982); *Margaret Bourke-White, Photographs*, ed. (Toronto: Jane Corkin Gallery, 1988; dist., Firefly Books Ltd.); *Children in Photography: 150 Years*, ed., text by Gary Michael Dault (Toronto: Firefly Books Ltd., 1990); *Photographs, Jane Corkin Gallery*, ed. (Toronto: Jane Corkin Gallery, 1989; dist., Firefly Books Ltd.); *André Kertész, Stranger to Paris*, ed. (Toronto: Jane Corkin Gallery, 1992; dist., Firefly Books Ltd.). EXHIBITIONS: *Children in Photography: 150 Years*, travelling exhibition (sponsor, Winnipeg Art Gallery), 1989-92; *Robert Bourdeau: The Mediated Image*, travelling exhibition, with curators James Borcoman & Shirley Madill, 1988; *Life Forces: Photographs by Carol Marino*, with curator Michael Bell, Agnes Etherington Art Centre, Queen's Univ., 1987; *Photography: The First Century, 1844-1900*, Winnipeg Art Gallery, 1984; *Brancusi, The Sculptor as Photographer*, Vancouver Art Gallery, 1984; *André Kertész: Lifetime of Perception, 1917-1982*, travelling exhibition, 1982-84. AFFIL: Association of International Photography Art Dealers,

N.Y. (Founder 1979; Dir. 1984-87); Professional Art Dealers' Association of Canada (Sec.); Power Plant Contemporary Art Gallery, Harbourfront, Toronto (Trustee); Arts Foundation of Greater Toronto (Trustee); Art Gallery of Ontario (Trustee, Foundation to the Bd.); Art Bank (Transition Advisory Committee 1985). HONS: Women Who Make a Difference, 1993; Toronto Branch Award, Queen's Univ. Alumni Assoc., 1995. MISC: speaker & lecturer.

Corley, Nora T., B.A.,M.A.,B.L.S. ■ ■ ▢ ▨
Librarian, Indexer, Bibliographer. Born Montreal. m. John T. Murchison. EDUC: McGill Univ., B.A.(Hons., Geog.) 1951, B.L.S. 1952, M.A.(Historical Geog.) 1961. HONS: Fellow, Arctic Institute of North America; Hon. Mbr., Polar Libraries Colloquy.

Corman, June, B.A.,M.A.,Ph.D. ■ ▨ ▨
Associate Professor, Sociology, BROCK UNIVERSITY, St. Catharines, ON L2S 3A1 (905) 688-5550, FAX 688-2789, EMAIL jcorman@spartan.ac.brocku.ca. Born Assiniboia, Sask. 1952. m. Harald Ensslen. 2 ch. Daniel Corman Ensslen, Christine Corman Ensslen. EDUC: Univ. of Regina, B.A.(Psych.) 1973; Univ. of Toronto, M.A.(Soc.) 1976, Ph.D.(Soc.) 1982. CAREER: Asst. Prof. with Tenure, Carleton Univ., 1984-91; Assoc. Prof. with Tenure, Brock Univ., 1992 to date. SELECTED PUBLICATIONS: *Recasting Steel Labour: The Stelco Story*, ed. with others; "Dissension within the Ranks: The Struggle over Employment Practices during a Recession" (*Studies in Political Economy* Spring 1990); "Unpacking Attrition: A Change in Emphasis," with others (*Canadian Journal of Higher Education* No. 3 1993). AFFIL: International Women's Day Organizing Committee, Niagara Reg.; Unemployed Help Centre (Advisory Committee). HONS: Ont. Grad. Fellowship, 1976; Canada Council Fellowship, 1977-80; Post-Doctoral Fellowship, 1982, 1983; Scholarly Achievement Award, Carleton Univ., 1986. INTERESTS: facilitating the careers of undergrad. students. COMMENT: *"I enjoy supporting women in their struggles to succeed and to promote social change by pushing the envelope."*

Corne, Sharron Zenith, B.Ped., B.F.A.(Hons.) ⊗ ✎
Artist. 207 Park Blvd. N., Winnipeg, MB R3P 0G6. Born Winnipeg. EDUC: Feminist Art Program, Women's Bldg., L.A.; Univ. of Manitoba, B.Ped., B.F.A.(Hons.); Univ. of Minnesota, Split Rock Arts Program; Banff Centre for the Arts, Residency, Leighton Colony. SELECTED PUBLICATIONS: "An Unfilling Cer-

emony" (*Response*, Brandeis Univ., 1975); "Art Education and Women" (*C.A.R./F.A.C.* 1977); "Pioneering Art Feminism on the Prairies" (*Branching Out* 1978); "Women Artists in Manitoba" (Prov. Council of Women of Manitoba, 1981); "Women Artists in Canada," in *Women Artists of the World* (New York: Midmarch, 1985); various other publications. **EXHIBITIONS:** 6 one-person exhibitions, incl. Powerhouse Gallery, Montreal (1981); Augsburg Coll., Minneapolis (1986); Gallery III, Univ. of Manitoba (1989); Winnipeg Art Gallery (1994); numerous group exhibitions, incl. *Canadian Women Artists*, U.N. Conference, Copenhagen (1980); *Contemporary Art in Manitoba*, Winnipeg Art Gallery (1987); Saskatchewan Cultural Exchange Society, Regina (1987); Thomas Gallery, Winnipeg (1987); Main Access Gallery, Winnipeg (1987); Plug In Gallery, Winnipeg (1988, 1996); Articule, Montreal (1988); Melnychenko Gallery, Winnipeg (1989); Women's Caucus for Art Conference, N.Y. (1990); Ace Art, Winnipeg (1990); Newzones, Calgary (1992); & Gallery on the Avenue, Winnipeg (1991). **AFFIL:** Women's Caucus for Art, US; Women's Art Resource Centre, Toronto; Mentoring Artists for Women's Art; Ace Art; Plug In; Fort Garry Women's Resource Centre; Manitoba Action Committee on the Status of Women. **HONS:** Woman of the Year Award, Arts, YWCA, 1980. **MISC:** subject of numerous reviews & articles incl. "Sharron Zenith Corne Explores Separation and Union," by Shirley Madil (*Tableau*, Winnipeg Art Gallery, 1994); "On The Edge: Connections, Disconnections," by Marian Yeo (Winnipeg Art Gallery, 1994); work reproduced in numerous publications, incl. *Atlantis* (Fall 1979), *Prairie Fire* (Fall 1986), *Women Artist News* (Fall 1988) & *Herizons* (Summer 1994); recipient of various grants; juror for grants & exhibitions; co-ordinated 1st nat'l juried exhibition of Cdn women artists, *Woman As Viewer* Exhibition, Winnipeg Art Gallery, 1975; consultant to fed. Advisory Council on Status of Women's Brief to Federal Cultural Policy Review Committee, 1981. **COMMENT:** "Woman as Viewer *was the first national exhibition at a major cultural institution to include depiction's of women's experiences–by women–and to use feminist criteria. Authored first provincial reports on inequities facing women in visual art (1976-81). Since 1970, pioneered new visual images of women's identity to counter destructive stereotypes.*"

Cornish, Mary, LL.B. ⚖ ✊

Senior Partner, CAVALLUZZO HAYES SHILTON MCINTYRE & CORNISH, 43 Madison Ave., Toronto, ON M5R 2S2 (416) 964-1115, FAX 964-5895. Born Toronto 1950. m. George Biggar. 2 ch. **EDUC:** Osgoode Hall Law Sch., LL.B. 1973. **BAR:** Ont., 1976. **CAREER:** Ptnr, Cornish, King and Sachs, 1976-81; Lawyer, Cornish Advocates, 1982-94; Sr. Ptnr, Cavalluzzo Hayes Shilton McIntyre & Cornish, 1994 to date; certified by Law Society of Upper Canada as a Specialist in Labour Law. **SELECTED PUBLICATIONS:** *Achieving Equality, A Report on Human Rights Reform* (June 1992); *Towards Service Equity, A Report of SOAR's Service Equity Committee* (Oct. 1994); *Getting Organized: Building a Union* (Toronto: The Women's Press, 1980); *Equal Pay: Collective Bargaining and the Law* (Ottawa: Labour Canada, 1987); *Organizing Together*, with others (Toronto: Second Story Press, 1994); "Women in Trade Unions" (*This Magazine,* 1975); various other publications. **AFFIL:** Canadian Bar Association; National Association of Women & the Law; Canadian Association of Labour Lawyers; Law Union of Ontario; County of York Law Association; Lawyers for Social Responsibility; Advocates' Society; International Foundation of Employee Benefit Plans; International Commission of Jurists; Skyworks (Dir.). **HONS:** Woman of the Year, Soroptimist Society of Toronto, 1979; "Aggie," YWCA Woman of Distinction, 1988; Law Society of Upper Canada Medal, 1993. **MISC:** frequent guest speaker; Co-founder & principal lobbyist, Equal Pay Coalition, 1974; Chair, Ont. Human Rights Code Review Task Force, 1992; Chair, Service Equity Committee, Society of Ontario Adjudicators & Regulators, 1993-94.

Cornish-Kehoe, Margaret, B.A.,M.Sc., M.B.A.,F.I.C.B. ■ $

Director, SCOTIAMCLEOD INC., Scotia Plaza, 40 King St. W., Box 4085, Stn. A, Toronto, ON M5W 2X6 (416) 863-2899, FAX 863-7003. Born Toronto 1948. m. James P. Kehoe. **EDUC:** Univ. of Toronto, B.A.(East Asian Studies–Chinese) 1971, M.B.A. 1988; London Sch. of Econ., M.Sc.(Int'l Econ.) 1975. **CAREER:** Dept. of External Affairs, 1971-79; Third Sec., U.N. Gen. Assembly, Ottawa, 1971; Second Sec., Cdn Embassy, Beijing, 1972-74; Ont. & Western Prov. Desk, Fed.-Prov. Rel'ns Div., Cdn Dept. of External Affairs, Ottawa, 1975-77; First Sec., Cdn Delegation to the European Communities, Brussels, Belgium, 1977-79; Mgr, Country Lending, Int'l Credit, Bank of Nova Scotia, 1980-82; Mgr, Sovereign Debt Rescheduling, 1982-85; Dir., Sovereign Debt Rescheduling, Int'l Dept., Toronto, 1985-87; VP & Dir., Equity Research (Industrial Products), ScotiaMcLeod Inc., Toronto, 1988 to date. **AFFIL:** Canada-Japan Society of Toronto (Dir.); Institute of Canadian Bankers (Fellow). **HONS:** Japan Study Trip, Mary Jane Hendrie Scholarship, 1988. **INTERESTS:** travel.

Cornwall, C. Gail, B.A.,LL.B.,Q.C. ⚖
Partner, GOODMAN PHILLIPS & VINEBERG, 250 Yonge St., Ste. 2400, Toronto, ON M5B 2M6 (416) 979-2211, FAX 979-1234. Born Toronto 1942. m. William J. Cornwall. **EDUC:** Univ. of Western Ontario, B.A.(Gen. Arts) 1963, LL.B. 1967. **BAR:** Ont., 1969. **CAREER:** Sr. Ptnr, Goodman Phillips & Vineberg. **AFFIL:** Canadian Tax Foundation (Ont. Tax Conference Planning Committee Mbr. 1991-93); Canadian Bar Association; Law Society of Upper Canada. **HONS:** Q.C., 1985. **COMMENT:** *"Currently, partner in Goodman Phillips & Vineberg. Law practice profile: general tax, including corporate and personal tax planning, with emphasis on corporate reorganizations and partnership and real estate taxation."*

Corrigan, Anne Marie, B.B.A. ■ ✏ 🗎 $
Vice-President, Journals and Design, UNIVERSITY OF TORONTO PRESS INCORPORATED, 5201 Dufferin St., North York, ON M3H 5T8 (416) 667-7838, FAX 667-7881, EMAIL corrigan@utpress.utoronto.ca. Born Toronto 1956. m. Cecil Leonard Bradley. 2 ch. Colin Bradley, Kathleen Bradley. **EDUC:** Univ. of Prince Edward Island, B.B.A. 1983. **CAREER:** Asst. Mgr, CN Hotels, 1986-87; Acctg Asst., 1987; Circulation Mgr, Univ. of Toronto Press, 1988-89; Journals Mgr, 1989-94; VP, Journals, 1994 to date. **SELECTED PUBLICATIONS:** *The Serials Librarian* (1995); Bus. Mgr for *Canadian Historical Review*; *Cartographica*; *Modern Drama*; *Canadian Theatre Review*; *Journal of Scholarly Publishing*. **AFFIL:** Association of American University Presses (Chair, Scholarly Journals Committee 1989-94); Canadian Association of Learned Journals; Conference of Historical Journals; Council of Editors of Learned Journals; Society for Scholarly Publishing; Canadian Magazine Publishers' Association. **INTERESTS:** travel; sewing; gardening; fitness; reading; World Wide Web exploration.

Corriveau, Sheila ■ $
Senior Consultant, BENCHMARK COMMUNICATIONS (public relations agency that focuses on the technology & entertainment industry), 73 Laird Dr., Ste. 207, Toronto, ON M4G 3T4 (416) 423-6605, FAX 423-5154. Born Kitchener-Waterloo, Ont. 1968. m. Ian Hudson. **EDUC:** Durham Coll. of Applied Arts & Technology, Public Rel'ns Diploma. **CAREER:** Supervisor, Tourist Info. Centre, Town of

Goderich, Ont., 1987; Public Rel'ns Coord., Barrow Communications Limited, 1988-89; Mktg & Comm. Coord., Retail Council of Canada, 1989-91; Public Rel'ns Mgr, The Dynacare Health Group Inc., 1991-96. **SELECTED PUBLICATIONS:** various articles in *Homes Magazine* & *Canadian Association of Retired Persons News.* **AFFIL:** International Association of Business Communicators; Canadian Public Relations Society; United Way of Greater Toronto (Chair). **HONS:** Publicity Appreciation Award, Big Brothers Association of Oshawa-Whitby, 1988; The Scheufelen Award of Design Excellence, Dynacare Inc. Annual Report, 1992. **INTERESTS:** to be an effective communicator; to remain active in the community. **MISC:** volunteers media-rel'ns expertise to publicize bone marrow searches for leukaemia patients. **COMMENT:** *"I am really enjoying the challenges and opportunities here. It has been an exciting switch from a corporate healthcare environment to a dynamic public relations consulting firm that is focused on technology and entertainment. I relish the pace and complexity of technology and entertainment which are both experiencing rapid change–like the healthcare industry."*

Cosman, Francene Jen, M.L.A. ■ ✿ 🏛 ⊕
Member of Legislative Assembly (Bedford-Fall River) and Deputy Speaker, GOVERNMENT OF NOVA SCOTIA, 1600 Bedford Hwy, Ste. 205, Bedford, NS B4A 1E8 (902) 835-9482, FAX 835-6223. Born Windsor, Ont. 1941. m. David. 2 ch. Lara, Andrea. **EDUC:** Saint John Gen. Hospital, R.N. 1962; Margaret Hague Sch., Jersey City, N.J., postgrad. admin. & teaching. **CAREER:** Nurse, Saint John Gen. Hospital, 1963; Head Nurse, Post-Partum Unit, Grace Maternity Hospital, 1968; Councillor, Halifax County Council, 1976-79; Mayor, Town of Bedford, 1979-82; Pres., Cricklewood Giftware Inc., 1987-90; Exec. Dir., N.S. Liberal Association, 1989-93; M.L.A., Bedford-Fall River, 1993 to date. **SELECTED PUBLICATIONS:** various reports, briefs, articles. **AFFIL:** Bedford Service Commission (Chair, Planning Committee 1975); Regional Parks Committee (1976-78); N.S. Advisory Council for the Status of Women (Pres. 1982-86); Bedford Village Homeowners' Association; City Centre Ministry (1986-88); Nova Scotia Art Gallery; Institute of Public Administrators of Canada. **INTERESTS:** hiking, swimming, cross-country skiing; painting; poetry.

Côté, Joanne, B.A.,M.A. ■ ⊗ 🎓 ✿
Education and Museum Consultant in private practice. Coordinator of internships for students enrolled in Masters Degree in Museum

Studies, UNIVERSITÉ DE MONTRÉAL. Born Montreal 1954 1 ch. Camille Côté. **EDUC:** Univ. du Québec à Montréal, B.A.(Art Hist.–Nat'l Heritage) 1979; John F. Kennedy Univ., San Francisco, M.A.(Museum Mgmt/Mktg) 1987; Doctoral Candidate, Educ. Studies, Univ. de Montréal. **CAREER:** Asst. Registrar, Collections Mgmt Svc., Montreal Museum of Fine Arts, 1979-84; Collections Mgr, Canadian Centre for Architecture, 1987; Mgr of Museum Move & Proj. Coord., Bldg Expansion & Reno. Proj., McCord Museum of Canadian History, 1988-92; Head of Special Projects, 1992; Head of Educ. Svcs & Cultural Programs, 1994-96. **SELECTED PUBLICATIONS:** "Moving a Museum: Nightmare or Opportunity" (*MUSE* Summer 1990). **AFFIL:** International Council of Museums; Canadian Museums Association; Société des musées québécois. **HONS:** various scholarships incl. Funds for Assistance, & Support to Research & Concerted Action, 1984-86; Canadian Museum Association, 1982-1993; The Banff Centre for Management, 1993; Joy Feinberg Scholarship, 1987. **INTERESTS:** developing public programs & cultural events in museums; teaching & developing training seminars for museum professionals or students in English or French; organizing cultural field trips in Canada, US or Europe. **MISC:** teaches grad. courses in museum studies, Univ. de Montréal & Univ. Laval; various grants. **COMMENT:** *"Resourceful, enthusiastic self-starter, skilled in project management, particularly in motivating people. Creative in developing public programs that are sensitive, flexible and responsive to the visitor's needs and expectations and abreast of new trends in museum education."*

Côté-Laurence, Paulette, B.Sc.,M.Sc., Ph.D. ■■ 🎓 ⚾

Associate Professor and Chair, Department of Physical Education, BROCK UNIVERSITY, St. Catharines, ON L2S 3A1 (905) 688-5550, ext. 4365, FAX 688-0541, EMAIL pcotelau@arnie.pec.brocku.ca. Born Sorel, Que. 1946. m. Gerard Michael. 3 ch. Jean-Christophe, Gabrielle, Benjamin. **EDUC:** Univ. de Montréal, B.Sc.(Phys. Educ.) 1968; Florida State Univ., M.Sc.(Phys. Educ.) 1972; Univ. of Wisconsin-Madison, Ph.D.(Phys. Educ.) 1985. **CAREER:** Lecturer, Univ. de Sherbrooke, 1969-72 & 1975-83; joined Brock Univ., 1983. **SELECTED PUBLICATIONS:** co-author with J.H. Bradford, "An application of artificial intelligence to the choreography of dance," (*Computers and Humanities*, 29, 233-240, 1995); co-author with J.H. Bradford, "Intégration de l'ordinateur dans la création chorégraphique" (*Actes du Congrès* "Arts et Technologies," Éditions Les Semaines de la Recherche, 27, Lyon, France, 1995); author, "Reflections on dance in higher education" (*Canadian Association for Health, Physical Education and Recreation Journal*, 58(4), 29-31, 1992); author, *La rhythmique à l'élémentaire* (Montreal: Presses de l'Univ. de Montréal, 1984, 135 pages). **EDIT:** Guest Ed., special issue on dance, author, "In pursuit of dance literacy," *Canadian Association for Health, Physical Education and Recreation Journal*, 55(4), 2-3, 1989). **AFFIL:** Canadian Association for Health, Physical Education, Recreation & Dance (Publication Officer 1986-91); American Association for Health, Physical Education, Recreation & Dance; Canadian Society for Psychomotor Learning & Sport Psychology; Association for Dance in Universities & Colleges in Canada; Brock Univ. (Bd. of Trustees 1989-91). **HONS:** invited keynote speaker, Newfoundland Association of Physical Education Conference, 1992. **INTERESTS:** dance & music as performing arts; piano; painting; gardening; sewing. **MISC:** recently successfully submitted an intensive program in phys. ed. to the Malaysian Ministry of Educ.; in Sept. 1996, 4 educators from Malaysia will come to Brock Univ. to attend the "Teaching Movement in primary & secondary schools" program, of which Paulette is the co-ordinator. **COMMENT:** *"Received an interdisciplinary Ph.D. from the University of Wisconsin-Madison, relating dance, music, cognitive psychology and motor learning. Is Associate Professor and Chair of the Department of Physical Education at Brock University, Ontario. Teaching/research interests are in motor learning, creative dance, Dalcroze Eurlythmics, and rhythm perception. In addition to teaching dance and motor learning in the department, has taught dance in the department of fine arts, Dalcroze Eurlythmics in the department of music, and elementary physical education in the faculty of education."*

Côté-O'Hara, Jocelyne, B.A. ■ $

Born North Bay, Ont. 1945. m. Tom O'Hara. 3 ch. **EDUC:** Univ. of Ottawa, B.A.(Social Sci.) 1967; Harvard Bus. Sch., Advanced Mgmt Program 1986. **CAREER:** various mgmt positions, Gov't of Canada, 1972-82; Special Advisor to the Chair, Petro-Canada International, 1982-84; Sr. Staff Mbr. to the Right Hon. Brian Mulroney, 1984-85; VP, Gov't Rel'ns, B.C. Tel, 1985-92; Pres. & CEO, Stentor Telecom Policy Inc., 1992-96. **SELECTED PUBLICATIONS:** *Beneath the Veneer* (1990); *Report by the Committee on Women and Economic Restructuring* of the Canadian Labour Market and Productivity Centre (1994). **DIRECTOR:** International Development Research Centre; Communications Research Centre; Xerox Canada; Northern Trust Company, Canada; Women's Television Network Foundation; Canadian Labour Market & Productivity Centre. **AFFIL:** Carleton Univ. (Gov.); Rideau Club; Canadian Women in Communications. **HONS:** "Canadian Business Successor" for outstanding leadership in business, 1988; Public Service Citation, APEX Award, 1990; Woman of the Year, Canadian Women in Communications, 1993. **INTERESTS:** tennis; skiing.

Coucill, Irma Sophia ✕

Portrait Artist. 393 Broadway Ave., Toronto, ON M4P 1X5. Born London, Ont. 1918. m. Walter Jackson Coucill, R.C.A.(dec.). 2 ch. John, Thomas. **EDUC:** St. Joseph's Convent Coll., 1934. **CAREER:** Ed. Artist, *The Globe & Mail*, 1958-60; Ed. Artist, *The Toronto Star*, 1960 to date; Syndicated Artist, The Toronto Star Syndicate, 1960-70; Ed. Artist, *Maclean's* Magazine, 1970-72; Contributing Artist, *Junior Encyclopedia of Canada*, 1990. **SELECTED PUBLICATIONS:** illustrator for: *Founders and Guardians* (2nd ed., 1982); *The Nation Makers* (1976); *The Journal Men* (1974); *Stories about 125 Years at Touche Ross* by Edgar Collard (20 illustrations); *The Canadian Prime Ministers*. **COMMISSIONS:** portrait artist for the following: Canadian Hockey Hall of Fame, Toronto (304 portraits); Canadian Aviation Hall of Fame, Reynolds/Alberta Museum Wetaskiwin (143 portraits); Canadian Business Hall of Fame, BCE Place, Toronto (99 portraits); Canadian Indian Hall of Fame, Woodland Indian Cultural Educational Centre, Brantford (30 portraits); United Way (portrait presented to Chair past 25 years); Cardiovascular Museum, Toronto Hospital (portrait of Dr. Wilfred Bigelow); portrait, Gov.-Gen. Edward R. Schreyer, Rideau Hall Collection, Ottawa; Terry Fox Canadian Youth Centre, Ottawa (portrait of Terry Fox); Canadian Press Collection, Toronto (past presidents, gen. managers, broadcast news managers); Canadian Medical Hall of Fame, London, Ont. (17 portraits). **INTERESTS:** photography; music; etymology; poetry; gardening; painting.

Cournoyer, Julie ■ ■ ⓐ

Paralympic Athlete. Sherbrooke, QC. **EDUC:** Univ. de Sherbrooke, current. **SPORTS CAREER:** mbr., Nat'l Cycling Team, 1996 to date; Paralympic Games: Bronze, Tandem Standing Kilo (ptnr Guylaine Larouche); Silver, Individual Pursuit; Gold, 50/60 km; Gold, 65K Tandem (ptnr Alexandre Cloutier), 1996. Défi Sportif: 1st, 21km, 1996. **MISC:** 1st year on nat'l team

Cournoyea, The Hon. Nellie J., MLA ■ ✲ ♂

Chair and Chief Executive Officer, INUVIALUIT REGIONAL CORPORATION (corp. mandated to receive the Inuvialuit lands & fin. compensation resulting from the 1984 land claim settlement), P.O. Box 2120, Inuvik, NT X0E 0T0 (403) 979-2737, FAX 979-2135. Born Aklavik, N.W.T. 1940. 2 ch. John Cournoyea, Maureen Cournoyea. **EDUC:** Federal Aklavik Day School. **CAREER:** Announcer & Stn Mgr, CBC Inuvik; land claim field work, Inuit Tapirisat of Canada; Founder Mbr., & later Administrator & land rights worker, Committee for Original Peoples' Entitlement (COPE); Mng Dir., Inuvialuit Development Corporation; Implementation Coord., Inuvialuit Final Agreement; elected M.L.A. (Nunakput), 1979-95; Premier, Gov't of the Northwest Territories, 1991-95. **HONS:** Woman of the Year Awards (Politics), NWT Native Women's Association, 1982; Wallace Goose Award, Inuvialuit Regional Corporation, 1986; National Aboriginal Achievement Award, 1994; LL.D.(Hon.), Lakehead Univ.; LL.D.(Hon.), Carleton Univ.; LL.D.(Hon.), Univ. of Toronto. **MISC:** Founding Mbr., Northern Games Association; 1st aboriginal woman to lead a gov't in Canada.

Coutts, Denise, B.P.E.,M.P.E. ⓐ ○

Executive Director, BADMINTON B.C., 1367 W. Broadway, Ste. 328, Vancouver, BC V6H 4A9 (604) 737-3030, FAX 738-7175. Born Vernon, B.C. 1957. m. Randy. 1 ch. Samatha. **EDUC:** Univ. of British Columbia, B.P.E.(Phys. Educ.), Masters in Sport Admin. 1982. **CAREER:** Program Coord., Basketball B.C., 1988-90; Exec. Dir., Squash B.C., 1990-91; Exec. Dir., Badminton B.C., 1992 to date. **AFFIL:** Sport B.C. (Rel'ns Committee; Professional Dev. Subcommittee); B.C. Luge Association (Gen. Mgr 1991-95); Meraloma Club; coach of numerous women's teams. **HONS:** numerous B.C. & nat'l championships in slow pitch, basketball & rowing; Harry Jerome Comeback Athlete of the Year Award, Sport B.C., 1990. **INTERESTS:** sewing; knitting; gardening; interior decorating; all sports. **MISC:** organizer for several sport championships & conferences. **COMMENT:** *"Have lived with the gastrointestinal disease, ulcerative colitis, for the past 18 years-can make life very difficult at times-your health really is one of your most important assets, never to be taken for granted."*

Cowan, Bonnie, B.A. ✎ ▢

Editor-in-Chief, CANADIAN LIVING MAGAZINE, 25 Sheppard Ave. W., North York, ON M2N 6S6 (416) 218-3546, FAX 733-3398. Born Chesley, Ont. 1943. d. 3 ch. Krista Baker, Jennifer Walker, David Cowan. **EDUC:** Wilfrid Laurier Univ., B.A.(English) 1965. **CAREER:** Secondary Sch. Teacher, 1965-71; Lifestyles Ed., *Burlington Post*; Columnist, *TheToronto Star*; Ed. & Coord. of Food Dept., *Canadian Living*, 1979-85; Mng Ed., 1985-88; Ed.-in-Chief, 1988 to date. **AFFIL:** Canadian Society of Magazine Editors (Founding Mbr.); Canadian Living Foundation for Families (Co-founder, Pres.); Breakfast for Learning. **COMMENT:** *"As editor of Canada's leading family magazine, Bonnie Cowan directs the content of 12 annual issues of* Canadian Living *magazine, which has a readership of 2.4 million Canadians."*

Cowling, Marlene, M.P. ♣ ♂

Member of Parliament (Dauphin-Swan River, Manitoba), **GOVERNMENT OF CANADA**, House of Commons, Centre Block, Rm. 549-D, Ottawa, ON K1A 0A6 (613) 992-3176, FAX 992-0930. Farmer. Born 1941. m. Doug Cowling. 5 ch. **CAREER:** Dir., local Co-op Bd., 1978-80; Sec.-Treas., Pleasant Valley Women's Institute, 1979-81; Census Quality Control Technician, 1979-81; Pres.-Elect, N.W. Reg., Manitoba's Women's Institute, 1983-84; Pres., 1984-85; Chair, District 11, Keystone Agricultural Producers, 1985-87; Exec. Mbr., 1987-88; Woman Rep. of Western Canada, Canadian Federation of Agriculture, 1987-90; 2nd VP, Keystone Agricultural Producers, 1988-91; Man. Women's Institute Exec. Officer, Federated Women's Institute of Canada, 1991-93; M.P. (Dauphin-Swan River, Man.), 1993 to date; mbr. of several Standing Committees incl. Agriculture & Agri-Foods, Transport & Aboriginal Affiars; Chair, Manitoba Liberal Caucus; Parliamentary Sec. (appointed by P.M.) to Min. of Natural Res. **AFFIL:** Manitoba Women's Institute (Life Mbr.); United Church Choir; Pleasant Valley Community Club; Pleasant Valley Women's Institute. **INTERESTS:** advocating the full participation of women in pol. process & in mainstream farm organizations; issues relating to educ., generally & particularly those issues directly related to the educ. of our own children; issues relating to the overall welfare of the agricultural community & particularly farm families at local, prov., nat'l & int'l level. **MISC:** has policed the by-laws & procedures of Keystone Agricultural Products to ensure that there were no procedural barriers to the full participation of farm women; instrumental in clarifying the role of the Eastern & Western Women Representatives to the Canadian Federation of Agriculture; 1st woman M.P. (Dauphin-Swan River); presently only woman in Manitoba Liberal Caucus.

Cox, Mae, B.Ed. ■■ ♥ ⊕

Executive Director, **ORGAN DONORS CANADA** (health info.) (403) 474-9363. Born Edmonton 1930. m. Philip Cox. 6 ch. Helen, James, Thomas, Charles, Gordon, Edward. **EDUC:** Univ. of Alberta, B.Ed.(with distinction). **CAREER:** teacher, elementary/ESL, mostly part-time, 1950 to date; Exec. Sec., Memorial Society of Edmonton & District, 1962-65 & 1968-78; Founding Sec., Memorial Society Association of Canada, 1971-74; Pres., 1974-75; Co-founder & Exec. Dir., Organ Donors Canada, 1974 to date; Co-ordinator, N. Alta., Lions Eye Bank, 1985-90. **SELECTED PUBLICATIONS:** *Human Transplants in Canada* (1978). **EDIT:** *A Teaching Unit on Death and Dying* (editor, 1976); *Transplant News* (editor, 1979-83); *Birding Around Edmonton* (pamphlet series, co-editor, 1983-86). **AFFIL:** Alberta Funeral Services Regulatory Bd. (Dir. 1993 to date); Edmonton Bird Club (founding mbr., various exec. positions, 1949 to date). **HONS:** Alberta Achievement Award (for community service), 1979. **INTERESTS:** teaching; writing; community service. **COMMENT:** *"As a stay-at-home mother, I was able to take part in many community service activities -school-related, Boy Scouts, handicrafts, and P.R./public information programs. This work is ongoing."*

Coxon, Helen C. ■■ 🍷 🏵

Conservator, **ROYAL ONTARIO MUSEUM**, 100 Queen's Park Cres., Toronto, ON M5S 2C6 (416) 586-5897, FAX 586-5863, EMAIL helenc@rom.on.ca. Born Leicester, UK 1960. m. Hugh Spencer. 2 ch. Simon, Evan. **EDUC:** Univ. of Durham, U.K., Gen. Arts (Archaeology, Music, Theology) 1982, Diploma (Archaeological Conservation) 1986. **CAREER:** Asst. Conservator, Royal Ontario Museum, 1987-88; Conservator, 1988 to date. **SELECTED PUBLICATIONS:** author, "Possibilities for the identification of polymeric materials used in conservation" (*Proceedings of the 14th Annual IIC-CG Conference*, May 27-30, 1988, Toronto); co-author with Julia Fenn, "Vulnerable Plastics" (paper presented at 17th Annual Meeting of American Institute for Conservation of Historic & Artistic Works, Cincinnati, May 31-June 4, 1989); author, "Practical Pitfalls in the Identification of Plastics" (in *Symposium '91: saving the twentieth century; the degradation and conservation of modern materials*, Canadian Conservation Institute, Ottawa, 1993). **AFFIL:** International Institute for Conservation of Historic & Artistic Works (IIC); Canadian Association for Conservation of Cultural Property (CAC); Orpheus Choir of Toronto; Orpheus Chamber Choir; Royal York Road United Church Sr. Choir (Pres. 1993-95).

INTERESTS: music, esp. singing; gardening; needlework/crafts; DIY. **MISC:** Grade 8 Vocal, Royal Conservatory of Music.

Crabtree, Linda, C.M.,O.Ont.,O.M.C., LL.D. ♡ ✎ ☝
Writer, Publisher, Entrepreneur and Disability Advocate. 1 Springbank Dr., St. Catharines, ON L2S 2K1 (905) 687-3630, FAX 687-8753, EMAIL emtint@vaxxine.com. Born 1942. m. G. Ronald Book. **EDUC:** Sir George Williams Univ. Sch. of Arts, Diploma (Fine & Commercial Art) 1966; Brock Univ., B.A.(with distinction) 1987. **CAREER:** Arnott, Rogers and Batten, Inc. (commercial art studio), Montreal, 1966-67; journalist,*The Standard*, St. Catharines, 1970-82; Founder, Pres. & Exec. Dir., CMT International, 1984; Pres., Phoenix Counsel Inc. (Founder, 1992 & Ed., 1992-95 of *It's Okay!* magazine, the first and only consumer quarterly written in N. America on sexuality, sex, self-esteem & disability); rehabilitation counselling specializing in neuromuscular disorders. **EDIT:** Prod., Ed. & journalist, *CMT International Newsletter*, a bimonthly 24-page publication going to 2,200 families in 44 countries, 1984 to date. **AFFIL:** Charcot-Marie-Tooth Disease/Peroneal Muscular Atrophy International Association (Chair & Founder). **HONS:** Ontario Medal for Citizenship (O.M.C.), 1987; Biennial Award to Women for work on disability awareness, YWCA, 1989; Canada Volunteer Medal, 1989; Hon. Mention for design of home & offices, Premier's Award for Accessibility, 1990; Order of Ontario (O.Ont), 1992; Breaking the Barriers Award for journalism regarding disability, Niagara Centre for Independent Living, 1992; Canada 125 Medal, 1992; "Women on the Move" Award, *The Toronto Sun*, 1993; Mbr. of the Order of Canada, 1994; Canada Peace Medal, YWCA, 1994 ; Beta Sigma Phi hon. int'l membership, 1995; Paul Harris Fellow, Rotary Int.'l, 1996; LL.D.(Hon.), Brock Univ., 1994. **INTERESTS:** husband; home; dog; all forms of creative art; publishing; architecture; photography; film making; horticulture; geology; animals; Studebakers; freelance writing. **MISC:** first consumer to enter & receive an award in "Premier's Award for Accessibility" competition previously open only to architects; featured on the Disability Network, CBC, Mar. 1992; founded St. Catharines Craft Guild, 1977; numerous public speaking & guest appearances, incl. *Morningside* with Peter Gzowski, CBC, Oct. 15, 1995. **COMMENT:** *"An entrepreneurial spirit, curiosity and a physical disability have led me to found two charities and a business, and shown me ways to meet and help others I never thought possible."*

Craig, Jane ✪ 🎓 ♡
General Manager, KIWANIS MUSIC FESTIVAL OF GREATER TORONTO, 100 Adelaide St. W., Ste. 501, Toronto, ON M5H 1S3 (416) 363-3238, FAX 363-2657. Born Toronto 1943. m. James. 2 ch. **EDUC:** Toronto Teachers' College, Music Specialist 1967. **CAREER:** Teacher, MacKay Centre for Deaf & Crippled Children, 1965-66; Teacher, Vocal & Instrumental Music, Deer Park Public Sch., Toronto, 1967-70, 1971-73; Admin. Asst., Timothy Eaton Memorial Church, 1986-89; Admin. Asst., Kiwanis Club of West Toronto, 1989-90; Gen. Mgr, Kiwanis Music Festival of Toronto, 1990 to date. **AFFIL:** Timothy Eaton Memorial United Church (Sr. Lay Officer); Toronto Children's Chorus (Sec. of the Bd. 1992-94); Roy Thomson Hall (Volunteer; Mbr., Award Committee); Toronto Board of Trade; Ontario Music Festivals Association (Exec.); Federation of Canadian Music Festivals. **INTERESTS:** choral music. **COMMENT:** *"Another interest of mine is supporting young Canadian talent and I feel I am doing that with my involvement with the Music Festival."*

Craig, Susan J., B.A.,M.A. ■■ $ ⊕ ✊
President, THE CRAIG CORPORATION (mgmt & career dev. & corp. staffing), 371 Berkeley St., Toronto, ON M5A 2X8 (416) 960-5062, FAX 960-6467, EMAIL cdndocs@istar.ca. President, MEDICAL RECRUITMENT SERVICES. Born Belleville, Ont. 1947. m. Dr. Brian Bustard, M.D. **EDUC:** York Univ., B.A.(English & Psych.) 1968; Goddard Coll., Vermont, M.A.(Human Studies) 1977. **CAREER:** Psychometrist, Clarke Institute of Psychiatry, Toronto, 1968-69; Dir. of Behavioral Lab., Green Valley Sch., Roscoe, N.Y., 1969-73; Social Worker, Belleville General Hospital, Belleville, Ont., 1973-76; Teaching Master, Loyalist Coll., 1976-80; Dir. of Staffing & Dev., Sonoco Limited, Brantford, Ont., 1980-82; Exec. Housekeeper, Yak and Yeti Hotel, Nepal, 1983; Pres., The Craig Corporation, Toronto, 1982 to date; Pres., Medical Recruitment Services, div. of The Craig Corporation (physician recruitment for hospitals & clinics in Canada, U.S. & overseas), 1992 to date. **SELECTED PUBLICATIONS:** co-author, *Creating Your Vision for Education.* **AFFIL:** Association for Creative Change & Organization Renewal & Development; Ontario Society for Training & Development; National Association of Physician Recruiters; Himalayan Institute of Canada (founder & Dir. 1984 to date); Warkworth Institution (Citizens' Advisory Committee 1991 to date). **MISC:** has taught numerous courses in training & organization effectiveness; frequent speaker on issues of physician recruit-

ment & retention to medical groups throughout Canada & U.S.; developed voluntary svc. group dedicated to educ. & health svcs for Cdns & internationally; originated ntwk of over 100 professional women in Belleville, The Women's Network; launched major community & organization dev. thrust established halfway houses for alcoholics, alternative schools, homes for battered women & outreach programs. **COMMENT:** *"Entrepreneur, educator and yogi. Founded the Himalayan Institute of Canada, Medical Recruitment Services and The Craig Corporation. Mentor of others. Growing into grace."*

Craighead, Joy, B.N.,M.Ed.,C.H.E. ✊ ⊕

Associate Director, Quality Management, COLLEGE OF PHYSICIANS AND SURGEONS OF ONTARIO, 47 Geneva Ave., Toronto, ON M5A 2J9 (416) 967-2600, ext. 415, FAX 967-2605. Born Campbellford, Ont. 1938. **EDUC:** Toronto Western Hospital, Diploma of Nursing 1959; McGill Univ., Bachelor of Nursing 1968; Queen's Univ., M.Ed. 1980. **CAREER:** Staff Nurse & Supervisor, Queen Elizabeth Hospital, Montreal, 1960-62; Asst. Head Nurse, Mount Sinai Hospital, 1962-65; Head Nurse, Toronto General Hospital, 1965-73; Instructor of Nursing, Univ. Teaching Hospital, Zambia, Africa, 1973-75; Teaching Master, Loyalist Coll., 1976-80; Dir., Quality Assurance Programs, The Wellesley Hospital, 1981-90; Program Dir., Independent Health Facilities, Coll. of Physicians & Surgeons of Ontario, 1990-92; Assoc. Dir., Quality Mgmt, 1992 to date. **SELECTED PUBLICATIONS:** *Accountability in Clinical Judgment and Decision Making* (New York: John Wiley and Sons, 1987); "Laying the Groundwork for a Board of Directors' Quality Assurance Program" (*Canadian Journal of Quality in Health Care* Nov. 1987); "Seven Steps for a Full Prevention Program" (*Dimensions in Health Service* May 1991); "Progress, Innovations and Directions for the Future" (*Members Dialogue*, Coll. of Physicians & Surgeons, May & Sept. 1993). **AFFIL:** Canadian Coll. of Health Service Executives (Certified Health Exec.); Canadian Association for Quality in Health Care (Exec. 1983-89; Pres. 1986-87); Quality Assurance Programs, Telemedicine Canada (Co-ordinating Chair & Moderator 1988-89); Himalayan Institute of Canada (Asst. Dir.); Toronto Flying Club (Membership Chair); The Ninety-Nines, International Women's Pilot Organization. **HONS:** Award in Recognition of Commitment & Contribution Through Service, Canadian Association for Quality in Health Care, 1990. **MISC:** yoga teacher, Himalayan Institute of Canada; previously a skydiver with more than 400 jumps; presently a private pilot. **COMMENT:** *"A dedicated, skillful healthcare executive with commitment to service in all aspects of life–spiritual, physical, emotional and material. Presently helping to build a teaching hospital in India."*

Cram, Lynne Muriel, B.A. $

Executive Vice-President, WINDJAMMER LANDING VILLA BEACH RESORT (subsidiary of Ellis-Don Limited), Box 5093, Stn. A, London, ON N6A 4M6 (519) 659-5407, FAX 455-2944. Born Canada 1953. d. 3 ch. Andrew, Robert, Nicole. **EDUC:** Univ. of Guelph, B.A.(Child Studies) 1974. **CAREER:** Catering Mgr & other positions, Four Seasons Hotel Yorkville, 1975-79; Sales Rep., Xerox Canada, 1979-81; Co-Owner/Mgr, Windjammer Clothing (St. Lucia), 1985-90; Exec. VP, Windjammer Landing Villa Beach Resort, 1991 to date. **SELECTED PUBLICATIONS:** published in *Financial Post Magazine* & *Boys Club Magazine*. **AFFIL:** Big Sisters of London (Dir.); London Club (Dir.; Chrm, Membership Rel'ns Committee). **INTERESTS:** tennis; skiing. **COMMENT:** *"I am a very determined individual who has taken on many new challenges, such as starting a manufacturing company in St. Lucia without any experience in export or manufacturing; promoted to Catering Manager at Four Seasons without hotel training; and have managed to be successful. Greatest challenge is balancing my work and travel with my family life."*

Cranston, Lynda S., B.Sc.N.,M.Sc.N. ■■ ⊕

President and Chief Executive Officer, B.C. WOMEN'S HOSPITAL & HEALTH CENTRE, 4500 Oak St., Vancouver, BC V6H 3N1 (604) 875-2151, FAX 875-2379. Clinical Instructor, Masters Program in Health Planning and Epidemiology, Faculty of Medicine, UNIVERSITY OF BRITISH COLUMBIA. President and CEO-Designate, B.C.'S CHILDREN'S AND WOMEN'S HOSPITALS AND HEALTH CENTRES (the result of a merger of B.C. Women's, B.C. Children's and Sunnyhill Hospital and Health Centre). **EDUC:** Univ. of Ottawa, B.Sc.N. 1970; Univ. of Western Ontario, M.Sc.N.(Admin.) 1975. **CAREER:** Staff Nurse, Hospital for Sick Children, Toronto, 1970-71; Nursing Teacher, Kingston Gen. Hospital Sch. of Nursing, Kingston, Ont., 1971-73; Dir. of Nursing, Queensway Carleton Hospital, Ottawa, 1975-80; Asst. Administrator, Patient Svcs, Calgary Gen. Hospital, 1980-82; Sr. VP, Oper., 1982-85; independent Health Care Consultant, Cranda Resources, Apr.-Sept. 1985; VP, Patient Care, Shaughnessy Hospital, Vancouver, 1985-87; VP, Professional Svcs, 1987-88; VP & Administrator, Shaughnessy Site, University Hospital, 1988-90; Pres. &

CEO, The Richmond Hospital, Richmond, B.C., 1990-94; Pres. & CEO, B.C. Women's Hospital & Health Centre, Vancouver, 1994-96; Pres & CEO Designate, Women's & Children's, 1996 to date. AFFIL: Canadian Coll. of Health Service Executives (V-Chair & Bd. mbr.; Health Product Review Svc.); American Coll. of Healthcare Executives (Regent's Advisory Council); Univ. of British Columbia (Dean's Advisory Council, Fac. of Commerce & Bus. Admin.); Hospital Administrators Association of B.C.; B.C. Health Risk Management Society (Bd. mbr.); Provincial Health Utilization Committee; Health Forum, San Francisco (Cdn Advisory Council); B.C. Reproductive Care Program (Bd. mbr.); Council of University Teaching Hospitals (Exec. mbr.); YWCA (Capital Campaign Chair 1993-96); Vancouver Symphony Orchestra (Bd. mbr. 1993 to date); Vancouver United Way Campaign (Acct. Exec. 1988-92; V-Chrm, Health Div. 1992; Chrm, Health Div. 1993); Ministry of Health, B.C. (Chrm, Prince George Reg'l Review Team 1993; Rural & Northern Task Force 1995); B.C. Mental Health Association (Chair, Workplace Awards 1996). HONS: Woman of Distinction Award (Mgmt & the Professions), YWCA, 1992; 125th Anniversary of Confederation Commemorative Medal for community contributions; B.C. Bus. Award, Univ. of B.C. Commerce Grad. Society, 1993. MISC: Guest Lecturer, Univ. of B.C. Bus. Sch., Course on Leadership Styles.

Cranton, Patricia, B.Ed.,M.Sc., Ph.D. ⌀
Professor, Faculty of Education, BROCK UNIVERSITY, St. Catharines, ON L2S 3A1 (905) 688-5550, FAX 892-9897, EMAIL pcranton@dewey.ed.brocku.ca. Born Hanna, Alta. 1949. d. EDUC: Univ. of Calgary, B.Ed. 1971, M.Sc. 1973; Univ. of Toronto, Ph.D. 1976. CAREER: Asst. Prof., Centre for Teaching & Learning Svcs, Dept. of Educ. Psych., McGill Univ., 1976-81; Assoc. Prof., 1981-86; Dir., Grad. Studies in Educational Psych., 1983-85; Assoc. Prof., Fac. of Educ., Brock Univ., 1986-90; Chair, Dept. of Grad. & Undergrad. Studies, Fac. of Educ., 1988-90; Prof., Fac. of Educ., 1990 to date; Dir., Instructional Dev. Office, 1991-94. SELECTED PUBLICATIONS: *Planning Instruction for Adult Learners* (Toronto: Wall and Thompson, 1989); *Working with Adult Learners* (Toronto: Wall and Emerson, 1992); *Understanding and Promoting Transformative Learning: a Guide for Educators of Adults* (San Francisco: Jossey-Bass, 1994); "Computer Models of Personality: Implications for Measurement" (*Journal of Personality Measurement* 1976); "Selecting Instructional Strate-

gies," with C. Weston (*Journal of Higher Education* 1986); "Self Directed and Transformative Learning" (*Journal of Higher Education* 1994); numerous other publications. AFFIL: American Education Research Association; Canadian Society for Studies in Education; Adult Education Research Association; Society for Teaching & Learning in Higher Education. HONS: Clarence Samson Medal in Educ., Alta., 1971; Distinguished Scholar, Brock Univ., 1990; Lieutenant Governor's Award for Teaching Excellence 1993. INTERESTS: reading; writing. MISC: recipient of various grants; numerous conference presentations. COMMENT: *"I have always wanted to be, and have become, a good teacher and known writer in my field."*

Crean, Susan, B.A.,M.A. 📖 ⌷ ⊕
Writer. 1916 W. 11th Ave., Vancouver, BC V6J 2C6 (604) 731-6866. Born Toronto 1945. m. B. Laurie Edwards. EDUC: Univ. of Toronto, B.A. 1967; Istituto della Storia dell'Arte, Università di Firenze 1966; Univ. of Toronto, M.A. 1969; École du Louvre, Paris, Diploma in Muséologie 1970. CAREER: appointments: Research Asst., Program in Arts Admin., York Univ., 1970-72; Tutorial Asst. & Lecturer, Dept. of Fine Art, York Univ., 1970-72; Assoc., Dixon, Moore & Associates, Arts Consultants, 1972-75; Exec. Sec., Canadian Artists' Representation, Ont., 1973-74; Program Consultant, CBC-2 Dev. Team, CBC English Svcs Div., 1980-81; Lecturer, Dept. of Pol. Studies, Univ. of Prince Edward Island, 1985; Guest Lecturer, Dept. of Pol. Sci., Univ. of Alberta, 1986; Maclean Hunter Chair in Creative Non-fiction & Bus. Writing, Dept. of Creative Writing, Univ. of British Columbia, 1989-90. SELECTED CREDITS: program research/interviewing, "The Politics of Culture," *The Great Canadian Culture Hunt*, Part 1, CBC-TV, 1978-79; Assoc. Prod., *There Never was an Arrow*, CBC-TV, 1980; Assoc. Prod., *Quarterly Report/Tel Quel*, CBC-TV, 1980-81; program research, *Eureka, eh?*, CBC-TV, 1980; program research/interviewing, *Airwaves*, CBC-TV, 1982. SELECTED PUBLICATIONS: *Who's Afraid of Canadian Culture?* (Toronto: General Publishing, 1976); *Deux pays pour vivre: un plaidoyer*, with Marcel Rioux (Montréal: Albert Saint-Martin, 1980); *Two Nations: an Essay on the Culture and Politics of Canada and Quebec in a World of American Pre-eminence*, with Marcel Rioux (Toronto: Lorimer, 1983); *Newsworthy: The Lives of Media Women* (Toronto: Stoddart, 1984); *In the Name of the Fathers: the Story Behind Child Custody* (Toronto: Amanita Publications, 1988); *Grace Hartman, A Woman*

for Her Time (Vancouver: New Star, 1995); *Twist and Shout. A Decade of Feminist Writing in This Magazine*, ed. (Toronto: Second Story Press, 1992); work in various anthologies, incl. "Taking the Missionary Position" in *Racism in Canada*, Ormond McKague ed. (Saskatoon: Fifth House, 1991); numerous papers & studies; articles, editorial & reviews in numerous journals incl. *This Magazine, Geist, FUSE, Quill & Quire* & *The Globe and Mail*, 1972 to date. EDIT: Ed. Bd., *Canadian Forum*, 1976-79; Contributing Ed., *Quill & Quire*, 1982-85; Ed. Collective, *This Magazine*, 1979-90, Contributing Ed., 1990 to date, Ed., "Female Complaints" column, 1986-91; Contributing Ed., *Canadian Art*, 1989 to date, "Female Gaze" column, 1988-90. AFFIL: Writers' Union of Canada (Chair 1991-92); CANCOPY (Dir.); International PEN; The Writers' Guild of Canada. MISC: Minister's Advisory Committee on the Status of the Artist in B.C., report entitled *In Spirit and in Law* released Feb. 1994.

Creary, Barbara, LL.B. 🎩 📖 ◁|▷
Publisher and Foreign Rights Director, LES ÉDITIONS DE LA COURTE ÉCHELLE INC., 5243 boul. Saint-Laurent, Montréal, QC H2T 1S4 (514) 274-2004, FAX 270-4160. Born Topeka, Kansas 1948. d. 1 ch. Ani Sara. EDUC: Univ. du Québec à Montréal, LL.B. 1981. BAR: Que., 1982. CAREER: Ptnr, Goyette, Cossette, Creary and Lefebvre, 1982-87; Publisher & Foreign Rights Dir., Les éditions de la courte échelle, 1987 to date. AFFIL: Groupe d'aide et d'information sur le harcèlement sexuel au travail, Montréal (Pres.); Association Nationale des Éditeurs de livres (Dir.); Association for the Export of Canadian Books (Dir.).

Creese, Gillian, B.A.,M.A.,Ph.D. ■ 🖋
Associate Professor, Department of Anthropology and Sociology, UNIVERSITY OF BRITISH COLUMBIA, 6303 N.W. Marine Dr., Vancouver, BC V6T 1Z1 (604) 822-2541, FAX 822-6161, EMAIL creese@unixg.ubc.ca. Born London, UK 1955. m. Donald Black. EDUC: Simon Fraser Univ., B.A.(Soc.) 1978; Queen's Univ., M.A.(Soc.) 1981; Carleton Univ., Ph.D.(Soc.) 1986. CAREER: Assoc. Prof., Anthropology & Soc., Univ. of British Columbia, 1986 to date; Chair, Women's Studies, 1993-96. SELECTED PUBLICATIONS: *Ups and Downs in the Ladder of Success: Social Mobility in Canada*, 1986, with Neil Guppy & Martin Meissner (Ottawa; Statistics Canada, 1991); *British Columbia Reconsidered: Essays on Women*, with Veronica Strong-Boag (Vancouver; Press Gang Publishers, 1992); "Sexual Equality and the Minimum Wage in British Columbia" (*The Journal of Canadian Studies*,

Vol. 26, No. 4, Winter 1991-92); "Power and Pay: The Union and Equal Pay at B.C. Electric/Hydro" (*Labour/Le Travail*, Vol. 32, Fall 1993); "Gender Equity or Masculine Privilege?: Union Strategies and Economic Reconstructing in a White Collar Union" (*The Canadian Journal of Sociology*, Vol. 20, No. 2, 1995); "Taking Gender Into Account in British Columbia: More Than Just Women's Studies" (*BC Studies*, No. 105-106, Summer 1995); "Making the News, Realizing Chinese Canadian," (*Studies in Political Economy*, no. 51, Fall 1996). EDIT: Ed. Bd., *Studies in Political Economy*, 1990 to date; Ed. Bd., *B.C. Studies*, 1993 to date; Ed. Bd., *Labour/Le Travail*, 1994 to date. AFFIL: MOSAIC, Multicultural Orientation Service Association for Immigrant Canadians (VP). INTERESTS: snow skiing; biking; travelling. COMMENT: *"I am a sociologist engaged in analyzing the processes of gender, race and class inequality in Canada and helping to communicate such knowledge to students and the broader community."*

Crépin, Denise, B.A.,B.Mus. ☺ ⊕ ♡
National Executive Director, EPILEPSY CANADA, 1470 Peel St., Ste. 745, Montreal, QC H3A 1T1 (514) 845-7855, FAX 845-7866. Born Châteauguay, Que. s. EDUC: Univ. of Montreal, B.A. 1963, B.Mus.(Piano) 1981; Nursing Sch., Hôpital Général de Verdun, 1964; various training & dev. courses. CAREER: Admin. Asst., Royal Victoria Hospital, 1964-71; Program Coord., Continuing Medical Educ., 1971-79; part-time position, Continuing Medical Educ., McGill Univ., 1976-79; Asst. Dir., N.E. Ont., The Muscular Dystrophy Association of Canada, 1981-82; Exec. Dir., Que. Div., 1982-88; Nat'l Exec. Dir., Epilepsy Canada, 1988 to date. AFFIL: Association des gestionnaires en philanthropie; Société canadienne des directeurs d'association; International Bureau for Epilepsy; Epilepsy Foundation of America; National Voluntary Health Agencies; National Voluntary Organizations; Canadian Centre for Philanthropy. INTERESTS: arts; music; opera; reading. COMMENT: *"My career has been focused on senior administration and fundraising positions because I am a cause-oriented individual with a great personal interest in promoting advancement within the voluntary health sector."*

Crewe, Katherine, B.Sc.,M.Eng. ■ 🏵 ☺ 🥄
Vice-President, MEDSTENT INC., 91 Kelfield St., Rexdale, ON M9W 5A3 (416) 242-6167, FAX 242-9481. Born Toronto 1958. m. D.M. Dixon. 2 ch. EDUC: Queen's Univ., B.Sc. (Chem. Eng.) 1981, McMaster Univ., M.Eng. (Biomedical Eng.). CAREER: Applications

Eng., Hayward Gordon Ltd., 1981-82; Plant Mgr, Vas-Cath Inc., 1985-91; Gen. Mgr, CYEX Medical Technologies, 1991-96; VP, MEDSTEND Inc., 1996 to date. **DIRECTOR:** CYEDORMEDIX. **AFFIL:** Professional Engineers Ontario; French Immersion Parents' Association; Queen's Univ. (Applied Science Advisory Council); Women in Science & Engineering. **HONS:** Young Engineers Award, Canadian Council of Professional Engineers, 1992; Order of Honour, Professional Engineers Ontario, 1993; Legacy of Achievement Award, Queen's Univ., 1995. **INTERESTS:** masters swimming. **MISC:** 1st woman to receive the Young Engineers Award. **COMMENT:** *"I have devoted much of my adult life to ensuring access and equality for women in engineering. My efforts have been recognized provincially and nationally by the engineering profession."*

Crocker, Anne, B.A.,B.L.S. 📖 ✊ ⚖

Head Law Librarian, Gerard V. La Forest Law Library, UNIVERSITY OF NEW BRUNSWICK, Bag Service 44999, Fredericton, NB E3B 6C9 (506) 453-4734, FAX 453-5186. President, CANADIAN ASSOCIATION OF LAW LIBRARIES. Born 1944. **EDUC:** Univ. of New Brunswick, B.A.(English) 1966; Univ. of Toronto, B.L.S. 1970; Univ. of California at Berkeley, Sch. of Library & Info. Studies, Certificate of Advanced Studies in Library Mgmt 1987. **CAREER:** Extension Svcs Librarian, York Reg'l Library, Fredericton, 1970-76; Head Law Librarian, Gerard V. La Forest Law Library, 1976 to date. **SELECTED PUBLICATIONS:** "INFOLEX and Beyond: A Research Agenda for Canadian Law Libraries" (*Canadian Law Libraries/Bibliothèques de Droit Canadiennes* (19)4, Oct. 1994); various book reviews, articles & presentations. **AFFIL:** Univ. of New Brunswick (Law Fac. Council; Chair, Law Library Assessment Committee; Mbr., ex officio, Law Library Committee; Senate User Library Committee; various other committees); Canadian Association of Law Libraries (Pres.; Chair, Statistics Committee; Academic Law Library Statistics; various other committees); Canadian Academic Law Library Directors; Muriel McQueen Fergusson Centre for Family Violence Research (Chair, Bd. of Dir.); Muriel McQueen Fergusson Foundation (Parliamentarian; V-Chair, Campaign Exec.; VP); Women in Transition (Hon. Pres.). **HONS:** Merit Award, Univ. of New Brunswick, 1994.

Crocker, Olga L., B.Ed.,M.B.A.,Ph.D. 🎓 $

President, CENTRE FOR WORKPLACE DYNAMICS, 272 North Talbot Rd., R.R. 2, Maidstone, ON N0R 1K0 (519) 723-2121, FAX 723-2400, EMAIL crocker@server.uwindsor.ca or olcrocker@aol.com. Professor, Faculty of Business Administration, UNIVERSITY OF WINDSOR. President and Chief Executive Officer, CROCKER EDUCATIONAL SERVICES. Chief Executive Officer, A^N ADVANTAGE. Born High Prairie, Alta. 1930. m. Leo Berl. 3 ch. Terence Lee, Kevin Barry, Nathan Bryce. **EDUC:** Univ. of Alberta, B.Ed. 1953, M.B.A. 1974; Univ. of Washington, Ph.D. 1977. **CAREER:** Adjunct Prof., Extended Degree Program, Central Michigan Univ., 1978-91; Adjunct Prof., Mgmt, Lawrence Technological Univ., 1991 to date; Chair, Organization & Mgmt, The Grad. Sch. of America, 1991 to date; consultant in hum. res., team bldg, change mgmt, 1991 to date. **SELECTED PUBLICATIONS:** *Experiential Exercises in Canadian Personnel Administration* (Toronto: Methuen, 1986); *Quality Circles: A Guide to Participation and Profitability* (New York: New American Library, 1986); "Conflict, an Overview," in *Organizational Communication*, S. Devereaux-Ferguson & S. Ferguson, eds. (New York: Transaction Books, 1988); "The Challenge For Women Expatriates and Spouses: Some Empirical Evidence" (*The International Journal of Human Resource Management* Dec. 1992); "Accountants React to Professional Misconduct" (*Canadian Journal of Criminology* 1983); various other publications. **HONS:** IODE Scholarship, 1948; Gov't of Alberta Teaching Bursary, 1948; Edmonton Women Teachers' Association Scholarship, 1972; Univ. of Alberta teaching assistantship & scholarship, 1974; Edna J. Benson Award, Univ. of Washington, 1977; Samuel Bronfman Foundation Sr. Fac. Research Award, 1978. **INTERESTS:** writing; "the farm" they live on. **MISC:** spent 3 yrs. in Kabul, Afghanistan, as a consultant for UNDP (United Nations Dev. Program); long involvement in the labour movement, incl. Pres., Univ. of Windsor Fac. Association; listed in *Canadian Who's Who* & *The World Who's Who of Women*; numerous conference presentations & proceedings. **COMMENT:** *"My life has been that of a juggler. At first it was trying to be an academic, a mother and a wife. I liked this so much that I added consulting and working for two additional universities. My greatest joys are my three grandchildren."*

Crocker, Susan, B.Sc. ■■ $

Senior Vice-President, Equities and Derivative Markets, THE TORONTO STOCK EXCHANGE, The Exchange Tower, 2 First Canadian Place, Toronto, ON M5X 1J2 (416) 947-4654, FAX 947-4708, EMAIL scrocker@tse.com. President, TORONTO FUTURES EXCHANGE. President, CANADIAN DEALING NETWORK. Born Brazil 1958. **EDUC:** Arizona State Univ., B.Sc.(Int'l

Econ.) 1981; Harvard Univ., Advanced Mgmt Program 1994. **CAREER:** various positions, becoming VP, Global Treasury & Money Mkts, CIBC, N.Y., 1982-92; Dir., Comcheq Services, 1993-95; Sr. VP, Corp. & Investment Bnkg, Toronto, 1993-95; Ptnr, Ernst & Young Mgmt Consulting, 1995-96; Pres., Toronto Futures Exchange, 1996 to date; Pres., Canadian Dealing Network, 1996 to date. **DIRECTOR:** Canadian Derivatives Clearing Corporation.

Crofford, Joanne, B.A. ✤
Member of the Legislative Assembly (Regina Lake Centre), GOVERNMENT OF SASKATCHEWAN, Legislative Building, Rm. 105, Regina, SK S4S 0B3 (306) 787-0892, FAX 787-7905. Born Regina, Sask. 1947. m. Victor Tiede. 2 ch. **EDUC:** Univ. of Regina, B.A.(Comm. & Soc. Studies) 1970. **AFFIL:** Canadian Parliamentary Association; Cathedral Village Arts Festival; Grey Cup 1995; Saskatchewan Association of Human Rights; N.D.P. **HONS:** Hon. Certificate, Saskatchewan Centre for International Languages. **INTERESTS:** arts; literature; canoeing; fitness; organizing community events; her grandchild. **COMMENT:** *"I strive to make my presence felt by bringing government closer to meeting the everyday needs in our communities for support and development, including economic development."*

Croft, Colleen, B.A.,LL.B. ○ ✋ ⚔
Consultant. 1716-22nd St., W., Vancouver, BC V7V 4E5 (604) 925-5072, FAX 925-5072. Born N. Vancouver 1958. m. Mark Cannuli. 3 ch. Liam, Zachary, Miguel. **EDUC:** McGill Univ., B.A.(English) 1982; Univ. of Saskatchewan, LL.B. 1987. **CAREER:** Proj. Coord., Public Legal Educ. Association of Saskatchewan, 1984; Researcher, 1985; Exec. Dir., Elizabeth Fry Society of Saskatchewan, 1985-87; Legal Researcher/Proj. Coord., Saskatchewan Association of Women & the Law, 1990-91; Researcher, Saskatoon Women's Resources, 1991; Prov. Coord., Prov. Association of Transition Houses of Saskatchewan, 1987-94; Cood., Vancouver Child Care Regional Delivery Models, 1995 to date. **SELECTED PUBLICATIONS:** *Exploring the Law: Three Programs on Law for Youth* (Public Legal Educ. Association of Saskatchewan, 1985); *Report of Pay Equity Conference* (Saskatchewan Association of Women & the Law, 1991); *Saskatchewan Women's Organizations: Current Funding Status and Potential Funding Sources* (Saskatoon Women's Charities, 1991). **AFFIL:** Open Door Society (Volunteer Tutor 1983-85); Campus Legal Services, Univ. of Saskatchewan (Volunteer Advocate 1984-86); Elizabeth Fry Society of

Saskatchewan (Dir. 1989-91); Planned Parenthood of Saskatchewan (Dir. 1993-94); B.C. Coalition to Eliminate Abuse of Seniors (Advisory Committee 1994-95); North Shore Community Services (Dir. 1994-96); North Shore Writers' Association; West Coast LEAF (Women's Legal Education & Action Foundation); B.C. Association of Community Law Offices (Dir. 1994-96). **HONS:** Bursary for Student Creative Writing, Canada Council, 1980; Senator John Hnatyshyn Scholarship, Coll. of Law, Univ. of Saskatchewan, 1984; Canada 125 Medal, 1993. **INTERESTS:** human rights issues; women's/children's issues; social/justice issues; writing; reading; music. **MISC:** appointed to Consensus Saskatchewan by Deputy Premier Pat Smith, 1990; appointed to Advisory Committee to the Cdn Panel on Violence Against Women by Fed. Min. Responsible for the Status of Women, Mary Collins, 1991-92. **COMMENT:** *"My role as a consultant/coordinator has allowed me the privilege to work with a number of truly fine associations and organizations. I particularly enjoy the challenges and mutual learning of organizational design and problem solving, strategic planning, board development and community partnerships."*

Cronenberg, Denise ⊗ ⛏
Costume Designer. Born Toronto. **SELECTED CREDITS:** *The Fly* (feature), Twentieth Century Fox, 1986-87; *The Long Road Home* (feature), Lauron Productions, 1987; *Murder Ordained* (miniseries), Interscope Productions, 1987; *Dead Ringers* (feature), Morgan Creek Productions, 1988; *The Guardian* (feature), Universal Pictures, 1989; *Naked Lunch* (feature), The Recorded Picture Co. Inc., 1990-91; 7 eps., *The Scales of Justice* (series), CBC, 1990-93; *M. Butterfly* (feature), Warner Brothers, 1992; *Child of Rage* (MOW), CBS, Republic Pictures, 1992; *How Could You Mrs. Dick?* (theatre), dir. Guy Sprung, 1992; *Moonlight and Valentino* (feature), Working Title Films Ltd., 1994; *Friends At Last* (MOW), Tristar Television, 1995; *Sam & Phyllis* (feature), HBO, 1995; *Crash* (feature), Recorded Picture Co., 1995; *Murder at 1600* (feature), Warner Bros., 1996. **AFFIL:** IATSE Local 873. **HONS:** nomination, Outstanding Costume Design (*How Could You Mrs. Dick?*), Dora Mavor Moore Awards, 1992. **COMMENT:** *"David Cronenberg's sister, not his wife!"*

Crook, Barbara, B.A.,M.A. ✐ ⊗ 📚
Theatre Critic, THE VANCOUVER SUN, 2250 Granville St., Vancouver, BC V6H 3G2 (604) 732-2122, FAX 732-2521. Born Montreal 1957. **EDUC:** Queen's Univ., B.A. (Hons.,

English Lit.) 1979; Univ. of Western Ontario, M.A.(Journalism) 1983; Southam Fellowship, 1996-97. CAREER: Bus. Writer, *The Ottawa Citizen*, 1983-85; Theatre Critic, 1985-90; Asst. Entertainment Ed., 1990-91; Event Marketer, *The Vancouver Sun*, 1991; Feature Writer, 1991-93; Theatre Critic, 1993 to date. AFFIL: Canadian Theatre Critics' Association (Dir. 1988-90, 1994 to date); KidSafe Society (Founding Dir. 1994); *Vancouver Sun* Children's Fund (Dir.). HONS: Finalist, Rhodes Scholarship, 1978; univ. scholarships, Univ. of Western Ontario, 1982-83; J.B. McGeachy Award, Univ. of Western Ontario Sch. of Journalism, 1983; Hon. Mention, Nathan Cohen Award for Excellence in Theatre Criticism, 1989; Finalist, B.C. Newspaper Awards, 1993, 1994; nominated, Critical Writing, National Newspaper Awards, 1994 & 1995. INTERESTS: marathon running; literature; music; swimming. MISC: numerous public speaking engagements yearly. COMMENT: *"I have been a professional journalist for 12 years and have tried to balance my newspaper career with strong community involvement and public speaking engagements that let young people know about career opportunities in journalism and media. Professionally, I am known as a fair and balanced critic who has educated readers about the local theatre community."*

Crooks, Charmaine, B.A. ⓐ ☖ ♔
Athlete. President, N.G.U. SPORTS & MEDIA CONSULTANTS. Co-owner, LE SPA DE MONTAGNE, Whistler, BC. Born Jamaica 1962. m. Anders Thorsen. EDUC: Univ. of Texas at El Paso, B.A.(Psych.) 1985. CAREER: Sports Commentator, CBC-TV; Co-Host, *CYCLE!*, CBC-TV, 1993 to date; Pres., N.G.U. Sports & Media Consultants. SPORTS CAREER: Olympic Games Team Mbr., 1980, 1984, 1988, 1992, 1996; World Cup Team Mbr., 1981, 1985, 1989, 1992; Commonwealth Games Team Mbr., 1982, 1986, 1994; World Championship Team Mbr., 1983, 1987, 1991, 1995; Pan-American Games Team Mbr., 1983; World Student Games Team Mbr., 1987; Int'l IAAF Mobil Grand Prix Circuit, 1989-95. SELECTED CREDITS: Co-Host, *CYCLE!* (series), CBC-TV, 1993 to date; Reporter, Canada Winter Games, CBC-TV, 1995; Commentator/Analyst, World Indoor Track & Field Championships, CBC-TV, 1993; Commentator/Analyst, World Outdoor Track & Field Championships, CBC-TV, 1993, 1995. AFFIL: International Olympic Committee (Athletes Council); Society of Composers, Authors & Music Publishers of Canada (SOCAN); Alliance of Canadian Cinema, Television & Radio Artists (ACTRA); Academy of Canadian Cinema & Television; Canadian Athletes' Association (CAA) (Bd. Mbr.); Canadian Centre for Drug-Free Sport (Bd. Mbr.); Canadian Youth Foundation (Hon. Committee Mbr.). HONS: Silver Medal, Nat'l Collegiate Athletic Association, 1981, 1984; Gold Medal, Commonwealth Games, 4x400m, 1982, 1986; Gold Medal, Pan-American Games, 400m, 1983; Silver Medal, Olympic Games, 4x400m, 1984; Gold Medal, World Student Games, 4x400m, 1987; Gold Medal, World Cup, 4x400m, 1989, 1992; B.C. Track & Field Athlete of the Year, 1990-91; John F. Bassett Award for outstanding community work & sporting excellence, 1991; Silver Medal, World Cup, 400m, 1992; Canada 125 Medal, 1992; Silver Medal, Commonwealth Games, 800m, 1994; Bronze Medal, Commonwealth Games, 4x400m, 1994; chosen to carry the flag, Opening Ceremonies, Olympic Games, Atlanta, 1996. INTERESTS: charitable events. MISC: 1st Cdn woman to break 2-minute barrier over 800m; 10-time Cdn champion; 5-time Olympian; corp. spokesperson for Nature Made Vitamins, featured in all Cdn advtg campaigns; professional motivational speaker; Creator & Prod., *No Laughing Matter™*, a comedy benefit/fundraiser for the Canadian Cancer Society, Breast Cancer Research & Programs, 1994, 1995. COMMENT: *"I am a five-time Canadian Olympian, a Silver Medallist (L.A. 4x400m) and was the 1996 Olympic Team flagbearer. I am the host of the nationwide CBC TV show CYCLE! and also run a sports & media consulting business and am a co-owner of Le Spa de Montagne, Whistler, BC. I am frequently sought after to speak to youth groups as well as major corporations."*

Crosbie, C. Patricia ◉ ○
Executive Director, NATIONAL ADVERTISING BENEVOLENT SOCIETY (NABS), 175 Bloor St. E., Ste. 307, S. Tower, Toronto, ON M4W 3R8 (416) 962-0446, FAX 944-3797. Born Toronto 1944. w. 2 ch. EDUC: North Toronto Collegiate Institute, 1963. CAREER: Asst. to the Pres., Magazines Canada, 1968-71; Exec. Dir., NABS, 1983 to date. SELECTED PUBLICATIONS: various articles, info. books, etc. AFFIL: The Granite Club. HONS: nominee, Women on the Move Award, *The Toronto Sun*, 1990. INTERESTS: her children; theatre; movies; her friends; travel. MISC: in 1966 travelled extensively throughout Europe, North Africa & Middle East; was "trapped" in Amman, Jordan during the Six Day War. COMMENT: *"I work hard, believe in honesty and ethics. My primary goal is to have my children emerge as happy and responsible adults."*

Crosbie, Evelyn ■■ $
Owner, EXCALIBUR EXECUTIVE (administrative-business consulting), 808 Muriel St., Winnipeg, MB R2Y 0Y3 (204) 888-8989, FAX 888-0944. Born Calgary 1937. m. Charles Reid. 2 ch. Donna Lynn, Diana Lynn. **EDUC:** Sturgeon Creek Regional, various courses incl. Bus. Admin., Acctg, Word Processing; U.S. Dept. of Transportation, Certificate (U.S. Fed. Motor Carrier & Hazardous Material Regulations) 1983; Canadian Trucking Association, Hazardous Materials Instructors' Course. **CAREER:** office admin., Bell Foundry; clerical duties, BFI; Office Mgr, Milwaukee Seasoning Canada Ltd., 1974; Sec., then Winnipeg Terminal Mgr, Melchin Auto Transport Ltd., 1974-79; Office Mgr/Bookkeeper, General Truck Sales and Leasing, 1979-80; Asst. Gen. Mgr, Manitoba Trucking Association, 1980-88; owner, Excalibur Executive. **SELECTED PUBLICATIONS:** articles in *Green Scene Gazette*, & *V.G.A.M. News*. **AFFIL:** Landscape Manitoba (Exec. Sec., Bd. of Dir.); Vegetable Growers' Association of Manitoba (Sec.-Treas., Bd. of Dir.); Habitat for Humanity - Jimmy Carter work project (1993); Winnipeg Humane Society; World Wildlife Fund; Bat Association of Manitoba. **INTERESTS:** walking; gardening; people; animals; bird watching; cross-country skiing. **MISC:** Commissioner of Oaths.

Cross, Amy Willard, B.A. 📖 ✎
Writer. 79 Walnut Ave., Toronto, ON M5V 2S1 (416) 703-0888, FAX 703-4988. Born Washington, D.C. 1960. m. Patrick Bermingham. **EDUC:** Wellesley Coll., Mass., B.A. 1982. **CAREER:** Sec. to novelist Stephen Z. Wendt, 1981; Asst. Ed., *Twenty-Five Years of Product Liability*; Creator, *Moxie Magazine*, 1986; Special Projects Ed., *Shape Magazine*, 1987; Lifestyle Ed., *Active Magazine*, 1994; Sr. Ed., *Chatelaine*. **SELECTED PUBLICATIONS:** *The Summer House: A Tradition of Leisure* (HarperCollins Canada, 1992); *Summer in America* (Key Porter, 1995); various articles in anthologies; articles published in *Working Woman*, *American Health*, *Woman*, *Women & Environments*, *Glamour*, *Self*, *In Fashion*, *Savvy*, *Washington Dossier*, *LA Weekly*, *San José Mercury News*, *Shape*, *The Globe & Mail*, *The Toronto Star*, & *Toronto Life Fashion*; Health Columnist, *Flare Magazine*, 1995 to date. **AFFIL:** Poets, Essayists & Novelists (PEN); Hamilton's Women's Trust.

Crouse, Elizabeth, B.Sc. ■ 🍁 🌾
Supervisor, 4-H and Rural Organizations, Nova Scotia Department of Agriculture and Marketing, GOVERNMENT OF NOVA SCOTIA, Box 550, Truro, NS B2N 5E3 (902) 893-6585, FAX 895-7963, EMAIL ecrouse@es.nsac.cs.ca. Born Montague, P.E.I. 1957. m. Brian M. Crouse. 2 ch. Megan, Timothy. **EDUC:** N.S. Agric. Coll., Diploma (Agric.) 1978; McGill Univ., MacDonald Coll., B.Sc.(Gen. Agric.) 1979. **CAREER:** Research Asst., Agriculture Canada, Charlottetown, 1976-79; Reg'l 4-H Rep., Hants-Kings Counties, N.S. Dept. of Agric. & Mktg, 1979-86; Supervisor, 4-H & Rural Org., Extension Svc Branch, 1986 to date. **AFFIL:** Canadian 4-H Council (Bd. of Dir.; Program Committee Chair; Public Rel'ns Committee; Resource Dev. Committee); Atlantic Advisory Committee on Social Economic Svcs; Atlantic 4-H Committee (Chair); N.S. Farm Health & Safety Committee (Sec.-Treas.); N.S. Exhibition Evaluation Committee; Provincial Extension Newsletter Committee; Atlantic Agricultural Hall of Fame (Sec.-Treas.); First Baptist Church, Truro (Bd. of Deacons); N.S. Agriculture Coll. Day Care (Dir.); N.S. Agric. & Mktg Staff Association (Pres.). **INTERESTS:** gardening; floral arranging; church & family activities. **COMMENT:** *"Extension work or the betterment of rural people has been my life-long goal. This began in my home province of Prince Edward Island and continues with my current career in Nova Scotia. It has also extended to the Czech and Slovak Republics. I developed an extension course, of which I led in the presentation, in the above two countries. I am also currently developing 4-H clubs in the former Communist countries. My strengths are in my belief in the importance of the development of leadership and life skills in rural adults and youth."*

Crowe Worthington, Carolyn, LL.B. ■■ ⚖
Associate Lawyer, GOWLINGS (law firm), 120 King St. W., Ste. 600, Hamilton, ON L8P 4V2 (905) 540-8201, FAX 528-5833, EMAIL worthin@gowlings.com or worthinc@freenet.hamilton.on.ca. Born Toronto 1954. m. Edward. 3 ch. Jeremy, Jeffrey, Joanna. **EDUC:** Ontario Institute of Law Clerks, Assoc. Certificate 1975, Fellowship Certificate 1980; Royal Conservatory of Music, Grade X Piano Certificate 1979 (continued to ARCT level); Ryerson Polytechnical Institute, TV Studio Production Certificate 1981; Univ. of Western Ontario, LL.B. 1983; Univ. of Toronto, Bus. Certificate (highest class average) 1984; Canadian Securities Institute, Canadian Securities Course Certificate 1993, Investment Mgmt Program, Part I 1994. **BAR:** Ont., 1985. **CAREER:** Law Clerk, Burt, Burt, Wolfe & Bowman, Toronto/Holden, Murdoch & Finlay, Toronto/Cassels, Brock, Toronto, 1972-80; worked part-time at 5 law firms while attending univ., 1980-83; tutorial leader, "Intro. to Law" undergrad.

course, 1982-83; part-time instructor, "Business Law II," Sheridan Coll., 1986-88; part-time instructor, legal secretarial course, Halton Business Institute, 1987-88; articled with O'Connor, Leitch, Hays, Oakville, Ont., 1983-85; Assoc. Lawyer, 1985-88; Legal Cnsl & Asst. Sec., Westinghouse Canada Inc., Hamilton, Ont., 1988-95; Assoc. Lawyer, Gowlings, 1995 to date. SELECTED PUBLICATIONS: "The Song You Write May Not Be Your Own! Proving Musical Copyright Infringement: A Review of *Gondos v Toth*" (*Intellectual Property Journal*, 29, 1984); "Disappearing Royalties - The Small User Exemption of the Canadian Copyright Act" (*Canadian Patent Reporter* (2d) 1984, 177). ASSISTANT SECRETARY: Westinghouse Canada Inc. AFFIL: Law Society of Upper Canada; Canadian Bar Association; Canadian Corporate Counsel Association (Subcommittee on Gender Equality); Hamilton Law Association; Christian Legal Fellowship (mbr.; Chair, Membership Committee 1983-85); Park Academy Chess Club (instructor). HONS: Victor Shield, Ontario Institute of Law Clerks, for outstanding achievement, 1975; scholarship, Ontario Institute of Law Clerks, for outstanding achievement, 1980; Frank Nicholson Beard Scholarship, Woodsworth Coll., top student in program, 1984; Excellent Service Award, Westinghouse Canada Inc., 1990. INTERESTS: chess; computers; decorating; fitness activities; investments; music; outdoor activities; piano; sports.

Crowley, Marilyn B., B.A. ■ ■ / ☺ ⌂
Associate Food Editor, CHATELAINE MAGAZINE, 777 Bay St., Toronto, ON M5W 1A7 (416) 596-5437, FAX 596-5516, EMAIL 75162.1315@compuserve.com. Born Alpena, Mich. 1946. m. Michael F. Crowley. 2 ch. Paul, Matthew. EDUC: State Univ. of N.Y., Cortland, B.A.(Biol.) 1969; George Brown Coll., Certificate (Culinary Mgmt) 1985. CAREER: Chef, 1985-91; freelance recipe tester & food writer, 1991-93; Assoc. Food Editor, *Chatelaine*, 1993 to date. AFFIL: Women's Culinary Network (founder 1990; Steering Committee 1990 to date); Cuisine Canada (Editor, mbr. newsletter 1994 to date); Women in Food Industry Management (mbr. 1994 to date). HONS: Needle Trade Management Award, 1985; Sven Erickson Award for Culinary Excellence, 1984. INTERESTS: Cdn regional & heritage cuisine; kayaking; hiking. COMMENT: *"In the food business since 1983, I spent 8 years working as a chef in restaurants ranging from an upscale neighbourhood grill to Italian fine dining then ended my commercial kitchen career with a year and a half of low-fat cooking and baking at King Ranch Spa. While at King*

Ranch, I wrote recipes for both guests and chefs and in 1990, founded the Women's Culinary Network. As a freelance food consultant, I have created low-fat recipes for commercial kitchens as well as domestic kitchens; food styled and recipe tested for both The Toronto Sun *and food writer, Lucy Waverman; and taught numerous cooking courses. I have written extensively for* Chatelaine, *as well as Canadian Living, and* The Toronto Sun. *I have appeared on "Eye on Toronto," CityTV's "Breakfast TV" and "Dini Petty" shows."*

Croy, Judy, B.A.(Hons.) ■ ⚘
President, JAC INTERNATIONAL, Box 8891, Saskatoon, SK S7K 6S7 (306) 934-6190, FAX 956-3042. Born UK. m. Calvin. 2 ch. Cameron Croy, Christopher Croy. EDUC: Univ. of Winnipeg, B.A.(Hons., Arts/Soc.) 1980; Univ. of Manitoba, M.A. in progress, Certificate in Adult & Continuing Educ. in progress. CAREER: Special Projects–research & comm. dev. initiatives, 1972-77; Oper. Mgr, Vibro Acoustics Western, 1978-80; Mgr/Trainer, Arris Centre, Stonewall, 1980-81; Exec. Dir., WASO Inc., 1981-83; Exec. Dir., The Abilities Network, 1983-93; Pres., JAC International, 1993 to date. SELECTED PUBLICATIONS: various research reports. AFFIL: Manitoba Society for Training & Development (Pres.); The Federation of Human Resource Development Associations of Canada (Dir.); Manitoba Association of Community-Based Education & Training Programs (VP); YM/YWCA, downtown (Pres., Advisory Bd.); Canadian Executive Services Organization (Volunteer Consultant); Independent Living Product Display Centre (Dir.). HONS: Volunteer Recognition Award, Stonewall Chamber of Commerce, 1975; Gold Medallist, Univ. of Winnipeg, 1980; Community Leadership Award, Society for Manitobans with Disabilities, 1993. INTERESTS: reading; travel; outdoor lifestyle/nature. MISC: Master Trainer, Skills Program, Manitoba Culture, Heritage & Citizenship. COMMENT: *"Striving to use the gift of each new day to contribute to a better world through everyday acts of kindness and community service."*

Crozier, Lorna, B.A.,M.A. ⚘ ⚘
Associate Professor, Department of Writing, UNIVERSITY OF VICTORIA, Box 1700, Victoria, BC V4N 1A6 (604) 721-7314. EDUC: Univ. of Saskatchewan, B.A. 1969, Professional "A" Teaching Certificate 1970; Univ. of Alberta, M.A. 1980. CAREER: High Sch. English Teacher, Glaslyn High Sch., 1970-72; High Sch. English Teacher & Guidance Councillor, Swift Current Comprehensive Sch., 1972-77; Composition Instructor, Univ. of Regina, 1976;

Instructor of Cdn Lit., Univ. of Alberta, 1978-79; Creative Writing Teacher, Saskatchewan Summer Sch. of the Arts, 1977-81, Red Deer Coll., 1988, Sechelt Writers' Festival, 1988; Writer-in-Residence, Cypress Hills Community Coll., 1980-81; Dir. of Comm., Dept. of Parks, Recreation & Culture, Regina, 1981-83; Book reviewer & writer, CBC Radio, Regina, 1986; Guest Instructor, Banff Sch. of Fine Arts, 1986-87; Special Lecturer in Cdn Lit. & Creative Writing, Univ. of Saskatchewan, 1986-91; Writer in Residence, Univ. of Toronto, 1989-90; Assoc. Prof., Dept. of Writing, Univ. of Victoria, 1991 to date. SELECTED PUBLICA-TIONS: *Inside Is the Sky* (Thistledown Press, 1976); *Crow's Black Joy* (NeWest Press, 1978); *No Longer Two People* (Turnstone, 1979); *Humans and Other Beasts* (Turnstone, 1980); *The Weather* (Coteau Books, 1983); *The Garden Going on Without Us* (McClelland & Stewart, 1985); *Angels of Flesh, Angels of Silence* (McClelland & Stewart, 1988); *Inventing the Hawk* (McClelland & Stewart, 1988); *Everything Arrives at the Light* (McClelland & Stewart, 1995); poetry appears in numerous literary magazines & anthologies; book reviews; non-fiction. EDIT: Ed., individual poetry books published by Coteau Books; Co-Ed. with Gary Hyland, *A Sudden Radiance*; Fiction Ed., *NeWest Review*, 1986-88; Western Ed., *Books in Canada*, 1991 to date; Poetry Ed., *Grain*, 1990-91. HONS: Univ. of Alberta Creative Writing Scholarship, 1979; Award for a Poetry Manuscript,The Saskatchewan Dept. of Recreation, Parks & Culture, 1979; Saskatchewan Writers' Guild Poetry Manuscript Award, 1983, 1987; Saskatchewan Arts Bd. Sr. Arts Award, 1983-83; Canada Council Arts Award, 1979-80, 1985-86; Prism International Poetry Contest, Second Prize, 1986; Saskatchewan Writers' Guild Poetry Manuscript Award, 1987; CBC Radio Nat'l Poetry Competition, First Prize, 1987; Nat'l Radio Awards, First Prize for Best Public Radio Program of the Year, 1987; Western Magazine Award, nonfiction, 1989; The Pat Lowther Award for the best book of poetry by a Cdn Woman, 1993; Canadian Authors' Association Award for Poetry, 1993; Gov. General's Award for Poetry, 1992; Nat'l Magazine Gold Medal for Poetry, 1994; Pat Lowther Award, 1996. MISC: Electronic Writer in Residence, a computer program for high sch. students across Canada, 1989-91; readings & lectures at universities, libraries, bookstores, & writing & teachers' conferences across Canada, in US & Europe; juror for various awards; until 1983, published under name "Lorna Uher." COMMENT: *"Lorna Crozier's one of the country's most accomplished and popular poets. She has per-*formed her work across the country and internationally in such places as Chile, Italy and the UK. Born on the prairies, she is a feminist, a populist and a respected teacher of poetry."*

Cruise, Margery, B.Math.,M.Sc., P.M.P. ■ 📖 🐟
President, CRUISE & ASSOCIATES, R.R. #1, Tottenham, ON L0G 1W0 (905) 936-3801, FAX 936-3847. Born Vancouver 1950. m. Bob Briscoe. 3 ch. Marisa Brisco, David Brisco, Carrie Brisco. EDUC: Univ. of Waterloo, B.Math.(Statistics) 1973; Stanford Univ., M.Sc.(Statistics) 1977; Professional Proj. Mgr Certification 1994. CAREER: Biostatistician, Syntex US, 1976-78; Mgr, Biostatistical Svcs, Wyeth Ltd., 1978-80; Prof., part-time, York Univ., 1981-84; Mgr, Statistics & Data Systems, Bayer Inc., 1985-90; Prof., part-time, Univ. of Montreal, 1988-90; Mgr, Nat'l Proj. Mgmt, 1990-95. SELECTED PUBLICATIONS: "Marketing Project Management at Miles Canada" (1993); "Role of Statistician in the Pharmaceutical Industry" (1990). AFFIL: CAWEE; Project Management Institute; Pharmaceutical Manufacturers Association of Canada (Bd. of Dir., Medical R.&D. Section 1988-90; Patent Committee 1991-92); Toronto Area Biostatistics Association (Founding Mbr. & First Pres. 1986); PMCO; Boy Scouts of Canada (Cub Leader, First Adjala Scouting). MISC: 1st biostatistician as Dir. on PMAC Medical R.&D. Council; began one of the first proj. mgmt groups in the Cdn pharmaceutical industry; began & built Statistics Depts. at Wyeth Ltd. & Miles Canada Inc.; workshop leader, Women of Tomorrow, 1991. COMMENT: *"Margery is an enthusiastic, intelligent and caring person. She has acted as a pioneer, starting up the Toronto Area Biostatistics Association and as a mentor for women in mathematics, eg. workshop at the 1991 Women of Tomorrow Conference for high school students. She switched careers in 1990 from biostatistics to project management."*

Cumming, Marie Novak, B.Sc., M.B.A. ■ 💲
Partner, CUMMING AND CUMMING WEALTH MANAGEMENT. Born Medford, Mass. 1954. m. Bruce D. Cumming. 2 ch. Jack, Kendall. EDUC: Boston Coll., B.Sc.(Chem.) 1976; New York Univ., M.B.A.(Fin.) 1978. CAREER: various positions, Exxon International Company, 1978-83; Dir., Mktg, Mary Kay Cosmetics Ltd., 1983-87; VP, Mktg, 1987-90; VP, Oper. & Admin., 1990-94; VP, Mktg & Sales, Careernet, 1994; Pres., Totallink International Group, 1994-96; Ptnr, Cumming & Cumming Wealth Mgmt, 1996 to date. AFFIL: United

Way of Peel Region (Sr. Volunteer, $6-Million Campaign 1990-93; Deputy Chair; Cabinet Mbr.; Comm. Chair; Special Events Chair); Mississauga Board of Trade (Dir. 1989-94; Treas. 1991; Sec. 1992); Canadian Association of Women Executives & Entrepreneurs (1987-94); Canadian Federation of University Women, Oakville Chapter (1987 to date); St. Vincent's Sch. Parent-Teacher Association (Chair, Fundraising Committee 1993 to date). INTERESTS: volunteer work; family activities. COMMENT: *"Committed to enabling clients to plan for and achieve financial independence at earliest date with the least amount of risk."*

Cumming, Marion M., B.A. ⊗ ◉
Heritage Artist, CANADIAN SCENES, 151 Sunny Lane, Victoria, BC V8S 2K6 (604) 598-9293. Born Toronto 1936. m. Prof. Bruce Cumming. EDUC: Principia Coll., B.A. 1959; Althouse Coll. of Educ., Univ. of Western Ontario, Ont. Teacher's Certificate 1966; univ. art & cultural studies in France, Mexico, Italy & Canada. CAREER: Social Worker, Children's Aid Society of Ont., 1959; Volunteer Art Therapist, Manicomio de Mixcoac, Mexico City, 1959-61; Social Sec., Argentine Embassy, Ottawa, 1961-64; Head, Art Dept. & UNESCO Program, Lisgar Collegiate Institute, Ottawa, 1966-69; Cdn Correspondent, Experiment in International Living (founded 1932), 1963-65; Group Leader; Community Rep.; Co-owner & Operator, Evergreen Farm, Fredericton, 1971-92; heritage artist, 1969 to date. SELECTED PUBLICATIONS: *London Heritage*, forward & contributing illustrator (London Free Press, four editions 1972-91). EXHIBITIONS: Landmark Gallery, Fredericton, 1979; Univ. of New Brunswick; York Sunbury Museum, 1985; various group shows incl. Marlowe Gallery, Canterbury, UK, 1979; Beaverbrook Gallery, Fredericton, 1987, King's Landing, N.B., 1996. AFFIL: Voice of Women; Amnesty International; World Federalists; Nature Trust of N.B.; Fredericton Heritage Trust (Patron; former Dir.); Sierra Club; Plan International (Foster Parents Plan); S.P.C.A.; Aboriginal Rights Coalition; Christian Science Church. HONS: MCC Campus Citizenship Award, Univ. of the Americas, Mexico City, 1960; Canadian Centennial Medal, 1967; National Heritage Award, 1992. INTERESTS: art; art sessions with street kids; culture; alleviation of poverty; animal rights; nature. MISC: subject of a national CBC film, *A Heritage to Draw Upon*, 1976; involved in Native Indian issues & culture; donated collection of antiques & artifacts to Kings Landing Historical Settlement. COMMENT: *"Working as an artist in all provinces and territories, I try*

to strive for protection of built, cultural and natural heritage, aboriginal rights and national unity."

Cunningham, Karen ■ ■ ♡ ⊕
President, AUTISM SOCIETY NEW BRUNSWICK (non-profit charitable organization), P.O. Box 635, Fredericton, NB E3B 5B4 (506) 363-3200, FAX 363-3200, EMAIL asnb@nbnet.nb.ca. Born Moncton 1952. m. David Cunningham. 4 ch. & foster ch. Jorah, Ross, Alana, Drew. EDUC: "life-long" learner, continually attending workshops, conferences & courses on autism & children with special needs. CAREER: Teacher Asst., District 18, Fredericton, 1992 to date; Karen Cunningham Consulting, 1996 to date. VOLUNTEER CAREER: mbr., District 18 Educ. Liaison Committee, 1994 to date; Pres., Autism Society N.B., 1994 to date; 2nd VP, Autism Society Canada, 1995 to date; Pres., Fredericton Association for Community Living, 1996; District Rep., N.B. Association for Community Living, 1996; Sec., Keswick Ridge Home & School Association, 1996; mbr., Foster Parent Association. INTERESTS: children; singing; community development. MISC: foster parent to child with autism. COMMENT: *"I am outgoing, enthusiastic and caring. I hope that I have made a difference to the parents and children I have come into contact with through school and my volunteer work and am able to empower parents with whatever means they need to assure their child the best future possible."*

Curran, Peggy, D.E.C.,B.A.,M.A. ✎ ▢
City Columnist, THE GAZETTE, 250 St. Antoine St. W., Montreal, QC H2Y 3R7 (514) 987-2529, FAX 987-2399. Born Montreal 1957. EDUC: Marianopolis Coll., D.E.C.(Lit. & Lang.) 1975; Concordia Univ., B.A.(Hist. & English) 1978; Univ. of Western Ontario, M.A.(Journalism) 1979. CAREER: Gen. Assignment Ed., *The Montreal Star*, 1979; Reporter, Assignment Ed., Parliamentary Correspondent (Ottawa Bureau), *The Gazette*, 1989-93; City Columnist, 1993 to date. AFFIL: Síamsa Sch. of Irish Music. HONS: O'Connor-O'Hearn Hist. Prize, Concordia Univ., 1978. MISC: Sec., Parliamentary Press Gallery, 1992-93.

Currie, Jane K., B.Sc.,M.Sc. ⊛ ⊗ ♡
Senior Environmental Associate, New Products, Fertilizer Marketing, VIRIDIAN, Edmonton, AB T0A 2W0 (403) 998-5832, FAX 998-6237. Born Hamilton, Ont. 1952. m. Dr. John C. Currie. EDUC: McMaster Univ., B.Sc.(Chem.) 1974; Colorado Sch. of Mines, M.Sc.(Chem. Eng.) 1991. CAREER: Sr. Research Chemist,

R.&D., Standard Oil, 1979-82; Proj. Leader, 1982-83; Group Leader, 1983-85; Research Scientist, R.&D., British Petroleum, 1985-88; Sr. Scientist, External Technology, Sherritt Gordon Ltd., 1991; Mgr, Environment, Safety & Transportation, Sherritt Inc., 1991-92; Dir. of Hum. Res. & Environment, 1993; IOL Acquisition Special Assignment, 1994; Sr. Environmental Assoc. for New Products in Fertilizer Mktg, 1995. **SELECTED PUBLICATIONS:** various journal articles on chemical research & environmental remediation; various conference papers; *House & Garden Tour Book*, 1995, 1996. **AFFIL:** Alberta Ballet (Bd. of Dir.); American Chemical Society; Association of Groundwater Scientists & Engineers; Edmonton House & Garden Tour (Co-Chair); Rotary International, Glenora chapter. **HONS:** Valedictorian, Glendale High Sch., Hamilton, 1970; Sherritt Gordon Ltd. Book Prize, 1970; Stelco Univ. Entrance Award, 1970-71; McGill Univ. French Prize, 1972; Research Assistantship, Colorado Sch. of Mines, 1989-91; United Way Certificate of Appreciation, 1993, 1994; Sherritt Inc. Loaned Rep. to the United Way, 1994. **INTERESTS:** skiing; finance; world events; fine arts; travel. **MISC:** holds seven US patents & four European patents; currently manages the first Canadian ind. Solar Aquatics™ facility in Fort Sask., AB. **COMMENT:** *"My career has evolved from chemicals research to plant environmental management to environmental business development. Personal work with community and arts organizations has balanced and enriched my professional life."*

Currie, Karen, B.Sc., M.B.A. ■ $

Vice-President, Human Resources and Environment, VANCOUVER CITY SAVINGS CREDIT UNION, 183 Terminal Ave., Vancouver, BC V6A 4G2 (604) 877-7621, FAX 877-8226. Born B.C. 1948. m. Alex. **EDUC:** Univ. of British Columbia, B.Sc.(Agric.) 1969; City Univ., M.B.A. 1989. **CAREER:** Industrial Hygienist, Algoma Steel Ontario, 1976-81; Occupational Health Scientist, B.C. Research, 1981-89; Asst. Mgr, Employee Dev., Vancouver City Savings Credit Union, 1990-92; Mgr, Community & Employee Dev., 1992-94; VP, Hum. Res. & Environment, 1994 to date. **AFFIL:** Canadian Mental Health Association (Dir., Vancouver/Burnaby); Human Resources Management Association of B.C. **COMMENT:** *"For the most part, I work hard, keep my eye on the future, think creatively and encourage others to do the same, laugh and enjoy my coworkers, and support and listen to everyone around me. My good fortune has been in finding a forward thinking, socially and ecologically conscious organization like VanCity, and finding my values in sync with theirs."*

Curry, Gwen J., M.F.A.,B.F.A. ✪

Visual Artist. 6807 Jedora Dr., Brentwood Bay, BC V8M 1A6 (604) 652-0096, FAX 652-0029. Born Victoria, B.C. 1950. m. Garry McKevitt. **EDUC:** Univ. of Victoria, B.F.A. 1974; Arizona State Univ., M.F.A. 1978. **CAREER:** Assoc. Prof., Univ. of Victoria, 1978-94. **SELECTED CREDITS:** cover, *The Whole Elephant* by Marlene Cookshaw (1989); cover of *Essays on Canadian Writing*, ed. Robert Lecker (McGill Univ.); *Two Portfolios of Prints*, for the 25th Anniversary of the Univ. of Victoria (1990); recipient of various fellowships & grants. **EXHIBITIONS:** 12 solo exhibitions incl. *Forms in Time*, Open Space, Victoria (1981); *Observations from the Edge*, Surrey Art Gallery, Surrey, B.C. (1985); *Icons: Images of Power and Transformation*, Open Space, Victoria (1987) & *Drawings*, Equinox Gallery, Vancouver (1991); over 50 group exhibitions, incl. *International Biennale of Graphic Art*, Ljubljana, Yugoslavia (1977, '79, '81, '89); *British International Print Biennale* (1979); *Interprint*, Ukrainian Independent Centre of Contemporary Art, Lviv, Ukraine (1992); *Premio Internazionale Biella per L'incisione*, Torino, Italy (1996); Cologne Art Fair (1990); L.A. Art Fair (1990); *Marks and Surfaces*, Surrey Art Gallery (1982). **COLLECTIONS:** Canadian Council Art Bank; Imperial Esso of Canada; Rothmans Pall Mall of Canada Ltd.; Burnaby Art Gallery; Art Gallery of Victoria; Skopje Museum, Yugoslavia; & others. **AFFIL:** Canadian Artists' Representation; Malaspina Printmakers' Society; Ground Zero Printmakers. **INTERESTS:** travel; ornithology; botany. **MISC:** affiliated with Equinox Gallery, Vancouver; listed in *Encyclopedia of Twentieth-century North American Women Artists, Canadian Who's Who*; in 1994 curated *DRAWING PLUS*, which brought together 9 artists from across Canada, catalogue written by Robin Laurence & produced by Open Space. **COMMENT:** *"Gwen Curry is an artist living near Victoria, B.C. who has shown her work in Canada, the U.S. and Europe. She is represented in numerous pubic and private collections and is represented by the Equinox Gallery in Vancouver and the Virginia Christopher Galleries in Calgary. She works mainly on large mixed media works on paper and board which often deal with issues of the environment. She was a professor in the Visual Arts Department at the University of Victoria from 1978 to 1994 when she resigned to work full time in the studio."*

Curtis, Kathleen ■ ✊

President, YUKON ASSOCIATION FOR COMMU-

NITY LIVING, Box 4853, Whitehorse, YT Y1A 4N6. Born Whitehorse 1963. s. 1 ch. EDUC: Yukon Coll., Food Svcs 1983, Early Childhood Dev. in progress. VOLUNTEER CAREER: Teey-ath'Ohzheh, support person to people with disabilities living in their own homes; VP, Yukon Association for Community Living, 1990-91; Pres., 1991 to date. AFFIL: People First of Canada; Canadian Association for Community Living. INTERESTS: sports; crafts; reading; working with people; educating people in community. COMMENT: *"I have been active in the community living movement since the birth in 1988 of my daughter, who was severely disabled. I envision a world where people with mental disabilities have the same rights and opportunities as others."*

Cusack Walsh, Elizabeth, B.A.,LL.B. ⚥
Barrister and Solicitor, ELIZABETH CUSACK WALSH & ASSOCIATES, 205 Charlotte St., P.O. Box 595, Sydney, NS B1P 6H4 (902) 564-8396, FAX 564-0030. Born Glace Bay, N.S. 1949. m. Gary Walsh. 2 ch. EDUC: Dalhousie Univ., B.A. 1971, LL.B. 1974. BAR: N.S., 1974. CAREER: High Sch. Teacher, Dunn Memorial High Sch., N.S., 1970-71; freelancing, CBC, mid-to-late 70s & on *Morningside*, 1991-92; part-time Instructor, University Coll. of Cape Breton, 1976-80; Articled Clerk, McInnes, Cooper & Robertson, 1973-74; Barrister & Solicitor, Elizabeth Cusack Walsh & Associates, 1974 to date. AFFIL: N.S. Advisory Council on the Status of Women (Advisor); Cape Breton Sexual Assault Services Coalition (former Advisory Committee); N.S. Transition Houses for Battered Women (Participant & Advisor, Conference for former residents); Transition House Association (Founding Mbr., Cape Breton); N.S. Barristers' Society (Bar Council; Discipline Committee; Admin. of Justice Committee; Lecturer, Bar Admission Course; Past Mbr., Council; Chair, Practice Assistance Committee 1990-91); L.E.A.F. (Women's Legal Education & Action Fund) (former mbr., Nat'l Bd.; former mbr., Nat'l Legal Committee); Learning Disabilities Association; Legal Profession Assistance Conference; N.S. Election Commission; Cape Breton Barristers' Society (Past Pres.); active lobbyist for human rights for women, lesbian, gay & bisexual persons, & for ethnic & racial equality. INTERESTS: gardening; cross-country skiing; golf; family; swimming; theatre; herbology; recreational reading. MISC: various lectures & public speaking engagements. COMMENT: *"I have had a general legal practice with a heavier concentration in areas of family law and civil litigation and have presented cases in every level of court within the province of Nova Scotia.*

Through service on the National Legal Committee of LEAF, I have participated in the committee process of factum preparation for cases before the Supreme Court of Canada and brief preparation for other levels of courts and tribunals in other Canadian jurisdictions."

Cushman, Hope C., B.A.,B.C.L., LL.B. ⚥ 💲
Counsel and Secretary, FORD MOTOR COMPANY OF CANADA LIMITED, The Canadian Rd., Oakville, ON L6I 5E4 (905) 845-2511, ext. 1390, FAX 845-5759. Born Morristown, N.J. 1951. m. David Cape. 3 ch. EDUC: Brown Univ., B.A.(Language/Lit.) 1974; McGill Univ., B.C.L.(Civil Law) 1979, LL.B. 1980. BAR: Que.; Ont. CAREER: Lawyer, Petro-Canada, 1982-86; Cnsl & Sec., Ford Motor Company of Canada, Limited, 1986 to date. AFFIL: Law Society of Upper Canada; Bar of Quebec; public sch. classroom volunteer; Brown Univ. (Recruiting). INTERESTS: skiing; tennis; running.

Cuthbert Brandt, Gail, B.A.,M.A., Ph.D. ■■ ⚥
Principal, Renison College, UNIVERSITY OF WATERLOO, Westmount Rd. N., Waterloo, ON N2L 3G4 (519) 884-4404, ext. 634, FAX 884-5135, EMAIL gcbrandt@renison.watstar.uwaterloo.ca. Born Ingersoll, Ont. 1946. m. Bernd Brandt. 3 ch. Nicole, Andrea, Gregory. EDUC: Univ. of Toronto, B.A.(Hons., Hist.) 1967; Carleton Univ., M.A.(Hist.) 1968; York Univ., Ph.D.(Hist.) 1977. CAREER: Teaching Asst., Glendon Coll., York Univ., 1969-72; Instructor, 1972-73; Visiting Lecturer, Erindale Coll., Univ. of Toronto, 1974-75; Visiting Lecturer, Glendon Coll., York Univ., 1975-76; Visiting Asst. Prof. of Hist., 1976-77; Asst. Prof. of Hist., 1977-80; Assoc. Prof. of Hist., 1980-81; Assoc. Prof., Hist. & Multidisciplinary Studies, 1981-92; Principal & V-Chancellor, Prof. of Hist. & Dir. of East Asian Studies, Renison Coll., Univ. of Waterloo, 1992 to date. SELECTED PUBLICATIONS: co-author: *Canadian Women: A History* (1988); *Canadian Women: A History*, 2nd ed. (1996); *Canadian Women: A Reader* (1995); numerous articles, & papers presented at scholarly meetings. AFFIL: Canadian Historical Association (Pres. 1991-92); Canadian Committee on Women's History; Ontario Women's History Network (founding mbr.); Kitchener-Waterloo YMCA (Bd. mbr.); Canadian Federation of University Women, Kitchener-Waterloo branch. EDIT: *Canadian Woman Studies/Les cahiers de la femme* (mbr., French Edit. Bd. 1987-94); *Labour/Le Travail* (mbr., Edit. Bd. 1986-92). HONS: Women of Distinction Special Award,

Metro Toronto YWCA, 1991; Citoyenne d'honneur, St. Christophe-des-Bardes, France, 1988; Hon. Mention, Marion Porter Award for Best Article of the Year, Canadian Research Institute for the Advancement of Women, 1986; several fellowships/scholarships. INTERESTS: travel; tennis; cycling. MISC: speaks French & German; recipient, numerous research grants.

Cynamon, Helena, B.Ed. ■ ⩗
Principal, Television Producer, FOREFRONT ENTERTAINMENT GROUP, 402 W. Pender St., Ste. 700, Vancouver, BC V6B 1T6 (604) 682-7910, FAX 682-8583, EMAIL 75031.1011@ compuserve.com. Born Oshawa, Ont. 1954. 1 ch. Martina. EDUC: Univ. of Alberta, B.Ed.(Special Educ.) 1978; Simon Fraser Univ., Diploma Program in Film 1982; Banff Sch. of Fine Arts, Electronic Film & Media 1982. CAREER: TV producer, film director, editor, public educator. SELECTED CREDITS: Exec. Prod., *The Adventures of Shirley Holmes*, eps. 1-13; Exec. Prod., eps. 1-52, *Madison* (series), Forefront Productions Corp., 1993-94; Writer/Dir., *A Balancing Act* (documentary), National Film Board, Studio D, 1992; Co-Prod., eps. 2-7, *Madison* (series), Forefront Productions, 1991-92; Co-Prod./Co-Writer, *Inside Stories: Journey Into Self-Esteem* (4-part series), Forefront Productions Corp., 1990; Exec. Prod./Co-Prod, "Working It Out," pilot for *Madison*, Forefront Productions Corp., 1990; Prod./Co-Dir., *Caught in a World of Pesticides* (documentary), 1988; Prod./Dir., *Women & Politics* (2-part series), Knowledge Network, 1987; Prod./Dir., *Women and the Nicaraguan Revolution*, 1987; Prod./Dir., *Learning Peace* (documentary), National Film Board, Studio G, 1985; Prod./Dir., *This Should Not Have Happened* (documentary), United Fishermen's Allied Workers Union, 1984. AFFIL: various boards of film associations, community & political organizations, women's groups. HONS: to date *Madison* has won 26 int'l awards; CALM Award, 1984 for *This Should Not Have Happened*; Finalist, American Film & Video Festival, *Inside Stories: Journey Into Self-Esteem*, 1991. MISC: part of many TV & film-related industry panels; *Women and the Nicaraguan Revolution* was chosen as an entry into the Chicago 1988 Women in the Director's Chair Film Festival. COMMENT: *"I continue to seek challenges, dreams and opportunities, both as a business partner in a TV production company and as a mother. I am also very proud to be one of the creators and producers of the award-winning TV series Madison. I have been blessed with the most incredible learning opportunity–not only of a professional nature, but of a personal one, working with partners that I truly admire and grow with daily."*

Cyr, Mary, B.A.,M.A.,Ph.D. ■ ⩗ ⊗
Chair, Department of Music, UNIVERSITY OF GUELPH, Guelph, ON N1G 2W1 (519) 824-4120 ext. 8452, FAX 767-2784, EMAIL mcyr@arts.uoguelph.ca. Born Fargo, N. Dakota 1946. EDUC: Univ. of California, Berkeley, B.A.(Music) 1968, M.A.(Music Hist.) 1970, Ph.D.(Music) 1975. CAREER: Prof., Music, McGill Univ., 1976-92; Dir. of Grad. Studies, Music, 1991-92; Prof. & Chair, Dept. of Music, Univ. of Guelph, 1992 to date. SELECTED CREDITS: recorded 4 CDs & 3 LPs as viola da gambist & dir. of early music ensembles. SELECTED PUBLICATIONS: *Performing Baroque Music* (Portland, Ore.: Amadeus Press, 1992); "Violin Playing in Late Seventeeth-Century England: Baltzar, Matteis and Purcell" (*Performance Practice Review* 8:1 1995); numerous articles in *The New Grove Dictionary of Music and Musicians*, 6th ed., ed. by Stanley Sadie (London, 1980); numerous other articles, book reviews, music reviews & CD notes. EDIT: English Ed., *Canadian University Music Review*, 1992-95. AFFIL: Canadian University Music Society (Bd. of Dir. 1983-85, 1992-95); Early Music Society (Bd. of Gov. 1990-92); American Musicological Society (Council 1978-81). HONS: Noah Greenberg Award for excellence in early music performance, American Musicological Society, 1983. COMMENT: *"My scholarly pursuits are divided between performing and research in the area of Baroque music, especially opera, and original performing techniques."*

D

acquay, Louise M. ■ ■ ✦

Speaker of the Legislative Assembly of Manitoba, PROVINCE OF MANITOBA, Legislative Building, Rm. 244, Winnipeg, MB R3C 0V8 (204) 945-3706, FAX 945-1443. Born Manitou, Man. 1940. m. Hubert (Bert). 2 ch. Daniel (Dan), Donald (Don). **EDUC:** Certified Bus. Teacher (credits toward degree in bus. educ.). **CAREER:** teacher, 17 yrs.; office mgr/property mgr/admin. asst./exec. dir./proj. coord./reg'l organizer, private industry, 10 yrs. **POLITICAL CAREER:** Councillor, Langevin Ward, City of Winnipeg, 1986-89; first elected to Manitoba Legislature, gen. election 1990; re-elected, 1995; Deputy Speaker of the Leg. Assembly, 1990-95; Speaker of Leg. Assembly, 1995 to date. **AFFIL:** Commonwealth Parliamentary Association (Pres., Cdn Reg'l Council; Pres., Man. chpt.); International Commonwealth Parliamentary Association; Midwestern Legislative Conference; National Conference of State Legislatures. **INTERESTS:** reading; knitting; cross-country skiing; travel; snow mobiling.

Dadson, Anita, B.A.,B.S.W. ♡ ✦

Volunteer. 954 Wentworth Ave., N. Vancouver, BC V7R 1R7 (604) 988-6966, FAX 988-6966. Born N. Vancouver 1929. m. Phillip. 2 ch. **EDUC:** Univ. of British Columbia, B.A. (Econ & Soc.) 1952; Univ. of Toronto, B.S.W. 1953. **CAREER:** Caseworker, Children's Aid Society of Toronto, 1953-55; Supervisor in Protection Dept., Children's Aid Society of Ottawa, 1955-59; Family Court Worker, 1959-62; mother & homemaker, 1962-86; operated bed & breakfast in own home, 1986-91. **AFFIL:** North Shore Disability Resource Centre (Founding Mbr., Bd. of Dir; Pres. 5 yrs);

Lionsview Sr. Planning Society (Bd. of Dir.); Kinsmen's Mothers' March (Area Captain); B.C. Association for Community Living (VP); B.C. Federation of Families for Community Living (Treas.); North Shore Transit Advisory Committee (Chair); Liberal Party of B.C. (Riding Past Pres., W. Vancouver-Capilano); B.C. Women's Liberal Commission (Pres. 1991-93); National Women's Liberal Commission (Reg'l Rep. for BC & YT); B.C. Association for Community Living (Pres. 1996-97).

Dagg, Anne Innis, B.A.,M.A., Ph.D. 📖 ⚘ ဪ
Academic Advisor, Independent Studies, UNIVERSITY OF WATERLOO, Waterloo, ON N2L 3G1 (519) 888-4567, ext. 2368, FAX 746-7326. Born Toronto 1933. w. 3 ch. Hugh Eric, Ian Innis, Mary Christine. EDUC: Univ. of Toronto, B.A.(Biol.) 1955, M.A.(Genetics) 1956; Univ. of Waterloo, Ph.D.(Zoology) 1967. CAREER: Lecturer, Wilfrid Laurier Univ., 1962-65; Asst. Prof., Univ. of Guelph, 1967-72; Academic Advisor/Dir., Univ. of Waterloo, 1978 to date; researcher & writer; Biological Sciences Consultant, *World Book Encyclopedia.* SELECTED PUBLICATIONS: *Canadian Wildlife and Man* (Toronto; McClelland and Stewart, 1974); *The Giraffe* (New York; Van Nostrand Reinhold, 1976);*The Camel* (Chicago: Univ. of Chicago Press, 1981); *Running, Walking and Jumping –the Science of Locomotion* (London: Wykeham Science Series, Francis and Taylor, 1977); *Harems and Other Horrors: Sexual Bias in Behavioral Biology* (Waterloo; Otter Press, 1983); *MisEducation and Canadian Universities* (Toronto: OISE Press, 1988); *User-friendly University: What Every Student Should Know* (Waterloo: Otter Press, 1994). AFFIL: Harold Innis Foundation (Pres. 1990-96). HONS: Gold Medal in Hons. Biol., Univ. of Toronto, 1955; Kitchener-Waterloo Status of Women Human Rights Award, 1984. INTERESTS: tennis; hiking; canoeing; bird watching. COMMENT: *"My primary interest has been writing, doing research and teaching in the areas of mammalogy and women's studies."*

Dahl, Marilyn O., B.Sc.,M.A., Ph.D. ■ 🌫 ⊕ ✪ ♿
Executive Director, WESTERN INSTITUTE FOR THE DEAF AND HARD OF HEARING, 2125 W. 7th Ave., Vancouver, BC V6K 1X9 (604) 736-7391 (voice) 736-2527 (TTY), FAX 736-1381, EMAIL mdahl@unixg.ubc.ca. Born Broderick, Sask. 1931. m. Lloyd T. 3 ch. Dr. Marshall Dahl, Howard Dahl, Valerie Dahl. EDUC: Victoria Hospital Sch. of Nursing, Diploma (Nursing) 1953; Univ. of British Columbia, B.Sc. 1979, Ph.D. 1995; Simon Fraser Univ., M.A.

1988. CAREER: Nursing Supervisor, Victoria Hospital, 1953-55; Staff Nurse, Medicine & Obstetrics, Union Hospital, 1955-56; Obstetrics Nurse, University Hospital, 1956; Charge Nurse, Dr. Rygiels Hospital for Children with Multiple Handicaps, 1969-71; Nurse Clinical II, Riverview Psychiatric Hospital, 1971-77; Instructor, Psychiatric component, Nursing Fac., Douglas Coll., 1980-89; Researcher, Health Svcs Div., Post-Secondary Dept., Ministry of Educ. of B.C., 1981; Nursing Consultant, Hearing Awareness, 1981-89; Researcher, Psychiatric Nursing Dept., Douglas Coll., 1987-88; Interim Administrator, Steering Committee to Develop Cdn Deaf & Hard of Hearing Forum, 1989-90; Pres., MDEnterprises, 1990-95; Researcher, Study of Comparative Oper. of Three Nat'l Disability Organizations, Health & Welfare Canada/Cdn Deaf & Hard of Hearing Forum, 1992-93; Proj. Coord., TO HEAR AGAIN, 1992-94; Exec. Dir., Western Institute for the Deaf and Hard of Hearing, 1995 to date. VOLUNTEER CAREER: Advisory Committee to Message Relay Svcs, B.C. Tel, 1989 to date; Focus Group–Strategy to Coordinate Disability Issues in B.C., 1994; Ad-hoc committee on Live Captioning Svcs in Post-Secondary Educ. in B.C., 1994 to date; Canadian Deaf & Hard of Hearing Forum (Pres.; VP 1989-92); Ad-hoc committee on Hearing Accessibility, Univ. of British Columbia, 1992 to date; Advisory Committee on Fed. Policy Regarding Communication Needs for Deaf, Hard of Hearing & Deaf-Blind People, 1986-92; Steering Committee to Develop Mental Health Svcs for the Deaf & Hard of Hearing in Greater Vancouver, 1989-90; CHHA Rep. to Cdn Disability Rights Council, 1989-91; Focus Committee for Dev. of Disability Resource Centre, Univ. of British Columbia, 1989-90. SELECTED PUBLICATIONS: *A Self-Help Guide for Better Hearing* (Ottawa, CHHA, 1990, 1991); *Jerusalem 92 Congress Report: 4th International Congress of Hard of Hearing People,* ed. with Howard Dahl (Port Coquitlam, MDEnterprises, 1993); "Putting Patients Back in Patient Care" (*Nursing,* Oct. 1976); "Noise Annoys - It Also Damages Your Hearing" (*IFHOH Journal,* 14(2) 1993); "The Will to Act" (*Listen/ Écoute* 3(3), 1994); various other publications & presentations. EDIT: *IFHOH Journal* (International Federation of Hard of Hearing People), 1990-92. AFFIL: Institute for Hearing Accessibility Research [IHEAR], Univ. of British Columbia (Coord. Committee; Core Committee); International Federation of Hard of Hearing People (Pres. 1992-94; VP 1988-92); Hearing International (Exec. & member-at-large 1992-94); Canadian Hard of Hearing Association (Acting Pres., B.C. Chapter 1992-

93; Pres. & Chair, Health Professionals Committee 1986-92); B.C. Elks Family Resource Centre (Steering Committee); Registered Nurses' Association of B.C. HONS: Clinical Proficiency Award, Nursing, 1952; Gen. Proficiency Award, Nursing, 1953; nominee, YWCA Women of Distinction Award, 1992; Distinctive Svc. Award, Canadian Hard of Hearing Association, 1992; Alice E. Wilson Award, Canadian Federation of University Women, 1992; B.C. Elks Scholarship; Canada 125 Medal, 1993; Order of British Columbia, 1993. INTERESTS: author & actor, children's TV program weekly, CBC, Medicine Hat, 1967-69; author & actor, *Caring for the Patient Who is Hard of Hearing*, video, 1982; listed in *Canadian Who's Who* & *Who's Who in International Organizations*; Marilyn Dahl Award of Merit was created in 1994 by Canadian Hard of Hearing Association; first woman president of International Federation of the Hard of Hearing; first woman to lead an int'l disability organization. MISC: photography; sketching; hiking; gourmet cooking. COMMENT: *"Has probably done more than any other individual Canadian to contribute to a national identity for hard of hearing people in Canada. Credited with being Canada's foremost advocate for the hard of hearing, she has worked tirelessly to change attitudes and legislation affecting two million Canadians of all ages."*

Dahl, Veronica, Ph.D.

Professor and Director, Logic and Functional Programming Group, Centre for Systems Science, Laboratory for Computer and Communications Research, School of Computing Science, SIMON FRASER UNIVERSITY, Burnaby, BC V5A 1S6 (604) 291-3372, FAX 291-3045, EMAIL veronica@cs.sfu.ca. Born Buenos Aires 1950. m. Rob Turner. 4 ch. EDUC: Buenos Aires Univ., unconcluded studies (Lit., 14 subjects incl. Linguistics) 1974, Computador Cientifico 1974; Aix-Marseille II Univ., Diplôme d'études approfondis (Intelligence Artificielle) 1976, Doctorat 1977. CAREER: English teacher, various primary & secondary schools, Buenos Aires, 1968-72; Teaching Asst., Exact Sciences Fac., Buenos Aires Univ., 1973-75; Researcher, Argentine National Institute of Hydrological Science & Technique, 1974-75; Head of Teaching Assts., Centre for Advanced Studies in Exact Sciences, 1975; Adjunct Prof., Math. Dept., Univ. of Buenos Aires, 1977-82; Head of the Systems Div., Vialidad Nacional, 1978-79; Adjunct Researcher, Argentine National Council for Scientific & Technological Research, 1979-82; Visiting Assoc. Prof., Southern Univ., Argentina, 1981; Visiting Assoc. Prof., Univ. of Kentucky, 1982; Assoc. Prof., Simon Fraser Univ., 1982-91; Dir., Logic & Functional Programming Group, 1986 to date; Consultant, Int'l Artificial Intelligence, 1987-88; Prof., Sch. of Computing Sci., Simon Fraser Univ., 1991 to date. SELECTED PUBLICATIONS: *Understanding and Translating Language–challenges of the 90s* (AI Communications); "Characterizing Logic Grammars–a substructural approach," with J. Andrews & F. Popowich (*Journal of Logic Programming*); "Fact updates in logic databases," with Y.N. Huang & J.W. Han (*International Journal of Software Engineering and Knowledge Engineering*, in press); *Logic Programming for Constructive Expert Systems* (Benjamin/Cummings, 1986); *Logic Grammars*, with H. Abramson (Springer-Verlag, 1989); *Natural Language Understanding and Logic Programming*, ed. with Saint-Dizier (North-Holland, 1985); *Natural Language Understanding and Logic Programming II*, ed. with Saint-Dizier (North-Holland, 1988); "Translating Spanish into Logic through Logic" (*American Journal of Computational Linguistics* 1981); "Discontinuous Grammars" (*Computational Intelligence* 1989); "Analysis of Female Underrepresentation in Computing Sciences Departments: What Can Be Done?" (*Society for Canadian Women in Science and Technology News* 1992); "What the Study of Language Can Contribute to AI" (*AI Communications* 1993); "Natural Language Processing and Logic Programming" (*The Journal of Logic Programming* 12(1) 1994); numerous other publications. EDIT: Edit. Advisor, *Journal of Logic Programming*, 1984-91; Guest Ed., "Special Issue: Knowledge Systems," 1986; Guest Ed., "Special Issue: Computational Linguistics and Logic Programming," 1994; Area Ed., 1991 to date; Ed. Bd., *Computational Intelligence*, 1985 to date; Assoc. Ed., *International Journal of Expert Systems: Research and Applications*, 1987-90; Ed. Bd., 1990 to date; Guest Ed., "Special Issue: Constraint Reasoning for Expert Systems," *International Journal of Expert Systems*, 1992. AFFIL: Canadian Society for Computational Studies in Intelligence; American Association for Artificial Intelligence; Association for Computing Machinery; Association for Logic Programming; Society for Canadian Women in Science & Technology; Science for Peace (former Bd. Mbr., B.C. chapter; Publications Dir. 1994 to date); Society for Text & Discourse. HONS: Third Prize for Scientific Production in Eng. Sciences, "Algoritmo de Grafos para la Operacion Optima de Aprovechamientos Hidraulicos" (Hydric Resources Optimisation through Graph Theory) in *Proceedings, VII National Conference on Water*, Argentina, Gran Buenos Aires area,

Educ. Ministry, Argentina, 1978; Calouste Gul-benkian Award for Science & Technology, 1994; Women Professorship Award, Queen's Univ., 1995. **MISC**: recipient of numerous grants from various agencies; recipient of various scholarships; referee for various journals & conferences; grant reviewer for NSERC, NSF(US), & FCAC.

Dahl Rees, Carolyn, B.A.,M.A., LL.B. ■■ ⚛ Ⓢ

General Counsel, TRANSALTA UTILITIES CORPORATION (investor-owned electric utility), 110 - 12 Ave. S.W., Calgary, AB T2P 2M1 (403) 267-2563, FAX 267-3734, EMAIL Carolyn_Dahl_Rees.transalta@Notes_SMTP.transalta.ab.ca. Born Manhattan, Kansas 1953. m. Gregory P. Gallelli. 2 ch. **EDUC**: Rice Univ., B.A. (cum laude) 1975; Univ. of Toronto, M.A. 1976, LL.B. 1980. **CAREER**: Lawyer, McCarthy Tétrault, 1982-95; Ptnr, 1988-94; Cnsl, 1994-95; Gen. Cnsl, TransAlta Utilities Corporation, 1995 to date. **SELECTED PUBLICATIONS**: co-author with K.R. Smith, G.A. Yarranton & C.H. Weir, *Decision Report, Application to Construct Recreational and Tourism Facilities in the West Castle Valley near Pincher Creek, Alberta* (Application 9201 - Vacation Alberta Corporation, NRCB, Dec. 1993); co-author with G.J. DeSourcy, G.A. Yarranton & C.H. Weir, *Decision Report, Application to Construct a Recreational and Tourism Project in the Town of Canmore, Alberta* (Application 9103 - Three Sisters Golf Resorts Inc., NRCB, Nov. 1992). **AFFIL**: Alberta Natural Resource Conservation Board (acting mbr.); Macleod Institute Inc., Univ. of Calgary (Chrm of the Bd.); Environmental Research Centre, Univ. of Calgary (Exec. Committee of Advisory Bd.); Calgary Opera Association (1988-95; Exec. Committee 1990-93; Exec. VP & Chrm, Budget & Fin. Committee 1991-93). **HONS**: Open Fellowship, Univ. of Toronto, 1975-76. **INTERESTS**: opera; hiking; reading; skiing. **MISC**: participated as one of five core members of legislative drafting team for Alberta Electric Utilities Act, S.A. 1995, Ch. E-5.5, royal assent, May 17, 1995; seminar presentations in sustainable dev. & advanced environmental law, Univ. of Calgary.

Dahlstrom, Helen, A.R.C.T., L.M.U.S. ■■ ⊗ ⌂ Ⓞ

1604 Park St., Rossland, BC V0G 1Y0 (305) 362-5786, FAX 362-7250. Born Regina 1917. m. Alton R. Dahlstrom (1941-93, deceased); John W. Nystuen (1994 to date). 2 ch. Carol Dahlstrom, David Dahlstrom. **EDUC**: Royal Conservatory of Music, A.R.C.T.(Piano Teacher's & Performer's); Univ. of Saskatchewan, L.M.U.S. (Piano Performer's). **CAREER**: private studio, 1941 to date; exec. positions with numerous music-related groups. **SELECTED PUBLICATIONS**: *Canada Music Week* magazine (Editor & Publisher, 1969-92); *Mini-biographies of Canadian Composers* (1978-92); now working on 2 books, *Canadian Music History & Anecdotes of Music Examiners: Laughs & Sighs*. **AFFIL**: Canada Music Week (Nat'l Chrm 1969-92); Royal Conservatory of Music, Coll. of Examiners (Sr. Examiner); Canadian Federation of Music Teachers' Association (former Pres.); Canadian Music Centre (voting mbr.); European Piano Teachers' Association. **HONS**: Hon. Life Mbr., Canadian Federation of Music Teachers Association; Trail's Home of Champions, 1989. **INTERESTS**: teaching; education; family; friends; gardening; travel. **MISC**: listed in *Encyclopedia of Music in Canada* & in *Women of Note*. **COMMENT**: *"I have spent a lifetime in various fields of music as student, performer, teacher, accompanist, examiner, adjudicator, judge, clinician, choral conductor, organist, and administrator, locally, provincially and federally. Over the long span of my musical career, I have attempted to infuse an all-encompassing love of music in my students, not only for the joy of learning, performing, developing discipline and achieving excellence, but also to open the vistas of self-expression, awareness and beauty of all facets of living. It is my hope that they in turn are carrying on my concept of 'music in life.' You might consider it a holistic approach. I have endeavoured to extend this vision throughout the community through my work with numerous arts organizations within the province and the nation. My achievements are varied: I feel I have made some contribution to the musical world through my students and the organizations with which I have been associated. My reward is knowing the majority of my students over the years have continued their interest and activity in music in manifold ways, both in Canada and abroad."*

Dale, Jennifer ⊗ ⌂ ♥

Actor. c/o Oscars and Abrams, 59 Berkeley St., Toronto, ON M5A 2W5 (416) 860-1790. Born Toronto. d. 2 ch. **EDUC**: National Theatre Sch., 1974-77. **SELECTED CREDITS**: May, *Fool for Love*, Toronto Free Theatre; Hero, *Much Ado About Nothing*, Stratford; Juliet, *Romeo and Juliet*, Stratford; Cressida, *Troilus and Cressida*, NAC; lead, *The Calendar Girl*, CBC; guest star, *Night Heat*, "Jane the Ripper" (series), CBS; lead, *Vanderberg* (miniseries), CBC; lead, *Empire Inc.* (mini-series), CBC; lead, *Love and Larceny*, CBC; lead, *No Place Like Home* (series), syndicated; lead,

Grand Larceny, CBC; guest star, *Street Legal* (series), CBC; guest star, *E.N.G.*, "Pandora's Box" (series), CTV; guest star, *Forever Knight*, "If Looks Could Kill" (series), CBS; guest star, *ROBOCOP* (premiere & series), syndicated/Paul Lynch; guest star, *Kung Fu* (series); lead, *Family Passions* (series), *Tek War* (series), *Taking The Falls* (series) CTV; lead, *Ticket to Heaven*, UA Classics; lead, *Stone Cold Dead*, George Mendeluk; lead, *Suzanne*, 20th Century; lead, *Side Effects* (series) CBC, 1995; lead, *The Adjuster* (film), Family Viewing Productions; lead, *Cadillac Girls* (film), Overdrive Motion Pictures; lead, *Whale Music*, Whale Music Productions; lead, *Martha, Ruth and Edie* (film), Sunrise Films. **AFFIL:** Women in Film (Bd. Mbr.); Television-Toronto. **HONS:** nominee, Best Actress (*Night Heat*, "Jane the Ripper"), Genie Awards, 1981; nominee, Best Actress (*Suzanne*), Gemini Awards, 1986; nominee, Best Actress (*Thunder In My Head*), Gemini Awards, 1990; nominee, Best Performance in a Continuing Role (*No Place Like Home*), Gemini Awards, 1992. **INTERESTS:** the study of theosophy & the mysteries of being; salsa! **MISC:** co-founder of workshop for actors, writers & directors; currently co-prod. first short film. **COMMENT:** *"At this stage of mid-life, I'm a woman who believes my best work and contributions are still to come; one who is grateful for so many blessed opportunities and one who continues to pursue vigorous dreams."*

Dale, Lisa ■■ 📖 ✎

Magazine Manager, WOMEN & ENVIRONMENTS MAGAZINE (quarterly; a project of The WEED Foundation), 736 Bathurst St., Toronto, ON M5S 2R4 (416) 516-2600, FAX 531-6214. Full Founding Member and Local Representative, EARTH APPEAL (workplace fundraising environmental charity). Born Downsview, Ont. 1953. m. Stephen Ellis. 2 ch. Robyn & Adrian Ellis. **EDUC:** York Univ., Music/Creative Writing/English. **CAREER:** Drednaught Press, Ontario Arts Council, *The Toronto Star*, 1974-75; Asst. to Publisher, *Content* magazine, 1975-76; freelance writer/poet, ongoing; Proofreader/Asst. to Mng Editor, *Descant* magazine, 1994 to date; freelance Proofreader, *Now* magazine. **INTERESTS:** gardening, both urban & rural; all literature & literary pursuits.

Dale, Maggie N., B.A.,M.A. $

National Marketing Director, PRICE WATERHOUSE, 1 First Canadian Place, Ste. 3300, Box 190, Toronto, ON M5X 1H7 (416) 365-2729, FAX 365-8885. Born Bangor, Wales 1950. m. Ian Monro Cartwright Dale. **EDUC:** Univ. of Nottingham, B.A.(Hist.) 1971; Univ. of Western Ontario, Diploma (Educ.) 1973, M.A. (Hist.) 1976, M.A.(Journalism) 1979; Chartered Institute of Marketing, UK, Certificate in Mktg Practice 1993, Diploma (Mktg) 1995. **CAREER:** Story Prod., *Metro Morning*, CBC, 1979; Ed. of Publications, Norcen Energy Resources, 1979-85; Asst. Dir. of Comm., Price Waterhouse, 1985-87; Dir. of Comm., 1987-90; Dir. of Mktg Comm., 1990-94; Nat'l Mktg Dir., 1994 to date. **SELECTED PUBLICATIONS:** "Matches Aren't Only Made in Heaven" (*Canadian Banker Magazine*, Feb. 1988). **AFFIL:** Canadian Institute of Marketing; Ontario Racquet Club; Adelaide Court Theatre (Dir.). **INTERESTS:** tennis; golf; photography; music; boating; dogs. **COMMENT:** *"A career-oriented, internationally minded, marketing driven individual who is focused on adapting the marketing concept to a professional services firm. This pioneering opportunity presents enormous challenge and is being attacked with considerable energy and enthusiasm."*

Dalglish, Brenda G., B.A. ■ ✎

Media Reporter, THE FINANCIAL POST, 333 King St. E., Toronto, ON M5A 4N2 (416) 350-6389, FAX 350-6301. Born Swift Current, Sask. 1954. m. John D.H. Partridge. **EDUC:** Univ. of Saskatchewan, B.A.(English) 1976. **CAREER:** worked for *The Vancouver Sun*, *The Victoria Times*, *The Goldstream Gazette*, *The Sidney Review*; Reporter, *The Canadian Press*, 1981-90; Nat'l Bus. Correspondent, *Maclean's* Magazine, 1990-95; Media Reporter, *The Financial Post*, 1995 to date. **HONS:** The Jack Wasserman Memorial Award, 1979; Southam Fellowship for Journalists, 1988-89. **INTERESTS:** reading; gardening; tennis.

Dalphond-Guiral, Madeleine, R.N., B.A.,M.P. 🍁

Member of Parliament (Laval-Centre), GOVERNMENT OF CANADA, Centre Building, Office 655-D, Ottawa, ON K1A 0A4 (613) 996-0864. Born Montreal 1938. w. 4 ch. **EDUC:** Hôpital Ste.-Justine, Licence d'Infirmière 1959; Univ. de Montréal, B.A. 1970, Certificat (Santé communautaire) 1974, Certificat (Éduc. et Organisation des soins) 1975. **CAREER:** Infirmière soignante en divers champs de spécialités et infirmière monitrice, Hôpital Ste.-Justine, 1959-74; Prof., Soins infirmiers, C.E.G.E.P. Montmorency, Laval, 1976-93; Députée (Laval-Centre), House of Commons, 1993 to date; Whip adjointe de l'Opposition officielle, House of Commons, 1993-94; VP, Comité référendaire, Bloc Québécois, 1993-94; Porte-parole du Bloc Québécois dans le dossier des nouvelles technologies de reproduction, House of Commons; VP, Association interparlementaire Canada-

France, 1994 to date. **AFFIL:** Parti Québécois (Prés., Laval-des-Rapides 1980-83); Bloc Québécois (Mbr. fondatrice, Laval-Centre 1991); Ordre des Infirmières et Infirmiers du Québec; Comité Arts-Pontmain. **INTERESTS:** ski de randonée; ski alpin; bicyclette; cuisine; théâtre; cinéma; musique; lecture. **MISC:** Organisatrice de trois colloques nationaux en soins infirmiers, 1988-90. **COMMENT:** *"Mon engagement socio-politique résulte d'une prise de conscience de deux réalités: la nécessaire autonomie économique des femmes et l'importance majeure de leur rôle dans la société; la nécessaire souveraineté du Québec, seul gage du maintien d'une société francophone dynamique sur un territoire défini et reconnu internationalement comme pôle de la francophnie en terre d'Amérique."*

Dalton, Marcia (Marty), B.A. ♡

Past President, National Chapter of Canada, IODE, 40 Orchard View Blvd., Ste. 254, Toronto, ON M4R 1B9 (416) 487-4416, FAX 487-4417. Born Pompton Lakes, N.J. m. Charles H. 2 ch. Karen Bumstead, Scott Dalton. **EDUC:** Elmira Univ., B.A.(Econ.) 1951. **CAREER:** Res. Dept., Procter & Gamble, 2 yrs.; numerous positions, IODE, 1966 to date; Pres., Mun. Chapter of London; Pres., Prov. Chapter of Ont., 1982-85; Pres., Nat'l Chapter of Canada, 1992-94. **HONS:** made Life Mbr. of Eldon House Chapter (London) IODE, Mun. Chapter of London IODE, Prov. Chapter of Ont. IODE, Nat'l Chapter of Canada IODE. **COMMENT:** *"My achievements can speak for themselves, and I endeavour to carry on and fulfill the mission of IODE wherever and whenever possible. The IODE is a Canadian charitable organization dedicated to improving the quality of life for children, youth and those in need, through education, social service and citizenship programs."*

D'Alton, Mary, B.A.,C.H.A. $ 🎭

Managing Director, WATERLOO INN, 475 King St. N., Waterloo, ON N2J 2Z5 (519) 884-0220, FAX 884-0321. Born Dublin. s. **EDUC:** Univ. of Toronto, B.A. 1978. **CAREER:** Asst. Gen. Mgr, Valhalla Inn; Gen. Mgr, Waterloo Inn; Mng Dir. **AFFIL:** American Hotel/Motel Association (C.H.A.); Meeting Planners International (Int'l Awards Bd.; Int'l Rel'ns Committee; Sales & Mktg Special Interest Group Bd.; Nominations Committee, Toronto chpt.); St. Mary's General Hospital (Bd. of Trustees; served on various committees); Kitchener-Waterloo Area Visitor & Convention Bureau (Bd.); Waterloo Economic Development (Committee Mbr.); Seagram Bond Warehouse Task Force; Univ. of Waterloo Campaigns (Chair, Svc. Club Sector); Ontario Hotel/Motel Association (VP, Fin.; Pres., Local Zone). **HONS:** Businesswoman of the Year, 1982. **MISC:** proj. mgr for social catering for Grand Prix, Montreal, Molson Indy, Econ. Summit & Canadian Open.

Dalton, Mary, B.A.,M.A. 📜 📖 🎓

Associate Professor, Department of English, MEMORIAL UNIVERSITY OF NEWFOUNDLAND, St. John's, NF A1C 5S7 (709) 737-5569, FAX 737-4569. Born Lake View, Harbour Main, Nfld. 1950. **EDUC:** Univ. of Toronto, B.A. (English) 1972; Memorial Univ., M.A.(English) 1975; Univ. of Liverpool, Canada Council Fellow (English) 1975-78. **CAREER:** Tutor, Univ. of Liverpool, 1976-77; Lecturer, Memorial Univ., 1978-89; Asst. Prof., 1989-95; Assoc. Prof., 1995 to date. **SELECTED PUBLICATIONS:** *The Time of Icicles* (Breakwater 1989, hardcover; 1991, paperback); *Allowing the Light* (Breakwater 1993); poems, essays, reviews, radio scripts & interviews in various nat'l & int'l journals. **EDIT:** Contributing Ed., *Books in Canada*; Co-Ed. & Co-Publisher, *TickleAce* (Nfld.'s literary magazine), 1980-86; Co-Ed., *Wild on the Crest: Sea-Poems–Newfoundland and Labrador* (Jeroboam Books 1995); Ed., *Newfoundland Studies* (interdisciplinary journal pub. by Memorial Univ.). **AFFIL:** Jury for the Pat Lowther Poetry Award (Chair). **MISC:** has given poetry readings in every province of Canada; launched both books with a cross-country Canada Council-sponsored tour; presently working on a scholarly & historical anthology of Nfld. poetry from the early 17th century to the present as well as a third collection of poems.

Dance, Faye, B.A.A. 📺 🎭

Broadcaster. c/o Talent Group, 401 Richmond St. W., Ste. 401, Toronto, ON M5V 3A8 (416) 408-3304, FAX 408-4867. Born Hanover, Ont. 1947. m. 2 ch. **EDUC:** Ryerson Polytechnic Univ., B.A.A.(Radio & TV Arts) 1969. **CAREER:** actor, broadcaster & host. **SELECTED CREDITS:** Host, *Wintario/Win TV*, Global TV/TVO/CFTO, ongoing; Host, National Santa Claus Parade, Global TV; Host, *Your Wealth*, CHCH TV; Guest Panelist, *Front Page Challenge*, CBC; Principal, *Model By Day* (telefilm), Alliance Entertainment; Principal, *E.N.G.* (series), Moviecorp XXIII; Principal, *Alfred Hitchcock Presents* (series), AHF Productions; various corp. videos. **AFFIL:** Ryerson Polytechnic Univ. (Gov.); Humber Valley United Church. **HONS:** Most Outstanding Grad., Radio & TV Arts, Ryerson, 1969. **INTERESTS:** reading; skiing; in-line skating. **COMMENT:** *"I have spent 25 years hosting* *television shows, parades, corporate videos, acting in movies and being a spokesperson for the Ontario Lottery Corporation (20 years). It's been a very rewarding career. I think my two boys are still my best accomplishment."*

Dance-Bennink, Terry, B.A.,M.Ed. 🐚 ✦
Vice-President Academic, SIR SANDFORD FLEMING COLLEGE, Brealey Dr., Peterborough, ON K9J 7B1 (705) 749-5544, FAX 749-5559, EMAIL tdance@flemingc.on.ca. Born UK 1948. m. Theodore Bennink. EDUC: Univ. of Toronto, B.A.(Phil.) 1970, M.Ed. 1987. CAREER: freelance journalist, 1970-72; Admin. Asst., East Asian Studies Program, York Univ., 1977-79; Counselling & Dev. Centre, 1973-77; Dir. of Adult Educ., Dixon Hall, Toronto, 1981-85; Chair, Community Outreach, George Brown Coll., 1985-89; Dean, Fac. of Access & Preparatory Studies, 1989-95; VP, Academic, Sir Sandford Fleming Coll., 1995 to date. SELECTED PUBLICATIONS: various papers & presentations. AFFIL: ACAATO (Heads of Access; Founding Mbr.; Prov. Chair); Coll. Standards & Accreditation Council (Generic Skills Council); Adult Preparatory Programs Articulation & Standards Committee (Steering Committee); Canadian Association for Adult Education; Canadian Vocational Association; Ontario Association for Continuing Education; Ontario Literacy Coalition; Canadian Congress for Learning Opportunities for Women (Ont. Dir. 1987-88); American Society for Training & Development; Association for Community-based Training & Education for Women (Founding Mbr., Bd. of Dir. 1984-88). INTERESTS: sailing; gardening; reading; the arts.

Dane, Nazla L. 👁
Retired Association Executive. 55 Belmont St., Toronto, ON M5R 1R1 (416) 921-3683. Born Indian Head, Sask. s. EDUC: Regina Collegiate Institute, Sr. Matriculation; Regina Normal Sch., teacher training. CAREER: Teacher, elementary & high sch., 1925-33; Sec., Simpsons, Regina/Copywriter, Advtg Dept., Hudson's Bay Company, Vancouver/Credit Operator, Vancouver, 1933-41; various positions, Dept. of Munitions & Supply, & Dept. of Transport, Ottawa, 1941-45; Dir., Women's Div. & Educ. Div., Canadian Life Insurance Association, 1945-71. VOLUNTEER CAREER: Pres., Toronto Business & Professional Women's Club, 1949-51; Pres., Inter-Club Council Women in Public Affairs; Sec., Toronto Public Relations Society; Mbr., Soroptomist Club of Toronto; Committee Mbr., YWCA of Canada; Mbr., Bd. of Dir., Victorian Order of Nurses (Metro Toronto Branch); Mbr., Bd. of Dir., Metro Tenants Legal Services, Toronto; Pres.,

Ontario Business & Professional Women's Clubs, 1958-60; VP, Canadian Federation of Business & Professional Women's Club, 1962-64; Pres., 1964-66; Pres., International Federation of Business & Professional Women, 1971-74. SELECTED PUBLICATIONS: articles in various women's publications; booklets on life insur. for schools & women's groups. AFFIL: Canadian Federation of Business & Professional Women (Life Mbr.; Hon. Pres. for Life); Toronto Business & Professional Women's Club. HONS: Queen Elizabeth Silver Jubilee Medal, 1977; Persons Award, 1985. INTERESTS: Canada; Cdn history; women's issues. MISC: written & overseen production of various film strips on life insur. for schools & women's groups; led International Federation of Business & Professional Women delegation to Habitat 7 NGO Forum, Vancouver, 1976; listed in *Canadian Who's Who.* COMMENT: *"I have always been active in organizations striving for equality for women. I like challenges and have always accepted them in my work and community endeavours. I am unable to be as active in such projects now, but do what I can."*

Daniels, Valsa, M.B.B.S.,M.D., FRCPC ⊕ 🐚
Director of Stroke Program, REHABILITATION HOSPITAL, Health Science Centre, 800 Sherbrook St., Winnipeg, MB R3A 1M4 (204) 787-1140, FAX 787-1476. Associate Professor, Rehabilitative Medicine, Faculty of Medicine, UNIVERSITY OF MANITOBA. Born Kerala, India. m. George. 1 ch. EDUC: Univ. of Mysore, M.B.B.S. 1972; Univ. of Manitoba, M.D. 1980, FRCPC 1984. CAREER: Assoc. Prof., Section of Rehabilitation Medicine, Fac. of Medicine, Univ. of Manitoba, 1983 to date; Medical Dir., Rehabilitation Medicine, Victoria General Hospital, 1983 to date; Active Medical Staff, Municipal Hospital, Winnipeg, 1983-88. SELECTED PUBLICATIONS: "Steady-state Response of Quadriplegic Subjects to Inspiratory Resistive Load" (*Journal of Applied Physiology* 60). AFFIL: Deer Lodge Centre (Bd. of Dir. 1992-95); Royal Coll. of Physicians & Surgeons of Canada (Fellow); Canadian Medical Association; Manitoba Medical Association; Canadian Association of Physical Medicine & Rehabilitation. INTERESTS: East Indian, Thai & French gourmet cooking; theatre; ballet; symphony; travel to exotic places.

Danis, Aimee 🖐
President and Co-Founder, VERSEAU INTERNATIONAL, 225 E. Roy St., Rm. 200, Montreal, QC H2W 1M5 (514) 848-9814, FAX 848-9908. Born Montreal 1929. d. EDUC: Univ. of

Ottawa, Licence (Educ.) 1949, Licence (Phil.) 1951. **CAREER:** Script Asst., Radio-Canada, 1960-67; Film Ed., Les Films Claude Fournier, 1967-68; Dir., Onyfilm & Verseau, 1968-85; Prod., Verseau International, 1985 to date. **AFFIL:** APFTQ (Pres. 1975-77, 1987-89); Banff Television Festival (Bd. 1992-95).

D'anna, Lynnette ☐ ⊗ ♙

Writer, Novelist, Poet, Publicist to the Arts, D'ANNA - HERSELF COMMUNICATIONS, Vancouver, BC. Born Steinbach, Man. 1955. s. 2 ch. **EDUC:** Univ. of Saskatchewan, Educ. 1985; Red River Community Coll., Diploma (Journalism/Creative Comm.) 1992. **CAREER:** Resource Dev. Officer, Saskatoon Planned Parenthood, 1985-86; Coord., Prov. Resource Guide to Self-Help Groups, Sask. Self-Help Dev. Unit, 1986; Coord., Prov. Women's Art Fair, 1986; Coord., AIDS Saskatoon, 1987-89; Publicist, Dance Collective, 1992-95; admin. support, Breaking the Cycle: Deaf, Hard of Hearing & Deaf-Blind Women & Family Violence Proj., 1994-95; publicist to the arts, 1994 to date. **SELECTED PUBLICATIONS:** *sing me no more*, novel (PressGang Publishers, 1992); *RagTimeBone*, novel (New Star Books, 1994); *fool's bells*, novel (New Star Books Ltd., 1996); poetry, reviews & interviews published in various literary journals, incl. *Grain, Prairie Fire, Poetry Canada, Zygote, subTerrain, Contemporary Verse 2, Prism international*; monthly books page of authors' profiles & reviews, *Interchange*, 1993-95. **AFFIL:** The Writers' Union of Canada; Vancouver Press Club; Prairie Fire Press Inc. (Pres., Bd. of Dir. 1993-95). **HONS:** Scholarship Award, Man. Community Newspaper Association, 1991; Hon. Mention, Winnipeg Press Club Awards, 1991; Finalist, The John Hirsch Award for Most Promising Manitoba Writer, 1993. **MISC:** Script Consultant, *Financial Post* Awards for Bus. in the Arts, May 1993; writers' grants awarded by the Man. Arts Council & the Canada Council; Coord., *hot shots erotic cabaret*, 1994; Founder, Post-Mennonite Survivors (PMS), 1992; various print & broadcast interviews; numerous public readings; first single parent accepted into Creative Communications program, RRCC; first to write & have a novel published while still a student; *sing me no more* originally published under surname "Dueck."

Danyluk, Vera, B.Ed. ■ ✦

Chair, Executive Committee, MONTREAL URBAN COMMUNITY, Les Cours Mont-Royal, 1550 Metcalfe St., 14th Fl., Montreal, QC H3A 3P1 (514) 280-3500, FAX 282-0241. Born Montreal 1944. m. Victor Danyluk. 1 ch.

Peter. **EDUC:** St. Joseph Teachers' Coll., Diploma 1963; McGill Univ., B.Ed. 1986. **CAREER:** Teacher, Granby Catholic Sch. Commission/Montreal Catholic Sch. Commission, 1961-68; Commissioner & mbr., Exec. Committee, Ste-Croix Sch. Bd., 1977-83; Councillor, Town of Mount Royal, 1983-87; Mayor, Town of Mount Royal, 1987-94. **AFFIL:** Federation of Canadian Municipalities (Chrm, Community Safety & Crime Prevention Committee 1996 to date; Nat'l Bd. of Dir. 1994 to date); La Chambre de Commerce française au Canada (Bd. mbr. 1996 to date); Union of Municipalities of Quebec (Bd. mbr. 1996 to date); Conseil régional de l'Île de Montréal (mbr. of Bd. & Exec. Committee 1996 to date); Montreal International Corporation (mbr., Founding Bd. 1996); McGill Univ. (Bd. of Gov. 1995 to date; Bldg & Property Committee 1995 to date); Bureau de transport métropolitain international (Chrm 1995-96); Montreal Urban Community (Chrm, Exec. Committee & Budget Committee 1994 to date); Société de transport de la Communauté urbaine de Montréal (Bd. mbr. 1994 to date); Canadian Club of Montreal (Bd. of Dir. 1996 to date); Conference of Montreal Suburban Mayors (Pres. 1992-94). **HONS:** Commemorative Medal for 125th Anniversary of Cdn Confederation, in recognition of significant contribution to compatriots, community & Canada. **INTERESTS:** classical music; arts; reading in areas of theology, philosophy & psychology; walking in nature reserves & bird conservatories. **COMMENT:** *"General interest in the well-being of society and in being a catalyst for human growth and development."*

Danzig, Etty ■■ ○ ☼

National President, NA'AMAT CANADA INC. (women's Zionist organization), 7005 Kildare, Ste. 6, Montreal, QC H4W 1C1 (514) 488-0792, FAX 487-6727, EMAIL na-amat@vic.com. Born Toronto 1937. m. Yehuda. 2 ch. Mark, Ian. **EDUC:** Toronto Teachers' Coll., 1957; Royal Conservatory of Music, ARCT (Diploma) 1960. **CAREER:** Teacher, Toronto Bd. of Educ., 1957-65; Piano Teacher, 1965-95; Breakfast Coord. & Caterer, United Jewish Appeal & Jewish Nat'l Fund campaigns, 1981-84; Teacher, kosher cooking course, Beth Tikvah Congregational Sch., 1983. **VOLUNTEER CAREER:** Pres., Na'amat Canada, Toronto Council, 1977-79; Chairperson, Music Committee, Jewish Community Centre, 1983-86; Pres., Jewish Women's Federation, Jewish Federation of Greater Toronto, 1988-90; Nat'l Pres., Na'amat Canada, 1993-96; mbr., Exec. Committee, Canadian Zionist Federation; mbr., Bd. of Gov., Jewish Federation of Greater

Toronto. INTERESTS: concerts; Beth Tikvah choir; cooking & baking; lavish entertaining; travel; reading. MISC: has planned and implemented local, nat'l & int'l colloquia, seminars & conferences; has designed advertising & fundraising campaigns related to admin. of nat'l organization with over 5,000 members. COMMENT: *"An innovative, highly motivated community leader who has developed excellent communication, mediation and interpersonal skills. Expertise in organizational planning, project development, logistics and presentation. Sound analytic and management skills combined with a flair for leadership."*

Daoust, Sylvia, R.C.A.,C.M., C.Q. ⊗
Sculpteure. 505 boul. Gouin O., Ste. 651, Montréal, QC H3L 3T2. Born Montréal 1902. EDUC: École des Beaux-Arts de Montréal, Diplôme (Enseignement) 1927. CAREER: Sculpteure; Prof., École des Beaux-Arts de Québec, 1930-43; Prof., 1943-68. COMMISSIONS: numerous medals, busts & religious works in wood & stone; *Monument Marie-Victorin*, Jardin botanique de Montréal, 1954; *Monument Père Viel*, façade du parlement du Qué., 1965; *Monument Edouard-Montpetit*, Univ. de Montréal, 1967; Mural en béton avec Fernand Paquette, sculpteur, édifice la Société Nationale de Fiducie, 1968; *Maternité*, Maison des Arts de Laval, 1986. EXHIBITIONS: Square Garden, N.Y. City (1930); *Exposition Hudon-Daoust*, École des Beaux-Arts du Québec (1938); *Exposition Beaugrand-Daoust*, Coll. Saint-Laurent (1946); *Fémina*, Musée prov., Qué. (1947); *First Exhibit of Liturgical Work*, Art Gallery of Hart House, Toronto (1963); Oratoire Saint-Joseph, Montréal (1973, 1979, 1991, 1993); Musée du Québec (1974); Centre culturel de Dorval (1975); Musée des Religions, Nicolet (1994); numerous group exhibitions. HONS: First Prize, Sculpture, Lord Willingdon Interprovincial Contest, 1928; Allied Arts Award, Sculpture, Royal Institute of Architecure of Canada, 1961; Médaille d'or, Conseil de la cité de Dorval, 1975; Décoration, Association d'éducation du Québec, 1975; Prix Philippe-Hébert, Société Saint-Jean-Baptiste, 1975; Order of Canada, 1976; Mérite diocésain Mgr Ignace Bourget, Archdiocese of Montréal, 1983; Chevalier, Ordre national du Québec, 1987; Médaille, Association québécoise des éducateurs et éducatrices specialisés en arts plastiques, 1992; Prix de l'excellence artistique de Laval, 1993; Prix spécial de l'Académie, 1994. MISC: numerous grants. COMMENT: *"Encore aujourd'hui, active à 94 ans, elle est à sculpter une Vierge et l'Enfant dans un bois d'acajou."*

Daoust-Roy, Jeannine, R.E.T., R. EEG T ⊕ ◐ ⊛
President, CANADIAN ASSOCIATION OF ELECTRONEUROPHYSIOLOGY TECHNOLOGISTS, INC. (CAET, Inc.), Children's Hospital, 840 Sherbrook St., Winnipeg, MB R3A 1S1 (204) 787-2544, FAX 787-4807. Born Winnipeg 1957. m. Louis. 1 ch. André. EDUC: Canadian Board of Registration of EEG Technologists, R.E.T. 1977; American Board of Registration of Electroencephalographic Technologists, R. EEG T. CAREER: EEG student & EEG Technologist, St. Boniface General Hospital, 1976-79; EEG Technologist, Winnipeg Clinic, 1979-83; Technologist II Gen. Duty, EEG Dept., Health Sciences Centre, Children's Hospital, 1983 to date; Coord., French Language Svcs, 1994 to date. SELECTED PUBLICATIONS: "A Waking 4 Hz Vertex Rhythm: 4 cps Vertex Spindles Revisited" (*American Journal of EEG Technology* 1989); "Epileptic Apnea in a Neonate," with A. Patton & S.S. Seshia (*American Journal of EEG Technology* 1991); "Benign Neonatal Sleep Myoclonus," with S.S. Seshia (*American Journal of Diseases of Children* 1992). AFFIL: CAET, Inc. (VP 1991-92; Pres. 1992-96); Manitoba Association of Electroneurophysiology Technologists, Inc. (VP 1991-92); ASET; Canadian Board of Registration of EEG Technologists (Aux. Bd. Mbr.; Assoc. Examiner 1994-95); French Language Services Committee, Children's Hospital, Winnipeg. HONS: Certificate of Award for Chemistry, 1975; Award for Excellence, Univ. of Manitoba Alumni Association, 1975; Academic Proficiency Scholarship, Univ. of Winnipeg, 1989; Best Poster Award, C.A.E.T., Inc., 1990. INTERESTS: reading; performing arts; travel; walking; cycling; skating. MISC: pursuing a degree in French-English/English-French translation, part time. COMMENT: *"You get out of life what you put into it, therefore I put a lot of thought and energy into everything I do. My motto: live, love and laugh!"*

Darcy, Judy ◑ ⬧
National President, CANADIAN UNION OF PUBLIC EMPLOYEES, 21 Florence St., Ottawa, ON K2P 0W6 (613) 237-1590, FAX 237-5508. Born Grinsted, Denmark 1949. m. Gary Caroline. 1 ch. Darcy Caroline. CAREER: Nat'l Sec.-Treas., Canadian Union of Public Employees, 1989-91; Nat'l Pres., 1991 to date. AFFIL: Canadian Labour Congress (Gen. VP). MISC: only woman to head a nat'l or int'l union in the Canadian labour movement. COMMENT: *"The President of Canada's largest union (with 460,000 members) is a dynamic and articulate leader speaking out on quality public services and social programs, equality and workers' rights."*

Darling, Betty Millins, B.A.,B.S.W., M.S.W. ⊕ ♡ ✊

Past President, OSTEOPOROSIS SOCIETY OF BRITISH COLUMBIA (OSTOP), 2110 W. 12th Ave., Vancouver, BC V6K 2N2 (604) 731-4997, FAX 222-8190. Born Nanaimo, B.C. 1922. m. G. Dudley Darling (dec.),. 4 ch. 3 stpch. S. Michael Fields, Daphne Fields, Darryl Ann Fields, Leslie Fields. **EDUC:** Victoria Coll., 1939; Univ. of British Columbia, B.A.(Econ.) 1944; Univ. of Toronto, B.S.W.(Social Work) 1946, M.S.W.(Psychiatric/medical social work) 1952. **CAREER:** Volunteer, Canadian Red Cross, 1944-45; Toronto Children's Aid Society, 1946-50; Staff Supervisor, Family Counselling, Homemaking Association (Red Cross), 1951-52; B.C. Ministry of Hum. Res./Vancouver Children's Aid Society, 1956-76; George Pearson Centre, B.C. Rehabilitation Society, 1976-87; Bd. of Dir., Osteoporosis Society of B.C., 1989 to date; Pres., 1991-93; Past Pres., 1994. **SELECTED PUBLICATIONS:** various public info. brochures for osteoporosis & brain injuries. **AFFIL:** Cheshire Home Society of B.C. (Dir. 1974-93); B.C. Association of Social Workers; Brock House Society for Seniors; Vancouver Lawn Tennis & Badminton Club; Univ. of British Columbia Fac. Women's Club; St. Anselm's Anglican Church. **INTERESTS:** gardening; ballet; family; tennis; reading biographies. **COMMENT:** *"Betty's professional and personal lives have revolved around the care of others, be they family, clients or the public in general. She has continually directed her energy into improving the world of others."*

Darling, Michèle Suzanne S., B.A., M.Ed. $ ☝

Executive Vice-President, CIBC, Commerce Court P.S., CCW-5, Toronto, ON M5L 1A2 (416) 980-5745, FAX 360-5271. Born Canada 1954. m. Michael Eagen. 2 ch. **EDUC:** Sydney Univ., B.A.(Pol. Sci.) 1975; Univ. of Toronto, M.Ed.(Adult Educ.) 1984; Univ. of Bath, Ph.D. current. **CAREER:** Dir., Hum. Res., The Oshawa Group, 1977-87; Dir., Hum. Res., Consumers Gas, 1987-89; VP, Hum. Res., CIBC, 1989-90; Exec. VP, 1990 to date. **SELECTED PUBLICATIONS:** various articles. **AFFIL:** Institute for the Prevention of Child Abuse (Chair, 1995 Fundraising Campaign); Univ. of Guelph (Dir.); Institute of Canadian Bankers (Chrm.). **INTERESTS:** tennis; sailing; skiing; enjoying her two small children. **MISC:** first female Exec. VP in Cdn bnkg history. **COMMENT:** *"Strong interpersonal and business skills, bringing a business perspective to the management of human issues in the workplace with particular expertise in accelerated change management."*

Dasko, Donna, B.A.,M.A.,Ph.D. ■ $ ⚛

Vice-President, ENVIRONICS RESEARCH GROUP LIMITED, 33 Bloor St. E., Toronto, ON M4W 3H1 (416) 920-9010. Born Winnipeg. m. Michael Adams. 2 ch. **EDUC:** Univ. of Manitoba, B.A. 1973; Univ. of Toronto, M.A.(Soc.) 1974, Ph.D.(Soc.) 1982. **CAREER:** Fac. Mbr. & Lecturer, Dept. of Soc., Univ. of Manitoba & Univ. of Toronto; VP, Environics Research Group Limited. **SELECTED PUBLICATIONS:** several articles in academic & bus. publications. **AFFIL:** United Way of Greater Toronto (Bd. of Dir.); Statistics Canada Advisory Council on Social Conditions. **MISC:** frequent commentator in the media on current pol. events. **COMMENT:** *"Donna Dasko is the Vice-President of Environics, one of Canada's leading public-opinion research firms. She is director of Environics' FOCUS CANADA Report, which is this country's largest regularly conducted public-opinion survey drawing on a database of national surveys going back to 1976. She specializes in the area of political and social trends."*

Dassinger, Janet, B.A. ✊ 🍁 🎓

Director of Training Programs and Policies and Assistant to the Canadian Director, National Training Fund, UNITED FOOD AND COMMERCIAL WORKERS INTERNATIONAL UNION (UFCW), 61 International Blvd., Ste. 300, Rexdale, ON M9W 6K4 (416) 675-1104, FAX 675-6919. **EDUC:** McMaster Univ., B.A.(Labour Studies). **CAREER:** Asst. Dir., Metro Labour Educ. Centre; Coord., Layoff & Closure Program, UFCW, 1991; Dir. of Training Programs & Policies. **AFFIL:** Canadian Labour Force Development Bd. (Standing Committee on Hum. Res. Planning); Ontario Federation of Labour (Subcommittee on Adjustment; Alternative, Educ. Committee); Canadian Labour Congress (Training Committee); Dufferin-Peel Association of the NDP (VP). **MISC:** is an ex-officio member of 2 joint labour training initiatives in grocery products mfg, & retail food & food distribution.

Daurio, Beverley Ann (née Hallard, later changed to Smith) ■ ■ 📖 📜

Editor in Chief, THE MERCURY PRESS (book publisher). President, THE MERCURY PRESS PUBLISHERS INC. Born Toronto 1953. m. Donald Daurio. 2 ch. Lydia Ann, Amelia Mary. **EDUC:** York Univ. & Univ. of Toronto, English Lit. **CAREER:** Asst. Ed., *Onion: The Toronto Paper on the Arts*, 1975-81; Asst. Ed., *Ichor* (fiction magazine), 1980-81; Fiction Reviews Ed., *Cross-Canada Writers' Magazine*, 1984-89; Ed. in Chief, Aya Press, 1985-89; Ed. in Chief, *Poetry Canada Review*, 1986-89; Ed. in

Chief, *Paragraph*, 1989-92; freelance Ed., *The Blue Pencil*, 1979 to date; Ed. in Chief, The Mercury Press, 1990 to date; Publisher & Acting Ed., *Paragraph: The Canadian Fiction Review*, 1993 to date. SELECTED PUBLICATIONS: *Hell & Other Novels*, fiction (Coach House Press, 1992); *Internal Document*, essay (Streetcar Editions, 1992); *His Dogs*, fiction (Underwhich Editions, 1990); *Justice*, fiction (Moonstone Press, 1988); *If Summer Had a Knife*, poetry (Wolsak & Wynn, 1987); *Next in Line*, fiction (Identity, 1982); Ed., *Hard Times: A New Fiction Anthology* (1990); Ed., *Vivid: Stories by Five Women* (1989); Ed., *Love and Hunger: New Fiction* (1988); Co-ed. with Luise von Flotow, *Ink & Strawberries: An Anthology of Quebec Women's Fiction* (1988); short fiction & poetry in magazines across Canada incl.: *Poetry Canada Review*; *Zymergy*; *Grain*; *Room of One's Own*; *Quarry*; *Best Canadian Stories*; *Snapshots: Short Short Fiction* (Black Moss Press); *This Magazine*; *Canadian Woman Studies*; also in publications in UK & Australia; in *The Wild Woman Reader* (The Overlook Press, US); non-fiction in: *Sub-Terrain*; *Thinking Through the Process of Writing* (McGraw-Hill); *Contemporary Literary Criticism*; *Language in Her Eye: Views on Writing and Gender by Canadian Women Writing in English* (Coach House Press); *The Globe and Mail*; *Books in Canada*; *Poetry Canada Review*; *Cinémag*; & others. EDIT: Ed. Bd., Underwhich Editions, 1989-91. AFFIL: Writers' Union of Canada; Association of Canadian Publishers; Ontario Book Publishers' Organization; Literary Press Group. HONS: nominated for Best First Book of Poetry in Canada (*If Summer Had a Knife*), Gerald Lampert Award, 1988; Barbara Deming Memorial Fund (Brooklyn, N.Y.) grant, 1991. MISC: readings, teaching & lectures at numerous conferences, galleries, bookstores, etc.

David, Cynthia, B.A. ⌣
Food Editor, THE TORONTO SUN, 333 King St. E., Toronto, ON M5A 3X5 (416) 947-2271, FAX 947-2446. Born Cochrane, Ont. 1956. s. EDUC: Queen's Univ., French 1975-76; Ryerson Polytechnical Institute (now Univ.), B.A.(Journalism) 1979; George Brown Coll., chef training 1985-86. CAREER: reporter, *London Free Press, Kingston Whig Standard, Windsor Star, Woodstock Sentinel Review*, CBC National Radio News, Radio Beijing, 1978-85; Food Ed., *The Toronto Sun*, 1989 to date. SELECTED PUBLICATIONS: freelance writing for *Canadian Living* magazine AFFIL: Association of Food Journalists, N.A.; Women's Culinary Network; Taoist Tai Chi Association. HONS: winner of a $7,000 schol-

arship from the International Foodservice Editorial Council to study food & wine in France for 6 months in 1986. INTERESTS: travelling; music; tai chi; cooking. COMMENT: *"Cynthia is a seasoned journalist and world traveler who shares her excitement about food and the food industry each week with her* Toronto Sun *readers."*

Davies, Christine, LL.B.,LL.M.,Q.C. ⌣ ⌓
Professor, UNIVERSITY OF ALBERTA, 468 Law Centre, Edmonton, AB T6G 2W5 (403) 492-5587. Born UK 1943. d. 3 ch. EDUC: Univ. of Wales, LL.B.(Law) 1964; Univ. of Pennsylvania, LL.M.(Law) 1966. CAREER: Assoc. Prof. of Law, Univ. of Windsor, 1972-75; Prof. of Law, Univ. of Alberta, 1975 to date. SELECTED PUBLICATIONS: *Family Law in Canada* (1985). AFFIL: Law Society of Alberta (Bencher 1990-96); Canadian Research Institute for Law & the Family (VP). HONS: Q.C., 1990. INTERESTS: swimming; opera; ballet.

Davies, Christine E., B.A.,M.B.,B.Ch., B.A.O.,C.C.F.P. ⊕
Physician. 28 King St., Ste. 3B, Saint John, NB E2L 1G3 (506) 634-7772, FAX 634-7101. Born Northern Ireland 1948. m. Dr. E. Colin Davies. 3 ch. EDUC: Trinity Coll., Dublin, B.A. 1970, M.B., B.Ch., B.A.O 1972. CAREER: Intern, Queen Elizabeth Hospital, Montreal, 1972-73; Emergency Rm. Physician, 1973-82; Lecturer, Family Medicine, McGill Univ., 1980-82; Lecturer, Family Medicine, Dalhousie Univ., 1982 to date; Active Staff, Family Medicine, Saint John Regional Hospital, 1982 to date; Active Staff, St. Joseph's Hospital, 1982 to date; Active Mbr., Family Medicine Teaching Unit, Saint John Regional Hospital, 1989 to date; Reproductive Clinic, 1993 to date; family practice, Saint John, 1982 to date. SELECTED PUBLICATIONS: "The Incidence of Chlamydia in an Urban Family Practice" (1985). AFFIL: Medical Coll. of Canada (Licentiate); Canadian Medical Association; Coll. of Family Physicians of Canada; Federation of Medical Women of Canada (Pres. 1987-88); Coll. of Physicians & Surgeons of N.B. (Council Mbr.); Region 2 Medical Staff (Exec. Mbr.); Society of Adolescent Medicine; Church of St. Andrew & St. David (Bd. Mbr.). INTERESTS: gardening; piano; reading; boating; cross-country skiing. MISC: Mbr., Sexual Assault Response Team, 1989 to date. COMMENT: *"I am a family physician with special interests in women's health issues and adolescent health. I have been working for many years to reduce the incidence of teen pregnancy by improving sex education and making birth control accessible to teens."*

Davies, Gwendolyn, B.A.,M.A., Ph.D. ■ ■ ☞ 📖

Head and Professor of English, ACADIA UNIVERSITY, Dept. of English, Wolfville, NS B0P 1X0 (902) 542-2201, ext. 1503, FAX 542-4727, EMAIL Gdavies@max.acadiau.ca. Born Halifax 1942. d. EDUC: Dalhousie-King's, B.A.(English/Hist.) 1963; Univ. of Toronto, Ontario Coll. of Education, Educ. Certificate (English/Hist.) 1964/69; Univ. of Toronto, M.A.(English) 1969; York Univ., Ph.D. (English) 1980. CAREER: secondary sch. teacher, East York Collegiate, 1963-67; Asst. Head of English, 1969-72; Asste. Associée canadienne, Univ. de Bordeaux III, 1974-75; joined Dept. of English, Mount Allison Univ., 1976; Asst. Dir. of Cdn Studies, 1980-81; Head of English, 1985-88; joined Dept. of English, Acadia Univ., 1988; Head of English, 1991-92 & 1994 to date. SELECTED PUBLICATIONS: scholarly edition of Thomas McCulloch's *The Mephibosheth Stepsure Letters* (1990); *Studies in Maritime Literacy History* (1991[2]); *Myth and Milieu: Atlantic Literature & Culture: 1918-1939*, ed. (1993); *Canadian Poetry: From the Beginnings Through the First World War*, co-ed. with Carole Gerson; "Gendered Responses: The Seccombe Diaries" in Margaret Conrad, ed., *Intimate Relations: Family & Community in Planter Nova Scotia, 1750-1800* (Fredericton: Acadiensis Press, 1995, pp. 132-140); "James DeMille's Inaugural Discourse at Acadia College, 1861," *University of Toronto Quarterly*, Vol. 64, No. 3, Summer 1995, pp. 431-443; "J.D. Logan and The Great Feud for Canadian Literature: 1915-1923," *Canadian Issues: Canadian Studies At Home and Abroad*, Vol. XVII, 1995, pp. 113-128; "Marshall Saunders and *Beautiful Joe: Education Through Fiction*," monograph, Dawson Lecture, N.S. Teachers' Coll., Truro, N.S. (29 Mar. 1995), pp. 1-29; "The Literary 'New Woman' and Social Activism in Maritime Literature, 1880-1920" in Janet Guildford & Suzanne Morton, eds., *Separate Spheres: Women's Worlds in the 19th-Century Maritimes* (Fredericton: Acadiensis Press, 1994, pp. 233-250). AFFIL: Acadiensis Press (Advisory Bd.); *Newfoundland Studies* (Advisory Bd.); *The Oxford Companion to Canadian Literature*, Second Edition (Advisory Bd.). HONS: Dawson Lecturer, N.S. Teachers' Coll., 1995; medal marking 125th anniversary of Cdn Confederation, for contribution to Cdn studies, 1993; Acadia Associated Alumni Award for Excellence in Teaching, 1992; W. Stewart MacNutt Memorial Lecturer, Univ. of N.B., 1992. INTERESTS: walking; local history; reading. MISC: has published & lectured widely on Maritime provinces' literature & culture. COMMENT: *"Interested in regional liter-*

ature, culture and history, I see myself as primarily a teacher and researcher of Atlantic Canada."

Davies, Jessie, B.A.,M.Phil. ☞ 🌿

Director, Environment and Sustainable Development Research Centre, UNIVERSITY OF NEW BRUNSWICK, Box 4400, Fredericton, NB E3B 5A3 (506) 453-4886, FAX (506) 453-4883, EMAIL enviro@unb.ca. Born Wyoming 1942. m. Huw. 2 ch. Llewellyn, Shiannon. EDUC: Cornell Univ., B.A. 1964; Cambridge Univ., M.Phil. 1989. CAREER: Ed. Asst., Houghton Mifflin Publishing Company, 1964-66; Teacher, Massachusetts Audubon Society, 1972-74; Consultant, Environmental Sciences & Planning Div., Jacques Whitford Environment Ltd., 1989-94; Dir., Environment & Sustainable Dev. Research Centre, Univ. of New Brunswick, 1994 to date. SELECTED PUBLICATIONS: *Manual for Handling Hazardous Materials in Institutions* (Office of Waste Mgmt Div., Hazardous Waste Mgmt Div., Environment Canada). AFFIL: N.B. Environmental Industries Association; Shell Environmental Fund (Atlantic Reg.); International Association of Impact Assessment (VP); Nature Trust of N.B. (Trustee; VP, Fundraising Committee); Conservation Council of N.B.; Association of Professional Engineers of N.B. (Lay Mbr. of Council 1991-94); Ecological Science Cooperative, Huntsman Marine Science Centre (Steering Committee); N.B. Environmental Industries Association (Dir.); Projet de Société (Chair, working group); N.B. Craft Council. HONS: Res. Assoc. (Hon.), Univ. of New Brunswick. INTERESTS: environment; women's rights. COMMENT: *"Jessie Davies has a strong commitment and interest in both the natural and the human environment. Her work focuses on working with people toward sustainable development."*

Davies, Laureen, B.Sc. ■ $

Vice-President, Commercial Services, AIR BC, 5520 Miller Rd., Richmond, BC V7B 1L9 (604) 273-2464, FAX 244-2676. Born Montreal 1956. m. Michael. 2 ch. EDUC: Marianopolis Coll., D.E.C.(Psych.) 1975; Concordia Univ., B.Sc.(Psych.) 1978; Univ. of Western Ontario, Exec. Dip. 1992. CAREER: Grad. Hire, Air Canada, 1978-79; Proj. Analyst, Strategy, 1979-81; Passenger Forecast Analyst, 1982-83; Product Planner, 1983-85; Mgr, Product Dev., Asia, 1985-86; Mgr, Product Dev., U.S., 1986-89; Dir., Int'l Routes, 1989-92; Dir., Product Mgmt, N.A. Short-Haul Routes, 1992-93; Gen. Mgr, Airport Customer Svc., B.C. & Pacific Rim, 1993-96. DIRECTOR: AirBC; 2776537 Canada Inc. (Vancouver

Airport De-icing Facility). **AFFIL:** Quality Council of B.C.; Vancouver Airline Operating Committee. **HONS:** Award of Excellence, Air Canada, 1989. **INTERESTS:** golf; cooking. **MISC:** involved, with spouse, in running a gourmet coffee business. **COMMENT:** *"I thrive on challenge, including balancing career and home life. My success is founded on the belief that our people are the true assets of our company. My achievements are a reflection of my leadership and teamwork skills that are necessary to reach and exceed our corporate vision and objectives."*

Davies, Patricia, B.A. 📖 ✏️
Writer, Editor, Communications Consultant. 11 Sparkhall Ave., Toronto, ON M4K 1G4 (416) 465-3081, FAX 465-8215. Born Toronto 1945. d. 2 ch. Evan, Elizabeth. **EDUC:** Univ. of Toronto, B.A.(English) 1968. **CAREER:** Prod. Asst., "As It Happens," CBC Radio, 1971-73; Copy Ed., *Miss Chatelaine* magazine, 1973-76; Staff Ed., *The Globe and Mail*, 1976-85; freelance writer, ed., comm. consultant, workshop leader, 1986 to date. **SELECTED PUBLICATIONS:** various articles in *The Globe and Mail, Report on Business Magazine, Toronto Magazine, Chatelaine, Canadian Business, Vista, Pathways*, Bank of Montreal's *First Bank News, Verve, Modern Women, The Financial Post's Small Business Magazine, Toronto Life*; newsletters & reports for various corporations & nonprofit agencies & institutions; video scripts for gov't ministries & corporations; speeches for professional associations. **AFFIL:** Bellefair United Church; St. Clair Club. **HONS:** National Magazine Award, Gold, 1989. **INTERESTS:** choral singing; tennis; quilting; reading; aerobics; cross-county skiing. **MISC:** presented writing workshop to Hum. Res. Mgmt Association, Brock Univ., 1995 and Faculty of Business, Ryerson Polytechnic Univ., 1996.

Davies, Rita, B.A.,M.A. ⊗ ❦
Executive Director, TORONTO ARTS COUNCIL, 141 Bathurst St., Toronto, ON M5V 2R2 (416) 392-6800, FAX 392-6920. Born Shanghai, China 1947. d. **EDUC:** Glendon Coll., York Univ., B.A.(English) 1971; Massey Coll., Univ. of Toronto, M.A.(Drama) 1972. **CAREER:** Exec. Dir., National Magazine Awards, 1980-82; Exec. Dir., Toronto Arts Council, 1982 to date. **AFFIL:** Toronto Arts Awards (Founding Bd. member); Toronto Artscape Inc. (Past Dir. & Founder); Community Arts Ontario (Steering Committee); City of Toronto Arts & Tourism Task Force; Univ. of Toronto Area Study (Reference Group); Arts & the Cities (Past Dir.); City of Toronto

Awards Nominating Committee (Past Mbr.). **INTERESTS:** arts; literature; sailing. **COMMENT:** *"During my tenure at the TAC, I have worked to expand municipal arts support in Toronto to all sectors of the arts, most recently to previously under-served artists from Toronto's many specific cultural communities. TAC is recognized as a national influence on progressive arts funding policies and practices across Canada; it has become Canada's fourth-largest arm's-length arts funding body."*

Davis, Ann, B.Sc.,C.A.,C.M.C. ■ $ ✿ ○
Partner, KPMG, Commerce Ct. Postal Stn, Box 31, Toronto, ON M2R 1W4 (416) 777-8587, FAX 777-3077. President, KPMG ENVIRONMENTAL SERVICES INC. **EDUC:** Queen's Univ., B.Sc. 1976; Canadian Institute of Chartered Accountants, C.A. 1979; Certified Management Consultant, C.M.C. 1994. **CAREER:** C.A., KPMG; Ptnr, 1987 to date; Sr. VP, KPMG Environmental Services Inc., 1992-95; Pres., 1995 to date. **AFFIL:** Canadian Standards Association (Tech. Committee); Canadian Institute of Chartered Accountants (Chair, Task Force on Consideration of Environmental Matters in a Fin. Statement Audit; Mbr., Study Group on Reporting on Environmental Performance; Co-Chair, Adv. Committee on Sustainable Dev.); Canadian Environmental Council (Operating Committee); Board of Trade of Metropolitan Toronto (Environment Policy Committee); Canadian Centre for Philanthropy (Treas. & Dir.); Variety Club (Fin. & Admin. Committee). **MISC:** Judge, *Financial Post* Environmental Reporting Awards; Chair, Judges Panel, *Financial Post* Environment Awards for Business.

Davis, Julie Diane ☺
Regional Director, CANADIAN UNION OF PUBLIC EMPLOYEES, 305 Milner Ave., Ste. 901, Scarborough, ON M1B 3V4 (416) 292-3999, FAX 292-2839. Born Brantford, Ont. 1957. d. 1 ch. **CAREER:** Staff Rep., Canadian Union of Public Employees, 1974-86; Exec. VP, Ontario Federation of Labour, 1986-88; Sec.-Treas., 1988-96. **AFFIL:** International Centre for Human Rights & Democratic Development, Montreal (Bd. Mbr.); Ryerson Polytechnic Univ. (Bd. Mbr. 1988-94; V-Chair 1993); Ont. NDP (Pres. 1991-94; Chair); Fed. NDP (VP 1987-95); Ontario Press Council; Action Canada Network (Founding Mbr.; Chair, Steering Committee). **HONS:** Women of Distinction Award, YWCA, 1988; Hon. Fellowship (Pol. & Public Admin.), Ryerson Polytechnic Univ., 1995. **COMMENT:** *"Longtime activist inside the labour movement–moving through the years from member to staff repre-*

sentative to full-time elected political office in 1986. Active in my political party of choice. Interested in women's issues, human rights issues and coalition work–all with a goal to building an economically and socially just society."

Davis, Marie, M.A. 🚪 ⬥ 🎓
Associate Editor, CANADIAN CHILDREN'S LITER-ATURE, Department of English, University of Guelph, Guelph, ON N1G 2W1 (519) 824-4120, ext. 3189, FAX 837-1315, EMAIL mdavis@bosshog.arts.uwo.ca. Professor, Department of English, UNIVERSITY OF WEST-ERN ONTARIO. Born St. Catharines, Ont. 1961. s. EDUC: McMaster Univ., M.A.(English Lit.) 1985. CAREER: Lecturer, Univ. of Western Ontario, 1991-96; Asst. Ed., *Canadian Children's Literature (CCL)*, 1990-92; Assoc. Ed., 1992 to date. SELECTED PUBLICATIONS: various articles incl.: "Walking on Revolving Walls: Coming of Age in Calgary" (*CCL*, Vol. 57/58, 1990); "Susan Musgrave: An Interview" (*CCL*, Vol. 68, 1992); "'The Big Adventure is Close-In': Jan Truss's Young-Adult Fiction" (*CCL*, Vol. 69, 1993); "Marie-Louise Gay: Canadian Author and Illustrator" (*Children's Literature Review*, Vol. 27, 1993); "Michael Bedard: An Interview" (*CCL*, 82, 1996); "An Interview with Paul Yee" (*CCL*, 83, 1996); "Parable or Parody: Tom King's *Coyote Columbus Story*" (*CCL*, 83, 1996). AFFIL: ACCUTE; Children's Literature Association; Canadian Society for Eighteenth-Century Studies; American Society for Eighteenth-Century Studies. HONS: Rotary Youth Leadership Award, 1981; Pan-Hellenic Council Teaching Award, Univ. of Western Ontario, 1993-94; Teaching Honour Roll, Univ. Students' Council, Univ. of Western Ontario, 1995-96; numerous univ. scholarships & book prizes. INTERESTS: contemporary children's lit.; 18th-century women's autobiographical writings; post structuralist & feminist theory & criticism; folklore. COMMENT: *"I am dedicated to improving the quality of Canadian children's literature through the kind of steady, clear-eyed critical assessment of it that our journal offers. I am also devoted to the task of understanding the intricacies and oddities of autobiographical writing and to the task of bringing literature to life for my students."*

Davison, Margaret L. (Peggy), B.A., B.Ed. ◯ ⊕
Chairman, Board of Directors, VICTORIA GEN-ERAL HOSPITAL FOUNDATION, 1278 Tower Rd., Halifax, NS B3H 2Y9 (902) 428-3932. Born Sydney, N.S. 1937. m. Justice John M. Davison. 2 ch. EDUC: Acadia Univ., B.A.(Biol.)

1957, B.Ed.(Educ.) 1958. CAREER: taught sch., Halifax & Winnipeg. AFFIL: Junior League of Halifax (Pres. 1972-74); Victoria General Hospital (VP, Bd. of Commissioners 1978-91); N.S. Association of Health Organizations (Chrm 1984-86); Canadian Hospital Association (Chair 1988-89). HONS: Silver Jubilee Award, 1977; Health Service Award, Bluenose Chapter, CCHSE, 1989; Hon. Membership, N.S. Association of Health Organizations, 1990; created, with the Bd. of Commissioners of Victoria General Hospital, the Davison Award to honour commitment to values of compassion, integrity, accountability & competence, 1994; Award of Excellence for Service & Leadership, Bd. of Dir. of the Canadian Healthcare Association, 1996. INTERESTS: golf; skiing; tole painting; bridge; needlework; reading. COMMENT: *"Through my volunteer involvement, I am constantly challenged to learn new things, meet new people and take on new endeavours. It has been an incredibly enriching 30-year journey."*

Davison, Rosena, B.A.,M.A.,Ph.D. ⬥
Associate Professor, Department of French, SIMON FRASER UNIVERSITY, Burnaby, BC V5A 1S6 (604) 291-3549, FAX 291-5932, EMAIL rdavison@sfu.ca. Born UK 1943. m. Douglas Bruce. 3 ch. EDUC: McGill Univ., B.A.(French) 1971, M.A.(French Lit.) 1974, Ph.D. 1981. CAREER: Asst. Prof., Simon Fraser Univ., 1982-90; Chair, Dept. of French, 1991-94; Assoc. Prof., 1990 to date. SELECTED PUBLICATIONS: *Diderot et Galiani: étude d'une amitié philosophique* (Oxford: Voltaire Foundation, 1985); Critical edition of Mme. d'Epinay's *Les Conversations d'Emilie* (Oxford: Voltaire Foundation, 1996); "A French Troupe in Naples in 1773: A Theatrical Curiosity" (*Theatre Research* 1985); "Diderot vu par ses contemporains italiens" (*Man and Nature* 1986); "Diderot, Galiani and Vico: un itinéraire philosophique" (*Diderot Studies* 1988); "Une source italienne de Jean-François Rameau" in *Studies on Voltaire and the Eighteenth Century* (Oxford: The Voltaire Foundation, 1989); "Mme. d'Epinay's Contribution to Girls' Education" in *Women Intellectuals of the French Eighteenth Century* (New York: Peter Lang, 1994); various other publications & papers delivered at conferences. EDIT: Co-Ed., *Man and Nature*, Vol. 8, 1990. AFFIL: Association Interdisciplinaire de Recherche sur l'Épistolaire; Canadian Society for Eighteenth Century Studies (Discipline Rep. in French); American Society for 18th Century Studies; Association des Professeurs de français aux Universités et Collèges canadiens; Canadian Society for Aesthetics; Modern Language Association.

INTERESTS: art hist.; contemporary lit.; theatre; opera. MISC: grant recipient. COMMENT: *"A late starter in the academic world, I have found two challenges particularly satisfying: 1) making students excited about learning, 2) the intellectual challenge of my research."*

Dawe, Mary E. $ ✋ 📖
Editorial Consultant and Writer. 8726 - 116 St., Edmonton, AB T6G 1P7 (403) 433-3017, FAX 439-4212. Born 1926. 2 ch. James, John. CAREER: Admin. Asst., Imperial Oil Ltd., 1948-56; Ed. & Publisher, *Canadian Author & Bookman*, 1969-75; Founding Ed., *Heritage* magazine, 1972-81; Ed., Worth Royal Commission Report on Educ., 1972; Instructor, Writing Workshops, Prov. of Alta. & others, 1972 to date; Co-Host & Writer, "Time of Your Life," CFRN TV, 1981-92; Broadcaster & Writer, "Alberta Legacy," CISN Radio, 1982; speech writer, various clients, 1984 to date; Ed., *Spectrum*, 1985-87; Lecturer, Univ. of Alberta, Grant MacEwan Coll., Lakeland Coll.; Pres. & CEO, Hugh J. Dawe Ltd., 1989 to date. SELECTED PUBLICATIONS: *A Choice of Futures*, Ed. (1972); *Edmonton Police Service–The First 100 Years*, Ed., 1993. AFFIL: Canadian Writers' Foundation (Dir.); Canadian Authors' Association Fund (Dir.); Cathedral Close Foundation (Dir.); Writers' & Publishers' Committee (Dir.); Young Alberta Book Festival Society (Founding Pres.); CANCOPY, Canadian Reprograpy Collective (Dir.); Canadian Authors' Association (Nat'l Pres. 1989-93). HONS: Silver Medal, Canadian Authors' Association; Alberta Achievement Award for Excellence in Lit.; Cultural Award, City of Edmonton; Allan Sangster Award for Service to Writers. INTERESTS: reading; music; travel.

Dawe, Shirley A. $
President and Owner, SHIRLEY DAWE ASSOCIATES INC., 119 Crescent Rd., Toronto, ON M4W 1T8 (416) 963-9446, FAX 963-8654. Born Vancouver 1946. m. John B. Dawe. 1 ch. EDUC: Univ. of British Columbia, Econ. 1964-67; McGill Univ., Econ. 1967-68. CAREER: Gen. Mgr, Merchandising, Hudson's Bay Company, 1969-84; Pres., Shirley Dawe Associates Inc., 1986 to date. DIRECTOR: Dominion Textile Inc; Gilmore's Inc., Specialty Stores, Michigan; Moore Corporation; Silcorp Ltd. AFFIL: Matinée Ltd. Fashion Foundation (Advisory Bd. Dir.); The Fashion Group International, Toronto Chapter (Founding Chair, Advisory Bd. 1989-95); Ontario Retail Sector Proj. (Working Group 1994-95); Retail Council of Canada; Children's Aid Society Foundation (Fundraising Exec. Committee 1989-93); Sch. of Fashion, Ryerson Polytechnic Univ. (Advisory Bd. 1988-93). INTERESTS: design; gardening; tennis; health & well-being issues. MISC: former dir. or affiliated with: C.B. Pak (1986-89), General Foods Canada Inc. (1986-89); Ontario Development Corp. (1991-96); Loeb Inc. (1992-93); Bus. Sch., Mount St. Vincent Univ., N.S. (1987-89). COMMENT: *"After a 15-year, high-profile career as a senior manager in the dynamic retail sector, Dawe has taken her knowledge of consumer marketing and product development into the consulting arena and corporate directorships."*

Dawson, Eleanor Ruth, B.Sc.,LL.B. ⚖ ♡
Partner, AIKINS, MACAULAY & THORVALDSON, 360 Main St., 30th Fl., Winnipeg, MB R3C 4G1 (204) 957-4682, FAX 957-0840. Born Burnaby, B.C. 1953. s. EDUC: Univ. of Manitoba, B.Sc.(Chem.) 1973, LL.B. 1976. CAREER: practised civil litigation with A.K. Twaddle, Q.C., 1977-84; Cnsl, Law Society of Manitoba, 1984-86; Ptnr, Aikins, MacAulay & Thorvaldson, 1986 to date. AFFIL: Canadian Federation of Humane Societies (Dir. 1985 to date; Pres. 1992 to date); Winnipeg Humane Society (Dir. 1983-95; Pres. 1989-92); Manitoba Law Reform Commission (Commissioner); The Advocates' Society; The Selden Society. HONS: appointed Q.C., 1988; Canada 125 Medal, 1992. MISC: Lecturer, Fac. of Law, Univ. of Manitoba, 1986-92. COMMENT: *"A lawyer in private practice who has endeavored to contribute to her profession through teaching and law reform and to her community through animal welfare."*

Dawson, Mary E., B.A.,B.C.L.,D.E.S.D., LL.B.,Q.C. 🍁
Associate Deputy Minister, Department of Justice, GOVERNMENT OF CANADA, 239 Wellington St., Rm. 650, Ottawa, ON K1A 0H8 (613) 957-4898, FAX 952-5279. Born Halifax 1942. m. Peter Dawson. 2 ch. David, Emily. EDUC: McGill Univ., B.A.(Hons., Phil.) 1963, B.C.L. 1966; Univ. of Ottawa, D.E.S.D. 1968; Dalhousie Univ., LL.B. 1970. BAR: Que., 1967; N.S., 1970; Ont., 1996. CAREER: Tax Researcher, Revenue Canada, 1967-68; Legal Cnsl, 1968-69; Teaching Fellow, Dalhousie Univ., 1969-70; Legislative Drafter, Dept. of Justice, 1970-79; Assoc. Chief Legislative Cnsl, 1980-86; Asst. Deputy Min., Public Law Sector, Fed. Dept. of Justice, 1986-88; Assoc. Deputy Min., 1988 to date. AFFIL: Parkdale United Church. HONS: Univ. Scholar, McGill Univ., 1960; Lyon William Jacobs, Q.C. Award, McGill Law, 1965; Queen's Counsel, 1978. INTERESTS: nordic skiing; swimming; theatre; reading. COMMENT: *"Legal and policy advisor to the Government of Canada espe-*

cially in constitutional, native, administrative, human rights areas. Drafter of many important laws, including the Constitution. Senior manager."

Dawson, T. Brettel, LL.B.(Hons), LL.M. ⌂ ⚖

Chair, Department of Law, CARLETON UNIVERSITY, Loeb Bldg., 1125 Colonel By Dr., C473, Ottawa, ON K1S 5B6 (613) 520-3690, FAX 520-4467, EMAIL bdawson@ccs.carleton.ca. Born Christchurch, New Zealand 1959. partner M.A. MacDonald. EDUC: Univ. of Canterbury, N.Z., LL.B.(Hons.) 1981; Osgoode Hall Law Sch., LL.M. 1988. CAREER: Barrister & Solicitor, Duncan Cotterill & Co., N.Z., 1982-83; Asst. Prof., Carleton Univ., 1986-91; Assoc. Dir., Women's Studies, 1991-92; Assoc. Prof., 1991; Senate, 1993 to date; Chair, Dept. of Law, 1994 to date. SELECTED PUBLICATIONS: various papers in refereed journals incl.: "Sexual Assault Law and Evidence of the Sexual Conduct of the Primary Witness: The Construction of Relevance" (*Canadian Journal of Women and the Law*, 2, 1987-88); "Estoppel and Obligation: The Modern Role of Estoppel by Convention" (*Legal Studies*, 9, 1989); "Legal Research in a Social Science Setting: The Problem of Method" (*Dalhousie Law Journal*, 1992); ed., *Women, Law and Social Change: Core Readings and Current Issues*, 2nd ed. (Toronto, Captus Press, 1993); numerous papers, book reviews & articles. AFFIL: Canadian Law & Society Association (Dir.); National Association of Women & the Law; Canadian Council of Canadian Law Deans; *Canadian Journal of Women and the Law* (Bd.). INTERESTS: feminist legal theory; writing; gardening; wine; travel; music. MISC: Mbr., Panel of Bds. of Inquiry (Ont.), 1987 to date. COMMENT: *"As an academic, I explore critical analysis of law; as an adjudicator, I plumb its application; as a teacher I encourage curiosity; as an administrator I seek to steward a pluralistic intellectual milieu."*

Day, Eileen B. 📖 $

Principal, BURGESS DAY COMMUNICATIONS, 7669 Endersby St., Burnaby, BC V3N 3Y8 (604) 520-7632, FAX 521-6929, EMAIL eday@unixg.ubc.ca. Born St. John's 1960. m. Terry C. Day. 2 ch. Bridget, Conor. EDUC: Memorial Univ. of Newfoundland, Liberal Arts 1977-81; Southern Alberta Institute of Technology, Diploma (Journalism) 1983-85; Univ. of British Columbia, Multimedia Studies, 1995 to date; ongoing writing, comm. & public rel'ns training. CAREER: Ed., *Emergency* (trade magazine for health care industry); Dir. of Comm., The Loewen Group Inc., 1989-96; Founder,

Burgess Day Communications, 1996 to date. AFFIL: International Association of Business Communicators; Editors' Association of Canada. HONS: awards for annual reports written: *AR100* (lists top 100 annual reports in North America), 1990; Monadock Award of Excellence, 1990; Gilbert Graphics Award of Excellence, 1990; Merit Award for Excellence, *Studio Magazin*, 1991; Bronze Award, *Financial Post*, 1992; Silver Birch Award, International Television Association of Canada, 1994. INTERESTS: reading; guitar; writing children's poetry.

Day, Peggy, B.A.,M.A.,M.T.S., Ph.D. ■ ⌂ ☼ 📖

Associate Professor and Chair, Department of Religious Studies, UNIVERSITY OF WINNIPEG, 515 Portage Ave., Winnipeg, MB R3B 2E9 (204) 786-9415, FAX 774-4134. Born Winnipeg 1954. EDUC: Univ. of British Columbia, B.A. 1975, M.A. 1977; Harvard Divinity Sch., M.T.S. 1979; Harvard Univ., Ph.D. 1986. CAREER: Teaching Fellow, Harvard Univ., 1981-86; Instructor in Biblical Hebrew, Harvard Divinity Sch., 1983-86; Asst. Prof. of Old Testament, Fac. of Divinity, Trinity Coll., Univ. of Toronto, 1986-89; Assoc. Prof. & Chair, Dept. of Religious Studies, Univ. of Winnipeg, 1989 to date. SELECTED PUBLICATIONS: *An Adversary in Heaven: śāṭān in the Hebrew Bible* (Atlanta: Scholars, 1988); *Gender and Difference in Ancient Israel*, ed. (Minneapolis: Fortress 1989); *The Bible and the Politics of Exegesis*, ed. with David Jobling & Gerald T. Sheppard (Cleveland: Pilgrim, 1991); various other publications. EDIT: Ed. Bd., *Journal of Biblical Literature*, 1992-95. AFFIL: SBL (Co-Chair 1994-95, ad hoc Committee on Women in the Profession; Steering Committee; Co-Chair, Hebrew Scriptures & Cognate Literature Section, 1992-95). INTERESTS: volleyball; baseball; gardening; canning. MISC: Co-Chair, Winnipeg Bible Colloquium, 1989-95; Head Coach, Varsity Women's Volleyball, Northeast Univ., 1983-85; Head Coach, Varsity Women's Volleyball, Boston Univ., 1978-79; Mbr., Canada's Nat'l Women's Volleyball Team, 1971-72.

De Cloet, Sharon, L.P.N. ⌂ $ ⊕

President, CAERAN, 25 Penny Lane, Brantford, ON N3R 5Y5 (519) 751-0513, FAX 751-3976. Born Midland, Ont. 1954. d. 2 ch. EDUC: Fanshawe Coll., L.P.N. 1974. CAREER: Pres., CAERAN, 1989 to date. SELECTED PUBLICATIONS: "Consumer Ethics" (*Growth Spurts* Spring 1994); "Knowing the Ingredients in Deodorants Can Make You Sweat!" (*Growth Spurts* Summer 1994).

AFFIL: Brant Community Futures Development Corporation (Dir.); Environmental Choice Program (Task Force Mbr.); Canada Trust Friends of the Environment, Brant County (Dir.); Brant County Environment Group; Brant County Toastmasters. HONS: HomePreneur of the Year, National Home Business Institute, 1992; InAward, National Women's Business Award for New Initiatives, 1993; Table Topics of the Year Award, Brant County Toastmasters, 1994. INTERESTS: raising her children; fitness; the environment; music; live theatre. MISC: gives lectures on environmental issues; various media appearances; gives workshops on running a home-based business. COMMENT: *"Primary pursuit: educating the public on the most important R in the environment: personal Responsibility!"*

de Gruchy, Eileen ⓖ Ⓢ
Executive Secretary, GRAPHIC COMMUNICATIONS INTERNATIONAL UNION, 1110 Finch Ave. W., Ste. 600, Downsview, ON M3J 2T2 (416) 661-9761. Born Montreal 1953. EDUC: Côte des Neiges Commercial Coll., Secretarial Degree 1971. CAREER: Graphic Communications International Union, 25 yrs. INTERESTS: country and community (in general); cross-country skiing; reading; music; arts & crafts; home decorating; dogs. COMMENT: *"Having worked my way up the ladder of life clearly gave me experience in many labour-oriented fields, and the opportunity to meet people from all walks of life. By today's standards, it is rare to have the same employer for 25 consecutive years which, in itself, is a testament to my survival instincts, not to mention capabilities. Technological change continues to run rampant throughout the world and, in some instances, has been merciless. No matter who we are; what type of work we do; or length of service we have been given; being appreciated for our skills, competency, and loyalty, should always be the motivating factors that keep us going strong. No machine will ever replace the human spirit!"*

de Souza, Anna Maria, C.A. Ⓞ Ⓧ
President and Founder, Brazilian Carnival Ball. 5689 2nd Concession B, R.R. 3, Stouffville, ON L4A 7X4. Born Brazil. m. Ivan X. de Souza. EDUC: Collegio Paula Frassinetti, Brazil, Teaching Degree; Escola Técnica de Comercio, C.A. CAREER: Curator, Henry Birks Antique Collection of Silver, 1976-80. VOLUNTEER CAREER: Founder & Pres., Brazilian Carnival Ball, 1966 to date; Convenor, *Madame Butterfly* Opera Ball (to celebrate Birk's 100th Anniversary); Co-Chair, Camp Oochigeas dinner; various fundraising activities for a number of charities. AFFIL: The Canadian Opera Women's Committee; The Breast Cancer Committee of Ontario; The Speech Foundation. HONS: Order of Rio Branco, presented by the Pres. of Brazil; Civic Award, City of Toronto; A ordem do Grande Colar do Brazaó, Brazil; Cidada Benemerita, Brazil; The Queen's Medal of Honour, The Gov. Gen. of Canada; Diamond Award, The Variety Club; The Arbor Award, Univ. of Toronto, 1996. INTERESTS: charitable work; tennis; gardening. MISC: Brazilian Carnival Ball is held every year for a different charity & her volunteer efforts have resulted in raising in excess of $16 million for various charities. COMMENT: *"She arrived in Canada from Brazil in 1965. For the past 31 years, she has involved herself and organized various fundraising activities."*

de Villiers, Priscilla, B.A. Ⓖ ⚔ Ⓧ ♦
President, CAVEAT (Canadians Against Violence Everywhere Advocating Its Termination), 3350 Fairview St., Ste. 3-164, Burlington, ON L7N 3L5 (905) 632-1733, FAX 632-3039. Born Pretoria, S. Africa. 1 ch. Etienne. EDUC: Johannesburg Coll. of Educ., Transvaal Teacher's Higher Educ. Diploma 1968; Univ. of Witwatersrand, B.A. 1968. CAREER: Asst. Stage Mgr, Performing Arts Council of Transvaal, & Stage Mgr, Alexander Theatre, Johannesburg, 1964-65; Secondary Sch. Teacher, King Edward VII High Sch. for Boys, Johannesburg, 1965-68; Foreign Svc. Cadet Diplomate, Pretoria, 1968-69; English Lecturer, Pretoria Normaal Kollege, 1969; English Teacher, Westerford High Sch., Cape Town, & English Lecturer, Johannesburg Coll. of Educ., 1975-76; Child Art Teacher, Ruth Prowse Art Centre, 1976; Artists-in-the-Schools Programme, Hamilton Separate Sch. Bd., 1990-91; Pres., CAVEAT, 1991 to date. SELECTED CREDITS: Interviewer, *Dundas Valley School of Art –An Overview*, video, Cable 14, Hamilton (1985); Interviewer, *Visit the Galleries*, video, Cable 14, Hamilton (1986); Prod. & Ed., *Newfoundlife*, video, Cable 14, Hamilton (1986); Prod. & Interviewer, *Ten Years Collecting, Ten Years Downtown*, video, Cable 14, Hamilton (1987). SELECTED PUBLICATIONS: *Student Teachers' Handbook* (Johannesburg: Johannesburg Coll. of Educ., 1964); art-related articles contributed to *Fusion, The Magazine of Clay and Glass, Hamilton This Month, Metro Magazine, Dundas Star Journal, Forum, Focus* (Ontario Craft Council) & *Artsbeat* (Hamilton Reg. Art Council); victim's rights & crime prevention-related articles contributed to *Association of Canadian Chiefs of Police Directory, CPA Express* (magazine of the Canadian

Police Association); *Hamilton Spectator* & *In Women's Voices: The Journal of Women in Educational Administration in Ontario*; "Afterword," *Fatal Mistakes: The Disturbing Events That Led to the Murder of Nina de Villiers*, by Kevin Marron (Doubleday, 1993). EDIT: Ed., *Kingston Potters' Guild Newsletter*, 1979-80; Asst. Ed., *Fusion, The Magazine of Clay and Glass*, 1982-85; Asst. Ed., *Edges*, International Clay Symposium, Toronto, 1986; Ed., *Stopwatch*, CAVEAT's newspaper, 1993-94. EXHIBITIONS: numerous group & juried exhibitions in Cape Town, South Africa & in S. Ont. (1974-92), incl. CKOC Juried Exhibitions (1983-85), *Exibitart* (1984-90) & Burlington Fine Art Association Juried Exhibitions (1984-89); various solo exhibitions incl. *Recent Works*, Carnegie Gallery, Dundas, Ont. (1984), *Faces of the Gardens*, Burlington, Ont. (1989) & *Mountains of My Mind*, Piano Nobile, Hamilton Place (1990). COLLECTIONS: paintings in many corp. & private collections incl. Hamilton & Region Conservation Authority Headquarters, Canada Trust Regional Head Office, K.N. Crowder, Mfg., & Remco Tire. AFFIL: CAVEAT (Pres.); Canadian Resource Centre for Victims of Crime (Dir.); World Society of Victimology; National Organization for Victim Assistance); National Crime Prevention Council; Conference on Victims & Corrections Services of Canada; Ministry of Justice (Intermediate Sanctions Committee; ad hoc Committee on Crime Prevention); Ministry of the Solicitor Gen. (ad hoc Committee on Dangerous Offenders); Hillfield-Strathallan Coll., Hamilton (Advisor to Educ. Committee). HONS: Woman of the Year in Public Affairs, Hamilton Status of Women Sub-committee, 1992; Distinguished Citizen of the Year Award, Advertising & Sales Club of Hamilton, 1992; Newsmaker of the Year, Woman on the Move Award, *The Toronto Sun*, 1993; Woman of the Year, Sigma Beta Phi, 1993; Paul Harris Fellow, Burlington Rotary, 1993; selected as one of "Canada's Top 50 Female Changemakers," *Chatelaine* Magazine, 1994; LL.D.(Hon.), McMaster Univ., 1995; *Maclean's* Hon. Roll, 1995; Meritorius Medal Award, Gov't of Canada, 1995; Woman of Achievement Award, Hadassah-WIZO Org. of Canada, 1996. MISC: 1st woman Foreign Svc. Cadet Diplomate, Pretoria, 1968-69; numerous submissions to fed. & prov. gov't; numerous speaking engagements; Preparatory Meeting on Workshops for the 9th U.N. Congress on Crime Prevention. COMMENT: *"On August 9, 1991, Nina de Villiers was abducted and murdered by Jonathan Yeo, a man out on bail who had a long history of violence. The de Villiers family decided to launch a petition to give Canadians a means of voicing the fear that society is not protected by the justice system, that victims and their families no longer count. CAVEAT, with Priscilla de Villiers, Nina's mother, as president, was incorporated on June 3, 1992, and became a designated not-for-profit, nongovernmental charitable organization in October 1992. Although the de Villiers petition, with 2.5 million signatures, was presented to the Justice Minister in 1994, the petition is still in circulation."*

Dean, Audrey, B.A.,B.S.W.,M.S.W., LL.B. ■■ ⚖ ✋
Legal Counsel, ALBERTA HUMAN RIGHTS COMMISSION, 187 Wakina Dr., Edmonton, AB T5T 2X5 (403) 481-8034, FAX 487-7260. EDUC: Univ. of Manitoba, B.A., B.S.W., M.S.W.; Univ. of New Brunswick, LL.B. CAREER: Caseworker, Child Protection Dept., Children's Aid Society, Toronto, 1960-61; Child Psychiatric Social Worker, Queen's Univ., Dept. of Child Psychiatry, 1961-63; Sr. Social Worker, Ruslyn House Home for Girls, Winnipeg, 1963-66; Sr. Social Worker, Dept. of Child Psychiatry, University Hospital, Saskatoon, 1966-69; Sr. Social Worker, Saskatoon Public Sch. Bd., 1970-71; Instructor, Institute of Child Guidance, Univ. of Saskatchewan, 1971-72; Asst. Dir., Mental Health Clinic, N.B. Dept. of Health, Fredericton, 1972-75; law student, 1975-78; Legal Consultant, N.B. Dept. of Social Svcs, 1978-80; Legal Consultant, Alta. Family & Social Svcs, 1980-83; articling student, Alta. Justice, 1983-84; Legal Consultant, Family & Social Svcs, 1984-86; Dir., Legislative Svcs, Alta. Educ., 1986-92; Legal Cnsl, Alta. Human Rights Commission, 1992 to date. AFFIL: Alberta Criminal Justice Association-Northern (Chair 1995; Bd. mbr. 1994); Canadian Association for Law & Education (Bd. mbr. 1989-92; VP 1992-93); National Organization for Law & Education (speaker & Chair, conference sessions); Canadian Institute for the Administration of Justice (workshop participant); Canadian Bar Association, Administrative Law subsection; Canadian Association of Social Workers, Prov. chpt. (former Bd. mbr.); Law Society of Alberta; Legal Resource Centre (Speaker's Bureau); Alberta Sch. Attendance Bd. (Tribunal mbr.); Planned Parenthood (former Bd. mbr.); Edmonton Olympic Track & Field (former Bd. mbr.); Canadian Mental Health Association (former Bd. mbr.); Foster Parent Association (former Bd. mbr.); Brownies/Guides.

Dean, Diana ⊗
Artist, DIANA DEAN STUDIO OF FINE ART, 135 Northview Place, Salt Spring Island, BC V8K 1A9 (604) 537-9587. Born 1942. 4 ch. Tom,

Max, Seth, Jacob. **EDUC:** Bath Academy of Art, Corsham, UK, Diploma in Art & Educ., Distinction in Sculpture. **EXHIBITIONS:** solo exhibits, incl. Sculpture Exhibition, Association of International Artists' Gallery, London, UK (1966); Studio Exhibit (1977); Vortex Gallery, Salt Spring Island (1991); *Hidden Values*, McMichael Gallery (1994-95); various exhibitions, Nancy Poole's Studio, Toronto; group exhibitions, incl. Association of International Artists' Group Sculpture Show, London, UK (1965); *Works on Paper*, London Regional Gallery, London, Ont. (1981); *BC Festival of the Arts* (1994,95,96); *Canadian Genre*, Memorial Univ. Gallery St. John's (1987); *Personal Vision in Landscape*, Cambridge Public Gallery (1987); *The Noble Gesture*, Art Gallery Mississauga (1994). **COLLECTIONS:** incl. Confederation Centre Museum & Art Gallery, PEI, Canada Council Art Bank, Northern Arts Association (British Arts Council), & Royal Bank of Canada Corp. Collection; DuPont Canada Inc.; Canadian Paraplegic Association; Norcen Corp. Collection; Owen's Art Gallery, Mount Allison Univ., N.S.; Texaco Canada Inc. Collection. **HONS:** First Prize, Association of International Artists' Group Sculpture Show, London, UK, 1965; Sculpture Commission, Castleford Civic Centre, UK, 1970; Purchase Prize, Mid-Pennine National Sculpture Exhibition, 1971; Jurors' Choice, *Look '94*, 1994.

DeBardeleben, Joan, M.A., Ph.D. ■ ⌖ ⌖
Professor, The Institute of Central/East European and Russian-Area Studies, CARLETON UNIVERSITY, Colonel By Dr., Ottawa, ON K1S 5B6 (613) 520-2888, FAX 520-7501, EMAIL j_debardeleben@carleton.ca. Born Park Falls, Wisc. 1950. 2 ch. **EDUC:** Univ. of Wisconsin-Madison, M.A.(Pol. Sci.) 1974, Ph.D.(Pol. Sci.) 1979. **CAREER:** Asst. Prof. & Lecturer, Colorado State Univ., 1978-80; Asst. Prof., McGill Univ., 1980-85; Assoc. Prof., 1985-91; Assoc. Prof., Carleton Univ., 1991-93; Prof., 1993 to date; Dir., Institute of Central/East European & Russian-Area Studies, 1992-95. **SELECTED PUBLICATIONS:** *Environmental Security and Quality after Communism*, ed. (with John Hannigan) & co-author (Boulder, Col.; Westview 1994); *Soviet Politics in Transition* (Lexington, Maine; DC Heath and Co. 1992); *To Breathe Free: the Environmental Crisis in Eastern Europe*, ed. & co-author (Washington, DC; Wilson Center Press & John Hopkins Press 1991); "The New Politics in the USSR: The Case of the Environment" in *The Soviet Environment: Problems, Policies, and Politics* (Cambridge, UK; Cambridge Univ. Press 1992); "Ecology and Technology in the USSR" in

Technology, Culture and Development: The Experience of the Soviet Model (Armonk, NY; M.E. Sharpe 1992); "'The Future has Already Begun': Environmental Damage and Protection in the German Democratic Republic" in *The Quality of Life in the German Democratic Republic* (Armonk, NY; M.E. Sharpe 1989); "Economic Reform and Environmental Protection in the USSR" (*Soviet Geography* Apr. 1990); *The Environment and Marxism-Leninism: The Soviet and East German Experience* (Boulder, Col.; Westview Press 1985); "Esoteric Policy Debate: Nuclear Safety Issues in the USSR and GDR" (*British Journal of Political Science* 1985); "The Meaning of Elections in Transitional Evidence from Russia and Ukraine," with Jon Pammett (*Electorial Studies*, no. 3 1996). **AFFIL:** Canadian Association of Slavists (Pres.); American Association for the Advancement of Slavic Studies (Bd. of Dir.). **HONS:** Phi Beta Kappa. **INTERESTS:** post-Soviet politics; Russian politics & pol. sociology; environmental policy & problems in the post-Soviet states. **MISC:** Project Dir., "Policy in Russia," a CIDA-funded assistance program, for Russian social scientists; initiator & principal investigator, "Russia's Move to the Market: The Human Factor in the Workplace," funded by a grant from SSHRCC (strategic research grant); "Russia's Regions," funded by the Univ. of Calgary Joint Trust Fund; on the Bd. of Advisors, Monitoring CIS Environmental Developments Proj., Monterey Institute of International Studies, California; has made numerous research visits to the Russian federation in the course of the past 6 yrs. **COMMENT:** *"I am a political scientist specializing in Russia and the post-Soviet states, with several published books and articles. I also comment on public affairs for the media and engage in consulting work."*

Deber, Raisa, S.B.,S.M.,Ph.D. ⌖ ⊕ $
Professor, Department of Health Administration, UNIVERSITY OF TORONTO, McMurrich Bldg., 2nd Fl., Toronto, ON M5S 1A8 (416) 978-8366, FAX 978-7350, EMAIL rdeber@medac.med.utoronto.ca. Born Toronto 1949. m. Charles Deber. 1 ch. **EDUC:** Massachusetts Institute of Technology, S.B. 1971, S.M. 1971, Ph.D. 1977. **CAREER:** Asst. Prof., Dept. of Pol. Sci., Univ. of Wisconsin at Madison, 1975-77; Asst. Prof., Dept. of Health Admin., Univ. of Toronto, 1977-82; Assoc. Prof., 1982-90; Prof., 1990 to date. **SELECTED PUBLICATIONS:** "Using Explicit Decision Rules to Manage Issues of Justice, Risk and Ethics in Decision Analysis: When is it not Rational to Maximize Expected Utility?" (*Medical Decision Making* July-Sept. 1990); "Overconfidence Among

Physicians and Nurses: the 'Micro-certainty, Macro-uncertainty' Phenomenon" (*Social Science and Medicine* 1991); "Canadian Medicare: Can it Work in the United States? Will it Survive in Canada?" (*American Journal of Law and Medicine* 1993); "The Patient-Physician Partnership: Decision Making, Problem Solving, and the Desire to Participate" (*Canadian Medical Association Journal* Aug. 1994); *Case Studies in Canadian Health Policy and Management* (Canadian Hospital Association Press, 1992); numerous other publications. AFFIL: American Political Science Association; Canadian Political Science Association; Society for Medical Decision Making; Policy Studies Organization; Canadian Health Economics Research Association; International Society for Technology Assessment in Health Care; Judgement/Decision Making Group; Phi Beta Kappa; Sigma Xi. INTERESTS: reading; computers; food. MISC: listed in *Canadian Who's Who*; recipient of numerous grants. COMMENT: *"Raisa Deber is a Professor in the Department of Health Administration, University of Toronto who has published and consulted widely on health policy."*

Debien, Maud, B.Ed.,B.A.,M.P. ♣

Deputée, Laval-Est, GOVERNMENT OF CANADA, House of Commons, 534 Confederation Building, Ottawa, ON K1A 0A6 (613) 992-0611, FAX (613) 992-8556. Born Qué. 1938. m. Léon Debien. 3 ch. Cyr-Marc, Etienne, Pascal. EDUC: École normale de Saint-Jérôme, B.Ed.; Univ. de Montréal, B.A.(Info.); Univ. du Québec à Montréal, B.A.(Info.). CAREER: Enseignante et animatrice pédagogique, Ministère de l'éduc. du Qué.; Animatrice et directrice-gén., Télévision de Laval, 1975-81; Attachée politique du député Jean-Paul Champagne, Assemblée Nationale du Qué., 1981-85; Députée (Laval-Est), House of Commons, 1993 to date; Porte-parole de l'Opposition officielle, Amérique latine et Afrique, Asie-Pacifique. AFFIL: Parti Québécois; Bloc Québécois; Centre des femmes de Laval; Centre de la Télévision de Laval; Société d'histoire de l'Île Jésus; Société Saint-Jean-Baptiste. INTERESTS: lecture; voyages; ski.

DeBruyn, Beverley A., B.Sc. ○ ⊕ ⊚

Executive Director, CANADIAN FOUNDATION FOR THE STUDY OF INFANT DEATH, 586 Eglinton Ave. E., Ste. 308, Toronto, ON M4P 1P2 (416) 488-3260. Born Brockville, Ont. 3 ch. EDUC: St. Mary's Univ., Halifax, B.Sc. 1976; York Univ., Voluntary Sector & Arts Mgmt Certificate 1986. CAREER: Officer Cadet, Royal Canadian Air Force, 1956-58; Unit Administrator, Don Mills Unit, Canadian Cancer Soci-

ety, 1979-81; Asst. Volunteer Coord., Women's College Hospital, Toronto, 1981; Volunteer Coord., Toronto Humane Society, 1981-84; Exec. Dir., Canadian Foundation for the Study of Infant Deaths, 1984 to date. AFFIL: Chartered Institute of Secretaries (A.C.I.S.); Institute of Chartered Secretaries & Administrators in Canada (Professional Administrator); National Society of Fundraising Executives; Canadian Society of Association Executives; Association of SIDS Program Professionals; SIDS International (Exec. Committee 1994-96). INTERESTS: antiques; theatre; travelling; gourmet cooking; charitable organizations.

Dedi, Barbara ⊚

President, SASKATCHEWAN ASSOCIATION ON HUMAN RIGHTS, 39 Springstein Ave., Regina, SK S4R 7J4 (306) 949-0787, FAX 949-0787. Born Regina 1953. sep. 3 ch. EDUC: Wascana Institute, Certified Nursing Assistant 1974, Registered Psychiatric Nurse 1975; Certificate in Clinical Psych. 1976; Hospital & Health Care Admin. Course, Certificate in Hospital & Health Care Admin. 1981. CAREER: Aide, General Hospital, Regina, 1974; Certified Nursing Asst., 1974-75; Psychiatric Nurse, Weyburn Psychiatric Centre, 1975; Psychiatric Nurse, Manitoba Sch., 1975-76; Registered Psychiatric Nurse, Valleyview Centre, Rehabilitation Cottage, Moose Jaw, 1976-78; Sr. Nurse, Psychiatry, Swift Current Union Hospital, 1978-79; Sr. Nurse, Adjunctive Therapy–Psychiatry, 1979-81; Community Mental Health Nurse, Swift Current Mental Health Clinic, 1981-90; Supervisor, Community Mental Health Nursing Dept., 1990-94. AFFIL: Sask. Psychiatric Nurses' Association; Library & Pioneer Lodge City Council Committee; Community Advisory Council Committee; Sask. Gov't Employees' Union; Swift Current Labour Coalition of Ten Unions (Pres. 1986-94; Chrm); Canadian Rights & Liberties Federation (Exec. Bd.); Sask. Association on Human Rights (Pres.); Multicultural Council of Sask. (Exec. Bd.); Swift Current Multicultural Council (Past Pres.). INTERESTS: human rights; labour; women's issues; rural & multicultural issues. MISC: has taught & given presentations on assertiveness training, harassment, discrimination, stress in the workplace, pay equity & communication, & women & labour issues; active within the Sask. New Democratic Party & was a delegate to NDP conventions, 1990-94; ran as a nominee for M.L.A.–Regina Sherwood; Bd. Mbr., United Way, representing labour; Bd. Mbr., Regina Union Centre. COMMENT: *"A few years ago, Barb realized in the struggle to obtain equality and justice in the labour movement, workplace and society, there were also many inequalities in the human rights movement. Barb is presently President of the Saskatchewan Association on Human Rights and an executive member of Canadian Rights and Liberties Federation in Ottawa. She has recently been elected as chairperson for the 800-plus devolved health-care workers from the Saskatchewan government to 30 individual health boards for that bargaining unit of Saskatchewan Government Employers' Union."*

Degler, Teri, B.A.,M.A. ✏ 📜

Writer and Freelance Journalist. (416) 429-2421, FAX 429-2421. Born Lafayette, Ind. 1948. m. Kaz Kobielski. 1 ch. Kasia. **EDUC:** Albertson Coll., B.A.(English Lit.) 1970; Univ. of New Mexico, M.A.(Special Educ.) 1971. **CAREER:** Ed., *Chimo–The Holistic Magazine*, 1978-80; Copy Supervisor/Copy Writer, AES Advertising, 1980-81; Creative Dir., Comm. Dept., *The Toronto Star*, 1984-87; freelance journalist & author, 1987 to date. **SELECTED PUBLICATIONS:** *Straight from the Horse's Mouth: And Other Animal Expressions* (Canada; Western Prod. Prairie Books, 1989; US: Henry Holt and Company, Inc. 1991); *Scuttlebutt: And Other Phrases of Nautical Origin* (Canada: Western Prod. Prairie Book, 1989; US: Henry Holt and Company, Inc., 1991); *Love, Limits and Consequences: A Positive Approach to Kids and Discipline* (Canada: Summerhill Press, 1990; Germany: Dommer Knaur, 1993); *Everything your kids ever wanted to know about dinosaurs and you were afraid they'd ask* (Canada: Western Prod. Prairie Books, 1991; US: Crown Publishing, 1992); *The Canadian Junior Green Guide*, with Pollution Probe (McClelland & Stewart, 1991); *The Kitchen Handbook: An Environmental Guide*, with Pollution Probe (McClelland & Stewart, 1993); articles on a variety of subjects published in many newspapers, & periodicals incl. *Family Circle*, *The Toronto Star*, *Today's Parent*, *Your Baby*, *à la carte Magazine* & *New Age Magazine*. **AFFIL:** PEN Canada; Writers Union; Pollution Probe; YMCA (volunteer for community fund drive). **HONS:** Our Choice Award (*The Canadian Junior Green Guide*), The Canadian Children's Book Centre; Award for accuracy & excellence in science writing about dinosaurs (*Everything your kids ever wanted to know about dinosaurs and you were afraid they'd ask*), The Dinosaur Society, US; winner of various advtg awards for copywriting & creative direction. **INTERESTS:** tai chi; yoga; swimming; environmental educ.; working for freedom of expression. **MISC:** various media appearances; has spoken widely on a variety of subjects, most recently on the relationship between creativity & spirituality. **COMMENT:** *"The mother of a preschooler, I have, in the past six years, authored or co-authored seven books, including the best-selling* Canadian Junior Green Guide, *done in conjunction with Pollution Probe."*

Degroot, Lois C., B.A.Sc., Dip.Bus.Adm. ■■ ⚛ $ 🎓

Scarborough, ON M1J 2C1 (416) 431-9418, FAX 431-2084. Born Detroit 1930. m. John M. 3 ch. Philip, Nancy, Eric. **EDUC:** Univ. of Toronto, B.A.Sc.(Mech. Eng.) 1952, Dip.Bus. Adm. 1977. **CAREER:** consulting eng., 1952-70; professional staff, Association of Professional Engineers of Ontario, 1976-80; Chrm, Environmental Appeal Board of Ont., 1978-87; Consultant in continuing educ. to the technological professions, 1980-82; Dir., Atomic Energy of Canada Ltd., 1987-92; Pres., Bridgings International Inc., 1986-94; Chair, Unemployment Insurance Commission Bd. of Referees, Scarborough, 1993-96. **VOLUNTEER CAREER:** Chrm, Scarborough Public Library Bd., 1974 & 1975; Dir., 1970-76; mbr., Governing Council, Sch. of Continuing Studies, Univ. of Toronto, 1977-82; Dir., Sandford Fleming Foundation, Univ. of Waterloo, 1981-86; Dir., Scarborough Unit, Canadian Cancer Society, 1980-85; Chair, Awards Committee, Association of Professional Engineers of Ontario, 1990-92; mbr., Bd. of Gov., Scarborough General Hospital, 1993 to date. **HONS:** Officer, Order of Honour, Professional Engineers Ontario, 1994.

Delage, Niquette, B.A.,BCL ✊ 🗳 ⚖

Executive Director, ADVERTISING STANDARDS COUNCIL (French Canada), 4823 Sherbrooke St. W., Ste. 130, Westmount, QC H3Z 1G7 (514) 931-8060, FAX 931-2797. m. Jacques G. Beauregard. 2 ch. Danielle, Gaëlle. **EDUC:** Collègue Marguerite-Bourgeoys, BAC ès-Arts 1965; McGill Univ., B.C.L.(Law) 1976. **BAR:** Que. **CAREER:** Dir., Women's Section, Dimanche Matin, 1967-70; Pres., RSVP Inc., 1970-72; Exec. Dir., Office de la protection du consommateur, Gov't of Que., 1972-75; Exec. Dir., Folk Arts/Canada's Birthday, Prov. of Que., 1976-81; Exec. Dir., Canada's Birthday, Que., 1982-83; Mbr., Human Rights Tribunal, 1978-91; Exec. Dir., Advertising Standards Council (French Canada), 1995 to date; Ptnr, Delage Beauregard, Barristers & Solicitors. **AFFIL:** Hôpital Ste-Jeanne-d'Arc (Pres., Bur. des Gouverneurs); Foundation Ste-Jeanne-d'Arc (Sec.); Centre hospitalier Ste-Jeanne-d'Arc (Bd. Mbr.); Comité provincial de prévention de la criminalité économique (Hon. Pres.); Phoenix Foundation (Sec.); Consumers' Association of

Canada (Volunteer). **MISC:** editor, columnist, broadcaster.

Delaney, Janet ■ ✊ $
President and General Manager, BETTER BUSINESS BUREAU OF WESTERN ONTARIO, 200 Queen's Ave., Ste. 616, Box 2153, London, ON N6A 4E3 (519) 673-3222, FAX 673-5966. Born Watford, UK 1935. d. 3 ch. Susan Cockshutt, Thomas Delaney, Jill Delaney. **CAREER:** Coord., Gallery Svcs, London Regional Art & Historical Museum, 1971-83; Pres. & Gen. Mgr, Better Business Bureau of Western Ontario, 1984 to date. **AFFIL:** Rotary Club of London; Western Fair Association (Bd.); London Community Small Business Centre (Bd.).

Delany, Sheila, B.A.,M.A.,Ph.D. 🎓 📜 📖
Professor of English, SIMON FRASER UNIVERSITY, Burnaby, BC V5A 1S6 (604) 291-3136, FAX 291-5737, EMAIL sdelany@sfu.ca. Born New Haven, Conn. 1940. 2 ch. Nicholas, Lev. **EDUC:** Wellesley Coll., B.A.(English) 1961; Univ. of California at Berkeley, M.A.(English) 1963; Columbia Univ., Ph.D.(English & Comparative Lit.) 1967. **CAREER:** Queen's Coll., City Univ. of New York, 1967-69; Columbia Univ. Summer Sch., 1970; Simon Fraser Univ., 1970 to date; writer & staff mbr., *Grape/Western Voice*, Vancouver political-cultural newspaper, 1972-73; Univ. of British Columbia, 1987. **SELECTED PUBLICATIONS:** *Counter-Tradition: The Literature of Dissent and Alternatives* (Basic Books 1970); *Chaucer's House of Fame: The Poetics of Skeptical Fideism* (Univ. of Chicago Press, 1972); *Writing Woman: Women Writers and Women in Literature, Medieval to Modern* (Schocken, 1983); *Medieval Literary Politics: Shapes of Ideology* (Manchester Univ. Press & St. Martin's Press, 1990); *Telling Hours and Other Journal Stories* (Vancouver: New Star, 1991); *A Legend of Holy Women*, translation of a late Middle English text by Osbern Bokenham, with introduction & notes (Univ. of Notre Dame Press, 1992); *The Naked Text: Chaucer's Legend of Good Women* (Univ. of California Press, 1994); various other published works of scholarship, journalism, fiction & poetry. **EDIT:** Consulting Ed., *Science & Society*, 1982 to date; Field Ed., *The Chaucer Encyclopedia*, 1987 to date; Advisory Bd., *Exemplaria: A Journal of Theory in Medieval and Renaissance Studies*, 1988 to date; Ed. Bd., *English Studies in Canada*, 1994 to date. **AFFIL:** Medieval Academy of America; Medieval Association of the Pacific; New Chaucer Society; Modern Language Association; Hagiography Society; Christine de Pizan Society; Association of Canadian Coll. & Univ. Teachers of English; Society of Canadian Medievalists. **HONS:** Woodrow Wilson Fellow, 1961-62; Fiction Award, Berkeley, 1963; Killam Sr. Research Fellowship, 1993-95. **INTERESTS:** swimming; billiards; music & theatre; gardening. **MISC:** recipient of Canada Council release time stipends, 1975-76, 1987-88, 1989-90; invited guest speaker at numerous conferences & universities in Canada, US, Australia, UK, Holland, South Africa & Italy; recipient of various grants & fellowships; founder (1988), organizer & mbr., Vancouver Medieval Symposium; referee for various journals, univ. presses & granting agencies. **COMMENT:** *"My two grown sons, my work in bringing historicist method and gender awareness into medieval studies, teaching and political activism have been my main endeavours and achievements."*

Delicaet, Anne Margaret, B.A.,B.Ed. $
President and Chief Executive Officer, THE KUNA INVESTMENTS GROUP, 21 Doncliffe Dr., Toronto, ON (416) 489-5351, CELL 704-2877, FAX 864-1174. Born Glace Bay, N.S. m. Leonard George. 3 ch. Mary-Kathleen, Kendra Anne, Leonard Jacques. **EDUC:** N.S. Teachers' College, Teacher "A" Certification 1956; Univ. of Toronto, B.A. 1964, B.Ed. 1966; Univ. of British Columbia, M. Ed. (in progress). **CAREER:** educator; Ont. Sch. Inspector, Ontario Teachers' Coll.; Supervisor, Primary Educ.; Supervisor, Phys. & Health Educ.; classroom teacher, 18 yrs., B.C., Ont. & N.S. **SELECTED PUBLICATIONS:** developed numerous texts for primary grades in Cdn Catholic schools; consultant to publishers of educational texts. **AFFIL:** Canadian Opera Company (Dir.; Past Pres., Women's Committee); Canadian Breast Cancer Foundation (Dir.); Providence Centre Foundation (Dir.); Remington Museum, N.Y. (Dir.); Ontario Teachers' Foundation (Exec.); Ontario Association for Curriculum Development (Exec.); Canadian Psychiatric Awareness Comm. (Exec.); Hospital for Sick Children - Operation Herbie (Exec.). **HONS:** Commemorative Medal for the 125th Anniversary of the Confederation of Canada. **INTERESTS:** opera; ballet; travel; gardening; theatre; reading. **MISC:** volunteer & fund raiser in numerous educ., religious, community, arts & cultural organizations; lay eucharistic minister; first communion teacher. **COMMENT:** *"I was brought up in a Catholic home with a Catholic education, which taught me that if you have gifts you have a responsibility to help others."*

Delisle, Margaret F., B.A. 🍁
Member of the National Assembly (Jean-Talon), GOVERNMENT OF QUEBEC, Hôtel du

Parlement, Bur. 3124, Quebec, QC G1A 1A4 (418) 646-6349, FAX 646-4385. Born Que. 1946. m. Pierre. 4 ch. **EDUC:** Laval Univ., B.A. 1967. **CAREER:** English teacher, 1968-73; City Councillor, Sillery, Quebec, 1982-85; Mayor, 1985-94; Pres., Federation of Canadian Municipalities, 1992-93; Mbr., Jean Talon, Nat'l Assembly, Gov't of Que., 1994 to date. **AFFIL:** Centraide Quebec (Pres.); United Way of Canada (Exec. Committee). **HONS:** Commemorative Medal for the 125th Anniversary of the Confederation of Canada. **INTERESTS:** reading; skiing; travelling.

Dell'Aquila, Tina, C.M.A.,B.Comm. 💲
Director of Corporate Accounting, DOMINION TEXTILE INC., 1950 Sherbrooke St. W., Montreal, QC H1E 3Z6 (514) 989-6164, FAX 989-6038. Born Italy 1962. **EDUC:** Concordia Univ., B.Comm.(Fin.) 1984; Certified Mgmt Acctnt 1991. **INTERESTS:** fitness; skiing; travel. **MISC:** fluent in English, French & Italian. **COMMENT:** *"Energetic, career-oriented individual; pursuing development activities in finance and information systems."*

Delong, Beverley J.T., B.A.,LL.B. ⚖ ○
President, LAWYERS FOR SOCIAL RESPONSIBILITY, 5120 Carney Rd. N.W., Calgary, AB T2L 1G2 (403) 282-8260, FAX 289-4272. **EDUC:** Univ. of Calgary, B.A.(Pol. Sci.) 1971; Queen's Univ., LL.B.(Law) 1974. **CAREER:** Edmonton Reg'l Office, Dept. of Justice, Gov't of Canada, 1975-79; Macleod Dixon, Barristers & Solicitors, 1979-86; Chairperson, Project Ploughshares Calgary, 1983-84; Exec. Mbr., 1984 to date; Pres., Lawyers for Social Responsibility, 1991 to date. **SELECTED PUBLICATIONS:** numerous articles on issues of peace & security building; *You Too Can Be a Peacemaker*, a children's workbook on conflict resolution. **AFFIL:** United Church of Canada. **HONS:** Peace Award, YMCA Calgary, 1994.

DeMarco, Jean Mary, B.A.,LL.B. ⚖
Partner, OSLER, HOSKIN & HARCOURT, 1 First Canadian Place, Box 50, Toronto, ON M5X 1B8 (416) 862-6603, FAX 862-6666. Born 1952. m. Christopher Desjardins. 4 ch. James, Jocelin, Juliann, Georgia. **EDUC:** Univ. of Windsor, B.A. 1973, LL.B. 1974. **BAR:** Ont., 1976. **CAREER:** articled, Osler, Hoskin & Harcourt, 1974-75; Barrister & Solicitor, 1976 to date; Ptnr, 1981 to date. **AFFIL:** Canadian Bar Association; Law Society of Upper Canada; Italian Advocates' Society; Women's Law Association. **HONS:** Income Tax Award for top standing in Income Tax, 1973; Harold Fox Award, 1973. **MISC:** Instructor, Bar Admission Course Program, 1980-82; Instructor, Pan-

ellist, misc. programs, Law Society of Upper Canada Continuing Legal Educ.

Dembe, Elaine, D.C. ⊕ ⌀
Doctor of Chiropractic. 200 St. Clair Ave. W., Ste. 308, Toronto, ON M4V 1R1 (416) 960-5353, FAX 960-0193. Born Hamilton, Ont. 1948. d. **EDUC:** Canadian Memorial Chiropractic Coll., D.C. 1978. **CAREER:** private practice, 19 yrs.; Chiropractor, The Toronto Blue Jays, 1985-86 & 1986-87 seasons; lecturer, motivational speaker, writer. **SELECTED PUBLICATIONS:** *Passionate Longevity–The 10 Secrets to Growing Younger* (Macmillan Canada, 1995); various articles on wellness, back pain, posture. **AFFIL:** Metropolitan YMCA (Health Advisory Bd.); United Way of Ont. (Voluntary Spokesperson); National Speakers' Bureau; Chief Protocol Office, Prov. of Ont. (Chiropractor on call). **HONS:** International Award for Amateur Sport, 1988. **INTERESTS:** running; tap dancing; gardening; public speaking; writing poems; performing rap songs. **MISC:** has appeared on numerous TV & radio programs; ranked 11th in Canada, marathon performance, 1982 (2:53:53). **COMMENT:** *"High energy healer whose mission in life is to make a difference in the world."*

Demers, Michèle, B.A. ⊙
Vice-President, PROFESSIONAL INSTITUTE OF THE PUBLIC SERVICE OF CANADA (PIPSC), 53 Auriga Dr., Nepean, ON K2E 8C3 800 267-0446, ext. 287, FAX 1-800-465-7477. Born Ville-Marie, Que. 1950. d. 2 ch. **EDUC:** Univ. of Ottawa, B.A.(Arts) 1972; Univ. of Montreal, B.A.(Social Work) 1974. **CAREER:** Social Worker, CSSMM, 1974-76; Social Worker, Veterans' Affairs, 1979-94; VP & Bd. Mbr., PIPSC, 1994 to date. **AFFIL:** Corporation professionnelle des Travailleurs Sociaux du Québec. **HONS:** Award of Merit, Korea Veterans' Association of Canada, 1989. **INTERESTS:** women's rights; collective bargaining; fighting discrimination in all areas. **COMMENT:** *"All my professional career as a social worker centred on working with the elderly. I soon became involved in union activities in a quest to defend employee rights, to bargain terms and conditions of employment and to try to contribute to the establishment of harmonious labour relations, through union management-consultation. My election as vice-president of the union has given me the opportunity to participate and contribute towards the challenging times ahead for public-sector unions. A lot is at stake for both the Canadian public and the professionals of the public service, and full cooperation is essential. Finally, as a female, single parent professional, the biggest challenge is to find a healthy*

balance between my professional and family responsibilities. My career would not be fulfilling if I could not devote quality time to my family."

Demeule, Lynne C. 🖉 ⚪
Supervisor, Life Enrichment Program, SASKATCHEWAN ABILITIES COUNCIL, 825 McDonald St., Regina, SK S4N 2X5 (306) 569-9048, FAX 352-3717. Born Winnipeg 1942. m. Roger. 3 ch. Michelle, Denise, David. CAREER: Voice of the Handicapped, 1980; Life Enrichment Supervisor, Saskatchewan Abilities Council, 1981; Vocational Training Centre Supervisor, 1982-83; Supervisor, Life Enrichment Program, 1984 to date. AFFIL: Saskatchewan Association for Community Living (Dir.); Early Childhood Intervention Program Provincial Council (Chair 1990 to date); Regina & Region Early Childhood Intervention Program (Bd. & Past Chair); Cheshire Homes of Regina (Bd. & Past Chair); City of Regina Paratransit Advisory Bd.; Regina Therapeutic Recreation Association. HONS: National Access Award for Community Development. INTERESTS: family; grandchildren (Andrea & Michael); outdoor activities; travel; camping. MISC: Co-Chair, Third Annual Western Canada Family Conference, Saskatoon, 1994. COMMENT: *"I am committed to assisting the disabled-consumer movement with a particular emphasis on children's services that are community-based and accessible to all."*

Dempsey, Catherine, B.A. 📜 🖉
Executive Director, NEWFOUNDLAND HISTORIC PARKS ASSOCIATION, Box 5542, St. John's, NF A1C 5W4 (709) 753-9262, FAX 772-2940. Born Ottawa 1952. m. Jim Dempsey. 2 ch. EDUC: Univ. of Victoria, B.A.(English) 1975, Certificate of Educ. 1976. CAREER: bookseller, 1979-81; Debt Counsellor, Personal Credit Counselling Service, 1987; Sales Mgr, Newfoundland Historic Parks Association, 1989-91; Exec. Dir., 1991 to date. AFFIL: Canadian Parks Partnership (Dir. & Sec.); Museum Association of Newfoundland & Labrador; St. John's Library (Bd.); Planned Parenthood of Newfoundland & Labrador. INTERESTS: travel; history; skiing; reading; family; dev. of cultural industries in Nfld. COMMENT: *"The refurbishment of two National Historic Sites in Newfoundland during the past few years has been the most satisfying achievement of my career since they have allowed the public to share Newfoundland's rich heritage and enhanced the local economies."*

Dempsey, Gaylene ■■ 🖉 💋 ✒
Executive Director, MANITOBA AUDIO RECORD-

ING INDUSTRY ASSOCIATION (music industry association), 100 Arthur St., Ste. 221B, Winnipeg, MB R3B 1H3 (204) 942-8650, FAX 956-5280. Born Winnipeg 1960. m. David Sherman. EDUC: Red River Community Coll., Creative Communications. CAREER: journalist (freelance news & entertainment); editor; writer; commentator on radio (CBC afternoon show, Winnipeg); music industry professional, MARIA, 5 yrs. SELECTED PUBLICATIONS: *SOCAN Words & Music*, Dec. 1995. INTERESTS: golf; music; travel; fine dining; budget eating; cooking; cartoons; animation; comic books; pop culture. COMMENT: *"Gaylene Dempsey is a communications and networking specialist. She has worked as a writer, journalist and editor for various publications and has been a regular pop culture commentator on CBC Radio. Currently, she is the executive director at MARIA, where she promotes and educates the Manitoba music industry."*

Dempsey, Karen Monnon, B.A., B.Ed. ■ 💲 🕸 🖉
Executive Director, OFFSHORE TECHNOLOGIES ASSOCIATION OF NOVA SCOTIA, World Trade and Convention Centre, Ste. 813, Halifax, NS B3J 3N8 (902) 425-4774, FAX 422-2332. Born Inverness, N.S. 1951. m. B.N. Dempsey. EDUC: Acadia Univ., B.A.(Hist.) 1972, B.Ed. 1973. CAREER: Substitute Teacher, King's County Sch. Bd.; various positions, Dalhousie Univ., Maritime Telephone and Telegraph, Grace Maternity Hospital; Exec. Sec. to the Gen. Mgr & Proj. Mgr, Offshore Atlantic Oper. Centre, Stone and Webster Canada Ltd, 1985-87; Exec. Dir., Offshore Technologies Association of N.S.), 1987 to date. AFFIL: Canadian Federation of University Women, Halifax Club (Pres.; 1st VP & Liaison Officer; 2nd VP & Program Chair 1990-91); Heritage Trust of Nova Scotia; Art Gallery of Nova Scotia; World Trade Centre, Halifax; Association of Atlantic Area Artists. INTERESTS: antiques; history; painting; collecting Nova Scotian art. MISC: paintings exhibited in juried & nonjuried shows; host & prod., limited series, Halifax Cablevision, 1989.

Denham, Elizabeth, B.A.,M.A.S. 🖉 📖
Archives Advisor, ARCHIVES SOCIETY OF ALBERTA, c/o 10416 Willowcrest Rd. S.E., Calgary, AB T2J 1P1 (403) 278-8083. Born Vancouver 1959. m. William Martin. 2 ch. Katherine, David. EDUC: Univ. of British Columbia, B.A.(Hist.) 1981, M.A.S.(Archival & Info. Studies) 1984. CAREER: Mun. Archivist, Municipality of Richmond, 1983-89; Sessional Lecturer, Simon Fraser Univ., 1988-89; City Archivist, City of Calgary, 1989-94; Archival

Consultant, Calgary Public Library & Calgary General Hospital, 1994-95; Calgary Regional Health Authority, 1994-96; Archives Advisor, Archives Society of Alberta, 1995 to date. **AFFIL:** Canadian Council of Archives (Dir. & Mbr., Exec. Bd. 1993-94); Alberta Archives Council (Pres.); B.C. Archives Council (Founding Mbr.); Legal Archives Society of Alberta (Bd.); Calgary Folk Festival Society (VP). **INTERESTS:** music; literature; running; reading; film. **MISC:** extensive teaching, training, advisory svcs in archival science. **COMMENT:** *"Responsible for the creation and development of local government archives programs in B.C. and Alberta; active in promoting public knowledge and interest in local history, medical history and awareness of the value of archives in Canada."*

Denham, Jill, B.A. ■ $
Managing Director, Origination and Structuring and Deputy Head of Europe, **CIBC Wood Gundy Plc**, Cottons Centre, Cottons Lane, London, UK SE1 2QL (44-171) 234-6145, FAX 234-6409. Born Welland, Ont. 1960. m. Stephen Marshall. 1 ch. **EDUC:** Univ. of Western Ontario, B.Sc. 1983; Harvard Bus. Sch., Bus. 1990. **CAREER:** VP & Dir., Wood Gundy Inc., 1983-88; Pres., CIBC Wood Gundy Capital, 1990-95. **DIRECTOR:** AT Plastics; Alliance Communications; Ensis Corp.; White Rose Crafts & Nurseries. **AFFIL:** Harvard Bus. Sch. Club of Toronto (Dir.). **INTERESTS:** skiing; golf.

Denis, Marielle, B.A.,C.A. $ 📺
Vice-President, Administration Services, **CFCF 12** (a division of CFCF Inc.)., 405 Ogilvy Ave., Montreal, QC H3N 1M4 (514) 495-6137, FAX 273-4488. **EDUC:** Univ. du Québec à Montréal, B.A.(Acctg) 1983; Ordre des comptables agréés du Québec, C.A. **CAREER:** Auditor, Price Waterhouse, 1984-88; Chief Acctnt, CFCF Inc., 1988; Cont., 1988-89; VP, Admin. (Div. CFCF 12), 1989 to date. **AFFIL:** Ordre des comptables agréés du Québec; Canadian Women in Communications. **INTERESTS:** finance; admin. **COMMENT:** *"I describe myself as being a very professional and dedicated person with strong interpersonal skills. My main achievements are the following: implemented a successful cash management system; created new management tools and reports, and increased computerized applications; contributed extensively and successfully to a major restructuring (downsizing); contributed to financing projects, initiated and completed a MIS strategic plan, actively involved in the company strategic and operational planning process."*

Dennett, Lauraine (Laurie), B.A., M.A. ■ 📖 📜 ♥
Writer and historian. 43 Andrewes House, Barbican, London, UK EC2. Born Toronto 1946. s. **EDUC:** Univ. of Toronto, B.A.(Hons., Modern Hist.) 1969; McMaster Univ., M.A.(Modern Hist.) 1971. **CAREER:** moved to the UK, 1971; began writing bus. hist., London, 1975. **SELECTED PUBLICATIONS:** *The Charterhouse Group* (1979); *Slaughter and May: The City Law Firm 1889-1989*; *Slaughter and May 1889-1989: A Short History*; *A Hug for the Apostle* (1987); contributor, *Macadam, Colossus of Roads* (1982); translator (from Spanish), *La Guiá del Peregrino* (author, Elías Valiña Sampedro, 1991); translator, *The Way of St. James: The Pilgrimage Route to Santiago de Compostela* (cartography created by Elías Valiña Sampedro, 1993). **AFFIL:** Confraternity of St. James (V-Chrm 1989; Chrm 1995); Multiple Sclerosis Society of Canada (Hon. Dir.). **HONS:** Confederation Medal, 1993. **INTERESTS:** walking; classical music; gardening; reading; looking at paintings. **MISC:** in 1986, raised nearly $100,000 for medical research for multiple sclerosis walking the ancient pilgrim roads from Chartres, France to Santiago de Compostela, Spain; in 1989, walked from London, UK to Rome, Italy along pilgrim routes to raise over $220,000 in 9 countries ($207,000 in Canada) for medical research for multiple sclerosis; went on a pilgrimage from Canterbury to Jerusalem (arriving Christmas Eve) for multiple sclerosis research in 1992; currently commissioned by the Prudential Corporation to write the history of the Prudential Assurance Company for its 150th anniversary in 1998. **COMMENT:** *"I am committed to literary excellence and compassion in the exercise of my vocation as a writer, and to aiding the fight against multiple sclerosis by whatever means I can. And although I work outside Canada, I still regard myself very much a Canadian."*

Dennison, Deanne, B.A. ■■ 🎓
Registrar, **University of New Brunswick**, P.O. Box 4400, Fredericton, NB E3B 5A3 (506) 453-4864, FAX 453-5016, EMAIL denn@unb.ca. Born Sydney, N.S. 1940. s. 1 ch. Sheila E. Dimas. **EDUC:** St. Francis Xavier Univ., B.A.(Pol. Sci.) 1977. **CAREER:** Registrar, University Coll. of Cape Breton, 1985-91; Registrar, Univ. of New Brunswick, 1991 to date. **AFFIL:** Atlantic Association of Registrars & Admissions Officers (former Pres.); Association of Registrars of the Universities & Colleges of Canada (Incoming Pres.); American Contract Bridge League. **INTERESTS:** special interest in governance of universities & enrolment issues. **COMMENT:** *"Typical background*

for a female of my age bracket. Began study for a degree after two children in school and then entered the world of university administration, which proved to be stimulating and challenging."

Dennys, Louise, B.A.,M.A. 📖 ⑤ ♙
Vice-President, RANDOM HOUSE OF CANADA, 33 Yonge St., Ste. 210, Toronto, ON M5E 1G4 (416) 777-9477, FAX 777-9470. Publisher, ALFRED A. KNOPF CANADA. Born Egypt 1948. m. Eric P. Young. EDUC: Oxford Univ., B.A./M.A.(English Lit & Lang.) 1969. CAREER: Bookseller, Blackwell's & Sons Ltd., Oxford, 1969-70; Mgr, Oxford Univ. Press Bookshop, London, UK, 1970-72; Ed. Asst., Clark Irwin Publishing Co., Toronto, 1972-74; Ed., 1974-75; Dir. & Ed.-in-Chief, Anson Cartwright Editions, 1975-78; Publisher, VP & Corp. Sec., Lester & Orpen Dennys, 1979-91; VP, Random House of Canada, 1991 to date; Publisher, Alfred A. Knopf Canada, 1991 to date. SELECTED PUBLICATIONS: *The Changing Resource* (O.I.S.E., 1975). DIRECTOR: Random House of Canada. AFFIL: PEN Canada (Past Pres.); Association of Canadian Publishers (Past Chair, Int'l Trade Committee). HONS: Woman of the Year Award, *Toronto Life* annual award. INTERESTS: varied. MISC: Lecturer, Banff Sch. of Fine Arts. COMMENT: *"A passionate believer in the importance of literature and language as a humane and humanizing force–one that connects us with each other, illuminates our daily lives and offers a coherent understanding of the world we live in. Pioneered book publishing in Canada as an international endeavour, being the first publisher to spearhead the publishing of Canadian books abroad, bringing the best of foreign writers to Canada and demanding, successfully, world recognition for Canada as a sovereign publishing territory."*

d'Entremont, R. Irene ■ ⑤ ⊛ ♙
President, M.I.T. ELECTRONICS INC., Box 514, Yarmouth, NS B5A 2G7 (902) 742-5555. President, WOMEN'S UP TO DATE SHOP INC. Secretary-Treasurer, WESMAR ELECTRONICS CANADA LTD. Born Yarmouth County, N.S. 1943. m. Theodore G. d'Entremont. 2 ch. EDUC: Diploma in Bus. Mgmt. CAREER: Sec.-Treas., Wesmar Electronics Canada Ltd., 1973 to date; Councillor (Alderman), Yarmouth Town, elected 1985; Pres., Women's Up to Date Shop Inc., 1988 to date; Pres., M.I.T. Electronics Inc., 1980 to date. DIRECTOR: Nova Scotia Power Inc. AFFIL: Yarmouth Chamber of Commerce (Pres. 1985); N.S. Chamber of Commerce (Chair 1987-93); Maritimes Marine Search & Rescue Council; Yarmouth Community Futures (Bd. of Dir.);

Univ. Ste. Anne (Bd. of Gov.); Atlantic Provinces/New England Business Council (Chair); Atlantic Provinces Chamber of Commerce (Chair); Canadian Chamber of Commerce (Dir. rep. Atlantic Canada 1992-94); N.S. Business Development Corporation; Gulf of Maine Council for the Marine Environment; Marine Atlantic (Bd. of Dir.). HONS: Dr. Stuart Peters Award, Chamber of Commerce, 1991; Canada 125 Medal, 1992; Woman's Entrepreneurship Award, Yarmouth Chamber of Commerce, 1994; N.S. Business Hall of Fame, St. Mary's Univ., 1994; Hon. Doctorate of Commerce, St. Mary's Univ., 1995. MISC: first female Pres., Yarmouth YMCA, 1983-84; listed in *Canadian Who's Who,* 1988 to date; elected, 1990, N.S. Rep., Council for Canadian Unity.

Deol, Monika ♙ ⊗ ♥
c/o Citytv, 299 Queen St. W., Toronto, ON M5V 2Z5. Born Beausejour, Man. EDUC: Univ. of Winnipeg, Psych. & English. CAREER: singer/songwriter/mgr, *Perfect Kiss* (Top 40 rock band); host, *Night Moves,* CKY-TV; former Entertainment Specialist, *CityPulse Weekends,* Citytv; former Entertainment Specialist, *CityPulse at 6;* former Host, *Electric Circus;* former Co-Host, *Fax,* MuchMusic; former Co-Host, *Ooh La La.* AFFIL: World Literacy of Canada; South Asian Women's Centre; Walk for AIDS; Urban Alliance on Race Relations; The United Way; Canadian Breast Cancer Foundation; Imran Khan Cancer Appeal; Metro Toronto Cultural Advisory Committee. INTERESTS: travel; writing poetry & short stories. MISC: small roles in *Just For Fun* (docudrama) & *Hostage for a Day* (feature & John Candy's directorial debut); works with Performers for Literacy & the Foundation for the Gift of Literacy; worked on *Flight for Freedom* Literacy TV special & a commercial spot for the Variety Club's "Gold Heart" day; speaks to numerous high schools & community groups promoting educ., race rel'ns & clean lifestyles.

DeRubeis, Maria, B.S.W. ⓐ ⊕
President, Board of Directors, BULIMIA ANOREXIA NERVOSA ASSOCIATION (BANA), 1407 Ottawa St., Unit G, Windsor, ON N8X 2G1 (519) 253-3100, FAX 253-0175. Clinical Social Worker, SEXUAL ASSAULT CRISIS CENTRE. Born Italy 1962. m. John. 2 ch. Kailey Elyse, Brycen Kane. EDUC: Univ. of Windsor, B.S.W.(Social Work) 1985. CAREER: Coord., BANA, 1986-88; Fac.-Based Instructor, Sch. of Social Work, Univ. of Windsor, 1988; Social Worker, Hiatus House, 1988-90; Clinical Social Worker, Sexual Assault Crisis Centre, 1990 to date; Pres., BANA, 1994 to date.

SELECTED PUBLICATIONS: stress mgmt manual, 1987; *BANA Newsletter*. AFFIL: Ontario Association of Social Workers (Bd. of Dir., Southwestern Branch); Ciociaro Club of Windsor. HONS: Miss Calabria, 1983. INTERESTS: reading; fitness; women's issues. COMMENT: "*I am a working mother juggling a career and home life. I have provided counselling services to women since 1986 and am dedicated to empowering women affected by all forms of violence. One of my endeavours is to go into a business partnership with a female colleague, combining our expertise in women's issues and providing a unique service for women.*"

Desautels, Suzanne ■ 📺 ✏

Host, *Travel, Travel* and *Simply Wine & Cheese*, CFCF TV, 405 Ogilvy Ave., Montreal, QC H3N 1M4 (514) 273-6311, FAX 273-6346. Born Washington, D.C. 1954. m. Ron Reusch. 3 ch. Samantha Claire, Katharine Theresa, Sarah Anita. EDUC: Univ. of Denver, Mass Comm. 1972-73; Concordia Univ., English Lit. 1975-76, TV & Radio 1982-83. CAREER: Intern, Radio News, CFCF Radio, 1983; joined morning & afternoon radio teams ("zoo" format), 1983; Statistician, Washington Capitals & Montreal Canadiens radio broadcasts, 1984-85; Co-Host, *Renovation Zone* (nat'l syndicated TV series); *Pulse News* Weather Forecaster, 1985 to date; Host, *Today's Magazine*, 1985-88; Host, *Travel, Travel* (series), 1987 to date; Host, *Suzanne* (daily TV column), 1988-89; Contributor, *Expos Summer '89* & *Expos Summer '90*, 1989-90; Host, *Suzanne Live*, 1990-91; *Pulse News* sportscaster & sports reporter, 1994; Co-Anchor, *Pulse Weekend*, 1995; Host, *Simply Wine & Cheese*, 1996 to date. SELECTED CREDITS: primary host, *Telethon of Stars* (Telethon for Research into Children's Diseases), 1987 to date; "Just for Laughs Festival," 1988-89; host, *Academy Awards Countdown*, 1988-91; Co-Host, Prix d'Été (harness race live broadcast); *Love and Human Remains* (feature), 1993. AFFIL: ACTRA; NABET; Families First. INTERESTS: scuba diving; skiing; walking; parenting; sports, music; laughter. MISC: ski instructor; energy-saving spokesperson for Hydro-Québec; daughter of Claude J. Desautels, Asst. to U.S. Presidents John F. Kennedy & Lyndon B. Johnson. COMMENT: "*A bright, well-respected versatile Montreal-based broadcaster. Has hosted travel documentaries, live sports broadcasts and own daily public affairs show. Devoted mother of three daughters, Samantha, Katharine and Sarah.*"

Desjardins, Alice, B.A.,LL.L.,LL.M. ⚖

Justice, FEDERAL COURT OF CANADA, APPEAL DIVISION, Supreme Court of Canada Building, Kent & Wellington, Ottawa, ON K1A 0H9 (613) 992-4992, FAX 952-1264. Born Montreal 1934. EDUC: Coll. Basile Moreau, Montréal; Univ. de Montréal, B.A. 1954, LL.L 1957; Harvard Univ., LL.M. 1967. BAR: Qué., 1958. CAREER: Asst. Prof., Fac. of Law, Univ. de Montréal, 1961-68; Assoc. Prof., 1968-69; Legal Cnsl, Privy Council, Ottawa, 1968-69; Dir., Advisory & Administrative Law, Dept. of Justice, Ottawa, 1974-81; Justice, Superior Court of Que., Montréal, 1981-87; Justice, Fed. Court of Canada, Appeal Div., 1987 to date; ex officio mbr., Fed. Court of Canada, Trial Div., 1987 to date; Justice, Court Martial Appeal Court of Canada, 1988 to date. AFFIL: Association de droit international; Association des juristes d'expression française de l'Ont.; Comité internationale de juristes; Conseil canadien de droit international; Conférence canadien des juges; Association du Barreau canadien; Institut canadien d'administration de la justice; Harvard Univ. Club of Ottawa; Association Henri Capitan; Harvard Law Sch. Association (Exec. Committee, Int'l Section). HONS: Mackenzie King Travelling Scholarship, 1958-59; Ford Foundation Scholarship, 1966; LL.D.(Hon.), Univ. of Ottawa, 1996.

Deslauriers, Roxanne, B.Sc.,Ph.D. ⚛ 🍁 $

Group Leader, Biosystems, Institute for Biodiagnostics, NATIONAL RESEARCH COUNCIL OF CANADA, 435 Ellice Ave., Winnipeg, MB R3B 1Y6 (204) 984-5146, FAX 984-6978, EMAIL deslauriers@ibd.nrc.ca. Born Montreal 1947. m. Rajmund Somorjai. 2 ch. EDUC: Laval Univ., B.Sc.(Experimental Biol.) 1968; Ottawa Univ., Ph.D.(Biochem.) 1972. CAREER: Mbr., Research Staff, National Research Council of Canada, 1972 to date; Adjunct Prof., Univ. of Ottawa, Univ. of Winnipeg, Univ. of Manitoba; Lecturer, Univ. of Toronto. SELECTED PUBLICATIONS: published over 150 scientific papers dealing with applications of magnetic resonance spectroscopy in biology & medicine. EDIT: Ed. Bd., *NMR in Biomedicine*; Ed. Bd., *Canadian Journal of Applied Spectroscopy*; Ed. *Newsletter of the Biophysical Society of Canada*; Ed., *Society of Magnetic Resonance Newsletter*, 1989-93. AFFIL: Biophysical Society of Canada (Sec.); Society of Magnetic Resonance (Fellow); International Society for Heart Research; American Heart Association; Biophysical Society of Canada. HONS: Bourse de perfectionnement du Ministèré de l'Éduc. du Qué., 1968-71; National Research Council Postgrad. Scholarship, 1968-71; Ont.-Que. Exchange Scholarship, 1970-71; Scholar in Residence, Queen's Univ., 1985. COMMENT: "*Current research interests focus on the use of magnetic resonance spectroscopy in the development of better methods of heart and brain protection during cardiac surgery."*

Desreux, Michell, B.Sc. Ⓢ ⬥ ⬧
Senior Vice-President, Operations, UNIGLOBE TRAVEL (INTERNATIONAL) INC., The Uniglobe Bldg., 1199 W. Pender St., Ste. 900, Vancouver, BC V6E 2R1 (604) 662-3800, FAX 662-3878, EMAIL mdesreux@uniglobe.com. Born Calgary 1955. EDUC: Univ. of Calgary, B.Sc. (Psych.) 1977. CAREER: Sales Svc. Rep., Wardair Canada, 1975; Agency Sales, 1977-78; Training Instructor, 1978-80; Bus. Dev. Consultant, W. Canada Reg., Uniglobe Travel, 1980-84; Asst. VP, 1985-87; VP, Program Dev., Uniglobe Travel (International), 1987-91; Pres., Uniglobe Travel (Information Services) Inc., 1988-91; Sr. VP, Oper., Uniglobe Travel (International) Inc., 1991 to date. SELECTED PUBLICATIONS: various articles for travel industry trade publications. DIRECTOR: Uniglobe Travel (Information Services) Inc.; B.C. Songwriters' Association; B.C. Society for Training & Development. INTERESTS: singing/songwriting; sports; fitness. COMMENT: *"My mission is to use whatever skills and talents I have acquired or developed through education, experience, trial and error to nurture and inspire growth and achievement in others."*

Desrochers, Gisèle, B.A. Ⓢ
Senior Vice-President, Administration and Human Resources, NATIONAL BANK OF CANADA, 600 de la Gauchetière W., 8th Fl., Montréal, QC H3B 4L2 (514) 394-8711, FAX 394-6658. Born Montréal 1949. m. Jean Ste.-Marie. 1 ch. EDUC: Univ. de Québec à Montréal, Baccalauréat (info. scolaire) 1972; École nationale d'administration publique, Maîtrise 1981. CAREER: divers travails, Gouv. du Qué., 1975-94; Sous-min., Ministère du Revenu du Qué.; Première VP, Ressources humaines et admin., National Bank of Canada, 1994 to date. AFFIL: la Caisse de dépôt et de placement du Québec (Prés., Comité de verification). HONS: Cadre d'excellence, Femme cadre, Banque Fédérale de développement, 1986. MISC: speaker at numerous conferences.

Desroches, Fabienne, B.A.,M.A. ⬥ ⬧
Présidente, ASSOCIATION POUR L'ÉDUCATION INTERCULTURELLE DU QUÉBEC, 7400 St.-Laurent, bur. 530, Montréal, QC H2R 2Y1 (514) 844-6403, FAX 343-2283. Born Qué. 1949. cl. Gilles Gauvreau. EDUC: Univ. de Montréal, B.A.(Speech Pathology) 1972, M.A.(Speech Pathology) 1974; McGill Univ., Scholarship (French as a Second Language) 1993. CAREER:

Speech Pathologist, schools, 1974-78; Counsellor in Educ. for Immigrants, Ministry of Educ., 1978-84; Coopérante, Senegal, Africa, 1984-90; Guest Lecturer, Univ. de Montréal, 1991-93; Coord., Global Educ. Proj., French Univ. in Canada, 1994 to date. SELECTED PUBLICATIONS: articles in *Bulletin de l'association canadienne de linguistique appliquée, Bulletin de l'AQEFLS, Revue Québec-Français.* AFFIL: Association pour l'éducation interculturelle du Québec (Pres. 1992 to date); Corporation des orthophonistes et audiologistes du Québec (Pres. 1986-90); Association des enseignants(es) du Québec (Conseil d'admin.); Coalition pour l'école publique. HONS: North American Folk Song Championship with les Contretemps, 1965. INTERESTS: immigration; education; peace; music; books; movies. COMMENT: *"Président de l'APEIQ et directrice générale du projet d'éducation planétaire, je m'efforce de convaincre les gens à mieux se comprendre et à mieux communiquer afin de vivre dans un monde de paix."*

Desrosiers, Gyslaine, B.Sc.N.,M.B.A. ⬥ ⊕
President, ORDRE DES INFIRMIÈRES ET INFIRMIERS DU QUÉBEC, 4200 Dorchester Blvd. W., Montréal, QC (514) 935-2501, FAX 935-8874. Born Montreal 1951. 3 ch. EDUC: Univ. de Montréal, B.Sc.N.(Nursing) 1972; École des Hautes Études Commerciales, Dipl.(Admin. Sci.) 1976, M.B.A. 1981. CAREER: Nurse, Montréal Sacré-Coeur Hospital, 1972-73; Teacher, Nursing Techniques, Edouard-Montpetit Coll., 1973-76; Coord., Nursing Dept., Montréal Sacré-Coeur Hospital, 1976-79; Coord., Health Programs, Community Health Centre, 1982-83; Dir., Health Programs, Quebec Hospitals Association, & Counsellor, 1983-89, 1989-92; Pres., Ordre des infirmières et infirmiers du Québec, 1992 to date. SELECTED PUBLICATIONS: *L'organisation des soins infirmiers: évolution et perspectives with Claire Thibault* (Montréal: AHQ, 1990); "La durée d'hospitalisation et l'allocation des ressources: les DRG sont insuffisants" (*Artère,* 20 1990); "Soins infirmiers: cadres et soignantes se concertent" (*Artère* 8 1991); "La mesure de l'intensité des soins infirmiers: pièce maîtresse de l'information clinico-administrative" (*Carnet de l'APIDES* 1 1992); *La gestion contemporaine des soins infirmiers à l'heure des DRG with Marie Valois* (Montréal: AHQ, 1993); "Les systèmes d'information clinico-administratifs en soins infirmiers: Une contribution majeure à la rationalisation des services" (*Le réseau informatique* Mar. 1994); editorials in *Nursing Québec & L'infirmière du Québec,* Jan. 1993 to date. AFFIL: American Organization of Nurse Executives; Association of Hautes Études

Commerciales Graduates; Professional Association of Higher Studies in Nursing Graduates. INTERESTS: healthcare system; women's educ. COMMENT: *"Recognized leader of a 65,000-member association, G. Desrosiers has developed a modern vision of the power of nursing expertise in the search for the most efficient health system. She has already convinced many influential people of the advantages of advanced nursing for the quality of care provided to the public."*

Deutscher, Maryann, CHRP ■ $ ⌺ ◉

Manager, Human Resources, CO-OPERATIVE TRUST COMPANY OF CANADA, 333 - 3rd Ave. N., Saskatoon, SK S7K 2M2 (306) 956-1890, FAX 652-7614. Born Humboldt, Sask. m. David. 2 ch. EDUC: Univ. of Saskatchewan, Bus. Admin. 1984, Certificate in Adult Educ. 1991. CAREER: hum. res., Co-operative Trust Company of Canada, 15 yrs. AFFIL: Saskatchewan Training & Development Association (Membership Dir., Saskatoon Chapter 1991-94; Pres. 1996); Avalon Community Association (Pres.); Saskatoon Human Resources Association. INTERESTS: organizational dev.; volunteer activities; group process; computers; family/work issues. MISC: guest speaker at conferences & seminars on work & family issues, & hum. res. dev.

Devanik Butterfield, Maureen ■ ◉ ▯ ⌣

Executive Editor, *PRAIRIE BOOKS NOW* and Director, ASSOCIATION OF MANITOBA BOOK PUBLISHERS, 100 Arthur St., Ste. 404, Winnipeg, MB R3B 1H3 (204) 947-3335, FAX 942-1555. Born Saint-Boniface, Man. 1957. CAREER: Dir., Association of Manitoba Book Publishers; Exec. Ed., *Prairie Books Now*; Dir. & Prod., Urban Picturers & Manitoba On-line Publishing Services. AFFIL: Manitoba Opera Association (Bd.); Canadian Magazine Publishers Association (Travelling Mktg Consultant). COMMENT: *"Devanik has worked in Winnipeg's cultural community for the past 11 years. She is an active publisher and filmmaker. In addition, she is the director of a trade association representing Manitoba's book publishers and a private marketing consultant."*

Devlin, Corinne (Margaret), MD,FRCS(C), FACOG,FSOGC,Dip.ABS,O.Ont. ⊕

Professor of Obstetrics and Gynecology, MCMASTER UNIVERSITY, 1200 Main St. W., HSC -4F1-8, Hamilton, ON L8N 3Z5 (905) 521-2100, ext. 6253, FAX 577-0471. Born St. Catharines, Ont. 1937. EDUC: Mack Training Sch. for Nurses, Grad. Registered Nurse 1958; Univ. of Western Ontario, MD 1967; McGill Univ. & McMaster Univ., FRCS(C)(Obs/Gyn)

1972; American Bd. of Sexology, Diplomate 1990. CAREER: Prof. of Obstetrics & Gynecology, McMaster Univ., 1984 to date. SELECTED PUBLICATIONS: "Postpartum Amenorrhea-Galactorrhea of Hypothyroidism," with R.A.H. Kinch & E.R. Plunkett (*American Journal of Obstetrics and Gynecology* Nov. 1969); "Preliminary Characterization of Two Types of Suppressor Cells in the Human Uterus," with S. Daya, D.A. Clark & J. Jarrell (*Fertility Sterility* Dec. 1985); "Successful/Unsuccessful Contraceptors: a Multivariate Typology," J.P. Hornick, M.K. Downey & P. Baynam (*Journal of Social Work and Human Sexuality* Winter 1985); "Evaluating and Treating the Menopausal Patient," with S. Psarakis (*Patient Care/Canada* May 1992); numerous other publications. AFFIL: Medical Council of Canada (Licentiate); Coll. of Physicians & Surgeons of Ontario (Fellow); Coll. of Physicians & Surgeons of Canada; Ontario Medical Association; Canadian Medical Association; Canadian Medical Protective Association; American Coll. of Obstetricians & Gynecologists (Fellow); Society of Obstetricians & Gynecologists of Canada (Fellow); Hamilton Academy of Medicine; Hamilton Academy of Medicine, Women's Section; Federation of Medical Women of Canada; Association of Professors of Obstetrics & Gynecology of Canada; Association of Professors of Obstetrics & Gynecology of USA; Canadian Sex Research Forum; Society for the Scientific Study of Sex; N.Y. Academy of Science; North American Menopause Society; American Board of Sexology; International Biographical Association, UK (Life Patron); American Biographical Institute Research Association, US (Life Fellow); Sch. of Nursing, McMaster Univ. (Assoc. Mbr.). HONS: Order of Ontario, 1995; Community Service Award, Zonta Club, 1990. INTERESTS: women's health care; the natural world. MISC: various consultancies, incl. ad hoc committee, Dept. of Health & Welfare, Health Protection Branch, Fertility Control in Canada, Fall 1986; listed in *Canadian Who's Who, World Who's Who of Women & International Who's Who in Sexology.* COMMENT: *"Women's health care in its breadth and depth continues to be my life's preoccupation, at the professional as well as personal level."*

Dewar, Marion, R.N.,B.Sc.N. ■ ○

Chairperson, OXFAM CANADA, 294 Albert St., Ste. 300, Ottawa, ON K1P 6E6 (613) 237-5236, FAX 237-0524. Born Montreal 1928. m. Kenneth. 5 ch. Bob, Elizabeth, Cathy, Paul, Elaine. EDUC: Registered Nurse 1949; Univ. of Ottawa, Certificate in Public Health 1968, B.Sc.N. 1972. CAREER: Nurse in hospitals, schools & communities; Mun. Councillor, 1972-85; Mayor, City of Ottawa, 1978-85; Pres., Canadian New Democratic Party, 1985-87; M.P. (Hamilton Mountain), Gov't of Canada, 1987-88; Exec. Dir., Canadian Council on Children & Youth, 1989-92; Chair, OXFAM Canada. **AFFIL:** Carleton Univ. (Bd. of Gov.); Centre for Studies of Children at Risk (Bd. of Gov.). **HONS:** Citizen of the Year Award, B'Nai Brith, 1982; Canadian Vietnamese Association Award, 1985. **COMMENT:** *"Active against proliferation of nuclear arms. Initiated municipal ballot on nuclear-free cities across Canada. Led a municipal organization to sponsor 4,000 Southeast Asian refugees to Ottawa in 1979. Assisted Aboriginal persons from "Constitutional Express" to be billeted and fed in Ottawa as they presented their request for protection in the Canadian Charter of Rights. Five thousand Aboriginals arrived in Ottawa in 1980 for a peaceful and strong presentation."*

Dewar, Susan E. ⊛ ✏ 🎭
Editorial Cartoonist, *THE OTTAWA SUN*, 380 Hunt Club Rd., Box 9729, Stn. T, Ottawa, ON K1G 5H7 (613) 739-5176, FAX 49-7296. Syndicated Cartoonist, UNIVERSAL PRESS, 4520 Main St., Kansas City, MO, 64112-7701. Born 1944. s. 1 ch. **EDUC:** Univ. of Western Ontario, Arts 1972; Toronto Teachers' Coll., 1973. **CAREER:** Tour Guide, Erlangen, Germany, 1975-79; Primary Teacher, Round Lake Reserve, 1980-81; Primary Teacher, Bayview Glen, 1981-84; Cartoonist, Archar Inc., 1981-84; Ed. Cartoonist, *Calgary Sun*, 1984-88; Ed. Cartoonist, *Ottawa Sun*, 1988 to date; Syndicated Cartoonist, Universal Press, 1995 to date. **SELECTED CREDITS:** Cartoon strip, "Us & Them," joint venture with cartoonist Wiley Miller, Iowa, syndicated by Universal Press, commenced July 1995. **SELECTED PUBLICATIONS:** work also appears in *Portfolio*, the Association of Canadian Editorial Cartoonists' annual anthology of cartoons in Canada, 1985 to date; monthly cartoon, *Modern Woman Magazine*. **AFFIL:** Association of Canadian Editorial Cartoonists (Pres. 1993, 1994). **HONS:** 5 Edward Dunlop Awards for editorial cartooning; 1 National Business Writing Award for editorial cartooning; 1 National Newspaper Award nomination for editorial cartooning. **INTERESTS:** "Anything I can put in a cartoon!" **COMMENT:** *"Single mom trying to beat the clock and the creditors with two full-time jobs. Primary pursuit: more time."*

Dewhurst, Margaret, B.Comm., R.S.W.(Alta.) ■ ✊ ♥
92 Fairway Dr., Edmonton, AB T6J 2C5. Born Widness, Lancs., UK 1933. m. William George Dewhurst. 2 ch. Timothy A., Susan J. **EDUC:** Univ. of Birmingham, B.Comm.(Hons.) 1955; Univ. of London, London Sch. of Econ., Certificate in Mental Health 1959. **CAREER:** various social work positions, UK, 1955-69; Sr. Social Worker, Edmonton General Hospital, 1971-77; Sr. Social Worker, Community & Family Svcs, City of Edmonton, 1977-78, Social Svc. Centre Supervisor, 1978-84; Dir., Personnel & Support Svcs, 1985-95. **SELECTED PUBLICATIONS:** *Effects of Late Onset Epilepsy*, co-author (1961); *The Canadian Health Care System with Special Reference to Mental Health Services*, co-author (1992); *On Track* (newsletter), ed. (1985-88); various articles & commentaries; reviewer. **AFFIL:** Community Organization Employee Benefit Society of Alberta (Past Pres.); Alberta Association of Social Workers (Past-Pres. 1985-89); Canadian Association of Social Workers (Pres, 1991-93); International Federation of Social Workers (Treas. 1992 to date); Regional Mental Health Advisory Committee, Edmonton (Chair 1995 to date). **HONS:** volunteer awards, United Way and Christmas Bureau of Edmonton; nominated for the Edmonton YWCA Women of the Year, 1989 & 1990. **MISC:** has made extensive presentations on social work, etc.; keynote speaker, Alberta Association of Social Workers, 1991; extensive exec. committee work.

de Wilde, Lisa, B.A.,LL.B. 📺 $ 🎭
President and Chief Operating Officer, TMN - THE MOVIE NETWORK/MOVIEPIX, BCE Place, 181 Bay St., Ste. 100, Toronto, ON M5J 2T3 (416) 956-2010, FAX 956-5399. Born Winnipeg 1956. m. Jim. **EDUC:** McGill Univ., B.A.(Pol. Sci.) 1977, LL.B. 1980; Law Society of Upper Canada, Bar Admission Course 1981. **BAR:** Ont., 1982. **CAREER:** Legal Cnsl, Canadian Radio-television & Telecommunications Commission, 1982-88; Exec. Asst to the Chair, 1988; Dir. Gen.-Cable, Pay & Specialty Svcs, 1988-89; Ptnr, Heenan Blaikie, 1989-92; Exec. VP, The Movie Network - First Choice Canadian Communications Corporation, 1993; Pres. & COO, TMN - The Movie Network/ MOVIEPIX, 1994 to date. **DIRECTOR:** Regal Greetings & Gifts Inc. **AFFIL:** Alliance for Canada's Audio-Visual Heritage (Dir.); Canadian Cable Television Association (Bd. of Dir.); Advanced Broadcasting Society of Canada (Chair, Mkt Impact Assessment Committee); Toronto Women in Film & Television; Academy of Canadian Cinema & Television; Canadian Bar Association; The Feature Film Project, an initiative of the Canadian Film Centre (Bd. of Dir.); Canadian Advanced Technology Association (Bd. of Dir.).

Dhruvarajan, Vanaja, B.A., Ph.D. ■ ■ ⟨⟩ ⊕
Professor of Sociology, UNIVERSITY OF WINNIPEG, Winnipeg, MB R3B 2E9 (204), FAX 786-1824, EMAIL Dhruvarajan-V@s.h.uwinnipeg.ca. Born Mosale, India 1939. m. Dr. P.S. Dhruvarajan. 2 ch. Raghu, Prabhu. EDUC: Univ. of Mysore, India, B.A.(Sociology, Econ. & Phil.) 1959; Univ. of Chicago, Ph.D.(Sociology) 1981. CAREER: Asst. Prof., Dept. of Sociology, Univ. of Winnipeg, 1973-81; Assoc. Prof., 1981-82; Prof., 1992 to date; Visiting Scholar, Univ. of Manitoba, 1985-86; Visiting Scholar, Carleton Univ., 1990; Visiting Scholar, St. Mary's Univ., 1990; Adjunct Prof., Dept. of Religion, Univ. of Manitoba, 1991-94; Ruth Wynn Woodward Endowed Chair in Women's Studies, Simon Fraser Univ., 1994-95. SELECTED PUBLICATIONS: 3 books, 7 refereed papers, 4 book chpts., book, manuscript & article reviews; invited presentations at numerous int'l, nat'l & community conferences/seminars, etc. EDIT: Assoc. Editor, *Canadian Review of Sociology and Anthropology*, 1992-94; mbr., Edit. Bd., *Atlantis: A Women's Studies Journal*, 1992-94. AFFIL: Immigrant Women's Association of Manitoba; U.N. Platform for Action Committee, Man.; Social Science Federation of Canada (Bd. mbr. 1986-89); Canadian Women's Studies Association (Pres. 1986-87; VP 1985-86); Canadian Research Institute for the Advancement of Women (Bd. mbr. 1986-89); Western Association of Sociology and Anthropology (VP 1985); National Council on Family Relations; Canadian Ethnic Studies Association; International Sociological Association; numerous admin. committees, Univ. of Winnipeg & others. HONS: YM/YWCA Woman of Distinction award, 1994; Ruth Wynn Woodward Prof. in Women's Studies, Simon Fraser Univ., 1994-95; nominated for Robin H. Farquhar Award for Excellence in contributing to self-gov't of Univ. of Winnipeg, 1990, 1992. INTERESTS: listening & singing Indian classical music; yoga & transcendental meditation. MISC: spending most of her time this yr. doing research & writing, focus of which is the popular print media; recipient, numerous grants. COMMENT: *"As long as I can remember, I have been interested in exploring ways and means of bringing about social change so that this world will be just and caring for all people. I have spent a significant part of my life in developing friendships among women of diverse background with interests similar to mine so that we can bring about such social transformation. Even though I generally take myself seriously, I have enjoyed bringing up two sons with my husband Raj, have experienced the joy of friendship and love with their*

wives and am enjoying the status of grandmother."

Di Domenico, Mina Ⓢ ◐ ⓔ
Human Resources Systems Consultant, Human Resources System Management, THE TORONTO-DOMINION BANK, T-D Tower, Toronto Dominion Centre, 18th Fl., Box 1, Toronto, ON M5K 1A2 (416) 982-7965, FAX 982-8498. Born Italy 1963. s. EDUC: Ryerson Polytechnic Univ.; Institute of Canadian Bankers. CAREER: Robert Simpson Company, 1980-84; IBM Canada Limited, 1984-85; Hum. Res. Asst., Toronto-Dominion Bank, 1985-88; Hum. Res. Officer, 1989-90; Special Projects, 1990-92; Hum. Res. Systems Consultant, 1992 to date. SELECTED PUBLICATIONS: "Canadian Women and Politics" (*IFBPW-YCW Newsletter*); "Canadian Women and Violence" (*IFBPW-YCW Newsletter*); "International Congress–Two Young Women Represent Canada" (*BP Women*); "International Young Career Women Move Ahead" (*BP Women*); "Natural Superiority of Women" (*BP Women*). AFFIL: Toronto Business & Professional Women's Club (Immediate Past Pres. 1996-98); Canadian Federation of Business & Professional Women (Chair, Personal Dev. & Young Career Women 1994-96); International Federation of Business & Professional Women (N.A. Rep., Twinning Chair 1996-99); High Park Ski Club; Bay/Bloor Bally Matrix Health Club. HONS: Award of Excellence, TD Bank, 1996. INTERESTS: weight lifting; hiking; skiing; computers; reading; languages; opera; classical music; travelling. MISC: Ambassador, Canadian Federation of Business & Professional Women, to represent Young Career Women Program, Int'l Congress, Nagoya, Japan, 1993.

Dick, Diana Davidson, R.N.,B.Sc.N., M.Ed. ⓔ ⊕
Executive Director and Chief Executive Officer, MANITOBA ASSOCIATION OF REGISTERED NURSES, 647 Broadway, Winnipeg, MB R3C 0X2 (204) 774-3477, FAX 775-6052. Born Picton, Ont. s. EDUC: Toronto General Hospital Sch. of Nursing, R.N.; Univ. of Ottawa, Diploma (Admin.) 1971, B.Sc.N. 1972; Queen's Univ., M.Ed.(Educ./Health Systems) 1983. CAREER: Staff Nurse, Emergency Dept., Toronto General Hospital, 1965-69; Staff Nurse, Hemodialysis Unit, Sunnybrook Medical Centre, 1969-70; Teaching Master, Nursing Div., Seneca Coll. of Applied Arts & Technology, 1974-83; Coord., Professional Svcs, Registered Nurses' Association of Ontario, 1983; Coord., Canada Health Act Proj., Canadian Nurses' Association, 1983-84; Coord., Profes-

sional Svcs, Registered Nurses' Association of Ontario, 1984-88; Exec. Officer, Educ., Pay Equity Commission, Gov't of Ont., 1988-91; Sr. Advisor, Ont. Training & Adjustment Bd. Proj., Gov't of Ont., 1991-92; Exec. Officer, Educ., Pay Equity Commission, Gov't of Ont., 1992-93; Exec. Dir. & CEO, Manitoba Association of Registered Nurses, 1993 to date. SELECTED PUBLICATIONS: articles published in *International Nursing Review, Canadian Nurse,* & *The Registered Nurse.* DIRECTOR: Women's World Finance; Higher Ground. AFFIL: Manitoba Association of Registered Nurses; Registered Nurses' Association of Ontario; Coll. of Nurses of Ontario; Provincial Nurse Administrators' Interest Group; Canadian Nurses' Association; International Council of Nurses; Sigma Theta Tau International; Nursing Economics Interest Group; Canadian Association of International Health; Manitoba Nursing Research Institute (Dir.); Manitoba Health Information Network (Dir.); Royal Winnipeg Ballet (Strategic Planning Committee); Women of Winnipeg Annual Retreat. HONS: nominated, Toronto Women's Health Award. INTERESTS: skiing; ballet; music; swimming; politics & issues, local to global; beach walking. MISC: Mbr., Ad Hoc Committee of Women on the Constitution, 1980-83, 1987-89; presented papers & speeches provincially, interprovincially, nationally & internationally; Winnipeg Symphony Orchestra Maestro Bramwell Tony composed & dedicated a musical composition for her cat Ron Peterson (Pete) entitled "A Tribute to Pete Mozart" performed in the 1996 Christmas Pops Series. COMMENT: *"20 years' experience in public sector and association work. Managed the development of proposals, broad public and private sector consultations, communications, education outreach and implementation of activities associated with major policy initiatives related to education, nursing, health, health care, training and systems."*

Dick, Susan, B.A.,M.A.,Ph.D. 🎨 📖 🖼
Professor of English, QUEEN'S UNIVERSITY, Kingston, ON K7L 3N6. Born Battle Creek, Mich. 1940. s. EDUC: Western Michigan Univ., B.A.(Liberal Arts) 1963; Northwestern Univ., M.A.(English) 1964, Ph.D.(English) 1967. CAREER: Dept. of English, Queen's Univ., 1967 to date. AFFIL: Royal Society of Canada. INTERESTS: reading; gardening. MISC: Mbr., Editorial Committee, *Shakespeare Head Press Edition of Virginia Woolf* (Blackwell Publishers).

Dickason, Olive Patricia, C.M.,Ph.D., D.Litt. ■ 🎨 🖼
Professor Emeritus, Department of History,

UNIVERSITY OF ALBERTA, Edmonton, AB T6G 2H4 (403) 437-5065, FAX 492-9125, EMAIL odickason@gpu.srv-ualberta.ca. Journalist. Born Winnipeg 1920. w. Anthony. 3 ch. Anne Dickason, Clare Trzeciak, Roberta Maron. EDUC: Notre Dame Coll., Sask., B.A.(French & Phil.) 1943; Univ. of Ottawa, M.A.(Cdn Hist.) 1972, Ph.D. 1977. CAREER: Teacher, Notre Dame Coll., 1943-44; Gen. & City-Hall Reporter, *The Leader-Post,* Regina, 1944-46; Reporter & Sub-Ed., *The Winnipeg Free Press,* 1946-47; Reporter, Sub-Ed. *The Gazette,* Montreal, 1950-55; Assoc. Women's Ed., *The Globe and Mail,* 1955-57; Women's Ed., *The Globe Magazine,* 1957-62; Women's Ed., *The Globe and Mail,* 1962-67; Chief of Info. Svcs, National Gallery of Canada, 1967-70; Sessional Lecturer, Univ. of Ottawa, 1971-75; Sessional Lecturer, Univ. of Alberta, 1975-76; Asst. Prof., 1976-79; Assoc. Prof., 1979-85; Prof., 1985-92; Prof. Emeritus, 1992 to date. SELECTED CREDITS: appeared in film, *The Learning Path* in the series *As Long as the Rivers Flow,* 1992; numerous interviews on radio & TV. SELECTED PUBLICATIONS: *Indian Arts in Canada* (Ottawa: Queen's Printer, 1972); *The Myth of the Savage and the Beginnings of French Colonialism in the Americas* (Univ. of Alberta Press, 1984); *The Law of Nations and the New World,* with Leslie Green (Univ. of Alberta Press, 1989); *Canada's First Nations: A History of Founding Peoples* (Toronto: McClelland & Stewart, 1992); ed. *The Native Imprint* (Athabaska Univ. Ed. Enterprises, 1995); co-ed with D.A. Long, *Visions of the Heart* (Harcourt Brace, 1996); various other publications; numerous reviews. EDIT: Ed. Bd., *American Indian Culture and Research Journal,* 1979 to date. AFFIL: Canadian Historical Association; Institut d'histoire de l'Amérique française; French Colonial Historical Society; American Society for Ethnohistory; Société française d'histoire d'outre-mer; Métis Nation of Alberta; Native Communications Program, Grant MacEwan Community Coll. (Bd. Mbr.); Ben Calf Robe Society (Bd. Mbr.); Institute for the Advancement of Aboriginal Women (Bd. Mbr.). HONS: D.Litt.(Hon.), Univ. of New Brunswick, 1993; Fellow, Ryerson Polytechnic Univ., 1994; D.Litt.(Hon.), Univ. of Alberta, 1995; LL.D.(Hon.), Univ. of Calgary, 1996; D.Litt.(Hon.), Univ. of Windsor, 1996; First Prize, Elizabeth Arden Award for fashion reporting, 1956; Second Prize (tie), Elizabeth Arden Award for fashion reporting, 1958; Judy Award for fashion reporting, 1959; Judy Award for editing women's section, 1962; MacLaren's Award for typography & layout, Women's Section, *The Globe and Mail,* 1965, 1967; Hon. Mention, Canadian Historical

Association, *The Myth of the Savage*, 1985; Hon. Mention, Alberta Writers' Guild, *The Myth of the Savage*, 1985; Hon. Mention, Society for Colonial Wars, *The Myth of the Savage*, 1986; Canada 125 Medal, 1992; Sir John A. Macdonald Prize, Canadian Historical Association, *Canada's First Nations*, 1992; Métis Woman of the Year, Women of the Métis Nation of Alberta; Medal of Honour, Nat'l Alumni, Notre Dame Coll. of Saskatchewan, 1992. **INTERESTS:** theatre; opera; ballet. **MISC:** recipient of grants & fellowships; numerous conference presentations & invited lectures; referee for various journals & granting agencies; Co-Chair, Conference on Women of the Métis Nation, 1987; Delegate for Women of the Métis Nation, First Ministers' Conference, 1987. **COMMENT:** *"I am now emeritus, and still very interested in developing the history of First Nations, not only for Canada but also for the hemisphere."*

Dickenson, June Chipman, B.A. ■ 📖 $ ✎
Advertising Manager, QUILL & QUIRE, 70 The Esplanade, Ste. 210, Toronto, ON M5E 1R2 (416) 360-0044, FAX 955-0794, EMAIL Quill@hookup.net. Born Edmonton 1963. m. Bob Dickenson. **EDUC:** Univ. of Alberta, B.A.(Soc.) 1985; Grad., Banff Pub. Workshop (Books, Magazines & Comp. for Publishing Program) 1985. **CAREER:** Sales Rep., Oxford Univ. Press, 1986-87; Sales Rep., Canadian Book Marketing Group, 1987-88; Advtg. Sales Mgr, *Quill & Quire*, 1988-91; Co-Publisher & Advtg Mgr, 1988-84; Advtg Mgr, 1994 to date.

Dickey Young, Pamela, B.A.,M.Div., Ph.D. ■ 🎓 ☸ 📜
Head, Department of Religious Studies, QUEEN'S UNIVERSITY, Kingston, ON K7L 3N6 (613) 545-6000, ext. 4324. **EDUC:** Dalhousie Univ., B.A. 1976; Atlantic Sch. of Theology, M.Div. 1978; Southern Methodist Univ., Ph.D. 1983. **ORDAINED:** Maritime Conference of the United Church of Canada, May 1978. **CAREER:** United Church Minister on Rawdon (NS) Pastoral Charge, 1983-85; Adjunct Asst. Prof., Atlantic Sch. of Theology, 1983-85; Asst. Prof., Queen's Theological Coll., 1985-91; Assoc. Prof., 1991-95; Prof., 1995 to date; Dean of Women, 1993-95; Head, Dept. of Religious Studies, 1996 to date. **SELECTED PUBLICATIONS:** *Feminist Theology/Christian Theology: In Search of Method* (Minneapolis: Fortress Press, 1990); *Theological Reflections on Ministry and Sexual Orientation* (Burlington: Trinity Press 1990); *Christ in a Post Christian World* (Minneapolis: Fortress, 1995); "Diversity in Feminist Christology" (*Studies in Religion/Sciences Religieuses* 1992); "An Introduction to the Study of a priori Christology" (*Toronto Journal of Theology* Spring 1985); "Feminist Theology: From Past to Future," in *Gender, Genre and Religion: Feminist Reflections*, ed. Joy Morny & Eva Neumaier-Dargyay (Waterloo: Wilfrid Laurier Univ. Press, 1995); "Beyond Moral Influence to an Atoning Life" (*Theology Today* 52(3), Oct. 1995); various other publications. **EDIT:** Coord., Ed. Bd., Women & Religion Series, Canadian Corporation for Studies in Religion, 1994 to date; Ed. Bd., *Gender in World Religions*, 1992 to date; Ed. Advisory Bd., *Toronto Journal of Theology*, 1993-96. **AFFIL:** Canadian Theological Society; Canadian Corporation for Studies in Religion; Canadian Society for the Study of Religion/Société canadienne pour l'étude de la religion; American Academy of Religion; American Theological Society; Canadian Women's Studies Association; Senior Women Academic Administrators of Canada. **HONS:** many scholarships & prizes. **COMMENT:** *"My twin goals at present are to advance feminist study in my own area (Religious Studies) and to advance the status of women in the university."*

Dickson, Jean, R.N. ✋ 📜
Chairman, Award Committee, STEPHEN LEACOCK ASSOCIATES, 203 Martin Dr., Orillia, ON L3V 3P4 (705) 325-6546. Born Toronto 1930. w. Dr. Lorne C. Dickson. 3 ch. Peter Dickson, Grant Dickson, Susan Both. **EDUC:** Toronto General Hospital, R.N. 1953; Univ. of Western Ontario, Diploma (Nursing Svc. Admin.) 1960. **CAREER:** nursing positions, Johns Hopkins Hospital, Baltimore, Le Roy Hospital, N.Y.C., Parry Sound General Hospital, St. Catharines General Hospital, & Soldiers' Memorial Hospital, Orillia; consultant, Mary Kay Cosmetics. **AFFIL:** Stephen Leacock Associates (Chair, Award Committee; Corresponding Sec.; Bd. of Dir., Leacock Museum 8 yrs.; Chair 6 yrs.); Stroke Recovery Association (Founder, Orillia Chapter 1977; Chapter Coord., Central Ont. 8 yrs.).

Dickson, Jennifer, R.A.,C.M. ■■ 🎓 🪶
Artist, Photographer and Garden Historian. 20 Osborne St., Ottawa, ON K1S 4Z9 (613) 730-2083, FAX 730-1818. Born Piet Retief, South Africa 1936. m. Ronald Andrew Sweetman. 1 ch. Bill Sweetman. **EDUC:** Goldsmiths Coll., Sch. of Art, Univ. of London, 1954-59; Atelier 17, Paris, 1960-65. **CAREER:** Teacher, Eastbourne Sch. of Art, 1959-62; directed & developed Printmaking Dept., Brighton Coll. of Art, 1962-68; Graphics Atelier, Saidye Bronfman Centre, Montreal, 1970-72; Visiting Artist, Ball State Univ. 1967, Univ. of West Indies 1968, Univ. of Wisconsin 1972, Ohio State Univ. 1973, Western Illinois Univ. 1973, Haystack

Mountain Sch. of Crafts 1973, Queen's Univ. 1977-78; Sessional Instructor, Concordia Univ. 1972-79, Univ. of Ottawa 1980-85; Head, Dept. of Art Hist., Saidye Bronfman Centre, 1985-88. SELECTED PUBLICATIONS: author, 29 suites of original etchings incl. 3 most recent: *The Haunted Heart* (1993), *Sanctuaries and Paradeisos* (1994), & *Old and New Worlds* (1995); author, *The Royal Academy Gardener's Journal* (1991). EXHIBITIONS: *The Last Silence*, toured Italy Feb.-May 1993, exhibited in Ottawa Nov. 1993-Jan. 1994 at Canadian Museum of Contemporary Photography. COLLECTIONS: represented in major int'l museums incl. Metropolitan Museum (N.Y.), Victoria & Albert Museum (London), Hermitage Museum (Leningrad), Canadian Council Art Bank, National Gallery of Canada. AFFIL: British Printmakers' Council (founding mbr.); Print & Drawing Council of Canada; Royal Society of Painter-Etchers & Engravers (Fellow). HONS: Prix des Jeunes Artistes (Gravure), Biennale de Paris, 1963; major prize, World Print Competition, San Francisco, 1974; Biennale Prize, 5th Norwegian Int'l Print Biennale, 1980; honorary LL.D., Univ. of Alberta, for contribution to Cdn culture, 1988; named Member of the Order of Canada, 1995. MISC: subject of CBC special TV programs, 1980, 1982, 1990 & 1995.

Dickson, Kimberly, B.A.,B.Ed. ✍ ⁄
Public Relations Director, ST. FRANCIS XAVIER UNIVERSITY, Box 5000, Antigonish, NS B2G 2W5 (902) 867-2489, FAX 867-5145. Born New Glasgow, N.S. 1956. m. Barry L. Campbell. 1 ch. Darcy Vance Dickson Campbell. EDUC: St. Francis Xavier Univ., B.A.(English) 1978, B.Ed.(English) 1979. CAREER: English teacher, East Pictou Rural High Sch., 1979-80; Public Rel'ns Officer, St. Francis Xavier Univ., 1980 to date; Interim Coord. of Univ. Advancement, May-Sept. 1993. SELECTED PUBLICATIONS: has written feature stories for the St. Francis Xavier Alumni magazine since 1980; Mng Ed., *Alumni News*; Ed., *Excerpts.*; articles published in N.S. weekly & daily newspapers during the past yr. AFFIL: St. Francis Xavier Univ. Alumni Association (Bd. of Dir.); Canadian Council for the Advancement of Education (Mbr.; Chair, Atlantic Conference 1994); Council for the Advancement of Post-Secondary Education; Antigonish Chamber of Commerce (Chair, Media Comm. 1992-95; Dir. 1990-95; Exec. 1995 to date); Pictou/Antigonish/Guysborough John Howard Society (Advisory Council); Antigonish Highland Games (volunteer, Public Rel'ns); Scotia Highland Dancers (Choreographer & publicity 1980-90); mbr., various univ. committees (Sta-

tus of Women; Presidential Committee on the Violence Against Women; Telecomm.; Staff Appreciation: Convocation & Institutional Analysis); Antigonish Highland Society (Bd. of Dir. 1995 to date). HONS: N.S. Highland Dancing Champion, 1972 & 1976; President's Award, Antigonish Chamber of Commerce, 1994; has won numerous dancing medals & trophies; has won nat'l awards for work with The Scotia Highland Dancers as part of a team of 3 choreographers. INTERESTS: highland dancing; creative writing; public speaking; travel; sports; drawing; tole painting. MISC: performed in the chorus in Theatre Antigonish productions; workshop leader on creative writing for Artstock, a provincial high sch. conference. COMMENT: *"Dickson is a university administrator who has dedicated the majority of her career to the development of the Public Relations Department at her alma mater, St. Francis Xavier University. She is a writer, editor, public speaker, university spokesperson, and events coordinator with a special love for creative writing. She is a wife, mother and an active member of the local community."*

Dion, Céline ■ ■ 🖋 ⊗ 🎵
Singer. c/o Productions Feeling Inc., 2540 boul. Daniel-Johnson, Ste. 755, Laval, QC H7T 2S3. Born Charlemagne, Que. 1968. m. René Angélil. CAREER: youngest of 14 children in highly musical family; gave first public performance at age 5; recorded demo tape, age 12 - led to recording of debut album (music entrepreneur René Angélil mortgaged house to finance recording). SELECTED CREDITS: *Unison* (1st English-language album; top 5 single in U.S. "Where Does My Heart Beat Now"), 1990; *Dion chante Plamondon*, 1991; *Céline Dion* (2nd English-language album, 4 hit singles), 1992; *The Colour of My Love* (triple Platinum, U.S.; singles "The Power of Love" & "Misled" topped Hot 100 & *Billboard* charts), 1994; *D'eux* (*The French Album* in US; sold more than 5 million copies worldwide; best-selling French-language album ever; best-selling album ever in France), 1995; *Falling Into You*, 1996; performed "The Power of the Dream" at opening ceremonies of Centennial Olympics, 1996. HONS: Gold Medal, Yamaha World Song Festival, Tokyo, 1982 (14 yrs. old); 1st Cdn to receive gold record in France, 1983; won Eurovision Song Contest, Dublin, 1988; Female Vocalist of the Year, & *Unison* named Album of the Year, Juno Awards, Canada, 1991 (1st French-Canadian to win in these categories); command performance for Prince Charles & Princess Diana, Ottawa, 1991; "Beauty and the Beast" (theme for Disney movie) won Academy Award for Best Song

Written for a Motion Picture or TV, 1992 - performed song with co-singer Peabo Bryson on Oscar telecast; Female Vocalist of the Year, Juno Awards, 1992; "Beauty and the Beast" named Best Pop Performance by a Duo or Group with Vocal, Grammy Awards, 1993; 4 Juno Awards incl. Female Vocalist of the Year (3rd consecutive yr.), 1993; hosted Juno Awards show, 1993; nominated for Grammy Award ("When I Fall in Love"), 1994; nominated for Best Female Pop Vocal Performance (for "The Power of Love"), Grammy Awards, 1995; Medal of Arts, French Gov't, 1996; 2 Victoires de la musique awards, France, 1996. **MISC:** only female artist ever to top UK single & album charts for 5 consecutive weeks; top-selling foreign artist in Japan - 1st non-Japanese performer in 12 yrs. to reach #1 on nat'l singles chart, 1995; biggest-selling artist of 1995 in Canada; 1 of only 4 female artists to sell more than 1 million copies of a single in the UK.

Dionne-Marsolais, The Hon. Rita, B.A., B.Sc.,M.A. ■ 🍁 $ 👍

Ministre déléguée à l'Industrie et au Commerce, GOUVERNEMENT DU QUÉBEC, 770, rue Sherbrooke O., 9e étage, Montreal, QC H3A 1G1 (514) 982-3004, EMAIL rita.dionne-marsolais@miscl.gouv.qc.ca. 710, Place D'Youville, 6e étage, Québec, QC G1R 4Y4 (418) 691-5650. Born Sherbrooke, Que. 1947. m. Jean Marsolais. **EDUC:** Univ. of Montreal, B.A. (Arts) 1967, B.Sc.(Econ.) 1970, M.A.(Econometric) 1971. **CAREER:** Asst. to Pres., Hydro-Québec; VP, Corp. Dev., Société générale de financement du Québec, 1979-82; Pres., Bio-Endo inc., 1982-84; Que. Agent Gen. in N.Y., 1984-87; Pres., les Consultants NUNC Inc., 1987-91; Sr. Mgr, Price Waterhouse, 1991-94. **AFFIL:** former affiliations: Science Council of Canada; Conseil de la science et de la technologie du Québec; Americas Society, N.Y. (Advisory Committee, Cdn Affairs Program); Chambre de commerce du Montréal métropolitain (Chair, Committee on Free Trade); Montreal Symphony Orchestra; International Year of the Family (Chair, Rosemount riding); Maison grise de Rosemont (Fin. Committee); Optimist Club of Rosemount; Mbr., Bd. of Dir., Fondation de l'Hôpital Saint-Luc, Bytec-Comterm, Centre de recherche industrielle du Québec, Société d'exportation des ressources éducatives du Québec, Institut national de productivité, Univ. de Montréal (Doctoral Fellowship Fund, Econ.). **MISC:** 1st woman appointed to a sr. mgmt position, Hydro-Québec. **COMMENT:** *"Mme. Dionne-Marsolais is a leader in the Montreal community. She is well-known for her commitment to the advancement of women in business and politics."*

Dirks, Patricia, B.A.,M.A.,Ph.D. 🎓 📖

Associate Professor, History Department, BROCK UNIVERSITY, St. Catharines, ON L2S 3A1 (905) 688-5550, ext. 3503. Born Ont. 1941. m. Gerald E. **EDUC:** Queen's Univ., B.A. 1963, M.A. 1966; Univ. of Toronto, Ph.D. 1972. **CAREER:** Sessional Lecturer, State Univ. of New York at Buffalo, 1970-71; Lecturer, Hist. Dept., Brock Univ., 1971-72; Asst. Prof., 1973-90; Assoc. Prof., 1990 to date. **SELECTED PUBLICATIONS:** *L'Action libérale nationale: A Failed Attempt to Reconcile Modernization with Tradition* (Kingston: Univ. Press, 1991); "The Public Power Movement in Quebec City, 1929-1934" (*Urban History Review* June 1981); "Finding the Canadian Way: Origins of the Religious Education Council of Canada" (*Studies in Religion/Sciences Religieuses* 1987); "Canada's Methodists Respond to the 'Big Boy' Problem 1900-1925" (*Canadian Methodist Historical Society Papers* 1990); various other publications. **AFFIL:** Canadian Historical Association; Canadian Institute of International Affairs; Ontario Historical Society; Association of Canadian Studies. **MISC:** recipient, numerous grants. **COMMENT:** *"I was born in a northern Ontario mining community, moved to Orillia, Ontario as a teenager where I became interested in Canadian history. I have pursued this interest ever since and have been fortunate to be able to teach Canadian history at the university level since the early 1970s."*

Djwa, Sandra A., B.Ed.,Ph.D. 🎓 📖

Professor, Department of English, SIMON FRASER UNIVERSITY, Burnaby, BC V5A 1S6 (604) 291-3136, EMAIL djwa@sfu.ca. Born St. John's 1939. m. Lalit Srivastava. 1 ch. **EDUC:** Memorial Univ., Teacher A. Level (Educ.) 1956; Univ. of British Columbia, B.Ed. (English) 1964, Ph.D.(English) 1968. **CAREER:** elementary teacher, 1957-60; Prof. of English, Simon Fraser Univ., 1968 to date; Chair of English, 1986-94; SFU Senate, 1987-90; Mbr., SFU Bd. of Gov., 1990-96. **SELECTED PUBLICATIONS:** *Giving Canada a Literary History: A Memoir* author Carl F. Klinck, Ed. (Carleton Univ. Press for Univ. of Western Ontario, 1991); *Complete Poems of E.J. Pratt: A Definitive Edition*, two vols., co-ed. with Gordon Moyles (Univ. of Toronto Press, 1989); *The Politics of the Imagination: A Life of F.R. Scott* (McClelland & Stewart, 1987; pbk., Douglas & McIntyre, 1989); *On F.R. Scott: Essays on His Contributions to Law, Literature and Politics*, co-ed. with R. St.J. MacDonald (McGill-Queen's Univ. Press, 1983); *Saul and Selected Poetry of Charles Heavysege*, Ed. (Univ. of Toronto Press, 1976); *E.J. Pratt; The Evolu-*

tionary Years (Copp Clark & McGill-Queen's Univ. Press, 1974); numerous reviews & articles. AFFIL: Simon Fraser Univ. (Bd. of Gov.); Association of Canadian & Quebec Literatures (Co-Founder); Canadian Association of Chairs of English (Pres.); Association of Canadian Teachers of English; Royal Society of Canada (Mbr. 1994). HONS: Sr. Killam Research Fellow, 1981-83. INTERESTS: gardening; writing biographies. COMMENT: *"I am an educator, writer and teacher particularly interested in the development of English-Canadian culture."*

Doan, Helen McKinnon, B.A.,M.A., Ph.D. ■ ⌾

Master of Vanier College and Associate Professor of Psychology, YORK UNIVERSITY, 254 Vanier College, 4700 Keele St., North York, ON M3J 1P5 (416) 736-5192, FAX 736-5899, EMAIL hdoan@yorku.ca. Born Toronto 1938. m. Robert Routbard. 1 ch. Lara Helen. EDUC: Univ. of Toronto, B.A.(Psych.) 1959, M.A. (Psych.) 1961; Queen's Univ., Ph.D.(Psych.) 1966. CAREER: Clinical Psychologist, Mental Health Clinic, Whitby, Ont., 1961-62; Clinical Psychologist, Bawden Clinic, Kingston General Hospital, 1962-63; Lecturer, York Univ., 1965-66; Asst. Prof., 1966-71; Assoc. Prof., 1971 to date; Master, Vanier Coll., 1993 to date. SELECTED PUBLICATIONS: *Every Pregnancy: from Conception to Delivery* (Toronto: Stoddart Publishing Co., 1990); *Every Woman: Adapting to Midlife Change* (Toronto: Stoddart Publishing Co., 1987); *Every Girl: Learning About Menstruation*, with J. Morse (Toronto: Stoddart Publishing Co., 1985); various publications in refereed journals, reports, articles, book chapters, presentations & workshops. AFFIL: Canadian Psychological Association; American Psychological Association; American Association for the Advancement of Science; Ontario Association for Clinical Hypnosis; American Association for the Advancement of Behavior Therapy; Academy of Medicine.

Dobkin, Patricia Lynn, B.A.,M.Sc., Ph.D. ⊕ 🏵

Medical Scientist, Division of Clinical Epidemiology, THE MONTREAL GENERAL HOSPITAL, 1650 Cedar Ave., Montreal, QC H3G 1A4 (514) 937-6011, ext. 4717, FAX 934-8293, EMAIL mcdp@musica.mcgill.ca. Assistant Professor, Department of Medicine, McGILL UNIVERSITY. Born Buffalo, N.Y. 1954. m. Pierre Binette. 2 ch. Raymond Dobkin Binette, Justine Dobkin Binette. EDUC: McGill Univ., B.A. 1982; Univ. of Georgia, M.Sc. 1984, Ph.D. 1987. CAREER: Staff Psychologist, Montreal General Hospital, 1987; Staff Psychologist, Allan Memorial Institute, 1987-88; Medical Scientist, Royal Victoria Hospital, 1988; Postdoctoral Fellow, McGill Univ. & Douglas Hospital, 1989-91; Research Assoc., Douglas Hospital, 1989 to date; Asst. Prof., Univ. de Montréal, 1991-93; Chercheure titulaire, Groupe de recherche sur l'inadaptation psychosocial chez l'enfant, 1991 to date; Asst. Prof., McGill Univ., 1993 to date; Medical Scientist, Montreal General Hospital, 1993 to date. SELECTED PUBLICATIONS: "Individual and Peer Characteristics in Predicting Boys' Early Onset of Substance Abuse," with Tremblay *et al* (*Child Development*, 1995); "Labour Pain is Influenced by Physical as Well as Psychological Variables," with R. Melzack *et al* (*Canadian Medical Association Journal* 1984); "Assessment of Sexual Dysfunction in Oncology Patients: Review, Critique, and Suggestions," with I. Bradley (*Journal of Psychosocial Oncology* 1991); "Determining Baseline and Adaptation Periods in Stress Research," with C. Létourneau & C. Breault (*Psychotherapy and Psychosomatics* 1994); "Is Having an Alcoholic Father Hazardous for Children's Physical Health?" with R.E. Tremblay *et al* (*Addiction* 1994); numerous abstracts & communications; various other publications. AFFIL: Corporation professionnelle des psychologues du Québec; Canadian Psychological Association; Society of Behavioral Medicine (Sec.-Treas. 1993-95; Pres.-Elect 1996); American Psychosomatic Society. HONS: career award, Conseil québécoise de la recherche, 1996-99. INTERESTS: health psych. across the life cycle. MISC: recipient, various grants incl. Principal Investigator, "Family factors in boys at risk for substance abuse," & "Social Support: Defining and Reinforcing Its Role in Adult Substance Abuse Treatmen," Social Sciences & Humanities Research Council of Canada, & Co-PI, "Decreasing Costs and Improving Outcomes in Chronic Diseases: A Randomized Multi-site Trail of Group Psychotherapy for patients with Systemic Lupus Erythematosus," NHRDP; reviewer for various journals & granting agencies. COMMENT: *"My aim is to highlight the biopsychosocial nature of health and to ensure, through research and education, that medicine takes into account all aspects of the person in the treatment of various diseases across the life cycle."*

Dobko, Theresa, B.Sc. ■ ♥ ⊛ ♂

Self-employed consultant to charities and foundations on organizational development, service delivery and fundraising. FAX (416) 515-8128, EMAIL dobko@pathcom.com. Born Toronto 1958. EDUC: Univ. of Toronto, B.Sc.(Psych.) 1977; York Univ. (Masters in Clinical Psych., incomplete) 1977-81. **CAREER:** Crisis Intervention Unit, Toronto East General Hospital, 1984; Coord., AIDS Support Dept., AIDS Committee of Toronto, 1984-88; Coord., Women & AIDS Proj., AIDS Committee of Toronto, 1989-91; Exec. Dir., Toronto People with AIDS Foundation, 1991-93; Exec. Dir., Kumbaya Foundation, 1993-96. **VOLUNTEER INVOLVEMENTS:** Crisis Intervention Unit, 1980-83; Amnesty International, 1981; Ontario Coalition for Abortion Clinics, 1981-84; York Univ. Women's Centre, 1983-84; Casey House Hospice, 1985-85; Big Sisters of Metropolitan Toronto, 1988-89; The Women's Common of Metropolitan Toronto, 1989-94; Voices of Positive Women, 1995; Willow: The Ontario Breast Cancer Support & Resource Centre, 1995-96. **SELECTED PUBLICATIONS:** *AIDS: Words and Meanings*, AIDS Committee of Toronto, 1990; *Women and AIDS* (booklet), AIDS Committee of Toronto, 1988, revised 1990. **INTERESTS:** women's health; AIDS; community activism; child & youth issues; lesbian/gay rights; computer training for women; the Internet. **COMMENT:** *"In 1984, I became one of the first AIDS counsellors in Canada. In 1989, I began Canada's first Women and AIDS Project. From 1993-96, I helped raise more than half a million dollars for a national AIDS foundation. Currently I have expanded my efforts to breast cancer and youth organizations as well. After 12 years working in the nonprofit sector, I am more concerned than ever for the financial and organizational survival of charities across Canada. When not working, I'm pulling weeds in my garden and avoiding speed bumps on the information highway."*

Dobran, Beverly Anne, B.A., B.Sc.(M.E.) ■ ■ ∰

Graduate Student, Mechanical Engineering Department, UNIVERSITY OF MANITOBA, Winnipeg, MB R3T 2N2 (204) 474-9652, EMAIL umdobran@cc.umanitoba.ca. Born St. Paul, Minn. 1953. m. Mauro F. Dobran. 1 ch. Gina Julianna Dobran. **EDUC:** Univ. of Manitoba, B.A.(English) 1972, B.Sc.(Mech. Eng.) 1977. **CAREER:** Petroleum/Reservoir Eng., Amoco Canada Petroleum Ltd., 1977-80; Exploitation Eng., Dome Petroleum Limited, 1980-82; Reservoir Eng., Westcoast Petroleum Ltd., 1982-85; Marker, Tech. Communication course, Univ. of Manitoba, 1991 to date; grad. student, Metallurgical Dept., 1995 to date. **SELECTED PUBLICATIONS:** contributor, *The Manitoba Professional Engineer*, 1990 to date. **AFFIL:** Association of Professional Engineers of the Province of Manitoba; Girl Guides of Canada; Canadian Cancer Society. **INTERESTS:** stamp collecting. **COMMENT:** *"I am a*

person who has always had many interests (as reflected by my studies). Now, I am busy combining family with pursuits at university."

Dobson, Lyndsay ■ ■ ▯ ▤ ⊗

LYNDSAY DOBSON BOOKS (distributor of Cdn private press books & broadsides), P.O. Box 285, Grimsby, ON L3M 4G5 (905) 309-0309. Born Toronto 1949. d. **EDUC:** Ryerson Polytechnical Institute, Certificate (Library Techniques) 1972. **CAREER:** Children's Coord., Grimsby Public Library, 1972-81; Library Technician, Lincoln Co. Separate Sch. Bd., 1986 to date; Lyndsay Dobson Books, 1983 to date. **SELECTED PUBLICATIONS:** *The Canadian Private Presses in Print* (Lyndsay Dobson Books, 1984); *Backlist Catalogue* (Lyndsay Dobson Books, 1995); *Recent Arrivals and Other News* (Lyndsay Dobson Books, biannual, 1985 to date). **AFFIL:** Grimsby Historical Society (newsletter editor); Grimsby Cultural Action Network (exec. mbr.); Shaw Guild, Shaw Festival (volunteer); Mackenzie Heritage Printery Museum; Carnegie Gallery, Dundas, Ont. (volunteer); Canadian Book Binders & Book Artists Guild. **INTERESTS:** all of the arts. **COMMENT:** *"Since 1983, Lyndsay Dobson Books has encouraged, promoted and made distribution possible for Canadian private press printers of hand printed books and broadsides."*

Dobson, Wendy K., B.Sc.N.,M.P.A.,S.M., Ph.D. $ ✦ ⧉

Director, Centre for International Business and Professor, Faculty of Management, UNIVERSITY OF TORONTO, 246 Bloor St. W., Toronto, ON M5S 1V4 (416) 978-7792, FAX 928-6694. **EDUC:** Univ. of British Columbia, B.Sc.N. 1963; Harvard Univ., Kennedy Sch. of Gov't, M.P.A. 1971, Sch. of Public Health, S.M. 1972; Princeton Univ., Dept. of Econ., Ph.D. 1979. **CAREER:** various positions, Cdn public health, 1963-66; Reg'l Dir., Family Planning Proj., Christian Medical Association of India, CUSO assignment, India, 1967; Program Officer, Planning & Training Div., CIDA, 1966-69; Program Officer, Div. of Population & Health Svcs, IDRC, 1972-73; Special Asst. to the Pres., International Development Centre, 1973-75; Assoc. Econ., C.D. Howe Institute, 1979-80; Dir., Policy Analysis, 1980-81; Pres. & Exec. Dir., 1981-87; Assoc. Deputy Min., Dept. of Fin., Gov't of Canada, 1987-89; Visiting Fellow, Institute for International Economics, Washington, D.C., 1989 to date; Prof. & Sr. Fellow, Fac. of Mgmt, Univ. of Toronto, 1990-93; Dir., Centre for Int'l Bus., & Prof., Fac. of Mgmt, 1993 to date. **SELECTED PUBLICATIONS:** *Benchmarking the Canadian Business*

Presence in East Asia, co-ed, with A.E. Safarian (Univ. of Toronto, 1995); *Pacific Trade and Investment: Options for the 90s*, co-ed. with Frank Flatters (Kingston: John Deutsch Institute, Queen's Univ., 1995); *Japan in East Asia: Trade and Investment Strategies* (Singapore: The Institute for Southeast Asian Studies, 1993); *International Economic Policy Coordination: Requiem or Prologue?* (Washington, D.C.: Institute for International Economics, 1991); *Canadian-Japanese Economic Relations in a Triangular Perspective* (Toronto: C.D. Howe Institute, 1987); *Shaping Competitive Advantage*, co-ed. with Richard Lipsey (Toronto: C.D. Howe Institute, 1987). EDIT: Ed. Advisory Bd., Hongkong Bank of Canada Papers on Asia. DIRECTOR: TransCanada PipeLines; Pratt & Whitney Canada Inc.; The Toronto-Dominion Bank; Working Ventures Canadian Fund Inc.; University of Toronto Press; DuPont Canada Inc.; IBM Canada Ltd. AFFIL: Japan Society (Dir.); Institute for International Economics (Advisory Committee); Asia Pacific Foundation (Advisory Committee, Research Ntwk); Purvis Prize for Excellence in Economic Policy Analysis (Selection Committee); Pacific Trade & Development Ntwk (Int'l Steering Committee); Canadian Economic Association; American Economic Association. COMMENT: *"Wendy Dobson has a unique background, combining a rich mixture of research and practice in economics. She is active on the domestic and international scenes, encouraging innovation and an outward-looking perspective among Canadians."*

Doherty, Barbara R.C., B.Ed.,LL.B. 🔲
Partner, MILLER THOMSON, 20 Queen St. W., Ste. 2700, Toronto, ON M5H 3S1 (416) 483-1662. Born Deep River, Ont. 1950. m. Mr. Justice David H. Doherty. 1 ch. Katie. EDUC: McGill Univ., B.Ed. 1971; York Univ., LL.B.(Law) 1980. BAR: Ont., 1982. CAREER: lawyer, 1982 to date. SELECTED PUBLICATIONS: *Directors' Duties in Canada: Managing Risk* (CCH Canadian Limited, 1995). DIRECTOR: Proctor-Silex Canada Inc. AFFIL: Ontario Securities Advisory Committee (1992-95); Canadian Bar Association; Law Society of Upper Canada; Victorian Order of Nurses (former Dir.). INTERESTS: family; reading; the practice of law. COMMENT: *"I have practised corporate and securities law for 13 years. I have advised clients on the securities, corporate, competition and other regulatory implications of a wide range of transactions, including corporate acquisitions, divestitures and reorganizations. I have acted in private placements and prospectus offerings of various equity and debt instruments, as well as take-over bids."*

Doiron, Cheryl A. ■ ⊕ $
Vice-President, Operations and Planning, ATLANTIC HEALTH SCIENCES CORPORATION, Box 5200, Saint John, NB E2L 4L4 (506) 648-6701. EDUC: St. Joseph's Hospital, Sch. of Nursing, Diploma in Nursing 1965; McGill Univ., Diploma in Teaching & Supervision 1966, Bachelor of Nursing 1970; Univ. of Ottawa, Master of Health Admin. 1978; Canadian Coll. of Health Service Executives, Certified Health Exec. 1984. CAREER: Nursing Instructor, Psychiatry, Centracare, 1966-69; Head Nurse, Psycho Endocrine Research Unit & Psychiatric Day Care Centre, Montreal General Hospital, 1970-71; Staff Nurse, Emergency & Medicine, Mineral Springs Hospital, 1971-72; Asst. Dir. of Nursing, St. Joseph's Hospital, 1972-75; Staff Health & Infection Control Coord., 1975-76; Admin. Residency, Victoria Hospital, 1977; Asst. Exec. Dir., Admin./Hum. Res. & Labour Rel'ns, St. Joseph's Hospital, 1978-87; Asst. Exec. Dir., Clinical Svcs & Planning, 1987-92; VP, Oper. & Planning, Region 2 Hospital Corporation, 1993 to date. AFFIL: N.B. Health Care Association (Legislation Committee; Alternate, Hospital Standards Committee); N.B. Community Coll. (Medical Laboratory Program; Respiratory Therapy Program); Region 2 Hospital Corporation,Task Force on Rationalization of Services; United Way of Greater Saint John (Bd. of Dir.; Mktg Committee; Chair, Agency & Community Rel'ns); St. Vincent's Alumnae Association (Pres.); Canadian Coll. of Health Services Executives; Nurses' Association of N.B.; N.B. Nurse Administrators' Association; Canadian Red Cross; Canadian Mental Health Association.

Doleželová-Velingerová, Milena, M.A., Ph.D. 📝 📚
Professor of Chinese Language and Literature, Department of East Asian Studies, UNIVERSITY OF TORONTO, 130 St. George St., Rm. 14207, Toronto, ON M5S 1S3 (416) 978-5167, FAX 978-5711. Born Prague 1932. d. 2 ch. Markéta, Milena. EDUC: Charles Univ., Prague, M.A.(Chinese Studies) 1955; Oriental Institute, Prague, Ph.D.(Chinese Lit.) 1965. CAREER: Research Assoc., Oriental Institute, Czechoslovak Academy of Sciences, Prague, 1954-68; Research Assoc., Institute for Literature, Chinese Academy of Sciences, Beijing, 1958-59; Research Assoc., Centre for Chinese Studies, Univ. of Michigan, 1967-68; Assoc. Prof., Univ. of Toronto, 1969-75; Prof., 1975 to date. SELECTED PUBLICATIONS: *The Ballad of the Hidden Dragon*, translator, with James I. Crump (London: Oxford Univ. Press, 1971); *The Chinese Novel at the Turn of the Century*, ed. & co-author (Toronto: Univ. of

Toronto Press, 1980); *A Selective Guide to Chinese Literature 1900-1949*, ed. & co-author (Leiden: E.J. Brill, 1988); *Poetics East and West*, ed. & co-author (Toronto: Toronto Semiotic Circle, 1989); about 30 scholarly articles published 1958-94, incl. "An Early Chinese Confessional Prose: Shen Fu's *Six Chapters of a Floating Life*," with Lubomir Dolezel (T'oung Pao 1972); "Pre-Modern Theories of Fiction and Drama in China," *The Johns Hopkins Guide to Literary Theory and Criticism*, eds. Michael Gorden & Martin Kreiswirth (Baltimore & London: The Johns Hopkins Univ. Press, 1994); "Studies of Modern Chinese Literature in Europe," *Europe Studies China* (London: Han-Shan T'ang Publishers, 1995); various books & articles translated into Chinese. **EDIT:** Ed. Bd., *Modern Chinese Literature*, 1975-83; Ed. Bd., *A Selective Guide to Chinese Literature 1900-1949*, 1980-85; Ed. Bd., *The Semiotic Review of Books*, 1989-92; Ed. Bd., *Canadian Review of Comparative Literature*, 1987 to date. **AFFIL:** Association of Asian Studies; Toronto Semiotic Circle; Canadian Association for Comparative Literature. **HONS:** Sr. Research Visiting Fellow, Corpus Christi Coll., Cambridge Univ., 1984-85; Resident Scholar, The Rockefeller Foundation Study & Conference Center, Bellagio, Italy, June 1985; Visiting Scholar, Harvard Univ., John Fairbank Research Center for East Asian Research, 1990-91; Jaroslav Průšek Dintinguished Prof., Charles Univ., Prague, 1996-99. **INTERESTS:** literature; music; visual arts. **MISC:** recipient, various SSHRC grants; Pres., Ninth International Institute for Semiotic & Structural Studies, 1987. **COMMENT:** *"Enjoys challenging generally accepted interpretation of Chinese literature. Her studies, carried out in team projects, contributed to a reinterpretation of 20th century Chinese fiction and premodern Chinese theories of narrative."*

Dompierre, Louise M.T., B.A., M.A. ■■ 🕮 Ⓧ
Associate Director/Chief Curator, THE POWER PLANT ART GALLERY (contemporary art), Harbourfront Centre, 231 Queen's Quay W., Toronto, ON M5J 2G8 (416) 973-4939, FAX 973-4933, EMAIL louised@interlog.com. Born Hull, Que. m. Peter Morris. **EDUC:** Queen's Univ., B.A.(Hons., Art Hist.); Carleton Univ., M.A.(Cdn Studies, Art Hist.). **CAREER:** Arts Officer, The Canada Council, 1971-76; Assoc. Curator, Agnes Etherington Art Centre, 1980-85; Assoc. Dir./Chief Curator, The Power Plant Art Gallery, 1985 to date. **SELECTED PUBLICATIONS:** *Toronto: A Play of History* (Toronto: The Power Plant, 1985); *Michael Snow: Embodied Vision* (Toronto: The Power

Plant, 1994); *Press Enter: Between Seduction & Disbelief* (Toronto: The Power Plant, 1995); *The Age of Anxiety* (Toronto: The Power Plant, 1995); *Digital Gardens: A World in Mutation* (Toronto: The Power Plant, 1996). **AFFIL:** International Council of Museums; Univ. of Western Ontario (Advisory Council for the Visual Arts). **COMMENT:** *"Louise Dompierre is associate director and chief curator of The Power Plant. Since she joined the gallery in 1985, she has been curator and co-curator of numerous exhibitions, including* Toronto: A Play of History *(Jeu d'histoire),* Prent/Cronenberg: Crimes Against Nature, Robert Fones: From Material Life into Art History, In Between and Beyond: From Germany, Ann Hamilton: a round, Michael Snow: Embodied Vision, Yasumasa Morimura, Naked State, Spring Hurlburt: La Somnolence, Press/Enter: Between Seduction and Disbelief, *and* The Age of Anxiety. *She has taught, lectured and published widely, as well as collaborated, in various curatorial capacities, with a number of art institutions abroad, such as ICC Intercommunication Centre, Tokyo (1996), Queensland Art Gallery, Brisbane, Australia (1996), Le Magasin, Grenoble (1994), the Contemporary Arts Museum, Houston (1993), the Wurttembergischer Kunstverein, Stuttgart (1992), the Musea da Gravura, Brazil (1992) and others. Ms. Dompierre serves on many committees, including the Advisory Council for the Visual Arts of the University of Western Ontario."*

Donaldson, Lesleh Ⓧ 🐝 🗡
Actor. Born Toronto 1964. m. **EDUC:** Circle in the Square Theatre Sch., 1988-89; Royal National Theatre Sch. of Great Britain, 1993. **CAREER:** stage debut at age 15. **SELECTED CREDITS:** Emily, *Digging for Fire*, Factory Theatre; Evelyn Dick, *How Could You Mrs. Dick?*, Winter Garden & Tivoli; Anna, *Burn This*, MTC Warehouse; Sandy, *Criminals in Love*, Factory Theatre; Anne Frank, *The Diary of Anne Frank*, Manitoba Theatre Centre; Robin, *Special People* (TV feature), CBS; Kim, *On My Own* (TV), CBC; Norma, *Hurt Penguins* (feature), Cold Feet Productions; Heather, *Funeral Home AKA Cries in the Night* (feature), Columbia Pictures; *You Love Me, I Hate You* (short film). **AFFIL:** Canadian Actors' Equity Association; ACTRA; SAG. **HONS:** nominated, Best Actress (*Funeral Home*), Genie Awards, 1982; *You Love Me, I Hate You* nomiated as best short film, Genie Awards, 1995. **INTERESTS:** writing poetry; singing; reading; art. **MISC:** studied theatre makeup with George Abbot; studied voice at the Royal Conservatory of Music. **COMMENT:** *"I love to do it all...hire me, hire me!!!"*

Donato, Maria Helen ⊗ ☻

Executive Director, INTERNATIONAL NATIVE ARTS FESTIVAL, Box 502, Stn. M, Calgary, AB T2A 3E1 (403) 233-0022, FAX 233-7681. Born Toronto 1947. m. Ernie Whitford. 2 ch. EDUC: Toronto Teachers' Coll., Teacher's Educ. 1965; Univ. of Waterloo, Fine Arts 1966-69; Family Life Educ. Council, Facilitator 1991. CAREER: Teacher, Metropolitan Separate Sch. Bd., Wellington County Separate Sch. Bd., Dufferin-Peel Separate Sch. Bd., 1966-80; Mgr, Delta-Bow Valley Hotel, 1981-88; Exec. Dir., Career Advancement Training Systems, 1988-91; Facilitator, Family Life Educ. Council, 1991 to date; Exec. Dir., International Native Arts Festival, 1992 to date. COMMENT: *"Maria Donato taught for fifteen years in Ontario, working with many students in every level of learning. The most rewarding was working with special needs children (autistic, learning disabled, highly gifted and emotionally handicapped). Since coming to Calgary in 1979, she has done a multitude of jobs, which included: teaching the learning disabled; helping teenagers that were under pressure, young parents as well as immigrant women. In 1991, after surviving a head-on car collision, she went to Family Life Education Council (FLEC), where she became one of their top facilitators. Working with FLEC she has conducted a variety of workshops including those for inmates, the deaf and hard of hearing, battered women, divorcees and for those going through hardship and loss."*

Donegan, Rosemary, B.F.A., M.A. ■■ 📖 ⊗ 📰

Independent curator, writer, educator, ONTARIO COLLEGE OF ART, 100 McCaul St., Toronto, ON M5T 1W1 (416) 977-6000, ext. 347, FAX 537-9571. Born Pretoria, S. Africa 1949. s. EDUC: Univ. of Saskatchewan, B.F.A.(Art Hist.) 1971; Univ. of Toronto, M.A. (Art Hist.) 1973. CAREER: Curatorial experience: Curator, "Spadina Avenue: A Photohistory," A Space, Toronto, Aug.-Sept. 1984; Guest Curator, "Industrial Images/Images Industrielles," The Art Gallery of Hamilton, May-July 1987; Guest Curator, "Work, Weather and the Grid: Agriculture in Saskatchewan," Dunlop Art Gallery, Regina, May-June 1991 & Mendel Art Gallery, Saskatoon, July-Sept. 1991; Guest Curator, "Ford City/Windsor," Art Gallery of Windsor, July-Oct. 1994. Teaching experience: Liberal Arts Studies Dept., Ontario Coll. of Art, 1991 to date; Acting Chair, Liberal Arts Studies Dept., 1993-94. SELECTED PUBLICATIONS: co-author with D. Read & L. Martin, "But is it Feminist Art?" in *Still Ain't Satisfied: Canadian Feminism Today* (The Women's Press, Toronto, 1982); "Whatever Happened to Queen St. West? A History of Art Scenes & Communities in Toronto" (*Fuse*, Fall 1986, No. 42, pp. 10-24); "The Iconography of Labour: An Overview of Canadian Materials" (*Archivaria*, #27, Winter 1988-89, pp. 35-56); "The Site: A History" (*Kawamata Toronto Project*, Mercer Union, Toronto, 1991); "History and Real People" (interviewed by N. Tousley, *Canadian Art*, Winter 1991, pp. 60-65); "Legitimate Modernism: Charles Comfort and the Toronto Stock Exchange" (*Designing the Exchange: Essays Commemorating the Opening of the Design Exchange*, Toronto, Design Exchange, 1994, pp. 50-67); *Spadina Avenue* (Vancouver/Toronto, 1985, Douglas & McIntyre); *Industrial Images/Images Industrielles* (Art Gallery of Hamilton, 1988); *Work, Weather and the Grid: Agriculture in Saskatchewan* (Dunlop Art Gallery, Regina, 1992); *Ford City/Windsor* (Art Gallery of Windsor, 1994). EDIT: contributing editor, *Border/lines* Magazine, 1991 to date (founding mbr. 1984; edit. collective 1984-91). AFFIL: Ontario Heritage Foundation (Bd. of Dir. 1993 to date); The Euclid Theatre (Bd. of Dir. 1990-92); Canadian Women's Educational Press (founding mbr. 1972; collective mbr. 1972-79); Women's Cultural Building (founding mbr. 1982; Pres. 1982-84); Development Education Centre (Bd. of Dir. - VP 1979-88, Pres. 1988-90). HONS: Reg'l History Award, Canadian Historical Association, 1987; nominated for Toronto Book Award, 1986; B grant, Canada Council, 1987.

Donlon, Denise 📖 ⊗ 📻

Director of Music Programming, MUCHMUSIC, CITYTV and MUCHMORE MUSIC/M3. 299 Queen St. W., Toronto, ON M5V 2Z5 (416) 591-5757, FAX 591-6824. Born Ont. 1956. m. M. McLauchlan. 1 ch. EDUC: Univ. of Waterloo, Joint Honour Program, Environmental Studies & Psych. CAREER: Entertainment/Educ. Coord., Federation of Students, Univ. of Waterloo; Pres., Denise Donlon Publicity; various positions, Sam L. Feldman and Associates; Anchor, *Rockflash News*, MuchMusic/CityTV, 1985; Prod. & on-air Host, *The New Music*, 1986-93; Co-Host, *Outlaws and Heroes*, MuchMusic, 1988-93; Dir. of Music Programming, MuchMusic/CityTV/MuchMoreMusic/M3, 1993 to date. AFFIL: CARAS; Academy of Canadian Cinema & Television; TWIFT, CSIS. HONS: Gemini, Best Light Info. Series (Prod. *The New Music*), Academy of Canadian Cinema & Television; Gemini, Special Event Coverage (Prod., MuchMusic *Election '93*), Academy of Canadian Cinema &

Television; Broadcast Exec. of the Year, Canadian Music Week Industry Awards, 1994 & 1995; Best Host & Best Documentary (*The New Music*, "In Your Face: Violence in Music"), Yorkton Short Film & Video Festival, 1994; Peter Gzowski/ABC Canada Award for Literacy, 1993; Video Personality or Programmer of the Year, *The Record*, 1994, Hon. Patron, Dancers For Life. INTERESTS: birdwatching; ballet; books. MISC: produced 2 one-hr. *Rock 'n' Roll 'n' Reading* programs, aired on *The New Music* & MuchMusic, & distributed to educators free of charge.

Donner, Gail J., R.N.,B.Sc.,M.A., Ph.D. ■ ⬡ ⊕
Professor, Faculty of Nursing, UNIVERSITY OF TORONTO, 50 St. George St., Toronto, ON M5S 1A1 (416) 978-2861, FAX 978-8222. Born Winnipeg 1942. 2 ch. Elizabeth, Simon. EDUC: Winnipeg General Hospital Sch. of Nursing, R.N. 1962; Univ. of Pennsylvania, B.Sc.(Nursing) 1967; New York Univ., M.A.(Psychiatric/Mental Health Nursing) 1969; Univ. of Toronto, Ph.D. 1986. CAREER: Staff Nurse, Central Registry, Toronto, 1963; Staff Nurse, Regina Grey Nuns Hospital, 1963; R.N., Regina Community Health Clinic, 1964; Staff Nurse, Eastern Pennsylvania Psychiatric Institute, 1964-67; Instructor, Wellesley Hospital Sch. of Nursing, Toronto, 1970-73; Instructor & Coord., Certificate Program on Psychiatric Nursing, Ryerson Polytechnical Institute, 1974-76; Prof. & Chair, Dept. of Nursing, 1976-82; Exec. Dir., Registered Nurses' Association of Ontario, 1984-89; Dir. of Nursing Educ., Hospital for Sick Children, 1989-92; Assoc. Prof., Fac. of Nursing, Univ. of Toronto, 1989-95; Prof. 1995 to date. SELECTED PUBLICATIONS: *Towards an Understanding of Canadian Nurses' Home and Work Lives: Gender, Power and Control*, with D. Semogas & J. Blyth (Toronto: Quality of Nursing Worklife Research Unit, 1993); "Parenthood as a Crisis: A Role for Psychiatric Nurses" (*Perspectives in Psychiatric Care* 1972); "Helping Nurses Learn Assertiveness" (*Journal of Nursing Education* 1982); numerous other publications. AFFIL: Registered Nurses' Association of Ontario (Bd. of Dir. 1982-84; Exec. Dir. 1984-89; Hon. Life Mbr.); Coll. of Nurses of Ontario; National League for Nursing; Sigma Theta Tau International (Pres., Lambda Pi Chapter, Univ. of Toronto); United Way of Greater Toronto (Exec. Committee); Ontario Medical Association (Committee on Hospitals); Hospital for Sick Children Foundation (V-Chrm, External Grants Committee). HONS: Award of Merit, Registered Nurses' Association of Ontario, 1989; Woman

of Distinction, YWCA of Metropolitan Toronto, 1994. MISC: listed in *Canadian Who's Who*, 1988 to date; mbr., District Health Council Hospital Restructuring Committee, 1994 to date; Chair, Air Ambulance Review, Ont. Ministry of Health (prov. appt.); recipient, various grants. COMMENT: *"I have been involved in professional nursing, nursing education and community service for over 30 years. I am committed to improving the quality of life for nurses, women and all citizens through responsible and caring health and social policy."*

Doob, Penelope Reed, B.A.,M.A., Ph.D. ⬡ 🕮
Professor of English, Multidisciplinary Studies, Women's Studies, and Dance, and Academic Director, Centre for the Support of Teaching, YORK UNIVERSITY, Ross S834, North York, ON M3J 1P3 (416) 736-5754, FAX 736-5704, EMAIL prdoob@vm2.yorku.ca. Born Hanover, N.H. 1943. d. EDUC: Harvard Univ., B.A.(English) 1964; Stanford Univ., M.A.(English) 1967, Ph.D.(English/Medieval Studies) 1969. CAREER: Asst. Prof., Glendon Coll., York Univ., 1969-74; freelance writer for various publications incl. *The Globe and Mail, Dance Magazine, Ballet International, Ballet News, Dance in Canada*, 1973 to date; Assoc. Prof., Glendon Coll., York Univ., 1974-84; freelance Prod. for CBC Radio, *The Dance*, 1976-79; Assoc. Principal (Academic), Glendon Coll., York Univ., 1981-85; Prof. of English & Multidisciplinary Studies, 1985 to date; VP (Faculties), 1986-89; V-Chrm of the Bd., Therapeutic Peptides Inc., Baltimore, 1991-93; Pres., Reed MacFadden Ltd., Toronto, 1990-94; Academic Dir., Centre for the Support of Teaching, York Univ., 1994 to date; consultant in dance, lit., educ., clinical trials design & endpoints assessment. SELECTED PUBLICATIONS: *Nebuchadnezzar's Children: Conventions of Madness in Middle English Literature* (Yale Univ. Press, 1974); ed., *Handbook on Teaching and Learning at York* (1989); *The Idea of the Labyrinth from Classical Antiquity through the Middle Ages* (Cornell Univ. Press, 1990); co-ed. & contributor, *The Uses of Manuscripts in Literary Studies* (Western Michigan Univ. Press, 1992); co-author, *Karen Kain: Movement Never Lies* (McClelland & Stewart, 1994); more than 400 articles, reviews, abstracts & conference presentations in the fields of dance, medieval hist. & lit., women's studies, science & medicine (immunology; AIDS; Health-Related Quality of Life assessment); 3 patent applications pending in medicine. AFFIL: Actors' Fund of Canada (Dir.); Society for Teaching & Learning in Higher Education;

Physicians' Association for AIDS Care (1991); Senior Women Academic Administrators of Canada (1987); American Association for Higher Education; World Dance Alliance; Society of Dance History Scholars; Dance Critics' Association; Dance in Canada Association; New Chaucer Society; Medieval Academy of America; Modern Language Association. HONS: numerous grants, Social Sciences & Humanities Council of Canada, & Canada Council, 1972 to date; Guggenheim Fellow, 1974; Kent Fellow, Danforth Foundation, 1966-69; Woodrow Wilson Fellow, 1965-69; Medical Research Fellow, Nat'l Science Foundation, 1964 & 1965; elected to Phi Beta Kappa, 1964. INTERESTS: education; medicine (esp. AIDS research & clinical trials methodology); entrepreneurial activities; mgmt theory; film; dance; music; art; creativity of every sort in every field; downhill skiing; constructive risk-taking. COMMENT: *"I try to combine extensive generalist knowledge with intense specialization, to use that knowledge in constructive change and innovation, and to communicate the excitement of discovery and the values of collaboration."*

Dorning, Maggie, AOCA ■ ■ ⊗ ⋃

Artist, Writer, Multimedia Producer, CYBERNETIC CIRCUS, 680 Queen's Quay W., Toronto, ON M5V 2Y9 (416) 260-0949, FAX 260-0939, EMAIL maggie_dorning@goodmedia.com INTERNET http://www.goodmedia.com/maggie. Born Brantford, Ont. d. 4 ch. EDUC: Ontario Coll. of Art, AOCA (Photo Electric Arts) 1986; Digital Media Studios, Multimedia Production 1995. CAREER: Gen. Editor, Science Council of Canada, 1976-83; operator, own business, 1987 to date; Exhibit Planner & Researcher, National Museums; Science Ed., *The Canadian Global Almanac*, Macmillan Canada, 1992 to date; Multimedia Producer & Production Mgr, various companies; Teacher, Internet Design, International Academy of Design. SELECTED PUBLICATIONS: "The Rheims Journal" (*Artword Magazine*, Fall 1992). EXHIBITIONS: solo exhibits include: *BR Formis: Perfect Bureaucrat*, National Museum of Science & Technology, 1986; *BR Formis: Let's Have a Meeting*, National Museum of Science & Technology, 1989; numerous group shows incl.: *Les Machines sentimentales*, La Charteuse, Villeneuve-lez-Avignon, 1986; Centre Georges Pompidou, Paris, 1987; Théâtre municipale, Caën, 1987; *Guerilla Tactics*, A Space, Toronto, 1987; *Automates et Robots*, Le Manège, Reims, 1992; *Art + Technology*, Workscene Gallery, Toronto, 1994; *Myths from Cyberspace*, Koffler Gallery, Toronto, 1997. AFFIL: Visual Arts

Ontario. INTERESTS: travel; photography & pinhole cameras; gardens; her Mac & the Web. MISC: Canada Council Artist-in-Residence, National Museum of Science & Technology; juror on a number of grant panels; subject of various articles, reviews & interviews. COMMENT: *"I'm very curious about human beings, about the systems we create, and the machines we develop. Through my art, I explore our increasing integration with our technologies."*

Dorosz, Wanda M., B.Ed.,LL.B. $

President and Chief Executive Officer, QUORUM GROWTH INC., 150 King St. W., Ste. 1505, Box 5, Toronto, ON M5H 1J9 (416) 971-6998, FAX 971-5955. Born Regina 1950. m. Richard Dole. EDUC: Univ. of Regina, B.Ed. (Secondary) 1971; Univ. of British Columbia, LL.B. 1975. BAR: B.C., 1976; Ont., 1978. CAREER: Lawyer, Goodman & Goodman, Barristers & Solicitors, 1976-81; Ptnr, Dorosz, Barristers & Solicitors, 1981-87; Pres. & CEO, Quorum Growth Inc., 1987 to date. SELECTED PUBLICATIONS: author & lecturer on finance & growth capital. DIRECTOR: Home Products Inc. (Chrm); Promis Systems Corporation (Chrm); Atlantis Aerospace Corporation; China Trust Quorum Corporation; Dynatek Automation Systems; Home Products Inc.; International Systems Group Inc.; Investors Group; Newstar Technologies Corporation; OpTx 2000 Corp.; PC DOCS Group; Positron Fiber Systems; Promis Systems Corporation; Quorum Funding Corporation; Quorum Growth Inc.; Quorum Growth International Ltd.; Wildcard Technologies (formerly Puredata Ltd.). ADVISORY BOARD: Abitibi Price; Andersen Consulting. AFFIL: Univ. of Toronto (Bd. of Gov. & Bus. Bd.); Univ. of Toronto Innovations Foundation (Dir.); Toronto Stock Exchange (Investors & Issuers Advisory Committee); National Advisory Board on Science & Technology (former mbr.); Harbourfront Corporation (former Dir.); Ontario Centre for Microelectronics (former Dir.); Canadian Centre for Creative Technology (former Dir.). MISC: frequent guest speaker.

Dorsey, Candas Jane ▯ ▨ /

Writer, Editor and Publisher, WOODEN DOOR & ASSOCIATES, 10022 - 103 St., 3rd Flr., Edmonton, AB T5J 0X2 (403) 448-0192 or 449-0590, FAX 448-0192, EMAIL 74301. 2607@compuserve.com. Born Edmonton 1952. CAREER: 15 yrs.' experience as a freelance writer & ed., incl. journalism, magazine writing, magazine & book editing, & production, etc.; consulting on communication needs; Founding Ed., River Books imprint, Books Collective, Edmonton; Founding Ed., *Edmonton*

Bullet arts newspaper; Publisher, Tesseract Books. **SELECTED PUBLICATIONS:** *this is for you,* poetry (Vancouver: blewointmentpress, 1973); *Orion Rising,* poetry (Vancouver: blewointmentpress, 1974); *Results of the Ring Toss,* poetry (Vancouver: blewointmentpress, 1976); *Leaving Marks,* poetry (Edmonton: River Books, 1992); *Hardwired Angel,* with Nora Abercrombie (Vancouver: Pulp Press, 1987); *Machine Sex and Other Stories* (Victoria: Tesseract Books, 1988); *Tesseracts3,* ed. with Gerry Truscott (Victoria: Tesseract Books, 1990); *Dark Earth Dreams,* short stories with music by Roger Dugan (Edmonton: Tesseract Books 1996); *Black Wine,* novel (New York: Tor Books, Jan. 1997); work has appeared in numerous periodicals, incl. *New York Review of Science Fiction, Quill & Quire & NeWest Review* & in numerous anthologies, incl. *Writing Right, Tesseracts, Ark of Ice, The Norton Anthology of Science Fiction* & *The Penguin Book of Fantasy by Women.* **EDIT:** Ed., special double issue "Canadian Speculative Fiction," *Prairie Fire,* Summer 1994. **DIRECTOR:** The Books Collective; Tesseract Books. **AFFIL:** The Writers' Union of Canada; Periodical Writers' Association of Canada; Writers' Guild of Alberta (Past Pres.); SFCanada (Past Pres.); Editors' Association of Alberta; Alberta Association of Social Workers; Hromada Housing Cooperative (Bd. Mbr.). **HONS:** *Edmonton Journal* Literary Contest; Alberta Playwriting Competition; Pulp Press international Three-Day Novel-Writing Competition, *Hardwired Angel,* 1986; Best Short-Form Work in English, Canadian Science Fiction & Fantasy Award, "Sleeping in a Box," 1989; City of Edmonton Arts Award, 1988. **MISC:** Registered Social Worker (inactive); Delegate, Canada-Soviet Media Interchange, 1988; short story "Johnny Appleseed on the New World" included on *Visions of Mars* CD-ROM proj. **COMMENT:** *"Published writer of fiction, nonfiction and poetry. I have edited a number of literary and educational texts, and have 17 years' experience as a freelance writer and editor."*

Doruyter, Renee ⊗ ✎ ▯
Singer, Columnist and Copy-Editor, THE PROVINCE, 2250 Granville St., Vancouver, BC V6H 3G2. Born Rotterdam, Holland. **EDUC:** Vancouver Sch. of Art, 1 yr.; Univ. of British Columbia, 2 yrs.; Banff Centre for Cont. Ed. **CAREER:** various jobs in newspaper & radio; Asst. to the FM Program Dir., writer, ed., on-air reviewer, CHQM, 1973-77; freelance theatre critic & arts reporter, *The Province,* 1977; Reporter, *The Vancouver Express*; Reporter, lifestyle/women's pages, *The Province*; layout, copy editing & Acting Food Ed., food & fash-

ion pages; Fashion Ed., 1986-91; Columnist & Arts Writer, 1991 to date; solo performer at various venues around Vancouver incl. The Alma Street Cafe, The Blue Note, Rossini's, The Glass Slipper, 1986 to date. **SELECTED CREDITS:** *Everytime We Say Goodbye,* CD, 1993; *Hooked on Romance,* CD, 1996. **SELECTED PUBLICATIONS:** "Vancouver Letter," *The Jazz Report.* **AFFIL:** Vancouver Press Club (Dir. 1979-82); Women in Music. **INTERESTS:** jazz; the arts; raising funds for AIDS research, the Vancouver Food Bank & breast cancer research. **COMMENT:** *"I feel I am very fortunate to be able to earn my living writing about the things I enjoy - theatre and music - while pursuing the thing that I love - singing jazz. My new CD,* Hooked on Romance, *also marks my debut as a songwriter."*

Dotto, Lydia, B.Jour. ■ ✎ ❀ ❧
Freelance Science Writer and Editor. 599 Gilmour St., Peterborough, ON K9H 2K3 (705) 741-1476, FAX 741-4228, EMAIL ldotto@cycor.ca. Born Cadomin, Alta. 1949. **EDUC:** Carleton Univ., B.Jour. 1971. **CAREER:** *Edmonton Journal,* 1969; *The Toronto Star,* 1970-71; Staff Sci. Writer, *The Globe and Mail,* 1972-78; Exec. Ed., Canadian Science News Service, 1982-92; freelance, 1978 to date; Co-Dir., Space Net Canada. **SELECTED CREDITS:** Scriptwriter, *The First Canadian Astronaut,* CBC-TV, Oct. 1, 1984; Scriptwriter, *The Space Experience* (six-part series), TVOntario, Fall 1987; frequent radio & TV appearances as commentator. **SELECTED PUBLICATIONS:** *The Ozone War,* with Harold Schiff (New York: Doubleday, 1978); *Planet Earth in Jeopardy: The Environmental Consequences of Nuclear War* (London: Wiley, 1986); *Canada in Space* (Toronto: Irwin, 1987); *Thinking the Unthinkable: The Social Consequences of Rapid Climate Change* (Waterloo, Ont.: Wilfrid Laurier Press, 1988); *Asleep in the Fast Lane: The Impact of Sleep on Work* (Toronto: Stoddart, 1990); *Blue Planet* (New York: Abrahamson, 1991); *Ethical Choices and Global Greenhouse Warming* (Waterloo, Ont.: Wilfrid Laurier Press, 1993); *The Astronauts: Canada's Voyageurs in Space* (Toronto: Stoddart, 1993); numerous articles published in various periodicals, incl. *The Globe and Mail, Canadian Business, Equinox, University of Toronto Magazine, Challenges, enRoute.* **AFFIL:** Canadian Science Writers' Association (Pres. 1979-80); Marc Garneau Collegiate Institute (Advisory Bd.); Writers' Guild of Canada. **HONS:** National Newspaper Awards citation, 1974; Canadian Science Writers' Association awards, 1974, 1981, 1984, 1993, 1994, Honourable

Mention, 1989; Canadian Meteorological Society award, 1975; Honourable Mention, National Magazine Awards, 1978-81; Sandford Fleming Medal, Royal Canadian Institute, 1983. MISC: frequent speaker on the space program, sleep & work, global environmental issues, public awareness of science, science literacy & media science writing; using the internet; frequent teacher of science-writing workshops for scientific organizations; speaker, Women in Science & Technology seminar at Women's World nat'l conference, 1984; listed in *Canadian Who's Who, The World Who's Who of Women, Encyclopedia and Directory of the Environment, Contemporary Authors*; participated in zero-gravity training flight, Johnson Space Center, 1983; journalist aboard *Ticonderoga* during recovery of *Skylab* astronauts, 1973; private pilot's licence.

Doty, Irene ● ○ ⚶
Past National President, AIR CADET LEAGUE OF CANADA, 313 Rideau St., Ottawa, ON K1N 5Y4 (613) 991-4349, FAX 991-4347. Born Fort Frances, Ont. 1935. m. Jack. 3 ch. Shawn, Mark, Trevor. CAREER: Sec., Ont. Bd. of Educ., 1952-55; Credit Investigator, Stenographer, Finance Corp., 1955-61; various volunteer positions, Air Cadet League, 1974 to date; Nat'l Pres., 1994-95. AFFIL: Carlyle United Church (Pres., U.C.W.; V-Chrm, Official Bd.; Fin. Committee); Souris Valley United Church (Presbytery Exec.); Carlyle Co-operative (Bd.); Camp Wabimasquah United Church Camp (Bd.); various church & community organizations. HONS: Commemorative Medal for 125th Anniversary of Cdn Confederation; Canadian Forces Citation, Dir. of the Year, Dept. of Defence, 1994. INTERESTS: writing; painting; crafts. MISC: still active with No. 723, No. 30 & No. 675 Squadrons, Air Cadets; 1st woman Nat'l Pres., Air Cadets; for 35 yrs., has run a farm & farm equipment mfg bus. with her husband. COMMENT: *"I experience a tremendous personal satisfaction working as a volunteer for and with children, whether it is teaching Sunday school, or as a choir leader, school board member, leader of Canadian Girls in Training (CGIT) or with the Air Cadet movement. When I see young people achieve and succeed, it is so rewarding."*

Doucet, Vida ⊕ ⚶
Public Health Nurse, Dartmouth and Halifax, Department of Health, GOVERNMENT OF NOVA SCOTIA, 6061 Young St., Ste. 323, Halifax, NS B3K 2A3 (902) 424-3963, FAX 424-0727. Born Halifax 1943. m. Gerald. 7 ch. Michelle, Garry, Dana, Paul, Denise, Brian, Brad. EDUC: Payzant Memorial Hospital, Windsor, N.S.,

Registered Nurse Diploma 1965; Dalhousie Univ., Public Health Diploma 1966. CAREER: Community Health Nurse, Mulgrave, Dept. of Health, Prov. of N.S., 1966-69; Staff Nurse (float), St. Martha's Hospital, 1972-76; Psychiatric Nurse, Eastern Counties Mental Health Centre, 1976-78; Casual Nurse, Mulgrave, Dept. of Health, Prov. of N.S., 1980-82; Nurse, Comcare, 1982-83; Public Health Nurse, Dartmouth & Halifax, Dept. of Health, Prov. of N.S., 1983 to date. AFFIL: I.W.K.-Grace Hospital (Bd.); Salvation Army (Advisory Bd.; V-Chair, Reg'l Bd.; Council); St. John's United Church (United Church Women; Social Action Committee; Elder 1993); St. Leonard's Society (Bd.). COMMENT: *"Hard working and fun loving."*

Doughty, Wendy, B.A.Sc.,M.Ed., Ph.D. ■ ✦ ○
Executive Director, Corporate Marketing Office, GRANT MCEWAN COMMUNITY COLLEGE, 10700 - 104 Ave., Edmonton, AB T5J 4S2 (403) 497-5829, FAX 497-5426, EMAIL doughtyw@iadmin.gmcc.ab.ca. Born Stratford, Ont. 1956. m. Jim Klingle. 2 ch. EDUC: Univ. of Guelph, B.A.Sc.(Consumer Behaviour) 1978; Univ. of Alberta, M.Ed.(Educ. Admin.) 1985, Ph.D.(Educ. Admin.) 1995. CAREER: Research Asst., Ont. Ministry of Housing, 1976-77; Research Asst., Ont. Social Welfare Council, 1977-78; Mktg Coord., Costain Limited, 1978-80; various positions, Proj. Asst., Asst. to Dean, Coord., Acting Dean, Community Educ. Div., Grant McEwen Community Coll., 1980 to date; Exec. Dir., Corp. Mktg Office, 1995 to date. SELECTED PUBLICATIONS: *Consumer Education ESL Series*, "Consumer rights and responsibilities"; "Money management"; "Credit, investment and savings" (1984); "A Framework for Developing Partnerships," in *The Changing Landscape of Workplace Education*, M. Taylor, Ed. AFFIL: Alberta Diversity Network; Association of Canadian Community Colleges (Managing Diversity Committee); Alberta Association for Continuing Education (Issues & Research Committee 1993-95); Alberta Advanced Education & Career Development (invited participant, round table discussions 1993-95). HONS: Prov. of Alta. Grad. Fellowship, 1991-92. INTERESTS: educational partnerships; community educ.; multiculturalism; int'l educ.; crafts; hiking; travel. COMMENT: *"As an adult educator, my lifelong passion is the empowerment of learners as individuals and members of caring, forward-thinking communities."*

Douglas, Catherine Gay ■ ■ ○ ⊕ ⚶
LITERACY LINK NIAGARA, 15 King St., Ste.

301B, St. Catharines, ON L2R 3H1 (905) 682-2222, FAX 682-2298. Born St. Catharines, Ont. 1951. w. 2 ch. Aaron, Shannon. **EDUC:** Niagara Coll. of Arts & Technology, Social Svc. Worker Program 1987-89, Volunteer Mgmt 1989; numerous Kidney Foundation staff dev. workshops re media rel'ns, direct mail, residential campaign mgmt 1989-92; fundraising workshop 1992; Connexions Direct Marketing Resource Centre, Basics of Direct Mktg 1995. **CAREER:** Pharmacy Asst. & Postmistress, Crown Pharmacy, St. Catharines, 1971-86; Adult Protective Svc. Worker, Family & Children's Svcs, Niagara Reg., & Counsellor, Ausable Springs Family Svcs, St. Catharines, 1987-89; Exec. Dir., The Kidney Foundation of Canada, Niagara District chpt., St. Catharines, 1989-95; Dir. of Fundraising & Proj. Dev., Recycling Council of Ontario, Toronto, 1995; Dev. Mgr, Big Sisters Association of Ontario, Toronto, 1996; Exec. Dir., Literacy Link Niagara, St. Catharines, 1996 to date. **VOLUNTEER CAREER:** founding mbr. & Chair, St. Catharines Block Parent Program, 1975-82; Counsellor, Women's Place, 1982-84; Public Rel'ns Chair, Canadian Red Cross, St. Catharines branch, 1989-91; Bd. mbr., Big Sisters of Welland & Pelham, 1994-95; mbr., St. Catharines Strategic Planning Task Force, 1995; delegate, Conference Board of Canada: Business in the Community, 1995. **INTERESTS:** mass media; social & health issues; art; antiques; travel; organizational theory; literature; theatre. **MISC:** created Canada's 1st motor vehicle donation program to raise funds for the Kidney Foundation of Canada.

Douglas, Michelle, B.A. ■■ ⊕

President, FOUNDATION FOR EQUAL FAMILIES, 552 Church St., P.O. Box 500-74, Toronto, ON M4Y 2E3. Born Ottawa 1963. life ptnr. **EDUC:** Carleton Univ., B.A.(Law) 1985. **CAREER:** Canadian Armed Forces, 1986-89; employee, Fed. Public Svc., 1989 to date. **MISC:** fired by military in 1989 for being a lesbian, in spite of excellent svc. record (graduated at top of class in basic training & career-training courses); through court challenge forced an end to military's discriminatory policy against gays & lesbians; now committed to fighting for equality for gays & lesbians; Pres., Foundation for Equal Families, which intervenes in test cases that affect the rights of gays & lesbians in Canada; lobbies Cdn politicans & speaks to many groups in Canada & U.S.; has met with U.S. senators to encourage them to adopt Cdn example of equality for their armed forces.

Dow, Patti, BREC ■ ⊕ ⊘

Executive Director, BASKETBALL NOVA SCOTIA,

Box 3010 South, Halifax, NS B3J 3G6 (902) 425-5450, FAX 425-5606. Born Moncton 1968. s. **EDUC:** Dalhousie Univ., BREC (Sport Admin.) 1990. **CAREER:** Intramural Sports Supervisor & Ref., Dalhousie Campus Recreation, 1986-91; Exec. Dir., Basketball N.S., 1991 to date; Head Coach, Univ. of King's Coll. Women's Volleyball Team, 1993 to date. **AFFIL:** various committees & organizations, Dalhousie Univ.; Volleyball N.S. (Official). **HONS:** Big Brothers/Big Sisters Service Award, 1992.

Down, Jane L., B.Sc. ⊗ ⊛ ✦

Conservation Scientist, Environment and Deterioration Research Division, CANADIAN CONSERVATION INSTITUTE, Department of Canadian Heritage, 1030 Innes Rd., Ottawa, ON K1A 0M5 (613) 998-3721, FAX 998-4721. Born Leamington, Ont. 1950. m. Robin Souchen. 1 ch. Alex Souchen. **EDUC:** Queen's Univ., B.Sc. (Chem. & Math.) 1973. **CAREER:** Research Technician, Centre of Forensic Sci., Toronto, 1971-72 (summers); Research Technician, Biochem. Dept., Queen's Univ., 1973-74; Research Technician, Dept. of Pharmacology, Univ. of Ottawa, 1974-77; Research Technician, Chem. & Biol. Research Institute, Agriculture Canada, 1977-78; Sr. Conservation Scientist, Canadian Conservation Institute, 1978 to date. **SELECTED PUBLICATIONS:** "Properties of the Nicotinamide Adenine Dinucleotide Phosphate Dependent Aldehyde Reductase from Pig Kidney," with T. Geoffrey Flynn & Donald J. Walton (*Journal of Biological Chemistry* 1975); "A Preliminary Report on the Properties and Stability of Wood Adhesives," with Ray Lafontaine, in *Proceedings of the Furniture and Wooden Objects Symposium* (1980); "Epoxy Resin Adhesives: Report on High Intensity Light Aging," (*Studies in Conservation* 1986);"Adhesive testing at the Canadian Conservation Institute - An evaluation of selected poly (vinyl acetate) and acrylic adhesive," with M. MacDonald, J. Tétreault, R.S. Williams (*Studies in Conservation* 1996); *Descendants of the Bradfords of Eastbourne and Surrounding Areas of Sussex, England* (1993); various other publications. **AFFIL:** Canadian Association of Professional Conservators (Membership Chair); Canadian Association for Conservation of Cultural Property (Treas. 1985-86); The ICOM Committee for Conservation Resins Group. **HONS:** Russelo Bursary Scholarship Award, 1969, 1970, 1971, 1972; Fellow of the International Institute for Conservation of Historic & Artistic Works). **INTERESTS:** genealogy; piano; gardening. **MISC:** various conference presentations. **COMMENT:** *"I am a dedicated conservation scien-*

tist, an active genealogist, and a devoted wife and mother. I strive to be focused, positive, flexible and true to my feelings. Some achievements that make me proud are my adhesive research that helps conservators worldwide; my genealogical book on the Bradfords of East bourne, which was a labour of love for an appreciative family; and my son, who is a constant source of joy whom I thoroughly treasure. My endeavours over the past few years have brought me a peace and understanding that affords me much happiness."

Down, Nancy, B.A.,M.D.,F.R.C.S.(c), F.R.C.S.,F.A.C.S. ⊕

Physician, NORTH YORK GENERAL HOSPITAL, 1333 Sheppard Ave. E., Ste. 218, North York, ON M2J 1V1 (416) 491-0345, FAX 491-8476. Born Trenton, Ont. 1955. m. Dr. Ian Soutter. 2 ch. EDUC: Univ. of Western Ontario, B.A. (English) 1976; Univ. of Toronto, M.D. 1980; Gallie Course, Toronto, F.R.C.S.(c)(Gen. Surgery) 1986. CAREER: Surgical Internship, Wellesley Hospital, 1980-81; Surgical Residency, Gallie Course, Toronto, 1983-86; Fellowship in Gen. Surgery, St. Michael's Hospital, 1986; Dept. of Surgery, Etobicoke General Hospital, 1986-94; Dept. of Surgery, North York General Hospital, 1995 to date. SELECTED PUBLICATIONS: "Successful Treatment of a Traumatic Hepatic Artery-Portal Vein Arteriovenous Fistula by Interpositional Mescoaval Shunt," with L. Makowa, B. Langer, R. Colapinto & R. Wensel (*Canadian Journal of Surgery*, Mar. 1987); various abstracts & presentations. AFFIL: Ontario Medical Association; Canadian Trauma Association; Canadian Association of General Surgeons; Canadian Medical Association; Royal Coll. of Physicians & Surgeons (Fellow); American Coll. of Physicians & Surgeons (Fellow); Canadian Breast Cancer Fdn. (Med. Adv. Bd.); Toronto Fire Dept. (Med. Bd.); North York Gen. Hosp. Breast Diagnostic Centre (Dir.). HONS: Bd. of Gov. Admission Scholarship, 1973; Colgate-Palmolive Undergrad. Award, 1975; Mosby Publications Book Award, 1978; Lange Publications Book Award, 1979; Medical Society Honour Award, 1980; Elizabeth Ann Munro Gordon Medal & Prize, Univ. of Toronto, 1980. INTERESTS: skiing; gourmet cooking; windsurfing. MISC: was medical sch. graduating class Valedictorian, 1980.

Downe, Valerie, B.A.,CAE ■■ ♡ ⊕

Executive Director, P.E.I. Division, CANADIAN CANCER SOCIETY, 1 Rochford St., Ste. 1, Charlottetown, PE C1A 3T1 (902) 566-4002, FAX 628-8281. Born Charlottetown 1950. d. 2 ch. Elizabeth, Blake. EDUC: Univ. of P.E.I.,

B.A.(Pol. Studies) 1989; Canadian Society of Association Executives, CAE 1993.

Downie, Mary Alice Hunter, B.A. 📖 ✒ ✑

Freelance Writer and Editor. 190 Union St., Kingston, ON K7L 2P6 (613) 542-3464, FAX 545-6637 (attn: J. Downie). Born Alton, Ill. 1934. m. John Downie. 3 ch. Christine, Jocelyn, Alexandra. EDUC: Univ. of Toronto, B.A. (English Lang. & Lit.) 1955. CAREER: Reporter, *Marketing Magazine*, 1955-56; Editorial Asst., *Canadian Medical Association Journal*, 1956-57; Publicity Mgr, Oxford University Press, Toronto, 1958-59; freelance, 1959 to date. SELECTED PUBLICATIONS: *Sacred Sarah* (Toronto: Thomas Nelson, 1974); *The King's Loon/Un huart pour le Roi*, illus. by Ron Berg (Toronto: Kids Can Press, 1979); *And Some Brought Flowers: Plants in a New World*, with Mary Hamilton (Univ. of Toronto Press 1980); *Seeds and Weeds: A Book of Country Crafts*, with Jillian Gilliland (Toronto: Four Winds Press, 1981); *The Window of Dreams: New Canadian Writing for Children*, with Elizabeth Greene & M.A. Thompson (Toronto: Methuen, 1986); *Honor Bound*, with John Downie, illus. by Wesley Bates (Kingston: Quarry Press, 1991); *Snow Paws*, illus. by Kathy W. Naipler (Stoddart, 1996); numerous other books; stories in *Canadian Children's Annual*, 1978, 1979, 1987, *Quarry Magazine*, *The Christmas Log*, *Canadian Christmas Stories*, & others; articles & reviews in *The Hornbook Magazine*, *Pittsburgh Press*, *Kingston Whig-Standard Magazine*, *The London Free Press*; *Ottawa Citizen*, *The Globe and Mail*, *Montreal Gazette*, *Canadian Gardening*, *Century Home*, & others. EDIT: Book Page Ed., *Kingston Whig-Standard*, 1973-78; Ed., with E. Greene & M.A. Thompson, special children's issue of *Quarry* Magazine, Mar. 1985. AFFIL: Writers' Union of Canada (Chrm, Membership Committee 1987-88); PEN; Travel Media Assoc. of Canada. HONS: 2nd Prize, 4th CBC Literary Competition, Children's Section, *The Bright Paddles*, 1982; Dickson Scholarship, Trinity Coll., 1951; sev. Canada Council & Ontario Arts Council grants & awards. MISC: listed in numerous biographical references incl. *Canadian Who's Who*, *International Authors' and Writers' Who's Who*, *Who's Who of American Women*, *The World Who's Who of Women*. COMMENT: *"As a child, I dreamed of writing historical novels about ancient Britain and the Dark Ages. As an adult, I fell in love with Canada's past. Since then, it has been my passion to write about our history, folklore and traditions."*

Doyle, Dianne, B.ScN., M.S.N. ⊕
Chief Operations Officer, MOUNT SAINT JOSEPH HOSPITAL, 3080 Prince Edward St., Vancouver, BC V5T 3N4 (604) 877-8334, FAX 875-8733. Born Kingston, Ont. 1950. m. Ken Robinson. 3 ch. Ashley Robinson, Christopher Robinson, Melissa Robinson. EDUC: Univ. of Ottawa, B.Sc.N.(Nursing) 1973; Univ. of British Columbia, M.S.N.(Nursing) 1981. CAREER: Staff Nurse, Royal Jubilee Hospital, Victoria, 1973-75; Instructor, Royal Jubilee Sch. of Nursing, 1975-76; Staff Nurse (casual) & I.C.U. (full-time), St. Paul's Hospital, Vancouver, 1977-83; Medical Instructor, 1980-83; Head Nurse, 1983-85; Dir. of Patient Care, Mount Saint Joseph Hospital, 1985-88; VP, Svc., 1988-95; COO, 1995 to date. SELECTED PUBLICATIONS: "Crossing Cultures" (*B.C. Health Management Review*, Vol. 4, No. 2, Fall 1989). AFFIL: Catholic Health Association of B.C. (Dir.); B.C. Council of Licensed Practical Nurses (Dir.; B.C.H.A. Rep.); Canadian Coll. of Health Service Executives; Registered Nurses' Association of B.C. (mbr., numerous committees). INTERESTS: swimming; skiing. MISC: numerous prov. & nat'l speaking engagements on health care issues. COMMENT: "*As a career woman, wife and mother of three young children, I continually strive to balance and integrate professional and personal goals and to seek opportunities for challenge, growth and mentoring of others.*"

Doyle, Judith, B.A. ■ ⊗ ⌣ ⩙
Instructor, ONTARIO COLLEGE OF ART, 100 McCaul St., Toronto, ON M5T 1N1 (416) 504-7370, FAX 504-7370. Director, READING PICTURES. Born Toronto 1957. m. Ted Myerscough. 1 ch. EDUC: York Univ., B.A.(Writing) 1978. CAREER: independent film & video dir., 1982 to date; Instructor, Ont. Coll. of Art, 1985 to date. SELECTED CREDITS: Writer/Prod./Dir., *Wasaga* (feature), 1994; Dir., *Artists' Television* (documentary), 1992; Dir., *The Seventh Fire/Elders Teaching* (documentary), 1991; Dir., *Whitefish Bay: Self-Government* (documentary), 1991; Writer/Prod./Dir., *Lac La Croix* (documentary), 1988; Writer/Prod./Dir., *Eye of the Mask: Theatre/Nicaragua* (documentary), 1985; Writer/Prod./Dir., *Private Property/Public History* (experimental documentary), 1982; Writer/Prod./Dir., *Launch* (experimental documentary), 1982. SELECTED PUBLICATIONS: articles & fiction in: *Fuse, The Independent Eye, Impulse, Vanguard, The Idler, Parachute, Parallelogramme, Fireweed, Content, Stereo Morning* (CBC Radio), YYZ Books; *TE BWE WIN (TRUTH), Stories by an Ojibway Healer*, co-author with Ron Geyshick (Summerhill Press 1989); Ed., *Impulse* Maga-

zine, 1978-90; Ed., Rumour Publications, 1978-81. EDIT: Ed. Bd., *Fuse*. AFFIL: Liaison of Independent Filmmakers of Toronto; Trinity Square Video; Toronto Arts Council (Visual Arts Committee 1991-93). HONS: Special Jury Citation, Mannheim Festival; grants & awards from the Canada Council & the Ont. Arts Council. INTERESTS: community-based culture & activism. MISC: int'l festival screenings include: Toronto International Film Festival; Mannheim; Vancouver; Havana; gallery screenings & collections include: National Gallery; Power Plant; London Regional; Art Gallery of Ontario; visiting lecturer at selected universities incl. York; Queen's; Simon Fraser; Ryerson Polytechnic; NSCAD; Univ. of Toronto; Emily Carr Coll. of Art; visiting lecturer, Toronto Festival of Festivals & the National Film Board. COMMENT: "*I have produced community-based films and videos with the Lac La Croix First Nation, Whitefish Bay First Nation, Anishnawbe Health, Toronto, The Toronto Public Library Literacy Unit and Houselink Inc. My films are distributed by Cinema Esperanza, Toronto (Wasaga) and the Canadian Filmmakers Distribution Centre, Toronto (shorts). My upcoming* Fuse *feature is on 'zines, nets and outlets by artists: the late '70s and now.*"

Doyle-MacBain, Lisa Bridget, B.B.A. ◉ ✿
Executive Director, FEDERATION OF PRINCE EDWARD ISLAND MUNICIPALITIES, 1 Kirkdale Rd., Charlottetown, PE C1E 1R3 (902) 566-1493, FAX 368-1239. Born Charlottetown 1967. m. Robert MacBain. EDUC: Univ. of PEI, B.B.A. 1989. CAREER: Exec. Dir., Federation of PEI Municipalities, 1989 to date. AFFIL: Zonta Club of Charlottetown; Maritime Municipal Training & Dev. Bd.; P.E.I. Environmental Advisory Council; Transition House Association (Treas. 1990-92); numerous prov. advisory committees. HONS: Life Pres., Univ. of P.E.I. Class of 1989; Owen J. MacDonald Award for Student Excellence, 1989. INTERESTS: cooking; crafts; auctions; antiques; computers; Internet; biking; tennis. COMMENT: "*I am a proud Canadian who strives to be the best I can be. I live by the adage: 'What's worth doing is worth doing well.' I try to see the positive side of circumstances and I do what I can to make the world a little brighter for people who are less fortunate than I.*"

Doyle-Rodrigue, Jocelyne, B.A. 🗊
President and Founder, EXCELCOM TRANSLEX, 116 Albert St., 9th Fl., Ottawa, ON K1P 5G3 (613) 234-5312, FAX (613) 563-9100. Born Montreal 1951. m. Nelson Rodrigue. 2 ch. Andréane, Philippe. EDUC: Univ. of Montreal,

B.A.(Translation) 1973. **CAREER:** Translator, Fed. Gov't, 1973-77; VP, Canadian Union of Professional & Technical Employees, 1975; Head, Translation Svc., CRTC, 1977; Founder & CEO, Translex, 1980; CEO, Traductions Sautemet, 1987-89; Pres. & Owner, Excelcom Translex, 1989 to date. **AFFIL:** Association of Translators & Interpreters of Ontario (ATIO); Women's Business Network of Ottawa-Carleton; Regroupement des gens d'affaires de l'Outaouais; Club Omnigym d'Aylmer; Children's Aid Society of Ottawa-Carleton (Dir.); École Guigues (Fundraising Committee). **HONS:** Women's Achievement Award, Women's Business Network of Ottawa; Business Woman of the Year, 1992; prix d'excellence du Regroupment des gens d'affaire de l'Outaouais, 1996. **INTERESTS:** golf; music. **COMMENT:** *"Founder of a one-person company, now heading a medium-sized written-communications firm, Mrs. Doyle-Rodrigue is active in business, professional and charitable groups."*

Drainie, Bronwyn, B.A.,M.A. / 💄 📖
Writer, Broadcaster, Cultural Critic. c/o The Globe and Mail, 444 Front St. W., Toronto, ON M5V 2S9. Born Toronto 1945. d. 2 ch. Gabriel Martin, Sam Martin. **EDUC:** Univ. of Toronto, B.A.(English) 1967, M.A.(English) 1969. **CAREER:** Promo. Dir., Peter Martin Associates, & Readers' Club of Canada, 1967-68; Researcher & Story Prod., *The News Programme,* CJOH-TV, Ottawa, 1969-70; Story Prod., *Weekday Journal,* CBLT-TV, Toronto, 1970-71; Researcher, BBC Radio, London, UK, 1974-75; wrote & recorded freelance material for CBC Radio, 1974-75; Staff Announcer, CBC Radio, 1975-76; Co-Host, *Sunday Morning,* CBC Radio, 1976-81; News reader, CBC Radio, 1982-85; freelance writing for *The Globe and Mail* & various magazines, 1985 to date; Nat'l Arts columnist, *The Globe and Mail,* 1989-91, 1993 to date; Maclean Hunter Chair of Journalism Ethics, Ryerson Polytechnic Univ., 1995 to date. **SELECTED PUBLICATIONS:** *Living the Part: John Drainie and the Dilemma of Canadian Stardom* (Toronto: Macmillan, 1988); *My Jerusalem: Secular Adventures in the Holy City* (Toronto: Doubleday, 1994). **HONS:** Best Host-Interviewer on Radio, ACTRA Award, 1980; Gold Award for Service Journalism, National Magazine Awards, 1987; Ann Saddlemyer Prize, Association of Canadian Theatre History, 1988 Shortlisted, Trillium Award, 1994. **MISC:** regular book critic & panelist, *The Journal,* CBC-TV & *Imprint, TVOntario* (1989-91); Guest Host, 2 weeks, *As It Happens,* 1 week, *Morningside,* & 1 week, *The Arts Tonight,* CBC-Radio

(1994); lived in Crete, 1973-74 & 1981-82, UK, 1974-75, & Jerusalem, 1991-93. **COMMENT:** *"Bronwyn Drainie is a cultural journalist who works in many media: books, magazines, radio and television, and in her regular weekly column on Thursdays in* The Globe and Mail.*"*

Dranoff, Linda Silver, B.A., LL.B. 💄 📖 /
Barrister and Solicitor, LINDA SILVER DRANOFF AND ASSOCIATES, 1033 Bay St., Ste. 314, Toronto, ON M5S 3A5 (416) 925-4500, FAX (416) 925-5197. Author and Columnist. m. 1 ch. **EDUC:** Univ. of Toronto, B.A. 1961; Osgoode Hall Law Sch. (York Univ.), LL.B. 1972. **BAR:** Ont., 1974. **CAREER:** Barrister & Solicitor, 1974 to date; Columnist, "Ask a Lawyer," *Chatelaine,* 1979 to date. **SELECTED PUBLICATIONS:** *Women in Canadian Law* (1977); *Every Woman's Guide to the Law* (1985); *Everyone's Guide to the Law: A Handbook for Canadians* (HarperCollins, 1997); various feature articles in *Chatelaine* & guest columns in *The Toronto Star, The Globe and Mail* & others. **AFFIL:** Canadian Bar Association (Founding Chair, Feminist Legal Analysis Section 1992-95); Canadian Civil Liberties Association; National Association of Women & the Law; Osgoode Society; Planned Parenthood (Hon. Dir.); Alliance of Canadian Cinema, Television & Radio Artists (ACTRA); Women's Law Association of Ontario; Women in Educational Administration (Advisory Bd.). **HONS:** Distinguished Service Award, Canadian Bar Association, 1993; Woman of Distinction Award, YWCA, 1995. **MISC:** various TV appearances; frequent lecturer on women's, legal, & community issues; Exec. Mbr., Ont. (prov. gov't) Status of Women Council, Advisory Council 1979-82, V-Chrm 1980-82; instrumental in the passage of the Family Law Act, 1986.

Drapeau, Suzanne Elizabeth, B.Sc., BPR,M.B.A. ■ 🍁 🌿 🏵
Funding Analyst, NOVA SCOTIA COMMUNITY COLLEGE, 75 Brookside Rd., Hatchet Lake, NS B3T 1S2 (902) 424-5277, FAX 424-4225, EMAIL drapease@nscc.ns.ca. Vice-Chair, Board of Governors, MOUNT SAINT VINCENT UNIVERSITY. Born Halifax 1959. m. Spencer Phillips. 3 ch. Kenzie Phillips, Leah Phillips, Connor Phillips. **EDUC:** Mount Saint Vincent Univ., B.Sc.(Biol.) 1980, BPR 1983; Dalhousie Univ., M.B.A.(Hum. Res.) 1992. **CAREER:** Public Rel'ns Officer, Canadian Association for Community Living, N.S. Div., 1984-87; Exec. Officer, Students' Union of N.S., 1986-95; Fin. & Admin. Coord., Nat'l Post-Secondary AIDS

Educ. Proj. (under aegis of SUNS), 1988-90; Funding Analyst, Nova Scotia Community Coll., 1995 to date. **SELECTED PUBLICA-TIONS:** various papers incl. co-author of: *Student Debt in the 1990's* (Students' Union of N.S., Nov. 1994); *A Comprehensive Survey of the Financial Situation of University Students in Nova Scotia in 1990* (Students' Union of N.S., Sept. 1991). **AFFIL:** Hum. Res. Sector Committee (N.S. Voluntary Planning 1995 to date); Mount Saint Vincent Univ. (Bd. of Gov. 1991 to date; V-Chair 1994 to date) Mount Saint Vincent Alumnae Association (1983 to date; Pres. 1989-91; Past Pres. 1991 to date); Metro Area Family Planning Association (Public Rel'ns Committee 1986-89); World Cup of Wheelchair Basketball (Media Rel'ns Coord.); VII Pan Am Wheelchair Games (Media Rel'ns Coord.). **COMMENT:** *"My career and volunteer participation in the higher education public policy community in Nova Scotia allows me to make a contribution to the goal of a broadly accessible post secondary education system. I am able to focus a particular emphasis on the education of women by maintaining strong ties to Mount Saint Vincent University."*

Draycott, Anita, B.A. ■ ■ / 🗖
Editorial Director, *Chatelaine* Special Editions, MACLEAN HUNTER PUBLISHING LIMITED, 777 Bay St., Toronto, ON M5W 1A7 (416) 596-6052, FAX 593-3197. Born Toronto 1949. m. William Orr. **EDUC:** Univ. of Toronto, B.A.(Hons., Psych. & Sociology) 1972. **CAREER:** Editor, *Teen Generation*, 1974-82; Editor, *Program Guide*, 1982-84; Editor, *City & Country Home*, 1984-94; Editor, *Chatelaine* Special Editions, 1994 to date. **HONS:** several National Magazine Awards. **INTERESTS:** golf; tennis; travel.

Drew, Fay 🕙 ⊕ 🔾
President, NEUROFIBROMATOSIS SOCIETY OF ONTARIO, 923 Annes St., Whitby, ON L1N 5K7 (905) 430 6141, FAX 430-6141. Born Bombay 1938. w. Stuart Drew. 4 ch. Mark, Debra, Hayley, Adam. **EDUC:** schools in India & UK. **CAREER:** VP, Neurofibromatosis Society of Ontario, 1989-91; Pres., 1991 to date. **SELECTED CREDITS:** produced 2 plays for community theatre, Whitby. **SELECTED PUB-LICATIONS:** pamphlets & other materials for the Neurofibromatosis Society. **HONS:** award for Beaver float in local parade. **INTERESTS:** working with people; working with children; crafts; my 4 grandchildren (Amanda, Victoria, Drew, Daniella). **MISC:** has lived in India, UK, & Cyprus; represented Ont., Neurofibromatosis Association of America gen. meeting, N.Y., 1993; Neurofibromatosis Society of Ontario is

twinned with Lincoln-Continental Owners' Club of Ontario, which helps raise funds for & awareness of the Society; est. various awards within the Society, incl. the Stuart Drew Achievement Award; recently directed the allocation of a grant for neurofibromatosis research in Canada. **COMMENT:** *"Proud mother of two boys and two girls. I was widowed at 55 very suddenly, but my goal is to fulfil my husband's and my dream to help find a cure for neurofibromatosis, to raise awareness of this condition, and to be there for the people who need me."*

Driedger, Florence Gay, B.A., M.S.W. 🔾 ☆ 🖑
Social Development Consultant and Lay Pastor, PEACE MENNONITE CHURCH, Regina, SK (306) 586-8718, FAX 586-4352. Born Roland, Man. 1933. m. Otto Driedger. 2 ch. Joan Boldt, Karen Driedger-Simes. **EDUC:** Bethel Coll., Newton, KS, B.A.(Social Svc.) 1954; McGill Univ., M.S.W.(Social Work) 1958. **CAREER:** Social Worker, Family Services Association, Montreal, summer 1958; Social Worker, Saskatchewan Social Services, 1958-59; Social Work Supervisor, 1959-60, 1961-62; Proj. Officer, 1965-68; Staff Dev. & Training Coord., 1968-80; freelance Social Dev. Consultant, 1980-83; Sessional Lecturer, Fac. of Social Work, Univ. of Regina, 1983 to date; Exec. Dir., Family Service Bureau of Regina, 1983-95. **VOLUNTEER CAREER:** Bd. & Exec. Mbr., Canadian Mennonite Bible Coll., 1971-80; Bd. & Exec. Committee, Mennonite Central Committee, 1980-90; Mbr., Family Life Saskatchewan, 1971-82; Bd. mbr. & Chair, Regina Plains Community Coll., 1980-83; Chair, Saskatchewan Association of Social Workers (S.A.S.W.), 1981-83; Exec. Committee & Codes of Ethics Committee, Canadian Association of Social Workers, 1982-84; Moderator, Gen. Conference, Mennonite Church of North America, 1986-92; Chair, Exec. Dir. Sub-Committee, Family Service Saskatchewan, 1988-93; Accreditation Committee, Family Service Canada, 1988 to date; Accreditation Committee, Canadian Association of Schools of Social Work, 1989-95; Mbr., integration Committee of the 2 major Mennonite denominations of North America, 1989-95. **SELECTED PUBLI-CATIONS:** "Reconciliation Through Brother-Sisterhood," & "Summary Report," *Jesus Christ Reconciles, Proceedings of the Ninth Mennonite World Conference*, Ed. C.J. Dyck (Nappanee, Ind.: Evangel Press, 1972); *Proceeding of the Family Policy Conference March 1979 Regina*, Ed. (Regina: Family Life Saskatchewan, 1979); "Native Ministries in the 80's: Where are we Headed" *(Mennonite*

Reporter, Aug. 4, 1980); *No More Dreams, a proposal for action in support of farm families in Saskatchewan,* F. Dreidger *et al* (Family Service Bureau of Regina); "Facts About Today's Families" (*Mennonite Reporter,* Sept. 16, 1991). AFFIL: Family Service Canada (Bd.); Family Service Canada/Family Service Ontario (Accreditation Committee); Conference of Mennonites in Canada (Chair, Ministries Commission); Saskatchewan Association of Social Workers; Canadian Council on Social Development; National Association of Poverty Organizations; Regina Social Development Council; Vanier Institute on the Family. HONS: Distinguished Service Award, Saskatchewan Association of Social Workers, 1985; Canada 125 Medal, 1993; 60th Anniversary Family Service Bureau of Regina Recognition, 1991; Women of Distinction Award, Community/Humanitarianism Service, Regina YWCA, 1994. INTERESTS: int'l travel; music; entertaining; reading; bridge; providing a home to new Canadians & int'l students & guests. MISC: 1st woman to make a presentation to the World Conference of Mennonites (held in Curitiba, Brazil, 1972); 1st woman to hold the position of Moderator, Gen. Conference of the Mennonite Church of North America; ongoing consultation with educational & social svcs agencies in Odessa, Ukraine; involved in social service/work research & dev. COMMENT: *"Coming from a family and community rich in care, love and resources and having been given many opportunities, I count it a privilege to serve my church, community, the disadvantaged at home and abroad. I have walked ahead into many organizations where no women had served and now am followed by many. Friends of all races abound."*

Driedger, Myrna, R.N. ◐ ○

Executive Director, CHILD FIND MANITOBA, 1181 Portage Ave., Ste. 294, Winnipeg, MB R3G 0T3 (204) 945-5735, FAX 948-2461. Born Benito, Man. 1952. m. Helmut Driedger. 2 ch. Rhys, Curtis. EDUC: Winnipeg General Hospital Sch. of Nursing, R.N. 1972; Red River Community Coll., Health Care Mgmt Certificate 1977. CAREER: Staff Nurse, Neurosciences Unit, St. Boniface General Hospital, 1974-75; Clinical Instructor, Continuing Educ., 1975-86; Special Projects Nurse, 1986-92; Nursing Supervisor, 1992 to date; Exec. Dir., Child Find Manitoba, 1991 to date; Pres., Child Find Manitoba, 1993-96; Second VP, Child Find Canada, 1993-95; First VP & Chair, Child Find Canada, Case Mgmt Committee, 1995. SELECTED PUBLICATIONS: "Neurofibromatosis" (*L'Axone* Dec. 1984); "Patient Focused Charting" (*Canadian Journal*

of Nursing Administration 1988); "Impact of Computerization On Nursing: Automated Order Entry, Care Planning, and Implications for Recruitment"(*Canadian Journal of Nursing Administration* May/June 1993). AFFIL: Social Planning Council of Winnipeg; Manitoba Association of Registered Nurses; Manitoba Coalition on the Rights of the Child; Neighbourhood Watch; United Way; Canadian Association of Neurological & Neurosurgical Nurses. HONS: Student of the Year, Benito Collegiate, 1969; Winnipeg General Hospital Award for Outstanding School Citizenship, 1972; Manitoba Nursing Research Institute Award for recognition of scholarly contribution to nursing research, 1991. INTERESTS: reading; travelling; cross-country skiing; horseback riding; photography; golfing; piano. MISC: facilitated the dynamic growth & profile of Child Find Manitoba over the past 9 years; Child Find Manitoba recognized with the 1994 Min. of Justice & Attorney Gen. Award for Outstanding Contribution to Crime Prevention in Manitoba, & the 1994 Program Dev. Award from Child Find Canada. COMMENT: *"I am an energetic, innovative individual who believes that a child has the right to be safe and that all people have the capability to make a difference in this world."*

Driver, Deana (née Pacholok) ✎

Writer and Photographer, FIRST-RATE FREE-LANCING, 91 Minot Dr., Regina, SK S4X 1B6 (306) 545-5293, FAX 545-5293. Born Athabasca, Alta. 1956. m. Al Driver. 3 ch. David, Lisa, Danielle. EDUC: Southern Alberta Institute of Technology, Diploma of Applied Arts, Journalism Admin. 1973-75. CAREER: Invoice Typist, Barber-Ellis of Canada, 1975-76; Advtg Mgr, Woolco Dept. Stores, Regina, 1976-78; Branch Sec., Dover Corporation, 1978; Advtg Copy Writer, Buffalo Broadcasting, 1978-79; Clerk Typist II (temp), Prov. Mediation Bd., 1979-80; Advtg Supplement Ed., *Regina Leader-Post,* 1980-81; Reporter, Weekender section, 1981-83; freelance journalist & photographer, 1983 to date; Sask. Correspondent, *The Medical Post,* 1984 to date; Writer, Saskatchewan Tourism & Small Business, 1984-85; Sask. Contributing Ed., *United Church Observer,* 1985 to date; Sask. Contributor, *The Journal,* Addiction Research Foundation, 1986-93; Sask. Correspondent, *The Bottom Line,* 1987 to date; Writer, *Profile* newsletter, Saskatchewan Health Programs Branch, Alcohol & Drug Svcs, 1988-96; Contributor, *Maclean's* magazine 1988-90; Sask. Correspondent, *Pharmacist News,* 1993 to date; Youth Pages Ed., *United Church Observer,* 1994 to date; self-employed photographer, 1995 to date. **SELECTED PUBLICATIONS:** contributed 1 chapter to *The First Book of Saints* (United Church Publishing House 1988). **AFFIL:** Heritage United Church; Prairie View Community Association (Exec. 1988-91); Heart Foundation; United Way; Carmichael Outreach Inc. (Bd. 1996-97); parent helper for Scouts, Brownies, soccer, hockey & some sch. programs. **INTERESTS:** photography; desktop publishing; reading; drama; sewing; crafts; dancing; bowling. **COMMENT:** *"I am a freelance journalist who works out of my home in Regina. For the past 12 years I have been a correspondent for various publications, bringing Saskatchewan stories and viewpoints to a national audience. Photography is my second love and has become my secondary business."*

Drover, Mary, B.A. ■■ ✊ 📕 ♥

Executive Director, SASKATCHEWAN WRITERS GUILD (prov. svc. organization for writers, 700 mbrs., non-profit), P.O. Box 3986, Regina, SK S4P 3R9 (306) 791-7743, FAX 565-8554, EMAIL swg@sk.sympatico.ca. Born London, Ont. 1949. d. **EDUC:** McMaster Univ., B.A. (Hist.) 1971. **CAREER:** Educ. Officer, Canadian Museum of Civilization, Ottawa, 1975-78; Reg'l Coord., Museum Assistance Programme, 1978-81; Museum Consultant & volunteer coord., Sask. Gov't, Regina, 1981-90; freelance cultural consultant, 1990-91; Exec. Dir., Saskatchewan Writers Guild, 1991 to date. **AFFIL:** Canadian Breast Cancer Network (Chair; founding mbr.); Allan Blair Cancer Centre (Lay Advisory Committee); Breast Cancer Action Saskatchewan (founding mbr.); Breast Cancer Info Link, Prairies/NWT (Advisory Panel); Saskatchewan Arts Alliance. **COMMENT:** *"Cultural administrator for 21 years, in Ottawa and Saskatchewan; an active member of the Saskatchewan cultural community; 12-year breast cancer survivor and activist, currently chairing the Canadian Breast Cancer Network."*

Dubin, Anne R., B.A.,LL.B.,Q.C. ⚖

Partner, TORY TORY DESLAURIERS & BINNINGTON, Toronto Dominion Centre, Box 270, Toronto, ON M5K 1N2. Born 1926. m. Hon. Charles L. Dubin. **EDUC:** Univ. of Toronto, B.A., LL.B. 1948; Osgoode Hall Law Sch., 1951. **BAR:** Ont., 1951; Queen's Counsel, 1962. **CAREER:** articled, McMaster Montgomery & Co., 1948-51; Ptnr, Kimber, Dubin, 1953-72; Ptnr, Tory Tory DesLauriers & Binnington, 1972 to date. **AFFIL:** Osgoode Excellence Fund & Trust Advisory Committee (Chair); York Univ. (Hon. Gov.); Toronto Hospital Foundation (Trustee); Law Reform Commission (Advisory Bd.); Toronto Hunt Club; Breakers Club, Palm Beach.

Dubsky, Fiona J.O., B.A. $

Senior Manager, Multinational Sector, Quebec, ROYAL BANK OF CANADA, 1 Place Ville-Marie, C.P. 6001, Montreal, QC H3C 3A9 (514) 874-2816, FAX 874-5315. Born Montreal 1950. m. 2 ch. **EDUC:** Loyola Coll., B.A.(Pol. Sci./Econ.) 1972. **CAREER:** joined Royal Bank of Canada, 1973; Corp. Acct Mgr, 1978-84; Nat'l Acct Mgr, 1984-89; Sr. Mgr, Multinat'l Sector, Que., 1989 to date. **AFFIL:** Scouts Canada; various home & sch. organizations.

Duchesnay, Isabelle J., C.L.H. y

Professional Figure Skater. Born 1963. s. **EDUC:** Univ. of Ottawa, Psych. 2nd yr.; private tutoring in piano, 10 yrs. **SPORTS CAREER:** Bronze Medal, Cdn Championships, 1984 & 1985; Nat'l French Champions (ice dancing with brother), 1985-92; 12th place finish, World Championships, Geneva, 1986; 9th place finish, World Championships, Cincinnati, 1987; 6th place finish, World Championships, Budapest, & 8th place finish, Olympic Games, Calgary, 1988; Bronze Medal, World Championships, Paris, 1989; Silver Medal, World Championships, Halifax, 1990; Gold Medal, World Championships, Munich, 1991; Silver Medal, Olympic Games, Albertville, 1992; professional skater, numerous skating tours & shows, incl. Tour of Olympic & World Figure Skating Champions, 1990-95. **SELECTED CREDITS:** lead role, "The Planets," TV special, 1994; biographical TV mini-series, "Fire and Ice," 1993-94; Christmas TV special, Reno, Nev., 1993; benefit show for Children's Hospital, Calgary; TV special for opening of Eurodisney, Paris, 1992; nat'l, int'l & private TV & radio announcing, France, Germany & Canada (e.g. 1994 Olympics). **AFFIL:** Pavillon du Parc Foundation (Hon. Pres. 1996); Star97 ballroom & competitive dancing (Hon. Pres. 1996). **HONS:** French Legion of Honour; hon. mbr., several skating & other clubs; Duchesnay name used for ice rink in Proville, France, & street in Aylmer, Que. **INTERESTS:** music; golf; tennis; cycling; horseback riding; interior decoration; fashion. **MISC:** mgmt of skating tours in Europe; seminars on leadership & stress with Bouygues, largest construction consulting firm in Europe; Cdn & French citizenship; speaks English, French, German & Spanish.

Dudek, Dorothy ✊ $ ✊

Executive Director, MANITOBA CHILD CARE ASSOCIATION INC., 364 McGregor St., Winnipeg, MB R2W 4X3 (204) 586-8587, ext. 5, FAX 589-5613. Born Stonewall, Man. 1953.

d. 2 ch. **EDUC:** Red River Community Coll., Diploma (Child Care Svcs) 1973; Univ. of Manitoba, Certificate Program in Non-Profit Organization Mgmt 1993. **CAREER:** Child Care Centre Dir. & front-line Staff Person, Family Day Care Provider, Family Day Care Coord., Prov. of Man., 1973-85; Private Child Care Consultant, 1985; part-time Instructor & Practicum Supervisor, Red River Community Coll., 1983-86; Coord., Child Care Svcs, Residential Child/Youth Care, Foster Care & Activity Worker Certificate Programs, Continuing Educ., 1983-86; Exec. Dir., Manitoba Child Care Association Inc., 1986 to date. **AFFIL:** Canadian Child Care Federation (Founding Dir. 1987-89); Provincial Council of Women (Fed. Rep. 1994-96). **HONS:** Child Care Service Recognition Award, 1982; Hon. Dip. (Adult Ed.), Red River Cmmunity Coll. 1989; YM/YWCA Woman of the Year nomination for Outstanding Achievement in the Professional Category, 1990. **INTERESTS:** interior design; reading; gardening. **MISC:** Advisory Bd., Nat'l Child Care Resource Dev. Proj., 1992-95; Advisory Bd., Nat'l Child Care Info. Ntwk Proj. (3-yr. proj.), 1991-93. **COMMENT:** *"I am fortunate to have chosen a career that constantly challenges and fulfills my passion regarding quality child care as a service and profession."*

Duff, Ann MacIntosh ⊗

Watercolour Artist and Printmaker. 133 Imperial St., Toronto, ON M5P 1C7 (416) 489-5957. Born Toronto 1925. s. **EDUC:** Central Tech. Sch. Toronto, Degree in Art 1945; Queen's Univ. Summer Sch. of Fine Arts, Diploma (Art) 1945. **SELECTED PUBLICATIONS:** *Pictures from the Douglas M. Duncan Collection*, Francis Barwick (Toronto: Univ. of Toronto Press, 1975); *Passionate Spirits* by Rebecca Sisler (Clarke Irwin and Co. Ltd, 1980); *Aquarelle!* by Rebecca Sisler (Porcupine's Quill, 1986). **EXHIBITIONS:** 16 solo exhibitions in Toronto; has exhibited in Japan, N.Y. City, London, Glasgow, Expo 67 Montreal; *Fifty Years of Water Colour* at the Art Gallery of Ontario (1975); *Graphex 1, 2, & 3*, London, Ontario Art Museum. **COLLECTIONS:** National Gallery of Canada, Art Gallery of Ontario, London Regional Gallery, Agnes Etherington Art Centre-Queen's Univ., City of Toronto Archives, OISE Collection, Toronto-Dominion Bank, Royal Collection of Drawings & Watercolours-Windsor Castle, CIBC Private Banking, Decima Research, Laurentian Univ., etc. **AFFIL:** Canadian Society of Painters in Water Colour (on exec. 1952-82; Treas.); Canadian Society of Graphic Art (on exec., several yrs.; Treas.); Royal Canadian

Academy of Arts (on council, 3 yrs). **HONS:** J. Grant Glassco Award, 1968; Loomis & Toles Award, 1969; John Labatt Ltd. Award, 1972 & 1973; Dofasco Award, 1976; Queen Elizabeth Silver Jubilee Medal, 1977; Curry Award, 1980 & 1981; Art Materials Association of Canada Award, 1983; Honour Award, Canadian Society of Painters in Watercolour, 1984. **COMMENT:** *"I am primarily a water-colour artist and also a printmaker. I paint strong paintings using rich liquid colours, of landscapes of the mind, including many things."*

Duffin, Jacalyn M., M.D.,F.R.C.P.(C), Ph.D. ■ ⊰ ⊕ ⬚

Hannah Professor of the History of Medicine, QUEEN'S UNIVERSITY, Kingston, ON K7L 3N6 (613) 545-6580, FAX (613) 545-6330, EMAIL duffinj@post.queensu. Born London, Ont. 1950. m. R.D. Wolfe. 2 ch. **EDUC:** Univ. of Toronto, M.D. 1974; Sorbonne, France, D.E.A. 1983, Ph.D. 1985; l'École Pratique des Hautes Études, Diplôme, IV Section 1985. **CAREER:** gen. practice locum tenens, Come-by-Chance, Nfld., 1977; internal medicine/haematology, Lac Mégantic, Que., 1979-80; haematology/oncology, Ontario Cancer Treatment & Research Foundation, Thunder Bay, 1980-82; médecin conseil, National Health & Welfare Canada, Cdn Embassy, Paris, 1983-85; internal medicine, Centre Hospitalier de Gatineau, Gatineau, Que., 1985-86; Hannah Postdoctoral Fellowship in Hist. of Medicine, Univ. of Ottawa, 1985-88; Consultant Physician, Haematology, Ottawa General Hospital, Hôpital St. Louis de Montfort, Ontario Cancer Foundation Civic Hospital Clinic, Ottawa, & Ontario Cancer Foundation General Hospital Clinic, 1985-88; Consultant Haematologist, Kingston General Hospital, 1988-94; Hannah Prof., Hist. of Medicine, Queen's Univ., 1988 to date; Assoc. Dean, Undergrad. Studies & Admissions, 1993-95. **SELECTED PUBLICATIONS:** *Langstaff: A Nineteenth-Century Medical Life* (Toronto: Univ. of Toronto Press, 1993); "Great Moments: Parke, Davis, and Co. and the Creation of Medical Art" with A. Li (ISIS, 1995); "In View of the Body of Job Broom: A Glimpse of the Medical Knowledge and Practice of John Rolph" (*Canadian Bulletin of Medical History* 1990); "The Death of Sara Lovell and the Constrained Feminism of Emily Stowe" (*Canadian Medical Association Journal* Mar. 1992); "AIDS, Memory and the History of Medicine: Musings on the Canadian Response" (*Genitourinary Medicine* 1994); various other publications. **EDIT:** Assoc. Ed., *Canadian Bulletin of Medical History*, 1987-90, Ed. Bd. 1990-93; Ed. Bd., *Journal of the History of Medicine and Allied Sciences*, Yale,

1991 to date. AFFIL: American Association for the History of Medicine; Canadian Federation of the Humanities (Bd. Mbr.); Canadian Society for the History of Medicine; Canadian Science & Technology Historical Association; History of Science Society. HONS: W.F. Connell Award for teaching excellence, Queen's Univ. Fac. of Medicine, 1992. INTERESTS: 19th-century medicine, esp. of France & of Canada; medical epistemology. MISC: various invited lectures incl.: "Laennec, his Stethoscope, and the Birth of Physical Diagnosis," *2nd Heberden Society Lecture*, the New York Hospital-Cornell Medical Center, Jan. 18, 1995 & *John Farquhar Fulton Lecture* in Medical History, Beaumont Club, Yale Univ., Jan. 19, 1995.

Duffy, Ann, B.A.,M.A.,Ph.D. ■■ ⩔ ▩
Professor, Department of Sociology, BROCK UNIVERSITY, St. Catharines, ON L2S 3A1 (905) 688-5550, ext. 3455, FAX 688-8337, EMAIL aduffy@paradigm.soci.brocku.ca. Born Ottawa 1948. m. Dusky Smith. 2 ch. Hermana, Mayra. EDUC: McMaster Univ., B.A.(Hons., Sociology) 1968, M.A.(Sociology) 1970, Ph.D.(Sociology) 1979. CAREER: Asst. Prof., Univ. of Toronto, 1979-85; Asst. Prof., Brock Univ., 1985-88; Assoc. Prof., 1988 to date. SELECTED PUBLICATIONS: co-author with N. Mandell & N. Pupo, *Few Choices: Women, Work and Family* (1988); co-author with N. Pupo, *The Part-time Paradox* (1992); author & co-author of a number of book chapters in academic texts; co-editor of several sociology texts. AFFIL: American Sociological Association; Canadian Sociology & Anthropology Association; Sex Information & Education Council of Canada. HONS: Teaching Award, Ontario Confederation of University Faculty Associations, 1995. INTERESTS: gardening; parenting. COMMENT: *"One of many women who worked to establish women's studies in academe and to ensure women's perspective and experience are reflected in academic texts."*

Duffy, Shirley Ⓢ
Corporate Secretary, ARMBRO ENTERPRISES INC., 25 Van Kirk Dr., Unit 8, Brampton, ON L7A 1A6 (905) 454-3737, ext. 305, FAX 454-5995. Born Lac-du-Cerf, Que. 1951. s. EDUC: Sir George Williams Univ., Collegial Studies Diploma 1972. CAREER: Sales Mgr, Drake International, 1975-80; various positions to Corp. Sec., Armbro Enterprises Inc., 1984 to date. DIRECTOR: Armbro Enterprises Inc. AFFIL: Ontario Highway Transport Board (Dir.); National Association of Women in Construction (Past Pres.); Minister's External Advisory Committee on Equity in Construction; Le Cercle canadien de Toronto (Past Pres.); La

Société d'histoire de Toronto (Pres.); numerous other committees & associations. INTERESTS: travel; reading; depression glass.

Duguay, Françoise, B.Sc.,M.Sc. ■ ▩ Ⓔ
President, ARCHÉOCENE INC., 104, 12e Rang Sud, St-Nazaire-D'Acton, QC J0H 1V0 (819) 392-2962, FAX 392-2962. Born La Malbaie, Que. 1956. s. EDUC: Univ. de Montréal, B.Sc. 1979, M.Sc. 1990. CAREER: freelance Archaeologist, 1978-80; Assoc. Archaeologist, Archéologie illimitée inc., 1981-86; freelance Archaeologist, 1986-89; Archaeologist/Pres., Archéocène inc., 1990 to date. SELECTED PUBLICATIONS: "Les autochtones de la période historique par l'archéologie: Contact et intéraction"(*Numéro thématique de Recherches amérindiennes au Québec* 1994); "Le schème d'établissement amérindien de la période historique à Fort McKenzie, Nouveau-Québec" (*Recherches amérindiennes au Québec* 1994); "Le domaine agricole d'un marchand aux XVIIe et XVIIIe siècles, le site LeBer à l'île des Soeurs: archéologie et histoire" (*Ministère de la Culture* 1993); " La Mission sulpicienne de Saint-Louis-du-Haut-de-L'lle" (*Mémoires Vives* 1992). EDIT: Coord., *Collection Paléo-Québec* 23, 1995; Publishing Committee Mbr., *Recherches amérindiennes au Québec*, 1990-96. AFFIL: Association des archéologues professionnels du Québec (Past Pres. 1994-95; Pres. 1990-94); concertation group, Que. Ministry of Culture & Communications (A.A.Q. Pol. Rep.); Social Sciences & Humanities Research Council of Canada (Advisor). INTERESTS: music; reading; sports; movies. MISC: gives both scientific & non-scientific conferences on archaeology. COMMENT: *"Since 1989, I have turned to historical urban archaeology (Montreal and region). I am also currently involved in archaeological politics, patrimonial conservation and anthropological-archaeological publications."*

Duhamel, Nathalie, LL.B.,M.P.A. Ⓞ ⚏
Executive Director, ELIZABETH FRY SOCIETY OF QUEBEC, 5105, chemin Côte St-Antoine, Montreal, QC H4A 1N8 (514) 489-2116, FAX 489-2598. Born Montreal 1951. s. 1 ch. Guillaume. EDUC: Univ. du Québec à Montréal, LL.B. 1977; École Nationale d'Administration, M.P.A. 1991. CAREER: Dev. Agent, CLSC Health & Social Services, 1980-87; Exec. Dir., Fondation Berthiaume du Tremblay, 1987-90; Exec. Dir., Elizabeth Fry Society of Quebec, 1990 to date. AFFIL: Quebec Federation of Women (VP); Quebec Association of Residential Centres (Dir.); Canadian Association of Elizabeth Fry Societies (Dir.). INTERESTS: women's issues; social justice; human rights.

Dukszta, Annette M., M.A.,M.B.A. ⊕ ☺
Executive Director, CANADIAN BRAIN TISSUE
BANK, 100 College St., Ste. 127, Toronto, ON
M5G 1L5 (416) 977-3398, FAX 964-2165.
Born Preston, UK 1950. m. Dr. Andrezej Duk-
szta. 1 ch. 3 stpch. EDUC: Univ. of Toronto,
B.A.(Modern Lang. & Lit.) 1972, M.B.A.
(Organizational Dev.) 1976. CAREER: Mgmt
Consultant, Ontario Hydro, 1980-82; Exec.
Dir., ALS Society of Canada, 1982-85; Exec.
Dir., Tourette Syndrome Foundation, 1989-94;
Exec. Dir., Canadian Brain Tissue Bank, 1985
to date. SELECTED PUBLICATIONS: *Tourette
Syndrome: A Handbook for Families* (1994);
Tourette Syndrome: A Guide for Educators
(1993); "Tourette Syndrome" (*RCMP Gazette*,
Vol. 55, No.3, 1993). DIRECTOR: Office Solu-
tions. AFFIL: Canadian Neurological Coalition
(Dir.); World Association for Infant Mental
Health (Conference Planning Committee);
Royal Canadian Yacht Club. HONS: Interna-
tional Order of Fellowship, Cambridge, 1995;
Tourette Syndrome Exceptional Achievement
Award, 1994. INTERESTS: travel; reading;
music; computers. COMMENT: *"An idealist at
heart, I have tried to dedicate my career to the
development of smaller, but necessary, support
services."*

Dumais, Michèle C., B.Comm.,C.A $ ✒
Vice-President, Finance, THE GAZETTE, 250 St.
Antoine St. W., Montreal, QC H2Y 3R7 (514)
987-2219, FAX 987-2244. Born Montreal
1955. EDUC: Concordia Univ., B.Comm.
(Acctg) 1977; McGill Univ., C.A. 1980.
CAREER: Auditor, Arthur Andersen & Co.,
1977-81; Fin. Analyst, Bank of Montreal,
1981-85; Cont., Sun Life Assurance Company
of Canada, 1985-89; Cont., Discus Music
World (1990) Inc., 1990-91; Cont., *The
Gazette* (div. of Southam Inc.), 1991-94; VP,
Fin., 1995 to date. AFFIL: Ordre des comptà-
bles agréés du Québec (Comite Régional de
Montréal). INTERESTS: cycling; gardening;
cross-country skiing.

Dumont, Daphne E., B.A.,M.A. ☺ ⚖ ⚥
Partner, MACNUTT & DUMONT, Box 965,
Charlottetown, PE C1A 7M4 (902) 894-5003,
FAX 368-3782. Born Charlottetown 1952.
EDUC: Queen's Univ., B.A.(Hist. & Phil.) 1974,
special concentration in Cdn Law 1976-77;
Oxford Univ., B.A.(Jurisprudence) 1976, M.A.
1983. BAR: P.E.I., 1978. CAREER: articled,
MacLeod & Carr, 1977-78; Lawyer, Camp-
bell, Mitchell, Lea & Cheverie, 1978-79;
Lawyer, James W. Macnutt Law Office, 1980-
82; Ptnr, Macnutt & Dumont, 1982 to date.
SELECTED PUBLICATIONS: "Matrimonial
Property Law in Prince Edward Island," articles

contributed to text *Matrimonial Property Law
in Canada* (1980, 1987, 1994); Mbr. of Com-
mittee to produce *P.E.I. Divorce Kit* (1984);
Mbr. of Committee to produce *P.E.I. Hand-
book for Battered Women* (N.A.W.L., 1982).
EDIT: Advisory Bd., *Canadian Journal of
Women and the Law.* AFFIL: Canadian Bar
Association (Pres., P.E.I. Branch 1986-87);
P.E.I. Law Society (Legal Aid; Teacher, Bar
Admission Course in Family Law); Women's
Legal Education & Action Fund (L.E.A.F.)
(Founding Mbr.; P.E.I. Branch Chair 1985-89;
Planning Committee, P.E.I. Person's Day Break-
fast); National Association of Women & the
Law (P.E.I. Caucus); P.E.I. Community Legal
Information Association; P.E.I. Women's Net-
work; Wadham Coll. Boat Club Society (Life
Mbr.); Kirk of St. James Presbyterian Church
(Elder; nominee to the Bd., the Charlotte Residence; nominee to the Cundall Trust); Salvation Army Advisory Board, P.E.I. (Chair, Family Svcs Committee); P.E.I. Rowing Association;
Hillsborough Rowing Club (Sec.); Rotary Club
of Charlottetown. INTERESTS: travel; cross-
country skiing; painting; poetry; art & architecture; P.E.I. history; languages; social & political
philosophy; law reform & public legal education; women's rights; yoga; ballet & opera;
rowing; theatre; reading; symphony; swimming.
MISC: Sessional Lecturer, Dept. of Pol. Studies,
Univ. of Prince Edward Island; lectures & radio
interviews on legal topics; regular commentator
on P.E.I. issues for CBC's *Morningside* &
Newsworld.

**Dumoulin, Françoise, B.A.,M.A.,
Ph.D.** ▯ ⚥ ▣
Author. Société des Auteurs, Recherchistes
Documentalistes, et Compositeurs, 1075 Jean-
Dumetz, Sainte-Foy, QC G1W 4K6 (418) 653-
8862. Born Québec City 1939. sep. 2 ch.
Claude Tessier, Marc Tessier. EDUC: Ottawa
Univ. Teachers' Coll., Standard I 1961; Laval
Univ., B.A.(Lit./Creative Writing) 1977,
M.A.(Lit.) 1981, Ph.D.(Dramatic Writing)
1984. CAREER: Teacher, Ottawa, 1961-62;
Documentaliste, Index Analytique, Centre de
documentation, Univ. Laval, 1966-67; French
Specialist, Ste.-Foy English Sch., 1969-71;
Teacher, Parkdale Sch., Kliptown, S.Africa,
1979; Instructor, Lit. & Creative Writing, Laval
Univ., 1980-81, 1985 to date; Analyste et cri-
tique littéraire, *Dictionnaire des oeuvres du
Québec*, 1980; Analyste et critique littéraire,
Livres et auteurs québécois, 1980-81; Concep-
trice de textes et publiciste, Plume-Habille enr.,
1986; Travail à la pige, Cossette Communica-
tion-Marketing, 1985-86; in charge of creative
writing work-groups, City of Ste.-Foy, 1984 to
date; Directrice littéraire et sociétaire, Produc-

tions Quatram Inc., 1987; Author. **SELECTED CREDITS:** Création et interprétation, 10 textes radiophoniques dramatiques, *Paroles*, CKRL-MF, 1974-76; La mère, *Léonie est en avance de Feydeau*, Théâtre de la Cité universitaire, 1975; Anna, *Anna*, de Suzanne Paradis, CKRL-MF, 1976; Fricka, *L'or du Rhin*, de Richard Wagner, CKRL-MF, 1976; Écrivain, *Antoine et Sebastien*, Radio-Canada, 1976; Écrivain, *Elise ou le temps d'aimer*, Radio-Canada, 1977; Écrivain, *Dernier acte,* pièce de théâtre, 1979; Écrivain, *La femme aux portraits*, pour la TV, 1983; *Écrivain*, Vol 535, pour la TV, 1984. **SELECTED PUBLICATIONS:** *Le Salon Vert* (Montréal: Cercle du Livre de France, 1980); *Visions d'amour* (Montréal: 1981); *Quatre jours...pas plus!* (Montréal: Cercle du Livre de France, 1983); intro. & analysis, *Marie Laberge*, 1990. **AFFIL:** Cercle d'écriture de l'Univ. Laval (Exécutif; responsable des affaires externes 1988-89); Société des Études anciennes; SARDEC; Association des Écrivains de langue française. **HONS:** Prix Littéraire Esso, 1980; Prix du Cercle du Livre de France, 1980; *Antoine et Sébastien*, presented as best realization of Radio-Canada Réseau, Festival of french speaking televisions at Prague, 1981. **MISC:** numerous readings; recipient of numerous grants; numerous conference presentations. **COMMENT:** *"Writing is the most important, exciting thing and challenge in my life. I am extremely moved when I see my 'paper characters' alive for a while in a play, through actors. I would like to work as a scriptwriter for a film."*

Duncan, Arlene 🎬 📺 🎭

Actor, Singer, Songwriter. The Core Group, 3 Church St., Ste. 507, Toronto, ON M5E 1M2 (416) 955-0819. Born Oakville, Ont. d. 2 ch. Matthew, Yuri. **EDUC:** Sheridan Coll., Music Theatre Program; Mohawk Coll., Music Theory/Jazz Harmony; CAST (Centre for Actors' Study in Toronto); Theatreworks, Scene study; Edward Johnson, Voice Instruction; Bill Vincent, Voice Instruction. **SELECTED CREDITS:** Co-host, *DuMaurier Search for Stars* (series); Cdn Rep., *Pacific Song Festival*, 1980; Host via satellite to 8 countries, *Pacific Song Festival*, 1981; Beneatha, *A Raisin in the Sun* (theatre); Henry, *The Club*; Charlaine, *Ain't Misbehavin* (musical); Phyllis, *Sophisticated Ladies* ; Darlene Love, *Leader of the Pack* ; Aunt Martha/Mrs. Willis, *The Good Times Are Killing Me*; Erzulie, *Once on this Island*; Acid Queen/Swing, *The Who's Tommy*, Elgin Theatre, Toronto, 1995; Harriet Tubman, *Sing Out Freedom Train* (musical/docudrama); TV & film credits include *The Wayne and Schuster Comedy Hour*, *The Palace with Jack Jones*, *The Littlest Hobo*, *An American Christmas Carol*, *Katts & Dog*, *Missing Treasures*, *Top Cops*, *Car 54 Where Are You*, *The Liberators*, *FXII*, *Extreme Measures*. **SELECTED DISCOGRAPHY:** "Only Time"/"I Wanna Groove" (12-inch single), 1982, Arlene Duncan/Bruce Ley/Willie Morrison (Wee Records); records under the name Kairene: "I Need a Man" (single), Contraband/Quality Records, co-written with Falconer Abraham & Gene King; "Glamourous Life" (Prince), *REMIX* CD, compilation (Contraband/Quality Music). **HONS:** Winner, DuMaurier Search for Stars, 1979; Artistic Merit Award, Pacific Song Festival, 1979; Female Vocalist of the Year, Black Music Awards, 1983; commercial spots for Suzy Shier Stores won Gold Marketing Award, 1988; ACTRA nomination for *All For One* TV special; Outstanding Achievement in Dance/House Music, Black Label Artist Coalition (BLAC), 1994. **INTERESTS:** children; African art; interior decorating; computer technology; clothing design. **MISC:** her single, "I Need a Man," went to No. 1 in the dance pools in Canada & the video was shown regularly on Much Music's *Extend-A-Mix* & *Electric Circus*.

Duncan, Muriel, B.A. ✎ ☼

Editor, *THE UNITED CHURCH OBSERVER*, 478 Huron St., Toronto, ON M5R 2R3 (416) 960-8500, FAX 960-8477. **EDUC:** Univ. of Western Ontario, B.A.(Journalism). **CAREER:** Assoc. Ed., *The United Church Observer*, 1978-81; Mng Ed., 1981-89; Ed., 1989 to date. **SELECTED PUBLICATIONS:** monthly column & 20 yrs. of articles & news stories, *The United Church Observer*. **HONS:** various writing awards for Feature, News & Humour categories, Canadian Church Press & Associated Church Press; Doctor of Divinity (Hon.), United Theological Coll. **COMMENT:** *"A full-time journalist with a very part-time farm in Bruce County."*

Duncan, Patricia Jane, B.A. 🍁 $ ♡

1507A Birch St., Whitehorse, YT Y1A 3X1 (403) 633-2652. **EDUC:** Carleton Univ., B.A.(Pol. Sci.) 1983; Certified General Accountants' Association, Correspondence Program 1988-89. **CAREER:** Special Asst., Constituency Affairs, Hon. Erik Neilsen, Deputy PM, 1984-86; Office Admin., Total North Communications Ltd., 1987-90; Mgr., Whitehorse Chamber of Commerce, 1990-94; Yukon Liberal Party Candidate, Porter Creek South; Yukon Legislative Assembly. **AFFIL:** Girl Guides of Canada (Prov. Commissioner, Yukon Council; National Exec. Committee); Yukon Health and Social Svcs Council; Women's Business Network (Founding Mbr.); Northern Resources Conference (Planning Committee); City of Whitehorse Environment. **MISC:** was the Yukon Mbr. for Canadian Advisory Council on the Status of Women, 1988-91.

Dundas-Matthews, R. Louise, B.Com., F.C.G.A. 🍁 [$]
Director, Financial and Management Services, GOVERNMENT OF THE NORTHWEST TERRITORIES, Box 1320, Yellowknife, NT X1A 2L9 (403) 873-7641, FAX 873-0173. Born 1954. m. Steven B. Matthews. 3 ch. Bredan, Andrew, Bryana. **EDUC:** McMaster Univ., B.Com. 1977; Certified General Accountants Program. **CAREER:** Inspector, Toronto-Dominion Bank, 1977-79; Auditor, Audit Bureau, Gov't of the Northwest Territories, 1979-81; Dir., Fin. & Mgmt Svcs, 1981 to date.

Dunlop, Marilyn E., B.A. ✒ [+] ⚛
Medical Columnist, *THE TORONTO STAR*, 1 Yonge St., Toronto, ON M5E 1E6 (416) 367-2000, FAX 869-4410. Science Writer. Born Detroit 1928. d. 2 ch. **EDUC:** Univ. of Western Ontario, B.A.(Journalism) 1949. **CAREER:** Reporter, *Toronto Telegram*, 1949-54; Reporter, *The Toronto Star*, 1964-67; Medical Reporter, 1967-77; London, UK, Correspondent, 1977-79; Medical Reporter, 1980-92; Medical Columnist, 1981 to date. **SELECTED PUBLICATIONS:** *Understanding Cancer* (1985); *Body Defences: Immunology* (1987); *Biography of Dr. William Mustard* (1989). **HONS:** Canadian Science Writers' Awards, 1976, 1980, 1985, 1993; National Newspaper Award, 1987; Sir Sandford Fleming Medal, Royal Canadian Institute, 1989-90. **AFFIL:** Canadian Science Writers' Association; Ontario Medical Association (Hon. Mbr.). **INTERESTS:** theatre; ballet; painting; literature. **COMMENT:** *"I am a proud mother, a journalist who always loved newspaper work and a perpetual student."*

Dunlop, Mary Jo, R.N. ■ [$] [+]
Vice-President and Chief Operating Officer, DYNACARE MANAGED HEALTH SERVICES, 339 Wellington Rd. S., London, ON N6C 4P8 (519) 667-4030, FAX 432-3731. Vice-President, Government Relations, THE DYNACARE HEALTH GROUP INC. Born London, Ont. 1957. m. James C. Dunlop. 1 ch. **EDUC:** Fanshawe Coll., R.N.; Univ. of Western Ontario, currently enrolled in B.A. program. **CAREER:** various positions, Staff Nurse, acute long-term & community health care, Canada & US; various positions from Nursing Supervisor to VP, COO, Med+Care Health Services, a div. of DMHS, 1987 to date; VP, Gov't Rel'ns, Dynacare, 1995 to date. **AFFIL:** St. Joseph's Pall Mall Rehabilitation Clinic (Dir.); Ontario Home Care Providers' Association (VP 1994-95); Ontario Palliative Care Association; Canadian Intravenous Nurses' Association; Indian & Inuit Nurses of Canada, Ontario Home Health Care Providers' Association (Standards Committee); Canadian Home Care Association; Home Support Canada. **INTERESTS:** future of health care in Ont. & Canada; role of private sector in health care; politics; reading; equestrian events. **COMMENT:** *"A diverse nursing background that eventually lead me to community health nursing. Joined Med+Care in 1987 as a Nursing Supervisor and have held five positions of increasing responsibility with company and its parent company, the Dynacare Health Group."*

Dunn, Barbara MacNaught, 🍁 ✊ 👍
President, CANADIAN SOCIETY OF AIR SAFETY INVESTIGATORS, 139 W. 13th Ave., Vancouver, BC V5Y 1V8 (604) 874-4806, FAX 874-7204. Born Victoria, B.C. 1948. s. **CAREER:** Working Flight Attendant, Air Canada, 1971 to date; Founder & Planning Committee mbr., Int'l Cabin Safety Symposium, Southern California Safety Institute, 1984 to date; Aviation Safety Consultant, 1989 to date; Fac. Mbr., Extension Programs, Aviation Safety Programs, Univ. of Southern California, 1989-95; Researcher, *The Invisible Injury*, video on Post-Traumatic Stress Disorder, Canadian Airline Flight Attendants' Association, 1989; Mbr., S-9 Committee (Cabin Furnishings), Society of Automotive Engineers, 1990 to date; Pres., Canadian Society of Air Safety Investigators, 1994 to date. **SELECTED PUBLICATIONS:** *Flight Attendant Training and Qualification Study* (Transport Canada 1990); *Accident Investigation Procedures for Cabin Issues* (Transportation Safety Board of Canada, 1992). **AFFIL:** Canadian Airline Flight Attendants' Association. **HONS:** Aviation Safety Award, Transport Canada, 1994 (first woman and first flight attendant to receive award). **MISC:** expert witness, passenger legal action re cabin baggage, 1994; expert witness, US Dept. of Justice re the Northwest Airlines collision in Detroit, 1994; consultant to Hum. Res. Branch, investigation into the VIA Rail accident in Hinton, Alta., 1986; consultant to Human Factors Chrm, investigation into the Air Ontario Fokker-F28 accident in Dryden, Ont., 1989; represented Canadian Airline Flight Attendants' Association, Royal Commission of Inquiry into Aviation Safety, 1979-80; represented flight attendants, Nat'l Transportation Safety Bd. (US) Public Inquiry, Air Canada Douglas DC-9 inflight fire, Cincinnati, Ohio, 1983; represented flight attendants, Royal

Commission of Inquiry, Air Canada Boeing 767 fuel starvation incident, Gimli, Man., 1983.

Dunn, Sonja, B.A.,M.Ed. 🗋 📚 ⛶
Children's Author and Drama Specialist. 335 Mill Rd., Ste. 401, Etobicoke, ON M9C 1Y6 (416) 626-8283. Born Toronto 1931. m. William J. 2 ch. Paul Walter, Kevin Joseph. **EDUC:** Laurentian Univ., B.A.(English), 1971; Teaching Degree 1949; Ont. Institute for Studies in Educ., M.Ed. 1975. **CAREER:** Prof., Univ. of Toronto; Prof., Laurentian Univ.; drama specialist; literary critic; TV broadcaster, *Sonja Dunn and Company*, Rogers Community 10; writer; prod.; author. **SELECTED PUBLICATIONS:** *Sonja Dunn on Tape* (recording); *Butterscotch Dreams; Crackers and Crumbs; Primary Rhymerry; Rapunzel's Rap; Beauty and the Beast Rap; Gimme a Break, Rattlesnake; Chanting with Sonja Dunn; Alphamagnets* (1996). **AFFIL:** Writers' Union of Canada; League of Canadian Poets; Toronto Musicians' Union; Canadian Society of Children's Authors, Illustrators & Performers (former Pres.); Council of Drama in Education (VP); Canadian Poetry Association. **HONS:** Sister Maris Stella Award, Northern Ontario Council of Teachers of English. **INTERESTS:** theatre; ballet; opera; film; literature; tennis; snorkeling; travelling.

Dunnet, Tamarin, B.A.,LL.B. ■■ ⚖
Judge, SUPREME COURT OF ONTARIO, Osgoode Hall, Toronto, ON M5H 2N5. Born 1949. 2 ch. Frederick Sagel, Tiffany Sagel. **EDUC:** Dalhousie Univ., B.A. 1971, LL.B. 1974; Law Society of Upper Canada, certified as Specialist in Civil Litigation. **CAREER:** Ptnr, Thomson, Rogers, Barristers & Solicitors, Toronto, 1976-90; appointed Judge of the Supreme Court of Ont., Mbr. of High Court of Justice for Ont. & *ex officio* Mbr. of Court of Appeal for Ont., 1990. **SELECTED PUBLICATIONS:** "The Family Law Reform Act, 1978: Changes in Procedure in Personal Injury Litigation" (*The Advocates' Quarterly*, Vol. 1, 1977-78); "The Family Law Reform Act, 1978: Changes in Procedure in Personal Injury Litigation - An Update" *(The Advocates' Quarterly*, Vol. 4, 1983); "The Ontario Family Law Reform Act: The Changing Attitude of the Courts with Respect to Post-Limitation Amendments Adding Derivative Claims" (*The Advocates' Quarterly*, Vol. 6, 1986); "Leaders Among the Women Lawyers of Ontario" (*The Law Society of Upper Canada Gazette*, Vol. XX, No. 3, 1986); "The Ontario Family Law Act, 1986: Procedural Changes and Post-Limitation Amendments Revisited" (*The Advocates' Quarterly*, Vol. 8,

1987); "Expert Testimony Must Be Limited to Areas Outside Common Knowledge" (*Construction Law Letter*, Nov./Dec. 1994). **AFFIL:** Canadian Bar Association (Nat'l Council 1982-90; Nat'l Exec. Committee 1987-89); Canadian Bar Association Ontario (mbr. of Council 1982-90; Chair, Prov. Judiciary Committee 1986; Mbr.-at-Large, Exec. Committee 1989-90); The Advocates' Society; County of York Law Association (Pres. 1990); The Lawyers' Club; Medico-Legal Society of Toronto (Dir. 1983-86); Women's Law Association of Ontario (Pres. 1980-83); Mississauga Golf & Country Club; Ontario Racquet Club. **INTERESTS:** skiing; golf; tennis; hiking; figure skating (silver medallist); piano. **MISC:** numerous lectures to CBA Ontario, The Advocates' Society, The Law Society of Upper Canada, & other groups.

Dunsmore, Rosemary, B.F.A. ⊗ ⛶ 🐝
Actor, Director, Teacher. c/o Pamela Friendly, Premier Artists, 671 Danforth Ave., Ste. 305, Toronto, ON M4J 1L3 (416) 461-6868, FAX 461-7677. Born Edmonton 1952. **EDUC:** York Univ., B.F.A.(Theatre) 1973. **CAREER:** actor; dir.; teacher, Centre for Actors' Study; teacher, Equity Showcase; guest teacher, Workshop for Professional Actors in Vancouver, Langara Coll., Univ. of British Columbia; guest teacher, Univ. of Toronto & Canadian Film Centre. **SELECTED CREDITS:** actor, *Total Recall*, Carolco; actor, *Liar Liar*, CBC; actor, *Undue Influence*, CBS; lead, *Mom P.I.* (series), Atlantis Films; actor, *Anne of Green Gables –The Sequel*, Sullivan Productions; actor, *Fallen Angels*, The Monument, Canadian Stage; actor, *Single* (one-woman show), Toronto & Montreal; actor, *A Midsummer's Night Dream*, Stratford; actor, *A Streetcar Named Desire*, Stratford; actor, *As You Like It*, Stratford; actor, *Straight Ahead/Blind Dancers*, Toronto Free Theatre & Edinburgh Festival, 1981; dir., *Two Rooms*, Paramour Productions; dir., *Love of the Nightingale*, Frederick Wood Theatre. **DIRECTOR:** Paramour Productions. **HONS:** Best Acting Performance in a Leading Role (*Blind Faith*), 1983; ACTRA; Best Leading Actress (*Straight Ahead/Blind Dancers*), 1982; Dora Mavor Moore Theatre Awards; selected as Best Performance, Edinburgh Festival, London Daily Telegraph, 1981; *Maclean's* magazine Honor Roll, Acting, 1990; nominated, Best Supporting Actress (*Skate*), Gemini Awards, 1988; nominated for a Toronto Theatre Alliance Dora Performance Award for *Fallen Angels* (1992) & *Single* (1984).

DuPont, Bonnie, B.S.W.,M.Ed. 🌿
Director, Human Resources and Administra-

tion, ALBERTA WHEAT POOL, 505 - 2nd St. S.W., Calgary, AB T2P 2P5 (403) 290-4846, FAX 290-4839. Born Swift Current, Sask. 1946. d. 1 ch. Kathryn Anne Buck. EDUC: Univ. of Regina, B.S.W.(Program Planning & Evaluation) 1975; Univ. of Calgary, M.Ed.(Hum. Res. Admin.) 1989. CAREER: Mgr, R.&D., Saskatchewan Wheat Pool, 1982-85; Mgr, Tech. Svc., City of Calgary, 1985-87; Dir., Hum. Res., Foothills Hospital, Calgary, 1987-90; Dir., Hum. Res. & Admin., Alberta Wheat Pool, 1990 to date. AFFIL: Nickle Arts Museum (V-Chair); Univ. of Calgary (Mgmt Advisory Council); The Associates (support group to Mgmt Fac., Univ. of Calgary); Calgary Olympic Development Association (Dir. 1990-94); YMCA Calgary (Dir. 1987-92). HONS: Most Distinguished Grad., Spring Convocation, Univ. of Regina, 1975. INTERESTS: art; antiques; golf; skiing. COMMENT: *"Labour and industrial relations main professional area. Expertise in broad range of human resource areas as well as administration."*

Dupont, Diane P., B.A.,M.A., Ph.D. ⚘ 🏵

Associate Professor, Department of Economics, BROCK UNIVERSITY, St. Catharines, ON L2S 3A1 (905) 688-5550, ext. 3129, FAX 988-9388, EMAIL ddupont@spartan.ac.brocku.ca. Born Ottawa 1955. m. Steven Renzetti. 2 ch. Allie, Nicholas. EDUC: Carleton Univ., B.A.(Econ. & German) 1978; Univ. of Toronto, M.A.(Econ.) 1979; Univ. of British Columbia, Ph.D. 1988. CAREER: Lecturer, Univ. of British Columbia, 1987-88; Visiting Prof., 1989; Asst. Prof., Univ. of Guelph, 1988-90; Asst. Prof., Brock Univ., 1990-93; Assoc. Prof., 1993 to date. SELECTED PUBLICATIONS: "Distributional Consequences of Fisheries Regulation," with Shelley A. Phipps (*Canadian Journal of Economics* 1991); "An Investigation into Sunset Chemicals and the Economic Dimension," with Steven Renzetti (Report for Pollution Probe, Oct. 1993); "Measuring the Benefits of Better Recreational Opportunities Using the Contingent Valuation Method" (McMaster Univ. Ecowise Seminar Sales Reports, 1994); "Limited entry fishing programs: theory and Canadian practice," in *Fisheries and Uncertainty: A precautionary approach to resource management*, eds. D.V. Gordon & G.R. Munroe (Calgary: Univ. of Calgary Press., 1996); "The Role of Water in the Canadian Food and Beverage Processing Industry," with Steven Renzetti (Brock Univ. Discussion Paper, 04, 1996); various other publications. AFFIL: Association of Environmental & Resource Economists (Int'l Correspondent for Canada); American Economics Association;

Canadian Economics Association; Resource Modeling Association; American Agricultural Economics Association; Committee on the Status of Women in the Economics Profession; International Association for Feminist Economics; Association for Women in Agricultural Economics. HONS: C.J. MacKenzie Entrance Scholarship, Carleton Univ., 1974-75; Francis Lynch In-Course Scholarship, Carleton Univ., 1975-76; Program in Natural Resource Economics Scholarship, Univ. of British Columbia, 1980-81. INTERESTS: tap dance; nature walks; reading; gardening. MISC: numerous conference papers; grant recipient; referee for various journals & granting agencies. COMMENT: *"I like to think of myself as a renaissance person–academic endeavours are wonderful, but I enjoy other pursuits, as well as time with my family. My only complaint is there is not enough time!"*

Dupuy, Diane, C.M. ■■ 🌐 💛 👍

President and Founder, FAMOUS PEOPLE PLAYERS (integration of developmentally challenged people into the community), 33 Lisgar St., Toronto, ON M6J 3T3 (416) 532-1137, FAX 532-6945. Born Hamilton, Ont. 1948. m. Bernard. 2 ch. Jeanine, Joanne. AFFIL: Windreach Farm for Disabled People (Bd. mbr.). HONS: B'nai Brith Woman of the Year, 1981; Member of the Order of Canada, 1981; Ernest C. Manning Award for Innovation, 1984; hon. degrees, Trent Univ., Univ. of Windsor, & Univ. of Calgary. INTERESTS: swimming; music; children. MISC: featured in: *Special People* (movie based on her life); 1-hr. special on *Phil Donahue Show; Adrienne Clarkson Presents; Regis & Kathy Lee; CBC Morningside; A Little Like Magic* (documentary). COMMENT: *"Through Diane's vision and love of theatre, she created a unique role for developmentally challenged people, whom she molded into a professional, dynamic theatre troupe. In 1994, the first theatre centre in the world dedicated to people with special needs was opened in Toronto."*

Durieux-Smith, Andrée, B.Sc.,M.A.Sc., Ph.D. ■■ ⚘ ⊕

Professor, Audiology and Speech-Language Pathology Program, Faculty of Health Sciences, UNIVERSITY OF OTTAWA, 545 King Edward, Ottawa, ON K1N 6N5 (613) 562-5254, FAX 562-5256, EMAIL adurieux@uottawa.ca. Research Coordinator, Audiology, CHILDREN'S HOSPITAL OF EASTERN ONTARIO. Born Montreal 1943. m. Roger. 2 ch. Dominique, Michel. EDUC: McGill Univ., B.Sc.(Genetics, Zoology) 1964, M.A.Sc.(Audiology) 1968, Ph.D.(Audiology) 1974. CAREER: founding Dir., Audiology, Children's Hospital of Eastern Ontario, 1974-91; Dir., Communication Disorders, 1991-92; Research Coord., Dept. of Communication Disorders, 1993 to date; founding & active mbr., CHEO Research Institute, 1985 to date; Asst. Prof., Otolaryngology, Fac. of Medicine, Univ. of Ottawa, 1978-85; Assoc. Prof., Otolaryngology, 1986-92; mbr., Sch. of Grad. Studies & Research, Univ. of Ottawa, 1992 to date; founding Dir. & Prof., Audiology & Speech-Language Pathology Program, Fac. of Health Sciences, 1993-96; Prof., Audiology & Speech-Language Pathology Program, 1996 to date; Adjunct Prof., Dept. of Psych., Carleton Univ., 1982-85. **SELECTED PUBLICATIONS:** 30 papers in refereed journals; 20 abstracts; 13 chpts. in books; 2 journals edited; 15 invited presentations; other misc. publications. **AFFIL:** Institute for Clinical Evaluative Sciences in Ontario (Advisory Committee, Ventilation tube study 1996); Univ. of Toronto (External Reviewer, Grad. Program in Speech-Language Pathology 1994); *Journal of Speech-Language Pathology and Audiology* (Edit. Consultant 1993 to date; Assoc. Edit. 1990-93); Canadian Association of Speech-Language Pathologists & Audiologists (mbr.; VP, Gov't Affairs 1988; Pres. 1987); Ontario Speech & Hearing Association; American Speech-Language & Hearing Association. **HONS:** honoured for outstanding scholarly contribution, Canadian Association of Speech/Language Pathologists & Audiologists, 1987; award for outstanding paper (co-author, "The Crib-o-gram in the NICU: An Evaluation Based on Brainstem Electric Response Audiometry"), American Auditory Society, 1986. **INTERESTS:** alpine skiing; running. **MISC:** reviewer, Ont. Ministry of Health, Ontario Mental Health Foundation, National Health Research & Dev. Program, & others, 1981 to date.

Durocher, Claudette, B.A.C. $

Vice-President, Administration, Financial and Trust Services, DESJARDINS TRUST, 2 Complexe Desjardins, Box 9000, Montreal, QC H5B 1H5 (514) 286-3100, ext. 2885, FAX 286-7876. Born Montreal 1942. **EDUC:** Univ. of Montreal, B.A.C.(Major Ind. Rel'ns) 1986, M.A. (Andragogy) 1995. **CAREER:** Supervisor, Mortgage Loans Centre, Bank of Montreal, 1974-76; Sales Supervisor, MasterCard Centre, 1976-79; Asst. Mgr, RRSP Admin., Desjardins Trust, 1979-83; Mgr, Trust Svcs, 1983-89; VP, Admin., Svcs aux Caisses, 1989-94; VP, Admin., Fin. & Trust Svcs, 1994 to date. **AFFIL:** Desjardins' Women's Association; Quebec Business Womens' Association. **INTERESTS:** music; movies; theatre; reading; sports. **COMMENT:** *"Known as a dynamic leader capable of motivating employees towards a goal and as a person who likes to take up challenges. To be in charge of a vice-presidency consisting of four departments which administer over one million savings accounts (mainly registered savings plans) for total assets of $15 billion, offering high quality service at the lowest possible costs to 1,500 Caisses popularies in a highly competitive context and ensuring the efficiency, as well as a high level of productivity and the dynamic participation of over 125 employees, that is the type of challenge that motivates me."*

Durr, Pat (Patricia), B.A.Ed. ✪ ✊ 🎓 ☝

Artist. 167 First Ave., Ottawa, ON K1S 2G3 (613) 232-8755. Born Kansas City, Mo. 1939. m. Laurence. 2 ch. Tanya, Sean. **EDUC:** Univ. of Kansas, B.A.Ed. 1961; Univ. of Southampton, UK, 1-yr. exchange fellowship 1961-62; Kansas City Art Institute, painting 1962-63; Ottawa Sch. of Art, painting 1965-66. **CAREER:** Coord. of Fine Arts, Teaching Master, Visual Arts Dept., Algonquin Coll. of Applied Arts, 1975-82; designed & presented lectures/workshops across Canada, 1984-91; Chair, Visual Arts Advisory Committee, City of Ottawa, 1985-91; Guest Instructor, Ottawa Sch. of Art, 1986-87; Instructor, Alpen Sch. of Art, Vankleek Hill, Ont., 1987; Art Consultant, Status of Women Person's Award Art Exhibition, 1987, 1988; Art Consultant, Peat Marwick, Ottawa, 1989; commissioned mural, City of Ottawa Heron Road Multiservice Centre, 1990; commissioned mural, frieze & ceiling, Churchill Alternative Sch., 1991; commissioned, mural & walkway insets, O.C. Transpo Heron Road Transitway Station, 1992-95; Guest Curator, Ottawa Art Gallery, 1992-93; Art Consultant, Canadian Institute of Planners' 75th Anniversary, 1994; Art Consultant, Central Canada Exhibition Association, Agrifest, 1994; Commission Adv., RMOG, 1992-94. **SELECTED CREDITS:** Royal Trust Anniversary Portfolio, silkscreen print, 1980; Canadian Conference of the Arts, publication cover, 1986. **SELECTED PUBLICATIONS:** "CARFAC, You and Revenue Canada Taxation" (*Visual Arts* Newsletter Fall 1983); "Death Taxes and the Arts" (*Articles* Jan./Feb. 1988); "The National Gallery's Wright" (*Extension* Summer 1994); visual arts reviews, & *Arts Atlantic* (1988 to date); various other publications. **EXHIBITIONS:** 24 solo shows, incl. Sisler Gallery, Toronto (1975), Acadia Univ. Art Gallery, Wolfville, N.S. (1986), Confederation Centre Art Gallery, Charlottetown (1989) & Robertson Galleries, Ottawa (1995); over 40 group shows, incl. Agnes Etherington Art Centre, Regional Juried Art Exhibition, Kingston

(1981), *When I Was a Cowboy*, organized by Off Centre Centre, Calgary (1985-86), *Twelve Ottawa Painters*, Arts Court Gallery, Ottawa (1990); *Canadian Printmakers*, Missouri Western States Coll. (1992); *Woman Printmakers*, Waldorf Coll., Iowa (1995). COLLECTIONS: works in various private collections & over 25 corp. collections, incl. Canada Council Art Bank, Ottawa Art Gallery at Arts Court, Canadian Embassy in Kiev, & Royal Bank of Canada, Montreal. HONS: First Prize, Painting, Loomis & Toles Regional Juried Exhibition, 1983; Victor Tolgesy Arts Award, City of Ottawa, 1989; Artist Grant, Ontario Arts Council, 1992; Artist 'A' Grant, Reg. Municipality of Ottawa-Carlton, 1992; Whitton Award for Arts and Culture, City of Ottawa, 1996. INTERESTS: gardening; reading. MISC: recipient of various grants & commissions; subject of numerous articles & reviews; first woman CEO of CARFAC. COMMENT: *"Born in the US, Durr studied there and in the UK before coming to Canada. Since the early 1980s, she has taught workshops from Alberta to PEI. She currently resides in Ottawa."*

Duval Hesler, Nicole ■ ■ ⚖

Judge, SUPERIOR COURT OF QUEBEC, 1 rue Notre-Dame E., Cabinet 14.26, Montréal, QC H2Y 1B6 (514) 393-2222, FAX 873-4760. Born Quebec City 1945. m. William Hesler. 2 ch. EDUC: Marianopolis Coll., B.A.(magna cum laude) 1964; Univ. de Montréal, law degree 1967. BAR: Que., 1968. CAREER: Ptnr, McAllister, Blakely, Hesler & LaPierre (now Blakely, Gascon), 1968-92; mbr. & presiding mbr. of Tribunals under the Cdn Human Rights Act, 1978-92; Special Cnsl appointed by Que. Consumer Protection Office for prosecution of claims relating to urea-formaldehyde foam insulation; teaching sessions, Que. Human Rights Commission; appointed to Que. Superior Court, 1992. SELECTED PUBLICATIONS: 26 publications incl. conference proceedings, seminars, lectures. AFFIL: Osgoode Society (Bd. of Trustees); Canadian Bar Association (served on Special Committee on Cameras in the Courts; Bd. of Trustees, Law for the Future Fund 1994); Canadian Institute for the Administration of Justice (Bd. of Dir. 1990-94; Sec.-Treas. 1992-94); Corporation Professionnelle des Médecins du Québec (Bd. of Dir. 1990). MISC: mbr. of task force and co-author, *Report of the Quebec Task Force on Spinal Disorders*, Feb. 1986; invited lecturer, Canadian Bar Association, Canadian Institute for the Administration of Justice, The Canadian Institute, Insight, Institute for International Research, The National Judicial Institute, & others.

Dvorsky, Margaret Ann (née Shavrnoch), L.H.S. ☺ ☯ ☼

President, SLOVAK CANADIAN NATIONAL COUNCIL, 50 McIntosh Dr., Ste. 210, Markham, ON L3R 9T3 (905) 513-1214, FAX 513-1215. Born Montreal 1933. m. John Dvorsky. 3 ch. EDUC: Outremont Business Coll., Grad. (Secretarial, Budget & Acctg) 1952; Comptoir Capponi of Montreal, Certificate (Design/Dressmaking) 1956; Univ. of Montreal, Certificate (French Language). CAREER: Long Distance & Overseas Operator, Montreal Head Office, Bell Canada, 1949-52; Cont. & Recorder of Box Car Movements, Canadian National Railways, 1952-54; Export Dept. Cont., Canadian Industries Ltd., 1954-56; Interpreter, Canada Manpower & Immigration, 1969-70; Curator, Ethnic Mosaic Pavilion, "Man and His World," 1969-71; Administrator, Canadian Slovak Building Ltd., 1976-83; Administrator, La Maison Slovaque Inc., 1983-85; Administrator & Office Mgr, Janovski Counter Tops, 1983-85. VOLUNTEER CAREER: Coord., Slovak Cultural Activities for the Prov. of Que., 1954-85; various positions incl. Pres., Canadian Slovak League, Local Assembly, Women's Lodge Branch 4 in Montreal, 1954-85; Founder, Dir. & Choreographer, LIPA Canadian Slovak Folk Ensemble, 1956-85; VP, Que. Ethnic Folk Arts Council, 1961-85; Dir., Promethean Society, 1963-68; Founder/Coord., Slovak Refugee Action Committee, 1968-70; VP, Quebec Multicultural Theatre Association, 1976-85; Pres., Youth Committee, Slovak World Congress, 1978-84; Exec. Bd. of Dir., Montreal Citizenship Federation, 1980-83; VP, Children for Peace Movement, 1981-83; Nat'l Pres., Canadian Slovak League Central Assembly, 1981-84; VP, Slovak World Congress, 1981-90; Pres., Montreal Citizenship Council, 1983-85; Dir., Canadian Ethno-Cultural Council, 1985-90; Bd. of Pres., Canadian Ethno-Cultural Council, 1985-90; Treas., Canadian Ethno-Cultural Council, 1986-90; Pres., Slovak Canadian Nat'l Council, 1985-90, 1994 to date; Dir., International Red Cross, 1994 to date; Chair, Pastoral Committee, Cathedral of Transfiguration Parish Council, Markham, 1996 to date; Chair, Keswick by the Lake Ratepayers' Association, 1996 to date. SELECTED PUBLICATIONS: various articles in the *Canadian Slovak* nat'l Slovak language weekly; numerous articles in cultural & souvenir program books. AFFIL: Saints Cyril & Methodius Choir; Slovak Theatre Group. HONS: Hamilton Builders Bonnet, 1977; Certificate of Recognition for Participation on the Canadian Multicultural Council, 1985-87; Canada 125 Medal; numerous citations, plaques & medals from youth folk groups &

fraternals in Canada, US & Slovakia. INTER-ESTS: classic culture; theatre; folk tradition culture; genealogy, demography & immigration patterns; Slovak & Canadian history; preservation of family unit & Christian ethics. MISC: recognized by the Church (Rome) & invested as Lady (Dame) of the Equestrian Order of the Holy Sepulchre of Jerusalem, Sept. 25, 1982. COMMENT: *"My lifestyle and activities involve the family unit, concern for my fellow man, civic mindedness, commitment to God and country, with an ambition to broaden the horizons for my children and all youth and then to document the experience."*

Dwarka, Diane ■■ ☗ ○ ☼ ♌

President, COMMUNITY LEGAL EDUCATION ASSOCIATION, CLEA (MANITOBA), 294 Portage Ave., Ste. 501, Winnipeg, MB R3C 0B9. Multicultural Information Specialist, Education and Training, GOVERNMENT OF MANITOBA, Box 3, 1181 Portage Ave., Winnipeg, MB R3G 0T3 (204) 945-4015, FAX 945-8756, ddwarka@minet.gov.mb.ca. Born Fyzabad, Trinidad 1937. m. Adrian P. Dwarka. 3 ch. Robin, Damon, Dane. EDUC: Naparima Teachers' Coll., Trinidad, Teacher's Diploma 1965; Red River Community Coll., Winnipeg, Library Technician's Diploma 1984. CAREER: Teacher, Trinidad, 1959-77; Info. Asst., High Commission of Malaysia, Ottawa, 1977-81; Library Technician, Reference Svcs, Library, Man. Educ. & Training, Winnipeg, 1984-92; Multicultural Info. Specialist, 1992 to date. SELECTED PUBLICATIONS: "Aboriginal Resources: a Selected Bibliography" (*CM: a Reviewing Journal of Canadian Materials for Young People*, Vol. XX, No. 4, Sept. 1992); "Together We Can Eliminate Racism" (*Education Manitoba*, Vol. 19:4, Feb. 1993); "Year for Racial Harmony" & "Let's Celebrate: February is Black History Month" (*Education Manitoba*, Vol. 20:2, 1994); "Racism and Education: Different Perspectives and Experiences" (*Equality News*, Vol. 3:2, May 1994, Manitoba Teachers' Society); compiler of bibliographies re human rights educ., anti-racist educ., the Holocaust, etc. AFFIL: Manitoba Association for Multicultural Education, MAME (Pres.); Canada Council for Multicultural & Intercultural Education (Sec.-Treas.); Council of Caribbean Organizations of Manitoba (VP); Black Educators' Association of Manitoba (Bd. of Dir.); Trinidad & Tobago Society of Manitoba (Bd. of Dir.); Coalition for Human Equality (Co-Chair); Manitoba Association of Library Technicians (former Pres.); Chair, 25th Anniversary Committee); Holocaust Awareness Committee (mbr.; Newsletter Committee); United Church (has served on local, reg'l &

nat'l committees). HONS: Women of Distinction Award, YM-YWCA, 1996; participant, int'l "Holocaust and Hope Tour" to Germany, Poland & Israel, 1994; scholarship to Michigan State Univ. (Prof. Youth Leadership Educators course). INTERESTS: reading; gourmet cooking; travel. MISC: presenter, numerous local & nat'l conferences; 1st non-educator to be pres. of MAME; 1st non-lawyer to be pres. of CLEA.

Dyke, Doris Jean, B.A.,B.Ed.,M.Ed., M.A.,Ed.D. ☼ ☗

Professor Emeritus, EMMANUEL COLLEGE, 82 Admiral Rd., Toronto, ON M5R 2L6 (416) 922-2323. Born Ont. 1930. m. Donald Milne. 5 ch. EDUC: Queen's Univ., B.A. 1959; Univ. of Toronto, B.Ed. 1961, M.Ed 1963; Columbia Univ. & Union Theological Seminary, M.A. 1962, Ed.D. 1967. CAREER: sch. teacher, Ont., 12 yrs.; Lecturer to Assoc. Prof. of Phil. of Educ., Coll. of Educ., Univ. of Saskatchewan, 1964-72; part-time Lecturer, Religious Educ., St. Andrew's Theological Coll., 1966-70; Head, Dept. of Educational Foundations, Univ. of Saskatchewan, 1967-72; Visiting Summer Sch. Prof., Univ. of British Columbia, 1971; Visiting Summer Sch. Prof., Univ. of Calgary, 1972; Assoc. Prof., Joint Appt. with Dept. of Phil. & the Sch. of Educ., Univ. of Louisville, 1972-73; Prof. & Dean of Educ., Dalhousie Univ., 1973-77; Prof. & Dir. of M.R.E. Studies, Emmanuel Coll., 1977-95; Visiting Summer Sch. Prof., Dalhousie Univ., 1978; Visiting Prof., Wesley Theological Seminary, 1989; Dir. of M.Div. Studies, Emmanuel Coll., 1990-93. SELECTED CREDITS: *Women and Holy Writ*, CJRT series (Summer 1989); *Man Alive*, CBC TV (1983). SELECTED PUBLICATIONS: *Crucified Woman* (Toronto: The United Church Publishing House, 1991); *Education and Social Policy: Local Control of Education*, co-ed. (New York: Random House, 1969); "God's Grace on Fools, God's Pity on God" (*Canadian Women's Studies* Fall 1987); "World, Religion and Peace: God as Mother" (*Women's Concerns* Fall 1985); various other publications. AFFIL: Canadian Theological Society; Association of Professors & Researchers in Religious Education; Canadian Corporation for Studies in Religion; ATS Case Study Institute (Fellow); Royal Society of the Arts (Fellow); Philosophy of Education Society (Fellow). HONS: Sr. Research Award, ATS, 1989. MISC: frequent speaker.

Dyson, Rose Anne, B.A.,R.P.N.,M.Ed., Ed.D. ■■ ☺ ☗ ☖

Chair, CANADIANS CONCERNED ABOUT VIOLENCE IN ENTERTAINMENT (research/public educ.), 167 Glen Rd., Toronto, ON M4W 2W8

(416) 961-0853, FAX 929-2720, EMAIL
rdyson@oise.utoronto.ca. Media Consultant.
Born 1940. m. Mr. Justice Norman Dyson. 2
ch. Anna Helen Dyson, Arthur Wm. Dyson.
EDUC: Univ. of Saskatchewan, R.P.N.(Psychiatric Nursing) 1961; Univ. of Toronto,
B.A.(English Lit.) 1980; OISE, Univ. of
Toronto, M.Ed.(Adult Educ./Counselling)
1986, Ed.D.(Adult Educ.) 1995. CAREER:
Public Rel'ns Asst., Maclaren Advertising Company Limited, 1965; Real Estate Agent, Canada
Permanent Trust, 1966-68; Psychodramatist,
Oshawa General Hospital, 1973-74; Seminar
Series Co-ord., Psychiatric Nurses Association
of Canada, 1974-75; Gen. Mgr, Dykos Corporation, 1977-95; Dir., Rosendee Corporation,
1988 to date; writer, lecturer, community
activist, 1985 to date; media consultant, 1995
to date. SELECTED PUBLICATIONS: numerous publications, book reviews, papers given.
EDIT: Edit. Bd., *Peace* magazine, 1992 to date.
AFFIL: Canadian Chemical Producers Association (Nat'l Advisory Panel 1990 to date); Canadian Association for the Study of Adult Education (Bd. Dir. 1996 to date); Cultural Environment Movement (Steering Committee, Bd. of
Dir. 1996). HONS: various scholarships.
INTERESTS: community dev. & social activism;
sailing; cross-country skiing.

E

Eagan, Trudy ✎ ♡ $
Vice-President, Corporate Affairs and Human Resources, THE TORONTO SUN PUBLISHING CORPORATION (communications - media), 333 King St. E., Toronto, ON M5A 3X5 (416) 947-2201, FAX 368-0374. **CAREER:** various positions incl. VP, Corp. Affairs, The Toronto Sun Publishing Corporation, 1974-96; VP, Corp. Affairs & Hum. Res., 1996 to date. **DIRECTOR:** The Toronto Sun Publishing Corporation. **AFFIL:** Sheena's Place (Chair & Co-founder); Edward Dunlop Foundation; several committees of charitable organizations. **INTERESTS:** fitness; charitable work. **MISC:** Sheena's Place is a transition centre for people living with eating disorders, their families, caregivers & community svc. providers.

Earle-Lambert, Beth, C.M.A. ■■ ✊ $
President, INNKEEPERS' GUILD OF NOVA SCOTIA (prov. association representing the interests of operators of fixed-roof accommodation in N.S.), P.O. Box 504, Digby, NS B0V 1A0 (902) 245-5841, FAX 245-2277, EMAIL mtngap@isisnet.com. Born Middleton, N.S. 1961. sep. 3 ch. Emily, Alexandra, Greyson. **EDUC:** Society of Management Accountants, C.M.A. 1990. **CAREER:** Fin. Mgr, Mountain Gap Resort, 1988-93; Gen. Mgr, 1993 to date. **AFFIL:** Southwest Regional Sch. Bd. (Bd. mbr. 1996 to date); Digby District Sch. Bd. (Bd. mbr. 1991-96); N.S. Sch. Bd. Association (Bd. of Dir. 1991-93); Society of Management Accountants; Digby & Area Board of Trade (2nd VP); Land of Evangeline Committee (Chair); Tourism Industry Association of N.S. (ex officio Bd. mbr.). **INTERESTS:** spending time with her children; swimming; walking; seakayaking.

MISC: instructor, Automated Acctg, 1992. **COMMENT:** *"I try always to apply integrity, intelligence and humour to my endeavours."*

Eastman, Barbara C., B.A.,M.A.,D.Phil. $
President and Director, PROBYN & COMPANY LIMITED, 95 King St. E., 2nd Fl., Toronto, ON M5C 1G4 (416) 777-2800, FAX 777-1190. President, ROSTAND INC., Treasurer, CANADIAN ENVIRONMENTAL ENERGY CORPORATIOn., Secretary, ENSERVE POWER CORPORATION. Born Toronto. cl. A. Stephen Probyn. **EDUC:** Trinity Coll., Univ. of Toronto, B.A.(Arts) 1968; York Univ., M.A.(English Lit) 1971; St. Hilda's Coll., Oxford Univ., D.Phil.(English Lang. & Lit.) 1978. **CAREER:** European Space Agency, Netherlands, 1978-80; Imperial Oil Limited, 1981-82; Royal Bank of Canada, 1982-89; Probyn & Company Limited, 1990 to date. **SELECTED PUBLICATIONS:** *Ezra Pound's Cantos: The Story of the Text* (1977); scholarly articles in US, UK & Europe. **DIRECTOR:** Enserve Power Corporation; Probyn & Company Inc.; Probyn & Company Limited. **AFFIL:** Couchiching Institute on Public Affairs (Dir.; Pres. 1989-90); Oxford Society of Southwestern Ontario (Membership Sec. 1987-89); Board of Trade of Metropolitan Toronto (Exec. Forum Committee 1983-88); York Univ. (Post Grad. Fellow 1970-72); Sr. Common Room, Trinity Coll. (Hon. Mbr. 1987-89); Royal Canadian Yacht Club. **INTERESTS:** art; literature; business; Canada's future. **MISC:** Dir. Gen., Prov.-Mun. Secretariat, 1988 Toronto Econ. Summit (of G-7 Countries); Guest Lecturer, Univ. of California, Berkeley, 1977; Prov. of Ont. Grad. Scholar, 1970-72; Doctoral Fellow, Canada Council, 1972-75.

Easton, Carol, R.N.,B.Sc.N.,M.Sc.(A), C.H.E. ■ ⊕
Administrative Leader–Surgical Services, Inpatients Preoperative Assessment Clinics and Acute Pain Services, CALGARY REGIONAL HEALTH AUTHORITY, Peter Lougheed Centre, 3500 - 26th Ave. N.E., Calgary, AB T1Y 6J4 (403) 291-8719, FAX 291-8766. Born Bancroft, Ont. 1951. m. Dr. Paul Easton. **EDUC:** McMaster Univ., B.Sc.N.(Nursing) 1974; McGill Univ., M.Sc.(A)(Nursing) 1987. **CAREER:** Bedside Nurse & Team Leader, McMaster Univ. Medical Centre, 1974-76; Teaching Master & Nursing Coord., St. Lawrence Coll. of Applied Arts & Technology, 1976-80; Nursing Clinical & Classroom Teacher, Red River Community Coll., 1980-82; Coord., Diploma Nursing Program, Red River Coll., 1982-84; Nursing Research Asst., Jewish General Hospital, 1986; Nurse Clinician Teacher, Royal Victoria Hospital, 1986-87; Nursing Research Asst., 1987; Nursing Educ. Consultant/Educ. Consultant–Medical Units, Jewish General Hospital, 1987-88; Dir. of Nursing–Medicine, 1988; Dir. of Medical/Surgical Nursing, Calgary General Hospital, 1988-91, 1991-93; Acting VP, Patient Svc., 1991; Dir. of Surgical Nursing, 1993-96; Administrative Leader–Surgical Svcs, Inpatients Preoperative Assessment Clinics & Acute Pain Svcs, Calgary Regional Health Authority, 1996 to date; Adjunct Asst. Prof., Univ. of Calgary. **SELECTED PUBLICATIONS:** "I.C.U. psychosis: delirium in the intensive care unit" (*Heart and Lung: The Journal of Critical Care*, 3, 1988); "Transition team guides hospital through change" (*Healthcare Advocate*, 3. 1994); several student modules for nursing programs, Royal Victoria Hospital & St. Lawrence Coll. **AFFIL:** Canadian Coll. of Certified Health Executives (Certified Health Exec.); Canadian Coll. of Health Service Executives; Alberta Association of Registered Nurses; Canadian Association of Registered Nurses; Coll. of Nurses of Ontario. **INTERESTS:** photography; travel; downhill skiing. **MISC:** Co-organizer, Annual Transcultural Festivals to enhance understanding of culture related to hospitalization & health care. **COMMENT:** *"As a nursing leader, I am excited about patient-focused, family-centred care. My interests are in the development of people- and patient-compliant resolution and cultural interfaces with health care."*

Eaton, Heather, B.A.,M.Div., Ph.D. ■ ☼ 🎓 ✋
Theologian, Ecologist and Feminist. 3 Holborne Ave., Toronto, ON M4C 2P8 (416) 696-0102, FAX 696-0102, EMAIL heaton@epas.utoronto.ca. Born Southampton, Ont. 1956. **EDUC:** Queen's Univ., 1975-78; Univ. of Toronto, B.A.(Psych. & Ethics) 1984; Toronto Sch. of Theology, M.Div. 1988; Ph.D. 1996. **CAREER:** L'Arche, France, 1978-83; Richmond Hill, Ont., 1983-85; Chaplain, Newman Centre, Univ. of Toronto, 1988-92; Chaplain, Covenant House, part-time, 1992 to date; Fac. of Theology, Univ. of St. Michael's Coll., 1992; Sessional Lecturer, 1993 to date; Fac. of Environmental Studies, York Univ. **SELECTED PUBLICATIONS:** "Why is Ecology a Religious Concern?" (*Roundtable: The Coalition of Concerned Canadian Catholics* 1994); "Ecological-Feminism" (*Voice of Women for Peace* 1994); "Ecofeminist Spiritualities: Seeking the Wild or the Sacred" (*Alternatives: Perspectives on Society, Technology and Environment* Feb. 1995); "Ecofeminist Theology," *Theology for Earth Community*, ed. Deiter Hessel (Maryknoll: ORBIS, 1995); various other publications. **AFFIL:** Women, Environment, Education,

Development (WEED) (Bd. Mbr.); Canadian Society for the Study of Religion; Canadian Theological Society; American Academy of Religion; Environmental Studies Association of Canada; Women for a Just & Healthy Planet; International Coordinating Committee for Religion & the Earth; Canadian Coalition on Ecology, Ethics & Religion; Holy Cross Centre for Ecology & Spirituality. HONS: Hunsaker-Irwin Scholarship, 1986-87; Mary Ward Scholarship, 1986-87; Toronto Office of Lay Ministry Award, 1987-88; Loretto Sisters' Bursary for Canadian Women in Religion, 1993-94; Mary Rowell Jackman Award for Feminist Scholarship in Religion, 1993-94. INTERESTS: feminism; ecology; spirituality; ethics; music; sailing; chocolate! MISC: numerous conference presentations. COMMENT: *"Worked for 20 years in spirituality, religion and culture and theology with a focus on social justice, feminism and ecology. Teaching, traveling, presentations; academic and activist. Greatest concern is the magnitude of the socio-ecological crisis. Interested in comprehensive response–theory and praxis, including increasing spiritual/religious sensitivity to the earth community."*

Eaves, Connie Jean, B.A.,M.Sc., Ph.D. ⊕ 🏵 🐟
Deputy Director, THE TERRY FOX LABORATORY FOR HEMATOLOGY/ONCOLOGY, 601 W. 10th Ave., Vancouver, BC V5Z 1L3 (604) 877-6070, FAX 877-0712. EDUC: Queen's Univ., B.A.(Biol. & Chem.) 1964, M.Sc.(Biol.) 1966; Univ. of Manchester, UK, Ph.D.(Immunology) 1969. CAREER: Visiting Fellow, Paterson Laboratories, Christie Hospital & Holt Radium Institute, Manchester, UK, 1969-70; Postdoctoral Fellow, Ontario Cancer Institute, Toronto, 1970-73; Demonstrator, Dept. of Histology, Univ. of Toronto, 1971-72; Hon. Asst. Prof., Medical Genetics, Univ. of British Columbia, 1973-79; Assoc. Prof., Medical Genetics, 1979-84; Assoc. Mbr., Pathology, 1981 to date; Prof., Medical Genetics, 1984 to date; Assoc. Mbr., Medicine, 1987 to date; Deputy Dir., Terry Fox Lab., 1986 to date. SELECTED PUBLICATIONS: "Clonal Hematopoiesis Demonstrated by X-linked DNA Polymorphisms after Allogenic Bone Marrow Transplantation," with Turhan *et al* (*New England Journal of Medicine* 320, 1989); "Functional Characterization of Individual Human Hematopoietic Stem Cells Cultured at Limiting Dilution on Supportive Marrow Stromal Layers," with Sutherland *et al* (*Proc. National Academy of Science* 87, 1990); "Rapid Decline of Chronic Myeloid Leukemic Cells in Long-Term Culture due to a Defect at the Stem Cell Level," with Udomsakdi *et al*

(*Proc. National Academy of Science* 89, 1992); "Unresponsiveness of Primitive Chronic Myeloid Leukemia Cells to Macrophage Inflammatory Protein-1d, an Inhibitor of Primitive Normal Hematopoietic Cells," co-author (*Proc. National Academy of Science* 90, 1993); "Characterization and Purification of a Primitive Hematopoietic Cell Type in Adult Mouse Marrow Capable of Lympho-myeloid Differentiation in Long-Term Marrow "Switch" Cultures," with Lemieux *et al* (*Blood* 89, 1995); "Self-Renewal of Primitive Human Hematopoietic Cells (Long-Term-Culture-Initiating Cells) In Vitro and Their Expansion In Defined Medium," with Petzer *et al* (*Proc. National Academy of Science* USA 93,1996); more than 200 articles in journals, conference proceedings & as chapters in books. EDIT: Ed. Bd., *Experimental Hematology*, 1978-81, 1984-87; Ed. Bd., *Blood*, 1978-83, 1992-95; Assoc. Ed., 1995-97; Ed. Bd., *Stem Cells/International Journal of Cell Cloning*, 1980-90; Assoc. Ed., *Developmental Biology*, 1987-95; Ed. Bd., *Cell Transplantation*, 1991-94; Bd. of Reviewing Eds., *Journal of Laboratory and Clinical Medicine*, 1991 to date; Ed. Bd., *Leukemia*, 1991 to date; Ed. Bd., *Canadian Journal of Oncology*, 1991 to date; Ed. Bd., *Bone Marrow Transplantation*, 1991 to date; Assoc. Ed., *Biology of Blood and Marrow Transplantation*, 1994 to date; Ed. Bd., *British Journal of Haematology*, 1995 to date. AFFIL: Canadian Society for Cell Biology; Canadian Society for Immunology; Canadian Hematology Society; American Society for Blood & Marrow Transplantation (Bd. Mbr. 1994-98; Chair, Hematopoiesis Subcommittee 1995-97); American Society for Cell Biology; American Society for Hematology; International Society for Experimental Hematology; American Association for Cancer Research, Inc.; International Society of Differentiation, Inc.; International Society for Hematotherapy & Graft Engineering; B.C. Cancer Foundation; National Cancer Institute of Canada (Mbr. at Large & Bd. Mbr. 1992-2000; VP 1994-96; Chair, Committee on Planning & Priorities 1994-96; Pres. 1996-98); Royal Society of Canada (Fellow); Canadian Society for Improvements to our System of Education (Dir. for B.C.). HONS: Queen's Univ. Entrance Scholarship, 1961; Prov. of Ont. Scholarship, 1961; Edgar Forrester Scholarship, 1962; W.W. Near & Susan Near Scholarship in Genetics, 1964; National Research Council Bursary, 1965; Ruben Wells Travelling Scholarship, 1966; National Research Council Special Scholarship, 1966-68; National Research Council Studentship, 1968-69; National Cancer Institute of Canada Research Scholarship, 1973-78; National Cancer Institute of Canada Research Associateship, 1978-85; National Cancer Institute of Canada Terry Fox Cancer Research Scientist, 1985-97; Hall of Fame, B.C. Health Research Foundation, Science World, 1993; Killam Research Prize, Univ. of B.C., 1993. MISC: numerous invited lectures & presentations in Canada, US & Europe; recipient of various grants; various conference presentations; reviewer for various journals & granting agencies; various consultancies.

Eberl-Kelly, Katherine, B.A.,B.Ed. ■■ ⊕ ℗
Board Chair, EAST PRINCE HEALTH REGIONAL BOARD, Summerside, PE (902) 888-8028, FAX 888-8023, EMAIL kelpiks@atcon.com. President, CANADIAN ASSOCIATION OF HEALTH CARE AUXILIARIES, 17 York St., Ottawa, ON K1N 9J6 (613) 241-8005, FAX 241-5055. Born Arcola, Sask. 1952. m. Dr. Paul Kelly. 2 ch. Ian, Sean. EDUC: Univ. of Saskatchewan, B.A.(Psych.) 1973; Univ. of Regina, B.Ed. (English) 1975. CAREER: CUSO cooperant teaching English as a 2nd language, Botswana, Africa, 1975-77; Teacher of English, Campbell Collegiate, Regina, Sask., 1978-80; Substitute Teacher, Three Oaks Sr. High Sch., Summerside, P.E.I., 1980-85. AFFIL: Prince County Hospital Foundation (VP 1993-96); Summerside YMCA (Sec., Bd. of Dir. 1993-95); Provincial Health Agency Board (mbr. 1993 to date); East Prince Health Regional Board (Chair); Canadian Association of Health Care Auxiliaries (Pres. 1996-98). HONS: Harry T. Holman Award for exemplary volunteer contribution to Prince County Hospital & the people it serves, 1991. INTERESTS: fitness; family activities; how we can manage our health & educ. systems to really make a difference in the quality of life for all. COMMENT: *"My CUSO experience was the catalyst for a life of trying to look beyond the trivial—regional, provincial differences are small when one is far, far away in a continent unknown. I have found that once we get beyond the petty issues of turf and power, we can begin to have an impact."*

Eccles, Robin Christina, M.D.,FRCS, FRACS ⊕ ⊛
Pediatric Surgeon, ALBERTA CHILDREN'S HOSPITAL, 1820 Richmond Rd. S.W., Calgary, AB T2T 5C7 (403) 229-7807, FAX 229-7634. Clinical Assistant Professor, Department of Surgery, UNIVERSITY OF CALGARY. Born St. Boniface, Man. 1956. m. 3 ch. Alexandra, Molly, Genevieve. EDUC: Univ. of Western Ontario, Chem. 1973-75; Univ. of Toronto, M.D.(Medicine) 1979. CAREER: Rotating Internship, North York General Hospital, 1979-80; Gen. Surgery Residency, Univ. of Alberta, 1981-86; Teaching Fellowship, Royal

Alexandra Hospital, Edmonton, 1986-87; Gen. Surgeon, Fort McMurray Regional Hospital, 1987-89; Sr. Surgical Registrar, Royal Alexandra Hospital for Children, Sydney, Australia, 1989-91; Research Fellow, Alberta Children's Hospital, 1991-92; Pediatric Surgeon, 1992 to date; Clinical Asst. Prof., Dept. of Surgery, Univ. of Calgary, 1992 to date. SELECTED PUBLICATIONS: "Validation of a Compact System for Measuring Gas Exchange," with Swinamer D.L., Jones R.L., King E.G. (*Critical Care Medicine*, Sept. 1986); "Muscle Function Testing and 31P-NMR Spectroscopy in Fasted Healthy Volunteer," with Swinamer D.L., *et al* (*Journal of Clinical Care*, Sept. 1987); "An Evaluation of the Effect of Fasting on the Exercise-Induced Change in pH and P1IPG from Skeletal Muscle," with Lunt J.A., Allen P.S., Swinamer D.L., *et al* (*Magnetic Resonance in Medicine*, June 1986). AFFIL: Canadian Association of Pediatric Surgeons; Canadian Medical Association; Alberta Medical Association; Alberta Association of General Surgeons; Medical Women's Federation; Association of Women Surgeons; Royal Coll. of Surgeons (Fellow); Royal Australasian Coll. of Surgeons (Fellow). HONS: Resident Research Award, American Coll. of Surgeons, Alta. Chapter. INTERESTS: ballet & dance; Australian wines. COMMENT: *"Surgery is a male-dominated field but one that is slowly changing to accept women. I enjoy the practice of general surgery and have limited it to pediatric surgery after a further three years of training in pediatric surgery."*

Edmonds, Erin O'Brien, B.Sc.,LL.B. ⚖ ⊘
Lawyer, MADDALENA HILL & EDMONDS, Clayton Professional Centre, 255 Lacewood Dr., Ste. 106, Halifax, NS B3M 4G2 (902) 445-5511, FAX 443-2600. Born Moncton, N.B. 1959. m. Timothy. 2 ch. EDUC: Dalhousie Univ., B.Sc.(Biol.) 1980; LL.B. 1983. BAR: N.S., 1984. CAREER: Articling Clerk, Crowe Thompson, Halifax, 1983-84; Assoc. Lawyer, Crowe Dillon Robinson, Halifax, 1984-90; Ptnr, Walker Schurman Edmonds, Halifax, 1991-95; Maddalena Hill & Edmonds, Halifax, 1995 to date. SELECTED PUBLICATIONS: *Opening Doors: Buying and Selling Real Estate-Your Lawyer's Role Explained*, brochure (Catherine S. Walker & Erin O'Brien Edmonds). AFFIL: Halifax Metro Exec. Group (Dir. 1994-95); Canadian Bar Association; N.S. Barristers' Society (Bar Council 1994-95); Halifax Women's Network (Pres. 1990-91). INTERESTS: swimming; skiing; reading; gardening & all outdoor activities. MISC: numerous seminars & speaking engagements on real estate law & estate planning; N.S. Synchro-

nized Swimming Duet Champion; N.S. Synchronized Swimming Team Champion. COMMENT: *"I am an individual who loves a combination of team work and independence. I am persistent and determined with any job I undertake. My family is most important to me, but I love my work too. I endeavour to strike a balance between work and family life. I have been able, with family support, to become a partner in my own law firm and raise two young boys, now ages five and eight."*

Edmondson, Sheila M. ■■ $ Ⓒ
Managing Partner, HSW MANAGEMENT ASSOCIATES LIMITED (multiple association mgmt), 10435 Islington Ave., P.O. Box 294, Kleinburg, ON L0J 1C0 (905) 893-1689, FAX 893-2392, EMAIL kleinbrg@netrover.com. Born Kent, UK. sep. 2 ch. Wendy Helen, Alistair Stuart. CAREER: Show Mgr, Canadian Toy & Decoration Fair, 1983 to date; Show Mgr, Toronto Int'l Art Exposition, 1990; Show Mgr, Cottage Show, 1987-92; Exec. Dir., Canadian Truck Trailer Association, 1989-92; Exec. Dir., Building Maintenance Contractors' Association, 1986-90. SELECTED PUBLICATIONS: *Canadian Toy & Decoration Fair Guide* (annually); *Canadian Toy Association Newsletter* (3x/year). AFFIL: Canadian Toy Association (Dir. 1993 to date); Gifts in Kind International, Cdn chpt. (Dir.); Canadian Association of Exposition Managers (mbr.; former Dir., Exec. Committee); Canadian Association of Association Management Companies. INTERESTS: decorative art painting; walking; reading; charitable activities; golf. COMMENT: *"Sheila Edmondson is Managing Partner of HSW Management Associates Limited, which provides full management services to trade and professional associations and exhibitions. She is currently Executive Director of the Canadian Toy Association."*

Edwardh, Marlys Anne, B.A.,LL.B.,LL.M. ⚖
Lawyer, RUBY & EDWARDH, 11 Prince Arthur Ave., Toronto, ON M5R 1B2 (416) 964-9664, FAX 964-8305. Born Lethbridge, Alta. 1950. 1 ch. EDUC: Carleton Univ., B.A.(with distinction) 1971; Osgoode Hall Law Sch., LL.B. 1974; Univ. of California (Berkeley), LL.M. 1983. CAREER: Assoc. Commission Cnsl, Commission of Inquiry into the Facts of Allegations of Conflict of Interest Concerning the Hon. Sinclair M. Stevens, 1987; Cnsl to Donald Marshall, Jr., Royal Commission on the Donald Marshall, Jr., Prosecution, 1989; Cnsl, Commission of Inquiry on the Blood System in Canada, 1994 to date. SELECTED PUBLICATIONS: "Political Offences: Extradition and Deportation," co-authored with J.G. Castel

(*Osgoode Hall Law Journal* June 1975); "Media Access to Refugee Proceedings in Canada" co-authored with Daniel Brodsky (*Alberta Law Review* Vol. 29, No. 3, 1991); Ed., *Canadian Rights Reporter*, 1982 to date. AFFIL: Criminal Lawyers' Association (Dir. 1989 to date); The Ontario Legal Aid Plan (Area Committee); Civil Liberties Association. HONS: Millvain Chairholder, Univ. of Calgary, Fac. of Law, 1990. MISC: part-time Lecturer, Osgoode Hall Law Sch., York Univ.; Special Lecturer, Fac. of Law, Univ. of Toronto.

Edwards, The Hon. Anne, B.A.,M.A. ■ ✦ $
Minister, Ministry of Employment and Investments, GOVERNMENT OF BRITISH COLUMBIA, Legislative Office, Parliament Buildings, Victoria, BC V8V 1X4 (604) 387-5295, FAX 356-5587. Born Tisdale, Sask. 1935. m. Russell Edwards. 4 ch. EDUC: Univ. of Saskatchewan, B.A.(English) 1955, M.A.(English) 1958. CAREER: journalist; college instructor; Mbr. for Kootenay, Gov't of B.C., 1986; Critic, Tourism, Recreation & Culture; Critic, Energy, Mines & Petroleum Resources; Min., Ministry of Energy, Mines & Petroleum Resources 1991 to date. SELECTED PUBLICATIONS: *Exploring the Purcell Wilderness*, co-author (1978). INTERESTS: various cultural & social organizations in the community; Cranbrook Archives, Museum & Landmarks Foundation. MISC: has also worked with the Bd. of Referees for UIC & Reg'l Bd. of Variances; as Min., is responsible for the B.C. Utilities Commission. COMMENT: *"In her position as Minister, Ms. Edwards launched B.C.'s first Mineral Strategy, designed to develop new opportunities for growth in the mining sector. She has overseen the negotiations over the sale of British Columbia's share of the downstream benefits under the Columbia River Treaty, the establishment of a long-term electricity export policy and the development of an energy strategy for the province."*

Edwards, Elizabeth, B.A.,M.A.,Ph.D. ⚐ ▤
Director, Contemporary Studies Program, UNIVERSITY OF KING'S COLLEGE, Halifax, NS B3H 2A1 (902) 422-1271, EMAIL eedwards@ ac.dal.ca. Born N. Vancouver 1955. m. 2 ch. EDUC: Dalhousie Univ., B.A.(English) 1979, M.A.(English) 1986; Cambridge Univ., Ph.D.(Middle English) 1996. INTERESTS: feminism; literary theory; medieval subjects.

Edwards, Mary-Jane, B.A.,M.A., Ph.D. ■ ⚐ ▤ ▤
Professor of English, and Director, Centre for Editing Early Canadian Texts, CARLETON UNIVERSITY, 1125 Colonel By Dr., Ottawa, ON

K1S 5B6 (613) 520-2365, FAX 520-3544, EMAIL mary-jane-edwards@carleton.ca. **EDUC:** Trinity Coll., Univ. of Toronto, B.A. 1960; Queen's Univ., M.A. 1963; Univ. of Toronto, Ph.D. 1969. **CAREER:** Lecturer, English Dept., Acadia Univ., 1961-63; Instructor II, English Dept., Univ. of British Columbia, 1966-69, Asst. Prof., English Dept., 1969-70; Asst. Prof., English Dept., Carleton Univ., 1970-73; Assoc. Prof., 1973-82; Prof., 1982 to date. **SELECTED PUBLICATIONS:** *The Evolution of Canadian Literature in English: Beginnings to 1867* (Toronto: Holt, Rinehart and Winston, 1973); *The Evolution of Canadian Literature in English: 1867-1914* (Toronto: Holt, Rinehart and Winston, 1973); *Canadian Literature in the 70's* (Toronto: Holt, Rinehart and Winston, 1980); "Early Canadian Literature in English: A Survey and a Challenge" (*College English* 51 1989); various other scholarly publications; contributed articles to *Ottawa Citizen*, *Ottawa Journal*, & *This Week* (Carleton). **EDIT:** Gen. Ed., CEECT 1981 to date; Ed. Bd., *Papers of the Bibliographic Society of Canada*, 1986-88; Ed. Bd., *English Studies in Canada* 1987-93; Contributing Ed., *Canadian Storytellers*, 1991 to date; Ed. Committee, Collected Works of Northrop Frye Proj., Victoria Coll., Univ. of Toronto, 1993 to date. **AFFIL:** Bibliographical Society of Canada; Shastri Indo-Canadian Institute (Dir.). **MISC:** numerous conference presentations; recipient of various grants; referee for various journals & grants.

Edwards, Nancy, C.G.A. 🎓 $ ✊
Secretary-Treasurer, SCHOOL DISTRICT NO. 48 (HOWE SOUND), 37866 Second Ave., Box 250, Squamish, BC V0N 3G0 (604) 892-5228, FAX 892-1038. Born N. Vancouver 1955. m. Brian. 2 ch. Tyson, Skai. **EDUC:** Duffus Coll., Sec. Svcs 1974. **CAREER:** Clerical Asst., Sch. District No. 48 (Howe Sound), 1974-76; various positions in acctg, 1976-81; Dir. of Fin., 1981-85; Asst. Sec.-Treas., 1985-89; Sec.-Treas., 1989 to date. **AFFIL:** Certified General Accountants' Association of B.C. (C.G.A.); Certified General Accountants of Canada; Rotary Club of Squamish (Dir., Youth Exchange Program); Squamish Health Foundation (Dir.); B.C. Secretary-Treasurers' Association. **HONS:** Silver Medal for highest average fourth-level marks in Canada, Certified General Accountants of Canada; two scholarships, Public Practice Committee, Certified General Accountants' Association of B.C., 1979; Barbeau Medal for highest marks in taxation in B.C., Certified General Accountants' Association of B.C., 1981; Gold Medal for highest marks in last 3 yrs. of CGA program in Canada, 1981; Valedictorian, graduating class of 1981. **INTERESTS:** squash; basketball; running; weight training. **COMMENT:** *"A certified general accountant, who has worked in both public practice and nonprofit fields. Currently working in business administration overseeing finance, labour relations and external development projects."*

Edwards, Viviane, B.A.,B.Ed.,M.Ed 🎓 📜
Director, Second-Language Education Centre, UNIVERSITY OF NEW BRUNSWICK, Faculty of Education, Fredericton, NB E3B 6E3 (506) 453-5136, FAX 453-4777, EMAIL vedwards@unb.ca. Born Charlo, N.B. 1941. m. John Edwards. 1 ch. Mark. **EDUC:** Univ. of New Brunswick, B.A. 1963, B.Ed.(Educ.) 1966, M.Ed.(Educ.) 1985. **CAREER:** Coord., Second Language Svcs, Prov. of New Brunswick, 1972-85; Prof., Fac. of Educ., 1985 to date; Dir., Second-Language Educ. Centre, 1985 to date; Ed., *Canadian Modern Language Review*, 1989-95. **SELECTED PUBLICATIONS:** "French Immersion: Process, Product and Perspective" (*Canadian Modern Language Review* 1992); "Touch of...Class!" (*Canadian Modern Language Review* 1994). **AFFIL:** Canadian Association of Immersion Teachers; Canadian Association of Second-Language Teachers. **HONS:** Plaque, in recognition of 20 yrs.' service to the people & gov't of N.B., 1989; Merit Award, Univ. of New Brunswick, 1990. **COMMENT:** *"Through hard work and dedication as well as enjoyment, I have been effective in influencing the growth of second-language education in New Brunswick and in Canada."*

Eeson, Cynthia, B.A.,LL.B. $
President, KIDS ONLY CLOTHING CLUB INC., 5775 - 11 St. S.E., Calgary, AB T2H 1M7 (403) 252-9667, FAX 252-9846. Born Toronto 1952. m. Ralph. 3 ch. **EDUC:** Univ. of Winnipeg, B.A 1973; Univ. of Manitoba, LL.B. 1978. **BAR:** Alta., 1979. **CAREER:** Corp. Lawyer, Beaumont Proctor, Petro-Canada, 1979-82; Pres., Kids Only Clothing Club Inc., 1988 to date. **DIRECTOR:** Kids Only Clothing Club. **AFFIL:** Direct Sellers Association of Canada; Young Presidents' Organization. **HONS:** Finalist, Woman Entrepreneur of the Year, 1992; Pinnacle Award, 1993; Western Canada Finalist, Entrepreneur of the Year, 1994.

Egan, Deborah, B.A. ■ ♡
Executive Director, CHATS (COMMUNITY HOME ASSISTANCE TO SENIORS), 628 Davis Dr., Newmarket, ON L3Y 8P8 (905) 898-3967, FAX 898-3626. Born Newmarket, Ont. 1959. m. Paul Sheardown. 2 ch. Samuel, Rachel. **EDUC:** York Univ., B.A.(Psych.) 1985, Volun-

tary Sector Mgmt Program (Hons.) 1988. **CAREER:** various positions in the not-for-profit/voluntary sector, 1977-85; Exec. Dir., CHATS, 1985 to date. **AFFIL:** York Region District Health Council (Long-Term Care Planning Committee); Ontario Community Support Association; various other prov. bd. & local service advisory group memberships. **INTERESTS:** yoga; outdoor & family activities; learning new things. **COMMENT:** *"Committed to innovation and creativity with a common sense approach in the reform of long-term care services in the community. We can all make a difference."*

Egan, M. Joan, B.A.Sc.,M.A.Sc. ■ $ ⚛
Manager, Business Resumption Planning, ROYAL BANK OF CANADA, 320 Front St. W., 16th Fl., Toronto, ON M5V 3B6 (416) 348-6903, FAX 348-6951. Born Toronto 1956. s. **EDUC:** Univ. of Toronto, B.A.Sc.(Mech. Eng.) 1978, M.A.Sc. 1980. **CAREER:** Consulting Eng., H.H. Angus & Associates Ltd., 1980-84; Central Plant Operator, Bramalea Limited, 1984-87; Consulting Eng., H.H. Angus & Associates Ltd., 1987-90; Sr. Eng., Royal Bank, 1990-95; Mgr, Bus. Resumption Planning, 1995 to date. **AFFIL:** Professional Engineers Ontario; Ordre des ingénieurs du Québec. **INTERESTS:** golf; cross-country skiing; reading; environment. **COMMENT:** *"I am a hard-working individual who prides herself on balancing managerial responsibility with employee enjoyment."*

Ehm, Erica, B.A. ■ 🎭 📖 📺 👍
Broadcaster, Actor, Songwriter, ERICA EHM COMMUNICATIONS LTD. (416) 533-4047, FAX 533-4047. **EDUC:** Ottawa Univ., B.A.(Comm.). **CAREER:** VJ & Correspondent, Citytv/MuchMusic, 1985-94; Songwriter, for Cassandra Vasik, Eleanor McCain, Joel Feeney, Don Nielson & Tim Thorney; Ptnr, Them Records; Music Publisher, Ehmusic; Hon. Spokesperson, Jeunesse UNICEF Youth Program, 1993 & 1994; Host, *Real Life*, Life Network, 1996. **SELECTED CREDITS:** reporter, *Entertainment Now*, Baton Broadcasting, 1996 to date; series regular, *The Company*, TVO, 1996; Host, *Powerplay*, Discovery Channel, 1995-96; Host, *World Music Video Awards*; Host, Hospital for Sick Kids Annual Telethon, 1990-95; Benita, *Unidentified Human Remains and the True Nature of Love*, National Art Centre, Ottawa, 1991 & Manitoba Theatre Centre, Winnipeg, 1992; series regular, *Robocop*, Skyvision; various other film & TV credits. **SELECTED PUBLICATIONS:** *She Should Talk: Conversations with Exceptional Young Women About Life, Dreams & Success* (HarperCollins). **AFFIL:** ACTRA; Equity; C.A.R.A.S; Canadian Country Music Association. **HONS:** 3 SOCAN Awards, country music, for "It Comes Back to You," "Diamonds" & "Fortune Smiled on Me." **MISC:** 1st woman on air on MuchMusic. **COMMENT:** *"I am probably best known as an on-air personality. I was the first female on air at Canada's National Music Channel, and for the past decade have become a role model for young people, particularly women."*

Eichler, Margrit, M.A.,Ph.D. ■ 🎓 ⚛
Professor of Sociology, Department of Sociology in Education, ONTARIO INSTITUTE FOR STUDIES IN EDUCATION OF THE UNIVERSITY OF TORONTO (OISE/UT), 252 Bloor St. W., Toronto, ON M5S 1V6 (416) 923-6641, FAX 926-4751, EMAIL meichler@oise.utoronto.ca. 1 ch. Jens Köhler. **EDUC:** Univ. of Goettingen, Germany, 1962-65; Free Univ. of Berlin, 1965-66; Duke Univ., M.A. 1968, Ph.D. 1972. **CAREER:** Lecturer, Dept. of Soc., Univ. of Waterloo, 1971; Asst. Prof., 1972-75; Assoc. Prof., Dept. of Soc., OISE, 1975-80; Dept. of Educational Theory, Univ. of Toronto, 1975 to date; Prof., Dept. of Soc., OISE/UT, 1980 to date; cross-appointed to Dept. of Soc., Univ. of Toronto, 1981 to date; Distinguished Visiting Prof., Univ. of Alberta, Fac. of Extension, 1985; Visiting Scholar, Canadian Research Institute on Law & the Family, Univ. of Calgary, 1990-91; Nancy Rowell Jackman Chair in Women's Studies, Mount Saint Vincent Univ., 1992-93. **SELECTED PUBLICATIONS:** *Martin's Father* (Lollipop Power Press, 1971); *The Double Standard: A Feminist Critique of Feminist Social Science* (London: Croom Helm, 1980); *Women in Futures Research* (Oxford: Pergamon Press, 1982); *Canadian Families Today: Recent Changes and their Policy Consequences* (Toronto: Gage Publishing, 1983); *Non-Sexist Research Methods: A Practical Guide* (Boston: Allen and Unwin, 1988); *Misconceptions. The Social Construction of Choice and the New Reproductive and Genetic Technologies* Vol. 1 (Hull: Voyageur, 1993); *Misconceptions. The Social Construction of Choice and the New Reproductive and Genetic Technologies* Vol. 2 (Hull: Voyageur, 1994); *Change of Plans* (Toronto: Garamond, 1995); numerous other publications. **EDIT:** Co-ed., *Resources for Feminist Research*, 1972-80; Advisory Bd., *Atlantis. A Women's Studies Journal*, 1975; Bd. of Eds., *Series on Dialectics in Society*, Van Gorkum, Holland, 1975-77; Cdn Correspondent, *Signs, Journal of Women in Culture and Society*, 1977 to date; Ed. Bd., *Women's Studies International Forum*, 1978-86; Consulting Ed., *Interchange*, 1978 to date; Ed., *CRIAW Papers*, 1981; Ed. Bd., OISE Press, 1982-83.

AFFIL: Royal Society of Canada (Fellow); American Sociological Association; Canadian Research Institute for the Advancement of Women; Canadian Sociology & Anthropology Association; International Sociological Association. **HONS:** Woman of Distinction Award, YWCA, 1990; LL.D.(Hon.), Brock Univ., 1991; Outstanding Contribution Award, Canadian Sociology & Anthropology Association, 1996. **MISC:** Social Sciences & Humanities Research Council, Committee on Nonsexist Research, 1984-85; recipient of numerous grants; numerous public talks & papers presented at conferences.

Elder, Michele (Shelley), R.N. ⊕ ✊ ♡

Registered Nurse, Neonatal I.C.U., ROYAL UNIVERSITY HOSPITAL, 114 Waterloo Cres., Saskatoon, SK S7H 4H5 (306) 955-1847. Secretary, SPINA BIFIDA ASSOCIATION OF CANADA. Born Grostenquin, France 1958. m. David T. Elder. 2 ch. **EDUC:** Saskatoon Bus. Coll., Secretarial Diploma 1979; Kelsey Institute of Applied Arts & Sciences, Nursing Diploma 1984. **CAREER:** bank teller; R.N., Royal University Hospital. **AFFIL:** Spina Bifida Association of Canada (Research Chair; Sask. Bd. Rep.); Spina Bifida Association of Saskatchewan (First VP; Past Pres., Saskatoon Chapter). **INTERESTS:** prevention of Spina Bifida; step aerobics; sewing. **MISC:** helped develop an educational resource kit entitled *Folic Acid and the Prevention of Neural Tube Defects*. **COMMENT:** *"I love being a mom to a 10-year old with Spina Bifida and a typical six-year old. I love working on the National Board for the Spina Bifida Association and I endeavour to help new parents of Spina Bifida infants in my work in the NICU."*

Elekes, Julie L., B.Sc.,M.S.W. $

Consultant, ELEKES RESOURCE CONSULTANTS, 628 Coach Grove Rd. S.W., Calgary, AB T3H 1C6 (403) 242-5008, FAX 246-5241. Born Brampton, Ont. 1953. m. James. 3 ch. **EDUC:** Univ. of Waterloo, B.Sc.(Health Sci./Kinesiology); Wilfrid Laurier Univ., M.S.W.(Clinical Counselling); Banff Centre for Management, Gov't Affairs 1992. **CAREER:** Mgr, Burns Memorial Foundation; Community Investment Program Mgr, Amoco Canada Petroleum Company Limited. **AFFIL:** Alberta Science Centre (Dir.); YMCA Calgary (Dir.; Corp. Advisor); YWCA Calgary; I.D.P.A.R. (Chair, Western Advisory Committee); Banff Centre for Management (Corp. Advisor). **INTERESTS:** skiing; golf; theatre; art. **MISC:** Foundation Fundraiser, Alberta Science Centre; Calgary Women's Emergency Shelter; Alberta Women's Enterprise Initiative, Alberta Sport Council. **COMMENT:** *"Julie is a high-energy, achievement-oriented individual with standard-setting expertise in public affairs, government relations, strategic fundraising and event management."*

Eliadis, F. Pearl, B.Sc.,LL.B.,B.C.L., B.C.L.(Oxon) ■ 🍁 ⚖ ♡

Director, Public Policy and Public Education, ONTARIO HUMAN RIGHTS COMMISSION (416) 314-4522. Past President, CANADIAN HUMAN RIGHTS FOUNDATION. Born Montreal 1959. m. Rob Yalden. **EDUC:** McGill Univ., B.Sc.(Biol.) 1981, LL.B.(Law) 1985, B.C.L.(Law) 1985; Univ. of Oxford, B.C.L.(Oxon) 1986. **CAREER:** Dept. of the Solicitor Gen. of Canada, 1983-84; Law Reform Commission (Canada), 1984; Commission of Inquiry on War Criminals (Canada), Canadian Jewish Congress, 1985; Stikeman Elliott, 1987-93; Pres. & CEO, Canadian Human Rights Foundation, 1990-95; Citizenship & Immigration Canada (NHQ), 1991-93. **SELECTED PUBLICATIONS:** "The Quebec Immigrant Investor Program: A Distinct Scheme" (1990) 9 *Imm. L.R.* (2d) 197; "The Right to Work: Policy Alternatives for Spouses with Pending Permanent Residence Applications" (1990) 11 *Imm. L.R.* (2d) 197; "The Regulation of Encrypted Satellite TV Signals," Eliadis and McCormack (1992) 3 *Media & Communications L.R.* 211; *International Human Rights Law: Theory and Practice*, Cotler & Eliadis (eds.) (Montreal: CHRF, 1992, Carswell dist.); "Immigration and Employment" in Stikeman, Elliott (*Executive Employment Law*, Butterworths 1993); "The Charter and Canada's Borders" (1994) 1 *Charter and Human Rights Litigation* 18; "Access to Courts: The Supreme Court of Canada's Decision in *Reza*" (1994) 1 *Charter and Human Rights Litigation* 50. **EDIT:** Ed. Bd., *Charter and Human Rights Litigation Quarterly* (Federated Press). **AFFIL:** Moot Court Canada (Bora Laskin Moot Competition); Quebec Bar Association; Canadian Bar Association (Quebec) (Past Chair, Immigration Section); Law Society of Upper Canada; Canadian Human Rights Foundation (Bd. of Dir.). **HONS:** Fac. Scholar, McGill Univ.; Rosa B. Gaultieri Prize, McGill Univ., 1985; John W. Cook Prize (shared), McGill Univ., 1985; Commemorative Medal for the 125th Anniversary of the Confederation of Canada, 1992.

Elie, Catherine, B.A.,B.Sc. ■■ ✏ 📖

Editor-in-Chief, *CHÂTELAINE* MAGAZINE, Éditions Maclean Hunter, 1001 de Maisonneuve O., Montréal, QC H3A 3E1. Born Montréal. **EDUC:** Coll. Marie-de-France, B.A. 1967; Univ. de Montréal, B.Sc.(Anthro.) 1970. **CAREER:** *Decormag*; Founding Ed., *Clin D'Oeil* (fashion magazine); Mbr., start-up team, *Santé* (health publication); created & launched, *Vous* (upscale women's magazine); Ed., *Retail/Detail* (French/English apparel trade magazine), 1990; Fashion Ed., *Châtelaine* Magazine, 1991-93; Ed.-in-Chief, 1993 to date. **MISC:** *Clin D'Oeil* broke publishing records by printing issues offering up to 450 pages of award-winning fashion photgraphy, edit. content & upscale, nat'l advertisements.

Ellerbeck, Karen Marie, B.A. ■ 📜 ♡

Consultant and Appraiser to museums and insurance companies. Born Calgary 1946. m. Douglas E. 2 ch. **EDUC:** Univ. of British Columbia, B.A.(Religious Studies) 1994. **CAREER:** Consultant & Appraiser to museums & insurance companies in antiques & art (area of specialty Northwest Coast Indian art), 1975 to date. **AFFIL:** Canadian Museum of Civilization (Trustee 1990-95); Elizabeth Foundation (Founding Mbr.; Sec.); White Rock Historical Society (Pres. & Dir. 1976-92); White Rock Festival of Strings (Dir. 1987-90); Rivers Canada; Univ. of British Columbia Museum of Anthropology (Advisory Committee); Vancouver Museum Commission (Commissioner); Surrey Museum (Advisory Committee). **COMMENT:** *"In order to achieve maximum results in my life I have integrated social, economic, political, and cultural endeavours."*

Elliot, Dawn, B.S.W. ■■ ♡ $

President, D.S. ELLIOT & ASSOCIATES INC. (non-profit mgmt consultant), 161 Manse Rd., Scarborough, ON M1E 3V2 (416) 284-9277, FAX 284-9458, EMAIL 73671.1751@compuserve.com. Born Ont. 1954. m. Stewart Elliot. 4 ch. Loralee, Lance, Jeremy, William. **EDUC:** Ryerson Polytechnical Institute, B.S.W.(Social Work) 1979. **CAREER:** Consultant, D.S. Elliot & Associates Inc., 1979 to date; Dir., Admin. & Resource Dev., St. Christopher House, Toronto, 1980-88. **DIRECTOR:** D.S. Elliot & Associates Inc. **AFFIL:** Lupus Canada (Sec.); Ontario Lupus Association (VP); The Canadian Women's Foundation (founder; Dir.); Ability OnLine (Dir.; Chief Host); Ontario Coll. of Professional Social Workers; Ontario Association of Professional Social Workers. **HONS:** Woman of Distinction for community svc., YWCA, 1992; Donna Chu Award for community svc., 1992. **INTERESTS:** camping; music; canoeing. **COMMENT:** *"As a woman with Lupus, I have learned to balance my entire career—volunteer work, family life and livelihood—to fit around my disability."*

Elliott, Mary Anne ■ $

Senior Vice-President, Corporate Services, THE MUTUAL LIFE ASSURANCE COMPANY OF CANADA, 227 King St. S., Waterloo, ON N2J 4C5 (519) 888-3472, FAX 888-3899. Born Toronto 1955. m. Brad. 2 ch. **EDUC:** Univ. of Toronto, B.Comm. 1978. **CAREER:** Mgr, Work-Out & Customer Satisfaction, G.E. Canada, 1978-91; Mgr, Fin., G.E. Plastics Canada, 1989-91. **DIRECTOR:** The Mutual Group (US); The Mutual Trust Company.

Elliott, Shirley Burnham, B.A.,M.A., S.B. 📖 ✎ 📜

Librarian. 15 Queen St., Box 342, Wolfville, NS B0P 1X0. Born Wolfville, N.S. 1916. **EDUC:** Acadia Univ., B.A.(English) 1937, M.A.(English) 1939; Simmons Coll., S.B.(Lib. Sci.) 1940. **CAREER:** Ref. Asst., Brookline Public Library, MA, 1940-46; Asst. Librarian, Univ. of Rhode Island, 1946-49; Asst. Ed., Canadian Library Association, 1949-50; Chief Librarian, Colchester-East Hants Regional Library, 1950-54; Legislative Librarian, Prov. of N.S., 1954-82. **SELECTED PUBLICATIONS:** *Province House* (1966); *Nova Scotia Book of Days* (1980); *The Legislative Assembly of Nova Scotia, 1758-1983*, A Biographical Directory (1984); *Nova Scotia in London, A History of its Agents General, 1762-1988* (1988); contributor to the *Dictionary of Canadian Biography*. **AFFIL:** Atlantic Provinces Library Association; Bibliographical Society of Canada; Heritage Trust of N.S.; Royal Nova Scotia Historical Society; Canadian Federation of University Women. **HONS:** Merit Award, Atlantic Provinces Library Association, 1981; Merit Award, CASLIS, 1988; Commemorative Medal for the 125th Anniversary of the Confederation of Canada; D.C.L.(Hon.), Acadia Univ., 1984; LL.D.(Hon.), Dalhousie Univ., 1986. **INTERESTS:** reading; travel; community volunteer work (particularly dealing with libraries & books). **COMMENT:** *"The initial establishment of the Colchester-East Hants Regional Library and the organization of the Nova Scotia Legislative Library from an uncatalogued collection of 40,000 volumes to a functioning institution."*

Elliston, Inez, B.A.,M.Ed.,Ph.D. 🍁 🎓 ✋

Career and Life Planning Consultant. National Director, "BUILDING THE BRIDGES TO PROSPERITY" (a foundation of CCMIE/CCEMI dedicated to youth training & development). Past President, CANADIAN COUNCIL FOR MULTICULTURAL AND INTERCULTURAL EDUCATION/CONSEIL CANADIEN POUR L'ÉDUCATION MULTICULTURELLE ET INTERCULTURELLE. s. **EDUC:** Univ. of the West Indies, Diploma in Educ. 1962; London Univ., B.A. 1961; Boston Univ., M.Ed.(Counselling Psych.) 1964; Univ. of Toronto, Ph.D.(Educ.) 1976. **CAREER:** Educ.

Officer, Ministry of Educ. & Training, Ont.; Coord., Multicultural & Race-Rel'ns, Bd. of Educ., 1987-92; Teacher/Administrator, Bd. of Educ., 1975 to date; Pres., CCMIE/CCEMI, 1993-95; Past Pres. 1995 to date; Educ. Officer: Special Proj., Ministry of Educ. & Training, 1994-95; Nat'l Dir., "Building the Bridges to Prosperity." SELECTED PUBLICATIONS: *Visible Minorities and Employment in Canadian Schools: Strategies for Affirmative Action*, with P. McCreath (1986); "Multicultural Centres: A Focus for Intercultural Learning" in *Multiculturalism in Canada, Social and Educational Perspectives*, ed. by Ronald J. Samuda *et al* (Toronto: Allyn and Bacon Inc., 1984); "Counselling West Indian Immigrants: Issues and Answers" in *Intercultural Counselling*, ed. by Ronald J. Samuda & Aaron Wolfgang (Toronto: C.J. Hogrefe, 1985); "Guidelines for Training Students in Race Relations" in *Multicultural Education Programs and Methods*, ed. by Ronald J. Samuda & Shiu Kong (Toronto: Intercultural Social Science Publishing, 1986); "Reforming Education for Diversity" in *Multicultural Education: The Challenges and the Future*, ed. Keith McLeod (State of the Art National Study Report #4, 1996); other papers & publications. AFFIL: Ontario Multicultural Association/AssociationMulticulturelle de l'Ontario (Dir.; Pres. 1991-93); International Association for Intercultural Educations; Association for Supervision & Curriculum Development; Council for Exceptional Children; Ontario Secondary School Teachers' Federation. HONS: 15-yr. volunteer service award, Ont. Ministry of Citizenship, 1987; Citation for Citizenship, Gov't of Canada, 1989; Outstanding Contribution Award, CCMIE, 1990; various other awards. INTERESTS: youth leadership dev.; cultural events. MISC: Co-Chair, CCMIE/CCEMI 5th Nat'l Conference on Multiculturalism, Intercultural & Anti-racism Educ., Vancouver, 1993; numerous lectures & conference presentations, incl. Int'l Conferences of Principals & of School Trustees, 1994 & 1995. COMMENT: *"Teacher, administrator, community development educator, writer, researcher and public speaker whose contributions are well known locally and nationally. Energetic, strong leadership qualities. Commitment to citizenship education and social justice."*

ElMaraghy, Hoda A., B.Sc.,M.Sc., Ph.D. 🐿 ❀ ♿

Dean of Engineering, UNIVERSITY OF WINDSOR, Essex Hall, 401 Sunset Ave., Rm. 242, Windsor, ON N9B 3P4 (519) 253-4232, ext. 2566, FAX 973-7053, EMAIL hae@ims.uwindsor.ca. m. Dr. Waguih ElMaraghy. 2 ch. EDUC: Cairo

Univ., B.Sc.(Mech. Eng.) 1967; McMaster Univ., M.Sc.(Mech. Eng.) 1972, Ph.D.(Mech. Eng.) 1976; Association of Professional Engineers of Ontario, Specialist Designation (CAD/CAM) 1985. CAREER: CAD/CAM Consultant, U.N., Summer 1982; CAD/CAM Consultant, Westinghouse Canada, 1982-83; Prof., Dept. of Mech. Eng., McMaster Univ., 1976-94; Assoc. Mbr., Dept. of Computer Sci. & Systems, McMaster Univ., 1986-94; Dir., Centre for Flexible Mfg Research & Dev., McMaster Univ., 1986-94; Dir., Intelligent Mfg Systems Centre, Univ. of Windsor, 1994 to date; Dean of Eng., Prof. of Mech. & Industrial Eng., 1994 to date. SELECTED PUBLICATIONS: "A Knowledge-Based Synthesizer for Flexible Manufacturing Systems," with T. Ravi (*CIRP Journal of Manufacturing Systems* 1991); "Dynamic Coordination of Multiple Robot Arms with Flexible Joints," with K.P. Jankowski (*International Journal of Robotics Research* 1993); "A Concurrent Engineering Approach to Robust Product Design," with M.H. Gadallah (*Concurrent Engineering Research Journal* 1994); "GAPP: A Generative Assembly Process Planner," with L. Laperriere (*Journal of Manufacturing Systems*, vol.15/no.4, pp.282-293); "Data Fitting using Dual Kringer and Genetic Algorithms," with A. Limaiem, A. Nassef (*CIRP Annals*, Vol.45/1/1996, pp.129-134); "Constraint Formulation for Invariant Hybrid Position/Force Control of Robots," with K. Jankowski (*Transactions of the ASME, Journal of Dynamic Systems, Measurements and Control*, Vol. 188, pp. 290-299); numerous other publications. EDIT: serves or has served on the ed. bds. of 4 refereed journals. AFFIL: Natural Sciences & Engineering Research Council; Ontario Premier's Council Project on Innovation & Entrepreneurship; Technology Ontario (Scientific Assessment Panel, Ontario's Research Industry Program); Institute for Robotics & Intelligent Systems (Principal Investigator & Proj. Leader; Assoc. Dir., Mgmt Bd. 1992-94); Manufacturing Research Corporation of Ontario (Principal Investigator); Flexible Manufacturing Centre (Dir.); Professional Engineers Ontario; Institute of Electrical & Electronics Engineers; Canadian Society of Mechanical Engineers (Fellow); International Institute for Production Engineering Research (CIRP) (Chair, Scientific Tech. Committee on Assembly); American Society of Mechanical Engineers; Society of Manufacturing Engineers. HONS: Woman of the Year, "Women in the Workplace" category, City of Hamilton, 1990; APEO Medal in R.&D., 1992. INTERESTS: intelligent automation; robotics; assembly; flexible mfg. MISC: 1st woman elected to CIRP since its inception in

1950; serves or has served on various organizing committees of refereed conferences & on grant selection committees; 1st woman Dean of Eng. in Canada, 1994. COMMENT: *"Dr. ElMaraghy has pioneered in making flexibility and adaptability important concepts in designing, fabricating and assembling products. These elements are now crucial to manufacturing competitiveness."*

Elton, Heather, B.F.A. ■ 📖 ⊗ ✎
Freelance Editor and Writer. 135 - 26th Ave. S.W., Ste. 3, Calgary, AB T2S 0M2 (403) 288-5780. Editor, BANFF CENTRE PRESS. Born Calgary 1957. cl. Kevin Brooker. EDUC: Concordia Univ., B.F.A.(Theatre) 1979. CAREER: Publisher & Ed., *Last Issue Magazine*, 1983-87; various capacities on feature film sets, for various companies, incl. Prod. Asst. & Third A.D., in Montreal, N.Y., Vancouver & Calgary, 1977-82; Publishing Consultant, Environmental Design Fac., Univ. of Calgary, Sept.-Dec. 1987; Contributing Ed., *Theatrum*, 1987-95; Publisher & Ed., *Dance Connection*. SELECTED PUBLICATIONS: essays, features & reviews for *Theatrum*, *High Performance*, *C Magazine*, *Dance Connection*, *Last Issue* & *Vanguard*. EXHIBITIONS: photography & videos exhibited in various art galleries across Canada & UK. AFFIL: Canadian Magazine Publishers' Association; Alberta Magazine Publishers' Association (Dir.). HONS: Queen Elizabeth Scholarship; First Year Fine Arts Scholarship, Concordia Univ.; Dean's List, Concordia Univ. INTERESTS: travel; backcountry skiing. MISC: photography credits include *Saturday Night*, *Western Living*, & *Flare*; recipient of various grants & fellowships. COMMENT: *"Of art, Heather Elton believes profoundly in its transformative power and its ability to originate in unexpected places. As such she is a leading exponent of culture in the Canadian West."*

Embleton, Sheila Margaret, B.Sc.,M.Sc., Ph.D. 🎓 📖
Associate Professor, Department of Language, Literatures and Linguistics, YORK UNIVERSITY, 4700 Keele St., North York, ON M3J 1P3 (416) 736-5260, ext. 22566, EMAIL embleton@yorku.ca. Born Ottawa 1954 1 ch. Anne. EDUC: Univ. of Toronto, B.Sc. 1975, M.Sc. 1976, Ph.D. 1981. CAREER: Sessional Lecturer, Dept. of Languages, Literatures & Linguistics, York Univ., 1980-81; Sessional Asst. Prof., 1981-82; Asst. Prof., Grad. Program in Interdisciplinary Studies, 1983-84; Asst. Prof., Dept. of Languages, Literatures & Linguistics, York Univ., 1982-84; Assoc. Prof., Grad. Program in Interdisciplinary Studies, 1984-87; Vis-

iting Scholar, Dept. of Linguistics, Univ. of California at L.A., 1986-87 & 1994; Fellow, Bethune Coll., 1986-88; Visiting Prof., Vilém Mathesius Centre, Charles Univ., Prague, 1994; Assoc. Prof., Dept. of Languages, Literatures & Linguistics, York Univ., 1984 to date; Assoc. Dean, Fac. of Arts, 1994-97. SELECTED PUBLICATIONS: *Statistics in Historical Linguistics* (Bochum: Brockmeyer Verlag, 1986); "Mathematical Methods of Genetic Classification" in *Sprung From Some Common Source: Investigations into the Prehistory of Languages* (1991); "Lexicostatistics applied to the Germanic, Romance, and Wakashan families" (*Word* April, 1985); "On the Origin of Suomi, Finland" (*Scandinavian-Canadian Studies* vol. 7 1994). EDIT: Review Ed. & mbr. of Ed. Bd., *Word*, 1989 to date; Ed. Bd., *Onomastica Canadiana*, 1989 to date; Assoc. Ed., *Diachronica*, 1991 to date; Advisory Ed. Bd., Amsterdam Classics in Linguistics book series, 1993 to date; Assoc. Ed. & Mbr. of Ed. Bd., *Journal of Quantitative Linguistics*, 1993 to date; Ed. Bd., *Musikometrika*, 1994 to date; Bd., Intercontinental Dictionary Series, 1994 to date. AFFIL: Canadian Society for the Study of Names; Finno-Ugric Studies Association of Canada; International Society for Historical Linguistics; American Name Society; Canadian Linguistic Association; Linguistic Society of America; Linguistic Association of Canada & the U.S.; International Linguistic Association; Atlantic Provinces Linguistic Association; Association for the Advancement of Scandinavian Studies in Canada; International Council of Onomastic Sciences; Canadian Friends of Finland; Canadian Friends of Finland Education Foundation. HONS: Queen Elizabeth II Scholarship, 1979-80; Gov.-General's Gold Medal, 1975; Mary H. Beatty Scholarship, 1971-75; Dickson-Cartwright 3TO Scholarship, 1974-75; Archibald Young Scholarship, 1973-74; Dr. Harold C. Parsons Scholarship, 1972-73; Colling Scholarship, 1972-73. MISC: recipient of various grants & fellowships; conference presentations; referee for various journals.

Emilio, Alison ⚘ 💲 ⊗
Toronto Film Commissioner and Marketing Agent, ONTARIO FILM DEVELOPMENT CORPORATION, Raleigh Studios, 650 North Bronson Ave., Bungalow 130, Los Angeles, CA 90004 (213) 960-4787, FAX 960-4786. Manager/Director. EDUC: Ryerson Polytechnic Univ., Film & Photographic Arts; York Univ., Film/English Studies. CAREER: Dir. of Advtg, Publicity & Promo., Norstar Releasing, Toronto, 1983-85; Dir. of Nat'l Advtg & Publicity, Atlantic Releasing, N.Y., 1985-87; Dir. of Publicity & Promo., Lorimar Film Entertain-

ment, Toronto, 1987-88; Sr. VP, Mktg & Publicity, New Line Cinema Corporation, N.Y./L.A., 1988-92; Toronto Film Commissioner, Mktg Agent, Ontario Film Development Corporation, L.A., 1992 to date. SELECTED CREDITS: Producer, *Dinner at Fred's* (Handmade Films/Paragon); Creative Consultant (on screen credit) on 3 feature films: *Heavy, Spanking the Monkey* & *Memory Run* (Meridian Entertainment); Prod., *Crash & Burn–The Freddy Kreuger Story*, MTV; Prod., *Women Make Movies*, Toronto Women in Film; Prod., Special Report Television (SRTV) with Joan Lunden, Whittle Communications, Channel One. AFFIL: Academy of Canadian Cinema & Television; Ted Danson's American Oceans Campaign (Advisory Bd; Co-Chair, Mktg Committee). MISC: *Heavy* won the Special Jury Prize, Sundance 1995 Film Festival; *Spanking the Monkey* won the Audience Award, Sundance 1994 Film Festival.

Empey, Charlotte E. ■■ / ▥

Editor, *Modern Woman* magazine, MACLEAN HUNTER PUBLISHING LIMITED, 777 Bay St., 8th Fl., Toronto, ON M5W 1A7 (416) 596-5824, FAX 593-3197. Born Hamilton, Ont. 1950. m. Larry Grzebinski. 1 ch. Ashley Jones. EDUC: Humber Coll., Journalism 1974. CAREER: Health & Beauty Editor, *Flare* magazine, Maclean Hunter Publishing, 1979-82; Sr. Communications Officer, City of Toronto, 1982-85; Creative Dir., MacLaren Advertising, 1985-87; Editor, *Images* & *HealthWatch* magazines, Telemedia Publishing, 1987-89; Ed., *Expression* magazine, 1989; Fashion & Beauty Dir., *Canadian Living* magazine, 1989-90; Exec. Ed., Svcs, *Chatelaine* magazine, Maclean Hunter Publishing, 1990-91; Chair, Continuing Educ., Applied Arts & Creative Arts, & Prof., Sch. of Journalism, Humber Coll. of Applied Arts & Technology, 1992-93; Founding Editor, *Modern Woman* magazine, Maclean Hunter Publishing, 1992 to date. SELECTED CREDITS: regular guest, *Real Life Show*, The Life Network; frequent appearances on radio talk shows across Canada. AFFIL: Canadian Society of Magazine Editors (VP). HONS: National Magazine Award. MISC: was Communications Consultant, City of Toronto Olympic Task Force; speaker, community groups & professional women's organizations. COMMENT: *"This has been my credo since I was about 18—and it has served me well, personally and professionally: 'Never retreat, never explain, never apologize - get the thing done and let them howl'* — *Nellie McClung."*

Eng, Brenda, B.S.N.,M.N. ■■ ⊕ ○

Founder and Clinical Specialist, CANUCK PLACE (hospice for children), 1690 Matthews Ave., Vancouver, BC V6J 2T2 (604) 731-4847, FAX 739-4376. EDUC: Univ. of British Columbia, Sch. of Nursing, B.S.N. 1984; Univ. of Washington, Sch. of Nursing, M.N.(Clinical Specialist, Pediatric Oncology) 1988. CAREER: Gen. Duty Nurse, Pediatric Oncology-Hematology Unit, B.C. Children's Hospital, Vancouver, 1984-86; Gen. Duty Nurse (per diem), 1986 to date; Community Health Nurse, City of Vancouver Health Dept., 1988-89; clinical internship, Helen House, hospice for children, Oxford, England, Aug.-Dec. 1988; Nursing Consultant, Nursing Respite Program, Community Support & Family Health, Ministry of Health, Burnaby, B.C., 1989-90; Research Asst., Div. of Nursing, B.C. Children's Hospital, 1990-92; Assoc., Program & Dev., Canuck Place, 1993-94; Clinical Specialist, 1994 to date. SELECTED PUBLICATIONS: author/co-author, many articles incl.: "Special issues in bereavement and staff support" in D. Doyle, G. Hanks & N. McDonald (eds.), 2nd Edition, *Oxford Textbook of Palliative Medicine* (Oxford: Oxford Univ. Press, 1995); "Pediatric palliative care" (*Progressive Palliative Care: A British Journal for Health Care Professionals*, 1995). AFFIL: Sigma Theta Tau int'l hon. society of nursing, Xi Beta chpt., Univ. of B.C. & Psi chpt., Univ. of Washington; Canadian Nurses' Foundation; Children's Hospice International; Pediatric Nurses' Group; Oncology Nursing Society; Association of Pediatric Oncology Nurses; B.C. Oncology Nursing Interest Group; Canadian Nurses' Association; Registered Nurses' Association of B.C.; Association for the Care of Children's Health (lifetime mbr.); Vancouver Palliative Care Coordinating Group, Canadian Cancer Society, Vancouver (Camp Nurse/Head Nurse, Camp Goodtimes, & Chair, Childhood & Family Program, Patient Svcs, B.C./Yukon Div. 1993 to date). HONS: Univ. of B.C. scholarship, 1981; Eleanor Jean Martin Nursing Award, Canadian Nurses' Foundation/Univ. of Washington Fellowship, 1986-87; Maurice Legault Fellowship, Canadian Cancer Society/Adria Grad. Scholarship, Oncology Nursing Foundation/Univ. of Washington Fellowship, 1987-88; Outstanding Master's Student Award for academic achievement, Univ. of Washington, 1988; Young Alumnus Award, Univ. of B.C. Nursing Alumni Div., 1993; Humanitarian Award, Ridge Hospital Foundation, 1994; Award of Excellence, Association of Pediatric Oncology Nurses, 1995. MISC: numerous presentations; special skills include children's art & drawings, kinetic family drawings with children who have cancer, puppet therapy, folk art painting, & pet therapy. COMMENT: *"Brenda Eng is clinical spe-*

cialist and founder of Canuck Place, the first free-standing hospice for children in North America."

Engel, Joyce, B.Ed.,M.Ed. ⌘ ⊕
Dean, Division of Applied Sciences, MEDICINE HAT COLLEGE, 299 College Dr. S.E., Medicine Hat, AB T1A 3Y6 (403) 529-3905, FAX 529-2437. Born Calgary. m. Stan. 5 ch. **EDUC:** Galt Sch. of Nursing, Nursing Diploma 1971; Univ. of Calgary, B.Ed. 1978, M.Ed. 1985, Ph.D. in progress. **CAREER:** Clinical Nurse in community health, psychiatry & medicine, 1971-78; Instructor of Nursing, Foothills Hospital Sch. of Nursing, 1978-79; Dir. of Educ., Medicine Hat & District Hospital, 1979-81; Instructor of Nursing, Medicine Hat Coll., 1981-86; Asst. Prof. of Nursing & Lecturer, Univ. of Lethbridge, 1987-92; Dean of Health & Allied Sciences, Medicine Hat Coll., 1992 to date. **SELECTED PUBLICATIONS:** various articles, chapters & presentations incl.: "Diagnostic and laboratory tests (all sections)," *Principles and Practice of Adult Health Nursing,* Ed. P. Beare & J. Meyers (St. Louis: C.V. Mosby, 1993); *Pocket Guide to Pediatric Health Assessment* (St. Louis: C.V. Mosby, 1993); *Instructor's Manual for Principles and Practice of Adult Health Nursing* (St. Louis: C.V. Mosby, 1991). **AFFIL:** Health Workforce Education Project Advisory Committee; Alberta Nurse Educator Administrator (ANEA) group; Committee on Nursing Education (Coll. Rep.); Alberta Association of Registered Nurses (various exec. positions); Regional Alberta Mental Health Committee (AARN Rep. 1979-80); Holy Cross Staff Nurses' Association (V-Chair 1973-74); Church Vestry (Mbr. 1984-85). **HONS:** Heritage of Service Award for Overall Nursing Excellence, 1994; nominated, Instructor of the Year, 1982, 1983; Gold Medal for gen. proficiency in nursing class, 1971. **INTERESTS:** family; singing; drawing; writing; bowling. **MISC:** has been involved in research & workshop presentations; NSERC small research grants, 1987, 1989. **COMMENT:** *"I view myself as energetic, enthusiastic, collegial, innovative, creative, and a professional who has a vision of nursing and of education. I have been fortunate to be able to translate these skills into rearing children; teaching, leading and caring for others; and into articulating a vision of nursing and health care. I believe that I am seen as a credible professional, not only by local nurses, but provincially and by professionals from other disciplines."*

Engel, June, B.Sc.,M.Sc.,Ph.D. ⌘ ⊕ ▯
Editor, HEALTH NEWS, University of Toronto, Medical Faculty, Medical Science Bldg.,

Toronto, ON M5S 1A8 (416) 978-5411, FAX 978-1774. Born London, UK 1930. 1 ch. **EDUC:** Univ. of London, B.Sc. 1950; University Coll., M.Sc. 1951, Ph.D. 1954. **CAREER:** Research Fellow, McGill Univ., 1957-59; Educ. Officer & Science Advisor to the BBC, & later Rediffusion TV, 1959-68; teaching (high sch. Biol.), writing & medical journalism, TV/film production for CBC, National Film Board of Canada & TVOntario, 1968-72; univ. lecturer, writer, medical journalist, TV Prod., on staff at the Univ. of Toronto's Fac. of Medicine, 1972-83; Writer, Ed., & supervisor of *Health News,* 1983 to date. **SELECTED CREDITS:** *Darwin and Evolution,* 13-part series, CBC Radio; *Infection and Immunity,* NFB; *Cosmic Zoom,* NFB. **SELECTED PUBLICATIONS:** *The Stuff of Life* (Dent & Co., 1964); *The Complete Canadian Health Guide* (Key Porter, 1993); *The Complete Breast Book* (Key Porter, 1996); contributed articles to *New Scientist* (1959-68); "We all begin female" (*Chatelaine,* 1976); "Latest news in mammography" (*Medical Post,* 1979); "Food additives" (*Chatelaine,* 1980); "Superbaby Kit: breeding healthier basics" (*Cinemedie,* 1981); numerous other publications. **HONS:** Media Award, The American Medical Association, for *African Histoplasmosis,* video, 1973; Canadian Science Writing Award, "How men react to women's operations" (*Chatelaine*), 1979; AAMC Award, American Association of Medical Colleges, "Melanoma" (*Health News*), 1988; Media award, Canadian Breast Cancer Foundation, 2 articles on breast cancer (*Health News*), 1991; Enid MacLeod Award for work (written & broadcast) on women's health issues, Federation of Medical Women of Canada, 1996. **INTERESTS:** music; art; swimming; sport; hiking; grandchildren; theatre. **MISC:** recipient of various grants. **COMMENT:** *"Dedicated to increasing awareness of science in young people and public at large, in promoting more self responsibility in looking after health and wellness."*

English, Hilde, B.A.,LL.B. ⌷
Partner, WHITE JENKINS DUNCAN & OSTNER, Waterloo, ON N2J 4B5 (519) 886-3440, FAX 886-8651. Born Germany. m. John English. 1 ch. Jonathan. **EDUC:** Univ. of Waterloo, B.A. (Languages) 1967; Univ. of Western Ontario, LL.B. 1974. **BAR:** Ont., 1975. **CAREER:** practice of law, White Jenkins Duncan & Ostner, 1975 to date; Ptnr, 1979 to date. **AFFIL:** Kitchener-Waterloo Chamber of Commerce (Dir.; VP 1991-93); Grand River Conservation Foundation (Bd.); Canadian Bar Association (Dir., Ont. 1990-94; V-Chair, Judges' Spouses & Judges' Salaries Pensions Committee); Cana-

dian Advocates' Society (Dir. 1990-94; Mbr.); Canadian Institute of International Affairs (Dir. Kitchener-Waterloo Branch); Clay and Glass Museum (Dir.); Opera Ontario (Dir.). **INTERESTS:** cooking; travelling; politics. **COMMENT:** *"I am a lawyer specializing in civil litigation, with particular specialization in family and libel law."*

Ens, Rosa Freda ■ ♡

Executive Director, VANCOUVER POLICE & NATIVE LIAISON SOCIETY, 324 Main St., Vancouver, BC V6A 2T2 (604) 687-8411, FAX 682-2967. Born Prince Rupert, B.C. 1957. s. 2 ch. Juanita, Billy. **EDUC:** Vancouver Native Education Centre, GED Certificate 1990; Certificate (Family Violence & Community Counselling) 1990. **AFFIL:** Canadian Association of Chiefs of Police (Policing with Aboriginal Peoples Sub-Committee); Minister's Advisory Council on Income Assistance; Vancouver Wife Assault Committee; Justice Sub-Committee; Native Women's Issues Sub-Committee. **HONS:** 1989/90 Achievement Award, Native Family & Community Counselling, Native Education Centre, Vancouver, B.C. **INTERESTS:** bike riding; long walks; doing puzzles; reading; spending time with her children, Billy & Juanita. **MISC:** on the planning committees for "Forum on Wife Assault" in Native Communities conference & "Justice Extending the Vision" conference on victimization & recovery; panel participant in the Criminal Justice System's Conference on Violence Against Women in Relationships; provided input for the B.C. Association on Specialized Victim Assistance Programs Records Mgmt Guidelines Training & the Ministry of the Attorney General's Sexual Assault Policy Aboriginal Discussion Group. **COMMENT:** *"I am a single parent of two beautiful children. Since leaving my husband, I returned to school, attained my GED and a certificate in Counselling. Spent two years on welfare, one year as a student. Began working as a support worker for two years and for the past year, Executive Director of the Vancouver Police & Native Liaison Society."*

Enser, Maureen Bronwyn ✊ $

Executive Director, URBAN DEVELOPMENT INSTITUTE, 717 W. Pender St., 3rd Fl., Vancouver, BC V6C 1G9 (604) 669-9585, FAX 689-8691. Managing Director, INTERNATIONAL CENTRE FOR SUSTAINABLE CITIES FOUNDATION. Born Winnipeg 1948. d. 2 ch. Allison, Stephen. **EDUC:** Ohio State Univ. (Wright State), Pol. Sci. 1968. **CAREER:** Asst. to the Min. of Environment; Canadian Team mbr., U.N. FAO Conference; Liaison Officer to Jacques Cousteau (on special assignment to the Cdn Gov't); Exec. Dir., Urban Development Institute, Pacific Region & Canada. **SELECTED PUBLICATIONS:** *Planning for Tomorrow: The Next Generation* (1992); co-authored a newspaper column in Nelson, B.C.; various articles on urban dev. issues, bus. & educ. **AFFIL:** International Centre for Sustainable Cities Foundation (Mng Dir.); Building Safety Advisory Council, Prov. of B.C.; Minister's Advisory Committee on Affordable Housing, Prov. of B.C.; Univ. of British Columbia (Advisory Bd., Canadian Real Estate Research Bureau); Lambda Alpha; Vancouver Resource Society for the Physically Disabled (Treas.; Past Pres.); Canadian Society of Association Executives; American Society of Association Executives; British Urban Renewal Institute; Urban Land Institute. **INTERESTS:** travel; city growth & planning issues; ancient history; reading; gardening; tennis. **COMMENT:** *"Ms. Enser is recognized as an authority on establishing partnerships for resolving urban issues and serves on numerous government and private sector committees dealing with urban planning and development, social and economic issues."*

Epp, Juanita Ross, B.Ed.,M.Ed.,Ph.D. 🎓

Associate Professor of Education, LAKEHEAD UNIVERSITY, Thunder Bay, ON P7B 5EI (807) 343-8722, FAX 344-6807, EMAIL juanita.epp@lakeheadu.ca. Born Lloydminster, Sask. 1949. m. Walter Epp. 3 ch. Nathan, Anthony, Jonathan. **EDUC:** Univ. of Saskatchewan, B.Ed. 1973, M.Ed. 1981, Ph.D. 1990. **CAREER:** Teacher, Canada, former Yugoslavia, & UK, 1968-90; Asst. Prof., Educ. Admin., 1990-91; Assoc. Dir., Saskatchewan Educational Leadership Unit, 1990-91; Visiting Prof., Univ. of Victoria, 1991; Asst. Prof. of Educ., Lakehead Univ., 1991-94; Assoc. Prof. of Educ., 1994 to date. **SELECTED PUBLICATIONS:** "Systematic Violence: How Schools Hurt Children" (Falmer Press); "Systematic Violence in Education: Promise Broken," (SUNY); "Strategies for Promoting Participation" (*Education Canada* 1993); "Gender Equity" (The NASSP Bulletin 1993); "Leadership Qualities Valued in Principal Selection" (*Canadian School Executive* 1993); "Pseudo-participation, Participation, and Shared Governance" (*The Canadian Journal of Educational Administration and Foundations*, 1993); "Re-examining Androcentric Bias in the Educational Administration Quarterly" (*Educational Administration Quarterly* 1994); "Women's perceptions of master's level education administration programs" (*Canadian Journal of Higher Education* 1994); various other publications; numerous conference papers. **EDIT:** Ed. Bd., *Canadian Journal of Educational Administration and Policy*, electronic journal, 1994. AFFIL: Canadian Association for the Study of Women in Education (Past Pres.); Ontario Council of Univ. Fac. Associations (Status of Women Committee). HONS: Landsdown Fellowship Award, Ph.D. Level, 1989; Saskatchewan Teachers' Federation Scholarship, 1990; Univ. of Saskatchewan Scholarship, 1988-90. MISC: speaker & workshop leader in democratic leadership, sch. improvement, inclusive pedagogy; part of int'l research team studying sch. effectiveness. COMMENT: *"Teacher (in Canada, Yugoslavia and UK) turned researcher and professor at Lakehead University specializing in gender issues, democratic leadership styles, school improvement, child advocacy, inclusive pedagogy and international studies."*

Epperly, Elizabeth ■ ■ ⊲ 🕮

President, UNIVERSITY OF PRINCE EDWARD ISLAND, PE, EMAIL eepperly@upei.ca. CAREER: Prof. of English, specialist in Victorian Literature; former Chair of English, Memorial Univ. of Newfoundland; 1st woman Pres., Univ. of P.E.I.; founder, L.M. Montgomery Institute, Univ. of P.E.I. SELECTED PUBLICATIONS: *The Fragrance of Sweetgrass: L.M. Montgomery's Heroines and the Pursuit of Romance* (Univ. of Toronto Press).

Erb-Campbell, Heather Lynn ◐ ⊕ ♂

Executive Director, HEART AND STROKE FOUNDATION OF NEW BRUNSWICK, 110 Crown St., Ste. 340, Saint John, NB E2L 2X7 (506) 634-1620, FAX 648-0098. Born Saint John 1956. m. Malcolm Albert Campbell. EDUC: Saint John Sch. of Nursing, R.N. 1976; McMaster Univ., Nurse Practitioner (NP) 1979; Dalhousie Univ., Bus. Mgmt Certificate 1989. CAREER: Emergency Room Nurse, Saint John Hospital, 1976-78; Emergency Cardiac Care Coord., Heart & Stroke Foundation of N.B., 1980-85; Dir. of Educ., 1985-93; Exec. Dir., 1993 to date. SELECTED PUBLICATIONS: "Position Statement–Emergency Cardiac Care Guidelines" (*Canadian Medical Association Journal*, Sept. 1993); *CPR Resource for Basic Life Support* (Heart & Stroke Foundation of Canada, 1993); script & content for "CPR–You Can Do It!" (Heart & Stroke Foundation of Canada, video, 1994). AFFIL: Nurses' Association of N.B.; Ontario Coll. of Nurses. INTERESTS: kayaking; cross-country skiing; piano. COMMENT: *"High achiever, energetic, self-motivated, committed to excellence in myself and others, knowledgeable in my field. First Emergency Nurse Practitioner in Canada. One of the pioneers in the development of CPR (cardiopulmonary resuscitation) network in Canada. Committed to the work of the Foundation."*

Eriksen, Maria, B.A.,M.A.,Ph.D. ■ ■ ⊕☺♡

Psychologist, ERIKSEN & WEBB (private practice as psychotherapist), 933 - 17th Ave. S.W., Ste. 403, Calgary, AB T2T 5R6 (403) 228-4777, FAX 245-1208. EDUC: Galt Sch. of Nursing, Lethbridge, Alta., Diploma in Nursing 1960; Univ. of Calgary, B.A.(Psych.) 1966, M.A.(Psych.) 1967, Ph.D.(Psych.) 1980. CAREER: Pediatrics Nurse, Medicine Hat General Hospital, Medicine Hat, Alta., 1960-63; Psychologist & Nursing Instructor, Calgary General Hospital, 1968-76; Acting Head, Dept. of Psych., 1975-77; private practice, Clinical Psych., M.K. Eriksen & Associates, 1977; Coord., Employee Assistance Program, City of Calgary, 1982-85; Sr. Organizational Analyst, 1985-86; Adjunct Prof, Fac. of Gen. Studies, Univ. of Calgary, 1992; private practice, Eriksen & Webb. SELECTED PUBLICATIONS: co-author with D. Gibson, "Cardiovascular Change and Mental Task Gradient" (*Psychonomic Science*, Vol. 6(6), 1966); co-author with C.G. Costello, "Heart Rates During Performance of a Mental Task Under Noise Conditions" (*Psychonomic Science*, Vol. 8(10), 1967); "Reality Therapy" (*Journal of Canadian Physiotherapy Association*, 1969); co-author with L. Dick, "A Comparison of Therapy Drop-outs and Continuers in Casework Counselling in a Family Service Agency" (*The Social Worker*, 1970); "Rehabilitation Nursing Skills" (*The Canadian Nurse*, May 1975); "The Effect of Women's Issues on Psychology" (*Alberta Psychology*, Vol. 13(4), 1984); co-author with M.R. Webb & V.K. Corfield, *Depression in Women: An Integrated Approach* (paper presented at Psychologists' Association of Alberta 1986 conference & workshop, Oct. 1986). AFFIL: Psychology Association of Alberta (Sec.-Treas. 1986); Legal Education & Action Fund (Pres. 1985); Canadian Psychology Association; YWCA; United Way; Canadian Advisory Council on the Status of Women. HONS: Alberta Achievement Award, Excellence category, 1984; co-recipient, Woman of the Year Award, Health & Fitness, YWCA, Calgary, 1981; several grants. MISC: headed City Council Committee to ensure that employment equity program was implemented; helped found many organizations incl. Legal Education & Action Fund of Alberta, Calgary Status of Women, & Famous 5 Foundation...COMMENT: *"After graduating in 1967 I worked at the Calgary General Hospital for 10 years, then returned to university to complete a PhD. At that time I established a private practice. I've served on the executive of the Psychology Assoc. of Alberta and started an annual conference "Women Helping Women" where women professionals present scholarly papers."*

Ernest, Rosemarie ⊕
Nurse Consultant. 165 Hickson Dr., Kitchener, ON N2B 2H8 (519) 576-1846. Born Dryden, Ont. 1934. d. 3 ch. Suzanne Hess, Paul, Jacqui Blowes. **EDUC:** Conestoga Coll., Diploma (Nursing) 1973, Nursing Certificate (Diabetic Nurse) 1975, Nursing Certificate (Intravenous Nursing) 1980; George Brown Coll., Certificate to Teach Basic & Advanced Foot Care 1987. **CAREER:** Registered Nursing Asst., 1967-73; Rehabilitation Nurse (RNA & RN), 1969-80; Intravenous Nurse (RN), 1980-92; private nursing practice (nursing foot care & entrepreneurial workshops), 1986 to date. **SELECTED PUBLICATIONS:** "Group fosters innovative nurses," co-author (*Registered Nurse Journal*, Oct./Nov. 1993). **AFFIL:** Registered Nurses' Association of Ontario; Coll. of Nurses of Ontario; Canadian Association of Nurses in Independent Practice (Pres. 1993-94); Ontario Association of Nurses in Independent Practice; IODE, Princes Richard & Michael Chapter (volunteer 30 yrs.; present position Regent). **INTERESTS:** curling; health education; travel; piano; singing; acting; sports. **MISC:** past volunteer positions include: Worker, Anselma House (a home for battered women); Camp Nurse, Stanley Park Sr. Public Sch.; Treas., Huntington Park Home & School Association; since 1988, has been providing community visits for nursing students at Conestoga Coll.; as a member of RNAO, was 3 times elected a voting delegate at its AGM as well as a volunteer voting delegate to 3 biennial conventions of the Canadian Nurses' Association. **COMMENT:** *"Successful entrepreneurial nurse; energetic and caring; dedicated and committed; loyal, fair-minded; flexible to change; role model; mentor and consultant–these are all reflective of my personality not only to my professional colleagues, but to my family and friends."*

Etherington, Lois, B.Ed.,M.B.A., Ph.D. 🎓 $
Associate Professor, Faculty of Business Administration, SIMON FRASER UNIVERSITY, Burnaby, BC V5A 1S6 (604) 291-3638, FAX 291-4920, EMAIL ethering@sfu.ca. Born Mundare, Alta. 1932. m. Michael Seals. 2 ch. Leslie, Murray. **EDUC:** Univ. of Alberta, B.Ed. 1956; Univ. of Washington, M.B.A. 1973, Ph.D.(Bus.) 1977. **CAREER:** High Sch. Teacher, Edmonton, Yellowknife, & Cold Lake, Alta., 1956-59; Predoctoral Teaching Assoc., Univ. of Washington, 1973-76; Asst. Prof., 1977-80; Invited Guest Prof., Fac. of Commerce, Nihon Univ., Tokyo, Fall 1979; Visiting Assoc. Prof., Queen's Univ., Fall 1987; Prof., San Francisco State Univ., 1984-85; Asst. Prof., Simon Fraser Univ., 1980-84; Assoc. Prof., 1986 to date. **SELECTED PUBLICATIONS:** *Internal Control in Canadian Corporations: A Management Perspective*, with I. Gordon (Toronto: Canadian Institute of Chartered Accountants & Society of Management Accountants, 1985); *Managing Budget Conflict: A Field Study*, with D. Tjosvold (Society of Management Accountants of Canada, 1992); "Theories and Beliefs About Efficient Markets" (*Mid-Atlantic Journal of Business* 1981); "Establishing a Measure of Airline Preference for Business and Non-Business Travellers," with T. Var (*Journal of Travel Research* 1984); "Institutional Pressures on Accounting Education," with A. Richardson (*Contemporary Issues in Accounting* 1994); various other publications. **EDIT:** Ed. Bd., *Issues in Accounting Education*, 1990 to date; Ed. Bd., *Journal of International Accounting, Auditing and Taxation*, 1994 to date. **AFFIL:** Canadian Academic Accounting Association (VP); American Accounting Association (Int'l Rep. on Exec., Mgmt Section; Cdn Rep., Acctg Behavior & Organizations Section); Pi Beta Phi; Beta Gamma Sigma. **HONS:** Univ. Scholarship in Educ., Univ. of Alberta; Harry Ainlay Scholarship in Educ., Univ. of Alberta; Meritorious Performance & Professional Promise Award, San Francisco State Univ., 1985. **INTERESTS:** research in internal control of organizations; acctg educ.; acctg ethics. **MISC:** recipient of various grants. **COMMENT:** *"Accounting faculty at Simon Fraser University, where she has served as University Senator, head of accounting faculty, SFU faculty Association President, etc. Researches in internal control, accounting ethics, and accounting education."*

Evans, Nancy Remage, B.A.,M.A., Ph.D. ■ ⚛ 🎓
Astrophysicist, SMITHSONIAN ASTROPHYSICAL OBSERVATORY, 60 Garden St., Cambridge, MA 02138, EMAIL nevans@cfa.harvard.edu. Born Mass. 1944. m. Martin G. Evans. 2 ch. **EDUC:** Wellesley Coll., B.A.(Astronomy) 1966; Univ. of Toronto, M.Sc.(Astronomy) 1969, Ph.D. (Astronomy) 1974. **CAREER:** Post-doctoral Research Asst. (part-time), Univ. of Toronto, 1975-82; Asst. Prof., Erindale Coll., Univ. of Toronto, 1982-83; Resident Astronomer, Int'l Ultraviolet Explorer Satellite, 1983-86; Resident Assoc., Univ. of Toronto, 1986-88; Assoc. Scientist, Space Astrophysics Lab, Institute for Space & Terrestrial Science, 1988-91; Adjunct Prof., York Univ., 1988 to date; Asst. Dir., Space Astrophysics Lab, Institute for Space & Terrestrial Science, 1991-94; Astophysicist, AXAF Satellite, Harvard-Smithsonian Center for Astrophysics, 1995 to date. **SELECTED PUBLICATIONS:** numerous. **AFFIL:** Canadian

Astronomical Society; American Astronomical Society; International Astronomical Union; Canadian Association for Women in Science (Treas.). HONS: numerous scholarships as student. COMMENT: *"Active astronomer (grantee in field) particularly in satellite astronomy, including the Hubble Space Telescope."*

Everatt, Ann (née Robertson), B.A. ✿

Director, Program and Staff Development, NORTHERN COLLEGE OF APPLIED ARTS AND TECHNOLOGY, Box 3211, Timmins, ON P4N 8R6 (705) 235-3211, FAX 235-7279, EMAIL everatar@kirk.northernc.on.ca. Born Clydebank, Scotland 1955. m. Robert Everatt. 1 ch. Blaxeny Paige Walin. EDUC: Concordia Univ., B.A.(Adult Educ.); Athabasca Univ., Master of Distance Educ., in progress; Nipissing Univ., M.Ed., in progress. CAREER: Computer Clerk, Iron Ore Company of Canada, 1976-78; Instructor, Thebacha Coll., Tuktoyaktuk, N.W.T., 1978-82; Dir., Calgary Bus. Coll. 1982-86; Mgmt Consultant, Fanshawe Coll., 1986-88; Chair, Mgmt Studies Dept., Arctic Coll., Iqaluit, N.W.T., 1988-91; Dir., Native Studies Dept., Northern Coll., 1992-93; Dir., Program & Staff Dev., 1994 to date. DIRECTOR: Timmins Videoconference Corporation. AFFIL: YMCA, Timmins (Bd. of Dir.; VP 1994); Distance Education Association. HONS: Award for Excellence in Bus. Educ. Partnerships, Prov. & Nat'l, Conference Board of Canada, 1991. INTERESTS: skiing; golf; instructional technology & the pursuit of realizing new means of providing access to college programs to remote areas. MISC: in 1984 was responsible for the establishment of the Calgary Bus. Coll. for Women. COMMENT: *"Born in Scotland and arrived in Canada at age 10. Grew up in Labrador City and attended university in Thunder Bay, Ottawa and Montreal. Spent many years in the high Arctic as an adult educator with the Inuit peoples where a series of training programs were developed by the college to allow the Inuit people to enter the labour market. While at Arctic College was also the NRC representative for the Industrial Research Assistance Program."*

Ewasyshyn, Mary Elizabeth, B.Sc.,Ph.D. ⬡ ⊕

Director of Microbiology and Senior Research Scientist, CONNAUGHT LABORATORIES LTD., Connaught Centre for Biotechnology Research, 1755 Steeles Ave. W., Willowdale, ON M2R 3T4 (416) 667-2800, FAX 661-7960. Born Windsor, Ont. 1955. s. EDUC: Univ. of Windsor, B.Sc.(Biol.) 1977, Ph.D.(Virology) 1983. CAREER: NSERC Postdoctoral Fellow, Connaught Research Institute, 1983-85; Assoc.

Research Scientist, 1985-88; Research Scientist/Group Leader, 1988-89; Asst. Dir., Virology, Connaught Centre for Biotechnology Research, 1992-94; Head & Sr. Research Scientist, 1992-94; Dir., 1994 to date. SELECTED PUBLICATIONS: "Protease Susceptibility of Human A Influenza Virus Polypeptides," with L.R. Sabina *et al* (*Acta Virology* 1981); "Prospects for Immunization Against Respiratory Syncytial Virus," with M.H. Klein (*Vaccine Research* 1993). AFFIL: American Society for Microbiology; American Society for Virology; American Association for the Advancement of Science. HONS: Norah Cleary Scholarship, 1973-77; Nat'l Sciences & Engineering Scholarship, 1977-81. INTERESTS: ballet; theatre; reading. MISC: involved in 4 vaccine-related patent applications. COMMENT: *"As a senior research scientist with a major vaccine manufacturer, my research activities have focused on developing efficacious vaccines capable of protecting infants against viral-induced bronchiolitis and pneumonia. Our integrated project team is striving to produce vaccines that will reduce the mortality and morbidity caused by these viral pathogens."*

F

agan, Christine A. ⚖️

Lawyer, CHALKER, GREEN AND ROWE, 10 Fort William Place, 5th Fl., Box 5939, St. John's, NF A1C 5X4 (709) 722-8735. Born Moncton 1950. EDUC: St. Francis Xavier Univ., B.A.(Soc.) 1972; Univ. of New Brunswick, M.A.(Soc.) 1974, LL.B. 1977. BAR: Nfld., 1978. CAREER: part-time fac., Dept. of Soc., Univ. of New Brunswick & St. Thomas Univ., 1974-76; Course Developer, Memorial Univ. Extension Dept., 1978-79; private practice of law, Chalker, Green and Rowe, 1978 to date; part-time fac. mbr., Fac. of Bus. Admin., Memorial Univ. of Newfoundland, 1979-83; Asst. to City Solicitor, St. John's, 1979-83; Gen. Cnsl, Canadian Offshore Vessel Operators' Association, 1985-88. DIRECTOR: National Life Assurance Company of Canada. AFFIL: Law Society of Newfoundland; Canadian Bar Association; Arbitration & Mediation Institute of Canada Inc.; Panel of Arbitrators accredited by the Newfoundland & Labrador Labour Management Committee; City Arts Jury (Chair); Newfoundland Historic Parks Association (Dir.); Battle Harbour Historic Trust Inc. (Dir.); VOCM Cares Foundation (Dir.); Women's Enterprise Bureau (Dir.); Y.M.C.A. Enterprise Board (Dir.).

Fagnan, Isabel, B.Ec.,M.B.A. 💲

Director, Process and Business Development Sales, AIR CANADA, C.P. 14000, Saint-Laurent, QC H4Y 1H4 (514) 422-5749, FAX 422-5055. Born Montreal 1958. EDUC: McGill Univ., B.Ec. 1983; Univ. of Ottawa, M.B.A. 1987. CAREER: Product Mgr, Info. Technology, Air Canada, 1987-90; Asst. Mgr, Corp. Product - Info. Technology, 1990-91; Principal,

Planning & Bus. Process Redesign, 1991; Mgr, Travel Agency Sales, 1991-93; Dir., Agency Sales, 1993-95; Dir., Process & Bus. Dev. Sales, 1995 to date. **AFFIL:** International Airline Transportation Association (Chrm, Agency Liaison Working Group; Delegate, Mktg Info. Working Group); BSP Canada Steering Panel (Delegate; Advisory Exec. Group); Alliance of Canadian Travel Associations Bd. of Dir.). **HONS:** Employee Performance Award, 1990. **INTERESTS:** classical music; opera; theatre; downhill skiing; swimming; tennis. **COMMENT:** *"A proactive fluently bilingual leader, attacking issues in an effort to find solutions and obtain results with over eight years' experience in sales and information technology."*

Fair, Penny M., C.G.A. $

Proprietor, Penny M. Fair - Certified General Accountant, Box 1122, Yellowknife, NT X1A 2N8 (403) 920-4250, FAX 920-7519. Owner and Secretary-Treasurer, Dolittle Services (1991) Ltd. Born Powell River, B.C. 1962. m. Charles. 1 ch. Ashley. **EDUC:** Certified General Accountants' Association, C.G.A. 1988. **CAREER:** Compt., Saskatoon Wholesale Auto Auction/Shannon Imports, 1984/86; Mgr, MacKay Computing Limited, 1986-89; Sr. Acctnt, Avery, Cooper & Co., 1989-91; Owner & Sec.-Treas., Dolittle Services (1991) Ltd., 1991 to date; Proprietor, Penny M. Fair–Certified General Accountant, 1993 to date. **AFFIL:** Certified General Accountants' Association of the NWT (Pres. 1993-94; VP 1992; Treas. 1990-92; Chair, Prof. Dev. Committee, & Policy & Procedures Committee 1989-90; Chair, Public Practice Committee, 1994-96); Kids' Help Phone Committee (V-Chair); YK Zone Bowling Association (Treas. 1992). **INTERESTS:** sports; crafts; outdoors; winemaking. **COMMENT:** *"I have worked hard to get where I am today and have achieved far more than I ever dreamed."*

Fairbairn, The Hon. Joyce, B.A. 🍁 ✏ ☝

Senator, Leader of the Government in the Senate and Minister with Special Responsibility for Literacy, Government of Canada, The Senate, Rm. 275-S, Ottawa, ON K1A 0A4 (613) 996-4382, FAX (613) 995-3223. Born Lethbridge, Alta. m. Michael Gillan. **EDUC:** Univ. of Calgary, B.A.(English) 1960; Carleton Univ., B.A.(Journalism) 1961. **CAREER:** news staff, *Ottawa Journal*, 1961-62; news staff, Parliamentary Press Gallery, United Press International, 1962-63; reporter, Parliamentary Bureau, F.P. Publications (*Winnipeg Free Press, Calgary Albertan, Lethbridge Herald, Vancouver Sun, Victoria Times, Ottawa Journal*), 1964-70; Legislative Asst. & Sr. Legal Advisor to Prime Minister Pierre Trudeau, 1970-84; Comm. Coord., Prime Minister's Office, 1981-83; Senator, 1984 to date; Co-Chair, Nat'l Campaign Committee, Liberal Party of Canada, 1991; Leader of the Gov't in the Senate & Min. Responsible for Literacy, 1993 to date. **AFFIL:** National Liberal Caucus (V-Chair 1984-91); Western & Northern Liberal Caucus (V-Chair); Univ. of Lethbridge (Senate); 18th Air Defence Regiment, RCA (Hon. Lt.-Col.). **MISC:** as Senator has served on several committees incl. the Special Senate on Youth, & Senate Standing Committees on Transportation & Comm., Legal & Constitutional Affairs, Foreign Affairs, & Agriculture & Forestry; Founding Mbr., Senate Standing Committee on Aboriginal Peoples; in 1990 was inducted into the Kainai Chieftainship of the Blood Nation & given the name Morning Bird Woman; 1st woman to be named Leader of the Senate.

Fairclough, Right Hon. Ellen Loucks, P.C., C.C.,F.A.C.,LL.D.,FRCGS,UE 🍁 ☺ ☝

25 Stanley Ave., Hamilton, ON L8P 2K9. Born Hamilton, Ont. 1905. m. D.H. Gordon Fairclough. 1 ch. (dec.). **EDUC:** Hamilton public & secondary schools; C.A. 1962. **CAREER:** public acctg practice, 1935-57; Sec., Canadian Wholesale Grocers' Association, 1942-54; Alderman, Hamilton City Council, 1946-49; Cont. & Deputy Mayor, 1950; M.P., Hamilton-West, Gov't of Canada, 1950-62; Mbr., Cdn Delegation to the U.N., 1950; Delegate, Conference of Parliamentarians from NATO Countries, Paris, July 1955; Cdn Delegate, Inauguration of the Federation of the West Indies Parliament, April 1958; Ambassador Extraordinary to the Inauguration of Pres. Frondizi of Argentina, May 1958; sworn to Privy Council & appointed Sec. of State of Canada, 1957; Min. of Citizenship & Immigration, 1958; Postmaster Gen., 1962; defeated in gen. election, 1963; Sec-Treas. then VP, Hamilton Trust and Savings Corporation; on amalgamation with Canada Permanent, served as a Dir. until 1980, & 1 more yr. on the Hamilton Advisory Committee. **AFFIL:** Institute of Chartered Accountants of Ontario (Fellow & Life Mbr.); Royal Geographical Society (Fellow); Girl Guides of Canada (Life Mbr.); Provincial IODE (Life Mbr.); Margaret Gage Burkholder Chapter, IODE (Life Mbr.); Zonta Club of Hamilton I; Zonta International (Hon. Mbr.); Canadian Club of Hamilton; Albany Club of Toronto; Hamilton Club; Advertising & Sales Club of Hamilton (Hon. Mbr.); Fac. Club, McMaster Univ.; The Huguenot Society of Canada (Patron); United Empire Loyalists' Association, Hamilton Branch (Patron); American Marketing Association (Hon. Mbr. 1959);

Advertising & Sales Executives' Club, Montreal (Mbr., Orateurs du Mont Royal 1959). **HONS:** Hall of Fame, Boston Conference on Distribution, 1958; "Woman of the Year," Canadian Business & Professional Women, 1963; honoured by the Six Nations Indian Band Council, named Princess Au Wa Ha Da Go (Bright Flower) of the Cayuga Tribe, Six Nations, 1962; elected by Blackfoot Tribe as Chief Pe Ta Ke (Eagle Woman), 1962; Sales Person of the Year, Canadian Advertising & Sales Association, 1969; Human Rel'ns Award, Canadian Council of Christians & Jews, 1979; honoured by the Prov. of Ont. among 25 women who made outstanding contributions to community or country, 1975; Officer of the Order of Canada, 1978; recipient, Eleanor Roosevelt Humanitarian Award, State of Israel, 1984; elected to the Hamilton Gallery of Distinction, 1985; Dame, Order of St. John Hospitallers, 1985; Steel Sculpture: presentation by Hamilton Status of Women Committee, 1988; recipient, "Persons Award," Ottawa, 1989; Hamilton Multi-Cultural Award, 1991; invested with the title "The Right Honourable" in the presence of H.M. Queen Elizabeth II, 1992; honoured by the Churchill Society for the advancement of parliamentary democracy, 1993; Companion of the Order of Canada, 1995; LL.D.(Hon.), McMaster Univ., 1975; LL.D. (Hon.), Brock Univ., 1996. **MISC:** bronze portrait by Elizabeth Bradford Holbrook was accepted by the Speaker of the House of Commons in 1967 & is placed in the Speaker's Gallery of the House of Commons to commemorate Fairclough's swearing-in to the Privy Council as the 1st woman Cabinet Min. in Canada; Ont. Gov't Bldg in Hamilton named the Ellen Fairclough Bldg, 1982; Mbr., Ont. Bicentennial Advisory Commission, 1984 (appointed by the Prov. of Ont., 1983).

Fairhead, Patricia, M.A.,M.Ed.,R.C.A., C.S.P.W.C.,O.S.A.,S.C.A. ■ ⊗

Painter. 34 Claremont St., Ste. #106, Toronto, ON M6J 2M4 (416) 603-0616. Born Hull, UK 1927. 2 ch. (from first marriage) John G. Fairhead, Judith A. Crich. **EDUC:** Forest Hill Village Sch., Art Base/Academic 1938-45; Ont. Coll. of Art, Commercial Art 1946; Ont. Institute for Studies in Educ., M.Ed.(Adult Educ.) 1972; Goddard Coll., Vermont, M.A.(Adult Educ.) 1975. **CAREER:** taught art & leadership dev. courses, various bds. of educ., community groups & art galleries, 1964-72; Coord., Centre for Women, Humber Coll., 1971; Coord. of Programs, Learning Resources Centre, Toronto Public Libraries, 1972; Dir. of Ntwk Proj., The Ont. Association for Continuing Educ., 1974-74; Coord., Resource Centre,

Ontario Crafts Council, 1975-76; Coord. of Community Art Proj. (developed its *ON AIR* Arts Programming Model), TVOntario, 1976-79; full-time painter, 1979 to date. **SELECTED PUBLICATIONS:** *Teaching Art with Television: a teacher's manual* (TVOntario 1979); *Youth, Environment and Art, a manual for young people, leaders & teachers* (Ministry of Educ., 1976); *Continuing Education Councils*, graphics & design format (Ont. Association for Continuing Educ., 1974); *Colour and Composition, a manual for adult students* (Ministry of Community & Social Services, 1966). **COMMISSIONS:** Alexander Park Housing Co-op, 1979; Aviva Art Show, 1981; Mason, McLeod, Lyle, Smith, Calgary, 1982; I.P. Sharp Associates Ltd., 1982; Novacor, Calgary, 1983; Paterson McDougall, 1984. **EXHIBITIONS:** numerous solo exhibitions incl.: Sobot Gallery, Toronto (1966, 67); Art Gallery of Edmonton (1970); Pollock Gallery, Toronto (1981); Roberts Gallery, Toronto (1982, 84, 86, 88, 90, 92, 94, 96); Queen Charlotte Islands Museum (1986); Fraser Galleries, Halifax (1991); Lydon Fine Art, Inc., Chicago (1992); Mabey Gallery, Virginia (1992, 93, 96); Wallace Galleries, Calgary (1996); various group exhibitions incl.: Canadian Society of Painters in Water Colour (1965-69, 1981-84, 1986-92); *Arts in Canada*, Midwest Museum of American Art, Indiana (1980) & The Jesse Besser Museum, Michigan (1981); Ontario Society of Artists (1983, 84, 85, 89, 90); Peterborough Art Gallery, Art Auction (1984-91); *Crucifixion of the Feminine*, Martha Mabey Gallery, Virginia (1994). **COLLECTIONS:** The Royal Collection of Drawing & Watercolours, Windsor Castle; Ontario House, London, UK; Market Gallery, City of Toronto Archives; numerous corp. collections incl.: Alcan Wire & Cable; Canadian Imperial Bank of Commerce; Bell Cellular; Coll. of Nurses of Ontario; Fuji Bank Canada; IBM; Northern Telecom; Royal Bank of Canada; The Printing House; Toronto Star Newspapers Ltd.; The Wool Bureau. **AFFIL:** Royal Canadian Academy of the Arts (elected 1993); Canadian Society of Painters in Water Colour (elected 1966; Exec. Committee 1980; VP 1981); Ontario Society of Artists (elected 1986); Ontario Coll. of Art Alumni; Society of Canadian Artists (Past Pres.; Founding Mbr.); The Art Gallery of Ontario; The Arts & Letters Club of Toronto (elected 1985; Exec. Committee & Chrm., Art Committee 1987-88); Ont. Institute for Studies in Educ. (Fellow). **HONS:** Proficiency Prize, Ont. Coll. of Art, 1946. **MISC:** painting trips to numerous locations incl.: California, Queen Charlotte Islands, UK, Australia, the Amazon jungle, Paris & Egypt. **COMMENT:** *"Painter, adventurer, feminist.*

Currently I'm excited about painting at the deepest level yet, speaking out about women in the arts, getting strong positive response!"

Faith, Karlene, B.A.,Ph.D. 🎨 ⚖

Associate Professor, School of Criminology, SIMON FRASER UNIVERSITY, Burnaby, BC V5A 1S6 (604) 291-3018, FAX 291-4140. Born Aylsham, Sask. 1938. 4 ch. David Craig, Kimberly Dawn, Christopher Todd, Brent "Woody" Arthur. EDUC: Univ. of California, Santa Cruz, B.A.(Anthropology) 1970, Ph.D. (Hist. of Consciousness) 1981. CAREER: Admin. Asst., US Peace Corps, Eritrea, 1965-67; Asst. Coord., Field Program, Univ. of California, 1969-70, 1974-75; Instructor, 1970-80; Program Dir., Distance Educ., Simon Fraser Univ., 1982-89; Criminology Fac., 1989 to date. SELECTED PUBLICATIONS: "Gendered Imaginations: Female Crime and Prison Movies" (*The Justice Professional: Special Issue on Mass Media and Criminal Justice* Summer 1993); *Seeking Shelter: A State of Battered Women* with Dawn Currie (Vancouver: Collective Press, 1993); *Unruly Women: The Politics of Confinement and Resistance* (Vancouver: Press Gang Publishers, 1993); "Santa Cruz Women's Prison Project" (*Schooling in a Total Institution*, ed. Howard Davidson, Westport: Greenwood Publishing, 1994); "Resistance: Lessons from Foucault and Feminism" *in Power/Gender: Social Relations in Theory and Practice* ed. L. Radtke & H. Stam (London: Sage, 1994); "Aboriginal Women's Healing Lodge: Challenge to Penal Correctionalism?" (*Journal of Human Justice*, 6(2) 1995). AFFIL: Canadian Women's Studies Association; Simon Fraser Univ. Feminist Institute for Studies on Law & Society (Dir. 1993-95); Western Assoc. of Sociology & Anthropology; American Society of Criminology (Chair, Women in Prison Task Force; Ethics Committee). HONS: Danforth Fellow, 1970-74; J.S. Woodsworth Resident Scholar, Simon Fraser Univ. Institute for the Humanities, 1990; B.C. Book Prize, for Unruly Women, 1994. INTERESTS: social justice; music; feminist theory & activism; pol. commitment to closing down prisons. MISC: has consulted & given talks on five continents. COMMENT: *"My life is blessed with children, grandchildren, good friends, and work I care about. I'm committed to social, political and economic equity for all."*

Falardeau-Ramsay, Michelle, B.A., LL.B.,Q.C. ✹ ⚖

Deputy Chief Commissioner, CANADIAN HUMAN RIGHTS COMMISSION, Ottawa, ON K1A 1E1. Born Montreal. m. EDUC: Coll. Bourgeoys, B.A.; Univ. of Montreal, LL.B.;

McGill Univ. BAR: Que. CAREER: Lawyer, Massicotte, Levac and Falardeau; Sr. Ptnr, Levac and Falardeau; Deputy Chrm, Public Svc Staff Rel'ns Bd., 1975-82; Chrm, Immigration Appeal Bd., 1982-88; Deputy Chief Commissioner, Canadian Human Rights Commission, 1988 to date.; consultant on human rights, U.N. Oper. in Somalia, 1993; mbr., Cdn delegation, Conference on Security & Cooperation, Warsaw; mbr., Cdn delegation participating in the bilateral observer mission for the S.African elections, 1994. SELECTED PUBLICATIONS: various articles & chapters incl.: "Recent Developments in Immigration Law," *Recent Developments in Administrative Law* (Toronto; The Carswell Co. Ltd., 1987); "L'évolution récente du droit de l'immigration," *Développements récents en droit administratif* (Cowansville, Que.; Yvon Blais Inc., 1987); "Collegiality and Decision Making in the Aftermath of the Consolidated-Bathurst Decision," *Canadian Journal of Administrative Law and Practice* (Toronto: The Carswell Co. Ltd., 1987); "The Changing Face of Human Rights in Canada" (*Constitutional FORUM Constitutionnel*, Edmonton, Vol. 4, No. 3, 1993); "Human Rights Laws need Reinforcement," (*Canadian Speeches: Issues of the Day*, a national forum of diverse views, Fredericton, Vol. 8, No. 5, 1994). AFFIL: International Day Committee for the Eradication of Poverty (Co-Pres.); Canadian Human Rights Foundation (Dir.); National Institute for Administrative Tribunals; Association of Professional Executives of the Public Service of Canada; Quebec Bar Association; Canadian Bar Association; Canadian Institute for the Administration of Justice; Société du droit administratif du Québec; Council of Canadian Administrative Tribunals; International Commission of Jurists; International Bar Association; International Law Association; Fédération des femmes du Québec; l'Association des civilistes; Council of Canadian Administrative Bureaus (Founder, Past Co-Pres. & Dir.); Canadian Association of Statutory Human Rights Agencies (Pres. 1992). MISC: instructor, Univ. of Ottawa, Univ. of Quebec, Sir George Williams Univ. (Concordia) & Algonquin Coll.; has led numerous seminars & workshops for various Cdn & foreign professional groups; regularly invited to give conferences, appear on panels & participate at conferences dealing with issues on human rights & administrative law.

Falk, Gathie ⊗

Artist. Equinox Gallery, 2321 Granville St., Vancouver, BC V6H 3G3. Born Alexander, Man. 1928. EDUC: Univ. of British Columbia. CAREER: artist; principal works include paintings, environmental sculpture, sculptured paintings, prints, sculpture, performance art & video performance art. COMMISSIONS: include two murals for the Lester Pearson Bldg, Ottawa, 1973; sculptured painting for the B.C. Credit Union Bldg, 1979; mural for the Cdn Embassy, Washington, 1988; Odeon Cineplex IV, Vancouver, 1988. EXHIBITIONS: solo exhibitions include Canvas Shack, Vancouver (1965); Douglas Gallery, Vancouver (1968); Canadian Cultural Centre, Paris (1974); Bau-Xi Gallery, Vancouver (1976); National Gallery Tour (1976-77); Forest City Gallery, London, Ont. (1977); Edmonton Art Gallery (1978); Artcore Vancouver (1978); Univ. of British Columbia (1980); Univ. of Southern Alberta (1980); Glenbow Museum, Calgary (1980); Equinox Art Gallery, Vancouver (1981, 82, 83, 85, 1987 to date); Isaacs Gallery, Toronto (1982, 84, 87, 88, 90); Wynick-Tuck Gallery, Toronto (1992); Victoria Art Gallery, touring painting retrospective (1985-86); Vancouver Art Gallery, *Retrospective 1962-85* (1985); 49th Parallel, N.Y. (1987); group exhibitions include Vancouver Art Gallery; Seattle Art Museum; Montreal Museum of Fine Arts; Australian National Library; Art Gallery of Ontario; National Gallery of Canada; Museum of Modern Art (Toyoma, Japan). COLLECTIONS: various public & private collections. HONS: Sun Award, 1968; Gershon Iskowitz Award, 1990; many commendations. MISC: recipient of many Canada Council grants; many art performance presentations; cited in numerous magazines, journals & books since 1968.

Farley, Donna ■ ■ 📖 / ☼

Writer. 9642 - 139 St., Surrey, BC V3T 5H3. Born East York, Ont. 1955. m. Lawrence. 2 ch. Rhiannon, Magdalen. EDUC: Univ. of Toronto, incomplete B.A. 1979. CAREER: Assoc. Editor, *Saskatchewan Anglican*, 1981-84; writer, science fiction, fantasy, young adult fiction, poetry & non-fiction, 1987 to date; Columnist, *Christian Vision*, 1991-93; Poetry Editor & Columnist, *The Handmaiden*, 1996 to date. SELECTED PUBLICATIONS: 13 works of short fiction incl.: "It Must Be Some Place" (*Catfantastic*, DAW Books, 1989); "The Passing of the Eclipse" (*Universe 2*, BantamSpectra, 1992); "Light One Candle" (*On Spec*, Vol. 4, No. 2, 1992); "Father Vadim's Angel" (*Worlds of Fantasy & Horror*, #3, Summer 1996); also non-fiction, poetry & a play. AFFIL: SF Canada. HONS: *Dreams & Visions* readers' award, Best Story of the Year, 1992; hon. mention, Sask. Year of the Child Literary Competition, 1979. INTERESTS: singing; birdwatching; karate; armchair travel (more affordable than the real thing); discovering new things of all kinds. MISC: has led writers' critique groups, judged literary contests, given writing workshops & women's retreats; now preparing to edit an anthology of Orthodox poetry. COMMENT: *"Convert to Orthodox Christianity and priest's wife Donna Farley writes uniquely religious SF and fantasy, humorous fiction and poetry. She calls her work not a "career" but a pilgrimage."*

Farlinger, Esther Ruth, R.N. ■ ■ ◐ ⊗

Volunteer/Fundraiser. Interior Designer. m. CAREER: Pres., ERA Designs, 1973-78; Pres. & CEO, Justme & Designs Associates Ltd, 1978 to date; Designer/Construction Chair, 21 McGill Club, Toronto, late 1970s. VOLUNTEER CAREER: Chair, over 10 special fundraising events incl.: The Gov. Gen.'s Horse Guards tribute dinner for Hon. H.N.R. Jackman, Nov. 1996; Hon. Chair, North York Symphony Gala, May 1996; Chair, Canadian World Olympic Culinary Association, Apr. 1996; Design Chair & Chairperson, Opera Ball; has chaired or co-chaired various functions to raise money for: Cystic Fibrosis; Parkinson's Foundation; Alzheimer's; The Kidney Foundation; Equine Research; Yellow Brick House; Kid's Help Phone; Duke of Edinburgh's Award; chair, Sandra Post Golf Tournament for Easter Seals, 6 yrs.; founder & Chair, Mixed Canadian Seniors' Golf Association (with annual tournament to benefit a charity - 8th Annual); Committee, annual Mike Harris Golf Tournament. AFFIL: McMichael Canadian Art Collection (Gov.); St. Joseph's Health Centre Foundation (Dir. 1993 to date); ROM Foundation (Dir. 1994 to date); Kidney Foundation (Bd. mbr. 1985-87); North York Symphony Association (Advisory Bd. 1996); Canadian Opera Company (Women's Committee 1 yr.); Beacon Hall Golf & Country Club; Country Club of Florida; Founders' Club; Lambton Golf & Country Club; Mississauga Golf & Country Club; St. Andrew's Golf & Country Club, Fla. MISC: Chair of St. Joseph's 20's Evening, raising over $400,000; Chair, Tribute to J.J. Barnicke, 1996. COMMENT: *"Volunteer fundraiser. Using her professional design qualifications and varied interests in golf, the arts, culture, etc. to raise funds to benefit many worthwhile organizations in Toronto."*

Farlinger, Shirley Ruth Tabb, B.A., B.A.A. ■ / ⏱ ✿

Freelance Writer and Peace Activist. 122 Hilton Ave., Toronto, ON M5R 3E7 (416) 532-0220, FAX 532-8009. Born Toronto 1930. d. 5 ch. (1 dec.). EDUC: Univ. of Toronto, B.A.(English) 1950; Ryerson Polytechnical Institute, B.A.A.(Journalism) 1980.

CAREER: Ed., Sunday School resources, United Church of Canada, 1975-83; Fed. Green Party candidate, Rosedale Riding, 1984; Fed. New Democrat candidate, Wellington-Grey-Dufferin-Simcoe Riding, 1988; Election Observer, Nicaragua, 1990; Chair, Toronto hearings of the Citizens' Inquiry into Peace & Security, 1991. **SELECTED PUBLICATIONS:** *A Million for Peace: The Story of the Peacemaking Fund of the United Church of Canada* (United Church Publishing House, 1995); chapter on human rights & gender equity in *United Nations Reform: Looking Forward after 50 Years*, ed. by Eric Fawcett & Hanna Newcombe (Dundurn Press/Science for Peace, 1995); *Children for Peace* (United Church); various other publications. **EDIT:** Writer & Ed., *Peace Magazine*; Bd. Mbr., *Disarmament Times*, United Nations. **AFFIL:** Canadian Federation of University Women; United Nations Association of Canada; United Church Peace Network; Voice of Women for Peace; National Action Committee on the Status of Women; Science for Peace; Canadian Association of Journalists; Group of 78; Rotary Club of Toronto-Eglinton (Past Sec.); World Federalist Foundation; New Democratic Party. **INTERESTS:** peace; children's rights; women's equality; global econ. issues; the environment; civil society. **MISC:** discussion of Canada's defence policies, *Between the Lines*, TVOntario (Jan. 23 & 24, 1992); appearances on Vision TV on Nicaragua, Canada's defence policy, & peace groups in former Yugoslavia; Mbr., City of Toronto Peace Committee, 1986; Mbr., Consultative Group for the Ambassador for Disarmament, 3 yrs.; former Bd. Mbr., Peacefund Canada; numerous int'l tours & conferences, incl. U.N. NGO Forum on Landmines, Nov. 1994; Quality of Life, Univ. of Northern B.C., Aug 1996. **COMMENT:** *"I count raising four children as one of my achievements. This led me into the areas of religious education, the peace movement, and advocacy journalism."*

Farr, Moira, B.A.,B.A.A. ■ ✎ 📖

Freelance Writer and Editor. Born Barrie, Ont. 1958. d. **EDUC:** Univ. of Toronto, B.A.(English & Hist.) 1982; Ryerson Polytechnic Univ., B.A.A.(Journalism) 1985. **CAREER:** Asst. Ed., *Canadian Architect*, 1985-87; Sr. Ed., Financial Post *Moneywise Magazine*, 1987-90; Freelance Writer, 1990 to date; Mng Ed., *This Magazine*, 1992-93; Sr. Ed., *Equinox*, 1994-96. **SELECTED PUBLICATIONS:** articles, essays & reviews in various publications incl. *Toronto Life*, *Canadian Business*, *FLARE*, *Utne Reader*, *The Globe and Mail*, *BRICK*, *This Magazine*, *Equinox*; "Where the Boys Aren't" (*Equinox*, Apr. 1995); "Welcome to Family Values World" (*This Magazine*, Dec. 1994); "The Death of Nature Writing" (*BRICK*, Winter 1993-94); essays reprinted in anthologies incl. *The Thinking Heart*, *The Broadview Reader*, *Twist & Shout*, *Far and Wide*. **EDIT:** Ed. Bd., *This Magazine*, 1991 to date. **HONS:** Protége Award, Toronto Arts Foundation, 1991; Hon. Mention, Culture Category ("The Last Dinner," *Toronto Life*, Nov. 1990), National Magazine Awards, 1991; Hon Mention, Arts & Entertainment ("Women Beware Critics," *This Magazine*), National Magazine Awards, 1996. **INTERESTS:** women's issues; mental health; environment; literature.

Farrell, Brenda $ ✎

President, FARRELL RESEARCH GROUP LTD., Marine Building, 355 Burrard St., Ste. 1230, Vancouver, BC V6C 2G8 (604) 682-7626, FAX 682-2977. Born UK 2 ch. Romina Farrell, Francesca Farrell. **EDUC:** France Hill, UK, O Levels. **CAREER:** VP, Campbell Farrell Inc., 1984; Pres., Farrell Research Group Ltd., 1985 to date. **SELECTED PUBLICATIONS:** writes a monthly column in *BC Business* Magazine, 1993 to date. **EDIT:** *BCAMA Newsletter*, 1995-96. **AFFIL:** American Marketing Association (Bd., B.C. Chapter). **HONS:** for service to the youth community through volunteer work. **INTERESTS:** people & cultures; classical music; art; reading; travel. **MISC:** often asked to speak at conferences, colleges & universities. **COMMENT:** *"I believe that vital ingredients for a successful and fulfilling life include a positive attitude, a healthy lifestyle, laughter and a genuine desire to help others reach their personal and career goals."*

Farrell, Ruby Violet Marilyn, B.A.,B.Ed., M.Ed. ■ 🎓 📖

Assistant Professor, Faculty of Education, LAKEHEAD UNIVERSITY, Thunder Bay, ON P7B 5E1 (807) 343-8020, FAX 343-6807. Born Whitewater Lake, Ont. m. 3 ch. Rosanna Mae, Amy Lynn, Lindsay Lee Amber. **EDUC:** Lakehead Univ., B.A.(Hist.) 1988, B.Ed. 1989, M.Ed. 1993. **CAREER:** Asst. Prof., Fac. of Educ., & Coord., Native Teacher Educ. Program, Lakehead Univ.; author (as Ruby Slipperjack). **SELECTED PUBLICATIONS:** *Honour the Sun* (Winnipeg: Pemmican Publications, 1987); *Silent Words* (Saskatoon: Fifth House Publishers, 1992). **INTERESTS:** native arts & crafts, instruction & research; oil painting. **COMMENT:** *"I am a member of the Eabametoong (Fort Hope) First Nations and I was born and raised at my father's trapline at Whitewater Lake in Northwestern Ontario. I now live in Thunder Bay with my husband and three children."*

Farrow, Maureen Anne, B.Sc. ■■ $
Executive Vice-President and Director of Economics and Equity Strategy, LOEWEN, ONDAATJE, MCCUTCHEON LIMITED (fin. svcs, brokerage), Hazelton Lanes, E. Tower, 55 Avenue Rd., Ste. 2250, Toronto, ON M5R 3L2 (416) 964-4486, FAX 964-4490. President, ECONOMAP INC. Born UK 1943. m. John Farrow. 1 ch. Karl. **EDUC:** Univ. of Hull, UK, B.Sc.(Hons., Econ.) 1966; York Univ., post-grad. studies in Econ. **CAREER:** mkt research, General Electric, UK, 1966-69; VP, Singer Associates Ltd., 1970-80; Ptnr, Coopers & Lybrand Consulting Group, 1980-92; Pres., C.D. Howe Institute, 1987-89; Pres., Economap Inc., 1992 to date. **SELECTED PUBLICATIONS:** numerous presentations at conferences & papers in technical journals re econ. policy issues & competitiveness; contributing ed. & author, several C.D. Howe publications. **DIRECTOR:** Dylex Limited; The Equitable Life Insurance Company; National Trustco Inc.; Penreal Advisors Ltd.; Schneider Corporation. **TRUSTEE:** Pension & Savings Plans, Imperial Oil Limited. **AFFIL:** Canadian Association of Business Economists (Pres. 1983-85); Toronto Association of Business Economists (Pres. 1979-80); British North American Committee; Canadian Chamber of Commerce (Dir. 1990-96). **HONS:** Fellow, Institute of Management Consultants of Ontario; Commemorative Medal for the 125th Anniversary of Cdn Confederation. **INTERESTS:** econ. policy; ballet; travel; gardening. **COMMENT:** *"My early training as a ballet dancer developed a skill set of independence, concentration, hard work and discipline, which has proven useful and instrumental in my subsequent professional life in the business world."*

Fehr, Beverley, B.A.,M.A.,Ph.D. ■ 🎓 ⊕
Associate Professor, Department of Psychology (on leave), UNIVERSITY OF WINNIPEG, 515 Portage Ave., Winnipeg, MB R3B 2E9. Born MacGregor, Man. 1958. m. Marvin Gresbrecht. 1 ch. Genevieve. **EDUC:** Univ. of Winnipeg, B.A.(Psych.) 1980; Univ. of British Columbia, M.A. 1982, Ph.D. 1986. **CAREER:** Asst. Prof., Univ. of Winnipeg, 1986-91; Adjunct Prof., Univ. of Manitoba, 1991 to date; Assoc. Prof., Univ. of Winnipeg, 1991 to date. **SELECTED PUBLICATIONS:** "Severe Wife Battering as Deindividuated Violence," with D. Dutton & H. McEwen (*Victimology* 1982); "Theories of Friendship: The Analysis of Interpersonal Attraction," in *Friendship and Social Interaction*, edited by V.J. Derlega & B.A. Winstead (New York: Springer-Verlag, 1986); "Prototype Analysis of the Concepts of Love and Commitment" (*Journal of Personality and Social Psychology* 1988); "Prototype-Based Assessment of Laypeople's Views of Love" (*Personal Relationships* 1994); *Friendship Processes* (Sage Publishers, 1996); various other publications. **EDIT:** Contributing Ed., *International Society for the Study of Personal Relationships Bulletin*, 1989-92; Assoc. Ed., *Journal of Social and Personal Relationships*, 1992-95; Ed. Bd., *Personal Relationships*, 1993 to date; Ed. Bd., *Journal of Personality and Social Psychology*, 1996 to date. **AFFIL:** American Psychological Association; Canadian Psychological Association; International Society for the Study of Personal Relationships (Co-Coord., Social Cognition Special Interest Group); Iowa/International Network on Personal Relationships; Society for Personality & Social Psychology; Society of Experimental Social Psychology. **HONS:** The MacBean Foundation Entrance Scholarship, 1976; Dr. A. Cragg Scholarship in Psych., 1979; Univ. Gold Medal in Psych. in Memory of Prof. C.J. Robson, 1980; Iowa International Network Dissertation Prize, 1988; Psych. Dept. 1st Annual Teaching Award, 1990. **MISC:** currently organizing the conference of the International Society for the Study of Personal Relationships, to be held in Aug. 1996; reviewer for various journals & grants; various conference presentations; recipient of various grants & fellowships. **COMMENT:** *"I am a social psychologist whose research interests lie in the field of close relationships. I am currently writing a book on friendship and have been awarded a 3-year Social Sciences and Humanities Research Council of Canada grant to study interaction patterns in close relationships."*

Fekete, Hazel ■■ 🎓 ♡
Retired Dean of Developmental Studies, YUKON COLLEGE. Born Nortondale, N.B. 1936. m. Anthony. 4 ch. Mark, Arthur, Gregory, Marion. **HONS:** Dean Emeritus, Yukon Coll., 1995; Yukon Women's Award in Educ., 1994. **INTERESTS:** amateur geology; history & genealogy; Canada's Depression era; rural community dev.; motivational theory; northern gardening. **COMMENT:** *"Retired in 1995 from 30 years in adult education; volunteer activities included, literacy learning disabilities, Canadian Parents for French, and family services. Presently preparing for teaching assignment abroad."*

Feld Carr, Judy ♡ ☺ 🎓 ☝
Educator and Community Volunteer. 114 Kilbarry Rd., Toronto, ON M5P 1L1 (416) 489-4168, FAX 489-3453. Born Montreal, raised in Sudbury, Ont. first marriage to Dr. Ronald Feld (deceased); m. Donald Carr, Q.C. 6 ch.

Aaron Carr, Jonathan Carr, Adam Carr, Alan Feld, Gary Feld, Elizabeth Feld. **EDUC:** Ontario Coll. of Education, Univ. of Toronto, Honour Diploma Specialist in Instrumental & Vocal Music, 1961; Univ. of Toronto, Mus.Bac 1960; Mus.M. 1968. **CAREER:** Visiting Lecturer, Sephardic Music, Yeshiva Univ., New York; Music Specialist, instrumental & vocal music, Toronto Secondary Sch. Bd.; full-time parenting and active community organization involvement, 1976 to date; Schermer Scholar in Residence, Youngstown State Univ., Ohio, 1988. **VOLUNTEER CAREER:** Mbr., Nat'l Exec., Canadian Jewish Congress, 1978-95; Pres., Beth Tzedec Congregation, Toronto, 1982-83; Mbr., Advisory Bd., United Synagogue of America, New York, 1985-92; V-Chair, Canadian Jewish Congress, Ont. Reg., 1989-92. **SELECTED PUBLICATIONS:** articles in *Encyclopedia Judaica*, Decennial Edition, 1982-93. **AFFIL:** American Joint Distribution Committee, N.Y. (Int'l Bd.); Hebrew Immigrant Aid Society, N.Y. (Int'l Bd.); Canadian Jewish Congress (Chair, Canadian Nat'l Task Force for Syrian Jews). **HONS:** Nominee, Woman of the Year, *Chatelaine* Magazine; Honouree, Sephardic Community of Toronto (Jews originally from Spain), Magen David Sephardic Congregation, 1983; Co-Honouree, Jewish National Fund Negev Dinner (largest Jewish Community dinner in Canada); Honouree, Beth Tzedec Synagogue, State of Israel Bonds Dinner; Ben Gurion Univ. Negev Award, Canadian Association of Ben Gurion Univ., 1993; honoured, American Joint Distribution Committee, Luncheon, N.Y., 1995; National Achievement Award, B'Nai Brith Women of Canada, 1995; Honoured by the Gov't of Israel "for being the leading force in the release & the rescue of the Jewish Community of Syria," Jerusalem, 1995; Saul Hayes Human Rights Award, Canadian Jewish Congress, 1995; Special Award of the United Synagogue of America, for the Rescue of Jews of Syria, Biennial Convention, Washington, 1995; honoured by World Jewish Agency, Tel Aviv, 1995; Humanitarian Award of Merit, Univ. of Haifa, Israel, 1996; Statement of praise in the House of Commons for "Canadian, Judy Feld Carr for earning a place in the history of humanity," Ottawa, March 14, 1995; Woman of Achievement Award, Hadassah-Wizo Org. of Canada, 1996. **INTERESTS:** music; piano performance; community involvement; volunteer interests; concerts; opera; ballet; reading, travel. **MISC:** first woman president of the Beth Tzedec Congregation; speaks frequently before large audiences in Canada and the US on a variety of int'l issues; advisor & speaker with Interfaith Women of Toronto; has appeared on radio programs addressing human rights issues;

consultant & advisor to the 1990 award-winning film *In the Shadows–The Tragedy of Syrian Jews.* **COMMENT:** *"An educator, a mother and now a grandmother who believes with a passion that one person can make a difference. In Jewish philosophy it states,* He who saves one life, saves an entire world.*"*

Fennell, Hope-Arlene, B.Ed.,M.Ed., Ph.D. ☜
Associate Professor and Chair, Preservice Teacher Education Program, LAKEHEAD UNIVERSITY, Faculty of Education, 955 Oliver Rd., Thunder Bay, ON P7B 5E1 (807) 343-8712, FAX 344-6807, EMAIL hfennell@sky.lakehead.ca. Born Indian Head, Sask. 1948. m. George Terrence Fennell. 1 ch. Jason T. **EDUC:** Univ. of Saskatchewan, B.Ed.(Educ. of Exceptional Children) 1977, M.Ed.(Curriculum Studies) 1986, Ph.D.(Educ. Admin.) 1990. **CAREER:** teacher, various schools, Sask., 1969-84, 1985-88; Sessional Lecturer, Univ. of Saskatchewan, 1984-85, 1989-90; Asst. Prof., 1991-94; Coord., Field Experiences, 1993; Asst. Coord., Field Experiences, 1994; Assoc. Prof., 1994 to date; Chair, Preservice Teacher Educ. Program, 1994 to date. **SELECTED PUBLICATIONS:** "An Alternate View of Values in the Framework for School Leadership" (*The Saskatchewan Administrator* 1989); "Preparing Students for Internship: Could We Do More?" in *WestCAST Proceedings,* edited by L. Kozey & L. Kurtz (Regina: Fac. of Educ., Univ. of Regina, 1992); "An Investigation of the Relationships between Organizational-Cultural Linkages and the Teachers' Stages of Concern Toward a Policy Implementation" (*The Alberta Journal of Educational Research* 1992); "Leadership for Change: Principals and Power-Sharing" (*The Canadian Administrator* 1992); "Organizational-Cultural Linkages: Expanding the Metaphor" (*The Journal of Educational Administration* 1994); "Cooperative Learning in Professional Education: Students' Perceptions and Preferences" (*Lakehead University Teachers* 1994); "Woman Principals as Leaders: A Case Study" (*The Journal of School Leadership,* 1994); various other publications. **AFFIL:** Phi Delta Kappa; American Educational Research Association (Special Interest Group for Teacher Educ.); Association for Supervision & Curriculum Development (Assoc.); Canadian Society for Studies in Education; Canadian Association for the Study of Educational Administration; Canadian Association for Teacher Education; Federation of Women Teachers' Associations of Ontario (Affiliate); United Church of Canada - St. Paul's United Church, Thunder Bay; Thunder Bay Symphony Orchestra Chorus. **HONS:** Lowensborough

Memorial Scholarship, 1988-89; Saskatchewan Teachers' Federation Bursary, 1990; Univ. of Saskatchewan Grad. Scholarships, 1988-89, 1989-90. **INTERESTS:** research in the areas of women in leadership & teacher educ.; music & choral work; reading on a variety of topics; community work. **MISC:** numerous invited lectures, presentations & consultations; recipient of 5 grants. **COMMENT:** *"My 26-year career in education has included teaching students from grades 1-12, students with various exceptionalities, undergraduate and graduate students as well as many leadership and administrative experiences. My main interests now are in research and scholarly work related to leadership and teaching as well as continued participation in church, musical, and community activities."*

Fenton, Jane ✎ ♡ ⊕
Research Associate, New Media, THE TORONTO SUN PUBLISHING CORPORATION, 333 King St. E., Toronto, ON M5A 3X5 (416) 947-2222. Director and Co-founder, SHEENA'S PLACE (416) 947-2365. **CAREER:** The Toronto Sun Publishing Corporation, 1991 to date. **COMMENT:** *"Sheena's Place is a recently established charitable organization whose purpose is to develop and run a transition centre for people living with eating disorders, their families, caregivers and community service providers. Sheena's Place will offer its programs and services in a comfortable house, accessible by public transit and close to supportive services. It will be non-institutional, non-residential, warm, welcoming and supportive."*

Fenton, Patricia, B.A.,M.S.W. ■■ ✊ ♡
Executive Director, Adoption Resource Centre, ADOPTION COUNCIL OF ONTARIO (adoption info. & support svcs), 3216 Yonge St., Toronto, ON M4N 2L2 (416) 482-0021, FAX 484-7454, EMAIL pfenton@netcom.ca. Born Markham, Ont. 1944. m. Aaron. 2 ch. Sara, Katherine. **EDUC:** Univ. of Toronto, B.A.(Languages) 1966, Hon. Psych. equivalent 1976, M.S.W.(Social Work with individuals, families & small groups) 1978. **CAREER:** Pres., Parent Co-operative Preschools International, 1991-94; Pres., Adoption Council of Ontario, 1991-95; Pres., Association of Canadian Childcare Co-operatives, 1995 to date. **AFFIL:** Ontario Association of Social Workers; Ontario Coll. of Certified Social Workers; Adoption Council of Canada (Bd. mbr.). **HONS:** Adoption Activist Award, North American Council on Adoptable Children, 1995. **INTERESTS:** music –singing, playing piano; reading; computer technology. **MISC:** mbr., Fed. Advisory Committee on Co-operatives, advisory to Min. Charles Mayer then Min. Ralph Goodale, 1992-95; co-founder, Families in Adoption, adoption support group for adoptive parents & their children; founding mbr., Deer Park Extended Program, childcare co-operative. **COMMENT:** *"Mrs. Fenton is a tireless worker with a strong commitment to improving services to children and families and to enhancing the lives of all who are touched by adoption–adoptees, birth parents, adoptive and pre-adoptive parents. Her impact has been felt in the adoption community and the co-operative childcare movement in Canada."*

Ferguson, Marnie H., B.A. ■■ $
Vice-President, People, Quality and EH&S, MONSANTO CANADA INC., 2330 Argentia Rd., Mississauga, ON L5N 2G4. Vice-President, Innovation and Change, MONSANTO COMPANY, 800 N. Lindbergh, St. Louis, MO. Born Lindsay, Ont. m. Gary S. 3 ch. Michael, Samuel, Christopher. **EDUC:** Ryerson Polytechnic Univ.; Waterloo Lutheran, Univ. of Waterloo, B.A. **CAREER:** various hum. res. mgmt positions incl. labour rel'ns, org. dev. & design; org. transformation in consumer packages goods ind.; Dir., Hum. Res., Monsanto Canada Inc., 1989-91; Gen. Mgr, Monsanto Incite Consulting Div., 1991 to date; Dir., Continuous Improvement, Monsanto Canada; Sr. Consultant, Incite Div., Monsanto; global responsibility for leading innovation & change, 1994 to date. **AFFIL:** Personnel Association of Canada; Council on Total Quality Management, Conference Board of Canada (Past Chair); American Management Association; R.C. Diocese of Hamilton (Dir., Marriage Preparation/Marriage Enhancement 1973 to date). **INTERESTS:** gardening; music; travel.

Ferguson, Tracey ■■ ⚾
Paralympic Athlete. Markham, ON. **EDUC:** Univ. of Illinois, Chem. student. **SPORTS CAREER:** mbr., Nat'l Wheelchair Basketball Team. Paralympic Games: Gold, 1996; Gold, 1992. World Championships, 1st, 1994. Stoke Manville Games: 1st, 1991. **HONS:** recipient, Terry Fox Humanitarian Award; Wheelchair Basketball Scholarship, Univ. of Illinois. **MISC:** one of the best shooters in the world; motivational speaker.

Fernandes, Teresa ■ ✲ ✎ 📺
Art Director, VISUAL ENTERPRISE, 34 Lincoln Ave., Greenwich, CT 06830 (203) 622-6329, FAX 622-2988, EMAIL America On Line: seventy8. Born Portugal 1958. m. Barry Blitt. 1 ch. Samuel Fernandes Blitt. **EDUC:** Dawson Coll., Montreal, Graphic Design 1974-77;

Univ. of Toronto, Hist. of Art 1984-86. **CAREER:** Layout Artist, T. Eaton Company, 1977-80; Sr. Art Dir., Vickers & Benson Advertising Agency, 1980-83; Art Dir., *Executive Magazine* & Assoc. Art Dir., *En Route* Magazine, Airmedia Publishing Ltd., 1983-85; Assoc. Art Dir., *Report on Business Magazine*/Art Dir., *Forum* Magazine/Art Dir., *Wardair* Magazine/Art Dir., *CA* Magazine, 1985-87; Art Dir., *Toronto Life* Magazine, Key Publishers Co. Ltd., 1987-90; Deputy Art Dir., *Sports Illustrated* Magazine, Time-Warner, 1990; freelance Art Dir., 1990-91; Art Dir., *Travel Holiday* Magazine, 1991-92; Art Dir., & Consultant, various publications, 1992 to date; Art Dir., *Selling* Magazine, 1993-95; Design Dir., *Popular Science* Magazine, Times Mirror Corp., 1995. **SELECTED PUBLICATIONS:** *ISSUE* Magazine, The Voice of the Art Directors Club of Toronto, a quarterly publication, founder, co-ed. & art dir.; *The Business of Illustration*, co-author (New York; Watson-Guptill Publications, 1995); *Magazines: Inside & Out*, co-author (New York: PBC International, Inc., 1995). **AFFIL:** The American Institute of Graphic Arts; The Society of Publication Designers (SPD); The Association of Magazine Editors; The Type Directors' Club; The Art Directors' Club of Toronto (Exec. Committee 1984-89). **HONS:** over 200 awards for art direction & design from various institutions incl.: National Magazine Awards Foundation of Canada, Graphic Designers of Canada, *American Photography Annual*, SPD; *Communication Arts Annual*. **INTERESTS:** graphic design theory; interior design; the arts from the '20s & '30s; travel; typography; art history. **MISC:** guest speaker, various colleges, seminars & conferences; judged the Western Magazine Awards, 1988 & 1989, the *American Illustration Annual*, 1992, the SPD annual competition, 1994, & the American Society of Magazine Editors' National Magazine Awards, 1995. **COMMENT:** "*Teresa Fernandes has been art directing since she was 18 years old. For the past 20 years, she has specialized in magazine art direction, working at such publications as* En Route, Toronto Life, Report on Business, Sports Illustrated, Allure, Mirabella, Travel Holiday, Men's Journal, Selling *&* Popular Science."

Ferrante, Angela, B.Jour.(Hons.) $ ✏ 🍁

Executive Vice-President and Chief Operating Officer, C.D. HOWE INSTITUTE, 125 Adelaide St. E., Toronto, ON M5C 1L7 (416) 865-1904, FAX 865-1866. Born Italy 1949. m. Michael Gerard. 1 ch. Christopher. **EDUC:** B.Jour. (Hon.), Carleton Univ., 1971. **CAREER:** journalist, *The Montreal Star*, *The Montreal Gazette*, *Maclean's*; Asst. Mng Ed., *Maclean's*. **SELECTED PUBLICATIONS:** *Out of Iran* (1987). **AFFIL:** The Ontario Institute for Studies in Education (O.I.S.E.) (Chair 1992-94; V-Chair, Bd. of Gov. 1990-92).

Ferron, Madeleine 📖

Writer. 1130, de la Tour, Québec, QC G1R 2W7 (418) 524-0313. Born Trois-Rivières, Qué. 1922. w. 3 ch. **CAREER:** author. **SELECTED PUBLICATIONS:** *La fin des loup-garous* (1966); *Le baron écarlate* (1971); *Sur le chemin Craig* (1983); "Coeur de sucre" (1966); "Le chemin des dames" (1977); "Histoires édifiantes" (1981); "Un singulier amour" (1987); "Le grand théâtre" (1989); "Quand le peuple fait la loi" (1972); "Les Beaucerons, ces insoumis" (1974); "Adrienne" (1993); numerous other short stories & essays. **AFFIL:** La Fondation Robert-Cliche pour la protection du patrimoine des Beaucerons (Prés. 1979 to date); L'Union des écrivains Québécois; Société des écrivains de la Mauricie. **HONS:** prix, Éditions la Presse, 1982; finalist, Prix France-Québec, 1987; finalist, Grand Prix Littéraire de Montréal, 1971, 1987. **INTERESTS:** flowers; bird-watching; rural scenery; wildlife.

Fershko, Jane S., B.A.,M.A.,M.B.A. $

Vice-President, Cardholder Services, ROYAL BANK OF CANADA, 200 Bay St., Toronto, ON M5J 2J5. Born Newark, N.J. 1949. m. Dr. Gary Taylor. 2 ch. **EDUC:** Univ. of Wisconsin, B.A.(Econ.) 1971; Columbia Univ., M.B.A. (Curriculum Design/Teaching) 1972; Wharton Sch., Univ. of Pennsylvania, M.B.A.(Mktg/Mgmt) 1975. **CAREER:** Dir. of Mktg, Merchandising/Packaging Div., The Mead Corporation, Atlanta, GA, 1975-86; VP, Retail Mktg & Sales, Royal Bank of Canada, 1991-94; VP, Cardholder Svcs, head office, 1995 to date. **SELECTED PUBLICATIONS:** published in various trade publications; student newspaper ed. **AFFIL:** Atlanta Lawn Tennis Association (Team Captain); Wharton Alumni Club (VP, Membership); Lawson Park Tennis Club (Pres. 1994-96). **HONS:** Standard Oil Fellowship, Wharton Sch. **INTERESTS:** tennis; politics; music. **MISC:** 2 US patents for point-of-sale gravity feed injection molded merchandising display.

Fichman, Ina, B.A. 🎭 $ 📺

Vice-President/Producer, MAXIMAGE PRODUCTIONS, 350 Grosvenor, Westmount, QC H3Z 2M2 (514) 485-6595, FAX (504) 481-6645, EMAIL inaf@maximage.interax.net. Born Montreal 1961. m. Howard Goldberg. 1 ch. Joshua Maxwell Fichman-Goldberg. **EDUC:** Carleton Univ., B.A.(Comm.) 1984. **CAREER:**

journalist, CBC Radio & Television, 1984-88; Prod./VP, Maximage Productions, 1988 to date; Assoc. Prod., La Fête Productions, 1993-94. SELECTED CREDITS: *Tokugawa* (1989); *Moving Mountains* (1990); *Moise* (1991); *Okanada* (1993); *La Force de l'âge* (1994); Assoc. Prod., *The Return of Tommy Tricker* (1994); *Longshots* (1994); *The Last Trip* (1995). AFFIL: Auberge Shalom...pour femmes (Recording Sec. & Exec. Mbr. 1993-96); Femmes du cinéma, de la télévision, et de la vidéo à Montréal (Pres., Founding Mbr.; Treas. 1991-94); Canadian Independent Film Caucus (Co-Chair 1994-95). HONS: CTV Fellowship, Banff TV Festival, 1988; Certificate of Merit, Houston Film Festival; Silver Apple Award for *Moving Mountains*, National Educational Film & Video Festival (California) 1990; Mentorship for Women Award, C.F.T.P.A./Global, 1993; Chris Award; New York Festivals; Hot-Docs - Special Jury Member; Gemini nomination. INTERESTS: travel; reading; cycling; skiing; music; theatre; cooking. MISC: attended The Canadian Film Centre's Producers' Program, 1993; Supervising Prod. of CD-ROM *The Return of Tommy Tricker*. COMMENT: *"Ina Fichman began her career in media more than 10 years ago, as a journalist for CBC TV and radio. In 1988, she became a partner in Maximage Productions where she produces films for television."*

Field, Leigh (Lanora), B.Sc.,M.A., Ph.D. ⚛ ⊕ ☸

Professor, Department of Medical Genetics, UNIVERSITY OF CALGARY, Health Sciences Centre, 3330 Hospital Dr. N.W., Calgary, AB T2N 4N1 (403) 220-3051, FAX 283-4841, EMAIL field@acs.ucalgary.ca. Born Sault Ste. Marie, Ont. 1949. EDUC: Univ. of British Columbia, B.Sc.(Zoology) 1974; Univ. of Toronto, M.A. (Phys. Anthro.) 1975, Ph.D.(Population Genetics) 1980; Univ. of California at L.A. (UCLA), postdoctoral training in medical genetics 1979-81. CAREER: Asst. Researcher in Genetics, Dept. of Psychiatry, UCLA, 1981-82; Asst. Prof., Depts. of Paediatrics & Community Health Sciences, Univ. of Calgary, 1982-87; Alberta Heritage Medical Scholar, 1985-90; Assoc. Prof., 1987-92; Visiting Prof., Div. of Medical Genetics, UCLA, 1989; Visiting Prof., Dept. of Human Genetics, Medical Coll. of Virginia, 1990; Alberta Heritage Medical Scientist, Dept. of Paediatrics, Univ. of Calgary, 1990-94; Prof., 1992-94; Visiting Prof., Dept. of Integrative Biol., Univ. of California at Berkeley, 1994; Prof. & Alberta Heritage Medical Scientist, Dept. of Medical Genetics, Univ. of Calgary, 1994 to date. SELECTED PUBLICATIONS: "Non-HLA Region Genes in Insulin-Dependent Diabetes Mellitus" (*Baillière's Clinical Endocrinology* 1991); "Report of the Committee on the Genetic Constitution of Chromosome 6: Eleventh International Workshop on Human Gene Mapping, 1991," with A. Ziegler & A.Y. Sakaguchi (*Cytogenetics and Cell Genetics* 1991); "Nonsyndromic Cleft Lip with or without Cleft Palate in West Bengal, India: Evidence for an Autosomal Major Locus," with A.K. Ray & M.L. Marazita (*American Journal of Human Genetics* 1993); "Transforming Growth Factors Alpha (TGFA): A Modifying Locus for Nonsyndromic Cleft Lip with or without Cleft Palate?" with A.J. Ray & M.L. Marazita (*European Journal of Human Genetics* 1994); "A Locus on Chromosome 15q26 (*IDDM3*) Produces Susceptibility to Insulin-Dependent Diabetes Mellitus," with R. Tobias & T. Magnus (*Nature Genetics* 1994); "Susceptibility to Insulin-Dependent Diabetes Mellitus Maps to a Locus (IDDM 11) on Human Chromosome 14q24.1-q31," with R. Tobias, G. Thomson & S. Plan (*Genomics* 1996); numerous other publications. AFFIL: Genetics Society of Canada (Chair, Human Genetics Interest Group 1986-88; Western Dir. 1991-94); Canadian Federation of Biological Sciences; Canadian Association of Physical Anthropologists; American Society of Human Genetics; European Society of Human Genetics; International Genetics Epidemiology Society; Human Genome Organization. HONS: Gold Star Letter for Excellence in Teaching, the medical students of the Univ. of Calgary, 1988. INTERESTS: cat genetics; flying light aircraft; kayaking; Amerindian culture; ethnic music; travel. MISC: reviewer for various journals & granting agencies; recipient of various grants & fellowships; numerous presentations at scientific meetings. COMMENT: *"I am a researcher in human genetics attempting to identify the genes which predispose to juvenile diabetes, cleft lip and palate and dyslexia; I have discovered three new diabetes genes."*

Fielding, Joy, B.A. 📖 $ ⌣

Writer. c/o Stoddart Publishing, 30 Lesmill Rd., Toronto, ON M3B 2T6. Born Toronto 1945. m. Warren. 2 ch. EDUC: Univ. of Toronto, B.A.(English) 1966. CAREER: former actress, various TV programs incl. *Gunsmoke* & the Cdn film *Winter Kept Us Warm* (1965); regular book reviews for 8 yrs. on *The Radio Show*, CBC; writer. SELECTED CREDITS: 2 scripts for the CBC; *Dream Baby* (film script); *Golden Girl–The Silken Laumann Story* (TV film script). SELECTED PUBLICATIONS: *The Best of Friends* (1976); *Trance* (1978); *Kiss Mommy Goodbye* (1980); *The Other Woman* (1982); *Life Penalty* (1984); *The Deep End*

(1986); *Good Intentions* (1989); *See Jane Run* (1991); *Tell Me No Secrets* (1993); *Don't Cry Now* (1995); numerous magazine articles, short stories for *Chatelaine* & other magazines. **HONS:** Book of the Year (*Kiss Mommy Goodbye*), Periodical Association of Canada, 1980. **INTERESTS:** reading; tennis; golf; bridge; swimming; movies; travel.

Filer, Diana Mary, Livingston, B.A., N.D.C. 📺
Broadcasting Consultant. 847 Hornby St., Apt. 301, Vancouver, BC V6Z 1T9, EMAIL diana_filer@mindlink.bc.ca. Born Vancouver 1933. d. 1 ch. **EDUC:** Univ. of British Columbia, B.A. 1954; National Defence Coll., Kingston, Ont., Diploma 1982. **CAREER:** joined CBC, 1961; Prod., radio features & current affairs, 1967-74; Prod., *24 Hours*, CBC-TV, 1975-77; Head, Radio Variety, CBC, 1977-81; Exec. Asst. to Asst. MD, English Ntwks, 1982-83; Dir., CBC London, 1984-86; Dir., Corp. Int'l Rel'ns, CBC, 1986-92. **SELECTED CREDITS:** prod. & writer, numerous radio documentaries during the 70s incl. *Tribute to Mahalia Jackson*, 1972, *David Livingston*, 1973. **AFFIL:** Music in the Morning Concert Society (Bd. Mbr.; Pres.); Writers' Development Trust (Bd.); Ballet BC (Bd.); Vancouver Symphony Orchestra (Mktg Committee); Performing Arts Lodges of Canada; International Institute of Communications; Royal Television Society; Canadian Institute of International Affairs; Vancouver Institute; Georgia Club; National Press Club; North American National Broadcasters' Association (Advisory Council 1988-93); Ottawa Writers' Development Trust (Committee Mbr. 1986-92). **HONS:** Commonwealth Rel'ns Bursary, 1972; National Defence Coll., 1981-82. **INTERESTS:** music; theatre; walking; reading. **MISC:** originated *Quirks and Quarks*, CBC Radio; Jury Chair, Prix Italia, 1973; Premios Ondas Jury, 1984; organizer of the Canada/Japan Television Executives' Conference, Toronto, 1987.

Filipovic, Dusanka, P.Eng. ■ $ ⚛ ☝
Chairman of the Board, BLUE-ZONE TECHNOLOGIES INC., 4 Forest Lane Way, Ste. 1201, Toronto, ON M2N 5X8 (416) 733-1169, FAX 733-1169. Born Belgrade, Yugoslavia 1948. sep. 2 ch. George, Mark. **EDUC:** Univ. of Belgrade, B.Eng.(Chem. Eng.) 1971. **CAREER:** Asst. to Prof., Dept. of Chem. Eng., Univ. of Belgrade, 1971-74; Commercial Eng., Foreign Trade Bus., Jugolaboratorija, Export-Import Co., Belgrade, 1971-74; Tech. Rep., Linde Div. for Industrial, Medical & Specialty Gases, Union Carbide Canada Ltd., 1974-76; Product Specialist, 1976-80; Accts Mgr, 1980-85; Mgr, New Bus. Dev., Linde Technologies Inc. (subsidiary wholly owned by Linde), 1985-91; Pres. & CEO, Halozone Technologies Inc., 1991-94; Deputy Chrm, 1994-96; Chrm, Blue-Zone Technologies Inc., 1996 to date. **SELECTED PUBLICATIONS:** *Recovery of Halogenated Hydrocarbons from Discharge Streams*; *CFC Emissions Management, Recovery and Reclamation–The Halozone Global Choice*; *Strategies for Successful Equity Financing*. **AFFIL:** Professional Engineers Ontario; Licensing Executives' Society, US/Canada; Water Pollution Control Federation, WPCF (Dir., PCAO Bd.); American Water Works Association (Trustee, Ont. Section 1990-94); Air & Waste Management Association; Canadian Environment Industry Association, (Dir.); Ontario Centre for Environmental Technologies Advancement (Dir.); Committee of Ontario Deans of Engineering (Advisory Council); Pollution Control Association of Ontario, PCAO (Dir. 1990-94). **HONS:** The Engineering Medal for R.&D., Association of Professional Engineers of Ontario, 1991; *The Financial Post* Environmental Award for Bus., Green Product Category, 1991; Women on the Move Award, The Toronto Sun Publishing Co., 1992; the prestigious 1993 Manning Principal Award for Cdn Innovation; 1993 Ont. Waste Minimization Award; Nat'l 1994 Skills for Change New Pioneers Award for Science & Technology. **INTERESTS:** sightseeing; travel; music; reading; public speaking. **MISC:** 1st person to serve simultaneously on the bds. of Pollution Control Association of Ontario & American Water Works Association, Ont. Section; Judge, Environmental Science & Eng. Awards Program; recognized as one of Canada's famous women inventors by the National Museum of Science & Technology for the invention of a portable device to recapture chlorofluorocarbons (CFCs) from refrigerators, air conditioners & industrial processes; Patent: Process for the Separation & Recovery for Reuse & Recycling Halogenated Hydrocarbons in a Gas Stream–Worldwide Protection. **COMMENT:** *"A graduate from the University of Belgrade. Co-invented a Blue Bottle Technology while working for the Linde Div. of Union Carbide, which has worldwide patent protection. I was granted exclusive licence by Linde to commercialize the process worldwide. In December 1991, co-founded Halozone, which is now publicly traded on the TSE."*

Finamore, Brenda ✪ $ ✏
Graphic Designer, BRENDA FINAMORE DESIGN, 2305 St. George St., Port Moody, BC V3H 2G3 604) 939-6534, FAX 939-6534. Born Vancouver 1963. m. Randy. 2 ch. Cicely,

Jacob. **EDUC:** Okanagan Coll., Fine Arts Diploma 1983; Emily Carr Coll. of Art & Design, Graphic Design Diploma 1986. **CAREER:** graphic designer, Cochrane & Cassidy Design, 1986-94; self-employed graphic designer, Brenda Finamore Design, 1994 to date. **SELECTED PUBLICATIONS:** graphic designer, *Dance International* Magazine, 1993 to date. **AFFIL:** Graphic Designers' Association of Canada; S.P.C.A. (fundraising; literature design). **HONS:** first place, Staedler Graphics Poster Design Award; Graphex Award, Graphic Designers' Association. **INTERESTS:** painting; photography; parenting; piano; child psych.; hiking; cycling; camping. **COMMENT:** *"Including nonprofit work, graphic design was the main focus of my life for eight years. The birth of my two children created a need for balance. Freelancing has allowed me financial, creative and maternal balance, because I work mainly at night while my children sleep. This is my greatest achievement, the best of both worlds."*

Finestone, Karen, R.N.,B.N.,M.Sc.(A.) ⊕
Clinical Nurse Specialist, SIR MORTIMER B. DAVIS JEWISH GENERAL HOSPITAL, Institute of Community and Family Psychiatry, 4333 Côte Ste.-Catherine Rd., Montreal, QC (514) 340-8120, FAX 340-7507. Born Montreal 1950. m. Kenneth Simmons. 3 ch. Sarah, Keith, Benjamin. **EDUC:** Montreal General Hospital, R.N. 1972; McGill Univ., B.N.(Nursing) 1972, M.Sc.(A)(Nursing) 1979. **CAREER:** Clinical Nurse Specialist, Montreal General Hospital, 1979-81; Nursing Instructor, Univ. of British Columbia, 1981-85; Head Nurse, Douglas Hospital, 1986-89; Clinical Nurse Specialist & Nursing Coord., External Psychiatric Svcs, Jewish General Hospital, 1989 to date. **SELECTED PUBLICATIONS:** "Group support for the families of psychiatric patients" with others (*Journal of Psychosocial Nursing* No. 12 1985). **AFFIL:** Canadian Federation of Mental Health Nurses (Dir.); Canadian Clinical Nurse Specialist Group (Que. Rep.); Health Canada: Health Promotion and Programs Branch (Self Care Proj., Advisory Group); Corporation des Infirmières et Infirmiers de la Région de Montréal (Dir. 1992-94); Registered Psychiatric Nurses' Association of B.C. (Standards Committee). **HONS:** Prize of Excellence, Fondation de la recherche en science infirmières du Québec, 1992; Marjorie Hiscott Keyes Award, Canadian Mental Health Association, 1993. **INTERESTS:** mental health; families coping with illness. **MISC:** researcher, standards of practice. **COMMENT:** *"I believe that nurses have an important role in the provision of mental health services. I have been able to facilitate the devel-*opment of psychiatric and mental health nursing practice standards, a nursing certification exam and to work with other health care providers to define mental health services."*

Finestone, The Hon. Sheila, P.C., M.P. ✦ ◉
Member of Parliament (Mount Royal), GOVERNMENT OF CANADA, 533 Confederation Building, House of Commons, Ottawa, ON K1A 0A6 (613) 995-0121, FAX 992-6762. Born Montreal 1928. m. Alan Finestone. 4 ch. **EDUC:** McGill Univ., B.Sc. **CAREER:** Pres., Women's Div., Combined Jewish Appeal, 1965-66; Pres., Corporation du Neighbourhood House, 1967-70; Exec. Committee & Community Rel'ns Committee, Canadian Jewish Congress, 1970-83; VP, Allied Jewish Community Sv.c, 1970-74; Pres., Fédération des femmes des services communautaires juifs de Montréal; Exec. Committee, L'Association de l'âge d'or, 1972-75; VP, Résidence Caldwell Inc., 1972-75; Co-Pres., Univ. de Montréal Multicultural Conference "Volontariat de demain"/"Tomorrow's Volunteers," 1974-75; VP, Young Men & Young Women's Hebrew Association (YM/YWHA) 1974-79; Official Hostess, Canadian Olympic Games, Widows of the Munich Olympics, 1975; Bd. of Dir., Nouveau Départ - Orientation pour les femmes, 1976-79; Entraide aux veuves, Qué., 1979-81; Bd. of Dir., Centre de Référence du Grand Montréal, 1979-83; Exec. Committee for "No" to the Referendum, 1980; Bd. of Dir., La Fondation de l'Institut de Cardiologie de Montréal, 1980-84; Policy Advisor to the Leader of the Opposition, Nat'l Assembly of Que., 1980-84; Bd. of Dir., Alliance Québec, 1982-84; Bd. of Dir., Coalition for Pension Reform for Women, 1982-84; Bd. of Dir., Musée des Beaux-Arts de Montréal, 1982-84; Treas., Fondation Thérèse F. Casgrain, 1983; Bd. of Gov., "La Bible et les Arts," YM-YWCA & NHS Svcs, 1983-86; MP (Mount Royal), 1984 to date; Official Opposition Critic, Status of Women & Youth, 1984-93; Official Opposition Critic for Comm. & Culture, 1985-93; Sec. of State for Multiculturalism & Status of Women, 1993-96;Chair., Standing Committee on Human Rights and the Status of Persons with Disabilities, 1996 to date. **AFFIL:** The Canadian Association of Gerontology; Retirement Planning Association; Canada-Europe Parliamentary Association; Canada-France Parliamentary Association; Canada-Greece Parliamentary Association; Commonwealth Parliamentary Association, Cdn Branch; Canadian NATO Parliamentary Association; Canada-China Friendship Group; Canada-Germany Friendship Group; Canada-Israel Friendship Group; Canada-Italy Friend-

ship Group; Canada-Japan Inter-Parliamentary Group; Inter-Parliamentary Union (V-Chrm); Committee on Soviet & Syrian Jewry; Liberal Party Caucus (Chair, Social Policy Committee). HONS: Barkoff Award for Young Leadership, 1956; Samuel Bronman Award for exceptional service to the Montreal Jewish Community, Federation CJA, 1996; Jackie Robinson Special Award, Montreal Assoc. of Black Business People, 1996. INTERESTS: skiing; bridge; art; golf. COMMENT: *"Mrs. Finestone has been involved in community development, ranging from cultural issues to those dealing with minorities in the province of Quebec. She has been active in protecting anglophone rights in Quebec and francophone rights throughout Canada."*

Finlay, A. Joy, B.A.,Dip.Ed., M.Ed. ■ 🐦 🐝 🖑
Naturalist and Educator. 270 Trevlac Place, Victoria, BC V8X 3X1. Born Davidson, Sask. 1932. m. J. Cam Finlay. 3 ch. Barton Brett, Warren Hugh, Rhonda Marie. EDUC: Brandon Coll., Univ. of Manitoba, B.A. 1954; Univ. of Alberta, Dip.Ed. 1974, M.Ed.(Curriculum & Instruction) 1978. CAREER: Social Worker, Children's Aid, Brandon, Man., 1954-55; Foster Home Worker, Social Svcs, Prov. of Sask., 1955-56; Foster Home Worker, City of Edmonton, 1958-59; Naturalist, City of Edmonton, 1965-74; Lecturer in Environmental Educ. & Curriculum, Univ. of Alberta, 1970s; teacher, consultant, administrator, Edmonton Public Sch. Bd., 1974-88; conservation educ. & interpretation for numerous projects, 1965 to date. SELECTED CREDITS: consultant/script writer, various nature, hist., environmental educ. & other topics, *ACCESS*, prov. radio & TV. SELECTED PUBLICATIONS: *Winter Here & Now*; *Parks in Alberta*, co-author (1987); *Ocean to Alpine, A.B.C. Nature Guide* (1982); *A Nature Guide to Alberta*, sr. author (1980); *Alberta Junior Atlas*, contributor; *Elementary Science Curriculum Guide, Alberta*, contributor; for more than 10 yrs., regular Nature Columnist for the *Edmonton Journal* & *The Calgary Herald*. AFFIL: American Nature Study Society (Past Pres.); Alberta Teachers' Association (Founding Pres., Environment & Outdoor Educ. Council); Canadian Nature Foundation (Dir.; VP 1984-90); North American Environmental Education Association (Dir. 1983-89); Federation of Alberta Naturalists (former Dir.); Banff Sch. of the Environment (former Dir.); Alberta Task Force on Environmental Educ.; Environmental Council of Alberta (Past Chair, Energy Conservation Study Group Public Advisory Commission); Outdoors Unlittered Alberta (Past Chrm). HONS: Commemorative Medal for the 125th

Anniversary of the Confederation of Canada, 1992; Reeves Award of Distinction, County of Strathcona, 1991; Douglas Pimlot Award, Canadian Nature Federation, 1991; Member of the Order of Canada, 1990; Canada Parks Service Heritage Award, Environment Canada, 1990; Ralph D. Bird Award, Manitoba Naturalist Society, 1988; Environment Canada presentation by H.R.H. Prince Philip, 1987; Order of the Bighorn Award, Alberta, 1987; Loran Goulden Award, Federation of Alberta Naturalists, 1979; "Woman of the Year," *Chatelaine* Magazine, 1975. INTERESTS: pottery; nature; photography. MISC: Nat'l Chair for Wildlife '97, a year-long celebration, which she helped to initiate, develop & implement, of Canada's 100th anniversary of wildlife conservation; helped establish the first city-run nature centre in Canada, the John Janzen Nature Centre in Edmonton; was involved in planning the Blue Lake Centre near Hinton, Alta. COMMENT: *"A true environmentalist, Joy Finlay has never slowed in her dedication to making our world a better place. She is one of the first urban environmentalists and was into recycling and reusing long before it ever became popular. Her innovative approach to education has made a significant impact on many students, teachers and leaders in the Edmonton region, the rest of Alberta and many other provinces in Canada and several U.S. states."*

Finlayson, Thelma, B.A. 🐝 🐦 ☯ 🖑
Professor Emerita, Department of Biological Sciences, SIMON FRASER UNIVERSITY, Burnaby, BC V5A 1S6 (604) 291-4220, FAX 291-3496. Born Oshawa, Ont. 1914. w. L. Roy Finlayson (dec.). EDUC: Univ. of Toronto, B.A.(Biol.) 1936, Ont. Coll. of Educ., Teaching Certificate (Sci.) 1937; American Registry of Professional Entomologists, Certificate in Entomology 1971. CAREER: Tech. Officer, Fed. Dept. of Agric., Institute for Biological Control, 1937-40 & 1942-59; Research Officer, 1959-64; Research Scientist, 1964-67; Asst. Prof., Simon Fraser Univ., 1967-71; Assoc. Prof., 1971-76; Prof., 1976-79; Prof. Emerita, 1979 to date. SELECTED PUBLICATIONS: 38 research papers in refereed journals incl.: "Taxonomy of cocoons and puparia, and their contents of Canadian parasites of some native Diprionidae (Hymentoptera)" (*Canadian Entomologist* (95) 1963); "The cephalic structures and spiracles of final-instar larvae of the subfamily Campopleinae, tribe Campoplegini (Hymenoptera: Ichneumonidae" (*Ent. Soc. Can. Mem. 94*, 1975); "The systematics and taxonomy of final-instar larvae of the family Aphidiidae (Hymenoptera)" (*Ent. Soc. Can. Mem. 152*, 1990); various monographs & chapters. AFFIL:

Entomological Society of B.C. (former Dir. & Pres.; Hon. Life Mbr.); Entomological Society of Canada (Hon. Mbr. 1989; Fellow); Entomological Society of America; Professional Pest Management Society of B.C. (Hon. Mbr.); Sigma Delta Epsilon (honour society of women scientists). HONS: C.D. Nelson Memorial Prize, Simon Fraser Univ., 1986; Association of Donors to Simon Fraser Univ. named "The Thelma Finlayson Society"; 2 species of insects have been named after Finlayson; Doctor of Laws honoris causa, Simon Fraser Univ., 1996. INTERESTS: music; travel; golf. MISC: became the university's first Prof. Emerita in 1979.

Finley, Diane Dennis, B.A.,M.B.A. ■ Ⓢ
Director of Strategic Planning and Development, LAIDLAW TRANSIT LTD., 3221 North Service Rd., Box 5028, Burlington, ON L7R 3Y8 (905) 336-1800, FAX 335-8662. Born Hamilton, Ont. 1957. m. EDUC: Univ. of Western Ontario, B.A.(Admin. Studies) 1979, M.B.A. (Policy & Mktg) 1982. CAREER: Strategic & Mktg Planner, Lawson Graphics, 1982-84; Bus. Analyst, Westeel Rosco, 1984; Mgr, Planning & Analysis, Manitoba Liquor Control Commission, 1985-90; independent mgmt consultant & teacher, 1990-92; Dir., Strategic Planning, Laidlaw Transit, 1992 to date. AFFIL: The Planning Forum. COMMENT: *"A hands-on internal consultant with experience in the public and private sectors of manufacturing, service, distribution and education."*

Finnigan, Joan, B.A. 📖 ⊗ 🖊
Writer. Hartington, ON. Born Ottawa 1925. w. Dr. Charles Grant MacKenzie. 3 ch. Jonathan MacKenzie, Roderick MacKenzie, Martha MacKenzie. EDUC: Queen's Univ., B.A.(English & Econ.) 1949; Sch. of Journalism, Carleton Univ. CAREER: teacher, journalist, wife, mother, writer. SELECTED CREDITS: Writer, *The Best Damn Fiddler from Calabogie to Kaladar*, NFB; various scripts for NFB & CBC Radio during 1960s & 1970s; *Up the Vallee!*, Tarragon Theatre Workshop Production, prod. Bill Glassco, 1976; *Songs From Both Sides of the River*, National Arts Centre, prod. Andis Celms, 1987; *Wintering Over*, Museum of Civilization, Hull, prod. David Parry, 1988. SELECTED PUBLICATIONS: *It Was Warm and Sunny When We Set Out*, poetry (Toronto: Ryerson, 1970); *Laughing All the Way Home*, oral hist. (Toronto, Deneau, 1984); *Some of the Stories I Told You Were True*, oral hist. (Ottawa: Deneau & Greenberg, 1981); *The Dog Who Wouldn't Be Left Behind*, children's (Toronto: Groundwood Books, Douglas & McIntyre, 1989); *The Watershed Collection*, poetry (Kingston:

Quarry Press, 1992); *Witches, Ghosts and Loups-Garous*, scary tales (Kingston: Quarry Press, 1994); *Dancing at the Crossroads*, fiction (Quarry Press, 1995). HONS: Genie, screenplay, *The Best Damn Fiddler from Calabogie to Kaladar*; shortlisted for Trillium Award, *Wintering Over* (poetry collection); shortlisted for the Stephen Leacock Award for humour, *Laughing All the Way Home*. MISC: *Wintering Over*, play commissioned for the opening of the Museum of Civilization, Hull, 1988, performed almost continuously at the museum for 4 yrs; pioneer in oral history in Canada, having innovated her own lifestory format for her five oral/social histories of the Ottawa Valley; her seven other books on this unique indigenous region of Canada also include some oral/social history; together all 12 books make up what she likes to call "history by osmosis" of the valley. COMMENT: *"Canadian poet, playwright, oral historian, short story writer, Joan Finnigan has published 26 books since her husband's death in 1965 pushed her into the bread-winning role for her three young children. During the first decade of walking the tight-rope of freelance writing in Canada, her bread-and-butter was garnered from the CBC and NFB. When these markets dried up for the freelancer, she turned to books, particularly those illuminating the Ottawa Valley."*

Fiorillo, Frances, B.A. Ⓢ
Vice-President, Inflight Service, CANADIAN AIRLINES INTERNATIONAL LTD., 6001 Grant McConachie Way, YVR 0510, Richmond, BC V7B 1K3 (604) 270-5305, FAX 276-3973. Born Vancouver 1952. m. George Heinmiller. EDUC: Univ. of British Columbia, B.A.(Psych.) 1974. CAREER: Flight Attendant, Canadian Pacific Air Lines, Limited, 1974-81; Supervisor, Standards & Procedures, Inflight Svc., 1981-84; Mgr, Standards & Procedures, Inflight Sv., 1984-87; Mgr, Flight Attendant Admin., Inflight Svc., Canadian Airlines, 1987-90; Dir., On-Bd. Svcs, 1990-93; VP, Inflight Svc., 1993 to date. AFFIL: Canada's Business Operating Group on Total Quality Management (Conference Bd.); Vancouver Board of Trade; Point Grey Golf & Country Club; Canadian Airlines Joint Union/Mgmt Committee. INTERESTS: golf; gardening. MISC: keynote speaker at various trade conferences. COMMENT: *"I believe in the necessity of striking an equitable balance between one's career and family. I attribute the success I have enjoyed in business to my being flexible and amenable to change, which has been a constant characteristic of both our company and the industry in which it operates. I feel strongly about the need*

for corporate involvement in the community as an essential means by which to express thanks in some small measure for public support of our company."

Firth, Beatrice (Bea), R.N. ■■ ✦
Member of Legislative Assembly, Riverdale South (independent), GOVERNMENT OF THE YUKON TERRITORIES, P.O. Box 2703, White-horse, YT Y1A 2C6 (403) 667-5420, FAX 667-4499. Born Yorkton, Sask. 1946. m. Thomas P. Firth. EDUC: Winnipeg General Hospital Sch. of Nursing, R.N. 1967. CAREER: Gen. Duty Nurse/Out-Patient Supervisor/Acting Head Nurse/Acting Asst. Dir. of Nursing/ Clinical Teacher & In-Svc. Educ. Coord., Whitehorse General Hospital, 14 yrs. POLITI-CAL CAREER: elected to Yukon Legislative Assembly as P.C. candidate for Whitehorse Riverdale South, 1982 gen. election; re-elected 1985, 1989, 1992; cabinet positions in Educ. & Tourism, & Heritage & Cultural Resources portfolios, 1982-84; unsuccessful attempt at running for leadership of Yukon P.C. Party; reappointed to cabinet responsible for Health & Hum. Res., 1985; left P.C. Party to form Independent Alliance, 1991; currently leader of the Independent Alliance & vocal opposition MLA.

Firus, Karen, B.A.,M.F.A. 🐾⊗ 🏺
Artist, Filmmaker, Renegade, RENAISSANCE WOMAN, 4101 Grace Cres., N. Vancouver, BC V7R 3Z9 (604) 987-1999, FAX 258-9107. Born Vancouver. s. EDUC: Univ. of British Columbia, B.A. 1981, M.F.A. 1986. CAREER: independent filmmaker, writer, dir., prod., 1981 to date; freelance art dir. & set designer for film & TV, 1984 to date; mixed-media artist & performer, 1990 to date. SELECTED CREDITS: Prod./Dir./Host, "Bustin' Into Art" segments, *The Creators* (series); Set Designer, *Demovision* (TV variety series); *Fashion 99* (film) 1986; *SpectrumSpectrumSpectrum* (film) 1981. SELECTED PUBLICATIONS: various short nonfiction for the *Vancouver Sun* & *Vancouver Magazine*. EXHIBITIONS: artwork featured in various group & solo exhibitions & found in private collections. HONS: various awards for film work incl.: Genie nomination, 1988; Norman McLaren Award, 1986; Silver, Houston International Film Festival, 1987; Sony Award for Excellence, Festival of Canadian Fashion, 1987; Kodak Canada Award, 1981; recipient of 2 U.B.C. Grad. Fellowships, 1981 & 1982. INTERESTS: history of clothing & cosmetics; Egyptology; Fellini; purple colours; accessory hoarding & being a "fabulous babe." MISC: ongoing donations of original artwork for invitational charity live-auc-

tions supporting the Canadian Craft Museum (Endeavour Auction) & Vancouver's Arts Umbrella for Children. COMMENT: *"I am the ultimate Renaissance Woman and visual vigilante.I do it all! My work enlivens people's lives with colour, humour and high-energy entertainment. My art is inspired by fashion, film, Cleopatra and the almighty lipstick tube, resulting in haute couture artifacts. My objective? To knock the socks off the world!"*

Fischman, Sheila, M.A. 🎋 📖 🏺
Literary Translator. 3640 Clark St., Montreal, QC H2X 2S2 (514) 842-1674, FAX 842-3998. Born Moose Jaw, Sask. EDUC: Univ. of Toronto, M.A. CAREER: literary translator; prepared & presented documentaries for CBC-Radio ntwk on Que. writers & publishers, 1975; Book Review Ed., *The Montreal Star*, 1977; Book Columnist, *The Gazette* & *The Globe and Mail*. SELECTED PUBLICATIONS: approx. 60 translations from French to English, principally of novels by such contemporary Que. writers as Yves Beauchemin, Lise Bissonnette, Marie-Claire Blais, Roch Carrier, François Gravel, Anne Hébert, Hélène Le Beau, André Major, Jacques Poulin, Michel Tremblay, Élise Turcotte; has translated short stories by those writers, as well as Monique Proulx, Louis Dantin & others. AFFIL: Literary Translators' Association of Canada (Founding Mbr.); PEN, Canadian Centre. HONS: Canada Council Translation Prize, 1974, 1984; finalist, Gov. General's Translation Prize, 1990, 1991, 1992, 1993, 1994, 1995; Félix-Antoine Savard Translation Prize, Translation Center, Columbia Univ., 1989, 1990.

Fisher, Valda, B.A.,B.Ed. 🙂 ⊕
President, SPINA BIFIDA AND HYDROCEPHALUS ASSOCIATION OF NEW BRUNSWICK, 325 Mountain Rd., Moncton, NB E1C 2T9 (506) 857-9941. Born Toronto 1925. m. Edward. 3 ch. EDUC: Univ. of Toronto, B.A. 1948; Mount Allison Univ., B.Ed. 1964. CAREER: war svc., Women's Royal Canadian Naval Svc., 1943-45; elementary sch. teacher, Sackville, N.B., 1968-88. AFFIL: Spina Bifida & Hydrocephalus Association of N.B. (Pres.); Canadian Diabetes Association (former Pres., Sackville & District Branch); IODE Sackville, N.B. (former Regent & Treas.); St. Paul's Anglican Church. COMMENT: *"My main interest in life has been my family and children. I have always loved children and striven to be a part of their development and education."*

Fitch, Catherine, B.F.A. ⊗ 🐾 🏺
Actor. c/o Caldwell & Company, 165 Danforth Ave., Toronto, ON M4K 1N2 (416) 465-

6168, FAX 465-0955. Born Balcarres, Sask. s. **EDUC:** Univ. of Calgary, B.F.A.(Acting) 1990; National Theatre Sch. of Canada, Diploma (Acting) 1990. **SELECTED CREDITS:** *The Arrow* (miniseries), Straight Arrow Prod./CBC; *Mama's Boys* (feature), Global; Lead, *Butterbox Babies* (telefilm), Sullivan Films; Guest Star, 3 eps., *Road to Avonlea* (series), Sullivan Films; 2 eps., *Kids in the Hall* (series), CBC; Lead, *South of Wawa* (feature), Accent Ent.; Janine, *2000*, Tarragon Theatre; Meggie, *Glorious 12th*, Neptune Theatre; Amanda/Helen, *The Wooden Hill*, Canadian Stage; Carol, *Oleanna*, Citadel Theatre; Armless Annie, *Freaks*, Atelier Theatre, NAC; Rose, *Dancing at Lughnasa*, Theatre Calgary, Canadian Stage; The Baroness, *The Baroness and the Maid*, NAC, Atelier Theatre. **AFFIL:** ACTRA; Canadian Actors' Equity Association. **HONS:** Best Supporting Actress (*Butterbox Babies*), Gemini Awards 1996. **INTERESTS:** gardening; photography; collecting folk art. **COMMENT:** *"Since graduating from the National Theatre School and the University of Calgary, Catherine has worked in major theatres across the country as well as performing feature roles in several television and film projects. She hopes to continue her commitment to the burgeoning Canadian arts scene."*

Fitch, Pamela L., B.A.,R.M.T. ⊕ ✊ ♥

Past President, ONTARIO MASSAGE THERAPIST ASSOCIATION (OMTA), 365 Bloor St. E., Ste. 1807, Toronto, ON M4W 3L4. Registered Massage Therapist/Massage Therapist Consultant, METCALFE MASSAGE THERAPY CLINIC, 180 Metcalfe St., Ste. 607, Ottawa, ON K2P 1P5 (613) 235-2377. **EDUC:** Carleton Univ., B.A. 1979; Sutherland-Chan Massage Sch. & Teaching Clinic, 1988. **CAREER:** Cultural Events Coord., Sask. Dept. of Culture & Youth, 1980; Intergov't Affairs Reporter during the Constitutional Accord Hearings, Gov't of Sask., 1980; researcher, Applebaum-Hébert Commission on the Arts, 1980-81; Astrolabe & Winterlude Entertainment Coord., National Capital Commission, 1981-82; Info. Officer, National Capital Commission, 1982-86; Registered Massage Therapist in private practice, 1988 to date. **SELECTED CREDITS:** choral singer with Cantata Singers of Ottawa, New Chamber Singers; writer & performer, "Letters from Magda," Ottawa (1992, 1994, 1995); Guest Host, *In Good Faith*, CHRO TV, Ottawa (1994); lyricist for "In the Beginning," a composition by Gary Hayes, performed by Cantata Singers of Ottawa (1995). **EDIT:** Contributing Ed., *Journal of Soft Tissue Manipulation*. **AFFIL:** OMTA (Dir. 1990-91; Pres. 1991-95); Centre for Treatment of Sexual Abuse & Childhood Trauma, Ottawa (Inter-Professional Committee). **MISC:** conference presentations & consulting on ethics, boundaries & post-traumatic stress. **COMMENT:** *"I am committed to heightening awareness about the wide-ranging benefits of and need for better access to massage therapy and ethical touch. Through my work in the OMTA, in my private practice and in my personal life, I try to embody the qualities of honesty, trust and respect, which are so integral to healing and personal growth."*

FitzGerald, Daphne J. ■ $

President, Group Insurance Division, ZURICH CANADA, 200 University Ave., 9th Fl., Toronto, ON M5H 4B8 (416) 597-5799, FAX 597-5555. Born Regina 1947. m. Brian FitzGerald. 1 ch. Casey. **EDUC:** Univ. of Toronto, Certificate in Personnel & Industrial Rel'ns 1979. **CAREER:** Personnel Supervisor, Zurich Canada, 1974-76; Superintendent, Personnel Svcs, 1976-82; Personnel Mgr, 1982-87; Fac. Mbr., Sch. of Continuing Studies, Univ. of Toronto, 1983-89; VP, Corp. Dev., Zurich Canada, 1987-88; Sr. VP, Corp. Dev., 1988-91; Sr. VP, Field Oper., 1991-92; Sr. VP, Personal Insur., 1992-94; Pres., Personal Insur. SBU, 1994; Pres., Group Insur. SBU, 1994 to date. **SELECTED PUBLICATIONS:** "Insurance Boring? The Insurance Institute of Canada Guide to Insurance Education" (*Canadian Underwriter* 1991); "How Performance Appraisal Links to Corporate Strategy" (*Canadian HR Reporter* Mar. 1989). **DIRECTOR:** MultiServices Canada; World Travel Protection. **AFFIL:** Canadian Chamber of Commerce (Chair, Hum. Res. Committee 1991-94); Ryerson Sch. of Bus. (Bus. Advisory Committee); Institute of Corporate Directors; Human Resources Professionals of Ontario; Ontario Society for Training & Development; Insurance Institute of Ontario; Out of the Cold; The United Way; The Easter Seals Foundations; Canadian Council for Native Business; Insure-Run; YWCA; Toronto Blue Jays Fan Club; The Granite Club. **HONS:** nominee, Women Who Make a Difference Award, 1992. **INTERESTS:** reading; baseball; computer hacking. **MISC:** frequent public speaker; Bd. Mbr., Ontario Workers' Compensation Bd., 1991-94.

Fitzgerald, Judith, B.A.,M.A. ■ 📖 ✎ 🎭

Poet, Editor, Critic. Box 876, Sundridge, ON P0A 1Z0 (705) 386-2771, FAX 386-2772. Born Toronto 1952. **EDUC:** York Univ., B.A. 1976, M.A. 1977; Univ. of Toronto, doctoral studies in English 1978-81. **CAREER:** Asst. Ed., *The English Quarterly*, 1976-77; leader, 12 creative writing workshops for students (4 for secondary, 8 for elementary) sponsored by Ont.

Arts Council, various cities in Ont., 1976-84; Teaching Asst., Erindale Coll., Univ. of Toronto, 1978-81; Poetry Acquisitions Ed., Black Moss Press, Windsor, 1980-86; regular contributor, book pages, *Windsor Star*, 1981-87; Host, *For/Words*, weekly TV book & interview feature, Windsor, 1981-82; Asst. Prof., Laurentian Univ., 1981-83; regular contributor, book pages, *The Globe and Mail* & *Quill & Quire*, 1981-84; Asst. Prof., Algoma Univ. Coll., Summer 1982; Entertainment Critic & literary journalist, *The Globe and Mail*, 1983; regular contributor, book pages, *Kingston-Whig Magazine, Books in Canada* & *Canadian Literature*, 1983-87; Sr. Lecturer, Glendon Coll., York Univ., Fall 1983; Poetry Critic & literary journalist, *The Toronto Star*, 1984-88; regular contributor, book pages, *Canadian Forum*, 1984-86; Sr. Lecturer, Algoma Univ. Coll., Spring 1984; Writer-in-Residence, Algoma Univ. Coll., Spring 1984; Writer-in-Residence, Hamilton Public Library, Fall 1984; Ed., General Publishing, 1985; Columnist, *Windsor Star*, 1985-86; Toronto Literary Correspondent & columnist, *Ottawa Citizen*, 1985-87; columnist, *Innings*, 1985-87; founder, Women'Speak, 1986; Assoc. Ed., Black Moss Press, 1987; Sr. Writer/Contributing Ed., *Country: The Canadian Country Music Authority*, 1990-91; Writer-in-Residence, Laurentian Univ., Fall 1992; syndicated columnist, "CountrySide," *The Toronto Star* & Southam Star Network, 1991-93; creator & Features Ed./Sr. Writer, *Today's Country*, SRN, 1992-93; Writer-in-Residence, Univ. of Windsor, 1993-94; Prof., Univ. canadienne en France, Villefranche-sur-mer, France, 1994-95; Ed., *Country Wave*, 1995 to date. **SELECTED PUBLICATIONS:** *Victory* (Couch House, 1975); *Lacerating Heartwood* (Coach House, 1977); *Split/Levels* (Coach House, 1983); *Given Names: New and Selected Poems 1972-1985* (Black Moss, 1985); *walkin' wounded* (Black Moss, 1993); *River* (ECW, 1995); *My Orange Gorange*, illustrated by Maureen Paxton, children's poetry (Black Moss, 1985); numerous other poetry books & chapbooks; *Un Dozen: Thirteen Canadian Poets*, edited with introductions (Black Moss, 1982); *SP/ELLES: Poetry by Canadian Women/Poésie de femmes canadiennes*, edited with an introduction (Black Moss, 1986); numerous anthologies & periodicals, incl. *Fiddlehead, Saturday Night, This Magazine,* & *Oxford Book of Poetry by Canadian Women*, Rosemary Sullivan, ed. (Oxford, 1989); criticism, feature articles & profiles in a variety of periodicals & newspapers, incl. *artmagazine, Academy of Canadian Literature,* & *The Globe and Mail.* **AFFIL:** League of Canadian Poets; SOCAN. **HONS:** Fiona Mee

Award, 1983; Writers' Choice Award, *Given Names: New and Selected Poems 1972-1985,* 1986; short-listed, Pat Lowther Award, *Given Names,* 1987; short-listed, Poetry, Gov.-General's Award, *Rapturous Chronicles,* 1991; Best Regularly Scheduled Music Program, International Radio Competition Citation, New York Festival, *Today's Country,* 1994; Silver Medal, Best Regularly Scheduled Music Program, *Today's Country,* Satellite Radio Network, Int'l Radio Competition, New York Festival, 1995; short-listed, Trillium Award, *River,* 1995. **INTERESTS:** world hist.; birding; photography. **MISC:** recipient of various grants from the Toronto Arts Council, Ontario Arts Council, Canada Council & other agencies; jury member, judge or panelist for various literary events & competitions, 1980 to date; manuscripts & archival material on deposit at McLennan Library, McGill Univ.; listed in *Canadian Who's Who, Contemporary Authors, Contemporary Literary Criticism, International Authors and Writers Who's Who, Who's Who in Canadian Literature, Who's Who in North American Poetry,* & *World Book Encyclopedia.* **COMMENT:** *"Internationally respected poet, editor, critic, and mentor to aspiring writers, Judith Fitzgerald nears completion of,* The Words that Came Between Us.*"*

Fitzgerald, Patricia A., B.B.A.,M.A., Ph.D. Ⓢ ⌇ ✿
Professor of Management, Department of Management, SAINT MARY'S UNIVERSITY, Halifax, NS B3H 3C3 (902) 420-5771, FAX 420-5119, EMAIL pfitzger@shark.stmarys.ca. Born N.S. **EDUC:** St. Francis Xavier Univ., B.B.A.(Acctg) 1967; Univ. of North Dakota, M.A.(Bus. Educ.) 1970; Univ. of Northern Colorado, Ph.D.(Mgmt) 1974. **CAREER:** Prof. of Mgmt, Saint Mary's Univ., 1976 to date; foreign expert, mgmt consultant, Beijing Univ. of Int'l Bus. & Econ., Beijing, P.R.C., 1983-84; Assoc. Prof., MBA Program, Univ. of Zimbabwe, 1987; Sr. Lecturer, Mgmt, Chinese Univ. of Hong Kong, Shatin, H.K., 1990-91; Program Consultant on Grad. Studies in Entrepreneurship, Queensland Univ. of Technology, Brisbane. **AFFIL:** Henson Coll., Dalhousie Univ.

Flaherty, Martha, R.N.A. ■ Ⓔ ⊕ ✐
President, PAUKTUUTIT INUIT WOMEN'S ASSOCIATION, 192 Bank St., Ottawa, ON K2P 1W8 (613) 238-3977, FAX 238-1787. Born Inukjuak, Que 1950. cl. Gordon Spence. 3 ch. **EDUC:** Fort Smith, Certificate of Nursing 1972; Univ. of Ottawa, Certificate of Journalism 1985. **CAREER:** interpreter/translator; politician; nurse; journalist; photographer; Pres., Pauktuutit Inuit Women's Association.

SELECTED CREDITS: suicide prevention video. SELECTED PUBLICATIONS: "I Fought to Keep My Hair, Inuit Women, Equality and Leadership" (*Canadian Women's Studies* Fall 1994). AFFIL: nuit Tapirisat of Canada (Interim VP); Canadian Panel on Violence Against Women; Indigenous Women of the Americas (Commission). INTERESTS: social issues; volleyball; throat singing; econ. dev.; human rights. COMMENT: *"Ms. Flaherty is a popular speaker, who is frequently asked to address family violence, health and social issues. As a result of her tireless work on behalf of Inuit women, she has become one of the most well-respected Inuit leaders in Canada."*

Flanagan, Catherine, B.A.,M.A.,LL.B. ■ ⚖
Lawyer, CROWN ATTORNEY'S OFFICE, Box 2000, Charlottetown, PE C1A 4J9 (902) 368-4595, FAX 368-5812. Born Charlottetown 1956. s. EDUC: Univ. of Prince Edward Island, B.A.(English) 1977; Dalhousie Univ., M.A. (English) 1982; Osgoode Hall Law Sch., York Univ., LL.B.(Law) 1982. BAR: Ont., 1984; P.E.I., 1989. CAREER: Lawyer, Litigation Dept., Woolley, Dale & Dingwall, Toronto, 1984-88; Lawyer, Farmer & MacLeod, Charlottetown, 1988-90; Sessional Lecturer, English, Univ. of Prince Edward Island, 1990 to date; Lawyer, Macnutt & Dumont, 1990-95; Crown Attorney's Office, 1995 to date. AFFIL: Law Society of P.E.I.; Charlottetown Yacht Club (Past Commodore); Boys & Girls Clubs of P.E.I. (Pres.); United Way of P.E.I. (Dir.); AIDS P.E.I. (Dir.). INTERESTS: sailing; gardening; reading. COMMENT: *"I am an eighth-generation Islander who is very proud of her community, enjoys practising law, teaching at the university and being involved in every aspect of competitive sailing locally."*

Flanders, Ellen, B.A.,M.A., M.F.A. ■ ▯ ▤ ⊗
Director, INSIDE/OUT, TORONTO LESBIAN AND GAY FILM FESTIVAL, 114 Brunswick Ave., Toronto, ON M5S 2M2 (416) 926-0499, FAX 926-0499. Chief Executive Officer, GRAPHIC PHOTO. Born Montreal 1966. EDUC: York Univ., B.A.(Feminist Studies & Fine Arts) 1988; Goddard Coll., M.A.(Cultural Studies) 1991; Rutgers Univ., M.F.A., 1996; Whitney Fellow, Whitney Museum of American Art. CAREER: Course Dir., Goddard Coll., 1990-91; Ed. Mbr., *Fireweed*, 1992-95; Film Programmer, 1993; Course Dir., Rutgers Univ., Mason Gross Sch. of Fine Arts, 1994-95; Photographer/Filmmaker; Dir., Inside/Out Toronto Lesbian and Gay Film Festival, 1996 to date. SELECTED PUBLICATIONS: photo-essay on lesbian sexuality (*Rites Magazine* 1991); photo-essay on Jew-

ish identity & location (*Fireweed* 1992); "Beyond Identity: Coalition Initiatives from the Left" (*Fireweed* 1992); "Lesbian Peep Show," in *The Girl Wants To*, edited by Lynn Crosbie (Toronto: Coachhouse Press, 1993); "Inqueery" (*Border/Lines* 1994); "All For You," *Tangled Sheets*, ed. by Karen Tachinsky (Woman's Press, 1995); freelance photography has appeared in *Xtra*, *Rites*. EDIT: Ed. Collective Mbr., special issue on Jewish women, *Fireweed*, 1991-90. EXHIBITIONS: solo, *Women and Images*, Concordia Univ. Fine Art Gallery (1984); solo, *The Eye of the Camera: Woman as Beholder?*, Concordia Univ. Fine Art Gallery (1985); solo, *Images from the Intifada*, Women's Common, Toronto (1989); solo, *Crossing Borders, Israel/Palestine: a photographer's peace initiative*, Tangle Gallery, Toronto (1991); solo, *Beyond Identity: Coalition Initiatives from the Left*, Tangle Gallery, Toronto (1992); group exhibitions at York Univ. Art Gallery (1986, 1988, 1991) & *Lacking Desire*, Walter's Gallery, Rutgers Univ., NJ; solo, *Lacking Desire*, Rutgers Univ., Mason Gross Gallery 1996; group, *Lacking Desire*, Whitney Studio Show, Whitney Museum of American Art, 1996. AFFIL: Jewish Feminist Anti-Fascist League. COMMENT: *"I am an artist and activist and have exhibited internationally."*

Foley, Joan, B.A.,Ph.D. ▭ ▦ ▯
Professor of Psychology, UNIVERSITY OF TORONTO, Division of Life Sciences, Scarborough Campus, 1265 Military Trail, Scarborough, ON M1C 1A4 (416) 287-7424, FAX 287-7642, EMAIL foley@psych.toronto.edu. Born Sydney, Australia. d. 2 ch. Brian, Colin. EDUC: Univ. of Sydney, B.A.(Hons., Psych.) 1957, Ph.D.(Psych.) 1960. CAREER: Scientific Officer, Defence Research Medical Laboratories, 1960-62; Prof., Psych., Univ. of Toronto, 1963 to date; Assoc. Dean, Fac. of Arts & Sci., 1971-74; Principal, Scarborough Coll., Univ. of Toronto, 1977-84; VP (Academic) & Provost, 1985-93. SELECTED PUBLICATIONS: various articles in scientific journals on learning, visual perception & spatial memory. AFFIL: Canadian Psychological Association (Fellow); Association of Universities & Colleges of Canada (Int'l Rel'ns & Programs Committee); International Development Research Centre (Bd. of Gov.). HONS: Civic Award of Merit, City of Scarborough, 1986; Fac. Award, Univ. of Toronto Alumni Association, 1985. INTERESTS: gardening; tennis; skiing; music; theatre; literature. COMMENT: *"After a lengthy career in academic administration (the first woman to be the university's chief academic officer), I have returned to full-time academic work."*

Fontaine, Nicole ♣ ⊕

Deputy Minister, Citizens' Relations and Immigration, GOVERNMENT OF QUEBEC, 360 McGill, Montréal, QC H2Y 2E9, FAX (514) 873-1810. EDUC: Hôpital Ste-Justine, Dip.(Nursing) 1966; Univ. of Ottawa, B.H.Sc.(Nursing) 1972, Master of Health Svcs Mgmt 1978. CAREER: nurse, various hospitals, Que. & Europe, 1966-72; Sec., Bd. of Dir., Outaouais Regional Nurses' Corporation, 1972-73; teacher, Paediatric Nursing Techniques, Hull CEGEP, 1972-73; Bd. of Dir., Outaouais Health & Social Svcs Council, 1972-76; Chrm, Bachelor of Health Sciences Program Committee, Univ. du Québec, 1973-74; Coord., Community Health Certificate Program, Univ. du Québec à Hull, 1973-75; Consultant-Summer trainee, Outaouais Region Health & Social Svcs Agency, 1976; Commissioner, Varennes Sch. Bd., 1978; Mgmt Consultant, Montreal Reg'l Union, Caisses populaires Desjardins, 1978-79; Mgmt Consultant, Montérégie Reg'l Health & Social Svcs Agency, 1979-84; mbr., Que. Mental Health Ministerial Committee, 1983-86; Sr. Mgr, Metropolitan Montreal Reg'l Health & Social Svcs Agency, 1984-90; mbr., Ministerial Steering Committee for Public Curatorship, 1987-88; mbr., Ministerial Prov. Advisory Committee on accessibility to social & health svcs for cultural communities, 1989-90; Curatrice publique, Le Curateur public du Québec, 1990-96. SELECTED PUBLICATIONS: book & articles published in Cdn & European journals. DIRECTOR: Groupe Innovation. AFFIL: Univ. de Montréal (Bd. of Trustees); Institute of Public Administration of Canada; The Order of Chartered Administrators of Quebec; Montreal Board of Trade. INTERESTS: skiing; sailing; tennis; cycling; swimming; travel; reading. MISC: numerous conference presentations.

Fonteyne, Karen ■■ ⓟ

Olympic Athlete. c/o Canadian Olympic Association. Born Calgary 1969. EDUC: currently working on M.B.A. SPORTS CAREER: mbr., Cdn Nat'l Synchronized Swimming Team, 1987 to date. Olympic Games: Silver, team, 1996. World championships: 2nd, team, 1994; 2nd, team, 1991. World Cup: 2nd, team, 1995; 2nd, team, & 3rd, duet, 1993; 2nd, team, 1991; 2nd, team, 1989. Pan Pacific championships: 2nd, duet, 1993. Pan American Games: 2nd, team, 1995. Canadian championships: 1st, team, & 2nd, duet, 1994; 1st, duet, & 1st, team, 1993. HONS: Petro-Canada Olympic Torch Scholarship, 1990-91, 1991-92. INTERESTS: rollerblading; tennis; puzzles.

Forand, Liseanne, B.A. ♣ ⊙

Director General, CANADIAN COUNCIL OF MIN-ISTERS OF THE ENVIRONMENT, 326 Broadway, Ste. 400, Winnipeg, MB R3C 0S5 (204) 948-2090, FAX 948-2125, EMAIL lforand@ ccme.ca. Born Montreal. EDUC: Concordia Univ., B.A.(English) 1980, program of study for M.A. in English, course work completed 1982. CAREER: Writer/Ed., *OPCAN-Katimavik*, 1983-85; Comm. Coord., House of Commons, 1985-86; Media Asst./Legislative Asst./Exec. Asst., Office of the Min. of Fisheries & Oceans, Gov't of Canada, 1986-87; Int'l Fisheries Officer, East Bloc Countries, 1987-88; Int'l Fisheries Officer, France, 1988-89; Fisheries Coord., Canada-France Maritime Boundary Arbitration, 1989-90; Dir., Atlantic Div., Int'l Directorate, 1990-93; Exec. Dir., Canadian Association of Prawn Producers, 1993-94; Dir. Gen., Canadian Council of Ministers of the Environment, 1994 to date. HONS: Deputy Minister's Commendation, 1989; Commemorative Medal for the 125th Anniversary of the Confederation of Canada, 1994; DFO Merit Award, 1994. MISC: awarded research grants ($12,000 over 2 yrs.), 1982 & 1983.

Forbes, Joyce, B.A.,M.A.,Ph.D. ⊰ ▤

Professor, Department of English, LAKEHEAD UNIVERSITY, 955 Oliver Rd., Thunder Bay, ON P7B 5E1 (807) 343-8375, FAX (807) 346-7764, EMAIL jforbes@flash.lakehead.ca. Born Trinidad, West Indies 1932. m. Percival G.A. Forbes. 2 ch. EDUC: Howard Univ., B.A. (English) 1961; Queen's Univ., M.A.(English) 1964; Univ. of the West Indies, Ph.D.(English) 1977. CAREER: Chair, Dept. of English, Lakehead Univ., 1989-92. SELECTED PUBLICATIONS: "William Golding as Essayist" in "British Essays 1880-1960," *Dictionary of Literary Biography*, Robert Beum ed. (South Carolina: Buccoli Clark, 1990); "The Tears of Things" (*Arts & Literary Review* Fall 1972); "Wilson Harris's Guyana Quartet: The Outsider as Character and Symbol" (*Laurentian University Review* Feb. 1986); "Teaching and Learning in Higher Education" (*Newsletter of STLHE* May 1988); "Recollections: The Impact of a University Strike" (*Dianoia: A Liberal Arts Interdisciplinary Journal* Spring 1991); various other publications. AFFIL: Canadian Association of University Teachers (Status of Women Committee 1989-94); Lakehead Univ. Fac. Association (Exec. 1987-94; VP 1989-90); Ont. Confederation of Univ. Fac. Associations; Sr. Women Academic Administrators of Canada; Association of Canadian University & College Teachers of English; Society for Teaching & Learning in Higher Education; Canadian Research Institute for the Advancement of Women; Thunder Bay Multicultural Association (Exec. Mbr., Bd. of Dir. 1988-92); Caribbean African Association (Pres.). HONS: Canadian Commonwealth Scholar, 1961-63; OCUFA Teaching Award, 1987; 3M Canada Teaching Fellowship for Outstanding Contribution to Univ. Teaching, 1988. INTERESTS: travelling; creative writing; storytelling. MISC: numerous conference presentations & workshops; CAUT/SWC Delegate, Renewal of Canada Conference, Institutional Reform, Calgary, 1992. COMMENT: *"A pioneer in quiet, determined self-assertion, an innovator challenged by the demands of circumstances, and a tactician who measures success through the transforming of principles into learned experiences."*

Ford, Christina ■ ■ 𝖍 $

President and Owner, IMPORTED ARTISTS FILM COMPANY (representation of int'l directorial talent for Cdn commercial film production), 49 Spadina Ave., Ste. 100, Toronto, ON M5V 2J1 (416) 971-5915, FAX 971-7915, EMAIL imported@passport.ca. m. Richard D'Alessio. 1 ch. Samantha Christina D'Alessio. CAREER: Pres. & owner, Christina Ford Cosmetics, 1982-85; Exec. Prod./Gen. Mgr, McWaters Film Company International, 1986-90; Pres. & owner, Imported Artists Film Company, 1991 to date; company now one of top five largest commercial production companies in Canada; opening feature film div., early 1997. HONS: Imported Artists has won over 100 domestic & int'l awards incl.: Marketing Awards, The Bessies, Int'l Broadcast Awards, Clios, N.Y. Art Director Show Awards, N.Y. One Show Awards, London Int'l Advertising Awards, & Playback Top Spot Awards. COMMENT: *"Married to Richard D'Alessio, a very successful commercial and documentary filmmaker. They are the proud parents of Samantha Christina D'Alessio. Christina and husband Richard together produced and directed two documentary films,* America the Beautiful, *a chronicle of the motorcycle subculture, and* Inside Schizophrenia, *an in-depth look at the struggles of families dealing with schizophrenia."*

Forgay, Margery Grace Elaine (Marnie), B.A.,B.Ed.,M.A.,LL.D. ⊕ ⊕

Past President, CANADIAN DENTAL HYGIENISTS ASSOCIATION. Born Rosetown, Sask. 1932. w. 3 ch. Donald, David, Alison. EDUC: Eastman Dental Centre, Diploma in Dental Hygiene 1952; Univ. of Saskatchewan, B.A.(Biol.) 1955; Univ. of Manitoba, B.Ed. 1976; Univ. of British Columbia, M.A.(Adult Educ.) 1980. CAREER: public health, Prov. of Sask., 1952-54; Founding Dir., Sch. of Dental Hygiene, Univ. of Man-

itoba, 1962-76; Acting Dir., 1982-83; Dir., Sch. of Dental Hygiene, Dalhousie Univ., 1985-90; Acting Dir., Sch. of Dental Hygiene, Univ. of Manitoba, 1990-92; Prof., 1990-94; Advisor, Canada-Mozambique Dental Proj., 1992-93. SELECTED PUBLICATIONS: "The Effects of Pulsing Gama Radiation Dose on the Frequency of Chromosome Breakage," with T.J. Arnason & D.V. Cormack (*Proceedings of the Genetic Society of Canada* 1957); "Attitude of Canadian Dental Hygienists to Mandatory Continuing Education" (*Canadian Hygienist* Winter 1981); "The Clinical Practice Standards for Canadian Dental Hygienists," with S.J. Feller (*Probe* 1989); "Canadian Students in US Dental Hygiene Programs," with M.E. Kinnear (*Probe* 1992); "Long-Term Effects of Meridol and Chlorhexidine Mouthrinses on Plaque, Gingivitis, Staining and Bacterial Vitality," with M. Brecx, L.L. MacDondald, & M. Cheang (*Journal of Dental Research* 1993); various other publications. AFFIL: Canadian Dental Hygienists' Association (Founding Mbr.; Pres.-Elect 1994-95; Pres. 1995-96; Life Mbr.); Manitoba Dental Hygienists' Association (Life Mbr.); Manitoba Kidney Association; Coalition of Organ Donor Associations - N.S. HONS: Albert Stevenson Gold Medal, Eastman Dental Centre, 1952; T. Copeland Prize, Univ. of Saskatchewan, 1955; LL.D.(Hon.), Dalhousie Univ., 1994; Prof. Emerita, Univ. of Manitoba, 1995. INTERESTS: Inuit art; western Cdn landscape art; music; reading; hiking; swimming. MISC: organizer, 1st conference on dental hygiene research ever held; Chair, Fed. Working Group on the Practice of Dental Hygiene, 1981-88. COMMENT: *"Education, service and caring were valued in my family. I have been fortunate personally and in having career opportunities in an important developing health profession."*

Forrest, Diane, B.A. ⬚ ✎ 𝖍

Writer and Editor. 1365 Yonge St., Ste. 200, Toronto, ON M4T 2P7 (416) 969-9514, FAX 323-1063. EDUC: Trinity Coll., Univ. of Toronto, B.A.(cum laude) 1977; Sch. of Fine Arts, The Banff Centre, Radio Writing Workshop 1990; SCS, Univ. of Toronto, Master Writer's Class–Anne Michaels 1994-95. CAREER: Ed., Holt, Rinehart and Winston, 1977-79; Copy Ed., *The Canadian Magazine/Today Magazine*, 1979-80; Mng Ed., *Imperial Oil Review*, 1980-83; Researcher, *Venture*, CBC-TV, 1985-86; Researcher, Story Ed., *Chasing Rainbows*, CBC-TV, 1986-87; reader & consultant, CBC-TV, Cinexus Famous Players, Cineplex Television, Daystar Productions, 1987-90; freelance writer/ed., magazines, books, corp. projects, 1983 to date.

SELECTED CREDITS: *The Interview*, staged reading, Solar Stage "Word Works '94" festival of new works; *Market to Market*, produced by the Discovery Players, Jan. 1993; "Down the Drain," *Love and Marriage*, CBC-TV anthology series, 1996. **SELECTED PUBLICATIONS:** *Where the Jobs Are*, with principal author Colin Campbell (Macfarlane, Walter, Ross, 1994); *Vintage McClure*, co-author with Dr. Robert McClure (Welch Publishing Company Inc., 1988); *The Adventurers* (Cdn ed. Woodlake Press, 1983/US ed., Abingdon Press, 1984); regular contributor to *Cottage Life*, *Moneywise* (Financial Post Magazine); articles in *Canadian Business*, *Canadian Living*, *Chatelaine*, *The Globe and Mail*, *The Toronto Star*; newsletter writing for the MS Society of Canada. **AFFIL:** PAL Reading Service (reader); Theatre Passe Muraille. **HONS:** Second Prize, Corp. Category, Canadian Petroleum Association, 1983; Calgary Press Club Energy Writing Awards, 1983; Silver Award, Reporting/Public Svc., International Regional Magazines Association, 1994; Bronze Award, Reporting/Public Svc., International Regional Magazines Association, 1995; Silver Award, Public Issues, National Magazine Awards, 1995; Silver Award, Svc. Journalism, National Magazine Awards, 1995; Gold Award, Reporting/Public Svc., International Regional Magazines Association, 1996.

Forrester, Helen, D.Litt. 📖 🔖
Writer. c/o Writers' Union of Canada, 24 Ryerson Ave., Toronto, ON M5T 9Z9. Born Cheshire, UK 1919. **SELECTED PUBLICATIONS:** *Alien There Is None* retitled *Thursday's Child* (London: Hodder and Stoughton, 1959); *The Latchkey Kid* (Longman's Canada, 1971); *Twopence to Cross the Mersey* (London: Jonathan Cape Ltd., 1974); *Minerva's Stepchild* retitled *Liverpool Miss* (Toronto: Clarke Irwin, 1979); *Liverpool Daisy* (Toronto, London: Robert Hale Ltd., 1979); *By the Waters of Liverpool* (London: The Bodley Head, 1981); *Three Women of Liverpool* (London: Robert Hale Ltd., 1984); *Lime Street at Two* (London: The Bodley Head, 1985); *The Moneylenders of Shahpur* (London: HarperCollins, 1987); *Yes, Mama* (London: HarperCollins, 1987); *The Lemon Tree* (London: HarperCollins, 1990); *The Liverpool Basque* (Toronto: HarperCollins, 1993); *Mourning Doves* (London: HarperCollins, 1996). **AFFIL:** Writers' Union of Canada; Society of Authors, London, UK; Canadian Association of Children's Authors, Illustrators & Performers; The Authors' Lending & Copyright Society Ltd., London; CANCOPY, Toronto; Chester Literature Festival (Patron). **HONS:** Beaver Award, Hudson's Bay

Company, 1970, 1977; Hon. Mention, *Edmonton Journal* Literary Competition; Distinguished Honouree, City of Edmonton, 1977; Achievement Award for Literature, Gov't of Alberta, 1979; Alberta Culture's Literary Award, 1986; Woman of the Arts, YWCA, 1987; D.Litt.(Hon.), Univ. of Liverpool, 1988; Guild Fiction Award, 1989; D.Litt.(Hon.), Univ. of Alberta, 1993. **MISC:** Canadian citizen; travelled extensively; lived in India, Edinburgh, UK, Edmonton & others.

Forrester, Maureen, C.C.,LL.D.,D.Litt., D.Mus. • ⊗ ⊰ ☺
Contralto, Teacher, Consultant. Born Montreal 1930. 5 ch. Paula, Gina, Daniel, Linda, Susanna. **EDUC:** student of Bernard Diamant. **CAREER:** professional debut at age 21, Montréal Elgar Choir; sang with Lois Marshall, Bach Aria Group, 1965-74; numerous concerts & recitals; Chrm, Canada Council, 1984-89; teacher; conducted series of workshops in China. **SELECTED CREDITS:** has performed with many leading conductors incl. Herbert von Karajan, Leonard Bernstein, Zubin Mehta, James Levine; has performed with symphony orchestras in N. America, Europe, Australia, Israel, Russia/USSR, China & Japan; numerous recitals & TV appearances. **SELECTED CREDITS:** numerous recordings incl. Rodgers & Hammerstein's *Carousel*; Handel, *Roman Vespers*; Mahler, *Symphony No. 2*; *Meet Me In St. Louis*. **SELECTED PUBLICATIONS:** *Out of Character*, biography (1986). **AFFIL:** Sigma Alpha Iota. **HONS:** Nat'l Award in Music, Banff Sch. of Fine Arts, 1967; recipient, Harriet Cohen Int'l Music Award, 1967; Companion of the Order of Canada, 1967; Molson Prize, 1971; Samuel Simons Sanford Award, Yale Sch. of Music, 1983; Toronto Arts Award, 1989; Fellow, Stong Coll., York Univ.; LL.D.(Hon.) Bishop's Univ.; LL.D.(Hon.), Carleton Univ.; LL.D.(Hon.), Dalhousie Univ.; D.Litt.(Hon.), Lakehead Univ.; D.Litt.(Hon.), McGill Univ.; LL.D.(Hon.), McMaster Univ.; D.Litt.(Hon.), Mount Allison Univ.; D.Litt.(Hon.), St. Mary's Univ.; LL.D.(Hon.), Sir George Williams Coll.; LL.D.(Hon.); D.Litt.(Hon.); Trent Univ.; Univ. of Manitoba; LL.D.(Hon.), Univ. of Prince Edward Island; LL.D.(Hon.), Univ. of Victoria; D.Mus.(Hon.), Univ. of Western Ontario; LL.D.(Hon.), Univ. of Windsor; LL.D.(Hon.), Wilfrid Laurier Univ.; D.Litt.(Hon.), York Univ. **MISC:** *Five Songs for Dark Voice*, written for her by Cdn composer Harry Somers; one of the world's great interpreters of Mahler.

Forsyth, Cecilia, B.A. ■ ■ ♥ ☺ ✿
National President, **REAL WOMEN OF CANADA**

(nat'l lobby group–equality for all women), P.O. Box 8813, Stn T, Ottawa, ON K1G 3J1 (819) 682-3937, FAX 682-3938, EMAIL forsyth@sask.usask.ca. Born Santa Fe, New Mexico 1943. m. George. 4 ch. James, David, Gavin, Grant. EDUC: Midwestern State Univ., B.A.(Bus. Admin.) 1965. VOLUNTEER CAREER: various positions, community, sch. & church groups, 1973-89; Pres., Office Mgr & Volunteer Coord., Saskatoon Pro-Life, 1973-91; Admin. Coord., Pregnancy Crisis Line, 1984-94; Sask. Dir., Tom Wappel Liberal Party leadership campaign, 1990; committee mbr., Focus Group on Women's Issues Conference, City of Saskatoon, 1992-93; NGO-UN Observer for REAL Women of Canada, Cairo 1994, Beijing 1995, Istanbul 1996. AFFIL: REAL Women of Canada (Nat'l Pres. 1994 to date; VP/Comm. Dir., Sask. chpt. 1992 to date); Campaign Life Coalition-Sask. (Prov. Bd. 1990 to date); Pregnancy Crisis Line (Advisory Bd. 1994 to date); Saskatoon Action Circle on Youth Sexuality (Group Rep. 1994 to date). HONS: Volunteer Recognition & Award, Saskatoon Pro-Life Association, 1991; Volunteer Recognition & Award, Brevoort Park Community Association, 1989. INTERESTS: family farm; gardening; handicrafts; camping; hiking. COMMENT: *"My career as full-time homemaker permits me to use my business administration skills to benefit school, community, church, local, provincial, national and international pro-life, pro-family groups. My interest in social justice issues began in the late 1960s and remains the focus of my life today in addition to my family. Working to make the world a better place for all people is my goal."*

Forsyth, Heather, MLA ✦
Member of the Legislative Assembly, Calgary-Fish Creek, GOVERNMENT OF ALBERTA, 503 Legislative Building, 10800 - 97th Ave., Edmonton, AB T5K 2B6 (403) 427-1851, FAX 422-0351. Constituency Office, 13 Deer Valley Shopping Centre, 1221 Canyon Meadows Dr. S.E., Calgary, AB T2J 6G2 (403) 278-4444, FAX (278-7875. Born Saskatoon, Sask. m. Gordon. 2 ch. Thomas, Scott. EDUC: Mount Royal Coll.. CAREER: various positions, advtg industry, 15 yrs.; elected MLA, Calgary-Fish Creek, 1993; Mbr., Professions & Occupations Bureau, 1994 to date; Mbr., Standing Policy Committee on Community Svc, Health Workforce Rebalancing Committee (Chair), the MLA Implementation Team on Sch. Bd. Funding, 1993 to date. AFFIL: Calgary Stampede (Prov. Rep.); Parent Support Association (VP, Gov't Liaison 1990-94); Children's Wish Foundation (Dir. 1988-93); Community League (Pres.); Alberta Social Services Appeal (former

mbr., Advisory Bd.); Calgary Board of Health; Alberta Specialty Advertising Association (Pres. 1989); Youth Justice Committee; Calgary Board of Health (former mbr.). HONS: Silver Marketing Award; 1989 President's Award. INTERESTS: baseball; figure skating; power skating; reading; working with families & youth. MISC: served as Chair, Task Force on the Young Offenders Act; Mbr., All Party Panel for the Freedom of Info. & Privacy Act Legislation; Chair, Juvenile Prostitution Task Force; Chair, Provincial Mental Health Review; Street Teams (Hon. Mbr); served on at least 13 committees in first 18 months as MLA. COMMENT: *"I believe strongly in the democratic process and that my job is to represent the wishes of my constituents, regardless of my own beliefs or the government's position."*

Forsyth, Phyllis, A.B.,M.A., Ph.D. ■ 🐿 📷 ⊛
Professor of Classical Studies, History, and Fine Arts, UNIVERSITY OF WATERLOO, University Ave., Waterloo, ON N2L 3G1 (519) 885-1211, FAX 746-7881, EMAIL forsyth@watarts.uwaterloo.ca. Born Brookline, Mass. 1944. m. James J. Forsyth. EDUC: Mount Holyoke Coll., A.B.(Classics) 1966; Univ. of Toronto, M.A. (Classics) 1967, Ph.D.(Classics) 1972. CAREER: Teaching Fellow, Trinity Coll., Univ. of Toronto, 1967-69; Lecturer to Full Prof., Univ. of Waterloo, 1969 to date; Founding Chair, Dept. of Classical Studies, 1979-88; Acting Chair, Dept. of Classical Studies, 1994 to date. SELECTED PUBLICATIONS: *Atlantis: The Making of Myth* (Montreal: McGill-Queen's Univ. Press, 1980); *The Poems of Catullus* (Univ. Press of America, 1986); *Labyrinth: A Classical Magazine for Secondary Schools*, editor 1973-84, 1988-94. EDIT: *Phoenix Magazine* (Ed. Board 1979-81, 1986-88, 1992-94). AFFIL: American Philological Association; Ontario Classical Association (Exec. Council 1975-77); Classical Association of Canada (Exec. Committee 1978-80, 1994-96; Programme Committee 1979); Canadian Federation for the Humanities (Corresponding Mbr., Univ. of Waterloo 1980-83); Archaeological Institute of America; Canadian Mediterranean Institute; Phi Beta Kappa (elected 1966); Professional Women's Association (Past Pres., Univ. of Waterloo); Univ. of Waterloo (Gov.); Advisory Council on Academic Human Resources (Chair 1992-94; Chair, Status of Women Subcommittee); Dept. of Classical Studies Promotion Committee (Acting Chair); Waterloo-Wellington Science & Engineering Fair Committee (Volunteer); Host Committee, Canada-Wide Science Fair, Univ. of Guelph (Universities & Colleges Co-Chair). HONS:

Distinguished Teaching Award, Univ. of Waterloo, 1977; Teaching Award, O.C.U.F.A., 1994. INTERESTS: volcanoes; science fairs; science fiction; science & society; Atlantic Canada; classical music. COMMENT: *"Through teaching, research and service to the nonacademic community, I have tried to show the relevance of Greco-Roman culture to the modern world."*

Forsythe, Janice T., B.A. ■■ ⦾ ⊕ ○
Executive Director, CANADIAN COUNCIL ON SMOKING AND HEALTH (NGO), 170 Laurier Ave. W., Ste. 1000, Ottawa, ON K1P 5V5 (613) 567-3050, ext. 303, FAX 567-2730, EMAIL jforsythe@ccsh.ca. Born Kingston, Ont. 1956. d. EDUC: Queen's Univ., B.A. (Hons., French/French Cdn Studies); Univ. of Ottawa, currently enrolled in the Exec. M.B.A. program; numerous courses/seminars on mgmt, fundraising, strategic planning, acctg, etc. CAREER: Asst. to the Coord., Allied Medical Educ. & Accreditation, Canadian Medical Association, Ottawa, 1979-84; Exec. Dir., Canadian Junior Chamber/Jaycees, Kanata, 1984-86; Assoc. Dir., Professional Councils, Canadian Dental Association, Ottawa, 1986-89; also Exec. Sec., Canadian Fund for Dental Education, 1987-89; Divisions Mgr, Canadian Real Estate Association, 1989-92; Exec. Dir., Canadian Council on Smoking and Health, 1992 to date. AFFIL: Business & Professional Women's Association of Ottawa (VP, Pol. Action 1995-96); Canadian Society of Association Executives (mbr.; former mbr., Membership Committee, Ottawa chpt.). INTERESTS: travel; reading mysteries & prof. dev. books; cooking; swimming; collecting Canadiana antiques & French Impressionist art. COMMENT: *"Senior association manager with diversified experience in operational planning, administration, and staff direction. Proven skills in advocacy, media relations, coalition-building, conference and meeting planning, newsletter editing, fundraising and membership development. Strong track record for nurturing productive working relationships in the public, private and association sectors. Values: personal commitment to causes in which I believe; strong work ethic; thirst for ongoing self-improvement; the synergy of teamwork; high regard for humour in the workplace."*

Foster, Christine M., B.A. ♨ 📚 ⊗
Vice-President and Director, FATA MORGANA INC., 46 Chine Dr., Scarborough, ON M1M 2K7 (416) 264-4081, FAX 264-4081. Born London, UK 1950. m. Gerald Holmes. 1 ch. Gwenneth. EDUC: Univ. of Toronto, B.A.(Anthropology/Archaeology) 1990.

CAREER: Apprentice/Journeyman, Stratford Festival, 1971-73; Writer-in-Residence, Tarragon Theatre, Toronto, 1976; VP & Dir., Fata Morgana Inc., 1980 to date; freelance Writer, 1976 to date. SELECTED CREDITS: Story Ed., *The Littlest Hobo* (series), CTV, 1980-83; Story Consultant, *Shadow Dancing* (feature) Source Productions, 1988; Interim Story Ed., *The Legend of White Fang*, 1993. SELECTED PUBLICATIONS: *Everything but Anchovies* (Playwrights' Union Press, 1983); *Raptures* (Playwright's Copyscript Publication, 1986); feature articles for *The Toronto Star* Insight & Travel sections. DIRECTOR: Fata Morgana Inc. AFFIL: Writers' Guild of Canada; Playwrights' Union of Canada. HONS: Silver Medal, N.Y. Int'l Film & TV Festival, 1983; Gold Medal for Academic Achievement, Victoria Coll., Univ. of Toronto, 1990; winner, New Script Competition, Storybook Theatre, Calgary, 1994. INTERESTS: archaeology; travel; history. COMMENT: *"Writing for radio, TV and film includes* Friday the 13th–the Series *and* Top Cops *and feature film story consulting. Stage productions include book and lyrics for five musicals and hit play for lunchtime theatre (Solar Stage in Toronto,) as well as the comedy murder mystery* The Death of Me *first produced at Lighthouse Festival, Ft. Dover, Ontario in 1996."*

Foster, Julia Elizabeth, B.A. ■■ ○ Ⓢ ♦
President, THE OLYMPIC TRUST OF CANADA (raising funds for Cdn Olympic athletes; administers fin. assets of Canadian Olympic Association), 21 St. Clair Ave. E., Ste. 900, Toronto, ON M4T 1L9 (416) 967-6681, ext. 224, FAX 967-4902. Born Toronto 1946. m. 4 ch. EDUC: McGill Univ., B.A.(Hons., Sociology & Pol. Sci.) 1968. CAREER: Research Mgr, CHFI Radio, Rogers Broadcasting, 1968-69; Mkt Research Analyst, Martin Goldfarb Consultants, 1970-73; founder & Pres., Foster Research Consultants, 1973-76; VP, Dir. of Mkt Research Svcs, & Co-Chrm, Strategic Planning Committee, McCann-Erickson Advertising of Canada Limited, 1976-83; Sr. Assoc., Environics Research Group Ltd., 1985-87; Pres., Olympic Trust of Canada, 1993 to date. DIRECTOR: Brascan Limited; Canada Post (Exec. Committee & Chrm, Compensation Committee), Canada Post Corporation, Ottawa. AFFIL: Hospital for Sick Children, Toronto (Bd. of Trustees 1996); Stratford Festival, Stratford, Ont. (Immed. Past Pres., Bd. of Gov.; Exec. Committee; Past Chrm, Mktg, & Audience Dev. Committees 1988-96); CN Tower, Toronto (Bd. of Dir. 1987-95); World Film Festival of Toronto (Bd. of Dir., Exec. Committee, Chrm, Capital Fund, & Compen-

sation Committees 1988-93); C.M. Hincks Training, Research & Resource Institute, Toronto (Bd. of Dir. 1987-91); Shaw Festival, Niagara-on-the-Lake, Ont. (Bd. of Dir. 1978-80). **MISC:** Nomination Campaign Mgr (1983), Election Campaign Mgr (1984) & Election Campaign Chrm (1988) for Barbara McDougall, M.P. for St. Paul's, Min. of Employment & Immigration, & Min. of Foreign Affairs; 1st woman pres. of Stratford Festival. **COMMENT:** *"Mrs. Foster brings a strong background in marketing and strategic planning to her current endeavours which include leadership positions in sport funding, the arts and corporate boards."*

Foster, Sandra, C.H.R.P.,C.F.P.,R.F.P., CIM,FCSI ■■ $ ✎ ☝
Author and Financial Advisor, EQUION SECURITIES CANADA LIMITED, 4936 Yonge St., Ste. 252, North York, ON M2N 6S3 (416) 223-4605 or 494-1380, FAX 494-9530, EMAIL fosters@idirect.com. Born Thunder Bay, Ont. 1955. m. David Foster. 4 ch. **EDUC:** Univ. of Toronto, B.A. 1976, Fac. of Mgmt, Advanced Program in Hum. Res. Mgmt 1991; Canadian Institute of Financial Planning, Chartered Fin. Planner 1994; Canadian Securities Institute, Certified Investment Mgmt 1995. **CAREER:** Computer Programmer, Crown Life Insurance Company, 1979-83; full-time homemaker, 1983-85; Computer Consultant (Crown Life, Zurich Life, Seneca Coll. & others), 1984-92; Instructor, Labour Econ., Seneca Coll., 1992-94; Fin. Advisor, Equion Securities Canada Limited, 1992 to date; author & public speaker. **VOLUNTEER CAREER:** Job Placement Officer, North York Volunteer Centre, 1983-84; Group Leader, Metro Parents of Twins, 1985-86; Chair, Personnel Committee, Kids' Haven Child, 1987-90; Hum. Res. Subcommittee, Alzheimer Society of Canada, 1991-93. **SELECTED PUBLICATIONS:** *You Can't Take It With You: The Common-Sense Guide to Estate Planning for Canadians* (John Wiley & Sons, 1996 - best seller); numerous articles on personal fin. & investing for newspapers & magazines; quarterly newsletter, *Personal Economic Reporter*. **DIRECTOR:** Carat Communications Inc. **AFFIL:** Canadian Securities Institute (Fellow); Canadian Association of Financial Planners (Registered Fin. Planner); Human Resource Professionals' Association of Ontario; North York Chamber of Commerce; Women in Capital Markets. **MISC:** 1st person to write an all-Cdn estate planning book. **COMMENT:** *"Ms. Foster believes that, in these changing times, knowledge and co-operation are necessary for individual survival and community betterment."*

Fouriezos, Carolyn, B.A. ■■ ✎ ✪
Columnist/Writer, *THE SUDBURY STAR* (newspaper), 33 Mackenzie St., Sudbury, ON P3C 4Y1 (705) 674-5271, FAX 674-7632. Born Tisdale Twp., Timmins, Ont. 1934. m. Charles. 5 ch. Charles, Wendy, Sylvia, Nicole, Barbara. **EDUC:** Univ. of Toronto, Victoria Coll., B.A. 1953. **CAREER:** Columnist, *Northern Life*, 1976-87; Contributor, *The Anglican Churchman, Ontario Craft News, Northward Journal, Inco Triangle*, 1976 to date; Writer/Editor, Laurentian Univ. publications, 1982-88; Arts & Entertainment Writer, *The Sudbury Star*, 1988-92; "Talk of the Town" Columnist, 1990 to date. **SELECTED CREDITS:** Book Reviewer, CBC Radio summer series, 1980. **SELECTED PUBLICATIONS:** newspaper columns/articles, 20-yr. span. **AFFIL:** National Film Board of Canada (Trustee); Cinefest Inc. (founder; Bd. mbr.); Laurentian Univ. Museum & Arts Centre (Advisory Bd.); Ontario Film Development Corp. (Exec. Bd. mbr. 1988-94); Sudbury Theatre Centre (founding mbr. 1970; Bd. mbr. 1970-86). **HONS:** Thorneloe Coll., Laurentian Univ., Hon. Fellowship 1995; Volunteer Svc. Award, Prov. of Ont. Ministry of Culture & Communications. **INTERESTS:** reading; filmgoing; aerobics; walking. **COMMENT:** *"As an arts advocate, both in my writing and board involvements, I have steadfastly promoted regional visual and performing arts and artists. In my role as a founder of two invaluable community assets–the professional theatre company and northern film festival–plus my participation in provincial and national film boards, I hope to have fostered awareness of the north's vibrant cultural scene."*

Fourmy, Sally J., B.S. $
Founder, SALLY FOURMY & ASSOCIATES, 30 Duncan St., Toronto, ON M5V 2C2. 2304 State St., Santa Barbara, CA 93105 (805) 898-9929, FAX 898-9429. Born Columbus, Ohio 1934. 2 ch. **EDUC:** Northwestern Univ.; Ohio State Univ., B.S. 1956; Univ. of California at Berkeley (1959) & Columbia Univ. (1962-63), post-grad. studies. **CAREER:** various positions during the '50s as Asst. Fashion Dir., Bloomingdale's; public sch. teacher; Flight Attendant, Pan Am World Airways; founded company offering seminars to women in bus., '60s; Fashion Coord. & Fac. Mbr., LaSalle Coll., '70s; Founder, Sally Fourmy & Associates, 1979 to date. **AFFIL:** Pi Beta Phi; Toronto Fashion Group; Ryerson Polytechnic Univ. (Advtg Committee); Profit Sharing Council of Canada (Dir.). **HONS:** Canadian Women Entrepreneur of the Year Award, Quality Plus Div., 1992; First Place Award, Hotel & Restaurants Competition, 1983 (won by her company).

Fournel, Jocelyne, B.A. ✇ 📜 ✏
Art Director, *L'ACTUALITÉ*, Maclean Hunter Ltd., 1001 de Maisonneuve O., Montréal, QC H3A 3E1 (514) 843-2546, FAX 845-7503. Born Montreal 1953. m. Philippe Brochard. 1 ch. Hugo Brochard Fournel. **EDUC:** Univ. du Québec à Montréal, B.A.(Design Graphique) 1977. **CAREER:** Art Dir., *Montréal Ce Mois-Ci*, 1982-85; freelance graphic designer in London, UK, 3 yrs.; Art Dir., *MTL* Magazine, 1988-93; Art Dir., *Qui Hebdo*, 1993-94; Art Dir., *L'actualité*, 1994 to date. **HONS:** Best Art Direction for Entire Issue, *L'actualité*, AQEM, 1995; Gold Award, Best Cover, *MTL*, National Magazine Awards, 1993; Gold Award, Best Cover, *MTL*, AQEM, 1993; Silver Award, Best Cover, *Montréal Ce Mois-Ci*, National Magazine Awards, 1985. **INTERESTS:** art in general; literature; travel. **MISC:** owned own company from 1988 to 1993 during which time was the art dir. for *MTL* Magazine as well as designing for other magazine & book covers. **COMMENT:** *"I like working with visual artists (photographers, illustrators, designers, etc.) to find graphic solutions. I am very challenged by new technology and happy to live near the turn of the century. I will continue to work for magazines but wish to broaden my artistic expression."*

Fournel, Lise, B.Sc.,M.Sc.,D.S.A. $ ⚛
Vice-President, Information Technology and Chief Information Officer, AIR CANADA, Air Canada Centre, Zip 045, Box 9000, Saint-Laurent, QC H4Y 1C2 (514) 422-4822, FAX 422-4899. Born Montreal 1953. m. F. Boisvenue. 2 ch. Julie Boisvenue, Étienne Boisvenue. **EDUC:** Univ. of Montreal, B.Sc.(Statistics) 1974, M.Sc.(Statistics) 1978; École des Hautes Études Commerciales, D.S.A.(Admin.). **CAREER:** Statistical Analyst, Dept. of Public Works, Gov't of Canada, 1975-76; Fin. Analyst, Univ. of Montreal, 1976-79; Sr. Analyst, Oper. Research, Air Canada, 1979-83; Mgr, Customer Svc., Info. Svcs, 1983-84; Mgr, Dev. Svcs, 1984-86; Mgr, Strategic Planning, 1986-87; Dir., Strategic & Tactical Planning, Info. Svcs, 1987-91; Sr. Dir., Pricing & Yield Mgmt, 1991-95. **AFFIL:** Operation Research Airline Association; Le Cercle des Chefs Mailleurs du Québec Inc.; Montreal Statistical Association. **HONS:** Dominion Bridge Scholarship, 1971-74. **INTERESTS:** computer science; working with university students; skiing. **COMMENT:** *"Person with high level of energy who needs ongoing challenges. Have succeeded in two very different fields: information technology and marketing."*

Fournier, Lili, B.A. 🎬 📖 🎭
Producer, Director and Writer, ZOLAR ENTERTAINMENT CORP., 131 Bloor St. W., Ste. 515J, Toronto, ON M5S 1R1 (416) 927-8587, FAX 927-8588. Born Transylvania. m. Gerard Fournier. 2 ch. David, Lisa. **EDUC:** York Univ., B.A.(Urban Geography) 1972. **CAREER:** various positions in TV & feature films incl.: Writer, Columnist, Asst. Dir., Script Supervisor, Prod. Mgr; owner of retail shops; Real Estate Agent; Prod., Writer & Dir., Zolar Entertainment, 1992 to date. **SELECTED CREDITS:** Prod./Dir., 2 hrs., *Women in the Arts*, WTN; Prod./Dir., *The Quest...Discovering Your Human Potential* (2, 1-hr. documentaries); Prod./Dir., *Living in the Light with Shakti Gawain* (1-hr. special), TVO; Prod./Exec. Prod., *Expulsion & Memory* (documentary); Assoc. Dir., *Pygmalion* (telefilm), 20th Century Fox; *El AL, Yellow Brick Road* (series); Prod./Dir., CBC Newsworld/TVO; *The Creators*, TWN; Moderator/Prod., *The Portrayal of Women in the Media*. **SELECTED PUBLICATIONS:** was Lifestyle Columnist ("Toronto Flavour"), *The Toronto Sun*; contributing author to cookbooks, gourmet magazines; freelance travel writer for major Cdn newspapers. **AFFIL:** Toronto Women in Film & Television, TWIFT (Chair, Community Liaison); Directors' Guild of Canada; has chaired numerous charity events & founded several organizations. **HONS:** Hon. Ambassador of Tourism to Israel, 1989; honoured by the Chinese Businessman's Association & the Champagne Society of France for her column "Toronto Flavor."; Best Screenplay, Houston Film Festival, 1996. **INTERESTS:** travel; the portrayal of women in the media. **MISC:** has traveled to over 80 countries around the world; coordinated the nat'l effort for interventions on behalf of Global CanWest's application for a "woman's network" specialty licence for T'Elle'Vision; Prod. & Moderator for a 2-hr. live/broadcast symposium on the issues & challenges facing women in the industry, Toronto Film Festival & TWIFT; Prod. of the TV production of the Universal Spiritual gathering held in Toledo, for Spain's Quinto Centenario, commemorating the 500th year expulsion of the Jews; her company presently develops, produces and distributes programming promoting wellness, spirituality & personal development. **COMMENT:** *"Lili Fournier has enjoyed a diversified career as a journalist, lifestyle columnist, producer and director. An active participant in both television and feature films in Toronto since the 70s, she has also worked in various supporting capacities. Always the inquisitive adventurer, she has with her life partner traveled to over 80 countries around the world, and created a number of enterprises. Her company is presently producing television productions*

that explore the nature and meaning of contemporary life, and lead the way in exploring the ongoing revolutions in the field of health, personal growth, the environment, spirituality and social change."

Fournier, Suzanne N., B.A. ✎ 📺
Journalist and Author, *VANCOUVER PROVINCE* NEWSPAPER, Pacific Press Ltd., 2250 Granville St., Vancouver, BC V6H 3G2 (604) 732-2089, FAX 732-2720. Born Calgary 1952. m. Art Moses. 2 ch. Naomi F. Fournier Moses, L. Zev Fournier Moses. **EDUC:** Univ. of Calgary, B.A.(English Lit. & Phil.); Univ. of British Columbia, 4th yr. B.A. & 1 yr. grad. sch. (Phil.). **CAREER:** freelance journalist, *The Globe and Mail*, *Maclean's*, *The Toronto Star*, *The Georgia Straight* Newspaper, CBC Radio; Reporter, *Vancouver Province*, 1977 to date. **SELECTED PUBLICATIONS:** 20 yrs. of reporting on social issues, child & family issues, aboriginal affairs; book on aboriginal children to be published in 1997. **AFFIL:** Newspaper Guild. **INTERESTS:** reading; hiking; gardening. **MISC:** communications & research consultant to aboriginal groups on heritage & fishing issues. **COMMENT:** *"I have been a journalist for 20 years, beginning with community radio in Vancouver. I have covered social and political events as a freelance journalist for major Canadian newspapers and magazines. A book on aboriginal family history in Canada will be published by Douglas & McIntyre in the spring of 1997, co-authored by myself and Sto:lo aboriginal leader Ernie Crey."*

Fowke, Helen Shirley, B.A. ■ ■ 📖 📺 📜
Writer. General Delivery, Lunenburg, NS B0J 2C0. Born Oshawa, Ont. 1914. s. **EDUC:** Bishop Bethune Coll./Univ. of Toronto, B.A. (Modern Languages-French & German) 1935. **SELECTED CREDITS:** numerous half-hour radio plays, children's TV series & hour-long radio play, CBC; several plays produced in U.S. & Canada by univ. & other stage groups. **SELECTED PUBLICATIONS:** *Joe, or A Pair of Corduroy Breeches* (self-published, N.S. best-seller based on historic character, 1971); article on N.S. in *Illustrated London News* (1961). **AFFIL:** N.S. Writers' Federation. **HONS:** 2 int'l playwriting awards incl. Maxwell Anderson Award for play in blank verse; University Coll. scholarships & Gov.-Gen.'s Medal in Modern Languages, Univ. of Toronto. **INTERESTS:** books; reading; painting; writing; golf; wildlife conservation.

Fowler, Libby, B.A. ■ ■ 🎓 ☝
Chair, Board of Governors, UNIVERSITY OF WESTERN ONTARIO. Member, NATIONAL ASSOCIATION OF UNIVERSITY BOARD CHAIRS. Citizenship Court Judge. Born London, Ont. 1941. m. Dr. Peter J. Fowler. 4 ch. Tim, Megan, Cameron, Peter. **EDUC:** Univ. of Western Ontario, B.A. 1962; Althouse Coll., grad. 1963. **AFFIL:** Univ. of Western Ontario (Chair, Bd. of Gov. (first woman) 1994 to date; mbr. of Bd. 1985 to date; mbr., Strategic Planning Task Force); Ontario Council of University Board Chairs; Univ. of Western Ontario Foundation (V-Chair); London Regional Art & Historical Museums (Chair of the Bd. 1985-86); Roberts Research Institute (Bd. 1995 to date); London Co-operative Research Council (Chair 1995 to date); various other community activities from politics to the arts. **HONS:** award for work, Ministry of Culture, 1988.

Fowler, Marian, B.A.,M.A.,Ph.D. ■ 📜 📖
Writer. 77 St. Clair Ave., Apt. 503, Toronto, ON M4T 1M5. Born Newmarket, Ont. 1929. d. 2 ch. **EDUC:** Univ. of Toronto, B.A.(Hons., English) 1951, M.A.(English Lit.) 1965, Ph.D. (English Lit.) 1970. **CAREER:** promotional work, Clarke, Irwin & Co., 1951-53; Advtg Copywriter, T. Eaton Co., 1953-54; Course Dir. & Lecturer (part-time), Atkinson Coll., York Univ., 1970-82; full-time writer, 1982 to date. **SELECTED PUBLICATIONS:** *The Embroidered Tent: Five Gentlewomen in Early Canada* (1982); *Redney: A Life of Sara Jeannette Duncan* (1983); *Below the Peacock Fan: First Ladies of the Raj* (1987); *Blenheim: Biography of a Palace* (1989); *In a Gilded Cage: From Heiress to Duchess* (1993); *The Way She Looks Tonight: Five Women of Style* (1996). **AFFIL:** Writers' Union of Canada; International P.E.N.; Anglican Church. **HONS:** Gov. General's Gold Medal in English, 1951; Biography Award, Association for Canadian Studies, 1979. **INTERESTS:** travel; birdwatching; antique collecting. **COMMENT:** *"Marian Fowler's first book appeared when she was 52; now, 14 years later, she is an internationally acclaimed author who has been called one of Canada's best biographers."*

Francis, Diane ✎ $ 📖
Editor, *THE FINANCIAL POST*, 333 King St. E., Toronto, ON M5A 4N2 (416) 350-6350, FAX 350-6166. Born Chicago 1946. 2 ch. Eric, Julie. **CAREER:** Contributing Ed., *Canadian Business* Magazine, 1979-81; Columnist, *Quest Magazine*, 1981-83; Fin. Columnist, *The Toronto Star*, 1981-87; Columnist, *The Sun* newspapers, *Maclean's* Magazine, 1987 to date; Ed., *The Financial Post*, 1991 to date; Commentator, CFRB Toronto, CKNW Vancouver. **SELECTED PUBLICATIONS:** *Controlling Interest: Who Owns Canada*; *Contrepreneurs*; *The*

Diane Francis Inside Guide to Canada's 50 Best Stocks; *A Matter of Survival*; *Underground Nation*. **AFFIL:** Clarke Institute of Psychiatry (Foundation Committee); Canadian Foundation for AIDS Research (Bd.); *The Financial Post* (Advisory Bd.); Canada-Ukraine Chamber of Commerce (Dir.); York Univ. East/West Enterprise Exchange Program. **HONS:** Bus. Writing Award, Royal Bank; 3 National Newspaper Awards; Edward Dunlop Award of Excellence; National Business Writing Award; Woman of the Year, *Chatelaine*, 1992; Woman of the Year, Zonta Club of Charlottetown, 1992; Women Who Make a Difference, *Toronto Life*, 1993; Hon. Mbr., Women's Press Club, 1993; Journalist of the Year, Ukrainian Canadian Congress, 1994; Women of Influence, *Chatelaine*, 1995; Nat'l Leadership Award, Our Lady of Lourdes High Sch. Forum, 1995; Nat'l Citizens' Coalition Freedom Award, 1995; Hon. Fellow, Canadian Sch. of Mgmt, 1995. **INTERESTS:** golf; tennis. **COMMENT:** *"Newspaper editor, award-winning columnist, well-known broadcaster, author of five best-selling books, and* Chatelaine *Magazine's Woman of the Year for 1992."*

Francis, Dorothy Delores 🎨 ♡
Artist. Qualicum Beach, BC V9K 1N7 (604) 752-3665. Born Dinsmore, Sask. 1923. m. Harold. 5 ch. (1 dec.). Kent (dec.), Randi, Timothy, Lisa, Mark. **EDUC:** Nutana Collegiate, Saskatoon, 1939; Vancouver Art Sch., 1957. **SELECTED PUBLICATIONS:** Aaron Ashley Inc., NY, 1959-72; Lawson Graphics Ltd., Vancouver, 1966-78; Canadian Gallery Prints Ltd., Port Moody, 1979-89; Arctic Art Gallery, Yellowknife, 1990 to date; D.H. Ussher Ltd., Vancouver, 1992 to date; U.N.I.C.E.F., NY, 1994. **EXHIBITIONS:** numerous solo exhibitions in Canada & abroad; small piece in the Smithsonian Museum, Washington, DC; permanent display, Gonzaga Univ., Spokane, Wash. **AFFIL:** Qualicum Cultural Centre. **HONS:** Commemorative Medal for the 125th Anniversary of the Confederation of Canada. **INTERESTS:** family; career; community. **MISC:** greeting card entitled *Is Our Side Winning*, was the top-selling U.N.I.C.E.F. card in Canada, 1994. **COMMENT:** *"Artist, wife, mother, with a compulsion to paint while raising five children to adulthood. Have endeavoured to fight racism with my paintbrush."*

Frank, Anne, M.A. ■■ 🎭
Producer and Script Consultant, FOX-FIRE FILMS (film production), 190 Bayview Heights Dr., Toronto, ON M4G 2Z2 (416), FAX 696-6009. **EDUC:** Univ. of Alberta, M.A.(Drama) 1972. **AFFIL:** Academy of Canadian Cinema & Television; Women in Film & Television. **COMMENT:** *"Anne Frank is an independent producer and script consultant. She has been executive story consultant for Atlantis Films on such television movies as* The Diviners, *the Emmy Award-winning* Lost in the Barrens, Tom Alone *and* Race to Freedom. *Frank has won numerous awards as producer of such CBC films as* A Change of Heart, Harvest, Seer Was Here, A Far Cry From Home *and* A Matter of Choice. *She has been story consultant on the television mini-series* The Arrow *starring Dan Ackroyd, on features such as* Never Too Late, *starring Olympia Dukakis and Cloris Leachman. She is currently script consultant on the feature film* Marine Life, *and the television movie* Atanajuat: The Fast Runner. *Frank has been consulting executive producer for the National Screen Institute and was a member of the National Advisory Committee (Academy of Canadian Cinema and Television) that led to the design of the Academy's "National Story Editor Training Program" and the popular "Understanding Story" workshop. She is editor of the book* Telling It: Writing for Canadian Film and Television *co-published by the Academy of Canadian Cinema and Television and Doubleday Canada Limited."*

Frank, Ilana, B.A. 🎭 $ 📺
Senior Vice-President, Production and Development, NORSTAR ENTERTAINMENT INC., 86 Bloor St. W., Ste. 400v, Toronto, ON M5S 1M5 (416) 961-6278, FAX 961-5608. Born Toronto. m. Peter R. Simpson. 2 ch. **EDUC:** York Univ., B.A. **CAREER:** VP, in charge of Prod., Norstar Entertainment Inc., 1982 to date. **SELECTED CREDITS:** has acted as Prod., Exec. Prod., Co-Prod. or Exec. in Charge of Prod., of over 20 films incl. *Iron Eagle IV*, *Jungleground*, *Boulevard*, *The Club*, *Oh What a Night*, *Cold Comfort*.

Frank, Roberta, B.A.,M.A.,Ph.D. ■ 🎓 📜 📖
University Professor, Department of English, and Director, Centre for Medieval Studies, UNIVERSITY OF TORONTO, 39 Queen's Park Cres. E., Toronto, ON M5S 1A1 (416) 978-5422. Born 1941. m. Walter Goffart. **EDUC:** New York Univ., B.A. 1962; Harvard Univ., M.A. 1964, Ph.D. 1968. **CAREER:** Asst. Prof., Dept. of English & Centre for Medieval Studies, Univ. of Toronto, 1968-73; Assoc. Prof., 1973-78; Prof., 1978 to date; Univ. Fellow, Institute of Social & Econ. Research, Rhodes Univ., S.Africa, 1979; Visiting Sr. Fellow, Linacre Coll., Oxford, 1979-80; Dir., Grad. Studies, Dept. of English, Univ. of Toronto, 1980-85; Distinguished Visiting Prof. of Medieval Studies, Univ. of California, Berkeley, 1992; Distin-

guished Visiting Prof., Università degli Studi di Roma "La Sapienza," 1993; Dir., Centre for Medieval Studies, Univ. of Toronto, 1994 to date; appointed Univ. Prof., 1995. **SELECTED PUBLICATIONS:** *Old Norse Court Poetry: The Drv. of Toronto,* (Ithaca: Cornell Univ. Press, 1978); *Computers and Old English Concordances*, edited with Angus Cameron & John Leyerle (Toronto: Univ. of Toronto Press, 1970); *The Politics of Editing Medieval Texts*, Twenty-seventh Conference on Editing Problems: Univ. of Toronto, 1-2 Nov. 1991, Ed. (New York: AMS Press, 1993); "A Plea for the Dictionary of Old English," with Angus Cameron (Toronto, Univ. of Toronto Press, 1973); "Old Norse Memorial Eulogies and the Ending of *Beowulf*" (ACTA, 1979); "Did Anglo-Saxon Audiences Have a Skaldic Tooth?" (*Scandinavian Studies,* 1987); "The Search for the Anglo-Saxon Oral Poet" (*Bulletin of the John Rylands University Library of Manchester,* 1993); "On a Changing Field: Medieval Studies in the New World" (*The Southern African Journal of Medieval and Renaissance Studies,* 1994); numerous other publications. **EDIT:** Gen. Ed., *Toronto Old English Series*, Univ. of Toronto Press, 1976 to date; Ed. Bd., *Speculum Anniversary Monographs*, 1984-87; Chrm, 1987; Gen. Ed., *Publications of the Dictionary of Old English*, Pontifical Institute of Mediaeval Studies, 1985 to date; Ed., *Anglo-Saxon England*, 1986 to date; Ed. Bd., *Speculum*, 1989-93; Ed. Assoc., *The Southern African Journal of Medieval and Renaissance Studies*, 1990 to date. **AFFIL:** Royal Society of Canada (Fellow); Association for the Advancement of Scandinavian Studies in Canada (Liaison Officer 1982 to date; Sec. 1985-88); Medieval Academy of America (Fellow; Councillor 1981-84; Chair, Fellows Nominating Committee 1994-95); South African Society for Medieval & Renaissance Studies (Corresponding Fellow); International Saga Society (Advisory Bd. 1988-92); International Society of Anglo-Saxonists (Advisory Bd. 1981-88; 1st VP 1982-85; Pres. 1986-88); Modern Language Association of America (Div. on Old English Language & Lit. - Exec. Committee 1974-78, Sec. 1975/1977, Chair 1978; Div. on Comparative Studies in Medieval Lit. - Exec. Committee 1989-94, Chrm 1993). **HONS:** Bowdoin Prize in the Humanities, Harvard Univ., 1968; Elliott Prize, Medieval Academy of America, 1972. **MISC:** "The Fifteen Joys of Marriage," videotape, Univ. of Toronto Media Centre (1972); recipient, various grants & fellowships, incl. a Guggenheim Fellowship, 1986-87; reviewer, various journals & granting agencies; mbr., Int'l Advisory Committee, *Dictionary of Old English*, 1987 to date.

Frank, Tema, B.Comm.,M.B.A., F.I.C.B. $ ✏ 📖

President, FRANK COMMUNICATIONS, 253 College St., Ste. 200, Toronto, ON M5T 1R5 (416) 591-7191, FAX 591-7202, EMAIL temafrank@titan.tcn.net. Born Winnipeg 1960. m. John M. Shaw. 2 ch. Benedict, Oriana. **EDUC:** Univ. of Alberta, B.Comm. 1982; Univ. of Toronto, M.B.A.(Mktg & Corp. Strategy) 1987. **CAREER:** Parliamentary Intern, House of Commons, 1982-83; Gov't Rel'ns & Public Affairs, Canadian Bankers' Association, 1983-88; Mktg Mgr, National Bank of Canada, 1988-90; Pres., Frank Communications, 1990 to date. **SELECTED PUBLICATIONS:** *Canada's Best Employers for Women: A Guide for Job Hunters, Employees and Employers*; numerous magazine articles. **AFFIL:** Institute of Canadian Bankers (Fellow); Toronto Employment Equity Practitioners' Association (Comm. Committee); Canadian Public Affairs Association (newsletter contributor); Univ. of Toronto Fac. of Mgmt Alumni Association (Dir.); Peggy Baker Dance Projects (Dir.); Dancemakers (Dir. 1988-91); Financial Women's Association of N.Y. **INTERESTS:** dance; travel; books; theatre; film; cycling. **MISC:** Volunteer Info. Officer, French delegation, 1988 Toronto Econ. Summit. **COMMENT:** *"My goal, as a writer, lecturer and consultant, is to help employers recruit and retain the best employees, including their fair share of the best women."*

Franklin, Melissa B., B.S.,Ph.D. 🎓 ⚛ ☝

Professor of Physics, HARVARD UNIVERSITY, Lyman Laboratory of Physics, Cambridge, MA 02138 (617) 495-2909 or 495-1189, FAX 496-5144, EMAIL franklin@physics.harvard.edu. s. **EDUC:** Univ. of Toronto, B.S. 1977; Stanford Univ., Ph.D. 1982. **CAREER:** Summer Research Assoc., Univ. of Toronto at Fermilab, 1975-76; Summer Research Assoc., Columbia Univ. at CERN, 1977; Research Assoc., Stanford Linear Accelerator, 1977-82; Postdoctoral Fellow, Lawrence Berkeley Lab., 1983-86; Asst. Prof., Univ. of Illinois, 1986-87; Jr. Fellow, Society of Fellows, Harvard Univ., 1987-89; Asst. Prof., Harvard Univ., 1989-91; John Loeb Assoc. Prof. of the Natural Sciences, 1991-92; Prof. of Physics, 1992 to date. **HONS:** Fellow, Alfred P. Sloan Foundation, 1988; Fellow, American Physical Society. **MISC:** 1st female Prof. of Physics, Harvard Univ.

Franssen, Margot, B.A. $ ✊

President and Partner, THE BODY SHOP, 33 Kern Rd., Don Mills, ON M3B 1S9 (416) 441-3202, FAX 445-2763. Born Holland 1952. m. Quig Tingley. 3 ch. **EDUC:** York University, B.A.(Phil.) 1979. **CAREER:** Sec., McLeod,

Young, Weir (now ScotiaMcLeod); Pres. & Ptnr, The Body Shop. **DIRECTOR:** CIBC. **AFFIL:** York Univ. (Bd. of Trustees). **HONS:** hon. fellowship, Ryerson Polytechnical Institute (now Ryerson Polytechnic Univ.), 1990; Henry Singer Award "for people who demonstrate exceptional leadership in retailing & services," Canadian Institute of Retailing & Services, Univ. of Alberta, 1993; LL.D.(Hon.), Univ. of Windsor, 1994; Hon. Degree of Humane Letters, Mount St. Vincent Univ., 1995. **INTERESTS:** human rights; the environment; Tetris. **MISC:** The Body Shop was chosen by *The Financial Post* as: 1 of the 100 best companies to work for in Canada, 1990; winner of the Environment Award for Business, Consumer Product Award, Green Product Category, 1991; 1 of the 50 best managed private companies in Canada, 1993; Women of Distinction Award, 1994.

Fraser, Joan, B.A. ■ / ▯
Former Editor-in-Chief, *The Gazette*. Born Halifax 1944. m. Michel Faure. 2 ch. **EDUC:** McGill Univ., B.A.(French & Spanish Lit.) 1965, sabbatical yr. studying economics 1976-77; Cdn Securities course. **CAREER:** gen., women's & fin. reporting, *The Gazette*, 1965-67; reporter/news editor/editor, Financial Times News Svc./editorial pg. editor/Que. bureau chief, *Financial Times of Canada*, Montreal, 1967-78; editorial pg. ed., *The Gazette*, 1978-93; Ed.-in-Chief, 1993-96; regular radio & TV broadcaster, English & French. **HONS:** Nat'l Newspaper Award for editorial writing, 1982, 1991; Citation, 1986, 1987, 1990; Southam Newspaper Group Prize for Journalism (Commentary), 1987; runner-up, 1989; Southam Inc. President's Prize for work as co-chair of company's task force on the status of women, 1990.

Fraser, Joan, B.A. ■ ■ ○ ⊕
Executive Director, HEART AND STROKE FOUNDATION OF NOVA SCOTIA (voluntary health organization), 5523 Spring Garden Rd., Ste. 204, Halifax, NS (902) 423-7530, FAX 492-1464. Born Saint John 1934. m. David. 3 ch. Peter, Susan, Janice. **EDUC:** Acadia Univ., B.A.(Econ.) 1954; Henson Coll., Dalhousie Univ., Certificate in Centre of Philanthropy (Voluntary & Non-Profit Sector Mgmt) 1993. **CAREER:** homemaker, 1962-73; Fed. Coord. for N.S., International Women's Year, 1973; contract positions with Statistics Canada, Women's Employment Outreach, 1973-82; Judge, Court of Canadian Citizenship, N.S., 1982-85; Exec. Dir., Heart & Stroke Foundation of N.S., 1986 to date. **AFFIL:** Mount St. Vincent Univ., Halifax (mbr., Human Ecology Advisory Bd.); Acadia Univ. (Bd. of Trustees,

Divinity Coll.; Bd. of Gov. 1973-79; mbr. of Senate 1976-79); Q.E. II Health Sciences Centre, Halifax (mbr. of Bd.); First Baptist Church, Halifax (Chair, Stewardship Committee 1994 to date; Chair, Bd. of Deacons 1990-92; Chair, Bd. of Mgmt 1982-85; mbr., Refugee Committee 1992 to date); Beta Sigma Phi chapter (Chair, 20-Chapter Council 1967); Canadian Centre for Philanthropy (N.S. Advisory Committee 1988-93); Multi-Cultural Association of N.S. (Prov. Council 1982-85; Chair, Strategic Planning Committee 1984); YWCA, Halifax (Chair, Nominating Committee, Women's Recognition Committee 1981-84); Fed. Advisory Committee, Status of Women (N.S. Rep. 1973-76, 1979-81); PTA Chebucto Sch. (Chair 1974-75); Oxford Community Sch. (Chair 1977-78). **HONS:** Woman of the Year Award, YWCA, 1979; Outstanding Community Service Award, City of Halifax, 1988; Volunteer Outreach Program Recognition, 1994. **INTERESTS:** gardening; walking; advocacy; politics. **COMMENT:** *"I am energetic and enthusiastic and love life. I care most about things that make a positive difference in people's lives. Working to improve the quality of life for people in my community is important and there are many opportunities when the commitment is there."*

Fraser, Joanna, B.Sc.,M.Sc., Ph.D. ▮ ⬧ ✿
Research Scientist (Forage Agronomy & Physiology), AGRICULTURE & AGRI-FOOD CANADA RESEARCH CENTRE, Box 3000, Lethbridge, AB T1J 4B1 (403) 327-4591, ext. 450, FAX 382-3156, EMAIL fraser@abrsle.agr.ca. Born Dartford, UK 1950. **EDUC:** London Univ., UK, B.Sc.(Botany/Geography) 1974; Aberdeen Univ., Scotland, M.Sc.(Soil Sci.) 1975; Lincoln Univ., New Zealand, Ph.D.(Agronomy/Crop Physiology) 1978. **CAREER:** Research Fellow, Dept. of Plant Science, Lincoln Univ., 1976-78; Postdoctoral Research Assoc., Dept. of Agronomy, Univ. of Kentucky, 1979-81; Postdoctoral Fellow, Dept. of Plant Sci., Univ. of British Columbia, 1981-82; Asst. Prof., Dept. of Plant Sci., Nova Scotia Agricultural Coll., 1982-86; Assoc. Prof., 1986-89; Research Scientist, Agriculture & Agri-Food Canada, 1989 to date. **SELECTED PUBLICATIONS:** "Floral Development in Sonja White Clover (*Trifolium repens* L.), a Papilionoid Legume," with B. Rettallack & N. Walker (*Annals of Botany* 1990); "Factors Required to Sustain Pastoral Farming Systems and Forage Supply in Winter-Cold Zones in Canada," with H.T. Kunelius (*Journal of Korean Grassland Science* 1992); "Panicle, Spikelet and Floret Development in Orchardgrass," with E.G. Kokko (*Canadian Journal of*

Botany 1993). **AFFIL:** Canadian Society of Agronomy; International Herbage Seed Production Research Group; American Society of Agronomy; Canadian Seed Growers' Association (Assoc.). **INTERESTS:** Scottish country dancing; hiking; gardening; cross-country & downhill skiing; travelling; reading; photography.

Fraser, Sylvia L., B.A. 🎨 ✒
Author. c/o Key Porter Books (416) 703-7030, FAX 703-3824. Born Hamilton, Ont 1935. **EDUC:** Univ. of Western Ontario, B.A.(English & Phil.) 1957. **CAREER:** feature writer, *The Toronto Star Weekly*, 1957-68; lecturer; author. **SELECTED PUBLICATIONS:** *Pandora* (1972); *The Candy Factory* (1975); *A Casual Affair* (1978); *The Emperor's Virgin* (1980); *Berlin Solstice* (1984); *My Father's House: a Memoir of Incest and of Healing* (1987); *The Book of Strange: a thinking person's guide to psychic and spiritual phenomena* (1992), published in US as *The Quest for the Fourth Monkey* (1994); *The Ancestral Suitcase* (1996). **AFFIL:** Writers' Development Trust (VP). **HONS:** Award for Canadian Journalism, Women's Press Club, 1967 & 1968; President's Medal for Cdn Journalism, 1968; Non-Fiction Book Award, for *My Father's House*, Canadian Authors' Association, 1987; Booklist Medal, for *The Quest for the Fourth Monkey*, American Library Association, 1994; National Magazine Award for Essays, 1995.

Frazer, D. Suzan, B.Sc.,LL.B. ■ ✒
Partner, PATTERSON PALMER HUNT MURPHY, Box 247, Halifax, NS B3J 2N9 (902) 492-2000, FAX 429-5215. Born New Glasgow, N.S. s. **EDUC:** Dalhousie Univ., B.Sc.(Math.) 1976, LL.B.(Law) 1979. **CAREER:** Ptnr, Patterson Palmer Hunt Murphy, 17 yrs.

Frazer, Robbin, B.A. 🎓 $ 🖋
President, LIFELONG LEARNING HORIZONS & ASSOCIATES, 7352 Goddard St., Powell River, BC V8A 5N7 (604) 483-2015, FAX 483-8963. President, SPECTRUM THREE CONSULTING; WORLD BESTRAVEL ASSOCIATES. Born Elnora, Alta. 1920. d. **EDUC:** Ottawa Univ., B.A. (Social Comm. & Public Rel'ns) 1982. **CAREER:** Media Rel'ns Officer, Public and Industrial Relations Ltd., Vancouver, 1956-67; Dir. of Public Rel'ns, Banff Sch. of Fine Arts & Mgmt Centre, 1961, 1962; various support positions, House of Commons, 1963-82; Supervisor of Public Info., Conference Board of Canada, 1973-75; Pres., Spectrum Three Consulting, 1976 to date; Alta. Prov. Info. Officer, Canada Mortgage and Housing Corporation, 1978-79; Exec. Asst. to Asst. Deputy Min. of

SPACE, Dept. of Comm., Gov't of Canada, 1982; Telecomm., Personnel & Policy Analyst, Gov't Telecomm. Agency, 1986, 1987; Pres., World Bestravel Associates, 1988 to date; Fac. Mbr., Algonquin Coll. of Applied Arts & Technology, 1988-91; Admin., Nat'l Office, Canadian Public Personnel Management Association, 1990; Dir., Nat'l Client Svcs, Gov't Leaders Training Institute/Custom Learning Systems, 1991-93; Pres., Lifelong Learning Horizons & Associates, 1994 to date; Consultant, Second Global Conference on Lifelong Learning, 1995-96. **SELECTED CREDITS:** freelance broadcaster & commentator for the CBC, 1961-69 & for *Report from Parliament Hill*, C.A.B. (Canadian Association of Broadcasters), 1966, 1967. **SELECTED PUBLICATIONS:** *Welcome to Greater Vancouver* (Vancouver Newcomers' Association, 1969); various gov't publications & reports; contributor to chapters for *Canada Handbook* & *Canada Yearbook* (Statistics Canada, 1975). **EDIT:** Founding Ed., *Performing Arts and Entertainment in Canada*, 1961, Assoc. Ed., 1962-71, Special Projects Ed., 1972-88; Banff/Jasper Ed., *Skiing Illustrated*, 1962-63; Contributing Ed., *Canadian Geographic*, 1974; Contributing Ed., *Communique Magazine*, 1975; Cdn Bureau Chief, *DPL–The Magazine of World Diplomacy*, 1976-78; Section Ed., *Petroleum Magazine*, 1982; Space Ed., *Aero Mag*, 1983-84; Contributing Ed., *Access Magazine*, 1984. **EXHIBITIONS:** consultant to: *Arctic Islands Centennial Celebration*, Canadian Museum of Civilization (1981); *SCC'83* (first Cdn domestic & int'l satellite comm. conference) (1983); "Women in Science Pavilion," *Women's World '84* (1984); *Canada in Space*, N.M.S.T. (1985). **AFFIL:** Canadian Public Relations Society; Business & Professional Women's Association of Ottawa; Canadian Association for Distance Education; Ottawa Distance Learning Group (Program Committee); Canadian Association of Home-Based Business; Media Club of Canada; Editors' Association of Canada; Ottawa Distance Learning Group; United Nationals Association in Canada (Ottawa & Vancouver) (Publicity Dir.); Royal Commonwealth Society (Publicity Committee); Canadian Study of Parliament Group (Founding Mbr.); World Federalists of Canada. **HONS:** Complimentary Membership in WILL (World Initiative of Lifelong Learning), 1995; events & int'l conference coord. include Canada Public Rel'ns Consultant to First Global Conference on Lifelong Learning in Rome, 1994 & First Global Conference on Educational Tourism, 1990. **INTERESTS:** lifelong learning; telecomm., science & technology; distance educ.; travel; the arts; training; swimming. **MISC:** frequent speaker; listed in

Who's Who in Canadian Business (1997), *Who's Who of American Women* (1966-94), *Who's Who in Public Relations* (1992), *The Capital List* (*Who's Who in Ottawa*, 1978), *Dictionary of International Biography* (1966), *Leading Ladies Canada* (1971), *Who's Who in Arts and Antiques* (1970), *2000 Women of Achievement* (1969), *Who's Who in the West* (1963). **COMMENT:** *"Futurist, citizen ambassador for Canada, interested in lifelong learning and humanity and a multiplicity of other concerns, Robbin Frazer has crusaded globally for causes intended to awaken mankind to our myriad possibilities. She has sought a modern Renaissance that might yet build peace on earth, goodwill to all men. In the Canadian House of Commons, served as executive, special and research assistant to cabinet ministers and as editor in the committees' secretariat. Internationally renowned writer/editor (magazines, newspapers, reports) and public relations consultant in communications, Information Highway, telecommunications, space, multiculturalism, environment, arts and travel. Faculty member, education–including teaching, training and distance education, plus volunteerism achievements across Canada."*

Fréchette, Sylvie ⊘ $

Athlete, Marketing Representative, Public Relations, NATIONAL BANK OF CANADA, 770 Sherbrooke St. W., Ste. 1600, Montreal, QC H3A 1G1 (514) 843-7171, FAX 843-7214. Born Montreal 1967. **EDUC:** Univ. of Montreal, Phys. Educ., 1988-91. **CAREER:** Mktg Rep., Speaker, in charge of support program for young Que. Athletes, National Bank of Canada, 1992 to date; sports commentator, incl. Winter Olympics, Lillehammer, 1994 & Commonwealth Games, Victoria, 1994; **SPORTS CAREER:** began swimming & synchronized swimming, 1974; 1st synchronized swimming competition, Cdn Jr. Championships, 1979; Cdn Jr. Champion, solo, duet & team, 1981; Cdn Jr. Champion, solo & team, 1982; 1st, team, FINA World Cup, 1985; 1st, solo & duet, Australian Games, 1985; Gold Medal, solo, Commonwealth Games, Edinburgh, 1986; 1st, solo, Soviet Union Meet, 1986; 2nd, team, FINA World Cup, 1987; Silver Medal, solo, Pan-Am Games, Indianapolis, 1987; 1st, solo, duet & team, Synchro Roma, 1988; 1st, solo, *Soviet Women's Magazine* Competition, Moscow, 1989; Cdn Sr. Champion, solo, 1989, 1990, 1991, 1992; 1st, solo, Majorca Synchro, 1989; 2nd, solo, 3rd, duet, & 2nd, team, World Cup, Paris, 1989; Gold Medal, solo, Commonwealth Games, Auckland, 1990; 1st, solo, Coupe Loano, Italy, 1990; 1st, solo, Roma Synchro, 1990, 1991, 1992; 1st, solo,

Swiss Open, Lancy, 1990; 1st, solo, German Open, 1990, 1992; Gold Medal, solo, world record, World Championship, Perth, 1991; 1st, solo, World Cup, Bonn, 1991; 1st, solo, Swiss Open, Lichtenstein, 1991; 1st, solo, Pre-Olympic Competition, 1991; 1st, solo, int'l competition, Czechoslovakia, 1991; 1st, solo, Japan Synchro, 1992; Gold Medal, solo, Summer Olympics, Barcelona, 1992; retired, 1992; returned to training for team synchronized swimming, Dec. 1994; 2nd, team, Cdn Championships, 1995; 2nd, team, FINA World Cup, Atlanta, 1995; 2nd, team, Summer Olympics, Atlanta, 1996. **SELECTED PUBLICATIONS:** *Sans Fausse Note*, biography, co-author (in English *Gold At Last*). **AFFIL:** Synchro Montréal (Hon. Chair 1993). **HONS:** numerous prizes & honours; Athlete of the Year, Quebec Federation of Synchronized Swimming, 1985; Elaine Tanner Trophy, 1986; Peg Seller Prize for Most Outstanding Competitive Synchronized Swimmer in the Prov. of Que., 1986; Cdn Athlete of the Year in Aquatic Sports, 1989, 1990, 1991, 1992; Sylvie Fréchette Award, Canadian Sports Federation, 1992; Que. Sportsmanship Award, High-Level Competition category, 1992; Personality of the Year, Courage, Humanism & Personal Accomplishment Category, *La Presse*, 1992; Grace Under Pressure prize, Canadian Association of the Advancement of Women in Sports & Physical Activity, 1993; *Per Ludos Fraternitas* Award, International Association for Non-Violent Sports, 1993; Olympic Order of Canada, 1994. **INTERESTS:** music; reading; biking; movies. **MISC:** at the 1992 Barcelona Olympics, a judging error (incorrectly registered points in compulsory figures) initially cost Sylvie Fréchette the Gold Medal, as the chief referee refused to correct the mistake, despite the protests of witnesses, which resulted in her taking the Silver Medal; in Oct. 1993, following a review, the International Amateur Swimming Federation recommended to the International Olympic Committee that she be awarded the Gold Medal & that her 1st-place finish be recorded in the official Olympic books; IOC presented her with the Gold Medal, Dec. 1993; Canadian Sports Federation created the Sylvie Fréchette Award in 1993, to be presented to athletes who overcome great difficulties to triumph in their sports, Sylvie Fréchette, Silken Laumann & Yves Laroche were the 1st recipients; among the 1st 5 recipients of the Olympic Order of Canada; world record, 7 perfect 10s, World Aquatic Games, Australia, 1991; designer, swimsuit collection. **COMMENT:** *"After returning from Barcelona, where I won the 1992 Olympic Gold Medal in synchronized swimming, I began a career as an ambassador* *for the National Bank, travelling across Canada as a motivational speaker encouraging young people to strive to reach their goals. I returned to competitive swimming in December 1994, to complete my Olympic dream. I am very proud to have been a member of the Synchronized Swimming Olympic Team that won a Silver Medal at the Centennial Olympic Games in Atlanta in 1996."*

Frederickson, Elinore G., B.Ed. $ ♡

Instructor, Developmental Studies, YUKON COLLEGE, Box 2799, Whitehorse, YT Y1A 5K4. Born Flin Flon, Man. 1944. m. Robert Frederickson. 1 ch. Jason. **EDUC:** Univ. of Saskatchewan, B.Ed. 1978; Univ. of British Columbia, Adult Educ. Diploma (Instructional Skills) 1990; Yukon Coll., Instructional Skills Workshop Facilitator 1996. **CAREER:** primary teacher, 3 yrs.; special educ. teacher, 6 yrs.; primary teacher, 5 yrs.; Play & Learn Store Mgr, 3 yrs.; kindergarten teacher, 5 yrs.; Instructor, Yukon Coll., 10 yrs. **SELECTED PUBLICATIONS:** helped design & write: *Employing People with Learning Disabilities is Good Business* (1989); *Job Interview Tips for People with Learning Disabilities* (1990). **AFFIL:** Learning Disabilities Association of Canada (Past Pres.); Learning Disabilities Association of Yukon (Past Pres.); The Coalition of National Voluntary Organizations (Bd.); American Association of Higher Education; Canadian Congress for Learning Opportunities for Women; National Study Group of Employment & Disabilities; Yukon Coll. President's Committee of Women's Studies Programs; Stay-in School Initiative Committee (Founding Mbr.); Barrier-free Housing Committee for Yukon. **HONS:** Canadian 125 Medal, 1993; Outstanding Service Award, LDAY, 1995; Canada Volunteer Award, 1996; Certificate of Honour, 1996. **INTERESTS:** volunteering; gardening; reading; sharing. **MISC:** keynote speaker on "Learning Disabilities and Mental Health," Surrey, B.C., 1993; appointed by the Min. of Educ. to the Yukon Curriculum Advisory Committee; appointed by Min. of Justice to the Employment Equity Advisory Bd.; participant in the Council of Ministers of Educ. Forum of Educ.; workshop presenter & facilitator at numerous reg'l & prov. conferences & workshops. **COMMENT:** *"An ardent advocate for the rights of persons with disabilities, Elinore was first introduced to learning disabilities while experiencing the frustration of watching the school system fail to recognize and accommodate her teenage son. For the last 10 years, she has been committed to utilizing every waking moment to share her knowledge and experience to ensure that persons with learning disabilities and their families are given the opportunity to reach their full potential in a positive and non-threatening environment."*

Freeman, Barbara M., B.A., M.A. ■ 🎓 📖 ✏

Assistant Professor, Journalism and Communication, CARLETON UNIVERSITY, 1125 Colonel By Dr., Ottawa, ON K1S 5B6 (613) 520-2600 Ext. 7437, FAX 520-6690, EMAIL freeman@ccs.carleton.ca. Born St. John's. **EDUC:** Carleton Univ., B.Journalism 1969, M.A.(Cdn Studies) 1988; Concordia Univ., doctoral candidate in Hist. **CAREER:** various positions as a journalist, broadcaster & news editor, Canada & the UK, 1967-80; Instructor, Journalism, Carleton Univ., 1980-89; Asst. Prof., Journalism & Comm., 1989 to date; occasional freelance radio documentaries & articles, 1980 to date. **SELECTED PUBLICATIONS:** *Kit's Kingdom: The Journalism of Kathleen Blake Coleman* (Ottawa, Carleton Univ. Press 1989). **AFFIL:** Amethyst Women's Addiction Centre, Ottawa (Dir.). **INTERESTS:** historical & contemporary perspectives on women in journalism; the media & gender; media, society & culture.

Freeman, Carolyn, M.B.,B.S., FRCP(C) 🎓 ⊕ ⚛

Chairman, Department of Oncology, Division of Radiation Oncology, MCGILL UNIVERSITY, 1650 Cedar Ave., Rm. D5-400, Montreal, QC H3G 1A4 (514) 934-8040, FAX 934-8220. Born Kettering, UK 1950. m. Juan Carlos. 2 ch. **EDUC:** Westminster Medical Sch., London Univ., UK, M.B., B.S. 1972. **CAREER:** House Surgeon, Professorial Surgical Unit, Westminster Hospital, London, UK, 1972; House Physician to Drs. F. Gibberd & R. Tonkin, Westminster Hospital, 1973; Sr. House Officer to Drs. T.M. Prossor & K.A. Newton, Dept. of Radiotherapy & Medical Oncology, Westminster Hospital, 1973; Registrar, 1974; Rotating Intern, Montreal General Hospital, 1974; Resident II, Therapeutic Radiology, Dept. of Therapeutic Radiology, McGill Univ., 1975; Resident III, Medical & Surgical Oncology, McGill Univ. Hospitals, 1976; Chief Resident, Therapeutic Radiology, Dept. of Therapeutic Radiology, McGill Univ., 1977; Asst. Prof., Dept. of Radiation Oncology, 1978-79; Assoc. Prof., 1979-80; Assoc. Prof., McGill Cancer Centre, 1980-83; Assoc. Prof., Dept. of Pediatrics, McGill Univ., 1983-86; Prof., Dept. of Radiation Oncology, 1986; Prof., Dept. of Pediatrics, 1990. **SELECTED PUBLICATIONS:** "A simple isocentric technique for irradiation of the breast, chest wall and peripheral lymphatics," with E.B. Podgorsak *et al* (*British Journal of*

Radiology 57, 1984); "Clinical experience with a single field rotational total skin electron irradiation technique for cutaneous T-cell lymphoma," with S. Suissa *et al* (*Radiotherapy and Oncology* 24, 1992); "Final results of a study of escalating doses of hyperfractional radiotherapy in brain stem tumors in children: a Pediatric Oncology Group study," with J.P. Kirscher *et al* (*International Journal of Radiation Oncology, Biology and Physics* 27, 1993); "Stereotactic external beam irradiation in previously untreated brain tumors in children and adolescents," with L. Souhami *et al* (*Medical and Pediatric Oncology* 22, 1994); "Tumors of the Central Nervous System," with R.L. Heideman *et al, Principles and Practice of Pediatric Oncology*, eds. P.P. Pizzo & D.G. Poplack (J.P. Lippincott, 1993); over 100 other scholarly publications. **EDIT:** Assoc. Ed., *International Journal of Radiation Oncology, Biology and Physics*, 1987 to date. **AFFIL:** National Cancer Institute of Canada; American Society for Therapeutic Radiology & Oncology; European Society for Therapeutic Radiology & Oncology (Bd.); Société Internationale d'Oncologie Paediatrique; Canadian Association of Radiation Oncologists (VP 1987-89; Pres. 1991-93); American Radium Society (Exec. Committee 1991-93). **HONS:** Chadwick Prize in Medicine, Surgery & Pathology, Westminster Medical Sch., 1972; Rosenbloom Chair in Radiation Oncology, McGill Univ., 1990. **MISC:** Chrm, Specialty Committee on Radiation Oncology, Royal Coll. of Physicians & Surgeons of Canada, 1992-96; numerous invited lectures, talks & presentations; reviews for *Cancer, Radiology, European Journal of Oncology, Journal of the Canadian Association of Radiologists*, & other journals; grant recipient. **COMMENT:** *"Dr. Freeman's research activities relate to clinical research in paediatric tumours especially brain tumours; altered radiotherapy dose fractionation schedules; prediction of response to radiotherapy; and development of new radiotherapy treatment techniques."*

Freeman, Linda, B.A.,PGCE,M.A.,Ph.D. ☜ ✿
Associate Professor, Department of Political Science, CARLETON UNIVERSITY, Ottawa, ON K1S 5B6 (613) 233-0370, FAX 520-4064, EMAIL ifreeman@web.apc.net. Born Vernon, B.C. s. **EDUC:** Univ. of British Columbia, B.A.(Int'l Studies) 1965; Univ. of London, UK, PGCE(Educ.) 1969; Univ. of Toronto, M.A. (Pol. Economy) 1971, Ph.D.(Pol. Economy) 1978. **CAREER:** Asst. Prof., Univ. of Guelph, 1978-80; Asst. Prof., Carleton Univ., 1980-85; Assoc. Prof., 1985 to date. **SELECTED PUBLICATIONS:** "Contradictions of Independence:

Namibia in Transition" (*Transformation*, 17, 1992); "Canada, Aid and Peacemaking in Southern Africa," *Aid as Peacemaker–Canadian Development Assistance and Third World Conflict*, ed. Robert Miller (Ottawa; Carleton Univ. Press, 1992); "The Effect of the World Crisis on Canada's Involvement in Africa" (*Studies in Political Economy*, 17, 1985); various other journal articles, book chapters, reviews, magazine & newspaper articles. **AFFIL:** Canadian Research Consortium on Southern Africa, (Founding Mbr. & Chair, Program Co-ordinating Committee); Canadian Association of African Studies; Canadian Political Science Association (Dir. 1983-85). **HONS:** recipient, Scholarly Achievement Award, Dept. of Pol. Sci., Carleton Univ., 1983. **INTERESTS:** hiking; skiing; music; cinema; riding; cooking. **MISC:** grant recipient; regular commentator on Cdn radio & TV on S.Africa; consulted regularly by newspapers, magazines, radio & TV; Mbr., Africa 2000 Consultative Group advising the Min. for External Affairs, Monique Landry, from Feb. 1987 until its disbanding in 1991. **COMMENT:** *"A professor; widely travelled; active in the anti-apartheid movement; founding member of an inter-university research consortium on Southern Africa; frequent commentator on television; forthcoming book,* The Ambiguous Champion: Canada & South Africa in the Trudeau & Mulroney Years.*"*

Freeman, Risa, M.D.,M.Ed., C.C.F.P. ■■ ⊕ ☜
Program Director, Undergraduate Education, and Assistant Professor, Department of Family and Community Medicine, Faculty of Medicine, UNIVERSITY OF TORONTO, 620 University Ave., Ste. 801, Toronto, ON M5G 2C1 (416) 978-1896, FAX 978-3912, EMAIL r.freeman@utoronto.ca. Born Hamilton, Ont. 1962. s. **EDUC:** Univ. of Toronto, B.Sc.(Human Biol.) 1984; McMaster Univ., M.D. 1988; Univ. of Toronto, Residency in Family Medicine 1990, M.Ed.(Higher Educ., specializing in Medical Educ.) 1993. **CAREER:** Chief Resident, Postgrad. Family Medicine Program, North York Gen. Hospital, 1989-90; Academic Fellow, Assoc. Staff, Dept. of Family Medicine, 1990-91; Clinical Fellow, Dept. of Family & Community Medicine, Sunnybrook Health Science Centre, 1990-91; Instructor, Dept. of Family & Community Medicine, Univ. of Toronto, 1990-91; Medical Consultant, Dept. of Occupational Health, Bloorview Children's Hospital, 1990 to date; Active Staff, Dept. of Family Medicine, North York Gen. Hospital, 1991 to date; Lecturer, Dept. of Family & Community Medicine, Univ. of Toronto, 1991; Staff Physician, Teen Clinic, North York Gen. Hospital,

1992 to date; Asst. Prof. (part-time), Dept. of Family & Community Medicine, Univ. of Toronto, 1993-94; Asst. Prof. (full-time), 1994 to date; Co-Chair, Dept. of Family Medicine, Div. of Obstetrics, & Undergrad. Program Dir., Dept. of Family Medicine, North York Gen. Hospital, 1994-95; Medical Advisor, Heart & Stroke Foundation of Ontario, 1995 to date; Program Dir., Undergrad. Educ., Dept. of Family & Community Medicine, Univ. of Toronto, 1995 to date. SELECTED PUBLICATIONS: *Mental Health in the Workplace* (Handicapped Employment Program monograph, Ont. Ministry of Labour, 1984); co-author, *Adolescent Health Questionnaire & Physician Guidelines* (Child Welfare Committee, Ontario Medical Association, 1992); co-author with V. Rachlis & E. Franssen, "Young Family Physicians Support Hospital-Based Activities" (*Canadian Family Physician*, Vol. 41, Feb. 1995); co-author with J. Tipping & A. Rachlis, "Using Faculty and Student Perceptions of Group Dynamics to Develop Recommendations for PBL Training" (*Academic Medicine*, Vol. 70, No. 11, Nov. 1995); co-author with S. Dunn, "Risky Business: Teaching Medical Trainees about the Potential for Abuse in the Doctor-Patient Relationship" (STFM monograph on Family Violence Education, Spring 1995). AFFIL: Ontario Medical Association (Focus Group, Women in Organized Medicine 1993; Working Group on Adolescent Health Care, Committee on Child Welfare 1991-92); Boyd Academy (mbr. of Council 1994 to date; Coll. of Family Physicians of Canada; Society of Teachers of Family Medicine, U.S.A.; Coll. of Physicians & Surgeons of Ontario; Canadian/Ontario Medical Association; Canadian Medical Protective Association. HONS: several scholarships; Academic Fellow in Family Medicine, North York Gen. Hospital, 1991; Best Poster Presentation, 35th Nat'l Annual Scientific Assembly, Coll. of Family Physicians of Canada, Halifax, 1993; Boyd Academy Director's Award for leadership in organizing & developing new Family Medicine Clerkship, Univ. of Toronto, 1995. MISC: numerous presentations. COMMENT: *"I feel very fortunate to be able to describe myself professionally as a clinician (community-based family physician, including primary care obstetrics and palliative care), educator (medical students and residents), researcher (medical education, women's and adolescent health), and administrator (Program Director, Undergraduate Education, Dept. of Family and Community Medicine, Faculty of Medicine, University of Toronto). My greatest achievement has been to juggle all of this (most days) with a meaningful private life that includes a loving family, strong and lasting friendships and a modest amount of self-improvement activities including fitness, gardening and puttering around in the kitchen and at the cottage."*

Freemark, Kathryn Elizabeth, B.Sc., Ph.D. ■ ❀ ♣ ✔
Songbird Research Ecologist, ENVIRONMENT CANADA, Canadian Wildlife Service, National Wildlife Research Centre, 100 Gamelin Blvd., Hull, QC K1A 0H3 (819) 997-1410, FAX 953-6612, EMAIL freemarkk@msm1s6.ncr.doe.ca. Born Renfrew, Ont. 1953. m. Timothy Holden Freemark. 3 ch. Christine Elizabeth, Sarah Kathryn, Leo Timothy EDUC: Queen's Univ., B.Sc.(Biol.) 1977; Carleton Univ., Ph.D.(Biol.) 1984. CAREER: Inland Waters Directorate, Water Quality Branch, Fisheries & Environment Canada, Ottawa/Hull, 1977; Cdn Wildlife Svc., Migratory Birds Conservation Branch, 1977-78; Scientific Consultant Svcs, Ottawa/Hull, 1978; Research Grants Directorate, Natural Sciences & Eng. Research Council of Canada, Ottawa, 1984-85; Planning & Budgeting Directorate, 1985; Strategic Grants Officer, Targeted Research Directorate, 1985-86; Songbird Research Ecologist, Migratory Bird Populations Div., Environment Canada, Cdn Wildlife Svc., National Wildlife Research Centre, Ottawa/Hull, 1988 to date; assignment to US Environmental Protection Agency, Corvallis, Ore., 1992-96; Songbird Research Ecologist, Canadian Wildlife Service, 1996 to date. SELECTED PUBLICATIONS: "Habitat Selection and Environmental Gradients: Dynamics in the 'Stable' Tropics," with J.R. Karr (*Ecology* 64(6) 1983); "Impacts of agricultural herbicide on terrestrial wildlife in temperate landscapes: A review with special reference to North America," with C. Boutin (*Agriculture, Ecosystems & Environment* 52(2) 1995); "Assessing the Effects of Agriculture on Terrestrial Wildlife: Developing a Hierarchical Approach for the US EPA" (*Landscape & Urban Planning* 31(1-3) 1995); numerous other publications. AFFIL: Ecological Society of America; Society of Environmental Toxicology & Chemistry; International Association of Landscape Ecology; International Association of Landscape Ecology (US Chapter); Society of Canadian Ornithologists; Canadian Nature Federation. HONS: Renfrew County Scholar, Univ. Women's Club Scholarship, 1972. INTERESTS: aerobics; alpine skiing; cross-country skiing; community theatre; horseback riding. MISC: numerous conference presentations; recipient of various grants; listed in *Who's Who in Science and Engineering*, *World Who's Who of Women* & *Registry of Canadian Women in Engineering, Science, Technology & Trades*. COMMENT: "*Interna-*

tional assignment with EPA as scientific lead on study of agricultural impacts on terrestrial wildlife and their habitats as part of a co-operative, multi-agency (EPA, USDA) research program in the midwestern United States."

Freiman, Ruth, B.A.,O.P.M. ⊗

Owner and Director, ROBERTSON GALLERIES, 162 Laurier Ave. W., Ottawa, ON K1P 5J4 (613) 235-2459, FAX 232-3017. Born 1950. m. A.J. Freiman. 2 ch. EDUC: Loyola Univ., B.A.(cum laude, Arts) 1974; Harvard Univ., Exec. O.P.M. Course 1993. CAREER: responsible for preparing ministerial speeches, Dept. of Industry, Trade & Commerce, Gov't of Man., 1974-75; responsible for V.I.P., PC Leadership Convention, 1975-76; Research Office, PC Party, 1976; owner & Mgr of a real estate holding co., 1977 to date; owner & Dir., Robertson Galleries, 1977 to date. AFFIL: National Gallery of Canada (V-Chair & Mbr., Bd. of Dir.); Ottawa Congress Centre (Bd.); Museum of Civilization (Committee Mbr., Civic Promo.); Professional Art Dealers' Association of Canada; Hillel Academy (Bd.). INTERESTS: theatre; music; tennis; swimming; skiing; foreign travel; visiting galleries.

French, Doris, B.A.,M.Sc. ⊲⊱ ☺

Retired Teacher and Union Activist. 140 Walton St., Box 364, Arthur, ON N0G 1A0. Born Arthur, Ont. 1939. s. EDUC: Waterloo Lutheran Univ., B.A.(Geography) 1971; Niagara Univ., M.Sc.(Educ.) 1983. CAREER: public elementary teacher, 1958-66; secondary sch. teacher, 1966-68, 1969-75; Academic Dir. in Adult Educ., 1968-69; elementary sch. teacher, 1975-80; V-Principal & teacher in elementary schools, 1980-93. UNION CAREER: Pres., North Wellington, Women Teachers' Association, 1964-66; Chief Negotiator for Teachers of Wellington County, 1978-81; Pres., Wellington County Women Teachers' Association, 1980-81; Pres./VP/Rep., Wellington County Women Teachers' Association, 1983-93; Chief Negotiator, Federation of Women Teachers' Associations of Ontario (F.W.T.A.O.), Bd. of Dir., 1984-86; P.A.R. (Positions of Added Responsibility) Rep., Wellington County Women Teachers' Association, 1988-93; Q.E.C.O. Councillor, 1989-91; Prov. Chair, Loans Fund Committee, F.W.T.A.O., 1989-93. SELECTED PUBLICATIONS: *In Terms of the Law – a teacher's glossary*, co-author (1983); on various writing teams for the Wellington County Bd. of Educ. for language arts & supervision of teachers. AFFIL: Ontario Teachers' Federation (Bd. of Gov. 1986-89); Federation of Women Teachers' Associations of Ontario (Dir. 1982-89; Exec. 1986-89); Arthur United Church (Choir Dir.; Chair, Official Bd. 1989-94); Heart & Stroke Canvass for Arthur, Ont. (Co-Chair 1989-96); Arthur Horticultural Society (Dir.); Arthur United Church Women (1st VP); Arthur Sr. Citizens' Club (Pres.); Bible Society for Arthur (Treas.); North Wellington Superannuated Women Teachers (2nd VP); Councillor, S.T.O. District, 1996. HONS: Diamond Jubilee Award, for distinguished service to educ. & community, F.W.T.A.O., 1978; Distinguished Service Award for 35 yrs. of teaching, F.W.T.A.O., 1994; Hon. Membership, F.W.T.A.O., 1996. INTERESTS: woodworking; photography; golfing; music; cadets; community work. MISC: became 2nd Lieut. in the R.C.A.F. in 1969 & promoted to Lieut. in 1994; trained Army Cadets, Air Cadets & presently training No. 1943 Palmerston Army Cadets; conducted several workshops throughout the province in math., poetry, leadership & sch. law. COMMENT: *"I am committed to helping women achieve equal pay for work of equal value, equal work and promotion opportunities in the workplace and political fairness."*

French, Mary ■■ ♡ 🖺

Owner and operator, VICTORIA MANOR HERITAGE HOUSE MUSEUM, P.O. Box 284, Harbour Grace, NF A0A 2M0 (709) 596-2085. Born St. John's 1921. m. Gordon L. French. 1 ch. Joyce Mary (Joy). EDUC: Centenary Hall, Council of Higher Educ., Nfld., 1934; Salvation Army Coll., St. John's, 1937. CAREER: beauty consultant; Bowring Bros.; Charles of the Ritz; Dorothy Grey Fashion Sales; modelling; Ayre & Sons Ltd.; millinery designer; self-employed. AFFIL: Carbonear Ladies Hospital Auxiliary (VP, Public Rel'ns 1994); Women's Institute of Newfoundland (former Bd. mbr.; former District Rep.; founding mbr., 2 branches); Anglican Church Women (mbr.; Public Rel'ns W.I. 1987-96); Harbour Grace Library Auxiliary (former VP, Public Rel'ns); Anglican Young People's Association (former Pres.); YMCA Menettes (founding mbr.). HONS: invited (with husband & daughter) to attend Buckingham Palace Garden Party, 1996 (after publication about Victoria Manor was sent to Queen Elizabeth); Appreciation Award for loyal & devoted svc., both Carbonear Hospital Auxiliary & Women's Institute; Red Cross Volunteer Award for work with the war effort, 1941-45. INTERESTS: travel; swimming; poetry; reading; volunteer work; social gatherings (afternoon teas); knitting/crafts. MISC: selected by CBC Radio to be interviewed for TV spot to commemorate CBC's 60th anniversary of radio; interviewed by "Here & Now," CBC TV re Buckingham Palace Garden Party & follow-up interview at Government House Garden Party, St. John's. COMMENT: *"I am a 75-year-old woman, very active. I enjoy meeting people and feel I am an ambassador of goodwill for my province of Newfoundland and my country, Canada."*

Frick, Elizabeth A., B.A., M.S.L.S. ■ ᭡ ▯ ⑤
Professor (retired), DALHOUSIE UNIVERSITY, 790 Washington, #1210, Denver, CO 80203 (303) 832-2981. Born Ottawa 1936. m. Stephen. 3 ch. EDUC: Trinity Coll., Univ. of Toronto, B.A.(Phil. & English) 1958; Syracuse Univ., M.S.L.S.(Library & Info. Sci.) 1967. CAREER: Reference Librarian, Sch. of Industrial & Labor Rel'ns, Cornell Univ., 1967-72; Reference Librarian, Olin Research Library, Cornell Univ., 1972; Reference Librarian, Earlham Coll., 1972-76; Head, User Svcs, Library, Univ. of Colorado, Colorado Springs, 1976-83; Prof., Fac. of Mgmt, Dalhousie Univ., 1983-94. SELECTED PUBLICATIONS: "Teaching Information Structure: Turning Researchers into Self-Teachers" (*Theories of Bibliographic Education: Designs for Teaching* ed. Cerise Oberman & Katina Strauch, New York: Bowker, 1982); "Humanizing Technology Through Instruction" (*Canadian Library Journal* Oct. 1984); "Information Structure and Bibliographic Instruction" (*User Instruction in Academic Libraries: A Century of Selected Readings* comp. Larry Hardesty & John Mark Tucker, Metuchen, NJ: Scarecrow Press, 1986); "Professional Training for User Education: the UK" (*Journal of Education for Library and Information Science* Summer 1987); *A Place to Stand: User Education in Canadian Libraries: A Collection of Original Essays* ed. (Ottawa: Canadian Library Association, 1988); "Survey or Standards? Teaching User Services as a Policy Issue" (*The Reference Librarian* 25/26 1987); "Qualitative Evaluation of User Education Programs: The Best Choice?" (*Research Strategies* Winter 1990); "Critical Analysis as a Pivotal Act" (*Judging the Validity of Information Sources: Teaching Critical Analysis in Bibliographic Instruction* ed. Linda Shirato, Ann Arbor, MI: Pierian Press, 1991); "The Think Tank Papers: Are We in the Ball Park?" (*The Evolving Educational Mission of the Library* ed. Betsy Baker & Mary Ellen Litzinger, Chicago: Association of College & Research Libraries, 1992); *Library Research Guide to History* (Pierian Press, 1995); "Faculty Support Information Literacy" with Fran Nowakowski (*C&RL News* Mar. 1993); numerous other papers, reviews & reports. AFFIL: Canadian Library Association; Canadian Association of Library Schools (Sec.-Treas. 1984-85); Ameri-

can Library Association; Association of Coll. & Research Libraries (Taskforce on Strategic Options for Professional Educations; President's Program Planning Committee; Committee on Educ. for Bibliographic Instruction (Nominating Committee); Atlantic Provinces Library Association (Committee on Library Instruction; Publications Committee). HONS: Library Service Enhancement Program Grant, Council on Library Resources, 1977-78; Travel Grant, British Research Council, 1986; Research Dev. Grant, Dalhousie Univ., 1989-91, 1991-93, 1992; Canada 125 Medal. INTERESTS: Internet; Internet training; info. access training; reference training. MISC: research papers presented & workshops given throughout Canada, US & UK; mbr., several editorial bds. COMMENT: *"Professor Frick moved from years of practice to teaching at the graduate level in one of Canada's major universities. She is particularly well-known for her teaching and writing in both Canada and the US."*

Fried, Myra I., B.F.A. ▯ Ꭾ
Writer, Director and Producer, LIGHTSHOW COMMUNICATIONS INC., 322 Clinton St., 2nd Fl., Toronto, ON M6G 2Y8 (416) 537-8154, FAX (416) 537-8624. Born Montreal 1953. m. Steve Wright. EDUC: Concordia Univ., B.F.A. 1975. CAREER: writer, dir., prod., currently in dev. on a number of film & TV projects. SELECTED CREDITS: Prod., *You Love Me I Hate You* (half-hour), 1994; Writer/Co-Dir./Co-Prod., *Hurt Penguins* (feature), 1992. DIRECTOR: Lightshow Communications Inc. (with partners Robert Bergman & Gerard Ciccoritti). AFFIL: ACTRA; WGA; EQUITY; SOCAN. MISC: co-wrote the songs *Not What You Need* & *Middle of a Dream* for *Hurt Penguins*; co-wrote *Cause He's A Boy* (closing song) for *You Love Me I Hate You.*

Friedland, Judith, B.A.,M.A., Ph.D. ⊕ ᭡ ○
Associate Professor and Chair, Department of Occupational Therapy, Faculty of Medicine, UNIVERSITY OF TORONTO, 256 McCaul St., Toronto, ON M5T 1W5 (416) 978-5936, FAX 978-4363, EMAIL friedland@medac.med. utoronto.ca. Born Toronto 1939. m. Martin Friedland. 3 ch. Tom, Jenny, Nancy. EDUC: Univ. of Toronto, Dip.(Phys. & Occupational Therapy) 1960, B.A.(Arts & Sci.) 1976, M.A .(Special Educ.) 1981, Ph.D. 1988. CAREER: Occupational Therapist, Fulbourn, Psychiatric Hospital, UK, 1960-61; Occupational Therapist, Toronto Psychiatric Hospital, 1961-63; Occupational Therapist, Toronto Achievement Centre, 1975-77; Lecturer, Rehabilitation Counselling Program, Seneca Coll., Toronto,

1976-78; Occupational Therapist, Community Occupational Therapy Associates, Toronto, 1977-82; Asst. Prof., Dept. of Occupational Therapy, Univ. of Toronto, 1982-93; Acting Dir., Div. of Occupational Therapy, 1990; Dir., 1991-93; Assoc. Prof. & Chair, Dept. of Occupational Therapy, 1993 to date. **SELECTED PUBLICATIONS:** "A Group Approach in Psychiatric Occupational Therapy," with M. Murphy (*Canadian Journal of Occupational Therapy* 1965); "When Doing Is Not Enough: The Relationship Between Activity and Effectiveness in Anorexia Nervosa," with M. McColl & A. Kerr (*Occupational Therapy in Mental Health* 1986); "Diversional Activity: Does It Deserve Its Bad Name?" (*American Journal of Occupational Therapy* 1988); "Accessing Language in Agraphia: An Examination of Hemiplegic Writing" (*Aphasiology* 1990); "Social Support Intervention After Stroke: Results of a Randomized Trial," with M. McColl (*Archives of Physical Medicine and Rehabilitation*, 1992); "Coping and Social Support as Determinants of Quality of Life in HIV/AIDS," (*AIDS Care*, 1996); various other publications. **AFFIL:** Canadian Association of Occupational Therapists; Coll. of Occupational Therapists of Ontario; Ontario Society of Occupational Therapists; World Federation of Occupational Therapists; Davisville Home & Sch. Association (VP 1971-73; Pres. 1973-75); West Park Hosp. (Gov.). **HONS:** Ontario Society of Occupational Therapists Prize, 1960. **INTERESTS:** family; opera & ballet; travel; gardening; reading. **COMMENT:** *"I have had several careers in my adult life: student (intermittently until age 49); wife and mother; community activist; occupational therapist; university teacher and researcher."*

Friendly, Lynda 🎭 $ 📺

Executive Vice-President, LIVENT INC., 165 Avenue Rd., Ste. 600, Toronto, ON M5R 3S4 (416) 324-5484, FAX 324-5520. Born Toronto 1949. s. **EDUC:** Ryerson Polytechnic Univ., Hotel, Resort & Institutional Admin. 1970. **CAREER:** comm./hospitality; Exec. VP, Comm., Cineplex Odeon Corporation, 1979-89; Exec. VP, Livent Inc., 1989 to date. **DIRECTOR:** Livent Inc.; Toronto Theatre Alliance. **AFFIL:** Ryerson Polytechnic Univ. (Gov.); Metro Toronto Convention & Tourist Association (Dir.). **INTERESTS:** theatre; art.

Friendly, Martha ■■ ✋ 🎓 ♡

Coordinator, Childcare Resource and Research Unit, CENTRE FOR URBAN AND COMMUNITY STUDIES, University of Toronto, 455 Spadina Ave., Ste. 305, Toronto, ON M5S 2G8 (416) 978-6895, FAX 971-2139, EMAIL martha@chass.utoronto.ca. Adjunct Professor, UNIVERSITY OF TORONTO. Born New York City 1943. m. Michael Friendly. 2 ch. Ethan, Abigail. **EDUC:** Hofstra Univ., B.A.(Psych.) 1965; Univ. of Connecticut, Ph.D. program (Social Psych.) 1966-68. **CAREER:** Research Asst., Educational Testing Svc., Princeton, N.J., 1968-69; Program Dev. Specialist, Dept. of Community Affairs, State of N.J., 1969-71; Research Officer, Ontario Institute for Studies in Education, Curriculum Dept., 1973-75; Researcher, Project Child Care, Social Planning Council of Metropolitan Toronto, 1975-76; Research Coord., Child in the City Program, Centre for Urban & Community Studies, Univ. of Toronto, 1977-82; Coord., Childcare Resource & Research Unit, 1982 to date; Adjunct Prof., 1992 to date. **SELECTED PUBLICATIONS:** author/co-author, numerous articles on child care, 1979 to date; *Child care policy in Canada: Putting the pieces together* (Don Mills, Ont.; Addison-Wesley Canada, 1994). **EDIT:** Guest Editor, *Child Welfare,* Child Welfare League of America/Canada, 1994. **AFFIL:** Human Resources Development Canada (Tech. Advisory Committee, Child Care Visions 1996; Steering Committee, Sectoral Study, Child Care 1996); Metro Toronto Children's Services Task Force (Expert Panel 1996); Ministry of Education & Training, Ont. (Expert Advisory Panel, Early Years Proj. 1994); Ministry of Community & Social Svcs, Ont. (Day Nurseries Act Review Panel 1994). **INTERESTS:** social policy; women's issues. **COMMENT:** *"Martha Friendly is currently the coordinator of the Child Care Resource and Research Unit at the Centre for Urban and Community Studies, University of Toronto and Adjunct Professor at the Urban Centre. She has written many articles on child care policy and has recently completed a book,* Child care policy in Canada: Putting the pieces together. *She has been active in child care advocacy for many years, supporting development of high-quality, non-profit child care for all families. She is a member of the Social Policy Working Group of the National Action Committee on the Status of Women and is on the Council of the Ontario Coalition for Better Child Care."*

Frith, Irene ■ ✋ ♡ 👍

Past President, GALIANO RATEPAYERS' ASSOCIATION, Site 4, Compartment 3, Galiano Island, BC V0N 1P0 (604) 539-3171, FAX 539-3171. Vice-President, GALIANO HEALTH CARE SOCIETY. Born Calgary 1933 m. Mel. 2 ch. Robert Howard, Roxanne Howard. 3 stpch. Michelle Frith, Debbie Frith, Bart Frith. **EDUC:** Magee High Sch. **CAREER:** founder & owner, Girl

Friday Service Ltd., 1965; Mgr, Richmond Chamber of Commerce, 1965-70; Alderman, City of Richmond, 1972-80; Commissioner, North Fraser Harbour Commission, 1985-95, Chair, 6 yrs.; Fraser River Mgmt Bd., 3 yrs. EDIT: *Galiano Ratepayers' Association Newsletter*. AFFIL: Richmond Chamber of Commerce (Hon. Life Mbr.); organizer & fundraiser for many organizations & events. HONS: Richmond Good Citizen Award, Kiwanis Club of Richmond, 1989; Canada 125 Medal, 1992; Hon. Life mbr., Pacific Coast Association of Port Authorities. INTERESTS: piano; golf; community. MISC: 1st woman Chair of a Harbour Commission in Canada; candidate, Nov. 1996 election for Trustee on the Islands Trust Council. COMMENT: *"For the past 40 years I have worked as a community volunteer, raising money and organizing many events."*

Fritz, Yvonne, R.N.,M.L.A. ✦

Member of the Legislative Assembly (Calgary Cross), GOVERNMENT OF ALBERTA, 204 Legislative Building, Edmonton, AB T5K 2B6 (403) 422-5375, FAX 422-5368. Born Calgary 1950. m. Lanny. 2 ch. EDUC: Calgary General Hospital Sch. of Nursing, R.N. 1973. CAREER: Occupational Health Nurse, Calgary General Hospital, 1973-88; Alderman, Ward 5, City of Calgary, 1988-93; M.L.A. (Calgary Cross), Prov. of Alta., 1993 to date. AFFIL: Calgary Bd. of Health; Carewest Foundation; Calgary District Hospital Group; Alberta Multiculturalism Commission (Chrm 1993 to date).

Frize, Monique, B.Sc.E.E.,M.Phil.,D.I.C., M.B.A. ⬅ ⚙

Professor and Nortel/NSERC Women in Engineering Chair, Department of Electrical Engineering, UNIVERSITY OF NEW BRUNSWICK, Box 4400, Fredericton, NB E3B 5A3 (506) 453-4561, FAX 453-4516, EMAIL mfrize@unb.ca. m. Peter Frize. 1 ch. Patrick M. Frize. EDUC: Ottawa Univ., B.Sc.E.E.(Elect. Eng.) 1966; Imperial Coll. of Sci. & Technology, London, UK, M.Phil. & D.I.C.(Eng. in Medicine) 1970; Univ. de Moncton, M.B.A. 1986; Erasmus Univ., Rotterdam, The Netherlands, Doctorate (Clinical Eng.) 1989. CAREER: Consultant Eng., Northern Electric, Montreal, 1966-67; Clinical Eng., Hospital Notre-Dame, Montreal, 1971-79; Dir., Reg'l Clinical Eng. Svc., Health Regions 1 & 7, Moncton, 1979-89; Prof., Elect. Eng. & Chair Holder (Nortel/NSERC Women in Eng. Chair), Univ. of New Brunswick, 1989 to date. SELECTED CREDITS: Prod., *Engineering: Design Tomorrow's World* (video). SELECTED PUBLICATIONS: 14 papers in refereed journals; 56 papers in refereed conference proceedings; 31 reports, papers (nonrefereed); 34 presentations (mostly invited) at professional & tech. meetings. AFFIL: Association of Professional Engineers of N.B.; Canadian Academy of Engineering (Fellow 1992); Institute of Electronics & Electronics Engineering (Sr. Mbr., Eng. in Medicine & Biology 1993); Canadian Medical & Biological Engineering Society (1973-90; 1992 to date). HONS: Ph.D.(Hon.), Ottawa Univ., 1992; Ryerson Fellowship, Ryerson Polytechnic Univ., 1993; Officer of the Order of Canada, 1993; Ph.D.(Hon.), York Univ., 1994; Ph.D.(Hon.), Lakehead Univ., 1995; Meritus-Tabouret, Alumni, Univ. of Ottawa, 1996. INTERESTS: reading; Scottish country dancing; cross-country skiing; hiking; music; gardening. MISC: on several nat'l committees & bds. COMMENT: *"Born of French Canadian parents, I loved math and science, even though in a literary family. This attraction led me to engineering and various higher degrees and an interesting career. My life is balanced with a son and husband whose interests are in the arts. I have never had a boring day since I was born."*

Frost-Rogers, Vivien ⊕ ○

Creative Spirituality Consultant. Box 5256, Airdrie, AB T4B 2B3 (403) 289-1440, FAX 955-3944. Peerspirit Circle Caller. Born Manchester, UK 1959. w. 2 ch. Tristan Rogers, Eric Rogers. CAREER: Legal Sec., Bull Housser and Tupper, 1979-81; marine sales, Quarterdeck, Vancouver, 1981-85; sightseeing bus owner/operator, Granville Island Express, 1985-88; Creative Spirituality Consultant, Peerspirit Circle Consultant. VOLUNTEER CAREER: Lower Mainland Coord., Kids First Parent Association of Canada, 1989-95; Nat'l Pres., 1993-95; Consultant, 1995 to date. SELECTED PUBLICATIONS: *Against the Tide*, Vancouver parent publication. AFFIL: Ladner United Church. INTERESTS: sailing; creative writing; travel; reading nonfiction. COMMENT: *"I am a proud activist/feminist at-home mom. As National President of Kids First, I have endeavoured to raise the awareness of the importance of the at-home choice to our children and society. My aim is that this option of childcare will always be available to Canadian women and men without discrimination, financial or otherwise."*

Fry, Margaret, B.A. ■ ⊕ 📖 ⊗

Program Officer, SASKATCHEWAN CULTURAL EXCHANGE SOCIETY, 2431 - 8th Ave., Regina, SK S4R 5J7 (306) 569-8966, FAX 757-4422. Born Kamloops, B.C. 1955. s. 1 ch. EDUC: Univ. of Regina, B.A.(Psych.) 1979; Banff Sch. of Fine Arts, Certificate of Admin. in the Arts

(1st level) 1987. **CAREER:** prior to 1986 held various jobs for community organizations; Exec. Dir., Saskatchewan Cultural Exchange Society, 1986-95; Program Officer, 1995 to date. **AFFIL:** Arts Sector Transition Team; Commonwealth Bd.; Parents for French Immersion; Sask. Arts Alliance. **INTERESTS:** arts; stitchery designs. **COMMENT:** *"It is difficult for me to describe myself, my endeavours and my achievements outside the context of the two roles, which at this point in time control my life. Those roles are: Executive Director of the SCES and Nathan's mother. Within those two roles, I have achieved a great deal. The SCES is currently a vibrant healthy organization, which has continually broken new ground in terms of the cultural community. My son is a happy, well-adjusted seven-year-old."*

Fukakusa, Janice, B.A.,M.B.A.,C.A.,C.B.V. $
Senior Vice-President, Financial Services, Multinational Banking, ROYAL BANK OF CANADA, Royal Bank Plaza, South Tower, Toronto, ON M5J 2J5 (416) 974-8540, FAX 364-7985. Born Toronto 1954. **EDUC:** Univ. of Toronto, B.A.(Pol. Sci.) 1976; York Univ., M.B.A.(Fin. & Acctg) 1979; Institute of Chartered Accountants, C.A. 1981, Chartered Bus. Valuator 1984. **CAREER:** C.A. & C.B.V., Price Waterhouse, 1978-84; various positions, Multinat'l Bnkg, Acct Mgmt, Corp. Fin., Treasury & Strategic Mgmt, Royal Bank of Canada, 1985-93; VP, Portfolio Mgmt, 1993-94; Sr. VP, Multinat'l Bnkg, 1995 to date. **DIRECTOR:** Royal Bank Capital Corporation. **AFFIL:** Institute of Chartered Accountants. **COMMENT:** *"As Senior Vice-President, Financial Services, Ms. Fukakusa has global responsibility for the planning and implementation of multinational banking portfolio management. These responsibilities encompass industry and large corporate risk assessment, loan syndication, asset trading, corporate finance products and asset securitization."*

Fulford, Mary Eileen, B.Sc.N. 🌿 ✊ ⊕
President, FULFORD FUNDY FISH FARM, 33 Bonavista Ave., Charlottetown, PE C1B 1L3 (902) 569-4475, FAX 569-5457. Born Charlottetown 1944. w. George. **EDUC:** Univ. of Ottawa, B.Sc.(Nursing) 1966. **CAREER:** Instructor, Prince Edward Island Sch. of Nursing, 1969-71; Asst. Dir., 1972-75; various positions, from Instructor to Dept. Head, Sir Sandford Fleming Coll., Peterborough, Ont., 1975-87; Pres., Fulford Fundy Fish Farm, 1987 to date; VP, Fulford Ingalls Seafood Holdings Inc. **DIRECTOR:** Fulford Fundy Fish Farm; Fulford Ingalls Seafood Holdings Inc. **AFFIL:** Canadian Cancer Society (Pres., P.E.I. Div.; Nat'l Dir.; Chrm of Patient Svcs, P.E.I. Div. 1989-94). **INTERESTS:** golf; curling; fishing; computers. **COMMENT:** *"Having left the field of nursing, I am now involved in operating salmon aquaculture companies in New Brunswick and Chile."*

Fulford-Spiers, Patricia, A.O.C.A.,D.A. ✻
Sculptor. 92 Yod Bet St., Safed, Israel 13201 06-974701. Born Toronto 1935. m. Raymond Spiers. **EDUC:** Ontario Coll. of Art, A.O.C.A.(Sculpture) 1957; Edinburgh Coll. of Art, D.A.(Sculpture). **CAREER:** Instructor, Ontario Coll. of Art, 1960-63; Instructor, Glendon Coll., York Univ., 1970-75; Instructor, Cariboo Coll., B.C., 1978-79; Harmon Sculpture Foundry, Vancouver, 1981-87; Instructor, Langara Coll., B.C., 1981-87; moved to Israel, 1987. **EXHIBITIONS:** solo exhibitions include Mazelow Gallery, Toronto (1972); New Brunswick Museum (1973); exhibitions with R. Spiers include Mirvish Gallery (1964); Mazelow Gallery (1967). **AFFIL:** Royal Canadian Academy of Arts; Canadian Sculpture Society; Israel Association of Painters & Sculptors; Safed Artists' Colony. **INTERESTS:** gardening; music. **COMMENT:** *"I am a professional sculptor who has worked in all traditional materials and several experimental ones. I have done a good deal of teaching, which I enjoy. Seven years ago, my husband, a painter, and I moved to Israel and opened a studio and gallery in Safed Artists' Quarter."*

Fuller, Heather A., B.Comm. $ ♡
Real Estate Broker and Owner, MARTIN & MEREDITH LIMITED, 191 Eglinton Ave. E., Ste. 201, Toronto, ON M4P 1K1 (416) 488-7000, FAX 488-7862. Born Toronto 1945. m. David G. 2 ch. Kathryn, Victoria. **EDUC:** Univ. of Toronto, B.Comm. 1967. **CAREER:** Systems Eng., IBM Canada, 1967-69; Consultant, C.G.I., 1969-82; Pres., First St. Ives Consulting Group, 1982-92; Real Estate Broker & owner, Martin & Meredith Limited, 1992 to date. **DIRECTOR:** Martin & Meredith Limited; First St. Ives Investment Corporation. **AFFIL:** West Park Hospital (Gov.; Exec. Committee); Centre for Management of Community Services (Bd.); World Association of Flower Arrangers (Cdn Mgmt Committee 1990-93); Garden Club of Toronto (Flower Show Chair 1984-85; Bd. 1980-85); Ladies' Golf Club of Toronto Limited (Pres. 1988); Kappa Kappa Gamma Foundation of Canada (Bd.); Toronto Real Estate Board; Society for Technical Communication; Toronto Golf Club. **INTERESTS:** gardening; golf; technology. **MISC:** Co-Chair of fundraising, Garden Club of Toronto's renovation of the Casa Loma Gardens, 1986-87; Chair of fundraising & pub-

licity for book, *The Canadian Flower Arranger* (Macmillan Canada, 1993).

Fulton, E Margaret, B.A.,M.A.,Ph.D., O.C. ■ ⌲
Education Consultant. 295 Lower Ganges Rd., Apt. 28, Salt Spring Island, BC V8K 1T3 (604) 537-5384. Born Birtle, Man. 1922. s. **EDUC:** Winnipeg Normal Sch., Teaching Certificate 1942; Univ. of Minnesota, Phys. Educ. Diploma 1946; Univ. of Manitoba, B.A. (English & Hist.) 1955; Univ. of British Columbia, M.A.(English) 1960; Univ. of Toronto, Ph.D.(English) 1968. **CAREER:** elementary & secondary sch. teacher, Man. & Ont., 1942-61; Prof. of English Lit., Wilfrid Laurier Univ., 1967-74; Dean of Women, Univ. of British Columbia, 1974-78; Pres., Mount Saint Vincent Univ., 1978-86; Adjunct Prof., Univ. of British Columbia, 1986 to date; Educ. Consultant, 1986 to date. **SELECTED PUBLICATIONS:** "The Status of Women in Canadian Universities" (*Peace Research*, 24(3) Aug. 1992); *The Kootenay Learning Culture*, Report of the Kootenay Post-Secondary Education & Training Review Panel (Ministry of Post-Secondary Educ., Prov. of B.C. 1993); "Revitalizing Community Learning," *Development Communication* Report No. 83 (Bureau for Research & Development, Arlington, 1993/94); numerous other articles & reports. **EDIT:** Ed. Bd., *Canadian Women's Studies, Women's EDUCATION des femmes* & *Atlantis.* **DIRECTOR:** Wellington Insurance Corporation. **AFFIL:** West Coast L.E.A.F. (past Bd. Mbr.); Voice of Women for B.C.; B.C. Gov't's Seniors Advisory Council (Chair); Univ. of Northern British Columbia (Bd. of Dir.); Green Coll., U.B.C. (Advisory Bd.); Women's World Summit Foundation (Bd. of Dir.); Association of Universities & Colleges of Canada; Association of Atlantic Universities; Association of Commonwealth Universities; Association of Canadian University Teachers of English; Canadian Council of Teachers of English; Canadian Society for the Study of Higher Education; Canadian Congress on Learning Opportunities for Women; Canadian Research Institute for the Advancement of Women; American Association for Higher Education; Canadian Futures Society; International Association of University Presidents; Inter-American Organization for Higher Education. **HONS:** Distinguished Educator Award, Ontario Institute for Studies in Education, 1987; Woman of Distinction Award, Vancouver YWCA, 1991; Officer of the Order of Canada, 1983; D.L.(Hon.), Univ. of British Columbia; Fellow (Hon.), Ryerson Polytechnic Univ.; D.Sc. de l'Éduc.(Hon.), Univ. de Moncton; LL.D.(Hon.), Univ. of Winnipeg; LL.D.(Hon.), Dalhousie Univ.; LL.D.(Hon.), Concordia Univ.; D.L.(Hon.), York Univ.; D.L.(Hon.), Lakehead Univ.; D.H.L.(Hon.), Mount Saint Vincent Univ.; D.E.D.(Hon.), Univ. of Victoria. **MISC:** numerous special projects & gov't appointments; subject of a documentary film to be released Jan. 1997. **COMMENT:** *"Dr. Fulton is an outspoken advocate for women's issues. She is much in demand by governments and corporations for her work on alternative administrative systems. She contends that traditional hierarchical structures no longer serve society effectively. To prepare citizens for the future, innovative learning systems, including developing the potential of electronic technologies, and community-based decision-making are needed. Both government and private sector corporations must restructure for a new Age of the Imagination and Information."*

Fulton, M. Jane, B.H.Ec.,M.Sc., Ph.D. ⊕ ♡ ∕ ♨
Principal, THE HEALTH GROUP, RR#1, Cobden, ON K0J 1K0. **EDUC:** University of British Columbia, B.H.Ec.(Nutrition) 1969, Dip. (Educ.) 1979, M.Sc.(Health Care and Epidemiology) 1982, Ph.D.(Bus. Admin. and Medicine) 1986. **CAREER:** Assoc. Prof., University of Ottawa, 1986-95; Faculty, Banff School of Advanced Management, Strategy and Business Policy, 1989-95; Deputy Min. of Health, 1995-96; Principal, The Health Group, 1996 to date. **SELECTED CREDITS:** weekly radio show, *Health Watch* (1988-92). **SELECTED PUBLICATIONS:** *Medical and Rehabilitation Programs in Workers' Compensation: An Administrative Inventory*, with J. Atkinson (British Columbia: Workers' Compensation Board, 1993); *Canada's Health System: Bordering on the Possible* (Washington: Faulkner and Gray, 1993); *Spending Smarter and Spending Less: Policies and Partnerships for Health Care in Canada*, with R. Sutherland (Ottawa: Health Group, 1994); "Screening for Congenital Dislocation of the Hip: An Economic Appraisal," with M.L. Barer (*Canadian Medical Association Journal* May 1984); "Previous Experience and Treatment Choice," with C.R. Kerr (*BC Medical Journal* 1989); "A Canadian Take on American Health Care" (*Financial Executive* Nov.-Dec. 1993); "Health and the Family," in *The New Canadian Family* (Montreal: The Vanier Institute, 1993); various other publications. **EDIT:** Ed. Bd., *Canadian Journal of Program Evaluation*, 1989-95. **HONS:** Excellence in Teaching Award, University of Ottawa, 1994; Gordon Henderson Memorial Lecturer, Faculty of Law, University of Ottawa, 1994; The Grieve Lecture, International Federation of Health Funds, Boston 1996. **INTERESTS:**

research **INTERESTS:** health policy in Canada and internationally; ethics; women in management; nonprofit organizations. **MISC:** recipient of various grants & fellowships; reviewer for various journals & granting agencies; 1st woman to give the Convocation Address at the Strich School of Medicine, Loyola Univ.

Fulton, Trish, B.A.,M.A.,Ph.D. ■■ 🎓 $
Associate Professor of Economics, HURON COLLEGE, 1349 Western Rd., London, ON N6G 1H3 (519) 438-7224, ext. 256, FAX 438-9981. Born Kamloops, B.C. 3 ch. Daniel, Geoffrey, Kate. **EDUC:** Univ. of British Columbia, B.A.; Univ. of Western Ontario, M.A., Ph.D. **CAREER:** mbr. of faculty, Huron Coll., 1977-96; areas of specialization include microecon. & public policy. **SELECTED PUBLICATIONS:** in various academic publications. **AFFIL:** London Acute Care Teaching Hospitals Restructuring Committee (mbr. 1994 to date); London Acute Care Teaching Hospitals (Restructuring Committee, Chair 1994-96; Governance Task Force 1993-94).

Fung, Lori ⚾ $ 👆
Co-Owner and Co-Head Coach, CLUB ELITE RHYTHMICS INC. (604) 327-9448. Born Vancouver 1963. s. **CAREER:** Mbr., Cdn Rhythmic Gymnastics Team; Cdn Grand Nat'l Champion, rhythmic gymnastics, 1982-88; Co-Owner & Co-Head Coach, Club Elite Rhythmics Inc. (formerly Lori Fung Rythmics), 1988 to date; Coach, Cdn Rhythmic Gymnastics Team, 1991 to date. **HONS:** Gold Medal, Rhythmic Sportive Gymnastics All-Around Event, Olympic Games, 1984; 4-time, 4-continent Gold Medalist; B.C. Athlete of the Year, 1984; mbr., Order of Canada; mbr., Order of British Columbia; mbr., Canadian Sports Hall of Fame; mbr., B.C. Sports Hall of Fame. **INTERESTS:** animals, esp. dogs. **MISC:** winner of the 1st Olympic Gold Medal awarded for rhythmic gymnastics, 1988; performed for their Royal Highness' Prince Charles & Princess Diana; performed for Pope John Paul during the B.C. Papal Visit; Coach of Camille Martens, 1994 & 1995 Cdn Champion & top medalist of the 1994 Commonwealth Games.

Furlong, Lynne, B.A. ■ $
Human Resources and Diversity Manager, HEWLETT PACKARD (CANADA) LTD., 5150 Spectrum Way, Mississauga, ON L4W 5G1 (905) 206-3327, FAX (905) 206-4155. Born Montreal 1954. m. Todd Sprague. 1 ch. **EDUC:** Concordia Univ., B.A.(Art Hist.), Diploma in Institutional Admin. **CAREER:** various positions, Personnel, Control Data; Personnel Mgr, Hewlett Packard Canada Ltd.; various sales & airline jobs. **AFFIL:** Information Technology Association of Canada (Mbr., Diversity Committee); Corporate Equal Opportunity Group; Ontario Resource Council (Steering Committee). **INTERESTS:** family & friends; the arts; skiing; cooking. **MISC:** published in *Human Resources Management in Canada* by Barbara Pope dedicated to Hewlett Packard Canada's efforts toward diversity; H.P.C.L. has received 2 Special Merit Awards in this field during Ms. Furlong's time as Diversity Mgr. **COMMENT:** *"My goal is to provide a value-added service to internal and external customers in the area of human resources management."*

Furtwangler, Virginia (writing as Ann Copeland), B.A.,M.A.,Ph.D. 📖 📜
Author. Born Hartford, Conn. 1932. m. Albert J. Furtwangler. 2 ch. **EDUC:** Coll. of New Rochelle, B.A.(English) 1954; Catholic Univ. of America, M.A.(English Lit.) 1959; Cornell Univ., Ph.D.(English Lit.) 1970. **CAREER:** Instructor of English, Coll. of New Rochelle, 1963-66; Asst. Prof. of English, Indiana Univ. Northwest, 1970-71; Instructor, extension courses, Mount Allison Univ., 1976-77; Asst. Prof. of English, 1976-77; Visiting fiction writer, Coll. of Idaho, Winter 1980; Visiting Prof. of English, Linfield Coll., 1980-81; extension, Mount Allison Univ., 1983-84; Distinguished visiting fiction writer, Univ. of Idaho, Winter 1986, Spring 1987; Bush Residency, Bemidji State Univ., Spring 1987; Distinguished visiting fiction writer, Wichita State Univ., Oct. 1988; Writer-in-residence, Mount Allison Univ., 1990-91; Writer-in-residence, St. Mary's Univ., 1993. **SELECTED PUBLICATIONS:** *At Peace*, short fiction (Ottawa: Oberon Press, 1978); *The Back Room*, short fiction (Ottawa: Oberon Press, 1979); *Earthen Vessels*, short fiction (Ottawa: Oberon Press, 1984); *The Golden Thread* (HarperCollins, 1989); *Strange Bodies on a Stranger Shore*, short fiction (Goose Lane Editions, 1994); *The ABC's of Fiction Writing* (Cincinnati: STORY Press, 1996); "The Pleasures of Revision" (*English Journal* 1980); "Notes from a Landed Immigrant" (*Wild East* 1989); 48 stories published in various journals in Canada & US, incl. *Canadian Fiction Magazine, Matrix, Southwest Review* & *Turnstile*; represented in 16 anthologies in Canada & US, incl. *Best American Short Stories, Best Canadian Stories* and *Best Maritime Short Stories*; various book reviews in Cdn journals & papers such as *Books in Canada* & *Catholic New Times*. **AFFIL:** Authors' Guild (US); Writers' Union of Canada; N.B. Writers' Federation; Associated Writing Programs; Intenational Women's Writing Guild. **HONS:** National Endowment for the Arts Fellowships, 1979,

1994; Contributors' Prize, *Canadian Fiction Magazine*, 1975; nominated, Gov. General's Award, Fiction, 1990; Ingram Merrill Award, 1990; Gemini Award, 1994. INTERESTS: music; piano. MISC: "Second Spring" adapted for TV by Atlantis Films, 1993; writes fiction under the pseudonym Ann Copeland; recipient of various grants; juror for various awards.

Fusca-Vincent, Martha, B.A. ■■ 丫 ♥
President, STORNOWAY PRODUCTIONS INC. (TV production), 160 Bloor St. E., Ste. 1220, Toronto, ON M4W 1B9 (416) 923-1104, ext. 304, FAX 923-1122. Born Italy 1955. m. Kitson Sr. 3 ch. Elena, Kitson, Francesco. EDUC: York Univ., B.A.(Hons., English) 1979. CAREER: Norfolk Communications (prod. co.); co-founded Stornoway Productions with Kitson Vincent, 1983; VP, 1987-93; Pres., 1993 to date. SELECTED CREDITS: Exec. Prod., *Yellow Brick Roads* (1993-95); Exec. Prod., *Dragons of Crime* (1993-94); Prod., *Out of the Shadows* (1991-92); Prod., *The Hunt for Red Mercury* (1991-92); Prod./Co-Dir., *Caught in the Crossfire* (1990-91); Producer, *Out of Control* (1990); Prod./Script Ed., *Promises to Keep* (1988). AFFIL: Canadian Women in Communications (Programming Chair 1996-97); The Academy of Canadian Cinema & Television; Toronto Women in Film & Television (ex officio mbr.); Canadian Film & Television Production Association; Juvenile & Canadian Diabetes Foundations (volunteer, fundraiser). HONS: 4 nominations for Gemini Awards, Academy of Canadian Cinema & Television; CINE Golden Eagle, Council on International Non-theatrical Events, Washington, D.C. (for *Caught in the Crossfire*), 1992; Bronze Plaque, Columbia Int'l Film & Video Festival, Ohio (for *Caught in the Crossfire*), 1993; Silver Screen Award, 2nd place, U.S. Int'l Film & Video Festival, Illinois (for *Caught in the Crossfire*), 1993; Bronze Award, Houston Int'l Film Festival (for *Out of Control*), 1991; Personal & Corp. Award for Entrepreneurial Excellence (Stornoway Productions), Canadian Film & Television Producers' Association, Toronto, 1992; numerous other awards. INTERESTS: reading; tennis. COMMENT: *"Martha Fusca is a dedicated television professional, but not at the expense of family and friends or causes that she supports wholeheartedly–The Canadian Diabetes Association and Sick Children's Hospital. Martha has been a tireless contributor to the advancement of women and women's issues."*

G

affney, Beryl M., M.P. ✦

Member of Parliament (Nepean), GOVERNMENT OF CANADA, House of Commons, Rm. 553-S Centre Block, Ottawa, ON K1A 0A6 (613) 992-2772, FAX 992-1209. Constituency Office, Greenbank Square, 250 Greenbank Rd., 2nd Fl., Nepean, ON K2H 8X4 (613) 990-8827, FAX 990-4178. Born North Bedeque, P.E.I. 1930. m. Cuthbert. 5 ch. **CAREER:** admin. branch, Parks & Recreation Dept., Nepean, 1967-78; elected to Nepean Council, 1978-88; elected to Reg'l Municipality of Ottawa-Carleton Council, 1980-88; Acting Mayor, 1984; elected MP, Nepean, Gov't of Canada, 1988-93; Liberal Party Critic, Nat'l Capital Commission, 1989; Liberal Assoc. Critic, Supply & Svcs, 1989; Liberal Party Critic, Human Rights, 1990; Liberal Assoc. Critic, Status of Women, 1990; Mbr., Standing Committee on Human Rights & Rights of the Disabled; Mbr., Subcommittee on Int'l Human Rights; re-elected MP, Nepean, 1993 to date; 1993/94 Chair, Standing Committee on Citizenship & Immigration. **SELECTED PUBLICATIONS:** co-authored a number of reports on human rights as well as on the disabled. **MISC:** in 1989, co-chaired the Nat'l Liberal Task Force on Mun. Infrastructure to look into the water, roads & sewage treatment crisis facing Cdn towns. **COMMENT:** *"In her first term in the House of Commons, Beryl held public discussions on the GST, pensions, the economy, social policy, sustainable development, the environment, the constitution and aboriginal peoples. Between 1988 and 1993 she introduced a number of Private Members' Bills in the House of Commons and was instrumental in ensuring that the Meme breast implant was removed from the* *market. The Private Member's motion on taxation of child benefits was passed in the House of Commons by the Justice and Finance Ministers."*

Gage, Frances Marie, RCA ⊗
Sculptor. Roseneath Landing, R.R. 2, Box 7, Roseneath, ON K0K 2X0. Born Windsor, Ont. 1924. EDUC: Oshawa Collegiate & Vocational Institute, 1943; Ontario Coll. of Art, Sculpture 1951; Arts Students' League, NY, 2-yr. scholarship; École des Beaux-Arts, Paris, 2-yr. scholarship. CAREER: served with W.R.C.N.S. during World War II; sculptor. COMMISSIONS: relief, Fanshawe Coll., London, Ont., 1962; Dr. Bertram Collip relief, Univ. of Western Ontario, 1963; life-size torso, Kitchener-Waterloo Art Gallery, 1964; life-sized walnut torso, Univ. of Guelph, 1966; Bear ciment fondu Wisneiwski, Newmarket, 1965; bronze bust Dr. Andrew Smith, Univ. of Guelph, 1967; 4 bronze portrait reliefs (A.Y. Jackson, Fred Varley, Healy Willen, Sir Ernest MacMillan), 1967; Rosamund twice-life bronze statue, Toronto, 1968; memorial, Song in the Wind, Music Bldg, Mount Allison Univ., 1968; Woman marble statue, Women's College Hospital, Toronto, 1969; bronze relief memorial, Robert Meredith James, Univ. of Toronto, 1969; Memorial, Charles Lake Grundy, Mt. Pleasant Cemetery, Toronto; commemorative medal, Samuel Bronfman, 1971; commemorative medal, Dr. Jason Hannah, Royal Society of Canada (also 5 commemorative busts), 1973; medal, John P. Carriere Award, Standards Council of Canada; bust, Dr. Gordon Nikiforuk, Univ. of Toronto, 1975; bronze Baby memorial, Kew Gardens, Toronto, 1975; portrait bust, Elmer Iseler, Roy Thomson Hall, Toronto, 1990; portrait head, late Col. R.S. McLaughlin, Ottawa Headquarters, Royal Coll. of Physicians & Surgeons, S. McLaughlin Foundation; Heritage Award Plaques, Guelph Arts Council (current); Mindemoya bronze dog L/S, Donald Forster Sculpture Park, Guelph, Ont., 1990. EXHIBITIONS: International Congress of Medallic Arts, Florence, 1984; Colorado, 1987; Helsinki, 1990; Fidem London, 1992. AFFIL: Royal Canadian Academy of Art (Council). HONS: recipient, Royal Society Scholarship (École des Beaux-Arts, Paris); Rothman Purchase Award, 1965. INTERESTS: music; conservation.

Gagnon, Nathaly, B.Sc.,M.A.,Ph.D. 🎨 🌸
Associate Professor and Chair, Leisure Studies, CONCORDIA UNIVERSITY, Loyola Campus, 7141 Sherbrooke W., HB 131, Montreal, QC H4B 1R6 (514) 848-3349, FAX 848-4200, EMAIL natgagn@vax2.concordia.ca. Born Montreal 1951. m. Babis Chronopoulos. EDUC: Univ. du Québec à Montréal, B.Sc.(Pol. Sci.) 1977, M.A.(Pol. Sci.) 1984, Ph.D.(Pol. Sci.) 1988; Univ. of Kent at Canterbury, UK, doctoral research, Social Admin. 1984-85. CAREER: Community Organizer, Que. Social Service Ntwk, 1976-86; Lecturer & Asst. Prof., Pol. Sci. & Soc. Work, Univ. du Québec à Montréal, 1986-88; Asst. Prof./Assoc. Prof., Leisure Studies, Univ. of Ottawa, 1988-91; Assoc. Prof., Chair, Dept. of Leisure Studies, Concordia Univ., 1991 to date. SELECTED PUBLICATIONS: *Un vol organisé: la discrimination envers les femmes* (Asticou, 1989); *Histoires d'amour,* ed. with Anne Froment & Nane Couzier (Asticou, 1990); "Women and Leisure: An Introduction" in *Recreation and Leisure in Canada,* L. Heywood & J. Singleton, eds. (Toronto: HJB-Holt, 1994); "Les MTS: l'occasion d'une contre-révolution sexuelle" (*Critiques Socialistes* 1989); "Femmes et pouvoir politique: les doubles allégeances" (*Medium-Sciences humaines* 1990); "Plaisir, liberté, égalité: une trilogie phallocentrique" (*Revue canadienne Droit et Société/Canadian Journal of Law and Society* Spring 1994); numerous other publications. AFFIL: CAHPER; M.U.R.S.; Centre des femmes la Moisson (VP 1987-93); WLRA. HONS: Fellowship, Nat'l Health Grant, Health & Welfare Canada, 1984-86; Prof. of the Year, Leisure Studies, Ottawa Univ., 1990, 1991. INTERESTS: music; literature; golf; gardening. MISC: *La Grèce: Découvrir le passé en explorant le présent,* audiovisual documentary (1990); various radio & TV appearances. COMMENT: *"Political scientist/feminist activist. Research endeavours: feminist political theory, sport culture and domestic violence, social policies and women's leisure. Author of the book* Un vol organisé: la discrimination envers les femmes *and many scientific articles on women's social conditions."*

Gagnon, Raymonde F., B.A.,M.D.,D.Phil., F.R.C.P.S.(C.) ⊕
Associate Physician, Division of Nephrology, MONTREAL GENERAL HOSPITAL, 1650 Cedar Ave., Montreal, QC H3G 1A4 (514) 937-6011, ext. 4034, FAX 934-8248. Born Montreal 1943. d. 1 ch. EDUC: Univ. of Montreal, B.A. 1962; Laval Univ., M.D. 1966; Oxford Univ., D.Phil.(Experimental Medicine) 1980. CAREER: Internist, 1971 to date; Nephrologist, 1973 to date. SELECTED PUBLICATIONS: 95 papers; 208 abstracts. AFFIL: Royal Coll. of Physicians & Surgeons of Canada (Fellow in Internal Medicine). HONS: Scholarship, Fonds de la Recherche en Santé du Québec, 1981-84, 1984-87, 1993-96. COMMENT: *"My primary research interests are dialysis biocompatibility*

and severe complications of chronic renal failure, particularly infection and anemia. My most productive work is related to infections associated with medical implants, such as peritoneal dialysis catheters and vascular access devices for hemodialysis."

Gagnon-Pratte, France, B.A., M.A. ■ ■ 🎨 ✦

President and Chairman, COUNCIL OF MONUMENTS AND SITES FOR QUEBEC, Heritage Quebec Foundation, 82 Grande-Allée W., Quebec, QC G1R 2G6 (418) 647-4347, FAX 647-6483. President and Chairman, HERITAGE QUEBEC FOUNDATION. Born Que. 1929. m. Claude Pratte. 2 ch. Cécile-Nathalie, Caroline-Anita. EDUC: Laval Univ., B.A.(Phil.) 1952; Univ. of Toronto, B.A. studies; Laval Univ., B.A.(Hist. of Art) 1978, M.A.(Hist. of Arch.) 1980. CAREER: private consultant; architectural historian, 1980 to date; VP, Continuité Press. SELECTED PUBLICATIONS: *L'Architecture et la nature à Québec aux XIXe siècle: les villas* (1980); *Maison de campagne des Montréalais, l'architecture de Edward et W.S. Maxwell* (1989); *Country Houses for Montrealers, the Architecture of Edward and W.S. Maxwell* (1989); co-author, *Chateau Frontenac: Hundred Years in a Castle* (1993); co-author, *The Architecture of Edward & William Maxwell* (1991). AFFIL: McGill Univ. (V-Chair, Maxwell Proj.); Coalition for Safeguarding the old Port of Quebec (Spokesman); Advisory Committee on Old Quebec (mbr. 1986-92); Heritage Policy Cultural Affairs (Advisory Group 1987-88); Heritage Montreal (Bd. of Dir.); C.D. Howe Memorial Foundation; National Capital Commission (Canadiana Fund); Canadian Mediterranean Institute; Quebec City Chamber of Commerce; Association for Preservation Techniques; National Trust for Historic Preservation, U.S.; International Council of Monuments & Sites; National Geographic Society, U.S. INTERESTS: reading; swimming; photography; travel.

Gagnon-Tremblay, Monique, B.A.,LL.B., M.N.A. ✦

Minister of the National Assembly (Saint-François), GOVERNMENT OF QUEBEC, Hôtel du Parliament, Bur. 2.68, Quebec, QC G1A 1A4 (418) 644-2817, FAX 646-6640. Constituency Office, 2140 King St. E., Bur. 102, Fleurimont, QC J1G 5G6 (819) 823-0498, FAX 823-2498. Born Plessisville, Qué. 1940. m. Jacques S. Adrien Tremblay. EDUC: Laval Univ., B.A. 1969; Univ. de Sherbrooke, LL.B. 1972, Degree in Notarial Law 1973. CAREER: Exec. Sec., notary's office, 1958-69; opened own notary office & became Teaching Asst., Notarial Law,

Univ. of Sherbrooke, 1973; Mbr., Mun. Council, Ascot Corner, 1979-85; Liberal candidate, Que. gen. election, 1981; M.N.A., Saint-François, 1985 to date; Min. Responsible for the Status of Women, Que. Gov't, 1985-89; Min., Cultural Communities & Immigration, 1989-94; VP, Que. Treasury Bd., 1989-94; Deputy Premier, Treasury Bd. Pres. & Min. Responsible for Admin. & Public Svc., 1994. AFFIL: Liberal Caucus (Pres. 1994 to date); l'Hôpital d'Youville, Sherbrooke (Mgmt Office); Centre Communautaire juridique de l'Estrie (Dir.); Fondation Mieux-Vivre (Dir.); Club de Réforme de Sherbrooke; Chamber Notaries Quebec; Fédération des notaires de la province de Québec; Société Saint-Jean-Baptiste du diocèse de Sherbrooke; Association québécoise de planification fiscale et successorale.

Gainsbourg, Gillian Kerby ■ ⊗

Co-Designer, The Basilisk Company, 1091A Yonge St., Ste. D, Toronto, ON M4W 2L6. Born Toronto 1958. EDUC; Ontario Coll. of Art, 3 yrs. CAREER: freelance illustrator & designer; Co-Designer, The Basilisk Company, 1994 to date. AFFIL: Bat Conservation International; Royal Ontario Museum; Metropolitan Toronto Zoological Society. INTERESTS: bats; the arts; theatre; film; laughter; paper things; antiques; all things dark & mysterious. COMMENT: *"There is so much much more to see in this world if you view it with an open mind and heart."*

Gajdel, Djanka 💲 ⊗

Business Consultant to the Photographic Industry. 260 Adelaide St. E., Studio 23, Toronto, ON M5A 1N1 (416) 535-4773. CAREER: Office Mgr & Admin. Asst., Calgary & Toronto, 1981-84; Bus. Consultant & Photographic Rep. to Edward Gajdel, 1985 to date; working rep., lecturer & creative consultant; extensive experience in the area of bus. practices for the photographic ind. AFFIL: Canadian Association of Photographers & Illustrators in Communication (active participant); American Society of Media Photographers (active participant). MISC: played a key role in advancing the career of top photographer, Edward Gajdel; managed & produced advertising photography projects for major corp. clients incl. Coca Cola, IBM, Royal Bank of Canada & others; developed unique & innovative promotional strategies allowing photographers to increase exposure & expand business. COMMENT: *"Recognized by the Canadian photographic community for exceptional expertise and resourcefulness in commercial facets of the profession; continually provides private consulting in all business areas to facilitate artists in achieving proper creative and financial recognition. I have assisted more than 100 photographers to date. I pride myself in having slain 1300 dragons in the last month alone.*"

Galiana-Brants, Henrietta L., B.Eng., M.Eng.,Ph.D. ⊛ ⊕ ⊛
Professor, Department of Biomedical Engineering and Department of Otolaryngology, Faculty of Medicine, McGILL UNIVERSITY, 3775 University St., Montreal, QC H3A 2B4 (514) 398-6738, FAX 398-7461. Born St. Lambert, Que. 1944. 2 ch. Isabel Marie, Francisco Enrique. EDUC: McGill Univ., B.Eng.(Elect. Eng.) 1966, M.Eng.(Biomed. Eng.) 1968, Ph.D. 1981. CAREER: Research Staff Eng., Man Vehicle Lab., Massachusetts Institute of Technology, 1967-70; Post-doctoral Fellow, Aerospace Medical Research Unit, McGill Univ., 1981-84; Asst. Prof., Dept. of Physiology, 1984-85; Assoc. Mbr., 1985 to date; Asst. Prof., Dept. of Biomedical Eng. & Dept. of Otolaryngology, 1985-90; Assoc. Mbr., Dept. of Elect. Eng., 1986 to date; Assoc. Prof., Dept. of Biomedical Eng. & Dept. of Otolaryngology, 1990-94; Medical Scientist & Co-Dir., Otolaryngology Research Lab., Royal Victoria Hospital, 1990 to date; Assoc. Mbr., McGill Centre for Intelligent Machines, 1992 to date; Prof., Dept. of Biomedical Eng. & Dept. of Otolaryngology, McGill Univ., 1994 to date. SELECTED PUBLICATIONS: "Gaze Control in the Cat: Studies and Modelling of the Coupling between Orienting Eye and Head Movements in Different Behavioral Tasks," with D. Guitton & D.P. Munoz (*Journal of Neurophysiology* 1990); "Evaluation of Three Template Matching Algorithms for Registering Images of the Eye," with R. Wagner (*IEEE Transactions of Biomedical Engineering* 1992); "Postural Instability on One Foot in Patients with Loss of Unilateral Peripheral Vestibular Function," with A. Katsarkas & H.L. Smith (*Journal of Vestibular Research* 1994); "Modelling Slow Correcting Gaze Movements," with P. Lefèvre & M. Missal (*Journal of Vestibular Research* 1994); numerous other publications. AFFIL: Society for Neuroscience; Canadian Medical & Biological Engineering Society; N.Y. Academy of Sciences; The Barany Society; IEEE Engineering in Medicine & Biology Society (Sr. Mbr.). HONS: Christie-Storer Chapter I.O.D.E. Scholarship, 1961-62; McGill Scholar, 1961-66; McGill Alumnae Helen R.Y. Reid Scholarship, 1962-63; Northern Electric Undergrad. Scholarship, 1964-65; Northern Electric Award, 1965-66; British Association Medal for Great Distinction in Electrical Engineering Honours, 1966; Ph.D. Dean's Honour List, McGill Univ., 1981. MISC: recipient, various grants & fellowships; reviewer for various journals & granting agencies; numerous invited papers & workshops.

Gallagher-LeBlanc, Karen, B.A. ■ ⊙ ♡ ⊛
New Brunswick Director, CANADIAN CONGRESS FOR LEARNING OPPORTUNITIES FOR WOMEN (CCLOW), Fredericton, NB (506) 462-0924. Born Fredericton 1954. d. 2 ch. EDUC: Univ. of New Brunswick, Bus. Certificate I 1988, B.A.(Soc.) 1990, M.Ed. in progress. CAREER: entrepreneur, Gallagher Originals, 1984; Mgr, Regent Craft Gallery, 1989; instructor, NB Craft Sch. & Centre, 1989; Gallery Mgr, 1985-90; Office Mgr, Amptech Ltd., 1990; Personal Care Attendant, Helping Hands Inc. (BC), 1991; Program Dir., Chimo Helpline Inc., 1992-94; Asthma Program Dev. Officer, N.B. Lung Association (working with a medical advisory committee to set up an asthma care & mgmt program in N.B.); N.B. Dir., Canadian Congress for Learning Opportunities for Women, 1992 to date. SELECTED PUBLICATIONS: "The Myth of Consenting Adults: The New Sexual Assault Provisions," with Gayle MacDonald (*University of New Brunswick Law Journal* 1993). EDIT: Co-Ed., *Atlantic Women and Jobs Network Bulletin*, 1994. AFFIL: Toastmasters International; CCLOW; Women Acting Today for Tomorrow (WATT); New Brunswick Lung Association (Project Office). HONS: Jack Longstaffe Memorial Bursary, 1989. COMMENT: "*Currently working on my M.Ed. in Adult Education. My thesis is on women's learning experiences in transitions. I am interested in facilitating seminars, conferences and courses, in consulting and/or counselling individuals or organizations, and in speaking to groups.*"

Gallant, Christel ⊛ ⊛
Professeure titulaire et Directrice du département de traduction et des langues, UNIVERSITÉ DE MONCTON, Moncton, NB E1A 3E9 (506) 858-4214, FAX 858-4166, EMAIL gallanc@ umoncton.ca. Born Troisdorf, Allemagne 1936. sep. Melvin. 3 ch. EDUC: Univ. de Mayence, Allemagne, Diplôme d'interprète 1959; École supérieure d'interprètes et de traducteurs, Sorbonne, Paris, Diplôme d'interprète de conférence 1960; Univ. de Neuchâtel, Suisse, Licence-ès-lettres 1969, Docteur ès lettres 1978. CAREER: en freelance, Interprète de conférence, 1960-64; instructeur, Univ. de Moncton, 1964-67; Prof. adjointe, 1969-72; Mise en place du programme de Baccalauréat spécialisé en traduction; Responsable du programme, 1972-74; Prof. agrégée, 1978; Prof. invitée à l'Univ. de Neuchâtel, Suisse, 1980; Prof. titulaire, Univ. de Moncton, 1985 à date; dir. du dépt., 1993-96.

SELECTED PUBLICATIONS: "L'Acadie, le berceau de la traduction officielle au Canada" (*Cultures de Canada français*, 2, 1985); "L'Influence des religions catholique et protestante sur la traduction des textes sacrés a l'intention des Micmacs dans les provinces Maritimes: du livre de prières de l'abbé Maillard (1717-1762) à la traduction des Évangiles par Silar Tertius Rand (1810-1889)" (*TTR– Études sur le texte et ses transformations* 3(2) 1990); "Paul Mascarene" (*Circuit*, automne 1995). AFFIL: Corporation des traducteurs, traductrices, terminologues et interprètes du Nouveau-Brunswick (Mbr. hon.). MISC: SSHRC bourse bénéficiaire.

Gallant, Margaret M. (Peggy), B.Sc.(P.E.), M.Sc.,B.Ed. ☜ ⓪
Professor, Department of Physical Education, ST. FRANCIS XAVIER UNIVERSITY, Antigonish, NS B2G 2P4 (902) 867-2234, FAX 867-2254. Born Stellarton, N.S. 1946. m. Les. 3 ch. L.T., Ian, Ray. EDUC: Nova Scotia Teachers' Coll., Diploma in Phys. Educ. 1966; St. Francis Xavier Univ., B.Sc.(Phys. Educ.) 1969, B.Ed. 1976; Dalhousie Univ., M.Sc.(Phys. Educ.) 1973. CAREER: teacher, Stellarton Sch. Bd., N.S., 1966-68; Instructor, Athletics & Intramurals, Mount St. Bernard, St. Francis Xavier Univ., 1969-70; Instructor, Dept. of Phys. Educ., 1969-71; Lecturer in Elementary Phys. Educ., Dept. of Phys. Educ. & Recreation, McGill Univ., 1970; Teaching Asst., Elementary Phys. Educ. & Dance, Sch. of Phys. Educ., Dalhousie Univ., 1970-71; Lecturer, Dept. of Phys. Educ. & Dept. of Educ., St. Francis Xavier Univ., 1971-74; Asst. Prof., Dept. of Phys. Educ., 1974-79; Assoc. Prof., 1979-91; Visiting Lecturer, Dept. of Recreation, Univ. of Glasgow, Fall 1980; Visiting Lecturer, Dept. of Phys. Educ. & Recreation, Univ. of Florida, Spring 1981; Prof., Dept. of Phys. Educ., St. Francis Xavier Univ., 1991 to date. VOLUNTEER CAREER: Coach, Antigonish Women's Volleyball, 1969-71 (Prov. Champions, 1970); Coach, St. Francis Xavier Univ. Women's Volleyball, 1969-74 (Intercollegiate "B" Champion, 1973); Coach, St. Francis Xavier Univ. Women's Varsity Soccer, 1981-90 (AUAA Champions, 1986); Coach, Antigonish Boys' Soccer Rep Teams, 1989-95 (Silver Medalists, 1995). SELECTED PUBLICATIONS: NCCP *Level III Theory Manuals* (Ottawa: CAC, 1990); "A Creative Approach to Traditional Folk Dance," with N. Mutrie (*Scottish Journal of Physical Education* Jan. 1981); "Sexism in Scottish Education," with N. Mutrie (*Scottish Journal of Education* May 1981); "Safety in Sports for Children" (*The Nova Scotian* June 1983); "Using Prepared Music as a Theme for

Movement" (*Tape Recorder* June 1985); "Expanding Your Curriculum Through Cooperatively Planned Fun Days" (*CAHPER Journal* Mar. 1991); "The Scooter" (*Canadian Intramural and Recreation Association Bulletin* Sept. 1990); numerous conference proceedings & papers; various other publications. AFFIL: CAHPER; AAHPER (Sec.; Pres.); AUAA (Sec.); NCCP (course conductor); Canadian Coaching Association (CAC) (Bd. of Dir.); Delta Kappa Gamma. HONS: Pictou County Sports Hall of Fame; Canada 125 Medal, 1992; St. Francis Xavier Univ. Outreach Award. INTERESTS: youth & coaching; gender equity. MISC: Teacher's Licence Class VII, Prov. of N.S.; Canadian Soccer Association "C" Licence; Nat'l Coaching Certification Program Master Course Conductor Level I, II, III & IV, Toronto; mbr., Nat'l Advisory Committee on Women's Soccer, 1989-90; choreographer, *Christmas from Sherbrooke*, video produced by Sherbrooke Historical Society (1987); recipient of various grants. COMMENT: "*Mother of three who spends a lot of volunteer time coaching and training coaches as a master course conductor.*"

Gallant, Mavis Leslie, C.C. • ▯ ▧
Writer. c/o McClelland & Stewart. Born Montreal 1922. CAREER: National Film Board; Feature Reporter, *Montreal Standard*, 1944; moved to France, 1950; writer, short stories, novels, essays & reviews, 1951 to date; Writer-in-Residence, Univ. of Toronto, 1983-84. SELECTED CREDITS: *What Is To Be Done?*, play, Tarragon Theatre, Toronto, 1982. SELECTED PUBLICATIONS: early stories published in Canada in *Preview* (1944), *Standard Magazine* (1946) & *Northern Review* (1950); many shorts stories published in *The New Yorker*; reviews & essays published in *New York Review of Books* & *The New York Times Book Review*; collections of short stories incl. *The Other Paris* (1956); *My Heart is Broken* (1964); *The Pegnitz Junction* (1973); *The End of the World and Other Stories* (1974); *From the Fifteenth District: A Novella and Eight Stories* (1979); *Home Truths: Selected Canadian Short Stories* (1981); *Overhead in a Balloon: Stories of Paris* (1985); *Paris Notebooks: Essays and Reviews*, non-fiction (1986); *Green Water Green Sky*, novel (1959); *A Fairly Good Time*, novel (1970); introduction, *The Affair of Gabrielle Russier* (1971). HONS: Officer of the Order of Canada, 1981 & Companion, 1993; winner, Gov. General's Award (*Home Truths: Selected Canadian Stories*), 1981; recipient, Canada-Australia literary prize, 1984; Fellow, Royal Society of Literature, 1989; LL.D.(Hon.), Queen's Univ., 1991; Trib-

utee, International Authors Festival, Harbourfront, Toronto, 1993.

Gallaway, Marguerite, B.A.,B.Ed., LL.D.(hon.),C.M. ■■ ⊗ ♡ ⬦
Born Birsay, Sask. 1929. m. Ronald Gallaway. 4 ch. Donald, David, Joan Gallaway, Eliza(beth) Gorchynski. EDUC: Univ. of Saskatchewan, B.Ed.(Bus. Ed.) 1973; Univ. of Regina, B.A.(Psych.) 1978. CAREER: Teacher, Estevan Collegiate Institute, 1949-51; Exec. Dir., Organization of Saskatchewan Arts Councils, 1974-87; owner/operator, The Craft Gallery of Estevan, 1987-91. AFFIL: Saskatchewan Order of Merit (Chair, Advisory Bd.); Saskatchewan Institute of Applied Science & Technology (Bd. mbr.); Saskatchewan Arts Board (Bd. mbr.); UNICEF of Saskatchewan (Exec. mbr.; former Chair); UNICEF Canada (Bd.); Souris Valley Theatre, Estevan (Exec. Producer). HONS: Saskatchewan Order of Merit, 1988; hon. LL.D., Univ. of Saskatchewan, 1989; Member of the Order of Canada, 1990; *Saskatchewan Report* Honour Roll, 1991. COMMENT: *"'Mrs. Gallaway transformed the Organization of Saskatchewan Arts Councils from seven affiliates into a cultural dynamo of sixty-two, launching concerts and visual arts tours into every nook of the province. Her gift of motivating people...organizational genius.' - Dr. Michael Jackson, Chief of Protocol. I am currently pleased to be developing the Souris Valley Theatre as an important tourist attraction."*

Gallimore, Robyn, B.A.,M.B.A. ⬦ ♡ ⬧
Executive Director, ASSOCIATION OF EARLY CHILDHOOD EDUCATORS, 40 Orchard View Blvd., Ste. 211, Toronto, ON M4R 1B9 (416) 487-3157, FAX 487-3758. Born Toronto 1950. s. 2 ch. Christopher Charles, Katherine Elizabeth. EDUC: Queen's Univ., B.A.(Math./ Psych.) 1972; Univ. of Toronto, M.B.A. (Econ./Fin.) 1975. CAREER: Fin. Analyst, Citibank Canada; Auditor, The Permanent; Researcher, Dance Program, Univ. of Waterloo; Grants Assoc., Trillium Foundation; Exec. Dir., Association of Early Childhood Educators, Ont. AFFIL: Society for Nonprofit Organizations; Sparrow Lake Alliance (Educ. Committee). INTERESTS: music; gardening. MISC: cellist; one of the earliest women to graduate with an M.B.A. from the Fac. of Mgmt, Univ. of Toronto. COMMENT: *"I believe in my role in leadership and as an agent of change in professional dealings. I believe in holding others accountable and being held accountable. Act as a role model for girls and women and believe in getting the job done. My children are first in all things, business is second and music is third."*

Ganoza, M. Clelia, B.Sc.,Ph.D. ■■ ⬦ ⊕
Professor, Banting & Best Department of Medical Research, UNIVERSITY OF TORONTO, 112 College St., Toronto, ON M5G 1L6 (416) 978-8918, FAX 978-8528, EMAIL m.ganoza@ utoronto.ca. Born Lima, Peru 1937. m. Andrew J. Becker. 1 ch. Monica Anne Becker. EDUC: Rollins Coll., Fla., B.Sc.(cum laude, Pre-Medics/Biol./Chem.) 1959; Duke Univ., N.C., Ph.D.(Biochem./Chem.) 1964. CAREER: Postdoctoral Fellow in Biochem., Rockefeller Univ., N.Y., N.Y., 1963-66; Research Assoc. in Biochem., 1966-68; Assoc. Prof., Banting & Best Dept. of Medical Research, Univ. of Toronto, 1968-74; Prof., 1974 to date; Prof., Microbiol. & Parasitology, 1979-96; Prof., Medical Genetics & Microbiol., 1996 to date; has served on several committees, Univ. of Toronto, 1968 to date. SELECTED PUBLICATIONS: numerous journal articles & book chapters; a symposium book, award lecture & symposium lecture; numerous scholarly addresses. AFFIL: American Federation of Biological Chemists; Canadian Federation of Biological Chemistry; N.Y. Academy of Sciences; Sigma Xi. HONS: numerous scholarships, grants & academic awards; Ayerst Award, Canadian Federation of Biological Chemists, 1976; Fellow, The Royal Society of Canada, 1983 to date; Visiting Scientist, National Cancer Institute, Biochem. Div., National Institutes of Health, Bethesda, MD, 1986; Visiting Prof., Max-Planck Institut Für Moleculare Genetik, Berlin, 1996 (open). INTERESTS: oil painting; classical music. MISC: The Medical Research Council of Canada: Assoc. 1969-74, Career Investigator 1974-94; referee of journals & grants. COMMENT: *"Interested in the structure and evolution of genetic information. Contributed to the solution of the genetic code and identification of the mechanisms of initiation and termination."*

Garber, Anne Theresa ■■ ⬚ ⁄
Author. Born Toronto 1946. d. 2 ch. Becky, Kit. CAREER: Deputy Supervisor, Public Rel'ns & Mkt Reports, Toronto Stock Exchange, 1968-70; Supervisor, Acct. Group, Dunsky Advertising Ltd., Vancouver, 1973-76; Head Writer, Films, Asta Productions Ltd., 1977-82; Commentator, *Consumers Report*, CBC-TV, 1983; Consumer Commentator, BCTV News, 1984; Prod., *Dave Barrett Show*; Talk Show Host, CJOR, 1984-87; Consumer Commentator, CKVU-TV, 1986-89; Communications Officer, Office of the Mayor, 1987-88; Film Commissioner, 1987-88; Exec. Dir., Associated Producers Bureau, 1988 to date; columnist, *The Vancouver Province*, 1989 to date. SELECTED PUBLICATIONS: *Vancouver Super Shopper #1*

(1982); *Shopping the World* (1990); *Rise and Shine, Vancouver* (1991); *Vancouver Out to Lunch* (1991); *Cheap Eats, Vancouver* (1991); *The Serious Shopper's Guide to Vancouver* (1992). AFFIL: Alliance of Canadian Cinema, TV & Radio Artists; Federation of B.C. Writers; Newspaper Guild; B.C. Motion Picture Association. INTERESTS: collecting advertising art, children's books & mail-order catalogues. MISC: Media Rel'ns Advisor, Commonwealth Summit Conference, 1987.

Garber, Eileen Epstein, B.A., B.S.W. ○ ☺
President, CANADIAN ASSOCIATION OF NEIGHBOURHOOD SERVICES, 129 Clansman Blvd., Toronto, ON M2H 1Y3 (416) 497-9129, FAX 497-2151. Born Montreal 1926. m. Ralph Garber. 7 ch. Jonathan David Jacob, Jeremy Simcha, Judah Barry, Jill Gita, Naomi Julie, Daniel Jeffrey, Jessica Louis. EDUC: McGill Univ., B.A.(Social Sci.) 1947, B.S.W.(Social Work) 1949. CAREER: Univ. Lecturer, Kansei Gakuin Univ., Japan; Program Outreach Coord., N.E. Community, Jewish Community Centre & Toronto Jewish Congress, 1977-82; Dir. of Adult Svcs & Special Projects, St. Christopher House, 1982-89. VOLUNTEER CAREER: Bd. Mbr., Ontario Council of Agencies Serving Immigrants, 1984-88; Bd. Mbr., Toronto Association of Neighbourhood Services; Pres., Canadian Association of Neighbourhood Services, 1990 to date; Cdn Rep., International Federation of Settlements & Neighbourhood Centres. INTERESTS: local, nat'l & int'l social welfare; social policy issues; dance; live theatre; films; educ.; welfare of children. MISC: elected Sch. Trustee, New Jersey, 1970s; chaired International Federation of Settlements Conference, Toronto, 1992. COMMENT: *"Interest in children and families led to leadership roles in social work, community development, education; then participation in national and international social development for peace and social justice."*

Garcea, Laurie, B.A. ☺ ○ ⌕
Executive Director, LEARNING DISABILITIES ASSOCIATION OF SASKATCHEWAN, 610 Clarence Ave. S., Ste. 26, Saskatoon, SK S7H 2E2 (306) 652-4114, FAX 652-3220. Born Moose Jaw, Sask. 1958. m. Joseph. 3 ch. Giustino, Michele, Maria. EDUC: Univ. of Manitoba, B.A. (English) 1981. CAREER: Research Asst., Learning Disabilities Association of Manitoba, 1981-82; Dir. of Camp, 1982-83; Admin. Asst., 1983-87; Exec. Dir., 1990 to date. COMMENT: *"Helped to revitalize a small nonprofit organization by focusing on the development of services."*

Garcia, Bertha (née Mispireta), B.Sc.,M.D., F.R.C.P.(C) ■■ ⊕ ⌕
Consultant Pathologist, UNIVERSITY HOSPITAL, Dept. of Pathology, Dental Sciences Building, 339 Windermere Rd., London, ON N6A 5A5 (519) 663-2954. Associate Professor, Department of Pathology, UNIVERSITY OF WESTERN ONTARIO. Born Lima, Peru 1946. m. 3 ch. EDUC: Peruvian Univ., "Cayetano Heredia," Lima, B.Sc. 1968, M.D.(with distinction) 1972; Educational Council Foreign Medical Graduates, U.S.A., E.C.F.M.G. 1971; L.M.C.C., Calgary, 1976; several internships & post-grad. training, 1974-80; Univ. of Calgary/Foothills Hospital, F.R.C.P.(C), 1980; American Bd. of Pathology, D.A.B.Path. 1982; Coll. of American Pathologists, F.C.A.P. 1983; International Academy of Cytology, M.I.A.C. 1988; continuing medical educ. at numerous conferences, etc. CAREER: gen. practice, Cartagena, Colombia, 1972-73; Asst. Prof., Div. of Pathology, Fac. of Medicine, Univ. of Calgary, & Anatomical Pathologist, Dept. of Pathology, Foothills Hospital, 1980-83; Clinical Asst. Prof., Dept. of Pathology, Fac. of Medicine, Univ. of Saskatchewan, & Assoc. Pathologist, Pasqua Hospital, Regina, Sask., 1983-85; Asst. Prof., Dept. of Pathology, Univ. of Western Ontario, 1985-90; Assoc. Prof., 1990 to date; Consultant Pathologist, University Hospital, London Psychiatric Hospital & Children's Psychiatric Research Institute, 1985 to date; Dir., Div. of Cytology, Dept. of Pathology, University Hospital, 1986 to date; Dir., Autopsy Svc., Dept. of Pathology, 1995 to date. SELECTED PUBLICATIONS: co-author, 54 articles in refereed journals (11 more in press); co-author, 110 abstracts. AFFIL: Coll. of American Pathologists; Canadian Medical Association; Ontario Medical Association; Canadian Association of Pathologists; Latin-American Pathology Foundation, New Orleans; Royal Coll. of Physicians & Surgeons of Canada; Ontario Association of Pathologists; International Academy of Pathology, U.S.A.-Cdn Div.; International Academy of Cytology; American Society of Cytology; International Society for Analytical Cytometry; Peruvian-American Medical Society; Royal Society of Medicine, London, U.K.; Society of Analytical Cytology, U.S.A. HONS: Best Thesis of the Year Award, Peruvian Univ., 1972; Gold Medallist, Peruvian Univ., 1972; Class of '62 Award, Medicine, Univ. of Western Ontario; nominated for Teaching Award, Fac. of Medicine, Univ. of Western Ontario, 1993; Dean's Award of Excellence, Fac. of Medicine, Univ. of Western Ontario, 1994; Hon. Class Pres., Medical Class of 1995, Fac. of Medicine, Univ. of Western Ontario. MISC: numerous univ. committee/task force appts.;

numerous extramural teaching assignments, conferences, etc.

Gardiner, Helen ■■ ⊗ ○
Chair, THE GEORGE R. GARDINER MUSEUM OF CERAMIC ART, 111 Queen's Park, Toronto, ON M5S 2C7 (416) 586-8080, FAX 586-8085. Born Ont. 1938. m. George. 1 ch. Lindy Catherine Barrow. EDUC: York Univ., 6 credits 1973-77; Christie's Fine Arts course, London, England, 1978-79. CAREER: Legal Sec. & Law Clerk, 1956-66; Media Buyer/Supervisor, Young & Rubicam Advertising, 1966-70; Media Research Dir., Grey Advertising, 1971-72. DIRECTOR: Gardiner Farms Limited. AFFIL: The George R. Gardiner Museum of Ceramic Art (Trustee 1984-94; Chair 1994 to date); Royal Ontario Museum (Trustee 1992 to date); The George R. Gardiner Charitable Foundation (Dir.); 28 (Ottawa) Medical Company (Hon. Lt. Col.); The National Ballet (Patron); The National Ballet Sch. (Patron). MISC: dressage rider. COMMENT: *"I am strongly committed to supporting and promoting cultural and artistic organizations, particularly in the Toronto area."*

Gardiner, Janet C., B.Comm.,F.C.A. Ⓢ
Treasurer, CHESTER DAWE LIMITED, Box 8280, St. John's, NF A1B 3N4 (709) 782-3104, FAX 782-0611. Born St. John's 1933. w. 3 ch. Dr. Jane A. Gardiner, Susan E. Gardiner, Steven J. Gardiner. EDUC: Dalhousie Univ., B.Comm. (Acctg) 1954. CAREER: Treas., Chester Dawe Limited. DIRECTOR: Chester Dawe Limited & associated companies. AFFIL: Fishery Products International (Hum. Res. Committee); Salvation Army (Past Chrm, Citizen's Advisory Bd.); Memorial Univ. of Newfoundland (Chair, Bd. of Regents); St. Thomas' Anglican Church (Chair, Fin. Committee); Institute of Chartered Accountants of Newfoundland (Fellow).

Gardiner, Susan, M.Sc., C.Psych. ■■ ✹ ⊕ ○
Director, Residential Programs, WOOD'S HOMES, 805 - 37th St. N.W., Calgary, AB T2N 4N8 (403) 270-4102, FAX 283-9735. EDUC: Univ. of Manitoba, B.H.E.(Family Studies, Family Econ. & Mgmt) 1975; Univ. of Calgary, Dept. of Educational Psych., M.Sc.(Clinical Program) 1983. CAREER: Clinical/Family Therapist, Wood's Homes, 1983-86; Clinical Supervisor, 1986-90; private practice, 1991-96; Exec. Dir., Calgary Women's Emergency Shelter Association, 1990-96; Dir. of Residential Svcs, Wood's Homes, 1996 to date. SELECTED PUBLICATIONS: author, "Putting An End to Family Violence" (*Family Health*, Winter 1991); author, "Out of Harm's Way: Interven-

tion With Children in Shelter" (*Journal of Child and Youth Care* (2), 1992); author, "Intervention With Children Who Witness Violence: Clinical Implications for Shelter-Based and Community Programs" (*Directions in Child and Adolescent Therapy* 2(2), 1995); co-author with Frank McGrath, "Wife Assault: A Systemic Approach That Minimizes Risk and Maximizes Responsibility" (*Journal of Systemic Therapies*, 14, 1995). AFFIL: Psychologists Association of Alberta (Chartered Psychologist); American Association of Marriage & Family Therapy (Clinical mbr.). HONS: Scottish Rite Foundation Bursary for $1,500, National Institute on Mental Retardation, 1982; Staff Appreciation award for Supervision, Wood's Homes, 1989; Peace Heroes Award for Discovery Toys, 1995; nominated for Woman of Distinction Award for Community Svc., YWCA, 1995. MISC: numerous presentations. COMMENT: *"Susan Gardiner is a chartered psychologist with more than 10 years of management experience in human services organizations. She is currently the Director of Residential Services at Wood's Homes in Calgary and was formerly the Executive Director of the Calgary Women's Emergency Shelter Association. Susan has extensive clinical, teaching and supervisory experience and has published in the area of adolescence and domestic violence."*

Gardner, M. Jane, B.A.,C.A. ■■ Ⓢ
Vice-President and Chief Financial Officer, LOMBARD CANADA LTD. (insurance), 105 Adelaide St. W., Toronto, ON M5H 1P9 (416) 350-4350, FAX 350-4417. Born Brantford, Ont. 1953. m. Bill Robinson. 3 ch. Bob, Danielle, Paul. EDUC: Wilfrid Laurier Univ., B.A.(Bus. & Commerce) 1975; Canadian Institute of Chartered Accountants, C.A.(Acctg & Fin.) 1977. CAREER: audit, KPMG Peat Marwick, 1975-79; acctg, Royal Insurance, 1979-86; fin., Lombard Canada, 1986 to date; CFO, 1994 to date. DIRECTOR: Lombard Canada Ltd. AFFIL: Canadian Insurance Accountants' Association; Canadian Institute of Chartered Accountants; Insurance Bureau of Canada (Fin. Affairs).

Gardner-Nix, Jacqueline, B.Sc.,Ph.D., M.R.C.P.(UK),L.M.C.C. ⊕
Program Director, SCARBOROUGH PALLIATIVE 'AT HOME' CARE TEAM (P.A.C.T.), 3030 Lawrence Ave. E., Ste. 205, Scarborough, ON M1P 2T7 (416) 439-6376, FAX 431-7273. Born Wanstead, Essex, UK 1950. m. Edward Nix. 3 ch. EDUC: University Coll., London, UK, B.Sc.(Biochem.) 1971; St. Bartholomew's Medical Coll., London, UK, Ph.D.(Biochem.) 1975, M.B./B.S.(Medicine & Surgery) 1979;

Royal Coll. of Physicians of UK, membership 1982. **CAREER:** Medical Intern, St. Bartholomew's Hospital, 1970-80; Surgical Intern, Whipps Cross Hospital, London, UK, 1980; Resident, Royal Northern Hospital, London, UK, 1980-81; Resident, St. Thomas Hospital, London, UK, 1981-82; Asst. Prof., Dept. of Radiation Oncology, Univ. of Western Ontario & Terry Fox Cancer Research Fellow, London Regional Cancer Centre, London, Ont., 1982-85; family physician, Scarborough, 1985 to date; Program. Dir., P.A.C.T., 1989 to date. **SELECTED PUBLICATIONS:** "Scarborough's Palliative 'At-Home' Care Team (PACT): A Model for a Suburban Physicians Palliative Care Team," with others (*Journal of Pain and Sympton Management* 1(5) May 1996); "Oral Methadone for Managing Chronic Nonmalignant Pain" (*Journal of Pain and Sympton Management* 1(5) May 1996). **AFFIL:** Scarborough Palliative Care Group; Scarborough General Hospital (Drug & Therapeutics Committee; Palliative Care Committee; Medical Exec.); Ontario Medical Association (Palliative Care Exec.). **HONS:** nominee, "Women on the Move" Award, *The Toronto Sun*, 1994. **INTERESTS:** her children, Katherine, Victoria & Elizabeth; tennis. **MISC:** has given many workshops & seminars on palliative care throughout Ont. & Canada; former mbr., Drug Quality & Therapeutics Committee, 1993-94; palliative care consultant, Drug Quality & Therapeutics Committee, 1994 to date. **COMMENT:** "*I am dedicated to ensuring that the dying have the choice of dying at home, with the attendance of physicians who are knowledgeable and properly funded to provide such care.*"

Garfield, Louise ⊗ 🗊 ⼝

Choreographer, Writer, Performer and Producer, TRIPTYCH MEDIA INC., 56 The Esplanade, Ste. 505, Toronto, ON M5E 1A7 (416) 955-8866, FAX 955-8867. Member, THE CLICHETTES. **EDUC:** York Univ., Fine Arts 1975; Canadian Film Centre, Resident 1991. **SELECTED CREDITS:** various theatrical production credits, incl. *Half Human, Half Heartache*, The Clichettes with Bill House, Horseshoe Tavern, Toronto, 1980, *The First Annual Five Minute Feminist Cabaret*, Horseshoe Tavern, Toronto, 1982, *Last Will and Testament of Lolita*, with Nightwood Theatre, Theatre Passe Muraille, Toronto, 1987, & *Mayworks Festival*, Toronto, 1991; Assoc. Prod., *The Making of Monsters* (feature), dir. John Greyson, Canadian Film Centre, 1991; Co-Prod., *Zero Patience* (feature), dir. John Greyson, 1992; performer, *Wisecracks* (feature), dir. Gail Singer, 1990; Co-writer/Performer, *She-Devils*

of Niagara, The Clichettes, dir. Bob White, 1985; Co-Writer/Performer, *Up Against the Wallpaper*, dir. Maureen White, Factory Theatre, 1988; Co-writer/Performer, *Out For Blood*, The Clichettes, dir. Peter Hinton, 1990; various writing, performance & choreography credits. **SELECTED PUBLICATIONS:** "Funny Girls: The Gender Strikes Back" (*Toronto Life Magazine* 1982). **AFFIL:** Danceworks; The Women's Cultural Building; National Action Committee on the Status of Women. **HONS:** National Lip Sync Championship, Houston, TX, 1984. **MISC:** recipient of various grants. **COMMENT:** "*Louise has been active as a choreographer, writer, performer and producer in feminist dance, theatre and media and a member of The Clichettes for 12 years. She is presently developing a feature film based on Susan Swan's novel* The Biggest Modern Woman of the World.*"

Garland, Kevin J., B.A.,M.Sc. ■■ Ⓢ ⊗ O

Senior Vice-President, Corporate Real Estate, CIBC DEVELOPMENT CORPORATION, Commerce Court E., 21 Melinda St., 12th Fl., Toronto, ON M5L 1G4 (416) 980-7361, FAX 861-3791. Born Toronto 1941. m. Roger Garland. 2 ch. Fiona, Caleigh. **EDUC:** Univ. of Toronto, B.A.(English) 1962, M.Sc.(Urban & Reg'l Planning) 1974. **CAREER:** Assoc., A.J. Diamond & Partners, Architects & Planners, 1975-83; Ptnr, 1983-86; Dev. Mgr, BCE Development Corporation, 1986-88; Dir. of Planning, 1988; VP, Planning, E. Reg., 1989; VP, Proj. Mgmt & Design, CIBC Development Corporation, 1989-93; Sr. VP, Corp. Real Estate, 1993 to date. **DIRECTOR:** Ontario Realty Corporation (1993-96). **AFFIL:** Canadian Urban Institute (Bd. of Dir. 1993 to date); National Ballet of Canada (Bd. of Dir. 1993 to date); United Way of Greater Toronto (Bd. of Trustees 1993 to date); Toronto Arts Awards Foundation (Bd. of Dir. 1988-92); Young People's Theatre Centre (Chrm, Bd. of Dir. 1976-83). **HONS:** Allen Prize in English Lit., Victoria Coll. (Univ. of Toronto), 1963; Ont. Grad. Fellowship, 1972-74. **MISC:** Lecturer (part-time), Dept. of Urban & Reg'l Planning, Univ. of Toronto, 1975; Guest Lecturer, Grad. Sch. of Design, Sch. of Architecture, Univ. of Texas, 1982.

Garneau, Céline, LL.L.,D.E.Sp. ⼐

Lawyer, LANGLOIS ROBERT, S.E.N.C., 1002 Sherbrooke St. W., 28th Fl., Montreal, QC H3A 3L6 (514) 842-9512, FAX 845-6573. Born St. Thuribe, Que. 1948. m. Raynold Langlois. 5 ch. **EDUC:** Univ. Laval, LL.L. 1979; Univ. de Montréal, D.E.Sp. 1987. **BAR:** Que., 1980. **CAREER:** acctg & admin., 1967-72; Pres.-Dir., Association des biologistes du

Québec, 1974-79; articling student, 1979; lawyer in private practice, 1980 to date; Ptnr, Langlois Robert, 1984 to date. **AFFIL:** Canadian Bar Association; Barreau du Québec; l'Association des Femmes de Carrières; Association of Family Lawyers of Quebec; La Fondation du Dr. Maurice Bertrand (1st VP, Bd. of Dir.); Country Club of Montreal. **INTERESTS:** skiing; tennis; golf; swimming. **COMMENT:** *"A member of the civil and commercial law team at Langlois Robert, she appears before all the civil courts, in the first instance and in appeal, as well as before hearing commissions."*

Garnett, Gale ⊗ 📖 💓

Actor, Writer and Director. c/o Great North Artists, 350 Dupont St., Toronto, ON M5R 1V7. Born Auckland 1949. s. **CAREER:** actor, writer, dir.; columnist, *The Toronto Star*, 1971-74, 1992-93; regular contributor, *The Globe and Mail*; Host, *In Touch*, CBC TV; Host, *City Show*, City-TV. **SELECTED CREDITS:** Principal, *Tribute*, dir. Bob Clark; Principal, *32 Short Films About Glenn Gould*, Rhombus Media; Principal, *Down Came a Blackbird*, Showtime; Principal, *The Queen of Mean*, CBS; Principal, *Mr. & Mrs. Bridge*, dir. James Ivory; One Woman Show, *Life After Latex*, Citadel Theatre; Luciana, *The Comedy of Errors*, Stratford Festival; Anne, Suzanne, Jane, *Sisters of Mercy*, Shaw Festival; Hoda, *Crackpot*, Alberta Theatre Projects; Gerutha, *Mad Boy Chronicle*, Alberta Theatre Projects; Improv., *Second City Review*, Ivar Theatre; Improv., The Jest Society, Toronto; Improv., The Groundlings, L.A.; Dir., *The Second Coming*, Hampstead Playwrights' Workshop; Dir., *Gale Garnett and Company*, various venues. **SELECTED PUBLICATIONS:** numerous essays, articles, columns & book reviews; excerpt from novel, *Visible Amazement* (*Exile*, Canada, Aug. 1995). **AFFIL:** Canadian Actors' Equity (VP, External 1991-94); ACTRA (Toronto Branch Council); US Actors' Equity (Councillor); Council of Canadians (Advisory Bd.). **HONS:** Best Folk Album, Grammy Award, 1964; Villager Award for Excellence in Solo Performance, Downtown Theatres, N.Y., 1979; nomination (*Tribute*), Genie Award, 1981. **MISC:** numerous books on tape, narrations & voice-overs; written 75 recorded songs; recorded 8 albums for RCA & Columbia Records. **COMMENT:** *"I've been a 'working actor' since age 13, and a writer since age 21. I try to promote Canadian arts and artists wherever in the world my own work takes me. I consider myself very lucky to make my living doing work I love to do."*

Garnier, Andrea, B.A.(Hons.) ⑤

Secretary-Treasurer, CANADIAN UNION OF PUB-LIC EMPLOYEES, Alberta Division, 925-19 Ave. N.W., Calgary, AB T2M 0Z6 (403) 289-7602. Archivist, **GLENBOW ARCHIVES**. Born Vancouver 1962. m. William Plettl. 1 ch. Zackary Simon Garnier Plettl. **EDUC:** Univ. of British Columbia, B.A.(Hons., Hist.) 1984. **CAREER:** Archivist, Glenbow Archives, 1987 to date. **AFFIL:** Canadian Union of Public Employees (Pres., Local 1645 1990-95; Sec.-Treas., Alta. Div. 1994-96); Archives Society of Alberta; Freedom of Information & Privacy Association of Alberta (Dir. 1993-94). **COMMENT:** *"My main goals in life are to empower people and facilitate positive change."*

Garossino, Virginia ⑤ ⓐ ⊕

President and Chief Executive Officer, **SUPERIOR VENTURES GROUP LTD.**, 1201 W. Pender St., 6th Fl., Vancouver, BC V6E 2V2 (604) 683-2165, FAX 683-2539. Past President, **ACOUSTIC NEUROMA ASSOCIATION OF CANADA**. Born Dawson Creek, B.C. 1935. m. Richard. 5 ch. Angela, Pam, Brenda, Brent, Candy. **EDUC:** Certified L.I.F.O (Life Orientation Survey), Analyst 1974. **CAREER:** Continuity Writer, CJDC Radio, Dawson Creek, 1950; Clerk, Unemployment Insur. Commission, 1951-53; contract employee, Canada Savings Bond campaign, Treasury Branches, 1968; Secretarial Administrator, Alberta Housing Corporation, 1969-71; Personal Asst. to the Pres., 1971-75; Mgr, Alberta Oper., Superior Ventures Group Ltd., 1975-79; VP, 1979-83; Pres., CEO & majority shareholder, 1983 to date. **DIRECTOR:** Superior Ventures Group Ltd. **AFFIL:** Acoustic Neuroma Association (Founder; Pres. until 1994); Northwest Reprographic Association of Canada (Past Pres.); Univ. of Alberta Visiting Committee; The Executive Committee. **HONS:** nominee, 1994 Canadian Woman Entrepreneur of the Year Awards; recipient, 1995 Lifetime Achievement Award, Canadian Woman Entrepreneur of the Year; Outstanding Woman, Commercial Reprographics Award, Xerox Engineering & The International Reprographics Association, 1996; Women of Distinction Award, Entrepreneur/Innovator, YWCA, 1996. **INTERESTS:** business; opera; family; holistic health. **MISC:** Virginia Garossino Fund est. in recognition of contribution in establishing Acoustic Neuroma Association of Canada. **COMMENT:** *"As a wife and mother of five, the co-owner of a successful business and a volunteer, I have dedicated my efforts to achieving the best in everything I do. I am especially proud of my involvement in the Acoustic Neuroma Association of Canada, which has brought assistance closer to home for people stricken with this debilitating disease."*

Garratt, Audrey ■ ○ ⊕

Chairman of the Board, VARIETY CLUB OF SOUTHERN ALBERTA, 1305 - 11 Ave. S.W., Ste. 305, Calgary, AB T2G 0X5 (403) 228-6168, FAX 245-9282. Born Calder, Sask. 1956. CAREER: Accts Receivable, 1974-79; Bank Teller, 1979-80; Sec., 1980-82; Graphic Arts Instructor, 1982-88; Graphic Arts & Sales Consultant, 1988-90; Graphic Sales Consultant, 1991 to date; owner, gift basket bus. (gift baskets for all occasions). AFFIL: Variety Club of Southern Alberta (Pres.; Chrm of the Bd. & Fundraising Organizer of Dev. of "Variety Park" in Calgary); Calgary Craftsman Club (Membership Chair; Organizer of Club Bulletin). HONS: Merit Award on *Craftsman Bulletin*, 1985; Craftsman of the Year, 1986. INTERESTS: golfing; swimming; hiking; art; camping; dancing; cooking; gardening. COMMENT: *"Energetic, organized, enthusiastic, love children, volunteering, socializing and enjoy helping others in any way."*

Garson, Joan H., B.A.,LL.B. ᗡᒪ

Partner, BLANEY, MCMURTRY, STAPELLS, FRIEDMAN, Barristers and Solicitors, 20 Queen St. W., Ste. 1400, Toronto, ON M5H 2C3 (416) 593-1221, FAX 593-5437. Born Halifax 1953. m. David Baskin. 2 ch. Jason Baskin, Rebecca Baskin. EDUC: Dalhousie Univ., B.A.(Pol. Sci.) 1974; Fac. of Law, Univ. of Toronto, LL.B. 1978. BAR: Ont., 1980. CAREER: Law Clerk to the Chief Judge, County & District Courts of the Prov. of Ont., 1980; Lawyer, Stapells & Sewell (predecessor firm to Blaney, McMurtry, Stapells), 1980-86; Ptnr, Blaney, McMurtry, Stapells, Friedman (then known as Blaney, McMurtry, Stapells), 1986 to date. SELECTED PUBLICATIONS: chapter, *Canadian Women's Legal Guide*. HONS: Bora Laskin Prize in Constitutional Law, Fac. of Law, Univ. of Toronto. COMMENT: *"Ms. Garson's present practice centres largely on secured transactions comprising a wide variety of national and international transactions, as well as equity financings. She heads the secured lending group in the corporate/commercial department."*

Gartner, Hana, * ᾝ ✎

Host, THE NATIONAL MAGAZINE, Canadian Broadcasting Corporation, Box 500, Stn A, Toronto, ON M5W 1E6. Born Prague 1948. EDUC: Loyola Univ., Concordia, Comm. Degree 1970. CAREER: broadcast journalist, CJAD, Montreal; Host, *The City at Six*, CBC, Montreal, 1974-75; Co-Host, *Take 30*; Co-Host, *the 5th estate*; Host, *The National Magazine*, 1995 to date. HONS: 3 Gemini Awards incl. Gordon Sinclair Award for excellence in broadcast journalism.

Gaskell, Jane, Ed.D. ᑫ

Professor and Associate Dean, Graduate Programs and Research, Faculty of Education, UNIVERSITY OF BRITISH COLUMBIA, 2125 Main Mall, Vancouver, BC V6T 1Z4 (604) 822-5513, FAX 822-8971, EMAIL janegask@ unixg.ubc.ca. EDUC: Swarthmore Coll., Pa., B.A.(Soc.) 1968; Harvard Univ., Ed.D.(Soc. of Educ.) 1973. CAREER: Lecturer & Asst. Prof., Fac. of Educ., Queen's Univ., 1971-74; Asst. Prof., Dept. of Social & Educ. Studies, Univ. of British Columbia, 1974-83; Assoc. Prof., 1983-88; Prof., 1988 to date; Head, 1988-93; Assoc. Dean, Grad. Programs & Research, Fac. of Educ., 1993 to date. SELECTED PUBLICATIONS: *Claiming an Education: Feminism and Canadian Schools*, with Arlene McLaren & Myra Novogrodsky (Toronto: Our Schools/Our Selves, 1989); *Women and Education* 2nd ed., ed. with Arlene McLaren (Calgary: Detselig, 1991); *Gender Matters from School to Work* (Philadelphia: Open Univ. Press, 1992); *Gender In/forms Curriculum: From Enrichment to Transformation*, ed. with John Willinsky (New York: Teachers' Coll. Press); *Secondary Schools in Canada* (Toronto: CEA, 1995); numerous other publications. EDIT: Ed. Bd., *Interchange*; Ed. Bd., *Educational Foundations*; Ed. Bd., *International Journal of Qualitative Studies in Education*; Ed. Bd., *Our Schools/Ourselves*; Ed. Bd., *Alberta Journal of Educational Research*, past; Ed. Bd., *Canadian Women's Studies*, past; Ed. Bd., *Working Teacher*, past. AFFIL: Canadian Society for Study of Education (VP 1986-88; Pres. 1988-90; Past Pres. 1990-92); Canadian Association for Foundations of Education (Pres. 1984-86); Social Science Federation of Canada (VP, External Comm. 1988-92); American Sociological Association; Social Sciences & Humanities Research Council (Chair, Educ. Research Grants Jury 1994-95; Bd. of Dir. 1995 to date; Canadian Education Association (Chair, Exemplary Schools 1993-95). HONS: Walter Izaac Killam Memorial Research Fellowship, 1987-88; Critics' Award, American Educational Studies Association, 1992.

Gaudet, Bérengère, B.A.,LL.B. ᑫ ᗡᒪ ♦

Secretary-General and Secretary, Board of Governors, CONCORDIA UNIVERSITY, 1455 de Maisonneuve Blvd. W., Montreal, QC H3G 1M8. Born Joliette, Que. 1938. m. Grégoire Tremblay. 2 ch. Guillaume, Anne-Marie. EDUC: Univ. de Paris, B.A. 1956; Univ. de Montréal, LL.B. 1960. CAREER: sworn in as Notary, 1960; private practice, Montreal, 1961-67; appointed to Royal Inquiry Commission on the Status of Women (research proj. on family law), 1967-70; Que. Bd. of Notaries,

1970-72; Legal Cnsl, Conseil du Patronat du Québec, 1977-81; private consulting firm, 1984-88; Sec.-Gen. & Sec., Bd. of Gov., Concordia Univ., 1988 to date. SELECTED PUBLICATIONS: author/co-author, 3 books. MISC: 1st woman to practise as a Notary in the Prov. of Que.

Gaulthier, Nathalie, B.F.A. ■ 🖖 ⊗
Founder and President, GAULTHIER ARTISTS INC. and N. GAULTHIER ONTARIO MANAGEMENT INC., 208 Carlton St., Loft, Toronto, ON M5A 2L1 (416) 922-8915, FAX 922-2580. Founder and President, LES PRODUCTIONS NATHALIE GAULTHIER INC., 538 Grosvenor St., Westmount, QC H3Y 2S4 (514) 931-9269, FAX 931-9246. Director and Acting Coach, KIDS IN ACT-ION EXCLUSIVE TRAINING/THEATRE COMPANY. Born Gaspé, Que. 1966. EDUC: John Abbott Coll., Creative Arts/Social Sciences 1984-86; Concordia Univ., B.F.A. 1991. CAREER: Dir./Acting Coach, Kids In Act-ion Theatre Company, 1984 to date; Talent Agent, Gaulthier Artists Inc. (Toronto) & Nathalie Gaulthier Productions Inc. (Montreal), 1988 to date; Entertainment Columnist, *The Chronicle*, Montreal, 1991 to date. SELECTED CREDITS: Writer/Prod., *Drugs. Answers Please* (on tour); Dir./Choreographer, *FAME*, Cdn premier, Centaur Theatre, 1995; Guest Star, *Are You Afraid of the Dark?* (series), Nickelodeon; Lead, *The Perfect Face* (feature), Future Classic Entertainment; Regular, *Drôle de Monde* (series), CFTM Telemetropole; Lead/Storyteller, *The Decameron* (theatre), J.A.C. Theatre; Snoopy, *You're a Good Man Charlie Brown* (theatre), St. Thomas Drama; various commercials. SELECTED PUBLICATIONS: *A Minor Consideration: A Parents Guide for Child Actors.* AFFIL: Talent Agent and Managers' Association of Canada (Bd. of Dir.; Head of Youth Actor–Union Liaison); ACTRA; Academy of Canadian Cinema and Television. HONS: Heart of Gold, Air Canada, 1990. INTERESTS: youth achievement. MISC: retired competitive gymnast, flying trapeze artist, choreographer; former child actor; her actors/clients have secured lead roles in such productions as *Clueless* (series lead-Paramount), *Batman Forever*; *Boys of St. Vincent, The Santa Clause*; *Legends of the Fall*; *Road to Avonlea*, Cirque du Soleil, *The Mickey Mouse Club*, & numerous series in the US, Europe & Canada. COMMENT: *"Having founded my companies at age 15 in Montreal, I encourage all young people to follow their dreams. Now 29, currently operating five companies in Toronto and Montreal, working in Canada, Europe and the US."*

Gay, Marie-Louise M.-L. 📖 ⊗ 📑
Author and Illustrator. 773 Davaar Ave.,

Montreal, QC H2V 3B3 (514) 273-0368. Born Quebec City 1952. 2 ch. Gabriel, Jacob. CAREER: author & illustrator; graphiste à temps plein, *Perspectives*, 1974-75; Graphiste à plein temps, *Décormag*, 1976-77; Directrice artistique et directrice de la production, Éditions la courte échelle, 1980-83; Chargée de cours, Univ. du Québec à Montréal, 1981-89; Chargée de cours, CEGEP Ahuntsic, 1985. SELECTED CREDITS: conception des marionnettes, des décors et costumes, *Ombrelles tu dors*, Théâtre de l'Oeil, Montréal, 1984; texte, décors, costumes et marionnettes, *Bonne Fête Willy*, touring show in Canada & Europe, 1988-91; décors illustrés, *La Boîte*, dir. Co Hoedmann, ONF, 1989; texte, décors, costumes et marionnettes, *Qui a peur de Loulou?*, Théâtre de l'Oeil, 1994. SELECTED PUBLICATIONS: numerous books written & illustrated, incl. *De Zéro à Minuit* (Montréal: Éditions la courte échelle, 1981); *Le Potager* (Éditions Ovale, 1985); *Moonbeam on a Cat's Ear* (Toronto: Stoddart Publishing, 1986); *Rainy Day Magic* (Toronto: Stoddart Publishing, 1987); *Angel and the Polar Bear* (Toronto: Stoddart Publishing, 1988); *Fat Charlie's Circus* (Toronto: Stoddart Publishing, 1989); *Willy Nilly* (Toronto: Stoddart Publishing, 1990); *Mademoiselle Moon* (Toronto: Stoddart Publishing, 1992); *Rabbit Blue* (Toronto: Stoddart Publishing, 1993); *Qui a peur de Loulou?* (Montréal: VLB, 1994); *Midnight Mimi* (Toronto: Stoddart Publishing, 1994); illustrations for numerous books, incl. Bertrand Gauthier, *Hou Ilva* (Montréal: Éditions le Tamanoir, 1976); Dennis Lee, *Lizzy's Lion* (Toronto: General Publishing, 1984); Louise Leblanc, *Ça suffit Sophie!* (Montréal: Éditions la courte échelle, 1990); Tim Wynne-Jones, *The Last Piece of Sky* (Toronto: Groundwood Books, 1993); Don Gillmor, *When Vegetables Go Bad* (Toronto: Doubleday Canada Limited, 1994); *The Three Little Pigs* (Toronto: Groundwood Books, 1994); Don Gillmor, *The Fabulous Song* (Toronto: Stoddart Publishing, 1996); illustration & design for numerous North American magazines & publishers. EXHIBITIONS: Terre des hommes, Pavillon de l'humour (1974); *Femmes et animaux*, Galerie 858, Montréal (1980); *Willy Nilly et cie*, Mable's Fables, Toronto (1990); numerous group exhibitions. HONS: Prix Claude Néon, 1972; Scholarship Award, Western Art Directors' Club, 1978; Award, Society of Illustrators of L.A., 1979; Silver Plaque Award, Intercom Film & Video, 1980; Merit Award, Toronto Art Directors' Club, 1982-83; Award, *Creative Source*, 1982-83; Award, *American Illustration Annual*, 1983-85; Award, *Print* Magazine, Chicago, 1984; Prix Alvin-Bélisle, l'ASTED,

1984; Prix du Conseil des Arts, Littérature-jeunesse, 1985; Canada Council Prize, Children's Literature, 1985; Amelia Frances Howard Gibbon Award, 1987, 1988; Prix du Gouverneur Général, 1988; Sélection "White Raven", Bibliothèque internationale jeunesse à Munich, 1993. MISC: recipient of various grants; numerous conference & workshop presentations; subject of various articles.

Gayle, Marlaina ✒ ⌂
Consumer Reporter, THE PROVINCE, 2250 Granville St., Vancouver, BC V6H 3G2 (604) 732-2010, FAX 732-2088. Consumer Columnist, CBC NEWSWORLD. Born Vancouver 1957. EDUC: B.C. Institute of Technology, Broadcast Communications Diploma 1977. CAREER: Legislative Reporter, CKNW Radio, 1978-80; gen. assignment, civic gov't reporter, 1980-82; Reporter, CBC, Vancouver, 1983; Reporter, CKNW Radio, 1984; Chef, Caribbean charter-boat, 1985; Consumer Reporter, CKNW Radio, 1986-88; Consumer Reporter, The Province, 1988 to date; Consumer Columnist, BCTV, 1990-92; Consumer Columnist, CBC Newsworld, 1992 to date. AFFIL: Vancouver Press Club (Pres. 1989-90); Mount Pleasant Safer Community Society (Founding Mbr.). HONS: Second Place, Bus. Reporting, B.C. Newspaper Awards, 1994; First Place, Best News Story, B.C. Newspaper Awards, 1989. INTERESTS: extensive travelling—Middle East, Asia, S.America, Europe, Africa, the Caribbean; Spanish language. MISC: Host for the Children's Development Centre Telethon, Trail, B.C., 1989-93. COMMENT: "'How hard can it be?' is my motto. It's taken me through six radio stations, three television networks, a stint as a Caribbean charter-boat chef and into newspapers as a consumer reporter. My most successful campaign saw the B.C. government introduce full disclosure on car-leasing contracts. 'How hard can it be?'–works with everything from learning to cook to speaking Spanish."

Gaynor, Kimberley, B.A., M.B.A. ■ ⊗ Ⓢ
Arts Administrator. 64 St. Georges Ave., London, UK N70AH (0171) 607-8350, FAX 700-6362. Born Hamilton, Ont. 1961. cl. Trevor Pinnock. EDUC: Univ. of Toronto, B.A.(Cdn Studies) 1983; York Univ., M.B.A.(Arts Admin.) 1989. CAREER: Mktg Dev. Officer, Canada Council, 1986-89; Dir. of Admin., Les Grands Ballets Canadiens, 1989-92; Sr. Mktg Officer, National Arts Centre, 1992-94; Head of Publications & Info. Svcs, Royal Opera House, 1994-96. HONS: Outstanding Progress & Achievement, York Univ. INTERESTS: cycling; travel; music & the performing arts.

Geddes, Carol, B.A. ⊗ ⌂ ♣ ⌂
Film/Video Producer and Writer. 61 Green Cres., Whitehorse, YT Y1A 4R8. Born Teslin, Y.T. (Tingit Nation). EDUC: Carleton Univ., B.A. 1978; Concordia Univ., grad. diploma in Comm. 1981. CAREER: Exec. Asst. to Chrm, Council for Yukon Indians, 1979-81; Prod., Studio One, National Film Board, 1991-93. SELECTED CREDITS: Doctor, Lawyer, Indian Chief (1988); Place For Our People (documentary); produced 20 videos on the lives of aboriginal people in Canada, their customs, arts & other current issues, 1986-90. SELECTED PUBLICATIONS: "Community Profiles: The Native Community," National Film Board Report, 1986. AFFIL: Canada Council (Dir.); Yukon Human Rights Commission; Banff Television Festival Board (Dir.); Women's Television Network Foundation (Dir.). HONS: Award (Doctor, Lawyer, Indian Chief), National Educational Film & Video Festival, 1988; Silver Award, essay Growing Up Native, National Magazine Awards Foundation. INTERESTS: films; wilderness; hiking; fishing; reading. MISC: 1st northerner & 1st aboriginal person appointed a Dir. of the Canada Council; currently working on films George Johnston, Tinglit Photographer & Dry Bay and Other Ideas.

Gee, Ellen M., Ph.D. ⊗ ▩
Professor and Chair, Department of Sociology and Anthropology, SIMON FRASER UNIVERSITY, Burnaby, BC V5A 1S6 (604) 291-3146, FAX 291-5799, EMAIL gee@sfu.ca. Born Vancouver 1950. m. Gordon K.W. Gee. 1 ch. Adrienne Pamela Gee. EDUC: Univ. of British Columbia, B.A.(Psych.) 1971, Ph.D.(Soc.) 1978. CAREER: Asst Prof., now Full Prof., Simon Fraser Univ., 1979 to date; Assoc. Dean of Arts, 1988-92; Acting Dean of Grad. Studies, 1992; Chair, Dept. of Soc. & Anthropology, 1994 to date. SELECTED PUBLICATIONS: Women and Aging, with Meredith Kimball (Toronto: Butterworths, 1987); "Marriage in Nineteenth Century Canada" (Canadian Review of Sociology and Anthropology 1982); "The Life Course of Canadian Women: An Historical and Demographic Analysis" (Social Indicators Research 1986); "Demographic Change and Intergenerational Relations in Canadian Families: Findings and Social Policy Implications" (Canadian Public Policy 1990); "Preferred Timing of Women's Life Events: A Canadian Study" (International Journal of Aging and Human Development 1990); "Pension Policies and Challenges: Retirement Policy Implications," with Susan A. McDaniel (Canadian Public Policy 1991); "Social Policy for an Aging Society," with Susan A. McDaniel (Jour-

nal of Canadian Studies 1993); numerous other publications. **AFFIL:** Canadian Population Society (VP 1994-95); Canadian Sociology & Anthropology Association (Status of Women Committee 1990-93); American Sociological Association; Population Association of America; Canadian Association on Gerontology (Chair, Social Sciences Div. 1989-91; Chair, Research Committee 1989-91); Gerontological Society of America; Committee for Family Research, International Sociological Association. **HONS:** Killam Predoctoral Fellowship, 1972-73; Canada 125 Medal, 1992. **MISC:** listed in *Canadian Who's Who*, 1991 to date; consultant to Statistics Canada, Health & Welfare Canada, Employment & Immigration Canada; grant recipient. **COMMENT:** *"I try to educate students about, and perform research on, important issues in Canadian society relating to demography (aging), families, and social policy."*

Geggie, Jan, B.H.Ec.,R.D. ⊕ ♡

Pediatric Clinical Dietitian, **ALBERTA CHILDREN'S HOSPITAL**, 1820 Richmond Rd. S.W., Calgary, AB T2T 5C7 (403) 299-7342, FAX 229-7086. Born Regina 1943. m. Peter Geggie. 2 ch. Kevin, Rodney. **EDUC:** Univ. of British Columbia, B.H.Ec.(Nutrition) 1965; Royal Victoria Hospital, Montreal, R.D.(Dietetics) 1966. **CAREER:** Admin. Dietitian, Royal Victoria Hospital, 1966-68; Clinical/Therapeutic Dietitian, Plymouth General Hospital, UK, Burnaby General Hospital, Vancouver General Hospital, 1968-70; Internship & Educ. Coord., Royal Victoria Hospital, 1970-72; Lecturer, Fac. of Dentistry, McGill Univ., 1972-75; private dietetic/nutrition counselling practice, 1973-77; Pediatric Clinical Dietitian, Alberta Children's Hospital, 1977 to date; Preceptor (Maternal & Infant Nutrition), Univ. of Calgary Medical Sch., 1988-90 & 1995-96. **SELECTED PUBLICATIONS:** "Intervention for a Non-Oral Feeder: Collaboration Between an Occupational Therapist and a Dietitian," in *Problems With Eating: Interventions for Children and Adults with Developmental Disabilities* (Rockyville MD, The American Occupational Therapy Association, Inc., 1987); "The Role of the Dietitian in the Follow-up of High Risk Infants," with R. Sauve (*Journal of the Canadian Dietetic Association*, Vol. 50, 1989); "Growth and Dietary Status of Preterm and Term Infants During the First Two Years of Life," with R. Sauve (*Canadian Public Health Association Journal*, Vol. 82, No. 2, 1991); "Feeding Problems in Continuing Care of Preterm Infants," with R. Sauve (*Canadian Journal of Pediatrics*, April 1992); book reviews, abstracts & other publications. **AFFIL:** Canadian Dietetic Association (Book Reviewer, J.C.D.A.); Alberta Registered Dietitians' Association (Speakers' Bureau); Alberta Lung Association (Respiratory Health Care Professionals' Section); American Academy of Pediatrics (Section on Perinatal Pediatrics of District VIII); Calgary Bd. of Educ. Nutrition Committee (Founding Mbr., Sch. Nutrition Incentive Program); Foothills Lutheran Church (Founding Mbr. of Doulos Kyriokos–caring ntwk); Varsity Community Association (Exec.; Past Pres.). **HONS:** Charlotte Large Gold Medal for Proficiency in Dietetic Internship, 1966; Hon. Mention & Recipient in Professional Achievement Award, Alberta Registered Dietitians' Association, 1996; nominee, Lifetime Achievement Award, YWCA Women of Distinction Awards, 1993; nominated for the 1989 & 1990 Ross Clinical Dietetics Award. **INTERESTS:** family; travel; cooking & entertaining; swimming; walking; outdoor sports & activities; gardening. **MISC:** various presentations. **COMMENT:** *"When I look back at my participation in so many avenues and accomplishments, I am thankful for my high energy level, my interest in helping people and for a totally supportive husband who has helped me keep a well-rounded balance in life. I delight in working with so many people in the various aspects of my life. I have been so very fortunate to have had challenging opportunities–both professionally and in my communities of neighbourhoods, schools and church."*

Geisler, Brigitte J., B.A.,LL.B. ■ ⚖ $

Assistant Vice-President, Securities Law, **CANADA TRUST COMPANY**, 161 Bay St., Toronto, ON M5J 2T2 (416) 681-2386, FAX 361-5465. Born Germany 1951. m. Carl V. Stacy. 3 ch. Vanessa, Mattison, Gisella. **EDUC:** Univ. of Guelph, B.A.(Phil.) 1972; Osgoode Hall Law Sch., LL.B. 1975. **BAR:** Ont., 1977. **CAREER:** private practice of law, 1977-81; Dir., Toronto Stock Exchange, 1981-83; VP, Compliance, Wood Gundy Inc., 1983-87; Dir., Corp. Sec., Sr. VP, Gen. Cnsl, Midland Walwyn Capital Inc., 1988-96. **AFFIL:** Canadian Bar Association; Law Society of Upper Canada. **INTERESTS:** music; int'l affairs; arts & crafts; phys. fitness. **COMMENT:** *"Ms. Geisler has many years of experience in securities regulation as well as corporate counsel. She brings excellent skills of evaluation, strategy and practicality."*

Gelber, Sylva M., O.C. 🍁

Retired Government Officer. Born Toronto 1910. **EDUC:** Havergal Coll.; Univ. of Toronto; Columbia Univ. **CAREER:** health & welfare organizations & gov't svc. abroad,

1932-48; Cdn Dept. of Nat'l Health & Welfare, 1950-68; Dir., Women's Bureau & Special Advisor, Cdn Dept. of Labour, 1968-78; Int'l Labour Organization Conferences, 1969, 1971, 1975, 1976; U.N. Commission on the Status of Women, 1970-74; Chrm of Working Party, Organization for Economic Co-Operation & Development, 1973-78; U.N. Gen. Assembly, 1976, 1978. **SELECTED PUBLICATIONS:** *No Balm in Gilead: A Personal Retrospective of Mandate Days in Palestine* (Ottawa: Carleton Univ. Press, 1989); numerous publications in several professional journals. **AFFIL:** Canadian Institute of International Affairs; Writers' Union of Canada; U.N. Association in Canada; Trent Univ. (Hon. Mbr., Bd. of Gov.). **HONS:** Gen. Service Medal, Palestine Bar; Centennial Medal, 1967; Officer of the Order of Canada, 1975; LL.D.(Hon.), Queen's Univ.; LL.D.(Hon.), Memorial Univ. of Newfoundland; D.Hum.L.(Hon.), Mount Saint Vincent Univ.; LL.D.(Hon.), Univ. of Guelph. **INTERESTS:** music; theatre; art; reading. **MISC:** Founder of the Sylva Gelber Music Foundation, which provides an annual award administered by the Canada Council, 1981.

Gelhorn, Carolyn, B.Ed. $

President, CARSHAW INC., 66 Edmonton St., Ste. 10, Winnipeg, MB R3C 1P7 (204) 944-9388, FAX 982-4665. Born Winnipeg 1944. m. 1 ch. **EDUC:** Univ. of Manitoba, B.Ed. 1976. **CAREER:** teacher, River East Sch. Div., Winnipeg, 1970-79; Mktg Rep. & Sales Team Mgr, Pitney Bowes of Canada, 1980-86; Pres., Carshaw Inc., 1986 to date. **SELECTED PUBLICATIONS:** *Street Smarts* (forthcoming); *Individual Instruction in Music Through Learning Centres*, ed. (1977). **DIRECTOR:** Carshaw Inc.; Unique Home Services. **AFFIL:** Women Inventors of Manitoba (Facilitator); Klinic Community Health Centre (sexual assault/crisis counsellor). **INTERESTS:** business; women's issues; personal growth; family; travel. **MISC:** developed an individualized in-house training system for mktg reps. of Pitney Bowes for use throughout Canada; guest lecturer on product dev., Univ. of Manitoba, Fac. of Mgmt. **COMMENT:** *"A highly organized business executive motivated by challenge, competition and achievement. Leadership and motivational skills coupled with experience in handling the challenges of entrepreneurial endeavours, result in my ability to achieve success. As president of Carshaw Inc., developed and patented a computerized vehicle data collection and reporting system."*

Geller, Elisabeth, B.A.,M.A. ♡ ✊

Director of Development, JEWISH HOME FOR THE AGED FOUNDATION, 1055 W. 41st Ave., Vancouver, BC V6M 1W9 (604) 261-9376, FAX 266-8722. Born St. Boniface, Man. 1964. 1 ch. **EDUC:** Univ. of Regina, B.A.(Advanced, Pol. Sci.) 1986, M.A.(Public Policy) 1989. **CAREER:** several yrs. in fundraising, mktg & dev., with Arts Club Theatre, West Coast Domestic Workers' Association, Canadian Craft Museum, Social Administrators' Research Unit (Univ. of Regina); Dir. of Dev., Jewish Home for the Aged Foundation. **SELECTED PUBLICATIONS:** numerous articles & news stories on social & public policy issues. **EDIT:** Ed. Bd., *Kinesis* Magazine. **AFFIL:** Vancouver Status of Women (Coord. Collective); Association of Fundraising Professionals of B.C. (Professional Dev. Committee); Association for Healthcare Philanthropy; North American Association of Jewish Communal Workers. **HONS:** Dean's Hon. Roll, Univ. of Regina, 1983, 1984, 1985, 1986; Shandoff Scholarship Award, Univ. of Regina, 1987.

Geneau, Rachelle M., B.A. ■ ⊛ ♡

Independent Curator and Visual Arts Consultant. 924 - 14th Ave. S.W., Ste. 1707, Calgary, AB T2R 0N7 (403) 209-1318. Born Grand Falls, N.B. m. Robert Schindelka. **EDUC:** Univ. of Regina, B.A.(Art Hist.) 1987. **CAREER:** Acct Exec., Vickers & Benson Limited, Vancouver, 1980-81; Acct Exec., Baker Lovick Limited, 1981-82; freelance advtg & mktg consultant, 1982-84; Acct Exec., Roberts & Poole Communications, Regina, 1984-85; Sales Consultant, Gallery Lynda Greenberg, Ottawa, 1989; Mktg Coord., Council for the Arts in Ottawa, 1989; Coord., Art for Public Places, City of Nepean, Ont., Parks & Recreation, 1990-91; Asst. Curator, The Canadian Craft Museum, Vancouver, 1991-93; Exec. Dir., Crafts Association of B.C., 1993-95. **AFFIL:** Canadian Craft Council (Prov. Alternate Dir. 1993-94); Canadian Craft Museum; Vancouver Art Gallery; Museum of Anthropology. **INTERESTS:** the promotion of Cdn craft nationally & internationally. **COMMENT:** *"Rachelle Geneau is currently working as an independent curator and visual arts consultant. Her experience includes: Coordinator of the Public and Corporate Art Program for the City of Nepean, Ontario; Assistant Curator at the Canadian Craft Museum, and Executive Director of the Crafts Association of British Columbia in Vancouver. She has worked extensively within Canada, and particularly in British Columbia's professional craft community. In the past year she has co-curated the exhibition* Metal Minded: a discovery of art jewellery and ornament *and curated* Venus & Vulcan: A

Union of Metal Myth and Beauty *and* Exterior Spaces: exploring sculpture.*"*

Gerriets, Marilyn, B.A.,M.A., Ph.D. 🕮 🏵 📖
Professor and Chair, Department of Economics, ST. FRANCIS XAVIER UNIVERSITY, Antigonish, NS B2G 2W5 (902) 867-3848, FAX 867-2448, EMAIL mgerriet@juliet.stfx.ca. Born Paterson, N.J. 1947. d. 2 ch. EDUC: San Francisco State Coll., B.A.(Econ.) 1970; Univ. of Toronto, M.A.(Econ. Hist.) 1971, Ph.D.(Econ. Hist.) 1978. CAREER: Lecturer, Glendon Coll., 1971-76; Lecturer, Mount Allison Univ., 1976-77; Lecturer, Wilfrid Laurier Univ., 1977-78; Asst. Prof., 1978-80; Asst. Prof., St. Francis Xavier Univ., 1980-83; Assoc. Prof., 1984-94; Full Prof., 1994 to date. SELECTED PUBLICA-TIONS: "Money among the Irish: coin hoards in Viking Age Ireland" (*Journal of the Royal Society of Antiquaries of Ireland* 115 1985); "Kinship and exchange in pre-Viking Ireland" (*Cambridge Medieval Celtic Studies* Summer 1987); "The King as Judge in early Ireland" (*Celtica* 20 1988); "The impact of the General Mining Association on the Nova Scotian Coal Industry, 1825-1850," in *Farm, Factory and Fortune: New Studies in the Maritime Provinces*, ed. Kris Inwood (Fredericton: Acadiensis Press, 1993); "The rise and fall of a free-standing company in Nova Scotia: The General Mining Association" (*Business History* July 1992); "Tariffs, Trade and Reciprocity: Nova Scotia 1830 to 1866," with Julian Gwyn (*Acadiensis*, forthcoming); "Comparison of the Relative Efficiency of Industry in the Provinces of Canada in 1871," with Kris Inwood (*Acadiensis*, forthcoming). AFFIL: Canadian Economic History Association; Eastern Economics Association (Pres.); Cliometric Society; Economic History Association of North America. INTERESTS: currently, exploring the econ. hist. of the Atlantic reg. in order to better understand the origins of current econ. difficulties & strengths. COMMENT: *"My primary goals have been to assist young people in developing their abilities to understand and interpret the world around them and to expand our understanding of the nature of the world we live in."*

Gersovitz, Sarah Valerie, M.A., R.C.A. ❂ 📖
Artist and Playwright. Montreal, QC. Born Montreal. m. Benjamin. 3 ch. Mark, Julia, Jeremy. EDUC: Concordia Univ., post-grad. Diploma (Comm.) 1978, M.A.(English) 1982; Montreal Museum of Fine Arts, art studies; Saidye Bronfman Centre, photography; Visual Arts Center, Rochester, photography; Univ. of Calgary, art studies. CAREER: artist (painter &

printmaker); playwright; taught art at Saidye Bronfman Centre, Pte. Claire Cultural Centre, Visual Arts Centre, & Sir Sandford Fleming Coll. SELECTED CREDITS: *The Picasso Affair*, Ottawa Little Theatre, 1983; staged readings, *Person-to-Person* & *Eh, Harry?*, Maxwell Anderson Playwrights Series, Greenwich, Conn., 1991; *Eh, Harry?*, Victoria Hall, 1991; *Survey Show*, Visual Arts Centre, Montreal, 1994; various other staged readings & performances in N.Y., Toronto, Montreal. SELECTED PUBLICATIONS: *A Portrait of Portia*, play (Texas: I.E. Clark, Inc.). EXHIBITIONS: participated in more than 65 int'l exhibitions worldwide incl. in France, Colombia, UK, Australia, Korea, Chile, Spain, Norway, Switzerland, Yugoslavia, Italy, Germany, Brazil, Peru, Venezuela, Taiwan, Czechoslovakia, Hungary, Bulgaria, Hong Kong, US & Canada; numerous solo exhibitions in galleries worldwide, incl. Universitat Kaiserslautern, Germany, l'Instituto Culturel Peruano, Lima, & 17 Cdn univ. shows; solo exhibitions in commercial galleries in Bogota, Lima, Montreal, Toronto, Winnipeg, & other cities. COLLECTIONS: work in numerous public & private collections in Germany, Peru, Brazil, Hungary, Venezuela, UK, US & Canada, incl. Library of Congress, National Gallery of Canada, National Gallery of South Australia, New York Public Library & Bibliothèque National du Québec. AFFIL: Royal Canadian Academy of the Arts (Mbr. of Council 1992-94); Dramatists' Guild, N.Y. HONS: Third Prize, Windmill Point Competition; Anaconda Award, Canadian Painter-Etchers & Engravers, twice; Graphic Art Prize, First Winnipeg Show Biennial; First Prize & Gold Medal, Seagram Fine Arts Exhibition; Hon. Mention, Miniature Painters, Sculptors & Gravers, Washington, DC; First Prize, Concours Graphique, l'Univ. de Sherbrooke; Int'l Jury Prize, Gabrovo, Bulgaria, 1989; Travel Award, House of Humor & Satire, Gabrovo, Bulgaria, 1991; Purchase Awards from La Fac. de droit, l'Univ. de Sherbrooke, The Thomas More Institute, Le Musée du Québec, National Gallery of South Australia, & Dawson Coll.; First Prize, National Playwriting Competition, Ottawa, *The Picasso Affair*, 1982; First Prize, Country Playhouse Playwriting Competition, Houston, *The Winding Staircase*, 1985; First Prize, Jacksonville Univ., Jacksonville, Fla., *Eh, Harry?*, 1988; 26 finalist, semi-finalist &/or hon. mention designations in competitions in L.A., N.Y. City, Toronto, Baltimore & others. INTERESTS: gardening. MISC: listed in various biographical sources, incl. *Canadian Who's Who, Who's Who in American Art* & *Who's Who in American Women*. COMMENT: *"I enjoy the tension of a dual career, tied together, I suppose, by the fact that I also write art-criticism."*

Getter, Ruth, B.Sc.,M.A.,Ph.D. $ ☝
Senior Vice-President and Chief Economist, THE TORONTO-DOMINION BANK, Toronto-Dominion Centre, Box 1, Toronto, ON M5K 1A2 (416) 982-2556, FAX 982-6884. Born Tel Aviv 1942. 2 ch. Aaron, Rebecca. **EDUC:** McGill Univ., B.Sc.(Genetics) 1964; Ohio Univ., M.A.(Econ.) 1973; Boston Univ., Ph.D.(Econ.) 1982. **CAREER:** Economist, Interindustry Svc., DRI/McGraw-Hill, Lexington, Mass., 1978-82; Mgr, Prod. Dev. & Special Studies, 1982-84; Sr. Economist & Dir., Prod. Dev., Economica, Inc., Cambridge, Mass., 1984-87; Sr. Economist, Ind./Reg. Group, Toronto-Dominion Bank, 1987-92; Dir., Econ. Research, 1992-93; VP, Econ. Research, 1993-94; Sr. VP & Chief Economist, 1994 to date. **MISC:** 1st woman to be appointed chief economist at any Cdn bank. **COMMENT:** *"Dr. Getter travels widely across Canada and abroad, speaking to bank clients and various business groups about the Canadian economy and its prospects, and she is frequently quoted in the media on economic issues."*

Ghauri, Yasmeen ■■ 🎭 📺
Super Model, NEXT MODEL MANAGEMENT, 23 Watts St., New York, NY 10013 (212) 925-5100, FAX 925-5931. Born Montreal 1971. s. **EDUC:** Royal West Academy, 1988. **CAREER:** campaigns incl.: Chanel, Versace, Valentino, Victoria Secrets; also appeared in *Sports Illustrated*; magazine covers incl.: *Vogue*, *Cosmopolitan*, *Elle*, *Marie Claire*; runway collections incl.: Dolce & Gabbana, Versace, Chanel, Isaac Mizrahi, Ralph Lauren, Victor Alfaro, Todd Oldham, Givenchy, Galliano.

Ghosh, Ratna, Ph.D. ■ 🎓
Macdonald Professor of Education, MCGILL UNIVERSITY, 3700 McTavish St., Montreal, QC H3A 1Y2 (514) 398-4493, FAX 398-4642, EMAIL in3g@musicb.mcgill.ca. **EDUC:** Univ. of Calcutta, B.A.(English) 1960; Trinity Coll. of Music, UK, Dip.(Pianoforte & Theory) 1961; Univ. of Calgary, M.A.(Educ. Found.) 1973, Ph.D. 1976. **CAREER:** Visiting Asst. Prof., Educ. Foundations, Univ. of Calgary, 1976-77; Visiting Prof., Sociology of Educ., Ont. Institute for Studies in Educ., 1977; Asst. Prof., Admin. & Policy Studies, McGill Univ., 1977-81; Instructor & Program Coord., Communist Systems of Educ., in E. Europe, through McGill Univ., 1978; Dir., Shastri Indo-Canadian Institute's Summer program for Cdn Teachers, India, 1979; Assoc. Prof., McGill Univ., 1981-88; Dir., Grad. Studies & Research, Fac. of Educ., 1981-82, 1983-86; Sr. Research Scholar & Resident Dir., Shastri Indo-Canadian Institute, New Delhi, 1982-83; Visiting Scholar, Cambridge Univ., 1985; Prof., McGill Univ., 1988 to date. **SELECTED PUBLICATIONS:** *Women in the Family and Economy: An International Comparative Survey*, ed. with G. Kurian (Westport, Conn.: Greenwood Press, 1981); *Educational Technology and Innovations*, ed. with G. Cartwright (New Delhi: Shastri Indo-Canadian Institute, 1984); *Education and the Process of Change*, ed. with M. Zachariah (New Delhi: Sage, 1987); *South Asian Canadians: Issues in the Politics of Culture*, ed. with R. Kanungo (New Delhi: SICI, 1991); *Redefining Multicultural Education* (Toronto: Harcourt Brace, 1996); "Overview on Women & Development," *Women's Studies Encyclopedia* (London: Harvester, 1996); "Multicultural Policy and Social Integration: South Asian Canadian Women" (*Indian Journal of Gender Studies*, 1994); various other publications. **EDIT:** Ed. Bd., *Canadian Journal of Education*; Ed. Bd., *Journal of Gender Studies*. **AFFIL:** Shastri Indo-Canadian Institute (Sec. 1984-86; Treas. 1986-88; Pres. 1988-90); Canadian Human Rights Foundation; National Advisory Committee on Development Education; Comparative & International Education Society, US (Bd.). **HONS:** Killam Predoctoral Scholar, Univ. of Calgary, 1974; Dame of Merit, Order of Saint John of Jerusalem, Knights of Malta, 1993; Women in Dev. Fellowship, Shastri Indo-Canadian Institute, 1994-95; Woman of Distinction, YWCA, 1996. **MISC:** several TV appearances, radio interviews, & newspaper writeups; numerous conference presentations; manuscript reviewer for various journals incl. *Journal of Comparative Family Studies*, *Canadian Ethnic Studies Journal*, & *Comparative Education Review*. **COMMENT:** *"Dr. Ratna Ghosh, Professor of Education, McGill University has published extensively on education and women. She serves on several boards and was President of Shastri Institute."*

Giacomazzi, Bruna $ ☝
Chief Credit Officer, HONGKONG BANK OF CANADA, 885 W. Georgia St., Ste. 300, Vancouver, BC V6C 3E9 (604) 641-1896, FAX 641-1909. Born B.C. m. Robert Burnett. **EDUC:** Vancouver Community Coll., secretarial; Stanford Univ., Fin. Mgmt Program; Univ. of British Columbia, Program for Exec. Dev. **CAREER:** various positions, Household Finance Corp. Ltd., 1965-71; various positions to VP, Corp. Fin., Mercantile Bank of Canada, 1971-87; VP, Special Credit, Hongkong Bank of Canada, 1987-88; VP, Personal Bnkg, 1988-92; Sr. VP, Special Credit, 1992-95. **AFFIL:** Vancouver Community Coll. Educ. Founda-

tion; Vancouver Community Coll. Alumni Association; Ellen Fairclough Foundation (Trustee); YWCA (Dir.); Vancouver Aquarium (Gov.); Committee for National Women's Retreat (Founding Mbr.); Vancouver Hospital & Health Sciences Centre Foundation (Bd.); Univ. of British Columbia, Fac. of Commerce & Bus. Admin. (Bd.). **HONS:** nominated, YWCA Women of Distinction Awards, 1984, 1990; Bus. Successor, *Canadian Business* Magazine, 1990; Canada 125 Medal, 1992. **INTERESTS:** golf; bridge; reading; gourmet food. **MISC:** featured in such publications as *Equity* Magazine (1984, 1991) & *Canadian Banker* (1993); Class Pres., Program for Exec. Dev., UBC, 1988; appointed by fed. gov't to "Friends of Kaon" Triumf Proj., 1989; 1st woman to hold the position of Chief Credit Officer of a bank in Canada.

Giangrande, Carole, B.A.,M.A. 📖 📺 📜
Writer. 18 Glenaden Ave. W., Etobicoke, ON M8Y 2L7 (416) 233-0833, FAX 233-4841. **EDUC:** Univ. of Toronto, B.A.(Pol. Sci.), M.A. 1968. **CAREER:** Instructor, Pol. Sci., Seneca Coll., Toronto, 1968-73; Broadcaster, co-hosted a daily program for 5 yrs., scriptwriting, research, editing, CBC Radio, 1973-89; Writer-in-Residence, Cobourg, Ont., Public Library, 1987; Writer-in-Residence, North York, Ont., Public Library, 1990; Instructor, Media Writing, Ryerson Polytechnic Univ., 1991-92. **SELECTED PUBLICATIONS:** *The Nuclear North: The People, The Regions and the Arms Race* (Toronto: Anansi Press, 1983); *Down to Earth: The Crisis in Canadian Farming* (Toronto: Anansi Press, 1985); *Missing Persons* (Cormorant Books, 1994); "Being Canadian," in *Not a Textbook: Issues in Canadian Life*, ed. by R.J. Fugere (Toronto: Garamond, 1989); "Allowing the Mind to Wander," in *The Broadview Reader*, 2nd ed., ed. by Herbert Rosengarten & Jane Flick (Peterborough, Ont.: Broadview, 1992); "Radio: The World Inside Your Head," in *Discovery*, Vol. 6 (Toronto: Nelson Canada, 1993); "Political Gardens," *Garden Voices*, eds. Pleasance Crawford & Edwinna von Baeyer (Toronto: Random House of Canada, 1995); articles, essays & reviews in various Cdn publications incl. *The Globe and Mail, The Toronto Star* & *Books in Canada*. **AFFIL:** The Writers' Guild of Canada; PEN. **HONS:** Third Prize, Postcard Story Contest, *Grain*, 1990; finalist, CBC Radio Literary Competition (Short Fiction), 1991. **MISC:** grant recipient; frequent reader & public speaker.

Gibb, Patricia, B.A.,C.H.R.P. $ ♥ ✊
President, INFINITUM MANAGEMENT SERVICES INC., 3582 W. 37th Ave., Vancouver, BC V6N 2V8 (604) 264-8646, FAX 266-0009. Born Lincoln, UK 1948. cl. Bruce Gillespie. 2 stpch. **EDUC:** Univ. of Edinburgh, B.A.(French/Italian/Art Hist.) 1970; Simon Fraser Univ., Diploma in Mgmt for Women 1984; Univ. of British Columbia, Mgmt Dev. Certificate 1986. **CAREER:** VP, Hum. Res. & Admin., CUE Datawest Ltd., 1983-90; Pres., Infinitum Management Services Inc., 1990 to date. **AFFIL:** B.C. Human Resources Management Association (Conference Chair 1991; Dir., Conferences 1990-92; Dir., Publications, VP, 1992-93; Pres. 1993-94; Dir., Special Projects 1994-95); Canadian Mental Health Association, B.C. Div. (Chair, Workplace Excellence Awards Program Committee 1992; Judge, Workplace Excellence Awards Program 1993-95); Canadian Craft Museum (Trustee; Chair, Personnel Committee); Canadian Council of Human Resource Associations (Founding Bd. 1994); YWCA Focus Program (Volunteer Presenter); Dunbar Soccer Association (Fundraiser). **HONS:** Good Citizen Award, Canadian Mental Health Association. **INTERESTS:** garden design & maintenance; creative cooking; wine; travel; crafts. **MISC:** Certified Hum. Res. Professional. **COMMENT:** *"A well-rounded, creative professional who uses her broad experience and natural talents to help organizations and individuals achieve excellence and harmony in the workplace."*

Gibson, Deborah Ruth, B.A. ■■ ✏ 📺 🏃
Publisher, CANADIAN ART MAGAZINE (Canada's quarterly nat'l contemporary visual arts), 70 The Esplanade, Toronto, ON M5E 1R2 (416) 368-8854. Born Toronto 1950. m. Sol Bienstock. 2 ch. Candice, Michael. **EDUC:** Queen's Univ., B.A.(Liberal Arts) 1971. **CAREER:** Publisher, *Toronto Life Fashion*, 1977-92; Co-Exec. Producer, *Fashion File*, 1989 to date; Pres., Toronto Life Ventures, 1992-94; Publisher, *Canadian Art Magazine*, 1994 to date. **AFFIL:** Canadian Stage Company (Bd. of Dir. 1989 to date); Fashion Group International (Reg'l Dir. 1994-95; Bd. of Advisors 1996); Canadian Art Foundation (Bd); P.A.D.A.C. (Bd.).

Gibson, Dyanne B., B.A., M.A. ■■ 🎓 ✏ $
President, DYANNE GIBSON & ASSOCIATES INC. (compiles & writes *Gibson's Student Guides to Universities in Canada*), 55 Sugar Millway, North York, ON M2L 4R5 (416) 444-8631. **EDUC:** Univ. of Toronto, B.A.(English); York Univ., B.A.(Hons., English), M.A.(Victorian Studies, English). **CAREER:** part-time faculty, York Univ., Fac. of Arts & Dept. of Humanities, Atkinson Coll., 1975 to date; Admissions

Office, Liaison, Adult Students & Community Rel'ns, 1980-83; Liaison/New Initiatives, 1983-84; Asst. Dir., Admissions/Liaison, 1984-87; Assoc. Dir., Admissions/Liaison, 1987-89; Ptnr, Weathers Inc., 1985 to date; Pres., Dyanne Gibson & Associates Inc., 1988 to date; Ptnr, Back on Track (subsid. of William Jeffery and Associates Ltd.), 1990 to date. SELECTED PUBLICATIONS: "Plan For Life As Well As Retirement" (*Financial Post Magazine*, Feb. 1996); *Gibson's Guide to Universities in Quebec and Atlantic Canada, Gibson's Student Guide to Universities in Western Canada & Gibson's Guide to Ontario Universities* (Dyanne Gibson & Associates, 1997 editions). AFFIL: York Univ. (Senate Committee on Teaching & Learning 1994-97; Co-Chair, Retirement Planning Centre 1991-95); Speakers' Bureau (1982-88); Canadian Advisory Council on the Status of Women (1989-92); Canadian Mental Health Association (Dir., Nat'l Bd. 1976-82; Programme Chrm 1979-82; Personnel Chrm 1976-79); Junior League of Toronto (Pres. 1975-76); Association of Junior Leagues Inc. (mbr. 1963 to date; Publications Chrm, Area II District Council 1973-74).

Gien, Lan, B.Sc.,M.Ed.,Ph.D. ■■ ⊕ 🦅
Professor, School of Nursing, MEMORIAL UNIVERSITY OF NEWFOUNDLAND, St. John's, NF A1B 3V6 (709) 737-6276, FAX 737-7037, EMAIL lgien@morgan.ucs.mun.ca. Born Thanh Hoa, Viet Nam 1942. m. Dr. Tran Trong Gien. 3 ch. Daniel, Lilian, Aileen. EDUC: Loretto Heights Coll., Denver, Colo., B.Sc.(Nursing) 1964; Univ. de Tunis, Certificat de Biol. Gén. 1965; Columbia Univ., N.Y., M.Ed.(Nursing Educ.) 1974; Univ. of London, England, Ph.D.(Community Medicine) 1991. CAREER: Staff Nurse, De Paul General Hospital, Cheyenne, Wyoming, 1964; Staff Nurse & Team Leader, Geoffrey St.-Hillaire Hospital, Paris, France, 1965-66; Instructor, Sch. of Nursing, General Hospital, St. John's, Nfld., 1966-71; Instructor, Sch. of Nursing, Memorial Univ. of Newfoundland, 1971-73; Lecturer, 1973-76; Asst. Prof., 1976-80; Assoc. Prof., 1980-94; Prof., 1994 to date; Assoc. Dir., Grad. Program & Research, 1989-93; cross-appointed to Gerontology Centre, 1989 to date. SELECTED PUBLICATIONS: numerous publications incl.: co-author with J.A.D. Anderson, "The impact of health education on the use of medication in elderly women" in S.J. Lewis, Ed., *Aging & health: Linking research and public policy* (Michigan: Lewis Publication, 1989); co-author with J.A.D. Anderson, "Medication and the elderly: a review" (*Journal of Geriatric Drug Therapy*, 4 (1), 59-90, 1989); author, "Evaluation of faculty teaching effectiveness:

Towards accountability in education" (*Journal of Nursing Education*, 30 (2), 92-94, 1991); co-author with M. Laryea, "The impact of HIV-positive diagnosis on the individual. Part I: Stigma, rejection and loneliness" (*Clinical Nursing Research: An International Journal*, 2 (3), 245-266, 1993); author, "Health education and the use of over-the-counter products in self-treatment of common minor ailments in elderly women: a randomized controlled trial" (in G. Gray & L. Mayner (Eds.), *Proceedings of the First International Conference-Nursing Research*, Proactive vs Reactive, Adelaide, S. Australia, 15-17 July, 1991, pp. 79-90). AFFIL: Canadian Commission for UNESCO (Exec. Committee); National Organization for Immigrant & Visible Minority Women of Canada (Reg'l VP; Prov. Rep.; Sec.); Canadian Association of University Schools of Nursing (Chair, Bd. of Accreditation; Pres., Atlantic Reg.). HONS: included in *Book of Experts*, 1996; recipient, several external grants for research; won numerous scholarships, grants for projects, travel, etc. INTERESTS: music; gardening; travel. MISC: reviewer of abstracts, grants, scholarships, manuscripts, promotion; conducted research workshops & presented briefs. COMMENT: *"Myself: I am a hard worker and enjoy meeting and working with people. My endeavours: try to excel in whatever I am involved in. My interests: diverse-there is so much to do. I like to help people to progress and advance to their fullest potentials. My achievements: have contributed to the intellectual growth of several thousands of university students, have succeeded in several research projects. Have contributed as much as possible to community by holding leadership positions in various organizations. "*

Giguère, Diane ■■ 📜🗂
Writer. 60, William Paul, #304, Nun's Island, QC H3E 1M6 (514) 762-0311. Born Montreal 1937. s. EDUC: Conservatory of Dramatic Arts, Theatre 1954-56. CAREER: leading roles in English & French, Mountain Playhouse/ Théâtre du Nouveau Monde/Brae Manor Playhouse/TV; announcer, CBC, French ntwk, 28 yrs.; writer. SELECTED PUBLICATIONS: *Le Temps des Jeux*, 1961 (published in English as *Innocence*); *L'eau est profonde*, 1965 (published in English as *Whirlpool*); *Dans les ailes du vent*, 1976 (published in English as *Wings in the Wind*); *L'abandon*, 1993– publishers: Tisseyre, McClelland & Stewart (Montreal & Toronto), Gollancz (London) & Laffont (Paris). HONS: 1st Prize in Acting, Conservatory of Dramatic Arts, 1956; Prix du Cercle du Livre de France for *Le Temps des Jeux*, 1961; Guggenheim Fellowship Award, N.Y., 1969;

Prix France Québec, 1977. **INTERESTS:** art; music; nature.

Gilbert, Jane ■■ ✏ ☒

Anchor, GLOBAL TELEVISION NETWORK, 81 Barber Greene Rd., Don Mills, ON M3C 2A2 (416) 446-5460, FAX 446-5447. Born Scunthorpe, UK 1957. m. Guy. 1 ch. Dominique. **EDUC:** Carleton Univ., Bachelor degree (Journalism & Law) 1980. **CAREER:** public rel'ns, Cdn Gov't Office of Tourism, summers 1979 & 1980; Intern, CKOC Radio, Hamilton, Ont., 1980-81; Video Ed./Videographer/Gen. Assignment Reporter/Anchor & Prod., Weekend Radio News (AM & FM)/Anchor & Producer, Weekend TV News, CKNX TV & Radio, Wingham, Ont., Jan.-Nov. 1981; Gen. Assignment Reporter/Anchor & Prod., CKVR TV, Barrie, Ont., 1981-82; Gen. Assignment Reporter/Host, Prod. & Writer, *Weekend Newsline*/Back-up Anchor, *Newsline* (6:00 news)/Host, Prod. & Writer, *Midday Newsline*, CJOH TV, Ottawa, 1982-89; Co-Host, *Newsworld Morning*, CBC Newsworld, Halifax, 1989-92; Co-Anchor, *The World Tonight* (11:00 news)/Anchor, *News at Six*, Global Television, Toronto, 1992 to date; freelance work with Lauron Productions, *Appreciating Your Wealth*, Toronto, 1992. **AFFIL:** Canadian Association of Journalists; Canadian Women in Communications (Ambassador mbr.); Carleton Univ. (President's Advisory Council); The ABCM Speakers' Bureau, Toronto. **HONS:** mbr., Hall of Fame, Carleton Univ. **MISC:** in addition to daily duties with Global News, balances schedule of public speaking engagements; Guest Lecturer, Sch. of Journalism-Ryerson Polytechnic Univ., Carleton Univ., Sch. of Journalism-Algonquin Coll., various high sch. programs & svc. clubs. **COMMENT:** *"Over the past 16 years, I have attempted to gain experience in many facets of broadcast journalism. The production and presentation of television news remains my key area of interest. Today I am fortunate to work with a growing and dynamic organization (CanWest Global), and still find time for the demands and challenges of family life."*

Gill, Judith, B.Ed.(PE),M.PE., Ph.D. ☒ ⊘ $ ☐

Co-Chair, Physical Education Department, JOHN ABBOTT COLLEGE, Box 2000, Ste-Anne-de-Bellevue, QC H9X 3L9 (514) 457-6610, ext. 410, FAX 696-4509. President, **106703 CANADA LIMITED**. Born Ottawa 1949. m. George Springate. **EDUC:** McGill Univ., B.Ed. (Phys. Educ.), Class I Teaching Certificate 1970; Univ. of Ottawa, M.PE.(Phys. Educ. Admin.) 1974; Univ. of Oregon, Ph.D.(Phys.

Educ. Admin.) 1979; Univ. of Sherbrooke, Collegial Teaching Certificate 1982. **CAREER:** Dir. of Women's Phys. Educ. & Athletics, John Abbott Coll. & MacDonald Coll., 1971-73; Coord., Phys. Educ., Kirkland Campus, 1973-77; Founder & operator, The Fitness Testing Centre, both campuses, John Abbott Coll., 1974-80; Pres., 106703 Canada Limited (umbrella company that runs numerous types of businesses incl. Palmquist Publications, Emergencies on Ice, Canadian Doodads, Dr. G. & Associates, etc.), 1976 to date; Co-Chair, Phys. Educ. Dept., John Abbott Coll., 1995 to date. **SELECTED PUBLICATIONS:** *Safe-Healthy Hockey*, co-authored with Gaetan Lefebvre, Head Trainer, Montreal Canadiens (Montreal: Palmquist Publications, 1992; 2nd edition, 1995); *Physical Training Manual for Police Technology Students* (Ste-Anne-de-Bellevue: John Abbott Coll., 1992; 2nd edition, 1993; 3rd edition, 1996); *A Guide to Building Fitness Trails* (Columbus, Ohio: Publishing Horizons, 1986); *Class Notes for Fitness* (Ste-Anne-de-Bellevue: John Abbott Coll., 5th edition, 1992-93); *PETS - Physical Fitness Testing Kit*, a computerized fitness testing system for men & women aged 15 to 60 yrs. (Montreal: Palmquist Publications, 1983); various articles for *Canadian Living* & *Homemaker's* magazines; syndicated fitness columns, Cdn & US newspapers for 17 yrs.; featured articles in various newspapers. **AFFIL:** YWCA (Nominations Committee, Women of Distinction Award, 1995); Quebec Major Jr. Hockey League (Co-Chair, educ. scholarship program 1993-95); Sun Youth of Montreal (Organizer, "Teens Talking to Teens"); Fitness Canada & the Women's Program (Advisor, "Female Youth & Physical Activity" program 1987-88); Association of Physical Educators of Quebec; Canadian Association for Health, Physical Education & Recreation; Canadian Society for Exercise Physiology; Canadian Research Institute for the Advancement of Women; Canadian Association for the Advancement of Women in Sport; National Strength & Conditioning Association; American Running & Fitness Association; Canadian Heart Foundation (CPR trained). **HONS:** Woman of Distinction Award, Sports & Leisure, YWCA of Montreal, 1994; Canada 125 Medal, 1993; Citizen's Award of Merit, for community work, City of Pierrefonds, 1993. **INTERESTS:** reading; travel; computers; antiques; various fitness-related activities, e.g. walking, jogging, weight-training, etc. **MISC:** Founder & 1st convenor, Montreal Women's Ice Hockey League, 1972-74; designed, financed & constructed the Macdonald-Abbott Fitness Trail, 1st bilingual fitness trail in Que.; designer & implementer of the

Westmount Fitness Trail, Westmount Park, Que., 1977; initiator of the computerized mass fitness testing programs at John Abbott Coll. used to test thousands of students yearly; administrator of the Sun League (hockey draft), a fundraiser for Sun Youth & the Quebec Society for Disabled Children, 1992 to date; consultant on the phys. training of Police Technology students, 1991 to date; organizer of safety clinics, "Emergencies on Ice – What to do until help arrives"; advisor to Fitness & Amateur Sport on the reorganization of Fitness Canada, 1987; mbr. of the committee to establish a certification program for fitness instructors in Que. COMMENT: *"Judy Gill, Ph.D., is a teacher, writer and broadcaster. She has degrees from four Canadian and US universities and has been teaching for 26 years. A recognized expert in fitness and health, she has written six books and is working on two more at present. She has received numerous awards for her community work."*

Gillam, Shirley, B.Sc.,Ph.D. ⌒ ⊕
Professor, Department of Pathology, UNIVERSITY OF BRITISH COLUMBIA, Research Centre, 950 W. 28th Ave., Rm. 309, Vancouver, BC V5Z 4H4 (604) 875-2474, FAX 875-4296. Born Chau-Chou, Taiwan 1935. m. Dr. Ian Gillam. EDUC: National Cheng-Kung Univ., B.Sc.(Chem. Eng.) 1959; Univ. of Kansas, Ph.D.(Biochem.) 1966. CAREER: post-doctoral training, Univ. of California, Davis, 1965-67, Univ. of Washington, Seattle, 1968-69, Univ. of British Columbia, 1970; Research Assoc., Univ. of British Columbia, 1971-81; Asst. Prof., Dept. of Pathology, 1981-86; Assoc. Prof., 1986-91; Prof., 1991 to date. SELECTED PUBLICATIONS: "Enzymatic synthesis of olignucleotides of defined sequence: Synthesis of a segment of yeast Iso-1-cytochrome C gene," with R. Rottman, P. Jahnke & M. Smith (*Proc. National Academy of Science*, Vol. 74, 1977); "Defined transversion mutations at a specific position in DNA using synthetic oligodeoxyribonucleotides as mutagens," with P. Jahnke, C. Astell *et al* (*Nucleic Acids Res.*, Vol. 6, 1979); "Oligodeoxyribonucleotides as site-specific mutagens," with M. Smith, *Genetic Engineering, Principles and Methods*, ed. J.K. Setlow & A. Hollander (New York; Plenum Press, Vol. 3, 1981); "Nucleotide sequence and in vitro expression of rubella virus 24 S subgenomic messenger RNA encoding structural proteins, C, E2 and E1," with D.M. Clarke, T.W. Loo, I. Hui & P. Chong (*Nucleic Acids Res.*, Vol. 15, 1987); "Role of N-link oligosaccharides in processing and intracellular transport of E2 glycoprotein of rubella virus," with Z. Qiu, T. Hobman *et al* (*Journal of Virology*, Vol. 66, 1992);

various other publications. AFFIL: The Genetic Society of Canada (Chair, Molecular & Biotechnology Committee 1985); The Canadian Society of Microbiologists (Educ. Committee 1985); The Canadian Biochemical Society; American Society for Microbiology; American Society for Virology; American Association for the Advancement of Science. HONS: B.C. Children's Hospital Foundation Research Award, 1988; Jeanne Mannery Fisher Award, The Canadian Society of Biochemistry & Molecular Biology, 1994. INTERESTS: molecular analysis of the structure & function of viral genes & proteins; interaction of virus & host cells; vaccine dev. MISC: MRC Scientist, Medical Research Council of Canada, 1981-86; B.C. Children's Hospital Foundation Investigatorship, 1986 to date. COMMENT: *"Productive career in basic medical research. Significant contribution to the development of site-directed mutagenesis and the understanding of the molecular biology of rubella virus (the etiologic agent of German Measles)."*

Gillese, Eileen, B.Com.,B.A., B.C.L. ■ ⌒ ⚖ ⌂
Dean, Faculty of Law, UNIVERSITY OF WESTERN ONTARIO, London, ON N6A 3K7 (519) 679-2111, ext. 8404, FAX 661-3790, EMAIL laweeg@uwoadmin.uwo.ca. Born Edmonton 1954. m. Robert Badun. 4 ch. Meghan Elizabeth Badun, David Robert Badun, Amy Evelyn Badun, Sarah Jean Badun. EDUC: Univ. of Alberta, B.Com. 1977; Oxford Univ., B.A.(Jurisprudence) 1979, B.C.L. 1980. BAR: Alta., 1981; Ont., 1988. CAREER: Sessional Lecturer, Fac. of Commerce, Univ. of Alberta, Sept.-Dec. 1981; Sessional Lecturer, Fac. of Law, Jan.-May 1983; Barrister & Solicitor, Reynolds, Mirth & Cote, 1980-83; Asst. Prof., Fac. of Law, Univ. of Western Ontario, 1983-88; Assoc. Dean (Student Affairs), 1988-89; Assoc. Prof., 1988-93; Barrister & Solicitor (on leave from UWO), McCarthy, Tétrault, 1989-91; Assoc. Dean (Admin.), Fac. of Law, Univ. of Western Ontario, 1992-95; Prof., 1993 to date; Dean, Fac. of Law, 1996 to date. SELECTED PUBLICATIONS: *Property Law* 2nd edition (Toronto: Emond Montgomery Publications Limited, 1990); *Text, Commentary, and Cases on the Law of Trusts* 4th edition, with A.H. Oosterhoff (Toronto: The Carswell Company, 1992); *Text & Materials on Pension Law in Canada* 4th edition (London, Ont.: Univ. of Western Ontario, 1996); various other publications. EDIT: Assoc. Ed., *Ontario Law Reports*, 1989-91; Assoc. Ed., *The Dominion Law Reports*, 1989 to date; Ed. Bd., *The Estates and Trusts Journal*, 1989 to date. AFFIL: Law Society of Alberta; Law Society of Upper Canada;

Canadian Association for Law Teachers; Society for Teaching & Learning in Higher Education; Pension Commission of Ontario (V-Chrm 1989-93; Chrm 1994-96). HONS: various academic awards & scholarships; Rhodes Scholarship, 1977; Outstanding Woman Award, Gov't of Canada, 1978; recipient of inaugural Fac. Excellence in Teaching Award, Legal Society, 1986; 3M Fellowship for Excellence in Teaching, 1987; Award for Excellence in Teaching, Fac. of Law, Univ. of Western Ontario, 1992; Edward Pleva Award for Excellence in Teaching, UWO, 1993. MISC: 1st Rhodes for women; 1st female Dean, Fac. of Law, UWO; 1st 3M Fellowship for Excellence in Teaching.

Gillett, Margaret, B.A.,M.A.,Ed.D. ■ ⌖
William C. MacDonald Professor Emeritus in Education, Department of Educational Studies, Faculty of Education, MCGILL UNIVERSITY, 3724 McTavish, Montreal, QC H3A 1Y2 (514) 398-6746, FAX 398-7436, EMAIL ingi@musicb.mcgill.ca. Born Wingham, Australia 1930. s. EDUC: Univ. of Sydney, B.A. 1950, Diploma in Educ. 1951; New South Wales Teacher's Certificate 1952; Russell Sage, Troy, NY, M.A. 1958; Columbia Univ., Ed.D. 1961. CAREER: teacher, English & Hist., Australia, 1951-53; supply teacher, London, UK, 1953-54; Educ. Officer, Commonwealth Office of Educ., Australia, 1954-57; Asst. Prof. of Educ., Dalhousie Univ., 1961-62; Registrar, Haile Sellassie I Univ., Addis Ababa, Ethiopia, 1962-64; Assoc. Prof. of Educ., McGill Univ., 1964-67; Chair, Dept. of Hist. & Phil. of Educ., 1966-68; Prof. of Educ., 1967-82; Chair, Dept. of Social Foundations of Educ., 1979-80; Coord., Women's Studies Minor, 1980-88; Macdonald Prof. of Educ., 1982-94; Founding Dir., McGill Centre on Research & Teaching on Women, Mar.-Dec. 1988; Prof. Emeritus, 1995 to date. SELECTED PUBLICATIONS: *A History of Education: Thought and Practice* (Toronto: McGraw-Hill, 1966); *We Walked Very Warily: A History of Women at McGill* (Montreal: Eden Press, 1981); *Dear Grace: A Romance of History* (Montreal: Eden Press, 1986); *Our Own Agendas*, with Ann Beer (McGill-Queen's Univ. Press, 1995); *A Fair Shake Revisited*, with Kay Sibbald & Elizabeth Rowlinson (1996); various other books; "Sexism in Higher Education" (*Atlantis* 1(2) Fall 1975); "Leacock and the Ladies of R.V.C." (*McGill Journal of Education* 16(2) Spring 1981); "Carrie Derick (1862-1941) and the Chair of Botany at McGill" in *Despite the Odds: Essays on Canadian Women and Science*, Marianne G. Ainley, ed. (Montreal: Vehicule, 1990); "The Heart of the Matter: Maude Abbott, M.D., 1869-1940" in *Despite*

the Odds: Essays on Canadian Women and Science, Marianne G. Ainley, ed. (Montreal: Vehicule, 1990); approx. 50 publications in professional journals or books; over 30 reviews in professional journals such as *Canadian and International Education, Journal of Asian and African Studies* & *Resources for Feminist Research*. EDIT: Founding Ed., *McGill Journal of Education*, 1966-77; Founding mbr., Ed. Bd., *Canadian and International Education*; Founding mbr., Ed. Bd., *Educational Studies*; Founding mbr., Ed. Bd., *Vitae Scholasticae*. AFFIL: Comparative & International Education Society of Canada (Hon. Life Mbr.); American Educational Studies Association; Canadian Society for the Study of Education (Hon. Mbr.); Canadian History of Education Association; Canadian Research Institute for the Advancement of Women; International Society for Educational Biography; Canadian Women's Studies Association; James McGill Society, McGill Univ. (Hon. Life Mbr.). HONS: 75th Anniversary Medal, for contribution to feminism & the higher educ. of women, Russell Sage, NY, 1991; Woman of Distinction (Educ.), YWCA, Montreal, 1994; LL.D.(Hon.), Univ. of Saskatchewan, 1988. MISC: 1st person to hold position of Registrar, Haile Sellassie I Univ., Addis Ababa, Ethiopia; numerous presentations to academic & civil groups; recipient of various scholarships & research grants; reviewer for SSHRCC & various journals; listed in numerous biographical sources, incl. *Canadian Who's Who, Who's Who in the World* & *International Who's Who in Education*. COMMENT: *"My academic career has been infused with a passion for trying to win recognition of women's achievements in the past and equity for the present and future. I am proud to have helped Women's Studies become a legitimate field of teaching and research."*

Gillham, Virginia, B.A.,M.S.L.S. ■■ ⬚ ⌖
University Librarian, WILFRID LAURIER UNIVERSITY, 75 University Ave. W., Waterloo, ON N2L 3C5 (519) 884-0710, ext. 3380, FAX 884-8023, EMAIL vgillham@mach2.wlu.ca. Born Hamilton, Ont. m. Robert Gillham. 1 ch. David. EDUC: McMaster Univ., B.A.(English Lit.); Univ. of Toronto, High Sch. Teaching Certificate, Sch. Library Specialists' Certificate; Univ. of Illinois, M.S.L.S.(Library Sci.). CAREER: Asst./Assoc. Librarian, Univ. of Guelph, 1984-92; Univ. Librarian, Wilfrid Laurier Univ., 1992 to date. SELECTED PUBLICATIONS: co-author with L. Cracknell, "Canadian Government Publications" (*Information Sources in Official Publications*, West Sussex, Bowker Saur, in press 1996); author/co-author, numerous articles, presentations, technical

reports & book reviews. **AFFIL:** Canadian Library Association; Ontario Library Association; American Library Association; Association of College & University Libraries; Ontario Council of University Libraries (Chair & Administrative Coord., Cooperative Documents Proj. 1980-88; Exec. mbr. 1996 to date). **INTERESTS:** classical music. **MISC:** Sessional Lecturer in Gov't Publication, Univ. of Western Ontario, Sch. of Library & Info. Sci., 1981, 1982, 1984; Visiting Lecturer on library public svc., Beijing Agricultural Univ., Sept. 1987; Judge & Referee, Canadian Figure Skating Association. **COMMENT:** *"Career has focused on academic library administration, library automation and information technology. Many publications and presentations. Considerable energy presently directed to information technology in a consortium environment."*

Gillis, Angela, R.N.,B.Sc.N.,M.Ad.Ed., Ph.D. 🏳️ ⊕ ♿

Professor and Chair, Department of Nursing, ST. FRANCIS XAVIER UNIVERSITY, Box 5000, Antigonish, NS B2G 2W5 (902) 867-3955, FAX 867-2448, EMAIL gillis@juliet.stfx.ca. Born Sydney, N.S. 1953. m. Phonse Gillis. 2 ch. **EDUC:** St. Rita Sch. of Nursing, R.N. Diploma 1973; St. Francis Xavier Univ., B.Sc.N. 1979, M.Ad.Ed. 1981; Univ. of Texas at Austin, Ph.D.(Nursing) 1993. **CAREER:** Staff Nurse, St. Martha's Hospital, Antigonish, 1973-75; Lecturer, Nursing, St. Francis Xavier Univ., 1977-78; Nursing Instructor, St. Martha's Sch. of Nursing, 1978-80; Lecturer, Dept. of Nursing, St. Francis Xavier Univ., 1980-82; Asst. Prof., 1982-86; Assoc. Prof. & Chair, 1987-95; Prof. & Chair, 1995 to date. **SELECTED PUBLICATIONS:** "Hazards and Complications of I.V. Therapy" (*Dimensions in Health Services* 61(2) 1983); "The Effects of Play on Immobilized Children in Hospital" (*International Journal of Nursing Studies* 26(3) 1988); "The Relationship of Exercise Practices to Measures of Health, Lifestyle, Well Being, Self-Esteem and Locus of Control in Mid-life Women," with A. Perry (*Nurse to Nurse* 1(6) 1990); "Determinants of Health-promoting Lifestyles in Adolescent Females" (*Canadian Journal of Nursing Research* 26(2) 1994); "Teens promote healthy lifestyles" (*Canadian Nurse* 92(6) 1996); "Priority women and smoking," with M.J. Stewart, G. Brosky *et al* (*Journal of Public Health* 87(4) 1996); "Adolescence: An opportunity for health promotion" in *Community Health Nursing: Community Nursing Promoting Canadians' Health*, ed. M. Stewart (Philadelphia: W.B. Saunders, 1996); "Exploring nursing outcomes for health promotion" (*Nursing Forum* 30(2) 1995); various

other publications. **EDIT:** Advisor, *RN Magazine*, 1986 to date. **AFFIL:** Canadian Nurses' Association; Canadian Nurses' Research Group; Canadian Association of University Schools of Nursing; Canadian Nurses' Foundation; Association for the Care of Children's Health; Society for Research on Adolescence; Registered Nurses' Association of N.S.; Women's Health Education Network; National Institute of Nutrition (Trustee); Atlantic Health Promotion Research Centre (Research Advisory Committee); R.K. MacDonald Nursing Home (Dir.); Phi Kappa Phi Honour Society; Sigma Theta Tau International (Epsilon Theta Tau Chapter). **HONS:** various academic scholarships; Gold Medal, St. Rita Hospital Sch. of Nursing, 1973; St. Francis Xavier Univ. Research, Publication, Teaching Award, 1987, 1985, 1989-94; Ross Award for Nursing Leadership, Canadian Nurses' Foundation, 1989; C.V. Mosby Book Award, Canadian Nurses' Foundation, 1991; Katherine E. MacLaggan Fellowship, Canadian Nurses' Foundation, 1991, 1992; Good Neighbour Scholarship, Univ. of Texas at Austin, 1992; Outstanding Graduating Nursing Student Award (Ph.D.), Univ. of Texas at Austin, 1993. **INTERESTS:** gardening; reading; dancing; family life. **MISC:** recipient of various grants; 1st recipient of Ross Award for Nursing Leadership, Canadian Nurses' Foundation; numerous conference presentations; consultant to various nursing associations. **COMMENT:** *"A natural leader on many institutional levels. Highly committed to her profession. Research interests include adolescent health promotion."*

Gillis, Patricia M., B.A. ■■ ⊛ ◯ ⊕

Director, Volunteer Services Department, B.C. CHILDREN'S HOSPITAL (pediatric tertiary care hospital), 4480 Oak St., Vancouver, BC V6H 3V4 (604) 875-2143, FAX 875-2292, EMAIL pgillis@wpog.childhosp.bc.ca. President, CANADIAN ADMINISTRATORS OF VOLUNTEER RESOURCES. Born Peterborough, Ont. **EDUC:** Univ. of Western Ontario, B.A.(English) 1978; Vancouver Community Coll., Certificate (Volunteer Mgmt) 1986. **CAREER:** Dir., Volunteer Svcs, Juan de Fuca Hospital Society, Victoria, B.C., 1979-91. **AFFIL:** Canadian Administrators of Volunteer Resources (Pres. 1996-97; 1st VP 1994-96; 2nd VP 1993-94; B.C. Prov. Rep. 1991-93); Canadian Association of Volunteer Bureaux & Centres (B.C./Yukon Rep. on Bd., Steering Committee 1993-96); B.C. Association of Volunteer Centres (Bd. mbr. 1989 to date; Pres. 1992; Past Pres. & Dir.); Western Association of Directors of Volunteers (Past Pres.; mbr. 1980 to date); Greater Victoria Volunteer Bureau Society (former Bd. mbr. & Pres.);

Camosun Coll., Victoria (Past Chrm & founding mbr., Advisory Committee, Volunteer Mgmt Certificate Program 1988-91). MISC: teaching/facilitating experience-volunteer mgmt courses & workshops-Camosun Coll., Vancouver Volunteer Centre, Western Association of Directors of Volunteers conferences, B.C. Association of Volunteer Centres conference, & others.

Gillson, Malca ⊗
Filmmaker, GLOUCESTER FILMS LTD., 105 Gloucester St., Ste. 1, Toronto, ON M4Y 1M2 (416) 920-0732. Born Yorkton, Sask. d. 1 ch. EDUC: Royal Conservatory of Music, ATCM, Performer/Singing 1951. CAREER: Opera Company (Royal Conservatory of Music); Music, Sound & Film Ed., over 90 National Film Board of Canada films; Dir.; Owner, Gloucester Films Ltd., 1989 to date. SELECTED CREDITS: Music Ed., *Helicopter Canada*; Dir./Ed. various NFB films incl.: *Alberta Girls, Musicanada*; *The Last Days of Living*; *Time for Caring*; *Reflections on Suffering*; *Singing: A Joy in Any Language*; *Musical Magic: Gilbert and Sullivan in Stratford*; Dir./Co-Prod., *The Joy of Singing*, Gloucester Films Ltd.; *Make The Words* Sing. HONS: Don Mullholland plaque for Music Ed. (*Helicopter Canada*); awards from various film festivals.

Gingell, The Honourable Judy ■■ ✦
Commissioner of the Yukon, GOVERNMENT OF THE YUKON, 211 Hawkins St., Whitehorse, YT Y1A 1X3 (403) 667-5121, FAX 393-6201. Born Moose Lake, Y.T. 1946. m. Don Gingell. 2 ch. Rick, Tina. EDUC: Selkirk St. Sch., Whitehorse; Yukon Vocational Sch., Whitehorse. CAREER: Band Mgr, Kwanlin Dun First Nation, 1969; Founding Dir., Yukon Indian Brotherhood, 1969; served on Exec., Yukon Indian Women's Association & Founding Dir., Northern Native Broadcasting, 1970s & 1980s; Pres., Yukon Indian Development Corporation, 1980-89; Chair, Council for Yukon Indians, 1989-95; Commissioner of the Yukon (first aboriginal Commissioner), 1995 to date. AFFIL: Yukon/B.C. Red Cross (Patron); Scouts Canada for Yukon (Patron); Girl Guides of Canada (Hon. Pres., Yukon Council); Rotary Club (Hon. mbr.). COMMENT: *"In 1973, travelled to Ottawa on team of leaders that included President of Yukon Indian Brotherhood to hand then Prime Minister Trudeau a document entitled "Together Today for our Children Tomorrow." This historic document contained a statement of grievances from all Yukon First Nations that launched comprehensive land claims negotiations in the Yukon. Under Mrs. Gingell's leadership, the Umbrella and four First Nations Final Land Claims and Self-Government Agreements passed into legislation in 1993 and became law on February 14, 1995."*

Givner, Joan, B.A.,M.A.,Ph.D. 📖 ⊜ ⌀
Professor of English (retired), UNIVERSITY OF REGINA. Born Manchester, UK 1936. m. David Givner. 2 ch. EDUC: London Univ., B.A. (English) 1958, Ph.D.(English) 1972; Washington Univ., St. Louis, M.A.(English) 1963. CAREER: high sch. teaching, US, 1959-61; Lecturer in English, Port Huron Jr. Coll., 1961-65; Lecturer in English, Univ. of Regina, 1965-70; Asst. Prof. of English, 1972-75; Assoc. Prof. of English, 1975-81; Prof. of English, 1981-95. SELECTED PUBLICATIONS: *Katherine Anne Porter: A Life* (Simon & Schuster 1982); *Tentacles of Unreason*, short fiction (Univ. of Illinois Press, 1985); *Unfortunate Incidents*, short fiction (Ottawa: Oberon Press, 1988); *Mazo de la Roche: The Hidden Life* (Oxford Univ. Press, 1989); *Scenes From Provincial Life*, short fiction (Ottawa: Oberon Press, 1991); *The Self-Portrait of a Literary Biographer* (Univ. of Georgia Press, 1993); *In the Garden of Henry James* (Oberon Press, Oct. 1996); "Katherine Anne Porter, Eudora Welty and Ethan Brand" (*International Fiction Review* 1(1) 1974); "The Eudora Welty Collection, Jackson, Mississippi" (*Descant* 23(1) 1978); various other publications. EDIT: Ed., *Wascana Review*, 1984-92. HONS: Mary Ingraham Bunting Fellowship, Radcliffe Coll., 1979-79; Herbert M. Umbach Award for best essay in volume of *Descant*, 1979; First Prize, Short Story, CBC Literary Award Competition, 1992; Award for Excellence in Research, Univ. of Regina Alumni Association, 1992. INTERESTS: gardening. MISC: recipient of various grants & fellowships; 1st recipient of the Award for Excellence in Research, Univ. of Regina Alumni Association. COMMENT: *"My life has been devoted to literature. I have been professor of English, editor of a literary journal, biographer, autobiographer and fiction writer."*

Glasco, Kimberly ■■ ⊗
Principal Dancer, THE NATIONAL BALLET OF CANADA, The Walter Carsen Centre for The National Ballet of Canada, 470 Queen's Quay W., Toronto, ON M5V 3K4 (416) 345-9686, FAX 345-8323, EMAIL info@national.ballet.ca INTERNET http://www.national.ballet.ca Born Eugene, Ore. EDUC: National Ballet Sch., grad. CAREER: joined corps de ballet, The National Ballet of Canada, 1979; promoted to Second Soloist, 1981; left to join American Ballet Theater, 1983; rejoined The National Ballet, 1984; First Soloist, 1986; Prin-

cipal Dancer, 1987 to date. **SELECTED CRED-ITS:** Hanna, *The Merry Widow*; title role, *Raymonda Act III*; Kitri, *Don Quixote*; The Swan Queen/Black Swan, *Swan Lake*; title role, *Giselle*; Princess Aurora, *The Sleeping Beauty*; Nikiya, *La Bayadere Act II*; title role, *Cinderella*; Natalia Petrovna, *A Month in the Country*; Juliet, *Romeo and Juliet*; lead roles in *Etudes, The Four Temperaments, Symphony in C, Serenade, Elite Syncopations, Tchaikowsky Pas de Deux, Divertimento No. 15, Forgotten Land, Diana and Acteon Pas de Deux, The Leaves Are Fading, Paquita, Alice*; featured role, *Dream Dances*; roles in *Voluntaries* & *La Ronde*; has performed with numerous other ballet companies; performed for an AIDS Benefit Royal Gala Performance at Covent Garden in London, England in presence of HRH The Princess of Wales; danced in CBC-TV/Primedia Productions 1989 filming of *La Ronde* & *Alice*, 1989; appeared in Norman Jewison's film *The January Man*, & in *Footnotes*, six-part series hosted by Frank Augustyn on BRAVO! channel. **HONS:** Silver Medal, Sr. Women's Category, Moscow Int'l Ballet Competition, 1981.

Glasgow, Janice I., Ph.D. ⬧ 🕸
Professor, Department of Computing and Information Science, QUEEN'S UNIVERSITY. **EDUC:** Univ. of Alberta, B.Sc.(Comp. Sci.) 1970; Univ. of Waterloo, M.Math.(Comp. Sci.) 1976, Ph.D. 1983. **CAREER:** Research Asst., Teaching Asst. & Lecturer, Dept. of Comp. Sci., Univ. of Waterloo; Asst. Prof., Queen's Univ., 1981-86; Assoc. Prof., 1986-93; Prof., 1993 to date; Visiting Scientist, Cambridge Crystallographic Data Centre, Cambridge Univ., 1995. **SELECTED PUBLICATIONS:** *Diagrammatic Reasoning*, ed. with H. Narayanan & C. Chandrasekaran (AAAI Press, 1995); "Computational Imagery," with D. Papadias (*Cognitive Science* 1992); "Molecular Scene Analysis: Crystal Structure Determination through Imagery," with S. Fortier & F.H. Allen, in *Artificial Intelligence and Molecular Biology*, L. Hunter ed. (AAAI/MIT Press, 1993); "Imagery and AI: Where Do We Go from Here?" (*Computational Intelligence* 1993); "The Imagery Debate Revisited: A Computational Perspective" (*Computational Intelligence* 1993); various other publications; numerous conference & workshop publications. **EDIT:** Ed. Advisory Bd., *Trends in Software*, 1995 to date. **DIRECTOR:** Information Technology Research Corporation of Ontario. **AFFIL:** Canadian Society for Computational Studies of Intelligence (VP 1990-92; Pres. 1992-94); Association for Computing Machinery; American Association for Artificial Intelligence (AAAI); International

Joint Conference on Artificial Intelligence (Int'l Advisory Committee); Brain & Behavioral Science (Assoc.); NSERC Grant Selection Committee for Computer Science (Chair 1995-96); IFIP Technical Committee for Artificial Intelligence (V-Chair 1996 to date). **MISC:** recipient of numerous grants; referee for various journals & granting agencies. **COMMENT:** *"Janice Glasgow is a professor of computer science who specializes in artificial intelligence and its application to molecular scene analysis."*

Glass, Helen Preston, O.C.R.N.,B.Sc.,M.A., M.Ed.,Ed.D.,LL.D. ⬧ ⊕ 🖊
Professor Emerita, School of Nursing, UNIVERSITY OF MANITOBA, Winnipeg, MB R3T 2N2. Born 1917. 1 ch. Susan Jane Glass. **EDUC:** Royal Victoria Hospital Sch. of Nursing, Montreal, R.N. 1939; Univ. of Manitoba, Certificate (Teaching & Supervision in Schools of Nursing) 1958; Columbia Univ., B.Sc.(Nursing Educ.) 1960, M.A. 1961, M.Ed. 1970, Ed.D. 1971; Univ. Paul Valery, France, Certificate (French Grammar & Conversation) 1980. **CAREER:** Supervisor, Anaesthetic Dept., Royal Victoria Hospital, Montreal, 1939-40; Staff Nurse, & supervisory positions, General Hospital, Dunnville, Ont., Abbotsford, B.C., & Victorian General (now Union) Hospital, Prince Albert, Sask., 1941-45; Clinic Nurse, Dr. Blair's Obstetric Clinic, Vancouver, 1952-53; Instructor, Sch. of Nursing, Victoria General Hospital, Winnipeg, 1958-59; Educational Sec., Manitoba Association of Registered Nurses (M.A.R.N.), 1961-62; Instructor, Sch. of Nursing, Univ. of Manitoba, 1962-66; Asst. Prof., 1966-71; Assoc. Prof., 1971-72; Prof., 1972-89; Dir., 1972-79; administrative leave incl. study visits to numerous nursing programs in Europe & attendance at various nursing conferences in N.America, 1979-80; Coord., Grad. Program in Nursing, 1979-84; Short-Term Consultant, World Health Organization & Danish Institute of Health & Nursing Research, 1980-84; Sr. Scholar, Sch. of Nursing, Univ. of Manitoba, 1987-89; Prof. Emerita, 1989 to date. **SELECTED PUBLICATIONS:** "Inferences of Physical Pain and Psychological Distress: II: In Relation to the Stage of the Patient's Illness and Occupation of the Perceiver," with Carrie Byrd Lenburg & Lois Jean Davitz (*Nursing Research* 1970); "Statements on the Expanded Role of the Nurse," with Sally Joy Winkler & Lesley F. Degner (*Nursing Papers* 1974); "Research: An International Perspective" (*Nursing Research* 1977); "Nursing's Vision: Dreams or Reality?" (*The Canadian Nurse* 1981); "Interventions in Nursing: Goal or Task-Oriented?" (*International Nursing Review* 1983); "Nursing Economics in

Canada," with J.A.M. Dick (*The Canadian Nurse/Infirmière Canadienne* 1992); numerous other publications. **AFFIL:** Manitoba Health (Chair, Advisory Committee on Community Nurse Research Centres 1993 to date); Canadian Association of University Schools of Nursing (CAUSN) (Hon. Mbr., Western Reg.); Sigma Theta Tau International Honour Society in Nursing (IOTA Omicron Chapter; Nominating Committee); Univ. of Western Ontario Nursing Honour Society; Kappa Delta Pi Honour Society in Education; Phi Lambda Theta Honour Society in Education; International Council of Nurses (1st VP 1985-89); Canadian Nurses' Association (Pres. Elect 1980-82; Pres. 1982-84; Chrm, Committee on Nominations 1984-86); Manitoba Association of Registered Nurses (Pres., Bd. of Dir. 1966-68); St. Amant Centre (Bd. of Dir.; Chair, Research Committee); Health Advisory Network, Gov't of Man. (prov. appointee, Steering Committee 1989 to date); Manitoba Hospice Association; MATCH; Canadian Health Services Research Association; Manitoba Public Health Association; Canadian Nurses' Foundation; Univ. of Manitoba Alumni Association; Univ. of Manitoba Nursing Educ. Alumni Association; Teachers' Coll., Columbia Univ., Nursing Educ. Alumni Association; World Future Society; North American Nursing Diagnosis Association; Canadian Association for the History of Nursing. **HONS:** Proficiency in Bedside Nursing, Royal Victoria Hospital Sch. of Nursing, 1939; Dr. Katherine E. MacLaggan Fellowship Award, Canadian Nurses' Foundation, 1968-70; Marion Woodward Award & Lecture, Univ. of British Columbia, 1974; Queen's Silver Jubilee Medal, 1977; Woman of the Year Award for Educ., YWCA, 1979; R. Louise McManus Medal, Teachers' Coll., Columbia Univ. Nursing Educ. Alumni, 1984; Award for Outstanding Achievement, Manitoba Association of Registered Nurses, 1987; Community Service Award, City of Winnipeg, 1987; Order of the Buffalo Hunt, Prov. of Man., 1987; Dr. Helen P. Glass Fellowship Award for Doctoral Study est. by the Canadian Nurses' Foundation, sponsored by the Manitoba Association of Registered Nurses & the Univ. of Manitoba Sch. of Nursing, 1987; Officer of the Order of Canada, 1989; Mary Tolle Wright Leadership Founder's Award, Sigma Theta Tau, 1989; Dr. Helen P. Glass Seminar Room dedicated, Univ. of Manitoba, 1990; Jeane Mance Award, Canadian Nurses' Association, 1992; Special Achievement Award, Manitoba Association of Registered Nurses, 1993; LL.D.(Hon.), Memorial Univ. of Newfoundland, 1983; LL.D.(Hon.), Univ. of Western Ontario, 1986; LL.D.(Hon.), St. Francis Xavier Univ., 1991;

LL.D.(Hon.), Univ. of Montreal, 1993; D.Sc. (Hon.), McGill Univ., 1995. **MISC:** 1st Cdn nurse to hold office in Sigma Theta Tau; fed. appointee to the Cdn Delegation to the World Health Assembly, 1983, 1985; numerous presentations & addresses; listed in *Canadian Who's Who* & *Dictionary of International Biography*.

Glass, Joanna McClelland ■ ■ ⊗
Playwright and Novelist. c/o Barbara Hogenson Agency, 19 W. 44th St., Ste. 1000, New York, NY, USA 10036 (212) 730-7306. Born Saskatoon, Sask. 1936. **SELECTED PUBLICATIONS:** *Canadian Gothic* and *American Modern* (2 one-act plays, published by Dramatists Play Service, N.Y., 1977; also in *Best Plays of 1978*, Richards/Chilton, Radnor, PA); *Artichoke* (full-length play, published by Dramatists Play Service, N.Y., 1979); *To Grandmother's House We Go* (full-length play, produced on Broadway, published by Samuel French, N.Y., 1981); *Play Memory* (full-length play, produced on Broadway, published by Samuel French, N.Y., 1981, & NeWest, Edmonton, 1987); *If We Are Women* (full-length play, published by Playwrights Union of Canada, 1994, Samuel French, London, Eng., 1995, & Dramatists Play Service, N.Y., 1996); *Reflections on a Mountain Summer* (novel, published by Alfred A. Knopf, N.Y., 1974; by McClelland & Stewart, Canada; Macmillan, England; & in Germany, Norway & Sweden); *Woman Wanted* (novel, published by St. Martin's Press, N.Y., 1985; & in England, Germany, Italy). **HONS:** Tony nomination, "Play Memory" Broadway production directed by Harold Prince.

Glass, Susan Jane, B.Comm. ⊛ ○
Volunteer. Born Vancouver 1945. m. Arni C. Thorsteinson. **EDUC:** Univ. of Manitoba, B.Comm. 1967. **CAREER:** Computer Systems mgmt & mktg, Air Canada, 1970-86. **VOLUNTEER CAREER:** Dir., Royal Winnipeg Ballet, 1987 to date; Gov., Univ. of Manitoba, 1988-94; Pres., Royal Winnipeg Ballet, 1995 to date; Dir., St. Boniface General Hospital; Dir., St. Boniface General Hospital Research Foundation; Dir., Canadian Club of Winnipeg; Dir., Univ. of Manitoba Alumni Association. **INTERESTS:** motorcycling; fishing; travel; ballet; theatre; art; interior design; women's issues; mentoring of young adults. **COMMENT:** *"As a full-time community volunteer, my commitment is to promoting and enhancing quality of life in Winnipeg."*

Glazer, Carol Lynn, B.Ed.,M.Ed. ■ ■ ⊲ ⊛ ○
Executive Director, EARLY CHILDHOOD INTER-

VENTION PROGRAMS SASKATCHEWAN INC. (home-based program), 3031 Louise St., Saskatoon, SK S7J 3L1 (306) 955-3344, FAX 373-3070. Born Port Radium, N.W.T. 1952. m. Doug. 1 ch. Drew. **EDUC:** Univ. of Saskatchewan, Coll. of Educ., Dept. for the Educ. of Exceptional Children, B.Ed. 1974, classes in teaching speech & language to children who are hearing impaired 1977-79, M.Ed. 1994. **CAREER:** Resource Therapist, Resource Centre for Children with Multiple Handicaps, Alvin Buckwold Centre, Saskatoon, 1974-77; Coord., SEECC Presch. Program, Institute of Child Guidance & Dev., Univ. of Saskatchewan, 1977-78; Coord., Interim Presch. Parent-Ptnr Program, Alvin Buckwold Centre, 1978-79; Family Support Officer, Saskatchewan Association for the Mentally Retarded, 1979-85; Child & Adult Educ. Coord., 1985-88; (educ. leave, grad. studies in educ., 1988-89); Prov. Exec. Dir., Early Childhood Intervention Programs Saskatchewan Inc., 1989 to date. **SELECTED PUBLICATIONS:** co-author with S. Jegard, L. Anderson & W. Zaleski, *A Comprehensive Program for Multi-Handicapped Children. An Illustrated Approach* (Saskatoon; Alvin Buckwold Centre, 1980, reprinted in 1981, published in French in 1984); contributor to 3 other publications. **AFFIL:** Saskatchewan Institute of Applied Science & Technology (Chairperson, Advisory Committee, Early Childhood Educ., Rehab. & Youth Worker Programs 1993 to date); Saskatchewan Action Plan for Children (Advisory Council on Children & Youth 1994 to date); Saskatchewan's Brighter Futures Community Action Program for Children (Advisory Committee 1993 to date); Canadian Association of Family Resource Programs (Sask. Rep. 1993 to date); National Early Childhood Intervention Steering Committee (Exec. Committee 1995 to date); Saskatchewan Parent Education Committee (mbr. 1993 to date); Univ. of Saskatchewan (Software Reference Group, Transition Co-Planner, Dept. of Educ. 1994 to date); Association for the Care of Children's Health; Council for Exceptional Children (Div. for Early Childhood & Div. on Mental Retardation); Family Service Canada; Saskatchewan Teachers' Federation (Early Childhood Educ. Council); Saskatchewan Child Care Association. **HONS:** *A Comprehensive Program for Multi-Handicapped Children* won Joan Kershaw Publication Award, Council for Exceptional Children, 1980.

Glover, Karen, B.A.,B.Ed.,M.B.A.,C.M.C. $

Partner, ERNST & YOUNG, Ernst & Young Tower, Toronto Dominion Centre, Box 251, Toronto, ON M5K 1J7 (416) 943-2351, FAX 943-3244. Born Toronto 1954. m. Chris Creed. 2 ch. **EDUC:** Univ. of Western Ontario, B.A. 1975, B.Ed. 1976; York Univ., M.B.A. 1980. **CAREER:** teacher, Scarborough Bd. of Educ., 1976-78; Consultant/Sr. Consultant, Urquhart Preger and Stern, 1980-83; Consultant, Ernst & Young, 1983-84; Sr. Consultant/Principal, 1984-89; Ptnr in Western Ont. Consulting Practice, 1989-95; Nat'l Dir., Hum. Res., 1995 to date. **AFFIL:** Institute of Management Consultants of Ontario (C.M.C.); Human Resources Professionals' Association of Ontario; Burlington Golf & Country Club; Toronto Board of Trade. **INTERESTS:** skiing; golf.

Glube, The Honorable Chief Justice Constance, B.A.,LL.B.,LL.D.(Hon.) ⚖ ☝

Chief Justice, SUPREME COURT OF NOVA SCOTIA, Law Courts, 1815 Upper Water St., Halifax, NS B3J 3C8 (902) 424-4900. Born Ottawa 1931. m. Richard Glube. 4 ch. John B. Glube, Erica D. Kolatch, Harry S. Glube, S. Joseph Glube. **EDUC:** McGill Univ., B.A. 1952; Dalhousie Univ., LL.B. 1955. **BAR:** N.S., 1956. **CAREER:** part-time retail, 1957-63; Barrister & Solicitor, Kitz, Matheson, 1964-66; Ptnr, Fitzgerald & Glube, 1966-68; Solicitor, Legal Dept., City of Halifax, 1969-74; City Mgr, City of Halifax, 1974-77; Puisne Judge, Supreme Court of N.S. (formerly Trial Div.), 1977-82; Chief Justice, 1982 to date. **SELECTED PUBLICATIONS:** *The Role of the Judge 1985: Justice Beyond Orwell* (Les éditions Yvon Blais Inc.); various published articles. **AFFIL:** Canadian Bar Association; Canadian Judicial Council (Chair, Equality Committee; Chair, Judicial Benefits Committee); Canadian Mental Health Association, N.S. Div. (Hon. Chair); Family Mediation of Canada (Advisory Council); Canadian Institute for the Administration of Justice (Hon. Bd. Mbr.); N.S. Chapter, Canadian Foundation of Ileitis & Colitis; John Howard Society; Cdn Div., International Commission of Jurists; Canadian Judges' Conference; Canadian Institute for the Administration of Justice; Conference of Chief Justices; Shaar Shalom Synagogue; Royal Nova Scotia Yacht Squadron; Halifax Hadassah-Wizo. **HONS:** Q.C., 1974; Award of Merit, City of Halifax, 1977; LL.D. (Hon.), Dalhousie Univ., 1983. **MISC:** various conference lectures; 1st woman City Mgr in Canada; 1st woman Chief Justice in Canada.

Goar, Carol, B.J. ✒

Washington Bureau Chief, *THE TORONTO STAR*, 529 - 14th St. N.W., Washington, DC 20045 (202) 662-7390, FAX 662-7388. Born Hamilton, Ont. 1951. s. **EDUC:** Carleton Univ., B.J. 1974. **CAREER:** Parliamentary Reporter, Canadian Press; Reporter, *Ottawa Citizen*; Reporter, FP News Service; Ottawa Bureau Chief, *Maclean's* Magazine, 1983-85; Nat'l Affairs Columnist, *The Toronto Star*, 1985-94; Washington Bureau Chief, 1995 to date.

Godard, Barbara Thompson, B.A.,M.A., Doct. 🐟 🏛

Associate Professor, English Department, YORK UNIVERSITY, 350 Stong College, 4700 Keele St., North York, ON M3J 1P3 (416) 736-5166, FAX 736-5412. Born Toronto 1941. d. 1 ch. EDUC: Univ. of Toronto, B.A.(English) 1964; Univ. de Montréal, M.A. 1967; Univ. de Paris VIII, Maîtrise 1969; Univ. de Bordeaux, Doctorate 3e Cycle (Littérature comparée) 1971. CAREER: Teaching Asst., Études anglaises, Univ. de Montréal, 1964-65; Toronto secondary schools, 1967-68; Chargée de cours, Univ. de Paris VIII, 1968-70; Visiting Asst. Prof., York Univ., 1971-76; Asst. Prof., 1976-81; Assoc. Prof., 1981 to date; Visiting Prof., Women's Studies, Univ. of Calgary, 1990; Scholar, Shastri Indo-Canadian Institute, 1990. SELECTED CREDITS: Academic Advisor, "The New Woman," CBC *Anthology* (Sept. 17, 1983); "English Canadian Feminist Writers," *In Her Own Eyes*, TV program for Carleton Univ. Women's Studies program (1985); "Alice Munro," Radio-Canada International (Feb. 1991); "Portrait d'Alice Munro," littérature actuelle, Radio-Canada FM (Feb. 17, 1991); news commentary, *Metro Morning*, CBC AM (Nov. 23, 1993); various other TV & radio appearances. SELECTED PUBLICATIONS: *These Our Mothers*, translation of Nicole Brossard's *L'Amer* (Toronto: Coach House, 1983); *Talking About Ourselves: The Literary Productions of Native Women* (Ottawa: CRIAW, 1985); *Bibliography of Feminist Criticism/Bibliographie de la critique féministe* (Toronto: ECW, 1987); *Gynocritics/gynocritiques: Feminist approaches to Canadian and Quebec Women's Writing*, ed. (Downsview, Ont.: ECW, 1987); *Audrey Thomas: Her Life and Work* (Toronto: ECW, 1989); translation of Nicole Brossard's *Picture Theory* (Montreal: Guernica, 1991); *Collaboration in the Feminine: Writing on Women and Culture from "Tessera"*, ed. (Toronto: Second Story Press, 1994); *Intersexions: Issues of Race and Gender in Canadian Women's Writing*, ed. with C. Vevaina (Delhi, 1995); "The Oral Tradition and Contemporary Fiction" (*Essays on Canadian Writing* Summer 1977); "Tales within Tales: Margaret Atwood's Folk Narratives" (*Canadian Literature* Summer 1986); "The Discourse of the Other: Canadian Literature and the Question of Ethnicity" (*Massachusetts Review* 1990); "La Ville en vol: Tracing Les-

bian E-motion through the City" (*Tessera* Summer 1994); more than 100 other publications. EDIT: Guest Ed., *Waves*, 1976-77; joint ed. of a series of French Cdn works in translation, Coach House, 1977-84; French Ed., *Fireweed*, 1978-80; lit. consultant, *New Canadian Encyclopedia*, 1981-82; Founding Co-Ed., *Tessera*, 1982-89, Mng Ed., 1989-93; Guest Ed., *Poetry Toronto*, May 1987; Contributing Ed., *Open Letter*, 1990 to date; Ed. Bd., *Resources for Feminist Research*; Ed. Bd., *Signature*; Ed. Bd., *Dalhousie Review*; Ed. Bd., *Social Semiotics*; Ed. Bd., *Topia: Canadian Cultural Studies*. AFFIL: Association for Canadian & Quebec Literatures (Exec. 1974-76; Chair, Research Committee 1982-88); Association of Canadian University & College Professors of English ; Canadian Comparative Literature Association; Canadian Semiotic Association; Toronto Semiotic Circle; Modern Language Association; Canadian Association of Translation Studies; Literary Translators' Association; Toronto Museum of Childhood; Canadian Amateur Musicians; Recorder Players' Society; Bruce Trail Association; P.E.N. International; CRIAW; Canadian Women's Studies Association. HONS: Archibald Lampman Scholarship in English, 1962; Sir Gilbert Parker Scholarship in English, 1963; Canada Council Doctoral Award, 1967-69; Gabrielle Roy Prize, Association for Canadian & Quebec Literatures, 1988; short list, Felix-Antoine Savard Translation Prize, Columbia Univ., 1991-92; Award of Merit, Association of Canadian Studies, 1995. INTERESTS: hiking; skiing; recorder playing. MISC: recipient, various grants & scholarships; jury mbr., various grants & awards; referee, various publishers & journals; numerous conference papers, guest lectures & invited addresses. COMMENT: *"Barbara Godard is Associate Professor of English, Women's Studies and Social and Political Thought at York University. She has published widely on Canadian and Quebec writers and on feminist literary theory. A translator, she has presented Quebec women writers, Louky Bersianik, Yolande Villemaire and Antonine Maillet, to an English audience."*

Godard, Mira M., C.M.,B.Sc.,M.B.A. ⊗

President, MIRA GODARD GALLERY INC., 22 Hazelton Ave., Toronto, ON M5R 2E2 (416) 964-8197, FAX 964-5912. Born Bucharest, Roumania 1932. m. Reginald Sydney Bennett. EDUC: École du Louvre, Art Hist. 1949; Sorbonne Univ., Sci.dipl. 1950; Concordia Univ., B.Sc. 1954; McGill Univ., M.B.A. 1960. CAREER: Metrology Eng., aircraft industry, Montreal, 1955-61; Founding Sec., Canadian Standards Association; Owner, Godard-Lefort

Gallery, 1961 to date; Owner, Marlborough-Godard Gallery, 1971 to date; Owner, Mira Godard Gallery, 1977 to date. **AFFIL:** Canadian Professional Art Dealers' Association (Founding Mbr. & First Pres.); Fed. Dept. of Public Works (Arts Advisory Committee); Canada Council Travelling Juries; Free Trade (Arts & Cultural Industries) (Sectoral Advisory Committee); Montreal Museum of Fine Arts (Patron); Art Gallery of Ontario (Trustee); Univ. of Western Ontario (Founding Mbr., Advisory Council for Visual Arts); Professional Art Dealers' Association of Canada (Bd. of Dir.); Design Exchange (Planning Committee & Bd. of Dir.). **HONS:** Member of the Order of Canada, 1988.

Godin, Carmen, B.S.W.,R.N.A. ⊕ 🍁
Social Worker, Department of Health and Community Services, GOVERNMENT OF NEW BRUNSWICK, 1175 Main St., Box 5002, Lower Neguac, NB E0C 1MC (506) 776-3833, FAX 776-3849. Born Halifax 1952. cl. Claude Savoie. 2 ch. Tara, Joël. **EDUC:** Dartmouth Community Coll., Registered Nursing Asst. 1971; Univ. of Moncton, Certificate in Gerontology 1985, enrolled, Master's in Social Work program 1996 to date; Univ. of Sherbrooke, B.S.W. 1989. **CAREER:** Nursing Asst., Activities Dir., Nursing Home "Les Résidences Monseigneur Chiasson," 1974-83; Coord., Community Social Day Care for Seniors, 1983-91; Social Worker, Community Svcs for Seniors, 1991-93; Social Worker, Intakes & Investigation, Dept. of Health & Community Svcs, 1993 to date. **AFFIL:** Centre de bénévolat de la Péninsule acadienne (Founding Mbr. 1979); Nursing Home "Les Résidences Monseigneur Chiasson" (Dir. 1986-92); Single Entry Point Program (Designing Committee); N.B. Association of Social Workers (Miramichi Chapter Pres. 1992-93); N.B. Gerontology Association; N.B. Acadian Society (Prov. Bd.). **HONS:** Dr. T. Leroy Creamer Memorial Medal for work in gerontology, 1989. **INTERESTS:** canoeing; cross-country skiing. **COMMENT:** *"I have completed studies while in the working force and raising two children. I believe in the importance of involvement in community and the ability to create change."*

Godkin, Celia, B.Sc.,M.Sc. ■ 🎓 ✿ ⚛
Freelance Author and Illustrator and Assistant Professor, Division of Biomedical Communications, Department of Surgery, Faculty of Medicine, UNIVERSITY OF TORONTO, Medical Sciences Bldg, 1 King's College Cir., Toronto, ON M5S 1A8 (416) 978-2659, FAX 978-6891, EMAIL celia.godkin@utoronto.ca. Born London, UK 1948. s. **EDUC:** London Univ., B.Sc.(Zoology) 1969; Ontario Coll. of Art, Assoc. of OCA (Fine Art) 1983; Univ. of Toronto, M.Sc.(Zoology) 1983. **CAREER:** Herpetologist, Reptile Breeding Foundation, 1974-76; Fisheries Biologist, Ont. Ministry of Natural Resources, 1976-81; freelance author & illustrator, 1983 to date; Asst. Prof., Univ. of Toronto, 1987 to date. **SELECTED PUBLICATIONS:** *Endangered Species: Canada's Disappearing Wildlife*, illus., Clive Roots, author (Toronto: Fitzhenry & Whiteside, 1987); *Wolf Island* (Toronto: Fitzhenry & Whiteside, 1989); *Ladybug Garden* (Toronto: Fitzhenry & Whiteside, 1995–published as *What About Ladybugs?* San Francisco: Sierra Club Books); "Problems of Species Identity in the Lake Ontario Sculpins *Cottus bairdi* and *C. cognatus*," with W.J. Christie & Don E. McAllister (*Canadian Journal of Fisheries and Aquatic Sciences* 1982); "Technique of Making Fish Illustration 8" (*Environmental Biology of Fishes* 1985); "Endangered Species; The Story Behind the Book" (*Guild of Natural Science Illustrators Newsletter* 1988); various other articles incl. many published in the *Guild of Natural Science Illustrators Canadian Newsletter*; approx. 1000 published illustrations. **EDIT:** Founder & Ed., *Guild of Natural Science Illustrators Canadian Newsletter*, 1985-91. **EXHIBITIONS:** solo exhibit, Royal Ontario Museum Staff Lounge, 1984; solo exhibit, Bancroft Art Gallery, 1994; numerous group exhibits incl. the Royal Ontario Museum Staff Lounge, 1984, 1989, 1990, Taiwan Museum, 1986, CANSCAIP Travelling Exhibit, 1992, & York Univ., 1996. **AFFIL:** Guild of Natural Science Illustrators; Canadian Society of Children's Authors, Illustrators & Performers (CANSCAIP); The Writers' Union of Canada. **HONS:** Best Information Book Award, *Wolf Island*, Children's Literature Roundtable of Canada, 1990; Excellence in Teaching Award, Sch. of Continuing Studies, Univ. of Toronto, 1992; Certificate of Appreciation for Excellence in Teaching, Div. of Biomedical Communications, 1994-95. **INTERESTS:** fine art; fostering an appreciation of the natural world in children through presentations in schools - with the long-term goal of creating environmental awareness & concern. **COMMENT:** *"An author/illustrator of children's information books, with a master's in zoology, Godkin teaches scientific illustration at the Division of Biomedical Communications, University of Toronto."*

Godfrey, Ellen, B.A. ■ $ 📖 ♡
President, SOFTWORDS RESEARCH INTERNATIONAL, LTD., 4355 Gordon Head Rd., Victoria, BC V8N 3Y4 (604) 727-6522, FAX 477-5958, EMAIL ellen@pinc.com. Born Chicago

1942. m. William David Godfrey. 2 ch. Rebecca, Samuel. EDUC: Stanford Univ., B.A.(Hist.) 1964. CAREER: freelance ed., copywriter & public rel'ns, 1968-73; Ed., Press Porcépic, 1973-75; Gen. Mgr, 1975-77; Pres., 1977-83; Founding Dir. & Pres., Softwords Research International, Ltd., 1981 to date. SELECTED PUBLICATIONS: *Case of the Cold Murderer*; *Murder Among the Well To Do*; *Murder Behind Locked Doors* (St. Martin, US; Penguin, Canada; Virago, UK; Todlicher Absturz, Germany); *Georgia Disappeared* (Penguin; Virago, UK; Todlicher Absturz, Germany); *By Reason of Doubt*, true crime. AFFIL: Crime Writers of Canada (Western Pres.; VP); Working Opportunity Fund (Advisory Bd.); Vancouver Island Technology Association (Bd.); Univ. of Victoria (Bd. of Dir., Co-op Educ. Council); B.C. Premier's Advisory Council on Science & Technology. HONS: Confederation of Canada Award; Special Edgar Award, Mystery Writers of America. INTERESTS: Medieval history; physics; literature; the French language; Cdn political life. COMMENT: *"Ellen Godfrey, author and businesswoman, co-founder of Softwords, a leading software research company, is also the author of four mystery novels and one true crime novel. Ellen's background in business and experience in consulting form the basis for her mystery novels."*

Godsoe, Dale Sullivan, B.A.,B.Ed., M.Ed. ■ ⌘ Ⓢ ○

WORLD YMCA EXECUTIVE COMMITTEE, 6560 Geldert St., Halifax, NS B3H 2C8 (902) 422-9416, FAX 423-0410. Co-Chair, IWK-GRACE HEALTH CENTRE FOUNDATION. Born Halifax 1944. m. Gerald. 3 ch. Suzanne, Stacey, Laura. EDUC: Dalhousie Univ., B.A.(Hist.) 1965, B.Ed. 1966, M.Ed. 1988. CAREER: teacher, Halifax District Sch. Bd., 1966-72. DIRECTOR:Maritime Telegraph and Telephone Company, Limited; Owl Communications; Viacom Canada. AFFIL: YWCA of/du Canada (Dir.; former Nat'l Pres.); Canadian Council for International Peace and Security (Dir. & Past Chair); Maritime Provinces Higher Education Commission (Council); Halifax Metro United Way Campaign (Chair, Leaders of the Way & Chair 1995); Halifax Metro United Way (Dir.); Atlantic Film Festival (Dir.); Canadian Centre for Philanthropy (Dir.); WTN (Women's Television Network) Foundation (Dir.); Drugs Directorate Expert Advisory Committee on Blood Regulation, Health Canada; Mount Saint Vincent Univ. (Bd. of Gov.; Chair 1987-94; Chair, Nominating Committee 1994); Canadian Journalism Foundation (Bd. Mbr.); Calmeadow Nova Scotia (Dir.); Halifax 1999 - Halifax's 250th Birthday (Chair, Culture Committee); Halifax City Committee to Promote the Arts (Mbr.); UNIFEM Canada (Cdn Bd.); Institute for the Study of Women, Mount Saint Vincent Univ. (Advisory Bd.); National Association of University Board Chairs & Secretaries (Hon. Officer; Bd. Mbr. 1991-94; V-Chair 1992-94); Mount Saint Vincent Univ. Alumnae (Hon. Alumna). PAST AFFIL: Halifax District Sch. Bd. (Mbr. 1977-80; Chair 1978-80); Canadian Parents for French (N.S. Alternate Nat'l Dir. 1979-81); Children's Aid Society of Halifax (Bd. Mbr & V-Chair 1980-85); Women's Employment Outreach (Bd. Mbr. 1982-87); YWCA of Halifax (Bd. Mbr. 1979-88; Pres. 1984-87); Public Legal Education Society (Bd. Mbr. 1986-89); Old Burying Ground Foundation (Bd. Mbr. 1988-91); CANFAR National Network (Chair, N.S. 1992-93); Halifax Grammar Sch. (Bd. Mbr. 1985-91; Chair 1992-93); Pure Gold, Symphony Nova Scotia fund raiser (Co-Chair, Fund Raising 1992). HONS: Canada 125 Medal, 1992; Canadian Volunteer Award of Distinction. MISC: weekly panellist, *Information Morning*, CBC (1988-93); Selection Committee, Peter F. Drucker Award; Imagine Awards Panel, Canadian Centre for Philanthropy. COMMENT: *"My work in education, communications and women's equality issues has led to work on a broad range of Boards. I have spent many years in the field of higher education, while my interest in communications has involved me in both the telecommunication and the communications fields. I work in women's equality issues, and am now adding an international security aspect to my work."*

Goerzen, Janice Lee Nicholls, R.N.,B.Sc.N.,F.R.C.S.C.,F.S.O.G.C., F.A.C.O.G.,M.D.,M.Sc. ■ ⌘ ⊕

Past Clinical Assistant Professor of Obstetrics, Gynecology and Pediatrics. Born Hayward's Heath, UK 1943. m. Cornelius Goerzen. EDUC: Galt Nursing Sch., Lethbridge, Alta., R.N. 1962; Univ. of Alberta, B.Sc.N. 1965; Univ. of Calgary, M.D., M.Sc. 1977; London, UK, grad. studies in Pediatric Gynecology 1984. CAREER: Pediatric Head Nurse, Lethbridge Municipal Hospital, 1962; Obstetric Head Nurse, Holy Cross Hospital, Calgary, 1964; Obstetric Nursing Instructor, Holy Cross Hospital Sch. of Nursing, Calgary, 1964-69; Assoc. Dir., 1969-72; Maternal-Child Nursing Instructor, Mount Royal Coll., Calgary, 1972; Obstetrician & Gynecologist, Foothills Hospital, Alberta Children's Hospital & Tom Baker Cancer Centre, Calgary, 1985-95; Head, Div. of Pediatric Gynecology, Alberta Children's Hospital, 1985-95; Clinical Asst. Prof., Obstetrics & Gynecology, Univ. of Calgary, 1985-96.

SELECTED PUBLICATIONS: *Review of Maternal and Child Nursing*, with P.L. Chinn (St. Louis: C.V. Mosby Co., 1975); "Blood Pressure: Physiologic Controls," with S.D. Abbott (*Canadian Nurse* 1976); "Ovulation Induction by Ambulatory Self Administration of Gonadotropin Releasing Hormone (GnRH)," with B. Corenblum, D. Wiseman & P.J. Taylor (*Fertility & Sterility* 1984); "Dysfunctional Uterine Bleeding in Adolescence" (*SOGC Journal* 1993); "Outcome of Surgical Reconstructive Procedures for the Treatment of Vaginal Abnormalities," with G.P. Gidwani *et al* (*Adolescent and Pediatric Gynecology Journal* 1994); various other publications. DIRECTOR: J.L. Goerzen, Professional Corporation. AFFIL: Royal Coll. of Physicians & Surgeons (Fellow); Alberta Coll. of Physicians & Surgeons; Alberta Medical Association; Society of Obstetricians & Gynecologists of Canada; Alberta Society of Obstetricians & Gynecologists; North American Society for Pediatric & Adolescent Gynecology (past Bd. Mbr.); American Coll. of Obstetricians & Gynecologists. HONS: St. John Ambulance Award Nat'l Scholarship for Post Grad. Study, 1975; Research Award, Alberta Heart Foundation, 1977; Best Resident Paper, International Society of Reproductive Medicine, 1985; Outstanding Resident, American Association of Gynecologic Laparoscopists, 1985. INTERESTS: music; art; dogs. MISC: numerous invited lectures. COMMENT: *"My major professional contribution has been in the development of a program to advance information, knowledge and service to children with gynecologic needs. I have also enjoyed teaching and the provision of obstetric and gynecologic medical care."*

Gold, Anne Judith Crozier, B.Sc.N., M.Sc.N. ■ ⊕ ♂
Manager, Adolescent Health Services, NORTH YORK GENERAL HOSPITAL, Teen Clinic - 4 South, 4001 Leslie St., North York, ON M2K 1E1 (416) 756-6776, FAX 756-6822. Born Oshawa, Ont. 1957. m. Jeffrey Gold. 2 ch. Rebecca Lauren, Aaron Marc. EDUC: Univ. of Toronto, B.Sc.N.(Nursing) 1979, M.Sc.N. (Nursing) 1982, Diploma (Acute Care Nurse Practitioner) 1995. CAREER: Staff Nurse, Hospital for Sick Children, 1979-82; Clinical Nurse Specialist, Bloorview Children's Hospital, 1982-84; Clinical Nurse Specialist, British Columbia Children's Hospital, 1984-86; Clinical Instructor, Univ. of Toronto, 1986-87; Clinical Instructor, Hospital for Sick Children, 1987-88; Nursing Unit Administrator, Mount Sinai Hospital, 1988-90; Clinical Nurse Specialist, Oncology Research, Mount Sinai Hospital, 1990-91; Clinical Nurse Specialist & Nurse

Practitioner, Adolescent Medicine, 1991-94; Mgr, Adolescent Health Svcs, 1994 to date. AFFIL: Canadian Association for Adolescent Health; Coll. of Nurses of Ontario. INTERESTS: adolescent sexuality; adolescent prenatal care; teen parents & parenting. MISC: 1st acute care nurse practitioner in a community hospital in Ont.; est. programs for teen prenatal care & teen parenting in collaboration with community physicians & health care practitioners; est. clinic for adolescent health in community hospital in collaboration with multidisciplinary health team. COMMENT: *"Committed to the promotion of adolescent health through clinical practice, community outreach and collaboration with teens, parents, schools and other youth-related agencies. Very proud mother of Rebecca and Aaron."*

Goldberg, Shirley, B.A.,M.A. ⊛ ♨
Instructor in Film Studies, MALASPINA UNIVERSITY COLLEGE, 900 Fifth St., Nanaimo, BC V9R 5S5 (604) 753-32450, EMAIL goldberg@ mala.bc.ca. Born Portland, Ore. 1923. d. 2 ch. EDUC: Reed Coll., B.A.(Lit. & Languages) 1945; Univ. of California, L.A., M.A.(English) 1949. CAREER: Instructor in English & Lit., L.A. City Coll., 1965-66; Instructor, Southwestern Oregon Community Coll., 1966-71; Instructor, Malaspina Coll., 1972-89; Instructor in Film Studies, Malaspina Univ. Coll., 1989 to date. SELECTED PUBLICATIONS: film reviews for *Canadian Dimension*; assorted film & drama reviews for various publications; *Fantastic Visions: Study Guide for Knowledge Network Course in Science Fiction Film and Literature*. AFFIL: Film Studies Association of Canada; Union for Democratic Communications; Global Village of Nanaimo (Bd.); Phi Beta Kappa (elected 1945). INTERESTS: film; society; culture; travel; hiking; camping; boating; cross-country skiing. MISC: Trustee, Barrett Memorial Award; mbr., Cine-Club Jury, Int'l Film Festival, Portugal, 1989; represented Canada, Int'l Film Society Association, East Germany, 1989. COMMENT: *"I have always been interested in too many things–pursued too many directions. But, overall, I have worked to encourage critical thinking and to preserve diversity in our culture."*

Goldblatt, Michaele-Sue, M.S.W.,C.S.W., R.S.W. ■■ ☺ ⊕
Vice President, ROYALE ACCOMMODATIONS and Former Executive Director, CFAS CHILD AND FAMILY ADOPTION SERVICES SOCIETY OF BRITISH COLUMBIA, W. Vancouver, (604) 921-6425, FAX 921-6427, EMAIL msg@cafe.net. Born Philadelphia, Penn. (grew up in Hamilton, Ont.) 1947. sep. 3 ch. Anthony, Daniel &

Matthew Gyra. **EDUC:** McMaster Univ., B.A.(English & Hist.) 1968; Univ. of Toronto, M.S.W., all course work for Doctor of Social Work 1978-80; Columbia Univ. Sch. of Social Work, N.Y. City, grad. studies; National Federation for Open Adoption Education, San Francisco, Open Adoption Professional Certification 1992; courses in Family Law, Psychopathology of Childhood, Divorce Mediation & Family Mediation. **CAREER:** Case Asst., Children's Aid Society of Pennsylvania, Philadelphia, 1968-70; Field Instructor, Univ. of Toronto, Fac. of Social Work, 1974-78; Reg'l Social Worker, Browndale residential treatment centre, 1972-75; Dir. of Info. Svcs, 1974-75; Intake Coord. & Sr. Social Worker, 1975-77; Sr. Clinical Social Worker, 1977; Consultant to agencies, individuals & families, 1977-79; Research Asst., Fac. of Social Work, Univ. of Toronto, 1979; private practice specializing in adoption, 1980-95; Social Work Consultant, CRCL Canadian Romanian Children's Link, 1990-92; Social Work Dir. & Consultant, International Orphans Support Group of Canada & ROSG Consulting Inc., 1992-93; Exec. Dir., CFAS, 1992-96; VP, Royale Accommodations, 1996 to date. **SELECTED PUBLICATIONS:** "Legal Considerations regarding Adoption" (*OASW Newsmagazine*, Vol. 22, No. 2, Toronto, Summer 1995). **AFFIL:** Association for Divorced, Separated & Remarried People (co-founder 1988). **MISC:** has given courses/workshops/seminars re adoption to various groups incl. Family Court Judges of Prov. of Ont., Adoptive Parents' Association of B.C., American Adoption Congress, Lionsgate Hospital. **COMMENT:** "*Truly, my boys have brought me the greatest happiness in my life and I would describe myself first as a mother, then as a daughter and only later would I define myself in terms of my professional activities. I believe I am well known as an advocate for children and have specialized in child welfare work, particularly with regard to adoption. I have tried to behave with integrity in both my personal and professional life and I believe I have done so.*"

Goldblatt, Rose, ARCM,FRSA ⊗ ⌘
Pianist and University Professor (retired). 342 Elm Ave., Westmount, QC H3Z 1Z5. Born Montreal 1913. m. Henry Finkel. **EDUC:** Royal Coll. of Music, London, UK. **CAREER:** began career as concert pianist at age six & continued for more than 50 yrs.; has concertized in Canada, US, UK; Assoc. Prof., Fac. of Music, & Chair, Piano Dept., McGill Univ. **AFFIL:** Royal Society of Arts, UK (Fellow); European Piano Teachers' Association (Cdn correspondent); Montreal Classical Music Fes-

tival (Artistic Dir.); Quebec Music Teachers' Association (Past Pres.); Canadian Federation of Music Teachers' Association (VP, Que.). **HONS:** at age 16 won the Montreal Strathcona Scholarship to study at the Royal Coll. of Music, UK; Scholarship, Ladies Morning Musical Club, Montreal; Diamond Jubilee Award for outstanding contribution to the association & to music in performance & teaching, Canadian Federation of Music Teachers' Association, 1995. **INTERESTS:** theatre; literature; science; geology; travel. **MISC:** among the 1st musical artists to perform when the CBC opened its TV svc.; studied with Kendall Taylor & Egon Petri; listed in the *International Who's Who of Music* & the *Canadian Encyclopedia of Music and Musicians.*

Goldbloom, Ruth M., B.Ph.Ed., C.M. ■■ ⚪ ⌘
President, PIER 21 SOCIETY, P.O. Box 611, Halifax, NS B3J 2R7 (902) 425-7770. Chancellor, TECHNICAL UNIVERSITY OF NOVA SCOTIA. Born New Waterford, N.S. 1923. m. Dr. Richard B. 3 ch. Dr. Alan Goldbloom, Barbara Hughes, Dr. David Goldbloom. **EDUC:** Mount Allison Univ., Arts 1940-42; McGill Univ., B.Ph.Ed. 1944. **VOLUNTEER CAREER:** numerous volunteer positions, The Izaak Walton Killam Hospital for Children, 1967-75; Regent, Mount Allison Univ., 1971-77 & 1987-91; mbr., Bd. of Gov., Mount Saint Vincent Univ., 1974-85 (2 terms); Chrm, Bd. of Gov., 1977-80; Dir., Voluntary Planning Association, 1978-87; Chrm, Project 1, Futures for Women, Mount Saint Vincent Univ., 1979-84; Chrm, Metro United Way Campaign, Halifax-Dartmouth, 1989-90; mbr. of Bd., Halifax Foundation, 1983 to date; Bd. mbr., Canadian Council of Social Development, 1988-90; mbr., Nat'l Advisory Council, IMAGINE, 1988-93; Chairperson, Dalhousie Univ. Annual Fund Drive, 1993 to date; Pres., Pier 21 Society, 1993 to date; Chancellor, Technical Univ. of Nova Scotia, 1994 to date. **HONS:** several incl. hon. Doctor of Humane Letters, Mount Saint Vincent Univ., 1985; hon. LL.D., Dalhousie Univ., 1987; Member of the Order of Canada, 1992.

Golden, Anne, B.A.,M.A.,Ph.D. ■ ⚪
President, UNITED WAY OF GREATER TORONTO (Canada's largest fundraising campaign), 26 Wellington St. E., Toronto, ON M5E 1W9 (416) 777-2001, FAX 777-0962. Born Toronto 1941. m. Ronald. 2 ch. Beth Golden, Karen Golden. **EDUC:** Univ. of Toronto, B.A. 1962, Ph.D. 1970; Columbia Univ., M.A. 1964. **CAREER:** Lecturer, American Pol. Hist., several universities incl. Univ. of Toronto & York Univ., 1964-74; Research Coord., Bureau

of Mun. Research, Gov't of Ont., 1973-78; Special Advisor to Leader of Opposition, 1978-81; Dir. of Allocations, United Way of Greater Toronto, 1982-86; Campaign Dir., 1986-87; Pres., 1987-95, 1996 to date. HONS: Award for United Way of Greater Toronto, Canadian Council of Christians & Jews.

Goldenberg, Bobbye, B.Sc.,M.A. ■ ⌖ ♡
Chief Executive Officer and Executive Director, Seneca Foundation, SENECA COLLEGE OF APPLIED ARTS AND TECHNOLOGY, 13990 Dufferin St., King City, ON L0G 1K0 (416) 491-5050, EMAIL bobbyeg@exec.seneca.on.ca. Born 3 ch. Bobbi D. Weichers, Jonathan Duncan, Amanda Duncan. 2 stpch. Stacy Goldenberg, Darin Goldenberg. EDUC: Appalachian State Univ., B.Sc.(English/Educ'l Media) 1965, M.A.(Higher Educ.) 1978. CAREER: teacher, various positions, high sch. & public sch., North Carolina, 1965-76; Instructor, English Dept., Appalachian State Univ., Boone, N.C., 1976-78; Instructor, Comm., Caldwell Community Coll., Continuing Educ., Boone/Lenoir, N.C., 1978-80; Coord., Credit Programs, Coll. of Continuing Educ., Appalachian State Univ., 1978-80; Prof., English Div., Seneca Coll., 1980-86; Chair, Arts & Sci., 1987-89; Dean, Liberal Studies, 1989-92; VP, Student Svcs, 1992-95; CEO & Exec. Dir., Seneca Foundation, 1996 to date. EDIT: est. prov. newsletter, General Arts & Science Association, 1988. AFFIL: National Society of Fund Raising Executives; Management Development Institute, (Steering Committee; Dir.); Student Federation Council, Inc. (Chair, Bd. of Dir. 1992-96); Academic Council, Seneca Coll. (Mbr. 1989-91; Mbr. ex-officio); SNY Sport Promotion (Bd. of Dir. 1995-96); United Way (Deputy Chair, Educ. Div., Metro Toronto 1994; Campaign Chair, Seneca Coll. 1993, 1994, 1995); Bethesda Lutheran Church (Bd. of Dir.). HONS: 3 teaching awards while teaching in N.C., 1965-76; Service in Professional Dev. Award, Central Region, Human Resource Development, 1988; Excellence Award for Achievement & Innovation, Seneca Coll., 1990; Int'l Excellence in Educ. Award, National Institute of Staff & Organizational Development, Univ. of Texas, 1991; Chair of the Year, United Way Employee Campaign, 1993. INTERESTS: fitness; writing; sports; music; Internet; puzzles of all kinds. MISC: Certified Ringette Coach; softball coach & player; Organist, Bethesda Lutheran Church, 1991 to date; workshop leader; frequent speaker; number of community bds.

Goldin Rosenberg, Dorothy,
M.E.S. ■ ☺ ⌖ ⊕
Women's Health and the Environment and

Global Education Consultant, Women for a Just and Healthy Planet, THE WOMEN'S NETWORK ON HEALTH AND THE ENVIRONMENT, 736 Bathurst St., Toronto, ON M5S 2R4 (416) 516-2600, FAX 531-6214. Born Montreal 2 ch. Pamela Rosenberg Vennin, Matthew Jay Rosenberg. EDUC: McGill Univ., Physiotherapy 1957; York Univ., M.E.S. 1992; Ont. Institute for Studies in Educ., doctoral studies (global transformative learning) in progress. CAREER: phys. therapist, public & private practice, Canada & US, 1957-67; Consultant, "Challenge for Change Program," Studio D, the Women's Unit, National Film Bd. of Canada, 1975-86; Dev. & Disarmament Coord., Canadian Council for International Cooperation, 1986-88; Proj. Dir., *A Directory of Women in Canada Specializing in Global Issues: development, environment, peace and the related areas of economics and social injustice*, 1988-90; Global Educ. Consultant, 1990 to date. SELECTED CREDITS: Research Consultant & Assoc. Prod., *Women's Health & The Environment with a Focus on Breast Cancer* (film). SELECTED PUBLICATIONS: "James Bay, Progress or Disaster" (*Our Generation* 1973); *The New Alchemists: A Resource Book*; *If You Love This Planet: A Resource Book*; *Disarmament and Development: A Roundtable Discussion in Preparation for the United Nations Conference on the Relationship between Disarmament and Development* (United Nations Association of Canada); "Feminism and Peace," in *Women and Men: Interdisciplinary Readings on Gender*, Greta Hoffman Nemiroff, ed. (Fitzhenry and Whiteside, 1987); *Les Femmes S'en Melent, Making a World of Difference: A Directory of Women in Canada Specializing in Global Issues*; chapters in *Collateral Damage: Environmental and Other Impacts of the War in the Gulf* (1991); "A Feminist Framework for Political Action on Peace and Global Transformation in Radical Adult Environmental Education," in *Proceedings of 12th Annual Conference of the Canadian Association for the Study of Adult Education* 1993; "Challenging the Impacts of New Technologies on Our Lives: Women and the Earth Connecting for Life," in *Theory and Practice* (Canadian Association for the Study of Adult Education, CASAE, 1994); *Women, Rape and War: Strategies for Education, Support to Women and Policy Change* (Canadian Research Institute for the Advancement of Women, 1994); "Feminist Transformative Learning and Advocacy in the Politics of Prevention," "Ecology and Health" (*CASAE*, 1995); "Integrating sectors in the platform for action" & "Peace, health and ecology: Relationships for feminist action" (*Canadian*

Women's Studies, post-Beijing issue, Summer 1996); various OP ED articles in newspapers & magazines incl. *TheGazette, The Toronto Star, The Globe & Mail, Le Devoir, Peace Magazine*, & *Contact*, the newsletter of the CCIC. AFFIL: Women, Environments, Education & Development Foundation (WEED) (Dir.); Women for a Just & Healthy Planet (Dir.); National Action Committee on the Status of Women (Environmental Committee); Canadian Coalition for Nuclear Responsibility; Ont. Energy Environment Caucus, Ontario Environment Network; Voice of Women for Peace/La Voix des Femmes; Project Ploughshares; Social Justice Committee of Montreal. HONS: Award for Environmental Stewardship, U.N. Environment Program, 1984; Gov. General Award; Canada 125 Medal, 1992. INTERESTS: int'l folkdancing; music; biking; walking; travelling; reading. MISC: principal research consultant, *Speaking Our Peace: Women, Peace and Power*, NFB; frequent public speaker; mbr., Beijing Preparatory Committee for 1995 UN Women's Conference, Voice of Women for Peace/La Voix des Femmes.

Gom, Leona, B.Ed.,M.A. 📜 ⊗
Writer. Born Alta. 1946. EDUC: Univ. of Alberta, B.Ed., M.A. CAREER: teacher, Univ. of Alberta, 2 yrs.; teacher, English & Creative Writing, Douglas/Kwantlen Coll., 14 yrs.; Ed. & Poetry Ed., *Event*, 10 yrs.; Writer-in-Residence, Univ. of Alberta, 1987-88; Writer-in-Residence, Univ. of Lethbridge, 1989; Writer-in-Residence, Univ. of Winnipeg, 1990; teacher, grad. & undergrad. creative writing courses, Univ. of British Columbia, 3 yrs. SELECTED CREDITS: writer, *The Inheritance* (radio play), CBC; writer, *Sour Air* (radio play), CBC. SELECTED PUBLICATIONS: poetry: *Kindling* (Fiddlehead Press, 1972); *The Singletree* (Sono Nis Press, 1975); *Land of the Peace* (Thistledown Press, 1980); *NorthBound* (Thistledown Press, 1984); *Private Properties* (Sono Nis Press, 1986); *The Collected Poems* (Sono Nis Press, 1991); novels: *Housebroken* (NeWest Press, 1986); *Zero Avenue* (Douglas & McIntyre, 1989); *The Y Chromosome* (Second Story Press, 1990); *After-Image* (Second Story Press, 1996; St. Martin's Press, 1996); various journals & anthologies in Canada, the US, the UK, Germany, the Czech Republic, Australia & New Zealand. HONS: Authors' Association Award for best book of poetry, for *Land of the Peace*, 1980; Ethel Wilson Award for Fiction for *Housebroken*, 1986. MISC: has given numerous readings & workshops on writing.

Gonzalez, Josefina, B.Sc.,M.S. ▦ Ⓢ
Research Scientist, FORINTEK CANADA CORP.,

2665 East Mall (UBC), Vancouver, BC V6T 1W5 (604) 222-5620, FAX 222-5690, EMAIL josefina@van.forintek.ca. Born Bataan, Philippines 1934. m. Jesus T. Gonzalez. 3 ch. EDUC: Univ. of Santo Tomas, Manila, B.Sc.(Chem. Eng.) 1955; State Univ. of New York at Syracuse, Coll. of Forestry, M.S. 1961. CAREER: Head, Chem. Composition Section, Forest Products Research Institute, Laguna, Philippines, 1957-66; Sr. Technologist, Columbia Cellulose Company Ltd., Annacis Island, B.C., 1966-67; Research Asst., Univ. of British Columbia, Jan.-May 1968; Research Technologist, Western Forestry Products Lab., Cdn Forestry Svc., Vancouver, 1968-79; Research Scientist, Forintek Canada Corp., 1979 to date. SELECTED PUBLICATIONS: several publications in wood science journals. AFFIL: Society for Canadian Women in Science & Technology (Pres. 1988-89); National Roundtable on the Environment & the Economy (Mbr. 1989-94);Canadian Tree Improvement Association (Chair, Wood Quality Working Group 1991-93); Vancouver Science & Technology Advisory Council (Chair). HONS: Outstanding Alumna Award, Univ. of Santo Tomas, 1987. MISC: recipient, Rockefeller Foundation Travel Grant, 1958 & Alice Wilson Grant, 1981; Mbr., Steering Committee, Conference on Women & Sustainable Dev., Canadian Perspectives, Vancouver, May 1994.

Good, Cynthia, B.A.,M.A. ▯ ▯ ◈
Vice-President, Publisher and Editor-in-Chief, PENGUIN BOOKS CANADA LIMITED, 10 Alcorn Ave., Ste. 300, Toronto, ON M4V 3B2 (416) 925-2249, FAX 925-0068. Born Toronto 1951. d. EDUC: Univ. of Toronto, B.A.(English Lit.) 1973, M.A.(English Lit.) 1974. CAREER: Co-Founder & Mbr., Menagerie Players, 1969-73; Ed., Dorset Publishing, 1978-80; Mktg Mgr, Doubleday Book Clubs, 1980-82; Ed. Dir., Penguin Books Canada Limited, 1982-87; VP & Ed.-in-Chief, 1987 to date. AFFIL: Canadian Centre for Studies in Publishing, Simon Fraser Univ. (Chair & Bd. Mbr.); Univ. of Toronto (University Coll. Committee). HONS: Reuben Wells Leonard Award; Univ. of Toronto Open Fellowship; Woodhouse Scholarship; Canada Council Doctoral Award; Ont. Grad. Scholarship.

Goode, Roslyn, B.Sc.N.,M.Sc.N. ▪▪ ⊕
Director of Professional Nursing Practice, NORTH YORK GENERAL HOSPITAL (acute care hospital), 4001 Leslie St., North York, ON M2K 1E1 (416) 756-6218, FAX 756-6364. Born Toronto. m. 4 ch. EDUC: Univ. of Toronto, B.Sc.N., M.Sc.N. CAREER: Public Health Nurse, City of Toronto; Childbirth Edu-

cator, Women's College Hospital; Dir., North Branch, Childbirth Education Association; Clinical Instructor, Univ. of Toronto, Fac. of Nursing & Sch. of Continuing Educ.; Clinical Nurse Specialist, Toronto General Hospital & St. Michael's Hospital; Dir. of Nursing, North York General Hospital. AFFIL: Sigma Theta Tau International Honour Society of Nursing; Registered Nurses' Association of Ontario (Chrm, CNSIG 1987-88); Association of Nurse Executives of Greater Toronto Area; Ontario Hospital Association (Reg. 3 Advocacy & Representation Committee); Canadian Coll. of Health Service Executives.

Goodreau, Ida, B.A.,B.Comm.,M.B.A. ■ $ Managing Director, TASMAN PULP AND PAPER CO. LTD., Box 2186, Auckland, New Zealand (649) 356-7809, FAX 356-7845. Born Ont. 1951. d. EDUC: Univ. of Western Ontario, B.A.(English/Econ.) 1980; Univ. of Windsor, B.Comm. 1981, M.B.A. 1986. CAREER: Union Gas Ltd., 1978-92; Fletcher Challenge Canada, 1992-94; Mng Dir., Tasman Pulp and Paper Co. Ltd., 1994 to date. DIRECTOR: Timberwest Forest Ltd. AFFIL: National Institute of Disability Management & Research; New Zealand Pulp & Paper Industry Association (Exec. Committee); Forest Industries Training & Education Council; United Way of Greater Vancouver (Bd. 1992-94). COMMENT: *"What has characterized my career has been variability. I have learned to be flexible, adaptable and quick, as I have moved through the disciplines of finance, operations, strategic planning, human resources and general management in the energy and forestry industries."*

Goodwin, Betty ■ ⊗ Artist. c/o Galerie René Blouin, 372 Ste. Catherine St. W., Montreal, QC H3B 1A2. Born Montreal 1923. m. Martin. 1 ch. (dec.) EXHIBITIONS: numerous solo exhibitions incl.: Penthouse Gallery, Montreal, 1962; Bau-XI Gallery, Vancouver, 1972; Galerie B., Montreal, 1974; Musée d'art contemporain, Montreal, 1976; Galerie France Morin, Montreal, 1981, 1982, 1983; Univ. of Vermont, 1984; Sable-Castelli Gallery, Toronto, 1985, 1987, 1988, 1989, 1991, 1993; Art Gallery of Ontario, 1987; Vancouver Art Gallery, 1987; New Museum, N.Y., 1987; Musée des Beaux-Arts, Montreal, 1988; Kunstmuseum, Berlin, 1989; Sao Paulo Biennale, 1989; Edmonton Art Gallery, 1990; Univ. Art Museum, Long Beach, Calif., 1992; Galerie René Blouin, 1986, 1989, 1990, 1991, 1992, 1993, 1995, 1996; *Icons*, Mackenzie Art Gallery, Regina, 1996; numerous nat'l & int'l group shows incl.: Fawbush Gallery, N.Y. 1993; La Ferme du Buisson,

France, 1994; *Signs of Life*, Art Gallery of Windsor, 1995; National Gallery of Canada, 1996; British International Print Show; National Gallery Canada; Bologna Art Fair; Art Cologne; Museum Van Hedendaagse Kunst Gent, Belgium. COLLECTIONS: numerous public & corp. collections incl.: National Gallery of Canada; Art Gallery of Ontario; National Museum of Women in the Arts, Washington, DC; various private collections. AFFIL: Ontario Coll. of Art (Fellow). HONS: Lynch-Stauton Award of Distinction, 1983; Banff Centre National Award Visual Arts, 1984; Prix Borduas, 1986; Guggenheim Foundation Fellowship, 1988; Ph.D.(Hon.), Univ. de Montréal, 1992; Ph.D.(Hon.), Univ. of Guelph, 1993. INTERESTS: friends; travel; reading; films. MISC: cited in numerous nat'l & int'l catalogues.

Goold, Susan R. ⊗ Artist, PETALS, 8 Carr Cres., Kanata, ON K2K 1K4 (613) 592-2476. Born San Diego, Calif. 1939. m. David W. 3 ch. Donna, Jeffrey, Karen. EDUC: Ottawa Teachers' Coll., 1959. CAREER: teacher, Buckhorn Sch. of Fine Art, 1992 to date; Creator/Ptnr, Petals, 1994 to date. EXHIBITIONS: Rideau Valley Art Festival, Westport, Ont.; National Capital Fine Art Festival (1995). AFFIL: Kanata Civic Art Gallery (Dir. 1992-95); Ottawa Watercolour Society (Fellow; Treas. 1992-95); Art Lending of Ottawa (Pres. 1991); Bells Corners Art League (Past Pres.); Kanata Art Club (Past Pres.). HONS: Volunteer Service Award, Prov. of Ont., 1989; Volunteer Recognition Certificate, City of Kanata, 1993; People's Choice Award, Ottawa Watercolour Society, 1993; Award of Excellence & Paraskeva Clark Award for most innovative piece, Bells Corners Art League, 1994. INTERESTS: watercolour; design; Cdn wildflowers & garden scenes. MISC: initiated Kanata Artists' Studio Tour. COMMENT: *"A watercolourist and, as a late bloomer, I created Petals, a business that markets casual wear featuring my designs. This wearable art is silk-screened onto clothing."*

Gordon, Alison ■ 📖 🖊 Crime Writer. 58 Playter Blvd., Toronto, ON M4K 2W3. Born New York City 1943. m. Paul Bennett. EDUC: primary & secondary educ., N.Y., Tokyo & Rome; Queen's Univ., 1960-65. CAREER: Program Asst., *The Way It Is*, CBC, 1968; Prod., *Up Against the Wall*, CJOH-TV, 1969; freelance broadcaster & writer, worked with Patrick Watson to develop a TV concept, *Earthrise*, 1970-74; Co-Host, *Here Today*, CBC, Halifax, 1974; freelance (incl. work as Story Prod., CBC Radio & regular appearances on *Up Canada*, CBC TV), Toronto, 1974-76; positions from Prod. to Nat'l Ed. & Sr. Assignment Ed., *As It Happens*, CBC Radio, 1976-78; freelance writer & novelist, 1978 to date; sports writer (baseball beat), *The Toronto Star*, 1979-83. **SELECTED PUBLICATIONS:** various articles & stories for major magazines incl. *National Lampoon & Weekend Magazine; Foul Balls: Five Years in the American League* (1984); *The Dead Pull Hitter* (1988); *Safe at Home* (1990); *Night Game* (1992); *Striking Out* (1995); *Prairie Hardball* (1997), all books published by McClelland & Stewart. **AFFIL:** International Association of Crime Writers (North American VP); PEN Canada (Bd. 1989-94; Pres. 1994); The Writers Union of Canada (Nat'l. Council 1990-92); Crime Writers of Canada (Chair 1990-92). **HONS:** National Newspaper Award Citation of Merit for Sportswriting, 1979; *Dead Pull Hitter* short-listed for the 1988 Stephen Leacock Award for Humour & the 1988 Toronto Book Award; *Striking Out*, short-listed for the Arthur Ellis Award for Best Canadian Crime Novel, 1995. **MISC:** frequent commentator on radio & TV; has led various writing workshops & was Writer-in-Residence with the City of York Public Library in 1993; first woman to cover baseball in the major leagues; a movie based on *Dead Pull Hitter* is currently in development.

Gordon, Dara, B.Comm.,LL.B. ■ ⚖
Partner, PALMER HUNT MURPHY, Box 247, Halifax, NS B3J 2N9 (902) 492-2000, FAX 429-5215. Born Halifax 1952. m. Gerald J. McConnell. 2 ch. Devon McConnell-Gordon, Ashley McConnell-Gordon. **EDUC:** St. Mary's Univ., B.Comm. 1972; Dalhousie Univ., LL.B. 1979. **BAR:** N.S., 1979. **CAREER:** Mgr, Newfoundland Telephone Company, Ltd., 1972-74; Mgr, Maritime Telephone and Telegraph Company, 1975-76; Assoc., Palmer Hunt Murphy, 1979-86; Ptnr, 1986 to date. **DIRECTOR:** Nova Scotia Gaming Corporation; Atlantic Lottery Corporation. **AFFIL:** Canadian Bar Association (Past Chair, Taxation Law Subsection; Mbr., Bus. Law Subsection); N.S. Barristers' Society; Canadian Tax Foundation; Dalhousie Law Sch. Alumni Association (Dir.); Hong Kong Canada Business Association (former Dir.).

Gordon, Elizabeth, B.S.H.Ec., M.C.Ed. ✋ ⌁
Career Counsellor, CYPRESS HILLS REGIONAL COLLEGE, 129 - 2nd Ave. N.E., Swift Current, SK S9H 2C6 (306) 778-5471, FAX 773-2384. Born Gull Lake, Sask. 1943. m. Melvin McNeill. 2 ch. **EDUC:** Univ. of Saskatchewan,

B.S.H.Ec.(Family & Consumer Studies) 1986, M.C.Ed. 1990. **CAREER:** owns & manages family farm, 1961 to date; Research Asst. (Farm Stress), Centre for Agricultural Medicine, Univ. Hospital, Saskatoon, 1986-87; Univ. Coord. & Career Counsellor, Cypress Hills Regional Coll., 1988 to date; Community Dev. Worker, Farm Stress Proj., Saskatchewan Agriculture & Food, 1992; Research Analyst, Rolling Hills Health District Needs Assessment, June-Aug. 1994. **SELECTED PUBLICATIONS:** "Stress in the farm family: Strategies for empowerment," *Agricultural Health and Safety: Workplace, Environment, Sustainability*, Ed. H. McDuffie (Boca Raton, Fla.: CRC Press, 1995); "Stress in the farm family: Implications for adult education," with B.J. Pain, *Proceedings of the 11th Annual Conference of the Canadian Association for the Study of Adult Education* (Saskatoon: Univ. of Saskatchewan, 1992); numerous conference presentations. **AFFIL:** Prairie Ecosystem Study (PECOS) (Community Rep., Mgmt Committee); Saskatchewan Education, Training & Employment (Working Group on Student Mobility); Saskatchewan Labour Force Dev. Bd. (Rural Women's Rep., Women's Reference Group); Univ. of Saskatchewan (Senate); Saskatchewan Women's Agricultural Network (Dir. 1992-95); Saskatchewan Association for Lifelong Learning; Canadian Association of College & University Student Services; Canadian Home Economics Association; Association of Saskatchewan Home Economists. **HONS:** Hannon Scholarship, 1985; Hope Hunt Post-Grad. Scholarship, 1986; First Prize, National Undergrad. Writing Competition, Canadian Home Economics Federation, 1986; Silver Jubilee Scholarship, Canadian Home Economics Association, 1987; Post-Grad. Scholarships, Coll. of Grad. Studies & Research, 1987, 1988; Distinguished Accomplishment Award, Student Affairs Div., Canadian Association of College & University Student Services, 1992; Professional Dev. Award, Student Affairs Div., Canadian Association of College & University Student Services, 1993. **INTERESTS:** farming; reading; knitting; sewing; gardening; cooking; watercolour painting; photography. **COMMENT:** *"My area of specialty has been farm stress and the difficult times inherent in modern farm life. My contributions have been to farm-stress literature and the design and delivery of educational programs for professionals, producer groups and farm families."*

Gordon, Irene M., Ph.D.,CGA ⌁ $
Associate Professor, Faculty of Business Administration, SIMON FRASER UNIVERSITY, Burnaby, BC V5A 1S6 (604) 291-4226, FAX 291-4920,

EMAIL irene_gordon@sfu.ca. Born Kansas City, Mo. 1951. **EDUC:** Simon Fraser Univ., B.A.(Econ. & Commerce) 1975, M.A.(Econ.) 1977, Ph.D. 1981; Certified General Accountant of B.C. (CGA) 1983. **CAREER:** Asst. Prof., Simon Fraser Univ., 1981-92; Assoc. Prof., 1992 to date; Dir. of Teaching, Fac. of Bus. Admin., 1992-96. **SELECTED PUBLICATIONS:** *Internal Control in Canadian Corporations: A Management Perspective*, with L.D. Etherington (Toronto: Canadian Institute of Chartered Accountants & the Society of Management Accountants of Canada, 1985); "Consumer's Surplus Measures and the Evaluation of Resources," with J.L. Knetsch (*Land Economics* Feb. 1979); "Criticizing Positive Accounting Theory," with L.A. Boland (*Contemporary Accounting Research* Fall 1992); various other publications. **EDIT:** Ed., *Canadian Accounting Education and Research News*, 1986-87. **AFFIL:** Canadian Academic Accounting Association (Mbr. of Exec. 1987-90; Pres. 1988-89; Past Pres. 1989-90; Chair, Haim Falk Contribution to Accounting Thought Award 1993-94); CGA-Canada (Educ. Advisory Council 1993-96; Research Committee 1984-96). **HONS:** Xerox Grad. Fellowship, 1979-80; Excellence in Teaching Award, Simon Fraser Univ., 1984-85. **INTERESTS:** reading mystery novels; travelling; learning about different cultures. **MISC:** numerous conference presentations; reviewer for various journals, publishers & granting agencies; recipient of various grants. **COMMENT:** *"I am committed to contributing to my discipline of accounting through three avenues. These are teaching, research and service."*

Gordon, Judy Dawn, M.L.A. ✦

Member of the Legislative Assembly (Lacombe-Stettler), **GOVERNMENT OF ALBERTA**, 503 Legislature Building, Edmonton, AB T5K 2B6 (403) 427-1807. Born Moose Jaw, Sask. 1948. m. Allan. 1 ch. Greg Gordon. **CAREER:** Acctnt, Olthius, Albach and Co., 1973-77; Acctnt/Office Mgr, Wagner's Stores Ltd., 1977-86; self-employed Acctnt, 1986 to date; Councillor, Town of Lacombe, 1986 to date; Mayor, Town of Lacombe, 1989-93; M.L.A. (Lacombe-Stettler), Gov't of Alta., 1993 to date; Mbr. of numerous Standing Policy Committees, Advisory Panels & Review Bds., Prov. of Alta., 1993 to date. **AFFIL:** Lord Lascelles Chapter I.O.D.E. (Past Regent); Kinette Club of Lacombe; P.C. Party of Alberta.

Gordon, Kayy ☼ ⊙

Founder and President, **GLAD TIDINGS ARCTIC MISSIONS SOCIETY**. Assistant Pastor, **GLAD TIDINGS FELLOWSHIP**, 3456 Fraser St., Vancouver, BC V5V 4C4 (604) 873-3621, FAX 876-1556. Born Maidstone, Sask. 1933. s. **EDUC:** Christian International Coll., Bach. Theol. 1978. **CAREER:** Missionary & Supervisor, Glad Tidings Missionary Society, Vancouver, 1956 to date; Founder & Pres., Glad Tidings Arctic Missions Society, 1980 to date; Founder & Principal, Glad Tidings Bible Sch., Rankin Inlet, N.W.T., 1980 to date; Asst. Pastor, Glad Tidings Fellowship, Vancouver, 1993 to date. **SELECTED PUBLICATIONS:** *God's Fire on Ice*, with Lois Neely (3 printings, Logos Publishers, 1977; Welch Punlishing Co., 1982, 1990); *Arctic Ablaze*, with Lois Neely (Welch Publishing, 1990). **HONS:** Northerner of the Year, *Up Here Magazine*, 1991. **INTERESTS:** people! **MISC:** travelled extensively in N.Am., preaching in many churches; visited over 30 countries & preached in most of them; travelled & resided extensively in the Arctic by various means. **COMMENT:** *"I see myself as an ordinary person called by an extraordinary God to fulfil a rather unusual and unique purpose as a pioneer missionary in the high Arctic privileged to work with the warmest-hearted people–the Inuit people of the north."*

Gordon, Lee ☒ ♥

President, **LEE GORDON PRODUCTIONS**, 4 Deer Park Cres., Ste. 2C, Toronto, ON M4V 2C3 (416) 925-6682. Born Shaunavon, Sask. **EDUC:** Iowa State Univ., Drama 1944; Columbia Univ., Writing 1946-47. **CAREER:** various positions from Prod. Asst. to Film Ed. to Prod., Films for Children, Inc., NY, 1949-56; Prod. Mgr, *Perspective Series*, NFB, 1956-57; Prod., Hollywood, CA, 1958-59; VP & Co-Owner, Westminster Films Limited, 1959-84; Consultant to Film Dept., Xerox, US, 1970-72; currently Prod. Assoc., Images Communication Arts Corp., N.Y.C.; Pres., Lee Gordon Productions, 1974 to date. **SELECTED CREDITS:** Script Supervisor/Film Ed./Assoc. Prod. various shows 1949-56 incl.: *Man Against Crime, The Guy Lombardo Show, Woman Without Shadow, Molly, Cop-Hater*; Prod., *The Lost Missile* (feature), 1959; Co-Prod, *Nikki, Wild Dog of the North* (feature), Westminster/Disney; Prod., *The Last Act of Martin Weston* (feature); Assoc. Prod., *Too Outrageous* (feature). **AFFIL:** Directors' Guild of Canada (Founding & Hon. Mbr.); Script Supervisors' Local, N.Y.C. (Founding Mbr.); St. Clair Club; Association of Motion Picture Producers & Laboratories of Canada (1959-84). **HONS:** Bronze Award (*Communication*), Int'l Film & TV Festival of N.Y., 1967; Bronze Plaque (*The Inner Mind of Milton Whitty*), Nat'l Committee on Films for Safety, Chicago, 1963; Bronze Plaque (*The Return of Milton Whitty*), Nat'l

Committee on Films for Safety, Chicago, 1966; Bronze Award (*The Trouble With Words*), Int'l Film & TV Festival of N.Y., 1968; Bronze Award (New Colleges), Int'l Film & TV Festival of N.Y., 1967; Bronze Medal (*A Way Out*), N.Y. Int'l Film Festival, 1972; Red Ribbon (*A Way Out*), American Film Festival, 1972; Best Public Rel'ns Film (*Shebandowan: A Summer Place*), ETROG, Canadian Film Awards, 1971; at the 1976 U.N. Habitat Conference, *Canwel* was 1 of the 4 (out of 220) films selected for exhibition & discussion; Bronze Award (*Nuclear Fuel Waste Management*), Houston Int'l Film Festival, 1979; Westminster's films won numerous awards from around the world. INTERESTS: Literature; films; theatre. COMMENT: *"Became one of the first and youngest women Hollywood producers. Has produced and/or directed 100 information and feature films and is currently developing film properties."*

Gorham, Deborah, Ph.D. 🐟 📜
Professor of History and Director, Pauline Jewett Institute of Women's Studies, CARLETON UNIVERSITY, Ottawa, ON K1S 5B6 (613) 788-6645, FAX 788-2154. Born New York City 1937. m. Toby Gelfand. 1 ch. David Keith. EDUC: McGill Univ., B.A.(Phil.) 1959; Univ. of Wisconsin, M.A.(Hist.) 1963; Univ. of Ottawa, Ph.D. 1982. CAREER: Asst. Prof., Carleton Univ., 1969-78; Assoc Prof., 1978-88; Prof., 1988 to date; Scholar, Center for Research on Women & Gender, Stanford Univ., 1991-92; Scholar, Beatrice M. Bain Research Group, Univ. of California at Berkeley, 1991-92; Dir., Pauline Jewett Institute of Women's Studies, Carleton Univ., 1994 to date. SELECTED PUBLICATIONS: *The Victorian Girl and the Feminine Ideal* (Bloomington: Indiana Univ. Press, 1982); *Vera Brittain: A Feminist Life* (Oxford & New York: Basil Blackwell, Publishers, 1996); *Up and Doing: Canadian Women and Peace*, ed. with Janice Williamson (Toronto: Women's Press, 1990); *Caring and Curing: Historical Perspectives on Women and Healing in Canada*, ed. with Diane Dodd (Univ. of Ottawa Press, 1994); "'The Friendships of Women': Friendship, Feminism and Achievement in Vera Brittain's Life and Work in the Interwar Decades" (*Journal of Women's History* Winter 1992). AFFIL: Canadian Committee on Women's History; Canadian Historical Association; Canadian Friends of Peace Now; Temple Israel (Bd. Mbr.). HONS: Carleton Univ. Scholarly Achievement Award, 1982, 1986; Carleton Univ. Arts Fac. Bd. Teaching Award, 1987; Carleton Univ. nominee for the Society for Teaching & Learning in Higher Education, 3M Canada Inc., 1987. MISC: numerous conference presentations. COMMENT: *"I am a feminist scholar and teacher who has been a faculty member of the Department of History at Carleton University for 25 years."*

Gosbee, Rebecca, R.N.,M.Sc.N. 🕘 ⊕
Executive Director and Registrar, ASSOCIATION OF NURSES OF PRINCE EDWARD ISLAND, 17 Pownal St., Charlottetown, PE C1A 3V7 (902) 368-3764, FAX 628-1430. Born Charlottetown 1951. s. EDUC: Prince Edward Island Sch. of Nursing, R.N. 1973; Dalhousie Univ., B.N.(Nursing) 1980; Univ. of Toronto, M.Sc.N.(Nursing) 1984. CAREER: Clinical Nurse Specialist, Critical Care, Toronto Western Hospital, 1985-86; Clinical Nurse Specialist, Respiratory, Queen Elizabeth Hospital, Charlottetown, 1986-90; Instructor, Univ. of New Brunswick Distance Educ., 1987-96; Exec. Dir., Association of Nurses of P.E.I., 1990 to date. AFFIL: Canadian Nurses' Association (Advisor); Clinical Nurse Specialist Interest Group (P.E.I. Rep.; Treas. 1989-93; Reviewer of Abstracts for Nat'l Biennial Conference 1989, 1993, 1995); Canadian Nurses' Respiratory Society (P.E.I. Rep. 1987-91); P.E.I. Lung Association (Sec. 1987-89; Health Educ. Committee 1987-90; Chair, Public Rel'ns Committee 1987-90; Coord., Adult Asthma Educ. Program 1987-90; VP 1989-91); P.E.I Salvation Army Red Shield Appeal (Campaign Coord.); Canadian Nurses' Foundation; National Health Action Lobby (Prov. Coord.); Prov. Gov't Advisory Committee on AIDS; Canadian Nurses' Protective Society (Dir.). INTERESTS: health care for elderly. MISC: numerous conference presentations & blind abstract reviews. COMMENT: *"Generally happy person enthusiastic about professional and personal life. Job opportunities have enabled me to accomplish more than I ever expected. Having passed the first 40 years of my life, I look forward with great anticipation to the next 40. Goal: doctorate in nursing."*

Goss, Joanne H., B.A.,LL.B.,C.Med. ■ 🪭
Lawyer, Chartered Mediator, Arbitrator, COOK, DUKE, COX, 2700 Commerce Place, 10155 - 102 St., Edmonton, AB T5J 4G8 (403) 429-1751, FAX 424-5866. CAREER: Lawyer, Mediator, Arbitrator, Cook, Duke, Cox; Sessional Instructor, Alternate Dispute Resolution, Fac. of Law, Univ. of Alberta, 1990 to date. SELECTED PUBLICATIONS: Ed., "Alternate Dispute Resolution" (*Alberta Law Review* Special Edition, 1995); *Consensus Building: The Canadian Perspective* (Tokyo Univ., Tokyo, Japan, 1995); *Grievance Mediation*, co-author (Canada Law Books Inc., 1994); *Alternate Dispute Resolution Teaching Materials* (Univ. of

Alberta, Fac. of Law, 1992); *Mediation Theory & Skills* (Alberta Arbitration & Mediation Society, Mar. 1990); "Mediation," Chapter 18, *Injury Evaluation: Medico-Legal Principles* (Butterworth Canada, 1991). **AFFIL:** Canadian Dispute Resolution Foundation (Dir.); Arbitration & Mediation Institute of Canada Inc. (Chartered Mediator Certification Committee; Past Pres.); Alberta Arbitration & Mediation Society (Chrm, Ethics Committee; Past Pres.); Alberta Family Mediation Society (Past Pres.); Canadian Bar Association, Alberta Branch (Past Chair, Alternate Dispute Subsection – Northern); Society of Professionals in Dispute Resolution; Int'l; The Network Interaction for Conflict Resolution; International Association of Public Participation Practitioners; Law Society of Alberta; Edmonton Bar Association. **HONS:** appointed Chartered Mediator by the Arbitrators' & Mediators' Institute of Canada, 1994. **INTERESTS:** her family; skiing; sailing; hiking. **MISC:** various local & int'l conference presentations. **COMMENT:** *"Joanne Goss is a lawyer practising mediation, facilitation, arbitration and dispute resolution systems design in the following areas: commercial, environmental, agriculture, discipline, labour relations, personal injury, family and multiple party. She is an active trainer teaching mediation, facilitation, negotiation and arbitration to both the public and private sectors."*

Gossen, Olinda ⦿ ♥

President, INTERNATIONAL WOMEN'S ASSOCIATION OF PRINCE EDWARD ISLAND, 105 Hunter's Creek Dr., Charlottetown, PE C1E 1X7 (902) 566-2854. Born Villa Barboza, Brazil 1951. m. George Gossen. 4 ch. **CAREER:** Owner/Operator, The Redwood Restaurant, Charlottetown, PEI, 1970-84; staff, various restaurants, Charlottetown, 1984-91; Customer Svc. Rep., Toronto-Dominion Bank, 1994-96. **AFFIL:** International Women's Association of P.E.I. (Pres.); P.E.I. Multicultural Council (Sec. & Bd. Mbr. 1995-96); Ethnocultural & Native Health Association of P.E.I. (Bd.); Canadian-Lebanese Association of P.E.I. **HONS:** Certificate of Appreciation for Volunteer Contribution, Educ. Race-Relation Committee, 1993; Certificate for Volunteer Contribution on Multiculturalism, Educ. Race-Relation Committee, 1994; Pin for Recognition for Volunteer Works on Multiculturalism, P.E.I. Multicultural Council, 1994; Certificate of Recognition for Volunteer Works in the Community, Mr. George Proud, M.P., 1994. **INTERESTS:** dancing; aerobics; travelling. **COMMENT:** *"I am friendly, hard-working, a good mother and adapt readily to any situation. What I have been working toward with our group is not only for homemakers and other women to socialize and learn new things relevant to their lives, but for them to have self-esteem and rights."*

Gossmann, Pamela, B.Sc.N. ⊕

Assistant Nursing Unit Manager, Orthopaedics, CALGARY GENERAL HOSPITAL, 841 Centre Ave. E., Calgary, AB T2E 0A1 (403) 268-9446, FAX 268-9222. Born Windsor, Ont. 1962. m. Dan. 3 ch. Randall, Emily, Garrett. **EDUC:** Univ. of Windsor, B.Sc.N. 1984. **CAREER:** Staff Nurse, Univ. of Alberta Hospitals, 1984-86; Unit Based Instructor, 1986-88; Asst. Nursing Unit Mgr, Calgary General Hospital, 1988 to date. **AFFIL:** Canadian Orthopaedic Nurses' Association (CONA). **HONS:** Depuy Continuing Educ. Award, Canadian Orthopaedic Nurses' Association, 1992. **INTERESTS:** family; continuing educ.; outdoors; biking; crafts. **COMMENT:** *"I work very hard at developing myself professionally to provide the best quality of patient care in the hospital setting. In my work I supervise staff, assist with educational requirements for staff, and work with patients and families to understand their health conditions and meet their needs for discharge or continued care."*

Gotlieb, Phyllis, B.A.,M.A. ▯ ▨ ▨

Writer. 19 Lower Village Gate, Ste. 706, Toronto, ON M5P 3L9 (416) 482-4509. Born Toronto 1926. m. Calvin Gotlieb. 3 ch. **EDUC:** Univ. of Toronto, B.A.(English) 1948, M.A. (English) 1950. **SELECTED PUBLICATIONS:** *Sunburst*, sf. (Fawcett Gold Medal Books, 1964; Berkely, 1978; Gregg Press (hc) 1978; transl. into Dutch, Norwegian & German); *Why Should I Have All The Grief?* (Macmillan of Canada, 1969); *Within the Zodiac*, poetry (McClelland & Stewart, 1964); *Ordinary Moving*, poetry (Oxford, 1969); *Doctor Umlaut's Earthly Kingdom*, poetry (Calliope Press, 1974); *Work of A.M. Klein*, essay (A.M. Klein Symposium, Ottawa, 1974); *O Master Caliban!*, sf. (Harper and Row, 1976; Bantam/Seal 1979; transl. into German, Italian & Japanese); *A Judgement of Dragons*, sf. (Ace, 1980); *Emperor, Swords, Pentacles*, sf. (Ace, 1982); *Son of the Morning and Other Stories* (Ace, 1983); *The Kingdom of the Cats*, sf. (Ace, 1985); *Tesseracts2*, co-ed. (Press Porcépic, 1987); *Heart of Red Iron*, sf. (St. Martin's Press, 1989); "Blue Apes" (*Tesseract*, Nov. 1995). **AFFIL:** Science Fiction Writers of America. **HONS:** nominee (*Ordinary Moving*), Gov. General's Award, 1969.

Gotlieb, Sondra ▪ ▯ ∕

Writer. 127 Roxborough Dr., Toronto, ON M4W 1X5 (416) 922-3304, FAX 924-8547.

Born Winnipeg 1936. m. Allan. 3 ch. **EDUC:** Univ. of Manitoba; Carleton Univ. **CAREER:** Co-Ed., *Where to Eat in Canada*; Columnist, *The Toronto Sun*; Columnist, *The Ottawa Sun*; Columnist, *The Financial Post*; Ed. Page Columnist, *Washington Post*; currently humour columnist, *The Globe and Mail*. **SELECTED PUBLICATIONS:** *The Gourmet's Canada* (Toronto: New Press, 1972); *Cross Canada Cooking* (North Vancouver: Hancock House, 1976); *True Confections* (Toronto: Musson, 1978); *Wife of; First Lady, Last Lady* (Toronto: McClelland and Stewart, 1981); *Washington Rollercoaster*; articles have appeared in various periodicals, incl. *Vanity Fair, New York Times, Saturday Night* Magazine, *Maclean's* Magazine, & *Ottawa Journal*. **HONS:** Leacock Prize for Humour, *True Confections*. **INTERESTS:** gardening. **COMMENT:** *"My principal current interests are as an essayist and humorist. I am also working on a novel."*

Gott, Carol, B.Sc.A. 🏵 ⌒

Executive Director, SOUTH EAST GREY COMMUNITY OUTREACH, Box 51, Markdale, ON N0C 1H0 (519) 986-3692, FAX 986-2022. Born Sault Ste. Marie, Ont. 1957. m. Richard Gott. 3 ch. William James Gott, Sean Patrick Gott, Benjamin Richard Gott. 1 foster ch. Susan Elizabeth Gallagher. **EDUC:** Univ. of Guelph, B.Sc.A.(Child Studies) 1980. **CAREER:** teacher, Rotary Children's Centre, Guelph, Ont., 1980-82; teacher, Tri-Ministry Proj., Barrie & District Association For People With Special Needs, 1982-86; Consultant, Infant Dev. Program, Wellington-Dufferin-Guelph Health Unit, Orangeville, Ont.; Coord., South East Grey Community Outreach, Markdale, 1986-91; Exec. Dir., 1991 to date. **SELECTED PUBLICATIONS:** *Rural Child Care Now. We're Worth It* background discussion paper (1995). **AFFIL:** Ontario Coalition for Better Child Care (Pres.); National Coalition for Rural Child Care (Sec.); Early Childhood Resource Network, Grey County; Ontario Rural Child Care Committee (Advocacy Chair 1994); Feversham Minor Ball Club (Little League Baseball Coach). **HONS:** Women of Change Award, Ontario Women's Directorate, 1994. **INTERESTS:** community volunteering; music; crafts; sewing. **MISC:** mbr., Implementation Committee, Ontario Coll. of Teachers, 1995. **COMMENT:** *"Carol Gott is actively involved in improving community services/supports to rural families locally, provincially and nationally. She strongly advocates for community ownership and participation of local services."*

Gourley, Ann, B.A.,LL.B. ■■ ⌐

Partner, BULL, HOUSSER AND TUPPER (Barristers & Solicitors), 3000 Royal Centre, 1055 W. Georgia St., P.O. Box 11130, Vancouver, BC V6E 3R3 (604) 641-4949, FAX 687-6575. **EDUC:** Queen's Univ., B.A.(Drama) 1972; Univ. of Ottawa, LL.B. 1980. **CAREER:** Ptnr, Marketplace International, Toronto, 1974-77; articled student, Ladner Downs, Vancouver, 1980-81; Assoc., Bull, Housser and Tupper, 1981-88; Ptnr, 1988 to date; area of practice: commercial incl. debt financing & restructuring, acquisitions & sales, business documentation.

Govier, Katherine, B.A.,M.A. 📖 ⌑

Writer. 54 Farnham Ave., Toronto, ON M4V 1H4 (416) 924-9704. Born 1948. 2 ch. Robin, Emily. **EDUC:** Univ. of Alberta, B.A.(Hons., English) 1970; York Univ., M.A.(English) 1972. **CAREER:** Instructor in English, Ryerson Polytechnic Univ., Toronto, 1973-75; Assoc. Ed., *Weekend Magazine*, 1978; Visiting Lecturer, Creative Writing, York Univ., 1982-86; Research Fellow, Leeds Univ., UK, 1987; Writer-in-Residence, Parry Sound Public Library, May-Sept. 1988; Writer-in-Electronic Residence, 1988-91; Coord., Writers in Electronic Residence, 1992-93; Writer-in-Residence, Toronto Public Library System, Oct. 1994-Apr. 1995. **SELECTED CREDITS:** participated onscreen & off in *Academy on the Short Story*, TVOntario; radio dramatization of 3 stories from *Before and After, Morningside*, CBC, Spring 1989; TV dramatization commissioned by CBC for *The Immaculate Conception Photography Gallery*. **SELECTED PUBLICATIONS:** *Angel Walk* (1996); *The Immaculate Conception Photography Gallery*, a collection of short stories (Little Brown Canada, 1994); *Hearts of Flame* (Viking Canada, 1991; paperback Penguin Canada, 1992); *Before and After*, a collection of short stories (Viking Canada, 1989; Penguin Canada, 1990); *Between Men* (Viking Canada, 1987; Penguin Canada, 1988); *Fables of Brunswick Avenue*, a collection of short stories (Penguin Canada, 1985; Penguin, UK, 1986); *Going Through the Motions* (Toronto: McClelland & Stewart, 1982; Toronto; Seal Books, 1983; New York; St. Martins Press, 1983); *Random Descent* (Macmillan of Canada, 1979; New American Library, 1980; Penguin Canada & UK, 1986); *Without a Guide*, contemporary women's travel adventures, anthology (McFarlane, Walter & Ross, 1994); feature articles in Cdn & British newspapers & magazines incl. *Maclean's, Saturday Night, Toronto Life, Chatelaine, Homemakers, The Canadian Forum, Flare, The Toronto Star, The Globe and Mail, Quest, This Magazine, Harpers & Queen* (UK); *New Society* (UK), *The Observer* (UK); short fiction & non-fiction in various magazines & anthologies. **AFFIL:** PEN Canada; The Writers' Union of Canada (former mbr., Status of Women Committee & Library Committee; Ont. Rep. 1987-88); Toronto Arts Awards (Lit. Jury 1986 & 1991); Writers' Development Trust (Chair 1989-92); Canadian Conference of the Arts (English-language Writing/Publishing Rep., Bd. of Gov. 1989-90). **HONS:** *The Immaculate Conception Photography Gallery*, shortlisted, Trillium Award, 1994; *Hearts of Flame*, City of Toronto Book Award, 1992; *Between Men*, shortlisted, Talking Book of the Year, Canadian Institute for the Blind, 1991; "The Immaculate Conception Photo Gallery" (short story), 3rd Prize, CBC Literary Contest, 1988; *Random Descent*, Author's Award, Periodical Distributors of Canada, 1980; "Radical Sheik," *Canadian Business*, National Magazine Award & Author's Award, Periodical Distributors of Canada, 1979; *Random Descent*, shortlisted, *Books in Canada* First Novel Award, 1979. **COMMENT:** *"Katherine Govier is a native of Edmonton who has lived in Calgary, Washington, D.C., and London, UK, and now lives in Toronto with her husband and two children. She has taught at Ryerson and York University in Toronto and at Leeds University in UK. Govier has previously published three collections of short stories and four novels. Her novel,* Hearts of Flame, *received the 1992 City of Toronto Book Award."*

Gowdy, Barbara ■ 🗋 📖 ☒
Writer. 19 Spruce St., Toronto, ON M5A 2H6 (416) 920-9365, FAX 920-9365. Born Windsor, Ont. 1950. d. **EDUC:** York Univ., Theatre Arts 1970-71. **CAREER:** Ed. & Mng Ed., Lester & Orpen Dennys, 1974-79; has taught creative writing at Ryerson Polytechnic Univ. & the Univ. of Toronto; critic & interviewer. **SELECTED PUBLICATIONS:** *The Rabbit and the Hare*, an anthology of poems & stories, published under the name of Barbara Purchase (1982); *Through the Green Valley* (Canada: General Publishing, 1988); *Falling Angels* (Canada: Somerville House, 1989; Random House, 1991); *We So Seldom Look on Love*, a short story collection (Canada: Somerville House, 1992); *Mister Sandman* (Canada: Somerville House, 1995); short stories in various magazines. **AFFIL:** Writers' Union of Canada; P.E.N. Canada; Toronto Humane Society. **HONS:** Finalist, Trillium Book Award, 1992; First Prize, Torgi Award, 1992; Annual Contributor's Prize, *Canadian Fiction Magazine*, 1992; chosen as one of Canada's Best 10 Young Canadian Novelists, *Quill & Quire*; Finalist, Giller Prize, 1995; Finalist, Governor General's Award for Fiction, 1995. **MISC:** has

been published in 13 countries including US, UK, France, Germany, Norway and Turkey.

Grace, Noëlle A.E., M.D.,F.R.C.S.(c), F.A.C.S.,F.A.A.P. ⊕
Paediatric Surgeon, NORTH YORK GENERAL HOSPITAL, 4001 Leslie St., Ste. 138, Willowdale, ON M2K 1E1 (416) 756-6223. Born London, Ont. m. Morris S. Shohet. 2 ch. Lara G. Shohet, Tegan S. Shohet. **EDUC:** Univ. of Western Ontario, M.D.(Medicine) 1965; McGill Univ., F.R.C.S.(c)(Gen. Surgery) 1971, F.A.C.S.(Gen. Surgery) 1974; Royal Coll. of Surgeons, Certificate of Special Competence in Paediatric Surgery 1976. **CAREER:** Intern, Montreal General Hospital, 1965-66; family practice, Kilifi, Kenya, July-Sept. 1966; Asst., Cardiovascular Surgery, Victoria Hospital, London, Ont., Sept.-Dec. 1966; Sr. House Officer, Cardiovascular Surgery, Brompton Hospital, London, UK, Mar.-May 1967; Resident, Montreal General Hospital, 1967-71; Paediatric Gen. Surgeon, Montreal Children's Hospital, 1971-80; Paediatric Gen. Surgeon, North York General Hospital, 1981 to date; part-time Instructor & Clinical Appointee, Fac. of Medicine, Univ. of Western Ontario, 1981 to date; Paediatric Gen. Surgeon, Consulting, Scarborough Centenary Hospital, 1984 to date; Paediatric Gen. Surgeon, Assoc. Staff, Hospital for Sick Children, 1994 to date; Lecturer, Dept. of Surgery, Univ. of Toronto, 1994 to date; VP, Medical Staff, North York General Hospital, 1994-96; Pres., Medical Staff, 1996 to date. **SELECTED PUBLICATIONS:** various articles incl.: "Making Water Skiing Safer" (*The Physician and Sports Medicine* (2)7, 1974); "Sports Medicine Section Position Paper: School Physical Education " (*Ontario Medical Review*, Mar. 1987); "A Woman and a Surgeon" (*Humane Medicine* 6, Spring 1990); numerous presentations. **AFFIL:** Royal Coll. of Surgeons of Canada (Fellow); American Board of Surgery; American Coll. of Surgeons; American Academy of Paediatrics (Surgical Section); Royal Coll. of Physicians & Surgeons; Canadian Association of Paediatric Surgeons (Dir. 1996); Canadian Medical Association; Ontario Medical Association; Association des Chirurgiens Généraux de la Province de Québec; Coll. of Physicians & Surgeons of Ontario; Federation of Medical Specialists of Quebec; Professional Corporation of Physicians of Quebec; North York General Hospital Medical Staff Association; Canadian Association of General Surgeons; Ontario Federation of Medical Women; Federation of Medical Women; Canadian Association of Sports Medicine; Association of Women Surgeons–American; various committees, North York General Hos-

pital; Devil's Glen Ski Club (Dir. 1992-95); Ministry of Tourism (Sport Safety Council 1989-95). INTERESTS: sports medicine; ethics in medicine; the fit child; tennis; skiing; travel; education. COMMENT: *"Proud mother of two great young women. Hard-working clinical paediatric surgeon contributing to areas of committee interests, boards, etc. Interested in all the challenges of life while enjoying all possible opportunities as they turn up."*

Grace, Sherrill E., B.A.,M.A.,Ph.D., F.R.S.C. ⌇ 🍵
Professor of English, THE UNIVERSITY OF BRITISH COLUMBIA, 1873 East Mall, Ste. 397, Vancouver, BC V6T 1Z1 (604) 822-4076/9824, FAX 822-6906, EMAIL grace@ arts.ubc.ca. 2 ch. Elizabeth Grace, Malcolm Grace. EDUC: Univ. of Western Ontario, B.A.(English) 1965; McGill Univ., M.A. (English) 1970, Ph.D.(English) 1974. CAREER: Asst. Prof., McGill Univ., 1975-77; Asst. Prof., Univ. of British Columbia, 1977-81; Assoc. Prof., 1981-87; Full Prof., 1991 to date; Assoc. Dean of Arts, 1991-94. SELECTED PUBLICATIONS: *Violent Duality: A Study of Margaret Atwood* (Montreal; Véhicule Press, 1980); *The Voyage That Never Ends: Malcolm Lowry's Fiction* (Vancouver; Univ. of British Columbia Press, 1982); *Margaret Atwood: Language, Text and System*, Co-Ed. with L. Weir (Vancouver: Univ. of British Columbia Press, 1983); *Regression and Apocalypse: Studies in North American Literary Expressionism* (Toronto; Univ. of Toronto Press, 1989); *Swinging the Maelstrom: New Perspectives on Malcolm Lowry*, ed. collection (with two contributions) (Montreal; McGill-Queen's Univ. Press, 1992); *Sursum Corda: The Collected Letters of Malcolm Lowry*, Vol. 1 (London; Jonathan Cape, 1995; Toronto; Univ. of Toronto Press, 1995), Vol. 2, 1996, scholarly edition; *Representing North*, ECW #59, guest edited collection with 2 contributions (Toronto: ECW Press, 1996); more than 100 scholarly articles, chapters in books & review articles. EDIT: Mbr., Ed. Bd.: *Canadian Review of American Studies; Essays in Theatre; Studies in Canadian Literature; Zeitschrift für Anglistik u. Amerikanistik.* AFFIL: Association of Canadian College & University Teachers of English; Canadian Association of American Studies; Association for Canadian Studies; Canadian Comparative Literature Association; Academic Women's Association (Pres. 1995-96); Univ. of British Columbia (Senate 1987-96). HONS: F.E.L. Priestley Award, 1993; Killam Research Prize, 1990; Killam Fac. Research Fellowship, 1990-91; elected Fellow, Royal Society of Canada. INTERESTS: visual arts; classical music; wilderness activities.

MISC: Canadian Federation for the Humanities Grants, 1982 & 1989; numerous research grants & fellowships. COMMENT: *"I have devoted my professional life to teaching and research, both of which I enjoy and believe in deeply. My research, published in books, editions and articles, always informs my graduate and undergraduate teaching and stimulates me to new discoveries and inquiries."*

Graff, Elyse, B.A.,P/IR 🔾 ⌇ 🕙
National Executive Director, CANADIAN COUNCIL OF CHRISTIANS AND JEWS, 44 Victoria St., Ste. 601, Toronto, ON M5C 1Y2 (416) 364-3101, FAX 364-5705. Born Toronto 1945. d. 1 ch. Jonathan Edward Graff. EDUC: Univ. of Toronto, B.A. 1966; Certification in Personnel & Industrial Rel'ns 1982. CAREER: Mgr, Personnel Dev., Peoples Jewellers Ltd., 1980-82; Dir., Hum. Res., Embassy Cleaners, 1982-84; Cadet Cleaners, 1984-86; Owner & Mgr, Elyse Graff & Associates, 1986-88; Sr. Mgr, Organizational Consulting, Laventhol & Horwath/ Price Waterhouse, 1988-91; Exec. Dir., Canadian Council of Christians & Jews, 1991 to date. AFFIL: Christian Jewish Dialogue of Toronto (Dir.); YWCA of Toronto (Nominating Committee; former VP); Metro Toronto Association for the Mentally Retarded (Past Pres., Young Women's Committee); King/ Bathurst Residents' Association (Exec. Committee); Human Resources Professionals' Association of Ontario (Instructor). INTERESTS: film; reading; volunteerism. COMMENT: *"A lifelong educator, bringing an understanding of sound human relations and business practices into the successful management of a high-profile, not-for-profit organization."*

Graham, Katherine Athol Hamilton, M.A. ■ ⌇ ♣
Associate Professor and Co-ordinator, Diversification Research Group, CARLETON UNIVERSITY, 1125 Colonel By Dr., Ottawa,, ON K1S 5B6 (613) 520-2600, ext. 2557, FAX 520-2551, EMAIL katherine_graham@carleton.ca. Born Winnipeg 1947. m. Andrew Graham. 1 ch. Katherine Lindsey Hamilton Graham. EDUC: Glendon Coll., York Univ., B.A.(Pol. Sci., Hons.) 1970; Queen's Univ., M.A.(Pol. Studies) 1978. CAREER: Consultant, Systems Research Group, Toronto, 1970-71; Proj. Mgr, 1972-73; Consultant, P.S. Ross & Partners (now Deloitte & Touche), Toronto, 1973; Sr. Consultant, 1974-76; Pres., 348151 Ontario Ltd. operating as Katherine A. Graham, C.M.C., Mgmt Consultant, 1976-78; Assoc. Dir., Institute of Local Gov't, Queen's Univ., 1978-80; Dir., 1980-83; Adjunct Asst. Prof., Sch. of Public Admin., Queen's Univ., 1981-

84; Asst. Prof., Sch. of Public Admin., Carleton Univ., 1984-90; Assoc. Prof., 1990 to date; Dir., 1992-96; Visiting Prof., Univ. of Alaska Southeast & Yukon Coll., 1992-93; Visiting Prof., Renmin Univ. & Lanzhou Univ., China, 1993. SELECTED PUBLICATIONS: *The Administration of Mineral Exploration in the Yukon and Northwest Territories*, with R.G. McEachern & C.G. Miller (Kingston: Centre for Resource Studies, Queen's Univ., 1978); *Regional Governments: A Selected Overview*, with Diane Duttle & Judith Mackenzie (Yellowknife: Western Constitutional Forum & Gov't of the N.W.T. Legislative Assembly, 1983); *An Overview of Socio-Demographic Conditions of Registered Indians Off-Reserve* (Ottawa: Indian & Northern Affairs Canada, 1987); "Intergovernmental Relations and Urban Growth: A Canadian View," with L.D. Feldman (*Local Government Studies* Jan. 1979); "Implementing Devolution: Learning from Experience" (*The Northern Studies Review* Summer 1990); *Soliloquy and Dialogue*, with Carolyn Ditlburner & Frances Abele (Ottawa: Royal Commission on Aboriginal Peoples, 1996, forthcoming); various other publications. EDIT: Ed., *How Ottawa Spends*, 1988-90; Ed. Bd., Case Program of the Institute of Public Administration of Canada, 1991 to date; Ed. Bd., *Canadian Journal of Urban Research*, 1992-96. AFFIL: Institute of Public Administration of Canada; Institute of Certified Management Consultants of Ontario; Canadian Political Science Association; Canadian Association of Programs in Public Administration (VP 1991-93; Pres. 1993-94); Carleton Univ. Senate (elected mbr. 1992-95); Centre for Resource Studies, Queen's Univ. (Research Advisory Committee). INTERESTS: urban & local gov't; Aboriginal policy; northern dev.; gov't organization & mgmt. MISC: active as a commentator & speaker, particularly on issues related to local gov't, on northern dev. & Aboriginal affairs; recipient of various grants; appointed by the Gov't of Ont. as Commissioner of Election Boundaries for the Regional Municipality of Ottawa-Carleton, 1990; sr. researcher & policy advisor, Royal Commission on Aboriginal Peoples, 1991-95. COMMENT: *"Katherine Graham's career has focused on academic and applied research and teaching about the Canadian public sector. She is a frequent media commentator on public policy issues. In her spare time, she co-manages a 245 acre beef farm."*

Graham, Kathleen Margaret (K.M. Graham) ■ ⊗
Painter. c/o Feheley Fine Arts, 45 Avenue Rd., Toronto, ON M5R 2G3. Born Hamilton, Ont.

1913. m. Dr. J. Wallace Graham. 2 ch. EDUC: Trinity Coll., Univ. of Toronto, B.A. SELECTED PUBLICATIONS: numerous drawings published in journals incl. *Canadian Forum* (1974); various works reproduced for book covers, incl. "Arctic Night #2", *From Ink Lake*, by Michael Ondaatje (Lester & Orpen Dennys, 1990). EXHIBITIONS: solo exhibitions include Carmen Lamanna Gallery, Toronto (1967), Trinity Coll., Univ. of Toronto (1968), Founders Coll., York Univ. (1970), Pollock Gallery, Toronto (1971, 1973, 1975), Art Gallery of Cobourg (1972), City Hall, Toronto (1974), David Mirvish Gallery, Toronto (1976), Klonaridis Inc., Toronto (1979, 1981, 1982, 1983, 1985, 1988, 1990), Galerie Elca London, Montreal (1983, 1985), Fran Wynans Gallery, Vancouver (1979), Watson Willour Gallery, Houston (1980), Downstairs Gallery, Edmonton (1980), Lillian Heidenberg Gallery, N.Y. (1981, 1986), Feheley Fine Arts, Toronto (1989), Douglas Udell Gallery, Vancouver (1993), Costin & Klintworth, Toronto (1994); solo survey exhibition originated at Memorial Univ. Art Gallery, Newfoundland & toured nationally (1984-85); solo survey exhibition originated at Memorial Univ. Art Gallery & went to Beaverbrook Art Gallery, Fredericton (1994); major group exhibitions include *Canada X 10*, originated Art Gallery of Ontario & toured (1974-75), *The Canadian Canvas*, organized by *TIME* Canada & toured (1975-76), *Changing Visions, The Canadian Landscape*, organized by Art Gallery of Ontario & Edmonton Art Gallery & toured (1976-77), *Four Canadian Painters*, Diane Brown Gallery, Washington, DC (1977), *14 Canadians*, Hirshhorn Museum, Washington, DC (1977), *Certain Traditions: Recent British and Canadian Art*, toured (1978-79), *Bolduc, Fournier, Graham: Recent Paintings*, London & Paris (1981); *The Heritage of Jack Bush*, originated at Robert McLaughlin Gallery, Oshawa & toured (1981-82), *Selections from the Westbourne Collection*, originated at Edmonton Art Gallery & toured (1982-83), *Hot off the Press*, Associated American Artists, N.Y. (1986), *Curators Choose*, Art Rental & Sales Gallery, Art Gallery of Ontario (1989), *C.I.L. Collection*, McMichael Canadian Collection, Kleinberg, Ont. (1993), *Hidden Values*, McMichael Canadian Collection, Kleinberg, Ont. (1994-95), *Prosperity Returns–The Oral Tradition in Painting*, Art Gallery of Hamilton (1994-95), *The Klonaridis Group*, The Moore Gallery, Hamilton (1995); Costin & Klintworth Gallery, 1995. COLLECTIONS: public collections include National Gallery, Ottawa; The British Museum, London, UK; The Art Gallery of Ontario, Toronto; The Agnes Etherington

Gallery, Queen's Univ., Kingston; Memorial Art Gallery, Newfoundland; Beaverbrook Art Gallery, Fredericton; Macdonald Stewart Art Centre, Guelph, Ont.; McMichael Art Gallery; represented in over 60 major corp. collections. **AFFIL:** Royal Canadian Academy of Arts. **HONS:** Fellow (Hon.), Trinity Coll., Univ. of Toronto, 1988. **MISC:** various radio & TV appearances; subject of numerous articles & reviews in journals such as *Arts Canada, Le Monde,* & *Art International.*

Graham, Patricia A., B.A.,LL.B. ■ /
Editorial Page Editor, THE VANCOUVER SUN, 2250 Granville St., Vancouver, BC V6H 3G2 (604) 732-2111. **EDUC:** Univ. of Windsor, B.A.(Phil.) 1970; Osgoode Hall Law Sch., LL.B. 1976. **BAR:** Ont., 1976. **CAREER:** Lawyer, Horsford & Lang, 1976-80; Reporter, *The Globe and Mail,* 1980-81; Instructor, North Island Coll., 1985-86; Copy Ed., *The Province,* 1986-87; Editorial Writer, 1987-89; Editorial Page Ed., 1989-91; Sr. Ed., *The Vancouver Sun,* 1991-93; Edit. Page Ed., 1993 to date. **AFFIL:** *The Vancouver Sun* Children's Fund (Dir.); Green Coll., Univ. of British Columbia; Dean's Advisory Committee, Fac. of Law, Univ. of British Columbia; Canadian Association of Journalists. **HONS:** Southam President's Award, 1990; Media Watch Award, 1990; First Place, Column Writing, B.C. Newspaper Award, 1990; Second Place, Column Writing, B.C. Newspaper Award, 1989. **MISC:** regular public speaking & TV engagements.

Graham, Wendy C., M.D. ⊕ ⊰ ✦
Physician. 111 Main St. W., Ste. 304, North Bay, ON P1B 2T6 (705) 476-7747, FAX 476-8201. Born North Bay, Ont. 1953. M. Alexander Graham. 4 ch. **EDUC:** Queen's Univ., B.Sc.(Physiology) 1976; Univ. of Toronto, M.D. 1980, Coll. of Family Practice, CCFP 1982. **CAREER:** attending physician for Canadore Coll. & Nipissing Univ. students, 1982-91; in private practice, 1982 to date; Head, Gen. & Family Practice, City of North Bay, 1989-91; Consultant, Canadian Medical Protective Association, 1989 to date; Asst. Prof., Dept. of Family Medicine, Univ. of Ottawa, 1994 to date; Chair, Primary Care Reform, Ministry of Health, 1996. **SELECTED PUBLICATIONS:** "Ontario Medical Association Response to the Ministry of Health Recommendations Re: Taking Action against Sexual Abuse of Patients," co-author, OMA position paper to address the CPSO Task Force on Sexual Abuse (1992); "The Politics of Women's Health," position paper for the National Retreat for Women (1993); co-author, *Primary Care Reform, A Strategy for Stability* (1996).

AFFIL: Coll. of Family Practice (Fellow); Delphi Panel, Sunnybrook Health Sciences Centre; Media Watch; American Women's Association; Ontario Medical Association (Chair, Women's Issues Committee 1991 to date; Joint Mgmt Appointment 1991-95); North Bay & District Medical Society (Pres. 1992-93); Canadian Medical Association. **INTERESTS:** women's health; primary care reform; dance; ballet; cooking; reading; aerobics; film; tennis. **MISC:** Preceptor, Northern Ont. Residency Program, 1992 to date. **COMMENT:** *"As a family physician, I strive to ensure that patients receive the highest quality health care that is cost-effective, comprehensive and compassionate, emphasizing prevention, continuous care and equal access."*

Graham-Fogwill, Loretta Advira, M.Sc., M.Ed.,M.P.A. ⊰ ❀
Instructor, Applied Sciences Department, RED RIVER COMMUNITY COLLEGE, 2055 Notre Dame Ave., Rm. A407A, Winnipeg, MB R3H 0J0 (204) 632-2171. Born Jamaica 1941. m. Douglas Fogwill. 1 ch. Roger Williams. **EDUC:** Univ. of the West Indies, B.Sc.(Hons.) 1966; Univ. of Manitoba, M.Sc. 1969, M.Ed. 1977, M.P.A. 1989. **CAREER:** technician, Agriculture Canada Grain Research Lab., 1966-67; high sch. science teacher & lab. instructor, univ., 1970-72; Instructor, Red River Community Coll., 1972 to date; Mgr, Int'l Educ., 1992-94. **AFFIL:** Agency for the Selection & Support of Individuals Starting Trade (A.S.S.I.S.T.), Jamaica; Congress of Black Women, Manitoba; Jamaican Society of Manitoba; Immigrant Women's Association of Manitoba. **INTERESTS:** travel; reading; music; horticulture; sports & the outdoors; interior decorating. **MISC:** various conference presentations on multicultural & racial issues & science educ. **COMMENT:** *"Goals: to maintain and enhance my activities in the areas of science education for women and to respond to the need for cultural diversity in educational institutions, international development educations and technology transfer to developing countries as required."*

Grant, Hon. Judith, B.A. ✦ ♂
Mayor/Préfet (Warden), MUNICIPALITY OF CHELSEA-MRC DES COLLINES DE L'OUTAOUAIS, 100 Chelsea Rd., Chelsea, QC J0X 1N0 (819) 827-1124, FAX 827-2672. Born Ottawa 1938. m. Norman. 3 ch. **EDUC:** Carleton Univ., B.A.(Journalism) 1958. **CAREER:** Councillor, Municipality of Chelsea, 1981-89; Mayor, Municipality of Chelsea, 1989 to date; Warden (Préfet), MRC des Collines de l'Outaouais, 1991 to date. **AFFIL:** Federation of Canadian Municipalities (Bd.); Lions Club International

(District Gov. 1993-94; Council Chair-Multiple District A 1994-95); Outaouais Transport Commission (Commissioner); Hôpital pour enfants de l'est Ontario (Conseil d'admin.); Union des municipalités régionales de comté du Québec (Conseil d'admin.). **HONS:** Citizen of the Year, Municipality of Chelsea, 1986; Melvin Jones Fellowship, 1993; 100% Gov., Pres. & Reg. Chair, Lions Club; Presidential Award for Drug Awareness, Lions Club. **INTERESTS:** community service work. **MISC:** Canada's 1st female Lions Club district gov.; 1 of 2 female Lions Club Council Chairs in the world. **COMMENT:** *"Tireless community worker who lives by ideal of service to others. Since becoming Mayor, have pushed to make Chelsea an ideal place to live, both environmentally and tax-wise."*

Grant, Rhondda Elaine Stout, B.A., LL.B. $ ⚖

Corporate Secretary and Associate General Counsel, NOVA CORPORATION, 801 - 7th Ave. S.W., Box 2535, Stn. M, Calgary, AB T2P 2N6 (403) 290-7745, FAX 290-6135. Born Edmonton 1957. m. Richard Grant. 2 ch. Morgan Ashley Grant, Dixon John Campbell Grant. **EDUC:** Univ. of British Columbia, B.A.(English) 1978, LL.B. 1981. **BAR:** Alta., 1982. **CAREER:** Student-at-Law/Assoc., Burnet, Duckworth and Palmer, Barristers & Solicitors, 1981-86; Assoc., Cook Snowden, Barristers & Solicitors, 1986-87; Assoc., Howard, Mackie, Barristers & Solicitors, 1987-89; Sr. Corp. Cnsl., NOVA Corporation of Alberta, 1989-94; Corp. Sec. & Assoc. Gen. Cnsl, NOVA Corporation, 1994 to date. **AFFIL:** Canadian Bar Association; Calgary Bar Association; Law Society of Alberta; Canadian Corporate Shareholder Services Association. **COMMENT:** *"I am a corporate finance and securities lawyer, primarily. I also manage a department of 15 assorted lawyers, administrators, paralegals and support staff, which fulfills the entire private and public corporate secretary function of NOVA and its subsidiaries."*

Grant, Trudy, B.A.,B.Ed. 🎭 📺

President, SULLIVAN ENTERTAINMENT INTERNATIONAL INC., 110 Davenport Rd., Toronto, ON M5R 3R3 (416) 921-7177, FAX 921-4322, 9465 Wilshire Blvd., Ste. 605, Beverly Hills, CA 90212 (310) 247-0166, FAX 247-1945. Born Ont. m. Kevin Sullivan. 3 ch. **EDUC:** Univ. of Western Ontario, B.A. 1976, B.Ed. 1977; Univ. Sorbonne, Paris, 1978. **CAREER:** Pres., Sullivan Entertainment International Inc., 1979 to date. **SELECTED CREDITS:** Prod., *The Fir Tree*; Prod., *Kreighoff*; Assoc. Prod., *Anne of Green Gables*; Prod., *Anne of Green Gables–The Sequel*; Prod., *Lantern Hill*; Exec. Prod., *Road to Avonlea*; Exec. Prod., *By Way of the Stars*; Exec. Prod., *Butterbox Babies*; Exec. Prod., *Under The Piano*.

Grattan, Patricia, B.A., B.F.A. 📜

Executive Director, ART GALLERY OF NEWFOUNDLAND AND LABRADOR, Memorial University of Newfoundland, St. John's, NF A1C 5S7 (709) 737-8210, FAX 737-2007. Born Sault Ste. Marie, Ont. 1944. m. Dr. M. Ian Bowmer. **EDUC:** Univ. of Western Ontario, B.A.(Hons., Journalism) 1966; Concordia Univ., B.F.A. (Printmaking & Art Hist.) 1974; Museum Management Institute, Berkeley, 1995. **CAREER:** Acting Chief Curator, Newfoundland Museum, 1980-81; Curator & Dir., Art Gallery, Memorial Univ. of Newfoundland, 1982-94; Exec. Dir., Art Gallery of Newfoundland & Labrador (formerly Memorial Univ. Art Gallery), 1994 to date; Mbr., Canada Council, 1995-98. **SELECTED PUBLICATIONS:** numerous Memorial Univ. Art Gallery catalogues; various articles for magazines incl. "Galleries and Museums in Newfoundland and Labrador–The Past Decade" (*MUSE*, Vol. X, No's. 2 & 3, Summer, Fall, 1992); "Rae Perlin as visual artist," intro. to *Not a Still Life–The Art and Writings of Rae Perlin*, ed. Marian Frances White (St. John's; Killick Press, 1991); "Newfoundland Yard Art: A personal discovery" (*Arts Atlantic* 18, Vol. 5, No. 2, Spring 1984). **EDIT:** Ed. Advisory Bd., *Arts Atlantic* Magazine, 1978-94. **EXHIBITIONS:** has curated & organized dozens of exhibitions, primarily of contemporary Nfld. & Cdn Art; exhibitions that have toured nationally include *Marlene Creates: Landworks 1979-1991* (1993); *Christopher Pratt: The Prints* (1992); *25 Years of Newfoundland Art* (1986). **AFFIL:** Canadian Art Museum Directors' Organization (Pres. 1993-95; Sec. 1990-93); Cabot Coll. of Applied Arts & Technology & Continuing Educ. (Advisory Committee, Textile Studies Program 1990 to date); Newfoundland Sound Symposium (Advisory Committee 1983 to date); Canadian Museums Association (Chair, Annual Conference 1989; Nat'l Council 1987-89); Gov't of Newfoundland & Labrador Art Procurement Program (Chair, Advisory Panel 1983-88). **HONS:** Univ. Gold Medal, Journalism, Univ. of Western Ontario, 1966. **INTERESTS:** travel; kayaking; ballet; folk art. **MISC:** Chair, City of St. John's Art Procurement jury, 1993 to date; juror & grants assessor, The Canada Council, & the Museum Assistance Programs, Dept. of Cdn Heritage.

Gravel, Line, B.A.,MAP 🍁

Committee Clerk and Executive Secretary to

the Canadian NATO Parliamentary Association, Committees and Private Legislation Directorate, THE SENATE OF CANADA, 140 Wellington St., Rm. 705, Ottawa, ON K1A 0A4 (613) 990-0088, FAX 995-0320. Born Chicoutimi, Que. 1953. m. Michael Zigayer. 2 ch. Philip Alexandre, Christine Jennifer. EDUC: Univ. de Montréal, Cert.(Public Rel'ns) 1980; Univ. of Ottawa, B.A.(Pol. Sci.) 1987, enrolled part-time, Ph.D. program (Pol. Hist.) 1996 to date; École nationale d'administration publique (ENAP), MAP (Maîtrise en admin. publique) 1991. CAREER: Deputy Registrar of Land Titles, Gov't of the N.W.T., 1982-85; Committee Clerk & Exec. Sec. to the Cdn NATO Parliamentary Association, Senate of Canada, 1986 to date. SELECTED PUBLICATIONS: "Au Sujet du Bénévolat" (Sources - ENAP Jul./Aug. 1993). EDIT: Founder & Mng Ed., Yellowknife French Cultural Association's monthly Newsletter, 1984-85. AFFIL: Professional Institute of the Public Service of Canada (Chair, Senate Legislative Clerk Group); Institute of Public Administration of Canada; Red Cross, Royal Lifesaving (Instructor). COMMENT: "My strengths are my planning and organization skills that serve me well in the work that I do. I am a high-energy person and I like to get things done leaving no loose ends, which is very helpful in my high-stress-level environment."

Graves, Gillian R., B.Sc.,M.D., F.R.C.S.(C) 🐟 ⊕ ⬩

Associate Professor, Department of Obstetrics and Gynaecology, DALHOUSIE UNIVERSITY, 5980 University Ave., Halifax, NS B3H 4N1 (902) 420-6726, FAX 425-1125. Active Staff, The Women's Clinic, GRACE MATERNITY HOSPITAL, Halifax, NS. Born Vancouver 1953. m. Don Williams. 2 ch. EDUC: Univ. of British Columbia, B.Sc.(Zoology) 1975, M.D. 1978. CAREER: Intern, Dalhousie Univ., 1978-79; gen. rural practitioner, 1979-81; active staff, Fisherman's Memorial Hospital, Lunenburg, N.S., 1979-81; Resident in Obstetrics & Gynaecology, Dalhousie Univ., 1981-85; Clinical Lecturer, Univ. of Western Ontario, 1985-88; Fellow in Reproductive Endocrinology, Univ. Hospital, 1985-88; active staff, Victoria General Hospital, Halifax, 1988 to date; active staff, The Women's Clinic, Grace Maternity Hospital, 1988 to date. SELECTED PUBLICATIONS: "Nonimmune Hydrops fetalis: Antenatal Diagnosis and Management," with T.F. Baskett (American Journal of Obstetrics and Gynecology 1984); "Rates and Outcomes of Pregnancies Achieved in the First Four Years of an In Vitro Fertilization Program," with A.A. Yuzpe et al (Canadian Medical Association Journal 1989); "Endometriosis and Infer-

tility: Are They Causally Related?" (Canadian Journal of Continuing Medical Education Jan. 1994); various other articles & abstracts. AFFIL: N.S. Medical Society; B.C. Medical Association; Canadian Medical Association; American Fertility Society; Canadian Medical Protective Association; Royal Society of Medicine; Royal Coll. of Physicians & Surgeons (Fellow); Society for the Study of Fertility; Society of Obstetricians & Gynecologists of Canada (SOGC) (Co-Chair, Reproductive Endocrinology Committee 1995); American Coll. of Gynecologists & Obstetricians; Canadian Fertility & Andrology Society (Nat'l Dir. 1995). HONS: Gold Medal, 1971; Norman MacKenzie Memorial Scholarship, 1971; B.C. Gov't Scholarship, 1971-75; Wyeth Postgrad. Award; Wyeth Centennial Award of Excellence, Society of Obstetricians & Gynecologists of Canada Annual Meeting, 1983; Wyeth Postgrad. Award, Society of Obstetricians & Gynecologists of Canada, 1984; Resident Research Day Award, 1985, 1986; Best Postgrad. Paper, 1985, 1986. INTERESTS: endometriosis; invitro fertilization; infertility; menopause.

Gray, Charlotte, B.A. 🐟 ✏ ⛏

Writer, Editor and Political Columnist. c/o 183 Mackay St., Ottawa, ON K1M 2B5 (613) 742-6262, FAX 742-6262. Born Sheffield, UK 1948. m. George R.M. Anderson. 3 ch. Alexander, Nicholas, Oliver. EDUC: Oxford Univ., St. Hilda's Coll., B.A.(Modern Hist.) 1969; London Sch. of Econ., Diploma in Social Admin. 1970. CAREER: teacher, Bristnall Hall Secondary Modern Sch., Birmingham, 1970-71; Research Asst. to Historical Advisor to the Foreign Sec., Foreign Office, Whitehall, 1972-74; Researcher, Daily Express, 1974-75; Asst. Ed. then Ed., Psychology Today UK Edition, 1975-79; Columnist, Evening Standard, 1978; freelance journalist in Canada, 1979 to date. SELECTED PUBLICATIONS: Contributing Ed., Saturday Night & Canadian Medical Association Journal. AFFIL: Parliamentary Press Gallery; PEN Canada (Bd. Mbr.); Children's Hospital of Eastern Ontario (V-Chair of Bd.). HONS: Catherine Pakenham Award, 1978; Asia-Pacific Foundation Fellowship, 1991; 2 Authors' Awards, Foundation for the Advancement of Canadian Letters; nominee, National Magazine Awards; Hon. Doctorate, Mount St. Vincent Univ., 1995. COMMENT: "I have tried to explore how and why things happen, not just what and when."

Gray, Victoria, B.Mus.,LL.B. ■ ⬩ ⊛ ♥

Partner, BULL, HOUSSER AND TUPPER, Barristers and Solicitors, 3000 Royal Centre, 1055 W. Georgia St., Box 11130, Vancouver, BC V6E

3R3 (604) 687-6575, FAX 641-4949, EMAIL nvg@bull.bht.com. Adjunct Professor, Faculty of Law, UNIVERSITY OF BRITISH COLUMBIA. Born Vancouver 1957. s. EDUC: Univ. of Victoria, B.Mus.(Music-Gen. & Oboe) 1978; Univ. of Toronto, LL.B. 1981. BAR: B.C., 1982. CAREER: articling student, Bull, Housser and Tupper, 1981-82; Assoc. & Jr. Ptnr, 1982-89; freelance musician, 1982 to date; active Ptnr, Bull, Housser and Tupper, 1989 to date; Adjunct Prof., Fac. of Law, Univ. of British Columbia, 1994 to date. SELECTED PUBLICATIONS: "Compensatory Damages" (*Remedies–Equitable and Common Law* 1989); "Remedies for Toxic Operations and Products" (*Toxic Land Purchases and Litigation Insight Educational Services* 1990); "Preservation of Property: Mareva Injunctions, Anton Piller Orders, Distress and Re-entry" (*Remedies* 1993); "Remedies Against Purchasers and Vendors" (*Real Estate Litigation* 1990, 1992, 1994). AFFIL: Vancouver Youth Symphony Orchestra Society (Dir. 1989-91); West Coast Women's Legal Education & Action Fund Association (Pres. 1986-89; Mbr., Nat'l Legal Committee 1989-91; Cnsl 1991; Local Legal Committee 1986-95); Vancouver YWCA (Dir.; Exec. Committee 1991-95; Dir. 1990-94; Sec. 1991-92; VP 1992-93; Pres. 1993-95; Past Pres. 1995 to date.); Continuing Legal Education Society (Guest Instructor 1989-95); Lower Mainland Orchestra Society (Pres. 1992-93); Elektra Women's Choir (Dir.). INTERESTS: law; music; equality; educ. MISC: various reports & comments given; Guest Instructor, Vancouver Professional Legal Training Course. COMMENT: *"Victoria Gray is a lawyer, musician and volunteer. She has been practising civil litigation at Bull, Housser and Tupper for 14 years. She is also a musician, freelancing as an oboist with groups such as the Victoria Symphony. Her volunteer work has focused largely on women's issues and music."*

Gray, Viviane, B.A. ■ 🎨 ♣ ⌂
Manager, INDIAN ART CENTRE, Department of Indian and Northern Affairs, 10 Wellington St., Rm. 928, Hull, QC K1A 0H4 (819) 994-1264, FAX 953-0165. Born Listuguj, Que. 1947. m. John Charles Clifford. 2 ch. EDUC: Coady International Institute, St. Francis Xavier Univ., Diploma in Social Leadership & Community Dev. 1965; Carleton Univ., B.A.(Anthro. & French) 1973; Nova Scotia Coll. of Art & Design, 1976-77; Parks Canada Historical Section, Halifax, Curatorial apprenticeship 1979-80. CAREER: Research Dir., National Indian Brotherhood (former Assembly of First Nations), Ottawa, 1974; Curator, Parks Canada Historical Research, Dept. of Environ-

ment, Halifax, 1978-81; Ptnr, Clifford-Gray Associates, Ottawa, 1983-89; Arts Admin., Indian Arts Centre, Dept. of Indian & Northern Affairs, Ottawa, 1988-95, 1996 to date; Dir., Listuguj Arts & Cultural Centre, 1995-96; artist, sculpture & fibre arts. SELECTED CREDITS: Exhibit Coord., *Things Made by Inuit* (1981); Coord./Curator, *First Native Artists Competition and Exhibition*, Canadian Canoe Festival, Ottawa (1983); Co-Curator, *l'Oeil Amerindien: Regard sur l'Animal*, int'l exhibition, Le Musée de la Civilisation, Québec (1990-91); Co-Curator, *Pe'l A'tukwey*, 17 contemporary Mi'gmaw & Maliseet artists, Art Gallery of Nova Scotia (1992-93); Conference Speaker, "Les Collections Exotiques et les Musées," int'l conference organized by the Office de Cooperation et d'Information Muséographiques, Dijon, France (1996). SELECTED PUBLICATIONS: "If You Could See Through Our Eyes," curator's essay in exhibition catalogue, *L'Oeil Amerindien: Regard sur l'Animal* (Quebec: Musée de la Civilisation, 1991); "Indian Artists' Statements Through Time," in exhibition catalogue, *In the Shadow of the Sun* (Ottawa: Canadian Museum of Civilization, 1993); curatorial essay in exhibition catalogue *Pe'l A'tukwey* (Halifax: Art Gallery of Nova Scotia, 1993); "Micmac (Gespeg, Gesgapegiag, Listuguj)," *Le Quebec Autochtone* (La Griffe de l'Aigle, Que., 1996); various other publications. EDIT: Guest Ed., special issue on Micmac of Eastern Canada, *Tawow*, 5(2), DIAND, 1976; Ed., *About Arts and Crafts*, DIAND, 1980-81; Ed. & Art Dir., *Nutrition Newsletter*, Health & Welfare Canada, 1984-88. EXHIBITIONS: 9 exhibitions 1991-95, incl. *Art Amerindian '81*, Gallery Montcalm, Hull, Que. (1981), *Keeper of Our Culture*, A Celebration of Native Women in the Living Arts, Woodland Indian Cultural Educational Centre (1985), *Hard and Soft*, collaborative works with Ron Noganosh, Lobby of Terrasses de la Chaudière, Hull (1990) & *The Kluane Expedition*, McMichael Canadian Art Gallery (1995). AFFIL: Committee for the Advancement of Native Employment (Founding Mbr.); Ottawa Native Arts Study Group (Founding Mbr.); Canada Council First People's Arts Committee. HONS: Jean Chalmers Award, 1986. INTERESTS: fibre arts; piano; singing; weight training; reading. MISC: Mi'gmac (Micmac) tribal affiliation, Listuguj, Que.; recipient of various grants; 1st woman to manage the nat'l program, The Indian Art Centre & the Indian Art Collection in its 26-year history. COMMENT: *"As we approach the millennium, it becomes increasingly evident that we must all work and survive together, no matter how different our approaches may be, to make this planet a better place for all life forms."*

Grayson, Eunice ■ ♡ 🎓 $
Executive Director, THE LEARNING ENRICHMENT FOUNDATION, 116 Industry St., Toronto, ON M6M 4L8 (416) 921-0387. **CAREER:** Exec. Dir., Learning Enrichment Foundation, 1980 to date. **AFFIL:** York Community & Agency Social Planning Council; Society of Mesopotamia Studies; St. Clement's Anglican Church. **HONS:** Canada 125 Medal. **COMMENT:** *"The Learning Enrichment Foundation is a leader in community economic development and offers a number of services including thirteen day care centres, a business incubator called The York Business Opportunities Centre, a Youth Employment Counselling Centre, Self Employment and various skill training courses, English as a Second Language, career planning and various employer services including employee selection and training."*

Greaves, Lorraine J., Ph.D. 🎓 ✋ ⊕
Director, CENTRE FOR RESEARCH ON VIOLENCE AGAINST WOMEN AND CHILDREN, 946 Wellington St. N., London, ON N6A 3S9 (519) 858-5033, FAX 858-5034, EMAIL lgreaves@julian.uwo.ca. Born Manchester, UK 1950. 2 ch. Lucas, Simon. **EDUC:** Univ. of Western Ontario, B.A.(Soc.) 1970, M.A. 1974; London Teachers' Coll., Teaching Cert. 1971; Monash Univ., Australia, Ph.D.(Soc.) 1994. **CAREER:** Group Home Worker, Family & Children Svcs of London & Middlesex, 1971-72; Prof., Soc., Fanshawe Coll., London, Ont., 1974 to date; Community Consultant, Addiction Research Foundation, 1982-83; Dir., Centre for Research on Violence against Women & Children, 1993 to date. **SELECTED CREDITS:** on Univ. of Western Ontario - Fanshawe Coll. video committee for "Chilly Climate" (1990) & "Backlash" (1994-95). **SELECTED PUBLICATIONS:** *Smoke Screen: Women's Smoking & Social Control* (Fernwood Books & Scarlet Press, 1996); "Wife Battering: An Emerging Problem in Public Health," with S. Nuttal & B. Lent (*Canadian Journal of Public Health* Sept./Oct. 1985); "What is the Relationship Between Academic & Activist Feminism?" in *Challenging Times: The Women's Movement in Canada and the United States*, eds. C. Backhouse & D. Flaherty (McGill-Queen's Univ. Press, 1992); "Herstories" (*World Smoking and Health* 1994); "History of Women's Tobacco and Drug Use in Canada," in *Women's Use of Alcohol, Tobacco and Other Drugs* (Addiction Research Foundation, 1995); *Taking Control: An Action Handbook on Women & Tobacco* (1989); *Mixed Messages: Women Tobacco & Media* (1995); *Background Paper on Women & Tobacco* (1990); various other publications. **EDIT:** Co-Ed., *Women and Tobacco*, World Health Organization, 1991. **AFFIL:** Coll. of Physicians & Surgeons of Ontario (Public Mbr. 1994); International Network of Women Against Tobacco; Canadian Sociology & Anthropology Association; London Status of Women Action Group; National Action Committee on the Status of Women (VP 1985-88); Women's Education & Research Foundation of Ontario Inc. (Dir.); Battered Women's Advocacy Clinic (Founder & Chair 1984-93). **HONS:** Augusta Stowe-Gullen Award, 1986; Outstanding Young Londoner Award, West London Jaycees, 1986; Outstanding Ont. Achievement Award, Ministry of Culture, Tourism & Recreation, 1994. **MISC:** listed in *Canadian Who's Who*; numerous lectures, speeches & media interviews; recipient of various grants. **COMMENT:** *"Dr. Greaves is an activist and researcher, interested in women's services and women's issues. She is a researcher, writer and speaker on women's tobacco use, violence against women and women's issues."*

Grebenc, Kelly D., B.Sc.,R.D.,C.D.E. ⊕
Clinical Dietitian, Outpatient Diabetes Clinic, Clinical Nutrition Services, ALBERTA CHILDREN'S HOSPITAL, 1820 Richmond Rd. S.W., Calgary, AB T2T 5C7 (403) 229-7340, FAX 229-7639. Born Elliot Lake, Ont. 1961. s. **EDUC:** Acadia Univ., B.Sc.(Nutrition) 1982; General Hospital Corporation, St. John's, Grad. Dietetic Internship 1983; Certified Diabetes Educator 1992. **CAREER:** Clinical Dietitian, St. Clare's Mercy Hospital, St. John's, 1983-85; Sr. Clinical Dietitian, 1985-87; Clinical Dietitian, Inpatients, Alberta Children's Hospital, 1988; Clinical Dietitian, Outpatient Diabetes Clinic, 1989 to date. **SELECTED PUBLICATIONS:** "Hyperlipidemia in children" (*Canadian Pediatric Nutrition Newsletter* 1992); "Development and use of laser disc in diabetes education" (*Canadian Pediatric Nutrition Newsletter* 1993). **AFFIL:** Canadian Dietetic Association; Alberta Registered Dietitians' Association; Canadian Diabetes Association (Program Chair for Nat'l Conference, Diabetes Educator Section 1993); American Association of Diabetes Educators; Church Parish Council (Chair); Calgary Diabetes Nutrition Committee. **INTERESTS:** church activities; choir; gardening; hiking; travel. **MISC:** numerous conference presentations; several research studies; camp for children with diabetes each summer 1989 to date. **COMMENT:** *"The gifts I have been given are meant to be shared. My patients and families continue to provide me, as an educator, with the enthusiasm to meet the*

challenge of improving my communication and teaching skills to make their lives just a little bit easier."

Greckol, Sheila J., B.A.,LL.B. ⚖ ♞
Partner, CHIVERS GRECKOL & KANEE, 10328 - 81 Ave., Ste. 30, Edmonton,, AB T6E 1X2 (403) 439-3611, FAX 439-8543. EDUC: Univ. of Alberta, B.A. 1972, LL.B. 1975. BAR: Alta., 1976. CAREER: articled with Court of Appeal of Alberta, & Wright Chivers & Company, 1975-76; Assoc., Wright Chivers & Company, 1976-77; Ptnr, 1978-85; Instructor of Labour Law, Univ. of Alberta Law Sch.; Ptnr, Chivers Greckol & Kanee, 1986 to date; mbr., City of Edmonton Police Commission, 1994 to date. AFFIL: Canadian Association of Labour Lawyers (Pres.); Canadian Bar Association; Legal Education Society of Alberta. MISC: mbr., weekly pol. panel, CBC Radio (1991-93); actively involved in pol. issues incl. representation of Morganthaler Clinic in Edmonton & co-chairing the City of Edmonton Mayor's Campaign, 1992 & 1995. COMMENT: *"Ms. Greckol has participated in continuing legal education in the areas of labour and human rights issues with a special interest in gender equity."*

Greek, Elizabeth, B.E.E.,B.Ed. ✤ ◉
Regional Representative, Atlantic Region, NATIONAL WOMEN'S LIBERAL COMMISSION, Moncton, NB E1E 1P9 (506) 389-3238. Born Cap-Pele, N.B. d. 2 ch. Glorie, Margot. EDUC: Univ. de Moncton, B.E.E.(Educ.), B.Ed. 1983. CAREER: teacher, Moncton Sch. District. AFFIL: Liberal Party of N.B. (Sec.; Pres., N.B. Women Liberals 1988-92; Women's Reg'l Dir.); Liberal Party of Canada (Reg'l Rep., Atlantic Reg., Nat'l Women's Liberal Commission); Curling Club (VP 1986-88, & 1996 to date); Muriel McQueen Fergusson Foundation (Treas., Moncton Chapter 1995 to date). COMMENT: *"Since I have to describe myself I will simply say that I enjoy meeting people, and at various stages in my life I have always welcomed a new challenge. My endeavours were not of great overtones; my involvement in various political activities was mostly done to sensitize, to help and to encourage people to take part and discuss issues that would have some effect on their daily lives. I would consider my daughters my greatest achievement."*

Green, Jane S., B.Sc.,M.Sc.,Ph.D. ⊕ ❀ ♞
Assistant Professor, Medical Genetics, Faculty of Medicine, MEMORIAL UNIVERSITY OF NEWFOUNDLAND, Health Sciences Centre, St. John's, NF A1B 3V6, EMAIL jgreen@kean.ucs.mun.ca. Born Vancouver 1943. m. John M. Green. 3 ch.

Teresa, Tim, Valerie. EDUC: Univ. of British Columbia, B.Sc.(Zoology) 1964, M.Sc.(Genetics) 1966; Memorial Univ. of Newfoundland, Ph.D.(Medical Genetics) 1996. CAREER: Research Asst., Fac. of Medicine, Memorial Univ. of Newfoundland, 1978-88; Lecturer, 1988-91; Asst. Prof., 1991 to date. SELECTED PUBLICATIONS: numerous articles in refereed journals. AFFIL: American Society of Human Genetics; International Collaborative Group on Hereditary Nonpolyposis Colon Cancer; International Society of Genetic Eye Disease; Canadian Association of Genetic Counsellors. HONS: Women of Distinction Award, YM-YWCA, Newfoundland, 1995; invited to be Principal Investigator for the Canadian Genetic Diseases Network. INTERESTS: softball, cross-country skiing; travel; classical music. MISC: collaborated on mapping & cloning a gene for colon cancer in 1993. COMMENT: *"As a medical geneticist at Memorial University of Newfoundland, I am involved in teaching, genetic counselling, development of clinical and genetic screening programs for hereditary cancers and collaborative research particularly on hereditary eye diseases and hereditary cancers–a particularly exciting area to be involved in as rapid advances in molecular genetics occur."*

Green, Janet-Laine, B.F.A.,M.F.A. ⊗ ⚰ ♥
Actor, Director. c/o Oscar & Abrams Inc., 59 Berkeley St., Toronto, ON M5A 2W5 (416) 860-1790, FAX 860-0238. President and Director, BRIEFCASE PRODUCTIONS INC. Born Prince Albert, Sask. m. Booth Savage. 2 ch. EDUC: Univ. of Saskatchewan, Theatre 1970; Univ. of Alberta, Edmonton, B.F.A.(Theatre) 1974; York Univ., M.F.A.(Theatre/Directing) 1995. SELECTED CREDITS: lead, *Diamond Fleece* (M.O.W.), U.S.A. Cable; Ellen, *Medicine River*, CBC; *End of Summer* (M.O.W.), Showcase; *Fighting For Justice* (M.O.W.), NBC; *The Believers* (feature); Principal, *When the Dark Man Calls* (M.O.W.), USA Ntwk; Tony, *Family Pictures* (miniseries), CBS; Annie, series regular, *Kung Fu* (series), Warner Bros.; Guest Star, *Road to Avonlea* (series), CBC; Lead/Assoc. Prod., *The Circle Game* (feature), B. Berman & J. Cohl; Lead, *The Shower* (feature), Norstar; regular, *The Beachcombers* (series), CBC; Lindsay Sutherland, *Cowboy's Don't Cry* (feature), Atlantis Films; Lisa, *Murder Sees the Light*; Regular, *Seeing Things* (series), CBC; Lead, *The Chautauga Girl* (telefilm), CBC; Medea/Dir., *Medea* (theatre), Showcase Productions; Mary, *Life Sentences* (theatre), Factory Theatre; Vicki, *Money and Friends* (theatre), Theatre London/Vancouver Playhouse; Lou/Prod./Dir., *Reversing Falls* (theatre), Factory Theatre; Blanche/Dir., *A Streetcar*

Named Desire (theatre), York Univ. Theatre; Janet, *A Mad World*, (masters) (theatre), St. Lawrence Centre; Candy, *O.D. in Paradise* (theatre), Quebec International Festival; Margot/Asst. Dir., *Transit of Venus* (theatre), Canadian Stage; Beatrice, *To Grandmother's House We Go* (theatre), Canadian Stage; *Hunter's Moon*, Theatre Passe Muraille; Viola, *Twelfth Night*, Skylight Theatre; Molly, *18 Wheels* (musical), Festival Lennoxville; lead roles for CBC radio programs incl. *Lucy Maud Montgomery*, CBC; *The Robber Bride*; *In The Skin of a Lion*, etc.; animation series *Ultra Force, Wild Cats, Little Bear, Never Ending Story*. AFFIL: ACTRA; Equity HONS: nominated, Best Actress, Dora Award, 1995; nominated, Best Actress (*The Shower*), Genie Award, 1993; nominated, Best Actress (*The Beachcombers*), Gemini Award, 1992; Best Actress (*The Beachcombers*), TV Week Award, 1990; nominated, Best Actress (*The Beachcombers*), Gemini Award, 1989; nominated, Best Supporting Actress (*Cowboys Don't Cry*), Genie Award, 1989; nominated, Best Actress, Comedy Series (*Seeing Things*), Gemini Award, 1986 & 1987; nominated, Best Actress, Special Drama Presentation (*Michael & Kitty*), Gemini Award, 1986; nominated, Best Actress (*The Chautauga Girl*), ACTRA Award, 1985.

Green, Joan M., B.A.,B.Ed., M.Ed. ■ ✦ ⟨⟩

Chief Executive Officer, Education Quality and Accountability Office, GOVERNMENT OF ONTARIO, 1 Dundas St. W., 25th Fl., Toronto, ON M5G 1Z3 (416) 325-2801, FAX 325-2956. Born Windsor, Ont. 1947. 2 ch. Erin Elizabeth, Caitlin Eleanore. EDUC: Univ. of Toronto, B.A. 1969, B.Ed. 1970, M.Ed.(Psycholinguistics & Curriculum) 1977. CAREER: secondary sch. teacher, 1970-77; Consultant & Lecturer, City of York Bd. of Educ., 1977-80; Curriculum Coord., 1980-81; Admin., Adult Day Sch., 1981-84; Principal & V-Principal, 1981-84; Sch. Superintendent, Toronto Bd. of Educ., 1984-89; Coord. Superintendent, 1986-89; Chief Superintendent of Field Svcs, 1989-90; CEO, Dir. & Sec.-Treas., 1990-95. SELECTED PUBLICATIONS: *In Your Own Words* I (1981), II (1982); *Your Voice and Mine* I (1986), II (1987); *The Interactive Classroom*, co-author (1989); various articles & professional dev. materials. AFFIL: Art Gallery of Ontario (Trustee); Canadian Education Association (VP); Women in Capital Markets (Advisor to the Bd.); Canadian Comprehensive Auditing Foundation (Bd.); The Learning Partnership (Founding Mbr.); Council of Ontario Directors of Education (Exec. Committee Mbr. 1992-94); Women in Educational Administra-tion in Ontario (Founding Mbr.); United Way of Greater Toronto (Chair, Educ. Committee); Phi Delta Kappa; Ontario Public Supervisory Officers' Association; Toronto Olympic Bid Committee; Voter Education South Africa Canada (Council). HONS: Theology Award, Univ. of Toronto, 1969; Woman of the Year, Organization for Women in Leadership, 1990; nominee, Woman of the Year, *The Toronto Sun*, 1991; Distinguished Educator, Ont. Institute for Studies in Educ., 1994. INTERESTS: the arts; cottaging; travel. MISC: subject matter expert on educational law text for sch. administrators; int'l public speaker. COMMENT: "*An energetic CEO in education with extensive leadership experience at the municipal and provincial levels.*"

Green, Susan L., B.A. ○ ⚙ ✦

Executive Officer, ALBERTA CANCER FOUNDATION and Vice-President, ALBERTA CANCER BOARD, 9707 - 110 St., 6th Fl., Edmonton, AB T5K 2L9 (403) 482-9322, FAX 488-7809, EMAIL susan.green@cancerboard.ab.ca. Born Prince Albert, Sask. m. Stewart A. Roth. 2 ch. John David Roth, Geoffrey Harding Roth. EDUC: Univ. of Alberta, B.A.(Recreation Admin.) 1974; Banff Sch. of Advanced Management, 1984. CAREER: Sr. Intergovernmental Officer, Dept. of Fed. & Intergovernmental Affairs, Alta., 1974-79; Exec. Asst. to Min. of Culture, Gov't of Alberta, 1979-83; Exec. Asst. to Min. of Hospitals & Medical Care, 1983-86; Sr. Policy Advisor to Min. of Hospitals & Medical Care, 1986-88; Exec. Officer, Alberta Cancer Foundation, 1988 to date; VP, Alberta Cancer Board, 1988 to date. EDIT: *Facing Cancer*, Alberta Cancer Board. DIRECTOR: Guardian Chemicals. AFFIL: P.C. Party of Alberta; National P.C. Women's Federation (Past Pres.); National Society of Fund-Raising Executives; Association of Health Care Philanthropists; La Confrérie de la Chaîne des Rôtisseurs; Holy Trinity Anglican Church; Univ. of Alberta (Senate); Edmonton Concert Hall Foundation (Seat Dedication Campaign). HONS: nominee, Woman of the Year Award, YWCA. INTERESTS: community service; politics; photography; fitness; theatre; reading; her children's innumerable activities. MISC: seeking nomination as P.C. candidate, upcoming prov. elections, 1997; Chair & Campaign Mgr for Nancy Betkowski Campaign for Leadership of Alberta P.C. Party; Chrm of 2 Prime Minister Dinners in Edmonton. COMMENT: "*A proactive, energetic individual with a high level of commitment to family, work and community. Strong organization, interpersonal and management skills have been assets in policy development, fund raising and politics.*"

Greenberg, Shirley, B.A.,LL.B. ⚖
Lawyer. 440 Laurier Ave. W., Ste. 330, Ottawa, ON K1R 7X6 (613) 235-7774, FAX 230-7356. Born Ottawa 1931. w. Irving Greenberg. 3 ch. EDUC: Carleton Univ., B.A.(Soc.) 1970; Univ. of Ottawa, LL.B.(Law) 1976. BAR: Ont., 1978. CAREER: Legal Sec., 1953-59; Lawyer, Greenberg & Associates, 1978-95. AFFIL: Law Society of Upper Canada; University Women's Clubs of Ottawa; Canadian Federation of University Women; National Association of Women & the Law (Founding Mbr.); Legal Education Action Fund (LEAF) (Founding Mbr.); Ottawa Women's Network (Founding Mbr.); Ontario Women's Lobby (Founding Mbr.); Federal P.C. Women's Caucus, Ottawa. INTERESTS: feminist activity; travel; outdoor sports incl. tennis, cycling & swimming; dining; theatre; developments for sr. adults. COMMENT: *"Activity in the law reform process was most gratifying and successful; also I was able to be of help to many people undergoing separation and divorce during my 15 years of active practice of law."*

Greene, Lucy G., M.B.A. $
Vice-President, Corporate Human Resources, SUN LIFE ASSURANCE COMPANY OF CANADA, 150 King St. W., 4th Fl., Toronto, ON M5H 1J9 (416) 979-6361, FAX 979-6002. Born Buchanan, Sask. 1932. m. Allan T. Thomas. EDUC: Univ. of Alberta, B.A. 1955; Univ. of Western Ontario, M.L.S. 1969; McMaster Univ., M.B.A. 1976; Chartered Life Underwriter (Canada), CLU 1980. CAREER: Library Administrator, Univ. of Western Ontario, 1969-75; Sales Rep., London Life Insurance Company, 1976-78, Mktg Officer, Indiv. Insur., Sun Life of Canada, 1978-84; Planning & Research Officer, 1984-85; Dir., Field Dev. of Canada, 1985-87; VP, Hum. Res., 1987; VP, Corp. Hum. Res. AFFIL: Canadian Association of Women Executives; Metropolitan Board of Trade; Life Underwriters' Association of Canada; Toronto Women's Network. INTERESTS: sailing; gardening.

Greene, Sandra ☻ ✿
President, FIRST NATIONS WOMEN'S GROUP, Box 921, Prince Rupert, BC V8J 4B7 (604) 624-3200, FAX 624-3322. Born Prince Rupert, B.C. 1951. m. Barry E. Greene. 1 ch. Nina Miller. EDUC: Ksan Art Sch., First Nations Art 1971; Univ. of Victoria, Diploma (Admin. of Aboriginal Gov'ts). CAREER: researcher, Prince Rupert & Skidegate; artist & craftswoman, 1975 to date; Sec., 1975 to date. SELECTED PUBLICATIONS: various research reports, incl. *Women in the Northwest*; *Human Rights in Prince Rupert*; *Training and Educa-*

tion Needs in Skidegate. AFFIL: Indian Homemakers' Association of B.C. (Past Pres. 1992-94; District VP 1990-91 & 1994); Ministerial Advisory Committee for Women's Health; Women's Hospital (Steering Committee); Transition House (Bd. 1994-95); Mental Health Committee (Bd. 1994-95); Community Action Committee (1994-95); Union of B.C. Indian Chiefs (Council 1993-94); currently working for the Ministry of Women's Equality as a Reg'l Program Coord. for the N.W.; Health Canada (Tobacco Reduction Committee). INTERESTS: beading jewellery; reading; painting; collage. MISC: involved in community events of the First Nations of Prince Rupert & the Northwest; have been in 2 Haida dance groups; facilitates workshops on First Nations history & culture of Northwest. COMMENT: *"Haida, First Nations Woman of the Eagle Clan. Concerned citizen for healthy communities within our First Nations at all levels. Main career–equality and equity for women, elders and youth."*

Greenglass, Esther Ruth, B.A.,M.A., Ph.D. ✑ ⊕ ♠
Professor, Department of Psychology, Faculty of Arts, YORK UNIVERSITY, 4700 Keele St., North York, ON M3J 1P3 (416) 736-5120, FAX 736-5184. Born Toronto. m. George Hiraki. 2 ch. EDUC: Univ. of Toronto, B.A. 1962, M.A. 1963, Ph.D. 1967. CAREER: Prof., York Univ., 1968 to date. SELECTED PUBLICATIONS: *After Abortion* (1976); *A World of Difference: Gender Roles in Perspective* (1982); over 150 book chapters, academic journal papers & professional reports in the areas of the status of women, the psych. of women, stress, burnout & coping. EDIT: Ed. Bd., *Applied Psychology: An International Review*. AFFIL: Internal Society of Health Psychology; National Action Committee on the Status of Women in Canada; Canadian Psychological Association (Fellow); American Psychological Association, Div. of the Psychology of Women; Canadian Research Institute for the Advancement of Women; Canadian Abortion Rights Action League; Academy of Management; International Association of Applied Psychology; Women's Health Care Advisory Committee, Women's College Hospital, Toronto. HONS: York Univ. Fac. of Arts Fellowship, 1985-86; Fellow, American Psychological Association; Fellow, Canadian Psychological Association. INTERESTS: movies; biographies; jogging; aerobics; animals. MISC: recipient, various grants from various agencies incl. SSHRC, Imperial Oil Ltd., & York Univ.; mbr., Ontario Confederation of University Faculty Association's Committee on the Status of Women Academics, 1971-74; numerous conference presen-

tations on the psych. of women, stress & coping in Canada, US & abroad; 1st to offer "psychology of women" course in Canada. COMMENT: *"Throughout my career in my teaching and in my research, I have devoted myself to the development of the psychology of women. I have also served on many committees for governments and at the university level that have worked for the improvement of the status of women in Canada."*

Greenhill, Pauline, Ph.D. ■ ⚛ 📖 ✿
Professor, Departments of Women's Studies and Anthropology, UNIVERSITY OF WINNIPEG, 515 Portage Ave., Winnipeg, MB R3B 2E9 (204) 786-9752, FAX 783-7981, EMAIL pauline.greenhill@uwinnipeg.ca. EDUC: Trent Univ., B.A.(Anthro. & English) 1976; Memorial Univ. of Newfoundland, M.A.(Folklore) 1981; Univ. of Texas at Austin, Ph.D.(Anthro.) 1985. CAREER: Asst. Prof., Cdn Studies (also Adjunct Fac. in English & Anthro.), Univ. of Waterloo, 1986-90; Assoc. Prof., 1990-91; Adjunct Fac., Religious Studies, Wilfrid Laurier Univ., 1990-91; Assoc. Prof., Women's Studies, Univ. of Winnipeg, 1991-96; Prof., 1996 to date; Coord., Women's Studies, Univ. of Winnipeg, 1992-94; Assoc. Prof., Anthro., Univ. of Winnipeg, 1995 to date. SELECTED PUBLICATIONS: *True Poetry: Traditional and Popular Verse in Ontario* (Montreal & Kingston: McGill-Queen's Univ. Press, 1989); *Ethnicity in the Mainstream: Three Studies of English Canadian Culture* (Montreal & Kingston: McGill-Queen's Univ. Press, 1994); *Undisciplined Women: Tradition and Culture in Canada* (Montreal & Kingston: McGill-Queen's Univ. Press. forthcoming); "'She Dwelt Among the Untrodden Ways': Nostalgia and Folk Poetry in Ontario" (*Journal of Folklore Research* 1989); "'25 Good Reasons Why Beer Is Better Than Women' and Other Qualities of the Female: Gender and the Non-seriousness of Jokes," with Kjerstin Baldwin *et al* (*Canadian Folklore canadien* 1993); "The Folk Process in Revival: 'Barrett's Privateers' and 'Barrat's Privateers,'" in *Transforming Tradition*, Neil V. Rosenberg ed. (Urbana: Univ. of Illinois Press, 1993); "Women and Traditional Culture," with Diane Tye, in *Changing Patterns: Women in Canada*, 2 ed., Sandra Burt *et al* ed. (Toronto: McClelland and Stewart, 1993); various other publications. EDIT: Ed. Bd., *Culture and Tradition* 4, 1979; Ed., *Canadian Centre for Folk Culture Studies*, selected & ed. numbers 36-39 & 50 of the Mercury Series, 1980-81; Guest Ed., Dossier on Folklore Studies, *Association for Canadian Studies Bulletin*, 1987; Ed. Bd. & English Book Review Ed., *Canadian Folklore canadien*, 1990-95; Guest

Ed., special issue on folk poetry, *Canadian Folklore canadien* 15 1, 1993; Guest Co-Ed., special issue on folklore, *Journal of Canadian Studies* 29 1, 1994. AFFIL: Canadian Women's Studies Association (Pres. Elect 1993; Pres. 1994; Past Pres. 1995); Folklore Studies Association of Canada (Co-Convenor, Ont. Section 1986-88); American Folklore Society (Women's Section); California Folklore Society; Canadian Society for Traditional Music; Association for Canadian Studies. HONS: Chicago Folklore Prize (2nd), *True Poetry*, 1990. MISC: recipient, various grants & fellowships; numerous conference presentations. COMMENT: *"I am interested in learning how women use traditional and popular culture in their everyday lives; we don't pay enough attention to the everyday."*

Greenley, Nora I., R.N.,B.N.,M.Sc. ⊕
Senior Operating Officer, Acute Care Services, CALGARY REGIONAL HEALTH AUTHORITY, 1820 Richmond Rd. S.W., Calgary, AB T2T 5C7 (403) 229-7841, FAX 229-7214. EDUC: Brockville General Hospital Sch. of Nursing, R.N. 1966; Univ. of Calgary, B.Nursing (with distinction) 1978, M.Sc. 1982. CAREER: Staff Nurse, St. Francis General Hospital, Smith Falls, Ont., 1966-67; Staff Nurse, Ottawa Civic Hospital, 1967-69; Staff Nurse, Dept. of Health & Social Svcs, Churchill, Man., 1969-70; Staff Nurse, Foothills Provincial General Hospital, Calgary, 1970-71; Asst. Head Nurse, 1971-73; Head Nurse, 1973-75; Medical Nursing Coord., 1975-79; Dir. of Nursing, Tom Baker Cancer Centre, 1981-84; Adjunct Assoc. Prof., Fac. of Nursing, Univ. of Calgary, 1982 to date; VP, Patient Care Svcs, Alberta Children's Provincial General Hospital, 1984-94; Sr. Operating Officer, Tertiary Academic Reg'l Svcs, Calgary Regional Health Authority, 1994-95; Sr. Operating Officer, Acute Care Svcs, 1995 to date. SELECTED PUBLICATIONS: "Patient Classification Systems: An Introduction" (*Alberta Association of Registered Nurses Newsletter* Mar. 1981); "Nursing Care of the Terminally Ill: State of the Art" (*Alberta Association of Registered Nurses Newsletter* May 1981); "Attitudes About Death, Dying, and Terminal Care: Differences Among Groups at a University Teaching Hospital" (*Omega* June 1983). AFFIL: Canadian Nurses' Association; Alberta Association of Registered Nurses; Canadian Coll. of Health Services Executives; Executive Nurses' Association of Alberta; Council of Teaching Hospitals of Alberta - Chief Nursing Officers; Canadian Association of Nurse Administrators. HONS: Gold Medal for Gen. Proficiency & Award for Professional Adjustment & Leadership, Brockville General

Hospital Sch. of Nursing, 1966. **MISC:** various conference presentations; Bd. Mbr., Hospital Privileges Appeal Bd., Gov't of Alta., 1986-92; Chair, Alberta Health Nursing Job Enhancement Advisory Committee, 1991-94; Bd. Mbr., Alberta Foundation for Nursing Research, Gov't of Alta., 1985-90.

Greenstone, Harriet A., M.A., C.P.P.Q. ⊕ ⌁ ○
Founding President, JUST FOR KIDS FOUNDATION (J.F.K.), 14770 Boul. Pierrefonds, Ste. 206, Pierrefonds, QC H9H 4Y6 (514) 624-4396. Psychologist in Private Practice and Director, MULTI DISCIPLINARY CARE CENTRE (M.D.C.). Born Montreal 1957. m. Warren. 5 ch. **EDUC:** Vanier Coll., D.E.C.(Social Sci.) 1976; Concordia Univ., B.A.(Hons., Psych.) 1979; McGill Univ., M.A.(Educ. Psych.) 1990. **CAREER:** psychologist in private practice; Dir., M.D.C.; consultant to a number of preschools & private schools; psychological collaborator on research proj. investigating long-term outcome of children with history of broncho-pulmonary diplasia with Dr. A. Majnemer and Dr. P. Riley. **SELECTED PUBLICATIONS:** "Factors Associated with Cigarette Smoking in Elementary School Children," with M. West, M. Subak & M. Carlin (*Canadian Family Physicians* 1983); "Discriminality between Three Risk Groups and Prediction to Later Mental Functioning," with D.M. Stack & M.S. Weiss, SRCD (Society for Research in Child Development) Abstract, Seattle, 1991; "Processing of Sequential Visual Auditory Events by 31-month-old Down Syndrome Babies," with M. St. Germain & C.L. Rogers, SRCD Abstract, Seattle, 1991; "Children's Reactions to parental separation: levels of anxiety and levels of self-esteem," with F. Cyr & J.L. Derevensky, workshop presented at the 2nd Int'l Conference on the Child, Organization of Children's Rights, 1992; many other workshops to parents & teachers on behaviour mgmt, learning disabilities, living disabilities, etc. **AFFIL:** Just for Kids (Founding Pres.); Montreal Children's Hospital (Mbr., Centre Bd., Foundation Bd.; Co-Chair, Task Force on Volunteers; Mbr., Task Force on Abuse): Lakeshore Sch. Bd. (Advisory Committee–students with special needs; rep. on Educ. Committee; Chair, Sch. Committee, Sunnydale Sch.); Hebrew Foundation Sch. (Mbr., Educ. Committee). **COMMENT:** *"I am a proud wife and mother, a psychologist and an individual who is interested in, and is working towards, bettering my community and other communities. My specific areas of work, both professionally and as a volunteer, focus on medical and education issues and institutions. J.F.K. is a volunteer group created to raise money to buy much-* *needed medical equipment for the Montreal Children's Hospital. There are more than 250 members and they have raised nearly $2,000,000 since 1987."*

Greer, Jan ○ ⌁
Executive Director, NEW BRUNSWICK COMMITTEE ON LITERACY, 88 Prospect St. W., Fredericton, NB E3B 2T8 (506) 457-1227, FAX 458-1352. Born Plaster Rock, N.B. 1953. d. 2 ch. Sean Linton, Carrie Linton. **EDUC:** New Brunswick Community Coll., Woodstock, Hons. Diploma (Journalism) 1988. **CAREER:** Writer/Researcher/Assoc. Prod./Prod./Dir., for *Information Morning* & *Mainstreet*, CBC Radio Fredericton; Public Rel'ns/Mktg for an employment agency for adults with mental handicaps; Exec. Dir., N.B. Committee on Literacy. **AFFIL:** Learning Disabilities Association of N.B. (Past Pres.); Fredericton Community Literacy Committee (Sec.); Canadian Celiac Association (VP, Fredericton Chapter). **INTERESTS:** music; theatre; reading; writing; sports. **COMMENT:** *"On my own and with two small children in 1986, I decided to further my education. Graduated from a journalism program two years later with honours. Reached many of my personal career goals with CBC and my current position with the New Brunswick Committee on Literacy. However, my greatest achievement likely has been, against many odds, successfully raising my two children, now 19 and 20 (both with learning disabilities), to healthy, happy adulthood."*

Gregory, Cristen, B.Mus. ⊗ ⍦ ⌕ ⟡
Professional Musician, Soprano. 92 Burnside Dr., Toronto, ON M6G 2M8 (416) 531-6120, FAX 530-4438. Born Toronto 1958. **EDUC:** Royal Conservatory of Music, Toronto, Voice/Piano; Univ. of Toronto, B.Mus. in Performance (Voice) 1980; Canadian Opera Company Resident Artists' Program, Grad. **CAREER:** professional vocalist, 1981 to date; operatic debut with Canadian Opera Company, 1981; performs opera, operetta & musical theatre worldwide; concert performer with symphony orchestras, worldwide; Program Coord., *Opus Classics*, classical music radio, WBFO, NY; Professional Entertainment Program Planner for concert series, orchestras, conventions, etc.; mbr, renowned soprano/cello duo, "Voci d'Amore." **SELECTED CREDITS:** Musetta, *La Boheme*, Canadian Opera Company; Rosina, *The Barber of Seville*, Canadian Opera Company; Suzel, *L'Amico Fritz*, Chicago Opera Theater; Alice Ford, *Falstaff*, Aldeburgh Festival, UK; Donna Elvira, *Don Giovanni*, Britten/Mozart Festival, London, UK; Countess Maritza, *Countess Maritza*, Sylva Varescu,

Gypsy Princess, Lisa, *Land of Smiles*, Angele Didier, *The Count of Luxembourg*, Toronto Operetta Theatre; Mabel, *The Pirates of Penzance*, Pacific Opera Victoria; Josephine, *H.M.S. Pinafore*, Rainbow Stage, Winnipeg; Nettie, *Carousel*, Greater Buffalo Opera Company; numerous other opera, operetta & musical theatre performances; concert appearances at the 1993 Rochester Bach Festival, Bermuda International Arts Festival, & the inaugural season of the Ford Centre for the Performing Arts, North York; broadcast credits include *Messiah*, WNIB Radio, a recital for *Music Around Us*, CBC Radio; *Death in Venice* (Cdn premier); *Texaco Saturday Afternoon at the Opera*, CBC Radio & *Johnson Over Jordan* (world premier) with the English Chamber Orchestra, BBC Radio; recitals, UK & France. **AFFIL:** Canadian Children's Opera Chorus (Dir. 1990-96; Artistic Advisory Committee); Canadian Actors' Equity Association; ACTRA; American Guild of Musical Artists ; Royal Canadian Coll. of Organists; Young Audiences of Western New York; Wednesday Morning Musicale, Buffalo, N.Y. **HONS:** Puccini Foundation Award; Concours International de Chant Loire-Atlantique, France; CBC Radio National Auditions; American Opera Awards, N.Y.; Jean Chalmers Award; Mendelssohn Foundation Scholarship. **MISC:** Voice Masterclass Specialist; 1st alumna of Canadian Children's Opera Chorus to become a director of same, 1992. **COMMENT:** *"Many accomplishments already highlight the career of Cristen Gregory. A dedicated professional, she seeks to contribute her artistry and abilities in cultural pursuits the world over."*

Grenier, Denise, B.A.,M.A. 🍁
Directrice de l'Ordre National du Québec, Ministère du Conseil exécutif, GOUVERNEMENT DU QUÉBEC, 885, Grand Allée E, Édifice "J", Rm. 24, Québec, QC G1A 1A2 (418) 643-8895, FAX 643-8638. Born Amqui, Que. 1941. m. Jean Grenier. 5 ch. **EDUC:** École normale d'Amqui, Certificate (Pédagogie) 1959; Hôpital du Saint-Sacrement, Nursing diploma 1962; Laval Univ., B.A.(Journalism) 1975; École nationale d'admin. publique, M.A.(Admin.) 1989. **CAREER:** Surgical & Obstetrical Nurse, 1962-67; Coord., courses for pregnant women throughout Que., Ministère des Affaires sociales, 1976; Ed. in chief, *Carrefour des affaires sociales*, 1978-81; Assoc. Chief of State for Min. of Social Affairs, 1981-84; Assoc. Chief of State for Min. of Cdn Affairs, 1984; Dir., l'Ordre National du Québec, 1984 to date. **SELECTED PUBLICATIONS:** many articles on health & social affairs in *Carrefour des affaires sociales, Les affaires sociales au Québec* & the official publication of the Ordre national du Québec; *La légion d'honneur: instrument ou miroir de l'histoire de l'État français*, report. **AFFIL:** Hôpital de l'Enfant-Jésus (Dir.); Association des hôpitaux du Québec (Dir.); Corporation du Théâtre du Trident (Dir.); Regie de la santé et des services sociaux, Qué. **INTERESTS:** history; travel; theatre; music. **MISC:** involved since 1990 in the organization of sports championships (speed skating); assisted Chef de mission, Calgary Olympics, 1988; volunteer Chair, Protocol & Reception Committee, Québec 2002; mbr., Selection Committee, Ordre des infirmières et infirmiers du Québec, 1987-93. **COMMENT:** *"Over the past few years, in working with numerous and varied clients, I have acquired in-depth knowledge of management and coordination information. Since 1984 as a director of the Ordre national du Québec, I have the greatest satisfaction in giving recognition to the men and women who are the true vectors of society's evolution."*

Grenier, Kathleen, M.Fisc.,C.A.,B.B.A. $
Director, Taxation, DOMINION TEXTILE INC., 1950 Sherbrooke St. W., Montreal, QC H3H 1E7 (514) 989-6065, FAX 989-6038. Born Sainte-Foy, Que 1959. 1 ch. Chloe Alexandra Parsons. **EDUC:** Bishop's Univ., B.B.A.(Acctg) 1981; McGill Univ., Diploma in Public Accountancy 1983; Sherbrooke Univ., Masters in Taxation 1988. **CAREER:** Dir., Taxation, Dominion Textile Inc. **SELECTED PUBLICATIONS:** "Détermination de la résidence fiscale des particuliers selon la convention fiscale Canada-États Unis" (*Canadian Tax Journal* Nov./Dec. 1988). **AFFIL:** Canadian Institute of Chartered Accountants; Canadian Tax Foundation. **HONS:** highest average in Commerce Program, Champlain Regional Coll., 1978; Douglas Carmichael Entrance Scholarship, Bishop's Univ., 1978. **INTERESTS:** watercolour painting; outdoor sports. **COMMENT:** *"I am a self-motivated, assertive individual with excellent interpersonal skills. I have spent the past 10 years working in taxation in a chartered accounting firm and in industry."*

Grey, Deborah C., B.A.,B.Ed./A.D., M.P. 🍁 🎓
Member of Parliament (Beaver River), GOVERNMENT OF CANADA, Ottawa, ON (613) 996-9778, FAX 996-0785. **EDUC:** Burrard Inlet Bible Institute, 1973; Univ. of Alberta, B.A. (Soc./English) 1978, B.Ed./A.D. 1979. **CAREER:** teacher, Frog Lake Indian Reserve, Alta., 1979-80; teacher, Dewberry Sch., Alta., 1980-89; candidate, Reform Party, Beaver River, Alta., 1988; M.P. (Beaver River), 1989 to date; Chrm, Reform Party, 1993 to date;

Deputy Parliamentary Leader, Reform Party, 1995 to date. **AFFIL:** Reform Party. **INTERESTS:** swimming; kayaking; canoeing; waterskiing; hiking; archery; camping; travelling; public speaking; drama. **MISC:** Foster Parent 1984-88.

Grierson, Lela Ⓢ

Regional Manager, VANCOUVER CITY SAVINGS, 3395 W. Broadway, Vancouver, BC V6R 2B1 (604) 877-7040, FAX 877-7904. Born Vancouver 1949. cl. Raymond Grierson. 1 ch. **CAREER:** Teller/Mbr. Svc., South Burnaby Credit Union, 1967-73; Teller, Bank of Nova Scotia, 1973-75; various positions, from Teller to Reg'l Mgr, Vancouver City Savings, 1976 to date. **AFFIL:** Learning Tree Daycare (Treas. 1987-89); Marpole Bus. Association (former Exec. Dir.); Kitsilano Business Association; Canadian Club of Vancouver. **INTERESTS:** golf; fishing; walking; reading. **COMMENT:** *"I am a positive, self-motivated, energetic person. I have achieved beyond my own expectations both personally and professionally with the support of family and colleagues."*

Griffin, Diane, B.Sc.,B.Ed.,M.Sc. ■ ■ ✦

Deputy Minister, Department of Environmental Resources, GOVERNMENT OF PRINCE EDWARD ISLAND, P.O. Box 2000, Charlottetown, PE C1A 7N8 (902) 368-5340, FAX 368-6488, EMAIL dfgriffin@gov.pe.ca. Born Summerside, P.E.I. 1947. m. Kevin. 1 ch. Sharleen. **EDUC:** St. Dunstan's Univ., B.Sc. 1969; Univ. of P.E.I., B.Ed.; Acadia Univ., M.Sc.(Biol.) 1973. **CAREER:** Supervisor of Interpretation, P.E.I. Dept. of Tourism, Parks & Conservation, 1973-77; Natural Areas Coord., Alberta Dept. of Energy & Natural Res., 1977-86; Exec. Dir., Island Nature Trust, 1986-95; Deputy Min., P.E.I. Dept. of Environmental Res., 1995 to date. **SELECTED PUBLICATIONS:** author, *Atlantic Wildflowers* (Oxford Univ. Press, 1984). **AFFIL:** Queen Elizabeth Hospital Foundation (V-Chair 1996 to date); UNESCO Program on Man & the Biosphere (Cdn Committee); Canadian Wildlife Foundation (Dir.); Parks Canada (Sci. Advisory Bd.); Strathgartney Foundation (Treas. 1995 to date). **HONS:** Douglas H. Pimlott Conservation Award, Canadian Nature Federation, 1992; Distinguished Alumna Award, Univ. of P.E.I., 1992; Gov. Gen.'s Conservation Award, Tourism Industry Association of Canada, 1989; Canadian Outdoorsman of the Year Award, 1986; Chair's Award, Nature Conservancy of Canada, 1996; Merit Award, Atlantic Society of Fish & Wildlife Biologists, 1990; National Parks Centennial Award, 1985. **INTERESTS:** travel; gourmet cooking; hunting. **COMMENT:** *"My*

interests have centred on environmental conservation, particularly wildlife habitat, and the integration of both environmental and economic concerns into decision-making."

Griffin, Lynne Ⓧ

Actor. c/o K.G. Talent, 55A Sumach St., Toronto, ON M5A 3J6 (416) 368-4866, FAX 368-2492. Born Toronto. m. Sean Sullivan. **SELECTED CREDITS:** featured, *True Identity* (feature), Touchstone; Co-Star, *Obsessed* (feature), Telescene Films; Lead, *Strange Brew* (feature), MGM; Lead, *Curtains* (feature), Simcom; series regular, *Wind At My Back* (series), CBC/Sullivan Films; Guest Star, *NYPD Blue* (series), ABC; Guest Star, *Picket Fences* (series), CBS TV, 20th Century; Lead, *How Do You Do?* (series), TVOntario; Lead, *Comedy Factory* (series), ABC TV; Lead, *A Class Affair* (telefilm), MGM TV; Guest Star, *The Magic of David Copperfield* (TV special), CBS TV; Hostess, *Drop In* (series); Macon, *Abundance* (theatre), Foothill Theatre; Mother, *Mr. A's Amazing Maze Plays* (theatre), Old Globe Theatre; Heidi, *The Heidi Chronicles* (theatre), Gaslamp Quarters; Violet, *Man and Superman* (theatre); South Coast Rep; Cordelia, *King Lear* (theatre), Stratford. **AFFIL:** ACTRA; CAEA; SAG; AFTRA; AEA. **HONS:** several Dramalogue Awards for stage performances in L.A. **COMMENT:** *"Actress for 30 years. Has appeared on stage and in film and television in Canada and the US. Has lived in L.A. for the past 12 years and has recently moved back to Canada."*

Griffin, Nonnie, A.R.C.T. ■ Ⓧ ♥

Actress. c/o The Characters, 150 Carlton St., Toronto, ON M5A 2K1 (416) 964-8522, FAX 964-8206. Born Toronto 1933. s. **EDUC:** Royal Conservatory, A.R.C.T.(Speech Arts & Drama) 1952. **CAREER:** Actor, Canadian Repertory Theatre, Ottawa, 1952-53; Leading Lady, Oakville Summer Theatre, 1952; Actor, numerous productions, 1954 to date. **HONS:** Best Actress Award (Gina Mallet), *The Toronto Star*, 1977, 1978; Finalist, Andrew Allan Award (Radio), 1983. **INTERESTS:** writing; singing; piano; cooking; canoeing; swimming; poetry; decorating; teaching youngsters (or anyone) the value of communication & good speech. **COMMENT:** *"Still vital after 40 years in show biz! Managed to stay alive in my career and portray every age and kind of human being on the globe. High standards have always been the goal. I am proud to be in such a challenging profession, especially in our country."*

Griffith, Gwyneth P., B.A.,M.S.W.,Ed.D., D.D. ◁

Educational Consultant. 154 Davisville Ave.,

Toronto, ON M4S 1E8 (416) 488-5074. Born Toronto 1932. s. **EDUC:** Univ. of Toronto, B.A.(Psych.) 1953, M.S.W. 1956, Ed.D. 1982. **CAREER:** Social Worker, Children's Aid Society of Ontario County, 1953-58; Social Worker, Children's Aid Society of Hamilton, 1958-62; Dir., Indiv. Svcs, YWCA of Metropolitan Toronto, 1962-64; Branch & Area Dir., 1965-69; Consultant for Leadership & Program Dev., YWCA of Canada, 1969-71; Exec. Dir., YWCA of Metropolitan Toronto, 1971-77; Extramural Instructor, Ontario Institute for Studies in Education, 1978-79; Academic Staff, Centre for Christian Studies, 1980-82; Principal, 1982-91; freelance Educational Consultant, 1991 to date. **SELECTED PUBLICATIONS:** "Images of Interdependence: Learning/Teaching for Justice and Peace" (*Religious Education* Summer 1984); "Power and Authority in Ministry: Differing Styles and Models" (*Practice of Ministry in Canada* Feb. 1985); "Workshops and Conferences: Planning for Adult Learning," in *Insight: A Resource for Adult Education* (Nat'l Office of Religious Educ., Cdn Conference of Catholic Bishops, 1988); "From Loneliness to Solitude: Reflections on Aloneness," in *Single Women: Affirming Our Reality*, ed. by Mary O'Brien & Clare Christie (Amherst, MA: Bergin & Garvey, 1993); several articles in *Exchange* (United Church of Canada publication). **AFFIL:** Union Theological Seminary, N.Y. (Fellow); Eglinton United Church; Toronto South Presbytery (Pastoral Rel'ns Committee); Canadian Churches' Forum on Global Ministries; 1998 Ecumenical Decade of Churches in Solidarity with Women in Church & Society event (Planning Committee); United Church TV Programming Bd.; Student Christian Movement of Canada; North Toronto ecumenical proj. on domestic violence; working as a consultant with various church organizations & courts–local, judicatories, nat'l esp. in the United Church of Canada. **HONS:** Queen's Silver Jubilee Medal, 1977; D.D.(Hon.), Univ. of Toronto, 1993; D.D.(Hon.), McGill Univ., 1993. **INTERESTS:** music; photography; women's spirituality/theology; cottage. **COMMENT:** *"I am a feminist educator, a lay woman involved in the institutional church, interested in exploring new theological understanding, passionate about justice, especially related to women. I love to sing."*

Griffiths, Linda 🕱 ▯ ⎍

Actor, Writer. 224 Markham St., Toronto, ON M6J 2G6, phone c/o Patty Ney, Chris Banks and Associates (416) 214-1155. Born Montreal 1956. **SELECTED CREDITS:** Maggie, Pierre and Henry, *Maggie & Pierre*, Theatre Pass Muraille, Toronto; Hilda, *The Master Builder*, Tarragon Theatre, Toronto; Alice, *Fen*, The Public Theatre, N.Y.; Ophelia, *Hamlet*, Theatre Pass Muraille, Toronto; She, *The Darling Family*, Theatre Pass Muraille, Toronto; principal, *Lianna*, John Sayles, dir.; principal, *Empire Inc.*, CBC-TV; principal, *The Marriage Bed*, CBC; principal, *Passion and Paradise*, NBC; principal, *The Darling Family*, Alan Zweig, dir.; various other film, TV & theatre credits. **SELECTED PUBLICATIONS:** *Maggie & Pierre*, play (Talon Books, 1980); "Prayer," poem (*The Prairie Journal of Canadian Literature* 1988); *The Book of Jessica*, prose with Maria Campbell (Toronto: Coach House Press, 1989); "Free Trade Election," poem in *Barbed Lyres* anthology (Toronto: Key Porter Books, 1990); "O.D. on Paradise," play in *Dangerous Traditions* anthology (Blizzard Publishing, 1991); *The Darling Family* (Blizzard Publishing, 1991); "The Speed Christmas," prose (*Journal of Canadian Women's Studies* 1993); "A Game of Inches," play in *Solo* anthology (Coach House Press, 1994); "Wallis Simpson," radio play in *Adventure Stories for Big Girls* anthology (Blizzard Publishing, 1994). **AFFIL:** Canadian Actor's Equity Association; Playwrights' Union of Canada; ACTRA. **HONS:** Outstanding New Play, *Maggie & Pierre*, Dora Mavor Moore Awards, 1980; Best Performance by an Actress in a Leading Role, *Maggie & Pierre*, Dora Mavor Moore Awards, 1980; Outstanding New Play, *O.D. on Paradise*, Dora Mavor Moore Awards, 1983; Outstanding New Play, *Jessica*, Dora Mavor Moore Awards, 1986; Chalmers Award, *Jessica*, 1986; Best Production, Quinzème Int'l Festival, Quebec City, *Jessica*, 1987; Best Actress in a Leading Role, *Empire Inc.*, Gemini Awards, 1983; A.G.A. Award, for performance, *Lianna*, 1984; nomination (*The Darling Family*), Gov. General's Award, 1991. **INTERESTS:** Tai Chi; baseball; politics. **COMMENT:** *"I'm a hybrid in the arts, between acting and writing, there is a schizophrenia. I call myself a 'writer/actor' or an 'actor/writer' depending on the job. I bristle when told I 'write parts for myself.' Somehow this implies a bogus attitude to the work."*

Griggs, Terry, B.A.,M.A. 📖

Writer. Born Little Current, Manitoulin Island, Ont. 1951. m. David Burr. 1 ch. Alexander Galen Griggs-Burr. **EDUC:** Univ. of Western Ontario, B.A.(English Lit.) 1977, M.A.(English Lit.) 1979. **CAREER:** writer. **SELECTED PUBLICATIONS:** *Harrier* (1982); *Quickening* (1990); *The Lusty Man* (1995). **HONS:** *Quickening* shortlisted for Gov. General's Award, 1991.

Grin, Gayle, B.A. ✏ 🕱 ⎍

Feature Design Director, THE GAZETTE, 250 St.

Antoine St. W., Montreal, QC (514) 987-2444, FAX 987-2399. Born Grand Rapids, Mich. 1949. cl. Jack Grin. 2 ch. Cedric Grin, Liam Grin. EDUC: Trinity Coll., Chicago, B.A.(Art/ Educ.) 1971; George Brown Coll., Graphic Design Certificate 1982. HONS: 22 nat'l & int'l design awards from The Advertising & Design Club of Canada, The National Magazine Awards, *Applied Arts* Magazine Awards & the Society of International Newspaper Design.

Grinspun, Doris R., R.N.,M.S.N. ■■ ⊕ ⊚

Executive Director, REGISTERED NURSES' ASSOCIATION OF ONTARIO, 438 University Ave., Ste. 1600, Toronto, ON M5G 2K8 (416) 599-1925, ext. 206, 1-800-268-7199, FAX 599-1926. EDUC: Hadassah Sch. of Nursing, Hadassah Medical Center, Jerusalem, R.N. 1974; Tel Aviv Univ., Post Baccalaureate (Nursing, magna cum laude) 1983; Univ. of Michigan, M.S.N. 1991; Univ. of Toronto, Fac. of Nursing, Ph.D. studies 1993-94; York Univ., Ph.D. studies (Sociology) 1995 to date. CAREER: Staff Nurse, Haematology Dept., Hadassah Medical Center, 1974-75; Staff Nurse, Surgical Dept. B, Meir Gen. Hospital, Kfar, Saba, Israel, 1975-78; Staff Nurse, Intensive Care Unit, Loewenstein Rehab. Hospital, Raanana, Israel, 1978-79; Staff Nurse, Amputee Patient Dept., 1979-80; Staff Nurse, Cranio-Cerebral Injury Dept., June-Oct. 1980; Asst. Head Nurse, Cranio-Cerebral Injury Dept., 1980-83; Staff Nurse, Adult Rehab. Unit, Univ. of Michigan Hospital, Ann Arbor, Mich., 1984; Clinical Nurse II for Brain-Injured Patients, Adult Rehab. Unit, 1984-85; Clinical Nurse III for Brain-Injured Patients, Adult Rehab. Unit, 1985-86; Asst. Head Nurse, Adult Rehab. Unit, 1986-89; Clinical Nurse Specialist, Rehab. Svcs, Queen Elizabeth Hospital, Toronto, 1989-90; Program Dir., Nursing (Chair, various nursing programs), Mount Sinai Hospital, Toronto, 1990-96; Exec. Dir., RNAO, 1996 to date. SELECTED PUBLICATIONS: author/co-author, 11 papers in refereed journals; 3 chpts. in books; over 25 other publications; more than 100 presentations. AFFIL: American Coll. of Health Care Executives (Assoc. 1995 to date); Coll. of Physicians & Surgeons of Ontario (RNAO Rep., Special Procedures Committee 1995-96); Canadian Nurses Association (Nominating Committee 1994-96; Voting Delegate 1994-95); Canadian Society for International Health; Canadian Nursing Research Group; Provincial Nurses Research Interest Group; Sigma Theta Tau (nat'l hon. society of nursing); National Association of Nurses in Israel; Heart & Stroke Foundation of Ontario (Chair, Stroke Educ. Task

Force 1991-93); Head Injury Association of Toronto (Bd. mbr. 1990-93; Pres. 1992-93); Metropolitan Toronto Acquired Brain Injury Network (Chair 1996 to date); Centre for Latin American & Caribbean Studies, York Univ. (Assoc. Fellow 1994 to date); World Health Organization (Assoc. mbr., Collaborating Centre, Mount Sinai Hospital 1992 to date); Centre for Health Promotion, Univ. of Toronto (Assoc. mbr. 1992 to date); Centre for Health Studies, York Univ. (Affiliate mbr. 1994 to date). HONS: Mgmt Leadership Award, Mount Sinai Hospital, 1993; Ella May Howard Award for Leadership in Nursing Admin., Mount Sinai Hospital Dept. of Nursing, 1992; Phys. Medicine & Rehab. Clinical Svc. Award, Univ. of Michigan Medical Center, 1989; numerous academic fellowships & awards. MISC: Clinical Consultant, brain injury programs, Michigan & London, Ont., 1986-92; int'l work through World Health Organization, Canadian International Development Agency, & others, in Chile, Ecuador, Mexico, Colombia & Nicaragua; fluent in Spanish & Hebrew.

Grisé, Yolande, B.A.,L.èsL.,M.èsL., D.èsL. de 3e cycle ⟨⟩ 🕮 ⊗

Professeure de littérature, Département des lettres françaises, et Directrice, Centre de recherche en civilisation canadienne-française, UNIVERSITY OF OTTAWA, 145, rue Jean-Jacques-Lussier, CP 450, Succ. A, Ottawa, ON K1N 6N5 (613) 562-5800, ext. 4010, FAX 562-5143. Born Montréal 1944. EDUC: Univ. de Montréal, B.A. 1965, B.Péd. 1965; Univ. Laval, Licence ès Lettres 1971; Univ. de Paris-IV, La Sorbonne, Maîtrise ès Lettres 1972, Doctorat ès Lettres de 3e cycle 1977. CAREER: Prof. d'hist. romaine, Dépt. d'Hist., Univ. Laval, 1978-79; Prof. adjointe, Dépt. des lettres françaises, Univ. d'Ottawa, 1980-83; Prof. agrégée 1983-90; Prof. titulaire, 1990 à ce jour; Prés., Conseil des arts de l'Ont., 1991-94; Dir., Centre de recherche en civilisation canadienne-française, Univ. d'Ottawa, 1985-88, 1989-91, 1991-94, 1994-97. SELECTED PUBLICATIONS: *Le Suicide dans la Rome antique* (1982); *Textes littéraires de l'Ontario français*, anthologie en 4 vols (1982); *Le Monde des dieux* (1985); *Les Textes poétiques du Canada français, 1606-1867*, Dir. et co-auteure, 12 vols; à date 9 vols ont paru (1987); *Les Arts visuels en Ontario français* (1990); *RSVP! Clefs en main/RSVP! Keys for the Future* (1991); *Mélanges de littérature canadienne-française et québécoise offerts à Réjean Robidoux*, co-Dir. (1992); *Émile Nelligan, Cinquante ans après sa mort*, co-Dir. (1993); *Les États généraux de la recherche sur la francophonie à l'extérieur du Québec*, éd. (1995); nombreux articles spécialisés en études anciennes et littérature canadienne-française parus que au Canada et en Europe. **AFFIL:** Fédération canadienne des études humaines (Dir. 1991-93); Société des études latines (Paris); Union des écrivains québécois; Association des études canadiennes; Association des littératures canadiennes et québécoise. **MISC:** boursière; participé à des jury académiques et littéraires; Prés., jury du Prix littéraire du Gouverneur général, catégorie "Études et essais," 1989; mbr. de la Société royale du Canada, Académie des lettres et des sciences humaines I, 1996.

Grist, Kari, B.Comm. ■ ⑤
Director, Special Projects, CANADIAN AIRLINES INTERNATIONAL LTD., 700 - 2nd St. S.W., Ste. 2800, Calgary, AB T2P 2W2 (403) 294-6134, FAX 294-6160. Born Edmonton 1959. m. Mark Grist. 1 ch. **EDUC:** Univ. of British Columbia, B.Comm.(Transportation & Mktg) 1983. **CAREER:** various positions, Mktg, Wardair, 1984-89; various positions, Mktg, Canadian Airlines, 1989-92; Dir., Customer Comm., 1992-96. **HONS:** President's Award, Canadian Airlines, 1994. **INTERESTS:** travel.

Grobety, Marcia ⑤
Independent Executive Senior Director, MARY KAY COSMETICS LTD., 29 Uplands Cres., Winnipeg, MB R2Y 0P7 (204) 837-1193. Born Sask. 1953. m. Pierre. 3 ch. **CAREER:** Salesperson, Mary Kay Cosmetics, 1979-81; Independent Sales Dir., 1981-93; Exec. Sr. Dir., 1993 to date. **AFFIL:** St. James Assiniboine Sch. Div. (Parents' Association for French Immersion); Heritage Victoria Community Club (Sec. 1987-88); Sturgeon Creek United Church. **HONS:** $500,000 Circle of Achievement, Mary Kay Cosmetics; Go-Give Award, Mary Kay Cosmetics; Court of Sales & Recruiting, 1986 & 1989. **INTERESTS:** travel; music; reading; golf. **MISC:** taught at annual Mary Kay convention, 1994; trained consultants & directors for Mary Kay England, Nov. 1994. **COMMENT:** *"One of Mary Kay's pioneers, having been with the company since its first year of operations in Canada."*

Groetzinger, Deanna, B.A.,M.A. ◑ ⊕ ⊚
National Director of Communications,, MULTIPLE SCLEROSIS SOCIETY OF CANADA, 250 Bloor St. E., Ste. 1000, Toronto, ON M4W 3P9 (416) 922-6065, FAX 922-7538. Born Ord, Neb. 1945. m. Paul Stuewe. 3 ch. Matthew Stuewe, Christina Stuewe, Sarah Stuewe. **EDUC:** Univ. of Nebraska, B.A.(Journalism) 1969; Univ. of Waterloo, M.A.(Pol. Sci.) 1977. **CAREER:** Educ. & Bus. Reporter, *Sioux City Journal,* 1969; Educ. & Arts Reporter, *Peterborough*

Examiner, 1970; Asst. to the Exec. Dir., Multiple Sclerosis Society, 1974-77; Dir. of Public Educ., 1977-87; Nat'l Dir. of Comm., 1987 to date. **SELECTED PUBLICATIONS:** numerous medical articles for lay readership. **EDIT:** MS/SP Canada. **AFFIL:** American Medical Writers' Association (Toronto Chapter); Palmerston Home & Sch. Association (Co-Chair 1987-88); Canadian Parents for French; Phi Beta Kappa; Kappa Tau Alpha. **INTERESTS:** raising happy, productive children; photography; gardening; reading; travelling. **COMMENT:** *"My professional goal of communicating clear, accurate information about a complex medical subject is attainable by working with others in a collaborative manner."*

Grogan, Liz, B.A. ⌣ ▯
Broadcaster, MCLELLAN GROUP, 119 Spadina Ave., Ste. 1203, Toronto, ON M5V 2L1 (416) 597-2020, FAX 597-9444, EMAIL mcledllan_group@magic.ca. Born Toronto 1949. m. Doug McLellan. 1 ch. **EDUC:** Univ. of Toronto, B.A.(Pol. Sci.) 1971; Institut de Français, Ville Franche sur mer, France, 1986. **CAREER:** TV prod., writer & performer. **SELECTED CREDITS:** *Live It Up,* CTV; *Lifetime,* CTV; Olympics, CTV; *For Kid's Sake,* BBS; *Hospital for Sick Children Telethon,* BBS. **AFFIL:** ACTRA; Kool-Aid for Kids, fundraiser for children's hospitals (Founder); UNICEF (Mother's Day Spokesperson); Toronto Hospital for Sick Children. **INTERESTS:** sailing; women's health issues; parenting; writing; life at the cottage. **COMMENT:** *"My current interests focus on the issues of child development and parenting skills and how I can use my broadcast experience and skills to spread the message."*

Grono, Marie ⓟ ⊛
Manager, SASKATCHEWAN FORESTRY ASSOCIATION, 969 - 1st Ave. E., Box 400, Prince Alberta, SK S6V 5R7 (306) 763-2189. Manager, TREEMENDOUS SASKATCHEWAN FOUNDATION INC. Born Winnipeg 1959. m. Fred. 2 ch. Jodi, Eric. **EDUC:** Univ. of British Columbia, Botany 1977-80; Malaspina Coll., Forest Resources Technology Diploma 1983. **CAREER:** Alta. Gov't Treasury Branch, 1980-81; Summer employment, B.C. Gov't Parks Branch, 1982 & 1983; Mgr, Saskatchewan Forestry Association, 1984 to date; TREEmendous Saskatchewan Foundation Inc., 1991 to date. **SELECTED PUBLICATIONS:** has developed & written numerous program brochures for both the Saskatchewan Forestry Association & TREEmendous Saskatchewan Foundation Inc.; 2 Annual Reports for TREEmendous Saskatchewan Foundation Inc.; *TREEmendous*

Trees and Shrubs Handbook (2 editions). **EDIT:** *Treelines* (Saskatchewan Forestry Association newsletter). **AFFIL:** Canadian Forestry Association; Canadian Institute of Forestry (1984-90). **HONS:** Credit Union Scholarship, 1983; Order of the Hoo/hoo Scholarship, 1982; Phys. Educ. Scholarship, 1977. **INTERESTS:** camping; cross-country skiing with her children; gardening; reading; cross-stitch. **COMMENT:** *"Worked in cooperation with the Saskatchewan Government to establish the TREEmendous Saskatchewan Foundation Inc. as an independent nonprofit organization, with a mandate to provide the opportunity for all people in Saskatchewan to improve the environment through the planting of free tree and shrub seedlings."*

Gross Stein, Janice, B.A.,M.A., Ph.D. ■■ ◁ ❖

Harrowston Professor of Conflict Management and Negotiation, UNIVERSITY OF TORONTO, Dept. of Political Science, 100 St. George St., Toronto, ON M5S 3G3 (416) 978-1048, FAX 978-5566, EMAIL jstein@chass.utoronto.ca. Born Canada 1943. m. Michael Stein. 2 ch. Isaac, Gabriel. **EDUC:** McGill Univ., B.A.(Hist., first class hons.) 1964; Yale Univ., M.A.(Int'l Rel'ns, Woodrow Wilson Fellow) 1965; McGill Univ., Ph.D.(Pol. Sci., McConnell Fellow) 1969. **CAREER:** Prof., Univ. of Toronto, 1982; Harrowston Prof., 1993; Univ. Prof., 1996. **SELECTED PUBLICATIONS:** co-author with Raymond Tanter, *Rational Decision Making: Israel's Security Choices*, 1967 (Columbus, Ohio: Ohio State Univ. Press, 1980) (winner of Edgar Furniss Award); co-author with Robert Jervis & Richard Ned Lebow, *Psychology and Deterrence* (Baltimore: The Johns Hopkins Univ. Press, 1985); co-author with Richard Ned Lebow, *We All Lost the Cold War* (Princeton: Princeton Univ. Press, 1994); co-author with Geoffrey Kemp, *Powder Keg in the Middle East: The Struggle for Gulf Security* (Washington, DC: Routledge and Kegan, 1995); co-editor with Louis Pauly, *Choosing to Cooperate: How States Avoid Loss* (Baltimore: Johns Hopkins Univ. Press, 1993). **EDIT:** mbr. Edit. Bd.: *Political Psychology*, 1989 to date; *Foreign Policy*, 1993 to date; *International History Review*, 1994 to date. **AFFIL:** Research Advisory Bd. to Min. of Foreign Affairs (Chair 1995 to date); American Academy of Sciences (Committee on the Middle East 1989 to date); Commission of the International Association of University Professors & the U.N. on Undergraduate Education (mbr. 1992 to date); International Society of Political Psychology (VP 1996-97); American Association for the Advancement of Science (Peace & Security Committee 1993-96). **HONS:** Fellow, Royal Society of Canada, 1989; elected to membership, World Association of International Relations, 1985; Edgar S. Furniss Jr. Award for a manuscript "making an outstanding contribution to the study of national security & civilian military education," The Mershon Center, 1978. **INTERESTS:** int'l conflict mgmt; negotiation; Middle East politics; Canadian foreign policy. **MISC:** commentator on CBC, Newsworld, CTV; regular panelist on *Studio 2*, TVO. **COMMENT:** *"I have an interest in conflict management, public policy and public education."*

Grosskurth, Phyllis M., B.A.,M.A., Ph.D. ■ 📖 ◁

Professor Emeritus, New College, UNIVERSITY OF TORONTO, Toronto, ON M5A 2J6 (416) 978-4274. Born Toronto 1924. m. R.J.H. McMullan. 3 ch. Christopher, Brian, Anne. **EDUC:** Univ. of Toronto, B.A.(English) 1946; Univ. of Ottawa, M.A.(English) 1960; Univ. of London, Ph.D. 1962. **CAREER:** Lecturer, Carleton Univ., 1964-65; Asst. Prof., Dept. of English, University Coll., Univ. of Toronto, 1965-69; Assoc. Prof., Dept. of English, Univ. of Toronto, 1969-72; Prof., 1972-89; Hon. Research Fellow, University Coll., London, 1978-82; Fac. Mbr., Humanities & Psychoanalytic Thought Program, 1987-95; Visiting Prof., Univ. of Tennessee, 1988. **SELECTED PUBLICATIONS:** *John Addington Symonds: A Biography* (London: Longmans, 1964); *The Woeful Victorian* (New York: Holt Rinehart, 1965); *Gabrielle Roy* (Toronto: Forum House, 1969); *Havelock Ellis: A Biography* (Toronto: McClelland & Stewart, 1980); Ed., *The Memoirs of John Addington Symonds* (Random House, 1982); *Melanie Klein: Her World and Her Work* (Toronto: McClelland & Stewart, 1986); *Margaret Mead: A Life of Controversy* (Penguin, 1989); *The Secret Ring: Freud's Inner Circle and the Politics of Psychoanalysis* (Toronto: MacFarlane Walter & Ross, 1991); "Search and Psyche: The Writing of Biography" (*English Studies in Canada* June 1985); various other publications. **EDIT:** Bd. Mbr., *The Canadian Forum*, 1973-76, Literary Ed., 1975-76; Advisory Bd., *English Studies in Canada*, 1975-76; Advisory Committee, *The Graduate*, 1975-76; Consultant, *Biological Psychiatry*, 1990; Ed. Advisory Bd., *The Dalhousie Review*, 1990 to date. **AFFIL:** American Academy of Psychoanalysis (Psychiatric Assoc.); F.E.L. Memorial Fund (Bd. Mbr.); P.E.N. International; Writers' Union of Canada; Toronto Psychoanalytic Society (Guest); A.C.U.T.E.; Center for Psychoanalysis & Humanities, Dept. of Psych., Univ. of Tennessee (Advisory Bd.).

HONS: Gov. General's Award for non-fiction, 1965; Univ. of British Columbia Award for Biography, 1965; short list, National Book Award (UK), 1981; finalist, Gov. General's Award for non-fiction, 1987; Hon. Research Fellow, Univ. of Kent, 1991; Doctor of Sacred Letters (Hon.) & Hon. Fellow, Univ. of Toronto, 1992. INTERESTS: biography; psychoanalysis; art; history of ideas. MISC: jury mbr., various grants; recipient, various grants & fellowships incl. 2 John Simon Guggenheim Fellowships, 2 SSHRCC grants, & a Killam Fellowship; Canada Council "A" Grant. COMMENT: *"One of Canada's leading biographers."*

Gryski, Camilla, B.A.,M.L.S. ■■ 🐾 ⊗ ⊕
Writer. EMAIL cgryski@io.org. Born Bristol, UK 1948. m. Chester Gryski. 2 ch. Mark, Damian. EDUC: Univ. of Toronto, B.A.(Hons., English Language & Lit.) 1971, M.L.S.(Library Sci.) 1976; Toronto Montessori Institute, Montessori Primary Teaching Certificate 1972. CAREER: Teacher, Toronto Montessori schools, 1972-74; Children's Librarian, Toronto Public Library at Hospital for Sick Children, 1977-95; Therapeutic Clown, Hospital for Sick Children, 1995 to date. SELECTED PUBLICATIONS: 9 children's books incl.: *Hands On, Thumbs Up* (ill. Pat Cupples, Kids Can Press, 1990); *Friendship Bracelets* (Kids Can Press, 1992); *Camilla Gryski's Favourite String Games* (ill. Tom Sankey, Kids Can Press, 1995); *Camilla Gryski's Cat's Cradle* (ill. Tom Sankey, Kids Can Press, 1995); *Let's Play: Traditional Games of Childhood* (ill. Dusan Petricic, Kids Can Press, 1995). AFFIL: Canadian Society of Children's Authors, Illustrators & Performers (Treas. 1985-87; VP 1991-93; Pres. 1993-95); International Board on Books for Young People (Councillor 1984-87); Canadian Children's Book Centre; Writers' Union of Canada; P.E.N. Canada; Arts & Letters Club; International Jugglers' Association; Toronto Jugglers' Club (Exec. 1995 to date). HONS: Notable Book (*Cat's Cradle, Owl's Eyes: A Book of String Games*), American Library Association, 1984; Information Book Award (*Hands On, Thumbs Up*), Children's Literature Roundtables of Canada, 1991; Notable Non-Fiction for Children (*Let's Play: Traditional Games of Childhood*), Canadian Library Association, 1995. INTERESTS: juggling; reading; Inuit art; clowning history & practice. COMMENT: *"I have always loved words, children and the particular creativity that happens when hands and simple materials come together. So for more than twenty years, I have taught children, written for them, helped them find books to read, and played with them as parent, friend, clown."*

Guarnieri, Albina, MP,B.A.,M.A. ✦
Member of Parliament (Mississauga East) and Parliamentary Secretary to the Minister of Canadian Heritage, GOVERNMENT OF CANADA, Confederation Building, Rm. 450, Ottawa, ON K1A 0A6 (613) 996-0420, FAX 996-0279. Born Faeto, Italy. m. EDUC: McGill Univ., B.A., M.A. CAREER: private sector experience, incl. *Time* Magazine, *The Globe & Mail*, Ontario Institute for Studies in Education, & Ontario Waste Management Corporation; Press Sec. to Solicitor-Gen. of Canada, to Ont. Liberal Leader Stuart Smith, & to Toronto Mayor Art Eggleton; elected MP (Mississauga E.), 1988; mbr., Special Joint Parliamentary Committee on a Renewed Canada; Cdn Delegation, Conference of the Association of S.E. Asian Nations, Jakarta, Indonesia, 1992; re-elected, 1993; mbr., Standing Committee on Cdn Heritage; Parliamentary Sec. to the Min. of Cdn Heritage; Standing Committee on Gov. Oper., 1996; Co-Chair, Joint Standing Committee on Official Languages, 1996. AFFIL: Liberal Party of Canada. HONS: Dame of Grace, Sovereign Order of St. John of Jerusalem.

Guay, Monique, M.P. ✦
Member of Parliament (Laurentides), GOVERNMENT OF CANADA (613) 992-3257. Born L'Île Bizard, Que. 1959. m. Michel Bergeron. 4 ch. Erick, Annie, Julie, Patrick. EDUC: Dawson Coll. & McGill Univ., Admin. CAREER: active professionally in the area of real estate, 12 yrs.; VP, property mgmt company, 1987-90; Founder-Proprietor & Pres., Monivest Immobilier Inc., 1988; Property Mgr, 1990-93; elected Bloc Québécois candidate, Laurentides, 1993; M.P. (Laurentides), Gov't of Canada, 1993 to date; V-Chair, Bloc Québécois Members' Caucus, 1993 to date; Critic, Public Works & Gov't, 1993-94; Critic, Environment & Sustainable Dev., 1994 to date. AFFIL: Association des femmes d'affaires du Québec; Corporation de développement des Laurentides. MISC: founding mbr., Bloc Québécois nat'l party, 1990, & for the riding of Laurentides; V-Chair, No Committee for the county of Prévost & Co-Chair for the county of Rousseau, 1992 referendum.

Guilford, Celia 🌾 🌐 🍃
Co-owner, GUILFORD'S ORGANIC SEED AND FEED, Box 70, Clearwater, MB R0K 0M0 (204) 873-2454, FAX 873-2454. Born Winnipeg 1962. m. Robert Guilford. 1 ch. Jessie Kate. EDUC: Assiniboine Community Coll., Agribus. Diploma 1989; Independent Organic Inspectors' Association, Certificate in Organic Form & Processor Inspection 1993; Univ. of Califor-

nia, Santa Cruz, Certificate in Ecological Horticulture 1994. **CAREER:** Farm Ptnr, Clearwater, Man., 1983 to date; Owner, Stains and Panes Stained Glass, 1984-89; Instructor, Agric. & Rural Enterprise, Assiniboine Community Coll., 1989 to date; Facilitator, Canadian Organic Advisory Board Accreditation Program, 1995-96. **AFFIL:** Organic Producers' Association of Manitoba (Pres. 1991-94; Marquis Proj. "El Salvador" Committee); Woodlot Association of Manitoba (Dir. 1992-94); Independent Organic Inspectors' Association (Chair, Forms Committee 1992-93). **HONS:** Award for Achievement & Excellence, Assiniboine Community Coll., 1988; Cargill Award for Highest Academic Achievement, Assiniboine Community Coll., 1989. **INTERESTS:** reading; writing; skiing; swimming; walking; gardening (organic). **MISC:** moving with family for 26 months to Indonesia to work as CUSO cooperants at an agricultural institute in West Timor, 1997-99. **COMMENT:** *"Celia's passion is the advancement of organic agriculture, as shown by her commitment to voluntary associations and her work in developing organic agriculture curriculum at Assiniboine Community College."*

Guillemin, Evelyn J., B.Sc.N.,M.A.,R.N., Ph.D. ■ ⊕ 🎓

Management Consultant. Calgary, AB. Born Saskatoon, Sask. 1941. **EDUC:** Saskatoon City Hospital, Dip.(Nursing) 1963; Univ. of Alberta, B.Sc.N. 1977, Ph.D.(Educ. Admin.) 1990; Univ. of Saskatchewan, Dip.(Hospital Health Care Admin.) 1981; Univ. of Calgary, M.A.(Educ. Policy & Admin. Studies) 1983. **CAREER:** Staff Nurse, various hospitals, Saskatoon & Calgary, 1963-71, 1977-78; Educ. Coord., Glenmore Park Auxiliary Hospital, 1978-81; Coord. of Continuing Educ. in Nursing, Fac. of Continuing Educ., Univ. of Calgary, 1981-83; Asst. Prof., Fac. of Nursing, 1983-86; Dir., Medical/Ambulatory Care Nursing, Calgary General Hospital, 1988-93; Adjunct Asst. Prof., Fac. of Nursing, Univ. of Calgary, 1992-96; Dir., Medical Nursing, Calgary General Hospital, 1993-96. **SELECTED PUBLICATIONS:** *Nursing Use of Computers and Information Science*, ed. with Kathryn J. Hannah & Dorothy N. Conklin (Amsterdam: North Holland, 1985); "Assessment of Learning Needs and Interest in Distance Education Technology of Southern Rural Alberta Non-Degreed Registered Nurses" (*Alberta Association of Registered Nurses Newsletter* May 1984); "Outreach Post R.N. Degree Program: A Demonstration Project" (*Alberta Association of Registered Nurses Newsletter* Jan. 1986); various other publications. **AFFIL:** Alberta Association of Registered Nurses; Alberta Health Care Educators' Interest Group; Canadian Association for Distance Education; Canadian Association for University Continuing Education; Canadian Association of University Schools of Nursing. **MISC:** numerous presentations; grant recipient. **COMMENT:** *"Dr. Guillemin's experience has included nursing practice, education and management responsibilities in various health care agencies and educational institutions. She has been actively involved in research and publication and has served on various committees of the provincial and national professional nursing associations. In addition, she has served as a consultant and workshop leader for a variety of organizations, most recently focusing on health aspects of the aging."*

Guillevin Wood, Jeannine, O.C. $ ✊ ♡

Chairman of the Board, GUILLEVIN INTERNATIONAL INC., 400 Montpellier Blvd., St-Laurent, QC H4N 2G7 (514) 747-9851, FAX 747-1568. Born Montreal 1929. m. Keith S. 1 ch. **CAREER:** Chrm & CEO, Guillevin International Inc., 1965-95; Chair of the Bd., 1995 to date; Pres., Copel Inc., 1969-82; Chrm & CEO, 1982-85. **DIRECTOR:** Laurentian Bank of Canada; BCE Inc.; Sun Life Assurance Company of Canada. **MEMBER:** Black & McDonald (Advisory Council) **AFFIL:** Conseil du Patronat du Québec (Chrm 1988-90; Bd. of Dir. & Bureau des Gouv.); Museum of Fine Arts of Montreal (Bd. of Dir.; VP, Exec. Committee; Chrm, Orientation Committee 1994); Fondation de l'Hôpital du Sacré-Coeur de Montréal (Bd. of Dir.); Asia Pacific Foundation of Canada (Bd. of Dir.); Canadian Electrical Distribution Association (Pres. 1975); Club Saint-Denis; Mount Royal Club. **HONS:** nominated Homme du Mois, The Electrical League of Montreal, 1974; nominated Homme du Mois, *Revue Commerce*, 1976; nominated Cdn Bus. Woman of the Year, "Veuve Clicquot," 1984; Mgmt Achievement Award, McGill Univ., 1989; chosen 1 of the 12 bus. personalities of the decade, *Le Journal de Montréal*, 1990; an award of distinction, Fac. of Commerce & Admin., Concordia Univ., 1991; Officer of the Order of Canada, 1995; Hon. Doctorate, Univ. of Laval, 1990; D.Comm.(Hon.), St. Mary's Univ.,1992. **MISC:** in 1965, following the death of her first husband, Mrs. Guillevin Wood assumed control of F.X. Guillevin & Fils; following several transactions, the company now operates under the name of Guillevin International Inc.; it is now under new control since Mrs. Wood sold her participation in Apr. 1995. **COMMENT:** *"Prior to 1965 I was family oriented and had a minimal* *interest in business. Following the death of my first husband, I took over his small business and built it into the second largest Canadian electrical distributor through an extensive expansion program. I have also become very involved in business associations as well as charitable and social organizations."*

Gulkin, Catherine ■ ⛤ ⊗ ⚘

Film and Video Editor, CATHY GULKIN FILM EDITING LTD., 11 Wilkins Ave., Toronto, ON M5A 3C2 (416) 368-6994, FAX 368-0229. Born Montreal 1954. s. 1 ch. Corinna Rose Gulkin. EDUC: Dawson Coll., Diploma of Collegial Studies (Social Sciences) 1972; London Int'l Film Sch., Diploma in the Art of Technique of Film-making 1976. CAREER: film & video editor, numerous award-winning programs, 1977 to date. SELECTED CREDITS: Ed., *Mum's the Word* (documentary), Mediatique/ONF, 1996; Ed., *The Pinco Triangle* (docu/drama), Upper Canada Productions, 1995; Ed., *Our Daughters' Pain: Female Genital Mutilation in Canada* (documentary), Whynot Productions, 1995; Ed., *Fiction and Other Truths: A Film About Jane Rule* (docu/drama), Great Jane Productions, 1994; Ed., *Cry of the Ancestors* (documentary), Breakthrough Productions, 1994; Ed., *Abby, I Hardly Knew 'Ya* (documentary), TVO, 1994; Ed., *Without Fear* (2 docu/drama), Breakthrough Productions, 1992; Ed., *And We Knew How to Dance* (documentary), NFB, 1992; Ed., *Forbidden Love* (docu/drama), NFB Studio D, 1991; Ed., *Caterpillar: The Story of a Plant Closure*, Venture CBC, 1991; Ed., *Flight for Freedom* (TV special), Forevergreen Productions, 1990; 1989; Ed., *No Looking Back* (documentary), Laszlo Barna, 1988; Ed., *Paul Strand: Under the Dark Cloth* (documentary), John Walker, 1986; Ed., *I Need a Man Like You to Make My Dreams Come True* (variety special), Daria Stermak & Kali Paakspu, 1986; Ed., *All of Our Lives* (documentary), Laura Sky & Helene Klodawsky, 1983; Ed., *Heart of Gold* (TV special), CBC, 1981; Ed., *Breakthrough*, Lauron Productions, 1980; Ed., *Houdini Never Died* ("docutainment" special), 1978. AFFIL: Academy of Canadian Cinema and Television; Canadian Independent Filmmakers' Caucus; Directors' Guild of Canada. HONS: Best Documentary Film Editing (*Forbidden Love*), Atlantic Film Festival, 1992; Best Editing in an information or documentary program or series (*Cry of the Ancestors*), Gemini Awards, 1996. INTERESTS: raising mher daughter; the arts; travel; wilderness activities. COMMENT: *"A film and video editor with a strong interest in feminism, lesbian and other social issues."*

Gullberg, Shannon R.W., B.Sc.,LL.B. ■ ⚖

Barrister and Solicitor. Box 818, Yellowknife, NT X1A 2N6 (403) 873-6370, FAX 873-2758. Born Edmonton 1960. m. Edward W. Gullberg. 3 ch. Erin, Sarah, Emily. EDUC: Univ. of Alberta, B.Sc.(Rehab. Medicine) 1983, LL.B. 1988. BAR: N.W.T., 1988; Alta., 1990. CAREER: Certified Speech-Language Pathologist; Barrister & Solicitor. AFFIL: Law Society of the N.W.T. (Sec. 1994; Pres. 1995); Law Society of Alberta; Canadian Speech & Hearing Association. INTERESTS: her family; continued dev. of the legal profession; rights of the physically & mentally handicapped. COMMENT: *"I continue to try and balance family and career ambitions. I am currently a student with the Justice Institute of British Columbia as I expand my career by developing an expertise in mediation."*

Gundersen, Sonja J., LL.B. ■■ ⚖ $ ❀

Vice-President, Law and Corporate Development, APPLE CANADA INC. (computers/hightech.), 7495 Birchmount Rd., Markham, ON L3R 5G2 (905) 513-5527, FAX 513-5872, EMAIL gundersen1@apple.com. Born Miami, Fla. EDUC: Univ. of Western Ontario, LL.B. 1983. CAREER: Assoc. Cnsl, IBM Canada, 1985-87; Gen. Cnsl, Apple Canada, 1987-90; VP, 1990 to date. AFFIL: George Brown Coll. (Bd. of Gov. 1987-93); Canadian Centre for Creative Technology (V-Chair, Bd. of Dir. 1993 to date); Intercom Ontario (Bd. of Dir. 1995 to date). COMMENT: *"Sonja Gundersen has been practising law in the computer industry since 1985. In her current role as Vice-President, Law and Corporate Development at Apple Canada, she manages the corporation's law department, government relations, strategic alliances, investment and sourcing activities in Canada."*

Gunter, Elaine E., B.A.,LL.B. ■ ✦ ⚖

Director, Legislative Services Branch, Department of Justice, GOVERNMENT OF NEW BRUNSWICK, Box 6000, Fredericton, NB E3B 5H1 (506) 453-2544, FAX 457-7342. EDUC: Univ. of New Brunswick, B.A. 1964, LL.B. 1978. BAR: N.B. CAREER: Dir., Legislative Svcs Branch, Dept. of Justice, Prov. of N.B.

Guptill, The Hon. Nancy E.,R.T., M.L.A. ✦

Member of the Legislative Assembly (5th Prince) and Speaker of the Legislative Assembly, GOVERNMENT OF PRINCE EDWARD ISLAND, Box 2000, Charlottetown, PE C1A 7N8 (902) 368-4310, FAX 368-5175. Riding Office, Summerside Regional Services Centre, 109 Water St., Summerside, PE C1N 5L2. Born Halifax

1941. m. Gregg. 3 ch. Krista, Nancy Beth, Peggy. EDUC: Queen Elizabeth High Sch.; Halifax Vocational Sch.; Victoria General Hospital Sch. of Radiotherapy, R.T. 1961. CAREER: Technologist, Victoria General Hospital, Halifax; Technologist & Instructor, Radiotherapy Dept., St. John's General Hospital, 1964; Town Councillor, Summerside, 1982 & 1985; M.L.A. (5th Prince), Gov't of P.E.I., by-election, 1987; re-elected 1989 & 1993; Min. of Tourism & Parks, 1989-91; Min. of Labour & Min. Responsible for the Status of Women, 1991-93; Speaker, 1993 to date. AFFIL: Kinettes (Pres.); Summerside Adult Dev. Centre; United Way (Reg'l Coord.); Heart Fund (Reg'l Coord.); volunteer for various nat'l sporting events. INTERESTS: reading; sports; fishing; travelling; music; volunteering.

Gurevitch, Sheila, R.R.L. ○
Volunteer. 8908 Bayridge Dr. S.W., Calgary, AB T2V 3M8 (403) 253-1101, FAX 259-2414. Born Calgary 1940. m. Dr. Ralph Gurevitch. 3 ch. Mrs. Illana Morton, Dr. Darryl Gurevitch, Dr. Jason Gurevitch. EDUC: St. Michael's Hospital, Registered Records Librarian 1960. CAREER: Registered Records Librarian, 1960-63; public rel'ns, 1987 to date. VOLUNTEER CAREER: Bd. Mbr., Jewish Family Svc., 1978-85; Bd. Mbr., United Jewish Appeal, 1983-87, 1989 to date; various volunteer positions, incl. Chair, Volunteer Advisory Committee, Alberta Children's Hospital, 1983-93; Chairperson, Life Memberships, Hadassah-Wizo, 1984 to date; Fundraiser, Calgary Centre for Performing Arts, 1985 to date; Bd. Mbr. & Coord. of Accommodation & Food, Calgary '86, Canadian Special Olympics Summer Games, 1986; Bd. Mbr., Calgary Jewish Community Council 1986-88, 1993 to date; Coord. of Volunteer & Spectator Svcs, Olympics '88, 1987-88; Telephones Coord., Alberta Children's Miracle Ntwk Telethon, 1987 to date; Bd. Mbr., Jewish Historical Society, 1993 to date; Bd. Mbr., Hospice Calgary Society, 1994 to date; Bd. Mbr. & Coord. of Accommodation & Food, Calgary '96, Canadian Special Olympics Winter Games, 1996; planned opening of Rosedale Hospice (cancer), 1996; Bd. mbr., Celebration of the 75th Anniversary, Alberta Children's Hospital, 1996-97. AFFIL: Beth Tzedec Synagogue (prep. & distribution of Jewish calendar 1981-85); Canyon Meadows Golf & Country Club (House Committee); Jewish National Fund (Dinner Committee 1992, 1994). HONS: Canada 125 Medal. INTERESTS: family; friends; golf; aerobics; mah-jongg; music travel; theatre; investment club. COMMENT: *"For the greater part of my life, I have been a volunteer. I have grown as a person through the many* experiences I have encountered and feel privileged to have been given these many opportunities. I am truly blessed with a husband, children and grandchildren."

Gurney, Janice, B.F.A. ⊗
Artist. 243 Macdonell Ave., Unit 2, Toronto, ON M6R 2A9 (416) 531-0950. Born Winnipeg 1949. m. Andy Patton. EDUC: Univ. of Manitoba, B.F.A.(Art) 1973. CAREER: artist; various teaching positions incl.: Sessional Instructor, Simon Fraser Univ., Centre for the Arts, 1984; Visiting Instructor, Photography, Ontario Coll. of Art, 1989; various work-related positions incl.: Co-Curator, *The Interpretation of Architecture*, YYZ Artists' Outlet, Toronto, 1986; Curator, *The Salvage Paradigm*, Wynick/Tuck Gallery & YYZ, Toronto, 1990. SELECTED PUBLICATIONS: various publications incl.: *The Salvage Paradigm*, pamphlet, YYZ & Wynick/Tuck Gallery, Toronto, 1990; "The Surface of Behaviour" (*Photo Communique*, Spring 1988); "Moveable Wounds (An Essay in Composition)" (*Art Metropole*, 1984). EXHIBITIONS: numerous solo exhibitions incl.: *Sum over Histories–10 Year Survey*, at Winnipeg Art Gallery, Power Plant (Toronto), Mackenzie Art Gallery (Regina), London Regional Art & Historical Museums (London, Ont.); Glenbow Museum (Calgary), 1992-94; *Name*, 49th Parallel, New York, NY; *For the Audience*, Mount St. Vincent Art Gallery, Halifax, 1986; *The Battle of the Somme*, YYZ, Toronto, 1981; numerous group exhibitions incl.: *Travelling Theory*, Jordan National Art Gallery (Amman, Jordan), McIntosh Gallery (London, Ont.), 1992; *Re-enactment: Between Self and Other*, Power Plant, Toronto, 1990; *Subjects in Pictures*, 49th Parallel (New York City, NY), YYZ (Toronto), 1984; *YYZ Monumenta* (YYZ, Toronto), 1982. COLLECTIONS: private & public collections incl.: The National Gallery, Ottawa; The Winnipeg Art Gallery. INTERESTS: reading books on phys. anthropology, primate studies, language, forensic science & mysteries. MISC: various Ontario Arts Council & Canada Council grants; represented by Wynick/Tuck Gallery, Toronto. COMMENT: *"Janice Gurney is a visual artist who pioneered the use of appropriated imagery and other artists' actual work to explore issues of originality and identity."*

Gusella, Mary M., B.A.,LL.B. ■ ✤
Commissioner, PUBLIC SERVICE COMMISSION OF CANADA, 300 Laurier Ave. W., Rm. 1931, Ottawa, ON K1A 0M7 (613) 992-2644, FAX 996-4337. Born Ottawa 1948. m. EDUC: Univ. of Toronto, B.A.(Pol. Sci.); Univ. of

Ottawa, LL.B. 1977. **BAR:** Ont., 1980. **CAREER:** Dir., Dept. of Energy, Mines & Resources, & Canada Oil & Gas Lands Admin., 1980-82; Dir., Dept. of Fin., 1982-83; Dir., Crown Corps., Treasury Bd., 1983-86; Asst. Sec. to the Cabinet (Comm.), Privy Council Office, 1986-90; Assoc. Under-Sec. of State, Sec. of State, 1990-91; Deputy Min., Multiculturalism & Citizenship Canada, 1991-93; Pres., Atlantic Canada Opportunities Agency & Enterprise Cape Breton Corporation, 1993-95. **AFFIL:** Law Society of Upper Canada. **HONS:** International Association of Business Communicators' Award, 1991. **MISC:** Canadian Securities Certificate. **COMMENT:** *"Advocate of value-oriented management that is client sensitive and responsive to the public environment. Focus on strategic communications and the development of public/private partnerships. Specialist in guiding corporate change."*

Gutman, Gloria M., Ph.D. ⬡ ⊕
Professor, Faculty of Arts and Director, Gerontology Research Centre and Program, SIMON FRASER UNIVERSITY, Harbour Centre, 515 W. Hastings St., Ste. 2800, Vancouver, BC V6B 5K3 (604) 291-5062, FAX 291-5066. Associate Member, Department of Health Care and Epidemiology, Faculty of Medicine, UNIVERSITY OF BRITISH COLUMBIA. Born 1939. 3 ch. Marina Gutman, Dr. Samuel J. Gutman, Marlene V. Gutman. **EDUC:** Univ. of British Columbia, B.A.(Psych. & English) 1961, Ph.D.(Dev. & Social Psych.) 1970; Univ. of Alberta, M.A.(Psych. of Aging) 1964. **CAREER:** Lecturer, Psych., Univ. of Calgary, 1964-65; Lecturer, Mount Royal Coll., Calgary, 1965; Lecturer, Psych., Univ. of British Columbia, 1970-74; Research Dir., Studies on Housing for Older People, 1973-76; Asst. Prof., 1974-80; Research Assoc., President's Committee on Gerontology, 1977-78; Research Assoc., Div. of Health Svcs R.&D., 1979; Coord., Gerontology Programs, Continuing Studies, Simon Fraser Univ., 1980-82; Assoc. Mbr., Psych. Dept., 1981-87; Dir., Gerontology Research Centre, 1982 to date; Assoc. Prof., 1982-90; Winegard-Harshman Visiting Prof., Coll. of Family & Consumer Studies, Univ. of Guelph, 1983; Visiting Prof., Coll. of Home Econ., Univ. of Saskatchewan, 1984; Assoc. Mbr., Dept. of Health Care & Epidemiology, Fac. of Medicine, Univ. of British Columbia, 1986 to date; Coord., 1983-88; Dir., Program in Gerontology, Simon Fraser Univ., 1989 to date; Prof., 1990 to date; Visiting Prof., Institute of Health Promo. Research, Univ. of British Columbia, 1990-91. **SELECTED CREDITS:** *Creating a Supportive Environment for the Elderly*, videotape, produced with M. Hood et

al, Biomedical Communications, Univ. of British Columbia, 1976; *Mental Health and the Elderly: Everyone's Tomorrow*, audiocassettes produced with M.A.S. Cowan-Buitenhuis, Simon Fraser Univ. Publications, 1982; & other audiocassettes. **SELECTED PUBLICATIONS:** *Canada's Changing Age Structure: Implications for the Future*, ed. (Burnaby: Simon Fraser Univ. Publications, 1982); *Fact Book on Aging in British Columbia*, G.M. Gutman et al (Burnaby: Gerontology Research Centre, Simon Fraser Univ., 1986; 2nd ed., 1995); *Health Promotion for Older Canadians: Knowledge Gaps and Research Needs*, ed. with A.V. Wister (Vancouver: Gerontology Research Centre, Simon Fraser Univ., 1994); "The Effects of Age and Extraversion on Pursuit Rotor Reminiscence" (*Journal of Gerontology* 1965); "Mortality Rates among Relocated Extended Care Patients," with C.P. Herbert (*Journal of Gerontology* 1976); "Forecasting Demand for Long-Term Care Services," with D. Lane et al (*Health Services Research* 1985); "On Fostering a Canadian Literature on Aging" (*GRC News* 1994); numerous other publications. **AFFIL:** Canadian Association on Gerontology (Pres. 1987-91); International Gerontology Association (Co-Chair, North American Reg'l Committee 1993-97; Chair, Organizing Committee, World Congress 2001); Gerontological Association of B.C. (Founding Pres. 1977-79); Gerontological Society of America (Fellow); American Psychological Association; Psychologists in Long-Term Care; Family Violence Institute of British Columbia (Chair 1994-96; Bd. of Dir.). **HONS:** Women of Achievement Award, State of Israel Bonds, 1985; Distinguished Service Award, Gerontology Association of B.C., 1987. **MISC:** recipient, numerous grants; reviewer, various journals, presses, granting bodies & other agencies; numerous conference presentations.

Guttman, Naomi, B.F.A.,M.F.A., M.A. ▪▪ 📖 ⬡ ⊗
Assistant Professor of English, HAMILTON COLLEGE, Clinton, NY 13323, EMAIL nguttman@hamilton.edu. Born Montreal 1960. m. Jonathan T. Mead. 1 ch. **EDUC:** Concordia Univ., B.F.A.(Music) 1985; Warren Wilson Coll., M.F.A.(Creative Writing-Poetry) 1988; Loyola Marymount Univ., M.A.(English Lit.) 1992; Univ. of Southern California, Ph.D. (English Lit.) in progress. **SELECTED PUBLICATIONS:** *Reasons for Winter*, a book of poems (London, Ont.; Brick Books, 1991). **HONS:** A.M. Klein Award in Poetry, Quebec Society for the Promotion of English-Language Literature, 1992; SSHRCC doctoral fellowship, 1994-96. **INTERESTS:** gardening.

Guy, Georgia, B.A.,M.A.,C.A.E. ■ ⊚
Executive Director, Ontario Council, GIRL GUIDES OF CANADA, 14 Birch Ave., Toronto, ON (416) 920-6666, FAX 920-1440. Born Red Deer, Alta. 1943. s. 1 ch. Cheryl Joanne Lee. EDUC: Univ. of Alberta, B.A.(English Lit.); Simon Fraser Univ., M.A.(English Lit.) 1972. CAREER: English Instructor, Vancouver City Coll., 1964-72; Exec. Dir., Girl Guides of Canada, Ont. Council, 1989 to date. AFFIL: Canadian Society of Association Executives, Toronto Chapter (Certified Association Exec.; Bd. Mbr.; Chair, Educ. & Training Committee). COMMENT: *"Always interested in education and personal development for women, I am enjoying working for an organization that is committed to offering opportunities for girls and women to achieve their full personal potential."*

Guyda, Patricia, R.N. ⟳ ⊕
President, CANADIANS FOR HEALTH RESEARCH, Box 126, Westmount, QC H3Z 2T1 (514) 398-7478, FAX 398-8361. Born Winnipeg 1941. m. Harvey. 2 ch. Marley, Evan. EDUC: Winnipeg General Hospital Sch. of Nursing, R.N. 1962. CAREER: Staff Nurse, Winnipeg General Hospital, 1962-63; Head Nurse, Psychiatry, 1963-64; Staff Nurse, Seton Psychiatric Institute, Baltimore, Md., 1968-69; Staff Nurse, Queen Elizabeth Hospital, Montreal, 1973. VOLUNTEER CAREER: Pres. & Dir., Canadians for Health Research, 1976 to date; Dir., Science Focus, 1980-82; Dir., Canadian Genetic Diseases Ntwk, Centre of Excellence, 1990 to date; Mbr., Science Policy Committee, Canadian Society for Clinical Investigation, 1991 to date; Ex-Officio Bd. Mbr., Coalition for Biomedical & Health Research, 1992 to date. SELECTED PUBLICATIONS: contributor to the dev. of Canadians for Health Research publications, such as *Future Health/Perspectives Santé* (1979); *The Diary* (1987); *A True Story/Histoire Vraie* (1989); *A Salute to Excellence* (1992); *The Road to Discovery/Sur la route du progrès* (1994). HONS: Distinguished Service Award, Canadian Society for Clinical Investigation, 1982; Member, Order of Canada, 1993. INTERESTS: travel; reading; walking. MISC: organized numerous conferences/workshops for C.H.R. & other groups; co-ordinates other projects & special events. COMMENT: *"Contributing to one's community was instilled in me by my mother. The bonus, particularly with regard to my leadership in C.H.R., is what I've learned in the process."*

Guzman, Carole, M.D.,M.Sc.,FRCPC ⊕ ⊚
Associate Secretary General, CANADIAN MEDICAL ASSOCIATION, 1867 Alta Vista Dr., Ottawa, ON K1G 3Y6 (613) 731-9331, FAX 731-7314. Born Toronto 1933. m. Antonio. 2 ch. EDUC: Univ. of Toronto, B.A.(Sci.) 1954, M.D. 1958; McGill Univ., M.Sc.(Experimental Sci.) 1965. CAREER: Assoc. Prof., Fac. of Medicine, Univ. of Ottawa, 1971-96; Dir., Respiratory Rehabilitation Program, Ottawa Rehabilitation Centre, 1974-92; Medical Dir., Canadian Thoracic Society, 1992-96; Assoc. Sec. Gen., Canadian Medical Association, 1992 to date. AFFIL: A.O.A. Medical Society ; Royal Coll. of Physicians & Surgeons of Canada (Fellow in Internal Medicine); Ontario Thoracic Society (Pres. 1978-80); Federation of Medical Women of Canada (Pres. 1981-82); Ontario Medical Association (Pres. 1989-90); Canadian Medical Association (Pres. 1991-92); Canadian Thoracic Society (Hon. Mbr.). HONS: Award of Excellence, Univ. of Ottawa, 1990. INTERESTS: classical music; reading; gardening; travel; cooking. COMMENT: *"I am a physician, a respiratory specialist who has been engaged in clinical service, education, research and administration, with a particular interest in health policy development."*

Gwyn, Alexandra (Sandra), B.A., LL.D. ⁄ ▯
Journalist and Author. 300 Carlton St., Toronto, ON M5A 2L5 (416) 921-4298, FAX 921-9133. Born St. John's 1935. m. Richard Gwyn. EDUC: Dalhousie Univ., B.A.(English) 1955. CAREER: Ottawa Ed., *Saturday Night* Magazine, 1975-80; Contributing Ed., 1980-87; self-employed journalist & author, 1987 to date. SELECTED PUBLICATIONS: *The Private Capital: Ambition and Love in the Age of MacDonald and Laurier* (1984); *Tapestry of War: A Private View of Canadians in the Great War* (1992). AFFIL: PEN Canada (Bd. of Dir.; Chair, Nat'l Affairs Committee 1993-95; Chair, Membership Committee 1995-96). HONS: Gov. General's Award (*The Private Capital*), Nonfiction, 1984; National Magazine Award, 1979, 1984; LL.D.(Hon.), Memorial Univ. of Newfoundland, 1991. INTERESTS: films; history; gardening.

H

aar, Sandra, AOCA ■ ⊗ 🗍
Co-ordinating Editor, *FIREWEED: A FEMINIST QUARTERLY OF WRITING, POLITICS, ART & CULTURE*, Box 279, Stn. B, Toronto, ON M5T 2W2 (416) 504-1339. Born Montreal 1967. **EDUC:** Ontario Coll. of Art, grad. (Media Arts Dept.) 1989. **CAREER:** writer; Ed., *Fireweed*, 1990-95; Teacher, Morris Winchevsky Community Sch., 1994 to date; Coord. Ed., *Fireweed*, 1995 to date. **SELECTED CREDITS:** cover, *Women's Education des Femmes* (8(1) 1990); cover design & artwork, *Ordinary Wonders: Living Recovery from Sexual Abuse*, by Lillian Green (Toronto: Women's Press, 1992); cover design, *The Bat Had Blue Eyes*, by Betsy Warland (Toronto: Women's Press, 1993); cover design, *Tangled Sheets: Stories and Poems of Lesbian Lust*, eds. Rosamund Elwin & Karen X. Tulchinsky (Toronto: Women's Press, 1995); cover design, *Pushing the Limits: Disabled Dykes Produce Culture* (Toronto: Women's Press, 1996). **SELECTED PUBLICATIONS:** "Addressing Spirituality, Congregation and the Community: Lesbian and Gay Jews Hold Conference in Toronto" (*Rites*, 1990); "Speaking Jewish: Women's Language," interview with Frieda Forman *(Fireweed*, 1994); "What (It) Is and What (It) Isn't: The Language of 'Tolerance'" *(Fireweed*, 1994); "Within and Without: Antisemitism in the Anti-Racist Context," with Susan Nosov (*Canadian Woman Studies/les cahiers de la femme*, 1994); "Seeds of Doubt: Constructing a Sephardi Identity" (*Bridges*, 1996); "All For You," with Ellen Flanders, in *Tangled Sheets: Stories and Poems of Lesbian Lust*, eds. Rosamund & Karen X. Tulchinsy (Toronto: Women's Press, 1995); 2 photo-text works are included in the anthology *The Girl*

Wants To: Women's Representations of Sex and the Body (Coach House Press, 1993). **EDIT:** Ed. Bd., *Fuse* Magazine, 1989-92; project initiator & Co-Ed., special issue on Jewish women, *Fireweed*, 1992. **EXHIBITIONS:** group shows incl.: Gallery 44: Centre for Contemporary Photography (1996); Artefact Gallery (1990, 1991); Gallery 76 (1990); Gallery 101, Ottawa (1992). **AFFIL:** Fireweed Inc. (Bd. of Dir.). **HONS:** Experimental Arts Fac. Award, Ontario Coll. of Art, 1989; Lazerline Desktop Publishing Prize, Ontario Coll. of Art, 1989; Student's Administrative Council Award, Ontario Coll. of Art, 1989; *The Toronto Star* Award, Ontario Coll. of Art, 1989. **MISC:** recipient, various grants; frequent speaker; numerous print & media interviews; gives workshops & presentations on sexuality, censorship, Jewish feminist issues & publishing.

Hackett, Barbara J., B.B.A.,M.B.A., C.M.A. ■ $
President, STRATHEDEN HOMES LIMITED, 3 Pine Forest Rd., Toronto, ON M4N 3E6 (416) 932-1909, FAX 489-7424. Born Welland, Ont. 1954. m. John H. Tory. 4 ch. John, Christopher, Susan, George. **EDUC:** York Univ., B.B.A.(Acctg & Fin.) 1979, M.B.A.(Fin.) 1980. **CAREER:** Fin. Analyst, Ontario Hydro, 1980-85; Mgr, Corp. Fin., MDS Health Group Limited, 1985-88; Dir., Fin. Svcs, MDS Health Ventures Inc., 1989-91; VP, Fin. & Admin., Bell & Howell Ltd., 1994-95; Pres., Stratheden Homes Limited, 1995 to date. **DIRECTOR:** YTV Canada Inc. **AFFIL:** Institute of Financial Executives; Society of Management Accountants of Ontario (C.M.A.); The Toronto French Sch. (Chair, Bd. of Dir. 1993-95); L.E.A.F. (Treas. 1987-90); M.B.A. Women's Association (Co-Founder & Pres. 1983-85). **HONS:** Gold Medalist, M.B.A. Grad. Thesis, York Univ., 1980; "Woman on the Move" Award, *The Toronto Sun*, 1990. **INTERESTS:** skiing; tennis; fitness.

Haddad-Forster, Mary Jo, R.N.,B.Sc. ⊕
Director, Paediatric Programs, HOSPITAL FOR SICK CHILDREN, 555 University Ave., Toronto, ON M5G 1X8 (416) 813-6489, FAX 813-5463. Born Windsor, Ont. 1956. m. James Forster. 3 ch. Stephen James Forster, Nicole Marie Forster, Jonathan Joseph Forster. **EDUC:** St. Clair Coll., Diploma (Nursing) 1976; Univ. of Windsor, B.S.N. 1984; Univ. of Toronto, M.H.Sc. in progress. **CAREER:** Patient Care Coord., Children's Hospital of Michigan, 1976-84; Ptnr, Parent Child Health Nursing, 1981-84; Program Admin., Critical Care & Neonatology, Hospital for Sick Children, 1990-95; Dir., Paediatric Programs, 1995 to date. **SELECTED PUBLICATIONS:** "Managing a neonatal intensive care unit" (*Intensive Care World*, 1995); "Private Practice Nurses" (RNAO, 1983). **AFFIL:** Registered Nurses' Association of Ontario (RNAC); Canadian Nurses' Association; United Way Hospital for Sick Children '95 (Chair). **HONS:** Nursing Excellence Award, Hospital for Sick Children; Employee of the Year, Hospital for Sick Children. **INTERESTS:** gourmet cooking (int'l); entertaining; sewing. **COMMENT:** *"I am an energetic healthcare administrator who strives for excellence in self and others. I am motivated by the challenges of a busy career and parenting three wonderful children. I have been blessed with a supportive husband and extended family. I am challenged each day to make a difference in my world."*

Haig, Susan E., B.A.,M.M.,D.M.A. ■ ✪ 📜
Music Director, WINDSOR SYMPHONY, 198 Pitt St. W., Ste. 172, Windsor, ON N9A 5L4 (519) 973-1238, FAX 973-0764. Born Summit, N.J. 1954. s. **EDUC:** Princeton Univ., B.A.(Music) 1976; S.U.N.Y., Stony Brook, M.M.(Piano) 1979, M.M.(Conducting) 1980, D.M.A.(Conducting) 1983. **CAREER:** Asst. Conductor, Minnesota Opera, 1983-84; Asst. Conductor, New York City Opera, 1984-86; Asst. Conductor, Santa Fe Opera, 1986; Resident Coach/Asst. Conductor, Canadian Opera Company, 1986-88; Resident Staff Conductor, Calgary Philharmonic, 1988-91; Music Dir., Windsor Symphony, 1991 to date. **AFFIL:** Arts Council of Windsor & Region (Bd.); Roseland Rotary; Heritage Windsor (Advisory Council); Arts for a Whole Community. **HONS:** Heinz Unger Conducting Award, 1992; Canada 125 Medal, 1992. **INTERESTS:** sports; theology; urban planning. **MISC:** Guest Conductor, National Arts Centre Orchestra, Toronto Symphony, Vancouver Symphony, CBC Vancouver Orchestra, Edmonton Symphony, Toronto Opera in Concert, Rhode Island Philharmonic, Pacific Opera Victoria, Minnesota Orchestra & others; Guest Host, *Stereo Morning*, CBC.

Haight, Lynn, M.A.,A.C.A.,C.A., F.C.M.C. $
Chief Accountant, MANULIFE FINANCIAL, 200 Bloor St. E., Toronto, ON M4W 1E5 (416) 926-6102, FAX 926-6285. President, MONTEVERDI: A CONSULTANCY. Born UK 1947. m. Dr. J. Haight. 2 ch. Emma, Adrian. **EDUC:** Oxford Univ., M.A. 1970; C.A. **CAREER:** Price Waterhouse Assoc., 1975-82; VP, Special Svcs, Scotiabank, 1986-93; Chief Acctnt, Manulife Financial, 1994 to date; Pres., Monteverdi: a consultancy, 1994 to date; Chair, Sectoral Advisory Group on Bus. & Professional Svcs to

Min. of Int'l Trade, 1993 to date. **DIRECTOR:** Hickling Corporation. **AFFIL:** Foundation for Responsible Computing (Dir.); Canadian Institute of Certified Management Consultants (Pres. 1994-95); Institute of Chartered Accountants of Canada. **HONS:** Women's Int'l Scholarship to London Bus. Sch. Exec. Program; Univ. of Jerusalem Educational Trust Scholar. **MISC:** U.N. Consultant for UNDTCD, World Bank & UNDP in a number of countries.

Hainer, Monica, B.Math. ■ $

President, LONDON LIFE REINSURANCE COMPANY, a div. of London Life Insurance Company, 1787 Sentry Parkway West., Ste. 420, Blue Bell, PA 19422 (215) 542-7200, FAX 542-1295. Born Toronto 1953. m. Ralph. 4 ch. **EDUC:** Univ. of Waterloo, B.Math. 1975. **CAREER:** Actuary, Manufacturer's Life, 1975-86; VP, London Life, 1988-95; Pres., London Life Reinsurance Co., 1996 to date. **AFFIL:** Society of Actuaries (Fellow); Canadian Institute of Actuaries (Fellow); American Academy of Actuaries. **HONS:** Descartes Scholarship, Univ. of Waterloo, 1971-74. **INTERESTS:** reading. **COMMENT:** *"I have helped to build a financially strong and rapidly expanding international reinsurance operation at London Life. I enjoy the technical challenges and the people internationally, with whom I work."*

Haines, Judith, B.F.A. ✎ 📖

Editor, *THIS COUNTRY CANADA*, One Mill St, Box 39, Pakenham, ON K0A 2X0 (613) 624-5000, FAX 624-5952. Born Vancouver 1951. m. Steve Mercer. 1 ch. Sophie. **EDUC:** Ottawa Civic Hospital Sch. of Nursing, R.N. 1972; Nova Scotia Coll. of Art & Design, B.F.A.(Photography & Fine Arts) 1983; Banff Publishing Workshop 1987, 1989. **CAREER:** Ed. Asst., *Vancouver Magazine*, 1978-79; Staff Writer, *Canadian Consumer*, 1985-86; English Ed., *The Canadian Nurse*, 1986-89; Acting Ed.-in-Chief, 1989-90, 1993-94, 1996; Ed., *This Country Canada*, 1994 to date. **EXHIBITIONS:** *The Art College Party Never Ends*, an exhibition of black & white, & colour prints, Anna Leonowens Gallery, Nova Scotia Coll. of Art & Design (1983). **HONS:** St. John Ambulance Award, Priory of Canada, 1994; The Eileen C. Flanagan Prize, Montreal Neurological Hospital, 1974. **INTERESTS:** old photographic processes; Celtic music; animals; health care issues. **MISC:** while attending the Nova Scotia Coll. of Art & Design, participated in the East Coast Art Colleges Exchange Program, spending 4 months in the photography program at Pratt Institute, Brooklyn, N.Y. **COMMENT:** *"Early on, a passion for reading and writing. Wanted desperately to travel, to do a 100 other things. Thus, a resumé with many twists and turns. Finally everything has converged."*

Hale, Marguerite (Grete), B.J.,G.C.L.J., F.H.S.C.,F.R.C.G.S. ■ $ ♡ ☝

Chairman, MORRISON LAMOTHE INC., 275 Slater St., Ste. 1603, Ottawa, ON K1P 5H9 (613) 238-8877, FAX 238-8340. Born Ottawa 1929. w. Reginald. **EDUC:** Carleton Univ., B.J.(Journalism) 1954. **CAREER:** 10 years' catering experience in UK, France, Scandinavia, Switzerland, & the US; Exec. VP, Morrison Lamothe Inc., 1972-78, Pres., 1978-89; Chrm of the Bd., 1989 to date. **SELECTED PUBLICATIONS:** *The Life and Times of G. Cecil Morrison, The Happy Baker of Ottawa* (1990). **DIRECTOR:** Morrison Lamothe Inc.; Consumer Gas Co.; Beechwood Cemetery. **AFFIL:** Univ. of Ottawa (Gov.); Community Foundation of Ottawa (Chrm); Royal Geographic Society (Dir. & VP); Friends of the National Library of Canada (Chrm); Salvation Army (Advisory Bd.); Military & Hospitaller Order of St. Lazarus of Jerusalem (Chancellor); Herald Society of Canada (Fellow); Royal Canadian Geological Survey (Fellow); 78th Fraiser Highlanders, Fort Glengarry Garrison (Hon. Col.); La Chaîne des Rotisseurs (V-Sénechale); Hospice of All Saints (Dir.); Macdonald Cartier Library (Chair); Canadian Association of Family Entrepreneurs (Pres., Ottawa Chapter); Institute of Palliative Care (Advisory Bd.); Kids Help Phone (Advisory Committee). **HONS:** Grand Cross, Order of St. Lazarus of Jerusalem. **INTERESTS:** cooking for friends; community service in volunteer organizations. **MISC:** was responsible for the catering to 40,000 at Canada's 100th Birthday party on Parliament Hill, July 1967, & for the 20-foot cake that Her Majesty Queen Elizabeth cut; 1st woman Pres., Bakery Council of Canada.

Haley, Carol, MLA ■ 🍁 🌾

Member of the Legislative Assembly (Three Hills-Airdrie) and Chairman, Standing Policy Committee on Agriculture and Rural Development, GOVERNMENT OF ALBERTA, 131 Legislature Building, Edmonton, AB T5K 2B6 (403) 422-5372, FAX 427-1320, Constituency Office, Box 5257, 209 Bower St., Airdrie, AB T4B 2B3 (403) 948-8741, FAX (403) 948-8744. Born Edmonton 1951 2 ch. **EDUC:** Edwin Parr Composite High Sch., Athabasca; various acctg, econ. & law courses through the R.I.A. program. **CAREER:** Co-Owner, Palliser Grain Co. Ltd., 1980-89; Co-Owner, Westar Farms Ltd., 1974-89; Owner, Carol Haley Consulting Inc.; elected MLA, Three Hills-Airdrie, 1993; Deputy Whip, Gov't Caucus, 1993-94; Mbr., Standing Policy Committee on Agric.

& Rural Dev.; Chair, Standing Policy Committee on Community Svc, 1991-96; Chair, Standing Policy Committee on Agriculture & Rural Dev; mbr., Public Accnts Committee, Member Svcs Committee, Leg. Review Committee, Health Svcs Funding Advisory Committee. SELECTED PUBLICATIONS: newsletter, *A Guide to Healthcare in Alberta.* AFFIL: Calgary General Hospital (Past Dir.; Past Chair, Fin., Audit & Hum. Res. Committee); Alberta Health Care Association (Past Dir.; Past Chair, Hum. Res. Committee); Canadian Hospital Association (Past Dir.).

Hall, Hon. Barbara, B.A.,LL.B. ■■ ✦
Mayor, CITY OF TORONTO, Mayor's Office, 100 Queen St. W., City Hall, 2nd Fl., Toronto, ON M5H 2N2 (416) 392-7001, FAX 392-0026, EMAIL mayor@city.toronto.on.ca. Born Ottawa 1946. m. Max Beck. EDUC: Univ. of Victoria, B.A.(Psych. & Sociology) 1969; Osgoode Hall Law Sch., York Univ., LL.B. 1978. CAREER: community worker; probation officer; teacher; lawyer.

Hall, Carol A., B.P.E.,B.Ed. ○ ⌇
Teacher and Volunteer. 2803 Canmore Rd. N.W., Calgary, AB T2M 4J7. Born Edmonton 1959. m. Jamie. 2 ch. Andrew, David. EDUC: Univ. of Calgary, B.P.E. 1980, B.Ed. 1981. CAREER: jr. high sch. PE/Math/Health teacher, 1981 to date. SELECTED PUBLICATIONS: *Moving to Inclusion* (series of documents for integrating children with disabilities into phys. educ., specifically Special Olympics); *Children With Intellectual Disability* resource; *Teaching Strategy for Children with Down Syndrome: A Resource Guide* (1994). AFFIL: PREP Program, a resource centre & pre-sch. for children with Down Syndrome (Chair); Moving To Inclusion (Nat'l Educ. Steering Committee); Ups & Downs, Calgary Down Syndrome Association (Exec.); Down Syndrome Program Team, Alberta Children's Hospital (Parent Rep.); Special Olympics (track & field volunteer); Canadian Intramural Recreation Association, CIRA (Dir. 1988-94; Exec. Committee 1992-94); Alberta Intramural Recreation Association (Dir. 1986-94; Pres. 1988-90); Active Living Alliance for Canadians with a Disability (CIRA Rep. 1989-94); Active Living Alliance for Children & Youth (CIRA Rep.). HONS: Marg Southern Award (for Outstanding Contribution to Athletics), Univ. of Calgary, 1980; Young Professional Award for Alberta, Canadian Association of Health, Phys. Educ./Recreation, 1989; Visiting Parent of the Year Award, Calgary Down Syndrome Association, 1994. INTERESTS: biking; skiing; running; golf; photography. COMMENT: *"The future is very bright*

for children with Down Syndrome and it is extremely exciting to be a part of it."

Hall, Judith G., B.A.,M.Sc.,M.D.,F.R.C.P.C., F.A.A.P.,F.C.C.M.G., F.A.B.M.G. ⊕ ⌇ ✿
Head, Department of Pediatrics, UNIVERSITY OF BRITISH COLUMBIA, British Columbia Children's Hospital, 4480 Oak St., Rm. 2D15, Vancouver, BC V6H 3V4 (604) 875-2315, FAX 875-2890. Born Boston 1939. d. 3 ch. EDUC: Wellesley Coll., B.A. 1961; Univ. of Washington, M.Sc. 1965, M.D. 1966; Johns Hopkins Hospital, Residency (Pediatrics) 1971. CAREER: Asst., Assoc. & Full Prof., Medicine & Pediatrics, Div. of Medical Genetics, Univ. of Washington Sch. of Medicine; Prof., Dept. of Medical Genetics, Univ. of British Columbia; Prof. & Head, Dept. of Pediatrics, Royal Coll. of Physicians & Surgeons; Study Leave, Genetics Lab, Oxford Univ., UK, 1988-89. SELECTED PUBLICATIONS: more than 250 peer-reviewed articles, 45 chapters & 4 books. AFFIL: American Society of Human Genetics; North Pacific Pediatric Society; Teratology Society; Western Society for Pediatric Research; Society for Pediatric Research; Physicians for Social Responsibility; Genetics Society of Canada; Canadian Pediatric Society; American Board of Medical Genetics (Founding Bd.); American Pediatric Society; Skeletal Dysplasia Group; Clinical Genetics Society; European Society of Human Genetics; International Society for Twin Studies; International Neurofibromatosis Society; Royal Coll. of Physicians & Surgeons of Canada (Fellow); American Academy of Pediatricians (Fellow); Canadian Coll. of Medical Genetics (Fellow); American Bd. of Medical Genetics (Fellow); American Coll. of Medical Genetics. HONS: Killam Research Prize, Univ. of British Columbia; Woman of Distinction Award, YWCA, 1994; Distinguished Medical Alumni Award, Univ. of Washington; Colonel Sanders March of Dimes Award for service in clinical genetics, John Hopkins Society of Scholars. INTERESTS: natural history of human genetic disorders; genetics of short stature; genetics of connective tissue disorders; etiology of congenital anomalies; delivery of genetic services; nontraditional inheritance; twins; neural tube defects; folic acid.

Hall, Mary C., B.A.,LL.B. ⌁
Partner, BAKER & McKENZIE, Barristers & Solicitors, BCE Place, 181 Bay St, Ste. 2100, Toronto, ON M5J 2T3 (416) 865-6917, FAX 863-6257. Born 1948. m. Glen F. Campbell. 3 ch. Jamie, Christopher, Callum. EDUC: Univ. of Guelph, B.A.(Pol. Sci.) 1969; Univ. of Windsor, LL.B. 1973. BAR: Ont., 1975. CAREER:

Lawyer, Baker & McKenzie, 1975-81; Ptnr, 1981 to date; Instructor, Environmental Law, Environmental Studies Dept., York Univ., 1991-92. **SELECTED PUBLICATIONS:** "Environmental Liability II: Protecting Yourself" (*Ontario Appraisal Quarterly*); "Toxic Real Estate and the Role of the Professional" (*Canadian Appraiser*). **AFFIL:** Law Society of Upper Canada; Canadian Bar Association; County of York Law Association; The Advocates' Society; Women's Law Association; American Bar Association (V-Chair, Environmental & Natural Resource Section 1993-94, 1994-95, 1996-97); Canadian Environmental Law Association. **MISC:** numerous conference presentations. **COMMENT:** *"Ms. Hall practised civil litigation for approximately 13 years and thereafter specialized in counsel and advisory work in the area of environmental law. She has served the local and international firm on various committees and is an active member of both litigation and environmental practice groups in the global firm."*

Hall, Pam, B.F.A.,M.Ed. ■■ ⊗ 📖 ⼿
Visual artist, author, filmmaker, designer. 36 Monkstown Rd., St. John's, NF A1C 3T3 (709) 754-7731, FAX 753-4471, EMAIL pamhall@nlnet.nf.ca. Born Kingston, Ont. 1951. m. Strat Canning. 1 ch. Jordan. **EDUC:** Sir George Williams Univ. (now Concordia), B.F.A.(Studio) 1973; Univ. of Alberta, M.Ed.(Art Educ.) 1978. **SELECTED CREDITS:** Production Designer, *The Elf* (TV drama), 1996; Production Designer, *Anchor Zone*, Red Ochre Productions, St. John's, 1993; Dir./Producer/Filmmaker, *Under the Knife-personal hystories*, 1992-94; Art Dir./Set Designer/Production Designer, several other projects; publicity stills, CODCO, various projects, early 1970s; publicity & poster stills, *Daddy, What's a Train?*; cover & liner note stills, 1st album, Rufus Guinchard; album/CD design, book design. **SELECTED PUBLICATIONS:** numerous publications, papers & lectures incl.: *On the Edge of the Eastern Ocean* (author & illustrator, GLC Publishers, Toronto, 1982); *Down by Jim Long's Stage* (illustrator, Breakwater Books, St. John's, 1977). **EXHIBITIONS:** numerous solo exhibitions incl.: "The Coil–a history in four parts–1988-93" (Thunder Bay, Ottawa, Lethbridge, 1995, & Art Gallery of the Cdn Embassy, Tokyo, 1994); "Tools of the Trade" (Cdn Mission, N.Y., 1993); "Inshore Artifacts" (St. John's, 1993); also numerous group exhibitions incl.: "When Cod Was King" (N.Y., 1995-96); "Canada at Bologna" (Bologna, Italy, 1990). **COLLECTIONS:** many corp., private & public collections incl.: Permanent Collection, National Gallery of Canada;

Dept. of Fisheries & Oceans, Canada; Hibernia Management Development Corporation; Fishery Products International; Toronto-Dominion Bank; Bank of Montreal; Dept. of External Affairs, Canada; Canada Council Art Bank. **AFFIL:** Atlantic Provinces Economic Council (Bd. of Gov. 1995); Art Gallery of Newfoundland & Labrador (Bd. mbr. 1994-95); Newfoundland Independent Filmmakers' Co-op (Bd. mbr. 1994-95); Multiculturalism & Citizenship Canada (Jury mbr., Arts Apprenticeship Program 1993); Queen's Univ. (Visiting Artist 1993); The Canadian Conference of the Arts (Bd. mbr. 1992); Canada Council Art Bank (Jury mbr. 1988); Canadian Society for Education through Art (Nat'l VP 1978-80); Association of National Non-Profit Artist-Run Centres (Nat'l Spokesperson 1986-87). **HONS:** Rex Tasker Award for Best Atlantic Cdn Documentary (for *Under the Knife: personal hystories*), Atlantic Film Festival, Halifax, 1995; Commemorative Medal for 125th Anniversary of Confederation of Canada, 1993; Amelia Frances Howard Gibbon Award for best Cdn illustration, for *Down by Jim Long's Stage*, Canadian Library Association, 1978; Newfoundland & Labrador Arts Council grant, 1996; other grants, awards & commissions. **INTERESTS:** home restoration (award-winning heritage home); beachcombing; gardening; serious walking in wilderness landscape of Nfld.

Hall, Patricia, B.A.,B.Comm.,C.A. ⑤
Controller, SASKATCHEWAN POWER CORPORATION, 2025 Victoria Ave., Regina, SK S4P 0S1 (306) 566-2621, FAX 566-2575. Born Regina 1949. s. **EDUC:** Univ. of Saskatchewan, B.A. (Math.) 1970; Univ. of Calgary, B.Comm. (Acctg) 1974. **CAREER:** Dir. of Computer Auditing, Prov. Audit, 1985-90; Mgr, Fin. Systems & Processing, Saskatchewan Power Corporation, 1990-92; Cont., 1992 to date. **AFFIL:** Saskatchewan Institute of Chartered Accountants (By-laws Committee); Speakers Corner Toastmasters (Treas.); Financial Executives Institute. **INTERESTS:** travelling; gardening; reading; theatre.

Hall, Sally A. ⑨ ⑤ ⵔ
Volunteer Consumer Advocate and Spokesman. Born Hamilton, Ont. 1933. m. Stanley B. 4 ch. **EDUC:** Central High Sch. of Commerce, Grade 13 1950. **VOLUNTEER CAREER:** Prov. Pres., Man., Consumers' Association of Canada, 1978-79; Prov. Pres., Alta., 1980-83; Nat'l Pres., 1984-88; Int'l Trade Advisory Committee, 1986-88; Consumer & Household Products, SAGIT, 1988-94; appointed by Fed. Gov't, Postal Svc Review Committee, 1988-90; public rep. on Bd. of Dir., Canadian Nurses'

Association, 1988-92; appointed to the Prov. of Alta. Committee on Fair Dealing in Consumer Savings & Investments, 1988; Chair, Prov. Task Force on Consumer Educ. in the Fin. Marketplace, 1989; appointed by the Fed. Gov't, Automotive Select Panel, 1989-92; Western Reg'l Council, Canadian Broadcast Standards Council, 1990-94; Chair, 1995 to date; Co-Chair, Task Force on Direct Access to Nursing Svcs, Alberta Association of Registered Nurses, 1992 to date; appointed to the Edmonton Convention Centre Authority (ECCA), 1992; appointed by ECCA as liaison to the Edmonton Convention & Tourism Authority, 1992; appointed to the Econ. Dev. Image/ Comm. Task Force, 1992; appointed to the JET Committee, 1992; Ground Transportation Advisory Bd., Edmonton Int'l Airport, 1992 to date; Bio-ethics Committee, Grey Nuns Hospital, 1992 to date; Waste Mgmt Task Force, City of Edmonton, 1992; appointed by Prov. Min. of Health, AARN Practice Review Committee, 1992 to date; est. structure for First Aid svcs & managed volunteers providing first aid for *The Greatest Show Unearthed*, 1993; Mbr of the Bd. & Chair, Event Coord. Committee, Edmonton 1994 Forestry Capital Society, 1993-94; Public Rep., Parking Svcs Restructuring Proj., Univ. of Alberta, 1994; Bd. Mbr. & Treas., Habitat for Humanity, Edmonton, 1994; appointed to Dues & Governance Task Force, Credit Union Central of Alberta, 1994. **DIRECTOR:** Capital City Savings and Credit Union Ltd. (Sec. of Bd.); Credit Union Central of Alberta. **HONS:** Canada Volunteer Medal of Honour, 1995. **INTERESTS:** all issues of medicare; computerized banking. **MISC:** consumer advocate & spokesman in print media, radio & TV; hosted several *Nightline Open Line* programs on CJCA Radio, 1991; acted as consumer commentator at CBC Radio, Edmonton, 1990.

Hallatt, Phyllis 🏵 🔾
President, CHILD FIND SASKATCHEWAN INC., 1002 Arlington Ave., Ste. 41, Saskatoon, SK S7H 2X7 (306) 955-0070, FAX 373-1311. Owner, HALLATT HOLDINGS. Born Winnipeg 1940. m. Michael. 2 ch. Catherine Mote, Donna Greenhorn. **EDUC:** Red River Coll., Bus. Law/Econ./Mktg 1964. **CAREER:** Bookkeeper, Robinson Little and Co., 1961-64; commission sales, 1968-79; Compiler, Statistics Canada, 1972-74; Acctnt, Simon and Co., 1976-78; Office Mgr, Interprovincial Concrete, 1979-83; Owner, Hallatt Holdings, 1983 to date. **AFFIL:** Child Find Saskatchewan Inc. (Treas. 1986-93; Pres.); Child Find Canada (Treas. 1987-91; Pres. 1991-93); Boomerang Connexions (Hon. Dir. 1994-96); A.C.T.

Ladies' Auxiliary (Dir. 1972-78; Pres. 1983-84; Treas. 1980-83, 1991-96). **HONS:** nominated Woman of the Year, 1991. **INTERESTS:** youth & their welfare. **COMMENT:** *"In the past 35 years I have been involved with children's issues. Child abuse and child abduction have been specific issues that I have addressed in the past several years."*

Hallis, Ophera, B.A. 🐟 🔯 🦋
Vice-President, HALLIS MEDIA INC., 122 de Touraine, St. Lambert, QC J4S 1H4 (514) 465-9571. Born Montreal 1949. m. Ron Hallis. 2 ch. Leandra Chivambo Hallis, Larissa Nehanda Hallis. **EDUC:** McGill Univ., B.A.(Phil. & Cinema) 1974, Dipl. in Educ.(E.S.L.) 1991. **CAREER:** public rel'ns, Radio-Canada, 1967-69; freelance film ed., 1971-78; Prod. Mgr, Cinéclair, 1976; Prod. Mgr, Cinélume Productions, 1977; Editing Instructor, National Film Institute of Mozambique, 1978-82; Instructor, Montage, Cinema Dept., Concordia Univ., 1986; Guest Lecturer, African Studies, Univ. du Québec, 1986-88; Sch. Commissioner, South Shore Sch. Bd., 1987-94; high sch. teacher, École Secondaire de Mortagne, Boucherville, Que.; VP, Hallis Media Incorporated. **SELECTED CREDITS:** Prod. Mgr, Olympic Newsreel, 1976; Sound Recordist, *Music from Mozambique*, volumes I, II & III, Folkways Records; translator of subtitles, French to English, *L'Ange et la femme*, Gilles Carle, Dir., 1977; translator of subtitles, Portuguese to English, *Mueda*, Ruy Guerra, Dir., 1980; photography has appeared in various films; Ed., *L'Ange et la femme*, feature, Gilles Carle, Dir., 1977; Co-Prod./Sound Recordist/Ed., *Women of OMM Village*, documentary, 1980; Co-Prod./Ed., *I Can Hear Zimbabwe Calling*, documentary, Zimbabwe Ministry of Educ., 1980; Ed., *Pamberi Ne Zimbabwe*, documentary, National Film Institute of Mozambique, 1981; Co-Prod./Co-Dir./Ed./Sound Recordist, *Nkuleko Means Freedom*, documentary, PBS, 1982; Researcher/Co-Prod./Sound Recordist, *Zimbabwe, the New Struggle*, PBS, 1984; Co-Prod/Ed., *Chopi Music of Mozambique*, documentary; various other film credits. **AFFIL:** Quebec Association of School Boards. **HONS:** finalist, various film festivals; various film awards; worked on *L'Ange et la femme*, which won Special Jury Award, Avoriaz Film Festival, 1978; worked on *Pamberi Ne Zimbabwe*, which won New Director's Prize, Leipzig Film Festival, 1982. **INTERESTS:** Educ.; language acquisition theory; cinema; paleontology; women's literature; cross-country skiing; dog breeding; horticulture. **MISC:** *I Can Hear Zimbabwe Calling* screened at Museum of Modern Art; *Chopi Music of Mozambique* screened at

Museum of Modern Art, 1988 & Royal Ontario Museum, 1990. **COMMENT:** *"I have developed my talents in various fields: film editor and producer, film teacher in Africa and in a Canadian university, full-time working mother, school trustee, an English (ESL) teacher in a high school sports-study program and now at École Secondaire St-Jean Baptiste."*

Halliwell, Janet, B.Sc.(Hons.),M.Sc.,D.Sc., D.Laws ■ ◔ ⌖

President, JEH ASSOCIATES INC., 125 Springfield Rd., Apt. 6, Ottawa, ON K1M 1C5 (613) 747-0569, FAX 747-0527, EMAIL jehall@cycor.ca. Born Que. 1945. m. Robin. **EDUC:** Queen's Univ., B.Sc.(Hons., Chem./Math.) 1967; Univ. of British Columbia, M.Sc.(Phys. Org. Chem.) 1970. **CAREER:** Academic Research Asst., Dept. of Microbiol., Univ. of British Columbia, 1969-74; Sessional Lecturer, Dept. of Chem., Queen's Univ., 1974-75; various positions, NSERC/NRC, 1975-83; Dir. Gen., Research Grants & Officer of Council, NSERC, 1983-90; Chair & CEO, Science Council of Canada, 1990-92; Chair, N.S. Council on Higher Education, 1992 to date. **AFFIL:** Humanist Association of Canada (Hon. Assoc.); Canadian Chemical Society; Canadian Association of Physicists; Canadian Association of University Research Administrators (Lifetime Mbr.); Canadian Association for the Club of Rome; Rhodes Scholarship Selection Committee, Maritime Reg.; Maritime Provinces Higher Education Commission (V-Chair); National Council of Education, Conference Board of Canada; Fields Institute of Mathematics (Bd. of Dir.); Statistics Canada (Advisory Committee on Science; Tech. Statistics & Advisory Bd.); Deputy Ministers of Education (Advisory Committee); Canadian Research Management Association (Mng Bd.). **HONS:** Walter Hitschfeld Prize, Canadian Association of University Research Administrators, 1991; National Research Council Scholarship, 1967-69; Golden Key of Merit, Canadian Institute of Chemistry/Chemical Industry, 1967; Medal in Chemistry, Queen's Univ., 1967; Queen's Univ. Scholarship, 1966; Ont. Scholarship, 1963; D.Sc.(Hon.), Memorial Univ. of Newfoundland, 1991; D.Sc.(Hon.), York Univ., 1991; D.Laws(Hon.), Brock Univ., 1991; D.Sc.(Hon.), Univ. of Western Ontario, 1992; D.Sc.(Hon.), The Univ. of Windsor, 1993; D.Sc.(Hon.), Univ. of Victoria, 1995; D.Sc.(Hon.), Queen's Univ., 1993. **COMMENT:** *"Extensive experience in post-secondary education policy and management, research administration management and policy, and science and technology policy. Active member of various national and regional standing committees, boards and advisory groups on education, training, and science and technology."*

Hallworth, Beryl, B.Sc. ■ ✾ ⌖

Botanist, Herbarium, UNIVERSITY OF CALGARY, Calgary, AB. Born Whitchurch, Cardiff, S. Wales 1911. m. Herbert Hallworth. 1 ch. Michael. **EDUC:** Univ. of Wales, B.Sc.(Botany) 1931, Hon. Botany 1932, Univ. Teaching Diploma 1933; USK Agricultural Coll., Student-Lecturer Diploma (Royal Horticulture Society Diploma) 1934-35. **CAREER:** taught Botany & Geography, UK, 1935-66; emigrated to Canada, 1966; Asst. Curator, Herbarium, Dept. of Biol., Univ. of Calgary, 1967-78; continues botanical work at the Herbarium, along with writing on the subject of botany, 1978 to date. **SELECTED PUBLICATIONS:** *Annotated Catalogue of Norman Sanson's Botanical Collection*, 9 volumes (Calgary: Univ. of Calgary Biol. Dept., 1978-82); contributor, *New Canadian Encyclopedia* 2nd Edition (Edmonton: Hurtig Publishers Ltd., 1988); *Pioneer Naturalists of the Rocky Mountains and Selkirks*, with M. Jackson (Calgary: Calgary Field Naturalists' Society, 1985); *Nose Hill: A Popular Guide*, ed. (Calgary: Calgary Naturalists' Society, 1988); *Plants of Kananaskis Country in the Rocky Mountains of Alberta*, with Dr. C.C. Chinnappa (Calgary: Univ. of Calgary Press & Univ. of Alberta Press, in press); "Nodding Thistle (*Carduus nutans*)," with M. Mychaijlvk (*Canadian Field Naturalist* Vol. 97 1985). **AFFIL:** Federation of Alberta Naturalists; Calgary Field Naturalists' Society (Hon. Mbr.); Canada Nature Federation; Friends of Nose Hill Society (Hon. Mbr.). **HONS:** Loren Goulden Award, Federation of Alberta Naturalists, 1995. **INTERESTS:** botany; geology; history; archaeology. **COMMENT:** *"My lifelong interest in biology and natural areas is now applied to the writing of books aimed at the preservation of natural areas in Western Canada."*

Halvorson, Marilyn, B.Ed. ▤ ▯

Writer. R.R. 2, Box 9, Site 14, Sundre, AB T0M 1X0. Born Olds, Alta. 1948. s. **EDUC:** Univ. of Calgary, B.Ed.(Social Studies) 1981. **CAREER:** teacher, County of Mountainview, 1968-90; writer; cattle rancher. **SELECTED PUBLICATIONS:** *Dare* (Toronto: General Publishing, 1988); *Let It Go* (Toronto: General Publishing, 1989); *Bull Rider* (Don Mills: Collier Macmillan, 1989); *Cowboys Don't Cry* (Toronto: Stoddart); *Cowboys Don't Quit* (Toronto: Stoddart); *To Everything A Season* (Toronto: Stoddart, 1991); *Brothers and Strangers* (Toronto: Stoddart, 1992); *Stranger on the Run* (Toronto: Stoddart, 1992); *But*

Cows Can't Fly and Other Stories (Toronto: Stoddart, 1993); *Nobody Said it Would be Easy* (Toronto: General Publishing, 1993). HONS: Alberta Culture/Clarke Irwin Writing for Youth Competition, 1984; Children's Literature Award, Writers' Guild of Alberta, 1987. INTERESTS: gardening; photography; ecology; horseback riding. COMMENT: *"I am an independent woman who enjoys a life of self-sufficiency close to the land and I have a deep appreciation of all living things. Most of my writing has been for teenagers. This comes from my years of teaching them and learning to appreciate their feelings and aspirations."*

Hamara, Olga Marian (née Ochitwa) ■ ■ 📖 ♥

President, Ontario Branch, UKRAINIAN MUSEUM OF CANADA. Born Gorlitz, Sask. 1919. m. William John Hamara. 2 ch. Gregory, Patricia. 5 grch. EDUC: Toronto Normal Sch., Elementary Sch. Teaching Certificate 1939; Ont. Dept. of Educ., summer courses (Art/Educ.) 1944. CAREER: elementary sch. teacher, 1939-83. AFFIL: Ukrainian Museum of Canada (Pres., Ont. Branch 1972 to date); Ontario Association of Superannuated Teachers (mbr.; Pres. 1989); Ukrainian Women's Association of Canada (active mbr.; VP 1969-74; held exec. positions, local, prov. & nat'l executives); Women Teachers' Association of Ontario (Exec. mbr., North York 1968-71 & Toronto 1951-54); St. Vladimir Institute, Toronto (V-Chair 1974-77); YWCA, North York (Pres. 1964-66); United Appeal, North York (Area Chair 1960); Ukrainian Orthodox Church (Choir; taught Sunday Sch. & children's choir); Anglican Young People's Association (active mbr.); Progressive Conservative Party (participated in electing G. Carton provincially & F. Stinson federally). HONS: 15-Yr. Service Award as Volunteer, Prov. of Ont., 1986; 50-Yr. Service Award, Ukrainian Women's Association of Canada, 1995; 25-Yr. Service Award, Ukrainian Museum of Canada, Ont. Branch, 1996. INTERESTS: volunteer work; church activities; bridge; cottage life; handicrafts; music. MISC: extensive travel to Europe, Asia, Africa, Middle East, South America & Far East. COMMENT: *"I have always held a positive attitude toward work, home life and extra-curricular activities. My family, my wide circle of friends and my professional associates have strongly contributed to the fulfilment of an exciting and interesting life."*

Hamilton, Doreen ✤

Member of the Legislative Assembly (Regina Wascana Plains), GOVERNMENT OF SASKATCHEWAN, 374 University Park Dr., Regina, SK S4V 0Y8 (306) 522-1027, FAX 522-4992. Born Regina 1951. m. Robert Hamilton. 2 ch. EDUC: Univ. of Regina, Educ. 1969-71. CAREER: teacher, 3 yrs.; elected Councillor, City of Regina, 1985, re-elected, 1988; Mayor, City of Regina, Oct.-Nov. 1988; elected M.L.A. (Regina Wascana Plains), 1991; Caucus Committee for Local Gov't & Educ.; Chair, Mun. Law Committee; Crown Corp. Committee; Admin. Committee; House Leader's Committee; Chair, Regina Caucus; re-elected, 1995. AFFIL: Canadian Parliamentary Association; Unified Board of Broadway United Church; Boothill Community Association; Regina Community Clinic. HONS: Canada 125 Medal, 1992. MISC: chosen as delegate, headed the Sask. delegation to Ottawa & presented the lead paper at the Canada Council Conference, *The Future of Work in Canada*, 1989; chosen to represent Sask. at int'l conference, Women, Power and Politics, Adelaide, Australia. COMMENT: *"I have always felt that becoming part of a community or organization also carries with it the responsibility to contribute in whatever way possible to enrich the quality of life for everyone. I firmly believe our world works best in partnership and that we must strive to be an example to women who would become involved in political life, to address the barriers and to allow men and women the opportunity to share in the nurturing of family and community. I have a particular interest in the quality of life issues (women's issues, hunger and poverty, full employment)."*

Hamilton, Ingrid ■ $ ⚒ 🐦

President, GAT PRODUCTIONS INC., 167 Gerrard St. E., Toronto, ON M5A 2E4 (416) 920-7789, FAX 920-2455. EDUC: Seneca Coll., Diploma (Comm.) 1977. CAREER: entertainment journalist & columnist, *The Toronto Sun*, 1982-89; instructor, Harris Institute for the Arts, 1992 to date; guest lecturer & speaker, 1994 to date; President & Founder, GAT Productions Inc., 1992. AFFIL: Women in Film & Television; Young ENTREPRENEURS of Ontario. HONS: nominated for Publicist of the Year, covering the music industry for all of Canada, 1993, 1994. COMMENT: *"I'm extremely driven and creative and have developed strong entrepreneurial skills. Since the growth of my company, it has been gratifying to see that I'm a pretty darn good boss too. I never miss out on a good opportunity and strive for challenges with successful results. There is nothing that satisfies me more than to see the hype created for my clients through media and public attention, and at the same time see my staff learn the ropes of the business. I get to feed off their enthusiasm and it's rewarding to know that they not only respect me as their boss, but also as their friend. I love the entertainment industry and look forward to new opportunities and endeavours currently leading me to producing television and film projects."*

Hamilton, M. Jill, B.A.,LL.B.,LL.M., Q.C. ■■ ⚖
Lawyer, DALEY, BLACK & MOREIRA (law firm), P.O. Box 355, Halifax, NS B3J 2N7 (902) 423-7211, FAX 420-1744. Born Halifax 1950. m. 1 ch. **EDUC:** Dalhousie Univ., B.A. 1971, LL.B. 1974; University Coll., Univ. of London, LL.M. 1975; Institute of World Affairs, London, Diploma (Air & Space Law) 1975. **BAR:** N.S., 1976. **CAREER:** lawyer in private practice. **AFFIL:** Canadian Bar Association; Canadian Tax Foundation; N.S. Barristers' Society (Pres. 1993-94; Exec. Committee 1991 to date; Chair, numerous committees 1991-93); Canadian Law Information Council (Chairperson 1987-88); Dalhousie Univ. (former mbr., Advisory Bd., Sch. of Bus. Admin.); N.S. Task Force on Investment & Taxation (former mbr.); Halifax Board of Trade (Dir. 1987-92); St. Andrew's United Church (Trustee 1991 to date); Salvation Army Grace Maternity Hospital, Halifax (Bd. of Mgmt 1992 to date); Beavers/Cubs (leader 1990 to date). **HONS:** Queen's Cnsl, N.S., 1992. **MISC:** lecturer, nat'l & local conferences, Canadian Tax Foundation; served as regular lecturer at bar admission course & prepared portion of materials for current course.

Hamilton, Margot, B.A.,M.C.I.P. $ ♡ 🍁
Urban Planner, CALGARY POLICE SERVICE, 1304 Baldwin Cres. S.W., Calgary, AB T2V 2B5 (403) 252-6539, FAX 252-6539. Born Winnipeg 1955. m. Duncan. 2 ch. Lise, Tess. **EDUC:** Univ. of Manitoba, B.A.(Psych.) 1976, Master of City Planning 1979. **CAREER:** Planner, Calgary Police Svc, 1989 to date; Principal, Hamilton and Associates, 1994 to date. **AFFIL:** YWCA (Pres., Bd. of Dir., Calgary 1991-93; Nat'l Bd. of Dir. 1993-95); Calgary Planning Commission (1993-96); Certified Law Enforcement Planner, 1993 to date; Child Friendly Calgary (Bd.); Canadian Institute of Planners; Sheriff King Home for Battered Women & their Children (Chair, Fund Dev. Committee 1987-90); World Police & Fire Games 1997 (Organizing Committee). **HONS:** Canada 125 Medal. **INTERESTS:** reading; travelling; sewing; cross-training. **COMMENT:** *"Through her extensive experience in law enforcement and land-use planning and in social issues, Margot is able to provide a balanced, down-to-earth contribution to organizations planning for the future. Margot is very active in community affairs, and is proud to be the mother of her two daughters."*

Hamilton, Muriel, B.Ed.,M.A.,Ph.D. ♡ ✊
President, PLANNED PARENTHOOD ALBERTA, 1220 Kensington Rd. N.W., Ste. 301, Calgary, AB T2N 3P5 (403) 283-8591, FAX 270-3209. Born Calgary 1926. w. 3 ch. **EDUC:** Univ. of British Columbia, B.Ed.(Secondary Educ.) 1971; Univ. of Calgary, M.A.(Educ.) 1981, Ph.D.(Educ) 1991. **CAREER:** teacher, rural sch., Spirit River Sch. Div. No. 47, Alta., 1945-56; Principal, Fort Nelson River Sch., 1957-60; teacher, ungraded sch., Sikanni Chief Sch., Alaska, 1960-63; English teacher, Dept. Head, Spirit River Secondary Sch., 1963-86; VP, 1974-75; Bd. Mbr., Planned Parenthood Alberta, 1992; Pres., 1993 to date. **SELECTED PUBLICATIONS:** various articles, book chapters & presentations. **EDIT:** Assoc. Ed., *Networks*, R-C-L, 1990-93. **AFFIL:** A.T.A. (Life Mbr.); English Language Arts Council (Life Mbr.); Canadian Council of Teachers of English; Phi Delta Kappa; Canadian Coll. of Teachers; Grande Prairie Business & Professional Women's Club. **HONS:** IODE scholarship, Fort Brisebois chapter, 1944; Queen's Jubilee Medal, 1977; Ves Thomas scholarship, 1987. **INTERESTS:** educ.; feminism; aboriginal interests; literature; local gov't; libraries. **COMMENT:** *"After a lifetime of teaching I am retired and can do volunteer work. PPA, with its strong educational and lobbying components, suited my needs."*

Hamilton, Patricia, B.F.A. ■■ 🎭 🎓
Actor. c/o Premier Artists Ltd., 671 Danforth Ave., Ste. 305, Toronto, ON M4J 1L3 (416) 461-6868. Born Regina, Sask. 1937. d. 1 ch. Ben Carlson. **EDUC:** Carnegie Institute of Technology, B.F.A.(Theatre) 1960; Central Sch. of Speech & Drama, London, England (Canada Council grant), 1961. **CAREER:** American Shakespeare Festival, Stratford, Conn., 1965-66; Seattle Rep. Co., 1969-70; Tarragon Theatre, Factory Theatre, Canadian Stage Company, reg'l theatres across Canada, 1970 to date; founding Producer, Masterclass Theatre, 1986; Dir., Advanced Actors Workshop, Banff Centre for the Arts, 1988-94; currently in 2-part drama *Angels in America*, The Canadian Stage Company. **SELECTED CREDITS:** Ruth, *If We Are Women*, Canadian Stage Co.; Lear, *King Lear*, Necessary Angel; Rachel Lynde, *Road to Avonlea*, Disney/CBC/K. Sullivan Prod.; Principal, *Street Legal*, CBC; numerous other stage, film & TV roles. **DIRECTOR:** The Canadian Stage Company. **HONS:** Brenda Donohue Award for distinguished contribution to Toronto theatre, 1989; Genie award for best

supporting actress *for A Bird in the House* (film), 1974; Dora award for best supporting actress for *I Am Yours* (theatre); Gemini award for best supporting actress in a series for *Road to Avonlea* (TV); Silver Ticket award for body of work. **COMMENT:** *"I have acted, directed, taught and produced in Canada and the U.S. for 35 years. I was the founding producer of Masterclass Theatre and later head of the Advanced Actors Workshop at the Banff Centre."*

Hamilton Lambie, Cathy, B.A.,M.B.A. $ ✎
Vice-President, Reader Sales and Service, THE GAZETTE, 25 St. Antoine W., Montreal, PQ H2Y 3R7 (514) 987-2401, FAX 987-2420. Born Montreal 1956. m. Rev. Dave Lambie. 3 ch. **EDUC:** McGill Univ., B.A.(Hons., English) 1978, M.B.A. 1988. **CAREER:** Retail Sales Rep., Advtg, *The Gazette*, 1978-83; Special Sections Coord., Advtg, 1984-85; Supervisor, Zoned Edition, Advtg, 1985-88; Asst. Mgr, Admin. & Dev., Advtg, 1988-89; Asst. Dir., Circulation, 1989-94; VP, Reader Sales & Svc, 1994 to date. **AFFIL:** Canadian Circulation Managers' Association. **INTERESTS:** Scouts Canada; reading; outdoors activities.

Hammell, Sue ■■ 🍁
Minister of Women's Equality, GOVERNMENT OF BRITISH COLUMBIA, Parliament Bldgs, Victoria, BC V8V 1X4 (604) 387-1223, FAX 387-4312. Born Vancouver. m. John Pollard. 1 ch. **EDUC:** Univ. of British Columbia, grad. **CAREER:** teacher, several sch. districts in B.C. **POLITICAL CAREER:** elected to B.C. legislature rep. Surrey-Green Timbers, 1991; served as Caucus Chair & on several legislative committees; Min. of Housing, Recreation & Consumer Svcs & Min. responsible for Co-operatives, 1995-96; Min. of Women's Equality, 1996 to date. **MISC:** environmental advocate, working to establish Green Timbers Forest as a "living" heritage site.

Hammond, Marie, M.A.Ed.,B.Ed., B.A. ■ ☺ ♡
Feminist, Peace Activist. 2118 Creighton St., Halifax, NS B3K 3R4 (902) 425-0563, EMAIL novaworx@fox.nstn.ca. Born Hamilton, Ont. 1962. m. Kevin Callaghan. 1 ch. **EDUC:** Burin District Vocational Sch., Nfld., Basic Drafting Certificate 1980; Mount Allison Univ., Hons. B.A. 1985, B.Ed. 1986; Univ. of Toronto, M.A.Ed. 1990. **CAREER:** Research Asst., Evaluation Branch, N.B. Dept. of Educ., 1986-87; Program Mgr, Work Orientation Workshop Program, School District No. 26, Fredericton, 1987; teacher, City of York & City of Toronto, 1988-91; Research Asst., Archives, Law Society, Osgoode Hall, Toronto, 1991-92; Program Trainer, YW-NOW, New Options for Women, Halifax YWCA, 1992-93; N.S. Bd. Rep., Voice of Women, N.S. Branch, 1992-95; Educ./Research Consultant, Halifax, 1993-95; Hist. teacher, Dartmouth High Sch., 1994-95; part-time Prof., St. Mary's, Mount St. Vincent & Dalhousie universities, 1996-97. **AFFIL:** Canadian Voice of Women for Peace; Women in Trades & Technology; Canadian Research Institute for the Advancement of Women; Canadian Committee on Women's History; YWCA, Halifax. **HONS:** Research Award, Dept. of Phil., Mount Allison Univ., 1985; B.Ed. Scholarship, 1986; Maritime Writers' Workshop Scholarship, 1987. **INTERESTS:** writing/teaching women's history; peace activism; aboriginal issues; environmental issues; social justice/human rights; new technology; Internet; history of Irish women & nationalism. **MISC:** composed & presented briefs to various gov't committees on social, justice & peace issues; presentation to the U.N. Conference on the Status of Women, Non-Governmental Organizations Forum, Vienna, Austria; developed seminars for schools/workplaces on gender & employment equity issues. **COMMENT:** *"I am an educator for gender equity in education and the workplace. I endeavour to bring perspectives on gender, class, race/ethnicity, and global peace/justice into every aspect of my profession."*

Hammond, Ruth (Bunting), ABC, APR. ✎ 🎓 ☺ ☝
President and Principal, RUTH HAMMOND PUBLIC RELATIONS, 33 Elmhurst Ave., Ste. 2410, Willowdale, ON M2N 6G8 (416) 226-5322, FAX 226-5322. Born Toronto 1920. w. (1st Lawrence J. Hammond, 2nd David W. Bunting). 2 ch. Gillian E. Silvester, John A. Hammond. **EDUC:** Victoria Coll., Univ. of Toronto, B.A.(English) 1943; Ont. Coll. of Educ., Teaching Degree, English Specialist Certificate 1944; International Association of Business Communicators, Accredited Bus. Communicator (ABC); Canadian Public Relations Society, Accredited Public Rel'ns (APR). **CAREER:** teacher, secondary schools, Ont. & Bahamas, 1943-46; daily broadcaster, women's morning show, CBC, Toronto, 1951; reporter, Women's Ed., *The Toronto Star*, 1946-51; Copy Ed., News Desk, 1946-51; Owner & Operator, Ruth Hammond Public Relations, 1952 to date; Dir., Public Rel'ns Div., Young and Rubicam Advertising Toronto, 1960s; Dir., Info. Svcs-Alumni Affairs, Ontario Coll. of Art. 1979-84; VP, Public Rel'ns Div., Vickers and Benson Advertising, 1984-85; course dir. & instructor, Ryerson Polytechnic Univ., York

Univ. & Univ. of Toronto, 1960s-95. SELECTED PUBLICATIONS: *Public Relations for Small Businesses*, with W. Forbes LeClair (Financial Post: McMillan and Gage, 1979); author of monograph on public rel'ns careers issued by Guidance Centre, Univ. of Toronto; many articles & speeches on public rel'ns. AFFIL: Canadian Women's Press Club, Toronto Branch (later, Media Club of Canada); Canadian Public Relations Society, Toronto; Humber CAAT (Founding mbr., & Chrm, Advisory Committee, Public Rel'ns Course); Centennial Coll. (Advisory Committee, Public Rel'ns Course); Toronto Press Club (Dir.). HONS: President's Medal, Canadian Public Relations Society, Toronto Chapter; Award of Attainment, Canadian Public Relations Society; Gold Quill Award, International Association of Business Communicators; Woman of Distinction, YWCA of Metropolitan Toronto; Philip A. Novikoff Memorial Award, Canadian Public Relations Society. INTERESTS: educ. in professional public rel'ns advtg; travel; politics. MISC: 1st female Women's Ed., 1st female Copy Ed., *The Toronto Star*; served on Gov't of Ont. Task Force on Comm. Educ. at CAATs; Ruth Hammond Scholarship set up in her name by Canadian Public Relations Society, Toronto. COMMENT: *"I am proud to have been a pioneer in women's journalism and in professional education for the communications field."*

Hammond, Susan, B.A.,A.R.C.T. ■■ ⊗ ♉
Producer and President, CLASSICAL KIDS (audio, live shows, video productions on classical music for children), 134 Howland Ave., Toronto, ON M5R 3B5 (416) 535-6649, FAX 535-2127. Born Toronto 1948. m. Michael. 2 ch. Sarah Hammond, Katie Hammond. EDUC: Royal Conservatory of Music, A.R.C.T.(Piano) 1966; Univ. of Toronto, B.A.(Sociology) 1970. CAREER: accompanist & teacher of piano, 1971-88; record producer, founder, Classical Kids, 1988 to date; writer, teachers' materials/workshop leader, 1988 to date; live symphony productions, 1991 to date. SELECTED CREDITS: *Mr. Bach Comes to Call* (CD, 1988); *Daydreams and Lullabies* (CD, 1992); *Beethoven Lives Upstairs* (CD, 1989; video, 1993; sym. show, 1993; book, 1994); *Mozart's Magic Fantasy* (CD, 1990; live opera performance, 1993-95); *Vivaldi's Ring of Mystery* (CD, 1991; sym. show, 1995); *Tchaikovsky Discovers America* (CD, 1993; sym. show, 1993; book, 1994); *Hallelujah Handel* (CD, 1995; live show, 1996). DIRECTOR: Classical Kids; The Children's Group. AFFIL: Pueblito Canada (supporter); Arts Foundation of Greater Toronto. HONS: Order of Canada,

1993. For recordings: 4 Junos for Best Children's Recording; 6 Awards of Excellence, Film Advisory Bd.; 6 American Library Association "Notable Children's Recording"; 4 Parents' Choice Awards. For "Beethoven Lives Upstairs" video: Emmy, Dove, Parents' Choice Classic Award. INTERESTS: singing; piano; skiing; tennis; golf. COMMENT: *"My aims are to introduce children to the world of classical music and to excite them about times past. My challenge: "Who would want to do the possible all their lives?" My gratitude for a wonderful family, the Order of Canada, Junos, and all those wonderful letters!"*

Hampson, Elizabeth M., B.A.,M.A., Ph.D. ■ ❀ ⊕ ♞
Associate Professor, Department of Psychology, UNIVERSITY OF WESTERN ONTARIO, London, ON N6A 5C2 (519) 661-2111, ext. 4675, FAX 661-3213, EMAIL ehampson@uwovax. uwo.ca. Born Kamsack, Sask. 1957. m. Richard Harshman. EDUC: Univ. of Saskatchewan, B.A.(Psych.) 1980; Univ. of Western Ontario, M.A.(Psychobiol.) 1982, Ph.D.(Clinical Neuropsych.) 1989. CAREER: Research Fellow, Hospital for Sick Children, Toronto, 1989-91; Asst. Prof., Univ. of Western Ontario, 1991-96; Assoc. Prof., 1996 to date. SELECTED PUBLICATIONS: "Hand movement asymmetries during verbal and nonverbal tasks" (*Canadian Journal of Psychology* No. 38 1984); "Sex differences and hormonal influences on cognitive functions in humans," with D. Kimura (*Behavioral endocrinology* ed. J.B. Becker, S.M. Breedlove, D. Crews, Boston: MIT Press/Bradford Books, 1992); "Cognitive pattern in men and women is influenced by fluctuations in sex hormones," with D. Kimura (*Current Directions in Psychological Science* No. 3 1994). AFFIL: Society for Neuroscience; International Neuropsychological Society; International Society for Behavioural Neuroscience; International Society of Psychoneuroendocrinology. HONS: Curt P. Richter Prize for Research in Behavioral or Neuro-Endocrinology, 1989. INTERESTS: gardening; cooking. COMMENT: *"Elizabeth is a faculty member in psychology and the interdisciplinary neuroscience program at the University of Western Ontario, where she does research in behavioral endocrinology."*

Hancock, Lorna, B.A. ■ ♡ ⊕
Executive Director, HEALTH ACTION NETWORK SOCIETY, 5262 Rumble St., Ste. 202, Burnaby, BC V5J 2B6 (604) 435-0512, FAX 435-1561. Born Gilbert Plains, Man. 1947. m. Brian. 3 ch. EDUC: Univ. of British Columbia, B.A. (English) 1969. CAREER: Social Worker, 1969-

74; Exec. Dir., Health Action Network Society. **EDIT:** *Health Action*, Health Action Network Society. **AFFIL:** Burnaby Girls' Soccer Club (Gen. Mgr). **INTERESTS:** family; friends; photography; writing; humour; passion; joy. **COMMENT:** *"Whoever nominated me thought I might deserve recognition simply for hanging onto a dream for 18 or so years–a dream of a public service (charitable) that would offer alternative health information, driven by the consumer."*

Hancock, Lyn (Beryl Lynette), B.Ed., M.A. ■ 🗊 ∕ ☺
Writer, Photographer, Lecturer., FRANKLYN ENTERPRISES, Box 244, Fort Simpson, NT X03 0N0 (403) 695-2328, FAX 695-2145, 8270 Sabre Rd., Lantzville (Nanaimo), BC V0R 2H0. Born East Fremantle, W. Australia 1938. m. Frank Schober. **EDUC:** Graylands Teachers' College, Diploma of Educ. 1956; Univ. of West Australia, A.S.D.A.(Speech & Drama) 1956, L.A.S.A. 1957; Trinity Coll., London, UK, L.T.C.L.(Speech & Drama) 1959; Royal Academy of Music, London, UK, L.R.A.M. (Mime & Movement) 1961, L.R.A.M.(Speech & Drama) 1961; British Columbia Teachers' Certificate 1977; Simon Fraser Univ., B.Ed. 1977, M.A.(Comm.) 1980; studied mime & movement, speech & drama with Rose Bruford & Peter Slade, in UK. **CAREER:** Principal, private Academy of Speech & Drama, W. Australia, 1954-59; teacher, 1956-70; filmmaker, 1963 to date; writer, 1964 to date; lecturer, 1964 to date; sec., animal caregiver, writer & filmmaker, Wildlife Conservation Centre, Saanichton, B.C., 1964-73. **SELECTED CREDITS:** Co-Prod., *Coast Safari*, feature film; Co-Prod., Pacific Wilderness (feature); 13 documentaries, *Klahanie* (nature series), CBC TV. **SELECTED PUBLICATIONS:** *There's a Seal in My Sleeping Bag* (Toronto: William Collins, 1972); *There's a Raccoon in My Parka* (Toronto: Doubleday, 1977); *Tell Me, Grandmother* (Toronto: McClelland & Stewart, 1985); *Looking for the Wild* (Toronto: Doubleday, 1986); *Alaska Highway: Road to Adventure* (Fort Nelson: Autumn Images, 1988); *Northwest Territories* (Toronto: Grolier, 1993) *Winging It in the North* (Lantzville, B.C.: oolichan Books, 1996); *Vancouver: Port City* (Minneapolis: Lerner Publications Company, 1997); contributor to *Great Canadian Fishing Stories that Didn't Get Away* (Ontario: Burns-Town, 1996); 7 other books; currently working on a series of children's books; photographs published in Coastal Canada (Toronto: Discovery Books, 1985), *The Last Wilderness: Images of the Canadian Wild* (Toronto: Key Porter Books, 1990); *Nunavut* (Minneapolis: Lerner

Publications Company, 1995); *Yukon* (Minneapolis: Lerner Publications Company, 1996) & others; currently working on a personal book of her life in the north in photographs; several thousand articles published internationally in newspapers & magazines such as *New York Times, Australian Women's Weekly, Canadian Geographic, Alaska Magazine* & *Up Here.* **AFFIL:** Writers' Union of Canada; Periodical Writers' Association of Canada; North West Outdoor Writers' Association; Outdoor Writers' Association; Canadian Nature Federation. **HONS:** numerous awards for literary & scholastic achievements, 1950-95; Francis J. Kortright Conservation Award for Excellence in Outdoor Writing (twice); American Express Travel Writing Award (twice); Pacific Northwest Booksellers' Award. **INTERESTS:** her work; the North; natural history; adventure travel; photography; reading; writing. **MISC:** listed in various biographical sources, incl. *Who's Who in Canadian Literature, World Who's Who of Women, International Authors and Writers Who's Who & International Who's Who of Distinguished Leadership.* **COMMENT:** *"Workaholic, enthusiastic, energetic, enjoys communicating her fascination for life's daily adventures and the people she meets, in words and photographs. Has written 13 books and thousands (literally) of lively articles. Likes travelling to the back of beyond and telling people about it."*

Hankins, Catherine, B.A.,M.D.,M.Sc., FRCPC ⊕
Public Health Epidemiologist, Infectious Disease Unit, MONTREAL PUBLIC HEALTH DEPARTMENT, 1616 René-Lévesque Blvd. W., 3rd Fl., Montreal, QC H3H 1P8 (514) 932-3055, FAX 932-1502, EMAIL md77@musica.mcgill.ca. Born Edmonton 1949. m. James Talmage Palmer. 2 ch. Andrea Hankins-Palmer, Althaea Hankins-Palmer. **EDUC:** Univ. of Calgary, B.A.(French, German) 1971, M.D.(Medicine) 1976; Univ. of London, UK, M.Sc.(Community health in developing countries) 1979; Royal Coll. of Physicians & Surgeons, FRCPC (Community Medicine) 1981. **CAREER:** Deputy Medical Officer of Health, Calgary Health Svcs, 1980-85; Dir., Reg. Sexually Transmitted Disease Program, Montreal Public Health Unit, 1986-89; Coord., Centre for AIDS Studies, 1989-90; Public Health Epidemiologist, Montreal Public Health Dept., 1986 to date; Assoc. Dir., McGill AIDS Centre, 1995; Assoc. Prof., Dept. of Epidemiology & Biostatistics, McGill Univ.; Prof. associée, Dept. de Médicine Sociale et Préventive, Univ. de Montreal. **SELECTED PUBLICATIONS:** "HIV: Evolution of a Pandemic" (*Canadian Medical Association Jour-*

nal, 153, 1995); "Confronting HIV infection in prisons" (Canadian Medical Association Journal, 151, 1994); "HIV and Women in Prison: Assessment of Risk Factors Using a Non-nominal Methodology," with Gendron S., Handley M., *et al* (*American Journal of Public Health*, 84, 1994); "Vulnerability and Access to Prevention: The Case of Injection Drug Use," *AIDS, Health, and Human Rights*, eds. J. Mann & C. Dupuy (Annecy, France; Merieux Foundation, 1993); "Towards an HIV/AIDS Research Agenda for the 1990s: A Background Discussion Paper" (Canadian Association for HIV research, 1992); "HIV Disease/AIDS in Women: Current Knowledge and a Research Agenda" (Journal of Acquired Immune Deficiency Syndrome, 5, 1992); numerous other publications. EDIT: ed. of two newsletters. AFFIL: U.N. Dev. Program (Consultant); Canadian Association for HIV Research (Pres. 1993-95); Canadian Society for International Health; Program for Appropriate Technology in Health (Dir.); Conseil médical du Québec. HONS: YWCA Women of Merit, Health, Montreal, 1994; National Rolleston Award for Harm Reduction, 1994; Canada 125 Medal, 1993; Distinguished Alumni Award, Univ. of Calgary, 1993. INTERESTS: travelling; photography; jogging; foreign cinema; music; art; theatre; fiction; mountaineering; ski-touring; cycling. COMMENT: *"In addition to my research and public policy interests in Quebec, I am coordinating a research capacity building initiative for the United Nations Development Program in four African countries."*

Hannon, Evelyn, B.A. ■■ 🗋 🗎 🗺
Editor and Publisher, *JOURNEYWOMAN TRAVEL MAGAZINE*, 50 Prince Arthur Ave., Ste. 1703, Toronto, ON M5R 1B5 (416) 929-7654, FAX 929-1433, EMAIL jwoman@web.net. Born Montreal 1940 2 ch. Erica Ehm, Leslie Ehm. EDUC: Macdonald Coll., Class III Diploma (Teaching Certificate); McGill Univ., B.A.(Film & TV) 1989. CAREER: primary sch. teacher, 1959-65; Dir., Camp Kennebec children's camp, 1966-73; Dir., 50 Plus Recreational Centre, Montreal, 1973-80; Dir., Sorties travel excursions for older adults, 1980-82; Producer, Cineve Film Production, 1990-92; Publisher & Editor, Journeywoman Travel Magazine, 1993 to date. SELECTED CREDITS: Middle East Production Coord., *Half the Kingdom* (NFB/Kol Ishah film); Researcher, *The New Nurses* (NFB film); Producer/Research Coord., *She Healers - East and West* (Cineve Film Production). SELECTED PUBLICATIONS: regular travel articles, *Journeywoman*. AFFIL: Canadian Magazine Publishers' Association; Travel Media Association of Canada; Artists for Art Literacy

in Canada (Nat'l Consultant 1992). HONS: graduated with Great Academic Distinction, McGill Univ., 1989; Apex Award of Excellence (magazine publishing), 1995 & 1996. INTERESTS: film; hiking; travelling solo; women's issues; graphology; all things Chinese. MISC: Coord., Canadian Women's Film Festival, Israel, 1989. COMMENT: *"Life is too short to be little. On to the next challenge!"*

Hannon, Heather M., B.A., LL.B. ■ ⚷ $
Counsel And Corporate Secretary, THE MARITIME LIFE ASSURANCE COMPANY, Box 1030, Halifax, NS B3J 2X5 (902) 453-7109, FAX (902) 453-7123. EDUC: Mount Allison Univ., B.A. 1975; Dalhousie Univ., LL.B. 1978.

Hanson, Alice, B.A.,M.L.A. ♣
Member of Legislative Assembly (Edmonton Highlands Beverly), Liberal Opposition, GOVERNMENT OF ALBERTA, 601, Legislature Annex, Edmonton, AB T5K 1E4 (403) 427-2293, FAX 427-3697. Born Edmonton 1927. w. 2 ch. Christopher Hanson, Lisë (Hanson) Niddrie. EDUC: Univ. of Alberta, B.A.(Psych.) 1949. CAREER: Teen Coord. Volunteer Action Centre, Edmonton, 1968-71; Exec. Dir., Boyle St. Community Svcs Co-op, 1972-79; Exec. Dir., Boyle McCauley Health Centre, 1980-86; Exec. Dir., Distinctive Employment Counselling Society, 1987-91; M.L.A. (Edmonton Highlands Beverly), Prov. of Alta., 1992 to date; Official Opposition Critic for Family & Social Svcs. AFFIL: Edmonton Inner City Housing (Bd. 1983-85); Boyle St. Community Svcs (Bd. & Exec.); *Boyle McCauley News* (Dir. 1987-89; Chair 1988-89); Liberal Party of Alberta; Edmonton Board of Health (Mbr. 1987-92; Chair 1990-91); WALN Foundation for Children & Families(1992 to date). HONS: Significant Contribution to Women in the Field of Legal, Political & Human Rights, City of Edmonton, 1975; Contribution to Better Understanding Between Edmonton Police Dept. & Community of Boyle St., 1979; Meritorious Contributions to the Community, Edmonton Social Planning Council, 1990. INTERESTS: reading; hiking; travel; family & friends; politics. COMMENT: *"My volunteer experience with youth in both Edmonton and inner city Vancouver prompted me to work to expand opportunities for people trapped in the poverty cycle."*

Hanson, Carla, E.M.C.A. $ ♡
President, Owner and Partner, CAN-AM MEDICAL, INC., HOUSE HELPERS INC. and HANSON'S INTERIOR DECORATING, 21 Ross St., Dryden, ON P8N 1T8 (807) 223-4489. Partner, Can Am Distributing. Born Virginia, Maine 1960.

m. Bruce. 2 ch. Natasha, Tristan. **EDUC**: Confederation Coll., Emergency Medical Care Asst. 1984; Ontario Real Estate Coll., Ont. Real Estate Bd. Certificate 1987; Sheffield Sch. of Design, Interior Design Program, 1995. **CAREER**: Emergency Medical Care Asst., Air Ambulance, Gov't of Ont., 1984 to date; Pres., Can-Am Medical Inc., 1985 to date; Owner, House Helpers Inc.; Ptnr, Hanson's Interior Decorating; Ptnr, Can Am Distributing, 1995 to date. **SELECTED PUBLICATIONS**: several articles for local newspaper; *Journal of Emergency Medicine*, 1985. **DIRECTOR**: Can-Am Medical, Inc. **AFFIL**: Dryden Inventor's Network (Co-Chair 1992-93); Dryden Child Abuse Prevention Council (Fundraising Chair, V-Chair 1990-94); Riverview Sch. Parent Advisory Committee (Fundraising Chair 1993-94). **HONS**: highlighted inventor in the "Women Invent" exhibition, Women Inventors' Network. **INTERESTS**: reading bus. publications; animal rights; child abuse prevention issues; spending time with my family. **MISC**: featured on the "Women of Change" poster produced by the Women's Directorate; patented inventor, C.P.R. Landmark®. **COMMENT**: *"I grew up a survivor of incest/alcohol in a small town, which instilled a drive for change in myself and my surroundings. I tend to be goal-minded, stubborn (which I consider a virtue) and creative. My motto is: 'Where there is a will, there is a way'."*

Hanson, Raymonde L., R.N.,B.N., M.Sc.N. ⌖
Vice-President, Academic, ALGONQUIN COLLEGE, 1385 Woodroffe Ave., Nepean, ON K2G 1V8 (613) 727-4723, ext. 7703, FAX 727-7773, EMAIL hansonr@algonquin.on.ca. Born Edmundston, N.B. 1944. m. Stephen. 2 ch. **EDUC**: Univ. of New Brunswick, B.N. 1966; Univ. of Western Ontario, M.Sc.N.(Educ.) 1976; Harvard Univ., Institute of Educational Mgmt, Grad. 1992. **CAREER**: Public Health Nurse, Dept. of Health, Moncton, N.B., 1966-67; Nursing Instructor, The Moncton Hospital, 1969-70; Chargé de cours (Lecturer), École des Sciences Infirmières, Univ. de Moncton, 1967-69, 1971-77; Asst. Prof., Sch. of Nursing, Univ. of Ottawa, 1977-81; Asst. VP, Nursing, Ottawa General Hospital, 1981-84; Dean, Sch. of Health Sciences, Algonquin Coll., 1984-87; VP, Academic, 1987 to date. **SELECTED PUBLICATIONS**: "Motor Skill Acquisition in Nursing" (Nursing Papers, Vol. 9, No. 21, Summer/Été 1977); "The Teaching of Nursing Motor Skills," paper presented at the Nurse Educators' Conference, Winnipeg, Mar. 1982. x. **AFFIL**: Registered Nurses' Association of Ontario; Cercle universitaire, Ottawa. **INTER-**

ESTS: gardening; movies; theatre. **COMMENT**: *"A committed academic leader who believes in the mission of the community colleges, the students who obtain a career-oriented education, and the staff who make it happen."*

Hanson, Tennys J.M., B.Sc. ○ ⌖
Campaign Director and Vice-President, UNIVERSITY OF TORONTO FOUNDATION, 27 King's College Circle, Toronto, ON M5S 1A1 (416) 978-0151, FAX 971-2442, EMAIL tennysh@dur.utoronto.ca. Born Winnipeg 1951. m. J. Douglas Hanson. **EDUC**: Univ. of Toronto, B.Sc. **CAREER**: Coord., Secondary Sch. Liaison, Erindale Coll., Univ. of Toronto, 1974-76; Coord., Community & Sch. Liaison, 1976-81; Dir., Campus Rel'ns, 1981-84; Exec. Dir., Campus Dev. & Public Affairs, 1984-89; VP & COO, Mount Sinai Hospital Foundation of Toronto, 1989-94; Acting Pres., 1994-95; Campaign Dir. & VP, Univ. of Toronto Foundation, Univ. of Toronto, 1995 to date. **AFFIL**: Mississauga Hospital (Dir. 1986-92); Junior Achievement of Peel (Dir. 1990-93); Univ. of Toronto (V-Chair, Coll. of Electors 1992-93; Dir., Alumni Association 1993-95); Sheridan Coll. (Gov.); Mississauga Board of Trade (Hon. Life Mbr.); Mount Sinai Hospital (Gov. 1995). **HONS**: Admissions & In-Course Scholarships, Erindale Coll., Univ. of Toronto, 1970-74; Gov. General's Silver Medal, Erindale Coll., 1973; Paul W. Fox Award for Distinguished Service, Univ. of Toronto, 1990. **INTERESTS**: opera; ballet; antiques; golf; dragon boat racing.

Harack, Joanne E., A.B.,M.A., Ph.D. ■■ ⊕ $ ⌖
Vice-President, Human Resources, Laboratory Services Division, MDS HEALTH GROUP LIMITED (health care), 100 International Blvd., Etobicoke, ON M9W 6J6 (416) 675-6777, ext. 2326, EMAIL jharack@mdshealth.com. Born Winnipeg 1947. m. Michael G. Kahan. **EDUC**: Indiana Univ., A.B.(Hons., English) 1968, M.A. (English) 1969; Univ. of Toronto, Ph.D. (English) 1978. **CAREER**: Coord., Programme Dev., Sch. of Continuing Studies, Univ. of Toronto, 1975-81; Program Dir., Mktg, Centre for Advanced Technology Educ., Ryerson Polytechnic Institute, 1984-88; Dir., Educ. & Training, Connaught Laboratories Limited, 1988-92; VP, Hum. Res., 1992-95. **SELECTED CREDITS**: has appeared in a number of training videos. **SELECTED PUBLICATIONS**: co-author with N. Pearson & P. Sweet, "Valuing Human Capital: Towards a Canadian Human Resource Industry" (discussion paper commissioned for the Skill Dev. Leave Task Force, Canada Employment & Immigration Commission, 1983); co-author with E.M. Christopherson,

"Re-Framing Continuing Professional Education" (*Canadian Journal of University Continuing Education*, Vol. IX, No. 2, 1983); "'Winners' and 'Losers': Skills Development Issues in a Canada-United States Free Trade Environment" (presentation to Ont. Cabinet Subcommittee on the proposed FTA, Nov. 1987); "University/Industry Cooperation in Continuing Education: A Discussion Paper" (commissioned by Canadian Association for University Continuing Education, & Employment & Immigration Canada, 1988); "Trained and Educated: Human Resource Development for Biotechnology Industries" (*Bionet*, Dec. 1990). **AFFIL:** Democracy Education Network (Dir. 1993 to date); Canadians for Health Research (Dir. 1991-95; Chair of the Bd. 1995); Liberal Party of Canada (Charter mbr., Dev. Council). **HONS:** Ford Foundation Fellowship, 1968-69; Ontario Grad. Fellowships, 1971-72; Award of Merit, Society of Manufacturing Engineers, 1986; Award of Recognition, Community Industrial Training Committee for North York & York Region, 1992. **INTERESTS:** gardening; sailing; detective fiction. **MISC:** Founding Pres., Cities in Schools, North York (a community-based network dedicated to keeping at-risk youth in school). **COMMENT:** *"An adult educator with more than twenty years' experience in the education, voluntary and private sectors; the author of numerous papers and monographs on human resource development; known for her progressive approach to industrial relations, employment equity, employee communications and educational partnerships."*

Harcourt, Joan, B.A. / 📖 📕
Poetry/Fiction Editor, QUEEN'S QUARTERLY, Queen's University, Kingston, ON K7L 3N6 (613) 545-2155, FAX 545-6822. Acquisitions Editor, MCGILL-QUEEN'S UNIVERSITY PRESS. Born Toronto 1930. d. 2 ch. **EDUC:** McGill Univ., B.A.(Hons.) 1954. **CAREER:** story researcher, J. Arthur Rank Studios & Warner Brothers Pictures, London, UK, 1955-63; freelance writer, London, UK, 1963-67; Ed. Asst., *Canadian Journal of Political Science*, 1968-71; Inhouse Manuscript Ed., McGill-Queen's Univ. Press, 1971-77; freelance ed., 1977-83; Sr. Correspondence Officer, Canadian Radio-Television & Telecommunications Commission, 1983-90; Manuscript Ed., *The Report of the Citizens' Forum on Canada's Future* (the Spicer Report), English-language edition, 1990-91; Fiction/Poetry Ed., *Queen's Quarterly* & Acquisitions Ed., McGill-Queen's Univ. Press, 1991 to date. **INTERESTS:** reading; films; some TV; walking. **COMMENT:** *"My endeavour: to find new Canadian writers. My achievement: to have been the first or an early publisher of a*

number of people whose work has since gained recognition."

Harder Mattson, Edna, R.N.,B.N. ■ ⊕ ✿
Past Provincial President, Manitoba Women's Commission, LIBERAL PARTY OF MANITOBA, 488 Christie Rd., St. Germaine P.O., St. Germaine, MB R0G 2A0 (204) 257-7761. Director of Administration and Nursing, MENNO HOME OF THE AGED. Born Gladstone, Man. 1943. m. James Mattson. 2 ch. Lisa-Jane Mattson, Heather-Anne Mattson. **EDUC:** Grace Hospital Sch. of Nursing, R.N. 1964; Univ. of Manitoba, Certificate, Teaching & Supervision 1966, B.N. 1970, Menno Simons Coll., currently pursuing B.A. in Conflict Resolution. **CAREER:** Gen. Duty Nurse, Portage la Prairie General Hospital, 1964-65; Teacher-LPN Program, Red River Community Coll., 1966-67; teacher/Asst. Dir. of Nursing Educ., St. Boniface General Hospital Sch. of Nursing, 1967-75; Nursing Supervisor, Community Resource Nurse, Asst. Head Nurse, Gen. Duty Nurse, Clinique Youville Clinic, St. Boniface General Hospital, 1983-85; Liberal candidate, provincial (Gladstone) 1986 (River East-Winnipeg) 1990; Nursing Coord., *In Vitro* Fertilization Program, Health Sciences Centre, St. Boniface General Hospital, 1985-87; Occupational Health Nurse, Manitoba Telephone System, 1987-88; Dir. of Nursing Practice, Medicine/Psychiatry, Seven Oaks General Hospital, 1988-95; Analyst, Home Care Appeal Process, Gov't of Man., 1995; Dir. of Admin & Nursing, Menno Home for the Aged, 1996 to date. **AFFIL:** Environment Canada (Partner's Fund); Canadian Mental Health Association (Dir.); Christian Health & Healing Council (Dir.); Manitoba Association of Registered Nurses; Bethania Mennonite Personal Care Home (Dir.); St. Philips Christian Wellness Centre; Liberal Party of Manitoba, Women's Commission (Past Pres.). **HONS:** Dean's Honour List, Univ. of Manitoba, 1970. **INTERESTS:** issues affecting women/family in Cdn society. **MISC:** registered nurse; frequent guest speaker; chaired Sheila Copps leadership campaign for Manitoba. **COMMENT:** *"I conduct conferences and workshops on various topics related to health and wellness to professional groups as well as the general public. In summary, I have held general duty, community health, teaching and administrative positions at several levels as well as engaged in private contract work. I have served as a board member of various agencies in health and education since 1984."*

Harding, Gladys Jane ◐ ☼
President, CHRISTIAN WOMEN'S CLUBS OF CANADA, Christian Business and Professional

Women, 121 Willowdale Ave., Ste. 305, P.O. Box 1200, Stn. A, Willowdale, ON M2N 5T5 (416) 222-0548, FAX 226-0540. Born Toronto 1926. m. Donald Nelson. 3 ch. **DIRECTOR:** H.M.S. Marketing; Stonecroft Ministries (US). **AFFIL:** Village Missions of Canada.

Harding, Gloria, LL.B. ⚖ ☝

Barrister and Solicitor, **NEWFOUNDLAND LEGAL AID COMMISSION**, 21 Church Hill, St. John's, NF A1C 3Z8 (709) 753-7860, FAX 753-6226. Born St. John's 1942. m. William Dalton. 1ch., 2 stpch. Carol Ann Harding Green, John Dalton, Colin Dalton. **EDUC:** St. Michael's & All Ages Sch., Grade XI Matriculation 1958; Dalhousie Univ., LL.B. 1979. **BAR:** Nfld., 1979. **CAREER:** Legal Sec., Bookkeeper, Office Admin., 1958-76; Course Lecturer, Cabot Institute, St. John's, 1982-84; gen. practice of law as a sole practitioner & in association with the firms of Hall and Harding; Learmonth, Harding; Parsons, Learmonth, Dunn and O'Hara; & Greene, Kelly, Harding and Fraize, 1979-91; Staff Solicitor, Newfoundland Legal Aid Commission, 1991 to date. **AFFIL:** Law Society of Newfoundland (Bencher; Hon. Sec.; Chair, Trust Accounting Committee); Canadian Bar Association (Dir., Legal Profession Assistant Committee). **INTERESTS:** painting; piano. **MISC:** V-Chair, Review Committee, Workers' Compensation of Newfoundland, 1987-88; Commissioner reviewing various municipal matters on a quasijudicial basis, 1983-88; 1st woman Hon. Sec. of the Law Society of Newfoundland. **COMMENT:** *"I endeavour to help my community and my profession by serving as a resource person, speaker for women's groups on self-direction and improvement, to encourage women to take a greater role in society and professionally and to help lawyers, suffering from stress, burnout or other conditions, access assistance programs.*

Harding, Judy ■ ♡ ⚖

Co-Founder, **CITIZENS CONCERNED WITH CRIME AGAINST CHILDREN (4C's)**, 100 Lancaster St. E., Kitchener, ON N2H 1M8 (519) 744-0904, FAX 744-5379. Born Sherbrooke, Que. 1949. m. Brian. 2 ch. **EDUC:** Sherbrooke High Sch., academic degree 1968; Sherbrooke Hospital, Nursing 1972. **CAREER:** Registered Nurse, Sexual Assault Team, St. Mary's General Hospital to date. **HONS:** Canadian Lifestyle Award, Health & Welfare Canada, 1984; The Service to Mankind Award from Prime Minister Brian Mulroney; Kitchener-Waterloo Woman of the Year, Humanitarian category, 1992; several local & reg'l awards. **INTERESTS:** public speaking; highland dancing; swimming. **MISC:** organization was featured *on The Nature of Things*, CBC, Oct. 1994. **COMMENT:** *"I feel very blessed to have the wonderful husband and two lovable children that I do. I truly believe the good Lord didn't put children on this earth to be sexually abused. In January 1981 I had no idea that 4C's would grow to the extent it has today. I would urge more Canadians to get OFF the couch because you really can make a difference."*

Harel, Louise, B.A.,LL.L. ■ 🍁

Member of the National Assembly (Hochelaga-Maisonneuve) and Ministre d'état de l'Emploi et de la Solidarité et ministre responsable de la Condition Feminine, **GOUVERNEMENT DU QUÉBEC**, Hôtel du Parlement, Québec, QC G1A 1A4 (418) 643-4810, FAX 643-2802. Born Ste-Thérèse de Blainville, Que. 1946 1 ch. **EDUC:** Séminaire Ste-Thérèse, B.A. 1967; Univ. de Montréal, LL.L. 1977. **BAR:** Qué., 1979. **CAREER:** VP, l'union générale des étudiants du Québec, 1968; permanente au secrétariat national du Parti Québécois, 1970-71; service des Coopératives, Conseil de développement social du Montréal métropolitain, 1971-74; Prés., région de Montréal-Centre, Parti Québécois, 1974-79; VP nationale, 1979-81; responsable du dossier de la condition féminine, Conseil des services sociaux du Montréal métropolitain, 1979-81; élue MNA (Hochelaga-Maisonneuve), 13 avril 1981; reélue déc. 1985, sept. 1989, sept. 1994; Min. de l'immigration et des communautes culturelles du Québec, 1984; Prés., Commission parlementaire de l'Éduc., 1989-94; Min. d'État à la Concertation et Min. de l'Emploi au sein du gouv. du Québec, 1994-96; min. d'État de l'Emploi et de la Solidarité et min. responsable de la Condition Feminine, 1996 à ce jour.

Hargrave, Diane, B.A. ■ $ 📖 📺

President, **DHPR COMMUNICATIONS INC.**, 73 Laird Dr., Ste. 305, Toronto, ON M4G 3T4 (416) 467-9954, FAX 467-0881, EMAIL dhprbks@interlog.com. Born Toronto 1951. s. **EDUC:** Univ. of Toronto, B.A.(English/Phil.) 1973. **CAREER:** more than 15 years' experience in the mktg & publicity sector of the book publishing industry; Mgr, Publicity & Advtg, Collins Publishing, 1986-89; Sole Proprietor, Diane Hargrave Public Relations, 1989 to date; Pres., DHPR Communications Inc., 1995 to date. **AFFIL:** Book Promoters' Association of Canada (Founding Exec.); Book Publishers' Professional Association; PEN Canada (Assoc.). **INTERESTS:** scuba diving; film; reading; travel. **COMMENT:** *"In all her wide-ranging projects, Diane Hargrave has used a stylish, well-organized, knowledgeable approach. Her flair and* *strengths have been displayed in conceiving and executing imaginative publicity campaigns for major events and awards, coordinating special launch events for new products, organizing national publicity for front-list authors and titles, and in the promotion of magazine features and specialty cookbooks."*

Harlan, Catherine, R.N.,B.Sc.N. ■■ ◉ ♡
Family Support Worker, THE FAMILY CENTRE (family-based svcs), 9912 - 106 St., Ste. 20, Edmonton, AB T5K 1C5 (403) 423-2831, FAX 426-4918. Born Calgary 1953. sep. 3 ch. Mark, Amanda, Timothy. **EDUC:** Grant MacEwan Community Coll., R.N.(Nursing) 1974; Univ. of Alberta, B.Sc.N.(Nursing) 1979; Loma Linda Univ., presently enrolled in M.Sc. program (Marriage & Family Therapy). **CAREER:** R.N., Edmonton General Hospital, 1974-75; R.N., Univ. of Alberta Hospital, 1975-78; Public Health Nurse, Grande Prairie Health Unit, 1979-80; Home Support Coord./ Postpartum Depression Support Program Coord., The Family Centre, 1987-96; Family Support Worker, 1996 to date. **SELECTED PUBLICATIONS:** "The Child with Tourette Syndrome" (*The Canadian Nurse*, May 1996); article on postpartum depression (*AARN Newsletter*, 1989). **AFFIL:** Alberta Association of Registered Nurses; Tourette Syndrome support group. **INTERESTS:** cross-stitch; travel; spending time with children. **MISC:** speaks to professional groups & the public about postpartum depression, & women & depression; TV appearances on local talk shows about postpartum depression; single parent of three children, one with Tourette Syndrome. **COMMENT:** *"Cathy is presently enrolled in the M.Sc. in Marriage and Family Therapy Program through Loma Linda University. This entails travelling three hours weekly to classes. Cathy is halfway through the program. Her area of interest is counselling people with depression, new parents and parents with children with special needs. Cathy has coordinated a PPD program in Edmonton for eight years. As part of this, she has attended conferences in Chicago, Washington and Toronto."*

Harnoy, Ofra, C.M. ■ ⊗ ♦
Cellist. c/o Suite Arts Management, 437 Spadina Rd, Box 23046, Toronto, ON M5P 2W0 (416) 863-1060, FAX 861-0191. Born Hadera, Israel 1965. m. Robert S. Cash. **EDUC:** studied with Jacob Harnoy, William Pleeth, London, Vladimir Orloff, Toronto; master classes with Mstislav Rostropovich, Pierre Fournier & Jacqueline Du Pre; Royal Conservatory of Music, Toronto. **CAREER:** professional debut, Dr. Boyd Neel & his orchestra, 1975; soloist with numerous major orchestras & in solo recitals in Canada, US, France, Germany, Austria, Belgium, UK, Japan, Israel, Holland, Denmark, Australia, Italy, Czechoslovakia, Taiwan, Hungary, Korea, Venezuela, Spain, Portugal, Hong Kong, Rumania, Poland, Turkey, Yugoslavia & Luxembourg; solo orchestral & recital debut, Carnegie Hall, 1982. **SELECTED CREDITS:** soloist, world premiere performance & commercial recording, *Cello Concerto* by Jacques Offenbach, Cincinnati Orchestra, 1983; presented the N.Am. premiere of Sir Arthur Bliss' Cello Concerto; world premiere recordings of Cello Concertos by Viotti, Myslivecek & several of Vivaldi's Cello Concertos; 40 classical solo albums for RCA Victor, London, EMI, Koch International, Pro Arte. **HONS:** First Prize, Montreal Symphony Competition, 1978; First Prize, Canadian Music Competition, 1979; youngest recipient in 42 yrs., International Concert Artists' Guild Award, 1982; Young Musician of the Year, Musical America Magazine, 1983; *Maclean's* 1987 Honour Roll; Best Classical Soloist, Juno Awards, 1988, 1989, 1991, 1992, 1993; Grand Prix du Disque, 1988; Member of the Order of Canada, 1995. **MISC:** for more information, visit the www/classical.mus.com website.

Harrington, Beth ■■ ☒ ✐ ♥
Host, CHATS & COMPANY (TV talk show– *Chatelaine*), 777 Bay St., Toronto, ON M5W 1A7 (416) 596-5425. m. 2 ch. **EDUC:** Berklee Coll. of Music, Boston, degree in music. **CAREER:** award-winning singer/songwriter; TV "variety" performer, several yrs.; TV hosting experience incl.: *Happy New Year Canada*, Live, Ottawa (1989), The Royal Visit of the Prince & Princess of Wales (1991), Toronto Festival of Festivals (1992); Entertainment Anchor, CBC Toronto news, 9 yrs.; created & hosted daily live on-location Toronto TV show *5:30 Live*, 1992-93; created & hosted *Cityscapes*, 1994-95; has also hosted various corp. & charitable public events. **COMMENT:** *"Skills range from hosting, interviewing and light-information reporting, to creating, writing and producing television programming. Beth's success results from her unique on-camera skills, combined with versatility, a natural ease and a witty, attractive style."*

Harris, Claire, B.A.(Hons.),Dip.Ed., Dip.Comm. ▯ ▱
Writer. 300 Meredith Rd. N.E., Ste. 701, Calgary, AB T2E-7A8 (403) 230-1781, FAX 230-1784. Born Trinidad 1937. s. **EDUC:** Univ. Coll., Dublin, B.A. 1961; Univ. of West Indies, Jamaica, Dip.Ed. 1963; Univ. of Lagos, Nigeria, Dip.Comm. 1975. **CAREER:** English

teacher, Calgary, 1966-94; writer, 1974 to date. **SELECTED CREDITS:** various short stories & poetry for CBC & National Public Radio (US) as well as others in Trinidad, Grenada & Jamaica. **SELECTED PUBLICATIONS:** *Dipped in Shadow* (New Brunswick: Goose Lane 1996); *Drawing Down a Daughter* (New Brunswick; Goose Lane, 1992, 1993, 1995); *The Conception of Winter* (Ontario; William-Wallace, 1989; Goose Lane, 1995); *Travelling to Find a Remedy* (New Brunswick; Goose Lane, 1986, 1995); *Translation into Fiction* (New Brunswick; Fiddlehead, 1984; Goose Lane 1995); *Fables from the Women's Quarters* (Ontario; William-Wallace, 1984, 1988; Goose Lane, 1995); *Kitchen Talk*, ed. with Edna Alford (Alberta; Red Deer College Press, 1992); various prose, fiction & poetry anthologies incl.: "Canadian Women Poets" (*Fireweed*, Summer 1986); *Caribbean Women Writers* (Calaloux, Mass.; 1990); *Grammar of Dissent* (New Brunswick; Gooselane, 1994); *Boundless Alberta* (NeWest, 1993); *Penguin Book of Caribbean Verse* (Great Britain; 1986); *Kanada* (Germany; Konigshausen/Neumann, 1991); *Poetry by Canadian Women* (Ontario; Oxford, 1989); Poetry Ed., Dandelion, 1981-89; Mng Ed., *blue buffalo*, 1984-87. **AFFIL:** Amnesty International; Inter Pares; Writers' Guild of Alberta; League of Canadian Poets; Women of Colour Collective, Alberta; Canadian Artist Network; Black Artists in Action. **HONS:** *Fables From the Women's Quarter* won a Commonwealth Reg'l Award; *Conception*, Alberta Special Award, 1989; *Travelling to Find a Remedy*, Award for Poetry, Writers' Guild of Alberta, 1987 & Alberta Culture Poetry Prize; Dragon Fly Award for Haiku, 1978, 1983; Alberta Achievement Award, 1987; *Drawing Down a Daughter* shortlisted for the Gov. General's Award, 1993. **INTERESTS:** travel; detective fiction. **MISC:** various panel discussions & readings at conferences in Europe, the West Indies & India; conducts an ongoing workshop for young writers of colour. **COMMENT:** *"I live the itinerant (semi-itinerant) life of a full-time writer. I write everyday or, in some way, work toward the writing. I travel to schools, universities to do readings. I read a great deal, work on juries and do odd jobs for the writing community. At the moment I find it a lovely life. When I master my computer, that will be an achievement."*

Harris, Marianne, B.Med.Sc.,M.D., C.C.F.P.C. ■ ⊕

Clinical Research Advisor, CANADIAN HIV TRIALS NETWORK, 1081 Burrard Street, Rm. 667, Vancouver, BC V6Z 1Y6 (604) 631-5060. Born Peace River, Alta. 1957. m. 2 ch. **EDUC:** Univ. of Calgary, Sci. 1974-77; Univ. of Alberta, B.Med.Sci. 1979, M.D. 1981. **CAREER:** family physician in private practice, Vancouver, 1983-91; sessional physician, Planned Parenthood Association of B.C., 1983-91; courtesy staff, Salvation Army Grace Hospital, Vancouver, 1985-91; family physician, Immune Deficiency Treatment Centre, Montreal General Hospital, 1992-94; Associateship training in HIV/AIDS clinical trials, Montreal General Hospital 1992-94; Sr. Postdoctoral Fellow, Canadian HIV Trials Ntwk, 1994-95; Clinical Research Advisor, 1995 to date. **SELECTED PUBLICATIONS:** "Helicobacter pylori Infection in an HIV-positive Patient," with J. Szabo (*AIDS* 6 1992); "A Phase I Study of letrazuril in AIDS-related Cryptosporidiosis," with G. Deutsch, J.D. MacLean & C.M. Tsoukas (*AIDS* 8 1994). **INTERESTS:** clinical trials involving combination antiretroviral therapy for HIV disease. **MISC:** various presentations & lectures.

Harris, Marjorie, B.A. ∕ ▯

Garden Writer. 199 Albany Ave., Toronto, ON M5R 3C7 (416) 531-3774, FAX 531-3384. Born Shaunovan, Sask. m. Jack Batten. 4 ch. **EDUC:** McMaster Univ., B.A.(English) 1959; Univ. of Toronto, M.A.(English) incomplete. **CAREER:** staff writer & Sr. Ed., *Maclean's* Magazine, 1966-71; freelance writer for various Cdn magazines incl. *Saturday Night, Chatelaine, Weekend, The Canadian, Artscanada, Quest, Toronto Life*, 1971-73; regular guest, *This Country in the Morning*, with Peter Gzowski, CBC Radio, 1971-73; Assoc. Ed., *Chatelaine*, 1973-77; writer & Ed., *The Toronto Star*, 1978; biweekly columnist, *The Canadian*, 1978-84; freelance writer with articles published in major magazines, 1979 to date; Garden Columnist, *Chatelaine*, 1988; regular, "The Urban Gardener," *Metro Morning*, CBC Radio, 1988; gardening articles, *Toronto Life, The Toronto Star*, 1988; writing & travelling across Canada for garden book, guest appearances on *Metro Morning* & *Morningside* on gardening, 1989; articles on gardening appearing in major magazines, incl. *Canadian Gardening, Toronto Life*, 1991 to date; Nat'l Garden Columnist, *The Globe and Mail*, 1991 to date; regular commentator on *Radio Noon Phone In* & *Gabereau!*, CBC Radio, 1992-93; regular appearances on *Freshair* & *Radio Noon*, CBC Radio, 1994; Co-Ed., *Toronto Life Gardens*, 1996 to date. **SELECTED PUBLICATIONS:** *Toronto: City of Neighborhoods; Historic Canada*, Co-author & Ed.; *Sciencescape*, Co-author David Suzuki; *Everyday Law: A Survival Guide for Canadians*, Co-author Jack Batten (1987); *The Canadian Gardener: A*

Guide to Gardening in Canada (Random House, 1990); *Ecological Gardening: Your Path to a Healthy Garden* (Random House, 1991); *Better House and Planet, Ecological Household Hints* (Key Porter, 1991); *The Canadian Gardener's Year* (1992); *The Canadian Gardener's Guide to Foliage & Garden Design* (Random House, 1993); *Marjorie Harris Favorite Garden Tips* (1994); *Marjorie Harris Favorite Shade Plants*; *Marjorie Harris Favorite Perennials*; *Marjorie Harris Favorite Annuals*; *Marjorie Harris Favorite Flowering Shrubs* (1994); *In the Garden: thoughts on changing seasons* (HarperCollins, 1995); *The Healing Garden* (HarperCollins, 1996); *Four Season Gardening* (Random House, 1996). AFFIL: Civic Garden Centre (Volunteer). INTERESTS: gardening; writing. MISC: numerous speeches to various groups on gardening. COMMENT: *"I have always been interested in the promotion and encouragement of Canadian talent, first in art galleries and magazines, then design and now gardening. We are an immensely gifted people."*

Harrison, Deborah, B.A.,M.A., Ph.D. ■ ⚙ 🐿 🌀
Professor of Sociology and Director, Muriel McQueen Fergusson Centre for Family Violence Research, UNIVERSITY OF NEW BRUNSWICK, Box 4400, Fredericton, NB E3B 5A3 (506) 453-3595, FAX 453-4788, EMAIL harrison@unb.ca. Born Toronto 1949. m. Walter Schenkel. EDUC: Queen's Univ., B.A. 1972; York Univ., M.A. 1974, Ph.D. 1979. CAREER: Research Advisor, Dept. of Social Svcs, Gov't of Sask., 1973-74; lecturer, York Univ., 1977-78; lecturer, McMaster Univ., 1978-79; Visiting Scholar, Ont. Institute for Studies in Educ., 1985-86; Asst. Prof., Dept. of Soc., Brock Univ., 1979-88; Assoc. Prof., 1988-95; Chair, 1994-95; Prof., Dept. of Soc., Univ. of New Brunswick, 1995 to date; Dir., Muriel McQueen Fergusson Centre for Family Violence Research, 1995 to date. SELECTED PUBLICATIONS: *The Limits of Liberalism: The Making of Canadian Sociology* (Montreal: Black Rose Books, 1982); *Fragile Truths: 25 Years of Sociology and Anthropology in Canada*, co-ed. with William Carroll, Linda Christiansen-Ruffman & Raymond Currie (Ottawa: Carleton Univ. Press, 1992); *No Life Like It: Military Wives in Canada*, with Lucie Laliberté (Toronto: James Lorimer and Company, 1994); "Octavio Paz: Revolution and Myth" (*The Canadian Forum* Sept. 1973); "The Terry Fox Story and the Canadian Media: A Case Study in Ideology and Illness" (*The Canadian Review of Sociology and Anthropology* Nov. 1985); "How Combat Ideology

Structures Military Wives' Domestic Labour" (*Studies in Political Economy* 1993); various other publications. EDIT: Reg'l Correspondent, *Society/Société*, 1991 to date. AFFIL: Canadian Sociology & Anthropology Association (Nat'l Chair, Annual Meeting Committee 1993-96); Ontario Association of Sociology & Anthropology; Canadian Women's Studies Association; Canadian Research Institute for the Advancement of Women; Canadian Society for Socialist Studies; Network Foundation of Educational Publishing (Founding Mbr.); Norman Bethune Coll., York Univ. (External Fellow); Legal Education and Action Fund (LEAF), New Brunswick. HONS: Ont. Scholarship, 1967; Queen's Univ. 125th anniversary Scholarship, 1967. INTERESTS: hiking; whale watching; cohousing. MISC: recipient, various grants & fellowships; various TV & radio interviews; various invited lectures, symposia, & workshop presentations; reviewer for various journals, presses & granting agencies. COMMENT: *"Deborah Harrison is Professor of Sociology and Director of the Muriel McQueen Fergusson Centre for Family Violence Research at the University of New Brunswick. Her latest book, which was co-authored with Lucie Laliberié, is No Life Like It: Military Wives in Canada (Toronto: Lorimer, 1994)."*

Hart, Evelyn Anne • ⊗
Dancer. Born Toronto 1956. EDUC: trained with teachers in London, Ont.; briefly trained at the National Ballet Sch.; attended the Sch. of the Royal Winnipeg Ballet. CAREER: entered Royal Winnipeg Ballet co., 1976; soloist, 1978; principal dancer, 1979. SELECTED CREDITS: has appeared around the world as a guest artist, & with other Cdn companies; Guest Artist, Odessa State Ballet, 1987. HONS: Gold Medal, Best Female Soloist, International Ballet Competition, Varna, Bulgaria, 1980.

Harvey, Anne, B.A. 🌀 ⊕
Chief Operating Officer, BRITISH COLUMBIA NURSES UNION, 4259 Canada Way, Ste. 100, Burnaby, BC V5G 1H1 (604) 433-2268, FAX 438-3149. Born Stockport, UK 1947. m. Gary Wayne Murray. 3 ch. EDUC: Manchester Metropolitan Univ., B.A.(Soc.); Cardiff Coll., Nat'l Union of Journalism apprenticeship courses; Salford Univ., 1st-yr. Bus. Admin. CAREER: reporter, *The Vancouver Sun* & Columbian newspapers, 1976-77; Pres., International Association of Business Communicators, 1977-79; Publications Ed., B.C. Hydro, 1977-79; Comm. Dir., Office & Tech. Employees Union (OTEU), 1979-80; Bus. Rep., OTEU, 1980-84; Pres., OTEU Local 378, 1984-90; VP, B.C. Federation of Labour, 1984-90; Chair,

Women's Rights Committee, 1984-89; Cdn Dir., Office & Professional Employees' International Union, 1986-90; Coord., Team & Organizational Effectiveness, B.C. Hydro, 1990-91; Coord., Environmental & Corp. Affairs, 1991-92; COO, B.C. Nurses' Union, 1992 to date. SELECTED PUBLICATIONS: various articles in *New Directions, Pacific Current* & *The Vancouver Sun.* AFFIL: B.C. Health Care, Labour Adjustment Agency (Dir.); Burnaby Multicultural Society; Women for Better Wages; CEIC Women in Trades & Technology National Network (Chair, Industrial Adjustment Committee 1990-94). HONS: Canada 100 Medal; 2 awards, Canadian Association of Labour Media. INTERESTS: travelling; exercising; walking; reading. COMMENT: *"A feminist by birth, a trade unionist by experience, a journalist by trade and a wife and mother by preference, underlying all other joys and commitments."*

Harvey, Carol, M.A.,L.èsL.,Ph.D. ⊗ 🗒

Professor of French, UNIVERSITY OF WINNIPEG, 515 Portage Ave., Winnipeg, MB R3B 2E9 (204) 786-9107. Born Heckmondwike, UK 1941. m. Albert Harvey. 2 ch. Alan, Stephanie. EDUC: Univ. of Edinburgh, M.A. 1963, Ph.D. 1969; Univ. de Caen, France, L.èsL. 1964. CAREER: lecturer, Univ. de Caen, 1963-64; Ed. Asst. (Lexicography), W.M. Collins, Glasgow, 1966-69; Asst. Prof., French Dept., Univ. of Winnipeg, 1970-76; Assoc. Prof., 1976-84; Prof., 1984 to date; Visiting Fellow, Corpus Christi Coll., Cambridge, 1989; Visiting Prof., Univ. de Perpignan, France, 1991-92. SELECTED PUBLICATIONS: *La littérature au féminin* (Montreal: Mondia éditeurs, 1995);*Le cycle manitobain de Gabrielle Roy* (Saint-Boniface: Editions des plaines, 1993); "Intertextuality in the Anglo-Norman Lyric" (*Journal of the Rocky Mountain Medieval and Renaissance Association* 1989); "Gabrielle Roy, institutrice: reportage et texte narratif" (*Cahiers franco-canadiens de l'Ouest* 1991); "Georges Bugnet et Gabrielle Roy: paysages littéraires de l'Ouest canadien" (*LittéRéalité* 1994); various other publications. AFFIL: International Courtly Literature Society; Canadian Society of Medievalists (Bd. Mbr.); Medieval Academy of America; Modern Language Association of America; Centre d'Études Franco-Canadiennes de l'Ouest (Bd. Mbr.); Alliance Française du Manitoba (VP). HONS: Chevalier, Ordre des Palmes Académiques, France. INTERESTS: literature; film; swimming. COMMENT: *"I endeavour to further (in myself and others) love and learning of French language, culture and literature and generally help students, especially women, to achieve their potential."*

Harvey, Dona Joan, B.A. ■ / ⊻

Writer and Communications Consultant. Kitchener, ON. Born Regina 1944. m. William Klassen. 3 ch. EDUC: Everett Jr. Coll., WA, Assoc. Arts 1963; Univ. of Washington, B.A. 1965; Banff Sch. of Advanced Management, Certificate 1979. CAREER: reporter, *Everett Herald*, WA, 1961-67; positions from reporter to Asst. to the Publisher, *Edmonton Journal*, 1967-76; Mng Ed., & Ed.-in-Chief, *Winnipeg Tribune*, 1976-80; Mng Ed., *Vancouver Province*, 1981-84; research work, Ecumenical Institute for Advanced Research, Jerusalem, 1984-86; Asst. VP, Public Affairs, Univ. of Toronto, 1987-89; Adjunct Prof., Grad. Sch. of Journalism, Univ. of Western Ontario, 1990-92; ed. writer, *Kitchener-Waterloo Record*, 1990-95. DIRECTOR: Ontario Hydro. AFFIL: Walter & Duncan Gordon Charitable Foundation (Trustee); National Newspaper Awards (Chair, Bd. of Gov. 1992-95); Westminster United Church. INTERESTS: Middle East affairs.

Harvey, Janice, B.Ed. ■ ✋ ⚘ ♣

Freelance Writer, Educator, Environmental Activist. R.R. 6, Waweig, St. Stephen, NB E3L 2Y3 (506) 466-4033, FAX 466-2911, EMAIL ccnbcoon@nbnet.nb.ca. Born Grand Manan Island, N.B. 1955. m. David Coon. 1 ch. Caroline Grace Harvey Moon. EDUC: Univ. of New Brunswick, B.Ed.(Hist.) 1977. CAREER: public sch. teacher, 1977-81; Mgr, small graphic arts bus., 1981-83; Exec. Dir., Conservation Council of N.B., 1983-89; Consultant, Institute for Sustainable Communities, 1989 to date; Public Affairs Columnist, *Telegraph-Journal*, Saint John; appointed to: Task Force on Consultation & Protocol (Environment Canada), 1985; Task Force on the Mgmt of Chemicals (Environment Canada), 1985-86; Public Advisory Committee on State of the Environment Reporting, Environment Canada, 1990-91; Nat'l Advisory Bd. on Science & Technology (PMO), 1994-95; Premier's Round Table on Environment & Economy, Prov. of N.B., 1994 to date. SELECTED PUBLICATIONS: "The Bay of Fundy Project" (*Environmental Assessment and Heritage in the Atlantic Region*, Occasional Paper No. 20, Heritage Resources Centre, Univ. of Waterloo, 1992); *Voices of the Bay: Reflections on Changing Times along Fundy Shores*, co-ed. R. Wilbur (Fredericton: Conservation Council of N.B., 1992); *Turning the Tide: A Citizen's Action Guide to the Bay of Fundy* (Fredericton: Conservation Council of N.B., 1994); "Sustainability in Atlantic Canada: The People's Agenda" (*National Round Table Review* Spring 1994); "Beyond Crisis in Fisheries: Ecological & Community-Based Management," (paper in press); weekly public affairs column, *Telegraph Journal*, Saint John. **AFFIL:** Conservation Council of N.B. (Exec. mbr.); Fundy Community Foundation (Past Pres.). **HONS:** Global 500 Roll of Honour Award, U.N. Environment Program, 1990 (presented to the Conservation Council of N.B.); Gulf of Maine/Bay of Fundy Visionary Award, Gulf of Maine Council on the Marine Environment, 1992-93. **INTERESTS:** local history & genealogy; rural living. **COMMENT:** *"Being born and raised in a fishing community, I have made my primary concern the survival of rural/regional environments and economies and the empowerment of people in small communities to assume leadership in these areas."*

Harvor, Elisabeth 📓 🗋 🗳

Writer. c/o English Department, Concordia University. 2 ch. Finn Harvor, Richard Harvor. **CAREER:** workshop organizer & instructor, Continuing Educ. Dept., Algonquin Coll., Ottawa, 1973-76; Sessional Lecturer, creative writing, Concordia Univ., 1986-87; Sessional Lecturer & Course Dir., Writing Program, York Univ., 1987-93; Writer-in-Residence, Ottawa Public Library, Summer 1993; Writer-in-Residence, Carleton Univ., Fall 1993; Writer-in-Residence, Univ. of New Brunswick, Fall 1994; Sessional Lecturer, Dept. of English, Univ. of New Brunswick, Spring 1995; Instructor, Extension Dept., Winter 1995; Instructor, Maritime Writers' Workshop, Summer 1995; Instructor, The Humber Sch. for Writers, Summer 1996; Writer-in-Residence, Concordia Univ., Spring 1997. **SELECTED PUBLICATIONS:** *Our Lady of All the Distances*, short prose (Toronto: HarperCollins, 1991); *If Only We Could Drive Like This Forever*, short prose (Markham: Penguin, 1988); *Fortress of Chairs*, poetry (Montreal: Signal Editions, Véhicule Press, 1992); poetry appears in various anthologies, incl. *More Garden Varieties* (Stratford: Aya/The Mercury Press, 1989) & *The Signal Anthology* (Montreal: Véhicule Press, 1993); *Let Me Be the One*, short prose (Toronto: HarperCollins, 1996); prose appears in various anthologies, incl. *The Best American Short Stories, 1971* (Boston: Houghton Mifflin, 1971), *The Penguin Book of Modern Canadian Short Stories* (Markham: Penguin, 1982) & *The Possibilities of Story* (Toronto: McGraw-Hill Ryerson, 1992); published in numerous journals & periodicals, incl. *The New Yorker, Prairie Fire, Event, The Hudson Review* & *Poetry Canada*; reviews & review essays appear in various journals & newspapers, incl. *Books in Canada, The Globe & Mail, Our Generation Against Nuclear War* & *Saturday Night*. **HONS:** First Prize, CBC's Young Writers' Award, 1965;

First Prize, Ottawa Short Story Competition, 1970; First Prize, League of Canadian Poets' Nat'l Poetry Prize, 1989, 1991; Malahat Long Poem Prize, *Afterbirth*, 1990; Confederation Poets Prize, 1991, 1992; Silver Medal (Poetry), National Magazine Award, 1991; Gerald Lampert Memorial Award for *Fortress of Chairs*, 1992. **MISC:** recipient, various grants & fellowships; juror, various competitions & grants; numerous public readings, Maritimes, Que., Ont. & BC.

Harwood, Vanesa, O.C. ■ 🏵 🗳

Dancer, Choreographer, Actor, Teacher. 328 Glencarr Ave., Toronto, ON M5M 1E6 (416) 780-9866, FAX 780-9867. Born Cheltenham, UK. m. Dr. Hugh Scully. 1 ch. Shannon Harwood Scully. **EDUC:** studied privately with Betty Oliphant; National Ballet Sch., 1959-64; received other training in France, Russia, UK & N.Y. **CAREER:** dancer, National Ballet of Canada, 1965-87; soloist, 1967; Principal Dancer, 1970; Artistic Dir. & Principal Dancer, Balletto Classico, 1989-93; Assoc. Artist, Theatre Plus, Toronto, 1992; guest artist with numerous ballet companies in N. Am. & abroad, incl. Munich Opera Ballet, Universal Ballet, Seoul, Korea, Dutch National Ballet, Matthew Nash Music & Dance, New York & Swan Lake, Australian Ballet, Sydney Opera House, 1978; numerous dance partners incl. Rudolf Nureyev, Alexander Godunov, Sergiu Stefansci, Fernando Bujones, Frank Augustyn & Patrick Bissell; guest teacher at numerous schools, incl. Univ. of Southern Florida, Waterloo Univ. Dance Workshop, Sean Boutilier Sch. of Dance, Opera Atelier, Georgia Ballet & Randolf Dance Theatre. **SELECTED CREDITS:** Lead, *Swan Lake*, National Ballet of Canada; Lead, *Cinderella*, National Ballet of Canada; Lead, *Romeo & Juliet*, National Ballet of Canada; Lead, *Giselle*, National Ballet of Canada; Lead, *Sleeping Beauty*, National Ballet of Canada; Lead, *La Fille Mal Gardée*, National Ballet of Canada; Lead, *La Sylphide*, National Ballet of Canada; Lead, *Coppelia*, National Ballet of Canada; Lead, *Nutcracker*, National Ballet of Canada; Lead, *Don Quixote*, National Ballet of Canada; Lead, *Cinderella*, Orlando Ballet, 1991; various shorter works, incl. *Dying Swan, Elite Syncopations, Kettentanz* & *Don Juan*; various original works, incl. *Slaughter on Tenth Avenue*, by Brian Foley; dancer, *Macbeth*, Andriana Lecouver, choreographer & dancer, André Chénier & Lead dancer, *Hamlet & The Merry Widow*, Canadian Opera Company; dancer & choreographer, *La Traviata*, Opera Hamilton; various other opera appearances; choreographer, *Stars on Parade*, Variety Club Convention (1986);

guest artist, various TV specials, incl. *Toller Cranston's Magic Planet*, ABC, 1982; dancer/actor, *Encore! Encore!*, Expo '86; actor, *The Mousetrap*, Kingston, Ont., 1989; actor, *The Road to Avonlea*, CBC-TV, 1993; actor, *Due South*, 1996; staged & danced, *Giselle*, Universal Ballet, Seoul, Korea, 1985; staged & danced, *The Merry Widow*, Dallas Opera, 1989. AFFIL: Toronto Arts Foundation (Bd. Mbr.; Trustee); Actors' Fund of Canada (Pres. 1996 to date); Theatre Plus (Dir.); Friend of Harbourfront; Canadian Actors' Equity Association; ACTRA; World Dance Alliance (Council). HONS: Officer of the Order of Canada, 1984; Canada 125 Medal, 1992. INTERESTS: acting; teaching. MISC: juror, New Choreography, Dora Awards; recipient, Canada Council Grant, 1969; coached Tracy Wilson & Robert McCall, Bronze Ice Dance champions, for the 1988 Olympics, Calgary & the 1988 "World's" in Budapest.

Haskell, Susan, B.Sc. 🖤 🏹
Actor. c/o Capital Cities/ABC, 77 W. 66 St., New York, NY 10023 (212) 456-3582, FAX 456-2755. Born Toronto. s. EDUC: Tufts Univ., B.Sc.(Biopsych.), cum laude); American Academy of Dramatic Arts, grad. 1991. CAREER: began modelling at age 16, cast in various commercials while still at sch.; int'l modelling assignments & nat'l commercials; actor. SELECTED CREDITS: various roles at the American Theatre of Dramatic Arts incl.: Elena, *Uncle Vanya*; Mandel, *Playing for Time*; Hazel, *Time and the Conways*; Patricia Winterbourne, *Mrs. Winterbourne* (feature), Tristar Productions; Pamela, *Fast Forward* (afterschool special), ABC; Elizabeth, *Danielle Steele's Zoya* (miniseries); Marty Saybrooke, *One Life To Live* (series), Capital Cities/ABC. AFFIL: National Head Injury Foundation Inc.; Lupus Foundation; Starlight Foundation; 'I Am Worth It'. HONS: Emmy for Best Supporting Actress (Marty Saybrooke), 1994; MVP, Soap Opera Update Award, 1994. INTERESTS: running; water sports; skiing. COMMENT: "*I pursued a degree in Biopsychology based on my interest in the human psyche and its relationship to the human body. I imagine this too explains my ultimate career choice in acting. I now have the opportunity to delve into the backgrounds of characters and try to honestly portray them. So far my involvement on One Life To Live as Marty Saybrooke and other various film and TV roles, has afforded me the opportunity to stretch my wings as an actor and reach out to the community around me in such varied causes as lupus, rape, domestic violence, alcoholism and most recently, traumatic brain injury.*"

Hatch, Mary S., B.A. Ⓢ
Vice-President and Manager, THE TORONTO-DOMINION BANK, St. Clair Commercial Banking Centre, 2 St. Clair Ave. E., Toronto, ON M4T 2V4 (416) 944-4006, FAX 975-1546. Born Windsor, Ont. 1948. m. David L. Stephens. 2 ch. EDUC: McGill Univ., B.A.(English) 1969; Canadian Securities Institute, Canadian Securities Course; Ptnrs, Dirs. & Officers Course. CAREER: various positions, Hum. Res., Commercial Acct Mgmt, & Supervision, leading to VP & Mgr, Toronto-Dominion Bank, 1970 to date. AFFIL: Toronto-Dominion Bank (Chair, Exec. Steering Committee on the Advancement of Women; Dir., Pension Fund Society); Rotary Club of Toronto (Eglinton); Girl Guides of Canada (Portfolio Review Committee); Downtown Churchworkers' Association (Past Bd. Mbr.). INTERESTS: cottaging; sailing; swimming; tennis; needlepoint; reading; gourmet cooking. COMMENT: "*I had the good fortune to be born into a family that encouraged dedication and commitment to any endeavour undertaken. I take great pride in my personal and professional accomplishments.*"

Hatley, Judith, B.A.,M.B.A. Ⓢ
Senior Vice-President, Sales, Personal Financial Services, ROYAL BANK OF CANADA, 123 Front St. W, 6th Fl, Toronto, ON M5J 2M2 (416) 974-2386, FAX 974-7747. Born Toronto 1949. m. Jeff. 2 ch. EDUC: Univ. of Western Ontario, B.A.(Zoology) 1971; York Univ., M.B.A.(Fin./Mktg) 1985. CAREER: Sr. Acct Mgr, Corp. Bnkg, Royal Bank of Canada, 1985-89; Mkt Mgr, Personal Bnkg, Metropolitan Toronto, 1989-90; VP, Mktg & Sales, Ont. District, 1991-92; VP, Mkt Segmentation, 1993-94; Sr. VP, Sales, Personal Fin. Svcs, 1994 to date. AFFIL: Kingsway Platform Tennis Club (Sec.); Toronto Symphony Orchestra (Bd.). INTERESTS: tennis; skiing; reading; family; community.

Haust, M. (Maria) Daria, MD,MSc, FRCP(C) ⊕ 🖋 🖐
Professor of Pathology and Paediatrics, UNIVERSITY OF WESTERN ONTARIO, Department of Pathology, Health Sciences Centre, London, ON N6A 5C1 (519) 661-2030, FAX 661-3370. Director of Pathology, CHILDREN'S PSYCHIATRIC RESEARCH INSTITUTE, London, ON. m. Dr. Heinz L. Haust. 2 ch. EDUC: Ruprecht-Karls-Univ., Heidelberg, M.D. 1951; Queen's Univ., M.Sc.(Med.) 1959; Royal Coll. of Physicians & Surgeons (Canada), Fellow (Anatomical & Clinical Pathology) 1959. CAREER: Rotating Intern, Kingston General Hospital, 1952-53; Resident, Pathology, 1955-59; Research Fellow, Queen's Univ., 1955-59; Post-

doctoral Fellow, Pathology, Children's Hospital, Cincinnati, 1959-60; Paediatric Pathologist, Children's Hospital, Kingston General Hospital, 1960-67; Asst. Prof. of Pathology, Queen's Univ., 1960-65; Assoc. Prof. of Pathology, 1967-68; Dir. of Pathology, Children's Psychiatric Research Institute, 1967 to date; Consultant, Paediatric Pathology, War Memorial Children's Hospital of Western Ontario & Victoria Hospital, 1967 to date; Hon. Lecturer in Paediatrics, Univ. of Western Ontario, 1968-72; Prof. of Pathology, 1968 to date; Prof. of Paediatrics, 1972 to date; Visiting Scientist, Sir William Dunn Sch. of Pathology, Oxford Univ., 1972-73; Staff Pathologist, University Hospital, London, Ont., 1973 to date; Consultant, Pathology, Hospital for Sick Children, Toronto, 1975 to date; Prof. of Obstetrics & Gynaecology, Univ. of Western Ontario, 1977 to date. **SELECTED PUBLICATIONS:** "Role of Mural Fibrin Thrombi of the Aorta in the Genesis of Arterio-sclerotic Plaques: Report of Two Cases," with R.H. More & H.Z. Movat (*Archives of Pathology* 1957); "A European Looks at the Status of Women in Canadian Medicine," (*Canadian Doctor* 1961); "Chromosomal Studies in Children with Mumps, Chicken Pox, Measles and Measles Vaccination," with T. Chun *et al (Canadian Medical Association Journal* 1966); "Platelets, Thrombosis and Atherosclerosis" (*Canadian Medical Association Journal* 1973); "Morphology of Fetal Placental Stem Arteries in Hypertensive Disorders ('Toxemia') of Pregnancy," with J. Las Heras & P.G.R. Harding (*Applied Pathology* 1983); "Fibrinogen Introduced into the Aortic Wall of Rabbits and Its Relevance to Intracellular Lipid Appearance" (*Czynniki Ryzyka* [Polish] 1994); over 240 other publications. **EDIT:** numerous ed. bds. incl. *Perspectives in Pediatric Pathology* 1973 to date, *Atherosclerosis* 1973 to date, *Pediatric Pathology: An International Journal* 1981 to date & *Canadian Medical Association Journal* 1987-90; Co-Ed., with G.W. Manning, "Atherosclerosis: Metabolic, Morphologic and Clinical Aspects," *Advances in Experimental Medical Biology* vol. 82 (New York: Plenum Press, 1977); Guest Ed., "Festschrift: Symposium on Cardiovascular Diseases and Neoplasia, in Honour of Dr. Robert Hall More," *Experimental Molecular Pathology*, 1979; Guest Co-Ed., with B.H. Landing, *Genetic Metabolic Diseases*, vol. 17 in *Perspectives in Pedatric Pathology*, H.S. Rosenberg & J. Bernstein, eds. (New York: Karger, Basel, 1993). **AFFIL:** American Heart Association (Council on Atherosclerosis; Council on Thrombosis); International Academy of Pathology, US/Canada Div.; Society for Pedriatric Pathology (Pres. Elect 1982-

83; Pres. 1983-84; Past Pres. 1984-85; Historian 1988 to date); International Paediatric Pathology Association (Sec. Gen. 1974-84; Pres. 1984-86; Chrm of Council 1984-87; Hon. Fellow); International Atherosclerosis Society (Sec.-Treas. 1978-85; Treas.); International Pediatric Association (IPA); Canadian Atherosclerosis Society (Pres. 1983-86; Past Pres. 1986-87; Historian; Chair, Long-Term Planning Committee; Exec. Committee); Canadian Society for Clinical Investigation (Historian); Royal Coll. of Physicians & Surgeons of Canada (Fellow); Royal Society of Medicine; Pathological Society of Great Britain & Ireland; American Association of Pathologists; Hungarian Society of Pathologists (Hon. Mbr.); Paediatric Pathology Society (of UK); European Atherosclerosis Group (Foreign-Corresponding, Hon. Mbr.); British Atherosclerosis Discussion Group (Foreign-Corresponding, Hon. Mbr.); Hungarian Arteriosclerosis Society (Hon. Mbr.); Univ. of Western Ontario Fac. Association; Chilean Society of Pathologists (Hon. Mbr.); Cuban Society of Pathologists (Hon. Mbr.); Academy of Sciences of Heidelberg (Heidelberger Akademie der Wissenschaften) (Hon. Foreign-Corresponding-Mbr.); Polish Society for Atherosclerosis (Hon. Mbr.); Coll. of Physicians & Surgeons of Ontario; Ontario Medical Association; Canadian Medical Association; Ontario Association of Pathologists; Canadian Association of Pathologists; Canadian Paediatric Society; Canadian Medical Protective Association. **HONS:** Best Teacher Award–Basic Sciences, Students' Evaluation Course Committee & Hippocratic Council, Univ. of Western Ontario, 1978; The Class of '62 Award, Hippocratic Council, Univ. of Western Ontario, 1982; Alexander von Humboldt Distinguished Service Award, 6th Int'l Symposium on Atherosclerosis, 1982; Hippocratic Council S.F.C.S.C. Teaching Award–Basic Sciences, Univ. of Western Ontario, 1984; Service Award, American Heart Association, 1986; Service Award to the First Pres., Canadian Atherosclerosis Society, 1986; Special Distinguished Colleague Award, Society for Pediatric Pathology, 1987; Gold Medal, International Atherosclerosis Society, 1988; Izaak Walton Killam Award in Health Sciences, Canada Council, 1990; Andreas Vesalius Medal, Univ. of Padova, Padua, Italy, 1993; Council on Arteriosclerosis Special Recognition Award, American Heart Association, 1993; Distinguished Achievement Award, International Atherosclerosis Society; numerous other hons. **INTERESTS:** classical music; nature walks; charities. **MISC:** 1st Pres., Canadian Atherosclerosis Society; more than 253 invited lectures & seminars worldwide; invited chair or co-chair, more than

135 scientific programs worldwide; recipient, various grants; Hon. Chair, 10th Int'l Symposium on Atherosclerosis, Montreal, Oct. 9-14, 1994; The Daria Haust Fellowship for Young Investigators est. by the International Atherosclerosis Society, 1994. COMMENT: *"I have been fortunate to be given the opportunity at Queen's (my alma mater) to enter, as the first and only female member, the academic world and life for generations with young people. Perhaps they kept one young at heart."*

Hawkeye, Lynn Aileen, CAH, CHHE ❀ ⟨⟩

Director, Housekeeping Services, HEALTH SCIENCES CENTRE, GF-117, 820 Sherbrook St., Winnipeg, MB R3A 1R9 (204) 787-1929, FAX 787-1650. Born St. Boniface, Man. 1963. s. EDUC: Certified Hospitality Housekeeping Exec. 1987; American Hotel/Motel Association, Univ. of Michigan, Certificate of Specialization in Housekeeping Mgmt 1988; Certified Administrative Housekeeper 1992; National Executive Housekeepers Association, Certified Exec. Housekeeper 1996. CAREER: Housekeeping Asst., The Westin Hotel, Winnipeg, 1980-85; taught courses in Supervisory Housekeeping, Educ. Institute of the American Hotel/Motel Association, Winnipeg, 1985; Calgary, 1988; Exec. Housekeeper, Marlborough Inn, Calgary, 1988-89; Housekeeping Mgr, Sheraton Winnipeg, 1985-87; Front Office Mgr, Sheraton Hamilton, 1987-88; Exec. Housekeeper, Radisson Suite Hotel, 1989-90; Dir. of Housekeeping, Misericordia General Hospital, Versa Services, 1990-94; Dir. of Housekeeping Svcs, Health Science Centre, 1994 to date; Instructor, Distance Delivery Course, *Cleaning Sciences and Environmental Applications*, Univ. of Manitoba, 1994 to date. SELECTED PUBLICATIONS: *Dancing with God*, Ed./Compiler. EDIT: *Quarterly Magazine*, Canadian Administrative Housekeepers' Association; Ed., CANFED newsletter. AFFIL: Canadian Administrative Housekeepers' Association (Dir., Public Rel'ns; Dir., Exec. Committee 1993-95); National Executive Housekeepers' Association; Manitoba Executive Housekeepers' Association; Certificate Program in Cleaning Sciences & Management, Univ. of Manitoba (Advisory Committee); American Society for Healthcare Environmental Services; Cleaning Management Institute; Manitoba Genealogical Society; Saskatchewan Genealogical Society; N.B. Genealogical Society; Manitoba Historical Society; Canada's National History Society; Canadian Federation of Genealogical & Family History Societies Inc. (CANFED). HONS: Distinguished Musician's Certificate for Recognition of Diligence, Dedication & Musical Excellence

as a Performing Bandsman & Soloist, Canadian Band Directors' Association; various awards incl. Cadet of the Year Award, Sr. Range Trophy & Strathcona Trust Ring from Sea Cadet Corps John Travers Cornwall V.C. INTERESTS: history (family & nat'l); music; needlecrafts; Stephen King books. MISC: belonged to the Sea Cadet Corps John Travers Cornwall V.C. for 7 yrs., left with rank Chief Petty Officer, 2nd Class; was an officer with the Dept. of National Defence – Reserve. COMMENT: `Energetic person, currently completing certification requirements for National Executive Housekeepers Association as well as a text book for the Environmental Cleaning Management from a Canadian perspective.'

Hawkeye, Patricia ◉ ○

Director of Finance and Administration, GIRL GUIDES OF CANADA, 50 Merton St., Toronto, ON M4S 1A3 (416) 487-5281, FAX (204) 222-2847. Born Pine Falls, Man. 1936. d. 4 ch. EDUC: M.I.M. Program, "Managing the Volunteer Board." CAREER: Office Mgr/ Acctnt, family owned mechanical contracting bus., 1962-90; Nat'l Treas., Girl Guides of Canada, 1983-88; Prov. Commissioner, Man. Council, 1989-94; Dir. of Fin. & Admin., 1994 to date. AFFIL: Manitoba Special Olympics (Treas.); Pax Lodge, World Centre, World Association of Girl Guides & Girl Scouts, London, UK (V-Chrm); Transcona Ladies' Curling Club (Past Pres.). HONS: Canada 125 Medal; Honorary Life Award, Girl Guides of Canada; Red River Care Award, Manitoba Girl Guides of Canada; Maple Leaf Award, Girl Guides of Canada. INTERESTS: fin. affairs; leadership; family; travel; crosswords. COMMENT: *"I strongly believe in the values and goals of the Girl Guides of Canada. I have spent 32 years with a strong commitment to support them. Satisfaction of being a member of a strong and vital organization that offers girls and young women in our country the opportunity to gain leadership skills and provide service."*

Hawley, Patricia, M.N.,R.N. ■ ⟨⟩ ⊕

Associate Professor of Nursing, ST. FRANCIS XAVIER UNIVERSITY, Box 5000, Antigonish, NS B2G 2W5 (902) 867-5175, FAX 867-2448, EMAIL phawley@juliet.stfx.ca. Born Antigonish, N.S. 1955. s. EDUC: St. Francis Xavier Univ., B.Sc.N. 1977; Dalhousie Univ., M.N. 1984. CAREER: Staff Nurse, Surgical Unit, Victoria General Hospital, Halifax, 1977-78; Staff Nurse, Emergency Dept., St. Martha's Regional Hospital, Antigonish, 1979-81; Teaching Asst., Sch. of Nursing, Dalhousie Univ., 1983; Clinical Instructor, 1984; Staff Nurse, Surgical Unit, Camp Hill Hospital, Halifax, 1984-85; Family

Practice Nurse, Dept. of Family Medicine, Dalhousie Univ., Halifax, 1985; Staff Nurse, Emergency Dept., Victoria General Hospital, Halifax, 1985-86; Staff Nurse, Neurosurgical Intensive Care Unit, Toronto General Hospital, 1986-88; Asst. Prof., Dept. of Nursing, St. Francis Xavier Univ., Antigonish, 1989-94, Assoc. Prof., 1994 to date. SELECTED PUBLICATIONS: "Sources of stress for emergency nurses in four urban Canadian emergency departments" (*Journal of Nursing* 1992); "Sexual Assault, Coping with Crisis" (*Canadian Nurse* 1993). AFFIL: St. Francis Xavier Univ. (mbr. of Senate; Fac. Advisor, Student Nurses' Society); N.S. Registered Nurses' Foundation (Chair, Selections Committee); International Association for Human Caring; Canadian Nurses' Foundation; ARCAUSN, Registered Nurses' Association of N.S.; RNANS Highland Region Branch; N.S. Nursing Informatics Interest Group. HONS: St. Francis Xavier Univ. Research, Publication & Teaching Award, 1992, 1993, 1994. INTERESTS: ice skating; recreational reading; cooking/baking; music; swimming; rollerblading. MISC: Registered Nurse, N.S.; mbr., St. Francis Xavier Univ. Task Force on Violence Against Women; various presentations; recipient, various grants. COMMENT: *"I describe myself as a gentle, caring and educated professional who is committed to excellence in nursing. I appreciate the richness of human experience and take advantage of the many different opportunities to enrich the human potential of others. In my relationships I am sincere, honest, loyal and sensitive to the needs of others."*

Hawrishok, Lorraine (née Swedberg) ■ $ ○ 🏵

Vice-President, I.L.S. LEARNING CORPORATION, 4609 Kilmarnock Dr., Courtenay, BC V9N 8H9 (604) 335-1881, FAX 335-1772. Born Regina 1950. m. Stephen Hawrishok. 3 ch. Shelley, Greggrey, Julie. EDUC: Univ. of Regina, Public Rel'ns 1993. CAREER: VP, Prairie Stonescapes Inc., 1981-84; freelance writer, 1982-85; writer, *Regina Leader Post*, 1985-88; public affairs, Gov't of Sask., 1988-89; Ministerial Asst., 1989-91; VP, I.L.S. Learning Corporation, 1991 to date. AFFIL: Beta Sigma Phi, Regina (Pres. 1982-84); Canadian Cancer Society (Dir.; Chair, Nat'l Public Rel'ns Committee; Fundraising Chair, Comox Valley Unit); 1995 B.C. Winter Games Society (Chair, Public Rel'ns Committee); Comox Valley Chamber of Commerce; Canadian Public Relations Society; Comox Valley Cultural Centre Society; Strathcona Rotary Club. COMMENT: *"A strong work ethic, a commitment to providing community service, and a supportive family*

have enabled me to pursue a varied and interesting career and volunteer life."

Hawthorn, Pamela, B.A.,M.F.A. ■ ✕ 🏵 ♨

Lecturer, Theatre Department, UNIVERSITY OF BRITISH COLUMBIA, 811 E. 15th Ave., Vancouver, BC V5T 2S1. Born Trail, B.C. 1939. m. Tom McBeath. 1 ch. Laura Hawthorn. EDUC: Univ. of British Columbia, B.A.(Arts) 1961; Yale Univ., M.F.A.(Drama) 1965. CAREER: Assoc. Dir., McCarter Theatre, Princeton, N.J., 1967-68; Assoc. Dir., Holiday Playhouse, Vancouver, 1969-70; Artistic & Mng Dir., New Play Centre, Vancouver, 1974-89; Mgr, Cultural Affairs, Telefilm Canada, 1989-95. AFFIL: Canadian Actors' Equity; Women in Film, B.C. Div.; Waterfront Theatre (Bd.). HONS: Queen's 25th Silver Jubilee Award; Vancouver Award, CKVU TV; Sam Payne Award, ACTRA. COMMENT: *"Best known in Canada for theatre directing and for the development of new scripts for the Canadian theatre."*

Hayes, Anna-Marie ⊕ ○ 🏵

Director, VALLEY FAMILY RESOURCE CENTER, Box 2268, Woodstock, NB E0J 2B0 (506) 325-2299, FAX 328-6220. Born Halifax 1956. m. Dr. Frank Hayes. 5 ch. Maria LeBlanc, Emily Beth LeBlacn, Marty Jane Hayes, Robert Cole Hayes, Matthew Hayes. EDUC: St. Mary's Univ., Dipl.(Criminology) 1979. CAREER: Recreation Coord., City of Halifax, 1976-78; Dir., Family Support Svcs, 1990-94; Dir., Valley Family Resource Centre, 1994 to date. SELECTED PUBLICATIONS: various articles & newsletters for parental involvement & educ.; research paper on child poverty for National Home & School Association. AFFIL: N.B. Federation of Home & School Associations (Past Pres.); Human Service Council (Pres.); National Home & School Association (Chair for Child Poverty); Vanier Institute of the Family. HONS: various awards of recognition at community & prov. levels. INTERESTS: educ.; women's issues; child poverty; social reform; family issues. MISC: Prov. Rep., steering committees & forums, N.B. Dept. of Educ.; Prov. Rep., steering committees & special projects, Dept. of Health; presented papers nationally & internationally; numerous interviews with radio, TV & press. COMMENT: *"My passion for children began when I was a child. I continue to work with children and families both at a professional and voluntary level. Children are our world's greatest asset!"*

Hayes, Carole-Ann, C.G.A. ■ ✐ $ 🦋

President, WHERE MAGAZINES INTERNATIONAL, 70 The Esplanade, Toronto, ON M5E 1R2 (416) 360-0044, FAX 941-9038, EMAIL carole-ann.hayes@where-int.com. Born Toronto 1957. m. Robert. 2 ch. Erica Hayes, Sean Hayes. EDUC: Certified General Acctnt, Queen's Univ., Exec. Program. CAREER: various positions, Key Publishers Co. Ltd., 1976-84; Cont., 1984-88; CFO, 1988-91; Pres., WHERE Magazines International, 1991 to date. DIRECTOR: Key Publishers Co. Ltd. INTERESTS: enjoying the outdoors; craft projects with children. COMMENT: *"Carole-Ann Hayes is the President of WHERE Magazines International, and has held a variety of positions through which she has acquired a comprehensive knowledge of all aspects of magazine publishing."*

Hayes, Linda, B.A. ■ 🖓 ❀ ✦

Editor, NATIONAL RESEARCH COUNCIL OF CANADA, Canadian Codes Centre, M-24 Montreal Rd., Ottawa, ON K1A 0R6 (613) 993-4078, FAX 952-4040, EMAIL hayes@irc.lan. nrc.ca. Born Erie, Penn. 1938. m. Dr. Don F. Mitchell. 5 ch. Mary S., Anne. E., Kathleen M., James C., Thomas M. EDUC: Saint Mary's Coll., South Bend, Ind., B.A.(English) 1960. CAREER: Ed., National Research Council of Canada, 1976 to date; Asst. to the Ed., *Canadian Journal of Microbiology*, 1976-84; Ed., Institute for Research in Construction, 1984-96. EDIT: *Rideau Trail Guidebook*; *National Building Code of Canada*. AFFIL: Ottawa Rideau Trail Club (Chair 1986-93); Rideau Trail Association (Dir. 1986-93; Trail Coord. 1996 to date); Professional Institute of the Public Service of Canada (P.I.P.S.C.) (Chair, Nat'l Research Council Info. Svcs Group 1990-96). COMMENT: *"I have raised five children as a single mother. I consider that my most significant achievement."*

Hayes, Nancy, R.N.,B.A.,M.N. ■ ⟳ ⊕

Vice-President, Organization, UNICEF CANADA, 1919 - 11th St. S.W., Calgary, AB T2T 3L9 (403) 245-8747, FAX 245-8742. Born 1941. m. Ross Hayes. 3 ch. Sarah Hayes, Michael Hayes, Erin Burnham. EDUC: Montreal General Hospital, R.N. 1962; McGill Univ., Diploma Public Health Nursing 1964; Concordia Univ., B.A.(Community Health Nursing) 1977; Univ. of Calgary, M.N.(Parent Child Nursing) 1990. CAREER: Gen. Duty Nurse, Obstetrics, Montreal General Hospital, 1962-63; Sch. Nursing Sister, UK, 1964-65; Public Health Nurse & Prenatal Educator, Victorian Order of Nurses, 1969-77; Nurse Practitioner, Pediatric Allergy, 1977-80; Nurse Coord., Pulmonary Clinic, Alberta Children's Hospital, 1980-88; Grad. Teaching Asst., Fac. of Nursing, Univ. of Calgary, 1988; Research Asst., Dr. Colleen Stainton, Fac. of Nursing,

1989-90; Clinical Instructor, Pediatric Nursing, Mount Royal Coll., 1991; Seminar Leader, Nursing Research, Athabasca Univ., 1991. SELECTED PUBLICATIONS: "The Lived Experience of Two Master of Nursing Students with a Phenomenological Study of Uncertainty in High Risk Perinatal Situations," co-author Sharon Oryschak (Int'l Maternity Nurse Researchers' Conference, Gothenburg, Sweden, 1990); "Caring for a Chronically Ill Infant Following NICU: A Paradigm Case of Maternal Rehearsal," with D. McNeil & C. Stainton (*The Journal of Pediatric Nursing*, Jan., 1994); "Severe Bronchopulmonary Dysplasia–An Interdisciplinary Approach to Helping Families Achieve Home Care," with M. Perry (presentation, Int'l Conference of the Association for the Care of Children's Health, 1986); "The Role of the Nurse in Early Intervention" (presentation to the annual meeting of the Canadian Association of Pediatric Hospitals, 1986). AFFIL: UNICEF Alberta (Chair; Mktg Committee; Educ. & Dev. Committee; Chair, Educ. for Dev. 1990-92); UNICEF Canada (Dir.; Dev. Liaison Program); VON (Dir., Calgary Branch); Alberta Lung Association (Chair, Nursing Advisory Committee 1983-84); Asthma & Allergy Association of Calgary (Founding Mbr.); Alberta Bay Friendly Hospital Action Committee; Canadian Parents for French (Chair, S. Alberta Branch 1979-80); Parents' & Children's Drop In Centre, Montreal (Founding Mbr. & Coord. 1975-77). COMMENT: *"Lifelong interest in children, particularly children's health and well-being. Committed to improving the health and development of children in the developing world through fundraising and awareness raising work with UNICEF."*

Hayes, Sharon Ruth, B.Math.,M.P. ✦ ⊕

Member of Parliament (Port Moody-Coquitlam), GOVERNMENT OF CANADA, House of Commons, Ottawa K1A 0A6 (613) 947-4482, FAX 947-4485. Born Toronto 1948. m. Douglas. 2 ch. EDUC: Univ. of Waterloo, B.Math .(Comp. Sci.) 1970. CAREER: actuarial trainee, Excelsior Life, 1965; Systems Eng. trainee, IBM Canada, 1966-67; Programmer/Analyst, Toronto Stock Exchange, 1968; Teaching Asst., Gen. & Tech. Math, North York Bd. of Educ., 1969; Programmer/Analyst, Fac. of Medicine, Univ. of British Columbia, 1970-71; Programmer/Analyst & Instructor, Institute of Comp. Sci., Univ. of Guelph, 1971-74; Sessional Instructor, Comp. Sci., Simon Fraser Univ., 1979-81, 1991-92; property mgmt; computer consulting; M.P. (Port Moody-Coquitlam), 1993 to date; mbr., Standing Committee on Health; mbr., Sub-Committee on HIV/AIDS; Assoc. mbr., Standing Committee on Human

Rights & the Status of Disabled Persons; Assoc. mbr., Standing Committee on Citizenship & Immigration; Chair, Reform Family Task Force; Deputy Critic for Health. **AFFIL:** Christian Women's Club; volunteer: preschool, school, youth work, church. **INTERESTS:** swimming; waterskiing; tennis; golf; walking; hiking; camping; reading; piano; sewing; crafts; gardening. **COMMENT:** *"An active member of the local community with priority given to the importance and positive role of family, women and youth in that community."*

Hazell, Cindy Dundon, Hons.B.Comm. ⚜

Dean, Faculty of Continuing Education, SENECA COLLEGE OF APPLIED ARTS AND TECHNOLOGY, 1750 Finch Ave. E., North York, ON M2X 2J5 (416) 491-5050, FAX 756-4360, EMAIL chazell@exec.senecac.on.ca. Born Kingston, Ont. 1956. m. Richard C. Hazell. 3 ch. **EDUC:** Univ. of Guelph, Hons.B.Comm.(with distinction) 1978; O.I.S.E., Univ. of Toronto, M.Ed.(Higher Educ.) in progress. **CAREER:** Tutorial Asst., Univ. of Guelph, 1977-78; Promotions Coord., CN Tower/CN Tower Restaurants Ltd., Toronto, 1978-80; Teaching Master, Centre for Individualized Learning, Seneca Coll. of Applied Arts & Technology, 1980-81; Conference Mgr, Int'l Society for Bus. Educ., 1981; Coord., Co-op Educ., Program Coord. & Academic Chair, Seneca Coll., 1982-86; Academic Negotiating Team, Ont. Council of Regents, 1987-90; Exec. Asst. to the Pres., Seneca Coll., 1986-90; Dean, Fac. of Continuing Educ., 1990 to date. **SELECTED PUBLICATIONS:** "A Collaborative Approach to Research," Metro Colleges Continuing Educ. survey, *Catalyst* (Virginia, 1994); "The College Council: A Status Report," *Ontario Journal of Higher Education* (Toronto, 1995). **AFFIL:** Association of Colleges of Applied Arts & Technology (Chair, Prov. Heads of Continuing Educ.); St. Margaret Church, North York (Leader, Children's Lit. Program). **INTERESTS:** squash; children's activities. **MISC:** active parent volunteer at St. Margaret Sch. **COMMENT:** *"Very energetic and enthusiastic, with a positive approach to all tasks. Rapid progression in academic career at Seneca to position of Dean at age 34."*

Heath, Michele, B.Sc.,Ph.D., F.R.S.C. ⚜ ⚜ ⚜

Professor, Botany Department, UNIVERSITY OF TORONTO, 25 Willcocks St., Toronto, ON M5S 3B2 (416) 978-6304, FAX 978-5878, EMAIL heath@botany.utoronto.ca. Born Bournemouth, UK. m. Ian Brent Heath. 1 ch. Lorraine. **EDUC:** Univ. of London, B.Sc.(Botany) 1966, Ph.D.(Plant Pathology) 1969. **CAREER:** Postdoctoral Fellow, Univ. of Georgia, 1969-71;

Post-doctoral Fellow, Univ. of Toronto, 1971-72; Lecturer, 1972-73; Asst. Prof., 1973-76; Assoc. Prof., 1976-81; Prof., 1981 to date. **SELECTED PUBLICATIONS:** more than 90 scientific publications incl. a book, book chapters, & original scientific papers. **EDIT:** Sr. Ed., A.P.S. Press, 1988-91; Sr. Ed., *Physiological and Molecular Plant Pathology*, 1982-89. **AFFIL:** Canadian Phytopathological Society (Fellow; VP 1993-94; Pres.-Elect 1994-95; Pres. 1995-96); American Phytopathological Society (Fellow); Royal Society of Canada (Fellow). **HONS:** Huxley Memorial Medal, 1979; Gordon Green Award, Canadian Phytopathological Society, 1984; Steacie Memorial Fellowship (1st woman recipient), Natural Sciences & Engineering Research Council of Canada, 1982. **INTERESTS:** lapidary; horseback riding. **COMMENT:** *"Dr. Heath is a world leader in the study of the cytology and evolution of the interactions between rust fungi (an important group of micro-organisms that cause diseases of crop plants) and their hosts."*

Heathcote, Isobel Winnifred, B.Sc., Ph.D. ⚜ ⚜

Director, INSTITUTE FOR ENVIRONMENTAL POLICY and Associate Professor, School of Engineering and Faculty of Environmental Sciences, UNIVERSITY OF GUELPH, Guelph, ON N1G 2W1 (519) 824-4120 x3072, FAX 836-0227, EMAIL heathcot@net2.eos.uoguelph.ca. Born Boston 1952. m. Alan F. Belk. 3 ch. Elspeth Evans, Zoë Belk, Edward Belk. **EDUC:** Univ. of Toronto, B.Sc. 1974; Yale Univ., M.S. 1975, Ph.D. 1978. **CAREER:** Phys. Limnologist, Acres Consulting Services Ltd., 1978-79; Phys./Chem. Limnologist, Water Resources Branch, Ont. Ministry of the Environment, 1979-80; Chief, Water Quality Systems, Water & Waste Water Mgmt Section, Water Resources Branch, Ont. Ministry of the Environment, 1980-84; Supervisor, Great Lakes Investigations & Surveillance, 1984-85; Dean of Women & Dir. of Residences, University Coll., Univ. of Toronto, 1986-90; Dir., Environmental Studies & Environmental Sciences, Innis Coll., 1985-91; Pres., Wyndham Research Inc., 1985 to date; Assoc. Prof., Environmental Eng. & Environmental Sciences, Sch. of Eng. & Fac. of Environmental Sciences, Univ. of Guelph, 1991 to date; Dir., Institute for Environmental Policy, Univ. of Guelph, 1994 to date. **SELECTED PUBLICATIONS:** *Environmental Problem Solving: A Case Study Approach* (New York: McGraw-Hill, 1997); "Canadian Water Resource Management" in *Environment and Canadian Society*, ed.T. Fleming (Toronto: Nelson Canada, 1996); "Low-waste technologies: If it is a low-hanging fruit, why doesn't the industry pick it?" with N.T. Yap in *Waste Management for Sustainable Development in India: Policy, Planning and Administrative Dimensions: A Case Study of Kanpur*, eds. N.T. Yap & S.K. Awasthi (Delhi: Tat-McGraw Hill, 1996); "Conflict resolution in Ontario waste resources policy" in *Water Quantity/Quality Management and Conflict Resolution*, eds. A. Dinar & E.T. Loehman (Westport, Conn.: Praeger, 1995); "An Integrated Water Management Strategy for Ontario: Conservation and Protection for Sustainable Use" in *Environmental Pollution: Science, Policy and Engineering*, eds. B. Nath *et al* (European Centre for Pollution Research, 1993); numerous other technical papers, conference presentations & policy analyses. **AFFIL:** MISA Advisory Committee, Ministry of Environment; Science Advisory Bd., International Joint Commission (Cdn Co-Chair, Parties Implementation Work Group); Canadian Institute for Environmental Law & Policy; Knowledge of the Environment for Youth Foundation. **INTERESTS:** gardening; cooking; travel. **MISC:** listed in *Canadian Who's Who*; numerous invited lectures & papers. **COMMENT:** *"Isobel Heathcote has a long history of interest in environmental management, particularly water policy and waste minimization. Her career spans work in government, universities, and private consulting."*

Heaton, Pauline R., B.A.A. ⛏ ⚜
President, WATERVISIONS UNDERWATER CAMERA SYSTEMS, 479 Shannon Way, Delta (Vancouver), BC V4M 2W6 (604) 943-2332, FAX 943-3608. Born Glen Williams, Ont. 1959. m. Brad Rota. 2 ch. **EDUC:** Ryerson Polytechnical Institute, B.A.A.(Motion Picture) 1984. **CAREER:** Dir. of Photography, film; professional scuba diver specializing in underwater cinematography. **SELECTED CREDITS:** *A Last Wild Salmon* (1995). **AFFIL:** IATSE 667 & 669. **HONS:** hon. by IATSE in Hollywood for tech. achievement & "tremendous accomplishments during the occasion of their 100th anniversary"; Genie Award, Best Cinematography; Finalist, Leo, for Cinematography, BCMPA; Hon. Mention, N.Y. Festival; Nominee, Columbus Festival; Best Documentary & Best Music, Yorkton Short Film Festival. **INTERESTS:** sons; scuba diving; environmental concerns; anything aquatic. **COMMENT:** *"Underwater cinematographer of feature films, MOWs etc. Rents underwater lighting and camera equipment to feature films. Recently completed producing 60-minute primetime documentary, A Last Wild Salmon."*

Hébert, Diane ⊕ ○ ◉
Président, FONDATION DIANE HÉBERT, 14 rue

Chatillon, Lorraine, QC J6Z 2ZS (514) 965-0333, FAX 965-0333. Born Montréal 1957. d. 1 ch. **CAREER:** Pres., Fondation Diane Hébert, 1987 to date. **SELECTED PUBLICATIONS:** *Un second souffle* (1986); *Second Chance* (1988). **AFFIL:** Québec Transplant (Dir.). **HONS:** Personnalité de la Semaine, *La Presse*, 1986; Ministre de l'Avenir, Salon de la Femme, 1986; reconnaissance, Clubs Optimistes Crémazie, 1986; reconnaissance civique, Ville de Lorraine, 1987; Prix de reconnaissance, Association pulmonaire du Québec, 1987; reconnaissance civique, Association des Citoyens de Lorraine, 1987; Gov. General's Award for English Lit. (*Second Chance* tr. M. Philip Stratford), 1988; reconnaissance, Ailes Québécoises Inc., 1989; Prix "Reconnaissance" du Docteur Paul David, Association Canadienne du Don d'Organes et de la Mutuelle du Canada, 1990. **INTERESTS:** music; oil painting; camping; fishing; computers. **MISC:** Chartered General Accountant, 1991 to date. **COMMENT:** *"En 1995, Diane Hébert fête le dixième anniversaire de sa greffe. Pour elle, cela représente dix ans de vie dont elle n'aurait jamais pu profiter, c'est sa fille qu'elle n'aurait jamais vue grandir, c'est dix ans de miracle. Il faut savoir que Diane Hébert détient le record de longévité Canadien en terme de greffe coeur-poumons. In 1995, Diane Hébert celebrated the 10th anniversary of her heart and lungs transplant. The 10 years since her operation have been a miraculous gift, allowing her to watch her daughter grow up. Diane Hébert holds one of the longest Canadian records for heart and lungs transplant patients."*

Hechtman, Lily, B.Sc.,M.D.C.M., F.R.C.P. ■■ ⊕ ⋰
Professor, Psychiatry and Pediatrics, and Head of Research, Division of Child Psychiatry, McGILL UNIVERSITY, Montreal Children's Hospital, Department of Child Psychiatry, Montreal, QC H3Z 1P2 (514) 934-4449, FAX 934-4337, EMAIL md43@musica.mcgill.ca. m. Peter. 2 ch. Kenneth, Jeremy. **EDUC:** McGill Univ., B.Sc.(Hons., Physiology/Psych.) 1963, M.D.C.M. 1967, F.R.C.P.(Psychiatry) 1972; Albert Einstein Coll. of Medicine, Psychiatric residency 1970-72. **SELECTED PUBLICATIONS:** co-author with Weiss, *Hyperactive Children Grown Up*, Second Edition (New York; Guilford Press, 1993); editor, *Long-Term Outcome of Childhood Disorders* (American Psychiatric Press, 1996); many articles in peer-reviewed journals. **AFFIL:** American Academy of Child-Adolescent Psychiatry (Chair, Program Committee); Canadian Academy of Child Psychiatry; Canadian Medical Association; Quebec Medical Association; Quebec Psychiatric

Association; International Society for Research on Child & Adolescent Psychopathology. INTERESTS: literature; classical music; ballet; theatre; boating; skiing; bicycling.

Heddle, Kathleen ■ ■ ⓐ
Olympic Athlete. c/o Canadian Olympic Association. Born Trail, B.C. 1965. SPORTS CAREER: full-time athlete; started rowing, 1985; mbr., Cdn Nat'l Rowing Team, 1987 to date. Olympic Games: Gold, 2x, & Bronze, 4x, 1996; Gold, 2-, & Gold, 8+, 1992. World championships: 1st, 2x, & 2nd, 4x, 1995; 2nd, 2x, 1994; 1st, 2-, 1991; 4th, 2-, 1990. Int'l regattas: 1st, 2x (Switzerland), 1995; 1st, 2-, & 1st, 8+ (Netherlands), & 1st, 2- (Germany), 1992; 1st, 2-, & 3rd, 8+ (Switzerland), 1991; 1st, 4- (Netherlands), 1st, 4- (Austria), & 1st, 8+ (US), 1990; 1st, 4+, & 1st, 8+ (UK), 1989. Pan Am Games: 1st, 2-, 1987. Canadian championships: 1st, 2-, & 1st, 8+, 1990. US championships: 1st, 2x, & 1st, 4x, 1995; 1st, 4-, & 1st, 8+, 1990. INTERESTS: volleyball; cycling; reading.

Heggie, Betty-Ann, B.Ed. ⑤
Senior Vice-President, Corporate Relations, POTASH CORPORATION OF SASKATCHEWAN INC. (PCS), 122 - 1st Ave. S., Ste. 500, Saskatoon, SK S7K 7G3 (306) 933-8521, FAX 933-8877. Born Regina 1953. m. Wade Heggie. 2 ch. Louise, Elizabeth. EDUC: Univ. of Saskatchewan, B.Ed. 1975. CAREER: teacher, Saskatoon Sch. Bd., 1975-76; Sales Rep., Claude-Neon Outdoor Advertising, 1976-78; Acct Exec., Xerox Ltd., 1978-81; Sr. Coord., Mkt Dev., Potash Corporation of Saskatchewan Sales, 1981-84; Mgr, Sales Promo., 1984-87; Dir., Mktg Svcs, 1987-89; VP, Corp. Rel'ns, Potash Corporation of Saskatchewan Inc., 1989-95; Sr. VP, 1995 to date. AFFIL: Canadian Public Relations Association (Dir. 1983-84); Twenty-Fifth Street Theatre (Dir. 1982-85); Western Canadian Fertilizer Association (Dir. 1985-89); National Fertilizer Solutions Association (Convention Chair 1986; Exec. Committee 1987-89); *Solutions Magazine* (V-Chair 1987-89); Fertilizer Institute Low Input Sustainable Task Force (1989-90); Junior Achievement of Northern Saskatchewan (Dir. 1993-94); National Advisory Committee on the Minerals & Metals Industry; Saskatoon Club; Riverside Country Club. HONS: President's Award, National Fertilizer Solutions Association, 1989. INTERESTS: public speaking; design.

Heidenreich, Rosmarin, B.A.,M.A., Ph.D. ⬧ 🎋
Professor, ST. BONIFACE COLLEGE, Winnipeg,

MB (204) 233-0210, FAX (204) 237-3240. d. 2 ch. EDUC: Moorhead State Univ., B.A. 1964; Univ. of Manitoba, M.A.(German Lit.) 1966, secondary teaching certificate 1968; Univ. of Toronto, Ph.D.(Comparative Lit.) 1983. CAREER: Prof., Dept. of German, Schiller Univ., Germany, 1968-69; Dept. of English, Univ. of Tübingen, Germany, 1969; Dept. of English, Univ. of Freiburg, Germany, 1969-74; Depts. of English & Translation, St. Boniface Coll. (Univ. of Manitoba), 1983 to date; Visiting Prof., Institute for Canadian Studies, Univ. of Augsburg, Germany, 1990; Visiting Prof., Dept. of English, Canadian Univ. in France, Villefranche-sur-mer, 1991; lecture tour in France, invitation issued by the French Association for Canadian Studies. SELECTED CREDITS: author & consultant, radio series, SWF, Frieburg, Germany, 1971; Moderator & Ed., *Telekolleg Englisch*, 13-episode TV series, SWF Baden-Baden, Germany, 1972; interviewer & researcher, *The Battle of Mons*, documentary, BBC-TV, London, 1972. SELECTED PUBLICATIONS: *The Postwar Novel in Canada: Narrative Patterns and Reader Response* (Waterloo, Ont.: Wilfrid Laurier Univ. Press, 1989); "Production et réception des littératures minoritaires: le cas des auteurs franco-manitobains" (*Francophonies d'Amérique* 1 1991); "Recent Trends in Franco-Manitoban Fiction and Poetry" (*Prairie Fire* 11(1) 1990); "Causer l'amour dans le Far-West du Canada," in *Poétiques de la Francophonie*, ed. P. Laurette (Paris: Harmattan, 1996); numerous other publications, mainly on Cdn writers. EDIT: Contributing Ed. for French submissions, *Prairie Fire*, 1986 to date; Ed., special issue on Franco-Manitoban lit., *Prairie Fire* 11(1), 1989; Ed. Bd., *Traduction, Terminologie et Rédaction*, 1988 to date; Ed. Bd., *Revue de l'association canadienne de linguistique appliquée*, 1989-94. AFFIL: Canadian Association of Comparative Literature; International Association of Comparative Literature; Canadian Association for Translation Studies (Western Rep.; mbr. of Exec.) Association for Canadian Studies; Conseil international d'études francophones; St. Boniface Coll. (Status of Women & Equity Committees). HONS: grant for higher educ., Gov't of Switzerland, 1966-67; Canada Council Doctoral Fellowship, 1976-79. MISC: reviewer, various journals & granting agencies; listed in *Canadian Who's Who*; various print & broadcast interviews; various conference presentations.

Heikkila, Sonja Chantal, CET, P.Eng. ■ ❀ ⓐ ♀
Former President, ONTARIO ASSOCIATION OF CERTIFIED ENGINEERING TECHNICIANS AND

TECHNOLOGISTS, 1396 Bourcier Dr., Orleans, ON K1E 3L1 (613) 824-3239. Born London, Ont. 1959. m. Art Heikkila. 2 ch. EDUC: Ryerson Polytechnic Univ., B.Tech.(Mech. Eng.) 1985; Licenced, Professional Engineers Ontario, P.Eng.; Ontario Association of Certified Engineering Technicians & Technologists, Certified Engineering Technologist (CET). CAREER: Proj. Coord., Kaptest Engineering Inc., Kapuskasing, Ont., 1982-85; Airworthiness Eng. Asst., Transport Canada–Aviation, Ont. Reg., 1985-90; Airworthiness Eng., Transport Canada–Aviation, H.Q., Ottawa, 1990-93; Fed. Gov't Career Assignment Program (CAP), 1993 to date. AFFIL: Ontario Association of Certified Engineering Technicians & Technologists (Dir.; Past Pres. & Chair, Hum. Res. Mgmt Committee 1994-95; Pres. & Chrm 1993-94); Ontario Council of Regents (appointed by Ont. Legislature, 1993-96); Girl Guide Leader. HONS: President's Equity Award for encouraging women to pursue technical careers, 1995. INTERESTS: her children; reading; fitness; crafts; sewing; cross-country skiing. COMMENT: "Having attended university in the late 70s I found it very common to be the only woman, or the first woman, to study a certain subject or to hold a specific type of job. In 1980, I was the first female 'Building Equipment Man' for Bell Canada, a summer job. I was one of the first women to study for a Mech.Eng. degree at Ryerson. I was also the second woman in Canada to be hired by Transport Canada to review aircraft modifications, and the first woman to travel the world reviewing aircraft designs as a member of the headquarters team. The current program for which I have been selected required that I successfully complete a challenging assessment. The CAP Program is an initiative that has been designed to provide individuals who meet certain criteria and who perform at an acceptable level in the 2.5 day role-play assessment, an opportunity to hone their leadership skills and to develop an overall appreciation for the mandate and function of the total federal public service, its departments and how they relate to the government's overall mandate. The program presents an opportunity to experience the unique challenges encountered in at least four different positions, within or outside (i.e. industry exchange), the federal public service. In addition, it is necessary to master both official languages early in the program. In my current assignment with the Office of the Auditor General of Canada, I have encountered many challenges and opportunities, which have provided me with a much clearer understanding of the machinery of government and the interrelationships therein. With so many changes taking place in the federal public service during the last few years of this century, I feel very fortunate to have the opportunity to observe and participate in the dynamics while part of the CAP program."

Heiman, Carolyn E., B.A.A. ✏ 📖
Editor, Living Section, VICTORIA TIMES COLONIST, 2621 Douglas St., Victoria, BC V8S 3C5 (604) 380-5343, FAX 380-5353, EMAIL timesc@interlink.bc.ca. Born Swan River, Man. 1955. m. H. Wayne Jensen. 2 ch. EDUC: Ryerson Polytechnic Univ., B.A.A.(Journalism). CAREER: Owen Sound Sun Times, 1976-78; Edmonton Journal, 1978-84; Southam Communications, 1984-85; Sr. Public Rel'ns Assoc., General Foods, 1985-86; freelance writer, 1986-88; Victoria Times Colonist, 1988 to date.

Heinrich, Katherine, B.Math., Ph.D. 🔬 ⚛ ⭕
Professor, Department of Mathematics and Statistics, SIMON FRASER UNIVERSITY, Burnaby, BC V5A 1S6 (604) 291-3378, FAX 291-4947, EMAIL heinrich@cs.sfu.ca. Born Australia 1954. m. Brian Alspach. EDUC: Univ. of Newcastle, B.Math. 1976, Ph.D.(Math.) 1979. CAREER: Asst. Prof., Univ. of Arizona, 1978-79; Asst. Prof./Assoc. Prof., Simon Fraser Univ., 1981-87; Prof., 1987 to date; Chair, Dept. of Math. & Statistics, 1991-96; Special Asst. to the VP, Academic for Academic Planning, 1996-99. SELECTED PUBLICATIONS: more than 60 research publications in discrete math. AFFIL: Univ. of Northern British Columbia (Dir. 1992-94); Canadian Math. Olympiad (Dir. 1993-95); Canada Youth Science Foundation (Dir. 1994-96); Canadian Mathematical Society (Dir. 1993-95; Pres. 1996-98); Society for Canadian Women in Science & Technology; Australasian Combinatorics Society; Association for Women in Math. HONS: Univ. Research Fellow, National Science & Engineering Research Council, 1981-91; Women of Distinction Award, Educ., Training & Dev., Vancouver YWCA, 1995; Gold Medal for Professional Excellence, Univ. of Newcastle, 1995. INTERESTS: math; reading; knitting; gardening. COMMENT: "An active promoter of the importance of mathematics and the need for numerate citizens, I encourage and support women in mathematics and university careers, and have assisted in building a strong and relevant department of mathematics and statistics at Simon Fraser University."

Heinrichs, Elfrieda Elizabeth, B.A., A.Music ⭕ 🖊 ✖
Volunteer. One Upper Brook St., London, UK

W1Y 1PA. Born Kitchener, Ont. 1936. m. Vern. 2 ch. Debra Cecile (1965-1975), Anne Marie. EDUC: Univ. of Western Ontario, A.Music (Piano) 1954; Univ. of Toronto, B.A.(Hons.) 1959. CAREER: secondary sch. teacher, 1959-64. AFFIL: Ceci Heinrichs Foundation for Developmentally Handicapped Children (Pres.); The Heinrichs Foundation (Pres); Association of Canadian Choral Conductors (Dir.); Ontario Choral Federation (Advisory Council 1993 to date; Pres. 1988-90); Art Gallery of Ontario; Royal Ontario Museum; McMichael Gallery; Stratford Festival; Shaw Festival; Elora Festival; Guelph Spring Festival; National Ballet of Canada; Maestro Club, Toronto Symphony Orchestra; President's Committee, Univ. of Toronto; Metropolitan Museum of Art, NYC; Metropolitan Opera Guild; English Speaking Union, London, UK; The Association of the Severely Handicapped (Int'l); Canadian Women's Club, London, UK; University Women's Club, London, UK; Royal Academy of Arts, UK; School House Concerts (1965-69); The Bayview Glen Foundation (1979-82); Ceci's Homes for Children (Pres. 1979-84); Oriana Singers (1985-89); Steering Committee, Podium '92 (1990-92); 150th Anniversary Committee, Little Trinity Church, Toronto (1991-92); Univ. of Toronto Foundation (Dir. 1994). INTERESTS: foreign travel; Iyengar yoga; collecting Mennonite quilts.

Helper, The Hon. Bonnie Merilyn, LL.B. ⚖
Justice, Court of Appeal, PROVINCE OF MANITOBA, Judges Chambers, The Law Courts, Winnipeg, MB R3C 0P9. 3 ch. Jeffrey A., Cara D., Steven R. EDUC: Univ. of Manitoba, LL.B. 1966. BAR: Man., 1966. CAREER: Librarian & Lecturer, Manitoba Law Sch., 1966-67; private practice, 1968-72; family law & civil litigation, Aikins, MacAulay & Thorvaldson, 1972-74; solicitor on consulting basis, Legal Aid Manitoba, 1975; family law & civil litigation, Walsh, Tadman & Yard, 1975-78; part-time appt., Family Div., Prov. Judges Court, 1978-80; full-time appt., 1980-83; Justice, Family Div., Court of Queen's Bench, 1983-89; Justice, Court of Appeal, 1989 to date. SELECTED PUBLICATIONS: "Does the Casual Connection Principle Enunciated in the Supreme Court Trilogy Apply to Payors under the Divorce Act, 1985?" (Canadian Family Law Quarterly, 1989). AFFIL: Manitoba Bar Association (Family Law Subsection); Provincial Judges' Association of Manitoba (Exec. Mbr.); Family Div. Provincial Court Judges (Rules Committee); Canadian Association for the Prevention of Crime; Canadian Bar Association; Canadian Society for Prevention of Cruelty to Children; Manitoba Association of Rights & Liberties;

Hadassah-Wizo of Canada (Life Mbr.). HONS: Isbister Scholarship, 1964; Wills & Trust Prize, 1965; Hon. Alexander Morris Exhibition Prize, highest aggregate standing in the full course in Law, 1966; Margaret Hypatia Crawford Scholarship, 1966; Gold Medal, Univ. of Manitoba, 1966; Gold Medal, Law Society of Manitoba, 1966.

Hemlow, Joyce, M.A.,Ph.D.,LL.D., F.R.S.C. 🖋 📚 ✒
Writer and Academic. 1521 LeMarchant St., Apt. 3-G, Halifax, NS B3H 3R2. Born 1906. EDUC: Queen's Univ., B.A. 1941, M.A. 1942, LL.D. 1967; Radcliffe Coll., A.M. 1944, Ph.D. 1948. CAREER: Marty Travelling Fellow, Queen's Univ., 1942-43; Nuffield Fellow, 1954; Greenshields Prof., McGill Univ., 1965; Emerita, 1975. SELECTED PUBLICATIONS: The History of Fanny Burney (1958); A Catalogue of the Burney Family Correspondence, 1749-1878 (1971); 12 volumes of an edition The Journals and Letters of Fanny Burney (Madame d'Arblay) 1791-1840 (1972-84); Selected Letters and Journals (1986); various articles, mainly about the Burneys. AFFIL: Canadian Federation of University Women (Fellow 1943-44); Guggenheim Memorial Foundation (Fellow 1951, 1967); Humanities Research Council of Canada (1957-61); Royal Society of Canada (Fellow); Phi Beta Kappa; IAUPE. HONS: Grad. Achievement Medal, Radcliffe Grad. Sch., 1969; The History of Fanny Burney received Gov. General's Award for Academic Non-Fiction, 1958; Rose Mary Crayshaw Prize; James Tait Black memorial book prize for the best biography in the UK, 1958.

Hénaut, Dorothy Todd ■ ⚰ 🌐 ✖
Freelance Filmmaker and Videomaker. 5045 Esplanade, Montreal, QC H2T 2Y9 (514) 276-5333, FAX 948-1832. Born Hamilton, Ont. 1935. d. 2 ch. Suzanne Hénaut, Marc Hénaut. EDUC: Bishop Strachan Sch., Sr. Matriculation 1953; the Sorbonne, Paris, French Hist. & Lit. 1954; Concordia Univ., Women in the Fine Arts 1989-91. CAREER: researcher & writer, Challenge for Change, National Film Board of Canada (NFB), 1968-76; Acting Dir., 1977-76; mbr., Studio D, NFB, 1977-89; filmmaker, NFB, 1989-96. SELECTED CREDITS: Co-creator, with Bonnie Klein, VTR St-Jacques, 1st video proj. "in the hands of citizens", Challenge for Change, NFB, 1968; Dir., The New Alchemists, NFB, 1974; Prod., Temiscaming, Québec, NFB, 1976; Dir., Sun, Wind and Wood, NFB, 1977; Dir., Horse-Drawn Magic, NFB, 1979; Prod., Not A Love Story, NFB, 1979-82; Dir., Fireworks, NFB, 1986; Dir., A

Song for Quebec, PBS/Global TV, 1988; Dir., *Un Amour naissant*, 1992; Dir., *You won't need running shoes, darling*, 1996. SELECTED PUBLI-CATIONS: articles published in *Arts/Canada*, *Radical Software*, *Studies in Canadian Communications*, *Femmes D'Action*, *Lumières*, *Visual Anthropology Review*, *Perforations*, *Broadside*, *The Womanist* & *Canadian Forum*; *Bringing It Home: Women Speak About Feminism in Their Lives*; drawings published in *Annals of Earth*. EDIT: Ed., *Access, Challenge for Change* newsletter, 1968-76. EXHIBITIONS: paintings in group exhibitions at Conceptart Outrement (1988, 1989), The Grey Gallery, Complexe du Canal, Montreal (1990) & the National Film Board, Montreal (1990). AFFIL: Voice of Women; SGCT/ONF; Femmes dans le cinema et la télévision de Montréal; Canadian Independent Filmmakers' Caucus; La Cinémathèque québécoise; NDP Canada, Section Quebec; Forum pour la création en cinéma et vidéo. HONS: films have won various awards. INTERESTS: peace & social justice; women; the environment; aging; the economy; Que. culture; Que.-Canada rel'ns; skiing; swimming; kayaking; painting; the role of media in society; the arts. MISC: Challenge for Change program experimented with the use of media as a tool in social change; frequent public speaker. COMMENT: *"An activist who believes in social justice, Dorothy Todd Hénaut makes films to encourage audiences to understand the world, to change it, and to enjoy themselves in the process."*

Hénaut, Suzanne ■ 💜 ⌷

TFO/TVONTARIO. Born Montreal 1956. s. 1 ch. Belkis Hénaut. CAREER: various positions in the film industry, 1975 to date; involved in set-up, Inuit Broadcasting Corporation, Iqaluit, 1978-81; Ptnr, Les Films Vision 4 inc., 1985-90; Pres., Les Productions Zann Inc., 1990-95; Co-prod. & preboys., Tfo/TVOntario, 1995 to date. SELECTED CREDITS: *Henri*, dir. François Labonté, 1986; *Pellan*, dir. André Gladu, 1986; *Candy Mountain*, dir. Robert Franck & Rudy Worlitzer, 1987; *Gaspard et fils*, dir. François Labonté, 1988; *Sous les draps les étoiles*, dir. Jean-Pierre Gariépy, 1989; *Cuervo*, dir. Carlos Ferrand, 1990; Line-Prod., *Scoop I*, dir. Georges Mihalka, 1991; *Aux Voleurs!*, short film, dir. Ghislaine Coté, 1992; *Baltic Fire*, documentary, dir. Zoe Dirse, 1993; *Héritage*, short film, dir. Najwa Thili, 1994. AFFIL: Canadian Conference of the Arts (Bd. of Dir. 1995 to date). MISC: founder, "Convergence," a forum on film & video technology, 1984-94; Treas., Cinémathèque Québécoise/Musée du Cinéma, 1988-94; Trainer for set-up, Inuit Broadcasting Corporation, Iqaluit, 1978-81.

Hendeles, Ydessa ■■ ⊗ ◐ ⌷ 🖉

President, YDESSA HENDELES ART FOUNDATION (art gallery/privately funded charitable organization), P.O. Box 757, Stn F, Toronto, ON M4Y 2N6 (416) 413-9400. Born Marburg, Germany 1948. 1 ch. Jason N. Hendeles. m. Max Dean. EDUC: Univ. of Toronto, B.A.(Social & Philosophical Studies) 1969; Toronto Art Therapy Institute, D.T.A.T.I. (M.A.) 1984. CAREER: owner, commercial gallery, Ydessa Hendeles Gallery Limited (The Ydessa Gallery), 1980-88. EXHIBITIONS: 20 nat'l & int'l contemporary art exhibitions curated, designed & funded by Ydessa Hendeles for the Ydessa Hendeles Art Foundation, 1988 to date (catalogues are forthcoming). AFFIL: Toronto Art Therapy Institute (Bd.); Canadian Society for the Weizmann Institute of Science (Bd., Toronto chpt.); Professional Art Dealers' Association of Canada; Ontario Association of Art Galleries (forwarded for nomination). HONS: honorary Doctorate of Fine Arts, Nova Scotia College of Art & Design, 1996. MISC: nat'l & int'l curatorial, critical & media acknowledgement for the foundation's exhibition program; first privately funded charitable organization in Canada that provides contemporary art exhibitions.

Henderson, Angela D., S.R.N.,B.S.N., M.S.N. 🖉 ⊕

Associate Professor, School of Nursing, UNIVERSITY OF BRITISH COLUMBIA, 2211 Westbrook Mall, Ste. T206, Vancouver, BC V6T 2B5 (604) 822-7426, FAX 822-7466. Born Nottingham, UK 1944. m. E. Harvey Henderson. 2 ch. EDUC: Norfolk & Norwich Hospital, S.R.N. 1965; Univ. of British Columbia, Sch. of Nursing, B.S.N. 1981, M.S.N. 1986. CAREER: Staff Nurse, Norfolk & Norwich Hospitals, 1965-67; Staff Nurse, Wellesley Hospital, Toronto, 1967-69; Staff Nurse, St. Paul's Hospital, Vancouver, 1969-73; part-time Relief Nurse, 1973-79; Sessional Lecturer, Univ. of British Columbia, 1981-83, 1986-89; Asst. Prof., 1989-94; Assoc. Prof., 1994 to date. SELECTED PUBLICATIONS: "Use of Social Support in a Transition House for Abused Wives" (*Health Care for Women International* 10(1) 1989); "The Experiences of New Fathers During the First Three Weeks of Life" (*Journal of Advanced Nursing* 16 1991); "Development of a Research Committee at a Community Hospital," with A.J. Brouse (*Canadian Journal of Nursing Administration* 5(1) 1992); "Abused Women's Perceptions of Their Children's Experience" (*Canada's Mental Health* 41(1) 1993); *Breaking the Cycle: A parenting guide for single mothers of children who have witnessed wife abuse*, manual, with J.R. Ericksen & M. Davidson (1990); various other publications. **AFFIL:** Canadian Nurses' Association; Registered Nurses' Association of B.C.; Nursing Network on Violence Against Women; North Shore Crisis Service Society (Bd. Mbr.). **INTERESTS:** gardening; skiing; travelling. **MISC:** numerous conference presentations & invited lectures. **COMMENT:** *"My primary ongoing interest is in improving the quality of care to abused women and their children by enhancing the ability of healthcare personnel to address this population's needs."*

Henderson, Ann Elizabeth Ludmilla Mary Zamoyska Buchanan ■■ ♡ ⊛ ☼
Volunteer. Born Plymouth, UK 1923. m. Lyman G. Henderson. 3 ch. Buchanan, Victoria, Antonia. **EDUC:** Sacred Heart Convent, London, England; London Univ., 1 yr. **CAREER:** Interpreter, Women's Royal Naval Svc., 1942-45. **VOLUNTEER CAREER:** founder & Pres., Woodbridge Unit, Canadian Cancer Society, 1964; founder & Pres., Central Counties District, 1968; founder & 1st Chair, Art Committee, Princess Margaret Lodge, 1968; Chair of Women's Svc. Committee, & Bd. mbr., Ont. Div., 1970-72; Chair, Art Acquisition Committee, Articipaction Art Sale, Arthritis Society, 1972; Dir., The National Ballet of Canada, 1973-76; Chair, Volunteer Committee, McMichael Canadian Art Collection, 1986-88; Hon. Chair (with husband), The National Ballet Ball, 1991; Chair, Benefactors of National Ballet Sch., 1992-95; Chair, McMichael Volunteer-Supported Autumn Art Sale, 1993-95. **AFFIL:** Canadian Cancer Society (Hon. Chair, Vaughan Unit; driver); National Ballet Sch. (Hon. Dir.); McMichael Canadian Art Collection (Membership Chair, Volunteers); McMichael Canadian Art Foundation (Gov. Mbr.); St. Margaret Mary's Roman Catholic Church, Woodbridge (Lector). **HONS:** War Svc. Medals, 1939-45; Ontario Volunteer Award, 10 yrs. **INTERESTS:** the arts incl. the performing & visual arts, & photography (along with her husband, is a private sponsor of several visual artists, musicians, dancers, actors & writers; has a large & eclectic collection of Cdn contemporary art). **COMMENT:** *"An English war-bride who brought up 3 children, worked enthusiastically with a dozen volunteer agencies, and enjoyed and supported many talented artists."*

Henderson, Anne, B.A. 🎬 ⊛
Film Director and Producer, ARCADY FILMS, 4121 de l'Esplanade, Montreal, QC H2W 1S9 (514) 845-0850, FAX 845-0850. Born Westmount, Que. 1948. **EDUC:** McGill Univ., B.A.(English Lit.) 1967. **CAREER:** film dir. & prod., 1975 to date; Lecturer, English Lit., Concordia Univ. **SELECTED CREDITS:** *And They Lived Happily Ever After* (1975); *Threads* (1976); *The Right Candidate for Rosedale* (1978); *Not a Love Story* (1982); *Attention! Women at Work* (1983); *Le Vent Dans Les Voiles* (1986); *The Impossible Takes a Little Longer* (1986); *Holding Our Ground* (1988); *A Song for Tibet* (1991); *The Gods of Our Fathers* (1994); "Body Politics" & "The Power Game," *Women: A True Story* (series), 1996; ed., various documentaries, short dramas, & 1 dramatic feature. **SELECTED PUBLICATIONS:** various articles. **AFFIL:** Academy of Canadian Film & Television; Canadian Independent Film Caucus; Directors' Guild of Canada; Playwrights' Workshop Montreal (Dir.). **HONS:** Red Ribbon, American Film Festival, 1976; Blue Ribbon Award, American Film & Video Association, 1985, 1992; People's Choice Award for Best Documentary, Hawaiian Film Festival, 1991; Best Short Documentary, Genie Award, Academy of Canadian Film & Television, 1992. **INTERESTS:** music; gardening. **MISC:** served as jury mbr. for several film awards committees.

Henderson, Anne, B.Comm., LL.B. ■■ ♡ 🎓 $
Instructor, Business Administration, NORTHERN ALBERTA INSTITUTE OF TECHNOLOGY (post-secondary education), 11762 - 106 St., Edmonton, AB T5G 3H1 (403) 471-7870. Born Dodsland, Sask. 1950. m. Tom Farrell. 4 ch. Bill, Adam, Tara, Lana. **EDUC:** Univ. of Alberta, B.Comm. 1973, LL.B. 1976. **CAREER:** lawyer, Edmonton, 1976-85; Instructor, Bus. Admin., Northern Alberta Institute of Technology, 1995 to date. **VOLUNTEER CAREER:** professional volunteer with positions incl. Chairperson, Bd. of Dir., Terra Association & Bd. mbr., Junior League of Edmonton, 1985-95. **AFFIL:** Law Society of Alberta (non-practising mbr.); Junior League of Edmonton (sustaining mbr.). **INTERESTS:** organizational dev.; communication skills; community dev. **COMMENT:** *"After obtaining business and law degrees from the University of Alberta, practised law for approximately nine years, followed by ten years of full-time parenting and volunteer involvement. Currently a business instructor at N.A.I.T., balancing professional, family and volunteer commitments."*

Henderson, Elfie ■ $
Assistant Vice-President, Investor Marketing Services, NATIONAL TRUST COMPANY, 55 City Centre Dr., 9th Fl., Mississauga, ON L5B 1M3 (905) 566-2457, FAX 566-2464. Born Cologne, Germany 1944. d. 1 ch. & 4 stpch.

EDUC: Trust Institute, M.T.I.(Lending) 1981; Appraisal Institute, tech. courses & various mgmt training; York Univ., will complete B.A.(Comm.) 1996. CAREER: law clerk, 1963-72; mortgage admin., Equitable Trust, 1972-73; income trust, 1975-76; Asst. Mgr, Mortgage Svcs, National Trust Company, 1976-78; Mgr, Mortgage Svcs, 1978-81; Reg'l Mgr, Mortgage Svcs, 1981-84; Mgr, Head Office Mortgage Svcs, 1984-85; Proj. Mgr, Lending, 1985-86; Dir., Investor Mortgage Svcs, 1986-89; Asst. VP, Investor Mortgage Svcs, 1989-94; Asst. VP, Admin. & Oper., Bnkg, 1994 to date; mbr., President's Advisory Committee, 1982-84. SELECTED PUBLICATIONS: segments of *Mortgage Services–Phase 1 & 2* (Trust Institute). AFFIL: United Way (Exec. Committee 1989-95; Co-Chair 1991 & 1993); Trust Institute (Curriculum Committee 1989 to date; Advisory Bd. 1994 to date); Canadian Bar Association (Standard Charge Committee 1983-86). HONS: David T. Appelt Award in recognition of outstanding contribution to the Trust Companies Institute & its work. INTERESTS: people; gardening; music; film; theatre; art; crafts; reading; volunteer activities; teaching; antiques.

Henderson, Judith, B.A. ⊗ ⌣

President, AIR TANGO, 2359 rue Duvernay, Ste. 200, Montreal, QC H3J 2X1 (514) 933-0232, FAX 989-8006. Born Montreal 1950. m. 2 ch. EDUC: Loyola Univ., B.A. 1972. CAREER: composer, film & advtg industry; Pres., Air Tango (music production company), 15 yrs. HONS: 5 Clio Awards; 3 International Hollywood Broadcasting Awards; 2 Gemini Awards; 1 Mobius; 1 Mondial. COMMENT: *"Song composer and lyricist. Won numerous awards for original compositions in advertising and film. Written songs for various artists."*

Henderson, Roxanne, C.E.B.,C.H.R.P. Ⓢ

Director, Human Resources, CREDIT UNION CENTRAL OF ONTARIO, 2810 Matheson Blvd. E., Mississauga, ON L4W 4X7 (905) 629-5520, FAX 238-3414. Born Newmarket, Ont. 1961. m. Douglas J. Henderson. 2 ch. Natalie, Samantha. EDUC: Humber Coll., C.E.B. 1986; C.H.R.P. designation; Heriot Watt Univ., M.B.A. current. CAREER: Asst. Mgr, Hum. Res., Crothers Limited, 1980-87; Div. Mgr, Hum. Res., Purolator Courier Ltd., 1987-90; Mgr, Hum. Res., Granada Canada Ltd., 1990-92; Dir., Hum. Res., Credit Union Central of Ontario, 1992 to date. SELECTED PUBLICATIONS: articles in *C.C.H., Canadian Business, Chatelaine* & *H.R.P.A.O.* publications. AFFIL: Human Resource Professional Association of Ontario (Certified Hum. Res. Professional);

Markham Board of Trade. INTERESTS: family; hiking; boating; interior decorating.

Hendry, Leona, B.A.,M.L.S. ▯ ▤

Chief Executive Officer, BELLEVILLE PUBLIC LIBRARY, 223 Pinnacle St., Belleville, ON K8N 3A7. Born Newmarket, Ont. 1948. EDUC: Univ. of Toronto, B.A. 1970, M.L.S. 1972. CAREER: Head of Cataloguing, Brampton Public Library, 1972-81; Head of Cataloguing, Voyageur (Northern Ont. Library Svc.), Sudbury, Ont., 1982-85; CEO, Belleville Public Library, 1985 to date. AFFIL: Canadian Library Association; Ontario Library Association; American Library Association; Hastings County Historical Society (Pres., Bd. of Dir. 1993-94; Treas. 1995-96); Quinte Arts Council (former mbr., Bd. of Dir.); Quinte Literacy (active in founding). INTERESTS: cross-stitch embroidery; local history; reading; cottage life; family activities.

Henley, Gail, B.A.,M.A., LL.B. ■ ⚔ ⌣ ♥

Legal Counsel, CANWEST GLOBAL SYSTEMS, c/o 180 Cottingham St., Toronto, ON M4V 1C5 (416) 967-7740, FAX 921-8877. Born Ont. m. Monte R. McMurchy. 1 ch. EDUC: McGill Univ., B.A.; Univ. of Toronto, M.A., LL.B. 1991. BAR: Ont., 1993. CAREER: Legal Asst., Bus. & Legal Affairs, First Choice Canadian Communications Corp., 1990-91; articles of clerkship, Heenan, Blaikie, 1991-92; Dir., Legal Affairs, Grosvenor Park, 1993-94; Policy Advisory, Canadian Musical Reproduction Rights Agency, 1994; Legal Cnsl, CanWest Global Systems, 1994 to date. SELECTED PUBLICATIONS: *Where the Cherries End Up*, novel (Canada; McClelland & Stewart, 1978); various legal publications incl.: "A Case For Statutory Damages in Canadian Copyright Law" (12 *Canadian Intellectual Property* 81, 1995); "Preferences about Preferences: A Positive Justification for Canadian Content Regulation" (3 *Media & Communications Law Review*, 127, 1993); "Significant Developments in the Canadian Law of Tenders" (18 *Canadian Business Law Journal* 382 1991); *Intellectual Property Casebook*, Co-Ed., 3 volumes: *Copyright, Trademarks, Publicity & Personality Rights* (Univ. of Toronto, Fac. of Law); various published articles on the film & TV industry incl.: "Quality Filmmaking on a Shoestring Budget" (*Playback*, Sept. 1987); "Ontario Feature Filmmaking Takes the ODFC Challenge" (*Cinema Canada*, Mar. 1986); "Women Decision-Makers in Canadian Television" (*Cinema Canada*, Nov. 1983). AFFIL: Writers' Guild of Canada; Canadian Bar Association; P.E.N.; Academy of Canadian Cinema & Television. HONS: *The*

Parable of the Leaven, National Screen Institute Award, Directing & Producing, Most Outstanding Short Film, Yorkton Film Festival, 1989. INTERESTS: competitive yacht racing. MISC: LORC Champion, 1989-94. COMMENT: *"Lawyer, published author, award-winning filmmaker, mother and wife. Specialist in entertainment law and Canadian broadcasting policy."*

Henley-Andrews, Janet, B.A., LL.B. 🐟 🐟 ⭘
Partner, STEWART MCKELVEY STIRLING SCALES, Box 5038, Cabot Place, St. John's, NF A1C 5V3 (709) 722-4270, FAX 722-4565. Born St. John's 1956. m. John P. Andrews. 3 ch. EDUC: Memorial Univ. of Newfoundland, B.A.(Math.) 1977; Univ. of Toronto, LL.B. 1980. BAR: Nfld., 1980. CAREER: articling student, Stewart McKelvey Stirling Scales (then Stirling, Ryan), June-Dec. 1980; Assoc., 1980-85; Ptnr, 1985 to date. AFFIL: Law Society of Newfoundland (Discipline Committee; Bar Admission Course Instructor in Civil Procedure); Catholic Education Council (Dir.); Newfoundland Workers Compensation Commission (Dir.); Girl Guides of Canada, Nfld. (Hon. Solicitor); Newfoundland Outport Nursing & Industrial Association (Pres.); St. Pius X Elementary P.T.A. (VP); Canadian Bar Association, Judicial Appointments Review Committee (Nfld.); Alliance for Choice in Education (spokesperson). INTERESTS: educ. issues; tennis; skiing; travel. COMMENT: *"I am an energetic mother of three who enjoys the practice of law full time and complements that with community involvement. I believe that it is important to give to the community and devote considerable time to volunteer activities."*

Hennessy, Ellen-Ray, B.F.A. ■ 🐟 🐟 🐟
Actor. c/o Butler, Rushton, Bell Talent Agency, 10 St. Mary St., Ste. 305, Toronto, ON M4Y 1P9 (416) 964-6660. Born Toronto 1958. d. EDUC: Univ. of Windsor, B.F.A.(Theatre) 1980; Banff Sch. of Fine Arts. CAREER: 20 years' experience as actor, singer, comedian, dancer, clown & voices in radio, TV, industrials, features, dramaturg; writer, dir., teacher, host & announcer; over 125 plays in Canada, US & Europe. SELECTED CREDITS: *Flash Forward* (TV series), Disney; *Trail Mix* (pilot), Discovery; *Shoemaker* (feature); *Goosebumps*, Fox Network; *FX* (TV series); *One Last Look in the Mirror*, Bravo; *Hardy Boys* (series); *Nancy Drew* (series); *Conspiracy of Fear* (feature); *It Takes Two* (feature); *Once Around This City* (live ent. workshop); *Taming of the Shrew* (theatre), World Stage Festival. AFFIL: foster parent; volunteer teacher of yoga classes for Multi-

ple Sclerosis & Muscular Dystrophy in Calgary; volunteer for sick & aged homes in Windsor; Ont.; gives to more than 30 charities in Canada & worldwide. HONS: 4 summer scholarships, Banff Sch. of Fine Arts; Dean's List, Univ. of Windsor, 1980; nominee, Dora Awards. INTERESTS: visual arts; design; sports; animals; children; music; cooking; skiing. MISC: runs 12 km. every day; creates store & restaurant displays; designs graphics & business letterhead; owns 4 cats, 1 dog & numerous fish; breeds Love Birds; a mystic. COMMENT: *"A walker on the wild side who revels in expressions, freedom, nature and creativity. Spirited and gutsy, the pursuit of happiness is a driving force. Optimistic and hopeful about mankind."*

Henry, Martha, B.F.A. ■ 🐟 🐟 🐟
Actor, Director. c/o Kathy Kernohan, Phoenix Artists Management, 10 St. Mary St., Ste. 810, Toronto, ON M4Y 1P9 (416) 964-6464, FAX 969-9924. Born Detroit 1938. m. Rod Beattie. 1 ch. EDUC: Carnegie-Mellon Univ., B.F.A. 1959; National Theatre Sch. of Canada, 1962. CAREER: actor with various theatre companies in Canada, US & UK, & for radio, film & TV, 1959 to date; has taught at National Theatre Sch., Univ. of Windsor, Tarragon Theatre's Maggie Bassett Studio & Prairie Theatre Exchange, Winnipeg; mbr., Advisory Committee, Canada Council, Theatre Section, 1985-87; Artistic Dir., The Grand Theatre, London, Ont., 1988-95; Bd. mbr., Canada Council, 1987-93; mbr., Exec. Committee, 1992-93. SELECTED CREDITS: Jennet, *The Lady's Not for Burning*, Manitoba Theatre Centre, 1961; Antigone, *Antigone*, Lincoln Center, 1971; Goneril, *King Lear*, Stratford Festival, 1980; Margaret, *Waiting for the Parade*, The Grand Theatre, 1983; Mary Cavan Tyrone, *Long Day's Journey into Night*, Stratford Festival, 1994-95; Regina, *The Little Foxes*, Stratford Festival, 1996; Princes Kosmonopolis, *Sweet Bird of Youth*, Stratford Festival, 1996; numerous other theatrical performance credits; actor, *The Manticore*, CBC-Radio; Sarah Bernhardt, *Memoir*, CBC-Radio; various other radio credits; actor, *The Wars* (feature), dir. Robin Phillips, 1984; actor, *Dancing in the Dark* (feature), dir. Leon Marr, 1986; actor, *Mustard Bath* (feature), 1994; numerous other film & TV credits; Dir., *Brief Lives*, Stratford Festival; Dir., *Top Girls*, Globe Theatre, Regina; Dir., *Oleanna*, The Grand Theatre, 1994; Mary Tyrone, *Long Day's Journey into Night* (feature), dir. David Wellington, 1996; various other directorial credits; various concert narrations. AFFIL: Canadian Actors' Equity Association; ACTRA. HONS: Best Actress, Genie Award, 1979, 1984, 1986; Officer of the Order

of Canada, 1982; Best Actress, Gemini Award, 1986, 1989; Best Guest Performance, Gemini Award, 1988; Toronto Drama Bench Award for Outstanding Contribution to Cdn Theatre, 1990; Companion of the Order of Canada, 1991; Gascon-Thomas Award, for inspirational work in Cdn Theatre, National Theatre Sch., 1992; Canada 125 Medal, 1992; Order of Ontario, 1994; Best Actress in a Supporting Role, Genie Award, 1994; D.F.A.(Hon.), Lawrence Univ.; D.Litt.(Hon.), York Univ.; LL.D.(Hon.), Univ. of Toronto; LL.D.(Hon.), Univ. of Windsor; D.Litt.(Hon.), Univ. of Guelph; D.Litt.(Hon.), Univ. of Western Ontario; Gov. General's Performing Arts Award, 1996. **MISC:** 1st grad. of the National Theatre Sch.; *Long Day's Journey Into Night* won award, Toronto International Film Festival, 1996.

Hérivel, Antoinette, B.F.A.,B.Ed., M.Ed. 🎨 🎓

Artist, Educator. Born UK. 1943. m. 4 ch. **EDUC:** Southlands Coll., London, UK,Teaching Certificate 1964; Univ. of Regina, B.F.A. 1986, B.Ed. 1992, M.Ed. 1996. **CAREER:** elementary sch. teacher, incl. full & part-time, 1964-92; instructor, painting, Univ. of Regina Extension Dept., 1985-90; Artist-in-Residence, Catholic Sch. Bd.–core area schools, 1990-94; Sessional Lecturer, Dept. of Fine Arts, Univ. of Regina, 1992; Artist-in-Residence, Univ. of Regina, 1992; Children's Festival Coord., 1993; Sessional Lecturer, Arts Educ., Univ. of Regina, 1993 to date; artistic collaboration with dancer Tracy Pfieffer, 1994. **COMMISSIONS:** cover *The Crew*, novel (Coteau Publishers, 1993); video prod., *Antoinette* (S.S.E.A., 1994). **EXHIBITIONS:** 16 solo exhibitions, Sask. & Alta., 1988 to date; more than 25 group exhibitions incl., *Women's Sensibilities, Contemporary Women in the Visual Arts*, W.A.R.M. Gallery, Minneapolis (1986); Articule Gallery, Montreal (1989); *Laughing Matters*, Mendel Art Gallery, Saskatoon (1992); *Regina Billboard Project*, Regina, Winnipeg, Toronto (1989-90); *Women And*, Gordon Snelgrove Gallery, Saskatoon (1994). **COLLECTIONS:** Sony Music Co., Toronto; Canada Council Art Bank; Sask. Arts Bd.; Coll. of Agriculture, Saskatoon; H.R.H. Prince Edward; represented in various other collections. **AFFIL:** CARFAC Saskatchewan; Canadian Society for Education through Art; Saskatchewan Society for Education through Art. **HONS:** Saskatchewan Teachers' Federation Purchase Award, 1981; Canadian Federation of University Women's Scholarship, 1984-85; Gene B. Ciuca Memorial Scholarship in Visual Arts, 1985; Margaret Messer Fellowship, Univ. of Regina, 1993, 1995. **INTERESTS:** modern dance (participant & supporting); theatre; music; gardening; reading; aerobics; travel; meeting people; working with young people. **COMMENT:** *"Artistic/academic career after age 43. Known as painter and promoter of arts and arts education in Saskatchewan. Creating resources/encouraging experimental art forms in all sectors of community."*

Heroux, Justine 📺 $

President and Producer, **CINEVIDEO PLUS**, 2100 Ste. Catherine St. W., Ste. 710, Montreal, QC H3H 2T3 (514) 937-7986, FAX 937-8332, EMAIL 103601.1036@compuserve.com. Born Montreal 1942. m. Denis Heroux. 1 ch. Marc-Antoine. **CAREER:** Script Asst., Radio-Canada, 1967; Script Asst., various motion pictures; Prod. Mgr; Assoc. Prod.; Prod.; Pres. & Prod., CINEVIDEO PLUS, 1990 to date. **SELECTED CREDITS:** Assoc. Prod., *Atlantic City* (feature), 1979; Prod., *The Plouffe Family* (feature & mini-series), Gilles Carle, 1980; Prod., *Little Gloria. Happy at Last* (mini-series), NBC & Edgar Scherick and Associates, 1982; Prod., *Murder in the Family* (feature & mini-series), Denys Arcand & Gilles Carle, 1983; Prod., *The Alley Cat* (feature & miniseries), Jean Beaudin, 1985; Prod., *In the Shadow of the Wind* (feature), Yves Simoneau, 1986; Co-Prod., *Dames Galantes* (feature), Jean Charles Tacchella, 1990; Co-Prod., *L'Homme de ma vie* (feature), Jean-Charles Tacchella, 1991; Co-Prod., *Monsieur Ripois* (telefilm), Luc Béraud, 1991; Co-Prod., *Connections* (MOW), Patrick Jamain, 1992; Co-Prod., *Flight from Justice* (feature), Don Kent, 1993; Co-Prod., *Meurtre en musique* (M.O.W.), Gabriel Pelletier, 1993; Prod., *Crosswinds* (MOW), Allan A. Goldstein, 1993; Exec. Prod./Prod., *Tales of the Wild* (six M.O.W.), Co-Prod. with Gaumont Television & Ellipse Programme, Dir. Gilles Carle, René Manzor, Arnaud Sélignac, 1994; *The Adventures of Smoke Belliou* (4 MOW), Co-Prod. with Ellipse Programme & Gaumont Television, Dir. Marc Simenon, 1995.

Herzog, Leona M., B.F.A. $

Manager, Residential/Small Commercial Markets, **CENTRA GAS MANITOBA INC.**, 444 St. Mary Ave., Winnipeg, MB R3C 3T7 (204) 925-0658, FAX 925-0630. Born Whitemouth, Man. 1952. s. 1 ch. Alexandra N. Herzog. **EDUC:** Univ. of Manitoba, B.F.A.(Ceramics/Printmaking) 1975, Certificate (Teaching) 1976, Certificate (Mgmt Dev. for Women) 1994. **CAREER:** Leisure Div. Mgr, The Real Canadian Superstore, Winnipeg, 1983-88; Consumer Mktg Mgr, Fin. Svcs Div., Comcheq Services Ltd., 1988-90; Mgr, Residential/Small Commercial Mkts, Centra Gas Manitoba Inc., 1990 to date. **AFFIL:** Canadian Gas Association (Chair, Residential Sub-Committee 1995-96); Home Expressions Mgmt Committee (mbr. 1990-92; Co-Chair 1993; Chair 1994); R2000 (Mgmt Committee); Carpathia Children's Day Care Centre (Dir. 1992-93); Winnipeg International Children's Festival (Dir. 1991-93). **INTERESTS:** quilt making as an art form (has exhibited work in US). **MISC:** Program Advisor & Mentor, Mgmt Dev. for Women Certificate Program, Univ. of Manitoba, 1994-95. **COMMENT:** *"Experienced manager with background in business environments within Canadian and international markets and within a provincially regulated industry. Academic program advisor and mentor for women with career aspirations in management. Leadership on committees and boards of directors related to industry and community events and organizations."*

Herzog, Shira, B.A.,M.A. ○
Vice-President, THE KAHANOFF FOUNDATION, Kanesco Holdings, 1235 Bay St., Ste. 500, Toronto, ON M5R 3K4 (416) 968-2109, FAX 968-0741. Born Israel 1953. d. 1 ch. **EDUC:** Hebrew Univ., B.A.(English/Hist.) 1974; York Univ., M.A.(English) 1978. **CAREER:** Dir. of Research, Canada-Israel Committee, 1978-81; Dir. of Public Affairs, 1982-84; Exec. Dir., Canada-Israel Committee, 1985-87; VP, The Kahanoff Foundation, 1988 to date. **SELECTED PUBLICATIONS:** *Canada-Israel Friendship, The First Thirty Years* (1978). **DIRECTOR:** The Kahanoff Foundation. **AFFIL:** Canadian Centre for Philanthropy (Dir.); Mount Sinai Hospital (Dir.); United Way of Greater Toronto (Dir.); York Univ. (Advisory Bd., Voluntary Sector Mgmt Program, Fac. of Administrative Studies); Canadian Women's Foundation (Advisory Bd.); Canadian Civil Liberties Association (Dir.); Canada-Israel Foundation for Academic Exchange (Dir.); Public Policy Forum (Dir.); Calmeadow Foundation (Dir.). **INTERESTS:** literature; politics; reading. **COMMENT:** *"I play a key role on a small executive team that has encouraged the role of 'venture philanthropist' for the Kahanoff Foundation. I believe that philanthropy is essential in a civil society and that foundations occupy a unique position at the crossroads of government, business and the community in strengthening the infrastructure of philanthropy."*

Hetherington, Linda ⊗
Artist. R.R. 2, 2078 Sunbury Rd., Inverary, ON K0H 1X0 (613) 353-6106. Born Lunenburg, N.S. 1945. m. Brian Hetherington. 2 ch.

EDUC: St. Lawrence Coll., Fine Arts Degree 1989. **CAREER:** professional artist, 1970 to date. **SELECTED PUBLICATIONS:** Magazine cover for *Enoteca* wine & food magazine. **EXHIBITIONS:** O'Keefe Centre; Evergreen Juried Art Exhibition; Rideau Valley Art Festival, Westport, Ont.; Buckhorn Wildlife Art Festival; Cobourg Cultural Celebration; Alumni Invitational Exhibition, St. Lawrence Coll.; Kingston Reg'l Arts Council Group Salon; Art Mode Gallery (1994); *Portraits of Nature*, Ottawa (1994); Lambeth Art Festival; *Affair With The Arts*, Kingston; solo exhibition, Libbey's of Toronto Gallery (1996). **COLLECTIONS:** Thorn; Ernst & Whinney; Beatrice Foods Inc.; Taylor Chev Olds Cadillac Ltd.; International Grocers Ltd.; DuPont Canada Art Collection; Connor Clark Investment Inc.; McCormick and Zock Inc.; Mitel Corporation; Dr. James Tripp; Midland Walwyn; Jet Form Corporation. **AFFIL:** Kingston Reg'l Arts Council. **HONS:** Gov. General's Award for Academic Achievement, 1990. **INTERESTS:** gardening; curling; quilting. **MISC:** galleries: Agnes Etherington Gallery, Kingston, Ont.; Gallery on the Lake, Buckhorn, Ont.; Libbey's of Toronto; Art Mode Gallery, Ottawa. **COMMENT:** *"In 1970 I began as a self-taught artist. With determination and study, my work progressed and is now represented in galleries and is in many private and corporate collections."*

Hewgill, Jody ⊗
Illustrator, JODY HEWGILL ILLUSTRATIONS, 260 Brunswick Ave., Toronto, ON M5S 2M7 (416) 924-4200. Born Brampton, Ont. 1961. **EDUC:** Ontario Coll. of Art, Comm. & Design 1984. **CAREER:** freelance illustrator, 1986 to date. **SELECTED PUBLICATIONS:** illustrations in numerous magazines & books published in Canada & the US. **HONS:** Communication Arts Award; Applied Arts Award; Canadian Business Press Award; Studio Magazine Awards; American Illustration; Communications Arts; The Society of Illustrators; The Advertising and Design Club of Canada. **INTERESTS:** cycling; alpine skiing; hiking; canoeing. **MISC:** illustrated the tribute to the nat'l anthem for the program of the opening ceremony of the Atlanta Olympic Games, the sole non-American contributor in the program. **COMMENT:** *"I have been working as a professional illustrator since 1986. Primarily interested in pursuing magazine and book illustration, as an expression of working with the written word, capturing the essence of a novel. I also have an expanding list of corporate clients, working with visuals in forms of annual reports, capabilities brochures, advertising, software/hardware packaging and interior murals."*

Hewitt, Jean D. (née Townsend), B.A., M.Ed.,Ed.D. ■■ 🎓

Founder, THE LEARNING CONNECTION, 23950 Fairview Rd., Thorndale, ON N0M 2P0, FAX (519) 461-0380. Born London, UK 1940. m. William Taylor. 2 ch., 3 stepch. Jonathan, James, Jeremy, Jon, Lisa. **EDUC:** Univ. of Western Ontario, B.A.(Psych.) 1967; Wayne State Univ., Detroit, M.Ed.(Applied Psych.) 1971; Ontario Institute for Studies in Education, Univ. of Toronto, Ed.D.(Phil.) 1981; Ministry of Educ., Ont., Supervisory Officer's Certification 1979; numerous other certificates/ diplomas in educ. **CAREER:** Teacher, England & Canada, 1960-74; Instructor, Fac. of Educ., Univ. of Western Ontario, 1975-76; Teacher, Special Educ. Intermed. Behavioural Classes, Lorne Avenue Public Sch., City of London, 1976-79; V-Principal, Sherwood Forest Public Sch., 1979-82; V-Principal, Lester B. Pearson Sr. Public Sch., 1982-83; Principal, 1983-86; Principal, Byron Northview Public Sch., 1986-88; self-funded leave, osbervations in sch. systems in many parts of the world, 1988-89; Superintendent of Schools, Bd. of Educ. of London, 1989-96; Sr. Proj. Officer–Violence-Free Schools, Ministry of Educ. & Training, Ont., 1994-96. **SELECTED CREDITS:** developed a number of training video-packs incl. "The Teacher of Tomorrow." **SELECTED PUBLICATIONS:** *Playing Fair: A Guide to the Management of Student Conduct* (1992); *Teaching Teenagers: Making Connections in the Transition Years* (1994); *The Crisis in Educational Leadership* (in progress, to be published 1997); numerous journal articles. **AFFIL:** Univ. of Western Ontario (Bd. of Gov. & Senate 1990-98); Lawson Museum of Archaeology (Bd. of Dir. 1992-98); St. Joseph's Hospital (Advisory Bd. 1992-96); Vanier Institute for Child & Adolescent Development (Bd. of Dir. 1992-98); Orchestra London (Bd. of Dir. 1980-88). **HONS:** Fred Bartlett Award, Ontario Public School Trustees, 1978; Woman of Distinction, City of London, YWCA, 1984; Florence Henderson Award, London Women Teachers' Association, 1988. **INTERESTS:** travel; writing; opera; gardening; committed to provision of increased opportunities for girls & women in every sphere of Cdn life. **MISC:** in progress, the dev. of a prov. leadership course for women educators; workshops & keynote addresses, 15 yrs.; extensive work with educators in Man., N.B., P.E.I., N.S. & Ont. **COMMENT:** *"I have been working in education for the past 37 years. In my capacity as a teacher and a school administrator, I have fought for educational change. I have a strong belief that human institutions exist to serve the needs of all people and that this value must always be reflected in their daily functioning. In my professional life, such a position has frequently led me into conflict and controversy. I have consistently challenged the dehumanizing and authoritarian tendencies found within large bureaucracies, the physical punishment of children, the stereotyping of females and minority groups, and the systemic misuse of power. I have worked hard to maintain the integrity of teaching as a profession. There have been times when I have felt isolated because of my refusal to compromise on value issues, or to allow myself to be seduced by the rewards of conformity. The support of family, friends and students, and my love of the vocation I am in, have always supported and energized me."*

Hickey, Bonnie, M.P. 🍁

Member of Parliament (St. John's East), GOVERNMENT OF CANADA, House of Commons, West Block, Rm. 491, Ottawa, ON K1A 0A6 (613) 995-3013, FAX 992-2178. Born St. John's. m. Gerry Hickey. 2 ch. **EDUC:** Our Lady of Mercy Coll. **CAREER:** M.P., St. John's E., Gov't of Canada, 1993 to date; past mbr., Standing Committeeon Nat'l Defence & Natural Resources; sat on fed. Hum. Res. Development's Task Force on Youth; sits on Standing Committee on Health; Chair, Nat'l Liberal Atlantic Caucus. **AFFIL:** Prov. Liberal Women's Commission; Liberal Party Exec.; St. Thomas of Villa Nova Parents' & Teachers' Association (Past Pres. & VP); Learning Disabilities Association of Newfoundland & Labrador (former volunteer). **MISC:** as a long-standing volunteer with the Liberal Party, she helped establish the Helena Squires Fund, which encourages women to seek election to the Nfld. House of Assembly.

Hill, Andrea ⊛ ✏ ⚖

Production Manager, *CANADIAN LAWYER*, 240 Edward St., Aurora, ON L4G 3S9 (905) 841-6480, FAX 841-5078. Born Belfast, Northern Ireland 1965. s. **EDUC:** Seneca Coll., Tourism Industry Admin. Diploma 1987; Int'l Bus. Educ. Centre, Basic Print Production Certificate 1988; Humber Coll., Advtg & Graphic Design Certificate Program 1990. **CAREER:** Asst. Coord., RMD Repro Images, 1987; Asst. Production Coord., Marovino and Associates (The Gill Promotion Company), 1988-89; Asst. Production Mgr, Camar Publications Ltd., 1989-91; freelance production, 1991; Production Mgr/Circulation Mgr, *Canadian Lawyer* Magazine Ltd., 1992 to date.

Hill, Bonny, B.Sc.,M.Sc. ■ $

Environmental Assessment and Mediation Consultant. 4043 Mars Place, Port Coquitlam, BC

V3B 6B9 (604) 942-5453. Born Winnipeg
1953. m. Ed. 2 ch. David, Lauren. EDUC:
Univ. of Manitoba, B.Sc. 1974; Memorial Univ.
of Newfoundland, M.Sc. 1984, Marine Archaeology Certificate 1980. CAREER: technician,
Dept. of Zoology, Univ. of Manitoba, 1973-
74; technician, Man. Dept. of Renewable
Resources & Environment, 1974-78; biologist,
Northland Associates Ltd. & Atlantic Biological Services Ltd., 1979-81; consultant, Nfld.
Dept. of Culture, Recreation & Youth, 1981-
84; consultant on public attitudes toward the
environment & resources, & environmental
impact assessment, 1982 to date; Nfld. Mbr.,
Fed. Environmental Assessment Review Office
(FEARO) Secretariat, 1985-86; Mgr of Public
Consultation & Analyst, various projects in
Nfld., 1987-90; Environmental Biologist, Envi-
ronmental Assessment Div., Dept. of Environ-
ment & Lands, 1990-94. SELECTED PUBLI-
CATIONS: "Encouraging Young Women into
Science and Engineering from Summer Jobs to
Career Choices–a Program Evaluation," in
*Contributions to the 6th International GASAT
Conference* Vol.II: Beyond Schooling (1991);
"Newfoundland/Labradorian Attitudes Toward
Wildlife and Environmental Issues" (*Canadian
Psychology Conference* 26(29) 1985); various
conference presentations & publications.
AFFIL: Human Dimensions in Wildlife Study
Group; International Association of Impact
Assessment; Canadian Society of Environmen-
tal Biologists; Women in Science & Engineering
(WISE); Home Emergency Response Organiza-
tion System (HEROS) (Area Rep.); B.C. Marine
Oil Spill Workforce.

Hill, Kathleen Louisa ■ ⊗ 🕮
Writer. c/o Victoria Hall Retirement Home,
Halifax, NS B3K 3B9. Born Halifax 1917. s.
EDUC: Halifax Academy Secretarial Sch.
CAREER: various secretarial & court reporting
jobs; freelance writer, 1935 to date. SELECTED
PUBLICATIONS: published in various newspa-
pers, magazines & anthologies; 5 books; scripts
for CBC Radio & TV productions. AFFIL:
Writers' Federation of N.S.; Authors' Guild;
Canadian Authors' Association; ACTRA.
HONS: various, incl. Vicky Metcalf Award;
Best Book of the Year for Children, Canadian
Library Association; Evelyn Richardson Award.
INTERESTS: oil painting; writing friends.
MISC: featured in *Scotia Storytellers* by Rose-
mary Bauchma. COMMENT: *"I'm 79 years
old, not writing much but doing some oil paint-
ing and enjoying life and the company of good
friends."*

Hill, M. Elizabeth, B.A.,B.A.A. ■ 🗋 ☺
Owner, M.E.H. PUBLISHING SERVICES, 28

Vradenberg Dr., Scarborough, ON M1T 1M6
(416) 497-6090, FAX 497-8890. Vice-Presi-
dent, East, TRANSPORT 2000 CANADA. Born
North Bay, Ont. 1940. m. Kenneth C. Hill. 3
stepch. EDUC: Ryerson Polytechnical Institute,
Dipl. (Radio & TV Arts) 1963, B.A.A.(Radio
& TV Arts) 1973; York Univ., B.A.(Hons.,
English) 1973, Certificate (Voluntary Sector &
Arts Mgmt) 1989. CAREER: Magazine Ed. &
Publishing Admin., Girl Guides of Canada,
Nat'l Council, 1971-89; Print Production
Coord., Scholastic Canada Limited, 1989-94;
owner, M.E.H. Publishing Services, 1995 to
date. VOLUNTEER CAREER: Girl Guides of
Canada (fundraising 1989-94; Nat'l Fundrais-
ing Committee); Kawagama Lake Cottagers'
Association (Treas. 1987-89); Ryerson Radio
& TV Arts Alumnae Association (Founding
Mbr. 1988-93); Transport 2000 Ontario (VP
1992-93; Pres. 1993-95). INTERESTS: reading;
photography; antique collecting; gardening;
environmental concerns; transportation concerns. MISC: interest in transportation, & rail
in particular, stems from having been born in
N. Ont., having lived on a school car (school-
on-wheels) for 1st 5 yrs. & having come from a
"railroad family." COMMENT: *"I have found
great satisfaction in the voluntary sector, either
as staff or as a volunteer. I believe in shared
leadership that results in more efficient and
empowered board members."*

**Hill, Marguerite F., C.M.,B.A.,M.A.,
M.D.,F.R.C.P.** 🕮 ⊕
Professor Emeritus, Faculty of Medicine, UNI-
VERSITY OF TORONTO, Toronto, ON M5S 1A1.
Born Toronto. s. EDUC: Univ. of Toronto,
B.A.(Psych.) 1940, M.A.(Psych.) 1941, M.D.
1952; FRCP (Internal Medicine) 1957.
CAREER: Capt., Personnel Selection, Canadian
Women's Army Corps, 1942-46; Staff Physi-
cian, Women's College Hospital, 1957-89;
Physician-in-Chief, 1968-84; Assoc Prof., Fac.
of Medicine, Univ. of Toronto, 1957-68; Full
Prof., 1968-84; Prof. Emeritus, 1984 to date.
DIRECTOR: Canadian Imperial Bank of Com-
merce (Dir. Emeritus). AFFIL: Ontario Medical
Society; American Coll. of Physicians; Royal
Coll. of Physicians & Surgeons of Canada (Fel-
low); Women's College Hospital, Toronto
(Trustee); Royal Canadian Institute (Council-
lor 1988-92); A.O.A. Honour Medical Society;
Ontario Art Gallery (Life Mbr.); Royal Ontario
Museum (Life Mbr.); Toronto Metropolitan
Zoo (Life Mbr.); Canadian Nature Federation;
Federation of Ontario Naturalists; Toronto
Federation of Naturalists; Kappa Kappa
Gamma Alumnae. HONS: LL.D. (Hon.),
Queen's Univ.,1984; Member of the Order of
Canada, 1994. INTERESTS: gardening; bird-

ing; snorkelling; reading; travelling. **COMMENT:** *"I have been primarily interested in the provision of good patient care, and teaching in medicine, plus support of Women's College Hospital."*

Hinton, Louisette ✊ 🍁 🎓 ☝
International Representative and Chairperson, Women's Advisory Committee, UNITED FOOD AND COMMERCIAL WORKERS INTERNATIONAL UNION (UFCW), 61 International Blvd., Ste. 300, Rexdale, ON M9W 6K4 (416) 675-1104, FAX 675-6919. **EDUC:** Univ. du Québec à Montréal, Technician (Genius Industriel); Univ. du Québec, Certificate (Admin. & Labour Rel'ns). **CAREER:** Air Force, 1959-61; mbr, UFCW, 1967; responsible for Women's Affairs, Que. Prov. Council, UFCE, 1983; Exec. Sec., 1984; elected & re-elected VP, Canadian Labour Congress (CLC), 1984 to date; Int'l Rep. & Coord. of Women's Issues, Nat'l Office, UFCW, 1992; Exec. VP, CLC, current; Pres.,NDP Fed.Section (Que.), current; VP, NDP Exec. Bd., Canada, current. **MISC:** 1st woman to be appointed Exec. Sec. of the Quebec Provincial Council of the UFCW. **COMMENT:** *"Louisette has participated on numerous working committees with the CLC–as well as the Ontario and Quebec Federations of Labour–that include women's and human rights issues, political action, pay and employment equity, balancing work and family, and pension and other legislative reforms. She understands both the moral and economic need of fighting for the rights of workers around the world and has been an active participant in international demonstrations, delegations and conferences in numerous countries."*

Hinz, Evelyn J., B.A.,M.A., Ph.D. ■■ 📜 📖 🎓
Distinguished Professor of English, UNIVERSITY OF MANITOBA, 208 Tier Building, Winnipeg, MB R3T 2N2 (204) 474-8597, FAX 261-9086. Born Humboldt, Sask. 1938. m. John J. Teunissen. **EDUC:** Univ. of Saskatchewan, B.A.(cum laude) 1961, High Hons. 1966, M.A. 1967; Univ. of Massachusetts, Ph.D. 1973. **CAREER:** Social Worker, Gov't of Sask., 1961-63; Writer-Producer, CFQC-TV, Saskatoon, 1963-65; Instructor, Univ. of Saskatchewan, 1966-68; Prof. of English, Univ. of Manitoba, 1972 to date. **SELECTED PUBLICATIONS:** author, *The Mirror and the Garden: Realism and Reality in the Writings of Anais Nin* (1971, rpt, enlarged 1973); over 90 critical articles & reviews in leading scholarly journals & books; Ed./co-ed., numerous publications incl.: *A Woman Speaks: The Lectures, Seminars, and Interviews of Anais Nin* (1975, 1978, 1979, US, Brit., German & French eds.; forthcoming in Penguin World Classics); *Death and Dying* (1982); *Henry Miller's World of Lawrence: A Passionate Appreciation* (US, British eds., 1980, 1985); *Idols of Otherness: The Rhetoric and Reality of Multiculturalism* (1996). **EDIT:** co-editor, *The Canadian Review of American Studies*, 1977-79; editor, *MOSAIC*, 1979 to date; mbr., Edit. Bd., *English Studies in Canada*, 1991 to date. **AFFIL:** Modern Language Association of America (Delegate Assembly 1989-91); Association of Canadian University Teachers of English; Humanities Association of Canada; Conference of Editors of Learned Journals (Pres. 1988-90). **HONS:** Authorized Biographer of Anais Nin & Second Literary Executor, Anais Nin Estate, 1977 to date; Gov. Gen.'s Medal for Academic Proficiency, 1957; Killam Post Doctoral Research Fellow, 1973-75; William Riley Parker Prize for outstanding essay publ. in PMLA, 1977; RH Institute Award for Interdisciplinary Scholarship, 1979; featured in "First & Best," Univ. of Saskatchewan promotion, 1993; Distinguished Univ. Prof., 1993. **INTERESTS:** painting; design; sewing; creative writing. **COMMENT:** *"My major endeavour is to explore and promote a holistic or interdisciplinary/interarts approach to life and learning, and here the international success of* MOSAIC *as a scholarly journal is my primary achievement."*

Hirji-Nowaczynski, Zabeen, M.B.A., F.I.C.B. $
Regional Manager, Central Card Centre, ROYAL BANK OF CANADA, 320 Front St. W., Toronto, ON M5V 3C8 (416) 974-5457, FAX 974-5393. Born Tanzania 1960. m. Mark Nowaczynski. 2 ch. Adam, Aliya. **EDUC:** Simon Fraser Univ., M.B.A.(Exec. Program) 1994. **CAREER:** numerous positions, Royal Bank of Canada, 1977-88; Mgr, Customer Svc., 1988; Mgr, B.C. Oper. Centre, 1988-90; Mgr, Oper. Ont. Processing Centre, 1992-93; Mgr, Organization & Planning, Oper., 1993-94; Reg'l Mgr, Central Card Centre, 1994 to date. **AFFIL:** Institute of Canadian Bankers (Fellow). **INTERESTS:** classical music; gardening. **COMMENT:** *"Began working at Royal Bank at the age of 17 as a teller. Have worked in Retail Banking, Processing Operations, Head Office roles and Card Services. Completed all my education as a part-time student while working full time."*

Hirou, Catherine, B.Eng. ■ ⚛ $
Transportation Advisor, Ministère de la Métropole, GOVERNMENT OF QUEBEC, Tour de la Place Victoria, C.P. 83, Montréal, QC H4Z 1B7 (514) 864-2570, FAX 864-4080. Born

Montreal 1960. d. 2 ch. Colin, Cédric. **EDUC:** École Polytechnique, B.Eng.(Civil Eng.) 1981. **CAREER:** Auxiliary Prof., McGill Univ., 1989 to date; Sr. Dev. Officer, Transport Canada; Transportation Advisor for City Council, City of Montreal, 1991-92; Dir.-Gen., Association québécoise du transport et des routes, 1992-96; Owner, franchise flower shop, 1993-96; Transportation Advisor, Min. de la Métropole, 1996 to date. **AFFIL:** Association Québécois des Transports et des routes (direction planification des transports et Dir. d'infrastructure); Ordre des ingénieurs du Québec; Canadian Ski Patrol System (First Aid Instructor); AIPCR Quebec (Dir. gén.). **HONS:** David Vaass Memorial Award, Organisation de la Patrouille Canadienne de Ski, 1987; Scholarship Award, Canadian Transportation Research Forum, 1989; Special Appreciation Award, Organisation de la Patrouille Canadienne de Ski, 1990. **INTERESTS:** nature; gardening; interior decoration. **MISC:** Pres., Nat'l Transportation Week, Québec, 1994, 1996; Organizing Committee Mbr., XXth World Road Congress; Prof., Transportation Eng., Kingston, Jamaica, 1992, Société canadienne de génie civil; various conferences & presentations to professional groups. **COMMENT:** *"Plan, organize, manage, travel, love and care for my children, help others and share my knowledge and experience; life is too short to waste time."*

Hislop, Barbara R., B.A. ■ ⑤ ❀

Group Vice-President, Coastal Operations, CANFOR CORPORATION, Box 49420, Bentall Post Stn., Vancouver, BC V7X 1B5 (604) 661-5234, FAX 661-5472. Born Vancouver 1954. m. John R. Hislop. 4 ch. Tyler, Kristy, Torylee, Scott. **EDUC:** Univ. of British Columbia, B.A.(Home Econ.) 1976. **CAREER:** Canfor Corporation, 1977 to date. **DIRECTOR:** Canfor Corporation; Hudson's Bay Company; Forintek Canada Corporation. **AFFIL:** York House Sch. (Bd.).

Histrop, Lindsay Ann, B.A.,LL.B., LL.M. ◁Ɪⷶ ⓐ ⭕

Partner, AIRD & BERLIS, Barristers & Solicitors, BCE Place, 181 Bay St., Ste. 1800, Box 754, Toronto, ON M5J 2T9 (416) 364-1241, FAX 364-4916. Born Toronto. m. Richard Martin. 2 ch. Lesley Caitlin, Connor Ryerson. **EDUC:** Glendon Coll., York Univ., B.A.(Hons., English Lit.) 1977; Osgoode Hall Law Sch., LL.B. 1980, LL.M.(Taxation) 1986. **BAR:** Ont., 1982. **CAREER:** freelance legal research, 1982-83; Assoc., Blaney, Pasternak, Smela & Watson, Barristers & Solicitors, 1983-84; Assoc., Borden & Elliott, 1985-88; Ptnr, Aird & Berlis, 1988 to date. **SELECTED PUBLICATIONS:**

Estate Planning Precedents, A Solicitor's Manual, co-author (Toronto: The Carswell Company Limited, 1995); "Proceedings Related to the Presumption of Death," *Estate Litigation* (Toronto: The Carswell Company Limited, 1995); "Taxation of US Resident Athletes and Artists Performing Services in Canada" (*Tax Management International Journal,* July 1987). **EDIT:** Ed. & regular contributor, *Deadbeat,* CBAO Trusts & Estates Section newsletter, 1983-88; Contributing Ed., "Personal Finance" insert, *Financial Times of Canada,* 1986; numerous presentations & lectures. **AFFIL:** County of York Law Association (Trustee); Canadian Bar Association (Ont.) (Past Chair, Trusts & Estates Section, & mbr. of Exec. 1983-92; Continuing Legal Educ. Committee 1990-94; Trust & Estates Section Committee on Paralegals; Committee on Charities; Family Law Act Committee); ALERT, Canadian Bar Association (Ont.) Legal Education & Research Trust (Dir.); North York General Hospital Foundation (Bd.; Chair, Planned Giving Advisory Council); Univ. of Toronto Planned Giving Committee (Chair, Law Sector 1990-93); Granite Club; Phi Delta Phi. **INTERESTS:** horseback riding; skiing; skating; theatre; music; literature; history. **MISC:** triple gold medallist, Canadian Figure Skating Association; gold medallist, U.S. Figure Skating Association; founder & sr. competitor, York Univ. Figure Skating Team, 1977-80; competitor in prov., nat'l & N.Am. events, 1969-74; currently involved in Masters events.

Hitchman, Carol, B.A.,LL.B. ◁Ɪⷶ

Partner, LANG MICHENER, BCE Place, 181 Bay St., Ste. 2500, Toronto, ON M5J 2T7 (416) 307-4010, FAX 365-1719. Born Toronto 1957. sep. 3 ch. Andrea, Philip, Emily. **EDUC:** Univ. of Toronto, B.A.(Hist./Econ.) 1979; Osgoode Hall Law Sch., LL.B. 1982. **BAR:** Ont., 1984. **CAREER:** Assoc., Lang Michener, 1984-89; Ptnr, 1989 to date. **SELECTED PUBLICATIONS:** "The Race to the Patent Office" (*In Brief* Fall 1990); "The Federal Court of Appeal: What's New Up There?" (*Canadian Bar Association Intellectual Property Law Update* Nov. 1992); "N.A.F.T.A.: Its Impact on the Patent Act" (*Federated Press Intellectual Property Quarterly* No. 1 1994); "The Prior Acquisition Exemption Under the Patent Act: What Does it Cover?" (*Federated Press Intellectual Property Quarterly* No. 3 1994); "Movie for Rent: The Rental Right Under the Copyright Act" (*Federated Press Intellectual Property Quarterly* Mar. 1995); "Corporate Software Management Policy," with Leonora Hoicka of IBM Canada Limited (*Federated Press Symposium,* June 1995); "To Tablet or

Not to Tablet, that is the Question" *(Federated Press Intellectual Property Quarterly*, Feb. 1996); "Software Transactions" (*Federated Press Intellectual Property Quarterly*, May 1996). **AFFIL:** Patent & Trade Mark Institute of Canada (Registered Patent & Trade Mark Agent); Law Society of Upper Canada (Intellectual Property Law Specialty Committee); International Trade Mark Association; Canadian Bar Association; Association of Intellectual Property Lawyers of America; Women's Law Association. **INTERESTS:** skating; running. **MISC:** numerous presentations given at seminars & meetings. **COMMENT:** *"I have developed an expertise in intellectual property law. I have written and spoken on intellectual property law topics. I am involved in the administration of the firm and I am on the executive of the PTIC. I also try to spend time with my three children!"*

Hobbs, Anna, B.Sc. ✏ 📖
Associate Editor, *CANADIAN LIVING* MAGAZINE, 25 Sheppard Ave. W., Ste. 100, North York, ON M2N 6S7 (416) 218-3545, FAX 733-3398. Born Montreal. m. William Hobbs. 2 ch. Susan Lynne Hobbs, Anna Margaret Hobbs. **EDUC:** McGill Univ., B.Sc.(Home Econ.) 1958. **CAREER:** teacher, 1959-66; lecturer, Univ. of Guelph, 1966-69; consultant, 1969-75; *Canadian Living*, 1975 to date. **SELECTED PUBLICATIONS:** *Glorious Christmas Crafts*, Ed.; *Canadian Living Christmas Book*, Co-Ed. **AFFIL:** Oakville Trafalgar Memorial Hospital (Gov.); Royal Agricultural Winter Fair (Exec.); Breakfast for Learning Foundation (Dir.); Canadian Home Economics Association; Fashion Group International.

Hochu, Carol, B.A.Sc.,M.B.A. ✊ $
President, CONFECTIONERY MANUFACTURERS ASSOCIATION OF CANADA, 885 Don Mills Rd., Ste. 301, Don Mills, ON M3C 1V4 (416) 510-8034, FAX 510-8044. Born Sault Ste. Marie, Ont. **EDUC:** Univ. of Guelph, B.A.Sc.(Consumer Studies) 1981; York Univ., M.B.A. 1990; Certified Association Exec. 1991. **CAREER:** Public Affairs Coord., Rothman, Benson and Hedges Inc., 1986-88; Pres., Confectionery Manufacturers Association of Canada, 1988 to date. **AFFIL:** Women in Food Industry Management; MBA Women's Association (Membership Committee); Canadian Society of Association Executives (Toronto Chapter Bd.); Foundation for Association Research and Education (Trustee). **INTERESTS:** tennis; golf; skiing; sailing; the arts. **COMMENT:** *"C.M.A.C. is the national trade association representing manufacturers of chocolate, candy, chewing gum and their suppliers."*

Hodgins, Kris ■■ ⚾
Paralympic Athlete. Edmonton, AB. Born 1 ch. **SPORTS CAREER:** mbr., Nat'l Track Team, 1994 to date. Paralympic Games: Bronze, discus, 1996. IPC World Athletic Championships: 1st, shotput, 2nd, discus & javelin, 1994. Windsor Classic Indoor Games: 1st, shotput, 1994. BC Games for the Disabled, 1st, discus, javelin & shotput, 1993. Nat'l Championships: 1st, discus, javelin & shotput, 1993. **MISC:** world record holder in shotput & discus.

Hodgson, Marianne, R.N.,B.N.,M.H.A., C.H.E. ✊ ⊕
Executive Director, SASKATCHEWAN REGISTERED NURSES' ASSOCIATION, 2066 Retallack St., Regina, SK S4T 7X5 (306) 757-4643, FAX 525-0849. Born Calgary 1936. m. Colin. 3 ch. **EDUC:** Winnipeg General Hospital, Diploma (Nursing) 1957; Univ. of Manitoba, B.N. 1980, M.H.A. 1985; Canadian Coll. of Health Service Executives, Certified Health Exec. 1988. **CAREER:** Gen. Staff Nurse, Winnipeg General Hospital, 1957-58; Asst. Head Nurse, 1958-59; Head Nurse, 1959-60; I.V. Therapist, 1961-67; Volunteer Sch. Nurse, 1967-75; Operating Rm. Staff Nurse, Children's Hospital National Medical Center, Washington, DC, 1975-77; Gen. Staff Nurse, Victorian Order of Nursing, 1979; Home-Care Coord., 1980; Instructor, Grace General Hospital Sch. of Nursing, 1980-81; Instructor, Ottawa Civic Hospital Sch. for Nursing Assistants, 1981-83; Summer Resident, Canadian Nurses' Association, 1984; Dir. of Nursing, Regina General Hospital, 1985-90; Exec. Dir., Saskatchewan Registered Nurses' Association, 1990 to date. **SELECTED PUBLICATIONS:** "Case Mix Management–Management Tool of the Future" (*Canadian Nurse* 81(10) 1985); "Minister Grants Approval in Principle to CNAs" (*ConceRN* 20(5) 1991); "Revitalizing SRNA's Grassroots" (*ConceRN* 20(6) 1991); "Bylaw Approval Denied Again" (*ConceRN* 20(6) 1991); "Registered Nurses: Dispelling the Myths" (*ConceRN* 21(5) 1992). **DIRECTOR:** Santa Maria Senior Citizens Home Inc. **AFFIL:** International Council of Nursing; Canadian Nurses' Association (Advisor to Bd. of Dir.); Canadian Association of Nurse Administrators; Canadian Coll. of Health Services Executives, Assiniboia Chapter; Canadian Nurses' Foundation; Canadian Association of Nurse Administrators; Saskatchewan Nurses' Foundation; Saskatchewan Health Advisory Committee on Technology (Advisory to the Min. of Health); Health Reform Advisory Committee (Advisory to the Deputy Min. of Health); Health Providers' Hum. Res. Committee (Advisory to

the Min. of Health); Advisory Committee on Home Care/Special Care Aide Program; Advanced Clinical Nursing Advisory Committee; Rotary International–Regina Chapter. HONS: Hon. Mention for Academic Performance in Diploma Program, Winnipeg General Hospital Sch. of Nursing, 1957; Esther Brina Erenberg Memorial Scholarship, Univ. of Manitoba, 1978; Nursing Educ. Alumni Award, Univ. of Manitoba, 1980; Nurses Celebrating Nurses Award, SRNA Regina Chapter, 1990. INTERESTS: summer home in Ont.; grandchildren; bridge; reading; travel. COMMENT: *"I've been able to combine a wonderful, fulfilling career in nursing with a marriage and raising three successful (now adult) children. Currently I enjoy a position in which I can influence the reform of the healthcare system in our province and nursing's role in the future."*

Hodgson, Marjorie Jane ⊗

Artist. 1 East Haven Dr., Scarborough, ON M1N 1L8 (416) 267-6749. Born Hamilton, Ont. 1932. Joshua. 3 ch. Mark Andrew, Joshua Clarke, Duncan Albert. EDUC: Hamilton Tech; studied privately in Hamilton with Hortense Gordon, ARCA, & John Sloan, ARCA; Artists' Workshop, Toronto; Ontario Coll. of Art; Doon Sch. of Fine Art. EXHIBITIONS: numerous exhibitions, incl. Nancy Poole's Studio, Toronto (1975), *Japan/Canada Watercolours*, exchange exhibition, Japan & Canada (1975-76) & Ontario House, 1986; regular exhibitor in Members' Exhibitions of Ontario Society of Artists & Canadian Society of Painters in Water Colour. COLLECTIONS: Union Gas; Molson Breweries; Henderson Hospital, Hamilton; Ellerslie Investments; Hiram Walker; Canada Permanent; The Royal Collection of Drawings & Watercolours, Windsor Castle, UK; many private collections. AFFIL: Canadian Society of Painters in Water Colour (Life mbr.); Ontario Society of Artists. HONS: Molson Purchase Award, *IMAGE/76*, 1976; Ellerslie Investments Purchase Award, *IMAGE/77*, 1977; Hiram Walker Purchase Award, *IMAGE/80*, 1980; Union Gas Purchase Award, *IMAGE/83*, 1983. INTERESTS: gardening. MISC: represented by Kingsmount Art Gallery, Toronto; listed in *International Who's Who of Women; Canadian Who's Who, International Who's Who, American Artists–An Illustrated Survey of Leading Contemporaries, International Who's Who of Professional and Business Women & International Who's Who of Contemporary Achievement.* COMMENT: *"Since I have spent my life honestly painting the Canadian landscape and urban scenes, my contribution to Canadian art is, I hope, unique."*

Hoecker-Drysdale, Susan, B.A.,M.A., Ph.D. ⊗ 🎓

Associate Professor, Sociology and Chair, Department of Sociology and Anthropology, CONCORDIA UNIVERSITY, 1455 de Maisonneuve W., Montreal, QC H3G 1M8 (514) 848-2141 or 2158, FAX 848-4548 or 4539, EMAIL hoecker@vax2.concordia.ca. Born Chicago 1936. m. John Philip Drysdale. 1 ch. David John Drysdale. EDUC: Northland Coll., B.A. 1958; Louisiana State Univ., M.A. 1961, Ph.D. 1969. CAREER: Asst. Prof., Social Sci., William Carey Coll., 1962-63; Special Lecturer, Soc., Louisiana State Univ., 1963-65; Asst. Prof., Soc., Eastern Kentucky Univ., 1965-66; Nat'l Teachers' Corps Instructor, Univ. of Kentucky, 1966-67; Asst. Prof., Home Econ. & Soc. Instructor, 1967-71; Asst. Prof., Soc., Loyola Univ. of Montreal, 1971-74; Dept. V-Chair, 1975-76; Asst. Prof., Soc., Concordia Univ., 1974-75; Assoc. Prof., 1975 to date; Chair, Dept. of Soc. & Anthropology, 1994 to date. SELECTED PUBLICATIONS: *The Sociology of Harriet Martineau*, manuscript being completed; *Harriet Martineau: First Woman Sociologist* (Oxford/New York; Berg Publishers, 1992); "Women Sociologists in Canada: The Careers of Helen MacGill Hughes, Aileen Dansken Ross and Jean Robertson Burnet," *Despite The Odds: Essays on Canadian Women and Science*, ed. Marianne G. Ainley (Montreal; Véhicle Press, 1990); "Sociologists in the Vineyard: The Careers of Everett Cherrington Hughes and Helen MacGill Hughes," *Creative Couples in The Sciences*, ed. Helena Pycior, Nancy Slack & Pnina Abir-Am (Rutgers Univ. Press, 1996); "The Enigma of Harriet Martineau's Letters on Science," *Women's Writing: The Elizabethan to Victorian Period* (vol. 2, n. 2, 1995); "On Understanding the Feminism of Harriet Martineau: How Do We Read Another's Life?" (*Le Bulletin*, Institut Simone du Beauvoir, Vol. 11, No. 1, 1991); "Toward an Understanding of Student Unrest" (*The Kentucky Alumnus Magazine*, Winter 1969-70); "Montreal Women in World War II: Their Work and Their Lives" Oral History Project, 1982-84, with K. Waters & G. Hochmann (tapes & indexes located in the National Library of Canada, & Concordia Univ.); various conference papers. AFFIL: Phi Kappa Phi (hon. scholastic fraternity); Institut Simone de Beauvoir (Fellow); Canadian Sociology & Anthropology Association; International Sociological Association; History of Science Society; Canadian Women's Studies Association; Canadian Committee on the History of Women; Midwest Victorian Studies Association; Northeast Conference of British Studies. HONS: National Science Foundation Summer Fellowship, 1962; Bobbs-Merrill Outstanding Grad. Student Award, LSU. MISC: recipient, SSHRC grants & various others. COMMENT: *"Currently I am a Department Chair and a university professor whose teaching, research and writing focuses on sociological theory, the history of sociology, and particularly the contributions of women in the development of sociology. Research on current SSHRC-funded project is The Feminist Tradition in Sociology."*

Hoegg, Lois, B.A.,LL.B. 🔳
Lawyer, CHES CROSBIE BARRISTERS, 169 Water St., 4th Fl., St. John's, NF A1C 1B1 (709) 579-4000, FAX 579-9671. Born N.S. m. Chesley Crosbie. 3 ch. EDUC: Acadia Univ., B.A.(German/Pol. Sci.) 1977; Dalhousie Univ., LL.B. 1982. BAR: Nfld., 1983. CAREER: Crown Attorney, Dept. of Justice, 1983-88; Legal Dir., Law Society of Newfoundland, 1988-92; private practice of law, Ches Crosbie Barristers, 1992 to date. AFFIL: Law Society of Newfoundland (Chair, Gender Equity Committee); Canadian Bar Association (VP, Nfld. Branch). INTERESTS: reading; travelling; family life. COMMENT: *"I spend the vast majority of my time working full time at the private practice of law and raising three children."*

Hoff, Rita, B.Comm. ■■ Ⓢ ⌂
President and Chief Executive Officer, FIRST CANADA SECURITIES CORPORATION (investment dealer), 2 First Canadian Place, The Exchange Tower, Ste. 3010, Toronto, ON M5X 1A4 (416) 365-3300, FAX 947-9490. Born Madras, India 1947. m. Eivind. 2 ch. Alexander, Sean. EDUC: Sydenham Coll., Univ. of Bombay, B.Comm.(Acctg/Econ.) 1966. CAREER: Bond Trader, Dominion Securities, 1970-76; Bond Salesperson, Mead & Co., 1976-80; VP, Bond Sales, First Canada Securities, 1980-86; Pres. & CEO, 1986 to date. DIRECTOR: C.A.A. Central Ontario; First Canada Securities Corporation; Trellcan Rubber Ltd. MISC: 1st woman bond trader in Canada; 1st woman Pres. of an invesment dealer.

Hoffmann, Ellen, M.A.,B.A. ■ 🔳 ◈
University Librarian, YORK UNIVERSITY, 4700 Keele St., North York, ON M3J 1P3 (416) 736-5601, FAX 736-5451, EMAIL hoffmann@yorku.ca. EDUC: Univ. of Wisconsin, B.A. 1965, M.A.(Library Sci.) 1966. CAREER: Asst. Librarian, Linonia & Brothers Library, Yale Univ., 1968-70; Public Svc. Librarian, Cross Campus Library, Yale Univ., 1970-71; Acting Dir. of Libraries, York Univ., 1983-84; Dir. of Libraries, 1984-90, Univ. Librarian, 1990 to date. SELECTED PUBLICATIONS:

"Complex Relationships: Libraries, Bibliographic Utilities and Automated System Vendors" (*Canadian Library Journal* Apr. 1987); "Information Technology: New Opportunities–New Problems," with Anne Woodsworth (*Journal of Library Administration* 9(2) 1988); "Management of Change," in *Library and Information Work Worldwide* 1994 (London: Bowker-Saur, 1994); various other publications. AFFIL: American Library Association; Association of Research Libraries; Canadian Association of Research Libraries; Canadian Library Association; OCLC, Research Library Advisory Committee. HONS: Vilas Fellowship 1966; Phi Beta Kappa, 1965. MISC: various conference papers.

Hoffman, Isabel 📇 🔳
President and Chief Executive Officer, I. HOFFMANN + ASSOCIATES INC. (multimedia training, consulting & production; produce interactive CD-ROMs for children), 34 Ross St., Toronto, ON M5T 1Z9 (416) 977-6732, FAX 977-0766, EMAIL hoffmann@h-plus-a.com INTERNET: http://www.h-plus-a.com or http://www.h-plus-a.com/nikolai/. Director, Information Technology Design Centre, and Associate Professor, UNIVERSITY OF TORONTO. EDUC: degrees in Math., Comp. Sci. & Educ.; Univ. of Toronto, completed most of the work required for Exec. M.B.A. CAREER: Lecturer, Dept. of Math. & Dept. of Comp. Sci., Univ. of Toronto, 5 yrs.; responsible for computer facilities for design students, Ontario Coll. of Art. AFFIL: Smart Toronto (founding mbr., Bd. of Dir.). HONS: teaching award, University Association of Part-time Undergraduate Students, Univ. of Toronto; nominated for teaching award, Ontario College & University Faculty Association; named one of Distinguished Alumni of 1995, Univ. of Toronto; named to Honour Roll, *Maclean's* magazine, 1995; Entrepreneur of the Year, Emerging Entrepreneur category, Ernst & Young, 1996. MISC: seminars, publications, presentations & committee work in design & multimedia production communities; regular appearances on *@discovery.ca.*, Discovery Channel, contributing reviews of latest CD-ROM titles.

Hoffmann, Susannah ⊗ 🔳 📇
Actor. c/o Oscars and Abrams, 59 Berkeley St., Toronto, ON M5A 2W5 (416) 860-1790. Born Montreal 1963. s. SELECTED CREDITS: *Vincent Black Shadow* (pilot), Cannell/Kim Manners; Jen Pringle, *Anne of Green Gables: The Sequel* (miniseries), Disney/Sullivan; Sheila Birling, *An Inspector Calls* (theatre), Royal Theatre/NYC; Jane Eyre, *Jane Eyre* (theatre), Young People's Theatre; Jessica, *The Merchant*

of *Venice* (theatre), Stratford; Rose, *The Shoe-maker's Holiday* (theatre), Stratford. **AFFIL:** ACTRA; Equity (Canada and US); SAG; Book Pals (reading for children). **HONS:** Tyrone Guthrie Award, Stratford Festival, 1989. **INTERESTS:** animals; gardening; art; running.

Hofstetter, Mary E., B.A., M.A. ■■ ⊗ ❦ ○
General Manager, STRATFORD FESTIVAL (performing arts, repertory theatre), 55 Queen St., P.O. Box 520, Stratford, ON N5A 6V2 (519) 271-4040, ext. 212, FAX 271-5957, EMAIL mhofstetter@stratford-festival.on.ca. Born Kitchener, Ont. m. R. David Riggs. **EDUC:** Banff Sch. of Fine Arts, Art, Theatre Arts 1966-67; Univ. of Guelph, B.A.(Hons., English, Art) 1968; Univ. of Western Ontario, M.A.(English) 1969; Univ. of Neuchâtel, French Language 1971; Sorbonne, Univ. of Paris, French Civilization 1973. **CAREER:** Teaching Fellow, Univ. of Western Ontario, 1968-69; Teacher, English, Brandwood Sch., Birmingham, UK, 1969-70; Teacher, English & Art, Neuchâtel Jr. Coll., Switzerland, 1970-72; freelance writer & student, Europe, 1972-73; Dir., Coll. & Community Rel'ns/Chair, Applied Arts/Assoc. Dir., Applied Arts & Bus., Conestoga Coll., 1973-84; VP, Academic, Mohawk Coll., 1984-88; Pres. & CEO, Sheridan Coll., 1988-96; Gen. Mgr, Stratford Festival, 1996 to date. **MEMBER:** Cdn Advisory Council, AT&T. **AFFIL:** Halton Industry Education Council (Bd. of Dir.); Living Arts Centre of Mississauga (Advisory Bd.); Canadian Clay & Glass Gallery (Bd. of Dir.); Round Table on Culture in the Toronto Region; Council of Ontario College Presidents (Past Chair); Canadian Bureau for International Education (Past Chair, Bd. of Dir.). **HONS:** Special Envoy for the Prov. of Ont.; various academic hons. incl.: Univ. Fac./Bd. Scholarship; Ont. Grad. Fellowship; Univ. Teaching Fellowship.

Hogan, Patricia, B.A.,L.M.S.,Ph.D. ⊗ 🕮
Professor of History, ST. FRANCIS XAVIER UNIVERSITY, Box 5000, Antigonish, NS B2G 2W5 (902) 867-3948. **EDUC:** St. Francis Xavier Univ., B.A. 1964; Pontifical Institute of Mediaeval Studies, Univ. of Toronto, L.M.S. 1967; Univ. of Toronto, Ph.D. 1971. **CAREER:** Asst. Prof., St. Francis Xavier Univ., 1970-75; Assoc. Prof., 1975-94; Prof., 1995 to date. **SELECTED PUBLICATIONS:** *Early Huntingdonshire Lay Subsidy Rolls*, with J.A. Raftis (Toronto: Pontifical Institute of Mediaeval Studies, 1976); "Medieval Villainy: A Study in the Meaning of Crime and Social Control in a Medieval Village" (*Studies in Medieval and Renaissance History*, 1987); "Clays, *Culturae* and The Cul-

tivator's Wisdom–Management Efficiency at Fourteenth-Century Wistow" (*British Agricultural History Review* 1988); "The Slight to Honor–Slander and Wrongful Prosecution in Five English Medieval Villages" (*Studies in Medieval and Renaissance History* 1991); "The Ability to Compromise–Informal Dispute Settlement in Five Medieval English Villages" (*Studies in Medieval and Renaissence History* 1995). **HONS:** Pontifical Institute of Mediaeval Studies Fellowships, 1965-67; Ont. Grad. Fellowship, 1967-69; Canada Council Doctoral Fellowship, 1969-70. **MISC:** Rhodes Scholarship Selection Committee (Maritime Reg.), 1988-93; Advisory Committee on Judicial Appointments, Prov. of N.S., 1994-96; recipient, various grants.

Hogan, Susan ■ ⊗ ❦
Actor. c/o The Characters Talent Agency, 1505 W. 2nd Ave., Vancouver, BC V6H 3Y4 (604) 733-9800. Born Toronto. m. Michael. 3 ch. Jennie Rebecca, Gabriel, Charlie. **EDUC:** Sir John A. Macdonald, 1966; National Theatre Sch., 1966-69. **SELECTED CREDITS:** Marlene, *Bordertown Cafe* (feature), Cinexus; Belinda, *White Fang* (feature), Disney/Touchstone; Kathryn, *Narrow Margin* (feature), Carolco; Marlene, *Golden Will* (M.O.W.), Carol Reynolds; Marie, *In Cold Blood* (M.O.W.), P.M.P.; Kate, *No Greater Love* (M.O.W.), N.B.C.; Claire, "Traitor," *Poltergeist* (series), Trilogy; Dr. Golding, *Outer Limits* (series), MGM/Trilogy; Esther, "Buying the Farm," *Jake and the Kid* (series), Hired Hand Prod.; series leads in: *Night Heat, Family Passions, Vanderberg, The Little Vampires, Ritters Cove*; Caroline, *True Mummy* (theatre), co-prod. with Playwrites Theatre, Vancouver Playhouse, East Cultural Centre; Regen, *King Lear* (theatre), Necessary Angel; Diane, *Escape From Happiness* (theatre), Factory Theatre. **AFFIL:** ACTRA; Equity. **HONS:** John Drainie Award. **MISC:** is a mbr. of *Sweet Lips*, an a capella singing group.

Hogarth, Marlene ◉ ✤
Immediate Past President, ONTARIO PROGRESSIVE CONSERVATIVE ASSOCIATION OF WOMEN, Thunder Bay, ON P7B 3K4 (807) 345-9181, FAX 344-5715. Born Port Arthur (Thunder Bay), Ont. 1943. m. William. 3 ch. Mary Hogarth, Christine Hogarth, William Hogarth (dec.). **EDUC:** Lakehead Teachers' Coll., Certificate 1962; Lakehead Univ., B.A.(Library Sci.) in progress. **CAREER:** teacher, Lakehead Sch. Bd., 1962-68; hotel staff/Mgr, New Ontario Hotel/Imperial Holiday Inn, 1970-75; Hotel/Restaurant Mgr, Hodder Ave. Hotel, 1980-88; teacher, Lakehead Bd. of Educ., Lake-

head District Roman Catholic Separate Sch. Bd., 1985 to date; Library Asst., Sch. of Educ., Lakehead Univ., 1988 to date; P.C. candidate, Thunder Bay Nip Redining, 1993 election; Mgr, Intercity Tan Jay Retail Store, current. **AFFIL:** Thunder Bay Historical Museum Society (Pres.; Co-Chair, Fundraising Committee, "New Museum Campaign"); St. John's Anglican Church (Pres., Anglican Church Women); Ontario P.C. Association of Women (Pres. 1989-94); Port Arthur Riding P.C. Association (Pres. 1991-93). **INTERESTS:** family & community as a whole. **COMMENT:** *"Through my active community involvement as an educator, advocate and political leader, I endeavour to support the efforts of women to challenge themselves to reach personal, professional and political goals."*

Hogg, Elspeth, B.A. ■■ ♡ ✊
Volunteer. Site 2, Box 1, R.R. #3, Utterson, ON P0B 1M0 (705) 385-2980. Born 1930. m. The Hon. Mr. Justice Stanton Hogg, Ontario Court of Justice. 3 ch. Dr. David Hogg, John Hogg, Andrew Hogg. **EDUC:** Univ. of Toronto, B.A. 1951. **CAREER:** Personal Loans & Mortgage Officer, CIBC, 1977-78; Reg'l Community Mbr., National Parole Bd., 1978-80; Ont. Ministry of Community & Social Svcs, Children's Svcs Div., 1978-81. **VOLUNTEER CAREER:** Bd. mbr., Ontario Association of Corrections & Criminology, 1962-68; mbr., Nat'l Committee, Canadian Corrections Association, 1963-67; Bd. mbr. & Pres., Junior League of Toronto, 1965-71; Bd. mbr. & Pres., Ont. Div., Canadian Mental Health Association, 1968-75; Bd. mbr. & Nat'l Pres., 1973-80; Bd. mbr. & Chair, Alliance for Children-Ont., 1981-84; Bd. mbr. & Chair, Muskoka Women's Advocacy Group/Bd. mbr., Muskoka Youth Counselling Centre/Bd. mbr., Muskoka Community Svcs Advisory Group, 1984-88; Chair, East Muskoka/Parry Sound District Health Council, 1988-94. **HONS:** Queen's Silver Jubilee Medal from Gov.-Gen. for exemplary community svc., 1977; Lifestyle Award, presented by Min. of Nat'l Health & Welfare, Ottawa, 1983; Canada Volunteer Award Medal, presented by Min. of Health, Ottawa, 1995.

Hohol, Linda $
Senior Vice-President, Personal and Commercial Banking, Alberta and Northwest Territories, **CIBC**, Bankers Hall, 855 - 2nd St. S.W., 11th Fl., Calgary, AB T2P 2P2 (403) 221-5800, FAX 221-5898. Born Nigeria 1952. m. Milt Hohol. 2 ch. **EDUC:** Institute of Canadian Bankers, Fellowship 1980; Kellogg Sch., Chicago, Exec. Dev. 1987; Int'l Banking Sch., Japan, Summer 1995. **CAREER:** teller, CIBC, 1972; VP, 1988; Sr. VP, 1993 to date. **AFFIL:** Glenbow-Alberta Institute (Bd. of Gov.); Calgary Opera (Dir.); Alberta Coll. of Physicians & Surgeons (Public Mbr., Council); Fac. of Mgmt, Univ. of Calgary (Advisory Council); Calgary United Way (Bd.); Calgary Economic Development Authority (Pres.'s Council); Calgary Chamber of Commerce (Bd. 1991-92); SAIT, Business Technology Centre (Leader of Fundraising Team); Rotary Club of Calgary; Petroleum Club of Calgary; Professional Club of Calgary; Canyon Meadows Golf Club; Pinebrook Golf Club. **HONS:** Woman of Distinction Award, Calgary YWCA, 1993. **INTERESTS:** golf; skiing; jogging; reading; travel. **COMMENT:** *"Strong advocate for women's issues. One of the first female executives at CIBC, a founder of a committee on women's issues that recommended changes to policy and practices at CIBC that had a profound and positive impact on the female employee population. Currently involved in a number of initiatives regarding aboriginals. Also a very committed and involved citizen of the Calgary community."*

Holberton, Pam, R.N.,B.Sc.,M.N. ■ ⊕
Clinical Nurse Specialist, Trauma Services, **CALGARY REGIONAL HEALTH AUTHORITY**, 841 Centre Ave. E., Calgary, AB T2E 0A1 (403) 268-9543, FAX 268-9515. Born Edmonton 1955 1 ch. **EDUC:** Royal Alexandra Sch. of Nursing, Diploma (Nursing) 1976; Univ. of Alberta, B.Sc. 1979; Univ. of Calgary, Masters of Nursing 1990. **CAREER:** Staff Nurse/Instructor, Intensive Care, Foothills Hospital, 1980-86; Asst. Nursing Unit Dir., Rockyview Intensive Care, 1986-90; Nurse Educator, Critical Care, Calgary District Hospital Group, 1990-92; Clinical Nurse Specialist, Trauma Svcs, & Reg'l Trauma Svcs Coord., Calgary General Hospital, 1992 to date. **AFFIL:** Emergency Nurses' Interest Group; Canadian Association of Critical Care Nurses; Society of Trauma Nurses; Alberta Association of Registered Nurses (Ward V Rep. 1980-82; District Info. Officer 1982; Prov. Council Rep. 1983-85; numerous ad hoc committees); Canadian Nurses' Association (Voting Delegate to Biennium 1982, 1984; Nursing Practice Conference, Planning Committee 1989; Alta. Rep. for Special Committee on Clinical Practice Issues 1993-95); Canadian Nurses' Foundation; Calgary Injury Prevention Coalition (Steering Committee). **HONS:** Scholarship, Royal Alexandra Hospital, 1977; Barry Vogel Award, Alberta Association of Registered Nurses, 1985; Betty Sellers Memorial Scholarship, Alberta Registered Nurses' Educ. Trust, 1989. **MISC:** numerous speaking engagements & presentations.

Holbrook, Elizabeth Bradford, C.M., R.C.A.,S.S.C.,O.S.A.,A.O.C.A., N.S.S. of N.Y. ⊛
Sculptor, Medallist, Designer. R.R. 3, 1177 Mineral Springs Rd., Dundas, ON L9H 5E3 (905) 648-3003. Born Hamilton, Ont. 1913. m. John Grant Holbrook, D.D.S. 3 ch. (1 dec.). Dr. J. David Holbrook, Jane E. Holbrook, Wm. H. Holbrook (dec.). EDUC: Hamilton Art & Tech. Sch., Art 1931; Ontario Coll. of Art, Assoc.(Sculpture) 1935; Royal Coll. of Art, London, UK, post grad. 1936; asst. to Carl Milles, sculptor, Cranbrook Academy of Arts, Bloomfield, Mich., 1948. CAREER: professional artist, sculptor, lecturer & teacher; disciplines include sculpture, relief, medals, monumental, liturgical, architectural, portraiture; works in bronze, wood, stone. COMMISSIONS: oak memorial altar, St. John's Church, Ancaster, Ont.; reredos panel, St. Mark's Anglican Church, Kitsilano, B.C.; architectural panels, stone, Fed. Bldg, Hamilton, Ont.; Royal Botanical Gardens sculpture, stone; Merriman Memorial; trophies for horse & sheep shows, Royal Agricultural Winter Fair, Toronto; numerous other works. EXHIBITIONS: numerous group & solo exhibitions; principal exhibitions include Art Gallery of Hamilton (1974), solo, McMaster Univ. Art Gallery (1989) & First Canadian Place Gallery, Toronto (1994). COLLECTIONS: National Gallery of Canada; National Portrait Gallery, Washington, DC; Art Gallery of Ontario; Art Gallery of Hamilton; London Regional Art Gallery, London, Ont.; Windsor Art Gallery; various other public collections; numerous works in private collections. AFFIL: Royal Canadian Academy of Arts; Ontario Society of Artists; Sculptors' Society of Canada; National Sculpture Society, N.Y.C.; Federation of International Medallists. HONS: Lt. Governor's Silver Medal, Ontario Coll. of Art, 1935; Gold Medal for Portraiture, National Sculpture Society of N.Y., 1969; Woman of the Year in Arts, City of Hamilton, 1987; Hamilton Gallery of Distinction, in Arts, 1994; Member, Order of Canada, 1995; Fellow, Ontario Coll. of Art, 1996. INTERESTS: equestrian; horse & pony breeding. MISC: listed in *Canadian Who's Who*, *Who's Who in America* (1980); *World Who's Who of Women* (1984) & *Climbing the Cold White Peaks*, by Stuart MacCuaig; Past Pres., Canadian Sport Horse Association; CHSA Judge. COMMENT: *"I am mainly a portrait sculptor having distinguished myself by creating portraits of such persons as Sir Winston Churchill, the Hon. Ellen Fairclough and the Hon. John D. Diefenbaker. I also carve wood and stone for liturgical, architectural and memorial pieces. My latest work is a monumental (6' 5") standing bronze figure of George Bernard Shaw for Niagara on the Lake, installed June 23, 1996."*

Holder, Rubi, M.T.I.,P.Mgr. ■ $
Business Development Representative, CO-OPERATIVE TRUST COMPANY OF CANADA, 10040 - 108th St., Edmonton, AB T5J 1K6 (403) 428-8488, FAX 424-7982. m. 2 ch. Michael, Christina. EDUC: Canadian Securities Course 1984; Trust Companies Institute, Mutual Funds (Hons.) 1990; Mutual Funds Compliance Officer Exam; Canadian Institute of Management, Certified in Mgmt designation; started Chartered Fin. Planner courses. CAREER: trust admin. positions, Canada Permanent Trust Company, 1976-82; acctg swing position, G.M.A.C., 1982-83; various temporary positions, Northwest Trust Company, 1983; Sr. Trust Statement Clerk, Canada Permanent Trust Company, 1983-84; R.R.S.P. Officer/Estate & Trust Administrator, National Trust Company, 1984-88; Accts Payable Supervisor, Pioneer Property Management, 1988; Dept. Mgr to Bd., Co-operative Trust Company of Canada, 1988 to date; Commissioner of Oaths for Alberta, 1991; Owner/Operator, sewing & designing business. AFFIL: Trust Companies Institute (Specialist, Fin. Svcs); Co-op Council of Edmonton (Past Chair; Co-op Week Coord. 1991-95); Canadian Institute of Management (Past Pres., Edmonton Branch); Trust Companies Association of Edmonton (Past Pres.). COMMENT: *"Happily married for the last 20 years, have two teenage children (one of each) and have started a small sewing/designing business from my home."*

Holland, Jane C., B.A. $ 📺
President, LEWIS CARROLL COMMUNICATIONS INC., 68 Scollard St., Toronto, ON M5R 1G2. Born Solihull, UK 1952. m. Clarence Poirier. 2 ch. EDUC: Sorbonne, France, Diploma in French Lit. 1972; Univ. of Bristol, UK, B.A. (French) 1973; Univ. of Birmingham, UK, Teacher's Certificate 1974; Harvard Univ., Diploma in Arts Admin. 1977. CAREER: publicity, Drama Dept., Univ. of Birmingham & BBC Radio, 1974-75; publicist, fundraiser & administrator, various theatre companies, Toronto, 1976-79; Promo. Mgr, Village by the Grange, Toronto, 1980; Public Rel'ns Dir., Ayliffe & Elias Advertising, Toronto, 1981; Pres., Lewis Carroll Public Relations, 1982-88; Pres., Lewis Carroll Communications Inc., 1988 to date. SELECTED PUBLICATIONS: writer of "Retirement Report," *Homes* Magazine. AFFIL: Juvenile Diabetes Foundation (Publicity Co-Chair 1984-86). HONS: First Runner-Up, William J. Wylie Award for Arts Administrators, Ontario Arts Council, 1976;

recipient, Wintario Grant to attend Harvard, 1976. **COMMENT:** *"With almost 20 years of hands-on experience in her field, Jane is an exceptionally energetic, independent business woman, whose approach marries the fresh enthusiasm of a 20-year old with the wisdom of her chronological age."*

Holland, Marie, B.Comm.,C.A. ■ Ⓢ
Partner, KPMG, Commerce Court W., Ste. 3300, Box 31, Stn. Commerce Crt., Toronto, ON M5L 1B2 (416) 777-8836, FAX 777-8818. Born Stratford, Ont. 1959. m. Edward Quan. 2 ch. **EDUC:** Univ. of Ottawa, B.Comm. 1982; C.A. **CAREER:** Acctnt, KPMG , 1982. **AFFIL:** Institute of Chartered Accountants of Ontario.

Hollingsworth, Margaret, A.L.A.,B.A., M.F.A 🎨 📖 📚
Associate Professor, Department of Writing, Faculty of Fine Arts, UNIVERSITY OF VICTORIA, Box 1700, Victoria, BC V8W 2Y2 (604) 721-7309. Born Sheffield, UK. **EDUC:** Loughborough Univ., UK, A.L.A.(Library Sci.); Lakehead Univ., B.A. 1971; Univ. of British Columbia, M.F.A.(Theatre & Creative Writing) 1974. **CAREER:** Ed., Sampson Low and Marston, publishers, Bucks, UK, 1962-63; freelance journalist & foreign correspondent, 1966-90; B.C. Ed., *Drama in Focus*, 1980-81; Asst. Prof., Creative Writing, Univ. of Victoria at David Thompson Univ., Nelson, B.C., 1981-83; Writer-in-Residence, Concordia Univ., 1985-86; Lecturer, Playwriting, Concordia Univ., 1986; Writer-in-Residence, Stratford Festival Theatre, 1987; founded Act One Press, 1988; Writer-in-Residence, Univ. of Western Ontario, 1989-90; Asst. Prof., Creative Writing, Univ. of Victoria, 1992-94; Assoc. Prof., 1994 to date. **SELECTED CREDITS:** acting, stage mng, directing & dramaturgy at numerous theatres in London (UK), B.C. & Ont.; author, *Numbrains*, Vancouver Fringe Festival, 1993; author, *The House That Jack Built*, Portland State Univ., 1993; author, *Ring of Fire*, Theatre Terrific, 1995; author, *In Confidence*, Firehall Theatre, Vancouver, 1994; author, *Alli Alli Oh*, Englisches Theater, Jülich, Germany, 1995; various other stage plays; various radio plays for CBC, BBC; writer, "Scene from a Balcony," *Airwaves*, CBC-TV, 1987; writer, "The Last Demise of Julian Whittaker," *Inside Stories*, CBC-TV, 1989; writer, "Saying It," *Performance*, CBC-TV, 1995; writer, *Blowing Up Toads*, ATP Calgary, Jan. 1996; 5 feature films in various stages of production. **SELECTED PUBLICATIONS:** *Alli Alli Oh*, play (Toronto: Playwrights Co-op, 1979); *Mother Country*, play (Toronto: Playwrights' Co-op, 1980);

Operators/Bushed, play (Toronto: Playrights' Canada, 1981); *Willful Acts*, anthology of plays (Toronto: Coach House Press, 1985); *Endangered Species*, anthology of plays (Toronto: Act One Press, 1989); *Smiling Under Water*, short stories (Vancouver: Lazara Press, 1989); *In Confidence*, play (Winnipeg: Scirocco, 1994); "Why We Don't Write: Where Are Our Women Playwrights?" (*Canadian Theatre Review* Summer 1985); "Collaborations: A Woman Playwright Works with a Male Director" (*Canadian Theatre Review* Fall 1991); "Musing on the Feminist Muse" in *Language in Her Eye*, L. Scheir, E. Wachtel & S. Sheard, eds. (Toronto: Coach House Press, 1991); "A Marriage in China" in *Frictions 2* (Toronto: Second Story Press, 1993) "Eva in Arles" (*Malahat Review* Fall 1993); *Numbrains* (Reference Press, 1994); plays have appeared in various anthologies; various other publications. **AFFIL:** Writers' Union of Canada; Playwrights' Union (mbr., Nat'l Caucus); ACTRA; Library Association, UK; PEN (Mbr. at Large); Betty Lambert Society. **HONS:** Jessie Award, 1995; Chalmers Award, drama, 1985; Dora Mavor Moore Award, drama, 1986, 1987; ACTRA Award, radio drama, 1986, 1988. **MISC:** numerous lectures, readings & seminars; recipient, various grants.

Hollo, Wendy, B.A. ◐ ⓔ
Executive Director, SKILLS TRAINING AND SUPPORT SERVICES ASSOCIATION, 705 Guardian Building, 10240 - 124 St., Edmonton, AB T5N 3W6 (403) 496-9686, FAX 482-6395. Born Blind River, Ont. 1954. d. 1 ch. **EDUC:** Univ. of Windsor, B.A.(Soc.) 1976. **CAREER:** Instructor, Grand Prairie Reg'l Coll., 1981-82; Clinic Consultant, Canadian Red Cross-Blood Donor Recruitment, 1982-86; Community Friends Program Coord., Canadian Mental Health Association, Edmonton Reg., 1986-88; Dir. of Programs, 1988-90; Administrator, Stage Polaris Theatre Company, 1990-91; Exec. Dir., Skills Training & Support Services Association, 1991 to date. **SELECTED PUBLICATIONS:** *But That's Not What My Mom Does–A Book About Volunteers* (Why Not Publishing Company); *The Service Standard* ed., biannual SKILLS publication. **DIRECTOR:** Creative Endeavours Inc. **AFFIL:** Council of Chief Executive Officers (V-Chair 1993-94); Family Support Task Force (Comm. Committee); Canadian Mental Health Association (Organizing Committee, Int'l Conference, "Women in a Violent Society," Banff, 1991); Business Women's Golf Association; Edmonton Learner Centre (Bd. Mbr.; Chair 1985). **INTERESTS:** golf; home renovations; fin. planning; discovering great new restaurants; spending time with

her daughter. COMMENT: *"I have to like who I am and what I'm doing. I'm lucky to have experiences that challenge me and good relationships that support me."*

Holmes, Barbara Una (née Dobbie), B.A. ✎
Senior Editor. Born 1931. 2 ch. Gillian, Kerry. EDUC: Univ. Of Western Ontario, B.A.(Journalism). CAREER: *Maclean's,* Maclean Hunter Publishing Limited; researcher, *The Pierre Berton Show*; props, *Polka-Dot Door*; Asst. to Alexander Ross, "Star Probe,"*The Toronto Star*; Travel Section; Assoc. Ed., *Toronto Life* Magazine; Assoc. Ed., *Canadian Business* Magazine,. 1977-92; Sr. Ed., 1992-96.

Holmes, Nancy, B.A.,M.A. 📜 🎓
Writer and English Professor, OKANAGAN UNIVERSITY COLLEGE, 583 Hastings Ave., Penticton, BC V2A 8E1 (604) 492-4305, FAX 492-5355. Born Edmonton 1959. d. 3 ch. Douglas, Ian, Alex. EDUC: Univ. of Calgary, B.A. (English) 1982, M.A.(Creative Writing) 1990. CAREER: English Prof., Okanagan University Coll., 1991 to date. SELECTED PUBLICATIONS: 2 collections of poetry, *Down to the Golden Chersonese* (Victoria, BC: Sono Nis Press, 1991); *Valancy and the New World* (Vernon, BC: Kalamalka New Writers' Society, 1988); various poems & short stories in Cdn periodicals incl.: *Saturday Night*, *Malahat Review*, *The Fiddlehead*, *The New Quarterly* & *Descant*. HONS: winner, Kalamalka New Writers' Society Nat'l Competition, 1987; winner, Alberta Culture Short Story Competition, 1987; winner, *Calgary Herald* Short Story Competition, 1984. MISC: has received grants from the Alberta Foundation for Literary Arts & the B.C. Culture Writing Grant, 1994.

Holmes, Vicki, M.D. ⊕
Family Practitioner. 39 - 23rd St. E., Ste. 301, Saskatoon, SK S7K 0H6 (306) 652-6260, FAX 655-0455. President, RCH HOLDINGS INC. Born Assiniboia, Sask. 1949. EDUC: Univ. of Saskatchewn, M.D., L.M.C.C. 1973. CAREER: Intern, St. Paul's Hospital, 1973-74; Casualty Officer, Misericordia Hospital, 1974-75; private practice, Winnipeg, 1975-77; family medicine, Saskatoon, 1977 to date; Active Staff, St. Paul's Hospital, Saskatoon; Courtesy Staff, Saskatoon City Hospital; Assoc. Staff, Royal University Hospital, Saskatoon. EDIT: Ed. Bd., *CME News*, 1982-86. AFFIL: Scientific Assembly Committee; Saskatoon Childbirth Education Association (Consultant); Teenage Pregnancy & Parenting Saskatoon (Bd. Mbr.); St. Paul's Hospital (Bd. of Mgmt; Chrm, Patient Care Committee). HONS: Hugh MacLean Medal in Surgery, Univ. of Saskatchewan, Coll. of Medicine, 1973; Pediatrics Award, Univ. of Saskatchewan, Coll. of Medicine, 1973. MISC: frequent speaker. COMMENT: *"I am devoted to improving health care in my community by providing direct care to patients, by being a member of the Board of Management at St. Paul's Hospital and by being involved in program development for obstetric services and early maternity discharge."*

Holroyd, Diane ♡ ⊕
Executive Director, Saskatchewan Branch, THE KIDNEY FOUNDATION OF CANADA, 2217 Hanselman Ct., Ste. 1, Saskatoon, SK S7L 6A8 (306) 664-8582, FAX 653-4883. Born Edmonton 1937. m. Gary Holroyd. 2 ch. Michael Dean Holroyd, Gillian Diane Hayes. EDUC: Univ. of Alberta, Arts (English & Drama) 1957-59. CAREER: Purchasing Clerk, Univ. of Alberta, 1959; Purchasing Clerk & mbr., Space Allocation Committee, 1960-62; Exec. Dir., Sask. Branch, The Kidney Foundation of Canada, 1988 to date. VOLUNTEER CAREER: Sunday sch. teacher, 1954-76; Dir., Dalhousie Community Association, 1969-72; Coord., Volunteer Program, Dalhousie Elementary Sch., 1969-77; Volunteer Committee, Calgary Public Sch. Bd., 1970; District Assoc. Exec., Girl Guides of Canada, Calgary, 1970-73; Captain, 1973-76; Volunteer Outlet Coord., UNICEF Alberta, 1979-81; Membership Committee, Women's Canadian Club, Calgary, 1981-85; Prov. Mktg Chair, UNICEF Alberta, 1981-82; V-Chair, 1981-82; Prov. Chair, 1982-85; Exec. Bd., UNICEF Canada, 1982-87; Nat'l Youth Programs Chair, 1985-87; Volunteer Committee Chair, UNICEF Sask., 1987-88. AFFIL: Volunteer Management Group, Saskatoon (Co-Chair, Educ. Committee); Reg'l Employment Dev. Program (Bd.); American Volunteer Association; Saskatchewan Coalition for Organ Donor Awareness (Past Chrm); Heath Care Public Relations Association (Past VP, Sask. Chapter); Mendel Art Gallery; Ukrainian Museum; Wanuskewin Heritage Park. HONS: Lawrence D. Bresinger Award, The Kidney Foundation of Canada. COMMENT: *"I was a career volunteer for 24 years before going back into the work force. I have been the Executive Director of The Kidney Foundation, Saskatchewan Branch since 1988. I give workshops in strategic planning, managing change, volunteer management, leadership. My greatest achievement is that all my volunteer experience and training provided me with the knowledge and the skills I need to work in a challenging and rewarding field."*

Holt, Linda, B.A. 🍁 $
Management Consultant, Department of

Finance, PROVINCE OF NEW BRUNSWICK, Box 6000, Fredericton, NB (506) 453-2692, FAX 444-5311, EMAIL lholt@gov.nb.ca. Born Saint John 1951. m. M. Douglas Holt. 1 ch. Jessica. EDUC: Univ. of New Brunswick, B.A.(Hist./Soc.) 1973. CAREER: Hum. Res. Mgr, Northern Telecom, 1981; Pres., Hum. Res. Mgmt, 1982-89. SELECTED PUBLICATIONS: personnel admin. chapter in *Maritime Premiers' Council Personnel Handbook for the Maritimes*. AFFIL: Univ. of New Brunswick (Gov.; Chair, Personnel Policy Committee; Hon. Degree Committee; Nominating Committee; Pres., Associated Alumnae 1992-96; Chair, Hon. Degrees Committee, Associated Alumnae; Chair, Scholarship Committee, Associated Alumnae; Chair, Awards Committee, Associated Alumnae); N.B. Cancer Society (Dir.; Chair, Hum. Res. Committee); N.B. Personnel Association (Pres.). INTERESTS: skating; horses; volunteer pursuits. MISC: mbr., first Canadian Winter Games, 1967 (speedskating); numerous speaking engagements on women & employment. COMMENT: *"In early 1970s pushed frontiers of employment for women through speaking engagements, groups and clubs, and continue to promote women in positions of equality and authority in the 1990s. Have made my own small strides–step by step."*

Holyk, Marcelene, B.A. ⊙

President, WOMEN'S INTERNATIONAL LEAGUE FOR PEACE AND FREEDOM. Born Thunder Bay, Ont. 1949. EDUC: Lakehead Univ., B.A. (English/French) 1970. CAREER: Transport Canada, Library & Research Svcs. EDIT: *The Canadian Women's Budget* (Women's International League for Peace & Freedom, 1993). AFFIL: Women's International League for Peace & Freedom (Pres., Ottawa Branch); Canadian Peace Alliance (W.I.L.P.F. Rep.); Social Science Employees' Association (Co-Chair, Joint Occupational Safety & Health Committee); Public Service Alliance of Canada (VP, Local 70703; Health & Safety Rep.); Canadian Union of Public Employees (VP, Local 2424; Co-Chair, Joint Occupational Safety & Health Committee; mbr., Negotiating Team). INTERESTS: peace; occupational health & safety; alternative health; dance; music; women's issues. MISC: has spoken regularly to media & Parliamentary Committees on peace & security; Rep. at US Biennial W.I.L.P.F. Conference. COMMENT: *"Marcelene (Marcy) Holyk is a long-standing peace activist and promoter of women's equality in Canada and throughout the world."*

Holzman, Hon. Jacquelin ✦

Mayor, CITY OF OTTAWA, 111 Sussex Dr.,

Ottawa, ON K1N 5A1 (613) 244-5380. CAREER: Councillor, Richmond Ward, City of Ottawa, 1982-91; Mayor, 1991 to date. AFFIL: Ottawa Planning & Econ. Dev. Committee (Chrm); Ottawa Civic Hospital (Bd. of Trustees); Central Canada Exhibition Association; Ottawa Hydro Electric Commission (Bd. of Dir.); City of Ottawa Superannuation Fund (Bd. of Trustees); National Arts Centre (Bd. of Trustees); Royal Ontario Hospital (Bd. of Trustees); Royal Ontario Hospital Foundation (Bd. Mbr.); Regional Homes for the Aged (Chrm, Bd. of Mgmt); LACAC; Westboro Business Improvement Association; District Health Council (Reg'l Council Rep.); Kidney Foundation of Canada, Ottawa Valley Chapter (Bd. Mbr.); Match & Share Program; Kiwanis Club of Ottawa. COMMENT: *"Since 1960 Jacquelin Holzman has been an activist who helped create and operate many social services in the Ottawa-Carleton Region."*

Honeyman, Ruth, B.A., M.A. ⊙ ⊛ ⊘

Executive Director, CANADIAN PONY CLUB, National Office, 1 Rideau St., 6th Fl., Ottawa, ON K1N 8S7 (613) 241-7429, FAX 241-2958. Born Ottawa 1952. s. 2 ch. Chelsea Victoria, Simon Alexander. EDUC: Carleton Univ., B.A. (English/Hist.) 1970; Georgetown Univ., M.A.(Hist./English) 1972. CAREER: Reg'l Chair, Canadian Pony Club, 1987-93; Nat'l Sr. Examiner, 1989-95; Nat'l V-Chair, 1989-93; Exec. Dir., 1993 to date. SELECTED PUBLICATIONS: various Canadian Pony Club brochures & info. pamphlets. EDIT: *Horse and Country Magazine*, Canadian Pony Club. AFFIL: Opera Lyra; Orpheus Operatic Society; Nepean Choir; Anglican Church of Canada. INTERESTS: opera; choral singing; the arts; Cdn film. COMMENT: *"I am particularly interested in the youth of Canada. My volunteer hours and work experience have solidified my belief that our future lies in well-rounded, caring, informed citizens."*

Hood, Barbara ⊙ ⊕

Executive Director, Northwest Territories Division, CANADIAN MENTAL HEALTH ASSOCIATION, Box 2580, Yellowknife, NT X1A 2P9 (403) 873-3190, FAX 873-4930. Born Stanley, N.B. 1949. d. 3 ch. Tammy Lynn O'Donnell, Sylvia Marie O'Donnell (McKinney); Stacey Lee Ann O'Donnell. EDUC: Arctic Coll., Certificate (Mgmt Studies) 1992. CAREER: Admin. Asst., Arctic Public Legal Educ. & Info., 1989-91; Acting Exec. Dir., 1991; Resource Coord., Northern Addiction Svcs, 1991-92; Exec. Sec. to CEO, Inuvik Reg'l Health Bd., 1992-93; Exec. Dir., Canadian Mental Health Association, N.W.T. Div., 1993 to date. **AFFIL:** Canadian Mental Health Association (Pres., N.W.T. Div. 1991-92; Dir.); Burnsville Presbyterian Church (Sunday Sch. Superintendent 1982-84; Youth Group Leader 1988-89). **INTERESTS:** women's rights; mental health; social action policy; pol. sci.; fishing; boating; outdoor activities; gardening. **COMMENT:** *"Knowledge is a wonderful tool to self awareness and growth. Life is a continuous classroom and all your life experiences can provide you with a wealth of opportunities. These opportunities can give you a truly fulfilled life."*

Hood, Hon. Suzanne M., B.A.,LL.B., Q.C. ■ ◁◻ ♂

Justice, SUPREME COURT OF NOVA SCOTIA, 1815 Upper Water St., Halifax, NS B3J 1S7 (902) 424-4900, FAX 424-0536. Born Windsor, N.S. 1950. m. Joseph Robichaud. 2 ch. Catherine Ann Robichaud, Claire Margaret Robichaud. **EDUC:** Acadia Univ., B.A.(English) 1971; Dalhousie Univ., LL.B., 1977. **CAREER:** Mgmt Trainee, Maritime Life Assurance Company, Halifax, 1972-74; Lawyer, Huestis Holm, 1977-81; Ptnr, 1981-93; City Solicitor, City of Dartmouth, 1993-95; appointed, Supreme Court of N.S., 1995. **AFFIL:** Grace Church United (Unified Bd.; Worship Committee). **HONS:** appointed Queen's Counsel, 1993; selected as 1 of the Dartmouth Heritage Museum's "Dartmouth's Memorable Women 1750-1994" & 1 of 24 to be profiled in its publication; Acadia Univ. hons.: J. Woodbury Williams & Univ. Scholarships; Class Valedictorian; Gold "A" for extra-curricular activities & academic achievement; Silver "A" for athletics; Dean's List. **INTERESTS:** community & volunteer work; family activities; literature. **MISC:** numerous papers & lectures on mun. law; founding mbr., 1st women's Kiwanis Club in Canada, the City of Lakes Kiwanis Club; appointed to the Interim Bd. of the Queen Elizabeth II Health Sciences Centre, Halifax, 1994-95. **COMMENT:** *"I have combined a demanding and interesting career with the rewards of raising a family and actively participating in community activities."*

Hood, Marilyn, B.A. Ⓢ

Director, Public Affairs, CREDIT UNION CENTRAL OF ONTARIO, 2810 Matheson Boulevard East, Mississauga, ON L4W 4X7 (905) 629-5535, FAX 238-5087. Born Oakville, Ont. 1958. s. **EDUC:** Sheridan Coll., Dipl.(Mktg); York Univ., B.A.(Comm.). **CAREER:** Exec. Asst. to Ken Robinson, M.P., 1982-84; Comm. Advisor to the Hon. Ian Scott, Attorney-Gen., Prov. of Ont., 1985-88; Comm. Mgr, Control Data Canada Ltd., 1988-89; self-employed

comm. consultant, 1990-93; Dir., Public Affairs, Credit Union Central of Ontario, 1993 to date. **AFFIL:** Peel Condominium Corporation No. 245 (Pres. 1990-93); International Association of Business Communicators; Canadian Public Relations Society. **INTERESTS:** precision skating; continuing educ.; music; theatre; reading; sports.

Hope, Kathryn, B.A.,M.B.A. ♥ ⰺ

Producer, KRH PRODUCTIONS, 100 Manor Rd. E., Toronto, ON M4S 1P8 (416) 322-5909, FAX 367-9803. **EDUC:** York Univ., B.A. (Hons., Film) 1974; Univ. of Toronto, M.B.A.(Exec. Program) 1987. **CAREER:** independent prod. & dir., film & TV, 1973 to date. **AFFIL:** Toronto Women in Film & Television; Fujiwara Dance Inventions (Bd.). **HONS:** several awards for production incl. Gold Plaque, Chicago Int'l Film Festival; Silver Medal, N.Y. Int'l Film & TV Festival. **INTERESTS:** political & cultural events; literature; music. **COMMENT:** *"Involved in productions related to the arts, drama and education; television and feature film experience."*

Hope, Louise, B.H.Sc. ▧ ◁

Owner/Operator, GENEALOGICAL RESEARCH SERVICES, R.R. 6, Claremont, ON L1Y 1A3 (905) 640-2667. Born Toronto 1931. m. Donald W. 3 ch. **EDUC:** Univ. of Toronto, B.H.Sc.(Home Econ.) 1954; Ont. Coll. of Educ., Certificate (Ont. High Sch. Teacher) 1960, Certificate (Home Econ. Specialist) 1963; York Univ., Certificate (Co-operative Educ. Specialist) 1982. **CAREER:** teacher, Ont. Ladies' Coll., 1960-61; Dept. Head, Home Econ., Uxbridge Secondary Sch., 1961-70; Dept. Head, Family Studies, Markham District High Sch., 1970-87; owner/operator, Genealogical Research Services, 1987 to date. **SELECTED PUBLICATIONS:** *Index to Niagara Conference Methodist Episcopal Church Baptismal Register 1849-1886:* a guide for genealogists; *Manx Freers in Canada; Beginners' Genealogy; A Canadian Colony in Kansas.* **AFFIL:** Ontario Genealogical Society (Dir.; VP 1990-92; Pres. 1992-94); Committee for the Preservation of Historical Land Registry Records, Ont. Ministry of Culture & Communication. **HONS:** Excellence in Educ. Award, York Reg. Bd. of Educ. **INTERESTS:** genealogy & local history. **MISC:** introduced the co-op educ. program into Markham District High Sch. **COMMENT:** *"A retired secondary school teacher who introduced co-operative education into a large Ontario secondary school. Continues by teaching seniors in community centres. Has developed hobby of genealogy into a research business."*

Hopkins, Barbara, B.A. ■ ✊ ⊕ 🎓

President, AUTISM SOCIETY OF NEWFOUNDLAND AND LABRADOR. Born Toronto 1936. m. Robert M. 4 ch. **EDUC:** Dalhousie Univ., B.A.(Hons., Psych.) 1955; Univ. of Maine, Fac. of Arts, Grad. Studies, Psych. 1957; Univ. of British Columbia, Fac. of Educ., Professional Year 1970. **CAREER:** Social Worker, Halifax Children's Aid Society, 1955-56; Counsellor, Algergrove Secondary Sch., B.C., 1970-73; Elementary Sch. Counsellor, Avalon Consolidated Sch. Bd., St. John's, 1973-77; Asst. Prof., Research, Diagnostic & Remedial Unit, Institute for Research in Human Abilities, Memorial Univ. of Newfoundland, 1977-83; Coord., 1977-83; Clinical Assoc., Div. TEACCH, Sch. of Medicine, The Univ. of North Carolina, during sabbatical, 1990; Dir., Diagnostic & Remedial Unit, Memorial Univ. of Newfoundland, 1983-91; Asst. Prof., Fac. of Educ., 1983-95. **SELECTED PUBLICATIONS:** various publications incl.: a review of *Nobody, Nowhere* (Rendezvous, 11); "Reflections about the TEACCH Center of North Carolina" (*Autism Society Canada Newsletter*, 9); *The Communication and Telecommunication Needs of the Cerebral Palsied Population in Canada*, with J. Green (Dept. of Comm., Gov't of Canada, 1984); *Functions of the School Counsellor and Educational Psychologists in Newfoundland Schools*, with E. Turpin, J. Harnett *et al* (Dept. of Educ., Gov't of Nfld. & Labrador, 1981). **AFFIL:** Autism Society of Newfoundland & Labrador (Charter Mbr.; Pres.); Autism Society Canada (Dir.; Pres. 1988-93; Past Pres. 1993 to date); Council for Exceptional Children, Nfld. Chapter (Membership Chair; VP 1992-94). **HONS:** Entrance Scholarship, Dalhousie Univ., 1951-52; Daughters of Israel Scholarship, Dalhousie Univ., 1953-54; Univ. Medalist, Arts & Sci. (Psych.), Dalhousie Univ., 1955; Entrance Scholarship, Univ. of Maine, 1957; B.C. Gov't Student Bursary, Univ. of British Columbia, 1969. **INTERESTS:** sailing; cross-country & downhill skiing; bridge. **MISC:** various research grants & contracts.

Hopkins, Elaine, B.A. ✊ 🎓

President, ONTARIO FEDERATION OF INDEPENDENT SCHOOLS, 2199 Regency Terrace, Ottawa, ON K2C 1H2 (613) 596-4013, FAX 596-4971. Born Iroquois, Ont. 1940. m. Herbert. 3 ch. **EDUC:** Ottawa Teachers' Coll., Certificate (Educ.) 1957; Carleton Univ., B.A.(Math./Soc.) 1962. **CAREER:** elementary sch. teacher/high sch. teacher/music teacher, Ottawa Bd. of Educ.; Principal, Bishop Hamilton Sch.; Principal, Orleans Christian Montessori Sch. **SELECTED PUBLICATIONS:** numerous articles for media & newsletters on independent sch. issues in Ont., Canada & the world. **AFFIL:** Federation of Independent Schools of Canada (VP & Dir. 1985-90; Pres.); Red Pine Camp (Chair, Operating Committee 1987-95); Dominion Chalmers United Church (Choir Dir. 1994-95). **INTERESTS:** music; leatherwork; stained glass. **COMMENT:** *"I have been a lifetime educator committed to alternatives in education providing choice for parents. As a Christian, I also integrate my faith into all aspects of my life, both professional and personal. Music is also integral to all my endeavours."*

Hopper, Carol ✊ $

Executive Director, NATIONAL SKI INDUSTRIES ASSOCIATION (NSIA), 8250 Decarie Blvd., Ste. 340, Montreal, QC H4P 2P5 (514) 737-1672, FAX 737-0724. Born Montreal 1952. m. Cedric Heimrath. 2 stpch. Natasha Heimrath, Erik Heimrath. **EDUC:** McGill Univ. Coll., Degree (Arts) 1971; Canadian Institute for Organization Management, Assoc. Mgmt 1991. **CAREER:** Asst., Ben Fuller Associates, 1973-89; Show Dir., NSIA, 1989-91; Exec. Dir., 1991 to date. **AFFIL:** Canadian Ski Council (Bd. of Dir.; V-Chair 1993, 1994); Sir Sandford Fleming Coll. (Advisory Committee, Sporting Goods Bus. Program 1994-96); Junior League of Montreal (mbr. of Bd. & Chair, 5 committees 1987-92); Canadian Society of Association Executives; Canadian Association of Exposition Managers; International Association of Exposition Managers. **INTERESTS:** skiing, cycling & other sports; reading; travel. **COMMENT:** *"I enjoy being with people, having fun and being happy. I strive to satisfy the changing needs of the members of the association by the provision of indispensable services."*

Hordyski, Sylvie E., R.N.,B.N. ⊕

Nurse Therapist, World Health Organization, CALGARY GENERAL HOSPITAL, 841 Center Ave. E., Calgary, AB T2E 0A1 (403) 268-9682, FAX 268-5205. Born Unity, Sask 1954. d. 3 ch. Erin, Nancy, Miles. **EDUC:** Kelsey Institute, Saskatoon, R.N. 1974; Univ. of Calgary, B.N. 1990, Hypnosis for Professions 1994; Univ. of Saskatchewan, Health Care Admin. Certificate, Community Health Focus 1996. **CAREER:** Staff Nurse, Calgary General Hospital, 1975 to date; Community Outreach Program Coord., World Health Organization, 1993 to date; private practice (counselling), 1994 to date; Eating Disorder Clinic, Western Canada Drug Investigation Unit, 1995 to date. **SELECTED PUBLICATIONS:** sexual abuse brochure (1993). **AFFIL:** Canadian Group Psychotherapy Association (Full Mbr.; Local Chapter Exec.); Alberta Association of Registered Nurses; Southern Alberta Mental Health

Nurses' Interest Group; U.N.A. (Ward Rep.); The Edit (volunteer with street people). **HONS:** Nurses Week Award, Calgary City, 1987; Southern Alberta Mental Health Contributor Award, 1994. **INTERESTS:** hiking; people; continuing educ.; reading; theatre; motivational speaking. **MISC:** numerous presentations at conferences; marriage prep. course coord., 1992 to date; Alberta Health-N.I.H.D. Round Table Talks, 1993 to date. **COMMENT:** *"I am a high-energy individual who uses a positive approach to my work and life. I have an interest in and enthusiasm for program development and motivational activities that promote mental wellness."*

Hore, Marlene ■ ■ (Ṡ) ㆔ ⬚
Founding Partner, THE ONGOING PARTNERSHIP INC., 81 Roxborough St. W., Toronto, ON M5R 1T9. Born Montreal. m. Ron. 2 ch. Seanna, Melissa. **EDUC:** McGill Univ.; McDonald Coll.; Sir George Williams Univ. (now Concordia). **CAREER:** Sr. Writer, CFCF Radio/TV, 1966-68; Copywriter, Vickers & Benson, 1968-69; VP & Creative Dir., J. Walter Thompson Co. Ltd., Montreal, 1978-83; VP & Nat'l Creative Dir., 1983-86; V-Chrm, 1986-92; Exec. VP & Creative Dir., BCP Advertising, 1993-95; founding Ptnr, The Ongoing Partnership Inc., 1995 to date; Prof., 3rd-yr. copywriting, Ontario Coll. of Art, 1995. **AFFIL:** Art & Design Club of Toronto (Dir. 1990-95); National Advertising Benevolent Society of Canada (Dir. 1991-95); Canadian Advertising Foundation (Dir. 1991-93).

Horinstein, Régine, B.A.,M.L.S. ⬚ O
Executive Director, CORPORATION OF PROFESSIONAL LIBRARIANS OF QUEBEC, 307 Ste.-Catherine St. W., Ste. 320, Montreal, QC H2X 2A3 (514) 845-3327, FAX 845-1618, EMAIL cbpq@interlink.net. Born Brussels 1951. **EDUC:** Haifa Univ., Israel, B.A.(Int'l Hist./French Lit.) 1974; Chiswick Polytechnic, Certificate (Proficiency of English) 1975; McGill Univ., M.L.S. 1983. **CAREER:** Exec. Dir., Corporation of Professional Librarians of Quebec, 1986 to date. **SELECTED PUBLICATIONS:** "The Mini Association: A Maxi Challenge" (*The Philanthropist* Fall 1992); "Réflexions à l'occasion des 25 ans de la C.B.P.Q." (*Argus* Summer 1994); annual reports of the Corporation of Professional Librarians of Quebec. **AFFIL:** Canadian Society of Association Executives (Treas., Montreal Chapter 1988-89); Centre pour l'avancement des associations du Québec (mbr.; Founding Bd. Mbr. 1990-91); Dialogue St. Urbain. **INTERESTS:** Middle Eastern politics; info. science trends; foreign film; travel. **COMMENT:** *"Self-motivated and*

good communicator. Monitors trends and technological changes in the information field, develops innovative continuing education programs to meet the needs of professional librarians."

Horner, Pamela O ⊕
President, Vernon Outreach, OSTEOPOROSIS SOCIETY OF BRITISH COLUMBIA, 1903 - 29 Cres., Vernon, BC V1T 1Y6 (604) 545-4990. Born Davidson, Sask. 1927. m. Ralph (Bill) Horner. 3 ch. James Douglas, Susan Jean, Gordon Hugh. **EDUC:** Univ. of British Columbia, gen. arts, in progress. **CAREER:** stenographer, sec., receptionist, various depts., fed. civil service, now retired; Vernon Community Music Sch. **SELECTED PUBLICATIONS:** *Osteoporosis –The Long Road Back* (Univ. of Ottawa Press, 1989); short stories & poems in local publications. **AFFIL:** NDP Constituency Association (Media Chair, Mbr. at Large); Osteoporosis Society of B.C., Vernon Outreach; North Okanagan Unitarian Fellowship (Exec. Mbr.). **HONS:** Canada 125 Medal, 1992. **INTERESTS:** bridge; current events; environmental concerns; elder hostels; home exchanges; travel; reading. **COMMENT:** *"Largely self-educated, active senior. Believe that learning (formal and informal) is a lifetime process. Try to do a night school course each year. Presently French–to become bilingual is a major goal. Sometimes feel an active social conscience is a curse!"*

Hornstein, Shelley, B.A.,D.E.A.,M.A., Ph.D. ⬨ ⊗ ᗡ
Chair, Department of Fine Arts and Associate Professor, Atkinson College, YORK UNIVERSITY, 4700 Keele St., North York, ON M3J 1P3 (416) 736-2100, ext. 66623, FAX 736-5103, EMAIL shelley@yorku.ca. **EDUC:** Univ. des Sciences Humaines de Strasbourg, Licence ès Lettres (Art Hist. & Archaeology) 1976, Diplôme des Études Approfondies, D.E.A.(Art Hist. & Archaeology) 1976, Maîtriste ès Lettres (Urban Murals in Montreal) 1978, Ph.D. 1981. **CAREER:** Visiting Lecturer, Art Hist. Dept., Laval Univ., 1982; Coord. of Public Conferences, Council of Historic Monuments & Sites of Que./Art Hist. Dept., Sch. of Architecture, Laval Univ., 1982-83; Instructor, Art Hist. Dept., Laval Univ., 1983; Instructor, Art Hist. Dept., Concordia Univ., 1983-84; Instructor, Art Hist. Dept., Laval Univ., 1984; Special Lecturer, Art Hist. Dept., Concordia Univ., 1984-85; Coord., Visual Arts Program, Dept. of Fine Arts, Atkinson Coll., York Univ., 1987-89; Chair, Dept. of Fine Arts, 1988-90; Assoc. Prof., 1988 to date; Assoc. Dean, 1990-92; Dir., Centre for Feminist Research, 1993-95; Chair, Dept. of Fine Arts, Atkinson Coll., 1995

to date. SELECTED PUBLICATIONS: "Interstices of Romance" (*C Magazine*, Vol. 9, Spring 1986); "The House That Jack Built" (*Canadian Woman Studies Journal*, 11(1) 1989); "Architecture on the Edge" (*Journal of Architectural and Planning Research*, Texas, London, 1989); "A Place to Die," *From Apartheid to Orchestras*, ed. Joseph Green & Jean Guiot (Toronto: Captus Press, 1990); "Art Nouveau as Surface Described," *Visual and Verbal Crossings 1890-1980*, ed. J.D. Hunt, Theo d'Haen & S.A. Varga (Amsterdam/Atlanta: Eds. Rodopi, 1990); "The Architecture of the First Montreal Teaching Hospitals of the 19th Century" (*The Journal of Canadian Art History*, Vol. XIII(2) & XIV(1) 1991); *Musings on Time and Space for Lyla Rye (with apologies to scholars of quantum physics)*, exhibition catalogue for Lyla Rye (Glendon Galerie, York Univ., 1995); *Capital Culture: A Reader on Modernist Legacies, State Institutions and the Value(s) of Art*, co-ed. with Jody Berland (McGill-Queen's Univ. Press, forthcoming); various professional reports, conference papers & invited talks. EDIT: Book Review Ed., *Revue Canadienne d'Art/Canadian Art Review*, 1983-86. EXHIBITIONS: guest curator, *The Wedding: A Ceremony or Thoughts about an Indecisive Reunion Revisited*, & author of accompanying catalogue, Art Gallery of York Univ. (1990; "Making Art Worth It," exhibition essay, *Rates of Exchange: The Changing Value(s) of Art* (Innis Coll., Univ. of Toronto, June 1995). AFFIL: Art Gallery of York Univ. (Bd. Mbr.); Centre for Feminist Research, York Univ. (Bd. 1993-94). MISC: reviewer, various granting agencies; Conference Dir. & Coord., *Conference on Feminist Issues: Post-Liberal Discourse and the Ethics of (Ms)Representation*, Centre for Feminist Research, York Univ., 1994; recipient, numerous grants from various agencies; coord. the visits & lectures of architect Daniel Libeskind & art historian, Eric Michaud; working on a book, with colleague Florence Jacobowitz (working title *Culture, Memory and Resistance: Representation and the Holocaust*).

Horsey, Jean S. ☯ ○
National President, THE ENGLISH-SPEAKING UNION OF CANADA, 485 Eglinton Ave. E., Ste. 101, Toronto, ON M4P 1N2 (416) 481-8648, FAX (416) 485-5562. Born Toronto 1925. s. EDUC: St. Mildred's Coll. CAREER: administrator for 40 yrs. with professional & educational organizations incl. John C. Beaton, Survey Consultant; Bursar, St. Joseph's Morrow Park High Sch.; Lawson Planning Consultants. AFFIL: International Council of The English Speaking Union, London, UK; The English Speaking Union of Canada, Toronto Branch

(Pres. 1987-92); The Young Women's Canadian Club (Pres. 1968-70); Granite Club; Art Gallery of Ontario; Empire Club; Royal Canadian Geographical Society; St. James Cathedral; Toronto Camera Club; during the 1970s, P.C. Women's Association of Metro Toronto; St. George's P.C. Women's Association; Eglinton Deanery, Anglican Church (Lay Sec.). INTERESTS: people; Canada; community; photography; art; lawn bowling; church. MISC: served Loyal Societies/Military Dinner Committees. COMMENT: *"My endeavours have been based on my values as expressed through my cultural and volunteer affiliations."*

Horsman, Karen, B.A.A. ■ ■ ⊻ ✎
Talk Show Host, TALK 640/Q107 (a division of WIC), 5255 Yonge St., Ste. 1400, North York, ON M2N 6P4 (416) 221-6400, FAX 512-4816. Born Weston, Ont. 1966. m. Chris Manderson. EDUC: Ryerson Polytechnical Institute (now Ryerson Polytechnic Univ.), B.A.A.(Radio & TV Arts) 1988. CAREER: Tape Editor/Traffic Reporter, CKO Radio News Ntwk; Sports Reporter, TSN, N.Y.; freelance Reporter, *Motoring '91* & *World of Horse Racing*, TSN; Producer/Host/News Anchor, CFNY; News Anchor/Reporter, CISS-FM; News Anchor/Talk Show Host, Talk 640/Q107. INTERESTS: various sports esp. biking, squash & skiing. COMMENT: *"I feel fortunate that I have always known what I've wanted to do with my career. It has become a passion. I live and breathe the news business and enjoy what I do for a living!"*

Hošek, Chaviva Malada, B.A.,A.M., Ph.D. ✦
Director, Policy and Research, Office of the Prime Minister, GOVERNMENT OF CANADA, Langevin Block, Rm. 129A, Ottawa, ON K1A 0A6. Born Chomutov, Czechoslovakia 1946. m. Alan Thomas Pearson. EDUC: McGill Univ., B.A. 1967; Harvard Univ., A.M. 1968, Ph.D. 1973. CAREER: Assoc. Prof. of English, Victoria Coll., Univ. of Toronto, 1978-87; Ptnr, Gordon Capital Corp., 1985-87; M.P.P. (Oakwood), Gov't of Ont., 1987-89; Min. of Housing, 1987-89; Sr. Policy Advisor to the Leader of the Opposition, & Dir., Nat'l Liberal Caucus Research Bureau, 1990-93; Dir., Policy & Research, Office of the Prime Minister, 1993 to date. SELECTED PUBLICATIONS: chapter in *And No One Cheered: Federalism, Democracy & The Constitution Act* (1983); chapter in *Oxford Companion to Canadian Literature* (1983); *Lyric Poetry: Beyond New Criticism*, ed. with Pat Parker (1985); *Circle & Labyrinth: Essays in Honour of Northrop Frye*, co-ed. (1983). AFFIL: Economic Council of Canada

(1986-87); National Action Committee on the Status of Women (1980-87). **HONS:** B'nai Brith Woman of the Year, 1984; YWCA Woman of Distinction, 1986.

Hoshizaki, Freda Stefania ✊

Founder, HOSHIZAKI HOUSE, 116 Queen St., Dryden, ON P8N 1A7 (807) 223-2137. Born Arnes, Man. 1919. w. 6 ch. **CAREER:** elementary sch. teacher; Asst. Librarian, 1980-84; Councillor, Town of Dryden, 1985-94; Trustee, Bd. of Educ., Dryden, 1994 to date. **AFFIL:** Hoshizaki House (Founder; Chair, Bd. of Dir. 1985-90; Hon. Life Mbr.); Royal Canadian Legion Ladies' Auxiliary, Dryden Branch No. 63 (Past. Pres. 1992-93; served as Sec. 14 yrs.); Multiple Sclerosis, Dryden Chapter (Pres. 1 yr.); Committee for Nonprofit Housing; The Mayor's Committee for the Prevention of Substance Abuse (1980-94); Committee for Northwestern Women's Conference; Northwestern Ont. Decade Council (mbr. 20 yrs.); Violence Committee (Advisory Bd.); Committee for the Economic Development for Women in Single-Industry Towns; Long-Term Care (Advisory Committee); Patricia Community Futures (Bd.); Dryden Race Relations Committee; Dryden AIDS Committee; Northwestern Ontario Women's Training Coalition (1994-95); Coll. of Physicians & Surgeons of Ontario (Bd. 1994-96). **HONS:** The Mayor's Alcohol Committee Award; The Substance Abuse Committee Award; Alcohol Research Foundation Award; Member Award, Decade Council; Special Achievement Award, Crimestoppers. **MISC:** helped to organize numerous conferences & workshops in Dryden. **COMMENT:** *"Freda formed and chaired the Committee for Battered Women. The Committee lobbied the provincial government to provide funding for the purchase of a house and for the funds to operate it. They also lobbied the municipal government for 20% operating funds. More important, the Committee began to educate the community regarding the need for a crisis centre, and also to educate the community regarding the myths surrounding battered women. Continual government lobbying has been necessary to implement ongoing counselling for women and children. Established and named after Freda, the Hoshizaki House was opened and incorporated on September 20, 1985, after five years of hard work and determination."*

Hosier, Ellen, B.Comm.,C.A. ■■ $

Corporate Secretary and Treasurer, FINNING LTD. (selling, servicing & financing Caterpillar machinery), 555 Great Northern Way, Vancouver, BC V5T 1E2 (604) 872-4444, FAX 331-4852. Born Burnaby, B.C. 1954. **EDUC:** Univ. of British Columbia, B.Comm. 1977; C.A. 1981. **CAREER:** Arthur Andersen & Co., 1977-80; Chief Acctnt, U.S. Oper., Finning Ltd., 1980-82; Treasury Mgr, 1982-90; Corp. Treas., 1990-93; Corp. Sec. & Treas., 1993 to date. **AFFIL:** Financial Executives Institute (Dir.); The Vancouver Playhouse (Bd. of Gov.).

Hospital, Janette Turner, B.A., M.A. ■ 📜 📖 🎓

Writer. c/o Knopf Canada, 33 Yonge St., Ste. 210, Toronto, ON M5E 1G4 (416) 777-9477, FAX 777-9470. Born Melbourne 1942. m. Clifford G. Hospital. 2 ch. **EDUC:** Univ. of Queensland, Australia, B.A.(English) 1965; Queen's Univ., M.A.(Medieval Lit.) 1973. **CAREER:** high sch. teacher, Queensland, Australia, 1963-66; Librarian, Harvard Univ., 1967-71; Lecturer in English, St. Lawrence Coll., & the maximum- & medium-security prisons for men, Kingston, Ont., 1971-82; full-time writer, 1982 to date. **SELECTED PUBLICATIONS:** *The Ivory Swing* (1982); *The Tiger in the Tiger Pit* (1983); *Borderline* (1985); *Charades* (1988); *The Last Magician* (1992); *Oyster* (1996); *Dislocations* (short story collection, 1986); *Isobars* (short story collection, 1990); *A Very Proper Death*, under pseudonym Alex Juniper (1991). **HONS:** an "Atlantic First," *The Atlantic*, 1978; First Prize, Magazine Fiction, Foundation for the Advancement of Canadian Letters, 1982; The Seal Award ($50,000) for *The Ivory Swing*, 1982; named in Canada's Best Ten Younger Writers, 1986; Fiction Award for *Dislocations*, Fellowship of Australian Writers, 1988; Finalist, the Miles Franklin Award, for *Charades*, Australia, 1989; Finalist, National Book Council Award, for *Charades*, Australia, 1989; *Best Short Stories 1990* & *Best Short Stories 1992*, UK (London; Heinemann, 1990 & 1992); Gold Medal for travel writing, National Magazine Awards, 1991; Doctor of the Univ., Griffith Univ., Brisbane, Australia, 1995. **COMMENT:** *"Novelist and short story writer; divides year mainly between Canada and Australia but is also frequently invited as writer-in-residence at universities in US, UK, Europe. Has won literary awards in Canada, Australia, US, UK; is translated into most European languages, and some Asian ones. Because Hospital's life has been unintentionally nomadic, her characters suffer from dislocations of various kinds (geographic, cultural, emotional) and tend to be caught in intractable moral dilemmas."*

Houda-Pepin, Fatima, B.A., M.N.A. 🍁

Deputée (La Pinière), GOUVERNEMENT DU QUÉBEC, Hôtel du Parlement, Bur. 2.38,

Québec, QC G1A 1A4. Born Meknes, Morocco 1951. m. Paul Pepin, 1978. **EDUC:** Univ. Laval, Baccalauréat (Sci. politique) 1976; Univ. d'Ottawa, Maîtrise (Rel'ns internationales) 1977; McGill Univ., Maîtrise (Biblio-théconomie-sciences de l'info.) 1981; Univ. de Montréal, Scolarité Ph.D. complétée (Science politique) 1981. **CAREER:** Consultante en éduc. interculturelle et relations internationales, 1981-94; Chargée de cours en sci. politique, Univ. du Québec à Montréal, 1990-93; Chargée de cours à l'Univ. de Montréal, 1993-94; Comité consultatif sur les relations interculturelles, Ville de Montréal, 1990-92; Pres., 1992-94; Députée (La Pinière), Assemblée Nationale du Qué., 1994 to date. **AFFIL:** Parti Libéral du Québec. **HONS:** Le Mérite, Office de la langue française, 1990; Prix d'honneur, Alliance des professeures et professeurs de Montréal, 1991; Canada 125 Medal; Personnalité de la Semaine, La Presse, 1992; Chevalier, Ordre de la francophonie et du dialogue des cultures, Assemblée internationale des parlementaires de langue française, 1994. **COMMENT:** *"Fatima Houda-Pepin considère le Canada comme un modèle d'harmonie et de paix sociale qu'il faut préserver et promouvoir, pour bâtir une société juste et équitable, pour des générations à venir."*

Hould, Claudette, L.èsL.,M.A., Ph.D. ■ ⊗ 🕮 ⋐

Professor of Art History, UNIVERSITÉ DU QUÉBEC À MONTRÉAL. Born Montreal 1942. **EDUC:** Univ. de Montréal, B.A. 1965, L.èsL. 1969, M.A. 1971; École des Hautes Études en Sciences sociales, Paris, Ph.D. 1990. **CAREER:** teacher, 1960-71; Curator, Montreal Museum of Fine Arts, 1975-76; Prof. of Art Hist., Univ. du Québec à Montréal, 1976 to date; Dir. of Dept., 1979-81, 1983-84, 1984-89; Dir., Maison des Étudiants Canadiens, 1992-96. **SELECTED PUBLICATIONS:** *Répertoire des livres d'artistes au Québec 1900-1980* (1982); *Code d'éthique de l'estampe originale*, co-ed. (1982); *L'image de la Révolution française* & *Images of the French Revolution*, transl. (1989); *Iconographie et image de la Révolution française*, ed.; *A Code of Ethics for the Original Print*, transl. (1990); *Codigo de Etica da Estampa Original*, traduit en portugais (1990); *Répertoire des livres d'artistes au Québec 1981-90* (1993). **AFFIL:** Montreal Museum of Fine Arts (Acquisition Committee); International Festival of Art Films (since inception in 1981; V-Chair then Chair 1986-89); Société d'histoire de l'art français; American Society for Eighteenth Century Studies; Conseil international des musées; Association d'art des universitiés canadiennes; National Gallery of Canada (Bd.

of Trustees 1990-93); Musée d'art contemporain de Montréal (Bd. of Trustees 1987-90); Musée du Québec (Bd. of Trustees 1984-85; Acquisition Committee 1989); National Museums of Canada (Bd. of Trustees 1985-90); UQAM (Trustee 1988-89). **HONS:** Prix d'excellence, Association de Musées canadiens, 1989; Remise de la médaille en argent du Bicentenaire de la Révolution française, 1989; Prix Publication, Association des Musées Québécois, 1990.

Houlden, Robyn, M.D. ■ ⊕ ⋐

Assistant Professor, Faculty of Medicine, QUEEN'S UNIVERSITY, Kingston, ON K7L 2V7 (613) 548-1379, FAX 548-6105, EMAIL houldenr@qucdn.queensu.ca. Staff Endocrinologist, KINGSTON GENERAL HOSPITAL. Born Canada 1958. m. Dr. David Yen. 1 ch. Joy Lily Yen. **EDUC:** Univ. of Ottawa, M.D.(cum laude) 1983. **CAREER:** Asst. Prof., Fac. of Medicine, Queen's Univ., 1990 to date; Staff Endocrinologist, Kingston General Hospital, 1990 to date. **SELECTED PUBLICATIONS:** "Diseases and Diabetes," *Medical Diagnosis and Therapy*, ed. M.G. Khan, J.G. Bartlett et al (Philadelphia; Lea & Febige, 1994); "Disorders of the Pituitary Thyrotroph," with R.L. Reid, *Reproductive Endocrinology, Surgery and Technology*, ed. E.Y. Adashi, J.A. Rock, Z. Rosenwaks (Raven Press, 1995). **AFFIL:** Canadian Society of Endocrinology & Metabolism (Chair, Educ. Committee). **HONS:** R. Samuel McLaughlin Fellowship, 1989; Aesculapian Society Lectureship Award, Queen's Univ., 1993, 1994, 1995, 1996; Pairo Trust Fund Travel Award, 1995. **INTERESTS:** diabetes mellitus & lipid disorders; medical educ. **MISC:** Program Dir., Queen's Univ./Univ. of Ottawa Conjoint Training Program in Endocrinology & Metabolism. **COMMENT:** *"Dr. Houlden is an Assistant Professor in the Faculty of Medicine of Queen's University and a Staff Endocrinologist at the Kingston General Hospital. She has a clinical practice devoted primarily to diabetes mellitus and disorders of lipid metabolism and is actively involved in medical research and education."*

Hould-Marchand, Valérie ■■ ⍈

Olympic Athlete. c/o Canadian Olympic Association. Born Rivière-du-Loup, Que. 1980. **SPORTS CAREER:** mbr., Cdn Nat'l Synchronized Swimming Team, 1994 to date. Olympic Games: Silver, team, 1996. World jr. championships: 1st, team, 1995. Int'l meets: 1st, solo, 2nd, team, & 3rd, duet (Switzerland), 1995. Canadian championships: 2nd, solo (15-17), 2nd, duet (15-17), & 2nd, team (15-17), 1995. Canadian jr. championships: 2nd, team (11-

14), & 1st, solo (11-14), 1994; 1st, solo (11-14), 1993; 1st, solo (11-14), & 2nd, team (11-14), 1992. INTERESTS: artwork, drawing.

Howard, (Helen) Barbara, RCA 🚫 🏛
Artist. 226 Roslin Ave., Toronto, ON M4N 1Z6 (416) 483-3954. Born Long Branch, Ont. 1926. m. Richard Daley Outram. EDUC: Ontario Coll. of Art, hons. grad. 1951. SELECTED PUBLICATIONS: *Twenty-Eight Drawings by Barbara Howard* (Toronto: Martlet Press, 1970). EXHIBITIONS: 22 solo exhibitions; numerous group exhibitions. COLLECTIONS: National Gallery of Canada; Art Gallery of Ontario; National Library of Canada; British Museum, London, UK; Bodleian Library, Oxford; Library of Congress, Washington, DC; Northern Telecom; Ont. Gov't Collection; Citibank Canada; numerous other public & private collections in Canada, UK & US. AFFIL: Royal Canadian Academy of Arts (Council 1980-82); Arts & Letters Club of Toronto; Art Gallery of Ontario (Hon. Artist Life Mbr.). HONS: Medalist, Ontario Coll. of Art, 1951. MISC: listed in *Canadian Who's Who, Who's Who in Ontario & Who's Who in American Arts*; subject of various reviews & profiles, incl. "Profile of Barbara Howard" (*Equinox* Magazine July-Aug. 1987) & *Passionate Spirits: a History of the Royal Canadian Academy of Arts, 1880-1980*, by R. Sisler (Toronto: Clark Irwin, 1980). COMMENT: *"Primarily a visionary artist–a painter, illustrator, wood-engraver and designer; recognized internationally, represented in important public and private collections in Canada, UK and US."*

Howard, Valerie J., B.Ed.,M.A., Ph.D. ■■ 💲 🐿
Owner/Manager, HOWARD INTERPERSONAL DYNAMICS INC. (mgmt & personal counselling), 519 - 2nd St. S.E., Medicine Hat, AB T1A 0C5 (403) 529-1226, FAX 529-1226. Professor of Psychology, MEDICINE HAT COLLEGE. Born Camrose, Alta. 1949. d. 2 ch. Sean, Kymberlei-Jane. EDUC: Univ. of Alberta, B.Ed.(Educational Psych.-Special Educ.) 1976, completed coursework for M.Ed.(Educational Psych.) 1978-80; Institute of Adlerian Studies, Chicago, Certificate of Professional Studies (Indiv. Psych.) 1985; Fielding Institute, Santa Barbara, CA, M.A. 1987, Ph.D.(Human & Organizational Systems) 1988. CAREER: Co-owner/Mgr, photographic oper. of 2 portrait studios, 1971-77; Teacher, Evelyn Unger Sch. for Language & Learning Dev., Edmonton, 1970-71; Teacher, Co. of Stettler, 1971-73; Teacher, Red Deer Public Sch. District, 1974-75; Teacher, Co. of Stettler, 1975-77; Teacher, Camrose Sch.

District, 1977-79; Administrator, 1979-81; Counsellor (part-time), Medicine Hat Community Counselling Association, 1981-86; part-time Educ. Instructor, M.Ed., Univ. of Lethbridge, 1987-88; part-time Educ. Instructor, Diploma of Special Ed. program, 1981-89; full-time Psych., Educ. & Communications Instructor, Dept. of Humanities & Social Sciences, Medicine Hat Coll., 1981 to date; owner & Mgr, Howard and Associates/Howard Interpersonal Dynamics Inc., 1987 to date. AFFIL: American Association for the Study of Mental Imagery; Carlson Learning Group-Management, Minneapolis; Medicine Hat Personnel Association; Human Resources Institute of Alberta; Canadian Mental Health Association, Medicine Hat branch (Bd. mbr.); Vocational Training Workshop for Handicapped Adults (Chairperson, Bd. of Dir.); McMann Group Home, Youth Services Association, Medicine Hat (Bd. mbr.); Woods Homes (Bd. mbr.); HRIA. HONS: Woman of Achievement, Business & Professional Women's Association of Medicine Hat, 1989; Distinguished Alumni Award, Augustana Univ. Coll., 1992. MISC: over 25 yrs.' experience in lecturing, training & dev., & mgmt consulting; consultant to gov't, business & industry; workshop facilitator; invited speaker, public & TV engagements.

Howard Coady, Jane, B.A. ⁄ 💲
Publisher/General Manager, PENTICTON HERALD, 186 Nanaimo Ave., Penticton, BC V2A 1N4 (604) 492-4002, FAX 492-4081. Born Louth, Lincolnshire, UK 1949. s. EDUC: Univ. of Bristol, UK, B.A.(Hons., Geography/English Lit./Pol. Sci.) 1970. CAREER: Hotel Mgr, Courtenay, B.C.; Event Coord., Filberg Festival; Dir., Mktg, Westerly Hotel, Courtenay; Promo./Circulation Mgr, *Comox District Free Press*; Publisher & Gen. Mgr, *Nanaimo Times*; Publisher & Gen. Mgr, *Penticton Herald*. AFFIL: Penticton Chamber of Commerce; Tourism Association of Vancouver Island (Tourism Dev. Task Force 1990-91); Mount Washington Community Futures (VP); Penticton Chamber of Commerce (VP 1992-94); Rotary Club of Penticton; Art Gallery of South Okanagan (Trustee). HONS: President's Merit Award, Comox Valley Chamber of Commerce. INTERESTS: gallery browsing; reading; gardening. COMMENT: *"Emigrated to Canada in 1973. Worked in numerous positions during early years in Canada, gaining a wide experience, which has been invaluable in better understanding the vagaries of public demand and their wide variety of interests. Being involved in the life of a community is integral to my life, on both a business and personal level. Working in the publishing business is a won-*

derful way to combine this. Arts, tourism and economic/community development issues are my primary interest areas."

Howell, Barbara C., B.A.,LL.B. ⚷ 🖐 Ⓢ ♦
Lawyer, FIELD & FIELD PERRATON, 200 Oxford Tower, 10235 - 101 St. N.W., Edmonton, AB T5N 3V2 (403) 423-3003, FAX 424-7116. Born Lucy Lake, Sask. 1953. m. Lorimer Dawson. 2 ch. EDUC: Univ. of Alberta, B.A.(Psych.) 1975, LL.B.(Law) 1978. BAR: Alta., 1979. CAREER: since 1979 has had a civil litigation practice including commercial & insurance litigation, & also practises as a mediator. SELECTED PUBLICATIONS: "The Constructive Trust Revisited" (1 *Estates & Trusts Reports* 309, 1978). EDIT: Ed. Bd., *Stevenson & Cote Civil Procedure Guide.* AFFIL: Law Society of Alberta; Canadian Bar Association; Edmonton Bar Association; Legal Equality Action Fund; Law Society & Civil Litigation Mentor Program; Alberta Arbitration and Mediation Society. HONS: Bd. of Gov. Prize in Law for highest academic standing in 1st yr. law class, 1976. INTERESTS: alternate dispute resolution, particularly mediation; women's issues incl. violence against women. MISC: has given lectures to various community groups on women's issues; 1st female ed. of the *Alberta Law Review*, 1977. COMMENT: *"I have worked full time as a lawyer in private practice for almost 17 years and also have a family - a husband who is also a lawyer and two children aged seven and 13. I am a committed feminist and have, together with several of my partners, started an annual fundraising breakfast for the legal community in Edmonton to support programs that combat family violence. The first breakfast was held in Dec. 1991 and attracted about 200 people. The event has grown each year and expanded beyond the legal community. In Dec. 1994, our guest speaker was the federal Minister of Justice, Allan Rock, and we attracted over 800 people to the breakfast."*

Howell, Doris, R.N.,B.Sc.N., M.Sc.N. ■ ■ Ⓢ ⊕
Cancer/Palliative Care Consultant. R.R. #2, P.O. Box 51, Lisle, ON L0M 1M0 (705) 435-7704, FAX 435-7704. 2 ch. Jess, Kaitlin. EDUC: Lambton Coll. Sch. of Nursing, Sarnia, Ont., R.N. 1975; Univ. of Ottawa, B.Sc.N. 1979; Univ. of Toronto, M.Sc.N. 1983. CAREER: Staff Nurse, Medical Unit, St. Anthony's Hospital, The Pas, Man., 1975-76; Staff Nurse, Medical Unit, Royal Inland Hospital, Kamloops, B.C., Apr.-Aug. 1977; Staff Nurse, Neurosurgery & Gynecology, Ottawa Civic Hospital, Ottawa, Ont., 1977-79; Staff Nurse, Palliative Care Unit, Toronto Grace Hospital, Toronto, 1979-81; Clinical Trials Nurse Symptom Mgmt, Princess Margaret Hospital, 1981-82; Palliative Care Coord./Clinician, Oshawa Gen. Hospital, Oshawa, Ont., 1981-82; Coord./Consultant, Community Palliative Care, Joseph Brant Memorial Hospital, Burlington, Ont., 1983-84; Clinical Nurse Specialist, Oncology/Palliative Care, Centenary Health Centre, Scarborough, Ont., 1984-90; Clinical Nurse Specialist, Oncology Research, Mount Sinai Hospital, Toronto, 1991-92; Nursing Unit Administrator/Clinical Nurse Specialist, Oncology, 1992-93; Cancer Care Consultant, independent practice, 1993 to date. SELECTED PUBLICATIONS: "Impact of Terminal Illness on the Spouse" (*Journal of Palliative Care* 2:1, 1986); co-author with M. Deachman, *Supportive Care at Home: A Guide for Terminally Ill Patients and their Families* (Knoll Pharmaceutical, 1991, reprint 1994); "Feeling Your Best During Cancer Therapy: A Patient Education Program Empowering People with Cancer" (*Oncology Advisor* 2:2, 1994); co-author with S. Burlein-Hall, "Feeling Your Best During Cancer Therapy: The Follow-Up" (*Oncology Advisor* 1:2, 1996); *A Comprehensive Guide to Breast Cancer* (1996); several works in progress. AFFIL: Canadian Association of Nurses in Oncology (Interest Group Rep., CNA 1993-96); The Council for the Advancement of Cancer Pain Management (Steering Committee 1993); Palliative Care Initiatives for Ontario (Educ. Task Force 1993); National Forum on Breast Cancer, Montreal (Educ./Support Working Group 1993); Registered Nurses' Association of Ontario/Canadian Nurses' Association (Independent Practice Nurses' Interest Group 1996). HONS: Imperial Oil Teagle Award for Higher Educ., 1973; Ont. Grad. Scholarship, 1980; Marie Bell Puzitz Award, 1981. MISC: numerous presentations, conferences across Canada, 1983 to date. COMMENT: *"I suspect one of my most notable achievements would be surviving as a nurse entrepreneur in the current economic environment in which we all find ourselves. I decided three years ago to seize the day and leave a secure position as a nursing unit administrator to independently position myself to make a greater impact on the quality of care of people living with cancer and their families. Quietly and humbly I continue to seek opportunities that will allow me to influence the care of people with cancer and particularly to raise the visibility of nurses in the health care system. I practice the art of nursing and I work to instill that art in others and to move our systems to be more humanistic in their approach to caregiving. Person by person I hope that I am making a difference."*

Howson, Elizabeth A., B.E.S.,MCIP, RPP ⚛ 🍁 🎾
Partner, MACAULAY SHIOMI HOWSON LTD., 293 Eglinton Ave. E., Toronto, ON M4P 1L3 (416) 487-4101, FAX 487-5489. Born Toronto 1951. m. Gregory Marlatt. 1 ch. Trevor Marlatt. **EDUC:** Univ. of Waterloo, B.E.S.(Urban & Reg. Planning) 1975. **CAREER:** Planner, James F. MacLaren Limited, 1975-78; Planner, City of London, 1979-81; Sr. Planner, Walker Wright Young Associates Limited, 1981-83; Ptnr, Macaulay Shiomi Howson Ltd., 1983 to date. **AFFIL:** Ontario Professional Planners' Institute (Examiner); Family Day Care Services (Dir.); Babypoint Club (VP); Toronto Chapter, Multiple Sclerosis Society (former Dir.); Canadian Association of Women Executives & Entrepreneurs. **HONS:** Honour Award, "Neighbourhood Plans," Canadian Institute of Planners, 1994. **INTERESTS:** tennis; cross-country skiing. **MISC:** initiated workshop for Ontario Professional Planners' Institute on "How to Hire & Manage Consultants" and "Zoning Problems and Answers."

Hoy, Alexandra (Alix), B.A.,LL.B. ■■ ⚖
Partner, LANG MICHENER (law firm), BCE Place, 181 Bay St., Ste. 2500, Toronto, ON M5J 2T7 (416) 307-4036, FAX 365-1719, EMAIL ahoy@toronto.langmichener.ca. Born N. Vancouver. m. Mark Feldman. 2 ch. Nicholas, Estée. **EDUC:** York Univ., Fac. of Fine Arts, B.A.(Hons., Film) 1975; Osgoode Hall Law Sch., LL.B. 1978. **DIRECTOR:** IKEA Limited. **COMMENT:** *"Represents major public and private corporations including leaders in the communications, entertainment and retail sectors. Involved in significant corporate transactions."*

Hrastovec, Denise Mayea , B.A.,B.Comm., C.A. ■■ $ ☝
Chair and Partner, COLLINS BARROW CHARTERED ACCOUNTANTS (public acctg), 441 Pelissier, Windsor, ON N9A 4L2 (519) 258-5800, FAX 256-2160. Born Windsor, Ont. 1957. m. Peter Hrastovec. 2 ch. **EDUC:** Univ. of Windsor, B.A.(English) 1977, B.Comm. (Acctg) 1979; Institute of Chartered Accountants of Ontario, C.A. 1981. **CAREER:** Ptnr, Meanwell Goodwin & Co., 1984-88; Ptnr, Collins Barrow, 1988 to date; Chair, 1996 to date. **AFFIL:** Big Sisters of Windsor & Essex County (Advisory Committee 1990 to date); Windsor Women's Incentive Centre (Advisory Committee 1996); Univ. of Windsor (Bd. of Gov. 1987 to date); Assumption Univ. (Bd. of Regents 1987 to date). **INTERESTS:** performing arts; travel. **COMMENT:** *"First woman to chair a top-10 Canadian accounting firm. Serves owner-managed businesses primarily in accounting, auditing, tax and management advisory fields."*

Hubley, Elizabeth Libbe, M.L.A. ■ 🍁
Member of the Legislative Assembly (4th Prince), GOVERNMENT OF PRINCE EDWARD ISLAND, Province House, Box 2890, Charlottetown, PE C1A 8C5. Born Howland, P.E.I. 1942. m. Richard Hubley. 6 ch. **EDUC:** Prince of Wales Coll.; Nova Scotia Coll. of Art & Design. **CAREER:** employed with various firms, Calgary, Montreal & Halifax; M.L.A., 4th Prince, 1989 to date; has served on the Standing Committee on Agric., the Standing Committee on Fisheries & Aquaculture, Tourism, Energy & Forestry, & the Special Committee on Maritime Econ. Integration. **AFFIL:** Kensington United Church. **MISC:** founded the "Stepping Out" Studio in Kensington, & has been choreographer & instructor of The Lady Slipper Step Dancers for the past 11 yrs.

Huddart, The Hon. Carol Mahood, B.A., LL.B. ■ ⚖
Judge, THE COURT OF APPEAL OF BRITISH COLUMBIA, The Law Courts, 800 Smithe St., Vancouver, BC V6Z 2E1 (604) 660-9563, FAX 660-5198. Born Peterborough, Ont. 1938. w. 3 ch. **EDUC:** Univ. of Toronto, B.A.(Pol. Sci. & Econ.) 1959; Osgoode Hall, LL.B.(Law) 1963.

Hudson, Susanne ■ 📖 $
President, SUSANNE HUDSON CONSULTING, 43 Castle Frank Rd., Toronto, ON M4W 2Z5 (416) 944-2536, FAX 944-0457. Born 1944. d. 2 ch. Julie Beattie, Stephanie Beattie. **CAREER:** Registered Nurse, 1966-78; Sales Mgr, T. Eaton Co., 1978-80; Buyer, 1980-81; nat'l advtg sales, *Harrowsmith* Magazine, 1981-82; nat'l advtg sales, *Toronto Life* Magazine, 1982-83; Advtg Dir., 1983-85; Publisher, *Your Money* Magazine, 1985-88; Publisher, *Canadian Geographic*, 1988-94; Pres., Susanne Hudson Consulting. **MISC:** Susanne Hudson Consulting specializes in mktg & magazine/catalogue publishing.

Huggan, Isabel, B.A. ■■ 📖
Writer. EMAIL i.huggan@cgnet.com. Born Kitchener, Ont. 1943. m. Robert Huggan. 1 ch. Abbey Clare. **EDUC:** Univ. of Western Ontario, B.A.(English & Phil.) 1965. **SELECTED PUBLICATIONS:** *The Elizabeth Stories* (short stories, Oberon 1984/HarperCollins, 1990); *You Never Know* (Knopf Canada, 1993). **AFFIL:** PEN. **HONS:** New Voice of the Year Award, Quality Paperback Bookclub (Book of the Month Club), 1987. **MISC:** creative writing workshops in Canada, Australia, France, Hong Kong &

the Philippines. **COMMENT:** *"Since 1987, I have lived outside Canada because of my husband's job. This expatriate existence is influencing my writing and teaching in unpredictable ways."*

Hughes, Barbara Dorothy, Q.C. $
Chair & Chief Executive Officer, EVANGELINE TRUST COMPANY, 535 Albert St., Box 10, Windsor, NS B0N 2T0 (902) 798-8326, FAX 798-3656. Born Bournemouth, UK. m. Gordon F. 1 ch. **EDUC:** Univ. of London, LL.B. 1949. **BAR:** Gray's Inn, London, UK, 1950; N.S., 1951. **CAREER:** legal practice, Windsor, N.S., 1951-94; Chair & CEO, Evangeline Financial Services Corporation & Evangeline Trust Company. **DIRECTOR:** Circuit Investment Ltd.; Maritime Telegraph & Telephone Co.; Ocean Co. Ltd. **AFFIL:** Investmental Dealers Association of Canada (Public Dir.); Participaction (Dir. 1972-85; Chrm 1977-82; Gov.); King's-Edgehill (Gov.); Royal Over-Seas League (Hon. Corresponding Sec.); Acadia Univ. (Gov.); Canadian Bar Association; N.S. Barristers' Society; N.S. Bar Council (1956-58); Hants County Barristers' Society (Pres. 1979). **HONS:** Queen's Counsel, N.S., 1971; Civic Award, Town of Windsor, 1978.

Hughes, Clara ■■ ⚾
Olympic Athlete. c/o Canadian Olympic Association. Born Winnipeg 1972. **SPORTS CAREER:** full-time athlete; mbr., Cdn Nat'l Cycling Team, 1991 to date. Olympic Games: Bronze, road ind. time trial, 1996. World championships: 2nd, road ind. time trial, 12th, ind. pursuit, & 30th, road race, 1995; 4th, road ind. time trial, 1994. Int'l tours/races: 1st, prologue, & 1st, time trial (Tour de l'Aude, France), 1995. World Cup: 1st, ind. pursuit, 1992. Pan Am Games: 2nd, road race, & 3rd, road ind. time trial, 1995. Commonwealth Games: 2nd, team time trial, 1994. Canadian championships: 1st, road ind. time trial, & 4th, road race, 1995; 1st, road ind. time trial, & 3rd, road race, 1994; 1st, ind. pursuit, & 1st, road ind. time trial, 1993; 1st, road race, 1992; 1st, ind. pursuit, 1990. **INTERESTS:** reading; drinking coffee.

Hughes, Linda, B.A. ✎ $
Publisher, *THE EDMONTON JOURNAL*, 10006 - 101 St., Box 2421, Edmonton, AB T5J 2S6 (403) 429-5129, FAX 429-5536. Born Princeton, B.C. 1950. m. George Ward. 2 ch. **EDUC:** Univ. of Victoria, B.A.(Hist./Econ.) 1972. **CAREER:** journalist, *Victoria Daily Times*, 1972-76; journalist, *The Edmonton Journal*, 1976-78; Ed. Bd., 1978 to date; Chief, Legislature Bureau, 1979-80; Asst. City Ed., 1980-81; City Ed., 1981-84; News Ed., 1984-85; Asst. Mng Ed., 1985-87; Ed.-in-Chief, 1987-92; Publisher, 1992 to date; Task Force on Equal Opportunities, Southam Newspapers; Task Force on Newspaper Readership, Southam Newspapers, 1992. **AFFIL:** National Newspaper Awards (Gov.); Canadian Committee to Protect Journalists. **HONS:** Southam Fellowship 1977.

Hughes, Margaret E., B.A.,LL.B.,LL.M., M.S.W. 🎓 ⚖ ☝
Professor, Faculty of Law, UNIVERSITY OF CALGARY, PF-B 4315, 2500 University Dr. N.W., Calgary, AB T2N 1N4 (403) 220-4012, EMAIL hughesm@aco.ucalgary.ca. Born Saskatoon 1943. m. John R. Hughes. 2 ch. Shannon M., Krista L. **EDUC:** Univ. of Saskatchewan, B.A. 1965, LL.B. 1966; Univ. of Michigan, LL.M. 1968, M.S.W. 1968. **CAREER:** Asst. Prof., Univ. of Windsor, 1968-71; Assoc. Prof., 1971-75; Cnsl, Exec. Interchange Program, Dept. of Justice, Gov't of Canada, Ottawa, 1975-77; Cnsl, Dept. of Justice, 1977-78; Prof., Univ. of Saskatchewan, 1978-84; Dean, Fac. of Law, Univ. of Calgary, 1984-89; Prof., 1989 to date. **SELECTED PUBLICATIONS:** contributed articles to professional journals & chapters of books. **AFFIL:** Centre for Higher Educational Research & Development for sr. univ. administrators, Univ. of Manitoba (Fac.); Industrial Relations Research Group, Univ. of Calgary (Bd. of Dir.); Annual Provincial Labour Arbitration Conference (Co-Chair); Law Societies of Alberta, Saskatchewan & Ontario; Canadian Council of Law Deans (Chair 1987-88); Canadian Research Institute for Law & Families (Founding Exec. Committee; Exec. Committee 1986-88; Bd. of Dir. 1986-89). **INTERESTS:** swimming; skiing; hiking. **MISC:** 1st female dean of a Cdn law sch. when appointed in 1984. **COMMENT:** *"Educator and specialist in employment and labour law. Special research interests in legal issues in university administration."*

Hughes, Monica 📜 📖
Writer. 13816 - 110A Ave., Edmonton, AB T5M 2M9 (603) 455-5602. Born Liverpool, UK. m. Glen Hughes. 4 ch. Liz, Adrienne, Russell, Tom. **EDUC:** educated in England & Scotland. **CAREER:** Women's Royal Navy Service during WWII; worked in a dress factory & a bank, Zimbabwe, 2 yrs.; emigrated to Canada, 1952; National Research Council, Ottawa, 1952-57; began seriously writing for young readers, 1971; writer, 1971 to date; short-term writer's residencies in Toronto Libraries, Windsor Library & Medicine Hat; Writer-in-Residence, Univ. of Alberta, 1 yr., 1984-85; mbr.,

Writers' & Publishers' Advisory Council, 1985-88; Henry Kreisel Lecture, 1987; Writer-in-Residence, Edmonton Public Library, 6 months, 1988-89. **SELECTED PUBLICATIONS:** *Gold-Fever Trail* (Edmonton: LeBel, 1974); *The Tomorrow City* (London, UK: Hamish Hamilton, 1978); *The Keeper of the Isis Light* (London, UK: Hamish Hamilton, 1980); *Hunter in the Dark* (Toronto: Irwin, 1982); *Blaine's Way* (Toronto: Irwin, 1986); *The Golden Aquarians* (Toronto: Harper Collins, 1994); *Castle Tourmandyne* (Toronto: HarperCollins, 1995); *Where Have You Been, Billy-Boy?* (Toronto: HarperCollins, 1995); 19 other novels; 2 picture books; short stories published in anthologies & collections incl. *Dragons and Dreams*, Jane Yolen ed. (New York: Harper, 1985) & *Mother's Day*, M. Hodgson ed. (UK: Methuen, 1992). **AFFIL:** Writers' Union of Canada; Writers' Guild of Alberta (Sec. 1988-89); Canadian Society of Authors, Illustrators & Performers; PEN International; SF Canada; International Board on Books for Young People (IBBY). **HONS:** Beaver Award (*Hunter in the Dark*), 1981; Alberta Culture Juvenile Novel Award (*Hunter in the Dark*), 1981; Vicky Metcalf Award, body of work, 1981; Vicky Metcalf Award, short story, 1983; Canada Council Prize for Children's Literature, 1981, 1982; Certificate of Honour (*Keeper of the Isis Light*), IBBY, 1982; Young Adult Novel Award (*Hunter in the Dark*), Library Association, 1983; R. Ross Annett Award, Writers' Guild of Alberta, 1983, 1984, 1987, 1992; Silver Feather Award, Germany (*Hunter in the Dark*), 1986; Alberta Achievement Award, Excellence Category, 1986; Boeken Leeuw (Book Lion), Belgium (*Hunter in the Dark*), 1987; City of Edmonton Cultural Creative Arts Award, 1988. **MISC:** recipient, Sr. Writing Grant, Alberta Foundation for Literary Arts, 1989; papers given at various conferences & meetings. **COMMENT:** *"Although I cannot remember a time when I was not either dreaming of being, or struggling to be, a writer, it was not until 1971 that I began seriously writing for young people. Between 1974 and 1995, I have had 27 novels published, about two-thirds of which are science fiction, as well as two picture books."*

Hughes, Pamela S., B.A.,LL.B.,LL.M. ⚖
Counsel, BLAKE, CASSELS AND GRAYDON, Commerce Court W., Box 25, Toronto, ON M5L 1A9 (416) 863-2226, FAX 863-3033, EMAIL ajp@blakes.ca. Born Winnipeg 1951. m. David P. Hughes. 3 ch. **EDUC:** McGill Univ., B.A. 1974, LL.B. 1977; Univ. of Toronto, LL.M. 1978. **BAR:** Ont., 1980. **CAREER:** corp./commercial bnkg & securities lawyer, Tory Tory

DesLauriers & Binnington, 1980-87; Solicitor, Corp. Fin. Branch, Ontario Securities Commission, 1987-88; Deputy Dir., Legal Corp. Fin. Branch, 1989-91; Dir., Capital Mkts & Int'l Mkts Branch, 1991-95; Cnsl, Blake, Cassels and Graydon, 1995 to date. **SELECTED PUBLICATIONS:** "Shelf Prospectus System Implemented" (*International Financial Law Review* June 1991); "International Securities Markets, Canada-US Multi-jurisdictional System" (*Practicing Law Institute* July 1991); "Canada revises proposed foreign issues prospectus system" (*International Financial Law Review*, June 1995). **AFFIL:** Law Society of Upper Canada; International Bar Association. **INTERESTS:** swimming; tennis; gardening. **COMMENT:** *"Pamela Hughes practises securities law with Blake, Cassels and Graydon in Toronto and teaches international securities regulation at the University of Toronto. As part of her distinguished career at the Ontario Securities Commission, Ms. Hughes was the primary negotiator of the multi-jurisdictional disclosure system between Canada and the US. She was also the OSC representative on the International Organization of Securities Commissions working groups on secondary markets and international equity offers."*

Hughes, Patricia, B.A.,M.A.,Ph.D., LL.B. ⚖ ⚖
Associate Professor, Mary Louise Lynch Chair in Women and Law, Faculty of Law, UNIVERSITY OF NEW BRUNSWICK, P.O. Box 4400, Fredericton, NB E3B 5A3 (506) 453-4738, FAX 453-4604. Born Bedworth, UK 1948. s. **EDUC:** McMaster Univ., B.A. 1970, M.A. 1971; Univ. of Toronto, Ph.D. 1975; Osgoode Hall Law Sch., LL.B. 1982. **BAR:** Ont., 1984. **CAREER:** Summer appointments, Social Sciences, Atkinson Coll., York Univ., 1980-81; Asst. Prof., Brandon Univ., 1971-71; Asst. Prof., Nipissing Univ. Coll., 1975-79; articling student, Laskin, Jack and Harris, 1982-83; researcher, Abella Commission on Equality & Equity in Employment, 1983; Cnsl, Ont. Ministry of the Attorney Gen., 1984-86; V-Chair, Ont. Labour Rel'ns Bd., 1986-89; Alternate Chair, Ont. Pay Equity Hearings Tribunal, 1989-92; Arbitrator, 1989 to date; Mary Louise Lynch Chair of Women & Law, Fac. of Law, Univ. of New Brunswick, 1992 to date. **SELECTED PUBLICATIONS:** "When Interests Collide: the Union's Duty of Fair Representation in the Workplace" (*Employment and Labour Law Reporter* 1986); "Feminism and Legal Education: Quandaries of Inclusion and Exclusion" (*University of New Brunswick Law Journal* 1993); "The Evolving Conceptual Framework of Sexual Harassment" (*Canadian*

Labour and Employment Law Journal, 1994); "Domestic Legal Aid: A Claim to Equality" (*Review of Constitutional Studies*, 1995); "The Evolution of a Concept: The Identity of 'Employer' For Pay Equity Purposes" (*Canadian Journal of Administrative Law & Practice*, 1995); "Women, Sexual Abuse by Professionals, and the Law: Changing Parameters" (*Queen's Law Journal*, 1996); various other publications. **EDIT:** Ed. Bd., *Canadian Labour Law Journal*; Ed. Bd., *Employment and Labour Law Reporter*; Ed. Bd., *Canadian Journal of Community Mental Health*. **AFFIL:** Law Society of Upper Canada; Law Society of N.B. (Gender Equality Committee); Canadian Bar Association; Canadian Bar Association, N.B. Branch (Implementation Committee for Wilson Report); LEAF-N.B. (Pres.); International Centre for Human Rights & Democratic Development. **INTERESTS:** feminist activism; gardening; cooking; running; art. **MISC:** referee for various journals & granting agencies; numerous conference presentations. **COMMENT:** *"In both my personal life and my professional work, I seek to communicate that feminist views and practice are a normal way of approaching the world."*

Hughes, Sherron J.L., B.A.,M.A., LL.B. ⚖ ✊ ☝

Lawyer, ATHEY, GREGORY AND HUGHES, 206 Rookwood Ave., Ste. 210, Fredericton, NB E3B 2M2 (506) 458-8060, FAX 459-8288. Born Winnipeg. m. Julian A.G. Dickson. **EDUC:** Univ. of Manitoba, B.A.(Psych.) 1971; Univ. of New Brunswick, M.A.(Psych.) 1973, LL.B. 1977. **BAR:** N.B., 1977. **CAREER:** Psychometrist, Dept. of Justice, Prov. of N.B., 1972-74; Lawyer, Garvie and Potter, Fredericton, 1977-78; Assoc., Atkinson and Atkinson, 1978-87; Lawyer, Sherron Hughes and Associates, 1987-88; Ptnr, Hughes Constable, 1988-93; Lawyer, Sherron J.L. Hughes, 1993-94; Ptnr, Athey, Gregory and Hughes, 1994 to date. **AFFIL:** Law Society of N.B. (Legal Aid Committee 2 yrs.; course leader & lecturer, Family Law Section, Bar Admission Course 1984-93; Chair, Bar Admission Course Committee 1990-93; Examination Committee 1991-93; Treas. 1993-94; VP 1994-95; Pres. 1995-96; Gender Equality Committee); Canadian Bar Association (mbr. of Council, N.B. Branch 1985-93; Chair, Family Law Subsection, N.B. Branch 1990-92); Legal Aid N.B. (Area Dir. for Fredericton 1986-90); Continuing Legal Education for N.B. (lecturer); York-Sunbury Law Society (Pres. 1989-90); N.B. Law Foundation, Univ. of New Brunswick, Fac. of Law Endowment Trust (Trustee); Family Enrichment & Counselling Svcs (Dir., Fredericton; Dir., Prov.); Women in Transition House, Fredericton (Dir.); United Way/Centraide Fredericton Inc. (Dir. 1983-89; Pres. 1988-89); Women's Legal Education & Action Fund (Dir. 1989-91); Mental Health Commission of N.B. (VP 1990-94). **HONS:** Queen's Counsel, Prov. of N.B., 1993. **COMMENT:** *"I was admitted to the New Brunswick Bar in 1977 and have been active in community and professional activities since that time. In 1993, I was the first woman elected to the executive of the Law Society of New Brunswick and will be its first woman president."*

Hughes Anthony, Nancy, B.A. ■ $

Vice-President, Group and Pension Services, METROPOLITAN LIFE INSURANCE COMPANY, 99 Bank St., Ottawa, ON K1P 5A3 (613) 560-6988, FAX 560-7668. Born Montreal 1949. m. Brian Anthony. 2 ch. **EDUC:** McGill Univ., B.A. **CAREER:** VP, Group Insur., Metropolitan Life Insurance Company. **AFFIL:** Ottawa General Hospital (V-Chrm, Bd. of Trustees); Life Insurance Institute of Canada (Dir.).

Huglo Robertson, Christine, B.A. ⚖ 🎓 ✊

Executive Director, CANADIAN INSTITUTE FOR THE ADMINISTRATION OF JUSTICE, Faculty of Law, Université de Montréal, CP 6128, Succ. Centre-Ville, Montréal, QC H3C 3J7 (514) 343-6157, FAX 343-6296. Born Marseille, France 1949. 3 ch. Alexandre, Kirsten, Anders. **EDUC:** Coll. Marie de France, Bacc.(Phil.) 1968; Univ. de Montréal, B.A.(Comm.) 1981. **CAREER:** Admin. Asst. to the Dir. of Studies, Goethe Institute, 1972-78; Info. Officer, Continuing Educ. Dept., Vanier Coll., 1978-81; Asst. to the Dir., Vanier Seminar Centre, 1982-85; Asst. to the Academic Dean, Vanier Coll., 1985-88; Asst. Exec. Dir., Canadian Institute for the Administration of Justice, 1988-93; Exec. Dir., 1993 to date. **AFFIL:** Institut canadien des affaires internationales; Association des parents du Coll. Jean-de-Brébeuf; Trésorière du comté électoral de Westmount; Association québécoise pour la formation et la performance; Société canadienne des Relations Publiques; Association québécoise des relationnistes; Publicity Club; Club des Relations internationales, Univ. de Montréal (VP; Sec.); Alliance française de Montréal (Conseil). **INTERESTS:** travel; photography; archaeology; reading; outdoor activities; arts and crafts. **MISC:** Chargée de l'organisation et de la planification de la Conférence sur la crise constitutionelle du Canada, 1991; Collaboration au Colloque Deauville IV, Montréal, 1981; Déléguée invitée à l'Organisation de l'Aviation civile internationale, Convention internationale à Montréal, 1970. **COMMENT:** *"She values freedom, harmony, integrity, trust, responsibil-*

ity, respect, cooperation, tolerance and creativity, and strives in her every endeavour to achieve the expression of these values. She is task-oriented and sees herself as a facilitator between people and organizations. Having an ability to organize, tries to convey information in the best possible manner to respond to the needs of the various people concerned."

Hume, Valerie, B.A.,Ph.D. ■ 🍁 ✊ ⚛
Policy Coordinator, Sustainable Development, Department of Indian Affairs and Northern Development, GOVERNMENT OF CANADA, Ottawa, ON K1A 0H4 (819) 997-9480, FAX 953-2590, EMAIL humev@inac.gc.ca. Born Auckland 1934. s. **EDUC:** Auckland Univ., B.A.(Geography) 1957, Dip.Ed.(Educ.) 1960; Edinburgh Univ., Ph.D.(Geography) 1970; National Defence Coll., 1975-76. **CAREER:** Asst. Prof., York Univ., 1969-76; Head, Policy & Planning of Northern Roads & Airstrips, Fed. Dept. of Indian Affairs & Northern Dev., 1976-87; Adjunct Prof., Carleton Univ., 1978-79; Head, Land Programs, Dept. of Indian Affairs & Northern Dev., 1987-88; Dir., Phys. & Mathematical Sciences, Natural Sciences & Engineering Research Council, 1989; Policy Coord. Sustainable Dev., Dept. of Indian Affairs & Northern Dev., 1989 to date. **SELECTED PUBLICATIONS:** "Planning of Scottish New Towns" (*Proceedings of the Annual Meetings of the Canadian Association of Geographers* 1970); "Northern Road Planning," with W.G. Cleghorn (*Proceedings of Northern Transportation Conference* Oct. 1982); "Sustainable Development in Canada's North" (*Visions 2020* background paper, 1990); "Northern Information Network" (*Polartech '92 Proceedings* Jan. 1992); "UNIFEM Supports Struggle for Equality" (*Peace and Environment News* Apr. 1994). **AFFIL:** Canadian Association of Geographers; Association of American Geographers; Canadian Institute of International Affairs (Chair, Nat'l Capital Branch 1984-86; Treas. 1988-92); Zonta International (various exec. positions incl. Pres., Zonta Club of Ottawa 1992-94; Area Dir. 1996 to date); Ottawa Field-Naturalists (Council Mbr. 1977-80); McLaughlin Coll., York Univ. (Fellow); Canadian Red Cross, Ottawa-Carleton Branch (Council Mbr.; Sec. 1992-94; VP); Canadian Association for the Club of Rome; Canadian Committee for UNIFEM (Founding Pres. 1993-95); Britannia Yacht Club; Canadian Power & Sail Squadron; Royal Over-Seas League. **HONS:** Deputy Minister's Outstanding Achievement Award, 1991-92. **INTERESTS:** tennis; badminton; walking; camping; travel; public speaking; cottaging; flute playing. **COMMENT:** *"A geographer working professionally toward sustainable development in the circumpolar regions. As a volunteer promoting UNIFEM in order to help women in the developing world to achieve their goals."*

Hummerstone, Jill ■■ ⚖ ✊
First Nations Programs Coordinator, Matsqui Institution, Correctional Service of Canada, GOVERNMENT OF CANADA, 33344 King Rd., Abbotsford, BC V2S 4P3 (604) 859-4841, FAX 850-8343. Born Den Hague, Netherlands 1946. m. Eric. 5 ch. Shawn, Bryce, Ellen, Debbie, Wendy. **CAREER:** Social & Cultural Dev. Officer; First Nations Program Coord. **COMMENT:** *"I am a non-Native person who has spent my career in Corrections devoted to making things better for First Nations men in jail. I have been accepted by Aboriginal inmates and honoured by them and the Elders."*

Humphreys, Gillian G., B.Tech.,M.Sc. $
Vice-President, CANADIAN FACTS, 1075 Bay St., Toronto, ON M5S 2X5 (416) 924-5751, FAX 923-7085. Born Liskeard, Cornwall, UK 1944. d. **EDUC:** Univ. of Bradford, B.Tech. 1966, M.Sc. 1967. **CAREER:** Process Eng., J. Lyons & Co. Ltd., 1967-69; Research Asst., Marplan, UK, 1969-70; Research Officer, H.J. Heinz Co. Ltd., UK, 1970-74; Mkt Research Mgr, Cadbury Ltd., UK, 1974-76; Mkt Research Mgr, General Foods Inc., Canada, 1976-79; VP, Canadian Facts, 1979 to date. **SELECTED PUBLICATIONS:** *Proceedings of Joint Symposium on Advances in Data Collection* (Statistics Canada/P.M.R.S., 1982); "Substantiating Claims: The Right Tests Done The Right Way," *Misleading Advertising: Advertising and the Law in the Electronic Age* (The Canadian Institute, 1995). **DIRECTOR:** CF Group Inc. **AFFIL:** Professional Marketing Research Society (Pres. 1980-81; Mbr., Nat'l Exec. 1977-78, 1979-80, 1981-82); Market Research Society, UK. **INTERESTS:** classical music; ballet; reading; politics.

Hundal, Nancy, B.A. 📜 📖
Author. 1517 W. 58th Ave., Vancouver, BC V6P 1W6 (604) 263-5970. Born Vancouver 1957. m. Derek Hundal. 3 ch. Joshua, Bianca, Lucas. **EDUC:** Univ. of British Columbia, B.A.(English/French) 1979; Teaching Certificate (Educ.) 1980. **CAREER:** teacher & teacher/librarian, Vancouver Sch. Bd., 1980-83, 1985 to date; children's author. **SELECTED PUBLICATIONS:** *I Heard My Mother Call My Name* (1990); *November Boots* (1993); *Puddle Duck* (1995); other stories & poems in children's magazines. **AFFIL:** Children's Literature Roundtable; Children's Writers & Illustrators of B.C. **HONS:** B.C. Book Prize (Sheila Egoff

Children's Prize) for *I Heard My Mother Call My Name*, 1990; shortlisted for Ruth Schwartz Award for *November Boots*, 1994. INTERESTS: singing in madrigal group; craftwork; reading. COMMENT: *"I am a mother, author and teacher, combining a love of children and literature with the goal of delighting and enriching my young readers."*

Hunter, Beatrice E. (née Cole), R.N., B.Sc. 🕲 ⊕ ▯
Past National President, NURSING SISTERS' ASSOCIATION OF CANADA. w. Vernon H. Hunter. EDUC: Regina General Hospital, R.N. 1944; Univ. of Alberta, B.Sc. 1953. CAREER: Lt. (N.S.), R.C.A.M.C., 1944-46; Lt. (N.S.) then Captain (Matron), R.C.A.M.C. (Reserve) 1950-60; Occupational Health Nurse, Imperial Oil, 1954-60; Sr. Sci. Instructor, St. Paul's Hospital Vancouver, 1960-66; Clinical Coord., Univ. Hospital, Edmonton, 1967-72; Dir., Nursing Educ., Misericordia Hospital Sch. of Nursing, 1974-82. SELECTED PUBLICATIONS: *Nursing Sisters' Association of Canada National Directory and Commemorative Issue* (1994). EDIT: Ed., *Newsletter, Leduc/Devon Oilfield Historical Society*, 1991 to date. AFFIL: Nursing Sisters' Association of Canada (Nat'l Pres. 1992-94); Leduc/Devon Oilfield Historical Society. HONS: Canada 125 Medal, 1992. INTERESTS: travel; writing; golf.

Hunter, Maureen, B.A. ■ 🖺
Playwright. c/o Christopher Banks & Associates, 6 Adelaide St. E., Ste. 610, Toronto, ON M5G 1H6 (416) 214-1155, FAX 214-1150. Born Indian Head, Sask. 1947. m. Gary Hunter. EDUC: Univ. of Saskatchewan, B.A. 1970. CAREER: journalist, *Saskatoon Star-Phoenix* & *Winnipeg Tribune*, 1968-73; Info. Officer/Exec. Asst. to the Bd./Sec. to Bd./Exec. Dir. of Admin., Canadian Wheat Board, 1973-83; full-time writer, 1983 to date; Playwright-in-Residence, Manitoba Theatre Centre, 1993 to date. SELECTED CREDITS: 6 full-length plays incl. *Footprints on the Moon*, premiered by Agassiz Theatre, Winnipeg, 1988; *Beautiful Lake Winnipeg*, Manitoba Theatre Centre, 1990; *Transit of Venus*, Manitoba Theatre Centre, 1992; *Atlantis*, Manitoba Theatre Centre & Theatre Calgary, 1996; numerous productions in Canada. SELECTED PUBLICATIONS: *Footprints On The Moon*, *Beautiful Lake Winnipeg*, *Transit of Venus*, *Atlantis* (all Blizzard Publishing); *Transit of Venus* in *3-D English: Contemporary Canadian Scripts*, Vol. 2 (Prentice Hall Canada); play extracts in various anthologies. AFFIL: Playwrights' Union of Canada; Manitoba Writers' Guild. HONS: *Footprints on the Moon* nominated for the

Gov. General's Award for Drama, 1988; nomination, Outstanding New Play (*Transit of Venus*), Dora Mavor Moore Award, 1995. MISC: translations in progress: *Transit of Venus* (Danish); *Atlantis* (Danish & French); *Transit of Venus* prod. by Royal Shakespeare Co., England, 1993-94 & by BBC Radio, 1996.

Huntsman, Elizabeth, B.A.,M.A.,Ph.D., R.Psych. ⊕
Head, Department of Psychology, BRITISH COLUMBIA'S CHILDREN'S HOSPITAL, 4480 Oak St., Vancouver, BC V6H 3V4 (604) 875-2147, EMAIL ehuntsman@wpog.childhosp.bc.ca. Born Calif. 1945. s. EDUC: Azusa Pacific, B.A.(Psych.) 1966; Pepperdine Univ., M.A. (Psych.) 1967; Univ. of Washington, Ph.D.(Psych.) 1973. CAREER: Instructor, Pepperdine Univ., 1967; Psychologist, Washington State Cerebral Palsy Center, 1967-70; Dir., Washington State Cooperative Program for the Multiply Handicapped, 1970; Instructor, Makah Indian Reservation, State of Washington, & Peninsula Coll., 1972; Research Asst., Dept. of Neurosurgery, Univ. of Washington, 1972-74; Psychologist, Children's Hospital, Vancouver, 1974-75; Acting Head, Dept. of Psych., 1975-76; Dir. of Programs & Instructor, Antioch Univ., Vancouver Centre, 1977-79; Sr. Consultant, Ryane Consulting, Inc., 1979-83; Instructor, Dept. of Music Therapy, Capilano Coll., N. Vancouver, 1980-81 & 1984-88; Psychologist, British Columbia's Children's Hospital, 1984-88; private practice in psych., 1986-88; Psychologist, Vancouver Health Dept., 1987; Head, Dept. of Psych., British Columbia's Children's Hospital, 1988 to date. AFFIL: Coll. of Psychologists of B.C. (Registered Psychologist); Canadian Psychology Association; B.C. Psychology Association; Canadian Register of Health Service Providers in Psychology. HONS: California State Scholar; Fellow, National Institutes of Mental Health, US Dept. of Health. INTERESTS: children's health care; health care ethics. COMMENT: *"I head a department of 25 professionals responsible for clinical service, consulting, research and training. I am interested in how children and families cope with acute and long-term health concerns and make decisions about the care they receive."*

Hurlbut, Spring ■■ ⊗
Artist. 245 Carlaw Ave., # 207, Toronto, ON M4M 2S1 (416) 469-2371, FAX 469-2396. Born Toronto 1952. EDUC: Ontario Coll. of Art, 1971-73; N.S. Coll. of Art & Design, 1974-75. SELECTED PUBLICATIONS: *Sacrificial Ornament*, Southern Alberta Art Gallery. EXHIBITIONS: numerous solo exhibitions incl.:

Lingual Consoles/La Somnolence, The Power Plant, Toronto, 1995; "Designer's Diary" (*International Contract,* Jan. 1993); *Sacrificial Ornament,* Southern Alberta Art Gallery (travelled across Canada), 1991; *Entablatures,* Sable/Castelli Gallery, Toronto, 1990; over 10 group exhibitions incl.: *Towards a New Vision,* John Weber Gallery, N.Y., 1993; *Currents,* The Institute of Contemporary Art, Boston, 1991. MISC: subject of numerous magazine & newspaper articles, & catalogues incl.: *Between Here and There: The Memory of Disruption* (exhibition catalogue, Sao Paulo, Brazil, 1986); "Opening Doors" (*Art in America,* Nov. 1994); "Spring Hurlbut at The Power Plant" (*Art in America,* May 1995); "Sans Demarcation, Cultural Exchange Between Ontario and Quebec" (*Vanguard,* Mar. 1988); "Ritual Ornament/Elemental Design" (*Parachute* magazine, Oct./Dec. 1993); "Spring Hurlbut at The Municipal Art Society" (*Art in America,* Jan. 1993); "Waking up to eerie presences, and absences around us" (*The Globe and Mail,* Feb. 27, 1995).

Hurley, Adèle M., A.M., B.A., M.E.S. ■ ✦ 🕸 🖐
Chair, INTERNATIONAL JOINT COMMISSION, 112 St. Clair Ave. W., Ste. 401, Toronto, ON M4V 2Y3 (416) 923-5200, FAX 923-4911. EDUC: Glendon Coll., York Univ., B.A. 1974; York Univ., Masters Degree in Environmental Studies 1975. CAREER: Researcher, Pollution Probe Foundation, 1977-78; Environment Portfolio Researcher, Opposition Party, Prov. of Ont., 1978-80; Exec. Dir., Canadian Coalition on Acid Rain, 1980-87; Assoc. Prof., Institute of Environmental Studies, Univ. of Toronto, 1985; Pres., Perley and Hurley Ltd., Environment Consulting, 1986-92; Pres., Hurley and Associates Inc., 1992-95; Int'l Trade Advisory Committee-Task Force on Environment & Trade; Chair, Environmental Health & Safety Committee, Ontario Hydro; Co-Chair, Nuclear Review Committee, Ontario Hydro; Chair, International Joint Commission. AFFIL: Walter and Duncan Gordon Charitable Foundation (Trustee). HONS: Conservation Achievement Certificate, Federation of Ontario Naturalists, 1984; "White Hat Award," Pennsylvania Fish Commission, 1986; Lieutenant-Governor's Conservation Award for Ontario, 1989; co-recipient, William Gunn Award in Conservation, Federation of Ontario Naturalists, 1990. MISC: 1st woman Chair, International Joint Commission.

Hurley, Audrey June, R.N., S.C.M., R.S.C.N. 🖐 ♥ 🐟
President, LAUBACH LITERACY COUNCIL OF NEWFOUNDLAND AND LABRADOR, c/o 16 Hamil-ton St., Gander, NF A1V 1V7 (709) 256-3348. Born New Delhi, India 1931. m. Michael. 5 ch. EDUC: high sch., UK, 1947; Victorian Children's Hospital, Liverpool, R.S.C.N. 1948-51; Softon General Hospital, S.R.N. 1954, State Certified Midwife 1956. AFFIL: Laubach Literary Council of Newfoundland & Labrador (VP 1 yr.; Pres. 3 yrs.); Gander & Area Laubach Literary Council; Amnesty International (fieldworker 2 yrs.); World Development & Peace; Catholic Women's League of Canada; St. Joseph Parish Council (Sec. 3 yrs.); Interfaith (Group Sec.). HONS: Lieutenant Governor's Award for Volunteerism in Literacy, 1989; Certificate for Volunteerism in Literacy, Town of Gander, 1992; Certificate for Volunteerism, Action Awareness Disabilities, 1993; Certificate for more than 1,000 hours volunteerism, Laubach Literacy, 1993. INTERESTS: reading; oil painting; walking; meeting people. COMMENT: *"In a short period of time, I found myself alone. I lost my husband. I retired (no job) and all my five children had left home. So I had to start a new life for myself. I had to get busy. So I joined the various organizations and gave of myself and talents. I got back a lot more in love and friendship. Hence the new ME."*

Husband, Vicky, B.A. 🕸 ♥
Conservation Chair, SIERRA CLUB OF BRITISH COLUMBIA, 1525 Amelia St., Victoria, BC (604) 386-5255, FAX 386-4453. Born Victoria 1940. EDUC: Univ. of British Columbia, B.A. (Fine Arts/Hist.) 1963. CAREER: Pres., Friends of Ecological Reserves, 1987-91; Chair, Sierra Club of B.C., 1992-95; Conservation Chair, 1995 to date. SELECTED PUBLICATIONS: *Ancient Rainforests at Risk* (Sierra Club publication, 1992). AFFIL: B.C. Wild (Dir.). HONS: Fred M. Packard Award for Conservation, IUCN, 1987; "Global 500" Award for Conservation, U.N. Environment Programs (UNEP), 1988; runner-up, Lifetime Achievement Award, Environment Canada, 1989. MISC: Dir., Vancouver Island satellite mapping proj.; mbr., B.C. Round Table on the Environment & Economy, 1989-91. COMMENT: *"Vicky Husband was born in British Columbia and has worked full time as a volunteer for the last 10 years. She is totally committed to the protection of B.C.'s outstanding natural heritage. Deeply involved in the successful struggle to save South Moresby, Queen Charlotte Islands/Haida Gwaii, as a National Park Reserve. Resource person for media on forestry, wilderness and environment issues and has worked with CBC's The Journal and The Nature of Things, BCTV, CBC Radio, local media and TVOntario. She has made a major*

contribution to changing the way forests are managed in B.C. and works to raise public awareness of environmental issues through research, education and the media."

Hushion, Nancy ⊛
President, N.L. HUSHION AND ASSOCIATES, 489 King St. W., Ste. 303, Toronto, ON M5V 1L3 (416) 351-0216, FAX 351-0217, EMAIL nhushion@inforamp.net. Born Hamilton, Ont 1941. **EDUC:** McGill Univ., Grad. in Art Hist. **CAREER:** Coord. of Extension Svcs, Art Gallery of Ontario; Head, Extension Svcs Div.; Visual Arts Officer, Ontario Arts Council; Pres., N.L. Hushion and Associates. **AFFIL:** Ontario Association of Art Galleries (Bd.); Canadian Museums Association (Fellow; Bd.; Pres. 1982-83); International Council of Museums (ICOM) (Pres., Cdn Committee; Pres., Bd. of Dir. 1992; Exec. Council); Public Art Commission, City of Toronto (Chair). **HONS:** Canada 125 Medal. **MISC:** instrumental in the designation of Quebec City as the site for the 1992 Triennial of ICOM.

Hussey, Valerie, B.A. 📖 $
Publisher and President, KIDS CAN PRESS LTD., 29 Birch Ave., Toronto, ON M4V 1E2 (416) 925-5437, FAX 960-5437. Born N.Y. 1950. m. James Ian Graham. 1 ch. **EDUC:** S.U.N.Y., Buffalo, B.A.(English) 1972. **CAREER:** Ed., Macmillan, N.Y.C., 1973-74; Ed., General Publishing, 1975-76; Ed., Harcourt, Brace, Jovanovich, N.Y., 1977-79; Co-owner, Publisher & Pres., Kids Can Press, 1979 to date; Fac., Banff Publishing Workshop, 1990-94. **SELECTED PUBLICATIONS:** various articles in professional journals incl. a piece for the collection *Writers on Writing*, ed. David Booth; book reviewer, *The Globe and Mail*, 1979-80. **AFFIL:** Canadian Women's Foundation (Bd.).

Hutcheon, Linda, B.A.,M.A.,Ph.D. ■ 🎓 📜
University Professor of English and Comparative Literature, UNIVERSITY OF TORONTO, 7 King's College Circle, Toronto, ON M5S 1A1 (416) 978-6616, FAX 978-2836. Born Toronto 1947. m. Michael Hutcheon. **EDUC:** Univ. of Toronto, B.A. 1969, Ph.D. 1975; Cornell Univ., M.A. 1971. **CAREER:** Asst. Prof. of English, McMaster Univ., 1976-82; Visiting Prof., Grad. Centre for Comparative Lit., Univ. of Toronto, 1980-82; Assoc. Fac., Centre for Comparative Lit., 1980-88; Assoc. Prof. of English, McMaster Univ., 1982-85; Visiting Prof., Grad. Centre for Comparative Lit., Univ. of Toronto, 1984-85; Prof. of English, McMaster Univ., 1985-88; Prof. of English & Comparative Lit., Univ. of Toronto, 1988-96; Univ. Prof., 1996 to date. **SELECTED PUBLICATIONS:** *Narcissistic Narrative: The Metafictional Paradox* (Waterloo: Wilfrid Laurier Univ. Press, 1980; London & New York: Methuen, 1984); *The Canadian Postmodern: A Study of Contemporary English-Canadian Fiction* (Toronto: Oxford Univ. Press, 1988); *The Poetics of Postmodernism* (London & New York: Routledge, 1988); *The Politics of Postmodernism* (London & New York: Routledge, 1989); *Splitting Images: Contemporary Canadian Ironies* (Toronto: Oxford Univ. Press, 1991); *A Postmodern Reader*, ed. with Joseph Natoli (Albany: State Univ. of New York Press, 1993); *Irony's Edge: The Theory and Politics of Irony* (London & New York: Routledge, 1995); *Opera: Desire, Disease, Death*, with Michael Hutcheon (Lincoln: Univ. of Nebraska Press, 1996); various other books, articles & reviews. **EDIT:** Co-ed., *Theory/Culture* series, Univ. of Toronto Press, 1990 to date; Assoc. Ed., *University of Toronto Quarterly*; Assoc. Ed., *Recherches Semiotiques/Semiotic Inquiry*, 1982-84; Ed. Bd., *PMLA*, 1990-92; Ed. Bd., *Modern Fiction Studies*, 1993 to date; Ed. Bd., *Texte*, 1982 to date; Ed. Bd., *Contemporary Literature*, 1992 to date; Ed. Bd., *English Studies in Canada*, 1984-95; Ed. Bd., *New Novel Review*, 1993-95; Ed. Bd., *Italian Canadiana*, 1984 to date; Ed. Bd., *Canadian Review of Comparative Literature*, 1986 to date; Ed. Bd., *Canadian Poetry*, 1987 to date; Ed. Bd., *Signature: Canadian Literature and Literary Theory*, 1989-92; Ed. Bd., *Arachne*, 1993 to date; Ed. Bd., *Fabula*, France, 1989 to date; Ed. Bd., *Essays in Canadian Writing*, 1992 to date; Int'l Advisory Ed., Utrecht Publications in General and Comparative Literature, 1987 to date; Advisory Ed., *Lexicon of Contemporary Literatures in English*, Netherlands, 1987 to date; Advisory Bd., *Encylopaedia of Literary Theory*, 1987-92; Advisory Bd., *Parallax*, 1994 to date; Sr. Ed. Committee, *Semiotic Review of Books*, 1990 to date; Int'l Advisory Bd., "Transatlantic Perspectives," Germany: Francke Publications, 1992 to date; Int'l Advisory Bd., *The Year's Work in Critical and Cultural Theory*, 1992 to date. **AFFIL:** Modern Language Association of America (Exec. Council); International Comparative Literature Association; American Comparative Literature Association; Canadian Comparative Literature Association; Association of Canadian College & University Teachers of English; Toronto Semiotic Circle; Centre for Italian Canadian Studies; International Research Institute for Postmodernism Studies, Beijing Univ. (Advisory Bd.); Association for Canadian & Québec Literatures; Canadian Semiotics Association; Royal Society of Canada (Fellow). **HONS:** 17 undergrad. fellowships &

awards; 4 grad. awards, incl. Woodrow Wilson Fellow, 1969-79; Killam Post-doctoral Fellow, 1978-79; John P. Robarts Chair in Cdn Studies, York Univ., 1988-89; Killam Research Fellow, 1986-88; Guggenheim Fellowship, 1992-93. INTERESTS: cycling; piano playing. MISC: numerous conference presentations; numerous invited lectures; reviewer, various journals, conferences, presses & granting agencies; listed in various biographical sources, incl. *Contemporary Authors* (1986), *Who's Who in the World* (8th ed.), *Who's Who of American Women* (1992) & *World's Who's Who of Women*; recipient, various grants & fellowships. COMMENT: *"A literary theorist and teacher, trying to make sense of our postmodern culture."*

Hutchings, Carol, B.A.,M.S.W. ◉ ○

Executive Director, ELIZABETH FRY SOCIETY OF EDMONTON, 10523 - 100 Ave., Edmonton, AB T5J 0A8 (403) 421-1175, FAX 425-8989. Born Calgary 1949. m. Andrew McCready. 2 ch. Andrew McCready, Heather McCready. EDUC: Univ. of Calgary, B.A. 1970; Wilfrid Laurier Univ., M.S.W. 1977. CAREER: Social Worker, Vanier Centre for Women, 1978-79; Acting Dir., Social Work Dept., 1979; Volunteer Coord., Vanier Centre for Women & Ontario Correctional Institute, 1979-80; Reg. Coord. of Volunteer Svcs, Calgary Region Correctional Svcs, 1981-82; Social Worker, Bissell Centre, Edmonton, 1983-85; Social Worker, Community & Family Svcs, 1985-86; Dept. Volunteer Coord., 1986-89; Instructor, Grant McEwan Community Coll., 1989; Exec. Dir., Elizabeth Fry Society of Edmonton, 1989 to date. SELECTED PUBLICATIONS: produced, directed & contributed to various Elizabeth Fry Society of Edmonton publications, incl. *Building Pathways: Employment Needs of Federally Sentenced Women* (1993), *Building Pathways: Employment Needs of Provincially Sentenced Women* (1993), *Common Threads: Women Who Have Been in Conflict Tell Their Stories* (1993) & *Nobody There: Making Peace with Motherhood* (1994). AFFIL: Edmonton Coalition on Family Violence; Advisory & Program Committee for Proposed Prairie Prison for Federally Sentenced Women; Inner City Task Force on Violent Crime; Victim Offender Mediation Program; Grant McEwan Community Coll. (Advisory Bd., Correctional Svcs Dept.). INTERESTS: making chocolate truffles; garage sales; raising socially conscious teenagers. COMMENT: *"I continue to struggle to provide opportunities for women in conflict with the law, who are some of the most disadvantaged women in society, and to change the criminal justice system so that these women are allowed to heal and move on."*

Hutchings, Geraldine, B.A.,LL.B. ⚖ ⊕ ♣

Barrister and Solicitor. 202-4133 4th Ave., Whitehorse, YT Y1A 1H8 (403) 633-4216, FAX 633-4223. Born Prince Rupert, B.C. 1961. cl. Raymond Breton. 3 ch. EDUC: Univ. of Victoria, B.A.(Psych.) 1984, LL.B. 1987. BAR: B.C., 1988; Yukon. CAREER: Assoc., Preston, Willis and Lackowicz, 1988-92; sole practitioner of law, 1993 to date. AFFIL: Mental Health Review Bd. (Chair); Yukon Human Rights Commission (Chair); Yukon Law Society (2nd VP 1995-96; Treas. 1996-97).

Hutchinson, Colleen G. ○ ⊕

President, THE HUTCHINSON FOUNDATION FOR RESEARCH (EWINGS SARCOMA), 1357 Peartree Circle, Oakville, ON L6M 2J3 (905) 847-5939. Born London, Ont. 1949. m. Lewis Hutchinson. 1 ch. EDUC: Waterloo Collegiate Institute, Jr. Matriculation 1965. CAREER: 25 yrs. in bnkg, various positions from teller to Mgr, Mortgage Dev., Ont. Central W. Div., The Toronto-Dominion Bank, 1967 to date; Pres., Hutchinson Foundation for Research (Ewings Sarcoma) 1994 to date. MISC: founded Hutchinson Foundation for Research (Ewings Sarcoma) after the 1994 death of her son, Dean Hutchinson, from Ewings Sarcoma, a rare form of bone cancer; the Foundation, which is currently being registered as a charitable organization, focuses on raising money to support research & patient comfort programs at Mount Sinai Hospital. COMMENT: *"I promised my son I would do my utmost to help other children and families, by trying to find a cure for this deadly disease. People need to become more aware of what kind of help families in need require."*

Hutchison, Peggy, B.A.,M.Sc.,Ed.D. ◁ ❀

Associate Professor, Department of Recreation and Leisure Studies, BROCK UNIVERSITY, St. Catharines, ON L2S 3A1 (905) 688-5550, FAX 688-0541, EMAIL phutchis@arnie. pec.brocku.ca. Born Kitchener, Ont. 1950. m. John Lord. 4 ch. EDUC: Queen's Univ., B.A. & B.P.H.E. 1973; Dalhousie Univ., M.Sc. 1974; Boston Univ., Ed.D. 1976. CAREER: lecturer, Acadia Univ., 1976; Asst. Prof., Univ. of Waterloo, 1978-85; researcher, Centre for Research & Education, 1985-90; Assoc. Prof., Brock Univ., 1990 to date. SELECTED PUBLICATIONS: *Listening: To People Who Have Directly Experienced the Mental Health System*, with J. Lord, H. Savage & A. Schnarr (Toronto: Canadian Mental Health Association, 1985); *Advocacy in Psychiatric Hospitals*, with J. Lord, S. Corlett & D. Farlow (Toronto: Ministry of Health, 1987); *Leisure, Integration and Community*, with J. McGill (Toronto:

Leisurability Publications, 1992); *Making Friends* (Toronto: G. Allan Rocher Institute, 1990); "The Voice of the People: Qualitative Research and the Needs of Consumers," with P. Schnarr (*Canadian Journal of Community Mental Health* 6(2) 1987); "Pitfalls of Increased Professionalism in the Field of Leisure," with J. McGill (*Recreation Canada* 49(3) 1991); "Double Jeopardy: Women with Disabilities Speak Out About Community and Relationships" (*Entourage* 7(2) 1992) "Work and Leisure: Paradoxes and Dilemmas for People With Developmental Disabilities" (*Journal on Development Disabilities* 3(1) 1994); numerous other books, articles & chapters in books. **EDIT:** Ed., *Journal of Leisurability*, 1981-82, 1994-96. **AFFIL:** Ontario Association for Community Living (Adjunct Mbr., Educ. Committee 1980-94); Kitchener-Waterloo People First (Advisor). **COMMENT:** *"Peggy Hutchison is a researcher, advocate, parent and writer who lives in Kitchener and works in St. Catharines at Brock University in Recreation and Leisure Studies and with a cross appointment in Education."*

Hyde, Darlene Kruesel, M.B.A.,B.A. $
Vice-President, Public Affairs and Road Safety, INSURANCE CORPORATION OF BRITISH COLUMBIA, 151 W. Esplanade, N. Vancouver, BC V7M 3H9 (604) 661-6103, FAX 661-6647. Born Regina 1947. m. Richard. 2 ch. **EDUC:** McGill Univ., B.A. 1969; Memorial Univ. of Newfoundland, M.B.A. 1982; Canadian Public Relations Society; International Association of Business Communication. **CAREER:** Mgr, Public Rel'ns & Advtg, Newfoundland Telephone Company, 1976-80; special assignment, Corp. Planning Dept., 1981; Dir., Corp. Affairs, Newfoundland and Labrador Housing Corporation, 1983-88; Mgr, Corp. Comm., TransAlta Utilities Corporation, 1988-93; VP, Public Affairs & Road Safety, Insurance Corporation of British Columbia, 1993 to date. **AFFIL:** Vancouver Board of Trade; Planning Forum, Vancouver Chapter; Conference Board of Canada (Council of Public Affairs Exec.); Fac. of Bus. Admin., Simon Fraser Univ. (Advisory Bd.); Canadian Public Relations Society, Vancouver Chapter; Canadian Council for Public Affairs Advancement; Traffic Injury Research Foundation of Canada (Bd.); Minister's Injury Prevention Advisory Committee (BC); Canada Safety Council (Bd.). **INTERESTS:** jogging; cross-country skiing; classical music; theatre; the arts. **COMMENT:** *"I have spent 25 years in marketing, public affairs and organizational communications fields. During this period, I have been extensively involved in the promotion of professional development and excellence for people in these fields. Currently, I am applying social marketing principles to the area of road safety in order to bring about positive attitudinal and behavioural changes on the roads of British Columbia."*

Hyland, Barbara, B.A.,B.L.S. ■■ 📖 $
Publisher, INVESTMENT EXECUTIVE (newspaper/magazine publisher), 90 Richmond St. E., Ste. 202, Toronto, ON M5C 1P1 (416) 366-4200, FAX 366-7846, EMAIL ienet@inforamp.net. Born Sherbrooke, Que. 1942. m. Geoffrey Armstrong. 2 ch. Mark, Patrick (Hyland). **EDUC:** Bishop's Univ., B.A.(Hist.) 1963; Univ. of Toronto, B.L.S. 1965. **CAREER:** Dir. of Electronic Publishing, The Globe and Mail, 1980-89; Publisher, *Financial Times of Canada*, 1989-92; Publisher, *Investment Executive*, 1992 to date.

I

ley, Sarah J.E., B.A. ■ ■ $ ⊗ ♡
President and Chief Executive Officer, THE
COUNCIL FOR BUSINESS AND THE ARTS IN
CANADA (nat'l bus. association serving arts
sponsors), 401 Bay St., P.O. Box 7, Toronto,
ON M5H 2Y4 (416) 869-3016, FAX 869-
0435. Born Kingston, Ont. 1956. m. Stephen.
2 ch. Sheila Meghan, Sarah Elizabeth. **EDUC:**
Queen's Univ., B.A.(Hons., English/Hist.) 1978;
Ryerson Polytechnical Institute, Mktg Certifi-
cate 1987. **CAREER:** Research Asst., The
Council for Business and the Arts in Canada,
1979-86; Communications Dir., 1986-91;
Administrator & Sec. to the Bd., Ontario Arts
Council Foundation, & Mgr, Developmental
Svcs, Ontario Arts Council, 1991-95; Pres. &
CEO, The Council for Business and the Arts in
Canada, 1995 to date. **SELECTED CREDITS:**
Exec. Producer, *Putting on the Arts* (4-part
series co-produced by TVOntario & Ontario
Arts Council, 1993). **SELECTED PUBLICA-
TIONS:** *Befriending Museums* (1991); *Business
Sponsorship of the Arts* (1986); *Developing
Effective Arts Boards* (1984); *Approaching
Corporations for Support* (1982); *Corporate
Art Collecting in Canada* (1980). **AFFIL:** Cana-
dian Association of Gift Planners (Bd. mbr.,
Exec. Committee 1995-97); Oakville Arts
Council (VP 1989 to date); Corporate Art Col-
lectors Group (former Co-Chair); Canadian
Public Relations Society (former Chair, Pro-
gram Committee). **INTERESTS:** all the per-
forming, visual & literary arts.

Imboden, Roberta, B.A.,M.A. ⊗ 📖
Professor, Department of English, RYERSON
POLYTECHNIC UNIVERSITY, 350 Victoria St.,
Toronto, ON M5B 2K3 (416) 979-5000, ext.

6148, EMAIL rimboden@acs.ryerson.ca. Born Buffalo, N.Y. 1934. m. J. David Grimshaw. EDUC: Mercyhurst Coll., B.A.(English) 1956, M.A.(English) 1961; Univ. of Toronto, M.A.(Comparative Lit.) 1977. CAREER: Instructor & Prof., Ryerson Polytechnic Univ., 1965 to date. SELECTED PUBLICATIONS: *From the Cross to the Kingdom: Sartrean Dialectics and Liberation Theology* (Harper and Row, 1987); *The Church, A Demon Lover: A Sartrean Critique of an Institution* (Univ. of Calgary Press, 1995). AFFIL: Delta Epsilon Sigma; Canadian Hermeneutical Postmodern Society (VP). INTERESTS: film; chamber music. COMMENT: *"I have always led an intellectual life dedicated to teaching literature. This teaching is intimately linked with research and writing which intertwines French philosophy, theology, and contemporary literature."*

Impey, Patrice, B.Sc.,M.B.A. ⑤

Controller, HEWLETT-PACKARD (CANADA) LTD., 5150 Spectrum Way, Mississauga, ON L4W 5G1 (905) 206-3471, FAX 206-4122. Born Winnipeg 1958. m. David Neiman. 2 ch. EDUC: Univ. of Manitoba, B.Sc.(Chem.) 1979; Univ. of Western Ontario, M.B.A. 1983. CAREER: Treasury Analyst, Hewlett-Packard (Canada) Ltd., 1985-88; Treasury Mgr, 1988-90; Mktg Svcs Mgr, 1990-91; Cont., 1991 to date. AFFIL: Lakeshore Yacht Club; Hewlett-Packard (Canada) Ltd. United Way campaign (Country Chairperson 1994, 1995).

Indra, Doreen Marie, B.A.,M.A., Ph.D. ⇔ ❀

Associate Professor of Anthropology, UNIVERSITY OF LETHBRIDGE, Lethbridge, AB T1K 3M4 (403) 329-2599, FAX 329-5109. Born Humboldt, Sask. m. Norman Buchignani. EDUC: Univ. of California, Berkeley, B.A.(Anthro.) 1974; California State Univ., Hayward, M.A.(Anthro.) 1974; Simon Fraser Univ., Ph.D.(Soc. & Anthro.) 1979. CAREER: Lecturer, Dept. of Soc., Univ. of Alberta, 1979-80; Lecturer, Grant MacEwan Coll., 1980-84; Visiting Prof. (Cdn Studies), Hokkaigakuen Univ., Sapporo, Japan, 1985; Asst. Prof., Dept. of Anthro., Univ. of Lethbridge, 1984-88; Assoc. Prof., 1988 to date; Visiting Fellow, Refugee Studies Program, Int'l Dev. Centre, Univ. of Oxford, 1988, 1989; Research Assoc., Centre for Social Studies, Dhaka Univ., Dhaka, Bangladesh, 1989-90, 1993 to date; Coord., Women's Studies Program, Univ. of Lethbridge, Jan.-July 1993; Acting Chair, Dept. of Anthro., Univ. of Lethbridge, 1994 to date. SELECTED PUBLICATIONS: *Continuous Journey: A Social History of South Asians in Canada*, with N. Buchignani & Ram Srivastava (Toronto:

McClelland & Stewart, 1985); *Uprooting, Loss and Adaptation: The Resettlement of Indochinese Refugees in Canada*, ed. with Kwok Chan (Ottawa: Canadian Public Health Association, 1986); *Ten Years Later: Indochinese Communities in Canada*, ed./author with Kwok Chan & Louis Jacques Dorais (Ottawa: Canadian Asian Studies Association, 1988); "Gender: A Key Dimension of the Refugee Experience" (*Refuge* 1987); "Some Anthropological Qualifications on the Effects of Ethnicity and Social Change on Mental Health" (*Santé Culture Health* 1991); various other publications, incl. chapters in books & book reviews. AFFIL: Canadian Asian Studies Association; Canadian Anthropology Association; Society of Applied Anthropology in Canada; American Anthropological Association; American Applied Anthropology Association. MISC: fieldwork in Canada, US, Bangladesh, Central America & S.E. Asia; recipient, various grants; numerous conference presentations & invited lectures; 1 of several organizers, Nat'l Symposium on Aboriginal Women in Canada: Past, Present and Future, Univ. of Lethbridge, 1989; referee, various journals, incl. *Anthropologica, Journal of Refugee Studies* & *Canadian Ethnic Studies*.

Ingram, Sandra, B.A.,M.Ed., Ph.D. ■■ ⇔ ❀ ❺

Instructor (Ph.D.), Department of Electrical and Computer Engineering, Faculty of Engineering, UNIVERSITY OF MANITOBA, Winnipeg, MB R3T 2N2 (204) 474-8450, FAX 261-4639, EMAIL umingramcc.umanitoba.ca. Born Winnipeg 1960. m. Sanjaye Ramdoyal. EDUC: Univ. of Winnipeg, B.A.(Hons., Anthropology) 1983; Univ. of Manitoba, M.Ed.(Educ. Foundations) 1985; Ontario Institute for Studies in Education, Univ. of Toronto, Ph.D.(Educational Sociology) 1993. CAREER: Lecturer, Fac. of Educ., Continuing Educ., Univ. of Manitoba & Univ. of Regina, 1987-94; Educational Consultant, Lifelore Ltd. (career dev. & employment counselling), Winnipeg, 1995; Instructor, Tech. Communications, Dept. of Electrical & Comp. Eng., Fac. of Eng., Univ. of Manitoba. AFFIL: Winnipeg Humane Society. INTERESTS: renovation of old homes; antiques; cats. COMMENT: *"My career and research interests are communication-centered. I've conducted studies at both the university and public school level. My specific areas of interest are gender issues, ethnography of communication and education as a social process."*

Ings, Joanne, B.A. ■■ ❸ ♡ ⊕

Executive Director, P.E.I. TRANSITION HOUSE ASSOCIATION (shelter for abused women), P.O. Box 964, Charlottetown, PE C1A 7M4 (902)

894-3354, FAX 368-7180, EMAIL tha@isn.net. Born P.E.I. EDUC: Univ. of P.E.I., B.A.(Pol. Sci.) 1975, Diploma (Public Admin.) 1981. CAREER: Production Asst., CBC Radio, 1977-81; contract writer/researcher, 1981-89; Planning Officer, P.E.I. Dept. of Health & Social Svcs, 1989-94. AFFIL: Rotary Club of Charlottetown Royalty; Univ. of P.E.I. Alumni Association.

Inkpen, Linda Louella, B.Sc.,B.Ed., B.Med.Sc.,M.D. ■ ⊕ 🎓 $

Physician. 2 Mount Cashel Rd., St. John's, NF A1A 1X7 (709) 753-1450, FAX 722-3576, EMAIL nladha@morgan.ucs.mun.ca. Born 1948. m. Dr. Nizar Ladha. 3 ch. EDUC: Memorial Univ. of Newfoundland, B.Sc. 1969, B.Ed. 1970, B.Med.Sc. 1972, M.D. 1974. CAREER: Host, CBC-TV youth current affairs program, 1966; Lab. Asst., Dept. of Math., Memorial Univ. of Newfoundland, 1968-70; Host, CBC-TV current affairs & music program, 1969; substitute teacher, St. John's, 1970-71; medical practice, St. John's, 1975 to date; Staff Health Physician, St. Clare's Mercy Hospital, St. John's, 1976-87; Staff Physician, Queen St. Mental Health Centre, Toronto, 1979-80; Commissioner, Royal Commission on Employment & Unemployment, Prov. of Nfld. & Labrador, 1985-86; Pres., Cabot Coll., 1987-93; physician, Planned Parenthood, St. John's, 1988 to date; Adjunct Asst. Prof., Fac. of Medicine, Memorial Univ. of Newfoundland, 1990 to date; Chair, Industrial Inquiry into the Labour Rel'ns Problems at Barry's Fishplant Ltd., Curling, Nfld., 1993; Chair, Health Industries Sector Strategy, Econ. Recovery Commission, 1994; Consultant, Sch. Incident Report, Avalon Consolidated Sch. Bd., St. John's, 1994; Chair, Review into Secure Custody Facilities for Juvenile Offenders, Nfld. & Lab. DIRECTOR: Fortis Inc.; Newfoundland Light & Power. AFFIL: Canadian Medical Association; Newfoundland & Labrador Medical Association; Women Interested in Science & Engineering; Law Society of Newfoundland (Lay Bencher); Fortis Education Foundation (Chair); Council for Canadian Unity (Prov. Dir.); Royal Newfoundland Yacht Club; Cabot 500. HONS: numerous scholarships & awards, 1954-65; Imperial Oil Univ. Entrance Scholarship, 1965; Jr. Jubilee Award, 1965; Dux Medal, 1965; Canadian Mathematical Congress Scholarship, 1965; Gov. General's Medal, 1965; Prov. Gov't Academic Scholarships, 1965-69; Miss Canadian Univ. Snow Queen Award, 1967; Fac. of Medicine Scholarship, 1988; Alumna of the Year, Memorial Univ. of Newfoundland, 1988. MISC: V-Chair, Nat'l Innovations Advisory Committee, Employment & Immigration Canada, 1990-95; mbr., Environmental Partnership Fund, Environment Canada, 1990 to date; Prov. Co-Chair, Nat'l Fundraising Campaign, Council for Canadian Unity, 1995.

Inkpen, Sarah, B.Math., M.Ed. ■■ ⚛ 🎓 ✊

Professor of Mathematics, Aviation Flight Technology Department, SENECA COLLEGE OF APPLIED ARTS AND TECHNOLOGY, 1750 Finch Ave. E., North York, ON M2J 2X5 (416) 491-5050, ext. 2398, FAX 778-5198, EMAIL sinkpen@oise.utoronto.ca. Born Wiltshire, England 1948. d. 1 ch. Carmen Maria. EDUC: Univ. of Waterloo, B.Math. 1970; Brock Univ., M.Ed.(Curriculum) 1993; Ontario Institute for Studies in Education, Univ. of Toronto, doctoral candidate (Virtual Reality & Calculus). CAREER: Teaching Master, Adult Training, Math. & English, Durham Coll., 1970-73; Prof., Aviation Flight Technology Dept., specializing in Applied Math., Calculus, Interactive Computer Labs, Multi-media dev. & other educational technologies, Seneca Coll. of Applied Arts, 1973 to date. SELECTED PUBLICATIONS: several incl. "Women and Mathematics" (*Advancing the Agenda of Inclusive Education*, June 1996); "Cyberspace Calculus Carnival" (*Technology and Communications: Catalyst for Educational Change*, Mar. 1996); "Jurassic Pedagogy in a Technocratic Park" (*Crucibles*, Sept. 1994). AFFIL: ATHENA, Association of Professional Women (founder & mbr. 1980-85); Seneca Faculty Association, SECOTEMAS (Pres. 1983 to date); Egrane International (Pres. 1983-85). HONS: Int'l Honoree, Computational Science Educ. Award, U.S. Dept. of Energy, Ames Lab., Iowa, 1995; winner, "Women on the Move," *The Toronto Sun*, 1994; Teaching Excellence Award, Association of Canadian Community Colleges, 1994; best paper presentation, American Society of Engineering Educators annual conference, 1992. INTERESTS: flying (private pilot); knitting; Internet surfing; reading; fitness; travel. MISC: presenter/keynote speaker/panel participant, numerous conferences, workshops; faculty exchanges, Singapore Polytechnic, Singapore, 1986 & Normandale Community Coll., Bloomington, Minn., 1988. COMMENT: *"As a mother, a feminist, a visionary and an educator, I realize that gender equity is attainable only if we as women become disciples of technological change."*

Iordanous, Freda ■■ $ ⊛

FREDA'S INC. (manufacture & sale of women's corporate apparel), 86 Bathurst St., Toronto, ON M5V 2P5 (416) 703-0304, FAX 504-

6048. Born Cyprus 1950. m. Demos. 2 ch. Paulina, Elaine. **AFFIL:** AHI business network; Step Up; AICI, Step Ahead; International Co-ordinating Committee (Founder). **HONS:** Gold Award for Small Business, Canada Awards for Business Excellence, Fed. Ministry of Industry, Science & Technology, 1991. **MISC:** chosen as official wardrobe designer of Expo '86, Vancouver; in 1987 was designated official designer by the Toronto Olympic Council in the bid to secure the 1996 Olympics. **COMMENT:** *"Award-winning fashion designer Freda Iordanous combines technical and creative ability with a professional winning sales and service philosophy that has secured new and repeat business for over twenty years. Over 200,000 Canadians have worn Freda's designs. Freda's Originals Inc. has a prestigious and extensive client base, ranging from airlines, governments, chartered banks, financial institutions, major sports and entertainment groups."*

Ip, Irene Kellow, B.A.,M.A. ■ $ 🍁
Research Adviser, Research Department, BANK OF CANADA, 234 Wellington St., Ottawa, ON K1A 0G9 (613) 782-8496, FAX 782-7163, EMAIL ireneip@bank-banque-canada.ca. Born London, UK 1934. m. Anthony K. Ip. 4 ch. Michael W. Ip, David W. Ip, Gregory W. Ip, Claire S. Kellow. **EDUC:** Toronto Teachers' Coll., Certificate 1958; Trent Univ., B.A. 1975; Univ. of Toronto, M.A. 1976. **CAREER:** elementary sch. teacher, 1958-64; Research Asst., Econ Dept., Trent Univ., 1973-74; Economist, Wood Gundy Inc., 1976-79; Chief Forecaster, 1979-88; Asst. VP, 1980-84; VP, 1984-88; Sessional Lecturer, Dept. of Econ., Univ. of Toronto, 1987; Sr. Policy Analyst, C.D. Howe Institute, 1988-93; Research Advisor, Bank of Canada, 1993 to date; Guest Lecturer, Brock Univ. **SELECTED PUBLICATIONS:** various C.D. Howe Institute studies, numerous articles & Woody Gundy publications. **EDIT:** Ed. Bd., *Canadian Business Economics*, 1992-95. **AFFIL:** Toronto Association of Business Economists (Dir. 1990-93); St. Joseph's Refugee Committee, Ottawa (Treas.); Taoist Tai Chi Society. **HONS:** various scholarships & prizes, Trent Univ., 1970-75; Special M.A. Scholarship, Canada Council, 1975-76. **INTERESTS:** hiking; cycling; tai chi; classical music; dev. econ.; family. **COMMENT:** *"I've changed careers many times, which has been very challenging but stimulating and fun. Since moving on often meant getting further education, continuous learning has now become a way of life."*

Ip, Maggie, B.A.,B.Ed.,M.Ed. 🍁
Councillor, CITY OF VANCOUVER, 453 W. 12th Ave., Vancouver, BC V5Y 1V4 (604) 873-7247, FAX 873-7750. Born Shanghai 1943. m. Kelly Ip. 2 ch. Pamela Ping Ping Ip, Che Kingston Ip. **EDUC:** Hongkong Baptist Coll., B.A.(Soc.) 1965; Univ. of Ottawa, B.Ed., M.Ed. 1967; Univ. of British Columbia, Certificate (English as a Second Language) 1971; Simon Fraser Univ., Teaching Certificate (P.D.P.) 1979. **CAREER:** statistician, Dept. of Nat'l Health & Welfare, 1967-69; Proj. Dir., Women in Training, Dept. of Manpower, 1971-72; real estate agent, Block Brothers Realty, 1973-77; teacher, Steveston Secondary Sch., 1980 to date; Councillor, City of Vancouver, 1993 to date. **AFFIL:** United Chinese Community Svcs Society (Founding Chair 1973-93); B.C. Heritage Language Association (Founding Chair 1982-89); United Way of Vancouver (Dir. 1977-78, 1991-93). **HONS:** Canada 125 Medal; Multicultural Educ. Award, Vancouver Multicultural Society, 1984; Nat'l Volunteer Award, Dept. of National Health & Welfare, 1987; Community Service Award, Rotary Club, 1989. **INTERESTS:** travel; reading; tai chi; yoga; food; music. **COMMENT:** *"Since coming to Canada in 1966, I have enjoyed a fulfilling personal, professional, social and family life through participation in a broad range of community-oriented services and organizations."*

Irish, Maureen, B.A.,LL.B.,LL.M., D.C.L. ⚖ 🎓
Professor, Faculty of Law, UNIVERSITY OF WINDSOR, 401 Sunset Ave., Windsor, ON N9B 3P4 (519) 253-4232, ext. 2950, FAX 973-7064, EMAIL mirish@uwindsor.ca. Born Simcoe, Ont. 1949. s. **EDUC:** Univ. of Toronto, B.A. 1970, LL.B.(Law) 1974; McGill Univ., LL.M.(Law) 1982, D.C.L.(Law) 1992. **BAR:** Ont., 1976. **CAREER:** Barrister & Solicitor, Ont., 1976 to date; Asst. Prof., Univ. of Windsor, 1980-84; Assoc. Prof., 1984-95; Prof., 1995 to date. **SELECTED PUBLICATIONS:** *Customs Valuation in Canada* (1985); *The Legal Framework for Canada–United States Trade*, co-ed. (1987); *International Trade and Intellectual Property: The Search for a Balanced System*, co-ed. (1994). **MISC:** mbr., Dispute Settlement Roster, Chapter 19, N.Am. Free Trade Agreement.

Irvine, Marie, LL.B. ■■ ⚖ ✊
Coordinator, BRITISH COLUMBIA ASSOCIATION OF COMMUNITY LAW OFFICES, 1140 W. Pender St., Ste. 1500, Vancouver, BC V6E 4G1 (604) 601-6048, FAX 682-7967. Born 1948. m. Bruce Renschler. 1 ch. Tracy. **EDUC:** Osgoode Hall Law Sch., LL.B. 1980; extensive continuing educ. in law & mgmt. **BAR:** Ont., 1982; B.C., 1996. **CAREER:** Exec. Dir., Justice for

Children & Youth, The Canadian Foundation for Children, Youth & the Law, Toronto, 1983-91; S. Alta. Dir., Children's Advocate Office, Dept. of Family & Social Svcs, Calgary, 1991-94; Coord., B.C. Association of Community Law Offices, Vancouver, 1994 to date. **SELECTED CREDITS:** Consultant, videos on children & the law. **SELECTED PUBLICATIONS:** articles in B.C. Association of Community Law Offices newsletter, Justice for Children & Youth newsletter & publications; contributor, *The Canadian Woman's Legal Guide* (1987). **AFFIL:** Canadian Bar Association; B.C. Law Society; Law Society of Upper Canada; Public Legal Education Association (Dir.). **INTERESTS:** reading; art. **COMMENT:** *"Achievements: promoting the legal interests of children and youth, and poverty law."*

Irving, Bonnie, B.A. ■ $ 📖 ✏

Editor, *BCBusiness* MAGAZINE, Canada Wide Magazines Ltd., 4180 Lougheed Hwy, Ste. 401, Burnaby, BC V5C 6A7 (604) 299-7311, FAX 299-9188. Born Winnipeg 1948. s. **EDUC:** Univ. of Manitoba, B.A.(Pol. Sci.) 1968; Vancouver Community Coll., Diploma in Journalism 1982. **CAREER:** Employment Counsellor, Drake Personnel, 1968-70; various positions to Reg. Dept. Mgr, The Bay, 1972-80; owner, The Gofers, 1980-81; Promo. Coord., *BCBusiness* Magazine, 1982-83; Mng Ed., *CitiBusiness*, Vancouver, 1983-84; Ed., *BCBusiness*, 1984 to date; Ed., *Pacific Golf Magazine*, start-up 1995. **AFFIL:** Western Magazine Awards Foundation (Dir. 1987; VP 1988); Vancouver Board of Trade; Langara Journalism Program (Advisory Committee). **HONS:** Scott Schill Memorial Award for best all-round graduating journalism student, 1982; nominee, YWCA Women of Distinction, Media & Public Affairs, 1990. **INTERESTS:** tennis; books; dogs. **MISC:** guest speaker &/or panelist for various media rel'ns courses at SFU & BCIT; judge for various awards programs incl. Junior Achievement's Canadian Business Hall of Fame (1994 & 1995). **COMMENT:** *"I have built two successful careers: one in retail, one in publishing. Under my stewardship,* BCBusiness *Magazine has acquired a reputation as a credible source of information about trends and issues affecting BC business."*

Irving, Catherine, B.A.,B.Ed.,TESL ♡ ✊

Executive Director, COORDINATING COUNCIL ON DEAFNESS OF NOVA SCOTIA, 1660 Hollis St., Ste. 803, Halifax, NS B3J 1V7 (902) 425-0240. Born Halifax 1965. 2 ch. Jeremy Gulliver, Jessica Gulliver. **EDUC:** Dalhousie Univ., B.A. (English) 1991, B.Ed.(English) 1992; TESL Adult Educ. Cert. **CAREER:** Residence Coord./Strategic Planner/Exec. Dir., Coordinating Council on Deafness of N.S. **SELECTED PUBLICATIONS:** "Needs Assessment in Health Care Service for Deaf, Deafened and Hard of Hearing People in Nova Scotia" (1993); Co-author, *Involving Consumers with Disabilities in Nova Scotia Reformed Health System: Challenges and Concerns* (pending publication Oct. 1996). **AFFIL:** National Access Awareness Week; Y.M.C.A. (Childcare Parents' Committee); Society for Deaf & Hard of Hearing Nova Scotians (Exec. Bd. 1993); Canadian Hard of Hearing Association (Dir.); Atlantic Sports Car Club. **HONS:** Award for Educ., Dalhousie Univ., 1992; John Frederick Knodell Award. **INTERESTS:** car racing & car slaloms; reading; creative writing; sign language. **COMMENT:** *"I am struggling to begin my career. As a severely hard of hearing woman, the barriers frequently seem insurmountable in each area of life. The achievements are savoured all the more. I enjoy my role as advocate for deaf, deafened and hard-of-hearing people."*

Irwin, Grace L., B.A.,M.A., D.Sac.Litt. ✱ 🎓 📜

Writer, Retired Teacher and Pastor. 33 Glenwood Ave., Toronto, ON M6P 3C7. Born Toronto 1907. s. **EDUC:** Victoria Coll., Univ. of Toronto, B.A.(Classics & English) 1929; Univ. of Toronto, M.A.(Greek) 1932. **CAREER:** teacher, Humberside Collegiate Institute, 1931-42; Head of Classics, 1942-69; Pastor, Emmanuel Church (Congregational Christian), 1974-86. **SELECTED PUBLICATIONS:** *Least of All Saints*, novel; *Andrew Connington*, novel; *Contend With Horses*, novel; *In Little Place*, novel; *Servant of Slaves*, novel; *The Seventh Earl*, novel; *Three Lives in Mine*, biography. **AFFIL:** Canadian Classical Association; Ontario Classical Association; University Women's Club. **HONS:** Centennial Medal, 1967; D.Sac.Litt.(Hon.), Univ. of Toronto, 1991. **MISC:** considerable public speaking in Canada & US. **COMMENT:** *"I seem to have spent my life doing what I had no desire to do, and enjoying it immensely. That goes for teaching, preaching, writing."*

Irwin, M. Eleanor, B.A.,M.A., Ph.D. 🎓 📜 ✱

Associate Professor, Scarborough College, UNIVERSITY OF TORONTO, 1265 Military Trail, Scarborough, ON M1C 1A4 (416) 287-7128, EMAIL irwin@macpost.scar.utoronto.ca. Born Toronto 1937. m. John W. 4 ch. John J., Marjorie (Robertson), Peter, Andrew. **EDUC:** Univ. of Toronto, B.A.(Classics) 1959, M.A.(Classics) 1960, Ph.D.(Classics) 1967. **CAREER:** Asst. Prof., Scarborough Coll., Div. of Humanities,

1968-73; Assoc. Prof., Scarborough Coll., 1973 to date; Assoc. Chair, 1980-82, 1994 to date; Assoc. Dean (Academic), 1985-89; V-Principal & Assoc. Dean, 1989-93. SELECTED PUBLICATIONS: *Colour Terms in Greek Poetry* (Toronto: Hakkert, 1974); "Evadne, Iamos and violets in Pindar's *Sixth Olympian*" (*Hermes*, 1996); numerous other articles & book chapters. AFFIL: Classical Association of Canada; Canadian Society of Patristic Studies; International Society for the Classical Tradition; International Service Fellowship (Chair of Cdn Council 1986-92, 1994-95); Canadian Baptist Ministries (mbr. of Council 1988-94; mbr. of Bd. 1995-97). HONS: D.R. Campbell Award for Outstanding Contribution to Scarborough Coll., 1984. INTERESTS: botany. COMMENT: *"Undergraduate education at the university is very important to me. I contribute to this through my discipline, Classics, and my interest in women in the ancient world."*

Irwin, Pat M., B.A. ■ $

Assistant Vice-President, Trust Operations and Administration, NATIONAL TRUST (416) 361-4123. EDUC: Univ. of Toronto, B.A. 1976. CAREER: Consultant, DMR Group, 1980-82; Consultant, Orenstein and Partners, 1982-84; Consultant, Hudson's Bay Company, 1984-85; Consultant, Peat Marwick and Partners, 1985-87; Nat'l Mgr, Central Guaranty Trust, 1987-92; Consultant, 1992-93; Asst. VP, Deposit Oper., Branch Support & Oper., & Asst. VP, Prod. & Oper. Support, Bus. Bnkg, National Trust, 1993 to date. AFFIL: Institute of Canadian Bankers (Assoc.); Institute of Management Consultants of Ontario (prospective mbr.); Toronto Mendelssohn Choir (singer & Dir. of Mktg). HONS: winner, with choir, Ont. Achievement Award for volunteer service, 1993 & 1994.

Irwin, Rita Louise, B.Ed.,Dip.Ed., M.Ed.,Ed.D. ⌾ ⊗ ◉

Associate Professor, Department of Curriculum Studies, UNIVERSITY OF BRITISH COLUMBIA, 2125 Main Mall, Vancouver, BC V6T 1Z4 (604) 822-5322, FAX 822-9366, EMAIL irwinr@unixg.ubc.ca. Born Lethbridge, Alta. 1955. d. EDUC: Univ. of Lethbridge, B.Ed. 1977, Diploma Program in Educ. 1985; Alberta Permanent Professional Teaching Certificate 1979; Univ. of Victoria, M.Ed. 1986; Univ. of British Columbia, Ed.D. 1988. CAREER: teacher, elementary schools, Lethbridge, Alta., 1977-84; Visual Arts Consultant, LSD No. 51, & also Art Dept. Head, Park Meadows Sch., Lethbridge, 1984-86; Visiting Asst. Prof., Visual & Performing Arts in Educ., Univ. of British Columbia, Summer 1989; Asst. Prof.,

Sch. of Educ., Lakehead Univ., 1988-92; Asst. Prof., Dept. of Curriculum Studies, Univ. of British Columbia, 1992-85; Assoc. Prof., 1995 to date. SELECTED PUBLICATIONS: *A Circle of Empowerment: Women, Education and Leadership* (New York: SUNY Press, 1995); "Visual Journals as an Integration Among Drawing, Art Appreciation, and the Writing Process" (*The CSEA Journal* 20(1) 1989); "Creativity in a Cultural Context" (*Canadian Journal of Native Education* 19(1) 1992); "Charismatic and Transformational Leadership Within A Community of Women Arts Educators" (*Canadian Review of Art Education* 20(2) 1993); various other publications. EDIT: Ed. Bd., *The Journal*, Canadian Society for Education Through Art, 1989-95; Ed. Bd., *CRAE*, Canadian Society for Education Through Art, 1990-95; Ed. Bd. *Journal of the Ontario Society for Education Through Art*, 1990-95. EXHIBITIONS: Dir., *Art's Alive and Well in the Schools*, children's art, Southern Alberta Art Gallery, Lethbridge, 1985, 1986; Dir., *Artist-in-Residence Installation*, permanent installation, Park Meadows Sch., Lethbridge, June 1985; Dir., *Centennial Mural*, permanent outdoor mural, Sch. Bd. Office, Lethbridge, 1986; exhibited own work in group shows at *Graduation Show*, A. Wilfrid Johns Gallery, Univ. of Victoria, 1985 & *Art Teachers' Show*, Bowman Arts Gallery, Lethbridge, 1986. AFFIL: Canadian Society for Education Through Art (Pres. 1992-96); National Art Education Association; Canadian Association for Curriculum Studies; Ontario Society for Education Through Art; International Society for Education Through Art; B.C. Art Teachers' Association. HONS: British Columbia Post Secondary Scholarship, 1987; John Walker Barnet Fellowship, Alberta Teachers' Association, 1987-88; Univ. of British Columbia Summer Grad. Fellowship, 1988. INTERESTS: Invited Visiting Researcher, Univ. of South Australia, Adelaide, 1993; numerous workshops & seminars; recipient, various grants; numerous conference presentations. COMMENT: *"My experience as a woman, artist, art educator, leader and researcher has offered me wonderful opportunities in my life. I have worked with all age levels of students, am actively involved in art advocacy efforts provincially, nationally and internationally, and am continually inspired by my ongoing work with women art educators and First Nations communities."*

Isaak, Leona, ANAPA ⊗ $

Owner, SPIRIT OF THE WEST PHOTO VENTURES, 31858 Hopedale Ave., Clearbrook, BC V2T 2G7 (604) 855-4848, FAX 859-6288. Born Rosetown, Sask. 1942. s. EDUC: Aldergrove

Secondary Sch. **CAREER:** Acctnt, various bus. firms, primarily in the floor covering industry; originator, "Horse Drive" photographic opportunities; Chair, Abbotsford Photo Arts Club Seminar, 1991, 1992, 1994. **AFFIL:** National Association of Photographic Art–Pacific Zone (Fraser Valley District Rep.); Abbotsford Photo Arts Club; National Association of Photographic Art (Treas., Bd. of Dir.). **HONS:** First in BC, BC Top Pictorial Club Slide, 1980; First, Fraser Valley Fine Arts Exhibition, 1986; Appreciation Award, dedication & svc., Abbotsford Photo Arts Club, 1992; Associateship, National Association of Photographic Art, recognition of substantial svc., 1994. **INTERESTS:** photography; the outdoors; cross-country skiing; cycling; walking. **MISC:** Abbotsford Photo Arts Club Seminar is the largest one-day seminar in Canada, held annually. **COMMENT:** *"My goal is to share my enthusiasm for photography, my techniques and my favourite locations with other photographers."*

Isinger, Lorraine K. (Lori), B.Ed. ■■ 🗋 🎯
Past President and Life Member, SASKATOON COUNCIL OF WOMEN, P.O. Box 9526, Saskatoon, SK S7K 2G1 (306) 373-9226, FAX 955-3590. Owner and Manager, MRI STUDIOS. **EDUC:** Univ. of Saskatchewan, B.Ed.(Hist. & English, with distinction). **CAREER:** Teacher &/or Librarian, several schools, elementary & high sch. level, Saskatoon; also taught pottery & ceramics to adults; Owner/Mgr, MRI Studios, retailer of limited-edition collectors' plates, figurines & lithographs. **AFFIL:** Friends of the Library (Chair of the Bd.); Saskatoon Public Library Bd. (Chair 1991-93); Saskatchewan Library Trustees' Association (Chair 1992-95); Canadian Library Trustees' Association (Chair, Handbook Revision Committee 1994); Saskatoon Council of Women (Pres. 1990-93); Provincial Council of Women of Saskatchewan (VP 1990-93); National Council of Women of Canada (Chair, Planning Committee, AGM '96; Chair, Task Force on Policy Dev. 1994-96); Royal University Hospital Foundation (Bd. mbr. 1983-86); Royal University Hospital (Pres., Auxiliary 1982-84); Univ. of Saskatchewan (V-Chair, Senate 1996-97; V-Chair, Exec. Committee, Senate 1995-96; Rep. to Senate from Sask. Library Trustees 1993-96); Saskatoon-Humboldt Fed. P.C. Association (Pres.); Saskatoon-Nutane Prov. P.C. Association (Pres.); P.C. Prov. Policy Formation Committee (Chair); P.C. Nat'l Policy Committee for Saskatchewan (Chair); City of Saskatoon Focus Group on Women's Issues (mbr. 1993-94). **HONS:** Life Mbr., Saskatchewan Library Association, 1995; Life Mbr., Saskatoon Council of Women, 1993; Life Mbr.,

Royal University Hospital Auxiliary, 1982. **MISC:** Returning Officer, several elections; Automation Coord., Saskatoon/Dundurn electoral riding, 1992.

Ivey, Beryl, B.A. 🎯 💲
Vice-President, THE RICHARD IVEY FOUNDATION, 630 Richmond St., London, ON N6A 3G6 (519) 673-1280, FAX 672-4790. President, BEEHIVE INVESTMENTS LIMITED. Born Chatham, Ont. 1924. m. Richard M. Ivey. 4 ch. **EDUC:** Univ. of Western Ontario, B.A. 1947; Ont. Coll. of Educ., 1948. **CAREER:** VP & Dir., The Richard Ivey Foundation, 1972 to date; Pres., Beehive Investments, 1973 to date. **VOLUNTEER CAREER:** Dir., Theatre London, 1965-67; Dir., London Art Gallery Association, 1969-80; Dir., Shaw Festival Theatre, 1969-75; Dir. & VP, 1977-82; mbr., National Theatre Sch., 1971-94; Dir., 1971-72; Trustee, Art Gallery of Ontario, 1974-77; Dir., Eskimo Arts Council, 1975-78; Dir., National Ballet Sch., 1975-80, 1983-84; Dir., Canadian Centre for Philanthropy, 1982-89; Dir., Trillium Foundation of Ontario, 1982-88; mbr., Advisory Bd., Parkwood Hospital, 1982-89; Dir., University Hospital, 1982-92; mbr., Arboretum Advisory Council, Univ. of Guelph, 1987-93; Pres., 1988-93; mbr., Inuit Art Committee, Art Gallery of Ontario, 1989-94. **DIRECTOR:** Ivest Corporation; Beehive Investments Limited. **PAST DIRECTOR:** Canada Trustco Mortgage Company, 1982-89; Galatea Art International Corporation, 1985-91; CT Financial Services Inc., 1987-89; Alcor Investments Limited, 1988-89. **AFFIL:** Canadian Medical Hall of Fame (Dir.); World Wildlife Fund (Canada) (Dir.); Foundation Western (Dir.); Canadian Association for Community Living (Hon. Advisory Bd. mbr.); Univ. of Western Ontario (Visual Arts Advisory Council); The 1001: A Nature Trust, World Wide Fund for Nature; 200 Canadians for Wildlife: A Conservation Trust, World Wildlife Fund, Canada; University Hospital Foundation (Dir. 1988-93; Pres. 1990-92; Hon. Patron). **HONS:** Canada 125 Medal, 1992; Centennial Award, Ontario Medical Association, jointly with Richard Ivey, 1993.

Ivey, Celese G., B.A.,C.H.R.P. 💲 ㄩ
Director, Human Resource Management, GLOBAL COMMUNICATIONS LIMITED, 81 Barber Greene Rd., Don Mills, ON M4G 1R1. Born 1957. m. Roger J. Ivey. 3 ch. Derrek, Fletcher, Leonard. **EDUC:** Victoria Coll., Univ. of Toronto, B.A. 1980; Certified Human Resources Professional 1992. **CAREER:** Ed. Asst./Writer, Global Communications Limited, 1979-80; Exec. Asst. to the VP, News & Current Affairs, 1980-81; Ed. Coord., News &

Info. Programming, 1981-83; Mgr, Program Admin. & Fin., News & Info. Programming, 1983-89; Dir., Hum. Res. Mgmt, 1989 to date. **AFFIL:** Ontario Human Resources Professionals' Association of Ontario; Canadian Association of Broadcasters (Hum. Res. Committee); Toronto Human Resource Broadcast Group; Goodwin Business Advisory Council (mbr., "work on track"). **INTERESTS:** music; swimming; art. **MISC:** presenter, Canadian Institute on Flexible Workplaces; presenter, Balancing the Multiple Roles of Women in the '90s, Girl Guides of Canada.

J

Jackman, Barbara Louise, B.A., LL.B. ■ ■ ⚖ ♡
JACKMAN & ASSOCIATES (private law practice), 196 Adelaide St. W., Ste. 200, Toronto, ON M5H 1W7. Born Toronto. EDUC: Univ. of Windsor, B.A.(Hons.) 1972; Univ. of Toronto, LL.B. 1976. BAR: Law Society of Upper Canada, 1978. CAREER: specialist in immigration & refugee law; Instructor/Bar Admission Lecturer, Law Society of Upper Canada, 1983-86; Lecturer, 1984-85, 1987-90; Fac. of Law, Queen's Univ., 1991-97; Fac. of Law, Univ. of Toronto, 1994-97. SELECTED PUBLICATIONS: author, various papers & articles; contributor to 4 books. AFFIL: Canadian Bar Association (Exec. mbr., Immigration Law 1989-92; Chair, Immigration Law, Ont. 1987-89; Exec. mbr., Ont. 1984-90); Canadian Civil Liberties Association (Dir. 1989-97); Working Women Community Centre (former Dir.); INTERCEDE (former Dir.); Law Union of Ontario; Canadian Council for Refugees. MISC: delegate, Trans-Atlantic Legal Exchange on Refugee Law, 1986-87; delegate, Northern Ireland Peace Process Fact-Finding Mission; Rep., Cdn Council of Churches, for monitoring Canada's participation before the U.N. Committee on the Rights of the Child, 1995 & the Human Rights Committee, 1990.

Jackman, Martha, B.A.,LL.B., LL.M. ■ ■ ⚖ 🎓 3
Associate Professor, Faculty of Law, UNIVERSITY OF OTTAWA, P.O. Box 450, Stn A, Ottawa, ON K1N 6N5 (613) 562-5800, ext. 3299, FAX 562-5124, EMAIL mjackman@uottawa.ca. Born Perth, Ont. 1959. m. Michael Langtry. 2 ch. Frances, Elizabeth. EDUC: Queen's Univ.,

B.A. 1981; Univ. of Toronto, LL.B. 1985; Yale Law Sch., LL.M. 1988. **CAREER:** Lecturer, École de droit, Univ. de Moncton, 1985-87; Asst. Prof., Fac. of Law, Univ. of Ottawa, 1988-91; Dir., Grad. Studies in Law, 1994-96; Assoc. Prof., 1991 to date. **SELECTED PUBLICATIONS:** numerous articles incl.: "Women and the Canada Health and Social Transfer: Ensuring Gender Equality in Federal Welfare Reform" (*Canadian Journal of Women and the Law/Revue Femmes et Droit*, 1996); "The Right to Participate in Health Care and Health Resource Allocation Decisions Under Section 7 of the Canadian Charter" (*Health Law Review*, 1995/96); "Constitutional Contact with the Disparities in the World: Poverty as a Prohibited Ground of Discrimination Under the Canadian Charter and Human Rights Law" (*Review of Constitutional Studies*, 1994); "The Constitution and the Regulation of New Reproductive Technologies" in *Overview of Legal Issues in New Reproductive Technologies*, Vol. 3 of Research Studies of Royal Commission on New Reproductive Technologies (Ottawa: Supply & Services Canada, 1994); "Rights and Participation: the Use of the Charter to Supervise the Regulatory Process" (*Canadian Journal of Administrative Law and Practice*, 1990); also numerous conference papers & presentations. **EDIT:** Co-Ed., *Canadian Journal of Women and the Law/Revue Femmes et Droit*, 1996 to date; mbr., Edit. Bd., 1989 to date. **AFFIL:** National Association of Women & the Law (mbr.; Consultant, Fed. Social Security Reform Proj. 1994-95); Law Society of Upper Canada; Canadian Bar Association (mbr.; Consultant, Health Care Task Force 1994); Association des juristes d'expression française. **MISC:** Cnsl, Women's Legal Education & Action Fund in *Falkiner et al v. Ontario*, 1996; Advisory Council mbr., Canadian Disability Rights Council, Income Security Reform Proj., 1994; Consultant, Royal Commission on New Reproductive Technologies, 1992-93.

Jacko, Esther Marie ✤ 📖 ☺

Community Historian and Lands Manager, WHITEFISH RIVER FIRST NATION, General Delivery, Birch Island, Ont. P0P 1A0 (705) 285-4334, FAX 285-4532. Born Little Current, Ont. 1954. m. Francis Jacko. 4 ch. **CAREER:** has worked for her First Nation Council, 15 yrs. **AFFIL:** Environmental Assessment Bd. (Advisory Committee); Mississauga Implementation Committee (Chair, Land Claim Settlement); Algoma-Manitoulin Native Women's Association (Co-Chair); North Channel Preservation Society. **INTERESTS:** lands mgmt for First Nations; environmental issues; Ojibwa traditional arts; history of Great Lakes aborigi-

nals. **MISC:** appointed by the Prov. Cabinet to sit as a mbr. on the Environmental Assessment Bd. of Ont., 1989-93; appointed by the Fed. Cabinet to sit as a mbr. on the Cdn Environmental Assessment Research Council, 1990-93; playwright; avid practitioner of Ojibwa cultural traditions particularly the Fast & Vision quest; has made various public & TV appearances in an on-going effort to raise awareness of the Ojibwa culture. **COMMENT:** "*I am also a well known traditional Ojibwa storyteller who has travelled across Canada and some parts of Europe. I have written plays performed by the De-Dah-Jeh-Ma-Jig Theatre from Wikwemikong, Ont.*"

Jacks, Evelyn ■ ■ $ 🗃 ▥

President and Owner, THE JACKS INSTITUTE (nat'l private career coll. for tax industry professionals), 167 Lombard Ave., Ste. 902, Winnipeg, MB R3B 0V3 (204) 956-7161, FAX 949-9429, EMAIL www.jackstax.com. Born Winnipeg 1955. m. Allan. 2 ch. Cordell & Donald Harrison. **EDUC:** Red River Community Coll., Bus. Teacher Educ. Diploma 1975; numerous tax industry seminars/courses over 20 yrs. **CAREER:** former Dir. of Educ. & VP, Admin. & Training, nat'l tax prep. chain. **SELECTED CREDITS:** fin. columnist for tax matters, CHUM Radio Ntwk (over 30 affiliates). **SELECTED PUBLICATIONS:** more than 15 books incl.: *Jacks on Tax Savings* (annual, 1984-97, Cdn bestseller); *201 Ways to Reduce Your Taxes* (1994-97); *Canadian Home Business Guide to Tax Savings* (1997); *Jacks on Personal Finance* (1994); *Jacks on GST* (1992). **EDIT:** Ed., *Jacks on Tax Update* (newsletter), 1992-97. **DIRECTOR:** The Jacks Institute. **MEMBER:** Customer Advisory Board, CIBC. **AFFIL:** Manitoba Public Insurance Commission (Bd. mbr.); Canadian Tax Foundation; Canadian Association of Financial Planners; Pan-Am Games 1999 (Chair, Tennis Venue); Winnipeg Chamber of Commerce (VP 1992-95). **HONS:** Gov. Gen. medalist, 1973; Woman of the Year, YM-YWCA, 1986; Entrepreneur of the Year, Women Business Owners category, Federal Business Development Bank, 1995. **INTERESTS:** business-education partnerships; int'l commerce; fishing; travel. **MISC:** has written over 50 tax-related certificate courses for individuals & professionals; panelist/keynote speaker/seminar leader, numerous groups; has developed internal training & policy/procedures manuals for companies; served as Grand Jury mbr., Federal Canada Awards for Business Excellence. **COMMENT:** "*I am greatly enjoying my career, which has taken me from teaching business law, economics and other business subjects at a high school level to owning*

Canada's leading correspondence school for tax preparation courses. I have hosted radio and TV shows, participated in CD-ROM products and commented on budgets of the federal government on virtually every media outlet in Canada. But I feel my greatest achievement is the raising of my two very fine sons."

Jackson, Margaret ✊ $

President, TORONTO AND AREA COUNCIL OF WOMEN, 45 Oakmount Rd., Ste. 205, Toronto, ON M6P 2M4 (416) 766-4695. Past President, CANADIAN FEDERATION OF BUSINESS AND PROFESSIONAL WOMEN'S CLUBS. Born Toronto 1922. s. **EDUC:** Western Commerce, Acctg 1942; Toronto Bus. Coll., 1944. **CAREER:** bookkeeping, Dental Co. of Canada, 1944-54; acctg/credit mgmt, United Dominion Investment Ltd., 1954-82. **AFFIL:** Canadian Federation of Business & Professional Women's Clubs (Pres. 1984-86; Life. Mbr.); Senior Talent Bank Association of Ontario (Treas. 1989-94); Toronto Mayor's Committee on Aging (Co-Chair 1990-95); UNESCO (Co-Chair, Status of Women 1990-94); Toronto & Area Council of Women (Pres.); Elsie Gregory MacGill Memorial Foundation (Treas. & Trustee); Canadian National Exhibition Association (Dir. 1990-95). **INTERESTS:** travel; music; volunteer work; equality for women. **COMMENT:** *"Since retirement, I do volunteer work at Runnymede Chronic Hospital, Women's College Hospital. I continue to work for Canadian Federation of Business and Professional Women's Clubs and enjoy meeting people."*

Jackson, Margaret A., B.A.,M.A., Ph.D. ■ 🎓 ⚖

Professor and Director, School of Criminology, SIMON FRASER UNIVERSITY, Burnaby, BC V5A 1S6 (604) 291-4040, FAX 291-4140. Born Columbia, Mo. 1942. d. **EDUC:** Univ. of California, B.A.(English) 1967; Univ. of Toronto, M.A.(Psych.) 1970, M.A.(Criminology) 1978, Ph.D.(Psych.) 1985. **CAREER:** Research Tech., Dept. of Physics, Univ. of California, 1966-69; Teaching Asst., Dept. of Psych., Univ. of Toronto, 1969-70, Research Asst., Comparative Psych., 1969-76; Special Lecturer, Comparative Psych., 1976-77; Sr. Research Asst., Centre of Criminology, 1979-81; Research Asst., Metropolitan Toronto Forensic Svc., Clarke Institute of Psychiatry, 1979-81; Sr. Research Assoc., Centre of Criminology, 1981-82; Research Scientist 1, Metropolitan Toronto Forensic Svc., 1982-83; Economist 2, Researcher, Ont. Ministry of Correctional Svcs, 1982; Instructor, Dept. of Criminology, Simon Fraser Univ., 1983-85, Acting Dir., Sch. of Criminology, 1985; Asst. Prof., 1985-88; Acting Dir., Institute for Studies in Criminal Justice Policy, 1986; Assoc. Dir., 1987-94; Co-Dir., 1994 to date; Assoc. Dir., Sch. of Criminology, Simon Fraser Univ., 1987; Assoc. Prof., 1988-96; Dir., 1995 to date; Prof., 1996 to date; Co-founder, Feminist Institute for Studies on Law & Society, 1990; Dir., Sch. of Criminology, Simon Fraser Univ., 1990-93; Acting Dean of Grad. Studies, 1991; Co-founder, Institute for Studies on Educ. in Corrections, 1992; Assoc. Mbr., Law & Psych. Program, Simon Fraser Univ., 1992; Bd. Mbr., Pres.'s Rep. & VP, International Centre for Criminal Law Reform & Criminal Justice Policy, 1992-94. **SELECTED CREDITS:** *House of Concord* Video (1990); *Sentencing Panel* Video (1991). **SELECTED PUBLICATIONS:** *Clinical Criminology* ed. with Z. Hilton & C.D. Webster (Toronto: Canadian Scholars Press, 1990); *Canadian Criminology: Perspective on Crime and Criminology*, ed. with C.T. Griffiths (Toronto: HBJ Holt Publishers, 1991; 2nd ed., 1995); "Legal and Medical Issues in Forensic Psychiatric Assessment," with R.J. Menzies & C.D. Webster (*Queen's Law Journal* fall 1982); "The Clinical Assessment and Prediction of Violent Behaviour" (*Criminal Justice and Behaviour* 1989); " Aboriginal Women and Self-Government: the Path of Self-Determination Leads to Self-Government" in *Implementation of Aboriginal Self-Government in Canada*, J. Hylton ed. (Saskatoon: Purich Publishing, 1994); *Ten Years Later: The Charter and Equality for Women*, co-ed. with N. Kathleen San Banks (Vancouver: SFU Continuing Studies Conference Proceedings, 1996); *The Keeps and the Kept: An Introduction to Canadian Corrections*, with J.W. Ekstedt (Toronto: Nelson Canada, 1996); *Impulsive People: Advances in Research and Treatment*, co-ed. C.D. Webster (New York: Guilford Press, 1996). **EDIT:** Book Review Ed., *Canadian Criminology Forum*, 1979-82; Ed., 1982-83; Advisory Bd., *Women and the Law*. **AFFIL:** American Society of Criminology; Canadian Psychological Association; Canadian Institute for the Administration of Justice; Western Society of Criminology; Canadian Law & Society Association; Mental Health, Law & Policy Institute; American Judiciary Society; National Association of Women & Law; Canadian Research Institute for the Advancement of Women; Langley Youth Resource Centre (Chair, Advisory Bd.). **HONS:** Ont. Grad. Fellowship, 1981; Centre of Criminology Fellowship, 1982; Research Fellowship, Univ. of Edinburgh Institute for Advanced Studies in Humanities; various academic awards & fellowships. **INTERESTS:** photography; writing of fiction; long-distance running. **MISC:** recipient, numerous grants & fellowships; reviewer for various journals, presses & grants; numerous conference presentations, keynote addresses & seminars; Convener, Cdn Law & Society Annual Conference, 1988. COMMENT: *"Person: academic criminologist. Interests: criminal justice decision-making; policy analysis; violence against women; aboriginal justice; women prisoners. Career achievements: Director, School of Criminology; founding member and Director, Feminist Institute; Co-Director, Policy Institute."*

Jackson, Margaret Rose, R.N.A. ■ ○ ⊕
Board Member, PEIGAN MENTALLY CHALLENGED SOCIETY, c/o Pincher Creek Municipal Hospital, Pincher Creek, AB T0K 1W0. Born Brocket, Alta. 1937. w. 5 ch. Marlene, Janet, Lorraine, Lorne, Brian. EDUC: AVC Calgary, Registered Nursing Asst. 1955; Foothills Hospital, Calgary, Alberta Operating Room Technician 1973. CAREER: Registered Nursing Asst.; Operating Room Technician; Operating Room Nurse, Pincher Creek Municipal Hospital, 1961-93; Alcohol Counsellor, Peigan Nation Alcohol Svcs, Brocket, Alta. AFFIL: Alberta Association of Registered Nurses Assistants (Life Mbr.); Napi Friendship Association, Pincher Creek (Pres. 1985-95); Peigan Minor Hockey (Bd. Mbr.); Peigan Nation Senior Centre (Bd. Mbr. 1994-95); Peigan Arts & Crafts Bd. (Bd. Mbr. 1994-95). HONS: Community Role Model, Peigan Nation, 1991; 25 Yrs. of Service, Dedication to AARNA, Chinook Chapter of AARNA, 1993. INTERESTS: prevention of substance abuse & sexual abuse of the youth. COMMENT: *"I am a member of the Blackfoot Confederacy. My mission in life was to become a nurse and help my Native people, which I achieved. My next goal is to help with prevention of substance abuse among the aboriginal people."*

Jackson, Sarah Jeanette, B.A., M.A. ■ ⊗
Artist. 1411 Edward St., Halifax, NS B3H 3H5 (902) 423-0670, FAX 494-2319, EMAIL jacksona@newton.ccs.tuns.ca. Born Detroit 1924. m. Anthony Jackson. 2 ch. Timothy Lynn, Melanie Naomie. EDUC: Wayne State Univ., B.A. 1946, M.A. 1948. CAREER: artist, working in sculpture, drawing, copier art & bookworks; lecturer, various universities, colleges, galleries in Canada, UK, Mexico; Artist-in-Residence, Technical Univ. of Nova Scotia, 1978-89; Dir., Art & Technology Program & associated annual festivals, 1979-89; Dir., Summer Arts Festivals & Copier Art Festivals, 1981-86; founder, Sarah Jackson Artwear, 1991. SELECTED PUBLICATIONS: numerous

limited edition books of poetry & images, incl. *Personae, Who is Sheba & Sheba Recalled;* contributor to newspapers & magazines. EXHIBITIONS: numerous solo exhibitions, incl. Apollinaire Gallery, London (1951), Roberts Gallery, Toronto (1961), Mount St. Vincent Univ. (1967, 1968, 1981), Pictura Museum, Sweden (1984), Micro Hall Art Centre, West Germany (1989) & "Copier Art Bookworks," WCBA, Minneapolis (1990); numerous group exhibitions in Canada, Europe & US, incl. *Women's Bookworks,* Powerhouse Gallery, Montreal (1982), *Mirrorings, Women's Art,* originated by Mount St. Vincent Art Gallery (1983) & Copier Art Festival, Technical Univ. of Nova Scotia (1989); Artistic Dir., Valentine's Day Copier Art Festival, Halifax (1991); Works Art Festival, Edmonton (1990); Copier Art Festival, Winnipeg (1993); International Biennal-Art Electro Images, Berlin (1994); Biennale d'Art Electro Images, Varsarely Museum, Budapest (1994); International Copy Art Expo, Seoul, Korea (1995); initiator & co-curator, International Mail/Copier Art Exhibition (with bookworks), London, UK (1987); guest artist & curator, International Mail/Copier Art Festival, Canadian Museum of Civilization, 1992; dir. of various other exhibitions & festivals. COLLECTIONS: Hirshorn Museum & Sculpture Garden; National Coll. of Fine Arts, Smithsonian Institute; National Gallery of Canada; Art Gallery of Ontario; Musée des Beaux-Arts de Montréal; Musée d'Art Contemporain Montréal; work in numerous other collections; "Sarah Jackson Mail-Copier Art Collection," acquired by National Postal Museum of Canada for their archives, to be housed in the Canadian Museum of Civilization, 1988; bookworks in numerous collections incl. National Library of Canada, National Museum of Women in the Arts, Washington, DC, Princeton Univ. Library, & Tate Gallery Library, London, UK. HONS: Award of Excellence, Art Museums Association of America, for bookworks catalogue, 1985; Copier Art Books Award, Minnesota Center for Book Arts, 1990. MISC: subject of film, *Sarah Jackson Halifax 1980,* NFB (1980); participant, *Substance,* NFB (1981); commissioned multidiscipline work based on her bookwork *Spirit Journey/Voyage de l'Esprit* & Margaret Harry's poetry (1983-85); dance choreographed by Pat Richards based on her copier art bookwork *Finding Herself,* 1984. COMMENT: *"Making copier art has been preoccupying me since 1973. It has become a direct means for making statements. I can control the final effects of images and contents. These become a very personal way of communication as a human vision through art."*

Jacobi, Joan 🕙

Executive Director, VERNON WOMEN'S TRANSITION HOUSE, P.O. Box 625, Vernon, BC V1T 6M6 (604) 542-1122, FAX 549-3347. CAREER: Exec. Dir., Vernon Women's Transition House Society, 1980 to date; Instructor, Okanagan Coll., Native Bands, Lifeskills group. SELECTED PUBLICATIONS: articles for various newspapers. AFFIL: John Howard Society (Bd., 12 years); Okanagan Coll., Kalamalka campus (Personnel Advisory Committee); Community Law Board; CCDA (Bargaining Committee); sponsored and trained many community support groups incl. Mom's Morning Out, the Native Skills Group and a sexual abuse Group. HONS: Woman of the Year, Vernon Women in Business, 1996/97. MISC: guest speaker at many community groups, both professional and non-professional; involved in fundraising that helped build an 11-bedroom Transition House (over $600,000 was raised within 3-1/2 months); helped establish a native network in association with First Nations Friendship Centre and the Okanagan Band #1; has designed and implemented many programs through the Transition House including: Pregnant Teen live-in group; Probation Teen (six month live-in); Specialized Victim Assistance; childcare programming for Children Who Witness Violence; Native Outreach Counsellor Program; Battered Women Outreach Counselling; Senior Women in Motion Program (work in the community to empower other elderly women). COMMENT: *"I would say my passion has always been to empower women and children. I am able to assess a need, involve the community and empower people to make it happen, be it a course, a group or a project. My ability to establish rapport with people is excellent."*

Jacobi, Nancy, B.A. ■ ⊗ $

Owner and President, THE JAPANESE PAPER PLACE, 887 Queen St. W., Toronto, ON M6J 1G5 (416) 703-0089, FAX 703-0163. Born Toronto 1943. s. EDUC: Univ. of Toronto, B.A.(English) 1965; Ont. Coll. of Educ., Teaching Certificate. CAREER: teacher, high sch. English, Toronto, Calgary & Winnipeg, 8 yrs.; English teacher, Japan, 1975; actor, children's theatre, 1 yr.; CUSO, incl. Papua, New Guinea, contract 5 yrs; owner & Pres., The Japanese Paper Place, 1982 to date. AFFIL: Canadian Bookbinders'–Book Artists' Guild; Friends of the Thomas Fisher Library; AGO. COMMENT: *"From 1979 until present I have focused on visiting the diminishing papermaking villages of Japan, documenting the people and processes and buying their beautiful papers, made in many cases, as they were 1,400 years ago. In 1982, I opened the Japanese Paper*

Place. In 1993 the store, and almost all the stock, was destroyed by fire. Now we are rebuilt, offering papers worldwide and I travel extensively to lecture about the paper and its potential for artists. It is my mission to support both the traditional papermakers in Japan and the artists in Canada who use the papers–through exhibitions, selling their works and organizing workshops in which they teach their particular way of working with this paper."

Jacobs, Jane, C.M. ■ ■ 🗐 ✎

Writer. c/o Random House of Canada, 33 Yonge St., Toronto, ON M5E 1G4. Born Scranton, Penn. 1916. m. Robert Hyde. 3 ch. James Kedzie, Edward Decker, Mary Hyde. EDUC: Columbia Univ. SELECTED PUBLICATIONS: contributor, *The Exploding Metropolis* (1958); author, *The Death and Life of Great American Cities* (1961); *The Economy of Cities* (1969); *The Question of Separatism* (1980); *Cities and the Wealth of Nations* (1984); *The Girl on the Hat* (children's fiction, 1989); *Systems of Survival: A Dialogue* (1993). HONS: Hon. Mbr., Ontario Association of Architects; Lifetime Achievement Award, Toronto Arts Awards; Member of the Order of Canada.

Jacobs-Moens, Maria, B.A., M.A. ■ ■ 🗐 🗐 👊

Co-Publisher, WOLSAK AND WYNN PUBLISHERS LTD. (publishers of Cdn poetry), 217 Northwood Dr., Willowdale, ON M2M 2K5 (416) 222-4690, FAX 736-5731, EMAIL genome@ yorku.ca. Born Bussum, The Netherlands 1930. EDUC: York Univ., B.A.(Math.) 1976, M.A.(English) 1979. CAREER: managed The Axle Tree Coffee House poetry reading series, 1977-83; Assoc. Ed., *Waves* (literary magazine), 3 yrs.; Literary Ed., *Canadian Woman Studies/Les Cahiers de la Femme*, 6 yrs.; Publisher/Ed., *Poetry Toronto*, 1979-88; Founder/Co-Publisher, Wolsak and Wynn Publishers Ltd., 1982 to date. SELECTED PUBLICATIONS: author: *Precautions Against Death* (Mosaic Press, 1983); *What Feathers Are For* (Mosaic Press, 1985); *Iseult, We Are Barren* (Netherlandic Press, 1987); author & translator: *Vijfenvijftig Sokken* (De Harmonie, Amsterdam, 1983); Dutch translation of *Precautions Against Death*. AFFIL: The League of Canadian Poets (mbr.; Pres. 1990-92; Ed., *Museletter* 1993-95); *Genome*, pub. by National Research Council of Canada (Asst. to Ed.); *Chromosoma*, pub. by Springer-Verlag, Heidelberg, Germany (Asst. to Editor); PEN International; Canadian Association for the Advancement of Netherlandic Studies. INTERESTS: sailing; gardening; reading. COMMENT:

"Brown eyes and hair, fair skin; small, vivacious. Writes poetry, biography, edits/publishes poetry. One husband, five children, eight grandchildren; loves life, men, women, reading and cats."

Jaczek, Helena, M.D.,M.H.Sc., M.B.A. ■■ ⊕ ✿

Commissioner of Health Services and Medical Officer of Health, REGIONAL MUNICIPALITY OF YORK, ONTARIO, 17250 Yonge St., Newmarket, ON L3Y 6Z1 (905) 895-4511, FAX 895-2631, EMAIL yrphu@hookup.net. Born London, UK 1950. w. 2 ch. Natasha, Nicholas. EDUC: Univ. of Toronto, M.D.(Medicine) 1973, M.H.Sc.(Community Health & Epidemiology) 1988; York Univ., M.B.A. 1994. CAREER: private practice as physician (on staff at Women's College Hospital, Toronto), 1974-82; physician, Windsor-Essex County Health Unit, 1983-85; Medical Dir., Clinical Svcs, 1986-87; Medical Officer of Health, Reg'l Municipality of York, 1988-96; Commissioner of Health Svcs & Medical Officer of Health, 1996 to date. SELECTED PUBLICATIONS: "Genital Chlamydia Trachomatis: Detection, Treatment and Patient Education" (*Canadian Family Physician*, Oct. 1985); "Screening Homosexual Men for Hepatitis B" (*Canadian Family Physician*, Apr. 1986); "Treating Gynecological Infections" (*Drug Protocol*, June 1987, Vol. 2, No. 6); co-author with G.M. Liss *et al*, "Improper Office Disposal of Needles and Other Sharps: An Occupational Hazard Outside of Health Care Institutions" (*Canadian Journal of Public Health*, Nov./Dec. 1990, Vol. 81, No. 6). AFFIL: Ontario Medical Association (Chair, Section of Public Health Physicians 1991 & 1992; mbr. of Exec. 1989-93); Association of Local Official Health Agencies (Pres. 1993-94; Bd. of Dir. 1991-95); Coll. of Family Physicians of Canada; Canadian Public Health Association; Essex County Medical Society (Exec. mbr. 1985-86); Essex County District Health Council (mbr. 1986-87). HONS: Distinguished Svc. Award, Association of Local Official Health Agencies for "outstanding contribution to public health in Ontario," 1996. INTERESTS: people; continuous learning. COMMENT: *"I am a public health physician with administrative responsibilities for a staff of 465 full-time equivalents and a budget of $60 million. I am firmly committed to health promotion and prevention of disease through public health practice in Ontario."*

Jaffer, Mobina, LL.B. ■■ ◪⌕ ♂

Barrister and Solicitor, DOHM, JAFFER & COMPANY (law firm), 3316 Kingsway, Ste. 268, Vancouver, BC V5R 5K7 (604) 438-3369,

FAX 438-5576. Born Kampala, Uganda 1949. m. Nuralla Jeraj. 2 ch. Azool Jeraj, Farzana Jeraj. EDUC: Univ. of London, U.K., LL.B. 1972; Simon Fraser Univ., Exec. Mgmt Dev. Program. CAREER: articled with Fowkes & Sons, London, U.K., 1973-75; articled with The Hon. Thomas Dohm, 1975-78; Barrister & Solicitor, Dohm, Jaffer & Company, 1978 to date. AFFIL: Liberal Party of Canada (VP (English 1994 to date); candidate for N. Vancouver in fed. election 1993; mbr., Nat'l Exec. 1990-92); Duke of Edinburgh Award for N. Vancouver (Rep. 1987 to date); Women & Development (mbr. 1988 to date); Hastings Institute (mbr. 1990 to date); Law Society (Multicultural Committee 1992 to date); Trial Lawyers' Association of B.C.; Lions Gate Hospital (mbr. of Bd. 1995 to date); YWCA of Canada (Sec. 1996 to date). HONS: numerous honours incl.: Women of Distinction Award, YWCA, 1993; Justice Achievement Award, Law Courts Education Society of B.C., 1993; Congress of Black Women Award for recognition of work on equality, 1993; Award from Trial Lawyers of B.C. for outstanding service to the legal profession, 1995. MISC: extensive experience in refugee & immigration law; broad background in personal injury cases & matrimonial law; 30 yrs. of work in equality issues in Uganda, the U.S., U.K. & Canada; fluent in 6 languages. COMMENT: *"I was the first East Indian woman lawyer to practice in British Columbia. I am committed to equality and justice for women of colour and the struggle to end violence against all women."*

James, Karen A., B.B.A. ■■ ▯⌐ ⌣

Publisher, *Canadian Grocer* Magazine, MACLEAN HUNTER PUBLISHING LIMITED, 777 Bay St., Toronto, ON M5W 1A7 (416) 596-5000. Born Sault Ste. Marie, Ont. EDUC: York Univ., B.B.A.(Bus. Admin.) 1983. CAREER: Publisher, Maclean Hunter Limited, 1989 to date. AFFIL: Canadian Diabetes Association (Edit. Bd. 1993); Canadian Association of Food Banks (Exec. Bd.). HONS: delegate to G7 Conference, 1988, Toronto.

James, Vivianne M. ■ Ⓢ ⚘

President, CUMBERLAND COMMUNICATION CONCEPTS, 1340 Frank Kenny Rd., Cumberland, ON K4C 1N8 (613) 833-3553, FAX 833-3516, EMAIL vmjames@vivianne.com, INTERNET: http://www.vivianne.com. Born Kirkland Lake, Ont. 1944. m. Edward F. James. 1 ch. EDUC: Park Bus. Coll., Exec. Secretarial Degree 1963. CAREER: CIBC, 1963-64; Onéson and Sauvé Insurance Adjusters, 1965-66; various admin. positions, National Research Council, 1966-90; Comm. Officer,

Institute for Mech. Eng., Nat'l Research Council, 1990-94; Pres., Cumberland Communication Concepts, 1994 to date. **AFFIL:** Women in Science & Engineering (Past Pres., Ottawa Chapter 1995-96); Cumberland Chamber of Commerce (Dir. 1995-97); Women's Institutes, Cumberland Branch (Dir. & pianist); High Tech Entrepreneurs' Association (Mktg Dir. 1995-97); Eastern Region Women's Network; Concerts Cumberland; Le Business Club d'Orléans; Ottawa-Carleton Board of Trade; Hi Tech Cumberland; The HTML Writers Guild; Concerts Cumberland (Mktg Co-Chair 1996-97); Wagon Train Travelers. **HONS:** Canada 125 Medal. **INTERESTS:** positive action related to equity & diversity; encouraging young people (& adults) to continue with their educ., both formal & informal; motorhome; sewing; music. **COMMENT:** *"My concerns have always been toward women's equality and education. I hope to help people learn more about the world of business and politics and to become as informed as possible on numerous topics."*

Jamieson, Darlene A., B.A., LL.B. ■ ⚖ ♥ ✊

Partner, FLINN MERRICK, 1801 Hollis St., Ste. 2100, Box 1054, Halifax, NS B3J 2X6 (902) 429-4111, FAX 429-8215. Born Trenton, N.S. 1963. **EDUC:** Saint Mary's Univ., B.A.(Pol. Sci./French) 1985; Dalhousie Law Sch., LL.B. 1988. **BAR:** N.S., 1989. **CAREER:** Ptnr, Flinn Merrick, 1989 to date. **AFFIL:** N.S. Barristers' Society (Chair, Gender Equality Implementation Committee); Canadian Bar Association (V-Chair, N.S. Insurance Law Subsection); Atlantic Association of Women Business Owners (Bd. of Dir.); N.S. Association of Women & the Law (Sec.-Treas.); National Association of Women & the Law (Nat'l Steering Committee; Nat'l Coord. 1995-97); Halifax County Regional Rehabilitation Centre (Bd. of Dir.). **COMMENT:** *"The majority of my volunteer time is devoted to working with women's groups who strive to achieve equality for all women."*

Jamieson, Jamesina G.L., LL.B., LL.M. ⚖ 🍁 ☝

Retired Lawyer and Civil Servant. Regina, SK. Born Regina. s. **EDUC:** Univ. of Saskatchewan, LL.B. 1958; Univ. of Ottawa, LL.M. 1989. **BAR:** Sask., 1960. **CAREER:** sole practitioner, private practice of law, Maple Creek, Sask., 1960-64; sole practitioner, private practice of law, Indian Head, Sask., 1964-67; Official Guardian of Infants, Sask. Dept. of Justice, 1967-82; Legislative Svcs, Sask. Dept. of Justice, 1982-84; Exec. Asst. to Chief Justice of Queen's Court Bench, Sask. Dept. of Justice, 1984-90; Special Legislation Proj., Sask. Dept. of Consumer & Corp. Affairs, 1990-91. **EDIT:** Ed. Bd., congregation magazine, Knox-Metropolitan United Church, Regina. **AFFIL:** Law Society of Saskatchewan (Nonpractising Mbr.); Knox-Metropolitan United Church, Regina (Bd. Mbr.). **INTERESTS:** travel. **MISC:** 1 of a small number of women lawyers practising in Sask. in early 1960s; 1st woman Official Guardian of Infants, Sask.; LL.M. thesis, "The Evolution of Executive Power in Saskatchewan 1944-1982," frequently referenced by researchers. **COMMENT:** *"In the early years, I was one of only perhaps four or five women lawyers practising in the province, and perhaps only one or two others had their own law practice. I recall only one other at the time who did court work. During my years as a practising member of the Law Society, I served for a number of years on the Regina Bar Association Executive and was the Canadian Representative on the Executive of the International Federation of Women Lawyers."*

Jamieson, Shelly, B.A. ■■ [$] ⊕

Executive Director, ONTARIO NURSING HOME ASSOCIATION (prov. long-term care association), 345 Renfrew Dr., Ste. 102-202, Markham, ON L3R 9S9 (905) 470-8995, FAX 470-9595, EMAIL onha@idirect.com. Born Toronto 1958. m. Douglas. 2 ch. Heather, Michael. **EDUC:** Univ. of Toronto, B.A.(Hons., Urban Studies) 1980. **CAREER:** Sr. Researcher, Associated Planning Consultants, 1980-82; Principal, Jamieson Research & Consulting Inc., 1982-86; Principal, Envirimed Inc., 1986-92; ONHA, 1992 to date. **AFFIL:** Health Services Restructuring Commission (Commissioner 1996 to date); Canadian Coll. of Health Service Executives (mbr. 1994-96). **COMMENT:** *"I have spent much of my career to date designing, analyzing and reforming services for senior citizens—from the most frail to the most active folk. Along this journey, I have learned how complicated a task this is and how massive our responsibility is to get it right. I'm still trying, hoping that my children inherit a better place."*

Jamison, Lorraine, B.F.A. 🎭 📺 📜

President, COMMUNICATIONS ENCOULEUR JAMISON INC., 364 Parc Cartier, Montreal, QC H4C 3A2 (514) 931-6263, FAX 931-6263. Born Montreal 1960. s. **EDUC:** Concordia Univ., B.F.A.(Art/Art Hist./Creative Writing) 1982. **CAREER:** Administrative Asst., John Howard Society, 1982-85; Acct Exec., David Novek Associates, 1985-89; Press Office Dir., Montreal World Film Festival, 1986-95; Dir. of Comm., Montreal World Film Festival, 1990; Nat'l Publicity Coord., National Film Bd. of

Canada, 1990-91; Pres., Communications encouleur Jamison inc., 1990 to date; Head of Comm., Ville Marie Social Service Centre, 1991-93; Publicist, *Just For Laughs* Montreal Int'l Comedy Festival, 1993 to date; Publicist, Hamptons Int'l Film Festival, 1993-95; Sr. Comm. Mgr, National Film Bd. of Canada, 1994-95. **SELECTED CREDITS:** Unit Publicist, *Murder at 1600*; Unit Publicist, *Lilies*; Unit Publicist, *Million Dollar Babies*; Unit Publicist, *The Valour and the Horror*. **DIRECTOR:** Jamison Incolour Communications Inc. **AFFIL:** Academy of Canadian Cinema & Television; Femmes du cinéma, de la télévision et de la vidéo Montréal (Dir. 1991-93); Ville Marie Foundation (Dir.); C.L.S.C. René-Cassin (Public Rel'ns Committee); Ville Marie Social Service Centre (Public Affairs Advisory Committee 1991-93). **INTERESTS:** the promotion of Cdn culture at home & abroad, but esp. in Canada, to Cdn audiences.

Janigan, Mary, B.A. ■■ ✎ 📖
Contributing Editor, *MACLEAN'S* MAGAZINE, Maclean Hunter Publishing Limited, 777 Bay St., 7th Fl., Toronto, ON M5W 1A7 (416) 596-5386. Born Kingston, Ont. 1948. m. Thomas Kierans. **EDUC:** Carleton Univ., B.A.(English) 1969. **CAREER:** *Kingston Whig-Standard*, 1971-72; *Montreal Gazette*, 1972-73; *The Toronto Star*, 1973-79; FP News Service, 1979-80; *Montreal Gazette*, 1980-81; *Maclean's* magazine, 1982 to date. **SELECTED PUBLICATIONS:** Co-ed. with Richard Simeon, *Toolkits and Building Blocks: Constructing a New Canada* (1990). **HONS:** National Newspaper Award (re constitution), 1981; Silver Medal, National Magazine Awards (re constitution), 1992. **INTERESTS:** gardening; scuba diving; hiking. **COMMENT:** "Maclean's *lets me write about issues ranging from fiscal federalism to national unity—often with a political slant. I love my job.*"

Jardine, Cherelle ■■ ✊ ✪
President, PACIFIC SONGWRITERS' ASSOCIATION, 349 W. Georgia St., P.O. Box 15453, Vancouver, BC V6B 5B2 (604) 872-7664, EMAIL psa@axionet.com. Born Toronto 1961. **EDUC:** Goderich District Collegiate. **EDIT:** Ed., *Hook, Line and Singer*, 1996. **AFFIL:** Pacific Songwriters' Association (Pres.; former Treas.); Salmon City Music Association (Exec. Dir. 1995 to date); Women in Music (Special Events Committee); SOCAN. **INTERESTS:** community service work; music; songwriting; performing. **COMMENT:** *"I am a singer/songwriter with an independent CD released in 1994. Am currently recording a second CD to be released fall/winter 1996. I am working to create a networking system for original artists to further their careers. I have done volunteer work in the music community for three years."*

Jarrett, The Hon. Laureen, B.P.E. 🍁 ⚛
Minister of the Legislative Assembly (Saint John Kings) and Minister of State for Mines and Energy, GOVERNMENT OF NEW BRUNSWICK, Box 6000, Fredericton, NB E3B 5H1 (506) 453-3030, FAX 457-7204. Born N.S. 1938. m. Thomas. 3 ch. Pamela, Nancy, Donald. **EDUC:** N.B. Teachers' Coll.; Univ. of New Brunswick, B.P.E. **CAREER:** teacher, elementary, jr. & sr. high sch., N.B. & Maine; coach, Univ. of New Brunswick. **POLITICAL CAREER:** elected M.L.A. (Kings West), Gov't of N.B., 1987; Bd. of Mgmt Cabinet Committee, 1987 to date; Min. of Income Assistance, 1987-91; re-elected 1991; Min. of Supply & Svcs, 1991-94; Min. of State for Mines & Energy, 1994 to date; re-elected (Saint John Kings), 1995. **AFFIL:** Jeux Canada Games (VP 1985); Saint John Boys & Girls Club (past Bd. of Dir.); Beta Sigma Phi; Salvation Army, Saint John Div. (Hon. Chair, Red. Shield Appeal Campaign).

Jay, Colleen E., B.B.A. $
Marketing Director, Paper Products, PROCTOR & GAMBLE INC., 4711 Yonge St., Box 355, Stn. A, Toronto, ON M5W 1C5. Born Barrie, Ont. 1962. m. Garth. 1 ch. Catherine. **EDUC:** Wilfrid Laurier Univ., B.B.A. 1985. **CAREER:** various positions, incl. Brand Mgr, Crest & Secret (2 yrs.), Mktg Mgr, Oral Care (1 yr.), Mktg Mgr, Detergents/Dishcare (2 yrs.), Mktg Dir., Paper Products, Procter & Gamble Inc., 1985 to date. **AFFIL:** Amadeus Choir of Greater Toronto (Corp. Advisory). **HONS:** Gold Medal, Wilfrid Laurier Univ. **INTERESTS:** running; sailing; travel; tennis. **COMMENT:** *"I graduated from Wilfrid Laurier University in 1985 and joined Procter & Gamble immediately. In the past 11 years, I have worked in every profit centre. I have been married for 11 years and last year we had our first child, Catherine. In our spare time we enjoy travelling, tennis and sailing."*

Jay, Shirley ■ ✊ 🎓
Executive Director, PRINCE EDWARD ISLAND HOME AND SCHOOL FEDERATION, Box 1012, Charlottetown, PE C1A 7M4 (902) 892-0664, FAX 628-1844. Born N.S. m. Allan. 3 ch. Stephanie, Adrian, Gregory. **CAREER:** office admin.; Exec. Dir., P.E.I. Home & Sch. Federation. **AFFIL:** P.E.I. Home & Sch. Federation (Life Mbr.). **INTERESTS:** music; church-related. **MISC:** various projects, incl. AIDS Info. for Parents Program, Smoke-Free Space Program, & Teacher/Staff Appreciation Week;

involved in ministry that helps troubled young adults aged 19-29. **COMMENT:** *"I have made my involvement with Home and School my career; I consider involvement with our children's education to be extremely important. Involvement is local, provincial, and national; have coordinated a variety of projects over the past 15 years."*

Jaye, Elisabeth Anne, B.A. $ ⚛
Vice-President and Director of Special Services, CREATIVE RESEARCH INTERNATIONAL, 4950 Yonge St., Ste. 1002, Toronto, ON M2N 6K1 (416) 250-8500, FAX 250-8515. Born London, UK 1945. m. Ivan Jaye. 2 ch. Paul Daniel, Naomi Ruth. **EDUC:** Univ. of Toronto, B.A. (English) 1995. **CAREER:** Advtg Mgr, Canadian Opera Company, 1969-71; Sales Exec., Xerox Canada, 1980-83; Product Mgr, 1983-84; Retail Sales Mgr, 1984-85; Dir. of Special Svcs, Creative Research International, 1985 to date; VP, 1990 to date. **AFFIL:** Professional Market Research Society (mbr.; Past Pres., Toronto Chapter); Holy Blossom Temple (Bd. 1990-92). **INTERESTS:** cycling; movies; concerts; reading. **MISC:** frequent public speaker. **COMMENT:** *"An active member of the market research community. Frequent public speaker on social trends and related topics."*

Jefferies, Glenna J., B.Sc.Eng.,P.Eng. $
Senior Production Engineer, CRESTAR ENERGY, Box 888, Calgary, AB T2P 4M8 (403) 231-6759, FAX 231-6750, EMAIL glenna@cadvision.com. Born Quebec 1958. m. David Genoud. 2 ch. **EDUC:** Univ. of Alberta, B.Sc.Eng.(Chem. Eng.) 1981. **CAREER:** Reservoir Eng., Dev. Eng., Gulf Canada Resources Ltd., 1981-83; Proj. Planner, Dev. Eng., 1984-86; Econ. Analyst, Corp. Econ., Husky Oil Operations Ltd., 1986-88; Prod. Eng., Conventional Oil & Gas, Crestar Energy, 1988-93; Sr. Production Eng., 1994 to date. **SELECTED PUBLICATIONS:** "How to Attract and Keep Women in the Sciences" (May 1992). **AFFIL:** Alberta Women's Science Network (Chair 1992-95); Association of Professional Engineers, Geologists & Geophysicists of Alberta; Association of Women in Engineering & Science. **INTERESTS:** alpine skiing & racing; hiking; sailing; paddling. **COMMENT:** *"I am enthusiastic about my career and volunteer activities. I believe mentorship and visibility to be very important to promoting career options."*

Jefferies, Marian, R.N. ■ ♡ ✊ ⊕
First Vice-President, Board of Directors and Director, Zone 3, CO-OP ATLANTIC, ATLANTIC PEOPLE'S HOUSING, ALTANTIC CO-OPERATIVE DEVELOPMENT FUND, FUNDY DEVELOPMENT CO-OPERATIVE, ATLANTIC CO-OPERATIVE BUILDING SUPPLIES and other CO-OP ATLANTIC SUBSIDIARIES, R.R. 1, Westfield, NB E0G 3J0 (506) 658-2733, FAX 757-2253, EMAIL marijeff@mi.net. Born Hamilton, Ont. 1951. m. Graham. 2 ch. **EDUC:** McMaster Univ., 1971-72; Saint John Sch. of Nursing, 1983. **CAREER:** Registered Nurse. **DIRECTOR:** Co-op Atlantic. **AFFIL:** N.B. Health Coalition (Chair); Topshee Council for Society Reform, St. Francis Xavier Univ. (1st VP); Community Health Promotion Network Atlantic (Mgmt Committee); Initiatives for Renewal (Past Chair); N.B. Farm Women (Assoc. Mbr.); Conservation Council of N.B.; N.B. Nurses' Union; N.B. Nurses' Association; Canadian Association for Studies in Co-operation. **INTERESTS:** water sports; camping; hiking; cycling; cross-country skiing; skating; reading, esp. science fiction; music. **COMMENT:** *"I believe that the quality of life for people can be improved if they are allowed the opportunity of self determination through control of their economic destiny. This can be accomplished through collective action and the application of co-operative values and principles. I hope that my efforts facilitate that process."*

Jefferson, Anne L., B.Ed.,M.Ed.,Ph.D. ■ 🎓
Professor, Educational Studies, UNIVERSITY OF OTTAWA, Ottawa, ON K1N 6N5 (613) 562-5800, ext. 4107, FAX 562-5146, EMAIL ajeffers@educ-l.edu.uottawa.ca. Born Saskatoon 1953. s. **EDUC:** Univ. of Alberta, B.Ed.(with distinction) 1975, M.Ed. 1979, Ph.D. 1982. **CAREER:** teacher, County of St. Paul No. 19, 1976-78; Fac. Consultant, Fac. of Educ., Dept. of Educ. Admin., Univ. of Alberta, 1978-79; teacher, Alberta Coll., 1979; Research & Admin. Asst., Fin., Statistics & Legislation Branch, Alberta Dept. of Educ., 1979-80; Research Asst., Fac. of Educ., Dept. of Educ. Admin., Univ. of Alberta, 1980-81; writer & researcher, *Canadian School Executive*, 1981-84; Sessional Lecturer, Fac. of Educ., Dept. of Educ. Admin., Univ. of Alberta, 1981-82; Private Consultant, Planning & Research Branch, Alberta Dept. of Educ., 1982; Invited Visiting Prof., Fac. of Educ., Dept. of Comm. & Social Foundations, Univ. of Victoria, 1982; Asst. Prof., Dept. of Educ. Admin. & Foundations, Fac. of Educ., Univ. of Manitoba, 1982-88; Assoc. Prof., Fac. of Educ., Univ. of Windsor, 1988-90; Invited Visiting Prof., Dept. of Educ., Univ. of Newcastle, Newcastle, Australia, 1990; Invited Visiting Prof., Fac. of Educ., Brandon Univ., 1992; Assoc. Prof., Educational Studies, Fac. of Educ., Univ. of Ottawa, 1990-94; Prof., Educational Studies, 1994 to date. **SELECTED PUBLICATIONS:** "Qualitative research: Impli-

cations for educational administration–A conference report" (*The University Council for Educational Administration Review* 22(3) 1981); "The unknown consequence of public support for private schools" (*Canadian Journal of Education* 31(1) 1988); "The impact early retirement plans have on university goals and objectives" (*Educational Considerations* 20(1) 1992); "Canadian universities: Publicly supported but not public institutions" (*Studies in Educational Administration* Summer 1994); "Federal Financing of Canadian Universities" (*University News*, July 1996); various other publications. EDIT: Consultant Ed., *Education and Society*, 1984-91; Consultant Ed. *New Education*, 1984-91; Consultant Ed., *Curriculum and Teaching*, 1984-91; Ed., *Journal of Educational Administration and Foundations*, 1985-91; Ed. Review Bd., *Journal of Educational Public Relations*, 1994 to date; Ed. Advisory Bd., *International Studies in Educational Administration*, 1996 to date. AFFIL: American Education Finance Association; Canadian Society for the Study of Higher Education; National Center for Educ., Statistics Technical Planning Panel, U.S. Dept. of Educ.; Commonwealth Council for Educational Administration; European Association for Institutional Research. HONS: Distinguished Service Award, American Education Finance Association, 1993; Merit Award, Univ. of Windsor, 1989; Phi Delta Kappa Award of Excellence in Research, 1982. INTERESTS: horseback riding & jumping; skiing (Alpine & Nordic); hiking; flying; canoeing; adventurous travel. MISC: listed in *Canadian Who's Who* (1994, 1995, 1996); reviewer for various journals; numerous presentations at nat'l & int'l conferences. COMMENT: *"Over the years I have been a teacher, consultant, researcher, editor, administrator and professor. Each has brought me in contact with diversified individuals from around the world. My love of adventure has taken me to Antarctica, to the plains of Africa, to the South Pacific, Europe, North and Central America, the Caribbean and Mexico."*

Jefferson, Christine, B.A.,M.A. ✆ ○ ⚖
Chair, HEALTH PROFESSIONALS REGULATORY ADVISORY COUNCIL, 2195 Yonge St., 4th Fl., Toronto, ON M4S 2B2 (416) 326-1550, FAX 326-1549. Born Digby, N.S. 1950. d. 1 ch. Jennifer Flora Jefferson. EDUC: Carleton Univ., B.A.(Soc.) 1972; Univ. of Ottawa, M.A.(Criminology-Applied) 1974. CAREER: Nat'l Consultant on Natives & the Criminal Justice System, Fed. Solicitor Gen., 1974-76; consultant, author, lecturer, 1976-77; Exec. Dir., Canadian Association of Elizabeth Fry Societies, 1978-84; Exec. Dir., Opportunity for Advancement,

1984-86; Exec. Dir., Women's Legal Education & Action Fund, 1986-92. VOLUNTEER CAREER: Pres., Carleton Univ. Day Care Association, 1970-71; Pres., Glebe Parents' Day Care Association, 1970-71; Pres. of the Bd., Friendship Concept, 1976; Nat'l Planning Committee, National Associations Active in Criminal Justice, 1978-84; Advisory Committee, Correctional Service of Canada Grant Review Committee, 1979-81; Women for Justice, 1979-84; Canadian Alliance of Prison After-Care Societies, 1979-84; Steering Committee, National Voluntary Organizations, 1981-83; work group chaired by Deputy Min. of Justice preparing a Cabinet document on purposes & principles of the Criminal Code of Canada, 1982; Justice Committee, National Action Committee on the Status of Women, 1982-83; Review Committee, Health & Welfare Sustaining Grants, National Voluntary Social Service Organizations, 1982-84; New Employment for Refugee Women, 1984-85; Women's Interagency Group on Housing, 1986; Network of National Women's Organizations, 1987-92; Coord. Committee, Equality Network, 1988-92; Advisory Committee, Court Challenges Program, 1988-92. SELECTED PUBLICATIONS: *Conquest by Law, Aboriginal Peoples Collection* (Solicitor Gen. of Canada, 1994). COMMENT: *"I have been instrumental in the development of a number of women's organizations in Canada and active in a number of coalitions and networks seeking social change and equality."*

Jeffery, Pamela Postian, H.B.A., M.B.A. ■■ Ⓢ
Principal, BURSTYN JEFFERY INC. (public affairs consulting), 155 University Ave., Ste. 1240, Toronto, ON M5H 3B7 (416) 361-1475, FAX 361-1652. Born London, Ont. 1961. m. William Ross Jeffery. 2 ch. William Stephen Jeffery, Samuel Postian Jeffery. EDUC: Univ. of Western Ontario, H.B.A.(Hons., Bus. Admin.), M.B.A.(Bus.-Gov't Rel'ns) 1988. CAREER: Special Asst. to Ont. Min. of Industry, Trade & Technology, 1985-87; Sr. Consultant, S.A. Murray Consulting Inc., 1988-94; Lecturer, M.B.A. Program, Fac. of Mgmt, Univ. of Toronto, 1993 to date; Principal, Burstyn Jeffery Inc., 1995 to date. AFFIL: The Donwood Institute (V-Chrm; Chrm, Exec. Committee; Bd. mbr. 1993 to date); Friends of Ontario Universities (Steering Committee 1991 to date); Office of the Ontario Liberal Finance Critic (Econ. Policy Advisory Committee 1995 to date); Ontario Women's Directorate (Co-Leader, Women Mentoring Proj. Team); Public Affairs Association of Canada; McGill Club; National Club. HONS: Leadership Award, Canadian

Cancer Society, Toronto, 1991. **INTERESTS:** current affairs; cooking; swimming; yoga; skiing; cycling; cottaging. **COMMENT:** *"My achievements are my mother's legacy. She taught me that family, work and community responsibilities can be balanced; it takes energy, humour and good friends."*

Jennings, Daphne G., B.Ed.,M.P. 🍁

Member of Parliament (Mission-Coquitlam), GOVERNMENT OF CANADA, House of Commons, 640C Centre Block, Ottawa, ON K1A 0A6 (613) 947-4613, FAX 947-4615. Born North Vancouver 1939. m. William Alan Jennings. 4 ch. **EDUC:** Univ. of British Columbia, B.Ed. (Hist./English/Phys. Educ.) 1973. **CAREER:** community worker; businesswoman; teacher, 1962-93; mbr., Sch. Budget Committee; Dept. Head, Inter-Sch. Dept.; Proj. & Prov. Facilitator, Year 2000. **POLITICAL CAREER:** M.P. (Mission-Coquitlam), 1993 to date; Chair, Reform Party Parliamentary Reform Committee, 1993-94; mbr., Gov't Oper. Committee, 1994 to date; Reform Senate Critic, June 1994-95; Reform Literacy Critic, June 1994 to date; mbr., Standing Committee on Transport; mbr., Standing Joint Committee on the Library of Parliament, June 1994-95; Deputy Critic, Hum. Res. (specialty seniors' programs), July 1995 to date; Deputy Critic for Environment, 1996 to date. **AFFIL:** B.C. Teachers' Federation; B.C. Ladies' Tennis League (former Dir.); Reform Party of Canada. **HONS:** Gold Medal in Tennis for Singles 55-59 Years, B.C. Seniors' Summer Games, 1994. **COMMENT:** *"The first year of my first term of office as a Member of Parliament was unusually successful for a member in Opposition. My Private Member's Motion 89 for freer votes was passed in the House, April 28, 1994 and, at present the government is exercising freer votes during Private Members' Business. As the lone M.P. to defend and keep lacrosse as a Canadian national sport, I was proud to defend our natural cultural heritage. And finally, my Grandparents' Rights Bill, C 232, received unanimous consent in the House and passed into Committee on May 4, 1995. I will keep working for the rights of children to have access to their families. Encouraging Canadians to recognize the value of literacy has been a challenge that I will continue to push. Literacy begins at birth and can play a major role in crime prevention. I firmly believe that by working together all Members of Parliament can achieve some goals for Canadians."*

Jennings, Dorothy, B.Sc.,M.B.A., R.P.N. ⊕ $

Manager, Clinical Support Services, BC REHABILITATION SOCIETY, 700 W. 57th Ave., Vancouver, BC V6P 1S1. Born Victoria, B.C. 1947. s. **EDUC:** Nova Scotia Hospital, Dartmouth, Certified Nursing Asst. 1968; Sch. of Psychiatric Nursing, Diploma of Psychiatric Nursing 1971; B.C. Institute of Technology, Health Care Certificate in Admin. 1978; City Univ., Vancouver, M.B.A. 1995. **CAREER:** Staff Nurse, Riverview Hospital, Essondale, 1971-71; Staff Nurse, Valleyview Hospital, Port Coquitlam, 1973-75; Asst. Head Nurse, 1975-77; Head Nurse, 1977-80; Acting Exec. Dir., Registered Psychiatric Nurses' Association of B.C., 1981-82; Exec. Dir., 1982-88; Dir. of Nursing, Continuing Treatment Program, Riverview Hospital, 1988-92; Dir., Educ. Svcs & Organizational Dev., 1992-95; Mgr, Clinical Support Svcs, BC Rehabilitation Society, 1995 to date. **AFFIL:** Registered Psychiatric Nurses' Association of B.C. (Pres.); Nurse Administrators' Association of B.C.; B.C. Gov't Managers' Association (Dir.); Psychiatric/Mental Health Nurses' Interest Group; B.C. Health Educators' Association; Psychiatric Nurses' Association of Canada (Exec. Committee); Nat'l Nursing Competencies Proj. (Psychiatric Nursing Rep., Mgmt Steering Committee). **HONS:** Min. of Health Cup, Excellence in Psychiatric Nursing Svcs, 1994. **COMMENT:** *"A highly energetic individual with a simple philosophy of life–to strive, to seek, to find, but not to yield. Endeavours have been directed toward the pursuit of excellence in the areas of clinical psychiatric service provision, education, psychiatric nursing practice and nursing administration. Achievements have been predicated on a belief that there is no such thing as failure, only varying degrees of success."*

Jensen, Maureen C., B.Sc. $

President, Chief Executive Officer and Director, NOBLE PEAK RESOURCES LTD., 50 Burnhamthorpe Rd. W., Ste. 906, Mississauga, ON L5B 3C2 (905) 897-9406, FAX 897-0669. Born Winnipeg 1956. m. Torben. 2 ch. Erik, Christopher. **EDUC:** Univ. of Toronto, B.Sc. (Geology) 1979. **CAREER:** B.P. Minerals, 1978-80; Terra Mining and Exploration, 1981; Canadian Mine Services, 1981-84; Jensen Mineral Services, 1984-86; Pres., CEO & Dir., Noble Peak Resources Ltd., 1986 to date. **DIRECTOR:** Noble Peak Resources Ltd.; Midasco Gold Corp. **AFFIL:** Prospectors' & Developers' Association of Canada (Dir.); Geological Association of Canada (Fellow); Canadian Institute of Mining, Metallurgy & Petroleum; American Geophysical Union; American Institute of Mining & Exploration.

Jensen, Susan, B.Sc.,Ph.D. ■ ⚛ 🎓

Professor and Chair, Department of Biological

Sciences, UNIVERSITY OF ALBERTA, Biological Sciences Bldg, CW 405, Edmonton, AB T6G 2E9 (403) 492-0672, FAX 492-2216, EMAIL susan.jensen@ualberta.ca. Born Edmonton 1950. m. Chris L. Jensen. **EDUC:** Univ. of Alberta, B.Sc.(Household Econ.) 1970, Ph.D. (Microbiol.) 1975. **CAREER:** Post-doctoral Fellow, Univ. of British Columbia, 1975-76; Research Assoc. & Sessional Lecturer, Univ. of Alberta, 1977-81; Asst. Prof., 1981-84; Assoc. Prof., 1984-90; Prof., 1990 to date; Chair, Dept. of Biological Sci., 1995 to date. **SELECTED PUBLICATIONS:** numerous articles in refereed publications, incl. "Functional analysis of the gene encoding the clavaminate synthase 2 isoenzyme involved in clavulanic acid biosynthesis in *Streptomyces clavuligerus*: gene disruption and transcriptional analysis," with A.S. Paradkar (*Journal of Bacteriology* (177) 1995); "Cloning, sequencing and disruption of a gene from *Streptomyces clavuligerus* involved in clavulanic acid biosynthesis," with A.K. Aidoo, A. Wong, D.C. Alexander & R.A.R. Rittammer (*Gene* (147) 1944). **AFFIL:** Canadian Society for Microbiology; American Society for Microbiology; Society for Industrial Microbiology. **COMMENT:** *"I am a university professor who conducts research on the biological production of antibiotics, with a goal of improving antibiotic production. In May 1995, I became Chair of the Department of Biological Sciences at the University of Alberta."*

Jérôme-Forget, Monique ■■ 🍁 ⊕ $

President, INSTITUTE FOR RESEARCH ON PUBLIC POLICY (think tank), 1470 Peel St., Ste. 200, Montreal, QC H3A 1T1 (514) 985-2461, FAX 985-2559, EMAIL IRPP@odyssee.net. Born Montreal 1940. m. Claude E. Forget. 2 ch. Elise, Nicholas. **EDUC:** Johns Hopkins Univ. & Univ. of London, England, 1961-65 (degree interrupted by birth of 2 children); Univ. de Montréal, Pol. Economy 1966-68; McGill Univ., B.A.(Psych.) 1970, Ph.D.(Psych.) 1976. **CAREER:** Psychologist, Royal Victoria Hospital, McGill Univ., 1975-79; Dir. of Professional Svcs, CLSC Metro (Centre local des services communautaires), 1979-82; Asst. Deputy Min., Policy Planning & Info., Nat'l Health & Welfare Canada, 1982-85; V-Rector, Fin. & Institutional Research, Concordia Univ., 1985-86; Chrm & CEO, CSST (Commission de la santé et de la sécurité du travail - Workers' Compensation Bd.), 1986-90; Pres., Institute for Research on Public Policy, 1991 to date. **SELECTED PUBLICATIONS:** *Health Care Reform Through Internal Markets: Experience and Proposals* (1995); "Les marchés internes dans le contexte canadien" (*Choices*, Vol. 1, No. 3, 1995). **DIRECTOR:** Canada Life Assurance Company; Premier Choix (Astral); Société d'investissement jeunesse. **MEMBER, QUEBEC ADVISORY BOARD:** SHL Systemhouse. **AFFIL:** McGill Institute for the Study of Canada (Bd. mbr.); National Statistics Council, Statistics Canada (Bd. mbr.); Queen's Univ., Institute of Intergovernmental Relations (Advisory Council); Social Sciences & Humanities Research Council of Canada (Bd. mbr.). **HONS:** Apex Public Service Citation, 1996.

Jerrard, Raye, S.R.N. ♡ ⊕

President, CANADIAN CYSTIC FIBROSIS FOUNDATION, 2221 Yonge St., Ste. 601, Toronto, ON M4S 2B4 (416) 485-9149 or 1-800-378-CCFF, FAX 485-0960. Born UK 1931. m. Roy. 2 ch. **EDUC:** Women's Royal Naval Svc. State Registered Nurse 1951. **CAREER:** Women's Royal Naval Svc. 1949-52; Bus. Mgr, Eaton's, Calgary Eaton Centre, 1989-95. **VOLUNTEER CAREER:** Pres., Calgary Chapter, Canadian Cystic Fibrosis Foundation, 1983-86; Reg'l Dir., 1986-89; Directors' Rep., Exec. Committee, 1989-91; Chair, Chapter Dev. Task Force, 1991-93; VP, Fundraising, & Dir.-at-Large, 1991-94; Pres., 1994 to date. **HONS:** Canada 125 Medal. **INTERESTS:** travel; volunteer work; gardening; knitting; reading. **COMMENT:** *"I have been involved with the Canadian Cystic Fibrosis Foundation since the day my granddaughter was diagnosed in 1980. I have found it to be a fulfilling, rewarding experience, with opportunities to meet other members of the cystic fibrosis communities worldwide."*

Jewett, Anne, B.B.A.,C.A. $

Tax Partner, DELOITTE & TOUCHE, 77 Westmorland St., Ste. 630, Fredericton, NB E3B 6Z3 (506) 458-8105, FAX 450-8126. Born Montreal 1954. m. Andrew Cook. 2 ch. Nicholas, Michael. **EDUC:** Univ. of New Brunswick, B.B.A. 1976; C.A. 1981. **CAREER:** Mgmt Training Program, The Toronto-Dominion Bank, 1977-78; Clarkson Gordon, Vancouver & Toronto, 1979-84; Deloitte & Touche, 1984 to date; Tax Ptnr, 1991 to date. **SELECTED PUBLICATIONS:** articles relating to tax aspects of marital settlement for Continuing Legal Education Association, NB Law Society. **AFFIL:** NB Institute of Chartered Accountants; Canadian Tax Foundation; Junior Achievement of Fredericton (Pres. 1995-96; Bd.). **INTERESTS:** skiing; golf; running. **MISC:** frequent speaker, CBC radio & TV re fed. & prov. budgets.

Jin Suen-Carter, Susan, B.A. $

Vice-President, Public and Corporate Affairs, NATIONAL TRUST COMPANY, One Financial

Place, 1 Adelaide St. E., Toronto, ON M5C 2W8 (416) 361-4486, FAX 361-4037. Born Sault Ste. Marie, Ont. m. Robin Charles Carter. 2 ch. EDUC: York Univ., B.A.(Theatre) 1981; Humber Coll., Certificate (Fundraising Mgmt) in progress. CAREER: freelance theatre designer, prod. & mgr, 1980 to date; Gen. Mgr, O'Neill's Dinner Theatre, 1981-82; Arts Administrator, Skylight Theatre Inc., 1982-84; Sr. Media Rel'ns Officer, Dept. of Comm., External Rel'ns, York Univ., 1985-88; Mgr, Special Events, American Express Canada Inc., 1988; Mgr, Public Affairs & Comm., 1989-91; Dir. of Public Affairs & Comm., American Express Canada Inc., American Express Bank of Canada, 1991-94; VP, Public & Corp. Affairs, National Trust Company, 1994 to date. AFFIL: Media Culture (Dir.); Canasian Artist Group (Patron); *Scrabble with the Stars* (Advisory Bd. Mbr.); Ontario Heart and Stroke (Chair, Comm., Aish Ha Torah Shares Tribute 1996). HONS: Theatre Proj. Award, Ont. Arts Council, 1984; Metropolitan Toronto Cultural Affairs Award, 1984, 1985; Toronto Arts Council Award, City of Toronto, 1986; Explorations Program Award, Canada Council, 1986; Wintario Proj. Award, Ont. Ministry of Citizenship & Culture, 1986; Mktg, Comm. & Outreach Awards, Multicultural Theatre Award & James Buller Award, Council for the Advancement of Education, 1984, 1987, 1988. INTERESTS: performing arts; good literature; tennis; biking; family-oriented outings. MISC: Judge, The Kids NETWORD, The Prism Awards. COMMENT: *"Ms. Carter's career ranges from numerous arts-related positions, academe, travel and card services to retail and restaurant, as well as the financial services sector."*

Jodoin, Shelley, B.A.,LL.B. ✦ ⚔

Labour Communications Specialist, WORKERS' COMPENSATION BOARD OF ALBERTA, Box 2415, Edmonton, AB T5J 2S5 (403) 498-4902, FAX 422-0972. m. Darrell Gilmar. 1 ch. EDUC: Univ. of Alberta, B.A. 1980, LL.B. 1983. BAR: Alta., 1984. CAREER: family law proj. worker, Student Legal Svcs, Fac. of Law, Univ. of Alberta, 1982; Assoc. Lawyer, Student-at-Law, Roderick W. Koski, Barrister & Solicitor, 1983-84; Mortgage Officer, Northwestern Funding II Corporation, 1985; research, Constituency Asst., Office of the New Democratic Official Opposition, Legislative Assembly, Edmonton, 1986-87; Assoc. Lawyer, Parker & Associates, Barristers & Solicitors, 1987-88; Legislative Officer, Casework & Outreach, Constituency Asst., Researcher, Office of the New Democratic Official Opposition, Legislative Assembly, 1988-93; contract researcher &

writer, Edmonton Social Planning Council & Premier's Council on the Status of Persons with Disabilities, 1994; Labour Comm. Specialist, Workers' Compensation Bd. of Alberta, 1995 to date. AFFIL: Law Society of Alberta; Sexual Assault Centre of Edmonton (Chair, Bd. of Dir.). HONS: Concordia Coll. Div. Social Sciences Academic Award, 1979; Prov. of Alberta Scholarships, 1977-80; Edmonton Public Sch. Bd. Honours Award, 1977. COMMENT: *"In my work and volunteer experience I have a strong commitment to matters of social justice."*

Joe, Rita 📖 🐿

Writer. 138 Shore Rd., Eskasoni C.B., NS B0A 1J0 (902) 379-2263. Born Whycocomagh 1932. 8 ch. EDUC: Indian Residential Sch.; Eskasoni Educ. Program, Grade XII, Bus. Ed. 2 yrs. CAREER: has been writing about the Native culture for 27 yrs. SELECTED PUBLICATIONS: *Poems of Rita Joe* (1979); *Song of Eskasoni* (1989); *LNU and Indians We're Called* (1992); *Kelusultiek* (1994); *Song of Rita Joe* (1997). HONS: Order of Canada, 1990; Privy Council, 1992; LL.D.(Hon.), Dalhousie Univ., 1993. INTERESTS: arts & crafts; writing, writing, writing. MISC: working on songs about culture. COMMENT: *"I am a widow and work on crafts and writing. I travel to schools, universities and gatherings when called upon–hopefully to enlighten others to Native culture."*

Johanson, Sue, R.N. ⊕ 🐿 ✂

Sex Educator, Counsellor, Radio Host, Author, Guest Speaker. Born Toronto. m. E.K. 3 ch. EDUC: St. Boniface Hospital, R.N. 1954; Toronto Institute of Human Relations 1984. CAREER: Dept. of Public Health, North York, 1970-86; est. Don Mills Birth Control Clinic, 1970; Clinic Coord., 1970-86; Counsellor, Planned Parenthood Toronto, 1971-75; started teaching "Sex & Sexuality" in schools; Instructor, Sexuality course, Humber Coll., 1982-87; Columnist, *Chatelaine* Magazine, 1985-87; Columnist, "Talking Sex," *Edmonton Sun,* 1985 to date; Columnist, "Health Line," *The Toronto Star,* 1996 to date. SELECTED CREDITS: *Pilot 1,* CBC TV, 1988-89; *Infotape,* CBC, 1988-89; *Sex, Drugs & Rock & Roll,* CHCH TV, 1989-91; *Talking Sex,* weekly, Rogers Cable TV, 1985 to date; *Sunday Night Sex Show,* Radio Q107, 1984 to date; *STDs,* video with Kim Martyn, Ontario Science Centre; Host, *The Sunday Night Sex Show,* WTN, 1995 to date. SELECTED PUBLICATIONS: *Talk Sex* (Penguin Books, 1988); *Sex is Perfectly Natural, But Not Naturally Perfect* (Penguin Publishers, 1991); *Sex, Sex, and More Sex*

(Penguin Books, 1995). **AFFIL:** Planned Parenthood (Bd. of Dir.); S.I.E.C.A.N.S. (Bd. of Dir.). **HONS:** Excellence in Educ. Award, OISE, 1990; Speaker of the Year, COCA, 1994, 1995, 1996. **MISC:** radio show syndicated across Canada; Guelph Conference, "Human Sexuality," 1979 to date. **COMMENT:** *"Canada's Answer to Dr.Ruth."*

Johns, Diane, B.Math.,F.L.M.I. ⚛ $
Director, Information Systems, THE CANADA LIFE ASSURANCE COMPANY, 330 University Ave., Toronto, ON M5T 1R8 (416) 597-1440, ext. 5510, FAX 597-0053. Born Toronto 1950. m. William Johns. 2 ch. Alison, Steven. **EDUC:** Univ. of Waterloo, B.Math. 1972. **CAREER:** Application/System Programmer, Canada Life, 1972-82; Mgr, Info. Systems, 1982-91; Asst. Dir., Info. Systems, 1987-91; Dir., Info. Systems, 1991 to date. **AFFIL:** Life Office Management Association (Fellow in Insur.; Cdn Systems Dev. Committee 1993; Exec., Cdn Systems Dev. Committee 1994-96). **COMMENT:** *"My career has been spent at Canada Life in computer systems, initially as an applications programmer, then as a systems programmer; office automation projects led to a management role."*

Johnson, Brooke 🎞 📺 🎭
Actor, Writer, Visual Artist. c/o Lorraine Wells & Company Talent Management Inc., 10 St. Mary St., Ste. 320, Toronto, ON M4V 1P9 (416) 413-1676, FAX 413-1680. Born Toronto 1962. cl. David Fox. **EDUC:** Sarah Lawrence Coll., N.Y.C., Humanities 1981-82; National Theatre Sch. of Canada, Grad. 1987. **SELECTED CREDITS:** Marie, *The Time and Place*, Theatre Smith-Golmour, 1995; Annie Sullivan, *The Miracle Worker*, dir. Martha Henry, Grand Theatre, London, Ont., 1994; Jhana, *Toronto, Mississippi*, Tarragon Theatre (original prod.), 1987 & Theatre Calgary, 1989; *The Sweet Hereafter* (feature), dir. Atom Egoyan; Marlene Moore, *Dangerous Offender* (telefilm), dir. Holly Dale, CBC, 1996; Loretta Bines, *For Those Who Hunt The Wounded Down* (telefilm), dir. Norma Bailey, 1996; Angie, *Conspiracy of Silence* (miniseries), CBC, 1992. **SELECTED PUBLICATIONS:** *Uh poo fem bon furtz*, writer & illustrator, children's book (1994). **AFFIL:** Canadian Actors' Equity Association; ACTRA; Academy of Canadian Cinema & Television; Theatre Smith-Gilmour (Bd. of Dir.). **HONS:** Best Performance in a Supporting Role (*Conspiracy of Silence*), Gemini Awards, 1993; nominated, Best Performance in a Leading Role (*Toronto, Mississippi*), Dora Mavor Moore Award, 1987 & *The Time and Place*, 1995. **INTERESTS:** constructive sculpture; the North; baseball; golf; canoeing. **MISC:** daughter of Mary (Johnston) & Bradley Johnson (C.S.L.A.,R.C.A.).

Johnson, Dorothy Charlotte (née Dodds) ✊ ♡
President, FEDERATED WOMEN'S INSTITUTES OF CANADA. Born Cochrane, Ont. m. Raymond Johnson. 5 ch. Peter Ross, Bryan Douglas (dec.); Annetta Martha, Ralph Edward, Kevin Charles. **EDUC:** Cochrane High Sch., Grade 13 1944; Northern Coll., Library Technician (incomplete) 1974. **CAREER:** taught sch. on letter of permit, 1944-47; substitute teacher for several yrs.; asst. sch. librarian, 12 yrs.; clerk & bookkeeper for family bus., Cochrane Sports & Marine Supply Ltd. **AFFIL:** Federated Women's Institutes of Ontario (Pres. 1983-86); Federated Women's Institutes of Canada (Pres.); Order of Eastern Star (Past Matron; Past District Deputy Grand Matron); Northern Ontario Ladies' Curling Association (Exec. Mbr. 1986-87); United Church of Canada (Commissioner, 33rd Gen. Council); Cochrane Recreation Committee (Chair, one term); Cochrane, Iroquois Falls, Black River, Matheson County Sch. Bd. (3rd term). **HONS:** Community Volunteer Award, Cochrane; Bicentennial Award, Ont. **INTERESTS:** curling; cross-country skiing; cycling; reading; sewing; church choir. **MISC:** led 4-H for over 30 yrs. in local rural community; helped draft constitutions for local church; undertook major revision of constitution & by-laws for Federated Women's Institutes of Ontario; former Treas., James Bay Tourist Association & Cochrane Figure Skating Club; Level One Curling Coach; served as a fully funded participant to the NGO Forum at the 4th U.N. World Conference for Women in Beijing, China. **COMMENT:** *"I have always worked with people and enjoyed it. My husband and I raised four sons and one daughter (one son dec. 1995). All have been successful. Two sons are in business for themselves, my daughter teaches and one son is a recreational therapist. Service to others is important to me and I hope for my family."*

Johnson, Elizabeth A., B.A.,LL.B. ⚖
Partner, LUCAS BOWKER & WHITE, Barristers & Solicitors, 1201 Esso Tower, Scotia Place, 10060 Jasper Ave., Edmonton, AB T5J 4E5 (403) 426-5330, FAX 428-1066, EMAIL lucas@supernet.ab.ca. Born Montreal 1951. **EDUC:** Univ. of Alberta, B.A.(English Lit.) 1973, M.A.(1st yr.) 1974, LL.B. 1979. **BAR:** Alta., 1980. **CAREER:** Ptnr, Lucas Bowker & White, 1985 to date; insolvency & foreclosures, admin. law, constitutional litigation, public inquiry litigation, & gen. appellate & cnsl

work. AFFIL: Law Society of Alberta; Canadian Bar Association; Edmonton Bar Association; Arbitration & Mediation Society; Canadian Bar Association (Alta. Branch) (Cdn Rights Subsection; Admin. Law Subsection; Environmental Law Subsection; Treas., Alternate Dispute Resolution Section 1993); Edmonton Food Bank (Bd. of Dir.; Chair 1993-94; Bus. Committee 1989-93); various community & charity fund-raising activities. MISC: participant in seminars on environmental liability & topics of interest to leaders.

Johnson, Hermine ■ ○ ✣

c/o Metro Toronto Housing, Toronto, ON. Volunteer. Born Westmoreland, Jamaica 1946. m. Baldwin (Barry). 3 ch. EDUC: Humber Coll., Commercial Stenographer Certificate; Pitmans Coll., London, UK, Acctg Certificate; York Univ.; Burnhamthorpe Collegiate, SSGD to Cdn Standard; Humber Coll., Registered Real Estate Certificate. CAREER: various clerical positions incl. Acctg/Statistical Clerk, Sec., Stenographer, Payroll/Acctg Clerk, Payroll/Benefits Coord.; Real Estate Sales Person. VOLUNTEER CAREER: Volunteer Probation Officer, Ministry of Correctional Svcs, 1982-85; Treas., Jamaican Canadian Association, 1982-85; Mbr., Miss Black Ontario Pageant Bd., 1985; Pres., Sickle Cell Association of Ontario, 1988-95; Treas., West Indian Volunteer Youth Program, 1989-92; Mbr., Supervisory Committee, C.C.A. Credit Union, 1990-94; Treas., Women for Peace Canada, 1991-93. AFFIL: Toronto Real Estate Bd.; Elmbank Community Centre (Advisory Bd.). HONS: Three Year Service Award, Ministry of Correctional Svcs; 10 Years Voluntary Service Pin, Prov. of Ont.; Service Awards, Elmbank Community Centre; Award, Humber Coll., 1969. INTERESTS: volunteering; people; reading; sewing; family & friends. COMMENT: *"Sympathetic, dedicated, compassionate and determined. Mother, wife and grandmother, likes doing things for others—I like to think that I'm well blessed with a lovely family, including parents and umpteen brothers and sisters, and feel that I should share my good fortune with others who are not so fortunate."*

Johnson, Hon. Beth, B.A. ✣ ⬗ ♙

Mayor, CORPORATION OF DELTA, 4500 Clarence Cres., Delta, BC V4K 3E2 (604) 946-3210, FAX 946-6055. Born Los Angeles 1957. m. Gary. 2 ch. EDUC: Scripps Coll., B.A. 1971; Univ. of British Columbia, Teaching Certificate 1974. CAREER: teacher, Richmond, B.C., 14 yrs.; Councillor, City of Delta, 7 yrs.; elected Mayor of Delta, 1990; re-elected, 1993; Chair, Delta Police Bd.; Chair, Sewerage, Drainage &

Air Committee, Greater Vancouver Regional District (G.V.R.D.); Mbr. Bd. of Dir.; Dir., Strategic Planning Committee; Dir., Intergov't & Comm. Committee. DIRECTOR: B.C. Transit (Chair, Strategic Planning & Client Svcs Committee). AFFIL: Federation of Canadian Municipalities (Dir.; various standing committees & task forces, incl. Policies & Resolutions, & Mun. Aboriginal Rel'ns; Chair, Standing Committee on Environmental Issues; Chair, FCM Tech. Committee on Electromagnetic Fields); Ladner Business Association; Tsawwassen Business Association; Delta Chamber of Commerce; Scott Road Business Association; Delta Youth Committee (Hon. Chair); Kennedy House Seniors' Recreation Centre (Council liaison). MISC: 1st woman elected Mayor of Delta.

Johnson, Margaret W., B.A.,M.A., B.Ed. ■ ✣

National Readiness Campaign, THE LIBERAL PARTY OF ALBERTA/NORTHWEST TERRITORIES. Born Sudbury, Ont. 1939. s. EDUC: Sir George Williams Univ., B.A.(Soc.) 1963; Univ. of Alberta, B.Ed. 1969, Grad. Diploma (Educ. Psych.) 1972, M.A.(Community Dev.) 1979. CAREER: Y.M.C.A. community worker, Montreal, 1961-67; teacher, Edmonton public schools, 1969-71; Sch. Counsellor, Edmonton public schools, 1974 to date. SELECTED PUBLICATIONS: *Election Readiness Manual-Walk, Knock and Talk* ed. (National Women's Liberal Commission, 1993). AFFIL: TERRA, The Association for Assistance to Unwed Mothers (Chair 1991-93); Break the Cycle Sexual Abuse Awareness Campaign (Co-Chair, Edmonton 1992); National Women's Liberal Commission (Reg'l Rep. Alta./N.W.T.; Election Readiness Chair 1993; Policy Co-Chair 1992-94; Liberal Policy Association Policy Committee); Edmonton Women's Liberal Policy Association (Chair, Women's Day Brunch Fundraiser 1991-93; Pres.); Alberta Teachers' Association (Pol. Action Committee 1994; Task Force, Public Educ. Works Campaign 1994). INTERESTS: camping; family cottage in N.Ont.; cross-country skiing; reading; political & women's issues discussions with friends. COMMENT: *"I am an educator and long-time community activist who finds the process of energizing others and facilitating change rewarding. I am committed to liberalism, working initially with community organizations and, more recently, empowering women to be full partners in the political decision-making process."*

Johnson, Nancy ♥ ⬥ ⊗ ♙

President, LOCKWOOD FILMS (LONDON) INC., 365 Ontario St., London, ON N5W 3W6 (519)

434-6006, FAX 645-0507. 3 ch. Christina Lorraine, Eileen Aldis, Matthew Magnus. **CAREER:** Promo. Dept., CFPL-TV, 1969-76; Founding Mbr., Women's Advertising & Sales Club, 1970-71; Ptnr, Creative Services, 1974; Principal, Pres., Prod., Writer, Dir., Lockwood Films, 1974 to date; Prod. of Record, General Motors Diesel Div., 1984 to date. **SELECTED CREDITS:** Prod., *Doctor Woman: The Life and Times of Elizabeth Bagshaw*, documentary, National Film Board, 1978; Prod./Writer, *Greg Curnoe*, documentary, CBC, 1980; Prod./Dir., *With Grace and Grit: A Conversation About Women and Cancer*; Prod., *Biomedical Research: Is It Really Necessary?*; Prod., *James Reaney: Listening to the Wind*, documentary, Vision TV; *The Home Office & Small Business Program* (8-week series), TVO; *The Business Plan* (13-week series), TVO. **AFFIL:** London Film Commission; Meals on Wheels; St. Andrew's United Church. **HONS:** company has won more than 40 awards at int'l, nat'l & reg'l competitions; Canadian Film & Television Award for Best Documentary, *Doctor Woman*, 1978; Woman of Distinction, London 1995; Hygeia Award for production excellence in program dealing with a medical subject, *With Grace and Grit*, 1994; Columbus Int'l Film & Video Award, *1993 (Biomedical Research)*, 1996 *(Cover Up)*. **INTERESTS:** theatre; history. **MISC:** one of the first woman to attend a meeting of the "men only" Ad & Sales Club of London. **COMMENT:** *"Nancy Johnson and partner Mark McCrudy have managed Lockwood from a two-person operation in 1974 into a business that has won over 40 international, national and regional awards. They have shot on-location in the UK, Peru, Bolivia, Puerto Rico, across Canada and the US, Broadcast on CBC, BBC, PBS, TVO, Vision and YTV."*

Johnson, Peggy, R.N.,B.V.E.,M.Sc.A. ○ ♦
Executive Director, NEWFOUNDLAND AND LABRADOR LUNG ASSOCIATION, 1 Campbell Ave., Box 5250, St. John's, NF A1C 5W1 (709) 726-4664, FAX 726-2550. Born Little Catalina, Nfld. 1940. m. John O'Brian. 2 ch. Valerie, Peter. **EDUC:** Sir Sandford Fleming Coll., R.N.D. 1977; Memorial Univ. of Newfoundland, B.V.E. 1984; Univ. of Notre Dame, M.Sc.A. 1989. **CAREER:** Principal, Red Bay, Labrador, 1957-58; teacher, LaScie, Nfld., 1958-60; mother, homemaker, wife, 1961-68; kindergarten teacher, Elmsdale, N.S., 1966-68; substitute teacher, City of Westmount, Que., 1970-71; Dir., Day Care Centre for Immigrant Children, Outremont, Que., 1970-71; sales clerk, Uptown Silk Shop, Peterborough, Ont., 1972-73; Psychiatric Nurse, General Hospital & Waterford Hospital, St. John's, 1977-80;

Educ. & Nursing Consultant, 1980-83; Coord., Program for Schools, St. John Ambulance, Nfld. Council, 1980-83, Coord., Healthy Aging Proj., 1980-83, Dir. of Programs & Mktg, 1986-94; Lecturer, part-time, Adult Educ. Dept., Memorial Univ. of Newfoundland, 1989 to date; Exec. Dir., Newfoundland & Labrador Lung Association, 1994 to date. **AFFIL:** Canadian Society of Safety Engineers (Nat'l Pres.); Canadian Federation of University Women; Newfoundland Liberal Party (Comm. Committee); St. John's Airport Regional Planning Group; School Health Agencies; Frecker Gerontological Association; Canadian Homemakers' Association; Gower Street United Church (Bd. of Dir.); Canadian Society of Fund Raising (Exec.). **HONS:** St. Joseph's Award for Most Compassion;Commander, Holy Order of St. John of Jerusalem. **INTERESTS:** reading; music appreciation; choir work & concerts; entertaining; time with family; travel. **MISC:** various scholarships. **COMMENT:** *"As a teacher, nurse, family councillor, adult educator, community organizer and nonprofit administrator, I have found tremendous meaning through my commitment to encouraging self-fulfilment, improving interpersonal relationships and enhancing quality of life."*

Johnson, Susan M., B.A.,Dip.Ed., M.A.,E.D. ❀ ⊕
Associate Professor of Psychology and Psychiatry, Department of Psychology, OTTAWA UNIVERSITY, Vanier Building, 11 Marie Curie, Ottawa, ON K1N 6N5. Director, Marital and Family Therapy Clinic, Department of Psychiatry, CIVIC HOSPITAL, Ottawa, ON. m. John Douglas. 2 ch. Timothy Douglas, Emma Douglas. **EDUC:** Hull-Yorkshire, UK, B.A.(English Lit.) 1968; London, UK, Dip.Ed.(Educ.) 1969; Univ. of British Columbia, M.A.(Educ.) 1980, Ed.D.(Counselling Psych.) 1984. **CAREER:** Counsellor & Ed. Dir., Maples Residential Treatment Centre, Vancouver; Asst. Prof., Psych., Univ. of Ottawa, 1984-88; Assoc. Prof., Univ. of Ottawa, 1988-91; Dir., Marital & Family Therapy, Civic Hospital, 1988-94; cross-appointee, Psychiatry, Univ. of Ottawa, 1990 to date. **SELECTED PUBLICATIONS:** *Creating Connection: The Practice of Emotionally Focused Couples Therapy* (N.Y.: Brunner Mazel, 1996); *Emotionally Focused Couples Therapy*, with L.S. Greenberg (New York: Guilford Press, 1988); *The Heart of the Matter: Emotion in marital therapy*, co-ed. with L.S. Greenberg (New York: Brunner/Mazel, 1994); "Emotionally focused couples therapy: Restructuring attachment," with L.S. Greenberg, *First sessions in effective psychotherapy: A casebook*, ed. S. Budman, M. Hoyt & S. Friedman (New

York: Guilford Press, 1992); "Facilitating intimacy: Interventions and effects," with M. Dandenau (*Journal of Marital and Family Therapy*, 20, 1994); various books, book chapters & numerous papers in refereed journals. **EDIT:** Ed. Review Bd., *Journal of Marital & Family Therapy*. **INTERESTS:** marital therapy–process & outcome; close relationships; emotion in therapy. **MISC:** recipient, various grants; Grant Application Evaluation, SSHRC, & Min. of Health, 1988 to date; reviewer, *Canadian Journal of Counselling*, 1988 to date; various lectures & workshops incl. lectures "Eating Disorder: A Family Affair" & "Infertility: A Couples Issue," & workshop "Emotionally Focused Couples Therapy." **COMMENT:** *"Innovative clinician, theoretician and researcher in marital therapy. Formulated emotionally focused therapy for couples, the second most empirically validated extant marital therapy."*

Johnson, The Hon. Janis Gudrun, B.A. 🍁 👆

Senator, THE SENATE OF CANADA, Rm. 356-E, Centre Block, Ottawa, ON K1A 0A4 (613) 943-1430, FAX (613) 992-5029. Born Winnipeg 1946. d. 1 ch. Stefan. **EDUC:** Univ. of Manitoba, B.A.(Pol. Sci.) 1968. **CAREER:** researcher, Office of Robert Stanfield, 1968; Policy Consultant & organizer to P.C. Party of Nfld. & Lab., 1970s; Founding Pres., P.C. Women's Caucus of Winnipeg, 1980-83; Consultant & Lecturer on Women's Programs, Fac. of Continuing Educ., Univ. of Manitoba, 1981-83; Dir., P.C. Party of Canada, 1983-84; Dir., Mulroney Leadership Campaign for Man., 1983; Dir., CN Railway, 1985-90; Senator, 1985 to date; Pres., Janis Johnson & Associates, 1985 to date; Sr. Consultant, Public Affairs Group, Peat Marwick, 1988-89; Sr. Strategist, P.C. Campaign, 1988. **AFFIL:** American Association of Political Consultants; Royal Winnipeg Ballet; Primus Theatre Group; Friends of Public Broadcasting; National Screen Institute; Albany Club; Icelandic Canadian Club; First Lutheran Church; Gimli Summer Club; fundraising work for: Brandon Univ., Univ. of Winnipeg, YM/YWCA; Manitoba Cancer Research Foundation. **HONS:** Velia Stern Award, outstanding contribution to student affairs, Univ. of Manitoba, 1968; Queen's Silver Jubilee Medal, 1977; Business & Professional Women's Award, 1985. **MISC:** 1st woman dir. of the P.C. Party of Canada.

Johnston, Carol Jean, R.N.,C.P.H.N., C.M. ■■ ♡ $ ✇

Volunteer. m. C.B. Johnston (Prof. & former Dean, Sch. of Bus. Admin., Univ. of Western Ontario). 5 ch. David, Jeffrey, Craig, Laura, Nancy. 12 grch. **EDUC:** Victoria Hospital Sch. of Nursing, R.N. 1953; Univ. of Western Ontario, Certificate of Public Health Nursing 1954, Teachers' Coll. 1972, Museology (audit course) 1976. **CAREER:** Public Health Nurse, City of Toronto, 1954-55; Supply Teacher, London Bd. of Educ., 1973-75; Exec. Dir. (founder), London Regional Children's Museum, 1975-90. **VOLUNTEER CAREER:** researcher with autistic children, Children's Psychiatric Research Institute, 1961-66; counselling single-parent women, Children's Aid Society, 1963-70; Classroom Asst., Madame Vanier Children's Services, 1968-70; Sec., Educ. Committee, Oak Park Home & Sch. Association, 1968-70; Auxiliary Chair, London French Sch., 1968-71; Program Committee, Sunday Sch. Teacher, First St. Andrew's United Church, 1965 & 1973-75; Founding Dir., London Regional Children's Museum, 1975-90; Bd. mbr., 1990 to date; Chrm of the Bd. (& Life Mbr.), Women's Christian Association, 1984-86; Bd. of Dir., London Int'l Children's Festival, 1989-94; developed Inuit Discovery Museum Kit, National Museum of Science, Tokyo, Japan, 1991; taught English as a 2nd language, UN Refugee Camp, Singapore, 1991; Consultant on dev. of children's museum, National Museum Singapore, 1991; mbr., Bd. of Dir., & Chair, Community Rel'ns Committee & Capital Campaign, Childreach, 1992 to date; mbr., Bd. of Dir. & Chair, Communications Committee, London Community Foundation, 1992-95; mbr., Bd. of Dir. & Sec. to the Bd., Madame Vanier Children's Services, 1994. **HONS:** Member of the Order of Canada, 1985; Mayor's New Year's Arts Award for outstanding contribution to the arts in London, 1983; Citizen of the Year, 1983. **MISC:** Guest Lecturer, Mgmt in the Arts Program, Banff Centre, 1982-83; Guest Lecturer, Museology Program, Univ. of Toronto, 1982-85; London Regional Children's Museum was used as a case study for Sch. of Bus. Admin., Univ. of Western Ontario, 1984.

Johnston, Elizabeth, B.Sc.,M.S.,Ph.D., P.Dt.,FCDA 🎓 ⚛ ⊕

Director, School of Nutrition and Food Science, ACADIA UNIVERSITY, Wolfville, NS B0P 1X0 (902) 542-2201, FAX 542-1454, EMAIL elizabeth.johnston@acadiau.ca. Born North Sydney, N.S. m. David S. 2 ch. J. Mark, Jennifer P. **EDUC:** Acadia Univ., B.Sc.(Home Econ.) 1968; Cornell Univ., M.S.(Nutrition & Food Sci.) 1970; Univ. of British Columbia, Ph.D.(Nutrition) 1975. **CAREER:** Fac., Acadia Univ., 1970-73; Fac., Univ. of British Columbia, 1973-75; Fac., Acadia Univ., 1975-85; Dir., 1984-87, 1993 to date. **SELECTED PUBLICATIONS:**

"Weight changes during pregnancy and the postpartum periods" (*Progress in Food & Nutrition Science*, 15, 1991). AFFIL: Canadian Dietetic Association; N.S. Dietetic Association; Canadian Institute of Food Science & Technology; Canadian Society for Nutritional Sciences; N.S. Nutrition Council. HONS: FCDA–Charter Fellow, Canadian Dietetic Association, 1989; Merit Award in recognition of outstanding achievement to the dietetic profession, N.S. Dietetic Association, 1991. INTERESTS: gardening; music; travelling. MISC: mbr., Council to the Congress, 16th Int'l Union of Nutritional Sciences; mbr., Advisory Committee on Nutrition for the Atlantic Committee on Food.

Johnston, Heather Erika, D.D. ☼ ◐ ♠
Ecumenist. 183 Chedoke Ave., Hamilton, ON L8P 4P2. Born Cölbe, Germany 1930. m. John Alexander. 3 ch. Andrew, Ian, Mary. EDUC: Early Childhood Educ., Frobel, 1946-48; English Institute, Heidelberg, Oxford, Interpreter 1953-55; Knox Coll., Toronto, D.D. 1984. CAREER: advisor to women's groups, Lagos, Nigeria, 1964-66; mbr., Family Life Committee, Presbyterian Church in Canada, 1967-74; Co-Founder & mbr., Multicultural Society of Hamilton, Ont., 1972-80; Ecumenical Rel'ns Committee, Presbyterian Church in Canada, 1973-91 (Chair 1976-84); mbr., Central Committee, World Council of Churches, Geneva, 1975-83; Pres., Canadian Council of Churches, 1979-82; Dir., Ecumenical Dev. Cooperative Society, Holland, 1984-90. AFFIL: Canadian Support Foundation of EDCS (Founder & Chair); Canadian Christian-Jewish Consultation (Chair 1986-92); Canadian Christian Festival IV, 1992-94 (Co-Chair). HONS: Woman of the Year Award, Hamilton, 1995; Order of Ontario, 1995. INTERESTS: family; friends; reading. MISC: nat'l & int'l guest speaker; mbr., int'l team to observe elections, Guyana, 1981; invited by China Christian Council, Shanghai, as Leader, Canadian Church Leaders, 1981. COMMENT: *"Dr. Heather Johnston's career has uniquely served the citizens of Canada in a myriad of ways. Trained as a teacher and interpreter, she served the World Council of Churches during the 1956 Hungarian uprising, arranging for the settlement of refugees in Canada and other nations. As the first lay president of the Canadian Council of Churches, she sought to widen the ecumenical base of Christendom in Canada. As president of the official Christian-Jewish Dialogue of Canada, she sought to widen the religious cooperative spectrum. She was the first woman to chair the Ecumenical Relations Committee of the Presbyterian Church in Canada and the first woman from Canada to serve on the Central Committee of the World Council of Churches."*

Johnston, Lynn, Ph.D.,LL.D. ⊛ ✒
Cartoonist and Creator, "For Better or Worse." c/o Universal Press Syndicate, 4900 Main St. E., Kansas City, MO 64112. Born Collingwood, Ont. 1947. m. J. Roderick Johnston. 2 ch. Aaron Michael Johnston, Katherine Elizabeth Johnston. EDUC: Vancouver Sch. of Art, 3 yrs. CAREER: animation studio ink & paint dept., Vancouver; medical illustrator, McMaster Univ., 5 yrs.; freelance designer & illustrator; cartoonist & creator of the comic strip "For Better or Worse," 1979 to date. SELECTED CREDITS: 7 animated films. SELECTED PUBLICATIONS: *David, We're Pregnant* (1972); *Hi Mom, Hi Dad* (1975); *Do They Ever Grow Up?* (1975); 16 books (collections). AFFIL: National Cartoonists' Society; 3 other cartoon societies. HONS: Reuben Award, National Cartoonists' Society, 1986; award, Children's TV Programming (*The Bestest Present*), Gemini Awards, 1987; Quill Award, Windsor Press Club, 1990; Inkpot Award, Outstanding Achievement in Comic Arts, San Diego Comics Convention, 1991; EDI Award (Equality, Dignity, Independence) for media efforts promoting EDI for people with disabilities, Easter Seals, 1992; Order of Canada, 1992; Paul Harris Fellow, Rotary Club of North Bay, 1992; Category Award, Best Strip, 1992; "The Order of Hirsch," 1993; "Crystal Ashtray" (a survival award), Past "Prez" National Cartoonists' Award, 1993; Ph.D. (Hon.), Lakehead Univ., 1990; LL.D.(Hon.), McMaster Univ., 1993. MISC: "For Better or Worse" appears in over 1500 papers worldwide. COMMENT: *"I always knew I would be a cartoonist. I never expected to make my LIVING as one!"*

Johnston-Aldworth, Tracey, A.O.C.A. ■ ▣
President, TRACES SCREEN PRINTING LTD., 145B Lexington Ct., Waterloo, ON N2J 4R2 (519) 746-3340, FAX 746-3478, EMAIL traces@ionline.net INTERNET: www.traces.com. Born Kitchener, Ont. 1957. m. Brian Aldworth. EDUC: Ontario Coll. of Art, A.O.C.A.(Fine Art) 1979. CAREER: Pres., Traces Screen Printing Ltd. EXHIBITIONS: Gallery Quest, St. Jacobs (1994). AFFIL: Zonta Club of Kitchener-Waterloo; Kitchener-Waterloo Chamber of Commerce; Federation of Independent Business; Waterloo Busker Carnival (Volunteer Exec.; Co-Chair 1991, 1994; Chair 1995). HONS: Zontian of the Year, Zonta Club, 1987; Environmental Achievement Award, Small Bus. Category, 1994; Women of the Year Award, Bus. Entrepreneur Category (Kitchener-Water-

loo & Cambridge), 1994; Environmental Award, Region of Waterloo, 1995. INTER-ESTS: fine arts. COMMENT: *"Traces Screen Printing and Tracey endeavour to support their community, be environmentally sensitive and continue excellence in quality, price, and service."*

Johnstone, Louise (Popsy) ⊗ Ⓢ
Art Consultant. 167 Major St., Toronto, ON M5S 2K9 (416) 925-5600, FAX 966-1133. Born Quebec City 1937. m. Robert. 4 ch. EDUC: Univ. of Ottawa, Art Hist. 1980-83; Hunter Coll., N.Y., Art Hist. 1984-86; New Sch. of Social Research, N.Y., 1986-88. CAREER: worked as & trained Museum Docents, Corcoran Gallery of Art, Washington, D.C., 1967-71; Co-founder & Operator, Gallery Graphics, Ottawa, 1973-80; Curator & Consultant, SAW Gallery & National Arts Centre, Ottawa, 1980-83; Dev. Office, New Museum of Contemporary Art, N.Y.C., 1984-88; Consultant, Dept. of External Affairs, Ottawa, 1989-91; Artexte Coord., Art Gallery, York Univ., 1989 to date; developed a membership strategy, Power Plant Art Gallery, Harbourfront, Toronto, 1991-92; Coord., major gala event for opening, Four Seasons Hotel, N.Y.C., 1992-93; Consultant on 2 public art commissions, Art & Architecture Div., Gov't of Ont., 1995. AFFIL: Ontario Coll. of Art (Order-in-Council appt.); Power Plant Art Gallery at Harbourfront, Toronto (Bd. of Dir.; Fin. Committee; Chair, Nominating Committee); Art Gallery of York Univ. (Advisory Bd.); Centre International de l'Art Contemporain, Montreal (Advisory Bd.); The American Friends of Canada, N.Y.C. (Advisory Bd.). HONS: Lescarbot Award, to recognize contributions to the promo. & dev. of cultural life in Canada, Communications Canada, 1992.

Johnstone, Rose, B.Sc.,Ph.D. ⊗ ⚛ ♦
Professor, Gilman Cheney Chair, Department of Biochemistry, MCGILL UNIVERSITY, 3655 Drummond, Ste. 810, Montréal, QC H3G 1V6 (514) 398-7264, FAX 398-7384, EMAIL mdrj@musica.mcgill.ca or johnstone@medcor.mcgill.ca. Born Poland 1928. w. Douglas F. 2 ch. Michael Trevor, M.D., Eric Stephen, M.Eng. EDUC: McGill Univ., B.Sc. 1950, Ph.D. 1953. CAREER: Postdoctoral Fellow, McGill-Montréal General Hospital Research Institute, 1953-54; Postdoctoral Fellow, Dept. of Bacteriological Chem., National Institute for Medical Research, London, UK, 1954-55; Fellow, National Cancer Institute of Canada, 1954-58; Postdoctoral Fellow, Chester Beatty Research Institute, London, UK, 1955-56; Postdoctoral Fellow, Strangeways Research Lab.,

Cambridge, UK, 1955-56; Research Assoc., McGill-Montréal General Hospital Research Institute, 1956-65; Asst. Prof., Dept. of Biochem., McGill Univ., 1961-66, Assoc. Prof., 1966-77; sabbatical leave, Weizmann Institute of Science, 1975-76; Prof., Dept. of Biochem., McGill Univ., 1977, Prof. & Chrm, 1980-90, Gilman Cheney Chair in Biochem., 1985 to date; sabbatical leave, National Institute of Health, Bethesda, 1985-86; Visiting Scientist, Harvard Univ. & Corpus Christi Coll., Oxford, 1991-92. SELECTED PUBLICATIONS: "Amino acid interactions in strict anaerobes," with J.H. Quastel (*Biochem. Biophys.* Acta. 12 1953); "Active transport of ascorbic acid in adrenal cortex and brain cortex in vitro and the effects of ACTH and steroids," with S.K. Sharma & J.H. Quastel (*Canadian Journal of Biochemical Physiology* 41 1963); "Na+-dependent amino acid transport in plasma membrane vesicles from Ehrlich ascites cells," with M. Colombini (*Journal of Membrane Biology* 15(3) 1974); "Fate of the transferrin receptor during maturation of sheep reticulocytes in vitro," with B.T. Pan (*Cell* 33,967 1983); "Vesicle formation during reticulocyte maturation," with M. Adam, L. Orr, J. Hammond & C. Turbide (*Journal of Biological Chemistry* 262 1987); "Origin of a soluble truncated transferrin receptor," with J. Ahn (*Blood* 81 1993); more than 100 other publications. AFFIL: American Society of Biological Chemists; Canadian Biochemical Society; Canadian Society for Cell Biology; Montréal Physiological Society; Royal Society of Canada. HONS: Moyse Traveling Fellowship, 1954; National Cancer Institute Post Doctoral Fellowship, 1954; Queen's Jubilee Silver Medal, 1977; Jean Manery Fisher Honorary Lecturer, Canadian Biochemical Society, 1988. MISC: referee, various journals & granting agencies; recipient, various grants; 1st woman Chair of basic sci. in medicine at McGill. COMMENT: *"I have sustained an independent research career of more than 30 years with continuous funding. Encouraged young women to ply personal careers without giving up their private lives. Was instrumental in getting the University to approve a daycare centre."*

Jolley, Jennifer, R.N. ■ / 🗐
Writer. R.R. 1, Goodwood, ON L0C 1A0 (905) 642-7444, FAX 642-7444. Born UK 1942. m. David. 2 ch. Bryan, Malcolm. EDUC: Richmond Hill High Sch., 1960; The Wellesley Hospital, R.N. 1963; York Univ., 1974. CAREER: R.N., Operating Room, Hospital for Sick Children, 1963; Head Nurse, Orthopaedic Operating Rm., 1965-67; Asst. Supervisor, Operating Rm., Orthopaedics & Neurosurgery, 1967-70; writer & Sales Mgr, Pagurian Press

Publishing, 1976-78; Sales Supervisor, *Toronto Calendar* Magazine, 1978-81; Advtg Dir., *Harrowsmith* Magazine, 1981-89; Advtg Dir., *Harrowsmith* Magazine & *Equinox* Magazine, 1989-94; Assoc. Publisher, *Harrowsmith Country Life* (North American), 1994-96. **SELECTED PUBLICATIONS:** *The First Toronto Catalogue* (Toronto: Penguin Press); *The First Toronto Arts and Crafts Catalogue* (Toronto: Penguin Press); *The First Toronto House and Garden Catalogue* (Toronto: Penguin Press). **HONS:** various sales awards. **INTERESTS:** Classical music; gardening; hobby farming; dog breeding; hiking; skiing; tennis; piano. **COMMENT:** *"I had never intended to pursue a career after having children, but after the break-up of my first marriage I had to go back to work! (and support my son!). I have always been a hard worker."*

Jolliffe, Lynn, B.A.,M.B.A. ■■ $ 🌾

Vice-President and Chief Financial Officer, WHITE ROSE CRAFTS AND NURSERY SALES LTD. (retail), 4038 Hwy 7 E., Unionville, ON L3R 2L5 (905) 477-3330, FAX 477-3902. Born Kitchener, Ont. 1952. m. Howard Hutchison. 2 ch. **EDUC:** Bishop's Univ., CEGEP (Gen.) 1971; Queen's Univ., B.A.(Sociology) 1973; Univ. of Toronto, M.B.A.(Fin.) 1979. **CAREER:** Sales & Mktg, Bell Canada, 1973-79; Hum. Res., Commercial & Corp. Bnkg, Bank of Montreal, 1979-85; VP, Cont. & MIS, 1985-87; VP, Hum. Res., 1987-91; VP, Gen. Mgr, 1991-92; Sr. VP & CFO, 1992-96, Holt, Renfrew & Co., Limited; VP & CFO, White Rose Crafts & Nursery Sales Ltd., 1996 to date. **SELECTED PUBLICATIONS:** Brown Public Sch. (volunteer). **DIRECTOR:** Sun Life Trust Company. **HONS:** nominee, "Women Who Make a Difference," Bus. Section, 1996. **INTERESTS:** family; biking; camping; canoeing; reading; skiing.

Jones, Barbara Ellen, B.A.,M.A., Ph.D. 🎓 ⊕ ⚛

Professor, Department of Neurology and Neurosurgery, MCGILL UNIVERSITY, Montreal Neurological Institute, 3801 University St., Montreal, QC H3A 2B4. Born Philadelphia 1944 m. John Gordon. 1 ch. James Gordon Jones Galaty. **EDUC:** Univ. of Delaware, B.A. 1966, M.A. 1969, Ph.D. 1971. **CAREER:** Predoctoral Fellow, Fac. de Médicine, Lyon, France, 1968-69; Postdoctoral Fellow, Coll. de France, Paris, 1970-73; Research Assoc., Univ. of Chicago, 1973-77; Killam Fellow, Montreal Neurological Institute, 1977; MRC Scholar, 1978-83; Asst. Prof., McGill Univ., 1977-82; Assoc. Prof., 1982-89; Visiting Scientist, Oxford Univ., UK, 1984-85; Prof., McGill Univ., 1989 to date; Invited Prof., Univ. de Genève, Switzerland, 1991-92. **SELECTED PUBLICATIONS:** numerous research reports, reviews in scientific journals & chapters in books. **EDIT:** Ed. Bd., *Sleep*, 1991 to date; Ed. Bd., *Neuroscience*, 1985 to date. **AFFIL:** American Association for the Advancement of Science; Sleep Research Society, US & Canada; Society for Neuroscience. **HONS:** Killam Scholarship, Montreal Neurological Institute, 1977-83; Canadian Medical Research Council Scholarship, 1978-83. **INTERESTS:** horseback riding. **MISC:** numerous lectures given on the subject of sleep.

Jones, Bernadette, B.A. ■■ 🎞 🎓 🎭

Artistic Director, THEATREWORKS PRODUCTIONS (independent theatrical production), 222 Coxwell Ave., Toronto, ON M4L 3B2 (416) 466-5385, FAX 466-1207. Born St. Catharines, Ont. s. 1 ch. Joshua Joudrie. **EDUC:** Concordia Univ., B.A.(English/Drama) 1978. **CAREER:** Prof., Theatre Dept., Vanier Coll., Montreal, 1979-82; Acting Head of Dept., 1981-82; Photo Researcher, *Executive* magazine, Toronto, 1983-84; Asst. (Theatre Ontario Award for study) to Michael Shurtleff, Los Angeles, 1984-86; Artistic Dir., Theatreworks Productions, Toronto, 1984 to date; teaching & private coaching, theatre, film & TV, 1985 to date; Prod., Master Class Workshops for Michael Shurtleff, Mar. 1991/93. **SELECTED CREDITS:** Dir., *Talking Story*, Edinburgh Fringe Festival & CBC Radio, 1988; Dir./Actor, *Italian American Reconciliation*, Off Broadview Theatre, Toronto, 1990; *Mirrors: Remount*, Theatre Centre, Toronto, 1992; Acting Coach, *Catwalk* (TV series), 1st & 2nd seasons, 1992-94; Writer/Prod./Dir., *Damaged Roses* (short film), 1993; Supervising Consultant, *Shurtleff: The Documentary* (film aired on Bravo! & on teaching video series, TVO), 1992. **AFFIL:** Canadian Actors' Equity; Toronto Women in Film; Liaison of Independent Filmmakers of Toronto; Equity Showcase; Theatre Ontario; Toronto Association of Acting Studios (Chairperson 1989-90); Anti-Drug Project, Prov. Anti-Drug Secretariat (Co-Dir. 1991). **HONS:** First Prize, *Damaged Roses*, Bowen Island Short Film Festival, 1995; Dora Mavor Moore nomination for direction, *Italian American Reconciliation*, 1991; Director's Observer Award, *By Way of the Stars*, Academy of Canadian Cinema & Television, 1992/93; Professional Dev. Award, Theatre Ontario, 1985. **INTERESTS:** tai chi practice; jazz; dance; photography. **MISC:** currently developing several film projects in Toronto. **COMMENT:** *"Bernadette has directed over thirty shows since she finished her studies at Concordia University, where she received a*

B.A. in English and Theatre. She has been artistic director of Theatreworks Productions of Toronto since 1984 and was nominated for a Dora Award for the direction of John Patrick Shanley's Italian American Reconciliation. Talking Story *aired on CBC Radio drama after a successful run at the Edinburgh Fringe Festival. She also directed the Summerworks 92 Toronto hit,* Mirrors - Short Plays by Joe Pintauro. *Bernadette directed* When Chickens Came Home To Roost *at Factory Theatre for Theatre Fountainhead and, most recently, directed Ms Satori Shakoor in her one-woman show* Who She Wasn't *at Factory Studio Café (Sept. 96). Bernadette also teaches actors and directors in Toronto, Vancouver and Montreal. Her own award-winning short film* Damaged Roses *can be seen on WTN's* Shameless Shorts."

Jones, Dorothy M., B.A.,A.Mus. ■ 🎓 ✪ ☝
Executive Director, CHILDREN'S TALENT EDUCATION CENTRE, 164 Albert St., London, ON N6A 1M1 (519) 679-2832, FAX 679-9659. Born Detroit 1939. m. Donald H. 3 ch. **EDUC:** London Teachers' Coll., Ontario Teaching Diploma 1958; Univ. of Western Ontario, B.A. (English) 1961, Diploma (Kodaly Music) 1971; Conservatory of Western Ontario, A.Mus. (Piano) 1962; Ont. Ministry of Educ., Diploma (Vocal Music) 1962; Royal Conservatory of Music, Toronto, Diploma (Carl Orff Music for Children) 1969; studied Suzuki in US & Japan with Haruko Katakao, Doris Koppelman, Constance Starr & Dr. Shin'ichi Suzuki. **CAREER:** elementary sch. teacher, Windsor & London, 1958-72; performer in numerous professional & community choirs, 1960 to date; consultant & workshop clinician for Suzuki & traditional music programs worldwide, 1975 to date; teacher, UWO Laboratory Presch., Dept. of Psych., Fac. of Social Sci., Univ. of Western Ontario, 1976-78; Teacher Trainer, registered with Suzuki Association of the Americas, 1981 to date; Adjudicator, music festivals in Oakville, Royal Conservatory, Toronto, & Guelph, 1988 to date; Founder, Exec. Dir. & Teacher Trainer, Children's Talent Education Centre, 1988 to date. **SELECTED PUBLICATIONS:** "Parent Teacher Relationships" (*American Suzuki Journal* 10(2) 1982); "Suzuki Parents: The Home Teacher" (*American Suzuki Journal* 13(5) 1985); "Reflections of a Suzuki Teacher" in *Oto no Sekai* (*Sounds of the Universe*, Haruko Kataoka (Japan: 1988); "Innovative Programs at the Children's Talent Education Centre, London" (*Ontario Suzuki Newsletter* 1(2) 1991); "ECE Teacher Training" (*Ontario Suzuki Newsletter* 2(3) 1993); parent educ. articles in *CTEC Communique*, bimonthly, 1989 to date; various other articles. **EDIT:** initiated & ed. quarterly newsletter, Suzuki Association of the Americas, 1988-90. **AFFIL:** International Suzuki Association (Exec. Bd.); Suzuki Association of the Americas (Pres. 1988-90; President's Advisory Committee); Ontario Suzuki Association (Chair of Bd. 1996); National Association for Education for Young Children; London Symphony Orchestra (Educ. Committee); First St. Andrew's United Church, London (Music Committee; Christian Educ. Committee). **HONS:** Outstanding Contribution Award, London Suzuki Parents' Association, 1980; Distinguished Service Award for vision, leadership & outstanding svc., Suzuki Association of the Americas, 1992. **INTERESTS:** flower arranging; Ikebana; gardening; reading; travel. **MISC:** Children's Talent Education Centre named 1st Centre for Suzuki Early Childhood Educ. Teacher Training in the world, 1993; 1st Cdn Pres., Suzuki Association of the Americas; featured in "Women Upfront," *London Magazine*, 1995. **COMMENT:** *"I believe that all children have the potential to become happy, successful lifelong learners. Our Centre provides nurturing family support and serves as a model for educators worldwide."*

Jones, Faye, B.A.,B.Ed.,M.B.A. ■ $
Vice-President, Affinity Markets, MANULIFE FINANCIAL, 5650 Yonge St., North York, ON M2M 4G4 (416) 229-3081, FAX 229-0566. Born Amherst, N.S. m. Dereck Jones. 3 ch. **EDUC:** Dalhousie Univ., B.A.(Pol. Sci.) 1970, B.Ed. 1975; Univ. of Toronto, M.B.A.(Mktg) 1986. **CAREER:** Mgr, Maritime Life, 1970-74; Mgr, Royal Trust, 1986-89; Dir., Corp. Mktg, North American Life Assurance Company, 1989-90; VP, Corp. Mktg, 1990-93; Sr. VP, Personal Mkts, 1993-96; VP, Affinity Mkts, Manulife Financial, 1996 to date. **DIRECTOR:** First North American Insurance Company.

Jones, Marsha, C.M.P. ■ $
President, MCC PLANNERS INC., 310 North Queen St., Ste. 201, Toronto, ON M9C 1K4 (416) 621-6622, FAX 621-0363. Born Brampton, Ont. 1951. m. Clive Richter. 1 ch. **EDUC:** Georgetown District High Sch., Bus. Course 1972. **CAREER:** Reg. Mgr, Tour Wholesale Company; Mgr, Destination Management Company; Pres., MCC Planners Inc., 1988 to date; VP, Travelmark Group Inc., 1994 to date. **SELECTED PUBLICATIONS:** articles *in Meeting & Incentive* Magazine, & *Meeting & Events* Magazine. **AFFIL:** Convention Liaison Council (C.M.P.); Meetings Professional International (MPI) (Chair, Cdn Council; Pres., Toronto Chapter); Canadian Hotel & Marketing Sales Executives; Metropolitan Convention & Visi-

tors Association (Dir. Affiliates). HONS: Supplier of the Year, MPI, 1990. INTERESTS: golf; skiing; baseball; entertaining; travelling; spending as much time as possible with my daughter. MISC: some speaking engagements; various quotes in publications. COMMENT: *"Over 20 years in the hospitality industry. I believe in hard work and providing top-notch service. I am committed to the meeting industry and will continue to see this profession grow and develop. A very active member of MPI, currently International Awards Committee member. Strongly promote Toronto and Canada in general as a great country and destination to visit."*

Jones, Merri L. ■■ Ⓢ
Vice-Chairman and Chief Operating Officer, T.A.L. PRIVATE MANAGEMENT LTD. (investment mgmt), The Exchange Tower, 130 King St. W., Ste. 2200, Toronto, ON M5X 1B1 (416) 364-5620, FAX 364-4472. Born Toronto 1950. m. Alan. 2 ch. Kelsey, Megan. CAREER: Royal Bank of Canada, 1973-78; Chemical Bank, 1978-83; First Interstate Bank, 1983-91; CIBC, 1991-96. AFFIL: Victorian Order of Nurses, Metro Toronto (Dir.). INTERESTS: family; golf; clients.

Jones, Phyllis, B.Sc.N.,M.Sc., D.N.Sc.(Hon.),R.N.,FAPHA ⬥ ⊕
Professor Emeritus, Faculty of Nursing, UNIVERSITY OF TORONTO, Toronto, ON. Born Barrie, Ont. 1924. s. EDUC: Univ. of Toronto, B.Sc.N. 1950, M.Sc.(Health Admin.) 1969. CAREER: Staff Nurse, Asst. Dir., Victorian Order of Nurses, Toronto, 1950-53; Staff Nurse, Asst. Supervisor, Public Health, Vancouver, 1953-57; Asst. Dir., Victorian Order of Nurses, Toronto, 1957-63; Asst. Prof./Assoc. Prof./Prof., Fac. of Nursing, Univ. of Toronto, 1963-89; Dean, 1979-88; Prof. Emeritus, 1989 to date. SELECTED PUBLICATIONS: *Nurses in Canadian Primary Health Care Settings: A Review of Recent Literature* (Toronto: Univ. of Toronto Faculty of Nursing Monograph Series, 1980); "The East York Public Health Nursing Project" (*Canadian Journal of Public Health* 1969); "Terminology for Nursing Diagnoses" (*Advances in Nursing Science* 1979); "Exploring the Prevalence of Nursing Diagnoses" (*Canadian Journal of Public Health* 1982); various other publications. EDIT: Hon. Consulting Ed., *International Journal of Nursing Studies*, 1979; Review Panel, *Canadian Journal of Public Health*, 1980-90; *Image: Journal of Nursing Scholarship*, *Nursing Diagnosis* (McGraw-Hill Ryerson, C.V. Mosby Co.). AFFIL: Registered Nurses' Association of Ontario (Mbr. Emeritus); Canadian Nurses' Association; Coll. of

Nurses of Ontario; Canadian Public Health Association; American Public Health Association (Fellow); North American Nursing Diagnosis Association (Charter Mbr.); Finnish Society of Professional Nursing (Hon. Mbr.); Sigma Theta Tau Honor Society of Nursing. HONS: D.N.Sc.(Hon.), Univ. of Turku, Finland. INTERESTS: history; gardening; skiing; cooking. MISC: as consultant with World Health Organization assisted Univ. of Turku, Finland, in planning for & establishing a degree program in nursing, 1985-86. COMMENT: *"Clinical area is community health nursing. Principal investigator of early demonstrations of nursing in primary health care settings. Contributed to the international ongoing effort to classify nursing diagnoses through longitudinal research supported by National Research and Development Programme, 1976-82."*

Jones, Sonia, B.A.,M.A.,Ph.D. ■■ ✔
Chief Executive Officer, PENINSULA FARM LTD. (dairy manufacturer), R.R. #3, Lunenburg, NS B0J 2C0 (902) 634-3844, FAX 634-8929. Born London, UK 1938. m. Gordon. 2 ch. Valerie, Victoria. EDUC: Bennington Coll., Vt., B.A.(French) 1961; Univ. of California at Berkeley, M.A.(Spanish)1963; Harvard Univ., Ph.D.(Romance Languages) 1971. CAREER: Chrm, Spanish Dept., Dalhousie Univ., 1972-80; full Prof. with tenure, 1980-91. SELECTED PUBLICATIONS: *It All Began With Daisy* (N.Y.: E.P. Dutton, 1987); *Alfonsina Storni* (Boston: G.K. Hall, 1979); *Spanish One* (N.Y.: D. Van Nostrand, 1974, 2nd ed. 1979); "From Culture to Culture" (*Los Angeles Times*, July 1987); "What's Wrong With My Baby?" (*Reader's Digest*, Nov. 1996). DIRECTOR: InNovaCorp. HONS: Canada Award for Business Excellence (awarded by IST), 1987; Successors Award for entrepreneurship, *Canadian Business* magazine, 1988; Canada Council Grant (travel & research in Argentina), 1975; Harvard Univ. grad. scholarship, 1966. INTERESTS: writing; travel; photography. COMMENT: *"I bought a cow in 1976 to graze the grass on my farm in Lunenburg. Since she gave too much milk for my family of four, I started making yogurt for a local health food store. My company is now the largest manufacturer of yogurt and frozen yogurt in the Maritime provinces, holding the second-largest market share and competing successfully with the giant multinationals."*

Jones, Susan ◑ 📖 ❀
Eco-tourism Trainer and Coordinator, WALK THE WILD SIDE (Ahousaht First Nation Women's Initiative), General Delivery, Ahousaht, Flores Island, BC V0R 1A0 (604)

670-9602. Born Sault Ste. Marie, Ont. 1961. m. Michael Rothe. 4 (blended family) ch. **EDUC:** one-on-one intensive training with distinguished experts in: ethno-botany, dendrochronology, wildlife habitat, forestry & Nuu-Chah-Nulth First Nation culture & language & Culturally Modified Tree Identification; numerous certificates towards CPM & RPA Property Mgmt Certification; workshops in volunteer organizational mgmt. **CAREER:** Lehndorff Property Management, Imperial Group of Properties, Dover Park Developments, 1982-92; advtg sales, Entertainment Columnist & Ed. Asst., *Calgary Downtown Magazine*, 1993; moved to Ahousaht, an isolated First Nations village on the west side of Vancouver, late 1993; Maaqtusiis Sch. substitute teacher, 1994; Coord. Trainer; co-founded Walk The Wild Side (a nonprofit Ahousaht First Nation Women's Initiative), 1994; developed Arts of Paawac Centre (art gallery); initiated & facilitated partnership between Ahousaht Band & Western Canada Wilderness Committee, early 1994 to date; Western Canada Wilderness Committee Ahousaht Office Coord., accomplishing numerous credible field research surveys & studies, incl. the joint Ahousaht First Nation & WCWC Ursus Culturally Modified Tree study, ed. & published landmark Ursus Valley CMT report; Coord. $400,000 CEIC Youth Service Canada grant awarded to develop a 30 km. Wild Side Heritage Trail & Eco-Tourism Proj. from Ahousaht to the Mount Flores Obelisk in cooperation between Ahousaht Chief & Council, WCWC & Walk The Wild Side with support from MacMillan Bloedel & the 17 districts within Port Alberni-Clayoquot area, Fall 1994-96. **HONS:** Recognition Award for commitment, dedication to excellence & entrepreneurial spirit & making it possible for many peoples to see what the world is like when nature takes care of itself, Ahousaht Band Council & Membership, 1994. **INTERESTS:** photography; writing; travel; hiking; exploring; history; learning & experiencing different cultures. **MISC:** Walk The Wild Side, a nonprofit Ahousaht Women's initiative, is an eco-tourism venture that creates employment & training while fostering inherent creative, entrepreneurial & adaptive abilities in partnership with the natural environment, which serves as the constant inspiration. **COMMENT:** *"My lifelong pursuit of knowledge of sustainable employment through conservation of the environment will continue. In our common interest to preserve and steward all creation, it is possible to lose a realistic perception of the expectations and needs of today's economic realities. As well, while fulfilling the demands of an aggressive consumer and industrial society, it is equally possible to lose sight of the need to both conserve and to encounter the natural environment. I will seek out opportunities, affiliations and directorships and volunteer with organizations that view their activities in relation to the integrity of the land and its people and culture as a priority."*

Jordan, Cally, B.A.,M.A.,B.C.L.,LL.B., D.E.A. ◼ ⚖

Lawyer, STIKEMAN, ELLIOTT (HONG KONG), China Building, 29 Queen's Rd. Central, Ste. 1103, Hong Kong (825) 2537-8211, FAX 2845-9076, EMAIL cj@tor.stikeman.com or 101610.2263@compuserve.com. Born Ottawa 1949. m. John Halbrook. 3 ch. Brooke, Daniel, Stephanie. **EDUC:** Carleton Univ., B.A.(with Distinction, English) 1970; Univ. of Toronto, M.A.(English) 1973; McGill Univ., Fac. of Law, LL.B. 1977, B.C.L. 1980; Univ. de Paris I, Panthéon-Sorbonne, France, D.E.A.(French Civil Law) 1978. **BAR:** Ont., 1981; Que., 1981; California, 1984; N.Y., 1986. **CAREER:** Lecturer, Dept. of English, Carleton Univ., 1971-72; Law Clerk, former Chief Justice Brian Dickson, Supreme Court of Canada, 1981-82; Lawyer, Stikeman, Elliott, 1982-83; Lawyer, O'Melveny & Myers, LA, 1983-86; Lawyer, Cleary, Gottlieb, Steen & Hamilton, NYC, 1986-89; Lawyer, Osler, Hoskin & Harcourt, Toronto, 1989-91; Assoc. Prof., Fac. of Law, McGill Univ., 1991-96; Consultant to Fin. Svcs Branch, Hong Kong Gov't, Review of Hong Kong Companies Law, 1995 to date. **SELECTED PUBLICATIONS:** *Canadian Corporate Law*, Welling, Rayner, Jordan, Smith (Toronto: Butterworths, 1996); "Regulation of Canadian Capital Markets in the 1990s: The United States in the Driver's Seat" (*Pacific Rim Law & Policy Journal*, 4 1995); "Lessons from the Bennett Affair" (*McGill Law Journal* (38) 1993); "The Problem with Banking on NAFTA" (*The Globe and Mail*, April 27, 1993); "Un nouveau raccourci pour les émetteurs: le prospectus préable," *Développements récents en valeurs mobilières* (Cowansville: Yvon Blais, 1992); various chapters in books; articles in various journals; various presentations. **EDIT:** Ed.-in-Chief, *North American Corporate Lawyer*, Federated Press, 1991 to date; Bd. of Ed., *Canadian Financial Services Alert*, Carswell, 1991 to date; Ed.-in-Chief, *McGill Law Journal*, Vol. 23, 1977. **AFFIL:** McGill Univ. (Law Coord., Law-MBA Program; Chair, Grad. Studies Committee; Chair, Meredith Lectures Committee; mbr., Senate Committee on Student Grievances); American Arbitration Association (Panel Mbr.); Law Society of Upper Canada; Quebec Bar; California Bar; New York State Bar; Canadian Securities Administrators (Task Force on Operational Efficiencies); Kings County Historical Society, N.S. HONS: Univ. Scholarship, McGill Univ.; Eugene Lafleur Scholarship, Clarkson, Tétrault; Social Services & Humanities Research Scholarship; Bourse Franco-québécoise, French Gov't; MacDonald Travelling Scholarship, McGill Univ. INTERESTS: reading; sports (skiing, cycling, hiking); Nova Scotia architecture; travel. COMMENT: *"I have combined my intellectual interests in law with an active international practice."*

Jordan, Colleen E., B.Ed. ✆
Secretary-Treasurer, CANADIAN UNION OF PUBLIC EMPLOYEES, British Columbia, 4940 Canada Way, Ste. 510, Burnaby, BC V5G 4T3 (604) 291-9119, FAX 291-9043. Born Pincher Creek, Alta. 1948. s. EDUC: Univ. of Alberta, B.Ed.(Secondary) 1973. CAREER: Media Librarian, Burnaby Sch. Bd., 1976-91; Sec.-Treas., Canadian Union of Public Employees, B.C., 1991 to date. AFFIL: Canadian Union of Public Employees (Pres., Local 379 1981-91; Reg'l VP); B.C. Federation of Labour (Exec. Council). INTERESTS: photography; spectator sports. COMMENT: *"Union involvement began in the 1970s with the issue of pay equity for women workers I have become increasingly involved in all aspects of representing and advocating improvements for women workers specifically and public sector workers in general."*

Josefowitz, Nina, B.A.,M.Sc.,Ph.D. ⊕ ⌖
Psychologist. 26 Wells Hill Ave., Toronto, ON M5R 3A6 (416) 736-5225, FAX 513-0899. Born US 1950. m. David Myran. 3 ch. Laura, Aaron, Daniel. EDUC: Brandeis Univ., MA, B.A. 1972; Univ. of London, UK, M.Sc. 1973; Ont. Institute for Studies in Educ., Ph.D. 1981. CAREER: Visiting Lecturer, Dept. of Psych., Universitas Gadjah Mada, Java, Indonesia, 1974-75; Research Coord., Prevention Subcommittee, North York Interagency Council, 1975-76; Lecturer in Psych., Seneca Coll. of Applied Arts & Technology, 1975-76; Lecturer, Canadian Memorial Chiropractic Coll., 1979-81; Asst. Prof. of Psych., 1982-84; Coord. of Student Counselling Svcs, Canadian Chiropractic Coll., Toronto, 1980-84; Dir., Glendon Coll. Counselling & Career Centre, 1984-87; Course Dir., Glendon Coll., York Univ., 1990; Assoc. Mbr., Grad. Dept. of Educ., Univ. of Toronto, 1983 to date; private practice, 1982 to date; Consultant, Counselling Centre, Atkinson Coll., York Univ., 1988 to date. SELECTED PUBLICATIONS: "N. Kerlinger's Theory of Social Attitudes: An Analysis," with K. Marjoribanks

(*Psychological Reports* 37 1975); "Assertion, Popularity, and Social Behaviour in Maximum Security Psychiatric Patients," with M.E. Rice (*Corrective and Social Psychiatry* 29 1983); "How Unassertive Women Perceive Emotional Expressions" (*Canadian Journal of Behavioral Science* 1 1989); "Making Computer Instruction Accessible: Familiar Analogies for Female Novices," with A. Russon & C. Edmonds (*Computers in Human Behaviour* 10 1994); "Flashback phenomena in survivors of childhood sexual abuse: A four-stage treatment model," with L. Musicar (*Journal of Contemporary Psychotherapy,* 26 1996); various other publications. AFFIL: American Psychological Association; Association for Behaviour Therapy; Canadian Association Against Sexual Harassment in Higher Education; Canadian Psychological Association; Canadian Association of College & University Social Services; Ontario Psychological Association; York Univ. Sexual Harassment Education & Complaint Centre (Bd. Mbr.); Coll. of Psychologists of Ontario (elected mbr. of council, 1994-97; Exec. 1995-97). INTERESTS: psych. of women; professional ethics; patient-therapist sexual abuse; sexual harassment. MISC: listed in *Canadian Who's Who* (1984 to date); expert witness on sexual & gender discrimination; numerous presentations at academic meetings; certified Psychologist, Coll. of Psychologists of Ontario, 1982. COMMENT: *"I am a Psychologist working in private practice, as well as university settings. I was recently elected to the Council of the College of Psychology and am interested in issues related to the regulation of health professionals."*

Josephson, Wendy, B.A.,M.A., Ph.D. ■ ⌖ ⊕
Associate Professor, Department of Psychology, UNIVERSITY OF WINNIPEG, 515 Portage Ave., Winnipeg, MB R3B 2E9, FAX (204) 774-4134, EMAIL josephso@io.uwinnipeg.ca. Born Virden, Man. 1953. m. Dr. Robert D. McIlwraith. 1 ch. Christopher McIlwraith. EDUC: Univ. of Manitoba, B.A. 1974, M.A. 1976, Ph.D. 1983. CAREER: Lecturer, Univ. of Winnipeg, 1980-83; Asst. Prof., 1983-89; Assoc. Prof., 1989 to date. SELECTED PUBLICATIONS: "Males, Females and Aggression," with N.L. Colwill in *The psychology of sex differences,* H. Lips & N.L. Colwill, eds. (Englewood Cliffs, N.J: Prentice-Hall 1978); "Attitudes, Beliefs, and Behavior," in *The New Partnership: Women and Men in Organizations,* N.L. Colwill (Palo Alto, Ca.: Mayfield, 1982); "A Cross-Cultural Analysis of Students' Sexual Standards," with D. Perlman, W.T. Hwang, H. Begum & T. Thomas (*Archives of Sexual Behaviour* 7

1978); "Movies, Books, Music, and Adult Fantasy Life," with R.D. McIlwraith (*Journal of Communication* 35(3) 1985); "Television Violence and Children's Aggression: Testing the Priming, Social Script, and Disinhibition Predictions" (*Journal of Personality and Social Psychology* 53 1987); "Attitudes Toward Equal Opportunity in Employment: The Case of One Canadian Government Department," with N.L. Colwill (*Business Quarterly* 48(1) 1983); *Television Violence: A Review of the Effects on Children of Different Ages*, report (Dept. of Canadian Heritage); various other publications. **EDIT:** Ed. Bd., *Canadian Psychology*, 1990 to date. **AFFIL:** Canadian Psychological Association (Sections on: Women & Psych.; Social & Personality Psych.; Industrial/Organizational Psych.). **INTERESTS:** teaching & research on mass media effects, violence & aggression, conflict, organizational psych., issues of sex & gender. **MISC:** numerous conference presentations; various invited lectures; recipient, various fellowships. **COMMENT:** *"As an academic psychologist, I do research on violence and other social issues. I try to share the knowledge that comes from that research not only through academic reports and university teaching, but through community involvement and research collaboration with community organizations."*

Joy, Jean Grahame (Nancy), AOCA ⊛ 🎓 ⊕

Medical Artist. Professor Emeritus, Faculty of Medicine, UNIVERSITY OF TORONTO, Toronto, ON. Born Toronto 1920. s. **EDUC:** St. Clement's Private Sch. for Girls, 1938; Ontario Coll. of Art, AOCA (Fine Art Diploma) 1942, Fellow (Hon.) 1984; Univ. of Toronto, special student 1942-44; Pupil-apprentice & then Asst. to Tom Jones, Prof. of Medical Illustration, Univ. of Illinois, 1944-47. **CAREER:** model-building, illustration, some teaching, Univ. of Illinois Medical Sch., 1944-47; Illustrator to Prof. John Charles Boileau Grant, M.D., M.B.,Ch.B., Head of Dept. of Anatomy, Univ. of Toronto, 1947-52; freelance illustrator, UK, 1952-54; Illustrator to Prof. J.C.B. Grant & minor part-time illustrator, Dept. of Radiology, Univ. of Toronto, 1954-56; Medical Illustrator, Dept. of Surgery, Fac. of Medicine, Univ. of Manitoba, 1956-59; Asst. Prof. of Medical Illustration, 1959-62; Assoc. Prof., Dept. of Art as Applied to Medicine, Fac. of Medicine, Univ. of Toronto, 1962-73; Assoc. Prof. 1973-85; Chrm, 1962-85; Dir., AAM Svcs, 1962-69; Dir., AAM program of study, 1962-86. **SELECTED PUBLICATIONS:** "Pictured Fact and Fancy in Current Medical Literature," editorial (*Annals of Surgery* 156(3) Sept. 1962); "Medical Illustration and Copyright" (*Medical and Biological Illustration* 13(2) Apr. 1964); "Synchronous Abdominoperineal Resection," with R.H. Thorlakson & T.K. Thorlakson (*Surgical Techniques Illustrated* 2(1) Winter 1977); "Positional Trauma," with B. Britt, M.D. & M. Mackay in *Complications in Anaesthesia*, eds. L.H. Cooperman & S.K. Orkin (J.B. Lippincott Ltd., 1978); ed., *Medical Illustration*, Cumulative Bibliography (AMI, 1969); various reviews, reports & other publications; contributed illustrations to *A Method of Anatomy*, 2nd through 7th editions, J.C.B. Grant (Williams & Wilkins Co.); contributed illustrations to *An Atlas of Anatomy*, 2nd through 5th editions, J.C.B. Grant (Williams & Wilkins Co.); contributed illustrations to *A Manual of Anatomy*, 5th ed., J.C.B. Grant (Williams & Wilkins Co., 1959); contributed illustrations to numerous other books published in US & UK (1950-78) & to numerous journal articles; illustrations contributed to various films produced by D.A. Gibson, Dept. of Photography, Children's Hospital, Winnipeg (1960-61), incl. *The Story of an Open Heart Operation* (1960) & *Resuscitation in a Children's Hospital* (1961); Prod. Coord., *Dizziness*, short film (1969). **EDIT:** author & ed., special bibliography issue, *Association of Medical Illustrators Newsletter* 2(2) 1961. **EXHIBITIONS:** medical art show, *A Fifty-year Retrospective Exhibit of Work Produced by Staff of AAM Department and Affiliated Teaching Hospitals*, Arts & Letters Club, Toronto (1976). **AFFIL:** Univ. of Medical Illustrators (Elected Mbr.); Ontario Coll. of Art Alumni Association (Charter Mbr.); Univ. of Toronto Fac. Association; Academy of Medicine (Assoc. Mbr.); Canadian Science Film Association; Univ. of Toronto Fac. Club; Bayfield-Nares Islanders' Association. **HONS:** Hughes Owens Prize, Ontario Coll. of Art, 1942; Medical Educ. Award, overall & Second Place, Clinical Category, Biocommunications '70, Houston (*Dizziness*), 1970; Second Place, Overall, International Medical Videotape & Film Festival, Williamsburg, Va. (*Dizziness*), 1970. **MISC:** designer of the curriculum for the conversion of the diploma course in AAM to a program leading to the degree of B.Sc. AAM, approved by Univ. of Toronto Statute No. 2975 (1967-3-9), 1964-67; co-inventor, Constudium Carrel, 1969.

Jubenville, Sheila J., B.S.W.,B.A. ⊕ $

Chief Executive Officer, RADVILLE MARIAN HEALTH CENTRE, Box 310, Radville, SK S0C 2G0 (306) 869-2289, FAX 869-2289. Born Virden, Man. m. Trevor J. Jubenville. **EDUC:** Univ. of Regina, B.S.W. 1983; Saskatchewan Association of Health Organizations, Certificate in Employee Rel'ns 1994; Univ. of

Saskatchewan, Fac. of Commerce: Acute Care Certificate 1989, Long-Term Care Certificate 1993, Community Health Care Admin. Certificate 1994. **CAREER:** various positions, CIBC, 1977-79; Admitting Dept./Operating Room Scheduler, South Saskatchewan Hospital Centre, Plains Health Centre, Regina, 1980-84; Psychiatric Social Worker, Lincoln Regional Center, Lincoln, Neb., 1983; Medical Social Worker, Providence Hospital, Moose Jaw, 1983-84; Medical Social Work Consultant, Dept. of Reg'l Svcs, South Saskatchewan Hospital Centre, 1984-88; CEO, Davidson Union Hospital, Davidson, Sask., 1988-92; CEO, Radville Marian Health Centre, 1993 to date. **SELECTED PUBLICATIONS:** articles on health care & health reform for local newspapers (rural). **AFFIL:** Saskatchewan Health Dispute Resolution Panel; Saskatchewan Association of Health Service Executives; Saskatchewan Association of Social Workers; Saskatchewan Gerontology Association; Saskatchewan Alliance for Agriculture Health & Safety; Rural Health Coalition, Sask. (Sec-Treas); Father Yandeau Memorial Foundation Inc. (Sec.-Treas.); Radville Chamber of Commerce; Radville Econ. Dev. Committee; Wascana Pistol Club, Regina; Saskatchewan Handgun Association; Quota International Club of Weyburn. **INTERESTS:** travelling; reading; gourmet cooking; piano; sports; writing; camping; hiking; french; spanish; target shooting; swimming. **MISC:** Certified Range Officer, Saskatchewan Handgun Association. **COMMENT:** *"I need the continued stimulation of a wide variety of interests and challenges in my daily life to feel fulfilled. I like the challenge of the unexpected and enjoy working under pressure. As other Canadian women do, I continue to grow toward my ever-expanding personal and professional capacity."*

Julien, Linda A., LL.L. ᓚ
Lawyer, Corporate Affairs Officer and Legal Counsel, CTI CAPITAL INC., 1 Place Ville Marie, Ste. 1635, Montreal, QC H3B 2B6 (514) 861-3500, FAX 861-3230. Born St-Timothée, Qué. **EDUC:** Univ. de Montréal, LL.L. 1976; Canadian Institute for Advanced Legal Studies, Cambridge Univ., UK, Comparative Law 1978; Canadian Securities Institute, Diplomas 1979; McGill Univ., Spanish Certificate 1989. **BAR:** Que., 1978. **CAREER:** criminal law articling student, 1977; Asst. Dir., Montreal Stock Exchange, 1978-81; Assoc. Lawyer, MacKenzie Gervais, Montréal, 1983-87; Liberal candidate, Fed. riding of Beauharnois-Salaberry, Que., 1988, 1993; Corp. Affairs Legal Cnsl & Officer, CTI Capital, 1990 to date. **SELECTED PUBLICATIONS:** numerous newspaper articles.

AFFIL: Union internationale des Avocats; Barreau du Québec; Judy Lamarsh Fund (Dir.); Univ. de Montréal Law Association; Châteauguay Valley Historical Society; Amnesty International; Environmental "ZIP" Group; Liberal Party of Canada (Nat'l Exec. Mbr.); National Women's Liberal Commission (Pres.); Quebec Heart & Stroke Foundation (Past Reg'l Pres.); Jeanne Sauvé Youth Foundation (Rresource person). **INTERESTS:** politics; humanities; reading; writing; alpine & cross-country skiing; music; cinema; riding; walking; travelling. **COMMENT:** *"I decided to enter politics because I have a dynamic personality, a strong voice and a caring heart. With a solid legal background and the capacity to influence, I believe I can (I have and will) make a difference, wanting to be a credible and worthwhile intermediary between the people and better government."*

Junor, Judy, R.N. ⊛ ⊕ ❀
President, SASKATCHEWAN UNION OF NURSES, 2330 - 2nd Ave., Regina, SK S4R 1A6 (306) 525-1666, FAX 522-4612. 2 ch. Dean Andrew, Heather Down. **EDUC:** St. Paul's Sch. of Nursing, R.N.; Saskatchewan Institute of Applied Science & Technology, Certificate in Intro. to Counselling; Credit Courses, Univ. of Saskatchewan & Univ. of Montreal. **CAREER:** Gen. Duty Nurse, Obstetrics & Gynecology, 25 yrs.; Local Union Pres., Local Sec.-Treas.; Pres., Saskatchewan Union of Nurses; VP, Saskatchewan Federation of Labour. **SELECTED PUBLICATIONS:** articles in SUNSPOTS, Saskatchewan Union of Nurses' internal newsletter and CONCERN, Provincial Registered Nurses' Association magazine. **AFFIL:** Minister of Health, Health Providers Human Resource Committee (V-Chair); Univ. of Saskatchewan (Advisory Bd., Labour Studies Program, Coll. of Commerce; Advisory Bd., Continuing Educ., Coll. of Nursing). **MISC:** participant, Gov. General's Study Conference, 1995; represents SUN on various gov't educ. and health committees. **COMMENT:** *"I am considered to be a clear thinker and a problem solver. I am a firm believer in positive action and a collaborative approach to conflict resolution."*

K

aegi, Elizabeth Ann, M.B.Ch.B.,M.Sc., C.C.B.O.M. ■ ■ ⊕ ⊚
Private Consultant, Medical Policy, Administration, Workshop Organization. c/o Canadian Cancer Society, 10 Alcorn Ave., Ste. 200, Toronto, ON M4V 3B1 (416) 961-7223, FAX 961-4189. Born Poona, India 1946. m. George Dutton. 2 ch. Simon Kaegi, Janet Dutton. **EDUC:** Univ. of Otago, N.Z., M.B.Ch.B. 1969; McMaster Univ., M.Sc. 1975; post-grad. medical training, N.Z. & Canada, 1970-75. **CAREER:** Asst. Prof., Univ. of Calgary Medical Sch., 1975-76; Pres., Western Health Services Research Ltd., 1976-79; Sr. Medical Consultant, Dept. of Labour, Gov't of Alta., 1979-80; Medical Dir., C-I-L Inc., 1981-86; Sr. VP & Chief Medical Officer, Ontario Workers' Compensation Board, 1986-92; Dir., Medical Affairs & Cancer Control, National Cancer Institute of Canada & Canadian Cancer Society, 1992-96. **SELECTED PUBLICATIONS:** numerous internal publications; co-author, several medical/policy publications. **AFFIL:** Ontario Workers' Compensation Board (Bd. of Dir. 1985-86); Min. of Labour's Advisory Committee on Occupational Health & Safety (mbr. 1984-85); Canadian Cancer Society (volunteer). **INTERESTS:** special interest in providing medical info. to the public (esp. cancer control issues) through print, radio & TV; travel in Canada & internationally; music; theatre; film; fitness; herbal medicine. **COMMENT:** *"Recently "retired." Just catching my breath before the next phase of my life."*

Kahn, Harriette Jean, M.B.Ch.B, FRCPath,FRCP(C) ⊕ ⊜
Research Director and Associate Chief, Depart-

ment of Pathology and Head, Immunochemistry Department, WOMEN'S COLLEGE HOSPITAL, 76 Grenville St., Toronto, ON M5S 1B2 (416) 323-6144, FAX (416) 323-6116. Professor, Department of Pathology, UNIVERSITY OF TORONTO. Medical Education Coordinator TELEMEDICINE CANADA/US. Born South Africa. m. Max. 3 ch. EDUC: Univ. of Witwatersrand, Johannesburg, M.B.Ch.B. 1961. CAREER: Intern, various hospitals, Johannesburg, 1962-63; various Pathology Registrar positions, South African Institute for Medical Research & Univ. of Witwatersrand, 1963-71; Pathology Staff, 1972-78; Pathology Resident, Princess Margaret Hospital, Toronto, 1979; Pathology Resident, Women's College Hospital, 1980; Temporary Staff Pathologist, 1981; Lecturer, Univ. of Toronto, 1981-82; Asst. Prof., Dept. of Pathology, 1982-87; Staff Pathologist, Women's College Hospital, 1982 to date; Head, Immunochemistry Dept., 1984 to date; Assoc. Prof., Univ. of Toronto, 1987-96; Full Prof., 1996 to date; cross appt., Dept. of Pathology, Hospital for Sick Children, 1987 to date; Head, Cytology Dept., Women's College Hospital, 1989-93; Research Dir., 1992 to date; cross appt., Dept. of Oncologic Pathology, Ontario Cancer Institute/Princess Margaret Hospital, 1994 to date; Medical Educ. Coord., Telemedicine Canada/US, 1996. SELECTED PUBLICATIONS: "Role of Antibody to S100 protein in diagnostic pathology," with A. Marks & R. Baumal (*American Journal of Clinical Pathology*, 1983); "Overexpression of p53 is a late event in the development of malignant melanoma," with N. Lassam & L. From (*Cancer Research*, 1993); "M1B1 proliferative activity is a significant prognostic factor in primary thick cutaneous melanomas," with J. Ramsay & N. Iscoe (*Journal of Investigative Dermatology*, 1995); "The Value of Immunohistochemistry in Increasing Diagnostic Precision of Undifferentiated Tumours by the Surgical Pathologist," with R. Baumal *et al* (*Journal of Histochemistry* 1984); "Distribution and Patterns of Staining of Neu-oncogene in Benign and Malignant Breast Disease," with W. Hanna *et al* (*Modern Pathology* 3(4) 1990); more than 100 abstracts; numerous other publications. AFFIL: Royal Coll. of Pathologists, London, UK (Fellow); Royal Coll. of Physicians & Surgeons of Canada (Fellow); Medical Council of Canada (Licentiate); Academy of Medicine; Ontario Medical Association; Coll. of Physicians & Surgeons of Ontario; International Academy of Pathology; Histochemical Society; American Association of Pathologists; Women's College Hospital (Research Ethics Committee; Research Committee of Board). HONS: Certificate of Appreciation for outstanding teaching,

Women's College Hospital, 1991-92; Colin R. Woolf Award for an outstanding continuing educ. course, Univ. of Toronto, 1992-93; J.B. Walter Teaching Award, Dept. of Pathology, Univ. of Toronto, 1994. MISC: participating in the joint venture between Women's College Hospital & the Univ. of Toronto to establish a centre for research in women's health; ad hoc reviewer for *American Journal of Pathology*, *Archives of Pathology and Laboratory Medicine*, *Laboratory Investigation*, & *Journal of Histochemistry and Cytochemistry*; numerous invited lectures; recipient, numerous research grants. COMMENT: *"Conscientious compassionate person striving for excellence in all endeavours, including teaching, research and service work. Dedicated to family as well."*

Kain, Karen, O.C. ■ ⊗
Principal Ballerina, NATIONAL BALLET OF CANADA, 470 Queen's Quay W., Toronto, ON M5V 3K4 (416) 345-9681, FAX 345-8323. Born Hamilton, Ont. 1951. m. Ross Petty. EDUC: National Ballet Sch. CAREER: joined the National Ballet of Canada, 1969; Principal Dancer, 1970 to date; major performances include: *The Mirror Walkers*, 1970; *Swan Lake* (Bruhn), *Fandango* (Tudor), *Autumn Song* (Comelin), 1971; *Intermezzo* (Feld), *Romeo and Juliet*, with Frank Augustyn (Cranko), *The Nutcracker*, with Frank Augustyn (Franca), *The Sleeping Beauty*, with Rudolph Nureyev (Nureyev), 1972; *Solitaire* (MacMillan), *Giselle*, with Frank Augustyn (Wright), *Les Sylphides* (Franca & Bruhn), 1973; *Don Juan* (Neumeier) & *La Sylphide* (Bruhn), both with Rudolph Nureyev, 1974; *Coppélia*, with Frank Augustyn (Bruhn), 1976; *Elite Syncopations*, with Frank Augustyn (MacMillan), 1978; *Sphinx*, with Frank Augustyn & Kevin Pugh (Tetley), 1983; world premiere, *Alice* (Tetley), *The Merry Widow*, with John Meehan (Hynd), 1986; *Impromptu* (Feld) & world premiere, *La Ronde* (Tetley), 1987; *Karen Kain 20th Anniversary Gala*, O'Keefe Centre, Toronto, 1989; *The Taming of the Shrew*, with Serge Lavoie (Cranko), 1992; world premiere, *Now and Then*, with Graeme Mears (Neumeier), 1993; world premiere, *The Actress* (Kudelka), 1994; world premiere, *Spring Awakening*, with Reid Anderson (Kudelka) 1994; company premiere, *A Month in the Country*, with Robert Conn, staged by Anthony Dowell (Ashton), 1995. SELECTED CREDITS: other leading roles in: *Afternoon of a Faun* (Robbins); *At Midnight* (Feld); *La Bayadère Act IV* (Valukin); *Carmen* (Petit); *Concerto* (MacMillan); *Daphnis and Chloë* (Tetley); *Don Quixote* (Beriozoff); *The Dream* (Ashton); *Études* (Lander); *La Fille Mal Gardée* (Ashton); *Forgotten Land*

(Kylian); *Four Schumann Pieces* (van Manen); *The Four Temperaments* (Balanchine); *Impromptu* (Feld); *Le Loup* (Petit); *A Month in the Country* (Ashton); *The Moor's Pavane* (Limon); *Napoli* (Schaufuss); *Nelligan Pas de Deux* (Ditchburn); *Onegin* (Cranko); *Raymonda Pas de Dix* (Balanchine); *Serenade* (Balanchine); *Song of the Earth* (MacMillan); *Symphony in C* (Balanchine); other original roles include: Albertine, *Les Intermittences du Coeur* (Petit, 1974); *Whispers of Darkness* (Vesak, 1974); *Inventions* (Patsalas, 1974); Louise, *Mad Shadows* (Ditchburn, 1977); *Nana* (Petit, 1976); *Quartet* (Peters, 1983); Chosen Maiden, *The Rite of Spring* (Patsalas, 1978); *Rape of Lucrece* (Kudelka, 1980); *The Seven Daggers/Los Siete Punales* (Susana, 1981); Guiletta, *Tales of Hoffmann* (Petit, 1982); *Oiseaux Exotiques* (Patsalas, 1984); *The Actress, La Ronde* (Tetley, 1987); *Pastorale* (Kudelka, 1991); *Musings* (Kudelka, 1991); *Cafe Dances* (House, 1991); *The Miraculous Mandarin* (Kudelka, 1993); guest performances include: *Giselle*, Bolshoi Ballet, Soviet tour, 1977; *The Sleeping Beauty*, with Rudolph Nureyev, London Festival Ballet, UK & Australia, 1975; *Swan Lake*, Vienna State Opera Ballet; various works, Le Ballet National de Marseille, 1972-82; "Makarova and Company," N.Y., 1980; teaching & performance tour with Frank Augustyn, China, 1981; Le Ballet National de Marseille, tours of Japan & Korea, 1981-82; *Nelligan Pas de Deux*, Spoleto Festival, 1982; *Onegin*, with Reid Anderson, Spoleto Festival & with the Stuttgart Ballet, 1984; various works with Eliot Feld Company, N.Y., 1984 to date; Grand Pas de Deux, *The Sleeping Beauty* with Rudolph Nureyev in Chicago & at 100th anniversary celebration of the Metropolitan Opera House, 1984; galas in Chicago, Monte Carlo & Florida; with Rudolph Nureyev in Australia, London, Vienna, Washington D.C.; with orchestras across Canada; Dancers for Life AIDS Gala, 1991, 1992, 1994; television performances include: *Giselle*, CBC, 1976; *Coppélia*, Roland Petit's The Ballet De Marseille, 1976; *La Fille Mal Gardée*, CBC, 1979; *Karen Kain Ballerina*, CBC, 1977; *The Littlest Hobo*, CTV, 1980; *100th Anniversary of the MET*, PBS, 1983; *The André Gagnon Television Special* & *The Jeff Hyslop Television Special*; British pantomime, *The Cinderella Gang*, with Ross Petty, CTV, 1987; *The Merry Widow*, Primedia Productions, CBC, 1987; Co-Host, *Competition for First Annual Erik Bruhn Prize*, CBC TV/Primedia Productions, 1988; *Live from the Met, Nureyev's 50th Birthday Party*, PBS, 1988; *La Ronde*, CBC, 1989; *Alice*, CBC, 1989; *Karen Kain Prima Ballerina*, CBC, 1989; *Making Ballet*, TVO, 1995; theatre perfor-

mances include: *Aladdin and His Wonderful Lamp*, 1982, 1988; *Dick Wittington and His Cat*, 1985; *The Cinderella Gang*, Hamilton Place, 1986; *Snow White*, Cdn tour, 1987. **SELECTED PUBLICATIONS:** *Karen Kain's Beauty and Fitness Book*, as told to Marilyn Linton (Doubleday, 1983); *Movement Never Lies: An Autobiography*, with Stephen Godfrey & Penelope Reed Doob (McClelland & Stewart, 1994). **AFFIL:** Dancer Transition Centre (Pres.). **HONS:** Silver Medal, Women's Category & Silver Medal, Best Pas de Deux, with Frank Augustyn, 2nd Int'l Ballet Competition in Moscow, 1973; Officer of the Order of Canada, 1976; Performing Arts Award, Toronto Arts Awards, 1992; Companion of The Order of Canada, 1991; a gala performance, "Celebrating Kain," held in honour of 20th anniversary with the National Ballet, 1988; The National Ballet of Canada's 1994/95 season dedicated to Karen Kain in honour of her 25 yrs. with the company, 1994; a gala evening held on Nov. 25 to honour her last performance of *Swan Lake*, 1994; Hon. degrees from: York Univ., Univ. of British Columbia, Trent Univ., McMaster Univ., Univ. of Toronto. **MISC:** *A Month in the Country* was acquired for Karen Kain's 25th anniversary with the National Ballet & was staged by Royal Ballet director Anthony Dowell, the first time the ballet was performed by a company other than Britain's Royal Ballet; numerous interviews, conversations & appearances on radio & TV; the subject of 3 books, *Kain and Augustyn* (Macmillan of Canada, 1977), *Karen Kain, Lady of the Dance* (McGraw Hill Ryerson, 1978) & *Karen Kain: Born to Dance* (Grolier Ltd., 1983).

Kaljuste, Kadi, B.A.A. $ ✎ ◉
Senior Vice-President, OEB INTERNATIONAL PUBLIC RELATIONS/PUBLIC AFFAIRS, 10 Lower Spadina Ave., Ste. 500, Toronto, ON M5Y 2Z2 (416) 260-6000, FAX 260-2708. Born Montreal. m. Bradley Ciccarelli. 1 ch. Dylon F. Kaljuste Ciccarelli. **EDUC:** Ryerson Polytechnic Univ., B.A.A.(Journalism) 1979. **CAREER:** tour guide, copy clerk, bookkeeper, reporter, *The Toronto Sun*, 1975-79; freelance reporter, Toronto & Montreal, 1979-80; Ed. Asst., Centennial Coll., Scarborough, Ont., 1980-81; Info. Officer, 1981-84; Mgr, Comm., George Brown Coll., Toronto, 1984-88; Acct Dir., Public Rel'ns, OPTIMUM (a Cossette company), Toronto, 1988-90; Acct Dir., Public Rel'ns, OEB International, Toronto, 1990-91; VP, Public Rel'ns, 1991-94; Sr. VP, 1994 to date. **AFFIL:** Habitat for Humanity Canada (media rel'ns/fundraising); Casey House Hospice (media rel'ns/fundraising).

Kallen, Evelyn, B.A.,Ph.D.,F.R.S.C. ⬧ 🏛
Emeritus Professor and Senior Scholar (Arts), YORK UNIVERSITY, 4700 Keele St., Toronto, ON M3J 1P3 (416) 736-5164, FAX 736-5892. Born Toronto 1929. m. Dr. David R. Hughes. EDUC: Univ. of Toronto, B.A. 1950, Diploma in Child Study 1953, Ph.D.(Social Anthro.) 1969. CAREER: Teaching Asst., Dept. of Anthro., Univ. of Toronto, 1966-68; Special Lecturer, Trinity Coll., 1969-70; Special Visiting Lecturer, Dept. of Soc., Queen's Univ., 1969-70; Asst. Prof., Div. of Social Sci., York Univ., 1970-74; Assoc. Prof., 1974-83; Full Prof., 1984-91; Chair, Human Rights Research & Educ. Centre, Fac. of Law, Univ. of Ottawa, 1989-90; Emeritus Prof. of Social Sci. & Anthro., & Sr. Scholar, Fac. of Arts, York Univ., 1991 to date. SELECTED PUBLICATIONS: *The Anatomy of Racism: Canadian Dimensions* with D.R. Hughes (Montreal: Harvest House, 1974); *Ethnicity and Human Rights in Canada* (Scarborough: Gage, 1982); *Ethnicity and Human Rights in Canada* 2nd edition (Toronto: Oxford Univ. Press, 1995); *Label Me Human: Minority Rights of Stigmatized Canadians* (Toronto: Univ. of Toronto Press, 1989); "Ethnicity and Collective Rights in Canada" in *Ethnic Canada: Identities and Inequalities* ed. L. Driedger (Toronto: Copp Clark Pitman Ltd., 1987); "Multiculturalism: Ideology, Policy and Reality" (*Journal of Canadian Studies* Spring 1982); "The Meech Lake Accord: Entrenching a Pecking Order of Minority Rights" (*Canadian Public Policy Special Issue* Sept. 1988); "Never Again!: Target Group Responses to the Debate Concerning Anti-Hate Propaganda Legislation" (*Windsor Yearbook of Access to Justice* Vol. XI); "Target for Hate: The Impact of the Zundel and Keegstra Trials on a Jewish Canadian Audience," with Larry Lam (*Canadian Ethnic Studies* #1 1993); "Aboriginal Rights and Cultural Autonomy" (*Key Issues in Peace Research Proceedings of the 9th Gen. Conference of the International Peace Research Association,* 1983); various other books, chapters in books, articles & papers in conference publications. AFFIL: Royal Society of Canada (Fellow); Canadian Ethnic Studies Association; Canadian Sociology & Anthropology Association; Canadian Human Rights Foundation (Nat'l Council). HONS: Panhellenic Prize, Univ. of Toronto, 1948-50; Annual Award, Canadian Human Rights Foundation, 1973. INTERESTS: human rights advocacy; reading; swimming; walking; loving companionship. MISC: recipient, numerous grants to support research & publication; Leave Fellowship, York Univ., 1991-92. COMMENT: *"University Professor of Social Science and Anthropology with abid-*ing research interests and extensive publication in human rights issues that focus on the rights of racial, ethnic and other stigmatized minorities in Canada and elsewhere."

Kamateros, Melpa, B.A. ☺
Executive Director, LE BOUCLIER D'ATHENA/ THE SHIELD OF ATHENA, 700 Cremazie Blvd. W., Montreal, QC H3R 3J1 (514) 274-8177, FAX 274-4309. Born Nicosia, Cyprus 1955. m. Apostolos Kamateros. 2 ch. Anne-Marie, Stamatis. EDUC: Concordia Univ., B.A.(Pol. Sci.) 1977, Grad. Diploma (Community Politics & the Law) 1993. CAREER: journalist, *Cyprus Mail*, Cyprus, 1977-78; Pres., Le Bouclier d'Athena/The Shield of Athena, 1991-93; Exec. Dir., 1993 to date. SELECTED CREDITS: prod. & dir., programs on family violence, CHCR, cable 24, *La Voie Hellenique de Montréal* (1993 to date); various radio appearances. SELECTED PUBLICATIONS: "Family Violence: A Greek Perspective" (*Vis-à-vis* Magazine 12(1) 1994); various articles on domestic violence in Greek. AFFIL: Hellenic Ladies' Benevolent Society, Montreal. INTERESTS: reading; writing; painting; appreciation of fine arts; music; languages. MISC: principal founding mbr. of Le Bouclier d'Athena/The Shield of Athena, an organization that deals with family violence in ethnic communities; numerous seminars & presentations. COMMENT: *"My main strengths are ones of an investigative nature, finding out if an injustice exists and then seeing what can be done to rectify it."*

Kambeitz, Sister Teresita (Rose Marie), O.S.U.,B.A.,B.Ed.,M.R.E.,M.Ed., Ph.D. ■■ ⬧ ☼ 🏛 ♦
Director of Religious Education Program, NEWMAN THEOLOGICAL COLLEGE, 15611 St. Albert Trail, Edmonton, AB T5L 4H8 (403) 447-2993, FAX 447-2685. Born Richmound, Sask. 1937. EDUC: St. Angela's Academy, Prelate, Sask., A.R.C.T.(Music) 1957; Teachers' Coll., Saskatoon, 1958-59; Univ. of Saskatchewan, B.A.(Great Distinction, English & Hist.) 1969, B.Ed.(Great Distinction, English & Hist.) 1969; St. Paul Univ., Ottawa, Theology 1969-70; St. Michael's Coll., Univ. of Toronto, M.R.E.(Religious Educ.) 1976; Ontario Institute for Studies in Education, Univ. of Toronto, M.Ed.(Phil. of Educ.) 1986, Ph.D.(Phil. of Educ.) 1988. CAREER: Teacher, various schools, Sask., 1959-64; Principal & Teacher, St. Patrick Sch., Swift Current, Sask., 1964-68; Teacher, Christian Ethics, Holy Cross High Sch., Saskatoon, 1970-85 (& Chaplain, half-time, 1983-85); taught various religion courses, Univ. of Saskatchewan & Univ. of Regina, 1976-87; Dir., Religious Educ. Program, Newman Theological

Coll., Edmonton, 1988 to date. **SELECTED PUBLICATIONS:** numerous articles, presentations, book reviews; monthly article, "Liturgy and Life," *The Prairie Messenger*, 1992 to date; monthly article in *Our Family* magazine, 1992-93; ed., *Ursulines Remember*, Vol. I (autobiographies of 83 Sisters), 1994, & Vol. II (biographies of 34 deceased Sisters), 1995; "Health Hazards of So-Called Low-Level Radiation" (brief prepared & presented to Eldorado Envir. Assessment Panel, Saskatoon), 1980; *Death and Dying* (teacher manual for use in Sask. high schools), 1979. **AFFIL:** Newman Theological Coll. (Exec. Committee, Senate 1991-95); St. Joseph's Coll., Univ. of Alberta (Bd. of Gov. 1992-95); Archdiocese of Edmonton (Adult Learning Commission 1992-95); Alberta Teachers' Association (Religious & Moral Educ. Council 1988 to date); Association of Professors & Researchers in Religious Education (mbr. 1988 to date); International Seminar on Religious Education & Values (Assoc. mbr. 1996 to date); Religious Education Association of the U.S. & Canada (Bd. of Dir. 1992 to date); Ursuline Congregation of Prelate (Gen. Council 1970-76, 1987-95). **HONS:** 5 piano scholarships; English scholarship, Teachers' Coll., Saskatoon, 1959; Sask. Gov't Educ. Bursary, 1968; hon. mention, Canadian Church Press, Spirituality category for article, "New Definition of Sin: Sleeping on the Bus," 1993; Peter Craigie Award for svc. to professional growth of religious & moral educ. in Alta., Alberta Teachers' Association, 1994. **INTERESTS:** music; travel; youth; social justice. **MISC:** mbr., Ursuline Congregation, Prelate, Sask.; has taught courses in Barbados, Latvia, Venezuela, & British Virgin Islands; keynote speaker, numerous teacher conferences, workshops, institutes, retreats, symposia & in-service days; pianist/organist, Newman Theological Coll. & Dir. of Convocation Choir, & Sunday organist, St. Charles Church, Edmonton; dir./pianist, 20 musical productions of campus singing group, Univ. of Saskatchewan, 1971-85; 1st woman (Roman Catholic) as Campus Chaplain & 1st woman to teach in the Sch. of Religious Studies, Univ. of Saskatchewan; established M.R.E. Degree Program at Newman Theological Coll.

Kaminsky, Barbara Anne, B.A.,M.S.W., M.Sc. ■■ ⊕ ♡ $

Chief Executive Officer, B.C. and Yukon Division, CANADIAN CANCER SOCIETY, 565 W. 10th Ave., Vancouver, BC V5Z 4J4 (604) 872-4400, FAX 879-4533. Clinical Assistant Professor, Health Administration Program, UNIVERSITY OF BRITISH COLUMBIA. Born Vancouver 1950. m. John Kaminsky. **EDUC:** Univ. of British Columbia, B.A.(English) 1971, M.S.W.(Social Work) 1973, M.Sc.(Health Svcs Planning & Admin.) 1982. **CAREER:** Proj. Coord., Social Svc. Dept., Vancouver General Hospital, 1973-77; Long-Term Care Administrator, Richmond Health Dept., 1977-84; independent consultant, 1984-85; VP, Mgmt Svcs, B.C. Health Care Systems, 1985-89; VP, Clinical Svcs, Surrey Memorial Hospital, 1989-94; CEO, Canadian Cancer Society, B.C. & Yukon Div., 1994 to date. **SELECTED PUBLICATIONS:** author, "Rational Planning Models for Resource Allocation in Health Care" (*Health Management Forum*, 5(4), Summer 1984, 43-57); co-author with L.A. Sheckter, "Abortion Counselling in a General Hospital" (*Health and Social Work*, 4(2), May 1979, 92-103). **EDIT:** *Health Management Forum* (edit. bd.). **AFFIL:** Canadian Coll. of Health Service Executives; Health Administrators' Association of B.C. (Pres. 1993-94); Canadian Foundation for Ukrainian Studies (Dir.); Ukrainian Manor Seniors' Residence (Dir.). **INTERESTS:** health & human svcs; Ukrainian culture (esp. folk dancing); golf; skiing; reading; karaoke. **MISC:** decades of volunteer work in the Ukrainian community & in the health care system. **COMMENT:** *"A health care executive with extensive and eclectic leadership and management experience in health care, non-profits and associations."*

Kane, Marion, B.A.,B.Ed. ✎ 📖

Food Editor, *THE TORONTO STAR*, 1 Yonge St., Toronto, ON M5E 1E5 (416) 869-4853, FAX 869-4410. Born Montreal 1946. d. 2 ch. **EDUC:** Univ. of Alberta, B.A.(Hons., Russian/French) 1968; Univ. of Toronto, B.Ed.(English/French) 1977. **CAREER:** Social Worker, Prov. of Alta., 1968-70; English as a Second Language Teacher, North York Bd. of Educ., 1977-79; freelance writer, 1978-83; Food Ed., *The Toronto Sun*, 1983-89; Food Ed., *The Toronto Star*, 1989 to date. **SELECTED PUBLICATIONS:** *The Enlightened Eater*, co-author; *Best Recipes Under the Sun*. **AFFIL:** American Institute of Wine & Food; International Association of Cooking Professionals; Association of Food Journalists. **HONS:** Food Editor of the Year, Canadian Food Writers Awards, 1985, 1986; Food Columnist of the Year, Canadian Food Writers Award, 1988. **INTERESTS:** exploring all kinds of music; low-key physical exercise; relaxing in Muskoka. **COMMENT:** *"I am one of those lucky people whose work revolves around a favourite pastime: the celebration, enjoyment and sharing of good food."*

Kaplan, Bonnie, B.A.,M.A.,Ph.D. ⊕ ⚛ 🎓

Professor of Pediatrics and Director, Behavioural Research Unit., UNIVERSITY OF

CALGARY, Alberta Children's Hospital Research Centre, 1820 Richmond Rd. S.W., Calgary, AB T2T 5C7 (403) 229-7365, FAX (403) 229-7221, EMAIL bonnie@ach.ucalgary.ca. Born Canton, Ohio 1947. m. Richard Conte. 1 ch. EDUC: Univ. of Chicago, B.A.(Psych.) 1968; Brandeis Univ., M.A.(Psych.) 1971, Ph.D. (Psych.) 1974. CAREER: Assoc. in Research, Dept. of Neurology, Yale Univ. Sch. of Medicine, 1973-74; Adjunct Fac., Div. of Special Studies, Univ. of New Haven, 1976; Research & Educ. Assoc., Neuropsych. Lab., West Haven VA Hospital, 1974-78; Research Assoc., Dept. of Neurology, Yale Univ. Sch. of Medicine, 1974-78; Research Assoc. (Fac. Rank), 1977-78; Assoc. Prof. (Adjunct), Dept. of Psych., Univ. of Calgary, 1979-84; Assoc. Prof. of Pediatrics & Psych., 1984-91; Dir., Behavioural Research Unit, Alberta Children's Hospital Research Centre, 1979 to date; Prof. of Pediatrics & Clinical Psych., Univ. of Calgary, 1991 to date. SELECTED PUBLICATIONS: 51 articles, four book chapters, 36 abstracts & reviews; "Malnutrition and mental deficiency" (*Psychological Bulletin* No. 78 1972); "Are families with reading difficulties at risk for immune disorders and nonrighthandedness?" with others (*Cortex*, vol. 30, 1994); "Subtyping of developmental motor deficits," with D. Dewey (*Developmental Neuropsychology*, vol. 10, 1994); "Use of the Bruininks-Oseretsky Test of Motor Proficiency in Occupational Therapy," with others (*American Journal of Occupational Therapy* vol. 49 1995). AFFIL: Grassroots ACH, Alberta Children's Hospital environmental committee (Chair). HONS: winner, Alberta Emerald Award for environmental work, 1995. INTERESTS: physiological causes & correlates of the developmental disorders. MISC: recipient, numerous research grants; mbr., Prov. Advisory Committee on Health Care Research, 1992 to date; Chair, Joint Faculties Research Ethics Committee, Univ. of Calgary. COMMENT: "*I am fortunate to be in a full-time research position, where I can pursue my interests in determining the causes of learning and attention disorders in children.*"

Kapoor, Manju, B.Sc.,M.Sc.,Ph.D. 🌸 ⚘
Professor, Department of Biological Sciences, UNIVERSITY OF CALGARY, Calgary, AB T2N 1N4 (403) 220-6788, FAX 289-9311, EMAIL mkapoor@acs.ucalgary.ca. Born Ferozepore, India 1937. m. Dr. Michael H. Benn. EDUC: Univ. of Delhi, India, B.Sc.(Botany) 1956, M.Sc.(Botany) 1958; Univ. of Manitoba, Ph.D. (Botany) 1963. CAREER: Research Assoc., Dept. of Biochem., Michigan State Univ., 1962-63; Research Assoc., Dept. of Genetics, Univ. of

Wisconsin, Madison, 1963-64; Asst. Prof., Dept. of Biol., Univ. of Calgary, 1964-69; Assoc. Prof., 1969-75; Prof., 1975 to date. SELECTED PUBLICATIONS: 98 full papers, 2 reports & 68 abstracts, incl.: "Development of thermotolerance in *Neurospora crassa* by heat shock and other stresses eliciting peroxidase induction," with G.M. Sreenivasan, N. Goel & J. Lewis (*Journal of Bacteriology* (172) 1990); "NAD-specific glutamate dehydrogenase of *Neurospora crassa*: cloning, complete nucleotide sequence and gene mapping," with Y. Vijayaraghavan, R. Kadonaga & K.E.A. LaRue (*Biochemistry and Cell Biology* (71) 1993); "Developmentally regulated expression of heat shock genes in *Leptosphaeria maculans*," with N.A. Patterson (*Canadian Journal of Microbiology* (41) 1995). AFFIL: Canadian Society of Microbiologists; Canadian Society for Biochemistry & Molecular Biology; American Society for Microbiology; International Society for Molecular Plant-Microbe Interactions; The Oxygen Society. INTERESTS: regulation of gene expression in filamentous fungi; studies of stress response of eukaryotic microbes; fungal-plant interactions; hiking; photography; travel. COMMENT: "*My initial training was in the field of botany. During the past 30 years, I have conducted research and teaching of undergraduate and graduate courses at the University of Calgary. My research has been supported by the NSERC of Canada. I have served on many administrative and academic committees, supervised several masters and doctoral students and held administrative positions within the department.*"

Kaprielian-Churchill, Isabel, Ph.D. ■ ⚘ 🏛
Visiting Scholar and Kazan Lecturer in Immigration History and Armenian Studies, CALIFORNIA STATE UNIVERSITY AT FRESNO (CSUF), Department of History, 5340 N. Campus Dr., Fresno, CA 93740 (209) 278-2153, FAX 278-2664, EMAIL isabel_kaprielian@csufresno.edu. Born Canada. m. Prof. Stacy Churchill. 3 ch. EDUC: Univ. of Toronto, O.I.S.E., Ph.D. 1984. CAREER: SSHRC Post Doctoral Fellow, Ontario Institute for Studies in Educ./Univ. of Toronto (OISE/UT), 1985-87; Research Assoc., 1989-94; Lecturer & Research Assoc., 1994-96; Kazan Lecturer in Immigration History & Armenian Studies, CSUF, 1996 to date. SELECTED CREDITS: Principal Investigator in prod. a video documentary in Armenian about the experience of Armenian refugee women in Ont., 1987; Principal Investigator in prod. a video documentary, "The Georgetown Boys: Armenian Orphans in Canada," 1987; Principal Investigator in writing & prod. a video doc-

umentary, "Rose's Triumph: The Story of an Armenian Refugee Girl," 1990. **SELECTED PUBLICATIONS:** *Les francophones hors Québec face au pluralisme. Facing Pluralism: The Future of Francophone and Acadian Communities in a Pluralistic Society, with Stacy Churchill* (Ottawa: Fédération des Communautés Francophones et Acadiennes du Canada, 1991); *The Pulse of the World: Refugees in Our Schools*, with Stacy Churchill (Toronto: O.I.S.E. Press, 1994); "Newcomers: The Women" (*Polyphony* Fall/Winter 1982); "Creating and Sustaining an Ethnocultural Heritage in Ontario: The Case of Armenian Women Refugees," in *Looking into My Sister's Eyes: An Exploration in Women's History*, Jean Burnet, ed. (Toronto: Multicultural History Society of Ontario, 1986); "Refugee Women as Domestics: A Documentary Account" (*Canadian Woman Studies Journal* Spring 1989); "Armenian Refugee Women: The Picture Brides: 1920-30" (*Journal of American Ethnic History* Spring 1993); various other publications. **EDIT:** Guest Ed., *Polyphony: Armenians in Ontario*, 1982; Guest Ed., *Canadian Woman Studies Journal*, Special Issue on Refugee Women, Spring 1989. **AFFIL:** Canadian Historical Association; International Council for Canadian Studies; Social Science History Association; Armenian Relief Society; Armenian International Women's Association; Ontario Women's History Network. **HONS:** The Ivey Award; Jewish Council of Women Scholarship; Gold Medal Essay Award for North America, Armenian Youth Federation; Armenian Youth Federation Scholarship; Henry Birks Medal; Marion Porter Prize, Canadian Institute for the Advancement of Women, 1986. **MISC:** various papers read at conferences & meetings.

Kartzmark, Elinor M., B.Sc.,M.Sc., Ph.D. 🎓 ⚛

Professor of Chemistry (retired), UNIVERSITY OF MANITOBA. Born Selkirk, Man. 1926. s. 1 ch. (by adoption) Richard Alan Kartzmark. **EDUC:** Univ. of Manitoba, B.Sc.(Sci.) 1949, M.Sc. (Chem.) 1950, Ph.D.(Chem.) 1952. **CAREER:** teaching & research, Univ. of Manitoba. **SELECTED PUBLICATIONS:** about 50 research papers. **AFFIL:** Altrusa Club of Winnipeg; Chemical Institute of Canada (Fellow). **INTERESTS:** travel; literature; theatre; music. **COMMENT:** *"35-year teaching career at the University of Manitoba, combined with research in physical chemistry."*

Kassie, Lynne, B.A.,LL.L. ⚖

Partner, ROBINSON SHEPPARD SHAPIRO, 800 Place Victoria, Ste. 4700, Montreal, QC H4Z 1H6 (514) 878-2631, FAX 878-1865. **EDUC:** McGill Univ., B.A.(Pol. Sci.) 1972; Univ. de Montréal, LL.L. 1975. **BAR:** Que., 1976. **CAREER:** Attorney & Ptnr, Robinson Sheppard Shapiro, 1976 to date. **SELECTED PUBLICATIONS:** many articles on various legal topics. **AFFIL:** Canadian Bar Association (Dir., Que. Div.); Montreal Bar Association (Sec. 1986-87); Barreau du Québec (Permanent Arbitrator; Dir., Disciplinary Committee); American Association of Lawyers; Association of Family Law Lawyers; Lord Reading Law Society (Pres. 1989-90); Reddy Memorial Hospital (Dir.); Jewish General Hospital Foundation (Dir.); Jewish Rehabilitation Hospital Foundation (Pres. 1991-94); McGill Univ. Graduates' Society (Dir.); McGill Univ. (Advisory Committee). **MISC:** frequent speaker & lecturer for various legal, acctg & professional groups.

Kastner, Kathy, B.A. $ 📺 🍼

Vice-President, Director of Programming, THE PARENT CHANNEL, The Health Television System, 62 Westmount Ave., Toronto, ON M6H 3K1 (416) 656-2402, FAX 654-4068. Born Toronto. m. Marvin Berns. 2 ch. Jessica, Julie. **EDUC:** Univ. of Toronto, B.A. **CAREER:** Copywriter, CityTV; TV Prod., CityTV; Entertainment Reporter/Prod., CityTV; Entertainment Reporter/Prod., CBC TV, 1985-89; Entertainment Reporter/Prod., Global Television Network, 1989-90; Prod. & Marketer of parenting videotapes (*Mom's The Word* series); VP, Dir. of Programming, The Parent Channel. **SELECTED CREDITS:** *You Be Safe*; *EnviroTeam*. **SELECTED PUBLICATIONS:** regular column in *Canadian Family* (multivision publishing); cover story, Thomson Press. **HONS:** Gold Medal for *You Be Safe*, N.Y. Int'l Film & TV Festival; Gold Medal for *You Be Safe*, I.T.V.A. Int'l; Silver Medal for *You Be Safe*, US Int'l Film & Video; Gold Medal for *You Be Safe*, Int'l TV Association Canada, 1993; Finalist for *EnviroTeam*, N.Y. Int'l Film & TV Festival, 1994. **INTERESTS:** yoga. **MISC:** The Parent Channel is the 1st nat'l in-hospital TV network. **COMMENT:** *"My combined skills are key to creating, sustaining and laterally expanding business and marketing concepts. My experiences have enabled me to focus, assess and act upon perceived or created opportunities."*

Katzenberg, Mary Anne, B.A.,M.A., Ph.D. 🎓 ⚛

Professor, Department of Archaeology, UNIVERSITY OF CALGARY, 2500 University Dr. N.W., Calgary, AB T2N 1N4 (403) 220-3334, FAX 282-9567, EMAIL katzenbe@acs.ucalgary.ca. Born Pittsburgh 1952. cl. David Coates. **EDUC:** Univ. of Cincinnati, B.A.

(Anthro.) 1974, M.A.(Anthro.) 1976; Univ. of Toronto, Ph.D.(Phys. Anthro.) 1983. **CAREER:** Asst. Prof., Anthro., Univ. of Toronto, 1983-85; Asst. Prof., Dept. of Archaeology, Univ. of Calgary, 1985-89; Assoc. Prof., 1989-95; Prof., 1995 to date. **SELECTED PUBLICATIONS:** *Chemical analysis of prehistoric human bone from five temporally distinct populations in Southern Ontario* (National Museum of Man, Mercury Series, No. 129, Archaeological Survey of Canada, 1984); *Skeletal Biology of Past Peoples: Research Methods*, ed. with S.R. Saunders (John Wiley & Sons, 1992) also chapter "Advances in stable isotope analysis of prehistoric bones"; "Nitrogen isotope evidence for weaning age in a 19th century Canadian skeletal sample," *Bodies of Evidence: Reconstructing History through Skeletal Analysis*, ed. Anne Grauer (New York: Wiley-Liss, 1995); "Stable isotope evidence for maize horticulture and paleodiet in southern Ontario, Canada," with H.P. Schwarcz, Martin Knyf & F.J. Melbye (*American Antiquity* 60(2) 1995); "Status and diet in precontact highland Ecuador," with D.H. Ubelaker & L.G. Doyen (*American Journal of Anthropology* (97) 1995); numerous articles in refereed journals, chapters in books. **EDIT:** Ed. Bd., American Association of Physical Anthropologists, 1995-98. **AFFIL:** Canadian Association for Physical Anthropology (Pres. 1993-95); American Association of Physical Anthropology; Sigma Xi, The Scientific Research Society (Univ. of Calgary Chapter, Pres. 1990); American Academy for the Advancement of Science; Society for American Archaeology; Society of Archaeological Science. **HONS:** Fulbright Scholarship, 1992. **INTERESTS:** hiking; skiing; classical music; piano. **MISC:** consultant for the Office of the Medical Examiner of Alberta in cases requiring identification of human skeletal remains. **COMMENT:** *"I feel fortunate to work in an active research university where I can have an impact in both teaching and research. My research interests are in reconstructing past human behaviour through the study of skeletal remains. My teaching includes courses on past and present human variation and thus deals with issues of race from a biological perspective. I hope that this information dispels some of the misunderstandings students have about variation."*

Kaufman, Donna Soble, B.C.L., LL.M. ■ ⚖ $

Barrister and Solicitor, Partner, STIKEMAN, ELLIOTT, Commerce Court W., Ste. 5300, Toronto, ON M5L 1B9 (416) 947-0866, FAX 869-5681. Born Toronto 1943. 2 ch. Leslie Ann, David Richard. **EDUC:** McGill Univ., B.C.L. 1984; Univ. de Montréal, LL.M.(Public Law) 1985. **BAR:** Que., 1985. **CAREER:** prod., researched & hosted various shows on CHCH-TV, Toronto-Hamilton, finally, Exec. Dir. of Public Affairs Programming, 1961-68; occasional freelance work for CBC Radio & CJAD, Montreal, 1968-72; Consultant, Commission of Inquiry on Equality in Employment (Abella Commission), 1983-84; Lawyer, Stikeman, Elliott, 1985-89; Ptnr, 1989 to date. **SELECTED CREDITS:** Prod./Host, *Spotlight* (series), CHCH-TV; Co-Prod./Co-Host, *People*, daily public-affairs show, CHCH-TV; Prod./Host, *The Mood of Quebec* (documentary), CHCH-TV. **SELECTED PUBLICATIONS:** *Broadcasting Law in Canada: Fairness in the Administrative Process* (Toronto: Carswell Company, 1987); "Oppression Remedies: Recent Developments," in *Corporate Structure, Finance and Operation*, vol. 3, Lazar Sarna, ed. (Toronto: Carswell Company, 1984); "Fiscal Residence of Corporations in Canada" (*Revue de Droit*, Univ. de Sherbrooke 1984); "Cabinet Action and the CRTC: An Examination of Section 23 of the Broadcasting Act" (*Les Cahiers de Droit*, Univ. Laval 1985); "Judicial Recourse and the CRTC" (*Administrative Law Journal* 1985); "How Exclusive is 'Exclusive'? An Examination of Section 18 of the Federal Court Act" (*Revue de Droit*, Univ. de Sherbrooke 1986). **EDIT:** Ed. Bd., *McGill Law Journal*, 1983-84; Ed. Bd., *Canadian Competition Record*. **DIRECTOR:** TransAlta Corporation; Southam Inc. **AFFIL:** The CRB Foundation (Dir.); International Development Research Centre (Bd. of Gov.); Canadian Bar Association (Chair, Int'l Competition & Trade Committee, Nat'l Competition Law Section); Bar of Quebec; American Bar Association. **HONS:** Canadian Association of Broadcasters Award, Best documentary about Que. by an English station (*The Mood of Quebec*); Fac. Scholar, McGill Univ., 1983-84; Award of Distinction for outstanding contribution to the world of bus. & the community, Fac. of Commerce & Admin., Concordia Univ., 1995.

Kaufman, Helena, B.A. 📖 📺 🎭

Director, *RETHINK: THE ECO-LOGICAL FAIR*/HLK COMMUNICATIONS, 938 Campbell St., Winnipeg, MB R3N 1C7 (204) 488-6141, FAX 488-6140. Born Poland 1955. s. 2 ch. **EDUC:** Univ. of Winnipeg, B.A. 1973; Red River Community Coll., Media Technician Certificate 1980. **CAREER:** professional writer; Principal, HLK Communications, 1982 to date; Dir., *Rethink: The Eco-Logical Fair*, 1992 to date. **SELECTED PUBLICATIONS:** more than 200 original pieces in print. **AFFIL:** Manitoba Writers' Guild; Winnipeg Chamber of Commerce; Canada Trust Friends of the Environment Fund, Manitoba Branch (Bd. Mbr.). HONS: awards for publications produced for clients. INTERESTS: racquet sports; cycling; reading; travel; language study; hearing the stories of people (professional & personal, a vocation!). COMMENT: *"Produces events serving the interests of environment and economy."*

Kaufman, Miriam, B.Sc.N.,M.D., F.R.C.P.(C) ■ ⊕
Physician and Medical Director, Complex Adult Problem Program, Division of Adolescent Medicine, THE HOSPITAL FOR SICK CHILDREN, 555 University Ave., Toronto, ON M5G 1X8 (416) 813-6657, FAX 813-5392, EMAIL miriam.kaufman@mailhub.sickkids.on.ca. Assistant Professor, Department of Paediatrics, UNIVERSITY OF TORONTO. Born Cleveland 1954. life partner Roberta Benson. 2 ch. Jacob Benson Kaufman, Aviva Rose Benson Kaufman. EDUC: Duke Univ., B.Sc.N. 1976; Queen's Univ., M.D. 1980. CAREER: Gen. Duty Nurse, Kingston General Hospital, 1976-80; Resident, Gen. Paediatrics, McMaster Univ. Medical Centre, 1980-82; Post Core Resident, Gen. Paediatrics, Hospital for Sick Children, 1982-83; Fellow, Div. of Adolescent Medicine, 1983-84; Sessional Physician, "The House" Planned Parenthood Clinic, 1984; Sessional Physician, Hassle Free Clinic, 1984-86; Medical Dir., Tots of Teens Program, Div. of Adolescent Medicine, Hospital for Sick Children, 1985-93; Active Staff Physician, 1985 to date; Asst. Prof., Dept. of Paediatrics, Univ. of Toronto, 1985 to date; Medical Dir., Adolescent Sexual Abuse/Assault Program, 1987-95. SELECTED PUBLICATIONS: *All Shapes and Sizes: Promoting Fitness and Self Esteem in Your Overweight Child*, with T. Pitman (HarperCollins Canada, 1994); *Easy for You to Say: Q's and A's for Teens Living with Chronic Illness and Disability* (Key Porter, 1995); "Menstrual Dysfunction" *(Paediatric Medicine Quarterly* 2(1) 1988); "Answering Parents' Questions about Homosexuality" *(Canadian Family Physician* 1991); "Discussing Sexuality with the Adolescent" *(Canadian Journal of Ob/Gyn and Women's Health Care* 4(3) 1992); "The Impact of the Ontario Consent to Treatment Act on Adolescent Health Care" *(Health Law in Canada* 15(2) 1994); "Recent Advances in the Diagnosis and Treatment of Some Chronic Illnesses Affecting Adolescents," in *Bailliere's Clinical Paediatrics*, R. Tonkin, ed. (1994). EDIT: Ed., Adolescent Section, *Canadian Journal of Ob/Gyn and Women's Health Care*, 1992. AFFIL: Royal Coll. of Physicians & Surgeons of Canada (Fellow); Coll. of Physicians & Surgeons of Ontario; Society for Adolescent Medicine; Canadian Paediatric Society (Chair,

Adolescent Medicine Committee); North American Society for Paediatric & Adolescent Gynaecology; Hassle Free Clinic (Bd. of Dir. 1987 to date); Karma Food Cooperative; Coalition for Services for Lesbian & Gay Youth; Coroner's Council (Gov't Appointee). HONS: Charles T. Fried Lecturer, Edmonton, 1993. INTERESTS: Claus Wirsig Humanitarian Award, HSC Foundation, 1996. MISC: "The Effects of War on Children," *W5*, CTV (Mar. 1991); listed in *Canadian Who's Who* & *Best Doctors in America*; grant recipient; numerous presentations & lectures; numerous media appearances. COMMENT: *"Miriam Kaufman's major work is in the field of public education regarding adolescent issues, with frequent television, radio and print media interviews. Her major interests are chronic illness and disability, body image, sexuality and teen parenting."*

Kavanagh, Els ■ ○ ⊛
Member of the Board, CARE CANADA, 6 Antares Dr., Ottawa, ON K1G 4X6 (613) 228-5602, FAX 226-5777. Born Amsterdam 1938. m. Kevin P. Kavanagh. 2 ch. EDUC: Fons Vitae, Amsterdam. VOLUNTEER CAREER: Chair, Manitoba Arts Council; Chair, Manitoba Historical Record Society; Trustee, St. John's Catholic Sch., Denver, Col.; Pres., Canada for Manitoba, Co-Host, *Holland Calling*, Channel 11 TV; Prod. & Host, Historical Program; former Chair & Mbr. of the Bd., CARE Canada; Past Pres., Canadian Club of Winnipeg (Men's); V-Chair, St. Boniface General Hospital. AFFIL: Canadian Museum of Nature; Manitoba Museum of Man & Nature (Capital Campaign); Local Action Committee "Imagine." INTERESTS: golf; tennis; boating; collecting sculptures.

Kealey, Linda, B.A.,B.L.S.,M.A., Ph.D. ⊛ ▨
Associate Professor of History, MEMORIAL UNIVERSITY OF NEWFOUNDLAND, St. John's, NF A1C 5S7 (709) 737-8420, FAX 737-2164. Born Rochester 1947. m. Gregory S. Kealey. 1 ch. EDUC: Univ. of Toronto, B.A.(Soc.) 1969, B.L.S. 1970, M.A.(Hist.) 1974, Ph.D.(Hist.) 1982. CAREER: Visiting Asst. Prof., Memorial Univ. of Newfoundland, 1980-81; Asst. Prof., 1981-86; Assoc. Prof., 1986 to date; Head, Dept. of Hist.,1994 to date; Co-Ed., *Canadian Historical Review*, 1994 to date. SELECTED PUBLICATIONS: *A Not Unreasonable Claim: Women and Reform in Canada, 1880s-1920s* , Ed. (Toronto: Canadian Women's Educational Press, 1979); *Beyond the Vote: Canadian Women and Politics*, Co-ed. with Joan Sangster & author of one chapter (Toronto: Univ. of Toronto Press, 1989); *Pursuing Equality: His-*

torical *Perspectives on Women in Newfoundland and Labrador* , Ed. & author of intro. (St. John's: ISER Books, 1993); "Canadian Socialism and the Woman Question 1900-14" (*Labour/Le Travail* Spring 1984); "Women and Labour During World War I: Women Workers and the Minimum Wage in Manitoba" in *First Days, Fighting Days*, ed. Mary Kinnear (Regina: Canadian Plains Research Centre, 1987); "The Status of Women in the Historical Profession in Canada, 1989 Survey" (*Canadian Historical Review* Sept. 1991); *Canadian Historical Review*, Ed., Special Issue on Women's History Dec. 1991; Ed./Compiler, *Newsletter, Women's History Month Issue*, Oct. 1992, Women's Policy Office, Gov't of Newfoundland & Labrador; various other publications. **AFFIL:** Royal Historical Society (Fellow); Canadian Historical Association; Canadian Women's Studies Association; Canadian Research Institute for the Advancement of Women; *Canadian Historical Review* (Bd. Mbr. & Chair); Atlantis (Advisory Bd.). **INTERESTS:** detective fiction; aerobics. **MISC:** Bd. mbr., Conference of Historical Journals; numerous lectures at nat'l & int'l conferences; recipient, numerous grants.

Keane, Kerrie, B.A. 🔲 ⊗ 🏛
President, WISHBONE PRODUCTIONS INC., 4400 Coldwater Canyon Ave., Ste. 110, Studio City, CA 91604 (818) 508-9244, FAX 760-7482. Born Toronto. m. **EDUC:** McMaster Univ., B.A.(Hist.) 1970. **CAREER:** actor, dir., writer. **SELECTED CREDITS:** Lead, *Distant Thunder* (feature), Paramount; Lead, support, *Steel* (feature), Warner Bros.; *Obsessed* (feature), Telescene Productions; Lead, *Divided We Stand* (TV), ABC; Lead, *Degree of Deception* (TV), NBC; Lead, *Dirty Work* (TV), CBS; Principal, *Mistress* (TV), CBS; Principal, *A Death in California* (TV), Lead, *Hot Pursuit* (series), NBC; Lead, *Studio 5B* (series), ABC; Lead, *The Yellow Rose* (series), ABC; recurring character, *Beverly Hills 90210* (series) FOX; *The Baby Dance* (theatre), San Jose Repertory; *Talley's Folley*, Theatre Plus, Toronto; *Rashomon*, Citadel Theatre, Edmonton; *By George* (musical review), The Royal Alex, Toronto. **AFFIL:** Academy of Canadian Cinema & Television (Chair, LA 1992); Gene Bua Theatre, L.A. (Assoc. Artistic Dir. 1992-95). **HONS:** nominee, Best Actress (*Obsessed*), Genie Awards, 1988. **COMMENT:** "*I have been lucky enough to earn my living as an actress for over 20 years. My move to Los Angeles 12 years ago afforded me a larger arena–working regular roles on three series, numerous movies of the week for television and creating challenging roles in feature films. During that time I have*

produced, directed and written for theatre and now endeavour to take the skills I've learned into the production of feature films.*"

Keating, Diane, B.A. 🔲 ⊗ 🏛
Vice-President, KEATING EDUCATIONAL TOURS, 240 Richmond St., Toronto, ON M5V 1V6 (416) 974-9600, FAX 974-9320. Born Winnipeg 1943. m. Christopher. 2 ch. Stephanie, Justin. **EDUC:** Univ. of Manitoba, B.A. (English) 1964. **CAREER:** VP, Keating Educational Tours. **SELECTED PUBLICATIONS:** *In Dark Places* (1978); *No Birds or Flowers* (1982); *The Optic Heart* (1984); numerous poems in anthologies. **AFFIL:** League of Canadian Poets. **HONS:** nominated for Gov. General's Award, 1982; nominated for Journey Prize, 1991. **INTERESTS:** reading; walking; thinking. **COMMENT:** "*I am a mother and a poet who works part-time as a wife and businesswoman. I have published three volumes of poetry and have completed writing a novel.*"

Keating, Lulu 🏛 ⊗ 🔲
President, RED SNAPPER FILMS LIMITED, 2125 Brunswick St., Halifax, NS B3K 2Y4 (902) 422-2427, FAX 492-2125. Born Antigonish, N.S. 1952. 1 ch. **EDUC:** Vancouver Sch. of Art, Fine Arts Diploma; Ryerson Polytechnic Univ., Film Studies Program 1976-77. **SELECTED CREDITS:** Co-Writer/Dir./Ed., *City Survival*, 1983; Dir./Ed., *Funny Things People Can Do To Themselves*, Red Snapper Films Ltd., 1984; Dir., *Rita MacNeil in Japan*, 1985; Researcher/Writer/Co-Dir., *Enterprising Women*, National Film Bd., 1987; Writer/Dir., *The Midday Sun* (feature), 1989; Dir., *Serendipity*, Atlantic Filmmakers' Cooperative Workshop Production, 1991; Dir./Co-Prod., *Ann and Maddy* (short film), 1992; Dir., *Come On In: Women's Centres in Nova Scotia*, 1994; Co-writer with Bryden MacDonald, *Panther's Moon*, feature secreenplay completed summer 1996; Winn, *John and the Missus*, dir. Gordon Pinsent, 1986; Principal, *The Housewife*, dir. Mark Curry, 1994; several other plays, skits, emcee performances; numerous dramatic, animated & documentary shorts, 1980-91. **SELECTED PUBLICATIONS:** "Paul Wong Can't Be All Wrong" (*Parallelogram* 1981); "The Independent Film Groups" (*Journal of Canadian Studies* 1981); "Lessons from an African Episode" (*Pottersfield Portfolio* 1987). **AFFIL:** Linda Joy Media Arts Society (Past Pres.); Academy of Canadian Film & Television; Writers' Federation of N.S.; Atlantic Filmmakers' Co-op; N.S. Film & Video Producers Association. **HONS:** numerous theatre & film awards; "Through Her Eyes," 4-hr. retrospective, WTN, 1995; Pioneer Award, CBC, 1995.

MISC: teaching experience, Film Production, Summer Enrichment Program, Oxford, UK, July 3-29, 1995. COMMENT: "*Lulu Keating is a director and screenwriter. Since 1980 she has been making films and videos, based in Nova Scotia but shooting in places such as Japan and Zimbabwe. Her production company has been in existence since 1983–Red Snapper Films Limited.*"

Keeler, Helen / ▯
Senior Editor, CANADIAN LIVING MAGAZINE, 25 Sheppard Ave. W., Toronto, ON M6C 1N2 (416) 733-7600, ext. 4441, FAX 733-3398. Born 1947. m. John Lavin. 2 ch. SELECTED PUBLICATIONS: articles for *Financial Post*; *Flare*; *Chatelaine*; *Your Baby*; *Investment Executive*; *Financial Post* Magazine. INTERESTS: fitness; health; finance; parenting; psychology; current affairs. COMMENT: "*I've spent 18 years as a writer and editor, for and with consumer magazines and business publications. I strive to serve the reader with the best information, in the most interesting manner.*"

Keeling, Nora, B.A.,M.A. ▯ ⊗
Author. London, ON. Born Owen Sound, Ont. 1933. m. Graham Ward Hall. 1 ch. James Graham Hall. EDUC: Royal Academy of Dramatic Art, London, UK, 1954; Univ. of Western Ontario, B.A. 1964, M.A. 1965. CAREER: various acting roles, Paris, France, 1956-61; Lecturer, French, Univ. of Western Ontario, 1966-71; Instructor, French & English, Fanshawe Coll., 1975-80. SELECTED PUBLICATIONS: *The Driver*, short stories & novella (1982); *chasing her own tail*, short stories (1985); *A Fine and Quiet Place*, short stories (1991); short fiction published in various anthologies; *London and Area Crime: Painful World*, non-fiction work in progress. COLLECTIONS: painting exhibition, Piccadilly Circus Gallery, London, UK, 1956. HONS: Best Actress Award, OSCVI, Owen Sound, *The Heiress*, 1951; CNE Girls' Public Speaking Championship, 1951; Chautauqua Scholarship, NY, Summer 1950; Bd. of Governors' Gold Medal in French Language & Lit., Univ. of Western Ontario, 1963; Best Actress Award, Dominion Drama Festival, Montreal, *Medea*, 1962. INTERESTS: nonfiction reading; legal procedure & the justice system in Canada; medical technology & admin.; police recruitment & procedure; architecture & real estate; bus. corporations & mgmt in S.W. Ont.; journalism; broadcasting & movie production; mun., prov. & fed. governments in Canada; photography; collecting fine art; antique furniture. MISC: recipient, various grants; research & personal papers deposited to Queen's Univ.

Archives, 1991, 1994. COMMENT: "*I am currently completing a work of non-fiction entitled London and Area Crime. My research papers are extensive. Due to the controversial nature of the subject, and difficulties with research assistants and funding, the work is progressing more slowly than anticipated.*"

Keeping, Lia $
Vice-President and Director of Sales, WEEKENDER LADIES WEAR, 29 E. Wilmot St., Richmond Hill, ON L5N 3V8 (905) 886-5990, FAX 886-0630. Born Toronto 1953. m. Gregg Keeping. 2 ch. Lyndsay, Ryan. CAREER: Customer Svc., Air Canada; Weekender Ladies Wear, 1985 to date; Sales Mgr, 1986; Sr. Sales Mgr, 1987; Exec. Sales Mgr, 1989; Nat'l Sales Mgr, 1990-93; VP & Dir. of Sales, 1993 to date. HONS: 1st Weekenders Million Dollar Sales Mgr (worldwide), 1988; 1st Three Million Dollars Sales Mgr (worldwide), 1989; No. 1 Sales Mgr, Weekender Canada, 1988, 1989, 1990; Mbr. of the Top Ten Sales Managers Club, 1987-93. INTERESTS: golf; travel; reading; photography. MISC: 1st Weekenders Exec. Sales Mgr (worldwide), 1989-90; 1st Weekenders Nat'l Sales Mgr (worldwide), 1990-93. COMMENT: "*I started my career with Weekenders like many other women to work around my full-time job and to spend more time with my young family. I soon realized the potential Weekenders offered and made Weekenders my full-time career. With hard work, determination and a desire to succeed, I worked my way to the top of the Weekenders sales organization and was promoted to corporate head office in 1993. I am now responsible for a sales force in excess of 5,000 and have increased revenues by 100% since joining the head office team in 1993.*"

Kehoe, Carol A., B.A.,M.A. ■ ⬚ / $
Internet Services Manager, BLACKBURN MEDIA GROUP, 369 York St., London, ON N6B 3M2 (519) 679-1111. Born Windsor, Ont. 1959. m. Gregory K.G. Clark. 1 ch. EDUC: Univ. of Western Ontario, B.A.(English Language & Lit.) 1982, M.A.(Journalism) 1984. CAREER: Copy Ed., *Regina Leader-Post*, 1984-85; Assoc. Ed., *City Woman* Magazine, 1985-86; Sr. Ed., *Your Money* Magazine, 1986-87; Copy Ed., *Encounter*, 1987-88; Ed., 1988-89; Supervisor, Specialty Publications, *London Free Press*, 1990-94; Gen. Mgr, Blackburn Magazine Group, 1994-96; Adjunct Prof., Univ. of Western Ontario Sch. of Journalism, 1994 to date. AFFIL: London Regional Art & Historical Museum (Dir.; Pres., Volunteer Committee 1994-96). HONS: winner, 1 of the 10 best advtg ideas (*Indoors* Magazine), Int'l Newspa-

per & Marketing Executives, 1992; winner, best special section by a multi-advertiser (*Indoors* Magazine), Newspaper Advertising Executives' Association, 1992; Certificate of Merit, best special section ("Home for the Holidays"), Newspaper Advertising Executives' Association, 1991.

Keillor, Elaine, A.R.C.T.,B.A.,M.A., Ph.D. ⌘ ⊗ ♧

Concert pianist, chamber musician, harpsichordist. Professor, School for Studies in Art and Culture–Music, CARLETON UNIVERSITY, 1125 Colonel By Dr., Ottawa, ON K1S 5B6 (613) 520-2600, ext. 3732, FAX 520-3905, EMAIL elaine_keillor@carleton.ca. Born London, Ont. 1939. m. Vernon McCaw. EDUC: Royal Conservatory of Music, Toronto, A.R.C.T.(Piano Performance) 1951; Univ. of Toronto, B.A.(Music) 1970, M.A.(Musicology) 1971, Ph.D. 1976. CAREER: Lecturer, York Univ., 1975-76; Instructor, Queen's Univ., 1976-77; Asst. Prof., Carleton Univ., 1977-82; Assoc. Prof., 1982-95; Visiting Prof., McMaster Univ., 1984; Prof., Carleton Univ., 1995 to date. SELECTED CREDITS: series of 4 piano recitals on CJSH-FM, 1951; soloist with Bayreuth Festival Orchestra, Germany, & Brantford Symphony Orchestra, piano solo recitals in Britain, Germany & more than 50 throughout Canada, 1959-60; solo recitals in Toronto, Hamilton, & on CBC-TV, soloist with Kitchener-Waterloo Symphony Orchestra, 1960-61; solo, duo performances with Christina Petrowska & chamber music groups mainly in Ottawa & Toronto area, but also solo recitals in Quebec, Montreal, Winnipeg & N.Y. (Sept. 28, 1984); many broadcasts on CBC Radio & TVOntario; National Gallery Sunday Afternoon Series, Nov. 8, 1992; recital of piano compositions in honour of the Year of Indigenous Peoples, Oct. 8, 1993; Viennese Piano Music, Ottawa, Jan. 5, 1996; numerous other recitals. SELECTED PUBLICATIONS: *Piano Music I*, ed. (Ottawa: The Canadian Musical Heritage/Le patrimoine musical canadienne, 1983); *Piano Music II*, ed. (Ottawa: The Canadian Musical Heritage/Le patrimoine musical canadienne, 1986); *Music for Orchestra II*, ed. (Ottawa: The Canadian Musical Heritage/Le patrimoine musical canadienne, 1994); *John Weinzweig and His Music: The Radical Romantic of Canada* (Metuchen, NJ: Scarecrow Press, 1994); *Music for Orchestra III*, ed. (Ottawa: The Canadian Musical Heritage/Le patrimoine musical canadienne, 1995); "Suites for Wind and Keyboard of the Early Classical Period" (*Winds Quarterly* Apr. 1981); "The Role of Dogrib Youth in the Continuation of Their Musical Traditions" (*Yearbook for Tra-*

ditional Music 1986); "La naissance d'un genre musical nouveau, fusion du traditional et du 'country'" (*Recherches amerindiennes au québec* hiver 1988-89); "Finding the Sounds of Canada's Musical Past" (*Fontes artis musicae* 1994); "The Emergence of Postcolonial Musical Expressions of Aboriginal Peoples Within Canada" (*Cultural Studies* 9(1) 1995); "Indigenous Music as a Compositional Source" in *Taking a Stand: Essays in Honour of John Beckwith*, ed. T. McGee (1995); numerous encyclopedia articles; various other publications. AFFIL: Canadian Musical Heritage Society (V-Chair); American Musicology Society; International Musicological Society; Society for Ethnomusicology (Council Mbr.); Canadian University Music Society (Rep. HSSFC); Association for Canadian Studies; International Council for Traditional Music; Canadian Society for Traditional Music; Association pour l'avancement de la recherche en musique du Québec. HONS: Chappell Medal, 1958; Merit Award, Fac. of Arts, Carleton Univ., 1981. INTERESTS: First Nations Music in Canada, particularly that of the Dene; Cdn concert music of the last 200 yrs.; piano music of the 19th & 20th centuries; gender issues in musicology. MISC: youngest A.R.C.T. ever awarded. COMMENT: *"My aim is to encourage as many as possible to participate in, relish and learn about the rich array of musical traditions that we have, particularly in Canada."*

Keith, Mildred J. ■■ ☺ ⚘

President Elect, FEDERATED WOMEN'S INSTITUTES OF CANADA (voluntary rural women's organization), R.R. #1, Havelock, NB E0A 1W0 (506) 534-2437, FAX 534-2437. Born Kinnear Sett., N.B. 1937. m. Ralph D. Keith. 4 ch. Martin (deceased), Stephen, Vance, Jonathan. EDUC: Petitcodiac Regional High Sch., 1955. SELECTED PUBLICATIONS: as Chair of the Rural Child Care Committee of F.W.I.C., was co-author of report based on survey of 3500 rural families. AFFIL: Federated Women's Institutes of Canada (Pres. Elect 1994-97; Pres. 1997-2000; Chair, Rural Child Care Committee); Associated Country Women of the World (Council mbr. 1994-2000); Maritime Agriculture Shows Corporation (former Dir.); Women's Institute Home for Senior Ladies (former Chair); Adelaide Hoodless Homestead Museum, St. George, Ont. (Bd. mbr.); local Library Bd. (mbr.). INTERESTS: agriculture; family life; gardening; reading; crafts. MISC: made presentations to Standing Committee on the Meech Lake Accord (on nat'l unity), & to National Committee on Social Reform (on rural child care & child poverty). COMMENT: *"I was president of the New*

Brunswick Women's Institute, 1987-1990. Council member of Associated Country Women of the World, attended world conferences in Kilarney (Ireland), Kansas City (U.S.), The Hague (Netherlands), and Christ Church (New Zealand), where I made Canada's presentation on the "Year of the Family" with emphasis on child poverty."

Keller, Betty, B.A. 📖 ⊗ ⋖

Writer. R.R. 1, Sandy Hook, C-23, Sechelt, BC V0N 3A0 (604) 885-3589. Born Vancouver 1930. d. 2 ch. Christopher Philip Keller, Perry Neil Keller. **EDUC:** Univ. of British Columbia, B.A.(English) 1967. **CAREER:** teacher, Drama & English, secondary sch., 1962-74; teacher, Creative Drama, Holiday Theatre, Vancouver, 1967-71; Fac. Assoc., Fac. of Educ., Simon Fraser Univ., 1975-76, 1978; teacher, Numan Women's Teachers' Coll., Gongola State, Nigeria, 1977-78; Sessional Lecturer, Creative Writing Dept., Univ. of British Columbia, Winter 1981-82, Summer 1985. **VOLUNTEER CAREER:** Founder & Chair, West Kootenay High Schools Drama Festivals, 1965-67; Chair, B.C. High Schools Drama Conference & Festival, 1977; Co-Chair, Canadian Child & Youth Drama Association Conference, 1979; Founder & First Pres., SunCoast Writers' Forge (Sunshine Coast writers' ntwk), 1983-85; Founder & Prod., Sunshine Coast Festival of the Written Arts, 1983-94. **SELECTED PUBLICATIONS:** *Trick Doors and Other Dramatic Sketches*, 14 short plays, used as a course book for Grades 11 & 12 Acting in B.C. schools from 1975-84 (November House, 1974); *Taking Off*, a handbook for secondary school teachers of creative drama (November House, 1975); *Opening Trick Doors*, a guide for teachers & directors using *Trick Doors and Other Dramatic Sketches* (November House, 1975); *Legends of the River People*, co-author Norman Lerman (November House, 1976); *Pauline: A Biography of Pauline Johnson* (Douglas & McIntyre, 1982); *Black Wolf: The Life of Ernest Thompson Seton* (Canada: Douglas & McIntyre, 1984; US: Salem House, 1984); *On The Shady Side: Vancouver 1886-1914* (Horsdal & Schubart, 1986); *Improvisation and Performance* (Colorado Springs, Col.: Merriwether Publishing and Contemporary Drama Service, 1988), a combination of *Trick Doors and Other Dramatic Sketches, Opening Trick Doors & Taking Off* in a single volume for high sch., coll. & amateur theatre trade in the US, UK, New Zealand, Australia & Canada; *Sea Silver: Inside British Columbia's Salmon-Farming Industry*, with Rosella M. Leslie (Horsdal & Schubart, 1996); *Bright Seas, Pioneer Spirits: The Sunshine Coast*, with Rosella

M. Leslie (Hosdale & Schubart, 1996); various magazine articles incl. "The Sechelt Hotel" (*The Sunshine Coast Journal*, June 1990); "Llama Lady: A Profile of Maggie Kreiger" (*B.C. Woman*, Sept. 1995); "Fire and Water: A Profile of Charmain Johnson" (*B.C. Woman*, Oct. 1995); "Game Over," short story (*Matrix*, Oct. 1987). **AFFIL:** B.C. Arts Board, Cultural Services Branch (Festival Advisory Committee 1993-94). **HONS:** The Canadian Biography Medal (*Pauline: A Biography of Pauline Johnson*), Canadian Literature, 1982; Gillian Lowndes Memorial Award for contributions to the cultural life of the Sunshine Coast, 1985; The Lescarbot Award in recognition of outstanding contributions to reg'l cultural activities, Communications Canada, 1991; Canada 125 Medal, 1992; the Talewind Book Award for literary contributions, 1996. **MISC:** recipient, various grants; acts as literary agent for a number of West Coast authors; provides mentorship for a total of 10 up-and-coming writers.

Kells, Catherine, M.D.,F.R.C.P.(C), F.A.C.C. ⊕ ⋖

Associate Professor, Department of Medicine, Division of Cardiology, Dalhousie University, VICTORIA GENERAL HOSPITAL, 1278 Tower Rd., A.C.C. Rm. 3055, Halifax, NS B3H 2Y9 (902) 428-7044, FAX 428-2271, EMAIL catherine. kells@dal.ca. Born Halifax 1960. m. David Kells. 1 ch. **EDUC:** Univ. Laval, French Immersion 1978; Dalhousie Univ., M.D. 1984. **CAREER:** Medical Asst., Cdn Armed Forces, Naval Reserves, 1977-84; Lt. (Medical Officer), 1984-89; Intern, Dalhousie Univ., 1984-85; Internal Medicine Resident, 1985-88; Cardiology Resident, 1987-89; Chief Resident, Cardiology, 1988-89; Postgrad. Fellow (Invasive Cardiology), 1989-90; Postgrad. Fellow in Cardiology (Heart Transplantation), Stanford Univ., 1990; Dir., Adult Congenital Heart Clinic, Victoria General Hospital, 1990 to date; Consultant Cardiologist, Izaak Walton Killam Hospital for Children & Grace Maternity Hospital, 1990 to date; Staff Cardiologist, Victoria General Hospital, 1990-95; Asst. Prof., Dept. of Medicine, Div. of Cardiology, Dalhousie, 1990-95; Dir., Coronary Care Unit, Victoria General Hospital, 1994 to date; Medical Dir., Cardiac Transplantation Program, 1995 to date; Assoc. Prof., Dept. of Medicine, Div. of Cardiology, Dalhousie Univ., 1995 to date. **SELECTED PUBLICATIONS:** "Evolving Acute Myocardial Infarction: Update in Therapy" (*Canadian Journal of CME* Jan./Feb. 1992); "Does the Speed of Balloon Deflation Affect the Complication Rate of Coronary Angioplasty?" (*American Journal of Cardiology* 73 1994); "Comparison of Fixed-Wire and Over-the-Wire Balloon Dilation Systems for Percutaneous Transluminal Coronary Angioplasty," with B.J. O'Neill *et al* (*American Journal of Cardiology* 73 1994); various other publications. **AFFIL:** N.S. Medical Society; Canadian Medical Association; N.S. Internal Medicine Society; Canadian Cardiovascular Society; Royal Coll. of Physicians & Surgeons of Canada (Fellow); American Coll. of Cardiology (Fellow); Maritime Heart Centre; Canadian Association of Interventional Cardiology; Society for Cardiac Angiography & Intervention; Canadian Adult Congenital Heart Network (Exec. Mbr.); International Society of Transplantation; Medical Research Council of Canada (Special Committee on Research & Women's Health Issues); Canadian Ski Patrol (Medical Advisor, Safety Committee). **HONS:** Entrance Scholarship, Dalhousie Univ., 1978; Resident's Research Award, Dalhousie Univ., 1988; Killam Postgrad. Scholarship, Dalhousie Univ., 1989. **MISC:** Mbr., Royal Coll. of Physicians & Surgeons of Canada Examination Bd.–Cardiology, 1994 to date; Steering Committee Mbr. & Reg'l Coord., Canadian Cardiovascular Collaboration Trials, CORE & OASIS, McMaster Univ., 1993 to date; recipient, various grants; various invited lectures.

Kells, Virginia C., APR ■ 📖 $

President, **VIPR COMMUNICATIONS**, 110 The Esplanade, Ste. 619, Toronto, ON M5E 1X9 (416) 777-9317. Born Toronto. **CAREER:** Exec. Dir., Performing Arts Lodges of Canada; Mktg Dir./Ed., Toronto Real Estate Bd.; Comm. Mgr, Tip Top Tailors; Advtg & Public Rel'ns Dir., Kuhl Construction Co.; Advtg & Public Rel'ns Dir., Unitrex of Canada Ltd.; Assoc. Ed., *Drug Merchandising* magazine; Ed., *Beauty Merchandising*; Ed., *Toronto Real Estate*; Pres., VIPR Communications, 1976 to date. **DIRECTOR:** Consort Communications Inc. **AFFIL:** Canadian Public Relations Society Inc. (Nat'l Chrm, Consultants' Institute 1983-86; Pres., Toronto 1984-85); *Who's Who International* (Exec. Gov. 1987-90); Toronto Press Club (Pres.). **HONS:** National Award of Excellence, Canadian Public Relations Society; Kenneth R. Wilson Editorial Award. **INTERESTS:** literature; music; theatre; art; sailing. **MISC:** 1st woman elected Nat'l Chair, Consultants Institute, Canadian Public Relations Society. **COMMENT:** "*Virginia Kells is a former journalist and business paper editor, with an extensive background in all aspects of communications, including public and government relations, advertising, and marketing. She established her own independent consulting firm in 1976 to provide total communications services and counsel.*"

Kelly, Gemey, B.A.,B.F.A. 📜 ✪ 🎓

Director and Curator, **OWENS ART GALLERY**, Mount Allison University, Sackville, NB E0A 3C0 (506) 364-2574, FAX 364-2575. Born Toronto 1948. m. D. John Murchie. **EDUC:** Univ. of Toronto, B.A.(English) 1972; Nova Scotia Coll. of Art & Design, B.F.A.(Fine Art) 1979. **CAREER:** Curator, Dalhousie Art Gallery, 1979-89; Lecturer, Dept. of Fine Arts, Mount Allison Univ., 1989 to date; Dir. & Curator, Owens Art Gallery, 1989 to date. **SELECTED PUBLICATIONS:** exhibition catalogues: *Arthur Lismer: Nova Scotia, 1916-1919*; *Rockwell Kent: The Newfoundland Work*; *J.E.H. MacDonald, Lewis and Edith Smith in Nova Scotia*; *Alex Colville, Selected Drawings*. **AFFIL:** Canadian Art Museums Directors' Organization; Atlantic Provinces Art Galleries Association (Past Pres.); Association of University Art Galleries; Canada Council (Arts Advisory Committee 1986-89). **MISC:** art critic & reviewer, CBC Radio's *Artsnational* (1980-81), & *ArtsAtlantic* & *Vanguard* magazines; served on Canada Council exhibition juries, 1984, 1986, 1991 & 1995.

Kelly, Nora Hickson, A.T.C.M. 📖 📜 ✏

Author. 2079 Woodcrest Rd., Ottawa, ON K1H 6H9 (613) 733-1700. Born Burton-on-Trent, Staffordshire, UK 1910. m. William Henry Kelly. **EDUC:** public & high sch. in N. Battleford, Sask.; First Class Teacher's Diploma; Certificate ATCM, Theory Harmony & Teaching Piano, Hist. of Music & Counterpoint. **CAREER:** taught public sch. in rural & urban Sask., 9 yrs. **SELECTED PUBLICATIONS:** *Highroads to Singing*, children's songs (School Publications Co., 1939); *The Men of the Mounted* (Dent., 1949); *The Royal Canadian Mounted Police–A Century of History*, co-author (Hurtig Publications, 1973); *Policing in Canada*, co-author (Macmillan of Canada, 1976); *The Horses of the Royal Canadian Mounted Police–A Pictorial History*, co-author (Doubleday, 1984); various children's plays & songs; school-help books in health, citizenship; operettas; shadow plays; presch. "Look and Learn"; teachers' manuals in literature; articles in *Maclean's*, *Red Cross Junior Magazine*, *Canadian Geographic* & trade journals. **AFFIL:** National Association for the Advancement of Coloured People (Life Mbr.); Voluntary Euthanasia Society (EXIT) of Great Britain (Life Mbr.); Rationalist Press Association, UK (Life Mbr.). **INTERESTS:** music; theatre. **MISC:** various talks for the CBC.

Kelly, Patricia ✊ ⊕ ♡

Breast Cancer Activist and President, **PISCES** (Partnering in Self-help Community Education and Support), 2021 Lakeshore Rd., Ste. 108, Burlington, ON L3R 1A2 (905) 637-2840, FAX 637-8536. Born Toronto 1952. d. 2 ch. EDUC: McMaster Univ., Fac. of Social Sci., 1991-95; York Univ., Voluntary Sector Mgmt Program 1995. CAREER: Research Technologist, reporting to Dr. John Kelton, Chief of Medicine, Chedoke-McMaster Hospitals, McMaster Univ., 1980-94; Project Coord., Halton Women's Self-Health Proj., 1990-91; Proj. Coord., The Ont. Breast Cancer Support Ntwk Proj., 1993-95; Founder & Exec. Dir., The Ont. Breast Cancer Support & Resource Centre (Willow), 1994-95; Pres., Pat Kelly Associates Limited, 1994-95; Pres., PISCES, 1995 to date. SELECTED PUBLICATIONS: *What You Need to Know About Breast Cancer* (1st edition, 1991, 2nd edition, 1993, 3rd edition, 1995); "Determinants of donor platelet variability when testing for heparin-induced thrombocytopenia" with T.E. Warkentin, C.P.M. Smith, C.M. Smith & J.G. Kelton (*Journal of Laboratory Clinical Medicine*, 1992); *Survey of Breast Cancer Survivors*, Health Canada sponsored Nat'l Forum on Breast Cancer (1993); regular contributor, *The Breast Cancer Network Newsletter*. AFFIL: Ontario Cancer Treatment & Research Foundation (Bd. of Dir.); The Ontario Cancer Institute/Princess Margaret Hospital (Bd. of Dir.); National Forum on Breast Cancer (V-Chair, Support Advocacy & Networking Committee 1993); Burlington Breast Cancer Support Services (Past Pres.). HONS: Nancy Brinker Awareness Award, Canadian Breast Cancer Foundation, 1989; Citizen Recognition Award, Women of the Decade, *Burlington Post*, 1990; Women on the Move Award, Women's Health Activist, *The Toronto Sun*, 1992; nominee, Woman of the Year, Hamilton Status of Women's Committee, 1993; Canada 125 Medal, 1994; Community Service Award, City of Burlington, 1995. MISC: numerous presentations; recipient, numerous grants; has presented testimony before the House of Commons Sub-committee on the Status of Women; has been profiled in numerous magazines & newspapers; profiled on *The Journal*, CBC Radio's *Sunday Morning* & *June Callwood's National Treasures*, Vision TV. COMMENT: *"Pat Kelly was employed in immunology research at McMaster University, when at the age of 35, she learned that she had breast cancer. As a direct result of her cancer diagnosis and treatment, Ms. Kelly became a founding member of numerous grass-roots cancer groups, as well as serving on the board of directors of The Ontario Cancer Treatment and Research Foundation (OCTRF) and The Ontario Cancer Institute/Princess Margaret Hospital (OCI/MPH). Ms. Kelly has provided testimony before the House of Commons and was a driving force at the 1993 National Forum on Breast Cancer. As well as nurturing the development of networks of self-help groups, Pat has written and published three editions of an information booklet for cancer patients, and edited a manual for self-help group facilitators. Pat Kelly has received public and private recognition for work as a social activist noted for community mobilizing, including the 1992 Governor General of Canada's Award. Pat Kelly was honoured to be among those Canadians identified by journalist June Callwood as a 'National Treasure.'"*

Kelly, Sheila, B.N.,M.N. ⊕

Nursing Unit Manager, CALGARY GENERAL HOSPITAL, Unit H4, Calgary, AB T2A 0E1 (403) 268-9409. Born Saskatoon 1959. m. James Kelly. 2 ch. Alexander, Samantha. EDUC: Univ. of Calgary, B.N.(Nursing) 1981, M.N.(Nursing) 1992. CAREER: Staff Nurse, Orthopedics, I.C.U., Gen. Relief, Calgary General Hospital, 1981-85; Sessional Nursing Instructor, Fac. of Nursing, Univ. of Calgary, 1985; Asst. Nursing Unit Mgr, Acute Orthopedics, Calgary General Hospital, 1985-88; Nursing Unit Mgr, 1988 to date. SELECTED PUBLICATIONS: "Patient Controlled Analgesia" (*Canadian Orthopedic Nurses' Association Journal*). AFFIL: Canadian Orthopedic Nurses' Association, Calgary Chinook Chapter (Publicity Chair 1989-91, 1993 to date; Nat'l 1995 C.O.N.A. Planning Conference Committee); East Meets West; Calgary Pain Interest Group. HONS: Academic Award of Merit, Univ. of Calgary, 1980; Howmedica Excellence in Orthopedic Nursing Practice Award, 1991; Isabelle Donaldson Scholarship Award, Calgary General Hospital, 1991; G.M. Hall Scholarship Award, Calgary General Hospital, 1992. INTERESTS: pain mgmt; discharge planning/care mapping; bike riding; golfing; swimming. MISC: various presentations at nursing conferences. COMMENT: *"In the current healthcare environment I strive to keep a flexible and optimistic outlook for the future. I encourage my staff to develop themselves both personally and professionally and become active participants in the changes ahead."*

Kelly, Sheila, B.A.,M.A. ♥ ⑳

Executive Director, SASKATCHEWAN SPORTS HALL OF FAME AND MUSEUM INC., 2205 Victoria Ave., Regina, SK S4P 0S4 (306) 780-9233, FAX 780-9427. Born Saskatoon 1962. m. David Kelly. 1 ch. EDUC: Univ. of Saskatchewan, B.A.(Archaeology) 1985, M.A. (Anthro.) 1988. CAREER: weekend front desk staff, Saskatoon Family Y.M.C.A., 1979-85;

Fitness Instructor & Coord., 1985-86; Grad. Teaching & Research Asst., Dept. of Anthro. & Archaeology, Univ. of Saskatchewan, 1985-88; Fitness Instructor, Field House, 1987-89; Archaeology Lab. Supervisor, Dept. of Anthro. & Archaeology, 1987-89; Lab. Technician, Dept. of Anthro. & Archaeology, 1988-89; Sessional Lecturer, Dept. of Anthro. & Archaeology, 1988-89; Receptionist/Office Mgr, Saskatchewan Sports Hall of Fame, 1989; Exec. Dir., Saskatchewan Sports Hall of Fame & Museum, 1990 to date. SELECTED PUBLICATIONS: "The Bethune Site: An Avonlea Burial From Saskatchewan" with G. Walker (*Saskatchewan Archaeology* Vol. 9 1988). AFFIL: Regina Museums Network (Rep. 1992-95); Museums Association of Saskatchewan (Rep., Conference Planning Committee); Canadian Museums Association Rep., Regina Conference, Local Arrangement Committee 1993); Canadian Association for Sport Heritage (Sec. 1992-93; Chair, Regina Conference Planning Committee 1993; VP of Comm. 1994-95; Exec. VP 1995; Pres. 1995-97); Univ. of Regina Cougar Wall of Fame (Rep, Planning Committee 1994); International Association for Sport Museums & Halls of Fame (Rep., Publications Committee 1994-95; Rep., Awards Committee 1995-96). HONS: Grad. Teaching Fellowship, 1987-88. COMMENT: *"A long-standing interest in history and sport has culminated in the directorship of a sport museum. Personal involvement in 'sport' was limited to extensive training through the advanced level of the Royal Academy of Dance."*

Kemeny, Lidia, B.A.,M.Sc. ⊕ ⍋
Director, Safe Start, BRITISH COLUMBIA'S CHILDREN'S HOSPITAL, 4480 Oak St., Vancouver, BC V6H 3G4 (604) 875-3273, FAX 875-2921. Born Budapest 1960. Dr. Joseph Finkler. 2 ch. Kate Finkler-Kemeny, Laura Finkler-Kemeny. EDUC: Queen's Univ., B.A./B.P.H.E.(Health) 1985; Dalhousie Univ., M.Sc.(Health Promo.) 1987. CAREER: Media Dir., PARTICIPaction, 1987-90; Comm. Proj. Coord., Family Service Association of Metropolitan Toronto, 1989-91; Nat'l Proj. Dir., Cdn Nat'l Literacy & Health Proj., Ontario Public Health Association, 1990-91; Dir., Safe Start, British Columbia's Children's Hospital, 1992 to date. SELECTED PUBLICATIONS: "Monograph on Youth in the 1990s" with A. Richards (Halifax: Dalhousie Univ. Press, 1986); "New Directions in Promoting Fitness to Young Women" (*The Starting Line*, Ottawa: 1988); "Fitness Promotion for Adolescent Girls: The Impact and Effectiveness of Promotional Material which Emphasizes the Slim Ideal" (*Adolescence* Fall 1989). AFFIL: Fitness Canada (Youth Task Force; Ado-

lescent Lifestyle Counselling); Ontario Public Health Association; Canadian Public Health Association; Canadian Association for Health, Physical Education & Recreation; Ontario Cancer Association (Task Force on Literacy); Ont. Ministry of Tourism & Recreation (Women in Active Living); B.C. Min. of Health Advisory Committee on Injury Prevention; Canadian Children's Safety Network (Steering Committee). COMMENT: *"Today I hope to: become a better listener, take myself less seriously, make my children feel capable and happy, and make B.C. safer for children."*

Kemp, Linda Patricia Frayne ⊗ ⍋
Artist and Owner, THE WATERCOLOUR GARDEN, 3797 Main St., Jordan, ON L0R 1S0 (905) 562-7844. Born St. Catharines, Ont. 1956. m. Barry James Kemp. 2 ch. Jamie Linn Kemp, Eric William Frayne Kemp. EXHIBITIONS: Grimsby Public Art Gallery (1982); Allen Gallery (1988); The Windpoppy (1988); Grimsby Art Gallery/Library (1988); Anthony Gallery (1988); Hennipen Gallery (1989); Royal Botanical Gardens (1989); Anthony Gallery (1990); Harbour Gallery (1991); The Townsend Gallery (1993); Grimsby Public Art Gallery (1995); numerous juried shows, incl. Rodman Hall Open Jury Show (1981); Beckett Gallery (1988); OSA (1989); Hamilton Art Gallery (1989); Society of Canadian Artists (1991); CSPWC Open Waters, J.B. Aird Gallery (1990, 1992, 1993,1994 & 1991 in Montreal); various group shows, incl. O'Keefe Centre CSPWC Members' Show (1990, 1995); Harbour Gallery Selected Artists (1991); Mitchell McNaught Watercolour Five (1994). AFFIL: Canadian Society of Painters in Watercolour (elected); Society of Canadian Artists (elected); Ontario Society of Artists (elected); Central Ontario Art Association (Past Pres.). HONS: Jurors' Choice, St. Catharines Art Association, 1981; Silver Medal, Osh Kosh International Photography Contest, 1986; Hon. Mention, Mississauga Visual Arts, 1989; Jurors' Choice, Rodman Hall Jury Show, 1989, 1991; BFA Gallery Award, Burlington Cultural Centre, 1990; Hon. Mention, HWAA Hamilton Art Gallery, 1990; Best in Show, Nassagaweya Valley, 1990, 1991, 1993; Best in Show, Homer Watson Gallery, COAA Crossections, 1990; Juror, First Choice, Nassagaweya Valley, 1992. INTERESTS: watercolour painting; printmaking; photography; ballet; hiking. MISC: recipient, Ont. Arts Council Grants, 1990, 1991, 1993, 1995; work included in *Color and Light for the Watercolor Painter* by C. Schink (Watson Guptill, 1995); TV program (cable), *Watercolour Workshop*, 1996. COMMENT: *"I am fortunate to spend my days*

doing what I love most. I paint, mostly watercolours. I also teach adults, organize workshops and run my studio/gallery."

Kemp, Lynda G. ■■ 🎭
President, THUNDER THIGHS COSTUMES LTD. (costume rentals for film, TV & theatre), 16 Busy St., Toronto, ON M4M 1N8 (416) 462-0621, FAX 462-0533. President, BUSY ST. HOLDINGS INC. Born Hamilton, Ont. 1953. m. Otta L. Hanus. 1 ch. Doane Hanus. **EDUC:** Ryerson Polytechnical Institute, Theatre program 1970-73; Royal Conservatory of Music, Singing Grade VIII, 1970-74. **CAREER:** actor after leaving Ryerson (before graduating) - offered an EQUITY contract, & then joined ACTRA; worked as actor/singer, 4 yrs.; Wardrobe Coord./Wardrobe Mistress/ Wardrobe Head/Costume Designer, numerous major film & TV productions, 1975 to date. **SELECTED CREDITS:** Costume Designer, numerous productions incl.: *Kissinger*, Paragon/Turner Broadcasting, 1995; *F/X*, TV pilot, 1995; *Lady Killer*, CBS/Kushner Locke Co., 1995; *Young at Heart*, Warner Bros./CBS, 1994; *Incident in a Small Town*, RHI Entertainment, Inc., 1993; *The Liberators*, Walt Disney Films, 1986; *Miracle at Moreaux*, PBS/ Atlantis, 1985.

Kempston Darkes, Maureen V., B.A., LL.B. $
President and General Manager, GENERAL MOTORS OF CANADA LIMITED, 1908 Colonel Sam Dr., Oshawa, ON L1H 8P7 (905) 644-5000, FAX 644-3830. Vice-President, GENERAL MOTORS CORPORATION. Born Toronto 1948. m. Larry J. Darkes. **EDUC:** Victoria Coll., Univ. of Toronto, B.A.(Hist. & Pol. Sci.) 1973; Univ. of Toronto Law Sch., LL.B. 1973. **BAR:** Ont., 1975. **CAREER:** joined Legal Staff, General Motors of Canada Limited, 1975; Asst. Cnsl, 1979; Legal Staff, General Motors Corporation, Detroit, 1979-80; headed Tax Staff, GM Canada, 1980-84; Treasurer's Office, GM Corp., N.Y., 1985-87; Acting Treas., GM Canada, 1987; Gen. Dir., Public Affairs, 1987-91; VP, Corp. Affairs & Dir., 1991-94; Gen. Cnsl & Sec., 1992-94; Pres. & Gen. Mgr, 1994 to date; VP, GM Corp., 1994 to date. **DIRECTOR:** CAMI Automotive Inc.; Hughes Aircraft Canada; General Motors of Canada Limited; CN Rail; Brascan Limited. **AFFIL:** National Quality Institute (Dir.); National Research Council (Dir.); Business Council on National Issues (Committee Mbr.); Motor Vehicle Manufacturers' Association; Natural Resources Canada (Minister's Advisory Council on Industrial Energy Efficiency); Ont. Gov't Educ. Accountability Bd. (Automotive Advisory Committee); Transportation Equipment Sectoral Advisory Group on International Trade (appointed 1994); New Directions (Bd.); Univ. of Toronto (Arts & Sciences Advisory Bd.); Univ. of Waterloo (Bd. of Gov.); Univ. of Western Ontario Bus. Sch. (Advisory Committee); Women's College Hospital (Chair for Major Gifts); Women's College Hospital Foundation; YMCA of Greater Toronto (Council of Advisory Gov.); YMCA of Durham Region (Chair, Healthy Returns fundraising campaign). **HONS:** Hon. Doctor of Commerce, St. Mary's Univ., 1995; LL.D.(Hon.), Univ. of Victoria, 1996; LL.D.(Hon.), Univ. of Toronto, 1996. **MISC:** fed. gov't appointee, Free Trade Agreement Automotive Select Panel, 1989.

Kendall, Gail Janice, B.P.E.,M.P.E. ■ ⚾ ✊
Executive Director, BASKETBALL MANITOBA, 200 Main St., Winnipeg, MB R3C 4M2 (204) 985-4119, FAX 985-4028. Assistant Coach, Women's Basketball Team, CALIFORNIA UNIVERSITY OF PENNSYLVANIA, 250 University Ave., California, PA 15419 (412) 938-4584, FAX 938-5849. Born 1956. m. Thomas John Kendall. 1 ch. **EDUC:** Univ. of Manitoba, B.P.E. 1977, M.P.E. 1988; Univ. of Winnipeg, Athletic Recreation courses 1978. **CAREER:** Team Capt., Univ. of Manitoba Women's Basketball Team, 1974-77; mbr., Cdn Nat'l Women's Basketball Team, 1975-80; Team Capt., Univ. of Winnipeg Women's Basketball Team, 1977-79; Asst. Coach, Univ. of Winnipeg Wesmen Women's Basketball Team, 1979 to date; Health Coord., City of Winnipeg Parks & Recreation Dept., 1980-82; Sport Admin., Univ. of Winnipeg, 1982-83; Sports Caravan Coord., City of Winnipeg Parks & Recreation, 1983-85; Exec. Dir., Basketball Manitoba, 1985 to date; Sport Psychologist, Western Canada Games, Resource Team, 1990; Asst. Coach, Women's Basketball Team, California Univ. of Pennsylvania. **SELECTED PUBLICATIONS:** "Psychological Skill Development," with C. Botterill (*Science Periodical on Research and Technology in Sport* 1984); "The Effects of an Imagery, Relaxation and Self-Talk Package on Basketball Game Performance," with D. Hrycaiko, G. Martin & T. Kendall (*Journal of Sport Psychology* 12 1990). **AFFIL:** Manitoba Softball Association; Manitoba Tennis Association; Synchro Manitoba; Athletics Manitoba; Manitoba Amateur Football Association; Manitoba Skeet Association; Canadian Skeet Association; Manitoba Trap Shooting Association; Manitoba Wheelchair Sport Association; Univ. of Winnipeg Wesmen Women's team. **HONS:** Great Plains Athletic Conference All Star–Basketball, 1975-79; Female Athlete of the Year, Univ. of Manitoba, 1976; Cdn

Inter Athletic Union All Star, 1978; Cdn Inter Athletic Union All Canadian, 1979; Cdn Sr. Women's Nat'l Championship All Star, 1983; MVP, Lakehead Univ. Invitational Tournament, 1983; Cdn Sr. Women's Nat'l Championship All Star, 1985; Univ. of Winnipeg Wesmen Classic All Star, 1987; inducted into the Grant Park High Sch. Hall of Fame as an athlete, 1993; inducted into the Basketball Manitoba Hall of Fame as an athlete, 1994 & as a part of the coaching staff for the Univ. of Winnipeg; Order of Sports Excellence Award, 1993, 1994; Order of the Buffalo Hunt, Prov. of Man., 1994. INTERESTS: basketball; personal fitness; time with her family. MISC: Asst. Basketball Coach, Univ. of Winnipeg Wesmen Women's Team, Cdn Univ. Nat'l Champions, 1992-93, 1993-94, team holds the N.Am. record for the most consecutive wins at 88; worked as sports psychologist with a number of amateur sports groups in Manitoba. COMMENT: *"I have been extremely fortunate to be involved in a sport that has, in turn, given me so much. Through my association with the many coaches, players and administrators, I have learned many life skills, which have made me more effective in my daily life."*

Kennedy, Arlene M., B.A.,M.A. ⊗
Director, McINTOSH GALLERY, University of Western Ontario, London, ON N6A 3K7 (519) 661-3059, FAX 661-3292. Born Toronto 1948. EDUC: Univ. of Western Ontario, B.A. (Fine Art) 1971; Memorial Univ. of Newfoundland, Dip.(Educ.) 1972; Nova Scotia Coll. of Art, M.A.(Art Educ.); Banff Sch. of Fine Art, Certificate (Arts Admin.) 1986. CAREER: Art Teacher, various schools in St. John's, 1971-74; Instructor, Visual Art, Fanshawe Coll., London, Ont., 1975; Art Teacher, Saunders Secondary Sch., London, Ont., 1976-77; various teaching positions in N.S., 1977-78; Art Teacher, A.B. Lucas Secondary Sch., London, Ont., 1979; Exhibition Coord., McIntosh Gallery, 1979-82; Dir., Oakville Galleries, Oakville, Ont., 1982-89; Dir., McIntosh Gallery, 1989 to date. SELECTED PUBLICATIONS: "Extending the Viewer's Awareness of Outdoor Sculpture" (*Dateline OAAG* Apr.-May 1983); "Thoughts on Acquisitions" (*Oakville-Burlington Arts Journal* June-July 1985); "What's the Percentage? A Public Percent for Arts Program" (*Arts Oakville* Fall 1985); "Reflections on a Theme: What Future the Creative Triangle?" (*Oakville-Burlington Arts Journal* Nov.-Jan. 1988); various other publications. AFFIL: London Arts Council (Dir.); Ontario Association of Art Galleries; Canadian Museums Association; McIntosh Gallery (Life Mbr.); Association of Cultural Executives; International Council of Museums; Oakville Galleries (Life Mbr.). INTERESTS: growing orchids; gardening; bonsai; collecting art.

Kennedy, Carole ■■ ♡ ⑤ ⑳ ⌀
Founder, CURL FOR CANCER. Realtor, BRIGHTSIDE REALTY, 237 University Ave., Charlottetown, PE C1A 4L8 (902) 894-5501, FAX 894-4055, EMAIL fbuell@atcon.com. Born St. John 1937. d. 4 ch. Catherine, Wesley, Susan, Carson. CAREER: realtor. AFFIL: Canadian Cancer Society (various volunteer positions with special events); Labatt 24-Hr. Relay (various positions); P.E.I. Real Estate Association (Bd. mbr.; Chair, Educ. Committee); Oshawa Information & Referral Centre (founding mbr.); G.L. Roberts Parent-Teachers Association (founding mbr.); church (Choir mbr.; Sunday Sch. Teacher; Office Mgr; Treas.; Chair, Bd. of Stewards; Chair, Women's Association). HONS: various certificates of achievement & of merit; Commemorative Medal for 125th Anniversary of Cdn Confederation; Citation of Merit, Canadian Cancer Society. INTERESTS: curling; golfing; oil painting; tai chi; walking; reading; easy-listening music; meditation; God; Curl for Cancer. MISC: Taoist Tai Chi instructor; organized 1st annual Kinsmen fundraising Funspiel. COMMENT: *"Have always been socially conscious, helping when I could. The so-far final culmination of this and the achievement I am most proud of was when, about 11 years ago, I came up with the idea of a fundraising curling bonspiel. I called it Curl for Cancer. It proved so successful that I started promoting it throughout the Atlantic provinces, then across Canada and, now, worldwide. This promotion is an ongoing process; when I get to the end of my list of curling clubs, I order an updated list and start again at A. Although the cancer society does not keep statistics on this special event, I've been told that Curl for Cancer raises millions. Curling recently became an Olympic sport and consequently is experiencing good growth. Along with curling's growth, Curl for Cancer is getting even bigger, raising more funds for the fight against a disease that, in one way or another, affects most of us. Some of the original Curl for Cancer material is in curling's Hall of Fame."*

Kennell, Elizabeth H., B.A.,M.A. ■ 📖 ⊙
Director of Development, McCORD MUSEUM OF CANADIAN HISTORY, 690 Sherbrooke St. W., Montreal, QC H3A 1E9 (514) 398-7100, FAX 398-5045. Born Montreal 1955. m. Robert Charles Kennell. 2 ch. Sarah Allison Kennell, Hannah Lucie Kennell. EDUC: Univ. de la Sorbonne Nouvelle, Diplôme de culture française

III 1977; Queen's Univ., B.A.(Art Hist./French) 1978; Concordia Univ., M.A.(Hist. of Cdn Art) 1985. CAREER: Asst., Travelling Exhibitions, Montreal Museum of Fine Arts, 1978-89; Head of Exhibition Svcs, McCord Museum of Canadian History, 1989-93; Consultant, Michael Lerch Design Inc., 1993-94; part-time Prof., Dept. of Visual Arts, Univ. of Ottawa, 1993-94; Dir. of Dev., McCord Museum of Canadian History. SELECTED PUBLICATIONS: "Edmond-Joseph Massicotte and F.S. Coburne," biographical entry in *New Canadian Encyclopedia* (Edmonton: Hurtig, 1985); "The McCord Museum's Inaugural Exhibition Program" (*Fontanus* 1992); "A low-tech interpretation: 1871 Composite Portraiture" (*Curator*, 1995); "The Painter as Illustrator," The Frederick Simpson Coburn Collection (Musée des beaux-arts de Sherbrooke, 1996); various other biographical entries & articles in the *McCord Museum Newsletter*. AFFIL: Société des musées québécois; Canadian Museums Association; Safdie Proj., Canadian Architecture Collection, McGill Univ. (Advisory Committee). HONS: Senator Frank Carrel Scholarship, 1978; Bourse du gouv. du Qué., ministère des Affaires culturelles, 1981. INTERESTS: sailing; travelling; family. MISC: numerous public & univ. lectures. COMMENT: *"I take great pride in what the McCord Museum has to offer. Three major collections of First Nations material, costumes and Notman photographs set us apart from all other museums, and make it easy for me to promote."*

Kent, Alia, B.A.,B.Ed.,M.A. ■■ ⨶ Ⓔ
President, WOMEN TEACHERS' ASSOCIATION OF OTTAWA, 275 Bank St., Ste. 204, Ottawa, ON K2P 2L6 (613) 235-0458, FAX 235-6900, EMAIL wtao@inasec.ca. Born India 1942. m. Darrel. EDUC: Osmania Univ., Hyderabad, India, B.A. 1962; Univ. of New Brunswick, B.Ed. 1968; Univ. of Ottawa, M.A.(English Lit.) 1972; Federation of Women Teachers' Associations of Ontario, Leadership Course, 1978-79; Ministry of Educ., Principals' Course, Part I 1983, Part II 1984; Computers in Educ., Part I 1989-90. CAREER: full-time teacher, 1964-74; Consultant in Language Arts, Grades 7-10, Ottawa Bd. of Educ., 1974-77; full-time teacher, 1977-87; V-Principal, 3 schools, 1987-95; Pres., Women Teachers' Association of Ottawa, 1995-96. AFFIL: Ottawa Elementary Vice-Principals' Association (Pres. 1993); Federation of Women Teachers' Associations of Ontario (Dir. 1994-96; Pilot Proj. Leader, Anti-Racist Educ. Committee 1993; Prov. Convenor, Anti-Racist Educ. Committee 1991-96); Women Teachers' Association of Ottawa (Pres. 1995-96; Exec. mbr. 1993-95); Ottawa Board

of Education (various committees 1970-86); International Reading Association (Pres., Ottawa-Carleton Council 1978-79). INTERESTS: gardening; travel; knitting. COMMENT: *"An educator for over 30 years, working for equity and equality for visible minority children and teachers–making an impact in the system."*

Kent, Judy, B.P.H.E.,B.Ed. ⨶ Ⓢ
President, KENT CONSULTING, 226 Bruyère St., Ottawa, ON K1N 5E3 (613) 241-2399, FAX 241-0978, EMAIL kentj@magi.com. Born Lethbridge, Alta. 1946. s. EDUC: Univ. of Toronto, B.P.H.E. 1970, B.Ed. 1972. CAREER: Phys. Ed. Teacher, Scarborough Bd. of Educ., 1972-74; Fac., Sch. of Phys. Educ., McMaster Univ., 1974-80; Sport Consultant, Ministry of Culture & Recreation, 1980-81; Sport Consultant, Sport Canada, 1982-84; Mgmt Consultant, 1984-95; Pres., Kent Consulting, 1986 to date. SELECTED PUBLICATIONS: *Applied Strategic Planning* (1991); *Sport: The Way Ahead* (1992); *Effective Organizations: A Consultant's Resource* (1992); articles, *Leader Resources Journal*, 1990-93; skills program workbooks on fin. mgmt, long & short term planning, volunteers working together, 1984-86. AFFIL: Commonwealth Games Association of Canada (Pres. 1994-98); Canadian Commonwealth Games Team (Chef de Mission 1994); Royal Life Saving Society of Canada (Pres. 1987-90); Canadian Association for the Advancement of Women & Sport. HONS: Volunteer Sport Leader of the Year, 1995; Woman of Distinction, Ottawa YM/YWCA, 1995; Service Cross & Bar to Service Cross, Royal Life Saving Society; Canada 125 Medal; Queen's Silver Jubilee Medal. INTERESTS: kayaking; cottaging; reading; nature; fulfilling life's potentials. MISC: keynote speaker in over 10 countries; has done strategic planning in several countries incl. Barbados, Sir Lanka, Zimbabwe, Belgium, Australia & the US. COMMENT: *"I have been very fortunate to have had many experiences. Learning from these experiences has shaped my belief that as a leader and role model, I am most effective when I enable others to address obstacles and opportunities–with energy and a belief in their own capacity to achieve results."*

Kent-Wilkinson, Arlene, R.N., M.N. ⊕ ⎐ ⌀
Forensic Nurse Consultant. 116 Martindale Close N.E., Calgary, AB T3J 2V3 (403) 293-1598, FAX 285-1760. Born St. Joseph Island, Ont. 1950. m. Dan. 2 ch. Kent, Grey. EDUC: Plummer Memorial Hospital, Sault Ste. Marie, Ont., R.N. 1971; Univ. of Victoria, B.S.N. 1990; Univ. of Calgary, M.N.(Family Nursing

& Addictions) 1993, doctoral studies (Community Health Sciences) in progress. **CAREER:** Staff Nurse, Memorial Hospital, Sudbury, Ont., 1971-72; Staff Nurse, Victoria Hospital, London, Ont., 1972-79; Shift Supervisor, Rest Haven Nursing Home, St. Thomas, Ont., 1979-80; Staff Nurse, Calgary Remand Centre, 1981-84; casual relief, Calgary General Hospital, 1982-84; Staff Nurse, Forensic Unit, 1984-86; casual relief–Nursing Supervisor II, Renfrew Recovery Centre, Alberta Alcohol & Drug Abuse Commission, 1986 to date; casual relief, Acute Care Psychiatry, Foothills Hospital, 1993 to date; Sessional Instructor, Hospital & Community Psychiatric/Mental Health Nursing, Fac. of Nursing, Univ. of Calgary, 1993-96; Forensic Nurse Consultant/Specialist, independent practice, 1994 to date; dev. Forensic Nursing Distance Courses, Mount Royal Coll., 1996 to date. **SELECTED PUBLICATIONS:** "What Brings Nurses Together?" (*Alberta Association of Registered Nurses Newsletter* 1990); "Politically Taking Action Column" (*Alberta Association of Registered Nurses Newsletter* 1992); "After the Crime, Before the Trial" (*The Canadian Nurse/L'infirmière canadienne* 89(11) 1993). **AFFIL:** Univ. of Calgary Alumni; Alberta Association of Registered Nurses (Chair, Pol. Action Committee 1993-94; Chair, Prov. Registration Committee 1993-94); Alberta Mental Health Nurses' Interest Group (Prov. Exec. Sec.); Canadian Federation of Mental Health Nursing; Canadian Mental Health Association; Canadian Nurses' Association; International Association of Forensic Nursing (Cdn Rep., Strategic Planning Council.); International Council of Prison Health Services. **HONS:** Gertrude M. Hall Scholarship, Calgary General Hospital, 1988-92; Nurse of the Year, G-8 Forensic Unit, Calgary General Hospital, 1989; Diane Davidson Scholarship, Alberta Registered Nurses' Trust Fund, 1989-90; Isobel Donaldson Scholarship, Calgary General Hospital, 1990; Award of Excellence, Canadian Federation of Mental Health Nursing, 1994; Exemplary Clinical Practice Award, Alberta Association of Mental Health Nurses, 1994. **MISC:** developed & is teaching 1st course ever on "Health Care in Forensic Populations: An Emerging Specialty"; reviewer for *Canadian Nurse/L'infirmière canadienne* & *Journal of Family Therapy*; numerous presentations; reviewer for *Journal of Psychiatric and Mental Health Nursing.* **COMMENT:** *"Arlene Kent-Wilkinson is a forensic nurse consultant. Her speciality area is forensic psychiatric nursing. Forensic refers to where the law overlaps with health care. Her goal is to develop and promote the speciality of forensic nursing. She developed and is teaching the first theoretical multidisciplinary course on forensic nursing called Health Care in Forensic Populations: An Emerging Specialty at the University of Calgary. Presently she is developing distance delivery courses in forensic nursing for Mount Royal College in Calgary."*

Keogh, Nina ■ ■ ♥

Proprietor, PUPPETEL (puppeteer/puppet creator for TV & film), 74 Walder Ave., North York, ON M4P 2S2 (416) 482-3242, FAX 482-9750, EMAIL n_keogh@tvo.org. Born Toronto 1946. m. David Burt. 1 ch. Matt. **EDUC:** Central Tech., Art Dept., Certificate. **CAREER:** puppet builder & puppeteer on hundreds of TV series, features, videos & commercials, 1968 to date; TV host, CBC & TVO, 1969 to date; 3rd-generation professional. **SELECTED CREDITS:** hosted several series incl. *Drop In,* CBC; *Polkadot Door,* TVO; *Whatever Turns You On,* TVO; *Calendar,* TVO; created &/or operated puppets for *Picoli & Lirabo,* TFO; *Today's Special,* TVO; *Bookmice,* TVO; *Mr. Dress Up,* CBC; Crystal, *Groundling Marsh*; Kitty, *Hello Mrs. Cherry-Winkle,* Family Channel; work with Peter Ustinov, Hanna Barbera, Jim Henson & others. **AFFIL:** ACTRA; Equity; UDA; The Alliance for Children & Television (Dir.). **HONS:** award for outstanding contribution to children's TV industry, Alliance for Children & Television, 1991; most of the series with which she's been involved have won major TV industry awards. **INTERESTS:** piano; painting; sculpting; carpentry/building; TV & film. **MISC:** parents, John and Linda Keogh, were pioneers in Cdn children's TV; they created & operated puppets & wrote for CBC since 1954 on many series & TVO. **COMMENT:** *"Since my puppeteering apprenticeship in 1958 on The Friendly Giant, I have worked steadily, particularly since 1968 as both TV series host and as a puppet creator and/or puppeteer on many series. The work has been varied and challenging and keeps my creative juices flowing at all times."*

Kepper, Shirley, B.H.Ec. 7

Provincial Executive Director, UNICEF BRITISH COLUMBIA, 536 W. Broadway, Vancouver, BC V5Z 1E9 (604) 874-3666, FAX 874-5411. Born Kamloops, B.C. 1943. m. Harvey Kepper. 1 ch. Corinne Kepper. **EDUC:** Univ. of British Columbia, B.H.Ec.(Home Econ./Nutrition) 1965, Certificate (Educ.) 1970; Univ. of Indiana Center of Philanthropy, Certificate (Fund Raising & Leadership) 1991. **CAREER:** secondary sch. teacher, School Districts No. 44 & No. 43, 1965-74, 1977; Program Coord., Family Support, Canadian Red Cross Society, 1982-90; Prov. Exec. Dir., UNICEF B.C., 1990 to date. **AFFIL:** Junior League of Greater Vancouver (Advisor); British Columbia Children's Hospital Auxiliary; Camp Goodtimes (Founder); Association of Fundraising Professionals (Treas. 1991-94). **HONS:** Volunteer Community Award, shared, for B.C. Family Support Program, 1989; Canada 125 Medal. **INTERESTS:** cross-country skiing; cooking; novels; fitness. **MISC:** various presentations. **COMMENT:** *"The focus of my professional and voluntary pursuits over the years has been the well-being of children and my belief that the protection and investment in their development is the foundation of a better future for mankind."*

Kermoyan, Mireille ■ ▯ ✿ ⌴
President and Chief Executive Officer, EDIROM INC., 384 Laurier W., Montreal, QC H2V 2K7 (514) 272-4363, FAX 272-8609, EMAIL edirom@socom.com. Born Nice, France. m. Ara Kermoyan. 2 ch. **EDUC:** educated in France. **CAREER:** Sec.-Treas., Art Global Inc.; Sec., Bd. of Trustees, National Film Bd.; Dir., Int'l Dev.; Dir. of Comm.; Gen. Mgr, EDIROM Inc. **AFFIL:** Club Gastronomique. **INTERESTS:** books; films. **COMMENT:** *"Has been involved for the past 25 years in different cultural fields. Currently addressing electronic publishing in view of developing highly creative cultural CD-ROM."*

Kérouac, Suzanne, B.Sc.,M.N., M.Sc. ⌖ ⊕
Dean, Faculty of Nursing, UNIVERSITÉ DE MONTRÉAL, CP 6128, succ. Centre-Ville, Montréal, QC H3C 3J7 (514) 343-6436, FAX 343-2306. Born Lislet, Que. 1941. s. 1 ch. **EDUC:** Hôtel-Dieu of Lévis, Nursing Diploma 1961; Univ. de Montréal, B.Sc.(Nursing) 1972, M.N.(Nursing Admin.) 1974; McGill Univ., M.Sc.(Epidemiology) 1981; Wayne State Univ., postgrad. studies in Transcultural Nursing 1990; Univ. of California, postgrad. studies in Theoretical Nursing 1990. **CAREER:** nursing instructor & nursing supervisor, Saint-Luc Hospital, Montreal, to 1980; Asst. Prof., Fac. of Nursing, Univ. de Montréal, 1980-86; Assoc. Prof., 1986-93; Dean, 1993 to date; Full Prof., 1994 to date. **SELECTED PUBLICATIONS:** *Introduction à la gestion des soins infirmiers*, with A. Duquette, S. Michaud & others (Montréal: Librairie de l'Univ. de Montréal, 1993); *La pensée infirmière*, with J. Pepin, F. Ducharme, A. Duquette & F. Major (Montréal: Éditions Études vivantes, 1994); "Portrait de la santé de femmes aux prises avec la violence conjugale," with M.É Taggart in *La violence conjugale au Québec: état de la recherche empirique*, M. Rinfret ed. (Québec: G. Morin, 1994); "Fac-

tors Relating to Nursing Burnout: A Review of Empirical Knowledge" (*Issues in Mental Health Nursing* 15(4) 1994); various other publications. **AFFIL:** Ordre des infirmières et infirmiers du Québec; International Council on Women's Health Issues; International Association for Human Caring; Transcultural Nursing Society; Association canadienne française pour l'avancement des sciences. **HONS:** Lieutenant Governor's Medal, 1961; Bursary, Warner-Chilcott, 1974; WHO Fellowship, 1990. **INTERESTS:** human caring; transcultural nursing; women & int'l health. **MISC:** recipient, various grants from various agencies; numerous conference presentations. **COMMENT:** *"Driven by desire for excellence in teaching, research and human resource management. I have acted as a consultant for such organizations as Price Waterhouse, Ministry of Social Services, hospitals and professional associations."*

Kerr, Kaye M., B.A.,M.A.,Ph.D. ⌖ ⊕
Associate Professor and Director, Developmental Studies, UNIVERSITY OF WINNIPEG, 515 Portage Ave., 4L39, Winnipeg, MB R3G 2E9 (204) 786-9130, FAX 786-1824, EMAIL uowmkk@ccu.umanitoba.ca or kerr@io.winnipeg.ca. Born Niagara Falls, Ont. m. Ian. **EDUC:** Univ. of Minnesota, B.A.(Zoology), M.A., Ph.D.(Child Dev.) 1974. **CAREER:** Instructor, Univ. of Minnesota, 1964-67; seminars, Tavistock Institute, UK, 1967; Psychologist, St. Lawrence County, N.Y., Mental Health Clinic, 1968; Sch. Psych. Practicum, American International Sch., New Delhi, 1968; Psychologist, Children's Svcs, Mid-Missouri Mental Health Center, 1968-69; Lecturer, Psych., Univ. of Winnipeg, 1969-70; Coord., Dev. Studies, 1970-89; Asst. Prof., 1970-77; Assoc. Prof., 1977 to date; Adjunct Asst. Prof., Psychiatry, Univ. of Manitoba, 1980-92; Visiting Colleague, Institute of Psychiatry, Univ. of London, 1982-83, 1990 to date; Dir., Dev. Studies, Univ. of Winnipeg, 1992 to date. **SELECTED PUBLICATIONS:** *Procedures for Meetings and Organizations*, 2 ed., with H.W. King (Toronto: Carswell Legal Publications, 1988; 3rd ed., 1996);*Concise Procedures for Meetings*, with H.W. King (Toronto: Carswell Legal Publications, 1996); "Child Abuse–Role of the Child, Family and Society" (*Today for Tomorrow* 1978); "Interpersonal Spacing and Behaviour in Children" (*Special Education in Canada* 1980); "Non-verbal Communication: Touching," with J.D. Godin (*Resources for Feminist Research* 1981); "Child Care Preparation Program for Early Childhood Special Education," with E. Polyzoi (*Canadian Journal of Special Education* 1991); "Special needs children: Sick children, a challenge for child care,"

in *Childhood Education: International Perspectives*, ed. Eeva Hujala-Huttunen (1996); "Issues and concerns of licensed family day care providers," with E. Polzol (*Canadian Journal of Research in Early Childhood Education*, 5, 1996); various other publications. EDIT: Sr. Journal Ed., Early Childhood Education Council of Manitoba, 1977-79. AFFIL: American Psychological Association; Association for Child Development & Psychiatry; Canadian Psychological Association; Council for Exceptional Children; Delta Kappa Gamma, International Honorary Society of Educators; International Society for Study of Behavioural Development; Manitoba Child Care Association; Psychological Association of Manitoba; Society for Research in Child Development; Univ. of Winnipeg Senate; Child Care Educ. Approval Committee (Prov. Min. of Educ. appointee). HONS: Outstanding contribution award, Canadian Mental Health Association, 1984; Clare Atchison Award for Outstanding Community Contribution, Univ. of Winnipeg, 1986; Queen's Univ. Visiting Woman Scholar, 1992. MISC: registered psychologist, Man., 1980; recipient, various grants; referee for *Child Development*, SSHRC & Canadian Mental Health Association; numerous conference presentations; Manitoba Adolescent Treatment Centre Bd. (Prov. Min. of Health appointee 1986-90; Pres. & Chair 1988-89); numerous workshops. COMMENT: "*A professional psychologist actively involved in the community, well-known for writing the* Kerr and King Procedures for Meetings and Organizations *which is used by prominent organizations, agencies and institutions.*"

Kerr, Krista L., B.Comm.,C.A., R.F.P. ■■ Ⓢ Ⓞ
Vice-President and Manager, Toronto Office, KERR FINANCIAL CORPORATION (personal fin. planning on a fee-only basis), 150 York St., Ste. 1808, Toronto, ON M5H 3S5 (416) 364-9447, FAX 364-0892, EMAIL kerrfintor@sympatico.ca. Born Montreal 1966. s. EDUC: Canadian Securities Course, C.S.C.(with Hons.) 1986; Queen's Univ., B.Comm.(Acctg/Fin.) 1988; Canadian Institute of Chartered Accountants, C.A. 1990; Canadian Association of Financial Planners, R.F.P. 1994. CAREER: Ernst & Young, 1988-93; VP & Mgr, Toronto office, Kerr Financial Corporation, 1993 to date. SELECTED CREDITS: numerous appearances on personal fin. TV & radio shows incl. CBC "Business World" & the AM 640 "Smart Money" show in Toronto. AFFIL: Canadian Children's Opera Chorus (Dir. 1989 to date; Pres. & Chrm of the Bd. 1993 to date); Evergreen Environmental Foundation (Dir. 1991 to

date; VP 1995 to date). COMMENT: "*Krista joined Kerr Financial Corporation in 1993 after several years with Ernst & Young, as a C.A. and an audit manager. Her past experience includes audit and financial consultation to entrepreneurs, small business owners, stock brokers and various financial services companies. Krista currently manages the Toronto office, with responsibility for corporate development as well as comprehensive financial planning for individuals and delivering financial and retirement planning seminars.*"

Kerr, Shelagh D., B.Sc. Ⓢ
Vice-President, Corporate and Environmental Affairs, COCA-COLA BEVERAGES LTD., 42 Overlea Blvd., Toronto, ON M4H 1B8 (416) 424-6342, FAX 424-6079. Chair, BEVERAGE RECOVERY IN CANADA. Born Fredericton 1955. m. Wolf Schrempf. EDUC: Univ. of Ottawa, B.Sc.(Dietetic) 1977; Calgary Gen. Hospital, Dietetic Internship Dipl. 1977. CAREER: Mgr, Prod. Dev., White Spot Ltd., Vancouver, 1979-81; Food Ed., *Nationale Pers.*, S. Africa, 1981-84; VP, Tech., Grocery Products Manufacturers of Canada, 1985-91; VP, Coca-Cola Ltd., 1991-94; VP, Corp. & Environmental Affairs, Coca-Cola Beverages Ltd., 1994 to date. DIRECTOR: Alberta Beverage Recycling Corporation; Encorp Atlantic. AFFIL: Canadian Foundation for Dietetic Research (Dir.); Canadian Dietetic Association; Canadian Institute of Food Science & Technology; Donalda Club, Toronto. INTERESTS: skiing; golf; cycling.

Kerr, Sheryl L., B.Comm. Ⓢ Ⓧ Ⓞ
President, STRATHFIELD CONSULTANTS LTD., 6 Glengowan Rd., Toronto, ON M4N 1E8 (416) 483-5842, FAX 483-8308. Born Montreal 1946. m. David W. Kerr. 2 ch. EDUC: McGill Univ., B.Comm. 1967. CAREER: IBM Canada & IBM Australia, 1967-71; independent computer consultant, 1971-75; Pres., Strathfield Consultants Ltd., 1975 to date. AFFIL: Toronto Symphony Orchestra (Dir.); Granite Club of Toronto (Dir.); Albert Coll., Belleville (Gov.); St. George's United Church (Bd. of Stewards); previously: Crescent Sch. (Gov.); Leaside Girls Hockey (Coach); YWCA of Canada (Dir. & Treas.). INTERESTS: symphony; riding; volunteer. COMMENT: "*I would describe myself as a straightforward, practical and resourceful person who enjoys working with others, and balances working priorities with personal life.*"

Kerrigan, Catherine ■■ ⬕ 📖
Professor of English, UNIVERSITY OF GUELPH, Guelph, ON N1G 2W1. CAREER: internationally known as one of the top people in her field;

guest lectures, Oxford Univ. (England), Queen's Univ. (Ireland), Yale Univ. (US), & others; frequent appearances on the BBC as a commentator. SELECTED PUBLICATIONS: several books & many articles on Scottish Literature. EDIT: Gen. Ed., *The Collected Works of Robert Louis Stevenson* (Univ. of Edinburgh Press); co-ed., *Scotlands*.

Kerslake, Susan 🕮 ⊕ ○

Writer. Born Chicago 1943. EDUC: St. Joseph's Children's Centre, Course (Child Care) 1975. CAREER: Kroch's and Brentano's Bookstore, Chicago, 1962-66; Dalhousie Univ. Libraries, 1966-73; St. Joseph's Children's Centre, 1973-80; Izaak Walton Killam Hospital for Children, 1980-85; freelance writer. SELECTED PUBLICATIONS: "Middlewatch" (1976); "The Book of Fears" (1984); "Penumbra" (1984); *Blind Date* (1989); appearances in various anthologies. AFFIL: Writers' Federation of N.S.; Writers' Union of Canada; Cystic Fibrosis volunteer, 1995 to date. HONS: shortlisted for Gov. General's Award, 1984. INTERESTS: reading fiction; balcony gardening; budgies; almost everything else. MISC: participant, "45 Below," CIBC.

Kert, Faye, B.A.,M.A. ■ 🕲 🕮

Past President and Chair, Awards Committee, CANADIAN NAUTICAL RESEARCH SOCIETY, 200 - 5th Ave., Ottawa, ON K1S 2N2 (613) 957-2989, FAX 941-5366. Born Ottawa 1948. s. EDUC: Queen's Univ., B.A.(Hist.) 1970; Carleton Univ., M.A.(Maritime Hist.) 1986. CAREER: Marine Archaeologist, Environment Canada, Underwater Archaeology Div., 1978-80; Archaeological Supervisor, Mary Rose Trust, Portsmouth, UK, 1981; Media Officer, Canadian Museum of Civilization, 1982-85; Chief, Info. & Educ., Canadian War Museum, 1985-89; Mgr, Media & Public Rel'ns, Revenue Canada, Customs & Excise, 1989-91; Coord., Environmental Analysis, Crisis Communication Task Force, 1991; Comm. Advisor, Info. Svcs Office, National Research Council of Canada, 1992; Chief, Public Rel'ns, Health & Welfare Canada, 1992 to date. SELECTED PUBLICATIONS: numerous educational kits & guidebooks for the National Museums of Canada. AFFIL: Canadian Nautical Research Society (Pres. 1993-96); North American Society of Oceanic History (Councillor 1993-96); International Maritime Economic History Association (VP 1995-98); Society for Historical Archaeology (Conference on Underwater Archeology); Canadian Museums Association. INTERESTS: maritime history & heritage; underwater archaeology; antiques; old houses. COMMENT: *"As a historian, underwater archaeologist, museum communicator and President of the Canadian Nautical Research Society, I have tried to encourage a love of history, especially Canada's maritime history."*

Key, Nancy L., LL.B. ⚖

Managing Partner, KEY AND McKNIGHT, Box 1570, Summerside, PE C1N 4K4 (902) 436-4851, FAX (902) 436-5063. Born Charlottetown 1957. m. Derek D. Key. 4 ch. EDUC: Dalhousie Law Sch., LL.B. 1981. BAR: P.E.I., 1982. CAREER: Justice of the Peace & Clerk of Court, Sir Louis Henry Davis Law Courts, Charlottetown, 1980; Articled Clerk, Farmer and Farmer, Barristers & Solicitors, 1981-82; Ptnr, Key and Key, Barristers & Solicitors, 1984-85; Ptnr, Key and McKnight, Barristers & Solicitors, 1985 to date. DIRECTOR: Professional Arts Investments Inc.; Ninety-Four Enterprises Inc.; Huntersfield Estates Inc.; Heronsfield Management Inc. AFFIL: Progressive Conservative Party of P.E.I.; Zonta Club of Summerside Area; Unit 2 Sch. Bd. (Trustee; Personnel Committee); Canadian Parents for French; Trinity United Church; Law Society of P.E.I.; Community School & Hospice Association. HONS: Dean's Hon. List, Univ. of Prince Edward Island, 1975-78; St. Dunstan's Basilica Diocese Bursary, Dalhousie Law Sch.; Mr. Justice Mark MacGuigan Entrance Scholarship, Dalhousie Law Sch. INTERESTS: skating; swimming; reading; horseback riding.

Keyserlink, Michaela 🕮 ⊗ 🕸

Senior Conservator, Textiles, CANADIAN CONSERVATION INSTITUTE, 1030 Innes Rd., Ottawa, ON K1A 0C8 (613) 998-3721, ext. 209, FAX 998-4721, EMAIL ela_keyserlink@pch.gc.ca. Born Breslau, Germany 1939. m. Robert Keyserlink. 4 ch. EDUC: Munich Univ., Teaching Diploma 1960; Algonquin Coll., Diploma (Museum Tech.) 1979. CAREER: teacher, Germany, 1960-62; archaeological digs, Italy, 1960-62; Asst. Curator, Chalice Well Trust, Glastonbury, UK, 1962-63; married, 4 ch., Ottawa, 1963 to date; Textile Conservator, National Museums of Canada, Ottawa, 1978-79; Textile Conservator, Canadian Conservation Institute, 1980 to date; special interest in painted textiles, flags & banners. SELECTED PUBLICATIONS: "The Question of Reversibility," *Preprints: Harper's Ferry Conference* (Washington, DC, 1992); "Case Histories of Textile Adhesive Treatments using Acrylic Resins Poly(n-butyl methacrylate," *Proceedings of the Symposium on the Use of Textile Adhesives*, New York (1993); "Approaches to the Conservation of Flags and Banners at the Canadian Conservation Institute," *Conservation of Flags, Symposium of the International Associa-*

tion of Arms and Military History (Stockholm, 1994 in press); various other presentations. EDIT: Contributing Ed., *AIC Textile Catalogue*. AFFIL: Canadian Association of Professional Conservators (Chair, Admissions Committee); ICOM Group Textiles (Asst. Coord.); *Art & Architecture Thesaurus* (Textile Consultant); International Institute for Conservation, Canadian Group. INTERESTS: textiles; upholstery; flower arranging; children; politics. COMMENT: *"A product of war, found a wonderful new life in Canada. Following motherhood, found a new and fulfilling career with practical work, research and travel."*

Keywan, Alicia, B.E.S.,B.Arch. ⊗ ⌣ ♥
Production Designer. 13 Castle View Ave., Toronto, ON M5R 1Z1 (416) 324-9730. 1 ch. Jelena. EDUC: Univ. of Illinois, Chicago, B.E.S.; Univ. of Waterloo, B.Arch. 1975. CAREER: Designer, Skidmore Owings and Merrill, Chicago, 1972; Arthur Erickson Architects, 1972-73; Carter and Greenberg Architects, 1974; Emiel van der Meulen Landscape Architects, 1977; Head of Interior Design, Arthur Erickson Architects, 1981-83; Art Dir. & Prod. Designer, 1980 to date. SELECTED CREDITS: Art Dir., *Silence of the North* (feature), Universal, 1980; Art Dir., *Dead of Winter* (feature), Dir. Arthur Penn, 1985; Prod. Designer, *Ray Bradbury Trilogy*, HBO, 1986; Prod. Designer, *Conspiracy of Love* (M.O.W.), CBS, 1987; Art Dir., *Stanley and Iris* (feature), MGM, 1988; Supervising Art Dir., *Dead Ringers* (feature), Morgan Creek, 1988; Art Dir., *The Freshman* (feature), Tri-Star, 1989; Art Dir., *M. Butterfly* (feature), Dir. David Cronenberg, 1992; Prod. Designer, "The Harry Oaks Murder," *The Scales of Justice* (series), CBC, 1993; Prod. Designer, "L'Affaire Belshaw," *The Scales of Justice* (series), CBC, 1994; Art Dir., *Tommy Boy* (feature), Paramount, 1994; Art Dir., *Bogus* (feature), Dir. Norman Jewison, 1995; Prod. Designer, *Jack Reed* (M.O.W.), dir. Brian Dennehy, ABC, 1996. AFFIL: Directors' Guild of Canada; United Scenic Artists' Local 829, NYC; ARIDO. HONS: Canada Council Award for the Arts, 1984. MISC: US work permit.

Khan, Shajia, M.B.,B.S.,FRCPC ⊕ ⊙ O
Physician and Past President, FEDERATION OF MEDICAL WOMEN OF CANADA, 1815 Alta Vista Dr., Ste. 107, Ottawa, ON K1G 3Y6 (613) 731-1026, FAX 731-8748. President, ASSOCIATION OF INDO-CANADIAN PHYSICIANS. Born India 1940. s. EDUC: Osmania Univ., Hyderabad, India, B.Med./B.Surg. 1965; Post Grad. training in Canada & US. CAREER: private practice in Internal Medicine & Endocrinology, Ottawa, 1972 to date; active staff, Grace Hospital & consultant staff, Ottawa Civic Hospital. AFFIL: Royal Coll. of Physicians & Surgeons of Canada (Fellow in Internal Medicine); Federation of Medical Women of Canada (Past Pres.; Bd. & Foundation Committees); Canadian Medical Association; Ontario Medical Association; Academy of Medicine Executive; Canadian Diabetes Association; American Diabetes Association; American Medical Women's Association; Association of Indo-Canadian Physicians (Pres); Professional Women's Association. INTERESTS: health promotion & patient educ.; women's health issues; computers in medicine; music; travel. COMMENT: *"Dr. Shajia Khan's practice of endocrinology includes treatment of Diabetes mellitus, thyroid and lipid disorders, menopause, and other endocrine problems, which gives her an opportunity to provide a continuum of care for her patients. She has promoted women's health issues at various levels of government and she has participated as a speaker and chaired workshops at women's health conferences."*

Khaner, Julie ■ ■ ♥ ⊗ ⌣
Actor. c/o A.C.I., 205 Ontario St., Toronto, ON M5A 2V6 (416) 363-7414, FAX 363-6715. Born Montreal. SELECTED CREDITS: Alana Newman (series regular), *Street Legal*, CBC, 6 yrs.; Emily (series regular), *Jake and the Kid*, Global; *In the Skin of a Lion* & *The English Patient*, CBC Radio; lead, *Deadly Love*, Lifetime Channel, U.S.A.; *Choices of the Heart: The Margaret Sanger Story*, Lifetime Channel, U.S.A. AFFIL: ACTRA; Equity; World Wildlife Fund.

Khetrapal, Shoba, B.A.,M.A. Ⓢ
Vice-President and Treasurer, MOORE CORPORATION LIMITED, First Canadian Place, Box 78, Toronto, ON M5X 1G5 (416) 364-2600, FAX 364-3364. Born India 1941. m. Ashok. 1 ch. Shivani. EDUC: B.A.(Hons., Econ.) 1961; M.A.(Econ.) 1963. CAREER: professional & managerial positions, Pension Investments & Treasury, Canadian Pacific Limited, 1965-77; Asst. Treas., 1977-79; Dir., Econ. & Planning, Canadian Pacific Enterprises, 1979-85; Asst. Treas., Canadian Pacific Limited, 1985-88; VP & Treas., Moore Corporation Limited, 1989 to date. DIRECTOR: Ontario Casino Corporation. AFFIL: Toronto Association of Business Economists; International Society of Treasurers; Toronto Society of Financial Analysts; Canadian Chamber of Commerce (Econ. Policy Advisory Committee). INTERESTS: swimming; theatre; cross-country skiing.

Kidd, Elizabeth M.E. ■ ■ ⊗ 📜 O
Museum and Curatorial Consultant. 1215

Pacific St., Ste. 313, Vancouver, BC V6E 3W6 (604) 683-7113, EMAIL ekidd@unixg.ubc.ca. **EDUC:** McGill Univ., B.A.(Art Hist.) 1966; École du Louvre, Paris, Diploma1969; École Pratique des Hautes Études 1969; Univ. of Toronto, M.A. 1973; various seminars & mgmt training, & ongoing research in issues affecting museums & art galleries. **CAREER:** Curator, Newfoundland Museum, St. John's, 1978-81; Art Gallery Curator/Dir., Whyte Museum of the Canadian Rockies, Banff, 1981-86; Chief Curator, The Edmonton Art Gallery, 1988-94; museum, art & admin. consultant, across Canada, 1979 to date. **SELECTED PUBLICATIONS:** numerous exhibition catalogues & several essays, articles. **AFFIL:** International Council of Museums (mbr. of Bd., ICOM-Canada; Pres., ICOM-Canada 1993-94; founding mbr., Int'l Committee of Exhibition Exchanges); Canadian Museums Association (Council mbr. 1985-88; 1996 Conference Programme Committee); American Association of Museums.

Kidder, Margot • 💓 ⊛
Actor. Born Yellowknife, N.W.T. 1948. **SELECTED CREDITS:** *Gaily, Gaily,* dir. Norman Jewison, 1969; Lois Lane, *Superman,* 1978; *The Amityville Horror,* 1979; *Heartaches,* dir. Don Shebib, 1981; Lois Lane, *Superman II,* 1983; *Trenchcoat,* 1983; *Keeping Track,* 1985; *Henry and Verlin,* 1994; *Honky Tonk* (M.O.W.), 1984; *Picking Up the Pieces* (M.O.W.), 1985; *Hoax* (M.O.W.), 1986.

Kieran, Sheila 📖 ✏
Writer and Editor. 66 Badgerow Ave., Toronto, ON M4M 1V4. Born Toronto. d. 7 ch. (1 dec.). **EDUC:** Columbia Univ., Dept. of Extension. **CAREER:** freelance writer & ed., 1970 to date; film reviewer for *The Globe & Mail, Homemaker's/Madame au Foyer,* CBC-FM & CBC-AM; Dir. of Public Participation, Royal Commission on Violence in the Communications Industry (LaMarsh Commission); Exec. Dir., Multiple Sclerosis Society of Canada; Dir., Book & Periodical Dev. Council; writer & ed., several studies & various Royal Commission reports; consultant to Chair, Ont. Social Assistance Review Committee; media strategist & writer, Social Assistance Review Committee - Public Awareness Campaign, 1989; writer, papers for Education for All initiative, sponsored by UNESCO, UNICEF, UNDP & World Bank; writer & consultant, Advisory Group on Working Time & Distribution of Work, Min. of Hum. Res. Dev.; ed. & writer, Royal Commission on the Future of the Toronto Waterfront; Mng Ed. & writer, *Waterfront Regeneration Trust Guidebook;* Sr.

Editorial Advisor & Mbr. of the Household, Right Hon. Ramon Hnatyshyn; writer, Fed. Dept. of the Environment, Dept. of Justice, the Rt. Hon. Romeo Leblanc, Gov. Gen. of Canada & many private-sector clients. **SELECTED PUBLICATIONS:** *The Non-Deductible Woman: A Handbook for Working Wives and Mothers* (Macmillan, 1970); *The Family Matters: Two Centuries of Family Law and Life in Ontario* (Toronto: Key Porter, 1986); chapter in *The Chatelaine Guide to Marriage,* Dr. B. Schlesinger, ed. (Macmillan, 1974); contributor, *Encyclopedia Canadiana* (Grolier, 1974); articles in all major Cdn publications, incl. *Saturday Night, The Canadian, Tamarack Review* & *The Globe & Mail;* various others. **AFFIL:** Ontario Prevention Clearing House (volunteer comm. consultant); Daily Bread Food Bank (volunteer comm. consultant). **MISC:** prod. & performer for CBC & TVO; ed. & writer, *Children and Their Prospects* report series, Laidlaw Foundation; writer & ed., *Rethinking Ontario's Health Care,* brochure, Ontario Nurses' Association; Ed., *Report of the Royal Commission on Education;* writer & ed., 2 educational handbooks. **COMMENT:** *"My life has been a balancing act between work and family: bringing up seven children (by myself) and doing the writing that, as well as my livelihood, has been essential to my sense of self. After all these years, I am still searching for ways to become a better writer. As naive and eager as I was to conform when I was young, I eventually realized that I wasn't on an even keel with my male co-workers, friends and family members; like many women, I did not learn feminism from Friedan, Greer or Steinem but from the men around me, especially from my ex-husband."*

Kilfoil, Anne, B.A.,M.L.S. 📖 ⊕
Director, Library Services, REGION 2 HOSPITAL CORPORATION, Saint John Regional Hospital, Box 2100, Saint John, NB E2L 4L2 (506) 648-6763, FAX 648-6764, EMAIL kilfoila@nbnet.nb.ca. Born Fredericton. **EDUC:** Univ. of New Brunswick, B.A.(Psych.) 1981; Dalhousie Univ., M.L.S. 1986. **CAREER:** Dir., Library Svcs, Region 2 Hospital Corporation. **AFFIL:** Canadian Health Libraries Association; Maritimes Health Libraries Association (Pres. 1992-94; Past-Pres.).

Killingbeck, Molly Elizabeth, B.A. ■ 🏃 🏆
Head Coach, Women's Track and Field and Cross-Country Team, YORK UNIVERSITY, School of Physical Education, North York, ON M3J 1P3 (416) 736-2100, ext. 20833, FAX 736-5774, EMAIL mkilling@yorku.ca. Associate National Relay Team Coordinator, ATH-

LETICS CANADA. Born Clarendon, Jamaica. m. Liam O'Connor. EDUC: York Univ., B.A.(Soc.) 1986. CAREER: Teacher's Aide, Tumpane Public Sch., 1988-89; Public Speaker, Ont. Ministry of Tourism, Culture & Recreation, 1985 to date. SPORTS CAREER: Gold Medal, 4x400 metre relay, Commonwealth Games, Brisbane, Australia, 1982; Silver Medals, 4x100 & 4x400 metre relay, 400 metres, World Univ. Games, 1983; 4th Place, 4x100 & 4x400 metre relays, World Championships, 1983; Silver Medal, 4x400 metre relay, Summer Olympics, L.A., 1984; Silver Medal, 4x400 metre relay, World Univ. Games, 1985; Gold Medal, 4x400 metre relay, Commonwealth Games, 1986; 4th Place, 4x400 metre relay, World Championships, 1987; Sprint Coach, Univ. of Windsor, 1989-95; Sports Info. Officer, 1990-93; Prov. Sprint Coach, Ont. Track & Field Association, 1990-95; Interim Head Coach, Track & Field, Univ. of Windsor, 1992; Sprint Coach, World Indoor Championships Team, Toronto, 1993; Head Coach, 17th World Deaf Games Team, Sofia, Bulgaria, 1993; Sprint Coach, World Univ. Games Team, Buffalo, 1993; Sprint/Relay Coach, Ont. Track & Field Team, Canada Summer Games, Kamloops, B.C., 1993; Head Coach/Gen. Mgr, Windsor Legion Track & Field Club, 1993-95; Sprint/Relay Coach, Commonwealth Games, Victoria, 1994; Assoc. Nat'l Relay Team Coord., Athletics Canada, 1994 to date; Head Coach, Women's Track & Field & Cross-Country Team, York Univ., 1995 to date; Sprint/Relay Coach, gold medal men's 4x100 metres relay team & men's 100m world record, Summer Olympics, Atlanta, 1996. SELECTED PUBLICATIONS: departmental handbooks for coaches, students & athletes; "Where Are They Now?" column (Athletics Magazine 1993 to date); "Women as Coaches" (NACACTFA Newsletter June 1994); various other publications. AFFIL: North America, Central America, Caribbean Track & Field Association; Coll. of Coaches, Athletics Canada; National Coaching Certification Program; Advisory Committee on Gender Equity in Sport & Physical Activity, Ont. Ministry of Culture, Tourism & Recreation; F.A.M.E. (Female Athletes Motivating Excellence); Athletics Canada (Banned Substances Solution Educ. Committee). HONS: Prov. Award for Sport Excellence at the nat'l & int'l level, Ont. Ministry of Tourism & Recreation, 1980-89; Sports Excellence Award, Gov't of Canada, 1983, 1985, 1987; Harry Jerome Award for Sport Excellence (Outstanding Black Cdn Athlete), 1984; Athlete of the Year, 1984, 1985; Outstanding Female Athlete, Canadian Interuniversity Athletic Association, 1985; Coach of the Year, Ont. Women's Interuniver-

sity Athletic Association, 1992, 1994; Fac. of Human Kinetics Award, Univ. of Windsor, 1993; Coach of the Year, Canadian Interuniversity Athletic Association, 1996. INTERESTS: helping & inspiring youth; modelling; shopping (esp. for bargains); Ginger & Silver, her cats. MISC: mbr. of the nat'l record 4x400m relay team; nat'l record holder 500m; former nat'l record holder 400m; 3 time Cdn nat'l champion, 1982, 1983, 1985; Team Captain, Cdn Track & Field Team, 1985, 1987, 1988; dir. & organizer of numerous track & field meets; numerous presentations to athletes, coaches, students (elementary, secondary & post-secondary); N.C.C.P. (Nat'l Coaching Certification Program) Level IV in progress. COMMENT: "As an athlete, Molly Killingbeck was a three-time Canadian 400m champion and former national record holder, and a member of 11 major international games teams, including three Olympic Games. She has made the transition from athlete to coach with great success. Her most recent accomplishment: sprint relay coach for the Olympic Champion men's 4x100m relay team in Atlanta this past summer."

Killinger, Barbara, B.A.,M.A.,Ph.D. ⊕ 🗋
Psychologist and Writer. 60 Pleasant Blvd., Ste. B, Toronto, ON M4T 1K1 (416) 968-2203. President, HENDERSON PUBLICATIONS INC. Born London, Ont. 1934. sep. 3 ch. Katherine, Michael, Suzanne. EDUC: Univ. of Western Ontario, B.A.(Secretarial Sci.) 1955; York Univ., Hons. B.A.(Psych.) 1972, M.A.(Psych.) 1974, Ph.D.(Psych.) 1977. CAREER: Intern, Psychological Services, York Univ., 1972; Intern, North York General Hospital, 1973-74; Intern, Toronto East General Hospital, 1974-75; Research Asst., York Univ., 1975-76; Clinical Psychologist, North York General Hospital, 1978-80; Clinical Psychologist in private practice, 1980 to date; writer, 1990 to date; Pres., Henderson Publications Inc., 1990 to date. SELECTED PUBLICATIONS: "The Place of Humour in Adult Psychotherapy" (It's a Funny Thing, Humour, ed. A.J. Chapman & H. Foot, Oxford: Pergamon Press, 1977); "Humour in Psychotherapy: A Shift to a New Perspective" in Handbook of Humor and Psychotherapy. Advances in the Clinical Use of Humor ed. W.F. Fry, Jr. & W.A. Salameh (Sarasota, Fla.: Professional Resource Exchange Inc., 1987); Workaholics: The Respectable Addicts (Toronto: Key Porter Books, 1991); The Balancing Act: Rediscovering Your Feelings (Toronto: Key Porter Books, 1995). AFFIL: Ontario Psychological Association; C.G. Jung Foundation of Ontario; University Women's Club of North York; Toronto Cricket, Skating

& Curling Club; Writers' Union of Canada. **INTERESTS**: skiing; tennis; swimming; bicycling; sculpture; reading club; gardening. **MISC**: numerous seminars & invited lectures; judged literary awards for Short Stories Writer's Award, 1987; numerous radio, TV & newspaper interviews on book *Workaholics: The Respectable Addicts*, 1991 & *The Balancing Act: Resdiscovering Your Feelings*, 1995; second-year student at Ontario Coll. of Art. **COMMENT**: *"A curious nature, a fascination with what makes people tick and why things work, leads me to diverse interests and a love of people and ideas. A pioneer in humour research and workaholism."*

Kimball, Mary A., B.Sc.,LL.B. 🗝 ♣ Ⓢ
Deputy Registrar General of Land Titles, NEW BRUNSWICK GEOGRAPHIC INFORMATION CORPORATION, 985 College Hill Rd., Box 6000, Fredericton, NB E3B 5H1 (506) 357-4066, FAX 357-4067. Born Fredericton 1950. m. Lorne A. Brown. 3 ch. Lorne P. Brown, Douglas T. Brown, Karin S. Brown-Harrison. **EDUC**: Dalhousie Univ., B.Sc.(Math.) 1971, LL.B. 1976. **BAR**: N.B., 1976. **CAREER**: Assoc. Lawyer, Stewart & Cooper, Moncton, N.B., 1976-81; Solicitor, Land Registration & Info. Svc., Halifax, 1981-83; Mgr, Land Titles Proj., Moncton, N.B., 1983-93; Deputy Registrar Gen. of Land Titles, N.B., 1986 to date; Registrar of Deeds/Land Titles, Albert County, N.B., 1992-93. **AFFIL**: N.B. Law Society (Council Mbr. 1984-86, 1991-92); Canadian Bar Association - N.B. Branch (Council; Exec. 1989-93); Canadian Bar Association (Chair, Constitution & By-Laws Committee 1994-95). **HONS**: Certificate of Outstanding Achievement, Council of Maritime Premiers, 1986; Canada 125 Medal; Certificate of Appreciation, Canadian Bar Association, 1994.

Kimball, Meredith M., B.A.,Ph.D. ■ 🐿 🏵
Professor in Psychology and Women's Studies, SIMON FRASER UNIVERSITY, Burnaby, BC V5A 1S6 (604) 291-4130, FAX 291-3427, EMAIL meredith_kimball@sfu.ca. Born Neb. 1944. **EDUC**: Macalester Coll., B.A.(Psych.) 1966; Univ. of Michigan, Ph.D.(Developmental Psych.) 1970. **CAREER**: Asst. Prof., Univ. of British Columbia, 1970-76; Asst. Prof., Simon Fraser Univ., 1976-82; Assoc. Prof., Simon Fraser Univ., 1982-96; Prof., 1996 to date. **SELECTED PUBLICATIONS**: "Women and success: a basic conflict?" in *Women in Canada* ed. M. Stephenson (Toronto: New Press, 1973); "Women and science: A critique of biological theories" (*International Journal of Women's Studies* No. 4 1981); "Science free of sexism: A psychologist's guide to the conduct of nonsexist

research," with C. Stark-Adamec (*Canadian Psychology* No. 25 1984); "Developing a feminist psychology of women: past and future accomplishments" (*Canadian Psychology* No. 27 1986); *Women and Aging* with E. Gee (Toronto: Butterworth's, 1987); "A new perspective on women's math achievement" (*Psychological Bulletin* No. 105 189); "The worlds we live in: Gender similarities and differences" (*Canadian Psychology* No. 35 1994); *Feminist Visions of Gender Similarities and Differences* (Binghamton, NY: Haworth Press, 1995). **EDIT**: Ed. Bd., *Canadian Psychology*, 1987-90. **AFFIL**: Association of Women in Psychology; Canadian Psychological Association (Fellow); Canadian Women's Studies Association. **COMMENT**: *"All of my professional accomplishments in teaching, research, and political work have been guided by visions of feminism that seek to eliminate domination and create a better world for all peoples."*

King, Charmion, B.A. ■■ ⊗ 🐿 ⼡
Actress. Born Toronto 1925. m. Gordon Pinsent. 1 ch. Leah Pinsent Capellupo. **EDUC**: Univ. of Toronto, B.A.(English & Hist.) 1947. **CAREER**: Actress. **SELECTED CREDITS**: *Rumours & Borders*, CBC Radio; *Anne of Green Gables* (TV); *St. Joan* (opening of Hart House), Univ. of Toronto; *Royal Family*, BBC; *Three Sisters, Cherry Orchard & MacBeth*, Crest Theatre; *Toys in the Attic, Impromptu at Outremont & Jitters*, Tarragon Theatre, Long Wharf Theatre & Centre Stage; *'Night Mother; Children; Cocktail Hour; Homeward Bound; Belfrey; Sweet Bird of Youth* (sesquicentennial), Univ. of Toronto; *Love Letters*, New Bastion Theatre; *Love & Libel*, Martin Beck Theater, N.Y. **AFFIL**: Canadian Actors' Equity Association; ACTRA (Pres., Performers' Guild 1992-93); Screen Actors' Guild; Actors' Equity Association, U.S. (Chair, Cdn Advisory Committee 1958-62). **HONS**: Jane Mallett award, Best Radio Actress. **INTERESTS**: everything, but esp. maintenance of actors in Canada; recognition of Cdn identity; music; cooking; gardens; art. **MISC**: co-produced original Straw Hat Players; started Canadian Equity Showcase. **COMMENT**: *"I am a liberal Torontonian, wife, mother and actress whose attempts to fulfill my aspirations are seldom fully achieved but the work put in results in knowledge and enlightenment that make life joyous."*

King, Jen Genia Ⓢ
President, WHITE SADDLE AIR SERVICES LTD., White Saddle Ranch, Box 44, Tatla Lake,, BC V0L 1V0 (604) 476-1182. Born Edmonton 1922. w. 3 ch. David, Michael, Brian. **EDUC**: MacDougall Commercial, Edmonton.

CAREER: Owner/Operator/Ptnr in business with husband, late 1950s to 1970s; Pres., White Saddle Air Services Ltd., since the mid-1970s. AFFIL: B.C. Mountaineering Club; *Canadian Alpine Journal* (Sponsor); Tatla Lake Rod & Gun Club & Community Club; Canadian Nature Federation; Canadian Wildlife Association; World Wildlife Fund; B.C. Wildlife Federation; Western Canada Wilderness; B.C. Aviation Council; Canadian Owners' & Pilots' Association. HONS: Canada 125 Medal. INTERESTS: reading; cross-country skiing; badminton; photography; gardening; 8 beautiful grandchildren. COMMENT: *"Lived in many cities. Retired in my early 50s to this wilderness, and changed from industrial-equipment business to an air charter. Built our own runway, developed our own hydro and power system, as well as water supply and telephone. None of these facilities was available in this valley. My husband was killed a few months after we moved from Victoria, and I kept this operation going with the help of my great sons."*

King, Karen A., B.A. 🖤 🐾

Producer. 593 Melita Cres., Toronto, ON M6G 3Y7 (416) 538-7165, FAX 538-6693. Born Trinidad, WI 1960. m. Okeluo Chigbo. 2 ch. Chicezie Karl King Chigbo, Chiemeka Andrew James Chigbo. EDUC: Simon Fraser Univ., B.A.(Pol. Sci. & English) 1982; various film-related workshops. CAREER: Asst. Prod./Writer/Host, *Cross Pulse* (weekly 1/2 hr. live magazine TV program), 1984-85; Asst. Prod. of Commercials, McWaters VanLint & Associates, 1986-87; Prod. of Commercials, Derek Vanlint & Associates, 1988-92; Host/Interview, *Issues in Education* (live panel discussion with hotline), TVOntario, 1992-93. SELECTED CREDITS: Prod. Asst., *The Top of His Head* (feature), 1985; Assoc. Prod., *Jennifer Hodge–The Glory & The Pain* (short documentary), 1992; Prod., *Wonderin' Where the Lions Are* (music video), 1992; Prod., *The Very Dead of Winter* (short film), 1993; Prod., *A Variation on the Key 2 Life* (short film), 1993; Assoc. Prod., *Underground to Freedom* (M.O.W.), Atlantis, 1993; Prod., *RUDE* (feature), 1995; Host & Interviewer, *Anti-Racist Teleconference*, TVO, 1993; Host & Interviewer, *The Safe Schools Teleconference*, TVO, 1993; Host, *Tobacco, Alcohol & Other Drugs*, TVO, 1995. AFFIL: Black Film & Video Network (Mbr., Founding VP); Feature Film Project (Prod.); Canadian Film Centre (Prod.); Women in Film & Television. HONS: Automotive Merit Award (Volkswagen "Blue Moon"), Bessie Awards, 1989; TV Single Merit Award (Volkswagen "Blue Moon"), Art Directors Club of Toronto Awards, 1989; Bronze Corporate Award (Noranda "Wrist"), Bessie Awards, 1990; best R&B Video (*Wonderin' Where the Lions Are*), Much Music Awards, 1992; Gold Plaque Award (*A Variation on the Key 2 Life*), Chicago Film Festival, 1993; Bronze Award, Short Dramatic Original (*A Variation on the Key 2 Life*), World Festival, Charleston, S.C., 1993; nominee, Best Movie or Mini-Series (*Race to Freedom: The Underground Railroad*), Cable ACE Awards, 1995; Best Canadian Drama (*RUDE*), Atlantic Films Festival, 1995; Best Ontario Film (*RUDE*), Sudbury Film Festival, 1995; Special Jury Citation (*RUDE*), Toronto International Film Festival, 1995; nominee, Best Picture (*RUDE*), Genie Awards, 1995. MISC: 1st black woman to produce a theatrically released dramatic feature film in Canada; *RUDE* had world premier at Int'l Festival of Film in 'Uncertain Regard' in Cannes '95 & the N.Am. premier as the Perspective Canada Opening Film, Toronto Int'l Film Festival, 1995; juror for various industry competitions; lecturer, panelist & moderator.

King, Lynn, B.A.,M.A.,LL.B. ⚖️

Judge, ONTARIO COURT OF JUSTICE (Provincial Division) - Family and Youth Court, 311 Jarvis St., Toronto, ON M5B 2C4 (416) 327-6891, FAX 327-6979. Born Canada 1944. m. M.T. Kelly. 2 ch. Jay Kelly, Max Kelly. EDUC: Univ. of Toronto, B.A.(Pol. Sci. & Econ.) 1967, LL.B. 1971; Fletcher Sch. of Law & Diplomacy, M.A.(Int'l Affairs) 1968. BAR: Ont., 1973. CAREER: Ptnr, Copeland, King, 1973-75; researcher-writer, Educ. Rel'ns Commission (Ont.), 1975-76; Lecturer, Osgoode Hall Law Sch., York Univ., 1975-76; Ptnr, King and Sachs (all women's law firm), 1976-86; Judge, Ont. Court of Justice (Prov. Div.), Family & Youth Court, 1986 to date. SELECTED PUBLICATIONS: *What Every Woman Should Know about Marriage, Separation and Divorce* (James Lorimer & Co., 1980); *Law, Law, Law* (Anansi Press); "Censorship and Law Reform: Will Changing the Laws Mean a Change for the Better?" in *Women Against Censorship* (Douglas and McIntyre); contributions to various journals, incl. *Today's Woman*. AFFIL: Ontario Family Law Judges' Association (Dir.). PAST AFFIL: Sexual Orientation & Youth Proj., Central Toronto Youth Services (Advisory Committee); Open Circle Theatre, Adelaide Court (Dir.); Film & Video Against Censorship (Legal Advisor); National Action Committee on the Status of Women (Dir.); Rape Crisis Centre (Dir.); Women's Habitat (Consultant & Dir.); Interval House (Consultant & Dir.); Casey House Hospital (Dir.). HONS: University Coll. Alumnae Scholarship, Univ. of

Toronto, 1965. INTERESTS: reading; children; wilderness canoeing & camping; wildflowers. COMMENT: *"I am interested in family and youth issues and my work allows me to play an active role in these matters."*

King-Leslie, Deardra ■■ ⊗

Director, STUDIO D (performing arts centre), 109 Ottawa St. S., Unit B, Kitchener, ON N2G 3S8 (519) 744-2600. Born Kitchener, Ont. 1953. CAREER: began dance (jazz, tap, ballet, musical theatre) & baton twirling at age 4; competed in dance & baton for 14 yrs., winning over 1000 awards; performed professionally with baton & dance act for 11 yrs. across Canada, North Pole & Europe; judging, teaching & coaching career for 27 yrs., across Canada, U.S.A., England, Ireland & France; CBTF & IBTA baton twirling teacher, coach, judge, coaches' course conductor & judges' course conductor; dir., choreographer, teacher, coach at Studio D. AFFIL: International Baton Twirling Association (Tech. Dir.); Kitchener-Waterloo Business Women's Association; Canadian Dance Teachers' Association; Canadian Baton Twirling Federation. HONS: Special Lifetime Achievement Award, Ontario Sports Federation; Lifetime Achievement Award, Canadian Baton Twirling Federation. INTERESTS: theatre; reading; travel; enjoying friendships. MISC: former Miss Majorette of Ontario, Miss Majorette of Canada, N.Am. Twirl Champion & World Champion; students & athletes have achieved high honours in dance & baton incl. Ont., Cdn, N.Am. & world awards; students have performed at Disneyworld, throughout Ont. COMMENT: *"I am a dreamer of dreams...I am a dance maker. I am a baton maker. I am a mover and shaker of the world forever, it seems."*

Kingston, Joan, B.N.,R.N.,MLA ✤ ⊕ ☺

Member of the Legislative Assembly, GOVERNMENT OF NEW BRUNSWICK, 108 MacIntosh Dr., New Maryland, NB E3C 1B7 (506) 462-0081, FAX 462-0082. Born Sussex, N.B. 1955. m. Jacques Roy. 2 ch. Stephanie Roy, Nicholas Roy. EDUC: Univ. of New Brunswick, B.N. 1978; Grace Maternity Hospital, Halifax, Certificate (Neonatal Intensive Care Nursing) 1984. CAREER: Staff Nurse, Mother & Baby Unit, Dr. Everett Chalmers Hospital, 1978-79; Staff Nurse, Labour & Delivery, 1982-84; Staff Nurse, Neonatal Intensive Care Unit, 1979-82; Nurse Mgr, Neonatal Intensive Care Unit, 1982-94; Chairperson, N.B. Advisory Council on the Status of Women, 1994-95; elected MLA (New Maryland), 1995 to date; Legislative Asst., Dept. of Educ. & Chair, Select Committee on Demographics, 1995-96. AFFIL:

Nurses' Association of N.B. (Exec. Committee 1989-94; Pres. 1993-94); Canadian Nurses' Association (Dir. 1993-94). HONS: Alumni Undergrad. Scholarship, Univ. of New Brunswick; Fanny Velensky Award for Clinical Excellence in Nursing, Univ. of New Brunswick Fac. of Nursing; Wyeth Section Award, Association for Women's Health, Obstetric & Neonatal Nursing. INTERESTS: politics; women's equality; advancement of nursing; public speaking on issues of health-care reform, nursing practice & women's equality. COMMENT: *"As a nurse, politician and a member of the largest professional group in Canada, I am acutely aware of how true equality for women could have a positive impact on issues as large as the nation's economy and health-care system and as personal as the quality of family life."*

Kinlough-Rathbone, Raelene Lorna, M.B., B.S.,M.D.,Ph.D. ■■ ⊗ ▯

Associate Vice-President, Faculty of Health Sciences, and Professor of Pathology, MCMASTER UNIVERSITY, 1200 Main St. W., HSC 2E5C, Hamilton, ON L8N 3Z5 (905) 525-9140, ext. 22184, FAX 546-0800. Born Adelaide, S. Australia 1936. EDUC: Univ. of Adelaide, M.B., B.S.(Medicine) 1961, M.D.(Medicine) 1967; McMaster Univ., Ph.D.(Medical Sciences) 1971. CAREER: Jr./Sr. Resident Medical Officer, Royal Adelaide Hospital/Adelaide Children's Hospital/Queen Elizabeth Maternity Hospital, Australia, 1961-63; Research Asst., National Heart Foundation of Australia, Dept. of Medicine, Univ. of Adelaide, & Hon. Clinical Asst., Medical Professorial Unit, Royal Adelaide Hospital, 1964-67; Post-doctoral Research Fellow, Medical Research Council of Canada, Dept. of Pathology, McMaster Univ., 1967-71; Prof. Research Asst., Medical Research Council of Canada (McMaster), 1971; Lecturer, Dept. of Pathology, 1971; Asst. Prof., 1973; Sr. Research Fellow, Ontario Heart Foundation (McMaster), 1974; Assoc. Prof., 1976; Research Assoc., Ontario Heart Foundation, 1980; tenured appt., Dept. of Pathology, McMaster, 1981; Prof., 1982; Chair, Grad. Programme in Medical Sciences, 1981-87; Acting Assoc. Dean, Educ., Fac. of Health Sciences, 1987-88; Assoc. VP, Fac. of Health Sciences, 1992 to date. SELECTED PUBLICATIONS: author/co-author, 161 journal articles, 40 book chpts, 173 abstract publications. EDIT: Edit. Bd., *Thrombosis Research*, 1994-96; *Platelets*, 1990 to date. AFFIL: International Society on Thrombosis & Haemostasis; American Heart Association (Council on Thrombosis); American Society for Investigative Pathology; American Society of Hematology; Canadian Society for Clinical Investigation; Canadian Artherosclerosis Society; American Association for the Advancement of Science; Senior Women Academic Administrators of Canada; Medical Research Council (Review Committee for the Michael Smith Award of Excellence 1994 to date); Centre for Studies of Children at Risk, Chedoke-McMaster Hospitals (Bd. of Dir. 1992 to date); Michener Institute of Applied Health Sciences, Toronto (Bd. of Dir. 1995 to date); Ontario Equestrian Federation; Canadian Equestrian Federation; Ontario Hunter, Jumper Association. **HONS:** Travel Award, National Heart Foundation of Australia, 1967; currently holds Medical Research Council grant in aid of research on the role of blood platelets in haemostasis & thrombosis. **INTERESTS:** horsemanship; opera; reading.

Kinnear, Kathy E., B.A. ■■ $
President, CRESFORD DEVELOPMENTS (real estate dev.), 155 Dalhousie St., Toronto, ON M5R 3C7 (416) 360-4223, FAX 360-5787. Born Cornwall, Ont. 1948. m. Alan Dean. 3 ch. Robert, Michael, Peter. **EDUC:** Carleton Univ., B.A.(English) 1970. **CAREER:** Research Analyst, Ontario Housing Corporation, 1970-73; Neighbourhood Planner, Planning Bd., City of Toronto, 1973-78; Sr. Planner, Planning & Dev. Dept., 1978-80; Proj. Mgr, Housing Dept., 1980-88; Mgr, Land Dev., 1988-89; VP, Dev., Centara Corporation, 1990-94; VP, Dev., Creson Corporation, 1994-96; Pres., Cresford Developments, 1996 to date. **AFFIL:** Canadian Construction Research Board (mbr. 1984-86); Urban Development Institute (mbr. 1991-96; Chair, Cityplan Subcommittee 1992-94); Toronto Rape Crisis Centre (Volunteer Counsellor 1975-79; Pres., Bd. of Dir. 1978-79); Hester How Day Care Centre (mbr., Bd. of Dir. 1983-87; Pres., Bd. of Dir. 1984-86); Red Cross (donor, Apheresis Programme 1989-96).

Kinsella, Sister Elizabeth A., M.A. ♡ ☼
Co-Founder and Executive Director, CENTRE YOUVILLE CENTRE OTTAWA-CARLETON INC., 19 Melrose Ave., Ottawa, ON K1Y 1T8 (613) 729-6748, FAX 729-3885. Born Ottawa 1928. Religious Sister of the Grey Sisters Congregation, Pembroke, Ont., 1947. **EDUC:** St. Patrick's Coll., B.A.(English/Hist.) 1957; High School Specialist, H.S.A.(English) 1958; Ottawa Univ., M.A.(English) 1967; St. Francis Xavier Univ.–Coady Institute, Co-op. Studies 1984. **CAREER:** elementary teacher, 1949-57; Principal, 1957-58; high sch. teacher, Dept. Head, English, 1957-79; high sch. teacher, part-time, 1979-83; Social Worker, part-time, 1979-83. **VOLUNTEER CAREER:** mbr., Co-op. Bd. & Interview Team, Dalhousie Nonprofit Housing Co-operative, 1980-83; Bd. & Interview Team, Daybreak Nonprofit Shelter (Ecumenical) Corporation, 1982-83; Co-Founder & Exec. Dir., Youville Centre, 1985 to date; Bd. Mbr., 1985 to date. **AFFIL:** Kiwanis Club of Ottawa (Hon. Chaplain). **HONS:** Canada Volunteer Award, 1992; Independent Learning Centre Award, 1992; Lamp of Learning Award, OSSTF, 1993; Award for Outstanding Contribution to the Community, Sigma Beta Phi, 1994; Charity Chapter Challenge Award, CSAE, 1994. **INTERESTS:** reading; meditating; music for relaxation; people. **MISC:** has worked–with youth groups–with Youville Centre Bd. & volunteers, responsible for setting up a high sch., an infant/toddler/presch. daycare, a residence, independent housing units & support systems for young high-risk single mothers & their children. **COMMENT:** *"The teaching of English helped me to reach out to the ideals, hopes and dreams of my students, as seen in literature. My life as a religious sister called me to work with the underprivileged in housing needs, sickness, prison and education. In my work at Youville Centre, I am able to help women and children become confident, self-sufficient citizens."*

Kinsley, Marnie, B.Comm.,C.A. $
Senior Vice-President and Chief Auditor, BANK OF MONTREAL, 55 Bloor St. W., 18th Fl., Toronto, ON M4W 3N5 (416) 927-6005, FAX 927-6024. Born Toronto 1954. m. Brian. 2 ch. Barbara, Raymond. **EDUC:** Univ. of Toronto, B.Comm.(Econ./Acctg) 1977. **CAREER:** audit staff & mgmt, Peat, Marwick, Mitchell & Co., 1977-85; Asst. Chief Auditor, Bank of Montreal, 1985-88; Sr. Mgr, Securities Svcs Centre, 1988-90; VP & Leader, Task Force on the Advancement of Women, 1991; VP, Corp. Electronic Bnkg, 1992-94; Sr. VP & Chief Auditor, 1995 to date. **SELECTED PUBLICATIONS:** "A Pragmatic Approach to Work Place Equality" (*Business & The Contemporary World*, Vol. V, No. 3, 1993). **AFFIL:** Canadian Institute of Chartered Accountants (C.A.; Dir., Criteria of Control Bd.); Foundation for International Training (Gov.); Bankers' Administration Institute (Audit Commission); Victoria Univ. at Univ. of Toronto (Chancellor's Council); Institute of Internal Auditors (Gov. 1989-94; Sec. 1992-93; Treas. 1993-94); The Hugh Macmillan Children's Foundation (Dir.); The Sch. of the Toronto Dance Theatre (Treas. 1984-86; Pres. & Chair 1987-88). **HONS:** Women of Distinction Award, YWCA of Metropolitan Toronto, 1995; Women on the Move Award, *The Toronto Sun*, 1994. **INTERESTS:** photography; classical music; travel. **COMMENT:** *"My belief in the strength of women and the needs of women in the work-*

place have driven me to address the inhibitors to their career advancement, through mentoring, advocating, public speaking and supporting the balance between work, family, education and community involvement."

Kinsman, Carolyn Marie (née Zagrosh) $ ⊛ ♂

Owner and President, AUTOMATED COMMUNICATION LINKS, INC., 2242 Malden Ct., Mississauga, ON L5K 1W5 (905) 855-0661, FAX (905) 855-2857. Born Toronto 1952. cl. Steven G. Kanyar. 1 ch. Leslie Kinsman. EDUC: Sheridan Coll., Diploma (Telecomm.) 1987. CAREER: Owner/Operator, Solo Wholesale Company, 1985-87; Corp. Ntwk Mktg, Northern Telecom, 1988-90; Customer Svc. Mgr, Nippon Electric Corporation, 1988-90; Nat'l Mktg Mgr, G.P.T. Plessy, 1988-90; Consultant, Ontario Hydro, 1988-90; Owner & Pres., Automated Communication Links, 1990 to date. SELECTED PUBLICATIONS: *The Automatic Meter Reading Handbook*; *Link Lingo*. EDIT: Ed., *The Link* quarterly industry newsletter. INTERESTS: navigating & piloting 38-foot motor cruiser. MISC: Keynote Speaker, Australian Utility Conference, 1992; official A.M.R. instructor for US Utility A.M.R.A. Association; chaired US Utility Conference for Fiber Installation & Services, California, 1995. COMMENT: *"Only consultant (ever) to successfully negotiate and manage a five-utility telecommunications and meter reading project; first to negotiate and manage an equally funded communications/energy management project between a cable company and a utility."*

Kirby, Sandra Louise, B.P.E.,B.Ed., M.A.,Ph.D. ⊛ ☺ ⋐

Professor, Department of Sociology, UNIVERSITY OF WINNIPEG, 515 Portage Ave., Winnipeg, MB R3B 2E9. Born Calgary 1949. EDUC: Univ. of British Columbia, B.P.E. 1971, B.Ed. 1972; McGill Univ., M.A. 1980; Univ. of Alberta, Ph.D. 1986. CAREER: Assoc. Prof., Dept. of Soc., Univ. of Winnipeg. SELECTED PUBLICATIONS: "Experience, Research, Social Change," co-author (1989); "Women Changing Academe," co-ed. (1992). AFFIL: Canadian Research Institute for the Advancement of Women (Pres.); Canadian Advisory Council for Drug-Free Sport; Fed.-Prov. Territorial Strategic Planning Sport Committee; Volunteer Home Support (Dir.); Sum Quod Sum; Univ. of Winnipeg Rowing Club (Founder & Coach). HONS: Canada 125 Medal. INTERESTS: rowing. MISC: mbr., 1976 Olympic Rowing Team. COMMENT: *"Areas of specialty are research methods and issues in sport as an Olympian, research in sports focuses mainly on sexual*

harassment issues; active feminist working on variety of issues to advance the status of women."

Kirk, Bernice ☺

President, British Columbia Division, CANADIAN UNION OF PUBLIC EMPLOYEES, 510-4940 Canada Way, Burnaby, BC V5G 4T3 (604) 291-9119, FAX 291-9043. Born Regina. m. Mervyn Kirk. 2 ch. CAREER: Sec. & Office Supervisor, Coquitlam Sch. Bd.; Sec.-Treas., Canadian Union of Public Employees, B.C. Div., 1979-91; Pres., 1991 to date. DIRECTOR: Insurance Corporation of British Columbia; Working Enterprises Financial; Working Opportunity Fund. COMMENT: *"I have been involved in the trade union movement for more than 20 years. During this time, I have worked for the rights of all workers–both men and women–to have safe, healthy workplaces, good working conditions, and benefits, and to provide decent wages so that they and their families can live comfortable lives. I have been in the forefront of the fight for pay equity in British Columbia."*

Kirkland, Lynn, B.Sc.,R.D. ■ ⊕ ○

Past President, ALBERTA REGISTERED DIETITIANS' ASSOCIATION, 445 Lessard Dr., Edmonton, AB T6M 1B6 (403) 487-8504. Owner, SIMPLY POWERFUL COMMUNICATIONS. Born Edmonton 1961. m. Paul Kirkland. 1 ch. Erin Kirkland. EDUC: Univ. of Alberta, B.Sc.(Home Econ./ Foods & Nutrition) 1985. CAREER: Dietetic Intern, Misericordia Hospital, 1986; Unit Supervisor, Cafeteria, Catering, Menu Formulation & Research, Misericordia Hospital, 1986-87; Dir., Dept. of Food Svcs, Fort Saskatchewan General Hospital, 1987-88; Educ. Coord., Dept. of Food Svcs, Misericordia Hospital, 1988-90; Coord. of Nutrition Programs, Club Fit, Edmonton, 1988-90; Mgr, Patient Svcs, Dept. of Food Svcs, Misericordia Hospital, 1990-92; Principal & Owner, Synerjoy Enterprises Ltd., 1992-95; Owner, Simply Powerful Communications, 1995 to date. SELECTED PUBLICATIONS: "Achieving Healthy Weights" (*Canadian Family Physician* Jan. 1993). AFFIL: Alberta Registered Dietitians' Association (Treas. 1987-88; Registrar 1990-91; Pres. 1993-94; Bd. of Dir. 1996-97); Canadian Dietetic Association (Chair, Public Rel'ns Conference 1989; Bd. of Dir. 1996-97). INTERESTS: food biotechnology; adult educ. COMMENT: *"I believe effective communications is essential to great leadership."*

Kirkland, Marie Claire, C.M.,C.Q., Q.C. ■ ✦ ☒ ♂

Legislator (retired) and Judge (retired),

PROVINCE OF QUEBEC, 2685 Rothesay Rd., T/H 14, Rothesay, NB E2E 5X9. Born Palmer, Mass. 1924. m. Wyndham Strover (d., P. Casgrain). 3 ch. Lynne-Marie, Kirkland, Marc. EDUC: McGill Univ., B.A. 1947, B.C.L. 1950. BAR: Que., 1952. CAREER: private practice of law, Montreal, 1952-61; elected Liberal M.N.A. (Jacques Cartier), by-election, Dec. 14, 1961; re-elected, gen. election, Nov. 14, 1962; Min. of State, Prov. of Que., 1962-64; Min. of Transport & Comm., 1964-66; elected Liberal M.L.A. (Marguerite Bourgeoys), gen. election, June 5, 1966; mbr., Liberal Opposition, 1966-70; re-elected, gen. election, Apr. 20, 1970; Min. of Tourism, Fish & Game, 1970-73; Min. of Cultural Affairs, 1973; Judge, Court of Quebec, 1973-90; Chrm, Minimum Wage Commission, 1973-80. AFFIL: Barreau du Québec; Canadian Bar Association; International Alliance of Women, Canadian Chapter (Founding Pres.); Quebec Safety League (Life Mbr.); Douglas Hospital Corporation (Life Gov.); Montreal General Hospital (Gov.); McGill Chamber Orchestra (Dir.); Phi Alpha Delta Law Fraternity (Life Mbr.). HONS: Queen's Counsel, 1969; Medal of Excellence for French Lit., Gov't of France, 1947; Member of the Order of Canada, 1992; Chevalier de l'Ordre National du Québec, 1985; Gov. General's "Persons" Medal, 1993; Grand Dame of the Order of St. John of Jerusalem (Knights of Malta), Priory of Quebec; LL.D.(Hons.), Univ. de Moncton, 1965; LL.D.(Hon.), York Univ., 1975. MISC: 1st woman to appear & plead before the Private Bills Committee, Legislative Assembly of Que.; 1st woman mbr., Que. prov. parliament, 1961; only woman mbr., Que. prov. parliament, 1961-73; 1st woman Cabinet Mbr., Que. prov. parliament, 1962; 1st Cdn woman to be appointed as Acting Premier of a province during the absence of the regular incumbent, 1972; 1st woman named Judge, Provincial Court of Quebec, 1973; sponsored Bill 16, which dealt with legal rights of married women in Quebec.

Kirschner, Teresa J., B.A.,M.A., Ph.D. ■ ⌒ 📖

Professor, Humanities Program, SIMON FRASER UNIVERSITY, Burnaby, BC V5A 1S6 (604) 291-4504, FAX 291-5950. Born Barcelona 1936. m. Dr. Don S. Kirschner. 2 ch. EDUC: Lycée Français de Barcelone, Baccalaureate Studies; Roosevelt Univ., Chicago, B.A.(French Lit.) 1962; Univ. of Chicago, M.A.(French Lit.) 1964, M.A.(Spanish Lit.) 1964, Ph.D.(Spanish) 1973. CAREER: Resident Lecturer, Spanish, Indiana Univ., 1966-67; Instructor, Simon Fraser Univ., 1967-74; Asst. Prof., 1974-81; Assoc. Prof., 1981-90; Spanish Lecturer,

Bureau of Cultural Rel'ns, Ministry of Foreign Affairs, Spain, 1989 to date; Prof., Simon Fraser Univ., 1990 to date. SELECTED PUBLICATIONS: *El protagonista colectivo en "Fuenteovejuna" de Lope de Vega* (Salamanca: Universidad de Salamanca, 1979); "Evolucie Vegactor, Simon Fr*Fuenteovejuna de Lope de Vega en el Siglo XX*" (*Cuadernos Hispanoamericanos* (Madrid) Feb.-Mar. 1977); "The Mob in Shakespeare and Lope de Vega," in *Parallel Lives: Spanish and English National Drama, 1580-1680*, Louise Fothergill-Payne, ed. (Lewisburg, PA: Bucknell Univ. Press, 1991); "The Staging of the Conquest in a Play by Lope de Vega" (*Pacific Coast Philology* Sept. 1992); "Typology of Staging in Lope de Vega's Theatre," in *The Golden Age "Comedia"* Text, Theory and Performance, Howard Mancing & Charles Ganelin, eds. (West Lafayette, Ind.: Purdue Univ. Press, 1994); various other publications. EDIT: Ed., *Homenaje a Jesús Lheory and Pe*, issue of *Revista Canadiense de Estudios Hispánicos*, Fall 1985; Ed. Bd., *Revista Canadiense de Estudios Hispánicos*, 1988 to date; Co-Ed., *Estudios hispánicos en el Canadá: Celebraciward Mancing & Charles Ganelin, eds. (West Lafayette, Ind.: Purdue Univ. Pres*, issue of *Revista Canadiense de Estudios Hispánicos*, Spring 1991; Ed., *The Two New Worlds Today: Constructions of Reality in Spain and Latin America*, issue of *Revista Canadiense de Estudios Hispánicos*, Spring 1994. AFFIL: Canadian Commission for UNESCO (mbr. of Exec. 1992-96); Social Sciences & Humanities Research Council of Canada (mbr. of Council 1988-91); Canadian Federation for the Humanities (Bd. of Dir. 1984-90; Exec. Committee 1985-87); Canadian Association of Hispanists (VP 1987, 1991; Pres. 1988-90); International Association Siglo de Oro; International Association of Hispanists; Modern Languages Association of America; North American Catalan Society; Canadian Association of University Teachers; Canadian Association of Latin American & Caribbean Studies; Association of Hispanic Classical Theatre; International Association of Spanish & Novohispanic Theatres of the Golden Age; Pacific Ancient & Modern Language Association. HONS: Univ. Fellow, Univ. of Chicago, 1965-66; Prize for best article, Canadian Association of Hispanists, 1978, 1983; Prize for best book, Canadian Association of Hispanists, 1981; Excellence in Teaching Award, Simon Fraser Univ., 1987; Killam Research Fellowship, 1995. MISC: recipient, numerous grants & fellowships; numerous conference presentations. COMMENT: "*Dr. Teresa J. Kirschner is a Professor of Humanities at Simon Fraser University. Her main interest in research is the* *relationship between literature and ideology, and theatre staging techniques."*

Kish, Ely 🏃 ⚛
Artist, **ELY KISH STUDIO**, R.R. 1, Lavigne, ON K0A 2A0 (613) 487-3348, FAX 487-3348. Born Newark, N.J. 1924. s. **EDUC:** Institute of Fine Art, Newark, Art 1942; Institute del Allende, San Miguel de Allende, Mexico, 1949-51. **SELECTED PUBLICATIONS:** *Country Splendor* & *Dinosaurs*, 2 calendars (Ottawa: Wyman & Son Publications Ltd., 1995); *Dinosaurs*, calendar (California: Portal Publications Ltd., 1995); *Stegosaurus* Book, Bones & Egg and Poster, *The Tiny Perfect Dinosaur* series, Illustrator (Toronto: Somerville House Publishing, 1995); *Brachosaurus* Book, Bones & Egg and Poster, *The Tiny Perfect Dinosaur* series, Illustrator (Toronto: Somerville House Publishing, 1994); *Leptoceratops* Book, Bones & Egg and Poster, *The Tiny Perfect Dinosaur* series, Illustrator (Toronto: Somerville House Publishing, 1991); *Dinosaur Babies*, Illustrator (National Geographic Society, Special Publications Div., Action Book, 1991); *Wonder and Mystery of Dinosaurs in Art*, 8 paintings (Japan: Gakken Publishing Co., 1990); *An Odyssey in Time The Dinosaurs of North America*, Illustrator (Toronto: Univ. of Toronto Press, 1989); *Dinosaurs an Illustrated History*, Illustrator (New York: Red Dembner Enterprise Corporation, 1983); *Thread of Life: The Smithsonian Looks at Evolution*, 1 painting (Washington, D.C.: Smithsonian Books, 1983); illustrations in various magazines incl.: *Equinox*; *Horizon, The Magazine of the Arts*, N.M.; *Art Impressions*; *Stern*, Germany; *Canadian Geographic*; *Sotheby's, Canada*. **EXHIBITIONS:** numerous solo & group shows incl. Gallery Five, Ottawa (1970); Univ. of Waterloo (1973); Travelling Exhibition, National Museums of Canada (1975); Den Art Gallery (1980, 1982); Museum of Natural Sciences (1983); New Mexico Museum of Natural History (1985); Kish Gallery, Albuquerque, N.M. (1985); Canadian Museum of Nature, Ottawa (1992); *Women Artists of the Nineties*, Raymer Art Gallery, Ottawa (1994); *Children's Book Fair Illustrators Exhibition*, Bologna, Italy (1995); Gallery Exhibit, Tokyo, Japan (1995); Arizona State Univ., Tempe, Arizona (April 1996). **COLLECTIONS:** National Museum of Ottawa; Canadian War Museum; New Mexico Museum of Natural History; Ronald McDonald House, Ottawa; Smithsonian Institution, Museum of Natural History. **HONS:** finalist (*An Odyssey in Time The Dinosaurs of North America*), Gov. General's Award for Non-Fiction, 1989; Member, Order or Canada, 1993; Silver Award (*Dinosaur Babies*), Dimensional Illustration Award, 1992. **MISC:** subject of numerous articles & TV programs in Canada, the US & Europe; The Ely Kish Studio opened in the Creative Discovery Museum in Chattanooga, Tenn., July 1995. **COMMENT:** *"Ely Kish is an internationally renowned painter, in the artistic tradition of the 18th and 19th centuries. She is one of Canada's foremost painters of wildlife and prehistoric landscapes and her murals are included in the permanent collections of various museums. Like the old masters, Ely's paintings are meticulous and accurate in every detail. They breathe."*

Kislowicz, Linda, B.S.W.,M.S.W. ■■ ✊ ⊕
Executive Director, **JEWISH FAMILY SERVICES OF THE BARON DE HIRSCH**. Born 1951. m. 2 ch. **EDUC:** McGill Univ., B.S.W. 1972, M.S.W. 1976 - area of concentration: child welfare. **CAREER:** various positions, YM-YWHA & NHS of Montreal, 1972-75; Researcher/Teaching Asst./Sessional Lecturer-Child Welfare Needs & Resources, McGill Univ., 1977-80 (part-time); Research Dir., Hospital Social Svcs Research Proj., Jewish Family Services Social Service Centre, 1976-80 (part-time); Researcher, Utilization of Small Groups in Montreal, Univ. de Montréal, 1981-82; Research Coord., Structural, Strategic Family Therapy Proj., & grad. student thesis supervisor, McGill Univ., 1982-85; Sessional Lecturer, Social Counsellor Program, Beth Jacob Teacher Seminary, 1988-92; Coord., Sch. Social Svcs, Jewish Family Services of the Baron de Hirsch, 1986-89; Coord., Program Mgmt, June-Nov. 1989; Branch Dir., Snowdon "Y", YM-YWHA & NHS of Montreal, 1989-93; "Y" Country Camp Dir., 1992-93; Exec. Dir., Jewish Family Services of the Baron de Hirsch, 1993 to date. **SELECTED PUBLICATIONS:** co-author, 8 articles/presentations incl.: "Teaching Child Welfare - Philosophy and Practice" (*Intervention*, Fall 1978); "Residential Care: The Impact of Institutional Policies, Structures and Staff on Residential Children" (*McGill University*, June 1979); "Étude Comparative de la Pratique du Service Social des Groupes à Québec" (*Service Social*, 1983). **AFFIL:** Corporation of Professional Social Workers of Quebec; Association of Jewish Centre Workers (former mbr.); Jewish Education Council (Planning Committee 1986; Bd. of Dir. 1993 to date); YM-YWHA & NHS (Mgmt Committee, Davis Branch 1986-87); Reconstructionist Synagogue (Committee Chairperson 1987-91); Batshaw Family & Youth Centres (Committee mbr. 1996 to date). **MISC:** speaks & writes French & Hebrew.

Kitchen, E. Ruth, B.A. ■■ ♡ $ ✊
1735 The Collegeway, #3, Mississauga, ON

L5L 3S7 (905) 828-5155, FAX 828-5867. **EDUC:** Univ. of Toronto, B.A.(Hons., Geol. Sci.); Ontario Coll. of Education, Type A Certificate; Canadian Securities Course; continuing educ. courses in computer skills, fin., public speaking & media rel'ns. **CAREER:** Payroll Administrator, Lansing Buildall, 1981-89; Mgr, Dev. of Design Centres, 1989-91; Exec. Dir., Living Arts Centre, Mississauga, 1993-95; consultant, Mississauga Int'l Children's Festival, 1995-96; Acting Gen. Mgr, The Toronto Mendelssohn Choir, 1996. **VOLUNTEER CAREER:** served on various bds. & committees incl. VP Strategic Planning, Treas., Chair, Sustaining Committee during membership, Junior League of Toronto, 1964 to date; Dir., Bloorview Hospital, 1978-79; Pres., United Way of Peel (Chair, Allocations Committee), 1977-82; Dir., United Way of Canada/Centraide, 1982-84; Chair, Scholarship Campaign, Principal's Club (1983-86)/Chair, Library Campaign (1986-89), Erindale Coll., Univ. of Toronto; Dir., Whiteoaks Lorne Park Community Association, 1989-93; Co-Chair, Leadership Giving Committee, United Way of Peel, 1991 & 1992; Dir., Mississauga Hospital Foundation, 1991 to date. **SELECTED PUBLICATIONS:** co-author, *Fare for Friends* (1983); co-author, *Good Friends Cookbook* (1991). **AFFIL:** Association of Cultural Executives; Junior League of Toronto; Alpha Phi Fraternity (Trustee). **HONS:** Citizen of the Year, Mississauga, & the Gordon S. Shipp Award, 1985; Paul W. Fox Award, Erindale Coll., Univ. of Toronto, for svc. to the coll., 1987; Award of Excellence, Junior League of Toronto, 1990; The 125 Commemorative Medal, Gov't of Canada, 1992; Margaret Rolph Award, Junior League of Toronto, for over 15 yrs. of voluntary leadership in the community, 1993. **MISC:** wide experience in event planning & fundraising, mktg & promotion, & strategic planning.

Kitson, Eleanor 🌸 ◐ ☼
Retired. 55 Charlotte Dr., Charlottetown, PE C1A 2N6 (902) 892-1581. Born Kingston, P.E.I. 1919. m. Norris. 5 ch. **CAREER:** Mgr/Ptnr, trucking company, 1956-80. **AFFIL:** Spring Park United Church (Pres., UCW General 1994-95; Pres., Unit 1, United Church Women 1975-79; Clerk of Session 1989-94; Hon. Elder; Life Mbr., United Church Women); North River Women's Institute (Life Mbr.); Provincial Women's Liberal Commission (Sec. 1978-82; Pres. 1983-85, 1995-96); P.E.I. Rose Society (Sec.). **HONS:** Service Industry Award, Atlantic Provinces Trucking Association, 1980; Canada 125 Medal; Transportation Person of the Year Award, Chamber of Commerce, 1994. **INTERESTS:** quilting; gardening, specializing in miniature roses. **COMMENT:** *"My retirement years have been full, and my business background assists me to complete all the activities due to strong organizational skills. I enjoy people, and my active involvement in politics, church and family keeps me youthful."*

Klassen, Sarah, B.A.,B.Ed. 📖 ⊲ ☼
Poet. 19 Del Rio Place, Winnipeg, MB R2G 1K9. Born Winnipeg 1932. s. **EDUC:** Univ. of Manitoba, B.A.(English) 1963, B.Ed. 1971. **CAREER:** teacher, 1952-90; poet. **SELECTED PUBLICATIONS:** *Journey to Yalta*, poetry collection (Turnstone Press, 1988); *Violence & Mercy*, poetry collection (Netherlandic Press, 1991); *Borderwatch*, poetry collection (Netherlandic Press., 1993). **AFFIL:** League of Canadian Poets (Nat'l Council 1991-95); Manitoba Writers' Guild (mbr.; Bd. 1993-95); River East MB Church. **HONS:** Gerald Lampert Award (*Journey to Yalta*), 1989. **INTERESTS:** reading; writing; theatre; walking; cycling. **MISC:** teaching English Lit. at the Liberal Arts Christian Coll., Klaipeda, Lithuania, 1995-96, 1996-97. **COMMENT:** *"I'm interested in all aspects of words and the Word–the potential for both truth and deception in language. I believe if I've done anything worthwhile, it's been a result of grace given by God."*

Klawe, Maria M., B.Sc.,Ph.D. ■ ■ ⊛ ⊲
Vice-President, Student and Academic Services, UNIVERSITY OF BRITISH COLUMBIA, 6328 Memorial Rd., Vancouver, BC V6T 1Z2 (604) 822-5075, FAX 822-8194, EMAIL vpsas@ unixg.ubc.ca. Born Toronto 1951. m. Dr. N. Pippenger. 2 ch. Janek, Sasha. **EDUC:** Univ. of Alberta, B.Sc.(Math.) 1973, Ph.D.(Math.) 1977; Univ. of Toronto, grad. (Comp. Sci.) 1979. **CAREER:** Asst. Prof., Dept. of Comp. Sci., Univ. of Toronto, 1979-80; Mgr, Almaden Research Center, IBM, San Jose, CA, 1980-88; Head, Dept. of Comp. Sci., Univ. of British Columbia, 1988-95; VP, Student & Academic Svcs, 1995 to date. **SELECTED CREDITS:** educational content design, "Counting on Frank," math CD-ROM game published by Electronic Arts, 1994. **SELECTED PUBLICATIONS:** co-author with B. Mumey, "Upper and Lower Bounds on Constructing Alphabetic Binary Trees" (*SIAM Journal of Disc. Math.* 8(4), 1995); co-author with K. Sedighian, "An Interface Strategy for Promoting Reflective Cognition in Children" (*Computer-Human Interaction '96 Conference Companion*, Vancouver, 1996); co-author with K. Inkpen & K.S. Booth, "Playing together beats playing apart, especially for girls" (*Proc. Computer Support for Collab-*

orative Learning '96, Indiana, 1995); author, "Superlinear bounds for matrix searching problems" (*J. Algorithms* 13, 1992); co-author with E. Philips, "A Classroom study: electronic games engage children as researchers" (*Proc. Computer Support for Collaborative Learning* '96, Indiana, 1995). **AFFIL:** B.C. Premier's Advisory Council on Science & Technology (mbr. 1992 to date); American Mathematical Society (Bd. of Trustees 1992-97); Computing Research Association (Bd. mbr. 1990-96); Science World, B.C. (Bd. of Gov. 1990 to date). **HONS:** Fellow, ACM, 1996; IBM Canada Award for contributing to univ.-industry rel'ns, 1992; IBM Outstanding Innovator Award, 1989. **INTERESTS:** art; running; ocean kayaking. **COMMENT:** *"As a mathematician, computer scientist and university educator and administrator, I am committed to creating effective learning environments that take full advantage of information technology."*

Kleihauer-Ward, Elke ■ ■ ⌲ ✦ ♙

Toolmaker/Technological Studies Teacher, NORTH LAMBTON SECONDARY SCHOOL, P.O. Box 40, Forest, ON N0N 1J0 (519) 786-2166, FAX 786-5250. Born Stratford, Ont. 1962. 2 ch. Erien, Xander, 2 stpch. Tina, Erica. **EDUC:** Stratford Central Secondary Sch., grad. 1980; apprenticed as toolmaker, F.A.G. Bearings, 1980-84; Univ. of Western Ontario, Fac. of Educ. 1988-89; currently working part-time on a degree. **CAREER:** 1st registered female toolmaker in Canada; 1st female machine shop teacher in Canada. **SELECTED CREDITS:** featured in local newspaper, *The Sarnia Observer*; seen on CKCO TV & broadcast across Canada, 1989; featured in Conestoga Coll. publications & high schools ads. **AFFIL:** Habitat for Humanity; Interval Home (women's shelter); Skills Canada Team (high-sch. level); Manufacturing Club (high sch.). **INTERESTS:** reading literature & human interest stories; writing–working on biographies of people with WWII experiences, & poetry; interior design & renovations; auditioning for Sarnia Little Theatre parts; experiencing what life has to offer. **MISC:** worked with Girls Exploring Technology Day Camp; worked on quality control for bearings used in Canadarm (that was a thrill, esp. when the arm worked); has worked on curriculum dev. for Conestoga Coll., Lambton County; set up shops for machining & manufacturing at Fanshawe Coll., Lambton County. **COMMENT:** *"I enjoy challenges. If someone believes I cannot achieve something, I try to find a way to prove that it can be done. There were many doubters when I began my apprenticeship. Working with my hands is a satisfying experience."*

Klein, Colleen J. (Chips) ■ ■ Ⓢ ◐

President, CHIPCO CANADA INC. (manufacturing/bus. consulting), 107 Holm Cres., Thornhill, ON L3T 5J4 (905) 771-6912 or (416) 243-0668, cell (416) 616-2438, EMAIL c.klein@utoronto.ca. Co-Director, WOMEN INVENTORS PROJECT, 1 Greensboro Dr., Ste. 302, Etobicoke, ON M9W 1C8 (416) 243-0668, FAX 243-0688. Born South Africa 1947. m. R. Paul. 2 ch. Lazar Victor, Talia Ruth. **EDUC:** completed educ. in South Africa. **CAREER:** Soloist, Mercedes Molina Spanish Dance Theatre, 1966; Ptnr, Enrique Segovia/Chiquita Albeniz Dance Duo, 1968; founder & Pres., Chipco Canada Inc. (manufacturer/distributor of The Eye Maker line of mirrors–designed, developed & patented by Chips Klein), 1982; Consultant, Women Inventors Project, 1986; Co-Dir., 1991; workshops, training & seminars to variety of organizations. **SELECTED CREDITS:** contributed to *What If? Women Inventors and Entrepreneurs* (video). **SELECTED PUBLICATIONS:** *Inventors Want to Know: A Reference Guide on Invention, Innovation and Entrepreneurship*; contributions to: *Venture Source* magazine & *Exchange* magazine; columnist, Small Bus. Section, *The Globe and Mail*. **AFFIL:** Council for Entrepreneurship Education of Ontario (Bd. of Dir.); Step Ahead One on One Mentoring Program for Women (Mentor & Treas.); Women's Rural Economic Development (Advisory Bd.); Inventors' Alliance of Canada; Toronto Board of Education (former mbr., Advisory Committee, Entrepreneurial Studies Curriculum); Hadassah-WIZO Organization of Canada (Life mbr.; former Pres.). **HONS:** nominated for Woman of Distinction Award, YWCA of Metro Toronto, 1990; Award of Commendation for work with mentally & physically challenged persons, Ontario March of Dimes. **INTERESTS:** fitness; water skiing; snow skiing. **MISC:** case study in *The Book for Women Who Invent or Want To*; interviewed on numerous major radio & TV talk & business shows in Canada. **COMMENT:** *"From professional flamenco dancer to inventor to business woman. Internationally recognized as a leading exponent and dynamic speaker on women's issues in business, invention, entrepreneurship and innovation."*

Klein-Lataud, Christine ■ ■ ⌲ 📖

Director, School of Translation, Glendon College, YORK UNIVERSITY, 2275 Bayview Ave., Toronto, ON M4N 3M6 (416) 487-6742, ext. 88392, FAX 487-6728, EMAIL klataud@venus.yorku.ca. Born Courbevoie, Hauts de Seine, France 1940. m. Michel. 2 ch. Mélusine, Alexis. **EDUC:** Sorbonne, L.ès L. 1961,

D.E.S.(Diplômes d'études supérieures) 1962; Paris X, Agrégation de lettres classiques 1963, D.E.A. de Sémiotique textuelle 1978. **CAREER:** Prof. titulaire/Directrice, École de traduction, Glendon Coll., York Univ.; appointed to Fac. of Grad. Studies, York. **SELECTED CREDITS:** Literary Reviewer, CBC, 1982 to date. **SELECTED PUBLICATIONS:** traduction, *Un Oiseau dans la maison* (Margaret Laurence); nouvelles traduites, *On ne sait jamais* (Isabel Huggan; Québec, Éd. L'instant même, 1996); nouvelles traduites, *Théâtre de revenants* (Steven Heighton; Québec, Éd. L'instant même, 1995); poèmes choisis traduits, *En guise d'amants* (Miriam Waddington; Montréal, Éd. du Noroît, 1994); co-editor, *Paroles rebelles* (Montréal, Éd. du remue-ménage, avril 1992); *Précis des figures de style* (Toronto, G.R.E.F., coll. TEL, 1991); 7 books; 5 chpts. in books; numerous articles & book reviews in refereed journals & conference proceedings. **AFFIL:** Association de traducteurs et traductrices littéraires du Canada (VP 1994 to date); la revue TTR (mbr. du comité 1992 to date); Conseil des arts du Canada/Canada Council (Évaluatrice de traductions & d'études critiques 1991 to date); Salon du livre de Toronto (mbr. du jury du Grand Prix 1995). **HONS:** Palmes académiques (highest French distinction for excellence in teaching), 1989; shortlisted for Gov. Gen.'s Award for *Un oiseau dans la maison*; Prix de l'Association des professeurs de français des universités et collèges canadiens for *Précis des figures de style*, 1992. **INTERESTS:** la traduction littéraire; les féministes françaises du XIXe siècle; la rhétorique. **MISC:** Évaluatrice, le Conseil de recherches en sciences humaines du Canada, 1994 to date; mbr. du jury, le Prix Trillium, 1992-94. **COMMENT:** *"Christine Klein-Lataud est spécialiste de traduction littéraire et de stylistique française. Elle a publié un Précis des figures de style, de nombreux articles sur la traduction et sur l'écriture des femmes ainsi que des traductions de recueils de nouvelles et de poèmes."*

Klodawsky, Fran, B.A.,M.A.,Ph.D. 🐦 🏵

Assistant Professor, Department of Geography and Pauline Jewett Institute of Women's Studies, CARLETON UNIVERSITY, 1125 Colonel By Dr., Ottawa, ON K1S 5B6 (613) 788-6645, FAX 788-2154, EMAIL klodawsky@ccs.carleton.ca. 2 ch. Noah, Gabriel. **EDUC:** Univ. of Toronto, B.A.(Geog.) 1973; Ohio State Univ., M.A. 1973; Queen's Univ., Ph.D. 1985. **CAREER:** Social Policy Research Consultant, 1982-83, 1984-85; Sessional Lecturer, Carleton Univ., 1983-85; Undergrad. Program Coord., Institute of Canadian Studies, 1984-85; Coord. for the Status of Women, 1986-91; Dir., Insti-

tute of Women's Studies, 1991-94; Asst. Prof., Dept. of Geography & Institute of Women's Studies, 1991 to date. **SELECTED PUBLICATIONS:** "Gender-sensitive Theory and the Housing Needs of Mother-led Families: Some Concepts and Some Buildings," with S. Mackenzie (*Feminist Perspectives* 1987); "New Families, New Housing Needs, New Urban Environments: The Case of Single Parent Families," with A. Spector, in *Life Spaces: Gender, Household, Employment*, Caroline Andrew & Beth Moore Milroy, eds. (Vancouver: Univ. of British Columbia, 1988); "The Housing Needs of Single Parent Families in Canada: A Dilemma for the 1990s," with A. Spector, in *Single Parent Families: Canadian Research and Policy Implications*, Joe Hudson & Burt Galaway, eds. (Toronto: Thompson Educational Publishing, 1993); "Women's Safety and the Politics of Transformation," with C. Andrew & C. Lundy (*Women and Environments* 14(1) 1994); "Feeling Safe on Campus: Women's Safety in the University Environment," with C. Lundy (*Journal of Architectural and Planning Research* 11(2) 1994); "Challenging Business as Usual in Housing and Community Planning: The Issue of Violence Against Women," with C. Lundy & C. Andrew (*Canadian Journal of Urban Research* 3(1) 1994); various other publications. **AFFIL:** Women's Action Centre against Violence (Bd. of Dir. 1992-93; Exec. Mbr., Bd. of Dir.); Canadian Association of Geographers; National Conference of Sexual Harassment Advisors; Canadian Women's Studies Association. **MISC:** recipient, various grants, fellowships & scholarships; various papers presented at conferences & meetings; founding mbr., City of Ottawa Women & Urban Safety Committee. **COMMENT:** *"Community activist, feminist geographer, teacher, writer, mother, daughter, friend. Founding member: Women's Action Centre Against Violence (Ottawa-Carleton). Research: socialist-feminist perspectives on housing and urban safety."*

Klodawsky, Helene, B.F.A. ⛏

Documentary Filmmaker. 5385 Durocher, Outremont, QC H2V 3X9, FAX (514) 270-5591. Born Toronto 1956. m. John M. Lucas. 2 ch. Simone Lucas, Yasmine Lucas. **EDUC:** Nova Scotia Coll. of Art & Design, Fine Arts 1977; Queen's Univ., B.F.A. **CAREER:** independent documentary filmmaker, researcher, writer & dir., 1979 to date; filmmaker, Sky Works Films, 1979-84; researcher, *Fraser's Edge*, CBC, 1983-84. **SELECTED CREDITS:** Prod./Writer/Researcher, *Women and the Church*, United Church of Canada; Asst. Dir./Researcher, *Moving Mountains*, Sky

Works Films, 1981; Asst. Dir./Researcher, *I See and I Am Silent*, Sky Works Films, 1982; *All of Our Lives/Chacune Sa Vie*, 1984; *Love's Labour*, TVOntario, 1986; *Painted Landscapes of the Times: The Art of Sue Coe*, TVOntario, 1986; *Shoot and Cry*, CBC, 1988; *No Time to Stop/Pas Le Temps D'Arreter*, 1991; *Motherland: Tales of Wonder*, 1994. **AFFIL:** Canadian Independent Film Caucus; Femmes de cinéma, de la télévision et de la vidéo à Montréal. **HONS:** numerous awards for films, incl. First Prize in Category (*All Of Our Lives*), Canadian Film & Television Awards, 1985; Gold Prize in Category (*Love's Labour*), Columbus Int'l Film Festival, Ohio, 1987; Gold Apple Award (*Painted Landscapes of the Times*), Nat'l Film & Video Festival, Oakland, Calif., 1986; Gold Ducat for Best Film (*Painted Landscapes of the Times*), Mannheim Int'l Film Festival, W. Germany, 1987; Best Documentary (*No Time To Stop*), La Mondiale de Films et Vidéos du Québec, 1991; nominee (*Motherland*), Hot Docs Documentary Film Festival, 1995; First Prize, 27th Nat'l Council on Family Rel'ns Media Awards, US, 1995; Bronze Apple Award, Nat'l Educ. Film & Video Awards, Oakland, Calif., 1995; nominee (*Motherland*), Best Feature Length Documentary, Genie Awards, 1996. **INTERESTS:** her children & partner; film; literature; feminism; novels; hiking. **COMMENT:** *"Working independently, as well as for broadcast television and the National Film Board, Helene is the recipient of many prestigious national and international film awards. Her films are distributed and televised in many countries."*

Klunder, Barbara ✖ ☺

Artist. 12 First St., Toronto Island, Toronto, ON M5J 2A6. Born Toronto 1948. d. 1 ch. Willem. **EDUC:** Ontario Coll. of Art, 1965-66. **CAREER:** 'making things' professionally since 1966; graphic artist, textile artist, protest artist. **SELECTED PUBLICATIONS:** self publications include *Falling in Love with Droplit Books* (1987); *Laura Secord, The Bitter Truth* (1991); *Buzzwords*, 27 original sayings (1992); *Snowspeak*, 21 new words for winter (1993); *Other Goose Rhymes*, environmental rhymes introducing a typeface designed by Barbara Klunder (1994) ; drawings have been featured in such publications as *Atlantic Monthly*, *The Globe & Mail*, *This Magazine*, *The Toronto Star*, *Pirhana*, *Casual/Casual Underground Comics*, *Saturday Night*. **COMMISSIONS:** include graphic illustration, ed. design, musical event & theatre posters, record jackets, stamps, billboards, T-shirt designs, costumes designed for theatrical prod. (many T-shirt designs were commissioned by such nonprofit organizations

as Canadian Physicians for African Relief, Temagami Wilderness Society, Greenpeace, 'Tools for Peace,' Nicaragua, shelters, community centres, breast cancer, teachers' groups, etc.); poster for Dora Mavor Moore Theatre Awards, 1991; Young People's Theatre poster & graphics for 1991-92 season; poster for Wise Cracks (documentary feature) 1990; T-shirt examples include Rolling Stones "Voodoo Lounge" T-shirt, 1994; Kumbaya AIDS Benefit T-shirt, 1995. **EXHIBITIONS:** various shows incl. *Tapestries for the Environment* (13 hand-hooked rugs depicting various mythical aspects of nature & humankind), Museum for Textiles (1990); *Laura Secord: The Bitter Truth* (oil painting, wearable art, constructions, Partisan Gallery, Toronto (1991); "Poultry in Motion" (an oil painting of former Prime Minister Brian Mulroney), *Lunch Bucket Art*, a Mayworks group show, Pages Bookstore Window, Toronto (1992); *Domestic Tea Off* (a musical miniputt in wood & copper), ABC Literary Benefit Show, Hazelton Lanes, Toronto (1992); *Voodoo Collages*, a gallery show of Rolling Stone collages & book covers, Vancouver (1994); painted medicine chest, *Survivors in Search of a Voice*, Breast Cancer show at ROM, Toronto (1995); *Women for a Just and Healthy Planet* Postcard Project, Partisan Gallery (1995); "wearable art" includes Planet Series (6 solid silver & 14K gold pieces of jewellery, depicting planets as faces), made in collaboration with Abel Barragan, Silversmith, Oaxaca, Mexico, 1993; *Sow's Ear: 25 Downsized Silk Purses for Frugal Times*, embroidered, hooked, ceramic, knitted, knotted, sewn, silver, gold, wool, silk purses that also carry a witty comment on cutbacks in the arts & social networks, Prime Gallery, Toronto (Nov. 1996). **INTERESTS:** music; live theatre; parade art. **MISC:** *Other Goose Rhymes* & Klunder-designed typeface were launched at the Design Exchange, 1994; proceeds for the auction of the rugs from *Tapestries for the Environment* benefited The Canadian Environmental Law Association & 4 other organizations. **COMMENT:** *"I know, not just believe, that there are solutions to most problems on this planet. It's implementing them that's proving difficult. My challenge is to be an effective visual messenger, helping these solutions to get 'up and working.' I'm very lucky to have had so many opportunities, but there's lots more to do."*

Knelman, Judith, B.A.,M.A.,B.Ped., Ph.D. ✑ ▤

Associate Professor, UNIVERSITY OF WESTERN ONTARIO, London, ON N6A 5B7 (519) 661-2111, ext. 6677, FAX 661-3848, EMAIL judith@gsoj.uwo.ca. Born Winnipeg 1939. d. 2

ch. **EDUC:** Univ. of Manitoba, B.Ped. 1959; Univ. of Toronto, B.A.(English) 1971, M.A.(English) 1972, Ph.D.(English) 1978. **CAREER:** Asst. Prof., Dept. of English, Bishop's Univ., 1979-80; writer & ed., Dept. of Comm., Univ. of Toronto, 1981-88; Asst. & Assoc. Prof., Univ. of Western Ontario, 1988 to date. **SELECTED PUBLICATIONS:** numerous newspaper, magazine & scholarly articles. **AFFIL:** Ontario Council on University Affairs. **COMMENT:** *"Teacher and journalist, author of many newspaper, magazine and scholarly articles, completing a book on women, 19th century English justice, and the press."*

Knight, Cheryl, B.A.,C.C.P. ⊗ $
Director, Human Resources, UNIVERSITY OF LETHBRIDGE, 4401 University Dr., Lethbridge, AB T1K 3M4 (403) 329-2276, FAX 329-2685, EMAIL knight@hg.uleth.ca. Born Moose Jaw, Sask. m. 1 ch. **EDUC:** Univ. of Calgary, B.A. (Psych.) 1980, Certificate (Mgmt Dev.) 1984; Univ. of Lethbridge, M.Ed.(Counselling) in progress. **CAREER:** Hum. Res. Officer, Royal Trust Corporation of Canada, 1982-85; Training & Dev. Consultant, 1985-87; Reg'l Mgr, Hum. Res., Royal Trust Corporation, 1987-90; Mgr, Compensation & Benefits, Canadian Tire Acceptance Limited, 1990-93; Mgr, Hum. Res., Univ. of Lethbridge, 1993; Dir., Hum. Res., 1993 to date. **AFFIL:** Canadian Compensation Association (Certified Compensation Professional). **INTERESTS:** swimming; aerobics; skiing; reading; camping. **MISC:** qualified as Canadian National Lifeguard; certified SCUBA diver.

Knight, Courtney ■■ ⊘
Paralympic Athlete. Prince George, BC. **EDUC:** Simon Fraser Univ., current. **SPORTS CAREER:** mbr., Nat'l Track Team. Paralympic Games: Silver, discus, 1996; 4th discus, 1992. IPC Athletic Championships: 2nd, pentathlon, 4th, discus, 5th javelin & shotput, 1994. **MISC:** earned a spot on B.C.'s able-bodied team, 1995 Canadian Nat'l Junior Track & Field Championships & Prov. Team, Western Canada Games

Knight, Florence ⊕ ○
President, Alberta Branch, CANADIAN GRANDPARENTS' RIGHTS ASSOCIATION, 5512 - 4th St. N.W., Box 64128, Calgary, AB T2K 6J1 (403) 284-3887, FAX 284-3887. Born Sask. 1930. m. Raymond. 3 ch. **CAREER:** Dept. of Math. & Dept. of Elec. Eng., Univ. of Calgary, 1972-90; upon retirement, founded the Alberta Branch, Canadian Grandparents' Rights Association, 1990; Pres., 1990 to date. **MISC:** a nonprofit society incorporated in Alta., formed

in 1990. **COMMENT:** *"Professional attitude, dedicated and committed to furthering the cause of grandparent involvement in the lives of grandchildren in order to provide the unconditional love and emotional support they require. I speak out for children's rights so they are not deprived of access to their heritage and relations. Lobbying federal and provincial government to amend legislation."*

Knowles, Valerie, B.A.,M.A.,B.J. ▤ ✎
Writer. 554 Piccadilly Ave., Ottawa, ON K1Y 0J1 (613) 722-4473, FAX 722-5792. Born Montreal 1934. m. David C. Knowles. **EDUC:** Smith Coll., B.A.(Hist.) 1956; McGill Univ., M.A.(Hist.) 1957; Carleton Univ., B.Journalism 1964. **CAREER:** Hist. Instructor, Prince of Wales Coll., 1958-59; Hist. Teacher, Elmwood Sch., Rockcliffe Park, Ont., 1959-60; Hist. Instructor, Carleton Univ., 1961; Archivist, Public Archives of Canada, 1961-63; Discussion Group Leader & Bibliographer, Hist. Dept., Carleton Univ., 1964-72; freelance writer, 1964 to date. **SELECTED PUBLICATIONS:** *Leaving With A Red Rose: A History of the Ottawa Civic Hospital School of Nursing* (Ottawa: commissioned work, 1981); *First Person: A Biography of Cairine Wilson, Canada's First Woman Senator* (Dundurn Press, 1988); *Strangers At Our Gates: Canadian Immigration and Immigration Policy, 1540-1990* (Dundurn Press, 1992); *Through The Chateau Door: A History of the Zonta Club of Ottawa 1929-1989* (Ottawa: commissioned work, 1994). **AFFIL:** Zonta Club of Ottawa (various exec. positions); Media Club of Ottawa (Chrm of Hospitality); Writers' Union of Canada; University Women's Club of Montreal; Humane Society of Ottawa-Carleton. **INTERESTS:** reading; theatre; walking; cross-country skiing; art; tennis; birdwatching; cooking; travel. **MISC:** various grants, Ontario Arts Council. **COMMENT:** *"Since the mid-70s my principal occupation has been that of freelance writer. This, plus a wide range of volunteer work, keeps me busy."*

Knowlton, Norma, B.A.,M.A.,R.N. ▧ ▤
Past President, ONTARIO ARCHAEOLOGICAL SOCIETY, 418 Bouchier St., P.O. Box 13, Roches Point, ON L0E 1P0 (905) 476-4747, Born Albany, NY 1931; d., 6 ch. **EDUC:** Dalhousie University, B.A.(Biology/History) 1952; Toronto General Hospital, Diploma (Nursing) 1955; Trent University, M.A. (Archaeology) 1992. **CAREER:** Private Duty Nurse, 1955-57; Archaeology Field Crew, Ontario Ministry of Culture and Recreation, 1978; Comcare and Riverglen Haven Nursing Home, 1979-87; Nurse, Cedarvale Lodge Nurs-

ing Home, 1991-96. **AFFIL**: Ontario Archaeological Society (Recording Sec. 1978-79; Corresponding Sec. 1980; Dir. 1986-87; Pres.); Society for American Archaeology; Royal Ontario Museum; Colege. of Nurses of Ontario; Toronto General Hospital Alumnae Association; Dalhousie Alumnae Association. **SELECTED PUBLICATIONS**: Chapter on Luna Polychrome in *Paths to Central American Prehistory*, ed. Frederick Lange, 1996. **HONS**: Governor-General's Bronze Medal, 1949; Entrance Scholarship, Dalhousie University, 1949; Scholarship, IODE, 1949; three Undergraduate Scholarships, Dalhousie University; Avery Prize, Dalhousie University, 1952; Graduate Scholarships, Trent University, 1991-92. **INTERESTS**: archaeology, especially Mesoamerica; travel; reading; gardening; astrology; camping; painting; handicrafts. **COMMENT**: *"Late bloomer and perennial student. Completed one career as wife and mother. Retired from nursing profession. New career in office support. Continued involvement in archaeology."*

Knutson, Susan Lynne, B.A.,M.A., Ph.D. 🐟 🕮
Associate Professor and Chair, Department of English, UNIVERSITÉ SAINTE-ANNE, Pointe-del'Église, NS B0W 1M0 (902) 769-2114, ext. 151, FAX 769-2930. Born Vancouver 1952. **EDUC**: Simon Fraser Univ., B.A.(English) 1975, M.A. 1983; Univ. of British Columbia, Ph.D. 1989. **CAREER**: Proj. Coord. & Ed., The Kootenay Community Printing Proj., Argenta, B.C., 1972; Ed. Asst., *New: West Coast*, Intermedia Press, Vancouver, 1977; Program Book Ed. & Administrator, Vancouver Folk Music Festival, 1978-80; Prod. & Script Writer, *WomanVision*, CFRO FM, 1980-81; writer & ed. of a variety of projects, 1981-87; Publicist, Vancouver Folk Music Festival, 1983; Prod. & Script Writer, *Women and Words on Air*, CFRO FM, 1985-86; Asst. Prof., Dept. of English, Univ. Sainte-Anne, 1988-93; Chair, 1992 to date; Assoc. Prof., 1993 to date. **SELECTED PUBLICATIONS**: "Challenging the Masculine Generic" (*Contemporary Verse* Spring/Summer 1988); "For Feminist Narratology" (*Tessera* Fall 1989); "'Imagine Her Surprise': The Debate Over Feminist Essentialism" (*Tessera* Summer 1991); "A Moral Exegesis of Chaucer's *Man of Law's Tale*" (*Revue de l'Université Sainte-Anne* 1991); "Not for Lesbians Only: Reading beyond Patriarchal Gender," in *Weaving Alliances: Selected Papers Presented for the Canadian Women's Studies Association at the 1991 and 1992 Learned Societies Conferences*, ed. Debra Martens (Ottawa: Canadian Women's Studies Association, 1993); various other publications. **EDIT**: Ed. Asst., *The*

Selected Literary Criticism of A.M. Klein, Univ. of Toronto Press, 1986; mbr. of the Ed. Collective, *Tessera*, 1987-91; Advisory Ed. Bd., *Studies in Canadian Literature*. **AFFIL**: Fac. Union (VP); Le Centre Préscolaire de la Baie Sainte-Marie (Bd. of Dir.); La Fanfare Régionale de Clare (Bd. of Dir.); Association for Canadian Studies; Canadian Women's Studies Association; Canadian Research Institute for the Advancement of Women; Association of Canadian University Teachers of English; Association for Canadian & Quebec Literatures; West Coast Women & Words Society. **HONS**: Morris & Tim Wagner Fellowship, 1984-85. **MISC**: panel discussion with Daphne Marlatt & Betsy Warland, *Worlds of Words*, CFRO FM (Apr. 28, 1987); *Les Femmes dans le jazz*, CIFA FM (July 6, 1991); recipient, various grants, fellowships & scholarships; mbr., Vancouver Committee, Third Int'l Feminist Book Fair, 1987-88; various conference papers.

Kobelsky, Janice, C.M.A. ■■ 🕮 $
Executive Director, SOCIETY OF MANAGEMENT ACCOUNTANTS OF ALBERTA (professional association), One Palliser Square, 125 - 9th Ave. S.E., Ste. 1800, Calgary, AB T2G 0P6 (403) 269-5341, FAX 262-5477. Born Moose Jaw, Sask. 1958. m. Del. 1 ch. Aaron. **EDUC**: Society of Management Accountants, C.M.A. (Prof. Mgmt Acctnt) 1984; City Univ., pursuing M.B.A. **CAREER**: Acct. Rec'l/Mgr, Acctg, Red Deer Coll., 1979-85; Utilities Dept. Supervisor, City of Red Deer, 1985-87; Area Mgr, John M. Fisher & Associates, Dale Carnegie Training, 1987-89; Dir., Professional Svcs, Society of Management Accountants of Alberta, 1989-91; Exec. Dir., 1991 to date. **AFFIL**: C.M.A. (registered mbr. 1984 to date). **INTERESTS**: yoga; reading; theatre; gardening; parenting. **MISC**: lived & travelled overseas in Algeria, Spain, Belgium, Malta & parts of France; speaks French & Spanish. **COMMENT**: *"I'm an enthusiastic, high-energy professional. My mission, 'making a difference,' underlies a track record of leadership, significant organizational progress and helping others achieve their best."*

Kofmel, Kim G., B.A.,M.L.S. ■ 📖 🕮 ⊗ ✎
Writer. EMAIL kkofmel@julian.uwo.ca. Instructor, Graduate School of Library and Information Science, UNIVERSITY OF WESTERN ONTARIO. Born Ottawa 1961. **EDUC**: York Univ., B.A.(Fine Art) 1984; Univ. of Western Ontario, M.L.S. 1985, doctoral studies in Library & Info. Sci., in progress. **CAREER**: Database Operator, Curry's Art Store, Toronto 1986; Ed., Trans-Canada Press, 1986-88; freelance writer & ed., 1988 to date; Sessional Lecturer, Grad. Sch. of Library & Info. Sci., Univ.

of Western Ontario, 1991, 1993, 1994; Instructor, 1996-97. SELECTED CREDITS: writer/dir., *Typefaces*, York Univ., 1981; writer/dir., *Making It Rich and Famous!*, York Univ. Cabaret, 1983; Co-writer & performer, *Mnemonic Steamrollers: A Play About Memories and the People They Flatten*, with Jen Frankel & Cass Wender, Forest City Gallery, London, Ont., 1994. SELECTED PUBLICATIONS: Ed., *Who's Who in Canadian Law* (Toronto: Trans-Canada Press, 1987, 6th ed.); Ed., *Who's Who in Canadian Finance* (Toronto: Trans-Canada Press, 1988, 10th ed.); Ed., *Who's Who in Canadian Business* (Toronto: Trans-Canada Press, 1989, 10th ed.); *Who's Who of Canadian Women* (Toronto: Who's Who Publications, 1995, 6th ed.); *Directory of College and University Librarians in Canada/Répertoire des Bibliothécaires des Collèges et Universitiés du Canada*, with Gloria J. Leckie (Toronto: OCULA, 1995; 2nd ed., 1996); contributor, *Magill's Guide to Science Fiction and Fantasy Literature* (Pasadena, Calif.: Salem Press); "Holiday" (*Hysteria* 2(1) 1982-83); "Mercy Killing" (*Endeavor* 3(1) 1986); "Cindercorp and the Fairy God-flop" (*The Toronto Star*, Aug. 1995); "Off the Request Line" (*The Blotter* 4, 1986); various book reviews in *Quill & Quire*, & *Epilogue*; various other publications. EDIT: Ed., *Cadre*, 1982-85; Ed., *Stardock*, 1984-85; Assoc. Ed., *Algorithm*, 1991-93. AFFIL: Association for Library and Information Science Education; Science Fiction Research Association; Friends of the Merril Collection. HONS: First, Prose, Poesis Arts Competition, 1983; President's Prize, Prose, York Univ., 1984; Judge's Choice, *The Toronto Star* Annual Short Story Contest, 1985; various competition awards for writing; Ont. Graduate Scholarship, 1991; Best Novice Fantasy Costume, ChiCon V, 19th World Science Fiction Convention, Chicago, *Masquerade*, 1991; various costume awards. INTERESTS: science fiction; reading; movies; photography; crafts; ephemera; collecting graveyards (photos); travelling with my companion, Carl Devore. MISC: various conference presentations; competitive costumer, Journeyman rank; various workshops; past & present mbr. and/or facilitator, various writers' groups; first recipient of the President's Prize for Prose, York Univ.; numerous public readings. COMMENT: *"I think the gods are trying to tell me something. I wish they'd speak English."*

Kogawa, Joy, C.M.,LL.D.,D.Litt. 🎨 📖
Writer. 25 The Esplanade, Ste. 2604, Toronto, ON M5E 1W5 (416) 214-9547. Born Vancouver 1935. d. 2 ch. Gordon, Deidre. SELECTED PUBLICATIONS: *The Splintered*

Moon, poetry (Univ. of New Brunswick, 1967); *A Choice of Dreams*, poetry (McClelland & Stewart, 1974); *Jericho Road*, poetry (McClelland & Stewart, 1977); *Obasan*, novel (Lester & Orpen Dennys, 1981; Penguin, 1983); *Woman in the Woods*, poetry (Mosaic, 1985); *Naomi's Road*, children's fiction (Oxford Univ. Press, 1986); *Naomi no Michi*, young adult fiction (Shogakkan, 1988); *Itsuka*, novel (Viking, 1992); *The Rain Ascends*, novel (Knopf, 1995). AFFIL: Canadian Civil Liberties Union (Dir.); Writers' Union of Canada; PEN International. HONS: First Novel Award, *Books in Canada*, *Obasan*; Book of the Year Award, Canadian Authors' Association, *Obasan*; Best Paperback Fiction Award, Periodical Distributors of Canada, *Obasan*; The American Book Award, Before Columbus Foundation, *Obasan*; Notable Book, American Library Association, *Obasan*; Order of Canada, 1986; Urban Alliance Race Rel'ns Award, 1994; Grace MacInnis Visiting Scholar Award, 1995; LL.D.(Hon.), Univ. of Lethbridge, 1991; Fellow, Ryerson Polytechnic Univ., 1991; D.Litt.(Hon.), Univ. of Guelph, 1992; LL.D. (Hon.), Simon Fraser Univ., 1993.

Koh, Poh-Chan, C.A. 💲
Executive Vice-President and Chief Financial Officer, HUSKY OIL LTD., 707 - 8th Ave. S.W., Calgary, AB T2P 3G7 (403) 298-6068, FAX 265-6599. EDUC: The Chartered Institute of Taxation, London, UK; Canadian Institute of Chartered Accountants, C.A.; Institute of Chartered Accountants in England & Wales, Fellow. CAREER: Sr. Consultant, Royal Bank of Canada; Dir., Int'l Taxation, Bank of Nova Scotia; Exec. VP & CFO, Husky Oil Ltd. DIRECTOR: Husky Oil Ltd. & subsidiaries. AFFIL: Canada-Hong Kong Business Association (Bd.); Calgary Chamber of Commerce (Corp. Rep.).

Kohut, Vera, B.Sc.,M.D. ⊕
Medical Doctor, BRAMALEA MEDICAL GROUP, 18 Kensington Rd., Ste. 500, Bramalea, ON L6T 4S5 (905) 791-7577, FAX 791-7110. Born Victoria 1954. d. EDUC: Univ. of Alberta, B.Sc.(Pharmacology) 1975; Univ. of Calgary, M.D. 1979. CAREER: Molecular Pharmacology Research, Univ. of Alberta, 1975-76; Rotating Internship, St. Michael's Hospital, Toronto, 1979-80; Residency, Internal Medicine, Women's College Hospital, 1980-81; Family Physician, Bramalea Medical Group, 1981 to date; various exec. positions, Peel Memorial Hospital, 1982 to date; Medical Dir., Southbrook Retirement Community, 1989-91. AFFIL: Region of Peel (Chair, Task Force on Women's Health 1991); Peel District

Health Council (mbr. 1989-91); Ontario Medical Association (Rep., Gen. Council 1988-89); Coll. of Family Practice; North Peel Medical Society; Federation of Medical Women; YMCA. HONS: Hospital Achievement Award, Peel Memorial Hospital, 1985; Certificate of Merit, Ont. Ministry or Health, 1991. INTERESTS: opera; film; literature; jogging; dancing; skiing. COMMENT: *"Enthusiastic about life, my interests and endeavours. Committed to my profession. A sense of obligation to give back to society for the privileges it has bestowed upon me."*

Kolber, Sandra, B.A.,C.M. $ ⊗ O
Director, CANADIAN BROADCASTING CORPORATION, 1170 Peel, 8th fl., Montreal, QC H3B 4P2 (514) 878-5245, FAX 392-4769. Born White Plains, N.Y. m. Senator E. Leo Kolber. 2 ch. Lynne Halliday, Jonathan. EDUC: McGill Univ., B.A. 1955. CAREER: writer, Anglo-Jewish Press, 1968-74; Consultant, Canadian Film Development Corporation (now Telefilm Canada), 1972-79; Dir., Creative Dev., Astral Film Productions Ltd., 1979-83; VP, Canadian International Studios Inc., 1983-86; Dir., Canadian Broadcasting Corporation, 1986 to date. SELECTED PUBLICATIONS: *Bitter Sweet Lemons and Love* (1967); *All There is of Love* (1968). DIRECTOR: Canadian Broadcasting Corporation. AFFIL: The Sandra & Leo Kolber Foundation (Pres.); Montreal Symphony Orchestra (VP; Exec. Committee; Co-Chair, Hon. Council); P.E.N. International; Composers, Authors, Publishers Association of Canada; Academy of Canadian Cinema & Television. HONS: Member of the Order of Canada, 1993; Ramon John Hnatyshyn Award for Support of the Arts, 1994.

Kome, Penney ✐ ▯ ✽
Author and Journalist. Calgary Contributing Editor, *NEWEST REVIEW*, EMAIL kome@ freenet.calgary.ab.ca. Born Chicago 1948. m. Bob Pond. 2 ch. Sanford Kome-Pond, Graham Kome-Pond. CAREER: author & journalist; freelance writer since 1971; Calgary Contributing Ed., *NeWest Review.* SELECTED PUBLICATIONS: *Somebody Has to Do It: Whose Work is Housework?* (McClelland & Stewart, 1982); *The Taking of Twenty-Eight: Women Challenge the Constitution* (Women's Educational Press, 1983); *Women of Influence: Canadian Women and Politics* (Doubleday Canada, 1985); *Peace: A Dream Unfolding*, co-ed. Patrick Crean (Canada: Lester & Orpen, Dennys; US: Sierra Club, 1986); *Every Voice Counts* (Canadian Advisory Council on the Status of Women, 1989); hundreds of features & columns in major Cdn publications, incl.

Homemaker's Magazine, *Calgary Herald, Maclean's, The Toronto Star, The Globe and Mail, Saturday Night, Quest, City Woman; Financial Post; Chatelaine* & *Toronto Life.* AFFIL: The Writers' Union of Canada; Writers' Guild of Alberta; Project Ploughshares; Inter Pares; Canadian Association of Journalists; Canadian Research Institute for the Advancement of Women (CRIAW) (Research Assoc.). HONS: Robertine Parry prize for outstanding female journalism, CRIAW, 1984; Women of Distinction Award, Comm., Metro Toronto YWCA, 1987; Canada 125 Medal, 1992. INTERESTS: cycling; parenting; Internet. MISC: listed in *Canadian Who's Who* since 1988.

Koniuck-Petzold, Margaret, B.A., C.G.A. ■ O $ ◉
Vice-President, Fundraising, UNICEF CANADA, 160 Stafford St., Winnipeg, MB R3M 2V8 (204) 477-4600, FAX 477-4040. Born Winnipeg 1959. m. Gregory Petzold. 2 ch. EDUC: Univ. of Winnipeg, B.A.(Econ.). CAREER: Officer in Charge of Oper., Asst. Mgr, Bank of Nova Scotia, 1987-90. VOLUNTEER CAREER: Treas., UNICEF Manitoba, 1991-92; Chair 1993; Dir & VP, Fundraising, UNICEF Canada. AFFIL: Certified General Accountant; Manitoba Historical Society. INTERESTS: children's rights; int'l dev.; travel. COMMENT: *"Travelling through Latin America, my heart went out to those children who live without many basic human needs. This spurred my involvement with UNICEF."*

Konnelly, Rhona ■ ◉ $ ✐
Founder, Director, THE ALEXANDRA WSA INTERNATIONAL, 1849 Chimo Place, Victoria, BC V8N 4Y1 (604) 721-5065. Born Glasgow 1955. m. Joel W. Konnelly. 2 ch. EDUC: Nelson High Sch., Burlington Ont.; Camosun Coll., Arts & Sci. Major. CAREER: Sales Supervisor, Sun Life Assurance Company of Canada, 1977-86; independent Insur. & Fin. Planning Consultant, PPI Associates, 1986-92; Researcher, R.A. Malatest and Associates Ltd., 1993-94; Dir., Mktg Mgr, Training Professional, Konnelly Communications Ltd., 1994 to date; Insur. Specialist, Investors Group, 1995 to date. SELECTED CREDITS: Host, *Westside Magazine* (a community-based variety show), Shaw Cable; Host & Prod., *Inner Views* (an arts documentary profiling local artists). SELECTED PUBLICATIONS: has been featured in, or written for publications incl. *Island Parent* Magazine, *Focus on Women* Magazine, *Sharing Ideas, Local Women* Magazine, *The Bachelor Book* & *Entrepreneurial Woman*; various other publications. EDIT: Publisher, *The Alexandra Quarterly* & *IMM Express.*

AFFIL: Network for Empowering Women & Men, Alexandria, Va. (Dir.); Life Underwriters' Association of Canada; Zonta International; Credit Women's International; Vancouver Island Training Association; Conscience Canada. **HONS:** Debate & Speaking Honours, Nelson High Sch.; Application Champion, Sun Life of Canada (8 yrs.). **INTERESTS:** family; fitness; gourmet cooking; walking; hiking; writing; public speaking; community work; helping people to become economically independent & self reliant; helping communities to heal; finding new ways to address the need for gender equity & peace to prevail in our socities. **MISC:** featured on *Conversations*, a 1/2-hr. community program; extensive media work; marketed & hosted 1st Cdn "Gender Reconciliation Conference," Victoria, 1995; The Alexandria WSA International is the 1st women's org. in Canada to offer insur. & pension plan benefits to its membership, which now includes both women & mem. **COMMENT:** *"My life's purpose is one that involves the healing of relationships, and hence our communities, through my professional and community endeavours. I would like to see more organizations join hands to address the very issues that come close to home for all of us, especially when it comes to the caring of our young people. Instead of so much emphasis being placed on 'gender' issues, there needs to be a union of all people, towards a common goal of mutual respect, understanding and peace."*

Kooluris Dobbs, Linda Kia, A.A., B.F.A. ⊗ ⊰
Artist. 1330 Spadina Rd., Ste. 1005, Toronto, ON M5R 2V9 (416) 960-8984, FAX 925-3001. Born Orange, N.J. 1949. m. Kildare Dobbs. **EDUC:** Pine Manor Coll., A.A.(Lib. Arts), 1968; Sorbonne & Academic Year Abroad Program, Diplôme Moyen (French) 1969; studied with Nicolas Manev, William T. Williams, Marshall Arisman & Gilbert Stone; Sch. of Visual Arts, N.Y., B.F.A.(Hons., Media Arts) 1972. **CAREER:** portrait commissions; Instructor, Dawson Coll., Montreal, 1975-78; Instructor, Ryerson Polytechnical Institute, 1980-94; Instructor, The International Academy of Merchandising & Design, Toronto, 1988-89; Instructor, George Brown Coll., 1994-95. **SELECTED PUBLICATIONS:** Contributor, *Northlight Book of Acrylic Techniques*, by Earl Glenville Killeen (1995); *Splash 3* (1994); *Splash 5* (1996); *Best of Flower Painting*; illustrations for over 80 clients in Canada, US & Europe, incl. *The Toronto Star*, *The Globe and Mail*, Sherrit Gordon Mines, *Enroute*, Drake Publications (US), RCA Records, & *Amerika* Magazine (USSR). **EXHI-BITIONS:** over 40 group & solo exhibitions, incl. group show, Pietrantino Gallery, N.Y. (1972), Canada's Discovery Train (1978-83), solo exhibition, The McGill Club (1985); Quan-Schieder Gallery (1989), art rental, Vancouver Art Gallery & Sarah Dobbs Gallery, Vancouver (1995, 1996). **COLLECTIONS:** work in over 100 private collections in Canada & abroad, incl. those of Bruce Cockburn, Joey & Toby Tanenbaum, the Hon. Barbara McDougall, & Moses Znaimer; works in over 32 corp. collections, incl. Artform (Norway), Mount Sinai Hospital, Probyn & Co., Midland Walwyn, Goodman & Goodman, & Temple Scott & Associates. **AFFIL:** Toronto Watercolour Society. **HONS:** Annual Art Purchase Prize, Pine Manor Coll., Boston, 1968; 2nd Prize (Paintings), *Financial Post* Annual Reports Awards, Mining Div. (1980), 1981; "Creative Decade" Merit Award, Toronto, *Studio* Magazine, 1986; Honourable Mention, Annual Fall Show, Toronto Watercolour Society, 1991; Best in Architecture, Annual Fall Show, Toronto Watercolour Society, 1994. **INTERESTS:** photography; travel; languages (French, English, Swedish, Spanish, Italian, Modern Greek). **MISC:** selected for *Ontario Living* Magazine, "Gallery," 1985; chosen for 2 covers featuring living painters in Canada, *Canadian Medical Association Journal*, 1985; featured in *Applied Arts* Magazine, Feb./Mar. issue 1993; *Business Quarterly* Winter, 1995. **COMMENT:** *"Known as an illustrator and portraitist, Kooluris-Dobbs has increasingly worked scenes from her travels into evocative, sun-drenched watercolour & acrylic paintings, and is collected worldwide."*

Kopansky, Charlene, B.Sc., B.Ed. ■■ ⊰ ⊘ ♙
President and Founder, CANADIAN AQUAFITNESS LEADERS ALLIANCE INC. (training & certification in aquafitness leadership & aquatic rehab.; membership; conferences, courses, workshops), 125 Lilian Dr., Scarborough, ON M1R 3W6 (416) 751-9823, FAX 755-1832. Born Toronto 1954. s. **EDUC:** Univ. of Guelph, B.Sc. (Hons., Biological Sci., Human Kinetics) 1977; Univ. of Toronto, B.Ed.(Sci. & Phys. Educ.) 1978. **CAREER:** high sch. Teacher, Biol., & Phys. & Health Educ., 1978-84; int'l fitness presenter, various organizations, 1980-86; Fitness Instructor, Granite Club, Fitness Institute, McGill Club, Elmwood Club & Sports Clubs, 1984-91; Employee Fitness Consultant, Kraft General Foods & Northern Telecom, 1985-91; Pres., Canadian Aquafitness Leaders Alliance (CALA), 1992 to date. **SELECTED CREDITS:** *Something Ventured* (National Film Board special, 1977). **SELECTED PUBLICATIONS:** various articles in *Club Direct* (1993); *Wavelink*

Newsletter (CALA quarterly publication, 1993-96); *CanFit Pro Newsletter* (1996); *Active Living Newsletter* & O.F.C., Canada (1992 to date); *Fitness Management Magazine*, Australia; *The Toronto Star; The Globe and Mail; Yukon News*. AFFIL: Ontario Fitness Council (Chairperson, NFLAC Exam Committee 1991); Network of Fitness Professionals, Australia; IHRSA; H2Oz Aqua Organization. HONS: Dean's Hon. Roll, Univ. of Guelph; Leadership Award, Ontario Fitness Council (O.F.C.), 1993; Volunteer Recognition Award, O.F.C., 1994; Top Specialty Presenter Award, International Bodylife Conference, Germany, 1996. INTERESTS: hiking; outdoor pursuits; travel; theatre; dance; the Tropics!. MISC: 1st woman to establish a nat'l training & certification membership-based organization for aquafitness & aquatic rehabilitation professionals in Canada. COMMENT: *"Fitness and wellness presentations including theoretical lectures (anatomy, physiology, biomechanics) and theory/practical workshops ("The Joy of Stretch," aerobics & "Step & Sculpt," aquafitness; numerous topics) across Canada and internationally: Brazil, 1982, 1985, 1988, 1991; Australia, 1992, 1993, 1994, 1995; Germany, 1995, 1996; Trinidad, 1986, 1988, 1989; Yukon & Northwest Territories, 1995, 1996; B.C., Alta., Sask., Man., Que., N.B., N.S., presented many times at regional conferences and organized workships since 1986."*

Korhonen, June M. (née Zimmerman) Ⓢ
Secretary-Treasurer and Office Manager, NORDEX EXPLOSIVES LTD., P.O. Box 790, Kirkland Lake, ON P2N 3K4 (705) 642-4265. Secretary, CANALEX RESOURCES. Born 1936. 4 ch. EDUC: Northern Coll. of Applied Arts & Technology. CAREER: admin. in acctg & mining offices. AFFIL: Canadian Institute of Mining, Metallurgy & Petroleum (CIMM); CIMM Kirkland Lake Branch (Chair); Business & Professional Women's Club, Kirkland Lake (Pres.); Kirkland Lake & District United Way (Pres.); Prospectors' Association; Prospectors' Association, Kirkland Lake & Cobalt Branch; Sir Harry Oaks Chateau, Museum of Northern History (Chrm 1980-95); Miners' Memorial Foundation (Dir.).

Korn, Alison ■■ ⑫
Olympic Athlete. c/o Canadian Olympic Association. Born Ottawa 1970. SPORTS CAREER: mbr., Cdn Nat'l Rowing Team, 1995 to date. Olympic Games: Silver, 8+, 1996. MISC: speaks English, French, German, Spanish.

Korper, Olga ⊗
Director and Owner, OLGA KORPER GALLERY,

17 Morrow Ave., Toronto, ON M6R 2H9 (416) 538-8220, FAX 538-8772. Born Konigsgraz, Czechoslovakia 1940. d. Leo Meyer. 1 ch. EDUC: Ontario Coll. of Art, 1963-67; Ontario Coll. of Education, 1967-69. CAREER: Art Instructor, Billings Composite High Sch., Northern Secondary Sch., Seneca Coll., 1969-73; Art Dealer, Gallery O & Olga Korper Gallery, 1973 to date. AFFIL: Canada Council Art Bank (Transition Advisory Committee); Canadian Cultural Property Export Review Bd. (Bd. Mbr.); past affiliations include CNE Arts Committee; Toronto Sculpture Garden (Bd.); Power Plant (Bd. of Dir.); Mayor's Committee for Art & Tourism; External Affairs Advisory Bd. for the 49th Parallel, NY; Professional Art Dealers' Association of Canada (VP 4 yrs.; Pres. 4 yrs.; Pres., PADAC Art Foundation; Bd. of Dir.); 49th Parallel (Programming Committee); Toronto Arts Awards Foundation (Trustee); Dundas Valley Sch. of Art (Trustee). INTERESTS: granddaughter Taiga; bridge; hiking. MISC: lecturer, 1980-93. COMMENT: *"My life's achievements revolve around my ambitions: to see my daughter Sasha, my granddaughter Taiga, my gallery and my bridge game grow to a magnificent level. I want to leave a fingerprint."*

Korzeniowski, Bonnie Catherine, B.S.W., R.S.W.,M.S.A. ⊕ ⊕ ⊙
Social Worker, Department of Psychogeriatrics, DEER LODGE CENTRE, 2109 Portage Ave., Winnipeg, MB R3J RG3 (204) 831-2184, FAX 885-1074. Born Winnipeg 1941. m. Gerald A. Korzeniowski. 4 ch. Karen, Kathryn, Ryan, Alexis. EDUC: Algonquin Community Coll., Ottawa, Social Service Worker Diploma 1974; Univ. of Manitoba, B.S.W. 1980; Central Michigan Univ., M.S.A. 1995. CAREER: Social Worker, North Bay Psychiatric Hospital, 1974-75; Juvenile Counsellor, Correctional Officer II, Manitoba Youth Centre, 1975-80; Parole Supervisor, John Howard & Elizabeth Fry Society, 1979-80; Social Worker, Medical Svcs Branch, Health & Welfare Canada, 1980-81; Social Worker, Brandon General Hospital, 1981-84; Social Worker, St. Boniface Hospital, 1984-87; Social Worker, Deer Lodge Centre, 1987 to date. AFFIL: Alzheimer Society of Manitoba (Bd.); Professional Institute of the Public Service of Canada (Nat'l Committees on Human Rights, Women's Issues, Policy, Steering-Group Advisory Council); Deer Lodge Centre (Winnipeg Branch Exec.; Chair, Health Care Professional Group); St. James NDP (Exec.); Deer Lodge United Church (Fin. Committee); Manitoba Institute of Registered Social Workers; Canadian Association of Psychosocial Oncology; Canadian Association of Gerontol-

ogy; Alzheimer Society of Canada. HONS: Recognition for Volunteer Work; Indian Friendship Centre, North Bay, 1974; Cancer Society, Brandon, Man., 1984; Alzheimer Society of Manitoba, 1994. INTERESTS: pottery; travel. COMMENT: *"I am a true Libra, struggling to balance family and career. Striving for personal and professional growth, I have borne children and furthered my education over a span of 20 years. Committed to helping others and making a difference, I fight for fairness when, where and however I can. My career choice and union role assist me in this endeavour. My 'joie de vivre' motivates and rewards me."*

Kosowan, Lynda, C.S.W.,M.S.W. ✿ ◐
Executive Director, SCARBOROUGH WOMEN'S CENTRE, 2100 Ellesmere Rd., Scarborough, ON M1H 3B7 (416) 439-7111, FAX 439-6999. Born Toronto 1953. d. EDUC: Univ. of Toronto, B.A.(Socio-Cultural Anthro.) 1976, M.S.W.(Social Policy, Planning & Admin.) 1980. CAREER: Admin. Mgr, The Boys Home, 1980-85; Exec. Dir., Scarborough Women's Centre, 1986 to date. AFFIL: SWAN Shelter for Women & their Children (Dir.); Canadian Executive Services Organization (Volunteer); Ontario Coll. of Certified Social Workers; Scarborough Community Safety Audit Committee (Chair); Scarborough Safety Council. HONS: Ont. Grad. Scholarship, 1979. INTERESTS: women's concerns; the arts. MISC: C.E.S.O. volunteer advisor to National Federation of Gypsies, Hungary, Fall 1994. COMMENT: *"I have worked toward women's equity and facilitation of women's full participation in the community."*

Kostash, Myrna, M.A. 📖 📚 🔖
Writer. 10415 - 87 Ave., Edmonton, AB T6E 2P4 (403) 433-0710. Born Edmonton. EDUC: Univ. of Toronto, M.A.(Russian Language & Lit.) 1968. CAREER: co-teacher, Women's Studies Program, Univ. of Toronto, 1972-74; teacher, various summer writing schools & writing workshops; Creative Writing Instructor, Mount Royal Coll., Calgary, 1989; Max Bell Prof., Sch. of Journalism, Univ. of Regina, 1989-90; Creative Writing Instructor, "My Town" Proj., Writer-in-Electronic-Residence, York Univ., 1993; Writer-in-Residence in Creative Nonfiction, The Loft, Minneapolis, 1994; Ashley Fellow, Trent Univ., 1996; Writer-in-Residence, Regina Public Library, 1996-97. SELECTED CREDITS: Writer, Edmonton, Workshop West, 1982; Writer, *No Kidding*, Vancouver, Green Thumb, 1988; Writer, *After the Fall: The Erotic Life of the Left*, Edmonton, Catalyst, 1992; Writer, "Reunion," CBC *Satur-day Stereo Theatre, 1984; Teach Me To Dance*, National Film Board, 1978; & others. SELECTED PUBLICATIONS: *This Magazine*, Contributing Ed.; *NeWest Review*, Contributing ed.; *Border Crossings*, Columnist; *Her Own Woman*, Contributor (Toronto: Macmillan, 1975); *All of Baba's Children* (Edmonton: Hurtig, 1977); *Long Way from Home* (Toronto: Lorimer, 1980); *No Kidding: Inside the World of Teenage Girls* (Toronto: McClelland and Stewart, 1987); *The Road Home*, contributor (Edmonton: Reidmore, 1992); *Bloodlines: A Journey into Eastern Europe* (Vancouver: Douglas and McIntyre, 1993); *Letters from Kiev*, by Solomea Pavlychko (translator) (New York: St. Martin's Press, 1992); short fiction & creative nonfiction in *Descant, The Camrose Review, Capilano Review, Prairie Fire, Literatura na swieciel Svesvit; Brick*; articles in *Saturday Night, Chatelaine, Maclean's* & various other magazines; stories in numerous anthologies, incl. *Kitchen Talk: Contemporary Women's Prose and Poetry* (Red Deer: Red Deer Coll. Press, 1992). AFFIL: Writers' Guild of Alberta; Writers' Union of Canada; ACTRA; PEN. HONS: Silver Citation, National Magazine Awards, 1985; Best Nonfiction, Alberta Culture Prize, 1988; Best Nonfiction, Writers' Guild of Alberta, 1988, 1994. MISC: several grants supporting writing & research; participant in Maclean Hunter Arts Journalism Seminar under direction of Alberto Manguel; guest lecturer in numerous classrooms worldwide; judge in various literary competitions; mbr. of several Canada Council & other arts council juries. COMMENT: *"For those who have yet to make her acquaintance, Myrna Kostash is something of an under-acknowledged national treasure. For the past two decades, she's been at the forefront of an unofficial movement to get the country's writing establishment to take more seriously the work of literary nonfiction"–Stan Persky*, The Globe and Mail, *1993.*

Koszo, Joan, B.Comm. $ ❀
Assistant Vice-President, Global Compensation, NORTHERN TELECOM LIMITED, 3 Robert Speck Pkwy, Mississauga, ON L4Z 3O8 (905) 566-3390, FAX 803-4652. Born Windsor, Ont. 1957. m. Joseph. 2 ch. EDUC: Univ. of Windsor, B.Comm.(Hum. Res./Fin.) 1983. CAREER: Fin. Administrator, Windsor Utilities Commission, 1975-80; Specialist, Hum. Res. Info. Systems, Northern Telecom, 1982-84; Specialist, Compensation Dev., 1984-86; Mgr, Benefits, 1986-88; Mgr, Hum. Res., 1988-89; Sr. Benefits Mgr, 1989-91; Dir., Compensation & Benefits, 1991-92; Asst. VP, Global Benefits, 1992-94; Asst. VP, Global Compensation, 1994 to date. SELECTED PUBLICATIONS: "Under-

standing Pension Administration" (*Benefits Canada*, Apr. & June 1992); "Empowerment" (*Canadian Healthcare* Dec. 1993); "Should Employers Continue to Cover Dependents?" exchange (*Benefits Canada* Sept. 1994). **AFFIL:** Conference Board of Canada (Compensation Research Centre Advisory Bd.); Information Technology Association of Canada; Canadian Pension & Benefits Conference (Past Co-Chair, Program Committee); Art Gallery of Mississauga (Immediate Past Pres., Bd. of Dir.). **INTERESTS:** performing arts; raising 2 young daughters. **MISC:** has developed & given lectures on benefits. **COMMENT:** *"I like to think of solutions that are 'outside of the box' and I have a preference for breaking away from established ways of doing things. I like challenge and have a strong preference for action–moving forward. Most recently I was involved in a major endeavour: North American flexible benefits for Northern Telecom."*

Kouri, Joan Lylian, B.A.,M.Ed. ■ ⊕ 🍁 ✊
Member, Convention Refugee Determination Division, IMMIGRATION AND REFUGEE BOARD OF CANADA. Born Cochrane, Ont. 1931. m. Robert Michael Kouri. **EDUC:** McGill Univ., B.A.(Soc. & English) 1952, M.Ed. 1979. **CAREER:** Program Dir. for Women & Girls, Young Men's Christian Association–Northmount Branch, 1953-59; Educator, Protestant Sch. Bd. of Greater Montreal, 1959-63; Lecturer, English as a Second Language, Univ. of Montreal, 1963-65; Educational Consultant/Remedial Therapist/Counsellor, Dept. of Psychiatry, Montreal Children's Hospital, 1969-94; Evaluator of Teachers of French as a Second Language, Montreal Catholic Sch. Commission, 1972-73; educ. consultant, 1989-94; mbr., Immigration & Refugee Bd. - Canada, 1994 to date; Pres., Working Group on Women and Children Refugees, 1995-96. **POLITICAL CAREER:** mbr., Liberal Party of Canada, 1959; mbr., Liberal Party of Que., 1969; Pres., Women's Commission, Fed. Liberal Association of St-Michel-Ahuntsic, 1981-86; mbr., Reform Committee, Liberal Party of Canada, 1983-86; Delegate, Leadership Convention, 1984; Pres., St-Michel-Ahuntsic Fed. Liberal Riding Association, 1985-89; Delegate, Reform Conference, Liberal Party of Canada, 1986; VP-Anglophone, Liberal Party of Canada (Que.), 1986-88; mbr. of the Exec. Council, Liberal Party of Canada (Que.), 1986-88; Co-Pres., Fin. & Membership Campaign, Liberal Party of Canada (Que.), 1987-88; Standing Committee on Comm., representing Nat'l Women's Liberal Commission, 1987-89; Chrm, Legislation Study Group, Lakeshore Univ. Women's Club, 1988-90; Dir., Interaction Pointe Claire, 1988-90; Pres., Nat'l Women's Liberal Commission, Liberal Party of Canada, 1990-94; Dir., Judy LaMarsh Fund, 1990-94; mbr., Nat'l Exec., Liberal Party of Canada, 1990-94; Delegate, Constitutional Conference, 1991; mbr., Nat'l Campaign Committee, 1992; mbr., Canada Yes Committee, 1992; Co-Pres., Leader's Special Task Force on Women in the Liberal Party of Canada, 1992-94; Liberal candidate (Brome Missisquoi, Que.), 1993. **SELECTED PUBLICATIONS:** co-author, *Multi-Medal Treatment of Hyperactive Children With and Without Learning Disabilities*. **INTERESTS:** golf; skiing; theatre & the arts; advocacy for women & children. **COMMENT:** *"My professional career in the past has focused on the challenge of helping youngsters, adolescents and young adults to better understand themselves and in so doing to help themselves. Their legacy to me was to better understand myself."*

Kovacs, Gail, B.P.E.,B.A.,C.C.R.C., A.R.P. $ ⊕ 🎓
President and Chief Executive Officer, CAREER PROBE INC., 775 Pacific Rd., Unit 31, Oakville, ON L6L 6M3 (905) 825-1900, FAX 825-1919. Born Hamilton, Ont. 1951. m. James. 1 ch. Maddie. **EDUC:** McMaster Univ., B.A. (French) 1974, B.P.E.(Phys. Educ.) 1974, Certificate in Hum. Res. Dev. 1986. **CAREER:** Dir., Sr. Citizens & Social Svcs, YWCA, 1974-76; Rehab. Counsellor, Workers' Compensation Bd., 1977-80; Researcher, 1980-82; Placement Specialist, 1982-84; Worksite Analyst, 1984-85; Team Coord., 1985-86; Reg. Proj. Specialist, 1986-88; Pres. & CEO, Career Probe Inc., 1988 to date; Consultant, Employment Services, 1990-93; Pres., The Rehabilitation Training Group, 1992 to date. **SELECTED PUBLICATIONS:** "Ergonomics and Job Placement of Workers Disabled Through Occupational Injury" (*Canadian Institute*, 1988); "Rehabilitation Counselling: The Canadian Experience" (*Canadian Institute*, 1994); "Ergonomics for Workplace Health and Safety" (Canadian Institute, 1994). **AFFIL:** National Rehabilitation Association, US; Job Placement Division, US; Vocational Evaluation & Work Adjustment Association, US; Canadian Vocational Association; Chamber of Commerce; Canadian Federation of Independent Business; Canadian Rehabilitation Council for the Disabled (Nat'l Professional Associations Committee); Canadian Guidance & Counselling Foundation; Canadian Association of Rehabilitation Professionals (Pres. 1992-94; Past Pres. 1994 to date); Ontario Society (Pres. 1990-92; Past Pres. 1992-93; Chair, Regulation Committee); Canadian Association for Vocational Evaluation & Work Adjustment (Pres.

1989-92; Past Pres. 1992-93). **INTERESTS:** boating; skiing; reading. **MISC:** Accredited Rehab. Professional, 1981; Canadian Certified Rehab. Counsellor, 1991. **COMMENT:** *"I have strived over the past 20 years to educate all parties on the appropriate techniques of placing people in work–with expertise on assisting people with disability."*

Kowaliczko, Béatrice, M.A. ○ ✦ ⊚
Consultant. 3844 Hôtel de Ville, Montreal, QC H2W 2G5 (514) 843-8289. Born Paris 1947. m. Brian Young. 1 ch. Julien Leloup. **EDUC:** Censier, Paris, Diplôme universitaire d'études littéraires (DUEL) 1971; Sorbonne, Paris, Licence de lettres modernes 1972; McGill Univ., M.A.(Que. Lit.) 1982. **CAREER:** writer & participant, radio broadcasts for youth, Radio-Tunis & Radio-Strasbourg, 1955-63; various duties, *Accueil de France*, Nice, 1965-68; Prof., French as a Foreign Language, Univ. de Nice, 1968-74; Prof., French, Ministry of Educ., France, 1975-82; Dir., Que. Office, Association for Canadian Studies, 1983-86; Assoc. Dir., Association for Canadian Studies, 1986-87; Exec. Dir., 1987-93; Exec. Dir., Royal Society of Canada, 1993-95; Exec. Dir. & Sec., Ordre des Architectes du Québec, 1995-96. **SELECTED PUBLICATIONS:** various publications. **EDIT:** Bd. of Dir., *Ecodecision: Revue environnement et politiques/Environment and Policy Magazine*, 1995 to date. **AFFIL:** Association for Canadian Studies; Conseil international d'études francophones (Bd. of Dir. Cdn Rep. 1989-91; VP 1991-83; Pres. 1993-94); l'association Québec dans le monde; United Way volunteer; Heritage Minutes/Minutes du patrimonie proj. (Committee Mbr. 1990-91). **HONS:** Lauréate du concours national de l'I.P.E.S., Nice, 1969; Lauréate du concours national du C.A.P.E.S., Paris, 1976; France-Quebec Scholarship, 1976; France-Canada Scholarship, 1980; Canadian Studies Award of Merit, 1996. **INTERESTS:** services to community; francophonie; nature; learning. **MISC:** listed in *Canadian Who's Who*; various conference presentations. **COMMENT:** *"Bilingual specialist in management of para-public organizations, writing and speaking. Since immigrating to Canada (at 35!) I was given a chance to play an active role in Canadian studies and professional postsecondary organizations."*

Kowalsky, Christina A., B.Sc.,D.E.S.S., Ph.D. ■ ⊕
Psychologist. 3101 Bloor St. W., Ste. 303, Toronto, ON M8X 2W2 (416) 231-7901, FAX 762-2076. Born Radville, Sask. 1952. m. Wiktor Moskaliuk. 2 ch. **EDUC:** Univ. of Toronto,

B.Sc.(Psych.) 1974; Univ. of Paris, France, D.E.S.S.(Psych.) 1976, Ph.D.(Psych.) 1981. **CAREER:** Ed. Asst., Shevchenko Scientific Society, Sarcelles, France, 1976-79; Psychologist, Dufferin-Peel Roman Catholic Separate Sch. Bd., 1981-96; Sr. Psychologist, 1996 to date; Psychologist in private practice, 1985 to date; part-time Consultant to French-Language Children's Programmes, TVOntario, 1988-89. **AFFIL:** West Park Hospital (Gov.; Continuing Care Committee); Ontario Psychological Association; Canadian Psychological Association; Canadian Register of Health Service Providers; Coll. of Psychologists of Ontario; Plast Youth Group (Nat'l Exec. 1981-83, 1994 to date); Second Wreath Women's Group, Toronto (Founding Mbr. 1987-89). **HONS:** St. George Medal for founding Plast Branches in Paris, France, Plast Youth Group, 1979. **MISC:** lecturer & presenter at numerous conferences, workshops: focus on women's issues, training sessions to youth counsellors, family violence & minority issues in the francophone & Ukrainian communities ; mbr. of Organizing Committee, Conference on Ukrainian Women: Tradition & Change, Oct. 1988. **COMMENT:** *"Feminist, fluent in English, French and Ukrainian; professionally, provide specialized services for French and Ukrainian communities; believe strongly in education and outreach programs in community, hence my involvement in workshops, lectures, etc."*

Kraft Sloan, Karen, B.A.,B.A.S.,M.E.S., M.P. ✦
Member of Parliament (York-Simcoe), **GOVERNMENT OF CANADA**, 466 Confederation Building, House of Commons, Ottawa, ON K1A 0A6 (613) 996-7752, FAX 992-8351. Born Kitchener, Ont. 1952. m. Tod Sloan. 2 ch. **EDUC:** Univ. of Windsor, B.A.(Comm. Studies) 1977; Brock Univ., B.A.S. 1982; York Univ., Masters in Environmental Studies 1990. **CAREER:** self-employed Consultant, Kraft Sloan Consulting; M.P. (York-Simcoe); Parliamentary Sec. to the Min. of the Environment. **SELECTED PUBLICATIONS:** "Each of our Voices: Equity and Discrimination in the University."

Krakauer, Renate, B.Sc.Phm.,M.E.S., C.H.R.P. ⊕ ⊲
President and Chief Executive Officer, **THE MICHENER INSTITUTE FOR APPLIED HEALTH SCIENCES**, 222 St. Patrick St., Toronto, ON M5T 1V4 (416) 596-3131, FAX 596-3156. Born Stanislawow, Poland 1941. m. Henry Lobbenberg. 3 ch. **EDUC:** Univ. of Toronto, B.Sc.Phm. (Pharm.) 1963; York Univ., Master of Environmental Studies (Social Change & Educ.) 1974.

CAREER: Pharmacist, 1963-72; part-time Instructor, Seneca, Sheridan & Humber Colleges, & York Univ., 1974-90; Program Consultant, Continuing Educ., Humber Coll., 1974-80; Deputy Commissioner, Hum. Res. Svcs, City of York, 1986-90; Commissioner, Hum. Res. Svcs, 1989-91; Dir., Hum. Res. Branch, Ministry of Health, Ont., 1991-94; Acting Asst. Deputy Min., 1994; Pres. & CEO, The Michener Institute, 1994 to date. AFFIL: Ontario Municipal Management Institute (Certified Mun. Mgr); Conference Board of Canada (Public Sector Executives Ntwk 1994); Human Resources Professionals' Association of Ontario (Certified Hum. Res. Professional); Ontario Coll. of Pharmacists (Registered Pharmacist). INTERESTS: reading; writing fiction; fitness; social issues. COMMENT: *"A dynamic, visionary senior executive with a varied generalist-management and educational background, dedicated to change management in the interests of creating effective organizations."*

Krause, Judith, B.A.,B.V.T.D. 🎭 ⟨⟩ 📖
Writer, Editor and Teacher. Born Regina 1952. EDUC: Univ. of Saskatchewan, B.A.(French/English) 1974; Univ. of Regina, B.U.T.D.(Adult Educ.) 1991. CAREER: Literary Arts Consultant, Saskatchewan Arts Bd.; Coord., Creative Writing Program, Saskatchewan Sch. for the Arts; Creative Writing Instructor, Univ. of Regina, Saskatchewan Sch. of the Arts at Fort San, & Sage Hill Writing Experience; Ed. Asst., *SALT* Magazine; Poetry Ed., *Windscript*; mbr., Thunder Creek Publishing Co-operative; Ed., *Grain*, 1993-94; Adult Educ. Instructor. SELECTED CREDITS: participant, *Tabloid Love* poetry performance, Poets' Combine, 1992-93. SELECTED PUBLICATIONS: *What We Bring Home* (Coteau Books, 1986); *Half the Sky* (Coteau Books, 1994); *Out of Place*, Co-ed. (1991); numerous anthology publications & poems in periodicals. AFFIL: Saskatchewan Writers' Guild; League of Canadian Poets; PEN International; The Poets' Combine. HONS: Robert Kroetsch Scholarship, Saskatchewan Sch. of the Arts, 1979; Major Poetry Prize, Saskatchewan Writers' Guild Literary Awards, 1982; Indiv. Assistance Grant, Saskatchewan Arts Bd., 1984, 1989; Honourable Mention, Poetry, Saskatchewan Writers' Guild Literary Awards, 1987; Writing Award, City of Regina, 1988; Honourable Mention, Nonfiction, Saskatchewan Writers' Guild Literary Awards, 1992; Finalist, National Poetry Contest, League of Canadian Poets, 1992; Study Grant, Saskatchewan Arts Bd., 1993; Finalist, Book of the Year, Saskatchewan Books Awards, 1994; Finalist, City of Regina Book Award, 1994. INTERESTS: writing & editing poetry; teaching

creative writing. COMMENT: *"I love teaching writing and have been lucky enough to be able to do so in a variety of educational settings for different kinds of learners."*

Krause, Margarida Oliveira, B.Sc.,M.Sc., Ph.D. ⚛ ⟨⟩
Professor, Department of Biology, UNIVERSITY OF NEW BRUNSWICK, Fredericton, NB E3B 6E1 (506) 453-4583, ext. 6207, FAX 453-3583, EMAIL mkrause@unb.ca. Born Lisbon 1931. m. Helmut H. Krause. 3 ch. Henry M. Krause, Edward A. Krause, George A. Krause. EDUC: Univ. of Lisbon, B.Sc.(Cytogenetics) 1953; Univ. of Wisconsin, M.Sc.(Botany) 1957, Ph.D.(Cell Biol.) 1960. CAREER: Postdoctoral Fellow, Cell Biol., Univ. of Wisconsin, 1961; Postdoctoral Fellow, Molecular Biol., Univ. of Toronto, 1963-66; Hon. Lecturer, Univ. of New Brunswick, 1967-70; Assoc. Prof., 1970-76; Prof., 1976 to date. SELECTED PUBLICATIONS: "Stimulation of transcription of chromatin by specific small nuclear RNAs," with M. Ringuette *et al* (*Gene* 8, 1980); "75-K nuclear RNA from simian virus 40-transformed cells has sequence homology to the viral early promoter," with U. Sohn, J. Szyszko & D. Coombs (*Proceedings of the National Academy of Science*, US, 80, 1993); "Changes in promoter utilization in human and mouse c-myc genes upon transformation induction in temperature-sensitive cell lines," with Y. Lou (*Journal of Cell Physiology* 160 1994); "Insecticdal activity of a recombriant baculovirus containing an antisense c-myc fragment" (*Journal of General Virology*, 1996); "C-myc deregulation during transformation-induction: involvement of 7SK RNA" (*Journal of Cell Biochemistry*, 1996); "Chromatin structure and function: the heretical path to an RNA transcription factor" (*Biochemistry & Cell Biology*, 1996). EDIT: Special Ed., *Perspectives in Cell Biology* 1988, special issue of *Canadian Journal of Biochemistry & Cell Biology*, June 1988; Special Co-Ed., Commemorative Issue on the 25th Anniversary of the Canadian Society for Cell and Molecular Biology, *Biochemistry and Cell Biology*, 1992; Assoc. Ed., *Biochemistry and Cell Biology*, 1993 to date. AFFIL: Canadian Society for Cell Biology (Dir. 1970-72, 1981-83; Pres.-Elect 1983-84; Pres. 1984-86; Past-Pres. 1986-87); International Federation of Cell Biology (NRC-selected Cdn Delegate 1984); International Union of Biological Sciences (NRC-selected Cdn Delegate 1985). INTERESTS: control of gene expression; role of small RNAs. MISC: grant reviewer for various agencies. COMMENT: *"My interests centre on the regulation of mammalian genes in the context of cancer transformation. I have uncovered a*

novel regulatory factor composed of RNA and detected its involvement in deregulating c-myc gene expression."

Kravtsov, Natasha, B.A. ■ ■ ⓟ ⊕
President, MANITOBA DENTAL HYGIENISTS ASSOCIATION (representation, gov't rel'ns, advocacy of dental hygiene), P.O. Box 307, Winnipeg, MB R3L 2H6. Born Kiev, Ukraine 1966. m. Sam Kravtsov. EDUC: Univ. of Winnipeg, M.A.(Soc.) 1988; Univ. of Manitoba, Diploma (Dental Hygiene) 1993. CAREER: private practice, 1993-96; DND, Dental Hygienist, 1996-97. AFFIL: Manitoba Dental Hygienists Association (Pres. Elect 1995-96; Pres. 1996-97); Jewish Women International of Canada (VP, Membership, Tzevah–local chptr. 1996-97). INTERESTS: sports; gardening; needlework. COMMENT: *"I am a young professional woman who is interested in finding ways of serving the community. I have been involved on a volunteer basis for the Canadian Heart & Stroke Foundation and Winnipeg Harvest. I enjoy spending my leisure time with family and friends."*

Krempien, Jennifer ■ ■ ⓠ
Paralympic Athlete. St. Albert, AB. EDUC: plans to complete a degree as a dietitian. SPORTS CAREER: mbr., Nat'l Wheelchair Basketball Team, 2 yrs. Paralympic Games: Gold, 1996; Gold, 1992. Canadian Wheelchair Basketball League (CWBL): 2nd, Women's Finals, 1995; 1st, Women's Finals, 1994; 1st, Women's Finals, 1993; 2nd, Women's Finals, 1992. World Championships: 1st, 1994. HONS: 1993 All-Star.

Kreuk, Mary, B.Comm. ⓢ
Vice-President, Marketing, PEOPLES JEWELLERS CORPORATION, 1440 Don Mills Rd., Don Mills, ON M3B 3M1 (416) 391-7837, FAX 391-7805. Born St. Catharines, Ont. 1959. m. Fred Levin. 2 ch. Joshua, Jacob. EDUC: Queen's Univ., B.Comm.(Mktg) 1982. CAREER: VP, Mktg, Peoples Jewellers Corporation, 1994 to date. INTERESTS: skiing; reading.

Kronberg, Jean, B.Sc.,M.Sc.,Ph.D.,M.D., F.R.C.P.(c) ⊕
Chair, Medical Advisory Committee and Anesthetist-in-Chief, WOMEN'S COLLEGE HOSPITAL, 76 Grenville St., Toronto, ON M5S 1B2 (416) 323-6008, FAX 323-6307. Born Toronto 1942. s. EDUC: Queen's Univ., B.Sc.(Chem.) 1963, M.Sc.(Phys. Chem.) 1965, Ph.D.(Phys. Chem.) 1969, M.D.(Medicine) 1980. CAREER: Chair, CUSO Thailand Committee, 1972-74; Lecturer, Dept., of Chem., Fac. of Sci., Chulalongkorn Univ., Bangkok, & appt. as Sr. CUSO

Volunteer, Gov't of Thailand, 1974-75; Anesthetist-in-Chief, Women's College Hospital, 1988 to date; Chair, Medical Advisory Committee, 1994-96. AFFIL: Canadian Anaesthestists' Society; American Society of Anesthesiology; Royal Coll. of Physicians & Surgeons of Canada (Fellow); Canadian Coll. of Family Practice; Ontario Medical Association; Anaesthesia Patient Safety Foundation; Society for Technology in Anaesthesia; Society for Obstetrical Aneasthesists & Perinatology; Clinical Teachers' Association of Toronto. COMMENT: *"I believe it to be important to support the continuing development of programs in institutions of learning so that others may experience the high quality of training that I have enjoyed in Canada."*

Kronick, Doreen, B.A.,M.A. ⓠ ⊕ ⓓ
Psychoeducational Consultant. 221 Broadway Ave., Toronto, ON M4P 1W1 (416) 489-7858. Born Winnipeg 1931. m. Joseph. 3 ch. EDUC: Skidmore Coll., B.A.(Special Educ.) 1974; York Univ., M.A. 1976. CAREER: Professional Dir., Integra Foundation, 1973-75; Dir., Developmental Clinic & Coord., Remedial Program, Wellesley Hospital, 1974-77; Consultant, Ont. Ministry of Educ., 1978-95; Asst. Prof., York Univ., 1981-83; Assoc. Prof., 1983-87. SELECTED PUBLICATIONS: *Learning Disabilities: its Implications to a Responsible Society* (Chicago: Argus Publications, 1969); *What About Me? The Learning Disabled Adolescent* (Novato, Cal.: Academic Therapy, 1975); *Social Development of Learning Disabled Persons* (San Francisco: Jossey-Bass, Inc., 1981); *New Approaches to Learning Disabilities: Cognitive, Metacognitive and Holistic* (Old Tappan, NJ: Allyn & Bacon/Simon & Shuster, 1988); *All Children are Exceptional* (Richmond Hill, Ont.: Scholastic-Tab Publications, 1993); "An Examination of the Psychosocial Aspects of the Learning Disabled Adolescent" (*LD Quarterly* 1(4) 1968); "The Importance of a Sociological Perspective Towards Learning Disabilities" (*Journal of Learning Disabilities* 9(2) 1976); "Divorce and Learning Disabilities" (*Academic Therapy* 20(3) 1985); "Relationships are Concepts" (*Review of Education* 1993); various other books; numerous other articles; various other publications. EDIT: Ed. Advisory Bd., *Journal of Learning Disabilities*, 1968 to date; Contributing Ed., *Academic Therapy*, 1966-88; Contributing Ed., *Perceptions*, 1978-83; Ed. Bd., *Techniques Journal*, 1985-89; Prof. Advisory Bd., *Australian Journal of Learning Disabilities*, 1996 to date. AFFIL: N.Y. Academy of Sciences; USA Council for Exceptional Children (Research Committee 1990-92); Learning Disability Association of

Ontario; Learning Disability Association of Canada (Professional Advisory Bd). IIONS: Outstanding Contribution Award, Learning Disabilities Association of Ontario, 1970, 1971, 1980; President's Award, International Learning Disabilities Association, 1973; Woman of the Year, Pioneer Women, Toronto, 1974; Founder's Award, Learning Disabilities Association of Canada, 1977; Loewen, Ondaatje, McCutcheon Award, 1980; Thérèse Casgrain Award, Health & Welfare Canada, 1983; Canada 125 Medal, 1994. INTERESTS: writing; music; art; travel; cooking. MISC: 1st recipient of Thérèse Casgrain Award for effecting social change; D. Kronick scholarship est. by Learning Disabilities Association of Canada, 1983; Ministers of Educ. in 9 provinces created D. Kronick scholarships to be awarded to recipients of LDAC Kronick scholarships, 1985; Co-founder of Learning Disability Association of Ontario (1963) & Learning Disability Association of Canada (1968); recipient, various grants; listed in numerous biographical sources, incl. *Who's Who of American Women, International Directory of Distinguished Leadership* (1994), & *International Who's Who of Business and Professional Women*. COMMENT: *"Started a university education when my oldest child was in university and became an associate professor. I am considered a theorist in learning-disability field, and have written extensively and toured internationally on psychosocial aspects of learning disabilities."*

Krowitz, Penny, CAE ⊛ O

Executive Director, JEWISH WOMEN INTERNATIONAL OF CANADA (formerly B'nai Brith Women of Canada), 638A Sheppard Ave. W., Ste. 210, Downsview, ON M3H 2S1 (416) 630-9313, FAX 630-9319. Born Toronto 1946. m. Barry. 3 ch. Charles, Marnie, David. EDUC: Toronto Teachers' Coll., Certificate (Elementary Teaching) 1965; York Univ., Certificate (Voluntary & Arts Sector Mgmt) 1988; Association Management Education (AME) Program, CAE Certificate. CAREER: Exec. Dir., Jewish Women International of Canada. AFFIL: Canadian Society of Association Executives; Beth Torah Congregation; Jewish Women International of Canada (Life Mbr.). COMMENT: *"My commitment to the profession of association management has led my organization into analytical and challenging directions. I am an excellent administrator and trainer, and use my well-developed skills in these areas to advance the cause of women."*

Krupa, Mary, B.Sc.,B.Ed. ■ ■ O ⫷ ⊛

Executive Director, CANADIAN FOUNDATION FOR THE LOVE OF CHILDREN (not-for-profit chil-

dren's charity), Midland Walwyn Tower, Ste. 1524, Edmonton, AB T5G 3G4 (403) 448-1752, FAX 441-9893. Born Vancouver 1958. m. Eugene Krupa. 4 ch. Joel, JoyAnne, Timothy, Jeffrey. EDUC: Univ. of Alberta, B.Sc. (Botany & Zoology) 1981, B.Ed.(Elementary) 1982. CAREER: Teacher, Njala Primary Sch., Sierra Leone, 1979; Lab. Instructor, Botany & Zoology, Univ. of Alberta, 1980; Camp Dir., Parks & Rec., City of Edmonton, 1980; Curriculum Developer & Naturalist, Devonian Botanic Garden, Univ. of Alberta, 1981-83; Teacher, Edmonton Public Sch. Bd., 1983-93; Exec. Dir., C.F.L.O.C., 1990 to date. SELECTED PUBLICATIONS: "Kids Kottage" corporate campaign package, 1995, 1996; co-author, *Science Directions 7* (text book used by most Grade 7 students in Alta., John Wiley & Sons, 1990); co-author with E. Krupa, *The Water We Use* (student text & teachers' guide for Grade 6, SEEDS/Alberta Environment Water Literacy Program, 1986); *Choices for Women and Their Children* (directory of svcs in Greater Edmonton area, Alberta Family & Social Services, 1993, 1994); "What a day we had!" (*Kinnikinnick*, Nov. 1982); "Did you ever see?" (*Kinnikinnick*, Aug. 1981). AFFIL: Alberta Association of Fundraising Executives; C.F.L.O.C. (Dir.); Alberta Human Services Association; Edmonton Public Sch. Bd. (Science Curriculum Advisory Committee); Alberta Teachers' Association (Environmental Educ. Council); Edmonton Child Poverty Action Group; Alpine Club of Canada; Women's Action Committee (Chairperson 1987-89). HONS: nominated by Premier Ralph Klein for Alberta Woman of Distinction for community svc., 1996; Edwin Parr Award, nominee for best 1st-yr. teacher in Alta., 1984; Louise McKinney Heritage Scholarship (highest standing in Fac. of Educ.), 1982; Queen Elizabeth Scholarship (outstanding academic performance), 1978, 1981, 1983. INTERESTS: mountains; many sports; birding; astronomy; botany. MISC: expertise in fundraising, public speaking, audio-visual production, mgmt; conference presentations re wildlife, science, environmental educ., volunteerism, sexuality & relationships, child abuse & neglect. COMMENT: *"I am an energetic, enthusiastic individual who sets her sights high and is not afraid to attempt seemingly impossible tasks. My achievements generally focus on envisioning and initiating projects and programs that benefit others."*

Kruse, Karen, B.Sc.,M.A., M.B.B.Chir. ⊕ $

Director, Corporate Health, BC TEL, 5 - 3777 Kingsway, Burnaby, BC V5H 3Z7 (604) 432-4013, FAX 432-9456. Born Vancouver 1942.

m. **EDUC:** Univ. of Alberta, B.Sc.(Biological Sci.) 1963; Duke Univ., M.A.(Biological Sci.) 1966; Univ. of Cambridge, B.Sc. 1974, M.B.B.Chir.(Medicine) 1979; Univ. of Southern California, M.A.(Sci.) 1980, M.A.(Human Factors) 1994. **CAREER:** Researcher in Microgenetics, Duke Univ., 1965-68; Clinical Counsellor, Adolescent Treatment Unit, Vancouver, 1968-70; Medical Advisor, Hoffmann La Roche, UK, 1970-74; Medical Officer, BC TEL, 1984-93; Dir., Corp. Health & Safety, 1993-97. **SELECTED PUBLICATIONS:** "Application of Karasek's Demand/Control Model in a Canadian Occupational Setting During a Period of Re-organization and Downsizing" (*Canadian Journal of Occupational Medicine* 1995). **AFFIL:** Amnesty International; B.C. Medical Association (Sec.-Treas., Occupational Medicine Section 1990-92). **INTERESTS:** opera; theatre; playing cello.

Kuhn, Lynda, B.A.,M.A. ■ $

Director of Corporate and Community Relations, PHILIP ENVIRONMENTAL INC., 100 King St. W., Hamilton, ON L8N 4J6 (905) 540-6658, FAX 521-9160. Born Trenton, Ont. 1955. d. 2 ch. **EDUC:** Dalhousie Univ., B.A. (Anthro.) 1978; McGill Univ., M.A.(Econ. Anthro.) 1982. **CAREER:** Dev. Consultant, Union of N.S., 1978-86; Band Dev. Coord., Chapel Island Band, 1978-86; Exec. Dir., Richmond County Industrial Commission, 1988-93; Adjunct Fac. Mbr., University Coll. of Cape Breton, 1992-93; Dir. of Corp. & Community Rel'ns, Philip Environmental Inc., 1993 to date. **SELECTED PUBLICATIONS:** *Chapel Island Community Profile/Community Plan*; *Philip Environmental Annual Report* (1993/94/95). **AFFIL:** Mohawk Coll. Foundation Bd.; Sherman Centre (Bd.); Industry Educ. Council (Bd., Hamilton); Hamilton & District Chamber of Commerce (Chair, Environmental Committee). **HONS:** Pinnacle Award, Canadian Public Relations Society, Hamilton Chapter. **INTERESTS:** writing; skiing; biking; cultural studies; first & foremost my children. **COMMENT:** *"Having been trained in community-based development strategies, I find my current position includes all aspects of communication, community and corporate relations for one of North America's leading environmental companies."*

Kukal, Olga, B.Sc.,M.Sc.,Ph.D. 🎓 ⚛

Assistant Professor of Biology, ACADIA UNIVERSITY, Wolfville, NS B0P 1X0 (902) 542-2201, FAX 542-3466. Born Prague 1956. m. Thomas Allen. **EDUC:** Carleton Univ., B.Sc. (Hons., Biol.) 1979; Univ. of Guelph, M.Sc. (Biol.) 1984; Univ. of Notre Dame, Ph.D.(Comparative Physiology) 1988. **CAREER:** Visiting Research Assoc., Dept. of Entomology, Michigan State Univ., 1988; Postdoctoral Fellow, Dept. of Entomology, Ohio State Univ., 1988-90; Postdoctoral Fellow, Dept. of Biol., Univ. of Victoria, 1990-91; Adjunct Asst. Prof., 1991-93; Asst. Prof., Dept. of Biol., Acadia Univ., 1993 to date; numerous contract positions as biologist & phys. scientist. **SELECTED PUBLICATIONS:** "Colonization of Snow Bunting nests by bumblebees in the High Arctic," with D.L. Pattie (*Canadian Field Naturalist* #10 1988); "Temperature and food quality influences feeding behaviour, assimilation efficiency, and growth rate of Arctic woolly-bear caterpillars," with T.E. Dawson (*Oecologia* 79 1989); "Role of chilling in the acquisition of cold tolerance and the capacitation of express stress proteins in diapausing eggs of the gypsy moth," with others (*Archives of Insect Biochemistry and Physiology* 27 1992); other refereed articles; "Behavioural and physiological adaptations to cold in a High Arctic insect," in *Insects at Low Temperature* ed. R.E. Lee, Jr., & D.L. Denlinger (New York: Chapman and Hall, 1991); "Caterpillars on ice" (*Natural History* 97 1988); "Jamaican caves and caving," with S.B. Peck (*Canadian Caver* 7 1975). **AFFIL:** Entomological Society of America; American Society of Zoologists; Arctic Institute of North America; American Association for the Advancement of Science; Northern Heritage Society; Society for Cryobiology; Sigma Xi; Entomological Society of Canada. **MISC:** recipient, numerous grants; numerous presentations at scientific meetings & invited lectures; subject of various newspaper in magazine articles & broadcast interviews; in *Canadian Who's Who in Science*, 1994; participant in exchange program between Carleton Univ. & Biological Research Institute, Leningrad State Univ., USSR, 1979-80.

Kulesza, Kasia ■■ 🎾

Olympic Athlete. c/o Canadian Olympic Association. Born Warsaw, Poland 1976. **EDUC:** currently studying Sociology. **SPORTS CAREER:** started synchro at age 10; mbr., Cdn Nat'l Synchronized Swimming Team, 1992 to date. Olympic Games: mbr. of team, 1996. World championships: 2nd, team, 1994. World jr. championships: 1st, team, 2nd, solo, & 2nd, duet, 1993; 10th, solo (Polish team), 1991. Canadian championships: 2nd, team, 2nd, duet, & 7th, solo, 1995; 4th, team, 4th, duet, & 6th, solo, 1994. Canadian jr. championships: 1st, solo, & 1st, duet, 1993. **HONS:** Helen Vanderburg Award for best overall 15-17-yr.-old synchro swimmer, 1993. **INTERESTS:** cycling; music; reading. **MISC:** moved to Canada at age 7; speaks English, French & Polish.

Kulesza, Kristine M., B.Comm.,C.A. ■ $
Vice-President, Merchandising, PEOPLES JEWELLERS CORPORATION, 1440 Don Mills Rd., Toronto, ON M3B 3M1 (416) 391-7765, FAX 441-1360. Born Toronto 1953. m. John. 2 ch. Adam, Jordan. **EDUC:** Univ. of Toronto, B.Comm.(Commerce/Fin.) 1976. **CAREER:** Public Acctnt, Deloitte Haskins and Sells, 1976-85; Pres., Liptons International Limited, 1985-93; VP, Merchandising, Peoples Jewellers Corporation, 1993 to date. **AFFIL:** Canadian Jewellers' Association (1995); Ontario Institute of Chartered Accountants (C.A.). **INTERESTS:** reading; physical fitness; camping; travelling. **COMMENT:** *"Senior executive with more than 20 years of business experience including strategic operational and financial experience, primarily in the retail industry."*

Kulhay, Katrina M., B.Sc.,B.Ed.,D.C. ■■ ⊕
Founder and Director, THE KULHAY WELLNESS CENTRE, 2 St. Clair Ave. W., Ste. 607, Toronto, ON M4V 1L5 (416) 961-1900, FAX 961-9578, INTERNET www.thewebpages.ca/kulhaywellness. Born Brampton, Ont. 1955. **EDUC:** Univ. of Toronto, B.Sc.(Hons., Biol./Nutrition) 1978, B.Ed. 1979; Canadian Memorial Chiropractic Coll., D.C.(Chiropractic) 1983. **CAREER:** Chiropractor, Nutritional Consultant; founder, The Kulhay Wellness Centre (with 38 health professionals), 1983; teacher & TV personality, 1983 to date. **SELECTED CREDITS:** "The Alternative Doctor" on *City-Line*, hosted by Marilyn Denis; regular expert on wellness & health care, CBC, CFTO, CTV, CFRB, CHFI, *City-Line*, *Pamela Wallin Live*. **SELECTED PUBLICATIONS:** "The Effect of Intravenous Sodium Clofibrate and Heparin on the Plasma Disappearance of Infused Intralipid in Rats" (*Journal of Clinical Investigation*, 1978). **AFFIL:** Ontario Chiropractic Association; Metro Toronto Police Force (Chiropractic Consultant 1989). **HONS:** Community Svc. Award, Ontario Chiropractic Association, 1985; known as "Canada's Pregnancy/Kid's Chiropractor." **INTERESTS:** sports; cooking; sewing. **MISC:** brings together eastern & western medicine to work harmoniously & in the best interests of patients. **COMMENT:** *"Dr. Kulhay is the "Doctor of the Future," advocating a total wellness approach combining traditional and complementary health care services for patient health. She is in private practice in Toronto with 38 health professionals and established Canada's first total health care facility."*

Kulyk Keefer, Janice, B.A.,M.A., D.Phil. 📜 🎓
Professor, Department of English, UNIVERSITY OF GUELPH, Guelph, ON N1G 2W1 (519) 824-4120, ext. 3825, FAX 766-0844. Born Toronto 1952. m. Michael Holland Keefer. 2 ch. **EDUC:** Univ. of Toronto, B.A.(English Lit.) 1974; Univ. of Sussex, UK, M.A.(Modern Lit.) 1976, D.Phil.(English Lit.) 1983. **CAREER:** Tutor & Seminar Leader, Univ. of Sussex, 1977-78; Teacher of Advanced Courses in English as a Second Language, Univ. de Dijon, 1979-80; Lecturer, Univ. Sainte Anne, 1981-82; Teacher of Extension Courses, 1982-83; Asst. Prof., English, 1983-84; Post-Doctoral Fellow, 1984-86; Writer-in-Residence, Douglas Coll., Vancouver, 1987; Visiting Fellow, Univ. of Sussex, 1988-89; Writer-in-Residence, Univ. of Prince Edward Island, 1989; Assoc. Prof., Univ. of Guelph, 1990-92; Prof., 1992 to date. **SELECTED PUBLICATIONS:** *The Paris-Napoli Express* (Ottawa: Oberon, 1986); *White of the Lesser Angels* (Charlottetown: Ragweed Press, 1986); *Under Eastern Eyes: A Critical Reading of Canadian Maritime Fiction* (Toronto: Univ. of Toronto Press, 1987); *Travelling Ladies* (Toronto: Random House, 1990); *Rest Harrow* (HarperCollins, 1992); *The Green Library*, novel (HarperCollins Canada, 1996); various other books; poetry, fiction & essays appear in numerous anthologies, incl. *More Stories by Canadian Women*, Rosemary Sullivan, ed. (Toronto: Oxford Univ. Press, 1987), *The Macmillan Anthology*, John Metcalf & Leon Rooke, eds. (Toronto: Macmillan, 1988), *Poetry by Canadian Women* (Toronto: Oxford Univ. Press, 1989), *Pens of Many Colours: A Canadian Reader*, Eva Karpinski & Ian Lea, eds. (Toronto: Harcourt Brace Jovanovich, 1993); "Fortunate Falls and Propitious Expulsions: Anglophone Fictions and the Acadian Question" (*International Journal of Canadian Studies Revue Internationale d'études canadiennes* 10, Fall/Automne 1994); "Mavis Gallant's World of Women: A Feminist Perspective" (*Atlantis* Spring 1985); "Another Country" (*Canadian Literature* Spring 1989); various other scholarly articles, fiction & poetry. **EDIT:** Advisory Bd., House of Anansi Press. **AFFIL:** Eden Mills Writers' Festival Committee. **HONS:** James Harris Entrance Scholarship, 1970-74; Woodhouse Scholarship, 1972, 1973, 1974; John King Scholarship, 1973; Gov. General's Gold Medal in English, 1974; Norma Epstein Award for Creative Writing, Univ. of Toronto, 1974; First Prize, Adult Poetry Collection, Second Prize, Adult Short Fiction, & Honourable Mention, Long Poem, N.S. Writers' Federation, 1984; First Prize, *PRISM* International Fiction Competition, 1984; First Prize, Adult Poetry & Top Prize, Novel, N.S. Writers' Federation, 1985; Honourable Mention, *PRISM* International Poetry Competition,

1985; First Prize, Fiction, CBC Radio Literary Competition, 1985, 1986; Honourable Mention, Magazine Fiction, Foundation for the Advancement of Canadian Letters Author's Award, 1986; Reg'l Winner, Canada & the Caribbean, British Airways Commonwealth Poetry Prize, 1987; Third Prize, Poetry, CBC Radio Literary Competition, 1988; Joseph B. Stauffer Prize, 1988-89; First Prize, Poetry, National Magazine Award Foundation, 1990, 1994; Winning Entry, *Malahat* Long Poem Competition, 1991. INTERESTS: multiculturalism, ethnicity & the formation of subjectivity; transcultural aesthetics; travelling; wildflower identification; looking at paintings. MISC: recipient, various grants, fellowships & scholarships. COMMENT: *"I have attempted, over the past 20 years, to lead a writer's life, incorporating into, rather than eradicating from my work those factors of ethnicity and gender that make me who I am."*

Kumi, Janna W., B.A.,M.Sc., R.P.F. ♣
Assistant Deputy Minister, Operations Division, Ministry of Forests, GOVERNMENT OF BRITISH COLUMBIA, 5 Pandora Ave., 4th Fr., Victoria, BC V8W 3E7 (604) 387-1236, FAX 953-3687. Born 1949. m. C.O. Kumi. 1 ch. Rebecca Kumi. EDUC: Concordia Univ., B.A.(Geography) 1972; Univ. of Munich, Germany, *Diplom Forstwirt* (Masters, Forestry) 1978; Univ. of British Columbia, M.Sc. (Forestry-Silviculture) 1984. CAREER: Research Asst., Fac. of Forestry, Univ. of Munich, 1974-78; Research & Teaching Asst., Fac. of Forestry, Univ. of British Columbia, 1979-81; Forest Biologist, 1981-82; Reg. Forest Pathologist, B.C. Forest Svc., Kamloops, 1982-83; Lecturer, Dept. of Biol., Univ. of Victoria, 1983-94; various positions, MacMillan Bloedel Limited, Nanaimo, B.C., 1984-94; Asst. Deputy Min., Oper. Div., Ministry of Forests, Prov. of B.C., 1994 to date. SELECTED PUBLICATIONS: articles in learned journals. AFFIL: Association of B.C. Professional Foresters (VP 1992; Pres. 1993). HONS: several scholarships & bursaries. MISC: Registered Professional Forester. COMMENT: *"Janna Kumi has been intensively involved in land-use planning issues, particularly nontimber resource inventories, environmental issues affecting forest land management, integrated research in silviculture and nontimber resources, research into alternatives to clear-cutting and developing and communicating forest land management and land-use policies. In her present position, Janna is responsible for 6 regional and 43 district offices, as well as the following branches: Protection, Resource Tenures and Engineering,* *Nursery and Seed Operations, Business Design and Compliance and Enforcement."*

Kuntz, Sister Dolores, B.A.,M.A., Ph.D. ■ ⌘
Principal, Brescia College, THE UNIVERSITY OF WESTERN ONTARIO, 1285 Western Rd., London, ON N6G 1H2 (519) 432-8583, FAX 679-6489. Born London, Ont. 1926. Mbr., Ursuline Community of Chatham Union. EDUC: The Univ. of Western Ontario, B.A. 1946; Univ. of Detroit, M.A. 1962; Queen's Univ., Diploma (Psych.) 1967, Ph.D. 1968. AFFIL: Ontario Psychological Association. HONS: Canada 125 Medal; Ont. Grad. Fellowship.

Kurbis Sereda, Rhonda, B.P.A.S. ■■ ⟐ ⊛
Executive Director, BOWLING FEDERATION OF SASKATCHEWAN INC. (non-profit sport organization), 438 Victoria Ave. E., Ste. 210, Regina, SK S4N 0N7 (306) 780-9412, FAX 780-9455, EMAIL bowling@sasknet.sk.ca. Born Regina 1962. m. Terry Sereda. 1 ch. Michelle Sereda. EDUC: Univ. of Regina, B.P.A.S.(Sport Admin.) 1987. CAREER: Admin. Asst., Regina Pats Hockey Club, 1986-87; Mktg/Public Rel'ns Dir., Weyburn Red Wings Hockey Club, 1987; Supervisor, Visitor Svcs, Saskatchewan Science Centre, 1988-90; Exec. Dir., Judo Saskatchewan, 1990-93; Exec. Dir., Bowling Federation of Saskatchewan, 1993 to date. VOLUNTEER CAREER: Mktg Committee, World Jr. Hockey Championships, 1990-91; Admin. Asst./Media Liaison, Labatt's Coupe de/Canada Cup, 1987. AFFIL: Wildlife Rehabilitation Society of Saskatchewan (Treas.); Canadian Nature Federation; Canadian Wildlife Federation; People for Animals Saskatchewan; Saskatchewan Sport Administrators Association. INTERESTS: family; sports; wildlife protection; animals; travel; fashion. COMMENT: *"Enthusiastic, people-oriented, compassionate, organized, self-motivated. The friendships I have made during my professional and volunteer endeavours have empowered me to achieve my professional and personal goals."*

Kussner, Sheila, B.A.,LL.D.,O.C. ♥ ⊕ ⊛
Founding Chairman, HOPE AND COPE, 2797 Graham Blvd., Montreal, QC H3R 1J5 (514) 340-8255, FAX 342-2482. Born Montreal. m. Marvyn. 2 ch. EDUC: McGill Univ., B.A.(Arts) 1953. VOLUNTEER CAREER: active as a volunteer in the service of many organizations & community institutions incl.: Quebec Heart Foundation, Youth Horizons, Canadian ORT, Alliance Quebec; Founding Chair, Hope & Cope, 1981 to date; Chair, Admin. Committee for the creation of a Dept. of Oncology, Fac. of Medicine, McGill Univ., 1988. AFFIL: McGill

Univ. (Bd. of Gov.); Jewish Community Foundation of Montreal (Exec. Committee); Montreal Symphony (Bd.). HONS: Eleanor Roosevelt Humanitarian Award, Gov't of Israel; President's Medal, Gov't of Israel; Certificate of Merit, Dept. of Health & Welfare; Member of the Order of Canada, 1983; Officer of the Order of Canada, 1995; Robert Fisher Fellowship Award, Memorial Sloan-Kettering Cancer Center, NY; mbr., Beaver Club, 1992; Canada 125 Medal; Medal of Courage, Canadian Cancer Society, 1995; Distinguished Service Award, Jewish General Hospital, 1995; LL.D.(Hon.), McGill Univ., 1990. INTERESTS: music; fundraising; volunteering in the health field. COMMENT: *"Mrs. Kussner is the founding Chair of Hope and Cope, a pioneering support system now comprising some 125 volunteers who provide a wide range of services to patients undergoing treatment for cancer at the Sir Mortimer Davis-Jewish General Hospital. Her concern with cancer medicine brought her to a position of leadership in the creation of a Department of Oncology in McGill's Faculty of Medicine. As Chair of the Administrative Council formed for the purpose, she played a key role and single-handedly raised $25 million for the development of the comprehensive Cancer Centre, which has combined research, physician training and patient treatment into a unified program within the hospitals of the McGill network."*

Kutrowski, Linda ■■ *Ⓤ*
Paralympic Athlete. Ottawa, ON. CAREER: fin. system mgr. SPORTS CAREER: mbr., Nat'l Wheelchair Basketball Team. Paralympic Games: Gold, 1996; Gold, 1992. Canadian Wheelchair Basketball League (CWBL): 1st, Women's Finals, 1995. World Championships: 1st, 1994. Stoke Mandeville Games, 1st, 1991. MISC: patient & methodical player.

Kuzyk, Mimi ⬥
Actor. c/o ACI Talent, 205 Ontario St., Toronto, ON M5A 2V6. Born Winnipeg 1 ch. SELECTED CREDITS: features/Movies of the Week incl. *Family of Cops II*, dir. David Greene, CBS; *A Maiden's Grave*, dir. Daniel Petrie Jr., HBO; *Men With Guns*, dir. Kari Skogland, Norstar; *Little Criminals*, dir. Steven Surjick; *Derby*, dir. Bob Clarke, Atlantis/ABC; *Malicious*, dir. Ian Corson, Ent. Secur./Keystone; *I Know My Son is Alive*, Dir. Bill Corcoran, NBC; *The Break Through*, dir. Piers Haggard, Filmline/USA; *Stormy Weathers*, dir. Ewil McKenzie, ABC; *False Arrest*, dir. Bill Norton, ABC; *Speed Zone*, dir. Jim Drake, Orion; *The Kiss*, dir. Pen Densham, Tri-Star; *Family Sins*, dir. Jerrold Freedman, NBC; *Miles to Go*, dir.

David Greene, CBS; *Blind Justice*, dir. Rod Holcolm, CBS; *Striker's Mountain*, dir. Allan Simmonds, NBC; TV series incl.: series regular, *The Hidden Room*, Lifetime; series regular, *Wolf*, CBS; series regular, *Hill Street Blues*, NBC; has appeared in hundreds of guest starring roles in US & Cdn series over the years; theatre work incl.: Mrs. Manningham, *Gaslight*, Room for Theatre, L.A.; various leads, *Just a Kommedia*, Cdn Tour; Panacea, *A Funny Thing Happened on the Way to the Forum*, St. Lawrence Centre; Laura, *I'll Be Back Before Midnight*, Solar Stage; Carlotta, *Love Rides the Rails*, Sudbury Theatre Co.; various roles, *Musical Story Children's Theatre*, Inner Stage, Canada. AFFIL: ACTRA; SAG. COMMENT: *"I moved back to Toronto in 1994. Since then, I've enjoyed a quality of life with family that I never experienced in LA, PLUS success as an actress."*

Kwok, Eva Lee, M.Sc. ■ Ⓢ
President and Chief Executive Officer, AMARA INTERNATIONAL INVESTMENT CORPORATION (real estate dev., investment, cross-cultural mgmt), 355 Burrard St., Ste. 408, Vancouver, BC V6C 2G8 (604) 681-8066, FAX 681-8012. President and Managing Director, MELCORP MERCANTILE INC. Born Penang, Malaysia 1942. m. Stanley Kwok. EDUC: Emily McPherson Coll., Australia, D.I.M.(Dietetics/Nutrition) 1964; Univ. of London, M.Sc.(Nutrition) 1967; Univ. of Western Ontario, Certificate in Sr. Admin. 1986. CAREER: Asst. Prof., then Assoc. Prof., Coll. of Home Econ., Univ. of Saskatchewan, 1968-80; Prof., 1980-88; Dean, 1986-88; Dir. & Ptnr, Sinfonia Travel Agency, Saskatoon, 1986 to date; Pres. & CEO, Saskatchewan Institute of Applied Science & Technology (SIAST), 1989-90; VP, Asia Pacific Foundation of Canada, 1990-91; Pres. & CEO, Amara International Investment Corp., 1992 to date. SELECTED PUBLICATIONS: more than 25 published works appearing in Cdn & int'l journals. DIRECTOR: Coca-Cola Beverages; Fletcher Challenge Canada Ltd.; Husky Oil (Chair, Employment Practices Steering Committee); The Mutual Life Assurance Company of Canada; Vancouver Board of Trade; Vancouver Arts Stabilization Team. AFFIL: Simon Fraser Univ. (Gov. 1994-96); Simon Fraser Univ. Foundation (Dir. 1992-94); Open Learning Agency Foundation (Dir. 1992-96); Vancouver General Hospital Foundation (Dir. 1992-94); Vancouver General Hospital (Dir., Vision 20/21 Eye Care 1992-93); B.C. Trade Development Corporation (Dir. 1992-93); Institute of Saskatchewan Enterprise (Dir. 1987-89); Canadian International Development Agency (Consultant, Int'l Dev. Research Centre

1972-76). **INTERESTS:** promotion of opportunities, strategic alliances & joint ventures for investors in Canada & the Asia Pacific region. **MISC:** numerous radio & TV interviews & guest appearances on CBC Radio & TV, CJWW Radio, & CFQC Radio & TV; nat'l & int'l lecturing & presentations focusing on investment, trade & Canada/Asia Pacific relations.

Kyrwa, Kelly ■■ ⍟

Paralympic Athlete. Revelstoke, BC. **CAREER:** owner, accessibility consultant bus. **SPORTS CAREER:** mbr., Nat'l Wheelchair Basketball Team, 2 yrs. Paralympic Games: Gold, 1996. Canadian Wheelchair Basketball League (CWBL): 3rd, Women's Finals, 1996; 3rd, Women's Finals, 1995. World Championships, 1st, 1994. **AFFIL:** Kamloops Wheelchair Sports Association (VP). **HONS:** All-Star, Aurora Light Tournament; All-Star at nat'l championships.

Labarge, Margaret Wade, B.A.,B.Litt., C.M.,F.R.C.S. ■■

Adjunct Research Professor, CARLETON UNIVERSITY. Born New York City 1916. w. Raymond C. Labarge. 4 ch. Claire Morris, Suzanne, Charles, Paul. **EDUC:** Harvard Univ., Radcliffe Coll., B.A.(Medieval Hist. & Lit.) 1937; Oxford Univ., St. Anne's Coll., B.Litt.(Medieval Hist.) 1939. **CAREER:** independent scholar, writer, historian & community volunteer. **SELECTED PUBLICATIONS:** *Simon de Montfort* (London, N.Y., Toronto: 1962; reprinted 1972, 1975); *A Baronial Household of the Thirteenth Century* (London, N.Y., Toronto, 1965; reprinted 1980); *Saint Louis* (London, Toronto, 1968; US title *Saint Louis: Louis IX, Most Christian King*, Boston, 1968); *Henry V, The Cautious Conqueror* (London, N.Y.: 1975); *Medieval Travellers: The Rich and the Restless* (London, N.Y.: 1982); *Women in Medievel Life* (London, Toronto, 1986; US title *A Small Sound of the Trumpet*, Boston, 1986; paperback 1988; Spanish translation, *Viajeros medievales*, 1992); *A Medievel Miscellany* (Carlton Univ., 1996); 5 shorter works incl.: *Court, Church and Castle/Cour, Eglise et Chateau* (Ottawa: National Gallery of Canada, 1972). **AFFIL:** St. Vincent Hospital (Bd. mbr. 1969-81; Chair 1977-79); Canadian Nurses' Association (Public Rep., Bd. of Dir. 1980-83); Carleton Univ. (Bd. of Gov. 1984-93); Council on Aging Ottawa-Carleton (mbr. 1986-93; Chair, Committee on Elder Abuse 1986-88; Pres. 1989-91); Canadian Society of Medievalists (Pres. 1993-94). **HONS:** Member, Order of Canada, 1982; Fellow, Royal Society of Canada, 1988; hon. D.Litt., Carleton Univ., 1976; hon. LL.D., Univ. of Waterloo, 1993. **INTERESTS:** travel; reading.

Labarge, Suzanne, B.A.,M.B.A. $

Executive Vice-President, Corporate Treasury, ROYAL BANK OF CANADA, Royal Bank Plaza, 200 Bay St., 15th Fl., S. Tower, Toronto, ON M5J 2J5 (416) 974-6849, FAX 974-8959. Born Ottawa 1946. s. EDUC: McMaster Univ., B.A.(Econ.) 1967; Univ. of British Columbia, Postgrad. (Econ.) 1968; Harvard Univ., M.B.A.(Bus. Admin.) 1971. CAREER: various positions, Royal Bank of Canada, 1971-84; VP, World Corp. Bnkg, Que. & Atlantic, 1984-85; Asst. Auditor Gen., Office of the Auditor Gen. of Canada, 1985-87; Deputy Superintendent, Regulatory Policy Sector, Office of the Superintendent of Fin. Institutions, 1987-92; Deputy Superintendent, Deposit-Taking Institutions Sector, 1992-95; Exec. VP, Corp. Treasury, Royal Bank of Canada, 1995 to date. AFFIL: Harvard Bus. Sch. Club of Toronto (Bd. Mbr. 1995); Univ. of British Columbia (Advisory Council. 1995); Carleton Univ. Foundation (Bd. Mbr.).

Labelle, Huguette, B.Sc.,B.Ed.,M.Ed., Ph.D.,LL.D. 🌼

President, CANADIAN INTERNATIONAL DEVELOPMENT AGENCY, 200 prom. du Portage, 12th Fl., Hull, QC K1A 0G4 (819) 997-7951, FAX 953-3352. Chancellor, UNIVERSITY OF OTTAWA. Born Rockland, Ont. EDUC: Univ. of Ottawa, B.Sc.(Nursing Educ.), B.Ed., M.Ed., Ph.D. (Educ. Admin.). CAREER: Dir., Vanier Sch. of Nursing, 1967-73; Lecturer, Sch. of Health Science Admin., Univ. of Ottawa, 1967-73; Principal Nursing Officer, Dept. of Nat'l Health & Welfare, 1973-76; Dir. Gen., Policy, Research & Evaluation, Indian & Inuit Affair Program, Health & Welfare Canada, 1976-78; Asst. Deputy Min., Corp. Policy, Dept. of Indian & Northern Affairs, 1979-80; Under Sec. of State, Dept. of the Sec. of State, 1980-85; Assoc. Sec. to the Cabinet & Deputy Clerk of the Privy Council, 1985; Chair, Public Service Commission of Canada, 1985-90; Deputy Min., Transport Canada, 1990-93; Pres., Canadian International Development Agency, 1993 to date. DIRECTOR: Export Development Corporation. AFFIL: Public Policy Forum (Dir.); International Development Research Centre (Dir.); International Centre for Human Rights & Democratic Development (Dir.); International Institute for Sustainable Development (Dir.); World Health Organization Working Group on Health & Development Policies (Dir.); numerous past affiliations. HONS: Officer of the Order of Canada, 1990; Vanier Medal, Institute of Public Administration of Canada, 1993; LL.D. (Hon.), Brock Univ., 1982; LL.D.(Hon.), Univ. of Saskatchewan, 1984; LL.D.(Hon.), Carleton Univ., 1986; LL.D.(Hon.), Univ. of Ottawa,

1986; LL.D.(Hon.), Univ. of Windsor; LL.D.(Hon.), Univ. of Manitoba; LL.D.(Hon.), Mount Saint Vincent Univ. MISC: Consultant to gov'ts of Haiti & Cuba on healthcare planning & health sci. educ., 1974-76; Co-Chair, World Health Organization's Expert Committee on Health Manpower Mgmt Systems, 1987.

Labelle, Micheline, Ph.D. 🍁 🏵

Professeure, Département de Sociologie, UNIVERSITÉ DU QUÉBEC À MONTRÉAL, CP 8888, Succ. A, Montréal, QC H3C 3P8, EMAIL labelle.m@uqam.ca. Born Montréal 1940. EDUC: Univ. de Montréal, Ph.D.(anthro.) 1975. CAREER: professeure titulaire, dépt. de sociologie, Univ. du Québec à Montréal; Dir. de recherche, Centre de recherche sur les relations ethniques et le racisme de l'UQAM; Titulaire, Chaire Concordia-UQAM en relations interculturelles, ethniques, et sur le racisme, 1993-96. SELECTED PUBLICATIONS: *Idéologie de couleur et classes sociales en Haïti*, 2e édition (Les Éditions du CIDIHCA et les Presses de l'Univ. de Montréal, 1987); *Histoires d'immigrées. Itinérairess d'ouvrières Colombiennes, Haïtiennes, Grecques, Portugaises de Montréal*, avec D. Meintel, G. Turcotte et M. Kempeneers (Montréal: Boréal, 1987); *Ethnicité et enjeux sociaux. Le Québec vu par les leaders de groupes ethnoculturels*, avec J.J. Lévy (Montréal: Liber, 1995); "La question nationale dans le discours des leaders d'associations ethniques de la région Montréal," avec B. Beaudet, F. Tardif et J. Lévy (*Cahiers de recherche sociologique* 20 1993); "Le discours des leaders d'associations ethniques de la région Montréal," avec M. Therrien et J. Lévy (*Revue européene des migrations internationales* 10(2) 1994); "Pluriethnicité, citoyenneté et intégration: de la souveraineté pour lever les obstacles et les ambiguïtés," avec F. Rocher et G. Rocher (*Cahiers de recherche sociologique* 25 1995); autre publications divers. EDIT: comité de rédaction, *Cahiers de recherche sociologique*. AFFIL: Association internationale de sociologie; Association canadienne des sociologues et anthropologues de langue française. HONS: Prix Thérèse-Casgrain, CRSH, 1990. INTERESTS: immigration; relations ethniques. MISC: boursière.

Labow, Rosalind S., B.Sc.,M.S., Ph.D. 🍁 ⊕ 🏵

Director, Taichman Laboratory, UNIVERSITY OF OTTAWA HEART INSTITUTE, 1053 Carling Ave., Ottawa, ON K1Y 4E9 (613) 761-4010, FAX 724-7921. Born Montreal 1942. m. Stanley. 2 ch. Dr. Brian Labow, Dr. Daniel Labow. EDUC: McGill Univ., B.Sc. 1962; Univ. of Michigan, M.S. 1964, Ph.D. 1966. CAREER:

Professional Research Asst., N.Y. State Dept. of Health, 1969-81; Research Assoc., Univ. of Ottawa, 1981-84; Mbr., Research Scientist, Ottawa Centre, Canadian Red Cross, Blood Transfusion Svc, 1984-88; Asst. Prof. of Surgery, Fac. of Medicine, Univ. of Ottawa, 1988-95; Assoc. Prof., 1995 to date; Asst. Prof. of Biochem., 1989-94; Assoc. Prof., 1995 to date; Scientific Research Active Staff, 1990 to date; freelance medical science writer, *Canadian Medical Association Journal*. **SELECTED PUBLICATIONS:** "Crystalline D-serine dehydrase," with W.G. Robinson (*Journal of Biological Chemistry* 1966); "The Transfer of Glucose to Steroids by Sheep Liver Microsomes," with D.G. Williamson & D.S. Layne (*Canadian Journal of Biochemistry* 1974); "Contamination of platelet storage bags by phthalate esters," with M. Tocchi & G. Rock (*Biomedical Polymers* 1987); "Neutrophil-mediated Degradation of Segmented Polyurethanes," with J.P. Santerre & D. Erfle (*Biomaterials*, 1995); "DEHP: Helpful and Harmful," with G. Rock (*New Biotech* Apr. 1987); "Mood Disorder Research" (*Canadian Medical Association Journal*, 1983); more than 75 other publications. **AFFIL:** Medical & Scientific Staff Association, Univ. of Ottawa Heart Institute (Sec. 1992 to date); American Association for the Advancement of Science; Sigma Xi; Canadian Biochemical Society. **MISC:** external reviewer for Medical Research Council, Heart & Stroke Foundation; grant reviewer for Miles/Canadian Red Cross.

Labrecque, Hélène ✏ 📖 ⚛

Editing Manager, ECODECISION MAGAZINE, Environment and Policy Society, 276 St.-Jacques St., Ste. 924, Montreal, QC H2Y 1N3 (514) 284-3043, FAX 284-3045. Born Montreal 1948. s. 1 ch. **EDUC:** Lycée Molière, Paris, Baccalauréat Lehres 1967. **COMMENT:** *"Since 1991 (first year of publication), I have developed and coordinated an international network of world-renowned authors, contributors, partners, freelancers and regular correspondents. I write regular columns, such as book reviews, calendars of events, international environmental awards, technological innovations in the field of the environment, ecological voyages. I represent* ECODECISION *at conferences, seminars and workshops specializing in the environment."*

Lacava, Lucie, B.F.A. ✇ ✏

Design Consultant, LUCIE LACAVA PUBLICATION DESIGN INC., 137 Mozart, Dollard-des-Ormeaux, QC H9G 3A2 (514) 626-0809, FAX 626-0809. Born Borgia, Italy 1958. m. Nicola Vannelli. 1 ch. **EDUC:** Concordia Univ., B.F.A.(Graphic Design) 1982. **CAREER:** Artist, *The Gazette*, 1982-84; Ed. Artist, *The Gazette*, 1984-86; Art Ed., *The Gazette*, 1987-92; Deputy Ed./Design Dir., *Le Devoir*, 1993-94; Design Consultant, 1992 to date. **AFFIL:** Society of Newspaper Design; La Société des designers graphique du Québec. **HONS:** Judges' Special Recognition, Société des designers graphique du Québec, 1989; Southam Inc. President's Award, 1990; Silver Award, Advertising & Design Club of Canada, 1994; Canadian National Newspaper Award, 1993, 1994; Best of Show Award, Judge's Special Recognition Award, 5 Gold Medals, 5 Silver Medals & 1 Bronze Medal, the Society of Newspaper Design, 1993-94; Applied Arts Magazine Award, 1993, 1994, 1995. **MISC:** mbr. of jury, various competitions; various engagements as guest speaker at workshops. **COMMENT:** *"Lucie Lacava is a newspaper architect. Held various positions for ten years at* The Gazette. *Launched her own business in 1992. Redesigned* Le Devoir, *later held the position of Deputy Editor/Design Director.* Le Devoir *has since earned her over thirty prestigious awards. Recent redesigns include* Le Soleil, The Gazette, *and* L'actualité. *Presently consulting for Southam Inc."*

Lacey, Roberta, B.F.A. [$]

Director, Communications, AVON CANADA INC., 5500 Trans-Canada Highway, Pointe-Claire, QC H9R 1B6 (514) 630-8328, FAX 630-5439. Born Toronto 1954. **EDUC:** Concordia Univ., B.F.A. 1976. **CAREER:** various positions, comm. field, 15 yrs.; Dir. of Comm., Avon Canada Inc. **AFFIL:** Breast Cancer International Centre, Toronto (Dir.). **HONS:** Pathfinder Award for Community Service, Avon Canada, 1994. **INTERESTS:** art; crafts; designing & marketing jewellery & accessories. **COMMENT:** *"Lectured globally on communications and catalogue design. In 1993, started Avon Canada's Flame Crusade against breast cancer, which has to date raised more than $2 million for research."*

Lacey, Veronica S., B.A.,M.A.,M.Ed. 🎓 🍁

Director of Education and Secretary-Treasurer, THE BOARD OF EDUCATION FOR THE CITY OF NORTH YORK, 5050 Yonge St., North York, ON M2N 5N8. **EDUC:** Univ. of Toronto, B.A. (Modern Languages & Lit.), M.A.(Comparative Lit.), M.Ed.(Admin.). **CAREER:** Dir. of Educ., Bd. of Educ. for the City of North York, 1989 to date. **AFFIL:** Advisory Council to the Information Highway; National Quality Institute (Dir.); Univ. of Toronto (Gov.); CANARIE (Dir.); National Council on Education (Conference Bd.); National Network for Learning;

Metro Action Committee on Public Violence Against Women & Children; United Way of Greater Toronto (Cabinet); United Nations' 50th Year Anniversary (Chair, Educ. Committee); National Total Quality Management; Canadian Council for Aboriginal Business; Commemmorative Services Board of Canada (Bd. of Dir.). **HONS:** Woman of the Year, Ontario Secondary Sch. Teachers' Federation, 1988, 1989; Women of Distinction Award, YWCA, 1991; Educator of the Year, Phi Delta Kappa, 1991; Distinguished Educator Award, Ontario Institute for Studies in Education, 1993; Gov. General's Award, 1993; IWAY AWARD, Canadian National (for leadership in information technology). **MISC:** invited as special guest of Mitsui Canada Foundation on 2-week study tour of Japan, 1993; organizer, forum on educ. reform, 1993; speaker at numerous conferences; co-founder, National Network for Learning, 1993. **COMMENT:** *"Veronica Lacey is a doer. She motivates people to action and takes action to benefit people. As Director of Education for the public school board in Canada's sixth largest city, Ms. Lacey has established a reputation for focusing on desired results in student achievement, measuring and accounting for outcomes, and taking bold, daring steps to elevate the standards and improve learning for all."*

Lachance, Gabrielle, M.A.,Ph.D. ■ ♡ ☼

Consultant (International Development). 6893 av. Guy, Anjou, QC H1K 2T8 (514) 352-0979, FAX 352-6773. Born Alma, Que. 1931. **EDUC:** Univ. Laval, M.A.(Soc.) 1978, Ph.D.(Soc.) 1984. **CAREER:** CEO, Institute O.M.M.I., 1968-74; Sr. Researcher, Confédération des Caisses populaires Desjardins, 1978-80; Sr. Researcher, Institut québécois de recherche sur la culture, 1980-88; Exec. Dir., Canadian Catholic Organization for Development & Peace, 1988-96. **SELECTED PUBLICATIONS:** *De l'aide au développement* (1979); *Le rapport industrie-culture* (1987); numerous articles. **AFFIL:** North-South Institute (Chair, Bd. of Dir.); Coady International Institute (Advisory Committee); Centre Justice et Foi (Bd of Dir.); Association canadienne d'études du développement international; Institut canadien des affaires internationales; Institut québécois des Hautes études internationales. **HONS:** Prize for Excellence, Gov't of Qué. **INTERESTS:** piano; reading; walking. **MISC:** numerous conferences. **COMMENT:** *"My life has been oriented toward promotion of justice and alleviation of poverty, which has brought me to working mainly in three fields: (1) international cooperation (2) women's issues and (3) peace issues."*

Lachapelle, Lise, B.A.A. ☺ $

President and Chief Executive Officer, CANADIAN PULP AND PAPER ASSOCIATION, 1155 Metcalfe St., Montreal, QC H3B 4T6 (514) 866-6621, FAX 866-3035. Born Montreal 1949. **EDUC:** Univ. of Montreal–École des Hautes Études Commerciales, B.A.A.(Bus.) 1971; Univ. of Western Ontario, Sr. Mgmt Program 1985; Harvard Bus. Sch., Advanced Mgmt Program 1987. **CAREER:** Commerce Officer, Fed. Trade & Industry Dept., 1970-76; Commercial Attaché, Cdn Embassy, Paris, 1976-79; Dir., Dir. Gen., Treasury Bd., 1979-85; Asst. Deputy Min., Fed. Dept. of Industry, 1985-88; Sr. VP, Montreal Exchange, 1988-90; Pres., Strategico Inc., 1990-94; Pres. & CEO, Canadian Pulp & Paper Association, 1994 to date. **DIRECTOR:** Russel Metals; l'Industrielle Alliance. **AFFIL:** National Institute for Scientific Research (Chair of the Bd. 1992-95); Sectoral Advisory Group for Fin. Svcs, reporting to Int'l Trade Min. (mbr. 1988-90); St. Luc Hospital (Bd. 1991-95); Defence Science Advisory Bd. (1992-94); Sectoral Advisory Group for Forest Products; National Council on Statistics; National Roundtable on the Environment & the Economy (V-Chair). **INTERESTS:** econ. & human dev. **COMMENT:** *"'Better' has replaced 'more' and 'higher' as my leitmotif in both career and personal life."*

LaCroix, Dana ■ ⊛

Singer, Songwriter. c/o The Brant Group, 25 Brant St., Toronto, ON M5V 2L9 (416) 703-5858, FAX 703-5892. Born Toronto 1966. s. **EDUC:** Birchmount Park C.I., Arts 1984; Carleton Univ., English 1984-85; Humber Coll., Honours Music 1989. **CAREER:** club singer, Toronto; played with Leroy Emmanuel; various bands & singer/percussionist with D'Tripp, N.Y., 1989-91; songwriting, Denmark, 1991-93; solo recording, Canada & US, 1993-94; Denmark tour, 1994; European tour, 1995. **AFFIL:** KODA (Danish Composers' Society); DMF (Danish Musicians' Union). **INTERESTS:** promoting, supporting & cultivating strong, successful independent female role models, & being one myself. **COMMENT:** *"Am an avid traveller. Have lived and performed in London, New York, Toronto, Copenhagen and Barcelona. Have also travelled extensively through Greece and Turkey. Speak three languages."*

Lacroix, Georgette 📖 ⊛

Poète et Écrivain. 694, rue St.-Jean, Ste. 2, Québec, QC G1R 1P8. Born Qué. 1921. 1 ch. Hélène Lacroix. **CAREER:** Archives Nationales, Ministère des Affaires Culturelles du Québec, 1972-84; Animatrice, Écrivain et Journaliste à la pige. **SELECTED PUBLICATIONS:** *Mortes Saisons* (Garneau, 1967); *Entre nous...ce pays* (Garneau, 1970); *Le Creux de la vague* (Garneau, 1972); *Aussi loin que demain* (Garneau, 1973); *Dans l'instant de ton âge* (Garneau, 1974); *Au large d'Eros* (Éditions La Minerve, 1975); *Vivre l'automne* (Garneau, 1976); *Québec 1608-1978* (Éditions La Minerve, 1978); *Québec capitale de la neige* (1979); *Québec* (Les Presses Laurentiennes, 1979); *Faire un enfant* (Éditions La Liberté, 1980); *Hommage au Québec*, Eugene Kedl photographe (Les Archives nationales du Québec, 1980); *Artistes du Québec* (Éditions La Minerve, 1980); *G. Larochelle, l'Homme, le Peintre* (1981); *Astrorama* (Ariès, 1982); *Tatoushak* (Comité du Patrimoine de Tadoussac, 1982); *Sports en Fête* (Éditions des Blés d'or, 1983); *Le Carnaval de Québec 1894-1984* (Éditions Québécor, 1984); *L'Acadie avec les yeux du coeur* (Les Presses Laurentiennes, 1984); *Les fermières d'Armagh* (Éditions La Minerve, 1984); *De Tadoussac à Mistassini* (Éditions J.C.L., 1984); *Le carnaval aux souvenirs* (Éditions La Minerve, 1985); *Tableaux-poèmes sur le temps d'autrefois* (Éditions Bellimage, 1986); *Charlevoix mes amours* (Club Lions de Baie St.-Paul, 1985); *Le salon de raconte* (Salon International du Livre du Québec, 1986); *Adieux du Québec à M. Yourcenar* (Les Presses Laurentiennes, 1988); *La Sinfonia, 25 ans de musique* (La Sinfonia, 1988); *La petite scène des grandes vedettes* (Les Éditions Spectaculaires, 1988); *Grands Peintres du Québec* (Éditions des Blés d'Or, 1990); *Les adieux du Québec à Alice Parizeau* (Guérin Éditeur, 1991); *Québec d'un carnaval à l'autre* (Éditions Vient de la Mer, 1995); various anthologies. **AFFIL:** Société des Poètes Canadiens-Français; Société des écrivains canadiens; Artistes associés du Québec; Salon international du livre de Québec. **HONS:** Prix de poésie au concours, La Société du bon parler français, 1963, 1969; Prix France-Québec, 1971; Certificat d'Honneur, La Ville de Québec, 1986; 1er Prix de Poésie, VIA Rail, 1990. **INTERESTS:** la lecture; le cinéma; les voyages; la peinture; les arts en général. **MISC:** 20 chansons. **COMMENT:** *"De 1944 à 1984, Georgette Lacroix, native de Québec, a été institutrice, discothécaire, rédactrice, speakerine, animatrice et réalisatrice à la radio et à la télévision de Québec."*

LaCroix, Lisa ■ ⊛ 📺 🎭

Actor, Producer, Multi-Media Artist. c/o Butler Rushton Bell, 10 St. Mary St., Toronto, ON M4Y 1Y4 (416) 964-6660, FAX 964-8979. Born Toronto. s. **EDUC:** Concordia Univ., Fine Arts 1985; acting training with C.A.S.T., Marriane Mclassic, Diana Reis, Janine Manatis, Kevin McCormack, Theresa Sear, David Switzer & others, 1986-93; intensive acting training, Circle in the Square Theater, N.Y., 1987. **CAREER:** actor, prod., dir., photographer; commercial & catalogue model; dramaturge; advertising photographers' sales rep. **SELECTED CREDITS:** Neggan (Lead), *Divided Loyalties*, CFTO/Baton Broadcasting, 1989; Kelly Longstreet (series regular) 18 eps, *E.N.G.*, Moviecorp XX (1992); Anita Harrison-Haley (contract player) 48 eps., *Family Passions*, NDF, Baton & J. Winther, 1993-94; Illiana Crow (lead), *Dance Me Outside* (feature), dir. Bruce McDonald, 1993; numerous stage plays, radio dramas, commercials & voice-overs, 1987-93; numerous principal roles in TV series, feature films & movies of the week, 1989 to date. **SELECTED PUBLICATIONS:** "Akkavalta," photographic series on Sumatran matriarchal community (*Me Naiset* Magazine, Finland, 1989). **DIRECTOR:** Elle Entertainment Incorporated. **AFFIL:** The Academy of Film & Television; Toronto Women in Film & Television; Liaison of Independent Filmmakers in Toronto; ACTRA; Canadian Actors' Equity Association; Full Screen. **INTERESTS:** deaf culture; running; canoeing; martial dance. **COMMENT:** *"Lisa LaCroix currently endeavours to produce her own work and contribute to the work of others, which expresses the complexity of the human experience and explores the identity unique to women of colour."*

Lacroix, Marie, B.Comm.,M.B.A. $

Vice-President and Area Manager, ROYAL BANK OF CANADA, 1 Place Ville Marie, Mezzanine 1, Montreal, QC H3C 3B5 (514) 874-2121, FAX 874-4709. Born St.-Georges de Beauce, Que. 1955. m. Guy Papillon. 2 ch. **EDUC:** Univ. Laval, B.Comm. 1976; Univ. of Western Ontario, M.B.A. 1979. **CAREER:** Acct Mgr, Commercial Bnkg, various branches, Royal Bank of Canada, 1979-86; Sr. Acct Mgr, Corp. Bnkg Centre, Que., 1986-89; Mgr, Corp. Lending, Corp. Bnkg Centre, Que., 1989-90; Area Mgr, Ste-Foy, 1990-93; VP & Area Mgr., Montreal W., 1993; VP & Area Mgr, Montreal Downtown, 1994 to date. **AFFIL:** Junior Achievement of Quebec; Montreal Chamber of Commerce; McGill University's Foundation of the Fac. of Educ. (Bd.).

LaCroix, Naomi Patricia (Patti) ■ ⊛

President, THE BRANT GROUP, 25 Brant St., Toronto, ON M5V 2L9 (416) 703-5858, FAX 703-5892. Born Vancouver 1938. m. Pat LaCroix. 2 ch. **EDUC:** St. Joseph's Sch. of Nursing, R.N. 1960; Univ. of Toronto (Hist.) 1970. **CAREER:** nursing, operating room specialist, Montreal General Hospital, Wellesley

Hospital, Princess Margaret Hospital, 1960-65; Gen. Mgr, Pat Lacroix Photography Limited, 1974 to date; Pres., The Brant Group, 1982 to date. **DIRECTOR:** Pat LaCroix Photography Limited; 1053716 Ontario Limited. **INTERESTS:** educ. & training of teenage mothers & their infant children to successful parenting. **MISC:** Cdn of Japanese ancestry, spent WWII in relocation camp in B.C.; leads seminars in business of photography. **COMMENT:** *"In 1982 I established The Brant Group as the business arm of Pat LaCroix Photography Limited, which is one of the most prominent photography studios in Canada. Presently we are in the process of directing our efforts toward establishing a very strong presence in the world of stock photography through our association with The Image Bank, one of the largest stock agencies in the world."*

Ladner, Cobi, B.A. ■■ 📖 ✏

Editor, *Canadian House & Home* magazine, CANADIAN HOME PUBLISHERS, 511 King St. W., Ste. 120, Toronto, ON M5V 2Z4 (416) 593-0204, FAX 591-1630, EMAIL homepub@inforamp.net. Born Ont. 1962. m. Robert Brehl. 1 ch. Aidan John Robert Brehl. **EDUC:** Ryerson Polytechnic Univ., B.A.(Radio & TV) 1984. **CAREER:** Asst. Decorating Editor, *Chatelaine* magazine, 1984-87; Fashion & Beauty Editor, *Canadian Living*, 1987-90; Decorating Editor, *Canadian House & Home* magazine, 1990-93. **AFFIL:** National Magazine Awards (Exec. 1995 to date); Canadian Society of Magazine Editors (Exec. 1993-95). **HONS:** Editor, Magazine of the Year, National Magazine Awards, 1996. **INTERESTS:** design; antiques; cottaging; travel. **COMMENT:** *"Editor of* Canadian House & Home *magazine. Spokesperson on home on nationally syndicated television shows and in appearances at home and trade shows."*

Ladner, Joanne, B.N.,R.N. ⊕

Nursing Unit Manager, CALGARY GENERAL HOSPITAL, Peter Lougheed Centre, 3500 - 26 Ave. N.E., Calgary, AB T1Y 6J4 (403) 291-8817, FAX 291-8739. Born Regina 1957. m. David. **EDUC:** Wascana Institute of Applied Arts & Sciences, Dipl.(Nursing) 1977; Univ. of Calgary, Bachelor of Nursing 1993. **CAREER:** Staff Nurse, Pediatrics, Pasqua Hospital, Regina, 1977-79; Staff Nurse, Pediatrics, Calgary General Hospital, 1979-93; part-time Sessional Instructor, Univ. of Calgary, 1989; Patient Care Coord., Post Partum, Calgary General Hospital, 1993-94; Nursing Unit Mgr for Pediatrics & Post Partum, 1994 to date. **AFFIL:** Alberta Association of Registered Nurses; Association of Women's Health & Neonatal Nurses; Community Block Watch (Captain). **HONS:** G.M. Hall Memorial Scholarship, Calgary General Hospital. **INTERESTS:** sports; travel; computers. **COMMENT:** *"Following 16 years as a staff nurse, I moved into a management role. I have been able to use my energy and apply it to this rewarding avenue of my career. I enjoy challenge, and today's health care is certainly a challenge."*

Laflamme, Diane, B.Ped.,B.B.A., A.I.I.C. 🎓 $

General Manager, L'INSTITUT D'ASSURANCE DE DOMMAGES DU QUÉBEC, 1200 McGill College Ave., Ste. 2230, Montréal, QC H3B 4G7 (514) 393-8156, FAX 393-9222. Born Que. 1949. s. 1 ch. **EDUC:** Univ. Laval, B.Ped.(Educ.) 1970, B.B.A.(Bus. Admin.) 1972; Univ. du Québec à Montréal, Grad. Diploma (Interdisciplinary Studies) 1993, Ph.D.(Applied Human Sciences) in progress. **CAREER:** insur.; Chair of Insur., Univ. Laval. **SELECTED PUBLICATIONS:** article in *Revue de l'association pour la recherche qualitative* (1995). **AFFIL:** Insurance Institute of Canada (Assoc.); Association d'entraide Ville-Marie (voluntary work with terminally ill persons who wish to stay at home). **MISC:** speaker at U.N. Conference on Trade & Dev., Lisbon, 1990; speaker at A.C.F.A.S. 62nd Convention, Montreal, 1994.

Lafrance, Carole M. $ 👍

Chief Executive Officer, CALA HUMAN RESOURCES COMPANY LTD., 63 de Bresoles St., Montreal, QC H2Y 1V7 (514) 288-9004, FAX 288-1689. Born Sudbury, Ont. 1944. s. **EDUC:** Univ. of Toronto, 1966; Laurentian Univ., 1972; Harvard Bus. Sch., 1988. **CAREER:** W.W. Incorporated, 1971-72; Nationwide Advertising Services, 1973-77; Founder/Pres., Cala Human Resources Company Ltd., 1978-95; CEO, 1995 to date. **DIRECTOR:** Canadian Commercial Corp. **AFFIL:** Public Policy Forum (Dir.; Exec. Bd.); Canadian Chamber of Commerce (Chair 1996); The Committee of 200 (First Cdn Mbr.); Young Presidents' Organization; Association of Human Resources Professionals of Québec; Montreal Chamber of Commerce; Les Amies du Ritz. **HONS:** Woman of the Year Award, Entrepreneurship. **INTERESTS:** classical music; opera; horseback riding; travel; nature. **COMMENT:** *"I founded Cala in 1978. It now operates in Montreal, Toronto, Calgary and Vancouver, with affiliates in New York, Europe and Australia. A continuing success story."*

Laing, Barbara, B.Math.,F.L.M.I. ■ $

Vice-President, Pension Systems, CROWN LIFE

INSURANCE COMPANY, 1901 Scarth St., Box 827, Regina, SK S4P 3B1 (306) 751-6205, FAX 751-7070. Born UK 1946. m. Robert. 3 ch. EDUC: Univ. of Waterloo, B.Math.(Comp. Sci.) 1969. CAREER: various systems positions, Crown Life Insurance; VP, Systems & Admin., 1992-94; VP, Tech. Direction, 1994-96; VP, Pension Systems, 1996 to date. AFFIL: Life Office Management Association (Fellow in Insur.); F.L.M.I. Society of Regina (Pres. 1994-96); St. Francis United Church (V-Chair of Bd. 1988-89); Regina Precision Teams (Gen. Mgr 1996 to date). INTERESTS: figure skating; church choirs. COMMENT: *"To be fully challenged is my goal. Balancing family life, church work and a career of successful progression through a number of positions at one company is an achievement."*

Lake, Suzy M., M.F.A. ⊗ ☜

Artist. Associate Professor, Fine Art Department, UNIVERSITY OF GUELPH, Guelph, ON N1G 2W1 (519) 824-4120. Born 1947. EDUC: Concordia Univ., Montreal, M.F.A. 1979. CAREER: part-time Instructor, Montreal Museum Sch. of Art & Design, 1969-70; full-time Instructor, 1970-73; Véhicule Art Galerie, Inc., 1971-76; part-time Instructor, Montreal Museum Sch. of Art & Design, 1973-76; Instructor, Technician, Concordia/Loyola Photography Workshop, 1975-78; sessional appointments, Concordia Univ., 1976-77; Summer Session Visiting Instructor, Banff Sch. of Art, 1980; sessional appointments, York Univ., 1980-81; sessional appointments, Ontario Coll. of Art, 1982-83; sessional appointments, Univ. of Guelph, 1983-88; Assoc. Prof., Univ. of Guelph, 1988 to date. SELECTED CREDITS: *Bisecting Space*, 1970; *Choreography with Myself*, Montreal Museum of Fine Arts, 1978; *It was a Classic Detroit Style Robbery*, 1987-88; various other performing credits; *Box Concert* (video), 1973-74; *A Natural Way to Draw* (video), 1975; *The Painter and the Paintee* (video), 1976; *Choreographies on the Dotted Line* (video), 1976. SELECTED PUBLICATIONS: contributor, *The Loyola Photographer's Workshop Album*, print portfolio (1975); contributor, *Olympic Posters*, print portfolio (Véhicule Press, 1976); *Jeux d'Image: 4 X 16 X 20*, print portfolia (1980). EXHIBITIONS: 35 solo exhibitions, incl. Vancouver Art Gallery, Vancouver (1978), Art Gallery of Ontario, Toronto (1978), Southern Alberta Art Gallery, Lethbridge (1982), Art Gallery of Hamilton (1982), *Authority is an Attribute #2*, MacDonald Stewart Art Centre, Guelph (1991) & *A Point of Reference* (retrospective), Canadian Museum of Contemporary Photography, Ottawa (1993); 14 two-person exhibitions incl.

Véhicule Art, Montreal (1973), Photo Union Gallery, Hamilton (1983) & Petro-Canada Exhibition Gallery, Calgary (1986); more than 90 group exhibitions, incl. *Photo and Idea*, Galleria Communale d'Arte Moderna, Parma, Italy (1976), *Identité/Identifications*, Centre d'Art Plastiques Contemporains, Bordeaux, France (1976), *Transparent Things*, Canadian Council Art Bank (1977), *Magma*, Museo Castelvecchio, Verona, Italy (1977), *Winnipeg Perspectives*, Winnipeg Art Gallery (1979), Vancouver Art Gallery (1990), *La Collection-Tableau Inaugural*, Musée d'Art Contemporain, Montreal (1992), *Beau* (inaugural exhibition), Canadian Museum of Contemporary Photography, Ottawa (1992) & *Corpus*, Mendel Art Gallery, Saskatoon (1993). COLLECTIONS: Canadian Museum of Contemporary Photography; Canadian Council Art Bank; Montreal Museum of Fine Art; Museum Lodz, Wroclaw, Poland; Art Gallery of Ontario; MacDonald Stewart Art Centre, Guelph; Musée d'Art Contemporain, Montreal; Vancouver Art Gallery; numerous other collections. AFFIL: Toronto Photographers' Workshop; U.A.A.C.; Ed Video; Society for Photographic Education; Art Gallery of Ontario (Hon. Life Artist Mbr.); Women's Art Resource Centre; A Space Gallery; C.A.R.O.; University Skating Club, Toronto. HONS: Open Studio Visiting Artist competition, 1994. INTERESTS: camping; canoeing; figure skating. MISC: recipient, various grants; subject of various articles & reviews. COMMENT: *"I make art to figure out how to come to terms with my world. This urgency not only provokes the visual exploration, but also the desire to communicate to others in the exhibition space or in the classroom."*

Laking, Hon. Janice, B.A. ♣ ☜

Mayor, CITY OF BARRIE, 70 Collier St., Barrie, ON (705) 739-4200, FAX 726-6941. Born Barrie, Ont. 1929. m. John. 7 ch. Wendy, Susan, Jane, Sandra, Paul, John, Ruth. EDUC: Univ. of Western Ontario, B.A.(Phys. Educ./Econ.) 1951; Univ. of Toronto, Fac. of Educ., Certificate (Secondary Sch. Teaching) 1953, Certificate (Specialist Phys. Educ.) 1964, Certificate (Guidance Specialist) 1968. CAREER: secondary sch. teacher, Petrolia, Ont., 1951-52; secondary sch. teacher, West Lorne, Ont., 1954-55; secondary sch. teacher, St. Thomas, Ont., 1955-56; secondary sch. teacher & Dept. Head of Girls' Phys. Educ. & Guidance, Barrie, 1961-88; Alderman, City of Barrie, 1972-88; Liberal candidate (Simcoe North), fed. election, 1974; Mayor, City of Barrie, 1988 to date; Public Utilities Commission, City of Barrie, 1988 to date; Chair, Police Svcs Bd., City of Barrie, 1988 to date; Barrie Hospital

Bd., 1988 to date; Barrie Chamber of Commerce Bd., 1988 to date; Barrie Nonprofit Housing Bd., 1988 to date; Liberal candidate (Simcoe Centre), fed. election, 1993. **AFFIL:** Royal Victoria Hospital (Bd.); Economic Development Committee; Simcoe County Homes for the Aged; Collier Street United Church; Barrie & District United Way (Past Chair); Tourism Study (Past V-Chair); University Women's Club (Past Pres.); Simcoe North Federal Liberal Association (Past Pres.); Liberal Party of Canada.

Lalumière, Donna A., B.A. ■ $

Vice-President and Director, Retail Distribution, Treasury, THE TORONTO-DOMINION BANK, Ernst & Young Tower, 222 Bay St., 7th Fl., Toronto, ON M5K 1A2 (416) 982-4741 or 1-800-387-1631, FAX 944-6821. Born Montreal 1957. **EDUC:** Concordia Univ., B.A.(Pol. Sci.) 1979. **CAREER:** joined The Toronto-Dominion Bank, Montreal, 1980 to date; VP, Treasury Svcs.

Lamb, Marjorie, B.A. ■ 📺 ✊ ♥

Writer Speaker and Consultant. 96 Highland Ave., Toronto, ON M4W 2A6 (416) 324-9342, FAX 924-2001, EMAIL mlamb@web.net. Born Tisdale, Sask. 1949. life partner Barry Pearson. 1 ch. Caroline Lamb. **EDUC:** Univ. of Saskatchewan, B.A.(English) 1972. **CAREER:** author; numerous keynote engagements speaking on the environment & personal environmental action; numerous guest appearances on TV & radio stations across Canada & the US; environmental consultant. **SELECTED CREDITS:** weekly appearances, *Metro Morning*, CBC Radio, Toronto, 1989-93; Host & Script Consultant, *Your Green Home* (6-part series), 1991; Writer & Performer, "Environmental Minute," weekly feature on *Midday* & CBC Newsworld, 1990. **SELECTED PUBLICATIONS:** *Two Minutes a Day for a Greener Planet* (HarperCollins, 1990; also published in the US & Australia); *Two Minutes a Day to Super Savings* (HarperCollins, 1991); monthly environmental column, "Greenscene," *Chatelaine* Magazine, 1990; monthly environmental column, *Select Homes* Magazine, 1993-95. **AFFIL:** Canadian Institute for Environmental Law & Policy (Dir.); The Pollution Probe Foundation (V-Chair); Women & Environments Education & Development Foundation (WEED) Foundation (Dir.); ACTRA, Wire Service Guild; Directors' Guild of Canada; The Urban Environment Centre (Dir.). **INTERESTS:** flying a Cessna 150; making clothes & jewellery; running; home renovation & repair. **COMMENT:** "*Environmental writer, speaker, activist; best known for book* Two Minutes a Day for a Greener Planet *and television series* Your Green Home. *Inspires audiences to help preserve the environment. Serves on the Board of Directors for four environmental organizations.*"

Lambermont, Jeannette, B.F.A. ■ ✪ 🎭 ☝

Director. 111 Fuller Ave., Toronto, ON M6R 2C4 (416) 543-1594. Born Dieren, The Netherlands 1956. d. 1 ch. Micaela Johanna L. Morey. **EDUC:** York Univ., B.F.A.(Theatre) 1978. **CAREER:** Dir., Stratford Shakespearean Festival, 1989-90; Dir., Citadel Theatre, 1990; Theatre Teacher, Univ. of Alberta, 1991, 1995; Theatre Teacher, Univ. of Victoria & Ryerson Polytechnic Univ. Theatre Sch., 1992; Theatre Teacher, Juilliard Sch., N.Y., 1993; Dir., Canadian Stage Company, 1993-94; Theatre Teacher, George Brown Coll., 1994; Dir., Paramour Productions, 1994; Dir., Theatre Ontario, 1992, 1993, 1994, 1996; Theatre Teacher, Ryerson Polytechnic Univ. Theatre Sch., 1995-96; Dir., Theatre Aquarius, 1995-96; Dir., Thousand Islands Playhouse, 1996; Dir., Factory Theatre, 1996; Theatre Teacher, York Univ., 1996-97. **AFFIL:** ACTRA; Canadian Actors' Equity Association; American Actors' Equity Association. **HONS:** Tyrone Guthrie/Jean Chalmers Award; Director Observer Award, Academy of Cinema & Television. **INTERESTS:** new Cdn works & artists; filmmaking; writing. **COMMENT:** "*The first Canadian woman to direct on the main stage at the Stratford Festival, Jeannette is devoted to nurturing and developing the work of new Canadian artists and writers.*"

Lambert, Phyllis, O.C.,C.Q.,OAL, FRAIC,FRSC,ARCA,LL.D. ■■ 📜 ✪

Director and Chairman of the Board of Trustees, CENTRE CANADIEN D'ARCHITECTURE/CANADIAN CENTRE FOR ARCHITECTURE, 1920, rue Baile, Montréal, QC H3H 2S6 (514) 939-7025, FAX 939-7020. **EDUC:** Vassar Coll., Poughkeepsie, N.Y., B.A. 1948; Illinois Institute of Technology, Chicago, M.S.(Architecture) 1963. **CAREER:** Dir. of Planning, Seagram Bldg, Joseph E. Seagram and Sons Inc., N.Y., N.Y., 1954-58; Architect, Saidye Bronfman Centre, YM-YWHA, Montreal, 1963-68; Chrm of the Bd. & Principal, Ridgway, Ltd., Architects/Developers, L.A., 1972-84; Architect, Jane Tate House renovation, Montreal, 1974-76; Architect-Developer, Biltmore Hotel renovation, L.A., 1976; Dir., archaeological & historical research & renovation, Ben Ezra Synagogue, Cairo, Egypt, 1981-93; Consulting Architect, Centre Canadien d'Architecture/Canadian Centre for Architecture, 1984-89; Dir. & Chrm of Bd. of Trustees, 1979 to date. Teaching: Adjunct Prof., Sch. of Arch., McGill

Univ., 1986 to date; Assoc. Prof., Fac. d'Aménagement, École d'Architecture et paysage, Univ. de Montréal, 1989 to date. SELECTED PUBLICATIONS: numerous incl. "How a Building Gets Built" (*Vassar Alumni Magazine* 44, no. 3, Feb. 1959); "Notes on Mies and His Drawings" in *Mies van der Rohe Drawings: From the Collection of A. James Speyer* (N.Y.: Max Protetch Gallery, 1986); ed. & wrote intro., "Towards an Interfaith Centre: Archaeology, Preservation and History" in *Fortifications and the Synagogue: The Fortress of Babylon and the Ben Ezra Synagogue, Cairo* (London: Weidenfeld & Nicolson, 1994). EXHIBITIONS: numerous incl. *Perspectives: The Architectural Heritage of Montreal*; paintings and photographs (McCord Museum, Montreal, 1975); co-curator with Richard Pare, *Photography and Architecture: 1839-1939* (Kunsthaus Lempertz, Cologne, 1982; Art Institute of Chicago, 1983; Cooper-Hewitt Museum, N.Y., 1983; Musée national d'art moderne, Centre Georges Pompidou, Paris, 1984; National Gallery of Canada, Ottawa, 1984); co-curator with Alan Stewart, *Opening the Gates of Eighteenth-Century Montreal* (Canadian Centre for Architecture, Sept. 1992-Feb. 1993). DIRECTOR: Hydro-Québec. AFFIL: Société du Vieux-Port de Montréal (Bd. of Trustees 1984 to date); Canadian Mediterranean Institute (Bd. of Trustees 1986 to date); Illinois Institute of Technology (Bd. of Overseers, Coll. of Arch., Planning & Design 1988 to date); Princeton Univ. (Visiting Committee, Dept. of Arch. 1990 to date); National Gallery of Canada (Special Advisor, Acquisitions Committee 1991 to date); Learning for a Sustained Future (Bd. of Dir. 1992 to date); Association of Art Museum Directors (mbr. 1994 to date); College Art Association, N.Y. (President's Advisory Committee 1994 to date); World Federation of Friends of Museums (Hon. Committee, representing Canada 1995 to date). HONS: Fellow, Royal Architectural Institute of Canada, 1983; Chevalier de l'Ordre national du Québec, 1985; Officer of the Order of Canada, 1990; Officer, Ordre des Arts et Lettres, Gov't of France, 1992; Fellow, Royal Society of Canada, 1995; several hon. degrees; Massey Medal for Arch. for the Saidye Bronfman Centre, Royal Architectural Institute of Canada, 1970; Award of Honor for excellence in design & execution for renovation of Biltmore Hotel, L.A., American Institute of Architects, S. Calif. chpt., 1978; Médaille de Mérite, Ordre des Architectes du Québec, 1981; Award of Merit, American Institute of Architects, N.Y. chpt., 1991; Gold Medal, Royal Architectural Institute of Canada, 1991; Lescarbot Award for outstanding contributions to the cultural life of Canada, Gov't of

Canada, 1993; Ordre de la Pléiade for exceptional contribution to cultural exchange, l'Assemblée internationale des parlementaires de langue française, 1995. MISC: numerous lectures.

Lambert, Valerie, B.A.,C.A. Ⓢ
Vice-President and Treasurer, B.C. GAS INC., 1111 W. Georgia St., Vancouver, BC V6E 4M4 (604) 443-6625, FAX 443-6929. Born Edinburgh, Scotland 1955. m. Duncan Farquharson. 2 ch. EDUC: Univ. of Toronto, B.A. (English/Commerce) 1976. CAREER: Mgr, Procedures & Compliance, Molson Companies Limited; Sr. Auditor, MacMillan Bloedel Limited; Fin. Analyst; Mgr, Investor Rel'ns & Fin.; Dir., Treasury Oper., B.C. Gas Utility Ltd.; Treas.; VP/Treas., B.C. Gas Inc. DIRECTOR: B.C. Transit. AFFIL: Institute of Chartered Accountants of B.C.; Institute of Chartered Accountants of Ontario; Canadian Institute of Chartered Accountants; Financial Executives Institute; Vancouver Board of Trade; Pacific Coast Gas Association; B.C. Women's Hospital (Dir.). INTERESTS: tennis; skiing. COMMENT: "*In my current role at B.C. Gas, I continue to endeavour to give recommendations to senior management and to the Board of Directors on matters of financial policy, and carry out all capital-raising transactions and insurance negotiations.*"

Lambrecht, Helga, B.Ed.,M.Ed. ■ ⓐ Ⓢ ⓦ
President, LAMBRECHT PUBLICATIONS, 1763 Maple Bay Rd., R.R. 5, Duncan, BC V9L 4T6 (604) 748-8722, FAX 748-8722, EMAIL helgal@cln.etc.bc.ca. Born Royce, Alta. 1943. m. Leonard Lambrecht. EDUC: Univ. of Alberta, B.Ed.(Home Econ./Phys. Sci.) 1967; Univ. of British Columbia, M.Ed.(Curriculum/Admin./Family) 1971. CAREER: secondary sch. teacher, Calgary, Drayton Valley, Cranbrook, Kamloops, Ladysmith, Duncan, 24 yrs.; Co-proprietor & VP, Genoa Bay Marina, 1971-88; Co-proprietor & VP, Lambrecht Properties, 1971-93; Author & Publisher, Lambrecht Publications, 1978 to date. SELECTED PUBLICATIONS: *Genoa Bay Reckonings*; *McMeekan's Yellowknife Blade*; *Man of the Land*; *Recipes We Love to Cook*; *Favorite Foods From Us to You*; *Specialties from our Kitchens*; *Recipes Plain and Fancy*; *Microcook Meals and Mixes*. AFFIL: Cowichan Spirit of Women (Founding Steering Committee); B.C. Teachers Federation; Canadian Home Economics Association (Hon. Life Mbr.); Canadian Authors' Association (Life Mbr.); German-Canadian Historical Association (Life Mbr.); Business & Professional Women's Club; Canadian Federation of University Women. HONS:

Award, Univ. of Alberta Undergrad. Society, 1961; Scholarship, Jewish Council, 1962; Pin of Recognition, Teachers of Home Economics Specialist Association, 1987. **INTERESTS:** home-catalogued library; swimming; walking; dancing; boating; vacationing with husband. **COMMENT:** *"Helpful, energetic, loving, generous, talented, Helga Lambrecht, multi-faceted Home Economist and Christian feminist, cherishes her rural upbringing and enjoys teaching, writing, publishing and community work."*

Lamon, Jeanne, B.A. 🧍 🎓 ○
Music Director, TAFELMUSIK, 427 Bloor St. W., Box 14, Toronto, ON M5S 1X7 (416) 964-9562, FAX 964-2782. Born New York City 1949. **EDUC:** Brandeis Univ., B.A.(Music) 1970. **CAREER:** Fac. Mbr., Royal Conservatory of Music & Univ. of Toronto. **HONS:** Doctor of Letters (Honoris Causa), York Univ., 1994. **COMMENT:** *"Leading from her position as first violinist, Jeanne Lamon has, since her arrival in 1981, developed the Tafelmusik Baroque Orchestra into an internationally acclaimed ensemble with a major recording contract, 50 concerts in Toronto and frequent tours worldwide."*

Lamont, Mary Susanne, B.A. ■■ $ ○ ✋
President, M.S. LAMONT AND ASSOCIATES LIMITED (financial counsel, investment mgmt), 25 Adelaide St. E., Ste. 1414, Toronto, ON M5C 3A1 (416) 364-1578, FAX 364-1578. Born Toronto 1947. s. **EDUC:** University Coll., Univ. of Toronto, B.A.(Modern Hist. & French) 1968. **CAREER:** stock cage, Wood Gundy, Toronto & London, U.K., 1968-69; Jr. Research Analyst, Investment Dept., Pitfield McKay Ross & Co. Ltd., Toronto, 1970-72; Fin. Analyst, Investment Dept., Wood Gundy, 1972-73; Analyst/Sr. Analyst/Asst. Mgr, Private Placements, Investment Dept., Royal Bank of Canada, Montreal & Toronto, 1973-78; Trainee, Int'l Corp. Credit, Toronto, 1978-79; Portfolio Mgr, Mortgage Insurance Corporation of Canada, 1980-83; Dir. of Investment, 1983-86; Pres., M.S. Lamont & Associates Limited, 1986 to date. **AFFIL:** Tarragon Theatre (Advisory Bd. 1984 to date); National Ballet Sch. (mbr. of Bd. 1986 to date); Havergal Coll. Foundation (Bd. of Trustees 1992 to date); Women's College Hospital (Bd. of Dir. 1992 to date). **HONS:** Women of Distinction Award, Bus./Entrepreneurship, YWCA, 1991. **INTERESTS:** reading; squash; tennis; golf; symphony; theatre; ballet; politics; travel.

Lamontagne, Mary, C.M.,B.Sc.A., B.A.,M.A. $ ✋ ○
Corporate Director, and Association Executive. Born Dayton, Ohio 1926. m. Gilles Lamontagne. 4 ch. **EDUC:** Laval Univ., B.Sc.A. (Chem.) 1948, B.A.(Phil.) 1974, M.A. (Phil.) 1982. **VOLUNTEER CAREER:** Treas., Symphonic Matinees for Children, 1960-65; mbr., Nat'l Committee on Educ., Canadian University Women, 1962; Founding Mbr., Que. Section, United Nations Association; mbr., Bd. of Gov., Laval Univ., 1970-74; Pres., Laval Alumni Association, 1971-72; Pres., Committee for the 125th Anniversary of the Canadian Institute of Quebec; Bd. Mbr., Vanier Institute of the Family, 1973-79; Founding Pres., S.O.S. Grosesse, 1974; Pres., Canadian Addiction Foundation, 1974-75; mbr., Medical Research Council of Canada, 1975-80; mbr., MRC Task Force on Human Experimentation, 1976-77; Chair, Centennial Sholarship Committee, MRC, 1977-80; Pres., United Way Fundraising Drive, Que. Reg., 1979; mbr., Nat'l Biotechnology Advisory Committee, 1983-88; mbr., MRC Standing Committee on Ethics in Experimentation, 1984-91; mbr., Société d'investissement Jeunesse, 1986-91; mbr., Orientation Committee, Science & Eng. Dept., Laval Univ.; mbr., Ethics Review Committee, Fac. of Medicine, Laval Univ. **DIRECTOR:** National Bank of Canada; CFCF Inc.; Quebecor; Société financière Bougie Ltée. **PAST DIRECTOR:** Allelix; Bio-Research Inc.; Canada Development Corporation; CDC Life Sciences Inc.; Connaught Laboratories; Lépine, Cloutier, Bourgie Ltd.; M. Loeb Ltée; North American Life Assurance Company; Quaker Oats of Canada. **AFFIL:** Laval Univ. Hospital (Bioethics Committee; Past Pres.); Maison Michel Sarazin (Ethics Committee). **HONS:** Member of the Order of Canada; Officer, Order of St. John.

Lamy, Martine ■■ 🧍
Principal Dancer, THE NATIONAL BALLET OF CANADA, The Walter Carsen Centre for the National Ballet of Canada, 470 Queen's Quay W., Toronto, ON M5V 3K4 (416) 345-9686, FAX 345-8323, EMAIL info@national.ballet.ca. Born Trois-Rivières, Que. **EDUC:** entered National Ballet Sch., 1975; dance studies in Europe & N.Y. **CAREER:** joined National Ballet of Canada, 1983; Second Soloist, 1985; First Soloist, 1987; Principal Dancer, 1990. **SELECTED CREDITS:** title role, *Manon*; Lise, *La Fille Mal Gardée*; Swanilda, *Coppélia*; Alice/Child Alice, *Alice*; Young Wife, *La Ronde*; Chloë, *Daphnis and Chloë*; title role, *Sphinx*; Kitri, *Don Quixote*; Swan Queen/Black Queen, *Swan Lake*; Princess Aurora, *The Sleeping Beauty*; Hanna, *The Merry Widow*; Katherina, *The Taming of the Shrew*; title role, *Giselle*; Tatiana, *Onegin*; title role, *Cinderella*; Snow Queen/Sugar Plum Fairy,

The Nutcracker; principal role, *Paquita*; Nikiya, *La Bayadère Act II*; leading roles, *Voluntaries, The Rite of Spring* & *Oracle*; *Sylvia Pas de Deux*; Stop-time Rag & Calliope Rag, *Elite Syncopations*. HONS: 3rd prize in Jr. Women's category & 1st prize for partnership with Serge Lavoie, 4th Moscow Int'l Ballet Competition, 1981; invited to dance with Jeremy Ransom at 66th Academy Awards show, 1994. MISC: film work includes CBC-TV/Primedia Production of Glen Tetley's *La Ronde*; appears in Rhombus Media documentary, *The Making of Blue Snake*, Ann Ditchburn's *A Moving Picture*, BBC documentary *Bold Steps*, Anthony Azzapardi's *Making Ballet*; host & writer for *Dimanche Classique*, 7 educational programmes on dance; guest artist, several dance companies.

Lancashire, Anne, B.A.,A.M., Ph.D. ■■ ⬧ 🍃 ♂
Professor of English, UNIVERSITY OF TORONTO, University College, Toronto, ON M5S 1A1 (416) 978-6270, FAX 971-2027, EMAIL anne@epas.utoronto.ca. Born Montreal 1941. m. Ian Lancashire. 3 ch. Susannah, David, Ruth. EDUC: McGill Univ., B.A.(Hons., English) 1962; Harvard Univ., A.M.(English) 1963, Ph.D.(English) 1965. CAREER: Lecturer, Univ. of Toronto, 1965-67; Asst. Prof., 1967-71; Assoc. Prof., 1971-76; Prof., 1976 to date; cross-appointed to University Coll. to Grad. Drama Centre, to Cinema Studies Program; Academic Sec., Dept. of Modern Languages & Literatures, 1969-70; Chair, 1970-71; VP, Women's Athletic Association Directorate, 1972-77; Asst. to the Dean, Sch. of Grad. Studies, 1974-76; Acting Chair, English Dept., 1983-84; Univ. V-Provost (Arts & Sci.) & V-Provost (Staff Functions), 1987-88; V-Principal & Program Dir., University Coll., 1990-93. SELECTED PUBLICATIONS: Editor, *Christopher Marlowe: Poet for the Stage* (author Clifford Leech, 1986); Author/Editor, *The Second Maiden's Tragedy* (1978); Author/Editor, *Gallathea & Midas* (1969); Ed., *Editing Renaissance Dramatic Texts: English, Italian and Spanish* (1976); numerous scholarly articles & papers. EDIT: Edit. Bd., *Medieval & Renaissance Drama in English*, 1990 to date; Edit. Bd., *Essays in Theatre*, 1991 to date; Ed. Bd., *The Internet Shakespeare*, 1996 to date. AFFIL: Shakespeare Association of America (Pres. 1988-89; Trustee 1984-87, 1989-91); Malone Society (Cdn Sec.-Treas. 1977-90); Modern Language Association of America; Film Studies Association of Canada; ACCUTE; Medieval & Renaissance Drama Society; Massey Coll. (Assoc.); Ontario Institute for Studies in Education (Bd. of Gov. 1988-91); Joint Council on

Educ., Univ. of Toronto/OISE (1981-84); 1st Etobicoke Central Scouts (Group Committee Chair 1985-89); St. Anne's Music & Drama Society (mbr. 1966-74); St. George's on-the-Hill (Sunday Sch. Teacher 1985-87). HONS: Canada Council Leave Fellow, 1971-72; SSHRCC Leave Fellow, 1986-87; Stratford Festival Celebrity Lecturer, 1983; Trafalgar-Ross Lecturer, 1987. INTERESTS: karate; gardening. MISC: 1st Cdn pres. of Shakespeare Association of America; 1st woman to be Acting Chair of the English Dept., V-Provost Staff Functions, V-Principal & Program Dir. of University Coll. COMMENT: *"As a professional scholar and teacher, also juggling administrative and family responsibilities, I have emphasized different professional and family goals at different points during my career."*

Lanctôt, Micheline, B.A. ⬧ ⬧
President, STOPFILM INC., 350 Birch, Saint-Lambert, QC J4P 2M6 (514) 465-9014, FAX 465-1367. Born Montreal 1947. s. 2 ch. EDUC: Coll. Jésus-Marie, B.A. 1966. CAREER: Maquettiste, Éditions du Jour, 1971. SELECTED CREDITS: *La vraie nature de Bernadette*, dir. Gilles Carle, 1972; *Squeeze*, Charlottetown Festival, 1972; *Souris, tu m'inquiètes*, dir. Aimée Danis, ONF, 1973; *Noel et Juliette*, dir. Michel Bouchard, ACPAV, 1973; *Comédienne, Jamais deux sans toi*, Radio-Canada, 1977-80, 1990-92; Comédienne, *Passage nuageux*, Radio-Canada, 1984; Tilly, Café de la Place, *Les Trompettes de la Mort*, 1992; Comédienne, *SCOOP III*, télévision, 1993; *L'Homme Laid*, Brad Fraser, Théâtre de Quat'Sous, 1993; Comédienne, *Triplex*, TQS, 1994; Comédienne, *Les Hérities Duval*, Radio-Canada, 1994; Comédienne, *SCOOP IV*, 1994; *Oleanna*, David Mamet, Théâtre de Quat'Sous, 1994; various animated films, incl. *Genèse*, ONF (1968); *Tiki-Tiki*, Potterton Productions (1969-70); *The Selfish Giant*, Potterton Productions (1971); *A Token Gesture*, ONF (1976); *Raggedy Ann and Andy*, ITT & Dick Williams (1977); roles in various films, incl. *Les corps célestes* (1973); *The Apprenticeship of Duddy Kravitz* (1974); *Ti-Cul Tougas* (1976); *Blood 'n' Guts* (1977); *Mourir à tue-tête* (1978); *Fun with Dick and Jane*, Columbia Pictures (1978); *Someone is killing the great chefs of Europe*, Lorimar (1979); *L'affaire Coffin* (1979); dir., *L'homme à tout faire*, Corporation Image (1980); dir., *Sonatine*, Corporation Image/Ciné II (1983); dir., *La poursuite de bonheur*, ONF (1987); dir., *Onzième spéciale* (1989); dir., *Deux Actrices* (1993); dir., *La Vie d'un Héros* (1994). SELECTED PUBLICATIONS: various illustrations for magazines & books, incl. Louis-

Philippe Hébert, *Le Petit Catechisme* (Montréal: l'Hexagone, 1971); *Le Roi Jaune* (Montréal: Éditions du Jour, 1972); *Le Cinéma de Petite-Rivière* (Montréal: Éditions du Jour, 1974); *Textes extraits de vanille* (Montréal: Éditions de l'Aurore, 1974); *Textes d'accompagnement* (Montréal: Éditions de l'Aurore, 1976); various novels, incl. *Armand Dorion, Homme à tout faire* (Éditions Beauchemin, 1980); *Garage Meo/Mina* (Éditions Inédit, 1981); *Les circonstances tragiques de sa mort* (Éditions de Quinze, 1986); *La Calepin* (Revue Ciné-Bulles, 1986); *La tentation du réalisme* (Éditions XYZ, 1993); numerous articles, *Lumières*, 1989-91. AFFIL: UDA; SACD-Québec (VP); ARRFQ (Pres. 1980-82); Cinémathèque Québécoise; SARDEQ; Fiducie Foncière Mont-Pinacle. HONS: Prix d'excellence pour l'ensemble d'oeuvre, Palmarès du film canadien, 1981. COMMENT: *"Have been working in films for almost 30 years, as film-animator, actress, writer, director and producer. Maintaining work in that field will be an achievement in itself in future years."*

Lande, Mildred Queene Bronfman, B.A., LL.D.,C.M. ✆ ○ ✉
President, JEWISH COMMUNITY FOUNDATION OF GREATER MONTREAL (514) 481-7897. Born 1913. m. Bernard Lande. 4 ch. EDUC: McGill Univ., B.A. 1936. VOLUNTEER CAREER: Gov. Emeritus, Concordia Univ.; Gov., Children's Hospital, Montreal; Gov. & Trustee, YM-YWHA; Officers' Bd., Exec. & Trustee, Allied Jewish Community Svcs; Exec. & Chair of Benefactors & Mothers in Israel, Youth Aliyah Hadassah-Wizo; Exec. & Sponsor Chair, Women's Div., Israel Bond Organization; Hon. Pres., Women's Auxiliary & Trustee, Jewish General Hospital; Pres., Shaar Hashomayim Synagogue; Gen. Chair, Combined Jewish Appeal & Israel Emergency Fund; Pres., Jewish Community Foundation; Chair, 150th Anniversary of Cong. Shaar Hashomayim. AFFIL: Elm Ridge Golf & Country Club; Association des Amis du Musée National Message biblique Marc Chagall; Holocaust Committee; Ben-Gurion Univ.; Bar-Ilan Univ.; Hebrew Univ. & Scholarship Endowment Fund; McGill Alumni Association; Museum of Modern Art, N.Y.C.; National Gallery, Ottawa; Art Auction Committee. HONS: Samuel Bronfman Medal for Meritorious Service, 1978; Medal, Jewish Theological Seminary of America, 1978; Citation as Woman of Achievement, Shaar Hashomayim Sisterhood & Women's League for Conservative Judaism, 1978; Member of Order of Canada, 1981; Eleanor Roosevelt Centennial Award, Israel Bond Organization, 1984; Endowment Achievement Award, Coun-

cil of Jewish Federations & Welfare Funds, 1986; LL.D.(Hon.), Concordia Univ., 1990. MISC: Chrm, Benefit Concert of Israel Philharmonic on behalf of Israel Emergency Fund after the '53 war.

Landolt, Gwendolyn C., LL.B. ✆ ⚖
National Vice-President, REAL WOMEN OF CANADA, Box 8813, Stn T, Ottawa, ON K1G 3J1 (819) 682-3937, FAX 682-3938. Born Rossland, B.C. m. 5 ch. Lydia, Phillip, Monica, Christian, Mark. EDUC: Univ. of British Columbia, LL.B. 1958. BAR: B.C., 1959. CAREER: gen. law practice, Vancouver, 1958-60; various positions, specializing in Citizenship & Immigration, & Native Affairs, Gov't of Canada, 1960-64; Legal Consultant for various voluntary organizations & private practice, 1964 to date; Founder & Pres., Right to Life Association of Toronto, 1971-75; VP, National Alliance for Life, 1973-75; Pres., 1975-78; Founder, York South Right to Life, 1974; Founder, Bd. Mbr. & Consultant, Campaign Life Canada, 1978-87; Bd. of Dir., Chair of Legislation Committee, Toronto Catholic Children's Aid, 1980-91; Founding Mbr., former Nat'l Sec., Canadian Advocates for Human Life, 1982; Founding Mbr., Ontario Chapter, Advocates for Human Life, 1982; Founding Mbr., currently VP, REAL Women of Canada, 1983 to date; Founder/Founding Mbr., Caucus on Stable Communities (to bring global involvement at U.N. on family issues), 1996 to date. SELECTED PUBLICATIONS: contributor, *Death Before Birth*, eds. Synan & Kremer (Griffiths Publishing Co., 1974); contributor, *Women Who Do and Women Who Don't Join the Women's Movement*, ed. Robyn Roland (London, UK: Routledge Kegan, 1984); numerous briefs, magazine & newspaper articles, with special emphasis on constitutional issues, & women & family issues. AFFIL: REAL Women of Canada; Caucus for Stable Communities; Canadian Advocates for Human Life; Toronto Right to Life; York South Right to Life. MISC: Delegate to the UN Conference on Population & Dev., Cairo, 1994; delegate to the 4th World Conference on Women in Beijing, 1995; UN Habitat II NGO Forum '96 Conference, Istanbul; NGO Delegate to the UN World Food Summit, Rome, Sept. 1996; guest speaker/commentator on radio & TV, Canada & abroad. COMMENT: *"I have founded and worked for several organizations on the political/education level to encourage and promote dignity and respect for all members of the human family and for the encouragement of traditional family life."*

Landsberg, Michele, B.A. ✏ ▢ ✆ ✉
Columnist, THE TORONTO STAR, 1 Yonge St.,

Toronto, ON M5E 1E6 (416) 869-4387. Born Toronto 1939. m. Stephen Lewis. 3 ch. EDUC: Univ. of Toronto, B.A.(English Language & Lit.) 1962. CAREER: reporter, *The Globe & Mail*, 1962-65; freelance writer for various publications incl. CBC & *Reader's Digest*, 1965-72; Ed., *Chatelaine*, 1972-78; Daily Columnist, *The Toronto Star*, 1978-83; Columnist, N.Y., *The Globe and Mail*, 1985-88; Columnist, *The Toronto Star*, 1990 to date. SELECTED PUBLICATIONS: *Women and Children First* (Macmillan, 1982, Penguin, 1983); *Michele Landsberg's Guide to Children's Books* (Penguin, 1986), published in the US as *Reading for the Love of It* (Prentice-Hall, 1987), published in the UK as *The World of Children's Books* (Simon & Schuster, 1987); *"This is New York, Honey!" A Homage to Manhattan with Love and Rage* (McClelland and Stewart, 1989). AFFIL: CARAL (Bd.); Opportunity for Advancement (Bd.); Lanark Interval House (Bd.); Women's Global Issues Directory (Bd.); PEN Canada (former Exec.); New Israel Fund; Peace Now; National Film Board (Women's Advisory Committee); Committee for '94 (Founding Mbr.); Judicial Appointments Advisory Committee (1989-90); United Appeal (New Admissions Committee, 1985). HONS: President's Medal for Journalism, Univ. of Western Ontario, 1972; winner, first National Newspaper Award for column-writing, 1980; winner, Feature Writing, National Newspaper Award, 1981; YWCA Women of Distinction Award, 1983; Robertine Barry Prize, Canadian Research Institute for the Advancement of Women, 1986; Special Achievement/Women in Media, Canadian Association of Journalists, 1990; Dodi Robb Award, MediaWatch, 1991; honorary degrees from Brock Univ., Acadia Univ. & Mount St. Vincent Univ. MISC: founder of the Feminist Succah-by-The-Water celebration, attended by 500 Jewish women annually; helped to organize the first multi-racial anti-apartheid committee in Toronto. COMMENT: *"I'm an activist for social justice, race and gender equality, peace and pluralism. I'm also a proud mother, devoted wife, reader, recent gardener, lifelong feminist."*

Lane, Elizabeth A., C.M.,B.A.,LL.D. 🌐 ⊗ ⭘
Treasurer, BRITISH COLUMBIA ARTS IN EDUCATION COUNCIL, Vancouver, BC. Born Vancouver 1928. m. William T. Lane. 2 ch. EDUC: Univ. of British Columbia, B.A.(Chem.) 1949. CAREER: Research Chemist, National Research Council of Canada, Royal Sch. of Mines, London, UK, & B.C. Research Council, Vancouver, 1949-56. VOLUNTEER CAREER: Pres., Community Arts Council of Vancouver, 1964-65; Pres., Vancouver Museums & Planetarium

Association, 1968-70; Convocation Mbr., Senate of the Univ. of British Columbia, 1969-78; mbr., Canada Council, 1970-73; First Chair, B.C. Arts Bd., 1974-78; Pres., Canadian Conference of the Arts, 1976-78; mbr., Fed. Cultural Policy Review Committee, 1980-82; Chair, Leon & Thea Koerner Foundation, 1981-86; Chair, 1986 World Conference on Arts, Politics & Bus. Society, 1985-87; Hon. Mbr. of the Bd., Leon & Thea Koerner Foundation; Treas., B.C. Arts in Education Council. AFFIL: B.C. Reg'l Council of the Canadian Music Centre. HONS: Member of the Order of Canada, 1979; Elsje Armstrong Outstanding Sustainer Award, Junior League of Vancouver, 1985; Canada 125 Medal; LL.D.(Hon.), Simon Fraser Univ., 1977. INTERESTS: furthering dev. of, & support for, arts & culture activities in Canada. COMMENT: *"My activities have been aimed at increasing community awareness of the importance of arts and cultural activities in Canada, and developing support for them."*

Lane, Patricia A., B.A.,M.A., Ph.D. 🍃 ⚘
President, LANE ENVIRONMENT LIMITED, 1663 Oxford St., Halifax, NS B3M 3Z5 (902) 423-8197, FAX 429-8089. Professor, Department of Biology, DALHOUSIE UNIVERSITY, Halifax, NS. Born Waterloo, N.Y. 1945. d. 4 ch. Kathryn, Suzanne, Jessica, David. EDUC: Hartwick Coll., NY, B.A.(Biol.) 1964; State Univ. of New York at Binghamton, M.A.(Biol.) 1966; State Univ. of New York at Albany, Ph.D.(Ecology) 1971; Ecological Society of America, Sr. Ecologist Certification 1985. CAREER: Post-doctoral Ford Fellow, Dept. of Biol., Univ. of Chicago, 1971-73; Research Assoc., W.K. Kellog Biological Station, Michigan State Univ., 1972-73; Asst. Prof., Summer 1973; Asst. Prof., Dept. of Biol., Dalhousie Univ., 1973-78; Adjunct Asst. Prof., W.K. Kellog Biological Station, Michigan State Univ., 1974-78; Assoc. Prof., Dept. of Biol., Dalhousie Univ., 1978-84; Visiting Assoc. Prof., Dept. of Population Sciences, Harvard Sch. of Public Health, Harvard Univ., 1980-82; Visiting Lecturer, 1982-96; Visiting Assoc. Prof., Grad. Sch. of Oceanography, Univ. of Rhode Island, 1982-84; Visiting Prof., 1984; Pres., P. Lane and Associates Limited, Halifax, 1983-93; Prof., Dept. of Biol., Dalhousie Univ., 1984 to date; Prof., Sch. of Resource & Environmental Studies, Dalhousie Univ., 1986 to date; Chair of Senate, 1987-92, Bd. of Governors, 1989-95, Dalhousie Univ.; Pres., Lane Environment Limited, Halifax, 1993 to date. SELECTED PUBLICATIONS: "A Winter-Spring Study of the Phytoplankton of Two New York Ponds" (*Journal of the Elisha Mitchell Science Society* 1969);

"The Evolutionary Strategy of Mimicry" (*American Biology Teacher* 1977); "Fish Versus Zooplankton Predation in Lakes" (*Nature* 1981); "Symmetry, Change, Perturbation and Observing Mode in Natural Communities" (*Ecology* 1986); "Phytoplankton Species and Abundance in Response to Eutrophication in Coastal Marine Mesocosm," with C. Oviatt, F. French III & P. Donaghay (*Journal of Plankton Research* 1989); numerous other publications. AFFIL: American Naturalists' Society; American Society of Limnology & Oceanography; Ecological Society of America; International Association of Theoretical & Applied Limnology; Rawson Academy of Aquatic Science (Dir. 1988-92); Society of Canadian Zoologists; Sch. of Resource & Environmental Studies, Dalhousie Univ. (Advisory Bd.); Superior Institute of Nuclear Science & Technology, Havana, Cuba (Hon. Mbr. & Prof. of the Environment 1994 to date); Dalhousie Women's Fac. Organization; Dalhousie Fac. Association; Canadian Association of University Teachers; Cuban Environment Agency (Advisory Bd.). HONS: named 1 of Top 10 Outstanding Campus Achievers, *Campus Canada*, 1985; Certificate of Merit, Professional Category, N.S. Environmental Awards, 1990; Woman of Distinction Award, Entrepreneur-Innovator Category, Halifax Cornwallis Progress Club, 1991. MISC: listed in numerous biographical sources, incl. *Canadian Who's Who*, *Who's Who in American Men and Women of Science*, *The World Who's Who of Women*, *Who's Who in Science and Engineering* & *Making a World of Difference: A Directory of Women in Canada Specializing in Global Issues*; recipient, numerous grants & fellowships; reviewer, various journals, granting agencies; numerous consultancies; frequent guest speaker; numerous conference presentations; Invited Mbr., Panel of Experts for the Bangladesh Flood Action Plan, World Bank, 1991-95. COMMENT: *"Dr. Lane is an internationally recognized environmental scientist and business woman. She is presently encouraging a major sustainable development effort in Cuba."*

Lang, Jessie, B.A.,B.S.W. ■ ■ O
Volunteer. Winnipeg, MB R3P 0R3. Born Calgary 1916. w. 1 ch. Signy Hansen (lost daughter to M.S. in 1993). EDUC: Univ. of Manitoba, B.A.(Math.) 1937, B.S.W.(Social Work) 1963. CAREER: Monarch Life Insurance Company, 1937-40; Child Guidance Clinic, 1964-70. AFFIL: Health Sciences Centre Foundation; St. Charles Country Club; Winnipeg Art Gallery (study group); The "20" Club. HONS: Nancy M. Perkins Award, Multiple Sclerosis Society of Canada, 1992; Distin-

guished Svc. Award, Univ. of Manitoba, 1982; honoured in National Volunteer Week by Free Press, 1994; twice nominated for Woman of the Year Award in volunteer svc. INTERESTS: art; golf; bridge. COMMENT: *"Have been involved in the advancement of health and education in Manitoba for over 50 years. Served two terms as representative of graduates on the University of Manitoba Board of Governors; 9 years on Health Sciences Centre Board, serving as Chairman in 1979-80. Was a Director of Manitoba Cancer Treatment & Research Foundation. Since 1980, involved with the Multiple Sclerosis Society of Canada."*

lang, k.d. (Katherine Dawn) · ♥ ⊗ ⊕
Singer & Composer. Born Consort, Alta. 1961. EDUC: Red Deer Coll. CAREER: singer, composer & Co-founder, *The Reclines*; has perfomed throughout Canada, US & Europe; numerous TV appearance. SELECTED CREDITS: *A Truly Western Experience*, 1984; *Angel with a Lariat*, 1986; *Shadowland*, prod. Owen Bradley, 1988; *Absolute Torch & Twang*, 1990; *Ingenue*, 1992; *All You Can Eat*, 1996; actor, *Salmonberries*, 1991. HONS: Best Country Singer, Juno Awards, 1987; Woman of the Year, *Chatelaine* Magazine, 1988; Entertainer of the Year, Canadian Country Music Awards, 1989; Album of the Year (*Absolute Torch and Twang*), Canadian Country Music Awards, 1990; Grammy Award, 1990.

Langevin, Suzanne, B.Tech. ■ ⊗
Photographer, SUZANNE LANGEVIN PHOTOGRAPHE, 5149 rue Marquette, Ste. 38, Montreal, QC H2J 3Z4 (514) 528-5046, FAX 528-6312. Born Montreal 1955. s. EDUC: Ryerson Polytechnical Institute, B.Tech.(Photo Arts) 1977. CAREER: freelance photographer. SELECTED PUBLICATIONS: photographs in numerous Cdn & US magazines. AFFIL: Advertising & Design Club of Canada. HONS: Gold Medal for Magazine Cover, National Magazine Awards, 1993; Gold Medal for Portrait, National Magazine Awards, 1994. COMMENT: *"Spent eight years in Los Angeles upon graduation. Returned to Montreal in 1986; now sharing time between Toronto and Montreal and wherever my work takes me."*

Langley, Elizabeth ⊗ ⊗
Professor, CONCORDIA UNIVERSITY, 7141 Sherbrooke St. W., Montréal, QC H4B 1R6 (514) 848-4740, FAX 848-4525. Born Melbourne, Australia 1933. d. 1 ch. CAREER: Modern Ballet Company, Australia, 1953-60; Martha Graham Sch. of Contemporary Dance, N.Y., 1960-65; Ottawa Univ. & Carleton Univ., 1965-78; Assoc. Prof., Concordia Univ., 1978-95; Prof.,

1995 to date. **AFFIL:** Dance in Canada Association; Society of Dance Research, London, UK; Society of Dance History Scholars, US; Danse Québec Dance; Association of Dance in University & Colleges in Canada. **HONS:** Award for Teaching Excellence, Concordia Univ. Students' Association, 1989. **INTERESTS:** reading; travel; history; present world political climates & developments. **MISC:** recipient, various grants. **COMMENT:** *"I value most my love of learning and teaching driven by my curiosity, energy and desire to sense progress and evolution. I have, with humour, tried to achieve whatever professional goals I have set for myself."*

Langlois, Lisa 🦋 🗡 🗋

Actor, Singer, Producer and Writer. c/o Maplewood Productions Inc., 1223 Wilshire Blvd., Ste. 242, Santa Monica, CA 90403-5400 (213) 960-5544. Born North Bay, Ont. m. Robert Ulrich. **EDUC:** Hamilton Collegiate Institute, Grade 13 1977; McMaster Univ., B.A.(French) ongoing. **CAREER:** actor, singer, producer, writer. **SELECTED CREDITS:** Actor, *Blood Relatives* (feature), dir. Claude Chabrol; Actor, *Violette Noziere* (feature), dir. Claude Chabrol; Actor, *Phobia* (feature), dir. John Huston; Actor, *The Slugger's Wife*, dir. Hal Ashby; Actor, *Class of 1984* (feature), dir. Mark Lester; Actor, *National Lampoon's Joy of Sex*, dir. Martha Coolidge; Guest Star, *Murder She Wrote* (series), CBS; Principal, *Doing Life* (telefilm), dir. Gene Reynolds; Actor, *Once in a Lifetime* (theatre), La Jolla Playhouse. **AFFIL:** Academy of Canadian Cinema & Television (Dir., LA Chapter 1992-94). **INTERESTS:** integrity; honesty; humour; health. **MISC:** 1 of 12 invited to participate in ABC-TV's talent dev. program, 1983.

LaPier, Sharon ■■ ⊘

Figure Skating Judge and Referee. Born Sarnia, Ont. w. 2 ch. Karolyn, Marianne. **EDUC:** Hallmark Business Institute, Detroit, Data Processing. **CAREER:** Customs Inspector, Bluewater Bridge, Sarnia, Ont.; in that role, was co-creator of programme to teach children in schools about drug use. **AFFIL:** Skate Ontario (Bd. mbr.); Canadian Figure Skating Association (mbr. of Bd.; Chrm, W. Ont. Section); Moore Figure Skating Club (former Pres.; former Chrm, various committees; hon. life mbr.); Moore Union Cemetery (former Dir.); Knox Moore Church (former mbr., Bd. of Mgrs; Co-Convenor, Christian Educ. Committee). **HONS:** honoured by Optimist Club of Moore for svc. to the community for public speaking to children about drugs; Canada 125 Medal for volunteer work with youth; community volunteer medal.

Larbi, Madonna O. ■■ ○ ⊛

Executive Director, **MATCH** INTERNATIONAL CENTRE (int'l dev. organization), 200 Elgin St., Ste. 1102, Ottawa, ON K2P 1L5 (613) 238-1312, FAX 238-6867. Born Ghana, W. Africa 1953. d. 1 ch. Kwesi Nketsia. **EDUC:** Ghana Institute of Journalism, Dip.(Journalism) 1974; Human Rights Summer Coll., Human Rights Research & Educ. Centre, Univ. of Ottawa, 1989; ongoing mgmt & dev. training. **CAREER:** Administrative & Liaison Consultant, U.N. Fund for Population Activities, Basic Needs Assessment, Team to Ghana, & Public Affairs Consultant, World Bank Office, Accra, Ghana, 1980-81; Communications Team Asst., Amnesty International, Ottawa, 1988-90; Exec. Dir., National Organization of Immigrant & Visible Minority Women of Canada, 1990-91; Programme Officer, English-speaking Africa & Asia, MATCH International Centre, 1991-92; Exec. Dir., 1992 to date. **AFFIL:** North-South Institute, Ottawa (Nat'l Bd. mbr. 1996 to date); YWCA of Canada (Nat'l Bd. mbr. 1994-96); SOS Children's Villages Canada (Nat'l Bd. mbr. 1993 to date); UNESCO (mbr., Status of Women Committee 1993 to date); MediaWatch (Nat'l Bd. mbr. 1992-94). **MISC:** numerous speeches, public presentations & int'l assignments; participation in int'l workshops & conferences.

Larlee, Hon. Madame Justice Margaret, B.A.,LL.B. ⚖

Judge, COURT OF QUEEN'S BENCH OF NEW BRUNSWICK, Trial Division, Justice Bldg, Box 6000, Fredericton, NB E3B 5H1 (506) 453-2952. Born Harvey Station, N.B. 1949. m. John D Larlee. 3 ch. **EDUC:** Mount Allison Univ., B.A. 1971; Univ. of New Brunswick Law Sch., LL.B. 1974. **BAR:** N.B., 1974. **CAREER:** Solicitor, N.B. Dept. of Justice, Law Reform Div., 1974-76; Lawyer, Dykeman and Delaney, Barristers & Solicitors, 1976; private practice, Larlee and Larlee, Campbellton, 1976-79; Acting Clerk of the County & Supreme Courts, 1977-79; Acting Judge of Probate, 1977; Clerk of the Court of Queen's Bench of N.B. Judicial District of Campbellton, 1979; Judge & Registrar of Probate for the County of Restigouche, 1979-84; appointed Admin. of the Family Div. Court of Queen's Bench, Judicial District of Campbell, 1983; Clerk of the Youth Court, Campbellton, 1984; Clerk of Probate Court, Campbellton, 1984; resigned as Clerk of the Court, July 1985; private practice with John D. Larlee, 1985; Judge, Court of Queen's Bench of N.B., Family Div., Campbellton, 1985-91; Judge, Court of Queen's Bench, Trial & Family Divisions, Campbellton, 1991-95; Judge, Court of Queen's Bench, Trial Div., Fredericton, 1995 to date. **AFFIL:** Christ Church Cathedral; Canadian Business & Professional Women's Club. **HONS:** Sharp Scholarship, 1971; Leonard Foundation Scholarship, 1974. **INTERESTS:** cross-country skiing; downhill skiing; piano. **MISC:** co-chaired with Mr. Michel Bastarache, CIAJ Conference, Work Employment, Justice, St. Andrew's, Oct. 1991.

Larochelle, Bernadette, B.A., M.Ed. ■■ Ⓢ 🐿 ▯

Directrice générale, CENTRE FRANCO-ONTARIEN DE RESSOURCES PÉDAGOGIQUES (non-profit organization, publisher & bookstore), Vanier, ON K1L 1A2 (613) 747-8000, ext. 251, FAX 747-2808. Born Mattice, Ont. 1939. s. **EDUC:** Univ. of Ottawa, B.A. 1971, M.Ed.(Counselling) 1973. **CAREER:** Teacher, 1961-74; Educ. Officer, 1974-86; Dir. Gen., CFORP, 1986 to date. **SELECTED PUBLICATIONS:** *Reflets d'un pays; Écrire avec la lumière*. **AFFIL:** Association des agents et agentes de supervision franco-ontariens (Dir.); Association des enseignantes et enseignants franco-ontariens; Association canadienne d'éducation de langue française; Association des auteurs de l'Ontario. **INTERESTS:** reading; gardening; arts & crafts; photography. **COMMENT:** *"Since 1986, director of the CFORP, a non-profit organization that publishes and sells French-language learning material throughout Canada. Staff of 40, annual budget of $4,500,000."*

La Rocque, Cheryl, B.A. ■ ✎ ⊕

Freelance Health Columnist, CAPE BRETON POST, 1913 Horison Dr., Kelowna, BC V1Z 3L3, FAX (604) 769-3619. Born Lac Mégantic 1959. m. Peter Kapyrka. 2 ch. **EDUC:** Vanier Coll., nursing studies 1976-78; Champlain Coll., Diploma (Social Studies) 1979; Bishop's Univ., B.A. 1982; Trent Univ., anthro. 1983-84. **CAREER:** Library Asst., Mount Saint Vincent University, 1984-85; Admin. Asst. & Sec., Robin Hood Multifoods Inc., 1987; Automation Intern, Barrie Public Library, Barrie, Ont., 1989; Chiropractic Asst., Barrie, Ont., 1989-90; freelance Health Columnist, *Cape Breton Post*, 1991 to date, *The Daily Courier*, Kelowna, B.C., 1996 to date. **SELECTED PUBLICATIONS:** columns & articles in various newspapers, incl. *Prince Albert Daily Herald, Sask. and Western Star*, Nfld., *The Canadian Chiropractic Association Newsletter*, 1996 to date. **HONS:** Award for Academic Standing, Grey Trust Company Bursary Fund; Award for Academic Standing, Beaver Food Service. **INTERESTS:** reading; yoga; walking; travelling. **COMMENT:** *"I am passionate in my beliefs. My goal is to promote accurate, readable and accessible health information. I feel that my enthusiastic attitude and outgoing nature prepare me for the challenges that life has to offer."*

LaRocque, Judith Anne, B.A.,M.A. ♣

Secretary to the Governor-General and Herald Chancellor, GOVERNMENT HOUSE, Ottawa, ON K1A 0A1 (613) 993-8200, FAX 993-1967. Born Hawkesbury, Ont. 1956. m. André Roland Lavoie. **EDUC:** Carleton Univ., B.A.(Pol. Sci.) 1979, M.A.(Public Admin.) 1992. **CAREER:** Procedural Officer & Committee Clerk, Committees Branch, House of Commons, 1982-86; Head of House Bus. & Legislative Asst. to Gov't House Leader, Pres. of the Queen's Privy Council for Canada, Min. Responsible for Regulatory Affairs, 1984-85; Exec. Asst. to the Min. of Justice & Attorney-Gen. of Canada, 1986-89; Chief of Staff to the Min. of State for Fed.-Prov. Rel'ns & the Leader of the Gov't in the Senate, 1989-90; Sec. to the Gov.-Gen. & Herald Chancellor for Canada. **HONS:** Commander, Royal Victorian Order; Officer, Order of Saint John of Jerusalem, Canada 125 Medal.

Larsen, Christine ■■ Ⓠ

Olympic Athlete. c/o Canadian Olympic Association. Born New Westminster, B.C. 1967. **EDUC:** currently part-time student. **SPORTS CAREER:** started in synchro at age 11; mbr., Cdn Nat'l Synchronized Swimming Team, 1986 to date (except 1993 & 1994). Olympic Games: Silver, team, 1996. World championships: 2nd, team, 1991. World Cup: 2nd, team, 1995; 2nd, team, & 3rd, duet, 1991. Commonwealth Games: 1st, duet, 1990. Canadian championships: 1st, team, & 5th, solo, 1995; 1st, duet, & 3rd, solo, 1991. **AFFIL:** Handicap Association (volunteer). **INTERESTS:** ocean swimming. **MISC:** aquatics leader.

Larue, Monique, B.A.,M.A.,Ph.D. 📗 ⊗ ▯

Écrivaine. 545 Rockland, Outremont, QC H2V 2Z4. **EDUC:** Coll. Marie-de-France, Baccalauréat (Enseignement secondaire) 1967; Univ. de Montréal, Baccalauréat (Phil.) 1970; Univ. de Paris, Maîtrise (Phil.) 1971, Doctorat de troisième cycle (Litt.) 1976. **CAREER:** collaboration régulière, *Littérature actuelle*, Radio-Canada FM, 1991-92, 1993-94; membre régulier du comité littéraires des Éditions du Boréal, 1993 to date. **SELECTED CREDITS:** *L'Enregistrement*, oeuvre radiophonique, Radio-Canada, 1984. **SELECTED PUBLICATIONS:** "Sur l'héroïne stéréotypée de la littérature enfantine" (*Le Devoir*, 10 May 1975); *La Cohorte fictive* (Montréal: Éditions de l'Etincelle, 1979); "Celles qui parlent" (*Spirales* May 1980); *Les Faux Fuyants* (Montréal:

Québec-Amérique, 1982); *Copies conformes* (Paris: Denoël, 1989); *Promenades littéraires dans Montréal* (Montréal: Québec-Amérique, 1989); *La démarche du crabe* (Éditions du Boréal, 1995). EDIT: ed. committee, *Spirale*, 1981-83; ed. committee, *Possibles*, 1989-90. HONS: Premier Prix (*L'Enregistrement*), Concours d'oeuvres dramatiques radiophoniques, Radio-Canada, 1984; Grand Prix du Livre de Montréal (*Copies conformes*), 1990; Grand Prix Littéraire du *Journal de Montréal*, 1995. MISC: invited speaker, numerous conferences; recipient, numerous grants; Comité Consultatif du Service des Lettres et de l'Édition du Conseil des Arts du Canada, 1986-89; participant, numerous award juries.

Latchford, Sandra, B.A.,M.Ed. ⚲
Associate Professor/Director of Learning Centre, Faculty of Education, UNIVERSITY OF NEW BRUNSWICK, Fredericton, NB E3B 6E3 (506) 453-3515, FAX 453-4765. Born Picton, Ont. 1949. m. Leslie Latchford. EDUC: Univ. of Guelph, B.A.(Child Psych.) 1972; Univ. of New Brunswick, M.Ed.(Learning Disabilities) 1980; Univ. of Groningen, The Netherlands, Ph.D.(Psych.) in progress. CAREER: Research Asst., Centre for Learning Disabilities, Univ. of Guelph, 1970-75; Learning Disabilities Consultant, Reg'l Mental Health Clinic, Moncton, N.B., 1975-76; Remedial Reading Consultant, Bd. of Sch. Trustees, Moncton, 1976-78; Special Educ. Teacher, Bd. of Sch. Trustees, Saint John, N.B., 1978-79; Psychometrist, 1980-84; Coord., Learning Centre, Fac. of Educ., Univ. of New Brunswick, 1984-92; Asst. Prof., Fac. of Educ., 1987-91; Assoc. Prof., 1991 to date; Dir., Learning Centre, Univ. of New Brunswick, 1992 to date; freelance Educational Consultant. SELECTED PUBLICATIONS: *An Open-Ended Research Database for Learning Centre Activity*, with D.J. van Eden, J.M. Fritz (1991); *Enhancing Accessibility: A Resource Guide* co-ed. (Dept. of Advanced Educ. & Labour, N.B., 1992); "Locus of Control and Teachers: A Preliminary Report of an Investigation of Locus of Control in Pre-Service Teachers," with Prof. M. Cashion & Dr. K. Radford (*Teacher Educator* Summer 1993). AFFIL: Fredericton Community Literacy Committee; Training Svcs for Persons with Disabilities (Program Advisory Committee); Premier's Council on the Status of Disabled Persons (Chairperson 1993-96); Council for Educational Diagnostic Services (Pres. 1994-96); Corrections Services Canada (Nat'l Advisory Committee on Learning Disabilities); National Access Awareness Week (Treas., Prov. Bd. of Dir. 1993-95); N.B. Special Education Subject Council (Hon. Life Mbr.). HONS: N.B. Award for Outstanding Personal & Professional Service to Disabled Persons, National Access Awareness Week. INTERESTS: hiking; baking; camping. COMMENT: *"I believe and act on the principle that all people, regardless of their mental or physical abilities, age, sex, religion, or culture, have the right to fair treatment."*

Latimer, Elizabeth Joan, B.Sc.N.,M.D., C.C.F.P.,F.C.F.P. ⊕
Palliative Care Physician. Professor and Administrator, HENDERSON GENERAL HOSPITAL, 711 Concession St. E., Hamilton, ON L8V 1C3 (905) 389-4411, ext. 2213. Born Hamilton, Ont. 1945. m. Willem Kamphorst. EDUC: McMaster Univ., B.Sc.N. 1967, M.D. 1979. CAREER: Public Health Nurse, Dept. of Public Health, Hamilton, 1967-68; Head Nurse, Surgical Unit, Mt. Sinai Hospital, Toronto, 1968-71; Nurse Practitioner, Dept. of Family Practice, McMaster Univ. Medical Centre, 1972-76; Lecturer, Dept. of Family Medicine, McMaster Univ., 1974-76; Chief Resident, Family Practice Program, 1980-81; Clinical Scholar, Dept. of Family Medicine, 1981-82; Dir., Palliative Care Program, Hamilton Civic Hospitals, 1982 to date; Asst. Prof., Dept. of Family Medicine, McMaster Univ., 1982-89; Assoc. Prof., Dept. of Family Medicine, 1989-95; Dir., Reg'l Palliative Care Program, Hamilton-Wentworth, 1984-96; Prof., Dept. of Family Medicine, 1995 to date. SELECTED PUBLICATIONS: "The Pain of Cancer: Helping Patients & Families" (*Humane Medicine* 1990); "Caring for Seriously Ill and Dying Patients: The Philosophy and Ethics" (*Canadian Medical Association Journal* 1991); "Caring for the Dying in Canada" (*Canadian Family Physician* 1995); numerous other refereed & nonrefereed articles, reviews, book chapters & letters to the editor. AFFIL: Coll. of Family Physicians of Canada; Ontario Coll. of Family Physicians; Ontario Coll. of Physicians & Surgeons; Ontario Medical Association; Medical Council of Canada; Hamilton Academy of Medicine; Ontario Palliative Care Association; International Working Group on Death, Dying & Bereavement; Canadian Bioethics Society; Society of Palliative Care Physicians of Canada. MISC: numerous invited presentations; recipient, numerous grants & awards; listed in *Canadian Who's Who*.

Latini, Sandra ⊗ /
Art Director, TORONTO LIFE MAGAZINE, 59 Front St. E., 3rd Fl., Toronto, ON M5E 1B3 (416) 364-3333, FAX 861-1169. Born Toronto 1960. m. Lewis Baios. 1 ch. Alexander A. Baios. EDUC: Sheridan Coll., Dipl.(Graphic Design) 1981. CAREER: Assoc. Art Dir.,

Toronto Life Magazine, 1990-92; Art Dir., 1992 to date. **AFFIL**: Art Directors' Club. **HONS**: several Art Dir. & magazine awards over the past yrs. **INTERESTS**: travelling (esp. N.Y. & Paris); visiting galleries; music; theatre; skiing; tennis. **COMMENT**: *"With the recent birth of my son Alexander, I've been inspired to take life on with a whole new direction–including designing the magazine."*

Lau, Catherine, B.Sc.,M.Sc.,Ph.D. ⊕ ❀ ♣

Director, Clinical Research, JANSSEN-ORTHO INC., 19 Green Belt Dr., Don Mills, ON M3C 1L9 (416) 442-1500, ext. 2427, FAX 449-7818. Born Hong Kong 1951. m. Sek Lun Yuen. 2 ch. Harold Yeun, Heidi Yeun. **EDUC**: Indiana Univ., B.Sc.(Physics) 1972; Yale Univ., M.Sc.(Biochem.) 1974, Ph.D.(Biochem.) 1976. **CAREER**: Mgr, Basic Research, Ortho-McNeil Inc., 1980-89; Dir., Discovery Research, R.W. Johnson Pharmaceutical Research Institute, 1989-95; Dir., Clinical Research, Janssen-Ortho Inc., 1995 to date.

Lauber, Anne, M.Mus.,D.Mus. ⊗ ⩗

Composer, Teacher. 5170 Hutchison, Outremont, QC H2V 4A9 (514) 279-7992, FAX 279-7992. Born Switzerland. m. André. 2 ch. Salomé, Augustin. **EDUC**: Département de l'Agriculture, de l'Industrie et du Commerce Lausanne, Certificat d'employée de commerce 1962; Conservatoire de Musique de Lausanne, Switzerland, Certificate 1965; Univ. of Montreal, M.Mus. 1982, D.Mus. 1986; studied with Serge Garant & André Prévost, Univ. of Montreal; studied conducting with Jacques Clément, Orchestre civique des Jeunes de Montréal. **CAREER**: public rel'ns, Orchestre civique des jeunes de Montreal, 1979-80; Que. area rep., Canadian League of Composers, 1980-82; mbr. of administrative council & VP, Canadian Music Centre, 1982-88; Pres., Quebec Area & mbr. of nat'l admin. council, 1988-92; more than 35 works premiered. **SELECTED CREDITS**: *Cantate 3* (prayer for peace), work bringing together the 3 major monotheistic religions–Judaism, Christianity & Islam (premier Nov. 1996); *Requiem* (1990); *L'Affaire Coffin*, orchestra & soloists (1979); *Violin concerto* (1988); *Jesus Christus: à la mémoire d'un grand homme: Le fils de l'Homme*, orchestra & soloists (1986); *Ouverture Canadienne*, orchestra (1989); *Cantate*, guitar & string quartet (1992); numerous other compositions; research & scripts, *Pour le clavier*, Radio-Canada (1981); hiring & supervising young musicians, *André Mathieu*, film (1992); music, *Les terribles vivantes*, Office National du Film, Dorothée Hénault, dir.; collaborator, with Paule Delorme, *Beyond the Sound Barrier*,

music, narration & staging; music for puppet shows, *Les Marionnettes Mérinat* (1976); various other film & stage music credits; several radio broadcasts; recording, *L'Affaire Coffin* (SNE-503); recording, *Fantasy on a known theme* (SNE 568); various other recordings. **SELECTED PUBLICATIONS**: *Sons d'aujourd'hui*, co-author & proj. initiator, teaching kit with tapes & manuals (Ed. Louise Courteau, 1990); *Divertimento for flute and guitar* (Ed. Doberman); *Mouvement pour flûte et piano* (Ed. Doberman); *Arabesque for solo guitar* (Ed. Doberman); *Mouvement pour alto et piano* (CMC); *Intermezzi* (Ed. Lanote). **AFFIL**: Musicians' Guild of Montreal; SOCAN; SODRAC; Canadian Music Centre. **INTERESTS**: literature; cinema. **MISC**: recipient, numerous grants; listed in *International Who's Who in Music*, 10th ed. & *Who's Who in American Music*, 2nd ed.; juror for many grants & competitions; various conference presentations.

Laumann, Silken, B.A. ■■ ⦾

Member, Canadian National Rowing Team. c/o The Landmark Group, 277 Richmond St. W., Toronto, ON M5V 1X1 (416) 593-1991, FAX 593-4984. Born Mississauga, Ont. 1964. m. John Wallace. **EDUC**: Univ. of Victoria, Science/English 1984-86; Univ. of Western Ontario, B.A. 1988. **SPORTS CAREER**: after ending career in competitive running entered competitive rowing, 1982; mbr., Nat'l Team, 1983 to date; 1st place finish, quadruple sculls, U.S. Championships; Gold, singles, Pan American Games; bronze (with sister Danielle), double sculls, Olympics, 1984; back injury nearly ended rowing career - took her out of competition for some time; Gold, single scull, Pan American Games, Indianapolis, 1987; 1st, single scull, Cdn Championship, 1989; 1st, Canadian Henley Regatta (3rd consecutive yr.), 1989; 1st, Cdn Championships, & 2nd, World Championships, 1990; World Cup Series Champion & World Champion, 1991; injury in May 1992 resulted in 5 operations in 10 days - again nearly ended career; went on to win–2 months later–Bronze medal, Olympics, 1992; took a year off to fully recover; placed 1st at first world cup race after returning to competition, 1994; disqualified (after winning semi-final heat) for 2 false starts, World Championships, 1994; Silver Medal, Olympics, 1996. **SELECTED PUBLICATIONS**: *Rowing* (Stoddart Publishing). **AFFIL**: The Clarke Courage to Come Back Campaign (Hon. Chairperson); Nike P.L.A.Y. Program (Spokesperson). **HONS**: Athlete of the Year, Victoria, Mississauga, & Ont., 1990; Canadian Airlines Athlete of the Month, May & Sept. 1991; Ont. Athlete of the Year, Cdn Female Athlete of the Year, & Cdn Athlete of the Year (Lou Marsh Award), 1991; Cdn Female Athlete of the Year, Ont. Athlete of the Year, *Sun*'s Athlete of the Year, & winner, Harry Jerome Comeback Award, 1992; Women Who Make A Difference, 1993; Hon. LL.B., Univ. of Victoria, 1994; Meritorious Service Cross, created by Her Majesty Queen Elizabeth to recognize the performance of an uncommonly high standard that brings great honour to Canada, 1994; street in Mississauga named Silken Laumann Way, 1995; Canadian Olympic Order, 1995. INTERESTS: outdoors; reading & writing; music (piano). MISC: movie made about her life, *Golden Will - The Silken Laumann Story*.

Laurin, Marice C. (née Gagné), B.A., M.Sc.Ed. ■ ☺ ⊕ ៉

National President, ADVOCACY GROUP FOR THE ENVIRONMENTALLY SENSITIVE (AGES), 1887 Chaine Ct., Orleans, ON K1C 2W6 (613) 830-5722, FAX 834-6699. Born Cornwall, Ont. 1940. w. 1 ch. Jean-Marc Laurin. EDUC: Ottawa Univ., Teacher's Certificate 1962, B.A.(Arts) 1974, B.A.(Litt. Français) 1976, Specialist (Special Educ.) 1979; Royal Conservatory of Music, Diploma (Theory II-Singing) 1966; York Univ., Reading Certificate 1981; Niagara Univ., N.Y., M.Sc.Ed.(Admin. & Supervision) 1984. CAREER: music teacher, voice & instrument, 1961-84; Special Educ. Teacher & Consultant, 1962-84; Publisher/Founder, Union Publications, 1972-84; Advocate, Counsellor, Legal Asst., 1970 to date; TV Prod., Cornwall Cable TV, 1973-79; Publisher, *Magazine Revue Le Trait d'Union & Realistic Learning* Magazine; Publisher, *AGES* Magazine, 1985 to date; Pres. & Founder, AGES, 1985 to date; Prod. & reporter, Rogers Cable 23, Ottawa, 1992 to date. SELECTED PUBLICATIONS: *On Roads to Love; For Women by Four Women; Allergies and Environmental Illness*; several prefaces & chapters in books; articles on health; plays in French for Ministry of Health; plays & monologues for seniors. EDIT: Ed., *Magazine Le Trait d'Union*, 1972-79; Ed., *Realistic Learning* Magazine, 1977-78; Ed., *AGES* Magazine, 1985 to date. AFFIL: Association des Allergies et des Maladies Environnementales; Ottawa-Carleton Housing (Dir.); Canadian Authors' Association; Centre Seraphin-Marion. HONS: Volunteer Recognition Award, City of Gloucester, 1991; Best Community Prod., Rogers Television Cable 23, 1993. INTERESTS: music; dance; theatre arts; writing; advocacy for seniors, the disabled & low-income earners. COMMENT: *"An educated and dedicated person to assist those in need. With experience as a missionary, I real-*

ized that those disabled as I am needed assistance in their plea to have their rights respected by a positive and fighter friend who knew their cause."

Lauzon, Jani ⊗ ☙

Musician, Actress and Puppeteer. c/o Ra Records, 1562 Danforth Ave., Box 72087, Toronto, ON M4J 5C1 (416) 462-0294, FAX 462-2857. Born Kimberley, B.C. 1959. s. CAREER: actress; puppeteer; musician; instructor, Claude Watson Sch. for the Arts, 1983-86. SELECTED CREDITS: Patsy, *Diva Ojibway*, Native Earth; Raven, *Whale*, YPT; Emily, *The Rose*, Native Earth; Andromache, *Andromache*, Orange Dog Theatre; Marie, *Conspiracy of Silence*, CBC; Tina, *Destiny Ridge*; Vocalist, Aboriginal Achievement Awards; Singer & Songwriter, Vancouver Folk Festival; Wabanakii Music Festival; Harbourfront Soul & Blues; *Blue Voice, New Voice* (record) (Ra Records, 1994). SELECTED PUBLICATIONS: "The Actor as Master" (*Canadian Theatre Review* Winter 1994). AFFIL: Native Theatre Sch.; Toronto Blues Society; SOCAN; ACTRA; Equity; AFOFM; Advisory Committee for Aboriginal Music Projects & Nightwood Theatre. HONS: nomination, Best Actress, Dora Mavor Moore Award, 1993; nomination, Best Aboriginal Music, Juno Award, 1995. INTERESTS: craft & fashion design; biking; hiking; natural medicine; painting; all things creative. COMMENT: *"I desire to enjoy expression in all things creative as a way of honouring the existence the creator has given me. I love my work on the stage, behind the puppet, in front of the camera. I live to perform, every minute of every day. I am also interested in bridging the native and non-native cultures that I belong to."*

Lavallée, Diane ■ ✦

Sous-ministre adjointe au Loisir et aux Sports, Ministère des Affaires municipales, GOUVERNEMENT DU QUÉBEC, 20, rue Chauveau, aile Cook, 3e etage, Québec, QC G1R 4J4 (418) 691-2096. Born Contrecoeur, Qué. 1956. EDUC: Univ. de Montréal, Certificat (Santé communautaire) 1981, Certificat (Organisation des soins et éduc.) 1983; École supérieure d'Acupuncture, Montréal, Diplôme (Acupuncture) 1986; École nationale d'admin. publique du Québec, Études de maîtrise en admin. publique 1991. CAREER: Infirmière, Hôpital Charles Lemoyne, 1977-78; Infirmière, Hôpital régional de Sion Valais, Suisse, 1978-79; Infirmière, Hôpital Hôtel-Dieu de Montréal, 1979-86; Première VP, La Fédération québécoise des infirmières et infirmiers, 1985-86; Prés., 1986-87; Prés., La Fédération des infirmières et infirmiers du Québec, 1987-93; Candidate du Parti

Québécois (Jean-Talon), élections provinciales, 1993-94; Secrétaire générale associée au Secrétariat à la condition féminine, 1994-96; Sous-ministre adjointe au Loisir et aux Sports, Ministère des Affaires municipales, 1996 à ce jour. **AFFIL:** Parti Québécois (Comité national des orientations politiques de la plate-forme électorale 1993-94; Comité national santé pour la plate-forme santé 1993-94); l'Ordre des infirmières et infirmiers du Québec; l'Association des femmes d'affaires du Québec. **HONS:** Prix spécial du jury, Salon de la femme de Montréal, 1990; Prix du Conseil d'intervention pour l'accès des femmes au travail, 1992. **INTERESTS:** la lecture; le sport; le cinéma; le théâtre; les spectacles; les voyages; la musique. **MISC:** nombreuses conférences; Membre de mission, Observation du processus électoral au Nicaragua, 1990; Jury de sélection, Salon de la femme, 1991-93; Membre de mission, Observation de la situation sociale, politique, et économique suite à l'embargo à l'application de la Loi Torricelli à Cuba, 1992.

Lavers, Leslie, A.R.C.T.,B.A.,M.Ed. ■ 🎓
Registrar, UNIVERSITY OF LETHBRIDGE, 4401 University Dr., Lethbridge, AB T1K 3M4 (403) 329-5129, FAX 329-5159, EMAIL lavers@hg.uleth.ca. Born Montreal 1953. m. Richard Shockley. 2 ch. Julia, Alanna. **EDUC:** Royal Conservatory of Toronto, A.R.C.T.(Performer) 1975; Univ. of Lethbridge, B.A. 1978; St. Francis Xavier Univ., M.Ed.(Adult Educ.) 1992. **CAREER:** Dir., Hire-A-Student Program, Canada Employment & Immigration Commission, Lethbridge, 1978; Coord., Adult Educ. Needs Assessment Survey, Alberta Dept. of Manpower, 1980; Facilitator, Career Planning Workshops, Alberta Dept. of Career Dev. & Employment, 1985-90; Coord., Applied Studies Program, Univ. of Lethbridge, 1980-84; Academic Advisor, Fac. of Arts & Sciences, 1984-88; Coord. of Academic Advising, Fac. of Arts & Sciences, 1988-90; Asst. Registrar, 1990-92; Assoc. Registrar, 1992-96; Registrar, 1996 to date. **AFFIL:** The Children's House Child Care Society (Personnel Chair; Chair 1982-85); Lethbridge & District Hire-A-Student Committee (Fin. Chair; Chair Advisory Council Rep. 1980-89). **HONS:** Certificate of Merit, American Coll. Testing/National Academic Advising Association, 1990; Career Dev. Award of Excellence, Alberta Career Dev. & Employment, 1990. **COMMENT:** *"Although it may sound like a cliché, my liberal arts background has equipped me to move in virtually any direction. I think that my ability to move from a 'warm and fuzzy' type of operation in advising to a highly technical environment in the Registrar's office is one of the achievements of which I am most proud."*

Laviolette, Julie M., B.Comm.,M.Sc. $
Director, Pricing and Yield Management, AIR CANADA, Air Canada Centre, Zip 255, Box 14000, St. Laurent, QC H4Y 1H4 (514) 422-5718, FAX 422-5509. Born Montreal 1963. m. Raymond T.M. Yong. **EDUC:** Concordia Univ., B.Comm.(with distinction) 1986; Univ. of British Columbia, M.Sc.(Strategic Mgmt) 1987 (Univ. Grade Point Average of 3.96/4, & First Class Standing in Master's Program at UBC). **CAREER:** Fin. Analyst, Profit Improvement & Fin. Analysis Dept., Canadian Airlines International Ltd., 1988; Proj. Leader, Advanced Productivity Programs Dept., 1988-89; Fin. Analyst, Fin. Planning & Reporting Dept., Air Canada, 1989-90; Strategic Planner, Strategic Planning Dept., 1990; Fin. Planning Analyst, Fin. Svcs-Tech. Oper., 1990-91; Mgr, Corp. Planning, Corp. Planning & Analysis Dept., 1991-93; Mgr, Commercial Strategy & Planning, 1993-94; Dir. & Branch Fin. Officer, Mktg & Sales, Fin. Planning & Cont. Div., 1994-95; Dir., Pricing & Yield Mgmt, 1995 to date. **AFFIL:** UBC Commerce Grad. Society; Côte de Liesse Racket Club; Riverview Badminton Club. **HONS:** Special Master's Scholarship, National Research Council of Canada, 1986-87; Woolco-Woolworth Academic Achievement Scholarship–Mktg, 1985; Concordia Univ. Academic Achievement Scholarships, 1983-85; mbr., Que. & Montreal Int'l Badminton Teams, 1981-84 (3 nat'l championships); 1994 West Island Racket Club Ladies Squash Champion. **INTERESTS:** racquet sports (squash, tennis, badminton); bicycling; skiing; hiking; listening to music; reading; travel. **COMMENT:** *"Time is valuable so I want to use it to make a difference. In so doing, I believe it is possible to pursue and achieve excellence in many aspects of life. Joined Air Canada senior management ranks at age 30."*

Lawrence, Delores, B.A., M.B.A. ■■ $ ⊕ ☺
President and Chief Executive Officer, NURSING & HOMEMAKERS INC. (provider of nursing & home health care), 2347 Kennedy Rd., Ste. 204, Scarborough, ON M1T 3T8 (416) 754-0700, FAX 754-4014. Born Jamaica, WI 1955. m. 2 ch. **EDUC:** C.A.A.T., Nursing diploma 1975; York Univ., B.A.(Bus./Social Sci.) 1984; Harvard Bus. Sch., Diploma (Bus. Admin.) 1990; Univ. of New Hampshire, Whittemore Sch. of Bus. & Econ., M.B.A. 1996. **CAREER:** critical care nurse, Toronto Hospital W. Div., 1975-78; nursing admin., Sunnybrook Health Science Centre, 1978-84; founder/Dir. of Nursing/Pres. & CEO, Nursing & Homemakers Inc., 1984 to date. **AFFIL:** African Canadian Entrepreneurs (Pres. 1993 to date);

Ethnocultural Training Advisory Council (Treas. 1992 to date); National Council of Ethnocultural Business & Professionals (Sec. 1993 to date); Canadian Italian Business & Professional Association; Empire Club; Canadian Club; Black Business & Professional Association (VP 1988-93); Bishop Strachan Sch. (Dir. 1993 to date). HONS: African Canadian Entrepreneur of the Year, 1996; African Canadian Woman of the Year, 1994. INTERESTS: travel; reading; weighlifting. COMMENT: *"Delores Lawrence is a very outgoing, vibrant, energetic woman who truly aspires to be the best that she can be. With 20 years of marriage, she combines family, business and community in a unique way."*

Lawrence, Karen, B.A.,M.A. 🐾 🗂
Author. 2153 Pine St., San Diego, CA 92103-1522. Born Windsor, Ont. 1951. m. Robert Gabhart. 1 ch. Devin Lawrence Gabhart. EDUC: Univ. of Windsor, B.A.(English Language/Lit.) 1973; Univ. of Alberta, M.A. (English) 1977. CAREER: writer. SELECTED PUBLICATIONS: *Nekuia: The Inanna Poems* (1980); *The Life of Helen Alone* (1986); *Springs of Living Water* (1990). AFFIL: Writers' Union of Canada. HONS: Special M.A. Scholarship, Canada Council; Writing Grant, Canada Council; First Novel Award, W.H. Smith/Books in Canada, 1987; First Novel Award, PEN Los Angeles Center, 1987. INTERESTS: reading; gardening; travel. COMMENT: *"In spite–or, perhaps, because–of having lived outside of Canada since 1979, I feel a strong sense of identity as a Canadian writer. I am here, thinking and writing about there."*

Lawrence, Minnie, B.A.,C.A. 💲 ⭕
Chartered Accountant. 60 Renfrew Dr., Ste. 210, Box 620, Markham, ON L3R 0E1. Born Yaas, Roumania 1955. m. Arthur Lawrence, C.A. 2 ch. EDUC: Univ. of Toronto, B.A. 1976; Canadian Institute of Chartered Accountants, C.A. 1981. CAREER: C.A., Rubinovich, Newton & Back, 1976-80; Tax Ptnr, Orenstein & Partners, 1980-93; sole practitioner specializing in taxation, 1993 to date; Lecturer, Ryerson Polytechnic Univ. for the Canadian Institute of Bankers. SELECTED PUBLICATIONS: contributing ed., various specialized texts for Richard DeBoo & Co., incl. *Retiring Right* & *Insure Sensibly*; author of numerous articles for Institute of Chartered Accountants of Ontario & Canadian Institute of Chartered Accountants. AFFIL: Canadian Institute of Chartered Accountants; Institute of Chartered Accountants of Ontario; Canadian Tax Foundation; United Jewish Welfare Fund (Professional Advisory Committee); UJWF/Toronto Jewish

Congress (Women's Endowment Committee); Canadian Weizmann Institute (Endowment Fund); Academy of Sports & Fitness (Exec. Bd.). INTERESTS: alternative medicine; psych.; reading; baseball; issues related to women in the workforce; travel. MISC: frequent speaker to various business groups; various press & broadcast interviews.

Lawrence, Susan A., B.A.,B.Educ. 🗂 ✒ ⊛
Writer, Editor. 21 Washington Ave., Toronto, ON M5S 1L1 (416) 593-5806, FAX 593-5806. Born Toronto 1946. EDUC: Queen's Univ., B.A. 1967; Univ. of Toronto, B.Educ. 1972. CAREER: Copy Ed., *Canadian Living* Magazine, 1983-85; Copy Chief, 1985-88; Sr. Ed., 1988-92. SELECTED CREDITS: script, *The Ride*. SELECTED PUBLICATIONS: *Back Roads and Getaway Places*, contributing ed. (Reader's Digest); articles published in *Canadian Living*, *Canadian Workshop*, *Cottage Life*, *Destinations*, *FirstBank News*, *Health Watch*, & *Homemaker's*, on topics ranging from health & travel to solar power & banking. AFFIL: Editors' Association of Canada. HONS: *The Ride*, hon. mention, National Film Board Writers' contest. INTERESTS: piano; folk music. COMMENT: *"18 years of experience writing, editing, researching, copy editing and proofreading everything from books to magazines."*

Lawson, Jane Elizabeth, B.A.,LL.B. ■ ■ 💲
Senior Vice-President and Corporate Secretary, ROYAL BANK OF CANADA, 1 Place Ville Marie, P.O. Box 6001, Montreal, QC H3C 3A9 (514) 874-6678, FAX 874-3890. Born Cornwall, Ont. 1946. s. EDUC: Univ. of New Brunswick, B.A. 1968, LL.B. 1971. CAREER: Sr. Cnsl & Cnsl, Law Dept., Royal Bank of Canada, 1974-87; VP & Corp. Sec., 1988-92; Sr. VP & Corp. Sec., 1992 to date. AFFIL: Barreau du Québec; N.B. Bar Association; Canadian Bar Association; Institute of Corporate Directors; American Society of Corporate Secretaries; Institute of Corporate Secretaries & Administrators, Canada; Canadian Breast Cancer Research Foundation (Mgmt Committee). INTERESTS: theatre; history; arts; music.

Lay, Marion, B.Sc.,M.Sc. Ⓓ 💲 ⛸
Program Director, PROMOTION PLUS, 1367 W. Broadway, Vancouver, BC V6H 4A9 (604) 737-3075, FAX (604) 738-7175. President and Chief Executive Officer, THINK SPORT LTD. Born Vancouver 1948. s. EDUC: California State Polytechnic Coll., B.Sc.(Phys. Educ.) 1970; California State, Hayward, M.Sc.(Soc. of Sport) 1972. CAREER: Tech. Sport Colour Commentator for Amateur Swimming, CBC, 1969-73; Teaching Asst., Grad. Studies, Univ.

of California, 1970-71; Lecturer, Dept. of Phys. Educ., Univ. of Western Ontario, 1971 & 1972; Sport Consultant then Proj. Officer, Fitness & Amateur Sport, Dept. of Nat'l Health & Welfare, 1974-76; Acting Mgr, Tech. Section, 1976-78; special assignment, 1978; Mgr, Sport Policy & Program Dev., 1978-79; various contract positions in sports & fitness, incl. Advisor to the Fed. Sports Min. & Pres. of Oper., Rick Hansen Man in Motion World Tour, 1981-94; currently, Dir. of Programs, ProMotion Plus, 1994 to date. **SPORTS CAREER:** mbr., Cdn Olympic Swimming Team, Japan, 1964; Cdn 100m Freestyle Champion, 1964-68; mbr., Cdn Nat'l Swimming Team, Europe, 1965; Team Captain, Cdn Commonwealth Swimming Team, Jamaica, 1966; US Long Course Nationals, Philadelphia, Pa., 1967; Cdn Nat'l Swimming Team, S.Africa, 1968; Team Captain, Cdn Olympic Team, Mexico, 1968. **AFFIL:** B.C. Games Society (Co-Chair); Canadian Association for the Advancement of Women in Sport & Physical Activity (C.A.A.W.S.) (Founding Mbr.; Co-Chair); Canadian Olympic Association ("A" Membership; Olympic Affairs Committee); Women Sport International (Founding Mbr. 1995). **HONS:** 2-time Gold Medalist, Commonwealth Games, Jamaica, 1966; Bronze Medalist, 100m freestyle, US Long Course Nationals, 1967; Bronze Medalist, 4 x 100m freestyle, Summer Olympics, 1968; Dean's Honour List, California State Polytechnic Coll., 1969, 1970; Scholarship, California Association of Health, Physical Education & Recreation, 1968-69, 1969-70; National Women in Herstory Award, C.A.A.W.S., 1994; YWCA Women of Distinction Award, Recreation & Sport, 1991; Bryce Taylor Memorial Award, Canadian Sport Council, 1995; Ottawa Business & Professional Women's Week Award, 1993; Leadership Award, ProMotion Plus Provincial Women in Sport, 1992. **INTERESTS:** women's spirituality; gardening; coffee with friends. **MISC:** lecturer & speaker on gender equity & women in sport, recreation & phys. educ. at prov., nat'l & int'l sports forums; conducts workshops on gender equity; former swimming coach. **COMMENT:** *"A proud feminist and spokeswoman, I am a part of a national network of individuals that takes risks, creates new models and dares to think differently to achieve gender equity in sport and physical activity."*

Lea, Nattalia, B.A.Sc.,P.Eng. ■■ $ ✎ ⚛
Manager of Business Development, EUCALYPTUS INTERNATIONAL LTD. (export mktg consortium of petroleum industry related products & svcs), 2323E - 3rd Ave. N.W., Calgary, AB T2N 0K9 (403) 283-0498, FAX 270-3023, EMAIL eucalypt@cadvision.com. President, PLATYPUS PUBLISHERS. Freelance Writer. Born Vancouver 1953. m. Godfried Wasser. 2 ch. Alisse, Cody. **EDUC:** B.C. Institute of Technology, Dip.T.(Bio-Sciences Technology) 1973; Univ. of British Columbia, B.A.Sc.(Bio-Resources Eng.) 1978. **CAREER:** Freshwater Biological Technician, Environment Canada, Vancouver, 1973-74; Design Eng., Reid Crowther & Partners Ltd., Calgary, 1979-80; Scheduling Eng., Fluor Daniel Inc., 1980-82; Well Testing Eng., Delta-P Test, 1983-84; Planning Eng., Husky Oil Operations Ltd., 1984-86; self-employed Publisher, Consultant, Writer, 1986 to date. **SELECTED PUBLICATIONS:** Author/Illustrator, *Miracles for the Entrepreneur* (Platypus Publishers, 1996); Contributing Writer, *Gender Issues - The Issues Collection* (McGraw-Hill Ryerson Ltd., 1993); "Mission: Japan" (cover story, *PROFIT magazine*, Fall 1993); "Women Engineers: Dismantling the Myths" (*The Globe and Mail*, Mar. 20, 1992); hundreds of other articles covering business, environment, educ., computers, etc., in over 50 journals & newspapers in Canada, US, Singapore & Malaysia incl. *Chatelaine, Financial Times of Canada, Oilweek, Vancouver Sun, CA Magazine, Canadian Lawyer, Woman Engineer*, & others. **EXHIBITIONS:** City of Calgary Devonian Gardens Joint Art Show with potter Gord Fulton, Calgary, 1984; Federation of Canadian Artists Juried Art Show, Muttart Public Art Gallery, Calgary, 1983; other juried shows, Calgary & Vancouver, 1963-83. **AFFIL:** Association of Professional Engineers, Geologists & Geophysicists of Alberta; Canadian Association of Professional Speakers; CanAsian Businesswomen's Network; Calgary Chamber of Commerce (Univ. of Calgary Fac. of Mgmt & Calgary Chamber Committee 1995-97); Malaysia Canada Business Council (Exec. mbr. 1996-97); Canada Indonesia Business Council; Engineering Institute of Canada. **HONS:** Shell Canada Scholar, Youth Science Foundation, 1971; top student in Food Technology, B.C. Institute of Technology, 1973; winner, First Int'l Solar Olympics, 1976. **INTERESTS:** public speaking; community fundraising; strategic alliances; wholistic health; relationship between humour & healing; hiking; cross-country skiing; interesting people; other cultures & travel. **MISC:** was sponsored in part by Cathay Pacific Airlines & Singapore Airlines to report on Asia; business articles have been used in mgmt classes at Univ. of Toronto; guest, CBC Newsworld, show re sexual harassment, Sept. 5, 1992; guest, numerous radio shows, addressing gender issues & entrepreneurship; has spoken on int'l export mkt consortia, freelance writing,

doing bus. in Asia, job search strategies, & humour, to journalism & bus. students, engineers, entrepreneurs & public; initiated & facilitated numerous job search strategy & entrepreneurship seminars for unemployed under auspices of Engineering Institute of Canada. **COMMENT:** *"First University of British Columbia Bio-Resources Engineering woman graduate, 1978. Journalist. Writer. Entrepreneur. Artist. Engineer. Cartoonist and humourist. Public speaker. Mother. Spouse. Human being. Optimist."*

Leahey, Dennice, B.A. $

Senior Vice-President and General Manager, Manitoba, ROYAL BANK OF CANADA, 220 Portage Ave., 16th Fl., Winnipeg, MB R3C 2T5 (204) 988-4258, FAX 942-5919. Born Edmonton. m. Stephen G. Leahey. 2 ch. **EDUC:** Mount Saint Vincent Univ., B.A. **CAREER:** various organizations, 1959-71; Asst. Mgr, Personnel & Corp. Lending Dept., Royal Bank of Canada, 1971-79; Branch Mgr, Westmount Square Branch, 1980-83; Sr. Acct Mgr, Corp. & Gov't Bnkg, Que., 1983-87; VP, Corp. Bnkg, Que., 1987-89; VP, Independent Bus., 1989; Sr. VP, Independent Bus. & Agric., 1989-92; Sr. VP & Gen. Mgr, Man., 1992 to date. **AFFIL:** Royal Winnipeg Ballet (Dir.); Heart & Stroke Foundation of Manitoba (Dir.); St. Boniface General Hospital; Chair, Technology 2000 Inc.); Crocus Investment Advisory Committee; Univ. of Manitoba (Dir., The Associates); Manitoba Quality Network (Dir.); Manitoba Canadian Banker's Association (Chrm).

Leaney, Cindy, B.A. ■ 📺 ✏ 🎭

President, VOYAGE MEDIA PRODUCTIONS INC., 1255 - 15 Ave. E., Ste. 14, Vancouver, BC V5T 2S7 (604) 879-7643, FAX 879-1444. President, NO TIME TO CRY PRODUCTIONS INC. Born Calgary 1959. m. Gerald Christenson. 1 ch. **EDUC:** Simon Fraser Univ., B.A.(Comm.) 1980, extended studies (Pol. Sci.) 1985. **CAREER:** Researcher, CBC TV, 1985-86; Prod. & Dir., CKVU TV, current affairs/documentary series, 1986-88; Field Prod., CBC TV, 1987-95; Prod./Dir., Shane Lunny Productions, 1988-90; independent Prod./Dir., 1990 to date. **SELECTED CREDITS:** Co-Writer, *Troubled Times*, Mission Community Services, 1989; Co-Writer, *Too Close for Comfort*, Wild Ginger Productions, 1991; Writer/Prod./Dir., *Earle Birney: A Maker of Words* (documentary), CKVU TV, Vancouver, 1987; Writer/Prod./Dir., *Working Together* (documentary), 1989; Writer/Prod./Dir., *East to West. The Goh Ballet* (documentary), 1991; various other documentary credits; Series Writer & Assoc Prod., *Perspectives on Human Rights* series, BC Human Rights Commission; Series Prod./Dir., *Newsmakers*, CKVU Television; Series Writer & Prod., *Press Conference*, CKVU TV, Vancouver, 1986-87; Contributing Writer & Unit Dir. (Western Canada), *OWL-TV*, OWL-TV Intenational, 1990; Line Prod., *Live & En Vie*, Health & Welfare Canada, 1990; various other broadcast credits; Prod./Ed., *Walking the Tightrope*, 1985; Co-Dir., *Unsung Lullabies*, 1995. **AFFIL:** Fire Hall Arts Centre (Past Pres.); Vancouver Women in Film & Video (Past VP); Academy of Canadian Cinema & Television; Women in Film & Video; Canadian Association of Journalists. **HONS:** Letter of Commendation, Children's Broadcast Institute (*Walking the Tightrope*), 1985; Canadian Health Association Video Award (*Barbara's Shift*),1991; Gemini nomination/TVO Award, Best Youth Program (*Too Close for Comfort*), 1992. **INTERESTS:** music; arts; film. **MISC:** juror for various awards. **COMMENT:** *"Voyage Media Productions Inc. was established to develop programs focusing primarily on social and health issues."*

Leatherdale, Linda ✏ $ 📖

Financial/Money Editor, *THE TORONTO SUN*, The Toronto Sun Publishing Corp., 333 King St. E., Toronto, ON M5A 3X5 (416) 947-2332, FAX 947-2041. Born Orillia, Ont. 1953. m. Ian R. MacDonald. 2 ch. **CAREER:** Ed., Key Publishers; Ed., *Ontario Business Magazine*; Bus. Ed., *The Ottawa Sun*; Bus. Ed., *The Edmonton Sun*; Fin./Money Ed., *The Toronto Sun*. **SELECTED CREDITS:** Commentary, "Bottomline," CBC Newsworld. **SELECTED PUBLICATIONS:** numerous articles on bus. & finance for newspapers & magazines. **AFFIL:** Canadian Taxpayers' Federation (Bd.). **HONS:** Edward Dunlop Award, 3 times. **MISC:** numerous seminars on fin. planning; TV & radio appearances. **COMMENT:** *"Linda Leatherdale, award-winning financial editor and columnist, is a regular commentator on business, political and personal finance issues. A believer in advocacy journalism, she has led highly charged campaigns on the GST, the high cost of credit cards and bank service charges, government fiscal policy, and writes regularly on taxation as well as real estate, consumer and small business issues. She was instrumental in the passage of the Ontario Loan Brokers Act (one of 3 Acts in North America to clamp down on upfront fees for bogus personal loans), known at Queen's Park as the Linda Leatherdale bill."*

Leatt, Peggy, B.Sc.N.,M.H.S.A., Ph.D. ⊕ 🎓

Professor and Chair, Department of Health

Administration, Faculty of Medicine, UNIVERSITY OF TORONTO, 12 Queen's Park Cres. W., Toronto, ON M5S 1A1 (416) 978-2736, FAX 978-7350. Born Skipton, UK. m. George Pink. 1 ch. EDUC: Univ. of Alberta, B.Sc.N. 1973, M.H.S.A. 1975, Ph.D. 1980. CAREER: Staff Nurse, Intensive Care, & Charge Nurse, Surgical Outpatients Dept., The General Infirmary, Leeds, UK, 1962-63; variety of managerial positions, Univ. of Alberta Hospital, 1967-73; Asst. Prof., Div. of Health Service Admin., Fac. of Medicine & Fac. of Nursing, Univ. of Alberta, 1975-79; Assoc. Prof., Dept. of Health Admin., Fac. of Medicine, Univ. of Toronto, 1980-84; Program Dir., M.H.Sc. (Health Admin.) Program, Dept. of Health Admin., 1983-87; Program Dir. M.Sc./Ph.D. (Health Admin.) Program, 1987-88; Assoc. Chair, 1983-88; mbr., Assoc. Scientific Staff, Dept. of Family & Community Medicine, Mount Sinai Hospital, Toronto, 1983 to date; Prof., Dept. of Health Admin., Fac. of Medicine, Univ. of Toronto, 1984 to date; Chair, Dept. of Health Admin., 1988 to date; Principal Investigator, Hospital Mgmt Research Unit, 1989 to date (funded by Ont. Ministry of Health). SELECTED PUBLICATIONS: *Strategic Alliances in Health Care: A Casebook in Management Innovations*, ed. with L. Lemieux-Charles, C. Aird, S. Leggat (Ottawa: Canadian Coll. of Health Service Executives, 1996); *Program Management and Beyond: Management Innovations in Ontario Hospitals*, ed. with L. Lemieux-Charles & C. Aird (Ottawa: Canadian Coll. of Health Service Executives, 1994); "Integrated Delivery Systems: Has their time come to Canada," with G. Pink & C. David Naylor (*Canadian Medical Association Journal*, 154(6), 1996). EDIT: Assoc. Ed., *Health Services Management Research Journal*, 1988-94. AFFIL: Canadian Coll. of Health Executives; American Coll. of Health Executives' Academy of Management; American Sociological Association; Association of University Programs in Health Administration; Accrediting Commission on Education for Health Science Administration; Association of Health Services Researchers; Academy of Management; Academy of Management, Health Care Div.; Canadian Coll. of Health Service Executives; Association of Young Health Executives; Society of Graduates in Health Admin., Univ. of Toronto; Health Svcs Admin. Alumni of the Univ. of Alberta. HONS: Eugene M. Stuart Award of Merit for Excellence in Teaching in Health Admin., 1993; Nat'l Health Student Fellowship, 1974-75, 1977-79; Canada Liquid Air Award, Univ. of Alberta, 1974; Prize for Medical Nursing, The General Infirmary, Leeds, 1962. INTERESTS: gardening; cooking. MISC:

recipient, numerous grants; numerous seminars & presentations; reviewer for *Administrative Science Quarterly, Human Relations, Academy of Management Journal* & *Health Care Management Forum*. COMMENT: "*To provide leadership in the education of individuals for senior management positions in Canada's healthcare system. To ensure there are continuous improvements in the delivery of health services to Canadians through research and education.*"

Le Blanc, Barbara, B.A.,M.A.,B.Ed., Ph.D. ■■ ⬠ 📖 ☻
Assistant Professor, Department of Education, UNIVERSITÉ SAINTE-ANNE, Pointe-de-l'Église, NS B0W 1M0 (902) 769-2114, ext. 318, FAX 769-2930, EMAIL barbaral@ustanne.ednet.ns.ca. Born Cheticamp, N.S. 1951. s. EDUC: Dalhousie Univ., B.A.(Théâtre) 1971, B.Ed. 1988; Laval Univ., M.A.(les arts et traditions populaires) 1986, Ph.D.(Ethnologie des francophones en Amérique du Nord) 1994. CAREER: Playground Leader/Program Coord., Recreation Dept., New Waterford, N.S., 1964-68; Sch. News Reporter, CBC, Sydney, N.S., 1967-68; Organizer, Youth Group, Association for the Mentally Handicapped, N.S., 1969; Coord., Group Home, 1972; teacher, schools in Italy, Mexico, Ireland, 1975-81; Lecturer, Dept. of History, Laval Univ., 1988; Lecturer, Dept. of Educ., Univ. Sainte-Anne, 1990; Dir., Grand-Pré Nat'l Historic Site, N.S., Dept. of the Environment, Parks Canada, 1989-92; Community Rel'ns Liaison Officer, Canadian Heritage, Atlantic Reg., 1994-95; Asst. Prof., Dept. of Educ., Univ. Sainte-Anne, 1995 to date. SELECTED PUBLICATIONS: "Changing Places: Dance, Society and Gender" in *Undisciplined Women*, ed. Pauline Greenhill & Diane Tye (Ontario: McGill-Queen's Univ. Press, forthcoming, 1997); *All Join Hands: The Traditional Acadian Dances of the Cheticamp Area* (with Laura Sadowsky. Wolfville: Éditions du Grand-Pré, forthcoming, 1997) - also being published in French as *Tous ensemble: les danses traditionnelles acadiennes de la région de Chéticamp*; "Tête à tête et Charivari à Moncton: Rencontre interculturelle entre les Acadiens et les Anglophones de Moncton" (*La société historique acadienne: les cahiers*, Vol. 27, No. 1, Jan.-Mar. 1996); "Candlemas in the Classroom: Relating Past Traditions to Present Realities" with Hilary Thompson in *Children's Voices in Atlantic Literature and Culture* (Guelph, Ont.: Canadian Children's Press, 1995); "Evangeline as Identity Myth" in *Femmes et traditions - Women and Tradition*, Revue d'ethnologie et de folklore, ed. Jocelyne Mathieu (Que.: Laval Univ., 1993); *L'Acadie*

en fête (book & cassette. London: BBC Educational Publishing & Longman Group Limited, 1993); "La découverte magique de nos racines: une trousse d'animation et d'apprentissage" with Mireille Baulu-MacWillie (*La société historique acadienne: les cahiers*, Vol. 23, Nos. 3 & 4, 1992). **AFFIL:** Fédération acadienne de la Nouvelle-Écosse (Pres. 1995-98); Folklore Studies Association of Canada/Association canadienne d'ethnologie et de folklore (Pres. 1996-98); Gorsebrook Atlantic Studies Research Institute (Bd. of Dir.); Helen Creighton Folklore Festival (Bd. of Dir.); Helen Creighton Foundation (Bd. of Dir.); American Leadership Study Groups, 1971-76/American Council for International Travel, 1976-87/American Educational Travel, 1986-88 (tour organizer/culture & civilization course teacher). **INTERESTS:** to participate fully in life. **MISC:** research asst., 2 films: *Acadie Liberté* (dir. Tim Radford, American Parks Service, Canadian Heritage, & Société Nationale de l'Acadie), 1994; *Evangeline's Quest* (dir. Ginette Pellerin, National Film Board), 1996; research re dance in Cape Breton, 1986-88; various responsibilities, incl. public rel'ns, acting, research, etc., several theatre companies in Italy, 1973-76; numerous presentations about Acadian history & folklore to a variety of audiences. **COMMENT:** *"Barbara Le Blanc has lived and worked in Canada, Europe and Mexico in such fields as management, ethnology and history research, teaching, theatre and tourism."*

Le Blanc, Huguette, B.A. 📖 ✏
Rédactrice en chef, MAGAZINE *UNIVERS*, 2269, chemin Saint-Louis, Sillery, QC (418) 687-9531, FAX 687-9051. Born Dugal, Qué. 1943. 2 ch. David, Caroline. **EDUC:** École-Normale Notre-Dame de Québec, Pédagogie B 1962; Univ. Laval, Baccalauréat ès arts (Théologie) 1969, B.A.(Gérontologie) 1982, B.A.(Journalisme) 1994. **CAREER:** Animatrice, Centre de loisirs pour jeunes filles, 1957-62; Prof., Coll. Bélanger, Vanier, Qué., 1962-64; Prof., Lomé, Togo, Afrique, 1964-66; Prof., Commission scolaire régionale Jean-Talon, 1966-71; Séjour en Algérie, Agence canadienne de développement international, 1971-73; Écrivaine, 1973 to date; Coordonnatrice des activités culturelles, Salon international du Livre de Québec, 1986-88; Directrice du Service d'animation (secteur des adultes), Oeuvres pontificale missionnaires, 1989-91; Directrice du Service des Communications et Rédactrice en chef du magazine *Univers*, 1990-95. **SELECTED PUBLICATIONS:** *Bernadette Dupuis ou la mort apprivoisée* (Montréal: Éditions Le Biocreux, 1980); *La nuit des immensités* (Montréal: Éditions HMH, 1983); *Alberto Kurapel, poésie et chant d'exil*

(Montréal: Éditions La Mêlée, 1983); "Les mémoires dupées" (*Bulletin Pantoute*, 1981); "L'homme emmuré" (*Châtelaine*, 1982); "De la rouille sur la cage dorée" (*Mouvements*, 1985); "Samina" (*Brèves*, 1987); "Le Bouchra" (*Nouvelles...nouvelles*, 1987); "Écrire pour survivre" (*Écrits du Canada français*, 1984); "Avons-nous vécu 1984?" (*Le Devoir*, 1984). **AFFIL:** Conseil de Presse du Québec; Fraternité de l'Épi; Association canadienne des périodiques catholiques. **HONS:** Lauréate, Salon international du livre de Québec, 1979, 1980; Premier prix, catégorie Nouvelle, Cercle d'écriture de l'Univ. Laval. **INTERESTS:** droits humains; défense des minorités, des exclus; la cause des Autochtones du Canada. **COMMENT:** *"Je suis une nomade qui aime installer sa tente au milieu des souffrants, là où la fragilité est grandeur et beauté. Un plongeon dans l'immensité pour y quêter la Joie."*

LeBlanc, Phyllis Evelyne, B.A.,M.A., Ph.D. ✎ 📖
Professor of History, UNIVERSITÉ DE MONCTON, Moncton, NB E1A 3E9 (506) 858-4060, FAX 858-4166, EMAIL leblanpc@bosoleil.umoncton.ca. Born Moncton, N.B. 1954. m. Jean-Valmond LeBlanc. **EDUC:** Univ. de Moncton, B.A.(Hist.) 1976, M.A.(Hist.) 1978; Univ. d'Ottawa, Ph.D.(Hist.) 1989. **CAREER:** Policy Advisor & Historical Researcher, Dept. of Indian Affairs & Northern Dev., Gov't of Canada, 1984-88; Asst. Prof. of Hist., Univ. of Winnipeg, 1988-90; Assoc. Prof., Univ. de Moncton, 1990-95; Prof., 1995 to date. **SELECTED PUBLICATIONS:** *Économie et société en Acadie, 1985-1950*, co-ed. with J.-P. Couturier (Moncton: Éditions d'Acadie, 1996); "Francophone Minorities: The Fragmentation of the French-Canadian Identity," *Beyond Quebec: Taking Stock of Canada*, ed. K. McRoberts (Montreal: McGill-Queen's Univ. Press, 1995); "The Vatican and the Roman Catholic Church in Atlantic Canada: Policies Regarding Ethnicity and Language, 1878-1922," *Papal Diplomacy in the Modern Age*, eds. P.C. Kent & J. Pollard (Conn.: Praeger Press, 1994); several articles in *Égalité & Histoire sociale/Social History*. **EDIT:** Ed. Bd., *Journal of History and Politics*, 1994. **AFFIL:** Univ. de Moncton (Chair, Dept. of Hist. & Geography 1992-95; Dir., Acadian Studies Centre 1994-95); Gorsebrook Institute for Atlantic Canada Studies, St. Mary's Univ. (Bd. of Dir. 1993-97); Association for Canadian Studies (Cdn Studies Program Admin.'s Committee; mbr., Jury, Award of Merit; Bd. of Dir. & mbr., Exec. Committee 1996 to date); Canadian Historical Association. **HONS:** Canada Council Special M.A. Scholarship, 1976;

Scholar in Residence, Center for Louisiana Studies, Univ. of South-Western Louisiana, 1995-96. INTERESTS: social & econ. hist.; women's hist. MISC: recipient, SSHRC doctoral grants, hist., 1981-83. COMMENT: *"Social historian interested in questions of modernity and its cultural implications. My chosen laboratory is the Acadian integration into the urban milieu of early 20th century maritimes."*

LeBlanc-Bridge, Theresa, B.A.,B.C.L., LL.B. ⚖ $

Senior Counsel, ROYAL BANK OF CANADA, Head Office Law Department, 1 Place Ville Marie, Montreal, QC H3C 3A9 (514) 874-7022, FAX 874-0241. Born Montreal 1953. m. Edward D. Bridge. 2 ch. Sarah Bridge, Jeremy Bridge. EDUC: Concordia Univ., B.A.(Hist./Cdn Studies) 1976; McGill Univ., B.C.L.(Civil Law) 1980, LL.B. 1980. BAR: Que., 1982; Ont., 1989. CAREER: Cnsl, Law Dept., Royal Bank of Canada, 1983-94; Sr. Cnsl, 1994 to date; Corp. Sec., Royal Bank Mortgage Corporation, 1992-93. AFFIL: Barreau du Québec; Law Society of Upper Canada; Canadian Bar Association; McGill Society of Montreal (Dir. 1994 to date; VP, Comm. 1996 to date); Catholic Community Services (Dir. 1992-94).

Leblon, Brigitte, Ph.D. 🏵 🗺

Assistant Professor, Faculty of Forestry, UNIVERSITY OF NEW BRUNSWICK, Box 44555, Fredericton, NB E3B 6C2 (506) 453-4924, FAX 453-3538, EMAIL bleblon@unb.ca. Born Bensberg, Germany 1960. m. Armand La Rocque. EDUC: Univ. Catholique de Louvain-la-Neuve, Belgium, Agricultural Eng. 1983; ENSA Montpellier, France, Ph.D. 1990. CAREER: Agricultural Eng., Dept. of Agric., Belgium, European Integration Policy Section, 1985-86; Research Asst., Institut National de la Recherche Agronomique, France, Bioclimatology Research Station, 1986-90; Lecturer, Univ. de Sherbrooke, Québec, Dept. of Geography & Remote Sensing, 1991-93; Research Asst. & Asst. Prof., Univ. of New Brunswick, Fac. of Forestry, 1994 to date. SELECTED PUBLICATIONS: "The Use of Remotely Sensed Data in Estimation of PAR Use Efficiency and Biomass Production of Flooded Rice," with M. Guérif & F. Baret (*Remote Sensing of Environment* 38 1991); "A Root Biomass Partitioning Function for Use in Models Which Predict Total Biomass from Absorbed Photosynthetically Active Radiation (PAR)," with M. Guérif (*European Journal of Agronomy* 1(3) 1992); "A Semi-empiral Model to Estimate the Biomass Production of Forest Canopies from Spectral Variables. Part 1: Relationship

Between Spectral Variables and Light Interception Efficiency," with H. Granberg, C. Ansseau & A. Royer (*Remote Sensing Reviews* 7 1993); various other publications. AFFIL: Association Québecoise de Télédétection; N.B. Remote Sensing Sub-Committee; Canadian Society of Remote Sensing. HONS: Rotary Foundations fellowship, 1986-87; Commissariat Général aux Relations Internationales fellowships, 1987-88, 1991-92; Association des Universités Partiellement ou Entièrement de Langue Française–Univ. d'Expression Française fellowship, 1992-93; Best Master of the Fac. of Agronomy of the Univ. Catholique de Louvain-la-Neuve, 1983. INTERESTS: travel. COMMENT: *"For me, it is highly important to know different languages (the vector of the culture!) and to have a broad training. For these reasons I don't believe in training our university students as if in a scientific and technical institute, but try to develop in my courses enthusiasm and a willingness to acquire broad knowledge."*

LeBreton, Hon. Marjory 🍁

Senator, THE SENATE OF CANADA, Victoria Building, Rm. 601, Ottawa, ON K1A 0A6 (613) 943-0756, FAX 943-1493. Born Nepean, Ont. 1940. m. Douglas. 2 ch. EDUC: Ottawa Business Coll., Dipl.(Bus. & Secretarial). CAREER: various admin. & organization positions, Progressive Conservative Party of Canada, 1962-84; Exec. Dir., Advance Planning & Camp Associates, Ottawa, 1984-86; Special Asst., Gov.-in-Council Appointments, Office of the Prime Minister, 1986-87; Deputy Chief of Staff to the Prime Minister of Canada, 1987-93; Senator, 1993 to date. AFFIL: P.C. Party of Canada; Albany Club; Kiwanis Club of Manotick. INTERESTS: political books & essays; gardening, indoor & outdoor.

Lecavalier, Louise ■■ ⊗ 🦋 ♂

Principal Dancer, LA LA LA HUMAN STEPS (dance company), 5655 ave. du Parc, Ste. 206, Montreal, QC H2V 4H2 (514) 277-9090, FAX 277-0862. Born Montreal. EDUC: CEGEP Bois de Boulogne, D.E.C.(Sci. Santé); studied classical ballet & modern dance, Montreal & N.Y. CAREER: professional dancer, 1977 to date; has danced with companies in Montreal & N.Y.; joined La La La Human Steps, 1981. SELECTED CREDITS: staged solo performance, *No.No.No. I Am Not Mary Poppins*, Montreal, 1982; roles in *Oranges* (1981), *Businessman in the Process of Becoming an Angel* (1985), *Human Sex* (1985), *New Demons* (1987), *Infante* (1991); performed with David Bowie in *Look Back in Anger*, at benefit concert at London's Institute of Contemporary Arts, 1988, & as part of *Wrap Around the*

World, broadcast in several countries; guest artist in N.Y. & Los Angeles as part of David Bowie's *Sound and Vision* tour, 1990; *Save the Last Dance for Me* (video, Carole Laure), 1989; performed in *The Yellow Shark* concert, Frank Zappa & the Ensemble Modern of Germany, Frankfurt, Berlin & Vienna, 1992; appeared in film *Strange Days*, L.A., 1994, & in *Pour tout dire* (National Film Board), 1994. **HONS:** Bessie Award for performance in *Businessman in the Process of Becoming an Angel*, N.Y., 1985 (1st Cdn to win Bessie); recipient, Canada Council grants for study in N.Y., 1982 & 1986; advanced study grant, Conseil des arts et des lettres, Que., 1994. **MISC:** Spokeswoman, La Semaine québécoise des arts, 1996. **COMMENT:** *Critics have been left speechless, in rapt amazement at this scintillating dancer whose talent, energy and presence are beyond compare. She has been called "the most tragically brilliant dancer alive today. A flame on legs."* (*Melody Maker*, London)

Leclair, Suzanne Bernard $

President and Chief Executive Officer, TRANSIT TRUCK BODIES INC., 3600 Boul. Industriel, Laval, QC H7L 4R9 (514) 382-0104, FAX 383-5636. **CAREER:** Pres. & CEO, Transit Truck Bodies Inc., 1978 to date. **DIRECTOR:** Natcan; National Bank of Canada. **AFFIL:** Foundation of the Hospital Cité de la Santé de Laval (Bd. of Dir. 1994-96); Youth Investment Society (Bd. of Dir. 1994-96). **HONS:** Businesswoman of the Year, 1984; Businesswoman of the Salon de la PME, 1987; Classic Bus., Salon de la PME, 1987; Dunamis, Large Bus. Category, Laval Chamber of Commerce, 1988; Canada Businesswoman, Veuve Clicquot Award, Schenley Canada, 1988; Businesswoman of the Year, Large Bus. Category, F.R.A.P.P.E., Québec BusinessWoman Association, 1989; Celebration, Fédération des Caisses Populaires Desjardins, 1989; Businesswoman of the Year, Hydro-Québec, Quebec Chamber of Commerce, 1989; Les Grande Entrepreneurs, Performance, 1995; Le Grand Prix de l'Entrepreneur, Manufacturer Category, 1995; Canadian Grand Prize for Leadership, Ernst & Young, LLP, 1995. **MISC:** frequent guest speaker.

Lederman, Marsha, B.A.A. ■■ 📺 ✏ ☝

Talk Show Host, "Horsman/Lederman", TALK 640 (radio), 5255 Yonge St., Ste. 1400, Toronto, ON M2N 6P4 (416) 221-6400, FAX 512-4816. Born Toronto 1966. s. **EDUC:** Ryerson Polytechnical Institute, B.A.A.(Radio & TV Arts) 1988; York Univ., working toward B.A.(Hons., English Lit.). **CAREER:** Assoc. Producer, ForeRunner Communications, 1988-91; News Anchor, CKBB, Barrie, Ont., Mar.-Sept. 1991; News Anchor/Reporter, K-Lite FM/Oldies 1150, Hamilton, Ont., 1991-93; City Hall Bureau Chief/News Anchor, Q107/AM640, 1993-94; Co-host, "Horsman/Lederman," 1995 to date. **SELECTED CREDITS:** Assoc. Producer, *How Will You Manage?* (TVOntario/ForeRunner Communications); Assoc. Producer,*Renovating: The Inside Story* (TVOntario/ForeRunner Communications); On-Air Host, *Canadian Jewish Focus* (VisionTV/AR Productions). **SELECTED PUBLICATIONS:** "Fair Treatment for the Fair Sex: A Woman's Guide to Auto Repairs" (*Toronto Life*, Oct. 1996); "Check Out" (*Canadian Retailer*, Summer 1996); "Child of Survivors" (*Voice of Radom*, 50th Anniversary Edition, Nov. 1995); "Talking Point" (*The Toronto Star*, Mar. 1995); "Communications Breakdown" (*Marketing* magazine, Nov. 1994). **AFFIL:** United Jewish Appeal (Co-Chair, Radio Committee, Arts & Entertainment Div. 1996). **HONS:** Dave Rogers Award for Best Feature Programming, Central Reg. ("Hate & Heroism: The Holocaust 50 Years Later," 5-part documentary), Radio-Television News Directors' Association; CHUM FM Award for Highest Aggregate Standing (2nd yr.), Ted Pope Memorial Award for Highest Standing in the Humanities (2nd yr.), & All Canada Radio & Television Award for Highest Aggregate Standing (1st yr.), Ryerson Polytechnical Institute. **INTERESTS:** reading literature; writing short stories & poetry; travel (lived in Dublin & worked on a kibbutz in Israel). **COMMENT:** *"As one of the hosts of the first talk show in Canadian commercial radio history to feature two female co-hosts, I feel proud as a woman and a journalist."*

Ledrew, Renee ■■ 🏀

Paralympic Athlete. Edmonton, AB. **CAREER:** former radio news anchor/reporter. **SPORTS CAREER:** mbr., Nat'l Wheelchair Basketball Team. Paralympic Games: Gold, 1996. Chanadian Wheelchair Basketball League (CWBL): 2nd, Women's Finals, 1995; 1st, Women's FInals, 1994; 1st, 1993; 2nd, Women's Finals, 1992. World Championships: 1st, 1994. **HONS:** All-Star, CWBL Women's Finals, 1994, 1995; All-Star, World Championships, 1994.

Leduc, Lyse, M.N.A. 🍁

Member of National Assembly (Mille-Îles), GOVERNMENT OF QUÉBEC, 800 Montrose St., 2nd Fl., Laval, QC H7E 3M5 (514) 664-3847, FAX 664-0107. Born Montreal 1938. w. 2 ch. **EDUC:** École normale Ignace-Bourget, Certificate (Teaching); Univ. de Montréal, Certificate (Hist. of Art). **CAREER:** Teacher, 1957-82;

Counsellor, Women Integration in the Job Market, 1982-84; Gen. Mgr, Conseil d'intervention pour l'accès des femmes au travail, 1984-94; Laval Reg'l Pres., Parti Québécois, 1988; Parti Québécois Candidate for Nat'l Assembly (Mille-Îles), Gov't of Qué., 1989; Pres., Parti Québécois Women's Nat'l Action Committee, 1991-93; M.N.A. (Mille-Îles), Gov't of Qué., 1994 to date; Mbr. of Parliamentary Commission on Social Affairs, 1994 to date; Mbr. of Parliamentary Commission on the Economy & Labour, 1994. **AFFIL:** Forum de l'emploi du Québec; United Way (Volunteer); Alliance des professeurs de Montréal (Union Delegate). **INTERESTS:** women's issues; Laval reg'l dev.

Leduc, Paule, B.A.,M.A.,Ph.D. ■ 🎓
Rector, UNIVERSITÉ DU QUÉBEC À MONTRÉAL, C.P. 8888, Succ. Centre-Ville, Montreal, QC H3C 3P8 (514) 987-3080, FAX 987-8424, EMAIL leduc.paule@uqam.ca. Born Bagotville, Que. 1936. m. Dr. Jacques Brunet. 1 ch. **EDUC:** Univ. de Sherbrooke, B.A. 1957; Univ. de Montréal, M.A. 1962; Univ. de Paris, Ph.D. 1965. **CAREER:** Head, Dept. of Lit., Univ. du Québec à Montréal, 1971-72; Asst. to V-Rector, Academic & Research, 1972-74; Exec. V-Rector, 1974-75; Asst. Deputy Min., Admin., Ministère des Affaires sociale du Qué., 1975-77; Pres., Conseil des univ. du Qué., 1977-81; Sec. Gen., Dév. social, Ministère du conseil exécutif du Qué., 1981-82; Deputy Min., Ministère des affaires culturelles du Qué., 1984-86; Dir., Centre for Policy Studies, École nationale d'admin. publique, 1986-88; Pres., Social Services & Humanities Research Council of Canada, 1988-94; Dir., Canada Council, 1992-94; VP, Academic & Research, Univ. of Québec, 1994-96; Rector, Univ. du Québec à Montréal, 1996 to date. **AFFIL:** Public Policies Research Institute; National Arts Centre, Ottawa (Bd. of Dir.); Musée au Québec (Pres., Bd. of Dir.). **HONS:** Diplômée d'honneur, Alumni Association, Univ. de Montréal, 1987; D.Litt.(Hon.), Univ. of Ottawa, 1989; D.Litt.(Hon.), St. Mary's Univ., 1990; LL.D. (Hon.), Queen's Univ., 1991; LL.D.(Hon.), Univ. of Manitoba, 1993; D.Litt.(Hon.), Royal Military Coll., Kingston, 1994. **MISC:** various lectures & presentations.

Lee, Lauren ("L.J."), B.A.(Hons.), M.A. ■■ 📺 ♥ ☝
Freelance TV/Radio/Video Announcer and Aviation Promoter. Bushhawk Creek, R.R. #1, Straffordville, ON N0J 1Y0 (519) 866-5294. Born Toronto 1959. m. Terry Lilliman. **EDUC:** Univ. of Toronto, B.A.(Hons., Pre-Journalism) 1985; Univ. of Western Ontario, M.A.(Journalism) 1986. **CAREER:** TV News Anchor/Reporter, CHEX-TV, Peterborough, 1986-88; TV News Anchor/Host/Reporter, CFPL-TV, London, Ont., 1988-93; freelance announcer, TV, radio, industrial video & Airshow, 1993 to date; Proprietor, Canadian Bushhawks. **SELECTED CREDITS:** announcer & aircraft performer, numerous airshows across N. America, 1992 to date. **SELECTED PUBLICATIONS:** various articles in Cdn & US aviation publications, 1992 to date. **AFFIL:** Canadian Bushhawks Liaison Squadron, int'l aviation heritage assoc. (Leader & Co-founder); Canadian Harvard Aircraft Association, Cdn aviation heritage (Past-Pres. & Life mbr.); Joint Liaison Formation Committee, N.A. advisory & certification assoc. (Co-Chair); Canadian Owners & Pilots Association; Experimental Aircraft Association; EAA Warbirds of America; International Council of Airshows; International Liaison Pilots & Aircraft Association. **HONS:** "Warbird Aviator," Experimental Aircraft Association, 1996; Silver Medal, Broadcast Journalism, Univ. of Western Ontario, 1986; various grad. scholarships, Univ. of Toronto, 1985. **INTERESTS:** aviation; broadcasting; restoration of antique furniture, homes & aircraft. **MISC:** author of *Canadian Bushhawks Liaison Squadron Formation Flight Syllabus*, a ground-breaking analysis & manual now in widespread use in aviation & air shows across N. America. **COMMENT:** *"Lauren freelances as a broadcast announcer in real life, while indulging in a life-long passion for aviation. Currently living on a farm, with airstrip and aircraft at her back door, she is recognized in aviation circles, North America-wide, for her promotion of aviation heritage."*

Lee, Mary ■■ $
President, LEE CONSULTING, Toronto ON. Born Vancouver 1954. m. 1 ch. David. **CAREER:** Founder & Pres., Lee Consulting.

Leeming, Virginia ✎
Fashion Reporter, *THE VANCOUVER SUN*, 2250 Granville St., Vancouver, BC V6H 3G2 (604) 732-2187, FAX 732-2521. Born Victoria, B.C. 1941. s. 1 ch. Victoria Leeming. **CAREER:** Teller, Bank of Montreal, 1962-72; Photo Coord. for various commercial studios, Montreal, 1962-68; Writer/Ed., *Ego* & *Femego* trade magazines, 1972-79; Acct Supervisor, public rel'ns agency, 1979-80; Fashion Reporter, *Vancouver Sun*, 1983 to date. **SELECTED PUBLICATIONS:** features for *Decormag*, *Elan*, *Canadian Architect*, *Renovation West*, *Vancouver* Magazine, *Vancouver Calendar*, *Montreal Gazette*, *Select Home Designs*, *Style* magazine, *Canadian Living*. **AFFIL:**

Kwantlen Coll. (Fashion Design Technology Program Advisory Committee); Fashion Group International (Exec., Montreal Chapter 1977-78); Helen Lefeaux Sch. of Fashion Design, Vancouver (Advisory Committee). **INTERESTS:** cooking; travel; photography; music; outdoors. **COMMENT:** *"I am optimistic, gregarious, eclectic, liberal, enthusiastic on the job, artistic, always ready to try something new, not afraid to learn from others, and try to balance work and home life."*

Lefebvre, Arlette, B.A.,M.D.,F.R.C.P.(C) ⊕
Staff Psychiatrist, HOSPITAL FOR SICK CHILDREN, 555 University Ave., Toronto, ON M5G 1X8 (416) 813-7526, FAX 813-5326, EMAIL arlette.lefebvre@ablelink.org. Born Montreal 1947. m. D. Yvan Bedard. 2 ch. **EDUC:** Univ. of Caen, France, B.A. 1964; Univ. of Toronto, M.D. 1970, F.R.C.P.(C) 1974, Dip.(Child Psychiatry) 1974. **CAREER:** Consultant, Catholic Children's Aid Society, 1973-74; Chief Resident, Dept. of Psychiatry, The Hospital for Sick Children, 1973-74; Teaching Fellowship in Child Psychiatry, 1974-75; Lecturer, Dept. of Psychiatry, Univ. of Toronto, 1974-78; Psychiatric Consultant, Learning Clinic, 1974-78; Team Leader, Dept. of Psychiatry, The Hospital for Sick Children, 1976-85; Psychiatric Consultant to the Child Dev. Clinic, 1978-80; Asst. Prof., Dept. of Psychiatry, Univ. of Toronto, 1978-84; Consultant to Health & Welfare Canada, 1989-90; Psychiatric Consultant for Plastic Surgery, The Hospital for Sick Children, 1975 to date; Psychiatric Consultant for the Burn Unit, 1980 to date; Assoc. Prof., Dept. of Psychiatry, Univ. of Toronto, 1984 to date; Team Leader, Phys. Disability Speciality Team, Dept. of Psychiatry, The Hospital for Sick Children, 1985 to date; Staff Psychiatrist, 1985 to date; Psychiatric Consultant for Bloorville Children's Hospital, 1988 to date; Psychiatric Consultant for The Hospital for Sick Children HIV & AIDS Comprehensive Care Team, 1989 to date. **SELECTED PUBLICATIONS:** "Psychosocial Impact of Craniofacial Deformities Before and After Reconstructive Surgery," with S. Barclay (*Canadian Journal of Psychiatry* Nov. 1982); "Ability OnLine: Promoting Social Competence in Adolescents with Disabilities" (*Rehabilitation Digest* June 1992); "Learning Disorders in Children and Adolescents," with W. Hawke in *Psychological Problems of the Child and His Family*, P.D. Steinhauer & Q. Rae-Grant, ed. (New York: Basic Books, 1983); various other publications. **AFFIL:** The Alliance for Children & Television (Bd. of Dir.); CANFAR (Bd. of Dir.); Canadian Medical Association; Ontario Medical Association; Canadian Medical Protective Association; Canadian Psychiatry Association; Ontario Psychiatry Association; Canadian Academy of Child Psychiatry; International Society of Craniomaxillofacial Surgery; AboutFace; Ability OnLine (Founder & Pres.); Easter Seal Society (Bd. of Dir.); Hasbro Toys International & Playskool (Advisory Panel); HSC Humour Library (Founder); Ability OnLine Support Network (Founder); HSC Fund for Children with AIDS (Founder). **HONS:** J. Franklin Robinson Memorial Award, American Academy of Child Psychiatry, 1975; Easter Seal Society Award, 1992; Women Who Make a Difference, Politics/Community Affairs category, 1993; Community Action Award, Office for Disability Issues, Ont. Ministry of Citizenship, 1993; Women On The Move Award, *The Toronto Sun*, 1993; Easter Seals Gold Award, 1995; HSC Family Advisory Committee Humanitarian Award, 1995; Order of Ontario, 1996. **MISC:** numerous media appearances, incl. "Computers and Women: Can the girls play too?" *Science Edition*, TVOntario (1991), *W5* (1994) & *CBC at Six*. **COMMENT:** *"For the past 20 years I have had the privilege of working with families dealing with disability and illness with tremendous courage and resourcefulness. I have learned much from them and created Ability OnLine to put children with disabilities in touch with the world."*

Legault, Jocelyne A., B.Sc.,M.Sc., Ph.D. ■ ◁ ❀
Associate Professor, Department of Earth Sciences, UNIVERSITY OF WATERLOO, Waterloo, ON N2L 3G1 (519) 888-4567, ext. 3233, FAX 746-0183, EMAIL jlegault@sciborg.uwaterloo.ca. Born Que. 1941. s. **EDUC:** Univ. of Ottawa, B.Sc.(Geol.) 1963, M.Sc.(Geol.) 1966; Univ. of Oklahoma, Ph.D.(Geol.) 1971. **CAREER:** Asst. Prof., Dept. of Geological Sciences, Univ. of Saskatchewan, 1971-76; Asst. Prof., Dept. of Earth Sciences, Univ. of Waterloo, 1976-82; Assoc. Prof., 1982 to date; Dept. Chair, 1986. **SELECTED PUBLICATIONS:** various papers published in learned journals. **AFFIL:** American Association of Stratigraphic Palynologists (Dir. 1978-79, 1982-84, 1995-97); Canadian Association of Palynologists; Geological Association Canada; Palaeontological Association; Canadian Association of Women in Science; Sigma Xi. **MISC:** Advisor to VP (Academic) on Interdisciplinary Programs, 1991-97.

Legge, Elizabeth M., B.A.,M.A., Ph.D. ⊗ ◷ ◁
University Art Curator and Assistant Professor, Fine Art Department, UNIVERSITY OF TORONTO, University College, Toronto, ON M5E 1A1.

m. George Meanwell. 2 ch. Max Meanwell, Lucy Meanwell. EDUC: Univ. of Toronto, B.A.(English) 1973; Mount Allison Univ., foundation year, studio art 1973-74; Cambridge Univ., B.A.(Hist. of Art) 1976; Courtauld Institute, Univ. of London, M.A. 1979, Ph.D. 1986. CAREER: Sessional Lecturer, Univ. of Winnipeg, 1979-81; Assoc. Curator, Winnipeg Art Gallery, 1979-81; Asst. Prof., Univ. of Winnipeg, 1985-87; Univ. Art Curator, Univ. of Toronto, 1988 to date; cross-appt., Fine Art Dept., Univ. of Toronto, 1992 to date; Asst. Prof., Fine Art Dept, 1996 to date. SELECTED PUBLICATIONS: *Max Ernst: The Psychoanalytic Sources* (Ann Arbor: UMI Research Press, 1989); "Max Ernst's Oedipus Rex and the Implicit Sphinx" (*Arts Magazine* Sept. 1986); "Posing Questions: Max Ernst's *Au rendezvous des amis*" (*Art History* June 1987); "Novalis's Fossils, Zeuxis's Grapes, Freud's Flowers, Max Ernst's Natural History" (*Art History* Mar. 1993); "Thirteen Ways of Looking at a Virgin: Picabia's 'La Sainte Vierge'" (*Word and Image* 1996); *Faded Allusions: Later Nineteenth Century Academic Painting*, catalogue (Winnipeg: Winnipeg Art Gallery, 1981); *Occurrences: Four Manitoba Painters*, catalogue (Winnipeg: Winnipeg Art Gallery, 1981); various other catalogues & publications. EDIT: Ed. Bd., *University of Toronto Quarterly*, 1990 to date. EXHIBITIONS: curator, *Faded Allusions: Later Nineteenth Century Academic Painting*, Winnipeg Art Gallery (1981); curator, *Occurrences: Four Manitoba Painters*, Winnipeg Art Gallery (1981). AFFIL: Institute for Contemporary Culture, Royal Ontario Museum (Curatorial Bd.); Gallery E (Curatorial Bd). HONS: Joseph Henderson Memorial Award, Trinity Coll., Univ. of Toronto, 1969-73; Raimaker Prize, Girton Coll., Cambridge Univ., 1976; Commonwealth Scholarship, 1981-84. MISC: External Advisor, Art Gallery of Ontario proj. team for the installation of the European Modern permanent galleries, 1995 to date; appointed to the 1st Manitoba Advisory Council on the Status of Women, 1980-81; juror, various granting agencies; various lectures; various papers & seminars, Univ. of Toronto; recipient, grants & fellowships; makes caricature dolls/puppets.

Leibovici, Karen, B.S.W.,M.S.W.,M.L.A. ✦
Member of Legislative Assembly (Edmonton Meadowlark), GOVERNMENT OF ALBERTA, 9544 - 163 St., Edmonton, AB T5P 3M7 (403) 484-4101, FAX 484-4107. Born Montreal 1952. m. Stephen I. Zepp. 1 ch. EDUC: McGill Univ., B.S.W. 1974, M.S.W. 1985, Dipl.(Mgmt) 1985. CAREER: Social Worker, Ville Marie Social Service Centre, 1975-78; Labour Rel'ns Consultant, Association of Ville Marie Social Service

Workers, 1978-80; Labour Rel'ns Officer/Equal Opportunity Officer, City of Edmonton, 1980-89; Labour Rel'ns Consultant, City of Edmonton & other organizations, 1989-93; Liberal candidate (Jasper Place), prov. elections, 1986; M.L.A. (Edmonton Meadowlark), Gov't of Alberta, 1993 to date. AFFIL: Western Industrial Research & Training Centre (Bus. Advisory Council; Bd. 1990-93); Edmonton Taxi Cab Commission (Bd. 1991; Chair 1992-93); Block Parent (Coord. 1990-92); West End Transportation Advisory Committee (Founding Mbr.); Social Planning Council; Youth Emergency Shelter; Alberta Liberal Party (Pres., Jasper Place 1986-88); Alberta Women's Liberal Commission (Treas. 1986-87); Alberta Liberal Party Convention (Policy Co-Chair 1987); Liberal Party of Canada (Dir., Edmonton S.W. 1986-88).

Leidl, Judith J., M.F.A. ■■ ⊗ ⌖
Fine Artist/Printmaker, JUDITH LEIDL FINE ART, 5211 Blowers St., Ste. 20, Halifax, NS B3L 1J6 (902) 422-6628, FAX 425-2468. m. Peter Wilson. 1 ch. Isobel Jane Winifred Leidl Wilson. EDUC: Kootenay Sch. of Art, Nelson, B.C., Diploma in Graphic Design 1982; N.S. Coll. of Art & Design, Halifax, B.F.A.(Studio major) 1986, M.F.A. 1994. EXHIBITIONS: 6 solo exhibitions, Halifax, Winnipeg, Windsor (Ont.), Toronto, 1986 to date; 18 group exhibitions overseas incl.: "Contemporary Canadian Bookworks," Cdn Embassy, Tokyo, 1995; Pacific Rim Int'l Print Exhibition, Univ. of Hawaii, 1995; Int'l Print Biennale, Varna, Bulgaria, 1993; others in Scotland, Taiwan, UK, The Netherlands, Japan, Slovenia, Germany, Spain & Ukraine; 36 group exhibitions in N.Am. incl.: *Collective Viewing: Selections from the Art Bank of Nova Scotia, 1975-1995*, Saint Mary's Univ. Art Gallery, Halifax, 1995; *Women Printmakers*, One West Contemporary Art Center, Ft. Collins, Colo., 1994; *The 44th North American Print Exhibition*, Boston Univ. Art Gallery, Boston, Mass., 1993; *Contemporary Artists in Nova Scotia*, Mount Saint Vincent Univ., 1992; *Medicine Hat Print Show*, Alta., 1991. COLLECTIONS: Art Gallery of Nova Scotia; Burnaby Art Gallery, B.C.; Canada Council Art Bank, Ottawa; Mount Saint Vincent Univ., Halifax; N.S. Art Bank, Halifax; Swan Hill Regional Art Gallery, New South Wales, Australia; Ukrainian Independent Centre for Contemporary Art, Lviv, Ukraine; various private collections in Canada & abroad. AFFIL: Visual Arts Nova Scotia (Bd. mbr., Reg. 4A); N.S. Printmakers' Association (Newsletter Coord. 1988-92; founding Bd. mbr. 1988 to date); College Art Association, N.Y.C.; Alberta Printmakers' Society, Calgary;

Association of Atlantic Women Business Owners, Halifax; Canadian Artists' Representation, Ottawa; CARFAC Copyright Collective, Ottawa; Canadian Bookbinders' & Book Artists' Guild, Toronto; Malaspina Printmakers' Society, Vancouver; National Museum of Women in the Arts, Washington, D.C. (Archives on Women Artists); Print Consortium, Kansas City, Miss.; Print & Drawing Council of Canada, Toronto; National Society of Painters, Sculptors & Printmakers, London, UK; N.S. Printmakers' Association, Halifax; NSCAD Alumni Association; Southern Graphics Council, Gainsville, Fla.; Windsor Printmakers' Forum, Windsor, Ont. HONS: Elizabeth Nutt Award, N.S. Coll. of Art & Design, 1986; short-listed for Commonwealth Fellowship in the Arts & Crafts (1 of 20), Commonwealth Institute, London, UK, 1992 & 1994; Best in Show award (1 of 5), Gulf Canada Exhibition: Work by the Alberta Printmakers' Society, 1992; Joseph Beuys Memorial Scholarship, N.S. Coll. of Art & Design, 1993; short-listed for Grand Prix of the City of Varna (1 of 5), Int'l Print Biennale, Varna, 1993; several grants. MISC: cover art: *Canadian Fiction* magazine, No. 89, 1995; *Equal/Opposites*, 1994; *Alberta Printmakers' Society, Newsletter* #12, 1992; *Visual Arts News*, Vol. 14, No. 3, Autumn 1992; *Quarry* Magazine, Vol. 41, No. 1, Winter 1992, & Vol. 38, No. 3, Summer 1989; cover art, *Engaged Elsewhere*, short stories by Canadian writers living abroad (Quarry Press, 1989); images used in feature film, *Two If By Sea*, 1995; Instructor, printmaking workshops, Continuing Educ. Dept., N.S. Coll. of Art & Design, 1986 to date; Visiting Artist, Windsor Printmakers Forum, Ont., 1991 & St. Michael's Print Shop, Nfld., 1993; Visiting Artist, *Engramme*, Quebec City, 1996. COMMENT: *"Dreams, desires, fears, fantasies and everyday experiences are the sources from which I derive my images. I then combine fragments from each, most often in an unconscious way, to form an alternate reality in which anything is possible. Within this "other" reality I am free to re-work my life experiences, to explore various possible endings to certain real-life scenarios, to experiment with different ways of seeing, and hopefully to present alternate solutions to current problems."*

Lem, Esther, B.A.(Hons.) ■■ ⑤

Vice-President, Personal Care, LEVER POND'S (manufacturer of home care & personal care products), 1 Sunlight Park Rd., Toronto, ON M4M 1B6 (416) 462-2225, FAX 462-2210. Born Toronto. EDUC: Univ. of Western Ontario, B.A.(Hons., Bus. Admin) 1978. CAREER: Acct Group, Ogilvy & Mather, 1978-

83; Brand Mgr, Warner Lambert, 1983-87; Mktg Mgr, Lever Pond's, 1987-90; Personal Products Coord., UK, 1991; VP, Personal Care, 1991-96. AFFIL: Canadian Congress of Advertising (Co-Chair, 1997 CASSIES); Non-Prescription Drug Manufacturers Advertising Task Force (1995 to date); Queen's Univ. (Mktg Case Judge, Inter-Collegiate Bus. Schools Competition 1990 to date); G.P.M.C. Marketing Council (1992-96); Canadian Cosmetics and Toiletry Association (Dir.); Print Measurement Bureau (Dir.). HONS: *Marketing* Award (Pears commercial), 1995; Unilever TV Award (Pears commercial), 1995; *Studio Magazine* Award (Q-tips), 1994. INTERESTS: sports, esp. golf, skiing, squash, volleyball; daily walks with the dog. COMMENT: *"I've progressed quickly in my career in three outstanding companies. I also maintain an active life outside of work. I just started golf and can finally boast about breaking 100 (honestly!)."*

Lemay, Patricia ■ ⑤

Director of Manufacturing, CULINAR MANUFACTURING, 1156 Dundas St. E., London, ON N6A 4R7 (519) 455-2250, FAX 455-1449. Born 1950. s. EDUC: Institut de Technologie Agro-Alimentaire, Tech. 1969. CAREER: Mgr, Flamingo, Quebec Poultry, 1969-75; Tech. Mgr, Grissol, Imasco, 1975-83; Owner, Reliure St.-Denis, 1983-86; Production Mgr, Grissol, Culinar Inc., 1986-91; Mfg Dir., Culinar, C.B.S., 1991-94; Mfg Dir., Culinar, McCormick's, London, 1994 to date. SELECTED PUBLICATIONS: "Profession directrice de production," career profile (*Revue agro-alimentaire du Québec* 1991). AFFIL: Canadian Institute of Food Science & Technology (1969-88); Big Sisters Montreal (1980-85). INTERESTS: theatre; skating; books (binding & literature); movies. MISC: various conference presentations. COMMENT: *"I am not a career person. I am doing what I have to do. Self-developed person in management. Skilled in achieving a 'change in an organization'; people-oriented."*

Lemieux, Diane ■ ⑥

Présidente, CONSEIL DU STATUT DE LA FEMME (CSF), 8 rue Cook, 3è etage, Québec, QC G1R 5J7 (418) 644-9269, FAX 644-0095. Born Sherbrooke 1961. EDUC: Univ. de Sherbrooke, Diplôme (Droit) 1983. CAREER: Coord. et porte-parole du Regroupement québécois des CALACS (Centres d'aide et de lutte contre les agressions à caractère sexuel), 1986-96; Prés., CSF, 1996 to date. SELECTED PUBLICATIONS: numerous conference papers. HONS: Prix de la Justice du Qué., 1991. INTERESTS: promotion & defence of the rights of Que.

women. **COMMENT:** *"Madame Lemieux à oeuvre plusieurs années dans le domaine de la violence faite aux femmes. Aujourd'hui, comme présidente d'un organisme gouvernemental de consultation et d'étude, elle s'intéresse à tout sujet touchant la condition féminine et particulièrement la promotion et la défense des droits des femmes et l'amélioration de leur situation économique."*

Lemieux, Julie, B.F.A.,M.F.A. ■ 🎞 🎭 📺
Actor. c/o Angela Wright, Edna Talent Management, Toronto, ON M4T 1W5 (416) 413-7800, FAX 413-7804. Born Asbestos, Que. 1960. s. **EDUC:** Concordia Univ., B.F.A.(Theatre Performance) 1983; York Univ., M.F.A. (Theatre Performance) 1986. **CAREER:** Rupert the Bear & other voices, Nelvana Productions; various programs, TVOntario; various roles, Théâtre Français de Toronto, Nightwood Theatre. **AFFIL:** ACTRA; Union des Artistes; Canadian Actors' Equity. **HONS:** Award of Excellence in Children's Programming, *Picoli and Lirabo*, Banff, 1990, 1991; 'A La Claire fontaine,' 1994. **INTERESTS:** professional: positive & realistic portrayal of women in the media; personal: passionate dog owner & avid toy collector. **MISC:** readings for 'Performers for Literacy'; participated in 'Share A Story' literacy event at Queen's Park, 1992. **COMMENT:** *"It's great to be rewarded for being a big kid instead of being told to grow up. I hope it never ends. The adult in me wants to direct and is presently writing a play."*

Lemire, Beverly, B.A.,M.A.,D.Phil. ■ 🎓 📜
Professor, Department of History, UNIVERSITY OF NEW BRUNSWICK, Fredericton, NB E3B 5A3 (506) 453-4621, FAX 453-5068, EMAIL lmre@unb.ca. **EDUC:** Univ. of Guelph, B.A. 1979, M.A. 1981; Balliol Coll., Oxford Univ., D.Phil. 1985. **CAREER:** Sessional Inst., Dept. of Hist., Wilfrid Laurier Univ., 1985; Sessional Instructor, Dept. of Hist., Univ. of Guelph, 1985; Asst. Prof., Dept. of Hist., Univ. of Lethbridge, Alberta, 1986-87; Assoc. Prof., Dept. of Hist., Univ. of New Brunswick, 1987 to date. **SELECTED PUBLICATIONS:** *Fashion's Favourite: The Cotton Trade and the Consumer in Britain, 1660-1800* (Oxford Univ. Press, 1991); *Dress, Culture and Commerce: The English Clothing Trade before the Factory* (Macmillan, 1997); "Developing Consumerism and the Ready-made Clothes Trade in Britain, 1750-1800" (*Textile History* 1984); "Reflections on the character of consumerism, popular fashion and the English market in the eighteenth century" (*Material History Bulletin* Spring 1990); "Peddling Fashion: Salesmen, Pawnbrokers, Taylors, Thieves and the Second-hand Clothes Trade in England, 1680-1800" (*Textile History* Spring 1991). **EDIT:** Guest Ed., "Surveying Textile History," *Material History Bulletin*, Spring 1990. **AFFIL:** Economic History Association, US; Economic History Society, UK; North American Conference of British Studies; Canadian Historical Association; Beaverbrook Art Gallery. **HONS:** D.C. Masters Prize in Hist., 1979; J.H. Steward Reid Memorial Fellowship, Canadian Association of University Teachers, 1980-81; Bryce & Reed Funds, Oxford Univ., 1983; Commonwealth Scholarship, 1981-84; Veronika Gervers Fellowship in Textile Studies, The Royal Ontario Museum, 1993. **MISC:** SSHRC research grant, 1989-91, 1992-95; various conference papers & public addresses.

Lemire-Rodger, Ginette, Ph.D. ■■ ⊕ $ 🍁
President, LEMIRE RODGER & ASSOCIATES (consultant–mgmt, health, nursing), 9938 - 86th Ave., Edmonton, AB T6E 2L7 (403) 439-5934, FAX 439-5934. Born Amos, Que. 1943. m. William. 3 ch. Robert, Philippe, Sabrina. **EDUC:** Univ. of Ottawa, B.Sc.N. 1966; Univ. de Montréal, M.A.(Nursing Admin.) 1971; Univ. of Alberta, Ph.D.(Nursing) 1995. **CAREER:** Dir. of Nursing, Notre-Dame Hospital, 1974-81; Exec. Dir., Canadian Nurses' Association, 1981-89; Pres., Lemire Rodger & Associates, 1989 to date. **SELECTED PUBLICATIONS:** several articles incl.: "Nurses: Partners in the changing health scene" in *Partners in change: Health care in Canada to the year 2000* (Ottawa: Pharmaceutical Manufacturers' Association of Canada, 1988); "Intraorganizational Politics," in *Nursing Management in Canada*, ed. by J. Hibbard & M. Kyle (Toronto: W.B. Saunders, 1994); co-author with S. Gallagher, "The shift toward primary health care in Canada from 1985-1995" in M. Steward (ed.), *Community Nursing: Promoting Canadians' Health* (Toronto: W.B. Saunders, 1995). **AFFIL:** Alberta Association of Registered Nurses (Chairperson, Strategy Committee, Task Force on Increased Direct Access to Svcs of RNs in Community 1992 to date); Canadian Nurses' Association, CNA; Canadian Nurses' Foundation, CNF; Canadian Nurses' Protective Society; Canadian Coll. of Health Service Executives; Registered Nurses' Association of Ontario, RNAO; International Council of Nurses; Sigma Theta Tau Int'l; *Journal of Advanced Nursing*, UK (Edit. Bd. 1983 to date). **HONS:** many, incl.: Officer, Order of St. John, 1981; Ryerson Fellowship Award in recognition of contribution to nursing & health policy, 1984; hon. mbr. for life in recognition of contribution to public health in Canada, Ontario Public Health Association, 1984; Com-

mander, Order of St. John, 1985; Ginette Lemire Rodger Scholarship in Nursing Admin. established by CNA, 1988; new wing of CNA headquarters named "Ginette Lemire Rodger Wing," 1988; hon. life mbr., RNAO, 1989; Dorothy Kergin Doctoral Scholarship, CNF, 1992; Helen Preston Glass Fellowship in recognition of excellence in nursing, CNF, 1993; hon. degrees: Univ. of New Brunswick, Queen's Univ., Univ. of Sherbrooke, Univ. of Calgary. INTERESTS: skiing; hiking; riding; jazz; opera.

Leonard, Christine, B.A.,M.A. ⊕ ○ ◁◻
Executive Director, JOHN HOWARD SOCIETY OF ALBERTA, 10523 - 100 Ave., 2nd Fl., Edmonton, AB T5J 0A8 (403) 423-4878, FAX 425-0008. Born Edmonton 1966. m. James Pepin. 1 ch. Julie Celine Faye Pepin. EDUC: Univ. of Alberta, B.A.(Criminology) 1988; Univ. of Toronto, M.A.(Criminology) 1989. CAREER: Sr. Research Asst., Addiction Research Foundation, 1989-90; Research Proj. Mgr, John Howard Society of Alberta, 1991-92; Research Mgr, 1992-93; Exec. Dir., 1993 to date. SELECTED PUBLICATIONS: "Selected References on Topics Related to Ethnicity and Adaptation," with Y.W. Cheung (*International Journal of the Addictions* No. 5A/6A 1990); "Young Offenders Act Amendments–Principled Reform?," with H. Sapers (*Issues and Perspectives on Young Offenders in Canada* ed. J. Winterdyk, Toronto: HBJ-Holt, 1995). AFFIL: Alberta Criminal Justice Association (Northern Bd. of Dir.); Canadian Criminal Justice Association; Alberta Status of Women Action Committee (Bd. 1991-94); Drug Policy Foundation; Association of Human Services in Alberta; Academy of Criminal Justice Sciences; Association for Safe Alternatives in Childbirth; Children's Services Working Group (Co-Chair); Edmonton Young Offender Centre (Citizen's Advisory Committee). HONS: Alexander Rutherford Scholarship for Outstanding Academic Achievement, 1984-85; Open Fellowship, Univ. of Toronto, 1988-89. INTERESTS: working in the service agencies involved in crime prevention; volunteering with feminist women's organizations. MISC: various conference presentations. COMMENT: *"I have a Master's Degree in Criminology and enjoy using my education in my work with the John Howard Society. Volunteering with criminal justice agencies and feminist women's organizations brings me great satisfaction."*

Leonard, Katherine A., M.D.,FRCP(C), FAAP ♥ ⊕ ◉
Medical Director, Teen Clinic, NORTH YORK GENERAL HOSPITAL, 4001 Leslie St., North York, ON M2K 1E1 (416) 756-6750, FAX

756-6822. Born Stamford, Conn. 1956. m. Garry Leonard. 2 ch. EDUC: Brown Univ., RI, B.A. 1979; Univ. of Florida, Coll. of Medicine, Gainesville, Fla., M.D. 1983; Univ. of Vermont Medical Sch., Marine Medical Center, Portland, Me., Pediatric Internship & Residency 1984-87; Hospital for Sick Children Fellowship, Adolescent Medicine, 1992-93. CAREER: Officer, US Navy, 1979-91; Staff Pediatrician, Pediatric & Adolescent Medicine Dept., Naval Hospital, Newport, RI, 1987-91; Dir., Lead Poisoning Screening Program, 1987-91; Chair, Family Advocacy Committee on Child & Spouse Abuse, 1988-91; Consultant to Family Practice Pilot Proj., 1989-91; Med. Dir., Teen Clinic, North York General Hospital, 1991 to date. SELECTED PUBLICATIONS: "Your Body: A Column of Questions and Answers by Dr. Katherine A. Leonard," continuing column in *Ingenue* Magazine, 1993 to date; "Firearm Mortality in Canadian Adolescents and Young Adults" (*Canadian Journal of Public Health*, Mar./Apr. 1994). AFFIL: Canadian Association for Adolescent Health; American Academy of Pediatrics (Section on Adolescent Health); Royal Coll. of Physicians & Surgeons of Canada (Fellow); American Academy of Pediatrics (Fellow); Society for Adolescent Medicine (Fellow). HONS: US Navy Achievement Medal, 1991. MISC: various presentations on firearm-related deaths in young people. COMMENT: *"I am a pediatrician with specialty training in adolescent medicine. I am also a researcher. My area of interest is injury prevention in adolescence and I am particularly interested in the subject of prevention of firearm-related deaths in young people. In Canadians between the age of 15 and 24, more die every year from gunshot wounds (suicides, homicides and accidental deaths) than from cancer or from falls, fires, and drowning combined. A good bit of my professional time in the past year has been spent writing and speaking publicly in favour of Bill C-68, the proposed Canadian gun control legislation. I believe that physicians have an important role to play in getting across the notion that deaths from firearms are a serious public health issue in Canada."*

Leonard, Mary, B.A. ○ ⊕ ◻
Chair, Board of Governors, SCARBOROUGH GENERAL HOSPITAL, 3050 Lawrence Ave. E., Scarborough, ON M1P 2V5 (416) 431-8100, FAX 754-9114. Born Peterborough, Ont. 1940. m. Paul Leonard. 3 ch. Michael W. Leonard, Suzanne E. Carson, Karen J. Leonard. EDUC: Queen's Univ., B.A.(Hist. & Pol. Sci.) 1962; Univ. of Toronto, Ontario Coll. of Education (now O.I.S.E.), Teaching Certificate 1963. CAREER: Chief Librarian & Hist.

Teacher, Hill Park Secondary Sch., Hamilton, Ont., 1963-66; Scarborough Coord., Heart & Stroke Foundation of Ontario, 1986-88; Panel Mbr., Canada Pension Plan Tribunal, 1992 to date; Council Mbr., Coll. of Optometrists of Ontario, 1996-99. **VOLUNTEER CAREER:** University Women's Clubs of Scarborough, 1969-86; Pres., 1981-82; City of Scarborough Bd. of Health, 1975-84; Chair, 1976-80; Chair, Liaison Committee of Local Boards of Health of Metro. Toronto, 1980; Metropolitan Toronto District Health Council, 1980-84; Chair, 1980-84; Chair, Scarborough Hospital's Coordinating Committee, 1988-90; Bd. of Gov., Scarborough General Hospital, 1988 to date; V-Chair, SGH Bd. of Gov., 1992-93; Chair, 1993 to date. **INTERESTS:** golf; bridge; politics; reading; travel. **MISC:** 1st Chair of the Metropolitan Toronto District Health Council; 1st female Chair, Bd. of Gov., Scarborough General Hospital. **COMMENT:** *"Although by profession I am a secondary school teacher, I have devoted considerable time over the past 20 years as a volunteer leader in the healthcare field. My interest in this area began with my appointment to the Scarborough Board of Health in 1975. I was truly honoured to be appointed by the Minister of Health, Dennis Timbrell, in 1980 as the first Chair of the Metropolitan Toronto District Health Council. Another highlight of my career was being elected first female Chair of the Board of Governors of the Scarborough General Hospital. My involvement in the healthcare field has been an exciting challenge."*

Leroux, Monique, D.E.S.,B.A.A.,C.A., C.M.A.,F.C.A. $

Senior Vice-President, Finance, ROYAL BANK OF CANADA, 1 Place Ville Marie, Montreal, QC H3C 3A9 (514) 874-5974, FAX 874-5891. Born Montreal 1954. m. Marc Leroux. **EDUC:** Conservatoire de musique du Québec, D.E.S. 1974; Univ. du Québec, B.A.A.1978; C.A. 1980; C.M.A. 1980; F.C.A. 1993; Univ. of Western Ontario, Exec. program 1994. **CAREER:** prior to joining the bank, Ptnr, Fin. Institutions, Caron Bélanger Ernst & Young; Royal Bank of Canada. **SELECTED PUBLICATIONS:** prepared & wrote briefs & discussion papers for the Ordre des comptables agréés du Québec on the following topics: the future of the acctg profession, public finances in Canada & Que. (Comprendre pour agir L'urgence d'agir); C.A.s' educ. in Que., the reform of the financial ind. in Que.; in charge of preparing the *Investors' Guide to Montreal* (1991); author of *Impôt et planification fiscale.* **AFFIL:** Chambre de commerce du Québec (Dir.); Hôpital Ste. Justine (Dir.); Fondation du Musée de Pointe à Callière (Dir.); Montreal Heart Institute Research Fund (Dir.); Ordre des comptables agréés du Québec (past Chrm; past Pres.; Fellow 1993); Canadian Institute of Chartered Accountants (past Gov.); Order des CMA du Québec; Club St. Denis. **HONS:** Medal, Univ. du Québec à Chicoutimi, 1994; received numerous scholarships & prizes (in music & in mgmt). **INTERESTS:** art; travel. **MISC:** was a prof. at H.E.C. for numerous yrs.

Lesser, Gloria, I.D.S.Q., I.D.C. ★ 🎓 📜

Freelance Interior Designer. 4870 Côte des Neiges, E-305, Montreal, QC H3V 1H3 (514) 733-6098. Professor, Art History and Design, CHAMPLAIN REGIONAL COLLEGE. Born Montreal 1936. d. 3 ch. **EDUC:** Chicago Sch. of Interior Decoration, Diploma 1963; Concordia Univ., B.A.(Art Hist./Studio Art) 1977, M.F.A.(Art Hist.) 1983. **CAREER:** elementary sch. teacher, 1956-60; substitute teacher, 1960-78; Founder, Gloria Lesser Interiors, 1970 to date; Research Asst., Montreal Museum of Fine Arts, 1979-80; Grad. Fellowship Lecturer, Concordia Univ., 1980-81; Reg'l Contributor, "News and Views" Column, *Canadian Collector*, 1982-84; teacher, Interior Decorating, Adult Educ. Svcs, Laurenval Sch. Bd., 1983; Prof., Art Hist. & Interior Design, Champlain Regional Coll., 1984 to date; teacher, John Abbott Coll., 1984-85, 1989; Guest Curator, Château Dufresne, Montreal Museum of Decorative Arts, 1988-89. **SELECTED PUBLICATIONS:** *École du Meuble 1930-50: Interior Design and Decorative Art in Montreal* exhibition catalogue (Montreal: Chateau Dufresne, Montreal Museum of Decorative Arts, 1989); "The Homes and Furnishings of R.B. Angus, Montreal" in *Living in Style*, ed. John R. Porter (Montreal: Montreal Museum of Fine Arts, 1993); "Biography and Bibliography of the Writings of Donald William Buchanan (1908-1966)" (*The Journal of Canadian Art History* 2 1981); "Karen Bulow, Masterweaver" (*Canadian Society of Decorative Arts Bulletin* Winter 1990); "Sources and Documents: The R.B. Angus Collection, Paintings, Watercolours and Drawings" (*The Journal of Canadian Art History* No.1 1994); "Carl Poul Petersen: Master Danish-Canadian Silversmith" (*Material History Review*, 43, Spring 1996); numerous other articles. **AFFIL:** Canadian Society of Decorative Arts (VP 1994-96); Interior Designers' Society of Quebec (I.D.S.Q.); Interior Designers of Canada (I.D.C.). **INTERESTS:** practises classical ballet. **MISC:** recipient, Canada Council grants, 1984, 1984-85; guest speaker at various associations; *Canadian Who's Who*, 1994, 1995.

Letheren, Carol Anne, B.P.E.,B.A.,M.B.A., LL.D. 🕐 ⊕ ♂
Chief Executive Officer and Secretary General, CANADIAN OLYMPIC ASSOCIATION, 21 St. Clair Ave. E., Ste. 900, Toronto, ON M4T 1L9 (416) 962-0262, ext. 230, FAX 962-2893. Born Toronto 1942. EDUC: Univ. of Toronto, B.P.E.(Phys. Educ.) 1963, B.A. (Psych./Anthro.) 1969; York Univ., M.B.A. 1977. CAREER: Assoc. Prof. & Lecturer, Sch. of Phys. & Health Educ., Univ. of Toronto, 1963-70; Assoc. Prof. & Coord. of Undergrad. Studies, Dept. of Athletics & Phys. Educ., York Univ., 1970-77; Consultant, Gov't of Canada, 1977-79; Sr. Ptnr, Mathieu Letheren Associates, 1979-94; CEO/Sec.-Gen., Canadian Olympic Association, 1993 to date. ATHLETIC ADMINISTRATION CAREER: Chair, Officiating Committee, National Volleyball Association, 1963-66; VP & Chair, Women's Tech. Committee, Ontario Gymnastics Federation, 1967-70; VP & Chair, Women's Tech. Committee, Canadian Gymnastics Federation, 1970-77; Women's Tech. Committee, International Gymnastics Federation, 1976-80; Chair, Women's Tech. Committee, Pan American Gymnastics Confederation, 1975-83; VP & Dir., Canadian Olympic Association, 1982-90; Pres., 1991-94; Trustee, Olympic Endowment Fund, 1987-92; Chef de Mission, Cdn Team, Olympic Games, Seoul, South Korea, 1988; Dir., Toronto Ontario Olympic Council, 1988-90; International Olympic Committee, 1990 to date; Press Commission, International Olympic Committee, 1992-94; VP, Commission for the International Olympic Academy & Olympic Educ., 1994 to date. AFFIL: Cavanagh Rehabilitation Program & Hospital (Dir.); YWCA (Hon. Chair, Run, Walk & Roll); George Brown Coll. (Sports Mktg Advisory Committee); Bishop Strachan Sch. (Dir.); Commemorative Services of Ontario (Dir.); Canadian Gymnastics Federation (Lifetime Hon. Mbr.); International Gymnastics Federation (Lifetime Hon. Mbr.). HONS: Official of the Year, Air Canada, 1978; Gold Pin for Service, Canadian Gymnastics Federation, 1985; Volunteer of the Year, McCain's, 1989; Women Who Make A Difference, *Toronto Life Fashion*/The Bay, 1992; Sports Hall of Fame, Univ. of Toronto, 1992; Public Contribution Award, York Univ. Fac. of Administrative Studies, 1992; Woman of Distinction, YMCA, 1992; LL.D.(Hon.), Univ. of Toronto, 1993. INTERESTS: running; cycling; music. MISC: mbr., various juries & selection committees; athlete; officiating coach; IOC mbr. of the Site Evaluation Commission for the XXVII Olympiad, 2004. COMMENT: *"She was a member of the International Gymnastic Federation's Women's Technical Committee, President of the Pan American Gymnastics Association, Chef de Mission for Canada's Olympic Team to Seoul in 1988, President of the Canadian Olympic Association–all as either the first female to hold the position or the first Canadian female."*

Letton, Sandra ■■ ⊕ ♥
Vice-President, ST. JOSEPH'S HEALTH CENTRE, 268 Grosvenor St., London, ON N6A 4V2 (519) 646-6100, FAX 646-6148. Clinical Associate, Faculty of Nursing, UNIVERSITY OF WESTERN ONTARIO. AFFIL: Canadian Coll. of Health Services Executives; London Intercommunity Health Centre (Bd. mbr.; mbr., Bd. Dev.); Mission Services, London (Bd. mbr.; Chair. Human Resource Committee). HONS: Award for Excellence in Nursing Admin., Sigma Theta Tau Int'l Honour Society of Nursing, Iota Omicron chpt., 1992.

Leuschner, Lizabeth, B.S.,J.D. ⚖ ♥
Lawyer, SHENNETTE LEUSCHNER McKAY, 700 - 4th Ave. S.W., Ste. 600, Calgary, AB T2P 3J4 (403) 269-8282, FAX 269-8295. Born Calgary 1956. m. 3 ch. EDUC: Texas A&M Univ., B.S.(Natural Resources & Conservation); Baylor Univ. Sch. of Law, Waco, Tex., Juris Doctor 1981. BAR: Texas, 1981; Alta., 1982. CAREER: Assoc. & Student, Fenerty, Robertson, Fraser and Hatch, 1981-83; Assoc., Howard, Mackie, 1983-94; Sessional Instructor, Fac. of Law, Univ. of Calgary, 1989-90; Lawyer, McLeod Ferner and Bruni, 1993-94; Lawyer, Shennette Leuschner McKay, 1995 to date. AFFIL: Law Society of Alberta; State Bar of Texas; Canadian Bar Association; American Bar Association; Canadian-American Bar Association; Certified Mediator; Phi Kappa Phi; Calgary Zoological Society (Trustee; Designated Legal Cnsl; Special Events Chair; V-Chair, Dev. Committee); Calgary Zoo Foundation (Founding Dir.); PALS Humane Society Senior Citizens' Visitation Program (participant); Fathers Alberta Shared Parenting Association (Approved Cnsl); Alberta Science Centre Society (Dir.; Dev. Committee); The Basement "Street Kids" Shelter (Dir./Legal Cnsl). HONS: numerous awards for academic excellence & advocacy while at university. INTERESTS: gourmet cooking; backpacking; skiing; travel; horseback riding; scuba diving.

Levenson, Jill ✎ 📖
Professor, Trinity College, UNIVERSITY OF TORONTO, 6 Hoskin Ave., Toronto, ON M5S 1H8 (416) 978-2886, FAX 978-4949. EDUC: Queens Coll. of the City, Univ. of New York, B.A. 1963; Harvard Univ., M.A. 1964, Ph.D. 1967. CAREER: Lecturer, Queens Coll. of the

City, Univ. of New York, 1964; Tutor, Harvard Univ., 1965-66; Asst. Prof. of English, Trinity Coll., Univ. of Toronto, 1967-74; Assoc. Prof. of English, 1974-82; Prof. of English, 1982 to date. **SELECTED PUBLICATIONS:** *Shakespeare in Performance: "Romeo and Juliet"* (Manchester: Manchester Univ. Press, 1987); *"The Weakest Goeth to the Wall": A Critical Edition* ed. (New York: Garland Publishing, Inc., 1980); "Romeo and Juliet before Shakespeare" (*Studies in Philology* Summer 1984); "The Narrative Format of Benoit's *Roman de Troie*" (Romania No. 1 1979); "Shakespeare's *Troilus and Cressida* and the Monumental Tradition in Tapestries and Literature" (*Renaissance Drama* No. 7 1976); numerous scholarly articles, book chapters, conference papers & reviews. **EDIT:** Chair, Ed. Advisory Bd., *Modern Drama* ; Ed. Bd., *Essays in Theatre*. **AFFIL:** Shakespeare Association of America (Pres. 1991-92); International Shakespeare Association (V-Chair 1996); American Society for Theater Research; Modern Language Association of America; Conference of Editors of Learned Journals. **HONS:** Special Certificate of Merit, Conference of Editors of Learned Journals, 1986; 25-Year Service Award, Univ. of Toronto, 1992; Outstanding Teacher Award, Fac. of Arts & Science, Univ. of Toronto, 1994. **MISC:** panel mbr., OGS Selection Committee, 1983; reviewer, various granting agencies, publishers & journals; recipient, various grants; numerous invited lectures. **COMMENT:** *"I have been doing research mainly in the field of English Renaissance drama."*

Lever, Andrina, B.A. $

President, Lever Enterprises, 89 Elm Ave., Toronto, ON M4W 1N9 (416) 920-5114, FAX 920-6764. Born Essex, UK 1950. m. Frank. 2 ch. **EDUC:** Texas Tech Univ., B.A. 1971; Polytechnic of Central London, UK, B.A.(Law) 1979. **BAR:** England & Wales, 1980; Victoria, Australia, 1981. **CAREER:** various positions, bnkg, advtg & corp. fin.; Founder & Mng Dir., Expansion International Advisory Inc.; Pres., Lever Enterprises, 1988 to date. **DIRECTOR:** Expansion International Advisory Inc.; JIT International Pty Ltd.; Make Mine Balloons! Pty Ltd. **AFFIL:** Canadian Stage Company (Dir.); Kids' Help Line (Chair, Mother's Day Breakfast 1995, 1996); Canadian Stage Theatre Ball (Chair 1994-95); Women Entrepreneurs of Canada (VP 1994; Pres. 1995-96); Bar Association of United Kingdom & Wales; Bar Association of Victoria, Australia; Honourable Society of Gray's Inn, UK. **HONS:** nominated for Veuve Cliquot Business Woman of the Year, 1988. **INTERESTS:** theatre; travel; reading. **MISC:** delegate & keynote speaker at both nat'l & int'l conferences; has developed & given various seminars, workshops & training programs across Canada, Europe, Asia & Asutralia. **COMMENT:** *"Mrs. Lever lived, studied and worked away from Canada for 20 years in Europe, Australia and the US, thus gaining a broad experience in living and dealing with other cultures, environments, and business and social practices."*

Levin, Deborah ■ 🎭 $ ☼

Clairvoyant. Owner and Operator, Maiden, Mother, Crone, 414 Ontario St., Apt. 2, Toronto, ON M5A 2W1 1-888-967-9447, FAX 1-888-967-9447. Born Toronto 1967. s. **EDUC:** Univ. of Toronto, Geol., Physics, Psych. **CAREER:** psychic & spiritual counsellor; perfumer; voice artist; owner & operator, Maiden, Mother, Crone, store & int'l occult mail-order company. **INTERESTS:** piano; collecting essential oils; paleontology; paranormal research; films; confectionery making; militant animal lover. **MISC:** travels extensively to counsel & conduct workshops; is a regular guest of numerous TV & radio programs, incl. CBC Newsworld, CityTV, CBC Radio, Women's Television Network, YTV, CFNY, 640AM, Q107, MuchMusic & many more. **COMMENT:** *"Deborah's emerging psychic sensitivity began at age five, when she showed remarkable psi abilities and is now considered by many to be one of the most talented Canadian psychics."*

Levine, Marlene, B.A. 🍁

Director General, Regional Operations Branch, Statistics Canada, Jean Talon Bldg., Tunney's Pasture, 6 B-8, Ottawa, ON K1A 0T6 (613) 951-9750, FAX 951-2105. Born Ottawa 1946. d. **EDUC:** Carleton Univ., B.A.(Soc.) 1966. **CAREER:** Dir., Labour Force Survey, Statistics Canada, 1981-85; Dir., Labour Div., 1985-87; Dir. Gen., Mgmt Practices Branch, 1987-89; Dir. Gen., Reg'l Oper. Branch, 1989 to date. **AFFIL:** CS Co-op (Chair, Credit Committee 1992-94).

Levine, Renee, B.A. ♡ ⊕ ✊

Chairperson, Aplastic Anemia Association of Canada, 22 Aikenhead Rd., Etobicoke, ON M9R 2Z3 (416) 235-0468, FAX 864-9929. Born Calgary 1957. m. Jeff. 2 ch. Michael, Stephanie. **EDUC:** McGill Univ., B.A.(Indust. Rel'ns) 1978; Seneca Coll., Certificate (Travel & Tourism) 1992. **CAREER:** various positions, Indust. & Labour Rel'ns, Pacific Western Airlines, 1978-85; Ptnr, Contemporary Conferences, 1986-87; Chair, Aplastic Anemia Family

Association of Canada, 1987 to date; Customer Svc., Insight Information. **AFFIL:** B'nai Brith Women of Canada. **INTERESTS:** volunteer work; cooking; travel; reading. **COMMENT:** *"As a result of personal experience, I established a national registered charity to deal with the rare disease of aplastic anemia. Through my work, I hope I have touched a few lives."*

Levy, Cathy, B.Sc.(Hons. Dance) 🎞 🎭
Producer, LEVY PRODUCTIONS, 490 Adelaide St. W., Ste. 201, Toronto, ON M5V 1T2 (416) 703-0848, FAX 504-8702. Born Montreal 1957. cl. Martin Bolduc. **EDUC:** Univ. of Waterloo, B.Sc.(Hons. Dance) 1980. **CAREER:** Admin. Tech. Asst., Mountain Dance Theatre, 1978-80; Researcher, Dance in Canada Association, 1980; Publicity Dir., Anna Wyman Dance Theatre, 1980-83; Publicity Dir., Vancouver East Cultural Centre, 1983-85; Asst. to Prod., Dance Theatre Workshop, N.Y.C., 1985; Special Events Coord., Canada Pavilion, Expo '86, 1986; Dir., Special Projects, Dance in Canada Association; Dir., Levy Productions, 1986 to date; Prod., Canada Dance Festival, 1988 to date; writer, various Cdn dance publications, 1988 to date; Dance Programmer, Harbourfront Centre, Premiere Dance Theatre, 1992 to date; Dir., Vancouver East Cultural Centre, 1994-96. **AFFIL:** Dancers for Life (Co-founder & Co-Chair, Toronto & Vancouver); First Night Toronto; 12 Alexander Street Selection Committee (Dance Rep.); Dance Ontario; Dance in Canada Association; Candance Presenters' Network; Toronto Theatre Alliance; *Dance Connection* Magazine (Advisory Committee). **INTERESTS:** biking; film; reading; performing & visual arts; summer sports; AIDS research. **MISC:** Co-founder & Coord., Vancouver Dance Week, 1983-84; Co-founder & Coord., First National Dance Critics' Seminar, 1983; mbr., various cultural delegations; recipient, 2 Canada Council grants. **COMMENT:** *"Ms. Levy is an active producer and presenter of the contemporary performing arts. Through her company, Levy Productions, she produces projects involving the presentation of both alternative and formal performing arts events."*

Levy, Julia, B.A.,Ph.D. ■■ ⚛ ⊕
Chief Executive Officer, Chief Scientific Officer and President, QLT PHOTOTHERAPEUTICS INC. (biotechnology), 520 W. 6th Ave., Vancouver, BC V5Z 4H5 (604) 872-7881, FAX 875-0001. Born Singapore 1934. m. Edwin. 2 ch. Benjamin, Jennifer. **EDUC:** Univ. of British Columbia, B.A.(Hons., Immunology) 1955; University Coll., London, Ph.D.(Experimental Pathology) 1958. **CAREER:** Prof., Dept. of Microbiol., Univ. of B.C., 1972 to date; VP, R.& D., QLT PhotoTherapeutics Inc., 1982-95; CEO, CSO & Pres., 1995 to date. **SELECTED PUBLICATIONS:** co-author, 165 papers/notes/communications in refereed journals, 31 full-length symposium papers, 1 book, & 7 chapters in books. **DIRECTOR:** QLT PhotoTherapeutics Inc.; Working Opportunity Fund. **HONS:** hon. doctorate, Univ. of Ottawa & Mount Saint Vincent Univ.; Gold Medal, B.C. Science Council, 1981. **INTERESTS:** tennis; gardens; cooking; grandchildren. **COMMENT:** *"Research in cancer has been a driving force. The opportunity offered by QLT to take basic scientific observations through to clinical testing is the best outcome I could dream of."*

Lewis, Harriet Isabel, B.A.,M.A., LL.B. ■■ ⚖ 🎓 ☝
University Counsel, YORK UNIVERSITY, Ross Building, 4700 Keele St., Ste. N945, North York, ON M3J 1P3 (416) 736-5310, FAX 736-5094, EMAIL hlewis@yorku.ca. Born Medicine Hat, Alta. 1947. m. Eldon J. Bennett. 2 ch. Daniel Lewis, Elliot James. **EDUC:** York Univ., B.A.(Hons., English) 1969, M.A. (English) 1971; Univ. of Toronto, LL.B. 1975; Law Society of Upper Canada, Barrister & Solicitor 1977. **CAREER:** law practice, Goodman & Goodman, 1977-78; Raymond & Honsberger, 1978-88; York Univ., 1988 to date. **AFFIL:** Law Society of Upper Canada; York Univ. (Exec. Committee, Budget & Policy Committee); Canadian Association of University Solicitors (Pres. 1995-96); Canadian Universities' Reciprocal Insurance Exchange (Advisory Bd. 1996 to date; Dir.); Institute of Contemporary Canadian Craft (VP; Dir.). **HONS:** York Univ. grad. scholarship, 1970-71. **INTERESTS:** reading; gardening. **COMMENT:** *"As the first University Counsel at York University, I have tried to support both the academic and administrative enterprise and assist in charting a course through the stormy seas of current university life. The challenge remains one of balancing dedication to work and achieving professional excellence with the pleasures and demands of family life...and maintaining perspective and a sense of humour throughout."*

Lewis, Judy, B.A. [$]
Executive Vice-President, STRATEGIC OBJECTIVES INC., 194 Front St. E., Ste. 701, Toronto, ON M5A 4N3 (416) 366-7735, FAX 366-2295. Born Montreal 1955. m. Stephen. 2 ch. **EDUC:** École Vincent D'Indy, Sr. Diploma of Music (Cello) 1970; McGill Univ., CEGEP Diploma (English) 1975, B.A.(with distinction, English Film & Comm.) 1977. **CAREER:** Prod. & Broadcaster, CBC Radio, 1977-81; Prod., Free

to Live Productions, 1981; Sr. Story Ed. & Story Prod., CTV Television, 1981-83; Prod. & Writer, DJW Communications, 1983; Exec. VP, Strategic Objectives, 1983 to date. **AFFIL:** International Association of Business Communicators (IABC); Canadian Public Relations Society (CPRS); International Public Relations Association (IPRA); YMCA of Metropolitan Toronto (former Mbr., Bd. of Gov.); United Jewish Appeal (Co-Chair 1994); Second Harvest (Comm. Committee). **INTERESTS:** music; theatre. **MISC:** Strategic Objectives Inc. has won numerous IPRA & CPRS awards for campaigns, incl.: Golden World Award, IPRA, 1996; Gold Quill Award, IABC, 1996; Special United Nations Award, IPRA, 1995; Golden World Award, IPRA, 1994; Gold Award, CPRS, 1994; Gold Quill Award, Community & Gov't Rel'ns, Multi-Audience Comm., IABC, 1994; various Certificates of Excellence & Certificates of Merit.

Lewis, Laurie, B.A.,F.G.D.C. 📖 ⌘
International Publishing Consultant and Teacher. Kingston, ON K7M 3R9 (613) 384-9487, FAX 384-2309. Born Vancouver 1930. m. Gary A. Lewis. 2 ch. Amanda Lewis, Delvalle Desilva Lewis. **EDUC:** Hunter Coll., CUNY, B.A.(Psych.) 1952; New York Univ., Graphic Arts Program, Certificate 1962; apprenticeship in graphic design from Carl Dair, 1965. **CAREER:** various positions from Prod. Asst. to Design Mgr, Univ. of Toronto Press, 1963-91; Instructor, Publication Design, International Rice Research Institute, Los Baelvalle Desilva Lewis. 95; Golden World Award, IPRA, 1994; Gold Award, CPRS, 1994; Gold Quill Textbook Proj., Min. of Educ. of Guyana, S. America, 1994. **SELECTED PUBLICATIONS:** *Sticks & Stones, Toronto Typographic*, ed. with John Gibson (1980). **EDIT:** Ed. Bd., *The Writers' Machine*; Ed. Bd., Roraima Publishing, Guyana, S. America; Ed. Bd., Longbird Press, Bermuda. **AFFIL:** Society of Graphic Designers of Canada (Fellow); Canadian Executive Service Organization; Canadian Organization for Development Through Education. **HONS:** Medal, Leipzig International Book Fair, 1972. **INTERESTS:** books, books & more books; Mac computers; grandchildren; gardening; teaching; writing. **COMMENT:** *"After an intense and satisfying career in the publishing business, I find a great deal of pleasure these days in assisting small publishers, particularly those in the third world; passing on my experience and skills and helping another generation fall in love with books."*

Lewis, Linda R., B.I.D. ■■ ⌘ 📖
Professor, RYERSON POLYTECHNIC UNIVERSITY,

350 Victoria St., Toronto, ON M5B 2K3 (416) 979-5000, ext. 6871, FAX 979-5139, EMAIL lrlewis@acs.ryerson.ca. Born Medicine Hat, Alta. 1943. m. Dr. Lorie Cappe. **EDUC:** Univ. of Manitoba, B.I.D.(Interior Design) 1970. **CAREER:** Interior Designer, R.J. Thom, Architects, 1966-67; Design Consultant, 1967-69; Prof., Ryerson, 1969 to date; Program Dir., Film Studies, 1984-89. **SELECTED CREDITS:** *I Object* (documentary), 1975 - exhibited at Sydney Film Festival, 1976, & Toronto Int'l Film Festival, 1994. **SELECTED PUBLICATIONS:** co-author with Peter Day, *Art in Everyday Life: Observations on Contemporary Canadian Design* (Summerhill Press, Toronto, 1988); contributor, *Changing Focus: The Future for Women in the Canadian Film & Television Industry* (T.W.I.F.T., 1991); numerous articles on Cdn design history for A.R.I.D.O. **EXHIBITIONS:** Exhibition Curator with Peter Day, "Art in Everyday Life: Aspects of Canadian Design, 1967-1987," The Power Plant, Toronto, June-Sept. 1988. **AFFIL:** The Design Exchange (founding Pres.; Chair, Hon. Bd.); National Design Alliance (founding mbr. 1992); Association of Registered Interior Designers of Ontario, A.R.I.D.O.; Visual Arts Ontario (Bd. mbr. 1986-88). **INTERESTS:** design; history; film; gardening. **MISC:** Pres., Group for the Creation of a Design Centre in Toronto, 1985-91; Chair, City of Toronto Bd. of Mgmt for the Design Exchange, 1987-96. **COMMENT:** *"I consider myself primarily an educator with a passionate interest in preserving Canada's design history. My proudest achievement is the establishment of The Design Exchange, a national centre for design and innovation, located in the old Toronto Stock Exchange at 234 Bay Street."*

L'Heureux-Dubé, Honourable Madame Justice Claire, B.A.,LL.L.,LL.D. ⚖
Puisne Judge, SUPREME COURT OF CANADA, Ottawa, ON K1A 0J1. Born Quebec City 1927. w. Dr. Arthur Dubé. 2 ch. (1 dec.). **EDUC:** Coll. Notre-Dame de Bellevue, Quebec, B.A. 1946; Laval Univ., LL.L. 1951. **BAR:** Qué., 1952; Queen's Counsel, 1969. **CAREER:** Ptnr, L'Heureux & Philippon, 1952-69; Sr. Ptnr, L'Heureux, Philippon, Garneau, Tourigny, St. Arnaud & Associates, 1969-73; Lecturer in Family Law, Cours de formation professionnelle du Barreau du Québec, 1970-73; Puisne Judge, Superior Court of Quebec, 1973-79; Commissioner, Inquiry into certain matters relating to the Dept. of Manpower & Immigration in Montreal, 1973-76; Judge, Court of Appeal of Quebec, 1979-87; Puisne Judge, Supreme Court of Canada, 1987 to date. **SELECTED PUBLICATIONS:** *Family*

Law–Dimensions of Justice, ed. with Rosalie S. Abella (Toronto: Butterworths, 1983); "La garde conjointe, concept acceptable ou non?" (*Revue du Barreau* 39 1979); "The Quebec Experience: Codification of Family Law and a Proposal for the Creation of a Family Court System" (*Louisiana Law Review* 44 1984); several contributions to *La Revue des Services du Bien-être à l'Enfance et à la jeunesse* & *Le Bien-être canadien*; various other publications. **EDIT:** Chrm, Ed. Bd., *The Canadian Bar Review*, 1985-88. **AFFIL:** Canadian Bar Association; Canadian Institute for the Administration of Justice; International Commission of Jurists (VP, Int'l Bd.); International Society on Family Law (Hon. Mbr., Bd. of Dir.); International Academia of Comparative Law; Canadian Human Rights Foundations; Association québécoise le droit comparé; International Federation of Women Lawyers; L'Association des Avocates de la Province de Québec; L'Association des Femmes diplômées d'université (Québec); Fédération Internationale des femmes juristes; Fondation Univ. Laval (Lifetime Gov.); 430 Tactical Helicopter Squadron, Canadian Forces Base, Valcartier (Hon. Lt.-Col.); American Coll. of Trial Lawyers (Hon. Mbr.); American Law Institute; Phi Delta Phi. **HONS:** Medal of the Lt. Gov., 1946; special awards in Civil Law & Labour Law, Univ. Laval, 1951; Medal of the Alumni, Univ. Laval, 1986; Medal of the Montreal Bar, 1994; LL.D.(Hon.), Laval Univ., 1981; LL.D.(Hon.), Dalhousie Univ., 1981; LL.D.(Hon.), Univ. de Montréal, 1983; LL.D. (Hon.), Univ. d'Ottawa, 1988; LL.D.(Hon.), Univ. du Québec à Rimouski, 1989; LL.D. (Hon.), Univ. of Toronto, 1994; Hon. Doctorate Degree, Gonzaga Univ., 1996. **MISC:** Counsellor, Bar of Québec, 1968-70; Cdn Delegate, IXe Congrès de l'Institut international de Droit d'expression française (IDEF), Tunis, 1974; various lectures.

Lichtman, Shelley $

Director, Group Marketing Development, THE GREAT-WEST LIFE ASSURANCE COMPANY, 60 Osborne St. N., Winnipeg, MB R3C 3A5 (204) 946-7778, FAX 946-8829. Born Winnipeg 1955. m. Edward. 1 ch. Mindy. **CAREER:** St. Boniface General Hospital; Turnbull and Turnbull, Consulting Actuaries; various positions, Great-West Life Assurance Company. **AFFIL:** American Contract Bridge League (Life Master). **INTERESTS:** family; reading; travel. **COMMENT:** *"Educated in the sciences and psychology, I have chosen a career in business where my aptitude for finance and interest in the health field have meshed. I am assertive and have furthered my career by seeking challenges and opportunities with Great-West Life."*

Lickley, Lavina A., A.R.C.T.,B.A.,M.D., FRSC(C),Ph.D.,F.A.C.S. ■■ ⊕ 🎓

Surgeon-in-Chief, WOMEN'S COLLEGE HOSPITAL, 60 Grosvenor St., Ste. 522, Toronto, ON M4W 3B5 (416) 323-6120, FAX 323-6535, EMAIL lavina.lickley@utoronto.ca. Professor of Surgery and Physiology, UNIVERSITY OF TORONTO. Born Toronto 1936. s. **EDUC:** Royal Conservatory of Music, Toronto, A.R.C.T.(Piano) 1958; Univ. of Toronto, Victoria Coll., B.A.(Physiology & Biochem.) 1958, Fac. of Medicine, M.D. 1962; Royal Coll. of Physicians & Surgeons of Canada, Fellow (Gen. Surgery) 1968; American Board of General Surgery, Diplomate (Gen. Surgery) 1969; McGill Univ., Ph.D.(Experimental Medicine) 1974; American Coll. of Surgeons, F.A.C.S.(Gen. Surgery) 1977. **SELECTED PUBLICATIONS:** 51 peer-reviewed published scientific papers in the fields of breast disease, & hormonal & metabolic responses to stress. **AFFIL:** American Coll. of Surgeons; Canadian Society of Endocrinology & Metabolism; American Diabetes Association; Canadian Society for Clinical Investigation; Ontario Medical Association; Royal Coll. of Physicians & Surgeons of Canada; Society for Academic Surgery; National Surgical Adjuvant Breast & Bowel Project (Principal Investigator, Women's College Hospital). **HONS:** Fellowship, Medical Research Council of Canada, 1971; Marion Hilliard Fund Award, Women's College Hospital, 1973; Travelling Fellowship, Royal Coll. of Physicians & Surgeons of Canada, 1973; F.N.G. Starr Memorial Grad. Scholarship, 1974; Hope Award for breast cancer research, Toronto Women's Breast Cancer Foundation, 1987; E.B. Tovee Award for excellence in undergrad. teaching, Dept. of Surgery, Univ. of Toronto, 1988; Professional Award, Canadian Breast Cancer Foundation, Ont. chpt., 1994; Arbour Award, Univ. of Toronto, 1995. **INTERESTS:** music; skiing; cottage in wilderness; reading. **COMMENT:** *"Main achievements in research in endocrine physiology and breast cancer."*

Lie-Nielsen, Anne, B.A. ♡ ✊ 🍁

Executive Director, PRINCE EDWARD ISLAND COUNCIL OF THE DISABLED, Box 2128, Charlottetown, PE C1A 7N7 (902) 892-9149, FAX 566-1919. Born Douglas, Ga. 1944. d. 3 ch. Perri Britt Shippien, Lara Christine Merritt, Morgan Butler Merritt. **EDUC:** Univ. of Maine, B.A.(Int'l Affairs) 1966. **CAREER:** Internship, Nat'l Aeronautics & Space Admin., 1966; Designer/Weaver, 1969-74; Exec. Asst., House of Commons, 1976-82; Prov. Sec., P.E.I. New Democratic Party, 1983-86; Exec. Dir., Arthritis Society of P.E.I., 1986-88; Exec. Dir., P.E.I.

Council of the Disabled, 1988 to date. **AFFIL:** New Democratic Party of Canada (Atlantic VP 1985-89); Rotary Club of Charlottetown; Queen Elizabeth Hospital Foundation (Dir. 1991-93); Phi Beta Kappa; Phi Kappa Phi. **HONS:** Int'l Scholarship, Rotary Club, 1962. **INTERESTS:** reading; yoga; cross-country skiing; biking. **COMMENT:** *"Involved social activist with goal of positive, peaceful social change. Believe that sharing strengths empowers self as well as others."*

Light, Marjatta A., A.I.I.C.,C.A.I.B. ■ $

National Personal Lines Manager, **ALEXANDER AND ALEXANDER** (Reed Stenhouse Ltd.), 20 Bay St., Ste. 2100, Toronto, ON M5J 2N9 (416) 868-5542 or 868-5500, FAX 868-5580. Born Helsinki 1954. m. Glen T. Light. 2 ch. Derek J. Light, Lisa L. Light. **EDUC:** B.A.(Bus. Admin.) in progress. **CAREER:** Client Svc. Rep., Baxter Insurance, 1979-80; Prod. Asst. Mgr, Riley Insurance, 1980-82; Client Svc. Rep., Computer Supervisor, Bonin Dobie Jackson Ltd., 1982-87; Prod. Sales Mgr, Lannon Insurance, 1987-90; Personal Lines Mgr, Reed Stenhouse Ltd., Thunder Bay, 1990-95; Nat'l Personal Lines Mgr, 1996 to date. **SELECTED PUBLICATIONS:** various insurance-related newspaper articles. **AFFIL:** Insurance Brokers' Association of Ontario (Cdn Accredited Insur. Broker; Past Sec., Thunder Bay); Insurance Institute of Ontario (Assoc.; Past Dir., Thunder Bay); Thunder Bay Insurance Women's Association (Past Pres.); Community Traffic Awareness Committee (Bd.); Insurance Community Awareness Committee; Crohn's & Colitis Foundation of Canada (Chair, Thunder Bay). **HONS:** Insurance Woman of the Year, Thunder Bay, 1982; Archie Frain Spirit Award, Insurance Community Action Committee, 1994. **INTERESTS:** travel; computers; tailoring; gardening. **MISC:** instructor, insur. courses; speaker at insurance seminars. **COMMENT:** *"Find my chosen field of insurance both exciting and challenging. Savour accomplishments, learn from defeats. Don't give up easily, and anticipate each day."*

Lightstone, Marilyn, B.A. 🎞 🎭 📺

Actor. c/o Caldwell & Company, 165 Danforth Ave., Toronto, ON M4K 1N2 (416) 465-6168, FAX 465-0955. Born Montreal. **EDUC:** McGill Univ., B.A. 1961; National Theatre Sch., 1964. **SELECTED CREDITS:** lead, *The Grand Tour*; co-star, *Anne of Green Gables*; lead, *The Tin Flute*, Cine St. Henri/Rose Films; lead, *In Praise of Older Women*, Avco Embassy; lead, *Lies My Father Told Me*, Columbia Pictures; various other film credits; recurring character, *Road to Avonlea*, CBC; guest star, *Street Legal*; guest star, *Cagney & Lacey*; lead, *King of Kensington*, CBC; lead, *The New Avengers*; lead, *Slow Dance on the Killing Ground*; various other TV credits; numerous radio dramas, narrations, voice overs, commercials, & voices for animated series; Aelis, *Tamara*, Tamara International, N.Y. & L.A.; Leah, *The Dybbuk*, The Mark Taper Forum, L.A.; one woman show, *Miss Margarida*, Toronto Workshop Productions; Goneril, *King Lear*, Lincoln Center, N.Y.; Hedda, *Hedda Gabler*, Crest Theatre, Toronto; Gwendolyn, *The Importance of Being Earnest*, Alley Theatre, Houston; various other theatre credits; writer, *The Littlest Hobo*; writer, *The Colours of Love*; writer & composer, *The Light Shines All Over the World*, music video. **SELECTED PUBLICATIONS:** lyrics & music, *Miss Lightstone Sings*, song collection. **AFFIL:** ACTRA; CAEA; AEA; AFTRA; SAG. **HONS:** Best Actress (*Lies My Father Told Me*), Canadian Film Awards; Best Film Actress (*Lies My Father Told Me*), ACTRA Awards; Best Supporting Actress (*In Praise Of Older Women*), Canadian Film Awards; Best Actress (*The Tin Flute/Bonheur D'Occasion*), Moscow Int'l Film Festival.

Lill, Wendy, B.A. 🎞 🎭 📺

Playwright/Film Writer. 20 Summit St., Dartmouth, NS B2Y 3A2 (902) 466-4699, FAX 461-0054. Born Vancouver 1950. m. Richard Starr. 2 ch. Samuel (Sam), Joseph (Joey). **EDUC:** York Univ., B.A. 1971. **SELECTED PUBLICATIONS:** *The Fighting Days* (Vancouver; Talon Books, 1984); *The Occupation of Heather Rose* (NeWest Plays for Women, Edmonton; NeWest Press, 1987); *Memories of You* (Winnipeg; Blizzard Publishing, 1989); *Sisters* (1989); *All Fall Down* (1993); *The Glace Bay Miner's Museum* (Talon Books, 1996). **AFFIL:** Writers' Guild of Canada; Playwrights' Union of Canada. **HONS:** Radio Drama Award, ACTRA, 1981; Radio Documentary Award, ACTRA, 1981; Golden Sheaf Award, Film Script, 1986; nomination, Chalmer's Canadian Play Award (*Memories of You*), 1989; nomination, Gov. General's Literary Award for Drama (*The Occupation of Heather Rose*), 1989; nomination, Gemini Award (*Sisters*), 1992; nomination, Gov. General's Literary Award for Drama (*All Fall Down*), 1994.

Limpert, Marianne ■■ ⚾

Olympic Athlete. c/o Canadian Olympic Association. Born Matagami, Que. 1972. **EDUC:** currently studying Phys. Educ. **SPORTS CAREER:** mbr., Cdn Nat'l Swimming Team, 1990 to date. Olympic Games: Silver, 200m

IM, 1996; 6th, 200m IM, & 8th, 4x100m free, 1992. World championships: 4th, 200m IM, 5th, 4x200m free, 6th, 4x100m free, & 15th, 100m free, 1994; 2nd, 4x50m free, 9th, 200m IM, & 12th, 50m back, 1991. Worlds (short course): 1st, 4x200m free, 1995. Pan-Pacific championships: 3rd, 4x200m free, 4th, 4x100m free, & 5th, 200m IM, 1995; 3rd, 4x100m free, 4th, 4x100 medley, 4th, 4x200m free, & 5th, 200m IM, 1993; 6th, 200m IM, 1991. Int'l meets: 1st, 200m IM, 3rd, 100m free, & 4th, 200m free (Canada Cup), 1996. Pan Am Games: 2nd, 200m free, 2nd, 200m IM, 2nd, 4x100m free 2nd, 4x200m free, 2nd, 4x100m medley, & 3rd, 100m free, 1995. Commonwealth Games: 2nd, 200m IM, 3rd, 100m free, 3rd, 4x100m free, 3rd, 4x200m free, 3rd, 4x100m medley, & 6th, 200m free, 1994. World University Games: 1st, 200m IM, 1st, 4x200m free, & 2nd, 4x100m free, 1993. Canadian championships: 2nd, 100m free, 2nd, 200m free, & 2nd, 200m IM, 1995; 1st, 4x100m free, 1st, 4x200m free, 2nd, 100m free, 2nd, 200m IM, & 2nd, 4x50m medley, 1994; 1st, 100m free, 1st, 200m IM, 2nd, 200m free, & 2nd, 4x100m free, 1993; 2nd, 200m IM, 1991; 5th, 200m IM, 1990. INTERESTS: reading; sewing; shopping. MISC: speaks English, German.

Lindley, Susan, B.Sc.,M.Sc.,Dip.Bact., M.D.C.M. ■ ■ ⊕
Clinical Director, Department of Ophthalmology, MONTREAL GENERAL HOSPITAL, 1650 Cedar Ave., #L4-309, Montreal, QC H3G 1A4 (514) 937-6011, ext. 4060, FAX 934-8223. Assistant Professor, Faculty of Medicine, McGILL UNIVERSITY. Born London, UK 1950. m. P. Charles Brown. EDUC: Univ. of New Brunswick, B.Sc.(Biol.) 1970, M.Sc.(Microbiol.) 1973; Univ. of Toronto, Dip.Bact.(Bacteriology) 1974; McGill Univ., M.D.C.M.(Medicine) 1980, residency (Ophthalmology) 1984. CAREER: Consultant, Centre Hospitalier Laurentien, 1984 to date; Asst. Ophthalmologist, Montreal General Hospital, 1985-90; Assoc. Ophthalmologist, 1990 to date; Clinical Dir., Dept. of Ophthalmology, 1994 to date; Lecturer, Fac. of Medicine, McGill Univ., 1985-90; Asst. Prof., 1990 to date; Consultant, Montreal Children's Hospital, 1994 to date. SELECTED PUBLICATIONS: co-author with K. Sindi et al, "Echographic versus computerized tomographic measurements of rectus muscles in thyroid related ophthalmopathy" (ARVO poster, 1996); co-author with M. Salvi et al, "Upper eyelid retraction in the absence of other evidence for progressive ophthalmopathy is associated with eye muscle autoantibodies" (*Journal of Clinical Immunology &*

Immunopathology 1995); co-author with B. Arthurs et al, "The value of ultrasound in the diagnosis of bilateral ocular myositis presenting as a paraneoplastic syndrome" (ARVO poster, 1994). AFFIL: Canadian Ophthalmological Society (Treas. 1995 to date); Association des médecins ophtalmologistes du Québec (Bd. mbr. 1991-95); American Academy of Ophthalmology; Quebec/Canadian Medical Association; International Society for Diagnostic Ophthalmic Ultrasound; Association for Research in Vision & Ophthalmology (ARVO). HONS: Outstanding Clinical Instructor, McGill Ophthalmology Program, 1993-94. INTERESTS: skiing; hiking; cycling. COMMENT: *"I fell in love with ophthalmology and have never regretted it. Although surgical and technological advances are exciting, my greatest satisfaction comes from my relationships with patients. Teaching and outreach eye care (northern Quebec and Ontario) add spice to the professional mix."*

Lindsay, Doreen, B.F.A.,M.A. ■ ⊗ 𝔖
Artist, Photographer, Curator. 483 Grosvenor Ave., Montreal, QC H3Y 2S5 (514) 932-6688. Born London, Ont. 1934. m. Gabor Szilasi. 1 ch. Andrea Doreen Szilasi. EDUC: Instituto Allende, Mexico, Dipl.(Painting) 1957; Concordia Univ., B.F.A.(Painting) 1965, M.A.(Art Educ./Fine Arts) 1969. CAREER: photographer of indigenous vegetation in the environment; pioneer electrographic artist in Canada; Instructor of Photography, Saidye Bronfman Centre for the Arts, 1974-96; Instructor of Photography, Coll. Marie-Victorin, 1985-92; Head of Photography Dept., Saidye Bronfman Centre for the Arts, 1986-96; Instructor of Photography, École Nationale de la Photographie, Arles, France, 1987-88; Instructor of Photography, Concordia Univ., 1988-91. SELECTED PUBLICATIONS: Publisher, various artists' books. AFFIL: Powerhouse Women's Art Gallery (Dir.); CARFAC Canadian Artists' Representation; Print & Drawing Council of Canada; Conseil québécois de l'estampe.

Lindsay, Gillian ■ 𝕎 ⊗ 𝕊
Principal, FOREFRONT ENTERTAINMENT GROUP, 402 W. Pender St., Ste. 700, Vancouver, BC V6B 1T6 (604) 682-7910, FAX 682-8583, EMAIL 7503.1011@compuserve.com. Born Victoria, B.C. 1952. s. EDUC: Vancouver Film Sch., Grad. (Film/TV) 1988; Capilano Coll., CGA Level I 1987. CAREER: TV Prod.; Exec in Charge of Prod.; Prod. Mgr. SELECTED CREDITS: Prod., *Behind the Scenes: Vancouver Aquarium* (in house), video display; Prod. Mgr, *Fire Attack* (TV documentary), 1988; Prod. Mgr, *Christmas Cowboy* (1/2 hr. TV drama),

1989; Co-Prod. & Co-Writer, eps. 1-4, *Inside Stories: Journey Into Self-Esteem* (TV series), 1990; Co-Prod., eps. 1-52, *Madison* (TV series), 1990-96; Prod. Mgr, *It's A Crime* (1/2 docu-drama), 1992; Prod. Mgr, *It's My Turn Now* (1/2 hr. documentary), 1993; Co-Exec. Prod., eps. 1-13, *The Adventures of Shirley Holmes* (TV series), 1996. **AFFIL:** Academy of Canadian Cinema & Television; Canadian Film & Television Producers' Association; B.C. Motion Picture Association. **HONS:** 30 int'l film awards for TV/educational programming for the youth series *Madison*. **INTERESTS:** skiing; gardening. **COMMENT:** *"Since joining Forefront in 1988 with my three wonderful female partners, I have enjoyed the financial and creative aspects of TV in my role as executive in charge of production."*

Lindsay Luby, Gloria, B.A.,M.Ed. ■ 🍁 $ ☝

President, GLORIA LINDSAY LUBY ENTERPRISES, 9 Timothy Ct., Etobicoke, ON M9P 3T8 (416) 235-1550, FAX 235-1501. Councillor, CITY OF ETOBICOKE. Born Thunder Bay, Ont. m. Larry. 3 ch. Alison, Ryan, Laura. **EDUC:** Univ. of Western Ontario, B.A.(Hist. & Econ.) 1967; Univ. of Toronto, M.Ed.(Adult Educ.) 1971. **CAREER:** Dir., Humber-York Campus, Humber Coll., 1971-73; Mgr, Strategic Planning, Canadian Institute of Chartered Accountants, 1980-86; Sch. Trustee, Etobicoke Bd. of Educ., 1982-85; Councillor, City of Etobicoke, 1985 to date. **SELECTED PUBLICATIONS:** numerous publications. **DIRECTOR:** Corporate Foods Limited (1985-95). **AFFIL:** Salvation Army (Metro Toronto Advisory Committee); The Planning Forum (Pres. 1987-88); Arts Etobicoke (Dir.). **HONS:** Excellence in Training Award, Ontario Municipal Management Institute, 1993. **INTERESTS:** business; politics; travel; golf. **MISC:** 1st woman Dir. of Corporate Foods; 1st woman Pres. of the Planning Forum; 1st Dir., Humber-York Campus of Humber Coll.; 1st Mgr, Strategic Planning, CICA.

Linton, Marilyn, B.A. 📖 ✏ ♡

Life Editor, *THE TORONTO SUN*, 333 King St. E., Toronto, ON M5A 3X5 (416) 947-2480, FAX 947-2446. m. 2 ch. Samantha, Tanya. **EDUC:** York Univ., B.A.(Urban Studies). **CAREER:** freelance writer, 1976-83; writer, *The Toronto Sun*, 1979-83; Assoc. Ed., *Homemaker's* Magazine, 1983-86; Life Ed., *The Toronto Sun*, 1986 to date. **SELECTED PUBLICATIONS:** author, 5 books, incl. *Taking Charge by Taking Care* (Macmillan, 1996). **AFFIL:** Canadian Breast Cancer Foundation (Bd.); Heart & Stroke Foundation (Chair, Women, Heart Disease & Stroke Initiative); The Canadian Club (Bd.); Women's College Hospital Nat'l Women's Health Research Institute (Advisor); Canadian Women's Foundation (Volunteer); The Migraine Association of Canada (Bd.). **COMMENT:** *"Special projects within the* Sun*: The creation and production of educational health supplements directed to specific target audiences: five, to date, in the areas of breast cancer, AIDS, women and heart disease, arthritis and eating disorders. Chair of the* Sun*'s annual Women on the Move Awards, which each Fall recognize the contributions of working women."*

Linton, Noreen, R.N.,B.N.,M.N., I.B.C.L.C. ■ ⊕

Transition Program Leader, CALGARY GENERAL HOSPITAL, 841 Centre Ave. E., Calgary, AB T2A 0E1 (403) 268-9896, FAX 268-9222. Born Taber, Alta. 1954. m. Robert Linton. 3 ch. **EDUC:** Holy Cross Sch. of Nursing, Dipl.(Registered Nurse) 1975; Grant McEwan Coll., Certificate (Gerontology Nursing); Univ. of Calgary, B.N. 1990, M.N. 1994. **CAREER:** Staff Nurse, Brooks General Hospital, 1975-76; Staff Nurse, Calgary General Hospital, 1976-78, 1980-88; Staff Nurse, St. Michael's General Hospital, 1978-80; Nursing Admin. Coord., Calgary General Hospital, 1988-90; Nursing Unit Mgr, 1990-92; Ambulatory Care Leader/Nurse Mgr, 1993 to date. **AFFIL:** Alberta Association of Registered Nurses; Association of Women's Health & Neonatal Nurses (V-Chair, Alta.-B.C. Section); Canadian Nurses' Association; Canadian Obstetrical Gynecological & Neonatal Nurses; Society for Ambulatory Care Professionals; R.T.S. (Resolve Through Sharing) Bereavement Services (Counsellor & Coord.); International Board Certified Lactation Consultant; Calgary Youth Orchestra (Chair, Fundraising Committee). **HONS:** Isabelle Donaldson Scholarship, 1991; Gertrude M. Hall Scholarship, 1992-93. **INTERESTS:** public speaking; education; crafts, incl. cross-stitching, needlework, knitting. **COMMENT:** *"As a nursing leader with extensive clinical and administrative health care experience, I assist healthcare workers in their transition to the new healthcare realities of the 1990s."*

Lipman, Nicola, B.A. ■ ✪

Actor. c/o The Sloan Agency, 10 Roden Place, Toronto, ON M5R 1P5 (416) 929-1915, FAX 929-9492. Born Vancouver. s. **EDUC:** Univ. of British Columbia, B.A.(Fine Arts) 1965; National Theatre Sch. of Canada, Grad. 1968. **CAREER:** actor, 1970 to date; mbr., Bd. of Dir., numerous theatres. **AFFIL:** ACTRA (former Council Mbr.); Canadian Actors' Equity (mbr. of Exec.). **HONS:** 2 "B" grants, Canada Council. INTERESTS: reading; some volunteer work (English as a Second Language teaching); physical fitness. COMMENT: *"Canadian actress 25 years; particular interest in new work and classical texts. Worked in most major theatres in Canada. Recipient of two Canada Council 'B' grants, one for personal study and one to produce a new work with Mary Vingoe and Wendy Lill."*

Lippert, Anne H., F.I.C.B. ■ Ⓢ ◯
Vice-President and Area Manager, Vancouver Downtown and West, ROYAL BANK OF CANADA, 1055 W. Georgia St., Vancouver, BC V6E 3S5 (604) 665-5200, FAX 665-8241. Born Berlin 1938. m. Wolfgang. 1 ch. CAREER: various positions, Royal Bank of Canada, 1971-88; VP & Area Mgr, 1989 to date; VP, Lippert Investments Ltd. SELECTED PUBLICATIONS: various short articles published in magazines & newspapers. AFFIL: Institute of Canadian Banking (Fellow); The Salvation Army (Advisory Bd.); KCTS Channel 9 Seattle (Advisory Bd.); Grace Hospital (Dir. 1991-94); B.C. Women's Hospital & Health Centre (Dir.); Women's Hospital Foundation (Past Chair, Bd. of Trustees); Group Bd.–B.C. Children's Hospital, B.C. Women's Hospital, Sunny Hill Health Centre for Children; Canadian Breast Cancer Foundation, BC Chapter (Chair, Unique Lives & Experiences Lecture Series 1996); B.C. Sports Hall of Fame (Trustee); Marine Drive Golf & Country Club; Leadership Vancouver; Western Indoor Tennis Club. HONS: nominee, Canadian Businesswoman of the Year Award, 1988; Woman of Distinction Award, Mgmt & the Professions, YWCA, 1990. INTERESTS: tennis; golfing; skiing. MISC: frequent speaking engagements. COMMENT: *"After a short career as interpreter in France, England & Germany, immigrated to Canada and started as Customer Service Representative with Royal Bank. Worked since in many different positions and promoted to Vice-President in 1989. Very involved in the business community. Frequently called upon for speaking engagements. A strategic thinker."*

Lippman, Abby, B.A.,Ph.D. ■ ◁ ▨
Professor, Department of Epidemiology and Biostatistics, McGILL UNIVERSITY, 1020 Pine Ave. W., Montreal, QC H3A 1A2 (514) 398-6266, EMAIL abbyl@epid.lan.mcgill.ca. Born Brooklyn, N.Y. 2 ch. EDUC: Cornell Univ., B.A. 1960; McGill Univ., Ph.D. 1979. CAREER: Lecturer, Dept. of Biol., McGill Univ., 1978; Postdoctoral Fellow, Dept. of Epidemiology & Health, 1978-79; Asst. Prof., Dept. of Epidemiology & Health, 1979-84; Asst. Prof., Centre for Human Genetics, 1979-84; Assoc.

Prof., Dept. of Epidemiology & Health, McGill Univ., 1984-92; Assoc. Prof., Centre for Human Genetics, 1984-92; Research Consultant, Dept. of Community Health, Montreal General Hospital, 1986-92; mbr., McGill Centre for Medicine, Ethics & Law, 1987 to date; mbr., McGill Centre for Research & Teaching on Women, 1988 to date; Visiting Int'l Scholar, The Hastings Center, Briarcliff Manor, NY, 1989; Adjunct Prof., Dépt. de médecine sociale et préventive, Univ. de Montréal, 1989 to date; Research Assoc., Dept. of Social Studies of Medicine, McGill Univ., 1990 to date; Membre Assoc., l'Institut de recherches et d'études féministes (IREF), Univ. du Québec à Montréal, 1991 to date; Prof., Dept. of Epidemiology & Biostatistics, McGill Univ., 1992 to date; Prof., Dept of Human Genetics, 1992 to date; Adjunct Prof., Union Institute Grad. Sch., 1994 to date; Acting Dir., McGill Centre for Research & Teaching on Women, 1994-95; Acting Co-Chair, Dept. of Epidemiology & Biostatistics, McGill Univ., 1995-96. SELECTED PUBLICATIONS: *Misconceptions: The Social Construction of Choice and the New Reproductive and Genetic Technologies*, co-ed. with G. Basen & M. Eichler (Hull: Voyageur Publishing, Vol. 1, 1993; Vol. 2, 1994); "Prenatal genetic testing and screening: Constructing needs and reinforcing inequities" (*American Journal of Law and Medicine*, XVII, 1 & 2, 1991); "Led (astray) by genetic maps: The cartography of the human genome and health care" (*Society of Scientific Medicine* 1992); "'Never Too Late:' Biotechnology, women and reproduction" (*McGill Law Journal* 40(4), 1995); "Resistance and adherence to the norms of genetic counseling" with F. Brunger (*Journal of Genetic Counsel* 4 (3)); over 125 other publications. EDIT: Epidemiology Ed., Ed. Bd., *Teratology*, 1989-92; Book Review Ed., Ed. Bd., *Woman and Health*, 1991-92; Ed. Bd., *Science and Engineering Ethics*, 1994 to date; Ed. Bd., *Eubios Journal of Asian and International Bioethics*, 1994 to date; Ed. Bd., *Ruptures*, 1993 to date. AFFIL: Canadian Coll. of Medical Geneticists; American Coll. of Epidemiology; Romanian Academy of Medical Sciences; Centre for Research & Teaching on Women (Advisory Bd.); American Society of Human Genetics; Society for Epidemiologic Research; American Public Health Association; Canadian Public Health Association; L'Association pour la santé publique du Québec; Society of Obstetricians & Gynaecologists of Canada; AAAS (Fellow). HONS: Alpha Epsilon Delta, Honorary Society, Cornell Univ., 1958-60; Dean's Honour List, Convocation, McGill Univ., 1978; Cornell Regent's Scholarship, 1956-60; Marion Porter Prize, Canadian

Research Institute for the Advancement of Women, 1991; Hon. Mbr., Romanian Academy of Medical Sciences. **MISC:** reviewer of journals & granting agencies; recipient of grants & fellowships; over 65 invited scientific presentations.

Lisson, Kathryn, B.Sc.,C.M.C. $
Partner Responsible for National Financial Institution Consulting, PRICE WATERHOUSE, 1 First Canadian Place, Ste. 3300, Box 190, Toronto, ON M5X 1H7 (416) 863-1133, FAX 365-8215. Born Montreal 1952. m. James H. 2 ch. **EDUC:** Carleton Univ., B.Sc. 1974. **CAREER:** Fin. Dept., Unemployment Insur. Canada, 1974-76; Consultant, Computer Svcs Group, Price Waterhouse Mgmt Consultants, 1976-82; VP, Info. Systems, Barclays Bank of Canada, 1982-86; Dir., Fin. Institution Consulting, Price Waterhouse, 1986; Ptnr, 1987-91; Ptnr Responsible for Nat'l Fin. Institution Consulting, 1991 to date; MCS Mgmt Committee, 1994; elected to Price Waterhouse Policy Bd., 1996. **AFFIL:** Institute of Management Consultants of Ontario (C.M.C.); Bishop Strachan Sch. (Gov.); Toronto Cricket, Skating & Curling Club; Donalda Club. **INTERESTS:** tennis; squash; skiing; reading.

Little, Judythe Patricia ⚖
Judge, ONTARIO COURT OF JUSTICE (Provincial Division), 216 Water St., Kenora, ON P9N 1S4 (807) 468-2882. **CAREER:** Mng Ptnr, Fraser and Little, 1976-86; Judge, Ont. Prov. Court, now Ont. Court of Justice (Prov. Div.), 1986 to date. **AFFIL:** Ontario Family Law Judges' Association (Bd. of Dir.; Pres. 1993-94); Ministry of the Attorney General Advisory Committee on Child Support Guidelines; Ontario Judges' Association; Canadian Bar Association; Association of Family & Conciliation Courts; Family Mediation Canada; Kenora Law Association. **MISC:** numerous public & professional legal educ. presentations on family law issues, incl. child representation, child abuse, young offenders & First Nations justice issues.

Ljubisic, Ljiljana ■■ ⚾
Paralympic Athlete. Coquitlam, BC. **CAREER:** full-time athlete & motivational speaker. **SPORTS CAREER:** mbr., Nat'l Track Team. Paralympic Games: Bronze, shotput & discus, 1996; Gold, discus, Silver, shotput, 1992; Bronze, shotput, 5th discus, 1988. Australian Nat'l Championships: 1st, discus & shotput, 1996. German Int'l Championships: 1st, discus & shotput, 1995. IPC World Track & Field Championships: 1st, discus, 2nd, shotput, 1994. German Int'l Games: 2nd, discus, 1993. Barcelona Invitational, 1st, discus, 1991. World Championships: 1st, discus, 3rd, shotput, 1990. **MISC:** Class B-1 record holder in discus since 1991; ranked no. 2 in the world in shotput.

Loat, Beverlee, B.A.,M.Comm. ■ $
Vice-President, Public Affairs, EDMONTON POWER, 10065 Jasper Ave., Edmonton, AB T5J 3B1 (403) 448-3195, FAX 488-3192, EMAIL 75127.313@compuserve.com. Born Columbus, Ohio 1954. m. Terry. **EDUC:** Ohio State Univ., B.A.(Behavioral Sci.) 1976; Georgia State Univ., M.Comm.(Public Rel'ns) 1987. **CAREER:** Mgr, Gov't Affairs, Cardinal Industries, 1984-89; Dir., Gov't Affairs, Atlanta Home Builders' Association, 1989-90; VP, Public Affairs, Edmonton Power, 1990 to date. **AFFIL:** Citadel Theatre (Dir. 1994-95); Junior Achievement of Edmonton & N.W.T. (Dir. 1994-95); Canadian Public Relations Society. **INTERESTS:** on-line computer comm.; travel.

Lobay, Mary, C.M.,B.Ed.,M.Ed., LL.D. 🎓 ✊ 👍
Retired Teacher. 638 Romaniuk Rd., Edmonton, AB T6R 1A6 (403) 430-6174. Born Wasel, Alta. 1920. m. William. 3 ch. **EDUC:** Univ. of Alberta, B.Ed.(Social Studies/English), Dipl.(Secondary English), M.Ed.(Secondary Educ.) 1966. **CAREER:** Teacher; Asst. Principal, sr. high sch., Edmonton; Coord. Consultant, jr. high sch., 1939-81; Sessional Lecturer, Univ. of Alberta, Proj.–Uganda Teachers, 1965-66. **SELECTED PUBLICATIONS:** "Ethnicity in a Modern City High School" (*Alberta Teachers' Association Magazine* May 1977). **DIRECTOR:** Heritage Savings and Trust Company (1984-87); North West Savings and Trust Company (1987-94). **AFFIL:** Phi Delta Kappa; Delta Kappa Gamma; Canadian Coll. of Teachers; Professional & Business Club (Hon. Life Mbr.); Alberta Coll. (Gov. 1984-94); Univ. of Alberta (Gov. 1986-92; Senate 1978-84 & 1986-92); Salvation Army (Dir., Advisory Bd.; Chair, Sunset Lodge); Edmonton Police Commission (Chair 1979-85); Capital Care Group Hospital Foundation (V-Chair 1987-92); Vanier Institute of the Family (Hon. Life Mbr.); Royal Alexandra Hospital Foundation (Dir.); Fort Edmonton Historical Foundation (Exec. & Dir. 1974-90; Hon. Chief Factor 1993-95); Ukrainian Cultural Heritage Village (Advisory Bd., Dir. & Chair). **HONS:** Alberta Achievement Award, 1980; Member of Order of Canada, 1988; Recognition (Mary Lobay Park), City of Edmonton, 1991; Lescarbot Award, Regional Cultural Activities, 1992; Canada 125 Medal; numerous others from City of Edmonton; LL.D.(Hon.), Univ. of Alberta, 1992. **INTERESTS:** history of the people of Alberta; education; Sunday visits with my chil-

dren & grandchildren. **MISC:** 1st woman Chair of the Edmonton Police Commission. **COMMENT:** *"Students often say that I was a true 'single educator.' Since my retirement I have put my efforts into many other activities, in organizations that help families in need and in historic research and preservation."*

Lochan, Katharine, B.A.,M.A.,Ph.D. ■ Ⓧ
Senior Curator, Prints and Drawings, ART GALLERY OF ONTARIO, 317 Dundas St. W., Toronto, ON M5T 1G (416) 979-6660, ext. 487, FAX (416) 979-6666. Born Ottawa 1946. m. George Yost. 2 stpch. **EDUC:** Univ. of Toronto, B.A.(Art Hist.) 1968, M.A.(Art Hist.) 1971; Univ. of London, Courtauld Institute, UK, Ph.D.(Art Hist.) 1982; Univ. of California at Berkeley, Museum Mgmt Institute, Certficate in Museum Mgmt 1987; Ryerson Polytechnic Univ., Certificate in Bus. Admin. 1991. **CAREER:** Curatorial Asst., European Dept., Royal Ontario Museum, 1968-69; Curatorial Asst., Art Gallery of Ontario, 1969-71; Asst. Curator, 1971-76; Volunteer Asst., British Museum, 1975-76; Curator of Prints & Drawings, Art Gallery of Ontario, 1976 to date; Fac., Dept. of Art Hist., Univ. of Toronto, 1992 to date. **SELECTED PUBLICATIONS:** *The Etchings of James McNeil Whistler* (1984); *Whistler's Etchings and The Sources of His Etching Style* (1987); *The Earthly Paradise: Arts and Crafts by William Morris and His Circle of Friends from Canadian Collections*, with Douglas Schoenherr & Carole Silver (1993); numerous exhibition catalogues, articles, papers & lectures. **AFFIL:** Canadian Museum Association; Master Print & Drawing Society of Ontario (Co-founder & Ex Officio Bd. Mbr.); Massey Coll., Univ. of Toronto (Assoc. Fellow); Print Council of America; William Morris Society of Canada; Opera Atelier (Bd. of Trustees); Toronto Historical Board (V-Chair). **HONS:** Ont. Scholar, 1964; Dean's List, Univ. of Ottawa, 1965; Scholarship, J. Paul Getty Trust, 1987; Award of Merit, Ryerson Polytechnic Institute, 1991. **INTERESTS:** historic preservation (architecture); gardening & farming; local history. **COMMENT:** *"Born in Ottawa and raised in London, UK (1954-61) where father was head of the National Film Board of Canada. He was Director of Culture and Aid to the Arts, Sec. State Dept., and instituted The Order of Canada and The Bravery Award at Government House. I am keen to build appreciation and resources in the field of arts and heritage in Canada, and to see our institutions and organizations receive international recognition."*

Lock, Margaret, B.Sc.,M.A.,Ph.D. ⚭ ⊕ ✿
Professor, Department of Social Studies of Medicine, MCGILL UNIVERSITY, 3655 Drummond St., Rm 416, Montréal, QC H3G 1Y6 (514) 398-6033, FAX 398-1498, EMAIL md65@musica.mcgill.ca. Born UK 1936. m. Richard. 2 ch. **EDUC:** Leeds Univ., B.Sc. 1961; Univ. of California, Berkeley, M.A. 1970, Ph.D. 1976; Stanford Inter-Univ. Centre, Tokyo, Dip.(Japanese Language) 1973. **CAREER:** Dir., Centre for East Asian Studies, McGill Univ., 1981-83; Assoc. Prof., Dept. of Humanities & Social Studies in Medicine, 1981-83; Prof., 1987-93; Chair, Dept. of Social Studies of Medicine & Dept. of Anthro., McGill Univ., 1988-93; Prof., 1993 to date. **SELECTED PUBLICATIONS:** *East Asian Medicine in Urban Japan: Varieties of Medical Experience* (Berkeley: Univ. of California Press, 1984); *Encounters With Aging: Mythologies of Menopause in Japan and North America* (California: Univ. of California Press, 1993); "The Concept of Race: An Ideological Construct" (*Transcultural Psychiatry Research Review* 1993); "Cultivating the Body: Anthropology and the Epistemologies of Bodily Practice and Knowledge" (*Annual Review of Anthropology* 1993); "Menopause in Cultural Context" (*Experimental Gerontology* 1994); numerous other publications. **AFFIL:** Royal Society of Canada (Fellow); Committee on Medical, Ethical, Legal & Social Issues, Canadian Human Genome Proj.; Population Health Program of the Canadian Institute for Advanced Research. **HONS:** Canada-Japan Book Award, 1994; Eileen Basker Memorial Prize, 1994; finalist, Hiromi Arisawa Award, 1993; Izaak Walton Killam Research Fellowship, 1993-95; Margaret Mead Lectureship, World Federation of Mental Health, 1993. **INTERESTS:** medical anthropological theory; comparative study of life cycle transitions; the anthropology of the body; the cross-cultural production & application of medical technologies. **COMMENT:** *"Originally trained as a biochemist, received Ph.D. in anthropology from University of California, Berkeley. Professor in Departments of Social Studies, of Medicine and Anthropology at McGill University. Wrote five books and numerous scholarly articles. Member of Canadian Institute for Advanced Research and a recipient of Canada Council Izaak Killam Fellowship for 1993-95."*

Lockert, Barbara L., B.Ed. Ⓢ
President and Chief Executive Officer, LOCKERT DISTRIBUTORS LTD., 9766 - 51 Ave., Edmonton, AB T6E 0A6 (403) 437-3134, FAX 438-5493. Born Edmonton 1958. m. Tim. 2 ch. **EDUC:** Univ. of Alberta, B.Ed.(Math./Phys. Educ.) 1979. **CAREER:** teacher, 1979-86; Pres., CEO & owner, Lockert Distributors Ltd., oper-

ating Bosch Kitchen Centre, Edmonton, 1986 to date; owner/operator, Bosch Kitchen Centre, Red Deer, Alta., 1991 to date. **AFFIL:** Retail Merchants' Association; Alberta Teachers' Association; Teen Time of Edmonton (Sec., Bd. of Dir.); Grant McEwan Coll. (Colleague). **HONS:** Entrepreneur of the Year, Retail, Western Reg. of Canada, 1994; Canadian Woman Entrepreneur of the Year, Quality Plus, Alta. Reg., 1994; many awards for trade show display booths. **INTERESTS:** cooking/baking; skiing; cycling; tennis; curling; camping; watching children play sports, esp. soccer. **MISC:** tests & writes recipes for classes & demonstrations; numerous TV presentations & speaking engagements. **COMMENT:** *"Barbara is a thoughtful and caring person who is highly focused, energetic and enthusiastic. She is self-motivated and committed to 'focusing on quality,' throughout balancing family life, business responsibilities and community involvement. Her plans for expansion for the Edmonton Bosch Kitchen Centre are to buy or build her own building, similar to her Red Deer Bosch Kitchen Centre expansion and relocation in September 1994. Excitement included the above listed Entrepreneur Awards."*

Lockie, Anne, B.A.Sc. ■ [$]

Senior Vice-President and General Manager, Saskatchewan, ROYAL BANK OF CANADA, 2010 - 11th Ave., Regina, SK S4P 0J3 (306) 780-2020, FAX 780-2029. Born Gateshead, UK 1950. m. Fred Promoli. **EDUC:** Univ. of Guelph, B.A.Sc. 1973. **CAREER:** Equitable Securities, 1974; Dominion Securities Ltd. (now RBC Dominion Securities Inc.), 1975-76; various positions from Branch Admin. trainee to positions in Admin., Recruiting, Sales Training, Fin. Mgmt & Employment Equity, Royal Bank of Canada, 1976-85; Mgr, Hum. Res. Planning, Montreal, 1985-88; Mgr, Mgmt Dev., 1988-89; Mgr, Organization Planning, Corp. Planning Group, 1989-90; Mgr, Mktg & Planning, Retail Bnkg, 1990-91; VP, Corp. Planning & Organization, 1991-93; VP, Quality Svc. & Planning, 1993-94; Sr. VP, Mktg & Planning, Personal Fin. Svcs, 1994-96; Sr. VP & Gen. Mgr, Sask., 1996 to date. **AFFIL:** Canadian Human Resource Planner (Past Pres.).

Lockitch, Gillian, M.B.ChB,M.D.,FRCPC ⊕

Director, Genes, Elements and Metabolism Program, BRITISH COLUMBIA'S CHILDREN'S HOSPITAL, Department of Pathology, 4480 Oak St., Vancouver, BC V6H 3V4 (604) 875-2394, FAX 263-1402, EMAIL kidsug@unixg.ubc.ca. Born Cape Town 1945. m. Robert. 3 ch. Michael, Keith, Amanda. **EDUC:** Univ. of Cape Town, M.B.ChB 1968, M.D. 1974; Royal Coll. of Physicians & Surgeons of Canada, FRCPC (Paediatrics) 1978, FRCPC (Medical Biochem.) 1980. **CAREER:** Sr. Research Officer, Div. of Medical Statistics & Epidemiology, Nutrition Research Institute, S.A. Medical Research Council, 1971-74; Lab. Physician, Children's Hospital, Vancouver, 1978-82; Program Head, Clinical Biochem., Dept. of Pathology, BC Children's Hospital & Consultant, Medical Biochemist, Grace Hospital, 1982-94; Dir., GEM Program, Dept. of Pathology, BC Children's Hospital & BC Women's Hospital, 1994 to date. **SELECTED PUBLICATIONS:** *Handbook of Diagnostic Biochemistry and Hematology in Normal Pregnancy*, Ed. & contributing writer (Boca Raton, Fla.; CRC Press, 1993); various scientific papers & reviews. **AFFIL:** Royal Coll. of Physicians & Surgeons of Canada (Fellow); Canadian Medical Association; B.C. Medical Association; Federation of Medical Women; Canadian Society of Clinical Chemists; B.C. Society of Clinical Chemists; Canadian Association of Medical Biochemists; Academy of Clinical Biochemistry; B.C. Association of Laboratory Physicians; Canadian Pediatric Society; N.Y. Academy of Science; International Society for Trace Element Research in Humans; American Association of Clinical Chemistry (Chair, Pediatric Clinical Chemistry Div. 1991-93). **HONS:** Annual Award Lectureship, Manitoba Society of Clinical Chemists, 1993; Outstanding Speaker Award, American Association for Clinical Chemistry, 1994. **INTERESTS:** gourmet cooking; wine; fitness; reading. **MISC:** Chair, Nat'l Committee for Clinical Laboratory Standards Subcommittee for NCCLS Consensus Document, "Control of Preanalytical Variation in Trace Element Analysis," 1993-95; Congress Chair, 6th Int'l Congress on Pediatric Laboratory Medicine Conference, Vancouver, July 1995. **COMMENT:** *"Wife, mother, mentor, teacher, researcher, writer, administrator, proud of my family, the achievements of my hospital department and happiest engaging in spirited debates with family, friends and colleagues over wonderful food and good wines."*

Lockyer, Debora ■■ ✎

Editor, *Windspeaker*, *Alberta Sweetgrass*, and *Saskatchewan Sage*, ABORIGINAL MULTI-MEDIA SOCIETY OF CANADA, 15001 - 112 Ave., Edmonton, AB T5M 2V6 (403) 455-2700, FAX 455-7639. Born Weston, Ont. 1959. m. Jim Steel. 2 ch. Richard, Nicole. **EDUC:** Grant MacEwan Community Coll., Journalism 1989. **CAREER:** Reporter-Photographer-Ed., *Spruce Grove* and *Stony Plain This Week* Newspapers, 1989-93; Ed., *Satellite Entertainment Guide*, 1993-94; Ed., *Windspeaker*, *Alberta Sweetgrass*, & *Saskatchewan Sage*, 1994 to date;

Windspeaker supplements include the "Classroom Edition," the "Guide to Indian Country," & the "Powwow Guide." **SELECTED PUBLICATIONS:** published in *Windspeaker, Alberta Sweetgrass, Indian Country Today, United Church Observer, Edmonton Journal, Grove Examiner, Stony Plain Reporter, Spruce Grove* and *Stony Plain This Week* Newspapers, *St. Albert This Week, Satellite Entertainment Guide, Edmonton Woman,* & *Edmonton City News.* **HONS:** Native American Journalism Association award for best news photo, 1994. **INTERESTS:** auctions & antiques; camping; reading; golf. **COMMENT:** *"The hottest ticket in journalism today is in the area of aboriginal affairs. The three newspapers published by AMMSA, most particularly* Windspeaker, *are extremely important reading for any person interested in Native issues in Canada."*

Lofthouse, Maureen, B.Sc.,M.B.A. ■■ ✦ ▒
Director, Enabling Technologies, TECHNOLOGY PARTNERSHIPS CANADA (fed. gov't), Journal Tower North, 300 Slater St., 10th Fl., Ottawa, ON K1A 0C8 (613) 954-2937, FAX 954-5654, EMAIL lofthouse.maureen@ic.gc.ca. Born Louth, UK 1939. s. 1 ch. **EDUC:** Univ. of Glasgow, B.Sc.(Mech. Eng.) 1963; McGill Univ., M.B.A. 1975. **CAREER:** Eng. (aircraft engine dev.), Pratt & Whitney Canada, 1968-76; Eng./Mgr (diesel engine dev.), Kloeckner Humboldt Deutz Canada, 1976-83; Sr. Proj. Mgr, Industrial Research Assistance Program, NRC, 1984-87; Sci. & Technology Counsellor, Cdn Embassy, Bonn, Germany, 1987-90; Asst. Dir., Space Stn Program, Cdn Space Agency, 1990-93; Sr. Advisor, Nat'l Advisory Bd. on Sci. & Technology, 1993-95; Coord., Functional Advisors Support Team, Industry Canada, 1995-96; Dir., Enabling Technologies, Technology Partnerships Canada, 1996 to date. **AFFIL:** Professional Engineers Ontario; Ordre des ingénieurs du Québec; Institution of Mechanical Engineers, U.K.

Logan, A Kirsten, LL.B. ◁ᴛᴀ ◉
Secretary and Co-Director of Administration, LAW SOCIETY OF SASKATCHEWAN, 2500 Victoria Ave., Ste. 1000, Regina, SK S4P 3X2 (306) 569-8242, FAX 352-2989. Born Regina 1956. d. 1 ch. Jessica Waller. **EDUC:** Univ. of Saskatchewan, LL.B. 1979. **BAR:** Sask., 1980. **CAREER:** articling student, Olive, Waller, Zinkhan and Waller, Barristers & Solicitors, 1979-80; Lawyer in gen. practice, 1980-82; Deputy Sec.-Treas., Law Society of Saskatchewan; Sec., 1991 to date; Acting Dir. of Continuing Legal Educ., 1992; Co-Dir. of Admin., 1992 to date. **AFFIL:** Regina Bar Association (Exec.); Regina Family YMCA. **HONS:**

C.H.A. Mair Highest Academic Award, Aden Bowman Collegiate Institute, 1974; Bursary, Prov. of Sask., 1974. **INTERESTS:** family; aerobics; reading. **COMMENT:** *"Graduated with a law degree at age 22, unsure as to career aspirations. After a period of time in general practice and at home, commenced employment with the Law Society of Saskatchewan. Performed various duties within the organization and now share the top administrative position in addition to the duties as Corporate Secretary."*

Logan, Kerrie, B.A.,LL.B. ■■ ◁ᴛᴀ
Partner, MACLEOD DIXON (law firm), 400 - 3rd Ave. S.W., Ste. 3700, Calgary, AB T2P 4H2 (403) 267-8340, FAX 264-5973. Born Saskatoon, Sask. 1956. m. 2 ch. **EDUC:** Univ. of Alberta, B.A.(with Distinction, Hist.) 1977, LL.B. 1980. **HONS:** Univ. of Alberta Matriculation Prize; Prov. of Alta. Scholarship, 1974-77. **COMMENT:** *"I articled with the Alberta Court of Appeal (1980-81) and became a Partner at Macleod Dixon in 1988. I was legal advisor to the Alberta government on the Finance Committee for the $2.4 billion OSLO Project."*

Lohans, Alison, B.A. ▒ 🗋
Freelance Writer. 76 Dolphin Bay, Regina, SK S4S 4Z8 (306) 586-4238. Born Reedley, Calif. cl. Stewart Raby. 2 ch. **EDUC:** California State Univ. at Los Angeles, B.A.(Music) 1971; Univ. of Victoria, Postgrad. Diploma (Elementary Educ.) 1976. **CAREER:** Instrumental Music Instructor, 1976-79; freelance writer; Correspondence Instructor, Writing for Children, Sask. Writers' Guild; Prose Ed., *WindScript* Magazine, 1990-91. **SELECTED PUBLICATIONS:** *Who cares about Karen?* (Scholastic Canada, 1983); *Can you promise me spring?* (Scholastic Canada, 1986/91); *Mystery of the Lunchbox Criminal* (Scholastic Canada, 1990); *Y a-t-il un voleur dans l'école,* French ed. of *Mystery of the Lunchbox Criminal* tr. Christiane Duchesne (Scholastic Canada, 1990); *The Secret Plan* (Scholastic Canada, 1995); *Le plan secret de Jérémie Jalbert* French ed. of *Germy Johnson's Secret Plan* tr. Francois Renaud (Scholastic Canada, 1992); *Foghorn Passage* (Stoddart, 1992); *Laws of Emotion* (Thistledown, 1993); *Nathaniel's Violin* (Orca, 1996); *Report on the Implementation of School-Based Program Evaluation Manual at Pilot Sites* published under the name Alison Pirot (Research Report No. 11, Sask. Instructional Dev. & Research Unit, Fac. of Educ., Univ. of Regina, 1988); 50 plus short stories, poems, articles, book reviews, & a song. **AFFIL:** Saskatchewan Writers' Guild (VP); Writers' Union of Canada; CANSCAIP; Canadian Children's Book Centre

(Sask. Rep.); Saskatchewan Children's Writers' Round Robin; Regina Young People's Literature Roundtable (Coord.). HONS: Student Creative Writing Contest Fiction Winner, *Canadian Author and Bookman*, 1985; Major Award, Saskatchewan Writers' Guild Literary Competition, 1989, 1991; "Our Choice" Award, Canadian Children's Book Centre, 1983, 1986, 1990 & 2 in 1992; Young Readers' Choice Award, South Saskatchewan Reading Council/Saskatchewan Writers' Guild, 1994, 1996; shortlisted for Young Adult Book Award (*Laws of Emotion*), Canadian Library Association, 1994; nominated, Manitoba Young Readers' Choice Award (*Foghorn Passage*), 1995. MISC: hundreds of author talks in schools & public readings; book sales have passed the 150,000 mark. COMMENT: *"Have been writing all my life; first published at age 12. Primary writing area: young adult fiction and children's. Very active in Saskatchewan Writers' Guild. Have done hundreds of author talks in schools and libraries."*

Long, Barbara A., S.D.T.,R.D.H. ⊙ ⊕
Past President, SASKATCHEWAN DENTAL HYGIENISTS' ASSOCIATION, 130 Saguenay Dr., Saskatoon, SK S7K 4G2 (306) 934-5268, FAX 934-5268. Born Prince Albert, Sask. 1955. m. Garth L. Drever. 3 ch. Danya Drever, Riley Drever, Ian Drever. EDUC: Univ. of Regina, Arts & Sci. 1975; Wascana Institute of Applied Arts & Science, Dental Therapy Dip. 1978, Dental Hygiene Dip. 1980. CAREER: Dental Asst., Sask. Dental Plan, Regina, 1975-76; Dental Therapist, Regina Rural, 1978-79; Dental Hygienist, offices of Drs. Finningely, Moore & Saganski, & Dr. D. Plosz, Saskatoon, 1980; part-time Dental Therapist-Hygienist, Reg'l Psychiatric Centre, Saskatoon, 1980-87; part-time Dental Hygienist, Private Consultation & Practice Unit, Coll. of Dentistry, Univ. of Saskatchewan, 1980-87; Dental Hygienist, Dept. of Diagnostic & Surgical Sciences, Coll. of Dentistry, Univ. of Saskatchewan, 1980 to date. SELECTED PUBLICATIONS: "Root Planing–A Primary Therapy in the Control of Periodontitis?" with J.N. Hoover & D.L. Singer (*Canadian Dental Hygiene Journal-Probe* 22(2) 1988); "The Gracey Curvettes–Their Design and Development" (*Canadian Dental Hygiene Journal-Probe* 25(3) 1991); "Evaluation of a New Periodontal Curet: an *In Vitro* Study," with D.L. Singer & S. Lozanoff (*Journal of Clinical Periodontology* 19 1992); "An Imaging Routine for Assessing the Efficacy of Instruments Used for Scaling and Root Planing," with S. Lozanoff, D.L. Singer & J.J. Deptuch (*Journal of Clinical Periodontology* 19 1992); various other publications. AFFIL: Saskatchewan Dental Therapists' Association (Hon. Life Mbr.); Saskatchewan Dental Hygienists' Association (Pres.); Canadian Dental Hygienists' Association (Research Fellowship Selection Committee); Saskatoon Bd. of Educ. (Citizens' Advisory Committee). INTERESTS: her children's activities take up any spare time she has. MISC: various invited lectures & invited conference presentations; patents granted for *Curet for Periodontal Treatment* USA Patent No. 5,169,314 & *Curet for Periodontal Treatment* Canadian Patent No. 2,012,433-4; grant recipient; registered Dental Hygienist, 1980 to present. COMMENT: *"As a highly motivated individual I have made significant contributions to all aspects of the dental hygiene profession, including instrument design, education, research and professional associations."*

Long, Wendy, B.A. ✎ ⓪
Sportswriter, THE VANCOUVER SUN, 2250 Granville St., Vancouver, BC V6H 3G2 (604) 732-2396, FAX 732-2524. Born Vancouver 1958. cl. Steve. EDUC: Vancouver Community Coll., Dipl.(Journalism) 1981; Simon Fraser Univ., B.A.(Comm./Pol. Sci.) 1991. CAREER: Gen. Reporter/Features Writer, *The Vancouver Sun*, 1980-85; Sportswriter, 1985 to date; Co-owner & Co-operator, *The Boarding Pass*, 1988-90. SELECTED PUBLICATIONS: *Celebrating Excellence: Profiles of Canadian Women Athletes* (Polestar, Fall 1995). AFFIL: Canadian Association of Journalists; B.C. & Yukon Heart & Stroke Foundation (Volunteer). HONS: mbr., *Vancouver Sun* team investigating Clifford Olson murders, which won a National Newspaper Award, 1982; Doug Gilbert Award, 1995. INTERESTS: jogging; swimming; cooking. MISC: mbr., committee choosing annual Sport B.C. Athlete of the Year Awards; mbr., selection committee for B.C. Sports Hall of Fame; ran & finished 4 marathons. COMMENT: *"I was one of those individuals who did a lot of different sports and was not outstanding in any. However, the experience has helped mightily, as I cover a lot of different sports for the newspaper."*

Lonsdale, Tanya, B.Sc.,M.Sc. ▩
Principal, BRAUN CONSULTING ENGINEERS LTD., 530 Willow Rd., Guelph, ON N1H 7G4. m. W. David Lonsdale. 1 ch. Michael David Lonsdale. EDUC: Seneca Coll., Dip.Eng.(Eng.Tech.); Univ. of Guelph, B.Sc.(Eng.) 1983, M.Sc.(Eng.) 1985. CAREER: Professional Eng.; Designated Consulting Eng. AFFIL: Professional Engineers Ontario; City of Guelph Chamber of Commerce (Dir.); Univ. of Guelph (Chair, Phys. Resources & Property Committee; V-Chair, Bd. of Gov.).

Loo Craig, Kathleen, B.A.,LL.B. ■ ■ ⚖
THE LAW OFFICE OF KATHLEEN LOO CRAIG, 295 Water St., Summerside, PE C1N 1C1 (902) 436-6696, FAX 436-0884. Born Charlottetown, P.E.I. 1960. m. Blake Craig. 3 ch. James, Kristen, Sandra. EDUC: Dalhousie Univ., B.A.(Pol. Sci.) 1981; Univ. of New Brunswick, LL.B. 1984. CAREER: Chairperson, Canada Pension Plan Review Tribunals, 1992-95. AFFIL: Western Sch. Bd. (Trustee 1995-96). COMMENT: *"My life at present can best be described as juggling the demands of a young family–children aged 7-1/2, almost 6 and 1-1/2, the two youngest of whom were diagnosed in 1995 with Cystic Fibrosis–with a sole law practice. Extra-curricular activities and volunteer associations have of necessity been sidelined for the time being."*

Loock, Christine Ann, M.D., F.R.C.P.C. ⊕ 🐟 ♂
Clinical Associate Professor, Faculty of Medicine, UNIVERSITY OF BRITISH COLUMBIA, Sunny Hill Health Centre for Children, 3644 Slocan St., Vancouver, BC V5M 3E8 (604) 434-1331, ext. 403, FAX 436-1743. Born Fort Worth, Tex. 1954. m. Ron Friesen. 3 ch. Dieter, Emma, Allegra. EDUC: Harvard Univ., M.D. 1981. CAREER: Resident, Pediatrics, Univ. of Washington, 1981-83; Chief Resident, Pediatrics, Univ. of British Columbia, 1983-85; Fellow, Medical Genetics, 1985-86; Clinical Assoc. Prof., 1994 to date; Harvard Macy Fellow in Medical Educ., 1996. SELECTED PUBLICATIONS: "Pharmacokinetics and bacteriological efficacy of moxalactarn, netilmicin, and ampicillin in experimental gram-negative enteric bacillary meningitis," with others (*Antimicrobial Agents and Chemotherapy* Mar. 1980); "Knowledge of Fetal Alcohol Syndrome among native Indians," with others (*Canadian Journal of Public Health* Sept.-Oct. 1993); "Upper body exercise capacity in youth with spina bifida," with others (*Adapted Physical Activity Quarterly* No.1 1993); "Effects of prenatal alcohol exposure on neuromotor and cognitive development during early childhood: a series of case reports," with others (*Physical Therapy* Sept. 1993); numerous chapters, articles, letters, reports & abstracts. AFFIL: American Board of Pediatrics (Diplomate); Royal Coll. of Physicians of Canada (Fellow in Pediatrics); B.C. Medical Association (Chair, Child & Youth Committee, Council on Health Promo.); B.C. Fetal Alcohol Syndrome Society (Pres. 1992-94); Canadian Pediatric Society; Canadian Medical Society on Alcohol & Other Drugs; Research Society on Alcoholism; International Fetal Alcohol Syndrome Study Group; North Pacific Pediatric Society; Phi Beta Kappa.

HONS: Phi Beta Kappa; N.C.A.A. Scholar, summa cum laude, 1976; Distinguished Alumni Award, S. Method Univ., 1996. MISC: 1st woman in the US to receive a varsity sport letter, 1975; Bronze Medalist, World Championship (Aquatics), 1975; Team mbr. (Diving), Pan Amerian Games, 1971. COMMENT: *"Academic and medical interest has focused on Fetal Alcohol Syndrome (FAS) and Fetal Alcohol Effects (FAE). This syndrome was first brought to the attention of the medical community in the early 1970s. Much of the research and attention given to this issue in British Columbia and Canada has been due to the efforts of Dr. Loock."*

Loos, Lynn ■ 📖 ✆ ⊗
Past President, ALBERTA CHAPTER OF THE REGISTRY OF INTERPRETERS FOR THE DEAF, 11337 - 61 Ave., Edmonton, AB T6H 1M3 (403) 488-6094, FAX 488-6094. Born Edmonton. EDUC: Grant MacEwan Community Coll., Certificate (Interpreter Training Program) 1987. CAREER: freelance Sign Language Interpreter, 1987 to date; Gen. Mgr, XII World Winter Games for the Deaf, Banff, 1989-91. AFFIL: Association of Visual Language Interpreters of Canada; Registry of Interpreters for the Deaf (Assoc. Mbr., USA.; Past Pres., Alberta Chapter); Alberta Association of the Deaf; Association of Visual Language Interpreters of Southern Alberta. HONS: Distinguished Alumni Award, Grant MacEwan Community Coll., 1994. COMMENT: *"I was born and raised in Edmonton, and still make it my home. After spending five years learning American Sign Language, I entered the Interpreter Training Program, and upon graduation became a freelance interpreter. I am involved in a number of volunteer activities within the Deaf and interpreting communities, which includes my work on the A.C.R.I.D. Board and volunteering for the World Winter Games before becoming General Manager."*

Lord, Shirley ☺ ✦ ✿
Community Organizer and Activist. c/o Choices! A Coalition for Social Justice, 275 Broadway, Ste. 503, Winnipeg, MB R3C 4M6 (204) 944-9408, FAX 956-70712. Born Winnipeg 1946. life partner George Harris. 3 ch. EDUC: Red River Community Coll., Lic. Practical Nurse 1970; Univ. of Manitoba, Labour Certificate Course 1976. CAREER: Licenced Practical Nurse, City of Winnipeg, 1970-81; community organizer & activist, 1972 to date. AFFIL: Winnipeg Folk Festival (Bd.); Canadian Dimension Collective ; Manitoba Federation of Labour (Political Educ. Chair); Working Group of the Choices!/CCPA Alternative Fed. Budget.

INTERESTS: travelling & sightseeing; eco tourism model. COMMENT: *"Committed to spending my life challenging a corporate agenda that puts profits before people. I want a world that protects our resources for generations to come. I believe that our work in social justice is done collectively and empowers all."*

Loren, Sandra, B.A.,M.Ed. ■ ✦ ◈
President, WOMEN'S COMMISSION OF THE BC LIBERAL PARTY, 705 - 3083 East Kent Ave., Vancouver, BC V5S 4R2 (604) 437-9301, FAX 924-1338. Born Vancouver 1962. EDUC: Univ. of British Columbia, B.A.(Pol. Sci./ English); Univ. of Southern Mississippi, M.Ed.(Educ. Admin.); Diplomas in Special Educ. & Small Bus. Mgmt. CAREER: teacher, mainstream & Special Educ., 1986 to date. AFFIL: B.C. Teachers' Federation (Special Educ. Association); Liberal Party of Canada, B.C. (Past Pres., Women's Commission; Fed. Exec. Rep. 1992-95); B.C. Liberal Party (Pres., Women's Commission; Prov. Exec. Rep. 1993 to date). INTERESTS: fed. & prov. politics; recruitment of women at all levels of the political process; policy dev.: educ., children/adolescents, social svcs.

Lorjé, Pat, B.A.,M.A.,M.L.A. ✦
Member of the Legislative Assembly (Saskatoon-Southeast), GOVERNMENT OF SASKATCHEWAN, 1945 McKercher Dr., Ste. 16, Saskatoon, SK S7J 4M4 (306) 955-8866, FAX 955-8836. Born Eastend, Sask. 1947. w. EDUC: Univ. of Saskatchewan, B.A.(Psych.) 1969, M.A.(Psych.) 1976. CAREER: Chief Psychologist, Saskatoon Mental Health Clinic, 1978-91; Mun. Councillor, City of Saskatoon, 1979-91; elected M.L.A. (Saskatoon-Southeast) 1991, re-elected 1995; Chair, Crown Corporations Committee; Chair, Gov't Caucus Employment & Economy Committee. AFFIL: Saskatoon NDP Caucus (Chair); Saskatoon Fringe Festival; Twenty-Fifth Street Theatre; Saskatoon Race Relations Committee (Founding Mbr.); Provincial Legal Aid Commission (former Mbr.); Saskatoon City Hospital (former Bd. Mbr.); 1989 Jeux Canada Summer Games (Organizing Committee). INTERESTS: marathon running.

Lothian, Pamela, B.A.,LL.B. ⚖ ◈ ♂
Partner, MCDOUGALL, READY, Barristers and Solicitors, 700 Royal Bank Building, 2010 - 11th Ave., Regina, SK S4P 0J3 (306) 757-1641, FAX 359-0785. Born Regina 1961. m. 2 ch. Kelsey Jade Lothian, Jasmine Paige Lothian. EDUC: Univ. of Saskatchewan, B.A.(Pol. Sci.) 1982, LL.B. 1985. BAR: Sask., 1986. CAREER: Police Constable, Saskatoon City,

1982; Youth Svcs Legal Educ. Proj., Ministry of the Solicitor-Gen., 1983; Legal Educ. for Youth & Professionals Program, 1984; articling student, McDougall, Ready, 1985; Assoc., 1986-92; Ptnr, 1992 to date. AFFIL: Big Sisters; Regina Bar Association (Dir.); Canadian Bar Association; Wesley United Church (Sec. to the Church Bd.). INTERESTS: music (previously taught piano & flute); sports; reading; movies; running. COMMENT: *"I am a mother of two pre-school girls, a wife, and a partner in a law firm of 26. In 1992, I became the first woman partner in the firm (established in 1891). My greatest accomplishment also continues to be my greatest challenge: balancing my family and my professional life, on my own agenda."*

Lottridge, Celia Barker, B.A.,M.A., B.Ed. ◳ ◯ ◈
Writer. 42 Vermont Ave., Toronto, ON M6G 1X9. Born Iowa 1936. EDUC: Stanford Univ., B.A.(Hist.) 1957; Columbia Univ., M.A. (Library Sci.) 1959; Univ. of Toronto, B.Ed.(Educ.) 1976. CAREER: Children's Librarian, Brooklyn Public Library & San Diego Public Library, 1958-61; elementary sch. librarian, N.Y.C., 1961-64; elementary sch. librarian, Providence, R.I., 1965-67; Cataloguer, Brown Univ. Library, 1969-72; Teacher Librarian, Toronto, 1976-77; Mgr, then Book Buyer, The Children's Book Store, Toronto, 1977-87; freelance storyteller, schools, libraries & community venues, 1982 to date; Dir., Parent-Child Mother Goose Program, 1986 to date. SELECTED PUBLICATIONS: *One Watermelon Seed*, illus. by Karen Patkau (Stoddart, 1986); *The Name of the Tree, a Bantu Tale*, illus. by Ian Wallace (Groundwood Books, 1989); *Mythic Voices, Reflections in Mythology*, ed. with Alison Dickie (Nelson Canada, 1990); *Ticket to Curlew* (Groundwood Books, 1992); *Ten Small Tales*, illus. by Paul Zwolak (Groundwood Books, 1994); *The Wind Wagon*, illus. by Daniel Clifford (Groundwood Books, 1995); *Letters to the Wind*, ed. (Key Porter, 1995). AFFIL: Writers' Union of Canada; Storytellers Sch. of Toronto (Founding Mbr.; Bd. Mbr. 1978-90); CANSCAIP; Canadian Children's Book Centre. HONS: Short List (*The Name of the Tree, a Bantu Tale*), Christie Award for Children's Books; Children's Book of the Year (*Ten Small Tales*), IODE Toronto Chapter; Book of the Year for Children (*Ticket to Curlew*), Canadian Librarians' Association; Honour Book for Canada (*Ticket to Curlew*), Int'l Bd. on Books for Young People; Geoffrey Bilson Award for Historical Fiction for Young People (*Ticket to Curlew*); Anne Izard Story Teller's Choice Award (*Ten Small Tales*). INTERESTS: travel; art; hiking the country;

walking in the city. **MISC:** The Parent-Child Mother Goose Program is a nonprofit, charitable organization, that runs supportive group programs for parents, infants & young children; the group activity focuses on the power of using rhymes, songs & stories within the family to encourage communication, comfort & fun. **COMMENT:** *"Story is at the centre of my life, from the beginning of my career as a librarian to my current varied freelance activities."*

Lougheed, Jeanne, B.A. $ ♡

Corporate Director. Calgary, AB (403) 298-3376. m. Peter. 4 ch. Stephen, Andrea, Pamela, Joe. **EDUC:** Univ. of Alberta, B.A. 1951. **DIRECTOR:** Sears Canada Inc.; Northwestern Utilities Limited; Canadian Western Natural Gas Co. Ltd.; CU Gas Ltd., Calgary. **AFFIL:** National Ballet of Canada (Gov.); Dancer Transition Centre (Advisory Council); Calgary Real Estate Charitable Foundation (Patron); Canadian Association for Community Living (Advisory Bd.); Calgary Philharmonic Society (Dir.); Calgary Art Gallery Foundation (Dir.).

Loughheed, M. Claire, B.A.,M.A. ■■ ⊛ 🎓

President, CHARIS ENTERPRISES/PARTNERS IN LEARNING (arts educ. programs & communications consultant), 70 Ray St. N., Hamilton, ON L8R 2X6 (905) 525-1352, FAX 525-1352. Born Sault Ste. Marie, Ont. 1960. m. James Jamieson. **EDUC:** Univ. of Guelph, B.A.(Theatre) 1983, M.A.(Theatre Hist.) 1986. **CAREER:** Instructor, Creative Arts Studio, Royal Ontario Museum, 1984-90; Asst. to Production, Shaw Festival, 1989; Programs & Publicity Coord., Oakville Arts Council, 1989; Educ. Programs Officer, Art Gallery of Hamilton, 1989-96; freelance Programs Consultant, Canada & U.S., 1996 to date. **SELECTED PUBLICATIONS:** "Canadian Theatre Archive Report" (*University of Guelph Archival Quarterly*, 1985). **EXHIBITIONS:** "Fabulous Fakes: Props from the Shaw Festival," Art Gallery of Hamilton, Kitchener-Waterloo Oktoberfest, Cultural Events, London Children's Museum, 1993. **AFFIL:** Big Brothers Association of Hamilton-Wentworth (Program Designer); American Association of Museums. **INTERESTS:** British fiction; rowing; artists' safety issues; textile arts; learning theory. **COMMENT:** *"My energies have seemingly always been focused on bringing the community and the arts together in engaging and enlightening ways. People's appreciation keeps me at it."*

Loughrey, Carol Elaine Ashfield, B.B.A., M.B.A.,F.C.A. ■ 🍁

Deputy Minister of Education, GOVENMENT OF NEW BRUNSWICK, P.O. Box 6000, Fredericton, NB E3B 5H1 (506) 453-2529, FAX 457-4810. Born Fredericton 1948. m. Ronald. 2 ch. Margaret, Katherine. **EDUC:** Univ. of New Brunswick, B.B.A. 1970; C.A. 1972; Univ. of Maine (Orono), M.B.A. 1982. **CAREER:** public practice, 1970-74; part-time consultant, 1974-77; various teaching & administrative positions to Assoc. Prof. & Asst. Dean (Grad.), Univ. of New Brunswick, Fac. of Admin., 1977-88; Compt., Prov. of N.B., 1988-96; Deputy Min. of Educ., 1996 to date. **SELECTED PUBLICATIONS:** author & co-author of various professional & academic articles. **EDIT:** Advisory Bd., *F.M.I. Journal*. **AFFIL:** N.B. & Ontario Institutes of Chartered Accountants (Pres. 1986-87; Fellow, Ont. 1994, N.B. 1989); Canadian Comprehensive Auditing Foundation (Gov.); Muriel McQueen Fergusson Foundation; N.B. Law Foundation; Canadian Institute of Chartered Accountants (Gov.; Chair & CEO 1994-95); Financial Management Institute of Canada; Institute of Public Administration of Canada; New Brunswick Breast Cancer Network Inc. (co-founder); Canadian Women's Foundation (Dir. & Sec.-Treas.); CCAF (Gov.); United Church; various charitable organizations; Univ. of New Brunswick (Bd. of Gov.). **HONS:** President's Award, Univ. of New Brunswick, 1987; Certificate of Achievement, Univ. of New Brunswick Fac. of Admin., 1992; Beta Gamma Sigma, 1982; Life Mbr., Ontario Institute of Chartered Accountants, 1996. **INTERESTS:** skiing; aerobics; walking.

Lovering, Mary Jane, Dip.P.T., B.L.A. ⊛

Principal Landscape Architect, VERTECHS DESIGN, INC., 131 Davenport Rd., Ste. 300, Toronto, ON M5R 1H8 (416) 927-6097, FAX 925-1782. Born Toronto. **EDUC:** Queen's Univ., Diploma in Phys. Therapy 1971; Univ. of Toronto, Bachelor of Landscape Architecture 1980. **CAREER:** Physiotherapist, Toronto Western Hospital, 1971-73; Physiotherapist, Arthritis Society, 1973-80; Physiotherapist, Home Care Program for Metropolitan Toronto, 1977; Landscape Architect, Humber Arboretum, 1980-81; Landscape Architect, E.D.A. Collaborative Inc., 1980-81; Principal Landscape Architect, Vertechs Design Inc., 1981 to date. **SELECTED PUBLICATIONS:** "Why Aren't Our Outside Spaces Being Used?" (*Ontario Association of Homes for the Aged Quarterly* 1 1984); "Planning Outdoor Spaces" (*Ontario Association of Homes for the Aged Quarterly* 3 1983); "Barrier-Free Design in Canada's National Parks" (*Landscape Architectural Review* 5 1983); "Design Opens Doors for the Elderly" (*Landscape Architecture* Nov./Dec. 1984); "Design for the Elderly, Some

Planning Considerations" (*Landscape Architectural Review* July 1985); "Alzheimer's Disease and Outdoor Space–Issues in Environmental Design" (*American Journal of Alzheimer's Care and Research* May/June 1990). **AFFIL:** West Park Hospital (Gov.); Toronto Symphony Orchestra (Volunteer Committee); Canadian Society of Landscape Architects; Ontario Association of Landscape Architects; American Society of Landscape Architects; Garden Club of Toronto. **HONS:** Jules Wegman Fellowship, Univ. of Toronto, 1980; Merit Award, Research Category, Ontario Association of Landscape Architects, 1983; Merit Award, Research Category, Canadian Society of Landscape Architects, 1983; Premier's Award for Accessibility, Design Category, for West Park Hospital, 1988; Merit Award, Design Category, Canadian Society of Landscape Architects, 1988; Award in Landscape Construction, Landscape Ontario Horticultural Trades Association, 1990. **MISC:** various guest lectures & conference presentations.

Lowenthal, Myra, A.O.C.A. ■■ ✪
Visual Artist. 84 Prue Ave., Toronto, ON M6B 1R5 (416) 789-2577 or 967-1268. Born Belgrade, Yugoslavia 1947. s. **CAREER:** Ontario Coll. of Art, A.O.C.A.(Advertising Art) 1968. **EXHIBITIONS:** Anomon Art Gallery, Toronto, 1976; McDowell Gallery, Toronto, 1981-83; Bonnie Kagan Gallery, Toronto, 1985-90; Edwards Gardens Civic Centre, Toronto, 1992; C'est What, Toronto, 1993; 11 group exhibitions. **COLLECTIONS:** ABN AMRO Bank Canada; Ambrose Carr Linton Kelly Inc., Toronto; Michel Biguett Gallery, Quebec; Davies Ward & Beck, Toronto; Gryphon Investment Counsel, Toronto; Kennedy & Associates, Toronto; Maclean Hunter Limited, Toronto; Milne & Nicholls Ltd., Toronto; Noma Industries Ltd., Toronto; Olympia & York Developments Ltd., Toronto; Paisley Products, Toronto; Precision Small Parts, Toronto; John Stratton Associates, Toronto; Toronto Star; Twentieth Century-Fox, Los Angeles; numerous private collections & commissions.

Lowes, Judith E., B.A.,M.C.A. ■■ $
Vice-President, Marketing, CO-OPERATORS INVESTMENT COUNSELLING LIMITED (investment mgmt), Priory Square, 130 Macdonell St., Guelph, ON N1H 6P8 (519) 767-3901, FAX 824-7040. Born Toronto 1952. m. Douglas Lynn. 2 ch. Heather, Kevin. **EDUC:** Univ. of Toronto, B.A. 1976; Univ. of Ottawa, M.C.A.(Criminology) 1979. **CAREER:** Sr. Consultant, SEI Financial Services; Dir. of Mktg, Bank of Montreal Investment Counsel. **AFFIL:** Association of Canadian Pension Management (Sec.-Treas.). **INTERESTS:** golf.

Lowey, Brenda, B.B.A.,C.A.,C.P.A. ■ $
Partner, DELOITTE & TOUCHE, Chartered Accountants, 2000 Manulife Place, 10180 - 101 St., Edmonton, AB T5J 4E4 (403) 421-3736, FAX 421-3782. Born Regina 1960. m. Ron Wild. **EDUC:** Univ. of Regina, B.B.A. 1982. **CAREER:** Office of the Prov. Auditor, Sask., 1980-81; various positions, leading to Ptnr, Taxation, Touche Ross & Co., later Deloitte & Touche, Chartered Accountants, 1982 to date. **SELECTED PUBLICATIONS:** various newspaper articles & papers for professional organizations. **AFFIL:** Canadian Institute of Chartered Accountants (C.A.; In-Depth Tax Accountant; In-Depth Tax Instructor 1991-94); Institute of Chartered Accountants of Alberta; Institute of Chartered Accountants of Saskatchewan; Canadian Tax Foundation; Junior Achievement (Past Pres.); Royal Lifesaving Society (Past Pres.); Business & Professional Women's Association (VP 1992-93); Saskatchewan Pension Plan (Trustee 1990-91). **HONS:** Recognition Badge, Royal Lifesaving Society Canada; Certificate of Thanks, Royal Lifesaving Society Canada; Commonwealth Award. **INTERESTS:** golf; waterskiing; ballroom dancing; soccer. **MISC:** guest on various TV & radio shows; numerous seminars & guest speaker appearances on tax. **COMMENT:** *"To provide professional planning advice to Canadian businesses expanding outside our borders and to provide foreign companies with tax planning in Canada. To encourage and contribute to growth of young people in business by support of Junior Achievement and teaching new tax professionals."*

Lowry, Cathie, B.Sc.(Agr.),M.Ag. $ 🌾 🎓
Partner, STRIVE!, 60 Ptarmigan Dr., Ste. 17, Guelph, ON N1C 2B8 (519) 836-0547, FAX 766-9098, EMAIL cathie@strive.com. Born Carleton Place, Ont. 1955. **EDUC:** Univ. of Guelph, B.Sc.(Agr.-Animal Sci.) 1978, M.Ag.(Agribus. Mgmt) 1988. **CAREER:** Credit Advisor, Farm Credit Corporation, 1978-86; Teaching & Research Assoc., Univ. of Guelph, 1987-89; Mng Dir., Ontario Agricultural Training Institute, 1989-92; Exec. Dir., 1992-95; Ptnr, Strive!, 1995 to date. **AFFIL:** Ontario Agricultural Leadership Alumni; Ontario Agricultural Coll. Alumni Association (Pres. 1988-89); Ontario Institute of Agrologists (Fin. Chair 1991-92; Pres. 1993-94; Professional Dev. Chair 1994-95); Women and Rural Economic Development. **HONS:** Outstanding Young Agrologist, Agricultural Institute of Canada. **INTERESTS:** swimming; skating; piano. **COM-**

MENT: *"A progressive individual who tends to be in leadership positions and/or involved in new ventures within the Ontario agricultural community."*

Lubinsky, Karen, F.L.M.I. $
Director, Variable Investment Products, THE CANADA LIFE ASSURANCE COMPANY, 330 University Ave., Toronto, ON M5G 1R8 (416) 597-1456, FAX 204-2300. Born Oshawa, Ont. 1952. m. Eli Lubinsky. 2 ch. Jason Lubinsky, Marla Lubinsky. **CAREER:** handicapped/mentally disadvantaged programs, Peel Recreation, 1968-71; Asst. Mgr, Town and Country Store, 1971-72; various positions, Canada Life Assurance Company, 1972 to date. **AFFIL:** Life Office Management Association (Chair, Group Pension Admin. Committee 1993-94; Fellow in Insur.); Canada Life Staff Association (Pres. 1981-82); Canada Life Daycare (Bd. of Dir. 1996 to date). **INTERESTS:** skiing; boating; tennis; spending time with family. **COMMENT:** *"I am a working woman who is married with two children. I enjoy both my career and family responsibilities. Although work/life balance can be a challenge at times, the rewards far outweigh the hard work and long hours."*

Lucas, Helen, D.Litt. 🎨
Artist. 14210 Seventh Concession, King City, ON L7B 1K4 (905) 859-4425. Born Weyburn, Sask. 1931. m. Derek Fuller. 2 ch. **EDUC:** Ontario Coll. of Art, 1950-54. **CAREER:** painting master, author/contributing artist, guest lecturer, panelist. **EDIT:** mbr., CARO Advisory Bd., Canadian Artists' Representation Ontario, *Guide to Professional Practice in the Visual Arts* publications. **EXHIBITIONS:** solo exhibitions held yearly from 1953, Canada & US. **COLLECTIONS:** represented in many corp. & private collections, Canada & overseas. **AFFIL:** CARO. **HONS:** Women of Distinction Award, YWCA, 1985; numerous other awards; D.Litt.(Hon.), York Univ., 1991. **MISC:** recipient, various grants; mbr., Steering Committee, Festival of Women in the Arts, Int'l Women's Year, Toronto, 1975.

Lucier, Mary Kaye, E.C.E.,B.S.W., M.S.W. ✊ ⊕
Clinical Director, BULIMIA ANOREXIA NERVOSA ASSOCIATION (BANA), 3640 Wells Ave., Windsor, ON N9C 1T9 (519) 253-7545, FAX 258-0488. Born Windsor, Ont. 1953. m. Dale. 2 ch. **EDUC:** St. Clair Coll., E.C.E. 1976; Univ. of Windsor, B.S.W. 1988, M.S.W. 1990. **CAREER:** Social Work Intern (Constituency Asst./Case Mgr), MP Constituency Office, Howard McCurty, Windsor, 1986-87; Social Work Intern, BANA, 1987-88; Social Work Intern, Windsor Western Hospital, 1988-89; Early Childhood Educator, ABC Day Nursery & Kindergarten, Windsor, 1973-85; Dir., BANA, 1989 to date; private practice, 1994 to date. **SELECTED PUBLICATIONS:** "Fat Oppression and the Relentless Pursuit of Thinness" (*Bulimia Anorexia Nervosa Association Newsletter* 1993); "Sexual Abuse and Eating Disorders" (*BANA Newsletter* 1992); various other articles in *BANA Newsletter*. **AFFIL:** Ontario Association for Professional Social Workers; Soroptimist International; Bulimia Anorexia Nervosa Association; Canadian Association of Schools of Social Work; National Eating Disorder Information Centre, Canada; National Eating Disorder Organization, US; Ontario Nutritional Education. **INTERESTS:** sewing; walking; bird watching; gardening; women's issues; her family. **MISC:** various workshops developed. **COMMENT:** *"I think knowledge is power and therefore like to think, talk, write and participate in the women's movement. I have a strong sense of justice and fairness, being able to consider many sides of an issue. I really enjoy being part of change."*

Ludlam, Mary Anne, A.O.C.A.,C.S.P.W.C., O.S.A.,N.F.W.S.,S.C.A. 🎨
Interior Designer and Visual Artist, DESIGNS BY MARY ANNE, 63 Oldham Rd., Etobicoke, ON M9A 2B9 (416) 239-5949. Born Oshawa, Ont. 1931. m. Arthur Walker Ludlam. 2 ch. **EDUC:** Ontario Coll. of Art, A.O.C.A.(Interior Design/Architecture) 1954; Fontainebleau Sch. of Fine Art & Music, Interior Design 1955. **CAREER:** Corp. Designer, Mitchell Houghton, Toronto, 1955-70; Sr. Designer, John C. Preston, 1970-78; self-employed visual artist, 1978 to date. **COMMISSIONS:** Christmas card commission, City of Etobicoke, 1986; Arts Etobicoke Annual Mayor's Luncheon commission, 1989; print commission, Canadian Institute of Chartered Accountants, 1989; British Airways commission, Terminal 3, Toronto, 1991. **EXHIBITIONS:** *Watercolours of Fontainebleau*, Ontario Coll. of Art (1956); McDowell Gallery (1981, 1982); Lindsay Gallery (1983); Rails End Gallery (1984); Beckett Gallery Ltd. (1986); Village Square Art Gallery (1987); Roberts Gallery (1988, 1990, 1992, 1994); Horizon Art Galleries (1991, 1993); included in numerous juried exhibitions. **COLLECTIONS:** represented in numerous permanent collections, incl. Bell Canada; City of Toronto; Fuji Film; Ontario Energy Bd.; Royal Collection of Drawings & Watercolours, Windsor Castle. **AFFIL:** Humber Valley Art Club; Etobicoke Art Group; Central Ontario Art Association; Niagara Frontier Watercolour Society (elected

1990); Canadian Society of Painters in Watercolour (elected 1983); Ontario Society of Artists (elected 1982); Society of Canadian Artists (elected 1981); Association of Registered Interior Designers of Ontario (elected 1956). HONS: Dunlop Scholarship, Ontario Coll. of Art, 1952; Third-Year Interior Design Prize, Ontario Coll. of Art, 1953; Gordon C. Leitch Travelling Scholarship, Ontario Coll. of Art, 1954; Best Painting Award, COAA Open Exhibition, 1980; Hiram Walker Purchase Award, OSA 108th Open Exhibition, 1980; Best Watercolour, Arts Etobicoke, 1980; Rowney Artists' Materials Purchase Award, CSPWC Open Exhibition; John Schlachter Memorial Award, COAA Open Exhibition, 1982; Best Painting Award, Central Ontario Art Association Open Exhibition, 1983; Anonymous Bank Purchase Award, CSPWC Open Exhibition, 1984; Award of Merit, Niagara Frontier Watercolour Society, 1990; Landscape Award, Nat'l Fine Art Competition, 1993; Award of Merit, Niagara Frontier Watercolour Society Nat'l Exhibition, 1994; Award of Excellence, Arts Etobicoke Open Exhibition, COAA, 1996. INTERESTS: travel; *antiques; music; drama; gardening.* MISC: listed in *Canadian Who's Who* 1991; subject of various magazine & newspaper articles; Feature Artist, Burlington Cultural Centre, June 1991. COMMENT: *"My years as a designer have much to do with the way I view the world. As a painter, I continue to use the principles of good design, i.e., order, structure and balance and how they influence people."*

Luke, Theresa ■ ■ ⑳

Olympic Athlete. c/o Canadian Olympic Association. Born Vancouver 1967. EDUC: currently studying Environmental Toxicology. SPORTS CAREER: mbr., Cdn Nat'l Rowing Team, 1993 to date. Olympic Games: Silver, 8+, 1996. World championships: 6th, 8+, 1995; 7th, 8+, & 8th, 4-, 1994. World University Games: 1st, 8+, 1993. Canadian championships: 1st, 2-, 1995. US championships: 1st, 8+, 1994. INTERESTS: horseback riding; cycling; hiking; swimming; hand drumming; dancing.

Lukkien (Van't Hof), Dorothy A., B.Ed. ■ ⑳ ⑳

Past President, SASKATCHEWAN BUSINESS TEACHERS' ASSOCIATION., 1905 Preston Ave., Saskatoon, SK S7J 2E9 (306) 683-7880, FAX 683-7857. Teacher, WALTER MURRAY COLLEGIATE. Born 1960. m. Joe Van't Hof. 2 ch. Marian, Alyssa. EDUC: Univ. of Alberta, B.Ed.(Secondary) 1987. CAREER: teacher, Walter Murray Collegiate, Saskatoon Bd. of Educ., 1987 to

date. AFFIL: Saskatoon Christian Sch.; Bethel Christian Reformed Church (Sunday Sch. & Catechism Teacher; Chair, Educ. Committee); LakeView Community Association (Basketball Coach); Saskatchewan Business Teachers' Association (Pres. 1992-94); Saskatchewan Teachers' Federation; Saskatoon Basketball Association. INTERESTS: basketball; fitness training; professional dev.; computer technology; spending time with her children & family. COMMENT: *"Commitment and dedication are the fabric of my persona. I deem it a privilege to share my knowledge and experiences with my colleagues and students."*

Lundman, Janis, B.A. ■ ⑳ ⑳

Director and Producer, BACK ALLEY FILM PRODUCTIONS LTD., 110 Spadina Ave., Ste. 800, Toronto, ON M5V 2K4 (416) 703-8825, FAX 703-1126. Born Alta. 1951. s. EDUC: York Univ., B.A.(Film) 1978. CAREER: Dir. & Prod., Back Alley Film Productions Ltd. SELECTED CREDITS: *Soul Survivor*, 1981; *Matinale*, 1982; *Las Aradas*, 1984; *Toronto 6:17*, 1985; *The Struggle for Choice*, 1985; *Close Your Eyes and Think of England*, 1988; *Talk 16*, 1991; *Talk 19*, 1993; *Lawn and Order*, 1994. AFFIL: Academy of Canadian Cinema & Television; Toronto Women in Film & Television. HONS: Honourable Mention (*Soul Survivor*), Greece Festival, 1981; Gold Winner (*Matinale*), Houston Film Festival, 1982; Canadian Short Film Showcase Winner (*Las Aradas*), 1985; Special Jury Prize (*Talk 16*), San Francisco Festival, 1991; Special Jury Prize (*Talk 16*), Cinéma du Reel, France, 1991; Best Documentary (*Talk 16*), Florida Film Festival, 1991; Jury Award (*Lawn and Order*), Yorkton Film Festival, 1994; Silver Plaque Award (*Lawn and Order*), Chicago Film Festival, 1994.

Lundrigan, Joanne, R.N. ⊕

Hospital Supervisor, CAPTAIN WILLIAM JACKMAN MEMORIAL HOSPITAL, 410 Booth Ave., Labrador City, NF A2V 2K5 (709) 944-2632, FAX 944-9341. Born St. Bride's, Placentia East, Nfld. 1952. s. 1 ch. EDUC: General Hospital Sch. of Nursing, R.N. 1985; CNA Certification in Emergency Nursing, 1996. CAREER: Sch. Sec., Fatima High Sch., 1973-76; Registered Nurse, Jackman Memorial Hospital, 1985-89; Hospital Supervisor, 1989 to date; Registered Nurse, Rehabilitation Hospital, Daytona Beach, Fla., 1993-94; R.N., East Pasco Emergency Center, Tampa area, Fla., 1995-96. AFFIL: Labrador West Status of Women (Dir.); Labrador West Well Women Clinic (Coord.); Big Brothers/Big Sisters (Steering Committee). HONS: Int'l Women's Day Award, 1992.

COMMENT: *"Survivor of abusive relationship. Single mom. Determined, strong willed, conscientious. Value family and friends. Began nursing training at 30 years of age, graduated with RN diploma in three years, working at Capt. Jackman Memorial Hospital since 1985. With two work teams in Florida. Daughter–independent, fun-loving, all around good person attending nursing school in Ottawa, Ont."*

Lundström, Linda ■■ $ ✪

President, LINDA LUNDSTRÖM LTD. (women's apparel design & mfg), 33 Mallard Rd., Toronto, ON M3B 1S4 (416) 391-2838, FAX 391-0788. President, LUNDSTRÖM RETAIL INC. Born Red Lake, Ont. 1951. m. Joel Halbert. 2 ch. EDUC: Sheridan Coll., Fashion Design 1970-72. CAREER: started bus., 1974; produces a complete family of products for women; all products are made in Canada; has maintained a 12% growth trend throughout the 1990s; designs are carried by independent boutiques across Canada & the U.S. HONS: numerous awards incl.: Order of Ontario, 1995; 3 Snow Country Awards, Las Vegas; Lifetime Achievement Award/Cdn Woman Entrepreneur of the Year, Univ. of Toronto, 1994; Outstanding Bus. Achievement Award, Ont. Chamber of Commerce, 1991. MISC: Judge, Canadian Council for Native Business Winds of Change Native Designer Competition; Judge, 1992 Canada Awards for Business Excellence; Sponsor, Faces and Stories, Breast Cancer Support Services; founder, "Kiishik Fund," which creates awareness of Native culture in classrooms in Red Lake district.

Lunn, Janet Louise Swoboda 📖 📜 ☝

Writer, Author. Born Dallas, Tex. 1928. w. Richard Lunn. 5 ch. Eric, Jeffrey, Alexander, Katherine, John. EDUC: Queen's Univ., 1947-50. CAREER: freelance reviewer & critic of children's lit., 1953 to date; Literary Consultant, Grades 2 & 3 sch. readers, Ginn & Co., 1968-78; Children's Ed., Clarke, Irwin & Co., Toronto, 1972-75; freelance ed., 1975 to date; Writer-in-residence, Regina Public Library, 1982-83; Writer-in-residence, Kitchener Public Library, 1988; Writer-in-residence, Univ. of Ottawa, Fall 1993; Bilson Memorial Lecturer, Univ. of Saskatchewan, 1993; Stubbs Memorial Lecturer, Friends of the Osborne Collection, Toronto Public Library, 1994. SELECTED PUBLICATIONS: *The County*, with Richard Lunn, history (Prince Edward County, 1967); *Double Spell* (Peter Martin Associates, 1968); *Larger Than Life*, collection (Press Porcepic, 1979); *The Twelve Dancing Princesses*, illus. by Laszlo Gal (Methuen, 1979); *The Root Cellar* (Lester & Orpen Dennys, 1981); *Shadow in Hawthorn Bay* (Lester & Orpen Dennys, 1986); *Amos's Sweater*, illus. by Kim LaFave (Groundwood, 1988); *Duck Cakes for Sale*, illus. by Kim LaFave (Groundwood, 1989); *One Hundred Shining Candles*, illus. by Lindsay Grater (Lester & Orpen Dennys, 1990); *The Story of Canada*, with Christopher Moore (Key Porter/Lester Publications, 1992); *The Unseen*, ed. anthology (Lester Publishing, 1994); various short stories for children, magazine articles, book reviews. AFFIL: IBBY Canada (Bd. of Dir. 1989); Canadian Children's Book Centre (Bd. of Dir. 1989; Pres. 1990); Writers' Union of Canada (2nd V-Chair 1979-80; 1st V-Chair 1983-84; Chair 1984-85); Canadian Society of Children's Authors, Illustrators & Performers; PEN International. HONS: Children's Book Award, Toronto Branch IODE, *The Twelve Dancing Princesses*, 1979; Vicki Metcalf Award, Canadian Authors' Association, body of work, 1981; Children's Book of the Year, Canadian Library Association, *The Root Cellar*, 1982; Award for Children's Lit., Canada Council, *Shadow in Hawthorn Bay*, 1986; Children's Book Award, Canadian Library Association, *Shadow in Hawthorn Bay*, 1986; Young Adult Book of the Year Award, Saskatchewan Library Association, *Shadow in Hawthorn Bay*, 1986; Children's Book of the Year, Nat'l Chapter IODE, *Shadow in Hawthorn Bay*, 1986; Ruth Schwartz Award, Canadian Booksellers' Association, *Amos's Sweater*, 1989; Mr. Christie Book Award, Christie Brown, *The Story of Canada*, 1993; Children's Book Award, Toronto Branch IODE, *The Story of Canada*, 1993; Info. Book Award, Children's Literature Round Tables of Canada, 1993; various other honours & recognitions; Order of Ontario, 1996; LL.D.(Hon.), Queen's Univ., 1992; Diploma (Hon.), Loyalist Coll. of Applied Arts & Technology, 1993. INTERESTS: gardening; reading; writing. MISC: writer, various radio talks & interviews; various writers' workshops with Ont. Arts Council & others; lecturer for International Reading Association, Ontario Reading Association & others; 1994 illustrated ed. of *The Root Cellar* chosen as the gift book for the Friends of Osborne Collection of children's books, a 1st for a book by a living Cdn writer.

Lustig, Terry, B.A. ■■ $ ♡

Senior Vice-President, Development, GOLDLIST DEVELOPMENT CORPORATION (land dev. & construction), 65 Overlea Blvd., Ste. 300, Toronto, ON M4H 1P1 (416) 421-3020, FAX 421-8408. Born N.Y. 1951. m. Alan Lustig. 2 ch. Jayme, Jonathan. EDUC: Pennsylvania State

Univ., B.A.(French) 1971. **CAREER:** Goldlist Development Corporation, 22 yrs. **AFFIL:** Urban Development Institute, Ontario (Bd. of Dir.); Ontario New Home Warranty Program (Tech. Committee); Canada Mortgage & Housing Corporation (Ont. Seniors Advisory Committee); North York Board of Education (Special Educ. Advisory Committee); Canadian National Institute for the Blind (Client Svcs Committee, Ont. Div.); VIEWS for the Visually Impaired (VP). **INTERESTS:** golf; tennis. **COMMENT:** *"I am proud of the contribution that I make every day, to the company that I work for and represent, to the various organizations that I participate in, and to teaching my children to be the best that they can be."*

Luther, Alice Hamilton, B.A.,M.A., Ph.D. ⊗ ⊰
Associate Professor, Department of Dramatic Arts, UNIVERSITY OF LETHBRIDGE, 4401 University Dr., Lethbridge, AB T1K 3M4 (403) 329-2688, FAX 382-7127. Born Newcastle, N.B. m. Scott Clark Luther. 2 ch. Kaitlin, Meghan. **EDUC:** Univ. of New Brunswick, B.A.(English) 1980; Univ. of Idaho, M.A.(Theater Arts) 1981; Univ. of Minnesota, Ph.D.(Theater Arts) 1985. **CAREER:** Teaching Assoc., Theater, Univ. of Minnesota, 1983; Instructor, English, Univ. of New Brunswick, 1984; Acting Coach/Dir., 1984; Artistic Dir., Anniston Community Theatre, Anniston, 1985; Artistic Dir., 1985-87; Asst. Prof. of Drama, Univ. of Saskatchewan, 1987-90; Asst. Prof., Dept. of Dramatic Arts, Univ. of Lethbridge, 1991-92; Assoc. Prof., 1992 to date; Acting Chair, 1992-93; Visiting Prof. of Cdn Studies, Hokkai-Gakuen Univ., Sapporo, Japan, 1995; Assoc. Prof. of English, Hiroshima Univ., Japan, 1995-96. **SELECTED CREDITS:** Mary, *The Return of A.J. Raffles*, Theatre New Brunswick/Neptune Theatre, 1979; Bonnie, *Free At Last*, Theatre New Brunswick, 1980; title role, *Sound Down*, Univ. of Idaho, 1981; Rita, *Educating Rita*, Holiday Inn Centre Stage Dinner Theatre, Saskatoon, 1988; numerous other film & stage performance credits; numerous ACTRA commercial credits; Dir., *Knights and Days* Univ. of Idaho, 1980; Dir., *Bus Stop*, Univ. of New Brunswick, 1984; Dir., *Crimes of the Heart*, Anniston Community Theatre, 1986; Dir., *On the Blueline*, 25th Street Theatre, 1988; Dir. *Sticks and Stones*, Univ. of Saskatchewan Mainstage, 1989; Dir., *Canadian Scenes*, Hokkai-Gakuen Univ., Sapporo, Japan, 1993; Dir., *Wind in the Willows,* The Univ. of Lethbridge Mainstage, 1991; Dir., *The Secret Garden*, Univ. of Lethbridge Performing Arts Series, 1994; *A Streetcar Named Desire*, The Univ.of Lethbridge Mainstage, 1997; numerous other

dir. credits; various TV appearances. **SELECTED PUBLICATIONS:** "The use of dramatic activity as an effective tool for teaching English in the Japanese university classroom" (*Studies in Language and Culture*, 1996); "Class Acts: Six Plays for Children," review (*Canadian Theatre Review* 78, 1994); "Mirror Game," review (*Canadian Theatre Review* 78, 1994); various other articles & reviews. **AFFIL:** ACTRA. **HONS:** Best Actress, N.B. Senior Drama Festival, 1976; Adjudicators' Award, director, N.B. Senior Drama Festival, 1978; Best Actress Award, N.B. Adult Drama Festival, 1979; Merit Award for Theatre, Univ. of New Brunswick, 1977-78, 1978-79, 1979-80; Grant for Advanced Studies, N.B. Dept. of Cultural Resources, 1980-81, 1982-83, 1983-84, 1984-85; O'Brien Foundation Fellowship, 1981-82. **INTERESTS:** travel; photography; drawing. **MISC:** various lectures & conference presentations; numerous consultancies; adjudicator for various drama festivals.

Luxton, Meg, B.A.,M.Phil.,Ph.D. ■ ⊰ ⊛
Professor, YORK UNIVERSITY, 4700 Keele St., North York, ON M3J 1P3 (416) 736-2100 ext. 33138, FAX 736-5103, EMAIL mluxton@ yorku.ca. Born Surbiton, Surrey, UK 1946. s. 2 ch. **EDUC:** Univ. of Toronto, B.A.(Social & Philosophical Thought) 1969, M.Phil.(Anthro.) 1973, Ph.D.(Anthro.) 1978. **CAREER:** Lecturer, Interdisciplinary Women's Studies Programme, Univ. of Toronto, 1971-78; Asst. Prof. of Anthro., 1978-80; Asst. Prof. of Soc., McMaster Univ., 1979-84; Assoc. Prof. with tenure, York Univ., 1984-90; cross-appointed to Grad. Fac., Dept. of Soc., York Univ., 1984-90; cross-appointed as Assoc. Mbr. of Grad. Fac., Univ. of Toronto, Ontario Institute for Studies in Education, 1989-90; Prof., Dept. of Social Science, York Univ., 1991 to date; Coord., Women's Studies Program, 1991-94; cross-appointed to Grad. Fac. of Social & Pol. Thought, Soc. & Women's Studies, 1991 to date. **SELECTED CREDITS:** Consultant/Participant, *All Day*, TVOntario, 1983; Consultant/Guest Speaker, "Feminism and Families," *Ideas*, CBC Radio, 1983; Consultant/Guest Speaker, Open Coll. Radio course on "Women and Money," CJRT FM, 1981-82; Consultant/Guest Speaker, Open Coll. Radio course on "The Family," CJRT FM, 1981. **SELECTED PUBLICATIONS:** *More Than a Labour of Love: Three Generations of Women's Work in the Home* (Toronto: The Canadian Women's Educational Press, 1980); *Through the Kitchen Window: The Politics of Home and Family*, with H. Rosenberg (Toronto: Garamond, 1986); *Feminism and Political Economy: Women's Work, Women's Struggles*, ed. with

H.J. Maroney (Toronto: Methuen, 1987); *Recasting Steel Labour: Stelco in the 1980s*, with J. Corman, D. Livingstone, W. Seccombe (Toronto: Fernwood, 1993); numerous book chapters, journal articles, reviews & conference papers. EDIT: Consulting Ed., *Canadian Review of Sociology and Anthropology*; Ed. Bd., *Canadian Woman Studies/les cahiers de la femme*. HONS: Teaching Excellence Award, Atkinson Coll. Alumni Association, 1992. MISC: recipient, numerous grants; participant, numerous conferences; Visiting Scholar, Social Policy Research Centre, Univ. of New South Wales, Sydney, Australia, 1993; Conference Organizer, "The Politics of Representation," Centre for Feminist Research, York Univ., 1993; Conference Organizer, "Sex, Race, Class Equity: In the Curriculum, In the Classroom," Atkinson Women's Studies, 1990-93; reviewer, various granting agencies, publishers & academic journals; consultant for a study of the impact of large-scale recreation & tourist dev. on local community & family networks in the Madawaska region, Ont.

Luz, Virginia ✕ ⚘

Artist. 113 Delaware Ave., Toronto, ON M6H 2S9 (416) 539-9665. Born Toronto 1911. EDUC: Central Tech. Sch., Grad.(Special Art) 1932; Ontario Training Sch. for Technical Teachers, Certificate 1939; McLane Art Institute, N.Y., 1940; Ontario Coll. of Education, Specialist Certificate (Vocational Art) 1956. CAREER: Commercial Artist, Toronto, 1932-38; Instructor of Illustration, Art Dept., Central Tech. Sch., Toronto, 1940-74; Asst. Dir., Art Dept., 1965-69; Dir., Art Dept., 1969-74. EXHIBITIONS: numerous group & solo exhibitions, 1945 to date, incl. Canadian Women Artists' Show, N.Y., 1947; Canadian National Exhibition Art Gallery Shows; *Tribute to 10 Women*, Sisler Gallery, Toronto, 1975; solo shows, 1948-76, 1981, 1993, 1994; group shows, 1951-53, 1954, 1981. COLLECTIONS: Robert McLaughlin Gallery, Oshawa, Ont.; London Regional Art Gallery, London, Ont.; J.S. McLean Collection; Dept. of External Affairs (Cdn embassies abroad); Huron Coll., London, Ont.; Etobicoke Bd. of Educ.; numerous private collections. AFFIL: Ontario Society of Artists; Canadian Society of Painters in Water Colours; Royal Canadian Academy of Arts. COMMENT: *"Virginia Luz, at 85, is a dedicated and prolific painter. She has clearly found her own voice. Her recent work has a unique, luminous and ethereal quality."*

Lychowyd, Sandra ■ ☺ ○ ⌙

Regional Director, Northwestern Ontario Region, THE KIDNEY FOUNDATION OF CANADA,

101 N. Syndicate Ave., Ste. 405, Thunder Bay, ON P7C 3V4 (807) 623-5437, FAX 623-9137. Born Minneapolis. m. Stephan. 2 ch. Dawn Marie, Troy Dylan. EDUC: Univ. of Minnesota, Psych./English. CAREER: Paralegal, Douglas, Jaycox, Trawick, McManus & Lippert, Minneapolis, 1975-77; Exec. Asst., Thunder Bay Community Auditorium, 1981-85; Dir. of Humane Educ., Shelter Supervisor, Ontario Humane Society, Thunder Bay, 1986; Gen. Mgr, Thunder Bay Emergency Shelter, 1988-90; N.W. Reg. Coord., The Easter Seal Society, 1990-92; Exec. Dir., N.W. Ont. & Sault Ste. Marie Chapters, The Kidney Foundation of Canada, 1992-95; Reg'l Dir., N.W. Ont. Reg., 1995 to date. SELECTED CREDITS: Prod./ Host, *Ask a Vet* (1-hr. open-line TV series), 1985 to date; Volunteer Host, Shaw Cable TV. AFFIL: Thunder Bay Chamber of Commerce; Thunder Bay Press Club; AIDS Committee; Lakehead Rotary Club; Thunder Bay Business Women's Network; Thunder Bay Association of Volunteer Administrators; Ontario Humane Society, Thunder Bay Branch (Past Pres.); St. Andrew's Presbyterian Church (Past Mbr., Bd. of Managers). HONS: Award of Merit recognizing commitment to improve quality of life for homeless individuals, 1990; Award of Merit recognizing 10 yrs. as volunteer host at Maclean Hunter Cable TV, 1994; Certificate of Recognition for leadership in the realization of the nat'l strategic plan, The Kidney Foundation of Canada, 1994; Chapter of the Year Award (for the N.W. Ont. Chapter), The Kidney Foundation of Canada, 1994; Wyn Tyler Award, The Kidney Foundation of Canada, 1996. INTERESTS: humane educ. & animal welfare; travel; music; football/sports. MISC: in 1995, represented the Kidney Foundation of Canada at the US Kidney Foundation conference in Washington, DC & was Honorary Guest Host of the reception at the Cdn Embassy during the conference; Facilitator, National Kidney Foundation Volunteer Dev. program, 1995-97; humane educ. consultant. COMMENT: *"The greatest joy of my life will always be my children. Their love, encouragement and belief in me provides me with the energy, passion and confidence to reach my professional goals and help other people."*

Lynch, Abbyann, B.A.,M.A.,L.M.S., Ph.D.,LL.D. ⚘ ⊕ ▤

Director, ETHICS IN HEALTH CARE ASSOCIATES, Box C35, Stn. Q, Toronto, ON M4T 2L7 (416) 932-8248, FAX 481-5075. Associate Professor, Faculty of Dentistry, UNIVERSITY OF TORONTO. Born N.J. 1928. m. Lawrence E. Lynch. 6 ch. Lisa, Emily, Edward, Martha, Paul, Christopher. EDUC: Manhattanville

Coll., NY, B.A.(Phil./Sci.) 1949; Univ. of Toronto, M.A.(Phil.) 1951, Ph.D.(Phil.) 1953, LL.D.(Bioethics) 1995; Institute of Mediaeval Studies, Toronto, L.M.S.(Mediaeval Studies) 1952. **CAREER:** Assoc. Prof., Medicine, Nursing, Dentistry, Social Work, Arts & Sci., Univ. of Toronto, 1974-94; Dir., Westminster Institute of Ethics & Human Values, London, Ont., 1986-90; Founding Dir., Dept. of Bioethics, Hospital for Sick Children, Toronto, 1991-94; Founding Dir., Ethics in Health Care Associates, 1994 to date. **SELECTED PUBLICATIONS:** "Publication of research: The ethical dimension" (*J. Dent. Res.*, Vol. 73, No. 11, 1994); "Ethical considerations in the care of newborn infants," *The Surgical Neonate*, Ed. D. Hatch, E. Sumner, J. Hellman (London: Edward Arnold, 1995); "Research use of individuals with Alzheimer's Disease," *Alzheimer's Disease Research*, Ed. J. Berg, H. Karlinsky, F. Lowy (Toronto: Carswell, 1991). **AFFIL:** National Council on Bioethics in Human Research (Pres.); Associated Medical Services, Inc. (VP); US Society for Bioethics Consultation (VP); WTN TV (Foundation Bd.); St. Elizabeth Health Care (Bd.); Ottawa Heart Institute (Ethics Committee). **HONS:** Order of Ontario, 1993. **INTERESTS:** piano performance; crime fiction writing; travel. **MISC:** 1 of 3 Canadians appointed by the Prime Minister to World Conference on Bioethics; Visiting Fellow, Univ. of Cambridge, UK; 10 named lectureships. **COMMENT:** *"I've tried to make a difference using personal abilities and effort; also, to encourage my children and students to do likewise–via teaching, writing, mentoring, challenging the status quo."*

Lynch, Jennifer, B.A.,LL.B.,Q.C. ■ [$] ⚖

President, PDG PERSONNEL DIRECTION GROUP (mgmt consulting & organizational development specializing in police hum. res. issues & alternative dispute resolution system design), 208 Russell Ave., Ottawa, ON K1N 7X5 (613) 565-6242, FAX 565-3875. Born Halifax 1950. s. **EDUC:** Queen's Univ., B.A. 1971; Osgoode Hall Law Sch., LL.B. 1975. **BAR:** Ont., 1977. **CAREER:** Barrister & Solicitor, F.J. Lynch & Associates, 1977-80; Ptnr, Honeywell Wotherspoon, 1980-83; mbr., Ont. Police Commission, 1985-88; V-Chair, External Review Committee, Royal Canadian Mounted Police, 1988 to date; Pres., PDG Personnel Direction Group, 1989 to date; Ptnr, Lang Michener, 1990-95; Acting Chairperson, External Review Committee, Royal Canadian Mounted Police, 1992 to date; alternatives dispute resolution systems design, for RCMP, 1995-96; Proprietor, multinat'l bus. in the distribution industry. **SELECTED PUBLICATIONS:** *Operation Identification: A Handbook*, with Dr. Ted Zaharchuk; *Police Programmes and Procedures Manual* Vol. I, II, & III, with Dr. Ted Zaharchuk (Fed. Ministry of the Solicitor-Gen. 1977); *Policing in Canada: A Bibliography*, with others (Toronto; Univ. of Toronto, Centre of Criminology 1979); "The Exigibility of Pensions" (1984, 36 R.F.L. (2d) 137); "Pensions, Tax and Trust: Considerations and Clauses" (1988, 15 R.F.L. (3d) 28); "A Checklist to Help You Avoid Writing a Cheque for your Deductible" (*Advocates' Society Journal* No. 1 1989); various manuals & papers. **AFFIL:** Law Society of Upper Canada; Canadian Bar Association; Women's Business Network of Ottawa; Rideau Club of Ottawa; Confederation Club (Dir.); National Progressive Conservative Women's Federation (Nat'l Pres. 1989-95); Algonquin Coll. (Advisory Committee, Law & Security Admin. Program); Legal Education Action Fund (Chair, fundraising event 1994-96); Saint Vincent's Hospital (Community Advisory Committee); Variety Club of Ottawa (Dir. 1994). **HONS:** Ottawa Business Women's Achievement Award, 1984; Queen's Counsel, Canada, 1990; Business & Professional Women's Award, Business & Professional Women's Club, 1991. **INTERESTS:** current affairs; phys. fitness; modern lit.; int'l travel.

Lynch, Kate 🎞 🎭 🎓

Actor, Teacher. 174 Crawford St., Toronto, ON M6J 2V4 (416) 536-8800. Born Toronto 1952. **EDUC:** Central Sch. of Speech & Drama, London, Post-Grad. Diploma 1993. **CAREER:** professional theatre, film, TV & radio actor, professional voice coach. **SELECTED CREDITS:** Juliet, *Stillborn Lover*, by Timothy Findley, Theatre Passe Muraille; Lady MacBeth, *MacBeth*, Equity Showcase; Del, *Fertile Imagination*, Nightwood Theatre; Constance Leadbelly, *Good Night Desdemona, Good Morning Juliet*, by Ann Marie Macdonald, Cdn tour; various other stage credits; various film and television credits including Sheila, *The Shower*, dir. Gail Harvey; Greta, *Lives of Girls and Women*, dir. Ron Wilson; Pauline Harris, *Anne of Green Gables: The Sequel*, Kevin Sullivan/CBC; Jordan, *Defcon Four*, dir. Paul Donovan; Roxanne, *Meatballs*, dir. Ivan Reitman. **AFFIL:** ACTRA; Equity. **HONS:** Genie Award, Best Actress, 1980; Genie nomination, Best Actress, 1988. **MISC:** voice coaching: The Shaw Festival, Equity Showcase, George Brown Coll., University of Toronto Drama program. **COMMENT:** *"The acting business has been very good to me for the past 20 years. In 1993, I took a year off to get a Postgraduate Diploma in Voice Studies at The Central School of Speech and Drama, in London UK. That has* *led to a great deal of teaching, which I find I love. In 1994, I directed my first play, Shakespeare's* Measure for Measure. *This year Nightwood Theatre is workshopping my first play,* Accidental Power.*"*

Lyon, Françoise E., B.A.A. ■■ $ 📖 ✏

Senior Consultant, CAI CORPORATE AFFAIRS INTERNATIONAL (private consulting firm specializing in gov't rel'ns), 1000 de la Gauchetière St. W., Ste. 3030, Montreal, QC H3B 4W5 (514) 861-9595, FAX 861-9596. Editor in Chief, *L'ÉCONOMIQUE* MAGAZINE. Born Montreal 1970. s. Richard Bolduc (ptnr). **EDUC:** Bath Univ., UK, Exchange Program (Int'l Bus.) 1992; École des Hautes Études Commerciales, B.A.A.(Mgmt & Int'l Bus.) 1993; McGill Univ., Certificate (Public Rel'ns Mgmt) in progress; C.M.C. accreditation in progress; Adm.A. accreditation in progress; seminars/short-term courses in entrepreneurship, Spanish language & bus. communications. **CAREER:** Immigration Officer, Cdn Immigration Centre, Philipsburgh, Que., summers 1991 & 1992; Research Asst., Zins Beauchesne & Associés, Montreal, 1993; Administrator & Export Dir., J.R. Wellington Export Corp., 1993; Sr. Consultant & Dir., Production & Creative Svcs, CAI Corporate Affairs International, 1994 to date; Editor in Chief, *L'Économique* magazine, 1995 to date. **SELECTED PUBLICATIONS:** several articles in *L'Économique* & in newsletter of Opera Guild, Montreal. **AFFIL:** Ordre des administrateurs agréés du Québec; Cooperative Housing Project (VP & mbr., Exec. Committee 1996-97); Big Brother/Big Sister Association (Big Sister 1995 to date); Opera 18-35, Opera Guild (Edit. Bd. 1993 to date). **INTERESTS:** opera; reading; languages; travel; windsurfing; rollerblading; Renaissance art. **MISC:** mbr. of winning group at prov. & nat'l levels for best student-managed public company, Junior Achievement program, 1987. **COMMENT:** *"Dynamic, multitasked, multilingual, network-driven woman, fired by a passion for learning, searching for new challenging experiences while always striving for excellence in all I do."*

Lyons, Harriet D., B.A.,M.Litt., D.Phil. 🎓 ⚛

Associate Professor, Anthropology, and Director, Women's Studies, UNIVERSITY OF WATERLOO, Waterloo, ON N2L 3G1 (519) 885-1211, ext. 2880, FAX 747-9149, EMAIL hlyons@watarts.uwaterloo.ca. Born N.Y. 1943. m. Andrew P. Lyons. 2 ch. Sean, Chantal. **EDUC:** Barnard Coll., Columbia Univ., B.A.(Anthro.) 1963; Oxford Univ., Diploma in Social Anthro. 1966, M.Litt.(Social Anthro.) 1970, D.Phil.(Social Anthro.) 1978. **CAREER:** Instructor, Dept. of Soc. & Anthro., Kent State Univ., 1973; Visiting Asst. Prof., Dept. of Anthro., Univ. of Massachusetts, 1973-74; Instructor, Dept. of Soc. & Anthro., Smith Coll.,1978-79; Asst. Prof., 1979-80; Asst. Prof., Wilfrid Laurier Univ., 1980-85; Chair, Dept. of Soc. & Anthro., 1983-89; Assoc. Prof., 1985-91; Assoc. Prof., Dept. of Anthro., & Dir. of Women's Studies, Univ. of Waterloo, 1991 to date. **SELECTED PUBLICATIONS:** "Anthropologists, Moralities, and Relativities: the Problem of Genital Mutilations" (*The Canadian Review of Sociology and Anthropology* 18 1981); "The Uses of Ritual in Sembène's Xala" (*The Canadian Journal of African Studies* Fall 1984); "Magical Medicine on Television: Benin City, Nigeria," with Andrew Lyons (*Journal of Ritual Studies* 1 1987); "Mass Media in Contemporary Urban Life: Benin City, Nigeria" (*Visual Anthropology* 3 1990); "A Sweet Hope of Glory in My Soul: Canadian and US Television Evangelism," with Andrew Lyons, in *The Beaver Bites Back*, Frank Manning & David Flaherty, eds. (McGill/Queen's Univ. Press, 1993); various other publications. **EDIT:** Co-ed. with Audry Wipper, Special Issue on Women in Africa, *The Canadian Journal of African Studies* 3 1988; Co-ed., *Anthropologica*, to date; Assoc. Ed, *Journal of African Studies*, to date. **AFFIL:** Canadian Association of Social & Cultural Anthropologists; American Anthropological Association; Canadian Association for African Studies; Royal Anthropological Association; Association of Feminist Anthropologists; Univ. of Waterloo (Women's Studies Advisory Bd.; Interdisciplinary Studies Bd.). **HONS:** Grace Anderson Memorial Fellowship, Wilfrid Laurier Univ., 1990; Distinction in Social Anthropology, Oxford Univ., 1966. **INTERESTS:** anti-racism; services for marginalized women; cinema; fiction. **MISC:** recipient, various grants; numerous conference presentations. **COMMENT:** *"I have spent my life trying to understand why race, religion, gender and sexual preference have been breeding grounds for hatred and oppression and, through teaching and research, to combat such oppression."*

Lyons, Keiko Margaret, B.A. 📺

Former Broadcasting Executive. P.O. Box 314, Thornhill, ON M1E 4R8 (416) 690-5565. Born Mission City, B.C. 1923. m. Edward R. Lyons. 1 ch. Ruth. **EDUC:** McMaster Univ., B.A. 1949. **CAREER:** Asst., French & Japanese Depts., BBC, 1951-54; Radio Prod., 1954-60; Prod., CBC Radio, 1960-62; TV & Radio Organizer, 1962-68; Exec. Prod./Ed., CBC Radio, 1968-72; Head, Current Affairs, 1972-76; Program Dir., 1976-81; VP, English Radio,

CBC, 1981-86; Dir., London Bureau, 1986-89. **AFFIL:** McMaster Univ. Foundation (Bd.); Soundstream (Bd.). **HONS:** D.Litt.(Hon.), McMaster Univ., 1996. **INTERESTS:** study of Japanese & Mandarin. **MISC:** volunteer teaching asst., Beginner's Japanese, Toronto Bd. of Educ. & experimental proj. for National Association of Japanese Canadians. **COMMENT:** *"Since retirement, have devoted myself to study and volunteer teaching, helping university fundraising in a limited way."*

M

acAlpine Foshay, Susan, B.A., M.A. ⊗ 📚
Exhibitions Curator, ART GALLERY OF NOVA
SCOTIA, Box 2262, Halifax, NS B3J 3C8 (902)
424-7542, FAX 424-7359. Born Montreal
1946. **EDUC:** Mount Allison Univ., B.A.
(French/Cdn Hist.) 1975; Univ. of Pennsylvania,
M.A.(Folklore/Material Culture) 1983.
CAREER: Info. Officer, Recreation Council for
the Disabled, Halifax, 1975-78; Archivist, Folklore Archive, Dept. of Folklore-Folklife, Univ.
of Pennsylvania, 1982; freelance writer/curator,
1983-86; Exhibitions Curator, Art Gallery of
Nova Scotia, 1986 to date. **SELECTED PUBLI-
CATIONS:** *Face Value: Nova Scotian Portrai-
ture*, with Greg Denton, Cliff Eyland & Patricia
Lee (Halifax: Art Gallery of Nova Scotia, in
progress, 1996); *Welcome to Our World: Con-
temporary Canadian Folk Art*, with Pascale
Galipeau & Nancy Fusley (Kleinberg:
McMichael Canadian Art Collection, 1996);
curator*, Deanne Fitzpatrick Hooked Mats–One
for Sorrow, Two for Joy*, with Robin E. Muller
& Doris Eaton (Halifax: Art Gallery of Nova
Scotia, 1996); "Aspects of Nova Scotia Folk
Portraiture," in *Spirit of Nova Scotia*, catalogue
(Halifax: Art Gallery of Nova Scotia, 1985);
Interior Decorative Painting in Nova Scotia,
catalogue, ed. (Halifax: Art Gallery of Nova
Scotia, 1986); *Vigour, Vitality, Innocence, and
Strength: Nova Scotia Folk Art* (Washington,
DC: Art Gallery of the Canadian Embassy,
1991); "Nova Scotian Portraiture: One Path of
Discovery" (*Bluenose* 1994); various other pub-
lications; writer, 30-min. Halifax Citadel Hill
walking tour script for the blind, Parks Canada
& Canadian National Institute for the Blind;
writer, 30-min. Nova Scotia Museum (tactile

displays) walking tour script for the blind, Nova Scotia Museum & Canadian National Institute for the Blind. **AFFIL:** Atlantic Provinces Art Gallery Association (Treas. 1990-91; VP 1991-92; Pres. 1992-94); Canadian Conference of the Arts; Halifax Rowing Club. **INTERESTS:** literacy; skiing; hiking. **MISC:** juror, various prov. & nat'l peer assessment juries. **COMMENT:** *"My commitment to the community is manifested in confirming the vital importance of our cultural heritage and to increase its accessibility."*

Macaulay, Catherine, B.A.,B.L.S. ⊗

Artist. 706 - 4th Ave. N., Saskatoon, SK S7K 2N1 (306) 665-6052. Born Swift Current, Sask. 1949. s. **EDUC:** Univ. of Saskatchewan, (Hist./Psych.) 1969, B.A.(Art/Art Hist.) 1986; Univ. of Alberta, B.L.S. 1971. **CAREER:** Asst. Librarian, Eastern Counties Reg'l Library, N.S., 1971-73; Branch Supervisor, Lakeland Library Reg., 1973-76; Reg'l Librarian, 1977-79; Head, Adult Svcs Dept., Regina Public Library, 1979-83; Registration Asst., Mendel Art Gallery, 1984; Gallery Coord., Saskatchewan Craft Gallery, 1985-88; Gallery Curator, Gordon Snelgrove Art Gallery, Dept. of Art & Art Hist., Univ. of Saskatchewan, 1986-90; Acting Curator, Permanent Collection, Art Committee of Council, Univ. of Saskatchewan, 1987. **COMMISSIONS:** Cover, *NeWest Review*, Aug./Sept. 1989; cover, *Herstory*, 1991. **EXHIBITIONS:** *Shadows and Light*, Yorkton Arts Centre (1988); *Growing Things*, McIntyre Street Gallery (1988); *The Flower Gardens at St. Peter's*, St. Thomas More Gallery (1989); *After the Frost*, McIntyre Street Gallery (1990); *Voice of Spring*, Dunlop Art Gallery (1991); *Summer Places*, McIntyre Street Gallery (1991); *Rhododendrons, Climate Change, and Plate Tectonics*, McIntyre Street Gallery (1992); *Travelogue: Mountain, Desert, Canyonland*, McIntyre Street Gallery (1994); *Studio Visit*, Mendel Art Gallery (1994); *Beauty and Age*, McIntyre Street Gallery (1995); *Looking West*, Galiano Lodge (1996); numerous group exhibitions incl. *Artists' Kites*, Rosemont Art Gallery (1989); *Figures of Speech*, Medicine Hat Museum & Art Gallery (1993); *Rosemont 20th Anniversary Salon & Show*, Rosemont Art Gallery (1996). **COLLECTIONS:** Saskatchewan Arts Bd.; Dunlop Art Gallery; Coll. of Agric., Univ. of Saskatchewan; Saskatchewan Government Insurance; Saskatchewan Oil and Gas Corporation; Saskatchewan Property Management Corporation; Armadale Communications; Credit Union Central of Saskatchewan; Collection of the Gov. General; Saskatoon Public Library; private collections throughout Canada. **AFFIL:** Canadian Artists' Representation;

A.K.A. Artists' Centre; Mendel Art Gallery; Saskatchewan Writers' Guild. **HONS:** Honours Scholarship, Univ. of Saskatchewan, 1984. **INTERESTS:** visual arts; hiking; backpacking; running; cross-country skiing; cycling; women's issues. **MISC:** subject of various catalogues, articles, reviews & interviews; recipient, various grants, incl. Saskatchewan Arts Bd. Indiv. Assistance Grant, 1989, 1990. **COMMENT:** *"After a 12-year career in public librarianship, I returned to university to study art and art history. I have been a full-time visual artist for the past six years, exhibiting across western Canada. My work is in several Canadian public and private collections."*

Macaulay, Linda D. ✿ ⊕

Development Coordinator, ALBERTA CHILDREN'S HOSPITAL FOUNDATION, 1820 Richmond Rd. S.W., Calgary, AB T2T 5C7 (403) 229-7646, FAX 228-1282. Born Kitchener, Ont. 1950. m. Doug. 2 ch. Brad, Greg. **EDUC:** Port Dover Composite High Sch., 1970. **CAREER:** fundraising, Cerebral Palsy Association in Alberta; Canadian Cancer Society; Alberta Lung Association; Alberta Children's Hospital Foundation. **AFFIL:** Children's Miracle Network. **INTERESTS:** crafts; motorcycling; camping. **COMMENT:** *"After an enjoyable 12 years at home with my boys, I re-entered the work force with a not-for-profit organization. Fundraising became a natural career for me and, as I have gained experience with various charities, I've found that for all I give, I get back even more from the people I work with and from the thanks that I receive. That appreciation is the greatest reward of all! In fundraising, a simple thanks is enough."*

MacCallum, Janice, B.B.A.,LL.B. ⚖

Lawyer, EVANS MACCALLUM, Barristers and Solicitors, 126 Richmond St., Box 714, Charlottetown, PE C1A 7L3 (902) 628-2025, FAX 628-8661. Born P.E.I. 1964. m. Allan MacEachern. **EDUC:** Univ. of Prince Edward Island, B.B.A.(Bus. Admin.) 1986; Dalhousie Univ., LL.B. 1989. **BAR:** P.E.I., 1990. **CAREER:** Ptnr, Evans MacCallum. **AFFIL:** P.E.I. Labour Relations Bd. (V-Chair); Cross Country P.E.I. (Treas.); Charlottetown Curling Club. **INTERESTS:** running; curling; fitness; cross-country skiing.

MacCaull, Wendy, B.Sc.,M.Sc.,Ph.D. ⬠ ⚘

Associate Professor, Department of Mathematics and Computing Sciences, ST. FRANCIS XAVIER UNIVERSITY, Box 5000, Antigonish, NS B2G 2W5 (902) 867-3989, FAX 867-2448, EMAIL wmaccaul@juliet.stfx.ca. Born Whycocomagh, N.S. 1953. m. Harley MacCaull. 4

ch. Andrew, Angus, Alexander, Aneill. EDUC: Mount Allison Univ., B.Sc.(Math.) 1974; Dalhousie Univ., M.Sc.(Mathematical Biol.) 1976; McGill Univ., M.Sc.(Math.) 1980, Ph.D. (Math.) 1984. CAREER: Asst. Researcher, Bedford Institute of Oceanography, Dartmouth, N.S., 1976-77; Lecturer, Dept. of Math., McGill Univ., 1981-84; Asst. Prof., St. Francis Xavier Univ., 1984-89; Assoc. Prof., 1989 to date; Visiting Mathematician, Univ. of Pennsylvania, 1990-91. SELECTED PUBLICATIONS: "On the Validity of Hilbert's Nullstellensatz, Artin's Theorem and Related Results in Grothendieck Toposes" (*Journal of Symbolic Logic* 1988); "Positive Definite Functions over Regular f-Rings and Representations as Sums of Squares" (*Journal of Pure and Applied Logic* 1989); "Tableau Method for Residuated Logic" (*Journal of Fuzzy Sets and Systems* 1995); "Kriptse Semantics for Logics with BCK Implication" (*Bulletin of the Section of Logic* 1996); various other publications. AFFIL: Atlantic Association for Research in the Mathematical Sciences (Bd. of Dir. 1996 to date); Canadian Mathematical Society (Bd. of Dir. 1991-93; VP, Atlantic Reg. 1993-95; Gov't Policy Committee; Nominating Committee 1996-2000); Atlantic Provinces Council on the Sciences (APICS) (V-Chair, Math. & Statistics Committee 1992-94; Chair, Math. & Statistics Committee 1994-96; Council Mbr.); American Mathematical Society; Association for Symbolic Logic; European Foundation for Logic, Language & Information; St. Francis Xavier Univ. (Sec. of Senate 1993-94; St. Francis Xavier Univ., Chair. Fac. of Science 1993-95). HONS: Plenary Speaker, APICS Math Days, 1994; Invited Speaker, Whycocomagh Schools Reunion, 1996. INTERESTS: singing; dancing; long solitary walks; activities of a mother of 4 school-age children who are all involved in music & sports. MISC: research involves theoretical aspects of reasoning, which are important for modelling natural language processing & system properties for computers; works to promote math., math. educ. & public awareness of math. at all levels; various conference presentations & lectures; recipient, various grants. COMMENT: *"Wife and mother of four children, advocate of small-university experience, teacher, researcher; mentor to students (especially female students) of mathematics; promoter of mathematics in Atlantic region; voice for women in a male-dominated field."*

MacCulloch, Carol, B.Comm. 🕐 💲
President, CONSTRUCTION ASSOCIATION OF NOVA SCOTIA, Box 47040, Scotia Drug RPO, Halifax, NS B3K 5Y2 (902) 429-6760, FAX 422-0471. EDUC: St. Mary's Univ., B.Comm.

1977. CAREER: Program Officer, Employment Opportunities Branch, N.S. Dept. of Dev., 1977-82; Research Analyst, Industrial Benefits Office, 1982-86; Sector Coord., Voluntary Planning, N.S. Dept. of Industry, Trade & Technology, 1986-88; Legislative Affairs Officer, Canadian Manufacturers' Association, 1989-91; Pres., Construction Association of N.S., 1991 to date. SELECTED PUBLICATIONS: various presentations & submissions. DIRECTOR: Marrin Brothers Limited, Winnipeg; Construction Technology Centre Atlantic, Fredericton. AFFIL: N.S. Advisory Council on Occupational Health & Safety; Canadian Society of Association Executives (Bd. Mbr., N.S. Div. 1993-94); Design & Construction Institute of N.S. (Bd. Mbr. 1992-93); Institute of Public Administration of Canada; N.S. Business Council on the Environment (Bd. Mbr.); Ad Hoc Industry Committee on Workers' Compensation (Co-Chair). INTERESTS: gardening; watercolour painting. MISC: Commissioner of Oaths, appointed 1991. COMMENT: *"My objectives are to serve as a catalyst for positive change and to continue in the search for quality and excellence as an individual and for our industry."*

Macdonald, Ellen, B.A.,LL.B. ⚖
Justice, ONTARIO COURT, General Division, 361 University Ave., Toronto, ON M5G 1T3 (416) 327-5824. Born Souris, P.E.I. 1949. m. Daniel Kavanagh. 1 ch. EDUC: St. Dunstan's Univ., B.A.(Econ.) 1969; McGill Univ., LL.B. 1972. BAR: Ont., 1974. CAREER: Justice, Ont. Court, Gen. Div., 1991 to date. SELECTED PUBLICATIONS: numerous journal articles on family law, advocacy, injunctions. AFFIL: Advocates' Society (Bd.); Ontario Association of Family Mediation (Bd.); Holland Coll. (Gov.); Dellcrest Children's Centre (Bd.); Canadian 4-H Club Foundation (Bd.); Canadian Judges' Conference; Ontario Superior Court Judges' Association.

MacDonald, Hon. Flora, O.C., LL.D. 🕐 ✦ 🛏 🍴
Chairperson, INTERNATIONAL DEVELOPMENT RESEARCH CENTRE, Ottawa, ON. Born North Sydney, N.S. 1926. s. EDUC: Empire Business Coll., Sydney, N.S.; National Defence Coll., 1-yr. course in Cdn & Int'l Studies 1971-72. CAREER: various secretarial positions, Canada & UK, 1943-56; Exec. Dir., Progressive Conservative Nat'l Headquarters, 1957-66; Nat'l Sec., P.C. Association of Canada, 1966-69; Admin. Officer & Tutor, Dept. of Pol. Sci., Queen's Univ., 1966-72; M.P. (Kingston & the Islands), 1972-88; as Opposition M.P., held critic's post for Indian Affairs & Northern

Dev., Fed.-Prov. Rel'ns, External Affairs, & Status of Women; Sec. of State for External Affairs, 1979-80; Min. of Employment & Immigration, 1984-86; Min. of Comm., 1986-88; Visiting Fellow, Centre for Canadian Studies, Univ. of Edinburgh, Sept.-Dec. 1989; Special Advisor, Commonwealth of Learning, 1990-91; Host, *Agenda 21* (originally *North South*), Vision TV, 1990 to date; Chair, International Development Research Centre, 1992 to date. DIRECTOR: Canada Trust Company; CT Financial Services. AFFIL: Canadian Crafts Council (Dir.); CARE Canada (Dir.); Centre for Refugee Studies, York Univ. (Dir.); Friends of the National Library (Dir.); Queen's Univ. Council (Dir.); Refugee Policy Group, Washington, DC (Dir.); Shastri Indo-Canada Institute (Dir.); Carnegie Corp. Commission on Prevention of Deadly Conflict; Commonwealth Human Rights Initiative (Patron); National Museums of Scotland (Hon. Patron for Canada). HONS: Officer of the Order of Canada, 1993; Order of Ontario, 1995; honorary degrees from a number of universities in Canada, US & UK. MISC: appointed by UN Sec.-Gen. as mbr., Eminent Person's Group to study Trans-National Corporations in S.Africa, 1989; 1st woman grad. from 1-yr. course in Cdn & Int'l Studies, National Defence Coll.

Macdonald, Janice, B.Sc.,M.Ed. 🎯 ⊕
Executive Director, BRITISH COLUMBIA DIETITIANS' AND NUTRITIONISTS' ASSOCIATION, 1755 W. Broadway Ave., Ste. 402, Vancouver, BC V6J 4S5 (604) 736-5606. Born P.E.I. 1958. m. Glen. 2 ch. EDUC: Acadia Univ., B.Sc. (Nutrition) 1979; Univ. of Manitoba, M.Ed.(Health Promotion) 1987. CAREER: Prov. Nutrition Specialist, Manitoba Health, 1981-87; Community Nutritionist, Vancouver Health, 1987-88; Exec. Dir., B.C. Dietitians' & Nutritionists' Association, 1989 to date; Health/Nutrition Consultant (Principal), Pacific Nutrition Consultants, 1993 to date; Mgr, Shop Smart Tours, 1993 to date. SELECTED PUBLICATIONS: numerous articles in *Nutrition Notes for Health Professionals, Manitoba Health, British Columbia Dietitians' and Nutritionists' Association Newsletter; Manitoba Association of School Trustees Newsletter; Organization of Manitoba Education Newsletter.* AFFIL: Canadian Dietetic Association (Professional Assoc.). HONS: Marion McColl Home Econ. Award, Acadia Univ., 1977; Dr. Moorehouse Award for Excellence in Diabetes Educ., 1980. INTERESTS: skiing; kayaking; reading. COMMENT: *"An energetic, enthusiastic, progressive and creative health professional with over 15 years' experience in the health and nutrition field, including association management & consulting."*

MacDonald, Lorna, B.M.,M.Music ■■ ⊗ ⟨᠊
Singer (Soprano). Associate Professor and Head of Voice Studies, Faculty of Music, UNIVERSITY OF TORONTO, Edward Johnson Bldg, 80 Queen's Park, Toronto, ON M5S 1A1 (416) 978-5777, FAX 978-5771, EMAIL lorna.macdonald@utoronto.ca Born Port Morien, N.S. s. EDUC: Dalhousie Univ., B.M.(Voice & Mus. Ed.) 1977; New England Conservatory of Music, Boston, M.Music (Vocal Performance) 1979; Florida State Univ. & Europe, post-grad. studies. CAREER: Artist in Residence, Fort Worth Opera, Texas, 1985-86; Assoc. Prof., Westminster Choir Coll., Princeton, 1988-94; Artist in Residence, Nat'l Festival of Music, Colorado, 1990-95; community concerts artist, N.Y., 1993; Assoc. Prof. & Head of Voice Studies, Univ. of Toronto, 1994 to date. SELECTED CREDITS: performances of chamber music, oratorio & opera & solo recitals throughout Canada & the U.S.;*Mostly Music, Music Around Us, All the Best* & *Arts National,* CBC-Radio; PBS radio & TV; soloist with symphonies in Edmonton, Forth Worth, Waco, Kitchener-Waterloo, Savannah, Halifax, Toronto, Oklahoma & Princeton; opera roles: Despina, Norina, Adele, Rose, Josephine, Mabel, Monica, Rosina, Susanna & Marie. AFFIL: National Association of Teachers of Singing; Canadian Voice Care Foundation; Canadian Music Festivals Adjudicators' Association. HONS: prizes from: Metropolitan Opera, Chicago Lyric Opera, N.S. & Canadian National Music Festivals, the Guilds of the Dallas, Fort Worth & San Antonio Operas, National Opera Association, National Association of Teachers of Singing, the Shreveport Opera, Oklahoma Symphony. INTERESTS: tennis. MISC: student of Philip May (N.S.) and Metropolitan Opera stars Eleanor Steber & Elena Nikolaidi, U.S.; has premiered numerous compositions in the U.S; clinician & judge, many vocal competitions incl. Metropolitan Opera auditions, Nat'l Finals of 1996 Eckhardt-Grammaté Competition, & Canadian Opera Company's Young Mozart Singers' Competition. COMMENT: *"It has been my goal to combine my love for singing with my passion for teaching and vocal research. The result continues to be a multi-faceted career in performance and academia, culminating in my current position at the University of Toronto. The joy of singing and the mysterious power of the human voice is at the centre of my musical life."*

MacDonald, Lynn M., B.A.,B.J. ✦ ⊗ $
Assistant Deputy Minister, Corporate Services, Ministry of Community and Social Services, GOVERNMENT OF ONTARIO, Hepburn Building,

80 Grosvenor St., 6th Fl., Toronto, ON M7A 1E9 (416) 325-5588, FAX 325-5615, EMAIL macdonl3@epo.gov.on.ca. Born Montreal 1951. EDUC: Carleton Univ., B.A.(Social Sci.) 1972, B.J.(Journalism) 1973. CAREER: various positions with Privy Council Office, Museums Corporation, Comm. Canada, Gov't of Canada; Dir. Gen., Cultural Policy & Programs, Comm. Canada, 1982-84; Dir. Gen., Strategic Planning, 1984-86; Asst. Deputy Min., Policy & Programs, Citizenship & Culture Ont., Gov't of Ont., 1986-88; Asst. Deputy Min., Policy & Programs, Citizenship Ont., 1988-90; Asst. Deputy Min., Culture & Comm., 1990-92; Asst. Deputy Min, Corp. Svcs, Ministry of Community & Social Svcs, 1992 to date. AFFIL: Public Sector Exec. Ntwk, Conference Board of Canada; Ryerson Polytechnic Univ. (Advisory Committee for Public Admin.); National Ballet Sch. (Scholarship Committee). INTERESTS: travel; languages; golf. COMMENT: *"Lynn MacDonald has served federal and Ontario public services for 23 years. Currently Assistant Deputy Minister, Community-Social Services, Ontario, she specializes in change management."*

Macdonald, Melanie, B.A.,B.S.W., A.M.C.T. ■ ■ ⊕
Executive Director, CUSO (int'l dev. agency), 2255 Carling Ave., Ste. 400, Ottawa, ON K2B 1B6 (613) 829-7445, ext. 214. Born Thunder Bay, Ont. 1948. m. David G. Macdonald. 2 ch. Joseph, Lucia. EDUC: Univ. of Guelph, B.A. (English & Sociology) 1970; McGill Univ., B.S.W.(Social Work) 1973; St. Lawrence Coll., A.M.C.T.(Municipal Mgmt) 1990. CAREER: Exec. Dir., Peterborough YWCA, 1978-82; Area Coord., YWCA Ont., 1982-88; CAO, Township of Cavan, 1988-91; CFO, The United Church of Canada, 1991-95; Exec. Dir., CUSO, 1995 to date. HONS: Woman of the Year in Peterborough for outstanding contribution to the advancement of women, 1988.

MacDonald, Norine A., B.A., LL.B. ■ ᗡᗡ ♥ ⊕
Barrister and Solicitor, 1055 W. Georgia St., Ste. 3000, Vancouver, BC V6E 3R3 (604) 641-4896, FAX 641-4949. Born Yorkton, Sask. 1956. EDUC: Univ. of British Columbia, B.A. 1978, LL.B. 1981. BAR: B.C., 1982. CAREER: Ptnr, Bull, Housser and Tupper. SELECTED PUBLICATIONS: "Tests for Capacity in Various Transactions" (*Continuing Legal Education* 1989); "GST and Your Estates and Trusts Practice," co-author (*Continuing Legal Education* 1990); *Probate Practice Manual*, Chapter 2, co-author (*Continuing Legal Education*, 1989); "Perpetuities Law in British Columbia" (*The*

Advocate Sept. 1990). AFFIL: Bencher, Law Society of B.C. (V-Chair, Credentials Committee; Chair, Special Compensation Fund Committee); Continuing Legal Education Society of B.C. (Chair); B.C. Library Foundation (Dir.); Simon Fraser Univ. Foundation (Dir.); National Retreat for Women (Committee); Estate Planning Council of Vancouver (Past Pres.). INTERESTS: advancement of women; environmental issues; legal profession; Third World travel. MISC: Course Coord., Asia Pacific Institute, 1990, Continuing Legal Educ., 1986-87; numerous lectures & presentations on charitable, trust, estate & family law matters.

Macdonald, Patricia C., B.Sc. Ⓢ ♥ ᄇ
Business Executive. 23 Dawlish Ave., North York, ON M4N 1J2 (416) 481-8150, EMAIL pmacdonald@netrover.com Born Dayton, Ohio. m. Ian M. Macdonald. 2 ch. Ian, Blake. EDUC: Ohio Univ., B.Sc.(Comm., summa cum laude) 1972; Levinson Leadership Institute, Sr. Mgmt Program. CAREER: brand mgmt, Procter & Gamble, Cincinnati, 1972-76; brand mgmt, H.J. Heinz Company, Pittsburgh, 1976-78; brand & category mgmt, Richardson-Vicks Inc., Wilton, Conn., 1978-81; Dir. of Hair Care, Skin Care & New Bus. Dev., Clairol Div. of Bristol-Myers Company, N.Y., 1981-85; freelance consultant, Bermuda, 1985-86; Dir., Bus. Dev., Palmer, Bonner BCP, Toronto, 1986-88; VP, Mktg & Sales Div., Paramount Canada's Wonderland, Toronto, 1988-95; Pres. & CEO, YTV Canada, Inc., 1995-96. AFFIL: Canadian Women in Communications (Bd.); Canadian Recording Artists' Association; American Marketing Association; Toronto Women in Film & Television; Women in Management (Founding Mbr.; former Bd. Mbr.); Attractions Council, Toronto (former Exec. Committee); Tourism Toronto (Mktg Committee). HONS: Lasher Award for most outstanding Journalism student, Ohio Univ.; several Scripps-Harvard Foundation Journalism Scholarships. MISC: attended numerous mgmt, comm., fin. & media rel'ns seminars; dual citizenship, Canada & US.

Macdonald, Ramuna, B.A.,B.Sc. ♥ Ⓢ ᄇ
President and Founder, DOOMSDAY STUDIOS LIMITED, 212 James St., Ottawa, ON K1R 5M7. President, THE "A" PICTURE COMPANY. Born Vilkaviskis, Lithuania. m. R. Douglas. 2 ch. EDUC: Univ. of Ottawa, B.A., B.Sc. CAREER: Pres. & Founder, Doomsday Studios Limited, 1978 to date; Pres., The "A" Picture Company, 1994 to date. SELECTED CREDITS: *God's Island; Spirits of an Amber Past; Sarah Jackson; Nobody's Perfect; Perspectives; Boundaries; Nuclear War; Spectrum;* various

others. AFFIL: Atlantic Film-makers' Cooperative; Ottawa Feature Film Production Association (Founding Mbr.). INTERESTS: nordic skiing. MISC: recipient, numerous grants.

MacDonald, Trudy, B.B.A.,C.I.M. ⊚
Executive Director, JUNIOR ACHIEVEMENT OF CAPE BRETON, 93 Johnstone St., Sydney, NS B1P 1T2 (902) 562-4040, FAX 567-6212. Born Glace Bay, N.S. 1953. m. Rod MacDonald. 1 ch. EDUC: University Coll. of Cape Breton, B.B.A. 1984. CAREER: Cost Analyst, Atomic Energy of Canada, 1973-85; Program Mgr, Junior Achievement of Cape Breton, 1989; Exec. Dir., 1989 to date. SELECTED PUBLICATIONS: various newspaper & magazine press releases. AFFIL: Rotary Club of Sydney (Vocational/Occupation Chair; Special Events Fundraising Chair 1996); Child Welfare Svcs (Pres., Advisory Bd.); Junior Achievement Atlantic (Chair); United Way Campaign (former Chair); N.S. Dept. of Econ. Renewal, Youth Entrepreneurial Skills-Mentor (Y.E.S.); church Sunday sch. (Values Educ. Instructor); "Men of the Deeps" 25th Anniversary Dinner (Chrm 1994); Univ. Coll. of Cape Britain (Technical Advisory Group 1996; Youth Advisory Group 1993-95). INTERESTS: reading; painting; music; art. MISC: subject of various radio & TV interviews. COMMENT: *"I firmly believe, as a business professional, mother, wife and a member of a community, that we have a responsibility to involve ourselves in programs or agencies that will improve the quality of life of all citizens and communities in which we live and work."*

MacDonald, Verna, B.Sc.N.,R.N., M.P.A. ■ ⌇
Alumni Affairs Officer, ST. FRANCIS XAVIER UNIVERSITY, Box 5000, Antigonish, NS B2G 2W5 (902) 867-2243, FAX 867-5145. Born North Sydney, N.S. 1957. m. Dr. Tom Mahaffey. 2 ch. Connor, Mia. EDUC: Aberdeen Hospital Sch. of Nursing, R.N. 1977; St. Francis Xavier Univ., B.Sc.N.(Nursing) 1980; Queen's Univ., M.P.A.(Public Admin.) 1988. CAREER: Staff Nurse, 1978-79, 1980-81; professional actor/singer/puppeteer, Mermaid Theatre, Wolfville, N.S., 1980; High Sch. Liaison Officer, St. Francis Xavier Univ., 1981-84; Alumni Affairs Officer, 1984 to date. EDIT: Mng Ed., *Alumni News* Magazine (with circulation of 22,000). DIRECTOR: Atlantic Broadcasters Ltd. AFFIL: Festival Antigonish (VP); St. Ninian Sr. Choir (Soloist); Council for Advancement & Support of Education; Canadian Council for Advancement of Education. HONS: Proficiency in Nursing Award, Aberdeen Hospital Alumnae Association, 1977;

Best Supporting Actor, One-Act Play Festival, Antigonish, 1980; M.P.A. Student Award for Outstanding Contribution, Queen's Univ., 1988; Guest Speaker, 'Heavy-Hitter' Designation, Council for Advancement & Support of Education, 1993. INTERESTS: music; amateur theatre; sports; cooking; entertaining; family holiday adventures. MISC: conference delegate & guest speaker; Chair, 1995 Canadian Council for Advancement of Education Awards of Excellence (Alumni Programs). COMMENT: *"A high-energy, enthusiastic achiever applying her varied talents, skills and experiences to develop and strengthen supportive relationships within a university community. Loyalty and financial commitment are the outcomes, essential to the institution's future advancement."*

MacDonald, Wilma, B.A.,M.A.S. ⬚ ⬚ ✦
Archivist, Manuscript Division, NATIONAL ARCHIVES OF CANADA, 344 Wellington St., Ottawa, ON K1A 0N3 (613) 996-7699, FAX 43-8112, EMAIL wmacdonald@archives.ca. Born Glace Bay, N.S. 1939. s. EDUC: Capilano Coll., Dipl.(Academic Studies) 1978; Simon Fraser Univ., B.A.(Anthro./Soc.) 1980; Univ. of British Columbia, M.A.S.(Archival Studies) 1995. CAREER: Legal/Academic/Corp./Union Administrative Asst., several Cdn cities & London, UK, 1956-80; Archivist, Rupert's Land Proj., 1984; Manuscript Archivist, National Archives of Canada, 1985 to date. SELECTED PUBLICATIONS: "Anglican Archives in Rupert's Land" (*Archivaria* Summer 1986); *Guide to the Holdings of the Archives of the Ecclesiastical Province and Dioceses of Rupert's Land* (Winnipeg: St. John's Coll. Press, 1986); Cdn Theses on Microfiche: "Archival History and Oral History Documents" (Vancouver, U.B.C., 1995). AFFIL: Association of Canadian Archivists (*Archivaria* Production Coord. 1986-90); Ontario Association of Archivists (Educ. Committee 1988-92); Canadian Oral History Association (Pres. & Newsletter Ed. 1989-94; Past Pres. & Archivist). INTERESTS: outdoor activities; reading; writing; photography; gardening; travelling; music; family history; Royal Scottish Country Dance Society dancing; interviewing; Scottish Gaelic. COMMENT: *"Someone who has played a small part in preserving the rich history of Canada and its people through working with textual archives, while, at the same time, encouraging those who do not create written records to leave behind their recorded memories."*

MacEachern, Antje ■■ ♡ ⊚ ⌇
Executive Director, CREATIVE CHILD CARE (special needs day care/kindergarten), P.O. Box 941, Cornwall, PE C0A 1H0 (902) 675-2876,

FAX 675-2876. Born Austria 1942. m. Dr. Gordon MacEachern. 3 ch. Garner, Kevin, Clifford. **EDUC:** Camousen Coll., Victoria, B.C., Early Childhood Dev. 1982-83; Holland Coll., Charlottetown, Early Childhood Dev. 1988. **CAREER:** Pres., Sprint Print, Ottawa, 1972-80; volunteer, G.R. Pearkes Centre, Victoria, B.C., 1981-83; Teacher, 1983-88; Exec. Dir./Owner, Creative Child Care, 1989 to date. **AFFIL:** P.E.I. Early Childhood Development Association; Canadian Child Care Federation; C.E.S.O. (Volunteer Advisor); P.E.I. Early Childhood Development Focus Group; P.E.I. Facilitation Bd. **COMMENT:** *"I have been extremely pleased to have worked in early childhood development (special needs) in B.C., P.E.I. and Guyana. It is the most rewarding and purposeful activity one can undertake. I believe I have been able to assist others to work effectively with special needs children and to enhance their professional development as well as that of the communities I have been a part of."*

MacGregor, Daune Lorine, M.D., FRCP(C) ■ ⊕
Clinical Director, Division of Neurology, Department of Paediatrics, HOSPITAL FOR SICK CHILDREN, 555 University Ave., Toronto, ON M5G 1X8 (416) 813-6332, FAX 813-6334, EMAIL dmacgreg@mailhub.sickkids.on.ca or daune.macgregor@utoronto.ca. Professor of Paediatrics (Neurology), UNIVERSITY OF TORONTO. Born Winnipeg 1947. s. 1 ch. Elizabeth Dru. **EDUC:** Coll. of Medicine, Univ. of Saskatchewan, M.D. 1971; Royal Coll. of Physicians, London & Royal Coll. of Surgeons, UK, Diploma in Child Health 1976. **CAREER:** Rotating Internship, New Mount Sinai Hospital, Toronto, 1971-72; Jr. Asst. Resident in Paediatrics, Hospital for Sick Children, Toronto, 1972-73; Sr. Asst. Resident in Paediatrics, 1974; Asst. Resident in Neurology, Sunnybrook Hospital & St. Michael's Hospital, Toronto, 1974-75; Registrar in Paediatric Neurology, Hospital for Sick Children, London, UK, 1975-76; Chief Resident in Paediatric Neurology, Hospital for Sick Children, Toronto, 1976-77; Clinical Fellow in Developmental Paediatrics & Mental Retardation, Children's Hospital Medical Center, & Fellow in Paediatrics, Harvard Medical Sch., & Boston, 1977-78; Active Staff, Div. of Neurology, Dept. of Paediatrics, Hospital for Sick Children, Toronto, 1978 to date; Asst. Prof. of Paediatrics (Neurology), Univ. of Toronto, 1978-83; Assoc. Prof. of Paediatrics (Neurology), 1983-95; Consultant Staff, Div. of Paediatrics, Dept. of Ob.&Gyn., Women's College Hospital, Toronto, 1984 to date; Assoc. Prof. (cross appt.), Dept. of Behavioural Sciences, Univ. of Toronto, 1984 to date; Dir.

& Head, Div. of Medical Educ., Dept. of Paediatrics, Univ. of Toronto & Hospital for Sick Children, 1985-87; Consultant Staff, Bloorview Children's Hospital, 1993 to date; Acting Head, Div. of Neurology, Dept. of Paediatrics, Hospital for Sick Children, 1994-96; Prof. of Paediatrics (Neurology), Univ. of Toronto, 1995 to date. **SELECTED PUBLICATIONS:** "A Case Report of Possible Valproate Teratrogenicity," with Ingrid Tein (*Archives of Neurology* 1985); "Influences on Maternal Responsiveness to Developmentally Delayed Preschoolers," with M. Lojkasek, S. Goldberg & S. Marcovitch (*Journal of Early Intervention* 1990); "Eye Problems in Children with Multiple Sclerosis," with M. Steinlin, S.I. Blaser & J.R. Buncic (*Pediatric Neurology* 1995); various other articles; numerous scholarly addresses, abstracts & invited presentations. **AFFIL:** Royal Coll. of Physicians & Surgeons of Canada (Fellow); American Academy of Neurology; American Academy of Paediatrics (Fellow); Canadian Association for Child Neurologists; Canadian Paediatric Society; Toronto Neurological Association; International Child Neurology Association; Child Neurology Association; Canadian Headache Society (Sec. 1991 to date); SafeHaven Group Home for Children (Dir. 1987-95); New Vision Homes for Children (Dir. 1988-96); Metropolitan Toronto Association for Community Living (Medical Advisory Bd.); Canadian Retts Syndrome Association (Medical Advisory Bd.); The Roeher Institute (Advisory Committee). **HONS:** Entrance Scholarship, Univ. of Saskatchewan, 1965; Saskatchewan Medical Scholarship, Univ. of Saskatchewan, Fac. of Medicine, 1968; Hoffman LaRoche Scholarship, Univ. of Saskatchewan, Fac. of Medicine, 1969; Horner Silver Medal & Prize in Paediatrics, Univ. of Saskatchewan, Fac. of Medicine, 1971; Hospital for Sick Children Foundation Fellowship, Univ. of Toronto, 1975; Harry Bain Award for Excellence in Clinical Teaching - Hospital for Sick Children/Univ. of Toronto, Fac. of Medicine, 1979, 1982; Teacher of the Year Award - Div. of Neurology, Hospital for Sick Children/Univ. of Toronto, 1992. **MISC:** reviewer for various granting agencies; numerous invited lectures & presentations; recipient of numerous grants from various agencies.

MacGregor, Mary L., B.A.,LL.B. ◁⏷
Partner, DICKSON, SACHS, APPELL & BEAMAN, 10 Alcorn Ave., Ste. 306, Toronto, ON M4V 3A9. m. John Rodger. 2 ch. Duncan Rodger, Caitlin Rodger. **EDUC:** B.A.; LL.B. **BAR:** Ont., 1974. **CAREER:** Lawyer, Woolley Dale and Dingwall, Toronto, 1974-76; Mgr, Trust Legal Svcs, Crown Trust Company, 1976-83; Mgr,

Personal Trust, Central Trust Company, 1983-85; Ptnr, Blaney, McMurtry, Stapells, Friedman, 1985-95; Lecturer, Osgoode Hall Law Sch., York Univ., 1988-92. **SELECTED PUBLICATIONS:** *O'Brien's Encyclopedia of Forms*, "Division V, Wills and Trusts" (Canada Law Book, 1988); *Wills and Powers of Attorney: First Interview to Final Report* (Canada Law Book, 1994); various other publications. **AFFIL:** Law Society of Upper Canada; Canadian Bar Association (Trust & Estates Section); Toronto Estate Planning Council; American Coll. of Trust & Estate Counsel (Fellow); Trust Companies Institute. **MISC:** seminars, TV & radio broadcasts on estate & personal planning, for bus. promo.

MacInnis, Janet G. ■■ ♡ ⊕ ☼
Volunteer. Born 1937. m. Garfield A. MacInnis. 4 ch. Iain, Lindsay, Alexandra, Heather. **AFFIL:** Women's College Hospital (hon. mbr., Bd. of Dir.; former mbr., Bd. of Dir.; V-Chair, Opening Windows Campaign; former mbr., various committees); Women's College Hospital Foundation (Bd. of Dir.); United Way of Greater Toronto (Past Chairs' Advisory Committee; Chair, Bd. of Trustees & Exec. Committee 1984-86; Campaign Chair 1982; former mbr., various committees); Mission Air Transportation Network (Advisory Committee); Jerusalem Foundation (Bd. of Dir.); International Sports Centre (Advisory Bd.); Deer Park United Church (Exec. Committee; Convenor, Pastoral Care Committee; Co-Chair, Rummage Sale; former mbr., various committees); Canadian Women's Foundation (Advisory Bd.); New Directions (Patron); United Way of Canada (Bd. of Trustees 1991-94); Victoria Univ., Univ. of Toronto (V-Chair, Bd. of Regents 1990-91; External Rel'ns & Dev. Committee 1988-94); Upper Canada Coll. (Bd. of Gov. 1985-89); Junior League of Toronto (former VP & Bd. mbr.); United Church of Canada (former Chair, Nat'l Church Property Mgmt & Planning Committee); Nelson Mandela Fund (former Dir., Bd. of Trustees). **HONS:** Certificate of Merit, Gov't of Canada, 1985; Civic Award of Merit, City of Toronto, 1988; Distinguished Svc. Award, United Way of Greater Toronto, 1988; Citation for Citizenship, Gov't of Canada, 1988; Woman on the Move Award, *The Toronto Sun*, 1989; Gardiner Award, Municipality of Metro Toronto, 1991; Margaret Rolph Award, Junior League of Toronto, 1992.

MacIntyre, Pamela J., B.A. ■ $
Vice-President, Human Resources, CROWN LIFE INSURANCE COMPANY, 1901 Scarth St., Regina, SK S4P 4L4 (306) 751-6058, FAX 751-6051. Born Val d'Or, Que. s. 1 ch. **EDUC:** Univ. of Western Ontario, B.A.(Psych.) 1966. **CAREER:** VP, Hum. Res., Crown Life Insurance Company. **DIRECTOR:** Marilyn Brooks Boutiques Inc., Toronto. **AFFIL:** Junior Achievement of South Saskatchewan (Dir.); Life Insurance Institute of Canada (Bd. of Dir.).

Mackaay, Carole, B.A.,M.A.,B.C.L. $
Corporate Secretary, VIA RAIL CANADA INC., 2 Place Ville Marie, Montreal, QC H3B 2G6 (514) 871-6155, FAX 874-0661. Born Montreal 1945. m. Ejan. 1 ch. **EDUC:** McGill Univ., B.A. 1966, M.A. 1969, B.C.L. 1973. **CAREER:** various positions, The Molson Companies Limited, 1969-82; Corp. Sec., VIA Rail Canada Inc., 1983 to date. **AFFIL:** Barreau du Québec; Canadian Bar Association. **INTERESTS:** fitness; horseback riding.

Mackay, Claire, B.A. 📜
Writer. 6 Frank Cres., Toronto, ON M6G 3K5 (416) 656-5277, FAX 656-3885. Born Toronto 1930. m. Jackson Mackay. 3 ch. Ian, Scott, Grant. **EDUC:** Univ. of Toronto, B.A.(Pol. Sci. & Econ) 1952; Univ. of British Columbia, 1 yr. post-grad. in social work 1968; Univ. of Manitoba, Certificate in Rehab. Counselling 1971. **CAREER:** Research Librarian, Polysar Corp., Sarnia, 1952-55; Medical Social Worker, Wascana Hospital, Regina, 1969-71; Research Librarian, United Steelworkers, Toronto 1972-78; full-time writer, 1978 to date; Consultant & Ed., Houghton Mifflin Canada, 1986-91. **SELECTED PUBLICATIONS:** *Mini-Bike Hero* (Scholastic, 1974); *Mini-Bike Racer* (Scholastic, 1976); *Exit Barney McGee* (Scholastic, 1979); *One Proud Summer*, co-author Marsha Hewitt (Women's Press, 1981); *Mini-Bike Rescue* (Scholastic, 1984); *The Minerva Program* (James Lorimer & Co., 1984); *Pay Cheques & Picket Lines: All About Unions in Canada* (Kids Can Press, 1987); *The Toronto Story* (Annick Press, 1990); *Touching All the Bases: Baseball for Kids of All Ages* (Boardwalk Books/Scholastic, 1994); *Bats About Baseball*, co-author Jean Little (Viking/Penguin, 1995). **AFFIL:** CANSCAIP (Canadian Society of Children's Authors, Illustrators & Performers) (Founding Mbr. 1977; Sec. 1977-79; Pres. 1979-81); Writers' Union of Canada (Chair, Grievance Committee 1979-80; Co-Chair 1984-85; Membership Committee 1988-89; Chair, Nominating Committee 1990-91); International PEN; Canadian Authors' Association; Canadian Children's Book Centre (Bd. of Dir. 1985-89); Friends of Osborne & Lillian H. Smith Collection of Rare Children's Books; International Board on Books for Young People (IBBY), Canada (Councillor

1991-93); Canadian National Institute for the Blind (Children's Book Selection Committee). HONS: Second Prize, *Toronto Star* Short Story Contest, 1980; Honourable Mention, Canada Council Children's Literature Prize, 1982; Ruth Schwartz Foundation Award for Best Children's Book, 1982; Vicky Metcalf Award for Body of Work for Children, 1983; Vicky Metcalf Short Story Award; Award of Excellence, Parenting Publications of America, 1990; Civic Award of Merit, City of Toronto, 1992. INTERESTS: birdwatching; dictionary collecting.

MacKay-Lassonde, Claudette, B.A.Sc., M.Sc.,M.B.A.,P.Eng. ■ Ⓢ ✿ ◉ ♃

President, FIRELIGHT INVESTMENTS LTD., 121 King St. W., Ste. 2525, Box 36, Toronto, ON M5H 3T9. Chairman, Chief Executive Officer and President, ENGHOUSE SYSTEMS LIMITED, 80 Tiverton Ct., Markham, ON L3R 0G4. m. Pierre Lassonde. 2 ch. Julie-Alexandra, Christian-Pierre. EDUC: Univ. of Montreal, B.A.Sc.(Chem. Eng.) 1971; Univ. of Utah, M.Sc.(Nuclear Eng.) 1973; Univ. of Toronto, M.B.A. 1983. CAREER: Design Eng., Bechtel Power Corporation, 1973-75; Nuclear Safety Compliance Eng., Atomic Energy of Canada Limited, 1975-76; Mgr, Load Forecasts Dept., Ontario Hydro, 1976-87; Dir., Premier Accts, Northern Telecom Canada, 1988-91; Asst. Deputy Min. (Trade & Int'l Rel'ns), Ont. Ministry of Industry, Trade & Technology, 1991-92; Asst. Deputy Min. (Comm.), Ont. Ministry of Culture & Comm., 1992-93; VP, Corp. Affairs, Xerox Canada Ltd., 1993-94; Chrm & CEO, Enghouse Systems Limited, 1994 to date; Pres., Firelight Investments Ltd., 1994 to date. DIRECTOR: Les Laboratoires Aeterna; AGF Management Limited; Abitibi-Price Inc; Clearnet Communications Inc. AFFIL: Sunnybrook Hospital (Dir.); Canadian Engineering Memorial Foundation (Chair 1989); Canadian Club of Toronto (Dir.); Professional Engineers Ontario (P.Eng.; Pres. 1986-87); Canadian Academy of Engineering (Fellow); Ryerson Polytechnic Univ. (Hon. Fellow). HONS: Young Achiever Award, 1988; Meritorious Service Award for Professional Engineers, Canadian Council of Professional Engineers, 1994; Order of Honour, Professional Engineers of Ontario, 1995; D.Eng.(Hon.),Univ. of Windsor, 1986; D. Eng.(Hon.), Carleton Univ., 1987; D.Sc.(Hon.), St. Mary's Univ. 1990; D.Sc.(Hon.), Univ. of Guelph, 1992; D.Eng. (Hon.), Technical Univ. of Nova Scotia, 1992; D.Sc.(Hon.), Queen's Univ., 1993; LL.D. (Hon.), Concordia Univ., 1996. INTERESTS: skiing; int'l travel; Cdn art. MISC: delivered over 100 speeches, some published.

Mackenzie, Lorna J., B.A.,LL.B. ◿ ✦

Legislative Solicitor, Department of Justice, PROVINCE OF NEW BRUNSWICK, Fredericton, NB E3B 5H1 (506) 453-2569, FAX 457-7342, EMAIL ljmack@gov.nb.ca. Born Duluth, Minn. 1942. m. Dr. David G. Likely. 3 ch. EDUC: McGill Univ., B.A.(Soc.) 1964; Univ. of New Brunswick, LL.B. 1981. BAR: N.B. CAREER: Legislative Solicitor, Dept. of Justice, Prov. of N.B. AFFIL: N.B. Law Society; Canadian Bar Association.

MacKenzie, Marilyn, B.A.,M.S.W. ■■ ◉

Consultant, Harassment and Discrimination in the Workplace, MACKENZIE & ASSOCIATE CONSULTING (educ., mediation, consultation, counselling, investigation, policy dev.), 67 Lakedale Place, Winnipeg, MB R3T 4L4 (204) 269-0355. Born Winnipeg 1946 2 ch. Julie, Reid. EDUC: Univ. of Manitoba, B.A.(Psych.) 1967, M.S.W.(Social Group Work) 1969, currently enrolled in Ph.D. program (Educational Psych.). CAREER: Child Care Worker, Children's Home of Winnipeg, 1967-69; Social Worker, Children's Aid Society of Winnipeg, 1969-74; Field Supervisor, New Careers Program, Gov't of Man., 1974-75; Sessional Lecturer, Univ. of Manitoba, Sch. of Social Work, 1974-85; Investigation Officer, Sexual Harassment Policy, Univ. of Manitoba, 1985-95 (Canada's 1st Sexual Harassment Officer); also small private practice specializing in "Women in Transition"; Educ. Coord., Hum. Res. Dept., 1995-96; Harassment & Discrimination Private Consultant, 1996 to date. SELECTED PUBLICATIONS: "Living the Changes - An Anthology of Contemporary Canadian Women" (Dec. 1990); "Sexual Harassment and Life - Just the Beginning" (Dec. 1990); "Feminism, the New "F" Word - A Response to the Montreal Tragedy" (*Lynx* magazine, 1990); "My View" (*Bulletin*, Univ. of Manitoba, Jan. 1990); *How to Avoid High Risk Situations* (handbook, 1990); *Instructor's Manual* (Univ. of Manitoba Sports Camps & Mini Univ., 1989); "Perspectives on Women in the 1980s" (*The Social Worker*, Vol. 50, No. 1, Spring 1982); "Children are People" (*Manitoba Day Care Association Newsletter*, 1979). AFFIL: Canadian Association Against Sexual Harassment (Pres.); Manitoba Association Against Sexual Harassment; National Conference of Sexual Harassment (Bd. of Dir.); Univ. of Manitoba (Women's Caucus); Manitoba Association of Social Workers; Manitoba Institute of Registered Social Workers; Winnipeg Business & Professional Women's Club; Media Watch; Choices. HONS: award for Meritorious Service in the Trenches, National Safe Schools Coalition Sexual Assault/Harassment Conference, Philadelphia, 1994. **INTERESTS:** golf; curling; downhill skiing. **COMMENT:** *"I have always been a major proponent of women's and children's rights. I am a feminist, and am committed to helping those in need. I am a strong advocate for equity both in and out of the workplace."*

Mackenzie, Suzanne, B.A.,M.A.,D. Phil. ■■ ⚛ 🎓
Associate Professor, Geography, CARLETON UNIVERSITY, Ottawa, ON K1S 5B6 (613) 788-2600, ext. 2561, FAX 788-4301. Born Vancouver 1950. m. Alan E. Nash. **EDUC:** Simon Fraser Univ., B.A.(Geog., Pol. Sci.) 1976; Univ. of Toronto, M.A.(Geog.) 1978; Sussex Univ., D.Phil.(Geog.) 1983. **CAREER:** Asst. Prof., Geog., Queen's Univ./Post-Doctoral Research Fellow, Social Science & Humanities Research Council of Canada, 1982-85; Asst. Prof., Geog., Carleton Univ., 1985-89; Assoc. Prof., Geog., 1989 to date (on extended leave, 1991 to date). **SELECTED PUBLICATIONS:** numerous incl.: *Visible Histories: Women and Environments in a Post-War British City* (Montreal: McGill-Queen's Univ. Press, 1989); co-editor, *Remaking Human Geography* (Boston: Unwin-Hyman, 1989); "Redesigning Cities, Redesigning Ourselves: Feminism and Environments" (Geraldine Finn, ed., *Limited Edition: Voices of Women, Voices of Feminism,* Halifax: Fernwood Publishing, 1992). **AFFIL:** Canadian Association of Geographers (Councillor, Nat'l Exec. 1988-90; Chair (co-founder), Women & Geography Study Group 1985-90); International Geographical Union (Int'l Exec., Women & Geog. Group 1989-91); Institute of British Geographers (co-founder, Women & Geog. Study Group 1978). **HONS:** Women & Geography Award for outstanding feminist scholarship, American Association of Geographers, 1990. **INTERESTS:** feminist perspectives on human-environmental rel'ns; responses to deindustrialization in Cdn resource-based communities, esp. creation of feminist-based econ. survival strategies. **COMMENT:** *"For the past quarter century, as I've tried to understand how gender and environmental relations change each other, I've worked both to make feminism a theoretical and political force in the academy and to make academic work available to women attempting to change their communities."*

MacKenzie-Nugent, Catherine Ann, B.A. $ ♡ ✋
Director and Fundraiser, 150 Duncan Mill Rd., Toronto, ON M3B 3M4 (416) 441-9933. Born Rio de Janeiro 1948. m. David Alan John. 3 ch. **EDUC:** York Univ., B.A.(Languages). **VOLUNTEER CAREER:** Canadian Opera Women's Committee; Toronto Symphony Women's Committee; Canadian Cancer Society; Canadian Women's Breast Cancer Committee; Inner City Angels; *Arts of Canada Magazine*; Canadian Mediterranean Institute; Canadian Museum of Photography; the Bach 300 Festival; Planned Parenthood; Operation Herbie (founder); Brazilian Ball (Chair 3 times); Opera Ball; Yves St. Laurent Fashion Extravaganza; Symphony Dream Auction; Ontario Judicial System (Interpreter). **SELECTED PUBLICATIONS:** "Panache," column, *The Toronto Sun* (ceased). **DIRECTOR:** Insignia Group of Companies. **HONS:** Canada 125 Medal, 1992. **MISC:** subject of various articles & photographs in newspapers & magazines; listed in *Toronto Who's Who*; travels extensively & works with husband, David A.J. Nugent.

MacKinnon, The Hon. Janice, MLA,B.A., M.A.,Ph.D. 🍁 $ ☝
Minister of Finance, GOVERNMENT OF SASKATCHEWAN, 312 Legislative Building, Regina, SK S4S 0B3 (306) 787-6060, FAX 787-6055. Born Ont. 1947. m. Peter. 2 ch. Alan, William. **EDUC:** Univ. of Western Ontario, B.A. 1969; Queen's Univ., M.A. 1970, Ph.D. 1977. **CAREER:** Prof., Univ. of Saskatchewan, 1975 to date; elected MLA (Saskatoon Westmount), 1991; Min. of Social Svcs & Min. Responsible for Seniors, then Assoc. Min of Fin., Min. Responsible for the Crown Investments Corp. & Min. Responsible for the Sask. Gaming Commission & for the Sask. Pension Plan, 1991-93; Min. of Fin., 1993 to date; re-elected MLA (Saskatoon Idylwyld), 1995. **SELECTED PUBLICATIONS:** all publications published under the name of J. Potter; *The Liberty We Seek: Loyalist Ideology in Colonial New York and Massachusetts* (Harvard Univ. Press, 1983); *While the Women Only Wept: Eastern Ontario Loyalist Women* (McGill-Queen's Univ. Press, 1993); "Loyalists and Community: The Eastern Ontario Loyalist Women" in *Loyalists and Community in North America*, ed. R.M. Calhoon, T.M. Burns & G.A. Rawlyk (Greenwood Press, 1994); various other books, chapters in books, review articles & papers in refereed journals. **AFFIL:** Women's Research Institute; Canadian Historical Association (Women's Committee). **HONS:** Canadian Historical Prize for Reg'l Hist., 1994; Riddell Award, for best article on Ont. hist., 1989; Killam Postdoctoral Research Fellowship, 1980-82; Canada Council Doctoral Fellowship, 1970-74; Ont. Grad. Fellowship, 1969-70; various scholarships & prizes, Univ. of Western Ontario & Vincent Massey Collegiate, 1960-69. **INTERESTS:** bridge; cross-country skiing;

hiking; jogging; biking; canoeing. MISC: 1st woman appointed as Fin. Min. in Canada.

Macklem, Anne Woodburne, B.A. 📖 $

Vice-President, MICHAEL, HARDY LIMITED (Operating division: Oberon Press), 350 Sparks St., Ste. 400, Ottawa, ON K1R 7S8 (613) 238-3275, FAX 238-3275. Born Ottawa 1928. m. Michael Kirkpatrick Macklem. 2 ch. Timothy, Nicholas. EDUC: Univ. of Toronto, B.A. (English Lang. & Lit.) 1950. SELECTED PUBLICATIONS: *Where to Eat in Canada* (Ottawa: Oberon Press), 26 editions, 1971-96 & continuing. INTERESTS: skiing; waterskiing; tennis; sailing; mountain climbing. COMMENT: *"I work as a representative for my company and sell books coast to coast. Travelling as I have for 25 years, I've seen the need of a national restaurant guide. Where to Eat in Canada is the result."*

Maclean, Heather, B.Sc.,Dip.Nutr.,M.Sc., Ed.D. ⊕ 🗇

Director, Centre for Research in Women's Health, UNIVERSITY OF TORONTO and WOMEN'S COLLEGE HOSPITAL FitzGerald Building, 790 Bay St., Toronto, ON M5G 1N8 (416) 351-3732, FAX 351-3746, EMAIL h.maclean@ utoronto.ca. Born Montreal 1947. d. 1 ch. EDUC: McGill Univ., B.Sc.(Home Econ.) 1968; Univ. of Toronto, Dipl.(Nutrition) 1972, M.Sc.(Nutrition) 1973, Ed.D.(Educ. Theory) 1979. CAREER: Dietitian, Toronto Western Hospital, 1969-71; Fac. Mbr., Univ. of Toronto, 1978 to date; Assoc. Prof. & Chair, Dept. of Nutritional Sci., Fac. of Medicine, 1992-96. SELECTED PUBLICATIONS: *Women's Experience of Breast Feeding* (Toronto: Univ. of Toronto Press, 1990); "The Food Problems of Low Income Single Mothers: An Ethnographic Study," with V. Tarasuk (*Canadian Home Economics Journal* 2 1990); "Junk Food and Healthy Food: Meaning of Food in Adolescent Women's Culture," with G. Chapman (*Journal of Nutrition Education* 25 1993); numerous other papers, book chapters, abstracts, reports & gov't publications. AFFIL: Canadian Public Health Association. MISC: reviewer, numerous granting agencies & academic journals; organizer, numerous conferences & workshops; numerous invited presentations. COMMENT: *"As an academic, I have interests in health-promotion research, women's health and fostering both practice-based research and interpretative research methods."*

MacLean, Margaret, B.A.,M.L.S.,B.Ed., M.Ed. ■ 🗇

Associate Professor and Chair, Department of Library and Information Studies, LAKEHEAD UNIVERSITY, 955 Oliver Rd., Thunder Bay, ON P7B 5E1 (807) 343-8398, FAX 343-8023, EMAIL mmaclean@sky.lakeheadu.ca. Born Hornepayne, Ont. 1944. m. A. Donald. EDUC: Lakehead Univ., B.A.(Anthro.) 1974, B.Ed. 1983, M.Ed. 1992; Univ. of Toronto, M.L.S. 1976. CAREER: Library Asst., Para-Professional Librarian, Waverley Resource Library, Thunder Bay, 1962-74; Reference Librarian, Brodie Resource Library, 1977-86; Reference Librarian, Waverley Resource Library, 1987; Lecturer, Fac. of Professional Studies, Sch. of Library Technology, Lakehead Univ., 1986-87; Asst. Prof. & Acting Dir., 1987-88; Asst. Prof. & Chair, Fac. of Arts & Sci., Dept. of Library & Info. Studies, 1988-94; Assoc. Prof. & Chair, 1994 to date. SELECTED PUBLICATIONS: "The Adult Educator's Library Shelf" (*The Lakehead University Teacher* 2(6) 1991); "Guides to the Literature" (*The Lakehead University Teacher* 3(2) 1992); various other publications. AFFIL: Association for Teacher-Librarianship in Canada; Australian Library & Information Association; Canadian Library Association; Ontario Association of Library Technicians; Ontario Association of Library Technician Instructors; Ontario Library Association; Thunder Bay Public Library Bd. (Trustee 1991; V-Chair; Chair); Lakehead Univ. (Senate); Cambrian Players; Eleanor Drury Children's Theatre. HONS: IODE Scholarship, Univ. of Toronto, 1974-75; Ont. Grad. Scholarship, 1975-76; Senate Committee on Teaching Award, Lakehead Univ., 1988. INTERESTS: reading; travel; handicrafts; sewing; knitting; petitpoint. MISC: various conference presentations. COMMENT: *"Throughout my life, both educationally and professionally, I have strived to achieve excellence and competency while still maintaining a 'joie de vivre'."*

Maclean, Victoria ✎ 🗇

Editor, THE EDMONTON SUN, 4990 - 92nd Ave., Ste. 250, Edmonton, AB T6B 3A1 (403) 468-0295, FAX 468-0139. Born Brockville, Ont. 1948. d. CAREER: various positions, *Brockville Recorder and Times*, 1970-73; Ed., *Hansard*, Gov't of Alta., 1975; Columnist/Mng Ed., *St. Albert Gazette*, 1976-80; Ed. Writer/Assoc. Ed./Ed., *The Edmonton Sun*, 1980 to date. HONS: Outstanding Columnist, Canadian Community Newspaper Association, 1980. INTERESTS: history; politics; gardening; cooking; news junkie; tyrannized by small house pets. COMMENT: *"I preside over Edmonton Sun's op-ed page/editorial page, and consider that these pages are home to some of the most interesting columnists around (ranging from centre to slightly left of Montana Militia)."*

MacLellan, Debbie, B.Sc.,M.Sc. 🎓 ⊕
Assistant Professor, Department of Home Economics, UNIVERSITY OF PRINCE EDWARD ISLAND, 550 University Ave., Charlottetown, PE C1A 4P3 (902) 566-0521, FAX 566-0777, EMAIL maclellan@upei.ca. Born Winnipeg 1955. m. J. Ronald. 4 ch. J. Darcy, Christopher, Heather, Megan. **EDUC:** Univ. of Prince Edward Island, B.Sc.(Home Econ.) 1976; Univ. of Alberta M.Sc.(Nutrition) 1979. **CAREER:** Asst. Dir., Nutrition Svcs, Providence Hospital, Moose Jaw, 1981-85; Dir., 1985-87; Dir. of Nutrition Svcs, Prince Edward Home, P.E.I., 1987-90; Asst. Prof., Dept. of Home Econ., Univ. of Prince Edward Island, 1990 to date. **SELECTED PUBLICATIONS:** "The Future is Ours. Let's Make It Happen Together" (*PEI Dietetic Association Newsletter* 14 1995); "Claims for Barley Green–Fact or Fiction" (*Golden Times* Winter 1994); various other publications. **EDIT:** Asst. Ed., Home Economics Publishing Collective, 1991; Asst. Ed., *Canadian Home Economics Journal*, 1995-98. **AFFIL:** Canadian Dietetic Association (Bd. of Dir. 1995-97); P.E.I. Dietetic Association (VP 1992-93; Pres. 1993-94; Past Pres. 1994-95); Canadian Home Economics Association; P.E.I. Home Economics Association (Publicity Chair 1991-94); Canadian Association for Research in Home Economics; Organization for Nutrition Education. **HONS:** Teaching Award, Univ. of Prince Edward Island, 1991-92. **INTERESTS:** nutrition educ.; home-delivered meal support for the elderly. **MISC:** recipient of various grants. **COMMENT:** *"As a professional dietitian and nutrition educator, I am interested in the areas of health promotion and illness prevention. Through my membership on the Health Policy Council of Prince Edward Island, I am attempting to influence healthy public policy. I also feel that I play an important role in the education of young people in the areas of nutrition and healthy eating. "*

MacMillan, Ann, B.A. ✏ 📺
European Correspondent, CANADIAN BROADCASTING CORPORATION, 45 Great Tichfield St., London, UK W1P 3DD (0171) 412-9200, FAX 323-5662. Born Tremadoc, North Wales 1946. m. Peter Snow. 3 ch. Daniel Snow, Rebecca Snow, Katherine Snow. **EDUC:** Univ. of Toronto, B.A.(English) 1968; Univ. of Florence, Italy, First Certificate (Italian & Fine Arts) 1969. **CAREER:** Program Supervisor, CHIN-FM Radio, Toronto, 1970-72; Co-Host, *New Direction*, CBLT Toronto, 1972-73; News Reporter, Global Television, 1973-75; News Reporter, CTV Television News, 1975-76; Bureau Chief, Montreal, 1976; Bureau Chief, London, UK, 1976-81; European Correspondent, CBC Television News, 1981 to date. **INTERESTS:** sailing; skiing; hiking; reading. **COMMENT:** *"As one of Canada's first female television news reporters, Ann MacMillan has covered a wide range of Canadian and international news stories."*

MacMillan, Carrie, B.A.,M.A.,Ph.D. 🎓 📜
Professor, MOUNT ALLISON UNIVERSITY, Sackville, NB E0A 3C0 (506) 364-2543, FAX 364-2543. Born Fredericton 1945. m. Peter W. Hicklin. 2 ch. Edward, Emma. **EDUC:** Univ. of New Brunswick, B.A.(English) 1967; Dalhousie Univ., M.A.(English) 1970; McMaster Univ., Ph.D.(English) 1977. **CAREER:** mbr., Dept. of English, Mount Allison Univ., 1977 to date; Head, Dept. of English, 1994 to date. **SELECTED PUBLICATIONS:** *Silenced Sextet: Six Nineteenth-Century Canadian Women Novelists*, with Dr. L. McMillan & Dr. E. Waterston (McGill-Queen's Univ. Press 1993). **AFFIL:** Association of Canadian College & University Teachers of English; Association of Canadian & Quebec Literatures; Centre for Canadian Studies (Assoc./Mbr. of Senate). **HONS:** Tucker Teaching Award, Mount Allison Univ., 1989; Research Grant, Social Sciences & Humanities Research Council of Canada, 1992-95.

Macmillan, Katherine E. [$]
Vice-President, Corporate Marketing, Public Affairs, BANK OF MONTREAL, 55 Bloor St. W., 4th Fl., Toronto, ON M4W 3N5 (416) 927-2660, FAX 944-7232. **EDUC:** Univ. of Western Ontario, Sch. of Bus. Admin., 1979. **CAREER:** Asst. Brand Mgr, Consumer Health Group, Warner Lambert Corporation, 1979-82; Group Product Mgr, Consumer Health Group, 1983-85; Dir., Consumer Products Mktg for Latin Am., Morris, N.J. headquarters, 1985-87; Trade Mktg Mgr, Adams Brand Div., 1987; Dir. of Mktg, Confectionery Products, UK, 1988-90; VP, Sales & Mktg, Adams Brands Div., Toronto, 1990-92; VP, Gen. Mgr, Grocery Brands, Campbell Soup Company, 1992-94; VP, Bank of Montreal, Corp. Mktg, 1994 to date. **AFFIL:** PMB (Bd. & V-Chair; Exec. Mbr.; Treas.); CAF Gender Portrayal Committee (Chair); Association of Canadian Advertisers (Bd., Exec. Mbr. & V-Chair); Canadian Congress of Advertising (Past V-Chair).

MacNeil, Rita * 👏
Singer and Songwriter. Big Pond, Cape Breton, NS. **CAREER:** singer & songwriter; recently signed with EMI Music Canada. **SELECTED CREDITS:** albums: *Born a Woman*, 1975; *Part of the Mystery*, 1981; *I'm Not What I Seem*, 1983; *Flying On Your Own*, 1987; *Reason to Believe*, 1988; *Now the Bells Ring*, 1988; *Rita*,

1989; *Home I'll Be*, 1990; *Thinking of You*, 1992; *Once Upon A Christmas*, 1993; *Volume One–Songs From the Collection*, 1994; *Porch Songs*, prod. Don Potter, 1996; Host, *Rita & Friends*, CBC. **HONS:** Female Vocalist of the year, Juno Awards, 1990; Country Female Vocalist of the Year, Juno Awards, 1991; Order of Canada, 1992; Canada 125 Medal, 1992; Best Performance in a Variety Program or Series, Gemini Awards, 1995; numerous East Coast Music Awards; Hon. Doctorate of Letters, Univ. of N.B., 1990; Hon. Doctorate of Letters, St. Mary's Univ., 1991; LL.D.(Hon.), St. Francis Xavier Univ., 1993; Hon. Doctorate of Letters, Mount St. Vincent Univ., 1993; Hon. Doctorate of Letters, University Coll. of Cape Breton, 1994.

MacPhail, Jannetta, B.S.N.,M.S.N.,Ph.D., LL.D.(Hon.),F.A.A.N. ⊕

Professor and Dean Emeritus, Faculty of Nursing, UNIVERSITY OF ALBERTA. Born Renfrew, Ont. 1923. s. **EDUC:** Victoria Hospital Sch. of Nursing, London, Ont., RN 1949; Columbia Univ., BSN 1952; Wayne State Univ., Detroit, MSN 1960; Univ. of Michigan, Ph.D.(Higher Educ. Admin.) 1966. **CAREER:** Staff Nurse, Obstetrics Dept., Victoria Hospital, 1949-50; Supervisor, Obstetrics Dept. & Instructor, Sch. of Nursing, Kitchener-Waterloo Hospital, 1950-54; Instructor & Coord., Maternal & Child Nursing, Univ. of Toronto, 1954-61; Asst. Prof. & Asst. Administrator, Gen. Nursing Program, Wayne State Univ., 1961-64; Dir., Nursing Demonstration Proj., Assoc. Prof. & Asst. Dean for Clinical Nursing, Case Western Reserve Univ., Cleveland & Assoc. Dir. of Nursing, Univ. Hospitals of Cleveland, 1966-71; Prof. of Nursing, Case Western Reserve Univ., 1971-82; Assoc. Dean, 1971-72; Dean, 1972-82; Prof. & Dean of Nursing, Univ. of Alberta, 1982-87; Prof. Emeritus, 1987 to date. **SELECTED PUBLICATIONS:** *Canadian Nursing: Issues and Perspectives*, with Janet Kerr (1988), 2nd ed. (1991), 3rd ed. (1996); *Concepts in Canadian Nursing*, with Janet Ross Kerr (1996); *Issues in Community Health Nursing in Canada*, with Janet Ross Kerr (1996); presented many papers & published many articles in nursing journals & several chapters in nursing textbooks. **AFFIL:** Community Church of Vero Beach, Fla. (Bd. of Trustees 1989-92); American Association of University Women (Pres., Vero Beach Branch 1991-94); Vero Beach Choral Society (Bd. of Dir.); Indian River Symphonic Association (Bd. of Dir.); Education Foundation of Indian River County (Bd. of Dir.); Canadian Nurses' Association; Florida Nurses' Association; American Nurses' Association; Alberta Association of Registered Nurses.

HONS: Hon Life Mbr., Alberta Association of Registered Nurses, Columbia Univ. Nursing Alumni Association & Frances Payne Bolton Sch. of Nursing Alumni Association; Fellow, American Academy of Nursing (FAAN); Sigma Theta Tau International Honour Society in Nursing; Luther Christman Award for Leadership in Nursing, American Assembly of Men in Nursing, 1981; Armiger Award for Distinguished Service to American Association of Colleges of Nursing, 1982; LL.D.(Hon.), McMaster Univ., 1986. **MISC:** recipient, various scholarships & fellowships. **COMMENT:** *"Since retiring and moving to Vero Beach, Fla., I have served as a consultant in nursing administration and organizational change and have continued professional writing. In addition, I have become involved in a number of organizations in the community with a view to adding variety and utilizing previous organizational experience and skills in writing and grantsmanship."*

MacPhail, The Hon. Joy K. ■ ✦

Member of the Legislative Assembly (Vancouver-Hastings), Minister of Health, Minister Responsible for Seniors and Government House Leader, GOVERNMENT OF BRITISH COLUMBIA, Parliament Buildings, Rm. 306, Victoria, BC V8V 1X4 (604) 387-5394, FAX 387-3696. Born Hamilton, Ont. 1 ch. Jack. **EDUC:** Univ. of Western Ontario; London Sch. of Economics, U.K. **CAREER:** Economist, B.C. Federation of Labour; M.L.A. (Vancouver-Hastings), Gov't of B.C., 1991 to date; Min. of Social Svcs, 1993-96; Min. of Health & Min. Responsible for Seniors, 1996 to date; Chair, Standing Committee on Fin., Crown Corporations, Gov't Svcs; V-Chair, Public Accts Committee; Co-Chair, Special Committee on Constitutional Matters; New Democratic Party Gov't Caucus Chair, 1992-93. **AFFIL:** Planned Parenthood of B.C.; VIEW Performing Arts Society; N.D.P. of B.C. **COMMENT:** *"Joy MacPhail was appointed Minister of Health and Minister Responsible for Seniors on June 17, 1996. As an economist with the B.C. Federation of Labour, Ms. MacPhail was responsible for policy development, communications and liaison with union affiliates. She worked previously with other unions and was a labour representative serving on the Provincial Apprenticeship Board."*

MacPhee, Medrie, B.F.A. ■ ⊗ ♡

Artist. 111 Bowery, New York, NY 10002 (212) 274-9428, FAX 334-4057. Painting Professor, COLUMBIA UNIVERSITY. Painting Professor, COOPER UNION. FOR THE ADVANCEMENT OF SCIENCE & ART. Born Edmonton 1953. m.

Harold Crooks. **EDUC:** Nova Scotia Coll. of Art, B.F.A.(Painting) 1976. **CAREER:** Painting Instructor, Nova Scotia Coll. of Art, 1985; Summer Studio Head, Visual Art Dept., Banff Sch. of Fine Art, 1986; Drawing Instructor, Cooper Union for the Advancement of Science & Art, 1987; Painting Instructor, Concordia Univ., 1989; Painting Instructor, Sarah Lawrence Coll., 1989-91; Painting & Drawing Instructor, Bard Coll., 1992-92; Drawing Instructor, New York Studio Sch., 1993; Artist-in-Residence, Emma Lake Artists' Workshop, Dept. of Art & Hist., Univ. of Saskatchewan, 1993; Painting & Drawing Instructor, Emily Carr Coll. of Art & Design, 1993 & 1995; Foundation Program Drawing Instructor, Rhode Island Sch. of Design, 1994; Visiting Sr. Painting & Drawing Instructor, Rhode Island Sch. of Design, 1994; Drawing Prof., Columbia Univ., 1995 to date. **EXHIBITIONS:** Linda Genereux (1995); Mira Godard Gallery (1980, 1981, 1983, 1985, 1986, 1988, 1990, 1992); 49th Parallel (1985, 1988); Concordia Univ. Art Gallery (1988); Phillipe Daverio Gallery (1991); Baldacci-Daverio Gallery (1993); Art & Living Gallery, Germany (1994); Paolo Baldacci Gallery (1994, 1995); numerous group exhibitions. **COLLECTIONS:** numerous collections incl. Metropolitan Museum of Art, N.Y.C.; Art Gallery of Ontario; Bank of Canada; Esso Resources; Deutsche Bank; various private collections. **AFFIL:** College Art Association. **MISC:** recipient, numerous grants; subject of numerous articles; numerous invited lectures.

MacPherson, Janet E., C.P.S. ■ 🎓 ✊ ♡
Instructor, Re-Entry Training, HOLLAND COLLEGE, 140 Weymouth St., Charlottetown, PE C1A 4Z1 (902) 566-9657, FAX 566-9505. Born P.E.I. 1945. m. Herb. 3 ch. Spenser, Bruce, Derek. **CAREER:** elementary sch. teacher, 1965-75; owner/operator, meat processing plant, 1967-75; Sec., Holland Coll., 1980 to date; Instructor, Holland Coll., 1987 to date; owner/operator, Port-A-Pit B-B-Q Sizzler. **AFFIL:** Multiple Sclerosis Society (various exec. positions; P.E.I. Rep., Atlantic Bd.; Atlantic Rep., Nat'l Social Action Committee); Zion Presbyterian Church; P.S.I.; Maritime Association of Life Skills Coaches; P.E.I. Council for the Disabled; Queen Elizabeth Hospital (volunteer). **HONS:** Certificate of Merit, Recognition Award, Multiple Sclerosis Society; Canada 125 Medal. **INTERESTS:** family; friends; grandchildren, Hailey & Bethany; meeting different people. **COMMENT:** "*I believe those of us who have like concerns deserve the help and support of others. This was my reason for helping to organize our three self-help groups on PEI for persons with multiple sclerosis. I am no professional, but consider that I have sensible approaches to most situations!*"

Macpherson, Jay, B.A.,M.A.,Ph.D. ■ 📜 🎓
Professor (retired). 17 Berryman St., Toronto, ON M5R 1M7 (416) 922-4458. Born London, UK 1931. s. **EDUC:** Carleton Univ., B.A. (Gen.) 1951; Univ. of Toronto, M.A.(English) 1955, Ph.D.(English) 1964. **CAREER:** Prof. of English, Victoria Coll., 1957-96. **SELECTED PUBLICATIONS:** *The Boatman*, poetry (1957); *Four Ages of Man*, high sch. text book of classical mythology (1962); *Poems Twice Told* (1981); *The Spirit of Solitude*, literary criticism (1982). **HONS:** Gov. General's Award for Poetry, 1958.

MacPherson, Sheila M., B.A.,LL.B. ⚖
Partner, JOHNSON, GULLBERG, WIEST AND MACPHERSON, Box 818, Yellowknife, NT X1A 2N6 (403) 669-5522, FAX 920-2206. Born Antigonish, N.S. 1960. **EDUC:** Carleton Univ., B.A.(Pol. Sci.) 1982; Dalhousie Univ., LL.B. 1987. **BAR:** N.W.T., 1988. **CAREER:** articling student, Cooper Johnson, 1987-88; Assoc., Cooper, Regel, Peach and Gullberg, 1988-92; Deputy Law Clerk, Legislative Assembly of the N.W.T., 1989-91; Law Clerk, 1991 to date; Ptnr, Johnson, Gullberg, Wiest and MacPherson, 1992 to date. **AFFIL:** Law Society of the N.W.T. (Social Committee 1987-88; Admissions Committee 1990-93; Legal Ethics & Practice Committee 1991; Treas. 1994; VP 1995; Pres. 1996); Canadian Bar Association (Chair, Family Law Subsection 1991-92); Arctic Legal Education & Public Information (Lawline Volunteer 1989 to date); Canadian National Institute for the Blind (Dir. 1987-93; Chair 1991-92; V-Chair 1993); Yellowknife Condominium Corporation 9 (Sec. 1994); Association of Parliamentary Counsel of Canada (Sec. 1995-96; Pres. 1996-97).

MacRae, Martha, B.A.,C.A. 💲
Vice-President, Management Reporting and Analysis, NATIONAL TRUST, One Financial Place, 1 Adelaide St. E., Toronto, ON M5C 2W8 (416) 361-5696, FAX 361-4114. Born Cape Breton, N.S. 1950. m. Michael J. Monteith. 1 ch. **EDUC:** Acadia Univ., B.A.(English/Phil., Reid Scholar); C.A.(Hons., 17th in Canada) 1978; C.F.A. program, Level II. **CAREER:** External Auditor/Computer Audit Specialist, Ernst & Young, 1975-79; Acctg Mgr, Hart House, Univ. of Toronto, 1980-85; Mgr of Research Admin., Univ. of Waterloo, 1985-86; Acctg Research Analyst/Acctg Analyst, The Toronto-Dominion Bank, 1987-89;

Mgr, Corp. Budgets/Dir., Corp. Fin. Analysis/Dir., Guaranteed Acctg/Mng Ptnr (VP) & Cont., Personal Fin. Svcs, Royal Trust, 1989-92; VP, Mgmt Reporting & Control/VP, Mgmt Reporting & Analysis, National Trust, 1993 to date. AFFIL: Canadian Institute of Chartered Accountants; Hart House, Univ. of Toronto (Hon. Mbr.). INTERESTS: riding; reading; hiking; family.

MacRury-Sweet, Karen E., R.N.,B.N.,M.N., M.Ed. ⊕
Director of Cardiac/Emergency Nursing, Queen Elizabeth II Health Science Centre, VICTORIA GENERAL HOSPITAL, 1278 Tower Rd., Halifax, NS B3H 2Y9 (902) 428-2261, FAX 428-3330. Born Sydney, N.S. 1958. m. Wayne Sweet. 1 ch. Allison. EDUC: Victoria General Hospital, R.N. 1978; Dalhousie Univ., B.N.(Nursing) 1983, M.Ed.(Adult Educ.) 1986, M.N.(Nursing) 1995. CAREER: Staff Nurse, Orthopedics, Intensive Care, Victoria General Hospital, 1978-87; Research Asst., 1980-81; Head Nurse, 1987-90; Asst. Dir. of Medical Nursing, 1990-91; Dir. of Clinical Nursing, Cardiac Sciences, 1991-95; Dir. of Cardiac/Emergency Nursing, QEII Health Sciences Centre, 1995 to date. AFFIL: Canadian Coll. of Health Service Executives; Canadian Council of Cardiovascular Services; Canadian Association of Critical Care Nurses (Sec., N.S. Chapter 1987-89); Canadian Council of Cardiovascular Nurses (Research Chair, N.S. Chapter 1991-92; Chair, Scholarship Committee). HONS: Bedside Nursing Award, Victoria General Hospital, 1978; W.B. Saunders Award, 1983; Scholarship, Canadian Council of Cardiovascular Nurses, 1990; Nurse's Scholarship, Victoria General Hospital, 1991. INTERESTS: painting; sports; singing. MISC: lecturer at conferences & in community on cardiac disease. COMMENT: *"I am an extremely outgoing, active individual who enjoys meeting new people. I have been active in my profession and taken on new challenges in my profession and personal life."*

Mactavish, Anne L., B.A.,LL.B. ■ 🖊 🖋
President, HUMAN RIGHTS TRIBUNAL, 473 Albert St., Ottawa, ON K1A 1J4 (613) 995-1707, FAX 995-3484. Born Montreal 1955. m. William Honeywell. 3 ch. EDUC: Bishop's Univ., B.A.(Pol. Sci.) 1977; Univ. of New Brunswick, LL.B. 1980. BAR: Ont., 1982. CAREER: Assoc., Perley-Robertson, Panet, Hill and McDougall, 1982-87; Ptnr, 1987-96. SELECTED PUBLICATIONS: "Mandatory Reporting of Sexual Abuse Under the Regulated Health Professions Act" (14 *Health Law in Canada* 89); "Tort Recovery for Economic Loss: Recent Developments" (21*Canadian*

Business Law Journal 395); *The Physicians' Legal Manual*, with others (Emond Montgomery Publications Limited, 1996); various articles on human rights & employment law issues for nonlegal publications. AFFIL: Law Society of Upper Canada; Canadian Bar Association; County of Carleton Law Association (Pres. 1995); Women's Law Association of Ontario; Advocates' Society; Medical Legal Society of Ottawa; Children's Hospital of Eastern Ontario (Bd. of Trustees). MISC: 1st woman to hold Presidency of the fed. Human Rights Tribunal.

MacTavish, Helen ■ ■ ○ ⊕
President, NEW BRUNSWICK ASSOCIATION OF HEALTHCARE AUXILIARIES (provincial auxiliary association), 280 Sewell St., Fredericton, NB E3A 3G6 (506) 472-7028. m. Boyd MacTavish. 3 ch. Richard, Judy, Nancy. CAREER: co-owner, Joe's Diner, Fredericton's north side, 34 yrs.; makes pies daily for the diner (& is renowned for her culinary skills). VOLUNTEER CAREER: volunteer, palliative care unit & info. desk, Dr. Everett Chalmers Hospital. AFFIL: N.B. Association of Healthcare Auxiliaries (Pres. 1994-96); Dr. Everett Chalmers Hospital Auxiliary Inc. (various positions on bd. incl. Pres. 1989-91); Victoria Health Centre; Gibson Memorial United Church (has served on various bds. & committees). HONS: Nashwaaksis Y's Men's Award for outstanding citizen, 1989; Confederation of Canada 125th Commemorative Medal, 1992; Distinguished Citizen Award, Fredericton Chamber of Commerce, 1993; Woman of the Year, Beta Sigma Phi, 1995. INTERESTS: hockey; baseball. MISC: selected for inclusion in Keith Minchin's book, *Faces of Fredericton*, 1988. COMMENT: *"Very thankful to have good health and happy marriage for 46 years. Two years after our marriage, my husband had polio (1952, before vaccine). This changed our life a little, as he always played hockey and baseball for Fredericton teams. We owned "MacTavish for Sports" sporting goods store for many years. Now my husband has retired and helps us at the diner we bought in 1962. We have 3 ladies who each have worked for us over 30 years. This makes it easier for me to volunteer. I find volunteering very rewarding, since I can help someone less fortunate. It is better to give than to receive."*

Maddocks, Judy, A.I.I.C. Ⓢ 🖋
President, Personal Insurance, ZURICH CANADA, 400 University Ave., Toronto, ON M5G 1S7 (416) 586-2905, FAX (416) 586-2990. Born Penticton, B.C. 1951. s. CAREER: Personal Lines Underwriter, Royal Insurance, 1975; Unit Supervisor, 1975-78; Personal Lines Asst. Mgr,

1978-82; Asst. Planning Mgr, Commercial Lines Div., 1982-84; Mgr, Commercial Lines Div., 1984-85; Mgr, Planning & Corp. Research, 1985-87; Deputy Mgr, Ont. Personal Lines, 1987-89; Reg'l Mgr, Ont., 1989-92; VP, Personal Insur., 1992-94; Pres., Personal Insur., Zurich Canada, 1994 to date. **AFFIL:** Insurance Institute of Canada (A.I.I.C.; Gov.); Insurance Institute of Ontario (Past Pres.); Minister's Advisory Committee for Employment Equity, Prov. of Ont. **HONS:** Employment Equity Award, Royal Insurance. **MISC:** 1st female Pres., Insurance Institute of Ontario. **COMMENT:** *"In her capacity as President, Personal Insurance, at Zurich Canada, Judy Maddocks has set her sights on designing products and services to meet customer needs."*

Madill, Shirley, B.A.,B.F.A.,M.A.
Curator, Contemporary Art and Photography, WINNIPEG ART GALLERY, 300 Memorial Blvd., Winnipeg, MB R3C 1V1 (204) 786-6641, FAX 788-4998. Born Selkirk, Man. 1952. 2 ch. Kassandra, Kirsten. **EDUC:** Univ. of Manitoba, B.A.(Hist.) 1976, B.F.A.(Art Hist.) 1978, M.A.(Hist.) 1982. **CAREER:** Curator, Winnipeg Art Gallery, 1979 to date; Instructor, Sch. of Art, Univ. of Winnipeg, 1981, 1993, 1995; Asst. Prof., Hist., 1982, 1984, 1986, 1988, 1992-96. **SELECTED PUBLICATIONS:** various articles & publications in conjunction with exhibitions. **EXHIBITIONS:** Curator, *A-Dress: States of Being*, 1996; *Colleen Cutshall: House Made of Stars*, 1996; *Quotation: Representing History*, 1995; *Aganetha Dyck*, 1995; *Swiss Paradigm: Contemporary Art from Switzerland*, 1994; *Janice Gurney: Sum over Histories*, 1992; *Private/Public: Art and Social Discourse*, 1992. **AFFIL:** Winnipeg Contemporary Dancers (Pres., Bd. of Gov.); Canadian Museums Association; International Council of Museums; Western Canadian Museums Association. **INTERESTS:** language. **MISC:** advisor & mentor, Manitoba Artists for Women's Art, 1994; juror & reviewer, 1994 Fotofest, Houston, Tex. & 1995 Photofest, Floating Gallery, Winnipeg; various panels. **COMMENT:** *"As a curator and writer, I am particularly interested in a global context of cultural and social issues as expressed in the visual and performing arts. International and collaborative exhibitions have been the most recent endeavours."*

Mady Kelly, Diana, B.A.,M.A. ⋐ ⊗
Director, School of Dramatic Art, UNIVERSITY OF WINDSOR, Windsor, ON N9B 3P4 (519) 253-4232, FAX 973-7050. Born Windsor, Ont. 1939. m. D.A. Park. 3 ch. Beverly Rilett, Colleen Park, Michael Park. **EDUC:** Assumption Univ., B.A.(English) 1960; Univ. of West-

ern Ontario, Secondary Sch. Teaching Certificate; New York Univ., M.A.(Theatre) 1982; Wayne State Univ., doctoral studies in directing, in progress; private study in mime &/or movement &/or voice with Mary Phillips, Molly Kenny & Trish Arnold, UK, Sonia Moore & Uta Hagen, N.Y., Viola Spolin, L.A. **CAREER:** acting teacher, secondary schools, universities, professional actors; actor, dir. & prod. for community & professional theatre companies; teacher, dir., founder, Theatre Arts Program, F.J. Brennan High Sch., 1960-69; Master Teacher, Althouse Coll. of Educ., Univ. of Western Ontario; Administrator, Prod., Mng Dir., Theatre Centre Windsor at Lapointe, 1972-73; Interim Dir., Sch. of Dramatic Art, 1991; Dir., Sch. of Dramatic Art, Univ. of Windsor 1993 to date. **SELECTED CREDITS:** Prod., *Matthew Locke's The Tempest*, a collaboration of performance & music, Windsor Symphony Society (1991); Dir., *Given to the Winds*, Workshop Production, Windsor Theatre Development Corporation (1993); narrator, *Carla Can Sing*, educational/creative work for children newly diagnosed with cancer; various other theatrical credits. **SELECTED PUBLICATIONS:** "Life Studies: Exercises in Characterization for the Actor-in-Training" (*Dramatics* Mar. 1986); "The People in Donald Sutherland's Head," with Sue Martin (*Dramatics* Dec. 1987); various other publications. **AFFIL:** Canadian Actors' Equity Association; Society of Stage Directors & Choreographers; Theatre Ontario Talent Bank; Arts Council, Windsor & Reg.; Canadian Association of University Teachers; Ontario Confederation of Faculty Association; Windsor Theatre Development Corporation (Artistic Dir.). **HONS:** OCUFA Teaching Excellence Award, 1992; Lieutenant Governor's Excellence in Teaching Award, 1993. **INTERESTS:** films; reading; psychology. **MISC:** recipient, various grants & fellowships. **COMMENT:** *"A dedicated and accomplished teacher, actress, director and administrator profoundly interested in the development of Canadian actors by providing them with artistic opportunities for innovative work."*

Maes, Sister Yvonne, B.A.,M.Ed., M.P.S. ■■ ☯ ☼ ⋐
HOLY NAMES CONGREGATION (founded in Canada), P.O. Box 399, Stn B, Happy Valley-Goose Bay, NF A0P 1E0 (709) 896-8862 or 896-2919, FAX 896-2588. Co-ordinator of Programs for Batterers and Sex Offenders, LABRADOR LEGAL SERVICES. Born on farm near Swan Lake, Man. 1939. **EDUC:** Univ. of Manitoba, B.A.(Hist. & English) 1968; Univ. of Botswana, Lesotho, & Swaziland, Africa,

M.Ed. 1973; Loyola Univ. of Chicago, M.P.S.(Pastoral Studies-Spiritual Direction) 1990. CAREER: Internship Coord., National Teachers' Training Coll., Lesotho, 1973; Headmistress, Mabathoana High Sch., Maseru, Lesotho, 1978-87. SELECTED PUBLICATIONS: *Agricultural Studies for Lesotho* (text for high schools); educational articles in Lesotho; awareness articles, weekly column of Mokami Status of Women in the *Labradorian*. AFFIL: Mokami Status of Women Council (Pres. 1995 to date); Canadian Guidance & Counsellors' Association (mbr. 1994 to date); Newfoundland Provincial Advisory Council on the Status of Women (mbr. 1996); Newfoundland & Labrador Writers' Alliance; Lesotho Headmasters' & Headmistresses' Association (Sec.-Treas. 1979-87); Lesotho Teachers' Association (founding mbr. 1983-87). HONS: small dam in Lesotho named Sister Yvonne Dam after her (she helped build the dam). INTERESTS: kayaking; needlework; women's issues. MISC: nearing completion of book, *The Cannibal's Wife*, the purpose of which is to expose the issue of clergy sexual abuse by using her personal story of clergy abuse & the disclosure process. COMMENT: *"I want the word "feisty" on my tombstone, so I am exposing the church for its complicity with clergy perpetrators of sexual abuse. Justice before charity was my motto in Africa with Apartheid and is now with batterers and sex offenders."*

Magee, Christine, B.A. ■■ ⑤
President, SLEEP COUNTRY CANADA (retailer-mattresses, boxsprings, frames), 2931 Viking Way, Unit 4, Richmond, BC V6V 1Y1 (604) 244-9171, FAX 244-9188. Born Ont. 1959. m. Allen Magee. EDUC: Univ. of Western Ontario, B.A.(Hons., Bus. Admin.) 1982. CAREER: Area Mgr, Ontario Place, 1978-82 (summer); Commercial Accts Mgr, Continental Bank, 1982-85; Sr. Mgmt, National Bank, 1985-94. AFFIL: Dealer Advisory Council (1996). HONS: Furniture Retailer of the Year, B.C. Home Furnishings Association, 1996. INTERESTS: sports; theatre; travel. MISC: featured in *BC Business Magazine* June 1996, "Reality Check" (article on retail in B.C.). COMMENT: *"Fortunately I have had the opportunity to complete my education and pursue my career aspirations through self determination and the support of family and colleagues. I was always confident that diligence, creativity and perseverance would create opportunities. Luckily I was correct!"*

Magnan, Nicole, B.Comm.,M.A.P. ⑨ ♥ ⊕
Executive Director, Quebec Division, CANADIAN CANCER SOCIETY, 5151 L'Assomption

Blvd., Montreal, QC H1T 4A9 (514) 255-5151, FAX 255-2808. Born Montreal 1940. m. Claude Magnan. 2 ch. Chantal, Patrice. EDUC: Concordia Univ., B.Comm.(Mktg) 1980; École nationale d'administration publique, M.A.P.(Public Admin.) 1988. CAREER: Public Rel'ns Officer, Air Canada, 1961-73; Public Rel'ns Asst. Dir., Canadian Red Cross, 1973-77; Public Rel'ns Dir., 1977-80; Programs Dir., 1980-83; Asst. Exec. Dir., 1983-85; Exec. Dir., Que. Div., Canadian Cancer Society, 1985 to date. SELECTED PUBLICATIONS: articles in internal publications of Canadian Red Cross, Canadian Cancer Society & Air Canada. AFFIL: Société canadienne des directeurs d'association (Que.); Partenaires santé/Health Partners (Que. Pres. 1989-92). INTERESTS: travel across Canada & abroad; playing piano; designing clothes. COMMENT: *"I am ambitious for the organization I work for and try to keep it ahead of the competition. A good challenge is always welcome in my books."*

Magnussen, Karen, O.C. ⑩
Figure Skater and Coach. 2852 Thorncliffe Dr., North Vancouver, BC V7R 2S8 (604) 988-9230 or (604) 980-5785. Born Vancouver 1952. m. Anthony R. Cella. 3 ch. Eric Cella, Kristopher Cella, Jennifer Cella. EDUC: Delbrook High Sch., N. Vancouver, 1968; Carson Graham High Sch., N. Vancouver, 1970; Simon Fraser Univ., 1971-73; coached by Linda Brauckmann. SPORTS CAREER: started skating at age 6; B.C. Coast Championship (at age 8), 1961; 1st, B.C. Coast Championship (reg'l), 1962; 2nd, B.C. Championship (sectional), 1962; 1st, B.C. Championship, 1963, 1964, 1965; Cdn Jr. Championship, 1965; 4th, Cdn Championship, 1966; 2nd, Cdn Championship, 1967, 1969; 4th, N.Am. Championship, 1967; 1st, Cdn Ladies Championship, 1968, 1970, 1971, 1972, 1973; 2nd, N.Am. Championship, 1969; due to injury, did not compete in World Championship, 1969; 4th, World Championship, 1970; 1st, N.Am. Championship, 1971; 3rd, World Championship, 1971; Silver Medal, World Championship, 1972; Silver Medal, Winter Olympics, Sapporo, Japan, 1972; Gold, compulsory figures, Gold, free-skating, & Gold, overall, ladies, World Championship, 1973; past star skater with Ice Capades; founder, Champions Way Skating Schools; founder, Karen Magnussen Foundation, 1973; professional figure skating coach, North Shore Winter Club, N. Vancouver. AFFIL: Friends of the Games, B.C. Winter Games 1996 (Dir.); B.C. Sports Hall of Fame (Bd. Mbr.; Trustee 1993); Emily Murphy House (Bd. Mbr.); Pacific National Exhibition (Hon. Life Mbr.);

Vancouver Parks & Recreation Bd. (Life Mbr.); N. Vancouver Recreation Commission (Life Mbr.); North Shore Winter Club (Life Mbr.); Swedish Canadian Club; Nordlandslaget; New Westminster Skating Club; B.C. Jockey Club, Vancouver (Life Mbr.); Beta Sigma Phi (Hon. Life Mbr.); United Church. **HONS:** B.C. Jr. Athlete of the Year, 1967; B.C. Sports Special Merit Award, 1970; B.C. Sr. Athlete of the Year, 1971, 1972; North Shore Jr. Athlete of the Year & Hall of Fame, 1971; Canada's Female Amateur Athlete of the Year, 1971, 1972; B.C. Over-All Athlete of the Year, 1972; Vanier Award, outstanding young Cdn, 1972; Special Achievement Award, Sons of Norway of America, 1972; named Top Female Athlete of Canada, 1972, 1973; Award of Merit, Canadian Figure Skating Association, 1973; First Freeman, District of North Vancouver, 1973; Hon. Citizen, Thunder Bay, Ont., 1973; B.C. Sports Hall of Fame, 1973; Canadian Sports Hall of Fame, 1973; Good Skate Award, Vancouver Rotary Club & Ice Capades, 1989; N. Vancouver Achievement Award of the Century, 1991; Athlete of Quarter Century, B.C. Sport Association, 1991; Citizenship Award, District of N. Vancouver, 1993; Canada 125 Medal, 1993. **INTERESTS:** golf; charities. **MISC:** biography, *Karen* (1973); Karen Magnussen Arena, Lynn Valley, N. Vancouver, named 1973; Hon. Coach, Figure Skating, Special Olympic Winter Games, Vermont, 1981; mbr., Advisory Bd., Calgary Dev. Committee for 1988 Winter Olympics.

Magwood, Kathleen ■ ⊗ ⊚
Past President, RUG HOOKING GUILD NOVA SCOTIA, Box 338, Bridgetown, NS B0S 1C0 (902) 665-4862. Born Dartmouth, N.S. 1932. w. 2 ch. **CAREER:** Medical Assessor; Rug Hooking Instructor, N.S. Annual Rug Sch., elder hostels; Demonstrator, Upper Clements Park. **SELECTED PUBLICATIONS:** numerous articles in newspapers & newsletters. **AFFIL:** Halifax Police Association (Past VP, Ladies' Auxiliary); Bridgetown Historical Society; Rug Hooking Guild of N.S. (Dir. 1991; VP 1992-93; Pres. 1994-95). **INTERESTS:** teaching & promoting rug hooking; restoration of a heritage home. **MISC:** interviewed on CBC *Mainstreet*; conducted an open house on rughooking, recommended by Dept. of N.S. Tourism. **COMMENT:** *"I enjoy all crafts and eagerly try new ideas. Most of my hooking goes to my two grandchildren; enjoy teaching others this enjoyable craft."*

Maharajh, Anna E., B.A. ⊗ ⊛
Program Co-ordinator, BRITISH COLUMBIA INSTITUTE OF TECHNOLOGY, 3700 Willingdon,

Burnaby, BC V5G 3H2 (604) 432-8586, FAX 432-042. President, LANTREK SERVICES LTD. Born B.C. 1939. m. Peter. 2 ch. **EDUC:** Univ. of British Columbia, B.A.(English & Fine Arts) 1972; B.C. Institute of Technology, Diploma (Bldg Econ.) 1975; Int'l Sch. of Estimating, Certificate of Construction Estimating; Canadian Institute of Quantity Surveying, Diploma of Quantity Surveying. **CAREER:** Epp Brothers Supply Ltd., 1963; Plan Checker, Bldg Dept., Municipality of Burnaby, 1974; Estimator & Proj. Mgr, Seaward Construction Co. Ltd., 1975-76; Architectural Drafter, Ed Dodson, Architect, 1975-76; Architectural Drafter, Campbell & Grill Co. Ltd., 1976-77; Developer/Designer/Contractor, Lantrek Services, 1975-90; Asst. Instructor, B.C. Institute of Technology, 1977-92; Program Coord., Part-Time Studies, Bldg Technology, 1986-92; Program Coord., Day Program, 1991-92. **DIRECTOR:** Nirvona Research Systems Inc. **AFFIL:** Canadian Institute of Quantity Surveyors; Quantity Surveyors' Society of B.C. (Pres. 1993-95); Canadian Construction Women (Founding Mbr.); Building Safety Advisory Council; Applied Science Technologists' & Technicians' Association. **INTERESTS:** design; art; music; sports; computers; gardening. **COMMENT:** *"A hard working woman trying to make a difference in the construction industry."*

Maheu, Hon. Shirley ■ ✦
Senator, THE SENATE OF CANADA, E. Block, Ste. 259, Ottawa, ON K1A 0A4 (613) 947-2212 or 1-800-267-7362, FAX 947-2215. Born Montreal 1931. m. Réne. 4 ch. Ronald, Richard, Daniel, Mark. **EDUC:** O'Sullivan Business Coll., Grad. **CAREER:** Mun. Councillor, City of Saint-Laurent, 1982-88; M.P. (Saint-Laurent-Cartierville), 1988-96; Official Opposition Critic for Multiculturalism & Citizenship, & Whip for Que., 1990-93; V-Chair, Standing Committee on Multiculturalism & Citizenship; Chair, Que. Caucus, Liberal Party of Canada, 1993-94; Deputy Chair of Committees of the Whole House, 1994-96; called to The Senate of Canada, 1996 (rep. the senatorial riding of Rougemont). **AFFIL:** Red Cross Society (Hon. Pres., Saint-Laurent Section); Insurance Brokers' Association of Quebec; Chamber of Commerce of Saint-Laurent; Carrefour Multi-Ethnique de Saint-Laurent; Fondation du Centre Hospitalier de Saint-Laurent; Liberal Party of Canada. **COMMENT:** *"Shirley Maheu was born in Montreal in 1931. She has a distinguished record of service as a parliamentarian."*

Mahoney, Kathleen E., LL.B., LL.M.(Cantab.) ⊗ ⚖
Professor, Faculty of Law, UNIVERSITY OF CAL-

GARY, 2500 University Dr. N.W., Calgary, AB T2N 1N4 (403) 239-8982, FAX 282-8325. Born 1947. m. Bryan E. Mahoney. 4 ch. **EDUC:** Univ. of British Columbia, LL.B. 1976; Univ. of Cambridge, LL.M. 1979; International Institute of Human Rights, Strasbourg, France, Diplôme (Int'l & Comparative Law of Human Rights) 1987. **BAR:** B.C., 1977; Alta., 1989. **CAREER:** Fac. Mbr. & Program Advisor, Western Judicial Educ. Centre, 1988 to date; Cnsl, Women's Legal Education & Action Fund (L.E.A.F.), in the Supreme Court of Canada in *R. v. Keegstra*; Prof., Fac. of Law, Univ. of Calgary, 1991 to date; Cnsl, Women's Legal Education & Action Fund, in the Supreme Court of Canada Intervention of *R. v. Butler*, 1992; Distinguished Visiting Scholar, Univ. of Adelaide, 1992; Visiting Fellow, Griffith Univ., Sch. of Law, 1993; Prof., Canadian Human Rights Foundation Int'l Cooperative Human Rights Training Program, Sherbrooke, Que., 1993; Cnsl & Advocate, International Court of Justice for Bosnia & Herzegovina in *Application of the Convention on the Prevention and Punishment of the Crime of Genocide* (Bosnia and Herzegovina v. Yugoslavia, [Serbia and Montenegro]), 1993 to date; Sir Allan Sewell Visiting Fellow, Sch. of Law, Griffith Univ., Brisbane, 1994; Visiting Prof., Fac. of Law, Australian National Univ., Canberra, 1994; Visiting Prof., Fac. of Law, Univ. of Western Australia, Perth, 1994; Visiting Prof., Law Sch., Univ. of Chicago, 1994; mbr., Canada-China Human Rights Research Proj., funded by CIDA, 1994-96. **SELECTED PUBLICATIONS:** *Women, The Law & The Economy*, ed. with E. Diane Pask & C.A. Brown (Butterworths, 1985); *Equality and Judicial Neutrality*, ed. with Sheilah L. Martin (Carswell, 1987); *Human Rights in the Twenty-First Century: A Global Challenge*, ed. with Paul J. Mahoney (Martinus, Nijoff, 1993); "The Constitutional Law of Equality in Canada" (*Journal of International Law & Politics* 24(2) 1992); "Gender Bias in Judicial Decisions" (*Judicial Review* 1(3) 1993); "Theoretical Perspectives on Women's Human Rights and Strategies for Their Implementation" (*Brooklyn Journal of International Law*, Vol. XXI 1996); "Hate Speech: Affirmation or Contradiction of Freedom of Expression" (*Univ. of Illinois Law Journal*, 1996); various other publications. **EDIT:** Ed. Bd., *Canadian Journal of Women and the Law*, 1987-89; Ed. Advisory Bd., 1989 to date; Bd. of Ed., *The National Journal of Constitutional Law*, 1990 to date; Bd. of Ed., *The University of New Brunswick Law Journal*, 1990 to date. **AFFIL:** International Centre, Univ. of Calgary (Advisory Bd.); Univ. of Calgary Group for Research & Education in Human Rights (Founding Mbr. & Chair); Alberta L.E.A.F. (Founding Dir. & Mbr.); Canadian Human Rights Foundation (Dir.); Canadian Institute for the Administration of Justice; Canadian Association of Law Teachers; Canadian Association of University Teachers; Dignity Foundation, Alberta (Co-Chair & Founding Dir.); Coalition Against Trafficking in Women, NGO, Consultative status with UNESCO (N.Am. Coord.). **HONS:** Peter Howard Memorial Scholarship, Fac. of Law, Univ. of British Columbia, 1976; Malcolm MacIntyre Memorial Trophy, First Place, Western Canada Trial Moot Court Competition, 1976; MacKenzie King Travelling Scholarship, 1978; Canadian Institute of Citizenship Scholarship, 1978; Law Foundation of B.C. Scholar, 1978; Woman of Distinction, Educ., YWCA, Calgary, 1985. **MISC:** Panelist & Back-Up Host, *Crossfire*, CBC-TV, 1985-90; Proj. Dir., CIDA-funded Int'l Proj. to Promote Fairness in Judicial Processes in South Africa, 1991-96; Olin Lectureship, Washington Univ., 1993; David C. Baum Mem. Lectureship, Univ. of Illinois, 1996; Special Rapporteur, Council of Europe Conference "Equality and Delivery," Strasbourg, France; numerous invited papers; numerous conference presentations. **COMMENT:** *"Professor Mahoney has published extensively on human rights, constitutional law and women's rights, as well as on gender and other forms of bias in the courts and in the legal profession. She lectures nationally and internationally, on topics related to human rights, constitutional law, gender, race and class bias in the courts and has appeared before the Supreme Court of Canada in a number of cases relating to freedom of speech, pornography and hate propaganda."*

Maidment, Karen, B.Comm.,C.A. ■ $
Vice-President and Chief Financial Officer, THE MUTUAL GROUP, 227 King St. S., Waterloo, ON N2J 4C5 (519) 888-3791, FAX 888-3899. Born Hamilton, Ont. 1958. m. David. **EDUC:** McMaster Univ., B.Comm. 1981. **CAREER:** Statements & Accts Officer, The Mutual Group, 1989-91; Fin. Exec., 1991-93; Dir., Corp. Fin., 1993-94; VP, Corp. & Capital Planning, 1994-96; VP & CFO, 1996 to date. **AFFIL:** Canadian Institute of Chartered Accountants (C.A.).

Maillet, Andrée, O.C.,G.O.Q. ■■ 📜 ✏ ☝
Author and Journalist. 28 Arlington Ave., Westmount, QC H3Y 2W4. Born Montreal 1921. m. Dr. L. Hamlyn Hobden. 3 ch. Dr. Roger Hobden, Dr. Alexandra Hobden, Dr. Christian Hobden. **EDUC:** post-grad. studies, N.Y. & Paris. **CAREER:** published first articles

at age 11; Correspondent in Paris, 1947-51; Journalist/Editorialist, *Petit Journal* & *Photo Journal*, Montreal; Publisher & Dir., *Amérique Française*; weekly column, *Le Devoir*. SELECTED PUBLICATIONS: novels: *Ristontac* (1945); *Le Marquiset têtu* (1965; Portuguese edit., 1972); *Le Chêne des Tempêtes* (1965 - 1st prize, Prov. of Que.); *Storm Oak* (children's stories, 1972); *Profil de l'Orignal* (1953, 1974, 1990); *Les Remparts de Québec* (1965, 1977, 1989); *Le Bois-pourri* (1971); *Le Doux Mal* (1972, 1991); *À la Mémoire d'un Héros* (1976); *Lettres au Surhomme* (1976, 1990); *Miroir de Salomé* (1977, 1990); poetry: *Elémentaires* (1964); *Le Paradigme de l'Idole* (1964); *Le Chant de l'Iroquoise* (1967); short stories: *Les Montréalais* (1963, 1987); *Le Lendemain n'est pas sans amour* (1963); *Nouvelles Montréalaises* (1966); *Le Bois de Renards* (1967); *Belle Gersende et l'Habitant* (1972); live theatre, radio & TV: *Souvenirs en Accords Brisés* (1969); *La Perdrière* (Radio Canada, TV, 1971); *La Dépendance* (1973); *Le Doux Mal* (1972); *Belle Gersende et l'Habitant* (Radio-Canada, radio); *Le Meurtre d'Igouille* (live, Que., 1965); *La Montréalaise* (1967); innumerable articles; translated into Portuguese, Welsh, Slovak & Danish. HONS: Officer of the Order of Canada, 1978; 'A' Award, Canadian Arts Council; Prix David, 1990 (officially stated that Andrée Maillet marks the beginning of modern lit. in French Canada); Grand Officier, Order of Quebec, 1991; Woman of the Year, Canadian Press, 1967, & Salon de la Femme, 1975; hon. mbr., PEN International, & Société des Écrivains Canadiens. MISC: First French-Canadian woman correspondant (accredited to French & British armies of occupation, Berlin).

Maillet, Antonine, C.C.,B.A.,M.A.,LL.D., Ph.D. ∎∎ 📖📁⊗
Writer. 355, rue Gilford, Montréal, QC H2T 1M6 (514) 845-0267, FAX 845-0712. President, LES PRODUCTIONS PÉLAGIE. Born Bouctouche, N.B. 1929. EDUC: Moncton Univ., B.A.(Lit.) 1950, M.A.(Lit.) 1959; Univ. de Montréal, LL.D.(Lit.) 1962; Univ. Laval, Ph.D.(Lit.) 1970. CAREER: Univ. Prof., Moncton, Laval, Montreal; Chancellor, Moncton Univ.; 33 books published in Montreal & Paris; more than 12 plays in Montreal theatres & more than 100 lectures in America, Europe & Africa. SELECTED CREDITS: *La Sagouine* (TV series); *GAPI* (film); *La Sagouine* (play); *Evangéline Deusse* (play); *La Contrebandière* (play); *William S.* (play); translator, *Jeanne La Pucelle* (musical). SELECTED PUBLICATIONS: *La Sagouine*; *Les Cordes de Bois*; *Pélagie-la-Charette*; *Le Huitième Jour*; *Les Confessions de Jeanne de Valois*; *Le Chemin St-Jacques*

(several translated into English & other languages). AFFIL: Union of Writers. HONS: 25 honorary univ. degrees; 10 literary prizes; Prix Goncourt, 1979; Member of the Privy Council of Canada; Companion of the Order of Canada; Commandeur de l'Ordre de Monaco; Officier de l'Ordre du Québec; Officier des Arts et des Lettres, France.

Mainprize, Daphne E.H. ∎∎ 📖📁
Director/Curator, STEPHEN LEACOCK MUSEUM/ARCHIVE, (nat'l historic site, tourist attraction, Leacock archives), 50 Museum Dr., P.O. Box 625, Orillia, ON L3V 6K5 (705) 329-1908, FAX 326-5578, EMAIL leacock@sparky.transdata.ca. Born Orillia, Ont. 1953. s. 2 ch. Anne E.M. Bristow, Craig R.L. Mainprize. EDUC: Wilfrid Laurier Univ., Hist. (degree incomplete) 1978; Ontario Museum Association, Museum Studies 1994. CAREER: Graphic Artist, *Orillia South* newspaper, 1987-89; sales, radio/newspaper, Telemedia Corp., 1989-91; owner, Gift Baskets Unlimited, 1989-93; Stephen Leacock Museum/Archive, 1991 to date. SELECTED CREDITS: Co-Producer with Jim Dykes, *A Sunshine Sketch* (Boathouse video, 10 mins., 1995); Dir., *The Voice of Stephen Leacock* (audio cassette). SELECTED PUBLICATIONS: currently working with J.A. McGarvey on book, *Leacock Picture Book*. EXHIBITIONS: Stephen Leacock's bedroom was recreated in the Leacock House with funds donated by the Rotary Club of Orillia; Leacock's Boathouse was rebuilt by the community as a "barnraising" in 24 hrs., Sept. 9/10, 1995; Leacock's study, where he did most of his writing, was also recreated. AFFIL: Rotary Club of Orillia; Orillia International Poetry Festival; St. George's Society of Orillia (VP; former Pres.); Leacock Heritage Festival; Simcoe North Progressive Conservative Association (Past Pres.); L.A.C.A.C., Orillia & East Gwillimbury (former mbr.); Sir Sam Steele Art Gallery (former VP); Downtown Management Bd. (former mbr.); Orillia & District Visitors & Convention Association (former mbr., Bd. of Dir.). HONS: Woman of Distinction, Orillia Business Women's Association, 1993 & 1994. INTERESTS: writing poetry; collecting antique books; reading; Leacock research. COMMENT: "*My love of history and literature has always drawn me to endeavours in the field of heritage and culture. In recent years, I have had the pleasure of developing my creative talents. My years at the Stephen Leacock Museum/Archives have been challenging, rewarding, exciting and, without a doubt, the best place to promote the best in Canadian culture. The support and encouragement of my family has allowed me the privilege of pursuing my dreams, in particular, my*

mother, who has always shown courage in her life, for which I have infinite respect. As Stephen Leacock wrote, "I am a great believer in luck; and I find the harder I work the more I have of it." I concur entirely."

Makus, Ingrid, B.A.,M.A.,Ph.D. ■ ■ ⬩ ❀
Assistant Professor, Department of Politics, BROCK UNIVERSITY, St. Catharines, ON L2S 3A1 (905) 688-5550, ext. 4077, FAX 988-9388. Born Canada 1958. m. Roger Lussier. 2 ch. Kira, Megan. EDUC: Univ. of Winnipeg, B.A.(Hons., Politics/English) 1981; Univ. of Toronto, M.A.(Politics) 1982, Ph.D.(Politics) 1993. CAREER: Lecturer, Dept. of Pol. Sci., Brandon Univ., 1986-93; Asst. Prof., Dept. of Pol. Studies, Univ. of Manitoba, 1993-94; Asst. Prof., Dept. of Politics, Brock Univ., 1994 to date. SELECTED PUBLICATIONS: *Women, Politics and Reproduction: The Liberal Legacy* (Univ. of Toronto Press, 1996). AFFIL: Canadian Political Science Association; American Political Science Association; Canadian Research Institute for the Advancement of Women; Canadian Women's Studies Association. HONS: Open Doctoral Fellowship, Univ. of Toronto, 1983-85. INTERESTS: political philosophy; Cdn politics; feminist theory. COMMENT: *"I teach and write in a university setting, about the relationship between political theory and feminist theory. My newly released book,* Women, Politics and Reproduction, *examines the roots of controversial political debates in Canada over reproductive rights and women's under-representation in politics."*

Malo, Nicole, B.A.,B.Sc.,M.Sc. ■ ❀
Sous-ministre, Ministère du revenu, GOUVERNEMENT DU QUÉBEC, 3800, rue Marly, Saint-Foy, QC G1X 4A5. Born Joliette, Qué. 1946. m. Bernard Ouimet. 2 ch. EDUC: Univ. de Montréal, B.Sc.(pédagogie) 1972; Univ. Laval, M.Sc.(sciences de l'éduc.-option admin. scolaire). CAREER: Éducatrice, Commission scolaire Chomedey-Laval, 1968-72; Agent de recherche et de planification, Direction générale de la planification, 1974-78; Chef du Service des politiques à l'enfance et à la famille, Ministère des Affaires sociales, 1978-81; Directrice de la réadaptation, Régie de l'assurance automobile du Québec, 1981-82; Directrice de l'indemnisation, 1982-84; VP à la planification et à la promotion de la sécurité routière, 1984-86; Prés., Office des ressources humaines, 1986-88; Sous-min., Ministère des Affaires culturelles, 1988-91; Sous-min., Ministère de l'Énergie et des Ressources, 1991-92; Sous-min., Ministère de l'Emploi, 1993-94; Sous-min., Ministère de la Sécurité du revenu, 1994-96; Sous-min., Ministère du Revenu, 1996 to date.

Malone, Deborah, B.Comm.,C.A. ■ $ ⊕
Director of Financial Services, SASKATOON DISTRICT HEALTH, 701 Queen St., Saskatoon, SK S7K 0M7 (306) 655-8444, FAX 655-5629. Born Montreal 1967. m. Tim. EDUC: Univ. of Saskatchewan, B.Comm.(Acctg) 1990. CAREER: Staff Acctnt, Deloitte & Touche, 1990-93; Sr. Acctnt, St. Paul's Hospital, 1994; Mgr of Fin. Svcs, 1994-96; Dir. of Fin. Svcs, Saskatoon District Health, 1996 to date. AFFIL: Basketball Saskatchewan (Bd. 1989-93); Saskatoon Chartered Accountants' Association; Canadian Institute of Chartered Accountants. INTERESTS: all sports; reading; coaching basketball. COMMENT: *"I am an outgoing and energetic person who works hard and plays hard. I pride myself on being a team player both in the office and out."*

Maloney, Sharon, B.A.,LL.B. ■ ⚖ ❀
Associate, MALONEY, GOTTLIEB & PEARSON GOVERNMENT RELATIONS, INC., The Madison Centre, 4950 Yonge St., Ste. 1800, North York, ON M2N 6K1 (416) 250-1550, FAX 250-7889. 1 ch. Alix Elin Rutsey. EDUC: Carleton Univ., B.A. 1973; McGill Univ., LL.B. 1979. BAR: Ont., 1981. CAREER: private practice of law, 1981-87; Exec. Dir., Canadian Shoe Retailers' Association, 1987-92; VP, Footwear, Retail Council of Canada, 1992-93; V-Chair & Secretariat, Footwear Council of Canada, 1993-94; Assoc., Gottlieb and Pearson, 1994 to date; Pres., Maloney, Gottlieb & Pearson Government Relations, Inc., 1994 to date. MISC: frequent public speaking engagements. COMMENT: *"Ms. Maloney has extensive experience in administration and government relations for trade organizations. She has acted on a variety of issues including market-value assessment in the City of Toronto, removal of imported pasta restrictions for Italian pasta importers and tariff rate quota for Canadian beef processors."*

Mamnguqsualuk, Victoria ⊗
Artist, BAKER LAKE FINE ARTS, Box 186, Baker Lake, NT X0C 0A0 (819) 795-2865, FAX 793-2000. Born Garry Lake, N.W.T. 1930. w. 9 ch. CAREER: artist. EXHIBITIONS: Mamnguqsualuk's work has been featured in more than 60 nat'l & int'l exhibitions; 3 solo exhibitions of work in Canada. COLLECTIONS: Amway Environmental Foundation Collection; Canadian Museum of Civilization; Inuit Cultural Institute, Rankin Inlet; Shell Canada Collections; Winnipeg Art Gallery; numerous other collections. HONS: Award for Craftsmanship & Design, 1974. MISC: accompanied Jessie Oonark to Ottawa for the presentation of the Sunday Missal of the Roman Catholic Church, 1976; presented one of her wallhangings on the

occasion of the transfer of Canadian Arctic Producers Ltd. shares from the fed. gov't to the Arctic Co-op, 1983; subject of numerous articles & monographs. COMMENT: *"Daughter of Jessie Oonark, one of Canada's foremost contemporary graphic artists. In early 1960s, Mamnguqsualuk abandoned her traditional nomadic lifestyle and settled permanently in Baker Lake. At age 33, she became involved in the community's embryonic art program. Over the past 30 years, she has become an accomplished graphic and textile artist, interpreting the old stories and legends told to her as a child."*

Mancuso, Maureen ■ ■ ⟨ ✤

Associate Professor and Department Chair, Department of Political Studies, UNIVERSITY OF GUELPH, Guelph, ON N1G 2W1 (519) 814-4120, ext. 6505/8939, FAX 837-9561, EMAIL Mancuso@css.uoguelph.ca. EDUC: McMaster Univ., B.A.(Hons., Pol. Sci. & Hist.-summa cum laude) 1982; Carleton Univ., M.A.(Pol. Sci.-with distinction) 1984; Nuffield Coll., Oxford, Ph.D.(Politics) 1991. CAREER: Cdn Parliamentary Intern (Research Asst. to Hon. Jean Chrétien & Hon. James McGrath, & Chrm's Asst., Special Committee on Reform of the House of Commons), House of Commons, Ottawa, 1984-85; Lecturer, Dept. of Pol. Sci., McMaster Univ., 1988; Asst. Prof., Dept. of Pol. Sci., Univ. of Windsor, 1989-91; Asst. Prof., Dept. of Pol. Studies, Univ. of Guelph, 1992-94; Assoc. Prof., 1994-96; Dept. Chair, 1996 to date; Visiting Research Fellow, Center for Congressional & Presidential Studies, American Univ., Washington, DC, Oct.-Dec. 1996. SELECTED PUBLICATIONS: *The Ethical World of British MPs* (McGill-Queen's Univ. Press, 1995); co-editor, *Leaders and Leadership in Canada* (Oxford Univ. Press, Mar. 1994); refereed articles, chpts. in books, papers, conference presentations; manuscript reviewer, Univ. of Toronto Press, *Canadian Public Administration, Governance, Canadian Journal of Political Science, Polity,* & Broadview Press; book reviewer, *Canadian Journal of Political Science, Canadian Public Policy.* AFFIL: Univ. of Guelph (mbr. of Senate 1994 to date); Auditor General of Canada (Consultant Mar. 1994); Ont. Grad. Scholarship Program (Assessor 1992-93); Ontario Legislature Internship Program (Selection Committee 1994-95);. HONS: "Popular Prof.," *Maclean's* magazine, "Guide to Universities," Jan. 1996; Teaching Award, Univ. of Guelph, Coll. of Social Sci., 1995-96; British Council Fellowship, 1985-91; various scholarships; numerous grants incl. SSHRC Major Research Grant, Apr. 1995. MISC: testimony to various parliamentary committees.

COMMENT: *"Political scientist, D.Phil., Oxford, specializing in comparative politics of industrialized states. Chair of Department of Political Studies, University of Guelph. Major research project on political ethics in Canada."*

Mandy, Pat, R.N.,B.A., M.P.A. ■ ⊕ ⟨

Vice-President, Patient Care–Community Hospital Services, HAMILTON CIVIC HOSPITALS, Henderson General Division, 711 Concession St, Hamilton, ON L8V 1C3 (905) 527-4322, ext. 2009, FAX 575-2641, EMAIL mandypat@hamcivhos.on.ca. Born Detroit 1945. m. Tom Mandy. 2 ch. Marilyn, Michael. EDUC: Hamilton Civic Hospitals Sch. of Nursing, R.N. 1965; McMaster Univ., B.A.(Soc.) 1978; Queen's Univ., M.P.A. 1990. CAREER: Gen. Duty Nurse, Hamilton General Hospital, 1965-67; Gen. Staff Nurse, Operating Rm., Henderson General Hospital, 1967-70; Asst. Operating Rm. Supervisor, 1970-73; Operating Rm. Supervisor, Chedoke Hospitals, Hamilton, 1973-78; Asst. Dir. of Nursing, Henderson General Hospital, 1978-81; Assoc. Dir., 1981-83; Dir. of Nursing, Hamilton Civic Hospitals, 1983-95; VP, Patient Care, 1995 to date; Educational Consultant, Nursing Mgmt Distance Educ. Program, 1985-87; Asst. Clinical Prof., Fac. of Health Sciences, McMaster Univ., 1994 to date. SELECTED PUBLICATIONS: "The Regulated Health Professions Act" (*Canadian Operating Room Nursing Journal* May/June 1992); "New Legislation in Ontario for Health Profession" (*Aboriginal Nurse* Nov. 1992). AFFIL: Canadian Nurses' Association; Registered Nurses' Association of Ontario (RNAO) (Prov. Nurse Administrators' Group); Aboriginal Nurses' Association of Canada; Academy of Chief Executive Nurses, Canada; Council of Nurse Executives, Ont.; Canadian Coll. of Health Service Executives (Certificate); Coll. of Nurses of Ontario (Council Mbr. 1987-94; VP 1989-91; Pres. 1991-94); Hamilton-Wentworth District Health Council (Chair; Past Chair, Mental Health Reform Planning Committee); Advisory Committee to the Advocacy Commission (Min. of Citizenship appointee); Hamilton Civic Hospitals Volunteer Association; Urban Native Homes Incorporated (Bd. Mbr.). HONS: Local 70 - Management Person of the Year Award, Ontario Nurses Association, 1985. INTERESTS: aboriginal health; health professions regulation; health policy. MISC: independent advisor to the Min. of Community & Social Services regarding the implementation of recommendations made by a Comprehensive Review Team of the Brantwood Centre; numerous presentations to conferences & professional meetings. COMMENT: *"Pat

Mandy is a member of the Mississauga, of the New Credit First Nation. She was the President of the College of Nurses of Ontario for three years during the proclamation and implementation of the Regulated Health Professions Act. Pat has been a member of several provincial and regional health planning and regulating committees."

Mangaard, Annette, AOCA 🎥 🖌
Filmmaker, THREE BLONDES INC., 72 Rusholme Rd., Toronto, ON M6J 3H6 (416) 537-8348, FAX 534-6542. Born Denmark 1956. cl. Don Truckey. 1 ch. Carson Mangaard. **EDUC:** Ontario Coll. of Art, AOCA (Fine Art) 1980. **CAREER:** independent filmmaker, 1984 to date; Resident, Canadian Film Centre, 1992-93. **SELECTED CREDITS:** Dir., Nothing by Mouth, 1984; Dir., She Bit Me Seriously, 1984; Dir., There Is in Power..Seduction, 1985; Dir., Her Soil Is Gold, 1985; Dir., The Tyranny of Architecture, 1987; Dir., The Iconography of Venus, 1987; Dir., Northbound Cairo, 1987, CBC Canadian Reflections, 1993; Dir., A Dialogue with Vision: The Art of Spring Hurlbut and Judith Schwarz, 1990, CBC Canadian Reflections, 1992; Dir., Let Me Wrap My Arms Around You, 1992, CBC Canadian Reflections, 1993; Dir., 94 Arcana Drive, 1993; Writer, Dir., & Co-Prod., Fish Tale Soup, 1996. **EXHIBITIONS:** Festival of Festivals, Toronto 1986, 1987, 1992; Grand opening of the National Gallery of Canada 1988; Kino Arsenal Cinémathèque, Berlin 1990; Vancouver Int'l Film Festival 1992; Atlantic Film Festival, Halifax 1993; numerous other festivals & screenings throughout Canada, US, Australia & UK. **COLLECTIONS:** A Dialogue with Vision: The Art of Spring Hurlbut and Judith Schwarz has been purchased for the collections of most major art galleries in Canada. **AFFIL:** Canadian Filmmakers' Distribution Centre (Past Bd. Chrm); IMAGES Festival of Independent Filmmakers of Toronto (Past Exec. Dir.); Liaison of Independent Filmmakers of Toronto (Past Bd. Mbr.); Toronto Women in Film & Television. **HONS:** Film Co-Production Award, Liaison of Independent Filmmakers of Toronto, 1989; Award of Merit, Charleston Film Festival, Houston, 1994. **MISC:** participated on panels & taught workshops on various aspects of independent filmmaking from fundraising & production to promotion; recipient of grants from various agencies, incl. Canada Council & Ontario Arts Council. **COMMENT:** "Annette Mangaard is an independent filmmaker who has written, directed and produced a number of acclaimed short dramas and documentaries, which have been screened at festivals and cinémathèques across Canada and Europe. "Fish

Tale Soup," starring Remy Girard, marks her debut as a feature film writer/director."

Mann, Susan, B.A.,M.A.,Ph.D. ■ 🎥 📚 🖊
President, YORK UNIVERSITY, 4700 Keele St., North York, ON M3J 1P3 (416) 736-5200, FAX 736-5641. Born Ottawa 1941. 1 ch. **EDUC:** Univ. of Toronto, B.A.(Modern Hist.) 1963; Univ. of Western Ontario, M.A.(Hist.) 1965; Laval Univ., Ph.D.(Histoire) 1970. **CAREER:** Lecturer in English, Tyo Eiwa Jogakuin, Tokyo, Japan, 1963-64; Chargée d'enseignement senior, Histoire, Univ. de Montréal, 1966-70; Asst. Prof., Hist., Univ. of Calgary, 1970-72; Asst. Prof., Hist., Univ. of Ottawa, 1972-74; Assoc. Prof., 1974-83; Chair, 1977-80; Prof., 1983-92; V-Rector, Academic, Univ. of Ottawa, 1984-90; Pres., York Univ., 1992 to date. **SELECTED PUBLICATIONS:** Stanley Knowles. The Man from Winnipeg North Centre (Western Producer Prairie Books, 1986); Dream of a Nation. A Social and Intellectual History of Quebec (Macmillan, 1982); The Twenties in Western Canada, ed. (Ottawa: National Museum of Man, 1972); Abbé Groulx, Variations on a Nationalist Theme, ed. (Copp Clark, 1975); Action Française: French Canadian Nationalism in the 1920s (Univ. of Toronto Press. 1975); "Feminist Biography" (Atlantis 10(2) 1985); "Thérèse Casgrain and the CCF in Quebec" (Canadian Historical Review 66(2) 1985); The Neglected Majority, ed. with Alison Prentice (McLelland & Stewart, vol. 1, 1977, vol. 11, 1985); "Gossip in History" (Canadian Historical Association, Historical Papers/Communications historiques 1985); numerous book reviews in scholarly journals; journalistic entries in Canadian Forum, Le Devoir, & New Canadian Encyclopedia; various other books & articles. **AFFIL:** Royal Society of Canada (Fellow); Senior Women Academic Administrators of Canada (Hon. Mbr.); Canadian Research Institute for the Advancement of Women (Hon. Life Mbr.); Council of Ontario Universities; Association of Universities & Colleges of Canada; Ontario Educational Communications Authority (TVOntario) (Bd. Mbr. 1994-97). **HONS:** Seagram Lecturer, Univ. of Toronto, 1984; Sec. of State Cdn Studies Prize for Excellence in Publication, Dream of Nation, 1984; LL.D.(Hon.), Concordia Univ., 1989; D.U.(Hon.), Univ. of Ottawa, 1994. **MISC:** 1st woman Pres. of York Univ.; 1st woman VP, Univ. of Ottawa; 1st woman Dept. Chair, Univ. of Ottawa. **COMMENT:** "An historian by training, a writer and teacher by avocation and a university administrator for fun."

Manning, Jo ⊗
Artist, R.R. 3, Blyth, ON N0M 1H0 (519)

523-4505. **EDUC:** Ontario Coll. of Art, Hons. Dipl.(Fine Art) 1945. **CAREER:** Etcher; Painter; Instructor, Printmaking, Univ. of Toronto, 1975; Instructor, Dundas Valley Sch. of Art. **SELECTED PUBLICATIONS:** illlustrations in numerous magazines & collections of poetry. **EXHIBITIONS:** Pollock Gallery, Toronto (1965-68); Univ. of Waterloo (1968); Gallery Pascal, Toronto (1974-80); Mira Godard Gallery, Montreal (1976); Calgary (1981); Bishop's Univ., Lennoxville, Que. (1990); numerous group shows. **COLLECTIONS:** many public, corp. & private collections. **AFFIL:** Canadian Society of Graphic Art (Past Pres.); Print & Drawing Council of Canada (Founding Mbr.); Blyth Festival Art Gallery; Huron Society of Artists. **INTERESTS:** concerns for the earth; emphasis on re-establishing the importance of the natural order; rebirth of primitive awe & fear of nature. **MISC:** numerous lectures & workshops. **COMMENT:** *"For the past six, seven years I have worked close to nature on an abandoned farm which is largely swamp. My work in oils, ink and drawing media pertains to the earth and our place within it."*

Manning, Lynne, B.A.,B.Ed. ⑤ ♂
Vice-President and Managing Director for Canada, KELLY SERVICES (CANADA) LTD., 1 University Ave., Ste. 300, Toronto, ON M5J 2P1 (416) 368-1058, FAX 368-3987. Born Edmonton. d. 3 ch. Lee Warren, Christine Warren, Patricia Warren. **EDUC:** Univ. of Alberta, B.A.(Modern Languages); B.Ed.(Educ.). **CAREER:** Mng Ptnr, Dunhill Temporary Systems, 1980-86; VP & Mng Dir. for Canada, Kelly Services (Canada) Ltd., 1987 to date. **DIRECTOR:** Kelly Services (Canada) Ltd. **AFFIL:** Federation of Temporary Help Services (Pres. 1989; Chrm, Gov't Liaison Committee 1995); Public Policy Forum (Dir. 1991 to date); Board of Trade of Metro Toronto (Labour Rel'ns Committee 1994-95). **HONS:** Leadership Award, Federation of Temporary Help Services, 1986; Exec. of the Year Award, Federation of Temporary Help Services, 1989; Bill Coke Award for Outstanding Contribution to the Temporary Help Industry, 1992. **INTERESTS:** reading; travelling. **COMMENT:** *"I am a Westerner by birth and have three daughters. I was a teacher before joining the staffing industry. The first woman to hold the positions of Vice-President and Managing Director for Kelly in Canada."*

Manzer, Alison R., B.Sc.,LL.B.,M.B.A. ■ ⚎
Partner, CASSELS BROCK & BLACKWELL, 40 King St. W., Ste. 2100, Toronto, ON M5H 3C2 (416) 869-5469, FAX 360-8877, EMAIL amanzer@casselsbrock.com. Born Saint John

1954. m. Glen Paul De La Franier. 2 ch. Amy Rose, Brian James. **EDUC:** Dalhousie Univ., B.Sc.(Chem. & Physics) 1974, B.Sc.(Biochem.) 1977, LL.B. 1977; Univ. of Toronto, M.B.A. 1984. **CAREER:** Assoc. Lawyer, Burt, Burt, Wolfe and Bowman, 1979-81; Assoc. Lawyer, Robins, Appleby & Taub, 1981-84; Ptnr, 1984-90; Exec. VP & Dir., Moyer Vico Corporation, 1987-89; Ptnr, Cassels Brock & Blackwell, 1990 to date. **SELECTED PUBLICATIONS:** more than 100 papers & lectures on bnkg, bankruptcy & insolvency, fin., gen. bus., insur. regulation, office mgmt, partnerships & shareholders, real estate & secured loan transactions, 1988 to date; *Bank Act Annotated*, text book; *A Practical Guide to Canadian Partnership Law*, text book; *CCH Commercial Law Guide–Banking and Negotiable Instruments*. **DIRECTOR:** Sottomayer Bank Canada. **AFFIL:** Canadian Bar Association–Ont. (Co-Chair, Paralegals Committee; Bus. Law Section Exec.; Program Chair, Continuing Legal Educ. Committee 1984-93; Chair, Fin. Institution Legislation Reform Committee); Canadian Bar Association (Chair, Fin. Institution Legislative Reform Committee; V-Chair, Continuing Legal Educ. Committee; Committee on Professional Liability; Council Mbr. 1984-94). **HONS:** Award, Contribution to Profession, Canadian Bar Association–Ont., 1991; various academic awards. **INTERESTS:** art collector; oenophile; horseback riding; hobby farming.

Manzer, Yvonne ■■ ⓔ ⚎ ◐
Administrative Co-ordinator, ELIZABETH FRY SOCIETY OF MAINLAND NOVA SCOTIA, (work with women in conflict with the law & women at risk), 2830 Agricola, Ste. 100, Halifax, NS B3K 4E4 (902) 454-5041, FAX 420-2873. Born Halifax 1953. s. 1 ch. Simon Manzer. **EDUC:** Saint Mary's Univ. & Univ. of New Brunswick, bus. courses; Dalhousie Univ., Maritime Sch. of Social Work, courses in Social Work 1991 to date. **CAREER:** Customer Asst., Xerox Canada Inc., 1974-82; Office Mgr, Co-operative Housing Federation of N.S., 1983-84; Group Leader, Katimavik, 1984-85; Counsellor, Bryony House (transition house), 1985-88; Research Asst., Psych., Dalhousie Univ., 1988; Program Coord., Canadian Book Information Centre, 1988; Admin. & Volunteer Coord., Alzheimer Society of N.S., 1989-93. **AFFIL:** OVO Housing Co-operative. **MISC:** vegetarian; single parent; lives in communal house in a housing co-op.

Maraden, Marti ⊗ ♥
Theatre Director and Actor. c/o Stratford Festival Theatre, Box 520, Stratford, ON N5A 6V2 (519) 271-4040. Born El Centro, Calif.

1945. EDUC: Univ. of Minnesota, 1963-64 & 1965-66; Michigan State Univ., 1966-68. CAREER: actor & dir.; Dir., Stratford Festival, 12 seasons; Assoc. Dir., Stratford Festival, 1992; Dir., The Young Company, Stratford Festival, 1992-93. SELECTED CREDITS: Dir., numerous Stratford prods. incl. *Macbeth, Alice Through the Looking Glass, The Illusion, Love's Labour's Lost, The Two Gentlemen of Verona, Les Belles Soeurs, The Merchant of Venice* (1996) & *Homeward Bound;* has appeared in more than 15 prods.; Dir., Shaw Festival prod. incl. *Getting Married, He Who Gets Slapped, Breaking the Silence* & *Tonight We Improvise* (co-dir. with Christopher Newton); played such roles as Cleopatra, *Caesar and Cleopatra* & Roxanne, *Cyrano de Bergerac;* other prod. dir. include: *Six Degrees of Separation, Fallen Angels* & *Homeward Bound* (Canadian Stage Company); *A Moon for the Misbegotten* (Theatre New Brunswick); *Waiting for the Parade* (Tarragon Theatre); *I Ought to be in Pictures* & *Hay Fever* (Grand Theatre); other stage appearances, include Bette Milner, *Number Our Days* (Mark Taper Forum, LA); Hermione, *The Winter's Tale* & Anna, *Barbarians* (off Broadway). AFFIL: Actors' Equity Association; American Federation of Radio & Television Artists; Canadian Actors' Equity Association; ACTRA. HONS: nominated, Outstanding Direction (*Fallen Angels*), Dora Awards, 1992; nominated, Outstanding Direction (*Six Degrees of Separation*), Dora Awards, 1995. MISC: dir. of *Homeward Bound* which won the Dora Award for Best Production, 1994.

Marchak, M. Patricia, B.A., Ph.D. ■ ⌇

Professor, Department of Anthropology and Sociology, UNIVERSITY OF BRITISH COLUMBIA, 6303 N.W. Marine Dr., Vancouver, B.C. V6T 1Z1 (604) 822-2548/2578, FAX 822-6096 or 822-6161, EMAIL marchak@arts.ubc.ca. Born Lethbridge, Alta. 1936. m. William. 2 ch. Gordon Eric Marchak, Lauren Craig Marchak. EDUC: Univ. of British Columbia, B.A.(Soc.) 1958, Ph.D.(Soc.) 1970. CAREER: part-time appointments as Sessional Lecturer, Instructor, Dept. of Anthro. & Soc., Univ. of British Columbia, 1965-72; Asst. Prof., 1973-75; Assoc. Prof., 1975-80; Prof., 1980 to date; Head, 1987-90; Dean of Arts, 1990-96; NDP prov. candidate, riding of Point Grey, 1983; Chair, B.C. Buildings Corporation, 1992-95. SELECTED PUBLICATIONS: *Ideological Perspectives on Canada* (Toronto: McGraw-Hill Ryerson, 1975); *Green Gold. The Forest Industry in British Columbia* (Vancouver: UBC Press, 1983); *The Integrated Circus. The "New*

Right" and the Restructuring of Global Markets (Montreal: McGill-Queen's Univ. Press, 1991); *Logging the Globe* (Montreal: McGill-Queen's Univ. Press 1995); *Racism, Sexism and the University: The Political Science Affair at UBC* (1996); "Women Workers and White Collar Unions" (*Canadian Review of Sociology and Anthropology* 10(2) 1973); "The Two Dimensions of Regionalism in Canada" (*Journal of Canadian Studies* 15(2) 1980); "The Re-Orientation of British Columbia Toward the Pacific" (*London Journal of Canadian Studies* 5 1988); "For Whom the Tree Falls: Restructuring of the Global Forest Industry" (*BC Studies* 90 1991); various other books, articles & other publications. EDIT: Ed., book review section, *Canadian Review of Sociology and Anthropology,* 1974-77; Ed. Bd., *Studies in Political Economy,* 1980-87; Ed. Bd., *Current Sociology,* Journal of the International Sociological Association, 1982-86; Assoc. Ed., *Canadian Journal of Sociology,* 1986-90; Ed. Bd., *BC Studies,* 1988-90. AFFIL: Canadian Sociology & Anthropology Association; Association for Canadian Studies; Canadian Political Science Association; International House of Japan, Tokyo; Royal Society of Canada (Fellow); Forest History Society; Ecotrust Canada (Bd. of Dir.); on boards of several community & professional associations. HONS: Kitsilano High Sch. Bursary, 1954; Senate Special Bursary, 1955; Canadian Women's Press Club Scholarship, 1956; MacMillan Family Fellowship, 1967-69; Research Fellowship, Institute of Industrial Relations, 1969; Inter-Univ. Consortium, Pol. Research Fellowship, Univ. of Michigan, 1967; John Porter Memorial Award, Green Gold, 1985; Outstanding Contributor Award, CSAA, 1990; Canada 125 Medal, 1993; invited participant, Deutscher Academischer Austauschdierst program, June 1993; Scholarship, Aspen Institute, Colorado, Aug. 1996. INTERESTS: hiking; swimming; skiing; painting; drawing; listening to music. MISC: Social Sciences & Humanities Research Council of Canada research funding, 1977-78; 1980-85; 1988-94, 1996-99; various consultancies; recipient, various grants; lecture tour of India, as Cdn Scholar, sponsored by Shastri Indo-Canadian Institute & Univ. Grants Commission, India, 1987; listed in various biographical sources, incl. *Canadian Who's Who, International Directory of Distinguished Leadership, Who's Where Among Writers* & *Who's Who in Sociology;* numerous keynote addresses & invited speeches. COMMENT: *"Professor of sociology of natural resource industries, ecology, especially forestry and fisheries; also writes about ideology and political economy, restructuring of world economy. Beginning new research project in South America starting in 1996 and continuing to 1999."*

Marchbank, Angela, B.Sc.(Kinesiology) ■ ■ ⓓ ⓞ

Executive Director, PRINCE EDWARD ISLAND SPECIAL OLYMPICS, (provides recreation, sport & fitness opportunities for persons with mental disabilities), P.O. Box 841, Charlottetown, PE C1A 7L9 (902) 368-4543, FAX 368-4542. Born Summerside, P.E.I. 1967. s. EDUC: Dalhousie Univ., B.Sc.(Kinesiology) 1989, Certified Fitness Appraiser 1990. CAREER: Fitness Leader/Strength Trainer, fitness studio, 1990-91; Active Living Coord., Town of Summerside (Pilot Proj.), 1992-94; Program Dir., Summerside YMCA, Apr.-Oct. 1994; Exec. Dir., P.E.I. Special Olympics, Oct. 1994 to date. AFFIL: Island Fitness Council (Pres. 1993-95; Past Pres. 1995 to date); Canadian Society of Exercise Physiology (CSEP); Fitness Appraisal Certification Accreditation Program of the CSEP; Certified Fitness Appraiser; Canadian Physical Activity, Fitness & Lifestyle Appraisal (course conductor). HONS: selected as one of three finalists for Coach of the Year, Sport PEI annual awards, 1993. INTERESTS: sports; reading; walking; cycling. COMMENT: *"Sincere, honest, easy listener, ambitious, organizer, healthy, volunteer, reliable, dedicated."*

Marcotte, Arlette, D.T.P.,M.B.A. ■ ■ ⓓ ⊕

Executive Director, ORDRE PROFESSIONNEL DES DIÉTÉTISTES DU QUÉBEC, (controls professional competency of its 2000 mbrs.), 1425 René-Lévesque Blvd. W., Ste. 703, Montreal, QC H3G 1T7 (514) 393-3733, FAX 393-3582, EMAIL opdq@opdq.org INTERNET http://www.opdq.org. Born Quebec City 1950. s. EDUC: Univ. of Montreal, B.Sc.(Nutrition) 1973; École des Hautes Études Commerciales, M.B.A. 1993. CAREER: Dir. of Nutrition Svcs, univ. teaching hospital, Montreal, 1991-95; int'l speaker. SELECTED PUBLICATIONS: "Diététique en Action" (*Scientific Journal of the OPDQ*); presentation on the professional health system in Que. & the place of the dietitian as a health provider, conference in Belgium, Oct. 1996. AFFIL: Canadian Dietetic Association; Dietitians of Canada; Sporting Club du Sanctuaire; Ste.-Justine Hospital for Sick Children (volunteer). HONS: Léo Scharry Award for Excellence in int'l mktg dossier, 1993. INTERESTS: nature & animals; gardening; meeting different people; English & Spanish languages. COMMENT: *"Dynamic and professional woman. I'm not afraid to take every opportunity to access new ways of doing things and to promote health and basic values in this era of change."*

Marcuse, Judith Rose ⊛ Ⓢ ㄷ

Artistic Director, JUDITH MARCUSE DANCE PROJECTS SOCIETY, 873 Beatty St., Ste. 402, Vancouver, BC V6B 2M6 (604) 606-6425, FAX 606-6432. Artistic Director, JUDITH MARCUSE DANCE COMPANY. Born Montreal 1947. m. Richard Frederick Marcuse. 1 ch. Rachel Katherine Marcuse. EDUC: modern & classical training with Elsie Salomons, Brian Macdonald, Sonia Chamberlain, Seda Zaré, 1950-62; National Ballet Summer Sch., 1960; Royal Ballet Sch., classes, with Barbara Feuster, Maria Fay, Pamela May, Clover Roope, Eileen Ward & others, 1962-65; classes, with Benjamin Harkarvy, Anthony Tudor, Hector Zaraspé, teachers of the Sch. of American Ballet, N.Y.C., various summer sessions; Banff Sch. of Fine Arts, classes with Vera Volkova, Brian Macdonald & others, 3 summers. CAREER: danced with various companies, incl. Les Grands Ballets Canadiens, Montreal, 1965-68; Bat-Dor Dance Company, Tel-Aviv, 1970-72; Ballet Rambert, London, UK, 1974-76; Artistic Dir., Judith Marcuse Dance Projects Society & Judith Marcuse Dance Company, 1980 to date; teacher, various classes in Canada, US & UK, 1972 to date; dir. & choreographer, 1974 to date. SELECTED CREDITS: choreographer, numerous dance productions incl. *Fusion*, Oakland Ballet, 1974; *Baby*, Ballet Rambert, UK 1975; *Four Working Songs*, Ballet Rambert, 1976 (remounted for Les Grands Ballets Canadiens, 1976); *Celebration*, Winnipeg's Contemporary Dancers, 1979; *Sadhana Dhoti*, Banff Festival, 1979 (remounted for Winnipeg's Contemporary Dancers, 1979); *Mirrors, Masques and Transformations*, Shaw Festival & the Judith Marcuse Dance Projects Society, 1980; *Spring Dances*, Les Grands Ballets Canadiens, 1981; *Cuts*, Dancemakers, 1981; *Playgrounds*, Judith Marcuse Dance Projects Society, 1981; *Transfer*, Nederlands Dans Theatre, The Hague, 1981; *In Concert: Judith Marcuse and Sacha Belinsky Dance* (program of solos & duets), World's Fair, Knoxville, Tenn., 1982; *Seascape*, Les Grands Ballets Canadiens, 1983 (remounted by Dance Projects Society; 1984 & the National Ballet of Portugal, 1987, 1994); *Hors d'Oeuvre*, Les Ballets Jazz de Montreal, 1983; *Currents*, Harbourfront Corporation, 1983; *Closed Circuit*, Dance Projects, 1985; *Playing Without Fire or The Final Flicker of the Flaming Ferromanganese Performers*, Dance Projects, 1987; *Moving Past Neutral*, Calgary Winter Olympics Arts Festival, 1988; *Tales from the Vaudeville Stage*, Dance Projects, 1991; *States of Grace*, Dance Projects, 1994; dir. & choreographer, numerous theatre & opera prods. incl. *Reflections on Crooked Walking*, Arts Club Theatre, Vancouver, 1982 (remounted 1983, 1987, 1992); *H.M.S. Pinafore*, Stratford Festival, 1981; Alcina, Vancouver Opera, 1994; choreographer for various film & video prods., incl. *H.M.S. Pinafore*, CBC TV, 1981; "Currents," *Canadance*, CBC TV, 1984; *Second Nature*, Rhodopsin Films, 1993; *At the Races*, Rhodopsin Films, 1994; *States of Grace*, CBC TV, 1994; Prod., *The Kiss Project* (a 5-week, multi-disciplinary festival), Dance Projects, Granville Island, B.C., 1995. **AFFIL:** Actors' Equity Association; ACTRA; Canadian Actors' Equity Association (Equity Council 1981-85); British Actors' Equity Association; Dance in Canada Association (Nat'l Bd. 1978-80); Vancouver Dance Centre Society (V-Chair & Bd. of Dir. 1992 to date); Cultural Svcs Branch, Prov. of B.C. (Dance Advisory Panel 1988-90). **HONS:** Chalmers Award for Choreography, 1976; Clifford E. Lee Award for Choreography, 1979; Woman of Distinction Award, Vancouver YWCA, 1985; Vancouver Award for Excellence in Theatre, 1986; Canada 125 Medal, 1992; Silver Juried Award (*Second Nature*) 1994 & (*At the Races*) 1995, New York City Int'l Dance Film & Video Festival; various other awards & grants. **INTERESTS:** cooking; travel; literature.

Margesson, Lynette, M.D.,FRCPC ⊕ 🐿

Assistant Professor of Medicine, QUEEN'S UNIVERSITY, 190 Wellington St., Ste. 400, Kingston, ON K7L 3E4 (613) 549-6660, FAX 547-2079. Born Toronto 1947. m. Dr. F. William Danby. 2 ch. **EDUC:** Univ. of Western Ontario, M.D. 1970; Univ. of Toronto, Dermatology Training 1975; American Board of Dermatology, Diploma 1975. **CAREER:** Dermatologist in private practice, Kingston, 1975 to date; Asst. Prof. of Medicine, Div. of Dermatology, Queen's Univ., to date; Lecturer in Obstetrics & Gynecology. **SELECTED PUBLICATIONS:** "Connective Tissue Diseases in the Skin–What You Would See and What You Would Order," with F.W. Danby (*Medicine of North America* 28 1982); "Vulvar Diseases: Common Problem, Difficult Diagnosis" (*Diagnosis* 2 1985); "11B-Hydroxyandrostenedione: A Marker of Adrenal Function in Hirsutism," with others (*Fertility and Sterility* 54 1990); "Porphyria Cutanea Tarda Due To Ferrous Gluconate," with others (*Canadian Medical Association Journal* Oct. 1990); "Erythema Multiforme with Ulcerative Stomatitis at Menstruation," with others (*The Canadian Journal of Ob/Gyn* Dec. 1990); "A Randomized, Double-Blind, Placebo-Controlled Trial of Ketoconazole 2% Shampoo Versus Selenium Sulfide 2.5% Shampoo in the Treatment of Moderate to Severe Dandruff," with others (*Journal of the American Academy of Dermatology* 29 1993). **AFFIL:** Canadian Dermatology Association (Past Dir.); Royal Coll. of Physicians & Surgeons of Canada (Fellow); American Academy of Dermatology (Fellow); Kingston District Wound Care Committee (Founder). **HONS:** Gold Award, St. Clements Sch., 1985. **INTERESTS:** skiing; fitness. **COMMENT:** *"For 20 years I have been in private practice in Dermatology in Kingston and an active teacher at Queen's University, and a continuous medical education lecturer in dermatology. I have set up a Kingston district Wound Care Committee, coordinating all institutions and nursing homes for the promotion of education and cost effectiveness in wound care. I have been very active in vulvar disease and helped organize a regional Vulvar Disease Clinic with Dept. of Ob/Gyn. I strongly feel that education of my community and my colleagues is my most important contribution."*

Markham, The Reverend Jean J. Burke, B.A. ■ ☼ 🛢

Pastor, THE BRITISH METHODIST EPISCOPAL CHURCH, (BME Church), 66 King St. W., Ste. 506, Mississauga, ON L5B 2H7 (905) 272-8207. Born Barbados, WI 1931. w. The Rt. Rev. Dr. A.S. Markham, M.Th.D.D., Bishop. **EDUC:** Albert Coll., Belleville, Ont., Bus. Admin. (Dip), Bus. 1958; Univ. of Toronto, B.A.(Gen. Arts) 1972; Ontario Theological Seminary, M.Div. program, incomplete, 1986-88, M.T.S. 1997. **CAREER:** teacher, shorthand, evening classes, Shaw's Bus. Sch., 1960s; owner & Mgr, Burke's Stenographic Services, 1960s; owner & Mgr, Burke's Employment Agency, 1960s; owner & Publisher, Rainbow Magazine, 1962-69; Exec. Sec., T. Eaton Co. Ltd., 1970-77; independent Real Estate Rep., 1980s; founder & Pastor, The Alexander S. Markham Memorial Methodist Episcopal Church, 1990-95; Present Min. (in charge) & Pastor, Peel Methodist Church (BME), 1995 to date. **SELECTED PUBLICATIONS:** various articles in *Apostle Magazine*. **EDIT:** Founding Ed., *Apostle Magazine*, Official Voice of the BME Church Conference, 1977 to date; Founding Ed., *Newsletter*, BME Church Conference, 1992 to date; ed. of several small booklets honouring women in church & community, 1975-89. **AFFIL:** BME Church Conference (Chair, Book & Publishing Committee; Founding Chair, Worship Manual & Hymnal Committee; Bd. of Christian Educ.; Historian); Canada Association of Ministers' Wives & Ministers' Widows (Founding Pres. & Pres. Emeritus); International Association of Ministers' Wives & Ministers' Widows (Life Mbr.; Central Chair, Int'l Annual Convention, Toronto,

1996); BME Conference Ministers' Wives League (Pres. Emeritus); Canada Sickle Cell Anemia (Life Mbr.; 1st Reg. Dir. 1970s); Ladies' League, Christ Church, BME (founding Pres. 1975-89). HONS: Plaque, Canada Association of Ministers' Wives & Widows, 1993; Plaque, Ladies' League, Christ Church, BME, Toronto; Plaque, Charter for Canada, International Association of Ministers' Wives & Widows, 1982; Certificate of Recognition, City of Mississauga, 1995; various real estate awards incl. Mbr. of Million Dollar Club, 1978, 1982. INTERESTS: selected social issues, esp. those that impact on the church family & its place in society; reading; writing; research; theatre; classical music; travel. MISC: 1st woman to found a BME Church in its 140-yr. history; 2nd woman to be ordained in the BME Church; presently writing the history of the BME Church from 1856 to present. COMMENT: *"A self-starter and pioneer of sorts. I seek justice, truth and order in every situation (they are necessary to my sense of well-being). A teacher by nature and example, challenging and encouraging others but stimulated by challenges, turning them into opportunities to chart a course so that others may follow with more or relative ease."*

Markowsky, Martha, A. (X) 📖
Artist. 216 Crichton St., Ottawa, ON K1M 1W4 (613) 749-6448. Born Lachine, Que. s. EXHIBITIONS: Gallery on the Lake, Buckhorn, Ont. (1993); Victoria Art Gallery, Toronto (1993); West End Gallery, Westmount, Que. (1995); Art Mode Gallery, Ottawa (1994), Galerie D'Art Vincent, Ottawa, (1995-96). COLLECTIONS: The Right Hon. Brian Mulroney; Ottawa Senators Hockey Association; The Sports Network; Fletcher Challenge Ltd.; Rockwell International; Canadian Museum of Civilization; Royal Ottawa Golf & Country Club; Yousef Karsh; Delta Ottawa Hotels; The Right Hon. Jean Crétien; CINRAM Toronto. AFFIL: Visual Arts Ontario. HONS: Loeb's Prize, Vanier Mural Competition; Best Oil Painting in Show, Westboro Fine Art Festival; MacDonald Club Scholarship. INTERESTS: walking; reading; skating; swimming. MISC: participant, 1995 Symposium de peinture de la Mauricie; participant, *Salon Biennal*, Société Nationale Des Beaux-Arts, Paris, France; represented by: Galerie d'Art Vincent, Ottawa; Art Mode Gallery, Ottawa; West End Gallery, Westmount; Galerie Art et Culture, Montreal; Diana Paul Gallery, Calgary; Adele Campbell Gallery, Whistler, BC; bibliographies appear in MagazinArt (1995), Canadian Artists' Guide (1996) & Guide Vallee III (1994). COMMENT: *"Martha Markowsky's career is dedicated to a world she deeply loves: the world of art. Painting in an intense manner, her works depict the activities of our lives–past and present–with subjects ranging from musical themes, cityscapes, barroom interiors, to the human figure."*

Marland, Margaret M., M.P.P. ✸ 👍
Member of the Provincial Parliament (Mississauga South) and Government Caucus Chair, GOVERNMENT OF ONTARIO, Queen's Park, Legislative Building, Rm. 169, Toronto, ON M7A 1A8 (416) 325-7731. Born St. Catharines, Ont. m. Dr. Kenneth Marland. 3 ch. CAREER: Bank Acctnt; Dental Asst.; Flight Attendant. POLITICAL CAREER: Trustee, Peel Bd. of Educ., 1974-78; Councillor, City of Mississauga, 1978-85; Councillor, Reg'l Municipality of Peel, 1978-85; elected, M.P.P. (Mississauga South), 1985; re-elected, 1987, 1990, 1995; in 1993 was appointed 1st female Chair, all-party Standing Committee on Gov't Agencies; past committee responsibilities include Gen. Gov't, Procedural Affairs, Resources Dev. Committee, Legislative Assembly Committee & as V-Chair on the Standing Committee on Estimates; Chair, Special Task Force on Gender in Sport; mbr., Select Committee on Educ., Select Committee on the Environment & PC Task Force on Extended Shopping Hours; past critic portfolios include, Culture & Citizenship, the Greater Toronto Area, Environment, Labour, Community & Social Svcs, Senior Citizens' Affairs & Women's Issues; served as Deputy House Leader for the PC Caucus. AFFIL: Rogers Community 10 (Advisory Bd.); United Way of Peel Region (1981-90); Mississauga Hospital Women's Auxiliary (former mbr.); St. Bride's Anglican Church (former mbr., Advisory Bd.); Peel Family Services (former bd. mbr.); Sheridan Coll. (Past Gov.); Oakville-Trafalgar Hospital (Past Gov.). INTERESTS: alpine skiing; photography; reading; flying. MISC: holds a private pilot's license & was the 1st female civilian to fly in the CF101 (Voodoo) jet fighter; sponsors an annual seniors' seminar & many public forums.

Marleau, The Hon. Diane, P.C.,M.P., B.A. ✸ ⊕
Minister, Public Works and Government Services Canada, GOVERNMENT OF CANADA, Parliament Buildings, Ottawa, ON K1A 0A6 (613) 957-0200, FAX 952-1154. Born Kirkland Lake, Ont. 1943. m. 3 ch. EDUC: Laurentian Univ., B.A.(Econ.). CAREER: Alderman, City of Sudbury, 1980-85; Reg'l Councillor, Sudbury Reg'l Council, 1980-85; mbr., Sudbury & District Health Unit Bd., 1981-82; mbr., Fin. Committee & Bd. of Dir., Laurentian Hospital,

1981-85; mbr., Ont. Advisory Council on Women's Issues, 1984; mbr., Northern Dev. Council, 1986-88; Chairperson, Bd. of Gov., Cambrian Coll., 1987-88; M.P., Liberal (Sudbury), Canada, 1988 to date; V-Chair, Nat'l Liberal Standing Committee on Policy, 1989; Chair, Ont. Liberal Caucus, 1990; Nat'l Exec., Liberal Party of Canada, 1990; Assoc. Critic for Gov't Oper., Liberal Party of Canada, 1990; Deputy Opposition Whip, Liberal Party of Canada, 1991; V-Chair, Standing Committee on Fin., 1992-93; Assoc. Critic for Fin., Liberal Party of Canada, 1992; Min. of Health, Gov't of Canada, 1993-96; Min., Public Works & Gov't Svcs Canada, 1996 to date. **HONS:** Paul Harris Award, 1996 **COMMENT:** *"On Nov. 4, 1993, Madame Diane Marleau was appointed Minister of Health in the Cabinet of the Right Hon. Jean Chrétien. In this capacity, she is responsible for maintaining a high-quality health system concerned with protecting and promoting the health of Canadians."*

Marois, The Hon. Pauline, MNA ■ ✦ ⬡
Member of the National Assembly (Taillon) and Minister of Education, GOVERNMENT OF QUÉBEC, 1035, rue De la Chevrotière, 16e etage, Quebec, QC G1R 5A5 (418) 644-0664, FAX 646-7551. Born Québec City 1949. m. 4 ch. **EDUC:** Univ. Laval, B.A.(Social Svc) 1971; École des hautes études commericales, Univ. de Montréal, M.B.A. 1976. **CAREER:** collaborated in setting up the ACEF de l'Outaouais, 1970-71; employed by Outaouais Reg'l Dev. Council, 197-73; Coord., social assistance tech. course, CÉGEP de Hull, 1973; Dir. Gen., CLSC de l'Ile-de-Hull, 1973-74; assisted in establishing social emergency svcs, CSS du Montréal metropolitain, 1974-76; Dir., specialized youth svcs, 1976-78; Press attaché to the Min. of Fin., Qué., 1978-79; Consultant, Association des CSS du Québec, 1979; Exec. Asst. to the Min. of State for the Status of Women, Qué., 1979-81; elected M.N.A. (La Peltrie), Apr. 1981; Min. of State for the Status of Women, 1981-83; V-Chrm, Conseil du trésor, 1982-85; Min. of Manpower & Income Security, 1993-85; Min. for Outaouais; placed 2nd at party convention to appoint new leader of the Parti Québécois, 1985; failed re-election, Dec. 1985; Consultant, Elizabeth Fry Society, 1988; Instructor, Univ. du Québec, 1988; program advisor, Parti Québécois, 1988; VP, Parti québécois, & Pres., exécutif national, 1988 to date; elected MNA (Taillon) Sept. 25, 1989; Chair, Committee on Social Affairs, 1989 to date; Opposition spokesperson on matters of industry & commerce, 1989-91; Opposition spokesperson on matters relating to the public admin. & integration of fed. public employees,

1991-93; Opposition spokesperson on matters relating to the environment, & integration of fed. public employees, 1993-94; re-elected MNA (Taillon) Sept. 12, 1994; Min. for Admin. & the Public Svc, 1994 to date; Chair of the Conseil du trésor, 1994 to date; Min. Responsible for Family Policy, 1994-96; Min. of Educ., 1996 to date. **AFFIL:** Amnesty International; Parti québécois.

Marr, Helen, B.A. ⬡ ○
President, INTERNATIONAL COUNCIL OF JEWISH WOMEN, 4700 Bathurst St., North York, ON M2R 1W8 (416) 633-5100, FAX 633-1956. Born Lindsay, Ont. 1934. m. Gerald. 3 ch. M. Shawn Marr, Pamela R. Marr, Peter S. Marr. **EDUC:** Univ. of Toronto, B.A.(Languages/Hist.) 1954; Ontario Coll. of Education, Certificate (Teaching); Royal Conservatory of Music, Vocal & Opera. **CAREER:** performer, Toronto Opera Company. **VOLUNTEER CAREER:** Past Pres., National Council of Jewish Women, Toronto Section; Past Pres., National Council of Jewish Women of Canada; VP, International Council of Jewish Women; VP, Baycrest Centre for Geriatric Care; Dir., Baycrest Centre Foundation; Committee Mbr., Skylight Theatre Seat Endowment Campaign; Sec., Canadian Associates of the Ben Gurion Univ. of the Negev; Delegate to U.N. Conference on Decade for Women, Nairobi, 1985; Chair, 14th Triennial Convention, International Council of Jewish Women, 1986; Pres., International Council of Jewish Women, 1990-93, 1993-96; Delegate to U.N.C.E.D., Rio de Janeiro, 1992; V-Chair, Bd. of Dir., Baycrest Centre; Exec. Mbr., Toronto Jewish Music Society. **HONS:** Community Service Award, National Council of Jewish Women of Canada, 1986; Hon. Chairperson, National Council of Jewish Women, Canada–Centenary Year, 1997. **INTERESTS:** family; art; music; travel. **COMMENT:** *"Committed to the improvement of the social, economic and legal status of all women worldwide under both Jewish and civil law, and to the best and highest interests of all humanity in the fields of international relations, government, social welfare and education; human rights."*

Marsden, Lorna, B.A.,Ph.D. ⬡ ✦ ⬡
President & Vice-Chancellor, WILFRID LAURIER UNIVERSITY, 75 University Ave., Waterloo, ON N2L 3C5 (519) 884-1970, FAX 746-2472, EMAIL marsden@mach2.wlu.ca. Born Sidney, B.C. 1942. m. Edward Harvey. **EDUC:** Univ. of Toronto, B.A.(Arts & Sci.) 1968; Princeton Univ., Ph.D.(Soc.) 1972. **CAREER:** Prof., Univ. of Toronto, 1972-92; Senator, Ont. (Toronto-Taddle Creek), 1984-92; Pres., Wilfrid Laurier Univ., 1992 to date. **SELECTED PUBLICA-**

TIONS: *The Fragile Federation: Social Change in Canada*, with E.B. Harvey (1979); *Lives of Their Own*, with Charles Jones & Lorne Tepperman (1990); over 50 other published chapters & refereed articles. DIRECTOR: Manulife Financial; Westcoast Energy; The Gore Mutual; Institute for Work and Health. AFFIL: The Laidlaw Foundation (Dir.); American Sociological Association; Canadian Sociology & Anthropology Association; Liberal Party of Canada; Canadian Federation of University Women; Business & Professional Women. HONS: Queen's Silver Jubilee Medal, 1978; Canada 125 Medal, 1993; Political Woman of the Year, Business & Professional Women, 1992; LL.D.(Hon.), Univ. of New Brunswick, 1990; LL.D.(Hon.), Univ. of Winnipeg, 1994; LL.D.(Hon.), Queen's Univ., 1995; LL.D.(Hon.), Univ. of Toronto, 1995. INTERESTS: women's movement; gardening; politics. COMMENT: *"Sociologist and university administrator, specializes in sociology of economic life, and is active in community."*

Marsden, Shirley A. ■■ ⊕ ♡ ♣ ♂
Volunteer. c/o Youthlink Agency, 34 Huntley St., Toronto, ON M4Y 2L2. Born Hamilton, Ont. 1927. w. 4 ch. Pamela Jane, Paul Carter, Geoffrey Alan, Hilary Anne. EDUC: sr. matriculation. CAREER: Prov. of Ont., 1944-47; International Harvester Company of Canada (1st woman selected for mgmt training course), 1947-54; Exec. Dir. for Prov. of Ont., Ontario Council, Canadian Figure Skating Association, 1979-88; Asst. to Mayor Lastman, City of North York, Metro Toronto Corporation, 1988-95; retired, 1995. AFFIL: Big Sisters Association of Metro Toronto (Pres., Big Sister Association, 1965 to date, operating Youthlink 1995-97; Bd. mbr. 1992 to date); Art Gallery of Ontario (volunteer, retail shop); Foundation of Metro Toronto Regional Conservation Authority (Bd. of Dir.); Black Creek Pioneer Village (Planning Committee); Metro Toronto Canadian National Exhibition Association (Co-Chair, Healthy Living Cluster); Canadian Olympic Association (Olympism in Action (formulating values & ethics) 1992 to date); P.C. Party, fed. & prov. (active mbr., P.C. Ont. Women's Association & P.C. Business Association, 1984 to date; Junior League of Hamilton (1957-66); Junior League of Toronto (various committees 1966 to date); Sport Ontario (Pres. & Treas. 1979-88); Ontario Association of Sports Administrators (Pres. & Treas. 1982-85); Women Active in Sports Administration (Pres. & Treas. 1982-88); Canadian Figure Skating Association (Bd. mbr. & Chair, Central Ont. Section 1976-79; Pres., Ont. Council 1976-79); Canadian Association for the

Advancement of Women in Sports (founding mbr., 1981 to date). INTERESTS: travel; knitting; gardening; reading.

Marshall, Geraldine, R.N.,B.A., B.Sc.N. ■ ⊕ ⊕
President, WORLD SCHIZOPHRENIA FELLOWSHIP, 3952 W. 18th Ave., Vancouver, BC V6S 1B7 (604) 222-0875, FAX 222-2662. Born Battleford, Sask. 1941. w. 2 ch. EDUC: Vancouver General Hospital, R.N. 1962; Univ. of Toronto, B.A.(Sci.) 1976; Ryerson Polytechnic Univ., B.Sc.N.(Psychiatry) 1986; Ph.D.(Mental Health Mgmt) in progress. CAREER: Therapist, Addiction Research Foundation; Therapist, Dept. of Psychiatry, Univ. of British Columbia; Coord. & Consultant, Family Svcs, Ministry of Health, B.C., & B.C. Schizophrenia Society. SELECTED PUBLICATIONS: *Education Manual for Families with Mentally Ill Members* (Geneva: World Health Organization; translated into 14 languages); "Partnership in Psychiatry," A Historical Event in Russian Psychiatry (*Russian Journal of Psychiatry*, Moscow, 1996). AFFIL: World Schizophrenic Fellowship (Pres.); World Association of Psychosocial Rehabilitation; B.C. Nurses' Association; B.C. Schizophrenia Society; Dr. R.N. Caulder Research Foundation (Dir); The Center for Education Training & Consultation in Mental Health, Seattle, Wash. (Dir.); World Association of Psychosocial Rehabilitation (Cdn Rep.); International Outreach for World Schizophrenia Fellowship (Dir. of Educ.). INTERESTS: miniature painting; short-story writing; sailing; adventure travel. MISC: founder, Canadian Emerald Ball, held annually in Vancouver, Winnipeg & Toronto; Founding Mbr., Russian Sch. of Social Work, Moscow & Arlangelisk. COMMENT: *"The past 10 years I have spent in major humanitarian endeavours around the world. The focus has been on developing educational partnership programs for professionals, families, consumers and governments. These programs are designed to alleviate the suffering of mental illness. Countries visited include Mexico, Japan, Bermuda, UK, Ireland, Singapore and several trips to Russia."*

Marshall, Heather, B.F.A.,M.B.A. ⊔ $
Deputy Director, Production Financing, Arts and Entertainment, CANADIAN BROADCASTING CORPORATION, Box 500, Stn. A, Toronto, ON (416) 205-6922, cell. (416) 464-3162, FAX 205-6923. Born London, Ont. 1952. m. Guenther Zuern. 1 ch. EDUC: York Univ., B.F.A. 1973, M.B.A. 1980. CAREER: film prod./owner, Marshall Business Affairs Inc.; Mgr, Program Contracts & Dev. of In-House Production, CBC, 1992-94; Deputy Dir., In-House

Production, Arts & Entertainment, 1994-95; Deputy Dir., Production Financing, Arts & Entertainment, 1996 to date. **SELECTED CREDITS:** bus. affairs svcs provider, *Inside Stories* (series), 1988; Exec. Prod., *Half the Kingdom* (documentary), National Film Board co-prod., 1989; Exec. Prod., *Shared Rhythm/Rythme du Monde* (documentary), NFB co-prod., 1990; Exec. Prod. & Prod., *Full Circle* (documentary), 1993; various other film & TV credits. **AFFIL:** Toronto Women in Film and Television

Marshall, Roz ⊗ ◁

Artist and Art Educator. Vancouver, BC Born Wales 1947. 2 ch. Kate, Tom. **EDUC:** Vancouver Sch. of Art, Grad.(Painting) 1970. **CAREER:** Alberta Coll. of Art, 1973-75; Teacher, Calgary Creative Sch., 1973-75; Art Teacher, York House Sch., Vancouver, 1975-78; Painting & Drawing Instructor, Langara Continuing Educ., 1981-93; Painting & Drawing Instructor, Arts Umbrella, Granville Island/Dunbar Community Centre, 1981 to date; Private Art Instructor, 1982-91; Univ. of British Columbia, Continuing Educ., 1982-94; Teacher, various Vancouver schools, 1987-92; Teacher, Summer Sch., Paradise Valley, N. Vancouver Sch. Bd., 1994. **EXHIBITIONS:** Bau-Xi Gallery, Toronto (1977, 1982, 1984, 1987, 1989, 1991); Bau-Xi Gallery, Vancouver (1977, 1978, 1980, 1982, 1983, 1985, 1986, 1988, 1990, 1992); Queen Elizabeth Theatre, Vancouver (1978); Prince George Art Gallery, Prince George, B.C. (1992); Still Life Installation, Buschlen-Mowatt Gallery (1993); One Woman's Journey, Buschlen-Mowatt Gallery (1994); Buschlen-Mowatt Gallery (1995); numerous group exhibitions incl. Emerging Canadian Artists, Muttart Gallery, Calgary (1981); Vancouver Arts and Artists, Vancouver Art Gallery, 1983; Trèsors d'Art, Singapore (1993); Art Auction, Vancouver Art Gallery (1994); one-woman show, John Ramsay Gallery (1996). **COLLECTIONS:** Canada Council Art Bank; Claridge Collection, Montreal; Esso; Univ. of Lethbridge; Husky Oil; many other public & private collections. **INTERESTS:** travel; fabric arts; ceramics; house renovation & decoration; furniture painting; gardening; reading. **MISC:** recipient, several grants; subject of numerous articles & documentaries. **COMMENT:** *"As a painter, I've become very interested in expressing femaleness because that is who I am. When I was starting out, there was no apparent tradition of a 'female way of expression' in the Visual Arts. To make it in a 'man's world' you had to express yourself as a man. I've been interested in finding a way for women."*

Martel, Shelley, D.M., M.P.P.,B.A. ✦

Member of the Provincial Parliament (Sudbury East), **GOVERNMENT OF ONTARIO**, Hanmer Valley Shopping Centre, Hanmer, ON P3P 1P7 (705) 969-3261, FAX 969-3538. Born Sudbury, Ont. 1963. m. Howard Hampton. 1 ch. **EDUC:** Univ. of Toronto, B.A.(Int'l Pol.) 1985; Univ. of Paris–Sorbonne (IV), Certificate of French Language 1986. **CAREER:** Claims Adjudicator, Workers' Compensation Bd., 1986-87; M.P.P. (Sudbury E.), 1987 to date; Min. of Northern Dev. & Mines, 1990-94; Gov't House Leader, 1990-91. **AFFIL:** Robin's Hill Aftercare Inc.; Sudbury Women's Centre; YWCA, Sudbury. **INTERESTS:** cross-country skiing; reading.

Martens, Debra, B.A.,M.A. ▯ ▤ ◁

Writer, Editor and Educator. Box 766, Stn. B, Ottawa, ON K1P 5P8. Born St. Catharines, Ont. 1957. m. Douglas Scott Proudfoot. 2 ch. **EDUC:** Univ. of Toronto, B.A.(English Lit./Hist.) 1981; McGill Univ., M.A.(English Lit.) 1986. **CAREER:** fiction writer; book reviewer/essayist; freelance ed.; adult educator; Contributing Ed., *Paragraph: The Canadian Fiction Review*. **SELECTED PUBLICATIONS:** "The Waterfight" (*Baker's Dozen: Stories by Women*, Toronto: Women's Press, 1984); "The Pip" (*Room of One's Own* 2 1987); *Bonne Chance: A Story* (Toronto: St.car Editions, 1989); "Afterwards" (*Paragraph Winter 93/Spring 94*); "Love Art," *Love's Shadow*, ed. Amber Coverdale (Sunrall, Freedom, Calif.: The Crossing Press, 1993); "The Past Projected: Mavis Gallant and Joseph Roth" (*Essays on Canadian Writing* 42 1990); "Laurence of Africa" (*Paragraph* Summer 1994); numerous other stories, essays, book reviews & ed. works. **AFFIL:** Canadian Authors' Association; Editors' Association of Canada; Indexing & Abstracting Society of Canada; Montreal Women's Literature Reading Group. **INTERESTS:** literature; education; feminism; the environment; Third World issues. **HONS:** Explorations Grant, Canada Council, 1988; Arts Writing Grant, Ont. Arts Council, 1992; Arts Grant, Reg'l Municipality of Ottawa-Carleton, 1994. **MISC:** lives in New Delhi.

Martens, Ethel, B.A.,M.P.H., Ph.D. ⊕ ◁ ▯

Consultant, Primary Health Care, **BAHA'I INTERNATIONAL COMMUNITY**, c/o Rideau Place, 550 Wilbrod St., Ste. 316, Ottawa, ON K1N 6N2 (613) 565-1959, FAX 565-1172, EMAIL av945@freenet.carleton.ca. Born Le Pas, Man. 1916. s. **EDUC:** Normal Sch., Winnipeg, Teacher's Certificate 1936; Univ. of Manitoba, B.A.(Econ. & Int'l Rel'ns) 1954; Univ. of California, Berkeley, M.P.H.(Health Educ.) 1957; Univ. of Saskatchewan, Ph.D.(Social & Preventative Medicine) 1973. **CAREER:** teacher, Man., 1936-41; teacher, Sci. & Math., Australia & England, 1948-51; health educator, Prov. of Man. Health Dept., 1954-58; Sr. Consultant, Health Educ., Health & Welfare Canada Medical Svcs Branch, 1958-73; Prof., Univ. Centre Health Sciences, Yaounde, Cameroon, Africa, 1973-76; Clinical Assoc. Prof., Univ. of North Carolina, 1976-78; Exec. Dir., Health & Social Svc Centre, Winnipeg, 1980-82; First Exec. Sec., Baha'i Int'l Health Agency, 1982-86; Consultant, Primary Health Care, Baha'i Int'l Community, 1985 to date. **SELECTED PUBLICATIONS:** "Canada: A Pilot Project" (*International Journal of Health Education*, Oct.-Dec. 1962); "Health Education and Health Development: A Baha'i Approach to International Health" (*Baha'i Studies Note Book*, Aug. 1985); "Primary Health Care and the Empowerment of Women," essay in *The Greatness Which Might Be Theirs–Reflections on the Agenda and Platform for Action for the United Nations Fourth World Conference on Women* (Baha'i Int'l Community Office for the Advancement of Women, Aug.-Sept. 1995). **DIRECTOR:** Intra Delta Management Consultants Inc. (Pres. of Bd.). **AFFIL:** Canadian Public Health Association; Association for Teachers of Community Health; Univ. of Saskatchewan (Alumni); Univ. of Manitoba (Alumni); Match International; Baha'i Faith; United Nations Association; Canadian Wildlife Federation. **INTERESTS:** phys. fitness; t'ai chi; reading; music; art; family & friends. **MISC:** mbr., Interdepartmental Committee on Community Dev., special planning secretariat, Privy Council, 1966-68; mbr., task force to study the reports of the Royal Commission on the Status of Women, five committees; many recommendations turned into law; presented papers at many nat'l & int'l conferences; 1st person to be bestowed Ph.D. in Social & Preventive Medicine from a Cdn univ. **COMMENT:** *"Innovative methods of health education, community development and training technology have enabled me to empower disadvantaged people to design and implement programs that help them to improve their lives socially and economically."*

Martens, Jean 🌸 ⚗️
President, BRITISH COLUMBIA AMATEUR SOFTBALL ASSOCIATION, Sunnyside Mall, Box 45570, Surrey, BC V4A 9N3 (604) 531-0044, FAX 531-8831. Born Matsqui, B.C. m. C. Neil Martens. 2 ch. J.C. Connors, A.D. Martens. **VOLUNTEER CAREER:** Coach/Team Mgr, B.C. Amateur Softball Association; Dir., B.C. Amateur Softball Association; Team Mgr, Canada Minor Summer Games; Registered Umpire; Pres., B.C. Amateur Softball Association; Instructor, Softball B.C. Summer Skill Dev. Schools. **AFFIL:** B.C. Summer Games; Sport B.C.; Canada Cup/Challenge Cup; Abbotsford/Matsqui Sports Facility Promotion; Int'l Training in Communication; Nat'l Coaching Certification Program (Certified 1978; Qualified Level 2 Instructor); Western Canada Amateur Softball Association; American Softball Association; International Softball Federation; Softball Canada (Jury Mbr., Skill Achievement Awards). **HONS:** Award for Outstanding Youth Service, Softball B.C./Softball Canada. **INTERESTS:** helping others to feel sense of purpose through recreation; cooking; crafts; sewing; outdoor activities; travel. **COMMENT:** *"The game of softball has given me direction and enjoyment. I am trying to give back to the sport and its participants the benefits I have received. I believe sport teaches life skills and gives youngsters opportunity."*

Martin, Carol 📖 📚
Writing and Publishing Consultant. Box 106, Thomasburg, ON K0K 3H0 (613) 478-1753, FAX 478-1756. Born Ottawa 1935. d. 3 ch. **EDUC:** Carleton Univ., Journalism 1958-59. **CAREER:** various positions, The Readers' Club of Canada Limited, 1959-78; Co-Founder & Sr. Ed., Peter Martin Associated Limited, 1965-77; Pres. & Publisher, 1977-81; Program Officer, Writing & Publishing Section, The Canada Council, 1981-88; independent consultant, writing, editing & publishing, 1988 to date. **SELECTED PUBLICATIONS:** *Martha Black: Gold Rush Pioneer* (Douglas & McIntyre, Aug. 1996); Ed., *Local Colour: Writers Discovering Canada* (Douglas & McIntyre, 1994); *Arthur Lismer* (Quarry Press, Fall 1995); "Textbooks of Our Own" (*The Canadian Forum*, Oct., 1994); "The Invisible World of Canadian Magazines" (*The Canadian Forum*, April 1993); *North: Landscape of the Imagination*, a catalogue for an exhibition of books, magazines and art at The National Library of Canada (1993); "A Torch for All Time," chapter, *McGill: A Celebration* (McGill-Queen's University Press, 1991); *Canadian Nomads: Travel Writing in the 20th Century*, catalogue, The National Library of Canada (1991); book reviews for *The Toronto Star* and the *Kingston Whig-Standard*, 1988-89. **EDIT:** Ed. Bd., *The Canadian Forum*. **INTERESTS:** gardening; reading. **MISC:** involved in the founding of the Children's Book Centre, the Independent Publishers' Association (later the Association of Canadian Publishers), the Association for the Export of Canadian Books, & the Belford Book

Distributing Company. COMMENT: *"My various job contracts have included coordinating special book projects, assisting with the development of a publishing program for large print books for the National Library of Canada, preparing a yearly statistical survey of book publishing for the Canada Council, and assessing grant applications and serving on juries for various government agencies and arts councils."*

Martin, Denny ■ ■ $

President and Owner, DENI M. ORIGINALS (direct sales, women's wear), 710 Cochrane Dr., Markham, ON L3R 5N7 (905) 940-3364, FAX 940-9071. Born Toronto. m. Al. 3 ch. Todd, Craig, Jaimi. CAREER: Sr. Sales Dir., Mary Kay Cosmetics, 1976-84; co-founder & Pres., Weekender Ladies Wear, 1984-94; Pres. & owner, Deni M. Originals, 1994 to date. AFFIL: Direct Sellers' Education Foundation (Bd. mbr.); Terry Fox Run; M.S. Society. HONS: many awards for top sales & leadership. INTERESTS: golf; cooking; gardening; travel. MISC: built company up to $40 million in sales in 8 yrs.; believes "success is a decision." COMMENT: *"Thousands of women have profited professionally and personally because of Denny's belief in their potential combined with her own business ethics and integrity."*

Martin, Eudel, B.A.,M.Min. ■ ■ ☼ ⟨ᔆ⟩

Regional Administrative Secretary, Global Missions, THE CHURCH OF GOD OF PROPHECY, P.O. Box 34753, Nairobi, Kenya, East Africa 011-254-2-47465 or P.O. Box 37320-2910, Cleveland, TN, USA 37320 (423) 559-5336. Born Jamaica 1945. m. Rev. Dr. Hubert. 1 ch. Ian D. Martin. EDUC: Humber Coll., Diploma (Nursing) 1978; Richmond Coll., B.A.(Psych. & Religion) 1982; Maryland Coll. & Seminary, M.Min.(Religious Educ./Counselling) 1990. CAREER: Religious Educ. Teacher & Dir., West-End Church of God of Prophecy, 1972-82; Instructor, Bible Training Institute, Church of God of Prophecy, 1982-90; Teen & Family Counsellor, Church of God of Prophecy, 1983-94; community nursing, Victorian Order of Nurses, 1986-89; part-time Nursing Supervisor, Casa Verde Health Centre, 1992-94. SELECTED CREDITS: *We Shall Be Changed* (album), Majestic label, 1978 - with West-End Church of God of Prophecy Concert Choir, of which she was organizer & director, 1975-85. SELECTED PUBLICATIONS: writer/reporter, church magazine with int'l circ. to 103 countries; editor/publisher, *The Regional Voice*, East Africa church publication, 1990 to date. AFFIL: Registered Nurses' Association of Ontario

(mbr. 1978 to date); Pan-Afric Community Development (Exec. Sec. 1993); Women's Ministries (Dir. 1990 to date). HONS: hon. doctorate in Humanities, Maryland Theological Seminary, 1992. MISC: designing & coordinating primary sch. proj. in Bubala, Uganda - many of the children are orphans whose parents were victims of the AIDS virus; coordinating building & dev. of orphanage & clinic for children who were orphaned during genocide in Rwanda in 1993-94. COMMENT: *"Canadian of African/Jamaican descent. Educated in Canada, Britain and the U.S. Registered nurse, Christian education instructor and counsellor. Speaker at women's conferences and Bible Training Institute in U.S., Canada, West Indies, Africa and Europe. Twenty-seven years as Minister's wife—presently a missionary in East Africa. Love people and have positively affected the lives of thousands. Very gratified with the gift of life and living!"*

Martin, Freda, D.P.M.,L.M.C.C., M.D. ⟨ᔆ⟩ ⊕ ◯

Executive Director, C.M. HINCKS TREATMENT CENTRE, 440 Jarvis St., Toronto, ON M4Y 2H4. 2 ch. Andrew Kenneth, Peter Charles. EDUC: Univ. of Toronto, M.D. 1956, L.M.C.C. 1957; Conjoint Examining Bd. for UK, D.P.M. 1960; Society of Analytical Psychology, Assoc. Professional Mbr. 1961, Full Professional Mbr. 1966; Royal Coll. of Psychiatrists (Founder Mbr. 1971; Fellow); Royal Coll. of Psychiatrists of Canada (Fellow). CAREER: Clinical Asst., Maudsley Day Hospital, London, UK, 1957-58; Clinical Asst., National Hospital for Nervous Diseases, London, UK, 1958-59; Registrar, Bethlem Royal & Maudsley Hospital, 1959-60; Registrar, Tavistock Clinic, Dept. for Children & Parents, 1960-62; Sr. Registrar, Tavistock Clinic, 1962-63; Consultant, Tavistock Institute of Human Rel'n, Sch. of Family Psychiatry & Community Mental Health, 1964-69; Consultant, Tavistock Clinic, 1969-72; Consultant & Chrm of Dept., 1972-75; Assoc. Prof., Dept. of Psychiatry, Univ. of Ottawa, 1975-80; full-time staff & Dir., Psychiatric Outpatient Dept., Children's Hospital of Eastern Ontario, 1975-80; Assoc. Prof., Dept. of Psychiatry, Univ. of Toronto, 1980 to date; Chief of Svc, Child & Family Studies Centre, Clarke Institute of Psychiatry, Toronto, 1981-84; Exec. Dir., C.M. Hincks Treatment Centre, Toronto, 1984 to date; Dir., C.M. Hincks Institute, 1986 to date. SELECTED PUBLICATIONS: 6 refereed publications; 5 chapters in books. EDIT: Ed. Bd., *Psychiatric Journal of the University of Ottawa*. AFFIL: Canadian Academy of Child Psychiatrists; Alpha Omega Alpha (elected 1955); Journal of

Family Therapy (Bd. of Assessors); Canadian Institute for Advanced Research (Advisory Bd.): Invest in Kids Foundation (Professional Advisor); Lawson Foundation. **MISC:** *Canadian Who's Who; Ontario Who's Who;* 30 presentations & lectures; 15 Int'l workshops.

Martin, Jane, B.A.,M.A. Ⓧ
Artist. **EDUC:** Bishop's Univ., B.A.(Hons., English/Hist.) 1965; Carleton Univ., M.A.(Cdn Studies) 1966. **CAREER:** Artist. **SELECTED PUBLICATIONS:** "Who Judges Whom?" (*Atlantis* 1 1979); various reports & appearances in catalogues; book & magazine covers. **EXHIBITIONS:** *Berkeley Castle Works 1984-87* Toronto (1987); *Gathie's Cupboard/Emblems/ Transfigurations,* Gallery 101, Ottawa (1989); *Wrapture,* Open Space, Victoria (1991); *Rose Show,* Toronto (1993); *The Four Show,* Toronto (1995); numerous other solo & group exhibitions. **COLLECTIONS:** Art Gallery of Greater Victoria; Agnes Etherington, Kingston, Ont.; Canada Council Art Bank; Canadian Advisory Council on the Status of Women; City of Ottawa; Memorial Univ. of Newfoundland Art Gallery; National Gallery of Canada; National Library of Canada; Robert McLaughlin Gallery, Oshawa, Ont.; Winnipeg Art Gallery. **AFFIL:** Canadian Reprography Collective (Founding Bd.); Canadian Artists' Representation (Exec.; Founder, Copyright Collective 1988; Dir., Copyright Collective, 1989-91; Nat'l Rep. 1989-91). **MISC:** subject of numerous newspaper & magazine articles. **COMMENT:** *"My concerns as an artist and arts activist have been with the analysis and achievement of love, truth and justice, which now, more than ever, seem a fool's errand."*

Martin, Marcia Ⓨ Ⓧ Ⓦ
Vice-President, Production, CITYTV, 299 Queen St. W., Toronto, ON M5V 2Z5 (416) 591-5757, FAX (416) 591-3545. Vice-President, CHUMCITY PRODUCTIONS. Born Portland, Me. **EDUC:** American Univ., Washington, DC, B.A.(Soc.). **CAREER:** various positions with Citytv & ChumCity, 1972 to date: incl. Mgr of Production Svcs; Dir. of News Oper.; currently VP, Production. **SELECTED CREDITS:** Supervising Prod., *I Am a Hotel;* Production Mgr, *Titans,* ChumCity Productions; Prod., *Toronto Trilogy;* Supervising Prod. of *FT-Fashion Television; MT-Movie Television; CityLine; Media Television; Life On Venus Ave.; Ooh La La; Ed's Night Party; The Originals; TVTV-The Television Revolution* & *Yo Canada.* **AFFIL:** Canadian Film & Television Production Association; Academy of Canadian Cinema & Television; Centennial Coll. (Advisory Bd.).

Martin, Mary-Lou, R.N.,B.Sc.N.,M.Sc.N., M.Ed. ■ ⊕
Acting Director of Nursing Practice and Clinical Nurse Specialist, HAMILTON PSYCHIATRIC HOSPITAL, 100 W 5th St, Hamilton, ON L8N 3K7 (905) 388-2511, FAX 336-0704, EMAIL martinm@fhs.mcmaster.ca. Born Toronto 1954. m. Robert W. Hill. 2 ch. Skyler Hill, Sierra Martin. **EDUC:** Ryerson Polytechnic Institute, R.N. 1975; Univ. of Toronto, B.Sc.N. 1980, M.Sc.N. 1986, M.Ed. 1994; McMaster Univ., doctoral studies in progress. **CAREER:** Staff Nurse, Queen St. Mental Health Centre, 1975-77; Charge Nurse, 1978-80; Community Nurse, Victorian Order of Nurses, 1979; Area Supervisor, Hamilton Psychiatric Hospital, 1980-85; Clinical Nurse Specialist, 1985 to date; Asst. Clinical Prof., McMaster Univ., 1987 to date; Acting Dir. of Nursing, 1994 to date. **SELECTED PUBLICATIONS:** "Thought Disorder and Aggression," with B. Johnson *et al* (*The Canadian Nurse,* 1995); "Sexual Knowledge Interview Schedule: Reliability," with C. Forchuk *et al* (*Journal of Intellectual Disability Research,* 1995); "Linking Research and Practice," with C. Forchuk (*International Nursing Review,* 1994); various other publications. **AFFIL:** Canadian Clinical Nurse Specialist Interest Group (Pres. 1993-95); Ontario Clinical Nurse Specialist Interest Group (Chair 1990-91); Sigma Theta Tau International Honour Society in Nursing; Wentworth Montessori Sch. (Mktg & Fundraising Committees). **HONS:** Kathleen Howe Mitchell Award, RNAO Foundation, 1996. **INTERESTS:** downhill & cross-country skiing; reading; photography; travel; my son's soccer games & dance activities; my daughter's kindergym activities. **COMMENT:** *"To Sierre, Skyler and Bob...who helped me experience the fun of motherhood and career, the unpredictability of life and a treasured discovery."*

Martin, Nancy, Ph.D. ■■ ❀ ⊕ ⊲
Assistant Professor, Department of Microbiology and Immunology, QUEEN'S UNIVERSITY, Kingston, ON K7L 3N6 (613) 545-2460, FAX 545-6796, EMAIL nlm@post.queensu.ca. Born Hamilton, Ont. 1959. m. John F. Ostrander. **EDUC:** Univ. of Guelph, B.Sc.(Zoology) 1982, M.Sc.(Microbiol.) 1984; Univ. of British Columbia, Ph.D.(Microbiol.) 1992. **CAREER:** Postdoctoral Fellow, Harvard Medical Sch., 1992-94; Research Assoc., Univ. of Calgary, 1994-95; Asst. Prof., Queen's Univ., 1995 to date. **SELECTED PUBLICATIONS:** author/co-author, 21 publications in scientific journals or texts on molecular mechanisms of protein folding, bacterial pathogenesis & antibiotic resistance mechanisms. **AFFIL:** Canadian Society of

Microbiology; American Society of Microbiology. **COMMENT:** *"I am a teacher and a researcher with a keen interest in understanding, at the molecular level, how bacteria survive and cause disease in their hosts."*

Martin, Nora, B.Sc.,M.Sc. ■ $

Senior Vice-President, UFL FOODS INC., 450 Superior Blvd., Mississauga, ON L5T 2R9 (905) 670-7726, FAX 670-7751. Born Toronto 1946. m. Robert Redbourn. **EDUC:** Univ. of Toronto, B.Sc.(Food Sci.) 1969, M.Sc. 1972. **CAREER:** R. & D., Gay Lea Foods, 1969-71; Dir., R. & D., Home Maid Foods Ltd., 1973; Dir., R. & D., Standard Spice Ltd., 1973-74; Consultant, Nado International & Alta. Dept. of Agric., 1975; Tech. Dir. & Gen. Mgr, Central Reg., Universal Foods Ltd., 1975-81. **DIRECTOR:** UFL Foods Inc. **AFFIL:** Canadian Institute of Food Science & Technology; Institute of Food Technologists; Women in Food Industry Management; Canadian Spice Association (Past Pres.); Agriculture & Agri-food Canada (Research Branch Advisory Committee); Food Institute of Canada.

Martin, Renée H., B.Sc.,Ph.D., F.C.C.M.G. 🎓 ⊕ ⚛

Professor, Department of Medical Genetics, UNIVERSITY OF CALGARY, Genetics Department, Alberta Children's Hospital, Calgary, AB T2T 5C7 (403) 229-7369, FAX 229-7624, EMAIL renee@ach.ucalgary.edu. Born Sweden 1948. m. Ken Maclean. 2 ch. Kyle Maclean, David Maclean. **EDUC:** Univ. of British Columbia, B.Sc.(Zoology) 1971, Ph.D.(Medical Genetics) 1975. **CAREER:** Instructor & Coord., Natural Sciences, Fraser Valley Coll., 1975-77; Asst. Prof., Univ. of Calgary, 1978-82; Assoc. Prof., 1982-88; Prof., 1988 to date; Scientist, Alberta Heritage Foundation for Medical Research, 1989-94. **SELECTED PUBLICATIONS:** more than 100 scientific publications, incl. "The effect of age on the frequency of sperm chromosomal abnormalities in normal men," with A.W. Rademaker (*American Journal of Human Genetics*, 41 1987); "Variation in the frequency and type of sperm chromosomal abnormalities among normal men," with Rademaker *et al* (*Human Genetics*, 77 1987); "A comparison of chromosomal aberrations induced by *in vivo* radiotherapy in human sperm and lymphocytes," with Rademaker *et al* (*Mutation Research*, 226 1989); "The distribution of aneuploidy in human gametes: comparison between human sperm and oocytes," with E. Ko & A. Rademaker (*American Journal of Medical Genetics*, 39 1991); "Effect of cryopreservation on the frequency of chromosomal abnormalities and sex ratio in human sperm," with A. Rademaker & J.E. Chernos (*Fertility Digest*, 4 1992); "Detection of aneuploidy in human interphase spermatozoa by fluorescence *in situ* hybridization (FISH)," with E. Ko & K. Chan (*Cytogenetic Cell Genetics*, 64 1993); "Analysis of sperm chromosome complements from a man heterozygous for a pericentric inversion of chromosome 1" (*Human Genetics*, 93 1994); "Multicolour fluorescence *in situ* hydridization analysis of aneuploidy and diploidy frequencies in 225, 846 sperm from 10 normal men," with E.L. Springgs & A. Rodemaker (*Biology Reproduction*, 54 1996). **AFFIL:** Medical Genetics Research Group (Chair); Canadian Fertility & Andrology Society (Chair, Ethics Committee); Canadian College Medical Geneticists (Bd.); Univ. of Calgary (Chair, Gender & Equity Issues Committee); American Fertility Society; American Society of Human Genetics; Genetics Society of Canada; European Society of Human Genetics; European Society of Reproduction & Embryology; Organ Sharing Canada (Genetics Consultant). **HONS:** Gold Star Letter for Teaching, Univ. of Calgary, 1988, 1990; Award of Excellence in Research, Univ. of Calgary, 1990. **MISC:** recipient, numerous grants; reviewed grants for various bodies, incl. NATO, the Medical Research Council of Canada, Health & Welfare Canada, & reviewed manuscripts for numerous journals incl. Human Genetics, Journal of Reproduction and Fertility, Environmental and Molecular Mutagenesis, & Proceedings of the National Academy of Sciences.

Martin, Sally E., R.N.,B.N.,M.H.Sc., C.H.E. ■■ ⊕

Vice-President, Surgical Programs, THE WELLESLEY CENTRAL HOSPITAL, 160 Wellesley St. E., Toronto, ON M4Y 1J3 (416) 926-7009, FAX 926-4908. Born Montreal 1945. s. **EDUC:** Montreal Gen. Hospital, R.N.(Nursing) 1966; McGill Univ., B.N.(Nursing Admin.) 1975; Univ. of Toronto, M.H.Sc.(Health Admin.) 1993. **CAREER:** Staff Nurse & Asst. Head Nurse, Surgical Intensive Care Unit, Montreal Gen. Hospital, 1966-70; Head Nurse, Surgical ICU, 1970-73; Head Nurse, Orthopedics, 1975-77; Nursing Coord., Huronia District Hospital, Midland, Ont., 1977-80; Asst. Dir. of Nursing, Toronto Western Hospital, 1980-85; Dir. of Nursing, Surgical Svcs, Toronto Western Div., The Toronto Hospital, 1985-90; Dir. of Nursing, The Toronto Hospital, 1990-92; Accreditation Coord., Oshawa Gen. Hospital, 1993; Proj. Coord., Central Hospital, Toronto, 1993-94; Asst. Administrator, Patient Care, 1994-96; VP, Surgical Programs, Wellesley Central Hospital, 1996 to date. **AFFIL:** Mid-Toronto Community Centre (Bd. mbr.;

Chair, Hum. Res.); Health Executive Forum (Exec. mbr.; Treas.); Canadian Coll. of Health Service Executives (Certified Health Exec.); Registered Nurses Association of Ontario (Professional Association mbr.). INTERESTS: computers; skiing; gardening; swimming. MISC: poster presentation, OHA convention, 1994 ("Reengineering in the OR and SPD"). COMMENT: *"I have been a health care executive for several years and have been involved in mergers and alliances, the most recent mergers being Central Hospital and The Wellesley Hospital, and The Wellesley Central Hospital's alliance with Women's College Hospital. We are faced with many challenges during this time of restructuring of the health care system."*

Martin, Sheilah, Q.C.,B.C.L.,LL.B.,LL.M., S.J.D. ⌘ ▱

Dean, Faculty of Law, UNIVERSITY OF CALGARY, 2500 University Dr. NW, Calgary, AB T2N 1N4 (403) 220-5447, FAX 282-8325, EMAIL smartin@ucdasvm1.admin.ucalgary.ca. Born Montreal 1957. m. John Courtright. 2 ch. EDUC: McGill Univ., B.C.L.(Civil Law) 1981, LL.B. 1981; Univ. of Alberta, LL.M. 1983; Univ. of Toronto, Doctor of Juridical Sciences 1991. BAR: Alta. CAREER: Asst. Prof., Fac. of Law, Univ. of Calgary, 1982-85; Visiting Prof., Osgoode Hall Law Sch., York Univ., 1986-87; Assoc. Prof., Fac. of Law, Univ. of Calgary, 1982-92; Prof. & Acting Dean, Fac. of Law, 1992; Prof. & Dean, Fac. of Law, 1992 to date. SELECTED PUBLICATIONS: *Quebec Laws* (Montreal: Guerin, 1983); *Defendez Vos Droits* with E. Grofier Atala (Montreal: Quebec Amerique, 1984); *Equality and Judicial Neutrality*, ed. with Kathleen E. Mahoney (Toronto: Carswell, 1987); "Canada's Abortion Law and the Canadian Charter of Rights and Freedoms" (*Canadian Journal of Women and the Law* 2 1986); "Women as Lawmakers" (*Alberta Law Review* 30 1992); "Some Constitutional Considerations of Sexual Violence Against Women" (*Alberta Law Review* 34 1994); numerous chapters, book reviews, reports & invited papers. AFFIL: Law Society of Alberta; Calgary Bar Association; Canadian Association of Law Teachers; Canadian Bar Association (Alta. Branch); Canadian Institute for the Administration of Justice; Canadian Research Institute for the Advancement of Women; National Association of Women & the Law; Women's Legal Education & Action Fund. HONS: Scholarship for Academic Excellence, McGill Univ., 1977-80; Fac. of Law Bursary, Univ. of Alberta, 1981; Superior Teaching Award, Univ. of Calgary Students' Union, 1985, 1988; Doctoral Fellowship, Social Sciences & Humanities Research Council of Canada, 1989; Women of Distinction Award for the Advancement of Women, Calgary YWCA, 1990; Distinguished Service Award for Legal Scholarship, Law Society of Alberta & Canadian Bar Association; Queen's Counsel, 1995. INTERESTS: swimming; cycling; running; baseball; reading. COMMENT: *"Most of my professional and personal life has been spent on issues relating to women, equality, and the law."*

Martin, Sue Ann, B.A.,M.A., Ph.D. ■ ⌘ ⊗ ▨

Professor of Dramatic Art, and Dean, Faculty of Arts, UNIVERSITY OF WINDSOR, 401 Sunset, Windsor, ON N9B 3P4 (519) 253-4232, ext. 2029, FAX 973-7050, EMAIL smartin@uwindsor.ca. Born Detroit 1940. 2 ch. Pamela Martin Campbell, David Harrison Martin. EDUC: Wayne State Univ., Detroit, B.A.(Pol. Sci.) 1961, M.A.(TV) 1963, Ph.D.(Speech) 1969. CAREER: Dir., Sch. of Dramatic Art, Univ. of Windsor, to 1991; (Full) Prof., to date; Dean, Fac. of Arts, to date. SELECTED PUBLICATIONS: *Sprouts: Projects for Creative Growth in Children*, with H. Green (Chicago: Good Apple, 1981); *Treasure Hunts: Creative Projects for Discovering the Classics*, with H. Green (Chicago: Good Apple, 1983); *Research Workout*, with H. Green (Chicago: Good Apple, 1984); "Techniques for More Effective Reading or Telling of Stories to Children" (*Elementary English Journal* 1968); "Using Developmental Drama with Brain-Damaged Children" (*Canadian Child-Youth Drama Association Journal* Feb. 1976); "How to Use Television as an Educational Tool" (*Alberta Teachers' Association Journal* 1978); "A Passion for Words: An Actor's Approach to Voice, Speech, and Interpretation" (*Dramatics Magazine* Mar. 1989); various other publications. HONS: Award for Teaching Excellence, Ontario Confederation of University Faculty Associations. INTERESTS: oral tradition & storytelling; interdisciplinary studies. MISC: various workshops & invited lectures; comm. consultant for bus. & industry; creative problem-solving consultant for bus. & academe. COMMENT: *"The Arts give each of us a space in which to stand back to ponder, to meditate and to think upon the human condition. The Arts core can illuminate every discipline in academe. The studio portion of the Arts core can raise a student's self-esteem, give the student an opportunity to fulfill the "making" urge. The Arts core nurtures an appreciation of the Arts and the cultures that produce them. Some of the Arts encourage teamwork and collaboration. And all of the Arts develop flexibility–a necessary skill for the student in the 21st*

Century who will have not one, but at least two, careers in her/his lifetime."

Martin Matthews, Anne, Ph.D. ■ 🎓

Professor, Department of Family Studies, UNIVERSITY OF GUELPH, Guelph, ON N1G 2W1 (519) 824-4120, ext. 8747, FAX 766-0691, EMAIL amm@uoguelph.ca. Born St. John's 1951. m. Dr. David Ralph Matthews. 2 ch. Adam, Leah. **EDUC:** Memorial Univ. of Newfoundland, B.A.(Soc. & Anthro.) 1971; McMaster Univ., M.A.(Soc.) 1974, Ph.D. 1980. **CAREER:** Lecturer, Dept. of Family Studies, Univ. of Guelph, 1978-80; Asst. Prof., 1980-84; Dir., Gerontology Research Centre, 1983-95; Assoc. Prof., 1984-91; Prof., 1991 to date; Visiting Research Scholar, Oxford Univ., 1992-93. **SELECTED CREDITS:** writer, narrator, interviewer for the instructional video "Aging in a Rural Environment," Office of Educational Practice, Univ. of Guelph (1983). **SELECTED PUBLICATIONS:** *Widowhood in Later Life* (Toronto: Butterworths, 1991); "Infertility and Involuntary Childlessness: The Transition to Non-Parenthood," with Ralph Matthews (*Journal of Marriage and the Family* 48(3) 1986); "Social Supports of the Rural Widowed Elderly" (*The Journal of Rural Health* 4(3) 1988); "Growing Old in Aging Communities," with Alun E. Joseph (*Journal of Canadian Studies* 28(1) 1993); "Widow and Widowerhood" (*Encyclopedia of Gerontology*, 1996); numerous other publications. **EDIT:** Social Sciences Ed., *Canadian Journal on Aging/Revue canadienne du vieillissement*, 1993-96; Ed.-in-Chief, 1996 to date. **AFFIL:** Canadian Association on Gerontology (Chair, Social Sciences Div. 1983-85); Gerontological Society of America (Elected Fellow); Gerontology Research Council of Ontario; International Sociological Association; Advisory Committee, Seniors Independence Research Program, Health Canada; Ontario Gerontology Association (1st VP 1981-85). **INTERESTS:** informal & formal supports of the elderly; policies related to aging in rural environments; widowhood; social psychological responses to infertility & its treatment. **MISC:** Co-Principal Investigator, The Canadian Aging Research Network (CARNET), funded by the Networks of Centres of Excellence Program, Gov't of Canada. **COMMENT:** *"Through my teaching, research and professional involvements, I am committed to advancing research and education on Canada's aging population, and its implications for social policy."*

Martinson, Jeanne $ 🎓

Partner, MARTRAIN CORPORATE AND PERSONAL DEVELOPMENT, 2320 Smith St., Regina, SK S4P 2P6 (306) 569-0388, FAX 781-7438. Born Assiniboia, Sask. 1962. d. **EDUC:** Southern Alberta Institute of Technology, Dipl.(Journalism Arts) 1982; Heriot-Watt Univ., M.B.A. in progress; Certified Practitioner, Neuro-Linguistic Programming 1993; Certified Practitioner, Hypnotherapy 1993; Certified Practitioner, Time Line Therapy 1993. **CAREER:** Acct Exec., Calgary Herald, 1980-83; Special Officer, Economics Laboratory, 1983-85; Comm. Officer, Ipsco Inc., 1985; Acct Exec., Southam Paragon Graphics, 1987-92; Ptnr & Trainer, MARTRAIN Corp. and Personal Dev., 1992 to date. **SELECTED PUBLICATIONS:** "Just Say No" (*Saskatchewan Training and Development Association Newsletter* Fall 1994); "Women Mentoring Women" (*Regina Business* Nov. 1994). **AFFIL:** Women Entrepreneurs of Saskatchewan Inc. (Pres.); Advisory Council for the Bridging Program for Women; Saskatchewan Business & Professional Women (Past Pres.); Canadian Federation of Business & Professional Women (Bd.; VP 1992-94); Saskatchewan Training & Development Association, Regina Chapter (Exec. member). **HONS:** Canada 125 Medal; Saskatchewan Outstanding Business & Professional Woman of the Year, 1994; nominated, Entrepreneur of the Year. **INTERESTS:** int'l travel; personal growth; educ.; psych. & mental health; studying other cultures & countries' social systems. **MISC:** developed "Women Mentoring Women" program for Univ. of Regina & community coll.; on Founding Bd., Women Entrepreneurs of Saskatchewan Inc. **COMMENT:** *"I am an entrepreneur, traveller and adventurer on the challenging path of becoming a superior communicator and trainer in the field of linguistics, communications and personal development."*

Martinuzzi, Bruna, B.A.,M.A. $

Manager of Administration and Human Resources, CANWEST GAS SUPPLY INC., 1285 West Pender St., 7th Fl., Vancouver, BC V6E 4B1 (604) 661-3331, FAX (604) 661-3347. Born Cairo, Egypt 1947. m. Saul Clamen. **EDUC:** Univ. of British Columbia, B.A.(English/French) 1981, M.A.(French) 1984, Ph.D. (partial completion) 1985-88. **CAREER:** various positions, from Exec. Asst. to the Chrm, to Mgr of Admin. & Hum. Res., British Columbia Petroleum Corporation (later CanWest Gas Supply Inc.), 1974 to date. **SELECTED PUBLICATIONS:** "Analyse spatiale d'Amphitryon" (*Papers on French XVII Century Literature* v.XI 1984); "Kid's Day," *Human Resources Management in Canada* (Prentice Hall, 1992). **AFFIL:** American Management Association International; Human Resources Management Association. **HONS:** Izaak Killam Predoctoral

Fellowship, 1987, 1988; B.C. Workplace Excellence Award, Canadian Mental Health Association, 1992. **MISC:** multi-lingual: Italian, German, French, Greek, Arabic. **COMMENT:** *"My achievements include pursuing a successful academic education up to the level of Ph.D. while maintaining a business career that helped me progress from Executive Assistant to a managerial position without neglecting the most important part of my life: my 24-year marriage to my husband, Saul."*

Mascoll, Beverly ■■ $ ♡

President, **MASCOLL BEAUTY SUPPLY LTD.**, (distributor of beauty products for Black consumers) and **THE BEVERLY MASCOLL COMMUNITY FOUNDATION**, 39 Orfus Rd., Toronto, ON M6A 1L7 (416) 256-2036, FAX 256-2025. Founder. Born Halifax, N.S. m. Emerson. 1 ch. Eldon. **CAREER:** Exec. Asst., major beauty supply co.; incorporated own co. specializing in products for Black consumers, 1970; Mascoll Beauty Supply Ltd. now one of Canada's leading beauty supply companies, mfg & distributing across Canada; holds seminars for professional hair stylists, beauty schools & beauty consultants. **AFFIL:** Dalhousie Univ. (Co-Chair, Toronto Campaign Committee, James Robinson Johnston Chair-1st Chair in Black Cdn Studies); Univ. of Guelph (Bd. of Gov.); Ryerson Polytechnic Univ. (Advisory Bd., Sch. of Bus. Mgmt); The Learning Partnership (Dir.); Ontario Video Gaming Corporation (Dir.); Allied Beauty Association (Dir.); Harry Jerome Scholarship Fund (Trustee); Black Educators (Hon. Patron); Eva Smith Bursary (Hon. Patron); The Canadian Club (VP); Ontario Black History Society; Barber & Beauty Supply Institute; Black Business & Professional Association; Ontario Science Centre (former Dir.); YMCA, Metro Toronto (former mbr., Youth Enterprise Advisory Committee); Women on the Move Awards, *The Toronto Sun* (Judge 1993). **HONS:** Achievement Award, Association of Black Women, 1985; Contrast-Black Achievement Award (Bus.), 1989; Harry Jerome Award for outstanding achievement in bus., 1991; Black Business Week Female Entrepreneur Award, 1992; Gov. Gen.'s Commemorative Medal for 125th Anniversary of Cdn Confederation, 1992; Woman of Distinction, Entrepreneurship, YWCA, 1993; Wall of Honour award, N.S. Black Cultural Centre, 1994; Canadian Black Achievement Award, Bus., 1994; Toronto Onyx Lions Club Award, 1995; Human Rel'ns Award, Canadian Council of Christians & Jews, 1995; City of North York Award, 1996. **INTERESTS:** fitness; reading; music; theatre. **MISC:** The Beverly Mascoll Community Foundation, non-profit charitable organization committed to raising funds to support community-enriching projects; mission & goals: to provide post-secondary educational scholarships; to promote the advancement of women; to assist in the dev. of youth & children.

Mascioli-Mansell, Josephina Lea (Jo Lee), B.Mus.,M.Mus. ■■ ♡ ✋ $

International Chairman and Chief Executive Officer, **YES! INTERNATIONAL** (Youth Empowered Solutions; not-for-profit corporation spearheaded by kids worldwide; cyberspace United Nations for youth; endorsed by the UN, UNEP & UNICEF), 13-135 The Royal York Hotel, Toronto, ON M5J 1E3 (416) 360-4898, FAX 861-9800, EMAIL curious@unicom.org. Born Timmins, Ont. d. **EDUC:** Univ. of Toronto, B.Mus.(Hons.); Univ. of Montreal, M.Mus. **CAREER:** narration & voice-overs, 1966-90; internationally known writer, lecturer & Emmy Award-winning dir., 1976-90; philanthropist, most notably with youth, 1985 to date; founder, YES! International. **AFFIL:** Angel Flight (L.A. Advisor 1992-96); Canadian American Society (San Francisco Advisor 1988-96); Global Peace (N.Y. Advisor 1995-96). **HONS:** Badge of Honour for Vocal Creative Range, Univ. of Montreal, 1972; Most Outgoing Personality in Daytime Writing, L.A., 1979; Best Foreign Creative Talent (Cdn in US), 1979; Best Dir., *General Hospital*, 1982; Outstanding Indiv. Contributor of the Year, AASK America, 1987; Woman of the Year, Northern California, 1989; Outstanding Rhythmic Narration in Children's Stories, Motion Picture & Film, US, 1992; Hottest Web Site of the Week, worldwide, *America On-Line*, 1996. **INTERESTS:** narration; skeet shooting. **MISC:** speaking engagements, mainly about growth & changes in TV industry, to int'l professional groups; lives in San Francisco & Toronto. **COMMENT:** *"'Jo Lee's ubiquitous meetings, her telephone high jinx and revolving door machinations of getting others to give - is unexplainable! If one were to sum up an impression of Jo Lee Mascioli-Mansell, it might best be done in the words of James M. Barrie: If you have it ("charm and brains") you don't need to have anything else and if you don't have it, it doesn't matter what else you have.'*–Gene Arceri (author of *Elizabeth Taylor* & Susan Hayward's *Red*)."

Masciuch, Sonia W., Ph.D. ■■ 🎓 ⊕

Associate Professor, Department of Education, and Coordinator, Master of Arts in School Psychology, **MOUNT SAINT VINCENT UNIVERSITY**, 166 Bedford Hwy., Halifax, NS B3M 2J6 (902) 457-6564, FAX 445-3960. **EDUC:** Univ. of

Alberta, B.Sc.(Psych.) 1967, Prof. Diploma (Educ.) 1970, M.Ed.(Applied Psych.) 1975; Univ. of Toronto, Ph.D.(Applied Psych.) 1986. **CAREER:** Clinician, Alberta Guidance Clinic, Edmonton, 1967-69; Teacher/Supervising Teacher, Alberta Sch. for the Deaf, 1970-72; Teaching Asst./Counsellor, Counselling Svcs Clinic, Univ. of Alberta, 1972-73; Itinerant Teacher, Hard-of-Hearing Classes, Edmonton Public Sch. Bd., 1973-75; Guidance Counsellor, elementary & jr. high sch., 1975-76; Teacher, Peel Bd. of Educ., Mississauga, Ont., 1977-80; Grad. Research Asst., Applied Psych. Dept., Ontario Institute for Studies in Education, Toronto, 1980-83; Psychoeducational Consultant, Halton Bd. of Educ., Oakville, Ont., 1981-82; Lecturer, Special Educ., Fac. of Educ., Univ. of Alberta, 1987; Psychologist, Assessment Team, Edmonton Public Sch. Bd., 1987; Assoc. Prof., Dept. of Educ., & Coord., Sch. Psych. Program, Mount Saint Vincent Univ., Halifax, 1987 to date; Lecturer, Dept. of Educational Psych., Ethics, Univ. of Alberta, Summer 1992 & Summer 1995; Visiting Prof., Dept. of Educational Psych., 1993-96; Psychologist, H.J. McLeod, Ph.D. & Associates Ltd., Edmonton, 1993-95; Psychologist, Anne Krane & Associates Limited, Halifax, 1995 to date. **SELECTED PUBLICATIONS:** author/co-author, 8 articles in research journals, incl.: "Preparing school psychologists for the future" (*Canadian Journal of School Psychology*, 11, 1995); "The disruptive student: The school psychologist's perspective" (*Education & Law: Education in the Era of Individual Rights*. Quebec: Imprimerie LISBRO, 1993); author, 9 contributions to professional journals; author/co-author, over 10 paper presentations & invited presentations. **AFFIL:** Association of Psychologists of N.S.; Canadian Association of School Psychologists (Sec., Membership Sec.); International Sch. Psychology Association; Psychologists' Association of Alberta.

Masini, Beatrice, M.B.A. $

Director of Marketing, HEWLETT PACKARD (CANADA) LTD., 5150 Spectrum Way, Mississauga, ON L4W 5G1 (905) 206-3165, FAX 206-4163. Born Rabastens, France 1951. m. Michel Masini. 1 ch. Camille. **EDUC:** National Engineering Sch., Lyon, France, Chemical Eng. 1975; École Polytechnique, Grenoble, France, Engineer (Pulp & Paper) 1976; York Univ., M.B.A. 1983. **CAREER:** District Sales Mgr., Hewlett Packard (Canada) Ltd., 1989-91; Channel Mgr, 1990-91; Area Sales Mgr, 1991-94; Dir. of Mktg, 1994 to date. **AFFIL:** Association of Professional Engineers. **INTERESTS:** travel; general fitness; movies; reading. **MISC:** frequent lecturer & counsellor to students on how educ. relates to the work & bus. environment. **COMMENT:** *"Beatrice Masini is the Director of Marketing for Hewlett-Packard (Canada) Ltd.'s Computer Systems Organization. In that capacity she is responsible for the programs that direct and support the company's national business information management systems sales efforts."*

Mason, Joyce, B.A. ✏ 🎞 📜

Editor and Publisher, C MAGAZINE, 988 Queen St. W., Ground Fl., Toronto, ON M6J 1H1 (416) 539-9495, FAX 539-9903. Director, C ARTS PUBLISHING AND PRODUCTION, INC. Born Hamilton, Ont. 1951. s. **EDUC:** Univ. of Western Ontario, Hons. B.A.(English & Drama) 1974; Univ. des Langues et Lettres de Grenoble, Diplôme d'Études Françaises 1978. **CAREER:** ed., writer, administrator & consultant; Distribution & "Challenge for Change" Officer, Atlantic Reg. Office, National Film Bd., Halifax, 1974-77; Film Program Administrator, Canada Council, 1979-80; Guest Ed., "After the Party's Over" (special section on Judy Chicago's The Dinner Party exhibit at AGO), *Fireweed*, Winter, 1992; Mng Ed., *FUSE* magazine, 1983-85; Interim Ed., *Parallelogramme*, 1988; filmscript consultant, 1986-90 (clients include OFDC, Telefilm, FUND & Breakthrough Films); freelance Ed., *Sans Souci*, short stories by Dionne Brand (Toronto: Williams Wallace, 1988); freelance ed., misc. contemporary art catalogues, Art Gallery of Ontario, 1988-90; Assoc. Ed., C magazine, 1989-90; Ed. & Publisher, 1990 to date. **SELECTED CREDITS:** camera & sound operator, *Born Near the USA* (video), by John Scott, 1989. **SELECTED PUBLICATIONS:** "Report on the Status of Women at the Ontario College of Art" (Ontario Coll. of Art, 1986-97); "Report on Working Conditions in Artist-run Centres" (Canadian Artists' Representation 1986-87); misc. features & reviews in various film, contemporary art & cultural magazines & journals. **AFFIL:** Toronto Women's Cultural Building Collective (Exec. Mbr.); Toronto Women in Film and Video; misc. art galleries. **COMMENT:** *"I have worked extensively in the film and visual arts communities of Canada, as a writer, consultant, editor and programmer."*

Mastin, Catherine M., M.A.,B.F.A. 🎞 📜 📖

Senior Curator of Art, GLENBOW MUSEUM, 130 - 9th Ave. SW, Calgary, AB T2G 0P3 (403) 268-4240, FAX 265-9769. Born Toronto 1963. **EDUC:** York Univ., B.F.A.(Visual Arts) 1986, M.A.(Art Hist.) 1988. **CAREER:** Curator, Cdn Historical Art, Art Gallery of Windsor, 1989-95; Sr. Curator of Art, Glenbow Museum, 1995 to date. **SELECTED PUBLICA-**

TIONS: *William G.R. Hind: The Pictou Sketchbook* (Windsor: The Art Gallery of Windsor, 1990); "The Talented Intruder: Wyndham Lewis in Canada, 1939-54," in *The Talented Intruder: Wyndham Lewis in Canada, 1939-54*, catalogue (Windsor: Art Gallery of Windsor, 1992); *New World–Old World: Eurocentric Perceptions of First Nations and the Landscape* (Art Gallery of Windsor, 1994); *Franklin Carmichael*, monograph (Kingston: Quarry Press, in progress). **AFFIL:** Boreal Forest Art Institute (Advisor); Artweek Calgary Biennial (Steering Committee); Alberta Museums Association; Ontario Association of Art Galleries; Alberta Equestrian Association. **HONS:** Curatorial Writing Award ("The Talented Intruder: Wyndham Lewis in Canada, 1939-54"), Ontario Association of Art Galleries, 1993; Curatorial Writing Award (*New World–Old World: Eurocentric Perceptions of First Nations and the Landscape*), Ontario Association of Art Galleries, 1995. **COMMENT:** "*Recently joined the staff of the Glenbow Museum as Senior Curator of Art. Prior to this appointment, she held the position of Curator, Canadian Historical Art at the Art Gallery of Windsor for six years. In addition, she has worked in art education, programming and teaching in public art gallery and university environments. She has curated more than 60 exhibits including co-curating the Alberta Biennial of Contemporary Art 1996 with Bruce Grenville and has authored and published several major exhibition catalogues.*"

Mastine, Susan C., B.A. ■ ▢ ◯ ⌂
Community Relations Manager and Columnist, THE RECORD, 2850 Delorme, Sherbrooke, QC J1K 1A1 (819) 569-9511, FAX 569-3945. Born St. Félix de Kingsey, Que. 1950. m. Russell Frost. 2 ch. Adam Mastine-Frost, Justin Mastine-Frost. **EDUC:** Bishop's Univ., B.A.(Soc.) 1972. **CAREER:** researcher, Prof. G. Caldwell, Bishop's Univ., 1972-73; researcher/journalist, Eastern Townships Social Action Group/*Townships Sun* (co-founder), 1973-75; teacher, Eastern Townships Sch. Bd., 1975-76; Coord., Women's Centre, 1976-78; Community Animator, Eastern Townships Sch. Bd., 1978-80; Mun. Councillor, Kingsey Falls, 1987-91; Page Design Artist, *Townships Sun*, 1988-90; Proj. Coord., Townshippers' Association, 1989-90; Exec. Dir., 1990-95. **SELECTED PUBLICATIONS:** page design for *The Townships Sun* (1988-90), *A Community with Deep Roots* (Sherbrooke, QC: Townshippers' Association, 1989). **AFFIL:** RRHS Sch. Committee; l'AFEAS (past Bd. mbr.); Regional Associations/Alliance Quebec Network (Sec. 1991-95); Townshippers' Association (Co-founder 1979;

Sec. 1980-81); CLSC (past Bd. mbr.). **INTERESTS:** writing; photography; hiking; gardening; attending meetings; collecting memorabilia. **MISC:** 1st woman Councillor, Kingsey Falls; helped introduce recycling program, Peace Candle Campaign; mbr., Cannon Committee, St. Félix de Kingsey, 1988-89, researched, wrote & designed commemorative panels. **COMMENT:** "*With a deep attachment to, and a rich heritage based in the Eastern Townships, I enjoy the dynamics of a bilingual, bicultural rural milieu. I thrive on involvement in community efforts and appreciate being able to contribute in creative ways toward the future of the Eastern Townships.*"

Matheson, Margaret, B.A. ■ ⊚
c/o 297 Dupuis St., Ste. 308, Ottawa, ON K1L 7H8 (613) 747-7339, FAX 747-8358. Born Toronto 1933. m. M.C. Murray Matheson. 2 ch. **EDUC:** Univ. of British Columbia, B.A.(Psych.) 1954. **CAREER:** Social Worker, Family & Children's Svcs, Victoria, 1954-56; Social Worker, Canadian Mental Health Association, Victoria, 1969-71; Mgr, Greater Victoria Art Gallery Gift Shop, 1977-80; Ptnr, Independent Book Store, 1985-90; Pres., Canadian Federation of University Women, 1990-92, 1992-94; Coord., Int'l Rel'ns, 1994-96. **SELECTED PUBLICATIONS:** chapter in *Only in Oak Bay* (1981); article in *Policy Options* Mar. 1993; numerous articles for Canadian Federation of University Women publications. **AFFIL:** University Women's Club, Victoria (Study Group Convenor 1961-63; Fed. Rep. 1970-73; VP, Membership 1973-75; Pres. 1975-77); Canadian Federation of University Women (VP, Constitution & By-Laws Committee, B.C. 1988-90); church; parent-teacher association; art gallery; museum. **INTERESTS:** music; gardening; natural history/environment; First Peoples. **COMMENT:** "*I have a long-term concern for women's issues as an integral part of society, and the need for personal commitment to voluntarism within the community.*"

Mathieu, Mireille, M.Sc., Ph.D. ■■ ⊰ 🕮 ⚘
Dean, Faculty of Arts and Science, UNIVERSITÉ DE MONTRÉAL, C.P. 6128, Succ. Centre-Ville, Montréal, QC H3C 3J7 (514) 343-6262, FAX 343-2185, EMAIL mathieum@umontreal.ca. Born Joliette, Que. 1944. m. Gilles Dupuis. 2 ch. Gabrielle, Jean-François. **EDUC:** Univ. de Montréal, M.Sc.(Psych.) 1967, Ph.D.(Psych.) 1969; Univ. de Lille, France, post-doctoral studies (Psych.) 1969-70; McGill Univ., post-doctoral studies (Clinical Psych.) 1974-75. **CAREER:** Asst. Prof., 1970-76; Assoc. Prof., 1976-82; Full Prof., 1982 to date; Dept. Head,

1983-87; V-Dean, Arts & Sci., 1987-94; Dean, Arts & Sci., 1994 to date; Assoc. Ed., *Canadian Psychology*, 1986-90. **SELECTED PUBLICA-TIONS:** "Adapter la formation professionnelle aux nouvelles réalités du Québec: une nécessité" (*Intervention*, 88, 1991); co-author with J. Langis & S. Sabourin, "Rôles sexuels et adaptation conjugale" (*Revue canadienne des sciences du comportement*, 23, 1991); "La résolution de problème comme stratégie d'intervention," in Wright et Sabourin (eds.), *L'intervention auprès du couple: diagnostic et traitement* (Montréal: Les Éditions Consultation, 1985); co-author with G. Bergeron, "Piagetian assessment of cognitive development in chimpanzee (Pan troglodytes)" in A.B. Chiarelli et R.S. Corrusini (eds.), *Primate behaviour and sociobiology* (Berlin: Springer-Verlag, 1981); co-author with N. Daudelin, Y. Dagenais et T. Décarie, "Piagetian causality in two house-reared chimpanzees" (*Canadian Journal of Psychology*, 1980); co-author with J. Wright & C. Valiquette, "Assertion et habiletés sociales" & co-author with J. Wright, "Problèmes de couple" in R. Ladouceur, M.-A. Bouchard et L. Granger (eds.), *Principes et applications des thérapies behaviorales* (St-Hyacinthe: Edisem, Paris: Maloine, 1977); numerous other articles & book chpts. **AFFIL:** Ordre des psychologues du Québec (Bd. mbr. 1985-89); Canadian Psychological Association (Bd. mbr. 1990-93); Canadian Conference of Deans of Science; Canadian Conference of Deans of Arts, Humanities & Social Sciences (Pres. 1994-97). **HONS:** Fellow, Canadian Psychological Association; Médaille de la Fondation Édouard-Montpetit. **INTERESTS:** music; science fiction; politics; books, books, books. **MISC:** numerous radio & TV interviews. **COMMENT:** *"Petite, très dynamique et déterminée. Passionnement impliquée dans ses activités professionnelles, orientées vers le changement des individus et des organisations pour amélioration de la formation universitaire. Très attachée à sa famille, nucléaire et élargie."*

Matis, Barbra ⊗ ⛏ ♥

Production, Set and Costume Designer. 222 Riverside Dr., Ste. 2D, New York, NY 10025 (212) 865-0239. Born Montreal 1952. **EDUC:** Sir George Williams Univ. (Concordia Univ.), Montreal, Fine Arts 1970; National Theatre Sch. of Canada, Design Grad. 1973. **CAREER:** Designer in theatre & film, 1972 to date; Co-Owner, Costumes Unlimited, Montreal, 1974-78. **SELECTED CREDITS:** as Production Designer: *Shadow Dancing* (feature), Source Productions; *The Return of Hickey* (2 hour-long telefilms); American Playhouse/Disney Channel; *Balconville* (TV drama), CBC; as Art Dir.: *Rescuing Desire* (feature), Pilgrims 4 Corporation; *Trial By Jury* (feature), Morgan Creek/Warner Bros.; *This Is My Life* (feature), 20th Century Fox; *New Jack City* (feature), Warner Bros.; *Road to Avonlea* (series), design of village, Sullivan Films/Disney; *Moonstruck* (feature), MGM/UA; *Children of a Lesser God* (feature), Paramount; as Set & Costume Designer: various theatre productions across Canada for Centaur Theatre, Montreal; Manitoba Theatre Centre, Winnipeg; Theatre Plus,Toronto; Theatre New Brunswick, Fredericton, etc. **AFFIL:** United Scenic Artists–Local 829 (NY); Directors' Guild of Canada; Associated Designers of Canada. **HONS:** 1st Dora Award for Set Design (*Balconville*), Toronto, 1980. **INTERESTS:** painting; all art forms; equestrian things; bridge. **MISC:** Interior Designer for the Manhattan Bridge Club & Ellen Christine in N.Y. **COMMENT:** *"After 25 years of working professionally–of many ups and downs–I believe that as an artist I have a place in this world and remain optimistic that the best is yet to come."*

Matte Packham, Mimi, B.F.A. ⊗ ▤

Painter. 425A Sackville St., Toronto, ON M4X 1T1 (416) 867-9102. Born Regina 1929. m. James Packham. 2 ch. Christine, Blair. **EDUC:** McGill Univ., B.F.A. 1951. **CAREER:** illustrator, Montreal, 1951-60; advtg mgr/graphic designer, Ottawa, 1960-65; painter/teacher, Toronto, 1965 to date. **SELECTED PUBLICATIONS:** newspaper reviews & feature articles; covers, illustrations & articles for magazines. **EXHIBITIONS:** Marlborough-Godard, Toronto (1975); Gairdner Estate Gallery, Oakville, Ont. (1977); Hart House, Univ. of Toronto (1978); More-Rubin Gallery, Buffalo, NY (1978); Bau-Xi Gallery, Toronto (1979; 1983; 1984; 1987; 1989; 1992; 1993; 1994); Shayne Gallery, Montreal (1981); Adley Gallery, Sarasota, Fla. (1982); Rosemont Gallery, Regina (1990); various group exhibitions. **COLLECTIONS:** Toronto French Schools; Imperial Oil Canada; Shell Oil Canada; Marcil Trust Co.; Southam collection; Unitel Communications, Toronto; Davies Ward and Beck, Toronto; Ingram and Schriver, N.Y.; New Life Vitamins, Toronto; Kinross Gold, Toronto; The Granite Club, Toronto; many private collections. **HONS:** Loomis and Toles Award, Ontario Society of Artists, 23rd Aviva. **INTERESTS:** computer graphics; writing. **COMMENT:** *"I consider myself an observer, one who can't help but find the human condition slightly comical. I've always used paint and visuals as a means of communication, but lately I've begun to use words. It's a whole new world for me to explore."*

Matthes, Mia ■■ ⊗ ▢

Photographer and Partner, MIA ET KLAUS, 805 boul. Ste-Croix, Ville St-Laurent, QC H4L 3X6 (514) 748-5352. m. Klaus Matthes. 4 ch. Johanne, François, Chantal, Stephan. CAREER: studio founded, Mia & Klaus, 1958. SELECTED CREDITS: photographs featured in NFB films *Entre amis, Canada du temps qui passe* & *Images*. SELECTED PUBLICATIONS: *Bonjour Québec*, 45 photographs with text by painter Alfred Pellan (McClelland & Stewart, 1967); *Québec et l'île Orléans*, text by Gatien Lapointe (les Éditions du Pélican, 1968); *Le Corps Secret*, in collaboration with Jacques Brault (Éditions du Jour, 1969); *Musique d'Été* (Éditions Fides, 1976); *Québec*, an album of 189 colour photographs accompanying the poem "Chorégraphie d'un Pays" by Gatien Lapointe (Éditions Libre Expression, 1980); *Montréal*, 151 colour photographs with text by François Barcelo (1983); *Canada*, 189 colour photographs with preface by The Hon. Jeanne Sauvé and text by Roch Carrier (1986); *Ciels de Saint-Jean*, text by Claude Sumner (Éditions Fides, 1988); *L'Architecture de Montréal* (1990); *Le Québec des Grands Espaces*, text by Mia Matthes (1991); *Charlevoix, Le Jardin Botanique* & *Îles de la Madeleine* (Sogides, Les Éditions de l'Homme, 1994); *Le chant de l'Eau/Sound of Waters* (soon to be pub.); their photographs have appeared in many magazines around the world incl. *Merian* (Germany), *Figaro* (France) & *Perspectives et Évasion* (Qué.). EXHIBITIONS: have exhibited at many places incl. Terre des Hommes, Place des Arts, Musée d'Art Contemporain & the National Library; many nat'l & int'l shows. HONS: awarded the Prix Edgar Lespérance, for most beautiful book (*Îles de la Madeleine*), 1995. MISC: has 13 grandchildren & 6 great grandchildren. INTERESTS: writing; collage.

Matthews, Victoria, B.A.,M.Div.,Th.M. ■ ☼

Bishop of the Credit Valley, Diocese of Toronto, ANGLICAN CHURCH OF CANADAA, 3210 Weston Rd., Box 95021, Weston, ON M9M 2H0 (416) 746-9963, FAX 746-9992. Born Toronto 1954. s. EDUC: Trinity Coll., Univ. of Toronto, B.A. 1976, Th.M. 1987; Yale Univ. Divinity Sch., M.Div.(Divinity) 1979. CAREER: Asst. Curate, Church of St. Andrew, Scarborough, Ont., 1979-83; Incumbent, Parish of Georgina, York-Simcoe, 1983-87; Incumbent, All Souls', Lansing, York-Scarborough, 1987-94; Reg'l Dean, Deanery of York Mills, Ont., 1989-94; Bishop of the Credit Valley, Diocese of Toronto, 1994 to date. HONS: North American Theological Fellowship, 1976-79. INTERESTS: reading; hiking; swimming; travel.

Matthiessen, Beverley D. ⊜ O

Executive Director, ALBERTA COMMITTEE OF CITIZENS WITH DISABILITIES, 10339 - 124 St., Ste. 707, Edmonton, AB T5N 3W1 (403) 488-9088, FAX 488-3757. Born Milden, Sask. sep. 2 ch. Darcie Lyn, Tracie Irene. EDUC: Grant MacEwan Community Coll., Volunteer Mgmt Certificate 1989, Nonprofit Agency Mgmt Certificate (with Distinction) 1993, Fundraising Mgmt Certificate (with Distinction) 1994, Nat'l Certificate in Fundraising Mgmt 1994, Social Work Dipl. (with Distinction) 1996; Univ. of Alberta, Supervisory Dev. Certificate 1991, Mgmt Dev. Certificate 1991; Ryerson Polytechnic Univ. & the Canadian Centre for Philanthropy, Nat'l Certificate in Voluntary & Nonprofit Sector Mgmt 1993. CAREER: Teller, Toronto-Dominion Bank, 1971-74; Asst. Mgr, Baldwin Hotel Company Ltd., 1975-78; Teller, CIBC, 1978-79; Mktg Officer, 1979-82; Personnel Officer, 1982-84; Asst. Office Mgr & Bookkeeper, Sprague Furniture, 1984-85; Discounts, CIBC, 1985-86; Coord. of Volunteers, Goodwill Rehabilitation Services of Alberta, 1985-87; Acctnt, Personal Dev. Centre, 1986-88; Educ. Dir., Personal Dev. Centre, 1986-87; Exec. Dir., 1987-91; Exec. Dir., Alberta Committee of Citizens With Disabilities, 1991 to date. AFFIL: Edmonton Art Gallery; Junior League of Edmonton; Laurier Heights Community League (Past VP); Robertson Wesley United Church; Royal Glenora Club; United Church of Canada; People Against Impaired Drivers; Volunteer Management Alumni Association; WIN House; Alberta Association of Fundraising Executives; Centre Club of Edmonton; Wild Rose Foundation; Federation of Community Leagues (Dir.); Valley Zoo Advisory Committee (Sec.); Valley Zoo Citizen's Action Committee (Co-chair); Festival of Trees; Chamber of Commerce; Edmonton Klondike Days Association. INTERESTS: reading; volunteer work; photography; travel. MISC: attended numerous conferences & workshops, facilitated conferences, campaigns & meetings; various media appearances. COMMENT: "*Beverley Matthiessen has worked in the volunteer and social service sector for more than 10 years. She developed and managed a Suicide Prevention Program, numerous educational courses, and presently works as Executive Director of Alberta's only cross-disability provincial advocacy organization. She is a strong advocate of human rights, fairness and equality for all.*"

Matusicky, Carol, B.A.,M.A., Ph.D. ⊜ O

Executive Director, BRITISH COLUMBIA COUNCIL FOR THE FAMILY, 2590 Granville St., Ste. 204, Vancouver, BC V6H 3H1 (604) 660-0675,

FAX 732-4813. Born Vancouver 1941. m. Leo. 2 ch. Catherine Lynn, Joseph (Joey) Paul. EDUC: Mount St. Vincent Univ., B.A. (Psych./Phil.) 1967; Univ. of Notre Dame, Indiana, M.A.(Phil.) 1972; Univ. of Toronto, Ph.D.(Adult Educ./Family Studies) 1982. CAREER: Asst. to the Academic Dean, Mount St. Vincent Univ., 1972; Coord., Family Life Institute, 1973-76; Consultant, Vancouver, 1980-84; Exec. Dir., B.C. Council for the Family, 1984 to date. SELECTED PUBLICATIONS: articles in quarterly newsletter *Family Connections*. AFFIL: Vanier Institute of the Family (Bd.); B.C. Coalition for Safer Communities; B.C. Min. of Health's Advisory Committee on Injury Prevention; Child-Friendly Housing Advisory Committee; Society for Children & Youth (Advisory Committee on the U.N. Convention on the Rights of Children); Canadian Mental Health Association (Youth Participation Advisory Committee); B.C. Medical Association (Child & Youth Advisory Committee); First Call: B.C. Coalition for Child & Youth Advocacy; B.C. Health Research Foundation (Peer Review Committee); Vancouver Foundation (Child & Family Advisory Committee); Kaiser Youth Foundation (Advisory Committee); Rogers Cablevision (Community Advisory Committee); Family Resource Coalition; National Council on Family Relations; International Council on Social Development; The Workplace Council; Directorate of Agencies for Sch. Health; Social Planning & Research Council of B.C. HONS: Canada Council Doctoral Scholarship, 1973-77. INTERESTS: walking; hiking; candle-making. MISC: Dr. Carol Matusicky Bursary for Family Educ. set up in 1994 to commemorate 10th anniversary as Exec. Dir. of B.C. Council for the Family; keynote presentations worldwide. COMMENT: *"I love what I do and have brought high energy and enthusiasm to my work, and a networking capability that reaches locally, provincially and internationally."*

Maunder, Maria ■■ ⓤ
Olympic Athlete. c/o Canadian Olympic Association. Born St. John's, Nfld. 1972. SPORTS CAREER: full-time athlete; mbr., Cdn Nat'l Rowing Team, 1992 to date. Olympic Games: Silver, 8+, 1996. World championships: 5th, 2-, & 6th, 8+, 1995; 7th, 8+, & 8th, 4-, 1994. Int'l regattas: 6th, 2- (Switzerland), & 3rd, 2- (Netherlands), 1994. World University Games: 1st, 8+, & 2nd, 4-, 1993. Canadian championships: 2nd, 2-, 3rd, 2x, & 5th, 1x, 1992. US championships: 2nd, 8+, & 2nd, 2-, 1995; 2nd, 4-, & 2nd, 8+, 1993. INTERESTS: swimming; reading; euchre; skiing. MISC: speaks English, French, Spanish.

Mawani, Nurjehan ✦ ⬥
Chairperson, IMMIGRATION AND REFUGEE BOARD OF CANADA, 240 Bank St., Ottawa, ON K1A 0K1 (613) 996-4752, FAX 947-5338. Born Mombasa, Kenya. m. Nizar Mawani. 2 ch. EDUC: Inns of Court Sch. of Law, London, UK. BAR: Lincoln's Inn, 1969; Solicitor of the Supreme Court of England & Wales, 1973. CAREER: Chair, Immigration & Refugee Bd. of Canada, 1992 to date. SELECTED PUBLICATIONS: "Introduction to the Guidelines on Women Refugee Claimants fleeing gender-related persecution" (*International Journal of Refugee Law*); chapter in 2nd vol. of *Human Rights in the Twenty-First Century: A Global Challenge*, ed. Kathleen E. Mahoney & Paul Mahoney. AFFIL: Laurier Institute (Bd.); Women's Legal Education & Action Fund. HONS: recognized for services to Ismaili community, His Highness the Aga Khan, 1983; honoured for volunteer service, Gov. General of Canada, 1991; Canada 125 Medal; Award for Outstanding Achievement, Vancouver Society of Immigrant & Visible Minority Women, 1992; Women of Distinction Award, YWCA, 1993; Human Rights Award, American Immigration Lawyers' Association, 1993; Humanitarian of the Year, Indo-Canadian Chamber of Commerce, 1993; Order of Canada, 1993. MISC: actively involved in community work in London; mbr. for Legal Affairs, National Council for the United Kingdom; speaker, various nat'l & int'l conferences; participated in Nat'l Symposium on Women, Law & the Admin. of Justice; Conferences of the Canadian Council of Administrative Tribunals; Women Towards the Millennium Conference; speaker to various associations, universities & non-governmental organizations. COMMENT: *"As chairperson, Mrs. Mawani's role is to oversee the management of the resources of the board, to ensure that the board achieves the goals and objectives established for it by the Parliament of Canada, and to manage the activities of members and senior staff."*

Maxwell, Judith, B.Comm. ■ ✦ ⓢ ⬢
President, CPRN INC., (Canadian Policy Research Networks), 250 Albert St., Ste. 430, Box 1503, Ottawa, ON K1P 6M1 (613) 567-7500, FAX 567-7640, EMAIL jmaxwell.cprn@idrc.ca. Born Kingston, Ont. 1943. m. Anthony Maxwell. 2 ch. EDUC: Dalhousie Univ., B.Com. 1960; London Sch. of Econ., London, UK, 1965-66. CAREER: researcher, Combines Investigation Branch, Consumer & Corp. Affairs, Ottawa, 1963-65; Econ. writer, Mbr. of Ed. Bd., Financial Times of Canada, Montreal, 1966-72; Dir., Policy Studies, C.D. Howe Institute, Montreal, 1972-80; Consul-

tant, Esso Europe Inc., London, 1980-82; Consulting Economist, Coopers and Lybrand, Montreal, 1982-85; Chrm, Economic Council of Canada, Ottawa, 1985-92; Assoc. Dir., Sch. of Policy Studies, Queen's Univ., Kingston, 1992-94; Adjunct Prof., Dept. of Medicine, Fac. of Health Sci. & Fac. of Admin., Univ. of Ottawa, 1994 to date; Fellow, Sch. of Policy Studies, Queen's Univ., 1994 to date; Pres., CPRN Inc., 1995 to date. SELECTED PUBLICATIONS: "The Social Role of the State in a Knowledge-based Economy," *Redefining Social Security* (Gov't & Competitiveness Project Discussion Paper, Sch. of Policy Studies, Queen's Univ., Kingston, 1995); *Social Dimensions of Economic Growth,* E.J. Hanson Memorial Lecture, Univ. of Alberta, Edmonton, 1966; various other publications. DIRECTOR: Bank of Canada; Mutual Life Assurance of Canada. AFFIL: Children's Aid Foundation of Ottawa-Carleton (Dir.); Institute on Governance (Dir.); L'Observatoire de l'administration publique (Dir.); Social Resarch & Demonstration Corporation (Dir.); Canadian Association for Business Economics; Council for Canadian Unity. HONS: LL.D.(Hon.), Dalhousie Univ., 1991; LL.D.(Hon.), Concordia Univ., 1992; LL.D. (Hon.), Queen's Univ., 1992; D.Comm.(Hon.), Lakehead Univ., 1993; D.Litt.(Hon.), York Univ., 1994. COMMENT: *"Judith Maxwell is a highly regarded independent communicator on the major social and economic issues of the day. She is a good communicator and has a capacity to organize large-scale, pioneering research projects."*

May, Elizabeth, LL.B. ■■ ⓔ 🏵
Executive Director, SIERRA CLUB OF CANADA (environmental organization), 1 Nicholas St., Ste. 412, Ottawa, ON K1N 7B7 (613) 241-4611, FAX 241-2292, EMAIL sierra@web.net. Born Connecticut 1954. m. Jeff Johnston. 1 ch. Victoria Cate. EDUC: Dalhousie Univ., Sch. of Law, LL.B. 1983. CAREER: Assoc., Kitz Matheson, Halifax, 1983-85; Assoc. Gen. Cnsl, Public Interest Advocacy Centre, Ottawa, 1985; Sr. Policy Advisor, Office of the Fed. Min. of the Envir., 1986-88; Exec. Dir., Sierra Club of Canada, 1989 to date. SELECTED CREDITS: Co-host, *Evergreen,* CJOH syndicated TV program, 1990-91; panel contributor on envir. issues to *Discovery,* CBC Radio, *Midday,* CBC TV. SELECTED PUBLICATIONS: *Budworm Battles* (N.S.: Far East Publications, 1982); *Paradise Won: The Struggle to Save South Moresby* (Toronto: McClelland & Stewart, 1990); contributed chpts. to *Endangered Spaces* (Key Porter Books, 1989) & *Rescue the Earth!* by Farley Mowat; *At the Cutting Edge: The Crisis in Canada's Forests* (Key Porter Books,

forthcoming 1997). AFFIL: National Round Table on Environment & Economy (V-Chair 1994 to date); International Institute for Sustainable Development (Bd. mbr.); Cultural Survival (Canada) (Exec. Dir. 1989-94); Earth Day 1990 (Bd. mbr.); Friends of the Earth Canada (former Bd. mbr.); Canadian Environmental Network (hon. mbr.); Canadian Environmental Defence Fund (founding mbr.); Women for a Healthy Planet (founding mbr.). HONS: Outstanding Achievement Award, Sierra Club of Canada, 1989; Int'l Conservation Award, Friends of Nature, 1990; UN Global 500 Award, 1990; Outstanding Leadership in Envir. Educ., Ontario Society for Environmental Education, 1996.

Mayda, Jacqueline E., B.Sc. ■ ✤ ⓔ
Survey Statistician, STATISTICS CANADA, R.H. Coats Bldg, 16-N, Ottawa, ON K1A 0T6 (613) 951-2250, FAX 951-3100, EMAIL dazejac@statcan.ca. Born Edinburgh 1965. m. Michael F. Mayda. EDUC: Carleton Univ., B.Sc.(Statistics) 1988. CAREER: Methodologist, Bus. Survey Methods Div., Statistics Canada, 1988-95; Sr. Methodologist, Household Surveys Methods Div., 1995 to date. SELECTED PUBLICATIONS: *A Multiple Frame Agricultural Survey Design: A Case Study from Statistics Canada,* with B.N. Chinnappa (United Nations Food & Agriculture Organization, 1994); "An Integrated Approach to Editing," with P. Whitridge & J.-M. Berthelot (*American Statistical Association,* Proceedings of the Section on Business and Economic Statistics 1990); *Variance Estimation and Confidentiality: They Are Related,* with C. Mohl & J.-L. Tambay (Statistical Society of Canada, Proceedings of the Section on Survey Research Methods, 1996); "Model-Based Estimation of Record Linkage Error Rates," with J. Armstrong (*Survey Methodology Journal* 19(2) 1993). AFFIL: American Statistical Association; Statistical Society of Ottawa; Professional Institute of the Public Service of Canada (Chair, Group Advisory Council; V-Chair, Math. Group; Chair, Advisory Committee of Women's Issues 1994). HONS: Employee Recognition Award, Statistics Canada, 1994. INTERESTS: reading, gardening. MISC: spent 8 weeks in Hungary working on a joint proj. with the Hungarian Bureau of Statistics. COMMENT: *"Jacqueline represents Statistics Canada in a professional manner. She participates in union activities in order to ensure that the rights of employees of the Public Service of Canada are taken into account in the decision-making process."*

Mayhew, Elza, B.A.,M.F.A.,R.C.A.
Sculptor. Born Victoria, B.C. 1916. w. 2 ch.

Anne, Alan. **EDUC:** Univ. of British Columbia, B.A.(French/Latin); Univ. of Oregon, M.F.A. 1963. **COMMISSIONS:** B.C. Archives & Museum (1967); Expo (1967); Bank of Canada, Vancouver (1968); Confederation Centre, Charlottetown, PEI (1973); Univ. of Victoria (1988). **EXHIBITIONS:** The Point Gallery, Victoria (1960); Venice Biennale, Canada Pavilion (1964); Equinox Gallery, Vancouver (1979); Wallack Gallery, Ottawa (1981); various other solo exhibitions; numerous juried & invited exhibitions. **COLLECTIONS:** Art Gallery of Greater Victoria; Univ. of Victoria; National Gallery of Canada; Simon Fraser Univ.; Brock Univ.; National Capital Commission. **AFFIL:** Royal Canadian Academy (Elected 1974). **HONS:** Sir Otto Beit Medal, Royal Society of British Sculptors, 1962; Purchase Award, B.C. Centennial Sculpture Exhibition, 1967; Hon. Doctorate, Univ. of Victoria, 1989. **MISC:** subject of various articles & a documentary; *Canadian Who's Who; Who's Who in American Art; 2,000 Notable American Women; International Who's Who of Women; Who's Who in the West; Dictionary of International Biography.* **COMMENT:** *"Elza Mayhew has been making sculpture in Victoria since the mid-fifties. Most of her work is bronze, cast in foundries in Ontario, the US and UK. The monumental pieces were cast at the Eugene Aluminum and Brass Foundry in Eugene, Oregon."*

Maynard, Rona, B.A. / ⬚
Editor, CHATELAINE MAGAZINE, 777 Bay St., Toronto, ON M5W 1A7 (416) 596-5424. m. Paul Jones, Executive Vice-President, Canadian Business Media Ltd. 1 ch. **EDUC:** Univ. of Toronto, B.A. 1972. **CAREER:** Ed. Officer, *Curriculum Theory Network,* 1976-77; Copy Ed., *Miss Chatelaine,* 1976-77; Assoc. Ed., *Flare,* 1977-80; Professions Ed., *Maclean's,* 1981-82; freelance writer for numerous nat'l magazines, 1982-93; Ed. Consultant, *Chatelaine,* 1987-93; Exec. Ed., Svcs, 1992-93; Ed., 1993 to date. **SELECTED PUBLICATIONS:** more than 150 publishing credits, spanning bus. trends, educ., social issues, medicine, family life & psych.; cover story, *Canadian Business;* 6 cover stories, *Report on Business* Magazine; 30 lead features in Cdn women's magazines, incl. *Chatelaine.* **AFFIL:** National Magazine Awards Foundation (Dir.); Banff Magazine Publishing Workshop (Fac. 1991-93); North York Bd. of Educ. (advisor, external evaluation); Univ. of Toronto (Fac. of Continuing Educ., Bus. Advisory Bd.; Fac. of Social Work, Campaign Exec. Committee); United Way of Metropolitan Toronto (Leading Women Committee). **HONS:** Woman of Distinction, Comm., YWCA of Metropolitan Toronto, 1992; Honourable Mention, editorial package, National Magazine Awards, 1992; Best Print Article, Canadian Nurses' Association Media Awards, 1990; Honourable Mention, bus. writing, National Magazine Awards, 1988; cited in *Best Short Stories* of 1966, ed. Martha Foley; 7 Scholastic Magazines Writing Awards (nat'l competition, US), 1962-66; Varsity Fund Scholar, Univ. of Toronto. **MISC:** has devoted most of her career to the issues that shape women's lives & aspirations.

Mazur-Melnyk, Mary, B.Sc.,M.Sc., Ph.D. ⓢ ❀
Director, Quality Assurance, CONNAUGHT LABORATORIES LTD., 1755 Steeles Ave. W., Willowdale, ON M2R 3T4 (416) 667-2916, FAX 667-3004. Born Toronto 1960. m. Walter Melnyk. 2 ch. **EDUC:** Univ. of Toronto, B.Sc.(Zoology) 1983; McMaster Univ., M.Sc.(Medical Sci.) 1985; York Univ., Ph.D.(Molecular Biol.) 1990. **CAREER:** Teaching Asst., Dept. of Nursing, McMaster Univ., 1983-85; Lab. Supervisor, York Univ., 1985-90; Mgr, Process Improvement, Connaught Laboratories Ltd., 1990; Asst. Dir., Viral Vaccines, 1990-92; Dir., Prod. Svcs, 1992-93; Dir., Quality Assurance, 1993 to date. **SELECTED PUBLICATIONS:** various publications, abstracts & conference presentations. **AFFIL:** Parenteral Drug Association; Pharmaceutical Sciences Group; American Tissue Culture Association; International Association of Biological Standardization. **HONS:** Lillian Massey Treble Gold Medal in Life Sciences, Univ. of Toronto, 1983; numerous scholarships. **INTERESTS:** music; travel. **COMMENT:** *"I am a highly motivated individual who is constantly seeking improvement through education. I achieve strength from my family, which has played an integral part in my education and career advancements."*

McAuley, Sharon, B.A. ⬚ / ⓢ
Publisher, QUILL & QUIRE MAGAZINE, Key Publishers, 70 The Esplanade, Ste. 210, Toronto, ON M5E 1R2 (416) 360-0044, FAX (416) 955-0794, EMAIL quill@hookup.net. Born Sault Ste. Marie, Ont. 1964. m. Brian Kendall. **EDUC:** Univ. of Toronto, B.A.(English Lit.) 1986; Banff Centre for the Arts, Grad.(Magazine Publishing Workshop) 1986, Grad.(Book Publishing Workshop) 1992. **CAREER:** Acct Exec., Saturday Night Publishing Services, 1986-87; Circulation Fulfillment Mgr, 1987-88; Circulation Mgr, 1988-89; CB Media Limited, 1987-89; Principal, Sharon McAuley Circulation Management, 1990 to date; Circulation Mgr, *Quill & Quire,* 1990-94; Mktg/ Circulation Mgr, 1994; Publisher, 1994 to date.

AFFIL: Circulation Management Association of Canada (Bd. 1991-93; Pres. 1993-94; Past Pres. 1994-95); Canadian Magazine Publishers' Association (Committee Mbr.; Newsstand Distribution Committee 1992 to date; Travelling Consultant 1993 to date; Postal Affairs Committee 1996 to date).

McAuliffe, Jane Dammen, B.A.,M.A., Ph.D. ✑ 📖 ☼
Chairman, Department for the Study of Religion and Director, Centre for the Study of Religion, UNIVERSITY OF TORONTO, 123 St. George St., Toronto, ON M5S 2E8 (416) 978-2395. 4 ch. Dennis James, Margaret, Katherine, Elizabeth. **EDUC:** Trinity Coll., Univ. of Toronto, B.A.(Classics/Phil.) 1968; Univ. of Toronto, M.A.(Religious Studies) 1979, Ph.D.(Islamic Studies) 1984. **CAREER:** Asst. Prof., Dept. of Study of Religion, Univ. of Toronto, 1981-86; Asst. Prof. to Assoc. Prof., Hist. of Religions & Islamic Studies, Candler Sch. of Theology, Emory Univ., Atlanta, GA, 1986-92; Assoc. Dean, 1990-92; Assoc. Prof., Dept. of Middle East & Islamic Studies, 1992 to date; Chair, Dept. for the Study of Religion & Dir., Centre for the Study of Religion, Univ. of Toronto, 1992 to date; Vatican Commission for Religious Rel'ns with Muslims, 1994 to date. **SELECTED PUBLICATIONS:** *Qur'anic Christians: An Analysis of Classical and Modern Exegesis* (1991); *Abbasid Authority Affirmed: The Early Years of al-Mansur* (1994); various articles in professional journals. **AFFIL:** American Society for the Study of Religion; American Academy of Religion; American Oriental Society; Canadian Society for the Study of Religion; Middle East Studies Association; Oriental Club of Toronto; Society for Values in Higher Education. **HONS:** Thesis Award, Middle Eastern Studies Association, 1985; Guggenheim Fellowship, 1996. **MISC:** numerous fellowships & research grants.

McBean, Marnie ■ ■ Ⓦ
Olympic Athlete. c/o Canadian Olympic Association. Born Vancouver 1968. **EDUC:** currently studying Kinesiology. **SPORTS CAREER:** started rowing, 1985; mbr., Cdn Nat'l Rowing Team, 1989 to date. Olympic Games: Gold, 2x, & Bronze, 4x, 1996; Gold, 2-, & Gold, 8+, 1992. World championships: 2nd, 4x, & 1st, 2x, 1995; 2nd, 2x, 1994; 2nd, 1x, 1993; 1st, 2-, & 1st, 8+, 1991; 4th, 4-, 1990; 4th, 4-, 1989. World junior championships: 3rd, 2-, 1986. World Cup: 1st, overall standings, 1994, 1st, 1x (UK), 1st, 1x (Germany), 2nd, 1x (Switzerland), & 5th, 1x (France), 1994. Int'l regattas: 1st, 2x (Switzerland), 1995; 1st, 2-, & 1st, 8+ (Netherlands), & 1st, 2- (Germany), 1992; 1st,

2- (Switzerland), 1991; 1st, 4- (Netherlands), & 1st, 4- (Austria), 1990. Pan Am Games: 1st, 2x, 1995. World University Games: 1st, 4x, & 1st, 1x, 1993; 2nd, 4-, 1989. Canadian championships: 1st, 2-, 1990; 1st, 2-, 1989. US championships: 1st, 2x, & 1st, 4x, 1995; 1st, 1x, & 1st, 4x, 1993; 1st, 4-, & 1st, 8+, 1990; 1st, 4+, & 1st, 8+, 1989. **AFFIL:** Kids Help Phone (Nat'l Spokesperson). **HONS:** Female Athlete of the Year, Univ. of Western Ontario, 1989; Female Athlete of the Year, Ontario Rowing Association, 1989; Centennial Medal, Canadian Amateur Rowing Association, 1991; Dick Ellis Memorial Trophy, 1991 & 1992; Meritorious Service Medal, 1995. **INTERESTS:** cycling; curling; coaching. **MISC:** coached Univ. of Western Ontario varsity women's heavyweight rowing team; Olympic team spare, 1988.

McCall, Christina, B.A. ✐ 📖
Author/Editor, SATURDAY NIGHT MAGAZINE, 184 Front St. E., Ste. 400, Toronto, ON M5A 4N3. Born Toronto 1935. m. Stephen Clarkson. **EDUC:** Univ. of Toronto, B.A.(English) 1956; Massey Coll., Univ. of Toronto, pst-grad. work in Pol. Sci. 1978. **CAREER:** Ed./Writer, *Maclean's, Saturday Night, The Globe and Mail*, late 1950s to mid-1990s. **SELECTED PUBLICATIONS:** *The Man from Oxbow* (1967); *Grits: A Portrait of the Liberal Party* (1982); *Trudeau and Our Times* vol. I (1990) vol. II (1994); hundreds of articles in periodicals. **AFFIL:** Writers' Union; PEN, Committee for '94; Univ. of Toronto (Hon. Degree Committee); Victoria Coll. (Chancellor's Council). **HONS:** President's Medal, Univ. of Western Ontario; National Magazine Awards, 1978 & 1980; Southam Fellowship, 1977-78; Book of the Year Award, Canadian Authors' Association, 1983; Gov. General's Award for Literary Non-Fiction, 1990; John W. Dafoe for Distinguished Writing, 1994. **INTERESTS:** literature; politics; travel.

McCallion, The Hon. Hazel * ✿ ♂
Mayor, CITY OF MISSISSAUGA, 300 City Centre Dr., Mississauga, ON L5B 3C1. Born 1921. **CAREER:** began political career, 1967; Councillor, 2 terms, & sat on numerous committees of the Region of Peel & the City of Mississauga; elected Mayor, City of Mississauga, 1978; currently serving 7th term. **AFFIL:** has served on the exec. of many committees & associations incl.: Association of Municipalities of Ontario; Canadian Federation of Municipalities; Advisory Committee on Local Government Management. **MISC:** became the 1st mayor of a major municipality to submit the annual operating budget to residents for input; established the GTA Mayor's Committee, 1992.

McCallion, Kathryn E., B.A. ■ 🍁 $
Assistant Deputy Minister, International Business and Communications, and Chief Trade Commissioner, Federal Department of Foreign Affairs and External Trade, GOVERNMENT OF CANADA, L.B. Pearson Building, 125 Sussex Dr., Ottawa, ON K1A 0G2 (613) 996-7065, FAX 996-0677. Born Toronto 1945. s. **EDUC:** Univ. of Waterloo, B.A.(Pol. Sci.) 1972. **CAREER:** Second Sec. (Commercial), Embassy of Canada, Mexico City, 1973-75; V-Consul & Asst. Trade Commissioner, Boston, 1975-77; Coord. for Enterprise Canada '77, Halifax Reg'l Office, Dept. of Industry, Trade & Commerce, 1977; Consul & Trade Commissioner, Boston, 1977-78; Pres., Professional Association of Foreign Service Officers, 1980-81; Officer, US Mktg & Oper. Div., Western Hemisphere Bureau, Dept. of Industry, Trade & Commerce, 1978; Deputy Chief, Commodity Arrangements Div., Office of Gen. Rel'ns, Dept. of Industry, Trade & Commerce, 1978-81; Exec. Asst. to the Deputy Min., 1981-82; Exec. Asst. to the Deputy Min. (Int'l Trade)/Coord., Int'l Econ. Rel'ns, Dept. of External Affairs, 1982-83; Dir., Agric., Fish, & Food Policy Div., 1983-84; Counsellor, O.E.C.D., Paris, 1984-87; High Commissioner, Kingston, Jamaica, 1987-90; Sr. Departmental Asst. to the Sec. of State for External Affairs, 1990-91; Dir.-Gen., Western Europe Bureau, Dept. of External Affairs, 1991-94; Asst. Deputy Min., Latin Am. & Caribbean Branch, Dept. of Foreign Affairs & Int'l Trade, 1994-96; Asst. Deputy Min., Int'l Bus. & Comm., & Chief Trade Commissioner, 1996 to date. **INTERESTS:** diving; golf; squash; skiing; reading; music.

McCallum, Lorna, M.A., Ph.D. ✏ ⊛
Dean, Faculty of Language, Literature and Performing Arts, DOUGLAS COLLEGE, Box 2503, New Westminster, BC V3L 5B2 (604) 527-5284, FAX 527-5095. Born Edmonton 1946. d.. **EDUC:** Univ. of Alberta, M.A.(English) 1971, Ph.D.(English) 1978. **AFFIL:** Mbr., Exec. Comm. for Event Management magazine; Exec. Prod., Technostyle (journal of the Cdn. Assoc. of Teachers of Tech. Writing); Mbr., Amelia Douglas Gallery Art Exhibit Committee; Mbr., Arts and Culture Advisory Committee, City of New Westminster; Admin. Liason, Women's Studies, Provincial Articulation Committee. **HONS:** Canadian Women's Press Club Scholarship; Isaac Walton Killam Memorial Fellowships, Canada Council Doctoral Fellowship. **INTERESTS:** Romantic and Victorian poetry, contemporary Canadian women writers, rhetorical theory, gender and cultural issues in language, art, antiques, poetry, women's issues, the restoration of a 1906 house. **COMMENT:** *"Much of my career has involved addressing the issue of the writing competence of post-secondary students - a controversial issue, particularly in the 80s.*

McCallum, Susan, A.O.C.A. ■ ⊛ 📖
Art Director. 674 Queen St. West, Toronto, ON M6J 1H1 (416) 703-2924, FAX 599-3404. Born Toronto s. **EDUC:** Ontario Coll. of Art, A.O.C.A.(Graphic Design/Photography) 1991. **CAREER:** Art Dir./Designer, *Steptext*, 1991-92; Art Dir./Designer, *C Magazine*, 1991 to date; Art Dir./Designer, *Ontario Craft*, 1993-95; Freelance Designer of Small Catalogues, Art Gallery of Ontario, 1993-95. **HONS:** Award of Excellence, O.S.G.D.A., 1991; 3 Silver Awards, Editorial Design, Advertising & Design Club of Canada, 1993, 1994; Gold Award, Best Cover (*C Magazine*), National Magazine Awards, 1994; Gold Award, Art Direction of an Entire Issue, National Magazine Awards, 1996. **MISC:** selected for Toronto Graphic Design Exhibition in Villeurbane, France, by the Society of Graphic Designers of Canada.

McCann, Penny ■■ 🎭 📺 ⊛
President, INDEPENDENT FILM & VIDEO ALLIANCE, 4550 Garnier, Montreal, QC H2J 3S7 (514) 522-8240, FAX 522-8011. **COMMENT:** *"Penny McCann is an independent video and filmmaker, residing in Ottawa, whose films and videos have appeared in festivals and on television networks, including the CBC and Women's Television Network."*

McCann-Beranger, Judith, B.A., B.Ed., M.A. ✊
Executive Director, ALZHEIMER PRINCE EDWARD ISLAND, 166 Fitzroy St., Charlottetown, PE C1A 1S1 (902) 628-2257, FAX 368-2715. Born Stephenville, Nfld. 1952. m. Gregory. 6 ch. **EDUC:** Memorial Univ. of Newfoundland, B.Ed.(Psych./Religious Studies) 1978, B.A.(Psych.) 1989; Regis Univ., Denver, Col., M.A.(Psych.) 1990. **CAREER:** teacher, sr. high sch., 1976-90; Dept. Head, 1987-90; Proj. Coord., HIV/AIDS Counselling Initiative, 1991; Prov. Coord., Ready or Not Parenting Program, 1991-93; Pres., People Concept, 1990 to date; Exec. Dir., Alzheimer P.E.I., 1991 to date. **SELECTED PUBLICATIONS:** "Family Strengthening Ideas" (*The Guardian* Mar. 1994). **EDIT:** Co-editor, *Alzheimer Prince Edward Island Provincial Newsletter,* Alzheimer P.E.I.; *Putting Families First*, Family Services Canada. **AFFIL:** Family Service Canada (Nat'l Bd.); P.E.I. Council for the Family (Prov. Chair); Mediation P.E.I. (Pres.); Canadian Certification Committee for Canadian Certified Family Education

(Cdn Certified Family Educator); National Family Education Committee (Co-Chair); Stepfamily Association of America (Bd. Mbr. representing Canada); Vanier Institute of the Family; Canadian Guidance & Counselling Association. **HONS:** Scholarship, Presentation Sisters, St. John's, 1988; Volunteer Award, Family Service Canada, 1990. **INTERESTS:** family; travel; reading. **MISC:** trained mediator. **COMMENT:** *"A caring and energetic educator, therapist, mediator and consultant, committed to improving the quality of life and performance of individuals, families and organizations."*

McCain, The Honourable Margaret Norrie, B.A.,B.S.W.,LL.D. 🍁 ♥

Lieutenant-Governor, PROVINCE OF NEW BRUNSWICK, 736 King St., Box 6000, Fredericton, NB E3B 5H1 (506) 453-2505, FAX 444-5280. Born Noranda, Que. 1934. m. George Wallace Ferguson McCain. 4 ch. **EDUC:** Mount Allison Univ., B.A.(Hist.) 1954; Univ. of Toronto, B.S.W.(Social Work) 1955. **VOLUNTEER CAREER:** Bd., Young Naturalist Foundation; Bd., Canadiana Fund of the National Capital Commission; Volunteer Music Asst., N.B. public schools; Co-Chair, Carleton Victoria Arts Council; Co-Chair, Florenceville Recreation Council; Dir., National Ballet Sch.; Dir., Muriel McQueen Fergusson Foundation; Canadian Battle of Normandy Foundation. **HONS:** Dame, Award, Muriel McQueen Fergusson Foundation Award, 1995; LL.D.(Hon.), Univ. of New Brunswick, 1993; LL.D.(Hon.), Mount Allison Univ., 1995; LL.D.(Hon.), St. Thomas Univ., 1995; LL.D.(Hon.), Univ. of Toronto, 1996; LL.D.(Hon.), Univ. of Moncton, 1996. **INTERESTS:** family; skiing; swimming; tennis; walking; reading. **COMMENT:** *"My family, and all related activities and events, have always been my greatest joy in life. I have four children, eight grandchildren. Since they have now left home, my primary focus has been on activities related to youth education, family value, and family violence."*

McCarthy, Doris, B.A.,R.C.A. ✪

Painter. Born Calgary 1910 **EDUC:** Ontario Coll. of Art, A.O.C.A.(Drawing/Painting/Sculpture) 1930; Univ. of Toronto, B.A.(English) 1989. **CAREER:** painter in oil & watercolour; teacher, Art Dept., Central Tech. Sch., Toronto, 40 yrs.; liturgical artist; graphic designer. **SELECTED PUBLICATIONS:** *A Fool in Paradise* (Toronto: MacFarlane, Walter and Ross, 1990); *The Good Wine* (Toronto: MacFarlane, Walter and Ross, 1991). **EXHIBITIONS:** *A Feast of Incarnation* (1991-94); *Crown of Time*, Banff (1992); Canadian Gallery, Calgary (1994); Wynick/Tuck Gallery, Toronto (1994, 1996); Canadian Gallery, Calgary (1995); Chapel Gallery, Bracebridge (1996). **AFFIL:** Ontario Society of Artists; Royal Canadian Academy; Canadian Society of Painters in Water Colour; Ontario Coll. of Art (Fellow). **HONS:** Award of Merit, City of Scarborough, 1982; Order of Canada, 1987; Order of Ontario, 1992; LL.D. (Hon.), Univ. of Calgary, 1995. **MISC:** Designer, City of Scarborough flag; subject of award-winning film *Doris McCarthy, Heart of a Painter.*

McCarthy, Francine, M.G., B.Sc.,M.Sc., Ph.D. ■ 🎓 ⚛ ♥

Associate Professor, Earth Sciences, BROCK UNIVERSITY, St. Catharines, ON L2S 3A1 (905) 688-5550, ext. 4286, FAX 682-9020, EMAIL francine@craton.geol.brocku.ca. Born Montreal 1961. s. **EDUC: EDUC:** Dalhousie Univ., B.Sc.(Geol./Biol.) 1984, Ph.D.(Earth Sci.) 1992; Univ. of Toronto, M.Sc.(Geol.) 1986. **CAREER:** Lecturer, St. Francis Xavier Univ., 1990; Lecturer, Brock Univ., 1991-92; Asst. Prof., 1992 to date; Dir., Radiocarbon Lab., 1992 to date; Research Assoc., Dept. of Botany, Royal Ontario Museum, 1993 to date. **SELECTED PUBLICATIONS:** "Global Warming Threatens Cities of the World" (*Niagara Falls Review* Feb. 29, 1992); "Pollen Transport Processes in the Western North Atlantic: Evidence from Cross-Margin and North-South Transects," P.J. Mudie (*Marine Geology* 1994); "A comparison of postglacial arcellacean ("Thecamoebian") and pollen succession in Atlantic Canada, illustrating the potential of arcellaceans for paleoclimatic reconstruction," with E.S. Collins, J.H. McAndrews, H.A. Kerr, D.B. Scott, F.S. Medioli (*Journal of Paleontology* 1995); various other publications. **AFFIL:** Geological Society of America; Canadian Association of Women in Science (Exec. Mbr., Niagara 1993-94); Brock Univ. (Chair, Status of Women in Science Committee 1994-95); Friends of Shopping Bag Ladies (Bd. Mbr.); American Association of Stratigraphic Palynologists. **HONS:** Undergrad. Prize, Canadian Society of Petroleum Geologists, 1983; Killam Memorial Scholarship, 1988-91. **MISC:** scholarship recipient; numerous conference publications. **COMMENT:** *"I teach undergraduate and graduate courses in Earth Sciences, especially environmental earth sciences. My research interests are paleoecology and paleoclimatology, especially of the last two million years (the Quaternary Period)."*

McCarthy, Grace, Mary, O.C., F.R.A.I.C. 🍁 $ ✊ ☝

Former Politician. Vancouver, BC. Born Vancouver 1927. m. Raymond B. McCarthy. 2 ch.

Mary, Calvin. **EDUC:** King Edward Senior Secondary Sch., Grade 12. **CAREER:** Pres., Grayce Florists Ltd., 1944-75; founded B.C. Sch. of Floral Design, 1953; V-Chrm & Commissioner, Bd. of Parks & Public Recreation, City of Vancouver, 1960-66; elected MLA 1966; re-elected 1969, 1975, 1979, 1983, 1986; Min. without Portfolio, 1966-72; Pres., B.C. Social Credit Party, 1973-75; Prov. Sec., Deputy Premier, Min. of Recreation & Travel Industry, 1975-78; Prov. Sec., Deputy Premier, Min. of Hum. Res. & Min. Responsible for the Insurance Corporation of B.C., 1978-79; Deputy Premier & Min. of Hum. Res., 1979-83; Min. of Hum. Res. & Min. Responsible for B.C. Transit, 1983-86; Prov. Sec. & Min. Responsible for B.C. Transit, 1986; Deputy Premier & Min. of Econ. Dev., 1986-88; Caucus Mbr., Legislative Assembly, 1988-91; Leader, B.C. Social Credit Party, 1993-94; retired from B.C. politics, 1994. **DIRECTOR:** B.C. Bearings; Health-Mor Industries Incorporated. **AFFIL:** Canadian Paraplegic Foundation (Dir., B.C. Div.); Kinsmen Rehabilitation Association (Bd. Mbr.); Salvation Army (Nat'l Advisory Bd.; Greater Vancouver Advisory Bd.; Chrm, Cultural Heritage Committee); BC CH.I.L.D. Foundation (Pres.); B.C. Lions Foundation for Children with Disabilities (Dir.); Osteoporosis Association of B.C. (Dir.); Swan-E-Set Golf & Country Club (Gov.); Canadian Music Competition (Hon. Patron, B.C. Society); Worldsphere Foundation (Patron); Variety Club, Tent 47; Daughters of BC (Native Daughter); Daughters of Nile; 3-H Society (Hon. Mbr.); ASTC Science World Society (Hon. Life Mbr.); Victoria A.M. Tourist Association (Hon. Life Mbr.); B.C. Travel Association (Hon. Life Mbr.); Vancouver A.M. Tourist Association (Hon. Life Mbr.); B.C. Motels, Resorts & Trailer Parks Association (Hon. Life Mbr.); B.C. Florists' Transworld Delivery Association (District 118) (Hon. Life Mbr.); Northwest Florists' Association (Hon. Life Mbr.). **HONS:** Award, Most Outstanding Contribution in Assisting the Mentally Handicapped, B.C. Association of Retarded Children, 1969; Svc Award, Kinsmen's Mothers' March, 1972, 1973; Harold J. Merrilees Award of the Year, Greater Vancouver Convention & Visitors' Bureau, 1977; Marketer of the Year Award, Northwest Council of Sales & Marketing, 1977; President's Award for Outstanding Contribution to Tourism in Greater Victoria, Greater Victoria Visitors' Info. Centre, 1977; Commendation, Outstanding Service in the Public Interest, Office of the Lieutenant-Gov. of the State of California, 1977; Appreciation Plaque, B.C. Aviation Council, 1978; Marketer of the Year Award, International Sales & Marketing Executives, 1978; Certificate of Recogni-

tion, B.C. Film & Video Industry Association, 1978; Marketer of the Year Award, B.C. Chapter, American Marketing Association, 1979; Award of Appreciation, Restaurant & Food Services Association of B.C., 1979; Plaque, Commitment to the Enhancement of Social Services, Catholic Community Services, 1980; Plaque, Signal Service, Salvation Army, 1980; Heart Award, Variety Club, Tent 47, 1981; Medal of Distinction, International Association of Lions Clubs, 1982; Gov't of Canada Silver Medal, outstanding achievement in tourism, 1982; Barker, Variety Clubs International, 1982; Commemorative Scroll for "Outstanding Contributions to the First Six *Timmy's Christmas Telethons for Handicapped Citizens*," B.C. Lions Society for Crippled Children, 1983; Fellow, Royal Architectural Institute of Canada, 1983; Mbr., Military Hospitaller Order of Saint Lazarus of Jerusalem, 1984; Recognition Plaque, Service to Tourism in Canada, Canadian Business Travel Association, 1985; Wake-up Award, Outstanding Contribution to Tourism & Hospitality Industry, Vancouver AM Tourist Association, 1987; Man of the Year Award, Brotherhood Interfaith Association, 1987; Dame Commander, Military Hospitaller Order of Saint Lazarus of Jerusalem, 1990; Service Award, Restaurant & Food Services Association of B.C., 1992; Golden Heart Community Achievement Award, Variety Club, Tent 47, 1992; Community Achievement Award, Vancouver Board of Trade, 1992; Jewish Nat'l Fund Honoree, 1993; Order of Distinguished Service, Worldwide, Salvation Army, 1993; Officer of the Order of Canada, 1993. **MISC:** initiated 1st toll-free help line for abused children, 1979; only Cdn MLA to be nominated for Gov't of Canada Silver Medal, 1982; 1st woman Pres. of any Chamber of Commerce (Hastings Chamber of Commerce) 1950-51; Canada's 1st woman Barker, Variety Clubs International, 1982; 1st woman mbr., Vancouver Chinatown Lions Club, 1989; 1st woman recipient, Golden Heart Community Achievement Award, Variety Club, Tent 47, 1992. **COMMENT:** *"Currently, I serve on several charitable and corporate boards, and am President of BC CH.I.L.D. Foundation (Children with Intestinal and Liver Disorders)."*

McCarthy, Sheila ⊗ ♥

Actor. c/o ACI Talent Inc., 205 Ontario St., Toronto, ON M5A 2V6 (416) 363-7414. Born Toronto m. Peter Donaldson. 2 ch. **EDUC:** Univ. of Victoria, Acting; National Ballet, Dance; studied with Uta Hagen, HB Studio, NYC, Acting. **SELECTED CREDITS:** Lead, *House Arrest* (feature), Savoy Pictures; Lead,

The Possession of Michael D. (MOW), Fox/Atlantis; Lead, *A Woman of Independent Means* (miniseries), NBC; Lead, *Adult Children of Alcoholics (The Musical),* CBC; Lead, *The Lotus Eaters* (feature), Mortimer & Ogilvey; Lead, *Stepping Out* (feature), Paramount; Support, *Die Hard II* (feature), Fox; Lead, *White Room* (feature), VOS Productions; Lead, *George's Island* (feature), Salter Street Films; Lead, *I've Heard the Mermaids Singing* (feature), VOS Productions; recurring role, *Picket Fences* (series), CBS; Guest Lead, *Hidden Room* (series), Lifetime Channel; Guest Lead, *Street Legal* (series), CBC; Guest Lead, *Mount Royal* (series), CTV/Alliance; Lead, *A Nest of Singing Birds* (MOW), CBC; Guest Star, 12 eps., *The Frantics* (series), CBC; Principal, *Waiting for the Parade,* dir. Robin Phillips, CBC/Grand Theatre; Helena, *A Midsummer Night's Dream,* Stratford, 1993; Toinette, *The Imaginary Invalid,* Stratford, 1993; Nora, *Wrong For Each Other,* Theatre London; Sally Bowles, *Cabaret,* dir. Brian McDonald, Stratford, 1987; Ophelia, *Hamlet,* dir. Guy Sprung, Toronto Free Theatre; Audrey, *Little Shop of Horrors,* dir. Marlene Smith, Crest Theatre; Rosie, *Really Rosie,* dir. Peter Moss, Young People's Theatre. AFFIL: Families for Children of Chernobyl (Bd. of Dir.); Willow, halfway house for women with breast cancer; ACTRA; CAEA. HONS: Best Actress (*Really Rosie*), Dora Mavor Moore Awards, 1983; nominated, Best Actress (*Waiting For the Parade),* 1985; Best Actress (*Little Shop of Horrors*), Dora Mavor Moore Awards, 1986; nominated, Best Actress (*A Nest of Singing Birds*), Gemini Awards, 1988; nominated, Best Actress, Series Guest (*Mount Royal*), Gemini Awards, 1988; Best Actress (*I've Heard the Mermaids Singing*), Genie Awards, 1988; Best Actress (*The Lotus Eaters*), Genie Awards, 1993; Charles Chaplin Award for Outstanding Performance (*I've Heard the Mermaids Singing*), Veve, Switzerland. INTERESTS: reading; cooking; my children; dancing. COMMENT: *"I am a working actor in Canada. I am raising two daughters. I have my work. I am blessed with good luck and a beautiful family. I will be doing this until I'm 90—I hope."*

McCawley, Deborah Joan, Q.C.,B.A., LL.B. ⚖ 🐝
Chief Executive Officer, LAW SOCIETY OF MANITOBA, 219 Kennedy St., Winnipeg, MB R3C 1S8 (204) 942-5571. Born Winnipeg 1951. m. Hon. Otto Lang. 2 ch. EDUC: Univ. of Manitoba, B.A. 1972; Osgoode Hall Law Sch., Toronto, LL.B. 1975. BAR: Man., 1976. CAREER: articling student, Aikins, MacAulay & Thorvaldson, 1975-76; Assoc., 1976-78;

Ptnr, Houston & McCawley, 1978-80; Deputy CEO, Law Society of Manitoba, 1981-88; Sessional Lecturer, Fac. of Law, Univ. of Manitoba, 1985-88; CEO, Law Society of Manitoba, 1988 to date. EDIT: Co-ed., *Legal Education in Canada.* AFFIL: Canadian Lawyers' Insurance Association (Advisory Bd); Lawyers' Excess Liability Insurance (Manitoba) Ltd. (Pres.); Federation of Law Societies (Chair, Committee on Indiv. Lawyer Mobility); Canadian Bar Association (Nat'l Council Mbr.); Manitoba Bar Association (Council Mbr.); Univ. of Manitoba (Special Admissions Committee, Fac. of Law); Manitoba Law Sch. Foundation (Sec.-Treas.); L.E.A.F.; Royal Winnipeg Ballet (Co-Chair, Capital Campaign); Manitoba Medical Services Foundation (Bd. Mbr.). HONS: Queen's Counsel, 1988.

McClare, Sharon, B.Comm. Ⓢ
Administrator, AMOCO CANADA PETROLEUM COMPANY LTD., 240 - 4 Ave. SW, Box 200, Calgary, AB T2P 2H8 (403) 234-4894, FAX 234-4433. Past President, DESK AND DERRICK CLUB OF CALGARY. Born Lethbridge, Alta. 1950. d. EDUC: Henderson Coll. of Business, Secretarial Program 1971; Univ. of Calgary, B.Comm.(Mktg) 1982, B.Comm.(Petroleum Land Mgmt) 1988; Mount Royal Coll., Certificate (Professional Speaking) 1995. CAREER: Sec., Gov't of Canada, 1971-72; Sec., Gov't of Alta., 1975-77; Administrator, Calgary Bd. of Educ., 1975-77; Life Underwriter, London Life Insurance Company, 1982-83; Administrator, Amoco Canada Petroleum Company Ltd., 1984 to date. AFFIL: Desk & Derrick Club of Calgary (Dir. 1989; 2nd VP 1992; 1st VP 1993; Pres. 1994; Past Pres. 1995; Chair, various committees); Canadian Association of Petroleum Land Administration (Dir. 1994). HONS: Gov't Rel'ns Commendation Award, Desk and Derrick Association, 1992. INTERESTS: theatre; opera; ballet; bridge; travel; hockey; public speaking. COMMENT: *"My employment at Amoco and association with Desk and Derrick Club provides me with recognition and the opportunity to interact on an educational level regarding the energy industry."*

McClellan, Hon. Shirley, M.L.A. ■ 🌿 ⊕
Member of Legislative Assembly (Chinook) and Minister of Community Development, GOVERNMENT OF ALBERTA, 127 Legislature Building, Edmonton, AB T5K 2B6 (403) 427-4928, FAX 427-0188. Born Hanna, Alta. m. 2 ch. CAREER: farmer; M.L.A. (Chinook), Gov't of Alta., 1987 to date; Agric. & Rural Affairs Caucus Committee; Educ. Caucus Committee;

Irrigation Caucus Committee; Ad Hoc Task Force on New Reproductive Health & Sexuality Programs in Alta. Health Units, 1987-88; Ad Hoc Task Force on Combined Birth Control & Sexually Transmitted Disease Screening Clinics, 1987-88; Water Supply Action Committee, 1988; Assoc. Min. of Agric., 1989-92; Min. Responsible for Rural Dev., 1992; Agricultural & Rural Economy Cabinet Committee; Econ. Planning Cabinet Committee; Legislative Review Committee; Min. of Health, 1992 to date; Min. Responsible for the Wild Rose Foundation, 1993 to date; Min. Responsible for the Alta. Alcohol & Drug Abuse Commission, 1993-96; Min. of Community Dev., 1996 to date; Treasury Bd.; Standing Policy Committee on Community Svcs; Min. Responsible for the Seniors Advisory Council, 1994 to date. **AFFIL:** Multicultural Commission; Alberta Parks Recreation; Alberta Foundation of the Arts; Alberta Association for Continuing Education (Dir.); Canadian Association for Continuing Education (Dir.); Big Country Further Education Council; Ministers' Advisory Committee on Further Education; Ministers' Advisory Committee on College Affairs. **COMMENT:** *"Shirley McClellan was born in Hanna and attended school in Cereal and Red Deer. Mrs. McClellan currently farms in New Brigden with her husband, Lloyd, and her son, Mick. Her daughter, Tami, is a school teacher."*

McClintock, Margaret ■ 📖 ⑤

Publisher, COACH HOUSE PRESS, 760 Bathurst St., Toronto, ON M5S 2R6 (416) 588-8999, FAX 588-3615. Born Jonquière, Que. 1954. m. James MacCammon. 1 ch. Tom MacCammon. **CAREER:** Ed., *Books for Everybody*, 1980-83; Assoc. Publisher, *Canadian Art* Magazine, 1984-85; Lit. Officer, Ontario Arts Council, 1986-89; Publisher, Coach House Press, 1990 to date. **DIRECTOR:** Coach House Press Inc.

McClure, Laurie ■■ ⑳ ♡

President, ONTARIO ASSOCIATION FOR VOLUNTEER ADMINISTRATION, (not-for-profit professional organization representing administrators of volunteers), 801 York Mills Rd., Ste. 201, Toronto, ON M3B 1X7 (416) 392-1347, FAX 392-0220. Born Toronto 1950 **EDUC:** Centennial Coll., Certificate (Recreation Leadership) 1970; Ryerson Polytechnic Institute, Diploma (Mgmt & Community Studies) 1989. **CAREER:** Community Rec. Mgr, City of Toronto Dept. of Parks & Rec., 26 yrs. **AFFIL:** Ontario Association for Volunteer Administration (Bd. mbr. 1990-94; VP 1994-96; Pres. 1996-98). **INTERESTS:** reading; travel; good wines. **COMMENT:** *"My greatest achievement*

will be in 1998 when O.A.V.A. successfully merges with Ontario Directors of Volunteers in Hospitals."

McCormack, Thelma ■■ ⑳ 凵 📖

Professor Emerita, YORK UNIVERSITY. **CAREER:** taught full-time at York Univ., 28 yrs. until recent retirement; areas of specialization: censorship, the media, mass communications, pornography, public policies, pol. issues, e.g. free trade & its implications for Canada, gender issues & feminism, reproductive technologies & ethics, & feminist research; Dir., Grad. Programme in Sociology, 1972-75; mbr., Bd. of Gov., 1977-79; Chairperson, Dept. of Sociology, 1980-83; Dir., Grad. Programme in Women's Studies; Acting Dir., Centre for Feminist Research (York), 1993-94. **SELECTED PUBLICATIONS:** 10 books or monographs for a variety of groups or sponsors incl. the Institute for Social Research, Canadian Research Institute for the Advancement of Women, a Metro Task Force subcommittee on Violence, the LaMarsh Research Program, York Univ., Ontario Medical Association, the CBC, & the Canadian Centre for Community Studies; 35 articles in Cdn, American, European & British journals of sociology, pol. economy, & women's studies, & cultural, univ. & professional publications; 14 papers printed/reprinted as chpts in books, encyclopedia & yearbook entries; more than 50 book reviews, various academic journals & news media. **EDIT:** served as mbr. of 4 ed. bds., professional & academic journals. **AFFIL:** Canadian Women's Studies Association (Pres. 1995-96); Canadian Sociology & Anthropology Association (former Pres.); Addiction Research Foundation (former mbr., Professional Advisory Group); Council of Ontario Universities (former York Univ. Academic Colleague). **HONS:** fellowships from Univ. of Wisconsin (the Vilas Award), Columbia Univ., the Canada Council; gave prestigious Sorokin Lecture, Univ. of Saskatchewan & Southam Lecture, Canadian Communications Association; Rep., Cdn Commission for UNESCO, 1989; honorary Doctor of Humane Letters, Mount Saint Vincent Univ., 1989; Distinguished Contribution Award, Canadian Sociology & Anthropology Association, 1991. **MISC:** participation in many academic conferences, & numerous lectures throughout Canada, the US & abroad; Visiting Prof., Hebrew Univ. of Jerusalem, 1975; Visiting Research Scholar, Univ. of California, L.A., 1980; Visiting Prof., Faculteit Massacommunicitaie, Univ. of Amsterdam, 1982; Resident Scholar & teacher, Nancy Rowell Jackman Chair in Women's Studies, Mount Saint Vincent Univ., 1990.

McCormick, Roxanne, M.A.,LL.B. (\$) ⚖
Partner, FASKEN CAMPBELL GODFREY, (Barristers & Solicitors), TD Bank Tower, Box 20, TD Centre, Toronto, ON M5K 1N6 (416) 865-4407, FAX 364-7813. Born Toronto 1952. m. Kevin McCormick. 2 ch. EDUC: Univ. of Glasgow, M.A.(Psych.) 1974; Univ. of Toronto, LL.B. 1980. BAR: Ont., 1982. CAREER: Assoc. Lawyer, Fasken Campbell Godfrey, 1982-87; Ptnr., 1987 to date. AFFIL: Canadian Bar Association; International Bar Association. HONS: Silver Medalist, Ont. Call to the Bar, 1982. INTERESTS: reading, music. COMMENT: *"I practise corporate commercial law in a firm of approximately 200 lawyers, focusing in particular on mergers and acquisitions, securities law and private and public financings."*

McCoubrey, Sharon, B.Ed.,M.Ed. ■ ⌘
Director, Bachelor of Education Program, OKANAGAN UNIVERSITY COLLEGE, 3333 College Way, Kelowna, BC V1V 1V7 (604) 762-5445, ext. 7306, FAX 470-6001, EMAIL slmccoub@okuc02.okanagan.bc.ca. Born Hanna, Alta. 1951. m. Robert W. McCoubrey. 2 ch. Sarah, Patrick. EDUC: Univ. of Victoria, B.Ed. 1981, M.Ed.(Art Educ.) 1986. CAREER: Classroom Teacher, District No. 23, Central Okanagan, 1972-74, 1981-83; 1984-87; Receptionist, Changing Images Audio-Visual Production Company, 1984; Sessional Instructor, Art Educ., Univ. of Victoria, Summer 1987, 1994, 1996; District Consultant, Fine Arts, District No. 23, Central Okanagan District, 1987-89; District Consultant, Primary Teaching & Fine Arts, 1989-90; Instructor, Art Educ., Okanagan University Coll., 1989-90; Prof., Art Educ. & Curriculum Studies, & Dept. Chair, 1990-94; Dir., B.Ed. Program, 1994-98. SELECTED PUBLICATIONS: *80 Art Lessons* (School District No. 23, 1989); *A Painter's Palette* (Vancouver: Creative Curriculum Incorporated, 1994); "Author-Illustrator, Students Making Books to Link Art and Writing" (*Journal of the BC Art Teachers' Association* 33(3) 1993); "To Think or Not to Think" (*Journal of the BC Art Teachers' Association* 34(1) 1994); "Honouring the Environment Through Art" (*Journal of the BC Art Teachers' Association* 34(2) 1994); "How to Teach Context in Art" (*PRIME AREAS*, Journal of the B.C. Primary Teacher's Association 38(1) 1995); *Treasures From Our Trees*, A Teaching Resource of the Tree Fruit Industry of British Columbia (B.C. Fruit Growers' Association, 1995); *Fabric and Fibre Art Works* (Vancouver, BC: Creative Curriculum Incorporated, 1996); "Decorated Mailboxes, A Disappearing Folk Art." (*BCATA Journal for Art Teachers* 36(2) 1996); various other publi-

cations. EDIT: Ed., "BC Report", Newsletter, Canadian Society for Education Through Art, 1988 to date; Ed., *Journal of the BC Art Teachers' Association*, 1990 to date. AFFIL: BC Art Teachers' Association; Canadian Society for Education Through Art; BC Arts in Education Council; National Art Education Association, US; International Society for Education Through Art; BC Provincial Primary Teachers' Association; BC Coll. of Teachers; Kelowna Art Gallery; Parents' Advisory Council (Pres. 1991-94); Church Bd. (Chair 1992-97); Community Shared-Use Facility (Consulting Committee); Lake Country Municipality Advisory Committee on Art in Public Places. HONS: BC Gov't Scholarship, 1969-71; Birk's Foundation Award, 1971; Univ. President's Scholarship, 1972; Maxwell Cameron Award, 1981; Art Educator of the Year, National Art Educators' Association, 1992. INTERESTS: watercolour painting & other art; reading; hiking; cross-country skiing; gardening; First Nations' art & culture; Regional Heritage. MISC: leader, numerous professional dev. workshops; guest speaker; various consultancies; various conference presentations. COMMENT: *"My life's goal is to balance involvement in my profession, community and family; to contribute to the learning of children; to share a rewarding life with my husband and to raise wise and happy children. Hard work, creativity and consideration of others have helped me meet this goal."*

McCracken, Kathleen Luanne, B.A.,M.A., Ph.D. ■ ⌘ ⊗ ▯
Lecturer in English and American Studies, UNIVERSITY OF ULSTER AT JORDANSTOWN, Shore Road, Newtownabbey, County Antrim, Northern Ireland, UK BT37 0QB 01 (232) 365131. Born Dundalk, Ont. 1960. cl. Arthur Aughey. 1 ch. Sky Blue McCracken Aughey. EDUC: York Univ., B.A.(English) 1983, M.A. 1984; Univ. of Toronto, Ph.D. 1989. CAREER: Visiting Author, League of Canadian Poets, Poets in the Schools program; various positions teaching lit. & writing, Univ. of Toronto, 1985-89; various positions teaching lit. & writing, Ryerson Polytechnic Institute, 1985-89; Course Dir., English, York Univ., 1988-89; Program Coord., Toronto Festival of Contemporary Irish Film, 1990; Ed., Wolfhound Press, Dublin, 1991; Visiting Poet, Annaghmakerrig, The Tyrone Guthrie Centre, Newbliss, County Monaghan, Ireland, May 1991; Tutorial Leader, Trinity Coll., Dublin, 1991; Lecturer, Sch. of Languages & Literature, Univ. of Ulster at Jordanstown, 1992 to date. SELECTED PUBLICATIONS: *A History of the Schools in Proton Township* (Markdale, Ont.: Grey County Bd.

of Educ., 1978); *Reflections* (Fredericton: Fiddlehead Poetry Books, 1979); *Into Celebration* (Toronto: Coach House Press, 1980); *The Constancy of Objects* (Kapuskasing: Penumbra Press, 1988); *Blue Light, Bay and College* (Waterloo: Penumbra Press, 1991); "Masks and Voices: Dramatic Personas in the Poetry of Paul Durcan" (*Canadian Journal of Irish Studies* 13(1) 1987); "A Northern Perspective: Dual Vision in the Poetry of Paul Muldoon" (*Canadian Journal of Irish Studies* 16(2) 1990); "Icon for a New Ireland: The Great Book of Ireland" (*The Ireland Fund of Canada Journal* 2(2) 1991); poetry has appeared in *Malahat Review, PRISM International, Poetry Canada Review, Waves, Canadian Woman Studies, Poetry Toronto, Literary Cavalcade, Vancouver Streets, Ariel, Moosehead Review* & others; various academic papers presented. **AFFIL:** Modern Language Association; Northeastern Modern Language Association; Association of Canadian University Teachers of English; Canadian Association for Irish Studies; British Association for American Studies; Irish Association for American Studies; American Conference for Irish Studies; League of Canadian Poets; Writers' Union of Canada; Ireland Fund of Canada; Canadian Alliance in Solidarity with Native People. **COMMENT:** *"I am a writer, primarily of poetry and literary criticism. My work is published in Canada, the US and the UK. Interests include painting, art history, film and photography, Native American literature and culture."*

McCready, Madge Evelyn ⊗ ☺
Vocalist, Choral Conductor. Edmonton, AB. 2 ch. Marla McCready-Kirilla, Patrick McCready. **CAREER:** vocal soloist; private vocal, piano & theory teacher, 1949-78; Dir. of Music, Trinity United Church, Edmonton, 20 yrs.; choral & vocal adjudicator, workshop leader & guest conductor throughout western Canada, 35 yrs.; mbr., Founding Bd. & Past Pres., Naramata Summer Sch. of Music Arts for Choral Musicians; mbr., Founding Bd., Association of Canadian Choral Conductors; mbr., Founding Bd. & Past Pres., Alberta Summer Music Workshop Association; mbr., Founding Bd., Alberta Choral Federation; Exec. Dir., 1978-94. **SELECTED CREDITS:** many leads in musical theatre productions in Edmonton. **AFFIL:** Alberta Choral Federation; Association of Canadian Choral Conductors; American Choral Directors' Association; International Choral Federation; Canadian Music Educators' Association; Musical Educators' Nat'l Conference. **HONS:** Distinguished Service Award, Association of Canadian Choral Conductors, 1994; Richard S. Eaton Award for Distinguished Service to Choral Music in Alberta, Alberta Choral Federation, 1994.

McCrone, Kathleen E., B.A.,M.A.,Ph.D. ⊗
Professor of History and Dean of Social Sciences, UNIVERSITY OF WINDSOR, Windsor, ON N9B 3P4 (519) 253-4232, ext. 2023, FAX 971-3659, EMAIL kem@uwindsor.ca. Born Regina 1941. s. **EDUC:** Univ. of Saskatchewan, B.A.(Hist.) 1963; New York Univ., M.A. 1967, Ph.D. 1971. **CAREER:** Lecturer, Univ. of Windsor, 1968-72; Asst. Prof., 1972-76; Assoc. Prof., 1976-84; Head, Dept. of Hist., 1978-81; Prof., 1984 to date; Dean, Fac. of Social Sciences, 1990 to date. **SELECTED PUBLICATIONS:** *Sport and the Physical Emancipation of English Women, 1870 - 1914* (London: Routledge, 1988); "William Thompson and the Appeal of One Half the Human Race" (*Atlantis* Spring 1980); "Play Up! and Play the Game! Sport at the Late Victorian Girls' Public School" (*Journal of British Studies* Spring 1984); "Class, Gender and English Women's Sport, 1890 - 1914" (*Journal of Sport History* Spring 1991); "Playing the Piano and Playing the Game: Culture and Physical Culture in Victorian and Edwardian Girls' Public Schools," in *The Private Schooling of Girls: Past and Present*, ed. Geoffrey Walford (London: Woburn Press, 1993); various other articles, book chapters, conference proceedings, & book reviews. **AFFIL:** Canadian Conference of Deans of Arts, Humanities & Social Sciences (Pres. 1994-95); Council of Deans of Arts & Science of Ontario (Exec. Committee 1993-95); Social Sciences Federation of Canada (Bd. of Dir. 1986-88); Canadian Historical Association (Council 1982-85); Windsor Symphony (Bd. of Dir., 1993 to date). **INTERESTS:** history of women in 19th-century England; music; travel; sport; reading. **MISC:** recipient of various grants. **COMMENT:** *"Throughout my career, I have been committed to academic excellence. My greatest satisfaction as a professor has come from my research and publications, and as an administrator from facilitating the achievements of others."*

McCullough, Marilyn Kay, B.A.,M.A. ■ ⊗
Director, Department of Continuing Education and Lecturer, History Department, MOUNT ALLISON UNIVERSITY, Sackville, NB E0A 3C0 (506) 364-2266, FAX 364-2216, EMAIL mmcullough@mta.ca. **EDUC:** Michigan State Univ., B.A.(Hist.) 1965; Cornell Univ., M.A.(Hist.) 1968. **CAREER:** Lecturer, Dept. of Hist., Oberlin Coll., 1970; Lecturer, Dept. of Phil. & Hist., Antioch Coll., 1970-71; Lecturer, Dept. of Hist., Univ. of Western Ontario, 1971-74; Lecturer, Humanities, Mount Allison Univ.,

1975-76; Lecturer, Religious Studies Dept., 1982 to date; Dir., Continuing Educ., 1984 to date; Lecturer, History Dept., 1995 to date. **AFFIL:** Atlantic Provinces Association of University Continuing Education (various executive positions); Canadian Association of University Continuing Education (Atlantic Rep. on Exec.); Phi Kappa Phi; Tau Sigma. **HONS:** NDFL (National Defense Foreign Language) fellowship, US, 1965-69; scholarship, NDFL; travel grant to Taiwan, London-Cornell Univ. **INTERESTS:** Asian hist., culture, phil. & religion; mature students. **MISC:** $24,500 grant to develop distance educ. teaching materials for 2 courses in world religions: Religions of the Near East & Religions of the Far East; extensive volunteer work, incl. prov. & local committees, mainly dealing with educ. & young people, the VON, Canadian Parents for French, Canadian Federation of University Women, Renaissance Sackville. **COMMENT:** *"I am also the mother of three and serve on a variety of volunteer organizations in my community."*

McDaniel, Susan A., PhD,FRSC 🎓 ⚛ ☝

Professor of Sociology, UNIVERSITY OF ALBERTA, Edmonton, AB T6G 2H4 (403) 492-0488, FAX (403) 492-7196, EMAIL susan.mcdaniel@ualberta.ca. Born New York City 1946. cl. Douglas Wahlsten. **EDUC:** Univ. of Massachusetts, B.A.(Soc.) 1968; Cornell Univ., M.A. 1970; Univ. of Alberta, Ph.D.(Social Demography) 1977. **CAREER:** Fac., Soc., Univ. of Waterloo, 1976-89; Visiting Prof., Soc., Univ. of Alberta, 1988-89; Prof., 1989 to date; Research Assoc., Population Research Lab., 1990 to date; Adjunct Prof., Human Ecology, 1994 to date. **SELECTED PUBLICATIONS:** *Social Problems Through Conflict and Order*, with Ben Agger (Don Mills, Ont.: Addison-Wesley, 1982); *Canada's Aging Population* (Toronto: Butterworths, 1986); *Family and Friends: General Social Survey Analysis Series* (Ottawa: Statistics Canada, 1994); *Families Function: Family Bridges from Past to Future* (Vienna: U.N., 1995); "Women and Aging: A Sociological Perspective" (*Journal of Women and Aging* Spring 1989); "Towards a Synthesis of Demographic and Feminist Perspectives on Fertility" (*The Sociological Quarterly*, 1996); "Serial Employment and Skinny Government: Reforming Caring and Sharing among Generations" (*Canadian Journal on Aging*, 1996); " Family/Work Challenges among Older Working Canadians," *Voices: Essays on Canadian Families*, ed. by Marion Lynn (Toronto: Nelson, 1996); more than 140 other publications. **EDIT:** Ed., *Canadian Journal of Sociology*, 1994-98; Ed. Bd., *Journal of Women and Aging*, 1987-93; Assoc. Ed., *Canadian Journal of Sociology*, 1989-91; Ed. Bd., *Canadian Journal of Health and Society*, 1990 to date; Ed. Bd., *Atlantis: A Women's Studies Journal*, 1991-93. **AFFIL:** Royal Society of Canada (Fellow); Canadian Sociology & Anthropology Association; Canadian Population Society (Exec. Council 1980-82; VP 1988-90; Pres. 1990-92); Population Association of America; International Union for the Scientific Study of Population (electee); Canadian Women's Studies Association; International Council on Women's Health Issues; Canadian Association of Gerontology; Canadian Research Institute for the Advancement of Women; Vanier Institute of the Family; International Sociological Association; National Statistics Council (fed. appointee). **HONS:** Award for Teaching Excellence, Fac. of Arts, Univ. of Alberta, 1994; Distinguished Teacher Award, Univ. of Waterloo, 1981; Casgrain Research Fellowship, 1987-88; Woman of the Year (Professional), Kitchener-Waterloo, 1988. **INTERESTS:** sociology; hiking; wildlife observation; photography. **MISC:** 1st recipient, Casgrain Research Fellowship; listed in Canadian Who's Who, 1993 to date; frequent keynote speaker at major nat'l & int'l conferences, incl. the United Nations Closing Conference on Int'l Year of the Family; gave 23 major keynote addresses in 1994; participated in Nov. 1994 in an int'l forum on social policy televised on CBC; Bd. of Dir., Canada Committee for the Int'l Year of the Family, 1993-94; appointed to the Expert Task Force on Women & Social Security, 1994; referee, numerous journals, presses & granting agencies. **COMMENT:** *"Sociology is more than what I do; it defines what I am. My success as a sociologist is attributable to my boundless curiosity about the social world."*

McDermid, Heather ■■ ⚾

Olympic Athlete. c/o Canadian Olympic Association. Born Calgary 1968. **SPORTS CAREER:** mbr., Cdn Nat'l Rowing Team, 1995 to date. Olympic Games: Silver, 8+, 1996. Canadian championships: 2nd, 4-, 3rd, 2-, & 3rd, 4x, 1994. **HONS:** MVP, women's track, Rice Univ., 1990; All-American, 1989 & 1990. **INTERESTS:** sewing & designing; tennis; hiking; reading. **MISC:** owns activewear business.

McDonald, Dorothy Zolf, B.Sc.,B.A., M.A.,Ph.D. ♡ $

Board of Directors, SHAW COMMUNICATIONS INC., Edmonton, AB. 3 ch. Janice, Patricia, Stephen. **EDUC:** Univ. of Alberta, B.Sc. 1953, B.A. 1971, M.A. 1973, Ph.D. 1984. **CAREER:** Researcher, Community TV Study Proj., Gov't of Alta. & Univ. of Alberta, 1971-72; Community Programming Coord. & Prod., Quality

Cable Television Ltd. (QCTV), Edmonton, 1973-74; Exec. Dir., Planned Parenthood Association, Alta., 1974-75; Mktg & Promo. Mgr, Oxford Group Development Ltd., Edmonton Centre, 1975-77; independent Mgmt Training & Comm. Consultant, 1977-82; Assoc. Prof., Admin., Athabasca Univ., 1980-82; Assoc. Prof., Comm. Studies, Univ. of Calgary, 1984-89; Supervising Prof. (Indiv. Study), Cdn Studies, Univ. of Alberta, 1990-91; Visiting Prof., Dept. of Mktg & Econ. Analysis, Univ. of Alberta, 1990-91; Mbr., Corp. Bd. of Dir., Shaw Communications Inc., 1991 to date. **SELECTED PUBLICATIONS:** "Educational Broadcasting: A Problem of Divided Jurisdiction" (*Canadian Journal of Communication* 12(2) 1986); "The Regulation of Broadcasting in Canada and in the United States: Straws in the Wind" (*Canadian Journal of Communication* 13(2) 1988); "Multiculturalism as a Public Policy Goal in Broadcasting: A Tale of Five Countries" (*Canadian Ethnic Studies* 21(2) 1989); "Canada-Mexico Co-Production Agreement on Film and Television Programming," with Colin Hoskins & Stuart McFayden, *NAFTA in Transition*, ed. by S.J. Randall & H. Kourdy; various other publications. **EDIT:** past mbr., Ed. Advisory Bd., Cable Communications Magazine. **AFFIL:** Alberta Cancer Bd. (Dir.); International Communication Association; Canadian Communication Association. **HONS:** Annual Research Award, Phi Delta Kappa (Alberta Chapter), 1984-85. **MISC:** recipient, various grants; referee, various journals; various conference presentations; various media appearances; various speaking engagements for private organizations regarding public broadcasting; various briefs & interventions before the CRTC for the Alberta Association for Public Broadcasting; listed in Who's Who of Canadian Jewish Women. **COMMENT:** *"I am presently involved with two directorships: Shaw Communications, which is in the private sector and directly relates to my area of expertise (broadcasting regulation and communications policy), and the Alberta Cancer Board, (the public sector) which administers the delivery of cancer care services for the entire province of Alberta, an Order-in-Cabinet appointment."*

McDonald, Katherine, LL.B. ✦ ⫯
President, NOVA SCOTIA ADVISORY COUNCIL ON THE STATUS OF WOMEN, Box 745, Halifax, NS B3J 2T3 (902) 424-8662, FAX 424-0573. Born Ottawa 1953. 1 ch. **EDUC:** Dalhousie Law Sch., LL.B. 1981. **BAR:** N.S., 1981. **CAREER:** Lawyer, Cooper and McDonald, Halifax, 1981-91; Exec. Dir., Public Legal Education Society of N.S., 1991-93; Pres., N.S. Advisory Council on the Status of Women, 1993 to

date. **AFFIL:** Planned Parenthood Federation of Canada (Past Pres.); International Planned Parenthood Federation (Bd., W. Hemisphere Reg.); Mount St. Vincent Univ. (Gov.); N.S. Association of Women & the Law; Tripartite Forum on Aboriginal Justice. **MISC:** numerous workshops & seminars on the legal rights of women.

McDonald, Lynn, B.A.,Ph.D. ■ ⫯ ❀
Professor, Department of Sociology and Anthropology, UNIVERSITY OF GUELPH, Guelph, ON N1G 2W1 (519) 824-4120, ext. 6527, FAX 837-9561, EMAIL lynnmcd@css. uoguelph.ca. Born New Westminster, B.C. 1940. s. **EDUC:** Univ. of British Columbia, B.A.(Pol. Sci./Slavonic Studies) 1961; Univ. of London, Ph.D.(Soc.) 1966. **CAREER:** Research Assoc. & Consultant, Commission of Inquiry into the Non-Medical Use of Drugs, Ottawa, 1970-71; various positions to Assoc. Prof., McMaster Univ., 1965-74; Visiting Prof., Göteborgs Universität, Sweden, 1973; Visiting Research Scholar, Paris, 1974; Prof. of Soc., Dalhousie Univ., 1975-77; M.P., 1982-88; Visiting Prof., Simon Fraser Univ., 1989; Prof. of Soc., Dept. of Soc. & Anthro., Univ. of Guelph, 1991 to date; Chair, 1991-96. **SELECTED PUBLICATIONS:** *Social Class and Delinquency* (London: Faber and Faber, 1969); *The Sociology of Law and Order* (London: Faber and Faber, 1976); *The Party that Changed Canada: The New Democratic Party Then and Now* (Toronto: Macmillan, 1987); *The Early Origins of the Social Sciences* (Montreal: McGill-Queen's Univ. Press, 1993); *The Women Founders of the Social Sciences* (Ottawa: Carleton Univ. Press, 1994); numerous articles. **AFFIL:** Social Science Federation of Canada (Treas. 1992-96); Campaign for Nuclear Phase-out (Steering Committee); Canadian Association of Former Parliamentarians (Bd., Educ. Foundation); Canadian Association of Transfused Hepatitis C Survivors (Bd.); Peace Magazine (Dir.); Canadian Council of Churches (Commission on Justice & Peace); Energy Probe (Bd.); C.R.T.C. Task Force on Sex-Role Stereotyping in the Broadcast Media. **INTERESTS:** birds; hiking; canoeing; cross-country skiing. **MISC:** author, Non-smokers' Health Act, 1988. **COMMENT:** *"Currently a professor of sociology and active environmentalist, McDonald is a former Member of Parliament and former president of the National Action Committee on the Status of Women."*

McDonald, Marci, B.A. ∕ ▯
Senior Writer, MACLEAN'S MAGAZINE, 777 Bay St., Toronto, ON M5W 1A7 (416) 596-5292, FAX 596-7730. Born Hamilton, Ont. 1945. d.

EDUC: Univ. of Toronto, B.A.(English Language & Lit.) 1967. **CAREER:** Reporter to Sr. Entertainment Feature Writer, *The Toronto Star*, 1967-74; Sr. Writer to Ed., *Maclean's* Magazine, 1974-76; European Correspondent, 1976-84; Washington Bureau Chief, 1984-92; Sr. Writer, 1992 to date. **SELECTED PUBLICATIONS:** "Roloff and the Shah of Iran," *Canada from the Newsstands: The Best Canadian Journalism From the Past 30 Years*, ed. Val Cleary (Macmillan of Canada, 1978); *Maureen Forester: Out of Character* co-author (McClelland & Stewart, 1986); *Yankee Doodle Dandy: Brian Mulroney and the American Agenda* (Stoddart, 1995); numerous articles in *Maclean's*, *Washington Post Magazine*, *Washington Monthly Magazine* & others. **AFFIL:** Writers' Dev. Trust; The McGill Club. **HONS:** Gold Medals in Business Writing, National Magazine Awards, 1977; Travel Writing, National Magazine Awards, 1979; Religious Journalism, National Magazine Awards, 1980; Silver Medal in Essays, National Magazine Awards, 1994; Author's Award, Personality Features, Foundation for the Advancement of Canadian Letters, 1995; Atkinson Fellowship in Public Policy, 1992-93. **MISC:** gave annual lecture, Canadian-US Fulbright Fellowship Program, Northwestern Univ. **COMMENT:** *"A journalist since the age of 16, when she began writing a high-school column, McDonald has written on entertainment, celebrities and politics in Europe, the Middle East, the US and Canada. She believes passionately in her profession."*

McDonald, Wendy Burdon $ 🍁 ✊ ☝

Chairman of the Board and Chief Executive Officer, **BC BEARING ENGINEERS LIMITED**, 8985 Fraserwood Court, Burnaby, BC V5J 5E8 (604) 433-6711, FAX 433-5473. Born North Vancouver 1922. w. 10 ch. (5 adopted). **CAREER:** 50 yrs. with BC Bearing Engineers Limited. **AFFIL:** Bearing Specialists' Association (former Pres.); Vancouver Board of Trade (Gov.; Past Chrm); Power Transmission Distributors' Association; Pacific Corridor Enterprise Council, PACE (Dir.); B.C. Paraplegic Foundation (Dir.); B.C. Institute of Technology (Gov.); Canadian Council for the Americas (B.C. Chapter); Lions Gate Hospital Foundation (Advisory Council); Fraser River Discovery Centre (Hon. Dir.); Swan-e-Set Bay Resorts (Hon. Gov.); Capilano Golf & Country Club; Terminal City Club; B.C. Club; Washington Athletic Club; Sunshine Coast Golf & Country Club; Schenley Awards (former Trustee); University Hospital (former Trustee); B.C. Sports Hall of Fame (former Trustee). **HONS:** Power Transmission Distributor of the Year, 1987; award, Vancouver Better Business Bureau, 1987; won Veuve Clicquot Award for 1st Cdn Bus. Woman of the Year, 1982; Woman of Distinction, Bus. Mgmt, YWCA, 1988; Businesswoman of the Year, B.C. Business Magazine, 1988; Canadian Woman of the Year for B.C., 1994; Hon. Doctorate, Simon Fraser Univ. **INTERESTS:** family; swimming; gardening; golf. **MISC:** Past Chrm, Pacific Advisory Reg'l Council for the Fed. Gov't; served as Chair, Task Force for Export of Svcs, Asia Pacific Initiative; participated for the Prov. of B.C. on the Int'l Trade Advisory Committee.

McDonnell, Mary Catharine, B.A.,M.S.W., R.S.W. ■■ ♥ ⊕

Past President, **THE KIDNEY FOUNDATION OF CANADA**, 5850 University Ave., P.O. Box 3070, Halifax, NS B3J 3G9 (902) 428-8173, FAX 428-3211. Social Worker, **IWK-GRACE HEALTH CENTRE FOR CHILDREN, WOMEN & FAMILIES**. Born Hamilton, Ont. 1953. m. Finbarr (Barry) McDonnell. **EDUC:** Univ. of Western Ontario, B.A.(Soc.) 1975; Wilfrid Laurier Univ., M.S.W. 1977. **CAREER:** Social Worker, St. Joseph's Hospital, Hamilton, 1977-81; Social Worker, Nova Scotia Hospital, 1981-82; Social Worker, IWK-Grace Health Centre for Children, Women & Families, 1982 to date. **AFFIL:** The Kidney Foundation of Canada (Chair, Nat'l Organ Donation Committee; former Chair, Nat'l Planning Team; former Chair, Research Council; Nat'l Pres. 1991-93; Nat'l Exec. Committee 1988-95; Chair, Nat'l Organ Donor Task Force 1994-95; Chair, Branch Patient Svcs Committee, N.S. Branch; former Pres., N.S. Branch); Canadian Organ Replacement Register (Bd. mbr. 1988 to date); N.S. Council for the Family (First VP; Steering Committee; Facilitator, Change Challenge 1995 to date); N.S. Association of Social Workers; Canadian Association of Nephrology Social Workers (founding mbr.); Canadian Foundation for the Study of Infant Deaths. **HONS:** Canada 125 Medal; Canada Volunteer Award & Certificate of Honour, 1993; Harold Ashenmiel Award, The Kidney Foundation of Canada, 1995; President's Award, The Kidney Foundation of Canada, 1989; Miss Dicks Award, Canadian Association of Nephrology Social Workers, 1995. **INTERESTS:** art; music; tennis; skiing. **COMMENT:** *"I have been privileged to work with The Kidney Foundation of Canada as this organization has made a positive difference, on a daily basis, in the life of patients and families with whom I work."*

McDonough, Alexa, B.A., M.A. * 🍁 ☝

Leader, **NEW DEMOCRATIC PARTY OF CANADA**.

Born Ottawa 1944. 2 ch. EDUC: Dalhousie Univ., B.A.; Maritime Sch. of Social Work, M.A.. CAREER: N.S. Dept. of Social Svcs; City of Halifax; teacher, Maritime Sch. of Social Work. POLITICAL CAREER: candidate, 1979 & 1980 fed. elections; elected M.L.A., Halifax Chebucto, Gov't of N.S., 1980; re-elected, 1984, 1988, 1993; Leader, New Democratic Party of Nova Scotia, 1980-94.; Leader, New Democratic Party of Canada, 1995 to date. HONS: D.C.L.(Hon.), University of King's Coll., 1995. MISC: 1st woman in Canada to lead a major political party.

McDougall, The Hon. Barbara, P.C.,C.F.A., LL.D. $ ✊ 🍁
8 King St. E., Ste. 300, Toronto, ON M5C 1B5 (416) 869-1598, FAX 366-4892. EDUC: Univ. of Toronto, B.A. CAREER: Economist, CIBC, 1960-62; Mkt Research Analyst, *The Toronto Star*, 1962-63; Bus. Writer, *The Vancouver Sun*, 1963-64; Investment Analyst, Odlum Brown Ltd., 1964-74; Portfolio Mgr, North West Trust & Seaboard Life Assurance Company 1974-76; Bus. Commentator, ITV News, 1974-76; VP, A.E. Ames and Co. Ltd. & its successor company, Dominion Securities Ames, Ltd. (now known as RBC Dominion Securities), 1976-82; Exec. Dir., Canadian Council of Financial Analysts and Bus. Columnist for various publications & CBC, 1982-84; elected, M.P. (St. Paul's), Gov't of Canada, 1984; Min. of State, Fin., 1984-86; Min. of State, Privatization, 1986-88; Min. of Employment & Immigration, 1988-91; Sec. of State for External Affairs, 1991-93. DIRECTOR: Avenor Inc.; E.L. Financial Corporation (& its affiliated companies Empire Life & Dominion of Canada General Insurance); National Trust; AT&T Canada Long Distance Services (V-Chair); Total Petroleum (North America) Ltd. AFFIL: York Univ. (Gov.; Advisor, Schulich Sch. of Bus.); Canadian Opera Company (Dir.); Canadian Institute of Strategic Studies (Dir.); The Lester B. Pearson Peacekeeping Training Centre (Dir.); The Japan Society (Dir.); Inter-American Dialogue, Washington, D.C. (Cdn Rep.); Int'l Crisis Group, London, UK (Dir.); Council on Foreign Relations, N.Y. (Advisor). HONS: LL.D.(Hon.), St. Lawrence Univ., Lawrencetown, N.Y., 1991. MISC: as Min. of State, Privatization, closed the sale of Canadair to Bombardier & oversaw the sales of Teleglobe Canada, RCI, Eldorado, & Air Canada, among others.

McEwen, Maryke, B.A. 📺 🎞 🎭 ☝
Producer, KINETIC PRODUCTIONS, 112 Willow Ave., Toronto, ON M4E 3K3 (416) 699-1517, FAX 699-3044. Born Oshawa, Ont. 1948. s. 1 ch. EDUC: Univ. of Toronto, B.A.(English Lit.) 1972. SELECTED CREDITS: Prod., *The Diary of Evelyn Lau* (telefilm); Prod. & Creator, *Street Legal* (series); Prod., *Shellgame* (pilot); Prod., *Tools of the Devil* (telefilm); Prod., *Rough Justice* (telefilm); Prod., *Ready for Slaughter* (telefilm); Prod., *Blind Faith* (telefilm); Assoc. Prod. & Script Ed. for various other films. AFFIL: Toronto Women in Film & Television; Academy of Canadian Cinema & Television. HONS: Best Drama, *Ready for Slaughter*, Banff Int'l Film Festival; Best Drama, *The Diary of Evelyn Lau*, Columbus Festival; various Gemini Awards & nominations; FIPA Award; various other festival awards. MISC: 1st woman Exec. Producer of a series. COMMENT: *"One of the first woman producers in television, Maryke McEwen enjoys creating and producing films that have meaning, can effect change in people's understanding and perception of one another. Enjoys reflecting Canadians to themselves."*

McFarlane, Betty ✊ ♥ 📜
President, SASKATCHEWAN ARCHAEOLOGICAL SOCIETY, 816 First Ave. N., Ste. 5, Saskatoon, SK S7K 1Y3 (306) 664-4124, FAX 665-1928. Vice-President, HARRIS AND DISTRICT MUSEUM INC. Born Leney, Sask. 1932. m. Edwin. 4 ch. Norman E., Lois A., Carol I., Lenore G. EDUC: Saskatoon Normal Sch., Certificate (Teaching) 1951. CAREER: sch. teacher, 1951-53; farmer, family farm, 1954 to date. VOLUNTEER CAREER: VP, Local Bd. Section, Saskatchewan School Trustees' Association, 1979-86; Pres., Eagle Creek Historical Society, 1986-90; Pres., National Farmers' Union Local 619, 1987-90; Sec., National Farmers' Union Local 619, 1990 to date; Pres., Harris and District Museum Inc., 1990-93; VP, Saskatchewan Archaeological Society, 1991-93; VP, Harris and District Museum Inc., 1993 to date; Pres., Saskatchewan Archaeological Society, 1993 to date. SELECTED PUBLICATIONS: *Harris Heritage and Homage History Book* co-ed. (1982); co-author/ed. of reports of Bents Bear Hills Proj., 1987, 1988, 1989; "The Ruby Rush of 1914" (*Western People, Western Producer* June 1994). AFFIL: Harris Tourism Committee; Heritage Saskatchewan (Bd.). HONS: Historical Award, Canadian Historical Association, 1991; various gardening awards. INTERESTS: protecting our environment & heritage; museums; archaeology; genealogy; architecture; family & grandchildren. COMMENT: *"Throughout my life I have set goals and worked toward them. First–to provide a happy home for my children and raise them to be successful, caring adults–which they are–and then to pursue my many other interests."*

McFarlane, E. Louisa, R.N.,B.N.Sc., M.H.Sc. ⊕

Clinical Nurse Specialist, Mental Health Centre, ABERDEEN HOSPITAL, 115 MacLean St., New Glasgow, NS B2H 4M5 (902) 755-1137. Therapist, CURRY, MCFARLANE ASSOCIATES, PO Box 344, 376 Cameron Ave., New Glasgow, NS B2H 5E3 (902) 755-9724. Born Lloydminister, Sask. 1941. s. EDUC: Univ. of Alberta, Jr. Educ. Certificate 1960; Royal Alexandra Hospital, R.N. 1965; McGill Univ., B.N.Sc. 1971; McMaster Univ., M.H.Sc.(Family Therapy) 1981. CAREER: Nursing Asst., Alberta Nursing Home, Medicine Hat, Alta., 1959-60; Team Coord., Health & Educ. Program, Alberta Sch. Hospital for Mentally Handicapped Children, Red Deer, Alta., 1960-62; Nursing Team Coord., Adolescent Svcs, 1976-70; Instructor, Nursing, Red Deer Coll., 1971-73; Staff Dev. Officer, North Eastern Reg'l Mental Health Centre, Timmins, Ont., 1973-74; Public Health Nurse, Porcupine Health Unit, Timmins, 1974-80; Nurse, Victorian Order of Nursing, Hamilton, Ont., 1980-82; Nat'l Steering Committee for the Dev. of a Canadian Association for Suicide Prevention, 1980-81; Research Proj. Coord., Hamilton Psychiatric Hospital, 1983; Community Mental Health Nurse, Yarmouth Regional Hospital, 1982-84; independent practice as therapist, Kingston, 1984-91; Lecturer, Sch. of Nursing, Queen's Univ., 1984-85; Asst. Prof., 1985-91; Cdn Coordinating Committee for the Dev. of Canadian Holistic Nurses' Association, 1986-87; Clinical Nurse Specialist, Dept. of Mental Health Svcs, Aberdeen Hospital, New Glasgow, N.S., 1991 to date; Therapist, in private practice, Curry, McFarlane Associates, New Glasgow, 1994 to date; Instructor, Nursing, Extension Program, St. Francis Xavier Univ. SELECTED CREDITS: Coord., *Health Life Styles* (series), Porcupine Region, Ont., 1976-79; "Grief in the Elderly," *Telemedicine*, 1986-87; "Depression in the Elderly," *Telemedicine*, 1986-87; "Stress and the Caregiver of the Elderly," *Telemedicine*, 1986-87; "Burnout of Professionals," *Telemedicine*, 1988; consultant, *Cry for Happiness* and *Right to Care*, Laura Sky Foundation films, 1988-91. AFFIL: American Holistic Nurses' Association; Canadian Association for History of Nursing; Canadian Foundation of Mental Health Nurses; Canadian Holistic Nurses' Association (Pres. 1990-94; Chair, Policy & Practice Committee); Provincial Nurses' Educators Group, RNAO; Provincial Psychiatric Nurses' Interest Group, RNAO; Clinical Nurse Specialist Group for N.S.; Registered Nurses' Association of N.S.; Canadian Nurses' Association (Advisory Council on Interest Groups); AIDS Awareness Formation Group, New Glasgow; Timmins Ontario Association for Developmentally Handicapped (Consultant); Tearman Society for Battered Women & Children (Chair, Bd. of Dir.); Pictou County Women's Centre Group Proj. on Sexual Assault. HONS: Proficiency in Nursing Award, Alta., 1966; Timmins Outstanding Citizen Award, Timmins, Ont., 1975; many public accolades for work with various associations; recognition for dev. of Canadian Holistic Nurses. INTERESTS: music; drama; reading; singing; outdoor sports; environmental & ecology issues; politics. MISC: Registered Nurse, Alta., Ont. & N.S.; currently involved in the dev. of N.S. Holistic Nurses' Association; numerous presentations & workshops. COMMENT: *"I am an innovative strong leader and a competent and compassionate person/professional. Have been at the beginning of many projects which are very grounded and still operative, such as the City Street Program for children and adolescents in trouble with the law, which I coordinated during my years in Alberta."*

McFarlane, Sheryl, B.Ed. 🎨 ✒ 📖

Writer. 168 Beechwood Ave., Victoria, BC V8S 3W5 (604) 598-5645, FAX 598-7322. Born Pembroke, Ont. 1954. m. John Hewitt. 3 ch. Ali, Cloe, Katie. EDUC: Univ. of British Columbia, B.Ed.(Elementary Sci./Cdn Studies) 1985. CAREER: child care worker, 1972-78; various positions, Agric. Canada, 1978-84; teacher, 1985-86; writer, 1986 to date. SELECTED PUBLICATIONS: *Waiting for the Whales* (Victoria: Orca Book Publishers, 1991); *Jessie's Island* (Victoria: Orca Book Publishers, 1992); *Moonsnail Song* (Victoria: Orca Book Publishers, 1994); *Eagle Dreams* (Victoria: Orca Book Publishers, 1994);*Tides of Change* (Orca Book Publishers, 1995); *Going To The Fair* (Orca Book Publishers, 1996). AFFIL: B.C. Coll. of Teachers; Writers' Union of Canada; CANSCAIP; Children's Writers & Illustrators of B.C.; Federation of B.C. Writers; Canadian Children's Book Centre; Vancouver & Victoria Children's Literature Roundtables (Steering Committee, Victoria Roundtable); Vancouver Island Reading Association. HONS: scholarship, Univ. of British Columbia; Ira Dilworth Prize for Most Promising Student of Cdn Lit.; Our Choice Award (*Waiting for the Whales*), Canadian Children's Book Centre, 1991; Elizabeth Mrazik-Cleaver Award (*Waiting for the Whales*), 1991; Amelia Frances Howard-Gibbon Award (*Waiting for the Whales*), 1991; Notable Book (*Waiting for the Whales*), Canadian National Library, 1991; Gov. General's Literary Award (*Waiting for the Whales*), 1991; Book Award (*Waiting for the Whales*), IODE

Nation Chapter, 1991; Our Choice Award (*Jessie's Island*), Canadian Children's Book Centre, 1992; Our Choice Award (*Moonsnail Song*), Canadian Children's Book Centre, 1994; Our Choice Award (*Eagle Dreams*), Canadian Children's Book Centre. INTERESTS: reading; gardening; kayaking; hiking; biking; travel. MISC: Cultural Svcs Grant for creative writing proj. assistance, 1994. COMMENT: *"Sheryl McFarlane was born in the Ottawa Valley and raised in Arizona, but she's a West Coast girl at heart. Her award-winning children's books celebrate the West Coast while exploring universal themes. Sheryl can't put a good book down, is always on the lookout for deer-proof plants, and steals away to her Gulf Island retreat with her husband and three daughters whenever possible."*

McFee, Oonah 🐾 ⊗ 🖐

Writer. 44 Jackes Ave., Ste. 2005, Toronto, ON M4T 1E5 (416) 929-3544. Born N.B. 1919. m. Allan. EDUC: Lisgar Collegiate Institute, Ottawa; Instituto Allende, San Miguel, Mexico; Royal Conservatory of Music, piano. CAREER: fiction writer; Writer-in-Residence, Trent Univ., 1979-80. SELECTED CREDITS: short story broadcast on CBC Anthology. SELECTED PUBLICATIONS: *Sandbars* (Macmillan, 1977); various short stories in *The Texas Quarterly*, *Redbook*, *Chatelaine*. HONS: First Novel Award, Books in Canada, 1978. MISC: various Canada Council & Ontario Arts Council grants; guest lecturer & readings at the Univ. of Toronto, Univ. of Western Ontario, Trent Univ., Univ. of PEI; invited contributor, Breadloaf Writers' Conference, Vermont. COMMENT: *"The subject of myself is not one I ever try to define. Achievements and endeavours seem to be in my case, just happenings. I don't mean to be elusive. It's just that I'm a 'background person.'"*

McGarry, Diane, E., B.Sc. 💲 ⬢

Chairman, President and Chief Executive Officer, XEROX CANADA INC., 5650 Yonge St., North York, ON M2M 4G7 (416) 733-6998, FAX 229-6826. Born Oakland, Calif. 1949 1 ch. EDUC: Univ. of Redlands, Calif., B.Sc.(Bus. Admin.) 1980. CAREER: various sales, mktg & exec. positions, Xerox, 1973-88; VP & Reg. Mgr, E. Coastal Reg., US, 1988-91; Dir., Sales Oper., UK, 1991-93; Chrm, Pres. & CEO, Xerox Canada, 1993 to date. AFFIL: C.D. Howe Institute (Dir.); National Quality Institute (Dir.); Univ. of Toronto (Dean's Advisory Council, Fac. of Mgmt); Conference Board of Canada (Dir.); Business Council on National Issues in Canada; Canada Post Learning Institute (Gov.); Earth Day Canada (Hon. Advisory Bd.).

McGeer, Edith G., B.A.,Ph.D.,O.C. ⊕ ⬩

Professor Emerita, Department of Psychiatry, UNIVERSITY OF BRITISH COLUMBIA. Born New York City 1923. m. 3 ch. Patrick Charles, Tad, Victoria Lynn. EDUC: Swarthmore Coll., Penn., B.A. 1944; Univ. of Virginia, Ph.D. 1946. CAREER: Lab. Asst., Squibb Institute for Medical Research, 1943; Research Chemist, Experimental Stn, E.I. DuPont de Nemours & Co., Wilmington, 1946-54; Research Assoc., Univ. of British Columbia, 1954-74; Assoc. Prof., 1974-78; Acting Head, Div. of Neurological Sciences, 1976; Prof., 1978-89; Head, Div. of Neurological Sciences, 1983-89; Prof. Emerita, 1989 to date; officially retired but still lecturing to Neurology residents. SELECTED PUBLICATIONS: *Molecular Neurobiology of the Mammalian Brain* with P.L. McGeer & Sir John Eccles (Plenum Press, 1978, 1987); 301 refereed papers & 102 chapters or invited papers, largely on neurochemistry & pathology in neurological diseases. EDIT: Ed. Bd., *Brain Research*; Ed. Bd., *Neuroscience Letters*; Ed. Bd., *Alzheimer Disease and Associated Disorders*; Ed. Bd., *Synapse*; Ed. Bd., *Neurobiology of Aging*; Ed. Bd., *Advances in Neuroscience* ; Ed. Bd., *Journal of Neurodegeneration*. AFFIL: Canadian Biochemical Society; Canadian Coll. of Neuropsychopharmacology (Fellow); International Brain Research Organization; International Society for Neurochemistry; Society for Neuroscience; American Neurochemical Society; Canadian Federation of BIological Societies; Sigma Xi; Phi Beta Kappa; Lychnos Society; North Pacific Society of Neurology & Psychiatry (Hon. Fellow); World Federation of Neurology Research Group of the Dementias (Exec. Committee). HONS: Sebring Scholarship, 1941-42; Swarthmore Open Scholarship, 1941-44; Merck Fellow, Univ. of Virginia, 1944-45; DuPont Fellow, Univ. of Virginia, 1945-46; Citation, Delaware Section, American Chemical Society, 1958; Distinguished Science Lecturer, Univ. of British Columbia, 1982; Teaching Award, First Year Residents in Psychiatry, 1982; D.Sc.(Hon.), Univ. of Victoria, 1987; Research Prize, Clarke Institute, 1993; Officer of the Order of Canada, 1995; Special Award for Lifetime Achievement, Science Council of B.C., 1995. MISC: Eccles Lectureship, First Cdn Symposium on the Organic Dementias, 1986; 4th McEwen Lecturer in Pharmacology, Queen's Univ., 1990; recipient, various grants; 5 patents in pharmaceutical field.

McGibbon, Hon. Pauline M., McGibbon, O.C.,C.C.,O.Ont.,B.A.,LL.D.,D.U., D.Hum.L.,D.Litt.S.,B.A.A., Hon. F.R.C.P.S.(C) ⋅ ♥ ⊗ 🖐

Former Lieutenant Governor, Province of

Ontario. Born Sarnia, Ont. 1910. m. Donald Walker McGibbon. EDUC: Univ. of Toronto, B.A.(Modern Hist.) 1933. CAREER: Lt. Gov., Prov. of Ont., 1974-80. VOLUNTEER CAREER: Pres., Children's Film Library of Canada, 1948-50; mbr. of Exec., Canadian Scene, 1951-59; Pres., Univ. of Toronto Alumni Association, 1952-53; Senate, Univ. of Toronto, 1952-61; Pres., Dominion Drama Festival, 1957-59; VP, Canadian Association for Adult Education, 1958-63; Nat'l Pres., I.O.D.E., 1963-65; Gov., Canadian Centenary Council, 1963-67; Bd., Elliot Lake Centre for Continuing Educ., 1965-71; Chrm, Bd. of Gov., National Theatre Sch., 1966-69; Chrm, Ontario Theatre Study, 1966-69; Hon. Sec., Women's Advisory Committee to Expo '67; mbr., Canada Council, 1968-71; Chrm, Women's College Hospital, 1970-74; Chancellor, Univ. of Toronto, 1971-74; Gov., Upper Canada Coll., 1971-74; Pres., Canadian Conference of the Arts, 1972-73; Dir., Donwood Institute, 1973-85; Chancellor, Univ. of Guelph, 1977-83; Chrm of the Bd. of Trustees, National Arts Centre, 1980-84; Dir., Massey Hall & Roy Thomson Hall, 1980-90; VP, 1988-90; Chrm, Toronto International Festival, 1984; Dir., Mt. Sinai Institute, 1981-86; Chrm, Ont. Selection Committee for Rhodes Scholarships, 1984-90; Mbr.-at-large, Bd. of Trustees, Toronto Sch. of Theology, 1984-87; Hon. Nat'l Co-Chrm, Canadian Council of Christians & Jews, 1986-93. DIRECTOR: George Weston Limited. AFFIL: du Maurier Council for the Arts (Hon. Chrm, 1980 to date); National Theatre Sch. (life mbr., Bd. of Gov.); I.O.D.E.(Hon. VP, Nat'l Chapter; Hon Pres., Municipal Chapter of Toronto); Royal Canadian Military Institute (Hon. life mbr.); Canadian Legion (Mbr., Fort York Banch); Toronto Symphony (Hon. mbr., Women's Committee); Volunteers of Roy Thomson Hall (Hon. Patron); Royal Canadian Yacht Club (Hon. mbr.); National Club (Hon. mbr.); Ganite Club (Hon. mbr.); Toronto Ladies Golf Club (Hon. mbr.); Boulevard Club (Hon. mbr.); Albany Club (Hon. mbr.); Toronto Ladies Club (Hon. mbr.); Business & Professional Women's Club (Hon. mbr.); Executive Women's Club (Hon. mbr.); Zonta Club (Hon. mbr.); University Women's Club of Toronto (Hon. mbr.); Ontario Chamber of Commerce (Hon. life mbr.). HONS: recipient, Canada Drama Award, 1957; Centennial Medal; Civic Award of Merit, City of Toronto, 1967; Dame, Order of St. Lazarus of Jerusalem, 1967; Award of Merit, Canadian Public Relations Society, 1972; Dame of Grace of the Order of St. John of Jerusalem, 1974; Queen's Jubilee Medal, 1977; Paul Harris Fellowship Award,

Rotary Club of Toronto/Forest Hill, 1977; Eleanor Roosevelt Humanities Award, State of Israel Bonds, 1978; Human Relations Award, The Canada Council of Christians & Jews; Ontario Teachers' Federation Fellowship, 1979; Humanitarian Award, B'nai Brith, 1980; Diplome d'honneur, Canadian Conference of the Arts, 1981; Prix au mérité, J-Louis Lévesque Foundation, 1982; Grand Prior of the Order of St. Lazarus, 1982-85; Dame Grand Cross, Order of St. Lazarus, 1982; Mbr., Order of Ontario, 1988; Fellowship Award, Rotary Club of Sarnia, 1989; Arbor Award, Univ. of Toronto Alumni, 1990; Canada 125 Medal, 1992; Hon. Fellow, Heraldry Society of Canada; LL.D.(Hon.); Univ. of Alberta, 1967; D.U. (Hon.), Univ. of Ottawa, 1972; LL.D.(Hon.), Univ. of Western Ontario, 1974; LL.D.(Hon.), Univ. of Toronto, 1975; D.U.(Hon.), Univ. of Laval, 1976; D.Hum.L.(Hon.), St. Lawrence Univ., Canton, N.Y., 1977; D.Litt.S.(Hon.), Univ. of Victoria, Toronto, 1979; Hon. F.R.C.P.S.(C), 1977; LL.D.(Hon.), McMaster Univ., 1981; LL.D.(Hon.), Carleton Univ., 1981; LL.D.(Hon.), Univ. of Windsor, 1988; D.Admin.(Hon.), Northland Open Univ., 1990. MISC: 1st woman Lt.-Gov., Prov. of Ont.; 1st Pres., Children's Film Library of Canada; 1st woman Pres., Univ. of Toronto Alumni Association; 1st woman Chancellor, Univ. of Toronto; 1st woman Pres., Canadian Conference of the Arts; 1st woman Chancellor, Univ. of Guelph; 1st woman Gov., Upper Canada Coll.; 1st woman Dir., IBM Canada, Imasco Limited & George Weston Limited; 1st woman Chrm, Bd. of Trustees, National Arts Centre; 1st Cdn woman, Hon. Col., 25 Toronto Service Battalion, 1975-83; 1st Hon. Life mbr., Ont. Chamber of Commerce, 1980; medal named in her hon., "Pauline McGibbon Honourary Award in Theatre Arts," presented by Prov. of Ont. annually since 1980; "Pauline McGibbon Lifetime Award in the Arts," 1981 to date.

McGill, Barbara J., R.N.,M.N. ■ ⊕
Vice-President, Patient Programs and Chief Nursing Officer, REGION 2 HOSPITAL CORPORATION, Box 5200, Saint John, NB E2L 4L4 (506) 648-6710, FAX 648-6364. Born Chatham, N.B. 1948. m. Peter. 4 ch. Charlotte, Corey, Ali, Emily. EDUC: St. Joseph's Hospital, Saint John, R.N. 1969; Univ. of New Brunswick, B.N. 1974; Dalhousie Univ., M.N. 1983. CAREER: Staff Nurse, Emergency Dept., St. Joseph's Hospital; Staff Nurse, Coronary/Surgical I.C.U., Victoria Public Hospital, Fredericton; Staff Nurse, Emergency Dept., Saint John General Hospital; Asst. Dir. of Nursing, Critical Care Areas, Emergency Dept. & Surgical Units; Staff Nurse, Adult ICU, Victoria Gen-

eral Hospital, Victoria; Implementation Coord., N.B. Cardiac Svcs Program, Saint John Regional Hospital; Program Mgr, N.B. Heart Centre; Program Mgr, Oncology; VP, Nursing & Patient Care Dev., Region 2 Hospital Corporation, 1993-95; VP, Patient Programs & Chief Nursing Officer, 1996 to date. **SELECTED PUBLICATIONS:** "Nursing Audit: Pragmatic Evaluation and Assessment," with M.A.H. Elbeik (*Dimensions in Health Services* Feb. 1985); "Nursing Environment Audits: An Empirical Study for Decision-Making Purposes," with M.A.H. Elbeik (*Dimensions in Health Services* June 1985). **AFFIL:** Canadian Council of Cardiovascular Nurses; Canadian Council of Health Services Accreditation (Surveyor); Canadian Institute of Health Information (committees); Heart & Stroke Foundation of N.B. (Hon. Life Mbr.); Nursing Workload Measurement/MIS Guidelines; Victoria General Hospital, Halifax (Cardiac Liaison Committee); Prov. Utilization Mgmt Coordinating Committee. **INTERESTS:** parenting; gardening; basketball, soccer & volleyball. **COMMENT:** *"Like to think of myself as a visionary, hard working, motivated, eager to make a difference; an immediate objective is to incorporate health promotion and wellness into the institutional health care setting."*

McGillis, The Hon. Donna, B.A.,LL.B. ⬟

Judge, Trial Division, FEDERAL COURT OF CANADA, Supreme Court Building, Wellington St., Ottawa, ON K1A 0H9 (603) 995-1278. Born Peterborough, Ont. 1951. m. Jean-Claude Demers, Q.C. 1 ch. **EDUC:** Queen's Univ., B.A.(French Lit.) 1972; Univ. of Windsor, LL.B. 1975; articled, Clayton C. Ruby, 1975-76. **BAR:** Ont., 1977. **CAREER:** private practice & criminal law research, 1977-79; Cnsl, Criminal Prosecutions, Toronto Reg. Office, 1980-86; Sr. Cnsl, 1986; Gen. Cnsl, Legal Svcs, R.C.M.P., 1986-88; Sr. Gen. Cnsl, Legal Svcs, Dept. of Indian & Northern Affairs, Gov't of Canada, 1988-92; appointed Judge, Fed. Court of Canada, 1992 to date. **EDIT:** Contributing Ed., *Canadian Lawyer Magazine*, 1977-80; Asst. Ed., *Canadian Rights Reporter*, 1983-84. **AFFIL:** Federal Court of Canada (Rules Committee; Judicial Educ. Committee). **HONS:** co-winner, Thomas Zuber Mooting Trophy, Univ. of Windsor, Fac. of Law, 1974; appointed Q.C., 1990. **MISC:** former instructor in various law & continuing educ. courses for Sir Sanford Fleming Coll., Osgoode Hall Law Sch. & the Law Society of Upper Canada.

McGonigal, The Honourable Pearl ✦ ⊙ ♦

301 Country Club Blvd., Ste. 30, Winnipeg, MB R3K 2E4 (204) 889-6448. Born Melville,

Sask. 1929. m. Norman L. Coghlan. 1 ch. **CAREER:** elected to the St. James-Assiniboia City Council, 1969; elected to the Greater Winnipeg City Council, 1971; Chair, Sub-committee on Centennial Celebrations, City of Winnipeg, 1972-74; re-elected 1974 (by acclamation) & 1977; Chair, Committee of Recreation & Social Svcs, 1977-79; elected Deputy Mayor & Chair, Exec. Policy Committee, 1979; re-elected 1980 (by acclamation); Lt.-Gov., Prov. of Man., 1981-86. **SELECTED PUBLICATIONS:** weekly food column, *The Winnipeg Free Press*, 1987-91; *Bringing It All Together*, cookbook, (1990); *Frankly Feminine Cookbook* (1975); weekly column in suburban newspapers, published by Reliance Press Ltd. (until appt. as Lt.-Gov.). **DIRECTOR:** Mediacom; CIBC; Royal Trust Company (Past Mbr., W. Advisory Bd.). **AFFIL:** Grace General Hospital Foundation (Chair); St. James Business & Professional Women's Clubs; Winnipeg Winter Club; St. Charles Golf & Country Club; Manitoba Club; Fac. of Dental Hygiene, Univ. of Manitoba (Past Mbr., Selection Committee); Grace General Hospital Sch. of Nursing (Past-Chair, Advisory Committee; Chair, Bd. of Mgmt 1987-93); Winnipeg Home Improvement Program (Past Mbr., Bd. of Mgmt); The Salvation Army, Catherine Booth Bible Coll. (Chair, Bd. of Reference 1983-91); United Way of Winnipeg (Campaign Chair 1990); Grey Cup Festival '91 (V-Chair, Special Events 1991); Salvation Army Ethics Centre (Bd. 1994); Winnipeg Lionelles (Past Pres.); St. James-Assiniboia Inter-Faith Immigration Council (Past Chair); St. Andrew's Anglican Church (Past Mbr. of Vestry). **HONS:** Toastmasters International Communication & Leadership Award Commendation Award, 1974; International Toastmasters Award, 1983; The Benevolent Protective Order of Elks of Canada, Winnipeg Lodge No. 10, 1975; Award, Manitoba Parks & Recreation Association Inc., 1983; Order of St. John, Dame of Grace, 1982; Silver Medal, Canadian Corps of Commissionaires, 1983; Univ. of Manitoba, LL.D.(Hon.) 1983; B'Nai Brith Canada Humanitarian Award, 1984; First Lady of the Year, Beta Sigma Phi International, 1986; Citizen of the Year, Knights of Columbus, 1987; Paul Harris Fellow; Distinguished Auxiliary Service Cross, Distinguished Auxiliary Order of the Salvation Army, 1991; Hadassah-Wizo Woman of the Year, 1994; Dame, The Military & Hospitaller Order of Saint Lazarus of Jerusalem, 1994; Order of Canada, 1995. **INTERESTS:** fishing; reading; bridge; cooking. **MISC:** 1st woman elected to St. James-Assiniboia City Council & the 1st woman elected as Deputy Mayor & Chrm of the Exec. Policy Committee of Winnipeg; the proceeds from *Bringing It All Together* were donated to The United Way & the proceeds from the *Frankly Feminine Cookbook* were used to establish a Scholarship Fund for Student Nurses at Grace General Hospital; Hon. Col., 735 Communications Regiment, 1982-86; Hon. Col., 402 City of Winnipeg Squadron, 1992 to date.

McGregor, Barbara, B.A.,LL.B. ⚖

Barrister and Solicitor, OSLER HOSKIN & HARCOURT, 1 First Canadian Place, Box 50, Toronto, ON M5X 1B8 (416) 862-6531, FAX 862-6666. Born Ottawa. **EDUC:** Univ. of Toronto, B.A. 1967, LL.B. 1972. **CAREER:** Ptnr, Osler Hoskin & Harcourt, 1979 to date. **SELECTED PUBLICATIONS:** numerous papers for the Canadian Bar Association & Law Society of Upper Canada. **AFFIL:** Canadian Bar Association; Law Society of Upper Canada; Rosedale Ratepayers' Association; Trent Univ. (Bd. of Gov.); Rosedale Tennis Club; Birchcliff Property Owners' Association of Douro Inc. (Past Pres.). **INTERESTS:** tennis; sailing; reading.

McHarg, Nancy, B.A. $

Director of Communications, WIC WESTERN INTERNATIONAL COMMUNICATIONS LTD., 505 Burrard St., Ste. 1960, Vancouver, BC V7X 1M6 (604) 687-2844, FAX 687-4118. Born St.-Eustache, Que. 1963. m. Hugh Wilson. 1 ch. **EDUC:** Concordia Univ., B.A.(Journalism) 1987. **CAREER:** Researcher, *Maclean's*, 1986-87; Reporter, *This Week in Business*, 1987-90; Assoc. Prod. (contract), Les Productions Affaires Mondiales, 1991; Public Rel'ns Officer, McGill Univ., 1991-92; Dir. of Comm., WIC Western International Communications Ltd., 1992 to date. **AFFIL:** Canadian Women in Communications.

McHugh, Fiona ■■ 📺 📜

Scriptwriter. c/o Agent, Krisztina Bevilacqua, 85 Roosevelt Rd., Toronto, ON M4J 4T8 (416) 463-7009, FAX 463-2206. **SELECTED CREDITS:** scriptwriter, *Lantern Hill* (TV movie), co-written with Kevin Sullivan, 1990 - top-rated movie on CBC, 1990; writer, *A Haunting Harmony* (original TV drama), CBC & Primedia Productions, 1990; writer/dir., *Waiting for You: Christiane Pflug 1936-1972* (documentary), CBC; writer, "The Hidden World of Bogs," *The Nature of Things*, CBC, 1993; writer, "Easy Targets" (TV documentary on child abuse), *The Nature of Things*, CBC, 1994; writer, "Sherri" (TV documentary), *Man Alive*, CBC, 1995; writer, "The Child Who Couldn't Play" (TV documentary on autism), *The Nature of Things*, CBC, 1996; co-writer, "Paul Ehrlich & The Population Bomb," *The Nature of Things*, CBC, 1996; numerous other documentaries, TV dramas, radio dramatizations, TV children's series, TV public educ. commercials. **SELECTED PUBLICATIONS:** 4 *Road to Avonlea* novels (HarperCollins); *Anne of Green Gables: The story book* (abridgement of L.M. Montgomery novel, Firefly Books, Toronto); collection of 21 original short stories for North York Bd. of Educ. literacy programme, grades 1-9; *Prime Time Parent* (handbook for leaders of media literacy workshops, Alliance for Children & TV, 1994). **HONS:** numerous awards incl.: Best Script & Best TV Documentary awards (*Hidden World of Bogs*), Missoula Wildlife Int'l Film Festival, 1994; Silver Hugo Award (*Getting Serious*), Chicago Film Festival, 1989; finalist (*Getting Serious*), Int'l Film & TV Festival of N.Y., 1988; finalist (*Getting Serious*), Yorkton Short Film Festival, Sask., 1988; Gold Medal (*Break The Silence*), Canadian Marketing Awards, 1986; Gold Plaque (*George Bernard Shaw and Women*), Chicago Film Festival, 1974.

McIlroy, Valerie $ 📺

Senior Vice-President, MEDIACOM INC., 250 Bloor St. E., Ste. 600, Toronto, ON M4W 1G6, FAX (416) 920-3042. Born New Waterford, N.S. 1948. d. 2 ch. **EDUC:** St. Francis Xavier Univ., Dipl.(Arts) 1967. **CAREER:** various sales & mktg positions, leading to VP, Mktg, Officer, Tele-Direct Publications Inc., 1969-94; Sr. VP, Sales, Mediacom Inc., 1994 to date. **AFFIL:** Royal Canadian Yacht Club; ABC (Literacy) Foundation (Committee of Mgmt; Bd.); Congress of Advertising (Bd.); Canadian Advertising Foundation (Bd); C&C 34 foot Yacht Owners (Sec.-Treas.). **HONS:** Canadian Direct Marketing Award. **INTERESTS:** sailboat racing; skiing; cycling; theatre; fast cars. **MISC:** selected to represent Gov't of Canada at U.N. Symposium on Substance Abuse, 1993; co-architect of National Literacy Awareness Program on behalf of Canadian Advertising Foundation & ABC Canada. **COMMENT:** "*I believe our Canadian business environment and community will be greatly advantaged by leaders who design and articulate break through vision supported by relentless attention to execution and endless positive energy. I hope to add vision, value and vitality to every activity, relationship or concept I am fortunate to be exposed to.*"

McInnes, Jennie E. ♡

Volunteer. Pictou, NS B0K 1H0, FAX (902) 485-8187. Born Scotch Hill, Pictou, N.S. 1933. m. Donald. 4 ch. **EDUC:** Nova Scotia Teachers' Coll.; St. Francis Xavier Univ. **CAREER:** dairy & hog farmer, 1956-83; teacher, Lyon's Brook

United Church Sunday Sch., 1957-78; various positions, various Women's Institutes, 1957 to date; various positions, 4-H, 1967-92; various exec. positions, Riverton Guest Home Corporation, 1972 to date; Mun. Councillor, Pictou County, 1974-78; Superintendent, Lyon's Brook United Church Sunday Sch., 1978-84; various positions, Pictou Presbyterial United Church Women, 1981 to date; mbr., Pictou Academy Educational Foundation, 1984 to date; mbr., Farm Debt Review Bd., N.S., 1986-91; Consumer Rep., Registered Nurses' Association of N.S., 1987-91; Chrm, Farm Debt Review Bd., N.S., 1988-91; Chair, Riverton Guest Home Corporation, 1990 to date; Founder & Pres., Betsey Heritage Society, 1992 to date; Chrm of Fund Raiser, Hector Arena Complex, 1993 to date. **SELECTED PUBLICATIONS:** *Cooking Collections*, ed. (Federated Women's Institutes of Canada); initiated & supervised the *Rural Child Care Survey* (Federated Women's Institutes of Canada). **DIRECTOR:** DeCoste Entertainment Centre. **AFFIL:** Lyon's Brook United Church (Treas.); Women's Institute, local (Hon. Life Mbr.; Pres. & Sec.); Women's Institutes of Nova Scotia (WINS) (Past Exec. Mbr.; Hon. Life Mbr.); Federated Women's Institutes of Canada (FWIC) (Pres. 1988-91; Hon. Life Mbr.); Associated Country Women of the World (ACWW); 4-H (former County Pres.; Nat'l Council 1970-73); Pictou Presbyterial United Church Women (Pres. 1985-87); Pictou Academy Educational Foundation (Chair); Betsey Heritage Society; Princess Rebekah Lodge (Past Nobel Grand; Past Degree Mistress); Hector Trust Museum; IODE; Pictou Golf Club. **HONS:** Int'l Women's Year Achievement Award, WINS, 1975; Outstanding Volunteer Service Certificate, 1982; Friend of 4-H Award, 1988; Cultural Dev. Award, Tourism Industry Association of N.S., 1992; Order of Canada, 1994; various other community & prov. volunteer awards. **INTERESTS:** sewing; crafts; golf; reading; painting; travel; gardening. **MISC:** licensed teacher in N.S.; delegate to over 5 int'l conferences, Associated Country Women of the World; chaired workshops on standard of living & quality of health, Associated Country Women of the World. **COMMENT:** *"Jennie McInnes: a woman with abilities to accomplish what she sets out to do and to motivate others. Longtime leader in the 4-H movement, the Women's Institute, Cultural and Heritage Organization, management and volunteer efforts. Served on the local, provincial and national executive of the Women's Institutes and on the projects committee of ACWW. Founded the Betsey Heritage Society, chaired a committee of citizens for funding for community arena/exhibition building; taught hundreds of girls to sew and compiled a national cookbook for FWIC; designed and made a daughter's wedding gown and decorated the family home."*

McInnis, Nadine, B.A.,M.A. 📖 📜
Writer. Born Belleville, Ont. 1957. m. Tim Fairbairn. 2 ch. Nadia Fairbairn, Owen Fairbairn. **EDUC:** Univ. of Ottawa, B.A.(English) 1981, M.A.(English) 1992. **CAREER:** poet; critic; short-story writer; Co-Ed., Arc Magazine; Teacher, Creative Writing, Univ. of Ottawa, 1987-93; Policy Writer, CBC, 1993 to date. **SELECTED PUBLICATIONS:** *Shaking the Dreamland Tree* (Coteau, 1986); *The Litmus Body* (Quarry, 1992); *Poetics of Desire: Nadine McInnis on Dorothy Livesay* (Turnstone Press, 1994); poems in various anthologies, incl. *Up and Doing: Canadian Women and Peace,* eds. Janice Williamson & Deborah Gorham (The Women's Press, 1989); *A Discord of Flags: Canadian Poets Write about the Persian Gulf War* ed. Stephen Heighton & Michael Redhill, 1992; *Kitchen talk* ed. Edna Alford & Claire Harris (RDC, 1992). **AFFIL:** League of Canadian Poets. **HONS:** First Prize (*Crossing Kurdistan*), National Poetry Contest, 1992; Second Prize, CBC National Literary Competition, 1993 & 1996; First Prize, Nepean Public Library Short Story Contest, 1993; shortlisted for Pat Lowther Award (*The Litmus Body)*, 1993; Ottawa-Carleton Book Award (*The Litmus Body*), 1993. **COMMENT:** *"I am a poet, critic, short-story writer, most interested in the inner lives of women."*

McIntosh, Jacqueline, B.A. $
Director, Corporate Properties and Facilities, CANADIAN AIRLINES INTERNATIONAL LTD., 700 - 2nd St. SW, Ste. 2800, Calgary, AB T2P 2W2 (403) 294-6055, FAX 294-6295. Born Oxford, UK. m. Bradley G. Jackson. 2 ch. **EDUC:** Univ. of British Columbia, B.A.(Geography) 1984. **CAREER:** Property Mgr, Transport Canada, Calgary Int'l Airport, 1985-88; Mgr, Properties & Facilities, Canadian Airlines International, 1988-91; Mgr, Airport Dev., 1991-93; Dir., Corp. Properties & Facilities, 1993 to date. **INTERESTS:** architecture; travel. **COMMENT:** *"Educated as an urban geographer, I have worked in both public and private sectors in the areas of real estate development and management, with a particular focus on airports and aviation-related property. I am currently responsible for Canadian Airlines' airport and commercial properties in Canada and throughout the world."*

McIntosh, Rosemary ■■ ♡ ⊕
Chair of the Board, THE HUGH MACMILLAN

CHILDREN'S FOUNDATION, Bloorview Macmillan Centre, 350 Rumsey Rd., Toronto, ON M4G 1R8 (416) 425-6220, EMAIL mchouse@interlog.com. Born Toronto 1948. m. John. 2 ch. Dale, Graeme.

McIntosh, The Hon. Linda Gwen, M.L.A. 🍁 🎓

Minister of Education and Training, GOVERNMENT OF MANITOBA, Legislative Building, Rm. 168, Winnipeg, MB R3C 0V8, FAX (204) 945-1291. Born Montreal 1943. m. Don. 2 ch. EDUC: Manitoba Teachers' Coll., Certificate 1964. CAREER: teacher, City of Winnipeg, several yrs.; Trustee, St. James-Assiniboia Sch. Bd., 1980-89; Pres., Manitoba Association of School Trustees, 1984; Illustrator, Rupertsland News, Anglican Church of Canada, 1985 to date; Special Asst. to Premier Gary Filmon, Gov't of Man., 1988-90; Weekly Panelist, CBC Week in Review, mid-1980s; M.L.A., Gov't of Man., 1990 to date; Min. of Cooperative, Consumer & Corp. Affairs & Min. Responsible for the Liquor Control Act, 1991-93; Treasury Bd., 1992-95; Min. of Urban Affairs & Min. of Housing, 1993-95; Min. of Educ. & Training, 1995 to date. AFFIL: Winnipeg Youth Orchestra (Dir.); Maple Leaf Toastmistress Club (Dir.); Boy Scouts of Canada (Service Scouter); Anglican Church of Canada.

McIntyre, Lynn, M.D.,M.H.Sc., F.R.C.P.C. ⊕ 🎓

Dean, Faculty of Health Professions, DALHOUSIE UNIVERSITY, Burbidge Building, 5968 College St., 3rd Fl., Halifax, NS B3H 3J5 (902) 494-3327, FAX 494-1966, EMAIL llmcinty@is.dal.ca. Born Peterborough, Ont. 1956. s. EDUC: Univ. of Toronto, M.D. 1980; M.H.Sc. (Community Health) 1984. CAREER: Rotating Internship, Mortimer B. Davis Jewish General Hospital, 1981; Clinical Fellowship, Tropical Medicine, Toronto General Hospital, 1982; Staff Physician, Sioux Lookout Zone Hospital, 1982-83; Community Medicine Residency, Univ. of Toronto, 1983-86; Hospital Epidemiologist, Izaak Walton Killam Children's Hospital, Halifax, 1986-91; Dean, Fac. of Health Professions, Dalhousie Univ., 1992 to date; Assoc. Prof., Schools of Recreation, Phys. & Health Educ., & Health Svc Admin., 1992 to date; numerous consultancies. SELECTED PUBLICATIONS: "Epidemiology of diabetes mellitus among Indians in Northeastern Manitoba and Northwestern Ontario," with others (*Canadian Medical Association Journal* 1985); "Exploratory analysis of children's nutrition programs in Canada," with J. Dayle (*Social Science Medicine* 1992); "The Dartmouth Health Promotion Study" with E.G. Belzer *et al* (*Journal of School Health* 66 1996); numerous other articles. AFFIL: Royal Coll. of Physicians & Surgeons of Canada (Fellow in Community Medicine); Canadian Society for International Health (Co-Chair 1994-96); Canadian Medical Association; N.S. Medical Society; Canadian Public Health Association; Public Health Association of N.S. (various exec. positions). HONS: numerous scholarships & research grants. INTERESTS: running; parrots; poodles. MISC: supervisor of numerous graduate students; speaker at many conferences. COMMENT: *"I am a entering my second term as Dean and plan to continue to work for social justice, consensus, group growth and the public good."*

McIvor, Jane, B.A. 📺 ✏ $

Managing Director, CORE GROUP PUBLISHERS INC., 1075 W. Georgia St., Ste. 270, Vancouver, BC V6E 3C9 (604) 688-0382, FAX 688-3105. Born Toronto 1963. s. EDUC: Columbia Broadcasting, Dipl.(Comm) 1989; Univ. of British Columbia, B.A.(Int'l. Rel'ns) 1992. CAREER: Mng Ed., *National Radio Guide*, 1993-95; Publisher, *Magazine of Magazines*, 1995; Jr. Consultant, Robertson Rozenhart, 1995 to date; Mng Dir., Core Group Publishers, 1995 to date. AFFIL: British Columbia Association of Magazine Publishers; Canadian Magazine Publishers Association.

McKay, Sharon, B.A.,M.S.W. ■ 🎓 ⊕

Dean and Associate Professor, Faculty of Social Work, UNIVERSITY OF REGINA, Regina, SK S4S 0A2 (306) 585-4563, FAX 585-4872, EMAIL sharon.mckay@uregina.ca. Born Edmonton 1940. m. Bruce. 3 ch. CAREER: full & part-time social work (primarily in child & family welfare & adult mental health), Canada, the US & UK, 1962-74; Assoc. Prof., Lakehead Univ., Thunder Bay, Ont., 1975-90; Dean & Assoc. Prof., Fac. of Social Work, Univ. of Regina, 1990 to date. SELECTED PUBLICATIONS: "Unemployment and Social Work Practice: Moving from Concern to Action," prepared for *Unemployment, Social Work and Social Policy: A Challenge for Human Services*, eds. Gordon Ternowetsky & Graham Riches, (Garamond Press, 1990); "Unemployment in a Northern Hinterland: The Social Impact of Political Neglect," with Stephen McBride & Mary Ellen Hill, in *Provincial Hinterland: Inequality in Northern Ontario*, Chris Southcott, ed. (Fernwood Publishing, 1992); various articles in refereed journals, professional publications & reports. AFFIL: Saskatchewan Association of Social Workers; Ranch Ehrlo Society (Bd. of Dir.); Ontario Association of Professional Social Workers (Life Mbr.). COM-

MENT: *"A modest record–I have been blessed with stellar colleagues, family and friends and more than my share of interesting and challenging opportunities."*

McKay, Shona, B.A. ✒

Writer. Toronto (416) 925-8672, FAX 920-2644. Born Edinburgh m. Warren Gerrard. 2 ch. **EDUC:** York Univ., B.A.(Art Hist.) 1978. **CAREER:** Staff writer, *Maclean's*, 1978-85; freelance writer, 1985 to date. **SELECTED PUBLICATIONS:** articles published in numerous newspapers & magazines, incl. *Maclean's*, *Report On Business*, *Financial Post Magazine*, *Canadian Business*, *Applied Arts Quarterly*, & *Advertising Age*; corp. clients include Hume Publishing, CIBC, Unisys, & Canadian Standards Association; speeches for cabinet ministers & sr. officials in various Ont. ministries, incl. Econ. Dev. & Trade, Culture, Tourism & Recreation, & the Pay Equity Commission; various other publications for Ont. gov't. **HONS:** Dean's List, York Univ.

McKean, Heather, LL.B. ■■ ⚖

Managing Partner, OSLER, HOSKIN & HARCOURT, First Canadian Place, P.O. Box 50, Toronto, ON M5X 1B8 (416) 862-6612, FAX 862-6666, EMAIL hmckean@osler.com. Born 1956. m. Edward Gettings. 2 ch. **EDUC:** Glendon Coll., York Univ., 1975-77; Osgoode Hall Law Sch., LL.B. 1980. **CAREER:** lawyer, Osler, Hoskin & Harcourt, 1982 to date; Ptnr, 1988; Mng Ptnr, 1996; while managing the various bus. & legal units within the firm, will continue legal practice in Corp.-Commercial Dept., advising on acquisitions, financings, restructuring & real estate. **SELECTED PUBLICATIONS:** various articles for legal publications. **AFFIL:** Canadian Bar Association.

McKee-Allain, Isabelle, B.A.,B.Sc.Soc., M.Sc.Soc.,Ph.D. ■ 🍁 ⚛

Doyenne par intérim, Faculté des sciences sociales, UNIVERSITÉ DE MONCTON, Pavillon Léopold-Taillon, Moncton, NB E1A 3E9 (506) 858-4183, FAX 858-4506, EMAIL mckeeai@umoncton.ca. Born Bouctouche, N.B. 1947. m. Greg Allain. 2 ch. Mélanie, Dominic. **EDUC:** Univ. de Moncton, B.A. 1967; Univ. Laval, B.Sc.Soc.(Soc.) 1970, M.Sc.Soc.(Soc.) 1975; Univ. de Montréal, Ph.D.(Soc.) 1995. **CAREER:** Researcher & Coord., research proj., N.B. New Start, 1971-73; Researcher & Host, Radio-Canada Atlantique (weekly TV series), 1975-77; Coord. & Co-Supervisor, research proj., Univ. of California in Santa Barbara, 1979-81; Prof., Dépt. de sociologie, Univ. de Moncton, 1982 to date; Chair, Dépt. de sociologie, 1993-95; V-doyenne, Fac. des sciences sociales, 1995-96; Doyenne par intérim, 1996 to date. **SELECTED PUBLICATIONS:** "Questionnement féministe en milieu minoritaire: des pistes offertes par l'étude des collèges classiques féminins en Acadie," dans L. Cardinal, dir., *Une langue qui pense: la recherche en milieu minoritaire francophone au Canada* (Ottawa: Presses de l'Univ. d'Ottawa, Collection Actexpress, 1993); " La société acadienne: lectures et conjonctures," dans *L'Acadie des Maritimes*, J. Daigle, dir. (Moncton: Chaine d'etudes acadiennes, 1993); "Les familles acadiennes des années 1990: profil et enjeux," dans *Famillies francophones: multiples réalités*, dir. C. Bernier, S. Larocque, M. Aumond (Sudbury, Ont.: Institut franco-ontarien Coll. fléur-de-trille, 1995); various chapters, articles & conferences. **EDIT:** Ed. Bd., *Recherches féministes*, 1993 to date; Ed. Bd., *Egalité*, 1983-86, 1993 to date; Ed. Bd., *Atlantis*, 1995 to date. **AFFIL:** CRIAW (N.B. Rep. on Bd. 1984-87); ACFAS/ACADIE (Bd.); Canadian Sociology & Anthropology Association; ACFAS; ACSALF; SAANB; Réseau des chercheur e.s. sur les communautés francophones minoritaires du Canada; various other associations. **HONS:** bourse du Conseil des gouverneurs, Univ. de Moncton, 1987-88; boursiére, Québec-Acadie, 1987-88, 1988-89. **INTERESTS:** books; travel; public speaking. **MISC:** was 1 of 3 students from N.B. chosen to host at the Canadian Pavilion, EXPO '67. **COMMENT:** *"Acadian women, youth and education have been my major fields of interest, both academically and through my involvement with various groups, and by combining my parental and my career responsibilities. I'm still very determined to continue working toward building a better society."*

McKenna, Joanne, B.Sc.,C.A. $ 🗳 🌷

President, CANWEST GLOBAL DEVELOPMENTS, 81 Barber Greene Rd., Don Mills, ON M3C 2A2 (416) 446-5557, FAX 446-5544. Born Toronto. **EDUC:** Univ. of Western Ontario, B.Sc. 1974. **CAREER:** Audit Group, Coopers and Lybrand, Toronto, 1974-78; Compt., CBS Records (Canada) Ltd., 1978-81; VP, Fin., V.K.S. Developments, 1981-85; VP, Fin., The Sports Network, 1985-88; Exec. VP, JLL Broadcast Group, 1988-93; Pres., CanWest Global Developments, 1993 to date. **AFFIL:** Institute of Chartered Accountants of Ontario; Canadian Institute of Chartered Accountants (C.A.).

McKenna, Seana ■ ✪

Actor. c/o Pamela Friendly, Premier Artists, Toronto, ON (416) 461-6868. Born Toronto 1956. cl. Miles Potter. **EDUC:** Trinity Coll., Univ. of Toronto; National Theatre Sch., Grad.

1979. CAREER: actor, 1979 to date. SELECTED CREDITS: Founding Mbr., FOOLSCAP (a new theatre co.), 1996; 1996 credits incl.: Jean-Louise, *To Kill a Mockingbird*, Huntington Theatre, Boston; Cleopatra, *Antony and Cleopatra*, Centaur Theatre; Maggie, *Cat on a Hot Tin Roof*, The Grand; various roles at the Stratford Festival, Stratford, Ont., incl. Lady Macbeth, *Macbeth*; Juliet, *Romeo and Juliet*; Helena, *A Midsummer Night's Dream*; Portia & Jessica, *The Merchant of Venice*; Viola, *Twelfth Night*; Cordelia, *King Lear*; other theatre incl. Blanche/Stella, *A Streetcar Named Desire*, Theatre New Brunswick, Boston's Huntington Theatre; Candida, *Candida*, Eliza Doolittle, *Pygmalion*, Shaw Festival; 1st Cdn productions of *The Baltimore Waltz*, Tarragon Theatre, & *The Search for Signs of Intelligent Life in the Universe*, Belfry Theatre, Manitoba Theatre Centre (M.T.C.), National Arts Centre, Neptune Theatre, Grand Theatre; Hedda, *Hedda Gabler*, Medea, *Medea*, Maggie, *Dancing at Lughnasa* & Billie Dawn, *Born Yesterday*, M.T.C.; *Educating Rita*, Belfry Theatre, Theatre New Brunswick; *Passion Play*, The Goodman Theatre, Chicago; *She Stoops to Conquer*, The Court Theatre, Chicago; *Alligator Pie* & *The Death of the Donnellys*, Theatre Passe Muraille; *In the Jungle of the Cities*, Toronto Free Theatre; *The Mac-Paps*, Toronto Workshop Productions; 2 seasons with the Blythe Festival; numerous film & TV appearances incl. *Margie Gillis, Wild Hearts in Strange Times*; *Street Legal, Side Effects,Grand Larceny*, CBC; *Glory Enough for All*, Gemstone; *Jimmy's Coming*, Bootleg Films; *Handel's Last Chance*, Devine Entertainment; Jane Urquhart's *"Away," "Between the Covers,"* CBC Radio. AFFIL: Canadian Actors' Equity; ACTRA; AEA. HONS: Dora Mavor Moore Award, (Joan in *Saint Joan*) Theatre Plus, Toronto, 1990; Dora Mavor Moore Award nominations: Elsa, *The Road to Mecca*, Canadian Stage, 1988 & Masha, *Three Sisters*, Banff/Equity Showcase, 1991. INTERESTS: gardening; travel.

McKenna, Sister Mary Olga, B.A.,M.A., Ph.D.,A.I.E.,LL.D. 〇 📖 🖎
Professor Emeritus, MOUNT SAINT VINCENT UNIVERSITY, 150 Bedford Hwy., Halifax, NS B3M 3J5 (902) 457-3500, FAX 457-3506. Born Charlottetown 1920. Sister of Charity of St. Vincent de Paul, Halifax, 1939. EDUC: Mount Saint Vincent Univ., B.A.(Hist.) 1947; Boston Coll., Chestnut Hill, Mass., M.A.(Phil.) 1957, Ph.D.(Educ.) 1964; Univ. of London, A.I.E. 1977. CAREER: sch. teacher, 1939-61; Supervisor of Educ., Archdiocese of Boston,

1961-64; Prof. of Educ., Mount Saint Vincent Univ., 1964-86; Congregational Historian, Sisters of Charity, Halifax, 1986 to date. SELECTED PUBLICATIONS: *Micmac by Choice: An Island Legend* (Formac, 1990); "Paradigm Shifts in a Women's Religious Institute: The Sisters of Charity, Halifax, 1950-79" (CCHA Historical Studies 61, 1995); *Women Witnessing to Love: Sisters of Charity*, St. Vincent de Paul, Halifax: 1950-1980 (to be published in 1996). EDIT: Guest Ed., "The Mi'kmaq," *The Abegweit Review*, UPEI, 1993. AFFIL: American Conference of Religious Women; Canadian Catholic Historical Association; Canadian Society for the Study of Education; Delta Kappa Gamma Society International. HONS: The Sister Mary Olga McKenna Diamond Jubilee Scholarship, Mount Saint Vincent Univ., 1985; ; LL.D.(Hon.), Univ. of Prince Edward Island, 1990. INTERESTS: women's studies; family genealogy; travel; card playing, particularly bridge; gathering & preserving various kinds of berries & other fruits. COMMENT: *"A member of a dedicated group of religious women, I am endeavouring to show through my writing how the Sisters of Charity are giving joyful witness to the love of God, of one another and of all persons in today's world as they minister to the unmet needs of society."*

McKenna, Suzanne, B.A.,B.Ed., B.S.W. 🖐 ⊕ 🖤
Executive Director, NEW BRUNSWICK ASSOCIATION OF SOCIAL WORKERS, Box 1533, Stn. A, Fredericton, NB E3B 5G2 (506) 459-5595, FAX 457-1421. Born Trois-Rivières, Que. 1947. m. Greg McKenna. 3 ch. Victoria Ann, Thomas Gregory, Janet Ellen. EDUC: St Francis Xavier Univ., B.A.(Math./Phil.) 1968; Dalhousie Univ., B.Ed. 1969; St. Thomas Univ., B.S.W. 1986. CAREER: teacher, East Pictou Rural High Sch., New Glasgow, N.S., 1969-70; supply teacher, Pictou County, N.S., 1970-71; supply teacher, District 26 (Fredericton & surrounding area), 1983; Social Worker, Post-Adoption Svcs, Dept. of Health & Community Svcs, N.B., 1987-88; Social Worker, Adolescent Parent & Children Svcs, 1988-90; Exec. Dir., N.B. Association of Social Workers, 1990 to date. AFFIL: Straight Area Literacy Council (Founding Mbr. & tutor 3 yrs.); Fredericton Area Coalition for Social Justice (F.A.C.S.J.); F.A.C.S.J. Legal Advice Clinic (Co-Chair); Diocesan Council of Dev. & Peace (VP, Nat'l Council of Dev. & Peace); Straight Area Music Committee (Founding Mbr.); Straight Area Hospital Auxiliary (Past Pres.); N.B. Association of Social Workers. INTERESTS: current affairs; social issues; environmental issues. COMMENT: *"I am a professional, working in*

an administrative position, very involved in social activism–committed to social justice."

McKennitt, Loreena ⊗ ⌣ ♥

Singer, Songwriter, Composer and Recording Artist. Founder and Managing Director, QUIN-LAN ROAD LIMITED (independent record label), Box 933, Stratford, ON N5A 7M3 (519) 273-3876, FAX 273-4553, EMAIL 75247.316@compuserve.com. Born Morden, Man. CAREER: actress in musical theatre; film, TV, concert composer & performer; touring musician, 1987 to date. SELECTED CREDITS: Recording Artist/Prod. of 5 albums on the Quinlan Road label: *Elemental*, 1985; *To Drive The Cold Winter Away*, 1987; *Parallel Dreams*, 1989; *The Visit*, 1991; *The Mask and the Mirror*, 1994; Cdn Rep., Canada Week, UNESCO, Paris, 1978; Composer/Performer, The *Two Gentleman of Verona*, Stratford Shakespearean Festival, 1984; Cdn Rep., Expo '85, Japan, 1985; Soundtrack Composer/Performer, *Women and Spirituality* (film series), National Film Board of Canada, 1989-92; Soundtrack Composer/Performer, *Léolo* (feature), Verseau, 1993; Segment Composer/Performer, *Highlander III* (feature), Miramax, 1995; songs licensed: *The Santa Clause* (feature), Walt Disney Pictures, 1995; *Jade* (feature), Paramount Pictures, 1995. AFFIL: American Federation of Musicians (Canada); Society of Composers, Authors & Music Publishers of Canada (SOCAN); Broadcast Music, Inc. (BMI); Canadian Academy of Recording Arts & Sciences (CARAS). HONS: Best Roots & Traditional Album, JUNO Awards, 1991 & 1994; Billboard Magazine International Creative Achievement Award, 1994. INTERESTS: travel; the natural world. MISC: since 1991, under contract for distribution worldwide via Warner Music International.

McKercher, Peggy, B.A., C.M. ■ ○ ⌥ ◉

Chancellor, UNIVERSITY OF SASKATCHEWAN, Administration Building, 105 Administration Place, E-204, Saskatoon, SK S7N 5A2, FAX (306) 975-1026. m. Robert. EDUC: Univ. of Saskatchewan, B.A., Certificate in Educ. CAREER: various positions in recreation & educ. incl. Boston YWCA; Ottawa sch. system; Hudson Bay Mining and Smelting Co., Island Falls, Man.; Fac. Mbr., Univ. of Saskatchewan; co-owner & co-operator (with husband Robert), grain & registered Aberdeen Angus farming operation. VOLUNTEER CAREER: Counsellor, Rural Municipality of Corman Park, 1978-81; Saskatoon District Planning Commission, 1978-81; various Council Committees, Rural Municipality of Corman Park,

1979-81; Deputy Reeve, 1979-80; Dir., Canadian Water Resource Association, 1979-81; Dir., Participaction, 1980-81; Chair, Meewasin Valley Authority, 1981-96; Dir., Jeux Canada Games, 1986 to date; Chair, Sherbrooke Community Centre Fund Raising Campaign, 1986 to date; Advisory Committee, Saskatchewan Order of Merit, 1988-90; Dir., Saskatchewan Medical Research Foundation, 1989 to date; Mayor's Task Force on South Downtown, Saskatoon, 1989-90; V-Chrm, Wanuskewin Heritage Park Bd. of Dir., 1989 to date; Exec. Mbr., Bd. of Dir., Canadiana Fund, National Capital Commission, 1990 to date; President's Advisory Committee on Community Rel'ns, Univ. of Saskatchewan, 1992 to date. AFFIL: St. Andrew's Presbyterian Church; Home & School Association; Mendel Art Gallery (Women's Committee); YWCA (Dir. Saskatoon; Dir. Ottawa); Riverside Golf Club (Women's Section); Wanuskewin Heritage Park (Dir.). HONS: Athletic Wall of Fame, Univ. of Saskatchewan; Rosalie Early Memorial Award; Citizen of the Year, City of Saskatoon, 1989; Award for Dedication & Excellence in Field of Endeavour, Saskatchewan Report, 1992; Canada 125 Medal; Socially Responsible Entrepreneur of the Year for Western Canada Award, 1994; Member of the Order of Canada, 1995. COMMENT: *"Peggy McKercher, homemaker and volunteer, has served as Chairman of the Meewasin Valley Authority since its inception in 1979. Her hours of devotion, perseverance and vision of the future of Saskatoon's riverbank along the South Saskatchewan River have enabled the city to achieve world recognition for its beautiful river corridor."*

McKinnon, Sherry L., B.A. ◉ ♡ ⊕

Executive Director, Saskatchewan Division, THE ARTHRITIS SOCIETY, 2078 Halifax St., Regina, SK S4P 1T7 (306) 352-3312, FAX 565-8731. Born Jonquière, Que. 1956. s. EDUC: Univ. of Western Ontario, B.A.(Soc.) 1979. CAREER: Dir. of Special Projects, Multiple Sclerosis Society, Atlantic Div., 1979-80 & Sask. Div., 1980-83; Admin. Asst., Wascana Home Care, 1983-92; Exec. Dir., The Arthritis Society, Sask. Div., 1992 to date. SELECTED PUBLICATIONS: numerous program-specific publications, incl. manuals, brochures & newsletters. AFFIL: Canadian Society of Association Executives; Canadian Association of Gift Planners; Progress Club. INTERESTS: people; travel; reading; painting; crafts. COMMENT: *"A creative, innovative program developer who enjoys the challenges of the nonprofit sector. My career has been one of building programs through a strong team approach with co-workers and volunteers. Fund-raising achievements have been numerous, as well as playing a key role in the development of the home-care program in Regina. At present, my energies and attention are being directed to the development of the Saskatchewan Division of the Arthritis Society and its programs."*

McKnight, Sandra, B.A. ✊ ♥
Chair of the Board, NOVA HOUSE WOMEN'S SHELTER, Box 337, Selkirk, MB R1A 2B3 (204) 482-7882, FAX 482-8483, EMAIL smcknight@co-operator.mn.ca. Born Stonewall, Man. 1947. m. William. **EDUC:** Univ. of Winnipeg, B.A.(Geography/Soc.) 1982. **CAREER:** Circulation Clerk, *Manitoba Co-Operator*, 1967-72; Home & Family Reporter, 1972-80; Copy Ed., 1980 to date. **AFFIL:** Canadian Farm Writers' Federation (various committees); Provincial Council of Women of Manitoba (Officers' Committee); National Council of Women of Canada (Chair, Image & Visibility Section, Revitalization Task Force); Univ. of Winnipeg (Regent); Nova House Women's Shelter (Chair). **INTERESTS:** travel; cooking; horses; reading; history

McLachlan, Sarah ■■ ✪ 🎭
Singer/Songwriter, Recording Artist, Visual Artist. c/o Nettwerk Productions, 1250 W. 6th Ave., Vancouver, BC V6H 1A5 (604) 654-2929, FAX 654-1993, EMAIL info@nettwerk.com. Born Halifax, N.S. 1968. **CAREER:** recording artist & touring musician, 1987 to date; corp. involvements include: Sarah McLachlan Entertainment Inc.; Never Get Off The Boat Touring Inc.; Amp Merchandising; and Lilith Fair Productions. **SELECTED CREDITS:** composer/recording artist, 3 full-length albums for Nettwerk Records (Arista/BMG outside of Canada): *Touch* (1988); *Solace* (1991); *Fumbling Towards Ecstasy* (1993) (all achieving Platinum status); songs licenced for use in film: *Boys on the Side*, *Bed of Roses*, & *Moll Flanders*; co-wrote hit single ("I Will Remember You") from *The Brothers McMullen*. **AFFIL:** SOCAN, Canada; BMI, US; CARAS; American Federation of Musicians, Canada. **HONS:** Best Video ("Into the Fire"), Juno Award, 1991; Female Vocalist of the Year, East Coast Music Awards, 1992; Pop/Rock Artist of the Year, East Coast Music Awards, 1994; Best Adult Contemporary Video ("Possession"), MuchMusic Awards, 1994; Favourite Female Performer ("Possession"), MuchMusic's *People's Choice*, 1994; Best Performance in a Music/Variety Special ("Fumbling Towards Ecstasy Live"), Gemini Award, 1995. **INTERESTS:** nature & the out-of-doors; humanitarian concerns of all sorts. **MISC:** Under recording agreement with Nettwerk Productions Ltd. (Arista/BMG Records for the world outside of Canada), Sarah is represented by Nettwerk Management.

McLachlin, The Hon. Madame Justice Beverley, B.A.,M.A.,LL.B. ⚖
Justice, SUPREME COURT OF CANADA, Ottawa, ON K1A 0J1 (613) 996-9174, FAX 996-3063. Born Pincher Creek, Alta. 1943. (w. Roderick McLachlin); m. Frank E. McArdle. 1 ch. **EDUC:** Univ. of Alberta, M.A. 1968, LL.B. 1968. **BAR:** Alta., 1969; B.C., 1971. **CAREER:** Lawyer, Wood, Moir, Hyde and Ross, Edmonton, 1969-71; Lawyer, Thomas, Herdy, Mitchell & Co., Fort St. John, 1971-72; Lawyer, Bull, Housser and Tupper, Vancouver, 1972-75; Lecturer, Assoc. Prof. & Prof., Univ. of British Columbia, 1974-81; appointed to County Court of Vancouver, 1981; Supreme Court of B.C., 1981; Court of Appeal of B.C., 1985; Chief Justice, Supreme Court of B.C., 1988; Justice, Supreme Court of Canada, 1989 to date. **HONS:** LL.D.(Hon.) Univ. of Alberta, 1991; LL.D.(Hon.), Univ. of British Columbia, 1990; LL.D.(Hon.), Univ. of Toronto, 1995.

McLaren, Patricia, B.Comm. ■ $
Vice-President and Area Manager, Calgary Central, ROYAL BANK OF CANADA, 335 - 8th Ave. SW, Ste. 301, Calgary, AB T2P 1C9 (403) 292-3975, FAX 292-3058. Born Weyburn, Sask. 1958. m. Brock Kaluznick. 2 ch. Hana, Nathalie. **EDUC:** Univ. of Saskatchewan, B.Comm. 1980; Sophia Univ., Ichygia Campus, Tokyo, Japan, 1985; Canadian Investment Finance, 1987. **CAREER:** Investment Advisor, Dominion Securities; Asst. VP, Mktg & Sales, Financial Trust Co.; Royal Bank of Canada, 1988 to date. **COMMENT:** *"Recognized as a leader who fosters change, takes risks and accepts responsibility for making it happen."*

McLaughlin, Audrey, B.A.,M.S.W., LL.D. 🍁 ✋
Member of Parliament (Yukon), GOVERNMENT OF CANADA, House of Commons, Ottawa, ON K1A 0A6 (613) 995-7224, FAX 992-8569. Born Dutton, Ont. 1936. d. 2 ch. **EDUC:** Univ. of Western Ontario, B.A. 1964; Univ. of Toronto, M.S.W. 1970. **CAREER:** teacher, Adisadel Coll., Ghana, 1964-67; Caseworker, Children's Aid Society of Toronto; Exec. Dir., Metro Toronto Branch, Canadian Mental Health Association; volunteer work with women & dev., Barbados, 1986; small bus. operator, admin. & community worker; Consultant, specializing in community dev. & aboriginal issues, Whitehorse; elected MP (Yukon),

by-election, July 1987; re-elected 1988, 1993; Leader, New Democratic Party of Canada, 1989-95; appointed to Privy Council, 1991; has been NDP critic & spokesperson on the Constitution, Northern Dev., Tourism, Revenue Canada, Health, & Status of Women. SELECTED PUBLICATIONS: *A Woman's Place: My Life and Politics* (Macfarlane, Walter & Ross, 1992). AFFIL: has been an active mbr. of many organizations within the women's movement, of the arts, environment community & anti-poverty groups. HONS: Knight, l'Assemblie internationale des parlementaires de langue française, 1991; LL.D.(Hon., Univ. of Toronto, 1995. MISC: 1st New Democrat to hold Yukon seat in House of Commons; 1st woman to lead a major fed. party in Canada; travelled extensively in Africa, Latin Am., Asia & the Caribbean. COMMENT: *"Throughout Audrey's career as a politician, businessperson and community activist, she has built a reputation as a skilled manager and a determined activist for working Canadian families."*

McLaughlin, Kathy, B.A. $ ⛑
Vice-President and General Manager, British Columbia, ROGERS CANTEL INC., 4710 Kingsway, Ste. 1600, Burnaby, BC V5H 4M5 (604) 431-1400, FAX 431-1542. m. 2 ch. EDUC: Univ. of British Columbia, B.A.(English) 1977; Univ. of Western Ontario, Exec. Mktg Program for Technology Companies 1989; Canadian Securities Course 1984. CAREER: Public Rel'ns Mgr, First City Financial Corporation/First City Trust, 1978-81; Public Rel'ns Dir. & Acct Dir., West-Can Communications Ltd. (now Scali, McCabe, Sloves), 1981-82; Gen. Mgr, Vancouver Branch, Burson-Marstellar Limited, 1982-84; Client Svcs Mgr, Toronto, 1984; Dir., Mktg, Toronto, Rogers Cantel Inc., 1984-88; VP, Nat'l Mktg, 1988-90; VP, Mktg & Merchandising, Owned Stores Div., 1990-91; VP, Mktg, Cantel West, Vancouver, 1991-93; VP & Gen. Mgr, B.C., 1993 to date. AFFIL: B.C. Kinsmen (Chair, Advisory Bd.). HONS: Achievement Award, Business in Vancouver "40 under 40", 1994; nominee, Marketer of the Year, American Marketing Association of Toronto, 1990.

McLaughlin, Mary ■ $
Vice-President, Corporate Communications, ONTARIO HYDRO, 700 University Ave., Toronto, ON M5G 1X6 (416) 592-2113, FAX 592-2174. Born Saint John 1944 EDUC: Ryerson Polytechnic Univ., Radio & TV Arts 1966. CAREER: various positions in TV incl. writer, researcher, prod. asst. & dir., CBC, CTV & *The Pierre Berton Show*, 1968-72; Press Sec./Special Asst. to the Hon. Marc LaLonde,

then Min., Health & Welfare, & Min. responsible for the Status of Women, Gov't of Canada, 1972-79; Public Affairs Officer, Mutual Life of Canada, 1977-79; Public Affairs Exec., 1979-86; VP, Public Affairs, 1986-95; VP, Corp. Comm., Ontario Hydro, 1995 to date. AFFIL: Council for Canadian Unity (Gov.); Conference Board of Canada (Public Affairs Council); International Association of Business Communicators.

McLean, Ellen, O.C.,B.A.,B.L.S., LL.D. ✍ ○ ✋
Dairy Farmer and Volunteer. R.R. 1, Eureka, NS B0K 1B0 (902) 923-2593. Born Winnipeg 1926. m. John A. McLean. 3 ch. EDUC: McGill Univ., B.A. 1947, B.L.S. 1948. CAREER: Int'l Labour Office, Geneva, Switzerland; Bus. Library, Bell Telephone Company of Canada, Montreal; Ptnr, family dairy operation. VOLUNTEER CAREER: Pres., Pictou County Council of Churches (1993-95); Pres., N.S. District, Canadian Bible Society (1990-92); Dir., International Centre for Ocean Development (1985-91); Chair, Advisory Bd., Pictou Campus, Nova Scotia Community Coll. (1985-91); Dir., N.S. Sch. Boards Association (1990-91); Mbr., Pictou District Sch. Bd. (1978-91); N.S. Consultation Committee on Sunday Shopping, Chair (1990-91); CBC Advisory Committee on Agriculture & Food (1985-89); Advisory Committee, Henson Coll., Dalhousie Univ.; Advisory Committee, Extension Dept., St. Francis Xavier Univ.; Pres., Women's Institutes of N.S. (1963-65); Pres., Federated Women's Institutes of Canada (1973-76); Pres., The Associated Country Women of the World (1983-89); Chair, N.S. Advisory Council on the Status of Women (1980-85); V-Chair, N.S. Royal Commission on Pensions (1981-83); Chrm, Pictou County Research & Dev. Commission; Mun. Councillor, Municipality of Pictou County; 4-H Leader for 24 yrs. HONS: Farm Leadership Award, Bank of Montreal, 1966; Centennial Medal, 1967; Queen's Jubilee Medal, 1977; Officer of the Order of Canada, 1981; Atlantic Agricultural Hall of Fame, 1986; Canadian Agricultural Hall of Fame, 1987; Canada 125 Medal; LL.D.(Hon.), St. Francis Xavier Univ., 1976. INTERESTS: agricultural concerns (future of the industry); women's issues worldwide; education. COMMENT: *"Over the years I have been very involved in all aspects of community activities, always trying to bring to whatever I am doing the point of view of rural people, of farm women, and of agriculture. My philosophy has always been to serve the community with whatever talents I might have, to help to make the community better."*

McLean, Marianne, B.A.,M.A., Ph.D. ■ ⬚ 🦫 🍁

Project Archivist, NATIONAL ARCHIVES OF CANADA, 344 Wellington St., Ottawa, ON K1A 0N3 (613) 996-7342, FAX 943-8112, EMAIL mmclean@archives.ca. Born Winnipeg 1949. m. Philip Goldring. 4 ch. Dimitri Goldring, Hugh Goldring, Alexander Goldring, Colin Goldring. EDUC: Univ. of Montreal, B.A. (Hist.) 1970; Carleton Univ., M.A.(Hist.) 1972; Univ. of Edinburgh, Ph.D.(Hist.) 1982. CAREER: Archivist, National Archives of Canada, 1982 to date. SELECTED PUBLICA-TIONS: *The People of Glengarry: Highlanders in Transition, 1745-1820* (Montreal & Kingston, 1991).

McLellan, The Honourable Anne, P.C., M.P. 🍁 🏵

Member of Parliament (Edmonton Northwest) and Minister of Natural Resources, GOVERN-MENT OF CANADA, Office of the Minister, 580 Booth St., Ottawa, ON K1A 0E4 (613) 996-2007, FAX 996-4516, House of Commons, Rm. 323 West Block, Ottawa, ON K1A 0A6. Born Hants County, N.S. 1950. EDUC: Dalhousie Univ., B.A. 1971, LL.B. 1974; King's Coll., Univ. of London, LL.M. 1975. BAR: N.S., 1976. CAREER: Asst. Prof., Fac. of Law, Univ. of New Brunswick, 1976-80; Acting Assoc. Dean, 1979-80; Assoc. Prof., Fac. of Law, Univ. of Alberta, 1980-89; Assoc. Dean, 1985-87; Prof., 1989-93; Acting Dean, 1991-92; elected MP (Edmonton N.W.), 1993; Min. of Natural Resources, 1993 to date; V-Chair, Cabinet Committee on Econ. Policy & mbr., Coordinating Group of Ministers on Program Review, to Jan. 1996; Chair, Social Dev. Policy Committee, mbr., Treasury Bd. Committee & mbr., Econ. Dev. Policy Committee, 1996 to date. AFFIL: N.S. Barristers' Society (non-practising member).

McLennan, Elizabeth (Betty), A.P.R. ■■ ⬚ ✒

Director, Regulatory Information, TELUS COR-PORATION (telecommunications), 10020 - 100 St., #21A, Edmonton, AB T5J 0N5 (403) 493-3215, EMAIL bmclenna@agt.net. Born Saint John, N.B. 1943. cl. Stanley Douglas Drake. 2 ch., 1 stch., Leanna Dawn McLennan, Leslie Adair McLennan, Brianna Leigh Drake. 2 grch. EDUC: Queen's Univ., Exec. Dev. Program 1994; Canadian Public Relations Society, APR designation/accredited status; various mgmt & public rel'ns courses. CAREER: Women's Dir./Host, CKCW-TV, Moncton, N.B., 1972-74; Copy Chief, Gordon Hill Advertising, Winnipeg, 1974-75; News Producer, CFAC-TV, Calgary, 1975-77; Public Rel'ns

Consultant/Freelance Journalist, 1977-84; Alta. & Prairie Ed., *Journal of Commerce*, 1984-86; Olympic Rel'ns Mgr, TELUS Corporation (formerly AGT Limited), 1986-88; Media Rel'ns Mgr, 1988-91; Public Affairs Dir., 1991-94; Dir., Regulatory Info., 1994 to date. AFFIL: Canadian Public Relations Society (Reg'l Examiner for accreditation process, B.C. & Alta.; mbr., Edmonton chpt.; formerly held several exec. positions, Edmonton chpt.); Canadian Women in Communications (VP, Edmonton chpt.); International Association of Business Communicators (former mbr.); Periodical Writers' Association of Canada (former mbr.); Maritime Reunion Association, Calgary (former Pres.); Pollution Probe, Moncton (former Coord.); Moncton Montessori Sch. (former Dir.); Women's Action Group, Moncton (founding mbr.). INTERESTS: reading; gardening; walking; holistic health; women's issues; watercolour painting; photography; quilting. COMMENT: *"I have been involved in the communications/information field for nearly 30 years. My career has included journalism (print and electronic), public relations consulting and corporate communications. I have set up and run my own company, and spent a number of years as a freelance journalist/writer. During the years that I worked for myself, I was a single parent. Flexibility in my work schedule was a priority during that time. I am proud of my daughters and the close relationship we've maintained. I have tried to maintain the highest ethical standards in my approach to both my work and my life."*

McLennan, Norma, B.Ed. 🌀 ○ 🦅

Regional Director, SASKATCHEWAN ABILITIES COUNCIL, 825 McDonald St., Regina, SK S4N 2X5 (306) 569-9048, FAX 352-3717. Born Regina 1950. m. Stuart. 2 ch. Heather, Patricia Jane. EDUC: Univ. of Regina, B.Ed.(Elementary) 1987. CAREER: elementary teacher, Buffalo Plains Sch., Div. 21; Adult Educ. Instructor, Saskatchewan Institute of Art, Science & Technology-Kelsey Institute; Reg'l Dir./Program Mgr/Vocational Evaluator, Saskatchewan Abilities Council. AFFIL: MacNeill Skipping Sensation Parent Group; Rotary Club. INTERESTS: developing new avenues for persons with intellectual disabilities to be competitively employed in Saskatchewan. MISC: Certified Life Skills Coach; developed Life Skills Curriculum for Saskatchewan Abilities Council; mbr., dev. team for "Whole People of God" Sunday Sch. curriculum, United Church of Canada.

McLeod, Catherine, B.A. ■■ $ 🖋

Chairman, ZEN INTERNATIONAL RESOURCES LTD. (mineral exploration & dev. in China),

625 Howe St., Ste. 328, Vancouver, BC V6C 2T6 (604) 684-0003, FAX 684-0007, EMAIL t.seltzer@direct.ca. Born Vancouver 1960. m. Tom Seltzer. **EDUC:** Trinity Western Univ., B.A.(Bus. Admin.) 1984. **CAREER:** Institutional Equities Trader/Acct. Exec., Yorkton Securities Inc., Vancouver, 1985-92; Oper. Mgr, Santiago, Chile, 1992; VP, Corp. Dev. & co-founder, Acuarios Minera y Exploradora (predecessor co. to Arequipa Resources), 1993-94; Pres. & CEO, Arequipa Resources Ltd., 1994-96; Chrm & co-founder, Zen International Resources Ltd., 1996 to date. **DIRECTOR:** Arequipa Resources Ltd.; Francisco Gold Corp.; Zen International Resources Ltd. **INTERESTS:** skiing; golf; travelling; reading. **COMMENT:** *"Entrepreneurial instincts combined with an upbringing in a third-generation mining family have led to a strong understanding of what it takes to build and finance a successful mining exploration company. Ms. McLeod successfully sold Arequipa Resources, her first endeavour in that field, to Barrick Gold in a transaction valued at over $1 billion, but, still interested in breaching new frontiers, has helped found her second exploration company, Zen International Resources Ltd., to develop gold properties in China."*

McLeod, Heleen Juliana, Ph.D. ■ ⊕

H.J. McLeod, Ph.D. & Associates Ltd., 11440 Kingsway Ave., Ste. 2, Edmonton, AB T5G 0X2 (403) 447-2614, FAX 455-8339. Born Athabasca, Alta. 1941. m. Rod D. McLeod. **EDUC:** Univ. of Alberta, B.A. 1961, B.Ed. 1968, M.Ed. 1972, Ph.D.(Counselling Psych.) 1980. **CAREER:** Teacher & Counsellor, Edmonton Public Sch. Bd., 1962-63, 1965-70; Consulting Psychologist, Westfield Diagnostic & Treatment Centre, 1971-73; Consulting Psychologist, Edmonton General Hospital, 1972-73; Acting Dir., Counselling Svcs Branch, Edmonton Public Sch. Bd., 1973-74; Supervisor, Teacher Staffing, 1974-75; Asst. Superintendent, Student Svcs Dept., 1975-81; Dir., Alberta Educ., Special Educ. Svcs Branch, 1981-87; Psychologist, H.J. McLeod, Ph.D. & Associates Ltd., 1987 to date; Instructor, Dept. of Educational Psych., Univ. of Alberta, 1987-88; Sr. Psychologist, Alberta Health, Mental Health Div., N.W. Reg., 1988-91; Expert Witness, Prov. Court of Alberta, Family Div., & Court of Queen's Bench, Alta.; Consulting Psychologist, Alberta Social Svcs & Community Health, N.E. Reg., 1988-92; Consulting Psychologist, Health Canada, Medical Svcs Branch, Edmonton, 1993 to date. **SELECTED PUBLICATIONS:** Sensory Multi-Handicapped Program Planning Project, with H. Finnestad (*Alberta Educ.*, Oct. 1979); "Counselling for the Integration of the Handicapped in Society" (*International Journal for the Advancement of Counselling* 5(2) 1982); "Special Education in the 1980s - A Decade of Crisis and Opportunity" (*BC Journal of Special Education* Fall 1983). **AFFIL:** Psychologists' Association of Alberta; Canadian Psychological Association; Society of Clinical Hypnosis (Alta.); Professional Examination Board in Psychology; Alberta Educ. (Attendance Bd.; Ministerial Review Committees); Employment Networks Bus. Advisory Council. **INTERESTS:** music; theatre; travel. **MISC:** Chair, Minister's Task Force on Gifted & Talented Pupils in Alberta, Alberta Educ., 1983; Alberta Teaching Certificate, Permanent Professional, 1966; Chartered Psychologist, Alberta, 1972; Registered Psychologist, N.W.T., 1988; Certified, Canadian Registry of Health Service Providers, 1991.

McLeod, Lorna, B.Comm.,C.A. ♡ ✊ $

Controller, Cotter Canada Hardware and Variety Cooperative Inc., 1530 Gamble Place, Winnipeg, MB R3T 1N6 (204) 453-9689, FAX 452-6615. National Treasurer, The Kidney Foundation of Canada. Born Cartwright, Man. 1964. s. **EDUC:** Univ. of Manitoba, B.Comm.(Acctg) 1986. **CAREER:** Audit Sr., Coopers & Lybrand, 1986-89; Mgr, Home Office Acctg, Macleod-Stedman Inc., 1989-91; Asst. Cont., 1991-92; Cont., Cotter Canada Hardware and Variety Cooperative Inc., 1992 to date. **AFFIL:** Institute of Chartered Accountants of Manitoba (C.A.); The Kidney Foundation of Canada (Nat'l Treas.; Dir., Nat'l Bd.; Chair, Fin. Committee; Exec. Committee; Personnel Committee; Man. Branch: Past Pres., Dir., Chair, Personnel & Nominating committees; Exec. Committee). **INTERESTS:** curling; baseball; skating; reading.

McLeod, Lyn, MPP, B.A., M.A. 🍁 ☝

Member of the Provincial Parliament (Fort William) and Interim Leader of the Official Opposition, Government of Ontario, Queen's Park, Legislative Building, Rm. 325, Toronto, ON M7A 1A4 (416) 325-7155, FAX 325-9895. Born Winnipeg 1942. m. Dr. Neil McLeod. 4 ch. Dana, Robin, Dara, Kristen. **EDUC:** Univ. of Manitoba, B.A.(English & French Lit.) 1965; Lakehead Univ., M.A.(Psych.) 1985. **CAREER:** Trustee, Lakehead Bd. of Educ., 1968-72, 1974-85; elected, MPP (Fort William), 1987; re-elected, 1990, 1995; Min. of Colleges & Universities, 1987; Min. of Energy, Mines & Natural Resources, 1989-90; Leader, Ont. Liberal Party, 1992-96. **HONS:** Alumni Honour Award, Lakehead Univ., 1993.

McMaster, Beverly, R.N. $ ⊕

President, WE CARE HEALTH SERVICES INC., 201 City Centre Dr., Ste. 601, Mississauga, ON L5B 2T4 (905) 949-9488, FAX 949-9717. Born Cornwall, Ont. 1946. m. George. 4 ch. **EDUC:** Hammersmith Hospital, London, UK, State Registered Nurse 1967; Misericordia General Hospital, Winnipeg, R.N. 1969. **CAREER:** community & acute care nursing, 1967-84; Pres. & Chair, We Care Health Services Inc., 1984 to date. **AFFIL:** Canadian Home Care Association; Canadian Franchise Association; Home Support Canada; Canadian Long-Term Care Association; National Association for Home Care, USA; Manitoba Association for Registered Nurses; Multiple Sclerosis Society; Ability Fund; Cancer Society (Bus. Committee); Heart Foundation (C.P.R. Committee); St. John Ambulance (C.P.R. Committee); Brandon United Way (Dir.); Westarc (Dir.); Venture Corporation Review Committee (Dir.). **HONS:** Business Person of the Year, Chamber of Commerce, 1988; Quality Plus Award, Assiniboine Credit Union/Women Business Owners of Manitoba, 1994; Woman Entrepreneur of the Year, Federal Business Development Bank/Women Business Owners of Manitoba, 1994; Nat'l Finalist, Woman Entrepreneur of the Year, 1996. **INTERESTS:** travelling; golf; skating; cross-country skiing; dancing; aerobics; classical music; reading. **MISC:** panelist & guest speaker, numerous conferences & associations; many appearances on local & nat'l TV, radio, & newspapers. **COMMENT:** *"I am motivated by a strong belief in quality health care choices for Canadians and in the power of people working toward common goals. My success is a direct result of a commitment to strong leadership, high standards and solid work ethics while fulfilling the We Care mission–providing the best possible care to the most people."*

McMaster, Juliet, B.A.,M.A., Ph.D. ■■ 🎓 📜

University Professor of English, UNIVERSITY OF ALBERTA, Dept. of English, Edmonton, AB T6G 2E5 (403) 492-4708, FAX 492-8142. Born Kenya 1937. m. Rowland D. McMaster. 2 ch. Rawdon, Lindsey. **EDUC:** Oxford Univ., B.A.(Hons., English) 1959, M.A.(English) 1962; Univ. of Alberta, M.A.(English) 1962, Ph.D.(English) 1965. **CAREER:** Asst. Prof. of English, Univ. of Alberta, 1965-70; Assoc. Prof., 1970-76; Prof., 1976-86; Univ. Prof., 1986 to date. **SELECTED PUBLICATIONS:** several books incl.: *Thackeray: The Major Novels* (Toronto: Univ. of Toronto Press, 1971, reprinted in paperback, 1976); *Trollope's Palliser Novels: Theme and Form* (London: Macmillan, 1978); *Dickens the Designer* (London: Macmillan, 1987); *Jane Austen the Novelist: Essays Past and Present* (London: Macmillan, 1995). **EDIT:** Edit. Advisory Bd., *Nineteenth-Century Literature*, *Eighteenth-Century Fiction*, *Victorian Review*; Gen. Editor, Juvenilia Press. **HONS:** Molson Prize in the Humanities & Social Sciences for "outstanding lifetime contributions to the intellectual life of Canada," 1994. **INTERESTS:** illustration; juvenile writing. **COMMENT:** *"Juliet McMaster, University Professor of English and winner of Canada's Molson Prize, is the author of books on Jane Austen, Thackeray, Trollope, Dickens, and the novel."*

McMaster, Susan, B.A. 📖 ✪ 📜

Poet. Senior Book Editor, NATIONAL GALLERY OF CANADA, 380 Sussex Dr., Box 427, Stn A, Ottawa, ON K1N 9N4 (613) 990-0531. Born Toronto m. Ian McMaster. 2 ch. Sarah Aven McMaster, Sylva Morel McMaster. **EDUC:** Carleton Univ., B.A.(English) 1970, grad. studies in Journalism 1975-80; Ottawa Teachers' Coll., Ont. Teaching Certificate (Elementary) 1971. **CAREER:** teacher, Edmonton Public Sch. Bd., 1971-72; freelance ed., writer & publisher, 1973-87; Sr. Book Ed., National Gallery of Canada, 1989 to date. **SELECTED PUBLICATIONS:** *Dark Galaxies*, (Ouroboros, 1986); *The Hummingbird Murders* (Quarry Press, 1992); *Learning to Ride* (Quarry Press, 1994); Pass This Way Again (1983) *North/South* (1987), (First Draft, published by Underwhich); *Dangerous Graces: Women's Poetry on Stage*, ed. (Balmuir 1987); poetry in various anthologies, incl. *Celebrating Canadian Women* (Fitzhenry &Whiteside, 1989) & *Vintage 93* (League of Canadian Poets, 1994); *Lisette Model*, ed. (Ottawa: National Gallery of Canada, 1990); *The Group of Seven*, ed. (Ottawa: National Gallery of Canada, 1995); various other publications. **EDIT:** Founding Ed., *Branching Out*, *Canadian Arts* and *Feminist Quarterly*, 1973-75; Contributing Ed., 1975-80; Contributing Ed., *Quarry*, 1986-89; Contributing Ed., *ARC*, 1992-93. **AFFIL:** First Draft (Dir.); League of Canadian Poets; Canadian Centre, PEN International; Religious Society of Friends. **HONS:** "Poet Laureate," Peter Gzowski's Golf Tournament for Literacy, 1989; finalist, CBC Literary Competition, 1986, 1990. **INTERESTS:** reading; riding; music; the outdoors. **MISC:** recipient, various grants; writing instructor for various institutions & workshops; co-host, Sparks 2, weekly poetry show, CHEZ-fm (1982-83); Wordmusic, audiotape, with First Draft & Open Score (1986); First Draft at Carleton, videotape, with First Draft (1992); more than 70 performances with First Draft & SugarBeat; numerous works performed by Open Score & Exposure; various other credits. COMMENT: *"Susan McMaster's publications include three books of poetry, a theatre script and two wordmusic books and an audiotape with the intermedia group First Draft. She was the founding editor of the feminist quarterly Branching Out. Her new manuscript is* How Chairs Pray. *She is currently performing with the contemporary jazz poetry group SugarBeat."*

McMechan, Sylvia Margaret, B.E.S., R.S.W. ☺

Executive Director, THE NETWORK: INTERACTION FOR CONFLICT RESOLUTION, Conrad Grebel College, Waterloo, ON N2L 3G6 (519) 885-0880, FAX 885-0806, EMAIL smmcmech@watserv1.uwaterloo.ca. Born Belfast 1955. 1 ch. Anna Jackman. EDUC: Algonquin Coll., Dipl.(Community Dev.) 1977; Univ. of Victoria, Certificate (Registered Social Worker) 1982; Univ. of Waterloo, B.E.S.(Environmental Studies) 1989. CAREER: Community Dev. Animator, Eastern Community Citizens' Planning Committee, 1975-77; Proj. Officer, Fed. Dept. of Energy, Mines & Resources, 1977-79; Community Dev. Consultant, Victoria, BC, 1979-80; Counsellor, Victoria Women's Transition House, 1980-84; Research Assoc./Teaching Asst./Outreach Coord., Dept. of Environment & Resource Studies, Univ. of Waterloo, 1986-90; Program Officer, Fund for Dispute Resolution, 1990-91; Administrative Dir., The Network: Interaction for Conflict Resolution, 1991-95; Exec. Dir., The Network, 1995 to date. EDIT: Ed. Bd., *Mediation Quarterly.* AFFIL: Canadian International Institute of Applied Negotiation (Advisory Committee); Lawson McMechan Philanthropic Fund (Trustee & Administrator). INTERESTS: photography; hiking; camping. COMMENT: *"My commitment to conflict resolution encompasses all aspects of my personal and professional activities."*

McMullan-Baron, Sharon, B.Ed., B.A. ☺ ◐ 🗋

Past President, ALBERTA LIBRARY TRUSTEES ASSOCIATION, 3 Caragana Court, Sherwood Park, AB T8A 1W6. m. Darryl Baron. 3 ch. EDUC: Univ. of Winnipeg, B.Ed. 1979, B.A. 1981. CAREER: elementary & jr. high sch. teacher, Winnipeg Sch. Div., 1979-81; Info. & Volunteer Centre, Strathcona County, 1996. VOLUNTEER CAREER: Coord., Sherwood Park Women's Book Club, 1993 to date; Pres., Sherwood Park Newcomers' Club, 1983-85; Coord., Madonna Presch. Playhouse Cooperative, 1984-85; Program Dir. & Publicity Coord., Beta Sigma Phi, Omega Chapter, 1986-

89; Volunteer Tutor, Strathcona County/Fort Saskatchewan Adult Literacy Program, 1987-90; Tutor Training Asst., 1988-90; "READ-IN" Coord., 1990; Chair, Early Childhood Svcs Advisory Committee, Sherwood Park Catholic Sch. Div., 1992; Telethon Comm. Committee, Edmonton Children's Health Foundation, 1992-93; Libraries Grant Review Task Force, 1993; Public Libraries Review Committee, 1994-95; Past Pres., Alberta Library Trustees' Association, 1994-95; Alberta Foundation For The Arts, 1995 to date; Advisory Bd., Strathcona County Permanent Art Collection, 1996. EDIT: Ed. Advisory Bd., Strathcona County This Week, 1995; AFFIL: Alberta Public Libraries Mktg Implementation Team; Strathcona County Mun. Library (Chair, Bd. of Trustees). INTERESTS: painting; reading; cross-country skiing. COMMENT: *"Volunteer public service has provided many opportunities to share my time and talents. These unique challenges have benefitted my communities and myself. My optimism, professional approach to volunteerism and dedication are my trademarks."*

McMullen, Lorraine, R.N.,B.Sc.N.,B.A., M.A.,Ph.D. ☜ 🖺

Adjunct Professor, Department of English, UNIVERSITY OF VICTORIA, MS 7236, PO Box 3070, Victoria, BC V8W 3W1 (604) 721-7236, FAX 721-6498. Professor Emeritus, Department of English, UNIVERSITY OF OTTAWA. EDUC: Royal Victoria Hospital, R.N. 1947; Univ. of Ottawa, B.Sc.N. 1948, B.A.(English) 1963, M.A. (English) 1967, Ph.D.(English) 1970. CAREER: Registered Nurse, 1947-63; high sch. teacher, 1963-67; instructor, Teachers' Coll., Univ. of Ottawa, 1968-69; lecturer, Univ. of Ottawa, 1969-72; Asst. Prof., 1972-74; Assoc. Prof., Dept. of English, 1974-79; Visiting Prof., Concordia Univ. Special Summer Institute of English Studies, Summer 1975, 1976; Prof., Dept. of English, Univ. of Ottawa, 1980-82; Visiting Scholar, Centre for Canadian Studies, Univ. of Edinburgh, 1982; Visiting Prof., Univ. of British Columbia, 1988-89, Summer 1991; Prof. Emeritus, Dept. of English, Univ. of Ottawa, 1992 to date; Adjunct Prof., Univ. of Victoria, 1993 to date. SELECTED PUBLICATIONS: *An Introduction to the Aesthetic Movement in English Literature* (Ottawa: Bytown Press, 1971); *An Odd Attempt in a Woman: The Literary Life of Frances Brooke* (Vancouver: Univ. of British Columbia Press, 1983); *Re(Dis)covering Our Foremothers: Nineteenth Century Canadian Women Writers* (Ottawa: Univ. of Ottawa Press, 1990); *Silenced Sextet: Six Nineteenth-Century Canadian Women Writers*, with Carrie MacMillan & Elizabeth

Waterston (Montreal: McGill-Queen's Univ. Press, 1993); "Leo Kennedy" (*The Golden Dog* 1(1) 1972); "Images of Women in Canadian Literature: Woman as Hero" (*Atlantis* 2(2) 1977); "Ethnicity and Femininity: Double Jeopardy" (*Canadian Ethnic Studies* 13(1) 1981); "Lily Dougall: The Religious Vision of a Canadian Novelist" (*Studies in Religion* 16(1) 1987); "A Checklist of the Works of May Agnes Fleming" (*Papers of the Bibliographical Society of Canada* 28 1990); numerous other books, articles & chapters in books. **EDIT:** Gen. Ed., *Reappraisal of Canadian Writers* Series, Univ. of Ottawa Press, 1975-94; Ed. Bd., *Short Story Library,* Univ. of Ottawa, 1975-80; Co-Ed., special issue "La Poésie depuis 1950/Poetry since 1950", *Laurentian University Review/Revue de l'université Laurentienne* 10(2) 1978; Guest Ed., special issue (selection of papers from Inter-American Women Writers' Conference, May 1978), *Atlantis* 4(1) 1978; Assoc. Ed., *Journal of Canadian Fiction,* 1978-85; Ed. Advisory Bd., *Atlantis,* 1979-94; Ed. Advisory Bd. *Canadian Poetry,* 1983 to date; Contributing Ed., *Feminist Companion to Literature Written in English,* V. Blaine, P. Clements & I. Grundy, eds. (Yale Univ. Press, 1990). **INTERESTS:** skiing; golf; travel. **MISC:** recipient, numerous grants from various agencies, primarily SSHRC & Canada Council; numerous papers read at conferences; reviewer/assessor for numerous journals, presses, Canada Council & SSHRC; Chair, Cdn Short Story Conference, Univ. of Ottawa, 1976. **COMMENT:** *"I have been directing my attention to early Canadian women writers, and, more generally, women in literature. I am also very interested in biography and am presently completing a biography of a Canadian woman writer of the late 19th and early 20th centuries."*

McMurray, Elaine, B.A. ■ ■ ○ ☼ ◉
Executive Director, PARENT SUPPORT ASSOCIATION, 805 - 37 St. N.W., Calgary, AB T2N 4N8 (403) 270-3251, FAX 270-1823. Born Calgary 1948. s. 2 ch. Lillian Assunta (Susie), Franceso Jesse (Frank). **EDUC:** Southern Alberta Institute of Technology, Chemical Technology 1969; Univ. of Calgary, B.A.(Sociology-Criminology) 1991; numerous workshops & courses on fundraising, public rel'ns, addictions, community dev., etc. **CAREER:** Clerk-Cashier, The Bay, Calgary & Toronto, 1978-82; Teacher-Aide, Calgary Catholic Bd. of Educ., 1982-86; Research Asst. (as summer student), Parent Support Association, 1990; Research Asst., Calgary McKnight constituency prov. MLA office, 1991; Exec. Dir., Parent Support Association, 1991 to date. **AFFIL:** Parent Support Association of Calgary (Pres., Bd. of Dir. 1987-91); Parent Resource Institute for Drug Education (volunteer 1988-89); John Howard Society of Calgary (Bd. of Dir. 1992-96; Chair, Issues Committee); Women's Policy Group-a political party; Calgary Police Commission (Prostitution Task Force); Family Foundation Association (Advisor); Elizabeth Fry Society of Calgary; Office for the Commissioner of Services for Children & Families (Steering Committee, Regionalization of Children's Svcs); Gov't of Alta. Task Force on Juvenile Prostitution (community mbr. 1996); St. Vincent de Paul Society; Exit Community Outreach (volunteer). **INTERESTS:** reading esp. spiritual literature; legal rights of parents; rights & responsibilities; walking; attending activities with the Sisters, Faithful Companions of Jesus. **MISC:** Companion, Sisters, Faithful Companions of Jesus with postulancy scheduled for 1997; currently preparing series of workshops for parents focusing on spirituality; active mbr. of parish in dev. of small Christian communities. **COMMENT:** *"I am an articulate, organized self-starter. After my divorce, I returned to university and established my career. I am a respected spokesperson for parents in Calgary, advocating for support for parents. My greatest achievement has been raising my two children and developing adult relationships with them. My life goal is to become a member of Sisters, Faithful Companions of Jesus, and to pursue social justice issues especially for parents."*

McNabb, Debra, B.A., M.A. ■ 🐿
Acting Director, NOVA SCOTIA MUSEUM OF INDUSTRY, 147 N. Foord St., Box 2590, Stellarton, NS B0K 1S0 (902) 755-5425, FAX 755-7045, EMAIL dmcnabb@fox.nstn.ca. Born Glace Bay, N.S. 1957. **EDUC:** Mount Allison Univ., B.A.(Geography) 1979; Univ. of British Columbia, M.A.(Geography) 1986. **CAREER:** freelance historical consultant; Registrar, Nova Scotia Museum of Industry; Mgr, Collections; Mgr, Exhibit Dev. **SELECTED PUBLICATIONS:** "Working Worlds," Plate 37, with Lynne Marks, *Historical Atlas of Canada,* vol. III (Toronto: 1990); "Pre-Loyalist Nova Scotia," Plate 31, with Graeme Wynn, *Historical Atlas of Canada,* vol. 1 (Toronto: 1987); *Old Sydney Town. Historic Buildings in Sydney's North End* (Sydney: 1986). **HONS:** undergrad. scholarship, Mount Allison Univ., 1975-79; Award of Academic Excellence, Champlain Geographical Society, Mount Allison Univ., 1979; Special M.A. Fellowship, Social Sciences & Humanities, Research Council of Canada, 1980-81; Grad. Fellowship, Univ. of British Columbia, 1982. **INTERESTS:** reading; N.S. history &

geography; hiking; kayaking. MISC: various conferences & presentations.

McNair, Noëlla, B.A. ⌘

Vice-President of Programs, NORTHERN COLLEGE, Bag 3211, Timmins, ON P4N 8R6 (705) 235-7218, FAX 235-7277, EMAIL mcnairnr@ kirk.northernc.on.ca. Born Timmins, Ont. 1937. m. Gerald. 4 ch. Joanne, Catherine, Neal, Michelle. EDUC: Univ. of Toronto, B.A.(Modern Lang. & Lit.) 1959, High Sch. Asst. Certificate 1960, Type A Specialist Certificate 1961; Provincial Academic Leadership Institute, 1990; Canadian Exec. Leadership Institute, 1993. CAREER: secondary sch. teacher, 1959-66; researcher & writer, Timmins Museum Nat'l Exhibition Centre, 1979; Prof. of Comm., Northern Coll., 1979-87; Chair of Comm., 1987-89; Dir., Bureau of Program & Staff Dev., 1989-94; VP, Programs, 1994 to date. SELECTED PUBLICATIONS: *Colleges Reaching Out: Report on the Status of Distance Education in Canadian Colleges and Technical Institutes* (May 1994); *Pick of the Crop: A Selection of Innovation Papers from Ontario College Faculty* (1994); *Final Report: Five–Year Action Plan for Human Resource Development in the Ontario Colleges of Applied Arts and Technology* (1994); *Twenty-five Years of Excellence in Staff, Program and Organizational Development* (1993). AFFIL: Coll. Committee on Hum. Res. Dev. (Past Chair, Prov. Exec. Committee); Comité provincial pour la formation des cadres francophones (Past Chair); Contact North (Sunset Review Committee); President's Exec. Committee; Porcupine Music Festival de Musique (former Pres.; Sec.; Exec. Committee); Porcupine Ski Runners. HONS: Certificate of Achievement for volunteer work related to the Porcupine Music Festival de Musique, Ont. Gov't. MISC: facilitator, participant, planning mbr., prov. dev. programs, in French & English, such as the First Prov. Curriculum Institute, Focus on Change, Great Teachers' Conferences, etc.

McNeil, Mary, B.A. ■■ ❦

Deputy Executive Director, APEC '97 (Asia Pacific Economic Cooperation) Canadian Coordinating Office, Department of Foreign Affairs and International Trade, GOVERNMENT OF CANADA, Vancouver, BC. m. 4 ch. Molly, Megan, Kate, Beth. EDUC: Univ. of British Columbia, B.A.(English) 1973. CAREER: Site Mgr, Commonwealth Heads of Gov't Meeting, Mar.-Dec. 1987; Sr. Mgr, Plans & Programmes, Toronto Econ. Summit, Jan.-July 1988; on contract, External Affairs Canada, Mar. 1990-May 1991; Capital Campaign Dir., Vancouver Public Library, Jan. 1990-Apr.

1993; Dir., Sites, Facilities & Svcs, Clinton/ Yeltsin Summit, Mar.-Apr. 1993; Special Advisor, Events/Logistics, The Halifax Summit, Jan.-July 1995; Deputy Exec. Dir., XI Int'l Conference on AIDS, Nov. 1995-Aug. 1996; Deputy Exec. Dir., APEC '97 Cdn Coordinating Office, Sept. 1996 to date. AFFIL: YWCA (Capital Campaign Exec. Committee; mbr. & former Chair, Inner Circle Committee); Endeavour Society (Bd. of Dir.); Vancouver Children's Choir (Bd. of Dir.); Prince of Wales' TREK Fundraising Program. HONS: Award of Merit, Dept. of External Affairs, Gov't of Canada, 1989; Award of Merit, Dept. of Foreign Affairs & Int'l Trade, Gov't of Canada, 1995. COMMENT: *"Consultant with a comprehensive background and experience in the administration and co-ordination of international summits, project and event management, and international public affairs, specializing in logistical preparations, program/scenario development, sponsorship and fundraising programs, and public/media relations."*

McNeill, Kim, M., B.B.A.,LL.B. ⚖

Partner, BIRT AND MCNEILL, Barristers and Solicitors, 12 Brackley Point Rd., Box 20063, Sherwood, PE C1A 9E3 (902) 566-3030, FAX 628-8820. Born Charlottetown 1962. m. Ensor J. McNeill. 2 ch. Joshua, Jacob. EDUC: Univ. of Prince Edward Island, B.B.A. 1983; Dalhousie Univ., LL.B. 1986. BAR: N.S., 1987; Ont., 1990; P.E.I., 1993. CAREER: Assoc. Lawyer, McGinty and Pillay, Halifax, 1987-88; Assoc. Lawyer, Simpson, Wigle, Hamilton, Ont., 1990-92; Sessional Lecturer, Sch. of Bus., Univ. of Prince Edward Island, 1992-95; Ptnr, Birt and McNeill, 1993 to date. AFFIL: N.S. Barristers' Society; Law Society of P.E.I.; Canadian Bar Association; Atlantic Association of Women in Business.

McNellis, Maryanne ✒

Editorial Director, THE FINANCIAL POST, (newspaper), 333 King St. E., Toronto, ON M5A 4N2 (416) 350-6300, FAX 350-6301. EDUC: Scripps Coll., Claremont, Calif.; Grad. Sch. of Journalism, Columbia Univ., Masters. CAREER: Gen. Assignments Reporter, *New York Daily News*; Police Reporter, *Daily News*; Founding Ed., *Investor's Business Daily*; Cdn Bureau Chief, Pacific-Basin Bureau Chief, *Business Week Magazine*; Ed., *Adweek* Magazine; Press Aide, N.Y. Senator; Ed., *The Financial Post Magazine*; Ed. Dir., *The Financial Post*. AFFIL: National Magazine Foundation (VP; Dir.); Sigma Delta Chi; Women in Communications. HONS: Post-Graduate Fellowship, Stanford Univ.; numerous awards for writing & editing, Canada & the US. COM-

MENT: *"Maryanne McNellis is the Editorial Director of* The Financial Post. *As such, she is responsible for the coordination and direction of all news operations of the national financial newspaper."*

McNicoll, Claire, B.A.,L.èsL.,M.A., Ph.D. ■■🖎

Vice-Rector, Public Affairs, UNIVERSITÉ DE MONTRÉAL, 2900 Édouard-Montpetit Blvd., Ste. H-401, P.O. Box 6128, Downtown Stn., Montréal, QC H3C 3J7 (514) 343-6488, FAX 343-2098. Born Montréal 1943. m. Jean-Claude Robert. EDUC: Univ. de Montréal, B.A. 1964, L.L.(Geog.) 1969, M.A.(Geog.) 1971; École des Hautes Études en Sciences sociales, Paris, Ph.D.(Geog.) 1986. CAREER: High Sch. Prof., Notre-Dame de l'Assomption Coll., Nicolet, 1964-66; High Sch. Prof., Geog., C.S.R. Maisonneuve, 1967-69; responsible for Socio-Cultural Activities, CEGEP de Joliette, 1969-71; Dir., Geog. Section, Dept. of Geog., Univ. du Québec à Montréal, 1974-77; V-Dean, Human Sci. Section, 1977-78; Dean, Undergrad. Studies, 1978-80; Asst. V-Rector, Teaching & Research, 1980-83; V-Rector, Comm., 1983-85; Dir., Teaching & Research, Télé-université, Univ. du Québec, 1986-88; Gen. Dir., Conférence des recteurs et des principaux des univ. du Québec, 1989-91; V-Rector, Public Affairs, Univ. de Montréal, 1991 to date. SELECTED PUBLICATIONS: *Montréal, une société multiculturelle* (Paris: Éditions Belin, 1993). AFFIL: Conseil supérieur de l'éducation (mbr. 1993 to date); Groupe de travail trilatéral Canada, E-U, Mexique (on student & prof. mobility within the ANENA, mbr. 1993 to date); Organisation universitaire interaméricaine (Treas. 1993 to date); Société pour la promotion de la science et de la technologie (Bd. 1994 to date); Canadian Club (Bd. 1995 to date); Nouvel Ensemble Moderne (Bd. 1993 to date); Télé-université (Bd. 1993 to date); Canadian Museum of Nature (Bd. 1990 to date); Canadian Society for the Study of Higher Education (Bd. 1992-95). MISC: several presentations to various groups, associations.

McPhedran, Marilou, C.M.,B.A.,LL.B., LL.D. ■ 🕭 ⊕ 🜋

Lawyer/Consultant. (416) 967-9485, FAX 967-1932, EMAIL marilou@web.net. Born Neepawa, Man. 1951. d. 2 ch. Jonathan, David. EDUC: Univ. of Toronto, B.A. 1973; Osgoode Hall Law Sch., York Univ., LL.B. 1976. CAREER: Owner, Health, Systems & Advocacy, providing advice & organizational effectiveness svcs to private & public sector clients which include Women's College Hospital, Liberty Health, the Pan American Health Organization. SELECTED PUBLICATIONS: *Canadian Medical Association Journal*, 1995 & 1996; *World Health Organization Statistics Quarterly*, 1996; Final Report, Task Force on Discharged Psychiatric Patients, 1984; Final Report, Independent Task Force on Sexual Abuse of Patients, 1991. AFFIL: Legal Education & Action Fund (Founding Mbr.); METRAC (Dir.; Pres., Bd. of Dir.); Gerstein Crisis Centre (Dir.). HONS: Special Citation, Women of Distinction, YWCA, 1981; Member of the Order of Canada, 1985; "Woman on the Move" Award, 1988; Woman of the Year, B'nai Brith Women, 1993; "Women Who Make a Difference" Award for Business, Toronto Life Fashion, 1996; LL.D.(Hon.), Univ. of Winnipeg, 1992. INTERESTS: playing with my children; walking; scuba diving; sleeping. MISC: Chairperson, Task Force on Sexual Abuse of Patients, Coll. of Physicians & Surgeons of Ontario, 1991. COMMENT: *"Dr. McPhedran was born and raised in Neepawa, Manitoba. Combining a high level of volunteerism with her consulting/law practice and single motherhood of two sons, Dr. McPhedran has interests that lie primarily in equality, health and organizational change."*

McPherson, Debra, R.N. 🕭 ⊕ ○

Vice-President, NATIONAL FEDERATION OF NURSES UNIONS, 377 Bank St., 2nd fl., Ottawa, ON K2P 1Y3 (613) 233-1018, FAX (604) 681-3711. Born Brantford, Ont. 1951. s. EDUC: St. Boniface Sch. of Nursing, R.N. 1972. CAREER: Registered Nurse, St. Boniface General Hospital, Winnipeg, 1972-75; Registered Nurse, numerous projects, Kinshasa, Zaire, 1975-77; Registered Nurse, Intensive Care Unit, Univ. of Alberta Hospital, 1977-80; Registered Nurse, Intensive Care Unit/Critical Care Unit, Univ. of British Columbia Hospital, 1980-85; Registered Nurse, Cardiac Surgery Intensive Care Unit, Vancouver Hospital, 1986 to date; Pres., B.C. Nurses' Union, 1990-94; VP, National Federation of Nurses' Unions, 1994 to date. AFFIL: Registered Nurses' Association of B.C.; CU&C Health Services Society (Bd. of Dir.); Women's Bank Society; N.A.C. INTERESTS: travel; politics; women's issues. COMMENT: *"Practising nurse, providing direct patient care in a critical care setting for 24 years, combined with being an activist for the advancement of the socioeconomic welfare of nurses and women in general for more than 15 years."*

McQuaig, Linda, B.A. ✏ 📖

Journalist and Author. c/o Penguin Books, 10 Alcorn Ave., Ste. 300, Toronto, ON M4V 3B2 (416) 925-2249, FAX 925-0068. Born

Toronto 1951. sep. 1 ch. Amy. **EDUC:** Univ. of Toronto, B.A. 1974. **CAREER:** Sr. Writer, *Maclean's* magazine; Nat'l Reporter, *The Globe and Mail*; Assoc. Producer, CBC Radio. **SELECTED PUBLICATIONS:** *Behind Closed Doors: How the Rich Won Control of Canada's Tax System* (Penguin, 1987); *The Quick and the Dead: Brian Mulroney, Big Business and the Seduction of Canada* (Penguin, 1991); *The Wealthy Banker's Wife: The Assault on Equality in Canada (Penguin, 1993); Shooting the Hippo: Death by Deficit and Other Canadian Myths* (Penguin, 1995). **HONS:** National Newspaper Award, 1989; Atkinson Fellowship for Journalism in Public Policy, 1991.

McQueen, Jennifer, Robertson, B.A. ✦
Retired Public Servant. Born Saskatoon 1930. s. **EDUC:** Univ. of Manitoba, B.A.(English & Phil.) 1951; Royal Coll. of Defence Studies, London, UK, Diploma 1980. **CAREER:** public svc, primarily in fed. gov't, 1957-93; final 3 positions: Public Svc Commissioner (1982-85); Deputy Min. of Labour, 1985-90; High Commissioner to Jamaica, Bahamas & Belize, 1990-93. **INTERESTS:** arts; theatre; opera; music; literature; gardening; travel; aid to Third World, esp. educ. **COMMENT:** *"Throughout career worked for greater equality of opportunity of women in the public service."*

McQueen, Shirley ♓ ♨
Radio Announcer, **Q107 FM**, 5255 Yonge St., Ste. 1400, North York, ON M4N 2P6 (416) 221-0107, FAX 512-4838. Born Regina 1961 **CAREER:** TV host: Life Channel; CFMT Channel 47; CHCH TV 11; radio host, Great Canadian Juno Party, 1993; host, 7pm-midnight, Q107 FM, Toronto. **SELECTED CREDITS:** Host, *Toronto Music Awards*, 1989-91; Host, *Talking Sex III*, Dir. Les Kottler (educational); Subject, *In The Dark*, Dir. Stuart Clarfield (docu.). **AFFIL:** ACTRA. **INTERESTS:** downhill skiing; bookbinding/making; white-water rafting; drama. **COMMENT:** *"I feel extremely lucky to be living at this exciting time in our history - the dawning of the second millennium and the information age offer such potential. Broadcasting and the dramatic arts are bursting with new ideas and I would like to think my work has made an impact 50 years from now."*

McTeer, Maureen A., B.A.,LL.B.,LL.M., D.Litt.(Hon.) ⚖ ☙ ♓
Adjunct Assistant Professor, Faculties of Law, Medicine and Nursing, **THE UNIVERSITY OF CALGARY**, 2500 University Dr. NW, Calgary, AB T2N 1N4 (403) 220-4635, FAX 284-4803. Coordinator, **CALGARY COALITION: CENTRES OF**

EXCELLENCE IN WOMEN'S HEALTH. Born Ottawa 1952. m. Rt. Hon. Joe Clark. 1 ch. Catherine McTeer Clark. **EDUC:** Univ. of Ottawa, B.A.(Gen. Arts) 1973, LL.B. 1977; Dalhousie Univ., LL.M.(Health Law) 1993. **BAR:** Ont., 1980. **CAREER:** articled with Paris, Mercier, Sirois & Paris, Ottawa, 1978-79; Lawyer, Lyons Goodman, Toronto, 1985-87; candidate, House of Commons in the fed. gen. election, 1988; mbr., Royal Commission on New Reproductive Technologies, 1989-91; Founder & Chair, Canadian Bar Association, Eastern & Central European legal/judicial programs, 1989-94; grad. LL.M., Dalhousie Univ., 1993; Visiting Scholar, Sch. of Public Health, Univ. of California at Berkeley, 1993-94; Adjunct Asst. Prof., Univ. of Calgary, Faculties of Law, Nursing & Medicine, & Coord., Calgary Coalition: Centres of Excellence in Women's Health, 1994-96. **SELECTED PUBLICATIONS:** *Residences: Homes of Canada's Leaders/Des maisons qui ont une histoire* (Prentice Hall/Editions Libre Expression); *Parliament: Canada's Democracy and How It Works/Le petit guide du système parlementaire* (Random House 1988/Editions Libre Expression, 1988); *The Tangled Womb: The Politics of Human Reproduction* (1992). **AFFIL:** Canada China Child Health Foundation (Bd.); Tianjin Children's Hospital, Tianjin, PRC (Foreign Advisor); PEN Canada. **HONS:** Canada 125 Medal; Rt. Hon. Louis St. Laurent Award for contribution to legal excellence, 1993; Small Cross of the President of Hungary for contribution to democracy & the rule of law; Woman of the Year, Berkeley Professional Women's Association, 1994; D.Litt.(Hon.), Athabasca Univ., 1995. **INTERESTS:** int'l human rights; maternal-child health; women's health; democratic institutions & rule of law–particular involvement in Eastern & Central Europe, China & S. Africa. **MISC:** led delegation of Canadian Bar to Eastern & Central European cities, incl. Warsaw, Budapest, Prague & Bratislava, to offer professional dev. seminars to lawyers in those cities, 1991-93. **COMMENT:** *"I am a Canadian lawyer who has spent the past 20 years involved in two main areas–public policy and social, political activism. My interests include reproductive and genetic issues and their challenge to the law and ethics. More broadly, I remain involved in institution building in emerging democracies and in health issues at the international level, where justice and health issues are linked and need advocates and a special focus."*

McTighe, Janice ♙
Executive Director, **RENFREW EDUCATIONAL SERVICES**, 1217 Center St. N., Calgary, AB T2E

2R3 (403) 276-2211, FAX 276-9875. Born Vancouver 1941. d. 4 ch. **CAREER:** 22 yrs. with Renfrew Educational Services. **INTERESTS:** gardening; cross-country skiing; hiking. **MISC:** Renfrew has 450 students in kindergarten to grade four. Half of those children have special needs. Renfrew employs 126 teachers, pathologists, child dev. facilitators, speech & language pathologists, occupational & physical therapists, social workers, office staff & bus drivers. Of the total staff, 118 are women. **COMMENT:** *"I'm surprised my name was submitted because, compared to others, I doubt I qualify. However, I am very proud of raising four children on my own and developing and creating a special, wonderful school for children with special needs and typical children. I'm also proud of creating an excellent workplace mostly for women—fair compensation, benefits, hours and flexible to family needs."*

Meagher, B. Margaret, B.A.,M.A.,O.C. ✲ ♂
Diplomat (retired). 6899 Armview Ave., Halifax, NS B3H 2M5. Born Halifax 1911. s. **EDUC:** Dalhousie Univ., B.A.(French, German & Pol. Sci) 1932, M.A.(French & German) 1935, postgrad. studies in Pol. Sci. 1937-38. **CAREER:** teacher, public schools, Halifax, 1932-42; Dept. of External Affairs, 1942-45; Third Sec., Cdn Embassy, Mexico, 1945-47; Second Sec., 1947-49; Dept. of External Affairs, Ottawa, 1949-53; First Sec., Cdn High Commission, London, UK, 1953-55; Counsellor, 1955-57; Charge d'Affaire, Tel Aviv, Israel, 1957; Cdn Ambassador to Israel, 1958-61; Cdn High Commissioner to Cyprus (concurrent assignment with Israel), 1961; Cdn Ambassador to Austria, 1962; Cdn Gov., Bd. of Gov., Int'l Atomic Energy Agency (IAEA), Vienna, 1962-64; Chair of Bd., IAEA, 1964-65; Cdn High Commissioner to Kenya, 1967; Cdn High Commissioner to Uganda, 1967; Cdn Ambassador to Sweden, 1969-73; Diplomat in Residence, Dalhousie Univ., 1973-74; retired, 1974; Trustee, Bd. of Trustees, National Museums Corporation, 1975-78; Bd. of Gov., Atlantic Sch. of Theology, 1976-82; Bd. of Gov., Nova Scotia Coll. of Art & Design, 1984-89. **AFFIL:** Dalhousie Alumni 1818 Society; Symphony N.S.; The Saraguay Club; Ashburn Golf Club; Royal Commonwealth Society; Royal United Service Institute. **HONS:** Officer of the Order of Canada, 1974; Dalhousie Univ., D.C.L.(Hon.), 1970; St. Francis Xavier Univ., D.C.L.(Hon.) 1974; St. Mary's Univ., D.C.L.(Hon.) 1975. **MISC:** 1st Cdn woman to be appointed an Ambassador.

Medina, Ann, B.A.,M.A. ☐ ⁄ ⊗
Independent Producer, MEDINA PRODUCTIONS

INC., 112 Alcina Ave., Toronto, ON M6G 2E8 (416) 656-8850, FAX 654-3209. **EDUC:** Wellesley Coll., B.A.(Phil.) 1965; Univ. of Chicago, M.A.(Phil.) 1967. **CAREER:** Network Prod., NBC, 1973; Correspondent & Prod., ABC News, 1973-75; Correspondent & Prod., *Newsmagazine*, CBC News, 1975-80; Exec. Prod., 1980-81; Sr. Journalist & Prod., *The Journal*, CBC News, 1981-86; Beirut Bureau Chief, 1983-84; Prod. Resident, Canadian Centre for Advanced Film Studies, 1988. **AFFIL:** Cultural Industries Council of Ontario (Chair 1995); TVO (Bd. of Dir.); Academy of Canadian Cinema & Television (Chair 1992 to date; V-Chair 1986-92); Canadian Women in Radio & Television (mbr. 1992 to date); Canadian Film & Television Production Association (mbr. 1991 to date); ACTRA (Nat'l Exec. Bd. 1987-89); Toronto Women in Film & Television (Bd. 1989-90). **HONS:** Herschel Fellow (Phil.), Univ. of Chicago, 1966; EMMY award, Outstanding Indiv. Achievement, 1972; Gold Medal (*Montage*), Columbus Int'l Film Festival, 1973; Broadcast Award, (*Montage*), San Francisco State Univ., 1974; Golden Sheaf Award (*Bhopal*), Yorkton Short Film Festival, 1985; Gold Hugo (*Bhopal*), Chicago Film Festival, 1985; Chris Plaque (*Like Fighting Death*), Columbus Int'l Film Festival, 1986; Kodak Award for outstanding achievement, Women in Film & Television, 1994; Hon. Doct. L.C.L., King's College, Halifax, 1994.

Medley, Sue ■ ♥ ⊗
Recording Artist, Singer, Songwriter. President, SUE MEDLEY MUSIC c/o Echo Park Studios, 2051 W. Vernal Pike, Bloomington, IN (812) 331-2762, FAX 331-2763. Born Nanaimo, B.C. 1962. s.. **CAREER:** Cdn recording artist, signed to Polygram Records, 1989; released *Sue Medley* album, 1990; 5 singles/4 videos released from that album; released *Inside Out*, 1992; 4 singles/3 videos released from that album; requested & obtained release from Polygram Record, 1994, citing creative differences. **SELECTED CREDITS:** *Sue Medley*, Polygram Records (1990); *Inside Out*, Polygram Records (1992). **AFFIL:** AFM; CARAS; SOCAN. **HONS:** Female Vocalist of the Year, West Coast Music Award, 1988, 1989, 1990; Country Vocalist of the Year, West Coast Music Award, 1989; Single of the Year, West Coast Music Award, 1989; Best Debut Recording, West Coast Music Award, 1990; Best New Female Artist, Juno Award, 1990; Gold Record, Sue Medley, 1990; Songwriter of the Year, SOCAN, 1991, 1992. **INTERESTS:** women's rights; reading; psychology.

Meehan, Denise P. ■■ $
President, LICK'S ICE CREAM & BURGER SHOPS INC., (fast food gourmet restaurant chain), Lick's Home Office, 1962A Queen St. E., Toronto, ON M4L 1H8 (416) 362-5425, FAX 690-0504. Born Sturgeon Falls, Ont. 1951. s. **EDUC:** high sch., completed grade 11. **CAREER:** entrepreneur; founder, Pres. & sole shareholder, Lick's, launched in 1978. **HONS:** Canadian Woman Entrepreneur, Quality Plus category, 1995; hon. degree, George Brown Coll.; Gold (1st place) winner, Readers' Voice Awards, categories of Best Burgers & Hot Dogs, *The Toronto Sun*, 1994 & 1995; voted #1 burger in 1st annual readers poll, *Now Magazine*, 1995. **INTERESTS:** business; the arts. **COMMENT:** *"As a self-made entrepreneur, I have devoted my life to creating a business that is not only financially profitable but is also successful in demonstrating the importance of developing self-confidence and growth in the people under my leadership. Mission statement: growth through caring."*

Meier, Shirley, B.A. 📖 ✋ 🎓
Writer, HEARTHSTONE INDEPENDENT ENTERPRISES, R.R. 2, Huntsville, ON P1H 2J3 (705) 789-7497, FAX 789-4940. Born Woodstock, Ont. 1960. life partner Karen Wehrstein. 1 ch. **EDUC:** Univ. of Western Ontario, B.A. 1991. **CAREER:** independent contractor & software consultant, 1985-91; writing teacher with Karen Wehrstein, independent workshops, 1991 to date; teacher with Karen Wehrstein, women's self-defence, 1993 to date; co-founder, with Karen Wehrstrein, *the other pages*, Muskoka's Guide to Alternative Goods & Services, 1995 to date. **SELECTED PUBLICATIONS:** *The Sharpest Edge*, with S.M. Stirling (New York: NAL, 1986); *The Cage*, with S.M. Stirling (New York: Baen Books, 1989); *Shadow's Daughter* (New York: Baen Books, 1991); *Sabre and Shadow*, with S.M. Stirling (New York: Baen Books, 1992); *Shadow's Son*, with S.M. Stirling & Karen Wehrstein (New York: Baen Books, 1991); "Trave," *Magic in Ithkar* IV; ed. Andre Norton; "Peacock Eyes," *Tales out of the Witch World* II, ed. Andre Norton; "The Witches Tree," *Northern Frights*, ed. Don Hutchison; "The Ice," *Northern Frights* II; ed. Don Hutchison "Tag," *Bolos Book 2: The Unconquerable*, ed. Bill Fawcett; *Flowers and Vice*, poetry collection, (Hearthstone Independent Press, 1990); *The Love Machine*, poetry collection (Hearthstone Independent Press, 1993). **EXHIBITIONS:** 3-dimensional artwork, Ad Astra Convention, 1994, 1995. **AFFIL:** Ad Astra Science Fiction Society (1987-93); Bunch of Seven Writers Group (Founding Mbr. 1985 to date); Costumers' Guild of Toronto (Journeyman 1993); Women's ReSource Centre, Muskoka (Bd. 1994-95). **HONS:** Black Belt in Karate (Tao Zen Chuan/Bumblebee Karate), Oct. 1992. **INTERESTS:** researching Goddess worship & its modern resurgence; martial arts & self-defense; natural birthing advocacy/midwifery support; stage combat; swords; dollmaking; paper mâché sculpture; costume; mask making; feminism; dogs, cats & kids. **COMMENT:** *"I'm a brunette with long reddish-brown straight hair, and dark brown eyes. I look forward to new projects, in writing, art and computer businesses, all of which are in progress right now, but my major focus of interest is my son."*

Meigs, Mary 📖 ✪ 📜
Writer and Painter. Born Philadelphia, Penn. 1917. s. **EDUC:** Bryn Mawr Coll., B.A.(English Lit.) 1939. **CAREER:** Instructor of English, Bryn Mawr Coll., 1940-42; W.A.V.E.S., US Navy, 1942-45; freelance writer & painter (1-woman shows in various cities). **SELECTED CREDITS:** actor, *The Company of Strangers*, NFB, 1988. **SELECTED PUBLICATIONS:** *Lily Briscoe: a Self-Portrait* (Vancouver: Talon Books, 1981); *The Medusa Head* (Vancouver: Talon Books, 1983); *The Box Closet* (Vancouver: Talon Books, 1987); *In "The Company of Strangers"* (Vancouver: Talon Books, 1990); various articles and reviews; French translations: *Lily Briscoe: un auto-portrait* (1983); *La Tête de Meduse* (1987); *Femmes dans un Paysage* (1995). **HONS:** Award for Non-Fiction (*In "The Company of Strangers"*), Quebec Society for the Promotion of English Language Literature, 1992. **INTERESTS:** nature; ecology; music; poetry; psychology; art; feminist writing & lesbian writing. **COMMENT:** *"When I began to write (in my middle 50s) my endeavour was to write as truthfully as possible about the experience of being a lesbian."*

Meister, Joan, B.A. ✊ ♡
c/o DISABLED WOMEN'S NETWORK CENTRE, 7785 Louis hebert, Montreal, QC H2E 2Y1. **EDUC:** Simon Fraser Univ., B.A.(English) 1977. **CAREER:** various positions, clerical & secretarial, 1974-80; Bus. Agent, Association of University & College Employees, Local 2, Simon Fraser Univ., 1980-81; instructor, "Learning About Disabilities", Vancouver Community Coll., 1987-89. **VOLUNTEER CAREER:** Organizing Committee, "Women and Words", 1981-83; Dir., B.C. Coalition of Persons with a Disability, 1983-84; Dir., West Coast Women & Words Society, 1983-84; Nat'l Advisory Committee & Chair, Media & Mktg Subcommittee, Independence '92 Conference, 1990-92; Advisory Committee, Cdn Panel on Violence

Against Women, 1991-92; Steering Committee, Sexual Abuse & Young People with Disabilities Proj., 1992-93; Advisory Committee, Women's Health Centre, Vancouver, 1992-93; Sec., Nat'l Action Committee on the Status of Women, 1992-93; Dir., Canadian Council on Rehabilitation & Work, 1986-94; Dir., Opportunities through Rehabilitation & Work Society, 1984 to date; Disabled Women's Network, B.C., 1985 to date; Supervisor, Safety Net/Work Projects, 1990 to date; Dir., Disabled Women's Network Canada, 1990 to date; Dir., Westcoast Aboriginal Network on Disabilities, 1992 to date; Premier's Advisory Committee on Disabilities. **HONS:** Award, Coalition of Provincial Organizations of the Handicapped, 1988; "Mother of DAWN" Award, Disabled Women's Network Canada, 1990; Canada 125 Medal; Award, Canadian Council on Rehabilitation & Work, 1992; Award, Univ. of British Columbia Sch. of Social Work, 1993; Award, The Women's Health Centre, 1994. **MISC:** delegate, 2nd Int'l Congress, Disabled Peoples' International, 1985; presenter, "Disabled Women in Development" Seminar, Dominica, 1988; panelist, "Women and Poverty" Panel, International Association of Official Human Rights Agencies 41st Annual Conference, 1989; Sustaining Grants Review Committee, Health & Welfare Canada, 1989-92. **COMMENT:** *"In 1981, I entered the G.F. Strong Rehabilitation Centre, stopped working and started using a wheelchair as a result of having multiple sclerosis."*

Melanson, Deborah A., B.A.,M.B.A., C.L.U.,CH.F.C. ■■ $

National Sales Manager, Retirement Planning Services. m. Michael Blaufus. **EDUC:** Univ. of New Brunswick, B.A. 1974; Chartered Life Underwriter 1980; Canadian Sch. of Management, Toronto, M.B.A. 1988; Chartered Fin. Consultant 1994; Investment Funds Institute of Canada, currently enrolled for completion 1996; various mgmt courses. **CAREER:** Field Exper. Sales Rep., 1974-80; Staff Dev. Asst., 1980-81; Mgr, Succession, Sales Mgmt Dev., 1981-84; Mgr, Dev. & Training, 1984-88; Reg'l Mgr, Montreal, 1988-91; Nat'l Sales Mgr, Retirement Planning Svcs, 1991 to date. **AFFIL:** Chartered Life Underwriters' Association (mbr., Toronto Bd.); Canadian Life & Health Insurance Association (Chrm, Training Officer's Section 1987-88; Exec., Training Officer's Section1986-87); Montreal Thistle Curling Club (Bd. mbr.); Westmount P.C. Association (Bd. mbr.); Life Underwriters' Association of Canada (former Chair, various committees); Canadian Life & Health Insurance Association (Atlantic Provinces Public Rel'ns Bd. 1975-76; former Chair, various committees); Life Insurance Management Association of Canada; Women's Fitness Club; National Ballet of Canada.

Melanson, Rosella, B.S.W.,M.A., D.E.A. ■ ✊ ✎

Director of Operations and Communications, NEW BRUNSWICK ADVISORY COUNCIL OF THE STATUS OF WOMEN, 770 Main St., Moncton, NB E1C 1E7 (506) 856-3252, FAX 856-3258, EMAIL acswcccf@nbnet.nb.ca. Born Moncton, N.B. 1952. m. Michael Guravich. **EDUC:** Univ. de Moncton, B.S.W. 1973; Univ. of Western Ontario, M.A.(Journalism) 1976; Univ. de Grenoble III, D.E.A.(Comm.) 1987. **CAREER:** Journalist, L'Evangeline daily, Moncton, 1977-78; Dir., Public Policy, Canada Post, NB-PEI, 1978-79. **SELECTED PUBLICATIONS:** "Citizenship and Acadie" in *Belonging–The Meaning and Future of Canadian Citizenship* (McGill-Queen's Univ. Press, 1993); *Every Woman's Credibility–Treatment of Women in the Justice System* (1992).

Melesko, Tracey ■■ ⚾

Paralympic Athlete. Kelowna, BC. **CAREER:** self-employed. **SPORTS CAREER:** mbr., Nat'l Track Team, 1994 to date. Paralympic Games: Silver, 200m & long jump, 1996; Silver, 200m & Bronze, 400m, 1992. World Special Olympics: Gold, 100m, 200m, long jump, 1995. Nat'l Special Olympics: 1st 100m, 200m, 400m, long jump, 1994. Int'l Special Olympics: 2nd, 200m.

Mella, Patricia Janet, B.A.,M.A.,B.Ed. 🍁 ☝

Member of Legislative Assembly (3rd Queen's) and Leader of the Official Opposition, GOVERNMENT OF PRINCE EDWARD ISLAND, Hon. George Coles Building, Box 338, Charlottetown, PE C1A 7K7 (902) 368-4360, FAX 368-4377. Born Port Hill, P.E.I. 1943. m. Angelo Mella. 3 ch. **EDUC:** St. Dunstan's Univ., B.A.(English) 1965; Catholic Univ. of America, M.A.(Medical Soc.) 1967; Univ. of Prince Edward Island, B.Ed. 1973. **CAREER:** teacher, Charlottetown, 1979-90; Leader, Progressive Conservative Party of P.E.I., 1990-96; M.L.A. (3rd Queen's), Prov. of P.E.I., 1993 to date; Leader of the Official Opposition, 1993 to date. **AFFIL:** Southport Recreation Commission. **INTERESTS:** golf, racquetball. **COMMENT:** *"First woman to be elected leader of a political party on Prince Edward Island. Teacher by profession."*

Meltzer, Susan, B.A. ■ $

Director, Risk Management and Insurance, BELL CANADA, 15 Asquith Ave., 4 Fl., Toronto,

ON M4W 1J7 (416) 215-4292, FAX 920-8335. Born Toronto 1954. s. 1 ch. Jeremy Meltzer. **EDUC:** Carleton Univ., B.A.(English) 1975. **CAREER:** Insur. Broker, Morris and Mackenzie Ltd., 1975-81; Coord., Risk & Insur., Canada Development Corporation, 1983-85; Risk Mgmt Officer, Gov't of Ont., 1985-87; Dir., Risk Mgmt & Insur., Bell Canada, 1987 to date; Community Instructor, Risk Mgmt & Risk Financing, Univ. of Toronto, 1988 to date. **SELECTED PUBLICATIONS:** frequently quoted in articles in insur. publications. **AFFIL:** Risk & Insurance Management Society (VP, Environmental); Institute of Risk management (Treas. & Bd. of Gov.) Insurance Institute of Canada (Certified Risk Mgr ; Fellow). **HONS:** Highest Marks, Certified Risk Manager Program, Insurance Institute of Canada; Runner-up for Highest Marks, Fellowship majoring in Risk Management, Insurance Institute of Canada. **INTERESTS:** sports; travel; reading. **COMMENT:** *"I began my career in a clerical function and have achieved a senior management position in a major corporation through hard work and academic achievement. Through participation in my professional society and teaching, I give back to my profession."*

Melville, Karen, B.A.,M.A.,M.L.S. 🎓 📖 $
Director of Professional Development, Faculty of Information Studies, UNIVERSITY OF TORONTO, 140 St. George St., Toronto, ON M5S 1A1 (416) 978-3035, FAX 978-5762, EMAIL melville@fis.utoronto.ca. Born North Bay, Ont. 1944. s. **EDUC:** Univ. of Toronto, B.A.(Hist.) 1966, M.A.(Hist.) 1989; Univ. of Western Ontario, M.L.S. 1971. **CAREER:** Sr. Reference Librarian, Metro Toronto Reference Library, 1973-81; Mgr, Corp. Library Svcs, Clarkson Gordon, 1981-84; Dir. of Placement & Public Rel'ns, Fac. of Info. Studies, Univ. of Toronto, 1985-94; Dir. of Professional Dev., Fac. of Info. Studies, 1994 to date. **AFFIL:** Canadian Library Association; American Library Association; Special Libraries Association.

Melvin, Ann Patricia Rothery, B.A.,M.L.S., D.L.S. 📜 ✪ $
President, ROTHERY ENTERTAINMENTS,, incorporating "Ann's Books" and "Mostly Mysteries," 225 Carlton St., Toronto, ON M5A 2L2. Librarian, ROYAL CANADIAN MILITARY INSTITUTE. Born Point-à-Pierre, Trinidad 1936. m. Lewis David St. Columb Skene-Melvin. **EDUC:** Univ. of Toronto, B.A.(English) 1959; Ontario Coll. of Education, OSST Certificate 1962; Univ. of Western Ontario, M.L.S. 1968; Wolfe's Univ., D.L.S. 1995. **CAREER:** librarian, researcher, writer, teacher, reviewer; formed own company to sell antiquarian books in fields of literary criticism, 19th & 20th century lit., modern first editions, & crime, mystery, spy fiction, science fiction, cookery, horticulture, Canadiana. **SELECTED PUBLICATIONS:** *Crime, Detective, Espionage, Mystery, and Thriller Fiction and Film: A Comprehensive Bibliography of Critical Writing Through 1979*, co-author (Westport, CT: Greenwood Press, 1980); *The River Within*, poetry (Toronto: Information Research Publishing, 1983). **AFFIL:** Arts & Letters Club; The Bookmakers of Toronto; The Adventuresses of Sherlock Holmes. **HONS:** Adventures of Sherlock Holmes (investiture awarded by the International Society of Women), for outstanding contribution to Sherlockianism. **INTERESTS:** bird watching; Sherlockiana

Menard, Louise, LL.L. ■ $
Vice-President, Corporate Affairs, Legal Affairs and Secretary, SODARCAN INC., 1801 McGill College Ave., Ste. 550, Montreal, QC H3A 3P2 (514) 288-0100, FAX 282-9841. **EDUC:** Univ. of Montreal, LL.L. 1973. **BAR:** Que., 1974. **CAREER:** private practice/Corp. Legal Cnsl, 1974-88; Corp. Sec., Sodarcan Inc., 1988; VP, Corp. Affairs, & Sec., 1989 to date; VP, Corp. Affairs & Sec., Dale-Parizeau Inc. **AFFIL:** Montreal Heart Institute Research Fund (Dir.).

Mendell, Marguerite, B.A.,Ph.D. 🎓 $
Associate Professor and Principal, School of Community and Public Affairs, CONCORDIA UNIVERSITY, 1455 Blvd de Maisonneuve W., Montreal, QC H3G 1M8 (514) 848-2580, FAX 848-2577, EMAIL mendell@vax2.concordia.ca. Born Paris 1947. m. Peter. 2 ch. Michael, Anika. **EDUC:** Concordia Univ., B.A.(Econ.) 1972; McGill Univ., Ph.D. 1983. **CAREER:** Lecturer, Econ. Dept., Vanier Coll., 1977-78; Lecturer, Dawson Coll., Montreal, 1982-83; Lecturer, Econ. Dept., Concordia Univ., 1982-83; Research Fellow, Sch. of Community & Public Affairs, 1984-86; Asst. Prof. & V-Principal, 1986-88; Acting Principal, 1988-89; Canada Research Fellow & Asst. Prof., Pol. Sci. Dept., 1988-92; Principal & Assoc. Prof., Sch. of Community & Public Affairs, 1991 to date; Professeure invitée, Institut national de recherche scientifique sur urbanisation, Univ. du Québec, 1993-95. **SELECTED PUBLICATIONS:** *The Legacy of Karl Polanyi: Market, State and Society at the End of the Twentieth Century*, ed. with Daniel Salée (New York: St. Martin's Press, 1996); "Social Determinants of Economic Activity: The Economy of Transfer" (*Journal of Economic Issues* June 1984); "Karl Polanyi: A Biographical Sketch,"

with Kari Polanyi-Levitt (*Telos* Fall 1987); "Market Reform or Market Failure: The Paradox of Convergence" (*Journal of Economic Issues* June 1989); "Democratizing Capital," with L. Evoy (*City Magazine* (Winnipeg) Spring 1993); various other publications. EDIT: Ed., *Bulletin de l'Association d'économique politique*, 1983-88; Ed. Committee, 1988-91; Ed. Committee, *Studies in Political Economy*, 1986 to date; Ed. Committee, *Alternatives*, 1990-91; Ed. Committee, *Lien social et politiques–RIAC*, 1994 to date; Ed. Bd., *Coopérative et developpement*, 1995. AFFIL: International Political Science Association; Society for the Advancement of Socio-Economics, US; Association pour le développement de la Socio-économie (ADSE-Québec); European Association of Evolutionary Political Economy; Association for Evolutionary Economics; Association d'économie politique (Prés. 1987-89); Association québecoise de science politique, Canadian Political Science Association; Karl Polanyi Institute of Political Economy, Concordia Univ. (Co-Founder & Co-Dir.); Fondation Léa Roback (Conseil d'admin.). INTERESTS: public policy formation & analysis; econ. theory; ethics & economics; comparative econ. systems; econ. democracy; local/community econ. dev.; social investment. MISC: Pres. & founding mbr., Montreal Community Loan Association, the 1st revolving investment fund in Canada; recipient, various grants & fellowships; numerous conference presentations & lectures; reviewer for various granting agencies; frequent contributions to TV, radio & written media on Cdn public policy & on transition in Eastern Europe & the former Soviet Union. COMMENT: *"In addition to my teaching, which deals primarily with critical economic analysis (in the tradition of political economy), my research is centred on the development of alternative democratic economic strategies. Through my empirical research, I have tried to formulate such alternatives and to establish appropriate institutions, for example, the establishment of micro credit."*

Menke, Ursula, B.Sc.,B.C.L. ⚖ Ⓢ
Vice-President, Counsel and Corporate Secretary, METROPOLITAN LIFE INSURANCE COMPANY, 99 Bank St., 13th fl., Ottawa, ON K1P 5A3 (613) 560-7918, FAX 560-7668. Born Bielefeld, Germany 1947. m. Konrad von Finckenstein. 2 ch. EDUC: McGill Univ., B.Sc. 1968, B.C.L.(Civil Law) 1976; Univ. of Alberta, Dipl.(Teaching) 1969. BAR: Quebec, 1977. CAREER: high sch. teacher, 1969-73; articling student, Dept. of Justice, 1977; lawyer, 1977-82, 1984-88; Compliance Officer, Dept. of Fin., 1982-84; Public Policy Consultant, Strategico Inc., 1989-90; Sr. Corp. Advisor, Office of the

Superintendent of Fin. Institutions, 1990-92; Inspector-Gen. of the Cdn Security & Intelligence Svc, Ministry of the Solicitor-Gen., 1992-93; VP, Cnsl & Corp. Sec., Metropolitan Life Insurance Company, 1993 to date. SELECTED PUBLICATIONS: "Restrictions and Limitations on Business Dealings Between Foreign Banks and Their Foreign Bank Subsidiaries" (*Banking Law and Practice* Vol. I, Insight, 1985); "The Bank Act" (*Commercial and Property Law Review* July 1986); "The Insurance Industry" (Conference Proceedings on the Financial Services Industry in Reform Insight, 1986); "New Regulatory Structure," with T. Laberge (Proceedings on How to Survive in the Financial Marketplace Insight, 1987). AFFIL: Barreau du Quebec; Ottawa Heart Institute Foundation (Bd.).

Mercer Clarke, Colleen S.L., B.Sc.,M.Sc., M.L.A. ■ ■ Ⓢ ⚛
Senior Environmental Manager, CBCL LIMITED (multidisciplinary consulting engineering), 1489 Hollis St., P.O. Box 606, Halifax, NS B3J 2R7 (902) 421-7241, FAX 423-3938, EMAIL colleenc@cbcl.ca. Born Gander, Nfld. 1951. m. John. 2 ch. Alexander, Lauren. EDUC: Memorial Univ. of Newfoundland, B.Sc. (Aquatic Ecology) 1972, M.Sc.(Marine Biol.) 1976; Univ. of Guelph, M.L.A.(Landscape Arch.) 1987. CAREER: Sr. Proj. Biologist, Applied Marine Research Limited, Halifax, 1974-76; Biologist, Environmental Protection Svc., Environment Canada, 1976-77; Mgr, Interdisciplinary Environmental Studies Div., Shawmont Newfoundland Limited, St. John's, Nfld., 1981-82; Principal, Polaris Consultants (private practice in envir. assessment & mgmt), 1977-81 & 1982-84; Principal, Lands End Consultants (private practice in environmental mgmt & design), Halifax, 1986-90; Mgr, Environmental Mgmt Div., Vaughan Engineering Associates, 1990-92; Dir., Environmental Mgmt, Halifax Harbour Clean-up Proj., Metro Engineering Limited (on assignment from Vaughan), 1991-92; founding Exec. Dir., N.S. Centre for Environmentally Sustainable Economic Development, 1992-94; Principal, Mercer Clarke Environments (private practice), 1994-96; Sr. Environmental Mgr, CBCL Limited, 1996 to date. SELECTED PUBLICATIONS: numerous papers & presentations incl.: "Environment and development in Canada - The pursuit of uncommon sense" (Cdn keynote address to first Canada-Thailand Conference on Sustainable Dev., Thailand, Nov. 1994); numerous radio, TV & magazine presentations on landscape architecture, east coast marine natural history, environmental stewardship & other environmental themes; numerous industry

reports. **AFFIL:** Oceans Institute of Canada (Bd. of Dir.; delegate, meetings of UN Commission on Sustainable Dev., Apr. 1996); Atlantic Provinces Association of Landscape Architects (Past Pres.); Canadian Society of Landscape Architects (Bd. of Gov. 1995 to date); N.S. Dept. of Transportation (mbr., Erosion & Sedimentation Control Round Table 1995 to date); N.S. Dept. of Environment (Min.'s Steering Group on Contaminated Land Mgmt 1994); City of Halifax (mbr., Lakes & Waterways Advisory Committee 1988-90 & 1995-96); N.S. Environmental Industry Association (Bd. of Dir. 1994-96); Canadian Society of Environmental Biologists (Dir., Atlantic Reg. 1988-93). **HONS:** recipient, Research Award, for research in water edge habitats design & mgmt, Landscape Architecture Canada Foundation, 1995. **INTERESTS:** outdoor recreation incl. hiking, canoeing, cross-country skiing; gardening; volunteer community activities.

Mercier, Eileen A., B.A.,M.A.,M.B.A., F.I.C.B. $

President, FINVOY MANAGEMENT INC., 77 Strathallan Blvd., Toronto, ON M5N 1S8 (416) 203-4759, FAX (416) 203-4903. Born Ont. 1947. m. Ernest C. 1ch., 4 stepch. **EDUC:** Wilfrid Laurier Univ., B.A. 1968; Univ. of Alberta, M.A. 1969; York Univ., M.B.A. 1977. **CAREER:** Mgr, Corp. Fin., The Toronto-Dominion Bank, 1972-78; Dir., U.S. Comm. Oper., Canwest Capital Corporation, 1978-81; Mgr, Corp. Fin., Gulf Canada Limited, 1981-86; VP, Pagurian Corporation Limited, 1986-87; Sr. VP & CFO, Abitibi-Price Inc., 1987-95; Finvoy Management Inc., 1995 to date. **DIRECTOR:** The CGI Group Inc.; C.I. Covington Fund Inc; Journey's End Corporation; Reko International Group Inc.; Winpak Ltd. **AFFIL:** Toronto Hospital Foundation (Dir.); York Univ. (Dir.); Workers' Compensation Board of Ontario (Dir.). **HONS:** Bus. Person of the Year, Wilfrid Laurier Univ., 1991. **INTERESTS:** travel; golf; family.

Mercier, Michelle, B.M.,M.A.A., M.B.A. ♡ ⊕ ✊

Executive Director, Quebec Branch, THE KIDNEY FOUNDATION OF CANADA, 2300 René-Lévesque Blvd., Montreal, QC H3H 2R5 (514) 938-4515, FAX 938-4757. Born Sherbrooke, Que. m. Robert Spickler. **EDUC:** Ècole de musique Vincent d'Indy, B.M.(Piano) 1971; Univ. de Montreal, Master of Musicology 1973; Indiana Univ., M.A.A. 1974; McGill Univ., M.B.A. 1986. **CAREER:** Production Studio Admin., The National Film Board of Canada, 1976-78; Administrator, Le Tritorium (Cégep du Vieux-Montreal), 1978-79; Admin. Svcs Mgr, ICS Export Inc., Super Steel Structures, 1979-81; Asst. Mgr, Budget Dept., La Société de Radio-Télévision du Québec, 1981-84; Mgr, Budget Dept., 1984-87; Exec. Dir. & Artistic Mgr, La Société du Grand Théâtre du Québec, 1987-93; Exec. Dir., Que. Branch, The Kidney Foundation of Canada, 1995 to date. **AFFIL:** Association des MBA du Québec; International Society of Performing Arts Administrators ; Association of Performing Arts Presenters; Board of Trade of Montréal-Métro; Ovetigo Dance Bd.; Association Québécoise de l'industrie du disque, du spectacle et de la vidéo (various juries); Musica Camerata Montreal (Chair 1985-87).

Meredith, Val, M.P. 🍁

Member of Parliament (Surrey-White Rock-South Langley), GOVERNMENT OF CANADA, House of Commons, 683 Confederation Building, Ottawa, ON K1A 0A6 (613) 947-4497, FAX 947-4500. Born Edmonton 1949. d. 4 ch. Ian, John, David, Paul. **CAREER:** Town Councillor, Slave Lake, Alta., 1973-77; Mayor, Slave Lake, 1977-80; owner & operator, Val's Flower and Gift Shop, Slave Lake, 1975-81; Sr. Administrator, Improvement District, Dept. of Mun. Affairs, Gov't of Alberta, 1982-85; Realtor, 1985-93; Reform Party candidate (Surrey-White Rock-South Langley), fed. election, 1988; M.P. (Surrey-White Rock-South Langley), 1993 to date; Justice & Legal Affairs Standing Committee, 1994 to date; Sub-committee on Nat'l Security, 1994 to date; Solicitor-Gen. Critic, Reform Party of Canada, 1994-95; Critic, Immigration & Citizenship, 1995 to date. **AFFIL:** Reform Party of Canada; Peace Arch Rock Musical Theatre Association; Semiahmoo Professional Women's Group; White Rock & Area Chamber of Commerce; Peace Portal Alliance Church. **INTERESTS:** reading; politics; walking; equestrian; flying; theatre. **COMMENT:** "*Val is one of nine children of Dr. J. Donovan and Lillian Ross. Dr. Ross was a member of the Alberta Legislature from 1952 until 1971. He served as a cabinet minister for 15 years. Val's great-grandmother was Charlotte Whitehead Ross, one of the first female doctors in Canada. Val's great-great-grandfather, Joseph Whitehead, was elected to the House of Commons in 1867, serving a five-year term.*"

Merikle, Mary, B.A. ✏ $

Managing Editor & Fiction Editor, *THE NEW QUARTERLY*, University of Waterloo, ELPP, PAS 2082, Waterloo, ON N2L 3G1 (519) 885-1211, EMAIL mmerikle@watarts.uwaterloo.ca. Born Decatur, Ill. 1940. m. Philip. 2 ch. **EDUC:** Knox Coll., Galesburg, Ill., B.A. 1962.

CAREER: public sch. teacher (grades 5 & 7), Charlottesville, Va., 1962-65; Sec., Univ. of Waterloo Early Childhood Educ. Centre, 1972-74; supply teacher, Waterloo County Bd. of Educ., 1977-78; tutor, English Language Proficiency Program, Univ. of Waterloo, 1978-95; assisted with organization of Writing Skills in Ont. Conference, 1979-80; sr. tutor, English Language Proficiency Program, Univ. of Waterloo, 1980-85; Edit. Asst., *The New Quarterly*, 1984-85; Mgr, English Language Proficiency Program, Univ. of Waterloo, 1985-95; Mng Ed. & Fiction Ed., *The New Quarterly*, 1995 to date. **INTERESTS:** reading; cycling; knitting; bridge. **MISC:** judge & workshop presenter, Waterloo County Bd. of Educ. English Awards, 1985-89. **COMMENT:** *"Primarily an editor and teacher, not a published writer, I help others (students and aspiring authors) improve their writing, and I continually look for new and promising writers."*

Meronowich, Florence ✋ ♡ 🎓
President, LAUBACH LITERACY CANADA, ALBERTA ASSOCIATION, 10010 - 105 St., Edmonton, AB T5J 1C4 (403) 424-5514, FAX 425-5176. Chairperson, THE LEARNING LINK. Born Cardston, Alta. 1933. m. John. 8 ch. **CAREER:** interviewer, consumer research, 1965-74; supervisor/interviewer, City of Calgary Transportation Dept., 1969-72; Canada Post, 1974-76; County Councillor/Sch. Bd. Trustee, Strathcona County, Alta., 1980-83; Local Issues Columnist, 2 Strathcona County newspapers, 1983-89; Founder & Mgr, County Clothesline, 1984-91; Exec. Dir., Proj. Adult Literacy Society, 1991-94. **AFFIL:** Laubach Literacy Canada (Bd. Mbr. 1991-95); The Learning Link (Chairperson 1993 to date); Alberta Association of Adult Literacy. **HONS:** Award of Excellence, Strathcona County, 1987; First Runner-Up, Edmonton Area Citizen of the Year Award, 1987; Canada Literacy Volunteer Award, 1990; Canada Volunteer Award (Health & Welfare) 1992. **INTERESTS:** family; avid reader; educ. & personal dev.; writing; community betterment. **COMMENT:** *"My work to help the socially disadvantaged is a payback to my country for the right to live comfortably in a democratic society."*

Merriman, Brenda Dougall, A.R.A.D.,B.A., C.G.R.S.,C.G.L. 📖 🎓
Independent Genealogist and Author. 110 The Esplanade, Apt. 201, Toronto, ON M5E 1X9. Born Port Arthur, Ont. 1939. m. Jonas Ancevich. 3 ch. **EDUC:** Royal Academy of Dancing, A.R.A.D.(Ballet) 1958; Univ. of Manitoba, B.A.(French/Phil.) 1960; Bd. for Certification of Genealogists, Certified Genealogical Records Specialist 1979, Certified Genealogical Lecturer 1987. **CAREER:** Post-Grad. Fellow, St. Michael's Coll., Univ. of Toronto, 1961; Ed., *Puslinch Pioneer*, 1976-78; professional genealogist, 1978 to date; columnist/writer, *Early Canadian Life*, 1978-80. **SELECTED PUBLICATIONS:** *Genealogy in Ontario: Searching the Records* (1984); *The Emigrant Ancestors of a Lieutenant-Governor of Ontario* (1993); numerous articles in genealogical periodicals. **AFFIL:** Association of Professional Genealogists (Trustee); International Society of British Genealogy & Family History (Trustee); Canadian Federation of Genealogical & Family History Societies (Past Pres.); Ontario Genealogical Society (Manuscript Advisory Committee). **HONS:** Citation of Recognition, Ontario Genealogical Society, 1986. **MISC:** Lecturer on genealogical research at numerous conferences.

Merrin Best, Patrice E., B.A. ■ $
Vice-President, Corporate Affairs, SHERRITT INTERNATIONAL CORPORATION, 5 Hazelton Ave., 2nd fl., Toronto, ON M5R 2E1 (416) 924-4551, FAX 924-5015. Born Toronto 1948. m. Anthony G. Best. 3 ch. **EDUC:** Queen's Univ., B.A.(Drama/Politics/Psych.) 1970. **CAREER:** Exec. Dir., Planned Parenthood of Toronto, 1971-74; Consultant on Public Affairs, YWCA of Canada, 1974-76; Special Asst. to the Hon. Marc Lalonde, Ottawa, 1976-79; Sr. Public Affairs Analyst, Canadian Pacific Limited, 1979-81; Asst. Mgr, Fin. Reporting & Analysis, 1981-82; Mgr, Toronto Life Ventures, Key Publishers, 1987-88; Dir., Corp. Affairs, & Asst. to the Chrm, The Molson Companies Limited, 1989-94; VP, Corp. & Investor Rel'ns, Lac Minerals Ltd., 1994; VP, Corp. Affairs, Sherritt Inc. (now Viridian Inc.), 1994-96; VP, Corp. Affairs, Sherritt International Corporation, 1996 to date. **AFFIL:** Canadian Investor Relations Institute; Queen's Univ. (Bd. of Trustees); Toronto Lawn Tennis Club; Friends of Drama, Queen's Univ.

Merry, Susan A., B.A.,B.L.S. ■■ 📖 $
Director, Business Information and Records Management, Corporate Governance Group, CIBC, Head Office, Commerce Ct. N., 7th Fl., Toronto, ON M5L 1A2 (416) 980-2899, FAX 861-3666, EMAIL merry@cibc.ca. Born Toronto 1938. m. Christopher W.E. 2 ch. Martha, Sarah. **EDUC:** Univ. of Toronto, B.A. 1959, B.L.S.(Library Sci.) 1962. **CAREER:** Univ. of Toronto Library, 1962-67; Chief Librarian, Dept. of Sec. of State, Gov't of Canada, Ottawa, 1967-70; multiple contract appts, Univ. of Toronto Library, 1974-78; Asst. Librarian, Tech. Svcs, Info. Centre, CIBC, 1978-83; Mgr, 1983-89; Sr. Mgr, 1989; Dir.,

1989 to date. **AFFIL:** Special Libraries Association (Copyright Committee 1986 to date; Chair, Gov't Rel'ns Committee, Toronto chpt. 1988 to date); Society of Copyright Consumers (Dir. 1995 to date); Univ. of Toronto (Fac. of Library & Info. Sci. Council 1992-94). **HONS:** Chrm's Award for outstanding svc. to CIBC, 1993; Mbr. of the Year, Special Libraries Association, Toronto chpt., 1994. **INTERESTS:** golf; skiing; music; reading. **MISC:** frequent presenter, panelist & author on copyright & info. svcs issues; Adjunct Lecturer, Fac. of Info. Studies (on the mgmt of corp. & other special info. centres), Univ. of Toronto, 1987 to date.

Mersereau, Marilyn, B.A. $

Director of Communications, IBM CANADA LTD., 3600 Steeles Ave. E., Markham, ON L3R 9Z7 (905) 316-4500, FAX 316-2268. Born Saint John 1953 **EDUC:** Univ. of Western Ontario, B.A.(Phys. Educ.) 1976. **CAREER:** Dir. of Mktg, Brands, Coca-Cola (Canada); Burger King International; Dir. of Comm, IBM Canada. **AFFIL:** Advertising Standards Council (Bd.); Broadcast Exec. Society (Bd.). **MISC:** Judge, Strategy's "Agency of the Year". **COMMENT:** *"I have had a unique mix of packaged goods and retail marketing experience, having worked for Coca-Cola in Canada for eight years as Director of Marketing, Brands, and in the UK and US for Burger King International. The combination of this experience has positioned me very well to face the future challenges in information technology that we face at IBM."*

Meschino, Wendy, M.D.,C.C.F.P., F.R.C.P.C.,F.C.C.M.G. 📺

Clinical Geneticist and Director, Clinical Genetics Service, Department of Genetics, NORTH YORK GENERAL HOSPITAL, 4001 Leslie St., Rm. 392, North York, ON M2K 1E1 (416) 756-6345, FAX 756-6727. Born Toronto 1954. m. Dr. Jim Sugiyama. 2 ch. Michael Sugiyama, Jaime Sugiyama. **EDUC:** Univ. of Toronto, M.D. 1979. **CAREER:** Dir., Predictive Testing Program for Huntington's Disease & Dir., Clinical Genetics Diagnostic Centre, North York General Hospital, 1988 to date; Lecturer, Dept. of Pediatrics, Univ. of Toronto, 1988 to date; Sr. Consultant, Outreach Genetics Clinic, Ministry of Health, Timmins, Ont., 1994; Consultant, Toronto-Sunnybrook Regional Cancer Centre & Clinical Geneticist, Familial Breast Cancer Clinic, 1995. **SELECTED PUBLICATIONS:** "Proceed with care: Direct predictive testing for Huntington disease," with C. Benjamin *et al* (*American Journal of Human Genestics*, vol. 55, 1994); "Molecular Genetic Predictive Testing for Alzheimer's Disease: Deliberations and Preliminary Recommendations, " with A. Lennox, H. Karlinsky, J. Buchanan, M. Percy & J. *Berg (Alzheimer's Disease and Associated Diseases Journal*, no. 8, 1994); numerous papers, abstracts & presentations. **AFFIL:** Canadian Coll. of Medical Geneticists (Bd. of Dir.; Treas.; Ethics & Public Policy Committee; Chief Examiner for examination in Clinical Genetics 1990-91); Association of Genetic Counsellors of Ontario (Pres. 1991-92); Royal Coll. of Physicians & Surgeons (Fellow; Examinations Committee in Medical Genetics); Canadian Pediatric Society; Hospital for Sick Children Alumnae Association; American Society of Human Genetics; Association of Genetic Counsellors of Ontario; Canadian Medical Protective Association; Ontario Medical Association; Canadian Medical Association. **HONS:** Ann Shepard Memorial Scholarship for Biol., 1974; Ann Shepard Memorial Scholarship for Zoology, 1975; Summer Scholarship, Pediatric Psychiatry, Clarke Institute of Psychiatry, 1976; Summer Scholarship, Pediatrics, North York General Hospital, 1977. **INTERESTS:** parenting & family; perennial gardening; photography; needlepoint. **COMMENT:** *"I am fortunate to have grown up with a caring, nurturing family who have encouraged and supported my successes. My husband and children are equally supportive. It has been my privilege as a physician to care for people with genetic problems, and to participate in the rapid unfolding of what to me is the most exciting of all sciences - the world of genetics."*

Mesley, Wendy, B.A.A. 📺 ✎

Journalist/Host, *Sunday Report* and Journalist/Host, *Undercurrents*, CANADIAN BROADCASTING CORPORATION, (television broadcasting), 205 Wellington St., Toronto, ON M5W 1E6 (416) 205-7865, FAX 466-7458. Born Montreal 1957 **EDUC:** Ryerson Polytechnic Univ., B.A.A.(Journalism) 1979. **CAREER:** Reporter/Newscaster, CHUM Radio, CHIN Radio, CKFM Radio, CFRB Radio, 1976-79; Reporter/Host, *As It Is*, CFCF-TV, 1979-81; Bureau Chief, CFTO-TV Montreal, 1981-82; local news, CBC-TV Montreal, 1982; Nat'l Assembly Correspondent, CBC-TV Montreal, 1983-85; Parliamentary Correspondent/Nat'l Affairs Correspondent, 1986-92; Anchor/Interviewer, CBC Newsworld, 1992-93; Journalist/Host, *Sunday Report*/Back-Up Host, *Prime Time News*, CBC-TV, 1994 to date. **INTERESTS:** travel; windsurfing; skiing. **COMMENT:** *"Raised by my mother; inspired by Barbara Frum; cut my political reporting teeth in Quebec 1980 Referendum; covered National Affairs on Parliament Hill–now an anchor/interviewer in Toronto who spends all her spare time* *searching for adventure on the slopes and the seven seas!"*

Messenger, Margaret, B.A.,B.Ed., M.A. 🐝 📖
Past President and Secretary-Treasurer, ARCHELAUS SMITH HISTORICAL SOCIETY, Box 190, Clark's Harbour, NS B0W 1P0. Born Newellton, N.S. 1922. s. EDUC: Acadia Univ., B.A. 1942, B.Ed. 1943, M.A.(Math) 1963. CAREER: Principal, Great Village Sch., 1943-45; teacher, Edgehill Sch. for Girls, 1945-47; teacher, Shelburne Sch., 1947-50; Principal, LaHave Sch., 1950-56; teacher, Yarmouth schools, 1956-78; Head of Math. Dept., Yarmouth schools, 1970-78. VOLUNTEER CAREER: Clerk, Newellton United Baptist Church, 1985-96; Chair, Personnel Committee, Western Counties Reg'l Library Bd., 1988-95; Pres., Archelaus Smith Historical Society, 1986-94; Past Pres./Sec.-Treas., 1994 to date. AFFIL: Retired Teachers' Association; Acadia Alumni; N.S. Genealogical Association; Shelburne County Genealogical Society; Yarmouth County Historical Society. HONS: Award for Outstanding Contribution to the Community, Mayor of Clark's Harbour. INTERESTS: local history; genealogy; church activities; gardening; needlework. COMMENT: *"I spend much time answering genealogical inquiries and researching local history in order to promote an awareness and appreciation of Cape Sable Island's past."*

Messing, Karen, B.A.,M.Sc.,Ph.D. ■ ⊕ 🐝
Professor of Biology and Researcher, Centre pour l'étude des interactions biologiques entre la santé et l'environnement (CINI/BIOSE), UNIVERSITÉ DU QUEBEC À MONTR´AL, Succ. Centre-Ville, C.P. 8888, Montreal, QC H3C 3P8 (514) 987-3334, FAX 987-6183, EMAIL messing. karen@uqam.ca. 2 ch. Daood Aidroos, Mikail Al-Aidroos. EDUC: Harvard Univ., B.A. 1963; McGill Univ., M.Sc. 1970, Ph.D.(Biol.) 1975. CAREER: Prof., Univ. du Quebec à Montréal, UQAM, 1976 to date; Dir., Centre pour l'étude des interactions biologiques entre la santé et l'environnement, 1990-95. SELECTED PUBLICATIONS: *Occupational Health and Safety Concerns of Canadian Women; Invisible: Issues in Women's Occupational Health,* with B. Neis & L. Dumais; numerous articles in peer-reviewed journals. EDIT: Ed. Bd., *Recherches féministes;* Ed. Bd., *Salud y Trabajo.* AFFIL: UQAM; Association canadienne d'ergonomie (mbre. titulaire); Association canadienne-français pour l'avancement des sciences; American Public Health Association; Regroupement québécois du chercheuses féministes. HONS: Woman of Distinction (with Donna Mergler),

Science & Technology, YWCA de Montreal, 1994; Prix Jacques-Rousseau, ACFAS, 1993; Conseil québécois de recherche sociale (Distinguished Fellow, 2-yr. fellowship, 1995-97). COMMENT: *"Karen Messing has been a professor of biological sciences at the University of Quebec in Montreal since 1976. She started her career as a geneticist and became involved in occupational health through an agreement between the university and Quebec trade unions."*

Metz, Luanne Marie, MD,FRCPC ⊕ 🐝
Director, Multiple Sclerosis Clinic, CALGARY GENERAL HOSPITAL, 841 Central Ave E, M4-022, Calgary, AB T2E 0A1 (403) 268-9746, FAX 268-9544. Assistant Professor, Department of Clinical Neurosciences, Faculty of Medicine, UNIVERSITY OF CALGARY. Born Maple Creek, Sask. 1957. d. 2 ch. EDUC: Univ. of Calgary, MD 1983, FRCPC(Neurology) 1988. CLINICAL CAREER: Intern, Wellesley Hospital, Univ. of Toronto, 1983-85; Neurology Resident, Univ. of Calgary, 1985-88; Neuroimmunology Fellow, 1988-89; Gen. Neurologist, Calgary General Hospital, 1989 to date; Dir., Multiple Sclerosis Clinic, 1992 to date. ACADEMIC CAREER: Asst. Clinical Prof., Dept. of Clinical Neurosciences, Univ. of Calgary, 1989-92; Asst. Prof., 1992 to date. SELECTED PUBLICATIONS: "Migraine and Intracerebral Hemorrhage," with A. Shuaib & T. Hing (*Cephalalgia* 1989); "Causalgia and the Sympathetic Dystrophies" (*Medicine North America* 35(3) 1989); "A Population Based Twin Study of Multiple Sclerosis in Twins: Update," with A.D. Sadovnick et al (*Annals of Neurology* 1993); "Interferon Beta Treatment of Multiple Sclerosis," letter, with R. Bell & D. Zochodne (*Neurology* 44(1) 1994); various other publications. AFFIL: Canadian Neurological Society; American Academy of Neurology; Canadian Headache Society; Consortium of Multiple Sclerosis Centres; Canadian Cooperative Multiple Sclerosis Study Group; Alberta Neurological Society; Royal Coll. of Physicians & Surgeons of Canada; Coll. of Physicians & Surgeons of Alberta; Canadian Medical Association; Alberta Medical Association; Multiple Sclerosis Society of Canada; Canadian Medical Protective Association. HONS: Alberta Lung Association Christmas Seal Scholarship, 1983; Gold Star Letter for excellence in teaching, Class of 1992, Univ. of Calgary; Vis Vitae Award, Calgary General Hospital Medical Staff, 1994. INTERESTS: children; books; hiking; walking; food; music. MISC: frequent public speaker. COMMENT: *"I have been blessed with good friends and colleagues, a loving and supportive family and 2 wonderful children. These people*

support my efforts to improve a small part of the world we live in."

Meyer, Doris, C.G.A. ■ $ ⚛
Vice-President, Finance, Chief Financial Officer and Corporate Secretary, QUEENSTAKE RESOURCES LTD., 1111 Melville St., Ste. 250, Vancouver, BC V6E 3V6 (604) 684-1218, FAX 684-9959. Born Vancouver 1952. d. 1 ch. CAREER: Acctg Mgr, Queenstake Resources Ltd., 1982-85; Cont., 1985-87; VP, Fin., 1987 to date. DIRECTOR: Golden Sitka Resources Inc. AFFIL: Certified General Accountant. COMMENT: *"As the CFO and Corporate Secretary of a Toronto Stock Exchange-listed mineral exploration and development company, I have gained a variety of skills and acquired specialized knowledge of all facets of the precious-metals mining company."*

Meyers, Marlene, O., B.Sc.M., M.Sc. ⊕ $ ✊
President, MEYERS AND ASSOCIATES, Healthcare Management and Education, 139 Coleridge Rd. NW, Calgary, AB T2K 1X5 (403) 282-4598. Born Saskatoon m. Eugene. 3 ch. Lori Forand, Lisa Gibbins, Dean Meyers. EDUC: Univ. of Saskatchewan, B.Sc.N. 1962; Int'l Summer Sch., Univ. of Oslo, Norway, 1973; Univ. of Calgary, M.Sc.(Medical Sci.) 1976; Harvard Univ., Contemporary Psychiatry Program 1980; Banff Sch. of Mgmt, Healthcare Exec. Program 1985; Univ. of Western Ontario, Western Bus. Sch., Western Exec. Program 1993. CAREER: various nursing positions, Alta. & BC, 1962-69; Mount Royal Coll., 1969-82; Coord., Psychiatric Nursing; Chair, Allied Health Dept.; Dir., Post Basic Mental Health Nursing Program; Asst. Exec. Dir., Nursing, Rockyview Hospital, Calgary, 1982-85; Adjunct Assoc. Prof., Nursing, Univ. of Calgary, 1983 to date; VP, Patient Svcs, Calgary General Hospital, 1985-91; Pres. & CEO, 1991-95; Surveyor & Fac., Canadian Council on Health Services Accreditation, 1987 to date; Adjunct Assoc. Prof., Community Health Svcs, Fac. of Medicine, Univ. of Calgary, 1993 to date. SELECTED PUBLICATIONS: "The Optimal Use of Nursing Homes in the Care of the Mentally Disturbed Person," with Mary McIntosh, Alta. Gov't (June 1980). AFFIL: Canadian Coll. of Health Service Executives; Alberta Association of Registered Nurses; American Hospital Association; Canadian Executive Services Organization; Alberta Mental Health Review Panel. HONS: Woman of the Year, Health, YWCA Calgary, 1982; Heritage of Service Award, Alberta Association of Registered Nurses, 1992; Nursing Honour Society, Mu Sigma Chapter of Sigma Theta Tau International, Univ. of Alberta, 1992; Life mbr., Alberta Association of Registered Nurses, 1996.

Micallef, Gabriella, B.A.A. 📺 📖 ✪
Director and Producer, I-SIS PRODUCTIONS, 172 Glenholme Ave., Toronto, ON M6E 3C4 (416) 651-2828, FAX 651-5101. Born Valetta, Malta 1960. cl. Debbie. 1 ch. EDUC: Vancouver Community Coll., Studio 54 (Theatre: Tech. & Production) 1980; Ryerson Polytechnic Institute, B.A.A.(Media Studies/Film) 1988. CAREER: Ryerson Film & Photography Dept., 1986-87; Elizabeth Fry Society, 1987-89; Ernestines Shelter, 1989-90, 1991; Promotions Coord., V-Tape Distribution, 1990; Writer, Dir. & Prod., I-Sis Productions, 1990 to date; Co-Dir., Full Frame Film and Video Distribution, 1993-95. SELECTED CREDITS: Camera, *Multi-Cultural Issues in the Classroom*, City of York Sch. Bd. (1988); Daily Grip/Asst. Ed., *Zero Patience*, Independent (1993); Co-Writer/Dir., *An Other Love Story* (1990); Prod./Co-Writer, *My Mom's A Dyke and Other Stories* (1992); Co-Writer, *Sticks and Stones* (1992); Co-Dir.,*Tama Ba? Tama Na! Enough is Enough* (1993); Co-Writer/Dir.,*Resisting Venus* (1994). AFFIL: Shirley Sameroo House; CKLN Community Radio; Trinity Square Video; Charles Street Video; Toronto Women in Television. HONS: New Journalism Prize (*An Other Love Story*), Buffalo, NY. MISC: Artist-in-Residence, Film Production in Toronto, Students' Sch., 1991. COMMENT: *"I live in Toronto with my partner Debbie Douglas and our daughter Siobhan. As lesbian-feminists, our work is a reflection of our commitment to furthering the struggle to gain equality for women and other minority groups."*

Michaels, Anne, B.A. 📖 📜
Writer. c/o McClelland & Stewart, 481 University Ave., Toronto, ON M5G 2E9. Born Toronto EDUC: Univ. of Toronto, B.A.(English Specialist) 1980. CAREER: freelance writer; Creative Writing Instructor, Univ. of Toronto, 1989 to date; Writer-in-Residence, Douglas Coll., Vancouver, 1993; Writer-in-Residence, York Univ., 1994; Writer-in-Residence, Univ. of New Brunswick, 1995. SELECTED PUBLICATIONS: *The Weight of Oranges* (Coach House Press, 1986); *Miner's Pond* (McClelland & Stewart, 1991); *Fugitive Pieces* (McClelland & Stewart, 1996); numerous selections in anthologies, some translated into Chinese, Gujarati & Hebrew. AFFIL: Writers' Union of Canada; League of Canadian Poets. HONS: Epstein Award for Poetry, 1980; Commonwealth Poetry Prize for the Americas, 1986; First Prize for Poetry, Canadian Authors' Asso-

ciation, 1991; First Prize for Poetry, National Magazine Awards, 1991; nominated for Trillium Award, 1991; nominated, Gov. General's Award for Poetry, 1991. MISC: *The Weight of Oranges* (Talking Book Series, Music Gallery/Coach House Press, 1989).

Michaud, Monique ⊗ ✦ ♂
Retired Cultural Agency Executive. Ottawa, ON. Born Ottawa 1929. d. 1 ch. EDUC: Congrégation de Nôtre-Dame. CAREER: United Nations; various positions with Canada Council, incl. Arts Award Officer, Asst. Head of Theatre Section, Head of Dance Section, Asst. Dir., Arts Div.; est. Dance Section, 1972; retired, 1990. MISC: 1st Head of Dance, Canada Council, 1972. COMMENT: *"Apart from giving dance its legitimate place at the Council, I produced in 1980 a major policy document for the development of the art form; my reign at the Council was very controversial. I believe that through determination, in spite of enormous political pressure, I managed to accomplish what I had set out to do. Some people would agree, some would not."*

Michener, Gail R., B.Sc.,Ph.D. ⊛ ⊴ ♂
Professor, Department of Biological Sciences, UNIVERSITY OF LETHBRIDGE, Lethbridge, AB T1K 3M4 (403) 329-2568, FAX 329-2082, EMAIL michener@hg.uleth.ca. Born Wisbech, UK 1946. m. Dan Michener. 1 ch. Rory Michener. EDUC: Univ. of Adelaide, B.Sc.(Zoology) 1966; Univ. of Saskatchewan, Ph.D.(Behaviour) 1972. CAREER: Lecturer, Univ. of Cape Coast, Ghana, W. Africa, 1972-74; Isaac Walton Killam Memorial Postdoctoral Fellow, Univ. of Alberta, 1974-76; Visiting Prof., Univ. of Lethbridge, 1977-81; NSERC Univ. Research Fellow, 1981-85; Assoc. Prof., 1985-90; Prof., 1990 to date. SELECTED PUBLICATIONS: "Notes on the Breeding and Young of the Crest-tailed Marsupial Mouse, Dasycercus cristicauda" *(Journal of Mammalogy* 1969); "Tail Autotomy as an Escape Mechanism in Rattus rattus" *(Journal of Mammalogy* 1976); "Differential Costs of Reproduction for Male and Female Richardson's Ground Squirrels," with L. Locklear (*Canadian Journal of Zoology* 1990); "Ethical Issues in the Use of Wild Animals in Behavioural and Ecological Studies" in *Animal Care and Use in Behavioural Research: Regulations, Issues and Applications,* J.W. Driscoll, ed. (1989); "Sexual Differences in Over-Winter Torpor Patterns of Richardson's Ground Squirrels in Natural Hibernacula" (*Oecologia* 1992); various other publications. EDIT: Assoc. Ed., *Journal of Mammalogy,* 1983-88; Ed. Bd., *Canadian Journal of Zoology,* 1987-96. AFFIL: Animal Behavior Society

(Pres. 1992-93); American Society of Mammalogists; Canadian Society of Zoologists. HONS: Distinguished Teacher Award, Univ. of Lethbridge, 1993; C.H. Merriam Award for Distinguished Contributions to Mammalogy, American Society of Mammalogists, 1994. INTERESTS: Scottish country dancing. COMMENT: *"Teaching animal physiology and animal behaviour to undergraduates. Research on behavioural ecology of native prairie animals."*

Mickelson, Norma I., B.Ed.,M.A., Ph.D. ⊴
Professor Emeritus, UNIVERSITY OF VICTORIA, Victoria, BC V8W 2Y2 (604) 477-5711, FAX 721-4118. Born Victoria, B.C. m. Harvey. 2 ch. Irene Ann, Richard Paul. EDUC: Victoria Coll., Univ. of British Columbia, B.Ed.(Hist. & Educ.) 1963; Univ. of Victoria, M.A.(Educ. Psych.) 1968; Univ. of Washington, Ph.D.(Educ. Psych.) 1972. CAREER: teacher, Sooke, Victoria, Vancouver; Supervisor of Instruction, Sooke, Saanich; Prof., Univ. of Victoria. SELECTED PUBLICATIONS: *Evaluation of Literacy: A Perspective for Change* (Heinemann, 1991); numerous journal articles. AFFIL: P.E.O. (Past Pres., Chapter AB). HONS: Sarah Shorten Award, Canadian Association of University Teachers, 1991; Canada 125 Medal; Distinguished Alumnus Award, Univ. of Victoria, 1995; Life Membership, Distinguished Founder, Whole Language Umbrella. INTERESTS: reading; travel; bridge. COMMENT: *"Established equity program at University of Victoria–active in community."*

Mickelson, Rhona ■ ○ ⊗ ⊴
Founder and Executive Director, STAR TRACKS PERFORMING ARTS CENTRE FOR THE DISABLED, c/o The Performing Arts Lodge, 110 The Esplanade, Ste. 207, Toronto, ON M5E 1X9 (416) 868-6568, FAX 368-5587. Born UK 1954. s. CAREER: Founder & Exec. Dir., Star Tracks Performing Arts Centre & Talent Agency for the Disabled. SELECTED PUBLICATIONS: "Images of Women with Disabilities: From Fashion to Film" (*Rehabilitation Digest,* Mar. 1993). AFFIL: Toronto SkyDome Access Committee for the Disabled (Bd.); Able/Disable Creative Art Centre (former Bd. Mbr.); North York Access Committee for Persons with Disabilities (former Mbr.). HONS: Certificate of Appreciation, Ontario March of Dimes, 1993; Certificate of Appreciation, Toronto Head Injury Association, 1994; Canada 125 Medal; Toronto Award of Merit, 1995; King Clancy Award (highest award given in Canada to persons who have outstanding achievements in the disabled community),

Canadian Foundation for the Physically Disabled, 1996; The Gardiner Award, Metro & Toronto Junior Board of Trade, 1996 INTERESTS: live theatre; music; classic movies. MISC: delivered several papers on disability issues. COMMENT: *"I feel in living life, we are all here for a reason. It is our duty to be the best we can be and to improve society for our fellow citizens. I hope that through my work with Star Tracks, I have made, and will continue to make, some small improvement for humankind."*

Mickleborough, Lynda L., B.Sc.,M.D.C.M., F.R.C.S.(C.) ⊕ ⌖

Professor of Surgery, UNIVERSITY OF TORONTO, 200 Elizabeth St., Toronto, ON M5G 2C4. Born Regina 1947. m. William B. 4 ch. Lisa, Jennifer, Stephen, Christopher. EDUC: McGill Univ., B.Sc. 1969, M.D.C.M. 1973. CAREER: Resident, Royal Victoria Hospital, Montreal, 1973-80; Research Fellow, Dept. of Cardiology & Cardiovascular Surgery, McGill Univ., 1975-76; Clinical & Research Fellow, Cardiovascular Surgery, Toronto General Hospital, 1980-81; Sr. Research Fellow, Ontario Heart & Stroke Foundation, 1981-88; Cardiac Surgeon, Toronto General Hospital, 1981 to date; Lecturer, Dept. of Surgery, Univ. of Toronto, 1981-84; Asst. Prof., 1984-89; Assoc. Prof., 1989-94; Prof. of Surgery, 1994 to date. SELECTED PUBLICATIONS: numerous scientific papers; clinical & basic lab. research related to coronary artery disease, ventricular arrhythmias, ventricular aneurysms & surgical treatment of heart failure. EDIT: Advisory Ed. Bd., *Journal of Thoracic and Cardiovascular Surgery*. AFFIL: Royal Coll. of Physicians & Surgeons of Canada (Fellow in Gen. Surgery; Fellow in Cardiovascular & Thoracic Surgery); Coll. of Physicians & Surgeons of Ontario; Ontario Medical Association; American Association of Thoracic Surgery; Society of Thoracic Surgery; Canadian Cardiovascular Society; North American Society of Pacing & Electrophysiology; Institute of Medical Science; various other nat'l & int'l committees. HONS: various scholarships, 1965-72; Campbell Keenan Prize, 1973; Mona B. Scheckman Prize, 1973; Alexander D. Stewart Prize, 1973; Annual Research Award, Canadian Cardiovascular Society, 1976; Lister Prize, 1994; Outstanding Service Award, Heart & Stroke Foundation of Ontario, 1994. INTERESTS: music; boating; skiing; windsurfing. MISC: recipient, numerous research grants; mbr., various nat'l & int'l review boards, incl. Scientific Review Executive Committee, Canadian Heart & Stroke Foundation; invited speaker at numerous associations & conferences.

Mielitz, Sandra J., B.A.,M.B.A. ■ $

Vice-President, Grain and Western Canada, CANADIAN NATIONAL, (transportation), 360 Main St., Ste. 890, P.O. Box 832, Winnipeg, MB R3C 2P8 (204) 988-8251, FAX 988-8517, EMAIL mielitz.cn.ca. Born B.C. m. Ronald. EDUC: Univ., B.A.(English) 1969, M.B.A.(Fin.) 1978. CAREER: Officer, CN, 1978 to date, in several parts of Canada & in a variety of areas incl. Public Affairs, Treasury, CN Hotels, Planning & Admin., & Mktg; previous position was Asst. VP in charge of Grain & Grain Products, a Bus. Unit of Mktg Dept. AFFIL: Royal Winnipeg Ballet (Dir. 1994 to date); Canadian Club of Winnipeg (Dir. 1994 to date); Univ. of Manitoba Transport Institute (Advisory Committee 1993 to date). INTERESTS: reading; music; antiques; languages. COMMENT: *"One of very few women in North America to have attained executive-level line responsibilities in a railroad. Diverse general management background."*

Mikhael, Nadia ■ ■ ⊕ ⌖ ✺

Professor and Chair, Department of Pathology and Laboratory Medicine, UNIVERSITY OF OTTAWA, Faculty of Medicine, 451 Smyth Rd., Ottawa, ON K1H 8M5 (613) 562-5422, FAX 562-5442, EMAIL nmikhael@danis.med.uottawa.ca. Born Cairo, Egypt 1944. m. Dr. Boushra Mikhael. 2 ch. Sam, Joseph.

Miller, Elizabeth, M.A.,Ph.D. ⌖ 📖 ♆

Professor of English, MEMORIAL UNIVERSITY OF NEWFOUNDLAND, St. John's, NF A1C 5S7 (709) 737-8276, FAX 737-4528, EMAIL emiller@morgan.ucs.mun.ca. Born St. John's 1939. d. 1 ch. Dennis W. Miller. EDUC: Memorial Univ. of Newfoundland, M.A.(English) 1974, Ph.D.(English) 1988. CAREER: high sch. teacher, 1958-64; high sch. principal, 1964-68; Dir. of Comm., Newfoundland Teachers' Association, 1968-70; Fac. Mbr., English, Memorial Univ. of Newfoundland, 1970 to date; currently full Prof. of English. SELECTED PUBLICATIONS: *The Life and Times of Ted Russell* (St. John's: Jesperson Press, 1981); *Banked Fires: An Anthology of Newfoundland Poetry*, ed.with Tom Dawe (St. John's: Harry Cuff Publications, 1989); *The Frayed Edge: Norman Duncan's Newfoundland* (St. John's: Harry Cuff Publications, 1992); *'Arms and the Newfoundlander': An Anthology of Poetry of the Great War*, ed. (St. John's: Harry Cuff Publications, 1994); ed. 6 collections of Ted Russell's work; "Newfoundland Literature in the Dirty Thirties" in *Myth and Milieu: Atlantic Literature and Culture 1918-1939*, ed. Gwendolyn Davies (Fredericton: Acadiensis, 1993); "Death by Text: Narrative Strategies in Stoker's Dracula" (*Udolpho* Sept. 1994); "The World Dracula Congress" (*Locus*, 1995); various other publications. **AFFIL:** Association of Canadian College & University Teachers of English; International Association for the Fantastic in the Arts; World Dracula Congress, Romania (Organizing Committee); Transylvanian Society of Dracula, Cdn Chapter (Pres.); International Bram Stoker Society; British Gothic Society; "Dracula '97: A Centennial Celebration" (Co-organizer). **HONS:** President's Award for Outstanding Dissertation (Ph.D.), Memorial Univ. of Newfoundland, 1988; President's Award for Distinguished Teaching, Memorial Univ. of Newfoundland, 1992; Baroness of the House of Dracula, 1995.. **INTERESTS:** Gothic fiction; travel; swimming. **MISC:** numerous conference presentations on 19th century Gothic lit., both in N.Am. & Europe. **COMMENT:** *"For many years, a specialist in Newfoundland literature, I now devote most of my efforts to scholarly papers (and books-in-progress) on Dracula and related works."*

Miller, Helen, S.E., B.A. 🏠
Archivist, CITY OF ST. JOHN'S, Box 908, St. John's, NF A1C 5M2 (709) 576-8226, FAX 576-8474. Born St. John's 1963. s. **EDUC:** Memorial Univ. of Newfoundland, B.A. (Anthro./Archaeology) 1985. **CAREER:** Archival Asst., Prov. Archives of Newfoundland & Labrador, 1986-87; Acting Gov't Records Archivist, 1988-89; Asst. Archivist (Contract), City of St. John's, 1989-90; Archivist, 1990 to date. **AFFIL:** Provincial Organization of Records Officers (Dir. 1989-91; Chair 1991-92); Association of Newfoundland & Labrador Archivists (Dir. 1990-91; VP 1991-92; Pres. 1992-94); Association of Newfoundland & Labrador Archives (Nfld. Rep. to the Cdn Council of Archives 1994-96); Newfoundland & Labrador Council of Archives (Dir. 1989-91; Chair 1991-92); Canadian Council of Archives (Dir. 1994-96; V-Chair, 1996 to date); Association of Canadian Archivists (Chair, Mun. Archivists' Special Interest Section 1994-95). **INTERESTS:** travel; heritage preservation. **MISC:** in conjunction with City of St. John's & the Federation of Canadian Municipalities, served as Cdn Advisor to the City of Accra, Ghana, 1994 & 1995. **COMMENT:** *"Dedicated to the preservation of Newfoundland's and Canada's archival heritage. Major career achievement: the design and implementation of an Archives and Records Management program for the City of St. John's."*

Miller, Jean, R.N., B.Sc.N., M.A. ■ ⊕ 🖎
Coordinator, Gerontology Certificate Program, Centre for Health Studies, MOUNT ROYAL COLLEGE, 3223 Kenmare Cres. SW, Calgary, AB T3E 4R4 (403) 240-6816, EMAIL jmiller@mt.royal.ab.ca. President, CANADIAN GERONTOLOGY NURSING ASSOCIATION. Born Kelvington, Sask. 1945. m. Leighton. 1 ch. April. **EDUC:** Univ. of Saskatchewan, R.N.(Nursing) 1967, B.Sc.N.(Nursing) 1968; Univ. of Calgary, M.A.(Educ.) 1987; Univ. of Alberta, Ph.D. current. **CAREER:** Staff Nurse, Home Care Liaison, Victorian Order of Nurses, 1968-71, 1972-74; Instructor & Coord., Diploma Nursing Program, Mount Royal Coll., 1974-86; Coord. & Instructor, Gerontology Certificate Program, 1987 to date. **SELECTED PUBLICATIONS:** numerous papers & articles in refereed journals, incl. "Gerontological nursing education for Alberta nurses," with S. Hirst (*Alberta Association of Registered Nurses Newsletter*, (49)9, 1993); "Nurses in pursuit of a gerontology certificate," with S. Hirst (*The Canadian Geronotolgical Nurse* (9)5, 1992); "Women and Aging: An inter-related experience," with S. Hirst (*AGNA Newsletter* (2)1, 1992; various reports, research projects, presentations & workshops. **AFFIL:** Canadian Gerontological Nursing Association (Pres.); Alberta Council on Aging (Bd.); Alberta Gerontological Nursing Association (Sec., South Central Chapter 1991-93); Alberta Association on Gerontology (Bd. 1986-89) Alberta Association of Registered Nurses; Association for Gerontology in Higher Education (Institutional Rep.); Canadian Association on Gerontology; Canadian Nurses' Association; Canadian Nurses' Foundation; Calgary Aquabelles Swimming Club (Grievance Committee Mbr.; Parent Volunteer); Woodcliff United Church. **HONS:** nominee, Distinguished Fac. Award, 1984, 1990, 1991; Canadian Nurses' Foundation Scholarship, 1995-96, 1996-97. **MISC:** currently Ph.D. student **COMMENT:** *"I am a nurse educator with extensive involvement in gerontological nursing. I am on study leave from my position as coordinator of a successful gerontology program. As well, I am President of the Canadian Gerontogical Nursing Association."*

Miller, Mary Jane, B.A., M.A., Ph.D. 🖎 ⊗ 🖂
Professor, Department of Film Studies, BROCK UNIVERSITY, St. Catharines, ON L2S 3A1 (905) 688-5530, ext. 3584, FAX 682-9020, EMAIL mjmiller@spartan.ac.brocku.ca. Born Beamsville, Ont. 1941. m. Dr. Jack Miller. **EDUC:** Univ. of Toronto, B.A.(English) 1963, M.A.(English) 1964; Univ. of Birmingham, UK, Ph.D.(Drama) 1973. **CAREER:** Lecturer, Univ. of Western Ontario, 1964-66; Asst. to Assoc. to Full Prof. in Drama Lit., & Radio & TV

Drama, Dept. of Film Studies, Brock Univ., 1968 to date; Chair of Dept., 1975-79, 1988-89. **SELECTED PUBLICATIONS:** various articles on contemporary plays, radio & TV drama; *Turn Up the Contrast: CBC Television Drama Since 1952* (UBC Press/CBC, 1987); *Rewind & Search: Makers and Decision Makers of CBC TV Drama* (McGill/Queen's Univ. Press, 1996). **AFFIL:** Association for the Study of Canadian Radio & Television (Co-Founder & Pres.); Association of Canadian Theatre History; Association of Canadian Studies; Canadian Communications Association; Concordia Univ. Centre for Broadcast Studies (Fellow). **HONS:** Hon. Award for Scholarship, ASCRT/ACRTC. **INTERESTS:** theatre; science fiction; gardening; walking; music; travel. **MISC:** various SSHRC grants; Canada Council Research Grant, 1973-74. **COMMENT:** *"I love teaching. I enjoy research and writing about both plays, and radio and television dramas–the process of production and the ethics and policy decisions which shape them. We love to travel to unusual places, food of all kinds, the family cottage and the endless surprises of gardening–and owning cats. I am a life-long member of the Presbyterian Church."*

Miller, Sherry ✪ 📺 🎭

Actor. Born Ponoka, Alta. 1955. sep. 3 ch. Shanda Bezic, Carlyn Bezic, McKenzie Bezic. **SELECTED CREDITS:** Simone, *Bedfull of Foreigners*, Stage West Edmonton; Fran, *The Only Game in Town*, Variety Theatre; Lead, *Rent-A Kid*, Viacom Prods.; Lead, *E.N.G.*, CTV/Alliance; Principal, *Johnny Mnemonic*, 20th Century Fox; Lead, *Sabrina The Teenage Witch* (series), Showtime; regular, *FX: The Series*, CTV, syndicated. **AFFIL:** Easter Seal Society (M.C. of Gala Ball 1991-93). **HONS:** nominated, Best Supporting Actress in a Dramatic Series, Gemini Awards, 1990, 1991. **COMMENT:** *"I guess I'm proudest of having made a living doing what I love without having to leave the country I love. Canada is my home and my children's home, and I endeavour to keep it that way."*

Millichamp, Barbara, B.A.,M.B.A., C.F.A. $

Vice-President and Director, First Marathon Securities Limited, 2 First Canadian Place, Ste. 3200, Box 21, Toronto, ON M5X 1J9 (416) 869-6672, FAX 869-3277. **EDUC:** Univ. of Toronto, B.A., 1976, M.B.A. 1980; Chartered Financial Analyst (C.F.A.) 1984. **CAREER:** Research Analyst, Pitfield Mackay Ross, 1978-79; Research Analyst, First Marathon Securities Limited, 1979-84; Corp. Fin., 1984 to date. **INTERESTS:** dressage; piano.

Milligan, Dianne, B.A. ■ ☺ ✪

Executive Director, Dance Nova Scotia, 1809 Barrington St., Ste. 901, Halifax, NS B3J 3K8 (902) 422-1749, FAX 422-0881, EMAIL dance@fox.nstn.ca. Born Halifax 1952. m. Tim Milligan. 1 ch. Alexiis. **EDUC:** Banff Centre for the Arts, Certificate (Arts Admin.) 1982; Mount St. Vincent Univ., B.A.(English) 1990. **CAREER:** actress, 1972-75; Registrar/Bus. Mgr, Halifax Dance, 1977-82; Co. Mgr, Nova Dance Theatre, 1983-84; Exec. Dir., Dance Nova Scotia, 1985 to date. **SELECTED PUBLICATIONS:** *Four on the Floor: A Guide to Teaching Cape Breton Square Sets in Public Schools*, with others; *Make Your Dancing Safe and Strong*. **AFFIL:** Association of Cultural Executives (Bd. 1992-93); Dance in Canada Association (Bd. of Dir. 1982-84); Partnerships in Arts Education (Steering Committee 1993-94). **INTERESTS:** dance; music; theatre; literature; cross-country skiing; hiking. **COMMENT:** *"I see myself as a catalyst, bringing experts with like interests together and providing the administrative support needed to make things happen."*

Millman-Floyd, Cynthia, A.R.C.T. 🎓 ✪

Professor, Department of Music, University of Ottawa, 50 University, Ottawa, ON K1N 6N5 (613) 562-5800, ext. 3418, FAX 562-5140. Born Toronto 1938. m. Rowland Winslow Floyd. 1 ch. Margaret Elise. **EDUC:** Royal Conservatory of Toronto, A.R.C.T. 1958; State Academy for Music & the Performing Arts, Vienna, Pedagogical Dipl. 1963, Concert Dipl. 1968. **CAREER:** private piano teacher & coach; lecturer, Univ. of Ottawa, 1970-73; Asst. Prof., 1973-80; Assoc. Prof., 1980-94; Prof., 1994 to date; soloist & chamber musician; fortepianist. **SELECTED CREDITS:** recital, National Gallery, Ottawa, May 5, 1985; recital, 18th Century Keyboard Sonatas, National Museum of Natural Sciences, Ottawa, Oct. 17, 1986; recital with Ingemar Korjus & Sandra Graham, Tianjin, China, May 18, 1988; premiere performance with Sandra Graham of Steven Gellman's "So that you may hear me," Univ. of Ottawa, broadcast by CBC, Jan. 10, 1992; numerous other concerts & recitals. **SELECTED PUBLICATIONS:** various lectures and papers. **AFFIL:** Canadian University Music Society; American Federation of Musicians. **HONS:** Graduating Prize, State Academy for Music & the Performing Arts, Vienna, 1968; Merit Award, Univ. of Ottawa, 1978. **INTERESTS:** reading; walking; swimming. **MISC:** grant recipient; visiting foreign expert, Conservatory of Music, Tianjin, China, 1988; mbr., numerous award & competition juries; *Cana-*

dian Who's Who; American Keyboard Artists; Canadian Encyclopedia of Music.

Mills, Claire, B.Sc.N.,LL.B. Ⓔ ⊕
Executive Director, ALBERTA LONG TERM CARE ASSOCIATION, 10004 - 104th Ave., Ste. 910, Edmonton, AB T5J 0K1 (403) 421-1137, FAX 426-0479. Born New Waterford, N.S. 1949. m. Joe. 3 ch. Michael, Lindsay, Sheena. EDUC: St. Francis Xavier Univ., B.Sc.N.(Nursing) 1971; Univ. of Calgary, LL.B. 1989. BAR: Alta., 1992. CAREER: Staff Nurse, Medicine, Intensive Care Unit, Halifax Infirmary Hospital, 1971-73; Acting Dir. of Nursing, Mineral Springs Hospital, Banff, Alta., 1974; Instructor, Sch. of Nursing, Foothills Hospital, Calgary, 1975-81; Instructor, Nursing Program, Mount Royal Coll., Calgary, 1981-83; Nursing Instructor, Rural Hospital Program for Sr. Students, Foothills Sch. of Nursing, 1984-86; Coord., Home Care Div., Calgary Health Services, 1986-93; articling student, Ebbert and Company, Barristers & Solicitors, 1991-93; Exec. Dir., Alberta Long Term Care Association, 1993 to date. AFFIL: Alberta Association of Registered Nurses; Canadian Nurses' Association; Canadian Bar Association; Canadian Society of Association Executives. COMMENT: *"I am intensely aware of the paradigm shift in health care away from a provider-driven focus to a consumer-driven model. This shift is presenting many challenges to me, the association and the industry. Tracking the issues emerging in the external environment and predicting their potential impact on members of our association is, in essence, my present endeavour."*

Mills, Jacqueline, B.A.,LL.B. ⚖
Partner, LANG MICHENER, 181 Bay St., Ste. 2500, P.O. Box 747, Toronto, ON M5J 2T7 (416) 307-4002, FAX 365-1719. Born Much Wenlock, UK (home of the modern Olympic games) 1956. m. James Musgrove. 2 ch. Alex, Max. EDUC: Queen's Univ., B.A.(Econ.) 1979, LL.B. 1984. BAR: Ont., 1986. CAREER: articling student, Lang Michener; Assoc., Lang Michener, 1986-91; Ptnr, Lang Michener, 1991 to date; appointed as a Dispute Resolution Officer of the Ont. Court (Gen. Div.), two-yr. term, 1996-98. SELECTED PUBLICATIONS: contributor to *The Financial Litigation Review,* 1987-89; *Ontario Family Law Guide,* ed. (CCH, 1996); "Structuring the Equalization Payment," co-authors A. Burke Doran & Marni Whitaker (Canadian Bar Association - Ontario, Annual Institute on Continuing Legal Educ., 1987); "Vocational Assessments: Will they Work for You?" (Canadian Bar Association, Institute of Continuing Legal Educ., 1997); "Limitation Periods in Family Law," co-

author A. Burke Doran (*Family Law,* 1(2) 1994); "Property Tracing Rules Under the Family Law Act are Tricky to Apply (Part I)," co-author A. Burke Doran & Marni Whitaker (*Family Law,* 1(3) 1995); "Tax Impact of New Support Guidelines Benefits Government. But Problems Remain," co-author Marni Whitaker (*The Lawyers Weekly,* 16(2) 1996) AFFIL: Canadian Bar Association (Ontario) (Exec. mbr., Family Law Section); County of York Law Association; Women's Law Association; Advocates' Society. INTERESTS: my children; reading; swimming; quilting. MISC: taught Family Law, Bar Admission Course, 1988-92; certified as a Specialist in Family Law, Law Society; Chair, "Matrimonial Homes Revisited," Canadian Bar Association, Ont. dinner meeting, Sept. 16, 1992; Chair, "Following the Rules," Canadian Bar Association, Ont. dinner meeting, March 25, 1996.

Mills, Josephine, MCSP ■■ ♡ ⓟ ⊕
Executive Director, DOWN SYNDROME RESEARCH FOUNDATION (charitable organization; info., research & educ.), 3580 Slocan St., Vancouver, BC V5M 3E8 (604) 431-9694, FAX 431-9248, EMAIL josephin@sfu.ca. Coordinator, INTERNATIONAL DOWN SYNDROME FEDERATION. Born Stoke on Trent, UK 1942. m. Michael D. Mills. 4 ch. Damien, Simon, Catherine, Rachel. EDUC: Middlesex Hospital, London, UK, MCSP (Physiotherapy) 1964. CAREER: Sr. Physiotherapist, Alberta Children's Hospital, Calgary; founder & Exec. Dir., Canadian Down Syndrome Society; co-founder & Exec. Dir., Down Syndrome Research Foundation; Bd. mbr. & Coord., International Down Sydrome Federation, 1994 to date. SELECTED PUBLICATIONS: *Adults with Down Syndrome* (1993). AFFIL: Simon Fraser Univ. (Dept. of Kinesiology); Institute for Human Factors & Interface Technology. HONS: recognition: for 10 yrs.' svc., from Alberta Children's Hospital; for svc., from Ups and Downs Calgary; for svc., from Canadian Down Syndrome Society. INTERESTS: sailing; walking; classical music; reading. COMMENT: *"A concerned individual who has always wanted to help the underdog. Family of most importance and supported by a close family wanted to help others, forming parent support groups, organizing conferences to inform and encourage, and finally giving leadership with the development of organization to meet current needs."*

Milne, Rose Eleanor ⊗
Sculptor. 229 Powell Ave., Ottawa, ON K1S 2A4, FAX (613) 234-4783. Born Saint John 1925. EDUC: Montreal Museum Sch. of Fine Art/McGill Univ. Sch. of Medicine, Certificate

(Lab. Anatomy) 1946; London County Council Coll. of Graphic Art, UK, Certificate (Wood Engraving) 1947; École des Beaux Arts, Montreal, Certificate (Wood Engraving & Bookbinding/Sculpture) 1949; Univ. of Syracuse, NY, Certificate (Monumental Sculpture) 1952. CAREER: Sculptor to the Fed. Gov't of Canada, retired 1993. AFFIL: Royal Canadian Academy of Arts (elected mbr.). HONS: named to the Order of Canada; D.Litt.(hon. causa), Carleton Univ.; D.Let.(hon. causa), Windsor Univ.; LL.D.(hon. causa), Queen's Univ.; D.Humanities(hon. causa), York Univ.

Milot, Louise ■ ■   ◴ 📚
Vice-rectrice aux études, UNIVERSITÉ LAVAL, Québec, QC G1K 7P4 (418) 656-2591, FAX 656-3300. Born 1942. m. 1 ch. EDUC: Univ. Laval, L.ès. L. 1968, M.A. 1972; Univ. de Paris VIII-Vincenne, Doctorat 1976. CAREER: Directrice adjointe, Dépt. des littératures, 1977-80; Directrice, *la Revue Études littéraires*, 1982-86; Directrice par intérim, Dépt. des littératures, 1985-86; Prof. titulaire depuis 1986; Vice-doyenne aux ressources de la Fac. des lettres, 1986-88; Vice-rectrice aux études, 1992- SELECTED PUBLICATIONS: 11 volumes en collaboration; 20 articles; 27 compte rendus critiques; 14, la Revue *Études littéraires publiés*. AFFIL: la Conférence des recteurs et des principaux des universités du Québec (Prés., Comité des vice-recteurs aux affaires académiques 1993-96); le Centre hospitalier universitaire de Québec (Comité d'implantation 1995-96; Conseil d'admin. provisoire 1996-); la Régie régionale de la santé et des services sociaux de Québec (Conseil d'admin. 1995-); Salon du livre de Québec (Prés. & mbr. du jury Prix Robert-Cliche 1991-92); Établissement de nouveaux chercheurs (Comité de programme 1990-91); la revue *Protée* (Comité de rédaction 1990); Conseil de recherches en sciences humaines du Canada (Comité d'éval. des Grandes subventions 1989-90).

Milway, Katie, Smith, B.A.,M.A., M.B.A. ⓒ 🔱
Consultant, BAIN & COMPANY CANADA, 162 Cumberland St., Ste. 300, Toronto, ON M5R 3N6 (416) 929-1888, FAX 929-3470. Born Conn. 1960. m. Michael D.S. Milway. 1 ch. EDUC: Stanford Univ., B.A.(English) 1982; Free Univ. of Brussels, M.A.(Int'l Rel'ns) 1985; European Institute of Business Administration, France, M.B.A. 1993. CAREER: Admin. Trainee, European Communities Commission, Brussels, 1984-85; Copy Ed., *The Wall Street Journal*, Brussels, 1985-86; Bus. Reporter, *The Gazette*, Montreal, 1986-87; Sr. Research Asst. to the Dean, John F. Kennedy Sch., Harvard

Univ., 1987-89; Int'l Program Coord., Food for The Hungry International, 1989-92; Consultant, World Vision International, 1993; Consultant, Bain & Company International, 1994 to date. SELECTED PUBLICATIONS: *Growing Our Future: Food Security and the Environment*, ed. with T. Yamamori (West Hartford, Conn.: Kumarian Press, 1992); *Future Value: Enterprise and Sustainable Development*, ed. with O. Cadot & M. Milway (Fontainebleu, France: INSEAD Press, 1993); *The Human Farm: A Tale of Changing Lives and Changing Lands* (West Hartford: Kumarian Press, 1994); articles in newpapers & magazines incl. *New York Times & Time*; various other publications. EDIT: Ed., *Inside Story*, newsletter, 1986-87; Ed., Opinions Section, *Stanford Daily*, 1981-82. AFFIL: Toronto Network for Women in Business & Development, Toronto (Founder); European Institute of Business Administration International Development Organization, Fountainebleau (Co-Founder). HONS: Rotary International Foundation Journalism Scholarship, 1993; European Community Administrative Trainee Fellowship, 1984; Rotary International Foundation Grad. Scholarship, 1983; Stanford Cap & Gown Honor Society, 1981-82.

Minard, Kathryn, Christine, B.A. ■ ■ ✘ ⓒ
Principal and President, CONTEMPORARY FINE ART SERVICES INC., (corp. art collection mgmt & fine art appraisal), 413 Dundas St. E., Toronto, ON M5A 2A9 (416) 366-9770, FAX 366-8541, EMAIL 75263.2530@compuserve.com. EDUC: York Univ., B.A.(Hons., Fine Art Hist.) 1975; American Society of Appraisers, Personal Property Appraisal, Principles of Valuation I-IV 1993-95, Uniform Standards of Professional Appraisal Practice Certificate 1995; International Society of Appraisers, Personal Property Program, Cdn Core Courses 101, 102, 103 1996. CAREER: Consultant, Fine Art Consultants of Canada Ltd., 1976-80; Co-founder, Contemporary Fine Art Services Inc., 1981. AFFIL: International Society of Appraisers (Accredited Mbr.); American Society of Appraisers (Candidate Mbr.); The Arts & Letters Club of Toronto. MISC: has served as juror, several art exhibitions, & taken part in several conferences/seminars re corp. art collecting.

Minna, Maria, B.A.,M.P. ■ ✿
Member of Parliament (Beaches-Woodbine), GOVERNMENT OF CANADA, Confederation Building, Rm. 784, Ottawa, ON K1A 0A6 (613) 992-2115, FAX 996-7942. Born Italy 1948. m. Robert MacBain. 2 ch. EDUC: Univ. of Toronto, B.A.(Soc.) 1976. CAREER: Chair,

Commission on Ontario Workers' Compensation Bd.; Dir., National Council of Welfare; Pres., COSTI Immigrant Svcs; Pres., Nat'l Congress of Italian Canadians; M.P. (Beaches-Woodbine), Gov't of Canada; Parliamentary Sec. to Min. of Citizenship & Immigration.

Mirabelli, Marilyn, B.A.,B.A.A. $

President, EXCELLENCE IN/EN COMMUNICATION, 115 Alcina Ave., Toronto, ON M6G 2E7 (416) 658-5518, FAX 658-8032. EDUC: McGill Univ., B.A. 1969; Ryerson Polytechnic Institute, B.A.A.(Journalism) 1984. CAREER: Flight Attendant, Air Canada, 1969-84; Min. Asst., Ottawa, 1984-89; Pres., Excellence in/en Communication, 1990 to date. AFFIL: Girl Guides of Canada (Nat'l Council); McGill Society of Toronto (Dir.); Alpha Omicron Pi International Sorority; The Strategic Leadership Forum; Board of Trade of Metropolitan Toronto; Canadian Club of Toronto (Bd.). HONS: Canada 125 Medal.

Mirkopoulos, Carole Rose, B.Sc., M.Ed. ■ ⊕ ⦿

President, C.R.M. ASSOCIATES, 198 Old Bloomington Rd., Aurora, ON L4G 3G8 (905) 773-2392, FAX 773-6714. Born Sudbury, Ont. 1954. m. Steve. 2 ch. EDUC: Univ. of Toronto, B.Sc.(Occupational Therapy) 1975, M.Ed.(Measurement & Evaluation) 1981. CAREER: Occupational Therapist, York County Hospital, Newmarket, Ont., 1975-77; Occupational Therapist, Addiction Research Foundation, 1977-79; Pres., Ontario Society of Occupational Therapists, 1980-82; Consultant & Private Ptnr, Aurora, Ont., 1981-85; Exec. Dir., Ontario Society of Occupational Therapists, 1983-85; Pres., C.R.M. Associates, Aurora, Ont., 1986 to date; Pres., Canadian Association of Occupational Therapists, 1992-94. AFFIL: Healthy Communities Coalition, York Reg.; York Reg. District Health Council (Health Promo. Committee); Hellenic-Canadian Community of York Reg. (Dir., Youth Advisor); Coalition for Prevention of Falls in Seniors, York Reg. INTERESTS: choir; skiing; dancing; reading; gardening. COMMENT: "As an active member of the community of York Region, I am interested in creating a healthy community for my children, family and friends to live in. As an occupational therapist, I am working to optimize the ability of my clients to function as independently as possible in the living situation of their choice, in the prevention of injury, and the promotion of well-being and following illness or injury."

Mironowicz, Maria ⍁ /

Executive Producer, CBC NEWSWORLD, 205 Wellington St. W., Toronto, ON M5V 3G7 (416) 205-2409, FAX 205-2516. Born Jerusalem, Palestine 1947. m. David Getz. 1 ch. EDUC: Carleton Univ., Journalism 1969. CAREER: Reporter, CBOT, CBC Ottawa, Ed. & Writer, Nat'l News, CBC TV; Nat'l Reporter, News, CBC TV; Supervising Prod., *Canada A.M.*; Nat'l Reporter, CTV News; Daily Ed., *Midday*, CBC TV; *Quick Turnaround* Documentary Ed., *The Journal*, CBC; Sr. Prod., *Marketplace*, CBC; Exec. Prod., CBC Newsworld Weekends.

Mirosh, The Hon. Diane, R.N.,M.L.A. ♣ ⦿

Member of the Legislative Assembly (Calgary-Glenmore) and Minister Responsible for Science and Research, GOVERNMENT OF ALBERTA, 423 Legislature Building, Edmonton, AB T5K 2B6 (403) 427-2294, FAX 422-5366. Born Edmonton. EDUC: Royal Alexandra Sch. of Nursing, R.N. CAREER: Intensive Care Nurse, Royal Alexandra Hospital, Edmonton, & Rockyview Hospital, Calgary; owner & operator, Access Health; M.L.A. (Calgary-Glenmore), 1986 to date; numerous caucus committees, Progressive Conservative Party of Alberta; Min. of Community Dev., 1992-93; Min. Without Portfolio responsible for Alberta Health Planning Secretariat & the Alberta Alcohol & Drug Abuse Commission, 1993; Min. Without Portfolio responsible for Alberta Opportunity Company, Alberta Research Council & Western Econ. Partnership Agreements, 1993-94; Min. Responsible for Science & Research, 1994 to date. SELECTED PUBLICATIONS: *Starting Points: Recommendations for Creating a More Accountable and Affordable Health System*, co-author (Alberta Health Planning Secretariat); *A New Vision for Long-Term Care: Meeting the Need*, co-author (Caucus Committee on Econ. Affairs & Long Term Care, P.C. Party of Alberta). AFFIL: P.C. Party of Alberta. COMMENT: "As Minister Responsible for Science and Research, she will be responsible for a Science and Research Authority. The Authority is led by a Board of Management, reporting directly to the Minister."

Misener, Adeline, B.H.Sc.,M.Ed. $

President, JOB ORIENTED TRAINING INC., 60 Bishop Dr., Fredericton, NB E3C 1B2 (506) 458-1351, FAX 453-7060, EMAIL jotinc@nbnet.nb.ca, internet: http://www.jot.nb.ca. Born Ireland 1946. m. Dr. Gerald Misener. 3 ch. Carmen, Veronica, Becky. EDUC: Univ. of Guelph, B.H.Sc.(Home & Family Studies) 1968; Univ. of New Brunswick, M.Ed.(Adult Educ.) 1985. CAREER: various positions: teacher, Nutrition Consultant, Research Asst., to 1989; Pres., Job Oriented

Training Inc. (JOT), 1989 to date. **DIRECTOR:** Incutech; GlobeTec. **AFFIL:** N.B. Information Technology Alliance; N.B. Training Industry; Advisory Committee for the Information Highway for N.B.; N.B. Community Coll. Curriculum Task Force; IT Event '95 (Bd.); Software Publishers' Association; Fredericton Chamber of Commerce; Scouts Canada; N.B. Home Economics Association; St. Andrew's Presbyterian Church; Int'l Student Organization, Univ. of Illinois (Program Coord.). **HONS:** Reg'l Finalist, Canadian Woman Entrepreneur of the Year, 1993, 1994, 1995; N.B. Woman Entrepreneur of the Year, 1993; Finalist, Ernst & Young Entrepreneur of the Year, 1994, 1995; Atlantic Canada Woman Entrepreneur of the Year, 1994, 1995. **INTERESTS:** gardening; interior design; piano; theatre. **COMMENT:** *"JOT is a full service company, that offers performance based results in corporate consultation, training, multimedia production and computer network application. The company's drive is to increase efficiency by helping people add value to their performance and by assisting with the development of employee expertise."*

Misner, Judy ♡ ⊕ ☝
Founder and President, PSORIASIS SOCIETY OF CANADA, National Office, Box 25015, Halifax, NS B3M 4H4 (902) 443-8680, FAX (902) 457-1664. Born Halifax 1940. m. Herbert. 3 ch. Stephen, Darren, Charmaine. **EDUC:** Dalhousie Univ. **CAREER:** medical sec., 20 yrs.; nurse, various hospitals & doctors' offices, 1975-83; Founder & Pres., Psoriasis Society of Canada, 1983 to date. **SELECTED PUBLICATIONS:** *A Handbook: A Guide to Understanding Psoriasis* (Halifax: Psoriasis Society of Canada); a cookbook for fundraising. **EDIT:** Ed., Psoriasis Society of Canada Newsletter, to date. **AFFIL:** Psoriasis Society of Canada (Pres.). **HONS:** Volunteer of the Year, City of Halifax, 1990; Canada Volunteer Award, Gov't of Canada, 1994. **INTERESTS:** providing growth & dev. for the Psoriasis Society of Canada; forming support groups in each province to assist those who have psoriasis. **COMMENT:** *"I enjoy people very much and this was one reason I wanted to be a nurse. My greatest achievement was having three children and next was forming the first national psoriasis organization in Canada 12 years ago. I have not missed one day of working for the cause, in the knowledge that I have made a difference in people's lives so they know they are very important people to the Psoriasis Society of Canada."*

Mitchell, Adrienne, B.A.A. 📺 ✪
Filmmaker, BACK ALLEY FILM PRODUCTIONS, 110 Spadina Ave., Ste. 800, Toronto, ON M5V 2K4 FAX (416) 703-8825. Born Sudbury, Ont. 1960. m. **EDUC:** Ryerson Polytechnic Univ., B.A.A.(Motion Picture Studies). **CAREER:** filmmaker, Back Alley Film Productions, 1989 to date. **SELECTED CREDITS:** *No Place Like Home* (1986); *Close Your Eyes and Think of England* (1986); *Life Revolution* (1987); *Checkpoint Charlie* (1985); *Heart of the Forest* (1988); *Ken Dryden's Home Game* (1989); *Talk 16* (1991); *Lawn and Order* (1991). **AFFIL:** Toronto Women in Film & Video; Academy of Canadian Film. **HONS:** Honourable Mention (*Heart of the Forest*), Children's Film Festival, Adelaide, Australia, 1988; Best Documentary (*Talk 16*), Florida Film Festival, 1991; Special Jury Prize (*Talk 16*), Cinema du Reel, France, 1991; Special Jury Prize (*Talk 16*), San Francisco Festival, 1991; Silver Plaque Award (*Lawn and Order*), Chicago Film Festival, 1994; Jury Award (*Lawn and Order*), Yorkton Film Festival, 1994. **COMMENT:** *"Adrienne Mitchell is an award-winning producer, director and writer of highly original Canadian films. In 1989, she joined forces with Janis Lundman to create Back Alley Film Productions Ltd."*

Mitchell, Camille ■■ $
Vice-President, INTERCONTINENTAL PACKERS, LTD., P.O. Box 850, Saskatoon, SK S7K 3V4 (306) 382-4366, FAX 931-4315. Born Santa Monica. **EDUC:** L'Institut Montesano, Diplôme 2e degré; Central Sch., London, England. **AFFIL:** National Theatre Sch. of Canada, Montreal (Bd. of Gov.). **HONS:** Jessie Richardson Award.

Mitchell, Carol R., B.A.,M.B.A. ■■ $
Senior Vice-President and Director, MIDLAND WALWYN INC., (investment dealer), BCE Place, 181 Bay St., Ste. 500, Toronto, ON M5J 2V8 (416) 369-3902, FAX 369-7508, EMAIL carol.mitchell@midwal.ca. Born Toronto 1956. m. Richard Venn. 1 ch. Madeleine Venn-Mitchell. **EDUC:** York Univ., B.A.(Phys. Ed.) 1979; McMaster Univ., M.B.A.(Int'l Fin.) 1982; Grade II (Hons.), Piano Theory; Grade V Piano. **CAREER:** VP, Retail Sales, Wood Gundy, 1982-87; Sr. VP & Dir., Equity, Institutional Sales, Midland Walwyn, 1987 to date. **INTERESTS:** music; dance; reading; canoeing; skiing; gymnastics; jogging; tennis; swimming; piano. **COMMENT:** *"I am blessed with a wonderful family, great friends and a career that is demanding and stressful, but highly rewarding. We have a beautiful escape for weekends in the country."*

Mitchell, Gay, B.A.,M.B.A.,F.I.C.B. $
Executive Vice-President, Human Resources,

ROYAL BANK OF CANADA, Royal Bank Plaza, N. Tower, 200 Bay St., 11th Fl., Toronto, ON M5J 2J5 (416) 955-5806. Born Port Credit, Ont. m. Archie McIntosh. 2 ch. EDUC: Queen's Univ., B.A.(Econ,) 1984; Univ. of Alberta, M.B.A.(Bus.Policy/Fin.) 1986. CAREER: various positions in Retail Bnkg, Royal Bank, 1974-79; Personnel Officer, Ont. District, 1978-80; Asst. Mgr, Admin., 1980-82; Acct Mgr, Corp. Bnkg, 1982-89; Head Office Corp. Lending/Head Office, Special Loans Group, 1989-90; Mgr, Corp. Bnkg Centre, 1990-93; VP, Head Office, Lending, Bus. Bnkg, 1993; VP, Bus. Bnkg, Ont. District, 1994-96; Exec. VP, Hum. Res., 1996 to date. AFFIL: Institute of Canadian Bankers (Fellow; Bd. of Gov.); Ontario Centre for Materials Research (Dir.); Humber Coll. (Gov.; Chair, Fin. Committee; Chair, Audit Committee); Fac. of Bus., Univ. of Alberta (Bus. Advisory Council); Canadian Bankers Association (Hum. Res. Committee); Conference Board of Canada (Hum. Res. Committee). INTERESTS: reading; boating; skiing.

Mitchell, Johanna ■ Ⓢ
Chairwoman of the Board, INTERCONTINENTAL PACKERS LIMITED, Box 850, Saskatoon, SK S7K 3V4 (306) 382-2210, FAX 931-4315. Born Recklinghausen, Germany 1917. d. 3 ch. EDUC: Reinhardt Seminar, Vienna, Language 1941; bus. schooling, N.Y., 1943-45. CAREER: Pres., Intercontinental Packers Limited, 1970; Chair of the Bd., 1976 to date. AFFIL: Riviera Country Club; Riverside Golf & Country Club; Saskatoon Board of Trade; Mendel Art Gallery (Hon. Chrm). HONS: Sask. finalist for Canadian Woman Entrepreneur of the Year Award (for lifetime achievement), 1992. INTERESTS: writing; art collecting; cattle breeding; swimming; travelling. COMMENT: *"My father, F.S. Mendel, founded Intercontinental Packers Ltd. in 1940. He appointed me President of the company in 1970. I was appointed Chairwoman in 1976 and currently hold that position."*

Mitchell, Jone, B.A.(Hons.),C.F.R.E. Ⓢ
Director of Alumni, Development, and Public Relations, UNIVERSITY OF KING'S COLLEGE, 6350 Coburg Rd., Halifax, NS B3H 2A1 (902) 422-1271, ext. 129, FAX 423-3357, EMAIL jmitchel@kilcom1.ucis.dal.ca. Born Toronto 1950. m. Charles Edwards. 2 ch. Lisa, Jeffrey. EDUC: Carleton Univ., B.A.(Hons., Geography) 1973. CAREER: Dir. of Alumni, Dev. & Public Rel'ns, Univ. of King's Coll. AFFIL: Canadian Cancer Society (Fundraising Coord., N.S. Div.); C.S.F.R.E. (C.F.R.E.; Treas.; various exec. positions, N.S. chapter); C.A.S.E.; C.C.A.E.; N.S.

Gymnastics Association (Pres. 1992-94). INTERESTS: skiing; golfing; reading; running

Mitchell, Joni • ♥ ❀ 🎵
Singer and Songwriter. Born Ft. McLeod, Alta. 1943. SELECTED CREDITS: *Song to a Seagull*; *Clouds*; *Ladies of the Canyon*; *Blue*; *For the Roses*; *Court and Spark*; *Miles of Aisles*; *The Hissing of Summer Lawns*; *Hejira*; *Don Juan's Reckless Daughter*; *Mingus*; *Shadows and Light*; *Wild Things Run Fast*; *Dog Eat Dog*; *Chalk Mark in a Rainstorm*; *Night Ride Home*; *Turbulent Indigo*; *Joni Mitchell Hits & Joni Mitchell Misses*. HONS: Female Vocalist of the Year, Juno Awards, 1976; Jazz Album of the Year & Rock-Blues Album of the Year (*Mingus*), *Downbeat* Magazine, 1979; Juno award for special achievement, 1981; Century Award, *Billboard* Magazine, 1995; Polar Music Prize, Stig Anderson Music Prize Fund, The Royal Swedish Academy of Music, 1996; Best Pop Album, *Mood Indigo*, & Best Album Packaging, Grammy Awards, 1996; Best Performance in a Performing Arts Program or Special, *Intimate & Interactive with Joni Mitchell* (MuchMusic), Gemini Awards, 1996; Orville H. Gibson Award; Gov. General's Performing Arts Award, 1996; to be inducted into the Rock & Roll Hall of Fame, 1996.

Mitchell, Margaret T., A.A.,B.A. Ⓢ
President, THE THOMAS-MITCHELL ASSOCIATES INC., 18A Hazelton Ave., Toronto, ON M5R 2E2 (416) 926-1860, FAX 960-3921. Born Baltimore, Md. 1946. d. 1 ch. Jeb. EDUC: Centenary Coll. for Women, A.A., Liberal Arts, 1966; Univ. of Kentucky, B.A., 1969. CAREER: Assoc., E.L. Shore & Associates, 1975-79; Ptnr, The Caldwell Partners, 1979-82; Pres., The Thomas-Mitchell Associates, 1982 to date; research, The Nat'l Geographic Society. SELECTED PUBLICATIONS: Contributing Ed. for Supplement "A Salute to the New Canadian Woman" (*Business Quarterly* Spring 1984); "Profile of the Canadian Woman Director" (*Business Quarterly* Spring 1984). COMMENT: *"Executive search firm specializing in director recruitment for Canadian boards; particular emphasis on the recruitment of women directors."*

Mitchelson, The Hon. Bonnie, R.N., M.L.A. ✦
Minister of Family Services, GOVERNMENT OF MANITOBA, Legislative Building, Rm. 357, Winnipeg, MB R3C 0V8 (204) 945-4173, FAX (204) 945-5149. Born Winnipeg 1947. m. Don. 2 ch. EDUC: Health Sciences Centre Sch. of Nursing, R.N. 1968, Certificate(Intensive Care Nursing) 1969. CAREER: M.L.A. (River

East), Prov. of Man., 1986 to date; Min. of Culture, Heritage & Recreation/Min. Responsible for Lotteries, 1988-93; Min. Responsible for Multiculturalism, Citizenship, & the Status of Women, 1990-93; Min. of Family Svcs, 1993 to date. AFFIL: Manitoba Heart Foundation.

Mitchinson, Wendy, B.A.,M.A., Ph.D. ⌂ 📖 ♻
Professor of History, Department of History, UNIVERSITY OF WATERLOO, Waterloo, ON N2L 3G1. Born Hamilton, Ont. 1947. m. Rex Lingwood. EDUC: York Univ., B.A.(Hist.) 1970, M.A.(Hist.) 1971, Ph.D.(Hist.) 1977. CAREER: Lecturer & Asst. Prof., Mount Saint Vincent Univ., 1975-77; Asst. to Assoc. Prof., Univ. of Windsor, 1977-85; Assoc. to Full Prof., Univ. of Waterloo, 1985 to date. SELECTED PUBLICATIONS: *The Nature of Their Bodies: Women and Their Doctors in Victorian Canada* (Toronto: Univ. of Toronto Press, 1991); *Canadian Women: A Reader*, co-ed. (Toronto: Harcourt Brace Jovanovich, 1996); *Canadian Women: A History*, co-author (Toronto: Harcourt Brace Jovanovich, 1988; 2nd. ed., 1996); *Essays in Canadian Medical History*, co-ed. (Toronto: McClelland & Stewart, 1988); *The Proper Sphere: A Woman's Place in Canadian Society* (Toronto: Univ. of Toronto Press, 1976). AFFIL: Canadian Historical Association; Ontario Historical Association; Ontario Women's History Network; Canadian Society for the History of Medicine; International Society for the History of Medicine; Canadian Studies Association; American Society for the History of Medicine; Kitchener-Waterloo YWCA; Kitchener-Waterloo Art Gallery; Canadian Clay & Glass Gallery. HONS: Hannah Visiting Prof., McMaster Univ., 1988-89; Woman of Distinction Award, (Group Category for *Canadian Women: A History*), Metro Toronto YWCA, 1988; Honourable Mention, Sir John A. Macdonald Prize, 1991 Best Book in Cdn Hist., 1992; Thérèse Casgrain Fellowship, 1993-94; 1994 Scholar in Residence, Rockefeller Study Centre, Bellagio, Italy. INTERESTS: gardening; cross-country skiing.

Mock, Karen R., Ph.D., C.Psych. ✿ ⌂ ✾
National Director, LEAGUE FOR HUMAN RIGHTS OF B'NAI BRITH CANADA, 15 Hove St., Downsview, ON M3H 4Y8 (416) 633-6224, FAX 630-2159. Born Toronto 1945. m. Dr. David Mock. 2 ch. EDUC: Univ. of Toronto, B.A.(Psych.) 1967, M.A.(Applied Psych.) 1970, Ph.D. 1975. CAREER: Research Asst., Dept. of Applied Psych., Ontario Institute for Studies

in Education (OISE); Research Officer, 1969-71; Lecturer, Hamilton Teachers' Coll., 1971; Fellow, Learning Clinic & Neuropsych. Research Unit, Hospital for Sick Children, 1974-75; Post-Doctoral Fellow, 1975-76; Asst. Prof., Fac. of Educ., Univ. of Toronto, 1975-78; Practicum/Theory Coord. & Acting Principal, 1977-83; Sessional Fac., Dept. of Early Childhood Educ., Ryerson Polytechnic Institute, 1978-82; Consulting Psychologist, Intercultural Associates, 1982-85; Lecturer, Dept. of Psych. & Fac. of Educ., York Univ., 1982-89; Psychoeducational Consultant, North York Bd. of Educ., 1983-84; Educ. Psychologist & Principal, Masemann and Mock Consulting, 1985-89; Nat'l Dir., League for Human Rights of B'nai Brith Canada, 1989 to date; Exec. Dir., Centre for Educ. & Training (the League's consulting & educational facility), 1989 to date. SELECTED PUBLICATIONS: "Effects of Interpolated Extinction after Partial Delay of Reward Training on Subsequent Reacquisition and Extinction," with C.T. Surridge & A. Amsel (*Quarterly Journal of Experimental Psychology* 1968); "The Successful Multicultural Teacher" (History and Social Science Teacher 19(2) 1983); "The Child Care Needs of Cultural and Racial Minorities" (*Canadian Journal for Research in Early Childhood Education* 1988); "Combatting Hate: Canadian Realities and Remedies" (*Forum, Canadian Human Rights Commission* Spring/Summer 1992); "Anti-Semitism in Canada Today: Realities, Remedies and Implications for Anti-Racism," in *Readings on Anti-Racist Organizational Change*, eds. C. James & A. Minors (United Way of Greater Toronto, 1994); various other publications. AFFIL: Ontario Multicultural Association (Pres. 1988-89; Presidents' Advisory Council); Univ. of Toronto (Advisory Committee on Racism & Anti-Racist Initiatives); Association for Ontario Universities (Bd. of Dir.); Anti-Racist & Multicultural Educators' Network of Ontario (AMENO) (Assoc.); Science Centre Anti-Racism Advisory Committee; Urban Alliance on Race Relations Anti-Racism Response Network; Ontario Board of Examiners in Psychology; Ontario Multicultural Association (OMAMO). HONS: Wm. Lyon MacKenzie Academic Proficiency Award, 1963; Maurice Hutton Scholarship, Univ. of Toronto, 1963-66; Arbour Award, Univ. of Toronto, 1992; Honourable Mention, YWCA Woman of Distinction, 1993. INTERESTS: human rights & inclusive educ.; antiracist & diversity training; curriculum dev. & coalition building; mediation & conflict resolution. MISC: Ontario Teacher's Certificate; Registered Psych., Ont.; Coord. & Leader, Holocaust & Hope Educators' Study Tour & Seminar Program on Holocaust Educ.; recipient, numerous grants; numerous invited workshops, addresses & papers. COMMENT: *"Karen Mock is widely acknowledged as one of the foremost Canadian experts on antiracist education and is well known as a dynamic lecturer and workshop coordinator to school boards, social service agencies, policing services and community groups."*

Modlich, Regula, B.A.,M.E.S., M.C.I.P. ■ ⑳ ꙮ

Planning Consultant. 72 Southwood Dr., Toronto, ON M4E 2T9 (416) 690-6644, FAX 690-5456, EMAIL modlich@inforamp.net. Born Zurich 1939. m. Nikos Evdemon. 2 ch. EDUC: Univ. of Toronto, B.A.(Soc.) 1962, Diploma in Urban & Reg'l Planning 1964; York Univ., Fac. of Environmental Studies, M.E.S.(Urban Planning) 1980. CAREER: Village Dev. Worker, CUSO, India, 1962-63; Planner, Project Planning Association, 1964-66; Planner, City of Toronto Planning Bd., 1966-69; Sr. Planner, 1969-72; Sr. Planner, City of Oshawa, Planning & Dev. Dept., 1972-75; Sch. Community Rel'ns Worker, Toronto Bd. of Educ., 1983-85; Mgr & Planning Coord., Women Plan Toronto, 1985-90; Course Dir., York Univ. Fac. of Environmental Studies, 1990; Sr. Planner, Long Range, Town of Aurora, 1990-94; Planning Consultant. SELECTED PUBLICATIONS: "Planning Implications of Women Plan Toronto" (*Plan Canada* July 1988); "Planning Policies for Doing 'Women's' Work and Being a Woman" (*Prospects for Planning: Coming to Grips with New Realities*, Proceedings of the 1982 Nat'l Conference of the Canadian Institute of Planners); "Women's Needs in Urban Form and Function" (*Women and Planning, Proceedings of a Conference*, May 1, 1982); "Design and the Home" (*Status of Women News* Winter 1979); "Women Plan Toronto," with Birgit Sterner (*City Planning* Fall 1988); *Women Plan Toronto, Shared Experiences and Dreams*, ed. (Toronto: Women Plan Toronto, 1986); *Women's Community Planning Manual* (Toronto: Women Plan Toronto, 1990). AFFIL: Canadian Institute of Planners; American Planning Association; Ontario Professional Planners' Institute; Women Plan Toronto; Women & Environments. HONS: Constance Hamilton Award, City of Toronto, 1995; various other articles on gender-related planning. INTERESTS: sustainable & diverse communities & their planning. MISC: speaking, reading & writing ability in English, German, French & to a lesser extent Greek, Spanish, Hindi & Russian; presented papers & conducted workshops at conferences; guest lecturer at York Univ.,

Univ. of Toronto & Ryerson Polytechnic Univ. COMMENT: *"Pioneered gender implications in Canadian planning theory and practice and helped build Women Plan Toronto, a grass-roots organization to encourage and empower women to present their needs and participate in local planning decisions."*

Moeser, Diana R.E., B.A,M.A., MHSC ■ ⊕ ♡ ꙮ

Vice-President, Community Health and Planning, WELLESLEY CENTRAL HOSPITAL, 160 Wellesley St. E., Toronto, ON M4Y 1J3. Born Toronto. EDUC: St. Clements Sch., Head Girl, 1962-63; Univ. of Toronto, B.A.(Pol. Sci.) 1966, M.A.(Pol. Sci.) 1970, MHSC(Health Admin.) 1984. CAREER: Reporter, Toronto Citizen, 1973-74; Bus. Mgr, Grad. Asst. Association, 1975-76; Exec. Asst., Univ. of Toronto Fac. Association, 1976-77; Concert Prod., Toronto Benefit, Oxfam Canada, 1978-79; freelance writer & ed., 1979-82; Consultant, Rehab. Through Educ. Program, 1982; Community Planning Consultant, York Community Svcs, 1983; Dir. of Community Health Planning, Doctors Hospital, Toronto, 1984-89; Dir. of Ambulatory & Community Health Svcs, 1989-91; VP, Ambulatory & Community Health Svcs, 1991; VP, Ambulatory & Community Health Svcs, Wellesley Hospital, Toronto, 1992-96, VP, Community Health & Planning, Wellesley Central Hospital, 1996 to date. AFFIL: Canadian Coll. of Health Service Executives; Society of Graduates in Health Administration; Women's Network of Health Care Directors; Canadian Society for International Health (Treas. & Bd.); Centre for Health Promotion, Univ. of Toronto (Assoc.); Min. of Health, Advisory Committee on the Community Health Framework (1995). HONS: Robarts Fellowship; Univ. of Toronto 'T' holder (badminton). INTERESTS: canoeing; hiking; painting. MISC: est. 1st detox for women in Toronto & was 1st Chair of the Advisory Bd., 1991; recipient, Canada Council Research Grant, 1973-75.

Moffat, Jeanne, B.A. ■■ ⑳ ♡

Executive Director, GREENPEACE CANADA, (non-profit environment & peace advocacy), 185 Spadina Ave., Toronto, ON M5T 2C6 (416) 597-8408, FAX 597-8422. Born Paris, Kentucky 1940. m. Robert Fugere. 2 ch. Katherine Moffat, Melanie Moffat-Lindzon. EDUC: Bethany Coll., B.A.(Sociology & Religion) 1962; Goethe Institute, German studies 1965; Univ. of Waterloo, French studies 1979; Univ. of Toronto, French studies 1987; Centre Linguistique, French studies 1988. CAREER: Program Worker, North Toronto YWCA, 1962-

63; Branch Dir., 1963-65; Resource Coord., Global Community Centre, Kitchener, Ont., 1977-78; Special Consultant, YWCA of Canada, 1980-81; Program Facilitator, Ten Days for World Development, 1981-85; Nat'l Coord., 1985-92; Exec. Dir., Greenpeace Canada, 1993 to date. **SELECTED PUBLICATIONS:** "New Challenges for Development Education in Canada in the Nineties" (theme address, *Canadian & International Education*, Vol. 20, No. 1, 1991); chapter in *Coalitions for Justice* (Novalis Press, 1993). **AFFIL:** Stitchting Greenpeace Council (Greenpeace Int'l) (Cdn Trustee); World Council of Churches (N.Am. Ntwk Coord. of Dev. Educ. 1986-92); Canadian Council of Churches (1st VP 1982-85; mbr. of Bd. 1979-85). **INTERESTS:** music (was in Toronto Chamber Society Choir for 9 yrs.); travel. **MISC:** numerous TV interviews on world dev. & human rights issues. **COMMENT:** *"My passion is justice — justice for victims of injustice caused by misuse and abuse of power and blind and unquestioning greed. My commitment is unflinching in this pursuit of justice."*

Mogford, Mary, B.A. ■ $ ☝
Partner, MOGFORD CAMPBELL ASSOCIATES INC., 3715 Lakeshore Rd., R.R. 8, Newcastle, ON L1B 1L9 (905) 987-3587, FAX 987-5133. Born UK 1944. m. Tom Campbell. 2 stepch. **EDUC:** Univ. of Wales, B.A. 1966; Coll. of William and Mary, Williamsburg, Va., 1967-68. **CAREER:** various positions, Ont. Public Svc, 1968-85; Deputy Min. of Natural Resources, Gov't of Ont., 1985-87; Deputy Treas. of Ont./Deputy Min. of Econ., 1987-89; Pres., Mogford Campbell Associates, 1989 to date. **SELECTED PUBLICATIONS:** "Governance: Emerging Issues and Trends" (Sept. 1992). **DIRECTOR:** Credit Suisse Canada; Falconbridge Limited; Battle Mountain Gold; Altamira Advisory Council; Greystone Prepaid Hospital Insurance; Teranet Land Information Systems. **AFFIL:** Hospital for Sick Children (V-Chair); Jane Austen Society (Toronto Pres. 1991-93); Trent Univ. (Gov. 1991-95; Hon. Gov. 1995 to date); Toronto Symphony Foundation (Trustee); Nature Conservancy of Canada (Trustee); Canadian Policy Research Network (Bd.). **HONS:** Lady Astor Scholarship, 1967-68; 1st recipient, Lieutenant-Governor's Medal for Distinction in Public Admin., 1990. **INTERESTS:** sailing; skiing; reading widely; public affairs; music. **MISC:** 1st woman in Canada to hold position of Deputy Min. in areas of either Fin. or Natural Resources. **COMMENT:** *"Mary Mogford is a corporate director and a partner with Mogford Campbell Associates Inc., which provides advice and assistance to corporations in the areas of finance, business and public policy."*

Moir, Nicole Trudel ■ ✊ ♡ ☝
Executive Director, QUEBEC FEDERATION OF SENIOR CITIZENS, (QFSC), 4545 ave. Pierre-De Coubertin, CP 1000 Succ. M, Montreal, QC H1V 3R2 (514) 252-3017, FAX 252-3154. Born Montreal 1940. m. Lewis E. Moir. 4 ch. Ian, Susan, Gail, Neil. **EDUC:** Coll. des Ursulines, Qué., Diploma (Rhetoric) 1959. **CAREER:** Agent de traitement de données, Centre de recherche pour le défense nationale, Valcartier, 1959-62; Dev. Agent, Quebec Federation of Senior Citizens, 1984-87; Programs Dir., 1987-90; Exec. Dir., 1990 to date. **AFFIL:** Fédération internationale des Associations de Personnes Âgées (FIAPA) (Scientific Committee); Regroupement Loisir Québec (RLQ) (Pres., Social & Educational Sector 1982-86; Sec.); Fondation Réussite Jeunesse inc. (Sec. 1990-95; VP 1995 to date). **HONS:** Bronze Beaver, Girl Guides of Canada; Harfang des Neiges, Guides & Scouts of Que. **INTERESTS:** music; swimming; travelling; camping; bicycling. **MISC:** 1st woman Exec. Dir. of the QFSC. **COMMENT:** *"I have been involved at the community level for more than 30 years: schools, youth movements, senior citizens. To facilitate people to get involved has also been an objective of my involvement. Seniors are now my work priority: their well being and the services adapted to them."*

Molot, Maureen Appel, B.A.,M.A., Ph.D. ■ 🎓 $
Professor of Political Science and Director, The Norman Paterson School of International Affairs, CARLETON UNIVERSITY, 1125 Colonel By Dr., Ottawa, ON K1S 5B6 (613) 520-2600, ext. 6658, FAX 520-2889, EMAIL mmolot@ccs.carleton.ca. Born Ottawa 1941. m. Henry. 2 ch. Alexander, Edie. **EDUC:** McGill Univ., B.A.(Pol. Sci. & Soc.) 1962, M.A.(Pol. Sci.) 1964; Univ. of California (Berkeley), Ph.D.(Pol. Sci.) 1972. **CAREER:** Asst./Assoc. Prof. of Pol. Sci., Carleton Univ., 1973-89; Prof. of Pol. Sci. & Int'l Affairs, 1989 to date; Dir., The Norman Paterson Sch. of Int'l Affairs, Carleton Univ., 1993 to date. **SELECTED PUBLICATIONS:** *State Capitalism: Public Enterprise in Canada*, with J.K. Laux (Ithaca: Cornell Univ. Press, 1988); *Driving Continentally: National Policies and the North American Auto Industry* (Ottawa: Carleton Univ. Press, 1993); *Democracy and Foreign Policy: Canada Among Nations* 1995 ed. with Maxwell A. Cameron (Ottawa: Carleton Univ. Press, 1995); *A Part of the Peace: Canada Among Nations* 1994 ed. with Harald von Riekhoff (Ottawa: Carleton

Univ. Press, 1994); "Insiders and Outsiders: Defining 'Who is Us' in the North American Auto Industry," with Lorraine Eden (*Transnational Corporations* Dec. 1993); "The Challenge of NAFTA: Canada's Role in the North American Auto Industry" with Lorraine Eden (*Canada-US Outlook* Nov. 1994); "Canada's National Policies: Reflections on One Hundred and Twenty-Five Years," with Lorraine Eden (*Canadian Public Policy* Sept. 1993). **AFFIL:** Community Foundation of Ottawa-Carleton (Dir.); Jewish Community Council of Ottawa (Pres. 1991-93). **MISC:** research grants, Social Sciences & Humanities Research Council.

Molzahn, Anita, R.N.,M.N.,B.Sc., Ph.D. ■ ⟨⟩ ⊕

Dean, Faculty of Human and Social Development, UNIVERSITY OF VICTORIA, Box 1700, Victoria, BC V8N 5G6 (250) 721-8050, FAX 721-7067, EMAIL amolzahn@hsd.uvic.ca. Born Edmonton 1955. m. Nigel Scott. 2 ch. Wesley Scott, Laurel Scott. **EDUC:** Royal Alexandra Hospital Sch. of Nursing, R.N. 1974; Univ. of Alberta, B.Sc.(Nursing) 1980, M.N. 1986, Ph.D.(Soc.) 1989. **CAREER:** Special Projects Nurse/Nephrology Nurse Clinician/Nursing Instructor/Staff Nurse, Univ. of Alberta Hospitals, 1974-87; Asst./Assoc. Prof., Fac. of Nursing, Univ. of Alberta, 1987-92; Dir., Sch. of Nursing, Univ. of Victoria, 1992-96; Dean, Fac. of Hum. & Social Dev., 1996 to date. **SELECTED PUBLICATIONS:** "Reliability and validity of a quality assurance instrument for a dialysis unit" (*Nephrology Nurse* 5(6) 1983); "Should quality of life measures be used to assess quality of care?" (*American Nephrology Nurses' Association Journal* 19 1991); "Research critique: Quality of life of hemodialysis patients" (*American Nephrology Nurses' Association Journal* 20 1993); numerous other refereed articles, book chapters, conference papers & abstracts; "Towards a clarification of the scope of practice of registered nurses and licensed practical nurses" (*Alberta Association of Registered Nurses' Newsletter* 48(3) 1992); other articles in professional & gen. publications. **AFFIL:** American Nephrology Nurses' Association (Chair, Research Committee; Ed. Bd., Journal, 1991-94); Kidney Foundation, BC Branch (Dir.; Organ Donor Awareness Committee). **HONS:** Mosby Times Book Award for highest GPA, Fac. of Nursing, Univ. of Alberta, 1986; MN Alumnae Award for professional excellence, Univ. of Alberta, 1986; Research Abstract Award, American Nephrology Nurses' Association, 1993; Nephrology Nurse Researcher Award, American Nephrology Nurses' Association, 1993; 2nd Prize, Writing Competition, American Nephrology

Nurses' Association Journal; 2nd Prize, Writing Competition, Nephrology Nurse; Award for Educ., Writing Competition, American Nephrology Nurses Assocation Journal, 1996. **INTERESTS:** family; sailing; skiing; biking. **COMMENT:** *"My career has moved from that of a staff nurse in a renal dialysis unit through a variety of positions to that of a university faculty member and administrator. My research interests relate to quality of life and chronic illness."*

Monk, Lorraine Althea Constance, B.A., M.A.,D.Litt.,C.M.,O.C. ▯ ⊗ ⌂

Author and Photographer. Born Montreal m. John McCaughan Monk. 4 ch. Leslie Ann, John, David, Karyn. **EDUC:** McGill Univ., B.A. 1944, M.A. 1946. **SELECTED PUBLICATIONS:** *Canada: A Year of the Land* (1967); *Ces Visages qui sont en pays* (1967); *Stones of History* (1967); *Call Them Canadians* (1967); *A Time to Dream–Reveries en Couleurs* (1971); *Canada* (1979); *The Female Eye* (1975); *Between Friends/Entre Amis* (1976); 10 books in the "Image" series; 3 books in the "Signature" series; *The Robert Bourdeau Monograph* (1980); *Canada With Love/Canada avec amour* (patriation of the Constitution of Canada) (1982); *Celebrate our City, 150th Anniversary of Toronto* (1983); *Ontario: A Loving Look* (1984); *Photographs That Changed the World* (1989). **HONS:** Centennial Medal, 1967; Excellence of Service Award, Federation internationale de l'art photographique; Gold Medal for outstanding contribution to photography, National Association of Photographic Art; Silver Medal (Canada), "Most Beautiful Book in the World" Award, Leipzig Book Fair, 1975; *Between Friends/Entre Amis* won many int'l awards, incl. Best Printed Book Award, Int'l Gallery of Superb Printing, US, & the 1st recipient of Gold Medal, 1977, in honour of her extraordinary achievement in the art of book creating, Int'l Book Fair, Leipzig, Germany; First Prize (*Canada With Love/Canada avec amour*), Int'l Craftsman Guild, 1983; York Univ., D.Litt.(Hon.), 1982; Carleton Univ., D.Litt.(Hon.), 1985. **MISC:** produced 1st major exhibition, *The Incredible Journeys–Photographs of the Canadian Far North 1947-52*, by Richard Harrington, Toronto, 1987.

Monroe, Jessica ■ ■ ⓦ

Olympic Athlete. c/o Canadian Olympic Association. Born Palo Alto, Calif. 1966. **SPORTS CAREER:** mbr., Cdn Nat'l Rowing Team, 1988-92. Olympic Games: Silver, 8+, 1996; Gold, 8+, & Gold, 4-, 1992. World championships: 1st, 8+, & 1st, 4-, 1991. Int'l regattas: 3rd, 8+, & 1st, 4- (Switzerland), & 3rd, 8+, &

1st, 4- (Germany), 1992. Canadian championships: 1st, 8+, & 3rd, 1x, 1990. INTERESTS: mountain biking; skiing; hiking. MISC: moved to Canada, 1972; currently a student.

Montagnes, Carol, B.A., M.A. 👁 🔱

Executive Director, ONTARIO NATIVE COUNCIL ON JUSTICE, 2 Carlton St., Ste. 1004, Toronto, ON M5B 1J3 (416) 592-1393, FAX 592-1394. Born Winnipeg 1945. m. Dr. Jan Musil. EDUC: Carleton Univ., B.A.(Soc.) 1971; Univ. of Toronto, M.A.(Criminology) 1978. CAREER: Case Historian, Mental Health Centre, Penetanguishene, Ont., 1968-70; Case Worker, Metro Toronto Community & Social Svcs, 1974-76; Researcher, Centre of Criminology, Univ. of Toronto, 1976-77, 1979-80; Mental Health Planner, Metropolitan Toronto District Health Council, 1982-84; Dir. of Policy & Program Dev., Ont. Native Council on Justice, 1984-89; Exec. Dir., 1989 to date. SELECTED PUBLICATIONS: *Planning for Progress: The Co-Ordination of Mental Health Care Services in Metropolitan Toronto* (1984); "Indian Children in Ontario's Juvenile Justice and Child Welfare Systems" (1985); "The Disproportionate Incarceration of Native People in Ontario" (1990). AFFIL: Aboriginal Legal Services of Toronto (VP); Canadian Criminal Justice Association. INTERESTS: contemporary native art; Cdn poetry; cuisine from around the world. COMMENT: *"I approach life with enthusiasm and determination, and hope that I will be found to have used the talents given to me wisely."*

Moon, Barbara Ethel ✏ 🗂

Editor-at-Large, SATURDAY NIGHT MAGAZINE, 184 Front St. E., Ste. 400, Toronto, ON M5A 4N3. Born St. Catharines, Ont. 1926. m. Wynne Thomas. EDUC: Trinity Coll., Univ. of Toronto, B.A. 1948. CAREER: Asst. Ed. & Staff Writer, *Maclean's*, 1948-52, 1956-64; Asst. Ed., *Mayfair*, 1953-56; Feature Writer, *The Globe and Mail*, 1964-66; Ed., *Toronto Calendar*, 1980-82; Sr. Ed., *Saturday Night*, 1986-90; Ed.-at-Large, *Saturday Night*, 1990 to date; Fac., Arts Journalism Program, Banff Centre for the Arts, 1992 to date. SELECTED CREDITS: writer & broadcaster of arts & science TV documentaries. SELECTED PUBLICATIONS: various books, incl. *The Canadian Shield* (1970); reviews, newspaper & magazine columns, numerous magazine articles. AFFIL: ACTRA (Life Mbr.); Writers' Guild of Canada (Life Mbr.). HONS: President's Medal, Univ. of Western Ontario, 1962; Award for Outstanding Achievement, The National Magazine Foundation, 1993.

Moor, Deborah L., B.A.,M.B.A. ■ $

Director, Product Planning, CANADIAN AIRLINES INTERNATIONAL LTD., 700 - 2nd St. SW, Ste. 2800, Calgary, AB T2P 2W2 (403) 294-6243, FAX 294-6014. Born Brantford, Ont. 1963. EDUC: Univ. of Waterloo, B.A.(Econ.) 1986; Univ. of Western Ontario, M.B.A. 1989. CAREER: Research Assoc., The Canada Consulting Group, 1986-87; Fin. Analyst, Canadian Airlines International Ltd., 1989-90; Investor Rel'ns Mgr, 1990-93; Dir., Insur., 1993-95; Dir., Product Planning, 1995 to date. AFFIL: Canadian Investor Relations Institute (Pres., Calgary Chapter, 1992-93). HONS: Dean's Honour List, Univ. of Western Ontario, 1987-88, 1988-89. INTERESTS: reading; skiing.

Moore, Carole, A.B.,M.L.S. 📖 🗂

Chief Librarian, UNIVERSITY OF TORONTO, 130 St. George St., Toronto, ON M5S 1A5 (416) 978-2292, FAX 971-2099. Born Calif. 1944. EDUC: Stanford Univ., A.B.(Spanish) 1966; Columbia Univ., M.L.S. 1967. CAREER: Reference Librarian, Columbia Univ., 1967-68; Reference Librarian, Univ. of Toronto, 1968-78; Head of Cataloguing, Reference & Chief Librarian, 1986 to date. AFFIL: Research Libraries Group (Dir.); Canadian Library Association; Canadian Association of Research Libraries (Pres.); Univ. of Toronto Press (Dir.). HONS: Distinguished Alumnus, Columbia Univ.

Moore, Cynthia, B.Ed. 👁 🗂 ⊗

Vice-President, CANADIAN SOCIETY FOR EDUCATION THROUGH ART, 2840 Arens Rd. E., Ste. 604, Regina, SK S4V 1N8 (306) 789-5000, FAX 584-5995. Born Moose Jaw, Sask. 1954. m. R. Randy McLeod. 4 ch. EDUC: Univ. of Regina, B.Ed.(Arts Educ.) 1985, M.Ed.(Educ'l Admin.) in progress. CAREER: teacher, Cochrane High Sch., Regina, Sask., 1985-90; Sessional Lecturer, Fac. Advisor, Fac. of Educ., Univ. of Regina, 1990-92; Sessional Lecturer, Dept. of Indian Educ., Saskatchewan Indian Federated Coll., Jan.-Apr. 1991; Sessional Lecturer, Saskatchewan Urban Native Teacher Educ. Program, Gabriel Dumont Institute, Univ. of Regina, 1991-92; teacher, Herchmer Community Sch., Regina, 1992 to date; teacher leader, Visual Arts, Arts Educ. Curriculum implementation team, (K-5) Regina Public Sch. Bd., 1994 to date. SELECTED PUBLICATIONS: various articles published in Saskatchewan Society for Education through Art Newsletter, *SCENES: Saskatchewan Council of Educators of Non-English Speakers* & *The Arts Educator*. AFFIL: Saskatchewan Society for Education through Art (Pres. 1992-94); Canadian Society for Education through Art (VP); United States

Society for Education through Art; International Society for Education through Art; Dance Saskatchewan Inc.; Multicultural Council of Saskatchewan; Saskatchewan Middle Years Association; Saskatchewan Science Centre; Saskatchewan Teachers' Federation; Univ. of Regina (Alumni Association; Faculty Club); North Central Community Play Advisory Committee, Regina; Middle Years Curriculum Advisory Committee, Regina Public Bd. of Educ. **HONS:** Margaret Messer Fellowship for Grad. Studies, 1991. **INTERESTS:** downhill skiing; drawing; clothing design; gourmet cooking. **MISC:** Chair, Canadian Society for Education through Art Assembly, 1990; developed & conducted many arts courses/workshops for teachers & students; various conference presentations; Cooperating Teacher, Internship/Preinternship, Univ. of Regina, Gabriel Dumont Institute & Saskatchewan Indian Federated Coll. **COMMENT:** *"I have been an arts educator at all levels from elementary to university. I am a graduate student in Educational Administration and a Grade 6/7 teacher. Past President of the Saskatchewan Society for Education through Art, I have recently been elected Vice-President of the Canadian Society for Education through Art."*

Moore, Dorothea D. (Tedde) Mavor ⊗ � ♥

Actor. Born Toronto 1947. life partner. Don Shebib. 3 ch. Zoë Carter, Suzanna Shebib, Noah Shebib. **EDUC:** Royal Academy of Dramatic Arts, London, UK, grad. Acting with Hons. 1966; continuing workshops in stage & film performance. **CAREER:** performing as Tedde Moore since 1950; appearing on stage, radio, commercials, TV & feature films; The Stratford Shakespearean Festival; St. Lawrence Centre for the Performing Arts; Necessary Angel Theatre; National Arts Centre; Neptune Theatre; CBC Radio (also newscaster & host on such programs as *Morningside*, *As It Happens*, *Sunday Morning* & *Radio Noon*); Assoc. Prod., Nothing Sacred Corporation, 1994; Creative Consultant on feature films; Script Ed., 4 feature scripts, 3 produced; independent radio producer, CBC, for such programs as Ideas; writer; parent. **SELECTED CREDITS:** *A Christmas Story* (feature), dir. Bob Clark; *Murder By Decree* (feature), dir. Bob Clark; *Second Wind* (feature), dir. Don Shebib; Ann, *The Castle*, dir. Richard Rose, Toronto Free Theatre; Anne Whitefield, *Man and Superman*, dir. Peter Dewes, National Arts Centre; Hermia, *A Midsummer Night's Dream*, dir. John Hirsch, Stratford Festival; Heritage Theatre (TV), My Country Prod. **SELECTED PUBLICATIONS:** *Canadian Actor's Anecdotes*, with actor Linda Mason Green (Oxford Univ. Press, 1997).

AFFIL: ACTRA (various positions 1988-93); Ontario Puppetry Association (Bd. Mbr. 1990-93); Citizens' Forum on Canada's Future (the Spicer Commission) (Nat'l Coord. for the Arts 1991); Lampoon Puppet Theatre (Bd. Mbr.); The National Party of Canada (mbr. 1993). **HONS:** Principal's Medal of Excellence, RADA, 1966; Best Supporting Actress (Second Wind), Canadian Film Awards, 1976; nominated, Best Supporting Actress (*A Christmas Story*), Genie Awards, 1983. **INTERESTS:** the arts; education; politics; nature; crafts. **COMMENT:** *"I am a soul, not in the Arts but of the Arts. I feel Art all around me. In nature and in the diverse populations of this country. I attempt to show by example that life is no life without Art, that our country is no country without culture."*

Moore, Linda ⊗ ♥ face

Artistic Director, **NEPTUNE THEATRE**, 1593 Argyle St., Halifax, NS B3J 2B2 (902) 429-7300, FAX 429-1211. Born Winnipeg 1950. m. Victor A. (Sandy) Moore, composer. 1 ch. Lorca. **CAREER:** Artistic Assoc., Manitoba Theatre Centre, 1984-86; Asst. Dir., Stratford Festival, 1985; Guest Dir. & Instructor, National Theatre Sch., 1987-89; freelance stage dir., Centaur, Citadel, TNB, Belfry, Theatre Plus & numerous other Cdn theatres. **MISC:** directed the 1st non-RSC production of *Les Miserables*, with a special licence from Cameron McIntosh for Neptune Theatre's 30th anniversary season, 1993-94 (an extraordinary success seen by 44,000 people). **COMMENT:** *"Currently, I am deeply involved in the completion of the Neptune renovation and expansion project, which will include provision of a new studio theatre, theatre school teaching studios, rehearsal halls and entirely new audience amenities."*

Moore, Shelia ⊗ face ♥

Actor. c/o L. Bonnell, The Characters Talent Agency (Vancouver) LTD., 1505 W. 2nd Ave., Ste. 200, Vancouver, BC V6H 3Y4 (604) 733-9800, FAX 733-6000. Born Wilkie, Sask. d. 1 ch. **SELECTED CREDITS:** *X-Files* (series)(2 eps.) *Circumstances Unknown*, *Bye Bye Blues*; *North of 60*; "The Day It Rained Forever," *Ray Bradbury Theatre*; *And The Sea Will Tell* (mini-series); "Harvey," *Hallmark Hall of Fame* (TV); *The Reflecting Skin* (feature); Bonnie Beachem, *Homeward Bound* (theatre); Vancouver Playhouse; Aurelie, *Aurelie, Ma Soeur* (theatre), Centaur; Eleanor, *Love and Anger* (theatre), Vancouver Playhouse/MTC; Amanda, *The Glass Menagerie* (theatre), Magnus Theatre; Barbara, *Pack of Lies* (theatre), Grand Theatre; *Three Tall Women* (theatre), Vancouver Playhouse. **AFFIL:** Canadian Actors' Equity; ACTRA; UBCP (Union of B.C. Performers). **HONS:** nomination, Best Actress, Jessie Awards, 1996; nomination, Best Female Performance (*Ray Bradbury Theatre*), AMPIA, 1991; Award, Best Ensemble Cast (*Love and Anger*), Jessie Awards, 1991; nomination, Best Acting/Supporting Role, *Homefires* (CBC TV), ACTRA, 1983; nomination, Best Acting Performance/Continuing Role, *Homefires*, (CBC TV), ACTRA, 1982; nomination, Best Acting Performance/Continuing Role, *Homefires*, (CBC TV), ACTRA, 1981; nomination, Best New Performer in TV, *Homefires*, (CBC TV), ACTRA, 1981.

Moore, Valerie A., B.A.,LL.B. ■ ⚖
Crown Attorney, CROWN ATTORNEY'S OFFICE, 40 Great George St., Charlottetown, PE C1A 4J9 (902) 368-4595, FAX 368-5812. Born Charlottetown 1959. s. 1 ch. Brennan Michael Moore. **EDUC:** Univ. of Prince Edward Island, B.A.(English/Psych.) 1980; Dalhousie Univ., LL.B. 1983. **BAR:** P.E.I., 1984. **CAREER:** lawyer in private practice, Charlottetown, 1984-87; Sessional Lecturer, Politics & Law, Univ. of Prince Edward Island, 1986-92; Departmental Solicitor, Gov't of P.E.I., 1987-91; Crown Attorney, 1991 to date. **AFFIL:** Law Society of P.E.I. (Sec.-Treas. 1990-91; VP 1994-95; Council 1989-90, 1991 to date; Pres. 1995-96; Past Pres. 1996 to date); Canadian Bar Association (Chair, Young Lawyers' Div., PEI Branch); Liberal Party of P.E.I. (Policy Chair 1986-87). **HONS:** Full-Tuition Scholarship, Univ. of Prince Edward Island; Scholarship, N.S. Law Foundation. **INTERESTS:** writing; cooking; playing guitar; roller-blading; cross-country skiing. **MISC:** Instructor, P.E.I. Bar Admission Course, 1992-95.

Moore-Ede, Carol, B.A.(Hons.) ■ ⛺ ⊗ ♥
Executive Producer, CBC-TV (416) 205-6872, FAX 205-6887. Born Tunbridge Wells, Kent, UK 1943. m. David Morris Clark. 2 ch., 2 stepch. Jill Clark Johnny, Julia Clark, Amelia Myers, Michael Clark. **EDUC:** Univ. of Toronto, B.A.(Hons., Fine Art) 1966. **CAREER:** author; photographer; film & TV dir., CBC-TV, PBS, BBC, Atlantis Films; Prod./Dir., 1967 to date; Exec. Prod. **SELECTED CREDITS:** Prod./Dir., *The Jonah Look* (drama), CBC-TV; Exec. Prod., *Adrienne Clarkson's Summer Festival*, CBC-TV; Exec. Prod., *Performance* & *Sunday Arts Entertainment*, CBC-TV; Dir., National Film Board; Dir., NHK Japan; Dir., Czechoslovakian TV. **SELECTED PUBLICATIONS:** *Canadian Architecture 1960-1970*; photographs in various magazines incl. *Time, Arbitare, Moebel Inte-*

rior Design & *Readers' Digest*, as well as in numerous books. **AFFIL:** Toronto Women in Film & Television; Directors' Guild of Canada; Academy of Canadian Cinema and Television. **HONS:** Gemini Award; Chris Award, Columbus Int'l Film Festival; Gabriel Award; Prix Italia; San Antonio Festival; Prix Anik; Certificate of Merit, Golden Gate Awards; Best Canadian Book of the Year (*Canadian Architecture 1960-70*). **INTERESTS:** architecture; photography; literature; art; science; sailing; skiing. **COMMENT:** *"I am committed to public broadcasting and exposing the arts to all Canadians from all parts of Canada. Through art and history we learn more about who we are and who we want to be, and strengthen our Canadian identity as a result."*

Morel, Sylvie, B.A. 📜 ❀ ♣
Director, Exhibitions and Programs, CANADIAN MUSEUM OF CIVILIZATION, Box 3100, Stn. B, Hull, QC J8X 4H2 (819) 776-8302, FAX 776-8300, EMAIL sylvie.morel@cmcc.muse.digital.ca. Born Ottawa 1950. m. Richard Garner. **EDUC:** Univ. of Ottawa, B.A.(Math.) 1972. **CAREER:** Loans Officer, Nat'l Educ. Program, National Museum of Man, 1974-76; Head, Circulation Section, Nat'l Programs Div., National Museum of Man, 1976-79; Chief, Exhibitions Div., Canadian Museum of Civilization, 1979-89; Dir., Exhibitions & Programs Branch, 1989 to date. **AFFIL:** International Council of Museums; Canadian Museums Association; American Association of Museums; National Association of Museum Exhibitionists. **INTERESTS:** travel; oenology; cooking; sailing; dogs. **COMMENT:** *"For 22 years I have been working to help develop the Canadian Museum of Civilization into a major national institution and tourist site. I have travelled extensively. My great loves are oenology, creative cooking and my dogs."*

Morey, Tracy, B.A. ◉
Communications Officer, CANADIAN UNION OF PUBLIC EMPLOYEES, 21 Florence St., Ottawa, ON K2P 0W6 (613) 237-1590, FAX 237-5508. Born Ottawa 1945. m. Philip Paquette. 3 ch. **EDUC:** Univ. of Ottawa, B.A. **CAREER:** newspaper reporter; radio & TV prod.; Comm. Officer, Canadian Union of Public Employees. **EDIT:** Ed. Bd., *Canadian Forum*, 1988 to date. **AFFIL:** New Democratic Party; Ottawa South Community Association; Canadian Association of Labour Media. **HONS:** Award for Radio Documentary, Ottawa, ACTRA, 1975. **INTERESTS:** 3 children; Cdn lit. & culture. **COMMENT:** *"I'm an Irish Catholic who grew up in a little French town in Ontario. I am a fanatical nationalist who replaced religion with*

feminism and 60s peace-love values. Although a little weary of the struggle, I'm trying to figure out whether my goal of saving this country from corporatist and philistine values might be better achieved by my three astute and wonderful children."

Morgan, Alison, B.Comm.,M.A. ⌲ $
University Secretary and Instructor in Economics, QUEEN'S UNIVERSITY, Kingston, ON K7L 3N6 (613) 545-6095, FAX 545-2793. Born Kingston, Ont. 1939. m. I.G. Morgan. 2 ch. EDUC: Queen's Univ., B.Comm. 1961; Univ. of Western Ontario, M.A.(Econ) 1969. CAREER: Research Asst. in Econ., Harvard Univ., 1963-65; Research Asst., McGill Univ., 1965-67; Agent de recherche et de planification, Ministère de l'Agric. de Qué., 1974-75; Agent de recherche et de planification, Office de Planification et du développement, Qué., 1975-78; Consultant, Gouv. du Qué., 1978; Instructor in Econ., Queen's Univ., 1978 to date; Sr. Administrative Asst., Queen's Univ., 1979-84; Visiting Asst. Prof., Econ., Univ. of British Columbia, 1984-85; Sec., Bd. of Trustees, Queen's Univ., 1985-88; Registrar, 1988-95; Univ. Sec., 1995 to date. SELECTED PUBLICATIONS: several publications in applied econometrics & income distribution. AFFIL: Kingston Tai Chi (Dir. 1993-95). HONS: Medal in Commerce, Queen's Univ., 1961.

Morgan, E. Louise ■ ■ $
Chairman of the Board and Director, CANADIAN GENERAL INVESTMENTS, LIMITED, (closed-end investments), 110 Yonge St., Ste. 1601, Toronto, ON M5C 1T4 (416) 366-2931, FAX 366-2729. President and Director, MAXWELL MEIGHEN & ASSOCIATES. Born Summerside, P.E.I. 1929. d. 3 ch. Scott, Vanessa, Jonathan. EDUC: Summerside Business Coll., Bus. 1947. DIRECTOR: Canadian World Fund Limited (Chrm); Third Canadian General Investment Trust Limited (Chrm). AFFIL: Canadian Opera Company (Dir.); Autism Society of Ontario; The Catherine and Maxwell Meighen Foundation (Pres. & Dir.). INTERESTS: gardening; reading; theatre; hiking; cross-country skiing; fishing; dollhouse miniatures. COMMENT: *"Joined the aforementioned closed-end funds in 1955 as Corporate Secretary and appointed a Director of CGI in 1982, and Third in 1967. Chairman of CGI in 1993 and Chair of Third in 1989, and a major shareholder of both funds. Was involved in incorporating Canadian World Fund and elected Chairman and Director in 1994."*

Morgan, Nicole, M.A.,Ph.D. ⌲ ❀
Visiting Professor, MCGILL CENTRE FOR MEDICINE, ETHICS AND LAW, McGill University, Montreal, QC H3A 1W9 (514) 398-7406, FAX 398-4668. Born France 1945. m. Alan Morgan. 2 ch. Ingrid, Eric. EDUC: Univ. de Dijon, M.A.(Phil.) 1968; Univ. Aix-en-Prov., M.A.(Soc. & Anthro.) 1971; Ottawa Univ., Ph.D.(Phil.) 1993. CAREER: Research Asst., Futuribles International, Paris; Policy Analyst, Gov't of Canada, 1981-85; Asst. Prof., Queen's Univ., 1991-94; Expert-in-Residence, CMHC, 1994. SELECTED PUBLICATIONS: *Nowhere to Go*; *Implosion, an Analysis of the Growth in the Canadian Federal Public Service, 1945-1985*; *The Equity Game*; *Le sixiéme Continent* (Paris: J. Vrin, 1995). HONS: Queen's Nat'l Scholar, 1991-94. INTERESTS: painting. COMMENT: *"Nicole Morgan is a Visiting Professor at the McGill Centre for Medicine, Ethics and Law in Montreal and is the Canadian representative for Futuribles International, Paris, France. She has recently completed three scenarios on future economic conditions with implications for the housing sector, as an Expert-in-Residence for Canada Mortgage and Housing Corporation. In 1991 she was named Queen's National Scholar and in that capacity taught public administration for three years while completing her doctoral dissertation on Renaissance political philosophy, which is being published in Paris (France). Her interest in the 15th-16th centuries is integrated to her general research on global trends: death of states, new and old forms of conflict, redistribution of resources and redefinition of the concept of humanity."*

Morgan-Silvester, Sarah A., B.Comm., F.I.C.B. ■ $
Senior Vice-President, Marketing and Ombudsperson, HONGKONG BANK OF CANADA, 885 W. Georgia St., Ste. 400, Vancouver, BC V6C 3E9 (604) 641-1965, FAX 641-1925. Born Victoria, B.C. 1959. EDUC: Univ. of British Columbia, B.Comm.(Hons. Fin.) 1982. CAREER: Mortgage Broker, Morguard Trust Company, 1982-85; various positions to Acct Mgr, Commercial Bnkg, CIBC, 1985-87; Mgr, Special Credit, Hongkong Bank of Canada, 1987-88; Mgr, Commercial Credit Training, 1988-89; Sr. Acct Mgr, 1989-92; Asst. VP & Branch Mgr, 1992-94; VP, Personal Credit, 1994-95; Pres., Hongkong Bank Mortgage Corporation, 1994-95; Sr. VP, Mktg & Ombudsperson, 1995 to date. AFFIL: Institute of Canadian Bankers (Fellow); Univ. of British Columbia Alumni Association. HONS: Gold Medal for Scholastic Achievement, Kiwanis Club, 1982.

Morin, Francyne, B.A. ✂ ♥
Freelance Producer. 1530 Bernard St. W., Ste.

8, Outremont, QC H2V 1W8 (514) 270-0760, FAX 270-8234. Born Montreal 1952. s. EDUC: Ravensbourne Coll. of Art & Design, B.A. 1976; Univ. of Montreal, Hautes Études Commerciales, Certificates in Continuing Educ.(Advtg Mgmt & Creative Mgmt). CAREER: Designer, GSM Design Inc., 1976-79; Dir. of Advtg & Promo., Les Films René Malo Inc., 1979-83; Gen. Mgr, Publifilms Inc., 1983-86; VP, Distribution, Malofilm Group Inc., 1986-88; Exec. VP, Distribution & Prod., 1988-91; Comm. Consultant, 1991-93; VP, Comm., Malofilm Communications Inc., 1994-95; Dir. of Comm., Télé-Québec, 1995 to date. SELECTED CREDITS: Prod., *The Revolving Doors*, Francis Mankiewicz; Prod., *Tinamer*, Jean-Guy Noel; involved in the mktg of more than 200 films incl. *Cruising Bar* and *The Decline of the American Empire*; creative dev. of the concept, content & branding for the Parents Channel. SELECTED PUBLICATIONS: several articles in major Que. magazines. AFFIL: Academy of Canadian Cinema & Television; Publicité Club de Montreal. MISC: *The Revolving Doors* has won more than a dozen int'l awards & was in Official Selection at the 1989 Cannes Film Festival.

Morin, Lyne ■■ ⊛ ✦ ⊕

Member of the Board of Directors, PROFESSIONAL INSTITUTE OF THE PUBLIC SERVICE OF CANADA, 53 Auriga Dr., Nepean, ON K2E 8C3 (514) 457-3440, ext. 2212, FAX 228-9048, EMAIL lmorin@rocler.qc.ca. Born Montreal 1956. d. 2 ch. Louis, Pierre-Yves. EDUC: Univ. Laval, B.H.Sc.(Occupational Therapy) 1977. CAREER: Occupational Therapist consultant in psychiatry, Ste. Anne's Hospital, Dept. of Veterans Affairs, 1980 to date. AFFIL: Ordre des Ergothérapeutes du Québec. INTERESTS: reading; walking; gardening. COMMENT: *"Active in the union movement since 1985, I have had different roles and functions over the years: member of the second largest union of the Public Service, Chair of the Occupational and Physical Therapy Group, Group Advisory Council Director, member of the bargaining team etc.. My main achievement: as the chairperson of the Equal Pay Task Force, I coordinate the activities to achieve equal pay for work of equal value for the three female-dominated groups in the professional categories in the Public Service of Canada. Equal pay was achieved in 1995, for dietitians, nurses, occupational and physical therapists, after a battle that lasted more than 15 years. This Equal Pay settlement is the largest to date in North America. Chairperson of the Committee on Human Rights in the workplace for the past two years, we coordinate activities, develop position papers, poli-*

cies and briefs on all human rights issues, such as employment equity, same benefits for same-sex partners, harassment, discrimination, balancing work and family, etc. Harassment is a major concern and a lot of work has been done with employers and with our own members to increase awareness of the consequences of such behaviour. I am also actively involved in the representation of members in work related situations. I also was the president of the board of directors of a nonprofit day care centre for two years."

Morissette, Alanis Nadine · ♥ ⊗

Singer, Songwriter. c/o Maverick Records. Born Ottawa 1974. CAREER: child actor; featured performer, *You Can't Do That on Television*, Nickelodeon, 1986; released self-financed single, "Fate Stay with Me," Lamor Records, 1987; signed with MCA Canada & released 2 albums; signed with Maverick Records, 1994. SELECTED CREDITS: *Alanis*; *Now Is the Time*; *Jagged Little Pill*, Maverick Records, co-writer & co-prod. Glen Ballard, 1995 (1st single "You Oughta Know," 2nd single "Hand in My Pocket"). HONS: Most Promising Female Artist, Juno Awards, 1991; Album of the Year & Best Rock Album (*Jagged Little Pill*), Best Female Rock Vocal Performance & Best Rock Song, Grammy Awards, 1996; Album of the Year & Best Rock Album (*Jagged Little Pill*), Single of the Year ("You Oughta Know"); Female Vocalist of the Year & Songwriter of the Year, Juno Awards, 1996. MISC: *Alanis* awarded platinum status in Canada; *Jagged Little Pill* has reached double-platinum status.

Morley, Patricia, B.A.,M.A.,Ph.D., D.S.Litt. ⊗ 📓 ⊲

Professor Emeritus, Department of English, CONCORDIA UNIVERSITY, Montreal, QC H3G 1M8. Born Toronto 1929. d. 4 ch. Laurence, Patricia, Christopher, David. EDUC: Trinity Coll., Univ. of Toronto, B.A.(English) 1951; Carleton Univ., M.A.(English) 1967; Univ. of Ottawa, Ph.D.(Modern English Lit.) 1970; Thornloe Coll., Laurentian Univ., D.S.Litt. 1992. CAREER: writer, 1967 to date; Lecturer, Univ. of Ottawa, 1971-72; Asst. Prof., Dept. of English, Sir George Williams Univ. (now Concordia Univ.), 1972-75; Assoc. Prof., Dept. of English, Concordia Univ., 1975-80; Prof., 1980-89; Prof. Emeritus, 1991 to date. SELECTED PUBLICATIONS: *The Mystery of Unity: Theme and Technique in the Novels of Patrick White* (McGill-Queen's Univ. Press, 1972); *The Immoral Moralists. Hugh MacLennan and Leonard Cohen* (1972); Robertson Davies (Gage, 1977); *The Comedians: Hugh*

Hood and Rudy Wiebe (Clarke Irwin, 1977); *Morley Callaghan* (McClelland & Stewart, 1978); *Kurelek. A Biography* (Macmillan Canada, 1986); *Margaret Laurence. The Long Journey Home* (McGill-Queen's Univ. Press, 1991); *As Though Life Mattered. Leo Kennedy's Story* (McGill-Queen's Univ. Press, 1994); approximately 60 articles *in Canadian Forum, Journal of Canadian Studies, Atlantis, Saturday Night* & other journals; approx. 800 book reviews in *Ottawa Journal, Ottawa Citizen* & *Birmingham News* (1971 to date) on lit., art & women's studies; various other books & publications. **AFFIL:** Simone de Beauvoir Institute, Concordia Univ. (Lifetime Hon. Fellow); The Writers' Union of Canada. **HONS:** Ottawa Citizen Award, Nonfiction, 1987; Ottawa Carleton Literary Award, 1988; Ottawa Carleton Literary Award, 1991. **INTERESTS:** travel; gardening. **MISC:** recipient, various grants & fellowships, incl. Japan Foundation Fellow, 1991; numerous conference presentations worldwide. **COMMENT:** *"Post-secondary education and the care of four children occupied the first 20 years of my adult life; writing and university teaching the next 20. I am now a full-time writer, my special interests are women's lives and women's writing in Canada and Japan."*

Morosoli, Joëlle ⊗ 🖺

Sculptor, Writer, Editor. 3385 rue Geoffrion, Saint-Laurent, QC H4K 2V1 (514) 337-3349. Born Strasbourg, France 1951. s. **EDUC:** Univ. Laval, Baccalauréat spécialisé en arts plastiques 1975; Univ. du Québec à Hull, First Grade Certificate in Educ. 1980. **CAREER:** sculptor; writer; Co-Mgr., Comme Galerie, Québec, 1975-77; Art Teacher, Outaouais Reg'l Sch. Bd., 1976-83; Art Teacher, Univ. du Québec à Hull, 1977-80; VP, Conseil de la sculpture du Québec, 1985-87; co-founder, Espace magazine, 1987; Asst. Ed., Espace, 1987 to date. **SELECTED PUBLICATIONS:** *Traînée rouge dans un soleil de lait,* poetry (Sherbrooke: Naaman, 1984); *Avec l'angoisse pour sablier,* novel (1986); *Le ressac des ombres,* novel (Hexagone, 1988); various art articles. **COMMISSIONS:** exterior mural, Bibliothèque de Pierrefonds (1990); suspended sculpture, Centre de Recherche Fernand-Seguin, Montreal (1992); exterior sculpture, Parc Marie-Victorin, Longueuil (1995); various others. **EXHIBITIONS:** 18 solo exhibitions incl. Musée régional de Rimouski, Rimouski (1989); Musée du Bas-St-Laurent, Rivière-du-Loup (1991); Saint Mary's Univ. Art Gallery, Halifax (1991); A Space, Toronto (1996); 48 group exhibitions in Que., Canada & France, incl. Les Machines sentimentales, Centre Georges Pompidou, Paris

(1987); Galerie d'art Lavalin, Montreal (1989), *Sculpture: Six Artists from Quebec* Leo Kamen Gallery, Toronto (1989) & Art Expo, N.Y. (1989). **AFFIL:** Espace (Treas., Bd. of Dirs.); Conseil de la Sculpture du Québec. **HONS:** 2e Prix Robert Cliche, *Avec l'angoisse pour sablier,* 1986. **MISC:** subject of numerous print & broadcast articles, reviews & interviews; recipient, various grants. **COMMENT:** *"I am particularly interested in kinetic sculptures, installations, murals and environments."*

Morrice, Betty-Lynn, B.Sc.P.T., M.Sc. ■ ⊕

Director, Rehabilitation, CALGARY GENERAL HOSPITAL, 841 Centre Ave. E., Calgary, AB T2E 0A1. Born Pouce Coupe, B.C. 1927. m. David Sevalrud. 4 ch. Robert, Clark, Austin, Kevin. **EDUC:** Univ. of Alberta, B.Sc.(Phys. Therapy) 1979; Univ. of Calgary, Master of Medical Sci. 1988. **CAREER:** Phys. Therapist, Univ. of Alberta Hospital, 1980-85; Research Asst., Univ. of Calgary, Dept. of Clinical Neurosciences, 1988-90; Program Coord., Outpatient Rehab, Program for M.S., 1992-93; Research Officer, Rehab., 1993-95; Dir., Rehab., 1995 to date; Research Enhancement Appt., Univ. of Alberta, Dept. of Phys. Therapy, 1993 to date. **SELECTED PUBLICATIONS:** "Manual Tracking Performance in Patients with Cerebellar Incoordination," with others (*Canadian Journal of Neurological Science* 17 1990); "Multi-Joint Reaching Movements and Eye Hand Tracking in Cerebellar Incoordination: Investigation of a Patient with Complete Loss of Purkinje Cells," with others (*Canadian Journal of Neurological Science* 18, 1991); "Modulation of the Soleus H-Reflex in Normal Humans and in Patients with Spinal Spasticity," with others (*Journal of Neurology, Neurosurgery and Psychiatry* 55 1992). **AFFIL:** Coll. of Physical Therapists of Alberta (Council; Chair, Educ. Committee 1986-91); Multiple Sclerosis Society, Alberta Div. (Dir.; Chair 1984-85); Canadian Evaluation Society. **HONS:** Alberta Achievement Award for nat'l badminton title, 1974; Research Grant, Physiotherapy Foundation of Canada, 1985-87; Studentship, Alberta Heritage Foundation for Medical Research, 1986-88. **INTERESTS:** outdoor pursuits with family; reading; travel; golf.

Morrison, Cathleen, B.A. ■ ◐ ⊕

Executive Director, CANADIAN CYSTIC FIBROSIS FOUNDATION, 2221 Yonge St., Ste. 601, Toronto, ON M4S 2B4 (416) 485-9149 & 1-800-378-CCFF, FAX 485-0960. Born Brantford, Ont. 1943. 2 ch. **EDUC:** Univ. of Toronto, B.A.(English/French) 1965. **CAREER:** Teacher of English Language & Lit., Staatliches Nicholaus Cusanus Gymnasium, Bonn/Bad

Godesberg, Germany, 1965-66; Teacher of English, National Ballet Sch., 1966-69; Researcher, Pollution Probe Foundation/Atkinson Charitable Foundation, 1974; Consultant, National Film Board of Canada, 1974-75; Exec. Dir., Ontario Association of Children's Mental Health Centres, 1976-81; Exec. Dir., Canadian Cystic Fibrosis Foundation, 1981 to date. SELECTED PUBLICATIONS: "National and International Cystic Fibrosis Associations" reference book chapter (*Current Topics in Cystic Fibrosis* Volume I, UK: John Wiley and Sons, 1992). AFFIL: National Voluntary Health Agencies (Chair 1988-90); Coalition of National Voluntary Organizations (Exec. Mbr. 1988-90); Ontario Law Reform Commission Proj. on Genetic Testing (Advisory Bd.); Healthpartners Fund (Rep. of the Canadian Cystic Fibrosis Foundation). HONS: Walter Massey Scholarship, Victoria Coll., Univ. of Toronto, 1961; Canada 125 Medal. MISC: extensive public speaking (English & French) within Canada & internationally.

Morrison, Claudia, B.A.,M.A.,Ph.D. 🎨 📖
Instructor, JOHN ABBOTT COLLEGE, Box 2000, Ste. Anne de Bellevue, QC H9X 3L9 (514) 694-4782. 2 ch. EDUC: American Univ., B.A. (English) 1957; Univ. of Florida, M.A.(English) 1958; Univ. of North Carolina, Ph.D.(English) 1963. CAREER: Asst. Prof., Sweetbriar Coll., 1965-66; Asst. Prof., Youngstown State Univ., 1966-69; Assoc. Prof., Univ. of Waterloo, 1969-72; Instructor, John Abbott Coll., 1972 to date. SELECTED PUBLICATIONS: *From the Foot of the Mountain* (Cormorant, 1990); short fiction in numerous magazines. AFFIL: Federation of English Writers of Quebec. HONS: shortlisted for Prize for Best English Fiction in Quebec (*From the Foot of the Mountain*), Quebec Society for the Promotion of English Language Literature, 1991. INTERESTS: photography; environmental & dev. issues; writing. COMMENT: *"A teacher of social issues, an environmental and peace activist, a mother of two daughters, a writer of engagé fiction."*

Morrison, Gabrielle, B.Sc.,B.Eng.,P.Eng., C.H.E. ⊕ $
Vice-President of Professional Services, IWK/GRACE HEALTH CENTRE FOR CHILDREN, WOMEN & FAMILIES, 5980 University Ave., Halifax, NS B3H 3E2 (902) 420-6652, EMAIL gmorrison@ccmail.gracehosp.ns.ca. Born N.S. 1953. s.. EDUC: Dalhousie Univ., B.Sc.(Eng.) 1974; Technical Univ. of Nova Scotia, B.Eng.(Industrial) 1976. CAREER: Mgmt Eng., Halifax Infirmary Hospital, 1976-80; Dir., Mgmt Eng., 1980-85; Asst. Exec. Dir., Grace Maternity Hospital, 1985-91; VP, Planning &

Oper., 1991-95; VP, Professional Svcs, IWK/Grace Health Centre for Children, Women & Families, 1995 to date. AFFIL: Association of Professional Engineers of N.S. (P.Eng.); Canadian Coll. of Health Service Executives (Certified Health Exec.); Technical Univ. of Nova Scotia (Gov.; Exec. Committee, Bd. of Gov.). INTERESTS: horseback riding (dressage). COMMENT: *"Gabrielle Morrison, P.Eng., is a results-oriented senior executive with 15 years' experience in planning, development and management in the health-care sector. She is a member of the Executive Committee of the Board of Governors of the Technical University of Nova Scotia and is an avid equestrian."*

Morrison, Nancy, Q.C.,B.A., LL.B. ■ 🎨 ✿ ✆
Judge, SUPREME COURT OF BRITISH COLUMBIA, Vancouver, BC. Born Estevan, Sask. 1937 EDUC: Univ. of British Columbia, B.A.(Pol. Sci.) 1958; Osgoode Hall Law Sch., Toronto, LL.B. 1961. BAR: Ont., 1963; B.C., 1970; Sask., 1996. CAREER: office worker; Social Welfare Worker, Sask. Dept. of Welfare; reporter, *Yorkton Enterprise*; Ptnr, LaMarsh & LaMarsh, Niagara Falls, Ont., 1963-66; Ptnr, Morrison, MacDonald & Morrison, Yorkton, Sask., 1966-70; Asst. City Prosecutor, Vancouver, 1970; est. own law firm, Vancouver, 1971; Ptnr, Deverell, Harrop, Morrison & Wood, Vancouver, 1972; Judge, Criminal Div., Prov. Court, B.C., 1972-81; V-Chrm, BC Labour Rel'ns Bd. & Labour Arbitrator,1973-76; Hon. Lecturer in Family Law, Univ. of British Columbia, 1980-81; resigned as Judge from the Prov. Court Bench, 1981; private law practice, 1981-96; appointed Judge, Supreme Court of B.C., 1996 to date. SELECTED PUBLICATIONS: "Separation & Divorce" in *The Canadian Woman's Legal Guide* (Doubleday, 1987). AFFIL: BC Motion Picture Appeal Bd.; Vancouver Safer City Task Force (Chair). HONS: Citizen of the Year Award, Vancouver Rotary Club, 1981; Woman of Distinction Award, YWCA, 1986. MISC: frequent public speaker.

Morrisroe, Sharon J., B.A.,LL.B. 🎨
In-house Counsel, CONNOR CLARK & LUNN INVESTMENT MANAGEMENT LTD., 925 W. Hastings St., Ste. 1200, Vancouver, BC V6C 3L2, FAX (604) 643-2003, EMAIL alex-campbell@mindlink.bc.ca. Born Calgary. m. Alex Campbell. 3 ch. Brian A., Laura E., Sarah C. EDUC: Univ. of Alberta, B.A.(with distinction) 1976; Osgoode Hall Law Sch., LL.B.(Law) 1979. CAREER: practised Corp./Securities Law, Swinton & Co., Barristers & Solicitors, 1980-92. AFFIL: Canadian Bar Association

(Securities & Bus. Law Subsections); Hollyburn Country Club, W. Vancouver; Christ the Redeemer Catholic Church, W. Vancouver.

Morrow, Joanne, B.A. ✕
Director, Arts Division, THE CANADA COUNCIL, 350 Albert St., Box 1047, Ottawa, ON K1P 5V8 (613) 237-3400, FAX 567-9507. EDUC: Trinity Coll., Univ. of Toronto, B.A.(Modern Languages & Lit.) 1971. CAREER: Soprano, The Festival Singers of Canada, 1971-72; Jr. Officer, then Grants Coord., The Touring Office, The Canada Council, 1972-76; Chef de Productions, Les Productions Internationales Albert Sarfati, Paris, France, 1977-80; Music Administrator, The National Arts Centre, 1981-85; Music Prod., 1985-89; Head, Music & Opera Section, The Canada Council, 1989-93; Dir., Arts Div., 1993 to date.

Morrow, Joy, B.Sc.,M.Sc.,LL.B. ◻ ❁
Partner, SMART & BIGGAR and FETHERSTONHAUGH & CO., P.O. Box 2999, Stn. D, Ottawa, ON K1P 5Y6 (613) 232-2486, FAX 232-8440. Born Montreal 1949. m. A. David Morrow. EDUC: McGill Univ., B.Sc.(Genetics/Zoology) 1970; Queen's Univ., M.Sc.(Cell Biol.) 1974, LL.B. 1977. BAR: Ont., 1979. CAREER: Registered Cdn Trade-Mark Agent, 1979 to date; Registered Cdn Patent Agent, 1982 to date; Ptnr, Smart & Biggar, 1987 to date; Ptnr, Fetherstonhaugh & Co., 1987 to date. SELECTED PUBLICATIONS: numerous - on various intellectual property & biotechnology patenting issues. DIRECTOR: Industrial Biotechnology Association of Canada. AFFIL: Canadian Bar Association; Patent & Trademark Institute of Canada (Chrm, Biotechnology Prosecution Liaison Committee); American Intellectual Property Law Association (Chrm, Int'l Subcommittee, Biotechnology Committee); International Association for the Protection of Industrial Property; Women's Business Network; Women in Science & Engineering; Canadian Animal Germplasm (Tech. Experts Bd.). INTERESTS: downhill skiing; long-blade & in-line skating; hiking; gardening; reading; travelling. MISC: invited speaker at numerous conferences. COMMENT: *"Fortunate to have been able to combine background in science and law in a career on the forefront of the latest developments in biotechnology."*

Morse, Elizabeth, B.Sc.,M.A. ■ ◐ ⊕
Member, Support Services Committee, AMYOTROPHIC LATERAL SCLEROSIS SOCIETY OF CANADA (800) 267-4257, Manitoba Region (204) 949-0387. Retired Director, Department of Communication Disorders, DEER LODGE CENTRE, 2109 Portage Ave., Winnipeg, MB

R3J 0L3 (204) 837-1301, FAX 897-7376. Born Mass. 1934. m. Wes Phippen. 6 ch., 4 stepch. EDUC: State Univ. of New York, Albany, B.Sc.(summa cum laude, Speech Language Pathology) 1973; George Washington Univ., M.A.(Speech Language Pathology) 1981. CAREER: Speech Language Pathologist, 1974 to date. EDIT: *Resources for A.L.S. Healthcare Providers*, A.L.S. Society of Canada. AFFIL: Canadian Association of Speech-Language Pathologists & Audiologists; Manitoba Speech & Hearing Association; American Speech-Language-Hearing Association; Board Certified in Neurologic Communication Disorders in Adults; Amyotrophic Lateral Sclerosis Society of Canada (Chair, Support Svcs Committee). HONS: 3 A.C.E. awards. INTERESTS: family; biking; sailing; canoeing. MISC: numerous appearances as guest speaker to various organizations & universities; collaborated with ALS Society of Canada compiling & editing *Resources For ALS Healthcare Providers*; initiated the ALS Team at Deer Lodge Centre in 1986 which formalized in 1989 as a self-directed team of rehab. specialists working with community health care to provide a continuum of service to persons with ALS. COMMENT: *"I started my career in Speech Language Pathology when I was in my late 30s while raising a family of six children. I worked in school systems for six years and then began a specialized career working with adults. I met my first ALS client in 1980 in graduate school. I worked at Deer Lodge Centre in Winnipeg, Manitoba from September 1984 until December 1995. I have served persons with ALS for the past 11 years."*

Mortil, Janne ■ ■ ✕ ♀
Actress. c/o Characters Talent Agency (Vancouver) Ltd., 1505 W. 2nd Ave., Ste. 200, Vancouver, BC V6H 3Y4 (604) 733-9800, FAX 733-6000. CAREER: began acting at age 5 with recurring role in *Huck Finn and Friends*; roles in TV series, movies of the week, feature films, commercials & on stage. SELECTED CREDITS: Film: Lead, *The Composer's* "Rossini's Ghost"; Lead, *Tokyo Cowboy*; Principal, *Little Women*; Lead, *Clan of the Cave Bear*; Principal, *Chaindance*; Principal, *The Changeling*. Movies of the week: Co-Star, *The Titanic* (mini-series); Supporting, *Mixed Blessings*; Supporting Lead, *Johnny's Girl*; Supporting Lead, *Friends to the End*; Principal, *The Valour and the Horror*; other roles. TV series: Guest Star, *The X-Files*; Series Regular, *Side Effects* (2 seasons); Guest Star, *Viper*; Guest Star, *Two*; Guest Star, *Poltergeist*; Guest Star, *North of 60* (3 eps.); Series Regular, *Street Justice* (2 seasons); Guest Star, *Mom P.I.*; Principal, *21 Jump Street* (3

eps.); Principal/Co-Star, *Beachcombers* (6 eps.); roles in numerous other series. Theatre: Abigail, *The Crucible*; Tracy, *Seascape With Sharks and Dancer*; Karen, *The Kite*; 4 other roles. HONS: nomination, Gemini Award (for *Side Effects*), 1996.

Morton, Kathleen, B.A. 🐝 📖 ☟
President, BETHANY HISTORICAL SOCIETY, RR 1, Bethany, ON L0A 1A0 (705) 277-2636. Born Peterborough, Ont. 1948. s. EDUC: Trent Univ., B.A.(Soc./Anthro.) 1977; Lacombe Sch. of Auctioneering, Certificate 1981; Sir Sanford Fleming Coll., Certificate (Bus.) 1986. CAREER: public sch. teacher, 1969 to date; auctioneer, 1981 to date; store owner, 1982 to date; Sch. Trustee, Victoria County, 1988 to date. SELECTED CREDITS: video record of Southern Ont. charting history from Ice Age to settlement (1982). AFFIL: Ontario Public School Trustees' Association; Ontario Women Teachers' Federation (Unit & County Pres.); Bethany Outdoor Theatre (site owner); Manvers Historical Society (Pres. & Founding Mbr.). HONS: Certificate of Outstanding Teaching Performance, Durham Bd. of Educ., 1984; Bicentennial Medal, Community Service, 1984. INTERESTS: local history; charting unwritten history from Ice Age to settlement; archeology; gardening; collecting antiques; art; music. MISC: grant for video to celebrate 200 yrs. of settlement in Ont., Gov't of Ont., 1982. COMMENT: *"Education; pilot and research projects to aid children with learning problems or gifted students. Mentor for youth, local historian, betterment of community life and cultural awareness."*

Mosher, Cathy, B.S.W. 📇 🐝 ⭕
Nephrology Social Worker, Social Work Department, VICTORIA GENERAL HOSPITAL, 1278 Tower Rd., Halifax, NS B3H 2Y9 (902) 428-4087, FAX 428-4429. Born Windsor, N.S. 1952. m. Michael Mosher. 2 ch. EDUC: N.S. Institute of Technology, Social Svc Worker (Social Work) 1977; Maritime Sch. of Social Work, Dalhousie Univ., B.S.W. 1991. CAREER: Health Care Social Worker, 1977 to date. AFFIL: The Kidney Foundation of Canada (Chair, Organ Donation Committee, N.S. Branch; Dir.-at-Large, Lunenburg County Chapter; Atlantic Rep., Nat'l Patient Svcs Committee; Atlantic Rep., Nat'l Awards Committee; Branch Strategic Planning Implementation Committee; Dir., Nat'l Bd. 1992-95; Chair, Nat'l Patient Svc Committee 1992-94; N.S. Branch: Immediate Past Pres.; Pres. 1993-95; VP 1990-93; Patient Svcs Chair 1986-91); Health Partner Fund (Immediate Past Pres., N.S. Div.); The N.S. Association of Social Workers (Registered Social Worker); The Canadian Association of Nephrology Social Workers; HONS: Community Service Award, Metro Area Community Service Bd. for the Deaf, 1985; Dr. A.J. MacLeod Scholarship, N.S. Branch, The Kidney Foundation of Canada, 1989; President's Award, N.S. Branch, The Kidney Foundation of Canada, 1990. INTERESTS: working with my hands; gardening; sewing; cross-stitch; camping; canoeing; hiking; reading. MISC: various presentations & workshops; began Master of Social Work degree (part-time), Maritime School of Social Work, Sept. 1996. COMMENT: *"I tend to be rather passionate about life and am not satisfied with doing things halfway. I've worked hard to achieve my goals and dreams, both in my personal and professional life. I get a great deal of satisfaction from my volunteer work and believe I get more from it than I give. I look forward to new challenges and plan to complete my Master of Social Work degree in the future."*

Mosher, Edith M. 📕 📖
Author, Poet. Hants County, NS. Born Hants County, N.S. 1910. w. 3 ch. Frederick George Mosher, Hazel Rita Mosher (dec.), Ernest Eldon Mosher. EDUC: high sch.; Acadia Univ., journalism & creative writing; self-taught. CAREER: worked as nurse's aide. SELECTED PUBLICATIONS: 10 books published by Lancelot Press; *The Family Book of Fact and Fiction* (West Hants Historical Society). AFFIL: SPCA. HONS: various awards for poetry. INTERESTS: amateur theatricals. MISC: operates amateur bird sanctuary. COMMENT: *"I live beside the sea and have much interest in things associated with the tides, the sea shore and the ships."*

Mossman, Mary Jane, B.A.,LL.B., LL.M. ☟ ◻
Professor, Osgoode Hall Law School, YORK UNIVERSITY, 4700 Keele St., North York, ON M3J 1P3 (416) 736-5547, FAX 736-5736. Born Halifax 1946. m. Brian D. Bucknall. EDUC: McGill Univ., B.A.(Hons. English) 1967; Queen's Univ., LL.B. 1970; Univ. of London, UK, LL.M. 1971. BAR: New South Wales, 1975; Ont., 1977. CAREER: Lecturer, Fac. of Law, Univ. of New South Wales, Australia, 1972-75; Sr. Lecturer, 1975-76; Assoc. Prof., Osgoode Hall Law Sch., York Univ., 1977-89; Acting Dir., Parkdale Community Legal Svcs, 1978; Clinic Funding Mgr, Ont. Legal Aid Plan, 1979-82; Asst. Dean, Osgoode Hall Law Sch., 1983-85; Visiting Fellow, Fac. of Law, Univ. of New South Wales, 1986; Assoc. Dean, Osgoode Hall Law Sch., 1986-

87; Visiting Prof., Fac. of Law, Univ. of Windsor, Jan. 1989; Prof., Osgoode Hall Law Sch., 1990 to date; Visiting Woman Scholar, Sch. of Public Admin., Queen's Univ., Feb. 1990; Visiting Prof., Fac. of Law, Queen's Univ., 1990-91; Parsons Visitor, Sydney Law Sch., 1992; Visiting Prof., Columbia Law Sch., Fall 1992; Gordon Henderson Chair in Human Rights, University of Ottawa, Fall 1995. SELECTED PUBLICATIONS: "The Ontario Board of Review: An Examination of Some Decisions" (*Bulletin, Canadian Welfare Law* 1972); "'Otherness' and the Law School: A Comment on Teaching Gender Equality" (*Canadian Journal of Women and the Law* 1985); "The Use of Non-Discriminatory Language in Law" (*Canadian Bar Review* 1994); "Running Hard to Stand Still: The Paradox of Family Law Reform" (*Dalhousie Law Journal* 1994); numerous other publications. EDIT: Ed. Bd., *Canadian Journal of Family Law*, 1979-81; Ed. Bd., *Australian Journal of Law and Society*, 1982 to date; Advisory Bd., *Canadian Journal of Women and the Law*, 1985-88; Ed. Bd., 1988-89; Advisory Bd., *Journal of Law and Social Policy*, 1985-90. AFFIL: Min. of Health, Psychiatric Patient Advocacy Program (Advisory Committee); Canadian Association of Law Teachers; Bloor St. United Church. HONS: McGill Univ. Entrance Scholarship, 1964; Queen's Univ. Entrance Scholarship, 1967; various undergrad. prizes, both universities; OLSA Gavel Award; Commonwealth Scholarship (UK), 1970; Distinguished Service Award, Canadian Bar Association–Ont., 1987; Supporter of the Year Award, Advocacy Resource Centre for the Handicapped, 1988; Medal of the Law Society of Upper Canada, 1990. MISC: numerous conference presentations.

Moulden, H. Julia Ⓢ 🗍
President, MOULDEN COMMUNICATIONS, 175 Elm St., Ste. 602, Toronto, ON M5T 2Z8 (416) 598-0370, FAX 598-7808. Born Toronto 1956. s. CAREER: Pres., Moulden Comm, 1985 to date. SELECTED PUBLICATIONS: *Green is Gold: Business Talking to Business About the Environmental Revolution*, with Patrick Carson (Toronto: HarperCollins, 1991); "Making a Better Butter" (*Marketing* May 19, 1993); "Portable compressor recycles CFCs" (*The Globe and Mail* Dec. 1, 1992); "Whitewash" (*Harrowsmith* Oct. 1992); "One Minute Workout" (*Toronto Life* Oct. 1988); "Porn: New Battle, Old War" (*MS. Magazine* Nov. 1987). AFFIL: Writers' Union of Canada; Charles Hastings Co-operative (Dir. 1990-93); Outward Bound (Fundraising/Mktg Committee 1992-93). HONS: Gold, Environmental Report, International Arc Awards (for writing

Abitibi Price's 1994-95 Environmental Progress Report). INTERESTS: women (okay, men too); words; wine; outdoors; opera. COMMENT: *"Autodidact feminist generalist. Speechwriter to the stars. Have called Canada, Germany, US and Mexico home. Operating theory: self-in-relation; no woman is an island."*

Moulder, Cathy, B.A.,M.L.S. 🗍 📖 🐟
Curator, Lloyd Reeds Map Collection, MCMASTER UNIVERSITY, 1280 Main St. W., Hamilton, ON L8S 4L6 (905) 525-9140, ext. 24745, FAX 546-0625, EMAIL moulder@ mcmaster.ca. EDUC: McMaster Univ., B.A. 1971; Univ. of Toronto, M.L.S. 1991. CAREER: Documentalist, Urban Documentation Centre, McMaster Univ., 1971-93; Curator, Lloyd Reeds Map Collection, McMaster Univ., 1986 to date. SELECTED PUBLICATIONS: "Acquisition of Municipal Documents" (Canadian Association of Special Libraries & Information Services/*Toronto Newsletter* Apr. 1977); *Canadian Urban Affairs Collections: A Directory* (C.A.S.L.I.S & Information Services, Urban Affairs Subcommittee, 1980); "Will Your Library be the Spatial Data Centre of the Future?" (*A.C.M.L.A. Bulletin* 83 1991); "Training Student Assistants for Reference Service in a Map Library" (*A.C.M.L.A. Bulletin* Dec. 1992); "Fire Insurance Plans as a Data Source in Urban Research: An Annotated Bibliography of Examples" (*Art Reference Services Quarterly* 3 1993); "Resource Sharing Projects of the O.C.U.L. Map Group" (*A.C.M.L.A. Bulletin* Mar. 1994); "GIS and Libraries: Issues and Implications" (*A.C.M.L.A. Bulletin,* Fall 1995). AFFIL: Association of Canadian Map Libraries & Archives (Exec.; Pres. 1993-95); Council of Planning Librarians (Exec. 1991-94); Ontario Council of University Libraries (Chair, Map Group 1990-92); Canadian Library Association; Canadian Association of Special Libraries & Information Services. HONS: Paper Award, Association of Canadian Map Libraries & Archives, 1992.

Moulton, Mary Elspeth Catherine 🕾 🛇 O
Executive Director, NEPTUNE THEATRE FOUNDATION, 1593 Argyle St., Halifax, NS B3J 2B2 (902) 429-7300. Born Montreal 1948. m. Maxwell Moulton. 2 ch. Allan Ross Moulton, Brian Douglas Moulton. EDUC: Codrington High Sch., Barbados, O Levels 1965; Univ. of King's Coll., Halifax, B.Sc. program 1965-66. CAREER: Mgr, Mktg Svcs, Central Trust, 1983-86; Asst. VP, Central Guaranty Trust, 1986-90; Dir., Univ. Rel'ns, Mount Saint Vincent Univ., 1990-94; Pres., Schooner Bluenose Contractors Limited, 1994-95; Mng Dir., Schooner Bluenose Foundation, 1994-95.

AFFIL: Rotary Club of Halifax (Bd. of Dir.); St. Margaret of Scotland Church Choir; Advisory Committee on Postulants for Ordination (Assessor). **HONS:** George Knudson Award, 1992. **INTERESTS:** travel; family; sports; current affairs. **COMMENT:** *"During a 19-year career in both the public and private sector, I developed strategies and directed the successful implementation of communications, sales, marketing and fund-raising programs. I enjoy people and working toward achieving results."*

Mowatt, E. Ann, B.A.,LL.B. ■ ⚖ ♡

Partner, PATTERSON PALMER HUNT MURPHY, One Brunswick Square, Ste. 1600, Box 1324, Saint John, NB E2L 4H8 (506) 632-8900, FAX 632-8809. Born Saint John 1962. cl. Robert D. McLardy. **EDUC:** Dalhousie Univ., B.A.(History) 1982, LL.B. 1985. **BAR:** N.B., 1986. **CAREER:** Lawyer, Patterson Palmer Hunt Murphy, 1986 to date; Ptnr, 1991 to date. **SELECTED PUBLICATIONS:** New Brunswick Chapter, *Matrimonial Property Law in Canada* eds. McLeod & Mamo (Carswell, 1994). **AFFIL:** Canadian Bar Association (N.B. Council 1986-89); Law Society of N.B. (Legal Aid Committee 1989-92); YWCA of Canada (Dir. 1989 to date; Pres. 1995); Saint John YM-YWCA (Pres. 1991); Multiple Sclerosis Society of Canada (Dir. & Pres., Atlantic Div.); Coalition of National Voluntary Organizations (Dir. 1994). **HONS:** Pace Setter Award, Saint John YM-YWCA, 1992; Canada 125 Medal. **INTERESTS:** reading; films; camping; canoeing; theatre; aquacise. **MISC:** Bar Admission Course Lecturer; presenter at Continuing Legal Educ. conferences. **COMMENT:** *"I am a lawyer who is very active in the voluntary sector at local, regional and national levels. I have been honoured to be a young woman in leadership roles with the YWCA and Multiple Sclerosis Society."*

Moyer, Janice M., B.Sc. ■ $ ⚛

President and Chief Executive Officer, APPLIED COMMUNICATIONS CANADA, INC., 155 University Ave., Ste. 1900, Toronto, ON M5H 3B7 (416) 216-3025, FAX 867-3945. Born Hamilton, Ont. 1952. m. Wes. **EDUC:** McMaster Univ., B.Sc.(Math) 1974. **CAREER:** various positions incl. Exec. Asst. to Chrm of the Bd., & Branch Office Mgr, IBM Canada, 1974-87; Pres., McCormack and Dodge Systems Canada Limited, 1987-90; Pres. & CEO, Information Technology Association of Canada (ITAC), 1990-95. **DIRECTOR:** Allstate Canada; Proctor and Redfern. **AFFIL:** ITAC (Bd. of Gov.); Ryerson Polytechnic Univ. (Fellow; Gov.). **INTERESTS:** country living; scuba diving; swimming; entertaining; reading; gardening. **MISC:** Past Chair, Nat'l Selection Committee for the Prime Minister's Awards for Teaching Excellence in Science &Technology; past mbr., Council of the Ontario Information Infrastructure, Science Network Ont. & Boards of Education; numerous articles & presentations on the role & importance of info. technology.

Mrazek, Margaret L., R.N.,B.Sc.N., LL.B. ⚖ ⊕

Partner, REYNOLDS, MIRTH, RICHARDS AND FARMER, 3200 Manulife Place, 10180 - 101 St., Edmonton, AB T5J 3W8 (403) 425-9510, FAX 429-3044. Born Alta. w. 1 ch. Monique Mrazek. **EDUC:** Misericordia Hospital Sch. of Nursing, R.N. 1960; Univ. of Edmonton, B.Sc.N.(Nursing) 1962; Univ. of Alberta, Masters in Health Service Admin. 1970, LL.B. 1986. **BAR:** Alta., 1987. **CAREER:** Staff Nurse, Misericordia Hospital, 1960; Staff Nurse, Wetaskiwin General Hospital, 1960; various Fac. positions, Misericordia Hospital Sch. of Nursing, 1962-68; Exec. Asst. to the Exec. Dir., Misericordia Hospital, 1970-76; Asst. Exec. Dir., Patient Care Svcs, 1976-77; VP, Patient Care Svcs, 1977-83; part-time, 1983-87; Student-at-Law, Reynolds, Mirth, Richards and Farmer, 1986-87; Assoc., 1987-93; Ptnr, 1993 to date. **SELECTED PUBLICATIONS:** numerous articles relating to health care field. **AFFIL:** American Coll. of Healthcare Executives; Canadian Coll. of Health Service Executives (Certified Mbr.; Health Executives' Forum, Northern Chapter); Catholic Health Association of Alberta; Alberta Association of Registered Nurses; Law Society of Alberta; Edmonton Bar Association; Canadian Bar Association (Health Law Subsection; Labour Law Subsection); Medico-Legal Society; Alberta Heritage Foundation for Medical Research (Trustee; V-Chair 1991-97). **HONS:** Gen. Proficiency Award, Misericordia Hospital Sch. of Nursing, 1960; scholarship, Misericordia Hospital Women's Auxiliary, 1960; bursary, Misericordia Nurses' Alumni Association, 1961; Fellowship, Canadian Nurses' Foundation, 1969-70. **MISC:** numerous speaking engagements & seminars.

Mulhallen, Karen, B.A.,M.A., Ph.D. 🎓 📜 📖

Professor, Department of English, RYERSON POLYTECHNIC UNIVERSITY, 350 Victoria St., Toronto, ON M5B 2K3 (416) 979-5000, ext. 6136. Editor-In-Chief, *DESCANT* MAGAZINE, Toronto, ON (416) 593-2557. Born Woodstock, Ont. 1942 **EDUC:** Waterloo Lutheran Univ., B.A.(English & Soc.) 1963; Univ. of Toronto, M.A.(English) 1967, Ph.D.(English) 1975. **CAREER:** Lecturer, Ryerson Polytechnic Institute (now Ryerson Polytechnic Univ.),

1966-70; Prof., 1970 to date; Summer Lecturer, Univ. of Toronto, 1971. SELECTED PUBLICA-TIONS: *Sheba and Solomon* (1984); *Modern Love, Poems 1970-1989* (Windsor, Ont.: Black Moss Press, 1990); *In the Era of Acid Rain*, fiction/travel (Windsor, Ont.: Black Moss Press, 1993); *Paper Guitar; 27 Writers Celebrate 25 Years of Descant*, ed. (Toronto: HarperCollins, 1995); *A Sentimental Dialogue* (Pas de Loup, 1996); *War Surgery* (Windsor, Ont.: Black Moss, 1996); various articles on literary & visual arts; poetry in various small magazines, incl. *Blewointment, Quarry* & *The White Wall Review*; various other publications. EDIT: Asst. Ed., *Descant*, 1971-72; Publisher & Ed.-in-Chief, 1973 to date; Ed., various special issues; Poetry Review Ed., *The Canadian Forum*, 1974-79; Arts Features Ed., 1975-88. AFFIL: Descant Arts & Letters Foundation (Dir.); ASECS; CMPA; CSECS; PEN; Writers' Union of Canada; ACCUTE; Friends of the Fisher Library. HONS: Ont. Scholar, 1960; Michelle Scholarship, Univ. Coll., Univ. of Toronto, 1960; Gen. Academic Scholarship, Waterloo Lutheran Univ., 1962-63; Finalist, poetry, CBC Literary Awards, 1989; Finalist, poetry, CBC-*Saturday Night* Literary Awards, 1994; Maclean Hunter Arts Journalism Fellowship, 1994. INTERESTS: art; book collecting; cooking; gardening; theatre; music. MISC: recipient, various grants & fellowships; adjudicator for various grants & competitions; numerous public readings; various broadcast appearances, incl. "Prison Poetry–Pancho Aguila," Rogers Cable TV 1974 & "Marshall McLuhan's Legacy," CJRT Radio, 1981. COMMENT: *"Editor, teacher, poet, literary journalist and writer, Karen Mulhallen makes her living professing English literature in Toronto. She is a scholar in the art of England in the 18th century and an editor and promoter of contemporary Canadian literature."*

Mulligan, Lois, B.Sc.,Ph.D. ■■ ❀ ⤳
Associate Professor, Department of Paediatrics, QUEEN'S UNIVERSITY, Kingston, ON K7L 3N6 (613) 545-6310, FAX 548-1348, EMAIL Mulligal@qucdn.queensu.ca. Born Saint John, N.B. 1959. m. R.W. McCleave. EDUC: Univ. of New Brunswick, B.Sc.(Biol.) 1981; Queen's Univ., Ph.D.(Biol.) 1986. CAREER: Postdoctoral Fellow, Ludwig Institute for Cancer Research, Montreal, 1986-90; Sr. Research Assoc., Cambridge Univ., 1990-93; Asst. Prof., Paediatrics, Queen's Univ., 1993-96; Assoc. Prof., Paediatrics, 1996 to date. AFFIL: Genetics Society of Canada; American Society of Human Genetics. COMMENT: *"Lois Mulligan is a researcher in the area of cancer genetics. Her work has included involvement in the*

Human Genome Mapping Project and particularly in identification of genes that cause inherited cancer syndromes. She is dedicated to the promotion of women in science."

Mullins, Sister Patricia, B.A.,M.Sc., Ph.D. ■ ☼
Head, SISTERS OF CHARITY, Mount St. Vincent Motherhouse, 150 Bedford Hwy., Halifax, NS B3M 3J5. Born Boston 1930; Sisters of Charity, 1951 EDUC: Mount Saint Vincent Coll., B.A. 1951; Univ. of Notre Dame, M.Sc. 1963, Ph.D. 1968. CAREER: high school teacher, N.S., 1951-65; Asst. Prof. of Chem., Mount St. Vincent Univ., 1968; Assoc. Prof., 1972; Visiting Postdoctoral Research Assoc., Univ. of Notre Dame Radiation Lab., 1975-76; Chair, Chem. Dept., 1977-79; Prof. of Chem., 1978-88; Dean of Humanities & Sci., 1979-88; Gen. Asst. & Treas., Sisters of Charity, 1988-96; Head, 1996 to date. SELECTED PUBLICA-TIONS: author/co-author of various articles in chem. publications. INTERESTS: reading; music. MISC: recipient, NRC, NSERC University Operating Research Grant, 1969, 1970, 1972-79.

Mumford, Cheryl A., B.A. ☻
Assistant to the Director, Communications, UNITED FOOD AND COMMERCIAL WORKERS INTERNATIONAL UNION (UFCW), 61 International Blvd., Ste. 300, Rexdale, ON M9W 6K4 (416) 675-1104, FAX 675-6919. EDUC: McMaster Univ., B.A.(Hist.) 1968. CAREER: various positions in sales, mktg & mgmt for organizations such as Maclean Hunter, Imperial Life, C.B.S. Educational Publishing, The United Way, Society for Visual Education; Asst. to the Dir., Comm., United Food & Commercial Workers' International Union, 1993 to date. AFFIL: Centre for Advancement in Work & Living (Bd. of Dir. 1994-97); Dorothy Ley Hospice (Public Rel'ns Committee 1992-93).

Mungall, Constance, B.A. ⛫ ☻ ⤳
Freelance writer. 946 Wilmer St., Victoria, BC V0S 4B7 (604) 592-3753. 2 ch. Robert Taylor Mungall, Alexander Mungall. EDUC: Univ. of Toronto, B.A. 1954. CAREER: Economist, Gov't of Ont., 1954-55; housewife & mother, 1955-80; various writing, editing & broadcasting positions incl., Contributing Ed., *Chatelaine*, Contributing Ed., *Maclean's*, & Producer of CBC documentaries, 1961-77; Ed., *GEOS Magazine*, 1977-87; freelance writer, 1988 to date. SELECTED PUBLICATIONS: *Probate Guide for British Columbia* (Vancouver: International Self Counsel Press 1975 & 13 eds. through 1995); *Changing Your Name in Canada* (Vancouver: International Self Counsel

Press 1976); *Yes We Can: Organizing Citizen Action* (Toronto: Synergistics Consulting Ltd. 1980); *More Than Just a Job: Worker Co-op Movement in Canada* (Ottawa: Steel Rail Publishing 1988); *Planet Under Stress*, ed., Royal Society of Canada (Toronto: Oxford University Press 1990); *La Terre en Péril* (Toronto: Oxford University Press 1990); *Taking Action* (Vancouver: International Self Counsel Press 1993). **AFFIL:** Religious Society of Friends (Quakers); Super Sch. of Toronto (founder & Dir., 1967-69); Victoria Sch. of Writing (Bd. of Dir. 1996 to date). **HONS:** many Association of Earth Science Editors & Media Club awards for content & design of GEOS. **INTERESTS:** change–personal, social, spiritual. **COMMENT:** *"Trying to make a constructive contribution to the planet while supporting self and two children and nourishing all three, being a decent friend and lover = doubletime job."*

Munro, Alice • 📖 🎭 ✏

Writer. c/o McClelland and Stewart. Born Wingham, Ont. 1931. m. 3 ch. Sheila, Jenny, Andrea. **SELECTED PUBLICATIONS:** *Dance of the Happy Shades* (1968); *Lives of Girls and Women* (1971); *Something I've Been Meaning to Tell You* (1974); *The Moons of Jupiter* (1982); *The Progress of Love* (1986); *Friend of My Youth* (1990); *Open Secret* (1994). **HONS:** Gov. General's Award for Literature, *Dance of the Happy Shades*, 1968 & *Who Do You Think You Are*, 1978; Canadian Booksellers Award (*Lives of Girls and Women*), 1971; winner, Canada-Australia Literary Prize; 1st recipient of the Marian Engel award.

Munro, June E., B.J.,B.L.S.,M.L.S. 📖 ✒ ⭘

Librarian (retired). 35 Towering Heights, Apt. 710, St. Catharines, ON L2T 3G8. Born Echo Bay, Ont. 1921. s. **EDUC:** Carleton Univ., B.J. 1961; Univ. of Toronto, B.L.S. 1962, M.L.S. 1972. **CAREER:** Head, Children's Library Svcs, Sault Ste. Marie Public Library, 1941-51; Children's Librarian, London Public Library, 1951-53; Head, Children's Library Svcs, Leaside Public Library, 1953-56; Asst. to Exec. Dir. & Publications Prod. Ed., Canadian Library Association, 1956-61; Supervisor, Extension Svc & Ed., Ontario Library Review, Ont. Provincial Library Service, 1961-70; Book Acquisitions Advisor, Coll. Bibliocentre, Toronto, 1970-72; Chief, Public Rel'ns Div., National Library of Canada, 1972-73; Dir. of Library Svcs, St. Catharines Public Library, 1973-82; Sessional Lecturer, Sch. of Librarianship, Univ. of British Columbia, 1983. **SELECTED PUBLICATIONS:** author, various library publications; Ed., *Ontario Library Review*, 1961-70; Ed., *National Library News*,

1972-73. **AFFIL:** Canadian Library Association; Ontario Library Association; Shaw Festival Guild; Carousel Players; University Women's–St. Catharines; Protestant. **INTERESTS:** church library & service; theatre; music; dance; Cdn literature. **COMMENT:** *"A career in library service, at local, provincial and national levels. A pioneer in some areas–concentration on children's library services. Some publishing and public relations and administration."*

Munroe-Blum, Heather, B.A.,B.S.W., M.S.W.,Ph.D. 🎓 ✚ ❀

Professor and Vice-President, Research and International Relations, UNIVERSITY OF TORONTO, 27 King's College Circle, Toronto, ON M5S 1A1 (416) 978-4984, FAX 971-2647. Born Montreal 1950. m. Leonard Solomon Blum. 1 ch. Sydney Rebecca Munroe Blum. **EDUC:** McMaster Univ., B.A. 1974, B.S.W. 1974; Wilfrid Laurier Univ., M.S.W. 1975; Univ. of North Carolina at Chapel Hill, Ph.D.(Epidemiology) 1983. **CAREER:** various administrative & program dev. at mental health facilities in Hamilton, Ont., 1976-89; Clinical Lecturer, Dept. of Psychiatry, McMaster Univ., 1976-79; Asst. Clinical Prof., 1979-84; Asst. Prof., Dept. of Social Work, Atkinson Coll., York Univ., 1982-84; Asst. Prof., Depts. of Psychiatry & of Clinical Epidemiology & Biostatistics, McMaster Univ., 1984-89; Adjunct Prof., 1989 to date; Prof., Fac. of Social Work, Univ. of Toronto, 1989 to date; Dean, 1989-93; Prof., Fac. of Medicine, 1990-96; Prof., Dept. of Psychiatry, 1991-97; Prof. & VP, Research & Int'l Rel'ns, 1994-99. **SELECTED PUBLICATIONS:** over 50 peer-reviewed scholarly publications incl. *PDQ Epidemiology*, with D. Streiner & G. Norman (Burlington, Ont.: B.C. Decker 1989); *Borderline Personality Disorder: An Empirical Perspective*, ed. with J.F. Clarkin & E. Marziali (New York: Guilford, 1992); *Schizophrenia in Focus: A Psychosocial Approach to Treatment Rehabilitation*, with D. Dawson & G. Bartolucci (New York: Human Sciences Press, Div. of Behavioral Publications, 1993); *Interpersonal Group Psychotherapy for Borderline Personality Disorder*, with E. Marziali (Basic Books, 1994); "Pharmacologic and Psychosocial Integration in the Treatment of Schizophrenia," with E. Collins (*Contemporary Psychiatry* 1993); "Canadian Study of Health and Aging: Study Methods and Prevalence of Dementia" (*Canadian Medical Association Journal* Mar. 1994); "Symposium of Epidemiology," co-ed. with N. Kates (*Canadian Journal of Psychiatry*, 35(5) 1990). **AFFIL:** American Association for Clinical Psychosocial Research (Fellow); Massey Coll. (Assoc. Fellow

1990-93); Delta Omega, American Public Health Honor Society; Society for Psychotherapy Research; The Canadian Institute for the Weizmann Institute of Science; Canadian Mental Health Association; Canadian Psychiatric Association; Canadian Public Health Association; Canadian Academy of Psychiatric Epidemiology; Ontario Cancer Institute/Princess Margaret Hospital (Bd. Mbr. 1994-97; Chair, Research Committee); The United Way Campaign (Co-Chair 1994-96); Nestlé Canada Advisory Bd. (Dir. 1995-97); Canadian Institute for Advanced Research (Research Council); Sunnybrook Health Science Centre (Bd. of Trustees); Institute for Work & Health (Bd.); Premier's Council on Health, Well-being & Social Justice, Ont. (Child & Youth Policy Issues Committee); Laidlaw Foundation (Child & Family Advisory Committee); Manitoba Centre for Health Policy & Evaluation (Advisory Bd.); Ontario Council on University Research (Chair 1995-96); Univ. of Toronto (Gov.; Co-Chair, United Way Campaign 1994-96); Industry Canada (Chair, Univ. Advisory Bd.). HONS: Outstanding Alumni Award, Sch. of Public Health & Dept. of Epidemiology, Univ. of North Carolina, 1992; McMaster Distinguished Alumni Award for the Arts, 1995; inducted as mbr., McMaster Alumni Gallery, McMaster Univ., 1996. INTERESTS: social-psychiatric epidemiology. MISC: recipient, numerous grants, incl. major grants from the National Institute of Mental Health, US; numerous invited lectures & conference presentations; reviewer for various granting agencies.

Murdoch, Sarah, B.A.A. ■■ /
Associate Editor, THE GLOBE AND MAIL, 444 Front St. W., Toronto, ON M5V 2S9, EMAIL smurdoch@globeandmail.ca. Born London, UK 1946. m. Douglas Marshall. EDUC: Ryerson Polytechnical Institute, B.A.A.(Journalism) 1974. CAREER: Reporter, The Ottawa Citizen, 1974-78; Editor, The Grad Post, 1979; Staff Writer, The Graduate & The Bulletin, Univ. of Toronto, 1980-81; Features Editor, Toronto Life magazine, 1982-85; Editor, Successful Executive magazine, 1986; Features Editor, Financial Times of Canada, 1987-90; Focus Editor/Assoc. Editor, The Globe and Mail, 1990 to date. AFFIL: The Women of the Royal Canadian Military Institute (founding mbr.). INTERESTS: food & drink; good conversation; non-taxing strolls; mystery novels.

Murphy, Beverle Elaine Pearson, B.A., M.D.,M.Sc.,Ph.D. ⊕ ⬦ ♂
Professor of Medicine, MCGILL UNIVERSITY, 845 Sherbrooke St. W., Montreal, QC H3A 2T5, FAX (514) 937-2455. Senior Physician, MONTREAL GENERAL HOSPITAL. Born Toronto 1929. w. David Raymond Murphy. 2 ch. Madeleine Louise Murphy, Catherine Elaine Murphy. EDUC: Univ. of Toronto, B.A.(Sci.) 1952, M.D. 1956; McGill Univ., M.Sc.(Experimental Medicine) 1960, Ph.D.(Investigative Medicine) 1964. CLINICAL CAREER: Rotating Intern, Toronto General Hospital, 1956-57; Resident in Medicine, Royal Victoria Hospital, Montreal, 1959-61; Dir., Endocrinology Lab., Queen Mary Veterans Hospital, Montreal, 1964-78; Consultant in Endocrinology, 1970-73; Asst. Physician, then Assoc., & Asst. Obstetrician & Gynecologist, then Assoc., Montreal General Hospital, 1972-79; Sr. Physician, & Sr. Obstetrician & Gynecologist, 1979 to date. ACADEMIC CAREER: Research Fellow, Royal Victoria Hospital, 1957-59; Research Fellow, Queen Mary's Veterans Hospital, 1961-64; Fellow, Medical Research Council, 1963-64; Lecturer, then Asst. Prof, then Assoc. Prof., McGill Univ., 1964-74; Research Assoc., Clinical Investigation Unit, Queen Mary Veterans Hospital, 1964-70; Scholar, Medical Research Council, 1965-67; Career Investigator, 1968-94; Dir., Reproductive Physiology Unit, Montreal General Hospital Research Institute, 1972-94; Prof. of Medicine, McGill Univ., 1975 to date; Prof. of Obstetrics & Gynecology, 1979 to date; Medical Scientist, Royal Victoria Hospital, 1981 to date; Assoc. Mbr., Dept. of Physiology, McGill Univ., 1981 to date; Prof. of Psychiatry, 1985 to date. SELECTED PUBLICATIONS: "The Determination of Thyroxine Utilizing the Property of Protein Binding," with Chauncey J. Pattee (Journal of Clinical Endocrinology & Metabolism 1964); "Some Studies of the Protein-Binding of Steroids and Their Application to the Routine Micro and Ultramicro Measurement of Various Steroids in Body Fluids by Competitive Protein-Binding Radioassay" (Journal of Clinical Endocrinology & Metabolism 1967); "The Chorionic Membrane as a Source of Fetal Cortisol in Human Amniotic Fluid" (Nature 1977); "Does Sex Hormone-Binding Globulin (SHBG) Play a Role in the Transport of Estradiol in vivo?" with Anie Philip (American Journal of Obstetrics and Gynecology 1984); "Steroids and Depression" (Journal of Steroid Biochemistry and Molecular Biology 1991); "Stress and Anxio-Depressive Syndromes" (Medicographia 1994); "Coping with Menopause: A Guide to Hormone Therapy" (Canadian Journal of Continuing Medical Education 1994); more than 125 other published articles; more than 100 published abstracts. EDIT: Ed. Bd., Journal of Clinical Endocrinology & Metabolism, 1975-79; Ed. Bd., Journal of Steroid Biochemistry and Molecular Biology (formerly Journal of Steroid

Biochemistry), 1976-94; Ed. Bd., *Journal of Immunoassays*, 1979 to date. AFFIL: American Coll. of Physicians (Fellow); American Society for Clinical Investigation (Fellow); Royal Society of Canada (Fellow); Endocrine Society; Canadian Association of Medical Biochemists; Canadian Society of Clinical Investigation; Canadian Society of Endocrinology & Metabolism (Sec.-Treas. 1984-89); Canadian Investigators in Reproduction; Canadian Biochemical Society; Montreal Physiological Society (Pres. 1972-74); Quebec Association of Laboratory Physicians; Society of Obstetricians & Gynecologists of Canada; Syndicat Professionel des Médecins Endocrinologues du Québec; Association for Women in Science. HONS: Warner-Chilcott Lectureship in Diagnostics, 1973; Pharmacia Diagnostics Award, US, 1978; Corning Award in Clinical Biochemistry, UK, 1986; Officer of the Order of Quebec, 1987. INTERESTS: interrelationship between hormones & the brain; premenstrual syndrome, psychological changes in pregnancy & the menopause, steroids & depression; breast cancer; drawing & painting; piano playing; cross-country skiing. MISC: the 1964 & 1967 articles listed above were among the 100 most cited in clinical research according to *Science Citation Index* in its study of articles published 1961-78 (see *Current Contents* Feb. 11, 1980); the 1967 article was the most frequently cited scientific article from a Cdn institution & the most frequently cited single-author scientific article in the world for the same period; 1 of 2 Cdn women, 1 of 12 Canadians, & 1 of 27 women worldwide included in a list of the 1000 most-cited contemporary scientists (see *Current Contents* Oct. 12, 1981); reviewer for numerous journals & granting agencies; patent, *Method for the Determination of Thyroxine*, with Chauncey J. Pattee, 1966; patent, *Use of Estradienolone for the Maintenance of Pregnancy*, with Anie Philip, 1987; has organized various symposia; numerous invited lectures worldwide.

Murphy, Debora, B.N.,R.N. ⊕
Director, Perioperative Nursing, QUEEN ELIZABETH II HEALTH SCIENCE CENTRE, Victoria General Site, Tower Rd., Halifax, NS B3H 2Y9 (902) 428-3572. Born Halifax 1953. m. Dr. Michael F. 3 ch. EDUC: Dalhousie Univ., B.N. (Nursing) 1976. CAREER: Head Nurse, Victoria General Hospital, 1979-82; Mgmt, Training & Dev. Educator, 1984-85; Asst. Dir., Medical Nursing, 1985-88; Dir., Ambulatory Nursing, 1988-89; Dir., Critical Care Nursing, 1989-92; Dir., Perioperative Nursing, 1992 to date. AFFIL: Registered Nurses' Association of N.S.; Operating Room Nurses' Association of N.S.

INTERESTS: skiing; travel; family. COMMENT: *"Functioned in various management roles over the past 10 years and have enjoyed the many and constant challenges in each. Nursing is a career on the edge of numerous horizons that will provide for expansion of what a nurse is and does in the health-care system of the future. I hope to influence this future."*

Murphy, Marion, M.L.A. ✦
Member of Legislative Assembly, GOVERNMENT OF PRINCE EDWARD ISLAND, Box 2000, Charlottetown, PE C1A 7N8 (902) 368-4330, FAX 368-4348. Born P.E.I. 1941. m. Elmer. 4 ch. EDUC: P.W.C., Certificate (Teaching). CAREER: teacher; school secretary; M.L.A., Gov't of P.E.I., 1989 to date. AFFIL: Liberal Party of P.E.I.; Central Queens Funeral Home Coop (Founding Dir.); St. Ann's Community Centre Coop (Founding Dir.); St. Ann's 4-H Club (Leader); St. Ann's Church Women's League (Pres.); St. Ann's Pastoral Council (VP); Canadian Red Cross (Water Safety Committee 1970s-90s). HONS: Canada 125 Medal; various plaques & certificates from above organizations. INTERESTS: people (young & old); reading; sewing; cooking; being near the water; time & food with others. COMMENT: *"I aim to find a teachable moment and use it to find the good in each individual and to enjoy every day to the fullest, at whatever task presents itself. An eternal optimist."*

Murphy, Michele M., B.A.,LL.B. ■ ⚖
Lawyer, MICHELE M. MURPHY AND ASSOCIATES, 129 Queen St., Charlottetown, PE C1A 7K4 (902) 368-2276. Born 1962. EDUC: Univ. of New Brunswick B.A.(Pol. Sci.) 1983, LL.B. 1986. CAREER: Assoc. Lawyer, MacNutt and Dumont, 1986-88; Lawyer, Michele M. Murphy, 1988-91; Lawyer, Michele M. Murphy and Associates, 1991 to date. AFFIL: Kinkora & Area Business Corporation (Dir.); P.R.I.D.E. PEI Inc (Dir.); PEI Law Society (Tariff of Fees Committee); Charlottetown Area Chamber of Commerce (Dir.); PEI Law Foundation (Bd of Gov.); P.E.I. Law Society (Council Mbr.); Canadian National Institute for the Blind (Dir.). HONS: Royal Canadian Regiment Milton Fowler Gregg Scholarship, 1982. INTERESTS: politically active

Murray, Anne, C.C. ■■ 🎵
Singer. c/o Bruce Allen Talent, 406-68 Water St., Vancouver, B.C. V6B 1A6 (604) 688-7274.Born Springhill, N.S. 1945. m. Bill Langstroth 2 ch. Dawn, William. EDUC: Univ. of New Brunswick, Phys. Educ. CAREER: joined *Singalong Jubilee*, TV series, 1966; recorded 1st album, 1968; signed with Capitol

Records Canada, 1969. **SELECTED CREDITS:** 30 albums incl.: *What About Me* (1968); *This Way Is My Way* (1969); *Danny's Song* (1973); *Love Song* (1974); *Keeping in Touch* (1976); *Let's Keep It That Way* (1978); *Christmas Wishes* (1981); *Something to Talk About* (1986); *Greatest Hits Vol II* (1989); *Croonin'* (1993); *The Best...So Far* (1994); *Now & Forever* (1995); *Anne Murray* (1996). **HONS:** 4 Grammy Awards; 3 American Music Awards; 25 Juno Awards; inducted into Juno Hall of Fame, 1993; 3 Country Music Association Awards; 3 Canadian Country Music Association Awards; 1 Academy of Country Music Awards; 1 ACTRA Award; 1 Gemini Award; Officer of the Order of Canada, 1975; Walkway of Stars, Country Music Hall of Fame, 1975; LL.D.(Hon.), Univ. of New Brunswick, 1976; LL.D.(Hon.), Saint Mary's Univ., 1978; Star on the Hollywood Walk of Fame, 1980; Companion of the Order of Canada, 1984; inducted into Canadian Music Hall of Fame, 1993; Gov. Gen.'s performing arts award, 1995.

Murray, Catherine A., Ph.D. ⬡ ❀
Associate Professor, SIMON FRASER UNIVERSITY, 515 W. Hastings St., Vancouver, BC (604) 291-5204, FAX 291-5641, EMAIL catherine_murray@sfu.ca. Born Kitchener, Ont. 1952. m. Larry Buchan. 1 ch. **EDUC:** Queen's Univ., Ph.D.(Pol. Studies) 1985. **CAREER:** Sr. Proj. Dir., Decima Research, 1985-89; VP, 1989-91; Assoc. Prof., Simon Fraser Univ., 1992 to date; Dir., Centre for Policy Research on Science & Technology, Simon Fraser Univ., 1993-96. **SELECTED PUBLICATIONS:** "Information Security: At Risk?" with M.A. Kirby (*Global Networks* 1993); "Privacy Potholes on the Information Highway," with Ray Straatsma (*Issues in Canadian Communications* ed. David Taras, 1996); co-author, *Making Our Voices Heard: The Future of the CBC, NFB and Telefilm* (Report of the Mandate Review Committee, Jan. 1996). **AFFIL:** P.M.R.S.; I.I.C.; WTN Foundation (Bd.); Owl Children's Trust (Bd.); BC Film (Bd.); Broadcast Standards Council.

Murray, Heather, B.A.,M.A., Ph.D. ⬡ 📖 ▢
Associate Professor of English, Trinity College, UNIVERSITY OF TORONTO, Toronto, ON M5S 1H8 (416) 978-8249, FAX 978-4949. Born Weston, Ont. 1951. m. Prof. David Galbraith. 1 ch. Sarah. **EDUC:** Victoria Coll., Univ. of Toronto, B.A.(English) 1973; York Univ., M.A.(English) 1977, Ph.D.(English) 1984. **CAREER:** Asst. Prof. & Postdoctoral Fellow, Queen's Univ., 1985-87; Assoc. Prof., Trinity Coll., Univ. of Toronto, 1987 to date; Dir.,

Women's Studies Program, 1993-96. **SELECTED PUBLICATIONS:** *Working in English: History, Institution, Resources* (Univ. of Toronto Press, 1996); numerous articles on women authors, history & criticism, & the history of English studies. **INTERESTS:** current work on literary culture of nineteenth-century Ont. **COMMENT:** "*I am particularly interested in the position of women in higher education–now, and historically–and in access and equity issues in contemporary universities.*"

Murray, Jacqueline, B.A.,M.A., Ph.D. ⬡ 📖 ▢
Associate Professor of History and Director, Humanities Research Group, UNIVERSITY OF WINDSOR, Windsor, ON N9B 3P4 (519) 253-4232, ext. 3509, FAX 971-3620. Born Trail, B.C. 1953 **EDUC:** Univ. of British Columbia, B.A.(Hist.) 1978; Univ. of Toronto, M.A. 1979, Ph.D.(Medieval Studies) 1987. **CAREER:** Curator, Centre for Reformation & Renaissance Studies, Victoria Univ., Univ. of Toronto, 1985-87; Sr. Fellow, 1988-92; Asst. Prof., Dept. of Hist., Univ. of Windsor, 1988-91; Assoc. Prof., 1991 to date; Dir., Humanities Research Group, 1991 to date; Visiting Fellow, Clare Hall, Cambridge Univ., 1994-95; Visiting Fellow, Pontifical Institute of Medieval Studies, 1994-95. **SELECTED PUBLICATIONS:** *Domestic Society in Mediaeval Europe: A Select Bibliography*, compiled with Michael M. Sheehan (Toronto: Pontifical Institute of Medieval Studies, 1990); *Agnolo Firenzuola's On the Beauty of Women*, translated, introduced & notated with Konrad Eisenbichler (Philadelphia: Univ. of Pennsylvania Press, 1992); *Constructing Sexualities*, ed. (Windsor: Humanities Research Group, Univ. of Windsor, 1993); "Our Secret Weapon: The Humanities Must Be Brought Back from the Margins" (*Bulletin of the Canadian Federation of the Humanities* Summer 1993); various other publications. **EDIT:** Ed., *Canadian Society for Renaissance Studies Newsletter*, 1988-92; Ed., "Sexuality in the Renaissance / La Sexualité à la Renaissance," special issue of *Renaissance and Reformation/Renaissance et Réforme*, 24(1) 1988. **AFFIL:** American Historical Association; Ecclesiastical History Society, Britain; Canadian Society for Medieval Studies; Medieval Academy of America; Society for Medieval Feminist Scholarship (Pres. 1991-93); Canadian Society for Renaissance Studies (Exec. Mbr. 1988-92). **INTERESTS:** needlework; theatre; travel. **MISC:** video, *Women in the Middle Ages*, Centre for Medieval Studies & Media Centre, Univ. of Toronto (1991); various fellowships. **COMMENT:** "*In both my academic research into women in the Middle Ages and*

my work as a university administrator, I promote the inclusion of women in all areas of life and the importance of the study of the humanities to the cultivation of a humane society and the educated citizen."

Murray, Joan, B.A.,M.A.,F.R.S.C. ✪
Director, THE ROBERT MCLAUGHLIN GALLERY, 72 Queen St., Oshawa, ON L1H 3Z3 (905) 576-3000, FAX 576-9774. Born New York City 1943. m. W. Ross Murray. 3 ch. **EDUC:** Univ. of Toronto, B.A.(Fine Art) 1965; Columbia Univ., M.A.(Modern Art) 1966. **CAREER:** Head of Educ., Art Gallery of Ontario, 1968; Research Curator, 1969; Curator of Cdn Art, 1970-73; Acting Chief Curator, 1973; Dir., The Robert McLaughlin Gallery, 1974 to date. **SELECTED PUBLICATIONS:** *The Beginning of Vision: The Drawings of Lawren S. Harris*, with R. Fulford (Vancouver: Douglas and McIntyre, 1982); *The Best Contemporary Canadian Art* (Edmonton: Hurtig Publishers, 1987); *The Best of Tom Thomson* (Edmonton: Hurtig Publishers, 1986); *Daffodils in Winter: The Life and Letters of Pegi Nicol MacLeod* (Moonbeam, Ont.: Penumbra Press, 1984); *The Last Buffalo: The Story of Frederick Arthur Verner* (Toronto: Pagurian Press, 1984); *Northern Lights: Masterpieces of Tom Thomson and the Group of Seven* (Toronto: Key Porter, 1995); *Tom Thomson: The Last Spring* (Dundurn Press, 1995); *Confessions of a Curator* (Dundurn Press, 1996); *Tom Thomson: Design for a Canadian Hero* (Quarry Press, 1996); various other books on Cdn art. **AFFIL:** Canadian Art Museum Directors' Organization; Bata Shoe Museum Foundation (Advisory Council); Royal Society of Canada (Fellow). **HONS:** numerous scholarships & awards for short stories & poetry, incl. Award for Short Story Broadcast, CBC, 1965; Fellowship, Columbia Univ., 1965; Woodrow Wilson Fellowship, 1965; grant, Ontario Arts Council, 1986; Award for Sr. Cultural Mgr, Association of Cultural Executives, 1993. **MISC:** W.L. Morton Lecture, "The World of Tom Thomson," Trent University, 1991.

Murray, Judith A., R.N.,M.N. ⊕
Clinical Nurse Specialist and Nurse Practitioner in Gerontology, NORTH YORK GENERAL HOSPITAL, 4001 Leslie St., North York, ON M4K 1E1 (416) 756-6329, FAX 756-6384. Born Toronto 1941. s. **EDUC:** Kingston General Hospital, Sch. of Nursing, 1963; Dalhousie Univ., B.N. 1980, M.N. 1987; Univ. of Toronto, Diploma, Nurse Practitioner, 1995. **CAREER:** Staff Nurse, Pediatric Unit, Joseph Brant Memorial Hospital & Kingston General Hospital, 1963-65; Staff Nurse, H.N. & A.H.N., Emergency Dept., The Hospital for Sick Children, 1965-70; Staff Nurse, I.V. Team, 1972; Office Nurse, Pediatric Practice, R.L. Rodgers and Associates, 1972-73; Staff Nurse, Victorian Order of Nurses, Grey-Bruce Owen Sound Branch, 1974-78; Supervisor (part-time) & Unit Coord. (relief), Northwoodcare Inc., Halifax, 1978-80; Clinical Coord., Ambulatory Svcs, Halifax Infirmary, 1980-82; Staff Nurse–Casual, Victorian Order of Nurses, Halifax Branch, 1982-85; Consultant to the Nursing Dept., Northwoodcare Inc., Nursing Home Complex, 1985-86; Research Asst., Dalhousie Univ., 1986-88; Consultant, Registered Nurses' Association of N.S., 1987-91; Clinical Nurse Specialist, Gerontology, North York General Hospital, 1991 to date. **AFFIL:** Canadian Nurses' Foundation; Coll. of Nurses of Ontario (CNO); Registered Nurses' Association of Ontario (RNAO); Canadian Gerontological Nursing Association (CGNA); Gerontological Nursing Association of Ontario; Heritage Canada; Friends of the Public Gardens, a National Historic Site, Halifax (former Pres. & Life Mbr.). **HONS:** O.M. Wilson Prize for kindness to patients & proficiency in bedside nursing, 1963; Frances MacDonald Moss Award for Study at the Masters Level, Registered Nurses' Association of N.S., 1983; Dalton & Iris Bales Research Fund, North York General Hospital, 1992; Dr. E.W. Wright Memorial Scholarship, North York General Hospital, 1995. **INTERESTS:** jazz & classical music; swimming; tennis; cycling; skiing; Cdn heritage; antiques. **COMMENT:** *"My practice is based on the belief that the role of the nurse is to provide advocacy and coordination in health care. Through leadership, education and research, I will continue to motivate for change in healthcare delivery."*

Murray, M. Lynn, B.B.A.,LL.B. ⚖
Partner, MATHESON AND MURRAY, Box 875, Charlottetown, PE C1A 7L9 (902) 894-7051, FAX 368-3762. Born Charlottetown 1958. s. **EDUC:** Univ. of Prince Edward Island, B.B.A. 1980; Dalhousie Univ., LL.B. 1983. **BAR:** P.E.I., 1984. **CAREER:** Ptnr, Matheson and Murray. **AFFIL:** Law Society of P.E.I. (Discipline Policies & Procedures Committee); Rules Committee; Canadian Bar Association (Nat'l Civil Litigation Committee).

Murray, Susan A., B.A. $ 🍁 ♡
President, SAMCI, (nat'l gov't rel'ns consulting firm), 49 Jackes Ave., 1st Fl., Toronto, ON M4T 1E2 (416) 922-5152. Born 1953. **EDUC:** Univ. of Western Ontario, B.A.(Pol.Sci.); Nat'l Defence Course for Senior Officers' Professional Dev., Kingston, 1990. **CAREER:** Policy

Analyst, Ont. Legislature; Corp. Affairs Dir. for a private sector company; Pres. SAMCI (formerly S.A. Murray Consulting Inc.), 1982 to date. DIRECTOR: Irwin Toy Limited. AFFIL: National Ballet Sch. (Dir.); Canadian Opera Company (Dir.); Cabbagetown Community Arts Company Foundation (Trustee); Executive MBA Program, Queen's Univ. (Advisory Bd.); Rideau Club, Ottawa; Albany Club, Toronto. INTERESTS: folk art. MISC: SAMCI employs 29 people & has offices in Toronto, Ottawa & Vancouver; frequent public speaker. COMMENT: *"Susan Murray has practised exclusively in the area of government relations since 1980. She has a strong background in business, government and politics, and is acknowledged by elected officials, senior public servants and business leaders as one of the country's leading government relations professionals."*

Murray, Suzanne, M.A., M.L.A. ■ ✸
Member of the Legislative Assembly (Regina Qu'Appelle Valley), GOVERNMENT OF SASKATCHEWAN, 6845 Rochdale Blvd., Regina, SK S4X 2Z2 (306) 781-9100, FAX 781-4727. Born Rotterdam 1943. m. Christopher. 2 ch. EDUC: Univ. of Victoria, Early Childhood Educ. 1963. CAREER: Educator in B.C., Sask. & the UK. SELECTED PUBLICATIONS: weekly newspaper articles; pol. book reviews. AFFIL: New Democratic Party; library bd.; Girl Guides; community coll. bd. HONS: various scholarships, bursaries & volunteer awards. INTERESTS: reading; outdoor activities such as riding, skiing, sailing, gardening, cycling; golf. COMMENT: *"I hope I have energy, commitment, a sense of humour, love for people, a willingness to help and a sense of justice."*

Murray-Weber, Kay, A.O.C.A.,R.C.A., O.S.A. ⊗
Painter and Printmaker, 11 Linden St., Toronto, ON M4Y 1V5 (416) 922-0352. Born Ayr, Ont. 1919. m. Dr. L. George Weber. 2 ch. Mark, Krista. EDUC: Ontario Coll. of Art, A.O.C.A.(Drawing & Painting) 1959. CAREER: self-employed painter/printmaker. EXHIBITIONS: numerous solo & 2 or 3 person exhibitions, incl. *New Silkscreens*, Gallery Moos, Toronto (1980); *Under the Sun*, Gallery Pascal, Toronto (1983); *Masters of their Media*, Miriam Perlman Gallery, Chicago (1985); numerous group exhibitions, incl. *Contemporary Canadians*, Albright-Knox Gallery, Buffalo, NY (1971); *World Print Competition*, San Francisco Museum (1973); *2nd Vienna Graphic Biennale*, Vienna (1975); *100 Years of Evolution of Ontario College of Art*, Art Gallery of Ontario (1976). COLLECTIONS: numerous public, corp. & private collections,

incl. Albertina Art Museum, Vienna; Art Bank, Canada Council. AFFIL: Royal Canadian Academy (elected 1977); Ontario Society of Artists (elected 1971); Canadian Society of Graphic Art (elected 1961); Society of Canadian Painter-Etchers & Engravers; Arts & Letters Club of Toronto (elected 1987). HONS: Jurors' Award, Burnaby Print Show, 1977; Editions Award, Ontario Arts Council, 1978. INTERESTS: photography; animals; astronomy. MISC: set up & conducted workshops for Ontario Bureau of Culture & Recreation, & Fanshawe Coll., London, Ont. COMMENT: *"I'm a painter and printmaker and love doing this work."*

Musgrave, Susan ■ ❑ ▨ ⼷
Author. PO Box 2421, Stn. Main, Sidney, BC V8L 3Y3 (250) 656-5037, FAX 656-5037, EMAIL smusgrave@pinc.com. Born 1951. m. Stephen Reid. 2 ch. Charlotte Musgrave, Sophie Musgrave Reid. CAREER: professional writer, 1970 to date; Writer-in-Residence, Univ. of Waterloo, 1983-85; Instructor, Camosun Coll., 1988-94; Writer-in-Residence, Univ. of Western Ontario, 1992-93; Writer-in-Electronic-Residence, York Univ. & the Writers' Development Trust, 1991-96; Univ. of Toronto Presidential Writer-in-Residence Fellowship, 1995. SELECTED CREDITS: *Gullband*, prod. & dir. by Paully Jardine, Theatre Passe Muraille, Toronto (Christmas 1976) & Touchstone Theatre, Vancouver (Christmas 1977); "The Wages of Love", *State of the Arts*, CBC Radio (1987); Book Panel reviewer, *The Journal*, CBC (1989-91); writer, 7 essays, *Morningside*, CBC Radio (1994); poems have been broadcast on numerous radio shows, incl. *Anthology*, CBC & *Poetry Now*, BBC; many radio & TV appearances. SELECTED PUBLICATIONS: *Songs of the Sea-Witch*, poetry (Sono Nis Press, 1970); *A Man to Marry, A Man to Bury*, poetry (McClelland & Stewart, 1979); *The Charcoal Burners* (McClelland & Stewart, 1980); *The Dancing Chicken* (Methuen, 1987); *Great Musgrave*, non-fiction (Prentice-Hall, 1989); *Musgrave Landing: Musings on the Writing Life*, non-fiction (Stoddart, 1994); *Forcing the Narcissus*, poetry (McClelland & Stewart, 1994); 9 other books of poetry; 3 books for children, incl. *Gullband*, poetry, illus. by Rikki Ducornet (J.J. Douglas, 1974); *Clear Cut Words: Writers for Clayoquot*, ed. (Hawthorne Society for Reference West, 1993); *Because You Loved Being a Stranger: 55 Poets Celebrate Patrick Lane*, ed. (Harbour Publishing, 1994); *In the Small Hours of the Rain*, poetry chapbook (Victoria: Reference West, 1991); numerous pamphlets & broadsides; poetry has appeared in various anthologies, incl. *The Norton Introduction to*

Literature, 6th Edition (1994); short fiction has appeared in various anthologies, incl. *Without a Guide: Contemporary Women's Travel Adventure*, Katherine Govier, ed. (Macfarlane Walter & Ross, 1994) & *Best American Erotica*, 1995, Susie Bright, ed. (Simon & Schuster); essays included in *Horizons*, Ken Roy, ed. (Harcourt Brace, 1994) & *Far and Wide*, Sean Armstrong, ed. (Nelson, 1994); poetry published in numerous periodicals in Canada, US, UK & Australia, incl. *Queen's Quarterly, Poetry Canada Review, Prairie Schooner, Ambit* & *Poetry Australia*; columnist for various newspapers & magazines, incl. *The Toronto Star* & *Cut To: Magazine*. **AFFIL:** Writers' Union of Canada; B.C. Federation of Writers; Stephen Leacock Poetry Awards (Advisory Committee); Writers in Electronic Residence (Advisory Committee & Exec. Committee); Life Profiles Advisory Committee). **HONS:** Silver, National Magazine Awards, 1981; 3rd Prize, R.P. Adams Short Fiction Award, *The Remains of Edward* (Negative Capability, Mobile, AL), 1989; 1st Prize, b.p. nichol Poetry Chapbook Award, *In the Small Hours of the Rain*, 1991; Readers' Choice Award for poems published in the Winter edition of *Prairie Schooner*, 1993; Recipient, CBC/Tilden Award for Poetry, 1996; Vickey Metcalfe Short Story Editor's Award, 1996. **MISC:** material on deposit, McMaster Univ. Archives; recipient, various grants; judge &/or jury mbr., various awards & grants; 6 poetry reading tours to Europe & UK; numerous poetry readings, lectures & speeches across Canada & US. **COMMENT:** *"Susan Musgrave was raised on Vancouver Island and has spent extended periods living in Ireland, UK, the Queen Charlotte Islands, Panama and Colombia. She currently lives near Sidney, BC, where she works as a poet, novelist, columnist, reviewer, and non-fiction writer."*

Mushinski, Valerie, R.P.N.,B.Ed., M.A.Ed. ■ ⌖ 丫
Director, Developmental Office, Wascana Institute, SOUTHERN ALBERTA INSTITUTE OF SCIENCE AND TECHNOLOGY, (SAIST), Box 556, Regina, SK S4P 3A3 (306) 787-0450, FAX 787-0157. Born Tisdale, Sask. 1949. m. John. 2 ch. Oren Wade, Kasia Nicole. **EDUC:** Sch. of Psychiatric Nursing, N. Battleford, Sask., Diploma in Psychiatric Nursing 1970; Univ. of Regina, Applied Certificate in Psychiatric Nursing 1984, Advanced Certificate in Continuing Studies 1984; Univ. of Regina, B.Ed. 1985; St. Francis Xavier Univ., M.Ed. 1992. **CAREER:** Psychiatric Nurse, Saskatchewan Hospital, 1970-72; Sr. Psychiatric Nurse, Regina General Hospital, 1973-76; Nursing Instructor, Health Sciences Div., Wascana Institute, SAIST, 1976-82;

Admin. Asst. to the Chair, 1982-83; Acting Coord., Program & Staff Dev., 1983-85; Facilitator, Program & Staff Dev., 1985-87; Program Supervisor, Emergency Medical Technician Health Sciences Div., 1987; Conference Coord., 1988-89; Exec. Asst. to the Principal, 1989-90; Acting Dean, Health Sciences Div., 1990-91; Dean, Extension Div., 1991-94; Dean, Health Sciences Div., 1994-96; Dir. of Dev., 1996 to date. **AFFIL:** Registered Psychiatric Nurses' Association of Saskatchewan (Chair, Educ. Committee; Degree Committee); Canadian Congress of Learning Opportunities for Women; Entrepreneurial Foundation Board; Wascana Institute Trust Foundation; Saskatchewan Special Olympics (Bd.). **INTERESTS:** reading; music; needlework; walking; yoga; golf. **COMMENT:** *"The primary force throughout my life has been one of learning in order to achieve a better way of being. This fundamental belief has enabled me to achieve in all aspects of my personal and professional life. All my post secondary education occurred after I was married and began a family. As my resumé reflects, I have had numerous jobs within the educational sector. The majority of these positions were new positions, thus requiring me to be creative and innovative in their evolvement, or they were positions requiring intensive collaborative decision-making. My successes have been achieved through the use of collaboration and consensus."*

Mussallem, Helen Kathleen, C.C.,B.N., M.A.,Ed.D.,LL.D.,D.Sc.,F.R.C.N., M.R.S.H.,D.St.J. 丫 ⊕
Special Advisor to National and International Health Organizations. 20 Driveway, Ste. 1706, Ottawa, ON K2P 1C8 (613) 234-5408. Born Prince Rupert, B.C. **EDUC:** Vancouver General Hospital, Nursing Diploma; Univ. of Washington, Seattle, Diploma (Teaching, Supervision & Admin.); McGill Univ., B.N.; Teachers' Coll., Columbia Univ., M.A.; Columbia Univ., D.Ed. **CAREER:** Lt. (Nursing Officer), Royal Canadian Army Medical Corps, active svc, Canada & overseas, 1943-46; Staff Nurse/Head Nurse/Supervisor, Vancouver General Hospital; Instructor/Sr. Instructor/Dir. of Nursing Educ., Vancouver General Hospital, Sch. of Nursing, 1947-57; Dir., Pilot Proj. for Evaluation of Schools of Nursing in Canada, Canadian Nurses' Association, 1957-60; Dir., Special Studies, 1960-63; seconded to Royal Commission on Health Svcs for Study of Nursing Educ. in Canada, 1962-63; Exec. Dir., Canadian Nurses' Association, 1963-81; Sec.-Treas., Canadian Nurses' Foundation, 1966-81; Proj. Dir., Int'l Study on "Group Action by Nurses", 1980-85; mbr., Bd. of Dir., Interna-

tional Council of Nurses, 1981-85; special advisor to nat'l & int'l health organizations, 1981 to date. **SELECTED PUBLICATIONS:** *Spotlight on Nursing Education* (1960); *Path to Quality, a plan for the development of nursing education within the general education system of Canada* (1964); *Succeeding Together, Group Action by Nurses* (International Council of Nurses, 1983); *Nursing Education in Canada* (Royal Commission on Health Servces, 1965); "A Pilot Project for Evaluation of Schools of Nursing" (*Canadian Journal of Public Health* 8(8) 1958); "Changing Role of the Nurse" (*American Journal of Nursing* 69(3) 1969); "The Nurse's Role in Policy Making and Planning" (*International Nurse Review* 20(1) 1973); over 40 articles in professional journals, incl. editorials, chapters in books & forwards. **AFFIL:** Royal Coll. of Nursing of the U.K. (Fellow); Victorian Order of Nurses (Past Pres.); Association of Nurses of P.E.I. (Hon. Life Mbr.); Alberta Association of Registered Nurses (Hon. Life Mbr.); Manitoba Association of Registered Nurses (Hon. Life Mbr.); Saskatchewan Registered Nurses' Association (Hon. Life Mbr.); N.B. Association of Registered Nurses (Hon. Life Mbr.); Registered Nurses' Association of Ontario (Hon. Life Mbr.); N.W.T. Registered Nurses' Association (Hon. Life Mbr.); Canadian Council of Health Service Executives (Hon. Life Mbr.); Canadian Nursing Students' Association (Hon. Life Mbr.); Canadian Nurses' Foundation (Hon. Life Mbr.); Aboriginal Nurses' Association of Canada (Hon. Life Mbr.); Canadian Public Health Association (Life Mbr.); Univ. of British Columbia Alumni Association (Hon. Life Mbr.); mbr. of &/or advisor to numerous nat'l & int'l organizations, incl. Canadian Nurses' Association, International Council of Nurses, Commonwealth Nurses' Federation, Canadian Society of Health Executives, & Law Reform Commission of Canada; Friends of the National Gallery of Canada; Friends of the National Museum of Civilization; Friends of the National Art Centre; Orpheus Society (patron). **HONS:** Rockefeller Foundation Travelling Scholarship, 1957; Centennial Medal, 1967; Officer, Order of Canada, 1969; Special Citation of Recognition, Canadian Red Cross Society, 1974; Award of Distinguished Achievement in Nursing Research & Scholarship, Columbia Univ., 1977; Queen's Silver Jubilee Medal, 1977; Medal for Distinguished Service, Columbia Univ., 1979; Canada's National Nursing Library designated "The Helen K. Mussallem Library," 1980; Commonwealth Foundation Lectureship Award, 1981; Florence Nightingale Medal, International Red Cross Society, 1981; Jeanne Mance Award,

Canadian Nurses' Association, 1981; Dame of Grace, Order of St. John, 1982; Award of Merit, Registered Nurses' Association of B.C., 1983; Miembro de Honor, Cuban Nurses' Society, 1984; Award for Service, International Council of Nurses, 1988; Canada 125 Medal, 1992; Companion, Order of Canada, 1992; LL.D.(Hon.), Univ. of New Brunswick, 1968; D.Sc.(Hon.), Memorial Univ. of Newfoundland, 1969; LL.D.(Hon.), Queen's Univ., 1983; LL.D.(Hon.), McMaster Univ., 1989; LL.D.(Hon.), Univ. of British Columbia, 1994. **MISC:** travelled to Nigeria, Ghana, Liberia, the Gambia, Sierra Leone, Malta & Cyprus on Commonwealth Foundation Lectureship Award, 1981; numerous major int'l assignments & missions in over 30 countries, incl. WHO Consultant, Survey of Nursing Educ. in the Commonwealth Caribbean, 1971 & World Health Organization Study of Nursing Svcs in Cyprus, 1980; numerous conference presentations; listed in *Who's Who in Canada* & *Outstanding Women of the 20th Century.*

Mutala, Catherine, LL.B.,LL.M. ⚖️

Partner, OYEN WIGGS GREEN & MUTALA, Barristers and Solicitors, Registered Patent and Trademark Agents, 480 - The Stn., 601 W. Cordova St., Vancouver, BC V6B 1G1 (604) 669-3432, FAX 681-4081, EMAIL baro@unixg.ubc.ca. **EDUC:** Univ. of Manitoba, LL.B. 1980; New York Univ., LL.M. 1982. **BAR:** Man., 1981; B.C., 1984. **CAREER:** articled in Winnipeg, 1980-81; articled Vancouver, 1983; Ptnr, Oyen Wiggs Green & Mutala; Adjunct Prof., Trademark Law, Univ. of British Columbia, 1985 to date; former mbr., Patented Medicine Review Bd. **SELECTED PUBLICATIONS:** "Trademarks, Copyright and Industrial Designs–What Are They and How Are They Created?" (*Technology, Design and the Law* 1994); "Acquisition of Intellectual Property Rights–Assignment and Licensing" (*Technology, Design and the Law* 1994); "Creation of Intellectual Property" (*Intellectual Property* 1(1) 1995); various other publications. **AFFIL:** Patent & Trademark Institute of Canada; Patent & Trademark Association of BC. **HONS:** Rotary Foundation of Rotary International Full Scholarship, 1981. **MISC:** Registered Trademark Agent; firm's practice restricted to intellectual & industrial property law.

Muzzi, Michèle, B.F.A.,B.Ed. ■ ⊗ 🍷 🎭

Actor and Teacher. c/o A.C.I. Talent Agency, 205 Ontario St., Toronto, ON M5A 2V6 (416) 363-7414, FAX 363-6715. Born Parry Sound, Ont. 1963. m. Mark Adilman. 1 ch. Nicola Rose Muzzi Adilman. **EDUC:** Univ. of Alberta, B.F.A.(Acting) 1987; trained with the Stratford

Young Company; Univ. of Toronto, B.Ed. 1996. CAREER: professional actor, 1987 to date; also interested in pursuing directing & producing in film, television, and theatre. SELECTED CREDITS: lead, *Hurt Penguins*, Cold Feet Productions; principal, *Street Legal* (two hour finale), CBC TV; series regular, *Taking the Falls*, Alliance; various other film and television credits; Carnelle, *Miss Firecracker Contest*, Phoenix Theatre; Second Witch, *Macbeth*, Stratford Festival; Peggy, *Jitters*, National Arts Centre; Tilly/Fern, *Grandad Upanishad*, Theatre Centre/McManus Studio; various other theatre credits; various commercials. AFFIL: Canadian Actors' Equity Association; Alliance of Canadian Television and Radio Artists. HONS: Amelia Hall Award, Stratford Festival; nominated for Sterling Award, Best Actress, Edmonton. INTERESTS: canoeing; playing hockey; swimming; figure skating; gardening; time with family & friends.

Mychan, Laura J. (\$) ♣

Strategic Projects Consultant. Saskatoon, SK. Born Saskatoon 1961. m. Mel. 2 ch. EDUC: Walter Murray Coll., Dipl.(Bus. Educ.) 1984. CAREER: shareholder, Cavalier Enterprises, 1972-86; Mktg Rep., Saturday Nite Styles Inc., 1987-90; Campaign Coord. for Reform Candidate Bob Head, Reform Party of Canada, 1993; Sask. Reg'l Mgr, Reform Party of Canada, 1993-95. AFFIL: Our Lady of the Prairies Foundation (Jr. Advisor, Grants Committee). COMMENT: *"Highly motivated, people-oriented person with a keen sense of current events and the ability to work on any subject in a strategic manner."*

Myers Avis, Judith Kathleen, B.A.,M.S.W., Ph.D. ✑ ⊕

Professor, Department of Family Studies, UNIVERSITY OF GUELPH, Guelph, ON N1G 2W1 (519) 824-4120, ext. 3970, FAX 766-0691, EMAIL jmyersav@uoguelph.ca. Born Toronto 1944. d. 2 ch. Andrew, Michael. EDUC: Queen's Univ., B.A.(Psych.) 1966; Univ. of Toronto, M.S.W. 1968; Purdue Univ., Ph.D. (Marriage & Family Therapy) 1986. CAREER: Social Worker, Ont. Dept. of Reform Institutions, 1968-69; Psychiatric Social Worker, Fredericton Mental Health Clinic, 1971-74; Social Worker, N.B. Dept. of Social Services, 1974; Lecturer, Dept. of Social Work, St. Thomas Univ., Fredericton, 1974-75; Sr. Social Worker, Life Line Crisis Centre, Melbourne, Australia, 1975-76; Asst. Prof., Dept. of Social Work, St. Thomas Univ., 1977-86; Therapist, private practice, Fredericton, 1977-83; Therapist, private practice, Guelph, 1986 to date; Assoc. Prof., Dept. of Family Studies, Univ. of

Guelph, 1986-92; Prof., 1992 to date. SELECTED PUBLICATIONS: *Group Treatment for Sexually Abused Adolescents*, with A. Crowder (Holmes Beach, Fla.: Learning Publications, 1993); "The Politics of Functional Family Therapy: A Feminist Critique" (*Journal of Marital and Family Therapy* 1985); "Integrating Gender into the Family Therapy Curriculum" (*Journal of Feminist Family Therapy*, Vol. 1); "A Study of the Role of Gender in Family Therapy Training," with S.B. Coleman & M. Turin (*Family Process* 1990); "Violence and Abuse in Families: The Problem and Family Therapy's Response" (*Journal of Marital and Family Therapy*, 18, 1992); "Working with Men in Family Change: Report of a Delphi Study," with A. Dienhart (*Journal of Marital and Family Therapy* 20(4) 1994); "Advocates Versus Researchers–A False Dichotomy?" (*Family Process*, 33, 1994); "Deconstructing gender in family therapy," *A Family Therapy Sourcebook*, 2nd ed., edited by F.P. Piercy, D.H. Sprenkle, J. Wetchler (New York: Guilford Press, 1996); "Feminist lenses in family therapy research: Gender, politics, and science," with J. Turner, *Family Therapy Research: A handbook of methods*, edited by S.M. Moon, D.H. Sprenkle (New York: Guilford Press, 1996); "Parallel journeys," *Bedtime Stories for Tired Therapists*, edited by L. Anderson (Adelaide, S. Australia: Dulwich Centre Publications, 1996). EDIT: Book Review Ed., *Feminist Family Therapy*, 1987-92; Ed. Advisory Bd., *Journal of Marital and Family Therapy*, 1990 to date; Ed. Bd., Journal of Feminist Family Therapy, 1991 to date; Ed. Bd., *Contemporary Family Therapy*, 1991 to date. AFFIL: Honour Society of Phi Kappa Phi (Elected Mbr.); Guelph/Wellington Women in Crisis (Consultant 1988 to date); American Family Therapy Academy; American Association for Marriage & Family Therapy; Ontario Association for Marriage & Family Therapy. HONS: Ontario Reform Institutions Training Fellow, 1966-67; Nat'l Welfare Doctoral Fellow, 1983-86; Mrs. R.S. Stewart Teaching Award for the Coll. of Family Studies, Univ. of Guelph, 1987; Distinguished Prof. Teaching Award, Univ. of Guelph, 1989; Down Under Family Therapy Scholar, Australia & New Zealand, 1992-93; Significant Contributions to Family Therapy Award, American Association for Marriage & Family Therapy, 1996. INTERESTS: travel; yoga; meditation; antiques; photography; biking; hiking. MISC: recipient, various grants; reviewer, various journals & granting agencies; numerous conference presentations; listed in Canadian Who's Who. COMMENT: *"An educator, researcher and therapist specializing in developing feminist, gender-conscious approaches to therapeutic training and practice. Has influenced consciousness in the international field of family therapy on issues of gender, power, abuse and violence."*

Myers Johnson, Nancy, R.N.,B.N., M.Ed.,C.H.R.P. ■ Ⓢ 🕐 ⊕
Vice-President, Human Resources, DATA BUSINESS FORMS, 2 Shaftesbury Lane, Brampton, ON L6T 3X7 (905) 791-3151, FAX 791-3277. Born Palmerston, Ont. 1945. m. Robert G. Johnson. 7 ch. Carla, Rebecca, Meredith, Stacey, Braden, Rennie, Gabrielle. **EDUC:** Toronto Western Hospital, Dipl.(Nursing) 1966; McGill Univ., B.N. 1969; Brock Univ., M.Ed. 1986; Univ. of Toronto, Advanced Diploma in Hum. Res. Mgmt 1988. **CAREER:** Clinical Instructor, Toronto Western Hospital, 1969-72; Registered Nurse Tutor, Hammersmith Hospital, London, UK, 1972-74; Teaching Master, Health Sciences, Centennial Coll., 1974-76; Nursing Educ. Coord., Doctors Hospital, 1977-81; Dir. of Educational Svcs, The Mississauga Hospital, 1981-88; VP, Hum. Res., 1988-94; VP, Hum. Res., Data Business Forms, Brampton, 1995 to date; Past Pres., Human Resources Professionals' Association of Ontario. **AFFIL:** Human Resources Professionals' Association of Ontario (Certified Hum. Res. Professional 1990; VP, Professional Standards 1989-93; Pres. 1993-94); Covey Leadership Centre (Trainer 1994); Canadian Council of Human Resources Associations (Founding Mbr. 1994 to date); Executive Advancement Resource Network. **HONS:** nominated for Woman of Distinction in Health/Educ. Award, YWCA, 1985; Award, Brock Univ., 1986; Hennigar Award, Human Resources Professionals' Association of Ontario, 1989. **MISC:** numerous speaking engagements. **COMMENT:** *"Bringing together a health-care background and human-resources management has given me the opportunity to help people with personal transitions, and organizations with workplace transitions. I have passion for my work and compassion for people."*

N

Nagel, Linda J., B.S.,M.S.S.A. ■ ♡ $ 📺
President and Chief Executive Officer, CANADIAN ADVERTISING FOUNDATION 350 Bloor St. E., Ste. 402, Toronto, ON M4W 1H5 (416) 961-6311, FAX 961-7904. Born Cleveland, Ohio 1949. m. Stan Solomon. **EDUC:** Boston Univ., B.S. 1971; Case Western Reserve Univ., M.S.S.A. 1974. **CAREER:** Coord. for Continuing Educ., American Academy of Pediatrics, Chicago, 1974-79; Assoc. Dir., Dev. & Training, Joint Commission on Accreditation of Hospitals, Chicago, 1979-82; Dir. of Educ. Products, 1982-83; Professional Svcs Consultant, Comprehensive Care Corporation Canada Ltd., 1984-85; Pres., Bakery Council of Canada, 1986-94; Pres. & CEO, Canadian Advertising Foundation, 1994 to date. **AFFIL:** Canadian Society of Association Executives Foundation for Association Research & Education (Trustee 1996).

Nakashima, Katrin ■■ $ ⚖
Secretary and Senior Counsel, IMASCO LIMITED (consumer products & svcs), 600 de Maisonneuve Blvd. W., 20th Fl., Montreal, QC H3A 3K7 (514) 982-6410, FAX 982-9320. Born Montreal m. Doron Altman. **EDUC:** McGill Univ., Diplôme d'études collégiales (Sci.) 1974, B.Sc.(Hons., Psych.) 1977, Bach. of Common Law 1980, Bach. of Civil Law 1981. **CAREER:** Assoc., Montreal law firm, 1982-87; Ptnr, 1987-91; Mng Ptnr, 1990-91; Sr. Cnsl, Imasco Limited, 1991 to date; Sec., 1995 to date. **EDIT:** Edit. Advisory Bd., *Canadian Lawyer* magazine, 1995 to date. **AFFIL:** Council of Senior Legal Executives, Conference Board of Canada (Advisory Bd. 1994 to date); Canadian Bar Association; Les Grands Ballets Canadiens,

Montreal (Dir. 1996 to date). HONS: several scholarships & prizes, McGill Univ.

Nash, Raylene ☺ 🏌

Manager, WILD BLUEBERRY PRODUCERS ASSOCIATION OF NOVA SCOTIA, Box 2439, Springhill, NS B0M 1X0 (902) 597-8484, FAX 597-2819. Born Lorneville, N.S. 1938. m. Robert Nash. 4 ch. Gerald Douglas Nash, Janet Carol Nash Glen, Cheryl Lynn Nash Harrison, Gregory Keith Nash. CAREER: Sec., Wild Blueberry Producers' Association of N.S., 1981-87; Promo. Coord., 1983-87; Mgr, 1987 to date; owner/operator, Christmas tree & wreath retail bus. AFFIL: Wild Blueberry Association of North America (Cdn Promo. Committee; Chrm 1992); Wells Heritage Foundation (Chair); IODE; Chamber of Commerce; ZONTA. INTERESTS: arts & crafts; travel; reading; hiking. COMMENT: *"Learned the wild blueberry industry from the ground up. In 1983, hired to promote wild blueberries within Nova Scotia. Have developed a flare for promotion."*

Nash, Terre, B.A.,M.A.,
Ph.D. ▪▪ ⊗ 🎞 ⼐

NASHFILM INC. (film & video production), 2024 Grey Ave., Montreal, QC H4A 3N4 (514) 489-4512, EMAIL rambler@total.net. Born Nanaimo, B.C. EDUC: Emily Carr Sch. of Art & Design (Vancouver Art Sch.), special sessions (Film Animation & Photography) 1968-70; Simon Fraser Univ., B.A.(English & Sociology) 1969, M.A.(Behavioural Sci. & Comm. Studies) 1973; McGill Univ., Ph.D.(Comm.) 1983. CAREER: Teaching Asst., Mass Media & Social Psych., Simon Fraser Univ.; Dir., Videotape Feedback Workshops for Teachers; Teaching Asst., Interpersonal Comm., Simon Fraser Univ.; Teaching Asst., Behavioural Sci. & Comm.; archival research/film research/Dir./ Ed., National Film Board of Canada. SELECTED CREDITS: Dir./Ed., *If You Love This Planet*; Co-Dir., *Speaking Your Peace*; Dir./Ed., *Russian Diary*; Dir./Prod./Ed., *Mother Earth*; Dir./Ed., *Who's Counting? Marilyn Waring on Sex, Lies and Global Economics*; & others. SELECTED PUBLICATIONS: *Images of Women in National Film Board of Canada Films During World War II and the Post-War Years: 1939-1945* (McGill Univ.); co-author, *Women at the National Film Board: An Equal Opportunity Study*; *The Effects of Videotape Feedback on Changes in Self-Perception* (Simon Fraser Univ.). HONS: Film: Academy Award; Blue Ribbon (First Prize), American Film Festival, N.Y.C.; Liepzig Peace Prize, Germany; Atom Award, Brazil; Karlovy Vary Diploma, Prague; Silver Medal, Melbourne; First Prize, John Muir Festival, San Francisco; Silver

Plaque, Chicago Film Festival; Bronze Plaque, Columbus; Best Editing, Ecocine, Prefettura de Sao Sebatio; 2nd Prize, Vermont World Peace Film Festival; & others. Academic: 6 undergrad. scholarships; Canada Council Doctoral Fellowship, McGill Univ.; Fonds F.C.A.C. Que. Doctoral Fellowship, McGill Univ.; President's Grad. Award, & Alumni Award, Simon Fraser Univ.; special 70th anniversary lecture, Emily Carr Sch. of Art & Design, 1996. MISC: subject of CBC documentary, *If You Love Free Speech: An Unguided Tour Through the Twilight Zone* (on testimony to US Congressional Committee on Free Speech, 1990).

Nathoo, Tazeem, B.A. ⓢ

Senior Vice-President, Operations, VANCOUVER CITY SAVINGS CREDIT UNION, 515 W. 10 Ave., Vancouver, BC V5Z 4A8 (604) 877-7624, FAX 877-7639. Born Tanzania 1946. m. Saleem. 2 ch. EDUC: Univ. of Leicester, UK, B.A.(Liberal Arts) 1968; Queen's Univ., Grad.(Exec. Dev. Program) 1994. CAREER: Staff Mgr, Harrods, Knightsbridge, London, UK, 1969-72; Placement Mgr, Insurance Corporation of British Columbia, 1973-78; Sr. Hum. Res. Mgr, BC Hydro, 1980-92; Sr. VP, Oper., Vancouver City Savings Credit Union, 1992 to date. SELECTED PUBLICATIONS: monthly column on social, cultural & ecological issues, *British Columbia Woman to Woman Magazine*, 1993. AFFIL: Family Services of North Shore (Advisory Bd.); Simon Fraser Univ. (Gov.; President's Club); Simon Fraser Univ. Foundation; Aga Khan Foundation, Canada; Human Resources Management Association. HONS: recipient, Woman of Distinction Award, Mgmt & Professions, YWCA, 1995. INTERESTS: fitness; literature; drama; the field of educ. MISC: frequent speaker. COMMENT: *"Career woman who has balanced work and family effectively; strategic thinker; good communicator; has taken a leadership role on highlighting people issues; fair and just treatment of employees."*

Natividad, Alicia, B.A.,LL.B. ⚖

Barrister, Solicitor and Notary Public, 99 Bank St., Ste. 600, Ottawa, ON K1P 6B9 (613) 566-7045, FAX 233-7045. Born Manila 1950. m. Donald Ballard Clarke. EDUC: Carleton Univ., B.A.(Law & Pol. Sci.) 1977; Univ. of Ottawa, LL.B. 1981. BAR: Ont., 1983. CAREER: Assoc., Brennan, Tunney, 1983-85; Assoc., Soloway, Wright, 1985-89; Assoc., Gowling, Strathy & Henderson, 1989-91; Ptnr, 1991-95; sole practitioner, 1995 to date. SELECTED PUBLICATIONS: Ed., *Directory of Women's Groups in Ottawa-Carleton*, 1981; contributor to various newsletters of legal articles & Op.

Ed. on issues dealing with women; contributor, various legal topics, *Ottawa Living*, 1993-94; contributor, Bar Admission Course real estate reference materials & other legal seminars, 1987 to date. **AFFIL:** Canadian Bar Association (Chair, Mun. Law, E. Ont. Section); Law Society of Upper Canada (Lecturer, Bar Admission Course); Ottawa Civic Hospital (Trustee); Filipino-Canadian Business & Professional Association (Co-Chair); Ottawa-Carleton Board of Trade (Downtown Bus. Dev. Network); Canada-Philippines Science & Technology Advisory Council (Legal Cnsl); Multicultural Council of Professional Women (Legal Cnsl); Canadian Tribute to Human Rights (Legal Cnsl); Nelson House of Ottawa-Carleton (Legal Cnsl). **HONS:** The Business & Professional Women's Week Award, 1992; nominated, Women of Distinction Award, YM-YWCA, 1994. **INTERESTS:** biking; cross-country skiing; travelling; the arts. **MISC:** speaker to various groups. **COMMENT:** *"Highly motivated, positive, spiritual and creative individual with a strong belief that any person can accomplish anything he or she wishes so long as there exists the will and the courage."*

Nault, Heather, B.Sc.,C.M.A. $

Vice-President, Corporate and Regulatory Affairs, MANITOBA TELEPHONE SYSTEM, 489 Empress St., Box 6666, Winnipeg, MB R3C 3V6 (204) 941-6147, FAX 775-9255. Born Winnipeg. **EDUC:** Univ. of Manitoba, B.Sc.(Math. & Statistics) 1964. **AFFIL:** Society of Management Accountants (C.M.A.); Alzheimer's Society of Manitoba; United Way of Winnipeg. **INTERESTS:** golf, travel.

Nebenzahl, Donna, B.A. ✎ 📖

Editor, Woman's News, *THE GAZETTE*, 250 St. Antoine St. W., Montreal, QC H4A 2M3 (514) 987-2501, FAX 987-2638. Born Trinidad 1949. m. Mark W. Swift. 2 ch. Katrina, Devin. **EDUC:** McGill Univ., B.A.(Cdn Hist.) 1976. **CAREER:** Ed., Book & Travel, *Ottawa Journal*, 1980-81; Press Attaché, Commission of the Delegation of the European Communities, 1981-82; Ed., various sections, *Montreal Gazette*, 1982 to date. **SELECTED PUBLICATIONS:** features in *McGill News*, *Montreal Gazette*, *Montreal Star*; *Maclean's*. **EDIT:** Ed., Portraits, *Woman News Agenda*, 1994-97. **AFFIL:** Willingdon Sch. Committee (Chair). **HONS:** Woman of Achievement, Business & Professional Women's Club, 1995; Remarkable Woman, Chambre du Commerce de Montréal, 1996.

Neidhardt, Anne, B.Sc.N.,B.A. ⊕

Program Director, Genetics Program, NORTH YORK GENERAL HOSPITAL, 4001 Leslie St., Rm. 392, North York, ON M2K 1E1 (416) 756-6349, FAX 756-6727. Born Scotland 1942. m. Wilfried Neidhardt. 2 ch. **EDUC:** Univ. of Western Ontario, B.Sc.N. 1967; York Univ., B.A.(Eng.) 1981; additional courses at the Univ. of Iowa & Baylor Coll. of Medicine. **CAREER:** Teacher, Sch. of Nursing, Toronto General Hospital, 1967-72; Teaching Fac. (sessional), Sch. of Nursing, Seneca Coll., 1972-78; Nurse-Teacher, Maternal Infant Program, North York General Hospital, 1978-84; Genetic Counsellor/Supervisor, Clinical Genetics Diagnostic Centre, 1987-94; Program Dir., Genetics Program, 1994 to date. **SELECTED PUBLICATIONS:** "Why Me? Second Trimester Abortion" (*American Journal of Nursing*, Oct. 1986); "Support Services in Genetics," with K. Boucher & B. Yousson *(Canadian Family Physician*, April 1988); various abstracts & presentations. **AFFIL:** Canadian Association of Genetic Counsellors (Past Pres. 1992-94; Pres. 1992-93; Exec. 1991-92; Certification Bd.); International Society of Nurses in Genetics; Registered Nurses' Association of Ontario; North York General Hospital (Pres., Advisory Council); Regional Genetics Service (Mgmt & Clinical Advisory Council).

Neil, Dolores ✊ $ 🎓

Past President, CANADIAN HOME AND SCHOOL AND PARENT-TEACHER FEDERATION. m. Harvey Neil. 4 ch. Ken, Dawn, Gary, Alynn. **CAREER:** Fin. Chair & Membership Chair, Saskatchewan Federation of Home & School Associations (SFHSA), 1980-86; Pres., 1986-88; Councillor, Village of Harris, 1988 to date; Western VP, Canadian Home & School & Parent-Teacher Federation, 1989-91; Pres., SFHSA, 1990-92; Pres., Canadian Home & School & Parent-Teacher Federation, 1992-94; SFHSA Rep., Saskatchewan Education Council, 1993 to date; Saskatchewan Federation of Home & School Associations Rep., Parent & Community Involvement Working Committee, 1995 to date. **AFFIL:** Harris Ruby Rush Days Committee (Chair & events organizer 1996); Sask. Gov't Educ. Boundaries Commission; Harris Credit Union Advisory Bd. (Committee Chair, Scholarships & Bursaries); Eagle Creek Rural Development Corporation (Sec.-Treas.); Small Business Loans Association, Village of Harris (Sec.-Treas.); Harris Tourism Committee (Chair 1990-95); Prairie Schooner Travel Region Tourism Bd.; Regional Waste Management Committee (1992-94); Harris Home & School Association; figure skating club (Exec. 1972-84); rink bd.; recreation bd.; community coll. committee (Chair 1978-88); Harris Museum & Heritage Society (2nd VP); United Church Sch.

(Teacher 1965-78; Superintendent 1972-78). INTERESTS: figure-skating instructor. MISC: P.A.L.S. (Parents Assist Learning & Schooling) Master Trainer.

Neiman, Joan B., Q.C.,B.A.,LL.B. ■ ✪ ✤
Born Winnipeg 1920. m. Clemens Michael. 3 ch. Dallis, Patricia, David. EDUC: Mount Allison Univ., B.A.(Hons. English) 1941; Osgoode Hall Law Sch., LL.B. 1954. BAR: Ont., 1954. CAREER: Women's Royal Canadian Naval Svc, ret'd Lt. Cdr., 1942-46; Asst. Office Mgr, Montreal Shipping Company, 1947-48; Comm. Administration, National Research Council, 1948-49; Ptnr, Neiman Bissett and Seguin, Toronto, as later Neiman Bissett in Brampton & Bolton, Ont., 1954-86; therafter Cnsl.; Senator, The Senate of Canada, 1972-95; Mbr., various Senate & joint committees; Chrm, Legal & Constitutional Affairs Committee; Chrm, Special Senate Committee on Euthanasia & Assisted Suicide, report published (*Of Life and Death*); Mbr., Inter-Parliamentary Union, 1975-95 & Int'l Chrm of it's Hum. Rights Commission, 1987-92. AFFIL: Canadian Corps of Commissionaires of Ottawa (Hon. Gov.); Admiral's Medal Foundation (Bd. of Selection). HONS: Queen's Counsel, 1982. INTERESTS: human rights; literature; music; Cdn antiques; history; politics; golf; swimming; hiking. COMMENT: *"While some progress has been made in the observance of human rights, serious violations which continue to occur in many parts of the world are not being adequately addressed. Canada's efforts, both federal and provincial, in settling the justifiable land claims of its Aboriginal peoples have improved but are still too slow and sporadic."*

Nellis, Zonda ■■ ⊗ $
President, ZONDA NELLIS DESIGN INC. (fashion designer), 2203 Granville St., Vancouver, BC V6H 3G1 (604) 736-5668, FAX 736-3534. Born Woodstock, Ont. 1950. m. David Robinson. 1 ch. Alexandra Robinson. COMMENT: *"Internationally known for her sophisticated handwoven separates and for her sumptuous sought-after evening wear. Has her own store in Vancouver and sells to approximately 30 high-end stores in the U.S. and Canada."*

Nesbitt, Patricia, B.Comm.,C.F.A. $
Director, Canadian Equities, G.W.L. INVESTMENT MANAGEMENT LTD., 100 Osborne St. N., Winnipeg, MB R3C 3A5 (204) 946-8433, FAX 946-8818. Born Neepawa, Man. 1964. EDUC: Univ. of Manitoba, B.Comm. 1986; C.F.A. 1989. CAREER: various analyst positions, Great-West Life Insurance, 1986-92; Asst. Mgr, Capital Mkts Group, 1992; Mgr, Capital Mkts

Group, 1993; Dir., Cdn Equities, G.W.L. Investment Management, 1994 to date. AFFIL: Association for Investment Management & Research; Winnipeg Society of Financial Analysts (Pres. 1992-94; Past Pres. 1994-95).

Ness, Kim G., B.A.,M.Litt.,M.M.St. ⊗ ⌇
Director and Curator, MCMASTER MUSEUM OF ART, McMaster University, 1280 Main St., Hamilton, ON L8S 4M6 (905) 525-9104, ext. 23081, FAX 527-4548, EMAIL nesskg@ mcmaster.ca. Born Hamilton, Ont. 1955. EDUC: McMaster Univ., B.A.(Art & Art Hist.) 1977; Univ. of Edinburgh, M.Litt.(Fine Art) 1982; Univ. of Toronto, M.M.St.(Museum Studies) 1983. CAREER: freelance Lecturer, National Gallery of Scotland, 1978-81; Intern, Admin. Asst. & Lecturer, 1979; Researcher, 1980; Admin. Asst., 1980; Lecturer, Extramural Dept., Edinburgh Univ., 1980-81; Intern/Museum Studies Course Requisite, Art Gallery of Ontario, 1982; Intern & Volunteer, Educ. Div., 1983; Intern, George R. Gardiner Museum of Ceramic Art, 1983; Educ. Officer, Adult Programs, Art Gallery of Ontario, 1983-84; Dir. & Curator, McMaster Museum of Art (formerly McMaster Univ. Art Gallery), 1984 to date. SELECTED PUBLICATIONS: *Levy Legacy, A commemorative book to highlight the contributions of the Levy Family and the gifts of Dr. Herman Levy, O.B.E.* (McMaster Museum of Art, Oct. 1996); *with minimal means: John Hartman Prints 1985-1995*, exhibition catalogue for eight-itinerary Cdn tour (McMaster Museum of Art, Aug. 1995); *York Wilson, The Geometric Works 1966-71*, exhibition catalogue (McMaster Museum of Art, Nov. 1994); *This object, that object... to reveal the hidden meaning of things*, exhibition catalogue (McMaster Museum of Art, Sept. 1994); *Beneath a Canopy of Blue*, exhibition catalogue (McMaster Univ. Art Gallery, June 1991); *Joyce Wieland: Quilts in Context*, exhibition catalogue (McMaster Univ. Art Gallery, Nov. 1990); *The Art Collection of McMaster University* (McMaster Univ. Press, 1987); "The Hand Holding the Brush," review (*MUSE*, Summer 1984); "Silk Roads–China Ships," exhibit review (*Quarterly*, Jan. 1984); numerous exhibition catalogues & exhibit reviews. AFFIL: Canadian Art Museum Directors' Organization; Ontario Association of Art Galleries (Bd. of Dir.; Membership Committee); Bay Area Arts Collective, Hamilton; Hamilton & Region Arts Council (Visual Arts Committee 1984-93); McMaster Univ. New Gallery Proj., 1988-94 (Architect Selection Committee; Art Gallery Users' Committee; ArtQuest Fundraising Committee). HONS: nominee, Woman of the Year, The Hamilton Status of Women, 1995; nomi-

nee, Chalmers Award, Ont. Arts Council, 1995. MISC: recipient, various grants from Dept. of Cdn Heritage, Ont. Arts Council & others; Univ. of Toronto Fac., Sch. of Grad. Studies, Museum Studies Program, 1988-89, 1989-90, 1990-91 & 1991-92. COMMENT: *"My professional career has been dominated by the belief that art can play a central and meaningful role in our everyday lives and that the excitement and interest of working in this field is the opportunity it provides to create a meaningful, personally relevant or challenging encounter between artist and viewer."*

Neuman, Shirley, B.A.,M.A.,Ph.D. ■ ⌾
Dean of Arts and Professor of English, UNIVERSITY OF BRITISH COLUMBIA, 1800 Main Mall, B130, Vancouver, BC V6T 1Z1 (604) 822-3751, FAX 822-6096, EMAIL shirley.neuman@ubc.ca. Born Edmonton 1946. EDUC: Univ. of Alberta, B.A.(English) 1968, M.A. (English) 1969, Ph.D.(English) 1976. CAREER: Sessional Lecturer, Univ. of Alberta, 1976-77; Asst. Prof., 1977-81; Assoc. Prof., 1981-86; Prof. of English, 1986 to date; Chair, Women's Studies, 1987-89; McCalla Research Prof., 1989-90; Chair, Dept. of English, 1992-95; Dean of Arts & Prof. of English, Univ. of B.C., 1996 to date. SELECTED PUBLICATIONS: *Gertrude Stein: Autobiography and the Problems of Narration* (Victoria: English Literary Studies Monograph Series, 1979); *Some One Myth: Yeat's Autobiographical Prose* (Dublin: The Dolmen Press, 1982); *Labyrinths of Voice: Conversations with Robert Kroetsch*, with Robert Wilson (Edmonton: NeWest Press, 1982); *A Mazing Space: Writing Canadian Women Writing*, ed. with Smaro Kamboureli (Edmonton: NeWest, Longspoon Presses, 1986); *ReImagining Women*, ed. with Glennis Stephenson (Toronto: UTP, 1994); numerous books, chapters in books, & articles on theory of autobiography, gender & autobiography, & Cdn literature. EDIT: Founding Mbr., Bd. of Dir., NeWest Press, 1976-87; Gen. Ed., Western Canadian Literary Documents Series, NeWest Press, 1981-88; Founding Ed., Longspoon Press, 1980-90; Ed. Bd., *Journal of Canadian Poetry*, 1986-89; Ed. Bd., *Prose Studies*, UK, 1984 to date; Ed. Bd., *Auto/biography*, US, 1984 to date; Ed. Bd., *Line*, Canada, 1986-90; Ed. Bd., *Signature*, Canada, 1988-92; Ed. Bd., *West Coast Review*, Canada, 1988-90; Ed. Bd., *West Coast Line*, Canada, 1990 to date. AFFIL: Academy of Humanities & Social Sciences, Royal Society of Canada (Pres. 1994-96); Canadian Association of Chairs of English (Pres. 1993-94); Association of Canadian University Teachers of English (Pres. 1990-92). HONS: Gabriel Roy Critical Essay Award,

Association of Canadian & Québecois Literature, 1984; Fellow, Royal Society of Canada, 1989. MISC: recipient, various grants; numerous presentations & invited talks; reviewer for various journals, conferences, presses & granting agencies. COMMENT: *"Primary areas of research and teaching: autobiography; Canadian literature; women's literature."*

Neustaedter, Annette K. ✦ ⍓
Director of Prince Albert Provincial Correctional Centre, SASKATCHEWAN DEPARTMENT OF JUSTICE, Prince Albert, SK S6V 6G1 (306) 953-3003, FAX 953-3030. Born Saskatoon, Sask. 1953. m. Prof. Ronald J. Schriml. EDUC: Univ. of Regina, B.S.W. 1974; Saskatchewan Institute of Art, Science & Technology/Natonium, Life Skills Coach 1982. CAREER: Dir. of Prince Albert Prov. Correctional Centre, Sask. Justice; Sessional Lecturer, Univ. of Regina. AFFIL: Saskatchewan Criminal Justice Association (Pres.); Canadian Criminal Justice Association (Bd.); Justice 2001 Interagency (Founding Mbr.); RCMP Citizens' Advisory Committee; Marysberg Organic Farming Chapter. HONS: YWCA Woman of the Year; Gov. General's Cdn Study Tour. INTERESTS: gardening; the environment. MISC: conference/workshop presentations relating to justice & gender issues, building community/restorative justice, harmony in the workplace.

Newall, Joy ■ ⍓ ☺ ✒
Past President, CONSCIENCE CANADA (PEACE TAX FUND), Box 8601, Stn. Central, Victoria, BC V8W 3S2 (604) 384-5532, FAX 383-9155. Born Australia 1929. m. Robert Newall. 3 ch., 4 stepch. EDUC: Sydney Kindergarten Training Coll., Certificate 1948. CAREER: Teacher, Sydney, Australia, 1948-49; Dir. of Pre-Sch., 1950-54; Radio Host & Writer, Kindergarten of the Air, Australian Broadcasting Commission, 1951-52; various positions from Script Asst. to Asst. to the Prod., Children's TV Dept., Canadian Broadcasting Corporation, 1955-57; freelance Writer, CBC Children's TV, 1957-90; Occasional Guest Lecturer, Ryerson Polytechnical Institute & Sheridan Community Coll., 1960-80; Lyricist, 1967; Playwright for Children in BlackBox & Mime, 1975; Prod., Griffin House Publishers, 1976-77; Workshop Leader, Children's Broadcast Institute, 1982-83; Consultant, Campbell-Methun Advertising Co., Minneapolis, Minn., 1987; Founder/Pres., Breakthrough Productions Ltd., 1987 to date; Ptnr, Breakthrough Distributing Ltd., 1987 to date; Guest Lecturer, Malaspina Community Coll., 1991; Columnist on Peace/World Issues, *Nanaimo Free Press*, 1994 to date. SELECTED CREDITS: Writer, *Nursery School Time* (series);

Writer, *Butternut Square* (series); Writer, *Mr. Dressup* (series), 1967-90; Writer, *Sesame Street* (series); Writer, Chetwynd Films Ltd., films for CBC programs; Prod./Writer, *I Wish You Peace!*, TV, taped in USSR; Artistic Consultant, *Free to Fly*, TV; Writer, *The Parks People*, BC Gov't; Prod./Writer, *Casey and Finnegan*, home videos; Prod./Writer, *Take-Off to the USSR*, travel video; Author, *Junk for Joy*, play for children; Prod./Writer, *Play-Replay*, commercial video; 2 educ. music records (*We Walk with the Lord*) for the Canadian Catholic Education Office, Griffin House Publishers. **AFFIL:** SOCAN; ACTRA; Girl Guides (Brownie Pack Leader); Sunday sch. leader; Parent-Teacher Association; Victoria Meeting Religious Society of Friends (Quakers) (Peace/Earth/Social Action Committee); Zagreb Trust Fund to Support Women of Bosnia-Herzegovina; Conscience Canada-Peace Tax Canada Inc. (Pres.). **INTERESTS:** peace & justice action; home & family; gardening; reading; travel; discussions; pottery; spiritual healing techniques; swimming/snorkelling; walking. **MISC:** has travelled extensively in most Cdn provinces, Australia, Fiji, New Zealand, USSR, many of the US states incl. Hawaii, Europe, UK; grant recipient. **COMMENT:** *"A perpetual optimist, I choose to work toward a better future though I may not see its fruition in my lifetime."*

Newbury, Jennifer, B.Sc.,LL.B. ■ ⟐
Associate, MARTIN, WHALEN, HENNEBURY AND STAMP, 15 Church Hill, Box 5910, St. John's, NF A1C 5X4 (709) 754-1400, FAX (709) 754-0915. Born Grand Falls, Nfld. 1968. s. **EDUC:** Memorial Univ. of Newfoundland, B.Sc.(Math) 1990; Osgoode Hall Law Sch., LL.B. 1993. **BAR:** Nfld., 1994. **CAREER:** Assoc., Martin, Whalen, Hennebury and Stamp, 1994 to date. **AFFIL:** Law Society of Newfoundland; Canadian Bar Association (Exec. Committee, Nfld. Branch; Nat'l Young Lawyers' Exec.).

Newbury, Mary V., B.A.,LL.B., LL.M. ■ ⟐ ✦
Justice, COURT OF APPEAL OF BRITISH COLUMBIA, 800 Smithe St., Vancouver, BC V6L 2E7 (604) 660-2957. **EDUC:** Univ. of British Columbia, B.A. 1971, LL.B. 1974; Harvard Univ., LL.M. 1975. **BAR:** B.C., 1976. **CAREER:** Assoc., then Ptnr, Ladner Downs, 1975-84; Ptnr, Mawhinney and Kellough, 1984-90; Ptnr, Fraser and Beatty, 1990-91; Justice, B.C. Supreme Court, 1991-96; Justice, Court of Appeal of B.C., 1996 to date. **SELECTED PUBLICATIONS:** various papers on continuing legal educ. **AFFIL:** BC Courthouse Library Society (Dir.); The Hamber Foundation; P.A. Woodward Foundation. **INTERESTS:**

gardening; music. **COMMENT:** *"Formerly practised corporate law; now on Court of Appeal of B.C. bench. Enjoy writing and therefore judgment writing tends to swallow all my time."*

Newcombe, Hanna, B.A.,M.A., Ph.D. ◑ 📖 ♥
Director, PEACE RESEARCH INSTITUTE, 25 Dundana Ave., Dundas, ON L9H 4E5 (905) 628-2356. Born 1922. m. Dr. Alan Newcombe. 3 ch. **EDUC:** McMaster Univ., B.A.(Chem.) 1945; Univ. of Toronto, M.A.(Chem.) 1946, Ph.D.(Inorganic Chem.) 1950. **CAREER:** Scientific Translator; Instructor, Chem., McMaster Univ., 1946; abstracted peace/war lit. for Peace Research Institute, 1962; Ed., Peace Research Abstracts Proj.; co-produced *Peace Research Reviews* with Dr. Alan Newcombe, 1967; Pres., World Law Foundation, 1974; Invited Mbr., World Federal Authority Committee, Oslo, 1975; Tutor, McLaughlin Coll., York Univ., 1976; Nat'l Pres., World Federalists of Canada, 1981-82; Mbr., Official Cdn Delegation to the 2nd Special Session of the U.N. on Disarmament, 1982; Prof., Institute of Mundialist Studies, La Lambertie, France. **SELECTED PUBLICATIONS:** *United Nations Reform: Looking Ahead After Fifty Years*, co-ed. Eric Fawcett (Toronto: Dundurn Press, 1995); *Design for a Better World*; several books; many articles. **EDIT:** Ed., Peace Research Abstracts. **AFFIL:** World Federal Authority Committee (Pres.); International Peace Research Association (Mbr. of Council); Women's International Relations Club; World Federalists of Canada; U.N. Association; University Women's Club of Hamilton (Chair, Int'l Affairs Group); Voice of Women. **HONS:** Chancellor's Gold Medal for Academic Achievement, Univ. of Toronto; World Federalists of Canada Peace Award, 1972; Lentz Int'l Peace Research Award, 1974; Canadian Peace Research & Educ. Award, 1983; Woman of the Year (Public Affairs), Hamilton Status of Women Committee, 1985; Peace Messenger Award, U.N., 1987 (to the Peace Research Institute-Dundas); World Citizen Award, Hamilton Mundialization Committee, 1989. **INTERESTS:** swimming; walking; writing poetry. **MISC:** founded Canadian Peace Research & Education Association, one of Canada's Learned Societies, 1965; received Hon. LL.D. from McMaster with husband, Dr. Alan Newcombe. **COMMENT:** *"I am a bookish kind of person, trying to promote peace through writing, teaching, editing, research and occasional public speaking."*

Newell, Jacqueline, B.A.,M.Sc. ◔ ⊗ ♛
Sound Editor, NATIONAL FILM BOARD OF

CANADA, 3155 Côte de Liesse, St. Laurent, QC H4N 2N4 (514) 283-9586, FAX 283-5487. Born Ottawa 1946. m. Jean-Pierre Joutel. **EDUC:** McGill Univ., B.A.(English) 1968; Syracuse Univ., M.Sc.(Radio/TV) 1969. **CAREER:** freelance Sound Ed./Location Mgr, 1972-77; Sound Ed., National Film Board of Canada, 1977 to date. **SELECTED CREDITS:** Sound Ed. on numerous films, incl. the IMAX film *Circus World* (1972); animated films *Why Me* (1978); *Black Fly* (1991); experimental films *End Game in Paris* (1982); *Mother Earth* (1990); fiction feature films *Rubber Gun* (1977); *For the Moment* (1993); and numerous National Film Board of Canada documentaries, incl. the Academy Award-winning *If You Love This Planet* (1981). **AFFIL:** Academy of Canadian Cinema & Television; Syndicat Général de Cinéma et de la Télévision. **HONS:** Fellow, Syracuse Univ., 1968-69; Golden Sheaf for Best Sound Editing, Yorkton Film Festival, 1982. **MISC:** long association with Studio D, the women's studio of the National Film Board, & has sound edited many of its productions. **COMMENT:** *"I'm a second-generation film craftsperson (both my mother and father worked in film) and I'm married to a film mixer. I'm interested in film as a tool for social change and film for art's sake. Technical quality of and creative use of sound on film are my more immediate concerns."*

Newman, Elizabeth, B.A. $

Director of Marketing, R.C.R. RESTAURANTS, 5426 Portland Place, Halifax, NS B3K 1A1 (902) 454-8533, FAX 429-8516. Born Summerside, P.E.I. m. Gary F. 1 ch. **EDUC:** Saint Mary's Univ., B.A.(Pol. Sci.) 1980. **CAREER:** Dir. of Sales, Exec. Travel Apartments, 1986-89; Gen. Mgr, A.M.J. Campbell Van Lines, 1989-94; Dir. of Mktg, R.C.R. Restaurants, 1994 to date. **AFFIL:** Transportation Club of Halifax/Dartmouth (Dir. 1993, 1994; Pres. 1994-95); Abilities Foundation of N.S. (Bd. 1994-95); Rotary Club of Harbourside Halifax (Bd. 1994-95).

Newton, Carolyn, B.A. ♡ ✪

Director of Development, CALGARY PHILHARMONIC ORCHESTRA, 205 - 8th Ave. S.E., Calgary, AB T2G 0K9 (403) 571-0270, FAX 294-7424. Born Nottingham, UK 1961. m. Bruce Elliott. **EDUC:** Univ. of Calgary, B.A.(Pol. Sci.) 1988. **CAREER:** Proj. Mgr, Haines Elliott Marketing Services, 1988-91; Dir., Resource Dev. & Public Rel'ns, YWCA of Calgary, 1991-94; Mgr, Fund Raising Svcs & Membership Dev., Reform Party of Canada, 1994 to date; Dir. of Dev., Calgary Philharmonic Orchestra, 1996 to date. **AFFIL:** Calgary Zoological Society (Bd. 1989-92); Churchill Park Day Care Society (Bd.; V-Chair); YWCA of Calgary (Bd.); National Society of Fund Raising Executives. **INTERESTS:** jazz & blues music; walking; reading; wine tasting. **COMMENT:** *"Born in UK, moved to Canada in 1980. Over a seven-year period, have developed and implemented fund raising strategies for eight major campaigns raising in excess of $28 million."*

Newton-White, Muriel Elizabeth, A.O.C.A. ■■ ✪ 📜 📖

Painter and Writer. P.O. Box 950, Englehart, ON P0J 1H0 (705) 544-2144. Born Robillard Twp. near Charlton, Ont. 1928. s. **EDUC:** Ontario Coll. of Art, A.O.C.A.(Drawing & Painting) 1949. **SELECTED PUBLICATIONS:** *Rabbit Tales in Temiskaming* (1972); *Backhouses of the North* (1972); *Pumpkin Pussycat* (1984); *The Cold Wind in the Winter* (1987); *No, Susie, No* (1991); about 20 other titles (all published by Highway Book Shop). **EXHIBITIONS:** solo shows: Timmins Museum, July 1983; Algonquin Art Gallery, Bancroft, Aug. 1983; Temiskaming Art Gallery, Nov. 1984 & Sept. 1986; group shows: Englehart Museum, Aug. 1991; Centre Culturel, Chapleau, Sept. 1993. **AFFIL:** Englehart/Charlton Anglican Church (layreader; working on Sunday Sch. curriculum). **HONS:** several Ontario Arts Council grants; Doctorate of Canon Law (honourir causa), Thorneloe Univ., Sudbury. **INTERESTS:** landscape painting; writing & illustrating for children; work in the church. **MISC:** has done a lot of volunteer art teaching in schools, taken part in a few "Artists in the Schools" programs, & taught evening & weekend art classes. **COMMENT:** *"I don't know how to describe myself other than as a lover of God, His people and His creation. I have "endeavoured" a great deal and "achieved" little! As far as I know my only claim to fame, other than locally, is a small book* Backhouses of the North, *published by Highway Book Shop, Cobalt."*

Nexhipi, Gjylena, B.A.,M.Ps., Ed.D. ■■ ⊕ ⚖

Consulting Psychologist, Correctional Services, GOVERNMENT OF CANADA, and Staff Psychologist, ONTARIO CORRECTIONAL INSTITUTE, 109 MCLAUGHLIN RD. S., P.O. BOX 1888, BRAMPTON, ON L6V 2P1 (905) 457-7050 FAX 452-8606. **EDUC:** York Univ., B.A.(Hons., Psych.) 1983; Univ. of Ottawa, M.Ps.(Clinical Psych.) 1986; Ontario Institute for Studies in Education, Univ. of Toronto, Ed.D.(Applied Psych.) 1993; Coll. of Psychologists of Ontario, P.Psych. 1995. **CAREER:** Psychometrist, Ontario Correctional Institute, Brampton, Ont.,

1983-84 & May-Sept. 1986; Instructor, Introductory Psych./Psych. in Everyday Life, Continuing Educ., Sheridan Coll., Oakville, Ont., 1986-90; Neuropsychometrist, Peel Memorial Hospital, 1988-89; Neuropsychometrist, Toronto General Hospital, Toronto, 1989-90; Psychologist, HealthServ, Mississauga, Ont., 1990-93; Consulting Psychologist, Ministry of Solicitor Gen. & Correctional Svcs, Probation & Parole, Etobicoke, Ont., 1993-94; Psychologist, assoc. in private practice with Dr. C. Parrott, 1993-95; Psychologist, private practice, 1995 to date; Staff Psychologist, Ontario Correctional Institute, 1994 to date; Consulting Psychologist, Correctional Services Canada, 1996 to date. **AFFIL:** Ontario Correctional Institute (3 yrs. as volunteer in Psych. Dept.). **HONS:** Community Service Award, Gov't of Ont. **MISC:** internship experience at Ontario Correctional Institute, Mount Sinai Hospital, Ontario Institute for Studies in Education, Royal Ottawa Hospital.

Nicholas, Cindy, B.Sc.,LL.B. ■■ ᐰ ♂
Barrister and Solicitor, 2891 Kingston Rd., Scarborough, ON M1M 1N3 (416) 266-3080, FAX 264-2330. Born Toronto. m. Raymond LeGrow. 1 ch. Leahanne LeGrow. **EDUC:** Univ. of Toronto, B.Sc. 1979; Univ. of Windsor, LL.B. 1982. **CAREER:** Programme Officer, Max Bell Foundation & Donner Canadian Foundation, 1984-87; Member of Provincial Parliament, Ont. Legislature, 1987-90; law firm, sole practitioner, 1990 to date. **HONS:** Member of the Order of Canada, 1979; elected into Canada Sports Hall of Fame; first recipient, City of Scarborough Award of Merit. **COMMENT:** *"Record swim crossing of Lake Ontario, 1974, 15 hours, 10 minutes. Nineteen successful crossings of the English Channel. First woman to do the two-way crossing of the English Channel in 19 hours, 55 minutes in 1977, breaking men's record by 10 hours, 5 minutes."*

Nichols, Eva, B.Sc. ᐰ ☺
MESE CONSULTING LTD, 30 Roydawn Ct., West Hill, ON M1C 3C7 (416) 283-4447, FAX 283-1322. Born Budapest. m. Michael. 2 ch. Sarah, Emma. **EDUC:** Univ. of London, B.Sc.(Zoology/Chem.) 1965, postgrad. diploma (Genetics) 1966, postgrad. diploma (Immunology) 1968. **CAREER:** Instructor, Univ. of Toronto, 1974-78; Trustee, Scarborough Bd. of Educ., 1974-82; Coord., Client Svcs, Learning Disabilities Association of Ontario, 1983-84; Exec. Dir., 1984-94; Consultant, 1994 to date. **SELECTED PUBLICATIONS:** *Did You Ever Wonder Why? A Probation Officer's Handbook on Learning Disabilities* (1987); *Still*

Putting The Pieces Together, a Parent's Guide to Special Education in Ontario (1994); *Design for Success, an Employer's Guide to Learning Disabilities* (1994); *Tools for Transitions, a Counsellor's Guide to Learning Disabilities* (1994); *Links in Learning* (1995); *Learning Assessment Profile for Adults, an employment training manual* (1996); various other publications. **AFFIL:** Integra (Bd. of Dir.) Ministry of Educ. Advisory Council on Special Educ. (Chair); General Educ. Council; Educ. Task Force, Sparrow Lake Alliance; George Brown Coll. (Special Needs Advisory Bd.); York Univ. Learning Disabilities Program (Advisory Committee); Interministerial Working Group on Learning Disabilities, Ministry of Citizenship. **COMMENT:** *"I am known and recognized for my initiatives in advocating for and supporting persons with learning disabilities. My publications are widely used by and on behalf of persons with disabilities. Beyond that, I am viewed as an expert in special education issues and educational legislation."*

Nickel, Dianne ☺ ☯
Executive Director, ACCESSIBLE HOUSING SOCIETY, 2003 - 14th St. N.W., Ste. 103, Calgary, AB T2M 3N4 403) 282-1872, FAX 284-0304. Born Calgary 1940. m. Herschel. 2 ch. Marshal, Heather. **CAREER:** Sec.-Treas., Heathmar Industries Ltd., 1975-80; part-time employment, 1981-82; Asst. Mgr, Ethier Associates, 1984-85; Bus. Mgr, Accessible Housing Society, 1985-88; Exec. Dir., 1988 to date. **AFFIL:** Calgary Housing Committee. **HONS:** Honorable Mention for Process & Mgmt, "Independence Through Housing" Awards, Canada Mortgage and Housing Corporation, 1992; Chairman's Gold Pin, Canada Mortgage and Housing Corporation, 1994. **INTERESTS:** gardening; hiking; cross-country skiing. **COMMENT:** *"Endeavoured to raise awareness of the need to coordinate funding, housing and support services for people with physical disabilities. Synthesize diverse elements to achieve solutions."*

Nicks, Joan Patricia, B.A., M.A. ■ ᐰ ☒ ㅂ
Associate Professor, Department of Film Studies, Dramatic and Visual Arts, BROCK UNIVERSITY, St. Catharines, ON L2S 3A1 (905) 688-5550, ext. 4278, FAX 688-2789, EMAIL jpnicks@spartan.ac.brocku.ca. Born Cudworth, Sask. 1937. d. 2 ch. **EDUC:** Brock Univ., B.A.(Film Studies) 1979; Carleton Univ., M.A.(Cdn Studies/Film Studies) 1984. **CAREER:** Elementary Sch. Teacher, Welland County Separate Sch. Bd., 1956-57; Elementary Supply Teacher, Lincoln County Bd., 1960-61; Seminar Leader, Drama & Film,

Brock Univ., 1978-79; Sessional Lecturer, 1980-81; Lecturer, 1981-84; Asst. Prof., Fine Arts, 1984-93; Assoc. Prof., Film Studies, Dramatic & Visual Arts, 1993 to date; Chair, 1993-96. SELECTED CREDITS: Script Dev. Advisor/Co-Dir./Screen Ed., *Let's Talk About Sex*, video, McMaster-Chedoke Hospitals, Hamilton, Ont., 1987; Prod. Mgr, *The Suzie Show*, THEA (1987); keynote performance presentation, *Expressive Mind, Body, Voice*, Niagara Region Int'l Women's Day, 1995. SELECTED PUBLICATIONS: "Aesthetic Memory in Mourir à tue-tête: Fragments from *Screens From Silence*," in *Responses*, Blaine Allen, Michael Dorland & Zuzana Pick, eds. (Kingston, Montreal, Ottawa: Responsibility Press/Les Editions La Responsabilité, 1992); "sex, lies, and landscape: meditations on vertical tableaux in Joyce Wieland's *The Far Shore* and Jean Beaudin's *J.A. Martin, photographe*" *(Canadian Journal of Film Studies* 1, 2-3 1993); "Crossing into Eden's Storehouse" *(Textual Studies in Canada* 2 Spring 1992); book reviews; various other publications. EXHIBITIONS: "See..r..ing Through Godard," mixed media installation, Brock Fine Arts Faculty Exhibition (1986). AFFIL: Niagara Artists' Centre (Bd. of Dir., VP 1983-85); St. Catharines Community Co-Op (Educ. Committee 1896); Niagara North Condominium Corporation (Bd. of Dir. 1992-95); Film Studies Association of Canada (Pres. 1992-93). HONS: Kinnear Estate Scholarship, Brock Univ., 1977-78; Harding Book Prize, Brock Univ., 1977-78; Gov. General's Medal, Brock Univ., 1978-79; Sophia Gampel Memorial Scholarship, Brock Univ., 1978-79; Dr. Marion B. Smith Book Prize, Brock Univ., 1978-79; Senate Award for Outstanding Grad. Work, Carleton Univ., 1984; Alumni Association's Excellence in Teaching Award, Brock Univ., 1994; Students' Union Teaching Excellence Award, Brock Univ., 1994. INTERESTS: cinema & popular culture; writing fiction & criticism; jazz; dance; the arts; power-walking; travel; cooking; dining with friends; sewing & design. MISC: committees to found & steer Brock's programs in Cdn Studies, 1981-86, Comm. Studies, 1982-86 & Women's Studies, 1989-90; numerous conference presentations; recipient, various grants; reviewer for various journals & granting agencies. COMMENT: *"I have endeavoured to link interdisciplinary teaching, research, and academic roles, fruitfully and creatively. I am concerned with people, and with how the processes of acquiring knowledge, and maintaining curiosity, can be vital—for myself, for students, and as cultural contribution. It is difficult to measure achievement in all this, but it feels right and vital."*

Nijssen-Jordan, Cheri, M.D., F.R.C.P.C. ⊕ ⍥
Director of Emergency Services, ALBERTA CHILDREN'S HOSPITAL, 1820 Richmond Rd. S.W., Calgary, AB T2T 5C7 (403) 229-7295, FAX 229-7649. Assistant Professor, UNIVERSITY OF CALGARY. Born Saskatoon, Sask. 1958. m. K. Peter Nijssen. 3 ch. Anthony, Kathryn, Marta. EDUC: Univ. of Saskatchewan, M.D. 1981. CAREER: Medical Staff, Turtleford Hospital, Sask., 1981; Pediatric Resident, Univ. Hospital, Univ. of Saskatchewan, 1982-83; District Medical Officer, Gov't of Lesotho, Mohale's Hoek Gov't Hospital, Lesotho, Africa, 1983-85; Pediatric Resident, Izaak Walton Killam Children's Hospital, 1986-88; Chief Resident, 1988-89; Lecturer, Dalhousie Univ., 1989-91; Active Staff, Izaak Walton Killam Children's Hospital, 1989-91; Asst. Prof., Univ. of Ottawa, 1991-93; Active Staff, Children's Hospital of Eastern Ontario, 1991-93; Asst. Prof., Univ. of Calgary, 1993 to date; Dir., Emergency Svcs, Alberta Children's Hospital, 1993 to date; Examiner in Emergency Medicine, Royal Coll. of Physicians & Surgeons of Canada, 1993 to date. SELECTED PUBLICATIONS: "Vaccine Failure: Haemophilus Influenzae type B Polysaccharide Vaccine," with R. Bortolussi & R. Ozere *(Canadian Diseases Weekly Report*, May 2, 1987); "Bacterial Tracheitis Associated with Respiratory-Syncytial Virus and Toxic Shock Syndrome," with S.A. Halperin & J.D. Donaldson *(Canadian Medical Association Journal*, Feb., 1990); "Epiglottitis in Canada: A Multiregional review," with B.J. Law *et al (Canadian Journal of Infectious Diseases*, May 1990); "Nocardia Brasiliensis: A Primary Cutaneous Infection," with S.J. Pegg *et al (Canadian Journal of Pediatric*, Feb. 1991). AFFIL: Ontario Medical Association; Royal Coll. of Physicians & Surgeons of Canada (Fellow in Pediatrics); American Academy of Pediatrics (Fellow; Task Force on APLS Pediatric Emergency Medicine Course; Canadian Pediatric Society (Pediatric Emergency Section; Exec. Mbr. at Large); Canadian Association of Emergency Physicians (Chair, Pediatric Emergency Section); American Board of Pediatrics (Certification in Pediatrics; Certification in Pediatric Emergency Medicine). HONS: Gov. General's Medal, 1975; W.P. Thompson Scholarship, Univ. of Saskatchewan, 1976. INTERESTS: skiing; folk music; reading; marriage preparation; choir. MISC: numerous invited addresses. COMMENT: *"Since completion of my pediatric specialty training, I have been working in the pediatric emergency medicine subspecialty. Together with many of my colleagues, we are working toward Royal College recognition of the subspecialty. Outside my*

medical work, I am occupied with family, sports and work within our church group."

Noble, Kimberley, B.A.A.,B.A. ✎ 📖 $

Reporter, "Report on Business," *THE GLOBE AND MAIL*, 444 Front St. W., Toronto, ON M5V 2S9 (416) 585-5387, FAX 585-5695. Born Sudbury, Ont. 1957. cl. Dan Westell. 2 ch. **EDUC:** Univ. of Guelph, B.A.(Fine Art/English) 1980; Ryerson Polytechnic Univ., B.A.A.(Journalism) 1984. **CAREER:** Toronto Correspondent, Fairchild News Service, 1983-84; Reporter, *The Globe and Mail*, 1984 to date; Adjunct Prof., Grad. Sch. of Journalism, Univ. of Western Ontario, 1991-92. **SELECTED PUBLICATIONS:** *Bound and Gagged: Libel Chill and the Right to Publish* (HarperCollins, 1992). **AFFIL:** Canadian Association of Journalists; Southern Ontario Newspaper Guild; Writers to Reform the Libel Law. **HONS:** National Newspaper Award for Business Reporting, 1990, 1991; Citation of Merit, Business Reporting, National Newspaper Awards, 1993, 1995. **INTERESTS:** freedom of expression & access to info. issues; the rise & fall of Cdn corp. conglomerates; the growth of the medical bus.; long-distance cycling; urban gardening; child care; travel.

Noel-Bentley, Elaine, B.A.,M.A. ■ $ 🍁

Senior Director, Total Compensation, PETRO-CANADA, P.O.Box 2844, Calgary, AB T2P 3E3 (403) 296-4343, FAX 296-7719. Born Toronto 1943. m. Peter Noel-Bentley. 2 ch. Karen Noel-Bentley, Matthew Noel-Bentley. **EDUC:** Univ. of Toronto, B.A.(Math/Actuarial Sci.) 1964; Univ. of Manitoba, M.A.(English) 1972. **CAREER:** Supervisor, Group Accts, Great-West Life Insurance, 1975-82; Mgr, Pension Svcs, Alberta Treasury, 1982-87; Instructor, Pensions & Benefits, Univ. of Alberta, Northern Alberta Institute of Technology, Mount Royal Coll., 1984 to date; Mgr, Employee Benefits, Petro-Canada, 1987-95; Mng Principal, The Alexander Consulting Group, 1995-96; Sr. Dir., Total Compensation, Petro-Canada, 1996 to date. **SELECTED PUBLICATIONS:** "Jane Austen and Regina Maria Roche" (*Notes and Queries* Sept. 1975); "A Further Note on Jane Austen and 'Thorough Novel Slang'" (*Notes and Queries* Mar. 1976); "Are You Ready For Retirement?" (*Mid-Canada Commerce* Feb. 1982). **AFFIL:** Association of Canadian Pension Management (Dir.); Advisory Committee to Certified Employee Benefits Specialist Program; Canadian Pensions & Benefits Conference (former Nat'l Sec.-Treas.); Calgary Chamber of Commerce (Arts & Bus. Committee); Alberta Health Workforce Rebalancing Committee; Advisory Committee to Alberta Superintendent of Pensions (Chair). **HONS:** Reuben Wells Leonard Fellowship, 1961; Grad. Fellowship, Canada Council, 1972-75. **INTERESTS:** health issues; pensions & fin. planning; educ. **MISC:** speaker at numerous conferences & associations. **COMMENT:** *"My endeavours have been in the broad field of compensation, pensions and benefits, managing programs, educating practitioners, influencing government policy and presenting issues to many groups."*

Noonan, Cathy, B.Sc.,B.A.Sc. $

Vice-President, Customer Service, COLGATE-PALMOLIVE CANADA INC., 99 Vanderhoof Ave., Toronto, ON M4G 2H6 (416) 421-6000, FAX 421-6913. Born Quebec City 1956. m. Robert Tays. 2 ch. **EDUC:** Univ. of Ottawa, B.Sc. (Biochem.) 1977, Certificate (Bus. Admin.) 1979, B.A.Sc.(Chem. Eng.) 1981. **CAREER:** Transportation Analyst/Bus. Advisor/Supervisor, Customer Svc, Shell Canada Limited, 1986-90; Mgr, Preferred Supplier/Dir., Logistics, Pillsbury Canada Limited, 1990-94; VP, Customer Svc, Colgate-Palmolive Canada Inc., 1994 to date. **AFFIL:** Canadian Association of Logistics Management; Grocery Products Manufacturers' Council. **INTERESTS:** jogging; reading; skiing. **COMMENT:** *"My objective has always been to elevate the profile of the logistics discipline within the corporate community through the identification of customer satisfaction as a key element of improved sales, profit margin and market share."*

Noonan, Donna, B.F.A. 🎭 ✪

Film Designer, Director, 155 - 52 Ave., Lachine, QC H8T 2X1 (514) 639-1079, FAX 639-1079. Born Port Arthur, Ont. 1955. m. Gabor L. Vadany. 2 ch. Christopher, Benjamin. **EDUC:** Confederation Coll., Diploma in Radio/Theatre/TV 1975; Concordia Univ., B.F.A.(Theatre Scenography) 1979. **CAREER:** various capacities in the film industry, 1979 to date; film proj. dev., Docuvision, to date; interior decorator, private sector, to date. **SELECTED CREDITS:** Prod. Designer, *Dead Innocent* (feature); Prod. Designer, *La Presence des Ombres* (feature), Allegro Productions; Prod. Designer, *Solo, The Legend Begins* (feature), Cinepix Productions; Prod. Designer, "L'Etrange Demoiselle," *Arsene Lupin*, Allegro Productions IV; Art Dir., *Princes in Exile*, TV, Cinepix Productions; Art Dir.,*Vanished*, TV, Films IV Productions (NBC); Art Dir., *Stalked*, feature film, Allegro Productions III; Art Dir., *Whispers* (feature), Cinepix Productions; Art Dir., *Snake Eaters Revenge* (feature), Cinepix Productions; Art Dir., *Ghost Town*/Cheap Trick (rock video), Warner Bros.; Art Dir., various industrial/corp. videos & TV commercials; Head Decorator, *Embrasse-Moi*; Native Crafts Consultant, *Black Robe*, feature film; various other film & TV credits; Stage Mgr, *October Stranger*, Association for Native Development in the Performing & Visual Arts, 6th World Amateur Theatre Festival, Monaco. **AFFIL:** Directors' Guild of Canada; Syndicat des Techniciennes/Techniciens du Cinema du Quebec; The Native Friendship Centre of Montreal (Past Chair); Society of Canadian Artists of Native Ancestry (Co-Chair). **MISC:** Coord., Urban Aboriginal Economic Development Colloquy, 1993; jury mbr., Canadian Native Arts Foundation, 1993. **COMMENT:** *"My film work intertwines itself with my identity as an aboriginal person. My knowledge of the native community extends into the work I have done for film. I have established many working relationships and friendships that blend well with the work I perform within the film realm."*

Norrie, The Hon. Eleanor, M.L.A. ■ ♣ ⚛
Member of the Legislative Assembly (Truro-Bible Hill), Minister of Natural Resources, Minister Responsible for the Women's Directorate and Minister Responsible for Administration of the Advisory Council of the Status of Women Act, GOVERNMENT OF NOVA SCOTIA, Box 698, Halifax, NS B3J 2T9 (902) 424-4037, FAX 424-0594. Born Tatamagouche, N.S. 1942. m. Roderick 3 ch. **EDUC:** Nova Scotia Provincial Normal Coll., Teacher's Certificate 1961. **CAREER:** Teacher, Prov. of N.S.; co-owner & co-operator, family restaurant bus. **VOLUNTEER CAREER:** V-Chair, Colchester Regional Hospital Foundation; Chair, N.S. Sport Heritage Centre; Pres., Truro Centurion Swim Club; Pres., Truro Attic Painters; Pres., Truro Play Sch.; Pres., Colchester North Liberal Auxilary; Exec., Truro Home & Sch. **POLITICAL CAREER:** M.L.A. (Truro-Bible Hill), Gov't of N.S., 1993 to date; Min. of the Dept. of Hum. Res., Min. Responsible for the Advisory Council on the Status of Women, Min. Responsible for the N.S. Sport & Recreation Commission, 1993-95; Min. of Housing & Consumer Affairs, 1995-96; Min. Responsible for the Advisory Council on the Status of Women, 1995 to date; Min. Responsible for the N.S. Gaming Control Commission, Min. Responsible for the Liquor Control Act, 1995; Min. of Natural Res. & Min. Responsible for the Women's Directorate, 1996 to date. **AFFIL:** Liberal Party of N.S. **INTERESTS:** painting; travel; swimming; music. **COMMENT:** *"As a woman of the 90s, I am committed to dedicating my life to my family, community and province. I endeavour to become a role model for women to follow. Achievements include a 30-year marriage, mother of three daughters, volunteer work and successful political candidate and Cabinet Minister.*

Northcote, Ann L., B.A. ✊
Past President, WORLD YWCA and YWCA OF/DU CANADA. Born Winnipeg 1932. m. W. Bruce. 2 ch. **EDUC:** Univ. of Manitoba, B.A. 1953. **AFFIL:** YWCA of Metro Toronto; Canadian National Institute for the Blind (Bd. 1988-93; V-Chair 1991-93); Family Service Association of Metro Toronto (Bd. 1988-94; Placement Coord. Svc Chair 1994 to date). **HONS:** Member, Order of Canada, 1987; Queen's Jubilee Medal; Canada 2000 Medal. **MISC:** has given numerous keynote addresses & guest lectures around the world; has visited refugee camps, rural dev. projects & health-care projects throughout the world.

Northey, Margot, B.A.,M.A.,Ph.D. 🎓 $ ☝
Dean, School of Business, QUEEN'S UNIVERSITY, Kingston, ON K9L 3N6 (613) 545-2305, FAX 545-2013, EMAIL mn6@qsilver.queensu.ca. Born Toronto 1940. m. Patrick Northey. 3 ch. Rodney, Scott, Brenda. **EDUC:** Univ. of Toronto, B.A.(Arts) 1960; York Univ., M.A. (English) 1969, Ph.D.(English) 1974. **CAREER:** Visiting Asst. Prof., English Studies, Erindale Campus, Univ. of Toronto, 1976-78; Assoc. Prof. & Dir. of The Writing Program, 1978-88; Assoc. Prof. & Dir. of Comm., Western Bus. Sch., Univ. of Western Ontario, 1988-95; Visiting Prof., Helsinki Sch. of Econ., 1993; Dir., Lac Minerals, 1993-94; Prof. & Dean, Sch. of Bus., Queen's Univ., 1995 to date. **SELECTED PUBLICATIONS:** *The Haunted Wilderness: The Gothic and Grotesque in Canadian Fiction* (Toronto: Univ. of Toronto Press, 1976); *Impact: A Guide to Business Communication* (Toronto: Prentice-Hall, 1986; 3rd ed., 1994); *Making Sense in the Social Sciences*, with Lorne Tepperman (Toronto: Oxford Univ. Press, 1986; 3rd ed., 1994) *William Kirby* (Toronto: ECW, 1989); "Sportive Grotesque: Carrier's *La Guerre, Yes, Sir!*" (*Canadian Literature* Autumn 1976); "Freedom and Control: Swinburne's Novels" *(English Studies in Canada* Fall 1980) "The Need for Writing Skills in Accounting Firms" (*Management Communication Quarterly* May 1990); case studies; various other publications. **EDIT:** Ed. Bd., *Journal of Business Communication.* **AFFIL:** Association for Business Communication (VP, Canada); Badminton & Racquet Club (Dir. 1987-90). **INTERESTS:** music; theatre; tennis; swimming. **MISC:** comm. consultant & seminar leader with diverse organizations across Canada; fellowships; 1st female Dean of a major bus. coll. **COMMENT:** *"A management communications*

specialist and university professor with varied experience as a consultant, researcher, teacher and speaker. An author or co-author of six books and many articles."

Nother, Joanne ✊ 🎓

Coordinator, Centre for Equity and Human Rights, CAMBRIAN COLLEGE OF APPLIED ARTS AND TECHNOLOGY, 1400 Barrydowne Rd., Sudbury, ON P3A 3V8 (705) 566-8101, ext. 7235, FAX 566-5847, EMAIL jxnother@venus.cambrianc.on.ca. **EDUC:** Cambrian Coll., Revenue Canada Taxation Acctg Certificate 1985; McMaster Univ. & Univ. of Waterloo, B.A. in progress. **CAREER:** Proj. Worker, Timmins Women's Centre, 1976; various clerical positions, Hamilton District Taxation Centre, 1977-80; Clerical Assessor, Assessing Div., Sudbury Taxation Centre, 1980-83; Appeals Officer, Appeals Div., 1983-84; Taxroll Section Head, Taxroll Div., 1984-87; Field Internal Auditor, Mgmt Controls Div., 1987-89; Acting Records Mgmt Officer, Fin. & Admin. Div., 1989-90; Mail & Records Section Head, Fin. & Admin. Div., 1990-91; Employment Equity Coord., Personnel Div., 1991-92; secondment to Cambrian Coll. from Sudbury Taxation Centre, 1991-92; Employment & Educ. Equity Coord., Cambrian Coll., 1992 to date. **AFFIL:** Multiple Sclerosis Society of Ontario (Sudbury Chapter); National Access Awareness Week Committee; Regional Social Services Research Advisory Group (Sudbury & Manitoulin Steering Committee); Persons United for Self-Help in N.E. Ontario (Chair); Sudbury Women's Centre; City of Sudbury Advisory Committee on Transportation for the Physically Disabled; Provincial Games for the Physically Disabled (Organizing Committee 1992); Legal Education Action Fund (Sudbury Chapter Committee); Laurentian Univ. (Community Midwifery Transition Committee); Sudbury-Manitoulin & District Health Council (Long-Term Care Consultation Committee); Sudbury & District Health Unit (Advisory Committee on the Integrated Homemaker Program); Manitoulin & Sudbury District Health Council (Supportive Housing Committee); Laurentian Hospital (Community Rep., Ethics Committee); Ministry of Citizenship, Queen's Park, Toronto (Advisory Council on Advocacy Commission); Coll. Committee on Equity in Educ. & Employment (Past Chair). **COMMENT:** *"Joanne is committed to promoting advocacy for persons with disabilities. She also very actively advocates equity and human rights for all people."*

Novak, Marie, M.Sc.,Ph.D. ■ 🎓 ⊕

Professor, UNIVERSITY OF WINNIPEG, 515 Portage Ave., Winnipeg, MB R3B 2E9 (204) 786-9296, FAX 786-1824, EMAIL mnovak@io.uwinnipeg.ca. Born Prague 1940. d. **EDUC:** Univ. of Manitoba, M.Sc.(Zoology) 1972, Ph.D.(Zoology) 1974. **CAREER:** Asst. Prof., Dept. of Biol., Univ. of Winnipeg, 1974-79; Assoc. Prof., Dept. of Biol., 1979-85; Prof., Dept. of Biol., 1985 to date; Adjunct Prof., Dept. of Anatomy, 1994 to date. **SELECTED PUBLICATIONS:** numerous refereed journal articles incl. "Long-term exposure effects of cold and heat on mouse peripheral leucocytes," with M.H. Howlader & I. Krampetz (*Journal of Thermal Biology*, no. 14, 1989); "An improved method for staining mouse mast cells," with S. Nombrado (*Canadian Journal of Zoology*, no. 67, 1989); "Hymenolepis nana induced mastocytosis in mice," with R.B. Sokolies & E. Pip (*Canadian Journal of Zoology*, no. 68, 1990); "Metabolic alterations in organs of Meriones unguiculatus infected with Echinococcus multilocularis," with A. Modha & B.J. Blackburn (*Comparative Biochemistry and Physiology*, 1993); "Proton nuclear magnetic resonance analysis of liver metabolites from mice infected with Mesocestoides vogae,"" with B.J. Blackburn & C. Hudspeth (*International Journal for Parasitology*, no. 23, 1993); "Phosphate metabolites of Tenebrio molitor (Coleoptera: Tenebrionidae) infected with metacestodes of Hymenolepis diminuta," with A. Modha *et al* (*Journal of Medical Entomology*, 1995). **AFFIL:** American Society of Parasitologists. **MISC:** reviewer of manuscripts submitted to *Canadian Journal of Zoology*, *International Journal for Parasitology*, *Journal of Parasitology*; recipient, various NSERC grants.

Novick, Catherine, H.B.A.,C.A. ■ $

Chief Financial Officer, CIBC INSURANCE, 5150 Spectrum Way, Mississauga, ON L4W 5G8 (905) 306-5173, FAX 306-5201. Vice-President, Personal and Commercial Bank, CIBC. m. Gordon Ray. **EDUC:** Univ. of Western Ontario, Sch. of Bus. Admin., H.B.A. 1977. **CAREER:** Gen. Practice Mgr, Coopers & Lybrand, Toronto, 1977-87; Exec. Dir., Fin., The Imperial Life Assurance Company of Canada, 1987-90; VP & Corp. Cont., Laurentian Financial Inc., 1990-91. **AFFIL:** Institute of Chartered Accountants (C.A.). **COMMENT:** *"Focused on working at the leading edge of change in the financial services industry in Canada."*

Nunn, Mary Margaret ✽ 🎓

Artist. 2056 Blackfriars Rd., Ottawa, ON K2A 3K8 (613) 722-6687. Born Toronto 1947. m. Ian. 2 ch. Danielle, Richard Damien. **CAREER:** artist; water-media workshop leader; art juror.

SELECTED PUBLICATIONS: art in magazines, newspapers, limited edition prints, cards & art calendars. COMMISSIONS: Art in Public Places, City of Ottawa (1996). EXHIBITIONS: Greenbank Gallery, Nepean (1984); Metropolitan Life Bldg, Ottawa (1986); MacDonald Club, Ottawa (1986); Atrium Gallery, City of Nepean (1992); A Source of Art Gallery, Ottawa (1994); Carleton Univ. Fac. Club (1995); Sante Art Gallery, Ottawa (1995); numerous group exhibits, reg'l, nat'l & int'l. COLLECTIONS: paintings have been purchased by gov't & univ. depts., art galleries, embassies, & private collections in many countries; work is on every continent but Antarctica. AFFIL: Ottawa Watercolour Society (Exhibition Coord.); Friend of the National Gallery. HONS: a purchase award, City of Ottawa, presented to Mayor of the Hague as part of the VE Day celebrations, 1995; numerous awards from Watercolour Societies. INTERESTS: active YM/YWCA mbr.; yoga; reading; observing. COMMENT: *"Making the transition from painting objects to painting ideas. Excited by the magic and enchantment of the natural and unseen world. Enjoy sharing my discoveries with (mentoring) others on the creative path."*

Nunn, Wendy, B.A.,C.H.R.P. ■ $

Corporate Director, Organizational Development, LAIDLAW INC., 3221 North Service Rd., Burlington, ON L7R 3Y8 (905) 336-1865, ext. 301, FAX 336-0670. EDUC: Queen's Univ., B.A.(English/French) 1970; Sheridan Coll., Certificate (Mgmt Studies). CAREER: Membership Clerk, Ontario Motor League, 1971-73; Admin. Asst. to the Pres., Tricil Limited, 1973-80; Personnel Administrator, Tricil Limited, 1981-86; Mgr, Personnel Programs, 1986-89; Mgr, Hum. Res., Laidlaw Inc., 1990-93; Dir., Employment Equity & Gov't Compliance, 1993-96; Dir., Organizational Dev., 1996 to date. AFFIL: Personnel Association of Ontario (Certified Hum. Res. Professional). COMMENT: *"Human Resources practitioner for 15 years. Generalist with specific expertise in policy development, equal opportunity, training, recruitment, performance management and salary administration. Designs and delivers train-the-trainer programs in harassment investigation and affirmative action."*

Nutaraluk Aulatujut, Elizabeth ⊗

Sculptor, c/o Arctic Co-operatives Limited, 1645 Inkster Blvd., Winnipeg, MB R2X 2W7 (204) 697-1625, FAX 697-1880. Born 1913 EXHIBITIONS: *Sculpture/Inuit: Masterworks of the Canadian Arctic*, Canadian Eskimo Arts Council, Ottawa, int'l tour (1971-73); *Annual Exhibitions of Eskimo Sculptures and Prints*,

Lippel Gallery, Montreal (1974); *The Mulders' Collection*, Winnipeg Art Gallery (1976); *The Coming and Going of the Shaman*, Winnipeg Art Gallery (1978); *The Circle is the Home*, The Inuit Gallery of Eskimo Art, Toronto (1982); *Eskimo Point/Arviat*, Winnipeg Art Gallery (1982); *The Beat of the Drum*, The Arctic Circle, L.A. (1982); *Grasp Tight the Old Ways: Selections from the Klamer Family Collection of Inuit Art*, Art Gallery of Ontario, Toronto, int'l tour (1983-85); *The Bond Between Mother and Child*, The Arctic Circle, L.A. (1987); *Arctic Forms–Inuit Sculpture*, Arctic Inuit Art Gallery, Richmond, VA (1988); many presentations by L'Iglou Art Esquimau, Douai (1989-92); *Three Women of Arviat: Sculpture by Elizabeth Nutaraluk, Lucy Tasseor & Joy Halluk*, The Isaacs/Inuit Gallery, Toronto (1992); *The Collector's Eye, Inuit Art from Private Collections*, Albers Gallery, San Francisco (1995). COLLECTIONS: Twomey Collection, Winnipeg Art Gallery; Swinton Collection, Winnipeg Art Gallery; Klamer Family Collection; Art Gallery of Ontario; Canadian Museum of Civilization; McMichael Canadian Art Collection. MISC: attended the opening of the exhibition "Sculpture/Inuit: Masterworks of the Canadian Arctic," Philadelphia, 1973.

O

Oakes, Jennifer J., B.A.,LL.B. ⚖ Ⓢ
Partner, FIELD & FIELD PERRATON, 2000
Oxford Tower, 10235 - 101 St., Edmonton, AB
T5N 3V2 (403) 423-3003, FAX 428-9329.
Born UK 1956 **EDUC:** Univ. of Alberta,
B.A.(Arts) 1976, LL.B.(Law) 1979. **CAREER:**
articled with Field & Field Perraton, 1979;
Assoc., 1980-84; Ptnr, 1984 to date; practice in
residential & commercial real estate, with
emphasis on condominium dev. **SELECTED
PUBLICATIONS:** *Builder and Buyer Beware–
Selected Issues in New Home Construction*
(1994); *New Residential Condominium Transactions* (1994); *New Homes Construction and
the Builders' Lien Act* (1994); Conflict Situations in the Practice of Residential Real Estate
(1994); *New Home Buyers Guide Seminar*
(1996). **AFFIL:** Fort Edmonton Historical
Foundation (Past Pres.); 1996 du Maurier Ltd.
Classic (Fin. Committee); Legal Education Society of Alberta (Lecturer, Bar Admission
Course); Greater Edmonton Home Builders'
Association. **HONS:** City of Edmonton Community Service Award, 1992. **INTERESTS:** golf;
spending time in the mountains; travelling.
COMMENT: *"I feel fortunate to have found
myself in a career that, while demanding, has
been very rewarding."*

Oaks, Ann, B.A.,M.A.,Ph.D. ■■ ✿ ✑
Professor of Botany (Adjunct), UNIVERSITY OF
GUELPH, Department of Botany, Guelph, ON
N1G 2W1 (519) 824-4120, ext. 6002, FAX
767-1991, EMAIL aoaks@uoguelph.ca. Pro-
fessor of Biology (Emeritus), MCMASTER UNI-
VERSITY. Born Winnipeg 1929. **EDUC:** Univ. of
Toronto, B.A.(Biol.) 1951; Univ. of Saskat-
chewan, M.A.(Biol.) 1954, Ph.D.(Plant Physiol-

ogy) 1959; post-doctoral studies in Germany & US 1959-63. **CAREER:** Asst. Prof., Biol., McMaster Univ., 1965-68; Assoc. Prof., 1968-74; Prof., 1974-89; Prof. Emeritus, 1989 to date; Prof., Botany, Univ. of Guelph, 1989-96; Adjunct Prof., 1996 to date. **SELECTED PUBLICATIONS:** numerous publications in refereed journals, & invited papers. **MISC:** main thrust of research proj. has been to understand nitrogen assimilation in cereals; has served as a reviewer of scientific papers, as a reviewer of research grants, & on several edit. bds.

O'Brien, Sheila, B.A. $

Senior Vice-President, Human Resources, NOVA CORPORATION, 801 - 7th Ave. S.W., Calgary, AB T2P 2N6 (403) 290-7503, FAX 290-7175. **EDUC:** Univ. of Calgary, B.A. 1969; Univ. of Western Ontario, Mgmt Training Course 1986. **CAREER:** various positions incl. Sr. Landman & various hum. res. roles, Amoco Canada Petroleum Co. Ltd.; Gen. Mgr, Admin. & Mgr, Employee Rel'ns, Panarctic Petroleum, 1980-84; Mgr, Cdn Benefits, Petro-Canada Resources, 1984-86; Dir., Public Affairs, Petro-Canada Inc., 1986-91; Dir., Public Affairs, NOVA Corporation, 1992-93; VP for People & Community, 1993-95; Sr. VP, Hum. Res., 1995 to date. **AFFIL:** Human Resources Development Canada (Advisory Group on Working Time & the Distribution of Work 1993); Alberta Vocational Coll. (Women in Science & Technology Advisory Committee 1993-94); Univ. of British Columbia (Dean's Advisory Council, Fac. of Commerce & Bus. Admin.); Calgary Petroleum Club. **HONS:** Advancement of Women category, Women of Distinction Award, 1988; Citation for Citizenship, Gov't of Canada Award for Community Leadership, 1989. **MISC:** Organizing Committee, "Women Celebrate Women" (dinner commemorating the 50th anniversary of women being legally declared as "persons"), 1979; Co-host, *Four Tonight*, weekly TV program, CFAC, Calgary, 1977-78.

O'Callaghan, Shelley, B.Ed.,LL.B. ⚖

Partner, BULL, HOUSSER AND TUPPER, Barristers and Solicitors, 3000 Royal Centre, 1055 W. Georgia St., Vancouver, BC V6E 3R3 (604) 687-6575, FAX 641-4949. Born Vancouver 1948. m. Patrick. 2 ch. Kevin, Michael. **EDUC:** Univ. of British Columbia, B.Ed. 1970; Univ. of Calgary, LL.B. 1985. **BAR:** B.C., 1987. **CAREER:** teacher, Canadian University Services Overseas, Zambia, 1970-72; Ptnr & Head of Environmental Practice, & Ed., *Environmental Brief*, Bull, Housser and Tupper. **AFFIL:** Vancouver Board of Trade (Chair, Taskforce on the Environment 1993-95; Committee on Economic Dev. & the Environment). **INTERESTS:** skiing; tennis; enjoying the outdoors. **MISC:** Stakeholder Advisory Committee mbr. drafting new B.C. Environmental Protection Act. **COMMENT:** *"Recognized for leadership in both community and professional endeavours."*

O'Connor, Lila J., M.L.A. 🍁

Member of the Legislative Assembly (Lunenburg), GOVERNMENT OF NOVA SCOTIA, Mahone Bay, NS B0J 2E0 (902) 624-9320, FAX 424-0539. Born Washington, D.C. 1940. m. Michael J. 3 ch. **CAREER:** owner/operator, small antique bus., 1986-93; Town Councillor, Town of Mahone Bay, 1988-93; M.L.A. (Lunenburg), Prov. of N.S., 1993 to date. **AFFIL:** Liberal Party of N.S. (various local & prov. exec. positions; past Campaign Mgr); Mahone Bay Business Association (Dir. 1989-92); South Shore Tourist Association (Treas. & Dir. 1990-92); Victorian Order of Nurses (Pres., Lunenburg County 1989-92); Home & School, numerous organizations; local museum (Dir.). **HONS:** Volunteer Award W.A.Y.S. (We Appreciate Your Service), Lunenburg County; N.S. Prov. Volunteer Award. **INTERESTS:** sailing; reading; knitting; antiques; grandchildren; bridge. **COMMENT:** *"Was brought up in the tourist industry, married, brought up three children, involved in organizations that involved the community, love politics, enjoy the grandchildren and volunteering in the community."*

Oda, Beverley J., B.A ■ $ 📺

Senior Vice-President, BATON BROADCASTING INCORPORATED, Box 9, Stn. O, Toronto, ON M4A 2M9 (416) 299-2028, FAX 299-2386. Born Thunder Bay, Ont. 1944. s. **EDUC:** Univ. of Toronto, B.A.(English & Psych.); Lakeshore Teachers' Coll., Permanent Teaching Certificate. **CAREER:** TVOntario, 1973; community channel Program Dir. & Admin. Asst. to the VP of Programming, Rogers Cable Television, Toronto, 1974-76; Program Dir., Multilingual Television (Toronto) Ltd., 1976-79; Prod., Global Television; independent prod.; Dir., Gov't & Public Affairs, Rogers Broadcasting Inc., CFMT-TV, Toronto, 1987; Commissioner, Canadian Radio-television & Telecommunications Commission, 1987-93; Chair, FUND, The Foundation to Underwrite New Drama, 1993-95; Sr. VP, Baton Broadcasting Inc., 1995 to date. **AFFIL:** Canadian Women in Radio & Television (Chair); Canadian Women in Communications (Chair 1993-95); Renison Coll., Univ. of Waterloo (Bd. of Gov. 1993-95); Banff International Television Festival (Bd. 1995-96); National Screen Institute (Bd. 1995-96); Canadian Film Centre (Bd. of Dir. 1994-96); Academy of Film & Television Arts (1993-

96); Ontario Film Review Bd. (1986-87); Anglican Church of Canada (past mbr., Nat'l Steering Committee for Multiculturalism); Toronto Japanese Canada Citizens' Association (past mbr.); Japanese Canada Cultural Centre (past Bd. mbr.).

Odam, Pamela $

Director, Human Resources Plans and Programs, IBM CANADA LTD., B2/186, 3600 Steeles Ave. E., Markham, ON L3R 9Z7 (905) 316-2393, FAX 316-2407. Born Toronto 1952. m. Tom 2 ch. David, Jonathan. **EDUC:** Certified General Accountant (C.G.A.) 1978. **CAREER:** various positions, Office Products Div., IBM Canada Ltd., 1971-80; Mktg, Plans & Controls, Vancouver, 1980-81; Mgr, Accts Payable & various fin. mgmt positions, 1982-85; Personnel, Toronto Mfg, & various positions, 1985-88; 2nd Line Mgmt, 1988-90; M&D Personnel Programs Mgr, 1990-92; Mgr, Tech. Dev. & Hum. Res., Toronto Software Lab., 1992-94; Mgr, Hum. Res. Oper., 1994-95; Dir., Hum. Res. Plans & Programs, 1995 to date. **AFFIL:** York Central Hospital, Richmond Hill (Trustee; Fin. & Community Rel'ns Committee); Richmond Hill Minor Ball; Youth Ministry Support Team, St. Mary's Anglican Church; Human Resources Professionals' Association of Ontario; Advisory Council on Women in IBM & Diversity Council (Chair 1993-96). **HONS:** Canada Excellence Award, IBM Canada Ltd., 1993, 1995. **INTERESTS:** activities with children eps. hockey, baseball; ceramics; reading.

Odjig, Daphne, C.M.,R.C.A. ⊗

Artist, Box 111, Anglemont, BC V0E 1A0 (604) 955-2974. Born Wikwemikong, Ont. 1919. m. Chester Beavon. 2 ch. **CAREER:** Founder & Pres., Indian Prints of Canada, 1970; Arts Instructor, Manitou Arts Foundation, Ont., 1971; Co-Founder, Professional Native Indian Artists Inc., 1973; Owner & Mgr, Warehouse Gallery, Winnipeg, 1974; Juror, Shuswap Lake Festival of the Arts, Sorrento, B.C., 1984; resource person, Society of Canadian Artists of Native Ancestry, Ottawa, 1985; Bd. Mbr., Canadian Native Arts Foundation, 1986; Lansdown Scholar & Discourse, "Arts in Education," The Lansdown Lectures, Univ. of Victoria, 1993. **SELECTED PUBLICATIONS:** writer & illustrator, "The Nanebush Series," 10 children's books (Toronto: Ginn & Co., 1971). **COMMISSIONS:** Earth Mother, Expo '70, Osaka, Japan, 1970; Creation of the World mural, Peguis High Sch., Hodgson, Man., 1971; mural depicting the Indian legend "Creation of the World," Manitoba Museum of Man & Nature, 1972; From Mother Earth

Flows the River of Life, painting, "Canadian Indian Art '74," Royal Ontario Museum, 1973; The Jerusalem series of paintings and prints, commissioned to tour & paint her interpretation of Jerusalem El Al (Israel Airlines), 1975; The Indian in Transition, on loan to the National Arts Centre, National Museum of Man, 1978; limited ed. serigraph, CKFM "Children's Fund" campaign, Hospital for Sick Children, 198; Salmon Arm Savings & Credit Union project, 1984; greeting cards for fundraising, Hospital for Sick Children, Toronto, 1984, 1988, 1991; Spiritual Renewal, Laurentian Univ. Museum & Art Centre, Ottawa, 1984; Tomorrow will hold our past & We dance through time, Glenview Corporation, Ottawa, 1986; limited ed. portfolio, Kamloops Art Gallery, 1996. **EXHIBITIONS:** numerous solo exhibitions incl. Lakehead Art Centre, Port Arthur, Ont. (now Thunder Bay) (1967); Int'l Peace Gardens (1970); Smotra Folklore Festival, Yugoslavia (1971); Jerusalem Series, Bashford & Schwartz Gallery, Calgary (1976); Images for a Canadian Heritage, Vancouver (1977); Pollock Gallery, Toronto (1979); Time Passages, Gallery West, Vancouver (1979); Parallels with Nature, Assiniboia Gallery, Regina (1980); Behind the Mask, Robertson Gallery, Ottawa (1980); Childhood Memories, Children of the Raven Gallery, Vancouver (1981); Shayne Gallery, Montreal (1983); Daphne Odjig, A Retrospective 1946-1985, organized by the Thunder Bay National Exhibition Centre & Centre for Indian Art, also exhibited at the McMichael Canadian Collection, the Woodland Indian Cultural Centre, Brantford, & Laurentian Univ. (1985); Wilfret's Hambleton Galleries, Kelowna (1990, 1991); Wallace Galleries Ltd., Calgary (1993); Gallery Phillip, Toronto (1995); numerous group exhibitions incl. Treaty Numbers 23, 287, 1171, Winnipeg Art Gallery (1971); Canadian Indian Art '74, Royal Ontario Museum (1974); Indian Art '75, Woodland Indian Cultural Educational Centre, Brantford (1975); From Women's Eyes: Women Painters in Canada, Agnes Etherington Art Centre (1976); Indian Art '76, Woodland Indian Cultural Educational Centre (1976); Contemporary Native Art of Canada–The Woodland Indians, Royal Ontario Museum, travelling show (1976); Links to a Tradition, Dept. of Indian Affairs & Northern Dev., travelling show (1977); Contemporary Indian Arts–the trail from the past to the future, Mackenzie Gallery, Trent Univ. (1977); One Hundred Years of Native American Painting, Oklahoma Museum of Art (1978); Renewal, Masterworks of Contemporary Indian Art from the National Museum of Man (1982); Contemporary Indian & Inuit Art of

Canada, Dept. of Indian Affairs & Northern Dev., U.N. Bldg, NYC (1983); *Contemporary Indian Art at Rideau Hall*, Dept. of Indian Affairs & Northern Dev. (1983); *Canada's First People: A Celebration of Contemporary Native Visual Arts*, touring Canada & Tokyo, Japan (1992-93); *Voices of Vision–Resurgence*, En'owkin Centre & the Art Gallery of the South Okanagan, Penticton, B.C. (1995). COLLECTIONS: numerous collections incl. Art Bank, Canada Council; Gov't of Israel; Laurentian Univ. Museum & Art Centre; McMichael Canadian Collection; Ojibwe Cultural Foundation, Ont.; Sir Wilfrid Laurier Univ.; Thunder Bay National Exhibition Centre & Centre for Indian Art; Tom Thomson Gallery; Winnipeg Art Gallery; Nova Corporation; Imperial Oil; Petro-Canada; Norcen Energy Ltd.; Gulf Canada Resources Ltd. AFFIL: B.C. Federation of Artists; Royal Canadian Academy of Art (R.C.A.); Canadian Heritage Foundation (Hon. Bd. Mbr.). HONS: Swedish Brucebo Foundation Scholarship & Resident Artist, The Foundation Studio, Visby, Island of Gotland, Sweden, 1973; Queen's Silver Jubilee Medal, 1977; presented Eagle Feather by Chief Wakageshig on behalf of the Wikwemikong Reserve, in recognition of artistic accomplishments–an honour previously reserved for men to acknowledge prowess in hunt or war, 1978; elected member, Royal Canadian Academy of Art, 1989; Member of the Order of Canada, 1986; Canada 125 Medal, 1992; Eagle Feather by SCANA (Society for Canadian Artists of Native Ancestry) at the 5th Nat'l Native Symposium, 1993; Certificate of Honour, En'Owkin Centre & Canada's Drug Strategy Program, 1994; D.Litt.(Hon.), Laurentian Univ., 1982; LL.D. (Hon.), Univ. of Toronto, 1985; Doctor of Educ.(honoris causa), Nippissing Univ. MISC: subject of the films, *Colour of Pride* (National Film Bd., 1973*), Spirits Speaking Through* (*Spectrum*, CBC, 1981*), Window on Canada–Daphne Odjig/Painter* (Tokyo TV, 1989); subject of book, *A Paintbrush in My Hand* by R.M. Vanderburgh & M.E. Southcott (Toronto: Natural Heritage/Natural History Inc., 1992); subject of numerous articles & chapters in books; Keynote Speaker, 20th Anniversary of the Thunder Bay Art Gallery, 1996; juror for Canadian Arts Foundation (grants & scholarship applications), 1996.

Ogilvie, M.H., B.A.,LL.B.,M.A., D.Phil.,F.R.S.C. ◻ Ⓢ ⟁
Barrister and Solicitor, Ottawa, ON K1S 5B6. Professor of Law, CARLETON UNIVERSITY. Born Falkirk, Scotland 1948. m. Dr. David Lindsay. EDUC: Trinity Coll., Univ. of Toronto, B.A.

1971; St. Hilda's Coll., Oxford Univ., D.Phil. 1974, B.A. 1976, M.A. 1976; Dalhousie Univ., LL.B. 1977. BAR: N.S., 1978; Ont., 1984. CAREER: articling student, Daley, Black and Moreira, Halifax, N.S., 1977-78; Asst. Prof. of Law, Carleton Univ., 1978-81; Assoc. Prof., 1981-86; Lecturer in Law, Fac. of Law (Common Law Section), Univ. of Ottawa, 1982-83, 1985-86; Prof. of Law, Carleton Univ., 1986 to date; articling student, Osler, Hoskin and Harcourt, Toronto, 1984; Dir. of Research, Fasken and Calvin, 1986-88; Visiting Prof., Faculties of Law & Divinity, Univ. of Edinburgh, 1989; Scholar in Residence, Law Dept., Royal Bank of Canada, 1992-93; Visiting Scholar, Fac. of Law, Univ. of Toronto, 1992-93; Sr. Visiting Fellow, Massey Coll., Univ. of Toronto, 1992-93; Visiting Fellow, St. Hilda's Coll., Oxford Univ., 1993. SELECTED PUBLICATIONS: "Historical Introduction to Legal Studies" (1982); "Banking: The Law in Canada" (1985); "Consumer Law: Cases and Materials" (1989; 2nd ed., 1993); "Banking Law Cases" (1990; 2nd ed., 1996); "Canadian Banking Law" (1991); "Churches and Religious Institutions" (1994); "Religious Institutions and the Law in Canada" (1996); numerous articles, comments & reviews. EDIT: Ed. Bd., *Banking and Finance Law Review*, *Canadian Business Law Journal*; Cdn Contributing Ed., *Journal of Business Law*. AFFIL: Canadian Bar Association; N.S. Barristers' Society; Law Society of Upper Canada; Canadian Association of Law Teachers; Osgoode Society; Selden Society; Stair Society; Canadian Law & Society Association; Royal Society of Canada (Fellow 1993; Sec., Academy II 1995-98).

O'Grady, Diane, P.Eng. ■ ■ ⟁ ⟁
Olympic Athlete. c/o Canadian Olympic Association. Born North Bay, Ont. 1967. CAREER: Engineer. SPORTS CAREER: started rowing competitively at age 21; mbr., Cdn Nat'l Rowing Team, 1994 to date. Olympic Games: Bronze, 4x, 1996. World championships: 2nd, 4x, 1995. Pan Am Games: 1st, 2x, 1995. Canadian championships: 1st, 1x, 1st, 4x, & 1st, 4-, 1994. US championships: 1st, 4x, & 4th, 2x, 1995; 1st, 4x, & 3rd, 2x, 1993. HONS: Centennial Award, Canadian Amateur Rowing Association, 1995; Female Sculler of the Year, Canadian Amateur Rowing Association, 1994. INTERESTS: cross-country skiing; designing activewear; walking her dog. MISC: former competitive fencer.

O'Grady, Jean, B.A.,M.A.,Ph.D. ■ ⟁
Assistant Editor, Collected Works of Northrop Frye, Victoria College, UNIVERSITY OF TORONTO, 73 Queen's Park Cres., Toronto,

ON M5S 1K7 (416) 585-4514. Born 1943. m. Dr. Walter O'Grady. 3 ch. Elizabeth, Jennifer, Caroline. EDUC: Univ. of Toronto, B.A. (English) 1964, Ph.D.(English) 1978; Yale Univ., M.A.(English) 1965. CAREER: Lecturer, York Univ., 1965-66; Lecturer, Univ. of Toronto, 1967-69; Lecturer, Ryerson Polytechnic, 1980; Post-Doctoral Fellow, Collected Works of John Stuart Mill, 1981-90; independent scholar, researching R.E. Knowles, 1990-93; Research Assoc., Collected Works of Northrop Frye, 1994 to date. SELECTED PUBLICATIONS: Indexes to the Collected Works of John Stuart Mill, Vol. 33 of *The Collected Works of John Stuart Mill*, with J.M. Robson (Toronto: Univ. of Toronto Press, 1991); *Special Writer: an Annotated Bibliography of the Writings of R.E. Knowles in the Toronto Daily Star and Star Weekly* (Toronto: Colombo & Co., 1993); "A Pocket Guide to the Peerage" (*Newsletter of the Victorian Studies Association* Spring 1988); contributor to *Oxford Companion to Canadian Literature, Canadian Encyclopedia*, & *Victorian Britain: an Encyclopedia*; various other publications. EDIT: Ed., *Newsletter of the Victorian Studies Association of Ontario*, 1990-94. AFFIL: Victorian Studies Association of Ontario (Sec.-Treas. 1987-90); Recycling Council of Ontario; Task Force to Bring Back the Don. HONS: Gov. General's Gold Medal in English, 1964; Yale Univ. Fellowship; Woodrow Wilson Fellowship; Canada Council Doctoral Award, 1978. INTERESTS: bicycling; gardening. COMMENT: "*I work both as an editor and as an independent scholar, publishing in the fields of Victorian literature and Canadiana.*"

Oh, Jane (Kyung Jin), D.E.C.,B.C.L., LL.B. ■ 🐾 ⚎ ●
Canadian Youth Program Coordinator, THE INTERNATIONAL CHILDREN'S INSTITUTE, Montreal, QC, EMAIL joh@lavery.qc.ca. Born Seoul 1972. EDUC: Marianopolis Coll., D.E.C. 1991; McGill Univ., Law, Nat'l Program, LL.B.(with Distiction). CAREER: Canadian Youth Program Coord., The International Children's Institute, 1992 to date; Student-at-Law, Lavery de Billy, 1996 to date. AFFIL: The Couchiching Institute on Public Affairs; National Association of Women & the Law (Que. Gen. Reg'l Rep., Nat'l Steering Committee); Students' Society of McGill Univ.; Joint Senate/Bd. Committee on Equity; Senate Sub-Committee on Women; Senate Sub-Committee on Race Rel'ns; McGill Women & the Law Caucus (Coord.); Jeanne Sauvé Youth Foundation (Cdn Delegate to 2nd Int'l Conference 1994). HONS: Andrew O'Connor Award for Humanities, Marianopolis Coll.; Sydney J.

Hodgeson Scholarship, McGill Univ.; James McGill Entrance Award, McGill Univ. INTERESTS: skiing; photography; travel; languages.

Ohama, Kendra ■ ■ ⓠ
Paralympic Athlete. Calgary, AB. CAREER: goldsmith. SPORTS CAREER: mbr., Nat'l Wheelchair Basketball Team, 1991 to date. Paralympic Games: Gold, 1996; Gold, 1992. Canadian Wheelchair Basketball League (CWBL): 1st, Women's Finals, 1994. HONS: All-Star, CWBL Women's Finals, 1995.

O'Hara, Catherine • 🐾 ⊗ ⛌
Actor and Comedienne. Born Toronto 1954. m. Bo Welch. CAREER: actor & writer, Second City, Toronto, 1974; co-founder, SCTV, 1976. SELECTED CREDITS: actor/co-writer, *SCTV*; numerous features incl. *Beetlejuice*, 1988; *Dick Tracy*, 1990; *Home Alone*, 1990; *Home Alone II*, 1993; Sally & various voices, *Nightmare Before Christmas*; *Waiting For Guffman*, 1996. numerous TV appearances; Dir., *Dream On*. HONS: EMMY (*SCTV*).

O'Hara, Jane, B.A. ■ ✎
Journalist, 32 Summerhill Ave., Toronto, ON M4T 1A8. EDUC: Univ. of Toronto, B.A. (English) 1974. CAREER: sports reporter, *The Toronto Sun*, 1975-78; European Bureau Chief, FP News Service, 1979-80; various positions incl. Nat'l Ed., *Maclean's* Magazine, 1980-88; Sports Ed., & columnist, in both sports & politics, *The Ottawa Sun*, 1988-93; regular sports panellist, Newsworld's *Week's End* & CBC Radio, 1988-93; pol. columnist, *The Vancouver Province*, 1992-93; pol. commentator, CBC Radio & CKNW Vancouver, 1992-93; Fellow, Massey Coll., Univ. of Toronto, Southam Fellowship, 1993-94; Max Bell Visiting Prof., Univ. of Regina, Sch. of Journalism, 1994-95. SELECTED PUBLICATIONS: *British Columbia, The Lampoon* (1986); *Union Jack: Labour Leader Jack Munro* (1988); *Bryan Adams* (1989); *Marjorie Nichols: A Very Political Reporter* (1992); various other publications. HONS: Southam Fellowship, 1993-94; Dunlop Award for Sportswriting 1990 & 1992. MISC: Canada's top-ranked tennis player, 1975; played on Canada's nat'l tennis team, 1968-75; competed in Wimbledon & the US Open.

O'Hara, Maggie Blue ■ 🐾 ⊗ ⛌
Actor, c/o Kirk Talent Agencies Inc., 304 W. Cordova St., Ste. 303, Vancouver, BC V6B 1E8 (604) 689-6861, FAX 684-9040. Born Victoria, B.C. 1975. s. CAREER: professional actor for over 16 yrs.; voice work for cartoon series, CD-ROM's commercials & radio dramas. SELECTED CREDITS: Guest Principal, *X-Files*

(series), FOX; Wanda, *Other Women's Children* (telefilm), O.W.C. Prods.; Nicole Williams (series reg.), *Northwood* (series), CBC, 4 yrs.; Jill Wheelock (guest star), *Neon Rider* (series), AVR; Principals, CD-ROM, Airwaves; Sweetheart (voice), *My Little Pony Tales* (cartoon series), Sunbow International; Megan/little girl (voice*), Barbie and the Rockers* (cartoon series pilot); Helga (voice), *Debts*, NFB; various TV commercials & CBC radio productions. **AFFIL:** UBCP. **INTERESTS:** writing; snowboarding; dancing; photography; independent films. **MISC:** has participated in Theatre Sports & actors' workshops; mbr., Kidco Dance Company, 1983-85. **COMMENT:** *"I have wanted to be an actress all my life and it is what I have worked for and at since I was four. My goal is to land a great character lead in a Canadian independent film."*

Oland, Linda Lee, LL.B. ■ ⚖
Partner, MCINNES COOPER AND ROBERTSON, Cornwallis Place, 1601 Lower Water St., Box 730, Halifax, NS B3J 2V1 (902) 425-6500, FAX 425-6386. **EDUC:** Dalhousie Univ. Law Sch., LL.B. 1976. **BAR:** N.S., 1977. **CAREER:** Ptnr, McInnes Cooper and Robertson; part-time Fac., Dalhousie Univ. Law Sch. **AFFIL:** N.S. Barristers' Society (Council; Discipline Committee; Fin. Committee); Continuing Legal Education Society of N.S. (Dir. 1989-92); Canadian Bar Association; Hong Kong Canada Business Association (Dir., N.S. Chapter); Asia Pacific Foundation of Canada (Dir. 1988-94); Chinese Society of N.S. (former Exec. Committee mbr.).

Olasker, Patricia, LL.B. ■ ⚖
Co-Managing Partner, MCMILLAN BINCH, Royal Bank Plaza, Ste. 3800, S.Tower, Toronto, ON M5J 2J7 (416) 865-7114, FAX 865-7048, EMAIL polasker@mbbinch.com. Born UK 1954. m. Brett Ledger. 1 ch. **EDUC:** Univ. of Alberta, 1974; Institute on International & Comparative Law, Institut Supérieur des Sciences Économiques et Commerciales, Paris, France, Dipl.(Int'l & Corp. Law) 1976; Osgoode Hall Law Sch., LL.B. 1977; Univ. of California at Berkeley, LL.M. 1981 (abt). **BAR:** Ont., 1979. **CAREER:** articling student, Lang Michener, 1978-79; Law Clerk to the Chief Justice of Ont., 1979-80; Asst. Cnsl, Mississauga Railway Accident Inquiry, 1980; Legal Advisor to the Chrm, Ont. Securities Commission, 1984-85; Assoc., McMillan Binch, 1982-86; Ptnr, 1986 to date. **SELECTED PUBLICATIONS:** "Understanding and Negotiating Underwriting Documents" (The Canadian Institute, 1987); "Realizing on Public Company Assets and Shares" (*Some Securities Law Issues*

for Lenders, Insight Press, 1992); "Understanding and Negotiating Underwriting Documents" (Canadian Bar Association, 1994); "Parent/ Subsidiary Conflicts in Cross-Border Mergers" (Osgoode Hall Law Sch., Professional Dev. Program, 1996). **AFFIL:** Law Society of Upper Canada; Canadian Bar Association (Past Chair, Securities Law Subcommittee, Bus. Law Section); International Bar Association; Canadian Foundation for AIDS Research (Co-Chair, Legal Aid for AIDS). **INTERESTS:** cycling; skiing; jogging. **MISC:** frequent lecturer at conferences; participant as a judge of the Corporate Securities Law Moot. **COMMENT:** *"Practice areas include corporate finance and mergers and acquisitions, representing both US and Canadian investment banks and Canadian public companies. Co-Managing Partner of McMillan Binch and former manager of the Securities Law Department, and co-chair of McMillan Binch's Gender Task Force, a committee studying the issue of gender bias within the firm and the profession."*

Olenek, Lynn, R.N.,B.Sc.N., M.S.A. ■ ⊕ ⚛ ⌖
In-Patient Program Manager, Northern Alberta Regional Geriatric Program, CAPITAL HEALTH AUTHORITY, Glenrose Rehabilitation Hospital, 10230 - 111 Ave., Edmonton, AB T5G 0B7 (403) 474-8814, FAX 474-8837. Born Edmonton 1953. m. Donald. 2 ch. **EDUC:** Edmonton General Hospital/Grant MacEwan Coll., R.N. 1973; Univ. of Alberta, B.Sc.N.(Nursing) 1976; Central Michigan Univ., M.S.A.(Admin./ Health) 1990. **CAREER:** various nursing positions, 1974-85; Dir. of Nursing, St. Mary's Health Care Centre, Trochu, Alta., 1985-89; Asst. Exec. Dir., Patient Care Svcs, Stanton Yellowknife Hospital, 1989-90; Acting Exec. Dir., 1990-91; Exec. Dir., 1991-94; In-Patient Program Mgr, N. Alberta Reg'l Geriatric Program, Edmonton General Hospital, 1994-96; In-Patient Program Mgr, N. Alberta Reg'l Geriatric Program, Capital Health Authority, 1996 to date. **AFFIL:** Canadian Coll. of Health Service Executives (Exec. Mbr.); Canadian Hospital Association (Advisor, Long-Term Care Mgmt Program); Alberta Association of Registered Nurses (various exec. positions); various community, school, sports committee involvements.

Oliphant, Betty, C.C.,LL.D.,D.Litt.,F.I.S.T.D. (C.S.B.-S.B.) ✪ ⌖ ⌂
Founder, THE NATIONAL BALLET SCHOOL, c/o 105 Maitland St., Toronto, ON M4Y 1E4 (416) 964-3780, FAX 964-3632. Born London, UK 1918. d. 2 ch. **EDUC:** Queen's Coll. Sch., London, UK; St. Mary's Coll. Sch., Lon-

don, UK; studied classical ballet in UK under Tamara Karsavina & Laurent Novikoff. **CAREER:** est. sch. for professional dancers, London, UK, & created & directed dance sequences in West End theatres prior to immigrating to Canada in 1947; principal, Betty Oliphant Sch. of Ballet, Toronto, 1948-59; Ballet Mistress, National Ballet of Canada, 1951-62; Founder, Dir. & Principal, National Ballet Sch., 1959-89; Assoc. Artistic Dir., National Ballet of Canada, 1969-75. **AFFIL:** Imperial Society of Teachers of Dancing (C.S.B.-S.B.) (Fellow, Examiner); Canadian Dance Teachers' Association (Charter Mbr., Past Pres); Canadian Association of Professional Dance Organizations (Founding Mbr.). **HONS:** Officer, Order of Canada, 1977; Molson Prize, 1978; National Dance Award, Canadian Dance Teachers' Association, 1981; Diplôme d'honneur, Canadian Conference of the Arts, 1982; Distinguished Educator, Ontario Institute for Studies in Education, 1985; Companion, Order of Canada, 1985; Lifetime Achievement Award, Toronto Arts Foundation, 1989; Order of Napoleon, Maison Courvoisier, France, 1990; Paul Harris Fellow of the Rotary Foundation of Rotary International, 1992; Canada 125 Medal, 1992; LL.D.(Hon.), Queen's Univ., 1978; LL.D.(Hon.), Brock Univ., 1978; LL.D.(Hon.), Univ. of Toronto, 1980; D.Litt. (Hon.), York Univ. **INTERESTS:** reading; swimming; theatre; concerts. **MISC:** one of the 1st 2 women & only the 3rd Cdn to receive the Order of Napoleon, Maison Courvoisier, France, 1990; well-known & internationally respected teacher; undertook reorganization of Ballet Sch. of the Swedish Opera at invitation of Erik Bruhn, 1967; undertook reorganization of Sch. of Royal Danish Ballet, at invitation of Henning Kronstam, 1978; guest of the USSR on 4 occasions; a guest of honour, First National Ballet Concours, Moscow, 1969; jury mbr., various int'l competitions.

Oliver, Bobbie ✪

Artist, New York, NY. Born Windsor, Ont. 1948. m. Frank F. Kitchens. **EDUC:** Center for Creative Studies, Detroit, 1966-68; St. Alban's Sch. of Art, UK, 1968. **CAREER:** Assoc. Prof., Rhode Island Sch. of Design, 1980 to date; Banff Sch. of Fine Art, 1981; Acting Head, Painting Dept., Rhode Island Sch. of Design, 1982-83; Head, Summer Program, Painting, Banff Sch. of Fine Arts, 1985; Visiting Artist, Lecturer, Painting, Anderson Research, Aspen, Col., 1989. **EXHIBITIONS:** 15 solo exhibitions, incl. York Univ., UK (1970), Canada House, London, UK (1970), Wolff Gallery, N.Y. (1985) & Olga Korper Gallery, Toronto (1994); more than 50 group exhibitions, incl. London Group Show, Royal Academy, London, UK (1970), *Making a Fresh New Thing: 10 Painters*, Harbourfront Gallery, Toronto (1979), *Artists from the Edward Albee Foundation*, Guild Hall Museum, East Hampton (1982), *Parallel and Boundaries*, Powerhouse Gallery, Montreal (1984) & *In a Meditative Manner*, E.S. Vandam Gallery, N.Y. (1995). **HONS:** Pollock/Krasner Award. **MISC:** subject of various articles & reviews; recipient, various grants.

Oliver, Carol R., FAHP,CFRE ■■ ♥ ✊

President and Chief Executive Officer, COMMUNITY FOUNDATION OF GREATER TORONTO (public foundation–granting & fund raising), 1 Dundas St. W., P.O. Box 78, Toronto, ON M5G 1Z3 (416) 204-4082, FAX 204-4100. Born Barrie, Ont. 1940. m. Peter. 2 ch. Karen, Mark. **CAREER:** Personnel Officer, Queen's Univ., Kingston, 1967-73; Personnel Officer, Canada Life Assurance Company, Toronto, 1973-79; Dir. of Personnel, Canadian Red Cross, Ont. Div., 1979-80; Exec. Dir., York County Hospital Foundation, 1980-86; Exec. Dir., North York General Hospital Foundation, 1986-96. **AFFIL:** Association for Healthcare Philanthropy (Dir., Cdn Educ. Foundation; former Chair, Int'l Bd.; Fellow); Council on Foundations; National Society of Fund Raising Executives (Certified Fund Raising Exec.); Canadian Centre of Philanthropy (Assoc. mbr.); Metropolitan Toronto Board of Trade. **HONS:** "Outstanding Fund Raising Exec.," National Society of Fund Raising Executives, 1995. **INTERESTS:** family; reading; walking; music. **MISC:** frequent speaker, conferences, seminars & meetings, non-profit sector. **COMMENT:** *"In providing staff leadership in raising funds for worthy causes, I have the privilege and satisfaction of working with dedicated, caring volunteers who really make a difference in our society."*

Oliver, Diane, B.Ed.,M.B.A. ■■ $

Vice-President, Marketing, CHANEL INC. (manufacturer & distributor of fragrances, cosmetics & fashion), 55 boul. Marie-Victorin, Candiac, QC J5R 1B6 (514) 659-1981, FAX 659-0032. Born Montreal 1950. **EDUC:** Univ. du Québec à Montréal, B.Ed. 1971; Concordia Univ., M.B.A. 1990. **CAREER:** Training Dir., Herdt & Charton Inc., 1983-84; Communication Dir., 1984-85; Dir., Sales & Mktg, 1985-90; VP, Mktg, Chanel Inc., 1990 to date. **AFFIL:** Canadian Cosmetics, Fragrance & Toiletries Association (Trade Rel'n Committee; Que. Advisory Bd.); Quebec MBA Association (Bd. of Dir. 1994-95; Exec. Dir. 1993-94); American Marketing Association; Look Good, Feel Better

Program (Chair, Conferences Activities Committee). **HONS:** Marketing Award for best fragrance launch (*Egoiste* men's fragrance), 1991. **INTERESTS:** arts; golf; music (opera); gardening. **COMMENT:** *"Dynamic; shows a great deal of leadership and is committed to excellence. Contributed greatly to the rebirth of Chanel brand in the last six years. A very strong corporate individual, capable of working in a group—a team player."*

Oliver, Karen 🎭 ✊ ♡
Executive Director, ASSOCIATED MANITOBA ARTS FESTIVALS, INC., 424-100 Arthur St., Winnipeg, MB R3B 1H3 (204) 945-4578, FAX 948-2073. Born Holland, Man. 1952. d. 3 ch. Jeffrey, Brent, Andrew. **EDUC:** Banff Sch. of Management, Certificate (Arts Admin.) 1988. **CAREER:** Exec. Dir., Tiger Hills Arts Association, Inc., 1986-88; Exec. Dir., Associated Manitoba Arts Festivals, Inc., 1988 to date. **AFFIL:** Manitoba Arts Council; Manitoba Music Educators (Advisory Council); Coalition of Custodial Parents; Art Space Inc. (Bd.); Federation of Canadian Music Festivals (Fin. Committee; Chair, Public Rel'ns Committee 1992-95); Community Arts Manitoba (Bd.). **INTERESTS:** music; theatre; dance; women's issues. **COMMENT:** *"Ms. Oliver has worked extensively to develop the community arts in Manitoba. She is recommended as a facilitator, speaker, administrator and innovative programmer in the field of arts development."*

Olivieri, Nancy F., B.Sc.,M.D., F.R.C.P.C. ⊕ 🎓
Director, Comprehensive Care Program for Thalassemia and Sickle Cell Disease, THE HOSPITAL FOR SICK CHILDREN, Toronto, ON M5G 1X8 (416) 813-6823, FAX 813-5346. Associate Professor, Pediatrics and Medicine, UNIVERSITY OF TORONTO. Born Hamilton, Ont. 1954. s. **EDUC:** Univ. of Toronto, B.Sc.(Biol.) 1975; McMaster Univ., M.D. 1978. **CAREER:** Research Fellow, Harvard Univ., 1984-86. **SELECTED PUBLICATIONS:** numerous refereed journal articles, incl. "Survival in medically treated patients with homozygous ß thalassemia" (*New England Journal of Medicine*, 1994); "Iron chelation therapy with oral deferiprone in thalassemia major" (*New England Journal of Medicine*); numerous book chapters & reviews. **AFFIL:** Royal Coll. of Physicians & Surgeons of Canada (Fellow in Internal Medicine; Fellow in Haematology); American Society of Hematology; American Society of Pediatric Hematology/Oncology; Society for Pediatric Research; Cooley's Anemia Foundation of America; Ontario Sickle Cell Association; American Society for Clinical Investigation. **INTERESTS:** travel. **COMMENT:** *"My goal is better provision of care and research leading to a cure for the two most common single-gene disorders in the world (sickle cell disease and thalassemia). Program is leading research efforts toward this goal."*

Olney, Miriam, B.A. $ ✊
Chair of the Board, INSURANCE CORPORATION OF BRITISH COLUMBIA, 151 W. Esplanade, N. Vancouver, BC V7M 3H9 (604) 661-6019, FAX 661-6647. President, OLNEY AND SAUNDERS ENGINEERING LTD. Born Toronto 1941. d. 2 ch. Shauna Lynne Olney, Cheryl Anne Olney. **EDUC:** Univ. of British Columbia, B.A. (English/Classical Studies) 1964; Honeywell Information Systems Education Centre, Dipl. (Systems Analyst) 1979. **CAREER:** various positions, United Food & Commercial Workers' Union, Local 1518, 1965-87; Dir. & Ptnr, Towncraft Builders Ltd., 1972-82; Dir. & Sec., Midlake Estates Ltd., 1975-85; Dir., Pensions & Benefits Dept., United Food & Commercial Workers' Union, Local 1518, 1987 to date; Dir. & Bus. Ptnr, Olney and Saunders Engineering International Inc., 1989-93; Dir., Insurance Corporation of British Columbia, 1992 to date; Chair of the Bd., 1993 to date; Pres., Olney and Saunders Engineering Ltd., 1993 to date; Trustee, Insurance Corporation of British Columbia Retirement Plans, 1993 to date. **DIRECTOR:** Insurance Corporation of British Columbia. **AFFIL:** National Institute of Disability Management and Research (Bd. of Dir.); North Shore Crisis Services Society (Bd. of Dir.); B.C. Federation of Retired Union Members (Dir.; Co-Founder); B.C. Federation of Labour (Exec. Council; V-Chair, Pension Committee; Legislative & Research Committee); International Foundation of Employee Benefit Plans; Canadian Association of Pre-Retirement Planners; Canadian Pension & Benefits Conference; Vancouver Board of Trade; Parthenon Place Owners' Association (Pres.; Dir.); University Women's Club, Vancouver; Legal Education & Action Fund. **INTERESTS:** reading; travel; golf.

Olsen, Charlotte A., LL.B. ⚖
Partner, LANG MICHENER LAWRENCE & SHAW, Bentall III, 595 Burrard St., Ste. 2500, P.O. Box 49200, Vancouver, BC V7X 1L1 (604) 691-7458, FAX 685-7084. Born St. Paul, Alta. 1949. s. **EDUC:** Univ. of British Columbia, LL.B. 1985. **BAR:** B.C., 1986. **CAREER:** Legal Sec., to 1975; Paralegal, 1975-80; Assoc., Lang Michener Lawrence & Shaw, 1986-93; Ptnr, 1993 to date. **SELECTED PUBLICATIONS:** various humour articles for *The Ubyssey*, Univ. of British Columbia; critique of Ont. Securities

Commission decision. **AFFIL:** Vancouver Bar Association; Canadian Bar Association; Inter-Pacific Bar Association; Rocky Mountain Mineral Law Foundation. **HONS:** various scholarships in law sch. **INTERESTS:** travel; reading; skiing. **MISC:** taught Securities Regulation for 3 semesters on voluntary basis at Univ. of British Columbia Law Sch. **COMMENT:** *"Best achievement: returning to university at 30 and obtaining my law degree."*

Olsen, Susan, R.N.,B.Sc.N.,M.P.A., C.H.E. ■ ■ ⊕ ✿ ○
Vice-President, NORTH YORK GENERAL HOSPITAL (acute care hospital), 4001 Leslie St., Toronto, ON M2K 1E1 (416) 756-6129, FAX 756-6958. Born Montreal 1946. s. **EDUC:** Univ. of Toronto, B.Sc.N.(Nursing) 1968; Coll. of Nurses of Ontario, R.N. 1968; Queen's Univ., M.P.A.(Public Admin.) 1991; Canadian Coll. of Health Service Executives, C.H.E. (Health Admin.) 1994. **CAREER:** various nursing positions, Mount Sinai Hospital, Toronto, 1968-75; Dir. of Nursing Practice, Perinatology, 1975-88; Acting VP, Nursing, 1988-89; VP, North York General Hospital, 1989 to date. **AFFIL:** International Congress of Nurses; Canadian Nurses' Association; Registered Nurses' Association of Ontario; Coll. of Nurses of Ontario; Canadian Coll. of Health Service Executives; American Coll. of Health Executives.

O'Malley, Patricia L., B.Comm.,C.A. ■ Ⓢ
Partner, KPMG PEAT MARWICK THORNE (professional svcs/chartered accountants), Scotia Plaza, 40 King St. W., Box 122, Toronto, ON M5H 3Z2 (416) 777-3499, FAX 777-3969, EMAIL tomalley@kpmg.ca. Born Winnipeg 1949. m. Ronald S. Hikel. **EDUC:** Univ. of Manitoba, B.Comm.(Hons.) 1971, C.A., Ont. 1976. **CAREER:** Supervisor, KPMG, 1977; Mgr, 1979; Ptnr, 1982 to date. **SELECTED PUBLICATIONS:** "Ethics and Positive Accounting Theory," monograph with Gordon D. Richardson (Centre for Accounting Ethics, Univ. of Waterloo). **AFFIL:** Multiple Sclerosis Society of Canada (Pres., Ont. Div.; Nat'l Bd. of Dir.); Ontario Securities Commission (Chair, Fin. Disclosure Bd.). **HONS:** FCA, Ont. 1991.

Omer Hashi, Kowser, R.N.,B.B.A. ⊕ ⛨ ◉
Community Health Educator and Counsellor, BIRTH CONTROL/VD INFO CENTRE, 2828 Bathurst St., Toronto, ON M6B 3A7 (416) 789-4541, FAX 789-0762. **EDUC:** Mogadishu Professional Sch. of Nursing, Somalia, Registered Nurse Diploma 1974; Hargeisa Sch. of Nursing, Somalia, Certificate of Midwifery 1976; Ohio Univ., B.B.A. 1983. **CAREER:** R.N.

(Head Nurse) Hargeisa Group Hospital, Hargeisa, Somalia, 1974-76; Midwife, 1976-78; Asst. Hospital Administrator, Dubai Hospital, Dubai U.A.E., 1983-86; Community Health Educator/Counsellor, Birth Control/VD Info. Centre, Toronto, 1987 to date. **SELECTED PUBLICATIONS:** "Female Genital Mutilation" (*Treating the Female Patient* 7(2) 1993); "Female Genital Mutilation: Overview and Obstetrical Care" *(Canadian Journal of Ob/Gyn & Women's Health Care* 5(6) 1993); "Commentary: Female Genital Mutilation: Perspectives from a Somalian Midwife" (*Birth* 21(4) 1994); "No Words Can Express: Two Voices on Female Genital Mutilation," with Joan Silver (*Canadian Woman Studies* 14(3)). **AFFIL:** Women Working with Immigrant Women (Bd. Mbr.); Cross Cultural Communication Centre (Bd. Mbr.); Toronto Birth Centre (Bd. Mbr.); Women's College Hospital (Advisory Committee on Community Action); Intergenerational Project for Somali Families (Advisory Committee); Family Service Association (Advisory Committee on Violence against Women for Somali Families); Ont. Female Genital Mutilation Prevention Task Force (Co-Chair, Subcommittee on Health). **HONS:** award for community work dedication; New Pioneers Education & Training Award, 1995. **INTERESTS:** community volunteering. **MISC:** mbr., Advisory Committee to the Women's Health Bureau on the report "Immigrant, Refugee and Racial Minority Women and Health Care Needs"; conducts workshops, seminars, presentations, consultations & public forums to educate about Female Genital Mutilation; lectures to various groups & institutions; frequent media appearances; various TV documentaries, incl. *The Fifth Estate.* **COMMENT:** *"I am a Somalian woman dedicated to empowering and educating women about reproductive function rights and healthy sexuality. I am an advocate against Female Genital Mutilation (FGM); my vision is the global eradication of FGM. By my putting my face, voice and energy into the public, women are getting better health care from health providers, but there is still a very long way to go."*

Ommer, Rosemary, M.A., Ph.D. ■ ⛨ 📗 ✿
Professor, Department of History and Project Manager, Eco-Research Program, MEMORIAL UNIVERSITY OF NEWFOUNDLAND, St. John's, NF A1C 5S7 (709) 737-7551, FAX 737-2041, EMAIL iser@morgan.ucs.mun.ca. Born Glasgow 1943. d. 4 ch. Andrew Delaney, Keith Delaney, Kenne Delaney, Catriona Girotti. **EDUC:** Glasgow Univ., M.A. 1964; Notre Dame Coll. of Education, Teaching Certificate

1965; Memorial Univ. of Newfoundland, M.A. 1974; McGill Univ., Ph.D. 1979. CAREER: high sch. Teacher & Head, Geography Dept., Scotland, 1965-66; emigrated to Canada, 1967; McConnell Fellow, McGill Univ., 1974; Asst. Research Prof., Memorial Univ. of Newfoundland, 1978-83; Econ. Historian, Hist. Dept., 1983-85; Prof., Dept. of Hist., 1985 to date; background research, Maritime Boundary Arbitration between Canada & France, 1989-90; Research Dir., Institute of Social & Economic Research, 1991-96; Principal Investigator, Eco-Research Program, Memorial Univ., 1994-97. SELECTED PUBLICATIONS: *Volumes Not Values*, Co-Ed. (1979); *Working Men Who Got Wet*, Co-Ed. (1980); *Merchant Credit and Labour Strategies in Historical Perspective*, Co-Ed. & Contributor (1990); *From Outpost to Outport* (1991). EDIT: Mng Ed., Royal Commission on Employment & Unemployment, Nfld., 1986; Review Ed., *Newfoundland Studies*, 1985-89; Ed. Advisory Bd., *Canada History Review*, 1986-89. AFFIL: sits on committees for nat'l funding bodies as well as univ. committees; SSHRCC (Council Mbr.); Vanier Institute of the Family (Chair, Program Committee; VP); Canadian Historical Foundation (Council); Canadian Global Change Program (Bd. of Dir.). INTERESTS: piano; choir directing.

Ondrack, Esther S. (nee Nielsen), B.A. Ⓢ
Senior Vice-President and Secretary, CHIEFTAIN INTERNATIONAL INC., 1201 Toronto Dominion Tower, Edmonton Centre, 10205 - 101 St., Edmonton, AB (403) 425-1950, FAX 429-4681. Born Edmonton 1940. m. Jack W. Ondrack. EDUC: Univ. of Alberta, B.A.(Social Sciences) 1963. CAREER: Canadian Chieftain Petroleum Ltd./Tidal Petroleum Corporation Ltd., 1963-64; Exec. Sec. to the Pres., Chieftain Dev. Co. Ltd., 1964-66; Exec. Sec. to Gerald Caplan, M.D., Dir. of the Lab. of Community Psychiatry, Harvard Medical Sch., 1966-67; various positions, Chieftain Dev. Co. Ltd., 1967-86; Sr. VP, Admin. & Corp. Sec., 1986-88; VP & Sec., Chieftain International, Inc., 1988-95; Sr. VP & Sec., 1995 to date. DIRECTOR: AGT Limited; Chieftain International, Inc.; TELUS Corporation. AFFIL: Edmonton Arts Council; Univ. of Alberta (Bus. Advisory Council); General Hospital (Grey Nuns) of Edmonton (Hospital Foundation Bd.); Edmonton YMCA (Foundation Bd.); Edmonton Petroleum Golf & Country Club; Centre Club; South Alberta Light Horse Officers' Club. HONS: Canada 125 Medal. INTERESTS: music; gardening; golf; canoeing; hiking.

O'Neil, Maureen, B.A. ■■ ✚Ⓐ
Interim President (Sept. 15–Dec. 15, 1996),

INTERNATIONAL CENTRE FOR HUMAN RIGHTS AND DEMOGRAPHIC DEVELOPMENT. Director, INSTITUTE ON GOVERNANCE, 122 Clarence St., Ottawa, ON K1N 5P6 (613) 562-0090, FAX 562-0097. EDUC: Carleton Univ., B.A.(Sociology) 1964. CAREER: various positions in policy analysis & program dev., fed. gov't, Gov't of Man. & Carleton Univ., 1964-73; Chief, Social Programs, Social Policy & Programs Branch, Communications Canada, 1973-74; Sr. Policy Analyst, Policy Research & Strategic Planning Branch, Social Programs Analysis Directorate, Health & Welfare Canada, 1974-76; Dir., Policy Research & Strategic Planning Branch, 1976-78; Coord., Status of Women Canada, 1978-86; Sec. Gen., Cdn Human Rights Commission, 1986-87; Deputy Min., Ministry of Citizenship, Gov't of Ont., 1987-89; Pres., North-South Institute, 1989-95; Dir., Institute on Governance, 1995 to date. AFFIL: Carleton Univ. (mbr., Bd. of Gov. 1989 to date; Chair 1993-95); Canadian Foundation for the Americas (mbr., Bd. of Dir. 1994 to date; Chair 1995 to date); Advisory Bd. to the Min. of Foreign Affairs (1995 to date); International Centre for Human Rights & Democratic Development (Chair 1996 to date); University Partnerships in Cooperation and Development, CIDA (Chair, Selection Committee 1994 to date); Institute for Women, Law and Development, Washington (Bd. of Dir. 1993 to date); U.N. Research Institute for Social Research (mbr. of Bd. 1989-95); U.N. Committee for Development Planning (mbr. of Bd. 1990-94); Institute for Research on Public Policy (Council of Trustees 1982-86). HONS: The Maureen O'Neil Scholarship, Carleton Univ., est. 1985; recipient, The A.D. Dunton Alumni Award, Carleton Univ., 1986. MISC: fluent in French, some Spanish & German.

Opheim, Eloise, C.M.B.A. Ⓞ
National Executive Director, PRIDE CANADA INC. (Parent Resources Institute for Drug Education), c/o College of Pharmacy and Nutrition, University of Saskatchewan, 110 Science Place, Saskatoon, SK S7N 5C9 (306) 931-9692, FAX 975-0503. Born Saskatoon. m. Ken. 2 ch. EDUC: Univ. of Saskatchewan, B.A.(Int'l Studies) 1991. CAREER: Nat'l Exec. Dir., PRIDE Canada Inc., 1983 to date. SELECTED PUBLICATIONS: *Youth and Drugs: What Parent Groups Can Do*; "Drug Abuse Prevalence in Western Canada and the Northwest Territories: A survey of students in Grades 6-12," with Dr. K.W. Hindmarsh (*International Journal of Addiction*, 1990); "The Use of Licit and Illicit Drugs by Junior and Senior High School Students in Rural Communities: 1990," with others (*Canadian Journal of Forensic Science*,

1991); "Alcohol and Other Substance Abuse by Canadian Youth," with others *(Canadian Pharmaceutical Journal*, Dec. 1992/Jan. 1993); "Perception and Attitudes with Respect to Drug Use Among Grades 4-5 Students: 1992," with others *(International Journal of Addiction*, 1994); "Alcohol and Drug Use by Students from Western Canada in Grades 6 through 12: have there been any changes over the past 5 years?," with others *(International Journal of Addiction*, 1994). **AFFIL:** Rotary Club; Canadian Society of Executive Directors. **HONS:** International Parent Award for Adolescent Drug Prevention; Woman of the Year, YWCA; Citizen of the Year, CFQC; Order of Canada. **INTERESTS:** family; down-hill skiing; cycling; reading. **MISC:** numerous lectures; interviewed for electronic & print media. **COMMENT:** *"In her 10 years with PRIDE Canada Inc., Eloise Opheim has given leadership in the drug prevention field, particularly in the area of the expansion of the parent and youth movement to reduce the use of psychoactive drugs among children."*

Orenstein, Elise, B.A.,M.Phil.,LL.B. ⚖ $
Partner, LANG MICHENER, BCE Place, 181 Bay St., Ste. 2500, Box 747, Toronto, ON M5J 2T7 (416) 307-4083, FAX 365-1719. Born Montreal m. Graham W. Savage. 2 ch. Coby Oren Savage, Caley Jessica Savage. **EDUC:** McGill Univ., B.A. 1976; Oxford Univ., M.Phil. 1978; Osgoode Hall Law Sch., LL.B. 1981. **BAR:** Ont., 1983. **CAREER:** Dir. of Bus. Affairs, CityTV, MuchMusic & ChumCity; Ptnr, Lang Michener, 1990 to date; Sec., SCOR Canada Reinsurance Company; Adjunct Prof., York Univ. Bus. Admin. Program, 1991, 1993. **DIRECTOR:** SCOR Canada Reinsurance Company. **AFFIL:** Canadian Bar Association (Media, Comm., & Bus. Law Sections); International Trademark Association; Patent & Trademark Institute of Canada (Fellow); Canadian Literary & Artistic Association Inc.; Interactive Multimedia Arts & Technologies Association; Licensing Executives' Society; Dancemakers (Dir.; former VP); N.A.A.M.A.T. **INTERESTS:** dance; music; sports. **MISC:** speaker at various seminars.

Ormerod, Mary, B.A.,LL.B. ⚖
Partner, PERLEY-ROBERTSON, PANET, HILL AND MCDOUGALL, 99 Bank St., Ottawa, ON K1P 1C1 (613) 238-2022, FAX 238-8775. Born Kingston, Ont. 1955. m. H. Blakeney. 2 ch. **EDUC:** Queen's Univ., B.A.(English/Psych.) 1976, LL.B. 1979. **BAR:** Ont., 1981. **CAREER:** practice of law, various firms & sole practice, 1981-85; Assoc., Perley-Robertson, Panet, Hill and McDougall, 1985-88; Ptnr, 1988 to date.

AFFIL: Women's Business Network Association of Ottawa; Women's Law Association (Ottawa Exec. 1992-96); Business & Professional Women's Association; Infertility Awareness Association of Canada (Pres., Ottawa Chapter 1994-96; Dir. 1994-95); Glebe Community Association (Dir. 1987-88); Law Society of Upper Canada. **HONS:** Order of Canada, 1996. **MISC:** Instructor, Bar Admission Course, Law Society of Upper Canada, 1991-92, 1995.

Ormsby, Margaret A., B.A.,M.A., Ph.D. ⚖ 📖
Professor Emerita, History Department, UNIVERSITY OF BRITISH COLUMBIA. Born Quesnel, B.C. 1909. s. **EDUC:** Univ. of British Columbia, B.A.(Hist.) 1929, M.A.(Hist.) 1931; Bryn Mawr Coll., Ph.D.(Hist.) 1937. **CAREER:** Head of Hist. Dept., Sarah D. Hamilton Sch., San Francisco, 1937-39; Special Lecturer in Hist., McMaster Univ., 1940-43; Lecturer in Hist., Univ. of British Columbia, 1943-46; Asst. Prof., 1946-49; Assoc. Prof., 1949-52; Prof. & Head of Dept., 1965-74; Visiting Prof., 1974-75; Visiting Prof., Hist. Dept., Univ. of Western Ontario, 1977; Visiting Prof., Hist. Dept., Univ. of Toronto, 1978. **SELECTED PUBLICATIONS:** *British Columbia: A History* (Macmillan, 1958, 1959, 1962, 1964; 1971; pbk. 1971); *A Pioneer Gentlewoman in British Columbia: the Recollections of Susan Allison* (UBC Press, 1976, 1994); *Fort Victoria Letters 1946-1851*, Intro. (Hudson's Bay Record Society, XXXII, 1979); *Coldstream–Nulli Secundus* (Friesen, 1990); biographies in *the Dictionary of Canadian Biography*, vol. IX, X, XI, XII. **AFFIL:** Canadian Historical Association (Pres. 1965-66; Life Mbr.); B.C. Historical Association (Life Mbr.); Okanagan Historical Association (Life Mbr.); Royal Society of Canada (Fellow); Historic Sites & Monuments Bd. of Canada (1960-68); B.C. Heritage (Advisory Bd. 1971-83); Okanagan Coll. (Bd. of Gov. 1980-85). **HONS:** D.Litt.(Hon.), Univ. of British Columbia, 1974; LL.D.(Hon.), Univ. of Manitoba, 1960; LL.D. (Hon.), Univ. of Notre Dame of Nelson, B.C., 1968; LL.D.(Hon.), Simon Fraser Univ., 1971; LL.D.(Hon.), Univ. of Victoria, 1976; LL.D. (Hon.), Univ. of Northern British Columbia, 1995. **INTERESTS:** fruit growing. **COMMENT:** *"As a professor, my teaching fields have been European medieval, American intellectual and post-Confederation Canadian history. Over the years I have emphasized provincial history in the hope that the Canadian experience will be seen with a less myopic view. With the expansion of graduate work, new and important interpretations have emerged; their exposition in a readable and attractive style have aroused public interest and modified stagnant theories."*

O'Rourke, Danielle J., B.Comm. ✊ $ 🍁
President, TEA COUNCIL OF CANADA, 885 Don Mills Rd., Ste. 301, Don Mills, ON M3C 1V9 (416) 510-8647, FAX 510-8044. Born Ottawa 1965. **EDUC:** Univ. of Ottawa, B.Comm. (Mktg/Int'l Bus.) 1987. **CAREER:** Small Bus. Consultant, Ont. Ministry of Industry, Trade & Technology, 1987-88; part-time Lecturer, Sheridan Coll., 1988; Int'l Mktg Consultant, Ont. Ministry of Industry, Trade & Technology, 1988-90; Mkt Research Analyst, Ministry of Industry, Trade & Technology, 1990-91; Ministerial Analyst, Office of Francophone Affairs, Gov't of Ont., 1991-92; Exec. Dir., Tea Council of Canada, 1992-93; Pres., 1993 to date. **SELECTED PUBLICATIONS:** articles on tea in US & UK trade publications. **AFFIL:** Cercle canadien de Toronto (Dir. 1994-95); International Tea Committee, UK (Dir. 1995); Business Women's Advisory Committee to the Ont. Min. Responsible for Women's Issues (1994-95); Association des femmes d'affaires francophones (Pres. 1991-92). **INTERESTS:** travel; golf; skiing; aerobics; public speaking; softball. **COMMENT:** *"Leadership of a Canadian organization that has a national focus, but operates in an international environment, corresponds to both my personal and professional aspirations. My academic, government and industry experiences have all had a global element. This is something I will continue to pursue."*

Orr, Nancy K., B.Comm.,LL.B., Q.C. ■ ⚖ 👍
Provincial Court Judge, PROVINCE OF PRINCE EDWARD ISLAND, Box 2290, Charlottetown, PE C1A 8C3. Born P.E.I. 1956. s. **EDUC:** Dalhousie Univ., B.Comm. 1976; Univ. of Ottawa, LL.B., 1979. **BAR:** P.E.I., 1979. **CAREER:** Staff Lawyer, P.E.I. Legal Aid, 1980-95; Prov. Court Judge, 1995 to date. **AFFIL:** Canadian Association of Provincial Court Judges (P.E.I. Rep. on Exec.; Atlantic Educ. Committee); P.E.I. Prov. Court (Chair, Educ. Committee); Federation of Law Societies (N.B. & P.E.I. Rep., Bd. of Dir. 1991-95; Chair, Committee on Women in the Legal Profession 1992-95); Canadian Bar Association, P.E.I. Branch (Exec. 1982-89; Pres., 1987-88; P.E.I. Rep., Nat'l Exec. 1988-89; Council 1982 to date); Law Society of P.E.I. (Sec.-Treas. 1985-89, 1990; VP, Pres. then Past Pres. 1989-92; various committees); Cavendish 4-H Club (Club Leader); P.E.I. 4-H Council (Bd.; Chair, P.E.I. 4-H Trust; Pres., VP & Past Pres. 1982-86); Canadian 4-H Foundation (Patron "500 Club"); Maritime Jr. "A" Hockey League (VP); Cdn Jr. "A" Hockey League (Eastern VP); Charlottetown Outlaws (lawyers) Hockey Team. **HONS:** appointed Q.C., 1992. **INTERESTS:** playing & watching hockey; downhill skiing; travel. **MISC:** 1st woman appointed to the P.E.I. Prov. Court; Course Instructor, Discipline component, Bar Admission Course, 1993 to date.

Orr, Sherry $ ✊ 👍
President, TRANS-MUTUAL TRUCK LINES LTD., 4503 - 78th Ave. S.E., Calgary, AB T2C 2Y9 (403) 279-7581, FAX 279-8716. Born Calgary 1962. m. Gordon. 2 ch. Mitchell, Ryan. **CAREER:** Pres., Trans-Mutual Truck Lines, 1984 to date. **AFFIL:** Alberta Trucking Association (2nd VP); Young Entrepreneurs' Association. **HONS:** Successor Award, *Canadian Business* Magazine, 1989; Alta. Exec. of the Year, Institute of Certified Management Consultants, 1990; Hon. Chair in Bus., Grant MacEwan Community Coll., 1992; 1 of the Top 100 Entrepreneurs Under 30, Association of Collegiate Entrepreneurs, 1994; Finalist, Entrepreneur of the Year program, 1994. **INTERESTS:** travelling; sailing; being involved with my children's activities. **MISC:** Sherry Orr & Trans-Mutual Truck Lines Ltd. have been the subjects of numerous newspaper articles & TV & radio programs across Canada. **COMMENT:** *"I enjoy challenges and seeing the results of our hard work and goal setting. One of my strongest traits is being positive and looking at challenges as opportunities."*

O'Shannacery, Karen ■ ✊ ♡
Executive Director, LOOKOUT EMERGENCY AID SOCIETY, 429 Alexander St., Vancouver, BC V6A 1C6 (604) 255-0340, FAX 255-0790. Born Vancouver 1950. m. Mike Landiak. 1 ch. **EDUC:** Vancouver Technical, 1968. **CAREER:** Outreach Worker, Connolly House Youth Hostel, 1969-70; Youth Counsellor, Connolly House Youth Hostel, 1969-78; Lookout Street Worker & Asst. Dir., Lookout Emergency Aid Society, 1970-71; Exec. Dir., Lookout Emergency Aid Society, 1974 to date; Coord., Multi Svc. Ntwk, 1987-88. **AFFIL:** Community Worker Association (Chair 1972); Vancouver Eastside Recreation & Sports Society (Pres. & Treas. 1983); Vi Fineday Society (V-Chrm 1985); Inter-agency Mental Health Council (Chrm, Housing Committee 1986 to date); Vancouver Urban Core Community Workers' Association (Chrm 1993-94). **HONS:** Canada 125 Medal, 1992; Gastown Lions Medal, 1993. **INTERESTS:** hiking; canoeing; softball; volleyball; reading. **MISC:** Vancouver delegate, Nat'l Urban Core Support Ntwk Annual Conference (1981, 1983 & 1984); forum speaker, Cdn Conference to observe UN Int'l Year of Shelter for the Homeless, Ottawa (1987). **COMMENT:** *"Advocate for the homeless and disenfranchised for 23 years in DTES. Found-*

ing member of Lookout Emergency Aid Society. Community oriented. Was founding member of the Vancouver Urban Core Workers' Association. Has served on the board of a number of agencies."

Osted, Annette ⊙ ⛨

Executive Director, REGISTERED PSYCHIATRIC NURSES' ASSOCIATION OF MANITOBA, 1854 Portage Ave., Winnipeg, MB R3J 0G9 (204) 888-4841, FAX 888-8638. Born Notre Dame de Lourdes, Man. 1946. d. 2 ch. EDUC: Sch. of Psychiatric Nursing, Selkirk, Man., Dipl.(Psychiatric Nursing) 1967; Canadian Institute of Organization Management, Certificate (Association Mgmt Issues) 1982. CAREER: Registered Psychiatric Nurse, Dept. of Psychiatry, Health Science Centre, Winnipeg, 1967-69; Registered Psychiatric Nurse, Chemical Withdrawal Unit, 1973-74; Primary Therapist, Alcohol Treatment Unit, 1974-76; Exec. Dir., Registered Psychiatric Nurses' Association of Manitoba, 1976 to date. AFFIL: Winnipeg Region Mental Health Council (Min. Appointee); Mental Health Review Bd. (Min. Appointee); Canadian Mental Health Association; Canadian Society of Association Executives; Manitoba Association for Continuing Educ.; Psychiatric Nurses' Association of Canada; World Federation for Mental Health. HONS: Marjorie Hiscott Keyes Award, Canadian Mental Health Association, 1992. INTERESTS: genealogy; music; reading; language. MISC: various presentations over past 10 yrs. COMMENT: *"A professional association manager with more than 18 years' experience as the CEO of a professional organization whose mandate includes statutory functions, corporate functions, membership services, resource development and lobbying."*

Ostry, Sylvia, C.C.B.A.,M.A.,Ph.D.,LL.D., D.M.Sc.,F.R.S.C. ▒ ⊲ ✦

Economist, 170 Bloor St. W, 5th Fl., Toronto, ON M5S 1T5. Chairman, Centre for International Studies, UNIVERSITY OF TORONTO. Chancellor, UNIVERSITY OF WATERLOO. Born Winnipeg 1927. m. Bernard Ostry. 2 ch. EDUC: McGill Univ., B.A.(Econ.) 1948, M.A. 1950, Ph.D. 1954; Cambridge Univ., Ph.D. residence 1950-51, 1954. CAREER: Lecturer & Asst. Prof., McGill Univ., 1948-54; Research Officer, Institute of Statistics, Univ. of Oxford, 1955-57; Assoc. Prof., Univ. of Montreal, 1962-64; Dir., Special Manpower Studies, Dominion Bureau of Statistics, 1965-69; Dir., Economic Council of Canada, 1969-72; Chief Statistician of Canada, Statistics Canada, 1972-75; Deputy Min., Consumer & Corp. Affairs Canada, 1975-78; Chrm, Economic Council of

Canada, 1978-80; Special Advisor, Privy Council Office, Gov't of Canada, 1979-83; Head, Econ. & Statistics Dept., Organization for Economic Co-operation & Development, Paris, France, 1979-83; Deputy Min. (Int'l Trade) & Coord. for Int'l Econ. Rel'ns, Dept. of External Affairs, 1984-85; Ambassador for Multilateral Trade Negotiations & Personal Rep. of the Prime Minister for the Econ. Summit, Dept. of External Affairs, Ottawa, 1985-88; Volvo Distinguished Visiting Fellow, Council on Foreign Relations, N.Y., 1989; Sr. Research Fellow, Univ. of Toronto, 1989-90; Chrm, National Council of the Canadian Institute for International Affairs, 1990-95; Chrm, Centre for International Studies, Univ. of Toronto, 1990 to date; Western Co-Chair, the Blue Ribbon Commission for Hungary's Economic Recovery, 1991-94; Chancellor, Univ. of Waterloo, 1991 to date. SELECTED PUBLICATIONS: "International Economic Policy Coordination," with Michael Artis (a Chatham House paper 1986); "Interdependence: Vulnerability and Opportunity" (Per Jacobsson Lecture, 1987); "Regional Trading Blocs: Pragmatic or Problematic Policy?," with Michael Aho in *The Global Economy: America's Role in the Decade Ahead* (New York: American Assembly, 1990); *Governments and Corporations in a Shrinking World: The Search for Stability* (New York: Council on Foreign Relations, 1990); "The Domestic Domain: The New International Policy Arena" (*Transnational Corporations* 1(1) 1992); "The Threat of Managed Trade to Transforming Economies" (*Occasional Papers* No. 41, Group of Thirty, Washington, 1993); *Technonationalism and Technoglobalism: Conflict and Cooperation*, with Richard Nelson (Brookings Institution, Washington, 1995); *Rethinking Federalism: Citizens, Markets and Governments in a Changing World*, with eds. Karen Knop, Richard Simeon, Katherine Swinton (Univ. of British Columbia, Vancouver, 1995); "New Dimensions of Market Access (*Occasional Papers* No. 49, Group of Thirty, Washington, 1995); *The Halifax G-7 Summit: Issues on the Table*, with ed. Gilbert R. Winham (The Centre for Foreign Policy, Dalhousie Univ., Halifax, 1995); *Who's on First? The Post Cold War Trading System* (Twentieth Century Fund, N.Y., 1997 forthcoming); numerous other publications since 1956, incl. over 80 publications on empirical & policy-analytic subjects. DIRECTOR: Power Financial Corporation. CHAIRMAN: Int'l Advisory Council, Bank of Montreal. AFFIL: InterAmerican Development Bank/Economic Commission for Latin America & the Caribbean Proj. (Advisory Committee); United Nations Univ./World Institute for

Development Economics Institute, Helsinki (Bd. Mbr.); Commission on Transnational Corporations, UN, N.Y. (Expert Advisor); Centre for European Policy Studies, Brussels (Int'l Advisory Council); Institute of International Economics, Washington (Advisory Bd.); American Economic Association; American Statistical Association (Fellow); Centre for European Policy Studies, Brussels (Founding Mbr.); Group of Thirty, Washington. **HONS:** Isbister Scholarship, Univ. of Manitoba, 1943-44, 1944-45; Alkin Scholarship, Univ. of Manitoba, 1943-44, 1944-45; Alexander MacKenzie Scholarship, McGill Univ., 1947-48; Cherry Prize, McGill Univ., 1948-49; Arthur Tagge Fellowship, McGill Univ., 1948-49; Moyse Travelling Fellowship, McGill Univ., 1950-51; Officer of the Order of Canada, 1978; Outstanding Achievement Award, Gov't of Canada, 1987; Companion of the Order of Canada, 1990; Honouree, Public Policy Forum Testimonial Dinner, 1991; Hon. Assoc. Award, Conference Board of Canada, 1992; LL.D.(Hon.) from: York Univ., 1971; Univ. of New Brunswick, 1971; Queen's Univ., 1972; Univ. of Western Ontario, 1973; McMaster Univ., 1973; Univ. of British Columbia, 1973; Queen's Univ., 1975; Brock Univ., 1975; Mount Allison Univ., 1975; Acadia Univ., 1981; American Coll. of Switzerland, 1983; Univ. of Winnipeg, 1984; Univ. of Manitoba, 1986; Concordia Univ., 1986; Univ. of Windsor, 1987; D.M.Sc.(Hon.), Univ. of Ottawa, 1976; D.Litt.(Hon.), Laurentian Univ., 1977. **INTERESTS:** films; theatre; books; art galleries; museums; travel. **MISC:** In 1992 the Sylvia Ostry Foundation annual lecture series was launched; gave The Per Jacobsson Foundation Lecture, Washington, DC, 1987; recipient, various grants.

Oswald, Linda L., ("Toby") ■ $

Vice-President, Public Relations and Government Affairs, CANADA SAFEWAY LTD., 1020 - 84 Ave. N.E., Calgary, AB T2E 7V8 (403) 730-3511, FAX 730-3902. 2 ch. Tamara, Krista. **EDUC:** Univ. of Manitoba, Bachelor of Home Econ. 1970; Univ. of Manitoba, Certificate (Educ.) 1972. **CAREER:** Teacher, Steinbach Jr. High, 1972-75; Teacher, Family & Community Nutrition, Steinbach Reg'l Secondary Sch., 1975-80; Home Economist, Penner Foods Ltd., 1980-89; Dir. of Public Affairs, Canada Safeway Ltd., 1990-95; VP, Public Rel'ns & Gov't Affairs, 1996 to date. **DIRECTOR:** EnCorp Pacific; Multi Material Stewardship Corporation. **AFFIL:** Home Economists in Business (Founding Mbr.); Grocery Retailers for Recycling Manitoba (Chrm); Variety Club (Advisory Council, Tent 58); Kids Help Phone (Bd.). **HONS:** 2-time recipient, Donald J. Smith Exceptional Achievement Award, 1991-93; Corp. Citizen of the Year, 1991-93. **INTERESTS:** gourmet cooking; sewing; crafts; curling; skiing; golf.

Oughton, Libby, B.A.,M.A. ✪ 📖 📜

Artist, Writer and Herbalist, R.R. 1, Pleasantville, NS B0R 1G0. Born Toronto 1938. d. 2 ch. Gillian Robinson (writer), Andrew Robinson (woodsman). **EDUC:** Queen's Univ., B.A. 1959; Cornell Univ. & Rutgers Univ., M.A. 1964. **CAREER:** Lab. Tech., Cornell Univ., 1960-63; Mng Ed., *This Magazine is about Schools*, 1965-67; Researcher & Writer, *Natural History of Canada*, McClelland & Stewart, 1967-69; Prod., Coach House Press, 1970-73; Info. Officer, Association of Canadian Publishers, 1973-75; Rights Mgr, Books Canada (UK), 1975-77; Asst. Dir., Association of Canadian Publishers, 1977-80; Ptnr, Ragweed Press, 1980-81; Council, Association of Canadian Publishers, 1981-86; Pres. & owner, Ragweed Press & gynergy books, 1981-89; freelance journalist, CBC Radio, 1984-87; Mng Ed., The Ayurvedic Press, 1993 to date. **SELECTED PUBLICATIONS:** *Island Women*, co-ed. (1982); *getting the housework done for the dance* (1988). **AFFIL:** Atlantic Publishing Association; Literary Press Group; Great George St. Gallery; P.E.I. Voice of Women; Writers' Union of Canada; League of Canadian Poets; Printmakers' Council of P.E.I.; P.E.N. (Exec. Council); Canadian Learning Materials Centre; New Democratic Party of Canada; *Atlantic Provinces Book Review*. **HONS:** Annual Alumni Achievement Award, Queen's Univ., 1987; Milton Acorn Award for Poetry, 1987; Semi-Finalist, Alumni of the Year Award, Council for the Advancement & Support of Educ., 1988; Carl Sentner Award (Fiction), 1988; Outstanding Contribution to the Literary Arts, 1992. **INTERESTS:** wood & clay sculpture; woodblock prints; herbology; the Greek Island of Lesbos; Cdn women writers & artists; buddhism; archaeology of women's artifacts; alternative communities for aging women; natural healing. **COMMENT:** *"My focus has always been on a better quality of life for women–from publishing Canadian women writers, to concentrating now on joyful alternatives to aging–through art, community, and natural healing. Survival with some grace!"*

P

aabo, Iris 🛏️ ⊗ 📜

Multimedia Artist, IRIZ STUDIOS, 564 Logan Ave., Toronto, ON M4K 3B7 (416) 465-2188, FAX 466-0626. m. Peter Faulkner. 2 ch. Jason Faulkner, Maxeen Paabo. **CAREER:** theatre musician, composer & performer, 1968 to date; designer of sets, costumes, puppets & posters, 1970-91; animator, ed. & broadcast illustrator, 1982 to date; multimedia artist, 1984 to date. **SELECTED CREDITS:** theatre performer, *Heaven Will Protect the Working Girl*, Pears' Cabaret, 1979; *Nursecapades*, RNAO, 1985; *Ten Lost Years* & other plays, Toronto Workshop Productions, 1973-84; various other performance credits; filmmaker, *I've Got A Little Brother*, 1982; *My Quill Clicks When I Walk*, 1983; *Bon Vivant*, 1985; *Wake Up/Wake Up*, 1990; *Leaving the Poisons Behind*, 1991; *Teknicly Inkorect*, 1996; composer & co-playwright of *Cab Array*, Group of Several, Du Maurier Theatre, 1985; *Projections*, Group of Several, Nathan Cohen Studio, 1987; playwright, *4Bags2Stones*, Broomstick Productions, Theatre Centre, 1992; voice-over narration for *Oh, Dad!*, film by Jonathan Amitay, 1987; various other theatre & film credits; music composition *for Nova Scotia Brothers*, CBC Radio, 1982; *Everybody's Children*, TVOntario, 1982; *Where the Heart Is* (broadcast video), Pax Productions, 1991; *The Swan*, by Elizabeth Lewis, 1992; various other music composition credits; children's illustrations for *Crossings* (Academic Press, 1985); *And I'm Never Coming Back* (Annick Press, 1986); broadcast animatics for TVOntario, 1987 to date; ed. illustrations for *The Globe and Mail*, *Starweek*, NFB, Southam Publishing, *Enroute* magazine & others, 1990 to date; animator for *It Starts With A Whisper* (feature), Bay of Quinte Productions, 1991; animator & illustrator, *History of Women* (broadcast video), Skyworks/TVO, 1992; various other clients, incl. CD-ROM publishers, software developers, *Sesame Street*, Electrosol, UPS, Northern Telecom; Co-Prod./Dir., *The Media Monitor* (educ. video), 1996; Co-writer/Composer, *DIEF*, 1996-97; Audio Art, *NO MO PO MO*, CIUT Radio, 1996; creator of interactive encaustic installation, *Leaving the Poisons Behind, Part II*, Scarborough Arts Centre, 1996 & *Documenting the Nineties*, mixed-media on ragboard & acrylic on canvas, 1990 to date. AFFIL: Toronto Animated Image Society; Visual Arts Ontario; Canadian Filmmakers' Distribution Centre; SOCAN. MISC: recipient, various grants & commissions; various lectures & public speeches; print & broadcast interviews; mbr., various juries & panels. COMMENT: *"It used to bother me to work in so many disciplines: now I just do it."*

Paakspuu, Kalli, B.A.,M.A. 👄 🗂 ⊗
Producer, Director, Writer and Videographer, CALIPIX PRODUCTIONS, 4 Cathedral Bluffs Dr., Scarborough, ON M1M 2T7 (416) 261-7889. Born Vancouver 1952. d. 2 ch. Virginia Paakspuu Hughes, Gareth Hughes. EDUC: Univ. of British Columbia, B.A.(English) 1975; Univ. of Toronto, M.A.(Soc.) 1985, Ph.D. in progress. CAREER: Film & Video Prod.–est. the following film production companies, October Alms Productions, Vancouver, 1978; Kalli Paakspuu Films, Toronto, 1978; Womenfilm/Womenart, Toronto, 1981; Bedroom Colony Inc., Toronto, 1988; Calipix Productions, Scarborough, Ont., 1995; part-time Fac., Fine Arts, York Univ., 1989 to date; Coord., "Women's Perspective in Cinema" film series at OISE, 1994-96. SELECTED CREDITS: *Solstanz* (1975); *Sacred Circle* (1976); *Passage* (1978); *October Alms* (1978); *Maypole Carving* (1981); *I Need a Man Like You to Make My Dreams Come True* (1986); *Goodbye Two Day Weekends* (1988); *When East Meets East* (1996); *The Colonizing Gaze*, in progress; *A Thousand and One Cuts*, in progress; *A Safe Place in Academia*, in progress; *Zoom* (feature film), in progress. SELECTED PUBLICATIONS: photographs in *Photographs Dance: A Collection* (Toronto: 15 Dance Lab), Cinema Canada. EXHIBITIONS: CBC Canadian Reflections; TVO; ACCESS: Knowledge Network; PBS (Seattle & Buffalo); films have been exhibited extensively in theatrical & nontheatrical venues in Canada, the US, Australia, Europe, China & Hong Kong. AFFIL: Canadian Filmmakers' Distribution Centre; Womenfilm/Womenart Inc.; Canadian Independent Film Caucus (CIFC); LIFT; Charles Street Video; Women Make Movies;

AIFA. HONS: Best Mixed Media Award, Scarborough Arts Council Members' Juried Show, 1992; Genie Award for Best Live Action Short Drama, 1987; Chicago Film Festival Award, Satire, 1986; Bronze Award for Drama, Int'l Film & TV Festival of N.Y., 1978. INTERESTS: fiction & drama; post-colonial culture; migration stories. MISC: recipient, numerous grants incl. Canada Council Film Production Grant, 1994; York Univ. Research Grant, 1993; Ontario Arts Council Film Production Grant, 1986; other Ontario Arts Council & Canada Council grants. COMMENT: *"Born of Estonian parents in Vancouver, I grew up knowing the world through our family-run global news and bookstore."*

Pace Lindsay, Kate ■ ■ ⊘
Downhill Skier. c/o International Management Group, 1 St. Clair Ave. E., Ste. 700, Toronto, ON M4T 2V7 (416) 960-5312, FAX 960-0564. Born North Bay, Ont. 1969. SPORTS CAREER: mbr., North Bay Ski Racers, 1988 to date; has competed in more than 20 int'l competitions, incl. 1994 Winter Olympics & 2 World Championships, & 9 World Cups; World Champion, Downhill, 1993; Cdn Champion, Downhill, 1994. HONS: Female Cdn Athlete of the Year, Canadian Press, 1993; Canadian Skier of the Year, *Ski Racing Magazine*, 1993.

Packer, Katherine Helen 🖘 🗍 ⊙
Professor Emerita, Faculty of Library and Information Science (now Faculty of Information Studies), UNIVERSITY OF TORONTO, 140 St. George St., Toronto, ON M5S 3G6 (416) 978-7111 (messages only). Born Toronto 1918. m. William A. Packer. 1 ch. Marianne Katherine Packer. EDUC: Univ. of Toronto, B.A.(Arts) 1941; Univ. of Michigan, A.M.L.S. 1953; Univ. of Maryland, Ph.D.(Library & Info. Sci.) 1975. CAREER: Cataloguer, William L. Clements Library, Univ. of Michigan, 1953-55; Cataloguer, Univ. of Manitoba Library, 1956-59; Cataloguer, Univ. of Toronto Library, 1959-63; Head Cataloguer, York Univ. Library, 1963-64; Chief Librarian, Ontario Coll. of Education, 1964-67; Asst. Prof., Fac. of Library Science, Univ. of Toronto, 1967-75; Assoc. Prof., 1975-78; Prof. & Dean, 1979-84; Prof. Emerita, 1984 to date. SELECTED PUBLICATIONS: *Early American Books. A Bibliography Based on the Boston Booksellers' Catalogue of 1804* (Ann Arbor, Mich.: Univ. of Michigan, 1954); various articles in professional journals. AFFIL: American Library Association; American Society for Information Science; Canadian Library Association; International Federation of Library Associations (Statistics Committee);

FID/ET; Canadian Association of Library Schools; Association for Library & Information Science Education; Amnesty International; Metropolitan Toronto's Solid Waste Environmental Assessment Plan (Public Caucus); Assessment Reform Working Group, City of Toronto; Working Group on Property Taxes, Ont. Gov't's Fair Tax Commission; Deer Park Ratepayers' Group, Inc. (Chrm); Phi Kappa Phi Honor Society. HONS: Howard Phalin/World Book Grad. Scholarship for Library Science, Canadian Library Association, 1972; Distinguished Alumnus Award, Univ. of Michigan, Library Sci., 1981. INTERESTS: literacy movement (tutor); protection of the environment, with special reference to native flora & the protection of wildlife preserves; birdwatching & photography; municipal affairs. MISC: has made depositions on the issue of reforming the property tax assessment system in Ont. before the councils of the City of Toronto & Metro. Toronto & before a subcommittee of the Gov't of Ont. COMMENT: *"Since my retirement, I have made an effort to contribute to the community by participating as a volunteer in a number of social, governmental and charitable organizations. I write Urgent Action letters for Amnesty International and I earned a certificate as a Master Composter from the Recycling Council of Ontario. In recent years my major commitment has been to the reform of the property tax assessment system in Ontario."*

Packham, Marian A., B.A.,Ph.D. ⬡ ⬢
University Professor Emeritus, Department of Biochemistry, UNIVERSITY OF TORONTO, Toronto, ON M5S 1A8 (416) 978-8567, FAX 978-8548. Born Toronto 1927. m. James L. Packham. 2 ch. Neil Lennox, Janet Melissa. EDUC: Univ. of Toronto, B.A.(Biochem.) 1949, Ph.D.(Biochem.) 1954. CAREER: Sr. Fellow & Lecturer, Dept. of Biochem., Univ. of Toronto, 1954-63; Research Assoc., Dept. of Physiological Sciences, Ontario Veterinary Coll., Guelph, 1963-65; Research Assoc., Blood & Cardiovascular Disease Research Unit, Dept. of Medicine, Univ. of Toronto, 1965-66; Lecturer/Asst. Prof./Assoc. Prof./Prof., Dept. of Biochem., 1966-89; Acting Chair, 1983; Visiting Prof., Dept. of Pathology, McMaster Univ.; Univ. Prof., Univ. of Toronto, 1989 to date. EDIT: Cdn Ed., *Thrombosis Research*, 1974-79; Ed. Bd., *Atherosclerosis*, 1978-89; Ed. Bd., *Blood*, 1980-85; Ed. Bd., *Thrombosis and Haemostasis*, 1981-94; Ed. Bd., *Experimental and Molecular Pathology*, 1987 to date; Cdn Ed., *Platelets*, 1990-95. AFFIL: Royal Society of Canada (Fellow); Int'l Committee on Thrombosis & Haemostasis. HONS: J. Allyn Taylor Int'l Prize in Medicine, 1988.

Pacsu, Margaret, B.A. ■ ⬡ ╱ ⊗
Broadcaster and Journalist, CANADIAN BROADCASTING CORPORATION, Box 500, Stn. A, Toronto, ON M5W 1E7 (416) 323-0486. Born Princeton, N.J. 1938. m. Robert R. Campbell. 2 (adopted) ch. EDUC: Smith Coll., Mass., B.A.(French & Hist.) 1960; École Nationale de langues orientales, Paris, Linguistics/Hungarian (equivalent of an M.A.). CAREER: freelance broadcaster & writer, English & French, French Broadcasting Corporation, 1962-70; Field Supervisor & Dir., Paris Office, Burke Marketing Research, 1968-70; Focus Group Leader & Acct Exec., Toronto, 1970-72, 1995 to date; TV News Anchor, CBC TV, 1972-77; Radio Broadcaster, 1974 to date. SELECTED CREDITS: Co-Creator & Host, *Easy Street*, CBC Radio, 7 yrs.; Host, *Listen to the Music*, CBC Radio, 12 yrs.; Host, *On Stage*, CBC Radio, 1994-95; narrator for The National Film Board of Canada, TVOntario; CBC documentaries & *The Nature of Things*; narrator & dubbing artist, Radio-Télévision France; *I've Got to Sing a Torch Song*, 1-woman vocal & spoken presentation primarily regarding great women jazz singers of the past, YPT Toronto, 1986. AFFIL: ACTRA; U des Arts; Toronto Musicians' Association (TMA); Canadian Wire Guild; École Étienne Brulé (Parent-Teacher Association). INTERESTS: classical & jazz music; comedy; avid baseball fan. MISC: comedy "sidekick" to Glenn Gould both at CBC Radio & on his "Silver Jubilee Album" (Columbia Master Works, 1981); 1 of the 32 short films in *32 Short Films About Glenn Gould*; bilingual Master of Ceremonies at major gov't & arts functions, incl. the Chalmers Awards for the Arts; hosted the week-long int'l conference honouring the anniversary of the birth & 10th anniversary of the death of Glenn Gould, the Glenn Gould Foundation. COMMENT: *"When I came to Canada in 1970, I did not know it would be for a lifetime. CBC gave me many opportunities: to go to the Soviet Union for a TV documentary, to share my love of jazz and classical music with so many listeners, to feel part of a new country. My association with Glenn Gould was unique. My two adopted children have given me a focus and a feeling of belonging to this great land–in two official languages."*

Page, P.K. ⊗ ⬢
Writer. Artist (as P.K. Irwin). 3260 Exeter Rd., Victoria, BC V8R 6H6 (604) 592-1880. Born UK 1916. m. W.A. Irwin. 3 ch. SELECTED PUBLICATIONS: *The Sun and the Moon*, novel (1944); *As Ten as Twenty*, poetry (1946); *The Metal and the Flower*, poetry (1954); *Cry Ararat!–Poems New and Selected* (1967); *The*

Sun and the Moon and other Fictions (1973); *Poems Selected and New* (1974); *To Say the Least*, ed., anthology of short poems (1979); *Evening Dance of the Grey Flies*, poetry & short story (1981); *The Glass Air*, poetry, essays & drawings (1985); *Brazilian Journal*, prose (1988); *A Flask of Sea Water*, fairy story (1989); *The Glass Air–Poems Selected and New* (1991); *The Travelling Musicians*, children's book (1991); *Unless the Eye Catch Fire*, short story (Full Spectrum Press, 1994); *The Goat that Flew*, fairy story (Beach Holme, 1994); *Hologram–A Book of Glosas*, poetry (Brick Books 1994); text, *The Travelling Musicians*, music by Murray Adaskin (1984); text, *A Children's Hymn to the United Nations*, music by Harry Somers (1995); poems, short stories, essays, art criticism & drawings in various magazines & anthologies in Canada, Australia, US, UK, Italy, Israel, Holland & others. **EXHIBITIONS:** 1-woman shows in Mexico & Canada; various group shows. **COLLECTIONS:** National Gallery of Canada; Art Gallery of Ontario; many others. **AFFIL:** Writers' Union of Canada; League of Canadian Poets; SOCAN. **HONS:** Oscar Blumenthal Award, poetry, Chicago, 1944; Gov. General's Award for Poetry, 1954; Order of Canada, 1977; Hon. Citizen of the City of Victoria, 1977; Gold, poetry, National Magazine Awards, 1986; Literary Award for Poetry, Canadian Authors' Association, 1986; Hubert Evans Prize, BC Book Awards, *Brazilian Journal*, 1988; Banff Centre Sch. of Fine Arts National Award, 1989; Silver, poetry, National Magazine Award, 1990; *Prairie Schooner* Readers' Choice Award, 1994; D.Litt.(Hon.), Univ. of Victoria, 1985; LL.D.(Hon.), Univ. of Calgary, 1989; D.Litt. (Hon.), Univ. of Guelph, 1990; LL.D.(Hon.), Simon Fraser Univ., 1990. **MISC:** subject of the NFB film *Still Waters*, 1991; subject of a 2-part sound feature, "The White Glass," *Ideas*, CBC Radio, 1996.

Pageau-Goyette, Nycol, Adm.A. ■ $ ♥ ☝
President and Chief Executive Officer, PAGEAU GOYETTE AND ASSOCIATES, 500 Sherbrooke St. W., Ste. 900, Montreal, QC H3A 3C6 (514) 844-2648, FAX 844-7556. Born Montreal 1943. cl. Charles Bourgeois. 4 ch. Marc, Philippe, Sophie, Martin. **EDUC:** Univ. de Montréal, B.A.(Admin.) 1972. **CAREER:** Tech. Translator, Hydro-Québec, 1961-67; Asst. Dir., Int'l Youth Camp, Olympic Games, 1975-77; Pres. & CEO, Pageau Goyette and Associates, 1977 to date. **DIRECTOR:** Hydro-Québec International; Aéroport de Montréal; Total Containment Inc.; Stella Jones; Nouveler. **AFFIL:** Quebec Chamber of Commerce (Chrm of the Bd. 1994-95); Metropolitan Montreal Board of Trade (Chrm 1992-93); Ordre des administrateurs agréés (Dir.); Fonds de solidarité des travailleurs du Québec (Dir.); Société du Parc des Îles (Chair); Canadian Council for Competitivity (Dir.); World Productivity Institute (Fellow); Univ. de Montréal (Gov.). **HONS:** Gov. General's Medal; Médaillée, Les Entretiens Jacques-Cartier. **INTERESTS:** work; being a grandparent; swimming; travelling; being happy. **MISC:** more than 100 addresses & speaking engagements; 1st woman Pres. & Chair of the Montreal Chamber of Commerce. **COMMENT:** *"I believe I am a hard-working, intelligent and very generous person whose biggest achievements are her two sons and a company that does well in providing work to an increasing number of people."*

Paget, Gail ✊
Executive Administrator, ALBERTA FUNERAL SERVICE ASSOCIATION, 6715 - 8th St. N.E., Ste. 130, Calgary, AB T2E 7H7 (403) 274-1922, FAX 274-8191. Born Calgary 1947. m. Dallas. 3 ch. Twyla, Shari, Cindy. **EDUC:** Modern Coll. of Bus., Certificate (Bus., Secretarial & Acctg) 1965. **CAREER:** Proprietor, Paget's Secretarial Services, 1971 to date; Exec. Administrator, Alberta Funeral Service Association, 1971 to date. **DIRECTOR:** Key Mechanical Ltd. **AFFIL:** Dealing With Grief Committee (Sec.-Treas.; Registrar); Calgary Widow Services; Alberta Sch. of Mortuary Sciences; Autumn Gold Ladies' Curling Classic/Labatt Men's Brier (Volunteer). **INTERESTS:** reading; country music; travelling; cooking. **COMMENT:** *"Service to public of Alberta through public information lines, funeral follow-up service and involvement in organization of conferences assisting professionals/consumers in grief work. Involvement in new Distance Education Program for Mortuary Science Students in Alberta."*

Paikin, Marnie, B.A.,LL.D. ✊ 🎓 $ ☝
Volunteer. 67 Caroline St. S., PH. 1, Hamilton, ON L8P 3K6 (905) 525-9081, FAX 525-8501. Born Toronto 1936. m. Larry. 2 ch. Steven, Jeffrey. **EDUC:** Univ. of Western Ontario, B.A. (Hons., Psych.) 1958. **VOLUNTEER CAREER:** numerous positions, incl. Dir., Hamilton Philharmonic Orchestra, 1968-73; Pres., 1969-71; Dir., Hamilton Place, 1972-77; Chair, 1973-75; Governing Council, Univ. of Toronto, 1972-80, Chair, 1976-80; mbr., Ont. Council of Health, 1980-84; Trustee, The Toronto Hospital (Toronto General Hospital), 1980-87; mbr., Ont. Council on Univ. Affairs, 1981-87; Chair, 1983-87; mbr., Inflation Restraint Bd., Ont., 1982-86; Bd. of Regents, Mount Allison Univ., 1985-90, 1993; Bd. of Gov., McMaster

Univ., 1987 to date; V-Chair, 1988-90; Bd. mbr. & Chair, Evaluation Council, Canadian Educational Standards Institute, 1987-90; Bd. of Trustees, Chedoke-McMaster Hospitals, 1988-96; Chair, Hamilton Negev Dinner, Jewish Nat'l Fund, 1990; Chair, Ont. AIDS Advisory Committee, 1989-91; Community Advisory Committee, Centre for Arthritic Diseases, 1989-91; Nat'l Bd., Canadian Council of Christians & Jews; Advisory Council, Centre for Health Economics & Policy Analysis, McMaster Univ.; Bd. of Dir., Chedoke-McMaster Hospitals Foundation; Co-Chair, Grey Cup 1996 Hamilton. **DIRECTOR:** Atomic Energy of Canada (Acting Chair, 1988-90, 1992-93); Canadian Institute of Chartered Accountants (Public Gov.); Westcoast Energy, Inc. **HONS:** Outstanding Woman Award, Prov. of Ont., 1975; Her Majesty the Queen's Silver Jubilee Medal (Cdn), 1978; Excellence in the Arts Award for contribution to the artistic community, 1980; Citizen of the Year, Jewish Nat'l Fund Negev Dinner, 1980; Human Rel'ns Award, Canadian Council of Christians & Jews, 1985; Woman of the Year, Community Svc., Hamilton Status of Women, 1990; Cornerstone Award, Chedoke-McMaster Hospitals Foundation, 1994; LL.D.(Hon.), Univ. of Toronto, 1981; LL.D.(Hon.), Univ. of Western Ontario, 1988; LL.D.(Hon.), McMaster Univ., 1993. **MISC:** 1st woman Pres. of the Hamilton Philharmonic; 1st woman Chair, Univ. of Toronto; 1st woman Dir. of Southam Inc.

Palmer, Valerie, B.F.A. ⊗
Artist. Wawa, ON P0S 1K0. **EDUC:** Univ. of Manitoba, B.F.A.(Painting) 1973. **EXHIBITIONS:** various solo exhibitions, incl. Art Gallery of Algoma, Sault Ste. Marie, Ont., 1987; Nancy Poole's Studio (1987, 1989, 1992, 1995); numerous group exhibitions incl. Gallery III, Univ. of Manitoba (1973); *Ontario North Now,* Ontario Place (1980); Rodman Hall Juried Show, St. Catharines (1983, 1984); *Aspects of Contemporary Realism,* MacIntosh Public Gallery (1987); *Personal Vision in Landscape,* Cambridge Public Gallery (1987); Invitational '88, '89, '91, Nancy Poole's Studio; W.P.K. Kennedy Gallery, North Bay (1993); Wilfrid Laurier Univ. (1993). **HONS:** Jurors' Award, Nor Art Juried Show, 1982; Audience Award, Rodman Hall Juried Show, 1983; Best in Show, Rodman Hall Juried Show, 1984. **MISC:** *Virago,* cover painting for Alice Monro's *Lives of Girls and Women,* 1990; recipient, numerous Canada Council grants. **COMMENT:** *"I have to paint and realizing this (when I was 19), I have made all the choices in my life on the basis of whether they further my art."*

Pape, Patricia Lesley ■ ⑤
President, THE POWERPOINT GROUP, 131 Davenport Rd., Ste. 200, Toronto, ON M5R 1H8 (416) 923-1688, FAX 923-2862. Born Ghana, Africa 1955. s. **EDUC:** Univ. of Western Ontario, B.A.(Hons.) 1978. **CAREER:** various mktg positions (responsible for mktg brands such as Dial soap, Tenderflake & Nutriwhip), Grocery Products Group, Canada Packers; VP, Mktg (responsible for products such as Tampax & diversification into the home diagnostic mkt with the launch of First Response product line), Tambrands Canada Inc.; VP, Mktg (responsible for strategic focus & profitability of nat'l toy bus. & Nintendo), Mattel Canada Inc.; VP, Mktg & Sales, Domestic & Int'l Mkts, Infonet Media; Exec. Search Consultant, Spencer Stuart; Founder & Pres., The Powerpoint Group, responsible for the creation & promotion of the "Women of Influence" luncheon series, 1994 to date. **AFFIL:** Toronto International Film Festival (Mktg Advisory Bd.); Women Entrepreneurs of Canada (Bd. of Dir.); The Easter Seal Society (volunteer); Association of Canadian Advertisers (various positions, Bd. 1985-93); Broadcast Executive Society (Bd. of Dir. 1992).

Paquet, Suzanne, B.A.,M.B.A. ✎ ⑤ ⓟ
General Manager, Financial Publications, TRANSCONTINENTAL PUBLICATIONS INC., 1100 René-Lévesque Blvd. W., 24th Fl., Montreal, QC H3B 4X9 (514) 392-9000, FAX 392-1586. Born Sherbrooke, Que. m. Guy Bossé. 1 ch. **EDUC:** Univ. of Sherbrooke, B.A.(Econ.) 1971, M.B.A. 1973. **CAREER:** Asst. to the Mayor, Olympic Village, 1976 Olympic Games, 1973-76; sr. positions, Canada Mortgage and Housing Corporation, 1977-84; Gen. Mgr, Société québécoise d'information juridique, 1984-94; Gen. Mgr, Fin. Publications, Transcontinental Publications Inc., 1994 to date. **INTERESTS:** arts; literature; travel. **COMMENT:** *"People who know me well will say that I am a creative and very dynamic person. I believe that it is possible to be efficient and human at the same time. It is really important for me to succeed in my personal, family and professional life. I try to keep a good equilibrium."*

Paquin, Madeleine, H.B.A.,D.S.A. ■ ⑤
President and Chief Executive Officer, LOGISTEC CORPORATION, 360 St. Jacques W., Ste. 1500, Montreal, QC H2Y 1P5 (514) 844-9381, FAX 843-5217. Chairman, NORTEC MARINE AGENCIES INC. Born Quebec City 1962. m. Jacques Thevenoz. **EDUC:** Univ. of Western Ontario, H.B.A.(Bus.) 1984; Univ. de Montréal, D.S.A. (Bus.) 1989. **CAREER:** Pres., March Shipping Ltd., 1988-94; VP, Planning, Logistec Corpora-

tion, 1992-94; Pres., Nortec Marine Agencies Inc., 1994-95. DIRECTOR: Logistec Corporation; Sanexen Environmental Services. AFFIL: Shipping Federation of Canada (Dir.); Alliance of Manufacturers and Exporters (Dir.; Treas.; Co-Chair). INTERESTS: horse-back riding; golf; reading.

Paris, Erna, B.A. 🗐 🏛 ✎
Author and Journalist, 126 Felstead Ave., Toronto, ON M4J 1G4. Born Toronto 1938. m. Thomas M. Robinson. 2 ch. Michelle Paris, Roland Paris. EDUC: Univ. of Toronto, B.A.(Phil./English) 1960; Univ. de Paris, Cours de Civilisation Française 1961. CAREER: author, magazine feature writer; radio documentary; book reviewer; commentator, CJBC Radio (French language), 1972-75; columnist, *Chatelaine* magazine, 1979-80; regular contributor, *The Globe and Mail.* SELECTED PUBLICATIONS: *Jews: An Account of Their Experience in Canada* (Macmillan of Canada, 1980); *Stepfamilies: Making them Work* (Avon Books of Canada, 1984); *Unhealed Wounds: France and the Klaus Barbie Affair* (Toronto: Methuen Publications, 1985); *The Garden and the Gun: A Journey Inside Israel* (Toronto: Lester and Orpen Dennys, 1988); *The End of Days: A Story of Tolerance and the Expulsion of the Jews from Spain* (Toronto: Lester Publishing, 1995); contributor to *Her Own Woman: Profiles of Canadian Women* (Macmillan of Canada, 1975); *The Toronto Book* (Macmillan of Canada, 1975); *Shaping Identity in Canadian Society* (Prentice Hall, 1978); *The Spice Box: An Anthology of Jewish-Canadian Writing* (Lester and Orpen Dennys, 1981); *Beyond Imagination: Canadians Write About the Holocaust* (McClelland and Stewart, 1995). AFFIL: Canadian Periodical Writers' Association (Founding Mbr.); Writers' Union of Canada; PEN Canada (Bd.); Canadian Reprography Collective (CANCOPY) (Founding Mbr.). HONS: Feature Writing Award, Media Club of Canada, 1970, 1974; Radio Documentary Award, Media Club of Canada, 1973, 1974; Gold Medal, National Magazine Awards, 1983; included *in Best Canadian Essays of 1990*, Fifth House Press, 1990; White Award, Bronze Medal, N. America, City & Regional Magazine Competition, 1991; National Jewish Book Award (Hist.), 1995; Maclean-Hunter Fellowship Award, 1996. MISC: various guest lectures; mbr., various award & grant juries; listed in *Canadian Who's Who, World's Who's Who of Women.*

Parish, Barbara, B.A.,M.D., F.R.C.S.(C.) ■ 🐟 ⊕
Associate Professor, Department of Obstetrics

and Gynaecology, DALHOUSIE UNIVERSITY, 5980 University Ave., Halifax, NS B3H 4N1 (902) 420-3491, FAX 425-1125. Born Bristol, UK 1951. s. EDUC: York Univ., B.A.(Pol. Sci.) 1983; McMaster Univ., M.D. 1986. CAREER: Assoc. Prof., Dept. of Obstetrics & Gynaecology, Dalhousie Univ. SELECTED PUBLICATIONS: *Practice Guidelines for Obstetrical and Gynaecological Care of Women Living With HIV*, with others. AFFIL: Royal Coll. of Surgeons of Canada (Fellow in Obstetrics & Gynaecology); Canadian Medical Association; N.S. Medical Society; Society of Obstetricians & Gynaecologists of Canada (Social & Sexual Issues Committee); Supporters of FIGO; SOGC Peer Counselling Support Group; Physicians for Global Survival; Midwives' Association of N.S.; N.S. Rhododendron Society. HONS: Edward A. Beder Scholarship in Pol. Sci., York Univ. INTERESTS: obstetrics; women's reproductive health & sexuality; undergrad. medical educ.; interface between medical & social sci.; gardening; reading; walking; riding.

Parker, Anne, B.A.,LL.B. $ 𐤀
Legal Counsel and Director of Corporate Communications, IPSCO INC., Box 1670, Armour Rd., Regina, SK S4P 3C7 (306) 924-7390, FAX 924-7522. Born Regina 1959. s. EDUC: Univ. of Saskatchewan, B.A.(Hist.) 1982, LL.B. 1985. BAR: Sask., 1985. CAREER: Lawyer, McDougall Ready, Barristers & Solicitors, 1985-87; Legal Cnsl/Dir. of Corp. Comm., IPSCO Inc., 1987 to date. AFFIL: Globe Theatre (Chair); United Way of Regina (Dir.); Canadian Bar Association; Women's Legal Education & Action Fund.

Parker, Molly ■■ ⊗ 🍸
Actress. c/o Characters Talent Agency (Vancouver) Ltd., 1505 W. 2nd Ave., Ste. 200, Vancouver, BC V6H 3Y4 (604) 733-9800, FAX 733-6000. CAREER: trained as a dancer for 14 yrs. in Vancouver & with the Royal Winnipeg Ballet; lead & co-starring roles in features, movies of the week, & numerous guest spots on TV. SELECTED CREDITS: Films & movies of the week: Lead, *Intensity* (mini-series); Lead, *Kissed* (feature); Lead, *The Ranger, The Cook and a Hole in the Sky* (M.O.W.); Lead, *Paris or Somewhere* (M.O.W.); Co-star, *The Titanic* (mini-series); Co-Star, *Serving in Silence* (M.O.W.); numerous others. TV: Guest Star, *Poltergeist* (series); Guest Lead, *Lonesome Dove II* (series); Guest Star, *Neon Rider* (series); Principal, *The Outer Limits* (series); others. Theatre: Lead, *The Passion of Dracula.* HONS: nomination, Gemini Award (*Paris or Somewhere*), 1996; Artistic Award of Merit (*Kissed*), Women in Film and Video, 1996

Parkin, Margaret L., B.A.,B.L.S. 📖 ⚛ ☝
Retired Librarian. 60 McLeod St., Ste. 1005, Ottawa, ON K2P 2G1 (613) 238-5118. Born Toronto 1921. s. **EDUC:** Univ. of Toronto, B.A. 1942; Univ. Of Ottawa, B.L.S. 1960. **CAREER:** Commissioned Officer (Admin. (AE)), R.C.A.F., 1942-46, 1951-59; Jr. Research Officer, Div. of Mech. Eng., National Research Council of Canada, 1946-49; Asst. to the Scientific Adviser, Atomic Energy Control Bd., 1949-51; Eng., liaison activities, Aeronautical Eng. & Armament Div., R.C.A.F., 1951-59; Librarian in Circulation Dept., Ottawa Public Library, 1960; Tech. Writer, Northern Electric Research Establishment, 1960-61; Librarian, Econ. & Research Branch, Dept. of Labour, 1961-62; Librarian, Unemployment Insur. Commission, Ottawa, 1962-63; Librarian, Cataloguer, Carleton Univ. Library, 1963-64; Librarian, Canadian Nurses' Association, 1964-79; Cataloguer, Library, Canadian Council on Social Dev., 1979; Indexer, Canadian Periodical Index, Canadian Library Association, 1979-85; freelance indexer, 1979-92; contract librarian, to organize library & archives, Catholic Health Association of Canada, 1984-87. **SELECTED PUBLICATIONS:** "Information resources for nursing research" (*Canadian Nurse* 68(3) 1972); "Library services and the nursing profession in Canada" *(International Nursing Review* 16(1) 1969); "Library service for nurses: Current trends" (*Canadian Nurse* 64(3) 1968); "Resources and use of CNA Library" (*Canadian Nurse* 65(3) 1969); *Répertoire de titres française. Un guide d'utilisation des titres français dans l'international nursing index* (New York: American Journal of Nursing Co., 1970); *Index to Land Use By-Law Exceptions, City of Ottawa* (1982); index, *Aeronautical Research in Canada, 1917-1957: Memoirs of J.H. Parkin* (Ottawa: National Research Council of Canada, 1983); various other publications. **EDIT:** Ed., *Bulletin*, Div. of Mech. Eng., National Research Council, Vol. 1-3; Compiler, annual index, *Canadian Nurse*, 1964-78; Ed., Index of *Canadian Nursing Studies*, Compilations, 1964-78; Compiler, *Infirmière Canadienne*, Répertoire 1964-78. **AFFIL:** Victorian Order of Nurses (Past Sec.); Women's Canadian Club of Ottawa; Altar Guild, Christ Church Cathedral, Ottawa (Pres.). **MISC:** 1st permanent Sec., Assoc. Committee on Aeronautical Research & its 6 subcommittees.

Parkinson, E.A. (Dee), B.Sc.(Eng.), M.B.A. $
Executive Vice-President, Oil Sands Group, SUNCOR INC., Box 4001, Fort McMurray, AB T9H 3E3 (403) 643-6425, FAX 791-8321. Born Dartmouth, N.S. 1948. m. Michel Marcoux. **EDUC:** Queen's Univ., B.Sc.(Eng.-Metallurgy) 1970, M.B.A.(Oper.) 1976. **CAREER:** various positions, Imperial Oil Ltd., 1976-83; various positions to Gen. Mgr, Western Reg. Refining, Petro-Canada, 1983-91; VP, Supply & Svcs, Ontario Hydro, 1990-91; Exec. VP, Oil Sands Group, Suncor Inc., 1991 to date. **SELECTED PUBLICATIONS:** *Capital Cost Estimating for Mineral Processing* (1972). **AFFIL:** YWCA of Canada (Dir. 1989-93); Alberta Chamber of Resources (VP); 1989 Canadian Eng. Memorial Foundation (Dir.); appointed, Nat'l Round Table on the Environment & the Economy (NRTEE). **HONS:** Resources Person of the Year Award, Alberta Chamber of Resources, 1994. **INTERESTS:** amateur botanist; hiking; photography; writing. **COMMENT:** *"Curiosity is the key to leadership. An inquisitive mind prepares you for a world of change, and it provides you with the ability to change the world."*

Parks, Bev, B.A. ■■ ♡ ✊
Executive Director, TERRA ASSOCIATION (not-for-profit agency, meeting the challenge of teen pregnancy), 10435 - 76 St., Edmonton, AB T6A 3B1 (403) 465-9272, FAX 469-2185. Born Peace River, Alta. 1956. m. Gary. 2 ch. Megan, Mindy. **EDUC:** Univ. of Alberta, B.A. (Psych.) 1976. **CAREER:** Special Needs Employment Officer, CEIC, 1976-90; Social Worker, Social Svcs, 1990-92; Coord., Peace Country Crisis Association, 1990-93; Sr. Dev. Officer, Northern Dev., 1992-93; Exec. Dir., Terra Association, 1993 to date. **AFFIL:** Lansdowne Elementary Sch. (Chairperson, Sch. Council 1995-96); United Way Cabinet (Chair, Agency Liaison 1996-97); Vision 2005, Edmonton (mbr.). **HONS:** Community Svc. Citation, United Way, 1995. **INTERESTS:** local theatre; travel; music. **MISC:** instrumental in starting a women's shelter in Peace River. **COMMENT:** *"As a mother of two, dedicated wife and a human services provider, I have made a lifetime commitment to working towards helping to build healthy communities and in this regard, I firmly believe that prevention is the key."*

Parr, Joy, B.A.,M.Phil.,Ph.D. 🎓 📜
Farley Professor of History, SIMON FRASER UNIVERSITY, Burnaby, BC V5A 1S6 (604) 291-3406, FAX 291-5837, EMAIL joy_parr@sfu.ca. Born Toronto 1949. m. Gregory Levine. **EDUC:** McGill Univ., B.A.(Econ.) 1971; Yale Univ., M.Phil.(Econ. Hist.) 1973, Ph.D.(Hist.) 1977. **CAREER:** Asst. Prof., Univ. of British Columbia, 1976-78; Asst./Assoc./Full Prof., Dept. of Hist., Queen's Univ., 1979-92; Coord. of Women's Studies, 1989-90; Farley Prof. of

Hist. (endowed chair), Simon Fraser Univ., 1992 to date. **SELECTED PUBLICATIONS:** *Labouring Children* (1980); *Childhood and Family in Canadian History* (1982); *Canadian Women on the Move* (1983); *Still Running* (1986); *The Gender of Breadwinners* (1990); *A Diversity of Women 1945-80* (1995); *Gender and History in Canada* (1996). **AFFIL:** Uppsala Univ. (Swedish Institute Fellow 1991-93); Radcliffe Coll. (Bunting Fellow 1992); Royal Society of Canada (Fellow); All Souls Coll., Oxford, UK (Fellow). **HONS:** Harold Innis Award; Macdonald Prize; Berkshire Prize; Laura Jamieson Prize; Fred Landon Award. **INTERESTS:** industrial design, consumer goods, consumer organizations & macroeconomic policy in Canada & Sweden 1945-68.

Parr-Johnston, Elizabeth, B.A.,M.A., Ph.D. ■ 🎓 $

President and Vice-Chancellor, THE UNIVERSITY OF NEW BRUNSWICK, P.O. Box 4400, Fredericton, NB E3B 5A3 (506) 453-4567, FAX 453-4599. Born 1939. m. A.F. Johnston. 2 ch. **EDUC:** Wellesley Coll., B.A.(Econ.) 1961; Yale Univ., M.A.(Econ.) 1962, Ph.D.(Econ.) 1973; Harvard Bus. Sch., MISR Certificate 1986. **CAREER:** Instructor, Huron Coll., Univ. of Western Ontario, 1964-67; Instructor, Dept. of Econ., Univ. of British Columbia, 1967-71; Visiting Scholar, Dept. of Econ., Wesleyan Univ., 1971-72; Academic Research Assoc., Dept. of Econ., Carleton Univ., 1972-73; Sr. Analyst, Multinat'l Enterprises Sections, Statistics Canada, 1973-74; Chief, Inter-Reg'l Analysis, Dept. of Reg'l Econ. Expansion, Gov't of Canada, 1974-75; Dir., Econ. Dev. Analysis, Dept. of Reg'l Econ. Analysis, 1974-76; Sr. Policy Analyst, Public Affairs, Inco Limited, Toronto, 1976-77; Dir. of Gov't Affairs, 1977-79; Chief of Staff & Sr. Policy Advisor, Fed. Min. of Employment & Immigration, 1979-80; Mgr, Socio-Pol. Analysis, Corp. Planning, Shell Canada Limited, Calgary, 1980-81; Mgr, Macro Environment, Corp. Strategies, 1981-84; Mgr, Bus. Environment, Corp. Strategies, 1984-85; Mgr, Computer Svcs, 1985-86; Mgr, Info. & Computing Oper., 1986-87; Mgr, Info. Technology, Info. & Computing, 1987-88; Mgr, Products Strategic Systems, 1988-90; Pres. & V-Chancellor, Mount Saint Vincent Univ., 1991-96; Pres. & V-Chancellor, The Univ. of New Brunswick, 1996 to date. **DIRECTOR:** Bank of Nova Scotia; The Empire Company Ltd.; Fishery Products International Limited; Nova Scotia Power Incorporated. **AFFIL:** Council of Nova Scotia University Presidents (Chair 1993-94); Association of Atlantic Universities (V-Chair 1991-94; Chair); Association of Universities & Colleges in Canada (Bd. Mbr.); Social Sciences & Humanities Research Council; Canadian Economics Association; Canadian Association for Community Living (Hon. Advisory Bd.); Council for Canadian Unity (Dir.); North/South Institute (Dir.); Phi Beta Kappa. **HONS:** Woodrow Wilson Fellow, 1962; Canada 125 Medal, 1992; Women of Excellence Award, Progress Club, 1993.

Parrish, Carolyn, M.P. 🍁

Member of Parliament (Mississauga West), GOVERNMENT OF CANADA, House of Commons, 812 Confederation Building, Ottawa, ON K1A 0A6 (613) 995-7321, FAX 992-6708. Born Toronto 1946. m. David. 2 ch. **EDUC:** Ontario Coll. of Education, Certificate 1970. **CAREER:** secondary sch. teacher, Etobicoke & Peel; writer & artist; Trustee, Peel Bd. of Educ., 1985-88; Chair, 1988-92; M.P. (Mississauga W.), Gov't of Canada, 1993 to date. **AFFIL:** Liberal Party of Canada; Cancer Fund; Heart Fund; Streetsville Cenotaph Renovation Proj.; Cheshire House. **COMMENT:** *"Carolyn Parrish is Member of Parliament for the federal riding of Mississauga West, Canada's second-largest riding. Carolyn has always been an active member of her community. She is a widely published writer and artist."*

Parry, Caroline Balderston, B.A. 📜 📖 🎓

Author, Performer and Teacher. **EDUC:** Radcliffe Coll., Harvard Univ., B.A.(Am. Hist. & Lit.) 1966; Hull Coll. of Educ., Yorkshire, UK, Grad. Certificate in Educ. 1971. **CAREER:** Certified Re-Evaluation Counseling Teacher; Folktale Consultant, Houghton Mifflin Canada; Ed., *The Canadian Friend*, 1994; Correspondant, *The Ottawa Citizen*. **SELECTED CREDITS:** *Banana Split*, with other Mariposa in the Schools artists, 1984; *Circle of Friends*, with other Mariposa in the Schools Artists, 1990. **SELECTED PUBLICATIONS:** *Let's Celebrate Canada's Special Days* (Toronto: Kids Can Press, 1987); *Eleanora's Diary, The Journals of a Canadian Pioneer Girl* (Richmond Hill, Ont.: Scholastic Canada, 1994); various magazine articles; ed. of poems in *Zoomerang a Boomerang* (Toronto: Kids Can Press, 1991). **AFFIL:** Writers' Union of Canada; Toronto Musicians' Association; Mariposa in the Schools; Storytellers Sch. of Toronto; Multicultural Arts in Schools & Communities; CANSCAIP; Ontario Historical Society; Society of Friends (Quakers). **HONS:** Book Award, IODE Toronto, 1987; Info. Book Award, Children's Literature Roundtables, 1988. **MISC:** recipient, various grants. **COMMENT:** *"Folksinger, storyteller, non-fiction and poetry writer, editor, artist-in-residence, consultant, speaker, counselor, teacher, library lover; celebrator!"*

Parsons, Catriona Niclomhair, M.A. ✄ 🕮
Assistant Professor, Celtic Studies Department, ST. FRANCIS XAVIER UNIVERSITY, Antigonish, NS B2G 2W5 (902) 867-2206, FAX 867-2448. Born Isle of Lewis, Scotland 1940. m. Rev. W.E. Parsons. 1 ch. EDUC: Edinburgh Univ., M.A.(English Lang.) 1961, Grad. Dipl.(Gen. Linguistics) 1969. CAREER: Head of Gaelic Instruction & Programming/Dir., Jr. & Sr. Choirs/Organizer, Gaelic Segment of N.S. Gaelic Mòd, Gaelic Coll. of Arts & Crafts Summer Schools, 1978 to date; Lecturer then Sr. Lecturer, Dartmouth Coll., Hanover, NH, 1984-96; developer & writer, Gaelic course for high sch. & adult beginners in the language, *Gaidhlig troimh chomhradh (Gaelic Through Conversation)*, 3 volumes, each with 3 90-minute tapes, 1989, 1990, 1991, 1993; Asst. Prof., Celtic Studies, St. Francis Xavier Univ. SELECTED PUBLICATIONS: various articles in Gaelic & English, incl. "The Gaelic Songs of Lewis," "Gàidhlig ann a'Vermont," "Naidheachd na Gàidhlig bho Cheap Breatainn" (Comann luchd-Ionnsachaidh Cuairtlitir, Inverness, Scotland); poetry in *GAIRM*, Scotland's Gaelic Quarterly. AFFIL: North American Association of Celtic Language Teachers; Scottish Club of Twin States. HONS: twice Finalist, Mòd Gold Medal Competitions, National Mòd, Scotland; Lt.-Governor's Award, Solo Singing, Mòd Ont., 1984; Winner, Oran Mòr Competition, National Mòd, Scotland, 1989; Flora MacDonald Award for Svcs to Gaelic Educ., 1994. INTERESTS: languages; music; travelling; writing Gaelic poetry. COMMENT: *"My chief pleasure is in working to promote Gaelic language and culture (particularly Gaelic song) and to instill a love of both in my students, in North America and beyond."*

Pascall, Bonnie, B.A. ■ $
Manager, Corporate Communications, HUSKY OIL LTD., 707 - 8th Ave. S.W., Calgary, AB T2P 1H7 (403) 298-7188, FAX 298-6799. Born Haileybury, Ont. 1951. m. Terrence. 2 ch. Darcy, Stephanie. EDUC: Univ. of Calgary, B.A.(Comm.) 1989. CAREER: Comm. Consultant, Towers Perrin, 1989-92; Dir., Community Rel'ns, Carewest, 1992-94; Corp. Comm. Mgr, Husky Oil Ltd., 1994 to date. AFFIL: Petroleum Communication Foundation (Gov.); Mount Royal Coll. (Program Advisor, Public Rel'ns); International Association of Business Communicators (Past Pres., Calgary Chapter); Univ. of Calgary (Past Fac. Advisor, Gen. Studies Program). HONS: Gold Quill of Excellence, International Association of Business Communicators. MISC: presenter & speaker at various bus. conferences. COMMENT: *"After many years in the workforce, I returned to school in*

the 1980s. I am still pursuing my education and am just completing a Masters in Communication Studies at the University of Calgary."

Paschal, Ada G., C.M.,M.A.,B.S.W., R.S.W. ■■ ⊕ ♡
Director, AMANA HOUSE (centre for addictions recovery), 371 Dufferin Row, Saint John, NB E2M 2J7 (506) 635-5735. EDUC: Mount Carmel Academy, Hons. Secretarial 1943; Dalhousie Univ., B.S.W. 1986; Univ. of New Brunswick, post-grad. course in educ. 1987; Summit Univ. of Louisiana, M.A.(thesis: recovery from addictions) 1992; numerous workshops/courses on addictions, suicide prevention, assertiveness training, etc. CAREER: secretarial positions, Saint John, N.B. & Thunder Bay, Ont., 1967-80; Ridgewood Treatment & Rehabilitation Centre, 1980-85; founder & Dir., Amana House, 1985 to date. VOLUNTEER CAREER: experience with: Elizabeth Fry Society of Saint John (founding mbr.); Saint John Community-Based Coalition on Housing; Breast Cancer Research Committee; Friendship Hall; Mayor's Committee on Alcoholism, Saint John. AFFIL: N.B. Association of Social Workers; Saint John Council of Women; International Association of Residential & Community Alternatives; Canadian Association of Children of Alcoholics; Canadian Criminal Justice Association. HONS: Woman of the Year, Beta Sigma Phi sororities, 1988; Canada 125 Medal, 1992; Member of the Order of Canada, Gov't of Canada, 1992; Certificate of Recognition, U.N. Association, 1994; Spiritus Award, Advisory Council on the Status of Women, 1996; nominated for Persons Award & Royal Bank Award.

Passmore, Janet M., B.Sc. $
Vice-President, Group Marketing, MUTUAL LIFE OF CANADA, 227 King St. S., Waterloo, ON N2J 4C5 (519) 888-3927, FAX 888-2990. Born St. Thomas, Ont. m. Phil. 1 ch. EDUC: Univ. of Waterloo, B.Sc.(Kinesiology) 1978; Queen's Univ., Certificate (Exec. Bus.) 1992. CAREER: various positions to VP, Group Mktg, Mutual Life of Canada, 1978 to date. AFFIL: Parent Advisory Committee, local elementary sch. (Chair 1994 to date); Women's Institute. INTERESTS: continuous learning for self & others; athletics; agric.; educ.; children. COMMENT: *"Have benefited greatly from the counsel and coaching of others and strive to return to society and those I work with whatever I can to help them attain their goals."*

Paterson, Janet, B.A.,M.Ed.,Ed.D. ■■ ✄
Executive Dean, School of Applied Arts and Business, ALGONQUIN COLLEGE, 1385

Woodroffe Ave., Nepean, ON K2G 1V8 (613) 727-4723, ext. 5795, FAX 727-7659, EMAIL patersj@algonquinc.on.ca. Born Toronto 1947. m. 2 ch. Creighton, Heather. EDUC: Ryerson Polytechnic Institute, Diploma (Bus.-Sec. Sci.) 1968; York Univ., B.A.(Pol. Sci.) 1974; Univ. of Ottawa, M.Ed.(Psychopedagogy) 1982; Nova Southeastern Univ., Ed.D.(Higher Educ.) 1996. CAREER: Teacher & Asst. Dept. Head, Vincent Massey Collegiate, Etobicoke Bd. of Educ., 1968-71; Hum. Res., Microsystems International, 1971-72; Prof./Coord./Assoc. Registrar/Continuing Educ. Dir./Dean of Arts, Algonquin Coll., 1972-94; Exec. Dean, Sch. of Applied Arts & Bus., 1994 to date. SELECTED PUBLICATIONS: "The Development of an Alternative Approach to Curriculum Delivery" (*Adult Training Magazine*, Vol. 11, 1978); "Key Issues in Higher Education" (*Canadian Vocational Journal*, Vol. 28, No. 4, 1993). AFFIL: Ontario Heads of Applied Arts (Chair 1992 to date); TVOntario (Prov. Distance Learning Committee 1982 to date); Ottawa Carleton Research Institute (Co-Chair, Employability Skills Profile Committee 1994 to date); Youth Services Bureau, Ottawa (Pres., Bd. of Dir. 1996); Ottawa Board of Trade. HONS: Administrator of the Year Award, Algonquin Coll., 1991. INTERESTS: power boating; gardening; travel; reading. MISC: conducted seminars & needs analysis in countries such as South Africa, Thailand & Hong Kong; community work with City of Kanata, Girl Guides & St. Isidore's Church. COMMENT: "*Having completed three university degrees part time with a career and a family, the concept of balance and performance has become second nature. As an academic and now an administrator, the opportunity to move and assume various positions has provided a wide scope of experience and opportunity. Utilizing this background with information technology and international education helps position Canadian education (with several other Canadians) on the world scene. Continuous community involvement particularly with youth has provided a wonderful sense of purpose.*"

Paterson, Janet M., B.A.,M.A., Ph.D. ■ ◁ 🗎 ❀
Associate Dean, Faculty of Arts and Science, UNIVERSITY OF TORONTO, 100 St. George St., Rm. 2020, Toronto, ON M5S 3G3 (416) 978-3390, FAX 978-3887. Born Berne, Switzerland 1944. m. John A. Paterson. 3 ch. John, Neil, Danielle. EDUC: Univ. of Toronto, B.A. 1964, M.A.(French) 1975, Ph.D.(French Lit.) 1981. CAREER: Language Teacher, Reform Sch. for Girls, Toronto, 1965-70; Instructor, St. Michael's Coll., Univ. of Toronto, 1970-74;

Prof., Dept. of French, Univ. of Toronto, 1981 to date; Chair for Grad. Studies, Dept. of French, 1991-95. SELECTED PUBLICATIONS: *Anne Hébert: architexture romanesque* (Ottawa: Presses de l'Univ. d'Ottawa, 1985); *Moments postmodernes dans le roman québécois* (Ottawa: Presses de l'Univ. d'Ottawa, 1990); *Challenges, Projects, Texts: Canadian Editing*, co-ed. with John Lennox (New York: AMS Press, 1993); *Hubert Aquin: Trou de mémoire critical edition* ed. with Marilyn Randall (Montreal: Leméac, 1993); *Postmodernism and the Quebec Novel* tr. David Homel & Charles Phillips (Toronto: Univ. of Toronto Press, 1994); 35 articles & chapters in books. EDIT: *Theory/Culture* series, Univ. of Toronto Press, 1993 to date. AFFIL: Association for Canadian & Quebec Literature (VP 1982-84); Association for Canadian Studies (Sec.-Treas. 1987-91). HONS: Gabrielle Roy Prize for best French language critical work of the year, 1990. INTERESTS: cycling; hiking; skiing. COMMENT: "*Professor, literary critic and mother of three children. Has written and lectured extensively on contemporary Quebec fiction. Active in several national scholarly organizations.*"

Paterson, Jody ■ ✎ 🗎 ♦
Managing Editor, VICTORIA TIMES-COLONIST, 2621 Douglas St., Box 300, Victoria, BC V8W 2N4 (604) 380-5333, FAX 380-5353. Born Saskatoon 1956. d. 3 ch. Daniel, Regan, Rachelle. EDUC: Cariboo Coll., Certificate (Comm./Media) 1982. CAREER: piano teacher, Courtenay, B.C., 1974-81; reporter, *Kamloops Sentinel*, 1982-87; reporter, *Kamloops Daily News*, 1987-89; reporter, *Victoria Times-Colonist*, 1989-93; City Ed., 1993-95; Asst. Mng Ed., 1995-96; Mng Ed., 1996 to date. AFFIL: Canadian Association of Journalists. HONS: Best Editorial, B.C. Newspaper Awards, 1989; Runner-up for Best News Story, Jack Webster Awards, 1989. INTERESTS: singing opera & accompanying other singers on piano; body-building; pets & plants; writing; raising my kids. MISC: 1st woman Mng. Ed. of the *Victoria Times-Colonist*. COMMENT: "*Having had my first child at age 17, I'd like to be a reminder to young mothers that the options are always open. I like change and an element of unpredictability in my life, so I don't know where my career will lead. But I've got energy for anything.*"

Patkau, Patricia, M.Arch. ■ ■ ❀ ◁
Principal, PATKAU ARCHITECTS, 560 Beatty St., Ste. 100, Vancouver, BC V6B 2L3. Associate Professor, School of Architecture, UNIVERSITY OF BRITISH COLUMBIA. Born Winnipeg 1950.

EDUC: Univ. of Manitoba, Bachelor of Interior Design 1973; Yale Univ., M.Arch. 1978. CAREER: Principal, Patkau Architects; Asst. Prof., Sch. of Arch., Univ. of California, L.A., 1988-90; Assoc. Prof., Sch. of Arch., Univ. of British Columbia, 1992 to date. EXHIBITIONS: over 20 exhibitions incl.: travelling exhibition, London, RIBA Gallery/Edinburgh, Matthew Architecture Gallery/Barcelona, Collegi d'Arquitectes de Catalunya/N.Y., Architecture League, 1994; travelling exhibition, Boston, Harvard Univ./Toronto, The Design Centre/Ann Arbor, Univ. of Michigan/Halifax, Technical Univ. of N.S., 1995; travelling exhibition, Troy, Rensselaer Polytechnic Institute/Spokane, Chase Gallery, 1996. AFFIL: Architectural Institute of British Columbia; Royal Canadian Academy of Arts; Royal Architectural Institute of Canada (Fellow). HONS: Gold Medal, Univ. of Manitoba, 1973; numerous professional awards incl.: Gov. Gen.'s Award for Arch., 1986, 1990, 1992 & 1994. MISC: Juror, numerous design competitions; Visiting Critic, U.S. & Cdn universities; Visiting Prof., Grad. Sch. of Design, Harvard Univ., 1993, William Lyon Somerville Visiting Lectureship, Univ. of Calgary, 1994, & Eliot Noyes Prof. of Arch., Grad. Sch. of Design, Harvard Univ., 1995; numerous lectures, universities & architects' associations, internationally, 1980 to date; featured in many books & articles about architecture, 1993 to date, incl. *Patkau Architects: Selected Projects 1983-1993* (Brian Carter, ed., Halifax: TUNS Press, Documents in Canadian Architecture, 1994).

Patten, Monica, B.A. ■■ ○ ⦿

Executive Director, COMMUNITY FOUNDATIONS OF CANADA (nat'l membership organization supporting Canada's 75 community foundations), 150 Laurier Ave. W., Ste. 320, Ottawa, ON K1P 5J4 (613) 236-1616, FAX 236-1621, EMAIL cfcmp@ibm.net. Born London, UK 1945. w. 3 ch. Alan, Jeffrey, Jocelyn. EDUC: McDonald Coll., McGill Univ., Diploma in Educ. 1964; Carleton Univ., B.A.(Arts) 1987. CAREER: Exec. Dir., Volunteer Centre of Ottawa-Carleton; VP, United Way/Centraide Canada; Exec. Dir., Community Foundations of Canada. AFFIL: The Well/La Source (Chair, Mgmt Committee 1993 to date); Family Service Centre, Ottawa-Carleton (Bd. mbr.); Anglican Church of Canada (Fin. Mgmt & Dev. Committee); Anglican Diocese of Ottawa (Community Ministries Coordinating Committee); Univ. of Ottawa (Chair, Advisory Committee, Voluntary Sector Mgmt Program). HONS: numerous recognition (local & prov.) citations for volunteer & community work. INTERESTS: walking/hiking; cooking. COMMENT: *"I have a keen interest in promoting volunteerism and the contribution voluntary organizations make to community life. Frequently am guest speaker or workshop leader on issues related to community. Taught for 8 years at Algonquin College (Continuing Education). I believe passionately that citizens make a difference at the community level and I work hard to promote citizen participation."*

Patten, Susan H. Ⓢ ⦿

Chairman, A. HARVEY & CO. LTD., 87 Water St., St. John's, NF A1C 5V6 (709) 726-8000, FAX 726-9891. Born St. John's 1933. m. Charles N. 4 ch. CAREER: Chrm, A. Harvey & Co. Ltd.; A. Harvey and Co. Ltd.; Browning Harvey Ltd.; Harvey's Oil Ltd. AFFIL: World Association of Girl Guides & Girl Scouts (Treas.); Bank of Canada (Past Dir.).

Patten Di Giacomo, Rose ■ Ⓢ

Senior Vice-President, Corporate Services, BANK OF MONTREAL, First Canadian Place, Toronto, ON M5X 1A1 (416) 867-6800, FAX 867-6836. Born Nfld. 1945. m. Thomas A. Di Giacomo. EDUC: Memorial Univ., Psych. & Math. CAREER: VP & Gen. Mgr, Lloyds Bank, 1975-87; Sr. VP, Manulife Financial, 1987-91; Exec. VP & Dir., Hum. Res. & Organizational Mgmt, Nesbitt Burns Inc., 1991-95; Sr. VP, Corp. Svcs, Bank of Montreal, 1995 to date. SELECTED PUBLICATIONS: various case studies & articles in journals. DIRECTOR: CFCF Inc. AFFIL: Univ. of Toronto (Dir.); National Ballet of Canada (Dir.); Conference Board of Canada (Dir.; Advisory Group). INTERESTS: skiing; boating; running; gardening. COMMENT: *"I'm an agent of change. I can't develop my own niche. My world revolves around what the business needs. And when that changes, I have to adapt."*

Patterson, Linda ⦿

Chairperson, NEW BRUNSWICK BLOCK PARENT ASSOCIATION INC., 100 Howe Cres., Apt. 47, Oromocto, NB E2V 2R3 (506) 446-5992, FAX 446-5992. EDUC: QECVI, Kingston, Ont., Commercial 1973. CAREER: clerical support staff to the Dir., Kingston Interval House & Women's Training & Employment Program, 1982-83; gen. office work, Big Sisters, Kingston, Ont., 1983-84; Town Councillor, Town of Oromocto, 1987-92; Prov. Coord., Nat'l Access Awareness Week, 1992. AFFIL: N.B. Block Parent Association (Chair); National Block Parent Association of Canada. COMMENT: *"I took over the reins of the New Brunswick Block Parent Association at a time when it needed new ideas. We have been able to increase our funds and the number of com-*

munities offering the program in New Brunswick."

Patterson, Margaret (Peggy), Ed.D., M.A.,B.A. ■ ✑

Associate Vice-President (Student Affairs), THE UNIVERSITY OF CALGARY, 2500 University Dr. N.W., Calgary, AB T2N 1N4 (403) 220-6580, FAX 289-6800, EMAIL 62113@ ucdasvm1.admin.ucalgary.ca. Born Toronto 1948. d. 3 ch. EDUC: Univ. of Guelph, B.A. 1970, M.A. 1973; McMaster Univ., Clinical Behavioral Sciences, Selected Studies 1985; Univ. of Toronto, Ed.D. 1991. CAREER: Research Assoc. & Instructor, Royal Prince Alfred Hospital, Sydney, Australia, 1973-75; Sessional Lecturer & Researcher, Dept. of Psych., Univ. of Guelph, 1975-77; Learning Skills Advisor, Counselling & Student Resource Centre, 1977-88; Asst. to the Assoc. VP, Student Affairs, 1988-93; cross-appt., Course Instructor, Special Grad. Fac., 1990 to date; Dir., Educ. & Planning Svcs, Office of Student Affairs, 1993-96; Assoc. VP (Student Affairs), Univ. of Calgary, 1996 to date. SELECTED PUBLICATIONS: "Interaction Between Students in Multidisciplinary Health Teams," with Susan Hayes (*Journal of Medical Education* 50 1975); "Verbal Communication in Students in Multidisciplinary Health Teams," with Susan Hayes (*Medical Education* 1977); *Student Development Theory: An Overview (Student Services Monograph Series,* Univ. of Guelph, 1985); "Transition to University: An Opportunity for Growth," with K. Beatty & M. Eisenbach (*The School Guidance Worker,* Jan. 1993); "Exploring the Country in Not Climbing a Ladder," in *The Doctoral Thesis Journey,* A. Cole & D. Hunt, eds. (Toronto: OISE, 1994). AFFIL: Canadian Association of College & University Student Services; Council for the Advancement of Standards in Higher Education; Learning & Study Skills Association; American College Personnel Association. HONS: Canada 125 Medal, 1992; Award for Significant Contributions to the Profession, Canadian Association of College & University Student Services, 1987; Award for Svc., Canadian Association of College & University Student Services, for Professional & Personal Contributions to Student Svcs, 1986, 1994. INTERESTS: gardening. MISC: *Study Skills,* 3-part video series (Office of Educational Practice, Univ. of Guelph, 1982). COMMENT: *"I have been pursuing the study and application of research in human development in higher education for almost 30 years. I am one of a handful of Canadians holding a doctorate in this area and have used my training to lecture extensively, as well as to hold leadership positions in the field of student life in Canada."*

Pau, Janet, B.A.,C.F.A. ⓢ

Vice-President and Treasurer, CANFOR CORPORATION, 1055 Dunsmuir St., Ste. 2900, Box 49420, Vancouver, BC V7X 1B5 (604) 661-5275, FAX 661-5472. Vice-President and Treasurer, CANADIAN FOREST PRODUCTS LTD. m. I.F. MacPhail. EDUC: York Univ., B.A. (Econ.) 1979. CAREER: Asst. Portfolio Mgr/ Money Mkt Trader, Bank of Nova Scotia, 1979-83; various positions, Canfor Corporation, 1983-88; Treas. & Officer, Canfor Corporation & Canadian Forest Products Ltd., 1988-95; VP & Treas., 1995 to date; Treas. & Officer, Howe Sound Pulp and Paper Limited, 1989 to date. AFFIL: Vancouver Art Gallery (former Trustee); Vancouver Stock Exchange (former Public Gov.); Fac. of Commerce, Univ. of British Columbia (Advisory Bd. for the Bureau of Asset Mgmt); Vancouver Society of Financial Analysts (C.F.A.; Pres. 1995); Treasury Management Association of B.C. (Past Treas.); Financial Executives' Institute; St. Paul's Hospital (Trustee). INTERESTS: skiing; tennis; golf; reading.

Paul, Louise, LL.L. ⓢ

Vice-President, Legal and Secretary, CORBY DISTILLERIES LTD., 1002 Sherbrooke St. W., Ste. 2300, Montreal, QC H3A 3L6 (514) 288-4181, FAX 288-0749. Born Val d'Or, Que. 1950. d. 2 ch. EDUC: Univ. of Ottawa, LL.L. BAR: Que., 1978. CAREER: Attorney, Cnsl & Dir., Composers', Authors' & Publishers' Association of Canada, 1978-80; Assoc., Gourd et Brunet, Attorneys, 1980-81; Ptnr, Champagne, Boucher and Paul, Attorneys, 1981-84; private practice of law, 1984-86; Legal Cnsl, Dir. of Corp. Affairs & Asst. Sec., Atlantique Image et Son Inc., 1986-87; VP, Legal & Sec., Corby Distilleries Limited, 1987 to date. AFFIL: Bar of Quebec; Better Business Bureau; Board of Trade of Metropolitan Montreal.

Pauli, Lori, B.A.,M.A. ■ ⊗ 📖

Assistant Curator, Photographs Collection, NATIONAL GALLERY OF CANADA, 380 Sussex Dr., Ottawa, ON K1N 9N4 (613) 990-0600, EMAIL lpauli@ngc.cwn.gc.ca. Born Guelph, Ont. 1960. m. Bruce Pauli. EDUC: Univ. of Waterloo, B.A.(Dance) 1982; Queen's Univ., M.A.(Art Hist.) 1990. CAREER: Curator, York Sunbury Historical Society Museum; Teaching Asst., Dept. of Art, Queen's Univ.; Curatorial Asst., Dept. of European Art, National Gallery of Canada; Curatorial Asst., Photographs Dept. SELECTED PUBLICATIONS: "Disciple of the American Dream: Listte Model" (*The World and I* 4 vol.7); "Silent Communion: Christel Gang and Edward Weston" (*History of Photography* 2 vol.19); "A Few Hellers: Women at the Clarence H. White School of Photography," in *Margaret Watkins 1884-1969 Photographs*, ed. by Martha McCulloch (Glasgow: Street Level Gallery and Workshop, 1994). **AFFIL:** Coll. Arts Association. **HONS:** Educ. Award, Univ. of New Brunswick. **INTERESTS:** reading; writing; dance; films. **COMMENT:** *"My career as an arts historian is really only just beginning. My main goals are to find out more about women and their contributions to photography; to rescue their histories from oblivion."*

Pavey, Mary Gunilla, R.C.A. 🎨
Painter. Toronto, ON M6H 3Z2. Born Stockholm 1938. 2 ch. Karin Pavey (ceramist), Sven Pavey (wood worker). **EDUC:** Ontario Coll. of Art, Hons. Diploma in Fine Arts 1980. **CAREER:** Prod., commercials, Foster Advertising/Vickers & Benson/MacLaren Advertising, 1966-76; full-time painter since 1980. **SELECTED PUBLICATIONS:** work published by Posters International. **EXHIBITIONS:** various solo exhibitions, incl. Gustafsson Galleries, Toronto (1982, 1983); Thomas Gallery, Port Hope (1984); Belleville Public Library Gallery (1986); Quan-Schieder Gallery, Toronto (1986, 1987, 1988, 1989, 1990); Peel Regional Gallery, Brampton (1989); Shayne Gallery, Montreal (1990); Wallace Galleries, Calgary (1992); Gallery One, Toronto (1992, 1993); various group exhibitions, incl. Pauline McGibbon Cultural Centre (1981); O'Keefe Centre, Toronto (1988); Ontario Society of Artists, juried exhibition (1989); Shayne Gallery, Montreal (1992); exhibition & poster, Parkinson Foundation, 1988; exhibition, Belleville Public Library, together with an exhibition of works by David Milne at Baptiste Lake (1984). **COLLECTIONS:** Canaccord Capital Corporation; DuPont Canada Limited; General Electric Canada Limited; Sony Canada Limited; Famous Players; Four Seasons Hotels; Glaxo Canada Limited; McLean House; North York Board of Education; Parkinson Foundation; Partners Film Company; Teddington Properties Limited; various other corp. collections; many private collections in Canada & abroad, incl. the Alex Trebec collection. **AFFIL:** Royal Canadian Academy of Arts; Ontario Society of Artists. **HONS:** Award, Peel Region Juried exhibition, 1986. **MISC:** represented in Toronto by Gallery One, in Montreal by Shayne Gallery, in Calgary by Wallace Galleries, & in Vancouver by Horizon Gallery.

Pawlick, Linda, B.A. ■■ ♡ $
Owner/Operator, PURRFECTLY CATS (specialty retail outlet for cat lovers), 37 Lido Dr., Stoney Creek, ON L8E 5E8 (905) 643-0528. **EDUC:** McMaster Univ., B.A.(Psych.) 1976; Mohawk Coll., Small Bus. Mgmt Program 1992. **CAREER:** Info. Counsellor, Community Info. Svc., Hamilton-Wentworth, 1976-81; Resource Officer, 1981-83; Community Dev. Consultant, McQuesten Legal & Community Svcs, 1983-85; Community Rel'ns Worker, Hamilton-Wentworth Housing Authority, 1985-91; Property Mgr, Apr.-Dec. 1989; Retail Sales Clerk, The Body Shop, 1991; Owner/Operator, Purrfectly Cats, 1992 to date. **AFFIL:** Multiple Sclerosis Society of Canada, Hamilton chpt. (Pres./VP/mbr. 1985-90); United Way of Hamilton-Wentworth/Burlington (mbr., Budget Panel 1991); Social Planning & Research Council of Hamilton-Wentworth (V-Chairperson & mbr., Community Dev. Advisory Committee 1983-85); Hamilton Alcoholism Workers' Council (former Treas.); Social Assistance Resource Service (former Chairperson, Bd. of Dir.); Kenora Skills Through Activity and Recreation program (former Co-Sec.). **HONS:** Best Bus. Plan, Small Bus. Mgmt Program, Mohawk Coll., 1992.

Payette, Julie, B.Eng.,M.A.Sc. ■ ⚛
Astronaut, Canadian Astronaut Program, CANADIAN SPACE AGENCY. Born Montreal 1963. m. Francois Brissette. **EDUC:** McGill Univ., B.Eng. 1986; Univ. of Toronto, M.A.Sc. 1990. **CAREER:** Tech. Advisor, IBM Canada, 1986-88; Visiting Scientist, Comm. & Computer Sci. Dept., IBM Research Lab., Zurich, 1991-92; Speech Research Group, Bell-Northern Research, Montreal, 1992; Astronaut, Tech. Advisor, Proj. Mgr & Advisor on Human-Computer Interaction Activities, Canadian Astronaut Program, 1992 to date; participant, Cdn Astronaut Program Space Unit Life Simulation (7-day simulated space mission), 1994; military jet training (obtained her Captaincy & logged more than 95 hrs. on the Tutor CT-114 jet aircraft), Cdn Air Force Base, Moose Jaw, Sask, Fall 1995; deep-sea diving training program (certified as a NEWTSUIT Level 2 Pilot & logged 25 hrs. as a one-atmosphere diving suit operator), Vancouver, 1996; selected to attend NASA's Astronaut Candidate Training, Johnson Space Center, Texas, 1996-98. **AFFIL:** l'Ordre des Ingénieurs du Québec; Ninety Nines. **HONS:** scholarship, United World Coll. of the Atlantic, 1980; Greville-Smith Scholarship, McGill Univ., 1982-86; Fac. Scholar, Fac. of Eng., McGill Univ., 1983-85; Univ. Scholar, McGill Univ., 1986; NSERC Canada Scholarship, 1988-90; Science Award, Gala of le Salon de la Femme de Montréal, 1993; Distinction for Exceptional Achievement by a Young Engineer, Canadian Council of

Professional Engineers, 1994. **INTERESTS:** piano; vocal music; triathlons; cross-country running; skiing; racquet sports; scuba diving; licensed pilot; languages. **MISC:** 1 of 2 nominated Cdn specialists on the NATO Int'l Research Group on speech processing; remains active in HCI research and her work has been presented in several nat'l & int'l forums. **COMMENT:** *"Ms. Payette reported to the Johnson Space Center in August 1996 to begin two years of training and evaluation. Successful completion of this initial training will qualify her for various technical assignments leading to selection as a mission specialist on a Space Shuttle flight crew."*

Payne, Alice V., M.Sc.,B.Sc. ■ ⚛ $ ☝
President, ARCTIC ENTERPRISES LTD., Site 3, Box 16, RR 2, Calgary (Springbank), AB T2P 2G5 (403) 286-1816. Born Edmonton 1940. m. Robert Allin Folinsbee. 3 ch. Katherine, Stuart, Ian. **EDUC:** Univ. of Alberta, B.Sc. 1962, M.Sc. 1965. **CAREER:** Research Officer, Geological Survey of Canada, 1962-63; Consultant, Univ. of Alberta, Depts. of Geol. & Physics & others, 1966-78; Proj. Geologist, Dames and Moore, 1978-79; Geologist, Reg'l Exploration Section, Gulf Canada Resources Ltd., 1979-83; Sr. Geologist, 1983-88; Sr. Bus. Planner, 1988-91; Sr. Geologist, 1991-94; Sr. Liabilities Mgmt, 1994-95; Pres., Arctic Enterprises Ltd., 1995 to date. **SELECTED PUBLICATIONS:** "Potassium-argon dates of basic intrusive rocks of the District of Mackenzie, NWT" (*Canadian Journal, Earth Sciences* 1966); "Energy–Challenge of Man's Future, Part's 1 & 2," with R.E. Folinsbee (*Geoscience Canada* 1 1974); "Zipf coding of the world's and Canada's porphyry copper deposits," with R.E. Folinsbee & G.W. Walrond (*Abstracts*, International Association Geology Ore Deposits, Sept. 1982). **AFFIL:** Canadian Society of Petroleum Geologists; Association of Professional Engineers, Geologists & Geophysicists of Alberta; Canadian Institute of Mining, Metallurgy and Petroleum; Geological Association of Canada; Association of Women in Science and Engineering. **HONS:** Canada 125 Medal, 1992; Paul Harris Fellowship Award; nominee, Woman of Distinction Award, YWCA Calgary, 1993; Hall of Distinction Award, Havergal Coll., 1994. **INTERESTS:** riding horseback; reading books; hunting. **MISC:** 1st woman Pres., Canadian Society of Petroleum Geologists; 1st Chair, Alberta Science & Technology Leadership Awards Foundation; past mbr., Premier's Council on Science & Technology for Alberta. **COMMENT:** *"Alice V. Payne, geoscientist, has a wide background encompassing research, consulting, teaching and management. Through her community activities and her professional activities, she has shown that, especially to women, science is fun and meaningful."*

Payne, Marilyn, B.A.,B.Ed., M.B.A. ■ ⚾ ♡
Executive Director, BC SCHOOL SPORTS, 1367 W. Broadway, Ste. 330, Vancouver, BC V6H 4A9 (604) 737-3066, FAX 737-9844. Born Winnipeg 1954. s. **EDUC:** York Univ., B.A. (Phys. Educ.) 1977; Univ. of Toronto, B.Ed. 1979; Simon Fraser Univ., M.B.A. 1995. **CAREER:** Exec. Dir., Canadian Field Hockey Council, 1985-91; Exec. Dir., BC School Sports, 1991 to date. **AFFIL:** B.C. Minister's Advisory Council on Athlete Assistance Program (Co-Chair); B.C. Minister's Advisory Council on Sport & Recreation; Sport Medicine Council of B.C. (Dir.). **HONS:** Achievement Award, Canadian Women's Field Hockey Association, 1990. **INTERESTS:** active sport admin. volunteer, 25 yrs. **COMMENT:** *"Combining a lifelong love of sport and an interest in association management and business, I strive to bring a professional, service-oriented style to my career, and toward the member-based organizations for which I have worked."*

Peacock, H. Ingrid Perry, B.A. ♡ ⊕ ✊
President, WOMEN'S COLLEGE HOSPITAL FOUNDATION, 76 Grenville St., Toronto, ON M5S 1B2 (416) 813-4702, FAX 813-4721. Born Scarborough, Ont. 1959. m. Robert I. Peacock. 1 ch. Victoria ("Tori"). **EDUC:** Univ. of Western Ontario, B.A.(Hist.) 1980. **CAREER:** Public Rel'ns Officer, Toronto Western Hospital Campaign, 1980-81; Public Info. Officer & Association Dir. (Fundraising), St. Lawrence Centre for the Arts, 1981; Consultant, Gordon L. Goldie Co. Ltd., 1981-87; Campaign Mgr, Art Gallery of Ontario, 1987-90; Exec. Dir., St. Michael's Hospital Foundation, 1990-95; Pres., Women's College Hospital Foundation, 1995 to date. **AFFIL:** National Society of Fundraising Executives; Canadian Association of Gift Planners; Association for Healthcare Philanthropy (Exec. & Cabinet 1991-94); York Mills Progressive Conservative Association (Pres. 1988-89); Etobicoke Centre Progressive Conservative Association; Fac. of Administrative Studies, York Univ. (Advisory Bd., Non-Profit Mgmt & Leadership Program). **INTERESTS:** politics; gourmet cooking; volleyball. **COMMENT:** *"Dedicated to the advancement of the philanthropic voluntary sector, Mrs. Peacock has raised $85 million for organizations including St. Michael's Hospital, the Art Gallery of Ontario, St. Lawrence Centre, Edmonton Symphony Society and Victoria Hospital."*

Peacock, Lucy ■ 🎬 🎭 📜
Actor. c/o Gary Goddard & Associates, 10 St. Mary St., Ste. 305, Toronto, ON M4Y 1P9 (416) 928-0299, FAX 924-9593. Born UK 1960. m. R. Christopher Thomas. 2 ch. Harry, Ben. **EDUC:** National Theatre Sch. of Canada, Acting 1983. **CAREER:** actor, Stratford Festival, 11 seasons, theatres in Montreal, Toronto & Edmonton & some TV; VP, Hedgestone Management. **SELECTED CREDITS:** Viola, *Twelfth Night* (theatre), Stratford; Desdemona, *Othello* (theatre), Stratford; Titania, *A Midsummer Night's Dream* (theatre), Stratford; Yelena, *Uncle Vanya* (theatre), Stratford; Rosalind, *As You Like It* (theatre), Stratford; Masha, *Three Sisters* (theatre), Stratford; Eliza Dolittle, *My Fair Lady* (musical), Stratford; Ophelia, *Hamlet* (theatre), Stratford; Principal, *Kung Fu–The Legend Continues* (series), Warner Bros.; Amelia Sandhurst, *Road to Avonlea* (series), CBC; Principal, *Forever Knight* (series). **HONS:** nominated, Best Actress in a performance in radio *(Adventures of the Lady That's Known as Lou)*, 1985; Guthrie Award, Stratford Festival, 1985, 1989. **INTERESTS:** music; singing (pop-rock); horses. **COMMENT:** *"Lucy lives in an old stone house on a horse farm with her husband, Christopher, and their two sons Harry and Ben. She has completed 11 seasons at the Stratford Festival and has become particularly devoted to the works of Shakespeare and Chekhov."*

Peake, Jacqueline, B.A. $ 🎭
Principal, CORPORATE EVENTS MANAGEMENT INC. and YORK EXPOSITIONS INC., One Toronto St., Ste. 803, Toronto, ON M5C 2V6 (416) 869-0141, FAX 869-1660. Born Toronto 1947. m. Bob Peake. 1 ch. Robert Elliott. **EDUC:** York Univ., B.A.(Soc. & Psych.) 1988. **CAREER:** Asst. Mgr, tourism & hospitality industry, Australia, 1966-73; Student Counsellor, Canadian Certified General Accountants' Association, 1973-78; self-employed mkt research contractor, 1978-87; VP, Corporate Events Management Inc., 1987-91; Principal, Corporate Events Management Inc. & York Expositions Inc., 1991 to date. **AFFIL:** Canadian Association of Women Entrepreneurs; The Board of Trade of Metropolitan Toronto; Metro Toronto Convention & Visitors Association. **HONS:** Dean's Honours List, Glendon Coll., York Univ. **INTERESTS:** reading; music; theatre; skiing; camping; tennis; travel. **MISC:** widely travelled with early career experiences in W. Canada & Australia. **COMMENT:** *"Jacqui, entrepreneurial by nature, is a principal in two major event management companies. She balances a challenging career with family life and many diverse interests."*

Pearce, Elizabeth, B.A.,M.A.,M.Ed. 🎓 ✋
Professor, CENTENNIAL COLLEGE OF APPLIED ARTS AND TECHNOLOGY, Box 631, Stn A, Scarborough, ON M1K 5E9. Born 1943. m. Michael O. Pearce. 4 ch. **EDUC:** Victoria Coll., Univ. of Toronto, B.A.(Languages) 1957; Ontario Coll. of Education, Specialist Teaching Certificate 1958; Univ. of St. Michael's Coll., M.A.(Theology) 1993; Ontario Institute for Studies in Education, M.Ed. 1994, doctoral studies, Hist. & Phil. of Educ., in progress. **SELECTED PUBLICATIONS:** "The Philosophy of Alfred North Whitehead" (*Ontario Journal of Higher Education* 1994). **EDIT:** writes & publishes a regular bi-monthly newsletter for a small organization. **AFFIL:** Canadian Council of Teachers of English; Ontario Council of Teachers of English; OISE/Univ. of Toronto (Governing Council); SuperCan, The High Performance Computing Association of Canada (Past Pres.). **INTERESTS:** sailing; writing; cross-country skiing.

Pearl, Debbie, C.M.A.,R.F.P. $
President, PRIVATE INVESTORS MANAGEMENT INC., 30 St. Clair Ave. W., Ste. 705, Toronto, ON M4V 3A1 (416) 324-2277, FAX 922-4833. Born Toronto 1957. m. Ted Kotschorek. 2 ch. **CAREER:** various positions, 1977-83; Consultant, Corporate Planning Associates, 1983-84; Consultant, Heritage Financial Inc., 1984-87; VP & Sr. Consultant, 1987-91; VP, Mktg & Group Programs, Heritage Financial Inc./Rhodes Financial Inc., 1991-93; Pres., Private Investors Management Inc., 1993 to date. **AFFIL:** Society of Management Accountants (C.M.A.); Canadian Association of Financial Planners (R.F.P.); International Association of Financial Planners. **INTERESTS:** family; downhill skiing; fitness; reading. **COMMENT:** *"As a highly energetic and motivated professional, I thrive on the challenges of my current position. I also enjoy spending time with my family as well as pursuing my outside interests."*

Pearson, Hilary, B.A.,M.A. ■ $ ✋
Senior Director, SECOR, 555 René-Lévesque Blvd. W., 9th Fl., Montreal, QC H2Z 1B1 (514) 861-9031, FAX 861-0281. Born Paris 1954. m. Michael Sabia. 1 ch. Laura. **EDUC:** Univ. of Toronto, B.A.(Pol. Economy) 1976, M.A.(Pol. Economy) 1979. **CAREER:** Economist, Mgr & Comm. Strategist, Dept. of Fin., Gov't of Canada, 1981-90; Sr. Official, Priorities & Planning Secretariat, Fed. Cabinet, 1990-91; Dir. Gen., Strategic Policy & Planning, Dept. of Fisheries & Oceans, 1991-93; VP, Corp. Planning, Royal Bank of Canada, 1993. **AFFIL:** Lester B. Pearson Coll. of the Pacific (Trustee).

Pearson, Kathleen Margaret (Kit), B.A., M.A.,M.L.S. ■ 📖 📚
Writer. 3888 W. 15th Ave., Vancouver, BC V6R 2Z9 (604) 224-3260, FAX 224-3261. Born Edmonton 1947. s. EDUC: Univ. of Alberta, B.A.(English) 1969; Univ. of British Columbia, M.L.S. 1976; Simmons Coll. Centre for the Study of Children's Literature, M.A.(Children's Lit.) 1982. CAREER: Children's Librarian, St. Catharines & North York, Ont., & Burnaby, B.C., 1976-86; writer of children's fiction, 1986 to date. SELECTED PUBLICATIONS: *The Daring Game* (Penguin Books Canada, 1986); *A Handful of Time* (Penguin Books Canada, 1987); *The Sky is Falling* (Penguin Books Canada, 1989); *The Singing Basket* illustrated by Ann Blades (Groundwood Books, 1990); *Looking At The Moon* (Penguin Books Canada, 1991); *The Lights Go On Again* (Penguin Books Canada, 1993); *Awake and Dreaming* (Penguin Books Canada, 1996). AFFIL: CANSCAIP; Writers' Union of Canada; P.E.N.; Federation of B.C. Writers. HONS: Book-of-the-Year for Children Award, Canadian Library Association, 1987, 1989; Mr. Christie's Book Award, 1989; Geoffrey Bilson Award for Historical Fiction for Young People, 1989, 1991; Manitoba Young Readers Choice, 1991; Violet Downey Award, National IODE, 1993. INTERESTS: travel; birding; playing the piano; yoga. COMMENT: *"Kit Pearson was born in Edmonton in 1947 and grew up there and in Vancouver, BC. She worked for 10 years as a children's librarian in Ontario and BC and occasionally teaches and writes articles on children's literature and writing for children."*

Pearson, The Hon. Landon Carter, B.A., M.Ed.,LL.D.(Hon.) ✤ ⊕
Senator, THE SENATE OF CANADA, Rm 210, E. Block, Ottawa, ON K1A 0A4 (613) 947-7134, FAX 947-7136. Born Toronto 1930. m. Geoffrey. 5 ch. Hilary, Katherine, Anne, Michael, Patricia. EDUC: Trinity Coll., Univ. of Toronto, B.A. 1951; Univ. of Ottawa, M.Ed. (Psychopedagogy) 1978. CAREER: author; Liberal Senator, Ont., The Senate of Canada, 1994 to date. VOLUNTEER CAREER: Co-Founder & Chair, Children Learning for Living, 1975 to date; V-Chair, Cdn Commission for the Int'l Year of the Child, 1979; Pres. then Chair, Canadian Council for Children & Youth, 1984-90; Founder & Chair, Canadian Coalition for the Rights of Children, 1989-94; V-Chair, Centre for Studies of Children at Risk, 1995. SELECTED PUBLICATIONS: numerous articles on child dev. & social policy issues; *Children of Glasnost* (1990); *For Canada's Children: National Agenda for Action*, ed. (1979). HONS: Canada Volunteer Award, 1990; LL.D.(Hon.), Wilfrid Laurier Univ., 1995. INTERESTS: U.N. Convention on the Rights of the Child; child dev. & social policy issues; int'l dev.; educ.; women's issues; human rights; psychology; arts & lit.; photography; writing. MISC: rep. for NGO community on Cdn Delegation to World Summit on Children, Sept. 1990; Cdn delegate to the 4th World Conference on Women, Beijing, Sept. 1995; Advisor to the Min. of Foreign Affairs, May 1996; Cdn delegate to the 1st World Congress Against Commercial Sexual Exploitation of Children, Stockholm, Aug. 1996. COMMENT: *"Actively involved with children's issues and children's rights for more than 40 years."*

Peck, Mary Biggar, B.A.,M.A. 📚 ⊰ ⛏
Research Historian and Writer. Summer: Lambertville, Box 160, Deer Island, NB E0G 2J0 (506) 747-2211. Winter: 1-163 Mackay St., Ottawa, ON K1M 2B5. Born Montreal 1920. m. Geo. W. Peck. 4 ch. Brenda, Barbara, John, Alexander. EDUC: McGill Univ., B.A.(Hons., Hist.) 1941; Carleton Univ., M.A.(Cdn Studies) 1969. CAREER: Louisbourg Restoration Proj.; Cdn Inventory of Historic Buildings; Maritime Aboriginal Rights & Land Claims Commission; National Archives Canada; Historical Resources Admin., Prov. of N.B., until 1978; presenter, 24 TV programs on historic photographs, 1976-80; writer. SELECTED PUBLICATIONS: *From War to Winterlude: 150 Years on the Rideau Canal* (Public Archives Canada, 1982); *The Bitter with the Sweet: New Brunswick 1604-1984* (Halifax: Four East Publications, 1983); *A New Brunswick Album: Glimpses of the Way We Were* (Toronto: Hounslow Press, 1987); *Red Moon Over Spain: Canadian Reaction to the Spanish Civil War 1936-39* (Ottawa: Steel Rail Publishing, 1988); *A Nova Scotia Album: Glimpses of the Way We Were* (Toronto: Hounslow Press, 1989); *A Full House and Fine Singing: Diaries and Letters of Sadie Harper Allen* (Fredericton: Goose Lane Editions, 1992); articles in *Atlantic Advocate; Canadian Collector; Horizon Canada; Antique Showcase & Canadian Antiquer and Collector.* INTERESTS: souvenir pictorial china. MISC: listed in *Who's Who in Canada.* COMMENT: *"After 17 contented years at home with my four children, I returned to graduate school and then to a career of historical research, writing, speaking and half-hour presentations on television."*

Peers, Marilyn R., B.A.,M.S.W., LL.D.,R.S.W. ⊙ ⊕
Social Worker. Halifax, NS. Born Lion's Head, Ont. 1932. m. John Michael. 2 ch. EDUC: Univ. of Western Ontario, B.A.(Modern

Languages) 1956; Dalhousie Univ., M.S.W. 1970. **CAREER:** Lt., Exec. Branch, Royal Cdn Navy, 1956-62; Staff Officer-Intelligence, Directorate of Naval Intelligence, Nat'l Defence Headquarters, Ottawa, 1956-59; Staff Officer, Fin. Estimates, Directorate of Naval Training, 1959; Exec. Officer's Asst. & Sr. Wren Personnel Officer, HMCS Stadacona, Halifax, 1959-62; Protection Worker, Children's Aid Society of Halifax, 1966-68; Asst. Administrator, 1970-72; Branch Dir., Atlantic Child Guidance Centre, Dartmouth, N.S., 1973-80; Exec. Dir., Children's Aid Society of Halifax, 1980-95. **AFFIL:** Avanta Network (Dir., Gov. Council); Family Mediation N.S. (Bd. of Dir.); Halifax Youth Foundation (Bd. of Dir.); Maritime Sch. of Social Work, Dalhousie Univ. (Advisory Bd.). **HONS:** Life Mbr., N.S. Association of Homemaker Services; Life Mbr., N.S. Federation of Foster Parents; Recognition for years of dedicated service, Parent Finders of N.S., 1980; Recognition of Women Award, Halifax YWCA, 1984; Achievement of Excellence Award, N.S. Family & Child Welfare Association, 1989; Canada Volunteer Award, Certificate of Merit, Health & Welfare Canada, 1990; Canadian Association of Social Workers' Award, 1992; Fifth Living Treasure Award, Avanta Network, 1992; Women of Excellence Award, Progress Club, 1994; LL.D.(Hon.), Dalhousie Univ., 1991. **INTERESTS:** travel; photography. **COMMENT:** *"Known as a leader in the profession of social work and in the field of child welfare, Dr. Peers is active as a consultant, teacher, public educator and advocate."*

Pell, Barbara, B.A.,M.A., Ph.D. ■■ ⟨꜔ ☼
Associate Professor, TRINITY WESTERN UNIVERSITY, 7600 Glover Rd., Langley, BC V2Y 1Y1 (604) 888-7511, FAX 820-9228. Born Hamilton, Ont. 1945. m. Rev. Dr. A.J. 2 ch. Elisabeth Anne, James. **EDUC:** Univ. of Toronto, B.A. (English) 1966; Univ. of Windsor, M.A.(Cdn Lit.) 1972; Univ. of Toronto, Ph.D.(Cdn Lit.) 1981. **CAREER:** Asst. Prof., Redeemer Coll., Hamilton, 1983-85; Asst./Assoc. Prof., Trinity Western Univ., 1985 to date. **SELECTED PUBLICATIONS:** *A Portrait of the Artist: Ernest Buckler's "The Mountain and the Valley"* (Toronto; ECW Press, 1995); *Little Brown Handbook*, Cdn Ed. (Toronto; Gage, 1991); "The African & Canadian Heroines" (*Challenging Territory: The Writing of Margaret Laurence*, Edmonton, Univ. of Alberta Press, 1996); "MacLennan's New Theology" (*Hugh MacLennan*, Ottawa, Univ. of Ottawa Press, 1994). **AFFIL:** Association of Canadian College & University Teachers of English; Association of Canadian & Quebec Literatures; Canadian Commonwealth Language & Literature Society; Christianity & Literature Study Group (Chair); Institute for Christian Studies (Senate). **HONS:** Univ. of Toronto doctoral fellowship, 1976-77; 2 SSHRC (ASU) grants, 1991, 1996. **INTERESTS:** reading; skiing. **COMMENT:** *"Married with two children and two grandchildren. Canadian Literature professor for 15 years, with numerous books, articles and papers delivered. With husband (Anglican priest Rev. Dr. A.J. Pell), prominent spokespersons for Canadian Evangelical Anglicans."*

Pelletier, Annie ■■ ⓥ
Olympic Athlete. c/o Canadian Olympic Association. Born Montreal 1973. **EDUC:** Coll. André Grasset (current). **SPORTS CAREER:** mbr., Cdn Nat'l Diving Team, 1991 to date. Olympic Games: Bronze, 3m, 1996. Olympic trials: 2nd, 3m World championships: 3rd, 1m, & 12th, 3m, 1994. Grand Prix: 1st, 3m (Dive Canada), 9th, 3m (Rostock, Germany), & 18th, 3m (Spring Swallows), 1996; 8th, 3m (Alamo Int'l, US), & 3rd, 3m (Dive Canada), 1995. Int'l meets: 3rd, 3m (Germany), 5th, 3m (China), & 3rd, 3m (Dive Canada), 1994. Pan Am Games: 1st, 3m, & 2nd, 1m, 1995; 5th, 3m, & 10th, 1m, 1991. Commonwealth Games: 1st, 3m, & 1st, 1m, 1994. World University Games: 2nd, 1m, & semi., 3m, 1993; 4th, 3m, 1991. Winter Canadian championships: 1st, 3m, 1996; 1st, 1m, & 2nd, 3m, 1995; 3rd, 3m, 1993; 2nd, 3m, 1992; 2nd, 3m, 1991. Summer Canadian championships: 1st, 3m, & 1st, 1m, 1995; 1st, 3m, & 1st, 1m, 1994; 1st, 3m, 1993. **AFFIL:** "Spirit of Sport" campaign. **HONS:** Aquatic female athlete of the year, 1994. **INTERESTS:** golf; writing; music; movies; fashion; dance; shows. **MISC:** speaks French, English, Spanish.

Pelletier, Maryse, B.A. ■■ ⊗ 🍃 🖤
Comédienne, Auteure Dramatique et Scénariste. 89, St-Norbert, Montréal, QC H2X 1G5 (514) 284-2845. Born Qué. 1946. s. **EDUC:** Univ. de Moncton, B.A. 1968; Conservatoire d'art dramatique de Québec, Art Dramatique 1971. **SELECTED CREDITS:** comme auteure dramatique: *Un samourai amoureux* (1991); *La Rupture des eaux* (1989); *Duo pour voix obstinées* (1985); *Du Poil aux pattes comme les CWAC's* (1982); *À qui le p'tit coeur après neuf heures et demie?* (1980); en gestion et administration: direction artistique et gén. du Théâtre populaire du Québec, 1992-96; TV et cinéma, comme auteure et scénariste: *Graffiti* (Radio-Québec, 1991-92); *Iniminimagimo* (plusieurs contes; Radio-Canada, 1986-89); *Du Poil aux pattes comme les CWAC's* (Les Films

Stock, 1985); *Traboulidon* (Radio-Canada, 1983-84). HONS: Prix du Gouv. Gén. (pour *Duo pour voix obstinées*), 1986; Grand Prix du *Journal de Montréal* (pour *Duo pour voix obstinées*), 1985; Génie de la meilleure émission de télévision pour enfants de 2 à 10 ans (pour *Iniminimagimo*), l'Académie Canadienne du cinéma et de la télévision, 1988 et 1989; Génie de la meilleure émission de télévision pour enfants de 2 à 10 ans (pour *Traboulidon*), 1987. COMMENT: *"Tout m'intéresse: l'écriture, la gestion, la vie, les diverses formes que prend l'expression de l'émotion, surtout. C'est une source intarissable du surprise."*

Petitclerc, Chantal ■ ■ ⊘
Paralympic Athlete. Ste-Foy, QC. SPORTS CAREER: mbr., Nat'l Track Team, 1992 to date. Paralympic Games: Gold, 100m & 200m, Silver, 400m, 800m & 1500m, 1996; Bronze, 200m & 800m, 1992. Gasparilla Classic, 11th, 15k, 1996; 3rd, 15k, 1995. Oita Int'l Marathon: 3rd, 1995. IAAF Championships: 2nd, 800m, 1995. Stoke Games: 1st, 100m, 200m, 400m, 800m & 1500m, 1995. Los Angeles Marathon: 5th, 1995. IPC World Athletic Championships: 1st, 200m & 400m, 3rd, 800m, 4th, 1500m, 1994. Francophone Games: 1st, 100m & 800m, 1994. Nat'l Marathon Championships, 1st, 1993. MISC: holds the Cdn record in 100m, 200m, 400m, 800m & 1500m; has recorded the best time ever by a Cdn in the marathon. COMMENT: *"Canada's first female star of wheelchair athletics."*

Penick, Barbara, B.A.,B.Ed.,LL.B. ■ 🕸 ❂
Director of Discipline, NOVA SCOTIA BARRISTERS' SOCIETY, Halifax, NS B3J 1X3 (902) 422-1491, FAX 429-4869, EMAIL bpenick@ mail.ns.ca. Born Cambridge, Mass. 1947. m. Frank Van Wie Penick. 2 ch. EDUC: Wellesley Coll., B.A.(Phil.) 1969; Acadia Univ., B.Ed. 1973; Dalhousie Univ., LL.B. 1979. BAR: N.S., 1980. CAREER: computer programmer, Blue Cross, N.Y., 1970; farmer, Canning, N.S., 1971-72; English teacher, Cornwallis District High Sch., Canning, 1973-76; articled, Stewart MacKeen & Covert, 1979-80; Lawyer, Stewart McKelvey Stirling Scales, 1980-94; Dir. of Discipline, N.S. Barristers' Society, 1995 to date. AFFIL: N.S. Barristers' Society (Discipline Policies & Procedures Committee); Canadian Bar Association (Gender Equality Committee); Art Gallery of Nova Scotia (Gov.); Halifax Club (Mgmt Committee); Dalhousie Alumni Association (Bd. of Dir.); Victoria General Hospital Foundation (Bd. of Dir.; Exec. Committee). HONS: Eunice W. Beeson Memorial Prize, Dalhousie Univ., 1979. INTERESTS: gender equality.

Pennefather, Joan, B.A. ■ 🕸 ❂
Vice-President, THORNLEY FALLIS INC., Communications Counsel, 90 Sparks St., Ste. 606, Ottawa, ON K1P 5B4 (613) 231-3355, FAX 231-4515. Born Montreal. EDUC: Marianopolis Coll., Montreal, B.A.(Hist.) 1964; Concordia Univ., Grad. Diploma in Communication Arts. CAREER: Asst., Public Rel'ns Dept. & Teacher, Marianopolis Coll., 1966-67; various positions, Multiple Access Limited, CFCF-12 TV, Montreal, 1975-76; various positions, Canadian Cultural Centre, Paris, France, 1976-77; Sponsored Program Officer, National Film Board of Canada, 1977-81; Exec. Asst. to the Deputy Film Commissioner, 1981-83; Planning Coord. & Sec. to the Bd. of Trustees, 1983-85; Dir. of Planning & Vice Film Commissioner, 1985-86; Dir. of Corp. Affairs & Vice Film Commissioner, 1986-89; Gov't Film Commissioner & Chair, 1989-94; Exec. Dir., National Arts Centre, 1994-95. AFFIL: International Institute of Communications; Canadian Women in Communications; Banff Television Foundation; Sisters of Charity of Ottawa Hospital Services (Bd.); Fac. of Admin., Univ. of Ottawa (Advisory Bd.). HONS: Astral Award, Toronto Women in Film & Television, 1993. INTERESTS: music; visual & performing arts; film; history; writing; swimming; skiing; travel. MISC: Host, International Institute of Communications Conference, 1992; Co-Chair, "Women in Communications" Pre-conference, 1993; Co-Chair, "Women in News and Current Affairs" Pre-conference, 1994; Chair, Int'l Symposium on Women & the Media, sponsored by the Cdn Commission for UNESCO. COMMENT: *"Have always supported women's issues, especially regarding the arts, film and television. Media literacy is an important interest, as well as the role of the arts in social change."*

Pennington, Sheila, Ph.D. ⊕ 🕸
President, CENTRE FOR THE HEALING ARTS, INC., 491 Eglinton Ave. W., Ste. 2B, Toronto, ON M5N 1A8 (416) 488-5764, FAX 322-7195. 4 ch. Ann, Michael, Alex, Tim. EDUC: Univ. of Toronto, B.A.(Art/Archaeology) 1955, B.Ed. 1964, M.Ed.(Educ. Psych.) 1966, Ph.D.(Counselling Psych.) 1981; Toronto Teachers' Coll., Primary Sch. Specialist Certificate 1956. CAREER: Primary Sch. Specialist, teaching kindergarten for the North York Sch. Bd., 1956-59; Research Asst., Research Dept., Toronto Bd. of Educ., 1962-65; Psychotherapist, Crisis Intervention, Scarborough General Hospital Community Psychiatry, 1970-72; Psychotherapist, private practice, 1972 to date; Pres., Centre for the Healing Arts, Inc. SELECTED PUBLICATIONS: *Draw-A-Class-*

room *"Test" Manual and Scoring Categories* (Toronto: Bd. of Educ. for the City of Toronto, Research Dept., 1967); *The Effect of Classroom Social Structure and Processes on Creativity* (Toronto: Ontario Institute for Studies in Education, 1967); "Living or Dying: An Investigation of the Balance Point" doctoral thesis (Toronto: Univ. of Toronto, 1981); *Healing Yourself: Understanding How the Mind Can Heal* (McGraw Hill Ryerson, 1988). **AFFIL:** American Association of Marriage & Family Therapists (Clinical mbr.); Association of Humanistic Psychology; Toronto Nuclear Disarmament: Friends of the Earth; Canadian Centre for Arms Control; Amnesty International; Canadian Civil Liberties Association; Greenpeace; Writers' Union of Canada; World Federalists. **HONS:** Presidential Award for doctoral thesis, Ontario Psychological Association, 1981. **MISC:** numerous workshops, conference presentations & speaking engagements; quoted or featured in numerous newspapers, magazines & journals; frequently interviewed on TV & radio.

Penrod, Lynn, LL.M.,LL.B.,Ph.D.,MAT, B.A. ✦ ⚖ ✍
President, SOCIAL SCIENCES AND HUMANITIES RESEARCH COUNCIL OF CANADA, 350 Albert St., Box 1610, Ottawa, ON K1P 6G4 (613) 995-5488, FAX 995-5498, EMAIL lpenrod@ vm.ucs.ualberta.ca. Born Piqua, Ohio 1946. **EDUC:** Ohio State Univ., B.A. 1967, Ph.D. 1975; Yale Univ., MAT 1968; Univ. of Alberta, LL.B. 1980, LL.M. 1986. **BAR:** Alta., 1984. **CAREER:** Teacher, Paul Laurence Dunbar High Sch., 1968-69; Lectrice d'anglais, Lycée Dumont d'Urville, Toulon, France, 1969-70; Teacher of French (AP French), Oakwood Sr. High Sch., 1970-72; Adjunct Asst. Prof. of French, Wright State Univ., 1970-72; Grad. Teaching Asst., Ohio State Univ., 1972-75; Asst. Prof. of French, Univ. of South Carolina, 1975-77; Lecturer, Dept. of Romance Languages, Univ. of Alberta, 1977-79, Asst. Prof., 1979-83, Assoc. Prof., 1983-89; Lecturer, Fac. of Law, Univ. of Alberta, 1986 to date; Prof. of Romance Languages, 1989 to date; Student at Law, Durocher Maccagno Arès Lynass Manning Carr & Simpson, Barristers & Solicitors, 1983-84; Assoc., 1983-85; Barrister & Solicitor (sole practitioner), 1985 to date. **SELECTED PUBLICATIONS:** *Hélène Cixous: The Future Feminine* (Boston and New York: Twayne, 1994); *Expériences Littéraires* (Toronto: Holt Rinehart Harcourt Brace, 1989); *Canadian Children's Literature in French: An Annotated Bibliography* (Edmonton); "Focalization Without (Too Much) Fuss: Using Narratology to Teach Thérèse Desqueyroux" (*ADFL Bulletin*

19(2) 1988); "Structure sociale, stratégie textuelle: l'univers narratif de Monique Corriveau" (*Canadian Children's Literature/Littérature canadienne pour la jeunesse* 46 1987); "Écrire pour les enfants: l'oeuvre de Claude Aubry" (*Canadian Children's Literature/Littérature canadienne pour la jeunesse* 41 1986); "Divorce Mediation: Helping to Ease the Pain" (*Network of Saskatchewan Women*, 3(9) 1986); reviews; various other publications. **AFFIL:** The Law Society of Alberta; Phi Beta Kappa; Alpha Lambda Delta; Phi Eta Sigma; Alpha Mu Gamma; Association des Professeurs de Français des Universités et Collèges Canadiens; Modern Language Association of America; American Association of Teachers of French; American Council on the Teaching of Foreign Languages; Pacific Northwest Council on Foreign Languages; Canadian Comparative Literature Association; Association for Quebec & Canadian Literatures; American Literary Translators' Association; The Friends of Georges Sand; Simone de Beauvoir Society, US; La Société de Beauvoir, Canada; National Association for Women in Education; Senior Women Academic Administrators of Canada; Academic Women's Association, Univ. of Alberta; Law Society of Alberta; Canadian Bar Association; Family Law Subsection, Canadian Bar Association; Edmonton Bar Association; Canadian Association of Law & Society; Alberta Arbitration & Mediation Society; Canadian Association of Law Teachers; Canadian Comparative Law Association; National Association of Women & the Law; Women's Law Forum, Univ. of Alberta; Kappa Kappa Gamma Foundation of Canada (Bd. of Dir.); Kappa Kappa Gamma Scholarship Committee (Chair); Alberta Women's Secretariat, Stepping Stones Proj.; A Celebration of Women in the Arts (Advisory Bd.); Little Caesar's Pizza Scholarship Fund (Bd Mbr.); Alberta Heritage Scholarship Program (Adjudicator); Institute for Law Research & Reform (Translator). **HONS:** Outstanding Grad. Teaching Associate Award, Ohio State Univ.; Fullbright Fellowship (France); Hon. Fellow, Calhoun Coll., Yale Univ.; Novice G. Fawcett President's Gold Medal, Ohio State Univ.; Coll. of Arts & Sciences Council Gold Medal, Ohio State Univ.; Mary Louise Bennet Boyd Prize, Kappa Kappa Gamma; Mortar Board, Chimes & Mirrors Hon. Societies; Univ. Honours Scholar, Ohio State Univ.; Women's Panhellenic Scholarship Gold Medal, Ohio State Univ.; Nat'l Merit Scholar. **MISC:** numerous invited academic papers; numerous invited lectures. **COMMENT:** *"President of the Social Sciences and Humanities Research Council of Canada, Dr. Lynn Penrod has held various administrative,* *teaching and research positions at universities in Canada and the US since the commencement of her academic career in 1970.*

Pepall, Sarah E., B.A.,LL.B.,LL.M. ⚖
Managing Partner, MCMILLAN BINCH, S. Tower, Royal Bank Plaza, Ste. 3800, Toronto, ON M5J 2J7 (416) 865-7002, FAX 865-7008. 2 ch. Gillian, Fraser. EDUC: McGill Univ., B.A., LL.B.; Osgoode Hall, LL.M. BAR: Ont., 1978. CAREER: Civil & Commercial Litigation Lawyer; Mng Ptnr, McMillan Binch. AFFIL: Canadian Bar Association; American Bar Association; Advocates' Society (Dir.; Ed., *The Brief*); Multiple Sclerosis Society (VP; Dir.). COMMENT: *"Sarah E. Pepall practises in the area of civil and commercial litigation and is the co-managing partner of the firm."*

Pepe, Tracy A. ■ $ ⚘ ♦
Owner and Operator, CLASSIC AROMATICS LTD., 1 Regan Rd., Unit 9, Brampton, ON L7A 1B8 (905) 846-8355, FAX 846-9866. Owner, COSMO DISTRIBUTION INC. Born Hamilton, Ont. 1968. m. Jim. 1 ch. Adrian Pepe. EDUC: Lam Sch. of Advanced Esthetics, Esthetics 1986; The Babor Institute, Aachen, Germany, 1987; private Aromatherapy tutoring, Anne Robuck, Toronto, 1987; David Singer Training, Chiropractic Office Mgmt, Toronto, 1989; Pacific Institute of Aromatherapy, Toronto, 1993. CAREER: Paul King Salon, Toronto, 1987-88; office mgmt, Rosedale Chiropractic, 1988-89; Teacher, Seneca Coll., 1989; Educator, Chilly Company, 1990; Aesthetics Consultant & Educ. Advisor, Breukner Group Company, 1991; Educator, Sheridian Coll. Continuing Educ., 1990 to date; owner & operator, Body Works Aromatherapy, 1988-92; owner & operator, Classic Aromatics, 1992 to date; Educator, Marvel Beauty Sch., 1994. SELECTED PUBLICATIONS: "Aromatherapy in Canada" (*Esthetics*, Spring 1994); *Toronto Life Fashion* (Oct. 1995). AFFIL: Canadian Federation of Aromatherapists (founder; Pres. 1993-94); CAWEE; North American Aromatherapy Association. INTERESTS: horseback riding; psychology; reading; animals; gardening. MISC: Coord., "Aromatherapie 1994" Conference; grant recipient; subject of various periodical articles. COMMENT: *"Tracy Pepe is a modern day woman. She runs the only aromachology company in Canada. She is the main instructor for the Sheridan College Aromachology/Aromatherapy program."*

Pepino, N. Jane, Q.C.,LL.B.,LL.M. ⚖ ✿ ◐ ♦
Partner, AIRD & BERLIS, Barristers & Solicitors, BCE Place, 181 Bay St., Ste. 1800, Toronto, ON M5J 2T9 (416) 865-7727, FAX (416) 364-4916. m. James D. Pearson. 3 ch. Andrew Walter Rodger Pearson, Allison Blaine Pearson, Victoria Jane Pearson. EDUC: Victoria Coll., Univ. of Toronto, 1967; Osgoode Hall Law Sch., LL.B. 1970; Univ. of Texas, Austin, LL.M. 1971. BAR: Ont., 1973. CAREER: practice concentrates on mun., regulatory & planning, & land dev. law; Ptnr, Aird & Berlis, 1982 to date. AFFIL: Canadian Bar Association; Metro Action Committee on Public Violence Against Women (METRAC); Canadian Urban Institute (Bd.); Univ. of Toronto (Academic Tribunal); Princess Margaret Hospital Foundation (Bd.); Women's College Hospital (Bd.; Exec. Committee); Bishop Strachan Sch. (Bd.). MISC: 1st woman appointed to Metropolitan Toronto Bd. of Commissioners of Police; former mbr., Cdn Council on the Status of Women, Ont. Human Rights Commission; Chair of Fed. Inquiries on halfway houses, dangerous offenders & temporary absences; TV commentator on political issues.

Pepler, Debra, B.A.-B.P.H.E.,B.Ed., M.Sc.,Ph.D. ■ ❀ ⚘
Full Professor, Psychology Department, YORK UNIVERSITY and Director, LAMARSH CENTRE FOR RESEARCH ON VIOLENCE AND CONFLICT RESOLUTION, 4700 Keele St., North York, ON M3J 1P3 (416) 636-2100, ext. 66155 (LaMarsh) & 66212 (Psych.), EMAIL pepler@yorku.ca. EDUC: Queen's Univ., B.A.-B.P.H.E. (French, Psych., Phys. Educ.) 1973, B.Ed. (Educ.) 1974; Dalhousie Univ., M.Sc. (Phys. Educ.) 1976; Univ. of Waterloo, Ph.D.(Psych.) 1979. CAREER: Research Assoc., Centre for Research in Human Dev., Univ. of Toronto, 1978-84; Research Dir., Earlscourt Child & Family Centre, 1984-88; Prof., Psych. Dept., York Univ., 1988 to date; Psychologist, private practice, McWhinney, Metcalfe & Associates, 1990 to date; Consulting Psychologist, Adventure Place, 1992 to date; Dir., LaMarsh Centre for Research on Violence & Conflict Resolution, 1994 to date. SELECTED PUBLICATIONS: *The Development and Treatment of Childhood Aggression*, ed. with K. Rubin (Hillsdale, N.J.: Erlbaum, 1991); "Social skills training and aggression in the peer group," with W.M. Craig & W.R. Roberts, *Coercion and Punishment in Long-Term Perspectives*, ed. J. McCord (New York: Cambridge Univ. Press, 1995); "A developmental perspective on violence and youth," with R. Slaby, *Reason to Hope: A Psychosocial Perspective on Violence and Youth*, ed. L. Eron (Washington, DC: APA Publications, 1994–report of the American Psychological Association's Commission on Violence & Youth); "A peek behind the fence: naturalistic

observations of aggressive children with remote audio-visual recording," with W. Craig (*Developmental Psychology*, 31, 1995); "An evaluation of an anti-bullying intervention in Toronto schools," with W. Craig, S. Zeigler & A. Charach (*Canadian Journal of Community Mental Health*, 13, 1994); "The mental health of Portuguese children," with I. Lessa (*Canadian Journal of Psychiatry*, 38, 1993); "Research on children from violent homes," with T. Moore, B. Weinberg *et al* (*Canada's Mental Health*, 1990); various chapters in books, papers published in refereed journals, book reviews, papers, presentations & workshops. **AFFIL:** Canadian Psychological Association (Fellow; Exec. Committee of Dev. Section 1987-90); American Psychological Association; Society for Research in Child Development; Society for Research on Child & Adolescent Psychopathology; International Society for the Study of Behavioral Development. **HONS:** Contribution to Knowledge Award, Psychology Foundation of Canada. **COMMENT:** *"Dr. Pepler conducts two major research programs on children at risk. The first, on children in families at risk, examines the risk and protective factors associated with the adjustment of children in violent, homeless one-parent and two-parent families. The second research program addresses children's aggressive behaviours, particularly in the school and peer contexts. Dr. Pepler's clinical work is in the areas of family breakup, programming for high risk mothers and their children (as a consultant to early intervention programs) and children with emotional and behavourial problems."*

Percy Jackson, Mary, O.C.,MB.ChB., MRCS LRCP,LL.D. ⊕
Born Dudley, Worcs., UK 1904. w. Frank (dec. 1979). 2 ch. **EDUC:** Birmingham Univ., MB.ChB.(Medicine) 1927; Royal Coll. of Surgeons, UK, MRCS LRCP, 1927. **SELECTED PUBLICATIONS:** *The Homemade Brass Plate, the story of a pioneer doctor told to Cornelia Lehn* (1988). **AFFIL:** Canadian Medical Association; Coll. of Family Physicians of Canada (Life Mbr.). **HONS:** LL.D.(Hon.), Univ. of Alberta, 1976; Mbr., Alberta Order of Excellence, 1983; Officer of the Order of Canada, 1990. **INTERESTS:** medicine; music; gardening. **COMMENT:** *"Spent 45 years as a general practitioner in a remote area of northern Alberta treating Indians and Métis and immigrant homesteaders. Married a fur trader and cattle rancher in 1931 and have two children and eight grandchildren."*

Perri, Cathy ○ ◑
National President, KIDS FIRST PARENT ASSOCI-

ATION OF CANADA, Box 5256, Airdrie, AB T4B 3B3 (403) 289-1440, FAX 539-0630. Born Swift Current, Sask. 1963. m. Michael. 2 ch. Christine, Michael. **EDUC:** Medicine Hat Coll., Nursing Diploma 1983; Foothills Hospital, Calgary, Neonatal Intensive Care Nursery Cert. 1987. **CAREER:** full-time Staff Nurse, Colonel Belcher Hospital, Calgary, 1983-86; full-time Staff Nurse, Medicine Hat & District General Hospital, 1986; casual staff Nurse, Brooks General Hospital, 1987-88; casual staff Nurse, High Level General Hospital, 1988-89; full-time mother, 1989 to date; Sec., Kids First Parent Association, Airdrie Chapter, 1992-93; Asst. Coord., Presch. Religious Educ., St. Paul's Catholic Church, Airdrie, Alta., 1992-93; Pres., Airdrie Chapter, 1993-94; Nat'l VP, 1993-95; Nat'l Membership Sec., 1993 to date; Alta. Advisory Council on Women's Issues (appointed), 1994-95; Nat'l Pres., Kids First, 1995 to date. **SELECTED PUBLICATIONS:** *Choosing to Stay Home in Canada*, policy paper (Kids First); "The Importance of Nurturing: A Parent's Perspective," Fed. Gov't Standing Committee on Health; several articles in *Kids First Newsletter*. **HONS:** Service Award, Premier's Council in Support of Alberta Families, 1993-95. **INTERESTS:** her children; reading nonfiction; sports; Catholic theology. **COMMENT:** *"As a full time mother and president of KIDS FIRST, I aim to enhance the role of mothering so as to be seen, not as the antithesis of growing and contributing but as one of immeasurable value. Remember the hand that rocks the cradle rules the world."*

Perry, Kathleen, B.A.,M.L.S. ⬠ 🏛
Associate Dean, Communication and Advancement, Faculty of Fine Arts, CONCORDIA UNIVERSITY, 1455 de Maisonneuve Blvd. W., VA-250, Montreal, QC H36 1M8 (514) 848-4600, FAX 848-4599, EMAIL kperry@vax2.concordia.ca. **EDUC:** Univ. of Toronto, B.A.(Art Hist.) 1976; Univ. of Western Ontario, M.L.S. 1978. **CAREER:** Slide Librarian, Dept. of Art Hist., Fac. of Fine Arts, Concordia Univ., 1978-87; Employment Equity Coord., 1987-94; Acting Advisor to the Rector on the Status of Women, 1992-94; Assoc. Dean, Comm. & Advancement, Fac. of Fine Arts, 1995 to date.

Peszat, Lucille C., R.N.,B.Sc.N.,M.Ed., Ed.D. ■ ⬠ ⊕ $
Founder and Director, CANADIAN CENTRE FOR STRESS AND WELL-BEING, 141 Adelaide St. W., Ste. 1506, Toronto, ON M5H 3L5 (416) 363-3204, FAX 367-1014. Born Chatham, Ont. s. **EDUC:** St. Joseph's Hospital Sch. of Nursing, Chatham, R.N. 1958; Univ. of Western Ontario, B.Sc.N. 1961; Univ. of Toronto,

M.Ed.(Adult Educ.) 1969, Ed.D.(Adult Educ. & Mgmt) 1979. **CAREER:** Consultant, Ontario Hospital Association, 1962-65; CIDA Advisor in Trinidad & Tobago, 1965-66; Lecturer & Proj. Dir., Univ. of Ottawa, 1966-67; Coord., Formal Continuing Educ., Registered Nurses' Association of Ontario, 1969-71; Founding Dean, Health Sciences Div., Humber Coll., Toronto, 1971-80; Principal, Lifecor Resources Inc., 1980 to date; Dir., Canadian Centre for Stress & Well-Being, 1982 to date. **SELECTED CREDITS:** *The Calming Response* relaxation exercise (audiotape) (1983, 1995). **SELECTED PUBLICATIONS:** "Banishing Burnout" (*CGA Magazine* June 1990); *Stress-Management Self-Help Kit* (1993); numerous articles & resource tools on change mgmt & stress mgmt. **DIRECTOR:** Lifecor Resources Inc. **AFFIL:** Coll. of Nurses of Ontario; Registered Nurses' Association of Ontario; Canadian Nurses' Association; Canadian Adult Education Association; Women Entrepreneurs of Canada; Toronto 2000 Multicultural Council. **INTERESTS:** folk & ethnic music & dance; reading; computers; interior design; travel. **MISC:** seminar leader, facilitator, psychotherapist & consultant; coll. & univ. prof.; professional speaker in a wide variety of settings & functions. **COMMENT:** *"As an innovator, educator, psychotherapist and designer of creative educational and psychotherapeutic approaches, seminars and learning resources, my work is focused on helping individuals and organizations toward creative stress management, successful change management and corporate and personal well-being."*

Petersen Burfield, M. Jane, B.A. $ ♡ 🍁

Vice-President and Director, INVESTORS FINANCE CORP. LTD., 95 King St. E., Ste. 101, Toronto, ON M5C 1G4 (416) 594-0487, ext. 13, FAX 594-1071. Born Toronto 1948. m. Mark Edward Burfield. 3 ch. Miranda, Jennifer, Katharine. **EDUC:** York Univ., B.A.(English/Psych.) 1971; St. Godric's Coll., London, UK, Certificate (Bus.) 1972. **CAREER:** Asst. Ed., Canadian Real Estate Association, 1972-76; Lecturer in Comm., Humber Coll., 1977-82; mbr. of Bd. & Audit Committee, Commercial Financial Corp., 1984; mbr. of Bd., Wellington Trust Co., 1985; Pres., Griffund Holdings, 1985-90; Sec.-Treas., then VP & Dir., Investors Financial Ltd., Investors Capital Corp., 1991 to date. **SELECTED PUBLICATIONS:** *Bishop Strachan School Alumni Magazine* ed. (1978-80); *History of Bishop Strachan School*, with others, 1992. **AFFIL:** Junior League of Toronto; Y.M.C.A. (various local exec. positions, Etobicoke, Geneva Park & Nat'l Council); Proud to be Canadian Committee. **INTERESTS:** bridge; journalism; reading; sailing; travel; computers. **COMMENT:** *"My challenge is balancing career and home demands. I believe in ongoing education and in a tolerant and balanced life-view. Work, travel, children, volunteering and reading all contribute."*

Peterson, Shelley ■■ 🎭 📜 📺

Actress. c/o Penny Noble Talent Agent. Writer, c/o Porcupine's Quill, publisher. Born London, Ont. 1952. m. David. 3 ch. Ben, Chloë, Adam. **EDUC:** Dalhousie Univ., Hist. of Theatre 1971; Univ. of Western Ontario, Theatre & Phil. 1972. **CAREER:** Cdn actress, stage, TV & film, 25 yrs.; writer (1st novel launched Nov. 1996). **SELECTED CREDITS:** *The Housekeeper* (film); principal performer, *Doghouse* (TV series); *Love Letters* (stage); *Einstein - Light to the Power of Two* (film); *Ondine* (stage). **SELECTED PUBLICATIONS:** *Dancer* (The Porcupine's Quill, 1996). **AFFIL:** Writers' Development Trust (committee 1996); Eglinton Caledon Association (committee 1996). **INTERESTS:** her children; horses; painting; writing; performing; reading. **COMMENT:** *"A creative person strives to find expression and to grow as an artist while retaining a centre, which in my case is my family."*

Peterson, Susan, B.A,M.A. 🍁

Assistant Deputy Minister, Federal Provincial Fiscal Relations and Social Policy, Department of Finance, GOVERNMENT OF CANADA, E. Tower, 140 O'Connor St., Fl. 15, Ottawa, ON K1A 0G5 (613) 966-0735, FAX 992-7754. Born Montreal. m. Thomas d'Aquino. **EDUC:** Univ. of British Columbia, B.A.(Psych. & Soc.) 1965; Carleton Univ., M.A.(Phil.) 1970; Univ. of London, UK, doctoral work (Phil.); Harvard Bus. Sch., Advanced Mgmt Program (Bus. Mgmt) 1991. **CAREER:** Sessional Lecturer, Phil., Carleton Univ., 1970-72; Parliamentary Centre for Foreign Affairs & Foreign Trade, 1975-76; Conference Board of Canada, 1976-81; Privy Council Office, 1981-84; Sr. Advisor, Pension Policy, Fed. Dept. of Fin., 1985; Dir. of Social Policy, 1986-89; Gen. Dir., Fed.-Prov. Fiscal Rel'ns & Social Policy, 1990-92; Asst. Deputy Min., 1993 to date. **SELECTED PUBLICATIONS:** *Compensation of Chairmen of Boards of Directors* (The Conference Board of Canada, 1980); "Directors Restless in Traditional Role" (*The Canadian Business Review*, Winter 1978-79); *Canadian Directorship Practices: A Critical Self-Examination* (The Conference Board of Canada, 1977); "Boards of Directors: Their Own Yardsticks" (*The Canadian Business Review*, Autumn 1977); "The Special Joint Committee on Immigration Policy 1975: An Exercise in Participatory Democracy"

Behind the Headlines (Vol. XXXIV, No. 6, The Canadian Institute of International Affairs, Toronto, 1976). INTERESTS: art history; gardening.

Petrie, Anne, G., M.A. ■■ ⚊ ✎
Host, *Early Edition*, CBC Newsworld, CANADIAN BROADCASTING CORPORATION, P.O. Box 2640, Calgary, AB T2N 2M7 (403) 521-6064, FAX 521-6013. Born Toronto. partner Maurice Yacowar. EDUC: Univ. of British Columbia, M.A. 1975. CAREER: broadcaster, radio & TV; author (3 gen. interest books on Vancouver); occasional actor & commentator. SELECTED CREDITS: Co-Host, *3's Company*, CBC Radio, Vancouver, 1975-80; Anchor, *CBC Late Night News*, CBC TV, Winnipeg, 1985-89; Host, *Petrie in Prime*, CBC Newsworld, 1992-95; Host, *Early Edition*, 1996 to date. SELECTED PUBLICATIONS: *Ethnic Vancouver* (Hancock House, 1982); *Vancouver Secrets* (Key Porter, 1983); *More Vancouver Secrets* (Key Porter, 1985). AFFIL: ACTRA. INTERESTS: drawing; painting; cooking; reading; gardening. MISC: Sr. Programmer, Vancouver Centennial Commission, 1983-85. COMMENT: *"Starting as a freelancer for CBC Radio, I have pursued a love of broadcasting in radio and television. I was the first host hired for CBC Newsworld and now anchor the prime time news and feature programme, Early Edition. In my private life, I try to learn as much as I can about drawing and painting."*

Petrie, Doris, A.R.C.T. ■■ ⊗ ✇ ⚊
Actor. c/o Premier Artists Ltd., 671 Danforth Ave., Ste. 305, Toronto, ON M4J 1L3 (416) 461-6868, FAX 461-7677. Born N.S. m. Harry W. Petrie. 3 ch. Anne, Harry (deceased), Claire. EDUC: Halifax Academy, Secretarial Sch.; Royal Conservatory, A.R.C.T.(Speech Arts & Drama-Teacher) 1971. CAREER: stage, film, TV & radio acting, 25 yrs.; performed across Canada, twice in England, and at Edinburgh Festival; taught drama to sch. children & individuals. AFFIL: ACTRA (life mbr.); EQUITY (life mbr.). HONS: Etrog Award for best supporting actress, *Wedding in White* (film); Dora Mavor Moore Award for best actress, *'Night Mother* (stage); Book of the Year, Talking Books, 12 yrs. INTERESTS: community affairs; church (Anglican).

Petro, Trina ⚊ ✇
Co-Owner and Executive Vice-President, MONTAGE INC. CAREER: Booking Agent, Giovanni, 1985-90; Exec. VP & co-owner, Montage Inc., 1990 to date. AFFIL: FARHA Foundation, Montreal; Organization for AIDS Research. INTERESTS: travel; reading; horseback riding.

MISC: Judge, ITM Model Search, 1991; Judge, Access Annual Model Search, 1992-93; represents Rodrigue, 1995 Supermodel of Canada (Male); represents Claudia Barilla, 1994 Runway Model of the Year. COMMENT: *"I consider myself a motivated and driven individual with an entrepreneurial spirit that has contributed to developing Montage into a growing enterprise. I bring passion to my work and strive to build relationships of mutual trust with each client. I am committed to maintaining the highest ethical and moral standards in all working arrangements and to further developing the agency into a comprehensive and diversified one-stop shop, capable of servicing all sectors of the media, including fashion, film, television and radio."*

Petrone, Serafina (Penny), ATCM,B.A., M.A.,Ph.D. ⚔ ⊗ ⚊
Professor Emeritus, LAKEHEAD UNIVERSITY, Thunder Bay, ON P7B 5E1. Born Port Arthur (now Thunder Bay), Ont. s. EDUC: Univ. of Toronto, ATCM 1942; Univ. of Western Ontario, B.A. 1951; Lakehead Univ., M.A. 1970; Univ. of Alberta, Ph.D.(English Lit.) 1977. CAREER: teaching positions from ungraded rural sch. to graded elementary & urban secondary to teachers' coll. & univ. levels; taught secondary sch. in Germany & France; taught at Teachers' Coll. in Uganda; Instructor, Inservice Upgrading programs, Cdn Army, Germany; directed plays, musicals & phys. training demonstrations, choreography; educational film, radio & TV. SELECTED PUBLICATIONS: *Selected Short Stories of Isabella Valancy Crawford* (Ottawa: Univ. of Ottawa Press, 1975); *The Fairy Tales of Isabella Valancy Crawford* (Ottawa: Borealis Press, 1977); *First People, First Voices* (Toronto: Univ. of Toronto Press, 1983); *Northern Voices* (Toronto: Univ. of Toronto Press, 1988); *Native Literature in Canada* (Toronto: Oxford Univ. Press, 1990); *Breaking the Mould: A Memoir* (Toronto: Guernica Editions Inc., 1995); contributor, *The Oxford Companion to Canadian Literature* (Toronto: Oxford Univ. Press, 1983); contributor, *Dictionary of Literary Biography* (Ann Arbor: Edwards Brothers Inc., 1987); contributor, *The Routledge Encyclopaedia of Commonwealth Literature* (London, UK: Alison Barr, 1991); "Native Canadian Literature," in *Studies on Canadian Literature: Introductory and Critical Essays* (New York: Modern Language Association of America, 1991); articles in refereed journals; contributed to the *Dictionary of Canadian Biography*, Vol. 10 (not yet released). AFFIL: Canada Council (Explorations Sub-Committee 1982-85); Canadian Federation of University

Women, Thunder Bay; Magnus Theatre Bd. (Past Dir.); Thunder Bay Regional Arts Council (Past Dir.). HONS: Canada 125 Medal, 1992; Order of Ontario, 1992; "Excellence in Teaching," Lakehead Univ., 1989; Citizens of Exceptional Achievement Award, Thunder Bay, 1981, 1984, 1989; The Delta Kappa Gamma Society Int'l Educ. Award for First People, First Voices, 1984; Hon. Chief (Ojibwa), Tibaajimowinan Kaababaamaawadoonany (Gatherer of legends & stories); Outstanding Contribution to Univ. Teaching, The Ont. Confederation of University Faculties Associations. INTERESTS: travelling; reading; music, theatre; bridge. MISC: numerous presented & invited papers & lectures. COMMENT: *"From the age of 18 when I started to teach in a one-room rural school to the time I retired from teaching university students I tried to make my passion for learning and for excellence infectious."*

Pettifor, Jean L., B.A.,B.Ed.,M.Ed., M.A.,Ph.D. ■ 🐿️ ⊕ 👣
Associate Professor, Department of Educational Psychology and Programme in Clinical Psychology, UNIVERSITY OF CALGARY, 2500 University Dr. N.W., Calgary, AB T2N 1N4. Born Sask. 1922. w. Richard. 2 ch. EDUC: Univ. of Saskatchewan, B.A.(English) 1944; Univ. of Alberta, B.Ed. 1946, M.Ed.(Educ. Psych.) 1948, M.A.(English) 1948; Wayne State Univ., Ph.D.(Clinical Psych.) 1964. CAREER: high sch. teacher, 1942-46; various positions, Alberta Mental Health Services, 1948-82; Mgr, Alberta Social Service, 1982-89; Adjunct Assoc. Prof., Univ. of Calgary, 1986 to date. SELECTED PUBLICATIONS: *The Professional Practice of Psychology: Self-Evaluation*, with B. Bultz, M. Samuels, R. Griffin & G. Lucki (Edmonton: Psychologists' Association of Alberta); *Companion Manual to the Canadian Code of Ethics for Psychologists*, with S. Sinclair (Ottawa: Canadian Psychology Association, 1992); "Ethics and Social Justice in Program Evaluation: Are Evaluators Value-Free?" (*Canadian Journal of School Psychology* 10(2) 1994); "Ethics: Virtue and Politics in the Science and Practice of Psychology" (*Canadian Psychology*, 37(1) 1996); various other publications. EDIT: Ed., *Alberta Psychologist*, 1961-63; Ed., *Psychologists' Association of Alberta Newsletter*, 1972-80; Ed., *Newsletter*, Canadian Psychological Association, Applied Div., 1976-83; Assoc. Ed., 1983-89; Ed. Bd., *Canadian Psychology*, 1979-87. AFFIL: Psychologists' Association of Alberta (Hon. Mbr.; Life Mbr.); Canadian Psychological Association (Fellow; Hon. Life Mbr.; Pres.-Elect 1993-94; Pres. 1994-95; Chair, Committee on Status of Women in Psych. 1993-95); Canadian Psycho-

logical Association Section on Clinical Psych. (Fellow); Association of State & Provincial Psychology Boards; Canadian Research Institute for the Advancement of Women. HONS: 1st Yr. Scholarship, Coll. of Arts & Sciences, Univ. of Saskatchewan, 1942; Honorable Mention, Creative Talents Awards Program, American Institute of Research, 1965; Canadian Centennial Medal, 1967; Professional Service Award, 25th Anniversary, Canadian Mental Health Association, 1980; Award of Recognition, 25th Anniversary, Psychologists' Association of Alberta, 1983; Award for Outstanding Contributions to the Application of Psych. to Human Problems, Canadian Psychological Association Applied Div., 1984; Special Award, recognition of dedication & devotion, Psychologists' Association of Alberta, 1989; Merit Award, Canadian Mental Health Association, Alberta Div., 1989. INTERESTS: standards & ethics in human svcs; community psych.; women's issues. MISC: 1st recipient, Award for Outstanding Contributions to the Application of Psych. to Human Problems, Canadian Psychological Association Applied Div.; listed in various biographical sources, incl. *International Who's Who of Business and Professional Women, Dictionary of international Biography, & 2,000 Notable American Women*; numerous presentations on theme of professional standards & ethics. COMMENT: *"Dynamic and persistent in promoting value-based decision-making in professional, practice, science and teaching by means of stimulating and provocative presentations and publications."*

Pettinicchi, Sandra ■ ■ ⑦
Paralympic Athlete. Montreal, QC. EDUC: interior design student. SPORTS CAREER: mbr., Quebec's Canada Games team; mbr., Nat'l Wheelchair Basketball Team, 2 yrs. Paralympic Games: Gold, 1996. Défi Sportif: 1st, 1995. Canadian Wheelchair Basketball League (CWBL): 4th, finals, 1995. Canada Games: 4th, 1995.

Phénix, Elaine C. ■ $
Senior Vice-President, Equities, THE MONTREAL EXCHANGE, 800 Square Victoria, 4th Fl., Montreal, QC H4Z 1A9 (514) 871-3546, FAX 871-3579. Born Montreal 1948. m. Robert J. Phénix. 2 ch. Lysane Phénix, Carl Phénix. CAREER: Syndication Dept. & Corp. Fin., Lévesque Beaubien Geoffrion Inc., 1979-84; VP, Syndication Dept., 1984-86; Sr. VP & Dir., Syndication Dept., 1986-94; Delegate, Min. for Finances & Fin. Institutions, Prov. of Que., 1991-92; Sr. VP, Equities, The Montreal Exchange, 1994 to date. AFFIL: Canadian Investment Dealers' Association (Fellow; Pres.,

Que. District 1987-88; Nat'l Exec. Committee 1989-90); The Financial Institutions of Ms. Louise Robic (Pres., Consultation Committee); Saint-Justine Hospital Foundation (VP, Exec. Committee 1992-93); Registered Securities Rep.; Laval-sur-le-Lac Golf Club (shareholder); Jeune Chambre de Commerce (Gov.).

Philip, M. Nourbese, B.Sc.,M.A., LL.B. ▯ ▨
Poet, Author. c/o Mercury Press, 137 Birmingham St., Stratford, ON N5A 2T1. Born Tobago 1947. m. Paul Chamberlain. 3 ch. Bruce King, Hiesper Philip-Chamberlain, Hoodie Philip-Chamberlain. EDUC: Univ. of the West Indies, B.Sc.(Econ.) 1968; Univ. of Western Ontario, M.A.(Politics & Int'l Rel'ns) 1970, LL.B. 1973. BAR: Ont., 1975. CAREER: practice of law, 1975-82. SELECTED PUBLICATIONS: *Thorns*, poetry (1980); *She Tries Her Tongue; Her Silence Softly Breathes*, poetry (1988); *Harriet's Daughter* (The Women's Press, 1988); *Frontiers: Essays and Writings in Racism and Culture* (1992); *Showing Grit: Showboating North of the 44th Parallel* (1993); various other books; short stories, essays, reviews & articles have appeared in magazines & journals in Canada, UK & US; poetry & prose appears in numerous anthologies. AFFIL: Poetry Society of America; Authors' Society, UK. HONS: Casa de las Americas Award, *She Tries Her Tongue..*, 1988; Guggenheim Fellow, 1990; Macdowell Fellow, US; Lawrence Foundation Award, US, *Prairie Schooner*, "Stop Frame", 1994. INTERESTS: shortwave; hiking; embroidery. COMMENT: *"I am a poet and writer who lives in the City of Toronto with my husband and children. My supreme endeavour is to contribute to a more just and equitable society whenever I can. My achievement is to continue to have faith that this is possible and to face the obstructions to that goal with some equanimity and dignity."*

Philips, Elizabeth, B.A. ▨ ✎ / ▯ ▱
Writer and Editor, GRAIN MAGAZINE, Box 1154, Regina, SK S4P 3B4 (306) 242-5004, FAX 242-5004. Born Gimli, Man. 1962. cl. D. Larson. EDUC: Univ. of Saskatchewan, B.A. (English) 1985. CAREER: Poet, 1979 to date; Word-11 Asst., English Dept., Univ. of Saskatchewan, 1984-85; Arts Administrator, Saskatchewan Writers' Guild, 1987; Manuscript Reader, Fifth House Publishing, 1987-88; Proj. Coord., Saskatchewan Writers' Guild, 1988; Contributing Ed., *Western Living, Saskatchewan Business Magazine*, 1990-92; Office Mgr, *NeWest Review*, 1991; freelance Journalist/Ed., 1990 to date; Poetry Ed.,

Grain Magazine, 1991-93; Interim Ed.-in-Chief, 1993-95. SELECTED PUBLICATIONS: *Breaking Through Ice* (Turnstone, 1982); *Time in a Green Country* (Coteau, 1990); *Beyond My Keeping* (Coteau, 1995); articles in *Equinox, This Country Canada; Sask Report; NeWest Review*; various other magazines. EDIT: Ed. Comm., *NeWest Review*. AFFIL: Saskatchewan Writers' Guild; League of Canadian Poets. HONS: 1st Recipient, Saskatchewan Poetry Award (for the best book of poetry published in Sask.), 1995. INTERESTS: gardening; goldfish; terriers. MISC: recipient, various grants. COMMENT: *"I have diverted my energies to a career as a writer, despite the lack of monetary reward for doing so. I think my greatest achievement to date is my new collection of poetry, Beyond My Keeping, in which and through which I came to terms with the death of two friends from AIDS. This work was as hard to accomplish as digging ditches–a necessary labour in a world where death is denied its rightful place."*

Phillips, M. Jane, B.A.Sc.,M.A., Ph.D. ⊰ ❀
Professor, Department of Chemical Engineering and Applied Chemistry, UNIVERSITY OF TORONTO, Toronto, ON M4R 1P1 (416) 978-5872, FAX 978-8605. EDUC: Univ. of Toronto, B.A.Sc.(Chem. Eng.) 1953; Bryn Mawr Coll., M.A.(Phys. Chemistry) 1954; Johns Hopkins Univ., Ph.D.(Phys. Chemistry) 1960. CAREER: E.I. du Pont de Nemours, Central Research Dept., Wilmington, Dela., 1954-56; NRC Postdoctoral Research Fellow, Mines Branch, Ministry of Energy, Mines & Resources, 1960-61; Postdoctoral Research Fellow, Queen's Univ. of Belfast (British Petroleum Fellowship), 1961-62; Lecturer, Dept. of Chemistry, Univ. of Toronto, 1963-64; Lecturer, Dept. of Chem. Eng., 1964-72; Asst. Prof., Dept. of Chem. Eng., 1972-77; Assoc. Prof., Dept. of Chem. Eng., 1977-89; Prof., Dept. of Chem. Eng., 1989 to date; Assoc. Chair, Dept. of Chem. Eng., 1990-91, 1995-97; Assoc. Dean, Phys. Sciences, Sch. of Grad. Studies, Univ. of Toronto, 1991-94. DIRECTOR: Chemical Engineering Research Consultants Limited. AFFIL: AAAS; Sigma Xi (Pres., Univ. of Toronto Chapter); Chemical Institute of Canada/CSChE (Catalysis Div., Chair 1983-84); Canadian Catalysis Foundation; Professional Engineers Ontario (Pres. 1993-94); Canadian Council of Professional Engineers (Dir. 1995-97). HONS: FCIC, 1990. INTERESTS: swimming; 18th century porcelain. COMMENT: *"Research interests and publications focus on the kinetics and mechanism of heterogeneous catalytic reactions."*

Phinney, Elizabeth, B.A.,M.P. ✦
Member of Parliament (Hamilton Mountain), GOVERNMENT OF CANADA, House of Commons, Confederation Building, Rm. 713, Ottawa, ON K1A 0A6 (613) 995-9389, FAX 992-7802. Born Paradise, N.S. 1938. s. EDUC: Hamilton Teachers' Coll., Certificate; McMaster Univ., B.A.(Pol. Sci.) 1964. CAREER: English as a Second Language Teacher, Montreal, 1968-74; Supervisor of Program Dev./Instructor of Teachers, Que. Ministry of Educ., 1974-79; Special Asst. to the Min. of Reg'l & Econ. Dev., 1981; Sales Rep., Real Estate, 1982-88; M.P. (Hamilton Mountain), 1988 to date; Assoc. Critic for Industry, Science & Technology, Liberal Party of Canada; Assoc. Critic for Disabled Persons; Reg'l Whip for Central & S.W. Ont.; Reg'l Coord. for Liberal Goods & Svcs Task Force; Critic for Disabled Persons; Assoc. Critic for Health & Welfare; mbr., Standing Committee for Justice & Legal Affairs; V-Chair, Heritage Committee. INTERESTS: literacy; sports; gardening; travel; reading.

Picard, Claudette, M.A.,LL.L. ⌆ ⌂
Partner, STIKEMAN, ELLIOTT, 1155 René-Lévesque Blvd. W., Ste. 4000, Montreal, QC H3B 3V2 (514) 397-3053, FAX 397-3222. Born Windsor, Ont. 1945. m. Marc Régnier. 1 ch. EDUC: Univ. of Ottawa, M.A.(Hist.) 1968, LL.L. 1968. BAR: Que., 1971. CAREER: Assoc., Stikeman, Elliott, 1971-79; Ptnr, 1979 to date. SELECTED PUBLICATIONS: chapter on trusts in *Doing Business in Canada* (Richard De Boo). AFFIL: Quebec Bar (VP & Pres., Fin. Committee 1993-94; Bâtonnière du Québec (Pres. 1994-95); Canadian Bar Association; Union internationale des avocats (Nat'l VP). INTERESTS: reading; travel. COMMENT: *"After having practised law in a major Canadian law firm where I became the first woman partner, I became President (Bâtonnière) of the Law Society of Quebec (Barreau du Québec), which governs the practice of some 16,000 lawyers in Quebec."*

Picard, The Honourable Madam Justice Ellen I., B.Ed.,LL.B.,LL.M.,LL.D. ■ ⌆ ✦ ⌂
Justice, COURT OF APPEAL OF ALBERTA, Judges Chambers, Law Courts, Edmonton, AB T5J 0R2 (403) 422-2319, FAX 427-0334. Deputy Judge, SUPREME COURT OF THE NORTHWEST TERRITORIES. Born Blairmore, Alta. 1941. 1 ch. EDUC: Univ. of Alberta, B.Ed. 1964, LL.B. 1967, LL.M. 1980. BAR: Alta., 1968. CAREER: teacher, Edmonton, 1960-64; articling student, 1967-68; Barrister & Solicitor, Matheson & Company, Edmonton, 1967-72; Asst. Prof., Fac. of Law, Univ. of Alberta, 1972-75; Assoc. Dean, 1974-75; Assoc. Prof.,

1975-78; Founder & Dir., Health Law Institute, Fac. of Law, Univ. of Alberta, 1977-86; Prof., Fac. of Law, 1978-86; Assoc. Dean, 1980-81; McCalla Prof., Univ. of Alberta, 1982-83; Visiting Prof., Univ. of Auckland, 1985; Willis Cunningham Visitor, Queen's Univ., 1986; Justice, Court of Queen's Bench of Alberta, 1986-95; Deputy Judge, Supreme Court of the N.W.T., 1992 to date; Justice, Court of Appeal of Alta., 1995 to date. SELECTED PUBLICATIONS: *Law of Liability of Doctors and Hospitals: Legal Liability of Doctors and Hospitals in Canada* 2nd ed. (Carswell, 1984); *Manual on Dental Jurisprudence* (University Printing Services 1976); various book chapters; numerous articles in law journals, incl. *Alberta Law Review, McGill Law Journal, Osgoode Hall Law Journal* & *Oxford Journal of Legal Studies*; various articles in other publications, incl. *Canadian Hospital Association Journals, Journal of Law & Legal Medical Quarterly*; numerous articles in *Canadian Cases on the Law of Torts*. AFFIL: Canadian Association of Administrative Justice (Dir.); Canadian Judicial Council; Canadian Institute for the Administration of Justice; Canadian Bar Association; Canadian Bar Association (Alberta) Health Law Subsection (Co-founder); Edmonton Medical Legal Society (Hon. Mbr.); Phi Delta Phi (Hon. Mbr.); Univ. of Alberta (Hon. Prof. of Law; Hon. Prof. of Medicine). HONS: LL.D.(Hon.), Univ. of Alberta, 1992. MISC: founder & 1st Chair, Section on Law & Medicine, Canadian Association of Law Teachers, 1976-79; Bd. mbr. & Exec. mbr., Alberta Institute of Law Research & Reform, 1975-79; mbr., Task Force on the Status of the Foetus, Law Reform Commission of Canada, 1985-87; consultant to Law Reform Commission of Canada, 1987-89; VP, Law Reform Commission, 1991-92.

Piché, The Hon. Justice Ginette, B.A., LL.L ⌆
Judge, SUPERIOR COURT OF MONTREAL, 1 Notre-Dame St. E., Montreal, QC H2Y 1B6 (514) 393-2223, FAX 393-2773. Born Montreal 1945. m. Mtre. Pierre Messier. 1 ch. EDUC: Coll. Basile-Moreau, B.C.(cum laude, Arts) 1966; Univ. of Montreal, LL.L.(cum laude, Law) 1969. BAR: Que., 1970. CAREER: Assoc. & Ptnr, McDougall, Hemens, Harris, Thomas, Mason & Schweitzer; chargée de cours, Fac. of Law, Univ. of Montreal, 1981-83; appt. to the Bench, 1985.

Pickard, Audrey, B.Sc.N.,R.N. ■ ○
Volunteer. Thornhill, ON. Born Humberstone, Ont. 1932. m. Franklin G.T. Pickard. 2 ch. EDUC: St. Joseph's Hospital Sch. of Nurs-

ing, R.N. 1954; Univ. of Western Ontario, B.Sc.N. 1966. CAREER: Nursing Educator, St. Joseph's Hospital, Hamilton, 1957-58; Nursing Educator, Provincial Mental Hospital, Ponoka, Alta., 1959-60; Nursing Educator, St. Paul's Hospital, Vancouver, 1960-65; Nursing Educator, Sudbury General, Marymount Sch. of Nursing, 1966-67; Nursing Educator, Laurentian Univ. Sch. of Nursing, 1969-73; Supervisor, Port Colbourne General Hospital, 1954-56. AFFIL: Girl Guides of Canada, York South Div. (District Council, Thornhill W.); Ont. Progressive Conservative Party (Past Chair, Women in Nomination); Women's Association of Mining Industry of Canada, Toronto; Genesis (Research–Education) Women's Health, Toronto; Thornhill Recycling Association. HONS: MacDonald-Cartier Award, PC Party of Canada; Bicentennial Medal for Volunteer Services; Multicultural Award, Town of Markham, Ont. INTERESTS: golf; hiking; fly-fishing; Cdn history. MISC: Founding Chair, Achievement & Civic Recognition Awards, Town of Markham; election campaign organizer–mun., prov., fed. COMMENT: *"Promoting citizenship, encouraging women and youth to pursue, take responsibility, and be a role model in community, political and volunteer organizations."*

Pierre, Marlene ■ ■ ⊕
President and Chief Executive Officer, ONTARIO NATIVE WOMEN'S ASSOCIATION (Aboriginal women's prov. advocacy organization), 977 Alloy Dr., Unit 7, Thunder Bay, ON P7B 5Z8 (807) 623-3442, FAX 623-1104. Born Thunder Bay, Ont. 1944. 6 ch. Peter, Elizabeth, Rob, Chris, Jeordi, Amanda. EDUC: Confederation Coll., grade 12 1968; Lakehead Univ., Pol. Studies courses 1980. CAREER: Dir., Thunder Bay Indian Friendship Centre, 1970; Housing Mgr, Native People of Thunder Bay Development Corporation, 1976-79; Proj. Mgr, LEAP, Training & Dev., Fort William First Nation, 1982; Consultant, 1982-86; Exec. Dir., Thunder Bay Indian Friendship Centre, 1986-88; Pres. & CEO, Ontario Native Women's Association, 1996 to date. SELECTED PUBLICATIONS: "Native Women and the State" (*Perspectives on Women in the 1980s*, Univ. of Manitoba Press, 1980); "Women and the Constitution" (Statement by Native Women's Association of Canada on Native Women's Rights, Canadian Advisory Council on the Status of Women, Cdn Gov't Publishing Centre, 1981). AFFIL: International Indigenous Women's Committee of the Americas (founder & mbr. 1995 to date); Canadian Human Rights Foundation (1995-96); Native Women's Association of Canada (Bd. of Dir. 1994-96; Pres. 1980-81);

Ontario Native Women's Association (Bd. of Dir. 1973-89 & 1994-96; Pres. 1977-79 & 1994-96); Thunder Bay Native Women's Association (founding Pres. & mbr. 1971-94); Ontario Board of Parole (mbr., N.W. Reg. 1978-84). HONS: Canada 125 Medal; Native Woman of the Year award, Ontario Native Women's Association, 1981; Outstanding Young Person, Thunder Bay South Jaycees, 1975; honoured by Prov. of Ont. to celebrate Int'l Women's Year, 1975. INTERESTS: working with Native youth; organizing cultural events; reading; studying Ojibway history. COMMENT: *"Since age twenty, Marlene has been a strong activist and leader in the Aboriginal people's and women's movement, advocating to improve economic and social conditions and about other rights issues."*

Pierson, Ruth Roach, B.A.,M.A., Ph.D. ■ 🖋 ⋞
Professor, ONTARIO INSTITUTE FOR STUDIES IN EDUCATION (OISE), University of Toronto, 252 Bloor St. W., Toronto, ON M5S 1V6 (416) 923-6641, ext. 2742, FAX 926-4725, EMAIL rrpierson@oise.utoronto.ca. Born Seattle, Wash. 1938. EDUC: Univ. of Washington, B.A.(Hist.) 1960, M.A.(Hist.) 1963; Yale Univ., Ph.D.(Hist.) 1970. CAREER: Teaching Asst., Univ. of Washington, 1961-63; Asst. in Instruction, Yale Univ., 1966-67; part-time lecturer, Univ. of Maryland, College Park, 1968-69; Asst. Prof., Memorial Univ. of Newfoundland, 1970-76; Assoc. Prof., 1976-80; Assoc. Prof., O.I.S.E., 1980-90; Prof., 1990 to date. SELECTED PUBLICATIONS: *"They're Still Women After All": The Second World War and Canadian Womanhood* (Toronto: McClelland & Stewart, 1986); *Women and Peace: Theoretical, Historical and Practical Perspectives*, ed. (London: Croom Helm; New York: Methuen, 1987); *No Easy Road: Women in Canada 1920s to 1960s*, ed. with Beth Light, introductions by R.R. Pierson (Toronto: New Hogtown Press, 1990); *Delivering Motherhood: Maternal Ideologies and Practices in the Nineteenth and Twentieth Centuries*, ed. with Katherine Arnup & Andrée Lévesque (London: Routledge, 1990); *Writing Women's History: International Perspective*, ed. with Karen Offen & Jane Rendall (London: Macmillan; Bloomington: Indiana Univ. Press, 1991); *Strong Voices*, Vol. 1, Canadian Women's Issues, with Marjorie Cohen, Paula Bourne & Philinda Masters (Toronto: James Lorimer, 1993); *Bold Visions*, Vol. 2, Canadian Women's Issues, with Marjorie Cohen (Toronto: James Lorimer, 1995); numerous articles published in refereed journals & parts of books, book reviews; numerous papers & lectures. EDIT: Ed. Bd.,

Women's History Review, 1991 to date; Advisory Bd., *Resources for Feminist Research/Documentation sur la recherche féministe*; Advisory Bd., *Atlantis: A Women's Studies Journal.* **AFFIL:** Canadian Historical Association; Canadian Committee on Women's History; Canadian Committee for the History of the Second World War; Canadian Women's Studies Association; Canadian Research Institute for the Advancement of Women; Voice of Women; National Action Committee on the Status of Women (Friend); International Federation for Research in Women in History (VP 1990-95); Centre of Women's Studies in Education, O.I.S.E. (Head 1988-91). **INTERESTS:** addicted to feminist detective fiction & non-violent movies (attended every Toronto Film Festival since 1980); writing of poetry. **MISC:** numerous invited guest lectures; organizer of conference "Women, Colonialisms, Imperialisms and Nationalisms Through the Ages" at the 18th Int'l Congress of the Historical Sciences, Montreal, 1995; recipient, numerous research & conference grants. **COMMENT:** *"Ruth Roach Pierson is a feminist women's historian who has written, co-authored, and co-edited seven books and more than 25 scholarly articles. Her goal has been to make women's history academically legitimate and to make the academic world open and hospitable to women of all races and classes."*

Pigott, Jean Elizabeth Morrison, O.C. Ⓢ ♡ ⊛ ♂
Chairman, OTTAWA CONGRESS CENTRE, 55 Colonel By Dr., Ottawa, ON K1N 9J2 (613) 563-1984, FAX 563-7646. Born Ottawa 1924. m. Arthur Pigott. 3 ch. **EDUC:** Ottawa Ladies Coll.; Albert Coll. **CAREER:** Pres. & Chrm, Morrison Lamothe Inc., 1967-76; MP (Ottawa-Carleton), 1976-79; Advisor, Hon. Joe Clark, PM, 1979; Advisor, Hon. Brian Mulroney, PM, 1984; Chrm, Nat'l Capital Commission, 1984-92; Chrm, Ottawa Congress Centre, 1993 to date; Chrm, Centre for Studies of Children at Risk, Chedoke McMaster Hospital, Fac. of Health Science, McMaster Univ., 1993 to date; Co-Chrm, Expo 2005 Corporation, 1994-95; mbr., Commission to Review Allowances of Members of Parliament, 1994. **SELECTED PUBLICATIONS:** *Special Interest Advocacy - A Right, a Necessity or a Danger?* (Conference Board of Canada, 1980); *Feeding the Nation and the World*, Gov't Policy Committee working paper. **DIRECTOR:** Ontario Hydro (mbr. of Audit Committee); Canadian Development Corporation (mbr. of Audit Committee); Canadian Tire Corporation; Trillium Corporation; Ben's Bakery, Halifax. **MEMBER:** Advisory Bd., Arthur Andersen. **AFFIL:** Canadian Council of Christians & Jews (Dir.); MacDonald Cartier Library (Chair); Canadian Association Club of Rome; Ottawa General Hospital Foundation (Chair); Ottawa General Hospital (Trustee); Ottawa Cancer Unit (Hon. Chair); Ottawa Regional Hospital Planning Council & District Health Council (Founding Mbr.); Carleton Univ. (Gov.); National Council on Children & Youth (Advisory Bd.); Tim Horton Foundation (Dir.); Centennial Centre, Charlottetown (Dir.); Canadian Living Foundation (Patron); Ernest Manning Awards, Calgary (Patron); Amethyst, Women's Alcohol & Drug Centre (Patron); Ontario Association of Architects (Hon. Mbr.); Canadian International Institute of Applied Negotiations; Lambda Alpha International Society; 28th Service Battalion (Hon. Lt. Col.). **HONS:** Award for Distinguished Service to the Community, Ottawa; Centennial Medal, 1967; Queen's Silver Jubilee Medal, 1977; Knight of the Golden Pencil Award, 1978; Canada 125 Medal, 1992; Award of Merit, B'nai Brith Canada; Hon. Doctorate, Univ. of Ottawa; Hon. Doctorate, Univ. of Waterloo; Hon. Doctorate, Univ. of Concordia; Officer of the Order of Canada. **MISC:** 1st woman Dir., Ontario Hydro. **COMMENT:** *"Born in the National Capital Region, Jean Pigott has roots in the Ottawa Valley that go back four generations. She is from an old Ottawa family, owners of Morrison Lamothe Inc., the family frozen-food business, which, under her direction, became a substantial food-processing company."*

Pilarski, Linda M., B.Sc., Ph.D. ■ ⊕ ⊛ ⊰
Professor, Department of Oncology, UNIVERSITY OF ALBERTA, Edmonton, AB T6G 1Z2 (403) 432-8925, FAX 432-8928. Born Beaver Dam, Wisc. 1941. m. Eugene M. Pilarski. 1 ch. **EDUC:** Elmhurst Coll., Ill., B.Sc.(Biol.) 1961; Univ. of Adelaide, Australia, Ph.D.(Biochem.) 1972. **CAREER:** Postdoctoral Fellow, John Curtin Sch. of Medical Research, Australian National Univ., 1972-75; Asst., Assoc. to Full Prof., Dept. of Immunology, Univ. of Alberta, 1975 to date; Prof., Dept. of Oncology. **SELECTED PUBLICATIONS:** 109 articles, book chapters, reports & conference presentations, incl. "Analysis of peripheral blood lymphocyte populations and immune function from children exposed to cyclosporin A and/or azathioprine in utero," with B.R. Yacyshyn & A.I. Lazarovits (*Transplantation*, no. 57, 1993); "Circulating monoclonal B lineage cells expressing P-glycoprotein may be a reservoir of multi-drug resistant disease in multiple myeloma," with A. Belch (*Blood*, no. 83, 1994); "In Multiple Myeloma, Clonotypic B.

Lymphocytes Are Detectable Among CD19+ Peripheral Blood Cells Expressing CD38, CD56, and Monotypic Ig Light Chain," with P.L. Bergsagel *et al* (*Blood* 85(2) 1995). **AFFIL:** Canadian Society for Immunology (Pres. 1995-97). **INTERESTS:** gardening; bee keeping; opera; reading; genealogy research. **MISC:** recipient, numerous operating grants for research. **COMMENT:** *"My research has provided a whole new perspective on multiple myeloma, a cancer that is terminal by three years, post-diagnosis, by describing drug-resistant malignant lymphocytes in the blood as well as in the bone marrow of these patients, and the ways these cells traffic through the body. My current goal is to devise a means to clinically target these cells and, thus, I hope to halt or eradicate the cancer.*

Pilkington, Marilyn L., B.A.(Hons.),LL.B., LL.D. 🐝 ⚖️

Dean, Osgoode Hall Law School, YORK UNIVERSITY, 4700 Keele St., North York, ON M3J 1P3 (416) 736-5199, FAX 736-5251. Born Edmonton 1947. m. Wayne E. Shaw. 2 ch. **EDUC:** Univ. of Alberta, B.A. Hons. 1968; Univ. of Toronto, LL.B. 1975. **BAR:** Ont., 1977. **CAREER:** Law Clerk to The Hon. Mr. Justice Judson, Supreme Court of Canada, 1975-76; Litigation Assoc., Tory Tory DesLauriers & Binnington, 1976-80; Assoc. Prof., Osgoode Hall Law Sch., 1980 to date; Dean, 1993 to date. **SELECTED PUBLICATIONS:** *Canadian Business Corporations*, with others (1975); various articles on constitutional litigation topics. **AFFIL:** Canadian Human Rights Tribunal; NAFTA Dispute Resolution Panel; Law Society of Upper Canada (Certification of Specialists Bd.); Ontario Council for University Affairs; Institute for Research on Public Policy; University Club; Granite Club. **HONS:** various scholarships, Univ. of Alberta, 1964-68; Grad. Fellowship, Prov. of Alberta, 1970-71; Professional Fellowship, Canadian Federation of University Women, 1975; Chief Justice Gale Mooting Trophy, 1975; Dean's Key, Univ. of Toronto, 1977; LL.D.(Hon.), Law Society of Upper Canada, 1994. **MISC:** numerous conference presentations.

Pinder, Leslie Hall, B.A.,LL.B. ⚖️ 📖 ⊗

Partner, MANDELL PINDER, Barristers & Solicitors, 111 Water St., Ste. 300, Vancouver, BC V6B 1A7 (604) 222-1574, FAX 222-1294. Born Elrose, Sask. 1948. s. **EDUC:** Univ. of Saskatchewan, B.A.(English) 1968; Univ. of British Columbia, LL.B.(Law) 1976. **BAR:** B.C., 1977. **CAREER:** articled, Ladner Downs, 1977; Ptnr, Mandell Pinder, Barristers & Solicitors, 1978 to date; writer, 1984 to date.

SELECTED CREDITS: Writer, *Isabel* (theatre), 1990; Writer, *Emma Storrow* (theatre), 1991; Libretto, *The World is Sharp as a Knife* (opera), music by Bruce Ruddell, 1992. **SELECTED PUBLICATIONS:** *Under the House* (Canada: Talon Books, 1986; UK: Bloomsbury, 1987; US: Random House, 1988); *On Double Tracks* (Canada: Lester & Orpen Dennys, 1990; UK: Bloomsbury, 1990); "June Brides," *Women in Words: The Anthology* (Harbour, 1984); "Nightmare" (*Saturday Night Magazine*, Nov. 1990); "The Fourth Wall," *Vancouver Forum, Old Powers, New Forces* (Douglas & McIntyre, 1992); *35 Stones*, poems (Lazara Publications, 1982). **AFFIL:** Federation of B.C. Writers; Writers' Union of Canada; PEN International; Westwater Research, Univ. of British Columbia (Dir. 1989-92); VIEW The Performing Arts Society; Law Society of B.C. **HONS:** shortlisted, Fiction (*On Double Tracks*), Gov. General's Award, 1990. **MISC:** various lectures & presentations; *On Double Tracks* has been optioned for film; Mandell Pinder has worked almost exclusively for native people & has been involved in major litigation involving native people for over 15 yrs.

Pinkus, Wilma, B.A. ■■ ⊗

Watercolour Artist. 296 Clemow Ave., Ottawa, ON K1S 2B8 (613) 235-2560. Born Toronto 1929. m. Philip. 3 ch. Paul, David, Mark. **EDUC:** Carleton Univ., B.A.(Hons., Art Hist.) 1981. **CAREER:** Art Teacher/Head, Art Dept., High Sch. of Commerce, 1989-90; Canterbury High Sch., Sch. of the Arts, 1992; retired from Ottawa Bd. of Educ., 1994. **EXHIBITIONS:** *Summer in Winter: A Visit to Provence*, A Source of Art, Ottawa, Feb. 1992; *My Love - Provence - Mon Amour*, A Source of Art, Ottawa, Oct. 1994; paintings from Italy, France & Canada, Nancy Poole's Studio, Toronto, from Aug. 1996; *Home and Abroad*, Philip K. Wood Gallery, Almonte, Ont., Sept.-Oct. 1996. **AFFIL:** Ottawa Watercolour Society (Fellow); C.A.R.O.; Delta Kappa Gamma; M.S. Society. **HONS:** numerous awards for paintings in Watercolour Society over the years since 1969. **INTERESTS:** swimming & water exercise; reading; cooking & entertaining; theatre; music; films. **MISC:** featured in *A Captor of Colour*, by Anita Lahey, *Ottawa* magazine, 1994; interviewed on *Rockburn and Company*, CBC TV, Nov. 1994; support person for those living active & constructive lives with M.S. and ignoring it or considering it a nuisance and having no time for it. **COMMENT:** *"Art has been my life, as an educator, mentor and watercolour artist. With a passion for colour, I've travelled worldwide in search of the special quality of light for painting in situ."*

Pip, Eva, B.Sc.,Ph.D. ⚲ ✳ ⊕
Professor, UNIVERSITY OF WINNIPEG, 515
Portage Ave., Winnipeg, MB R3B 2E9 (204)
786-9319, FAX 786-1824. Born Winnipeg
1950. s. EDUC: Univ. of Manitoba, B.Sc.(Biol.)
1972, Ph.D.(Ecphisiology) 1977. CAREER:
Asst. Prof., Univ. of Manitoba, 1977-78;
NSERC Postdoctoral Fellow, 1978-79; Instructor, Univ. of Winnipeg, 1979-80; Asst. Prof.,
1980-85; Adjunct Prof., Univ. of Manitoba,
1984-91; Assoc. Prof., Univ. of Winnipeg, 1985-
91; Full Prof., 1991 to date. SELECTED PUBLI-
CATIONS: *Urban Drinking Water Quality*
(Winnipeg: Institute of Urban Studies, 1993);
*Ukrainian Ritual Calendry Songs, with Musical
Scores and Choreography* (Winnipeg: Trident
Press, 1987); "A Stratigraphic study of Mol-
lusks in Lake Manitoba sediment" (*Walkerana*
4 1990); "Mollusc-macrophyte communities in
a meteor crater lake on the Precambrian Shield"
(The Canadian Field-Naturalist 105 1992);
numerous other papers in refereed journals;
numerous gov't reports; various published
abstracts; many conferences; numerous publica-
tions in Ukrainian. AFFIL: Hawaiian Malaco-
logical Society; International Association of
Aquatic Vascular Plant Biologists; International
Society for Medical & Applied Malacology;
Manitoba Conservatory of Music & Arts (Bd.
of Dir.); Rawson Academy of Science, Ottawa.
HONS: NRC Postgrad. Scholarships, 1972-76;
NSERC Post Doctoral Fellowship; Exceptional
Merit Award, Univ. of Winnipeg, 1984, 1986,
1988, 1990, 1992; Clarence Atchison Award
for Excellence in Community Service, Univ. of
Winnipeg, 1987; Manitoba Naturalists' Society
Award for outstanding contribution to natural
hist. in Man., 1992; Order of the Ram,
Ukrainian Professional Business Men's Associa-
tion, 1993; YW-YMCA Woman of Distinction
Award nominee, 1994; Univ. of Manitoba
Alumnae Alpha Omega Woman of the Year
Award, 1994. INTERESTS: composing music
& giving concerts for piano; largest private shell
collection in Canada; collecting rocks & fossils;
gardening, reading; canoeing; horseback riding.
MISC: Univ. of Winnipeg & Music Performance
Trust Fund International Concert Series, full-
length concert of original piano compositions
(1991); Registered Consultant, Center for
Aquatic Plants, Univ. of Florida; recipient, various grants; numerous invited public lectures &
seminars; tech. consulting & identification for
various private, public & media companies;
more than 300 media interviews on environment & public health issues. COMMENT: *"I
worry about what is happening to our environment. Although just one person does not make
much difference, I have tried to satisfy my own
conscience."*

Piquet, Rita-Anne, B.A. ■ ⊗ ⓔ
Artist. Born Toronto 1953. s. EDUC: Univ. of
Toronto, B.A.(Phil. & Soc.) 1974; Ballinakill
Studios, Ireland; Three Schools of Art, Toronto.
CAREER: professional artist & art instructor;
Co-ordinating artist & designs, International
Festival of Trees, Dufferin Mall, Toronto,
1994, 1995. SELECTED PUBLICATIONS:
included *in L'Art au Feminin/The Feminine
Viewpoint: Works by Contemporary Women
Artists* (Montreal: Jacob, 1994). COMMIS-
SIONS: Amnesty International Christmas Card
(1989); "Silences", illustration, *Late Harvest
Journal of Creative Culture* (Winter 1994);
cover, *Canadian Journal of Women's Health
Care*, April 1995; cover, *Canadian Treasurer*,
Feb. 1996. EXHIBITIONS: solo, Arts Cafe,
Artsweek, Toronto (1991); solo, Leah Posluns
Theatre, Toronto (1993); solo, *The Spectator
Gallery*, Hamilton (1993); various group exhi-
bitions, incl. Rose Noir Gallery, Welland
(1990), Koffler Gallery, Toronto (1992) & *The
Feminine Viewpoint*, Boutique Jacob, Toronto
(1994); Dufferin Mall Charity Art Auction
(1996). COLLECTIONS: Law Society of Upper
Canada; Cassels, Brock & Blackwell. AFFIL:
Amnesty International; Canadian Foundation
for the Study of Infant Deaths (Past Pres., Bd.
of Dir.). INTERESTS: art; theatre; dance; music.
MISC: recipient, various grants.

Piros, Joanna, B.A. ⟋ ⛫ ⚘
President, PIROS PRODUCTIONS, 3614 Rutherford Cres., N. Vancouver, BC V7N 2C7 (604)
988-2981, FAX 988-2910. Born Warsaw
1955. 5 ch. Matthew, Mark, Georgia, Wysia,
Isabella. EDUC: Carleton Univ., B.A.(Journalism) 1977. CAREER: Public Info. Officer,
Canadian Radio-television & Telecommunications Commission, 1975-77; News Reporter,
CKO-FM, 1977-79; News Reporter, CKVU-
TV, 1979-81; News Anchor, CKVU-TV Vancouver, 1981-88; Pres., Piros Productions, 1988
to date. SELECTED CREDITS: Media Consultant, Canada 125/Participaction; Media Consultant, Vancouver Int'l Film Festival; Prod. &
Writer, *Spilled Milk*; Principal, *The Outer Limits* (series); Principal, *The X-Files* (series); Prod.,
RealLife (Knowledge Network/OLA); *Year in
Review* (1984-86); *Sweet Young Thing* (1986-
87); *A Matter of Conscience: A Matter of Policy* (1987); *The Quality Series* (Knowledge Net-
work/OLA, 1993). AFFIL: Leadership Vancouver. MISC: various M.C. & moderator
engagements, live, televised, radio broadcast;
media trainer, UBC Residential Exec. Program,
ICBC, Justice Institute of B.C.

Pitcher, Patricia Cherie, B.A.,Ph.D. ■ ⚲
Professor of Leadership and Dean of the Doc-

toral Program, L'ÉCOLE DES HAUTES ÉTUDES COMMERCIALES, 5255 Decelles Ave., Montreal, QC H3T 1V6 (514) 340-6730, FAX 340-5635. Born Tillsonburg, Ont. 1950. m. Jean-Jacques Bourque. EDUC: Trent Univ., B.A.(Politics) 1973; McGill Univ., Ph.D.(Mgmt) 1992. CAREER: Research Assoc., New Democratic Party Leader Stephen Lewis, 1973; Chief Economist, Toronto Stock Exchange, 1979-80; Sr. VP, Canadian Federation of Independent Business, 1984-90; Prof. of Leadership, Écoles des Hautes Études Commerciales, 1990 to date. SELECTED PUBLICATIONS: *L'artiste, l'artisan, et le technocrate* (Montréal: Québec/Amérique, 1994); *Artists, Craftsmen, and Technocrats* (Toronto: Stoddart 1995); *The Drama of Leadership* (New York: John Wiley & Sons, 1996). INTERESTS: tennis; swimming; snowshoeing.

Piternick, Anne B., B.A.,F.L.A. 📖 ⬧
Professor Emerita, School of Library, Archival and Information Studies, UNIVERSITY OF BRITISH COLUMBIA, Vancouver, BC V6T 1Z1. Born Blackburn, UK 1926. m. George Piternick. EDUC: Manchester Univ., B.A.(English) 1948. CAREER: various positions, Library, Univ. of British Columbia, 1956-66; Asst. Prof., Sch. of Library, Archival & Info. Studies, UBC, 1966-73; Assoc. Prof., 1973-78; Prof., 1978-91; Assoc. Dean, Fac. of Arts, 1985-90. SELECTED PUBLICATIONS: various writings on info. systems & svcs, Cdn bibliography, scholarly communication. AFFIL: British Library Association (F.L.A.); National Library (Advisory Bd. 1978-84); Social Sciences & Humanities Research Council (Advisory Academic Panel 1981-84; various other committees); Canadian Library Association (Pres. 1976-77); Council on Library Resources (Fellow 1979-80); National Advisory Committee on Culture Statistics (1985-90); UBC Senate (1969-72). HONS: Queen's Silver Jubilee Medal, 1977; Award for Special Librarianship in Canada, Canadian Association for Special Libraries & Information Sciences, 1987; UBC 75th Anniversary Medal, 1990; Canada 125 Medal, 1993. INTERESTS: music; cuisine. MISC: organizer of conferences on the state of Cdn bibliography, 1974 & 1981. COMMENT: *"Promoted and helped develop programs to support the infrastructure of research in Canadian studies; worked to advance the standing of my professional field in academia."*

Pizano, Beatriz, B.A. ⬧ ⬧ ⬧
Actor, Writer and Video Artist, 99 Bertmount Ave., Toronto, ON M4M 2X8. Born Colombia, S. America 1960. EDUC: Univ. of British Columbia, B.A.(Psych.) 1986; Emily Carr Coll. of Art & Design, 1987. CAREER: Research

Asst., Psych. Dept., Univ. of British Columbia, 1982-84; Research Asst., Shaughnessy Hospital, Psychiatry Outpatient Dept., 1985-86; actor, film/TV/theatre, 1988 to date. SELECTED CREDITS: Spanish Dialogue Coach for film & TV, *MacGyver* (series), Paramount Pictures, 1990-92; translation, *Learning About AIDS*, Shane Lunny Productions, 1990-92; Spanish translation & subtitles, *Speaking of Courage*, Gemini nominee, Condor Productions Ltd., dir. Vladimir Bondarenko, 1990-92; Principal, *Spenser* (series), M.O.W. Norstar; Lead, *City of Dark* (feature), October Films & National Film Bd., dir. Bruno L. Pacheco; Prod., *In Between* (feature), 1993-96; Writer/Dir./Prod., *Poetry in the Americas* (documentary), 1994; Co-writer, *Tangueratas* (stage play), Sur Theatre, 1995; Prod., *For Sale: Tobacco, English Spoken, Manuelita Saenz* (theatre), 1996. AFFIL: Southern Currents; ACTRA; EQUITY. INTERESTS: photography; equestrian; ballet; modern dance. MISC: recipient, various grants. COMMENT: *"As a woman and an actor, I have seen it necessary to expand my artistic possibilities into other creative areas, such as writing and video production."*

Platts, Diana, B.A.,B.A.A. ■■ ✎ ⬧ ⬧
Co-Producer and Host, TWISTED PAIR PRODUCTIONS (TV production), ON (416) 690-5340, EMAIL 74252.2331@compuserve.com. Born Toronto 1962. s. EDUC: Univ. of Toronto, B.A.(English, French) 1988; Ryerson Sch. of Journalism, Grad. Program in Journalism, B.A.A. 1991; various seminars re scriptwriting, video journalism, & mktg. CAREER: TV producer/host/reporter; freelance magazine reporter; professional actor; Exec. Asst., Public Affairs & Corp. Communications Dept., National Public Relations, 1994-95. SELECTED CREDITS: co-prod./host/reporter, *Clickstreams* (Cdn/Dutch/Banff Centre for the Arts co-production, TV series on culture & technology, 12 eps.); co-host/reporter, *Lifestyle* (nat'l daily, magazine-format), 1992-94; host/aerobics instructor, *The Fitness People*, CBLT-TV, daily, 1988-90; mbr., original Cdn cast, *CATS*, 1985-87; roles in *Spencer for Hire* (TV M.O.W.), *Darkman III* (feature film), *Catwalk*, *Boogie's Diner*. SELECTED PUBLICATIONS: freelance writer, *CyberStage Magazine* (Cdn quarterly on arts & technology); health & fitness article, *You Magazine*, Feb. 1990; health & fitness article, *Verve Magazine*, cover story, Fall 1986. AFFIL: ACTRA (Chairperson, Nat'l Women's Committee; Chairperson, Toronto Women's Committee; Nat'l Councillor, Performers' Guild); Canadian Labour Congress (Women's Committee 1996 to date); Equity; Canadian Association of Journalists; Women

in Film & Television; The McLuhan Program in Culture & Technology, Univ. of Toronto (Jr. Research Assoc.). **HONS**: CityTV scholarship for excellence in broadcast journalism, 1990. **MISC**: aerobics instructor (OFC certified). **COMMENT**: *"Facing the paucity of employment opportunities in the biz, I became concept originator, co-producer, host, field reporter, writer, researcher, P.A. (chasing waivers), camera operator, off-line editor, audio mixer and on-line producer for my own series, currently in international distribution with Raymond International."*

Playdon, Kathy Carol, B.Sc. 🌐 🎓 ⬛
President, CANADIAN FINNSHEEP BREEDERS' ASSOCIATION, R.R. 4, Box 10, Site 10, Stony Plain, AB T0E 2G0 (403) 963-0416. Born Dryden, Ont. 1955. m. Ralph Playdon. **EDUC**: Univ. of Alberta, B.Sc.(Agric.) 1976, Forage Utilization 1978. **CAREER**: Animal Nutritionist, Norwest Labs, Edmonton, 1976-84; Instructor, Grant MacEwan Coll., 1980-82; Purebred Finnsheep Breeder, Stony Plain, Alta., 1981 to date; Level II English Coach, Canadian Equestrian Federation. **AFFIL**: Alberta Sheep & Wool Commission (Dir.; Chrm 1990-93); North Central Sheep Breeders; Canadian Finnsheep Breeders' Association (Pres.); Northwest Sheep Producers' Association; Canadian Cooperative Woolgrowers; Alberta Agriculture Research Institute (Bd.); Edmonton Northlands (shareholder); Alberta Horse Trials Association. **INTERESTS**: equestrian. **COMMENT**: *"I am the first woman to Chair any agricultural commission."*

Plouffe-Pinel, Suzanne, B.Sc.N., C.M. ▪▪ 📖 🌱
President and owner, LES ÉDITIONS CLOWN SAMUEL INC. (publishing house, children's songs), C.P. 506, Orléans, ON K1C 1S9 (613) 745-2871, FAX 745-2871. Born Ottawa 1945. 3 ch. Anne-Marie, Patrick, Pierre-Louis. **EDUC**: Univ. of Ottawa, Diploma (Public Health Nursing) 1966, B.Sc.N. 1967. **CAREER**: Teacher, Psych. of Growth & Dev., Pediatrics, Nursing Sch., Ottawa Gen. Hospital, 1967-70; Animator/Lecturer, Musical Expression & Musical Pedagogy courses, Fac. of Educ., Univ. of Ottawa & Laurentian Univ., 1977-82; Creator/Writer/Producer/Actor, children's TV program, *Marie-Soleil*, 1987-93. **SELECTED CREDITS**: 130 eps. *Marie-Soleil*, syndicated series, YTV, BBS; 4 50-min. video-cassettes each with 20 songs for children & activity notes for parents/educators; 15 audio-cassettes of songs composed & recorded for children, 1979-95; *Musique s'il vous plaît*, Vol. 1 (1989) & Vol. 2 (1993), musical activities program for

primary sch. children, for int'l distribution; "My Best Friend/Mon copain préféré" (bilingual children's game, created & distributed internationally for Elections Canada to foster understanding about elections, 1987). **DIRECTOR**: Les éditions Clown Samuel Inc. **AFFIL**: Ottawa District Referee Board on Employment Insurance (Pres. 1995 to date); Children's Hospital of Eastern Ontario Foundation (Chair, Exec. Admin. Bd. 1996 to date); Gloucester Arts Council (Bd. of Dir. 1996 to date); Ottawa-Carleton Children's Aid Society Foundation (Hon. Chair 1994-95); UNICEF (Prov. Ambassador 1991-94); Canadian Parents for French (Hon. Chair 1995-96). **HONS**: Member of the Order of Canada, 1991; Media Award in Children's Educ., Solicitor General of Ont., 1993; 2 Gold Can-Pro Awards for *Marie-Soleil*; Graham Spry Award, ACTRA; Escarbot Award for outstanding contribution to community cultural activities, Communications Canada; President's Award for svc. to health & welfare of the community, Ontario Medical Association; nominated for Best Children's Program of the Year, ACTRA, 1991 & 1993; Personality of the Year, City of Gloucester, 1990; Woman of Vision, Association des enseignants franco-ontariens, 1990; Salon de l'enfant de l'Ouest québécois/Ottawa-Carleton Preschooler Services Association (Hon. Chair, "Say no to drugs" campaign); Outstanding Achiever Award for singing/composing, City of Gloucester; Hon. Mom, Caisses populaires de l'Ontario Week; Citizenship Judge, several Citizenship Ceremonies, 1995 & 1996. **INTERESTS**: family; music; cooking; ice skating; leisure cycling; reading children's publications. **COMMENT**: *"This Ottawa-born composer/producer/performer touches the lives of children everywhere. Wholly dedicated to their well-being and healthy development, Suzanne Pinel beckons them, through music and artistic expression, to explore their worlds and the wonders of life. Her career, which now spans over three decades, has been an unwavering commitment to children and their pursuit of happiness. Awarded the Gold Can-Pro Award for her Marie-Soleil TV series and the coveted ACTRA Graham Spry Award, Suzanne Pinel has been a member of the Order of Canada since 1991."*

Poff, Deborah C., B.A.,B.A.,M.A., Ph.D. ▪ 🐦 ✏
Professor and Vice-President, Academic, UNIVERSITY OF NORTHERN BRITISH COLUMBIA, 3333 University Way, Prince George, BC V2N 4Z9 (604) 960-5610, FAX 960-5791. Editor, *JOURNAL OF BUSINESS ETHICS*. Co-Editor, *TEACHING BUSINESS ETHICS*. Born Toronto 1950. m. Alex Michalos. **EDUC**: Univ. of Guelph,

B.A.(Psych.), Ph.D.(Phil.) 1987; Queen's Univ., B.A.(Phil.) 1977; Carleton Univ., M.A.(Phil.) 1979. **CAREER:** Ed., *Journal of Business Ethics*, 1981 to date; Asst. Prof., Phil. Dept., Univ. of Alberta, 1983-84; Chair, Women's Studies & Asst. Dir., Institute for the Study of Women, Mount St. Vincent Univ., 1984-87; Co-Ed., *Atlantis: A Women's Studies Journal*, 1985-90; Assoc. Dir., Institute for the Study of Women, & Assoc. Prof., Mount St. Vincent Univ., 1987-90; Dir., Institute for the Study of Women, & Assoc. Prof., 1990-93; Ed.,*Atlantis*, 1990-94; Prof. & Dean, Fac. of Arts & Sci., Univ. of Northern British Columbia, 1993-96; Acting VP, Academic, 1994-96. **SELECTED PUBLICATIONS:** General series ed., *Canadian Issues* (Montreal, Association for Canadian Studies, 1988); *Business Ethics in Canada*, ed. with W. Waluchow (Prentice-Hall, Inc., Mar. 1987, 2nd edition 1991); numerous refereed book chapters & articles, incl. "The Poff-Michalos Feminism Scale" (*Social Indicators Research*, 1988); "A Feminist Conception of the Classroom and Classroom Discussion" (*Philosophy of Education: Introductory Reading*, ed. J. Portelli & W. Hare, Calgary: Diselig Press, 1988); "Reproductive Technology and Social Policy in Canada" *in The Future of Human Reproduction* ed. C. Overall (Toronto: The Women Press, 1989); "The high cost of keeping women poor: Female-headed, lone parent families" (*Canadian Women's Studies Journal*, Summer 1992); numerous reports, non-refereed articles, & reviews. **EDIT:** Ed. Bd., *Canadian Journal of Human Sexuality*; Ed. Bd.,*International Journal of Value-Based Management*; Ed. Bd., *Canadian Women's Studies*. **HONS:** Hon. Lifetime Membership, "in recognition of outstanding contribution to feminist research," Canadian Research Institute for the Advancement of Women, 1995. **MISC:** recipient, numerous grants & fin. awards; selected as Cdn rep. to H.R.H. The Duke of Edinburgh Commonwealth Study Tour, 1992; numerous scholarly addresses & lectures. **COMMENT:** *"I am a feminist scholar, teacher and administrator with a commitment to equity issues."*

Pohl, Tanya, CPPB,CPPO ■■ $ ⊕

Director, Medical/Surgical Services, JOINT HOSPITAL PURCHASING SERVICES (on behalf of The Hospital for Sick Children, Princess Margaret Hospital, Mount Sinai Hospital & The Toronto Hospital Corporation), c/o The Hospital for Sick Children, 555 University Ave., Toronto, ON M5G 1X8 (416) 813-7062, FAX 813-7985, EMAIL tanyapohl-lew@mailhub.sickkids.on.ca. Born Montreal 1962. m. Ivan Lew. 2 ch. Kyle, Meiping. **EDUC:** George Brown Coll., Labour Studies 1988; National Institute of Government Purchasing, Certified Professional Public Buyer 1990, Certified Public Purchasing Officer 1992; Univ. of Toronto, part-time B.Comm. studies ongoing; several hospital-related mgmt courses & accompanying certification. **SELECTED PUBLICATIONS:** several articles related to purchasing, internal & external procurement-related magazines; author, several strategic procurement practice reference materials on behalf of Joint Hospital Services. **AFFIL:** Ontario Public Buyers' Association (Dir. of Public Awareness; mbr. of Exec. 1994 to date; Consultant on Course Dev.); Cubs (leader 1994 to date). **INTERESTS:** knitting; music; the arts; baseball; reading. **MISC:** speaker & facilitator on behalf of Jackson & Associates. **COMMENT:** *"Tanya has a broad range of experience as a Certified Public Purchasing Officer, administrator and consultant in health care reform. She has been critical in the re-engineering of health care within the four institutions (HSC, MSH, TH and PMH). She is one of the principal negotiators and controls well over 200 million hospital dollars."*

Poirier, Leigh A. ■■ ♥ ✊

Executive Director, CANADIAN TOY TESTING COUNCIL (evaluation of children's toys, non-profit organization), 22 Hamilton Ave. N., Ottawa, ON K1Y 1B6 (613) 729-7101, FAX 729-7185. Born Halifax, N.S. 1955. m. Maurice Poirier. 2 ch. Tasha, Justin. **EDUC:** Algonquin Coll., Recreation Leadership (Hons.) grad. 1976; Ottawa Univ., Therapeutic Recreation Course 1977; fed. gov't, Admin. & Fin. Mgmt programs 1980 & 1982. **CAREER:** initiated & implemented recreation & fitness programs, various groups incl. private resorts, hospitals, communities, etc., 1975-85; administered, researched & consulted with nat'l sports organizations in areas of contribution programs, amateur athletes, publications & projects for disabled, Fitness and Amateur Sport, 1977-88; Exec. Dir., Canadian Toy Testing Council; teacher, special needs children, Ottawa educational system. **SELECTED PUBLICATIONS:** Editor, 1994 *Toy Report*; prepared biographical info. for "Jasper Talks" proceedings, 1986; collaboration with Advisory Committee in production of *Physical Activity for Canadians with a Disability: Blueprint for Action*, 1988. **AFFIL:** Recreation Advisory Committee, Goulbourn Township (mbr. 1993 to date). **INTERESTS:** travel; participating in sports (skating, skiing, tennis, fencing, martial arts, rollerblading) with family; photography; statistics; writing; innovative gardening. **MISC:** media tour for the promotion of the 1994 *Toy Report*; initiated annual gala "Toy Auction" held in conjunction with the media launch of the Canadian Toy Testing Council's *Toy Report* & 10 Top Toys of the Year–fundraising event with long-term goal to generate funds to enable Council to undertake a project on the adaptability of toys for special needs children. COMMENT: *"I always aspire to a challenge. I try to find the most effective method to successfully complete a project and if there isn't one, I'll create a new way. My personal commitment is to give 120 percent and to approach each situation with integrity."*

Poirier, Nicole ■ ⊕ ⊕
Directrice, SOCIÉTÉ D'ALZHEIMER DE LA MAURICIE, 1765 boul. St. Louis, Trois Rivières, QC G8Z 2N7 (819) 376-3538, FAX 376-7063. EDUC: Univ. du Québec à Trois-Rivières; Univ. du Montréal. CAREER: Propriétaire d'une résidence privée pour personnes âgées, 1984-91; Promotrice, Centre d'hébergement, de soins et de services spécialisés pour les personnes atteintes de la maladie d'Alzheimer, 1985-89; Fondatrice, la Société d'Alzheimer de la Mauricie, 1985-93; Coord., Conseil Régional de la Santé et des services sociaux, 1989-90; Consultant, Ministère de la Santé et des services sociaux, 1989; Mbr. du conseil d'admin., Fédération québécoise des sociétés Alzheimer, 1989 to date; Prés., 1991-93; Coord., l'équipe de psychogériatrie, 1990-94; Mbr., conseil d'admin. la Société d'Alzheimer du Canada, 1992-93; Mbr., assemblée régionale, Mauricie-Bois-Francs, 1992-93; VP, conseil d'admin. unifié des centres d'acceuil Joseph-Denys, 1992-93. HONS: Prix Spécial Cascades, 1987; Lauréate avec mention d'Honneur, 1988. MISC: divers communications à conférences.

Poirier, Thelma ◻ ▯ ▧
Author, Fir Mountain, SK S0H 1P0 (306) 266-4750. SELECTED PUBLICATIONS: *Double Visions* (Coteau Books, 1984); *Grasslands* (Coteau Books, 1990); *The Bead Pot* (Pemmican Publications Inc., 1993). AFFIL: Wood Mountain Historical Society. COMMENT: *"Lifelong interest in prairie history and ecology, particularly in the southwest area of Saskatchewan. Have tried to combine ranching and conservation and promote awareness of environmental concerns."*

Polivy, Janet, B.S.,M.A.,Ph.D. ▧ ⊕
Professor, Department of Psychology, Erindale College, UNIVERSITY OF TORONTO, Mississauga, ON L5L 1C6 (905) 828-3959. Born 1951 3 ch. Lisa, Eric, Saretta. EDUC: Jackson Coll., Tufts Univ., B.S. 1971; Northwest Univ., M.A. 1973, Ph.D. 1974. CAREER: Asst. Prof., Dept. of Psych., Loyola Univ. of Chicago, 1974-76; Visiting Asst. Prof., Dept. of Psych., Univ. of Toronto, 1976-77; Research Assoc., Clarke Institute of Psychiatry, Psychosomatic Med. Unit, 1977-83; Prof., Dept of Psych., Univ. of Toronto, Erindale Coll., 1983 to date; Prof., Dept. of Psychiatry, 1983 to date; Research Assoc., Toronto General Hospital, Dept. of Psychiatry, 1983 to date. SELECTED PUBLICATIONS: *Breaking the Diet Habit: The Natural Weight Alternative*, with C.P. Herman (New York: Basic Books Inc., 1983); *Psychology*, 3rd ed., with H.L. Roedger III, E. Capaldi & S.G. Paris (New York: HarperCollins, 1991); "Psychological effects of radical mastectomy" *(Public Health Reviews* 1975); "Effects of smoking status on perceived attractiveness," with R. Hackett & P. Byclo *(Personality and Social Psychology Bulletin* 1979); "On the induction of emotion in the laboratory: Discrete moods or multiple affect states?" *(Journal of Personality and Social Psychology* 1981); "Food perception in dieters and non-dieters," with G. King & C.P. Herman *(Appetite* 1987); "Food restriction and binge eating: A study of former prisoners of war," with S.B. Zeitlan, C.P. Herman & A.L. Beal *(Journal of Abnormal Psychology* 1994); numerous other publications. EDIT: Assoc. Ed., *Journal of Personality*, 1981-86; Consulting Ed., *Journal of Abnormal Psychology*, 1979 to date; Consulting Ed., *International Journal of Eating Disorders*, 1988 to date; Consulting Ed., *Journal of Consulting and Clinical Psychology*, 1985-86. AFFIL: Ontario Coll. of Psychologists (mbr. of Council 1994-97); American Psychological Society (Fellow); Association for Advancement of Behaviour Therapy; Canadian Psychological Association; Canadian Register of Health Service Providers in Psychology; Society for the Study of Ingestive Behaviour; Society for Personality & Social Psychology. HONS: US Public Health Svcs Fellowship, 1971. MISC: recipient, various grants; reviewer for various professional journals; various conference presentations; numerous invited addresses.

Pollock, Lorraine Marie ■■ ▧ ⊕ $
President, NEW BRUNSWICK HOME ECONOMICS ASSOCIATION, c/o Sussex Regional High School, P.O. Box 5003, Sussex, NB E0E 1P0 (506) 432-2017, FAX 432-2613. Born Sussex, N.B. 1949. m. Norman. 2 ch. Alaina, Robert. EDUC: N.B. Teachers' Coll., Home Econ. 1969; Univ. of New Brunswick, B.Ed.(Home Econ.) 1972, degree in Guidance in progress. CAREER: teacher, 1969 to date. AFFIL: N.B. Teachers' Association (has served on numerous provincial & local committees); N.B. Home Economics Association (Pres. 1996; former Chairperson, Educ. & Scholarship Committees); Canadian Home Economics Association

(Int'l Dev. Proj.); Sussex Vale Transition House (Chairperson, Bd. of Dir.); Sussex Lioness; Sussex Women's Network; Saint John's United Church. **HONS:** Outstanding Home Economist "Rheta Inch Award of Recognition," N.B. Teachers' Association; Gender Equity Award in Educ., 1993; Rouse Scholarship, 1993. **INTERESTS:** upholstery; reading; bridge; travel. **MISC:** Acting Consultant, Family Studies, N.B. Dept. of Educ., Curriculum & Implementation Div., 1994; various presentations; Hospitality teacher, Canberra, Australia, 1995-96; mbr., 2 curriculum dev. advisory committees, Sr. High Home Econ. & Broad-Based Technology, Dept. of Educ., 1995 to date. **COMMENT:** *"Intensely involved in community and professional affairs. Energetic and outgoing, enabling me to juggle personal and public life effectively. I often find myself acting counsellor to troubled teens, parents or helping grieving parents, lonely seniors, visiting sick and shut-ins. In recent months, I have been used as an after-dinner speaker. Speaker for 3 professional workshops. I guess I'm recognized as the one "in the know" re home economics and broad-based technology (as it applies to Home Economics in New Brunswick)."*

Pomerleau, Jeanne, B.A. 📖 📜

Writer. Sainte-Foy, QC. Born Saint-Séverin, Beauce, Que. 1937. m. Jean-Claude Dupont. 2 ch. Luc Dupont, Marie Dupont. **EDUC:** Univ. de Moncton, B.A.(Lit. & Hist.) 1971; Univ. Laval, Certificat en création littéraire 1986. **CAREER:** writer & researcher, 1980 to date. **SELECTED PUBLICATIONS:** *Les Grandes corvées Beauceronnes* (1987); *Le Montreur d'ours* (1988); *Métiers ambulants d'autrefois* (1990); *Les coureurs de bois. La traite des fourrures avec les amérindiens* (1994); *Arts et métiers de nos ancêtres 1650-1950* (1994); *Les chercheurs d'or des Canadiens français épris de richesse et d'aventure* (1996). **AFFIL:** Union des écrivains québécois, Montréal. **INTERESTS:** dessin; peinture; histoire de l'art. **COMMENT:** *"I am currently doing research on French Canadian culture. I am particularly interested in rural and family life. I write especially on folk crafts."*

Pontbriand, Chantal, B.A. ■ ✪ ✎

Curator, Writer and Consultant. 4060 boul. Saint-Laurent, Ste 501, Montreal, QC H2W 1X9 (514) 842-9805. Born Montreal 1951. m. Raymond Gervais. 1 ch. **EDUC:** Univ. du Québec à Montréal, B.A.(Art Hist.) 1991. **CAREER:** independent Curator & Consultant, 1970 to date; mbr., galerie Véhicule Art, 1973-75; Founder, Ed., *Parachute*, contemporary art magazine, 1975 to date; Founder, Pres. & Dir., Festival International de Nouvelle Danse, 1985 to date. **SELECTED PUBLICATIONS:** has published more than 150 articles. **EXHIBITIONS:** organizer, 03 23 03, exhibition & festival, Montreal (1977); organizer, *Performance*, exhibition, festival & conference, Montreal (1980); guest curator, *Pluralities*, National Gallery of Canada, Ottawa (1980); curator, *La ruse historique*, Power Plant, Toronto (1988); curator, *Geneviève Cadieux*, Canadian Pavilion, Venice Biennial (1990). **HONS:** "Personalité de la semaine," *La Presse*, 1991; Grand Prix of the Conseil des Arts de la Communanté urbaine de Montréal, 1995 (for the F.I.N.D.). **INTERESTS:** contemporary art; art museums; music; dance; architecture; modern lit.; social & cultural trends. **MISC:** listed in *Les femmes qui ont bâti Montréal* (Éditions du Remue-Ménage, 1994); recipient, various Canada Council grants.

Poole, Nancy Geddes, B.A., LL.D. ■ ✪ 📜 ☝

Management and Development Consultant. 420 Fanshawe Park Rd., London, ON N5X 2S9 (519) 660-0634, FAX 660-0634. Born London, Ont. 1930. m. William R. Poole, QC. 1 ch. Andrea Geddes Poole. **EDUC:** McGill Univ., Diploma 1949; Univ. of Western Ontario, B.A. 1955. **CAREER:** Prod., weekly classical music programme, CFPL Radio, London; Writer, Interviewer & Prod., series on London artists, CFPL-TV, London; founded & operated Nancy Poole's Studio, London, 1969-77 & Toronto, 1971-77; Chrm, Governing Council, Ontario Coll. of Art, 1972; mbr., Bd. of Gov., Univ. of Western Ontario, 1974-85; Interim Dir., London Regional Art Gallery, 1981; Exec. Dir., 1985-96. **SELECTED PUBLICATIONS:** *Jack Chambers*, ed. of autobiography (1985); *The Art of London 1830-1980* (1984). **HONS:** Woman of Distinction Award, London YM-YWCA, 1984; Mayor's New Year's Honours List, London, 1984; Award of Merit, Univ. of Western Ontario Alumni Association, 1985; LL.D.(Hon.), Univ. of Western Ontario, 1990; Fellow(Hon.), Ontario Coll. of Art. **MISC:** 1st woman to chair Property & Fin. Committee, Bd. of Gov., Univ. of Western Ontario; received 1st Woman of Distinction Award given by London YM-YWCA. **COMMENT:** *"Administrator, art gallery owner, art historian, author, publisher and broadcaster."*

Poole, Suzanne, B.A.,M.B.A. ■ $ ☝

Vice-President and Regional Manager, THE TORONTO-DOMINION BANK, 1130 Sherbrooke W., Montreal, QC H3A 2M9 (514) 594-4073, FAX 289-0022. Born Toronto 1953. s. **EDUC:** York Univ., B.A.(English Lit.) 1978; Univ. of Toronto, M.B.A.(Fin./Mktg) 1982. **CAREER:**

Stanley/de Maisonneuve, Montreal, The Toronto-Dominion Bank, 1987-89; Branch Mgr, Cavendish Hall, Montreal, 1989-91; Branch Mgr, Greene Ave., Westmount, 1991-92; Reg'l Mgr, Central Que. Reg., 1992-95; VP & Reg'l Mgr, 1995 to date. INTERESTS: cycling; reading; theatre. MISC: regular guest on local radio phone-in show to discuss banking & other fin. matters; 1st woman VP for TD in Que. COMMENT: *"As the daughter and sister of entrepreneurs, and as a woman, I know how unfriendly banks can seem. My goal as a banker is to humanize the face of our profession."*

Popil, Irene ✪

Administrative Secretary, BRITISH COLUMBIA ASSOCIATION OF HEALTH CARE AUXILIARIES, 1333 W. Broadway, Ste. 600, Vancouver, BC (604) 734-2423, FAX 734-7202. Born Evansburg, Alta. 1940. m. Rudolf. 2 ch. Lesley Kim Mercado Ruano, Nicholas Rudolf Popil. EDUC: Vancouver Vocational Institute, Grad.(Bus./Office) 1961. CAREER: Typist/ Office Clerk, Parsons Brown Co. Ltd., 1963-66; Office Clerk, Westwood Shipping Agencies Ltd., 1983-84; Administrative Sec., B.C. Association of Health Care Auxiliaries, 1987 to date. AFFIL: Burnaby Hospital Auxiliary (volunteer); John Norquay Sch. (Kindergarten Asst.; Library Aide). INTERESTS: needlecraft; reading; volunteering; cooking; sewing; walking; music; swimming; gardening. COMMENT: *"I feel that I am compassionate, helpful, concerned, sincere, honest, hard-working, giving, discreet and able to accept almost any challenge. I have raised two productive children and run the B.C.A.H.A. office; organize conferences and assist the president."*

Porac, Clare, B.A.,M.A.,Ph.D. ⬧ ❀ ⑤

Professor of Psychology, Department of Psychology, UNIVERSITY OF VICTORIA, Box 3050, Victoria, BC V8W 3P5 (604) 721-7537, FAX 721-8929, EMAIL hand@castle.uvic.ca. President, EDVEST MANAGEMENT ASSOCIATES LTD. Born Pittsburgh 1945. m. Wilfred Oppel. EDUC: Duquesne Univ., Pittsburgh, B.A.(Soc.) 1967; The Grad. Fac. of the New Sch. of Social Research, N.Y., M.A.(Psych.) 1971, Ph.D.(Psych.) 1974; Institute for Behavior Genetics, Univ. of Colorado, Post-doctoral Fellow 1975. CAREER: Therapeutic Activities Worker, Mayview State Hospital, Bridgeville, Pa., 1967-68; Recreation Therapist, Coney Island Hospital, Brooklyn, N.Y., 1968-69; Sessional Lecturer, Univ. of Victoria, 1974-75; Asst. Prof., Psych., 1975-80; Assoc. Prof., 1980-83; Prof., 1983 to date. SELECTED PUBLICATIONS: *Sensation and Perception*, with S. Coren & L.M. Ward (New York: Academic Press, 1979; 2nd edition Orlando, Fla.: Academic Press, 1984); Instructors' manual to accompany *Sensation and Perception* (New York: Academic Press, 1981; 2nd edition, Orlando, Fla.: Academic Press, 1984); *Lateral preferences and human behavior*, with S. Coren (New York: Springer-Verlag, 1981); numerous published papers incl. "Hand preference and the incidence of accidental unilateral hand injury" (*Neuropsychologia* (31) 1993); "Are age trends in adult hand preference best explained by developmental shifts or generational differences?" (*Canadian Journal of Experimental Psychology* (47) 1993); "Comparison of wings-in, wings-out and Brentano variants of the Mueller-Lyer illusion" (*The American Journal of Psychology* (107) 1994); "Attempts to switch the writing hand: Relationships to age and handedness" (*Canadian Psychology* (35)2a, 1994); "Decrement and the illusions of the Mueller-Lyer figure" (*Perceptual and Motor Skills* (79) 1994); "Anomalous dominance, incidence rate studies and other methodological issues" (*Brain and Cognition* (26) 1994). EDIT: Ed. Bd., *Journal of Experimental Psychology*: Gen. Ed., 1991 to date; Ed., Canadian Psychological Association, Section on Women and Psychology (SWAP) Newsletter, 1995-97; Ed. Bd., *Canadian Journal of Psychology*, 1980-85. AFFIL: American Psychological Association (Fellow, Div. 3, Experimental Psych.); American Psychological Society (Fellow); Canadian Psychological Association (Fellow); Univ. of Victoria Faculty Association (Pres. 1994-95); Canadian Psychological Association (Status of Women Committee 1994-95).

Porteous, Tracy ■ ⓗ ❂ ⬧

Consultant, BRITISH COLUMBIA ASSOCIATION OF SPECIALIZED VICTIM ASSISTANCE COUNSELLORS PROGRAMS, 620 View St., Ste. 505, Victoria, BC V8W 1J6 (604) 995-2166, FAX 995-2167. Born Winnipeg 1959. CAREER: Proj. Worker, Women & Economic Hard Times, Victoria, 1984; Proj. Mgr, Need Crisis & Info. Line, Victoria, 1984; Publications Coord., Victoria Women's Sexual Assault Centre, 1983-87; Volunteer Coord., 1985-87; Exec. Dir., 1987-95; Program Mgr, Ministry of Women's Equality, Gov't of B.C., 1992-93. SELECTED PUBLICATIONS: *Working with Survivors of Sexual Assault*, with others (Victoria: Victoria Women's Sexual Assault Centre, 1986); *Let's Talk About Sexual Assault*, with others (Victoria: Victoria Women's Sexual Assault Centre, 1983); *Sexual Assault. A Victim Support Worker's Handbook*, with S. Alexander (Gov't of B.C., Ministry of Attorney Gen. & Ministry of the Solicitor Gen., 1989); *Sexual Assault and Counselling Skills,* curriculum modules for the Victims Asst. Program (Justice Institute of B.C. on behalf of the Gov't of B.C., Ministry of Attorney Gen. & Ministry of the Solicitor Gen., 1991). **AFFIL:** B.C. Association of Clinical Counsellors; Mayor's Advisory Committee on the Prevention of Violence (Co-Chair); Interministry Committee for the Dev. of Prov. Sexual Assault Policy; Victoria Interministerial Committee on Sexual Abuse & Sexual Assault; Disaster Response, Victoria Mental Health Association (Psychological Support Volunteer). **HONS:** Nat'l Solicitor Gen. Award for Crime Prevention, *Let's Talk about Sexual Assault,* 1983; Canada 125 Medal, 1993; Hon. for Significant Contribution, B.C. Attorney Gen., 1995; nominated, Women of Distinction, YWCA, 1996. **MISC:** Registered Clinical Counsellor, B.C.; Co-Chair, "Justice: Extending the Vision. A National Conference on Victimization and Recovery," Victoria, 1992; Co-Chair, "Triumphs and Challenges: Victim Services in the '90s," prov. conference, 1995; field practicum supervisor, Sch. of Social Work, Univ. of Victoria. **COMMENT:** *"Tracy Porteous is a longtime feminist and advocate for justice and social change for women. She has co-authored numerous resources regarding sexual assault and abuse and has provided training and assistance to groups and organizations throughout the province."*

Porter, A. Helen Fogwill 🗋 🐾
Writer, 51 Franklyn Ave., St. John's, NF A1C 4L2. Born St. John's 1930. w. John K. Porter. 4 ch. Kathryn Victoria, Margaret Anne, John Robert, Stephen Francis. **EDUC:** Prince of Wales Coll., St. John's, graduated 1947. **CAREER:** various jobs; professional writer since 1965. **SELECTED PUBLICATIONS:** *A Long and Lonely Ride,* short story collection (Breakwater Books, 1991); *January, February, June or July,* novel (Breakwater, 1988); *Below the Bridge,* memoir (Breakwater, 1980); many short stories, poems, plays & reviews published & performed across Canada & overseas. **AFFIL:** NDP; Newfoundland Writers' Guild; Writers' Alliance of Newfoundland & Labrador; The Writers' Union of Canada; International PEN; St. John's Status of Women Council; The Longside Club. **HONS:** shortlisted, W.H. Smith/ Books in Canada First Novel Award, 1989; winner, Young Adult Canadian Book Award, Canadian Library Association, 1989; Lifetime Achievement Award, Newfoundland & Labrador Arts Council, 1993. **INTERESTS:** reading; walking; writing & thinking in restaurants; movies; theatre; discussing books; writing; spending time with my friends & family.

COMMENT: *"Ever since I can remember, I've wanted to write. I've been writing one thing or another all my life and continue to do that."*

Porter, Anna, B.A.,M.A. 🗋 $
Publisher and Chief Executive Officer, KEY PORTER BOOKS LIMITED, 70 The Esplanade, Toronto, ON M5E 1R2 (416) 862-7777, FAX 862-2304. Chairman, LESTER PUBLISHING LIMITED. Born Hungary. m. Julian Porter, Q.C. 2 ch. **EDUC:** Canterbury Univ., Christchurch, New Zealand, B.A.(English & Modern Languages) 1964, M.A.(English Lit.) 1965. **CAREER:** Jr. Ed., Cassell and Company, London, UK; Coll. Sales Mgr, Collier Macmillan Limited, London, UK, 1967-69; Ed., Collier Macmillan Canada Limited, 1969; VP, Ed.-in-Chief, McClelland & Stewart Limited, 1969-78; Pres., McClelland-Bantam Inc., 1978-92; Pres. & Publisher, Key Porter Books Limited, 1981 to date; Exec. Chrm, Doubleday Canada Ltd., 1986-91. **SELECTED PUBLICATIONS:** *Hidden Agenda,* novel; *Mortal Sins,* novel. **DIRECTOR:** Alliance Communications; Argus Corporation Limited; Key Porter Books; Key Publishers. **AFFIL:** Association of Canadian Publishers; Association for the Export of Canadian Books; Book Publishers' Professional Association; Mystery Writers of America; Mystery Writers of Canada; P.E.N. International; Council of Canadians; Unicef Canada (Advisory Bd.); World Wildlife Fund Canada (Exec. Bd.); Schulich Sch. of Business (Dir.); Information Highway Council. **HONS:** Officer, Order of Canada, 1992; hon. degree, Canadian Sch. of Management, Toronto; hon. degree, Ryerson Polytechnic Institute; D.Litt.(Hon.), St. Mary's Univ. **MISC:** lectures & speeches throughout Canada about culture & publishing. **COMMENT:** *"Key Porter Books is one of Canada's leading book publishing houses, with a wide-ranging and varied list of authors. Anna Porter is well-versed in the publishing field worldwide, and regularly attends the Frankfurt International Book Fair, the American Booksellers' Association Convention, the London Book Fair and other book conventions."*

Potts, Nadia ✕ 🎴
Director, Dance Program, RYERSON POLYTECHNIC UNIVERSITY, 350 Victoria St., Toronto, ON M4E 1Y8 (416) 979-5086, FAX 979-5275. Born London, UK 1948. m. Harold Gomez. 2 ch. Alexander, Natalya. **EDUC:** National Ballet Sch., Grad. **CAREER:** Corps de Ballet, National Ballet of Canada, 1966; Soloist, 1967-69; Principal Dancer, 1969-86; Teacher, 1986 to date (has led numerous master classes & workshops); Dir., Dance Program, Ryerson Polytechnic Univ., 1989 to date. **SELECTED CRED-**

ITS: leading roles in *The Nutcracker, Cinderella, Swan Lake, La Sylphide, Sleeping Beauty, Giselle, La Fille Mal Gardée, Romeo and Juliet, Don Quixote, La Bayadere, Don Juan, Etudes*; principal & soloist roles *in The Dream, Serenade, Spectre de la Rose, Four Schumann Pieces*; *Four Temperaments*; *Symphony in C*; *Concerto Barocco, Monotones, Black Angels, Kettentanz* & others; various guest & TV appearances. **AFFIL:** Royal Academy of Dancing; Association for Dance in Universities & Colleges in Canada; Dance Ontario; Sch. of Classical & Contemporary Dance (Artistic Advisor); Canadian Actors' Equity Association; ACTRA. **HONS:** Bronze Medal & Prize for Best Pas de Deux, Int'l Ballet Competition, Varna, Bulgaria, 1970. **MISC:** recipient, Canada Council Study Grant, 1971; listed *in Who's Who in Canada, Who's Who in America, International Who's Who of Professional and Business Women, Concise Oxford Dictionary of Dance*; entries & pictures included in *Karsh's Canadians, Baryshnikov at Work, Women of Canada, Dance in Canada, Canada's National Ballet, The National Ballet of Canada* & numerous other dance books; during career was partnered with Mikhail Baryshnikov, Peter Schaufuss, Peter Martins, Fernando Bujones, Gary Norman, Rudolph Nureyev, Anthony Dowell, Erik Bruhn, Stephen Jeffries, Jean Charles & the principals of the National Ballet of Canada. **COMMENT:** *"Nadia Potts, formerly a dancer with the National Ballet of Canada, is currently director of the Dance program at Ryerson Polytechnic University. Ms. Potts has taught at the National Ballet School, York University and the Banff Centre of Fine Arts, and has led numerous master classes and workshops. During her 20-year stage career, she performed internationally and was partnered with some of the most renowned dancers of our time."*

Poudrette, Danielle, B.Sc.,M.B.A.,C.G.A. $
Senior Director, Product Management, AIR CANADA, Box 14000, St.-Laurent, QC H4Y 1H4 (514) 422-5847, FAX 422-6439. Born Montreal 1956. s. **EDUC:** École des Hautes Études Commerciales, B.Sc.(Acctg) 1980; McGill Univ., M.B.A.(Int'l Bus./Mgmt Policy) 1985. **CAREER:** External Auditor, Maheu, Noiseux, Roy et Associés, 1974-76; Internal Auditor, Head Office, National Bank of Canada, 1977-80; Internal Auditor, Que. Divisions, St. Lawrence Cement Inc., 1980-83; Consultant, McGill Bus. Consulting Bureau, 1984; Coord., Charter Programs, Air Canada, 1985-86; Int'l Strategy Analyst, 1986-89; Mgr, New Product Dev., 1990-93; Mgr, Int'l Product, 1993-94; Dir., Int'l Product, 1994-95; Sr. Dir., Product Mgmt, 1995 to date. **AFFIL:** Certified General Accountants' Association of Quebec (C.G.A.); Canada-Korea Business Council. **INTERESTS:** sailing; tennis; skiing. **MISC:** various appearances as guest speaker & lecturer. **COMMENT:** *"I am proud to be part of Air Canada's senior management team, challenged with turning the corporation into a profitable airline positioned to compete effectively with other international carriers globally. I am a persevering action-oriented team worker, possess a good sense of humour and high level of energy, am enthusiastic, optimistic and care for the well-being of others."*

Powell, Anna, C.S.W.,B.S.W. ⊕ ♡
Employment and Education Counsellor, CANADIAN PARAPLEGIC ASSOCIATION (SASKATCHEWAN) INC., 4401 Albert St., Ste. 210, Regina, SK S4S 6B6 (306) 584-0101, FAX 584-0102. Born Tipperary, Ireland 1947. d. 3 ch. John Powell, Paul Powell, Julie Powell. **EDUC:** Univ. of Regina, C.S.W. 1991; B.S.W.(Social Work) 1992. **CAREER:** Childcare Worker, 1980-83; Income Security, Saskatchewan Social Svcs, 1993; Shelter Counsellor, Isabel Johnson Shelter, YWCA, 1994 to date; Employment & Educ. Counsellor, Canadian Paraplegic Association (Saskatchewan) Inc., 1994 to date. **AFFIL:** Canadian Hard of Hearing Association (Regina Branch) Inc. (Sec. 1990-91, 1994-95; Pres. 1991-93; VP 1993-94); Canadian Hard of Hearing Association (Nat'l Dir.); Saskatchewan Deaf & Hard of Hearing Svcs (Pres. 1993-94; Past Pres. 1994 to date); Regina Deaf & Hard of Hearing Community Centre (VP 1993-95). **INTERESTS:** theatre; reading; walking; volunteer work; family; travelling overseas. **COMMENT:** *"Immigrated to Canada in 1979 from London, UK. 1987 was a significant year for me, a turning point in my life. I turned 40, became a grandmother, and entered university. Education and community service has helped me reach my potential and I look forward to more challenges in the future."*

Power, Rosalie ■■ 🍁 ♡ 👍
Administrative Assistant to Mayor David Lovell, CITY OF YELLOWKNIFE, P.O. Box 580, Yellowknife, NT X1A 2N4 (403) 920-5693, FAX 920-5649, EMAIL www.city.yellowknife.nt.ca. Born St. John's 1947. cl James Gill. 2 ch. Jason Power, Aasha Gill. **EDUC:** Coll. of Trades & Technology, Bus. Admin. Certificate 1968. **CAREER:** Office Clerk, Macleods Dept. Store, Peace River, Alta., 1973-74; Office Clerk, Aquatine of Canada, Rainbow Lake, Alta., 1975-76; Gov't of N.W.T., 1976-95; Sec., part-time, Bank of Montreal, 1986-89; Chapter III Bookstore, 1989 to date.

AFFIL: North of 60 Block Parent Program (Chairperson 1983 to date; Sec. 1979-83); Block Parent Program of Canada Inc. (Newsletter Editor 1991-93; Delegate for the N.W.T. 1984 to date); Society for the Prevention of Cruelty to Animals, Yellowknife (Sec. 1986-88). HONS: award from Solicitor Gen. of Canada for Operation Family Identification, 1986; award from RCMP, Yellowknife for crime prevention program, 1986; Suggestion Award, Gov't of the N.W.T., 1990; City of Yellowknife Award for coordinating Physical Activity Week, 1986; certificates of appreciation from Canadian Cancer Society & various Block Parent programs. INTERESTS: reading; fishing; hunting; gardening; volunteer work; providing an orphanage in Jamaica with books & clothing. COMMENT: *"My interest in volunteering began in high school and my commitment to my community and safety of children has resulted in the first finger printing in the N.W.T."*

Praeg, Irene ■ ☺

President, PARENT FINDERS NEW BRUNSWICK, 16 Grove Ave., Box 263, Rothesay, NB E2E 5K3 (506) 847-8098, FAX (506) 847-5798. Born Kitchener, Ont. 1928. m. Aldo. 3 ch. CAREER: office, sec. & supervisory positions in mfg company in Kitchener, auto sales firms in Toronto & Vancouver, C.P.R. Telegraph, Vancouver. VOLUNTEER CAREER: Pres., Parent Finders N.B.; Dir., Parent Finders Canada. AFFIL: Riverside Country Club, Saint John; IODE; A.A.R.P.; Canadian Snowbird Association; Saint John Volunteer Centre; Family Services. HONS: presented with The Victoria Leach Award for lengthy & outstanding svc. to the adoption community, The Adoption Council of Canada, 1996. INTERESTS: people; reading; puzzles. COMMENT: *"I am an unpaid volunteer who uses investigative techniques to bring people together. I estimate I have helped 4,000 people in 19 years."*

Prata, Gabrielle, B.A. ⊗

Opera Singer. Affiliated with the Canadian Opera Company. Born Toronto 1960. m. Robert Longo. 2 ch. Nicholas, Adriana. EDUC: York Univ., B.A.(Psych.) 1983; Univ. of Toronto, Opera Diploma 1986. CAREER: Mezzo Soprano; trained with the Company Ensemble, Canadian Opera Company; frequent performer with the Canadian Opera Company; N.Y. debut with National Grand Opera, 1990; concert singer, frequent soloist. SELECTED CREDITS: Cinderella, *Cinderella*, Bermuda Festival, 1987; Dryade, *Ariadne auf Naxos*, Canadian Opera Company, 1988; Maddalena, *Rigoletto*, Calgary Opera, 1989; Rosina, *Il barbiere di Siviglia*, National Grand Opera, 1990; Meg

Page, *Merry Wives of Windsor*, Anchorage Opera, 1991; Hansel, *Hansel and Gretel*, Nevada Opera Theater, 1992; title role, *Carmen*, Opera North, 1992; Anita, *West Side Story*, Sherbrooke Symphony, 1993; Suzuki, *Madame Butterfly*, Canadian Opera Company, 1994; *Rosina*, Opera Hamilton, telecast, 1994; *Adalgisa*, Gold Coast Opera, 1995; *Verdi's Requiem*, Saskatoon Symphony, 1996; various other opera credits; various oratorio & concert performances; *La Forz del Destino*, "Making Opera," telecast, 1988; *The Makrapoulus Case*, telecast, 1989. HONS: Winner, Young Canadian Mozart Singers Competition, 1986; Winner, Edward Johnson Music Foundation Vocal Competition, 1987; Herman Geiger-Torel Award for "Outstanding Achievement," Canadian Opera Company Ensemble, 1987; Winner, Metropolitan Opera District Finals, 1988; Montreal Int'l Vocal Competition, 1989; Floyd Chalmers Grant, 1989, 1991; Winner, Ismaele Voltolini Int'l Competition of Opera Singers, Mantova, Italy, 1989. INTERESTS: family; keeping fit; mastering the art of singing. MISC: grant recipient. COMMENT: *"Of my endeavours, I am committed to being the best person, mother, wife, singer, friend, etc., that I can be. I feel my achievements to date have been largely due to good fortune, support and a willingness to learn. I hope that the real achievements of my career are ahead of me."*

Pratt, Mary Frances (née West), B.F.A. ■■ ⊗

Painter and Printmaker. 161-1/2 Waterford Bridge Rd., St. John's, NF A1E 1C7 (709) 726-5355, FAX 726-4007, EMAIL npratt@new-comm.net. Born Fredericton, N.B. 1935. m. Christopher Pratt. 4 ch. John, Anne, Barbara, Ned. EDUC: Mount Allison Univ., Certificate (Fine Arts) 1956, B.F.A. 1961. SELECTED PUBLICATIONS: co-author, *Across the Table* (Prentice-Hall, 1985). EXHIBITIONS: solo, prov. touring exhibition, *Mary Pratt: A Partial Retrospective*, Memorial Univ. of Newfoundland Art Gallery, 1973; group show, *Survey of Canadian Art Now*, Vancouver Art Gallery, 1974; group show, *Some Canadian Women Artists*, The National Gallery of Canada, Ottawa, 1975; group nat'l touring exhibition, *Aspects of Realism*, The Gallery, Stratford, 1976; group show, *Strictly People*, Cdn Consulate Gen., Chicago/Boston/Atlanta, Cdn Embassy, Washington, D.C., 1978; solo, *Mary Pratt*, London Regional Art Gallery, London, Ont., 1981; group nat'l touring exhibition, *Survivors in Search of a Voice: The Art of Courage*, Royal Ontario Museum, Toronto, 1995; solo nat'l touring exhibition, *The Art of Mary Pratt: The Substance of Light*, The

Beaverbrook Art Gallery, Fredericton, 1995 (travelling to Vancouver, Victoria, Toronto, Winnipeg, St. John's, Halifax, & ending in Corner Brook, Nfld., Aug. 1997). Regular exhibitions at: Mira Godard Gallery, Toronto; Equinox Gallery, Vancouver; Douglas Udell Gallery, Edmonton. COLLECTIONS: Public: National Gallery of Canada, Ottawa; Canada Council Art Bank, Ottawa; New Brunswick Museum, Saint John; Art Gallery of Nova Scotia, Halifax; Canada House, London, UK; Vancouver Art Gallery; CBC, Calgary; Art Gallery of Ontario, Toronto; & others. Universities: Memorial Univ. of Newfoundland; Univ. of Toronto, Erindale Coll.; Univ. of Guelph; Univ. of N.B.; Acadia Univ.; Mount Allison Univ.; & others. Corporate: Dofasco Inc., Hamilton, Ont.; C-I-L Inc., Toronto; Canada Packers, Toronto; Petro-Canada; Irving Oil; McCain Foods; Northern Telecom; Manufacturers Life, Toronto; & others. AFFIL: Gov't Task Force on Educ., St. John's, Nfld. (Bd. mbr. 1973); Fishing Industry Advisory Bd. of Newfoundland (mbr. 1978); Law Society of Newfoundland & Labrador (Bencher 1980); Applebaum-Hebert Cultural Review Committee, Ottawa (mbr. 1981); Grace Hospital, St. John's (Bd. of Dir. 1981); Mount Allison Univ. (Bd. of Regents 1983-89); Arts & Cultural Industries Sectoral Advisory Group on Int'l Trade, Ottawa (mbr. 1988); Canada Council (Rep. 1987-93); Memorial Univ. of Newfoundland Art Gallery (Advisory Committee 1994); Royal Canadian Academy of the Arts (Atlantic Rep. 1994); Friends & Lobbyists of the Waterford (F.L.O.W.) River, St. John's (Hon. Patron 1995 to date); Children's Hospital of Western Ontario, London (Acquisitions Chairperson, Pediatric-Oncology Art Therapy Program 1995-96); General Hospital Health Foundation, St. John's (Hon. Spokesperson 1993 to date). HONS: Fellowship Award, Ontario Coll. of Art, 1990; Commemorative Medal for the 125th Anniversary of Cdn Confederation, 1993; inducted into Newfoundland & Labrador Arts Council Hall of Honour, 1994; 6 honorary degrees, Dalhousie Univ., Memorial Univ. of Newfoundland, St. Thomas Univ., Univ. of Toronto, Mount Allison Univ., & Univ. of Victoria. MISC: books about her: *Mary Pratt* (by Sandra Gwyn & Gerda Moray, McGraw-Hill, 1989) & *The Art of Mary Pratt: The Substance of Light* (by Tom Smart, Goose Lane Editions, 1995); documentaries: "Infused with Light," *Adrienne Clarkson Presents*, CBC TV, 1996; *Originals in Art*, Bravo! Channel, Sleeping Giant Productions, 1996.

Pratt, Patrice 🖰 ✤
Director, Contract and Resource Services,

BRITISH COLUMBIA GOVERNMENT AND SERVICE EMPLOYEES' UNION, 4911 Canada Way, Burnaby, BC V5G 3W3 (604) 291-9611, FAX 293-1369, EMAIL patrice_pratt@bcgeu.bc.ca. Born Akron, Ohio 1948. d. 1 ch. Jordana. CAREER: various positions, Manitoba Health Svcs Commission, 1969-74; Employee Rel'ns Officer, Man. Gov't Employees' Union, 1974-76; Staff Rep., Administrative Support Component, B.C. Gov't & Svc Employees' Union, 1976-79; Negotiations & Arbitration Dept., 1979-80; Asst. Dir., Membership Svcs, 1980-83; Solidarity Coalition Coord., 1983-85; Educ. Officer, 1985-88; Coord., Lower Mainland/Fraser Valley Reg., 1988-89; Dir., Contract & Resource Svcs, 1989 to date. SELECTED PUBLICATIONS: position papers & articles in union & NDP publications. AFFIL: Canadian Association for Williams Syndrome; C.A.W.S. (B.C. Dir.); Centre for Labour & Management Studies (Dir.); Medical Services Foundation (Dir.); B.C. Federation of Labour (Exec. Council; V-Chair, Women's Committee); New Democratic Party of B.C. (Past Pres.); New Democratic Party of Canada. HONS: Joe Morris Award, United Way, 1993. INTERESTS: unionism; politics; community service; travel; gardening; reading. COMMENT: *"As the eldest child in a large family, I learned at an early age that I am 'my brother's (and sister's) keeper'. My work as a trade unionist, community organizer, and in the political arena, is undertaken to this end."*

Pratte, Lise, LL.B.,M.B.A.,F.C.I.S., Adm.A. ■ ⚖ 💲
Lawyer and Administrator. Born Laval, Que. 1950. m. 1 ch. EDUC: Laval & Sherbrooke Universities, LL.L. 1976; Montreal Univ., École des Hautes Études Commerciales, M.B.A. (Hum. Res. & Fin.) 1988. BAR: Que., 1977. CAREER: Asst. Sec., Malouf Inquiry Commission on the 21st Olympiad, 1977-79; Asst. Sec., Des Manoirs Sch. Bd., Terrebonne, Que., 1979-82; Legal Cnsl & Mgmt Consultant, private practice, 1981-82; Corp. Sec. & Legal Cnsl, Canadian Arsenals Ltd., Le Gardeur, Que., 1982-85; Asst. Sec. & Legal Cnsl, Imasco Limited, Montreal, 1985-88; Corp. Sec., Bombardier Inc., 1988-96. AFFIL: Laval Univ. Foundation (Bd. of Dir.); Quebec & Canadian Bar Associations; Institute of Chartered Secretaries & Administrators (Fellow); Canadian Shareholders' Services Association (Bd. of Dir.; Nominating Committee); American Society of Corporate Secretaries. INTERESTS: law; psychology; finance; computer-related matters. COMMENT: *"Has acted as a senior officer of public and parapublic corporations for 20 years. Specializes in securities law matters and corporate law and managing departments."*

Prentice, Alison, B.A.,M.A.,Ph.D. ■ ⊴ 🕮
Professor, Department of Theory and Policy
Studies in Education, ONTARIO INSTITUTE FOR
STUDIES IN EDUCATION (OISE), University of
Toronto, 252 Bloor St. W., Toronto, ON M5S
1V6 (416) 923-6641, ext. 2510, EMAIL apren-
tice@oise.on.ca. Adjunct Professor, Depart-
ment of History, UNIVERSITY OF VICTORIA.
Born Wilmington Del. m. James D. Prentice. 2
ch. (1 dec.) Douglas, Matthew (1963-79).
EDUC: Smith Coll., B.A.(Hist.) 1955; Univ. of
Toronto, M.A.(Hist.) 1958, Ph.D.(Hist.) 1974.
CAREER: Teacher of Hist., Bishop Strachan
Sch., 1955-57; Teaching Asst., Dept. of Hist.,
Univ. of Toronto, 1958-59; Teacher of Hist. &
French, Harbord Collegiate Institute, 1959-61;
Teaching Asst., Dept. of Hist., Univ. of
Toronto, 1962; Teacher of Hist. & French,
Harbord Collegiate Institute, 1963; Teaching
Asst., Dept. of Hist., Univ. of Toronto, 1964-
67; Teaching Asst., Dept. of Hist. & Phil. of
Educ., OISE, Summer 1970; Lecturer, then
Asst. Prof., Dept. of Hist., Atkinson Coll., York
Univ., 1972-73; Assoc. Prof., Dept. of Hist. &
Phil. of Educ., OISE, 1975-83; Visiting Scholar,
Centre for Research on Women, Stanford
Univ., 1981-82; Prof., Dept. of Hist. & Phil. of
Educ., OISE, 1983 to date; Founding Head,
Centre for Women's Studies, OISE, 1983-85;
Adjunct Fellow, Simone de Beauvoir, Concor-
dia Univ., 1986; Adjunct Prof., Univ. of Victo-
ria, 1996-98. SELECTED PUBLICATIONS: *The
School Promoters: Education and Social Class
in Mid-Nineteenth Century Upper Canada*
(Toronto: McClelland & Stewart, 1977); *Cana-
dian Women: A History*, with others (Toronto:
Harcourt, Brace, Jovanovich, 1988); *Schooling
and Scholars in Nineteenth Century Ontario*,
with Susan E. Houston (Toronto: Univ. of
Toronto Press, 1988); *Women Who Taught:
Perspectives on the History of Women and
Teaching*, ed. with Marjorie Theobald
(Toronto: Univ. of Toronto Press, 1991); *Gen-
der and Education in Ontario: An Historical
Reader*, ed. with Ruby Heap (Toronto: Cana-
dian Scholars Press, 1991); "The Feminization
of Teaching in British North America and
Canada, 1845-1875" (*Social History/histoire
sociale* May 1979); "Teachers' Work: Chang-
ing Patterns and Perceptions in the Emerging
School Systems of 19th and Early 20th Cen-
tury Central Canada," with Marta Danylewycz
(*Labour/le travail* Spring 1986); "Multiple
Realities: The History of Women Teachers in
Canada," in *Feminism and Education: A Canadian Perspective*, Freida Forman *et al*, eds.
(Toronto: Centre for Women's Studies in Education, OISE, 1990); "Bluestockings, Feminists,
or Women Workers? A Preliminary Look at
Women's Early Employment at the University

of Toronto" (*Journal of the Canadian Historical Association* 1992); various other publications. AFFIL: Canadian Committee on
Women's History; Canadian Historical Associ-
ation; Ontario Women's History Network;
Canadian Research Institute for the Advance-
ment of Women; Women's History Network
of B.C.; Canadian History of Education Association; History of Education Society; Ontario
Historical Society. HONS: Honourable Men-
tion, Marion Porter Prize, Canadian History of
Education Association, 1986; Founders' Prize,
Best Article, Canadian History of Education
Association, 1986; Hilda Neatby Prize, Best
Article, Canadian Historical Association, 1987;
Book Prize, Canadian Association for Foundations in Education, 1992; Distinguished Service
Award, Canadian Association for Foundations
in Education, 1992; Founders' Prize, best
anthology, Canadian History of Education
Association, 1992; D.Litt.(Hon.), Univ. of
Guelph, 1993. INTERESTS: canoeing; hiking;
cross-country skiing; cycling; birdwatching;
environmental issues; English-Canadian &
Que. lit.; the culture of France & of aboriginal
peoples; communities; family; gender & the
professions; history of women historians' work
in Canada. MISC: Distinguished Lecturer,
Simon Fraser Univ., Jan. 1982; Distinguished
Lecturer, Fac. of Educ., Univ. of Saskatchewan,
Mar. 1985; Distinguished Lecturer, Canadian
Studies Association, Univ. of Alberta,
Athabaska Univ., & Grant McEwan Community Coll., Nov. 1986; Distinguished Lecturer,
Canadian Historical Association Annual Meet-
ing, June 1991; Founding Chair, Ontario
Women's History Network, 1990-91. COM-
MENT: *"Developing scholarship in educational
history and women's history and disseminating
this scholarship to a wider public. Helping to
found feminist networks and communities."*

**Prepas, Ellie E., B.Math.,M.Env.,
Ph.D.** ⊴ ❀
Professor, Limnology, Department of Biological
Sciences, UNIVERSITY OF ALBERTA, Edmonton,
AB T6G 2E9 (403) 492-3463. Born Hamil-
ton, Ont. 1947. 1 ch. Natasha Solange. EDUC:
Univ. of Waterloo, B.Math. 1971; York Univ.,
M.Env. Studies, 1974; Univ. of Toronto, Ph.D.
1980. CAREER: Lecturer, McGill Univ., 1977;
Asst. Prof. of Limnology, Zoology Dept., Univ.
of Alberta, 1979-85; Co-Dir., Meanook Bio-
logical Research Stn, Univ. of Alberta, 1983-86;
Dir., 1986 to date; Assoc. Prof. of Limnology,
Zoology Dept., Univ. of Alberta, 1985-90; Act-
ing Dir., Environmental Research & Studies
Centre, Univ. of Alberta, 1990-91; Prof. of
Limnology, Zoology Dept., Univ. of Alberta,
1990 to date; Dir., Environmental Research &

Studies Centre, Univ. of Alberta, 1991-95; mbr., Evolution & Ecology panel, Natural Sciences & Engineering Research Council, 1990-94; V-Chair, 1992-94; mbr., Review Panel, Canadian Model Forest, 1995 to date. SELECTED PUBLICATIONS: "The Enigma of Daphnia death rates," with R.H. Rigler (*Limnology and Oceanography* 23 1978); "Comparison of the Phosphorus-Chlorophyll Relationships in Mixed and Stratified Lakes," with R.H. Ridler (*Canadian Journal of Fisheries and Aquatic Sciences* 42 1985); "Impact of lime on sediment phosphorus release in hardwater lakes: the case of hypereutrophic Halfmoon Lake, Alberta," with J. Babin *et al* (*Lake and Reservoir Management* 8 1994); "Nutrient dynamics in riverbeds: the impact of sewage effluent and aquatic macrophytes," with P. Chambers (*Water Research* 28 1994); "Chemical control of hepatotoxic phytoplankton blooms: Implications for human health," with A. Lam, D. Spink, S.E. Hrudey (*Water Research* 29 1995); numerous other publications. AFFIL: Alberta Lake Management Society; American Chemical Society; American Society of Limnology & Oceanography, Inc.; International Association on Water Pollution Research & Control; North American Benthological Society; North American Lake Management Society; Societas Internationalis Limnologiae; Society of Canadian Limnologists. HONS: Ont. Grad. Scholarship, 1973-74; Univ. of Toronto Open Scholarship, 1974-75; Postgrad. Scholarship, National Science Research Council, 1975-78; Technical Excellence Award, North American Lake Management Society, 1992; ITV Woman of Vision, 1995. MISC: Rigler Lecturer, Society of Canadian Limnologists' annual meeting, Saskatoon, 1994; recipient (Scientific Leader with over 100 scientists) of a Networks Centres of Excellence Award for Sustainable Forest Management, 1995; recipient of numerous grants & contracts. COMMENT: *"My research on the impact of land-use practices (including forestry) on water quality is part of a team program to understand and manage terrestrial and aquatic systems, including water quality and fisheries potential, in the boreal forest."*

Preston, Carol, B.A.,M.L.S. 📖 📚
Associate Editor, THE BEAVER: EXPLORING CANADA'S HISTORY, 167 Lombard Ave., Ste. 478, Winnipeg, MB R3B 0T6 (204) 988-9300, FAX 988-9309. Born Brandon, Man. 1945. m. Thomas Sinclair. EDUC: Univ. of Manitoba, B.A.(Hist. & English) 1966; Univ. of Toronto, Master of Library Science 1975. CAREER: reference work in public libraries in the Winnipeg area, 1966-73; Librarian, Histor-

ical Research Library, Hudson's Bay Company, 1975-77; Asst. Ed., *The Beaver*, 1977-85; Mng Ed., 1985-95; Assoc. Ed., 1995 to date. SELECTED PUBLICATIONS: *Manitoba: 125*, Vol. 1, a new history of Manitoba, Contributor (1993); *A Brief History of the Hudson's Bay Company*, Compiler & Ed., last 3 editions (1989, 1990, 1994); overseeing preparation of 2 cumulative indexes to *The Beaver*, 1920-85 & 1986-95. AFFIL: Canadian Club of Winnipeg; Women & History Association of Manitoba (W.H.A.M.); Canadian Magazine Publishers' Association. INTERESTS: history; astronomy; painting; gardening. MISC: *The Beaver* was originally published by the Hudson's Bay Company until 1994 when it was sold to Canada's National History Society, a not-for-profit society promoting interest in & knowledge of Cdn history. COMMENT: *"Professionally, my main endeavour has been to spread the gospel that Canadian history is far from boring, and that many ordinary men and women did extraordinary things that helped develop Canada."*

Preston, Joan, B.A.,M.A.,Ph.D. ■■ 📖 📚
Professor of Psychology and Communication Studies, BROCK UNIVERSITY, 500 Glenridge Ave., St. Catharines, ON L2S 3A1 (905) 688-5550, ext. 3447, FAX 688-6922, EMAIL jpreston@spartan.ac.brocku.ca. Partner, NORTHERN WEB DESIGN. Born St. Thomas, Ont. 1939. 2 ch. Eric, Stephen. EDUC: Univ. of Western Ontario, B.A.(Hons., Psych.) 1964, M.A. (Psych.) 1965, Ph.D.(Psych.) 1967. CAREER: Asst. Prof., Univ. of Toronto, 1967-71; developed Child Studies Program (1st concurrent B.A./B.Ed. degree), Brock Univ., 1976; co-founder, Communication Studies Program, 1984; Prof. of Psych. & Communications Studies. SELECTED PUBLICATIONS: numerous articles/papers on processing visual & verbal info., incl. TV, simulated environments. AFFIL: International Communications Association (Info. Systems); Canadian Psychological Association (Scientific Affairs Committee). HONS: Excellence in Teaching Award, Brock Univ., 1992; Teaching Award, Brock Univ. Faculty Association, 1992. INTERESTS: tierra encantada. MISC: producer, digital educational & entertainment material. COMMENT: *"Goals: to continue to explore and experience the symbolic, aesthetic, spiritual, emotional meanings of visuals."*

Preston, Valorie, B.A.,M.A. ■ 📖 📚
Artist. 19 Clarey Ave., Ottawa, ON K1A 2R6 (613) 231-5105, FAX 231-4212. Past President, BUSINESS AND PROFESSIONAL WOMEN'S ASSOCIATION OF OTTAWA. Born Winnipeg

1943. 1 ch. **EDUC:** Univ. of Saskatchewan, B.A.(Hist.) 1967; Northwestern Univ., M.A. (English Educ.) 1971; Univ. of Ottawa, French 1987-88. **CAREER:** Teacher, English, 1964-78; Special Asst. to Premier, Gov't of Sask., 1978; Exec. Dir., 1979-82; Nat'l Campaign Mgr, Audrey McLaughlin Leadership Campaign, 1989; Exec. Dir., Canadian Synchronized Swimming Association, 1990-92; self-employed artist, 1992 to date. **EXHIBITIONS:** Glebe Community Art Show (1995); Art Exhibit, Bella's Restaurant (1995). **AFFIL:** Business & Professional Women's Association of Ottawa (Past Pres.); Sussex Club of Ottawa (Founding Mbr.); Ottawa & District Association for the Mentally Retarded; International Women's Year Proj. (Asst. Dir. 1975-76). **HONS:** Award for Membership Recruitment, Canadian Federation of Business & Professional Women's Club, 1994; nominated, Women of Distinction Award, Ottawa, YWCA, 1996. **INTERESTS:** politics; art; music; reading; golf; evening skies; women's role in society. **MISC:** single mother of a mentally challenged, epileptic son, now an independent-living, gainfully employed happy adult. **COMMENT:** *"Women are walking where few have trod before. My network of family and friends strengthens my risk and "go for it" belief and gives me confidence in encouraging young women to reach beyond in politics, work and life. As individuals, we contribute our best: as a society, we must learn to accept and rejoice in that."*

Prevalnig, M. Joan, B.Com.,CLU $

Vice-President, Agencies, THE GREAT-WEST LIFE ASSURANCE COMPANY, 60 Osborne St. N, Winnipeg, MB R3C 3A5 (204) 946-7695, FAX 946-8533. Born Winnipeg. m. 1 ch. **EDUC:** Univ. of Manitoba, B.Com; Chartered Life Underwriter. **CAREER:** Dir., Agency Oper. & Dir., Hum. Res., The Great-West Life Assurance Company, 1981-86; VP, Agencies, 1992 to date. **SELECTED PUBLICATIONS:** contributions *to Customer Service in Insurance–Principles and Practices* (LOMA, 1991). **AFFIL:** Life Management Institute (Fellow); Canadian Pension Plan Advisory Bd. (Chair, Standing Audit Committee); Winnipeg Football Club (Mbr. of the Exec. Committee). **INTERESTS:** French-language training; continuous learning in all areas of the fin. svcs industry. **MISC:** subject of numerous periodical articles.

Price, Donna, F.C.G.A. $

Vice-President, Airports, AIR CANADA, L.B. Pearson International Airport, Terminal 2, Box 6002, Toronto A.M.F., ON L5P 1B4 (905) 676-4242, FAX 676-4210. Born Winnipeg 1951. m. Gordon. **CAREER:** various positions to Gen. Mgr, Customer Svc (Toronto), Air Canada, 1971 to date. **AFFIL:** Certified General Accountants' Association of Canada (C.G.A.; Past Dir.); Certified General Accountants' Association of Manitoba (Past Pres.; Fellow). **INTERESTS:** running; fitness; sports; reading; the cottage. **COMMENT:** *"I have enjoyed my 25-year career with Air Canada and have worked my way up from the mail desk to a senior management position. My C.G.A. designation was a most gratifying achievement. I have been married for 20 years and we enjoy our peaceful getaways to our cottage."*

Priddy, The Hon. Penny, R.N., M.L.A. ■ 🍁 $

Member of the Legislative Assembly (Surrey-Newton) and Minister of Small Business, Tourism and Culture, GOVERNMENT OF BRITISH COLUMBIA, Legislative Buildings, Rm. 133, Victoria, BC V8V 1X4 (604) 387-1683, FAX 387-4348. m. Rob Priddy. 2 ch. **CAREER:** Hum. Res. Consultant; CEO, N.S. Association for Community Living; Instructor, Hum. Res. Program, Douglas Coll.; M.L.A. (Surrey-Newton), Gov't of B.C., 1991 to date; Min. of Women's Equality, 1991-96; Social Policy Cabinet Committee, 1991-93; Sustainable Dev. Cabinet Committee, 1991-93; Crown Corporations Cabinet Committee, 1991-93; Planning Bd. Cabinet Committee, 1991-93; V-Chair, Treasury Bd., 1991-93; Min. of Labour, 1996; Min. of Small Bus., Tourism & Culture, 1996 to date. **AFFIL:** B.C. Association for Community Living; Surrey Association for the Mentally Handicapped; Surrey/White Rock Home Support Association; Boundary Unit Bd. of Health; Surrey Parks & Recreation; Surrey Women for Action. **COMMENT:** *"For many years, Penny has stood beside people with disabilities and their families."*

Priesnitz, Wendy ■ 🍁 ✎ $

Leader, GREEN PARTY OF CANADA, 272 Hwy 5, RR 1, St. George, ON N0E 1N0 (519) 448-4001, FAX 448-4411. Publisher, THE ALTERNATE PRESS. Coordinator, THE HOME BUSINESS NETWORK. Born Hamilton, Ont. 1950. m. Rolf Priesnitz. 2 ch. Heidi, Melanie. **EDUC:** Hamilton Teachers' Coll., Diploma, 1969; Ontario Elementary Teachers' Certificate 1969; Conestoga Coll. of Applied Arts & Sciences 1983; Univ. of Waterloo, Environmental Studies 1987-89. **CAREER:** elementary sch. teacher, Hamilton Bd. of Educ., 1969-70; freelance writer & journalist, 1976 to date; owner, Alternate Press, 1976 to date; Founder & Coord., The Home Business Network, 1985 to date; Ed., *Home Business Advocate*, 1986 to date; Ed., *York Region Business Journal*, 1987 to date; micro bus. dev. consultant, 1988 to date; self-employment trainer, Community Opportunities Development Association, Cambridge, Ont., 1994-96; elected Leader, Green Party of Canada, Aug. 1996. SELECTED PUBLICATIONS: *Women and Home-Based Business in Canada–An Investigation* (CRIAW) (The Home Business Network, 1988); *Home-Based Education in Canada - An Investigation (1989/90)* (The Alternate Press, 1990); *School Free* (Alternate Press, 1986); *North York–Realizing the Dream* (Windsor Publications Inc., 1988); *The Canadian Guide to Working at Home* (Alternate Press, 1990); *Metropolitan Toronto: Working Towards the Future* (Windsor Publications Inc., 1990); *Markham: A Contemporary Portrait* (Windsor Publications Inc., 1990); *Bringing It Home* (Alternate Press, 1995); articles have appeared in various periodicals, incl. *Tapestry*, *The Toronto Star* & *Natural Foods in Canada*. EDIT: Publisher, *Natural Life Newspaper*, 1976 to date; Ed., 1976-81, 1991 to date; Publisher, *Child's Play Magazine*, 1985-90; Publisher, *Home Business Advocate Newspaper*, 1986 to date; Ed., 1986-92; Ed., *York Region Business Journal*, 1987-90; Ed., *Markham Visitors' Guide*, 1989-90; Ed., *York Region Business Magazine*, 1990; Ed., *Toronto Business Age*, 1990. AFFIL: Canadian Alliance of Home Schoolers (Founder & Nat'l Coord.); Ontario Association of Alternative & Independent Schools (Pres. & Bd. Mbr. 1984-87). MISC: on-air host, *Doing Business*, weekly TV news feature, Markham, Ont., 1989-91; workshop leader & seminar presenter on micro & home-based business; mbr., Ontario Film Review Bd., 1992-93. COMMENT: *"A pioneer in the field of home business in Canada."*

Priest, Margaret, M.A.,R.C.A. ⊗ ⌁
Professor of Fine Art, UNIVERSITY OF GUELPH, Guelph, ON N1G 2W1. Born Tyringham, Bucks, UK 1944. m. Tony Scherman. 3 ch. EDUC: Maidstone Coll. of Art, Dipl.(Art & Design) 1967; Royal Coll. of Art, M.A. 1970. CAREER: Lecturer, Harrow Sch. of Art, 1970-74; Lecturer, St. Martin's Sch. of Art, 1972-76; Lecturer, Univ. of Waterloo, Sch. of Architecture, 1982-83; Lecturer, Univ. of Toronto, 1983 to date; Assoc. Prof., Dept. of Fine Art, Univ. of Guelph, 1983 to date; Visiting Critic to schools of art & architecture in UK, Canada & the US. COMMISSIONS: Bay/Adelaide Monument to Construction Workers (1993). EXHIBITIONS: mixed & solo exhibitions in Canada, US & abroad, 1970 to date. COLLECTIONS: works in numerous public & private collections in Canada & abroad. AFFIL: University Art Association of Canada; Gershon Iskowitz Foundation (Bd.). HONS: Award, Arts Council of Great Britain, 1969; John Minton Scholarship, 1970; Drawing Award, Ontario Arts Council, 1981; Gov. General's Award for Architecture with Baird/Simpson Architects, Milus, Bollenberghe, Topps, Watchorn Landscape Architects, 1994.

Prieto, Claire, B.A.A. ■ ⌂ ⊗
Producer, NATIONAL FILM BOARD OF CANADA (NFB), 150 John St., Ste. 207, Toronto, ON M5V 3C3 (416) 973-3012. Born Trinidad 1945. s. 1 ch. EDUC: Ryerson Polytechnic Institute, B.A.A.(Radio & TV Arts) 1977. CAREER: Program Prod., New Initiatives in Film, Studio D, National Film Bd., 1993-96; Prod., NFB, 1996 to date. SELECTED CREDITS: Prod./Researcher, *Different Timbres*, Film Arts/Black Communication Explorations, 1980; Dir./Researcher, *Older, Stronger, Wiser*, Studio D, 1988-89; Story Consultant, *Underground to Canada*, Atlantis Films Toronto, 1992; Co-Prod., *Last Dance First Steps*, Skyworks Charitable Foundation, 1993; *It's Not an Illness* (1979); *Home to Buxton* (1986-87); *Black Mother, Black Daughter* (1987-89); *Children Are Not the Problem* (1990-91); *Survivors* (1992); several other films as prod. or co-dir. AFFIL: Black Film & Video Network (Founding Mbr. & Pres. 1989-93); Caucus of Independent Filmmakers; Federation of Caribbean Filmmakers; Toronto Women in Film & Television; Black Filmmakers' Foundation. HONS: Fitness Award (*It's Not An Illness*), John Muir Medical Film Festival, 1982; Red Ribbon (*It's Not An Illness*), American Film & Video Festival, 1980; Honourable Mention (*Home to Buxton*), Gemini Awards, 1988; Kathleen Shannon Award, Golden Sheaf Awards (*Black Mother, Black Daughter*), Yorkton Film & Video Festival, 1990; Honourable Mention (*Black Mother, Black Daughter*), Int'l Film Festival, Sacramento, CA, 1991; Award of Merit, City of Toronto, 1991; First Place, Chris Statuette (*Survivors*), Columbus Int'l Film Festival, 1992; Woman of Distinction, YWCA, 1992; Golden Sheaf Award, Best Drama over 30 min. (*Survivors*), Yorkton Film & Video Festival, 1993. MISC: Immigrant Women's Job Placement Centre (Bd. of Dir. 1982-84); The Black Secretariat (Bd. of Dir. 1985-87); Film & Video Committee, 1992; SELAFI Int'l Conference of Artists, 1991. COMMENT: *"From 1977-1993, Claire Prieto produced films on different aspects of the black experience in Canada as a partner in Prieto-McTair Productions. At the same time, she volunteered with black community organizations. She is also the mother of a wonderful son, Ian."*

Pringle, Heather, B.A.,M.A. ✏ ▯ ⌘
Journalist and Author. 712 Robson St., Ste.

24, 3rd Fl., Vancouver, BC V6Z 1A2 (604) 688-4010, FAX 688-4010, EMAIL 71774. 442@compuserve.com. Born Edmonton 1952. m. Geoffrey Lakeman. **EDUC:** Univ. of Alberta, B.A.(Cdn Hist.) 1973; Univ. of British Columbia, M.A.(English Lit.) 1976. **CAREER:** Fiction & Poetry Ed., *Branching Out* magazine, 1977-80; Asst. Ed., Hurtig Publishers Ltd., 1978-79; freelance Journalist & Ed., 1979-89; Contributing Ed., *National Geographic Traveler*, 1989 to date; Assoc. Ed., *Equinox*, 1989-90; Sr. Ed., 1990-93; freelance Author & Journalist, 1993 to date. **SELECTED PUBLICATIONS:** articles have appeared in various publications incl. *Equinox, National Geographic Traveler, New Scientist, Omni, World, Financial Post Magazine, Saturday Night Magazine; In Search of Ancient North America* (1996). **HONS:** Author's Award, 1992; Gold, Science Journalism, National Magazine Award, 1988; Award, Canadian Science Writers' Association, 1989; Public Writing Award, Canadian Archaeological Association, 1988, 1989. **COMMENT:** *"I am a journalist interested in bringing worthy but often arcane scientific research to public attention."*

Prior, Roxanne V., LL.B. ■ ■ ⚖ ☮ ✿
Barrister and Solicitor. (self-employed; criminal law practice), R.R. #3, Wilson's Beach, Lacombe, AB T0C 1S0 (403) 782-6392, FAX 782-4902. Born Sarnia, Ont. 1954. m. Robert V. Chatwin. 1 ch., 1 stepch. ch. Lauren Chatwin, Christopher Chatwin. **EDUC:** Lambton Coll., Sarnia, Ont., Diploma (Process Oper.) 1976, Certificates (Basic & Advanced Fire Fighting) 1978; Univ. of Toronto, Fac. of Arts & Sci., under-grad. course work toward entry into law sch., 1980-82; Univ. of Calgary, LL.B. 1985. **CAREER:** catering truck driver, Bunsen Burner Restaurant, Sarnia, Ont., 1972-73; Mgmt Trainee, KMart, St. Catharines, Ont., 1973-75; Process Operator in ethylene extraction unit & fire fighter, Sarnia, Ont., 1976-79; made temporary dental crowns & bridges, York Dental Lab, Toronto, 1979-80; part-time teacher of parents of autistic children on behaviour mgmt techniques, Geneva Centre for Autistic Children, 1980-82; research, Calgary Legal Assistance, Summer 1984; student at law, gen. practice, 1986-87; private law practice, Red Deer, Alta., 1987-91; Crown Prosecutor, Alberta Attorney Gen., 1991-92; homemaker, Wilson's Beach, May-Dec. 1992; contracted lawyer, Woollard Hopkins & Company, Rocky Mountain House, 1993-94; self-employed, criminal law practice, 1994 to date. **AFFIL:** John Howard Society Alberta (Bd. mbr. 1990 to date; Pres. of Bd. 1995 to date); John Howard Society, Red Deer (Bd. mbr. & Pres. of

Bd. 1989-95); Red Deer Child Care Society (Bd. mbr. 1988-91); Calgary Legal Guidance (volunteer 1983-86). **MISC:** candidate, Alta. prov. election, Rocky Mountain House constituency, 1993, & Red Deer South constituency, 1989.

Profeit-LeBlanc, Louise ■ ☼ ⊗ ☯
Vice-Chairman of National Spiritual Assembly of Canada, NATIONAL BAHÁ'Í COMMUNITY OF CANADA, 18 Thompson Rd., Whitehorse, YT Y1A 5R2 (403) 667-3099, FAX 667-8023. Born Whitehorse 1951. m. Robert LeBlanc. 3 ch. **EDUC:** Yukon Tech. & Vocational Sch., Dipl.(Nursing Asst.) 1971; Life Skills Coach Training, Dipl. 1973. **CAREER:** Community Health Liaison Officer, Council for Yukon Indians; Native Mental Health Worker, Dept. of Health & Welfare Canada; Native Heritage Advisor, Dept. of Tourism, Heritage Branch. **SELECTED CREDITS:** 2 children's videos, written & co-produced; video documentary *Jan An Dah* (suicide prevention drama). **SELECTED PUBLICATIONS:** poetry, short stories; cultural materials for Univ. of British Columbia; children's story for primary curriculum. **AFFIL:** National Spiritual Assembly, National Bahá'í Community of Canada (Chrm); Council for Yukon Indians (Dir.); Society of Yukon Artists of Native Ancestry (Founding Dir.; Pres. 1994-95); Yukon Writers' Circle; Yukon International Festival of Storytelling (Co-founder); Canadian Bahá'í Studies (Dir.). **HONS:** Canadian Aboriginal Award for best documentary, 1986; Volunteer Arts Award, NWTEL, 1994. **INTERESTS:** performing arts; storytelling (traditional); visual arts; beading & traditional footwear construction; jogging; swimming. **COMMENT:** *"Louise Profeit-LeBlanc is a member of the Nacho N'y'uk Dun First Nation of the Northern Tutchone people of Mayo in the Yukon. She is married with three daughters and has two grandsons. Most of her life has been spent in the Yukon, but she has travelled extensively throughout the world."*

Proven, Bonnie Bachorcik, B.G.S. ■ 🖋 ⛺
Chairperson, Distance Education and Media, ASSINIBOINE COMMUNITY COLLEGE, 1430 Victoria Ave. E., Brandon, MB R7A 2A9 (204) 726-6615, FAX 727-6196, EMAIL proven@admin-net.assiniboinec.mb.ca. Born Midale, Sask. 1951. d. 3 ch. **EDUC:** Univ. of Regina, Teaching Certificate 1972, additional yr., Adult Educ. 1973-75; Brandon Univ., B.G.S. 1988. **CAREER:** various teaching & admin. positions in community adult-based educ., Sask. Dept. of Educ., 1971-74; career & employment counselling, Canada Manpower Office, Estevan, Sask., 1974-77; active as union Pres. in Public Service Alliance of Canada; lifeskills facilitator

& adult educator in various aboriginal communities in S.W. Man., Educ. & Training, Gov't of Man., 1981-85; Proj. Consultant Work, Assiniboine Community Coll., 1986-88; Agric. Training Branch, 1987-90; Reg. Mgr, Westman North Employment Svcs, Dept. of Family Svcs, Brandon, 1990-92; Coord., Distance Educ., Assiniboine Community Coll., 1992-95; Acting Chair, Agric. & Rural Ent. Div., 1992; Chair, 1992-94; Dean, Coll. Dev., 1994-95; Chair, Technologies & Environmental Industries, 1995-96. **AFFIL:** Association of Canadian Community Colleges (Man. Rep., Int'l Program Committee); Ministry of Post-Secondary Educ. (Assiniboine Rep., Distance Educ. & Tech. Sub-Committee); Brandon Univ. Alumni Association (Pres.); Brandon Chamber of Commerce; Minnedosa & Area Committee on Wife Abuse (Chair); Rural Development Resource Network, W. Man. (Committee); January Group (focus: sustainable dev./rural dev.)(Committee); Canadian Congress for Learning Opportunities for Women (Nat'l Action Committee on the Status of Women, Marquis Proj.–Int'l Dev. Proj.); Canadian Association for Distance Education. **INTERESTS:** distance educ.; sustainable community dev.; job creation through micro-enterprise; int'l dev. & educ.; rural agric.; her rural community, home & 3 wonderful children (18, 16 & 12). **MISC:** various presentations; is currently enrolled in a Masters in Educ. program at Brandon Univ.

Provencher, Diane M., M.D. ⊕

NOTRE-DAME HOSPITAL, 1560 E. Sherbrooke St., Montreal, QC H2L 4M1 (514) 876-6800 or 876-6600, FAX 876-5476 or 876-6814. Born Montreal 1955. m. **EDUC:** Univ. of Montreal, M.D. 1979. **CAREER:** Internship & Residency, Obstetrics & Gynecology, McGill Univ., 1979-83; Emergency Medicine, Haut-Richelieu Hospital, 1982-84; Assoc. Mbr. in Obstetrics & Gynecology, McGill Univ., Jewish Gen. Hospital, 1983-86; Assoc. Mbr. in Obstetrics & Gynecology, McGill Univ., Ste-Mary's Hospital, 1983-89; Affil. Staff in Obstetrics & Gynecology, McGill Univ., Montreal Gen. Hospital, 1983 to date; Fellow, Gynecologic Oncology, Univ. of Miami, 1986-88; research in ovarian cancer, Memorial Sloan-Kettering Cancer Center, N.Y., N.Y., 1988-90; Assoc. Mbr. in Obstetrics & Gynecology, Univ. of Montreal, Notre-Dame Hospital, 1989-96; Prof. agrégée in Obstetrics & Gynecology, Div. of Gynecologic Oncology, 1996 to date; clinical researcher, Centre de recherche Louis-Charles Simard/Institut du cancer de Montréal, 1989 to date; Master, Program of Molecular Biol., Univ. of Montreal, 1994 to date. **SELECTED PUBLICATIONS:** co-author with S.C. Rubin, C.L. Finstad *et al*, "Analysis of Antigen Expression at Multiple Tumor Sites in Epithelial Ovarian Cancer" (*American Journal of Obstetrics and Gynecology* 164, No. 2, 1991); co-author with C.L. Finstad, P.E. Saigo *et al*, "Comparison of Antigen Expression on Fresh and Cultured Ascites Cells and on Solid Tumors of Patients with Epithelial Ovarian Cancer" (*Gynecology Oncology* 50, 1993); co-author with H. Lounis, C. Godbout *et al*, "Primary Cultures of Normal and Tumoral Human Ovarian Epithelium: A Powerful Tool for Basic Molecular Studies" (*Experimental Cell Research* 215, 1994); co-author with A.-M. Trottier, A.-M. Mes-Masson *et al*, "Absence of Human Papillomaviruses Sequences in Ovarian Pathologies" (*Journal of Clinical Microbiology* 33, No. 4, 1995); co-author with F. Coutlée & H. Voyer, "Detection of Human Papillomavirus DNA in Cervical Lavage Specimens by a Nonisotopic Consensus PCR Assay" (*Journal of Clinical Microbiology* 33, No. 8, 1995); co-author with C. Pomel, J. Dauplat *et al*, "Laparoscopic Staging of Early Ovarian Cancer" (*Gynecology Oncology* 58, 1995); numerous book chapters, abstracts & non-refereed articles. **AFFIL:** Royal Coll. of Surgeons of Canada (Fellow); Quebec Federation of Specialist Physicians (Fellow); American Coll. of Obstetricians & Gynecologists (Fellow); Society of Obstetricians & Gynecologists of Canada; Fédération des médecins omnipraticiens du Québec; Society of Gynecologic Oncologists; International Federation of Gynecologic Oncology; Research Centre of Notre-Dame Hospital; American Society for Colposcopy & Cervical Pathology; Society of Canadian Colposcopy; Association of Diplomates & Professors of the Fac. of Medicine, Univ. of Montreal. **HONS:** award, William A. Little Ob./Gyn. Society, 1988; Esculape Prize, Notre-Dame Hospital, 1991; Promotion Merit, Univ. of Montreal, 150th anniversary of Univ. of Montreal, 1993; Best Poster Award, Gynecologic Oncologists of Canada, 1993; Best Abstract Award, Gynecologic Oncologists of Canada, 1993; Best Poster Award, Gynecologic Oncologists of Canada, 1996. **MISC:** various research grants; numerous conference presentations.

Provenzano, Diana, B.Comm.,C.A. ■ $

Company Secretary, BOC CANADA LIMITED, 5975 Falbourne St., Unit 2, Mississauga, ON L5R 3W6 (905) 501-1700, FAX 501-1717. Born Toronto 1958. m. Luigi. 1 ch. **EDUC:** McMaster Univ., B.Comm. 1980, Chartered Accountant 1982. **CAREER:** various positions, Coopers and Lybrand, 1980-84; Sec.-Treas., Canadian Oxygen Limited, 1984-88; Dir. of Fin. & Company Sec., 1988-90; Dir. of Fin. &

Admin. & Company Sec., 1990-95; Company Sec., BOC Canada Limited (formerly Canadian Oxygen Limited), 1994 to date. **AFFIL**: Canadian Institute of Chartered Accountants; Ontario Association of Chartered Accountants; Canadian Diabetes Association; Catholic Women's League; Camp Huronda (Treas.). **HONS**: Bronze Medal, Ontario Association of Chartered Accountants; placed 7th, Canadian Institute of Chartered Accountants. **INTERESTS**: travelling; cycling.

Pryde, Rosemary, B.A. ○ ⊛

Executive Director, VOICE FOR HEARING IMPAIRED CHILDREN, 124 Eglinton Ave. W., Ste. 420, Toronto, ON M4R 2G8 (416) 489-7719, FAX 487-7423. Born Kingston, Ont. 1945. s. **EDUC**: Queen's Univ., B.A.(English) 1967. **CAREER**: Counselling Consultant, Gov't of Canada, 1977-88; Coord., Women's Employment, 1980-88; Exec. Dir., Voice for Hearing Impaired Children, 1988 to date. **AFFIL**: Churchill Society (Dir.); Women's Business & Professional Club (VP, Toronto Chapter 1983); Canadian Hearing Society (Dir. 1987-90); Auditory-Verbal International Inc. (Dir.). **INTERESTS**: music; art; books; food. **COMMENT**: *"I am profoundly deaf yet communicate with regular speech; I am used as a role model for deaf children and their families. I believe that all disadvantaged people, given opportunities and support, can become contributing members of society. My role as creator and encourager facilitate their independence."*

Pryor, E. Jane, B.Sc.(H.Ec.),B.B.A., B.A.,C.I.M. ⊕

Director of Dietetics, DARTMOUTH GENERAL HOSPITAL AND COMMUNITY HEALTH CENTRE, 325 Pleasant St., Dartmouth, NS B2Y 4G8 (902) 465-8505, FAX 465-8461. Born N.S. 1961. s. **EDUC**: Mount St. Vincent Univ., B.Sc.(H.Ec.-Nutrition) 1983; Univ. Coll. of Cape Breton, C.I.M.(Bus.) 1988, B.B.A.(Bus.) 1993, B.A.(Community Studies) 1993. **CAREER**: Therapeutic Dietitian & Supervisor, Sydney City Hospital, 1985-87; Dir. of Dietary Svcs, Rush Communications: Breton Bay Nursing Home, Sydney, N.S., 1987-92; Dir. of Dietetics, Dartmouth General Hospital & Community Health Centre, 1993 to date. **SELECTED PUBLICATIONS**: "Nova Scotia Dietetic Association's Submission to the Blueprint Committee" (*Canadian Dietetic Association Journal*, Spring 1995). **AFFIL**: Canadian Dietetic Association (Dir.); N.S. Dietetic Association (Past Pres.); Consulting Dietitians of Canada; Canadian Hospital Association (Educ. Consultant, Advisory Committee for the Program in Food Svc. Supervision); Univ. Coll.

of Cape Breton (Alumni Association); Canadian Cancer Society (Sydney & Dartmouth Units); HeartBeats; Families of Persons with Eating Disorders. **MISC**: speaks to various schools & community groups on nutrition; involved with prov. & nat'l health system reform. **COMMENT**: *"In the 10 years that I have been a dietitian, I have been involved with my professional associations for both the personal and professional growth they have provided. I continue to strive to create an awareness of nutrition in the public I serve."*

Puder, Christine, B.A.,M.Ed., C.C.L.S. ■ ⊕ ⊛

Director, Child Life Department, BRITISH COLUMBIA'S CHILDREN'S HOSPITAL, 4480 Oak St., Vancouver, BC V6H 3V4 (604) 875-2345, ext. 7687, FAX 875-2292, EMAIL cpuder@ wpog.childhosp.bc.ca. Born Vancouver 1958. m. Gil. 2 ch. Jason, Brendan. **EDUC**: B.C. Institute of Technology, Psychiatric Nursing Program 1978; Univ. of Victoria, B.A.(Child & Youth Care) 1983; Univ. of British Columbia, M.Ed.(Educ. Psych.) 1991. **CAREER**: Registered Psychiatric Nurse, 1978-83; Child Care Counsellor, Eileen Corbett Reception Centre, Vancouver, 1983; Child Life Specialist (Neurology), Adolescent Module, Intensive Care Unit, British Columbia's Children's Hospital, 1983-88; Child Life Specialist (Special Projects), Community Outreach/School Liaison, 1988-90; Dir., Child Life Dept., 1990 to date; Sessional Fac., Dept. of ECE & CYC, Univ. Coll. of the Fraser Valley, 1995 to date. **SELECTED PUBLICATIONS**: *From hospital to school..a book for parents* (British Columbia's Children's Hospital, 1990); *From hospital to school..a handbook for teachers* (British Columbia's Children's Hospital, 1990); *Caring for Children and Families: Guidelines for Hospitals* with others (Bethesda, Md.: Association for the Care of Children's Health, 1992). **AFFIL**: Council of the Coll. of Dental Surgeons of B.C.; Canadian Association of Child Life Directors; Association for the Care of Children's Health; Child Life Council; C.C.L.S. Child Life Certification (1988 to date). **INTERESTS**: playing with my children; keeping fit in a variety of ways; gardening; cooking & entertaining for friends & family. **MISC**: numerous conference presentations. **COMMENT**: *"In my roles as health-care professional, community volunteer, and mother, I value, and strive to provide, healthy environments and activities that promote optimal development for children and adults."*

Pugen, Diane Fern ⊗ ⊛ ⊕ ⊡

Visual Artist, Freelance Curator, Faculty Member, ONTARIO COLLEGE OF ART, 100 McCaul

St., Toronto, ON M5T 1W1 (416) 977-5311, ext. 766, FAX 593-6178. Born Toronto 1943. cl. Barry Arthur Dickie. 1 ch., 1 stpch. **EDUC:** Sch. of Art, Institute of Chicago, Visual Arts 1962-64; Univ. of Chicago, Humanities 1962-64; Fenn Coll., Cleveland, Ohio, Educ., Psych. 1964; Arts Students' League of N.Y., Visual Arts 1964-65. **CAREER:** Instructor, Artists' Workshop, 1965-77; Instructor, New Sch. of Art, 1969-77; Instructor, Banff Sch. of Fine Art, 1975-76; Course Dir., Fac. of Educ., York Univ., 1980-82; Instructor, Sault Coll., Sault Ste. Marie, 1986-87; Instructor, Hart House, Univ. of Toronto, 1977 to date; founder & Fac. mbr., Arts' Sake Inc., 1977-83; Creative Artists in the Schools Program, Ont. Arts Council, 1981 to date; Instructor, Centennial Coll., 1987-91; Instructor, Glendon Coll., York Univ., 1986 to date; Instructor, Ontario Coll. of Art, 1970, 1990 to date; Acting Co-Chair, Foundation Studies Dept., 1993-94; various other positions as instructor. **SELECTED CREDITS:** subject of documentary, *Diane Pugen, Printmaker*, Rogers Cable TV (1982-83); participant, as mbr. of Isaacs Gallery Ensemble Mixed Media Concerts, coord. by Udo Kasemetts, 1966-70; various other experimental music performances. **SELECTED PUBLICATIONS:** "Denis Cliff at A.C.T." (*Artmagazine* 40 1978); "Who Are These CARFAC People, and What's All the Copyright Business About?" (*Work Seen* 1(2) 1989); "Peter Maqua: The Creation Cycle" (*Work Seen* 1990); various published drawings & reproductions; various other publications. **EDIT:** nat'l advisory council, *Matriart Magazine*. **COMMISSIONS:** 8 banners for show *This City Now*, Art Gallery of Ontario (1967); 6 designs for gold, silver & bronze medals, & reg'l logo, Ontario Gymnastics Federation, Metro E. Reg. (1982); original lithograph to honour 75th Anniversary of Hart House, Univ. of Toronto (1994); various other commissions. **EXHIBITIONS:** solo, Pollock Gallery, Toronto (1966); solo, Peter Whyte Gallery, Banff (1977); solo, *Diane Pugen: Notations*, Workscene Gallery, Toronto (1989); solo, *Recycled Transgressions*, Workscene Gallery, Toronto (1992); various other solo exhibitions; 2-person show, *Diane Pugen, Joan Van Damme*, Studio Three Gallery, Hamilton, Ont. (1979); group, The United Nations International Children's Emergency Fund group exhibition, UN Bldg, N.Y. (1968); group, *Black and White 1968*, travelling show sponsored & organized by Ontario Art Institute (1968); group, *Inaugural Exhibition: Survey of Contemporary Canadian Women Artists*, Pauline McGibbon Cultural Centre, Toronto, 1979; group, *Exportacion*, Cuba/Canada Cultural Exchange Exhibition,

Havana, Cuba (1990); group, *Via Renovatur–Nord-Sud/North-South*, Museo d'Arte Contemporaneo, Santiago, Chile & Glendon Gallery, York Univ. (1994); various other group exhibitions; curator, *Inaugural Exhibition: Survey of Contemporary Canadian Women Artists*, Pauline McGibbon Cultural Centre, Toronto, 1979; curator, *Our Home and Native Land* (1990); co-curator, *Okanata*, Workscene Gallery & A Space Gallery, Toronto (1991); curator, *Drawing the Future Close*, Workscene Gallery (1993); curated various other exhibitions. **COLLECTIONS:** McKenzie Art Gallery, Regina; Toronto-Dominion Bank Collection of Contemporary Art, Toronto; Art Gallery of Ontario; Peter Whyte Foundation, Banff; Tory Tory DesLauriers & Binnington, Toronto; Art Gallery of Algoma, Sault Ste. Marie; Univ. of Lethbridge; the late John B. Aird, former Lt.-Gov. of Ont.; various other collections. **AFFIL:** Canadian Artists Representation Ontario (Nat'l Council Rep.); Canadian Artists Representation, Federation des Artistes Canadiens (CARO Rep.); CARFAC Copyright Collective (shareholder); Artists Voice Legal Defence Fund, Toronto (Pres., Bd. of Trustees); Art Gallery of Ontario (Art Rental Service); Print & Drawing Council of Canada; Ontario Arts Council; Women's Art REsouce Centre/*Matriart Magazine* (Nat'l Advisory Council); Workscene Co-operative Corporation; Association for Native Development in the Performing & Visual Arts (VP, Bd. of Dir.); Centre for Indigenous Theatre (Incorporating Committee, Acting Bd. of Dir.); Arts & Education Coalition; A Space Gallery, Toronto; Mercer Union, Toronto (Assoc. Mbr.); Powerplant Gallery at Harbourfront, Toronto (Artist Mbr.); Canadian Conference of the Arts; Native Canadian Centre of Toronto; Anishnabe Health; Artword Centre. **HONS:** Medal of Service, City of Toronto, 1992. **INTERESTS:** arts generally; visual arts; literature; performing arts; indigenous cultures; history; geology; anthropology; world religions; earth sciences; social & political sciences; native studies. **MISC:** work in 1968 UNICEF group exhibition 1st Cdn work so chosen; recipient, numerous grants from the Canada Council & Ontario Arts Council; leader, numerous workshops; freelance consultant; subject of various print & broadcast articles, interviews & reviews; listed in *World Who's Who of Women*. **COMMENT:** *"Professional visual artist/curator/art instructor/lobbyist and activist. Continuous participation in the nonprofit arts, arts services organizations and arts funding agencies, municipally, regionally and nationally, in Native and non-Native arts groups. Politically outspoken on issues of the earth and our environment, social* *injustice and causes that relate to the human condition/survival. My art reflects these concerns."*

Pugliese, Olga (nee Zorzi), B.A.,M.A., Ph.D. ■ 🐿️ 📖 📖

Professor, Department of Italian Studies, UNIVERSITY OF TORONTO, Toronto, ON M5S 1A1 (416) 978-5573, FAX 978-5593, EMAIL pugliese@chass.utoronto.ca. Born Toronto 1941. m. Guido. EDUC: Univ. of Toronto, B.A.(Modern Languages & Lit.) 1963, M.A. (Italian/French) 1964, Ph.D.(Romance Languages & Lit.) 1969. CAREER: Fac. Mbr., Dept. of Italian Studies, Univ. of Toronto, 1967 to date; Undergrad. Sec., Dept. of Italian Studies, 1973-74; Fellow, Victoria Coll., 1978 to date; Grad. Coord., Dept. of Italian Studies, 1984-88, 1992. SELECTED PUBLICATIONS: Ed. & Translator, *Lorenzo Valla, The Profession of the Religious and Selections from The Donation of Constantine* (1985; 2nd ed. 1994); Co-ed., *Ficino and Renaissance Neoplatonism* (1986); Ed. & Translator, *Lorenzo Valla, La falsa donazione di Costantino* (1994); *Il discorso labirintico del dialogo rinascimentale* (1995); 32 articles on aspects of Italian lit. & culture of the Renaissance, incl. "Humour in Il libro del cortegiano" (*Quaderni d'italianistica*, No. 14, 1993); 24 book reviews. AFFIL: Canadian Society for Renaissance Studies; Renaissance Society of America; *Quaderni d'italianistica* (Book Review Ed. 1990-95); Canadian Society for Italian Studies; American Association of Teachers of Italian. COMMENT: *"Devoted university career to teaching classics such as Machiavelli's* Prince *and Castiglione's* Courtier, *writing on religious and other aspects of Renaissance culture, carrying out administrative duties."*

Pulleyblank, Millie, B.A.,M.L.S. 18 6

Corporate Archivist, THE TORONTO-DOMINION BANK, Toronto-Dominion Centre, Box 1, Toronto, ON M5K 1A2 (416) 982-8848, FAX 944-6609. Born Windsor, Ont. 1938. s. EDUC: Univ. of Toronto, Diploma (Public Health Nursing) 1971; Univ. of Windsor, B.A.(Fine Arts) 1971; Univ. of Western Ontario, M.L.S.(Info. Sci.) 1973. CAREER: Mgr, Employee Health Svcs, Hotel Dieu Hospital, Windsor, 1972; Librarian, Victoria Univ., 1973-77; Corp. Archivist, TD Bank, 1977 to date. AFFIL: Wellspring. INTERESTS: painting abstract expressionalism.

Purcell, Shelagh 🌀 ◐ ⊕

President, ONTARIO LUPUS ASSOCIATION, 250 Bloor St. E., Ste. 901, Toronto, ON M4W 3P2 (416) 967-1414, FAX 967-7171. Born Swift

Current, Sask. 1939. w. 4 ch. CAREER: News Reporter, *Swift Current Sun*; CKWS-TV; professional musician, Toronto. VOLUNTEER CAREER: Pres., Ontario Lupus Association. AFFIL: Toronto Musicians' Association. INTERESTS: music; quilting; books; gardening; people. COMMENT: *"Since two of my four children have been diagnosed with lupus, my focus has been as a volunteer with the Ontario Lupus Association, the Lupus Data Bank and the Arthritis Society, to raise money for research and to inform the public about lupus."*

Pyke, Sandra W., B.A.,M.A.,Ph.D. 🐿️ ⊕

Professor and Chair, Department of Psychology, YORK UNIVERSITY, 4700 Keele St., North York, ON M3J 1P3 (416) 736-5116, FAX 736-5814, EMAIL spyke@yorku.ca. Born Winnipeg 1937. m. Dale Pyke. 2 ch. Aryn Alexandra, Kyra Ellen. EDUC: Univ. of Saskatchewan, B.A.(Psych.) 1959, M.A.(Psych.) 1961; McGill Univ., Ph.D.(Psych.) 1964. CAREER: Proj. Supervisor, Psychological Research Centre, Saskatoon, Sask., 1960-62; Applied Research Coord., Psychological Research Centre, 1964-66; Lecturer, Univ. of Saskatchewan, 1965; Asst. Prof., York Univ., 1966-70; Program Coord., Dept. of Psychological Svcs, 1966-70; Assoc. Prof., 1970-82; Women's Workshop Coord., Counselling & Dev. Centre, 1973-79; Advisor to the Pres. on the Status of Women, 1980-81; Feminist Counsellor, Counselling & Dev. Centre, 1980-82; Prof., 1982 to date; Chair, Counselling & Dev. Centre, 1982-84; Dean, Fac. of Grad. Studies, 1987-92; mbr., Grad. Program in Women's Studies, 1991 to date; Chair, Dept. of Psych., 1994 to date. SELECTED PUBLICATIONS: *The Science Game: An introduction to research in the behavioural science* with N. McK. Agnew (Englewood Cliffs, NJ: Prentice-Hall, 1969, 1978, 1982, 1987, 1991); "Dichotomies: An alien perspective" (*Atlantis* 14(1) 1988, reprinted from *Newletter*, CPA Section on Women and Psychology 10(2), 1986); "Logistic regression analysis of graduate student retention," with P. Sheridan (*The Canadian Journal of Higher Education*, XXIII(2), 1993); "Sexual harassment and sexual intimacy in learning environments" (*Canadian Psychology* 37(1) 1996); "Menopause: A health hazard?" (*Alive: Canadian Journal of Health & Nutrition* 83, 1988); 4 book chapters; numerous articles in refereed & nonrefereed journals. AFFIL: Canadian Psychological Association (Fellow); American Psychological Association (Fellow); Social Science Federation of Canada (Dir.); Coll. of Psychologists of Ontario (Registered Psychologist); Senior Women Academic Administrators of Canada; Canadian Council of Departments of

Psychology; Canadian Research Institute for the Advancement of Women; Canadian Society for the Study of Higher Education. HONS: IODE Scholarship, 1955-59; Scholarship, Univ. of Saskatchewan, 1959-60; Distinguished Member Award, Canadian Psychological Association, Section on Women & Psych.; Award for Distinguished Contribution to Canadian Psychology as a Profession, Canadian Psychological Association, 1996. MISC: recipient, numerous grants; listed in *Canadian Who's Who; World Who's Who of Women*; numerous presentations at professional meetings; grant reviewer for SSHRC & Ontario Mental Health Foundation, among others. COMMENT: *"My personal and professional life has focused on efforts to understand the dynamics of the subordination of women and to enhance their status."*

Pyykkönen, Lea (nee Jokinen) ■■ ⊕ ⊕
Nursing Coordinator, THE HOSPITAL FOR SICK CHILDREN, 555 University Ave., Toronto, ON M5G 1X8 (416) 813-7508. Born Lahti, Finland 1934. w. Eero (deceased). 1 ch. Miriam. EDUC: Salisbury Gen. Infirmary, Diploma (Nursing) 1957; Univ. of Toronto, post-grad. Certificate (Hospital Nursing Svc.) 1961; York Univ., working part-time toward B.A.(Admin. Studies) 1982 to date. CAREER: Gen. Duty Nurse, Women's College Hospital, Toronto, 1957-58; Gen. Duty Nurse, Neonatal Ward, Hospital for Sick Children, 1958-60; Asst. Head Nurse, Infant Medical Ward, 1961-62; Head Nurse, Infant Medical Ward, 1962-65; Gen. Duty Nurse (casual), Pediatric Ward, Sudbury Memorial Hospital, Sudbury, Ont., 1965-68; Proj. Supervisor, Hospital for Sick Children, Toronto, 1968-72, 1973-76; Area Coord., Area 6, 1976-82; Staff Asst., Dept. of Nursing, 1982-86; Nursing Supervisor, Sr. Administrator, Night Tour of Duty, 1986 to date. AFFIL: Toronto Finnish-Canadian Seniors Centre, Suomi-Koti (founding mbr., Bd. of Dir. 1982 to date; V-Chair 1990 to date). HONS: 2nd Prize for Sr. Nursing, 1957; Certificate of Appreciation, Suomi-Koti, Toronto, 1988; Canada's Birthday Achievement Award, 1990; introduced to Legislative Assembly of Ont., 1992. INTERESTS: music; outdoor activities - bicycling, swimming, cross-country skiing. MISC: participated in Int'l Cardiovascular Risk Factor Study, 1988. COMMENT: *"Job related: as a project supervisor, pioneered (commenced 1969) with a colleague family-centred care at The Hospital for Sick Children. Until then, visiting hours were very restricted. Voluntary: 1991-92 Chairperson of the Suomi-Koti, Toronto Nursing Home Committee to develop plans and build 34-bed nursing home - opened in November, 1992."*

Q

uaife, Darlene Barry, B.A.(Hons.), M.A. 📖 📚 ⌂
Writer and Instructor. c/o Turnstone Press, 100 Arthur St., Ste. 607, Winnipeg, MB R3B 1H3 (204) 947-1555, FAX 942-1555. Born Calgary 1948. m. Ron. EDUC: Univ. of Calgary, B.A. (Hons., English) 1975; Univ. of Alberta, M.A.(English) 1986. CAREER: Instructor, Univ. of Calgary, 1976-94; Instructor, Mount Royal Coll., 1977-95; freelance writer for periodicals, newspapers, media & public rel'ns, 1978-92; Writer-in-Residence, The Calgary Public Library; Writer-in-Residence, Writers' Development Trust; Dir., Pan Canadian Wordfest '96, Banff/Calgary International Writers Festival. SELECTED PUBLICATIONS: *Death Writes: A Curious Notebook* (Arsenal Pulp Press, 1996); *Days & Nights on the Amazon*, novel (Winnipeg: Turnstone Press, 1994); *Bone Bird*, novel (Winnipeg: Turnstone Press, 1989); *I Ching of Shoes* (PRISM International Short Story Contest, Spring 1992); "Still Life & Nude" (*Border Crossings*, Spring 1994); "Bodymapping" (*The Malahat Review*, Winter 1993); "Word Made Flesh" *(Room of One's Own*, Spring 1993); "Pleasure Dome" (*Descant*, Winter 1992); "The Invisible Part of the Spectrum" (*Prairie Fire*, Winter 1991-92); *Pleasure Dome*, short story, CBC Literary Competitions (1990); *The Invisible Part of the Spectrum* (PRISM Int'l Short Fiction Contest, 1989); various other short stories, poems & plays. AFFIL: Writers' Guild of Alberta (Mbr.-at-Large 1989-90; VP 1994-95; Pres. 1995-96); PEN Canada (Writers' Guild of Alberta Rep.; Writer in prison "minder"): The Writers' Union of Canada. HONS: Banff Centre for the Arts Scholarship; Queen Elizabeth Prov. Scholarship;

Commonwealth Writers' Prize, Best First Book, Canada/Caribbean Reg., 1989; *I Ching of Shoes*, was runner up in the PRISM Int'l Short Story Contest, 1992; *Pleasure Dome* was shortlisted in the fiction category for the CBC Literary Competitions, 1991; *The Invisible Part of the Spectrum* was a finalist in the PRISM Int'l Short Story Contest, 1989; Petro-Canada Stage One Lunchbox Theatre Playwright, 1996. INTERESTS: community theatre; painting; paragliding; hiking; mountain climbing; skiing; dance. MISC: recipient, various Canada Council & Alberta Foundation for the Arts grants; guest speaker & reader. COMMENT: *"Internationally recognized, Darlene Quaife's first novel,* Bone Bird *won a Commonwealth Writers Prize. Her second novel,* Days & Nights on the Amazon, *appeared from Turnstone Press in the fall of 1995. She has published short stories (four prize winners), poetry and nonfiction in a variety of magazines. She has done many things to support the writing life from bank teller to freelance writer to writing instructor to President of The Writers' Guild of Alberta."*

Quinn, Louise, B.A.,M.Sc.,Ph.D. ■ ⌁ ✿
Associate Professor and Chair, Department of Geology, BRANDON UNIVERSITY, Brandon, MB R7A 6A9 (204) 727-9684, FAX 728-7346, EMAIL quinn@brandonu.ca. Born Glasgow 1959. m. Geoff Butler. EDUC: Cambridge Univ., B.A. 1980; Memorial Univ., M.Sc. 1985, Ph.D. 1993. CAREER: Lecturer, Univ. of Saskatchewan, 1988-89; Lecturer, Brandon Univ., 1989-93; Asst. Prof., 1993-95; Assoc. Prof., 1995 to date. SELECTED PUBLICATIONS: "The Landscape at Bonne Bay," in *Lise Sorenson: Gros Morne Paintings*, exhibition brochure (Memorial Univ. Gallery, 1985); "Distribution and Significance of Ordovician Flysch Units in Western Newfoundland," in *Current Research*, Part B (Geological Survey of Canada, 1988; "Sedimentology of the Silurian Clam Bank Formation, Western Newfoundland," abstract (Geological Association of Canada Program with Abstracts 19 1994); "Middle Ordovician Foredeep Fill in Western Newfoundland" (Geological Association of Canada, Special Paper 41, 1995). AFFIL: Canadian Society of Petroleum Geologists (Chair, Nat'l Liaison Committee). HONS: numerous grants & scholarships. INTERESTS: traditional (Celtic) music. MISC: founding coord. of 1st geology coop program, Brandon Univ.; recipient, various grants; various conference presentations. COMMENT: *"I am a female faculty member in a male-dominated discipline, and I try to maintain a balance between teaching activities and research. I enjoy opening new doors of opportunity for students and am involved in some new academic initiatives to achieve this. Most of my research field work is conducted in Newfoundland."*

R
abbani, Mary, Sutherland Maxwell (Mme. Rúhíyyih Rabbani) ☼ 🔲

Hand of the Cause, BAHÁ'Í FAITH, Box 155, 31001, Haifa, Israel (972) 4-358358, FAX 4-358659 or 972-4-358652. Member, INTERNATIONAL BAHÁ'Í TEACHING CENTRE. Born Montreal. w. Shoghi Effendi Rabbani, World Head of the Bahá'í Faith. **EDUC:** Montessori Sch.; primary schools in Montreal & Chevy Chase, Md.; high sch. in Montreal; McGill Univ.; privately taught. **CAREER:** on the death of her husband, managed worldwide affairs of Bahá'í Faith with eight other high-ranking officials, until election of the Universal House of Justice (Supreme Body of the Faith), 1957-63; travelled to visit Bahá'í centres worldwide, 1963 to date; crossed Africa, driving her own Landrover, 1969-73; expedition to Suriname, Guyana, & up the Brazilian Amazon, 1975; high-ranking officer of the Bahá'í Faith, Hand of the Cause; mbr., Int'l Teaching Centre, Haifa, Israel; public lecturer; author of books & plays. **SELECTED PUBLICATIONS:** *Prescription for Living* (Oxford: George Ronald, 1950); *The Priceless Pearl* (London, UK: Bahá'í Publishing Trust, 1969); *A Manual for Pioneers* (New Delhi: Bahá'í Publishing Trust, 1974); *The Desire of the World* (Oxford: George Ronald, 1982); *The Guardian of the Bahá'i Faith* (London, UK: Bahá'í Publishing Trust, 1988); *Poems of the Passing* (London: Biddles Ltd., Guildford and King's Lynn, 1996). **HONS:** given name of "Natu Ocsist" (Blessed Mother) by Blackfoot Indians of Canada; adopted by Eagle Tribe of Tlingit Indians, Alaska, & given name "Precious Lady"; adopted by grandson of Sitting Bull & given name "Princess Pretty Feather"; honorary Pres., Sacred Literature Trust, Manchester, U.K., 1989 to date; honorary mbr., International Centre for Peace, Peace Museum, Verdun, France, 1991 to date; honorary mbr., Club of Budapest, 1995 to date. MISC: travelled to 185 nations, dependencies & islands; numerous broadcast & print interviews throughout the world; opened to the public all existing Bahá'í Houses of Worship, Wilmette, Ill. (1953), Kampala, Uganda (1961), Sydney, Australia (1961), Frankfurt, Germany (1964), Panama City, Panama (1972), Apia, Western Samoa (1984) & New Delhi, India (1986); attended 1st Cdn Bahá'í Conference for Indians & Eskimos, Frobisher Bay, 1986; presented Bahá'í peace plan "The Promise of World Peace" to Sec.-Gen. of the United Nations, 1985; presented compilation on the environment from Bahá'í writings to Int'l Pres. of World Wide Fund for Nature, 1987; delegate to International Society for General Systems Research, Budapest, Hungary, 1987; principal speaker, European Bahá'í Women's Conference, Madrid, 1990; principal speaker, Bahá'í World Congress, London, 1963 & New York City, 1992; official speaker, World Forestry Charter Gathering, London, 1994; represented Bahá'í Faith as its leading dignitary at Summit on Religions & Conservations, Windsor Castle, U.K., 1995; keynote speaker, "The Fourth International Dialogue on the Transition to a Global Society," Univ. of Maryland, 1995; honoured guest speaker at special session of Brazilian Federal Chamber of Deputies, commemorating the 75th year of Bahá'í Faith in Brazil, 1996; principal speaker, Iberian Conference, Lisbon, Portugal, 1996; Prod., *The Green Light Expedition*, documentary (1976); Prod., *The Pilgrimage*, documentary (1980). COMMENT: *"Madame Rabbani—whose own marriage was a union of East and West—devotes her time and energies to promoting the cardinal principle of the Bahá'í Faith: universal peace."*

Rabinovitch, Marlene, B.Sc.,M.D. ⟨ᴕ ⊕ ❀
Professor of Pediatrics, Pathology and Medicine, UNIVERSITY OF TORONTO, 555 University Ave., Toronto, ON M5G 1X8 (416) 813-5918, FAX 813-7480, EMAIL mr@sickkids.on.ca. Director, Cardiovascular Research, THE HOSPITAL FOR SICK CHILDREN. Born Montreal 1946. EDUC: McGill Univ., B.Sc.(Physiology & Psych.) 1967, M.D. 1971. ACADEMIC CAREER: Instructor in Pediatrics, Children's Hospital Medical Center, Harvard Medical Sch., 1977-78; Asst. Prof. in Pediatrics, 1979-82; Assoc. Prof., Univ. of Toronto, 1982-88; Prof., Pediatrics & Pathology, 1988 to date; Prof. of Medicine, 1994 to date. CLINICAL CAREER: Intern in Pediatrics, Univ. of Colorado Medical Center, 1971-72; Resident in

Pediatrics, 1972-73; Pediatrician for the Ministry of Health & Central Hospital of the Negev, Beersheva, Israel, 1973-74; Clinical Fellow in Pediatric Cardiology, Texas Children's Hospital, Baylor Coll. of Medicine, 1974-75; Clinical Fellow in Pediatric Cardiology, Children's Hospital Medical Center, Harvard Medical Sch., 1975-76; Research Fellow in Pediatric Cardiology, 1976-77; Asst. in Cardiology, Dept. of Cardiology, Children's Hospital Medical Center, Boston, 1977-78; Assoc. in Cardiology, 1978-82; Sr. Assoc. in Pediatrics & Pathology, The Hospital for Sick Children, 1982 to date; Acting Dir., Cardiovascular Research Institute, 1986-88; Dir., Cardiovascular Research, 1988 to date. SELECTED PUBLICATIONS: "Blockade of very late antigen-4 integrin binding to fibronectin with CS1 peptide reduces accelerated coronary arteriopathy in rabbit cardiac allografts," with S. Molassi *et al* (*Journal of Clinical Investigation 95*, 1995); " Exogenous leukocyte and endogenous elastases can mediate mitogenic activity in pulmonary artery smooth muscle cells by release of extracellular matrix-bound basic fibroblast growth factor," with K. Thompson (*Journal of Cellular Physiology 166*, 1995); "Functional interplay between interleukin-1 receptor and elastin binding protein controls fibronectin synthesis in coronary artery smooth muscle cells" (*Experimental Cell Research 225*, 1996); "Elafin, a serine elastase inhibitor, attenuates post-cardiac transplant coronary arteriopathy and reduces myocardial necrosis in rabbits following heterotopic cardiac transplantation," with B. Cowan, O. Baron *et al* (*Journal of Clinical Investigation 97*, 1996); numerous other publications. EDIT: Ed. Bd., *Pediatric Pulmonary*; Ed. Bd., *American Journal of Physiology*; Ed. Bd., *Circulation Research*; Ed. Bd., *International Journal of Biochemistry and Molecular Biology*; Ed. Bd., *American Journal of Respiratory Cell and Molecular Biology*; Ed. Bd., *The Canadian Journal of Cardiology*. AFFIL: Royal Coll. of Physicians (Fellow); American Coll. of Cardiology (Fellow); Society for Pediatric Research; American Association of Investigative Pathology; American Thoracic Society; American Society of Cell Biology; American Society for Clinical Investigation; Canadian Society for Clinical Investigation (Exec. Councillor); Perinatal Research Society; Canadian Institute of Academic Medicine; Medical Research Council (Committee for Policy, Planning, Analysis & Evaluation); Heart & Stroke Foundation of Ontario (V-Chair of Research Policy); American Heart Association (Intercouncil Working Group, Molecular & Gene Therapy). HONS: Cushing Memorial Award in Pediatrics, McGill Univ., 1971; Research

Achievement Award, Canadian Cardiovascular Society, 1994; Julius Comroe Distinguished Lecturer, American Physiological Society, 1996. MISC: reviewer for numerous journals; recipient, various grants; frequent visiting professor.

Raby, Gyllian, B.A.,M.A. ■ ⊗ ▯ ⩘
Writer and Director of Theatre. Univ. Lecturer, DALHOUSIE UNIVERSITY, Halifax, NS. Born Shrewsbury, Wales 1959. m. Nigel Scott. 2 ch. Xavier, Nelly-Zoë. EDUC: Univ. of Manchester, B.A.(Drama) 1980; Univ. of Calgary, M.A.(Dramatic Lit.) 1982. CAREER: Founder, Artistic Dir., One Yellow Rabbit Performance Troupe, 1982-88; freelance Writer, Dir., 1982-83; Asst. Prof. for Theatre Studies, Univ. of Manitoba, 1983-84; Instructor, Univ. of Calgary, 1984, 1985, 1987, 1991 & 1992; Artistic Dir., Northern Light Theatre, Edmonton, 1988-92; Lecturer, Univ. of King's Coll. & Dalhousie Univ., 1992 to date. SELECTED CREDITS: "The Ecstacy and the Terror," drama, *Talkin' 'Bout AIDS*, CBC Radio, 1993; adaptor, *Something Wicked This Way Comes*, ballet theatre spectacle, Northern Light Theatre, 1989; various other adaptations & translations; *Music to Wreck Autos By*, performance poem, Eastern Front Theatre, 1994; *Treacheries of the Blue Angel*, music-video drama, Northern Light Theatre, 1990; writer/dir., *The Dog's Temper*, Northern Light Theatre, Mile Zero Dance, 1991; dir., *The Emperor's New Clothes*, 1994; various other works produced for stage & puppet theatre; dramaturge of various works; various other theatrical credits. SELECTED PUBLICATIONS: "The Creativity of Improvisors: Hip hop, Zip zop" (*Grenfell College Review: Creativity and Discourse*, a Multi-Disciplinary Conference Newfoundland, 1994); "Polygraph," by Robert LePage & Marie Brassard, translator (*Canadian Theatre Review* Fall 1990); "Weedkiller" and "Bluebeard's Wife," in *Womansong: Anthology of Canadian Women Poets* (Vancouver: Sandstone Press, 1981); various other publications. AFFIL: Playwrights' Atlantic Resource Centre (Past Chair); Playwrights' Union Canada (Atlantic Rep.); Halifax Ecology Action Group; Halifax Tai Chi Association; Canadian Institute of Theatre Technology. HONS: Grace Phillips Award for Creative Enterprise, 1976; Hanley Award for Scholarship, 1977; Univ. of Calgary scholarships, 1980-82; Alberta Culture Playwrighting Competition Prize; Alberta Culture Arts Study Award, 1980; Chalmers Award for New Canadian Plays, with R. LePage & M. Brassard, 1991; Michael Luchovich Heritage Trust Award for Career Recognition, 1992. INTERESTS: play & fiction reading/writing; hiking; skiing; world travel; swimming; classical guitar; mask construction; stiltdancing; Tai Chi. MISC: Calgary 1988 Winter Arts Festival Theatre Working Committee; recipient, Canada Council Explorations Grant. COMMENT: *"Raby has been creating cutting edge Canadian performance theatre for 15 years. Her concerns: to expose hidden cultural mythologies for discussion."*

Rached, Tahani ⩘
Filmmaker, NATIONAL FILM BOARD OF CANADA, Box 6100, Stn Centre-Ville, Montreal, QC H3C 3H5 (514) 283-9344, FAX 283-4300. CAREER: vidéos pour SUCO et Carrefour international, 1973-75; Réalisatrice, ONF, 1980 to date. SELECTED CREDITS: coréalise, *Les mesures de contrôle et une nouvelle société*, 1976; *Leur crise on la paye pas*, 1979; 6 emissions pour Radio Quebec dans *Planete*, 1979-80; *Les voleurs de job*, 1980; *La phonie furieuse*, 1982; *Beyrouth! "à défaut d'être mort,"* 1983; *Haïti-Québec*, 1985; *Bam pay a !* *Rends-moi mon pays*, 1986; *Au chic resto pop*, 1990; *Medecins de Coeur* (long metrage documentaire), 1993; *Quatre Femmes Egyptiennes* (long metrage documentaire), Sortie Prevue, Printemps, 1997.

Racine, Yolande, B.A.,M.F.A. ■■ ▨ ⊗
Curator, MUSÉE D'ART CONTEMPORAIN DE MONTRÉAL, 185 rue Ste-Catherine O., Montréal, QC H2X 1Z8 (514) 847-6282, FAX 847-6293. Born Montréal 1948. 2 ch. Marianne, Simon. EDUC: Coll. Jean-de-Brébeuf, B.A. 1969; Univ. de Montréal, B.F.A.(Art Hist.) 1972, M.F.A. 1980. CAREER: Researcher, Musée Ferme Saint-Gabriel, Montréal, 1971; Pre-archivist, Art Hist. documentation, Cégep Vieux-Montréal, 1972; Pedagogical Cons., Fine Arts Dept., 1978; Head of Educ., Animation & Communications Dept., Musée d'art contemporain de Montréal, 1973-74; freelance researcher, 1975-76; study trip, Asia, Middle East & N. Africa, 1977; Curator, Musée d'art contemporain de Montréal, 1978-82; Curator of Contemporary Art, Montreal Museum of Fine Arts, 1982-92; part-time Fac. Mbr., Dept. of Painting & Drawing, Concorida Univ., 1992-93; Dept. of Art Hist., 1994; Curator & Head of Multimedia Programme, Musée d'art contemporain de Montréal, 1993. SELECTED PUBLICATIONS: author, *Avant-scène de l'imaginaire/Theatre of the Imagination* (Montreal Museum of Fine Arts, 1984); *Betty Goodwin: oeuvres de 1971 à 1987/Works from 1971-1987* (Montreal Museum of Fine Arts, 1987); "Rebecca Horn: Anima" (*Parachute*, No. 73, Jan./Feb./Mar. 1994); "Kimio Tsuchiya: Un Autre Monde," in *Kimio Tsuchiya, Provenance - A Fragment of Silence* (La Galerie du Coll. Edouard-Mont-

petit, Longueuil, 1994); "La Vidéo, au-delà du récit," in *Jean-François Cantin: La Production du temps - Travaux vidéographiques, 1977-1994* (Collection Olive Noire, 1994); *Martha Townsend: Entre le silence et l'écoute* (Musée d'art de Joliette, 1995); "Dans le rôle principal: la caméra/Starring: The Camera," in *Michael Snow* (Musée d'art contemporain de Montréal, 1995); "Kim Adams: The Forest Behind the Trees," in *Kim Adams* (Centraal Museum, Utrecht, Holland, 1995); "Corps à la dérive," in *Luc Courchesne: Salon des Ombres* (Musée d'art contemporain de Montréal, 1996); "L'Esprit du collectionneur/The Spirit of the Collector," in *L'Oeil du collectionneur* (Musée d'art contemporain de Montréal,,1996); co-author, *L'Architecture traditionnelle, Le mobilier traditionnel, L'orfèvrerie traditionnelle, Les instruments d'artisanat* (1973); *Albert Dumouchel, rétrospective de l'oeuvre gravé* (1974); *Tendances actuelles au Québec* (1980); *Le Monde selon Graff* (1987); contributor, *The Dictionary of Art* (London, England 1988). EDIT: editor, Éditions Yolande Racine, published *Ricochets*, 1993. AFFIL: Canada Council, Ottawa (mbr. of Jury); Ministère de la Culture et des Communications du Québec (mbr. of Jury); Société des musées québécois; Canadian Museums Association; International Council of Museums; Artexte (mbr. of Bd. & Publication Committee). HONS: Award of Excellence, presentation category, Canadian Museums Association, 1988 (Betty Goodwin exhibition); Special Mention, Société des musées québécois, 1988 (Betty Goodwin exhibition); Award of Excellence, American Federation of Arts, 1988 (Betty Goodwin catalogue).

Radchuk, Leona, B.Paed.,B.Sc.,B.Ed., M.Ed. ●
Manager, UKRAINIAN FRATERNAL SOCIETY OF CANADA, 235 McGregor St., Winnipeg, MB R2W 4W5 (204) 586-4482, FAX 589-6411. Born Ukraine 1931. m. Serge. 2 ch. Julianna A., Natalie V. EDUC: Univ. of Manitoba, B.Sc. 1955, B.Paed.(Secondary Sch. Educ.) 1955, B.Ed.(High Sch. Chem. & Physics) 1958, M.Ed.(Educational Psych.) 1981. CAREER: high sch. Teacher, 1955-75; Sch. Trustee, Seven Oaks Sch. Div., 1968-77; Chrm, Seven Oaks Sch. Bd., 1975-77; Mgr, Ukrainian Fraternal Society of Canada, 1978 to date. AFFIL: St. Andrew's Coll. (Dir. 1985-91, 1993 to date; Chrm of the Bd. 1990, 1993 to date); St. Andrew's Coll. Foundation (Treas. 1985 to date); Alpha Omega Alumnae (Past Pres. & other exec. positions). INTERESTS: stamp collecting; Ukrainian embroidery book collection; reading. COMMENT: *"I have had three suc-

cessful careers so far in my life: teaching, parenting, and business administration. I am looking forward to a fourth career, that of stamp collecting and grandparenting."*

Radcliffe, Rosemary ■ ⊗ ♥ ⌣
Canadian Actor, Writer, Composer. c/o The Characters Talent Agency, 150 Carlton St., Toronto, ON. Born Stratford, Ont. 1946. d. J. Stephen Stohn. 1 ch. EDUC: Ryerson Polytechnic Univ., Diploma in Radio & TV Arts 1967; Royal Conservatory of Music, ARCT (Performance, Piano). CAREER: an original mbr. of Second City; has appeared on TV, on stage & in films. SELECTED CREDITS: *Coming Up Rosie* (series), CBC; Tina, *The King of Kensington* (series), CBC; Mrs. Barry, *Anne of Green Gables* & *Anne of Green Gables–The Sequel*, CBC; *The Events Leading Up to My Death* (feature), Bill Robertson; *Married Life* (series), US cable channel Comedy Central. HONS: nominee (*Married Life*), Gemini Awards. COMMENT: *"A graduate of the Royal Conservatory of Toronto, Miss Radcliffe and librettist/lyricist Nika Rylski were given the "Eric Harvie Award," for their original stage musical* Hello Gorgeous!, *created for the 1982 Charlottetown Festival. Miss Radcliffe continues to compose and entertain as an after-dinner speaker."*

Radke, Lori ■■ ⑦
Paralympic Athlete. Calgary, AB. CAREER: physiotherapist. SPORTS CAREER: mbr., Nat'l Wheelchair Basketball Team, 3 yrs. Paralympic Games: Gold, 1996. Canadian Wheelchair Basketball League (CWBL): 2nd, Women's Finals, 1996; Women's Finals, 1995. World Championships: 1st, 1994. HONS: All-Star, CWBL women's finals, 1995. MISC: has had many ligament reconstruction surgeries and is classified as "minimal disability."

Radloff, Laurie ⑤ ♂
President, UNIGLOBE TRAVEL (WESTERN CANADA) INC., 1199 W. Pender St., Ste. 800, Vancouver, BC V6E 2R1 (604) 681-9192, FAX 681-1047. Born Fort McLeod, Alta. 1956. m. Dave Radloff. 1 ch. CAREER: Travel Consultant & Office Supervisor, Four Seasons Travel, Cranbrook, B.C., 1974-81; owner, Uniglobe Baker Street Travel, Cranbrook, 1981-87; Pres. & owner, Uniglobe Travel (Western Canada) Inc., Vancouver, 1987 to date. AFFIL: Young Entrepreneurs' Association (1991-94); Executive Travel Network. HONS: Uniglobe Region of the Year, Uniglobe Travel (Western Canada) Inc., 1991, 1992, 1996; 1 of Top 40 Bus. People, Business in Vancouver Annual Achievement Awards, 1994. INTERESTS: walking;

cycling; gardening; travelling. **MISC:** Uniglobe's only female reg'l owner.

Rae, Barbara, M.B.A.,C.M. ■ $
Corporate Director. 2206 Folkestone Way, #3, W. Vancouver, BC V7S 2X7, FAX (604) 925-3259. Born Prince George, B.C. 1931. m. George Suart. 3 ch. James, Glen, John. **EDUC:** Simon Fraser Univ., M.B.A. 1972. **CAREER:** Pres. & CEO, Adia Canada Ltd., 1960-92; Chair, 1992-95; Chancellor, Simon Fraser Univ., 1986-92. **DIRECTOR:** Adia Canada Ltd.; B.C. Telephone Co.; B.C. Telecom Inc.; CIBC; Grosvenor International Holdings; Noranda Inc.; Xerox Canada Inc. **AFFIL:** KCTS Channel 9 Seattle (Dir.); Canadian Association for Philanthropy; Canadian Council of Christians & Jews (Nat'l Co-Chrm). **HONS:** Outstanding Alumnae Award, Simon Fraser Univ., 1985; Business Woman of the Year, YWCA, 1986; B.C. Entrepreneur of the Year, 1987; Canadian Volunteer Award, 1989; Order of B.C., 1991; Canadian Entrepreneur of the Year, 1992; Member of the Order of Canada, 1993. **COMMENT:** *"High energy and enthusiasm are gifts that have supported a broad and active involvement in a great variety of business and community activities."*

Raeburn Paul, Nancy Anne ■■ 🏃 $ ♥
President, ROLLINS RAEBURN INTERIOR DESIGN INC., 261 Davenport Rd., Toronto, ON M5R 1K3 (416) 923-5676, EMAIL rollins@accent.net. Born Canada 1947. w. 1 ch. E. Sarah Raeburn Paul. **EDUC:** Ontario Coll. of Art, Environmental Design Dept., grad. 1979; Sotheby Decorative Arts Program, London, U.K., 1980; Art Hist. of the Italian Renaissance, Palazzo Corsini, Florence, 1981. **VOLUNTEER CAREER:** health-related public svc. incl.: founder & founding Pres., Canadian Breast Cancer Foundation, Ont. chpt. & nat'l foundation; Pres., Peter Paul Charitable Foundation, 1985 to date; Co-Chrm, Brazilian Carnival Ball in support of Princess Margaret Hospital Breast Cancer Centre, 1994; Chrm, Bd. of Dir., Muki Baum Centre for Handicapped Children, 1988 & 1989. Arts & cultural public svc. incl.: Gov. Council, Ontario Coll. of Art, 1987-91; Chrm & founder, Toronto Friends of Stratford fundraising gala, 1981; mbr., Women's Committee, Canadian Opera Company, 1992 to date; Campaign Cabinet, The Design Exchange, 1994-95. **AFFIL:** Association of Registered Interior Designers of Ontario; Interior Designers of Canada; Canadian Antique Dealers' Association; American Society of Interior Designers. **HONS:** numerous awards/decorations incl. ARIDO award for excellence in residential design, 1983; Dame Commander of the Sovereign Military Order of St. John of Jerusalem Knights of Malta in recognition of services rendered, 1990; City of Toronto Award of Merit for community action, 1991; Gov. General's Confederation Medal for significant contribution to Canada in the field of public svc., 1992; Fellow, Ontario Coll. of Art, for outstanding contribution to the arts, 1995. **INTERESTS:** 18th- & 19th-century decorative arts, esp. ceramics, silver & furniture. **MISC:** public speaking: speeches, tapes, videos, TV appearances, publications.

Raffé, Alexandra 📺 🍁
Chief Executive Officer, ONTARIO FILM DEVELOPMENT CORPORATION, N. Tower, 175 Bloor St. E., Ste. 300, Toronto, ON M4W 3R8 (416) 314-6858, FAX 314-6876. Born Singapore 1955. s. **CAREER:** various positions, Xerox Corporation; Pres., Riffraff Films Inc., 1985-94; Co-Chair of the Advisory Committee for a Cultural Industries Strategy, 1993-94; CEO, Ontario Film Development Corporation, 1994 to date. **SELECTED CREDITS:** Exec. Prod., *Battle of the Bulge*, dir. Arlene Hazzan-Green; Exec. Prod., *I Love A Man In Uniform* (feature), dir. David Wellington, 1993; Exec. Prod., *Lotus Eaters* (feature), dir. Paul Shapiro, 1993; Exec. Prod., *Zero Patience* (feature), dir. John Greyson, 1993; Assoc. Prod., *Passion: A Letter in 16 mm*, 1985; Prod., *I've Heard the Mermaids Singing* (feature), 1987; Prod., *White Room* (feature), 1990. **AFFIL:** Human Rights Campaign (Dir.). **HONS:** Outstanding Achievement as a Producer, Toronto Women in Film & Television, 1995. **INTERESTS:** sailing; travel; reading. **COMMENT:** *"In June of 1994 Alexandra Raffé was appointed the CEO of the Ontario Film Development Corporation. Prior to that, Raffé was president of Riffraff Films Inc., an independent production company concentrating on the development and production of theatrical feature films."*

Rains, Elizabeth ■■ ✎ 🎭 📺
Managing Editor, *THE CAPILANO REVIEW* (literary magazine), 2055 Purcell Way, N. Vancouver, BC V7J 3H5 (604) 984-1712, EMAIL 72347.1140@compuserve.com or erains@capcollege.bc.ca. Journalism Instructor, LANGARA COLLEGE. Born Buffalo, N.Y. m. Al Hyland. 2 ch. Danielle Michael, Jessica Raya. **EDUC:** Selkirk Coll. (Kootenay Sch. of Art), Certificate (Graphic Design); Langara Coll., Accelerated Journalism Certificate (Dean's List); Simon Fraser Univ., Bach. of Gen. Studies (minor Sociology, Honour Roll). **CAREER:** Reporter, *Vancouver Sun*, 1986-87; Reporter, *Kamloops Daily News*, 1987-88; Ed., *BC Grocer Magazine*, Canada Wide Magazines, 1990; Public

Rel'ns Officer, Capilano Coll., 1990-94; Instructor, Institute of Communication Arts, 1991-94; Ed., *Arts Access* Magazine, 1994; Mng Ed., *The Capilano Review*, 1995 to date. SELECTED PUBLICATIONS: author, *Vancouver Parents Survival Guide* (Brighouse Press); freelance writer & ed., *West World, Home Office Computing, B.C. Business Magazine, Campus Canada,* & others; more than 800 published articles. AFFIL: B.C. Association of Magazine Publishers (Pres. 1996 to date). HONS: Dr. M. Sheila O'Connell Prize for Children's Lit.; B.C. & Yukon Community Newspapers Association Award for outstanding achievement in journalism. MISC: immigrated to Canada, 1972.

Rajan, Tilottama, B.A.,M.A.,Ph.D., F.R.S.C. 🐗 🐚
Director, Centre in the Study of Theory and Criticism, UNIVERSITY OF WESTERN ONTARIO, London, ON N6A 3K7 (519) 679-2111, ext. 5883, EMAIL trajan@bosshog.arts.uwo.ca. Professor, Department of English, UNIVERSITY COLLEGE. Born N.Y. 1951. s. EDUC: Univ. of Toronto, B.A.(English) 1972, M.A.(English) 1973, Ph.D.(English) 1977. CAREER: Asst. Prof., Huron Coll., Univ. of Western Ontario, 1977-80; Asst. Prof., Queen's Univ., 1980-83; Assoc. Prof., 1983-85; Visiting Prof., Univ. of California at San Diego, 1984; Prof., Univ. of Wisconsin at Madison, 1985-90; Prof., Dept. of English/Centre for Theory & Criticism, Univ. of Western Ontario, 1990 to date. SELECTED PUBLICATIONS: *Dark Interpreter: The Discourse of Romanticism* (Cornell Univ. Press, 1980/86); *The Supplement of Reading: Figures of Understanding in Romantic Theory and Practice* (Cornell Univ. Press, 1990); *Intersections: Nineteenth Century Philosophy and Contemporary Theory* co-ed. (State Univ. of New York Press, 1994). EDIT: Advisory Bd., *P.M.L.A.,* 1990-94; Ed. Bd., *The Wordsworth Circle,* 1993 to date; Ed. Bd., *European Romantic Review,* 1993 to date; Ed. Bd., *Clio,* 1995 to date. AFFIL: Modern Language Association (Exec. of Div. on Non-Fictional Prose 1985-88; Exec. of Div. on English Romantic Period 1993-98); North American Society for the Study of Romanticism (Founder & Pres.); Royal Society of Canada (Fellow). HONS: John Simon Guggenheim Fellowship, 1987-88; Research Fellowship, Social Sciences & Humanities Research Council of Canada, 1990-94. INTERESTS: feeding & observing squirrels. COMMENT: *"Theoretically oriented work in Romantic literature (both poetry and fiction); romantic philosophy and its connections to contemporary theory; phenomenology and deconstruction."*

Ralling, M. Jane, B.A.,B.Ed.,LL.B. ⚖ 🎓
Partner, CAMPBELL, LEA, MICHAEL, MCCONNELL AND PIGOT, 15 Queen St., P.O. Box 429, Charlottetown, PE C1A 7K7 (902) 566-3400, FAX 566-9266. Born Shawinigan, Que. 1951. m. Geoffrey Ralling. 2 ch. Kingsley, Alexandra. EDUC: Mount Allison Univ., B.A.(Psych./French) 1972, B.Ed. 1975; Univ. of Western Ontario, LL.B. 1982. BAR: Ont., 1985; P.E.I. 1986. CAREER: articling student, Ivey and Dowler, London, Ont., 1983-84; articling student, Campbell, Lea, Michael, McConnell and Pigot, 1986; Assoc., 1986-88; Ptnr, 1988 to date. AFFIL: Law Society of P.E.I. (Real Estate Committee 1990-95; Council Mbr. 1992-93); Canadian Bar Association (P.E.I. Chair, Constitutional Law Section 1991-95); P.E.I. Heart & Stroke Foundation (Bd. 1993-95; Advocacy Chair 1994); Friends of Confederation Centre (Bd.; Sec. 1987-90); Law Society of Upper Canada; Community Legal Information Association (Bd. 1990-92); Child Care Facilities (Bd. 1988-92). HONS: Undergrad. & Entrance Scholarships, Mount Allison Univ.; Giffen, Pensa Prize for 1st Place Standing Average, Ont. Bar Admission Course, 1985. INTERESTS: local hockey booster; sailing; cross-country skiing; sewing; reading; travel. COMMENT: *"Despite the temptations of the 'big city,' I have been able to return to my roots in the Maritimes and enjoy the small successes and daily pleasures of a balanced life."*

Ramkhalawansingh, Ceta, B.A.,Dip.C.S., M.A. ■ ✦ ◯ 🎓
Manager, Equal Opportunity, CITY OF TORONTO, 595 Bay St., 11th Fl., Toronto, ON M5G 2C2 (416) 392-7855, FAX 392-0006. Born Trinidad & Tobago 1951. EDUC: Univ. of Toronto, B.A.(Pol. Econ.), Dip.C.S.(Child Study) 1974, Certificate (Educ.) 1977, M.A.(Soc.) 1980, doctoral studies (Soc.) 1979-81. CAREER: Lecturer, Women's Studies, Univ. of Toronto, 1971-77; Researcher, Social Planning Council of Metro Toronto, 1973; Ed./Researcher, Canadian Women's Educational Press, 1973-74; Admin., Work Group on Multicultural Programs, Toronto Bd. of Educ., 1974-76; Lecturer, York Univ., 1974; Proj. Consultant, SCORE Proj., Toronto Bd. of Educ., 1977-78; Lecturer, McMaster Univ., 1978-81; Consultant, City of Toronto, 1981; Interim Coord., Sesquicentennial Celebrations for the City of Toronto, 1981; Policy Consultant, 1982-85; Mgr, Contract Compliance, 1986-92; Mgr, Svc. Equity, 1992-94; Acting Dir., Equal Opportunity, 1994-95; Chair, Employment Equity Committee; Mgr, Equal Opportunity, 1995 to date. SELECTED PUBLICATIONS: "Women During the Great War,"

in *Women at Work: Ontario 1850-1930* (Canadian Women's Educational Press, 1974); *(Un)Equal Pay: Canadian and International Perspectives* (Toronto: Resources for Feminist Research, 1979); *Equal Opportunity–Detecting Bias: Communications and Employment*, report, City of Toronto (1983); "Pay Equity–An Historical Perspective" (*The Pay Equity Practitioner* 1(5) 1988); extensively published in a variety of disciplines & subjects. **EDIT:** Mng Ed. & Contributing Ed., *Resources for Feminist Research*, 1977-76; Guest Ed., special issue on north-south rel'ns, *Women and Environments*, Apr. 1993. **AFFIL:** Learnxs Foundation (Pres.); Cecil Community Centre; MATCH International Centre (former Pres.); Committee for 94; Univ. of Toronto (Women's Studies Advisory Bd.); Commonwealth Women's Network Steering Committee (Cdn delegate); YWCA (Bd. Mbr.); Canadian National Committee for the 50th Anniversary of the U.N.; Grange Park Residents' Association; Grange Historical Society (VP 1988 to date); Arts Foundation of Greater Toronto (Trustee). **HONS:** City of Toronto Book Award, with the Women's Press, 1974; Scholarship, Harvard Grad. Sch. of Educ., 1977; OISE Fellowships, 1977-79; Doctoral Fellowship, SSHRC, 1979-81; Certificate of Honour, Friends of the Sesquicentennial Museum, 1990; Persons' Day Award, LEAF & Women's Intercultural Network, 1994; Award of Merit to Learnxs Foundation–publisher of *Art for Enlightenment*, Toronto Historical Bd., 1994. **MISC:** appointed by Ont. Cabinet to serve on the Ont. Advisory Council on Women's Issues, 1983-88; chaired Council Committees on Pay Equity & Employment Standards; co-founder of the Women's Studies Programs at the Univ. of Toronto, 1971; appointed by the Fed. Min. of Women as official Cdn delegate, Commonwealth Ministers' Conference on Women, 1993; various guest lectures. **COMMENT:** *"My personal goals include opening doors and eliminating disadvantage and making a contribution to my local community and the world at large."*

Ramsay, Susan ■ Ⓢ

President and Chief Executive Officer, THE MOVING STORE FRANCHISE SYSTEMS, INC., 39 Orfus Rd., Toronto, ON M6A 1L7 (416) 789-4185, FAX 789-0181, EMAIL moving@idirect.com. Born Summerside, P.E.I. 1949. life partner Bruce Davidsen. 2 ch. **CAREER:** Pres. & CEO, Rent A Boxx Moving Systems Inc., 1979 to date; Pres. & CEO, The Moving Store, 1983 to date. **MISC:** inventor of "Movetech," a world-wide patented shipping container. **COMMENT:** *"Susan's greatest accomplishment and*

endeavour, besides her two sons, of course, is her business, Rent-A-Boxx/The Moving Store. She has dedicated the past 18 years to the success of it and her invention, the Movetech box. 1997 brings franchising plans to fruition."

Randall, Janet, B.A.Sc.,M.Sc. ■ ♣ �※

Director, Cabinet and Corporate Services, PUBLIC WORKS AND GOVERNMENT SERVICES CANADA, Place du Portage, 11 Laurier, Rm. 15A1, Ottawa, ON K1A 0S5 (819) 956-9524, FAX 956-4962. Born Ottawa 1952. m. Edward. 2 ch. Jefferey, Bradley. **EDUC:** Univ. of Guelph, B.A.Sc.(Textile Sci.) 1974, M.Sc.(Textile Sci.) 1975. **CAREER:** Chemist, Product Safety Lab., Fed. Dept. of Consumer & Corp. Affairs, 1976-78; Program Officer, Product Safety Branch, 1978-81; Qualification Officer, Canadian Gen. Standards Bd., 1981-82; Sr. Standards Program Mgr & Program Officer, 1982-87; Acting Sec., 1985; Dir. of Standards, 1987-95; United Way/Healthpartners Campaign Leader, Public Works & Gov't Svcs Canada, 1994. **SELECTED PUBLICATIONS:** "Standard Time" (*CanadianTextile Journal* Apr./May 1993); "ISO Quality Standards: Recommendations for Canadian Companies" (*Consensus* Summer 1994); "Where Canada Stands on ISO" (*Canadian Textile Journal* Dec. 1994/Jan. 1995). **AFFIL:** Institute of Textile Science (Dir.; Treas. 1987-90; VP 1990-92; Pres. 1992-94); Ottawa Valley Textile Association (VP); Canadian Textile Federation (Past Treas.; Dir.); American Association of Textile Chemists & Colorists; Association of Professional Executives of the Public Service. **HONS:** Exemplary Customer Service Award, Fed. Deputy Min. for Public Works & Gov't Svcs. **COMMENT:** *"After a number of technical positions within the federal Public Service, I am now the Director of Cabinet and Corporate Services at PWGSC. I remain active within the textile industry and its associations."*

Randall, Joan R., B.A. ■ Ⓞ ※ ☞ ♂

Volunteer. 39 South Dr., Toronto, ON M4W 1R2 (416) 964-1588, FAX 964-1588. Chair of the Board, UNIVERSITY OF TORONTO ART CENTRE. Born Toronto w. 3 ch. **EDUC:** Univ. of Toronto, B.A.(Hist.) 1949. **CAREER:** Public Rep., Council of the Institute of Chartered Accountants for Ontario (ICAO). **VOLUNTEER CAREER:** Univ. of Toronto: Advisory Council, Sch. of Continuing Studies, Univ. of Toronto; Admissions Committee, Fac. of Medicine; Exec. Committee, Dean's Advisory Council, Fac. of Mgmt; mbr. & V-Chair, Univ. Coll. Committee; Art Committee; Chair, Bd. of Trustees, Univ. Coll./Univ. of Toronto Art Gallery; Chair, Task Force on Sr. Adult Learning; numerous past committees & exec. positions incl. Chair, Gov. Council 1989-90; Royal Ontario Museum: Curatorial Planning Committee, Institute of Contemporary Culture; Benefactor Mbr.; numerous past committees & exec. positions incl. Founding Chair, Volunteer Committee 1956-60, Chair, Touring Committee 1965; Chair, Travel Committee 1972-75; mbr. & Founding Pres., Rosedale Branch, The Arthritis Society of Ontario; Life Mbr.; Bd. of Trustees & Acquisitions Committee, Program & Mktg Committee 1990-93, The National Gallery of Canada; Trustee Section, American Associations of Museums; Chair of the Bd., Univ. of Toronto Art Centre; Advisory Council of the Dean of Eng., Univ. of Toronto. **AFFIL:** The Art Gallery of Ontario (Life Mbr.); The Metropolitan Museum of Art, N.Y.; The Canadian Club; The Muskoka Lakes Association; Timothy Eaton Memorial Church; The Muskoka Lakes Golf & Country Club. **HONS:** 1st Annual Award for Volunteerism, Ministry of Culture & Recreation, Prov. of Ont., 1986; The Arbor Award, Univ. of Toronto, 1990; Canada 125 Medal, 1993; LL.D.(Hon.), Univ. of Toronto, 1995.

Randoja, Ingrid, B.A. ■■ ✏ 🎞

Film Reviewer and Entertainment Writer, *NOW* MAGAZINE, 150 Danforth Ave., Toronto, ON M4K 1N1. Born Toronto 1963. s. **EDUC:** Wilfrid Laurier Univ., B.A.(Comm. Studies) 1986. **CAREER:** Film Reviewer & Entertainment Writer, *NOW* Magazine, 1991 to date; has appeared as film commentator, *Face-Off*, CBC Newsworld; *E-Now*, Baton; *Canada AM*, Baton; *Real Life*, Life Network; occasional reviewer, AM640 Talk Radio. **SELECTED CREDITS:** writer, *Mockingbird Hill*, screenplay. **SELECTED PUBLICATIONS:** reviews & interviews in *Sight + Sound* (June 1995); *Take One* (1992, 1995, 1996); various European film magazines (through writing agent). **INTERESTS:** canoeing; reading biographies. **COMMENT:** *"I'm lucky enough to make a living writing and talking about films. It's a good thing."*

Rankin, Linda M., B.A. ■■ 📺 $

Executive Vice-President and General Manager, WETV (Global Access Television Network), WETV House, 342 MacLaren St., Ottawa, ON K2P 0M6 (613) 238-4580, FAX 238-5642, EMAIL lrankin@wetv.com. Born Foam Lake, Sask. 1946. m. Guy Houdin. 2 ch. Alexandre, Jonathon. **EDUC:** Univ. of Saskatchewan, B.A.(Psych.) 1968; Columbia Bus. Sch., Exec. Mgmt Program 1987; L'Institut de Français, Villefranche, France, 1993. **CAREER:** various positions, Hum. Res. Mgmt, Policy Dev., & Customer Svc., Bell Canada, 1972-81; Dir. of Personnel & Public Affairs, Telesat Canada, 1981-83; VP, Admin., 1983-84; VP, Telecomm. Svcs, 1984-88; VP, Bus. Dev., 1988-93; Proj. Leader, Lifestyle TV, Moffat Communications Limited, 1993-94; Pres. & CEO, WTN - Women's Television Network, 1994-95; Exec. VP & Gen. Mgr, WETV - Global Access Television Network, 1996 to date. **DIRECTOR:** Akjuat Aerospace Limited; Cresset Investments. **AFFIL:** Advanced Broadcasting Systems of Canada (Chair 1988-95); Banff Television Festival Foundation (Dir. 1988-95); Canadian Satellite Users' Association (Dir. 1994-95); Canadian Women in Communications (Dir. 1994-96); Health Sciences Centre, Winnipeg (Dir. 1995). **HONS:** Gemini Special Award for outstanding tech. performance of the production in high-definition TV of 1991 All-Star Baseball Game, 1992; Award of Excellence, "Breakthrough Award," Telesat Canada, 1988. **COMMENT:** *"I have tried to give something back to my communities. I haven't quite finished."*

Rankin, Ragini V., B.Arch.,M.C.I.P. ⚛ 🍁

Urban Planner, PATTI RAO ASSOCIATES. Born Bilaspur, India 1952. m. Lee Rankin, City Councillor, Burnaby. **EDUC:** M.A. Coll. of Technology, Bhopal, India, B.Arch. 1975; Royal Danish Academy of Fine Arts, Copenhagen, Denmark, Certificate (Advanced Urban Planning Studies) 1980. **CAREER:** Urban Planner, Patti Rao Associates Planning Consultants; candidate for Vancouver City Council, 1993; candidate for Vancouver-Langara, Prov. Election, 1996. **AFFIL:** Planning Institute of B.C.; Canadian Institute of Planners. **INTERESTS:** music; painting. **COMMENT:** *"Patti Rao Associates has successfully completed 150 large-scale planning projects in British Columbia, the State of Washington, Malaysia, and Costa Rica."*

Raoul, Valerie, M.A.,Ph.D. ■ 🎓 📜

Professor, Department of French and Director, Centre for Research in Women's Studies and Gender Relations, UNIVERSITY OF BRITISH COLUMBIA, 1987 East Mall, Ste. 797, Vancouver, BC V6T 1Z1 (604) 822-2879, FAX 822-6675. Born Shrewsbury, UK. 1941. m. Yvon Raoul. 3 ch. **EDUC:** Girton Coll., Univ. of Cambridge, B.A.(Modern Languages) 1963, M.A.(Modern Languages) 1968; London Sch. of Econ., Diploma in Social Admin.(Social Work) 1964; Univ. of Bristol, Grad. Certificate in Educ.(French & German) 1966; McMaster Univ., M.A.(French) 1971, Ph.D.(French) 1978. **CAREER:** taught English in Thailand & France, taught French in UK before coming to Canada in 1970; part-time teacher, French, McMaster Univ., St. Michael's Coll. (Univ. of Toronto) & Ryerson Polytechnic Univ., 1970-79; Dept. of French, Univ. of British Columbia, 1979 to date; Women's Studies Coord., 1988-90; Head of Dept., 1991-96; Full Prof., 1992 to date; Visiting Prof., Univ. de Bourgogne, France, Fall 1996; Dir., Centre for Research in Women's Studies & Gender Rel'ns, 1996 to date. SELECTED PUBLICATIONS: *The French Fictional Journal: Fictional Narcissism/Narcissistic Fiction* (Univ. of Toronto Press, 1979); *Distinctly Narcissistic: Diary Fiction in Quebec* (Univ. of Toronto Press, 1994); *The Anatomy of Gender: Women's Struggle for the Body*, co-ed. (Carleton Univ. Press, 1988); articles & reviews in *The French Review, Texte, Atlantis, Mosaic, Yale French Studies, Voix et Images, New Comparison, Canadian Literature, Canadian Review of Comparative Literature, Tessera, Dictionary of Literary Biography*. AFFIL: Association of Professors of French in Canada Universities (Exec. Committee 1986-90); Association for Canadian & Quebec Literatures (VP 1987-89); C.F.H. (Publications Committee 1988-90); Academic Women's Association, UBC (Exec. 1987-90); Association of Chairs of French Departments in Canadian Universities (Pres. 1992-95; Women in French (delegate for West 1996). COMMENT: *"Introduced courses on literary and feminist theory and on women's writing in the department of French at UBC; fostered interdisciplinary studies by involvement with Women's Studies and Comparative Literature; supervised numerous graduate students working in these areas; contributed to setting up exchanges with France and Quebec and greater community involvement by the department."*

Rapoport, Janis, B.A. 📖 📕 ⊗
Author, Playwright, Editor. c/o The Writers Union of Canada, 24 Ryerson Ave., Toronto, ON M5T 2P3. 4 ch. Jeremy Seager, Sara Seager, Julia Seager, Renate Donegani. EDUC: Univ. of Toronto, B.A.(Phil.) 1967. CAREER: ed., author, poet, playwright & critic, 1966 to date; Ed. Asst., *Which?* magazine, London, UK, 1968-69; Asst. Ed., Paul Hamlyn Ltd., London, UK, 1969-70; Assoc. Ed., *The Tamarack Review*, Toronto, 1970-82; Ed., Heinemann Educational Books (Cdn subsidiary), Scarborough, Ont., 1971-73; Story Ed., TV Drama, CBC, Toronto, 1973-74; Playwright-in-Residence, Tarragon Theatre, Toronto, 1974-75; freelance writer, ed., creative-writing instructor, broadcaster, Toronto, 1975 to date; Playwright-in-Residence, Banff Centre, 1976; Assoc. Coord., Words Alive Reading Series, Toronto, 1980-84; Founding Ed., *Ethos* magazine, 1983-

86; Instructor, Creative Writing, Sheridan Coll., 1984-86; Writer-in-Residence, St. Thomas Public Library, St. Thomas, Ont., 1987; Writer-in-Residence, Beeton Public Library, Beeton, Ont., 1988; Instructor, Creative Writing, Sch. of Continuing Studies, Univ. of Toronto, 1988 to date; Instructor, Creative Writing, George Brown Coll., 1989; Writer-in-Residence, Dundas Public Library, Dundas, Ont., 1990; Writer-in-Residence, Toronto Bd. of Educ., 1991; Writer-in-Residence, North York Public Library, North York, Ont., 1991. SELECTED CREDITS: playwright, *And She Could Eat No Lean*, 1975; playwright, *Gilgamesh*, 1976; playwright, *Dreamgirls*, 1979; various works broadcast on CBC Radio, Pacific Radio Network, KAZU (California) & TVOntario, 1966 to date. SELECTED PUBLICATIONS: *Within the Whirling Moment* (Anansi, 1967); *Jeremy's Dream* (Press Porcepic, 1974); *Landscape*, co-ed. (Women's Writing Collective, 1977); *Winter Flowers* (Hounslow, 1979); *Dreamgirls*, play (Playwrights' Union of Canada, 1979); *Imaginings*, co-author (The Ethos Cultural Development Foundation, 1982); *Upon Her Fluent Route* (Hounslow, 1991); *After Paradise* (Simon & Pierre/Dundurn, 1996); poetry, drama, fiction & critical writing published in various magazines, anthologies & newspapers. AFFIL: ACTRA (Writers' Guild); League of Canadian Poets; PEN; Playwrights' Union of Canada; The Writers' Union of Canada. HONS: 2 Awards of Merit, N.Y. Art Directors' Club, 1983; Certificate of Excellence, American Institute of Graphic Arts, 1983; Outstanding Achievement, American Poetry Association, 1986. MISC: recipient, various grants; numerous workshops, readings & talks at public & educational institutions across Canada & in France & UK, 1973 to date; official Cdn participant (1 of 2), 14th franco-anglais festival de poésie, Paris, France, 1991; listed in various biographical sources, incl. *Canadian Who's Who, Contemporary Authors, International Authors and Writers Who's Who & World Who's Who of Women*.

Rappaport, Henny S., M.D.,C.C.F.P. ⊕ 🐉
Chair, Division of Family Medicine Obstetrics, NORTH YORK GENERAL HOSPITAL, 1333 Sheppard Ave. E., Ste. 232, North York, ON M2J 1V1 (416) 498-8999. Assistant Professor, Faculty of Medicine, UNIVERSITY OF TORONTO. Born Toronto 1951. m. Michael W. Burns. 4 ch. Lisa, Miriam, David, Jonathan. EDUC: Univ. of Toronto, M.D. 1975. CAREER: Instructor, Fac. of Medicine, Univ. of Toronto, 1986-89; Lecturer, 1989-94; Asst. Prof., 1994 to date; V-Chair, Dept. of Family Medicine, North York General Hospital, 1989-94. AFFIL:

Federation of Medical Women of Canada (Sec.-Treas., Toronto Branch 1984-85, 1985-86); Coll. of Family Physicians of Canada (C.C.F.P.; Examiner for the Certification Exams 1986, 1987, 1989); Canadian Medical Protective Association; Ontario Medical Association; North York General Hospital (Exec. Committee, Dept. of Family Medicine; Sub-Committee on Continuing Medical Educ. for Family Medicine 1989-93; Chair 1989-90). INTERESTS: mentor relationships; women's health; primary care obstetrics. COMMENT: *"Committed to the delivery of high quality comprehensive patient-centred primary care by family physicians. Actively involved in teaching the discipline of family medicine at the undergraduate and postgraduate level. Strong focus on multidisciplinary approach to achieving goals."*

Raptis, Leda Helen, M.Sc.,Ph.D. 🌸 ⫣ ⊕
Associate Professor, Department of Microbiology and Immunology, QUEEN'S UNIVERSITY, Kingston, ON K7L 3N6 (613) 545-2462, FAX 545-6796, EMAIL raptisl@post.queensu.ca. Born Athens 1950. m. Kevin L. Firth, P.Eng. 2 ch. Andromahi, Leif. EDUC: Agricultural Univ. of Athens, M.Sc.(Plant Sciences) 1973; McGill Univ., M.Sc.(Plant Virology) 1975; Univ. of Sherbrooke, Ph.D.(Microbiol.) 1979. CAREER: Postdoctoral Fellow, Cancer Research Centre of McGill Univ., 1979-80; Centennial Postdoctoral Fellow, Dept. of Biochemical Sciences, Princeton Univ., 1981-82; Centennial Postdoctoral Fellow, Pathology Dept., Harvard Medical Sch., 1982-84; Research Assoc., National Research Council of Canada, 1984-86; Asst. Prof., Dept. of Microbiol., Queen's Univ., 1986-92; Assoc. Prof., 1992 to date. SELECTED PUBLICATIONS: "Regulation of cellular phenotype and expression of polyoma virus middle T antigen in rat fibroblasts," with H. Lamfrom & T.L. Benjamin (*Molecular and Cellular Biology*, 5, 1985); "Cellular ras gene activity is required for transformation by polyoma virus," with R.C. Marcellus *et al* (*Journal of Virology*, 65, 1991); "A novel technique for the study of intercellular, junctional communication: electroporation of adherent cells on a partly conductive slide," with H.L. Brownell *et al* (*DNA and Cell Biology*, 13, 1994); numerous other refereed papers & abstracts. AFFIL: Association of Women Teaching at Queen's; American Society for Microbiology. HONS: Centennial Fellowship, Medical Research Council of Canada, 1981-84. INTERESTS: skin diving; reading; "lifting tonnes of feathers."

Rauhala, Ann, B.A.,B.A.A. ✐ ﻬ
Journalist, CANADIAN BROADCASTING CORPORATION, P.O. Box 500, Stn. A, Toronto, ON M5W 1E6 (416) 205-7486. Born Sudbury, Ont. 1954. m. Lorne Slotnick. 1 ch. EDUC: Univ. of Toronto, B.A.(English) 1977; Ryerson Polytechnic Institute, B.A.A.(Journalism) 1979. CAREER: Asst. Foreign Ed., *The Globe and Mail*, 1983-86; Reporter, Women's Issues, 1986-89; Foreign Ed., 1989-94; Columnist, 1993-94; Documentary Reporter, *The National Magazine*, CBC TV, 1994 to date. AFFIL: Y.M.C.A. Youth Substance Abuse Program (Dir.); Canadian Association of Journalists (Women in Media Conference Organizer). HONS: Robertine Barry Award, Canadian Research Institute for the Advancement of Women. INTERESTS: film; travel; literature.

Rauter, Rose Marie, B.Sc.,M.Sc.F. ◉ $
President, ONTARIO FOREST INDUSTRIES ASSOCIATION, 130 Adelaide St. W., Ste. 1700, Toronto, ON M5H 3P5 (416) 368-6188, FAX 368-5445. Born Toronto 1943. s. EDUC: Univ. of Toronto, B.Sc.(Forestry, cum laude) 1965, M.Sc.F.(cum laude) 1968; invited as post-doctoral student by Univ. of California, Berkeley, 1983. CAREER: Research Scientist—genetics, Ministry of Natural Resources, 1968-79; Supervisor, Tree Seed & Forest Genetics Unit, 1979-88; Adjunct Prof., Forest Genetics, Univ. of Toronto, 1975-85; Mgr, Ontario Forest Industries Association, 1988-92; Pres., 1992 to date. AFFIL: Wildlife Habitat, Ottawa (Bd. of Dir.); Canadian Pulp & Paper Association, Montreal (Bd. of Dir.); Univ. of British Columbia (Advisory Committee); Canadian Institute of Forestry; Ontario Forestry Association; Ontario Professional Foresters' Association. INTERESTS: gardening; woodworking.

Read, Cari ■ ■ ⍣
Olympic Athlete. c/o Canadian Olympic Association. Born Edmonton 1970. EDUC: currently studying Communications. SPORTS CAREER: started synchro at age 9; mbr., Cdn Nat'l Synchronized Swimming Team, 1988 to date. Olympic Games: Silver, team, 1996. World championships: 2nd, team, 1994; 2nd, team, 1991. World Cup: 2nd, team, 1995. Canadian championships: 3rd, solo, & 4th, team, 1995; 1st, team, 2nd, duet, & 3rd, solo, 1994; 1st, team, 1st, duet, & 2nd, solo, 1993. INTERESTS: cross-country skiing; hiking; jazz dancing; fly fishing.

Read, Merilyn ﻬ ﻬ ﻬ ✐
President, M.T.R. ENTERTAINMENT LIMITED, 47 Rockcliffe Way, Ottawa, ON K1M 1B4. Director of Development, LACEWOOD PRODUCTIONS. Born Bath, UK 1948. sep. 2 ch. EDUC: Hamilton Teachers' Coll., Certificate. CAREER: Photo Ed. & Reporter, The Canadian

Press, Ottawa Bureau; Reporter, CBOT-TV Ottawa; freelance Reporter, CBC-TV, CBC Radio, *Maclean's, Ottawa Journal*; Film Prod./ Pres., M.T.R. Entertainment Limited, 1984 to date. SELECTED CREDITS: Prod., *The Tom Green Show* (pilot), CBC-TV, 1996; Prod., 2 specials (animation), Lacewood Productions. SELECTED PUBLICATIONS: *Rainspoosh; What Is The Pretzel Doing in the Bathroom?*. AFFIL: Ottawa-Hull Film & Television Association; Children's Broadcast Institute. HONS: Best Animated Children's Film (*Babar and Father Christmas*), Gemini Award, 1987; Bronze Medal, N.Y. Film & Video Festival; Best Broadcast Award/Best Documentary Award (*Let Me Call You Sweetheart*). INTERESTS: travel; films; tennis; cross-country skiing; music; art; gardening; comedy; camping; interior design. COMMENT: *"Since forming M.T.R. Productions in 1984, I have produced award-winning broadcast productions. I have just completed 'Happy Birthday Bunnykins' based on the Royal Doulton Bunnykins china. I wish to continue to produce award-winning, high-quality family films."*

Reagh, Elizabeth Strong, B.A., LL.B. ⚖ 🏵 🏵 🖊

Barrister, Solicitor and Mediator, REAGH & REAGH, 17 West St., Charlottetown, PE C1A 3S3 (902) 892-7667, FAX 368-8629. Born Summerside, P.E.I. 1936. m. Theodore Reagh. 4 ch. Charles Strong Reagh, Jane Reagh Bruce-Robertson, Richard Reagh, Margaret Reagh. EDUC: Dalhousie Univ., B.A. 1957, LL.B. 1959. BAR: B.C., 1960; P.E.I., 1975. CAREER: articled with J.O.C. Campbell, QC, Charlottetown, 1958; articled, Bull Housser & Tupper, Vancouver, 1959; sole practitioner of law, then Assoc., Henry G. Castillou, Vancouver, 1960-61; Assoc., Donald S. McTavish, Salmon Arm, B.C., 1961-62; sole practitioner, Salmon Arm, 1962-64; Official Administrator, County of Yale-Salmon Arm, 1962-67; Ptnr, Reagh and Reagh, Salmon Arm, B.C., 1964-75; Ptnr, Reagh and Reagh, Charlottetown, 1975 to date. AFFIL: on Ad Hoc committees of Home and School Association, Child Abuse, on proposed Child Welfare Law Legislation, the 1978 Family Law Reform Act, the 1992 Adoption Act & Regulations; Society of P.E.I. (Chair, Alternate Dispute Resolution Committee 1991-95); Family Mediation Canada Inc.; Mediation P.E.I. Inc. (Pres. 1989-91; Past. Pres. 1991-92); Association of Family & Conciliation Courts; Tremploy, Inc. (Dir. 1989-95); P.E.I. Citizens' Council for Drug Abuse; Bd. of Review & Criminal Law Review Bd. for P.E.I. (Chair); P.E.I. Genealogical Society; Home & School Association; Social Work Registration Bd. (lay mbr.); P.E.I. Museum & Heritage Foundation (Life Mbr.); Canadian Bible Society, P.E.I. District (Dir.); Cathedral Church of St. Peter (Rep. to P.E.I. Diocesan Church Society Council 1995; Rep. to CBS, P.E.I. Dist.); Cathedral Church of St. Peter Choir. INTERESTS: music; local history; bicycling; aerobics. MISC: first lay mbr., Social Work Registration Bd., Child Support Guidelines (fed.); frequent speaker. COMMENT: *"Practised since 1989 as a lawyer-mediator serving private persons with comprehensive mediation, mainly in the Family Law area before and after separation; of late doing some employer-employee mediation, mediation re sexual harrassment; also using mediation with regard to wills and estates, powers of attorney, marriage contracts and personal injury matters."*

Reddy, Dianne, B.N. ■■ ✪

President, LEARNING DISABILITIES ASSOCIATION OF NEWFOUNDLAND AND LABRADOR (charitable organization, non-profit), P.O. Box 26036, St. John's, NF A1E 5T9 (709) 754-3665, FAX 754-3678. Born St. John's 1954. m. Donald. 3 ch. Angela, Darryl, James. EDUC: St. Clare's Mercy Hospital, Nursing Diploma 1975; Memorial Univ., B.N. 1996. CAREER: Nurse I, Janeway Child Health Centre, 1975-89; Nursing Administrative Supervisor, 1989-96; Div. Mgr, PICU, Child Health Programme, Health Care Corporation of St. John's, 1996 to date. AFFIL: Learning Disabilities Association of Newfoundland & Labrador (Pres. 1996 to date); Learning Disabilities Association Canada (Dir.); Girl Guides of Canada (Deputy Int'l Commissioner, Nfld. Council 1995 to date; Int'l Adviser, St. John's E. Area 1995 to date). HONS: Medal of Merit, Girl Guides of Canada. INTERESTS: reading; walking; family; Girl Guides; learning disabilities. COMMENT: *"As President of LDANL, I want to work toward increasing awareness of learning disabilities for both educators and the general public. I hope that, with increased awareness, understanding will increase and accommodations will be more readily available."*

Reddyhoff, Gillian, B.A.,M.A. ■■ 📖 ⊗

Curator, THE MARKET GALLERY OF THE CITY OF TORONTO ARCHIVES (art gallery), 95 Front St. E., Toronto, ON M5E 1C2 (416) 392-7604, FAX 392-0572. Born London, UK 1952. m. Joseph Fraser. EDUC: Maria Grey Coll., Univ. of London, England, Teaching Certification (Specialist in Studio Art-Ceramics) 1974; Univ. of Toronto, B.A.(Hons., with distinction, Art Hist.) 1985, M.A.(Art Hist.) 1993; ongoing educ. at meetings, workshops & seminars of Ontario Association of Art & Ontario Museum

Association. **CAREER:** Teacher, High Sch. Art & English, Hinde House Comprehensive Sch., Sheffield, England, 1974-78; Teacher of children with learning disabilities, Toronto Learning Centre, 1978-80 & 1985-87; Consultant, City of Toronto Archives, May-Sept. 1987; Guest Curator, The Market Gallery, City of Toronto Archives, May-Oct. 1988; Curator, 1989 to date. **EXHIBITIONS:** *Toronto Impressions: Historical & Contemporary Printmaking* (1993); *A Toronto Decade: Contemporary Paintings of the City* (1994); *A Century Ago: Art in Toronto 1890-1910* (1995); *Portrait of Toronto: The Work of Owen Staples, 1866-1949* (1996). **AFFIL:** Canadian Museums Association; Art Gallery Educators of Ontario. **HONS:** Open Master's Fellowship, Univ. of Toronto. **INTERESTS:** gardening; collecting English ceramics; art; caring for 2 Labrador Retrievers. **MISC:** Judge, Toronto Outdoor Art Exhibition & annual exhibitions administered by Toronto Historical Bd. **COMMENT:** *"I was originally trained to be a teacher of children with learning disabilities. In the mid-80s, I decided to change careers, returning to university to study art history at the undergraduate and graduate levels. Today I am a curator of art for the City of Toronto."*

Reed, Honourable Madame Justice Babara Joan, B.A.,LL.B.,LL.M. ■■ ⚖

Judge, Trial Division, FEDERAL COURT OF CANADA, Supreme Court Bldg, Ottawa, ON K1A 0H9 (613) 995-1364, FAX 954-7714. Born St. Catharines, Ont. 1937. m. Robert Barry Reed. 3 ch. Christopher, Bruce, Thea. **EDUC:** Univ. of Toronto, B.A.(Law) 1960; Dalhousie Univ., LL.B. 1968, LL.M. 1970. **BAR:** Ont., 1971. **CAREER:** Asst. Prof., Univ. of Ottawa, 1971-73; Legal Officer, Constitutional Law Section, Dept. of Justice, 1973-74; Constitutional Advisor, Privy Council Office & Fed.-Prov. Rel'ns Office, 1974-80; Dir., Legal Svcs, Fed.-Prov. Rel'ns Office, 1980-82; Legal Cnsl, Privy Council Office, 1982-83; Judge, Fed. Court of Canada, 1983 to date; Chrm, Competition Tribunal, 1986-92. **AFFIL:** Law Society of Upper Canada; Canadian Bar Association; Canadian Institute for the Administration of Justice; Canadian Judges' Conference; International Commission of Jurists (Cdn). **HONS:** Queen's Counsel, 1982. **INTERESTS:** cross-country skiing; volleyball; needlework; church work; photography; literature; drama.

Rees-Potter, Lorna K., B.A.,M.L.S., Ph.D. 🎓 📖 ⚛

Associate Professor, Graduate School of Library and Information Studies, MCGILL UNIVERSITY, Montreal, QC H3A 1Y1 (514) 398-4204, FAX 398-7193, EMAIL rees-potter@gslis.lan.mcgill.ca. Born Montreal 1942. **EDUC:** Univ. of New Brunswick, B.A.(Soc.) 1963; McGill Univ., M.L.S.(Library Studies) 1967; Univ. of Western Ontario, Ph.D.(Info. Studies) 1987. **CAREER:** Library Asst., *Montreal Star*, 1963-65; Dir., Document Centre, Canadian Council on Social Development, 1967-79; Research Dir., Canadian Law Information Council, 1982-85; Prof., McGill Univ., 1985 to date. **SELECTED PUBLICATIONS:** *Patterns of Authority* (1984); *Communicating Court Information* (1984); *Dynamic Thesaurus Generation* (1982). **AFFIL:** Association of Computing Machinery; American Society for Information Science; Canadian Association for Information Science; Institute of Electrical & Electronics Engineers.

Reeves, Lynda, B.A.,B.Ed. ✎ 📖 $

Publisher and President, *CANADIAN HOUSE AND HOME* MAGAZINE, Canadian Home Publishers, 511 King St. W., Toronto, ON M5V 2Z4 (416) 593-0204, FAX 591-1630. Founder, *GARDENING LIFE* MAGAZINE. Born Niagara Falls, Ont. 1953. d. **EDUC:** Trinity Coll., Univ. of Toronto, B.A. 1976; Fac. of Educ., Univ. of Toronto, B.Ed. 1977. **CAREER:** Teacher & Guidance Counsellor, East York Bd. of Educ.; Mng Ptnr, interior design firm; Pres. & co-owner, Canadian Home Publishers; Publisher,*Canadian House and Home* Magazine. **SELECTED PUBLICATIONS:** *Homestyle: A Hands On Guide to Decorating* (Random House, 1993). **AFFIL:** Museum for Textiles (Bd. of Dir.); CANFAR National Network, Magazines Canada (Bd.). **MISC:** regular contributor, *The Globe and Mail* & other media. **COMMENT:** *"Founder and publisher of* Canadian House and Home *Magazine. Author and spokesperson on home design and trends in home decorating and entertaining in Canada. TV home expert on nationally syndicated shows."*

Regan, Gail, B.A.,M.B.A.,Ph.D. $

President, CARA HOLDINGS, 230 Bloor St. W., Toronto, ON M5S 1T8 (416) 969-2712, FAX 969-2545. Born Canada 1944. m. Tim. 4 ch. **EDUC:** Univ. of Toronto, B.A. 1965, M.B.A. 1978; Ontario Institute for Studies in Education, Ph.D.(Educ. Theory) 1973. **CAREER:** Lecturer & Asst. Prof. of Educ., Univ. of Toronto, 1972-82; VP & Pres., Cara Holdings, 1982 to date. **SELECTED PUBLICATIONS:** various articles on educ. **DIRECTOR:** Cara Holdings; Cara Operations; Langar Co. Ltd.; other holding companies. **AFFIL:** Canadian Association of Family Enterprise; Family Firm Institute; Strategic Leadership Forum; Women's College Hospital (Dir.); Energy Probe (Dir.). **INTERESTS:** family bus.; preservation of Canada's health care system; social science; sports. **COMMENT:** *"I regard as my most important achievement my contribution to the preservation of the autonomy of Women's College Hospital. This is a unique institution that holistically serves women and provides academic leadership opportunities to women in medicine."*

Rehner, Maria, B.A.,M.L.S.,LL.B. ■■ ☺ ⚖
President, CANADIAN INDUSTRIAL TRANSPORTATION LEAGUE (lobby group), 1090 Don Mills Rd., Ste. 602, Don Mills, ON M3C 3R6 (416) 447-7766, FAX 447-7312, EMAIL citl@caspar.net. **EDUC:** Univ. of Western Ontario, B.A. 1968; McGill Univ., M.L.S. 1972, LL.B. 1979. **CAREER:** Attorney, Canadian Pacific Ltd., 1981-85; Assoc., Gottlieb Kaylor Stocks, 1987-88; Assoc., Clarkson Tétrault, 1988-90; Pres., CITL, 1990 to date. **SELECTED PUBLICATIONS:** "An Overview of the Rail Provisions in the National Transportation Act, 1987" (*Transportation Practitioners Journal*, Vol. 55, No. 1, 1987); "Canadian-Provincial Motor Carrier Legislation, Specifically the Truck Transportation Act (Ontario)" (*Transportation Practitioners Journal*, Vol. 57, No. 3, 1990). **AFFIL:** Law Society of Upper Canada; Massachusetts Bar Association; Association for Transportation Law (Cdn Ed., *Logistics & Policy*); Sectoral Advisory Group on Transportation Services to Min. of Int'l Trade (Chair). **HONS:** Award of Excellence, Nat'l Transportation Week, 1995. **INTERESTS:** theatre; walking the dog. **COMMENT:** *"A superb advocate specializing in regulatory law, with 14 years' experience in private law and public advocacy. Adroit at building consensus and possessing an uncanny ability to persuade. Excellent communication, interpersonal and leadership skills."*

Reid, Barbara ⊗ 🐌 🏠
Illustrator. 37 Strathmore Blvd., Toronto, ON M4J 1P1 (416) 461-9793, FAX 461-9759. Born Toronto 1957. m. Ian Crysler. 2 ch. **EDUC:** Ontario Coll. of Art, Certificate (Comm./Design) 1980. **CAREER:** illustrator, 1980 to date. **SELECTED PUBLICATIONS:** *Playing With Plasticine* (Toronto: Kids Can Press, 1988); *Zoe's Rainy Day, Zoe's Sunny Day, Zoe's Windy Day, Zoe's Snowy Day* (Toronto: HarperCollins, 1991); *Two By Two* (Toronto: Scholastic Canada, 1992); illustrations for various children's books, incl. *Have You Seen Birds?* by Joanne Oppenheim (Toronto: Scholastic-TAB Publications Ltd., 1986). **EXHIBITIONS:** The Merton Gallery, Toronto (1986); *Once Upon a Time* group show of Cdn illustrators, Vancouver Art Gallery (1988); *Canada at Bologna*, group show of Cdn illustrators, Bologna, Italy (1990); Mabel's Fables Book Store, Toronto (1991); Berthold Type Centre, Toronto (1992); Canadian Children's Book Centre (1994). **AFFIL:** CANSCAIP; Books for Young People (Int'l Bd.). **HONS:** Award for Children's Illustration (*Have You Seen Birds?*), Canada Council, 1986; Elizabeth Mrazik-Cleaver Award (*Have You Seen Birds?*), 1987; Ezra Jack Keats Award (*The New Baby Calf, Have You Seen Birds?*, & *Sing a Song of Mother Goose*), 1988; Mr. Christie Book Award (the Zoe series), 1991; Elizabeth Mrazik-Cleaver Award (*Two By Two*), 1993; Amelia Frances Howard Gibbon Medal (GIFTS), 1995. **COMMENT:** *"Working as a freelance illustrator in the advertising, editorial, educational and trade books fields, Barbara Reid is best-known for her three-dimensional plasticine illustrations for children's books."*

Reid, Diana R., B.Sc.,LL.B. ⚖
Consultant, LANG MICHENER LAWRENCE & SHAW, 595 Burrard St., Ste. 2500, Box 49200, Vancouver, BC V7X 1L1 (604) 689-9111, FAX 685-7084. Born Vancouver 1956. m. Mark R. Steven. 2 ch. **EDUC:** Dalhousie Univ., B.Sc.(Marine Biol./French) 1977; LL.B. 1980. **BAR:** B.C., 1981. **CAREER:** Assoc., Lawrence & Shaw, 1981-87; Ptnr, 1987-89; Ptnr, Lang Michener Lawrence & Shaw, 1989-91; Consultant to Lang Michener Lawrence & Shaw, 1991 to date. **CHAIRMAN:** British Columbia Pavilion Corporation (responsible for the mgmt & mktg of several facilities incl. the Vancouver Trade & Convention Centre, B.C. Place Stadium & the Bridge Film Studios). **AFFIL:** Canadian Bar Association (various committees); Law Society of B.C. (Comm. Committee 1991-92); B.C. Continuing Legal Education; Estate Planning Council. **INTERESTS:** the well-being of her family & the educ. of her children. **MISC:** numerous seminar & conference presentations relating to preferred area of practice, being estate planning incl. personal & family trusts, wills & the succession to bus. interests & other property generally. **COMMENT:** *"Energetic and committed lawyer and businesswoman who, through determination, has successfully combined a challenging career and rewarding family life."*

Reid, Fiona, B.A. ⊗ 👱 🌷
Actor. c/o Oscars and Abrams, 59 Berkeley St., Toronto, ON M5A 2W5. Born Kent, UK 1951. m. McCowan Thomas. 2 ch. **EDUC:** Lawrence Park Collegiate Institute, Ont. Scholar 1969; McGill Univ., B.A.(English) 1972; Banff Sch. of Fine Arts, 2 yrs. theatre.

CAREER: actor, theatre, film & TV in Canada, the US & UK. SELECTED CREDITS: *Second City* (improv/theatre), Toronto, 1973; *Cathy King, The King of Kensington* (series); *Waiting for the Parade* (theatre), Tarragon Theatre, Toronto & the Lyric Theatre, Hammersmith, London, UK; *Night & Day* (theatre), Toronto Free Theatre; *Automatic Pilot* (theatre), Toronto Free Theatre; Shaw Festival (theatre), 7 seasons, incl. *Private Lives, Hedda Gabler, Heartbreak House, Cavalcade; Comedy of Errors* (theatre), Stratford Festival; *Wild Oats* (theatre), Stratford Festival; *Fallen Angels* (theatre), Canadian Stage Company; *Hayfever* (theatre), Canadian Stage Company; *6 Degrees of Separation* (theatre), Canadian Stage Company; *The Importance of Being Earnest* (theatre), Huntington Theatre, Boston; *Three Tall Women* (theatre), Citadel Theatre; *Arcadia* (theatre), CSC; numerous film & TV projects. AFFIL: Canadian Actors' Equity Association; ACTRA; Toronto Arts Awards (Bd.); Canadian Stage Company (Exec. & Exec. Bd. Mbr.). HONS: Best Actress (*6 Degrees of Separation*), Dora Award, 1995; Best Actress (*Fallen Angels*), Dora Award; ACTRA award for radio. COMMENT: *"My family travelled a lot when I was a child as my father was a British army doctor. We immigrated to Canada when I was 13, having lived in the UK, Africa, Germany and the US. Canada is very much my home, and I feel very grateful for the opportunities it has presented me."*

Reid, Jill, B.A. ⓐ ⓧ

Executive Director, DANCE SASKATCHEWAN INC., P.O. Box 8789, Saskatoon, SK S7K 6S6 (306) 931-8480, FAX 244-1520. Born Hamilton, Ont. 1953. m. Derby Reid. 2 ch. EDUC: Seneca Coll., Certificate (Sports Admin./Gymnastics) 1972; Univ. of Saskatchewan, B.A.(Soc.) 1977. CAREER: Loans Officer, Watrous Credit Union, 1975-80; owner & operator, Reid's Shop-Rite, 1981-88; Exec. Dir., Dance Saskatchewan Inc., 1989 to date. AFFIL: Saskatoon East Sch. Div. (Past Trustee); Saskatchewan Gymnastics Association (Past VP). INTERESTS: landscaping; rural econ. dev. COMMENT: *"My goal has been to work in careers that are satisfying and to enjoy life to its fullest. I love life and my life has been particularly satisfying. I still have things to achieve and I will continue to work towards those goals."*

Reid, Linda, B.Ed.,M.A., MLA ■ ■ ✿ ❀

Member of Legislative Assembly (Richmond East), Official Opposition Critic for Science, Technology and Research, and Workers' Compensation Board, GOVERNMENT OF BRITISH COLUMBIA, Parliament Buildings, Rm. 201, Victoria, BC V8V 1X4 (604) 356-3056, FAX 387-2731. EDUC: Univ. of British Columbia, B.Ed., M.A. (specializing in educ. of exceptional learners, language acquisition & admin.). CAREER: worked on report about employment opportunities for the disabled, Human Res. Directorate, House of Commons, Ottawa; language therapist with autistic children; teacher/sch. administrator, Richmond Sch. District; mbr. of Legislative Select Standing Committees: Econ. Dev., Science, Labour Training & Technology, & Health & Social Svcs; formerly Official Opposition Critic for Attorney Gen., Health & Seniors, Skills & Training, & Women's Equality. AFFIL: Richmond Teachers' Association (former mbr.); Richmond Association of School Administrators (former mbr.); Richmond Chamber of Commerce; Asia Pacific Business Association; Richmond Chinatown Lions Club (founding mbr.); B.C. Youth Parliament (Chair of the Bd. 1986-91).

Reid, Margot, RN ⓞ ⓧ ⊕

Volunteer. 125 Rennie's Mill Rd., St. John's, NF A1B 2P2 (709) 753-4235, FAX 753-3820. Born St. John's 1927. m. Ian T. Reid. 5 ch. EDUC: Dalhousie Univ.; Royal Victoria Hospital Sch. of Nursing, RN 1950. CAREER: Ptnr, M K Crafts, 1978-90. VOLUNTEER CAREER: mbr., St. John's Unit, Canadian Cancer Society, 1952-74; mbr., Prov. Girl Guide Council, 1953-58; mbr., Prov. Lone Guide Committee, 1953-57; mbr., Community Svc. Council Bd.; mbr., Memorial Univ. Art Gallery Bd.; mbr., Newfoundland Symphony Orchestra Bd.; mbr., Dr. Charles A. Janeway Hospital Bd., 1964-73; mbr., Nfld. Div., Canadian Cancer Society, 1974-89; mbr., Nfld. Medical Bd., 1976-85; mbr., Federal Business Development Bank Bd., 1976-82; Pres., Nfld. Div., Canadian Cancer Society, 1982-84; mbr., Nat'l Bd. of Dir., Canadian Cancer Society, 1982-86; mbr., Bd. of Dir., Forum for Young Canadians, 1983-90; mbr., National Cancer Institute Bd., 1984-86; mbr., General Hospital Health Foundation, 1985-88; Nat'l Advisory Bd., Imagine, 1989-91. DIRECTOR: Churchill Falls & Labrador Corporation; Reid Newfoundland Company. MEMBER: Advisory Bd., Labatt's Newfoundland. AFFIL: Newfoundland & Labrador Art Gallery (Bd. of Dir.); Lakecrest Sch. (Advisory Bd.); St. John's & Mount Pearl Unit, Canadian Cancer Society (1951 to date). HONS: Award of Merit, Nfld. Div., Canadian Cancer Society; Canadian Cancer Society (Hon. Life Mbr.); Certificate of Merit, Nfld. Div., Canadian Cancer Society; Citizen of the Year Award, St. John's Jaycees, 1972; Merit Award, Dr. Charles A. Janeway Hospital; Canadian Volunteer

Medal, 1992. INTERESTS: tennis; skiing; gardening. COMMENT: *"Main endeavour: looking after my husband, raising 5 children, and devoting volunteer time and energy to the Canadian Cancer Society (provincially and nationally) for 43 years, and other organizations."*

Reid, Maureen, LL.B. ⚖

Partner, McInnes Cooper and Robertson, Summit Place, 1601 Lower Water St., Box 730, Halifax, NS B3J 2V1 (902) 425-6500, FAX 425-6350. EDUC: Dalhousie Univ., B.Sc. 1981; Dalhousie Univ., LL.B. 1984. BAR: N.S., 1985. CAREER: Ptnr, McInnes Cooper and Robertson. AFFIL: Canadian Association for the Practical Study of Law in Educ. (Past Pres.); Canadian Association of Univ. Solicitors; Association des juristes d'expression française de la Nouvelle-Écosse; Neptune Theatre Foundation (Dir.; VP of Dev.); Canadian Bar Association. COMMENT: *"Maureen Reid's areas of practice are labour and employment law, administrative law and education law. She represents public sector employers in the education and health-care sectors."*

Reimer, Marlene A., R.N.,M.N., CNN(C) ■■ ⊕ ☜

Associate Professor, Faculty of Nursing, THE UNIVERSITY OF CALGARY, 2500 University Dr. N.W., Calgary, AB T2N 1N4 (403) 220-5839/6262, FAX 284-4803, EMAIL mareimer@acs.ucalgary.ca. Born Alta. 1943. m. Ernie. 3 ch. Beth Gallup, Andrew Reimer, Jennifer Reimer. EDUC: Calgary Gen. Hospital Sch. of Nursing, Diploma in Nursing 1963; Univ. of Manitoba, B.N. 1970; Univ. of Calgary, M.N. 1984, Dept. of Community Health Sciences, Ph.D. candidate. CAREER: Staff Nurse, Calgary Gen. Hospital, 1963-64; Staff Nurse (part-time), Foothills Hospital, 1966-67, 1972, 1977, 1982; Clinical Asst. (part-time), Fac. of Nursing, Univ. of Manitoba, 1969-70; Nursing Instructor, Foothills Hospital Sch. of Nursing, 1972-73 & 1975-82 (part- & full-time); Relief Admin. Supervisor, Foothills Hospital, 1982-84; Rural Liaison Instructor, Foothills Hospital Sch. of Nursing, 1982-84; Grad. Teaching Asst., Fac. of Nursing, Univ. of Calgary, 1983-84; Sessional Instructor, May-June 1983/84; Asst. Prof., 1984-91; Assoc. Prof., 1991 to date; Assoc. in Nursing, Foothills Hospital, 1985 to date; Research Assoc., Alberta Lung Association Sleep Centre, Foothills Hospital, 1992 to date; Dir., Wellness & Lifestyle Div., Canadian Sleep Institute, 1995 to date. SELECTED PUBLICATIONS: 7 chapters in books incl.: author, "Clients with sleep disorders" in *Psychiatric Nursing*, 5th ed.,eds. H.

Wilson & C. Kneisl (Redwood City, California: Addison-Wesley, 1996); author, "Sleep and sensory disorders" in *Luckmann & Sorensen's medical-surgical nursing: A pathophysiological approach*, 4th ed., eds. J. Black & E. Matassarin-Jacobs (Philadelphia: W.B. Saunders Co., 1993); author, "Sleep and rest" in *Fundamentals of Nursing*, eds. R. Craven & C. Hirnle (Philadelphia: J.B. Lippincott Co., 1992); numerous articles, abstracts, & int'l, prov. & reg'l presentations. AFFIL: Canadian Nurses' Association (Special Committee on Certification 1995-97; Bd. of Dir. 1988-90); World Federation of Neuroscience Nurses (Pres. 1993-97; VP & Chair, Scientific Program Committee 1989-93); Alberta Association of Registered Nurses; Canadian Association of Neuroscience Nurses; American Association of Neuroscience Nurses (*Journal of Neuroscience Nursing* Manuscript Review Bd. 1992 to date); Head Injury Association of Alberta; Canadian Nurses' Respiratory Society; American Sleep Disorders Association; Alberta Lung Association (Respiratory Health Care Professionals Section); Suicide Prevention Training Programs (Advisory Committee 1994 to date); Alberta Primary Care Research Unit (Bd. of Dir. 1992 to date); Canadian Nursing Research Group. HONS: Nat'l Health Ph.D. Fellowship, Nat'l Health R.&D. Program, 1993-95; various fellowships/scholarships; Gold Medal, Calgary Gen. Hospital Sch. of Nursing, 1963. INTERESTS: hiking; camping. MISC: taught brain & spinal cord rehab. in Gaza Strip as part of Univ. of Calgary & CIDA-sponsored proj., summer 1993 & winter 1995 (3-4 weeks each time). COMMENT: *"Through my clinical practice and teaching, I have been facilitating the development of advanced practice roles in nursing. Much of my research is collaborative with other disciplines—medicine, physiotherapy, etc."*

Rein, Reet, B.A. ■ Ⓢ

President, SABRE CANADA, a div. of American Airlines, 5001 Yonge St., Ste. 1504, Toronto, ON M2N 6P6 (416) 218-5445, FAX 218-5474. Born Montreal 1953. sep. 2 ch. Katrina Muur, Brendon Muur. EDUC: Univ. of Toronto, B.A.(French/German) 1975. CAREER: various positions with American Airlines since 1975. AFFIL: Association of Canadian Travel Agents; Toronto Board of Trade; Tourism Industry Association of Canada; Association of Corporate Travel Executives. INTERESTS: walking; golf; sewing; skiing. COMMENT: *"I value honesty and hard work—although I do like to have fun, even at work. I support people who work hard and I will do my best to help others achieve their goals."*

Reinhold, Caroline ■■ ⊕ ⬸

Assistant Radiologist, Department of Diagnostic Radiology, and Section Chief, Body MRI, MONTREAL GENERAL HOSPITAL, 1650 Cedar Ave., Montreal, QC H3G 1A4 (514) 934-8003, FAX 934-8263, EMAIL reinhold@radiology.mgh.mcgill.ca. Assistant Professor of Diagnostic Radiology, McGILL UNIVERSITY. Born Zurich, Switzerland 1961. EDUC: McGill Univ., MD, CM 1984, Internal Med. Internship 1984-85, Residency in Diagnostic Radiology 1986-90; Yale Univ., Fellowship in Abdominal Imaging 1990-91. SELECTED PUBLICATIONS: co-author, *MRI of the Abdomen and Pelvis* (Wiley-Liss Inc., in press); co-author, "MRI of the biliary tree" & "MRI of the gallbladder," chpts. in book, *Medical Radiology - Diagnostic Imaging and Radiation Oncology* (Springer, in press); over 30 articles in peer-reviewed journals; book reviews; numerous abstracts & conference presentations. EDIT: Reviewer, *Canadian Association of Radiology Journal*, 1994 to date; Reviewer, *Radiology*, 1995 to date; Reviewer, *Abdominal Imaging*, 1996 to date. AFFIL: McGill Univ. (Chrm, Visiting Prof. Program 1995 to date); Society for the Advancement of Women's Imaging (Mbr.-at-large, Exec. Committee 1995 to date); Radiologic Society of North America; American Roentgen Ray Society; Canadian Association of Radiologists; International Society of Magnetic Resonance in Medicine; American Institute of Ultrasound in Medicine; American Coll. of Radiology; Canadian Medical Association; Corporation professionnelle des médecins du Québec; Federation of Medical Specialists of Quebec; Royal Coll. of Physicians & Surgeons of Canada. HONS: Fellowship Award ($30,000), Canadian Radiological Foundation, 1993; GE-AUR Scholarship ($100,000 US), 1996; numerous invited lectures outside the university, incl. several lectures as Visiting Prof., various universities, 1992-96. COMMENT: *"Current interests include Body MRI particularly the biliary tract and female pelvis. Am a member of team at Montreal General Hospital that helped develop MR cholangiopancreatography. Will return to university full time fall '96 to pursue a Master's thesis followed by a Ph.D. in technology assessment and cost-effectiveness research."*

Reisler, Susan, B.A. ■ ⬚ ✎

Host, *Tapestry*, CBC Radio and Senior Producer, Radio Current Affairs, CANADIAN BROADCASTING CORPORATION, P.O. Box 500, Stn. A, Toronto, ON M5W 1E6 (416) 205-6074, FAX 205-2371, EMAIL sreisler@toronto.cbc.ca. Born Port Hope, Ont. 1947. m. Nicholas Hirst. 1 ch. EDUC: Univ. of Toronto,

B.A.(Modern Languages & Lit.) 1970. CAREER: Features Ed., Canadian University Press, 1970-71; Parliamentary Reporter, United Press International, 1971-75; Ed., CBC Radio News, 1975-76; Documentary Reporter, *Sunday Morning*, CBC Radio, 1975-79; Washington Correspondent, CBC Radio News, 1979-81; Documentary Reporter, CBC TV *The Journal* & later, *Prime Time News*, 1982-94; Exec. Prod., *Morningside with Peter Gzowski*, 1994-95. SELECTED CREDITS: Prod., *Death of the Crippler*, Oct. 1993; Prod., *One Last Chance for Belfast*, Dec. 1993; Prod., *The Peasant Revolt*, Feb. 1994; various other documentaries. HONS: Documentary Awards from the N.Y. Film Festival & Columbus Film Festival. COMMENT: *"For more than two decades, I have covered revolutions, the birth of new democracies, the victories and defeats of people at home and abroad. I have worked with the best and the brightest, dedicated to a public broadcasting system that provides Canadians with the best information and entertainment possible."*

Rekai, Catherine (Kati), C.M. ⬚ ✎ ⬚

Writer, Journalist and Broadcaster. (416) 922-5841, FAX (416) 921-8322. Born Budapest, Hungary. w. Dr. John Rekai C.M., co-founder of Central Hospital. 2 ch. Julie, Judyth. CAREER: Contributor & Dir., Cdn Scene, Multilingual News Svc.; Contributor & Dir., *Performing Arts and Entertainment Magazine*; Contributor, *The Spark Magazine*; weekly radio commentator on cultural events & the arts; literary workshops in schools; Public Rel'ns Consultant, Central Hospital, Toronto. SELECTED PUBLICATIONS: *The Adventures of Mickey, Taggy, Puppo, and Cica, and how they discover...Toronto, Ottawa, Montreal, Kingston, Brockville, the Thousand Islands, the Gardiner Museum of Ceramic Art, France, Switzerland, Budapest, Vienna, the Netherlands, Italy, Greece, Toronto 200*. AFFIL: Writers' Union of Canada; CANSCAIP; P.E.N. International; Canadian Institute for International Affairs; Royal Ontario Museum; Heliconian Club; Museum of the History of Medicine; Canadian Opera Company; Hungarian Helicon Literary Society; Arts & Letters Club. HONS: Knighthood of St. Ladislaus, 1980; Certificate of Honour for Contribution to Canadian Unity, 1981; Award of Merit, American Biographical Institute, 1985; Prix Saint-Exupéry, Francophonie Valeurs-Jeunesse, 1988; Award for Preservation of the Historical & Cultural Heritage of the Magyars, Rakoczi Foundation, 1990; Cross of the Order of Merit of the Republic of Hungary for Contribution to the Dev. of Cdn-Hungarian Cultural Rel'ns,

1993; Member of the Order of Canada, 1993; Sierjey Khmara Ziniak Award for multilingual journalistic excellence, 1996. **INTERESTS:** everything; sports; travel; theatre; opera; children; movies; dogs; even TV. **MISC:** author, several puppet shows, incl. *Tale of Tutankhamen* & *The Boy Who Forgot*. **COMMENT:** *"I have had the best of both worlds, as I was born into a family of intellectuals in Hungary, married a highly intelligent and talented surgeon, have 2 daughters, 2 sons-in-law, 5 grandchildren as best friends, and most of all I have the privilege of living in Canada and being a Canadian."*

Renaud, Bernadette 📖 ✪ 🎓

Écrivaine, Scénariste, Aquarelliste, Contrecoeur. QC. Born Ascot Corner, Qué. 1945. **EDUC:** D.E.C.(Psych.), Montreal, 1972. **CAREER:** Assoc.-bibliothécaire scolaire, Waterloo, Que., 1964-67; Enseignante au primaire, Waterloo, 1967-70; Secrétaire-administrative, Association Médi-Tech-Science, Montréal, 1972-76; auteure professionelle, 1976 to date. **SELECTED CREDITS:** *Klimbo*, 4 émissions de TV, Radio-Canada, 1981, 1982; *Michou et Pilo*, 8 émissions de TV, Radio-Canada, 1984-85; *Le Ber*, pilote, Productions Téléscène, 1988; *Quand l'accent devient grave*, ONF, 1989; *Bach et Bottine*, Productions la Fête, 1986; *Watatatow*, 4 émissions de TV, Productions Publivision, 1991-92; auteure-conseil, 6 courts métrages d'animation, *Droits au coeur*, ONF, 1992; édition de 4 aquarelles en cartes de souhaits, 1994 et 1995. **SELECTED PUBLICATIONS:** *Le Chat de l'Oratoire*, roman jeunesse (Édition Fides, 1978); *Une boîte magique très embêtante*, pièce de théâtre pour la jeunesse (Éditions Leméac, 1981); *Bach et Bottine*, roman jeunesse (Éditions Québec-Amérique, 1986); *Bach and Broccoli*, children's novel (Montreal Press, 1987); contributor, *La littérature et la vie* (Éditions Modulo, 1991); *Un homme comme tant d'autres: Tome 1, Charles* (Éditions Libre Expression, 1992); *Un homme comme tant d'autres: Tome 2, Monsieur Manseau* (Éditions Libre Expression, 1993); *Un homme comme tant d'autres: Tome 3, Charles Manseau* (Éditions Libre Expression, 1994); various other publications. **EXHIBITIONS:** aquarelles, expositions depuis 1992; solo, Galerie Horizon, Tracy, Qué., 1995. **AFFIL:** Association des écrivaines et écrivans québécois pour la jeunesse; Société des Auteurs et Compositeurs Dramatiques; Société des Auteurs, Recherchistes, Documentalistes et Compositeurs; Union des Ecrivains Québecois; Communication-Jeunesse; Conseil Culturel de la Montérégie; Association des Artistes-Peintres Affiliés de la Rive Sud. **HONS:** 2 prix pour le premier livre, *Émilie la baignoire à pattes*; 16 prix lors de festivals internationaux pour le film *Bach et Bottine*; Prix spécial de l'UNESCO, pour l'année internationale de la famille en 1994, *Bach et Bottine*, 1993. **INTERESTS:** aquarelle; horticulture; ornithologie; archéologie. **MISC:** juror for various competitions, awards & grants; Prés. du jury int'l, Festival International du film pour Jeune Public de Laon, France, 1988; seminars, courses & workshops at various universities & schools across Que. & Canada & also in the US, France & Belgium; extensive travels. **COMMENT:** *"La création est l'élément le plus important de ma vie. Auteure professionnelle depuis vingt ans (littérature pour la jeunesse et pour adultes, théâtre, cinéma et télévision), je suis aussi devenue peintre, séduite par l'aquarelle. J'écris comme je peins, je peins comme j'écris, brossant des tableaux de vie quotidienne, y laissant un espace pour que le lecteur et le spectateur y coule ses émotions secrètes. Je crois profondément que la vie est un renouvellement constant et que chaque instant est le plus important, puisqu'il est le seul réel."*

Renault, Suzanne, B.C.L. $ ⚖

Vice-President Legal Affairs and Secretary, LE GROUPE VIDÉOTRON LTÉE, 300 Viger Ave. E., Montreal, QC H2X 3W4 (514) 985-8822, FAX 985-8834. Born Montreal 1954. m. François Matte. **EDUC:** McGill Univ., B.C.L. (Civil Law) 1976; Quebec Bar Sch., 1977. **BAR:** Que., 1977. **CAREER:** private practice of law, Ogilvy Renault, 1977-85; Dir., Legal Affairs, Le Groupe Vidéotron Ltée, 1985-88; VP, Legal Affairs & Sec., 1988 to date. **AFFIL:** Canadian Bar Association; Quebec Bar Association; Association of Canadian General Counsel; Association des secretaires et chefs de contentieux du Québec.

Render, Shirley, B.A.,M.A. 🍁 📖 👍

Member of Legislative Assembly, GOVERNMENT OF MANITOBA, 55 Victoria Cres., Winnipeg, MB R2M 1X5 (204) 945-0301, FAX 948-2092. Born Winnipeg 1943. m. Douglas. 2 ch. **EDUC:** Univ. of Manitoba, B.A.(Hist./French/Psych.) 1964, M.A.(Hist.) 1984. **CAREER:** social worker; teacher; aviation historian; author; M.L.A., Manitoba; Manitoba Constitutional Task Force; Legislative Review Committee; Regulatory Review Committee. **SELECTED PUBLICATIONS:** *No Place for a Lady, The Story of Canadian Women Pilots, 1928-1992*. **EDIT:** Ed., *Aviation Review*. **DIRECTOR:** Manitoba Hydro. **AFFIL:** Canadian Aviation Historical Society; Manitoba Historical Society; Western Canada Aviation Museum (1st woman Pres.); Canadian Club;

RCAF Association; International Organization of Women Pilots.; Western Canada Aviation Museum Foundation (Dir.); Canadian Bushplane Heritage Centre (Patron); Youville Centre (Dir., Advisory Committee). **HONS:** Prix Manitoba, 1990; Canada 125 Medal. **MISC:** Licensed Pilot.

Reno, Ginette, O.C. ■■ 🎭

Singer. c/o melon-miel inc., 1676 Sherbrooke E., Ste. 10, Montreal, QC H2L 1M5 (514) 523-5343. **CAREER:** singer, pop music, 35+ yrs.; best-selling recording artist of Que. **SELECTED CREDITS:** over 50 albums, most of them gold or platinum; *Je ne suis qu'une chanson* (1980) best-selling album ever in Que.; featured role, *Leolo* (feature), 1992; featured role, *Million Dollar Babies* (mini-series), CBS-CBC, 1994; shows throughout Canada & in U.S. & Europe; has appeared on several TV shows in U.S. & Canada. **HONS:** First Prize for best female singer & best song, Tokyo Song Festival; voted most popular recording artist, female performer, TV & radio personality numerous times; many professional awards in Que. & Canada; Officer of the Order of Canada.

Renouf, M.A. Priscilla, B.A.,M.A., Ph.D. 🎓

Associate Professor and Head, Department of Anthropology, MEMORIAL UNIVERSITY OF NEWFOUNDLAND, St. John's, NF A1C 5S7 (709) 737-8870, FAX 737-8686, EMAIL mapr @kean.ucs.mun.ca. Born St. John's 1953. s. **EDUC:** Memorial Univ. of Newfoundland, B.A.(Anthro.) 1974, M.A.(Anthro./Archaeology) 1976; Univ. of Cambridge, UK, Ph.D.(Archaeology) 1981. **CAREER:** Asst. Prof., Dept. of Anthro., Memorial Univ. of Newfoundland, 1981-89; Assoc. Prof., 1989 to date; Head, 1994 to date. **SELECTED PUBLICATIONS:** *Prehistoric Hunter-Fishers of Varangerfjord, Northeastern Norway* (Oxford: British Archeological Reports, Int'l Services, S487, 1989); *Newfoundland Studies* 9(2), special issue of *Newfoundland & Labrador Archaeology*, Ed., 1993; numerous papers & reviews. **EDIT:** Social Sciences Ed., *Studies in Polar Research* book series (Cambridge Univ. Press), 1988-92; Ed. Bd., *Newfoundland Studies*, Memorial Univ. of Newfoundland, 1992 to date; Ed. Bd., Institute of Social and Economic Research Books, Memorial Univ. of Newfoundland, 1994 to date; Ed. Bd., *Manuals in Archaeology* book series, Cambridge Univ. Press. **AFFIL:** Canadian Museum of Civilization (Trustee; Exec. Committee; Chair, Strategic Planning Committee; Co-Chair, Strategic Planning Working Committee); Summit of the Sea, Cabot 500 Corporation (Dir.); Smallwood Centre for Newfoundland Studies (Dir.). **HONS:** Canada Council Special M.A. Scholarship, 1974-75; Rothermere Fellowship, Rothermere Fellowship Trusts, Univ. Coll., London, UK, 1977-80; SSHRC Doctoral Fellowship, 1979-80; President's Award for Outstanding Research, 1992. **COMMENT:** *"Dr. Renouf is an archaeologist who has done field work in Arctic Norway, southern Labrador, Greenland and northern Newfoundland. Her current project is on the prehistory of Port au Choix, on the northern Peninsula of Newfoundland. In connection with this project she has done seven seasons of fieldwork, has published several papers, and has given many public lectures, as well as numerous professional presentations at international conferences. She is currently helping develop a new exhibition on the prehistory of Port au Choix, and is a key organizer in a group of collaborative archaeologists working in different areas of the North Atlantic."*

Renouf, Susan E., B.A. ■■ 📖

President and Editor-in-Chief, KEY PORTER BOOKS LTD., 70 The Esplanade, Toronto, ON M5E 1R2 (416) 862-7777, FAX 862-2304. Born New Glasgow, N.S. m. Scott G. Thompson. 3 ch. Matthew, Connor, Roisin. **EDUC:** Dalhousie Univ.; Univ. of Edinburgh, Scotland, B.A. 1975. **CAREER:** Exec. Dir., N.S. Drama League, 1977-79; Gen. Mgr, Penguin Theatre Co., Ottawa, 1979-80; Westcoast Actors, Vancouver, 1980-82; joined Douglas & McIntyre, 1983; Key Porter Books, 1985-87; Editorial Dir., Doubleday Books & Music Clubs Canada, 1988-91; Kids Can Press, 1991-92; Pres. & Editor-in-Chief, Key Porter Books Ltd., 1992 to date. **AFFIL:** Writers In Electronic Residence; Canada Book Day.

Reszel, Rozanne, B.A.,M.B.A.,C.A., C.F.A. $

Vice-President and Secretary, CANADIAN INVESTOR PROTECTION FUND, Toronto, ON (416) 866-8366. Born Eldorado, Sask. 1955. m. Ameen Karmally. 1 ch. Natalie Andrea. **EDUC:** Univ. of Waterloo, B.A.(Acctg/Econ.) 1976; Harvard Grad. Sch. of Bus., M.B.A. 1986. **CAREER:** Staff Acctnt, Touche Ross and Co., 1977-79; Examiner, Investment Dealers' Association, Toronto, 1979; Dir. of Compliance, 1980-84; various positions to VP, Client Svcs, Nesbitt Thomson Inc., 1985-90; VP & Sec., Canadian Investor Production Fund, 1990 to date. **AFFIL:** Institute of Chartered Accountants of Ontario (C.A. 1979 to date); Chartered Fin. Analyst (1991 to date); Boulevard Club (Bd. Mbr. 1991-96; Mktg & Fin. Committees); Providence Centre (Bd. Mbr. 1992-95; Chrm, Fin. Committee).

Rethy, Katherine, B.Sc.,LL.B., M.B.A. ■ ⚖ $
Vice-President, Transportation, NORANDA METALLURGY INC., 1 Adelaide St. E., Ste. 2700, Toronto, ON M5C 2Z6 (416) 982-3507, FAX 982-7498. Born Toronto 1956. m. George Rethy. 2 ch. **EDUC:** Univ. of Toronto, B.Sc.(Biol.) 1977; Univ. of Windsor, LL.B. 1980; York Univ., M.B.A. 1984. **BAR:** Ont., 1983. **CAREER:** Lecturer, York Univ., 1981-82; Judicial Law Clerk, Policy Advisor, Gov't of Ont., 1983-85; Legal Cnsl, Mkt Dev. Mgr, Sales Mgr, Supply Chain Project Mgr, Flooring Systems Bus. Mgr, Dir. Materials Logistics & Svcs, DuPont Canada Inc., 1985-96. **AFFIL:** Law Society of Upper Canada; Canadian Council on Logistics (mbr., Advisory Bd.). **INTERESTS:** music; travel; reading; gardening; the outdoors.

Reynolds, Barbara, B.A.,M.A. ■ ✊ 🍁
Executive Director, CENTRE FOR LEGISLATIVE EXCHANGE, 250 Albert St., 4th Fl., Ottawa, ON K1P 6M1 (613) 237-0143, ext. 306, FAX 235-8237. Born Windsor, Ont. 1947. m. Gregory Reynolds. **EDUC:** Univ. of Windsor, B.A.(Soc./Anthro.) 1970, M.A.(Soc.) 1971. **CAREER:** Research Officer, Library of Parliament, 1974-83; Assoc., Parliamentary Centre, 1983 to date; Exec. Dir., Centre for Legislative Exchange, 1983 to date. **AFFIL:** United Church of Canada (extensive involvement at local & reg'l levels). **HONS:** Bd. of Governors Award in Soc., Univ. of Windsor, 1970. **INTERESTS:** cooking; travel; reading. **COMMENT:** *"For almost 23 years, I have provided professional support to parliamentarians in their role as legislators here in Canada and in their role as Canadian representatives at international meetings."*

Reynolds, Carolann 🗳 👍
Vice-President, Corporate Development, REGAN PRODUCTIONS INC., 2 Berkeley St., Ste. 402, Toronto, ON M5A 2W3 (416) 364-6636, FAX 364-5951. Born Montreal 1948. d. 2 ch. Johanna Reynolds, Thomas Reynolds. **EDUC:** Royal Conservatory of Music, Univ. of Toronto, Voice 1969-70; Humber Coll., Early Childhood Educ. 1972; York Univ., Public Rel'ns 1990. **CAREER:** VP, Avenue Television, 1983-88; Pres., Challenge Media Productions Inc., 1989 to date; VP, Corp. Dev., Regan Productions Inc., 1992 to date. **SELECTED CREDITS:** Host, *Polka Dot Door*, TVOntario, eight years; Prod./Writer, *A Fragile Tree Has Roots* (documentary), CBC, 1985; Co-Prod., *Vid Kids* (series), CBC, 1986-87; Assoc. Prod., *Stress Point* (series), 1987; Prod./Writer, *Challenge Journal* (syndicated series), 1988-89; Prod./Writer, *Challenge Journal* (series II & III), TVOntario, 1990, 1993; Exec. & Creative Prod., *Fascinating Tales of Technology* (documentary), Discovery Channel, 1995; Prod., CD-ROM, Technology Ontario; Exec. & Creative Prod., *Chatelaine* series, *Chats & Company*, Life Network, 1997. **SELECTED PUBLICATIONS:** various poetry pieces, *Chickadee* Magazine, 1980-85; "The Sneeze," *Outside the Door* (Nelson Canada); "The Yellow Eyed Cat," *Timespinners* (Nelson Canada). **DIRECTOR:** Challenge Media Productions Inc.; Wiseguy Communications Inc.; Regan Productions Inc. **AFFIL:** ACTRA; National Association of Television Production Executives); Canadian Society of Children's Authors, Illustrators and Performers (Dir. of Public & Media Rel'ns, 1985-86); Board of Trade. **HONS:** *A Fragile Tree Has Roots*, Chris Award, Columbia Film Festival, 1986; Gemini Award, 1987; John Muir Film Festival, 1987; Superfest (Los Angeles) 1987; *Vid Kids* (pilot), Best Variety, CFTA, 1984; *Challenge Journal*: 1995 Winner, National Media Award, Canadian Association for Community Living; Finalist, Media Access Awards, US.; Nominee, International President's Award Council of Exceptional Children. **INTERESTS:** music; art; literature; travel; new technologies; writing; thinking. **MISC:** created & produced the 1st mainstream broadcast series in North America, *Challenge Journal*, that focused entirely on the issues of disabled persons & featured people with disabilities as hosts. **COMMENT:** *"Intelligent, creative and dedicated to making an enduring societal contribution using my talents in business, the arts and communications. I won't take no for an answer."*

Rhea, Celia, B.A.,LL.B. ⚖
Partner, GOODMAN PHILLIPS & VINEBERG, 250 Yonge St., Toronto, ON M5B 2M6 (416) 979-2211, FAX 979-1234. Born Montreal 1960. s. **EDUC:** Univ. of Western Ontario, B.A. (Hist./Phil.) 1980; McGill Univ., LL.B. 1984. **BAR:** Ont., 1986. **CAREER:** Ptnr, Goodman Phillips & Vineberg. **DIRECTOR:** Danone International Brands Canada Inc.; Haco Canada Inc. **AFFIL:** Law Society of Upper Canada; Canadian Bar Association.

Rhind, Katharine Elizabeth, B.A. ■■ ♡
Member, Board of Reproductions Association, ROYAL ONTARIO MUSEUM. Born 1923. m. John A. Rhind. 3 ch. **EDUC:** University Coll., Univ. of Toronto, B.A.(Modern Languages) 1944. **CAREER:** French Translator, National Life Assurance Company, 1944-48; French Translator, Mutual Benefit Health & Accident Association, 1948-49. **VOLUNTEER CAREER:** Junior League of Toronto: mbr., 1950 to date; various

bd. positions incl. Ed., "The Key"/VP/Pres. 1959-63. Royal Ontario Museum: founding mbr., Members' Volunteer Committee, 1957 (various exec. positions on this committee incl. Pres. 1968-69); Bd. of Trustees, 1977-83; Revenue Svcs Committee–mbr., 1974-78, Chair, 1978-83; Chair, Women's Special Names Committee, Renovation/Expansion Campaign, 1978; Bd. of Reproductions Association–mbr., 1987 to date, Pres., 1988-90; mbr., several other committees. Oolagen Community Services: V-Chair & Chair of the Bd., 1970-74. Canadian Red Cross Society: non-Red Cross mbr., Long-Range Planning Task Force, 1973. Sch. of Continuing Studies, Univ. of Toronto: mbr. of Council, 1977-78. St. James Cathedral: Chair of Tour Guides, 1977-79. Dixon Hall Music Sch.: fund-raising committee, 1982-88. Volunteer Centre of Metro Toronto: mbr. of Bd., 1983-85. Hillcrest Hospital: capital fund-raising committee, 1990-93. AFFIL: Badminton & Racquet Club; Osler Bluff Ski Club; Toronto Hunt Club.

Rice, Chick, B.F.A. ■ ⊗ ⌘
Artist. c/o Emily Carr Institute of Art and Design, 3267 W. Fifth Ave., Vancouver, BC V6K 1V3 (604) 736-8520. Born Macau 1954. EDUC: Univ. of British Columbia, B.F.A. 1976; Emily Carr Institute of Art & Design, Diploma (Photography) 1978; Banff Sch. of Fine Arts, Master Class (Photography) 1979. CAREER: photographic artist, 1975 to date; Photography Fac., Emily Carr Institute of Art & Design, 1992 to date. SELECTED PUBLICATIONS: photographs for articles on various literary, cultural & topical issues in bus., sci. & lifestyle periodicals. AFFIL: Contemporary Art Gallery (Bd. of Dir.); Vancouver Foundation (Arts & Culture Advisory Committee). HONS: Viva Award for Visual Arts, 1994. INTERESTS: languages; culture; cuisine; dogs; cats; hamsters; publishing; film-making; travel; fine art books. COMMENT: *"Steady contributor to the arts via photography and art education. Exhibitions in galleries and museums, lecturing about art and photography, publishing in periodicals and teaching photography."*

Rice, Marnie Elizabeth, B.A.,M.A,Ph.D. ⊕
Director of Research, MENTAL HEALTH CENTRE, Box 5000, Penetanguishene, ON L0K 1P0 (705) 549-3181, FAX 549-3652. 2 ch. Andrea Kathryn Rice, Austin David Rice. EDUC: McMaster Univ., B.A.(Psych.) 1970; Univ. of Toronto, M.A.(Psych.) 1971; York Univ., Ph.D.(Clinical Psych.) 1975. CAREER: Clinical Psychologist, Oak Ridge Div., Mental Health Centre, Penetanguishine, 1975-80; Research Psychologist, Research Dept., Mental Health

Centre, 1980-84; Acting Dir., Research Dept., 1984-86; Dir. of Research, 1988 to date; Consultant Psychologist, Advisory Committee for Persons with Developmental Disabilities who Exhibit Inappropriate Sexual Behaviour in Community Settings, York Behaviour Mgmt Svcs, 1992 to date; Assoc. Prof., Dept. of Psychiatry, Fac. of Medicine, McMaster Univ., 1992 to date; Adjunct Assoc. Prof., Dept. of Psych., Fac. of Social Sciences, Queen's Univ., 1992 to date. SELECTED PUBLICATIONS: *Violence in Institutions: Understanding, Prevention, and Control*, with G.T. Harris, G.W. Varney & V.L. Quinsey (Toronto: Hans Huber, 1989); *The Violence Prediction Scheme*, with C.D. Webster *et al* (Toronto: Centre of Criminology, Univ. of Toronto, 1994); "Empathy for the Victim and Sexual Arousal Among Rapists and Nonrapists," with T.C. Chaplin, G.T. Harris & J. Coutts (*Journal of Interpersonal Violence* 9 1994); "Psychopaths: Is a "Therapeutic Community" Therapeutic?" with G.T. Harris & C. Cormier (*Therapeutic Communities* 15 1994); "The Actuarial Prediction of Sexual Recidivism," with V.L. Quinsey & G.T. Harris (*Journal of Interpersonal Violence* 10 1995); numerous other publications. EDIT: Ed. Bd., *Journal of Interpersonal Violence*; *Law on Human Behavior*. AFFIL: Canadian Psychological Association (Fellow); Ontario Psychological Association; American Psychological Association; American Psychology-Law Society. HONS: Ont. Scholar, 1966; Dean's Honour List, Univ. of Western Ontario, 1967; Wellingford Hall Scholarship, McMaster Univ., 1968; Dean's Honour List, McMaster Univ., 1968-70; Catherine MacNeil Prize, McMaster Univ., 1970; Distinguished Contributions to Research in Public Policy Award, American Psychological Association, 1995. MISC: Registered Psychologist, Ont.; recipient, various scholarships, fellowships & grants; various invited presentations; reviewer for various journals & granting agencies. COMMENT: *"I am a research psychologist with an interest in the prevention, management, treatment and prediction of violence. I believe I have contributed to knowledge in these areas."*

Richards, Janet L., B.Sc.N.,R.N., M.Ed. ■■ ⊕ $ ☼
Registered Nurse/Counsellor/Psychotherapist. (private practice - indiv. & couples counselling; eclectic approach with a feminist perspective) (416) 588-2030, FAX 923-6431. Born Lachine, Que. 1962. EDUC: Univ. of Windsor, B.Sc.N. 1985; Univ. of Toronto, Ontario Institute for Studies in Education, M.Ed.(Counselling Psych.) 1993. CAREER: R.N., Forensic Psychiatry, Clarke Institute of Psychiatry,

Metropolitan Toronto Forensic Svc., 1985-87; R.N., GI Medicine/Surgery/Cardiology, Toronto General Hospital, 1987-90; R.N., Psychiatry/Surgery/Long-Term Care, West Coast General Hospital, Port Alberni, B.C., Summer 1989; R.N. (part-time), Dept. of Psychiatry, Toronto East General Hospital, 1990 to date; Counsellor (internship), Ajax Family Counselling Svc., 1991-92; Clinical Nursing Instructor, Sessional Professorship, Mental Health Component, Centennial Coll. of Applied Arts & Technology, Sch. of Health Sciences, Summer 1993; Counsellor, The 519 Church Street Community Centre, 1994-96; Counsellor/Psychotherapist in private practice, 1996 to date. **EDIT:** mbr., Edit. Bd., *Women & Environments.* **AFFIL:** Family Support Institute of Ontario; Coll. of Nurses of Ontario; Sex Information & Education Council of Canada; Ontario Association of Consultants, Counsellors, Psychometrists & Psychotherapists; The Council of Canadians; U.N. Association in Canada; Toronto Association for Community Living (volunteer); AIDS Committee of Toronto (volunteer); Windsor Community Living Support Services (volunteer). **MISC:** fully trained in the healing technique Therapeutic Touch - offered in private practice. **COMMENT:** *"I am a therapist in private practice and I use a feminist approach in my counselling. I am lesbian- and gay-positive and have counselling experience in the gay community in Toronto. I believe strongly in promoting individuals on their personal and spiritual paths; I am knowledgeable about many community contacts and provide referrals where necessary. I have special interests in and have done workshops in phychotherapy issues, creative writing and photography."*

Richardson, Beverley, M.D., F.R.C.P.C. ⊕ ⌒
Chief, Medical Staff Affairs, Women's College Hospital, UNIVERSITY OF TORONTO, Faculty of Medicine, 60 Grosvenor St., Ste. 422, Toronto, ON M5S 1B6 (416) 967-4335, FAX 967-4335. Born Montreal 1948. **EDUC:** Univ. of Toronto, M.D. 1972. **CAREER:** Lecturer, Dept. of Medicine, Women's College Hospital, Univ. of Toronto Fac. of Medicine, 1980-83; Asst. Prof., 1983 to date; Chief, Medical Staff Affairs, Women's College Hospital; Chair, Gender Issues Committee, Univ. of Toronto Fac. of Medicine, 1992 to date. **AFFIL:** Ontario Medical Association (Dir.); Council of Ontario Faculties of Medicine (Gender Issues Committee); Royal Coll. of Physicians & Surgeons of Canada (Fellow). **COMMENT:** *"Women's College Hospital is dedicated to meeting the health care needs of women. Advocacy for research*

and education in women's health is my primary professional focus."

Richardson, Marjolane Symington ■ ■ ⊗ ◗ ⊘
WOMEN'S ART ASSOCIATION OF HAMILTON (art & art scholarships), c/o Beverleigh Orchards, 3477 Hwy. 6 S., Mount Hope, ON L0K 1W0. Born Hamilton, Ont. 1924. w. 2 ch. Denise J. Walkinshaw, Dana W. Richardson. **EDUC:** Teachers' Coll.; Royal Conservatory of Music, Toronto, 1943. **CAREER:** taught art hist., drawing, painting, crafts, home econ. & family studies, Grades 9-12; private studio; porcelain painter & teacher, 1944 to date. **EXHIBITIONS:** Exhibitions Hamilton, Feb. & Mar. 1996; Royal Botanical Gardens, July 1996; Hamilton Art Gallery, Oct. 1996. **AFFIL:** Women's Art Association of Hamilton (Pres. 1955-57 & 1989-95; Chrm, Scholarship Committee 1983 to date); Art Gallery of Hamilton (Volunteer Committee); Canadian Figure Skating Association (35 yrs.); MacNab Presbyterian Church (Choir & Couples Club 50+ yrs.); Hamilton Opera Company; Royal Botanical Gardens. **HONS:** Life Mbr., Women's Art, 60 yrs.; nominated Woman of the Year in Art, 1994; Gold 25-yr. pin, Canadian Figure Skating Association; Wentworth Heritage Volunteer Award. **INTERESTS:** helping young people to achieve in skating & with art scholarships; gardening; sewing; genealogy. **COMMENT:** *"Music and art, fundraising for scholarships, convening events and trips to further art knowledge. Private art studio, specializing in porcelain painting. All I'm involved in keeps me extremely busy, plus driving 6 grandchildren to music, dance and skating lessons."*

Richardson, Mary Frances, B.S., Ph.D. ❀ ⌒
Professor of Chemistry, BROCK UNIVERSITY, St. Catharines, ON L2S 3A1 (905) 688-5550, ext. 3400, EMAIL mrichard@abacus.ac.brocku.ca. Born Barbourville, Kentucky 1941. **EDUC:** Univ. of Kentucky, B.S.(Chem.) 1962, Ph.D. (Chem.) 1967. **CAREER:** Research Assoc., Wright Patterson Air Force Base, Ohio, 1967-71; Asst. Prof., Brock Univ., 1971-75; Assoc. Prof., 1975-81; Chair, Dept. of Chem., 1979-82, 1995 to date; Prof., 1981 to date; Assoc. Fac. Mbr., Dept. of Women's Studies, 1991 to date. **SELECTED PUBLICATIONS:** more than 60 in professional chemistry journals. **AFFIL:** Chemical Institute of Canada (Fellow); American Chemical Society; American Crystallographic Association. **HONS:** Teaching Award, Ontario Confederated University Faculty Associations, 1990; Cdn Prof. of the Year, C.A.S.E., 1992. **INTERESTS:** out-of-doors; making &

judging beer. COMMENT: *"I enjoy teaching and doing research in solid-state chemistry."*

Richardson, Sheila, B.A. ✪ ✿

Executive Director, ONTARIO GOOD ROADS ASSOCIATION, 530 Otto Rd., Unit 2, Mississauga, ON L5T 2L5 (905) 795-2555, FAX 795-2660. Born Orangeville, Ont. 1950. s. EDUC: York Univ., B.A.(Geography) 1977. CAREER: Sec. of Land Div. Committee, County of Dufferin, 1972-77; Exec. Dir., Association of Counties & Regions of Ontario, 1977-82; Dir. of Mgmt & Membership Svcs, Association of Municipalities of Ontario, 1982-86; Exec. Dir., Ontario Good Roads Association, 1986 to date. AFFIL: Tri Committee on Utilization of Computers in Public Works (Dir.); Big Sisters of Peel (Dir. & First VP). HONS: Canada 125 Medal. INTERESTS: sewing; reading; travelling. COMMENT: *"Sheila Richardson has worked for the betterment of municipal government in Ontario throughout her working career, and for her community through her volunteer service with Big Sisters of Peel."*

Richler, Diane, B.A. ✪ ◐

Executive Vice-President, CANADIAN ASSOCIATION FOR COMMUNITY LIVING, Kinsmen Building, 4700 Keele St., North York, ON M3J 1P3 (416) 661-9611, FAX 661-5701, EMAIL drichler@orion.yorku.ca. Born Presque Isle, Me. 1950. m. Ronald M. Richler. 3 ch. EDUC: McGill Univ., B.A.(Psych.) 1971. CAREER: Dir., National Institute on Mental Retardation, 1984-87; Exec. VP, Canadian Association for Community Living, 1984 to date. SELECTED PUBLICATIONS: "Service Delivery Patterns in North America: Trends and Challenges" with J. Pelletier (*Mental Handicap: A Multi-Disciplinary* Approach ed. Michael Craft *et al*, UK: Baillière Tindall, 1985); "Changing Special Education Practice: Law, Advocacy, and Innovation" with G. Porter (*Canadian Journal of Community Mental Health* Fall 1990); "Emerging Realities: The Case for Community Living, The Case Against Segregation" (*abilities* Spring 1991); *Changing Canadian Schools: Perspectives on Inclusion and Disability* ed. with G. Porter (G. Allan Roeher Institute, 1991); "Organizing for Social Change: How to Get What We Want" (*entourage* Summer 1991); "The United Nations Convention on the Rights of the Child: A Tool for Advocacy" (*As If Children Matter: Perspectives on Children, Rights, and Disability*, L'Institut Roeher Institute, 1995). AFFIL: Confederation of the International League of Societies for People with Mental Handicap (Advisor); Willows, Ontario Breast Cancer Resource Centre (Founding Bd. Mbr.); Reference Group to Mainstream '92,

The Federal, Provincial & Territorial Review of Services Affecting Canadians With Disabilities; Min. of Transport (Chair, Advisory Committee on Accessible Transportation 1991-92); Independence '92 Int'l Conference (Co-Chair, Program Committee 1990-92); Advisory Bd. of the 2nd Int'l Conference on Family Support; 1998 Congress of Inclusion Int'l (Program Chair). COMMENT: *"Diane Richler was one of the major architects of a deinstitutionalization strategy for persons with an intellectual disability in Canada involving the federal and provincial governments and the national and provincial Associations for Community Living. She is active internationally promoting the participation of civil society in shaping policy based on human rights."*

Ricker, Marvi, B.Sc.,M.Sc. ◑ ◐ ❀

Executive Director, RICHARD IVEY FOUNDATION, 630 Richmond St., London, ON N6A 3G6 (519) 673-1280, FAX 672-4790. Born Parnu, Estonia 1943. m. John Carman Ricker. 3 stepch. EDUC: Univ. of Toronto, B.Sc.(Math/Physics/Chem.) 1966, M.Sc.(Organic Chem.) 1967. CAREER: Chem. Instructor, Univ. of Toronto, 1967-71; Administrator, 1971-77; Coord., Community Rel'ns, 1977-84; Dir., Public & Community Rel'ns, 1984-90; Exec. Dir., Richard Ivey Foundation, 1990 to date. SELECTED PUBLICATIONS: *The Public Institution in a Multicultural Society* (1983). AFFIL: London Health Sciences Centre (Patient Care Committee); Univ. of Western Ontario (Fac. of Eng. Sci. Advisory Council); Environment Canada (Biodiversity Advisory Group); Hungarian Research Institute of Canada (Dir.); Courtyard Concerts London (Dir.); London Club. HONS: Scholarship, National Research Council, 1967; Award, US Council for Advancement & Support of Education, 1980; Award, Estonian Arts & Letters Society, 1981; Publication Award, Canadian Council for Advancement of Education, 1986; Rakoczi Medal, 1990. INTERESTS: travel; hiking; music. COMMENT: *"I consider myself fortunate to be involved in philanthropy at this time of fundamental change in all sectors of Canadian society. What an opportunity to make a significant contribution!"*

Riddell-Dixon, Elizabeth M., B.A., M.Sc.,Ph.D. ◑ ❀

Associate Professor, Department of Political Science, UNIVERSITY OF WESTERN ONTARIO, London, ON N6A 5C2 (519) 661-3267, FAX (519) 661-3904. EDUC: Univ. of Toronto, B.A.(Hist. & Pol. Sci.) 1977, Ph.D.(Pol. Sci.) 1985; London Sch. of Econ. & Pol. Sci., UK, M.Sc.(Int'l Rel'ns) 1978. CAREER: Research

Assoc., Canadian Institute of International Affairs (CIIA), 1982-83; Lecturer, Politics Dept., Brock Univ., 1984-85; Asst. Prof., Dept. of Pol. Sci., Univ. of Western Ontario, 1985-90; Assoc. Prof., 1991 to date; Chair, 1993-96. **SELECTED PUBLICATIONS:** *The Domestic Mosaic: Interest Groups and Canadian Foreign Policy* (Toronto: CIIA, 1985); *Canada and the International Seabed: Domestic Determinants and External Constraints* (Montreal: McGill-Queen's, 1989); "The Preparatory Commission on the International Seabed Authority: New Realism?" (*International Journal of Estuarine and Coastal Law* 7(3) 1992); "Winners and Losers: Formulating Canada's Policies on International Technology Transfers" (*International Journal* Winter 1991-92); "The United Nations after the Gulf War" (*International Journal* 49(2) 1994); various other publications. **EDIT:** Ed. Bd., *Canadian Foreign Policy*, 1993 to date; Ed. Bd., *Global Governance*, 1994 to date. **AFFIL:** Canadian Political Science Association; CIIA; Academic Council on the United Nations System, Internation Studies Association. **MISC:** recipient, various grants; various conference presentations.

Righter, Julie, M.D.,FRCPC ■ ⊕

Psychotherapist. 150 Consumers Rd., Ste. 209, Toronto, ON M2J 1P9 (416) 782-5030. Born Hungary 1948. m. Raphael Schick. 2 ch. Ruth, Jonathan. **EDUC:** Univ. of Toronto, MD 1971, FRCPC(Medical Microbiol.) 1975. **CAREER:** Asst. Microbiologist, McMaster University Medical Centre, 1976-78; Head., Div. of Microbiol., Toronto East General Hospital, 1978-92; Asst. Prof., Dept. of Microbiol., University of Toronto, 1981 to date; Physician, Psychotherapist in private practice, 1992 to date; Certified Group Psychotherapist, 1996. **SELECTED PUBLICATIONS:** various conference presentations; numerous journal articles including: "Erythromycin: an update" (*Modern Medicine* 36, 1981); "Rapid diagnosis of catheter-associated infection," letter (*New England Journal of Medicine* 313, 1985); "Pneumococcal meningitis after intravenous ciprofloxacin therapy" (*American Journal of Medicine* 88, 1990); "View on labelling" (*Canadian Journal of Medical Technology* 53, 1991; *Canadian Journal of Infection Control* 6(4), Winter 1991). **AFFIL:** Drug Quality and Therapeutics Committee, Ontario Ministry of Health (1989-94; Acting Chair 1992-93; Chair 1993-94); Humanist Association of Toronto; American Group Psychotherapy Association. **INTERESTS:** classical music. **COMMENT:** *"I treat emotional problems with group psychotherapy, using a drug-free, holistic approach. I also do specialized psychotherapy for serious medical illness, using mind/body medicine techniques."*

Riley, Donna Bastien, M.H.A., C.H.E. ■ ⊕ 🎓

Director of Planning, McGILL UNIVERSITY HEALTH CENTRE, 2015 Peel St., Montreal, QC H3A 1T8 (514) 842-4680, ext. 754, EMAIL driley@po_box.mcgill.ca. d. 2 ch. **EDUC:** Rivier Coll., Nashua, New Hampshire, B.A. (English/Educ.) 1965-69; Univ. de Strasbourg, France, full-time studies in art hist., 1972-73; McGill Univ., Diploma in Mgmt, part-time studies, three courses, 1980-82, M.B.A. Program, completed 11 courses, 1982-83; Univ. de Montreal, Master's in Health Admin. 1983-85. **CAREER:** English Teacher, Handelschule Frenzel, Kaufbeuren, W. Germany, 1974-75; Medical Sec.-Sr. Level, Hitchcock Clinic, Dartmouth-Hitchcock Medical Center, Hanover, N.H., 1976-79; Medical Sec., Montreal Neurological Hospital, 1980; Admin. Asst., Office Supervisor, Fraser Wray Consultants, Montreal, 1980-82; Admin. residency, M.H.A. Program, Montreal General Hospital, 1984; Admin. Asst. reporting to Exec. Dir., 1985-86; Asst. to Dir. of Professional Svcs, 1986-87; Dir., Planning & Dev., 1987 to date; Dir., Planning & Dev. & Acting Dir., Tech. Svcs., 1994-95. **SELECTED PUBLICATIONS:** preliminary & final reports regarding the proposed merger of McGill Hospitals. **EDIT:** Edit. Bd., *Healthcare Management Forum*, 1992 to date. **AFFIL:** Canadian Coll. of Health Service Executives (C.H.E.; founding Mbr., Montreal Chapter 1990; Sec.-Treas. 1990-92); YWCA (Bd. of Dir., Montreal 1987); Christ Church Cathedral, Montreal (Mbr., Select Vestry 1986-89, 1991-93; Sec. to Select Vestry 1987-89; Sec. to Gen. Vestry 1990-93). **HONS:** Robert Wood Johnson Award for student most apt to make a significant contribution to the advancement of healthcare administration, 1985. **INTERESTS:** literature; holistic health & philosophy; art; fitness; travel. **MISC:** sang with a semi-professional choir, 1979-84. **COMMENT:** *"I am a 48-year old woman who took the leap, in 1982, after 13 years out of school, and with two small children, and pursued a Master's in Health Admin. I have been fortunate since then to work on progressively more exciting projects, of which the McGill merger is the most recent. I've never looked back."*

Rimell, Drude, B.Sc. ■■ $

Vice-President, Corporate Services, ALBERTA ENERGY COMPANY LTD. (oil & gas exploration, production, mktg & pipelines), 421 - 7th Ave. S.W., Ste. 3900, Calgary, AB T2P 4K9 (403) 266-8401, FAX 266-8100. Born Oslo, Norway 1945. **EDUC:** London Sch. of Econ. & Pol. Sci., B.Sc.(Hons., Econ.) 1966; Univ. of Calgary, grad. studies (Math.). **CAREER:** Tech. Systems Dev., Canadian Arctic Gas Study Ltd./ Union Oil/Canadian Pacific Oil and Gas (Pan-Canadian)/Honeywell Bull (France), 1967-77; Mgr, Application Systems, Petro-Canada, 1977-88; Mgr, Application Systems, Alberta Energy Company Ltd., 1988-91; Dir., Computer Svcs, 1991-94; VP, Corp. Svcs, 1994 to date. **AFFIL:** Univ. of Calgary (Leadership Diversity Committee, Fac. of Mgmt).

Rinaldo, Sandie 🖾 🗂
Anchor, *CTV News Weekend*, CTV TELEVISION NETWORK, 250 Yonge St., Ste. 1800, Toronto, ON M5B 2N8 (416) 595-4176. Producer and Reporter, *PORTRAIT*. Host, *W5*. Born Toronto 1950. m. Michael. 3 ch. **EDUC:** York Univ., B.A.(Hons., Fine Arts) 1973. **CAREER:** joined the CTV news dept., 1973; Prod. Coord. & Researcher, *W5*, 2 yrs.; Story Ed., *Canada AM*; Reporter, *CTV News*; back-up Co-Host, *Canada AM*; News Anchor, *Canada AM*, 1980; named alternate Anchor, *CTV National News*, 1981; Weekend Anchor, *CTV News*, 1985-89; backup Anchor, Prod. & Reporter, *CTV News*; Co-Anchor & Sr. Ed., *World Beat News*, CFTO, 1989-91; Weekend Anchor, *CTV News*, 1991 to date; Prod. & Reporter, CTV's *Portrait* series; Host, *W5*, 1996 to date. **HONS:** American Film & Video Award for her work prod. *Childbirth From Inside-Out*, a medical video, 1990; Silver Medal, Best Analysis of a Single Current Story, Houston Int'l Film Festival, 1990; Bronze Medal, Best News Anchor, Int'l Film & TV Festival of N.Y., 1990; Finalist Certificate, Best News Anchor, Int'l Film & TV Festival of N.Y., 1991; Silver Medal, Best Coverage of an Ongoing Story, Int'l Film & TV Festival of N.Y., 1991. **MISC:** 1st woman in Cdn TV history to anchor a daily ntwk newscast.

Ringuette-Maltais, Pierette, M.P., B.A. ■ 🌢 🗂
Member of Parliament (Madawaska-Victoria) and Assistant Deputy Chairman of Committees of the Whole House, GOVERNMENT OF CANADA, House of Commons, Ottawa, ON K1A 0A6. Born Edmundston, N.B. 1955. m. Laurent Maltais. 1 ch. Andrée Julie. **EDUC:** Univ. de Moncton, Edmundston Campus, B.A.(Admin./Social Sci.); Univ. Laval in Quebec, completed course work for a M.A. in Ind. Rel'ns. **CAREER:** Supervisor and Customer Svcs Officer for several Que. bus. firms; Lecturer, Univ. du Québec in Rivière-du-loup; Prof. of Continuing Educ., Univ. de Moncton; elected MLA (Madawaska South), Gov't of N.B., 1987; Deputy Speaker,

1987-91; mbr., standing committees on Crown Corporations, on Privileges and the Special Committee on Econ. Policy Dev.; appointed to the Min.'s Task Force on Housing & Legislative Assembly's select committee on Meech Lake, 1988; V-Chair, Assemblée internationale des parlementaires de langue française, NB section, 1988-93; mbr., Commonwealth Parliamentary Association, 1988-93; appointed to N.B. Commission on Canadian Federalism, 1990; re-elected 1991; elected MP (Madawaska-Victoria), Gov't of Canada, 1993; Co-Pres., Standing Joint Committee for Official Languages, 1994; Pres., Sub-Committee responsible to review comm. for the Committees of the House; nominated, V-Chair, Policy Dev. Committee, Liberal Party of Canada, 1994; appointed Asst. Deputy Chrm, Committees of the Whole House, 1996 to date. **AFFIL:** Cercle de Presse Internationale de la République (Former mbr.); Nurses Association of New Brunswick (former mbr. Discipline Committee); Family Enrichment Services (former Bd. mbr.); Edmundston Chamber of Commerce (former Exec. Dir.). **MISC:** 1st female pres. of Foire Brayonne, 1986; mbr. of the first bd., Compagnie des Jeunes Travailleurs du Nord-Ouest Inc.; seconded the motion on the speech from the Throne on the opening of the 35th Parliament of Canada, an honour bestowed by the Hon. Jean Chrétien.

Rioux, Marcia Hampton (née Gautschi), Ph.D. ♥ ☺ 🔻
Executive Director, THE ROEHER INSTITUTE, Kinsmen Bldg, 4700 Keele St, North York, ON M3J 1P3 (416) 661-9611, ext. 220, FAX (416) 661-5701, EMAIL mrioux@yorku.ca. Assistant Professor, Faculty of Environmental Studies, YORK UNIVERSITY. Born Trail, B.C. 1947. d. **EDUC:** Carleton Univ., B.A.(Soc.) 1968, M.A.(Soc.) 1973; Univ. of California at Berkeley, Ph.D.(Jurisprudence & Social Policy) 1993. **CAREER:** Research Asst., Royal Commission on the Status of Women, 1968-70; freelance researcher & policy consultant, 1968-74; Special Instructor, Carleton Univ., 1971-72; Dir. of Research, Canadian Advisory Council on the Status of Women, 1974-77; Policy Analyst, Law Reform Commission of Canada, 1977-79; freelance consultant, 1979-86; Visiting Scholar, The Roeher Institute, York Univ., 1986-87; Exec. Dir., 1987 to date; Asst. Prof., Fac. of Environmental Studies, 1991 to date. **SELECTED PUBLICATIONS:** *Disability Is Not Measles*, ed. (North York: Roeher Institute, 1994); "Poverty and Disability: Toward a New Framework for Community Mental Health" (*Canadian Journal of Community Mental Health* Fall 1990); "Toward a Concept of

Equality of Well-Being: Overcoming the Social and Legal Construction of Inequality" (*Canadian Journal of Law and Jurisprudence* Jan. 1994); "Social Policy, Devolutions and Disability: Back to Notions of the Worthy Poor," *Remaking Canadian Social Policy*, ed. by Pulkingham & Ternowetsky (1996); "Ethical and Socio-Political Considerations on the Development and Use of Classification" (*Canadian Journal of Rehabilitation* Winter, 1996); *Hacia un Cambio en Politica Sociol* (Prometeo: Fuego para el Propio Conocimiento, Primavera, 1996); numerous other publications. **EDIT:** Bd. of Dir., *Abilities* Magazine, 1991 to date; *European Journal on Mental Disability*, 1995 to date; *Tizard Learning Disability Review Journal*, 1995 to date; *Canadian Journal of Rehabilitation*, 1995 to date. **AFFIL:** Canadian Law & Society Association; National Institute of Disability Management & Research (Int'l Advisory Committee); Canadian Sociology & Anthropology Association; International Interest Group on Decentralisation, User Empowerment & Citizenship, Univ. of Wales, UK; Women's Research Network: An Int'l Interest Group on Research in the Area of Women & Disability (Organizer & Coord.); International League of Societies for Persons with Mental Handicaps (New Bio-ethical Issues Committee); International Association for the Scientific Study of Intellectual Disability (VP); Ont. Advisory Council on Disability Issues (Council Mbr. 1990-94); Caribbean Association for Mental Retardation & Other Developmental Disabilities (Advisor 1990 to date). **MISC:** various conference presentations; various consultancies; recipient, various grants; observor to the UNESCO Int'l Bioethics Committee on the Human Genome Proj. on behalf of the International League of Societies for Mental Handicap, 1994.

Ripley, M. Louise, B.A.,M.B.A.,Ph.D. 🎓 $

Associate Professor, Atkinson College, YORK UNIVERSITY, 4700 Keele St., North York, ON M3J 1P3 (416) 736-4210, FAX 736-5963, EMAIL lripley@yorku.ca. Born New York City 1946. m. Albert P. (Bert) Christensen. 1 ch. **EDUC:** Shimer Coll., Waukegan, IL, B.A. 1968; Loyola Univ. of Chicago, M.B.A. 1978; Univ. of Toronto, Ph.D.(Mgmt Studies) 1989. **CAREER:** teaching; small & large stock brokerages; int'l bnkg; research/consulting in fin. & mktg; Asst. Prof., Mktg & Coord. of Mktg Area, Atkinson Coll., York Univ.; Visiting Prof., St. Francis Xavier Univ.; Assoc. Prof. of Admin. Studies, of Women's Studies, & of Environmental Studies, York Univ. **SELECTED PUBLICATIONS:** articles in bus. journals on advtg & channels of distribution. **AFFIL:** Administrative Sciences Association of Canada; Shimer Coll., Waukegan, IL (Bd. of Trustees); Toronto Musicians' Association; Unitarian Universalist Church. **INTERESTS:** issues of women in bus., particulary women & risk taking; harp. **COMMENT:** *"A feminist, passionate about teaching and Peterbilt trucks, a PhD, wonderful husband and delightful son, three cats, a concert harp, and building a model railroad."*

Riske, Barbara, A.M.M.,A.R.C.T., B.A. ■ ⊛ ☝

Musician. 227 Deer Crossing Way, Henderson, NY 89012. 2 ch. Elizabeth Nicola, William Norman Malcolm. **EDUC:** Royal Conservatory of Music, Toronto, A.R.C.T. 1965; Univ. of Manitoba, Western Board, A.M.M. 1967, B.A. 1967. **CAREER:** Principal Pianist, Royal Winnipeg Ballet, 1966-96; Pianist, American Ballet Company, 1969; numerous recitals, 1969 to date; Pianist, American Ballet Theatre, 1970-72; mbr., Music Plus (chamber ensemble), 1979 to date; Keyboard Player, Winnipeg Symphony Orchestra, 1985-96; teacher & clinician. **SELECTED CREDITS:** numerous recitals & performances in Canada, the US & Europe; has played with many artists including Robert Aitken, Tracy Dahl, Guy Few, Susan Heppner, Walfrid Kujala, Josef Marx, Diana McIntosh, Zara Nelsova, Ramon Parocells, Francois Rabbath, Eugene Rousseau, Patricia Spencer & Alain Trudel. **AFFIL:** Aurora Musicale, a chamber music society (Co-Founder & Assoc. Artistic Dir.); Artists in the Schools program, Manitoba Arts Council (teacher); Manitoba Conservatory of Music and Arts (Bd. 1988-91); Junior Musical Club (Bd. 1984-90); Manitoba Arts Council (Music Advisory Committee, 1989); Woman's Musical Club (Bd. 1980-84). **HONS:** Isbister Scholarship for the highest marks, Sch. of Music, Univ. of Manitoba; Best Pianist, Int'l Ballet Competition, Helsinki, 1991. **MISC:** designed & supervised 1st year of Program of Preparatory Studies, Sch. of Music, Univ. of Manitoba.

Ritchie, Judith, R.N.,B.N.,M.N.,Ph.D., D.Sc.(Hon.) ⊕ 🎓 ✊

Professor, School of Nursing, DALHOUSIE UNIVERSITY, Halifax, NS B3H 3J5 (902) 494-2611, FAX 494-3487, EMAIL judith.ritchie@dal.ca. Director of Nursing Research, IWK-GRACE HEALTH CENTRE FOR CHILDREN, WOMEN & FAMILIES. Born Saint John 1943. s. **EDUC:** Univ. of New Brunswick, B.N.(Nursing) 1965; Univ. of Pittsburgh, M.N.(Nursing of Children) 1969, Ph.D.(Nursing of Children) 1975. **CAREER:** Camp Nurse, 1963-68; Staff Nurse, Montreal Children's Hospital, 1965-66; Lecturer, Asst. Prof., Assoc. Prof., Univ. of New

Brunswick, 1966-68, 1974-78; Hon. Research Instructor, Univ. of Pittsburgh, 1970-71; Clinical Nurse Specialist, Pittsburgh Children's Hospital, 1970-72; Assoc. Prof. then Prof., Dalhousie Univ., 1978 to date; Visiting Assoc. Prof., Univ. of California, San Francisco, 1982-83; Dir., Nursing Research, IWK-Grace Health Centre, 1986 to date. SELECTED PUBLICATIONS: approx. 50 articles & book chapters pertaining to children & their families in healthcare situations. AFFIL: Canadian Nurses' Association (Chair, Nursing Research Committee 1980-84; Mbr.-at-Large, Nursing Research 1982-84; Exec. Committee 1982-84; Pres.-Elect 1986-88; Pres. 1988-90); CAUT; RNANS; Canadian Nursing Research Group; Canadian Pediatric Nurses' Interest Group; National Forum on Health (1994-98). HONS: Canadian Nurses' Foundation Scholar, 1968, 1969, 1970; Medical Research Council Studentship, 1972, 1973; D.Sc.(Hon.), Univ. of New Brunswick, 1989; Inaugural Research Award, IWK Children's Hospital, 1993; Canadian Nurses Foundation/Ross Laboratories Award for Nursing Leadership, 1996. INTERESTS: singing - church choir. MISC: mbr., Prov. Health Council, 1990-93; Chair, Prov. Health Council Committee on Health Goals, 1991-92 & Technology Assessment Committee, 1993. COMMENT: *"Energetically committed to nurses and nursing, children and their families. Has had a long-standing research program focused on children and their families coping with major chronic health problems. Teaching, research and administrative work all focus on helping nurses find ways to improve children's health and advancing the use of research in nursing practice."*

Ritchie, Marguerite Elizabeth, Q.C.,B.A., LL.B.,LL.M.,LL.D. 🎭 ⚜ 🗡

President, HUMAN RIGHTS INSTITUTE OF CANADA, 246 Queen St., Ste. 303, Ottawa, ON K1P 5E4 (613) 232-2920 or 232-7477, FAX 232-3735. Born Edmonton 1919. s. EDUC: Univ. of Alberta, B.A. 1943, LL.B. 1943; McGill Univ., LL.M.(Int'l Air & Space Law) 1958. BAR: Alta., 1944; Q.C., Fed., 1963. CAREER: articled with Howard T. Emery Q.C., Newell, Lindsay, Emery and Ford, Edmonton, 1943-44; Combines Officer, Combines Investigation Commission, Ottawa, 1945-51; Sr. Advisory Cnsl, Fed. Dept. of Justice, Ottawa, 1952-72; mbr., Inter-Departmental Committee dealing with U.N., Int'l Law, Constitutional Law, Treaties, Hum. Rights questions, Status of Women, etc.; Departmental Specialist on all questions involving these issues & specific coord. with Departments of External Affairs, Labour, Transport on questions of Cdn reson-

sibility for laws & policies relating to treaties signed & ratified by Canada; Legal Advisor, Cdn Delegation, ICAO Conference on Warsaw Charter Amendments, The Hague, 1955; Legal Advisor, Cdn Delegation to UN Human Rights Committee, 1966; Exec. Asst. to Hon. E.D. Fulton & to Hon. Lionel Chevrier (Mins. of Justice); V-Chair, Fed. Anti-dumping Tribunal, Ottawa, 1972-79; Pres., Human Rights Institute of Canada, Ottawa, 1974 to date. SELECTED PUBLICATIONS: "How Canada Wastes its Woman Power" (*Saturday Night* Apr. 2, 1960); "Alice Through the Statutes" (*McGill Law Journal* Nov. 1975); "History versus Arab Claims to Homeland" (*Ottawa Journal* Dec. 25, 1975); "Revolutionary Violence and Canadian Policy: A Study of Middle East Politics" (*Dialogue* May 1976); "The Language of Oppression: Alice Talks Back" (*McGill Law Journal* Fall 1977); "Experimenting with Canadian Business: Anti-Dumping Protection in Canada" (*Canadian Business Law Journal* Aug. 1979); regular columnist, *DIALOGUE*, journal of informed commentary on Constitution, Quebec and human rights; numerous legal submissions to gov't organizations, submitted in the name of Human Rights Institute of Canada; various other publications. EDIT: ed., *Women's University Club Newsletter*, Ottawa, 1958-60. AFFIL: Alberta Law Society; International Commission of Jurists; legal advisor from time to time to native women, women's organizations, concerned citizens' groups, about Constitution, gov't responsibility under the law, gov't violations of rights of native peoples; advisor to native women about gov't violations of rights of women guaranteed under Charter of Rights & Freedoms, U.N. Charter & important U.N. Conventions; mbr., Special Cdn Committee advising S. African Chief Justice on drafting S. African Constitution; Advisor to External Affairs Dept. on Canada's obligations under U.N. Convention on the Rights of the Child. HONS: Centennial Medal, 1967; special necklace from Indian Rights for Indian Women, for work for Indian women during Lavell case before Supreme Court of Canada, 1973; Outstanding Woman Award, Prov. of Ont., 1975; 1st woman appointed Q.C. by Fed. Gov't; Hon. LL.D. received for work on human rights. INTERESTS: reading books related to equality & justice; meeting people with similar interests; travel; gardening. MISC: Human Rights Institute of Canada is a federally incorporated nonprofit corporation for the advancement of equality & justice in Canada. COMMENT: *"I have used my legal and government training to achieve changes in laws with respect to women, and to work for justice regardless of race, creed, colour or sex. In view of the many forms of injustice and inequality that women face around the world, I have been particularly involved in the promotion of justice and equality for women."*

Ritchie, Penny ⊘ ♥ ⊜

Partner, SKYDIVE UNLIMITED INC., Box 28, Stewiacke, NS B0N 2J0 (902) 639-2604, FAX 639-2604. Born Halifax 1959. cl. Robert Mowry. 1 ch. CAREER: various positions, retail fashion, 1979-87; Ptnr, Skydive Unlimited Inc., 1990 to date. AFFIL: N.S. Parachuting Association (Dir. 1992-94; Pres. 1993; VP 1994); Canadian Sport Parachuting Association (Certified Level One Instructor/Coach; 10-yr. mbr.). INTERESTS: skydiving; travel; fashion; needlepoint; family. COMMENT: *"Finished high school in 1979 and went to work in retail fashion. Began skydiving in 1983 as a hobby, became career path in 1987. Started Skydive Unlimited Inc. with husband in 1990."*

Rittinger, Carolyne ✎

Editor, THE KITCHENER-WATERLOO RECORD, 225 Fairway Rd. S., Kitchener, ON N2G 4E5 (519) 894-2231, FAX 893-7259. Born Swift Current, Sask. 1942. m. Robert Rittinger. 3 ch. Robert Rittinger, Angela Bieronski, Lisa Rittinger. CAREER: Reporter, *The Swift Current Sun, The Moose Jaw Times Herald*; City Ed., *Medicine Hat News*; Reporter, *The Kitchener-Waterloo Record*, 1973; numerous positions incl. District Ed., Entertainment Ed., City Ed., & Mng Ed., 1974-92; Ed., 1992 to date. AFFIL: Canadian Daily Newspaper Association (Ed. Div.). HONS: Kitchener-Waterloo Oktoberfest Professional Woman of the Year, 1992; Western Ontario Newspaper Award for Investigative Reporting (team award), 1973; Calgary Women's Press Club Award for Arts Reporting, 1970; Best News Story, Calgary Women's Press Club, 1969. INTERESTS: skiing; travel; the arts. COMMENT: *"As Editor, Mrs. Rittinger has overall responsibility for the editorial content of the paper. She leads a staff of 70, is a member of* The Record's *senior management team, helps to set strategic direction for the company and plays a key role in community relations."*

Rix, Brenda Diane (née Vardy), B.A., M.A. ⊗ 📖

Supervisor, Print and Drawing Study Centre, ART GALLERY OF ONTARIO, 317 Dundas St. W., Toronto, ON M5T 1G4 (416) 979-6660, ext. 261, FAX 979-6666. Born Belleville, Ont. 1956. m. Michael Rix. 2 ch. Matthew Rix, Geoffrey Rix. EDUC: Univ. of Toronto, B.A. 1978, M.A. 1980. CAREER: Teaching Asst.,

St. George Campus, Univ. of Toronto, 1979; Research Asst., Oakville Galleries, 1979; Slide Librarian, Erindale Coll., Univ. of Toronto, 1979-81; Teaching Asst., 1979-80, 1980-81; Research Asst., Art Gallery of Ontario, Summers 1980-81; Educ. Officer, Adult Program, 1980-81; Curatorial Asst., Print & Drawing, 1981-82; Asst. Curator, 1982-87; Guest Curator, Walter Trier Collection, Art Gallery of Ontario, 1988 to date; freelance art consultant, 1993 to date; Supervisor, Marvin Gelber Prints & Drawings Study Centre, Art Gallery of Ontario, 1993 to date. SELECTED PUBLICATIONS: *Pictures for the Parlour: The English Reproductive Print from 1775 to 1900*, catalogue (Toronto: Art Gallery of Ontario, 1983); *Our Old Friend Rolly: Watercolours, Prints, and Book Illustrations by Thomas Rowlandson in the Collection of the Art Gallery of Ontario*, catalogue (Toronto: Art Gallery of Ontario, 1987); *French Printmaking of the Eighteenth Century*, catalogue (Toronto: Art Gallery of Ontario, 1988); *"A Real Amateur". The Elizabeth E. Dales Collection of Nineteenth-century French Prints*, catalogue (Toronto: Art Gallery of Ontario, 1992); *"Prints" in The Earthly Paradise: Arts and Crafts by William Morris and his Circle from Canadian Collections*, catalogue (Toronto: Art Gallery of Ontario, 1993); "Original Prints: Unveiling the Mystery of Printmaking Techniques" (*Canadian Collector* 21(2) 1986); regular contributions to AGO publications; various other publications. EXHIBITIONS: curator, *"A Real Amateur" The Elizabeth E. Dales Collection of Nineteenth-century French Prints*, organized by the Art Gallery of Ontario & circulated provincially (1992); exhibition coord., *The Earthly Paradise: Arts and Crafts by William Morris and his Circle from Canadian Collections*, organized by the Art Gallery of Ontario & circulated nationally (1990-93). AFFIL: Print Council of America; William Morris Society of Canada; Friends of the Thomas Fisher Rare Book Library; Forest Ave. Public Sch. Parent-Teacher Association (Pres. 1994-96). MISC: numerous lectures on the history of prints. COMMENT: *"I am an art historian with a particular interest in the history of prints and drawings."*

Roach, Corry, R.N. ⊕

Independent Nurse Practitioner, C. ROACH AND ASSOCIATES, RR 4, Box 18, Site 2, Stony Plain, AB T7Z 1X4 (403) 963-9729. Born Fort Macleod, Alta. 1954. m. Gene. 3 ch. (1 dec.) Brandi, David, Lindsay. EDUC: Galt Sch. of Nursing, Lethbridge Municipal Hospital, R.N. 1975; certified practitioner, Neurolinguistic programming 1993; studied drawing interpretation with Elisabeth Kubler-Ross M.D. & Gregg Furth Ph.D., 1983-93. **CAREER:** Nurse, various institutions, 1975-87; private practice, specializing in Therapeutic Art Methods, 1987 to date. **SELECTED PUBLICATIONS:** "Coping When a Child Dies: A Personal Perspective" (*Victim's Advocate* 1984). **AFFIL:** Alberta Association of Registered Nurses; Canadian Association of Nurses in Independent Practice; Alberta Association of Nurses in Independent Practice; Bereavement Society of Alberta (Founder 1985); Compassionate Friends, Edmonton Chapter (Chapter Leader 1985-90, 1992-93). **HONS:** C. Dianne Davidson Memorial Award for mental health nursing. **INTERESTS:** kids; music; gardening; spiritual growth; personal growth; animals; learning new things; volunteering for bereaved parents & foster parents. **MISC:** Registered Nurse, Alberta; workshops & lectures to hospital staff, teachers, psychologists & physicians; developed unique method of therapy, which involves Therapeutic Art Methods, Jungian & Senoi Indian Dreamwork, Neurolinguistic programming, Therapeutic Touch & analysis of fairy tales & their use in psychodrama. **COMMENT:** *"I am a wife, mother, nurse, adoptive mother, birthmother, bereaved mother, owner of my own successful practice, which involves a method of therapy I've personally pioneered, which offers hope and resolution to anyone willing to accept responsibility for the unfinished business in their lives."*

Roback, Barbara, B.A.,M.A.,Ph.D., M.D. ■ ⊕
Family Physician, JAMES BAY COMMUNITY PROJECT, Victoria, BC (250) 388-6811, FAX 380-0244. Born Montreal 1950. m. Marc Fagen. 2 ch. **EDUC:** McGill Univ., B.A.(Psych.) 1971; Ontario Institute for Studies in Education, Univ. of Toronto, M.A.(Applied Psych.) 1975, Ph.D.(Applied Psych.) 1979; McMaster Univ., M.D. 1987. **CAREER:** Psychometrist, York Borough Child Guidance Clinic, Ont., 1976; Sch. Psychologist, Durham Bd. of Educ., Ont., 1977-80; Psychologist, Thistletown Regional Centre, Ont., 1980-82; Mgr, Research, Evaluation & Professional Educ. Div., 1982-84; Resident, Family Medicine, St. Mary's Hospital, Ont., 1990-92; Asst. Physician, Montreal General Hospital, 1992-94; Physician, Centre local de services communautive, N.D.G./MIL, Montreal, 1992-96. **SELECTED PUBLICATIONS:** "Children's Stimulus Appraisal Questionnaire," with Solveiga Meizitis (1976); "Depressive Symptoms in Children" (*Journal of Consulting and Clinical Psychology* 45(5) 1977); "Validation of a Self-Report Battery for Assessing Depression in Children and Adolescents," with Meizitis, Butler & Friedman in *Creating Alternatives to Depression in Our Schools*, Solveiga Meizitis, ed. (Toronto: Hogrefe and Huber, 1992); "Inconceivable," short story (*Family Medicine Newsletter*); various other publications. **AFFIL:** Academy of Hospice Physicians; Ontario Coll. of Physicians; Canadian Society of Palliative Care Physicians. **HONS:** Ont. Grad. Scholarship, 1975; Canada Council Fellowship, 1975-77; Medical Research Council Grant, 1985; Montreal General Hospital Award, 1993. **INTERESTS:** reading; sports; movies. **MISC:** grant recipient; various conference papers. **COMMENT:** *"I like challenges that take me beyond my comfort zone–beginning a second career in a new field or travelling in the Third World. But being a parent is by far the biggest challenge!"*

Roberge, Hélène
President and Director-General, LES PRODUCTIONS HÉLENE ROBERGE E.N.R., 1814 Sherbrooke St. W., Montreal, QC H3H 1E4 (514) 937-3310, FAX 937-3350. Born St. Georges, Que. 1932. **CAREER:** TV Prod. & Dir., CRCM-TV, Channel 6, Quebec City, 1954-60; TV Prod. & Dir., Société Radio-Canada Montréal, 1960-86; Dir. of Drama Dept., 1986-90; Dir. of Int'l Rel'ns, Société Radio-Canada, 1990-91; Dev. Prod., Coscient Inc., 1991-94; Pres. & Dir.-Gen., Les Productions Hélène Roberge, 1994 to date. **AFFIL:** Cinemathèque Québécoise (Bd. of Dir.); Academie du cinéma et de la télévision. **HONS:** Award, Children's Television Workshop, 1970. **INTERESTS:** TV; cinema; human rel'ns; anthropology; history. **COMMENT:** *"Pioneer of French-speaking television; still interested in my trade. I wish to take advantage of new technical developments to create new TV programs."*

Roberson, Gail, M.R.A. ■■
Executive Director, THE ALBERTA ASSOCIATION OF REHABILITATION CENTRES (umbrella association for organizations serving persons with disabilities). Born UK. d. 2 ch. Leishan, Jarett. **EDUC:** Univ. of Calgary, B.A.(Psych.) 1972, Educ. Certificate 1975; Canadian Securities Course 1974; Univ. of San Francisco, McLaren Sch. of Business, Master of Rehab. Admin. Certificate 1994. **CAREER:** Substitute Teacher, Calgary Public Sch. system, 1975-76; Counsellor, Calgary Women's Emergency Shelter, 1977-78; Dir. of Programs, Calgary Mental Health Association, 1978-84; Alberta Association of Rehabilitation Centres, 1984 to date. **AFFIL:** American Association on Mental Retardation (Alta. Bd.); Calgary Sexual Assault Centre (training volunteers 1975-84); Canadian Mental Health Association (training volunteers

1975-84; taught course, "As Parents Grow Older," through CMHA at Univ. of Calgary). INTERESTS: human rights particularly as they relate to women & persons with disabilities; sociology. MISC: as Exec. Dir. of AARC, makes regular presentations to students in Rehab. Practitioner courses, Grant MacEwan Coll., & at AARC conferences; has twice presented at AAMR conferences; presents at Caucus Committee meetings of Alta. Legislature; numerous other presentations; has participated in several collaborative curriculum dev. processes, Univ. of Calgary, Univ. of San Francisco, Alberta Vocational Coll., Grant MacEwan Coll., & Univ. of Alberta. COMMENT: *"I am a parent of 2 wonderful adult children. I am fortunate to work in the field of community rehabilitation, which is leading the way in providing supports to people with disabilities with strong ethics, values and professional skills."*

Robert, Hélène, M.N.A. ✦

Députée de Deux-Montagnes, Adjointe parlementaire et Secrétaire régionale des Laurentides, ASSEMBLÉE NATIONALE. Born Ste.-Scholastique, Que. 1945. EDUC: Baccalauréat (Pédagogie) 1965. CAREER: Enseignante, Commission des Écoles catholiques de Montréal, 1965-66; Enseignante, Commission scolaire Papineau, 1966-67; Enseignante, Séminaire Saint-Sacrement, 1967-68; Enseignante, Commission scolaire Les Écores, 1969-84, 1988-94; Productrice agricole en pomiculture, 1979-88; Députée (Deux-Montagnes), Assemblée Nationale, Prov. du Qué., 1994; Déléguée régionale des Laurentides et Adjointe parlementaire du premier-Ministre, 1994-96; Comité Spécial d'Initiative et d'Action sur le Grand Montréal; Adjointe parlementaire et Sec. régionale des Laurentides, 1996 à ce date; Commission de l'Assemblée Nationale sur l'Éduc. AFFIL: Parti Québécois de Deux-Montagnes (VP de l'executif 1988-89; Prés. 1989-93); Comité du "NON" (Prés., Deux-Montagnes 1992; Comité Provincial Provisoire des Femmes en Agriculture (Prés. 1986-87); Syndicat des Agricultrices, Outaouais-Laurentides (Prés. fondatrice 1985-87); Sommet socio-économique des Laurentides (Comité d'orientation); Fédération canadienne de l'agriculture (Administratrice 1986-87); Fédération régionale de l'UPA des Laurentides (Prés. du comité de crédit 1985). MISC: participante à un projet d'entraide et de solidarité entre agricultrices et agriculteurs du Qué., Sénégal et Burkina Faso, 1985-87; Rép. de secteur pour les enseignants et les enseignants de la commission scolaire Les Écores, 1977-78; Prés. du conseil d'administration de la polyvalente Georges-Vanier, 1990-92.

Robert, Lucie, B.A.,M.A.,Ph.D. ⊛

Professor, Departement d'Études Littéraires, UNIVERSITÉ DU QUÉBEC À MONTRÉAL, Box 8888, Stn Centre-Ville, Montreal, QC H3C 3P8 (514) 987-4296, FAX 987-8218, EMAIL robert.lucie@uqam.ca. Born Jonquière, Que. 1954. 1 ch. Jérémie. EDUC: CEGEP de Hull, D.E.C.(Lettres) 1973; Laval Univ., B.A.(Que. Lit.) 1976, M.A.(Que. Lit.) 1981, Ph.D.(Que. Lit.) 1987. CAREER: Research Assoc., *Dictionnaire des oeuvres littéraires du Québec*, Univ. Laval, 1978-86; Prof., Dept. d'Études Littéraires, Univ. du Québec à Montréal, 1986 to date. SELECTED PUBLICATIONS: *L'Institution du littéraire au Québec* (Québec: les Presses de l'univ. Laval, 1989); *Le Manuel d'histoire de la littérature canadienne-française de Mgr Camille Roy* (Québec: Institut québécois de recherche sur la culture, 1982); *La Vie littéraire au Québec (1763-1914)*, with Maurice Lemaire *et al*, multi-volume (Sainte-Foy: les Presses de l'univ. Laval, 1991, 1992, 1996); "Quelques réflexions concernant les femmes et le théâtre au Québec" (*Revue d'histoire littéraire du Québec et du Canada français 5* 1985); "Le Livre et l'État" (*Voix et images 41* 1989); "Towards a History of Quebec Drama" (*Poetics Today* 12(4) 1991); "Monsieur Quesnel ou Le Bourgeois anglomane" (*Voix et images 59* 1995); various other publications. EDIT: Ed. Bd., *Voix et Images*, 1982-92; Ed., 1988-92; Ed. Council, 1992. AFFIL: Centre de Recherches en Littérature Québécoise, Univ. Laval (Affiliate); Association Québécoise pour l'Étude de l'Imprimé (Bd. of Dir. 1993-95); Société Québécoise de Recherches Théâtrales; Fédération Internationale de Recherches Théâtrales; Association for Canadian & Quebec Literature; Association Canadienne des Professeurs de Français. HONS: Prix Edmond-De-Nevers, 1980-81; Prix Raymond-Klibansky, Fédérations des études humaines du Canada, 1989-90, 1991-92. COMMENT: *"Specializes in Quebec literature, drama in French and literary theory, sociology, sociocriticism, feminist criticism."*

Roberts, Barbara Ann, B.A.,M.A., Ph.D. ⊛ ❋ ◗

Professor, Women's Studies, ATHABASCA UNIVERSITY, Athabasca, AB T0G 2R0 (403) 675-6250, FAX 675-6186, EMAIL barbarar@cs.athabascau.ca. Born Riverside, Calif. 1941. m. F. David Millar. 2 ch. Michael Paul Hoffman, David Sean Hoffman. EDUC: Simon Fraser Univ., B.A.(Hist.) 1972, M.A.(Hist.) 1976; Univ. of Ottawa, Ph.D.(Hist.) 1980. CAREER: Visiting Prof. of Ethnic Studies, Dept. of Hist., Univ. of Winnipeg, 1980-82; Lecturer, InterUniversities North & Program Dev. Consultant to the VP, Academic, Univ. of Winnipeg, 1982-83; Asst. Prof., Dept. of Educ. Foundations, Univ. of Saskatchewan, 1983-84; Summer Lecturer, Dept. of Educ., Dalhousie Univ., 1986; Asst. Prof., Simone de Beauvoir Institute, Concordia Univ., 1987-88; Assoc. Prof., Women's Studies, Athabasca Univ., 1989-92; Prof., Women's Studies, 1992 to date. **SELECTED PUBLICATIONS:** *"A Reconstructed World." A Feminist Biography of Gertrude Richardson* (McGill-Queen's Univ. Press, 1996); *Strategies for the Year 2000: A Woman's Handbook* (Fernwood Press Network Basics Series, 1995–joint authorship); *A Decent Living: Women in the Winnipeg Garment Industry* (Toronto: New Hogtown Press, 1991–joint authorship); *Whence They Came: Deportation from Canada, 1900-35* (Ottawa: Univ. of Ottawa Press, 1988); various reports; numerous articles in refereed & non-refereed journals; numerous invited presentations. **AFFIL:** Canadian Research Institute for the Advancement of Women (Bd. of Dir.); Voice of Women. **INTERESTS:** gardening; reading; feminist mysteries & science fiction; walking.

Roberts, Eve, B.A.,LL.B., Q.C. ■ ⚖ ✊ ♡

Partner, Patterson Palmer Hunt Murphy, Box 610, St. John's, NF A1C 5L3 (709) 570-5510, FAX 726-0483. Born Chatham, Ont. 1939. m. Edward Roberts. 2 ch. **EDUC:** Univ. of Toronto, B.A.(English) 1960; Osgoode Hall Law Sch., LL.B. 1963. **BAR:** Alta.; Nfld. **CAREER:** Ptnr, Patterson Palmer Hunt Murphy; Legal Ed., *Western Weekly Reports*, 1978-81; Legal Ed., *Carswell's Practice Cases*, 1981-96; Chair, Newfoundland & Labrador Human Rights Commission, 1989-94. **AFFIL:** Memorial Univ. Botanical Gardens Inc. (Chair); YWCA of Canada (Dir.); Law Society of Alberta; Law Society of Newfoundland; Canadian Bar Association. **HONS:** Queen's Counsel, 1989. **INTERESTS:** reading; painting.

Robertson, The Hon. Brenda Mary, B.Sc., Ph.D. 🍁 👍

Senator, The Senate of Canada, 140 Wellington St., Ste. 401, Ottawa, ON K1A 0A4 (613) 998-5585, FAX 998-0916. Born Sussex, N.B. 1929. m. Wilmont Waldon Robertson. 3 ch. **EDUC:** Mount Allison Univ., B.Sc.(Home Econ.) 1950. **CAREER:** Home Econ., Prov. of N.B., 1950-52; M.L.A. (Riverview), Gov't of N.B., 1967-84; Min. of Social Svcs & Youth, 1971-74; Min. of Health, & Chair, Social Policy, 1976-82; Min. of Social Program Reform, & Chair, Treasury Bd., 1982-84; appointed to the Senate, Dec. 1984; former Deputy Chair, Senate Standing Committee on Social Affairs, Sci. & Technology; Chair, Senate Standing Committee on Standing Rules & Orders; mbr., Senate Standing Committee on Fisheries. **SELECTED PUBLICATIONS:** *Chère Sénateur*, co-author Hon. Solange Chaput-Rolland (1992). **DIRECTOR:** Imperial Life Assurance Company of Canada. **AFFIL:** Univ. de Moncton (Chair, Endowment Committee, Centre for Aging); Canada-Europe Parliamentary Association. **HONS:** Doctorate of Humane Letters (Hon.), Mount Saint Vincent Univ., 1974; Doctorate of Social Sciences (Hon.), Univ. de Moncton, 1983. **MISC:** 1st woman to be elected to the N.B. Legislature.

Robertson, Catherine, B.A.,B.J. $

President, Robertson Rozenhart Inc., 1075 W. Georgia St., Ste. 270, Vancouver, BC V6E 3C9 (604) 664-7638, FAX 688-3105. Born Canada. **EDUC:** Univ. of Saskatchewan, B.A.(Pol. Sci./English) 1967; Carleton Univ., Bachelor of Journalism 1968. **CAREER:** Chrm, Vancouver City Savings Credit Union; Pres., Robertson Rozenhart Inc.; Pres., Core Group Publishers Inc.; Pres., Robertson Telecom Inc. **DIRECTOR:** Core Group Publishers Inc.; Robertson Rozenhart Inc.; Robertson Telecom Inc. **AFFIL:** Canadian Public Relations Society (Past Dir.); Consultants' Institute (Past Chair); Vancouver Art Gallery (Trustee).

Robertson, Donna Lee, B.A.,B.L.S., M.L.S.,LL.B. ■ ⚖

Principal, Robertson & Co., Barristers and Solicitors, Trade Mark Agents, 1177 W. Hastings St., Ste. 2350, Vancouver, BC V6E 2K3 (604) 688-7151, FAX 685-7832, EMAIL dlr-law@direct.ca. Born Edmonton 1942. m. Ian Donald Robertson. 6 ch. **EDUC:** Univ. of Alberta, B.A.(English) 1963; Univ. of British Columbia, B.L.S. 1964, M.L.S. 1982, LL.B. 1982. **BAR:** B.C., 1983. **CAREER:** Gen. Cnsl, Ledcor Industries Limited, 1983-89; Ptnr, Lang Michener Lawrence and Shaw, 1989-95. **DIRECTOR:** D.L.R. Capital Corporation; NST Network Services Inc.; NS Telecom Group Inc.; Seacor Environmental Engineering Inc. **AFFIL:** Kappa Alpha Theta; Canadian Bar Association (Bus. Law Section); Canada Korea Business Association; Hollyburn Country Club; Phoenix Investment Club; Vancouver Bar Association; B.C. Chamber of Commerce (Gen. Cnsl 1993-94). **HONS:** Univ. Honours Prize, Univ. of Alberta, 1962. **INTERESTS:** skiing; golf; reading; bridge; piano. **COMMENT:** *"In private practice since 1989, I have practised as a corporate commercial solicitor advising on corporate organizations, acquisitions and mergers, corporate transfers and intellectual property issues. My work has involved extensive travel to Korea, Taiwan, and Hong Kong, where I* *have advised foreign clients on relocating to Canada and doing business in Canada."*

Robertson, Françoise, B.Comm., D.E.C. ■ ♨ ⊗

Actor. c/o Glenn Talent Management, 3981 St. Laurent Blvd., Ste. 730, Montreal, QC H2W 1Y5 (514) 499-3485, FAX 499-3491, c/o Bonnie Owens (US Mgr) (213) 654-1443. Born London, UK. s. EDUC: Vanier Coll., D.E.C.(Health Sciences); Concordia Univ., B.Comm.(Bus. & Mktg). CAREER: actor in TV, film & theatre. SELECTED CREDITS: Lead, *Primal Scream* (Showtime movie); Regular, *Jasmine* (French series), TVA; Guest, *High Incident* (series), ABC; Lead, *The Great Lover* (theatre), The MET Theatre, L.A. AFFIL: ACTRA (Council Mbr., Montreal Branch 1992-94); UDA; SAG. INTERESTS: reading; theatre; educ. programs; classical guitar. MISC: founded & was Pres. of the Vanier Coll. Drama Club; fluent in English, French & Spanish. COMMENT: *"British-born and Montreal-raised, Françoise Robertson gave up the pursuit of a medical career for that of an actor. Although she works extensively in Canada, she currently makes her home in Los Angeles, where she has met with continued success."*

Robertson, Heather, B.A.,M.A. ■ ▯

Writer. 12860 Dufferin St., King City, ON L7B 1K5. Born Winnipeg 1942. m. Andrew Marshall. 1 ch. Aaron. EDUC: University of Manitoba, B.A.(English) 1963; Columbia University, M.A.(English Lit.) 1964; Woodrow Wilson fellow 1963-64. CAREER: writer since 1964; reporter, *Winnipeg Tribune*, 1964-66; radio prod. and television story ed., public affairs, CBC Winnipeg, 1968-71; television critic and columnist, *Maclean's* magazine, 1971-75; columnist, *Canadian Forum*, 1990-92; feature writer for *Saturday Night, Toronto Life, Equinox* & other Cdn. magazines; book reviewer for *The Globe and Mail, The Toronto Star*. SELECTED PUBLICATIONS: *Reservations Are for Indians*, non-fiction (Lorimer, 1970); *Grass Roots*, non-fiction (Lorimer, 1973); *Salt of the Earth*, non-fiction (Lorimer, 1974); *A Terrible Beauty, the Art of Canada at War*, non-fiction (Lorimer, 1977); *The Flying Bandit*, non-fiction (Lorimer, 1981); *Willie, A Romance*, fiction (Lorimer, 1983); ed., *A Gentleman Adventurer, The Arctic Diaries of Richard Bonnycastle* (Lester, Orpen Dennys, 1984); ed., *I Fought Riel* by Major Charles Boulton (Lorimer, 1985); *Lily, A Rhapsody in Red*, fiction (Lorimer, 1986); *Igor, A Novel of Intrigue*, fiction (Lorimer, 1989); *More Than a Rose, Prime Ministers, Wives and Other Women*, non-fiction (Seal, 1991); *On the Hill, A People's Guide to Canada's Parliament*, non-fiction (McClelland & Stewart, 1992); *Driving Force: The McLaughlin Family and the Age of the Car*, non-fiction (McClelland & Stewart, 1995); various anthologies. AFFIL: ACTRA; Writers' Union of Canada. HONS: Fiction Prize, Canadian Authors' Association, 1984; Best First Novel, *Books in Canada*, 1983; Talking Book of the Year, CNIB, 1984; Second Prize, Best Book of the Year, fiction, Periodical Distributors of Canada, 1984; Second Prize, Best Book of the Year, non-fiction, Periodical Marketers of Canada, 1992; National Business Book Award, 1995. MISC: writer-in-residence, North York Public Library, June-Dec. 1987; Chair, non-fiction jury, Governor General's Literary Award, 1994.

Robertson, Heather-Jane, H.-j., B.A., M.Sc.Ed. ⊲ 📚 ⊻

Director, Professional Development Services, CANADIAN TEACHERS' FEDERATION (CTF)/ FÉDÉRATION CANADIENNE DES ENSEIGNANTES ET DES ENSEIGNANTS (FCE), 110 Argyle St., Ottawa, ON K2P 1B4 (613) 232-1505, FAX 232-1886. Born 1949. m. Dwight Renneberg. 2 ch. EDUC: Univ. of Saskatchewan, B.A. 1969; Univ. of Alberta, Post-Grad. Diploma in Educ. 1970; Univ. of Houston, M.Sc.Ed.(Future Studies) 1984. CAREER: classroom teacher, Saskatoon Public Bd. of Educ., 1970-76; Admin. Staff, Saskatchewan Teachers' Federation, 1976-85; Dir., Professional Dev. Svcs, Canadian Teachers' Federation, 1985 to date; Pres., Op-Ed Services Inc. SELECTED CREDITS: Exec. Prod., *Brother of Mine: Children and the Culture of Violence* (feature documentary), 1993; Proj. Dir., *Meeting the Needs of Immigrant and Refugee Students* (video-based teacher training proj.), 1995. SELECTED PUBLICATIONS: *Class Warfare: The Assault on Canada's Schools*, co-author Maude Barlow (Toronto: Key Porter, 1994); author of a number of articles, chapters & essays; author of a number of CTF publications. AFFIL: Canadian Education Association; Canadian Association for the Study of Educational Administration; Canadian Research Institute for the Advancement of Women; Canadian Congress for Learning Opportunities for Women; Association for Supervision & Curriculum Development; National Staff Development Council; Canadian Centre for Policy Alternatives (Exec. Mbr.); Coalition on the Rights of the Child; Coalition for Responsible Television (Exec. Mbr.); Campaign 2000 (child poverty); YWCA Task Force on Family Violence; CAVAW (Chair, Proj. on Youth Violence); National Network on Child Abuse; National Organization Proj. on Immigrant & Refugee Students (Chair); Canadian Association for School Health. **HONS:** nominated, the Montador Award for best Cdn nonfiction book of 1994. **MISC:** Proj. Dir., "The A Cappella Project," a multi-phase research, writing & action-oriented proj. on the quality of life of adolescent women, 1990-95; *Class Warfare: The Assault on Canada's Schools* now in its 6th printing; frequent invited expert on diverse educ. & public-policy topics.

Robertson, Linda, B.A.,LL.B.,LL.M. ⚖
Corporate Secretary and General Counsel, INSURANCE CORPORATION OF BRITISH COLUMBIA, Corporate Law Dept., 151 W. Esplanade, North Vancouver, BC V7M 3H9 (604) 661-6280, FAX 661-2243. Born Vancouver 1952. m. Gordon Lee. 2 ch. **EDUC:** Univ. of British Columbia, B.A.(Hist.), LL.B. 1978; London Sch. of Economics, LL.M. 1983. **BAR:** B.C., 1980. **CAREER:** Law Clerk, B.C. Supreme Court, 1978-79; Solicitor, Insurance Corporation of British Columbia, 1980-82, 1985-87; Corp. Fin., Wood Gundy, London, UK, 1984; Contractor, Ombudsman's Office, B.C., 1985; Corp. Solicitor, Insurance Corporation of British Columbia, 1987-89; Gen. Cnsl, 1990-93; Corp. Sec. & Gen. Cnsl, 1993 to date. **AFFIL:** Law Society of B.C. (Gender Bias Committee Sub-Committee on Alternate Work Policies 1992); Canadian Bar Association; West Coast Legal Education & Action Fund; Canadian Corporate Counsel Association (Co-Chair, Spring Conference 1995). **INTERESTS:** travel; reading; ballet.

Robertson, Patricia Mary (née Howison), B.A.,M.C.S.,M.A.,Ph.D. 📖 ✎
Registrar, UNIVERSITY OF KING'S COLLEGE, Halifax, NS B3H 2A1 (902) 422-1271, FAX 423-3357. Born Winnipeg 1958. m. Neil Graham Robertson. **EDUC:** Univ. of Winnipeg, B.A. (English Lit.) 1978; Regent Coll., Univ. of British Columbia, M.C.S.(Biblical Lit.) 1980; Univ. of Ottawa, M.A.(English Lit.) 1981, Ph.D.(English Lit.) 1985. **CAREER:** Asst. Prof., Dept. of English, Dalhousie Univ./Univ. of King's Coll., 1985-86; Teaching Fellow, Univ. of King's Coll., 1986-87; Registrar, 1987 to date. **SELECTED PUBLICATIONS:** "Memory and Will: Selective Amnesia in Paradise Lost" (*University of Toronto Quarterly* Summer 1987); "John Donne's Sermons and the Rhetoric of Prophecy" (*English Studies in Canada* June 1989); "'The Baseless Fabric of this Vision': Expectation, Illusion, and Dream in Conrad's Victory" (*Conradiana* 3 1990). **AFFIL:** Association of Registrars, Universities & Colleges of Canada; Atlantic Association of Registrars & Admission Officers; Anglican

Church of Canada; St. Paul's Home (Bd. of Mgmt). **HONS:** Univ. medals, Univ. of Winnipeg, Regent Coll.; Ont. Grad. Scholarship, 1981-85. **INTERESTS:** music (voice); creative writing; literary interpretation of the Bible.

Robichaud, Dani Ann, LL.B.,LL.L. ■ ⚖ ⊙
Barrister & Solicitor. 28 Nicolet St., Hull, QC J9A 1J3 (819) 770-9503, FAX 771-8996. Born Ottawa **EDUC:** Univ. of Ottawa, 4 yrs. completed, B.Comm.(Mktg. & Int'l Bus.), LL.B., LL.L. **BAR:** Que., 1994. **SELECTED PUBLICATIONS:** "Lost Earning Capacity under the Divorce Act, Fact or Fiction?" (May, 1994). **AFFIL:** National Association of Women and the Law (Nat'l Steering Committee, 1994-96); Outaouais Chapter, Canadian Cystic Fibrosis Association. **COMMENT:** *"Sole legal practitioner dedicated to the practice of law and servicing her clientele in a professional and courteous manner. Enjoys spending her spare time acting in various capacities in the organizations with which she is affiliated."*

Robillard, The Hon. Lucienne, MP,B.A., M.A.,M.B.A. ✿
Minister of Citizenship and Immigration and Member of Parliament (St. Henri-Westmount), GOVERNMENT OF CANADA, House of Commons, Ottawa, ON K1A 0A6. Born Montreal. **EDUC:** Coll. Basile-Moreau, B.A. 1965; Univ. de Montreal, M.A.(Social Sci.) 1967; École des hautes études commerciales, Diploma in Admin. 1983, M.B.A. 1986. **CAREER:** Social Worker & Clinical Practitioner, Maisonneuve-Rosemont Hospital; Sr. Admin., Centre de services sociaux Richelieu; appointed Public Curator of Que., 1986-89; elected M.N.A. (Chambly), Gov't of Que., 1989; Min. of Cultural Affairs, 1989-90; Min. of Higher Educ. & Science, 1990-93; Min. of Educ., 1992-93; Min. of Educ. & Science, 1993-94; Min. of Health & Social Sciences, 1994; elected MP (St. Henri-Westmount), Gov't of Canada, 1995; Min. of Labour & Min. Responsible for the fed. campaign in the Que. Referendum, 1995. **AFFIL:** Corporation professionnelle des travailleurs sociaux du Québec; Association des practiciens de service social en milieu de santé du Québec (Pres. 1984-86); Conseil régionale de la Montérégie (Commission administrative des services de santé mentale 1983-86). **MISC:** consulting expert from the Mental Health Project of the Rochon Commission, 1986; worked as a youth leader on a kibbutz in Israel, 1969-72; in her term of office as Public Curator of Que., reformed the Act regarding the Public Curator by updating & humanizing this legislation to enable it to better meet the needs of the clients & their next of kin; was on the Ed. Committee

for the book, *Le travail social et la santé au Québec* (Behaviora, 1985).

Robillard-Frayne, Hélène, B.A.,B.Sc., M.Sc. ■■ 📺 $ ☝

Director of Radio Programming and Schedule Planning, SOCIÉTÉ RADIO-CANADA (broadcasting), 1400 René-Lévesque Blvd. E., 12th Fl., Montreal, QC H2L 2M2 (514) 597-4785, FAX 597-4794, EMAIL hrfrayne@montreal.src.ca. Born Quebec City 1946. m. Anthony Frayne. 1 ch. Isabelle. **EDUC:** Coll. Jésus-Marie, B.ès arts 1965; Laval Univ., B.Sc.(Pol. Sci.) 1968; Univ. of Montreal, M.Sc.(Pol. Sci.) 1976. **CAREER:** Trainee Research Exec., National Opinion Polls, London, England, 1969-70; Proj. Dir., Contemporary Research Centre Ltd., Montreal, 1970-72; Research Officer, Research Dept., Radio-Canada, 1973-80; Head, Research Dept., 1981-84; Asst. to Gen. Mgr of Radio Programming, 1984-87; Dir. of Radio Programming & Broadcasting, 1987-93 (responsible for int'l rel'ns, 1991 to date); Dir. of Radio Programming & Schedule Planning, 1993 to date. **AFFIL:** Parents' Association of Pensionnat du Saint-Nom-de-Marie, Outremont (Montreal) (Pres. 1996-97). **INTERESTS:** travel; photography; sports. **COMMENT:** *"I am a graduate in Political Science from the University of Montreal (1976). I have been involved in public opinion research, market research and audience research for 14 years both in private firms, in London, UK, and in Montreal, and then in the Research Department at Radio-Canada, where I was the Head from 1981 to 1984. I switched to radio programming in 1985 and have had since then various responsibilities concerning scheduling. Since 1991, I have also been responsible for the International Relations of Radio-Canada. Since I was a teenager I have often been the first woman president of different associations and the first woman to hold specific job positions."*

Robin, Shula ■■ ✪ 📜

Poet. 4383 Bathurst St., Apt. 1012, Toronto, ON M3H 3P8. Born Poland 1920. **EDUC:** Agricultural Coll., 1938; Teachers' Seminary, Home Econ. 1948. **CAREER:** Teacher, served during the war, A.T.S., 1941-45. **SELECTED PUBLICATIONS:** *Sunshine From Within* (poetry, 1996); *I Know Who I Am* (poetry, 1996). **DIRECTOR:** Robin's Artists Management. **AFFIL:** League of Canadian Poets; Canadian Friends of Ezrath Nashim-Herzog Hospital, Jerusalem (former Coord.); Mizrachi Women's Organization of Canada (former Dir. & Lecturer). **HONS:** poem, "To The German Tourist's Daughter" will be published in the anthology for permanent display at the Holocaust Museum in Washington. **INTERESTS:** classical music; literature; above all, people. **COMMENT:** *"Over the years, I was employed in a number of professions: home economics teacher, lecturer, fund raiser, impresario, and poet. Some poems were set to music and performed at a gala concert."*

Robinson, Ann Elisabeth, B.Pharm.,Ph.D., F.R.S.C.(UK),F.C.I.C.(UK & Ont.) ⊕ ⚛ 🎓

Consultant. 80 Quebec Ave., Ste. 601, Toronto, ON M6P 4B7 (416) 762-6488, FAX 762-6488. Born Ilford, Essex, UK 1933. w. **EDUC:** Univ. of London, B.Pharm. 1955, Ph.D. 1958. **CAREER:** Asst. Lecturer, Pharmaceutical Chem., Chelsea Coll., Univ. of London, 1957-59; Lecturer, 1959-64; Lecturer, Forensic Medicine, London Hospital Medical Coll., 1964-68; Sr. Lecturer, 1968-77; various consulting assignments in forensic medicine & toxicology, UK & abroad, 1965-77; Hon. Toxicologist, London Hospital, 1977; Chief, Occupational Health Lab. & Consultant in Toxicology, Ont. Ministry of Labour, 1978-80; Adjunct Prof., Univ. of Toronto, 1979-95; Asst. Deputy Min., Occupational Health & Safety Div., Ont. Ministry of Labour, 1980-87; Gov., Canadian Centre for Occupational Health & Safety, 1981-88; Sci. Policy Advisor, Occupational & Environmental Health & Safety, Ont. Ministry of Labour, 1987-91; Advisor, World Health Organization's Int'l Programme on Chemical Safety, 1991-93; mbr., Institute for Risk Research, Univ. of Waterloo, 1991 to date. **SELECTED PUBLICATIONS:** *Gradwohl's Legal Medicine* 3rd edition (1976); *Substance Abuse in the Workplace*, co-author (1992); numerous other scientific publications. **AFFIL:** Toronto Board of Health (Citizen Rep.); Soroptimist Foundation of Canada (Dir.); many learned societies in Canada, UK & US; Soroptimist International of Toronto.

Robinson, Emma ■■ ⚾

Olympic Athlete. c/o Canadian Olympic Association. Born Montreal 1971. **EDUC:** currently working on Ph.D. in Medical Genetics. **SPORTS CAREER:** mbr., Cdn Nat'l Rowing Team, 1993 to date. Olympic Games: Silver, 8+, 1996. Olympic trials: 1st, 2-, 1995. World championships: 6th, 8+, 1995; 7th, 8+, & 8th, 4-, 1994; 3rd, 4-, 1993. Int'l regattas: 1st, 4-, & 1st, 8+ (Ont.), 1994. World University Games: 1st, 8+, & 2nd, 4-, 1993. Canadian championships: 2nd, 2-, & 2nd, 8+, 1992. US championships: 2nd, 8+, 1995; 1st, 8+, & 1st, 2-, 1994. **HONS:** Canada Scholar, 1990-94; Petro-Canada Olympic Torch Scholarship, 1995. **INTERESTS:** road hockey; in-line skating; reading; cross-country skiing.

Robinson, Geraldine Gail Erlick, M.D.,
F.R.C.P.(C),Dip.Psych. ⊕ ⌘
Director, Program in Women's Mental Health,
General Division, Department of Psychiatry,
THE TORONTO HOSPITAL, 200 Elizabeth St.,
8EN - 231, Toronto, ON M5G 2C4 (416) 340-
3048, FAX 340-4198. Professor of Psychiatry
and Professor of Obstetrics and Gynaecology,
UNIVERSITY OF TORONTO. Born Toronto 1943.
sep. J. Michael Robinson. 2 ch. Alexandra
Catherine, Laura Elizabeth. EDUC: Univ. of
Toronto, M.D. 1966, Dip.Psych. 1970;
C.R.P.C.(C), Psychiatry 1971; F.R.C.P.(C), Psy-
chiatry 1972. CAREER: Rotating Internship,
Mount Sinai Hospital, Toronto, 1966-67; Resi-
dent, Douglas Hospital, Verdun, Que., 1967-
68; Resident, Clarke Institute of Psychiatry,
Toronto, 1968; Resident, Sunnybrook Hospi-
tal, Toronto, 1969; Resident, Toronto General
Hospital, 1969-70; Chief Resident in Psychia-
try, Toronto General Hospital, 1970-71; Staff
Psychiatrist, Toronto General Hospital (now
The Toronto Hospital), 1971 to date; Coord.,
Community Psychiatry, 1971-72; Dir., Ambu-
latory Care & Community Svcs, Dept. of Psy-
chiatry, 1972-78; Coord., Postgrad. Educ.,
Dept. of Psychiatry, 1976-85; Staff Psychiatrist,
Hospital for Sick Children, Toronto, 1977-82;
Consultant in Psychiatry, Women's College
Hospital, Toronto, 1977 to date; Dir.,
Women's Clinic, Dept. of Psychiatry, Toronto
General Hospital, 1982-90; Acting Dir., Ambu-
latory Care, Dept. of Psychiatry, 1985-86; Con-
sultant in Psychiatry, St. Michael's Hospital,
Toronto, 1987 to date; Consultant in Psychia-
try, Toronto Western Hospital, 1989 to date;
cross-appt., Dept. of Obstetrics & Gynaecol-
ogy, Toronto Hospital; Dir., Program in
Women's Mental Health, Dept. of Psychiatry,
The Toronto Hospital, 1990 to date. ACA-
DEMIC CAREER: Sr. Fellow, Psychiatry, Univ.
of Toronto, 1971-72; Lecturer, 1972-74; Asst.
Prof., 1974-82; Assoc. Prof., 1982-94; Assoc.
Prof., Obstetrics & Gynaecology, 1989-94; Co-
Dir., Program in Women's Mental Health,
Dept. of Psychiatry, Univ. of Toronto, 1990 to
date; Prof. of Psychiatry & Obstetrics &
Gynaecology, 1994 to date. SELECTED PUBLI-
CATIONS: "Management of a Rape Victim"
(*Canadian Medical Association Journal* 115
1976); "Autonomy in Mothers with Careers"
(*Canadian Psychiatric Association Journal* 27
1982); "Infertility by Choice or Nature," with
D.E. Stewart (*Canadian Journal of Psychiatry*
34 1989); "Fatal Attraction: The Ethical and
Clinical Dilemma of Patient-Therapist Sex,"
with M.L. Carr (*Canadian Journal of Psychiatry* 35(2) 1990); "Place of Psychoactive Drugs
in the Treatment of Premenstrual Syndrome"
(*CNS Drugs* 2 1994); more than 150 publica-

tions in total. EDIT: Ed. Bd., *Treating the
Female Patient*, 1991-94. AFFIL: American
Coll. of Psychiatrists (Ed. Committee, *Psychiatry Update*); Ontario Medical Association;
Canadian Medical Association; Ontario Psychiatric Association; Canadian Psychiatric Associ-
ation; American Society for Psychosomatic
Obstetrics & Gynaecology; International Soci-
ety for Psychosomatic Obstetrics & Gynaecol-
ogy; Association of Women Psychiatrists;
American Psychiatric Association (Chair, Com-
mittee on Women); American Fertility Associa-
tion; Marcé Society; Australian Society for Psy-
chosomatic Obstetrics & Gynaecology (Hon.
Mbr.); Task Force on Physician-Patient Sexual
Misconduct, American Medical Association;
Metro Toronto Action Committee on Public
Violence Against Women & Children (Bd. of
Dir.; VP); Arts & Letters Club. HONS: Lt.
Governor's Award for Excellence in Math. &
Science, 1959; Gov. General's Award for Gen.
Proficiency, 1960; Ontario Mental Health
Foundation Fellowship, 1971-72, 1972-73;
Civilian Citation, Commissioner of Police of
Metropolitan Toronto, 1984; Women of Dis-
tinction Award, Health, YWCA, 1993. INTER-
ESTS: acting; singing; travel; skiing. MISC: con-
tributor, *It's Your Decision*, educ. film, Cana-
dian Cancer Society; *No Means No*, teaching
film, Task Force on Violence Against Women
& Children; *Violence: Psychiatric Problems,
Psychiatric Solutions*, video, American Psychiatric Association (1993); various other audio-
visual credits; co-founder, Toronto Rape Crisis
Centre, 1st such centre in Canada; expert
adviser regarding physician-patient sexual misconduct for Coll. of Physicians & Surgeons of
Ontario & of Saskatchewan, & various courts,
1990 to date; Bernstein Lecturer on Psychiatric
Aspects of Obstetrics & Gynaecology, Univ. of
Minnesota, 1992; numerous conference presentations; numerous invited lectures; frequently
"visiting professor"; recipient, various grants;
reviewer for various journals & granting agencies; listed in *Who's Who in Toronto* (1984) &
Canadian Who's Who (1995). COMMENT:
*"My emphasis has been the initiation and
development of educational, clinical and
research programs concerning women's mental
health, violence against women and physician-
patient misconduct."*

Robinson, J. Jill, B.A.,M.A.,M.F.A. ▯ ⊗
Editor-in-Chief, GRAIN MAGAZINE, Box 3092,
Saskatoon, SK S7K 3S9 (306) 244-2828, FAX
665-7867, EMAIL grain.mag@sk.sympatico.ca.
Born Langley, B.C. 1955. life partner. Steven
Ross Smith. 1 ch. EDUC: Univ. of Calgary,
B.A.(Lit.) 1982, M.A.(Lit.) 1985; Univ. of
Alaska, Fairbanks, M.F.A.(Creative Writing)

1990. CAREER: Instructor, Dept. of English, Univ. of Calgary, 1985-88, 1992-94; Book Reviewer, *Edmonton Journal*, 1993 to date; Ed., *Grain*, 1995 to date. SELECTED PUBLI-CATIONS: *Saltwater Trees*, short story collection (Vancouver: Arsenal Pulp Press, 1991); *Lovely in Her Bones*, short story collection (Vancouver: Arsenal Pulp Press, 1993); *Egg-plant Wife*, short story collection (Vancouver: Arsenal Pulp Press, 1995); stories published in *Event, NeWest Review, Dandelion, Canadian Fiction Magazine, Prism International*. AFFIL: Writers' Union of Canada (Judging Team, New Fiction Contest 1995); Alberta Writers' Guild; Saskatchewan Writers' Guild; Cancopy. HONS: winner, Short Story Contest, *Prism International*, 1989; co-winner, Nonfiction Contest, *Event*; Alberta Writers' Guild Prize for short story collection, 1991; shortlist, Alberta Writers' Guild Prize for short story collection, 1993. MISC: grant to attend Banff Centre Writing Program, 1987, 1994; various Canada Council grants.

Robinson, Sheila A., B.Sc.N.,M.A., Ph.D. ⊕ ☜
UNIVERSITY OF CALGARY, 2500 University Dr. N.W., BI 570, Calgary, AB T2N 1N4. Born Boston 1945. m. Brian W. Unger. 2 ch. EDUC: Boston Coll., B.Sc.N. 1966; Univ. of Calgary, M.A.(Int'l Dev.) 1979, Ph.D.(Community & Int'l Health) 1987. CLINICAL CAREER: Staff Nurse, Boston City Hospital, 1966-67; Community Health Nurse, Int'l Jesuit Volunteer, Jamaica, 1967-69; Asst. Head Nurse, Boston City Hospital, 1969-70; Coord., Rural Health Projects, Social Action Centre, Kingston, Jamaica, 1971-72; Staff Nurse, Calgary General Hospital, 1972-73; Health Consultant in private practice, 1988 to date; Coord., Nepal Health Dev. Proj., Div. of Int'l Dev., Univ. of Calgary, 1989 to date. ACADEMIC CAREER: Clinical Nursing Instructor, Boston Coll., 1969-70; Instructor, Allied Health Dept., Mount Royal Coll., Calgary, 1973-82; Lecturer & Coord., Pearson Fellowship Program, Community Health Sciences, Univ. of Calgary, 1982-83; Adjunct Asst. Prof., 1989 to date; Adjunct Assoc. Prof., Fac. of Nursing, 1989 to date. SELECTED PUBLICATIONS: "The Primary Health Care Experience in the Developing World: Lessons for Canada?" (*Canadian Family Physician* Jan. 1990); "The Relative Influence of the Community and the Health System on Performance of Community Health Workers," with D. Larsen (*Social Science and Medicine* 30(10) 1990); "Estimation of Maternal Mortality in Mid-Western Nepal: Use of the Sisterhood Estimator," with S. Beaton (*Journal of the Nepal Medical Association* Jan.-

Mar. 1993); "The Nepal Health Development Project: Fit and Framework for Institutional Partnerships," with S. Dugan & P. Cox (*International Journal of Organizational Analysis* Fall 1995); various other publications. AFFIL: Alberta Association of Registered Nurses; Canadian Nurses' Association; American Public Health Association, International Health Section; Canadian Public Health Association; Canadian Society for International Health (Bd. Mbr.; Pres./Chair 1991-94); Arusha International Development Education Centre (Bd Mbr. 1974-82; Chair 1976-77; Chair, Personnel Committee 1981-83); Commonwealth Society; National Council for International Health, US; Society for International Development (SID); Yoga Association of Alberta; C.G. Jung Society of Alberta. HONS: Alumni Award (Gen. Excellence), Boston Coll., 1966; Euryclea Award (Nurse of the Year), Boston Coll., 1966. INTERESTS: yoga; Buddhism; dance; Jungian psych. MISC: various grants; various conference presentations. COMMENT: *"Energy, enthusiasm, mild idealism, good synthesizer of ideas and experience. Program planning, management evaluation, teaching and research in innovative approaches to health and development in Asia and Latin America. Provided effective leadership in the Canadian Society for International Health, a national professional organization."*

Robinson, Virginia, B.Sc.,M.D.,C.C.F.P. ⊕ ☜
General Practitioner of Medicine. 250 Lawrence Ave. W., Ste. 216, Toronto, ON M5M 1B2 (416) 785-5001, FAX 785-6539. Born Toronto 1953. m. Gregor. 2 ch. Alexandra, Esmée. EDUC: McGill Univ., B.Sc.(Biol.) 1976; Univ. of Toronto, M.D. 1980, C.C.F.P. 1986. CAREER: active staff mbr., North York General Hospital; Asst. Prof., Univ. of Toronto, Dept. of Family Medicine; Gen. Practitioner. AFFIL: North York General Hospital (Gov.; Foundation Bd.). HONS: Award of Merit, Dalhousie Law Alumni, 1986. INTERESTS: skiing; tennis. COMMENT: *"I have an extremely busy family practice in North Toronto with a considerable commitment to teaching family practice residents. I enjoy doing part-time emergency medicine. I endeavour to balance this with my family, friends and sports, as well as fundraising for North York General Hospital."*

Robitaille, Evelyne, A.R.C.T. ⊛ ⊕ ⊗ ♦
President, ORGANIZATION OF CANADIAN SYMPHONY MUSICIANS, Quebec City, QC G1S 4V5 (418) 688-0801, FAX 688-3447. Born St. Boniface, Man. w. 2 ch. Geneviève, Michel. EDUC: Royal Conservatory of Music, A.R.C.T.(Violin/Viola) 1959; Conservatoire de

musique du Québec, Certificate (Viola) 1960. CAREER: Violinist, Winnipeg Symphony Orchestra; Violist, L'Orchestre symphoniue de Québec. SELECTED PUBLICATIONS: a few articles in music-related publications. AFFIL: Organization of Canadian Symphony Musicians (Pres.); Guild des musiciens du Québec (Bd., Local 406); Association of Canadian Orchestras (Bd.). INTERESTS: the arts; encouraging artists & frequenting museums. MISC: 1st woman to be elected to the bd. of an American Federation of Musicians' Local (119 Québec) in Canada. COMMENT: *"I do not know why I have been nominated. I am an ordinary citizen passionately defending the present and future of our profession. Although it is not an easy task, it has become my life's work in spite of myself."*

Robson, Ann Wilkinson, B.A.,M.A., Ph.D. 🐿 🎋
Professor, UNIVERSITY OF TORONTO, Victoria College, Toronto, ON M5S 1K7 (416) 585-4573, EMAIL arobson@epas.utoronto.ca. Born UK 1931. m. John Robson. 3 ch. EDUC: Univ. of Toronto, B.A.(Hist.) 1953, M.A.(Hist.) 1954; Univ. of London, UK, Ph.D.(Hist.) 1958. CAREER: Prof., Hist. Dept., Univ. of Toronto, 1968 to date. SELECTED PUBLICATIONS: *A Moralist In And Out of Parliament* with J.M. Robson & Bruce Kinzer; *Sexual Equality* ed. with J.M. Robson. AFFIL: Victorian Studies Association; British Studies Conference. INTERESTS: golf; children & grandchildren.

Rochester, Helen, B.A. ✏️ 🗄️
Restaurant Columnist, THE GAZETTE, Montreal, QC H2X 3R7 (514) 987-2633, FAX 987-2638. Born Corner Brook, Nfld. 1933. m. Ian D. Rochester. 2 ch. EDUC: St. Francis Xavier Univ., B.A.(Phil.) 1954; Univ. of British Columbia, B.A.(Soc.) 1955. CAREER: Reporter, *Vancouver Sun*; Reporter & Columnist, *Montreal Star*; Columnist, *The Gazette*. SELECTED PUBLICATIONS: *Guide to Dining Out in Montreal* (1969-71, 1973); *Helen Rochester's 1995 Guide to Montreal Restaurants* (1995); articles in various magazines. COMMENT: *"I have been a journalist all my life, and covered just about every beat there is, plus training young cubs at the Star. In my younger years, I ran for Alderman in Westmount (unsuccessfully, but fun) and for 5 years ran, with my husband, a therapy group for parents of troubled adolescents at Douglas Hospital."*

Rock, Gail Ann, B.Sc.,Ph.D.,M.D., FRCPC ■ ⊕ 🐿️
Associate Professor of Pathology, UNIVERSITY OF OTTAWA, Ottawa, ON K1N 6N5 (613) 741-0174, FAX 749-6121. Chief of Hematology and Transfusion Medicine, OTTAWA CIVIC HOSPITAL. 2 ch. Jennifer, Christine. EDUC: St. Patrick's Coll., Ottawa, B.Sc. 1962; Univ. of Ottawa, Ph.D.(Biochem.) 1966, M.D. 1972; Univ. of Toronto, FRCPC(Hematopathology) 1991. CAREER: Commissioned Officer, Personnel/Admin., Canadian Armed Forces Officers' Training Sch., 1962; Post-Doctoral Fellow, Biophysics Dept., National Research Council, 1965-67; Post-Doctoral Fellow, Biochem. Dept., Fac. of Medicine, Univ. of Ottawa, 1968-69; Intern, Ottawa General Hospital, 1972-74; Medical Dir., Ottawa Centre, Blood Transfusion Svc., Canadian Red Cross, 1974-88; private medical practice, 1988-89; Consultant, Dept. of Agric., Gov't of Canada, 1990-95; Reviewer–New Drug Submissions, Drugs Directorate, 1990-92; Consultant, Office of the Surgeon Gen., 1991-95; Consultant on Fractionation, Armour Pharmaceuticals, 1992-93; Consultant, Dept. of Vascular Surgery, Ottawa Civic Hospital, 1992-94; Drug Reviewer, Bureau of Drugs, Health Canada, 1994-95; Asst. Dir., Hematology Laboratories, Hospital for Sick Children, 1994-95; Clinical Assoc. Prof., Dept. of Medicine, Univ. of Ottawa, to date; Adjunct Prof., Dept. of Biochem., to date; Adjunct Prof., Dept. of Lab. Medicine, to date; Consultant, Dept. of Medicine, Ottawa General Hospital, to date; Consultant, Dept. of Lab. Medicine, to date; Special Advisor, Hospital Blood Establishments, Bureau of Drugs, Health Canada, 1995 to date; Assoc. Prof. of Pathology, Univ. of Toronto, 1995 to date. SELECTED PUBLICATIONS: *The Platelet Membrane in Transfusion Medicine*, ed. with F. Décary (Basel: S Karger AG, 1988); *Quality Assurance in Transfusion Medicine*, ed. with J. Seghatchian (Boca Raton, FL: CRC Press, 1992); "Analysis of Contaminants in Factor VIII Preparations Administered to Hemophiliacs," with G. Farrah *et al* (*Canadian Medical Association Journal* 128 1983); "The Application of Protein A Immunoadsorption to Remove Platelet Alloantibodies" (*Transfusion* 33 1993); "Hematological and Lipid Changes in Newborn Piglets Fed Milk Replacer Diets Containing Vegetable Oils with Different Levels of n-3 Fatty Acids," with J.K.G. Kramer (*Lipids* 29 1994); more than 190 other publications. EDIT: Ed. in Chief, *Transfusion Science*, 1988 to date. AFFIL: American Association of Blood Banks; American Society of Hematology; American Society for Apheresis (Pres. 1987-88); Canadian Biochemical Society; Canadian Hematology Society; Canadian Apheresis Group (Chrm & Founding Mbr.); European Society for Haemapheresis; International Soci-

ety of Blood Transfusion; International Society of Thrombosis & Haemostasis (Subcommittee on Factor VIII & von Willebrand Factor 1985-86); World Apheresis Association (Pres. 1988-90); World Federation of Hemophilia; Gene Therapy Advisory Committee, Health Canada. HONS: Roche Award for Medical Students, 1969. MISC: more than 360 conference presentations; recipient, numerous grants & contracts; holds 7 patents (Canada, US, Europe, Japan), incl. Method of Obtaining Intermediate Purity Factor VIII, with D.S. Palmer (Cdn, 1982).

Rock, Virginia Jeanne, B.A.,M.A., Ph.D.,D.Litt. 📖 📖 🍴

Professor Emerita, English Department, YORK UNIVERSITY, 310 Stong College, 4700 Keele St., North York, ON M3J 1P3 (416) 736-5166, ext. 20333, FAX 736-5412. Born Detroit, Mich. 1933. s. EDUC: Univ. of Michigan, B.A.(English) 1944, M.A.(English) 1947; Univ. of Minnesota, Ph.D.(American Studies) 1961. CAREER: Instructor, Univ. of Michigan, 1947-48; Instructor, Univ. of Louisville, 1948-50; Asst. Prof., Lake Erie Coll., Ohio, 1951-53; Instructor, Univ. of Minnesota, 1956-57; Asst. Prof., Montclair State Coll., 1958-60; Asst. Prof., Michigan State Univ., 1960-65; Fulbright Prof., Jagiellonian Univ., Krakstructor, Univ. of Louisville, 1948-50; Asst. Prof., Lake Erie Coll., Ohio, 1951-53; Instructor, Univ. of Minnesota, 1956-57; Asst. Prof., Monclair State Coll., 1958-60; Asst. Prof., Michigan State Univ., 1960-65; Fulbright Prof., Jagiellonian Univ., Krakow, Poland, 1962-64; Prof., various ranks, York Univ., 1965-89; Master, Stong Coll., 1969-78; Prof. Emerita, York Univ., 1989 to date. SELECTED PUBLICATIONS: biographical essays, *I'll Take My Stand: The South and the Agrarian Tradition* (LSU Press, 1977); "They Took Their Stand: The Emergence of the Southern Agrarians," in *Prospects*, an Annual I (1975); "Bridging Cultures in Poland and Canada" in *Essays for Yvonne Grabowski, 1929-1989* (1993); publishes on Southern & Am. lit. & culture; articles in various journals incl. *The Georgia Review, Mississippi Quarterly, Southern Humanities Review.* AFFIL: Modern Languages Association; American Studies Association; Canadian Association for American Studies (Past Sec.; Past Pres.); Association of Canadian College & University Teachers of English; Society for the Study of Southern Literature; Canadian Women's Studies Association (Treas. 1995 to date). HONS: chosen as 1 of 16 academic women who "made a significant contribution" to the "positive image of women," Ont., OCUFA, 1974; D.Litt.(Hon.), York Univ., 1994. MISC: guest lecturer at universities in Poland, Finland, & Germany; 1st

woman Master, Stong Coll., York Univ. COMMENT: *"Throughout her three decades at York, her career came to focus on three commitments: on students, whom she delights to be with and to teach; on research into the wide field of American Studies and her area field, the American South; and finally, on Women's Studies, which continues to evoke her enthusiasm and her devotion."*

Rockett, Beverley ■ ■ ⊗

Photographer and Fashion Director, BEVERLEY ROCKETT PHOTOGRAPHY, P.O. Box 524, Niagara-on-the-Lake, ON L0S 1J0 (416) 482-6396, FAX 322-9085. Born Toronto. EDUC: Branksome Hall; Ontario Coll. of Art. AFFIL: Shaw Festival Theatre (Gov.'s Council; Auction Committee; V-Chair, Mktg Committee; fundraising); The Fashion Group International, Toronto (mbr. of Bd.); Art Directors Club of Toronto; Ontario Coll. of Art (President's Dinner Committee). COMMENT: *"For almost three decades, the name Beverley Rockett has been synonymous with creative and stylish photography. Since the late 1960s, her photographs have appeared in every major publication in Canada. She made a major contribution to establishing a presence for Canadian fashions in that decade. In the 1970s, she directed her camera to photographing famous faces in politics and the arts, winning awards along the way for her portraits of Pierre Trudeau, Jeanne Sauvé, Judy LaMarsh, Robertson Davies, Margaret Laurence, Anthony Quinn, David Susskind, Truman Capote and others. In 1981, Beverley was appointed fashion and beauty editor for City Woman Magazine and for the next three years established a different and leading approach to editorial fashion, winning gold and silver National Magazine Awards during the entire three-year period. From 1983 to 1990, in partnership with graphic designer, Theo Dimson, she produced trend-setting advertisements for Lipton International, a national retail fashion chain. She has been recognized by her peers with a Women Who Make a Difference Award in 1989, and is listed in Canadian Who's Who."*

Rodgers, Sanda, B.A.,LL.B.,B.C.L., LL.M. ■ ■ 📖 🔖

Dean, Common Law Section, Faculty of Law, UNIVERSITY OF OTTAWA, 57 Louis Pasteur, Ottawa, ON K1N 6N5 (613) 562-5927, FAX 562-5124, EMAIL srodgers@uottawa.ca. 1 ch. Shoshana. EDUC: Case Western Reserve Univ., B.A. 1969; McGill Univ., LL.B. 1974, B.C.L. 1975; Univ. de Montréal, LL.M. 1978. CAREER: Dean, Common Law Section, Fac. of Law, Univ. of Ottawa, 1994 to date; Adjudicator, Grandview Agreement, Ministry of the Attorney Gen., Ont., 1994 to date. **SELECTED PUBLICATIONS:** "Fetal Rights and Maternal Rights: Is There a Conflict?" (*Canadian Journal of Women and the Law* 456, 1986); "Canadian Blood Supply Delivery Systems: Liability and Compensation, for the Federal/Provincial/Territorial Review on Liability and Compensation Issues in Health Care" (*Ottawa Law Review*, 1990); "Juridical Interference with Reproductive Autonomy," in *Legal and Ethical Issues in New Reproductive Technologies: Pregnancy and Parenthood* (The Royal Commission on New Reproductive Technologies, Min. of Supply & Svcs, 1993); "Health Care Providers and Sexual Assault: Feminist Law Reform?" (*C.J.W.L.* 159, 1995); co-editor with C. Andrew, *Women and the Canadian State* (forthcoming, McGill Queens Press, 1996); and others. **AFFIL:** Law Society of Upper Canada. **HONS:** Wainwright Fellow, Fac. of Law, McGill Univ., 1975; SSHRC Sabbatical Leave Fellowship (declined), 1984.

Roeland, Rita L., B.A. 🌐 ✦ ○ ♿
Executive Director, MANITOBA SAFETY COUNCIL, 213 Notre Dame Ave., Ste. 700, Winnipeg, MB R3B 1N3 (204) 949-1085, FAX 956-2897. Born St. Boniface, Man. 1946. d. 4 ch. Noreen, Rhonda, Lana, Rena. **EDUC:** Univ. of Manitoba, B.A.(Econ./Pol.Sci.) 1990. **CAREER:** Liberal candidate, prov. election, 1977; Prov. Constituency Pres., Liberal Party, 1978-80; Fed. Constituency Pres., 1980-83; VP, Man. Prov. Council, Liberal Party, 1982-84; Insur. Agent & Fin. Planner, The Imperial Life Assurance Company, 1977-83; Exec. VP, Tourism Industry Association of Manitoba, 1983-89; Co-Chair–Man., John Turner Leadership Campaign, 1984; Exec. Dir., Manitoba Safety Council, 1990 to date. **SELECTED PUBLICATIONS:** several articles on safety. **EDIT:** ed., *Update*, tourism newsletter, 1985-89; ed., *Spotlight Safety*, 1992 to date. **DIRECTOR:** Rogers Broadcasting (Advisory Bd. Mbr. 1995 to date). **AFFIL:** Manitoba Historical Society (Council Mbr. 1994 to date); American Industrial Hygiene Association; Canadian Standards Association; Accident Prevention Association of Manitoba; Univ. of Manitoba (Health & Safety Certificate Program). **HONS:** Presidential Award, Manitoba Chamber of Commerce, 1976, 1980; National Quality Award, Life Underwriters' Association, 1981, 1982, 1983; Outstanding Young Manitoban Award, Jaycees, 1982. **INTERESTS:** golf; history; gourmet cooking; reading; family; Cdn politics; gardening; travel. **COMMENT:** "*I have held positions in many organizations, often as first or only woman and have never felt impeded in*

my progress. I relish challenges and finding solutions. I enjoy working with people and making things happen."

Rogers, Linda, B.A.,M.A. 📖 ✌ ♿
Poet, Children's Writer and Novelist. 1235 Styles St., Victoria, BC V9A 3Z6 (604) 386-8066. Born Port Alice, B.C. 1944. m. Rick Van Krugel. 3 ch. Sasha, Keefer, Tristan. **EDUC:** Univ. of British Columbia, B.A.(Fine Arts & Theatre) 1966, M.A.(Lit.) 1970. **CAREER:** Teacher of English, Univ. of British Columbia, Univ. of Victoria, Camosun Coll. & Malaspina Coll.; songwriter & performer for children; writer, poetry, fiction, articles. **SELECTED CREDITS:** for children: *Worm Sandwich*; *Brown Bag Blues*; *Harry Zapper and the Disappearing Teacher*; *The Magic Flute*; *Molly Brown is Not a Clown*; for adults: *Queens of the Next Hot Star*; *Witness*; *Singing Rib*; *Woman at Mile Zero, Letters from the Doll Hospital, Hard Candy, Love in a Rainforest, The Half Life of Radium*, novella; various reviews & criticisms for *Books in Canada, The Toronto Star, The Vancouver Sun, Monday Magazine, Victoria Boulevard, Poetry Canada Review, The Victoria Times Colonist, The Globe and Mail*. **AFFIL:** League of Canadian Poets (Exec. 1988-91); Federation of B.C. Writers (Pres. 1990); PEN; Pacific Opera (Exec.). **HONS:** Stephen Leacock Award for Poetry (*Wrinkled Coloratura*), 1994, 4th in 1995, 2nd in 1996; The Gov. General's Confederation Medal For Poetry & Performance; Canada Council arts awards; Cultural Services Arts Award; The B.C. Writers' Poetry Prize; Aya Poetry Prize; Cross Canada Writers' Quarterly Poetry Prize; The Seattle Arts Commission Poetry Award; Voices Israel Poetry Prize, 1995; Peoples Poetry Prize (Acorn), 1995; Dorothy Livesay Poetry Prize, 1995; finalist, Pat Lowther Award, Canadian Authors Award, League of Poets Nat'l Poetry Contest, *Malahat Review* Long Poem Contest, Hawthorne Poetry Award, Commonwealth Poetry Award & the CBC Poetry Contest. **INTERESTS:** opera; film; art; folk music. **MISC:** has served on various literary juries; has performed at many festivals, schools & libraries across Canada, as well as on TV & radio; does a children's show, songs & poems with her husband, illustrator & musician Rick Van Krugel; 1st recipient of the Stephen Leacock Prize for Poetry.

Rogers, Mickey, B.A. ■ ♿
Principal, FOREFRONT ENTERTAINMENT GROUP, 402 W. Pender St., Ste. 700, Vancouver, BC V6B 1T6 (604) 682-7910, FAX 682-8583. Born Toronto 1950. d. 1 ch. Tomas Bush. **EDUC:** Carleton Univ., B.A.(English/Journal-

ism) 1972. **CAREER:** Mgmt. Consultant, gov'ts of Alta. & Ont.; Journalist, Prod., Writer, Researcher & Broadcaster, CBC Radio; Prod., Writer & Principal, Forefront Entertainment. **SELECTED CREDITS:** Prod., Writer & Narrator, *The War We Fought on the West Coast*, feature radio documentary, CBC, 1987; Prod./Writer & Narrator, *Balancing the Costs* (three-part radio documentary), CBC, 1988; Co-Prod./Co-Writer, *Working It Out* (half-hour pilot for Madison), 1990; Co-Prod./Co-Writer, *Madison* (series), 1991-92, 1993-94; Co-Prod./Co-Writer, *Inside Stories: Journey Into Self-Esteem*, 1989-90; Prod./Writer, *It's My Turn Now* (half-hour video documentary), 1992; Prod./Writer, *It's a Crime*, 1993. **SELECTED PUBLICATIONS:** numerous magazine articles. **DIRECTOR:** Forefront Productions. **AFFIL:** Academy of Canadian Cinema & Television; Women in Film (Bd.); voluntary organizations. **HONS:** *The War We Fought on the West Coast* has won The Gabriel, The B'nai B'rith & The Major Armstrong awards & was nominated as one of the best radio shows, ACTRA, 1987; winner of over 25 int'l. awards for *Madison*; winner of a Gemini award; nominated, YWCA Woman of the Year. **INTERESTS:** hiking; writing; tap dancing.

Rohr, Peggy, B.Comm.,CFM $

Vice-President, Business Planning, MACKENZIE FINANCIAL CORP., 150 Bloor St. W., Toronto, ON M5S 3B5 (416) 922-5322, FAX 922-3385. **EDUC:** Univ. of Toronto, B.Comm.(Commerce & Fin.) 1976. **CAREER:** prior to 1986 worked in int'l trade & telecomm. industry; Mackenzie Financial Corporation, 1986 to date. **AFFIL:** International Facilities Management Association (IFMA).

Rooke, Constance, B.A.,M.A.,Ph.D. 🎓 📜

Associate Vice-President Academic and Professor of English, UNIVERSITY OF GUELPH, Guelph, ON N1G 2W1 (519) 824-4120, ext. 3880, FAX 767-1693. Born New York City 1942. m. Leon Rooke. 1 ch. Jonathan Rooke. **EDUC:** Smith Coll., B.A.(English) 1964; Tulane Univ., M.A.(English) 1966; Univ. of North Carolina, Ph.D.(English) 1973. **CAREER:** Dir., Learning & Teaching Centre, Univ. of Victoria, 1982-83; Lecturer to Prof., Dept. of English, 1969-88; Ed., *The Malahat Review*, 1983-92; Prof. & Chair, Dept. of English, Univ. of Guelph, 1988-94; Assoc. VP, Academic, & Prof. of English, 1994 to date. **SELECTED PUBLICATIONS:** *Reynolds Price* (1983); *A Grammar Book for Lawyers* (1985); *Night Light: Stories of Aging* ed. (1986); *Fear of the Open Heart: Essays in Contemporary Canadian Writing* ed. (1989); *Writing Away: The P.E.N. Canada Travel Anthology* ed. (1994); *The Clear Path* (1995); numerous books, scholarly articles, short stories, book reviews, interviews, & entries in reference works. **AFFIL:** Canadian Association of Periodical Publishers (Dir. 1985-88); Canada Council Advisory Committee on Writing & Publication (1986-90); Canadian Association of Chairs of English (Pres. 1991-92); Senior Women Academic Administrators of Canada (Exec. 1992-93); Canadian Federation of the Humanities (Exec. 1991-95; Chair, Gov't & Public Rel'ns Committee 1994); P.E.N. Canada (Dir.). **HONS:** grants, Social Sciences & Humanities Research Council of Canada; Teaching Fellow, 3-M, 1987; numerous awards associated with *The Malahat Review*. **INTERESTS:** travel. **MISC:** author of a computer program that teaches grammar & punctuation. **COMMENT:** *"Constance Rooke's academic interests lie principally in contemporary Canadian literature, feminism, old age, and pedagogy. She is an editor, short story writer, and academic administrator."*

Ropchan, Glorianne, B.Sc.,M.D., FRCS(C) ⊕ 🎓

Assistant Professor, QUEEN'S UNIVERSITY and Staff Surgeon, Cardiovascular and Thoracic Surgery, KINGSTON GENERAL HOSPITAL, 102 Stuart St., Kingston, ON K7L 2V6 (613) 549-6345, FAX 549-2902.. Born Kitchener, Ont. 1954. s. **EDUC:** Univ. of Toronto, B.Sc. (Math./Chem.) 1976, M.D. 1980, FRCS(C) (Gen. Surgery) 1985, FRCS(C)(Cardiovascular and Thoracic Surgery) 1989. **CAREER:** Asst. Prof., Queen's Univ.; Staff Surgeon, Kingston General Hospital & Hotel Dieu Hospital. **SELECTED PUBLICATIONS:** "Intermittent Percutaneous Infusion into the Hepatic Artery of Cytotoxic Drugs for Hepatic Tumors," with R. Falk, P. Greig & L. Larratt (*Canadian Journal of Surgery*, 25, 1982); "Aortic Valve Replacement with Stentless Porcine Aortic Bioprosthesis," with T.E. David & J.W. Butany (*Journal of Cardiac Surgery*, 3, 1988); "Ascending Aorta–Bifemoral Artery Bypass," with Baird & Oates, *Mastery of Surgery*, 2nd ed. (Nyhus, Baker, 1992); "Salvage of Ischemic Myocardium by Nonsynchronized Retroperfusion in the Pig," with C.M. Fiendel *et al (The Journal of Thoracic and Cardiovascular Surgery*, 104, 1992). **HONS:** Ontario Scholarship; Academic Gold Medal, Music Award & Senior Shield, Kipling Collegiate Institute; Billes Scholarship, 1972-77; Collins Scholarship, 1978-80; Univ. of Toronto Athletics Silver "T", 1979; Resident Award, Canadian Society of Cardiovascular & Thoracic Surgeons, 1988; Toronto General Hospital Teaching Award, 1989; First Prize, Univ. of Toronto Cardiovascular & Thoracic Surgery Residents' Competition, 1989. COMMENT: *"I have an extremely busy clinical practice, am involved extensively in teaching and have had previous research training that I hope to be able to implement. I have little "free time" but try to get to the ballet, concerts and read an occasional non-medical book as well as keeping up with my friends and family."*

Roper, Janice, B.Comm.,C.A. $

Tax Partner, DELOITTE & TOUCHE, 4 Bentall Centre, 1055 Dunsmuir St., Ste. 2000, Vancouver, BC V7X 1P4 (604) 669-4466, FAX 685-0395. Born UK 1960. m. Donald. 2 ch. EDUC: Univ. of British Columbia, B.Comm.(Acctg) 1982. CAREER: various positions, Deloitte & Touche, 1982-86; Tax Group, 1986-94; Tax Ptnr, 1994 to date. AFFIL: Canadian Institute of Chartered Accountants (C.A.); Institute of Chartered Accountants of B.C. (Professional Dev. Committee; G.S.T. Sub-committee); Deaf Children's Society of B.C. (Treas.); Vancouver Board of Trade. HONS: Gold Medal in Tax Course, Institute of Chartered Accountants of B.C., 1983. INTERESTS: reading; tennis; attending theatre. MISC: has spoken & been quoted in newspapers on G.S.T. & related matters. COMMENT: *"I am one of the top experts in G.S.T. in Vancouver and am often called upon to speak on G.S.T. matters. I provide sales tax advice to Deloitte & Touche clients in Western Canada."*

Rose, Elizabeth Stikeman, B.A., M.L.S. $ ❀

Vice-President, Employee Satisfaction and Environment, NORTHERN TELECOM LIMITED, 2920 Matheson Blvd. E., Mississauga, ON L4W 4M7 (905) 238-7344, FAX 238-7076, EMAIL elizabeth_rose@nt.com. EDUC: McGill Univ., B.A.(Geography) 1968, M.L.S. 1970. CAREER: Consultant, William M. Mercer Limited, 1975-84; Principal, Settler Services of New York, 1979-86; independent Mgmt Consultant, 1986-88; Pres., Cosult International, 1989-92; Asst. VP, Environmental Affairs, Northern Telecom Limited, Mississauga, 1992-95. SELECTED PUBLICATIONS: *Environmental Review* (Northern Telecom, 1992, 1993); *Energy Efficiency Guidelines* (Northern Telecom, 1991); "Corporate Environmental Action...Putting it on the Record" (*New Pacific* Spring 1994); various reports & case studies with environmental focus. AFFIL: International Cooperative for Ozone Layer Protection (Exec. Committee); World Environment Center (I.E.F. Committee); Canadian Organization for Development through Education (CODE), Ottawa (Bd. 1990-94); CODE International (Bd.); International Cooperative for Environmental Leadership (Chrm of the Bd.); Pollution probe (Bd.)

Rosenberg, Dufflet $ ❀

President, DUFFLET PASTRIES INC., 41 Dovercourt Rd., Toronto, ON M6J 3C2 (416) 536-1330, FAX 538-2366. Born Toronto 1954. cl. Martin Kohn. EDUC: Univ. of Toronto, one year Gen. Arts, 1974; Le Nôtre, 2 week program, Entremets & Pastry, 1978. CAREER: Pres., Dufflet Pastries, 1975 to date. SELECTED PUBLICATIONS: various recipes in magazines & newspapers. DIRECTOR: Great Cooks (a div. of Dufflet Pastries Inc.). AFFIL: McGill Club; Step Ahead; CFRA; Toronto Culinary Guild; James Beard Foundation; Bakery Production Club; CFIB; Knives & Forks; has volunteered on gala committees for CANFAR & WALADI; Interval House (Corp. Fundraising Team). INTERESTS: skiing; cycling; aerobics; food; travel; volunteer work; film; literature. MISC: The Great Cooks program, now in its seventh year, is a series of cooking classes featuring some of Toronto's finest chefs, caterers & food professionals. COMMENT: *"Dufflet Pastries was established in 1975 after Dufflet Rosenberg started baking desserts for the Cow Cafe. As more and more restaurants rushed to place orders, she quickly developed a product line produced out of her home. Soon she was winning raves as the 'Best Baker in Toronto.' When the kitchen operation outgrew itself in 1980, Dufflet Pastries established a manufacturing outlet then a retail outlet. Today Dufflet Pastries supplies over 350 restaurants and cafes, as well as fine food shops, hotels and caterers, with over 100 different products."*

Rosenberg, Monda, B.A. ✏ ▯

Food Editor, CHATELAINE MAGAZINE, 777 Bay St., Toronto, ON M5W 1A7 (416) 596-5439, FAX 596-5516. Born Brockville, Ont. EDUC: Univ. of Western Ontario, B.A.(Home Econ.) 1963. CAREER: Food Ed., *The Toronto Star*, 1973-78; Food Ed., *Chatelaine* Magazine, 1978 to date. SELECTED PUBLICATIONS: contributor to *Where to Eat in America*, William Rice (1982); features on Toronto (*Diversion* 1983, 1985); 2-part story on Cdn cheese (*Cuisine* 1984); *Chatelaine Cookbook: No Fuss Recipes for Family and Friends* (1992); *Vitality Cookbook* (1995). AFFIL: Toronto Home Economic Association (Pres. 1974-75); Ontario Home Economic Association (Pres. 1983-85). HONS: Elizabeth Chant Robertson Nutrition Writing Award, 1977; Nutrition Writing Award, General Foods, 1978; Award for Food Styling, N.Y. Art Directors, 1981; Food Ed. of the Year Award, *Nabisco Food Writers' Magazine*,

1985; Canadian Publishing Award for Excellence, Maclean Hunter, 1989; Silver Ladle Award, Toronto Culinary Guild, 1990. **INTERESTS:** dogs; gardens; antiques. **MISC:** frequent speaker on nat'l radio & TV programs.

Rosenfeldt, Sharon ♡ ✊ ⚖
President, VICTIMS OF VIOLENCE CANADIAN CENTRE FOR MISSING CHILDREN, 211 Pretoria Ave., Ottawa, ON K1S 1X1 (613) 223-0052, FAX 233-2712. Born Prince Albert, Sask. 1946. m. Gary. 2 ch. Jana Rosenfeldt, Darryl Rosenfeldt. **CAREER:** Counsellor, Poundmaker's Lodge, St. Albert, Alta., 1984-89; Pres., Victims of Violence Canadian Centre for Missing Children, 1991 to date. **AFFIL:** Canadian Police Association Victims' Resource Centre (VP); Ontario Criminal Injuries Compensation Board (Bd. mbr. 1996 to date). **COMMENT:** *"Parent of murdered child; well known as advocate for crime victims throughout Canada. Have made a significant change in regards to treatment of crime victims and in keeping dangerous violent offenders in prison. Regularly present to justice committees on these subjects and work with MPs to change laws for the better protection of society."*

Rosenfield, Ruth, B.A. ■ ✊ 🎓 👍
President, MONTREAL TEACHERS ASSOCIATION, 4260 Girouard, Ste. 200, Montreal, QC H4A 3C9 (514) 487-4580. Born Montreal 1950. s. **EDUC:** McGill Univ., B.A. 1971, Dip.Ed. 1973. **CAREER:** Teacher, 1973 to date; Exec. Asst., Montreal Teachers' Association, 1980-87; Pres., 1987 to date. **AFFIL:** Provincial Association of Protestant Teachers (Mbr. at Large). **INTERESTS:** music; reading. **COMMENT:** *"As the first ever female president of her union, she is considered to be intelligent, courageous, articulate, compassionate, literate, and humorous, as she represents strongly the over-2500 members of the Montreal Teachers' Association."*

Rosinger, Eva, M.Sc.,Ph.D. ⚛ $ 👍
Deputy Director, Environment Directorate, ORGANISATION FOR ECONOMIC CO-OPERATION AND DEVELOPMENT (OECD), 2, rue André-Pascal, 75775, Paris Cedex 16, France (33-1) 4524 9310, FAX 4524 7876, EMAIL eva.rosinger@oecd.org. Born Prague 1941. m. Dr. Herbert E. Rosinger. **EDUC:** Technical Univ., Prague, M.Sc.(Chem. Eng.) 1963, Ph.D.(Chem.) 1968; Univ. of Toronto, Post-doctoral Fellow (Chem. Eng.) 1970. **CAREER:** Tech. Info. Svcs, Technical Univ., Aachen, Germany, 1970-72; Research Scientist, AECL Research, Whiteshell Laboratories, 1973-79; Section Head, 1979-80; Scientific Asst. to the Dir. of the Waste Mgmt Div., 1980-84; Mgr, Environmental & Safety Assessment Branch, 1984-85; Exec. Asst. to the Pres., AECL Research, Ottawa, 1986-87; Dir., Waste Mgmt Concept Review, 1987-90; Dir. Gen. & CEO, Canadian Council of Ministers of the Environment, 1990-94; Deputy Dir., Environment Directorate, OECD, 1994 to date. **SELECTED PUBLICATIONS:** more than 40 scientific reports & papers on environmental issues, waste mgmt, environmental assessment, polymer science & chemical processes in nuclear industry. **AFFIL:** Univ. of Waterloo (Advisory Committee); Association of Professional Engineers of Manitoba (Council Mbr. 1992-94); Canadian Nuclear Society. **HONS:** several Man. & Ont. cross-country skiing & orienteering championships; Order of Sport Excellence, Man. Mininstry of Sports, 1986; Certificate of Merit for Contribution to the Community, Gov't of Canada, 1988; Woman of Distinction Award, YWCA Winnipeg, 1992. **INTERESTS:** cross-country skiing; orienteering; wilderness trekking; photography. **MISC:** holds 2 patents. **COMMENT:** *"Scientist and environmentalist with deep appreciation of global interplay of environmental, economic and social issues. Professional engineer who has followed a nontraditional path in the field of engineering and science."*

Ross, Anita K., B.A.(Hons.),M.A.,Ph.D. $
Vice-President, Management Services, IBM LATIN AMERICA, Route 9, Town of Mount Pleasant, North Tarrytown, NY 10591 (914) 332-3831, FAX 332-3835. Born Winnipeg. **EDUC:** Univ. of Manitoba, B.A.(French & Classics) 1965, M.A.(French Lit.) 1966, Ph.D.(French Lit.) 1972. **CAREER:** various mktg & mgmt positions, IBM Canada, 1973-83; Dir., Personnel Rel'ns, 1983-86; various special assignments, IBM Corp., 1986-88; VP, Hum. Res., IBM Canada, 1988-94; IBM Dir. of Transformation, IBM Corp., 1994-95; VP, Mgmt Svcs, IBM Latin America, 1995 to date. **AFFIL:** The Advisory Board Company (Corp. Leadership Council); Catalyst (Bd. of Advisors). **HONS:** Gov. General's Medal; Gold Medal in Classics, Univ. of Manitoba; numerous scholarships & fellowships. **INTERESTS:** cooking; needlework; photography; travel.

Ross, Catherine, M.A.,Ph.D., M.L.I.S. ■ 🎓 📖 📺
Professor of Library and Information Science and Acting Dean of Communications and Open Learning, UNIVERSITY OF WESTERN ONTARIO, Stevenson-Lawson Building, 149A, London, ON M6A 5B8 (519) 661-2102, Ext. 4636, FAX 661-3730, EMAIL ross@julian.uwo.ca. Born London, Ont. 1945. m. George Ross. 2 ch. **EDUC:** Univ. of Western Ontario,

B.A.(English) 1967, M.A.(English) 1968, Ph.D.(English) 1976, M.L.I.S.(Library & Info. Sci.) 1984. CAREER: high sch. Teacher, Lockerby Composite Sch., Sudbury, Ont., 1968-69; Teacher, Univ. of Western Ontario, 1973 to date; Assoc. Dean, Fac. of Grad. Studies, 1992-95; Prof., 1993 to date; Acting Dean, Fac. of Grad. Studies, 1995-96; Acting Dean, Fac. of Comm. & Open Learning, 1996-97. SELECTED PUBLICATIONS: *Communicating Professionally*, with Patricia Dewdney (New York: Neal-Schuman, 1989); *Alice Munro: A Double Life* (Toronto: ECW Press, 1992); *Triangles: Shapes in Math, Science and Nature* (Toronto: Kids Can Press, 1994); published more than 25 scholarly articles on reading for pleasure, Cdn lit., children's literatures & the reference interview; has also written non-fiction books for children published by Kids Can Press in Toronto. HONS: Canada Council Doctoral Fellowship, 1971-73. INTERESTS: leisure reading; canoeing; bicycling; writing non-fiction books for children. COMMENT: *"My current research interest is the ethnography of reading for pleasure."*

Ross, Lou 🐾 ⊕
Executive Director, S.O.S. SOCIETY OF SEXUAL ABUSE SURVIVORS, 6047 - 18th St. S.E., Calgary, AB T2C 0M2 (403) 236-0369. Born Sarnia, Ont. 1955. s. EDUC: Univ. of Alberta, Educ.(Special Needs), 1986. CAREER: Church Organist & Choir Director, Ogden United Church, Calgary, 1988 to date; Founder & Exec. Dir., S.O.S. Society of Sexual Abuse Survivors, 1992 to date; S.O.S. became a registered charity & society, Nov. 1993. SELECTED PUBLICATIONS: S.O.S. Survivor Series Handbook #1–*Calgary Support Groups* (Calgary: S.O.S.); *Sparrow* (a survivor self-help book) (Calgary: S.O.S. 1995). EDIT: Ed., *S.O.S. Survivors of Sexual Abuse Newsletter*, 1992 to date. INTERESTS: her animals (most found abandoned); singing; gardening; walking; visiting with family & friends. MISC: *A Conversation With the Selves*, video on MPD, S.O.S.; Volunteer, *Survivors of Challenge*, Shaw Cable, Calgary, 1992-96; public speaker; various media appearances; presently involved in creating a support group role model for prisoners who are survivors of sexual abuse. COMMENT: *"I live in Calgary. I am a survivor of childhood abuse by neighbours. I have struggled with severe self-inflicted violence and mood swings as a result, but have had a lot of help from my friends, family and therapist on this healing journey. My frustration at the lack of services for survivors of sexual abuse led to my forming the S.O.S. Society and Newsletter. We have support groups, which are free and which are accessible to the mentally and physically challenged survivor."*

Ross, Marie-Claire ■ ■ 🐾
Paralympic Athlete. Kingston, ON. EDUC: Ryerson Polytechnic Univ., current. SPORTS CAREER: mbr., Nat'l Swim Team, 1993 to date. Paralympic Games: Bronze, 100m butterfly, 50m & 100m freestyle, Gold, 100m IM &100m breaststroke, Silver, 100 backstroke, 1996; Silver, 100m breaststroke, Bronze, 50m freestyle, 4th, 100m freestyle & 100m backstroke, 1992. Int'l Paralympic Swim Trials: 1st, 100m freestyle, 100m breaststroke & 200m IM, 2nd, 50m & 400m freestyle, 100m backstroke, 1995. Atlanta Int'l Invitational: 1st, 100m, freestyle, 100m breaststroke & 200m IM, 1995. IPC World Championships: 1st, 100m breaststroke, 2nd, 200m IM, 3rd, 50m & 100m freestyle, 100m, backstroke & 100m butterfly, 1994. MISC: world record holder, 50m, 100m (1:21.4) & 200m breaststroke

Ross, Marsha ■ ■ 🐾 ♡ 🦅
Chief Commissioner, GIRL GUIDES OF CANADA/ GUIDES DU CANADA, 50 Merton St., Toronto, ON M4S 1A3 (416) 487-5281, FAX 487-5570. EDUC: Bennett Coll., Millbrook, N.Y., Diploma (Home Econ.); Ryerson Polytechnical Institute, Diploma (Presch. Educ.). CAREER: Teacher, Bayview Glen Jr. Schools, 1962-64; Asst. Dir., 1964-66; Teacher, presch. deaf & hard-of-hearing children, Society of Crippled Children & Adults of Manitoba, 1966-68; owner, retail antique business, 1974-81. AFFIL: Downtown Churchworkers' Association (Chair, Urban Committee 1981-84; mbr., Exec. 1979-84; mbr., Bd. of Dir. 1977-84; VP 1980-81; Chair, Nominations Committee 1979-80); Alliance for a Drug-Free Canada (Bd. of Dir. 1991-92); Junior League of Toronto (Sustaining mbr. 1984 to date; various committees); Havergal Coll. (volunteer 1981-83; Havergal-years Sec. 1986 to date); Diocese of Toronto, Anglican Church of Canada (Long-Range Planning Committee 1992 to date; Exec. Committee 1986-93; mbr. of Synod 1983-93; various committees); Girl Guides of Canada (Chief Commissioner 1991 to date; Acting Dir., Communication Svcs Group 1990-91; numerous committees).

Ross, Sandi 🐾 🐾 💌 🖌
Actor and President, Toronto Branch, ACTRA, 2239 Yonge St., Toronto, ON M4S 2B5 (416) 489-1311, FAX 489-1435. Born St. Paul, Minn. 1949. EDUC: San Diego State Coll., 1967-69; Univ. of Minnesota, 1969-72. CAREER: over 25 years' experience as a performer. SELECTED CREDITS: television credits

include *Race to Freedom: The Underground Railroad*, *Forever Knight*, *Tekwar*, *E.N.G.*, *Street Legal*, *The Judge* & *Night Heat*; film credits include *Trial by Jury*, *Camilla*, *Guilty as Sin*, *Where the Heart Is*, *Suspect* & *Adventures in Babysitting*; theatre credits include *Titus Andronicus*, *Joe Turner's Come and Gone*, *Farther West* & appearances at the National Arts Centre, Manitoba Theatre Centre, Magnus Theatre North-West, The Royal Alexandra Theatre, Toronto; appeared at Stratford Festival in *A Streetcar Named Desire*, *The Little Foxes* & *Sweet Bird of Youth*, 1996; radio credits include several CBC dramas such as *Famished Land* & *Death Downtown* and the voice of Shard on Fox Television's cartoon *X-Men*. **EDIT:** Founding Ed., *Into the Mainstream*. **AFFIL:** ACTRA (Pres., Toronto Performers Branch, 2nd Team; Toronto Branch Council; National Performers Guild; Chair, National Performers Guild Equal Opportunities Committee; Chair, Toronto Branch Equal Opportunities Committee 1988-94); Canadian Advertising Foundation's Race Relations Advisory Council on Advertising; Equity Showcase Theatre (Pres. of the Bd.); Ontario Advisory Committee for Cultural Industries Sectoral Strategies (ACCISS) (Mbr., Steering Committee; Chair, sub-committee on training & professional dev.); Laidlaw Foundation (Performing Arts Committee). **HONS:** New Pioneers Award for the arts for work on *Into the Mainstream*, sponsored by Skills for Change, 1993. **MISC:** became a Canadian citizen on April 5, 1993; 1st woman & 1st person of colour to be pres. of the Toronto Branch of ACTRA, which is 66% of nat'l membership. **COMMENT:** *"Specifically in the area of promoting cultural diversity I felt that there was a great deal of talent not being used. To that end I created Into the Mainstream, which is a talent directory of ACTRA and Equity members who are visible minorities, audible minorities or disabled performers. I've also become very involved with promoting the Arts as an industry and lobbying the provincial government for Status of the Artist legislation through ACCISS and ACTRA's lobby and legislature committee. As an actor, politician and cultural activist, I can only describe myself as very busy, very lucky and quite happy."*

Ross, Shannon, B.Comm. ■■ $ ⚛

Vice-President, Corporate Affairs, QUARTZ MOUNTAIN GOLD CORP. (mineral exploration) and Controller, FARALLON RESOURCES LTD., 800 W. Pender St., Ste. 1020, Vancouver, BC V6C 2V6 (604) 684-6365, FAX 662-7557. Born Edson, Alta. 1951. s. **EDUC:** Univ. of Alberta, B.Comm. 1976; C.A., Alta. 1979. **CAREER:** Cont./Treas./CFO, Cornucopia Resources Ltd., 1988-94; VP, 7557 Management Group Ltd., 1991 to date; Cont., Farallon Resources Ltd., 1996 to date. **AFFIL:** Institute of Chartered Accountants of B.C.; Canadian Institute of Chartered Accountants. **INTERESTS:** skiing; reading; travel; other sports & activities.

Ross, Val, B.A. ✎ ✪ 📖

Arts and Publishing Reporter, *THE GLOBE AND MAIL*, 444 Front St. W., Toronto, ON M5V 2S9 (416) 585-5528, FAX 585-5699. Born London, Ont. 1950. m. Morton Ritts. 3 ch. **EDUC:** Univ. of Toronto, B.A.(Urban Geography) 1974. **CAREER:** researcher, CBC TV, current affairs, 1972-75; freelance magazine writer, 1975-79; Sr. Writer, Section Ed. & Entertainment Ed., *Maclean's* Magazine, 1979-87; Mng Ed., *Toronto Magazine*, 1987-90; Reporter, Arts Section, *The Globe and Mail*, 1991 to date. **HONS:** Finalist, critical writing category; National Newspaper Award, 1991, 1994; winner, critical writing category, National Newspaper Award, 1992. **INTERESTS:** her family; karate; drawing; canoeing.

Ross, Veronica 📖 📜

Writer. Born Hannover, Germany 1946. m. Richard O'Brien. **CAREER:** writer; Writer-in-Residence, St. Mary's Univ., 1985; Writer-in-Residence, Thunder Bay Public Library, 1987; Writer-in-Residence, London Public Library, 1990; Association Ed., *The Antigonish Review*; Fiction Ed., *Canadian Author*. **SELECTED PUBLICATIONS:** *Goodbye Summer* (Oberon, 1980); *Dark Secrets* (Oberon, 1983); *Fisherwoman* (Potters Field Press, 1984); *Homecoming* (Oberon, 1987); *Order in the Universe* (Mercury, 1990); *Hannah B.* (Mercury, 1991); *Millicent* (Mercury, 1994); *The Anastasia Connection* (Mercury Press, 1996); numerous articles in literary journals & magazines. **AFFIL:** Writers' Union of Canada; Canadian Authors' Association. **HONS:** Writing Award, Benson and Hedges; 2 Awards, Periodical Writers of Canada; Kitchener-Waterloo Arts Award, 1991. **INTERESTS:** reading; life; cooking. **COMMENT:** *"I've written fiction almost all my life. To date, I've had seven books published. I conduct workshops and teach creative writing. Plans? To continue writing."*

Rossant, Janet, B.A.,Ph.D. ■■ ⚛ ⊕ 🎓

Senior Scientist, Samuel Lunenfeld Research Institute, MOUNT SINAI HOSPITAL, 600 University Ave., Toronto, ON M5G 1X5 (416) 586-8267, FAX 586-8588, EMAIL rossant@mshri.on.ca. Professor, Molecular and Medical Genetics, and Professor, Obstetrics and Gynaecology, UNIVERSITY OF TORONTO. Born Chatham, U.K. 1950. m. Alex Bain. 2 ch. Jennifer, Robert. EDUC: Hugh's Coll., Oxford, B.A.(Zoology) 1972; Darwin Coll., Cambridge, Ph.D.(Dev.) 1976. CAREER: Assoc. Prof., Biological Sciences, Brock Univ., 1981-85; Assoc. Prof., Medical Genetics, Univ. of Toronto, 1985-88; Prof., Molecular & Medical Genetics, 1988 to date; Prof., Obstetrics & Gynaecology, 1995 to date; Sr. Scientist, Samuel Lunenfeld Research Institute, Mount Sinai Hospital, 1985 to date; Joint Head, Program in Dev. & Fetal Health, 1994 to date. SELECTED PUBLICATIONS: co-editor with R.A. Pedersen, *Experimental Approaches to Embryonic Mammalian Development* (Cambridge Univ. Press, 1986); co-author with A. Gossler, A.L. Joyner & W.J. Skarnes, "Mouse embryonic stem cells and reporter constructs to detect developmentally regulated genes" (*Science* 244, 1989); co-author with S.-L. Ang, "HNF-3 is essential for node and notochord formation in mouse development" (*Cell* 78, 1994); co-author with T.P. Yamaguchi, K. Harpal & M. Henkemeyer, "Fgfr-1 is required for embryonic growth and mesodermal patterning during mouse gastrulation" (*Genes & Development* 8, 1994); co-author with F. Shalaby *et al*, "Failure of blood island formation and vasculogenesis in flk-1 deficient mice" (*Nature* 376, 1995). EDIT: Editor, *Development*. AFFIL: Society for Development Biology (Pres.); The Jackson Lab (Chair, Bd. of Scientific Overseers); International Society for Developmental Biology (Bd. mbr.); National Cancer Institute of Canada (Advisory Committee on Research). HONS: MRC Distinguished Scientist Award, 1996; Fellow, Royal Society of Canada, 1993; Howard Hughes Int'l Scholar, 1991-96; Terry Fox Cancer Research Scientist, NCIC, 1988 to date; NCIC Research Associateship, 1985-88; NSERC E.W.R. Steacie Memorial Fellowship, 1984-85; Alberta Heritage Fund for Medical Research Visiting Scientist Award, 1983. COMMENT: *"I am a research scientist interested in understanding the development of the early mammalian embryo. I have made several important contributions to understanding cell lineage development and the genetic control of early development in the mouse. My achievements have been recognized in the scientific community by awards, invitations to lecture and election to executive positions in professional societies."*

Rosser, Deborah, B.A.,B.Ed. ⑤
Vice-President and Director of Advertising Sales, CANADIAN BUSINESS MEDIA LTD., 777 Bay St., 5th Fl., Toronto, ON M5W 1A7 (416) 596-5932. Born Toronto. EDUC: Univ. of Toronto, B.A.(Hons.) 1976, B.Ed. 1977. CAREER: Prod. Traffic Mgr & Acct Mgr, Comac Communications Ltd., 1978-84; Nat'l Acct Mgr, *Saturday Night* Magazine, 1985-88; Nat'l Acct Mgr, *Small Business/PROFIT, The Magazine for Canadian Entrepreneurs*; Dir. of Advtg Sales, *PROFIT, The Magazine for Canadian Entrepreneurs*, Canadian Business Media Ltd., 1988-90; Dir. of Advtg Sales, 1990 to date; VP, 1995 to date. AFFIL: Heart & Stroke Foundation; Advertising & Sales Club, Toronto; Magazines Canada (Chair, Educ. Committee); Canadian Association of Women Executives & Entrepreneurs.

Roth, Katherine, B.A. ⑦ ⑤
Past President, WOMEN'S ECONOMIC FORUM. Associate Broker, BOB PEDLER REAL ESTATE, 300 Cabana Rd. E., Windsor, ON N9G 1A3 (519) 966-3750, FAX 966-0988. Born Windsor, Ont. 1953. m. Garry Cranston. EDUC: Univ. of Windsor, B.A.(Languages) 1974. CAREER: Assoc. Broker, Bob Pedler Real Estate Limited. AFFIL: United Way (Bd.; Bd. Chair 1996-97; Strategic Planning Committee; Nominating Committee; Year Round Revenue Committee; Campaign Committee; Women's Economic Forum (Founding Mbr. 1981; 2nd Pres. 1982; Pres. 1993-94). INTERESTS: sailing; kayaking; gardening; art; antiques. COMMENT: *"Highly motivated and customer-oriented, Katherine Roth has a 'super servant' business philosophy which has been instrumental in her success as top sales agent at Bob Pedler Real Estate Limited. Professionally and personally, Katherine 'puts people first'."*

Roth, Lorna, B.A.,M.A., Ph.D. ■ ■ ⑦ 📖 ⼿
Assistant Professor, Department of Communication Studies, CONCORDIA UNIVERSITY, Bryan Bldg, 7141 Sherbrooke St. W., Rm. 421, Montreal, QC H4B 1R6 (514) 848-2545, FAX 933-0853, EMAIL roth@odyssee.net. Born Montreal 1947. s. EDUC: McGill Univ., Certificate (Educ.) 1967; Concordia Univ., B.A.(Sociology, with Distinction) 1972, Diploma (Comm.) 1974; McGill Univ., M.A.(Comm.) 1983; Concordia Univ., Ph.D.(Comm.) 1994. CAREER: Elementary Sch. Teacher, Protestant Sch. Bd. of Greater Montreal, 1968-73; Cross-cultural Comm. & Educ. Consultant, private sector, 1977-93; part-time Lecturer, Comm. Studies, Concordia Univ., 1979-92, Creative Arts, CEGEP Champlain, 1991-92, & Dept. of English, Film/Comm. Program, McGill Univ., 1992; Lecturer, Comm. Studies, Concordia Univ., 1992-94; Asst. Prof., Comm. Studies, 1994 to date. SELECTED CREDITS: Narrator, *Moose Jaw* (film directed by Rick Hancox,

1993). SELECTED PUBLICATIONS: "Broadcasting North of 60" in H. Holmes & D. Taras (eds.), *Seeing Ourselves: Media Power and Policy in Canada* (2nd Ed. Toronto: Harcourt Brace Jovanovich Canada Inc., 1996); with B. Nelson & M. David, "Three Women, a Mouse, a Microphone, and a Telephone: Information (Mis)Management During the Mohawk/Canadian Governments' Conflict of 1990" in A. Valdivia (ed.), *Feminism, Multiculturalism, and the Media: Global Diversities* (Pennsylvania State Univ., Sage Publication, 1995); "The Politics and Ethics of 'Inclusion'" in V. Alla, B. Brennan & B. Hofmaster (eds.), *Deadlines and Diversity* (Halifax: Fernwood Press, 1995); several other book chpts.; "Mohawk Airwaves and Cultural Challenges: Some Reflections on the Politics of Recognition and Cultural Appropriation After the Summer of 1990" (*Canadian Journal of Communications*, Vol. 18, No. 3, 1993); "The Role of CBC Northern Service in the Federal Election Process" study commissioned by Royal Commission on Electoral Reform & Party Financing, F.J. Fletcher (ed.), *Election Broadcasting in Canada*, Vol. 21 (Toronto: Dundurn Press, 1991); book reviews; encyclopedia articles; handbooks & reports; conference proceedings. AFFIL: Centre for Research/Action on Race Relations (Bd. of Dir. 1984-96; Chair, Policy & Planning Committee 1994-96); Canadian Communications Association (Bd. of Dir. 1990-94 & 1995-97); Association of Canadian Universities for Northern Studies (Council mbr.); Waseskun House, halfway house for Native ex-prisoners (Advisory Bd.); WEB-TV project, Montreal Internet Project (Advisory Bd.); Concordia Univ. (mbr. of Senate; Rep., Comm. Studies & Journalism depts., Faculty Association; Fellow, Sch. of Community & Public Affairs (1992-97); Conseil de Presses du Québec (Comité de Recruitement et Selection); Union for Democratic Communications; Canadian Association of Journalists; Black Theatre Workshop, Montreal (Advisory Bd. 1991-94). HONS: numerous grants, scholarships, fellowships. INTERESTS: info. highway dev., particularly in remote areas; race/ethnicity/media; media & diversity; cross-cultural communications & humour; indigenous media history; gender issues; equity issues; race/gender/technology/dev.; photography; swimming as a graceful activity; collecting fragments of cultural artifacts; cultural geography. MISC: numerous radio & TV appearances incl.: *Morningside, The Journal, Newsworld,* & others. COMMENT: *"I am now at a place in my life where I can weave my interest in activism with my work of University teaching, service and reseach. My projects keep me very busy as I am in the process of writing two books in* addition to my career obligations and personal activities. One is on the history of First Peoples' television in Northern Canada and the other, which is a longer-range project and about which I am deeply impassioned, is about the history of technologies of colour."

Rothenburger, Janice, B.R.E. ■■ ○ ☼
Community Pastoral Care Worker, CHURCH ON THE STREET (YONGE STREET MISSION) (Christian ministry to the poor of the inner-city), 280 Gerrard St. E., Toronto, ON M5A 2G4 (416) 923-3392. Born Toronto 1959. s. EDUC: Ontario Bible Coll., B.R.E.(Pastoral Christian Ministry) 1996. CAREER: Promotional Coord., Sanofi Beauté Canada Inc., 1987-93; Youth Worker (volunteer & paid), Evergreen (for street youth), 1991 to date; Street Worker, Sanctuary (outreach to prostitutes), 1994 to date; Home Support Care Worker, Phillip Azziz Centre (AIDS homecare hospice), 1995 to date; Chaplaincy to female offenders, Metro West Detention Centre, 1995 to date; Community Pastoral Care Worker (was Head Usher, Church Elder; now part-time), Yonge Street Mission/Church on the Street, 1995 to date. HONS: upon graduating, Ontario Bible Coll., Delta Epsilon Chi Distinguished Scholastic Attainment Award & Joseph McDermott Scholarship in Evangelism. INTERESTS: writing poetry and short stories; cats (has two); performing stand-up comedy; drama; guitar playing; music; the arts. MISC: involved in inner-city ministry to the poor & troubled, beginning as volunteer in 1991; since graduating has been trying to raise funds to do work full-time; continues to do the work with or without the money; featured in articles, *The Connection* (Ontario Bible Coll. quarterly), Summer 1996; "Second careers that require a leap of faith," *The Toronto Star*, July 28, 1996. COMMENT: *"Left the business world to pursue full-time Christian ministry to the poor, street youth and people, prostitutes, prisoners, mental health patients, drug addicts, alcoholics, and others. My goals are to continue to work in the downtown southeast core and to help as many people as possible overcome their destructive lifestyles. To be the church outside the walls, and help bring people into a loving community."*

Rothman, Claire, B.A.,B.C.L.,M.A. 📖 ✏ 📚
Writer. 4643 Sherbrooke St. W., Ste. 17, Montreal, QC H3Z 1G2 (514) 935-2518, FAX 935-2518. Born Montreal 1958. m. Arthur Holden. 2 ch. EDUC: McGill Univ., B.A.(Phil.) 1981, B.C.L. 1988; Concordia Univ., M.A.(English Lit.) 1988. BAR: Que., 1985. CAREER: writer & translator (French to English); teacher of

English Lit. at Marianapolis Coll.; freelance literary critic for the *Montreal Gazette*. SELECTED PUBLICATIONS: author, *Salad Days and Other Stories* (Dunvegan: Cormorant Books, 1990); translator, *Influence of a Book*, by Philippe Aubert de Gaspé fils (Montreal: Robert Davies Publications, 1993); co-translator, *In the Eye of the Eagle*, by Jean-François Lisée (Toronto: HarperCollins, 1990); co-translator, *The Traitor and the Jew*, by Esther Delisle (Montreal: Robert Davies Publications, 1993). AFFIL: Federation of English-language Writers of Quebec; Literary Translators' Association; Barreau du Québec. HONS: McGill Scholar, 1980, 1981; James Darling Philosophy Award, McGill Univ., 1981; Wainwright law scholarship, McGill Univ., 1981; John Glassco Translation Award, 1994. INTERESTS: writing; French Que. culture. MISC: Master of Ceremonies, Canadian Cultural Programs (lit.), Montreal; occasional Master of Ceremonies, Books & Breakfast Reading Series, Montreal; Jury of Grand Prix du Livre de Montréal, 1995 to date.

Rousseau, Christiane, Ph.D. ⚥ 🏵
Full Professor and Chair, Département de mathématiques et de statistique, UNIVERSITÉ DE MONTRÉAL, C.P. 6128, Succ. Centre-Ville, Montréal, QC H3C 3J7 (514) 343-6710, FAX 343-5700, EMAIL rousseac@ere.umontreal.ca. Born Versailles, France 1954. m. Serge Robert. 1 ch. Olivier Rousseau. EDUC: Univ. de Montréal, B.Math. 1973, M.Math. 1974, Ph.D. (Math.) 1977. CAREER: NSERC Postdoctoral Fellow, McGill Univ., 1977-79; Prof. substitut, Univ. de Montréal, 1979-82; NSERC Research Fellow, 1982-87; Prof., 1987 to date; Prof. titulaire, 1991 to date; Directrice de Dépt. de mathematiques et de statistique, 1993 to date. SELECTED PUBLICATIONS: "Zeroes for complete elliptic integrals for 1:2 resonance," with H. Zoladek (*Journal of Differential Equations* 94 1991); "Hilbert's 16th problem for quadratic vector fields," with F. Dumortier & R. Roussarie (*Journal of Differential Equations* 110 1994); "Elementary graphics of cylicity 1 and 2," with F. Dumortier & R. Roussarie (*Nonlinearity* 7 1994); "Linearization of isochronous systems," with P. Mardesic & B. Toni (*Journal of Differential Equations* 121 1995). AFFIL: American Mathematical Society; Canadian Mathematical Society (VP). INTERESTS: mathematical research; math educ.; outdoor sports; handicrafts. MISC: presenter & organizer, numerous conferences; recipient, various grants; reviewer, numerous journals. COMMENT: *"Enthusiastic in discovering new things and meeting new challenges. Interested in communications: popularizing*

great currents of mathematics for students. I like to work with people: stimulate the enthusiasm of colleagues and students for hard and challenging work."

Routledge, Marie, B.A. ⊗
Associate Curator, Inuit Art, NATIONAL GALLERY OF CANADA, Box 427, Stn. A, Ottawa, ON K1N 9N4 (613) 990-1987, FAX 991-6522. Born Toronto 1951. m. Jeff Blackstock. 2 ch. EDUC: Univ. of Toronto, B.A.(Art Hist./French) 1975. CAREER: Cataloguer, Inuit Art Section, Dept. of Indian & Northern Dev., 1975-76; Curator, Inuit Art Section, 1976-79; Gallery Dir., Theo Waddington and Company, NYC, 1979-81; Research & Documentation Coord., Inuit Art Section, Dept. of Indian & Northern Affairs, 1981-84; Asst. Curator, Cdn Art (Inuit), National Gallery of Canada, 1985-93; Assoc. Curator, Inuit Art, 1993 to date. SELECTED PUBLICATIONS: "Contemporary Inuit Sculpture: An Approach to the Medium, the Artists and Their Work," in *The Shadow of the Sun: Perspectives on Contemporary Native Art* (Canadian Museum of Civilization, 1993); *Pudlo: Thirty Years of Drawing*, exhibition catalogue, with essay by Marion E. Jackson (Ottawa: National Gallery of Canada, 1990); *Inuit Art in the 1970s/L'art inuit actuel 1970-79* (The Agnes Etherington Art Centre, 1979). EXHIBITIONS: *Pudlo: Thirty Years of Drawing*, National Gallery of Canada (1990); *Contemporary Indian and Inuit Art of Canada*, travelling exhibition, Indian & Northern Affairs Canada (1993); *Inuit Art in the 1970s*, Agnes Etherington Art Centre (1979). AFFIL: Native Art Studies Association of Canada; Ottawa Native Art Study Group; Canadian Museums Association.

Roveto, Connie I., B.A.,B.Ed. ■ Ⓢ ⚥
Chief Operating Officer, THE TRUST COMPANY OF BANK OF MONTREAL, 302 Bay St., 11th Fl., Toronto, ON M5X 1A1 (416) 867-6487, FAX 956-2363. Senior Vice-President, Asset Management Services, BANK OF MONTREAL. EDUC: Univ. of Toronto, B.A.(English Language & Lit.), B.Ed. CAREER: VP, Central Capital Management Ltd., 1986-89; VP, Central Guaranty Trust, 1988-89; Exec. VP, United Financial Management Ltd., 1989-93; Pres. & CEO, 1993-95. AFFIL: St. Michael's Coll., Univ. of Toronto (Senate & Collegium); Queen Elizabeth Hospital Foundation (Dir.); Interlink Community Cancer Nurses (Dir.); Canadian Club of Toronto (Dir.). INTERESTS: films; reading; tennis; fitness.

Rovinescu, Olivia, B.Ed.,M.A. ■ ⚥
Associate Director, Centre for Teaching and

Learning Services, CONCORDIA UNIVERSITY, 7141 Sherbrooke St. W., Montreal, QC H4B 1R6 (514) 848-2495 or 848-4955, FAX 848-2497. Born Romania 1952. m. Clifton Ruggles. 2 ch. EDUC: McGill Univ., B.Ed. 1976, M.A.(Educ.) 1982. CAREER: high sch. English Teacher, Académie Michele Provost, 1981-83; Humanities Teacher, John Abbott Coll., 1983-84; Dir., Lacolle Centre for Educational Innovation, 1984-96; Sessional Lecturer, Centennial Coll., 1985-91; Sessional Lecturer, Active Retirement Program, Coll. Marie Victorin, 1985-91; Sessional Lecturer, Dept. of Religion & Phil., Fac. of Educ., McGill Univ., 1987-89, 1993. SELECTED PUBLICATIONS: *Expressions of Montreal's Youth*, children's poetry & photography (Montreal: Community Expressions, 1974); *Exploring the World of Work*, poetry (Montreal: Community Expressions, 1975); *Words on Work*, with Stanley Nemiroff & Clifton Ruggles, text & photography (Toronto: Globe Modern Circulation Press, 1981); "Thinking Critically about Critical Thinking," with Stanley Nemiroff (*Thinking and Learning* Jan. 1990); "Mentally Handicapped Students Join Workforce," with Clifton Ruggles (*Montreal Gazette* Jan. 1993); "The Combat Process," with Clifton Ruggles (*Montreal Serai* Spring 1993); *Dimensions of Literacy in a Multicultural Society*, with Riva Heft (Montreal: Concordia Univ., 1993); *Outsider Blues: A Voice from the Shadows*, with Clifton Ruggles (Halifax: Fernwood Books, 1996); various other publications. AFFIL: Youth in Motion (Bd. of Dir.); Leave Out Violence (Bd. 1994-95); Nomad Scientists' Exhibitions (Bd. of Dir.). HONS: McConnell Memorial Fellowship, 1979-80, 1980-81. INTERESTS: cycling; jogging; photography. MISC: various scholarships; numerous conference presentations; recipient, various grants; subject of various articles, incl. "Work Up Those Creative Powers" (*Thursday Report* Sept. 25, 1986). COMMENT: *"I'm passionate about ideas, social change, combatting racism. I value creativity and derive pleasure from generating ideas and implementing them. I enjoy helping individuals become life-long learners and critical thinkers. But best of all, I love being a mother to my daughters Amy and Ali."*

Rowe, Ebonnie ● ○ ♛ ♎

Co-Founder and Director, EACH ONE TEACH ONE MENTOR PROGRAM, Frontier College, 35 Jackes Ave., Toronto, ON M4T 1E2 (416) 923-3591, FAX 323-3522. Founder and Director, PHEMPHAT PRODUCTIONS. EDUC: George Vanier Secondary Sch., Hons. Grad.; Univ. of Toronto, English Lit. courses, three years. CAREER: Research Asst., Decima Research

Ltd., 1979-82; Asst., part-time, Tapestry Productions, 1982-89; Micro-Computer Salesman, Compucentre, 1982; Sec., Ian Roberts Inc., 1982-83; Sec. to the Publisher, Key Porter Books, 1983-84; Research Coord., Hay Management Consultants, 1984-88; Comm. Asst., Polysar Limited, 1988-89; freelance admin., sec., public rel'ns & proj. coord., 1989-90; Power of Sale Clerk, Gowling, Strathy & Henderson, 1990-93; freelance legal sec., 1993 to date. SELECTED CREDITS: Prod. Asst. & Researcher, B-Fun'n, *Wonderin' Where the Lions Are* (video). SELECTED PUBLICATIONS: *The Wedding Workbook* (1990); Fashion Ed., *Contrast Newspaper*, 1982-86. AFFIL: Each One, Teach One Mentor Program (Founder; Dir.); Black Film & Video Network. HONS: Award winner, "Women on the Move," *The Toronto Sun* 1995. MISC: volunteer researcher & organizer for charity & other events, incl. Expose '82, Expose '83, Freedom Fest '88 and Fashion Cares, 1989. COMMENT: *"Each One, Teach One, launched in February 1992, addresses the shortage of examples of successful Black role models that Black youth can see, identify with, learn from and emulate. Success nurtures success and Black youth need to see other Blacks in positions they would like to see themselves in. They need to see tangible examples that demonstrate that obstacles can be overcome. The program is run out of Frontier College, a national adult literacy and tutoring organization founded in 1899. Founder and Director of PhemPhat Productions, an entertainment company that promotes the advancement of women in all aspects of the music industry. Produced the first music seminar for women in urban music, as well as all-female talent showcases called HONEY JAMS."*

Rowe, Penelope M.,M.A., B.A., M.Sc. ● ○ ✒

Executive Director, COMMUNITY SERVICES COUNCIL, NEWFOUNDLAND AND LABRADOR, Virginia Park Plaza, Newfoundland Dr., Ste. 201, St. John's, NF A1A 3E9 (709) 753-9860, FAX 753-6112, EMAIL penelope_rowe@porthole. entnet.nf.ca. Born St. John's 1943. m. William N. Rowe. 2 ch. W. Dorian Rowe, Tory L. Rowe. EDUC: Emerson Coll., Boston, B.A. (Speech Pathology) 1965; Memorial Univ. of Newfoundland, Certificate (Bus. Admin.) 1985; London Sch. of Econ., M.Sc.(Social Policy) 1988. CAREER: Host & Journalist, CBC TV; Exec. Sec., Early Childhood Development Association; Exec. Dir, Community Housing & Support Svcs; Chairperson, Workers' Compensation Commission, Nfld. & Labrador; Exec. Dir., Community Svcs Council, Nfld. & Labrador; Chair, Social Policy Advisory Committee, Gov't of Nfld. & Labrador. **AFFIL:** National Volunteer Organization (Dir. 1986-94); Canadian Council on Social Development (Dir. 1978-86). **HONS:** Canada 125 Medal; named one of Canada's 50 most influential women, *Chatelaine* Magazine; recognized for outstanding contributions to the development of social policy in Canada, Canadian Council on Social Development, 1995. **INTERESTS:** integration of econ. & social dev. **COMMENT:** *"Penelope Rowe has been influencing public policy for 20 years. As a senior executive, consultant, policy analyst, researcher, journalist, social planner and speech therapist, she has dedicated her professional life to improving, expanding, and reorganizing social programs."*

Rowland, Beryl, M.A.,Ph.D.,D.Lit., D.Litt. 🐚 📚 ♂
Distinguished Professor Emerita, Department of English, YORK UNIVERSITY, North York, ON. Adjunct Professor, Department of English, UNIVERSITY OF VICTORIA, Box 1700, Victoria, BC V8W 2Y2 (604) 721-7236. Born Scotland. m. Dr. Edward Murray Rowland. **EDUC:** Univ. of London, UK, B.A., D.Lit. 1980; Univ. of Alberta, M.A. 1958; Univ. of British Columbia, Ph.D. 1962. **CAREER:** Asst. Prof., Dept. of English, York Univ., 1962-68; Assoc. Prof., 1968-71; Prof., 1971-83; Distinguished Prof. Emerita, 1983 to date; Distinguished Research Prof. Emerita; Visiting Scholar, Univ. of Victoria, 1987-89; Adjunct Prof., 1989 to date. **SELECTED PUBLICATIONS:** *Cressida in Alberta*, drama (1955); *Behold a Pale Horse*, drama, CBC (1956); *Companion to Chaucer Studies*, ed. (Oxford, 1968, revised ed., 1979); *Blind Beasts: Chaucer's Animal World* (Kent State Univ. Press and Allen & Unwin, 1971); *Animals with Human Faces* (Univ. of Tennessee Press, 1973); *Chaucer and Middle English Studies in Honor of Rossell Hope Robbins*, ed. (Kent State Univ. Press, 1974); *Birds with Human Souls* (Univ. of Tennessee Press, 1978); *Medieval Women's Guide to Health: The First Gynecological Handbook* (Kent State Univ. Press and Croom Helm Presses, 1981); *Earl Birney: Chaucerian Irony*, ed. (Univ. of Toronto Press, 1985); "Old English & Middle English Poetry with commentary, *Poetry in English* (Oxford Univ. Press, 1987); *The Artificial Memory, Chaucer and Modern Scholars* (Poetica, Tokyo, 1992); "The Chess Problem in The Book of the Duchess" (*Anglia* 80 1963); "Sitting up with a Corpse: Malthus According to Melville" (*Journal of American Studies* 1972); "Chaucer's Working Wyf: The Unraveling of a Yarn-Spinner" in *Chaucer in the Eighties*, Julian N. Wasserman & Robert J. Blanch,

eds. (Syracuse Univ. Press, 1986); more than 150 articles published in learned journals in Canada, Europe, Japan & US. **EDIT:** bibliographer, *Bulletin*, International Association of University Professors of English; Ed. Bd., *The Chaucer Review*; Ed. Bd., *Florilegium*; Ed. Bd., *Bestia*. **AFFIL:** Association of Canadian University Teachers of English; Humanities Association; International Association of University Professors of English (Int'l Consulting Committee); English Association; Modern Languages Association (Life Mbr.); Medieval Academy of America; New Chaucer Society; Epopée Animale; Victoria Golf Club. **HONS:** Alberta Golden Jubilee Drama Award, *Cressida in Alberta*, 1955; American Univ. Presses Book Award, 1974; Huntington Fellow, International Association of University Professors of English, 1976; D.Litt.(Hon.), Mount Saint Vincent Univ., 1982; Pres., International New Chaucer Society, 1984-86; Canada 125 Medal, 1993; reappointed to Fac. of Grad. Studies, York Univ., 1995-2002. **MISC:** numerous conference presentations; frequent guest lecturer: Ist woman Ph.D. in English, Univ. of B.C., 1962; 1st woman Pres., International New Chaucer Society.

Rowntree, Jessie-May Anna, B.F.A., B.A. 🐚 /
Director of Communications, YORK UNIVERSITY, 4700 Keele St., North York, ON M3J 1P3. Born Toronto 1956. m. Gordon Bontoft. 2 ch. Nicole Bontoft, Lindsay Bontoft. **EDUC:** York Univ., B.A.(Fine Arts) 1981, B.A.(English) 1984. **CAREER:** Prod. Asst., Canadian Institute of Chartered Accountants, 1979; Owner, Rowntree Assoc., 1980-83; Ed., *Gazette*, York Univ., 1984; Mng Ed., 1985; Asst. Dir., Comm., 1987-88; Dir. of Comm., 1989 to date. **SELECTED PUBLICATIONS:** *Modern Canadian Eloquence*, Ed. (1985); Publisher, *Profiles*. **AFFIL:** International Association of Business Communicators; Canadian Council for the Advancement of Education–Ontario (Dir.); Council for the Advancement & Support of Education; Ontario Universities Public Affairs Council (Past Chair 1994-95); Canadian Organization for Part-Time University Students (Ont. Coord. 1981-82; Pres. 1982-84; Past. Pres. 1984-85). **HONS:** Val Hudson Award for Outstanding contribution to college life, Atkinson Coll., York Univ.; Gold Medal Award, Best Univ. & Coll. Magazine in Canada (*Profiles*), CCAE. **INTERESTS:** karate; curling.

Rowsell, Sally Ann, B.Mus.,B.Mus.Ed., M.Mus,R.M.T. ■ ⊗ ☺ ☒
Classical Musician, Piano Teacher, Performer,

Organizer, Examiner & Clinician. 79 New Cove Rd., St. John's, NF A1A 2C2 (709) 726-2414. Past President, NEWFOUNDLAND REGISTERED MUSIC TEACHERS' ASSOCIATION. Born St. John's 1963. s. **EDUC:** Memorial Univ. of Newfoundland, B.Mus. 1985, B.Mus.Ed. 1985; GuildHall Sch. of Music, London, UK, 1984; Brandon Univ., M.Mus.(Performance & Lit.) 1987; Royal Conservatory of Music, Adjudicator's/Examiner's course 1990. **CAREER:** Teacher of Piano, Brandon Univ. Conservatory, 1986-88; Lecturer in Piano, Brandon Univ., 1987-88; Music Specialist, Dunne Memorial System, St. Mary's Bay, Nfld., 1988-89; Professional Accompanist, 1988 to date; Private Piano Teacher, private studio, St. John's, 1989 to date; Piano Fac., Eastern Music Camp, Mount Pearl, Nfld., 1994 to date; Royal Conservatory of Music Examiner & Clinician. **SELECTED CREDITS:** numerous recitals & concerts as soloist, Nfld. & Man., 1983 to date; accompanist with Jon Kimura Parker, 1992; official accompanist for numerous CIBC prov. & nat'l music festivals; frequent appearances on CBC Radio (local: *Musicraft*, Nat'l: *Arts National*) & CBC TV. **SELECTED PUBLICATIONS:** *A History of the Newfoundland Registered Music Teachers' Association* (Canadian Federation of Music Teachers' Associations, 1995). **AFFIL:** Newfoundland Registered Music Teachers' Association (Pres. Elect 1991-92; Pres. 1992-94; Past Pres. 1994-96); Canadian Music Festival Adjudicators' Association. **HONS:** Grad. Teaching Assistantship, Brandon Univ., 1986, 1987; A.L. Collis Limited Scholarship, Memorial Univ. of Newfoundland, 1982, 1983; Frederick & Isabel Emerson Memorial Scholarship, Memorial Univ. of Newfoundland, 1984. **INTERESTS:** classical music; arts; jazz; blues; gourmet cooking; interior design; reading; exercising; travelling. **MISC:** 1st Convenor, Canada Music Week in Nfld., 1990-91; rep. for Nfld., Canadian Federation of Music Teachers' Association annual meetings, 1993, 1994. **COMMENT:** *"I feel successful since I love what I do, am in control of my career as a self-employed individual, and am secure in an unstable financial time."*

Roy-Vienneau, Jocelyne, P.Eng.,B.Sc., M.P.A. ■■ ⚛ 🎓 ✊

Instructional Dean, NEW BRUNSWICK COMMUNITY COLLEGE - BATHURST, P.O. Box 266, Bathurst, NB E2A 3Z2 (506) 547-2187, FAX 547-2917, EMAIL vienneje@gov.nb.ca. Born Newcastle, N.B. 1956. m. Ronald Vienneau. 2 ch. Isabelle, Cédric. **EDUC:** Dept. of Advanced Educ. & Labour, Certificate (Adult Teaching) 1982; Univ. de Moncton, B.Sc.(Indust. Eng.) 1979, M.P.A. 1995. **CAREER:** Proj. Eng., Esso Imperial Refinery, Montreal, 1979-80; Instructor, Mech. Eng. Technology Program, N.B. Community Coll., 1980-82; Coord., CAD/CAM Centre, 1982-87; Dept. Head, CAD/CAM & Metal Training Programs, 1987 to date; Instructional Dean, Eng. Technology & Trade Programs, 1987 to date. **DIRECTOR:** *Ven d'Est* (bi-monthly magazine). **AFFIL:** N.B. Association of Professional Engineers; Société des Acadiens et Acadiennes du Nouveau-Brunswick (Pres., Pointe-aux-Pères section 1992-94); Caisse Populaire de Robertville Ltée (Bd. of Dir. 1984-87). **MISC:** guest speaker, various occasions incl. annual mtg of Les Dames d'Acadie; panelist, "A Question of Attitude" conference, Atomic Energy of Canada Limited, Nov. 1994; official reporter, Congrès Mondial Acadien, Aug. 1994.

Rozema, Patricia, B.A. 📺 🎬 🎭

Filmmaker, CRUCIAL PICTURES (film prod. company), 108 Bellevue Ave., Toronto, ON M5T 2N9 (416) 504-3992, FAX 504-8500. Born Kingston, Ont. 1958. 1 ch. Jacoba Lesley Rozema. **EDUC:** Calvin Coll., B.A.(English & Phil.) 1981. **CAREER:** Journalist, Global TV & *The Journal*, CBC, 1981-84; film writer & dir. **SELECTED CREDITS:** Dir./Writer/Ed./Prod., *Passion: A Letter in 16MM* (dramatic short); Dir./Writer/Ed./Co-Prod., *I've Heard the Mermaids Singing* (feature), 1987; Dir./Writer/Ed./Exec. Prod., *White Room* (feature), 1990; Writer/Dir., "Desperanto," *Montréal vu par...* (feature), 1991; Writer/Dir., *When Night is Falling* (feature), 1995. **AFFIL:** Amnesty International; Foster Parents' Association; Writers' Guild of Canada; ACTRA; PEN; Director's Guild of Canada. **HONS:** *I've Heard the Mermaids Singing* winner of Prix de la Jeunesse, 10 int'l awards, 9 Genie nominations; *White Room* winner of 4 int'l awards; received for *When Night is Falling*: Best Film, Melbourne Int'l Film Festival; Audience Prize, Sydney Int'l Film Festival; Best Film, Créteil Women's Film Festival; Audience Award, Berlin Film Festival (in official competition); Best Film, London Gay & Lesbian Int'l Festival, UK. **COMMENT:** *"I do what I can."*

Rozsa, Marilyn $

Vice-President, Independent Business and Agriculture, BANK OF MONTREAL, 55 Bloor St. W., 15th Fl., Toronto, ON M4W 3N5 (416) 927-2662, FAX 927-3006. **CAREER:** various positions, Personal & Commercial Bnkg, Montreal, Bank of Montreal, 1972-94; VP, Independent Bus. & Agric., Toronto, 1994 to date. **AFFIL:** York Finch Hospital Foundation (Past Dir. & Mbr. of Exec. Committee); Bank of Montreal, Our People's Fund (Bd. of Dir.); Canadian

Bankers' Association (Independent Bus. Committee).

Rubenstein, Gale, LL.B. ⚖️
Senior Partner, GOODMAN PHILLIPS & VINEBERG, 250 Yonge St., Ste. 2400, Toronto, ON M5B 2M6 (416) 979-2211, FAX 979-1234. Born Toronto 1953. m. Dr. Joseph Blankier. 3 ch. EDUC: Osgoode Hall Law Sch., LL.B. 1975. BAR: Ont., 1976. CAREER: Sr. Ptnr, Goodman Phillips & Vineberg. SELECTED PUBLICATIONS: "Conflicting Jurisdictions and Work-Out Arrangements" (*Journal on Creditor-Debtor Relations*); *Insolvency of Insurance Companies in Canada: An Overview.* AFFIL: Law Society of Upper Canada (Committee for the Certification of Insolvency Specialists); Canadian Bar Association (Subsections on Insolvency & Insur.); American Bar Association (Subsection on Tort & Insur. Practice); National American Association of Insurance Commissioners (Committee on Insur. Liquidations & Rehabilitations); International Bar Association (Subsection on Insur. & Insolvency & Creditor's Rights).

Rubes, Susan Douglas ■ ⊗ ♥
Actress, Producer. RR #3, Collingwood, ON L9Y 3Z2, EMAIL 74353,174@compuserve. com. Born Vienna 1925. m. Jan Rubes. 3 ch. Jonathan, Anthony, Christopher. EDUC: in Czechoslovakia & New York. CAREER: actress in radio, TV, theatre & film, 1945 to date; founded Young People's Theatre, Toronto, 1964; opened Young People's Theatre Centre, 1977; Head, CBC Radio Drama, 1982-86; Pres., Family Channel, 1987-89; film producer. SELECTED CREDITS: *He Who Gets Slapped*, Broadway theatre debut; lead, *Bell Ami*, United Artists; Kathy Grant, *The Guiding Light*; *The Outside Chance of Maximilian Glick*, feature film; *Street Legal*, TV. DIRECTOR: Haysett Ltd. HONS: Tony Award, best debut on Broadway; Drama Bench Award, 1974; Order of Canada, 1975; Woman of the Year Award, B'Nai B'Rith Women's Council of Toronto, 1979; New York Citation. INTERESTS: grandchildren; golf; tennis. MISC: Young People's Theatre renamed The Susan Douglas Rubes Theatre.

Rubess, Baṇuta N., B.A.,D.Phil. ■ ■ ⊗ 📖
Writer/Director/Theatre Artist. 40 Borden St., Toronto, ON M5S 2M9 (416) 929-9895, FAX 929-6146. Born Toronto 1956. m. Nicholas Gotham. 1 ch. Dzintars Gotham. EDUC: Queen's Univ., B.A.(Hons., Drama/Hist.) 1977; Univ. of Oxford, D.Phil.(Modern Hist.) 1982. CAREER: theatre company, 1982; Lecturer, Glendon Coll., York Univ., 1987-89; Assoc.

Artist, Theatre Passe Muraille, 1992-96; has been Playwright-in-residence, Univ. of Western Ontario, Great Canadian Theatre Company, Theatre Columbus, Theatre Direct, Mixed Company & Nightwood Theatre; has taught courses in playmaking, improvisation & collective creation workshops at universities & high schools across Canada & in Germany, 1985 to date; taught Creating Opera in the Schools, Canadian Opera Company, 1995; Communications Consultant, The Humphrey Group, 1994 to date. SELECTED CREDITS: director, all of her own work & several other plays incl.: *The Stillborn Lover* (by Timothy Findlay, Theatre Passe Muraille, 1995); *Nigredo Hotel* (chamber opera by Nic Gotham & Ann-Marie MacDonald, produced by Tapestry Music Theatre & Tarragon Theatre, 1992; tour to Great Britain, 1993, & to Victoria, Vancouver, Toronto, 1995; recorded for CBC Radio); *Goodnight, Desdemona* (by Ann-Marie MacDonald, several theatres across Canada). SELECTED PUBLICATIONS: more than 10 English-language plays incl.: *Head in a Bag*; *Pope Joan; Smoke Damage; Boom, Baby, Boom!, Thin Ice*; 4 screenplays (documentary, film, drama); 3 plays in Latvian; translations of short stories by Andra Neiburga, published in *Agni Review*, Boston; articles published in *Theatrum, Canadian Theatre Review, Broadside, Fireweed, Fuse & Latvian* literary journals. AFFIL: Writers' Guild; PEN; PUC; CAEA; Toronto Arts Council (Bd. of Dir. 1989-92); Nightwood Theatre (Bd. of Dir. 1986-88). HONS: Dora Mavor Moore Award & Chalmers Children's Play Award for *Thin Ice*; PBLA (World Federation of Free Latvians) Literary Award for *Tango Lugano*; Latvian Critics' Award for production in Riga of *The Avenging Woman*; Ont. Rhodes Scholar; Helen Simpson Lynett Scholarship; Susan Near Drama Prize; Gold Medal in Hist., Queen's Univ. INTERESTS: politics; literature; motherhood; Latvia. MISC: translator of Latvian prose. COMMENT: "*Baṇuta Rubess has written and directed more than 30 plays in English and Latvian. She has moved the hearts and minds of audiences across Canada and Europe.*"

Rubinsky, Holley, B.A., M.Ed. ■ 📖 ⊕ 📁
Writer and Master of the Usui System of Reiki Healing. 50 Prince Arthur Ave., Ste. 904, Toronto, ON M5R 1B5 (416) 960-3306. Born Los Angeles 1943. m. Yuri Rubinsky. 1 ch. EDUC: Univ. of California at L.A., B.A.(Motion Pictures) 1965, M.Ed. 1974. CAREER: teacher; short story writer; Writing Instructor, Banff Sch. of Fine Arts, 1986-87; Writing Instructor,

Continuing Studies, Univ. of Toronto, 1989-91; Reiki Practitioner. **SELECTED PUBLICATIONS:** *Rapid Transits and Other Stories* (Polestar, 1990); *Butcher, Baker: The People of Kaslo* (Buchanan, Loki, & True Blue Press, 1993); *At First I Hope for Rescue* (Knopf Canada, 1997); stories in numerous Cdn & American magazines & anthologies. **EDIT:** Ed. Bd., *Descant* Magazine, 1987-89. **AFFIL:** Writers' Union of Canada; PEN. **HONS:** Samuel Goldwyn Writing Award, Univ. of California at L.A., 1965; Finalist, Fiction, Western Magazine Awards, 1988, 1989; Gold Medal for Fiction, National Magazine Awards, 1989; Journey Prize, McClelland and Stewart, 1989. **INTERESTS:** photography; exploration of voice & personal sound for healing. **COMMENT:** *Yuri Rubinsky writes: "Holley Rubinsky combines compassion for other's suffering with a talent for stark narrative to create award-winning short stories; compassion with a talent for aiding healing in her practice of Reiki."*

Rubio, Mary, B.A.,M.A., Ph.D. ■ ✎ 📖 ✪
Professor, Department of English, UNIVERSITY OF GUELPH, Guelph, ON N1G 2W1 (519) 824-4120, ext. 3261, FAX 766-0844. Born Mattoon, Ill. 1939. m. Gerald J. Rubio. 2 ch. Tracy Katherine Rubio Siddall, Jennifer Joanna Rubio. **EDUC:** DePauw Univ., Ind., B.A. (English) 1961; Univ. of Illinois, M.A.(English Lit.) 1967; McMaster Univ., Ph.D.(English Lit.) 1982. **CAREER:** Lecturer, Univ. of Guelph, 1974-83; Asst. Prof., 1983-87; Assoc. Prof., 1987-96; Prof., 1996 to date. **SELECTED PUBLICATIONS:** *KANATA: An Anthology of Canadian Children's Literature*, ed. with Glenys Stow (Methuen, 1976); *The Genesis of Grove's "The Adventure of Leonard Broadus": A Text and Commentary*, ed. (Canadian Children's Press, 1983); *The Selected Journals of L.M. Montgomery*, Vol I: 1889-1910 (1985); Vol. 2: 1919-1921 (1987); Vol. 3: 1921-29 (1992), ed. with Elizabeth Waterston (Oxford Univ. Press); *Harvesting Thistles: The Textual Garden of L.M. Montgomery. Essays on Her Novels and Journals*, ed. (Canadian Children's Press, 1994); *L.M. Montgomery: Writing a Life*, with Elizabeth Waterston (ECW Press, 1995); "Subverting the Trite: L.M. Montgomery's 'Room of Her Own'" (*Canadian Children's Literature* 65 1992); various other publications. **EDIT:** Co-founder & Co-ed., *CCL: Canadian Children's Literature*, A Journal of Criticism and Review, 1975 to date. **AFFIL:** CAAS; IRSCL; Association of Canadian College & University Teachers of English; Modern Language Association; Children's Literature Association; Friends of the Osborne

Collection. **INTERESTS:** Cdn, American & children's literature. **MISC:** numerous Ontario Arts Council & SSHRCC grants; literary advisor to the estate of L.M. Montgomery, 1982-92. **COMMENT:** *"Mary Rubio has worked since 1975 to establish the field of children's literature in Canada; co-founder and co-editor of Canada's only academic journal about children's literature, she is also co-editor of the L.M. Montgomery journals. (Lucy Maud Montgomery wrote Anne of Green Gables.)"*

Runte, Roseann, B.A.,M.A.,Ph.D. ✎ 📖
President, VICTORIA UNIVERSITY, 73 Queen's Park Cres., Toronto, ON M5S 1K7 (416) 585-4510, FAX 585-4459, EMAIL rrunte@epas.utoronto.ca. Born Kingston, N.Y. 1948. m. Hans R. Runte. **EDUC:** State Univ. of New York at New Paltz, B.A.(French) 1968; Univ. of Kansas, M.A.(French) 1969, M.Ph. 1971, Ph.D.(French) 1974. **CAREER:** Lecturer & Language Lab. Dir., Bethany Coll., 1970-71; Lecturer, Adult Studies, Saint Mary's Univ., 1971-72; Lecturer, Dalhousie Univ., 1972-74; Asst. Prof., 1974-79; Assoc. Prof., 1979-83; Asst. Dean, Fac. of Arts & Sci., 1980-82; Chair, Dept. of French, 1980-83; Pres., Univ. Sainte-Anne, 1983-88; Principal, Glendon Coll., York Univ., 1988-94; Pres., Victoria Univ., 1994 to date. **SELECTED PUBLICATIONS:** *Studies in Eighteenth Century Culture* vol. VII, VIII & IX, ed. (Madison: Univ. of Wisconsin Press, 1977; 1978; 1979); *Brumes bleues*, poetry (Sherbrooke: Naaman, 1982); *Faux soleils* (Sherbrooke: Naaman, 1984); *Regional Economic and Cultural Development*, ed. (Nova Scotia: Univ. Ste. Anne, 1989); *Birmanie Blues* (Toronto: Editions du GREF, 1994); *The Idea of Beauty* (Tokyo: ICLA, 1996); numerous other publications. **EDIT:** Ed. Bd., *Œuvres et critiques*; Advisory Bd., *LittéRéalité*; Ed. Bd., *Dalhousie French Studies*, 1980-88; Advisory Bd., 1988 to date; Review Ed. (Lit. Hist. & Crit.), *The French Review*, 1988-94; Ed. Bd., *Mosaic*, 1994 to date; Ed., *Recherches littéraires/Literary Research*, 1994 to date. **AFFIL:** Canadian Commission for UNESCO (Pres. 1992-96); Club of Rome; Int'l Advisory Bd., Expo 2000, Hanover, Germany; Foundation for International Training (Bd. Mbr.; VP 1994-95, 1995-96; Chair of Bd. 1996 to date; Association of Universities & Colleges of Canada; Canadian Literary Research Foundation (VP); Canadian Society for Eighteenth-Century Studies; Atlantic Society for Eighteenth-Century Studies; American Society for Eighteenth-Century Studies; French Society for Eighteenth-Century Studies; International Society for Eighteenth-Century Studies; Canadian Comparative Literature Association; International Compara-

tive Literature Association; Modern Language Association of America; Association des Professeurs de Français des Universités et Collèges Canadiens; American Association of Teachers of French; Gardiner Museum (Bd. V-Chair); Northrop Frye Centre (Advisory Bd. Mbr.; Dir. 1994-95); The Canadian Club; Le cercle canadien; Phi Delta Kappa; Delta Kappa Gamma. **HONS:** Prisma Scholarship, 1965; Leslie Whitwright Award, 1968; French Gov't Award for Excellence in French, 1968; N.Y. State Regents' Scholarship, 1965-68; Merit Award, Dalhousie Univ., 1980, 1981; Chevalier des Palmes académiques, 1985; François Coppée poetry prize, Académie française, 1988; Dame Commander, Order of Saint John of Jerusalem (Malta), 1992; Chevalier, Ordre du mérite, 1994; D.Litt.(Hon.), Acadia Univ., 1989; D.Litt.(Hon.), Memorial Univ. of Newfoundland, 1990; D.Litt.(Hon.), Univ. Vest de Timisoara, Romania, 1996. **INTERESTS:** educ.; literature. **MISC:** Co-Host, French radio program, CHFX-FM, Halifax (1972-83); numerous conference presentations; numerous addresses, speeches & talks; numerous poetry readings; recipient, various grants. **COMMENT:** *"Educator, writer and scholar, Roseann Runte has devoted her career to international and intercultural understanding through education and communication."*

Rusch, Barbara, B.A.,M.A. 📖 ⊚ ⊰
Ephemerist. Founder and President, THE EPHEMERA SOCIETY OF CANADA, 50 Hallcrown Place, Ste. 100, Willowdale, ON M2J 1P7 (416) 492-5958, FAX (416) 492-5958. Born Toronto 1949. m. Donald Zaldin. 2 ch., 4 stpch. Corinne Rusch-Drutz, Adam Drutz, Matthew Zaldin, Elise Zaldin, Erin Zaldin, Ryan Zaldin. **EDUC:** Univ. of Toronto, B.A.(French Lit.) 1971, M.A.(French Lit.) 1976. **CAREER:** Founder & Pres., Ephemera Society of Canada, 1987 to date; writer & lecturer on subjects relating to 19th-century ephemera & social history. **SELECTED PUBLICATIONS:** "Canadian Printed Ephemera: An Historical Survey" (*A.B. Bookman's Weekly* Mar. 1988); "Collecting Victorian Ephemera" (*Journal of the Victorian Studies Association,* Univ. of Toronto Fall 1991); "Patterns of Alienation in 19th-Century Manuscript Ephemera" (*Ephemera Journal* 1992); "Blue Boxes Devour Paper Past" (*Ottawa Citizen* July 1993); "The Art of Persuasion: Images of Victorian Advertising Ephemera" (*Ephemera Canada,* 1994); "Factory View Trade Cards: Image of a New Social Order" (*Journal of the Trade Card Collectors' Association,* 1996). **EDIT:** Ed., *Ephemera Canada,* 1991 to date. **AFFIL:** Ephemera Society of America (Dir.

1992-96); Ephemera Society, UK; Ephemera Society of Australia; Bootmakers of Toronto (Sherlock Holmes Society of Canada) (Dir. 1987-91). **HONS:** Ont. Scholar, 1967; Varsity Fund Scholar, 1967-70; True Davidson Memorial Award for Excellence, Bootmakers of Toronto, 1986; Warren Carlton Memorial Award, Bootmakers of Toronto, 1988, 1989; Master Bootmaker Award, 1989; Maurice Rickards Award, Ephemera Society of America, 1989; Samuel Pepys Award, Ephemera Society, UK, 1992; Award for "Goddesses & Whores": The Socio-Sexual Implications of the Corset," Trade Card Collectors' Association, 1996. **INTERESTS:** collecting Victorian ephemera incl. advtg trade cards, chromolithographed photo albums, Queen Victoria memorabilia, personal letters & American Civil War letters, manuscript diaries, autograph albums, Judaica, dance cards, Valentines & Christmas cards, photographs & stereo views, tins, medicine bottles, boxes, newspapers, magazines, memento mori. **MISC:** articles written about Barbara Rusch in *The Toronto Star, The Globe and Mail, Canadian Living;* various other publications; various conference presentations; organizes exhibitions & symposia of ephemera; various media interviews, incl. CBC Radio *Gabereau* (1992); *Hunters and Gatherers,* a documentary about collectors (1994). **COMMENT:** *"As an ephemerist, I see myself as a custodian and interpreter of Canada's printed heritage, preserving the documents of popular culture, promoting and sharing with others the knowledge they reveal and passing on evidence of our social history to future generations. My continued goal is to see the word 'ephemera' accepted into popular English usage."*

Rusk, Sue ■ ⊗
Artist. 15 Kilburn Cres., Montreal, QC H3X 3B8 (514) 488-9541, FAX 342-1357. Born Montreal 1937. m. Marvin. 3 ch. Ilene Naomi, Bonnie, Peter. **EDUC:** Macdonald Coll., McGill Univ., Teacher's certification 1955; Saidye Bronfman Centre, Montreal, fine arts 1959-71; Concordia Univ., fine arts 1977-84. **CAREER:** elementary sch. Teacher, Protestant Sch. Bd. of Greater Montreal, 1955-61; fitness instructor, YMHA, Montreal, 1970-80; Dir. & Teacher, Creative Art Sch. for Children, Montreal, 1972-80; Instructor, painting & drawing, Saidye Bronfman Centre, 1984 to date; Dir. & instructor, Sue Rusk's Fitness for Women, 1989 to date. **EXHIBITIONS:** solo, Picture Hook Gallery, Winnipeg (1978); solo, Gallery CJS, Denver (1981); solo, Wallack Gallery, Ottawa (1982); solo, Angel Art Gallery, Ottawa (1984); solo, Galerie Daniel, Montreal (1985, 1988, 1989); solo, Leo Kamen Gallery, Toronto

(1989); solo, Galerie Estampe Plus, Quebec City (1990); solo, Galerie Barbara Silverberg, Montreal (1994); solo, Saidye Bronfman Centre for the Arts, Espace Trois, Montreal (1996); more than 70 group exhibitions, incl. *Printmakers '74*, Saidye Bronfman Centre, Montreal (1974), *Première Triennale Mondiale de l'Estampe*, Musée d'Art Contemporain, Chamalières, France (1988), *Int'l Print Bienniale 1993*, Japan (1993), & Pratt & Whitney Gallery, Les Femmeuses, Montreal (1987, 1988, 1992-96). COLLECTIONS: Bell Canada; Sony Music Ltd.; Bibliothèque Nationale de Québec; Corvallis Collection, Oregon Univ.; Collection Prêt d'Oeuvres d'Art, Musée du Québec; Cabo Frio Museum, Brazil; Alcan; Royal Bank; Pratt & Whitney; more than 15 other collections. AFFIL: Print & Drawing Council of Canada; Atelier Graphia Inc., Montreal; Conseil Québécois de L'Estampe; Conseil de la Peinture du Québec; Montreal Printmakers Society. INTERESTS: painting; drawing; printmaking; phys. fitness; teaching. MISC: listed in *Canadian Who's Who*; represented in Montreal by Dominion Gallery, Galerie Barbara Silverberg, Museum of Fine Arts Sales & Rental Gallery, & Guild Graphique. COMMENT: *"My art is about people, music, nature and colour. To me these are metaphors for history, the intrinsic power of organic life and consciousness. It is an ongoing quest."*

Rusnak, Anne M., B.A.,M.A., D.E.A. ■ 🎓 📖 ○

Instructor III, Department of French Studies, UNIVERSITY OF WINNIPEG, Winnipeg, MB R3B 2E9 (204) 786-9452, FAX 783-7981. Born Winnipeg 1954. m. Glenn Rusnak. 1 ch. EDUC: Univ. of Winnipeg, B.A.(Hons. 1st class, French Language & Lit.) 1977; Univ. of Manitoba, M.A.(French Lit.) 1984; Univ. de Bordeaux III, Diplôme d'études approfondies (Children's Lit.) 1987. CAREER: Coord., English Immersion Program for Québécois students, Univ. of Winnipeg, 1979; Lecturer, Dept. of French, 1980-81; Lab. Instructor II, 1981-83; Instructor II, 1983-88; Dir. of Language Laboratories, 1984-86; Instructor III, 1988 to date. AFFIL: Association des professeurs de français des universités et collèges canadiens; Association canadienne pour l'avancement de la littérature de jeunesse; Books for Youth (Int'l Bd.); Children's Literature Association; Canadian Children's Book Centre; Ukrainian Canadian Foundation of Taras Shevchenko; Ukrainian Canadian Congress (Canada-Ukraine Rel'ns Committee). HONS: Univ. of Manitoba Grad. Fellowships, 1978-79, 1979-80; Merit of Excellence Award, Univ. of Winnipeg, 1985, 1986; Clifford J. Robson Award

for Excellence in Teaching, Univ. of Winnipeg, 1986; Gov't of France Grad. Award, 1986-87. INTERESTS: reading; travel; cross-country skiing; cooking. MISC: "Popular Prof." in the *Maclean's Guide to Universities*, 1996. COMMENT: *"I feel indeed fortunate to have the opportunity to share my enthusiasm for learning with my students."*

Russell, Brenda M., A.M.C.T. ■ 🎓 📖 ✿

President, MUNICIPAL LAW ENFORCEMENT OFFICERS' ASSOCIATION (ONTARIO) INC., c/o City of Barrie, P.O. Box 400, Barrie, ON L4M 4T5 (705) 739-4241, FAX 739-4243. Born Orillia, Ont. 1958. m. J. Wallace Russell. 2 ch. EDUC: Georgian Coll., A.M.C.T. 1983, Certificate (Cdn Courts & Criminal Law) 1988, Certificate (Cdn Institute of Mgmt) 1988. CAREER: Sec., Nat'l Sales & Mktg, Dorr Oliver Canada, 1977-81; Sec., City of Barrie, 1981-87; Mun. Law Enforcement Officer Coord., City of Barrie, 1987 to date. AFFIL: Municipal Law Enforcement Officers' Association (Treas. 1989-92; Pres.); Canadian Institute of Management (Treas. 1987-89); Barrie Advisory Committee on Crime Prevention (Sec. 1988-90). INTERESTS: law; education; reading; ceramics; golf. COMMENT: *"My intense interest in municipal law led me to a career in this field, my involvement with the M.L.E.O. and ultimately to the position of President of this professional association."*

Russell, Hilary, B.A. 📖 ✿

Staff Historian, National Historic Sites Directorate, PARKS CANADA, Department of Canadian Heritage, 25 Eddy St., 5th Fl., Hull, QC K1A 0M5 (819) 997-0531, FAX 953-4909. Born Kingston, Jamaica 1947. m. Richard T. Russell. 1 ch. EDUC: Carleton Univ., B.A. (Hist.) 1969. CAREER: Proj. Historian, Elgin & Winter Garden Theatres, Ontario Heritage Foundation, 1985-89; Policy Analyst, Canadian Human Rights Commission, 1991-92; Staff Historian, National Historic Sites Directorate, Parks Canada, Dept. of Cdn Heritage. SELECTED PUBLICATIONS: *All That Glitters: A Memorial to Ottawa's Capitol Theatre and its Predecessors* (1975); *Double Take: The Story of the Elgin and Winter Garden Theatres* (1989). EDIT: Mng Ed., *Sandy Hill Image*, 1991-95. AFFIL: Action Sandy Hill (Dir. 1990-91); Home & School Association, Rockcliffe Park Public Sch. (Pres. 1988-89). HONS: Book Award, City of Toronto, 1990. INTERESTS: running; hiking; travel; reading. COMMENT: *"I am employed as a researcher and writer and use many of the same skills in my community work."*

Russell, Roberta J., Ph.D. ■■ ◆
Manager, Canadian Studies and Youth Programs, Citizens' Participation and Multiculturalism Branch, Department of Canadian Heritage, GOVERNMENT OF CANADA, Ottawa, ON K1A 0M5 (819) 994-2086, FAX 994-1314, EMAIL roberta_russell@pch.gc.ca. Born Woodstock, N.B. 1941. m. Ivan. 2 ch. Christopher, Jonathan. EDUC: Carleton Univ., B.A.(Psych. & Sociology) 1973, B.A.(Hons., Sociology) 1976; Univ. of Ottawa, M.Ed. 1977, Ph.D.(Educ. Admin.) 1993. CAREER: early yrs. of career spent as a secondary sch. teacher; Multiculturalism Educ. Officer, Multiculturalism Directorate, Dept. of the Sec. of State, 1978-85; Acting Chief, Citizenship Educ. & Promo., Citizenship Registration Branch, 1985-86; Policy Analyst, Corp. Policy Branch, 1986-91; Assoc. Dir., Corp. Secretariat, 1991-92; Dir., Ministerial Svcs & Exec. Dir., Cdn Multiculturalism Advisory Committee, Departmental Coord. & Reg'l Oper., Multiculturalism & Citizenship Canada, 1992-93; Special Advisor, Office of the Chief Policy Cnsl, Corp. Policy & Programs Sector, Dept. of Justice, Jan.-May 1993; Sr. Policy Analyst, Corp. Mgmt, Policy & Programs Sector, 1993-94; Eval. & Special Projects, Eval. Branch, Dept. of Hum. Res. Dev., Apr.-Dec. 1994; Mgr, Cdn Studies & Youth Programs, Dept. of Cdn Heritage, 1994 to date. SELECTED PUBLICATIONS: papers presented at numerous conferences, Canada & U.S. (on leadership, power, career dev., gender, literacy, women's hist., & multiculturalism); co-author with Ruth Wright, "The Socialization Experiences of Visible Minority Women in Educational Administration Positions" (*Canadian Ethnic Studies*, Summer 1993); "Learning from Survivors: Women Leaders Share Their Stories" (chpt. in book, *Women and Leadership in Canadian Education*, Reynolds and Young, eds., 1995); "Women Building Careers in a Diverse Society" (chpt. in book *Canadian Diversity: 2000 and Beyond*, 1995). AFFIL: Business & Professional Women's Association of Ottawa (Educ. Bursary, Program, & Communications Committees); American Society for Training & Development (Mgmt Dev., Women's, & Multicultural Ntwks); American Educational Research Association (Educ. in the Professions, Research on Women, & Research Utilization SIGS); Canadian Society for Studies in Education; National Council for the Social Studies, Washington. HONS: People Mgmt Award, Dept. of Cdn Heritage, 1996; Themis Award of Merit, Dept. of Justice, 1994; Grad. Award, Phi Delta Kappa, 1990; Grad. Research Fellowship, Univ. of Ottawa, 1990-91; National Award for contribution to multiculturalism in educ. in Canada, Canadian Council for Multicultural & Intercultural Education, 1984.

Rust, Helene, B.P.T.,M.Sc. ◉ O
Director, Clinical and Support Services, THE CAPITAL CARE GROUP INC., 9925 - 109 St, Ste. 500, Edmonton, AB T5K 2J8 (403) 448-2404, FAX 429-2217. Born Vancouver 1947. m. Raymond. 3 ch. Melanie, Randy, Geoffrey. EDUC: Univ. of Alberta, Diploma (Phys. Therapy) 1971, B.P.T.(Phys. Therapy) 1971; Central Michigan Univ., M.Sc.(Health Admin.) 1990. CAREER: Phys. Therapist, Lynnwood Extended Care, Capital Care Group, 1984-87; Dir., Rehab., 1987-91; Dir., Rehab. & Environment Svcs, 1991-93; Dir. of Housekeeping–Corp., 1993-95; Recruitment Coord., Hum. Res., 1994-95; Dir. of Support Svcs, 1995 to date. AFFIL: Canadian Coll. of Health Care Executives; Alzheimer Society of Edmonton (Pres. 1989-93; Past Pres. 1994 to date); Alzheimer Association of Alberta (VP 1993; Pres. 1994 to date); Alzheimer Society of Canada (Bd. of Dir. 1994 to date; Prov. Rep. 1995 to date); Alberta Baptist Women (Pres. 1979-81). HONS: Certificate of Merit for Saving a Life, St. John's Ambulance, 1972. INTERESTS: playing piano; singing in church choir. COMMENT: *"I was raised by a very liberated mother who truly made me believe I could do whatever I set my mind on, professionally as well as being a wife and mother. My endeavours and achievements include my family and their well-being.. hopefully I will have made a positive difference in someone's life. My motto seems to be, if I can't do it .. enable or help someone else to!"*

Rust, Velma Irene, B.Sc.,B.Ed.,M.Ed., Ph.D. ◁ ❀
Economic Researcher (retired). Born Edmonton 1914. w. Ronald Stuart Rust, Ph.D. EDUC: Univ. of Alberta, B.Sc.(Arts/Math & Sci.) 1934, Teacher's Diploma 1935, B.Ed.(Educ.) 1944; M.Ed.(Educ.) 1947; Univ. of Illinois, Champagne-Urbana, Ph.D.(Math. Educ. & Math.) 1959. CAREER: Teacher, high sch. math & sci., Alberta, 1936-44; Inspector, Inspection Board of the UK & Canada, Montreal, 1942-43; Admin. Sec., Dean of the Fac. of Educ., Univ. of Alberta, 1944-52; Asst. Prof. of Math. Educ., Univ. of Alberta, 1952-56; Dir. of Student Teaching, 1954-56; Grad. Asst., Univ. of Illinois, Champagne-Urbana, 1956-59; Sessional Lecturer (Calculus & Trigonometry), Carleton Univ., 1959-62; Researcher, Directorate of Personnel Planning, RCAF HQ, Ottawa, 1960-62; Chief of Staff Training, Inspection Svcs, Dept. of Nat'l Defence, 1962-65; Statistician, Aviation Statistics, Dept. of Transport, 1965-67; Policy Analyst, Health &

Welfare Canada, 1967-79. SELECTED PUBLI-CATIONS: "Factor Analyses of Three Tests of Critical Thinking" (*The Journal of Experimental Education*, Dec. 1960); "A Study of Pathological Doubting as a Response Set" (*The Journal of Experimental Education*, June 1961); "A Factor-Analytic Study of Critical Thinking," with R. Stewart Jones & Henry F. Kaiser (*The Journal of Educational Research*, Mar. 1962); "How do Canada's Older Women Fare?" (*Women Speaking*, Jan. 1969; published in Essex, UK); "Being Old and a Woman in Canada," with Freda L. Paltiel (*Women Speaking*, July to Sept. 1974). AFFIL: United Empire Loyalists' Association of Canada; MacKay United Church; University Women's Club of Ottawa; Public Service Recreation Association; American Contract Bridge League; many genealogical associations; Kappa Delta Pi. HONS: Volunteer Services Awards, Ont. Ministry of Citizenship & Culture, 1986, 1991. INTERESTS: golf; duplicate and contract bridge; genealogical research; gardening. MISC: Genealogist for the Sir Guy Carleton Branch, United Empire Loyalists, for about twenty years. COMMENT: "*My interests have been broad–all sports, different hobbies, piano playing (including duets), elocution and the French language. Mathematics and research provided a challenge, then came computers.*"

Ruth, Nancy, C.M.,B.A.,M.A., D.Hum.L.,LL.D. 💲 〇 ⊕

President, NANCY'S VERY OWN FOUNDATION, 10 Cluny Dr., Toronto, ON M4W 2P7 (416) 924-6961, FAX 924-2933, EMAIL webmom@web.net. President, 443472 ONT. LTD. President, 983963 ONT. LTD. President and Co-founder, COOL WOMEN. Born Toronto 1942 EDUC: London Sch. of Economics, 1962; Covenant Coll., Dipl.(Theology) 1967; York Univ., B.A. 1969; Whitworth Coll., M.A. 1977; Univ. of Toronto, Christian Theol. 1972-83, 1986-87. CAREER: extensive experience with religious, professional & educ. organizations in Canada, UK & US, 1972-80; Owner/Operator, Creativity–The Human Resource, 1978-82; VP, Gradenwitz Management Service, 1979-82; Pres., 443472 Ont. Ltd. (investment co.), 1980 to date; Pres., Nancy's Very Own Foundation, 1985 to date; Interim Min., Metro United Church, 1986; candidate for Ont. Prov. Legislature, 1990 (St. Andrew/St. Patrick), 1993 (St. George/St. David); Pres., 983963 Ont. Ltd. (land dev. co.), 1992 to date; Pres. & Co-founder, Cool Women (women's history web site), 1995 to date. VOLUNTEER CAREER: Staff Association, Naramata Centre for Continuing Educ., B.C., 1973-76; Mgmt Consultant to Archbishops of Canterbury & York,

Commission on Evangelism, UK, 1977; Canadian Women on the Constitution, 1981 to date; Charter Watch, Justice Committee, National Action Committee on the Status of Women, 1981-82; Co-founder & Mgr, The Charter of Rights Coalition, 1982-90; International Institute of Concern for Public Health, 1985-92; Gov., Mount St. Vincent Univ., 1986-92; Casey House AIDS Hospice, 1986-88; Leader, Women's Charter of Rights Issues, Ad Hoc Committee, Women on the Constitution (Ontario), 1987 to date; Canadian Centre for Global Security, 1988-93; Fullbright Foundation of Canada/US, 1990-93; Doctor's Hospital Foundation, 1992-94; has given major support to women's organizations & institutions, econ. dev., cultural, educational & community health & environment, int'l peace & disarmament. AFFIL: Women's Legal Education & Action Fund (Co-Founder & Dir. 1984-86); Legal Education & Action Fund Foundation (Dir., Pres. & Co-Founder 1990-93, 1995-98); Canadian Women's Foundation (Co-Founder 1989 to date); Economic Council of Canada (Dir. 1989-92); Massey Centre (Hon. Dir.); Iris Foundation; John Black Aird Gallery (Advisory Committee); Linden Sch. (Advisory Bd.); Friends of Shopping Bag Ladies; Canadian Society of Painters in Watercolour; Scarborough Women's Centre; Theatre Direct Canada; Rosedale P.C. Assocation (Hon. Dir.). HONS: Nancy R. Jackman Jubilee Scholarship, Mount St. Vincent Univ., 1986 to date; Woman of Distinction Special Award, Metro Toronto YWCA, 1988; Tribute Dinner announcing the LEAF Nancy Rowell Jackman Award, 1988; Nancy Rowell Jackman Chair in Women's Studies, Mount St. Vincent Univ., 1988; Nancy Rowell Jackman Child Care Centre, International Feminist Univ., Norway, 1988; Nancy's Part Time Day Care Centre, Univ. of Toronto; D.H.L.(honoris causa), Mount St. Vincent Univ., 1989; LL.D.(Hon.), York Univ., 1994; LL.D.(Hon.), Trent Univ., 1995; Member of the Order of Canada, 1994.

Rutherford, Sally, B.A.,M.A. 〇 🌾

Executive Director, CANADIAN FEDERATION OF AGRICULTURE, 75 Albert St., Ottawa, ON K1P 3E7 (613) 236-3633, FAX 236-5749. Born 1954. EDUC: McGill Univ., B.A.(Pol. Sci.) 1976; Univ. of Toronto, M.A.(Pol. Sci.) 1978. CAREER: Researcher, Library of Parliament, 1979-87; Policy Analyst, Canadian Federation of Agriculture, 1987-91; Exec. Dir., 1991 to date. COMMENT: "*I am committed and conscientious with a strong belief in the right and duty of citizens to influence and mold public policy at all levels. My achievements reflect these beliefs.*"

Ryan, Carey A., B.A.,B.Ed.,M.Ed. 🎓
Principal, ST. VINCENT'S HIGH SCHOOL, 1 Cliff
St., Saint John, NB E2L 3A8 (506) 658-5365,
FAX 648-9491. Born Saint John 1948. m.
Francis J. McHugh. EDUC: Univ. of New
Brunswick, B.A.(Pol. Sci.) 1970, M.Ed.
(Admin.) 1979; St. Thomas Univ., B.Ed. 1973.
CAREER: Teacher, Holy Trinity Sch., 1970-72;
Teacher, St. Vincent's High Sch., 1972-84;
Guidance Counsellor, 1984-88; Acting V-Prin-
cipal, 1988-89; V-Principal, 1989-92; Principal,
1992 to date. AFFIL: N.B. Teachers' Associa-
tion (various committees; Guidance Subject
Council; Principals' & V-Principals' Subject
Council); Canadian Foundation for Economic
Education; Canadian Guidance & Counselling
Association; Principals' & V-Principals' Council
(Districts 6 & 8); Delta Kappa Gamma Society
International; Association for Supervision &
Curriculum Development; National Association
of Secondary Schools' Principals; Junior
Achievement of Saint John Inc. (Bd. of Dir.);
Canadian Mental Health Association (Bd. of
Dir., Saint John Branch); Belfast Children's
Vacation–Saint John Inc. (Co-Chair); Birthright
(Dir. & Volunteer, Saint John Chapter); St.
Vincent's Alumnae Association (Exec. Dir &
Hon. Pres.); St. Peter's Parish Council; Univ. of
New Brunswick (Bd. of Gov.; Alumni Council);
Saint John Sch. of Nursing (Past Chair, Bd. of
Trustees); 1991 United Way Campaign (Cabi-
net Mbr.).

S

abiston, Carole, O.B.C.,D.F.A.,R.C.A. ⊗
Artist. 1648 Rockland Ave., Victoria, BC V8S
1W7 (604) 598-8139, FAX 382-2832. Born
UK 1939. m. Jim Munro. 1 ch. Andrew Sabiston. **EDUC:** Victoria Coll., Educ. 1957-59;
Univ. of Victoria, gen. studies; Univ. of British
Columbia, gen. studies. **CAREER:** art teacher,
secondary schools, 1959-72; artist, working in
textiles, 1972 to date; Instructor, London
Regional Art Museum, London, Ont., 1964-
66; workshops & lectures, B.C., Alta., Ont.,
Que. & N.S., 1967-77; Instructor, Univ. of Vic-
toria, 1974-76; Gov't appointee, B.C. Art Bd.,
1981-84; Instructor, Univ. of British Columbia,
1982; Artist-in-Schools, Cultural Svcs, Gov't of
B.C., 1983; Teacher & Founding Dir.,
Metchosin Int'l Summer Sch. of the Arts, Lester
B. Pearson Coll., 1985-87. **COMMISSIONS:**
Heathrow Airport, London, UK (1971); Christ
Church Cathedral, Victoria (1974); *Sunburst,*
Opening Ceremony Design, Expo '86, Vancouver (1986); 12 Banners, Victoria Public Library,
Victoria (1992); *Cape of Many Hands,* 1994
Commonwealth Games, Victoria (1994); logo
design, *Napoleon,* musical, Toronto (1994);
numerous other commissioned works; various
theatrical designs, Pacific Opera Victoria (1977-
88); various theatrical designs, Kaleidoscope
Theatre for Children (1977-87); various other
theatrical design credits; participant, *Hand and
Eye: Ties that Bind,* film series, CBC-TV
(1984); subject of video, *The Art of Carole
Sabiston* (1990). **EXHIBITIONS:** solo, Art
Gallery of Greater Victoria (1967, 1982, 1990);
solo, Shaw Rimmington Gallery, Toronto
(1974); solo, Centre des Arts Visuels, Montreal
(1979); solo, Winnipeg Art Gallery (1985);
solo, Memorial Univ. of Newfoundland (1989);

numerous other solo exhibitions; group, Royal Ontario Museum, Toronto, 1969; group, Vancouver Art Gallery, 1975; group, London Regional Art Museum (1981); group, *Restless Legacies*, Winter Olympics, Calgary (1988); group, *7th Montreal Tapestry Biennial* (1993); group, *Celebrating the Stitch*, toured US, Canada, UK & Japan, 1992-94; numerous other group exhibitions. COLLECTIONS: Canadian Museum of Civilization, Hull, Que.; Canada Council Art Bank; Confederation Art Centre, Charlottetown; Royal Trust Company; Bronfman Collection, Montreal; Ontario Gov't Travelling Exhibitions; various other corp. collections; numerous private collections in Canada, US, UK & Spain. AFFIL: Royal Academy of Arts; Art Gallery of Greater Victoria (Bd. of Trustees; Chair, New Bldg Committee); B.C. Cultural Foundation (Bd.). HONS: Nat'l Winner, Singer Sewing Machine competition, 1957; various awards, Canadian Guild of Crafts, 1965-67; theatre curtain design, Invitational Competition, Univ. of Victoria, 1981; 300 city street banners, Design Competition, City of Victoria, 1982; nominated, Allied Arts Medal, Royal Canadian Architectural Institute, 1986; Saidye Bronfman Award for Excellence, 1987; Order of B.C., 1992; Canada 125 Medal, 1993; Women of Distinction Award, 1995; D.F.A.(Hon.), Univ. of Victoria, 1995. MISC: subject of numerous articles & reviews; invited to meet HRH Queen Elizabeth II, Silver Jubilee Celebrations, Ottawa, 1977; 1 of 22 Cdn participants, Nat'l Invitational Crafts Exhibition, XIV Olympic Winter Games, Calgary, 1988. COMMENT: *"Carole Sabiston is an artist who works principally in textile and mixed media, constructing large-scale wall hangings, banners and three-dimensional space sculptures."*

Saddlemyer, Ann (Eleanor), O.C.,F.R.C.S., F.R.S.C.,B.A.,M.A.,Ph.D.,D.Litt., LL.D. ■ 🎭 📖 📱
Professor and Master Emerita, Massey College, UNIVERSITY OF TORONTO, 4 Devonshire Place, Toronto, ON M5S 2E1 (416) 978-2891, FAX 978-1759, EMAIL saddlemy@chass.utoronto. Born Prince Albert, Sask. 1932. s. EDUC: Univ. of Saskatchewan, B.A.(English & Psych.) 1953, D.Litt.(English) 1991; Queen's Univ., M.A. (English) 1956; Univ. of London, Ph.D. (English) 1961. CAREER: Lecturer, Victoria Coll., Victoria, 1965-68; Prof. of English, 1968-71; Prof. of English, Victoria Coll., & of Drama, Univ. of Toronto, 1971-75; Dir., Grad. Centre for Study of Drama, 1972-77; Berg Prof., New York Univ., 1975; Sr. Fellow, Massey Coll., Univ. of Toronto, 1975-88; Dir., Grad. Centre for Study of Drama, 1985-86; Master, Massey Coll., 1988-95. SELECTED

PUBLICATIONS: *The World of W.B. Yeats* (1965); *In Defence of Lady Gregory, Playwright* (1966); *Letters to Molly: Synge to Maire O'Neill* (1971); *Theatre Business, The Correspondence of the First Abbey Theatre Directors* (1982); *Lady Gregory Fifty Years After*, with Colin Smythe (1987); *Early Stages: Theatre in Ontario, 1800-1914* (1990); *Later Stages: Theatre in Ontario WWI to the 1970s* (1996); various other publications. EDIT: founding Co-Ed., *Theatre History in Canada*, 1980-86; Ed. Bd., *Modern Drama*, 1972-82; Ed. Bd., *English Studies in Canada*, 1973-83; Ed. Bd., *Themes in Drama*, 1974 to date; Ed. Bd., *Shaw Review*, 1977 to date; Ed. Bd., *Research in the Humanities*, 1976-90; Ed. Bd., *Irish University Review*, 1970 to date; Ed. Bd., *Yeats Annual*, 1982-86. DIRECTOR: Colin Smythe Ltd., Publishers. AFFIL: Royal Society of Canada (Fellow); Royal Society of Arts (Fellow); International Association for the Study of Anglo-Irish Literature (Chair 1973-76); Association of Canadian Theatre Research (Founding Pres. 1976-77); Canadian Association of Irish Studies; Association of Canadian University Teachers of English; Canadian Association of University Teachers; Association for Canadian & Quebec Literatures. HONS: Canada Council Scholar, 1958-59; Canada Council Fellow, 1968; Guggenheim Fellow, 1968, 1977; Sr. Research Fellow, Connaught, 1985; Rose Mary Crawshay Award, British Academy, 1986; Distinguished Service Award, Prov. of Ont., 1985; Award of Excellence, Univ. of Toronto Alumni, 1991; Women of Distinction, YWCA Toronto, 1994; Officer of the Order of Canada, 1995 LL.D.(Hon.), Queen's Univ., 1977; D.Litt. (Hon.), Univ. of Victoria, 1989; D.Litt.(Hon.), McGill Univ., 1989; D.Litt.(Hon.), Univ. of Windsor, 1990. INTERESTS: theatre; music; travel. MISC: selected as 1 of 12 women role models in the Royal Society of Canada, *Claiming the Future: Women in Scholarship/Se Batir un avenir: les femmes et le savoir*, 1990; 1 of the women featured in the feminist calendar *Herstory*, 1994; lectured extensively throughout Canada, US, Japan, Ireland, Germany, Yugoslavia, India & Austria.

Sadlier, Rosemary, B.A.(Hons.),M.S.W., B.Ed., ○ 📱 📖
President, Board of Directors, ONTARIO BLACK HISTORY SOCIETY, 10 Adelaide St. E., Ste. 202, Toronto, ON M5C 1J3 (416) 867-9420, FAX 867-8691. Born Toronto. m. Dr. Jay Carey. 3 ch. EDUC: York Univ., Glendon Coll., B.A. (Hons. Soc.); Univ. of Toronto, M.S.W., B.Ed. CAREER: Pres., Bd. of Dir., Ontario Black History Society, 1993 to date. SELECTED CREDITS: Exec. Prod., 5 nat'l Public Service

Announcements/Black History Bytes, *A Reflection of Canadian Heritage*, 1996. **SELECTED PUBLICATIONS:** *TUBMAN, Harriet Tubman and the Underground Railroad, Her Life in Canada and the United States* (Umbrella Press, 1996); *Mary Ann Shadd: Publisher, Editor, Teacher, Lawyer, Suffragette* (Umbrella Press, 1995); *Leading the Way: Black Women in Canada* (Umbrella Press, 1995); various other publications. **EDIT:** Ed., *Ontario Black History News.* **AFFIL:** Writers' Union of Canada; CAN:BAIA. **HONS:** Certificate of Recognition, Women for P.A.C.E.-Project for Advancement of Childhood Education (Canada), 1996; Volunteer Award for 10 Years of Service, Ministry of Citizenship, 1994; "Our Choice Award," for 1st book (*Leading the Way: Black Women in Canada*), The Canadian Children's Book Centre, 1994; chosen as "Local Hero," by Global Television, 1993; Volunteer Award, Ontario Black History Society, 1991. **INTERESTS:** travel; the arts. **MISC:** featured in "Gift of Family" segment, The Canada Day Show, CBC, July 1, 1996; Host, 6 eps., *Black in Ontario*, Rogers Cable 10 Metrowide TV, 1994. **COMMENT:** *"I am interested in seeing the emergence of a society that is inclusive of diversity for our children."*

Safran, Laura, B.A.,LL.B.,LL.M. ■ 🏛
Barrister & Solicitor, MILNER FENERTY, 237 - 4th Ave. S.W., 30th Fl., Calgary, AB T2P 4X7 (403) 268-7000, FAX 268-3100. Born Calgary. s. **EDUC:** Univ. of Alberta, B.A. 1973; Osgoode Hall Law Sch., LL.B. 1976; London Sch. of Econ. & Pol. Sci., LL.M. 1978; Columbia Univ., LL.M. 1981. **BAR:** Alta., 1977; B.C., 1996. **CAREER:** Solicitor, City of Calgary, 1978-80; Assoc. Lawyer, Conrad Blain, 1981-83; Dir., Law, Pacific Western Airlines Ltd., 1983-86; Sr. Dir., Law, 1986-87; Sr. Airline Cnsl, Canadian Airlines International, 1987-89; VP, Law & Corp. Sec., 1989-95; Davis & Company, 1995-96; Milner Fenerty, 1996 to date. **AFFIL:** Law Society of Alberta; Law Society of B.C.; Canadian Bar Association (various exec. positions to Chairperson, Air & Space Law Subsection 1991-92); Air Transport Association of Canada (Chair, Legal Div. 1986-87); International Bar Association (Bus. Law Subsection); American Bar Association (Assoc. Mbr.).

Sager, Hanni ■■ 📖 ⊗ ⊙
78 Shaftesbury Ave., Toronto, ON M4T 1A3 (416) 961-9967. Born Graenichen, Switzerland 1938. d. 1 ch. Charles Sager. **EDUC:** degree in fashion design. **CAREER:** own business in Canada, 1962-72, & 1 yr. in Melbourne, Australia; doll & toy collector, curator/organizer,

toy shows & exhibitions; artist; founder, toy workshop with street children, Canica, Oaxaca, Mexico, 1994. **SELECTED PUBLICATIONS:** working on a book about Mexican toy projects. **EXHIBITIONS:** *The Art of Playing*, toy collection, Hamilton Art Gallery, Hamilton, Ont., 1993-94; *Toys We Never Part With*, toys of well-known people such as Liona Boyd, Barbara McDougall & Erica Ritter, Harbourfront, Toronto, 1986; *Toyship Takeoff*, with artist Laura Kikauka, Harbourfront, 1985; *Year of the Child*, doll collection, Royal Ontario Museum, Toronto & McCord Museum, Montreal, 1979; *Straight from the Heart*, Creative Spirit Art Centre, Toronto, 1995; *Creative Visions*, Artist-in-Residence, McMichael Gallery, Kleinburg, Ont., 1994; *Images of Women*, group show, Creative Spirit Art Centre, 1994; *La Mano Magica*, guest artist, Oaxaca, Mexico, 1990; watercolour paintings & soft sculptures, Switzerland, 1990; curator/organizer, numerous other toy workshops, exhibits; facilitator, Paul Hogan's Spiral Garden, Hugh MacMillan Rehab. Centre, Toronto (designed for disabled children to use art as a form of physiotherapy), 1994-95. **HONS:** Ontario Medal for Good Citizenship, 1995. **MISC:** numerous lectures on dolls & toys, Toronto & Mexico; creator, *Toy Hospital*, Toronto Sick Children's Hospital, 1983; subject of documentary film, *The Art of Playing*, CBC, 1993; volunteer work at Creative Spirit Art Gallery with Paul, who had severe head injury 3 yrs. ago. **COMMENT:** *"When I work with the disadvantaged, the toys act as both an extension and reinforcement of my personal philosophy that playfulness, imagination and creativity are essential to living and health."*

St. Croix, Bernadette, B.Sc.,B.Ed. ⊛ ⊙
President, NEWFOUNDLAND ASSOCIATION FOR COMMUNITY LIVING, P.O. Box 5453, St. John's, NF A1V 1P3 (709) 256-3880, FAX 651-2939. Born St. Mary's, Nfld. 1942. m. Fintan. 2 ch. Lynn, Mark. **EDUC:** Mercy Coll. of Detroit, B.Sc.(Home Econ./English) 1973, B.Ed. 1973. **CAREER:** teacher, 1963-85. **EDIT:** Ed., *Gateway*, quarterly publication, Newfoundland Association for Community Living. **AFFIL:** Gander Association for Community Living (Past Pres.); Canadian Association for Community Living (Bd.); Newfoundland Association for Community Living (Pres.); St. Joseph's Home & School Association (Founding Pres. 1989-91); St. Paul's Home & School Association; Salvation Army; Newfoundland Arthritis Society; Boy Scouts of Canada; Catholic Women's League; Newfoundland & Labrador Retired Teachers' Association. **INTERESTS:**

music; reading; education. COMMENT: *"I enjoy being involved in many aspects of community. One of my main interests is in the area of education. I have worked as a teacher for many years and am now very much involved in advocacy efforts to ensure all children receive a quality education that meets their individual needs."*

St. Denis, Judith ■ ✦ ⊚

Co-President, Aboriginal Peoples' Commission, LIBERAL PARTY OF CANADA, 1447 Hornby St., Vancouver, BC V6Z 1W8 (604) 689-9776, FAX 444-5877. CAREER: salesclerk, Dalmy's, Burnaby, B.C., 1981-82; TQ1 & Fin. Clerk, Canadian Armed Forces, 1982-84; Acct Rep., Loomis Courier Services, 1983-88; Sales Rep., Canpar, 1988-90; Sales Rep., Greyhound Courier Express, 1990; Co-Owner, The Great Crate Company, 1990 to date; VP, Indian Commission, B.C. Liberal Party, 1990-94; Rep. to Exec., Aboriginal Peoples' Commission, B.C. Liberal Party, 1993-94; VP, Aboriginal Peoples' Commission, Liberal Party of Canada, B.C., 1990 to date. AFFIL: Burnaby Special Olympics (Volunteer Coord., Public Rel'ns); Kidney Foundation (Zone Captain); Burnaby Mentally Handicapped Association; Burnaby Voters' Association; Luma Native Housing Society.

St. George, Marie Elyse Yates ■ ⊗ 🖼 🐦

Artist, Poet, Saskatoon, SK S7H 2V1 (306) 653-2014. Born Merritton, Ont. (now St. Catharines) 1929. 2 ch. CAREER: visual artist; poet; lecturer; art advisor. SELECTED PUBLICATIONS: numerous book jackets & magazine illustrations; *White Lions in the Afternoon* (Coteau Books, 1990); *Voice*, in collaboration with Gov. General award winner Anne Szumigalski (Coteau Books/Mendel Gallery, 1996); poems in anthologies. COMMISSIONS: National Museums Discovery Train; Coteau Books; NeWest Press; private collectors. EXHIBITIONS: Latitude 53, Edmonton (1975); The Hett Gallery, Edmonton (1982); Susan Whitney Gallery, Regina (1993); Mendel Gallery, Saskatoon (1995); numerous group exhibitions incl. Expo 86; *Women and Peace*, Mount St. Vincent Univ. (1985); Glenbow Museum (1984). COLLECTIONS: Mendel Gallery, Saskatoon; Univ. of Saskatchewan, Printmaking Dept.; Saskatchewan Arts Bd.; numerous private collections in Canada & US. AFFIL: League of Canadian Poets; Canadian Artists' Representation; Saskatchewan Writers' Guild; PEN International; The Connaught Prose/Poetry Group, Saskatoon. HONS: Weston Associates Award, Currier Gallery, 1970; First Prize, Poetry, Saskatchewan Writers' Guild, 1989; shared Nat'l First Prize, League of Canadian Poets,

1989; Woman of Distinction Award, Sask. YWCA, 1995. INTERESTS: reading; music. MISC: writrer/participant, various multimedia performances & readings. COMMENT: *"As a person, wife, mother and grandmother, I'm interested in life's paradoxes. As a painter and a writer, I probe the mysteries we all carry unaware."*

Saint Pierre, Marie, D.E.C. ■■ ⊗ $ ♦

Designer, MARIE SAINT PIERRE DESIGN INC. (women's clothing), 4455 St-Denis, Montreal, QC H2J 2L2 (514) 281-5547, FAX 281-5675. Born Montreal 1961. m. François Lalonde. 1 ch. Étienne. EDUC: Coll. Brébeuf, D.E.C.(Arts & Communications) 1982; Univ. de Montréal, Arts 1984; Lasalle Coll., D.E.C.(Fashion Design) 1986. HONS: Hon. scholarship for excellent quality of work during apprenticeship, Montreal Fashion Group, 1986; 1st Que. designer to be chosen to participate at Fashion Coterie of N.Y., 1989; selected as one of Quebec's most promising women by *Chatelaine*, 1990; Woolmark Canada award, 1990; bronze medal, L.A. (over 250 competitors), 1990; selected by City of Montreal to represent fashion design in Montreal Top Mode campaign, 1990; Griffe d'Or for best collection, Prov. of Que., 1993; interviewed as a famous Montrealer, *Conde Nast Travelers* Magazine, 1993; chosen by prestigious store in Paris as one of its best collections for article in *Journal du textile*, France, 1993; "Designer Elle Québec 1994," *Elle Québec* magazine; "Personality of the Week," *La Presse* newspaper, 1994 & 1995; 1st Cdn to present collection in Paris, 1995; Vidal Sassoon Buyers' Choice Designer of the Year, Toronto Ready-to-Wear show, 1995; designer, Musée du Québec uniforms, 1996; presented collection in N.Y., 1996; Bursor, Yorkdale Shopping Centre. 1996; Canadian Designer Award of Distinction. INTERESTS: rollerblading; music; travel; visual arts; reading; food & wine.

Saj, Tami Leanne ■■ ⊘

Swimmer, Paralympic Athlete. 157 Crystal St., Thunder Bay, ON P7B 6H6 (807) 767-5143, FAX 767-5859. SPORTS CAREER: int'l swimming career, 1984-92; during that time, held numerous Cdn & Ont. swim records, some of which still stand; represented Canada in 2 Paralympic Games, 1988 & 1992; numerous int'l swim competitions incl. Stoke-Mandeville World Wheelchair Games, UK (3 times), World Open Swim Championships, Sweden, int'l swim competitions, Texas & Penn.; numerous Cdn & Ont. Games for the Physically Disabled; won over 34 medals in prov., nat'l & int'l competitions. HONS: chosen to represent all athletes to Prince Andrew & Sarah, Duchess of York, 1987 Ontario Games for the Physically Disabled; Exceptional Citizen Achievement Award, Thunder Bay, 4 times; inducted into Northwestern Ontario Sports Hall of Fame. **MISC:** invited speaker, numerous local & prov. functions; profiled in *Distant Voices* series, TVOntario.

Salamoun-Dunne, Marie, B.A., B.Ed. ■ ✊ ♥ ⊕

Past President, AMYOTROPHIC LATERAL SCLEROSIS SOCIETY OF PRINCE EDWARD ISLAND, Summerside, PE C1N 5S7, FAX (902) 436-1209, EMAIL wassims@cycor.ca. Born Antigonish, N.S. 1950. m. W. Salamoun. 2 ch. Cedric, Andrew. **EDUC:** St. Francis Xavier Univ., B.A. 1971, B.Ed. 1975; Univ. de Bordeaux, France, Diplôme d'Études Françaises 1974. **VOLUNTEER CAREER:** Pres., Prince County Hospital Auxiliary, 1991-93; Unit Dir., P.E.I., Amyotrophic Lateral Sclerosis Society of Canada, 1992-95; Pres., Amyotrophic Lateral Sclerosis Society of P.E.I., 1992-94; mbr., Confidentiality & Security Committee, P.E.I. Health & Community Svcs, 1994 to date. Pres., P.E.I. Association of Health Care Auxiliaries, 1995 to date; Bd. mbr., Canadian Association of Health Care Auxiliaries, 1995 to date. **SELECTED CREDITS:** lyricist, "Chrissie's Melody," 1996. **HONS:** Golden X Award, St. Francis Xavier Univ., 1971. **INTERESTS:** travelling. **MISC:** "Chrissie's Melody" was written to promote ALS awareness. **COMMENT:** *"I am particularly interested in our health care system and issues of privacy and confidentiality within it. My heart is given to the A.L.S. Society and the people it serves."*

Salcudean, Martha Eva, B.Eng.,Ph.D. 🎓 ⚛

Professor of Mechanical Engineering, UNIVERSITY OF BRITISH COLUMBIA, 2324 Main Mall, Rm. 2201, Vancouver, BC V6T 1Z4 (604) 822-2732, FAX 822-2403, EMAIL msal@unixg.ubc.ca. Born Cluj, Romania 1934. m. George Salcudean. 1 ch. Dr. Tim (S.E.) Salcudean. **EDUC:** Univ. of Cluj, B.Eng.(Mech. Eng.) 1956, Post-grad. diploma (Instrumentation & Control Systems) 1962; Institute of Polytechnics, Brasov, Romania, Ph.D.(Mech. Eng.) 1969. **CAREER:** Mech. Eng., Armatura, Cluj, 1956-63; Sr. Research Officer, Heat Transfer Lab., National Research Institute for Metallurgy, Bucharest, 1963-75; Sessional Lecturer, Institute of Polytechnics, Bucharest, 1967-75; Research Assoc., McGill Univ., 1976-77; Sessional Lecturer, Univ. of Ottawa, 1976-77; Asst. Prof., Mech. Eng., 1977-79; Assoc. Prof., 1979-81; Prof., 1981-85; Sabbatical, Dept. of Mech. Eng., Univ. of California at Berkeley, 1983-84; Head, Mech. Eng., Univ. of British Columbia, 1985-93; Prof., 1985 to date. **SELECTED PUBLICATIONS:** *Optimization of Casting Solidification and Heating Phenomena in Steel Ingots*, with J. Tripsa & M. Costescu (Bucharest: Editura Technica, 1975); "A Study of Heat Transfer during Arc Welding," with M. Choi & R. Greiff (*International Journal of Heat and Mass Transfer* 29(2) 1986); "Numerical Study of Czochralski Growth of Silicon in a Axisymmetric Magnetic Field," with P. Sabhapathy (*Journal of Crystal Growth* 113 1991); "Mathematical Simulation of Gas Bubble Transport in Moving Liquids in Low Gravity Environments," with Z. Abdullah (*Microgravity Quarterly* 1(3) 1991); "A Study of Bubble Ebullition in Forced-Convective Subcooled Nucleate Boiling at Low Pressure," with E. Bibeau (*International Journal of Heat and Mass Transfer* 37(15) 1994); more than 80 other refereed journal papers; numerous other publications. **AFFIL:** Canadian Society for Mechanical Engineering (Fellow); Professional Engineers Ontario; American Society of Mechanical Engineers; International Centre for Heat & Mass Transfer; Computational Fluid Dynamics Society of Canada; Advanced Systems Foundation (Bd. of Trustees); Dept. of National Defence (Defence Sci. Advisory Bd.). **HONS:** Sr. staff award, Univ. of Ottawa, 1983; award for best paper presentation, Int'l Heat Transfer Conference, 1986; Gold Medal in Applied Sci. & Eng., B.C. Science Council, 1991; Hon. Doctorate, Univ. of Ottawa, 1992; Killam Research Prize, Univ. of British Columbia, 1993; Canada 125 Medal, 1993; Julian C. Smith Medal, Engineering Institute of Canada, 1995; Fellow, Canadian Engineering Academy; Fellow, Royal Society of Canada. **INTERESTS:** reading; music. **MISC:** reviewer for various granting agencies; recipient, numerous grants & contracts; various invited lectures; various consultancies; 2 patents in Romania. **COMMENT:** *"Educated as a mechanical engineer; worked in industry and universities; began research work as an undergraduate and continued throughout my career; main research interests are modelling of industrial processes, computational fluid dynamics and heat transfer; have worked extensively in various organizations to promote technical education, research and partnerships between industry, government and academia."*

Salomon, Carole J., B.A.,M.B.A. ■ $

President, Residential Services, AT&T CANADA LONG DISTANCE SERVICES, 200 Wellington St. W., Toronto, ON M5V 3G2 (416) 345-3620, FAX 345-2854. Born Montreal 1948. m. David. 1 ch. Angela. **EDUC:** McGill Univ.,

B.A., M.B.A. CAREER: Mktg Mgr, Montreal Trust, 1971-77; VP, Mktg, Confectionery Div., Nabisco Brands, 1977-87; VP, Nat'l Sales & Mktg, Ronalds Printing, 1987-89; Sr. VP, Mktg, Purolator Courier Ltd., 1989-96. DIRECTOR: Laurier Life Insurance Company. AFFIL: Canadian Direct Marketing Association; The Founders' Club; Board of Trade; Elmridge Golf Club.

Salomon, Felicia, LL.B. ■ $ ⊕
Senior Vice-President and General Counsel, LOMBARD CANADA LTD. (formerly Continental Canada), 105 Adelaide St. W., Toronto, ON M5H 1P9 (416) 350-4408, FAX 350-4417. Born Toronto 1953. m. Edward Goldstein. 1 ch. EDUC: Osgoode Hall Law Sch., LL.B. 1978. BAR: Ont., 1980. CAREER: articling student, Benson Percival, Barristers & Solicitors, 1978-80; Lawyer, Cassels Mitchell, 1980-83; various positions to Sr. VP & Gen. Cnsl, Lombard Canada, 1983 to date. AFFIL: Law Society of Upper Canada; Superintendent's Special Committee on Insolvencies; Canadian Bar Association; Property & Casualty Insurance Compensation Corporation (Chair).

Saltman, Judith, B.A.,B.L.S.,M.A. ⊕ ▯
Associate Professor, School of Library and Information Studies, UNIVERSITY OF BRITISH COLUMBIA, 1956 Main Mall, Rm. 831, Vancouver, BC V6T 1Y3 (604) 822-4448, FAX 822-6006, EMAIL saltman@unixg.ubc.ca. Born Vancouver 1947. 1 ch. Anne Barringer. EDUC: Univ. of British Columbia, B.A.(English) 1969, B.L.S.(Library Sci.) 1970; Simmons Coll., M.A.(Children's Lit.) 1982. CAREER: Children's Librarian, Toronto Public Library, 1970-73; Coord. of Children's Svcs, W. Vancouver Memorial Library, 1973-79; Children's Librarian, New Westminster Public Library, Vancouver Public Library, 1980-82; Assoc. Prof., Children's Lit. and Librarianship, Univ. of British Columbia, 1983 to date. SELECTED PUBLICATIONS: Ed., The Riverside Anthology of Children's Literature, 6th ed. (Boston: Houghton Mifflin, 1985); Goldie and the Sea (Toronto: Groundwood, 1987); Modern Canadian Children's Books (Toronto: Oxford University Press, 1987); Co-author, The New Republic of Childhood: A Critical Guide to Canadian Children's Literature in English (Toronto: Oxford University Press, 1990). AFFIL: American Library Association: British Columbia Library Association; Canadian Library Association; Canadian Society of Children's Authors, Illustrators and Performers. INTERESTS: reading; drawing; writing. COMMENT: "I have worked as a children's librarian and professor of children's literature and librarianship. I have

written children's books and criticisms of children's literature, especially Canadian children's literature which I believe gives our children a sense of cultural identity."

Samuels, Barbara ♥ ⋈
Television Writer, Producer. c/o The Alpern Group, 4400 Coldwater Canyon Ave., Studio City, CA 91604 (818) 752-1877, FAX 753-1252. SELECTED CREDITS: writer & dir., numerous music videos, commercials, industrials & short films; writer, several scripts, Mount Royal (CTV); writer, Jim Henson Hour, NBC; Exec. Story Ed./Writer E.N.G., seasons 1 & 2; Co-Creator/Co-Exec. Prod., North of 60, CBC; Co-Creator & Co-Exec. Prod., Dark Eyes, ABC; Co-Creator/Co-Exec. Prod., Black Harbour, CBC; various other credits. MISC: co-creator, Convergence: An International Forum on the Moving Image, Montreal.

Sanders, Doreen McKenzie, C.M. ■ ⁄ ⊕ ♡ ♉
Editor, WOMEN IN MANAGEMENT NEWSLETTER, Richard Ivey School of Business, University of Western Ontario, London, ON N6A 3K7. President, DOREEN SANDERS COMMUNICATIONS, 248 Pall Mall St., Ste. 400, London, ON N6A 5P6 (519) 673-3089, FAX 433-6982. Born Portland, Ore. d. 1 ch. Peter McKenzie-Sanders. EDUC: Univ. of Western Ontario, B.A.(Journalism) 1961. CAREER: reporter & columnist, Vancouver Daily Province; Special Correspondent, Financial Post, 1961-63; Asst. Ed., Business Quarterly, Business Sch., Univ. of Western Ontario, 1963-68; Publisher & Ed., 1968-88; Adjunct Prof., Sch. of Journalism, Univ. of Western Ontario, 1975-95; Instructor, Publishing Procedures Course, Radcliffe Coll., 1979-87; Instructor, Banff Sch. of Fine Arts, 1981; Ed., Women in Management, Business Sch., Univ. of Western Ontario, 1989 to date. SELECTED PUBLICATIONS: Learning to Lead, publisher & ed. (London: Univ. of Western Ontario Business Sch., 1994). EDIT: Advisory Bd., Alumni Gazette, Univ. of Western Ontario; Advisory Bd., Who's Who Publications. AFFIL: Canadian Press Association; Walter J. Blackburn Foundation (Bd. Mbr.); Univ. of Western Ontario (Exec. Mbr., Advisory Committee, Women in Mgmt research program); Huron Coll. (Bd. Mbr.; Chrm, 1996 Courtyard Concerts); London Hunt Club; University Club of Toronto. HONS: Order of Canada, 1987; Alumni Award of Merit, Univ. of Western Ontario, 1987; Special Recognition Award for Distinguished Service to the Radcliffe Publishing Procedures Course, Harvard, 1988; Women of Distinction Award, YWCA London, 1989; Harvey S. Southam, Lifetime Achievement Ed.

Career Award, 1992; Alumni Honour Roll, Grad. Sch. of Journalism, Univ. of Western Ontario, 1992; Canada 125 Medal, 1993. INTERESTS: music; art; golf; camping. MISC: 1st woman Pres., Business Press Editors' Association of Canada (now part of Canadian Business Press Association), 1972; 1st woman elected to the Bd. of Dir., Canadian Business Press Association, 1973.

Sanderson, Marie, B.A.,M.A., Ph.D. 🐦 🏵 🖊

Director, The Water Network, Department of Geography, UNIVERSITY OF WATERLOO, Waterloo, ON N2L 3G1 (519) 885-1211, ext. 6902, FAX 746-2031. Born Chesley, Ont. 1921. w. 3 ch. Susan Martha, Robert Hardie, James William. EDUC: Univ. of Toronto, B.A.(Geography) 1944; Univ. of Maryland, M.A.(Geography) 1946; Univ. of Michigan, Ph.D.(Geography) 1965. CAREER: Prof., Univ. of Windsor, 1965-88; Dir., The Water Ntwk, Dept. of Geography, Univ. of Waterloo, 1988 to date. SELECTED PUBLICATIONS: *The Climate of the Essex Region, Canada's Southland* (Dept. of Geography, Univ. of Windsor, 1980); *Griffith Taylor: Antarctic Scientist and Pioneer Geographer* (Carleton Univ. Press, 1988); *UNESCO Source Book in Climatology–for Hydrologists and Water Resource Engineers* (Paris: UNESCO Press, 1990); *Letters From a Soldier*, co-author R.M. Sanderson (Escart Press, Univ. of Waterloo, 1993); *The Impact of Climate Change on Water in the Grand River Basin*, ed. (Dept. of Geography Publication Series, No. 40, Univ. of Waterloo, 1993); *Prevailing Trade Winds: Weather and Climate in Hawaii*, ed. (Honolulu: Univ. of Hawaii Press, 1993); various articles & chapters in books. EDIT: Ed., Canadian Water Resources Journal. AFFIL: Dept. of National Defence (Environmental Advisory Committee). HONS: Windsor Woman of the Year, 1988; hon. degree, Ryerson Polytechnic Univ., 1993. MISC: 1st female Pres., Canadian Association of Geographers.

Sandilands, Catronia, A.H., B.A., M.A. 🐦 🏵

Assistant Professor, Faculty of Environmental Studies, YORK UNIVERSITY, 4700 Keele St, North York, ON M3J 1P3 (416) 736-5252, FAX 736-5769, EMAIL essandi@orion. yorku.ca. Born Victoria, B.C. 1964. EDUC: Univ. of Victoria, B.A.(Soc.) 1987; York Univ., M.A.(Hons., Soc.) 1988, Ph.D.(Soc.) (ABD). CAREER: Sessional Lecturer, Women's Studies Program, Univ. of Victoria, 1989-92; Course Dir., Dept. of Soc., York Univ., 1992-93; Sessional Instructor, Dept. of Soc., Trent Univ., 1993-94; Asst. Prof., Fac. of Environmental

Studies, York Univ., 1994 to date. SELECTED PUBLICATIONS: "Lavender's Green? Some Thoughts on Queer(y)ing Environmental Politics" (*Undercurrents* May 1994); "Political Animals: The Paradox of Ecofeminism" (*The Trumpeter* Fall 1994); "From Natural Identity to Radical Democracy" (*Environmental Ethics* Winter 1995); various other publications. EDIT: Guest, Ed. Bd., "Women and the Environment" special issue, *Canadian Woman Studies* 1993; Toronto Ed. Collective, *Capitalism, Nature, Socialism* 1993 to date; Ed. Bd., *Women and Environments* 1994 to date; Guest Ed., *Alternatives*, special issues from ESAC, Calgary & Montreal, 1995, 1996; Ed. Bd., *City Magazine* 1995 to date. AFFIL: Environmental Studies Association of Canada; Canadian Sociology & Anthropology Association; Environmental Studies Association (Mbr. at Large, Bd. of Dir.); Women & Environments Education & Development Foundation (Bd. of Dir.); ACT for Disarmament. HONS: York Univ. Master's Thesis Prize, 1989; Gov. General's Gold Medal, 1989; Doctoral Fellowship, SSHRC, 1989-93; various other scholarships & awards. INTERESTS: gender; environments; community democracy; contemporary political theory; postmodernism; democracy; contemporary feminist theory; psychoanalysis; ecofeminism. MISC: Reviewer, *Capitalism, Nature, Socialism*; Reviewer, *Women and Environments*; various conference presentations; frequent speaker. COMMENT: *"I define myself primarily as a political/politicized theorist, who has a particular interest in gender, nature and democracy, and who tries to work in both academic and community milieux."*

Sandor, Anna, B.A. ■■ 🌱 📖 🖊

ZIVEG PRODUCTIONS INC. (TV & film writing & producing), c/o Steve Weiss, William Morris Agency, 151 El Camino Dr., Beverly Hills, CA 90212 (310) 859-4423, FAX 859-4317. Born Budapest, Hungary. d. 1 ch. Rachel Alice. EDUC: Univ. of Windsor, B.A.(Drama) 1971. SELECTED CREDITS: writer/co-writer, 15 TV movies incl.: *Amelia Earhart, The Final Flight*, TNT/Avenue Pictures; *Family of Strangers*, CBS/Alliance; *Miss Rose White*, Hallmark Hall of Fame, NBC/Marian Rees Assoc./Lorimar; *Mama's Going to Buy You a Mockingbird*, CBC; *The Marriage Bed*, CBC; *Charlie Grant's War*, CBC; has worked on 6 TV series/sitcoms incl.: *Seeing Things*, CBC; *Danger Bay*, Disney Channel/CBC; *For the Record*, CBC; *King of Kensington*, CBC. AFFIL: Writers' Guild of Canada; Writers' Guild of America; Academy of Television Arts & Sciences; Academy of Canadian Cinema & Television; Crime Writers of Canada (Co-Chair 1985-86). HONS: Margaret Collier Award for significant contribution to Cdn & int'l TV, Academy of Canadian Cinema & Television, 1996; Humanitas Prize (Long Form), 1993; Emmy nomination, Best Writer, Special/Mini Series, 1992; WGA nomination, Best Writer, Adapted Long Form, 1992; ACTRA Award, nominated 5 times as Best Writer, winner 1986; Gemini Award nomination, Best Writer, Special/Mini Series, 1987, 1994; Edgar Dale Award for Excellence in Screenwriting, Columbus Film Festival, 1989; Prix Anik, 4-time winner. **INTERESTS:** music; theatre; films; dance. **COMMENT:** *"A prolific, award-winning writer of movies, primarily for television, Sandor has found great success in her field, both in Canada and the United States, and is now branching into producing."*

Sands, Cara, B.A. ■ ✊ ♡

Director and President, FRIENDS OF THE DOLPHINS INC., P.O. Box 337, Thornhill, ON L3T 4A2, FAX (905) 508-5315, EMAIL 74164.3463@compuserve.com. Born Toronto 1967. m. **EDUC:** York Univ., B.A.(English) 1995. **CAREER:** freelance scriptwriter, 1989-93; Founder, Dir. & Pres., Friends of the Dolphins Inc., 1990 to date. **SELECTED PUBLICATIONS:** several articles & newsletters on marine mammals. **AFFIL:** Canadian Coalition for the Protection of Whales. **INTERESTS:** marine mammal conservation & welfare; environmental issues; driftnetting; tuna fishing. **COMMENT:** *"Founded Friends of the Dolphins in 1990; exposed cases of captive dolphin abuse; investigated, researched and produced videos to increase public awareness of marine mammal mistreatment."*

Sandwell, Carol, B.Math,C.A. $

Director of Finance and Administration, LAIDLAW RESOURCES, Reimer Tower, 5420 North Service Rd., 4th Fl., Burlington, ON L7L 6C7 (905) 336-1161, ext. 310, FAX 336-0515. Born Hamilton, Ont. 1963. m. Paul Lavergne. **EDUC:** Univ. of Waterloo, B.Math. (C.A. Option Coop.) 1986. **CAREER:** Audit Sr. II, Coopers & Lybrand, 1982-87; Fin. Analyst, Passenger Svc Group, Laidlaw Transit Ltd., 1988-89; Corp. Acctg Mgr, Laidlaw Waste Systems, 1989-91; Mgr, Budgeting & Analysis, 1992-93; Dir. of Fin. & Admin., Laidlaw Resources, 1994 to date. **AFFIL:** Canadian Institute of Chartered Accountants (C.A.); Ford World Cup Curling Championships (Dir. of Admin.); Oakville Curling Club (OLCA Rep.; Exec. 1993-95); Alzheimer Society of Hamilton-Wentworth (Treas. 1989-91). **HONS:** numerous scholastic achievements in high sch., incl. highest averages in grades 12 & 13. **INTERESTS:** golf; curling; travel; photography. **MISC:** selected for 4-month secondment to Auckland, N.Z. in 1987 while working at Coopers & Lybrand. **COMMENT:** *"I am a highly motivated individual who is committed to success in all areas of my life. All activities (academic, social or work-related) are undertaken with enthusiasm and commitment to meet and exceed my personal goals, and/or to ensure improved benefits are achieved for all parties involved. I enjoy becoming involved in management/leadership roles outside the workplace in support of my other interests."*

Sanger, Penelope, B.A. ■ ✊ 🎓 🍁

Execuitve Committee, CANADIAN FRIENDS OF BURMA, 145 Spruce St., Ste. 206, Ottawa, ON K1R 6P1 (613) 230-8056. Born Framingham, Mass. m. Clyde Sanger. 4 ch. Richard, Mathew, Tony, Daniel. **EDUC:** Univ. of Toronto, B.A.(English Language & Lit.) 1954. **SELECTED PUBLICATIONS:** *Blind Faith, the nuclear industry in one small town* (McGraw Hill, 1981). **EDIT:** Bd. Mbr., *The Canadian Forum*. **AFFIL:** Educating for Peace (Founder & Coord.). **INTERESTS:** fresh-water resources & public policy; the public educ. system in Canada. **COMMENT:** *"I am a writer/activist with a particular interest in international human rights and development, and the connections between this and social justice in our own communities."*

Sangster, Peggy, B.N.,M.Sc.(A.), R.N. ⊕ 🎓

Director, Nursing Staff Development, MONTREAL GENERAL HOSPITAL, 1650 Cedar Ave., Montreal, QC H3G 1A4 (514) 937-6011, ext. 4183, FAX 937-2455. Born Kingston, Jamaica 1943. w. 2 ch. **EDUC:** University Hospital of the West Indies, Jamaica, R.N. 1965; McGill Univ., B.N.(Nursing) 1977, M.Sc.(A.)(Nursing) 1979. **CAREER:** Staff Nurse, various hospitals, 1965-74; Clinical Instructor, Montreal General Hospital, 1979-82; Inservice Coord., 1982-84; Dir. of Nursing Staff Dev., 1984 to date; mbr., numerous committees, Montreal General Hospital, 1984 to date. **AFFIL:** L'Ordre des Infirmiers et Infirmières du Québec; South Shore Black Community Association. **HONS:** Marion Lindeburgh Scholarship, McGill Sch. of Nursing Alumnae Association, 1976; bursary, Montreal General Hospital, 1976. **INTERESTS:** music; theatre; adult educ.; women's health issues. **MISC:** resource person on nursing at youth seminar sponsored by Montreal Association of Black Business Persons & Professionals. **COMMENT:** *"I am an immigrant woman of colour who came to Canada in 1966. I seek to promote and support activities that foster* *individual learning and development, particularly in adults."*

Sansom, Brenda Jean, B.Ed. ■ ✊ 🍁
Chairperson, NEW BRUNSWICK ADVISORY COUNCIL ON THE STATUS OF WOMEN, 26 Fairlawn Court, Fredericton, NB E3B 2N9 (506) 457-6949, FAX 457-6948. City Councillor and Deputy Mayor, CITY OF FREDERICTON. Born St. Stephen, N.B. 1950. m. David. 2 ch. **EDUC:** Teachers' Coll., Bachelor of Teaching (1971); Univ. of New Brunswick, B.Ed. (French/Hist.) 1991. **CAREER:** sch. teacher, 1972-78; travel industry, 1978-89; City Councillor, City of Fredericton, 1989 to date; Exec. Dir., Junior Achievement of N.B., 1989-95; Deputy Mayor, City of Fredericton, 1995 to date. **AFFIL:** Rotary Club of Fredericton (Pres.); Big Brothers/Big Sisters (Hon. Mbr. 1994); Canadian Paraplegic Association (Hon. Chair, Paraskate '95); Portage Residential Youth Treatment Centre (Dir.); numerous committees & task forces. **HONS:** Atlantic Canada Entrepreneur Award for Advancement of Entrepreneurship, 1992. **INTERESTS:** promotion of youth; integrity in politics; fairness for all Canadians; protection of environment. **COMMENT:** *"I am respected for the integrity I bring to politics, the enthusiasm and sense of fairness I bring to women's issues, and my determination to ensure fairness and excellence prevails in all that I do."*

Santa Barbara, Joanna, B.Sc.,MB.BS., FRANZCP,FRCP(C) 🎓 ⊕ ✊
Assistant Professor, Department of Psychiatry and Centre for Peace Studies, MCMASTER UNIVERSITY, Hamilton, ON, EMAIL joanna@web.apc.org. Child Psychiatrist, 925 King St. W., Hamilton, ON L8S 1K7 (905) 529-9951, FAX 529-9951. Born Australia 1943. m. Jack Santa Barbara. 3 ch. **EDUC:** Univ. of Queensland, B.Sc.(Med.-Physiology) 1965, MB.BS. 1967; New South Wales Institute of Psychiatry, FRANZCP 1972, Diploma in Child Psychiatry 1974. **CAREER:** Resident Medical Officer, Royal Brisbane Hospital, Australia, 1969; Medical Officer, Bloomfield Hospital, Orange, Australia, 1969; Medical Officer, North Ryde Psychiatric Centre, Sydney, Australia, 1969-72; Training Fellow in Child Psychiatry, Avoca Clinic, Prince of Wales Hospital, Sydney, 1972-74; Staff Psychiatrist, Avoca Clinic, 1975-76; Staff Psychiatrist, Thistletown Region Centre for Children & Adolescents, Ont., 1977-79; Lecturer, Fac. of Medicine, Univ. of Toronto, 1977; Asst. Prof., 1978; Consultant, Sudden Infant Death Syndrome Groups, 1978-81; Staff Psychiatrist, Hamilton Psychiatric Hospital, 1979; Asst. Prof., Dept. of Psychiatry, Fac. of Medicine, McMaster Univ., 1979 to date; Psychiatrist, Chedoke Child & Family Centre, Hamilton, 1980-86; Dir., Children's Svcs, 1982-84; Consultant, Wentworth County Bd. of Educ., 1982 to date; Consultant, Family Practice Unit, McMaster Univ. Medical Centre, 1986 to date; private practice, 1986 to date. **SELECTED PUBLICATIONS:** "Psychological Impact of the Arms Race on Children" (*American Health Foundation–Preventative Medicine* 16(3) 1987); "Global Peace as a Professional Concern" (*Journal of Business Ethics* 8 1989); "Children and War, Children and Peace," in *Peacemaking for Canadians in the '90s*, Tom Perry, ed. (1991); *War Toys* (CPPNW Publications/Ploughshares Monitor, 1991); various other publications. **AFFIL:** Royal Coll. of Physicians of Canada (Fellow); Royal Australian & New Zealand Coll. of Psychiatrists (Fellow); Canadian Academy of Child Psychiatry; Ontario Psychiatric Association; Ontario Medical Association; Physicians for Global Survival–Canada (Pres. 1991); International Physicians for the Prevention of Nuclear War (Deputy Speaker); Centre for Peace Studies, McMaster Univ. (Council mbr.); War & Health Program, McMaster Univ. **MISC:** numerous presentations to conferences, associations, schools & public meetings. **COMMENT:** *"Day by day, I'm engaged in trying to use skill, knowledge and compassion to help my patients and my immediate community. I am trying to simplify my life to consume less, to "tread lightly on the earth." As an educator, I delight in opening young minds to issues of war and peace. As a physician activist, I try to contribute to preventing war and expanding peace."*

Sargent, Linda, B.S.,F.B.A.,M.B.A., C.H.R.P.,F.C.A.M. $
President, LINDA SARGENT ENTERPRISES INC., 260 Adelaide St. E., Ste. 177, Toronto, ON M5A 1N1. Born UK. m. William Basztyk. **EDUC:** Trinity College, University of Toronto, B.A.(Hons.)(Modern Lang. & Lit.) 1972; Canadian School of Management, F.B.A.(Bus. Admin.) 1982; Northland Open University, M.B.A. 1982. **CAREER:** Mgr., Mkt. Research, Loblaws Limited, 1974-80; Mgr., Manpower Planning, 1980-81; Dir., Training & Dev., 1981-85. VP, Human Resources and Dev., Loblaws Supermarkets Ltd. and National Grocers Co. Ltd., 1985-89; Assoc. Prof., Northland Open University, 1988 to date; Mng. Dir., Juvenile Diabetes Foundation Canada, Toronto Chapter, 1989-94; Pres., Linda Sargent Enterprises Inc., 1989 to date. **SELECTED PUBLICATIONS:** "People Planning–As Strategic as Business Planning" (*Professional Administra-*

tor, Summer 1986); "HR Ventures into EAP Monitoring Software" (*Human Resource Management in Canada*, April 1987); *Employee Assistance Program, Guide and Manual* (Food Marketing Institute, Washington, D.C., 1989). **AFFIL:** Human Resource Professionals of Ontario (C.H.R.P., 1989); Canadian Institute of Certified Administrative Managers (C.A.M., 1986; Fellow; Dir.); Ontario Centre for Management Studies (VP and Dir.); George Brown College (Chair, Retail Advisory Committee, 1981-90; Mktg. Advisory Committee); Cornell University (Food Industry Mgmt. Advisory Bd., 1988-89); Canadian School of Management (Pres., 1984-88); National Society of Fundraising Executives; Canadian Society of Association Executives. **HONS:** commissioned as Colonel on Staff of Governor of Kentucky, 1993. **MISC:** various conference and seminar presentations; recognized in *Canadian Who's Who*, 1994. **COMMENT:** *"A business professional with strong leadership ability and success in assisting and motivating organizations and individuals to establish and achieve their visions."*

Sarkar, Gerlinde, B.Ed.,B.A.,M.B.A. ■■ ⬏
Director, Research and Development, SASKATCHEWAN INSTITUTE OF APPLIED SCIENCE AND TECHNOLOGY (post-secondary educational/technical institution), 606 Spadina Cres. E., Ste. 1401, Saskatoon, SK S7K 2H6 (306) 933-7716, FAX 933-7334, EMAIL sarkar@ siast.sk.ca. Born Germany 1942. m. Dr. Kit Sarkar. 3 ch. Andrew, Robert, Christopher. **EDUC:** Univ. of Alberta, B.Ed.(French, German, Math.) 1964, B.A.(Linguistics) 1967; Univ. of Saskatchewan, M.B.A. 1986. **CAREER:** Teacher, Edmonton Sch. Bd., 1963-67; Lecturer, Univ. of Saskatchewan Coll. of Commerce, 1986-89; Pres., TARA Management Consulting, 1987-90; Research Officer, SIAST, 1990-93; Dir., R. & D., 1993 to date. **SELECTED PUBLICATIONS:** Agriculture Business Certificate Course, Modules 1-4 (Univ. of Saskatchewan, 1988, reprinted in subsequent yrs.); various articles, *Journal of the Association for Canadian Community Colleges*; *SIAST Retention Study* (presented & published in Proceedings of the Canadian Institutional Researchers Conference, Mar. 1993 & at Canadian Society for the Study of Higher Education Conference, June 1993); "Factors Affecting Retention of First Year Students in a Canadian Technical Institute of Applied Science and Technology" (*Resources in Education*, & included in ERIC database by Centre on Education & Training for Employment, Ohio State Univ., 1993). **AFFIL:** Saskatoon Business & Professional Women's Club (Pres. 1992-94);

Univ. of Saskatchewan (Women's Studies Research Unit; Bd. mbr., "Encouraging Enrolment in Engineering for Women"); Saskatoon YWCA (Bd. mbr.; Chair, Fin. Committee 1995-96; Pres.-Elect); Rotary Club, N. Saskatoon (mbr. 1995 to date); Saskatchewan Business & Professional Women's Club (Pres. 1996-97). **INTERESTS:** to promote women in science & technology; travel. **MISC:** developed & taught 4-week "Training Needs Assessment" course in Nepal, Nov.-Dec. 1993; developed Needs Assessment Plan for Universities of Notre Dame in Catabato, Mindanao & Midsayap in the Philippines to assess feasibility of college/institute system offering tech. skills programs, Dec. 1992; conducted workshops on research techniques, needs assessment & eval. studies, INNOTECH, Manila, Univ. of the Philippines, Dec. 1992; was instrumental in establishing Science Career Mentoring Program designed to encourage young women to pursue a career in the sciences; has travelled extensively in all 5 continents.

Sasges, Rita, Elaine ■ ⊗ $
Owner, SASGES DESIGN PARTNERSHIP, 640 - 8th Ave. S.W., Ste. 1100, Calgary, AB T2P 1G7 (403) 261-5650, FAX 261-5664. Born Kamloops, B.C. 1964. s. **EDUC:** Emily Carr Coll. of Art & Design, summer session in Italy, Photography 1991; Univ. of Alberta, B.F.A.(Visual Comm. Design) (2 courses to complete degree). **CAREER:** Jr. Designer, Calgraphika Ltd., 1987-89; Intermediate Designer, Strokes Design, 1989-90; Intermediate Designer, Taylor & Browning Design Associates, 1990-91; Sr. Designer, Kunz & Associates, 1991-93; Owner, Sasges Design Partnership, 1993 to date. **EXHIBITIONS:** *Design Works*, Triangle Gallery, Calgary (1992); *BFA Graduating Exhibition*, Univ. of Alberta (1986). **AFFIL:** American Institute of Graphic Artists (AIGA). **HONS:** Applied Arts Awards Annual, 1992, 1993, 1994, 1995, 1996; Communication Arts Design Annual, 1995, 1996; AR100, 1995, 1996; Potlatch Award of Excellence, 1994, 1995. **INTERESTS:** independent travel; archeology; art history; languages; photography.

Sasso, Julia ■■ ⊗
Assistant Artistic Director, DANCEMAKERS, 927 Dupont St., Toronto, ON M6H 1Z1 (416) 535-8880 FAX 535-8929. EMAIL dncemkrs@ interlog.com. Born Windsor, Ont. 1956. **EDUC:** York Univ., Fac. of Fine Arts, 1974-76. Dance training: Rose Marie Floyd Studio of Dance, 1963-74; Harkness House, N.Y. (Apprentice, Harkness Ballet); Carol Anderson, Serge Bennathan, Peter Boneham, Patricia Miner, Dianne Miller & others, 1987 to date;

training in voice, theatre, Pilates, SRT and Improvisation, 1985 to date. **CAREER:** Performing experience: The Contemporary Civic Ballet, Detroit, 1969-74; Dancemakers, and independently in works by Conrad Alexandrowicz, Carol Anderson, Serge Bennathan, Bill Coleman, David Earle, Christopher House, Bill James, James Kudelka, Lar Lubovitch and Jean-Pierre Perreault, 1984 to date. Teaching experience: Guest fac. at numerous institutions locally, nationally & internationally incl.: Dancemakers, The National Ballet Sch., the Sch. of the Toronto Dance Theatre, Canadian Children's Dance Theatre, Cornell Univ., Univ. of California and York Univ., 1984 to date. **SELECTED CREDITS:** Choreographer, *Sporting Life* (commissioned by Canada Dance Festival & CanDance Network), 1996; *Ripple* (commissioned by the Sch. of the Toronto Dance Theatre); *Maxine* (commissioned by Art Space, Peterborough), 1993; *The Theory & Practice of Rivers*, 1992; *Such Sweet Sorrow* (commissioned by the Contemporary Civic Ballet, Detroit), 1992; *The Outer Dark*, 1991; *dissolve/reveal*, DUNK and *Lost Weekend*, 1990; numerous other works, 1972 to date. **AFFIL:** Dancers for Life (Co-Chair 1993-95); Artistic Advisor/Dance Assessor for the Canada Council & Ontario Arts Council, Metro Arts Council, The Dora Mavor Moore Awards, First Night, fFrida & Dance Works/DanceTalks (1989 to date). **HONS:** numerous grants and awards from the Canada Council, Ontario Arts Council & Toronto Arts Council; scholarships from Cecchetti Council of America, American Ballet Centre (Joffrey Ballet), Harkness House, York Univ.; Paul Taylor Dance Co. & Chalmers Fund.

Sauer, Angelika, M.A.,Ph.D. ⚜ 🎓
Chair in German Canadian Studies, UNIVERSITY OF WINNIPEG, 515 Portage Ave., Winnipeg, MB R3B 2E9 (204) 786-9007, FAX 772-0472. Born Erlangen, W. Germany 1960. s. **EDUC:** Univ. of Augsburg, Germany, M.A.(Hist./Classics/Soc.) 1986; Carleton Univ., M.A.(Cdn Hist.) 1988; Univ. of Waterloo, Ph.D.(Cdn Hist.) 1994. **CAREER:** Chair in German Cdn Studies, Univ. of Winnipeg, 1994 to date. **SELECTED PUBLICATIONS:** "A Matter of Domestic Policy? Canadian Immigration Policy and the Admission of Germans, 1945-50" (*Canadian Historical Review* 74(2) 1993); "Christian Charity, Government Policy and German Immigration to Canada and Australia, 1947 to 1952," in *Immigration and Ethnicity in Canada*, eds. A. Laperrière, V. Limndström, T. Palmer Seiler (Montreal: Association for Canadian Studies, 1996) & (*Canadian Issues* VXIII, 1996); "Hopes of Lasting Peace: Canada

and Post-Hostilities Germany, 1945," *1945 in Canada and Germany: The Past Viewed Through the Present*, eds. H. Braun & W. Klooss (Schriftenreihe des Zentrums für Kanada Studien, vol. 5 & Kiel: l&f Verlag, 1996). **AFFIL:** Canadian Institute for International Affairs; Gesellschaft für Kanada-Studien, Germany; Committee for the History of the Second World War; Organization for the Study of the National History of Canada (Sec.-Treas.). **HONS:** Beaverbrook Prize, Carleton Univ., 1987; Award to Foreign Nationals, Gov't of Canada, 1988-92. **INTERESTS:** politics; sports; music; movies. **COMMENT:** *"I live what I teach: the immigrant experience. I hope for a world in which national borders will matter less and less. My work is my contribution."*

Sauer, Elizabeth, H.B.A.,M.A., Ph.D. ■ ⚜ 🎓
Associate Professor, Department of English, BROCK UNIVERSITY, St. Catharines, ON L2S 3A1 (905) 685-5550, ext. 3887, FAX 685-5550, ext. 4492, EMAIL emsauer@spartan. ac.brocku.ca. Born Kitchener, Ont. 1964. **EDUC:** Wilfrid Laurier Univ., H.B.A.(English) 1986; Univ. of Western Ontario, M.A.(English) 1987, Ph.D.(English) 1991. **CAREER:** Research Asst., Translator, Wilfrid Laurier Univ., 1982-86; Teaching Asst., Univ. of Western Ontario, 1986-90; Research Asst., Univ. of Western Ontario, 1990-91; Asst. Prof., Brock Univ., 1991-95; Assoc. Prof., 1995 to date. **SELECTED PUBLICATIONS:** *Barbarous Dissonance and Images of Voice in Milton's Epics* (McGill-Queen's Univ. Press, 1996); *Agonistics: Arenas of Creative Contest*, ed. Janet Lungstrum & Elizabeth Sauer (SUNY Press, 1997); *Milton and the Imperial Vision*, ed. Balachandra Rajan & Elizabeth Sauer (in progress); "The Politics of Performance in the Inner Theatre: "Samson Agonistes" as Closet Drama", *The Heretical Milton*, ed. John Rumrich & Stephen Dobranski (forthcoming); "Monstrous altercations and barking questions: The Prodigious Births of Scylla, Mris. Rump, and Milton's Sin," *The Ben Jonson Journal: Literary Contexts in the age of Elizabeth, James and Charles* (2, 1996); numerous conference presentations, incl. papers at MLA Convention (1993) & 5th Int'l Milton Symposium, Wales (1995). **AFFIL:** Milton Society of America; Canadian Society for Renaissance Studies (Program Chair 1996); Association of Canadian College & University Teachers of English; Renaissance Society of America; The Newberry Library, Centre for Renaissance Studies; Centre for Reformation and Renaissance Studies. **HONS:** SSHRC Research Grants, 1992-95, 1995-99; Canadian Federation for the Human-

ities Grant, 1994-97; SSHRC Doctoral Fellowships, Univ. of Western Ontario, 1988-91; Ontario Graduate Scholarships, Univ. of Western Ontario, 1986-88; Gold Medal for English, Wilfrid Laurier Univ., 1986

Saunders, Doris J., D.Litt.,O.C. / 🗍 🕮
Editor, *THEM DAYS*, Box 839, Stn. B, Happy Valley-Goose Bay, NF A0P 1E0 (709) 896-8531. Born Cartwright, Lab. 1941. w. 3 ch. CAREER: various positions in the fishing industry, 1956-57; sales clerk, short-order cook, waitress, 1958-59; housewife, 1960-75; Ed., *Them Days: Stories of Early Labrador*, 1975 to date. EXHIBITIONS: *Faces of Labrador*; *Grasswork of Labrador*; *Visions of Labrador*; single-threaded needle embroidery, *Lone Hunter*; various other award-winning single-threaded needle embroidery pieces. AFFIL: Heritage Foundation of Newfoundland & Labrador (Dir.); Labrador Craft Producers' Association; Embroiderers' Guild of Canada; Newfoundland & Labrador Craft Development Foundation; Labrador Heritage Society; Newfoundland & Labrador Archivists' Association; Moravian Women's Auxiliary; Canada Council; Moravian Church. HONS: Canadian Regional History Award; The Newfoundland Historical Society Award; Order of Canada, 1986; St. John's Guild of Embroiderers' Award; 3 other embroidery awards; D.Litt.(Hon.), Memorial Univ. of Newfoundland, 1994. INTERESTS: embroidery; fishing; hiking; canoeing. COMMENT: *"I am of Inuit and European white descent. My hope is to preserve the history of Labrador as told by the people; this I have been doing since March 1975."*

Savage, Candace, B.A. 🐾 🕮
Writer. 302 Albert Ave., Saskatoon, SK S7N 1G1 (306) 653-4595. Born Grande Prairie, Alta. 1949 1 ch. EDUC: Univ. of Alberta, B.A.(English) 1972. CAREER: Ed. Asst., Co-Operative Consumer Newspaper, 1972-74; Curriculum Dev. Officer/Audio-Visual Prod., Saskatchewan Indian Cultural Coll., 1975; freelance writer, ed. & consultant, 1975-84; Public Affairs Officer, Culture & Comm., Gov't of the N.W.T., 1984-87; Coord. of Info. & Educ., Science Institute of the N.W.T., 1987-89; freelance writer, 1989 to date; Writer-in-Residence, Saskatoon Public Library, 1990-91. SELECTED PUBLICATIONS: *A Harvest Yet to Reap: A History of Prairie Women* with Anne Wheeler, Lorna & Linda Rasmussen (Toronto: Women's Press, 1976); *Our Nell: A Scrapbook Biography of Nellie L. McClung* (Saskatoon: Western Producer Prairie Books, 1979); *Wolves* (Vancouver: Douglas and McIntyre, 1988); *Trash Attack!* (Toronto: Groundwood Books, 1990); *Eat Up! Healthy Food for a Healthy Earth* (Toronto: Groundwood Books, 1992); *Wild Cats* (Vancouver: Douglas and McIntyre, 1993); *Aurora: The Mysterious Northern Lights* (Vancouver: Douglas and McIntyre, 1994); *Bird Brains: Ravens, Crows, Magpies and Jays* (1995); *Cowgirls* (1996). AFFIL: Saskatchewan Writers' Guild; Writers' Union of Canada (Prairies/N.W.T. Rep. to Nat'l Council 1991-92); Science Culture Canada (Past Mbr., Evaluation Committee). HONS: Rutherford Gold Medal in English, Univ. of Alberta, 1972; Gov. General's Gold Medal, Univ. of Alberta, 1972; Honour Book Award, Children's Literature Roundtables of Canada, 1991; Honor Roll, Rachel Carson Institute, Chatham Coll., Pittsburgh, Pennsylvania, 1994. COMMENT: *"I became a single parent, through an untimely death, when my daughter was two. I am grateful that I could often support our household by doing things I loved."*

Savoie-Zajc, Lorraine, B.A.,M.Sc., Ph.D. ■ 🕮
Professor, UNIVERSITY OF QUEBEC IN HULL, C.P. 1250, Succ. B, Hull, QC J8X 3X7 (819) 595-3900, ext. 4406, FAX 595-4459, EMAIL lorraine.savoie@uqah.uquebec.ca. Born Trois-Rivières, Que. 1948. m. Mladen Zajc. 1 ch. Milena. EDUC: Univ. Laval, B.ès Arts (Lit.) 1968; Syracuse Univ., M. ès Sc.(Educ. Tech.) 1971; Indiana Univ., Ph.D.(Educ. Technology) 1987. CAREER: univ. Prof. since 1975; Secondary Language Instructor, Cdn Civil Svc; Media Coord., Que. Civil Svc. SELECTED PUBLICATIONS: *Les modèles de changement planifié en éducation* (Montreal: Éd. Logiques, 1993); "Le discours sur l'école de jeunes indentifiés à risque de décrochage scolaire," *L'abandon scolaire: on ne naît pas décrocheurs*, by L. Langevin (Montreal: Éd. Logiques, 1994); "Quelle recherche pour quel changement?" with A. Dolbec, *La recherche en éducation comme source de changement*, ed. J. Chevrier (Montreal: Éd. Logiques, 1994); "Les critères de rigueur de la recherche qualitative," *Actes du colloque de la Société de recherche de l'Abitibi-Témiscamingue*(SOREAT) (Rouyn, 1990); "Qu'en est-il de la triangulation: là où la recherche qualitative se transforme en intervention sociale (*Revue de l'Association pour la recherche qualitative*, vol. 8, 1993). AFFIL: Association pour la recherche qualitatif; Association francophone internationale de recherche scientifique en éducation; Conseil interinstitutionnel pour le progrès de la technologie éducative; American Educational Research Association. INTERESTS: reading; travelling; planned change in educ.; qualitative research methodology. MISC: currently head of master's degree

program in educ. **COMMENT:** *"Lorraine Savoie-Zajc has been a professor in education since 1975 at the University of Quebec in Hull. She has assumed various administrative roles regarding programs management, from baccalaureate level to Ph.D. She was elected president of the professional association in educational technology in Quebec and has been administrative secretary for the Association pour la recherche qualitatif."*

Sawatsky, Sarah ⊗ ⋈ ♥

Actor. c/o Tarlington Talent, 275 E. 8th Ave., Ste. 200, Vancouver, BC V5T 1R9 (604) 876-7600, FAX 876-7100. Born Vancouver 1976. **EDUC:** Burnaby Central Secondary; Circle in the Square Theater Sch., N.Y., Acting, Summer 1994; National Institute for Dramatic Art, Sydney, Australia, Acting 1995; studied with Carole Tarlington, 1986 to date; Vancouver Youth Theatre, 1986 to date. **CAREER:** acting since age 5. **SELECTED CREDITS:** numerous commercials; Principal ("Cupcake"), *Beans Baxter* (series), 1987; Principal, Tina Tonelli, *Paper Route*, CBC Family Series, 1988; Series Regular, Kathleen Danforth, *Murphy's Law*, ABC, 1988/89; Recurring Principal, Jess, *Danger Bay*, CBC, 1989; Principal, Jenny, *The Challengers* (feature), The Challengers Movie Inc., 1989; Recurring Principal, Lucy, *Bordertown*, Moviecorp, 1989-90; Principal, *The Girl from Mars* (feature), Atlantis/Family Channel, 1990; Series Regular, Sarah, *Northwood*, Soapbox Productions/CBC, 1990-93; Principal, *Needful Things* (feature), Needful Productions/Castle Rock, 1992; Actor, *Beyond Obsession* (M.O.W.), Green Epstein, 1993; Lead, "La Bounty," *Hawkeye*, Hawkeye Productions/US Syndicate, 1995; Principal, *Never Too Thin* (M.O.W.), 1995; Principal, *X-Files* (series), 1996; various other film & TV credits; various voice overs, incl. "Miss Popularity," *Captain Zed*, Animated City Editorial Services, 1991; Ensemble, *The Obsession Cabaret*, Vancouver Youth Theatre, 1992; various other stage credits. **HONS:** *TV Week* Award for Best Supporting Actor in a Local Series (*Danger Bay*), 1990; YTV National Youth Achievement Award in Acting, 1991; Youth in Film Award for Best Young Actor starring in a Cable Special, 1991. **INTERESTS:** singing; dancing; piano; writing

Scace, Susan M., B.A. ■■ ○

Born 1941. m. Arthur R.A. Scace. **EDUC:** Univ. of Toronto, B.A.(Psych.) 1962; continuing educ. courses in fundraising, public speaking, career dev., mgmt planning, French language, & English Lit. **CAREER:** Librarian, Glasgow Commission, 1960; Teacher, Oxford, England, 1962-63; Teacher, Branksome Hall

Sch., Toronto, 1963-64; Pres., Eagle's Publications, 1984 to date. **SELECTED PUBLICATIONS:** author, *Take Me With You - Please*. **AFFIL:** Univ. of Toronto (mbr., Bd. of Gov., Bus. Bd. & Campaign Cabinet 1995 to date); National Ballet of Canada (Dir., Exec. mbr. 1995 to date; Campaign Cabinet, Chair of Pace-Setting Gifts 1995 to date; Nominating Committee 1993 to date); North York General Hospital (Dir., mbr., Patient Care Committee, Grants Committee, & Seniors Health Centre Bd. 1992 to date); Trinity Coll., Univ. of Toronto (mbr. of Corporation 1970 to date; Exec. Committee 1990-96; Task Force mbr. 1991-92; V-Chrm, Exec. Committee 1992-93; Steering Committee 1992-93; Fin. Committee 1994 to date); Henry White Kinnear Foundation (Dir. 1983-95; VP 1996 to date); Timothy Eaton Memorial Church (Sanctuary Guild 1990-93; Congregational Bd. 1990-93); Royal Ontario Museum (Volunteer Committee 1987 to date; ROM Reproductions Committee 1988 to date; ROM Decor Committee 1988-94; V-Chair, Volunteer Orientation 1988-89; Chrm, ROM-MVC Workbook 1991-92); Serve Canada (Advisory Bd.); Wellspring (Advisory Bd.); Junior League of Toronto (sustaining mbr. 1981 to date). **HONS:** Arbour Award, Univ. of Toronto, 1996. **INTERESTS:** golf; tennis; travel; opera; ballet; music.

Schaan, Eloise ☆ ⊕ ○ ♂

President, LUTHERAN WOMEN'S MISSIONARY LEAGUE - CANADA, 7 Klein Court, Kanata, ON K2L 2X7 (613) 831-8317. Born Grenfell, Sask. 1937. m. Lloyd. 2 ch. **EDUC:** Grenfell High Sch., Grade 12 1955; Royal Conservatory of Music, ARCT (Piano) 1958. **CAREER:** private music teacher, piano & theory, 1955-83; Sec. to the Head of Psych. Svcs, North York Bd. of Educ., 1987-90; Sec., Lutheran Church of St. Matthew, Scarborough, Ont., 1987-90; Pres., Lutheran Women's Missionary League, 1993 to date. **AFFIL:** International Lutheran Women's Missionary League (Dir. 1984-88, 1989-91); Christ Risen Lutheran Church, Kanata (Music Dir. 1993 to date). **HONS:** Grade 12, Gov. General's Medal for Proficiency. **INTERESTS:** music; reading. **MISC:** has served on various committees & as seminar presenter, all church-related; served for several yrs. in the Guiding movement as a Brownie leader. **COMMENT:** *"As a committed Christian, I find it exciting to experience God at work in my life – opening doors and enabling one to meet the challenge."*

Schabas, Ann H., B.A.,A.M.,B.L.S.,M.A., Ph.D. ◁ ▯

Professor Emeritus, Faculty of Library and

Information Science, UNIVERSITY OF TORONTO, 63 St. Clair Ave. W., Ste. 907, Toronto, ON M4V 2Y9. Born 1926. m. Ezra Schabas. 5 ch. William, Richard, Margaret, Michael, Paul. EDUC: Univ. of Toronto, B.A.(Physics) 1948, B.L.S. 1964; Smith Coll., A.M.(Physics) 1949; Univ. of London, M.A.(Info. Sci.) 1970, Ph.D.(Info. Sci.) 1979. CAREER: Research Asst. (Chem.), Amherst Coll., 1949-50; Research Asst. (Physics), Smith Coll., 1949-50; housewife & mother, 1950-64; Reference Librarian, Educ. Centre Library, Toronto Bd. of Educ., 1964-66; Prof., Fac. of Library & Info. Sci., Univ. of Toronto, 1966-90; Dean, 1984-90; Prof. Emeritus, 1990 to date; freelance researcher, ed., 1990 to date. SELECTED PUBLICATIONS: "Trends in Indexing," in *Proceedings of the 69th Annual Conference of the Ontario Library Association* (May 14-16, 1971); "The Imprint Date in the Anglo-American Cataloguing Rules," with Katherine H. Packer (*Library Resources & Technical Services* 20 1976); "Post-Coordinate Retrieval: A Comparison of Two Indexing Languages" (*Journal of the American Society for Information Science* 33 1982); "Decision Logic for AACR2 Chapter 21: Choice of Access Points," with M.E. Cockshutt & C.D. Cook (*Library Resources and Technical Services* 27 1983); book reviews in *Canadian Library Journal, Cataloguing and Classification Quarterly, Indexing and Abstracting Society of Canada Newsletter* & *Journal of Library Automation*; various other publications. EDIT: Advisory Bd., *Canadian Periodical Index*, InfoGlobe, 1987-90. AFFIL: Canadian Association for Information Science; Indexing & Abstracting Society of Canada (Pres. 1984-86); Canadian Library Association; Canadian Classification Research Group; Sigma Xi, Ex Libris. HONS: Trustee Fellowship, Smith Coll., 1948-49; Naval Research Fellowship, US, 1949-50; Jr. Research Fellowship, Univ. of Toronto Research Bd., 1969, 1970; Postgrad. Scholarship in Sci. Librarianship & Documentation, National Research Council of Canada, 1969-70; Doctoral Fellowship, Canada Council, 1974-75. MISC: grant recipient; numerous lectures & addresses; various consultancies, incl. indexing consultant, British National Bibliography, 1969-70; reviewer for various journals & granting agencies.

Schacherl, Eva, B.A. ■ ○ ◉ ▒
Senior Communications Officer, CANADIAN MUSEUM OF CIVILIZATION/CANADIAN WAR MUSEUM. Born Saskatoon, Sask. 1960. m. Jean-Louis Chassin. 1 ch. EDUC: Univ. of Saskatchewan, B.A.(English) 1981; Univ. de Paris (Sorbonne), Magistère (Civilisation française) 1983. CAREER: Reporter, *Saskatoon Star-Phoenix*, 1978-81; Asst. Dir., Educational Exchanges, Canadian Bureau for International Education, 1984-87; Ed. & Fundraiser, Inter Pares, 1987-90; Exec. Dir., Canadian Environmental Network, 1990-96; Sr. Comm. Officer, Canadian Museum of Civilization/Canadian War Museum, 1996 to date.

Scheier, Libby, B.A.,M.A. ⊗ ▒ ▯
Writer. Toronto, ON. 1 ch. Jacob. EDUC: Sarah Lawrence Coll., B.A.(French & Phil.); State Univ. of New York at Stony Brook, M.A.(English). CAREER: Instructor, Toronto Poetry Workshop, 1984-86; Writer-in-Residence, Dunnville Public Library, Dunnville, Ont., 1987-88; Instructor, Women Writing, George Brown Coll., 1988-90; Course Dir., York Univ., 1988-95; Lecturer, Contemporary Fiction, Kaleidoscope series, Royal Ontario Museum, 1993; Founder/Dir., Toronto Writing Workshop, 1994 to date. SELECTED PUBLICATIONS: *Language in Her Eye–Writing and Gender* (Views by Canadian Women Writing in English), ed. with Sarah Sheard & Eleanor Wachtel (Coach House Press, 1990); *SKY–A Poem in Four Pieces* (Mercury Press, 1990); *Saints and Runner–Stories and a Novella* (Mercury Press, 1993); poetry in various anthologies, incl. *Women on War*, Daniela Gioseffi, ed. (Simon & Schuster US, 1988) & *Poetry by Canadian Women*, Rosemary Sullivan, ed. (Oxford Univ. Press, 1989); short fiction in various anthologies, incl. *Frictions - Stories by Women*, Rhea Tregebov, ed. (Second Story Press, 1989) & *By, For and About*, Wendy Waring, ed. (The Women's Press, 1994); criticism in various anthologies, incl. *In the Feminine: Women & Words Conference Proceedings* 1983, Ann Dybikowski, Victoria Freeman, Daphne Marlatt, Barbara Pulling & Betsy Warland, eds. (Longspoon Press, 1985) & *Twist and Shout–A Decade of Feminist Writing in This Magazine*, Susan Crean, ed. (Second Story Press, 1992); "Polarities and Polemics" (*Books in Canada* Oct. 1992); "Kicking the Dogma Under the Table: Some Thoughts on Phyllis Webb" (*West Coast Line* Winter 1991-92); various book reviews; short fiction in various journals incl. *Descant, Paragraph–The Fiction Magazine* & *Prairie Fire*; poetry in various journals incl. *This Magazine, Quarry, Malahat Review* & *Canadian Woman Studies*; various other publications. EDIT: Poetry Ed., *Poetry Toronto*, 1985-87; Contributing Ed., *Paragraph–The Fiction Magazine*, 1990 to date; Ed., *No Language is Neutral*, by Dionne Brand, poetry (Coach House Press, 1990); Literary Ed., *Canadian Woman Studies*, 1992-93; Ed., *Mother, Not Mother*, by Di Brandt, poetry

(Mercury Press, 1992). **AFFIL:** The Writers' Union of Canada; PEN International, Canadian Centre, English-Speaking; League of Canadian Poets; Modern Language Association; Canadian Union of Educational Workers. **HONS:** Third Prize, Poetry, Prism Int'l Contest, Univ. of British Columbia, 1986. **MISC:** recipient, various grants from Ontario Arts Council, Canada Council & Toronto Arts Council; more than 100 readings across Canada; various print & broadcast interviews; various conference presentations, incl. Panelist, *Strategies for Change*, After the Montreal Massacre–Canadian Perspectives on Violence Against Women, George Mason Univ., Fairfax, VA, Mar. 1993; juror for various grants. **COMMENT:** *"Libby Scheier is a writer and feminist who has published books in the genres of poetry, fiction and essays. She taught at York University from 1988 to 1995, and since 1994 has been founder/director of the independent Toronto Writing Workshop."*

Schelle, Susan ⊕

Sculptor. 50 Croft St., Toronto, ON M5S 2N9 (416) 868-6170, FAX 924-3185. Born Hamilton, Ont. 1947. partner Mark Gomes. **EDUC:** Sheridan Coll., 1972-76. **COMMISSIONS:** various commissions incl.: Arbour, Ont. Prov. Courthouse, Ottawa, 1986; Salmon Run, Tower Park W. Fountain Proj., The SkyDome, Toronto, 1991; Passage, Academic Science Complex, York Univ., Toronto, 1992; Hedge, Honeywell Limited, Toronto, 1992; 2 piece, David & Vivien Campbell Sculpture Terrace, Art Gallery of Ontario, Toronto, 1994; Whitby Psychiatric Hospital; Court House Square Park. **EXHIBITIONS:** numerous solo exhibitions incl.: Glendon Gallery, York Univ., 1978; Mercer Union, Toronto, 1981; P.S.I., Institute for Art & Urban Resources, N.Y., 1986-87; Cold City Gallery, Toronto, 1990; Susan Hobbs Gallery, Toronto, 1994; various group exhibitions incl.: *Performance*, 10th Int'l Sculpture Conference, Art Gallery at Harbourfront, Toronto, 1978; *Art and Audience*, Art Gallery of Northumberland, Cobourg, 1984; The Clocktower, N.Y., 1987; *Literati*, Toronto Sculpture Garden, 1988; *Body is a Loaded Word*, Evelyn Aimis Gallery, Toronto, 1989; *Survivors: In Search of a Voice*, various galleries & museums throughout Canada, 1995. **COLLECTIONS:** various collections incl.: Art Gallery of Ontario, Art Gallery of Hamilton; Canada Council Art Bank, Ottawa; London Life Insurance Company, London; McCarthy Tétrault, Toronto; Univ. of Lethbridge Art Gallery; Walter Phillips Art Gallery, Banff; Winnipeg Art Gallery. **AFFIL:** Power Plant Gallery (Bd.); Cold City Gallery (Founding Mbr.). **MISC:** Canada

Council Paris Studio & various other Canada Council grants. **COMMENT:** *"My work not only involves exhibiting in galleries but I am extensively involved in large public projects. Most of these projects are site-specific and I work in close contact with architects and designers, e.g. Toronto SkyDome Fountain project, Salmon Run, 1990 and York University Science Complex, Passage, 1992."*

Schiff, Daphne, BA,MA,PhD ⊲ ❀ ⼁

Associate Professor of Natural Science, Glendon College, **YORK UNIVERSITY**, 2275 Bayview Ave., Toronto, ON M4N 3M6 (416) 487-6732, FAX 487-6728, EMAIL gl250050@ venus.yorku.ca. Co-Director and Pilot, **AIR-O-SOLS**, c/o Gervase Mackay, Unisearch Associates, 222 Snidercroft Rd, Concord, ON L4K 1B5 (905) 669-3547, FAX 669-5132. Born Edmonton 1924. m. Harold. 2 ch. J. Michael Schiff, Ph.D., Prof. Sherry Schiff. **EDUC:** Univ. of Toronto, B.A.(Math./Physics/Chem.) 1945, M.A.(Phys. Chem.) 1947; York Univ., Ph.D. (Phys. Chem.) 1976; Fed. Ministry of Transport, Airline Transport pilot's licence 1986. **CAREER:** Research Chemist, National Research Council, 1943-45; Research Chemist, Chalk River Atomic Energy, 1946; Research Chemist, Defence Research Bd., 1947-50; Research Chemist, Univ. de Montréal, 1951-54; Asst. Prof., York Univ., 1969-80; Assoc. Prof., 1980 to date. **SELECTED CREDITS:** Prod., *Science: Live to Tell About It*, film; Prod., *The Ozone Story*, film; Prod., *CAPMON I*, film produced for Environment Canada (1990); Prod., *Questions*, film concerning science careers for girls below Grade 8 produced for Science Culture Canada; Prod., *The Northern Wetlands: Its Role in Global Warming*, film produced for the Canadian Institute for Research in Atmospheric Chemistry (1992). **AFFIL:** Association for Media & Technology in Education in Canada (AMTEC); The Ninety-Nines Inc.–International Organization of Women Pilots (Toronto exec. 1976; Chair, Amelia Earhart scholarship program); Canadian Association for Women in Science (CAWIS); Sigma Xi–The Scientific Research Society; CBC Advisory Bd. on Science & Technology (Chrm 1985-88); Space Science Centre, Ahmedabad, India; Operation Skywatch. **HONS:** award for sci. documentary film, National Committee on Safety, Chicago, 1980; award for sci. documentary film, Int'l Film & TV Festival, N.Y., 1981; award for sci. documentary film, Association for Media Technology in Education in Canada, 1982, 1989, 1993. **MISC:** Co-Captain, with Adele Fogle, in various air races incl. New York to Paris Air Race, 1985, Air Race Classic, 1989, 1990, Great Southern Air Race, 1992, 1993 Around-the-World Air Race, 1994, Air Race of the Americas, 1996. COMMENT: *"Daphne Schiff is a professor of Natural Science, teaching meteorology and aeronautics. She has an Airline Transport pilot's licence with 4,000 hours and has worked as a commercial pilot. Each year, she lands a light aircraft on the York campus, flies government-sponsored pollution-monitoring flights, and produces award-winning documentary science films. She is blessed with a son, daughter and son-in-law–all professionals–and four grandchildren."*

Schiller, Ruth Boswell, M.B. ⊗ ☜ ☺

Music Specialist. 461 McAllister Ave., Riverview, NB E1B 4H7 (506) 386-7842, FAX 734-3707. Founder and Choral Director, HILLSBOROUGH GIRLS' CHOIR. Born Victoria, B.C. 1931. m. John. 3 ch. Caroline, Leanne Delaney, Heidi Ruth. EDUC: Mount Allison Univ., Associateship of Music 1953; studied at McGill Conservatory of Music. CAREER: music teacher in 6 provinces, 35 yrs.; teaching staff, Hillsborough Girls' Sch., 1978 to date; Founder & Choir Dir., Hillsborough Girls' Choir, 1980 to date. AFFIL: N.B. Choral Federation (Bd.); Moncton Community Concert Series (Bd.); Association of Canadian Choral Conductors (Bd.); Dept. of Educ. (Bd., Music Curriculum); International Choral Federation (Bd.); American Choral Directors' Association (Bd.); National Music Educators' Association of Canada (Sec.-Treas., 2 terms); N.B. Teachers' Association (Program Chair, Music Council). HONS: Member of the Order of Canada, 1992; Paul Harris Fellow, 1996. MISC: instrumental & Orff specialist; Hillsborough Girls' Choir recipient of many awards & honours. COMMENT: *"Ruth Schiller exemplifies excellence in choir work and indeed in music education. She teaches children more than music. She teaches them about responding to life itself. She is truly outstanding as a Canadian educator and this heritage of music will live in our community, in our schools and in our hearts forever."*

Schlifer, Anne ○

Volunteer. Toronto, ON. EDUC: high sch. completion; courses in court reporting. CAREER: various office work positions for many companies, from filing to office administrator; worked in 2 universities; since retiring, active in various seniors' organizations & projects. AFFIL: Bernard Betel Centre for Creative Living (V-Chair, Mbrs' Council; former mbr., Bd. of Dir.); Ontario Coalition of Senior Organizations (Steering Committee); Association of Jewish Seniors (Co-Chair; former Pres.); Alliance of Seniors to Protect Canada's Social Programs (Steering Committee); Senior Care

(Bd. Mbr.; mbr., Service Review Committee). HONS: various honours for volunteerism; 3 pins; several certificates. MISC: panelist on issues of seniors' physical & mental health; performer in plays dealing with abuse of the elderly; appeared on TV regarding seniors' issues.

Schnitzer, Deborah, B.A.,M.A,Ph.D. ☜ ☝

Associate Professor, Department of English, UNIVERSITY OF WINNIPEG, 515 Portage Ave., Winnipeg, MB R3M 2E9 (204) 786-9292, FAX 984-4869, EMAIL schnitzer@ uwpg02uwinnipeg.ca. Born Sault Ste. Marie, Ont. 1950. m. Mendel. 2 ch. Ben, Zachary. EDUC: Univ. of Western Ontario, B.A.(English & Phil.) 1972; Univ. of Calgary, M.A.(Hons., English Lit.) 1973; Univ. of Manitoba, Teacher Certificate 1975, Ph.D.(English Lit.) 1986. CAREER: jr. & sr. high sch. teacher, language arts, Dept. of Indian & Northern Affairs, Fisher River Sch., Koostatak, Man., 1975-77; part-time lecturer, English Lit., Univ. of Manitoba, 1977-79, 1984-86; Curriculum Consultant, Post-Secondary Career & Dev., Man. Dept. of Educ., 1987-88; Dir., Writing Centre, Univ. of Winnipeg, Writing Program, 1988-91; Asst. Prof. of Lit., Dept. of English, 1991-94; Assoc. Prof., 1994 to date. SELECTED PUBLICATIONS: *The Pictorial in Modernist Fiction from Stephen Crane to Ernest Hemingway* (Ann Arbor: UMI Research Press, 1988); *English 300: A Community-Based University Entrance Curriculum* (Post-Secondary Career Dev., Man. Educ., 1989); "Reading the Classroom 'Set-up'" (*Inkshed* 11(3)); "Lot's Wife" (*Contemporary Verse* 2 16 Fall 1993); "Tricks: Artful Photographs and Letters in Carol Shields' *Stone Diaries* and Anita Brookner's *Hotel du Lac*" (*Prairie Fire* Spring 1995); *Uncommon Wealth: An International Anthology of Poetry in English*, with Neil Besner & Alden Turner (Oxford Univ. Press: forthcoming Dec. 1996); *Black Beyond Blue* (Staccato Press, Sept. 1996); various other publications. EDIT: mbr., *Inkshed*; mbr., *English Studies in Canada*; mbr. *Mosaic*. AFFIL: Association of Canadian College & University Teachers; Manitoba Teachers of English; Volunteer Home Support Services (Founding Mbr.); Manitoba Alternative Program Education; Temple Shalom Sch. (Bd. Mbr.); Hadassah Wizo Book Club (Facilitator); Judith Putler Book Club (Co-facilitator); Telecourse Program, Univ. of Winnipeg. HONS: Gold Medal, English & Phil., Univ. of Western Ontario, 1972; Univ. of Manitoba Grad. Fellowship, 1977-81; SSHRC Doctoral Fellowship, 1983-84; Merit Award, Univ. of Winnipeg, 1990; Finalist, with Writing Program Fac., Lt. Governor's Literacy Award, 1990; Red

River Valley Educ. Award, 1991; Clifford J. Robson Award for Excellence in Teaching, 1993; nominated for 3M Teaching Fellowship, 1994. INTERESTS: family; visual art; music; community initiatives. MISC: various consultancies; numerous conference presentations. COMMENT: *"I believe in ideas and our right to exchange them within diverse communities. I am inspired by processes that value learning as a lifelong movement toward understanding and genuine compassion."*

Schoemperlen, Diane Mavis, B.A. 🗎 📚 🐟
Writer. c/o The Writers' Union of Canada, 24 Ryerson Ave., Toronto, ON M5T 2P3 (416) 703-8982, FAX 703-0826. Born Thunder Bay, Ont. 1954. s. 1 ch. Alexander Tait Schoemperlen. EDUC: Lakehead Univ., B.A.(English) 1976; Banff Centre Sch. of Fine Arts, Creative Writing Program 1976. CAREER: Publicity Asst./Staff Writer, Banff Centre Sch. of Fine Arts, 1976-77; Newspaper Reporter, *Banff Crag and Canyon*, 1977-78; freelance writer, 1980 to date; Asst. Ed., *Quarry Magazine*, 1986-89; Summer Instructor in Fiction Writing, Kingston Sch. of Writing, Queen's Univ., 1986-93; Instructor, Frontenac County Bd. of Educ. Summer Institute, 1987-88; Instructor of Creative Writing, St. Lawrence Coll., 1987 to date; Writer-in-Residence, David Thompson Univ. Writing Workshop, 1991; Instructor of Fiction Writing, Univ. of Toronto Writers' Workshop, 1992; Instructor of Fiction Writing, 1000 Summer Sch. of the Arts, St. Lawrence Coll., 1994-95; Ed., *Coming Attractions* Oberon Press, Ottawa, 1994 to date. SELECTED PUBLICATIONS: *Double Exposures* (Coach House Press, 1984); *Frogs and Other Stories* (Quarry Press, 1986); *Hockey Night in Canada* (Quarry Press, 1987); *The Man of My Dreams* (Macmillan of Canada, 1990); *Hockey Night in Canada and Other Stories* (Quarry Press, 1991); *In the Language of Love* (Harper-Collins, 1994; Viking Penguin USA, 1996; Rabén Prisma/Arleskär, Sweden, 1996). AFFIL: Writers' Union of Canada. PEN. HONS: Writers' Guild of Alberta Award for Excellence in Short Fiction, *Frogs and Other Stories*, 1986; shortlisted, Gov. General's Award, *The Man of My Dreams*, 1990; shortlisted, Trillium Award, *The Man of My Dreams*, 1990; *In The Language of Love* shortlisted, Books in Canada/Smithbooks First Novel Award, 1995. MISC: recipient, various grants; judge, various fiction contests; numerous Ontario Arts Council juries; public readings across Canada.

Schon, Denise, B.A. ■ 🗎 💲 🐟
President, DENISE SCHON & ASSOCIATES, 80

Fuller Ave., Toronto, ON M6R 2C5, EMAIL daschon@aol.com. Born Woodstock, Ont. 1956. EDUC: Glendon Coll., York Univ., B.A.(English) 1979. CAREER: Ed. Asst., Deneau Publishers, 1979-80; Ed., Deneau Publishers, 1980-81; Literary Agent, Nancy Colbert and Associates, 1982-83; Sr. Ed., Doubleday Canada, 1983-85; Editorial Dir., Gen. & Professional Books, McGraw-Hill Ryerson, 1985-89; VP & Publisher, Macmillan Canada, 1989-95; Pres., Denise Schon & Associates, 1995 to date; Fac., Book Publishing Program, Ryerson Polytechnic Univ. AFFIL: Book Publishers' Professional Association (Pres. 1992-93); Canadian Book Publishers' Council (Dir., Trade Group 1992-94); Women's Legal Education & Action Fund (Nat'l Fundraising Committee 1991-92); United Way Leading Women program.

Schroedter, Linda 🌾 💲 🐝
Past President, MANITOBA SHEEP ASSOCIATION, P.O. Box 113, Moosehorn, MB R0C 2E0 (204) 768-3766, FAX 768-3766. Pres. Born Manitoba 1955. m. Peter. 1 ch. CAREER: banking industry, 1974-83; Mgr & Owner, P and L Ranch, 1974 to date; Asst. Ed., Sheep Canada Magazine, 1985-90; Co-Owner & Co-Mgr, Radio Shack store, 1987-90. DIRECTOR: Ramshead Publishing. AFFIL: Manitoba Commercial Lamb Producers Association (Dir.); Manitoba Sheep Association (Pres. 1993-94); Interlake Sheep Association (Pres. 1994-95); Manitoba 4-H. HONS: Award, Canadian Co-operative Wool Growers, 1985, 1987, 1992; Grand Champion Fleece, Manitoba Wool Show, 1984, 1994; Champion Range Wool, Royal Winter Fair (Toronto), 1995. INTERESTS: music; outdoors; travel; reading; women's issues. COMMENT: *"Rather than being concerned about becoming older, I enjoy the experience life brings and the opportunities of planning new projects."*

Schwartz, Judith, B.A., M.A. ⊗ 🐟 🐝
Director and Curator, Hart House, UNIVERSITY OF TORONTO, 7 Hart House Circle, Toronto, ON M5S 1A1 (416) 978-2453, FAX 978-8387, EMAIL judi.schwarz@utoronto.ca. Born Toronto 1949. s. EDUC: Univ. of Toronto, B.A.(Fine Art/Anthro.), M.A.(Fine Art). CAREER: Registrar, New Sch., 1970-75; Dir. & Curator, Hart House, 1975 to date. SELECTED PUBLICATIONS: exhibition catalogues; travel articles. AFFIL: Famous People Players (Chrm of the Bd.); Leading Tone Productions (Bd.); Toronto Hospitals Art Committee (Advisor); Committee on Arts-Related Activities, Association of College Unions Inter-

national (Reg. 2 Chrm). **INTERESTS:** art; dance; theatre; travel; gourmet cooking. **MISC:** designer of art mgmt computer program.

Scott, Cynthia, B.A. ■■ 🎞 🎭 📺
Film Director, NATIONAL FILM BOARD OF CANADA, P.O. Box 6100, Montreal, QC H3C 3H5 (514) 283-9510, FAX 283-5487. Born Winnipeg 1939 1 ch. Dylan Smith. **EDUC:** Univ. of Manitoba, B.A.(English Lit. & Phil.) 1959; Univ. of Manitoba Sch. of Art, painting classes 6 yrs.; studied piano & music theory. **CAREER:** Script Asst., CBC, Winnipeg, 1959-61; 2nd Asst. Dir., Manitoba Theatre Centre, 1962; Researcher, CBC, London, UK, 1963-65; Dir./Prod., *Take Thirty*, & directed film portraits for *Telescope*, & *Man Alive*, CBC, 1965-71; joined NFB, 1971. **SELECTED CREDITS:** Dir., *The Ungrateful Land: Roch Carrier Remembers Ste-Justine* (documentary, 1971); Co-Scenarist, *First Winter* (TV fiction, 1981); Co-Dir., *Gala* (theatrical, 1982); Dir./Co-Prod., *Flamenco at 5:15* (theatrical documentary, 1983); Dir., *Jack of Hearts* (TV fiction, 1986); Dir./Co-Scenarist, *The Company of Strangers* (fiction, 1990); numerous others. **EXHIBITIONS:** int'l film festivals in Venice, Toronto, London, Tokyo & Mannheim. **AFFIL:** Royal Canadian Academy. **HONS:** Oscar for *Flamenco at 5:15*; Oscar nomination for *First Winter*; numerous int'l prizes for *The Company of Strangers*. **INTERESTS:** nature; art; film. **MISC:** has travelled extensively in Canada, US & Europe.

Scott, Donna M., B.A. 🎞 🍁
Chair, THE CANADA COUNCIL, 350 Albert St., P.O. Box 1047, Ottawa, ON K1P 5V8 (613) 566-4414, ext. 4208, FAX 566-4411. Born Toronto. m. Hugh R. Farrell. 4 stpch. **EDUC:** Queen's Univ., B.A.(Personnel & Labour Rel'ns). **CAREER:** various positions, Eaton's; Dir. of Personnel, Maclean Hunter Limited; Gen. Mgr, Financial Post Conferences, Maclean Hunter Limited; Founder & Publisher, *Flare* Magazine, to 1994; VP, Maclean Hunter Publishing Company, to 1994; mbr., Mgmt Committee, Maclean Hunter Limited, to 1994; Chair, Canada Council, 1994 to date. **DIRECTOR:** The Royal Mutal Funds. **AFFIL:** Canadian Women in Communication (Bd. Mbr.); Canadian Foundation for AIDS Research (Bd. Mbr.); Salvation Army of Metropolitan Toronto (Bd. Mbr.); Queen's Univ. (Trustee). **HONS:** Women of Distinction in Communications, YWCA, 1984; Women Who Make a Difference in Toronto, 1989; Donna Scott Chair in Fashion Merchandising, endowed by International Academy of Merchandising & Design, 1989.

Scott, Jacquelyn Thayer, M.B.A., Ph.D. 🎓 $
President and Vice Chancellor, UNIVERSITY COLLEGE OF CAPE BRETON, Grand Lake Rd., Box 5300, Sydney, NS B1P 6L2 (902) 564-1333, FAX 562-0273, EMAIL jscott@sparc.uccb.ns.ca. Born Russell, Kansas 1945. d. 3 ch. **EDUC:** Univ. of Kansas, Undergrad. Studies (Journalism/Pol. Sci.) 1963-67; Univ. of Manitoba, M.B.A. 1980; Univ. of Colorado, Ph.D.(Public Admin.) 1992. **CAREER:** Lecturer, Fac. of Mgmt Studies, Univ. of Manitoba, 1979-81; Field Supervisor, Indian Mgmt Assistance Program, Sch. of Bus. Admin., Univ. of Western Ontario, 1980-86; Dir., Proj. Mgr, Continuing Educ. Div., Univ. of Manitoba, 1981-84; Asst. Prof./Head, Mgmt Studies Section, 1984-86; Consultant, 1984-89; Fac. Mbr., Voluntary Sector Mgmt Program, Fac. of Admin. Studies, York Univ., 1987-92; Dir., Sch. of Continuing Studies, Univ. of Toronto, 1987-92; Pres., Resourceworks, 1990-92; Pres. & V-Chancellor, University Coll. of Cape Breton, 1993 to date. **SELECTED PUBLICATIONS:** "Continuing Education and the Voluntary Sector" (*The Philanthropist/Le Philanthrope* 6(2) 1987); "Managing Change in Nonprofit Organizations," in *The Nonprofit Organization: Essential Readings*, David Gies, J. Steven Ott, Jay Shafritz, eds. (Pacific Grove, CA: Brooks/Cole, 1990); "Issues, Priorities and Structure of the Canadian Voluntary Sector" (*The Philanthropist/Le Philanthrope* 10(1) 1991); various other publications. **EDIT:** Ed. Advisory Bd, Series on Nonprofit Organization Management, Lyceum Books, 1989-93. **AFFIL:** Corporate Higher Education Forum (Bd. of Dir.); Advisory Council on Science & Technologies, Gov't of Canada; Novanet (V-Chair, Bd. of Dir.); National Educations Organization Committee (Chair); Canadian Association for University Continuing Education (Pres.); Council of Ontario Universities (Chair, Status of Women Committee); Association of Universities & Colleges (Rep. to NEOC); Canadian Centre for Management Development, Gov't of Canada (Bd. of Gov.); Management Consortium on Environmental Technology, Gov't of N.S. (Bd. of Gov.); Atlantic Institute for Market Studies (Bd. of Gov.); Cape Breton County Economic Development Authority (Bd. of Dir.); Cape Breton District Sch. Bd. (Strategic Planning Committee); Association for Research on Nonprofit Organizations & Voluntary Action; Canadian Society for the Study of Higher Education; Senior Women Academic Administrators of Canada; Canadian Association for University Continuing Education. **HONS:** Canada 125 Medal, 1992; Newsperson of the Year Award, B.C. School Trustees' Asso-

ciation, 1972; National Newspaper Award for Editorial Writing, Toronto Men's Press Club 1970; various awards & honourable mentions from the Canadian Association for University Continuing Education. **MISC:** frequent speaker; peer reviewer for Policy Sciences, Nonprofit Research Sector Fund, Washington, DC, & Univ. of Toronto Press. **COMMENT:** *"As an educational leader and manager, my focus is on restructuring models of Canadian higher education to meet the needs of a global economy, and provide a more secure future for my children and grandchildren."*

Scott, Karen, R.N. $

Designer, Marketing Director and Secretary-Treasurer, **Body Matters Ltd.**, 6428 Trans Canada Hwy., Montreal, QC H4T 1X4 (514) 738-1600, FAX 738-4114. Born Montreal 1948. m. John. 2 ch. **EDUC:** Jewish General Hospital, R.N.(Nursing) 1968. **CAREER:** nursing, 5 yrs.; Co-Founder, Designer & Mktg Dir., Body Matters Ltd. (est. 1988). **AFFIL:** Reddy Memorial Hospital, Jewish General Hospital (volunteer); McKay Centre for Deaf & Crippled Children (volunteer); O.R.T. **HONS:** First Place, Private Label Category, Giftpack for Clairol, 1995; Best Exhibitor, Canadian Gift & Tableware Show, Fall 1994; high sch. & nursing leadership character awards. **INTERESTS:** art; music; reading; theatre; creative crafts. **COMMENT:** *"My family always has and always will be my first interest. My other interests include creating beautiful things from everyday materials. At work we strive to maintain a family atmosphere and I have always believed it important to see some humour in even the most stressful situations–the interpersonal dealings are (beside the creative) very important to me. They help to bring out the best in everyone I deal with."*

Scott, Marianne Florence, B.A., B.L.S., LL.D. DLitt. 📖 🎓

Librarian and Educator, **National Library of Canada**, 395 Wellington St., Ottawa, ON K1A 0N4 (613) 996-1623, FAX 996-7941. Born Toronto 1928. s. **EDUC:** McGill Univ., B.A. 1949, B.L.S. 1952. **CAREER:** Asst. Librarian, Bank of Montreal, 1952-55; Law Librarian, McGill Univ., 1955-73; Lecturer in Legal Bibliography, Fac. of Law, 1964-75; Law Area Librarian, 1973-75; Dir. of Libraries, 1975-84; Nat'l Librarian, National Library of Canada, 1984 to date. **SELECTED PUBLICATIONS:** *Index to Canadian Legal Periodical Literature*, co-founder & ed., 1963 to date; contributed articles to professional journals. **AFFIL:** International Association of Law Libraries (Dir. 1974-77); American Association of Law Libraries; Canadian Association of Law Libraries (Pres. 1963-69); Canadian Library Association (Pres. 1981-82); Corporation of Professional Librarians of Quebec (VP 1975-76); Canadian Association of Research Libraries (Pres. 1978-79); Centre for Research Libraries (Dir. 1980-83); International Federation of Library Associations; Conference of Directors of National Libraries (Chrm 1988-92). **HONS:** Officer of the Order of Canada, 1995; LL.D.(Hon.), York Univ., 1985; LL.D. (Hon.), Dalhousie Univ., 1989; D.Litt.(Hon.), Laurentian Univ., 1990.

Scott, Mary M. ■ ✋ ♡

President, **Child Find P.E.I. Inc.**, P.O. Box 1092, Charlottetown, PE C1A 7M4 (902) 368-1678, FAX 368-1389. Born McAdam, N.B. 1947. d. 3 ch. **CAREER:** Sec., Gov't of Canada & private industry. **VOLUNTEER CAREER:** Founder/Pres., Child Find P.E.I. Inc., 1988 to date. **AFFIL:** Charlottetown Lioness Club (Pres.; Sec.-Treas.); Girl Guides of Canada (Guider); Child Find Canada (Dir.). **INTERESTS:** reading; music; dancing; basketball. **COMMENT:** *"I started Child Find P.E.I. about eight years ago as there was no branch on Prince Edward Island. I love working with children and could not understand how anyone could go through the experience of having a child abducted. I have a 9 to 5 job everyday. Child Find related work is done evenings and on-call 24 hours a day with supportive volunteers."*

Scott, Phyllis, B.P.E. ■■ ♡ ✋ 🎓

Past President, and Coordinator of International Relations, **Canadian Federation of University Women** (non-profit, non-partisan NGO providing educational opportunities for women & concerned about status of women), 297 Dupuis St., Ste. 308, Ottawa, ON K1L 7H8 (613) 747-7339, FAX 747-8358. Born Ottawa 1940. m. Stan. 1 ch. Richard. **EDUC:** Univ. of British Columbia, Bachelor of Phys. Educ. 1962, Diploma (Educ. of Children with Behaviour Disorders) 1972. **CAREER:** high sch. & elementary teacher, 1962-66 & 1972-93, Canada & US, incl. 21 yrs.' experience with mentally & physically challenged students, N. Vancouver. **AFFIL:** Canadian Federation of University Women (Bd. mbr. 1985 to date; Nat'l Educ. Chair 1985-90; VP 1990-94; Nat'l Pres. 1994-96; Dir. of Int'l Rel'ns 1996-98); Retired Teachers' Association of B.C.; Alpha Delta Pi Sorority; International Federation of University Women; B.C. Beijing Committee (mbr. 1994-95). **INTERESTS:** politics-all levels; downhill skiing; tennis; music; public sch. educ.; humane treatment of animals; wilderness preservation; environment. **COMMENT:** *"I believe in the worth and capacity to succeed inherent in all people, given the right opportunity. I believe that children are our most valuable resource. Developing a sense of humour is an invaluable asset in life. My career and voluntary work with CFUW have provided me wonderful opportunities to expand my personal horizons."*

Scott, Sheridan Elizabeth, B.ès.Sc.,B.A., LL.B. ■■ ⚖ $ 📺
Vice-President, Multimedia Law and Regulation, BELL CANADA, 105 Hôtel-de-Ville, 6th Fl., Hull, QC J8X 4H7 (819) 773-6026, FAX 778-3437. Born Vancouver 1950. m. David Zussman. 2 ch. Richard Frederic, Julianne Rebecca. **EDUC:** Coll. Marie de France, B.ès.Sc. 1970; McGill Univ., B.A.(Hons., Psych.) 1973; Univ. of Victoria, LL.B. 1981. **CAREER:** Social Sciences & Humanities Research Council, 1973-78; Sr. Cnsl, Canadian Radio-television & Telecommunications Commission, 1983-92; Asst. VP, Planning & Corp. Dev., Canadian Broadcasting Corporation, 1992-93; VP, Planning & Regulatory Affairs, 1993-94; VP, Multimedia Law & Regulation, Bell Canada, 1994 to date. **SELECTED PUBLICATIONS:** author, several articles on communications law. **AFFIL:** Canadian Women in Communications (Dir. & mbr., Exec. Committee 1994 to date); National Capital Association of Communications Lawyers (founding mbr. & mbr., Exec. Committee 1992 to date); Univ. of B.C. Centre for Communications Law (Steering Committee 1995 to date); Media Awareness (Advisory Bd. 1993 to date); Le Cercle Universitaire. **INTERESTS:** tennis; travel. **MISC:** Law Clerk to the Rt. Hon. Bora Laskin; part-time Prof., Fac. of Law, Univ. of Ottawa, 1990-91; part-time Prof., Dept. of Law, Carleton Univ., 1991-92.

Scott, Suzie, B.A.,LL.B. ✊ ⚖ 🎓
Executive Director, UNIVERSITY OF TORONTO FACULTY ASSOCIATION, 720 Spadina Ave., Ste. 419, Toronto, ON M5S 2T9 (416) 978-3351, FAX 978-6071. Born Bluffton, Ind. 1946. s. 1 ch. **EDUC:** York Univ., B.A.(Psych.) 1974; Univ. of Toronto, LL.B. 1977. **BAR:** Ont., 1979. **CAREER:** private legal practice (criminal law), 1979-85; Exec. Dir., Univ. of Toronto Fac. Association, 1985 to date. **SELECTED PUBLICATIONS:** *Offense/Defense: Survival Manual for Activists*, co-author. **AFFIL:** Law Society of Upper Canada; Canadian Bar Association; Law Union of Ontario. **INTERESTS:** political activism; old music; reading, esp. non-fiction; privacy issues & their relationship to computers/cyberspace. **COMMENT:** *"Born and raised in Indiana, I came to Canada as the wife of a draft-dodger in 1968. Started law school in 1977 with an infant daughter, on welfare. I survived and flourished."*

Schwartz, Nancy E, B.H.E., Ph.D. ■ ⊕ ♥ 🎓
Director, National Centre for Nutrition and Dietetics, THE AMERICAN DIETETIC ASSOCIATION, 216 West Jackson Blvd., Chicago, IL 60606-6995 (312) 899-0040, ext. 4761, FAX 899-1739. **EDUC:** Univ. of British Columbia, B.H.E.(Nutrition & Dietetics) 1968; Ohio State Univ., Ph.D.(Human Nutrition) 1973. **CAREER:** Therapeutic Dietician & Nutrition Instructor, Queen Elizabeth Hospital & Sch. of Nursing, Montreal, 1969-70; Teaching Asst., Ohio State Univ., 1970-72; Asst./Assoc. Prof., Dir. of Continuing Educ., Univ. of British Columbia, 1973-87; Pres. & CEO, National Institute of Nutrition, Ottawa, 1987-90; Dir., National Centre for Nutrition & Dietetics, Chicago, 1990 to date. **SELECTED PUBLICATIONS:** "Tracking Nutrition Trends: Canadians' attitudes, knowledge and behaviours regarding fat, fibre and cholesterol" with L. Beggs, S. Hendricks & K. Biro *(Journal of the Canadian Dietetic Association* 54 1993); "Narrowing the Gap: Practical Strategies for Increasing Wholegrain Consumption" *(Critical Review of Food Science and Nutrition* 34 1994); "Helping Americans Eat Right: Developing Practical and Actionable Public Nutrition Messages based on the ADA Survey of American Dietary Habits," with S.J. Morreale (*Journal of the American Dietetic Association* 95 1995); various other publications. **AFFIL:** Canadian Dietetic Association (Charter Fellow); American Dietetic Association; American Institute of Nutrition; Canadian Dietetic Association; Canadian Society for Nutritional Sciences; Chicago Nutrition Association; Society for Nutrition Education; Institute of Medicine Food Forum.

Seatle, Dixie 🎞 🎭
Actor. c/o Oscars and Abrams Associates Inc., 59 Berkeley St., Toronto, ON M5A 2W5 (416) 860-1790, FAX 860-0236. **EDUC:** Dawson Coll., CEGEP, 2nd yr. Arts 1971; National Theatre Sch., Grad. 1974. **SELECTED CREDITS:** Principal, *Glitterdome* (feature); Principal, *Ticket to Heaven* (feature); Co-Star, *Pure Escape* (feature); Mona (series regular), *Adderley* (series), CBS/Global; Sheila (series regular), *A Gift To Last* (series), CBC; Mistress Ford, *Merry Wives of Windsor* (theatre), Stratford; Lady MacDuff, *MacBeth* (theatre), Stratford; Emilia, *Othello* (theatre), Stratford; Jane Banbury, *Fallen Angels* (theatre), Citadel; Katherine, *The Secret Rapture* (theatre), Theatre Cen-

tre; Susan Traherne, *Plenty* (theatre), St. Lawrence Centre; Olivia, *Twelfth Night* (theatre), YPT; Anne, *Ashes* (theatre), MTC; extensive radio work incl. book reading, most recently Margaret Atwood's novel, *Alias Grace*. **AFFIL:** ACTRA; EQUITY. **HONS:** Best Performance, Continuing Dramatic Role (*Adderley*), Gemini Awards, 1987; nomination, Best Actress (*Population of One*), ACTRA Award, 1981; nomination, Best Supporting Actress (*Ticket to Heaven*), Genie Awards, 1982; nomination, Best Supporting Actress ("The Wedding," *A Gift To Last*), ACTRA Award, 1980. **INTERESTS:** painting (acrylic & watercolour); piano; cross-country skiing; gardening; yoga. **MISC:** taught acting at Maggie Bassett studio at the Tarragon Theatre at various times between 1981 & 1988. **COMMENT:** "*I have had a fulfilling career without having to leave Canada, and my greatest achievement is my happy family life.*"

Séguin, Yvonne Donna Marie 🌑 **○**
Directrice, GROUPE D'AIDE ET D'INFORMATION SUR LE HARCELEMENT SEXUEL AU TRAVAIL, 4229 de Lorimier, Montréal, QC H2H 2A9 (514) 526-0789, FAX 526-8891. Born Toronto 1953. 2 ch. Marie-Josée, Steven. **CAREER:** Cofondatrice en 1980 et dir. du Groupe d'aide, premier et seul organisme canadien spécialisé en intervention auprès des personnes victimes de harcèlement sexuel et en formation préventive en enterprises Organise le 1er Colloque au Québec sur le harcèlement sexuel au travail, 1994, et une vaste campagne de sensibilisation auprès des femmes immigrantes de Montréal, 1990; Invitée par le Min. de la Justice du Canada, présente un Mémoire sur le projet de loi C-126 (*Stalking Law*); Mbr. de la Table de concertation des agressions à caractère sexuel de la Communauté urbaine de Montréal depuis 1989; Mbr. de l'Association canadienne contre le harcèlement sexuel dans l'enseignement supérieur (CAASHHE), depuis 1989; Collabore à la rédaction du guide "Comprendre pour agir" publié par le Bureau de la main-d'oeuvre féminine du Canada; Invitée au Colloque de l'Association européenne contre les violences faites aux femmes au travail, Paris, 1987 et rencontre des représentantes européennes, Paris, 1996. **SELECTED PUBLICATIONS:** collabore à la rédaction des livres, *Ça fait pas partie d'la job!* (1989-90); réédité en 1996, *It's not part of the job!* (1996). **MISC:** collabore à la conception de la pièce de théâtre, "Le silence des autres," 1994; Consultée pour la conception de la vidéo de formation d'Emploi & Immigration Canada (loi C-105), 1993. **COMMENT:** "*Depuis déjà 15 ans, madame Yvonne Séguin oeuvre à l'amélira-*

tion des conditions de travail des femmes ainsi qu'à la défense des droits de celles-ci. Tantôt intervenante, tantôt conférencière, formatrice, militante, elle travaille d'arrache-pied pour contrer le harcèlement sexuel en milieu de travail."

Seiler, Tamara Palmer, A.A.,B.A., M.A. ■ 🐦 📜 🌸
Associate Professor, Faculty of General Studies, UNIVERSITY OF CALGARY, Calgary, AB T2N 1N4 (403) 220-5320, FAX 282-6716, EMAIL tseiler@acs.ucalgary.ca. Born Yerington, Nev. 1946. m. Robert M. Seiler. 2 ch. Tanya Palmer, Mark Palmer. **EDUC:** Cottey Coll., A.A. 1965; Brigham Young Univ., B.A.(English) 1968; York Univ., M.A.(Cdn Lit.) 1972; Univ. of Alberta, doctoral studies in Cdn Lit., in progress. **CAREER:** high sch. teacher, 1968-69; freelance ed. & writer, combined with childrearing, 1973-81; Instructor, now Prof., Fac. of Gen. Studies, Univ. of Calgary, 1981 to date; Dir., Cdn Studies Program, to 1995. **SELECTED PUBLICATIONS:** *Peoples of Alberta, Portraits of Cultural Diversity*, with Howard Palmer (Prairie Books, 1985); *Alberta, A New History*, co-author; writes on Alta. politics & society, & immigrant & ethnic experience in Canada; articles published in various journals incl. *Journal of Canadian Studies & Prairie Forum*; book reviews. **AFFIL:** Association for Canadian Studies (Nat'l Bd. Prairie Rep.); NeWest Institute (Past Pres.); Association of Canadian University Teachers of English; Phi Kappa Phi. **HONS:** Que. Advisory Committee to Premier Ralph Klein (mbr.); Teaching Excellence Award. **INTERESTS:** history; literature; music; theatre; film; hiking

Seip, Jo-Anne, Dip.Ed., B.A, M.Ed. 🐦 ○ 🌐
Chief Executive Officer, GATEWAY SOCIETY, 4807 Georgia St, Delta, BC V4K 2T1 (604) 946-3610, FAX 946-2956, EMAIL jseip@cln.etc.bc.ca. Administrative Officer, GATEWAY PROVINCIAL RESOURCE PROGRAM. Born Kitchener, Ont. 1942. m. Kenneth Rattray. 4 ch. Jeffrey Seip, Julie Seip, Shelley Robinson, Michael Rattray. **EDUC:** Univ. of Waterloo, B.A. (Soc./Hist.) 1972; Ontario Coll. of Teachers, Diploma (Educ.) 1973; Univ. of Western Washington, M.Ed.(Special Educ.) 1982. **CAREER:** Asst. Admin., Kitchener-Waterloo Habilitation Services for the Retarded, 1969-72; Dir., Summer Programs for Autistic Children, Reg'l Municipality of Waterloo, Dept. of Recreation, 1972-74; Teacher, Orthopaedic Unit, Waterloo County Bd. of Educ., Kitchener, Ont., 1973-74; Teacher, Autism Unit, 1974-76; Admin. Officer & CEO, 1976-95. **SELECTED CRED-**

ITS: *Education of Students with Autism*, Educational TV, U.B.C., 1982; *Services to the Autistic*, Delta Cable 10, Delta, B.C., 1984; Presenter, *Autism America International Conference*, 1993, 1994, 1995. SELECTED PUBLICATIONS: "Alternative Living Arrangements for the Severely Behaviourly Disordered," with D. McCoy in *Critical Issues in Educating the Severely Emotionally Disturbed* (Univ. of Washington, 1982); *Teaching Students with Autism & Developmental Disorders* (Gateway Press, 1982; revised 1995); Autism Module, M.H. Core Training, ed. with A. Emmons (Gateway Society, 1992); *Autism Module 1: Training and Inservice*, ed. with A. Emmons & L. Johl (Gateway Society, 1992); *Autism Screening Protocol*, with Kim McGunn *et al* (Gateway Society, 1992); *Autism Inservice & Training Manual*, with E. Smith, M. Mackenzie, B. Porco, L. Hansen (Gateway Press, 1996). AFFIL: Austism Society America; Autism Society Canada, Council for Exceptional Children; Council for Administrators of Special Education; Principals' Association of B.C.; Autism Society of British Columbia (Past Pres., Professional Advisory Bd.); Federation of Private Child Care Agencies, Prov. of B.C. (Past Pres.); Autism Council of B.C. HONS: Outstanding Educator, C.E.C., Int'l Award, 1982; Women of Distinction Nominee, Y.W.C.A., 1984. INTERESTS: music; gardening; interior decorating; writing. MISC: numerous conference presentations & workshops. COMMENT: *"Jo-Anne Seip is the Administrative Officer and Coordinator of Gateway Provincial Resource Program, which provides a range of school services to students with autism and pervasive developmental disorders throughout British Columbia. In addition, as the CEO for Gateway Society she has also coordinated and administered a continuum of residential, community and outreach programs for children and adults with autism for the past 18 years."*

Semple, Goldie ⊗ ⅄ ♥

Actor. c/o ACI, 205 Ontario St., Toronto, ON M5A 2V6 (519) 271-9967. Born Vancouver 1952. m. Lorne Thomas Kennedy. 1 ch. Madeline Elliot Kennedy. EDUC: Univ. of British Columbia, 1970-74; Bristol Old Vic Theatre Sch., UK, 1975-77. SELECTED CREDITS: Co-Founder/Prod., *Foolscap*, 1996; Prod/compiled, *George and Victoria Send Their Best*, 1996; Melissa Gardiner, *Love Letters*, Magnus Theatre & The Grand Theatre, London, 1994-95; Stella Kirby, *Eden End* (theatre), Shaw Festival, 1994; Dir., *Macbeth* (theatre), N.Y.U.; Shirle Deluca, *Blowin' on Bowen* (theatre), Arts Club; Cleopatra, *Anthony and Cleopatra* (theatre), Stratford, 1993; Constance, *King John* (theatre), Stratford, 1993; Chloe, *Lips Together, Teeth Apart* (theatre), Vancouver Playhouse; Hanna, *Not Wanted on the Voyage* (theatre), MTC/Canadian Stage; Beatrice, *Much Ado About Nothing* (theatre), Stratford, 1991; Lady MacBeth, *Macbeth* (theatre), Stratford, 1990; Maggie, *Cat on a Hot Tin Roof* (theatre), Stratford, 1989; Lorraine, *The Man Who Came To Dinner* (theatre), Theatre London; Kate, *The Taming of the Shrew* (theatre), Stratford, 1988; Ellen, *Calvalcade* (theatre), Shaw Festival; Lead, *To Save The Children* (telefilm), CBS; Lead, *Comedy of Errors* (teleplay), CBC; Lead, *The Taming of the Shrew* (teleplay), CBC; Principal, *Street Legal* (series), CBC; Principal, *Judge* (series), CBC; Principal, *The Beachcombers* (series), CBC; Principal, *Anthology* (radio), CBC Radio; Principal, *The Four Gated City* (radio), CBC Radio; Principal, *The Bright Red Herring* (radio), CBC Radio. AFFIL: Canadian Actors' Equity Association; ACTRA. COMMENT: *"I suppose my main achievement (other than my 19-year marriage and long-awaited child, Madeline Elliot Kennedy) has been to survive as a classical actress in Canada. I have been blessed with opportunity and gifted people as my colleagues."*

Serbin, Lisa A., B.A.,Ph.D. ⃠ ⊕

Professor of Psychology, Centre for Research in Human Development, CONCORDIA UNIVERSITY, 7141 Sherbrooke St. W., Montreal, QC H4B 1R6 (514) 848-2255, FAX 848-2815, EMAIL lserbin@vax2.concordia.ca. Born 1946. EDUC: Reed Coll., Portland, Ore, B.A.(Psych.) 1968; State Univ. of New York at Stony Brook, Ph.D.(Psych.) 1972. CAREER: part-time private practice, 1975 to date; Co-Dir., Butternut Hill Presch., Dept. of Psych. lab. sch., SUNY-Binghamton, 1974-78; Asst. Prof. of Psych., 1973-78; Assoc. Prof. of Psych., Concordia Univ., 1978-84; Dir., Centre for Research in Hum. Dev., Concordia Univ., 1981-91; Prof. of Psych., 1984 to date. SELECTED PUBLICATIONS: "Sex-role Stereotyping in Children's Television Programs," with S.H. Sternglanz (*Developmental Psychology* 10 1974); "Identification of Children at Risk for Adult Schizophrenia: A Longitudinal Study," with A. Schwartzman & J. Ledingham (*International Journal of Applied Psychology* 34 1984); "Gender, Ethnic and Body-type Biases: The Generality of Prejudice in Childhood," with K. Powlishta, A-B. Doyle & D. White (*Developmental Psychology* 30 1994); numerous other publications. EDIT: Ed. Bd., *Journal of Applied Behavior Analysis*, 1977-81; Ed. Bd., *Behavioral Assessment*, 1979-83; Ed. Bd., *Child Development*, 1979-84, 1986-90; Ed. Bd., *Sex Roles*, 1979 to date; Guest Ed., special issue "Social Change," *Sex Roles*, 1986; Ed. Bd., *Developmental Psychology*, 1980-86. **AFFIL:** American Psychological Association (Fellow) (Divisions: Developmental, Clinical, Psych. of Women); Canadian Psychological Association (Fellow); Society for Research in Child Development; Corporation Professionelle des Psychologues du Québec; Phi Beta Kappa. **HONS:** Woodrow Wilson Fellowship, 1968. **MISC:** Registered Psychologist, Que., 1979 to date; reviewer, various granting agencies; recipient, various grants; numerous conference presentations.

Sereny, Julia ■ ⬡ ♥
Producer, SIENNA FILMS INC., 110 Spadina Ave., Ste. 800, Toronto, ON M5V 2K4 (416) 703-1126, FAX 703-8825. Born Toronto 1956. m. Christopher Johnson. 1 ch. **CAREER:** as a prod. has worked independently on numerous dramatic & documentary films over the last 15 years & has worked for the Ontario Regional Production Office of the National Film Board, Atlantis Films & Rhombus Media; Prod., Sienna Films Inc., 1989 to date. **SELECTED CREDITS:** Project Dev., *The Bruce Curtis Story* (telefilm), Atlantis Films; Project Dev., *The Magic Hour* (13-part series), Atlantis Films; Prod. Consultant and Coord. Prod., *The Hand of Stalin* (documentary series); Co-Prod., *Stop the World, We Want To Get On* (two half-hour documentaries), CBC/Channel 4, U.K.; Prod., *April One* (feature); Prod., *Hidden Children* (documentary), Sienna Films Inc./October Films, UK. **AFFIL:** Academy of Canadian Cinema and Television. **HONS:** Gold Plaque (*Hidden Children*), Chicago International Film Festival; Nominated, Best Documentary (Hidden Children), Gemini Awards, 1995; Bronze Award, Independent Film Feature (April One) Worldfest Houston. **MISC:** has a number of other projects in development including a feature entitled *The Double*, a film on women's Erotica; *Man Overboard*, based on the book by Ian Brown, was recently completed; provides project consultant svcs. for CBC/independent production.

Service, Patricia Olive, B.A. ■ ⊗
Artist. 237 E. 4th Ave., Unit 111, Vancouver, BC V5T 4R4 (604) 877-1847, FAX 264-7856. Born Port Alberni, B.C. 1941. m. David Grant Nelson. 2 ch. David C. Nelson, Greer L. Nelson. **EDUC:** Univ. of British Columbia, B.A.(English & Latin) 1963; Glasgow Sch. of Art, 1966-67. **COMMISSIONS:** 40 monoprints for the Executive Life Insurance Co., Los Angeles, 1989. **EXHIBITIONS:** many solo exhibitions, including Buschlen-Mowatt Gallery, Vancouver (1983, 1990, 1991, 1992, 1994, 1996);

Wade Gallery (1985, 1986, 1988); The Gallery/Art Placement, Sask. (1985, 1987); Canadian Art Galleries, Calgary (1987, 1991); Waddington and Shiell Gallery, Toronto (1987, 1989); Wade Gallery, Los Angeles (1988, 1989); Miriam Shiell Fine Art, Toronto (1990); Gallery One, Toronto (1991, 1995, 1996); Kathleen Laverty Gallery, Edmonton (1994); Wallack Galleries, Ottawa (1995); recent group exhibitions include: *Lineart* (Buschlen-Mowatt), Ghent, Belgium (1994, 1995); *Art Asia* (Buschlen-Mowatt), Hong Kong (1994); *Tresors D'Art* (Buschlen-Mowatt), Singapore (1994); *Reflecting Paradise*, Selections from the Collection of the University of Lethbridge, Calgary (1994); *Artists in Bloom* (Buschlen-Mowatt), Vancouver (1994); *Recent Acquisitions*, The Mendel Art Gallery, Saskatoon (1994); *Landscape 96 Festival* (Painters on Site), Saskatoon (1996). **COLLECTIONS:** numerous corporate collections; many private collections in Canada, the US, the UK, Taiwan, Japan, Singapore & Hong Kong. **HONS:** Canada 125 Medal. **MISC:** profiled in the book *Drawn to the Edge: The Paintings of Pat Service* by Robert Christie, Charles Killam, Barrie Mowatt and Pat Service. **COMMENT:** *"I am a painter of landscapes, still life and other motifs, working in the medium of acrylic and oil on canvas, as well as watercolour and monotypes on paper. My starting point is nature, and from there I abstract, simplify or change as necessary. With my work being exhibited regularly, I sacrifice other community involvements to devote all of my time to painting."*

Sethi, Sarla, B.Sc.,M.A.,M.A., Ph.D. ■ ■ ⬡ ⊕
Associate Professor, Faculty of Nursing, UNIVERSITY OF CALGARY, 2500 University Dr. N.W., Calgary, AB T2N 1N4 (403) 220-4641, FAX 284-4803, EMAIL sethi@acs.ucalgary.ca. Born West Pakistan 1936. **EDUC:** Univ. of Delhi, B.Sc.(Hons., Nursing) 1957; Punjab Univ., M.A.(Psych.) 1960; New York Univ., M.A.(Public Health Teaching) 1964; Univ. of Colorado, Ph.D.(Nursing) 1994. **CAREER:** Asst. Prof., Univ. of Calgary, 1970-76; Assoc. Prof., 1976 to date. **SELECTED CREDITS:** *Complete Physical Examination of an Adult (Female)* (videotape, 57 mins., 1987). **SELECTED PUBLICATIONS:** "The dialectic in becoming a mother: Experiencing a postpartum phenomenon" (*Scandinavian Journal of Caring Sciences*, 9, 1995); "Convergence of spirituality and caring: Gandhi as an exemplar," in S. Roach (ed.), *Caring from the heart* (Paulist Press, in press); co-editor with M.C. Stainton, *Crossroad to the Future: Proceedings of International Conference of Maternity Nurse*

Researchers (1986); "Oxytocin Challenge Test: Nursing Implications" (*American Journal of Nursing*, Vol. 78, No. 12, 1978). **AFFIL:** Calgary Coalition, Centre of Excellence, Women's Health (Dean's delegate 1994 to date); Postpartum Support Services, Calgary (Bd. mbr. 1982-87); Planned Parenthood of Alberta (Bd. mbr. 1986-88); Family Life Education of Calgary (Bd. mbr. 1980-83). **HONS:** Superior Teaching Award, Student Union, Univ. of Calgary, 1982-83; award to produce videotape for teaching purposes, Univ. of Calgary & Fac. of Nursing, 1986-87. **INTERESTS:** reading & cooking (if time permits). **MISC:** referee, study titled "Postnatal Depression: Are Canadian Indian Women Immune?", Prov. Mental Health Advisory Council, 1986. **COMMENT:** *"I ventured to North America in 1961 with a dream of obtaining a Ph.D. in Nursing. I fulfilled this dream as well as raising two very fine children as a single parent and working full time as an academician."*

Sevigny, The Hon. Pierrette, B.A.,B.Ed., B.C.L.,Q.C.,J.S.C. ⬨⊤⬦
Judge, SUPERIOR COURT OF THE PROVINCE OF QUEBEC, 1 Notre Dame St. E., Rm 6.40, Montreal, QC H2Y 1B6. Born Montreal 1947. m. Richard McConomy. 1 ch. **EDUC:** Loyola Coll., B.A. 1967; McGill Univ., B.Ed. 1968, B.C.L. 1973. **BAR:** Que., 1975; Queen's Counsel, 1989. **CAREER:** teacher, Protestant Sch. Bd. of Greater Montreal, 1968-79; articled, Ogilvy, Cope, Porteus, Montgomery, Renault, Clarke & Kirkpatrick, 1974; articled, Reg'l Law Dept., St. Lawrence Reg., Canadian National Railways, 1974-75; Attorney, 1975-81; Ptnr, McConomy, De Wolfe, MacDougall, 1981-92; Prof., LaSalle Coll., 1981; Prof., Concordia Univ., 1983-89; Judge, Superior Court of the Prov. of Que., 1992 to date. **AFFIL:** Quebec Bar Association (1975-92); Montreal Bar Association (1975-92; Pres., Comité de la formation permanente 1990-91); Canadian Bar Association (Exec., Que. Section 1990-92); Residence Project Chance Inc. (Founder & former Pres.); SPCA Montreal (Dir.); Canadian Council of Christians & Jews (Dir. 1991-92); Montreal Association for the Blind (Dir. 1990-92; Hon. Treas. 1991-92); Montreal Thistle Curling. **INTERESTS:** skiing; golf; reading. **MISC:** Delegate, Nat'l Conference, Report on the Status of Women, Ottawa, 1978; Conference Delegate, Les Femmes et la Constitution, Ottawa, 1989.

Sévigny, Suzanne, B.A.,M.B.A. ■ Ⓢ
Associate Vice-President, Human Resources & Administration, Quebec Div., THE TORONTO-DOMINION BANK, 500 St. Jacques St., Montréal,

QC H9S 5N3 (514) 289-1478, FAX 289-0630. Born Montreal 1948. s. **EDUC:** Bishop's Univ., B.A.(Psych.) 1970; McGill Univ., M.B.A.(Fin.) 1982. **CAREER:** various locations abroad, Fed. Dept. of External Affairs, 1972-80; Acct Mgr, Commercial, Toronto-Dominion Bank, 1983-87; Mgr, Corp. & Investment Bnkg Group, 1987-93; Dir., Toronto-Dominion Securities Inc., 1992 to date; Mgr, Commercial Fin. Svcs, Que. Div., Toronto-Dominion Bank, 1993-95; Assoc. VP, Hum. Res. & Admin., 1995 to date. **AFFIL:** Bishops' Univ. Foundation (Investment Committee). **INTERESTS:** golf; travel.

Seward, Shirley B., B.Ed.,M.A. ■ Ⓢ ✿ Ⓒ
Chief Executive Officer, CANADIAN LABOUR MARKET AND PRODUCTIVITY CENTRE, 55 Metcalfe St., Ste. 1500, Ottawa, ON K1P 6L5 (613) 234-0505, FAX 234-2482. Born Montreal 1947. **EDUC:** McGill Univ., B.Ed. 1970; Carleton Univ., M.A.(Int'l Affairs) 1975. **CAREER:** various positions, with increasing responsibility at International Dev. Research Centre (I.D.R.C.), 1974-80; Sr. Program Officer, I.D.R.C., 1981-85; Acting Assoc. Dir., 1980-81; Sr. Policy Advisor, Prime Minister's Office, 1984; Dir., Studies in Social Policy, Institute for Research on Public Policy,1985-91; CEO, Canadian Labour Market & Productivity Centre, 1991 to date. **SELECTED PUBLICATIONS:** *Tourism in the Caribbean: The Economic Impact* ed. with Bernard Spinrad (Ottawa: I.D.R.C., 1982); "The Impact of Development Programs on Women and Fertility in Three Developing Countries" (*Resources for Feminist Research* 4 1983);*The Future of Social Welfare Systems in Canada and the United Kingdom* ed. (Halifax: Institute for Research on Public Policy, 1987); "Demographic Change and the Canadian Economy: An Overview" (*Canadian Studies in Population* Vol. 14, Number 2, 1987); "Immigration, the Canadian Labour Force, and Structural Change," *Canada-Japan: Views on Globalization* ed. K. Lorne Brownsey (Halifax: Institute for Research on Public Policy, 1990); *Alternatives to Social Assistance in Indian Communities* ed. with Frank Cassidy (Halifax: Institute for Research on Public Policy, 1991); various discussion papers & conference papers. **AFFIL:** Canadian Population Society; Canadian Economics Association; Canadian Sociology & Anthropology Association. **HONS:** Ronald Brigdon Memorial Scholarship, McGill Univ.; B'nai Brith Achievement Scholarship, McGill Univ.; Research & Travel awards, Carleton Univ. **INTERESTS:** travel; reading; music; the arts; nature; hiking. **COMMENT:** *"With broad national and international public policy experience, Shirley Seward is a major contributor to*

policy-related consensus-building, notably in labour market and economic issues."

Sexsmith, Gail (S) ⌇
Senior Vice-President, Customer Services, B.C. HYDRO, 6911 Southpoint Dr., Burnaby, BC V3N 4X8 (604) 528-3373, FAX 528-2970. Born Sask. 1949. m. Garry Sexsmith. 2 ch. EDUC: B.C. Institute of Technology, Certificate (Bus. Admin.); Univ. of Calgary, Certificate (Exec. Dev.). CAREER: Mgr, Hum. Res., B.C. Hydro; Mgr, Property Svcs; VP, Hum. Res.; Sr. VP, Customer Svcs. DIRECTOR: Powersmart Inc. AFFIL: Simon Fraser Univ. (Chair, Co-op Advisory Council).

Sexton, Rosemary ■ ☐ ﾊ
Columnist and Author. 211 Queen's Quay W., Ste. 1107, Toronto, ON M5J 2M6. Born Haileybury, Ont. 1946. m. J. Edgar Sexton. 2 ch., 3 stpch. Stephanie Black, John Beverley Robinson Black, Timothy Sexton, Christopher Sexton, Jennifer Sexton. EDUC: Laurentian University, B.A. 1968; College of Education interim high school assistant certificate Type B 1969; Specialist Guidance Certificate 1973; University of Toronto, B.A.(Hons) 1973; York University, M.A. 1976; Osgoode Hall Law School, LL.B. 1976. BAR: Ont., 1977. CAREER: English & Latin Teacher, New Liskeard Secondary School, 1968-69 & West Hill Secondary School, Owen Sound, 1969-72; articled, Holden Murdoch Finlay Robinson, 1976-77; Tax Ed., CCH (Canada) Ltd., 1977-78; Mbr., Ontario Censor Board, 1978-81; Society Columnist, *The Globe and Mail*, 1988-93; author. SELECTED PUBLICATIONS: *The Glitter Girls* (1993); *Confessions of a Society Columnist* (1995). AFFIL: has served on the boards of many organizations. INTERESTS: reading; travel; golf; roller-blading; ice-skating.

Seymoar, Nola-Kate, B.A.,M.A., Ph.D. ■■ (S) ✤ ◐
Deputy to the President, INTERNATIONAL INSTITUTE FOR SUSTAINABLE DEVELOPMENT (research & communications organization), 161 Portage Ave. E., Winnipeg, MB R3B 0Y4 (204) 958-7752, FAX 958-7710, EMAIL nkseymoar@iisdpost.iisd.ca. Born Edmonton 1944. d. 2 ch. Colleen Collar, Jeffrey Breitkreutz. EDUC: Univ. of Alberta, B.A.(Recreation Admin.) 1966, M.A.(Community Dev.) 1971; Union Grad. Sch., Ohio, Ph.D.(Social Psych.) 1972. CAREER: Lecturer & Counsellor, Univ. of Saskatchewan, 1970-75; Exec. Dir. of Reg'l Social Svcs, Saskatchewan Social Svcs, & Exec. Dir. of Departmental Svcs, Saskatchewan Public Service Commission, Gov't of Saskatchewan, 1976-84; Pres., Family Video Inc., 1984-85;

various assignments, Treasury Bd. of Canada, Dir. Gen. of Special Projects, Environment Canada, Special Advisor to the Pres., The Asbestos Institute, & Exec. Dir., Commission of Inquiry on Unemployment Insurance (Forget Commission), 1986-93; Exec. Dir., ECO-ED (World Congress for Education & Communication on Environment & Development), Toronto, 1991-93; Exec. Dir., "We the Peoples: 50 Communities Awards Program" (citizens' initiative in honour of 50th anniversary of UN), N.Y., 1993-95; Deputy to the Pres., IISD, Winnipeg, 1994 to date. SELECTED PUBLICATIONS: *Creating Common Unity* (in press); "The Dependency Cycle: Implications for Theory, Therapy and Social Action" (*Transactional Analysis Journal*, Spring 1977). AFFIL: "Smartrisk" Injury Prevention Foundation (founding Chair 1992; Bd. mbr.); American Academy of Psychotherapists; International Commission for Occupational Health; Centre for Days of Peace; Physicians for Global Survival (Canada); Manitoba Council of Women; Friends of the United Nations (Bd. mbr.); Governor General's Canadian Study Conference (former mbr.); Prince of Wales Business Leaders Forum (former mbr.). HONS: numerous awards & scholarships in undergrad. & grad. training; Global Citizen Award, 50th Anniversary of the UN. MISC: served as advisor in founding of women's collective responsible for *Herstory, the Canadian Women's Calendar*. COMMENT: *"A social entrepreneur interested in the well-being of communities, individuals and ecosystems. An innovator and advocate for multi-sectoral approaches to problem solving and conflict resolution."*

Sfeir, Marsha, B.A. ◉ ◑ ⌇
Educator and Trainer, EDUCATION WIFE ASSAULT, 427 Bloor St. W., Box 7, Toronto, ON M5S 1X7 (416) 968-3422, FAX 968-2026. Born Buffalo, N.Y. 1947. d. 2 ch. Joshua Cormie, Justin Cormie. EDUC: Canisius Coll., B.A.(Social Studies) 1970. CAREER: Supervisor of Student Teachers, Associated Colleges of the Midwest, Chicago, 1976-78; secondary sch. teacher, Chicago & Buffalo, NY, 1970-77; staff, Middle East Peace Educ. Program, American Friends Service Committee, Chicago, 1977-80; staff, Christian Movement for Peace, Toronto, 1981-85; Coord., Teacher Training Proj., Christian Movement for Peace, 1986-88; Cooperant, short-term, CUSO, Chile, 1988, 1989, 1990; Coord., Canada-Chile Cooperative Proj. on Overcoming Violence Against Women, 1988-92; Coord. of Public Educ. & Skillsharing, Education Wife Assault, Toronto, 1988 to date; Trainer, "Policing in a Multiracial Society," Charles Novogrodsky and

Associates, 1991 to date. **SELECTED PUBLICATIONS**: "Peace Pilgrimage: Responding to the Cry of the Poor in Central America" (*Calumet* Winter 1984); *A Compassionate Peace: A Future for the Middle East* prepared for the American Friends Service Committee by Mendelsohn, Day, Elder, Sfeir & Pressberg (N.Y.C.: Hill and Wong, & Toronto: McGraw Hill Ryerson Ltd., 1982); *As Women, Together with Bev Burke* (1991); *Political and Social Rights and Human Policy* (1985), *Work and Co-creation* (1982*) Economic Rights and Human Development* (1984), *Women and Human Wholeness*, 1983 (Hutley, Morin & Sfeir, Wm. C. Brown Co. Publishers, Dubuque, Iowa). **AFFIL**: Doris Marshall Institute (Dir.; Treas.); Metro Women Abuse Protocol Council (Educ. Committee); Metro Toronto Coordinating Committee Against Wife Assault; Match International; Council of Canadians; Education Against Homophobia. **HONS**: "Women Helping Women" Award, Soroptimist International, 1991. **INTERESTS**: photography; gardening; hiking/canoeing; spirituality; the struggles & celebrations of women internationally; music. **MISC**: regularly serve as a consultant to policy-makers in fed. & prov. gov't ministries; evaluate funding proposals, when they pertain to violence against women, for C.I.D.A., Sick Children's Foundation, etc. **COMMENT**: *"Mother, educator, activist, dreamer with 30 years' experience working locally, nationally, internationally on gender violence, racism, heterosexism, militarism and economic injustice. My goal is to continue in the struggle for justice with a sense of humour and an ability to dance!"*

Shack, Sybil F., C.M.,B.A.,B.Ed.,M.Ed., LL.D.,F.CCT,FOISE ■ ■ ✤ ○ ⊕

President, CANADIAN CIVIL LIBERTIES ASSOCIATION. Born Winnipeg 1911. s. **EDUC**: Univ. of Manitoba, B.A. 1929, B.Ed. 1945, M.Ed. 1946; Ontario Coll. of Educ., post-Master's courses in Supervision & Admin. 1950-52. **CAREER**: Teacher, various schools, Man., 1930-48; Principal, various schools, Winnipeg, 1948-76. **SELECTED PUBLICATIONS**: several book chpts., textbooks, gen. interest books; writer & broadcaster, School Radio Broadcasts, Dept. of Educ., Man., & CBC, 1950-80. **AFFIL**: Manitoba Association for Rights & Liberties (Hon. Pres.; former Exec. Chair); Creative Retirement, Man. (mbr. from inception; life mbr.); Manitoba Teachers' Society (hon. life mbr.); Canadian Education Association (hon. life mbr.); Jewish Child & Family Service (hon. life mbr.); Society of Manitobans with Disabilities (Advisory Committee); Canadian Coll. of Teachers (Nat'l Pres. 1967); Univ. of Manitoba (Bd. of

Gov. 1961-67); currently supporting mbr., many organizations & institutions incl. Shaarey Zedek Synagogue, Winnipeg Humane Society, Manitoba Theatre Centre, Manitoba Schizophrenia Society. **HONS**: numerous incl.: Centennial Medal, 1967; hon. LL.D., Univ. of Manitoba, 1969; John M. Brown Award for contribution to educ. in Man., Univ. of Manitoba, 1976; George Croskery Award for contribution to Cdn educ., Canadian Coll. of Teachers, 1982; Special Award for contribution to educ. at prov., nat'l & int'l levels, Canadian Teachers' Federation, 1980; Woman of the Year for community svc., YWCA, 1983; Person's Award (nat'l hon. given to only 5 women every year to record contribution to women's rights), 1983; Order of the Buffalo Heart (Man. gov't citizen's award), 1983; Order of Canada, 1984; Man. recipient, Model Educator, Quebec City, 1989; Canada 125 Medal, 1992; Manitoba Human Rights Achievement Award, 1995; Winnipeg Citizens' Hall of Fame, 1996; Fellow, Ontario Institute for Studies in Education. **INTERESTS**: animal welfare; human rights. **MISC**: mbr., Community of Inquirers, Fac. of Educ., Univ. of Manitoba, working in a project on Life in Manitoba Classrooms in the 1920s to 1940s. **COMMENT**: *"Sybil Frances Shack, retired Manitoba teacher and principal, continues to be active as a volunteer, a researcher, writer, feminist and civil libertarian."*

Shadd, Dolores ■ ■ ⊕ ⚘

Women's Advisor for Ontario, NATIONAL FARMERS UNION, 250C - 2nd Ave. S., Saskatoon, SK S7M 2M1 (306) 652-9465, FAX 664-6226. Born Detroit, Mich. 1926. m. Edwin. 3 ch. Duane, Terence, Darrell. **EDUC**: 2 yrs. of coll. educ. **CAREER**: farming; teaching (supply teacher, Kent County Bd. of Educ.); volunteer work. **SELECTED CREDITS**: *Older, Stronger, Wiser* (film, National Film Board of Canada). **AFFIL**: Chatham YMCA (Bd. of Dir.); Kent County Agriculture Hall of Fame (Pres.); Ontario Secondary School Teachers' Federation; Association of Country Women of the World (Life Mbr.). **HONS**: Grassroots Leadership Citation, National Farmers Union, 1995; first recipient, Kent County Peace Medal, YMCA; Women of Excellence Award, YMCA, 1996; inducted into Kent County Agriculture Hall of Fame, 1990; honoured by Kent County Farm Safety Association; ACWW life member. **INTERESTS**: agriculture; travel; people; lobbying; women's issues; showing slides of her travels; teaching Sunday Sch. **MISC**: founding mbr., Women's Development Day Program (now in 11th yr.). **COMMENT**: *"Husband Edwin Shadd is a sixth-generation farmer; married 48 years, with 3 sons and 3 grandchildren. Enjoy* *teaching physical education and health, and special education children. ACWW holds a conference every 3 years; I have been a delegate to 6 world conferences: Australia, 1974; Kenya, 1977; Vancouver, 1983; Kansas City, US, 1989; Holland, 1992; and New Zealand, 1995."*

Shaffer, Beverly, B.A.,M.Sc. 🎞 📺 🎓
Film Director and Producer, Documentary Studio, NATIONAL FILM BOARD OF CANADA, Box 6100, Montreal, QC H3C 3H5 (514) 283-9509, FAX 283-5487. Born 1945. **EDUC:** McGill Univ., B.A. 1966; Boston Univ., M.Sc. 1971. **SELECTED CREDITS:** Prod./Dir., *Children of Canada*, film series; Prod./Dir., *To a Safer Place*; Dir., *I'll Find a Way*; Prod./Dir., *Children of Jerusalem* (series). **HONS:** over 30 int'l awards incl. Academy Award, Best Live Action Short (*I'll Find a Way*), 1978.

Shafran, Grace, LL.B. ⚖ $ 📺
Vice-President and General Counsel, BATON BROADCASTING INCORPORATED, 9 Channel Nine Court, Scarborough, ON M1S 4B5 (416) 299-2218, FAX 299-2423. Born Toronto 1956. m. Edward John. 2 ch. **EDUC:** Univ. of Windsor, LL.B. 1980. **CAREER:** VP & Gen. Cnsl, Baton Broadcasting Inc. **INTERESTS:** travel; fitness.

Shamian, Judith, RN,Ph.D.,C.H.E. ✚ 🎓 ⚛
Vice-President, Nursing, and Head, World Health Organization (WHO) Collaborating Centre, MOUNT SINAI HOSPITAL, 600 University Ave, Toronto, ON M5G 1X5 (416) 586-5073, FAX (416) 586-8830, EMAIL jshamian@mtsinai.on.ca. Associate Professor, Faculty of Nursing, UNIVERSITY OF TORONTO. Born Hungary 1950. m. Chanoch. 3 ch. **EDUC:** Shaare Zedek Hospital, Jerusalem, R.N. 1971; Concordia Univ., B.A.(Community Nursing) 1978; New York Univ., M.P.H.(Int'l Health Educ.) 1984; Case Western Reserve Univ., Cleveland, Ph.D.(Nursing Exec. Track) 1988; American Coll. of Healthcare Executives, C.H.E. 1995. **MEDICAL CAREER:** Emergency Room Nurse, Shaare Zedek Hospital, 1971-74; Nurse Practitioner in a Kibbutz, Tirat-Zvi, Israel, 1974-75; Nursing Coord., Special Svcs & Research, 1980-86; Coord., Sir Mortimer B. Davis - Jewish General Hospital, Social Policy Committee, Canadian Nurses' Association, 1983-84; Researcher Nurse Consultant, Nursing Div. of First Consulting Group, California, 1986-92; Dir., Dept. of Nursing R.&D., Sunnybrook Medical Centre, Toronto, 1986-89; VP, Nursing, Mount Sinai Hospital, Toronto, 1989 to date; Head, World Heath Organization Collaborating Centre, 1992 to date. **ACADEMIC CAREER:** Lecturer, Sch. of Nursing, McGill Univ., 1980-86; Asst. Clinical Prof., Sch. of Nursing, Case Western Reserve Univ., Cleveland, 1989; Clinical Assoc., Fac. of Nursing, Univ. of Western Ontario, 1991; Postdoctoral Fellow in Mgmt, Wharton Sch., Univ. of Pennsylvania, 1992; Asst. Prof., Fac. of Nursing, Univ. of Toronto, 1989-93; Assoc. Mbr., Centre for Health Promotion, 1992 to date; Assoc. Prof., Fac. of Nursing, 1993 to date; Dozor Visiting Prof. of Nursing, Ben-Gurion Univ. of the Negev, Israel. **SELECTED PUBLICATIONS:** *Health Education in the Americas* (English Speaking Countries), ed. (Ottawa: International Union for Health Education, 1983); "An Evaluation of the Preceptor Model versus the Formal Teaching Model," with S. Lemieux (*Journal of Continuing Education* 15 1984); "Factors Affecting the Nurse as Teacher and Practicer of Breast Self-Examination" with L. Edgar (*International Journal of Nursing Studies* 21 1984); "Editorial: Global Enhancement of Nursing. WHO (World Health Organization) Will Lead the Way," (*Canadian Journal of Nursing Administration* 5(3) 1992); "Staff Nurses' and Nurse Managers' Perceptions of Job-Related Empowerment and Managerial Self Efficacy," with H.K. Laschinger (*Journal of Nursing Administration* 24(9/10) 1994); "Nurse effectiveness: Health and cost-effective nursing services," *Review of literature & policy & organizational recommendations*, J. Shamian & B. Chalmers (The Global Network of WHO Collaborating Centres for Nursing/Midwifery Development, 1996); numerous other publications. **EDIT:** Ed. Bd., *HYGIE: The International Journal of Health Education*, 1986 to date, Chair, 1988-90; Co-Ed., *HYGIE*, 5(3) 1986, 7(2) 1988; Ed., *HYGIE*, 7(4) 1988; Ed., "Ask an Expert" column, *Applied Nursing Research*, 1988-89; Ed. Bd., *Applied Nursing Research*, 1989 to date; Ed. Bd., *Canadian Journal of Nursing Administration*, 1990-94; Advisory Bd., *The Mount Sinai Health Report*, 1990 to date; Ed. Bd., responsible for mgmt articles, *NOVER* (Hungary), 1993 to date. **DIRECTOR:** Interhealth Canada Ltd. **AFFIL:** Canadian Association for History of Nursing; Canadian Society for International Health (Bd.); Academy of Chief Executive Nurses; American Coll. of Healthcare Executives; American Organization of Nurse Executives; Canadian Coll. of Health Service Executives; Canadian Nursing Research Group; Canadian Society for International Health; Lambda Pi Chapter, Sigma Theta Tau, Int'l Honour Society of Nursing at the Univ. of Toronto; International Union for Health Education; Registered Nursing Association of Ontario (Nursing Research Interest Group). **HONS:** Excellence in Leadership Award, Sigma Theta Tau, Univ.

of Western Ontario, 1992; J.&J. Wharton Fellowship, Univ. of Pennsylvania, 1992; Ella May Howard Award for Nursing Leadership, Gerald P. Turner Dept. of Nursing, Mount Sinai Hospital, 1993; Excellence in Nursing Admin. Award, Lambda Pi Chapter, Sigma Theta Tau, Univ. of Toronto, 1993; Ross Award for Nursing Leadership, Canadian Nurses' Foundation, 1995. **MISC:** numerous conference presentations; frequent speaker; recipient, various grants; numerous consultancies; reviewer, various journals & granting agencies; rep. of Canadian Nurses' Association on the Canadian Association of University Schools of Nursing Bd. of Accreditation, 1991 to date; mbr., World Health Organization Expert Advisory Panel on Nursing, 1994-98; mbr., World Health Organization Global Advisory Group on Nursing & Midwifery.

Shannon, Valerie, B.Sc.N.,M.S.N. ⊕ 🎓
Director of Nursing, THE MONTREAL GENERAL HOSPITAL, 1650 Cedar Ave., D6156, Montreal, QC H3G 1A4 (514) 934-6022, ext. 3088, FAX 937-8366. Associate Professor, School of Nursing, MCGILL UNIVERSITY. Born Montreal 1948. m. Dr. J. David Shannon. 2 ch. Christopher, Grant. **EDUC:** McGill Univ., BScN(Nursing) 1970; Univ. of British Columbia, MSN (Nursing) 1977. **CAREER:** Staff Nurse, Medical Ward & Coronary Monitoring Unit, The Montreal General Hospital, 1970-71; Head Nurse, Coronary Monitoring Unit, 1970-71; Staff Nurse, West Suffolk Hospital, Suffolk, UK, 1974-75; Asst. Prof., School of Nursing, Master's Program, McGill University, 1977-79; Head Nurse, Adolescent Ward, Montreal Children's Hospital, 1979-83; Nursing Dir., Surgical Areas, Royal Victoria Hospital, Montreal, 1983-84; Asst. Prof., School of Nursing, McGill University, 1979-87; Dir. of Nursing, The Montreal General Hospital, 1984 to date; Assoc. Prof., School of Nursing, McGill University, 1987 to date. **SELECTED PUBLICATIONS:** "Practising nurses identify concept central to the care of hospitalized adolescent" (*Nursing Montreal*, 6 1982); "Head nurse in primary nursing" (*Nursing Quebec*, 7 1987); "The Role of the enterostomal therapist in primary nursing" (*CAET Journal*, 8 1989); "The Head Nurse: Perception of Stress - Ways of Coping," with S.R. Frisch and P. Dembeck (*Canadian Journal of Nursing Administration*, 4(4) 1991); occasional reviewer, *Canadian Journal of Nursing Research* & *The Canadian Journal of Nursing Administration*; numerous conference papers & published abstracts. **AFFIL:** Sigma Theta Thau International (Nursing Honour Society); McGill University, School of Nursing (Joint Appointees Exec. Committee); Association of Directors of Nursing in the Province of Quebec (Exec. Committee of the Bd. of Dir.); Canadian Council of Health Service Executives; Academy of Chief Nurse Executives of Teaching Hospitals; Order of Nurses. **HONS:** Johnson & Johnson/Wharton Fellowship, Univ. of Pennsylvania, 1991. **INTERESTS:** hiking; bird watching; kayaking. **COMMENT:** *"Passionate advocate of the power of nursing to make a difference in people's lives. Have created a caring milieu where critical thinking is valued and patient and family focused care is practised."*

Shanoff, Nancy ■ ✇ 🗳 $
President, NANCY SHANOFF AND ASSOCIATES LTD., 950 Dupont St., Toronto, ON M6H 1Z4 (416) 535-7468, FAX 535-5559. Born Toronto 1952. m. Peter Weis. **EDUC:** Sheridan Coll., Dipl.(Photography) 1974. **CAREER:** photographer, 1974 to date; Pres., Nancy Shanoff and Associates Ltd. **HONS:** numerous awards incl. Cleo Award, London Advertising Award, Toronto Art Directors Club, The One Show, Maggies, Marketing Award.

Sharkey, Shirlee, B.Sc.N.,M.H.Sc., C.H.E. ■■ ⊕ $
President and Chief Executive Officer, SAINT ELIZABETH HEALTH CARE (integrated nursing & related health care), 10 Gateway Blvd., Ste. 320, Don Mills, ON M3C 3A1 (416) 429-1234, FAX 429-8244, EMAIL 545611@lcan.net. Assistant Professor, Faculty of Nursing, and Faculty of Medicine, Department of Health Administration, UNIVERSITY OF TORONTO. Born Windsor, Ont. 1955. 2 ch. Avi, Rebecca. **EDUC:** Univ. of Windsor, B.Sc.N.(Nursing) 1978; Univ. of Toronto, M.H.Sc.(Health Admin.) 1992; Canadian Coll. of Health Service Executives, Certified Health Exec. 1994. **CAREER:** Staff Nurse/Team Leader, Doctors Hospital, 1978-79 & Mount Sinai Hospital, 1979-80; Staff Nurse, Victorian Order of Nurses, 1980-82; Nurse Mgr, Geriatric Day Hospital, Sunnybrook Health Science Centre, 1982-83; Coord., Day Programs, 1983-84; Mgr, Ambulatory Care Svcs, 1984-87; Dir. of Nursing-Psychiatry, 1987-89; Dir. of Nursing-Surgery & Psychiatry, 1989-92; Pres. & CEO, Saint Elizabeth Health Care, 1992 to date; Asst. Prof., Fac. of Nursing, Univ. of Toronto, 1992 to date; Asst. Prof., Fac. of Medicine, Dept. of Health Admin., 1996 to date. **SELECTED PUBLICATIONS:** co-author with P. Leatt, L. Zagar, E. Meslin, *Perspectives on Physician Involvement in Resource Allocation and Utilization Management: An Annotated Bibliography* (Hospital Mgmt Research Unit, Dept. of Health Admin., Univ. of Toronto

& Clinical Ethics Centre, Sunnybrook Health Science Centre, 1991); author, "Strategic Alliances: A Competitive Strategy" (*Leadership in Health Services*, Canadian Healthcare Association, Mar./Apr. 1996). AFFIL: Canadian Association on Gerontology; Canadian Coll. of Health Service Executives; Coll. of Nurses of Ontario; Registered Nurses Association of Ontario, Provincial Nursing Administrators Interest Group; Ontario Nurse Executives (Past Pres. 1996; Pres. 1995; Bd. of Dir. 1995 to date); Catholic Health Association of Canada (Participating Observer 1994-96); Canadian Home Care Association (Pres. 1995 to date; Bd. of Dir. 1992 to date; Sec. 1993); Whitby Mental Health Centre (Community Advisory Bd. 1996). HONS: President's Roll of Scholars, Univ. of Windsor, 1973-78. INTERESTS: various sports esp. jogging & aerobics. MISC: profiled in *Who's Who Among Outstanding Business Executives* & *Who's Who Among Top Executives* (Cdn publications); Saint Elizabeth Health Care is featured in *Canada's Best Employers for Women*, ranked among top ten; numerous presentations, & board/committee memberships. COMMENT: *"Shirlee Sharkey has more than twenty years of progressively responsible health care management experience through previous positions at health care institutions and executive positions with provincial professional associations. Ms. Sharkey is a member of various committees related to community nursing and new directions in health reform."*

Sharom, Frances Jane, B.Sc.,Ph.D. 🐦 🏵

Professor, Department of Chemistry and Biochemistry, UNIVERSITY OF GUELPH, Guelph, ON N1G 2W1 (519) 824-4120, ext. 2247, FAX 766-1499, EMAIL sharom@chembio. uoguelph.ca. Born Newcastle-upon-Tyne, UK 1953. w. 2 ch. Jeffrey Roslan Sharom, Sofia Ellen Sharom. EDUC: Univ. of Guelph, B.Sc.(Chem.) 1975; Univ. of Western Ontario, Ph.D.(Biochem.) 1978. CAREER: Postdoctoral Fellow, Univ. of Guelph, 1979-80; Asst. Prof., 1980-87; Assoc. Prof., 1987-94; Prof., 1994 to date. SELECTED PUBLICATIONS: "A Glycosphingolipid Spin Label: Ca2+ Effects on Sphingolipid Distribution in Bilayers Containing Phospatidylserine," with C.W.M. Grant (*Biochemistry and Biophysics Research Communications* 67 1975); "Effects of Polychlorinated Biphenyls on Biological Membranes: Physical Toxicity and Molar Volume Relationships," with A. Mellors (*Biochemical Pharmacology* 29 1980); "Multidrug Resistance and Chemosensitization: Therapeutic Implications for Cancer Chemotherapy," with E. Georges & V. Ling (*Advances in Pharmacology* 21

1990); "Developmentally Regulated Changes in the Glycoproteins of the Equine Embryonic Capsule," with J.G. Oriol & K.J. Betteridge (*Journal of Reproduction and Fertility* 99 1993); "Biological Membranes," Chapter 12 in *Biochemistry* by Moran & Scrimgeour (Neil-Patterson Publishers/Prentice Hall, 1994); more than 108 publications in total. AFFIL: American Society for Biochemistry, Cell & Molecular Biology; American Association for Cancer Research; Canadian Society for Biochemistry & Molecular Biology; Canadian Society for Immunology. HONS: Special Merit Teaching Award, Univ. of Guelph Fac. Association, 1992; Teaching Award, OCUFA, 1992; Lt. Governor's Award for Teaching Excellence, 1993. INTERESTS: fitness; Asian cookery; gardening & plants; travel. COMMENT: *"I have a dual interest in teaching and training the next generation of scientists, and carrying out biochemical research to develop better treatments for cancer."*

Sharpe, Marjorie, B.A.,M.S. ■ 🜨 🏵

President, SHARPE & ASSOCIATES, 7 N. Sherbourne St., Toronto, ON M4W 2S9 (416) 962-6466, FAX 962-1165, EMAIL maris@ visionol.net. Born Toronto 1931. m. Alexander B. 1 ch. EDUC: Univ. of Toronto, B.A.; National Coll. of Education, M.S.(Mng. and Dev. Human Resources); graduate work at The Univ. of Toronto, York Univ. & J.L. Kellogg; Graduate Sch. of Management, Northwestern. CAREER: Secondary Educ. Teacher, North York Board of Education, 1959-68; various positions including Chrm, City of Woodstock Landmark Commission; 1st VP, Junior League of Chicago, Inc.; Chrm, Docents, Chicago Historical Society; Citizen's Advisory Committee, US Corps of Engineers; State of Illinois Arts Council, Advisory Panel of Lit.; Board Mbr., TRUST Inc., Flexible Careers & Chicago Youth Centres, 1968-74; Operating Officer & Natl. Bd. Mbr., Association of Junior Leagues, Inc., N.Y., 1973-77; Principal/Consultant, Marjorie J. Sharpe & Associates, Barrington, Ill., 1977-81; Exec. Dir. & CEO, American Dental Hygienists' Association, Chicago, 1981-84; Principal/Consultant, Sharpe & Associates, Barrington, Ill. 1984-85 & Toronto, 1985-87; Pres. and CEO, Community Foundation of Greater Toronto, 1989-96. AFFIL: Academy of Management (1985-97); Canadian Centre for Philanthropy (Chair, Foundations Committee); Council on Foundations, Washington, D.C. (Committee on Community Foundations); Community Foundations of Canada (Bd. of Dir.); Canadian Paraplegic Association of Ontario (Bd. of Dir.); Serve Canada (Bd. of Dir.); Badminton & Racquet Club; Toronto

Cricket, Skating and Curling Club. MISC: featured *in Who's Who in America, World Who's Who of Women* and *Canadian Who's Who.* COMMENT: *"Prior to joining CFGT in 1985, Marjorie J. Sharpe lived for several years in the Chicago area. Ms. Sharpe's background includes extensive experience with non-profit corporations in Canada and the US. As President of Sharpe & Associates, she has consulted with health care institutions in both countries on management training programs and management systems."*

Shatsky, Lily Frankel ○ ⊕ ⊚
Executive Director, JEWISH SUPPORT SERVICES FOR THE ELDERLY (JSSE), 5151 Cote St. Catherine St., Ste. 330, Montreal, QC H3W 1M6 (514) 343-3795, FAX 343-9983. Exec. Dir. Born Montreal 1931. w. 2 ch. Celia Harte, Maury Harte. EDUC: Chicago Sch. of Design, Interior Design, 1960; Concordia Univ., Sociology-Deviant Behaviour 1970, Community Health 1976; Institute of Community & Family Psychiatry, Jewish General Hospital, Family Therapy Program, 1974. CAREER: Community Worker, Peoples Youth Clinic, 1971-73; Community Health Worker, Cote St. Luc Community Project, 1973; Consultant/Group Counselling, Alternative Operant Drug Dependency Centre, 1974; Community Consultant, Town of Hampstead, 1976-77; Research, Jewish Family Services (Social Service Centre), 1979-80; Coord. of Community Dev., Golden Age Association, 1982-86; Supervisor of Individual Svcs, 1988-89; Exec. Dir., Jewish Support Services for the Elderly, 1989 to date. AFFIL: Federation CJA (Chair, Exec. Dir. Assoc., 1994); One Voice; Canadian Association of Gerontology; The National Council on the Aging, Inc. INTERESTS: politics; art; grandchildren. MISC: has led training programs & workshops; has lectured to many varied groups such as the National Council on Aging (Washington), Alliance Quebec, Intergenerational Conference, CBC, CJAD Radio, CTV, Golden Age Association Conference, various universities, colleges etc. COMMENT: *"Lifelong commitment to community and involvement in social issues provided me with many exciting career opportunities permitting creative, professional and social growth."*

Shaw, Gillian, B.A.,B.J. ■ ∕ ▯
Columnist, "The People's Business," THE VANCOUVER SUN, 2250 Granville St., Vancouver, BC V6H 3G2 (604) 732-2554, FAX 732-2320, EMAIL gishaw@wimsey.com. Born Canada 1957. m. Gerry Bellett. EDUC: Brock Univ., B.A. 1977; Laval Univ., 1 yr. French 1978; Carleton Univ., B.J. 1981. CAREER: Reporter (pol-

itics, consumer affairs, Asia Pacific), *The Vancouver Sun*; Bus. Ed. AFFIL: Canadian Association of Journalists; Society of American Business & Economic Writers. HONS: National Newspaper Award as mbr. of *The Vancouver Sun* team covering the Clifford Robert Olsen case. MISC: launched a mentor program through *The Vancouver Sun* to match leaders in the bus. & fin. community with unemployed people.

Shaw, Kim, R.N.,B.A. ⊚ ⊕
Director, Prairie Region and Secretary, Nursing Group Executive, PROFESSIONAL INSTITUTE OF THE PUBLIC SERVICE OF CANADA, 53 Auriga Dr., Nepean, ON K2E 8C3 (613) 228-6310, FAX 228-9048. Born Winnipeg 1959. m. John. EDUC: Red River Community Coll., R.N. 1979; Univ. of Winnipeg, B.A.(Psych.) 1989. CAREER: Registered Nurse, Stony Mountain Penitentiary, 1981 to date; Dir., Prairie Reg., Professional Institute of the Public Service of Canada, 1990-91, 1994 to date; Sec., Nursing Group Exec., Professional Institute of the Public Service of Canada, 1992 to date. AFFIL: Liberal Party of Canada (Dir., Portage Interlake Constituency; Sec., Gimli Riding Association); Manitoba Association of Registered Nurses; Professional Institute of the Public Service of Canada (Sec., Winnipeg Branch); Correctional Service National Labour Management Committee (Union Rep., Hum. Res. Committee). INTERESTS: politics. COMMENT: *"I enjoy challenges to seek redress of P.I.P.S.C. members' rights; won 1st adjudication which requires the employer to reimburse licensing fees for nurses, now a national policy. Nursing representative on the negotiating team which established the largest settlement of equal-pay complaints in Canada, a million-dollar operation."*

Shaw, M. Ann, B.A.,B.Ed. ■ ■ ○ ⑳
Vice-President, CANADIAN FIGURE SKATING ASSOCIATION. Born Toronto. m. 2 ch. Lindsay Shaw Lowy, Heather Lowy. EDUC: Univ. of Toronto, B.A. 1962; Ontario Teachers' Coll., B.Ed. 1963. CAREER: full-time Teacher, Hist. & Geog., Toronto Bd. of Educ., 1963-67; retired from teaching to devote time to volunteer skating activity; occasional Teacher, 1981-92. SPORTS CAREER: figure skater - Cdn Bronze Medallist in Ice Dance, 1958, 1959 & 1960; mbr. of Team Canada in Ice Dance, World Championships, 1959 & 1960; N. Am. Bronze Medallist, 1959; figure skating Judge & Referee, 1956 to date; Judge, 1984 & 1988 Olympics, 1983 & 1988 World Championships; Referee, 1993 & 1994 Jr. World Championships, 1995 European Champi-

onships, 1995 & 1996 World Championships; Mgr, Cdn World Team, 1992 (Asst.) & 1993; trainer of Cdn judges, 20 yrs.; mbr., Bd. of Dir., Canadian Figure Skating Association, 8 yrs.; Exec. Committee, 6 yrs.; VP (serving 3rd 2-yr. term); oversees 6 committees; mbr., Ice Dance Tech. Committee (2nd 4-yr. term), International Skating Union, Switzerland; mbr., ISU Dev. Commission (1st 4-yr. term); ISU championship referee, Olympic, world & int'l events. **AFFIL:** Junior League of Toronto (various community svc. positions 1967-80; Chrm, Communications Committee & Career Dev. Committee; Exec. VP 1978-79; Pres. 1979-80); Young Naturalist Foundation (former mbr. of Bd.); Balsam Lake Sailing Club (former Commodore); former canvasser, Salvation Army, Canadian Heart & Stroke Foundation, & Canadian Cancer Society.

Shaw, Maureen C. ■■ ✊ ⊕ ☝

President and Chief Executive Officer, INDUSTRIAL ACCIDENT PREVENTION ASSOCIATION (reducing Ontario's workplace injuries & illnesses), 250 Yonge St., Ste. 2800, Toronto, ON M5B 2N4 (416) 506-8888, ext. 220, FAX 506-9610, EMAIL mcshaw@istar.ca. Born Victoria, B.C. 1942. m. Norman Shaw. 2 ch. Christine L., Marc B. **EDUC:** Victoria Business Coll., various courses; various univ. courses. **CAREER:** Chairperson, Appeals Div., Alberta Occupational Health & Safety Council (AOHSC), 1983-86; Chairperson, AOHSC, 1986-89; Chair & Acting CEO, Canadian Centre for Occupational Health & Safety, 1989-92; owner/Pres., MCS International, 1992-95; Pres. & CEO, IAPA, 1995 to date. **AFFIL:** United Way of Greater Toronto (Chair, Mfg. Div.; Cabinet mbr.); Safe Communities Foundation (Dir.); Canadian Institute for Radiation Safety (Bd. of Gov.); Major Industrial Accident Council of Canada (former mbr., Exec. Committee); Canadian Injury Prevention Foundation (founding Dir.). **HONS:** Woman of Distinction, Business, Labour & the Professions, Calgary, 1993; Nat'l Achievement Award, Canada Safety Council, 1991; Cdn Medal of Merit (1st recipient), Canadian Society of Safety Engineering, 1989. **INTERESTS:** reading; futures scanning; classical & jazz music; supporting Cdn artists; gardening; politics. **MISC:** papers & keynote presentations, nationally & internationally, incl. all provinces of Canada, & countries such as Germany, Australia, Hong Kong, Italy, Switzerland; topics incl. workplace issues, mgmt & innovative approaches to old issues. **COMMENT:** *"Born in Victoria, B.C. and spent my childhood in Chemainus, a solid working town. Have had a full life, with many challenges and achievements..never afraid of a challenge! Have taken each opportunity as it arose, and learned from each. Am committed to working toward positive change in our society, at work, in education and in our communities. My children are an inspiration in their ability to master incredible personal and medical challenges. I continue to learn."*

Shaw, Sally, B.Sc. ⊕ ✊

Owner, VALLEY PHYSIOTHERAPY CLINIC, 70 Exhibition St., Kentville, NS B4N 4K9 (902) 678-2029. Born UK 1951. sep. 2 ch. **EDUC:** Univ. of Toronto, B.Sc.(Physiotherapy) 1974. **CAREER:** Staff Physiotherapist, Halifax Infirmary, 1974-75; Sole Charge Physiotherapist, The Arthritis Society, N.S., 1975-77; Staff Physical Therapist, Durham Rehabilitation Center, N.C., 1977-79; Asst. Chief Physical Therapist, 1979-80; Physiotherapy Supervisor, Soldiers' Memorial Hospital, Middleton, N.S., 1980-86; owner, Valley Physiotherapy Clinic, Kentville, N.S., 1986 to date. **DIRECTOR:** Valley Professional Centre. **AFFIL:** Annapolis Valley District Canadian Physiotherapy Association (Pres. 1989-91); N.S. Branch, Canadian Physiotherapy Association (Chair); N.S. Coll. of Physiotherapists (Chair, Licensing Bd.); Acupuncture Foundation. **INTERESTS:** horseback riding (dressage); gardening; travel. **COMMENT:** *"At midlife I have a successful and rewarding career and business. What is next? Gratitude, service and creating a sense of community come to mind."*

Shears, Mary-Deanne ✏

Deputy Managing Editor, *THE TORONTO STAR*, 1 Yonge St., Toronto, ON M5E 1E6 (416) 869-4404. Born St. John's, Nfld. 1944. **EDUC:** Carleton Univ., Journalism 1970. **CAREER:** Gen. Assignment Reporter, *The Toronto Star*, 1970-75; various positions from Chief of Rewrite Desk to Deputy City Ed., 1975-80; City Ed., 1980-83; Asst. Mng Ed., Ed. Admin., 1983-86; Asst. Mng Ed., Personnel & Training, 1986-92; Deputy Mng Ed., 1992 to date.

Sheehan, Barbara E., B.A., M.B.A. ■ [$]

Vice-President, Client Services, CASSELS BLAIKIE INVESTMENT MANAGEMENT LIMITED, 33 Yonge St., Ste. 200, Toronto, ON M5E 1S8 (416) 814-4071, FAX 814-4084, EMAIL cbim@ntrust.com. Born 1956. **EDUC:** Univ. of Toronto, B.A.(French) 1978; York Univ., M.B.A. 1987. **CAREER:** Asst. Registrar & Exec. Asst. to the Headmaster, Toronto French Sch., 1979-84; Exec. Asst., Barclays McConnell Limited, 1984-87; Asst. VP, 1987-93; VP, 1993-94; VP Client Svcs, Pension Investment

Mgmt, National Trust, 1994-96; VP, Client Svcs, Cassels Blaikie Investment Management Limited, 1996 to date. **AFFIL:** Canadian Pension & Benefits Institute; M.B.A. Women's Association; A.I.M.S.E.; Multiple Sclerosis Society (Bd. & Pres., Toronto Chapter; Bd., Ont. Div.). **INTERESTS:** travel; theatre; skiing; hiking; golf.

Sheets-Pyenson, Susan, B.A., Ph.D. ■ ⬡ 🕮 ⊕

Associate Professor of History, UNIVERSITY OF SOUTHWESTERN LOUISIANA, P.O Box 42531, Lafayette, LA 70504-2531 (318) 482-5412, FAX 989-4449, EMAIL srp5378@usl.edu. Born Toledo, Ohio 1949. m. Lewis Pyenson. 3 ch. **EDUC:** Univ. of Michigan, B.A.(Hist.) 1970; Univ. of Pennsylvania, Ph.D.(Hist. of Sci.) 1976. **CAREER:** Assoc. Prof. of Geography, Concordia Univ., 1977-95; Assoc. Prof., USL, 1996 to date. **SELECTED PUBLICATIONS:** *John William Dawson: Faith, Hope and Science* (Montreal: McGill-Queen's Univ. Press, 1988); *Cathedrals of Science: The Development of Colonial Natural History Museums during the Late Nineteenth Century* (Montreal: McGill-Queen's Univ. Press, 1988); *Index to the Scientific Correspondence of John William Dawson* (British Society for the History of Science Monograph 7) (Stanford in the Vale: British Society for the History of Science, 1992); various articles & chapters of books, incl. "Darwin's Data: His Reading of Natural History Journals, 1837-1842" (*Journal of the History of Biology* Fall 1981); "A Measure of Success: the Publication of Natural History Journals in Early Victorian Britain" (*Publishing History* 9 1981); "Popular Science Periodicals in Paris and London, 1820-1875: the Emergence of a Low Scientific Culture, 1820-1875" (*Annals of Science* 42 1985); "Horse Race: John William Dawson, Charles Lyell, and the Competition over the Edinburgh Natural History Chair in 1854-1855" (*Annals of Science* 49 1992); "Joseph Frederick Whiteaves" (*Dictionary of Canadian Biography* 1994); book reviews in *Isis, Earth Sciences History, Technology and Culture, American Scientist, Science, Nature Canada, Canadian Journal of History, Annals of Science, Times Higher Education Supplement.* **EDIT:** Advisory Ed., *Isis,* History of Science Society, 1992-94. **AFFIL:** History of Science Society; British Society for the History of Science; Society for the History of Natural History (advisory committee, N.Am. branch); History of Earth Sciences Society. **MISC:** recipient, various grants, incl. Hannah Institute for the History of Medicine; Social Sciences & Humanities Research Council research grant, 1978-88; referee, National Science Foundation,US, National Endowment of the Humanities,US, & Social Sciences & Humanities Research Council of Canada. **COMMENT:** *"Susan Sheets-Pyenson is a historian of science who writes and teaches in Louisiana, specializing in nineteenth-century natural history sciences."*

Sheffer, Andra, B.A.(Hons.) ⚭ ⬡

Executive Director, MACLEAN HUNTER TELEVISION FUND, 777 Bay St., 7th Fl., Toronto, ON M5W 1A7 (416) 596-5878, FAX 596-2650. Born Ottawa 1951. m. Denis Hamel. 1 ch. Kayla. **EDUC:** Carleton Univ., B.A.(Psych.) 1973. **CAREER:** Film Festivals Officer, Dept. of the Sec. of State, 1971-78; Film Certification Officer, 1974-77; Mng Dir., Toronto Int'l Film Festival, 1978-79; Exec. Dir., Academy of Canadian Cinema & Television, 1979-89; Arts Admin. Consultant, 1989-91; Exec. Dir., Maclean Hunter Television Fund, 1991 to date; Instructor, Film & TV Depts., Ryerson Polytechnic Univ. **SELECTED PUBLICATIONS:** *Making It: The Business of Film and Television Production in Canada,* Co-Ed. **AFFIL:** Banff Television Festival (Dir.); Performers for Literacy (Dir.). **HONS:** Award, Toronto Women in Film & Television, 1990. **INTERESTS:** cooking; cross-country skiing; looking after my 7-yr.-old daughter. **COMMENT:** *"Major achievement was the establishment of the Academy of Canadian Cinema and Television, as founding Executive Director, which is playing a key promotional and educational role in the Canadian film and TV industry."*

Shekter, Louise, B.A. ⚭ ⊗ 📖

President, MEDIA SOLUTIONS INC., 145 Hampton Ave., Toronto, ON M4K 2Z3 (416) 462-0124, FAX 778-6622, EMAIL lshekter@web.apc.org. Born Montreal 1950. m. Mark H. Shekter. 2 ch. **EDUC:** Ryerson Polytechnic Univ., B.A.(Film Prod.) 1984. **CAREER:** Pres. & Founder, Media Solutions Inc., 1985 to date. **SELECTED CREDITS:** *Making A Difference;* numerous other productions from children's drama to scientific documentaries for Cdn TV. **AFFIL:** Academy of Canadian Cinema & Television; Writers' Guild of Canada; International Multimedia Development Association; Toronto Women in Film & Television; Association for Computing Machinery (SIGGRAPH). **HONS:** Award for Documentary (*Making A Difference*), New York, San Francisco, Columbus, & Yorkton Film Festivals; several other awards. **INTERESTS:** productions on: science, new technologies, educational & children's programming, women's issues, & dev. issues. **COMMENT:** *"An award-winning, multi-talented writer/director/producer of high-quality dra-*

matic and documentary films and television programs in French and English."

Shenouda, Hannah-Mary, D. Pod.M., M.Ch.S., L.S.A.C. 🐾 ✦
President, SASKATCHEWAN WOMEN'S LIBERAL COMMISSION, 149 - 22nd St. W, Prince Albert, SK S6V 4J9 (306) 953-2446, FAX 764-7401. Born 1949. m. Emmanuel, Sarah-Mary. EDUC: The London Foot Hospital, Diploma of Podiatric Medicine & Registered State Chiropodist 1969; certificate obtained (local anaesthesia) 1974; North London Podiatry Post Grad. Enfield Hospital, certificate obtained 1975. CAREER: Chiropodist, Bedfordshire County Council, 1965-75; Ptnr, private practice, UK, 1968-75; Chiropodist, St Mary's Geriatric Hospital, 1970-74; Consultant, Chiropodist Diabetic Dept., Medical Coll., Univ. Hospital of London, UK, 1969-75; Asst. Podiatrist practicum, Podiatry Association of Great Britain, 1974-75; various positions, Saskatchewan Health, Dept. of Public Health, 1975-76; Clinic Chiropodist, Melfort Medical Clinic, 1976-80; Contract Chiropodist, North Park Centre, 1976-85; owner, private practice, Sask., 1985 to date; Podiatrist, Community Health Svcs, Prince Albert Health District, 1985 to date; Prov. Liberal candidate for Prince Albert Northcote, 1989; Reg'l Dir., Sask. Liberal Party, 1992-93; Chair, Subcommittee on Social Policy, 1993-94; Pres., Sask. Liberal Women's Commission, 1994 to date; presently seeking nomination for the new constituency of Prince Albert, Liberal Party of Canada. AFFIL: Western Canadian Immigrant Service Agencies (Past Pres.); Prairie International Economic Trading Foundation (Past Pres.); Canadian Friends of the International Christian Embassy of Jerusalem (Dir.); Society of Chiropodists & Podiatrists of Great Britain; Saskatchewan Association of Chiropodists; Holy Family Hospital (Bd.); Council of Women; Prince Albert Business & Professional Women's Clubs; Prince Albert Chamber of Commerce. INTERESTS: equestrian; tennis; racquet ball; golf; reading; music (classical & jazz). MISC: Coord./Prod./Councillor, It's a New Day Television Show, Betty & Williard Thiessen, 1979-84.

Shepherd, Helen Parsons, A.O.C.A., R.C.A.,LL.D. ⊗
Painter. Born St. John's, Nfld. 1923 1 ch. Scott Shepherd. EDUC: Memorial Univ. of Newfoundland, 1942; Ontario Coll. of Art, graduated with honours 1948. CAREER: co-founder & teacher, Newfoundland Academy of Art, 1949-61. EXHIBITIONS: *Maritime Art Exhibition*, Beaverbrook Gallery, with Purchase Award Honours (1963); Montreal Museum of Fine Arts (1968); Memorial Univ. of Newfoundland (1975); "Four Decades" with Reginald Shepherd, Memorial Univ. Art Gallery (1989). COLLECTIONS: numerous public, corp. & private collections, incl. portraits of the Presidents of Memorial Univ. & their Excellencies the Gov. General & Mrs. Schreyer. AFFIL: Royal Canadian Academy of Arts (R.C.A.). HONS: Newfoundland & Labrador Arts Hall of Honour, 1990; LL.D. (Hon.), Memorial Univ. of Newfoundland, 1988. MISC: painted for 6 months in Holland, 1957; numerous commissions. COMMENT: *"I enjoy painting in my own environment the things that I am familiar with and like. I feel pure enjoyment when interpreting the objects I see around me every day: the way light plays on white, the contrasting red of an apple, how light filters through glass."*

Sheppard, Marsha I., B.A.,M.A., Ph.D. ■ 🕸
Soil Scientist, Head, Ecological Research Section, Environmental Science Branch, Whiteshell Laboratories, AECL RESEARCH, Pinawa, MB R0E 1L0 (204) 753-2311, ext. 2718, FAX 753-2638, EMAIL sheppardm@wl.aecl.ca. Born 1947. m. Stephen C. Sheppard. 2 ch. EDUC: Carleton Univ., B.A.(Geog.) 1971, M.A. (Geotech. Sci.) 1973; Univ. of Guelph, Ph.D. 1977. CAREER: Pharmaceutical Chemist, Wampoles Pharmaceuticals, Perth, Ont., 1966; Biochemical Technologist, Fisheries Research Bd. of Canada, Arctic Biological Stn., 1967-69; Geomorphologist, Dept. of Indian Affairs & Northern Dev., Arctic, 1970; Geomorphologist, Energy, Mines & Resources, Geological Survey of Canada, Terran Sciences Div., N.W.T., 1971; Geotech. Eng., Carleton Univ., 1972-73; Computer Modeller, Dept. of Land Resource Sci., Univ. of Guelph, 1977-79; Soil Scientist, Head, Ecological Research Section, Environmental Research Branch, Whiteshell Laboratories, AECL Research, Pinawa, Man., 1979 to date. SELECTED PUBLICATIONS: "A Field or Laboratory Thermal Conductivity Probe" (as M.I. Joynt) (*Canadian Journal of Soil Science* 54 1974); "Uptake by Plants and Migration of Uranium and Chromium in Field Lysimeters," with S.C Sheppard & D.H. Thibault (*Journal of Environmental Quality* 13(3) 1984); "Volatilization: A Soil Degassing Coefficient for Iodine," with J.L. Hawkins & P.A. Smith (*Journal of Environmental Radioactivity* 25 1994); numerous other publications. AFFIL: American Society of Agronomy; Association of Women Soil Scientists; Soil Science Society of America. MISC: various conference presentations; reviewer for various journals.

Shepherd, Elizabeth, B.A. ■■ ⊛ 🎭 📺
Actor and Director. c/o 310 Manor Rd. E., Toronto, ON M4S 1S2 (416) 481-4070, FAX 481-4070. Born London, UK 1936 1 ch. Edmund Boys. **EDUC:** Bristol Univ., UK, B.A. (Gen. Arts incl. Drama) 1957. **SELECTED CREDITS:** Movies: *The Tomb of Ligeia* (with Vincent Price, Dir. Roger Corman); *Damien: Omen 2* (with William Holden); *Criminal Law* (with Gary Oldman, Kevin Bacon); *The End of Summer* (with Jacqueline Bisset, Peter Weller); 12 others. Over 500 TV appearances incl.: "The Duchess of Duke St." & "By the Sword Divided," *Masterpiece Theatre* (BBC); *All My Children* (ABC); star, *The Phoenix Team* (CBC); *Frost in May* (mini-series, BBC); *The Cleopatras* (mini-series, BBC); *Buddenbrooks* (mini-series, BBC); *Bleak House* (mini-series, BBC); *The Winter's Tale* (WNET/PBS); *The First Night of Pygmalion* (CBC); *The Cuckoo Bird* (CBC); *Street Legal* (CBC); *E.N.G.* (CTV); *The Road to Avonlea* (CBC); Judy Owens, R.N., *Side Effects*, 1994/95 (CBC); Peggy Holmes, *The Adventures of Shirley Holmes* (YTV); numerous other roles. Theatre: Marjorie Hasseltine, *Conduct Unbecoming* (Broadway); Maria, *The Jumping Fool* (off-Broadway); Melanie, *Adjustable Positions* (off-Broadway); Rachel Brown, *Inherit the Wind* (West End, London); Isabel Haverstick, *Period of Adjustment* (West End); Natasha, *War and Peace* (West End); Yvonne, *Les Parents Terribles* (Fringe, London); Queen Katherine, *Henry VIII* (Stratford Festival); Gertrude, *Hamlet* (Stratford); Cordelia, *King Lear* (Stratford); Eliza Doolittle, *Pygmalion* (Shaw Festival); Rebekka West, *Rosmersholm* (Shaw); Sweetie, *Too True to be Good* (Shaw); Mrs. Prentice, *What the Butler Saw* (Washington, DC); Blanche DuBois, A *Streetcar Named Desire* (Montreal); Lybov Ranevskaya, *The Cherry Orchard* (Toronto); Simone de Beauvoir, *Tête à Tête* (Toronto); Sara Turning, *Breaking The Code* (Toronto); Elaine, *Tartouffe* (Toronto); Virginia Sedgeway, *Immediate Family* (Toronto & Vancouver); Timothea, *Sea Marks* (Toronto - also producer); numerous other roles. Dir., *Masterpieces*; *Clean*. **AFFIL:** all actors' associations in Canada, UK & US; Women's Action Coalition, Toronto (founding mbr.); Nightwood Theatre (Advisor; former Bd. mbr. & Co-Chair). **HONS:** Anik Award for Best Actress (*The First Night of Pygmalion*); Gemini nominations as Best Actress (*The Cuckoo Bird* & *The Phoenix Team*); Emmy nomination (*The Winter's Tale*). **INTERESTS:** writing poetry; furthering of women's best interests, both in drama and through the legal system; travel, esp. in the Far East; The Leprosy Mission; Aung San Suu Kyi' brave leadership for democracy in Burma; my Burmese mountain dog, Pakokku. **MISC:** born of Methodist missionary parents, spent early years in Burma; motto: "It is my feeling that as we grow older we should become not less radical but more so" (Margaret Laurence). **COMMENT:** *"Became an actor as a vocation not a career. Proud to have always earned my living at it. Favourite roles: Blanche DuBois in* A Streetcar Named Desire *and Queen Katherine in* Henry VIII. *Newest venture: writing professionally. Greatest achievement: yet to come."*

Sheridan, Georgette, B.Ed.,LL.B., M.P. ■ 🍁
Member of Parliament (Saskatoon-Humboldt), GOVERNMENT OF CANADA, Confederation Building, House of Commons, Rm. 265, Ottawa, ON K1A 0A6 (613) 992-8052, FAX 996-9899. Born 1952. m. Mark Sheridan. 2 ch. David, Paul. **EDUC:** Univ. of Saskatchewan, B.Ed. 1975, LL.B. 1982. **BAR:** Sask., 1983. **CAREER:** Teacher, 1975-76; articling student, D.E. Gauley, Q.C., 1982-83; association, D.E. Gauley, Q.C., 1983-93; M.P. (Saskatoon-Humboldt), Gov't of Canada, 1993 to date; Chair, Northern & Western Liberal Caucus, Liberal Party of Canada, 1994-95; former mbr., Health Committee; mbr., Natural Resources Committee & Official Languages Committee, House of Commons; Dir., Parliamentary Centre, Ottawa; mbr., Gov't Task Force on Taxation of Child Support; mbr., Gov't Task Force on the Commercialization of C.N. Rail; Gov't Task Force on Youth. **AFFIL:** Meewasin Foundation (Dir.); Saskatoon City Hospital Foundation (Dir.); Liberal Party of Saskatchewan (Pres. Saskatoon-Broadway Constituency Association 1987; Committee Mbr., Lynda Haverstock Leadership Campaign; Chair, Leader's Fundraising Dinner 1989; Candidate Liaison/Special Events Coord., Prov. Liberal Campaign, 1991; various fund-raising events); Liberal Party of Canada (Dir. Saskatoon-Humboldt Riding Association; Comm. Dir., Dr. C.W. "Red" Williams Campaign 1988; various fund-raising events); Young Liberals (sponsor). **INTERESTS:** reading; art; skiing; sailing.

Sherk, Susan, B.A.,M.A. ■ $ ⚛
Senior Consultant, AGRA EARTH & ENVIRONMENTAL, 33 Kenmount Rd., P.O. Box 13309, Stn A, St. John's, NF A1B 4B7 (709) 739-7774, FAX 739-7775. Born New Haven, Conn. 1943. m. Miller Ayre. 2 ch. **EDUC:** Bradford Coll., Mass., A.A.(Liberal Arts) 1964; Wheaton Coll., Mass., B.A.(Soc.) 1966; Memorial Univ. of Newfoundland, M.A.(Anthro.) 1972. **CAREER:** Relocation Coord., Boston Redevelopment Authority, 1966-67; Sociologist, Inter-

national Grenfell Association, Labrador, 1967-68; Asst. Dir. of Admissions, Bradford Coll., 1968-70; Researcher & Writer, Memorial Univ. of Newfoundland Extension Svc, 1972-75; Head, Publications & Info., 1975-80; Nfld. Ed., *Atlantic Insight* Magazine, 1978-80; Staff Asst., Public Affairs, E. Coast, Mobil Oil Canada, St. John's, 1980-83; Sr. Staff Coord., 1983-87; Advisor, Community Affairs, Mobil Corporation, N.Y., 1987-88; Mgr, Corp. Comm., Michelin Tire (Canada), 1989; Commissioner, Economic Recovery Commission of Newfoundland & Labrador, 1990-94; Asst. Deputy Min., 1994-95; Sr. Consultant, AGRA Earth & Environmental, 1995 to date. **SELECTED PUBLICATIONS:** articles & photographs have appeared in *Weekend* Magazine, *The Globe and Mail*, various trade publications & text books. **DIRECTOR:** Investors Group. **AFFIL:** Newfoundland Symphony Orchestra (Dir.); Atlantic Centre for the Environment (Dir.); Fisheries & Marine Institute of Memorial Univ. of Newfoundland (Dir.); Memorial Univ. Botanical Gardens (Dir.). **HONS:** Mary C. Barrett Award for Outstanding Student, Bradford Coll., 1964; Award of Merit, Canadian Petroleum Association, 1985; Nat'l Silver Leaf Award, International Association of Business Communicators, 1982, 1983, 1985; Nat'l Award of Excellence, Canadian Public Relations Society, 1985; award from *Canadian Business* as 1 of 13 up-and-coming bus. leaders, 1990. **INTERESTS:** gardening; tennis; raising animals; hiking. **MISC:** commentator for CBC on prov. & nat'l public affairs, 1975-80; various speeches & conference presentations. **COMMENT:** *"Susan has worked for a university, private industry and government for the past 30 years in the fields of community development, socio-economics and public affairs in both the US and Canada. Her interest is in the rural economies and their adaptation to changing economic times. Through her work, she regularly brings together all three sectors to help solve problems facing rural economies."*

Sherman, Caren Harriet ■■ ♡ ⊕

Director and Past President, LEUKEMIA RESEARCH FUND OF CANADA (volunteer-driven fundraising charitable & funding institution) (416) 781-9888, FAX 781-8583, EMAIL caren@iplinknet. Born Toronto. m. Norman. 2 ch. Elizabeth Sherman-Graif, Stuart Sherman. **CAREER:** real estate salesperson, 1970-76; Registered Real Estate Broker, 1976 to date. **VOLUNTEER CAREER:** Pres., after many yrs. as volunteer, Crusade Against Leukemia, 1967-69; Pres., after many yrs. as volunteer, Leukemia Research Fund, Toronto, 1989-91; First Pres. & one of the founders, Leukemia Research Fund of Canada (CRFC), 1991-94; Pres., Parent-Teacher Association, Glen Rush Public Sch., 1975-78, & Forest Hill Collegiate, 1981-84. **AFFIL:** Leukemia Research Fund of Canada (Dir.; affiliated since 1961); Island Yacht Club. **INTERESTS:** sailing; symphony; reading; assisting leukemia patients. **COMMENT:** *"An optimistic humanitarian, motivating volunteers, developing new LRFC branches across Canada, refining the scientific review process to support the leading-edge of leukemia research in Canada; ensuring a treatment resource for Canadians until a cure is found."*

Shettler, Read Bonnie ■ $

Vice-President, Aboriginal Affairs, BANK OF MONTREAL, 55 Bloor St. W., 15th Fl., Toronto, ON M4W 3N5 (416) 927-6134, FAX 927-5523. **EDUC:** Harvard Business Sch., Grad., Int'l Mktg Program; Queen's Univ., Grad., Exec. Program. **CAREER:** 15 years experience in strategic planning, product dev. and intl. mktg.; Sr. Mgr., Mastercard Mktg., Bank of Montreal; Chair, Mktg. Committee, Mastercard Association of Canada, Bank of Montreal; VP, Aboriginal Affairs.

Shields, Carol, M.A. ■ 📜 🎓

Chancellor, UNIVERSITY OF WINNIPEG, Fletcher Avenue Building, Winnipeg, MB R3T 5V5 (204) 474-8147. Author and Professor, English, UNIVERSITY OF MANITOBA. Born Oak Park, Ill. 1935. m. Donald Shields. 5 ch. John, Anne, Catherine, Meg, Sara. **EDUC:** Univ. of Exeter, UK, exchange student, 1955-56; Hanover Coll., Indiana, 1957; Univ. of Ottawa, M.A.(Cdn Lit.) 1975. **CAREER:** author, 24 yrs.; Prof., Univ. of Manitoba, 1980 to date. **SELECTED PUBLICATIONS:** *Small Ceremonies*, novel (1976); *The Box Garden*, novel (1977); *Happenstance*, novel (1980); *A Fairly Conventional Woman*, novel (1982); *Various Miracles*, short stories (1985); *Swann*, novel (1987; published as *Mary Swann* in UK); *The Orange Fish*, short stories (1989); *The Republic of Love*, novel (Random House Canada, Viking US, Fourth Estate, UK 1992); *The Stone Diaries*, novel (Random House 1993); *Departures and Arrivals*, play; *Not Another Anniversary*, play; *Thirteen Hands*, play; *Women Waiting*, play; *Fashion Power Guilt*, play (with Catherine Shields). **AFFIL:** TWUC; PUC; PEN; Canada Council. **HONS:** Best Novel (*Small Ceremonies*), Canadian Authors' Association, 1976; First Prize (*Women Waiting*), CBC Drama Award, 1983; First Prize, National Magazine Award, 1985; shortlisted, Gov. General's Award, 1987; Arthur Ellis Award for best Cdn crime novel, 1987; Marian Engel Award, 1990; shortlisted (*The Republic of Love*),

Guardian Fiction Prize (finished 2nd place); Gov. General's Award (*The Stone Diaries*), 1993; Booker Shortlist (*The Stone Diaries*), 1993; Canadian Booksellers Award (*The Stone Diaries*), 1994; National Book Critics Circle Award, US, 1995; Hon. Doctorate, Univ. of Ottawa, 1995; The Pulitzer Prize for Lit., 1995; hon. degrees from Univ. of Ottawa, Hanover Coll., Queen's Univ., Univ. of Winnipeg. **INTERESTS:** France; contemporary fiction. **MISC:** *Swann* optioned for film rights, UK, 1992; *The Republic of Love* optioned for film rights, Canada, 1992; *The Stone Diaries*, rights sold to NFB; currently working on a novel titled *Larry's Party* & the filmscript for *The Republic of Love*. **COMMENT:** *"I'm a writer and teacher, living in Winnipeg and spending my summers in France."*

Shiff, Helaine ■ $ ✊ ♥

Partner, GLINA GROUP, 5001 Yonge St., Ste. 1501, North York, ON M2N 3A1 (416) 224-2317, FAX 224-2181. Partner, GGS SERVICES–FOCUS ON YOU. Born Toronto 1940. m. Allan. 2 ch. Lorne, Melissa. **CAREER:** acctg, Murray Grossman, C.A., 1961-70; Ptnr, Glina Group. **DIRECTOR:** Havenbrook Realty Company Ltd. **AFFIL:** Juvenile Diabetes Foundation (Founder, Toronto Chapter 1974; Pres., Toronto Chapter 1981-83; Nat'l Pres. 1988-92; Dir., Int'l 1992-97; Chair, Int'l Affiliates Committee 1994-96; Chair, Int'l Conference 1994); Secular Jewish Association (Dir. 1975-79); Hadesh Foundation (Dir.); Music Toronto (Dir. 1991-95); Canadian Foundation for Infectious Disease (Advisor 1993-95); Mount Sinai Hospital, Toronto (Bd. 1993-99). **HONS:** Canada Volunteer Award, 1987; Canada's Birthday Achievement Award, Metro Toronto, 1990; Volunteer of the Year, Juvenile Diabetes Foundation International, 1992. **INTERESTS:** hiking; skiing; music; reading. **MISC:** created North York Bd. of Educ. Multi-Aged Grouping Unit, 1970; created Learning Disability Proj., John Ross Robertson P.S. through Fed. Gov't grant, 1973. **COMMENT:** *"Self-driven, creatively goal-oriented person interested in health-related causes, working on many levels (local, national and international) using fundraising techniques and board development to achieve viable, successful organizations."*

Shilton, Elizabeth J., M.A.,LL.B., LL.M. ■■ ⚖ 🎓

Senior Partner, CAVALLUZZO HAYES SHILTON MCINTYRE & CORNISH (law firm), 43 Madison Ave., Toronto, ON M5R 2S2 (416) 964-1115, FAX 964-5895. Born Wolseley, Sask. 1948. m. David Mackenzie. 2 ch. Graeme, Christina. **EDUC:** Univ. of Toronto, M.A.(English) 1972; Dalhousie Univ., LL.B. 1977; Harvard Univ., LL.M. 1979. **CAREER:** certified as Specialist in Labour Law by Law Society of Upper Canada; founding Ptnr, Cavalluzzo Hayes Shilton McIntyre & Cornish & predecessor firm; practises & litigates in area of labour & employment law for trade unions & employees, human rights & equality law, educ. law & constitutional law. **SELECTED PUBLICATIONS:** co-author with M. Eberts *et al*, *The Case for Women's Equality: Federation of Women Teachers' Associations of Ontario and the Canadian Charter of Rights and Freedoms* (FWTAO: Toronto, 1991); book chpt., "Charter Litigations and the Public Policy Processes of Government: A Public Interest Perspective" (in *The Impact of the Charter in the Public Policy Process in Canada*, ed. Monahan & Finkelstein, Toronto, 1993); *Education Labour and Employment Law in Ontario* (Canada Law Book, 1996); several articles incl.: "Sex Equality and Sexual Assault: In the Aftermath of *Seaboyer*" (with Anne S. Derrick, 11 *Windsor Yearbook of Access to Justice* 107, 1991); "Organizing the Unorganized: Unionization in the Chartered Banks of Canada" (18 *Osgoode Hall Law Journal* 1977, 1980). **AFFIL:** Canadian Institute for Advanced Research Law Project (Advisory Committee); Canadian Bar Association; Harvard Law School Association (Exec. mbr.); Canadian Association for the Practical Study of Law in Education; Canadian Association of Labour Lawyers; Women's Legal Education & Action Fund (former Chair, Nat'l Legal Committee; former mbr., Bd. of Dir.; founding Dir., LEAF Foundation). **MISC:** frequent speaker, legal & professional continuing educ. functions, univ. guest lecturer.

Ship, Leona ♥ ⊕ ✊

Executive Director, Eastern Ontario Branch, THE KIDNEY FOUNDATION OF CANADA, 1335 Carling Ave., Ste. 212, Ottawa, ON K1Z 8N8 (613) 724-9952, FAX 722-5907. Born Montreal 1944. m. Bernie. 3 ch. Harold, Donna, Daniel. **EDUC:** Macdonald Coll., McGill Univ., Teacher's Diploma 1963; Carleton Univ., Mass Comm., current. **CAREER:** Kindergarten Teacher, Herbert Purcell Sch., Pierrefonds, Que., 1963-66; Asst. to the Dir. of Women's Div., U.J.A., Ottawa, 1979-80; Exec. Dir., Ottawa Valley Chapter, The Kidney Foundation of Canada, 1981 to date; Exec. Dir., E. Ont. Branch, 1993 to date. **SELECTED PUBLICATIONS:** *Trilogy on Volunteerism* (Kidney Foundation of Canada, 1990). **AFFIL:** The Kidney Foundation of Canada (Exec. Dir.'s Forum; Nat'l Fundraising Committee); Ottawa Fundraising Executives; Machzekei Hadas Synagogue. **HONS:** Lawrence D. Bressinger Award (nat'l staff award), 1985; Wyn Tyler Award (Ont. branch staff award), 1990; Chapter Staff Award, Ottawa Valley Chapter, 1989. INTERESTS: crafts; antiques; reading; travelling. MISC: The Ottawa Valley Chapter has won many awards for fundraising, contributions to research, etc.; the branch won the Peanut Campaign Award, 1995. COMMENT: *"I received my primary school specialist diploma at MacDonald College of McGill University in Montreal; and taught for three years. 1981 marked my first year in the field of fundraising as Executive Director of the Ottawa Valley Chapter of The Kidney Foundation of Canada. It was one of three part-time positions and along with a small group of dedicated volunteers, we raised $169,472. Today, the small group of volunteers has grown to thousands and the Chapter, now a Branch, raises close to $1.5 million. During this time my husband Bernie and I raised three children. Harold, a graduate in Hons. Math, Donna an English and History Hons. graduate and teacher, and Daniel, currently studying Mandarin and teaching English in Taiwan. During these years, I have been very fortunate to have had the opportunity to learn about the volunteer business world from a wide variety of professional, business, community and support people, who have taken the time to be thoughtful, sharing and caring in our fast-paced technological world."*

Shnier Moncik, Bonnie, B.A., C.H.R.P ■■ ⑤

President, GESCO INDUSTRIES INC. (floorcovering supplier of logistic and merchandising services), 1965 Lawrence Ave. W., Toronto, ON M9N 1H5 (416) 243-0040, FAX 243-1263. m. 2 ch. EDUC: Univ. of Toronto, B.A.; Certified Human Resources Professional (C.H.R.P). DIRECTOR: Gesco Industries Inc. AFFIL: National Association of Floor Covering Distributors (Dir. 1993-96); Univ. of British Columbia (mbr., Advisory Council, Fac. of Commerce & Bus. Admin., 1995-98).

Shohet, Linda, B.A.,M.A.,Ph.D. ⑤ ⑨

Director, THE CENTRE FOR LITERACY OF QUEBEC, 3040 Sherbrooke St. W., Montreal, QC H3Z 1A4 (514) 931-8731, ext. 1411, FAX 931-5181, EMAIL lshohet@dawsoncollege. qc.ca. Born Montreal 1946. m. Naim Shohet. 4 ch. EDUC: McGill Univ., B.A.(English) 1967, M.A.(English) 1970; Univ. de Montréal, Ph.D.(Études anglaises) 1980; Thesis: "Impact of the Holocaust on Canadian Jewish Writing". CAREER: high sch. Teacher (English/Secondary 5), 1967-68; Lecturer, Dept. of English, Concordia Univ., 1969-73; Fac. Mbr., Dept. of English, Dawson Coll., 1973 to date; mbr.,

Teaching Team, Career Plus Adult Re-Entry Program, 1980-82; Chairperson, Dept. of English, Dawson Coll./Lafontaine, 1980-84; Founder & Dir., The Centre for Literacy of Quebec, 1989 to date. SELECTED PUBLICATIONS: "For Sorrows Yet Unknown — Gabrielle Roy's Vision of Childhood" (*Canadian Children's Literature* Spring 1975); "An Essay on The History of Emily Montague," *The Canadian Novel — Beginnings. A Critical Anthology*, ed. John Moss (Toronto: New Canada Publications, 1980); "Pierre Berton: a Biographical Essay" (*Dictionary of Literary Biography* 1986); numerous articles on all aspects of literacy for magazines & journals & numerous reviews; *Literacy Across the Curriculum* (newsletter) developer & ed. AFFIL: Canadian Congress for Learning Opportunities for Women (Bd.); Literacy Partners of Quebec (Founding Mbr.; Pres. 1993-95, 1995-97); National Adult Literacy Database (Bd.; Chair, Nat'l Steering Committee); Association of Teachers of English of Quebec (Dir.). HONS: Lydia Burton Literacy Award, Freelance Editors' Association of Canada, 1992; Lionel Stein Award for Leadership, Montreal Jewish Community. INTERESTS: reading; writing; cooking; drawing; walking. MISC: multiple workshops, consultancies & presentations across Canada & US incl. conferences; mbr., Commission on Adult Educ., Que. Superior Council of Educ. (gov't advisory body), 1984-87; curriculum writer for a women's literacy curriculum, part of 15-mbr. team, nat'l proj. of C.C.L.O.W., 1994-95; recipient, various grants. COMMENT: *"I have devoted 20 years to teaching, writing and attempting to expand public understanding of literacy as the core of learning. I believe I've made a difference for many individual students. On the larger front, as one of many advocates worldwide, I would have more difficulty identifying an impact that I could call personal."*

Shore Hume, Penny ■■ 📖 🖂

President, PENTRON COMMUNICATIONS INC. (publishing-specializing in multi-media consumer educ. in fin., health/medical & parenting areas) (416) 972-1229, FAX 972-1147. Born Montreal 1948. m. Ronald C. Hume. 4 ch. Jayson, Amanda; Peter, Charron. EDUC: Carleton Univ., B.A.(Psych.) 1968; Algonquin Coll., Interior Design 1971; Univ. of Toronto, Grad. Certificate (Gerontology) 1984. CAREER: various middle mgmt position, Training & Dev., & Organization Dev., Gov't of Canada, 1968-73; Founding Ptnr & VP, Women Associates Consulting Group, 1974-82; Founding Ptnr, The Aevitas Corporation, 1983-84; VP, Hume Publishing, 1984-89; Pres.,

Pentron Publishing, 1989 to date. **AFFIL:** National Theatre Sch. (Bd. of Gov.); Canadian Foundation for AIDS Research (VP & Bd. mbr.); Toronto Women in Film & Television (Bd. of Dir.); CANFAR National Youth Network (V-Chairperson); Best Buddies Canada (V-Chairperson, Bd. of Dir.); Best Buddies International (Bd. of Dir.); Society for the Advancement of Gifted Education (Bd. of Dir.); YMCA of Greater Toronto (Bd. of Gov.); United Way of Greater Toronto (Women's Advisory Council); Canadian & Ontario Gerontology Associations (former mbr.); Canadian Association of Pre-Retirement Planners (former mbr.). **HONS:** Int'l Leadership Award, Best Buddies International, Washington, 1996; nominee, "Women Who Make a Difference" award, *Toronto Life*, 1995. **INTERESTS:** design; music; literature; sports. **COMMENT:** *"For the past 28 years, I have always gravitated to career moves that involved breaking new ground with innovation or entrepreneurial start-ups. This has by necessity involved an approach using "tabula rasa" concepts, usually focused on human rights and education in the areas of equal opportunity in employment, the patient's need for and right to quality medical information, seniors' retirement planning, and parenting skills. This approach applied to my work in the voluntary sector as well."*

Shortell, Ann M., B.A. ✏ 📖

Author. 24 Macpherson Ave., Toronto, ON M5R 1W8. Born Kingston, Ont. 1957. m. Herbert Solway. **EDUC:** Carleton Univ., B.A. (English) 1979. **CAREER:** writer, *Financial Post*, 1979-84; freelance writer & author, 1984 to date; Contributing Ed., *Maclean's* Magazine, 1986-88; Sr. Writer & Investment Ed., *Financial Times of Canada*, 1988-89; Contributing Ed., *Toronto Life* Magazine, 1990 to date. **SELECTED PUBLICATIONS:** Co-author, *A Matter of Trust* (1985); Co-author, *The Brass Ring* (1988); *Money Has No Country* (Macmillan Canada, 1991); "Hard Times at Castlehill" (*Toronto Life*). **HONS:** Inaugural Winner (*A Matter of Trust*), National Business Book Award, 1985; Best Bus. Book (*The Brass Ring*), Periodical Publishers Award, 1989; Japan Assignment, Asia Pacific Foundation, 1990; Bus. Writing Award ("Hard Times at Castlehill"), National Magazine Awards, 1994. **COMMENT:** *"As a writer, I like to jump off cliffs. I'm doing that right now, attempting my first novel. The satisfaction is in the stretch, not the safe landing."*

Shum, Mina, B.A. 🎭 ⊗ 🌐

Filmmaker. Secretary and Shareholder, FORTY-SEVEN FILMS INC., 2405 Franklin St., Vancou-ver, BC V5K 1X3 (604) 253-1873, FAX 251-6419, EMAIL buda64c@prodigy.com. Born Hong Kong 1965. s. **EDUC:** Univ. of British Columbia, B.A.(Theatre) 1988, Film & TV Diploma Program 1990. **CAREER:** filmmaker, 1989 to date. **SELECTED CREDITS:** Casting Dir./First Asst. Dir., *The Grocer's Wife* (feature), dir. John Pozer, 1989; Dir./Prod./Writer, *Picture Perfect* (short film), 1989; Dir./Prod./Writer, *Shortchanged* (short film), 1990; Dir./Prod./Writer, *Love In* (short film), 1991; Dir./Co-Prod./Writer/Ed., *Me, Mom and Mona* (documentary), 1993; Dir./Writer, "Hunger," *Breaking Up in Three Minutes* (Cineworks omnibus film), 1993; Writer/Dir., *Double Happiness* (feature), 1994. **DIRECTOR:** Thoughts From the Asylum Productions Inc.; 47 Film Inc. **AFFIL:** Directors' Guild of Canada (Dir. Mbr.); ACTRA; Cineworks Film Co-op (Bd.). **HONS:** Special Jury Citation for Best Cdn Short Film (*Me, Mom and Mona*), Toronto Int'l Film Festival (formerly Toronto Festival of Festivals), 1993; *Double Happiness* winner of numerous awards, incl. Special Jury Citation for Best Cdn Feature Film, Toronto Int'l Film Festival, 1994; tied for third place (with Krystof Kielowski's *Rouge*), Toronto Metro Media Prize; nominated for 7 Genies, incl. Best Picture, Best Direction, Best Screenplay; won the Wolfgang Staudt Prize for Best First or Second Feature, Berlin Film Festival, 1995 (attached was a $20,000 Deutsche Mark cash prize); selected among 56 scripts for the New Views 3 Program (a joint investment of the NFB, Telefilm & B.C. Film). **INTERESTS:** music: alternative, jazz & learning how to play it; Virtual Cop arcade game; Peepshow Comix by Joe Matt; food (as in good food). **MISC:** short films have been screened in various film festivals around the world; Sandra Oh won a Genie Award for Best Actress for her role in *Double Happiness* & Alison Grace won a Genie for Best Editing. **COMMENT:** *"I'm too young to take stock of my life right now. All I know is that I'm trying. Trying to do something, trying to be happy, trying not to be scared and I'm looking to feel right in a world that can make you feel wrong. I figure if I just move around fast enough, they can't catch me."*

Shuttleworth, Elaine M., R.N.,B.S.N., M.P.A. ■ ⊕ 📖

Nurse Practitioner, IMAGES OF WELLNESS, Box 1771, Minnedosa, MB R0J 1E0 (204) 867-2978, FAX 867-2978. Born Minnedosa, Man. 1937. d. 4 ch. **EDUC:** Winnipeg General Hospital, Grad. Nurse Diploma 1958; Canadian Hospital Association, Nursing Unit Admin. Diploma 1967; Univ. of Manitoba, B.N.(Community Health Nursing) 1976; Univ. of Winnipeg, M.P.A.(Public Admin.) 1990. CAREER: Public Health Nurse, St. Clair County Visiting Nursing Association, Ill., 1959-63; Head Nurse, Missouri Pacific Railway Hospital, St. Louis, Mo., 1963-66; Nursing Supervisor, Surgical Units, Deer Lodge Hospital, Winnipeg, 1966-73; Continuing Care/Public Health Nursing Coord., Neepawa Health Unit, Neepawa, Man., 1976-79; Dir., Outreach Svcs, Seven Regions Community Health Centre, Gladstone, Man., 1979-86; Quality Assurance/Staff Educ. Coord., Victorian Order of Nurses, Winnipeg, 1986-90; Exec. Dir., Registered Nurses' Association of N.S., 1990-94; hon. joint appt., Dalhousie Univ. Sch. of Nursing, 1992; Liberal candidate for Man. Legislative Assembly (Minnedosa), 1995; independent Nurse Practitioner, Images of Wellness, 1995 to date; Educ. Consultant, Health & Human Svcs Dept., Assiniboine Community Coll., 1995 to date. AFFIL: Registered Nurses' Association of N.S.; Institute of Public Adminstration of Canada; Canadian Public Health Association; Canadian Coll. of Health Services Executives; Alumni Association, Univ. of Manitoba, Sch. of Nursing; Alumni Association, Health Science Centre, Sch. of Nursing; Alumni Association, Univ. of Winnipeg. INTERESTS: gardening; stained glass design & manufacture of lamps. MISC: guest lecturer. COMMENT: *"In 1966, when my four children ranged from two to eight years of age, I was suddenly faced with the challenge of single parenting on the sole income of a Registered Nurse. My activities for many years directly focussed on these primary responsibilities. As a professional nurse, I was active in addressing workplace issues that interfere with care provision and quality of life."*

Siberry, Jane, H.B.Sc. ■■ 🎀 👜 🖼

Founder, SHEEBA RECORDS (record company with int'l distribution), 238 Davenport Rd., P.O. Box 291, Toronto, ON M5R 1J6 (416) 531-4151, FAX 531-7281, EMAIL sib@ sheeba.ca. Born Toronto 1955. s. EDUC: Univ. of Guelph, B.Sc.(Microbiol.) 1979. CAREER: singer/songwriter, A&M/Windham Hill label, 1984-86; Reprise/Warner Bros. label, 1987-96; Sheeba Records (own label), 1996 to date. SELECTED CREDITS: 8 mostly self-produced albums of original music; self-directed music film, *The Bird in the Gravel* (11 mins.); 5 self-directed music videos; songs included in: soundtracks for Wim Wenders' films, *Until the End of the World* (song "Calling All Angels") & *Faraway So Close* (song "Slow Tango"); *The Crow* soundtrack (song "It Won't Rain All The Time"); one song by invitation on 4 albums from Peter Gabriel's Real World Recording Week. DIRECTOR: Sheeba Records; Sib Pro-

ductions. HONS: Album of the Year & Producer of the Year, Casby Awards.

Sibson, Elaine Sabra, B.Comm.,C.A. $

Tax Partner, COOPERS AND LYBRAND, 1809 Barrington St., Ste. 600, Halifax, NS B3J 3K8 (902) 425-6190, FAX 425-1095. Born Saint John, N.B. 1952. m. Robert Risley. 1 ch. Hilary Risley. EDUC: Mount Allison Univ., B.Comm. 1974. CAREER: Clarkson Gordon, Saint John, N.B., 1974-77; Clarkson Gordon, London, Ont., 1977-78; Cont., General Bakeries, Dartmouth, N.S., 1978-79; Mgr, Clarkson Gordon, Halifax, 1979-82; Coopers and Lybrand, 1982-87; Tax Ptnr, 1987 to date. SELECTED PUBLICATIONS: *Donations and Receipts: A Guide for Charities* (Coopers and Lybrand); *Here and Hereafter* newsletter. AFFIL: Canadian Tax Foundation (Tax Specialist 1981; Gov.); Grace Maternity Hospital (Dir. 1989-95; Treas. 1991 to date); The IWK Grace Health Centre (Dir. 1995; Treas. 1995); Association of Atlantic Women Business Owners (Treas. & Dir. 1992-94); Technical Univ. of Nova Scotia (Gov.; Treas.); Voluntary Planning of N.S. (Bd. 1989-95); Institute of Chartered Accountants of N.S. (C.A.). INTERESTS: cooking. MISC: Chair of Coopers and Lybrand annual Tax Conference. COMMENT: *"I entered a primarily male-dominated profession in 1974 and was one of the first five women in the firm to be admitted to partnership and currently am one of 12 women partners out of 257 partners in Canada. I am active on a volunteer basis and in my area of specialty, taxation."*

Sidimus, Joysanne 🎭 🚫 👜

Executive Director, DANCER TRANSITION RESOURCE CENTRE, 66 Gerrard St. E., Ste. 202, Toronto, ON M5B 1G3 (416) 595-5655, FAX 595-0009. Born New York City 1 ch. EDUC: Barnard Coll.; Sch. of American Ballet. CAREER: dancer, New York City Ballet; soloist, London's Festival Ballet Company, London, UK; Principal Dancer, National Ballet of Canada; Principal Dancer, Pennsylvania Ballet Company; Ballet Mistress, Les Grands Ballets de Genève; Ballet Mistress, A.B.T. II, N.Y.; Instructor, American Ballet Theater Sch.; Instructor, Dance Theater of Harlem; Instructor, Briansky Saratoga Center; fac. mbr., North Carolina Sch. of the Arts, 7 yrs.; Instructor, York Univ.; Instructor, National Ballet Sch.; Instructor, George Brown Coll.; Instructor, Les Ballets Jazz; Guest Teacher, Canadian Dance Teachers' Association; Exec. Dir., Dancer Transition Resource Centre. SELECTED CREDITS: stagings of Balanchine works for various ballets, incl. Pennsylvania Ballet Company, Les Grands Ballets de Genève & the National Ballet

Sch.; Ballet Mistress for the National Ballet of Canada & the National Ballet Sch. whenever Balanchine repertoire is concerned. **SELECTED PUBLICATIONS:** *Exchanges: Life After Dance* (Press of Terpsichore, 1986). **AFFIL:** Dance Ontario (Advisory Council); Ontario Arts Network; Steering Committee to form an Artists' Health Clinic in Toronto (Co-Chair). **HONS:** Dance Ontario Award, 1989; Canada 125 Medal, 1993. **COMMENT:** *"Ms. Sidimus has been involved with the issue of career transition for dancers since 1981 when she started researching the subject for her book, Exchanges. After three years of intensive investigation, she became increasingly convinced of the need for a service to aid the retiring dancer. Her work and commitment to this idea led to the initiation of the Dancer Transition Project in 1984."*

Siebert, Evelyn, B.Sc.,M.B.A. ■■ $ ⚛
Vice-President, Compliance, Novopharm Ltd. (pharmaceutical products manufacturer & distributor), 5691 Main St., Stouffville, ON L4A 1H5 (416) 291-8888, FAX (905) 642-4591. **EDUC:** Univ. of Toronto, B.Sc.(Chem. & Biochem.) 1977; York Univ., M.B.A. 1989. **CAREER:** Supervisor, Analytical Svcs, Ortho Pharmaceutical (Canada), 1983-88; Dept. Head, Analytical Svcs, Eli Lilly, Toronto, 1988-89; Dept. Head, Quality Control, 1989; Dir., Quality Assurance, Novopharm Ltd., 1989-93; VP, Quality Assurance, 1993-96; VP, Compliance, 1996 to date. **AFFIL:** Pharmaceutical Sciences Group of Canada; Regulatory Affairs Professionals' Society; Stouffville Chamber of Commerce. **INTERESTS:** horseback riding; travelling; swimming. **MISC:** presentation on FDA/HPB process validation requirements, Drug Information Association conference, Bombay, India, Mar. 1996; presentation on FDA/HPB pre-approval inspections, Parenteral Drug Association conference, Mexico City, June 1995; presented GMP training sessions, 1994 Pharmaceutical Sciences Group GMP Workshop. **COMMENT:** *"I consider myself to be hard-working and goal-oriented but these attributes are tempered by a sense of humour and the enjoyment of working with others in a team-oriented environment to resolve critical issues. For most of my professional life, I have been involved in the pharmaceutical quality assurance/quality control areas. One of the things that I am most proud of is establishing the QA Department at Novapharm which has played a major role in raising the level of compliance with the Canadian and US Food and Drug Regulations. This has contributed to the receipt of new product approvals which, in turn, have provided Novopharm with a competitive advantage in the marketplace. Having now assumed responsibility for Regulatory Affairs, I am enjoying the challenge of working with the R&D team to bring our product to market first."*

Siebert, Traute, R.N. 📺 🎭 🎓
President and Owner, Eleanor Fulcher International Ltd., 615 Yonge St., Ste. 200, Toronto, ON M4Y 1Z5 (416) 922-1945, FAX 922-1874. President and Owner, Blast Models Inc. (416) 922-7205. Born Neumunster, Germany 1943. m. Dietrich E. Siebert. 1 ch. Clarrisa E. **EDUC:** Nursing Academy in Germany, R.N. 1963. **CAREER:** Registered Nurse, Germany; high fashion model, Canada, 1965; modelling teacher; VP, Eurocommerce Canada Inc.; Sch. Dir., Eleanor Fulcher International Ltd; VP, 1990; owner & Pres., 1991 to date; owner & Pres., Blast Models Inc. **DIRECTOR:** Eleanor Fulcher International Ltd.; Can-Am International Properties Inc.; Eurocommerce Canada Inc. **AFFIL:** International Model & Talent Association (Dir.); Women Entrepreneurs of Canada; Speakers' Forum (Corp. Sponsor). **HONS:** Award of Educational Excellence, International Model & Talent Association, 1991-96. **INTERESTS:** high fashion; sociology; charity work. **MISC:** speaker at fashion seminars & fashion shows; commentator on modelling & career opportunities on TV & radio shows. **COMMENT:** *"Immigrated to Canada from Germany in 1964. Graduate of Eleanor Fulcher Int. 1965. Followed by High Fashion Modellin, School Director and President and Owner of Eleanor Fulcher International Ltd. Modelling School and Agency."*

Sievwright, Georgia, B.A.,LL.B. ⚖ $
General Counsel and Secretary and Director of Corporate Relations, Hewlett-Packard (Canada) Ltd., 5150 Spectrum Way, Mississauga, ON L4W 5G1 (905) 206-3297, FAX 206-4122. Born Toronto 1956. m. Johnnie-Mike Irving. 1 ch. **EDUC:** York Univ., B.A. (Social Sci./Law) 1980; Osgoode Hall Law Sch., LL.B. 1983. **BAR:** Ont., 1985. **CAREER:** Asst. Cnsl, IBM Canada Ltd., 1985-88; Gen. Cnsl & Sec., Hewlett-Packard (Canada) Ltd., 1988 to date; Dir., Corp. Rel'ns, 1995 to date. **SELECTED PUBLICATIONS:** "Organizing the Small Legal Department," with Joyce Borden Reed *(Canadian Corporate Counsel Practice Manual)*. **AFFIL:** Information Technology Association of Canada (Chair, Legal Affairs Committee); Canadian Bar Association (Chair, Gender Issues Committee); International Computer Law Association; *Canadian Corporate Counsel (Ed. Advisory Bd.)*; *Canadian Society of Corporate Secretaries*; Law Society of Upper

Canada. INTERESTS: downhill skiing; water sports; cycling; golf.

Siggins, Maggie ■ ☐ 🐿 ⋈
Writer, MAY-SMITH ENTERPRISES, 2831 Retallack St., Regina, SK S4S 1S8 (306) 586-9505, FAX 585-3461, EMAIL 102246.1421compuserve.com. Born Toronto 1942. m. Gerald B. Sperling. 3 ch. Soshana Sperling, Adam Sperling, Carrie-May Haggart. EDUC: Ryerson Polytechnic Univ., Journalism 1965. CAREER: Reporter, Toronto Telegram, 1965-70; Pol. Reporter, Citytv, 1970-72; Prod. & Interviewer, CBC-TV, 1974-76; Prod., CityPulse News, 1978-80. SELECTED PUBLICATIONS: *Bassett: His Forty Years in Politics, Publishing, Business and Sports* (James Lorimer Publications, 1974); *Brian and the Boys: A Study of Gang Rape* (Lorimer, 1984); *A Canadian Tragedy, JoAnn and Colin Thatcher: A Story of Love and Hate* (Macmillan, 1985); *Revenge of the Land: A Century of Greed, Tragedy and Murder on a Saskatchewan Farm* (McClelland & Stewart, 1991); *Riel: A Life of Revolution* (HarperCollins, 1994). DIRECTOR: Four Square productions (VP). AFFIL: Writers' Union of Canada (Past Chair); ACTRA; Saskatchewan Writers' Guild; PEN (Bd.); Canadian Association of Journalists; Canadian Federation of University Women (VP). HONS: Southam Fellowship for Journalists, 1973-74; Max Bell Chair in Journalism, Univ. of Regina, 1983-84; Arthur Ellis Award (*A Canadian Tragedy, JoAnn and Colin Thatcher: A Story of Love and Hate*), Crime Writers of Canada, 1985; Gov. General's Literary Award for Nonfiction (*Revenge of the Land: A Century of Greed, Tragedy and Murder on a Saskatchewan Farm*), 1992; Best Book Award (*Riel: A Life of Revolution*), City of Regina, 1994. INTERESTS: reading; gardening; politics. COMMENT: *"A writer of books (eight so far), of television scripts, documentaries and variety shows, a teacher, a literary polisher and translator (Mandarin Chinese to English)."*

Signori, Céline, M.N.A. ♣
Member of National Assembly (Blainville), GOVERNMENT OF QUÉBEC, Hôtel du Parlement, Office 3.83, Quebec City, QC G1A 1A4 (418) 528-1349, FAX 646-6685. Born Saint-Jean-sur-Richelieu, Que. 3 ch. CAREER: Real Estate Agent, Royal LePage, 1981-87; Pres. & Gen. Mgr, Québec Federation of Single Parent Associations, 1985-92; Pres., Québec Federation of Women, 1992-94; M.N.A. (Blainville), Prov. of Qué., 1994 to date; mbr., National Assembly Parliamentary Commissions on Social Affairs & on the Institutions, 1994 to date. AFFIL: Parti Québécois; Quebec Family Council (VP

1992-94); National Family Week Organizational Committee (Pres. 1990-92); International Union of Family Organisations (Gen. Council); C.R.A.R. Reference Montréal Regional Centre (Dir. 1986-88); West Island Women's Shelter (Coord. 1987-88).

Sikorski, Paula A., D.D.S.,M.Sc., F.R.C.D.(C),Dip.A.B.O.M.R. ■ ■ ⊕ 👌
Oral Radiologist, 4211 Yonge St., Ste. 324, Toronto, ON M5P 2A9 (416) 226-3363, FAX 226-4377. Assistant Professor, UNIVERSITY OF TORONTO. Born Toronto 1953. m. Dennis. 3 ch. Evan, Trevor, Brett. EDUC: Univ. of Toronto, D.D.S.(Dentistry) 1977, M.Sc.(Oral Radiology) 1981. CAREER: self-employed oral radiologist & dentist; Asst. Prof., Univ. of Toronto. SELECTED PUBLICATIONS: co-author with K.W. Taylor, "The effectiveness of the thyroid shield in dental radiography" (*Oral Surgery, Oral Medicine, Oral Pathology* 58(2), 1984); co-author with M. Dagenais & M.J. Pharoah, "The radiographic characteristics of histiocytosis X (*Oral Surgery, Oral Medicine, Oral Pathology* 74, 1992); "Risk from dental radiography" (*Ontario Dentist*, Nov. 1994); co-author with M. Bourgeois & R. Wood, "Educational use of indirect digital imagery" (*C.D.A. Journal* 61(11), 1995). AFFIL: Canadian Academy of Oral & Maxillofacial Radiology (Pres.); Royal Coll. of Dentists of Canada (former Councillor; 1st woman Chief Examiner, Oral Radiology); American Academy of Oral & Maxillofacial Radiology (Media Rel'ns Committee); H.M. Worth Study Club (Sec.-Treas.); HARP Commission (former Chairperson, Dental Advisory Committee); Ontario Dental Association (former Oral Radiology Rep., Specialists Committee). HONS: James Branston Willmett Scholarship, Association of Women Dentists Scholarship, Oral Anatomy Scholarship.

Sillett, Mary J., B.S.W. ■ ♣
Interim President, INUIT TAPIRISAT OF CANADA, 170 Laurier Ave. W., Ste. 510, Ottawa, ON K1P 5V5. Born Hopedale, Lab. 1953 2 ch. Matthew Lougheed, Martin Lougheed. EDUC: Memorial Univ. of Newfoundland, B.S.W. 1976. CAREER: Researcher, Company of Young Canadians, Happy Valley, Lab., summer 1973; Student Placement Officer, Canada Manpower Centre for Students, Canada Employment & Immigration Commission, summer 1974; Researcher, Company of Young Canadians, summer 1975; Researcher, "Needs Among the Inuit," Nat'l Parole Svcs, St. John's, summer 1976; Researcher, Labrador Resources Advisory Council, 1976-77; Exec. Asst. to the Pres., Labrador Inuit Association, 1977-80;

Field Worker, contract position, Torngat Fish Producer's Co-operative, 1981; Coord., Inuit Committee on National Issues, 1981-82; Chief, Policy and Program Dev., Native Citizen's Directorate, Dept. of Secretary of State, 1982-86; Policy Analysts, Policy and Program Dev., 1986-89; Pres. and CEO, Pauktuutit (Inuit Women's Association of Canada), 1989-91; Commissioner, Royal Commission on Aboriginal Peoples, 1991-94; VP, Inuit Tapirisat of Canada, 1994-95; Interim Pres., 1995 to date.

Silliphant, Lorraine, B.Sc. ⊘ ○
Executive Director, NEW BRUNSWICK ASSOCIATION FOR COMMUNITY LIVING, 86 York St., Fredericton, NB E3B 3N5 (506) 458-8866, FAX 452-9791. Born P.E.I. 1939. m. David Silliphant. 3 ch. EDUC: Mount Allison Univ., B.Sc.(Home Econ.) 1961; Univ. of Saskatchewan, Educ. 1970-71. CAREER: Teacher, 1961-62; Pres., Fredericton Association for Community Living, 1977-79; Pres., N.B. Association for Community Living, 1979-81; Bd. Mbr. & Exec. Mbr., Canadian Association for Community Living, 19780-85; Exec. Dir., Int'l Year of Disabled Persons, N.B., 1981-82; Program Coord., N.B. Association for Community Living, 1982-90; Exec. Dir., 1990 to date. AFFIL: N.B. Labour Force Development Bd.; York Manor (Dir.); Jobs Unlimited (Dir.); Minister's Advisory Committee for the Family; Canadian Association for Community Living (Working Group on Employment); Fredericton Association for Community Living (Life Mbr.); N.B. Association for Community Living (Life Mbr.); Provincial Executive Directors for Disability; Grace-IWK Hospital (Bd. of Trustees). HONS: Canada 125 Medal, 1992. INTERESTS: skiing; gardening; reading; grandchildren. MISC: mbr., Canada Committee, Int'l Year of the Family, 1994; instrumental in closing the W.F. Roberts Hospital Sch., allowing formerly institutionalized children to integrate into the community. COMMENT: *"Worked co-operatively with volunteers and others to develop early intervention, inclusive education, vocational opportunities and social policy, which support people with disabilities to live meaningful productive lives in their families and in their communities."*

Sills, Judith, B.Mus.,Grad.Dip.Ed. ■ ◿ ⊗
Music Specialist/Curriculum Coordinator, EDMONTON PUBLIC SCHOOLS (403) 476-3969, FAX 478-1586. Born Stettler, Alta. 1946. m. Ron. 2 ch. Christopher, Erin. EDUC: B. Mus.; Professional Certificate in Educ.; Grad. Diploma in Education (music/French) 1990; Recorder Grade 8; Kodaly level 1 (French); Orff Schuelwerk Levels 1 through Master

Class(English), Level 111(French). CAREER: Music Specialist, Edmonton Public Schools, 1969-93; Dir., Edmonton Public Schools Enrichment Choir, 1981-95; Dir., Grace Martin Sch. Children's Choirs, 1985-93; Dir., numerous sch. choirs throughout career; Dir., Grace Martin Orff Ensemble (performers at nat'l conferences), 1987-93; Coord., Music Enrichment Program, Edmonton Public Schools, 1988-89; Music Consultant, Edmonton Public Schools, 1993 to date. SELECTED PUBLICATIONS: *Canadiana, Canadian Folk Songs orchestrated in the Orff Style* (Edmonton: Black Cat Publications, 1995); *Musica Activa: An Approach to Music Education–Rhythmic Expression, English Adaptation & Commentary* (New York: Schott Music Corporation 1994); *55 x Funtastic–55 Songs with Motion for Children*, Jos Wuytack, adapted by Judy Sills (Waterloo: Waterloo Music 1993); *Can You Canon? 55 Canons by Jos Wuytack* collected by J. Sills (Waterloo: Waterloo Music, 1994); various articles, Ostinato, 1987-91. AFFIL: Carl Orff Canada (Nat'l Past Pres./Founding Pres, Alberta Chapter); Fine Arts Council, Alberta Teachers' Association; Canadian Music Educator's Association; American Orff Schuelwerk Association; Alberta Choral Federation; Edmonton Symphony Orchestra (Educ. Committee); Kiwanis Music Festival (Advisory Bd.); Edmonton Opera (Educ. Committee). HONS: City of Edmonton Arts Achievement Award, for efforts in promoting music educ. in Edmonton & across Alta. INTERESTS: cyclist; walker; gourmet cook; symphony & opera. MISC: clinician, music workshops in Canada & US; course instructor in Canada. COMMENT: *"My lifelong goal is to instill in children an appreciation and love for music. As a teacher, it is my responsibility to provide children the necessary tool so that they can use music as a means of self expression."*

Silver, Florence, B.A.,M.Ed. ▨ ⊗
Vice-President, Exhibits and Marketing, ROYAL ONTARIO MUSEUM, 100 Queen's Park, Toronto, ON M5S 2C6 (416) 586-5541, FAX 586-8044. Born Toronto 1945. m. William Weiss. 2 ch. EDUC: York Univ., B.A.(Classical Studies) 1974; OISE, M.Ed. 1986. CAREER: V-Principal, North York Bd. of Educ., 1983-85; Principal, 1985-87; Admin. Asst., Community & Admin. Svcs, 1987-89; Supervisory Officer, 1989-93; VP, Exhibits & Mktg, Royal Ontario Museum, 1993 to date. SELECTED PUBLICATIONS: *ROM Wasn't Built in a Day* (1979); *Language Arts Guideline* (1990); *The Arts in North York Schools* (1992). HONS: Distinguished Educator Award, OISE, 1994. INTERESTS: music; cooking; gardening. COMMENT:

"I am thoroughly committed to the value of the arts, both for personal enrichment and as a powerful vehicle for learning. My life, as an educator and museum professional, has given me the great satisfaction that comes with service and constant learning."

Silverberg, Christine, B.A.,M.A., APR ■■ ⌀ 🕐

Chief, CALGARY POLICE SERVICE, 133 - 6th Ave. S.E., Calgary, AB T2G 4Z1. EDUC: York Univ., B.A.(Soc.); Univ. of Toronto, M.A. (Criminology); APR (Professional Accreditation in Public Rel'ns); Queen's Univ., Sch. of Bus., Exec. Dev. Course; numerous courses in police operations, mgmt & admin. from both Ont. & Cdn Police Colleges. CAREER: over 24 yrs. in policing; various positions to Inspector, Peel Regional Police Service, Ont.; Dir., Policing Svcs Div., Ont. Ministry of the Solicitor Gen. & Correctional Svcs, 2 yrs.; appointed Deputy Chief, Admin., Hamilton-Wentworth Regional Police, 1992-95; appointed Chief, Calgary Police Service, 1995 to date. AFFIL: Canadian Association of Chiefs of Police (Bd. of Dir.; mbr., Law Amendments Committee); Alberta Association of Chiefs of Police; International Association of Chiefs of Police; International Association of Women Police; Institute of Public Administration of Canada (Chair, Calgary Chapter); Police Executive Research Forum; Criminal Intelligence Services of Alberta (Chair); Arthritis Society of Canada (Nat'l Bd. of Dir.); Burns Memorial Police Fund (Chrm); Calgary Police Service Museum (Pres.); Port Credit Yacht Club, Ont.; Glencoe Club; Ranchmen's Club.

Silverman, Eliane Leslau, B.A., Ph.D. ⌀ 📗

Professor and Advisor to the President on Women's Issues, UNIVERSITY OF CALGARY, Calgary, AB T2N 1N4 (403) 220-7346, FAX 282-6716, EMAIL elsilver@acs.ucalgary.ca. Born France 1939. 2 ch. EDUC: Univ. of California, Berkeley, B.A.(Hist.) 1963; Univ. of California at L.A., Ph.D.(Hist.) 1973. SELECTED PUBLICATIONS: *We're Here, Listen To Us: A Survey of Adolescent Women in Canada* with Janelle Holmes; *The Last Best West: Women on the Alberta Frontier.* AFFIL: Canadian Women's Studies Association; Canadian Historical Association; Elizabeth Fry Society (Exec.); Grace Hospital Community Advisory Committee. HONS: Calgary Woman of the Year. COMMENT: *"I have devoted my life to improving the status of women, as a scholar and as an activist. The challenge of our historical moment is to enhance women's autonomy in every realm."*

Silverman, Leslee, B.A.,M.A. ⌀ ⌀ 🖊

Artistic Director, MANITOBA THEATRE FOR YOUNG PEOPLE, 89 Princess St., Winnipeg, MB R3B 2X5 (204) 947-0394, FAX 943-4129. Born Winnipeg 1952. m. David Warburton. EDUC: Univ. of British Columbia, B.A.(English) 1975; Univ. of Colorado, M.A.(Theatre) 1978. CAREER: Artistic Dir., Manitoba Theatre for Young People, 1982 to date; has directed over 75 productions. HONS: Canada 125 Medal, 1993. INTERESTS: the wilderness. MISC: her work has played on Cdn stages such as the National Arts Centre, Young People's Theatre, Toronto, & the Citadel, Edmonton; has established theatre schools, prov. drama programs, festivals; has extensive drama teaching experience; initiated the 1st permanent sch. touring in Man. & subscription mainstage theatre for children & adolescents. COMMENT: *"I've always worked in the interest of children—whether as a street worker or artistic director of a theatre."*

Simand, Harriet, B.A.,LL.B.,B.C.L. 🕐 ⊕ ⌀

Founder, D.E.S. ACTION CANADA, 5890 Monkland Ave., Ste. 203, Montreal, QC H4A 1G2 (514) 482-3204, FAX 482-1445. Born Montreal 1960. EDUC: Trent Univ., B.A.(Phil.) 1984; McGill Univ., LL.B. 1989, B.C.L.(Civil Law) 1989. BAR: Ont., 1991. CAREER: Pres. & Founder, D.E.S. Action Canada, 1982-91; Researcher, Law Reform Commission of Canada, 1988; bar admission & articling student, Cornish Advocates, 1989-91; Lawyer, Cornish Advocates, 1991-94; Lawyer, Cavaluzzo Hayes Shilton McIntyre and Cornish, 1994 to date. SELECTED PUBLICATIONS: "The Iatrogenic Effects of D.E.S." (*Misconceptions* 1995); "Religious Accommodation in the Workplace" (*Canadian Labour Law Journal* 2 1992); "1938-1988: 50 Years of D.E.S.- 50 Years too Many," *The Future of Human Reproduction,* C. Overall, ed. (Women's Press, 1989). AFFIL: Canadian Bar Association; Women & the Law; Toronto Women's Health Network; Equal Pay Coalition (spokesperson); Advisory Council to the Pay Equity Commission; Advisory Council to Women's Regional Health Centre; Health & Welfare Canada Conference on Changing Patterns of Health & Disease in Canadian Women (Chair). HONS: M. MacCormack Scholarship, Marianapolis Coll., 1979-80; Gadfly Prize, Trent Univ., 1982-83; Woman of the Year in the field of health (jointly with mother Shirley), Salon de la Femme, Que., 1983; Terry Fox Humanitarian Prize, 1983-84; Soroptimist Scholarship, 1983-84; Phil. Honours Bursary, 1983-84; Ogilvy Renault Entrance Scholarship, McGill Law Sch., 1985-86; Fac. Scholar, McGill Law Sch.,

1985-86; Feigelson Obligations Prize, McGill Law Sch., 1985-86; Molson Pioneer Award, McGill Law Sch., 1986; James McGill Scholarship, McGill Law Sch., 1986-87, 1987-88; Kark Klaxton Memorial Prize, McGill Law Sch., 1987-88; George S. Challies Memorial Award, McGill Law Sch., 1988-89; Univ. Scholar, McGill Law Sch., 1988-89; Canada Volunteer of the Year Award, Health Canada, 1991. INTERESTS: human rights; health issues. MISC: Canadian Women's Health Network–consultation to establish a nat'l network; various speaking engagements incl. Panel on Toxic Torts & Product Liability, Canadian Bar Association, 1994; Panelist, National Association of Women & the Law, 1993; Keynote Speaker, Conference on Corp. Crime, Queen's Univ., 1988; Speaker, U.N. Conference on Women, Nairobi, Kenya, 1985. COMMENT: *"I have been involved for many years in women's health issues. My experience founding D.E.S. Action motivated me to become a lawyer, and to try to effect change through the legal system."*

Simand, Shirley, B.A. ⊕ ⊕

President, **D.E.S. ACTION CANADA**, 5890 Monkland Ave., Ste. 203, Montreal, QC H4A 1G2 (514) 482-3204, FAX 482-1445. Born Montreal 1929. m. Leonard. 2 ch. **EDUC:** McGill Univ., B.A. 1949. **CAREER:** Public Rel'ns Sec., Canadian Jewish Congress, 1953-57; Exec. Sec., National Council of Jewish Women of Canada, 1953-57; Exec. Sec., International Council of Jewish Women, 1957-65; Credit Officer, M. Ross Displays Limited, 1965-72; Exec. Sec., United Synagogue, Eastern Canada Reg., 1972-90; Pres., D.E.S. Action Canada, 1991 to date. **AFFIL:** National Council of Jewish Women - Montreal Section, D.E.S. Action USA (Bd. Mbr. 1985-91). **HONS:** Woman of the Year Award (jointly with daughter Harriet), Salon de la Femme, Montréal, 1983; Canada 125 Medal, 1992. **INTERESTS:** classical music; reading; travel. **MISC:** Shirley Simand formed D.E.S. Action Canada with her daughter in 1982, after Harriet Simand had been diagnosed with a rare cancer caused by D.E.S. that was given to her mother to prevent miscarriage; D.E.S. Action is now a nat'l, nonprofit organization committed to identifying, educating, supporting & advocating for D.E.S.-exposed Canadians. **COMMENT:** *"I formed D.E.S. Action to address the lack of public information about the health hazards of the anti-miscarriage drug D.E.S. (diethylstilbestrol). I felt compelled to take action after taking D.E.S."*

Simand-Seidman, Carol, B.A., M.S.W. ■■ ⊕ ⊕

Director, Donor Relations, **MOUNT SINAI HOS-** **PITAL FOUNDATION**, 600 University Ave., Toronto, ON M5G 1X5 (416) 586-8661, FAX 586-8639, EMAIL cseidman@mtsinai.on.ca. Born Montreal 1951. m. Peter Seidman. 2 ch. Joshua, Sarena. **EDUC:** Loyola Coll., Montreal, B.A.(cum laude) 1972; State Univ. of N.Y., Buffalo, M.S.W. 1974; various mgmt courses. **CAREER:** Youth Dept. Supervisor, Jewish Center of Buffalo, 1974-76; Supervisor, Group Svcs Dept., Baycrest Centre for Geriatric Care, 1976-78; Social Worker, Family Svc. Dept. & Intake Dept. (part-time), Children's Aid Society of Metro Toronto, 1978-83 & 1984-86; self-employed seminar specialist (leadership dev. & effective communications), 1980 to date; Dir., Jewish Women's Federation/United Jewish Appeal Women's Campaign, Toronto Jewish Congress, 1987-89; Asst. Dean, Fac. of Social Work, Univ. of Toronto, 1989-96; Dir., Donor Rel'ns, Mount Sinai Hospital Foundation, 1996 to date. **AFFIL:** Canadian Association of Gift Planners (Bd. mbr., Roundtable Exec. 1996-98); *Canadian Jewish News* (Advisory Bd.); Univ. of Toronto (Bd. mbr., Jewish Students' Union; Academic Bd. Governing Council). **HONS:** Meloche Monnex Prize, Gold Medal, nominated for Case District 11 awards (Best Program, Alumni Rel'ns), The Canadian Council for the Advancement of Education, 1995. **MISC:** instructor, courses at: Centennial Coll. (1979-81), Skills Exchange (1980-83), Ryerson Polytechnical Institute, Continuing Educ. Div. (1983-87), Univ. of Toronto, Sch. of Continuing Educ. (1983-92); papers presented, 1996: *Private Funding - A Model for the New Economic Reality* (Joint World Congress, Int'l Association of Social Work & Int'l Schools of Social Work, Hong Kong), *Fundraising in the 90s: A Critical Imperative for Schools of Social Work* (Learned Societies Congress, Brock Univ., Canadian Association of Schools of Social Work). **COMMENT:** *"I feel grateful for the opportunities I have been given. I have been blessed with good health, lots of energy and have had excellent teachers and role models. I'd like to transform my feelings of gratitude to helping others."*

Simard, R.M. Louise, B.A.,LL.B. ⊶

Lawyer, **MACPHERSON LESLIE & TYERMAN**, 1874 Scarth St., Ste. 1500, Regina, SK S4P 4E9 (306) 347-8000, FAX 352-5250. Born Val D'or, Que. 1947. m. Dwain Lingenfelter. 5ch. in a blended family. **EDUC:** Univ. of Saskatchewan, B.A.(Phil.) 1969, LL.B. 1970. **CAREER:** articles of law, MacPherson, Leslie & Tyerman, Regina, 1970-71; lawyer, Mssrs. Gauley, Dierker & Dahlem, Saskatoon, 1971-73; Legis. Council & Law Clerk, Gov't of Sask., 1973-76; lawyer, own practice, 1978-85;

MLA, 1986-91; MLA & Min. of the Crown (Min. of Health & Min. Responsible for the Status of Women), 1991-95. AFFIL: Saskatchewan Registered Nurses Association (Hon. mbr.). HONS: Jurisprudence Award, 1970, LL.B. INTERESTS: biking; jogging; skiing; travel; gardening; reading; art & drama. COMMENT: *"I have been very active in the community and at the workplace. I practised law for a number of years both in the private and public sectors and eventually ran for public office. When I was Minister of Health in Saskatchewan, I spearheaded a totally comprehensive major health reform. Saskatchewan is perceived to be doing something very unique and leading the country in many aspects on health reform, according to some critics."*

Simard-Laflamme, Carole, B.A., M.Museumology ⊗
Artiste et Muséologue. 93 L'Espérance, St.-Lambert, QC J4P 1X4 (514) 672-4694, FAX 672-4699. Born Baie St.-Paul, Qué. 1945. m. Denis K. Laflamme. 3 ch. EDUC: Univ. Laval, B.A. 1966; Univ. de Montréal/Univ. du Québec à Montréal, M.Museumology 1991. CAREER: Prof., National Institute of Fine Arts, Bamako, Mali, 1968-70; Nat'l Dir., Conseil canadien de l'artisanat, 1975-79. EXHIBITIONS: 15 solo exhibitions in Que. & Ont., 1966-89; more than 22 gigantic pieces of art integrated into Que. architecture, 1972-85; various contests, incl. Paris, Grenoble, Strasbourg, Bruxelles, Luxemburg (1976); Vevey, Switzerland (1977); Paris, Bordeaux, Lyon (1981); Scandinavia & Spain (1983); London, UK (1983); Kyoto, Japan (1989); Tournai, Belgium (1990). COLLECTIONS: well-represented in collections in Canada & abroad. HONS: First Prize for Sculpture (La force de l'énergie), Gaz Metropolitan, 1989; 2ème Prix Duchamp-Villon, 1989. INTERESTS: textile art; architecture; musicology. MISC: only artist selected to represent Canada at Int'l Textile Competition, Kyoto, 1989; extensive travel in Europe, the Middle-East & the Orient, 1970-90; recipient, various grants; *Canadian Who's Who*.

Simbul-Lezon, Marita, B.A. ■ ■ ⑤
Executive Vice-President, FORTUNE FINANCIAL CORPORATION (investment & fin. planning), 2075 Kennedy Rd., Scarborough, ON M1T 3V3 (416) 412-4303, FAX 291-0791, EMAIL simbul@neocom.ca. INTERNET http://www.marita.com. Born Manila, Philippines 1955. m. Ronald Lezon. 2 ch. Christopher Andrew, Alexandra Rose. EDUC: St. Scholastica Coll., B.A.(Psych.) 1975; Ryerson Polytechnical Institute, Certificate (Bus. Admin.) 1978; Canadian Sch. of Management, Certificate (Bus. Mgmt)

1981; Cdn Securities Course & Registered Rep Exam 1985; Partners/Directors/Officers Qualifying Exam 1993. AFFIL: International Association of Financial Planners. COMMENT: *"Marita Simbul-Lezon is one of Canada's most successful financial planners. As Executive Vice-President at Fortune Financial, Marita has over 700 clients and manages assets in excess of $100 million, $75 million in mutual funds alone."*

Simeone, Marianna, B.A. ■ ■ ⑤ ⑨
Executive Director, THE ITALIAN CHAMBER OF COMMERCE IN CANADA (int'l business promotion), 550 Sherbrooke St. W., Ste. 680, Montreal, QC H3A 1B9 (514) 844-4249, FAX 844-4875, EMAIL camit@magnet.ca, INTERNET http://www.italchamber.qc.ca. Born Montreal 1960. m. Domenico Pappadia. 2 ch. Alessandro, Massimilano. EDUC: Istituto Italiano per Stranieri, Naples, Italy, 1983; Kanadische Schule in Deutschland, Kassel, Germany, 1984; Concordia Univ., B.A.(Hons., Italian) 1986. CAREER: TV Host, *Sunday Morning Italian Magazine*, CFCF 12, 1985-91; Special Projects Coord., Italian Chamber of Commerce in Canada, 1986; Exec. Dir., 1990 to date. AFFIL: Santa Cabrini Hospital Foundation (Bd. of Dir.; Pres., 1993-94 Fund Raising Campaign). MISC: fluent in English, French & Italian, & also speaks German.

Simmie, Lois ▯ ▯
Writer. 1501 Cairns Ave., Saskatoon, SK S7K 2H5 (306) 343-8313. Born Edam, Sask. 1932. d. 4 ch. Odell, Leona, Anne, Scott. CAREER: writer, 1972 to date; Writer-in-Residence, Saskatoon Public Library, 1987-88. SELECTED PUBLICATIONS: *Ghost House*, Chapter book of stories & poems (Coteau Books, 1976); *They Shouldn't Make You Promise That* (NAL, Signet, for Macmillan, 1981; trade pbk., Greystone Books, 1996); *Pictures*, short stories (Fifth House Ltd., 1984); *Auntie's Knitting a Baby*, children's poems, illus. by Anne Simmie (Western Producer Prairie Books, 1984); *An Armadillo Is Not a Pillow*, children's poems, illus. by Anne Simmie (Western Producer Prairie Books, 1986); *What Holds Up The Moon?*, picture book, illus. by Anne Simmie (Coteau Books, 1987); *Oliver's Chickens*, illustrated by Kim LaFave, a children's picture & early chapter book (Groundwood Books, 1992); *Betty Lee Bonner Lives There*, short stories (adult) (Douglas & McIntyre Ltd., Greystone Imprint, 1993); *Mister Got To Go*, picture book, illus. by Cynthia Nugent (Red Deer Coll. Press, 1995); *The Secret Lives of Sgt. John Wilson*, creative non-fiction (Greystone Books, 1995); adult fiction published in *Saturday*

Night, McCall's, various literary magazines & anthologies & read on CBC; Ed., 3 books incl. Cora Taylor's award-winning children's books, *Julie* & *The Doll.* AFFIL: Saskatchewan Writers' Guild; The Writers' Union of Canada; ACTRA. HONS: several children's books, Canadian Children's Book Centre Choices; won several writing awards for individual stories & poems; twice won a major award for a collection of short stories in the Saskatchewan Writers' Guild Competition & Dept. of Culture & Youth competition; *Mister Got To Go,* shortlisted for the City of Vancouver Book Award; winner, Non-Saskatchewan Children's Book of the Year, 1995; winner, Alberta Book Award, Children's Title of the Year and ABA Best Illustrated Book; *Secret Lives of Sgt. John Wilson,* winner of Arthur Ellis Award for Non-Ficton, Crime Writers of Canada. INTERESTS: reading; writing; going out for lunch. MISC: readings from *They Shouldn't Make You Promise That* featured on CBC Radio's *Morningside*; commissioned by *Morningside* to adapt 2 short stories for drama broadcast, June 1994; numerous readings from adult & children's work in Sask. & around the country; has conducted writing workshops for both children & adults; Stories from *Betty Lee Bonner Lives There* featured on *Between the Covers,* CBC, 1995. COMMENT: *"I didn't start to write until I saw 40 looming and will keep on as long the few brain cells hold out. My next project is a novel. My major achievement is that I seem to be making a living at this, albeit a precarious one."*

Simmie, Monica, B.A. Ⓢ
Assistant Corporate Secretary, ROGERS COMMUNICATIONS INC., Scotia Plaza, 40 King St. W., Ste. 6400, Box 1007, Toronto, ON M5H 3Y2 (416) 864-2364, FAX 864-2365, EMAIL msimmie@rci.rogers.com. Born Toronto. m. Grant Wilfrid Simmie. EDUC: Univ. of Toronto, B.A.(Econ.). CAREER: various positions up to Corp. Sec., Maclean Hunter Limited, 1975-95; Asst. Corp. Sec., Rogers Communications Inc., 1995 to date.

Simmons, Joyce Nesker, B.A.,M.Ed., Ph.D. ⌖ ✎ ⊕
Medical Consultative Staff, HOSPITAL FOR SICK CHILDREN, 555 University Ave., Toronto, ON M5G 1X8. Assistant Professor, Faculty of Medicine, UNIVERSITY OF TORONTO. EDUC: Univ. of Toronto, B.A. 1973, M.Ed. 1974, Ph.D. 1981; Dept. of Neurology, The Hospital for Sick Children, Clinical Residency 1974-75. CAREER: specialization in the dev. & educ. of children with complex learning problems, incl. blindness & multiple handicaps; in this area

consults to bds. of educ., courts & various prov. svcs throughout Ont., & int'l agencies. SELECTED PUBLICATIONS: *School Problems: Questions Parents Ask About Schools* (1996); *The Simmons-Davidson Developmental Profile; Teachers, Models of Excellence in Today's Classrooms,* co-author Walter Pitman (1994); *The Handbook For Parents of Young Blind Children; The Early Development of Blind Children: A Book of Readings;* Ed. Columnist, "School Problems," *The Toronto Sun.* AFFIL: W. Ross Macdonald Sch. for the Blind (Prov. Consultant, Psychological Svcs; Dir. of Research); Canadian National Institute for the Blind (Prov. Consultant, Children's Svcs). HONS: The Florence S. Dunlop Memorial Fellowship, 1976; Federation of Women Teachers of Ontario Open Fellowship; The Ontario Psychological Foundation Annual Education Award; Writing Award, Ontario Association for Continuing Education; Women of Distinction, Educ., YWCA of Metropolitan Toronto, 1995.

Simonds, Merilyn, B.A. ■■ ✎ ✍ ⌂
Writer. EMAIL simonds@adan.kingston.net. Born Winnipeg 1949. m. Wayne Grady. 2 ch. Karl J. Mohr, Erik Mohr. EDUC: Univ. of Western Ontario, B.A.(English) 1971. CAREER: freelance magazine writer, 1979 to date; Asst. Editor, Camden House Publishing Ltd., 1988; freelance book editor, 1989-93; Editor, *Sourcebooks* magazine, 1987-90; Assoc. Editor, *Harrowsmith* magazine, 1987, 1989; Sr. Contributing Editor, 1987-91; Founding Sr. Editor, *This Country Canada* Magazine, 1992. SELECTED CREDITS: Contributor, *Basic Black,* CBC-Radio, 1993 to date; Contributor, "Kingston Radio Writer's Project," 1995. SELECTED PUBLICATIONS: *The Convict Lover* (Macfarlane, Walter & Ross, Toronto, 1996); *The Valour and the Horror* (co-author, HarperCollins, Toronto, 1991); *Fit to Drink* (Groundwood, Toronto, 1995); *The Games Treasury* (Chapters Publishing, Vermont, 1993); *The Harrowsmith Salad Garden* (co-author, Camden House Publishing, Camden East, Ont., 1992); *A Chronicle of Our House* (Camden House Publishing, 1988); *Home Playgrounds* (Camden House Publishing, 1987); *Sunwings* (Camden House Publishing, 1985); *Canoecraft* (co-author, Camden House Publishing, 1983); *The Art of Soapmaking* (Camden House Publishing, 1979); included in several anthologies incl. *Living in Harmony; Nature Writing by Women* in Canada (ed. Andrea Lebowitz, Orca Books, Vancouver, 1996); numerous magazine articles; book reviews, *Books in Canada* & *The Montreal Gazette.* AFFIL: Writers' Union of Canada; Loyalist Coll. (Advisory Bd., Print

Journalism 1994-97). **HONS:** The Connaught Medal, 1996; Canadian Science Writer's Award, 1990; Greg Clark Award for outdoor writing, 1989; recipient, several grants; short-listed for the Governor General's Literary Award for Nonfiction, 1996. **MISC:** Judge, Bronwen Wallace Award, 1995, & Kingston Literary Award, 1996; Guest Lecturer, Queen's Univ., Carleton Univ., St. Lawrence Coll., Loyalist Coll. & Harbourfront, 1990-96; Instructor, Creative Nonfiction, Kingston Sch. of Writing, July 1988, 1989, 1990; Instructor, Freelance Writing, Loyalist Coll., 1995; Host, Printed Passage Reading Series, 1994, 1995. **COMMENT:** *"Born in Winnipeg, Manitoba in 1949, Merilyn Simonds spent her childhood in Brazil. She graduated in 1971 from the University of Western Ontario with a Bachelor of Arts degree in English. She taught film briefly at the University of Guelph before moving in 1976 to a 50-acre homestead near North Bay, Ontario, where she raised her sons, Karl and Erik. In 1978, she began freelancing for* Harrowsmith *magazine and ten years later moved to Kingston, Ontario, to become a columnist and associate editor, responsible for energy and architecture issues. Since 1991 she has devoted herself full-time to writing. She has published ten books and scores of articles under the names Merilyn Mohr and Merilyn Simonds Mohr in* Harrowsmith, Equinox, Saturday Night *and* Canadian Geographic *magazines. She has been heard on* Morningside *and* Gabereau, *and is a regular guest on* Basic Black. *She lives with writer Wayne Grady and divides her time between their house in Kingston, Ontario, and a log cabin on a lake north of the city."*

Simons, M.Y.C. (Peggy), B.A.Sc.,M.B.A., P.Eng. ■ $ ✋

Management Consultant. Box 32, Site 6, R.R. #1, Calgary, AB T2P 2G4 (403) 246-8887, FAX 246-0916. Born Sarnia, Ont. 1946. m. Frank H. 3 ch. Denis, Dan, Eden. **EDUC:** Univ. of Toronto, B.A.Sc.(Chem. Eng.) 1968, M.B.A. 1987. **CAREER:** various eng. & operating positions, Gulf Canada Product, 1968-86; Mgr, Western Reg. Product Supply, Products, Petro-Canada, 1987-88; Dir., Strategic Planning, Products, 1988-90; Gen. Mgr, Whitecourt Value Centre, Resources, 1991-92; Dir., Strategic Mgmt, Resources, 1992-93; VP, Western Canada Oil Bus. Unit, 1993-96. **AFFIL:** Univ. of Calgary (Chrm, Eng. Associates Program); Professional Engineers Ontario; Planning Forum (Calgary Chapter); National Advisory Bd. for Science & Technology (1994-95); Association of Professional Engineers, Geologists and Geophysicists of Alberta; Univ. of Toronto (Dean's Advisory Committee, Eng.). **HONS:** Meritorious Service Award, Univ. of Toronto Engineering Alumni Association.

Simpson, Lee, B.A. ✎ $

Vice-President and Group Publisher (responsible for *Chatelaine, Chatelaine Special Editions!,* & *Modern Woman*), **MACLEAN HUNTER PUBLISHING LIMITED**, 777 Bay St., Toronto, ON M5W 1A7 (416) 596-5408, FAX 593-3197. Born Toronto 1951. m. Paul McKenna. 1 ch. **EDUC:** Univ. of Toronto, B.A. 1974. **CAREER:** Maclaren Advertising, 1974-78; Independent Media Analysis Research, 1978-80; Bristol Myers Canada Inc., 1980-84; Maclean Hunter, 1984 to date; Publisher, *Chatelaine* Magazine, Maclean Hunter, 1988 to date. **AFFIL:** Magazines Canada (Bd. mbr.); Canadian Advertising Foundation (Bd. mbr.); Print Measurement Bureau (Exec. Committee; former Treas.); Canadian Advertising Research Foundation (former Dir.); Professional Marketing Research Society; Grocery Products Manufacturers' Marketing Council; Canadian Cosmetic, Toiletry & Fragrance Association; National Advertising Benevolent Society; Girl Guides of Canada; Arthritis Society (Bd. of Dir.). **INTERESTS:** painting (watercolour); bird watching (hawks); gardening (rosa rugosa).

Sims, Deborah ♡

President and Executive Director, **A WORLD OF DREAMS FOUNDATION**, 465 St. Jean, Ste. 708, Montreal, QC H2Y 2R6 (514) 843-7254, FAX 843-3822. Born Montreal 1949. m. John K. Sims. 3 ch. Paul, Matthew, Richard. **VOLUNTEER CAREER:** Founder, Children's Wish Foundation, 1984; Founder, Pres. & Exec. Dir., A World of Dreams Foundation, 1987 to date. **AFFIL:** Molson Pioneers Club; Muscular Dystrophy Association; Rotary Club; United Irish Societies; Lions Club; Majorette Corps; National Transportation Week. **HONS:** Canada 125 Medal. **COMMENT:** *"I feel that I have accomplished so far, in 47 years, the ability to give a helping hand, to think of others. I do not feel that I have achieved my potential yet; however, the fact that I was able to help many in need and to start two foundations for Canada on my own, is my largest achievement to date."*

Sims, Elizabeth (Betty), A.B. ■ $ 🎓

President and General Manager, **CHICOPEE MANUFACTURING LIMITED** (precision custom machine shop–primarily aircraft components), 975 Wilson Ave., Kitchener, ON N2C 1J1 (519) 893-7575, FAX 893-2025. Born Brunswick, Ga. 1934. m. Peter H, Sims, QC. 5 ch. **EDUC:** Duke Univ., A.B.(Econ.) 1956.

CAREER: Systems Mgr, Chicopee Manufacturing Limited, 1976-79; VP, Admin., 1979-83; Gen. Mgr & VP, Admin., 1983-84; Pres. & Gen. Mgr, 1984 to date. DIRECTOR: Chicopee Manufacturing Limited; Chicopee Securities Limited; Union Gas Limited (mbr., Independent Committee). AFFIL: Wilfrid Laurier Univ. (Chair, Bd. of Gov.). HONS: Queen's Silver Jubilee Medal, 1977; Oustanding Business Leader Award, Wilfrid Laurier Univ., 1989.

Sims, Mary-Woo ⚖ ✤ ◉
Vice-Chair, Boards of Inquiry - Human Rights, Pay Equity Hearings Tribunal, PROVINCE OF ONTARIO, 150 Eglinton Ave. E., 2/F, Toronto, ON M4P 1E8 (416) 314-0004, FAX 314-8743. CAREER: variety of non-traditional occupations; Mgr, Human Rights & Employment Equity Programs, Municipality of Metropolitan Toronto; V-Chair, Equity Tribunals, Prov. of Ont.; V-Chair, Bds. of Inquiry– Human Rights, Pay Equity Hearings Tribunal. AFFIL: Community Foundation for Greater Toronto (Advisory Committee, Safe City Awards). HONS: Award of Recognition for contribution to Project to Combat Lesbian & Gay Bashing, Metropolitan Toronto Police Services; Award of Recognition, Metropolitan Community Church; "Women on the Move," *The Toronto Sun.* INTERESTS: scuba-diving; movies; motorcycling. MISC: founding mbr., rape crisis centre; former Co-Chair, Min. of Citizenship's Anti-Racism Advisory Group; former mbr., Cabinet Round Table on Anti-Racism; former mbr., Ontario Civilian Commission on Police Services; former Co-Chair, Campaign for Equal Families. COMMENT: *"Prior to becoming an adjudicator, Mary-Woo Sims was a tireless activist in human rights issues. She attributes her sense of justice and belief in the dignity and worth of every individual to her late mother whose support and encouragement was invaluable."*

Simson, Claudine, B.Sc.,Ph.D. ■ Ⓢ ❀
Assistant Vice-President, Advanced Technologies, NORTEL TECHNOLOGY (formerly Bell-Northern Research Ltd.), 3500 Carling Ave., Ottawa, ON K1Y 4H7 (613) 763-4425, FAX 763-31275. Born Angers, France 1953. m. Moris Simson. 2 ch. Sylvia Simson, Mélissa Simson. EDUC: Institut National des Sciences Appliquées, Toulouse, France, B.Sc.(Elec. Eng.) 1975, Ph.D.(Semiconductor Physics) 1978. CAREER: Device Physicist, Bell-Northern Research, then 3 successive levels of mgmt positions, Bell-Northern Research & then Northern Telecom Electronics, 1978-86; Dir., Technology, Northern Telecom Electronics, with added responsibilities, 1986-93; Asst. VP, Telecom Microelectronics Centre, Northern Telecom Limited, 1993-94; Gen. Mgr, 1994-95; Asst. VP, Advanced Technologies, Bell-Northern Research Ltd., 1995 to date; Adjunct Prof., Dept. of Elec. & Computer Eng., Univ. of Toronto. AFFIL: Microelectronics Federal Network of Excellence (MICRONET) (Chair, Bd. of Dir.); National Research Council of Canada (fed. appointee to the Council); Fields Institute for Research in Mathematical Sciences (Bd.; V-Chair); Massey Coll., Univ. of Toronto (Assoc. Fellow); National Sciences & Engineering Research Council of Canada (Committee on Collaborative Research Initiatives); Univ. of Ottawa (Research Advisory Council); Queen's Univ. (Advisory Bd.); Canada Council (Killam Research Program Selection Committee); Canada Gold Medal for Science & Engineering (Selection Committee); Ottawa-Carleton Education-Business partnership program for Teacher Summer Internships in local businesses (Exec. Chair); Canadian Microelectronics Initiative (Exec. Committee); US Semiconductor Research Corporation (Bd. of Dir.). HONS: Doctorate Research Grant, Centre National de la Recherche Scientifique, France, 1975; President's Award, Mgr of the Year, Northern Telecom Ltd., 1991; Chairman's Award for Innovation, Northern Telecom Ltd., 1993; President's Award for Teamwork, Northern Telecom Ltd., 1994; 10-Year Contribution Award, ULSI Research Group, Univ. of Waterloo, 1995; Merit Award, Microelectronics Network of Centres of Excellence, BOD, 1996. INTERESTS: gourmet cooking; piano; arts; photography. MISC: founding participant, task force on int'l cooperation on science & technology, commissioned by Bd. on Science, Technology & Econ. Policy, US National Research Council; listed in *International Who's Who of Business* & *5,000 Personalities of the World.* COMMENT: *"Executive leader in Canada for the microelectronics and telecommunicatons sector, in charge of corporate worldwide external research and intellectual property and corporate global advanced technology R&D for Nortel's next-generation Broadcast Network's products. Device physicist, one of the youngest Ph.D.s in France in 1978. High professional ethics striving for excellence in all professional aspects (technical, business, financial, people). Participative management style practising empowerment and true leadership."*

Sinclair, Donna, B.A. ✎ ☼
Senior Writer, THE UNITED CHURCH OBSERVER, 478 Huron St., Toronto, ON M5R 2R3 (416) 960-8500, FAX 960-8477. 3 ch. David, Andrew, Tracy. EDUC: Univ. of Toronto, B.A. 1964; Ontario Coll. of Education, Certificate

1965. **CAREER:** secondary sch. Teacher, 1964-72; freelance writer, 1970-90; Contributing Ed., The United Church Observer, 1979-89; Teacher, Creative Writing, Canadore Coll., North Bay, Ont., 1982-94; Sr. Writer, The United Church Observer, 1990 to date. **SELECTED PUBLICATIONS:** *The Pastor's Wife Today* (Abingdon, 1981); *Worth Remembering* (Wood Lake Books, 1984); *Living Together in Marriage* (The United Church, 1985); *Christian Parenting with Yvonne Stewart* (Wood Lake Books, 1990); *Crossing Worlds: the Story of the Women's Missionary Society of the United Church* (United Church Publishing House, 1992); ed., *Dream of a New Life* (United Church Publishing House, 1992); *Getting Along: The ABCs of Human Relations*, illustrated by cartoonist Allan Hirsh (Wood Lake Books, 1993). **HONS:** various Associated Church Press & Canadian Church Press Awards for devotional/inspirational, theological reflection, news & fiction. **INTERESTS:** gardening; reading; camping; travel; cross-country skiing; cycling.

Sinclair, Helen K., B.A.,M.A. ■ $

Chief Executive Officer, BANK WORKS TRADING INC., 20 Adelaide St. E., Ste. 500, Toronto, ON M5L 1T6 (416) 362-2361, FAX 367-2188. Born Edmonton 1951. m. James S. Coatsworth. 2 ch. **EDUC:** York Univ., B.A.(Econ.); Univ. of Toronto, M.A.(Econ.); Harvard Business Sch., Advanced Mgmt Program. **CAREER:** Consultant, J.J. Singer Consulting Economists, 1974-75; supervisory positions, The Bank of Nova Scotia, 1975-80; Dir. of Public Affairs, Canadian Bankers' Association (CBA), 1980-85; sr. exec. positions incl. Sr. VP & Gen. Mgr, Planning & Legislation, The Bank of Nova Scotia, 1985-89; Pres., CBA, 1989-96; CEO, Bank Works Trading Inc., 1996 to date. **DIRECTOR:** Toronto Dominion Bank; Livingston Group Inc.; Stelco Inc. **AFFIL:** Canadian Institute for Advanced Research; Harvard Business Sch. Club of Ontario (Dir.); York Univ. (Bd. of Gov.); Social Sciences & Humanities Research Council of Canada; YMCA of Greater Toronto (Dir.); C.D. Howe Institute (Dir.) Ontario Financial Review Commission (V-Chair); The Ticker Club; York Club; Toronto Lawn Tennis Club; Rideau Club. **HONS:** Doctor of Civil Law (Hon.), Acadia Univ., 1992. **INTERESTS:** tennis; hiking; downhill & cross-country skiing; golf.

Singer, Sharon, B.A. ■ 📜 🎭 ☝

President, FIRST CANADIAN ARTISTS INC. Born Toronto. s. **EDUC:** Univ. of Toronto, B.A. (English); London Film Sch., Certificate in Film Production; Millenium Film Workshop, New Sch. for Social Research, N.Y. **CAREER:** Mgr, Montreal Office, Film Canada (film distribution) 1970; Mgr, Cinema Images Div., International Tele-Film Ent., 1972-74; Pres., Dabara Films (film distribution) 1975-82; Pres., First Canadian Artists, 1980 to date; Press Officer, Toronto Int'l Film Festival, 1987-88; co-founder, Grand Central Web (Web site creation & promotion), 1996. **SELECTED CREDITS:** Unit Publicist for *To Catch A Killer*, *Darkman: Durant Returns*, *First Degree*, *The Michelle Apartments*, *The Women of Windsor*, *Clearcut*, *The Outside Chance of Maximilian Glick*; Prod., *Economics* (short film), 1973; Prod., *Les Fables de Lafontaine* (educ. mixed media), 1975; Prod., *Not By Design Alone* (industrial), 1976; Assoc. Prod., *Comedy Tonight* (series), 1983-84; Interviewer, *The Entertainers*, CBC Radio, 1984-86; electronic press kits prod. for features *White Room*, *Clearcut*, *Bordertown Cafe*. **SELECTED PUBLICATIONS:** *Fire Rider*, a book of poetry (Fire Mountain Press, 1996; Web site: www.enterprise.ca/~ssinger/fire-rider); published poems "No Walls," "Eve," "Inukshuk"; articles published in various magazines & newspapers incl. *The Globe and Mail*, *The Toronto Star; The Toronto Sun*; *TV Guide*; *TV Times*; Reuters International (wire service); *Fangoria*. **DIRECTOR:** First Canadian Artists Inc. **AFFIL:** Jewish Genealogical Society; Crime Writers of Canada; Toronto Free-Net (Co-Chair, Publicity Committee 1993-95). **INTERESTS:** archaeology; ancient cultures; holistic philosophies; Eastern philosophies; psychology; art; travel; culture; dance. **MISC:** judge, Chicago Film Festival; listed in *Who's Who in Canadian Film and Television*; speaker, "Publicity in the '90s: The Internet Challenge," Canadian National Internet Show, 1996. **COMMENT:** *"My major life's work is in entertainment and the arts. In the motion picture business, I was the first woman in Canada to found and operate a motion picture distribution company (Dabara Films) which released such eminent films as Academy Award winner* Madame Rosa, Dona Flor and Her Two Husbands *and* The Innocent. *I have also done film marketing and publicity and produced for the television and educational markets. In August 1996 I started "Words in Concert" a live poetry reading series (Web site: www.enterprise.ca/~ssinger/words) which I am programming and hosting at the renowned Free Times Cafe. I have also been enthusiastically involved in using the Internet for marketing, promotion and publicity and all my endeavors now have Web sites."*

Singh, Monica Khhem K. ■ ☺ ♡

President, PROVINCIAL COUNCIL OF WOMEN OF

MANITOBA. Past President, IMMIGRANT WOMEN'S ASSOCIATION OF MANITOBA, 290 - 1dst St., Rm. 204, Winnipeg, MB R3B 2L9 (204) 989-5800, FAX 895-9058. m. Sobharam Singh. 3 ch. CAREER: Item Records Officer, Hudson's Bay Downtown, Winnipeg, 1975-87; Pres.-Elect, Provincial Council of Women of Manitoba, 1994; Pres., 1995 to date. VOLUNTEER CAREER: Host Program, Manitoba Intercultural Council, 1987-93; Volunteer Cook, Ethos Sr. Summer Camp, 1987; Volunteer Visitor, Mun. Hospitals, 1987-89; Volunteer Cooking Class Instructor, Age & Opportunity, 1988; Visitors' Program Volunteer, Age & Opportunity, 1989-94; VP, East Indian Support & Advocacy, 1991-93; Dir., Immigrant Women's Association of Manitoba, 1991 to date; Acting Pres., East Indian Support & Advocacy, 1992-93; VP, Immigrant Women's Association of Manitoba, 1992-93; Pres., 1993 to date; Pres.-Elect, Provincial Council of Women, 1995; Convenor of Committee on Citizenship & Immigration, National Council of Women, 1995; Bd. Mbr. & Man. Rep., Western Canada Association of Immigrant Serving Agencies, 1995-97; Bd. Mbr., National Organization of Immigrant & Visible Minority Women of Canada, 1995-97. AFFIL: Commonwealth Ladies' Association of Guyana (Sec. 1968; Treas. 1970; Pres. 1972); Caribbean Canadian Association of Manitoba; Indo-Caribbean Association; Legal Education & Action Fund; Board of Alpha House; Univ. of Manitoba Continuing Educ. Dept. (Women in Mgmt Committee); Social Planning Council (Employment Equity Committee); International Professional Association of Manitoba; City of Winnipeg Year of Racial Harmony & Human Rights Committees; Immigrant Awareness Week; End of Decade Committee. HONS: Certificate of Appreciation-Bridging Traditions, Winnipeg Boys & Girls Inc. of Manitoba, 1989; Certificate of Appreciation-Friendly Visitor Program, Mun. Hospitals of Winnipeg, 1989; Certificate of Appreciation-Convivial Symphony, ETHOS Multicultural Seniors, 1991; Certificate of Appreciation-Honours, ETHOS Multicultural Seniors Coalition, 1992; Certificate of Appreciation, Planned Parenthood of Manitoba Inc., 1992; Certificate of Appreciation - Outstanding Volunteer, Age & Opportunity Centre, 1993; Certificate of Recognition of Nomination for Women of Distinction Award, Y.M.-YWCA, 1994. INTERESTS: creation of a more equitable & fair society; preservation of the ecosystem, wildlife & nature; conservation of resources, recycling & reusing. COMMENT: *"I believe in the family and living in harmony with nature. I strive for justice and the pursuit of happiness for all the world's peoples."*

Singhal, Nalini, M.B.B.S.,DCH, M.D., FRCP(c) ⊕ ⌖ ☺
Medical Staff, Pediatrics, FOOTHILLS HOSPITAL, 1403 - 29 St. N.W., Calgary, AB T2N 2T9 (403) 670-1615, FAX 670-4892. Associate Professor, Pediatrics, UNIVERSITY OF CALGARY. 2 ch. Ashutosh, Deven. EDUC: Hindu Coll., New Delhi, India, Pre-Medicine 1965; All-India Institute of Medical Sciences, New Delhi, India, M.B.B.S. 1971; Kanpur Univ., India, DCH 1974, M.D.(Pediatrics) 1977. CAREER: Intern, All India Institute of Medical Sciences, 1970; Houseman, Pediatrics & Opthamology, 1971; Resident, Pediatrics, G.S.V.M. Medical Coll., India, 1973-76; Intern, Foothills Provincial General Hospital, 1977; Sr. Resident, 1978; Fellow, Neonatology, 1979-81; Medical Staff, Pediatrics, 1982 to date; Medical Staff, Pediatrics, Alberta Children's Hospital, 1982 to date; Asst. Prof., then Assoc. Prof., Univ. of Calgary, 1982 to date. SELECTED PUBLICATIONS: "Practical Use of Nitroblue Tetrazolium Test in Febrile Disorders of Children" (*Indian Journal of Pediatrics* May 1976); "'Long Term' Morbidity of Infants with Bronchopulmonary Dysplasia," with R.S. Sauve (*Pediatrics* Nov. 1985); "Conjoint Nursing/Physician Training Program in Neonatal Resuscitation: The Impact of Attitudes and Resources," with D.D. McMillan *et al* (*Neonatal Network* 4 1992); "Development of a Program for Case Room Resuscitation by Respiratory Therapists," with S.N.M Boucher (*Canadian Journal of Respiratory Therapy* 28 1992); "Nitric oxide in neonates" (*Neonatal Forum*, 1995). AFFIL: Indian Medical Association; Alberta Medical Association; Canadian Medical Association; American Academy of Pediatrics (Fellow); Royal Coll. of Physicians & Surgeons of Canada (Fellow); Canadian Pediatric Society; American Academy of Pediatrics; Alberta Thoracic Society; Medical Council of Canada (Licentiate); Alberta Coll. of Physicians & Surgeons (Licentiate). INTERESTS: improvement of care of newborn babies in dev. countries through educ. of mothers, alternate health care providers & health care professionals. MISC: recipient, various grants; frequent invited speaker; currently involved in educ. of physicians caring for newborn babies in Ukraine, Russia, Philippines & India.

Sirek, Anna, M.D.,M.A.,Ph.D. ⊕ ⌖
Professor Emeritus of Physiology, UNIVERSITY OF TORONTO, Medical Sciences Bldg, Toronto, ON M5S 1A8. Born Velke Senkvice, Czechoslovakia 1921. m. 4 ch. Ann, Jan, Peter, Terese. EDUC: Slovak Univ. of Bratislava, M.D. 1946; Univ. of Toronto, M.A. 1955, Ph.D. 1960. CAREER: Intern, Detska Klinika,

Bratislava, 1946-47; Research Fellow in Surgery, Kronprinsessan Lovisas Barnsjukhus, Stockholm, 1947-50; Research Fellow in Surgery, Hospital for Sick Children, Toronto, 1950-54; Research Assoc., Banting & Best Dept. of Medical Research, Univ. of Toronto, 1954-60; Lecturer, 1960-63; Asst. Prof. of Physiology, Univ. of Toronto, 1963-66; Assoc. Prof., 1966-72; Asst. Dir., Div. Teaching Labs, 1969-75; Prof., 1972-86; Dir., Div. Teaching Labs, 1975-86; Prof. Emeritus, 1986 to date. **SELECTED PUBLICATIONS:** more than 100 articles published in scientific journals & as chapters in books. **AFFIL:** Canadian Federation of Biological Societies; American Association for Advancement of Science; Canadian Association of University Teachers; Federation of Medical Women in Canada; International Diabetes Federation; Toronto Diabetes Association; Canadian Society of Endocrinology & Metabolism; Canadian Diabetes Association, Clinical & Scientific Section; Societa Italiana Di Diabetologia. **HONS:** Starr Medal, Univ. of Toronto, 1960; Centennial Medal, Hoechst Co. Frankfurt/M, Germany, 1966. **INTERESTS:** cooking; gardening; music; needlework. **MISC:** listed in numerous biographical sources, incl. *Canadian Who's Who, Canadian Achievers and Their Mentors, World Who's Who of Women, Who's Who in the Commonwealth* & *American Men and Women of Science.* **COMMENT:** *"On the basis of expertise in experimental surgery, Dr. Sirek has developed innovative procedures that have facilitated long-term metabolic studies, resulting in solutions to numerous basic problems in the study of diabetes in animals and humans."*

Sivers, Glendene ■■ [$] ⊕ ☼

Senior Vice-President, Investments, TORONTO MUTUAL LIFE INSURANCE COMPANY, 112 St. Clair Ave. W., Toronto, ON M4V 2Y3 (416) 960-3463, FAX 960-0082. Born Toronto 1942. m. 2 ch. **EDUC:** Canadian Business Coll., Matriculation 1959; Canadian Investment Finance II 1985. **CAREER:** Nesbitt, Thomson, Bongard, 1959-69; J.D. Dodge, Investment Counsel, 1980-81; McLeod Young Weir, 1981-83; Toronto Mutual Insurance Company, 1983 to date. **AFFIL:** Granite Club.

Skanes, Lois J., B.A.,LL.B. ■ ⚖

Partner, WILLIAMS, ROEBOTHAN, MCKAY AND MARSHALL, 209 Duckworth St., P.O. Box 5236, St. John's, NF A1C 5W1 (709) 753-5805, FAX 753-5221. **EDUC:** Memorial Univ. of Newfoundland, B.A.(Psych.) 1981; Univ. of Saskatchewan, LL.B. 1984. **BAR:** Nfld. 1985. **CAREER:** Lawyer, Mercer, Spracklin, Heywood, 1984-87; Lawyer, City of St. John's, 1987-93; Partner, Williams, Roebothan, McKay and Marshall, 1993 to date. **AFFIL:** Canadian Bar Association (Exec. Mbr., Nfld. Branch; Pres.); Canadian Mental Health Association (Exec. Mbr., Nfld. Branch 1988-90); P.R.E.P. (local affiliate of Canadian Mental Health Association) (Exec. 1985-92; Chair 1990-91).

Skeir-Armstrong, Odessa ✊ ☼

General Treasurer, BRITISH METHODIST EPISCOPAL CHURCH CONFERENCE OF CANADA, 30 Burnhill Rd., Ste. 509, Scarborough, ON M1L 4R8. Born Halifax 1924. d. 5 ch. **EDUC:** Halifax Academy, Commercial Diploma 1948; Adult Training Centre, Key Punch Certificate 1965, Bookkeeping Certificate 1965. **CAREER:** Post Office & Correctional Office, Civil Service; Prod. Coord., Southam Communications Ltd.; various positions, Office Overload; Sec., law office of Mr. Spencer Pitt. **AFFIL:** Grand Chapter of the Order of Eastern Stars, Prov. of Ont. & Juris (Past Grand Sec.); The Elks (Fin. Sec.); The Good Will Club (Fin. Sec.); BME Church Conference of Canada (Gen. Treas.); Women's Inter-Church Council of Metro Toronto. **HONS:** various certificates from Office Overload, Catholic Children's Aid Society, The United Way, Order of Eastern Stars, Prov. of Ont. & Juris, The Elks; Volunteer Certificate, The Prov. of Ont.; Award of Distinction, BME Church Conference of Canada. **INTERESTS:** promoting justice between the races: civil rights. **MISC:** honoured to be chosen to sing as a mbr. of the choir during the Royal Visit of the King & Queen in 1939 in Halifax. **COMMENT:** *"I am and will always be a devoted black Canadian. I have been in many parts of the world but none have proven better! Sure, we have discrimination–so do all peoples–whites included. But in Canada, as in ages past, blacks were given liberalism, they were supported, assisted and empowered. I have endeavoured to promote this feeling to others! I feel I have achieved these ideals within my immediate family. Therefore my association with programs that promote 'sisterly love' to mankind."*

Skelton, Ruta, B.A., B.Jour., A.B.C. [$] ✎ ♡

Canadian Communication Practice Manager and Principal, TOWERS PERRIN, South Tower, 175 Bloor St. E., Ste. 1501, Toronto, ON M4W 3T6 (416) 960-7493, FAX 960-2819. **EDUC:** Trinity Coll., Univ. of Toronto, B.A. (Pol. Sci./Hist.) 1975; Carleton Univ., B.Jour. (Journalism) 1976. **CAREER:** Sr. Copy Ed., Maclean's Magazine, 1976-80; Coord., Publications & Staff Comm., Ontario Hospital Association, 1980-86; Canadian Comm. Practice

Leader, Hewitt Associates, 1986-92; Canadian Comm. Practice Mgr & Principal, Towers Perrin, 1992 to date. **SELECTED PUBLICATIONS:** "Serving Up a First-Class Communications Campaign" (*Benefits Canada* Feb. 1988); "Back to School" (*Benefits Canada* Sept. 1990); "15 Years Young" (*Benefits Canada* Feb. 1992); *Canadian Handbook of Flexible Benefits* contributing writer & ed. (John Wiley and Sons, 1990). **AFFIL:** International Association of Business Communicators (A.B.C. 1984; various exec. positions incl. Int'l Chrm 1994-95; Pres., Toronto Chapter 1985-86); Health Care Public Relations Association (Canada) (Dir. 1984-86). **HONS:** Accolade for Writing, International Association of Business Communicators, Toronto, 1981; Int'l Award for Excellence of Chapter Mgmt, International Association of Business Communicators, 1986; Award of Excellence, E.B.C. Business Insurance, 1991; Hon. Gold Quill Award of Excellence, International Association of Business Communicators, 1992. **INTERESTS:** sailing; skiing; cooking; gardening. **MISC:** frequent writer & speaker on hum. res. & employee comm. issues. **COMMENT:** *"I look forward to growing personally and professionally, wherever the future takes me. Most of all, seeing my sons grow up happy, healthy and successful is my greatest aspiration."*

Skene, Jennie, R.N. ⊘ ⊕
President, FÉDÉRATION DES INFIRMIERES ET INFIRMIERS DU QUÉBEC, 2050 rue Bleury, 4ième étage, Montréal, QC H3A 2J5 (514) 987-1141, FAX 987-7273. Born Lac-Edouard, Que. 1950. s. **EDUC:** École des Infirmières de l'Hôpital de l'Enfant-Jésus, R.N. 1970. **CAREER:** Déléguée syndicale/Agente de griefs, Hôpital de l'Enfant-Jésus, 1976; Administratrice, trésorière et prés. par intérim, Syndicat Professionel des Infirmières et Infirmiers du Québec, 1976-85; Admin., trésorière et VP, Comité Exécutif de la Fédération des SPIIQ, 1978-87; Membre fondatrice/VP, Fédération des Infirmières et Infirmiers du Québec, 1987-93; Prés., 1993 to date. **AFFIL:** Ordre des Infirmières et Infirmiers du Québec. **INTERESTS:** voyages; lecture. **COMMENT:** *"En tant que présidente de la FIIQ, Jennie Skene assume la responsabilité politique de toutes les représentations publiques de la Fédération. Elle est également membre d'office de tous les comités. A ce titre, elle a prononcé plusieurs conférences traitant de différentes sujets touchant les infirmières. Elle a, entre autres, abordé lors de l'assemblée de fondation de l'Association des infirmières-bachelières du Québec et la santé communautaire québécoise devant le syndicat des infirmières du Nouveau-Brunswick."*

Skoke, Roseanne Marie, B.A.,LL.B., M.P. ✦ ⚖
Member of Parliament (Central Nova), GOVERNMENT OF CANADA, Confederation Bldg, House of Commons, Rm. 630, Ottawa, ON K1A 0A6 (613) 995-5822. Born New Glasgow, N.S. 1954. d. 2 ch. **EDUC:** Dalhousie Univ., B.A.(Pol. Sci.) 1973, LL.B. 1976. **BAR:** N.S., 1978. **CAREER:** Barrister & Solicitor, Prov. of N.S., 1978-93; M.P. (Central Nova), 1993 to date. **AFFIL:** Liberal Party of Canada. **COMMENT:** *"Graduated from Dalhousie University with two degrees at age 21; has practised 18 years and became actively involved in defending the rights of the oppressed and the 'common' folk. Was elected MP in a riding that was Tory for almost 40 years."*

Sky, Deanna ■ ⊗
Artist and Owner, MIN'S INDIAN CRAFT, R.R.#2, Ohsweken, ON N0A 1M0 (519) 445-2894. Born Six Nations Ohswehen, Ont. 1940. m. James. 5 ch. Lori Dale Martin, Bonnie Lee Hill, Susan Ann Issaces, Georgie James Sky, Cecelia Deanna Smith. **EDUC:** Hamilton RNA Centre, Registered Nursing Asst. **CAREER:** Registered Nursing Asst.; owner, Min's Indian Crafts, 1971 to date. **AFFIL:** Six Nation Tourism (Dir.); Mohawk Coll. (Native Peoples' Advisory Committee); Six Nation Fair (VP, Bd.); Grand River Pow Wow Committee. **HONS:** "EEDEE" Craft Design Award, Ministry of Industry & Tourism, 1973. **COMMENT:** *"Deanna took over the running of Min's Indian Crafts after her mother, who started the store in 1963, died in 1971. She makes many of the items sold, but specializes in making deer skin dresses, skirts, vests and jackets. Many people on the reserve have been helped by Deanna, as she purchases their crafts and places the items in her shop for sale. She has done some travelling with her husband, Jim, and his Indian dance troupe, as she also enjoys taking part in Indian dancing."*

Sky, Laura ■ ◿ ◯ ⊕
Film Producer and Director, SKY WORKS CHARITABLE FOUNDATION, 566 Palmerston Ave., Toronto, ON M6G 2P7 (416) 536-6581, FAX 536-7728. Born Montreal 1946. 1 ch. Adam Sky. **CAREER:** independent film Prod. & Dir., 1972 to date; Reg. Dir., Challenge for Change Program, National Film Bd., 1973-79; Assoc. Prof., Film Studies, Queen's Univ., 1979-81; Founder, Prod., Dir. & Writer, Sky Works Charitable Foundation, 1981 to date; health care researcher & analyst. **SELECTED CREDITS:** Prod./Dir., *Tomorrow's Children* (documentary), 1972; Dir./Prod., *The Artistic Woodworkers Strike Tape*, NFB; Prod., *A Long Way*

to Go, NFB; Writer/Dir., *Shutdown*, NFB; Prod./Dir., *Moving Mountains* (documentary short), Sky Works, 1980, 1982; Prod./Dir., *Good Morning Monday* (documentary short), Sky Works; Co-Prod./Dir., *All Our Lives*, Sky Works, 1983; Writer/Prod./Dir., *To Hurt and Heal* (documentary), Sky Works, 1986; Writer/Prod./Dir., *Crying for Happiness*, Sky Works, 1990; Prod./Dir., *The Right to Care*, Sky Works, 1991; Dir./Prod., *Working Lean* (documentary), Sky Works, 1994; Dir/Prod., *Jake's Life* (documentary), Sky Works, 1995; Host, *Shift Change*, weekly radio show for CJRT, Toronto; Contributor, CBC Radio's *Metro Morning* & *Morningside*; Prod., "Medical Management," CBC *Ideas*. SELECTED PUBLICATIONS: numerous reports & publications on health-related issues incl. "Lean and Mean Health Care–The Creation of the Generic Worker and the Deregulation of Health Care," (Ontario Federation of Labour, 1995); "Training for the Future," a teaching module for assertiveness and advocacy training (Ontario Senior Citizens' Coalition, 1995); "I Just Have to be a Mother Bear," A research report on women care givers at home (Trillium Foundation, 1996). AFFIL: Media People for Social Responsibility; Canadian Independent Film Caucus; Equal Pay Coalition; Toronto Women's Film Caucus; Canadian Liaison group with the Committee of Latin American Film Makers; Mayworks (Dir.); Coalition Against Bill C-54; McGill Centre for Ethics, Medicine & Law (Assoc. Mbr.); National Action Committee on the Status of Women (Nat'l Sec. 1995; sub-committee on Reproductive & Genetic Technologies); Women's Alliance on Reproductive Technology. HONS: Women of Distinction Award, Arts & Letters, YWCA, 1986. MISC: numerous lecturing & speaking engagements, guest teaching & consulting; on various juries. COMMENT: *"I am an independent documentary filmmaker, focusing on films that deal with social issues. These issues primarily concern work place concerns, health care, policy and women's realities. I integrate film production, public process and adult education."*

Slaight, Annabel / ✂ ▢
President and Chief Executive Officer, OWL COMMUNICATIONS, 179 John St., Ste. 500, Toronto, ON M5T 3G5 (416) 971-5275, FAX 971-5294. Born 1940. m. Brian W. Slaight. CAREER: Pres. & CEO, Owl Communications, 1975 to date; Co-Founder, *OWL* Magazine, 1976 to date; Co-Founder, *Chickadee* magazine, 1979 to date; Founding Ed., Tree House Family; Founder, OWL Books; Founder, OWL Television Inc. SELECTED CREDITS: Exec.

Prod. of a number of TV projects incl.: *OWL/TV* (series), *The Big Comfy Couch* (series), *Spirit Rider* (feature); *F.R.O.G.* (series), *Wacky Palms* (pilot), *The Max Show* (pilot), *What's The Big Idea?* (pilot). DIRECTOR: Key Publishers. AFFIL: Canadian Film & Television Production Association (Dir.); Alliance for Children & Television (Dir.); CFPTA (Chair, Children's Producer's Committee). HONS: 1995 Women Who Make a Difference, Media category; Order of Ontario; Sir Sandford Fleming Award as Outstanding Science Communicator, Royal Canadian Institute, 1991; YWCA Women of Distinction Award, 1990; the 1st Outstanding Communicator for Environmental Awareness Award, Environment Canada, 1989; the 1st Eve Orpen Award for outstanding contribution to Cdn publishing; Canada's Outstanding Magazine Award (*OWL* magazine), 1979; Runner-up, Golden Lamp Award (*Chickadee* magazine), 1992; Parent's Choice Gold Seal (*Chickadee* magazine), 1992; Edpress Golden Lamp Award, for outstanding N.Am. children's magazine (*OWL* magazine), 1992; Canada's Outstanding Magazine Award (*OWL* magazine & *Chickadee* magazine), 1993.

Slavin, Linda, B.A. ■ ■ ✆ ☺ ✿
Global Educator/Consultant, Kawartha World Issues Centre TRENT UNIVERSITY, 180 Bernardo Ave., Room 10, Peterborough, ON K9H 5V3 (705) 745-1380, FAX 745-9720, EMAIL lslavin@trentu.ca. Born Vancouver 1944. m. Alan J. 2 ch. Lisa Claire, Geoffrey Sean. EDUC: Univ. of Toronto, B.A.(English) 1966; Coll. of Education, Diploma (Secondary Sch. English, Theatre Arts) 1967; Univ. de Nancy, France, French study 1989-90; Spanish study in Guatemala (1 month), 1993, & Mexico (2 months), 1996. CAREER: secondary sch. teacher, English/Theatre Arts, Canada, 1967-68; English teacher, Cambridge, UK, 1969-70; potter, 1973-76; elementary French teacher, 1981-86; caterer, 1981-84; activist for peace, social justice & the environment, 28 yrs.; Global Educator, Int'l Dev. Educ. Proj., Sir Sandford Fleming Coll., Peterborough, 1987-89; Consultant, Facilitation & Mgmt, 1990-96; Global Educator, Kawartha World Issues Centre (KWIC), 1989-96. SELECTED CREDITS: Host, *Peterborough Insight*, weekly 1/2-hr. show (int'l focus on women), Cable 6, 1988-94; theatre dir./prod./actor (emphasis on Cdn playwrights & women's experiences), 1974-89. SELECTED PUBLICATIONS: consultant/sponsor/research/mgmt support, *Our Common Future Too* report; *Rainbow Immigrant Needs Assessment* (1995); *Food Security Policy Statement* (1996); *To Beijing & Beyond: Our*

Voices, Our Choices (1995); contract work reports on organizational mgmt, global educ., eval. & impact assessment & codes of ethics. **AFFIL:** Ontario Council for International Cooperation (Pres. 1995 to date); One World Fund (Chair, Bd. Mgmt Committee 1996 to date); Peterborough Coalition for Social Justice (Exec. /Steering Committee); Women Working for Change; Ten Days for Global Justice; Educating for Action Today; Food Policy Action Coalition; Kawartha Ploughshares; Council of Global Education Centres of Ontario; Committee Against Racism/Hate Crimes; Peterborough's Raging Grannies (initiator; songwriter). **HONS:** Development Education Award, Canadian International Development Agency, 1992; Hall of Honour, Norwood District High Sch., 1993; Canada 125 Medal, 1994. **INTERESTS:** methodology appropriate for social learning/social change; linking North/South issues - working toward global equity; theatre; travel; swimming; cross-country skiing; cooking; hosting community pot lucks. **MISC:** NDP candidate, prov., 1985 & 1987, & fed., 1984; organizer/facilitator/designer, "Our Common Future," community forum on sustainable dev., 1989, & "Our Common Future Too," community forum on sustainable dev. & globalization, 1991; ongoing workshops in global educ. (women, envir., food, militarism, etc.), facilitation, "popular" educ., organizational mgmt, media, etc., with schools, univ. students, professionals, svc. groups, community, prov. & nat'l organizations; work/study in: Mozambique (1989), China (1988), Guatemala (1992/93), El Salvador (1991/93), Nicaragua (1993), Mexico (1993/96); monitor, South African election, 1994. **COMMENT:** *"My interest and my work are directed toward redressing power imbalances, socially, economically and culturally, both at home and internationally. I work from a feminist analysis, which tries to be inclusive and consensual. Through KWIC, I have directed energy, support and skills to grassroots organizations (women, environment, peace, immigrants, food producers/consumers/retailers, and others) as a way of strengthening civil society and democracy. My achievements are but one part of a broad collective movement in grassroots organizing for change - change in community process, and in awareness of/commitment to social justice and peace. Regional, provincial, national and international associates are critical partners in the work of integrating local and global equity issues."*

Slawinski, Wanda, B.Sc.,F.L.M.I. ■■ $
Vice-President and Secretary, THE EMPIRE LIFE INSURANCE COMPANY (financial svcs), 259 King St. E., Kingston, ON K7L 3A8 (613) 548-1881, FAX 548-4104. Born Toronto. m. **EDUC:** Univ. of Toronto, B.Sc. 1964.

Sloot, Rosemary Alida Johanna, B.F.A., M.V.A.,B.E. ⊗ ⌖
Artist. London, ON. Born Simcoe, Ont. 1952. m. David Magee. **EDUC:** Humber Coll. of Applied Arts & Technology, Diploma in Painting 1974; Nova Scotia Coll. of Art & Design, B.F.A.(Painting) 1976; Univ. of Alberta, M.V.A.(Painting) 1978; Univ. of Western Ontario, B.E.(& O.T.C.) 1996. **CAREER:** teacher & coord., fine arts & film program for children, Lynnwood Arts Centre, Simcoe, Ont., 1976; supply teacher, Haldimand Norfolk Roman Catholic Sch. Bd. & Norfolk County Sch. Bd., 1978-79; sessional lecturer, Div. of Fine Arts, Lakehead Univ., 1981-84; painting & drawing instructor, London Regional Art Gallery, Fanshawe Coll., various art groups & galleries, London & area, Ont., 1985-94; sessional lecturer, spring intersession, Lakehead Univ., 1989, 1991, 1992, 1993; sabbatical replacement instructor, Wilfrid Laurier Univ., Fall 1991. **COMMISSIONS:** ceiling & wall murals, Children's Playroom, Pratten I, Children & Parents Resource Institute, London, Ont. **EXHIBITIONS:** solo, Norfolk General Hospital, Simcoe, Ont. (1977); solo, *Recent Paintings*, Nancy Poole's Studio, Toronto (1986); solo, *Definitely Superior*, Thunder Bay, Ont. (1993); solo, *Priority of Truth*, travelling exhibition, London Regional Art Gallery in collaboration with Kitchener-Waterloo Art Gallery, guest curator Sonya Halpern (1992); solo, *Anthrophy and Divinity*, Orchardside Gallery, St. Marys, Ont. (1995); 12 other solo exhibitions; group, *Young Contemporaries '78*, travelling exhibition, London Regional Art Gallery, London, Ont. (1978); group, *Australian Jesuit Mission in India*, St. Aloysius' Coll., Sydney, Australia (1981); group, *13 Women Artists from London, Ont.*, Premier's Office, Queen's Park, Toronto (1986); *Land Escapes*, London Regional Art & Historical Museums, London, Ont. (1995); numerous other group exhibitions. **COLLECTIONS:** Ivest Corp.; Canada Council Art Bank; Univ. of Alberta; VIA Rail Canada; Victoria Hospital, London, Ont.; various other corp. collections; private collections in Australia, Canada, UK, Germany, Japan, Netherlands, Nigeria, US. **AFFIL:** Visual Arts Ontario; Definitely Superior; Lynnwood Arts Centre; Thunder Bay Art Gallery; Amnesty International; Pollution Probe. **HONS:** Coll. Pin (highest academic standing in program), Humber Coll. of Applied Arts & Technology; Purchase Award, Annual Juried Exhibition, Lynnwood Arts Centre, Sim-

coe, Ont., 1982; Purchase Award, 40th Annual Western Exhibition, London Regional Art Gallery, 1987; Student Council Award for practice teaching excellence, Fac. of Educ., Univ. of Western Ontario. INTERESTS: travelling; reading; gardening; sewing/rug braiding; theatre; classical music; support a child in the third world. MISC: recipient, various grants from Canada Council & Ontario Arts Council; has visited USSR, Australia & Pacific Rim countries to study various types of art. COMMENT: *"Brown hair, grey blue eyes, 5'7, 116 lbs. Born 1952 in rural Ontario, two months after family arrived from Holland; five sisters, one brother. Professional Canadian artist. Painter. Also teacher, primarily university level."*

Smale, Joanne R., Muroff, B.A. 🖐

President, JOANNE SMALE PRODUCTIONS LIMITED (a film production co.), 51 Bulwer St., Main Level, Toronto, ON M5T 1A1 (416) 977-7118, FAX 977-8780. Vice-President, DARK LIGHT MUSIC LTD. Born Brooklyn, N.Y. 1949. EDUC: Univ. of Miami, B.A.(Psych.). CAREER: owner, Listening House Booking Agency, 1974-80; Pres., Joanne Smale Productions Limited, 1980 to date; associated with The Raleigh Group, Ltd, L.A.; production, publicity & promotion exec. working with a wide variety of people & projects, ranging from performers, cultural events, charities & benefits to industry conferences & awards. SELECTED CREDITS: *Tears Are Not Enough* launch gala, 1985; "Rekindle the Light" Festival, 1988; publicist, *Road Movies*, series, CBC TV; publicist, *In the Key of Oscar*, documentary, CBC TV, NFB & Elitha Peterson Productions Inc.; co-prod., *Mondo Moscow, The Un-Canadians*, TV documentaries; *The Juno Awards*; The Women's Television Network; clients include Caribana, Mariposa, The Women's Snooker Association of Canada, Ecofest, *Now Magazine, The Toronto Star*, The New Music Seminar (NY), EMI Music Canada, Molson Ontario Breweries Ltd., The Horseshoe, The El Mocambo, Shuffle Demons, Flying Bulgar Klezmer Band, Liona Boyd & many others; numerous other credits. AFFIL: VideoFact; Canadian Independent Recording Producers' Association (VP); International Federation of Festival Organizations; Canadian Women in Radio & Television; Toronto Women In Film & Television; Toronto Entertainment District Association. HONS: awarded 6 gold & 2 platinum albums for her work with Rough Trade, Murray McLauchlan & Bruce Cockburn.

Smalley, Katherine 💲 🖐 ⌣

President, ALLIED CORPORATE SERVICES INC., 368 Brunswick Ave., Toronto, ON M5R 2Y9

(416) 961-8907, FAX 324-8253. CAREER: independent film & TV producer; Pres., Allied Corporate Services Inc. SELECTED CREDITS: Prod., numerous programs, *Man Alive* (series), CBC;*So Many Miracles; All That Glistens; Pornography, The Double Message; A Glimpse of Heaven: Easter in the USSR.* HONS: Special Jury Award (*So Many Miracles*), San Francisco Film Festival; Gabriel Award (*So Many Miracles, A Glimpse of Heaven*); Gold Medal (*All That Glistens*), N.Y. Film Awards; Golden Eye Award (*Pornography, The Double Message*); Christopher Award (*Pornography, The Double Message*), Columbus Int'l Film Festival. COMMENT: *"Katherine Smalley is president of Allied Corporate Services Inc., a limited market dealer, licensed by the Ontario Securities Commission, specializing in investment banking and private-placement financing for national and international public and private companies."*

Smart, Joan, B.A.,LL.B. 💲 ✤ ⌐⍁

Vice-Chair, ONTARIO SECURITIES COMMISSION (prov. regulatory agency), 20 Queen St. W., 18th Flr., Toronto, ON M5H 3S8 (416) 593-3666, FAX 593-8241. Born Toronto 1952 1 ch. EDUC: Univ. of Western Ontario, B.A. 1974, LL.B. 1978. BAR: Ont., 1980. CAREER: Assoc., Harrison, Elwood; Assoc., McMillan Binch; Special Asst. to the Ont. Min. of Fin. Institutions & Consumer & Commercial Rel'ns, 1985-86; Policy Consultant, B.C. Securities Commission, 1986-88; Sr. Legal Cnsl, Capital Mkts Branch, OSC, 1988-89; Dir., Capital Mkts Branch, 1989-91; V-Chair, 1991 to date. AFFIL: Law Society of Upper Canada; Canadian Bar Association, Ontario (Exec. Committee, Bus. Law Section 1990-91).

Smart, Patricia, B.A.,M.A., Ph.D. ⍃ 🕮

Professor of French, CARLETON UNIVERSITY, Colonel By Dr., Ottawa, ON K1S 5B6, EMAIL psmart@ccs.carleton.ca. Born Toronto 1940. m. John Smart. 2 ch. Mary Ann, Michael. EDUC: Univ. of Toronto, B.A.(Modern Languages) 1961; Laval Univ., M.A.(French) 1963; Queen's Univ., Ph.D.(French) 1977. CAREER: Prof. of French, Que. Lit., Cdn Studies, Carleton Univ., 1971 to date; Distinguished Visiting Prof., Cdn Studies, Univ. of Alberta, 1981; Visiting Fellow, Cornell Univ., 1991. SELECTED PUBLICATIONS: *Hubert Aquin agent double* (1973); *Écrire dans la maison du Père: l'émergence du féminin dans la tradition littéraire au Québec* (1988); *Writing in the Fathers House: the emergence of the Feminine in the Quebec Literary Tradition* (1991); *The Diary of André Laurendeau*, transl. & ed. (1991); Ed., *Language, Culture and Values in*

Canada at the Dawn of the 21st Century (1996). **EDIT:** Ed. Bd., *The Canadian Forum*; Advisory Ed., *Dalhousie French Studies, Voix et Images: littérature québécoise*. **AFFIL:** Royal Society of Canada (Hon. Sec. & Fellow). **HONS:** Marion Porter Award for the best feminist article published in French, Canadian Research Institute for the Advancement of Women, 1986; Marston Lafrance Research Leave Fellowship, Carleton Univ., 1986-87; Gov. General's Award for Non-Fiction in French, 1988; Finalist, Gov. General's Award for Translation, 1991; Gabrielle Roy Prize for best work of criticism published in English, Association of Canadian & Quebec Literatures, 1991. **COMMENT:** *"My main interest, commitments and publications are in the area of Quebec and English Canadian literature and culture, in particular, women's contributions to them."*

Smiley, Alison, B.Sc.,M.A.Sc.,Ph.D. 🕸
President, HUMAN FACTORS NORTH INC., 118 Baldwin St., Toronto, ON M5T 1L6 (416) 596-1252. Born London, Ont. 1948. 2 ch. Christopher Shante-Smiley, Sarah Shante-Smiley. **EDUC:** Univ. of Western Ontario, B.Sc. (App. Math.) 1970; Univ. of Waterloo, M.A.Sc. (Systems Design Eng.) 1972, Ph.D.(Systems Design Eng.) 1978. **CAREER:** Research Officer I, National Research Council of Canada, 1972-74; Research Scientist, Southern California Research Institute, 1978-81; Design Eng., Ontario Hydro, 1981-82; Pres., Humanchine Incorporated, 1983-90; Pres., Human Factors North Inc., 1984 to date; Adjunct Prof., Dept. of Mech. & Industrial Eng. & Dept. of Chem. Eng., Univ. of Toronto. **SELECTED PUBLICATIONS:** "The Hinton Rail Crash" (*Accident Analysis and Prevention* 22(5) 1990); "Development of bilingual freeway exit signs," with R. Dewar, C. MacGregor *et al* (*Transportation Research Record,* 1456, 1994); *"Simulated driving performance in patients with obstructive sleep apnea,"* with C. George & A. Boudreau (*American Journal of Respiratory and Critical Care Medicine,* 154(1) July 1996) various other publications. **EDIT:** Ed., *Newsletter of the Human Factors Association of Canada,* 1973-77. **AFFIL:** Human Factors Association of Canada; Human Factors Society; US National Research Council (Chair, Vehicle User Characteristics Committee). **HONS:** Ont. Grad. Scholarship, 1966, 1975, 1976; National Research Council Scholarship, 1971; Univ. of Waterloo Bursary, 1976. **MISC:** expert witness on human factors issues in car accidents; consultant, traffic & public signing; Public Review Panel on Oil Tanker Safety, 1990; various conference presentations.

Smillie, Carol, R.N., B.Sc.N.,B.Ed., M.Sc. 🕸 ⊕
Associate Professor, School of Nursing, DALHOUSIE UNIVERSITY, 5869 University Ave., Halifax, NS B3H 3J5 (902) 494-2032, FAX 494-3487, EMAIL csmillie@kilcoml.ucis.dal.ca. Born Toronto 1935. m. Howard. 3 ch. Andrea, Nadine, Leticia. **EDUC:** Univ. of British Columbia, B.Sc.N 1958; Mount Saint Vincent Univ., B. Ed. 1971; Dalhousie Univ., M.Sc (Health Educ.) 1988; Ontario Institute for Studies in Education, doctoral studies in progress. **CAREER:** Gen. Duty Nurse, Vancouver General Hospital, 1957-58; Night Supervisor, 1958; Public Health Nurse, Metropolitan Health Dept., Vancouver, 1958-61; Gen. Duty & Relief Nurse, C.A.F. Base 4, Wing Baden, Soelingen, Germany, 1963-66; Staff Nurse, Victorian Order of Nurses, Dartmouth, 1966-68; Clinical Instructor, Grace Maternity Hospital, 1979; Clinical Instructor, Halifax Infirmary, 1981. **ACADEMIC CAREER:** Instructor, Mount Saint Vincent Univ., 1968-70; Instructor, Dalhousie Univ., 1972-75; Dir. of Nursing program, Mount Saint Vincent Univ., 1978-79; Asst. Prof., Dalhousie Univ., 1980; Consultant, Curriculum Evaluation, Hawkesbury Agricultural Coll. of Advanced Educ., Australia, 1987; Consultant, Lincoln Institute of Health Services, Australia, 1987; Guest Lecturer, Queensland Institute of Technology, Australia, 1987; Assoc. Prof., Dalhousie Univ., 1987 to date. **SELECTED PUBLICATIONS:** *Community Health Nursing in Canada* ed. with Stewart, Innes & Searle (Toronto: Gage Publishing Co., 1985); "Planning and Evaluation of Cross-Cultural Health Education Activities," with T. Nolde (*International Journal of Advanced Nursing* May 1987); "Primary Health Care Through a Community-Based Smoking Cessation Program," with K. Coffin, K. Porter & B. Ryan (*Journal of Community Health* Fall 1988); various other publications. **EDIT:** Ed. Bd., Canadian Public Health Association Journal, 1983-86, 1989. **AFFIL:** Registered Nurses' Association of N.S.; N.S. Div., Canadian Cancer Society (Pres.); Canadian Cancer Society (Bd. of Dir.); National Cancer Institute (Bd. of Dir.); Public Health Association of N.S. **MISC:** recipient, various grants; Canadian Volunteer Medal, 1996. **COMMENT:** *"I have interpreted my practice of nursing to focus on health education, program evaluation and health volunteering. A recognition of the power for good that is generated in our world by the act of volunteering to help your neighbour drives my practice, teaching and research activities."*

Smith, Angela, B.Comm. ■ ╱ 📖 💲
Publisher and Editor, *BUSINESS QUARTERLY,*

Richard Ivey School of Business, The University of Western Ontario, London, ON N6A 3K7 (519) 661-3309, FAX 661-3838, EMAIL bq@uwo.ca. Born Hamilton, Ont. **EDUC:** McMaster Univ., B.Comm.(Mktg & Acctg) 1984. **CAREER:** Davies Demonstrating Limited, 1984; Sr. Software Support Analyst, Union Gas Limited, 1985-88; Analyst, Advtg & Sales Promo., 1988-90; Mng Ed., *Business Quarterly*, 1990-95; Publisher & Ed., 1995 to date. **AFFIL:** Richard Ivey Sch. of Bus. Fac./Staff Social Committee (Past Chair); Canadian Magazine Publishers' Association; various charitable organizations. **HONS:** Mktg Achievement Award, American Gas Association, 1990; Print Advtg Award, American Gas Association, 1989; Comm. Award, Grand Prize, American Gas Association, 1989. **INTERESTS:** writing; photography; travel; cycling; skiing

Smith, C. Linda, B.A.A. ■ $

Senior Vice-President, Partner and General Manager, FLEISHMAN-HILLARD, 360 Bay St., Toronto, ON M5H 2V8 (416) 214-0701, FAX 214-0720. Born Montreal 1957. m. Robert White. 2 ch. **EDUC:** Ryerson Polytechnic Institute, B.A.A.(Journalism) 1981. **CAREER:** Reporter & Ed., *Broadcast News*, 1981-82; various positions to Sr. VP, Hill and Knowlton, 1982-93; Sr. VP & Gen. Mgr, Fleishman-Hillard, 1993 to date. **DIRECTOR:** Fleishman-Hillard Canada Inc. **AFFIL:** Planning Forum; Pharmaceutical Marketing Association of Ontario. **HONS:** John Hill Award for Excellence, 1989. **INTERESTS:** dogs; kids; tennis; skiing; running. **COMMENT:** *"Linda Smith is a career public relations professional. Her achievements include establishing a strong operation in Canada for the leading PR agency in the world, Fleishman-Hillard."*

Smith, Colleen, B.Comm.,M.B.A., C.G.A. 🎓

Director, Communications and Investor Relations, DOMINION TEXTILE INC., 1950 Sherbrooke W., Montreal, QC H3H 1E7 (514) 989-6012, FAX 989-6308. Born Montreal 1948. m. J. Thomson. 2 ch. Simon, Erika. **EDUC:** McGill Univ., B.Comm.(Fin./Mktg) 1977; York Univ., M.B.A.(Fin.) 1979; C.G.A. 1994. **CAREER:** Bus. Analyst, Canadian Pacific Ltd., 1980-84; Sr. Bus. Analyst, 1984-86; Mgr, Proj. Fin. Analysis, Dominion Textile Inc., 1986-91; Dir., Fin. Analysis & Strategic Planning, 1991-93; Dir., Comm. & Investor Rel'ns, 1993 to date. **AFFIL:** Canadian Investor Relations Institute; Jay Peak Ski Racing Sch.; Ordre des comptables généraux licenciés du Québec (C.G.A.). **INTERESTS:** skiing; golf; reading. **COMMENT:** *"Highly disciplined, organized and motivated; manage to strike perfect balance between career and family; went back to school at 44 to get an accounting designation; next career move: Vice-President."*

Smith, Corinne ■ ✎ 📺 $

Production Director, CANADA WIDE MAGAZINES LTD., 4180 Lougheed Highway, 4th Fl., Burnaby, BC V5A 6A7 (604) 299-7311, FAX 299-9188. Born Calgary 1957. s. **EDUC:** Alberta Coll. of Art, Dipl.(Visual Comm.) 1979. **CAREER:** owner & operator, The Banke Nightclub, Calgary, Alta.; Art Dir., Canada Wide Magazines Ltd.; Production Dir.; Session Instructor, Magazine Practicum, Kwantlen Coll., Richmond, B.C. **INTERESTS:** work-related educ.; travel; fitness; family; friends; continual professional growth & dev.

Smith, Cynthia M., B.A.,M.A.,B.L.S., M.L.S. 📖 🍁

Director, Legislative Research Service, ONTARIO LEGISLATIVE LIBRARY, 2520 Whitney Block, 99 Wellesley St. W., Toronto, ON M7A 1A2 (416) 325-3637, FAX 325-3696. Born Bracebridge, Ont. 1942. m. John T. McLeod. 2 ch. Andrew T. Price-Smith, Adrienne F. Price-Smith. **EDUC:** Univ. of Toronto, B.A.(Modern Hist.) 1964, M.A.(Cdn Hist.) 1966, B.L.S.(Library Info. Sci.) 1968, M.L.S.(Library Info. Sci.) 1979. **CAREER:** Archivist, Ont. Archives, 1965-67; Librarian, Trinity Coll. Library, 1976-77; Historian, Heritage Admin. Branch, Ont. Ministry of Culture & Recreation, 1977-78; Research Asst. for Prof. Kenneth Rea, Dept. of Pol. Economy, Univ. of Toronto, 1974-79; Head Librarian, Inco Metals Limited, Toronto, 1979-82; Dir. of Placement, Fac. of Library & Info. Sci., Univ. of Toronto, 1982-84; Co-Instructor, Grad. Course, 1982-85; Dir., Legislative Research Svc, Ont. Legislative Library, 1984 to date. **SELECTED PUBLICATIONS:** *Oxford Book of Canadian Political Anecdotes*, Assoc. Ed. with J.T. McLeod, Ed. (Toronto: Oxford Univ. Press, 1988); *The Anecdotal Life of Sir John A. Macdonald*, Ed. with J.T. McLeod (Toronto: Oxford Univ. Press, 1989); various short publications, articles in refereed & professional journals, articles & reviews. **AFFIL:** Institute of Public Administration, Canada; Univ. of Toronto Alumni Association (VP, Governance 1989-90; Pres. 1990-91); Univ. of Toronto (Coll. of Electors: mbr. 1987-90, Chair 1989-90; Academic Bd., Governing Council 1992-93; Univ. Affairs Bd., Governing Council 1991, 1993-95; Pres., FIS Alumni Association 1989-90; Co-Chair, FIS "Excellence 2000" fundraising campaign 1993-95); Special Libraries Association (Pres., Toronto Chapter 1984-85; Chair, Gov't Rel'ns 1985-

87); Chamber Players of Toronto (Bd. Mbr. 1977-89); Toronto Symphony (1974-75); Women's Musical Club of Toronto (Advisory Bd.); Toronto Symphony Junior Women's Committee (Chair 1974-75). HONS: Arbor Award for outstanding volunteer service, Univ. of Toronto, 1991; Jubilee Award for distinguished service to the library profession, Fac. of Info. Alumni Association, 1993. INTERESTS: writing; music; theatre; film; visual arts; tennis; cross-country skiing; fitness.

Smith, Deborah L. ☺ ✿ ⌘
International Representative, UNITED FOOD AND COMMERCIAL WORKERS INTERNATIONAL, 96 Norwood Ave., Ste. 306, Moncton, NB E1C 6L9 (506) 857-3226, FAX 858-7573. EDUC: Labour Coll. of Canada, Univ. of Ottawa, Certificate (Labour Studies) 1984. CAREER: employee & Union Steward, Halliday Craftsman, 1978-84; Bus. Rep., United Food & Commercial Workers Local 1973, 1984-85; Int'l Rep., United Food & Commercial Workers Int'l, 1985 to date. AFFIL: New Democratic Party of N.B.; New Democratic Party of Canada. INTERESTS: reading; horse-back riding; woodworking; antique reproduction of furniture. COMMENT: *"Have settled grievances, negotiated better working conditions and benefits, and organized workplaces. Seeing the positive difference that a union can make in people's lives has made me a believer. Knowing that I am helping workers and their families makes the time away from home worth the sacrifice."*

Smith, Frances K., B.A. ⊗ 🏛
Curator Emeritus, AGNES ETHERINGTON ART CENTRE, Queen's University, Kingston, ON K7L 3N6. Born Bolton, Lancs., UK 1913. m. Walter MacFarlane Smith. 2 ch. EDUC: London Sch. of Economics; Queen's Univ., B.A. CAREER: British Civil Service, various positions of admin. nature, particularly with Home Office during World War II (Civil Defence Precautions); employed at Agnes Etherington Art Centre, Queen's Univ., incl. Curator & Acting Dir. for 2 lengthy periods, 1955-79; Curator Emeritus, 1979 to date. SELECTED PUBLICATIONS: *André Bieler: An Artist's Life and Times*, biography (1980); numerous articles, reviews, exhibition catalogues; in-depth art studies of Cdn artists, notably Daniel Fowler, Fritz Brandtner, George Harlow White, & Kathleen Morris, in association with Agnes Etherington Art Centre; some poetry; currently writing various entries about Cdn artists for publication in *Allgemeines Kunster-lexicon* (Leipzig, SAUR). AFFIL: Canadian Museums Association; Ontario Museums Association;

Ontario Association of Art Galleries; Cataraqui Archaeological Research Foundation; MacLachlan Woodworking Museum, Pittsburgh Township; Canadian Club; Cataraqui Golf & Country Club. HONS: Award of Merit, Ontario Association of Art Galleries, 1980; Award of Merit, Canadian Museums Association, 1981; Distinguished Service Award, Queen's Univ. Council, 1987. INTERESTS: cultural & historical affairs; art history; local history; heritage preservation; writing; golf. COMMENT: *"I have been deeply involved with the visual arts, writing about Canadian artists and developing the role of the art gallery as a cultural focus for education and enjoyment."*

Smith, Janet Rosalea, B.Comm., Ph.D. ■ ✿
Principal, Canadian Centre for Management Development, GOVERNMENT OF CANADA, Canada Place, 9700 Jasper Ave., Ste. 1500, Edmonton, AB T5J 4H7 (403) 495-5772, FAX 954-1044. EDUC: Univ. of British Columbia, B.Comm. 1965; Univ. of California, Berkeley, Ph.D.(Bus. Admin) 1974. CAREER: Instructor/Asst. Prof., Dept. of Econ. & Commerce, Simon Fraser Univ., 1968-73; Coord., Office of Equal Opportunities for Women, Public Svc Commission, 1973-74; various positions, Anti-Inflation Bd., 1975-77; participant, National Defence Coll. of Canada, Kingston, Ont., 1977-78; Dir. Gen., Prices & Profits Branch, Anti-Inflation Bd., 1978-79; Dir. Gen, Monitoring, Nat'l Commission on Inflation, 1979; Policy Officer, Temporary Assignment Pool, Treasury Bd., 1979; Dir. of Oper., Econ. Policy, Privy Council Office, 1980-81; Asst. Sec. to the Cabinet, Econ. & Reg'l Dev. Policy, Privy Council Office, 1981-85; Assoc. Deputy Min., Dept. of Transport, 1985-86; Deputy Min., Office of Privatization & Regulatory Affairs, 1986-89; Exec. Dir., Royal Commission on Nat'l Passenger Transportation, 1989-93; Deputy Min., Consumer & Corp. Affairs, 1993; Deputy Min., Western Econ. Diversification, 1993-95; Principal, Cdn Centre for Mgmt Dev., 1995 to date. HONS: Univ. of California Fellowship, 1965; Charles Kofoid Eugenics Fellowship, 1966-67; Ernst and Ernst Travelling Fellowship, 1970; Data Processing Management Association Fellowship, 1971.

Smith, Jennifer, B.A.,M.A.,Ph.D. ⌘ ✿ 🏛
Associate Professor, DALHOUSIE UNIVERSITY, Halifax, NS B3A 4H6 (902) 494-6606, FAX 494-3825. Born Sudbury, Ont. 1950. m. Denis Stairs. EDUC: McMaster Univ., B.A.(Pol. Sci.) 1972; Dalhousie Univ., M.A.(Pol. Sci.) 1975, Ph.D.(Pol. Sci.) 1981. CAREER: Lecturer, Acadia Univ., 1978-80; Lecturer, Dalhousie Univ.,

1980-81; Asst. Prof., 1981-89; Deputy Chair, Fed. Electoral Boundaries Commission, Prov. of N.S., 1986-87; Assoc. Prof., Dalhousie Univ., 1989 to date; research, Royal Commission on Electoral Reform & Party Financing, 1989-90; Commissioner, Prov. Electoral Boundaries Commission, 1991-92; Chair, Advisory Committee on the Division of Powers & Gov't Institutions, Prov. of N.S., 1991. SELECTED PUBLICATIONS: "Representation and Constitutional Reform in Canada," *After Meech Lake: Lessons for the Future*, J. Courtney et al (Saskatoon: Fifth House, 1991); "The Franchise and Theories of Representative Government," *Democratic Rights and Electoral Reform in Canada*, ed. Michael Cassidy, Vol. 10 for the research studies of the Royal Commission on Electoral Reform & Party Financing (Dundurn Press, 1991); "Should Legislatures Legislate?," *Liberal Democracy in Canada and the United States*, ed. T.C. Pocklington (Peterborough: Broadview Press, 1994); "The Unsolvable Constitutional Crisis," *New Trends in Canadian Federalism*, eds. Miriam Smith & Francois Rocher (Peterborough: Broadview Press, 1995). AFFIL: Canadian Political Science Association. INTERESTS: tennis; gardening; sailing. COMMENT: *"I am an academic and therefore follow the old directive to pursue truth, in my case via the study and teaching of government and politics."*

Smith, Lynn, B.A.,LL.B.,Q.C. 🔱 ⌖

Professor and Dean, Faculty of Law, UNIVERSITY OF BRITISH COLUMBIA, 1822 East Mall, Vancouver, BC V6T 1Z1 (604) 822-2818, EMAIL lsmith@law.ubc.ca. Born Calgary. m. Jon Sigurdson. 2 ch. EDUC: Univ. of Calgary, B.A.(Phil.) 1967; Univ. of British Columbia, LL.B. 1973. BAR: B.C., 1974. CAREER: Clerk, Chief Justice of B.C., 1973-74; Articled Clerk, Shrum, Liddle and Hebenton, 1973-74; Assoc., 1974-79; Ptnr, 1979-81; Assoc. Prof., Univ. of British Columbia, 1981-90; Prof., 1990 to date; Dean, Fac. of Law, 1991 to date. SELECTED PUBLICATIONS: Ed.-in-Chief, *Righting the Balance: Canada's New Equality Rights* (Saskatoon: Canadian Human Rights Reporter, 1986); *Civil Jury Instructions*, with J.C. Bouck (Vancouver: Continuing Legal Education Society, 1989; Annual Supplements 1990-95); *A Feminist Guide to the Canadian Constitution*, with Eleanor Wachtel (Ottawa: Canadian Advisory Council on the Status of Women, 1992); numerous articles & chapters in books, incl. "The Legal Profession and Women: Finding Articles in British Columbia," with Marylee Stephenson & Gina Quijiano (*University of British Columbia Law Review* 1973); "An Equality Approach to Reproductive Choice: R.

v. Sullivan" (*Yale Journal of Law and Feminism* 1991); "Have the Equality Rights Made Any Difference?" (*Protecting Rights and Freedoms*, ed. Philip Bryden et al, Toronto: Univ. of Toronto Press, 1994, pp. 60-89); "The Equality Rights," with William Black, *Canadian Charter of Rights and Freedoms*, eds. Gerard Beaudoin & Errol Mendes (Toronto: Carswell, 1996); various factums, case comments, conference papers, reports of committees, review commentaries & teaching materials. AFFIL: Law Society of B.C.; Canadian Bar Association; Canadian Association of Law Teachers; Vancouver Institute (Dir.); B.C. Women's Hospital & Health Centre (Dir.); Law Foundation of B.C. (Chair); National Forum on Health; National Judicial Institute (Dir.). HONS: numerous scholarships as undergrad. & law student; Women of Distinction Award, Comm. & Public Affairs, YWCA, 1990; Queen's Counsel, Prov. of B.C., 1992. MISC: Chair, Working Committee on New Employee Organization in Health System, appointed by Min. of Health & Korbin Commission, 1992-93; Moderator, Women's Health Conference, Ministry of Health, 1993; consultation in judicial educ. programs, 1993 to date; numerous principal lectures, conference presentations, visits, judicial educ. presentations, lectures to professional groups, & panel discussions; recipient, various research grants.

Smith, Marva J., B.A.,L.L.B., L.L.M. 🔱

Counsel, Constitutional Law Branch, MANITOBA JUSTICE, 405 Broadway, Ste. 7, Winnipeg, MB R3C 3L6 (204) 945-1951, FAX 945-0053. Born 1949. m. 2 ch. EDUC: Univ. of Winnipeg, B.A.(Soc.) 1970; Univ. of Manitoba, LL.B. 1976; London Sch. of Econ. & Pol. Sci., Univ. of London, LL.M.(Labour & Company Law) 1977. BAR: Man., 1978. CAREER: children's librarian, River Heights Public Library, 1971-73; articled under Mel Myers Q.C., Swark, Myers, Winnipeg, 1977-78; Lawyer, Skwark, Myers, 1978-83; Asst. Prof., Fac. of Law, Univ. of Manitoba, 1981-83; Consultant on labour law, Man. Labour, Gov't of Man., Winnipeg, 1983-86; Cnsl, Man. Justice, Constitutional Law Branch, Winnipeg, 1986 to date. AFFIL: Canadian Bar Association (Exec. Mbr. at Large, Nat'l Constitutional & Human Rights Section); Manitoba Bar Association (Council; Equality Issues Section). HONS: Student of Distinction, Univ. of Winnipeg, 1970; Univ. Gold Medal in Law, Univ. of Manitoba, 1976; Hon. Alexander Morris Exhibition Scroll, Univ. of Manitoba, 1976; Margaret Hypathia Crawford Scholarship, Univ. of Manitoba, 1976; numerous other awards during law sch.; Canada Council Doctoral Fellowship, 1976-77; Mark of Distinction, Univ. of London, 1977. **MISC:** mbr., Manitoba Justice Lawyers' Working Group on Gender Equality, 1994.

Smith, Nancy ■ 🗳 ✏ 📖 ☝
President, NEXTMEDIA (media agency), 205 Richmond St. W., Ste. 402, Toronto, ON M5V 1V3 (416) 971-9973, FAX (416) 971-4828, EMAIL nextmedi@inforamp.net. Born Toronto 1949. m. Jeffrey Marshall. 2 ch. Jarett Smith, Crystal Smith. **EDUC:** York Univ. **CAREER:** teacher, high sch. & community coll.; writer & journalist for various magazines, incl. *Strategy*, *Playback*, *Image*, etc.; speaker, conferences, industrial associations, women's groups; Dir., Corp. Comm., Citytv/MuchMusic/Musique Plus, 1978-86; VP, Comm. Mktg, Global Television Network, 1986-93; Pres., "Tellevision," Women's Speciality Application. **SELECTED CREDITS:** Exec. Prod, *Women in the 90s*; consultant, video *Exercise Your Options*. **SELECTED PUBLICATIONS:** writer for various industry publications incl. *Playback*, *Strategy*, *Marketing Magazine*. **AFFIL:** Women in Film & Television (Bd.); Women in Capital Markets (Advisory Council); Canadian Film Centre (Advisory Council); Ryerson Polytechnic Univ. (Advisory Council); Brewers of Ontario (Chair, Gender Committee); Canadian Women in Communications (founder). **HONS:** Canpro Scroll of Honour; Broadcaster of the Year Award; Award of Excellence, Canadian Association of Journalists; Women of Distinction, YWCA; Astral Award of Excellence. **INTERESTS:** hiking; reading; writing; being with family & friends; travelling the globe. **MISC:** int'l broadcast consultant; teacher, Ryerson RTA Program. **COMMENT:** *"I left school at 16–went to university as an adult while building a career and raising two children as a single parent. First woman in 39 years to win Broadcaster of the Year award. I left a high profile broadcasting position to create my own media business,which is now billing over several million per year after only 3 years. Great transition lifestyle change."*

Smith, Nancy L., B.A.,M.B.A. $
Treasurer, PETRO-CANADA, 150 - 6th Ave. S.W., 28th Fl. W., Calgary, AB T2P 3E3 (403) 296-7960, FAX 296-7907. Born Sask. 1962. m. J.C. MacGillivray. 1 ch. Jane. **EDUC:** Univ. of Alberta, B.A.(Econ.) 1983, M.B.A.(Fin.) 1985. **CAREER:** commercial bnkg, Toronto-Dominion Bank, 1985-86; corp. bnkg, Bank of Montreal, 1987-90; Treas., Petro-Canada, 1990 to date. **DIRECTOR:** Oil Investment Corporation Ltd. **AFFIL:** United Way Campaign (Corp. Fund Raising). **INTERESTS:** sports; reading; travel.

Smith, Phyllis, B.A.,LL.B.,LL.M. ■■ ⚖ ♡
Partner, EMERY JAMIESON (law firm), Edmonton Centre, 1700 Oxford Tower, Edmonton, AB T5J 3G1 (403) 426-5220, FAX 420-6277. Born Ponoka, Alta. 1947. m. Patrick Smith. 3 ch. Morgan, Meredith, Michael. **EDUC:** Univ. of Toronto, B.A.(Hons., Pol. Sci. & Econ.) 1968; Univ. of Alberta, LL.B. 1974; Harvard Univ., LL.M. 1976. **CAREER:** Articling Student, Emery Jamieson, 1974-75; law, City Solicitor's Office, City of Edmonton, 1976-80; Assoc., Emery Jamieson, 1980-82; Ptnr, 1982 to date; Sessional Lecturer, Univ. of Alberta Law Sch., 1978-82, 1983-86 & 1994 to date. **AFFIL:** Law Society of Alberta (mbr.; Pres. 1991-92; Insur. Committee); Federation of Law Societies (Dir.; Pres. 1994-95); Canadian Lawyers' Insurance Association (Advisory Bd. - V-Chair 1994 to date; Chair, Claims Admin. Committee 1989 to date); American Coll. of Trial Lawyers (Fellow); Edmonton Bar Association; Canadian Bar Association. **HONS:** Distinguished Svc. Award, Edmonton Bar Association, 1993. **MISC:** involved over the years in numerous continuing educ. programs as instructor, incl. Canadian Bar Association, Legal Education Society of Alberta, Canadian Association of Members of Public Utility Tribunals, Canadian Institute for the Administration of Justice, Canadian Appraisal Institute, Alberta chpt.; mbr., Mgmt Committee, Emery Jamieson. **COMMENT:** *"I have had the good fortune of having developed a successful litigation practice with the support of my family and my colleagues. I have always considered it important to make whatever contribution I can to my profession and the community (while my focus today is on my profession, in the past I spent 10 years as a director of a non-profit community daycare, and six years as a director of the Alberta Cancer Board)."*

Smith, Rosalind, D.E.C.,B.Sc., M.H.Sc. ■■ ⊕ ⚛ ✊
District Manager, Institutional Health Group, Ministry of Health, GOVERNMENT OF ONTARIO (health care, hospital admin.), 5700 Yonge St., 4th Fl., North York, ON M2M 4K5 (416) 327-7296, FAX 327-4697, EMAIL smithro@health.moh.gov.on.ca. Born Montreal. s. **EDUC:** Vanier Coll., Montreal, D.E.C.(Health Sciences) 1976; Concordia Univ., B.Sc.(Biological Sciences) 1979; Univ. of Toronto, M.H.Sc.(Health Admin.) 1982. **CAREER:** Exec. Asst., Centenary Health Centre, Scarborough, Ont., 1983-86; Dir. of Strategic Planning, 1986-89; Hospital Consultant, Institutional Health Group, Ont. Ministry of Health, 1989-93; District Mgr, Institutional Health Group, 1993 to date. **AFFIL:** Ontario March of Dimes

(Bd. Dir.; Chair, Communications Committee); United Church of Canada (Nat'l Anti-Racism Task Group); Black Professionals Reaching Out (former Dir.); Flemingdon Health Centre (former Bd. mbr.). INTERESTS: playing tennis; writing poetry for special events; quilt making; sewing; out-of-country travel. MISC: former tutor & mentor with North York Bd. of Educ., African Heritage Educ. Ntwk; former volunteer, Each 1 Teach 1, Toronto East Women's Business and Professional Club. COMMENT: *"A health care executive who has worked with a number of communities–Hamilton, Guelph, Halton, Brant–restructuring the local health care system. Her community involvement relates primarily to anti-racism and volunteer development."*

Smithies, Marney ■ ■ ⓛ
Paralympic Athlete. Burnaby, BC. CAREER: Admin. Asst. SPORTS CAREER: mbr., Nat'l Wheelchair Basketball Team, 6 yrs. Paralympic Games: Gold, 1996; 4th, 1998. Canadian Wheelchair Basketball League (CWBL): 3rd, Women's Finals, 1996. Stoke Mandeville World Games: 1st, 1991.

Smith-Palmer, Truis, B.Sc.,M.Sc., Ph.D. ⓢ ⚙
Associate Professor of Chemistry, ST. FRANCIS XAVIER UNIVERSITY, Box 5000, Antigonish, NS B2G 2W5 (902) 867-2270, FAX 867-5153, EMAIL tsmithpa@juliet.stfx.ca. Born Sydney, Australia 1952. m. Howard Swaine. 2 ch. Suzanne, Ronald. EDUC: Auckland Univ., B.Sc.(Chem.) 1974, M.Sc.(Chem.) 1975, Ph.D. (Chem.) 1977. CAREER: Postdoctoral Fellow, Harvard Univ., 1977-78; Visiting Fellow, National Research Council, Halifax, 1978-80; Analytical Chemist, St. Francis Xavier Univ., 1980 to date; sabbatical, Univ. of Kentucky, 1991-92. SELECTED PUBLICATIONS: "The Effects of Cationic Polymers on Flocculation of a Coal Thickener Feed in Washery Water as a Function of pH," with C.W. Angle & B.R. Wentzell (*Journal of Applied Polymeric Science*, 1996); "Flocculation Behaviour of some Cationic Polyelectrolytes," with N. Campbell, J.L. Bowman & P. Dewar (*Journal of Applied Polymetric Science* 52 1994); "Fiber Optic Sensor for Ca2+ Based on an Induced Change in the Conformation of the Protein Calmodulin," with T.L. Blair, S.T. Yang & L.G. Bachas (*Analytic Chemistry* 66 1994); various other publications. AFFIL: Chemical Institute of Canada; Atlantic Provinces Council on the Sciences (Scribe, Chem. Committee). INTERESTS: outdoor activities with my family. MISC: recipient, various grants. COMMENT: *"As a chemistry professor, I carry out my chosen research and hope to inspire my chemistry students and children with a similar love of chemistry."*

Smith-Sauvé, Deborah, B.A. ■ ⚚ ⊗
Coordinator of Development, McCORD MUSEUM OF CANADIAN HISTORY, 690 Sherbrooke St. W., Montreal, QC H3A 1E9 (514) 398-7100, FAX 398-5045. Born Ottawa 1957. EDUC: Univ. of Ottawa, B.A.(Visual Arts) 1979. CAREER: Documentation Centre Coord., Slide Librarian, Indian & Northern Affairs, Canada, 1979-86; Gov't Liaison Officer, Avataq Cultural Institute, 1987; Coord. of Dev., McCord Museum of Canadian History, 1987 to date. SELECTED PUBLICATIONS: "Ottawa Collections Move North: Transfer of Artworks from Indian and Northern Affairs Collection to Avataq," with M. Craig (*MUSE* Summer 1990); Ed., *Development Opportunities for Native Professionals* (Ottawa: Canadian Museum Assembly/Association of First Nations Task Force, 1992). AFFIL: Native Arts Studies Association of Canada (Dir., E. Canada; Exec. Committee); Canadian Museum Association; Morgan Arboretum, McGill Univ. (Dev. Committe); Ste.-Anne-Bout-de-L'Île Historical Society. INTERESTS: community proj. mgmt; local & nat'l history; fed. & mun. politics; First Nations history & culture. MISC: frequent guest speaker, moderator & panelist; mbr., Canadian Museum Association/Assembly of First Nations Fed. Task Force mandated to develop guidelines on repatriation, access to museum collections & interpretation of aboriginal culture/history, 1990-92; mbr., selection committee representing Avataq Cultural Institute during disbanding & transfer of the Dept. of Indian & Northern Affairs' Inuit art collections, 1990; recipient, professional dev. bursaries from Ministère des Affaires culturelles, Québec & Banff Centre for Management, 1992. COMMENT: *"Active support of just causes, involved in municipal and federal projects, committed to projects and programs that ensure a better quality of life for everyone."*

Smits, Sonja ⊗ ⚘ ⓦ
Actor. c/o Great North Artists Management, 350 Dupont St., Toronto, ON M5R 1V9 (416) 925-2051. Born Sudbury, Ont. 1958. m. Seaton McLean. 2 ch. Avalon Saskia, Lian Michael. EDUC: Ryerson Polytechnic Univ., Acting Program 1974. SELECTED CREDITS: Co-Star, *Videodrome* (feature), Filmplan Int'l.; Lead, *That's My Baby* (feature), Gemini Films; Morag, *The Diviners* (telefilm), based on the novel by Margaret Laurence, Atlantis/CBC; Carrie, *Street Legal* (series), CBC, 6 yrs.; Sally, *Traders* (series), Global/Can West, 2 yrs.; Anna, *Nothing Sacred* (theatre), Wintergarden,

Toronto; Alma, *Summer in Smoke* (theatre), Theatre Calgary; Yelena, *Uncle Vanya* (theatre), Theatre Calgary; Helena, *A Midsummer Night's Dream* (theatre), Manitoba Theatre Centre. **AFFIL:** SAG; CAEA; ACTRA (Founding Mbr. of the ACTRA Women's Caucus). **HONS:** nomination, Best Performance by an Actress in a Leading Role in a Dramatic Program or Mini-Series (Morag, *The Diviners*), Gemini Awards, 1994; Blizzard Award for Best Actress in a Leading Role (Morag, *The Diviners*), 1994; nomination, Best Performance by an Actress in a Continuing Leading Dramatic Role (Carrie, *Street Legal*), Gemini Awards, 1993; Best Performance by a Lead Actress in a Dramatic Program or Mini-Series (Carrie, *Street Legal*), Gemini Awards, 1988; nomination, Best Performance by a Lead Actress (*War Brides*), ACTRA Awards; nomination, Best Performance by a Supporting Actress (*Videodrome*), Genie Awards, 1984; nomination, Best Performance by a Lead Actress (*That's My Baby*), Genie Awards, 1985.

Snee, Betty-Ann, R.N.A. ⊕ O

Past President & Executive Director, Pro-family Legal Defense, ALBERTA FEDERATION OF WOMEN UNITED FOR FAMILIES (AFWUF), 61 Princeton Cres. W., Lethbridge, AB T1K 4S5 (403) 381-1760, FAX 381-2957. Born Timmins, Ont. 1946. m. 6 ch. Lisa, Jennie, Alan, Kerri-Beth, Kyle, Caleb. **EDUC:** Scarborough General Hospital, R.N.A.; Small Bus. Admin. Dipl. 1996. **CAREER:** Sec. & Membership Chrm, Alberta Federation of Women United for Families, 1984-86; Treas., 1986-87; Pres., 1988-89 & 1993-94; Exec. Dir., Pro-family Legal Defense, 1994-97. **SELECTED PUBLICATIONS:** Publisher, *Reality* (newsletter of Real Women of Canada), 1992 to date; ed., *AFWUF Voice* (newsletter of Alberta Federation of Women United for Families), 1984-86. **AFFIL:** Canadian Health Care Guild; Real Women of Canada (Alberta Dir. 1987 to date); Univ. of Lethbridge (Early Childhood Svcs Bd.); The Church of Latter Day Saints; La Leche League of Canada (Lethbridge Leader 1970s-80s). **HONS:** Community Service Award, Alberta Federation of Women United for Families. **INTERESTS:** piano; alto saxophone; directing choral groups; desktop publishing, networking with other professionals who are involved politically. **COMMENT:** *"The most important thing in my life is my family. Lobbying for policies on the family and helping families to become strong is my goal. Motto: 'Strengthen the family, strengthen the nation'."*

Snell, Linda, M.D. ⊗ ⊕

Associate Dean, Continuing Medical Educa-

tion, MCGILL UNIVERSITY, Royal Victoria Hospital, 687 Pine Ave. W., A4.21, Montreal, QC H3A 1A1 (514) 843-1515, FAX 843-1676. **CAREER:** Assoc. Dean, Continuing Medical Educ., McGill Univ.; Dir., Div. of Gen. Internal Medicine, McGill Univ. **AFFIL:** Canadian Society of Internal Medicine (Pres. 1993-95).

Snider, Carol, B.B.A.,M.B.A., C.A. ■ $ ⌂

Senior Vice-President, Personal and Commercial Financial Services, BANK OF MONTREAL, 5151 George St., 15th Fl., Halifax, NS B3J 3C4 (902) 421-3403, FAX 421-3404. Born Toronto 1951. m. John. 2 ch. **EDUC:** York Univ., B.B.A. 1973, M.B.A. 1980; C.A.. **CAREER:** Acctg Fac., Commerce Dept., Univ. of Toronto, 1979-82; Sr. Mgr, Nat'l Acctg Standards Dept., Clarkson Gordon, 1982-84; Fin. Div., Bank of Montreal, 1984-92; VP, Community Bnkg, 1992-94; Sr. VP, Personal & Commercial Svc, 1994 to date. **AFFIL:** Atlantic Economic Council (Bd. of Gov.); Institute of Chartered Accountants of Ontario); Institute of Chartered Accountants of N.S.; "Our People Fund" Bank of Montreal Employee Fundraising Charity (Chair 1993-95); Junior Achievement of Metropolitan Toronto & York Region (Dir. 1993-95). **MISC:** 1st woman to hold the post of a div. Sr. VP at Bank of Montreal.

Soave, Luciana, B.A. ■■ O

General Director, QUÉBEC MULTI-ETHNIC ASSOCIATION FOR THE INTEGRATION OF HANDICAPPED PEOPLE, 6462, boul. St-Laurent, Montréal, QC H2S 3C4 (514) 272-0680, FAX 272-8530. Born Italy 1940. m. Silvio Caddeo. 2 ch. Ingrid Caddeo, Keven Caddeo. **EDUC:** Concordia Univ., B.A.(Psych.) 1984; Univ. de Montréal, Diploma 2nd cycle (Social Admin.) 1996. **SELECTED PUBLICATIONS:** L. Soave *et al*, *Adaptation and social integration of persons with disabilities from different cultural communities*, 1986; L. Soave *et al*, *Family and ethnocultural persons with disabilities*, 1994; L. Soave *et al*, *Intégration des élèves handicapées issus des différentes communautés culturelles* (brief), 1995. **AFFIL:** ACCESSS, Alliance des communautés culturelles pour l'égalité en santé et services sociaux (founding mbr.; Chair of the Bd.); Spina Bifida & Hydrocephalus Association of Quebec (founding mbr.; Pres.); Régie Régionale de la santé et des services sociaux de Montréal Centre (Dir.). **HONS:** Life Style Awards, Health & Welfare Canada, 1985; Citation for Citizenship, Sec. of State, 1988. **COMMENT:** *"Originally a very shy, insecure person, I have discovered and put into action my strengths. I have developed leadership and the capacity to help others."*

Soetaert, Colleen, B.Ed.,M.L.A. ✦
Member of Legislative Assembly (Spruce Grove-Sturgeon-St. Albert), Opposition Critic for Community Development and Women's Issues, GOVERNMENT OF ALBERTA, 420 King St., Ste. 24, Spruce Grove, AB T7X 2C6 (403) 962-6606/458-1393, FAX 962-1568. Born 1956. m. Raymond. 4 ch. EDUC: Univ. of Alberta, B.Ed., Secondary English dipl. CAREER: Teacher, Sturgeon Heights Sch.; Teacher, St. Albert, primary & elementary educ.; Teacher, Sturgeon Composite High Sch.; M.L.A., 1993 to date; Alberta Liberal Caucus Critic Responsible for Community Dev. & Women's Issues. AFFIL: Pastoral Council, St. Peters Villeneuve; Youth Group (Leader); Catholic Women's League (Pres.); Villeneuve Athletic Association; 4-H Club; Liberal Party of Alberta; Alberta Liberal Caucus Outreach (Chair). INTERESTS: fastball; St. Peter's Church Choir.

Sokolyk, Oksana T. (nee Bryzhun), ARCT ■■ ⊕ ⬥ ✎
President, WORLD FEDERATION OF UKRAINIAN WOMEN'S ORGANIZATIONS (umbrella organization uniting 22 women's organizations on 4 continents), 2336 Bloor St. W., P.O. Box 84578, Toronto, ON M6S 1T0 (416) 603-4299, FAX 536-0592. Born Humenne, Czechoslovakia (now Slovak Republic) 1927. m. Yaroslav. 2 ch. Wsevolod-Konstantin Ihor. EDUC: Handel Conservatorium, Munich, Piano 1946-48; Royal Conservatory of Music, Toronto, ARCT (Piano) 1950, ARCT (Vocal) 1958; Univ. of Toronto, Fac. of Music, Teacher's Diploma (Piano) 1955. CAREER: private piano studio, 1950-88; piano teacher, St. Michael's Choir Sch., Toronto, 1966; freelance reporter, CBC Radio Canada International, 1974. SELECTED CREDITS: co-prod., LP of the works of M. Fomenko. SELECTED PUBLICATIONS: author, over 500 articles on a wide variety of subjects in 2 languages; concert reviews; co-publisher, *Voschad* (by F. Odrach, 1972). AFFIL: Ontario Registered Music Teachers' Association (mbr., 1960 to date; mbr. of Exec. 1975-77; Pres., Central Toronto branch 1979-82; mbr., Prov. Council 1985-88; Chair, "Canada Music Week" 1985-88; Rep. to the Committee "International Year of Canada Music" 1985-88); Ukrainian Catholic Women's League of Canada (mbr. 1958 to date); World Federation of Ukrainian Women's Organizations, WFUWO (Chair, Educ. Committee 1981-87; VP 1987-92; mbr. of Exec., World Congress of Free Ukrainians (WCFU) 1988-93; Chair, Decade of Ukrainian Family (WFUWO & WCFU) 1985-90; Pres. 1992 to date; VP, Ukrainian World Coordinating Council 1992 to date; President's (Ukrainaine) 1932-33 Ukrainian Famine Remembrance Committee 1992-93; 2nd VP, Ukrainian World Congress (UWC, formerly WCFU) 1993 to date); International Society for Music Education (former mbr.). HONS: 2nd Prize, XIII WFUFO literary competition, 1972; Prov. of Ont. plaque recognizing outstanding contribution to the Cdn Ukrainian community in Ont., 1982; Metropolitan Sheptytsky Award (Ukraine) for community & educational work in the Diaspora, & for assisting the consolidation of the Ukrainian nation, 1993; recognized by Ukrainian Embassy in Canada for assistance to Ukraine, 1994. INTERESTS: gardening; reading; embroidering; opera; concerts; theatre. MISC: speaker on a variety of issues. COMMENT: *"Oksana Sokolyk is a teacher and community volunteer who became involved in community work at the grassroots level. She currently heads up an international women's organization with membership on four continents. In this capacity, she has global responsibility and was recently a delegate at the UN Women's Conference in Beijing. Her position has provided her with opportunities to meet with and work with a wide cross-section of community leaders—from missionary nuns in South America to President and Mrs. Kuchma of Ukraine."*

Soldan, Heather Jean (Heather Jean Glebe), B.Ed. ■ ⬥⊗ ⬥
Writer, Editor and Music Teacher. P.O. Box 29, Two Hills, AB T0B 4K0 (403) 657-2700. Born Edmonton 1946. m. Allan. EDUC: Univ. of Victoria, B.Ed.(Art/Hist.) 1971. CAREER: Teacher, Merritt & Penticton Districts, B.C., & Two Hills, Alta.; Reporter, Photographer & Ed., *Penticon Herald*; Writer & Ed.; part-time Music Teacher, Two Hills High Sch. SELECTED PUBLICATIONS: numerous articles in periodicals, 1975-90; *All Things Considered* (Martin Park, 1989); *Now That's an Egg! The Story of the Vegreville Pysanka* (Vegreville Chamber of Commerce, 1991); *Alberta Guide to Wild Fur Management* (Alberta Dept. of Fish & Wildlife); *Pens in Motion Anthology* ed. (1986); *Pulse to Pen, Remembering When* ed. (1992). AFFIL: Alberta Society of Fiddlers (Reg'l Dir. 1993-96); Federation of B.C. Writers (Reg'l Rep. for Okanagan 1986-88; VP 1988-89; Pres. 1989-90); Okanagan Summer Sch. of the Arts (Bd. 1989-90); Okanagan Writers' League (Founding Pres. 1984-90). INTERESTS: music (violin & piano); teaching violin; farm work. MISC: Founder/Dir. of "Fiddlin' Kiddlins." COMMENT: *"I remarried in 1992 after coming to Alberta from the Okanagan for a 'temporary' job as an editor. I am less involved in writing now, but more in music."*

Solowan, Barbara ⊗ ✦

Art Director, BERLIN STUDIO INC., Nine Ellis Park Rd., Toronto, ON M6S 2V1 (416) 604-2920, FAX 604-7080. Born Hamilton, Ont. EDUC: Ontario Coll. of Art, Diploma (Comm. & Design) 1974. CAREER: Art Dir., *City Woman* Magazine, 1982-85; Art Dir., *Cosmetics Magazine*, 1985-86; Art Dir., *Toronto Magazine*, 1985-87; Design Dir., *Chicago Magazine*, 1987-88; Art Dir., Berlin Studio Inc., 1987 to date; Art Dir., *Toronto Life* 'Homes', 1988-90; Art Dir., *City & Country Home*, 1991-94; Art Dir., *Active Magazine*, 1993-94. AFFIL: Advertising & Design Club of Canada (Bd. 1993-95). HONS: 1 Gold & 3 Silver Awards for Art Dir., National Magazine Awards; Gold Awards for Magazine Design, Art Directors' Club of Toronto; The White Award, 1988; Festival of Fashion Arts Award, 1986. MISC: travel, architecture, gardening, teaching, painting. COMMENT: *"In my professional career I have moved from magazines to studio to advertising and now back to magazines. This has given me the invaluable experience of working with editors, writers, photographers, illustrators, ad directors, account executives, production managers, as well as outside suppliers."*

Solvason-Wiebe, Ishbel ⊕ ○ ⧖

Executive Director, ELIZABETH FRY SOCIETY OF OTTAWA, 195A Bank St, Ottawa, ON K2P 1W7 (613) 238-1171, FAX 238-2873. 4 ch. (2 dec.) Catherine Ishbel Solvason, Kristin Heather Solvason, Colin Scott Solvason (1974-1987), Kenneth William Solvason (1980-1987). CAREER: Community Dev. Officer, John Howard Society of Manitoba, 1980-86; Exec. Dir., John Howard Society of Brandon, 1986-90; Reg'l Dir., Canadian Mental Health Association of S.W. Manitoba, 1990-91; Dir., Fergusson House, Elizabeth Fry Society of Ottawa, 1991-93; Exec. Dir., Elizabeth Fry Society of Ottawa, 1993 to date. SELECTED PUBLICATIONS: various written submissions to governments incl. Gov't of Canada, Panel on Violence Against Women; published poet. AFFIL: Judicial Council of Ontario (appointed as Lay Mbr. by an order in council, Feb. 1995 for a 6-yr. term); Ontario Half-Way House Association (Exec. Mbr.). HONS: YMCA Woman of the Year Nominee, 1988. MISC: est. the 1st Social Assistance Advisory Committee, Brandon, Man., 1986-88; frequent speaker & extensive program dev.

Soly, Geneviève, D.Mus. ■■ ⊗

Directrice artistique et générale (Artistic Director), LES IDÉES HEUREUSES (baroque music society), 3575 Saint-Laurent Blvd., Ste. 488, Montréal, QC H2X 2T7 (514) 843-5881, FAX 843-7091. Born Montreal 1957. m. Jean Letarte. 2 ch. Armnaud, Matthias. EDUC: Conservatoire de musique de Montréal, Organ (first prize) 1976; Univ. de Montréal, D.Mus.(interprètation harpsichord) 1992; private lessons with Kenneth Gilbert, Gustav Leonhardt (harpsichord), Marie-Claire Alain (organ); int'l summer academies in France, Austria, Italy, Belgium & Holland. CAREER: musician, contract with Analekta label - 6 CDs to date; recitalist (organ & harpsichord), baroque repertoire - over 200 solo recitals, half of them recorded for CBC/SRC; teacher, Centre musical CAMMAC, 1976-96 & Coll. Marie de France, 1982-96; founder, Artistic & Gen. Dir., Les Idées heureuses - producer of over 50 programs & more than 100 concerts, 1987 to date. AFFIL: Conseil Québécois de la Musique (Adm.). HONS: First Prize, John Robb Organ Competition, Royal Canadian Coll. of Organists, 1975; First Prize, unanimous, organ, Conservatoire de Musique de Montréal, 1976; Second Prize, Paul Hofhaimer Competition, Innsbruck, Austria, 1979. Scholarships: Canada Arts Council, 1977, 1978, 1979; Ministère des affaires culturelles du Québec, 1980; FCAR, 1990, 1991, 1992. INTERESTS: studies in general; arts in general; literature (esp. contemporary & XIXth-century French); museums; travel; wines & cheeses; swimming; flowers. MISC: Les Idées heureuses has received grants from Montreal Arts Council, Conseil des arts et des lettres du Québec, & Conseil des arts du Canada (Canada Arts Council). COMMENT: *"Very active, versatile (soloist and chamber music player, teacher with a very good sense of pedagogy, organist and harpsichordist, administrator), honest and rigorous, hard worker (but not workaholic). I am proud of my company, Les Idées heureuses, which is well-recognized among people in Quebec."*

Solymoss, Susan, B.Sc.,M.D.C.M., F.R.C.P.C. ⊕ ❀

Assistant Physician, Department of Medicine, MONTREAL GENERAL HOSPITAL, 1650 Cedar Ave., Montreal, QC H3G 1A4. Born 1954. EDUC: McGill Univ. Coll. Equivalent Program, Diploma of Collegiate Studies 1974; McGill Univ., B.Sc. 1977, M.D.C.M. 1981. CAREER: Straight Medical Intern, Montreal General Hospital, 1981-82; Resident in Internal Medicine, 1982-84; Resident in Hematology, McGill Univ. Hospitals, 1984-86; Fellow in Lab. Medicine, Hemostasis, Medical Center Hospital of Vermont, Univ. of Vermont, 1986-88; Asst. Prof. of Medicine, Depts. of Medicine & Oncology, McGill Univ., 1988-92; Asst. Physician, Depts. of Medicine & Laboratories, St. Mary's Hospital Centre, 1988 to date; Asst.

Physician, Dept. of Medicine, Royal Victoria Hospital (affiliate), 1988 to date; Asst. Physician, Dept. of Medicine, Montreal General Hospital, 1992 to date; Dir., Hematology Lab., St. Mary's Hospital Centre, 1993 to date. SELECTED PUBLICATIONS: numerous abstracts, incl. "Effect of aspirin intake on perioperative blood loss in prostatic surgery" with J. Caro (*Clin and Inv Med* 9 1986); "High dose etoposide and cyclophosphamide as cytoreductive therapy in refractory/relapsed lymphomas and leukemias- an update of 46 patients" with others (*Blood* 82 1993); various articles, incl. "Intravenous immunoglobulin therapy for refractory chronic idiopathic thrombocytopenic purpura" with others (*Canadian Medical Association Journal* 136 1987); "Les anticoagulants endogènes" (*L'Actualité Médicale* 13 1992); "Venous ischemia in skin flaps: Microcirculatory intravascular thrombosis" with others (*Plast Reconstructive Surgery* 93 1994). AFFIL: Quebec Medical Association; Royal Coll. of Physicians & Surgeons of Canada (Fellow in Internal Medicine 1985; Fellow in Hematology 1987); Canadian Society of Hematology; American Society of Hematology; American Heart Association: Council on Thrombosis. MISC: LMCC, 1981; Certificate of the National Board of Medical Examiners, 1982; Diplomate of Internal Medicine, American Board of Internal Medicine, 1984; Certificate of Internal Medicine, Que., 1985; Certificate of Hematology, Que., 1986; Diplomate in Hematology, American Board of Internal Medicine, 1986.

Sombrowski, Ingrid ⓢ
Co-Founder and Co-Head, SOMBROWSKI GROUP OF COMPANIES, P.O. Box 2560, Fernie, BC V0B 1M0 (604) 423-6008, FAX 423-7664. Born Paderborn, Germany 1940. m. Gotthardt Sombrowski. 3 ch. CAREER: Co-Founder and Co-Head, Sombrowski Group of Companies. VOLUNTEER CAREER: Co-Founder & Co-Head, Sombrowski Group of Companies. AFFIL: Chamber of Commerce; Downtown Revite Committee; Merchants' Association. INTERESTS: family; arts; interior decoration. COMMENT: *"Co-founder and co-head of the Sombrowski Group of Companies, primarily involved as head of financial affairs for a diverse group of businesses, including ventures in real estate, retail and hospitality."*

Somerville, Margaret Anne Ganley,
A.M.,F.R.S.C.,A.u.A.(pharm),LL.B.,
D.C.L.,LL.D. ■ ⚖ ⊕ ♂
MCGILL CENTRE FOR MEDICINE, ETHICS AND LAW, 3690 Peel St., Montreal, QC H3A 1W9 (514) 398-7401, FAX 398-4668. Born Adelaide, Australia. d. EDUC: Univ. of Adelaide,

A.u.A.(Pharm.) 1963; Univ. of Sydney, LL.B. 1973; McGill Univ., D.C.L.(Comparative Law) 1978. BAR: New South Wales, Australia, 1975; Que., 1982. CAREER: Registered Pharmacist, Birks Chemist Pty. Ltd., Adelaide, 1963-66; Locum tenens pharmacist, various pharmacies in Adelaide, rural South Australia & Melbourne, 1966-68; Locum tenens pharmacist, N.Z., 1969; Sci. teacher, Southland Boys' High Sch., Invercargill, N.Z.; Locum tenens pharmacist, Sydney, 1970-73; Messrs. Stephen, Jaques, Stone, James (now Mallesons), Sydney, Australia, 1974-75; Consultant, Law Reform Commission of Canada, 1976-86; Teaching Fellow, Fac. of Law, McGill Univ., 1976-77; Asst. Prof., Fac. of Law, Institute of Comparative Law, 1978; Assoc. Mbr., Dept. of Humanities & Social Studies in Medicine, Fac. of Medicine, 1979; Assoc. Prof., Fac. of Law, Institute of Comparative Law, 1979-84; Assoc. Prof., Dept. of Humanities & Social Studies in Medicine, Fac. of Medicine, 1980-84; Prof., Fac. of Law, Institute of Comparative Law, 1984 to date; Prof., Fac. of Medicine, 1984 to date; Medical Scientist, Dept. of Medicine, & Mbr., Research Institute, Royal Victoria Hospital, Montreal, 1985 to date; Founding Dir., McGill Centre for Medicine, Ethics & Law, 1986-95; Brockington Visitor, Queen's Univ., 1988-89; Gale Prof. of Law, Fac. of Law, McGill Univ., 1989 to date; Assoc. Mbr., McGill AIDS Centre, 1990; Assoc., Grad. Program in Comm., McGill Univ., 1993. SELECTED PUBLICATIONS: "Labels versus Contents: Variance between Philosophy, Psychiatry and Law in Concepts Governing Decision-Making" (*McGill Law Journal* 39(1) 1994); "Stigmatization, Scapegoating and Discrimination in Sexually Transmitted Diseases: Overcoming 'Them' and 'Us', " with N. Gilmore(*Social Science & Medicine* 39(9) 1994); "'Death Talk' in Canada: The Rodriguez Case" (*McGill Law Journal* 39(3) 1994); numerous other publications. EDIT: Contributing Ed., *Health Law in Canada*, 1979-87; Int'l Advisory Bd., *Bioethics Reporter*, 1983 to date; Int'l Advisor, *Medical Humanities Review*, 1987 to date; Advisory Ed., *Social Sciences and Medicine*, 1988-96; Ed. Bd., 1988-96; Ed. Bd., *Kennedy Institute of Ethics Journal*, 1990 to date; Int'l Review Essay Ed., *Journal of Law, Medicine & Ethics*, 1991 to date; Ed. Bd., *Health and Human Rights*, 1993 to date; Ed. Bd., *Ecosystem Health and Medicine*, 1993 to date. AFFIL: American Society for Pharmacy Law; Values Group, McGill Univ.; American Society of Law, Medicine & Ethics (Bd. of Dir.; Sec. 1992-93); Association Henri Capitant; Canadian Bar Association; Advisory Committee to the CBA Task Force on Health

Care; Canadian Pharmaceutical Association; World Association for Medical Law; Canadian Law Teachers' Association; Society for Health & Human Values; International Academy of Comparative Law; World Association of Law Professors of the World Peace Through Law Center; McGill Study Group for Peace & Disarmament; International Law Association; International Work Group on Death, Dying & Bereavement; World Jurist Association, Washington, DC (Mbr. of Council); National Research Council of Canada (Chair, Ethics Committee for Human Subject Research 1991 to date); Expert Advisory Committee on fate of stored serum samples, Canadian Red Cross Society (Chair); Task Force on Pain in AIDS, International Association for the Study of Pain; Royal Society of Canada (Fellow); Canadian Centre for Drug-Free Sport (Bd. of Dir.); National Institute on Mental Retardation, Toronto (Assoc.); Institute of Society, Ethics & the Life Sciences, The Hastings Center, Hastings-on-Hudson, NY (Int'l Fellow); Centro Studi e Ricerche Sui Problemi Etici Giuridici e Medicolegali Relativi All'AIDS, Milan, Italy (Int'l Advisory Bd.); Royal Victoria Hospital (Clinical Ethics Committee 1980-95); Montreal Association for the Intellectually Handicapped (Hon. Patron). **HONS:** Univ. of Sydney Medal, 1973; Women Lawyers' Association of New South Wales Prize, 1973; Canadian Commonwealth Scholarship & Fellowship Plan Grant, 1975; Joseph Dainow Prize, McGill Univ., 1976; Distinguished Service Award, American Society of Law & Medicine, 1985; Pax Orbis ex Jure, Gold Medal, Associates of the World Peace Through Law Center, Washington, DC, 1985; Mbr., Order of Australia, 1990; Woman of the Year Award, Zonta Club of Charlottetown, 1994; LL.D.(Hon.), Univ. of Windsor, 1992; LL.D.(Hon.), Macquarie Univ., Sydney, 1993; numerous other academic distinctions, scholarships, prizes & honours. **MISC:** 1st woman in Canada to hold a named chair in law; Co-Chair, First Int'l Conference on Health Law & Ethics in a Global Community, Sydney, 1986; listed in numerous biographical sources, incl. *Canadian Who's Who, International Who's Who of Intellectuals & Who's Who in Australia*; Registered Pharmacist, South Australia, Victoria, N.Z., New South Wales; reviewer, various journals & granting agencies; numerous consultancies; recipient, numerous grants; frequent guest lecturer, public speaker & participant in media; numerous conference presentations.

Sonberg, Melissa, B.Sc., M.H.A. $

Director, Customer Service Communication, Employee Involvement and Training, AIR CANADA, 14000, Saint-Laurent, QC H4Y 1H4 (514) 422-5681, FAX 422-6055. Born Montreal 1960. m. Ron Wigdor. 1 ch. Yalia Lindsay Wigdor. **EDUC:** McGill Univ., B.Sc.(Psych.) 1982; Univ. of Ottawa, M.H.A. 1984. **CAREER:** Coord., Hum. Res. Svcs, Montreal Neurological Hospital, 1984-86; Mgr, Educ. & Dev., Royal Victoria Hospital, 1986-90; Asst. Dir., Hum. Res., 1990-91; Lecturer, Hum. Res. Mgmt, McGill Univ., 1990 to date; Mgr, Employee & Organization Dev., Air Canada, 1991-93; Mgr, Corp. Educ. & Quality Dev., 1993-94; Dir., Customer Svc Comm., Employee Involvement & Training, 1994 to date. **AFFIL:** Auberge Shalom Pour Femmes (VP, Exec. Committee).

Songhurst, Ruth, B.A. ☼ $

President (and owner), MORTICE KERN SYSTEMS INC., 185 Columbia St. W., Waterloo, ON N2L 5Z5 (519) 883-4361, FAX 884-8861, EMAIL ruth@mks.com. Born Ingersoll, Ont. 1948. s. 2 ch. Harold Songhurst Soulis, Nicky Songhurst Soulis. **EDUC:** Univ. of Guelph, B.A.(Hist./Pol. Sci.). **CAREER:** Public Interest Group, Univ. of Waterloo, 1979-81; Coord., Institute for Computer Research, 1981-85; VP, Sales & Mktg, Mortice Kern Systems Inc., 1985-94; Pres., 1994 to date; owner. **INTERESTS:** travel; fitness; cottage; swimming; literature.

Sorensen, Linda ⊗ ⌣ ♥

Actor. c/o Oscars and Abrams, 59 Berkeley St., Toronto, ON M5A 2W5 (416) 860-1790, FAX 860-0236. **EDUC:** New York Univ., Sch. of Commerce, Retailing & Merchandising; American Conservatory Theater, San Francisco, 1968. **CAREER:** Buyer, T. Eaton Co.; Fashion Coord., Saba Bros., Vancouver; actor & writer. **SELECTED CREDITS:** *Native Strangers* (feature), USA Network; *Up To Now* (feature), Lifetime Channel; *Adventures in Baby-Sitting* (feature), Touchstone Films; *Joshua Then and Now* (feature), 20th Century Fox; *Draw!* (feature), First Choice; *McCabe and Mrs. Miller* (feature), Warner Bros.; Guest Star, *Robocop* (series), syndicated; Guest Star, *Murphy Brown* (series), CBS; Guest Star, *Road to Avonlea* (series), Disney Channel; Series Regular, *Material World* (series), CBC; Principal, *Miles From Nowhere* (telefilm), New World TV; Guest Star, *Street Legal* (series), CBC; Guest Star, *Our Man Flint* (series), ABC; Principal, *Family Reunion* (telefilm), CBC; Helen Hanf, *84 Charring Cross Road* (theatre), Centaur Theatre; Florence Unger, *The Odd Couple* (theatre), Stage West; Miss Lizzie, *Blood Relations* (theatre), MTC. **AFFIL:** AFTRA; SAG; Equity; ACTRA. **HONS:** nominated, Best Guest Performance in a Series ("Strictly Melodrama,"

Road to Avonlea), Gemini Award, 1995; Best Supporting Actress in a Feature Film (*Joshua Then and Now*), Genie Award, 1986; Best Supporting Actress in a Feature Film (*Draw!*), Genie Award, 1985; Best Writing for a Children's Film (*Christmas Lace*), Chris Award, 1979; Silver Award, Best Production, Children's Category (*Christmas Lace*), N.Y. Film Festival, 1979. **MISC:** presently attending UCLA.

South, Valerie, R.N. ■ ⊕ 📖 ○
Freelance Medical Writer and Lecturer. 120 Evans Ave., Etobicoke, ON M8Z 1H9 (416) 251-3501, FAX 251-9238, EMAIL valsouth@ aol.com. Co-ordinator, WORLD HEADACHE ALLIANCE. Born Toronto 1962. m. Robert South. 2 ch. **EDUC:** George Brown Coll., R.N. 1984. **CAREER:** Exec. Dir., The Migraine Foundation, 1991-93; Dir., Comm., 1994; freelance medical writer/lecturer, 1994 to date; Coord., World Headache Alliance, 1996 to date. **SELECTED PUBLICATIONS:** *Migraine* (Key Porter Books, 1994). **COMMENT:** *"Working in health care and later specializing in the field of migraine has allowed me to continue to fulfill my commitment to help others improve their total health, thereby achieving greater quality of life."*

Sparling, Mary, B.A.,B.Ed.,M.A., D.F.A. ⊗ 🐿 ✿
Cultural Executive, 6030 Jubilee Rd, Halifax, NS B3H 2E4. Part-Owner, VENTURE HYDRAULIC LTD. Born Collingwood, Ont. 1928. w. 2 ch. Margaret Dafoe, John Sparling. **EDUC:** Queen's Univ., B.A.(Pol./Econ.) 1949; Saint Mary's Univ., B.Ed. 1970; Dalhousie Univ., 1978. **CAREER:** high sch. teacher, Que., Ont. & N.B., 1961-68; Curator of Educ., Nova Scotia Museum, 1968-73; Dir., Art Gallery, Mount Saint Vincent Univ., 1973-94. **EXHIBITIONS:** organizer, *Africville: A Spirit That Lives On*, MSVU Art Gallery, toured nationally; organizer, *Terra Firma: Five Immigrant Artists in Nova Scotia*, MSVU Art Gallery (1993); organizer, *In Transit: Pier 21*, Halifax, Nova Scotia, MSVU Art Gallery (1994); during 21 yrs. with Mount Saint Vincent Univ. Art Gallery, organized approx. 500 exhibitions & associated programming, with emphasis on work by & about women, craft, work from indigenous peoples, & work from & about the region. **AFFIL:** Canadian Museums Association; Canadian Eskimo Arts Council; N.S. Coalition on Arts & Culture (Founding Mbr.); Neptune Theatre (Dir.); Pier 21 Society (Dir.). **HONS:** Queen's Silver Jubilee Medal, 1977; Woman of Distinction Award, Halifax Progress Club, 1990; Outstanding Cultural Exec.

Award, Cultural Federations of N.S., 1991; Warner-Lambert Award for Distinguished Arts Admin. in Canada, 1993; D.F.A.(Hon.), Nova Scotia Coll. of Art & Design, 1994. **COMMENT:** *"I believe that a strong presence of the artist and the arts is a fundamental necessity for a healthy, entrepreneurial, prosperous country, one that is respected at home and abroad."*

Sparling, Sharon, B.A.,M.A. 📖
Writer. Born Montreal 1951. m. Robert Graham. 3 ch. Morgannis, Max, Hadley. **EDUC:** McGill Univ., B.A. 1974; Concordia Univ., M.A. 1984. **CAREER:** Writer. **SELECTED PUBLICATIONS:** *The Glass Mountain* (1985); *The Nest Egg* (1991); *Homing Instinct* (1993). **HONS:** Author's Award for Magazine Fiction, 1983.

Speak, Dorothy, B.A.,M.A. ■ 📖
Writer. Born Seaforth, Ont. 1950. m. Paul LaBarge. 2 ch. Monica, Emily. **EDUC:** McMaster Univ., B.A.(English & Fine Art) 1973; Carleton Univ., M.A.(Cdn Studies) 1975. **CAREER:** Curator, Picture Div., Public Archives of Canada, 1973-75; Researcher & Curator, Inuit Art, Fed. Dept. of Indian & Northern Affairs, 1975-80; Instructor, Art Hist. Dept., Univ. of Calgary, 1980-82; Assoc. Curator, Glenbow Museum, 1980-83; Ed., Canadian Museums Corporation, 1983-84; Instructor, Creative Writing, Carleton Univ., 1983-86; freelance journalist, 1980 to date; freelance ed., 1981-96. **SELECTED PUBLICATIONS:** *Object of Your Love* (Somerville House, 1996); *The Counsel of the Moon* (Random House Canada, 1990); numerous short stories, incl. "Relatives in Florida" (*Journey Prize Anthology*, McClelland and Stewart, 1994); "Living with Women" (*The Fiddlehead* no.158 1988); "Tube" (*Room of One's Own* no.3 1987); "Homefree" (*Grain* no.1 1985); "Cracker Jack" (*Dandelion* no.2 1981); numerous non-fiction articles, incl. "Inuit Art: A Regional Perspective" (*Inuit Art Quarterly* Fall 1994); "Caryn Nuttall: New Paintings" (*Canadian Art* Fall 1987); "Picture Books Celebrate Obscure Canadian Art" (*Calgary Herald* Dec. 18, 1992); "Fine Art Printmaking" (*Interface* Apr. 1982); "Corporate Collections: Art and the Office Wall" (*Interface* Nov. 1981); *From Drawing to Print: Perception and Process in Cape Dorset Art* (exhibition catalogue) (Glenbow Museum, 1986). **AFFIL:** Rideau Tennis & Squash Club; Writers' Union of Canada. **INTERESTS:** tennis; skiing; jogging; travel. **COMMENT:** *"I am a full-time writer engaged in the creation of literary fiction. My stories have been published in Canadian and American literary magazines. My story collections include,* The Counsel of the Moon, *1990 and* Object of

Your Love, 1996. I am presently writing a novel."

Spencer, Elizabeth, A.B.,M.A., LL.D. 📖📗⊘

Writer. 402 Longleaf Dr., Chapel Hill, NC 27514 (919) 929-2115. Born Carrollton, Miss. 1921. m. John Rusher. EDUC: Belhaven Coll., Jackson, Miss., A.B.(English) 1942; Vanderbilt Univ., M.A.(English) 1943. CAREER: Instructor in English, Northwest Jr. Coll., Senatobia, MS, 1943-44; Instructor in English, Ward-Belmont Sch., Nashville, 1944-45; Reporter, *Nashville Tennessean*, 1945-46; Instructor in English, Univ. of Mississippi, 1948-53; Visiting Prof., then writer-in-residence, Writing Program, Concordia Univ., 1976-81; Adjunct Prof., 1981-86; Visiting Prof., Univ. of North Carolina, 1986-92. SELECTED PUBLICATIONS: *Fire in the Morning* (1948); *The Voice at the Back Door* (1956); *The Light in the Piazza* (1960); *Knights & Dragons* (1965); *Ship Island and Other Stories*, collection (1968); *The Snare* (1972); *The Salt Line* (1984); *For Lease or Sale*, drama (1989); *The Night Travellers* (1991); various other novels & short story collections; short stories published in various magazines incl. *The New Yorker*, *McCall's* & *Chatelaine*; articles & criticism for *The New York Times*, *The Washington Post* & others. AFFIL: American Academy of Arts & Letters; Fellowship of Southern Writers (Charter Mbr., V-Chancellor 1993 to date). HONS: Recognition Award, American Academy of Arts & Letters, 1952; Guggenheim Foundation Fellowship, 1953; Kenyon Review Fiction Fellowship, 1956-57; 1st Rosenthal Award, American Academy of Arts & Letters, 1957; McGraw-Hill Fiction Fellowship, 1960; Donnelly Fellowship, Bryn-Mawr Coll., 1962; Bellaman Award, 1968; National Endowment for the Arts Fellowship, 1983; Award of Merit Medal for the Short Story, American Academy of Arts & Letters, 1983; National Endowment for the Arts Sr. Fellowship in Lit. Grant, 1988; Salem Award for Distinction in Letters, Salem Coll., 1992; John Dos Passos Award for Lit., 1992; North Carolina Governor's Award for Lit., 1994; LL.D.(Hon.), Southwestern Univ. (now Rhodes), Memphis; D.L.(Hon.), Concordia Univ., 1988; Univ. of the South, Sewanee, Tenn., LL.D.(Hon.) 1992. COMMENT: *"Brought up in a pleasant home environment in Mississippi, I began to write by using Southern themes, characters and landscapes. Later, a writing fellowship enabled me to go to Italy, where I met my husband, John Rusher, an Englishman with Canadian connections. We came to Canada in 1958 and lived in Montreal for the next 28 years. I began there to write fic-* tion centred out of the South, and have so continued through a total output of nine novels and three volumes of short stories."

Spencer, Mary Eileen Stapleton, A.A.,B.A., M.Sc.,Ph.D. 🐿️ ⚘ ⊕

University Professor, Department of Agriculture, Food and Nutritional Science, UNIVERSITY OF ALBERTA, Edmonton, AB T6G 2P5 (403) 492-3843 (a.m.), 492-4265, EMAIL h.horvath@afns.ualberta.ca. President, ROOTRAINERS CORPORATION. Born Regina 1923. m. Henry A. Spencer. 1 ch. Susan Mary McLean. EDUC: Regina Coll., A.A.(Chem.) 1942; Univ. of Saskatchewan, B.A.(Chem.) 1945; Bryn Mawr Coll., M.Sc.(Chem.) 1946; Univ. of California, Berkeley, Ph.D.(Agricultural Chem.) 1951. CAREER: Chemist, Ayerst, McKenna & Harrison, Montreal, Summer 1945, 1946-47; Chemist, National Canners' Association, San Francisco, 1948-49; Lecturer, Univ. of California, Berkeley, 1951-53; Asst. Prof., then Assoc. Prof., then Acting Head, Dept. of Biochem., Univ. of Alberta, 1953-62; Assoc. Prof., Dept. of Plant Sci., 1963-64; Prof., 1964-83; Univ. Prof., 1984 to date; Emeritus, Dept. of Agric., Food & Nutritional Sci., 1990 to date. SELECTED PUBLICATIONS: "Methods for quantification of ethylene produced by plants," in *Modern Methods of Plant Analysis*, New Series, vol. 9, *Cases in Plant and Microbiology Cells* ed. by H.F. Linskens & J.F. Jackson (Berlin, Heidelberg: Springer-Verlage, 1989); "Effect of 2,4-dichlorophenoxyacetic Acid on Endogenous Cyanide, ß-cyanoalanin Synthase Activity and Ethylene Evolution in Seedlings of Soybeans and Barley" (*Plant Physiology*, 1990); "Ethylene Production during Degreening of Maturing Seeds of Mustard and Canola," with A.M. Johnson-Flanagan (*Plant Physiology* 106 1994); over 100 other publications; more than 100 published abstracts. EDIT: Ed. Bd., *Plant Physiology*, 1984-87. DIRECTOR: Spencer-Lemaire Industries Ltd. AFFIL: Canadian Society of Plant Physiologists; American Society of Plant Physiologists; Chemical Institute of Canada; Plant Growth Regulator Society of America; International Plant Growth Regulator Society; Canadian Federation of Biological Societies. HONS: Fellow, Chemical Institute of Canada; Fellow, Royal Society of Canada; Queen's Silver Jubilee Medal, 1977; Gold Medal, Canadian Society of Plant Physiologists, 1990; Canada 125 Medal, 1992. MISC: mbr., Premier's Council on Science & Technology, Prov. of Alta., 1990-93; Council Mbr., National Research Council of Canada, 1970-76; Council Mbr., Natural Sciences & Engineering Research Council of Canada, 1986-92; mbr., Bd. of Gov., Univ. of Alberta, 1976-79;

recipient, various fellowships; with Thérèse Decane, was one of 1st two women to be appointed to the National Research Council of Canada. COMMENT: *"Major research interest is in plant biochemistry, with emphasis on ethylene analysis and metabolism and alternative mechanisms of respiration."*

Spencer, Sally ■ ■ ○

Executive Director, YOUTH ASSISTING YOUTH (non-profit charity, serving children aged 6-15), 3080 Yonge St., Ste. 4080, Toronto, ON M4N 3N1 (416) 932-1919, FAX 932-1924. Born England 1956. partner. Barry Moffatt. EDUC: Centennial Coll., Social Svc. diploma (Social Work) 1976. CAREER: Youth Counsellor, Welfare Visitors, 1977-82; PT Passenger Svc. Rep., Wardair, 1981-87; Association for Community Living, 1983-88; Exec. Dir., Youth Assisting Youth, 1988 to date. AFFIL: Association for Community Living; Canadian Society of Association Executives. INTERESTS: sailing; horseback riding; running. MISC: has a hobby farm. COMMENT: *"I was born in England and immigrated with my family in 1968. We settled in Orillia, where I lived until moving to Toronto to attend school. I put myself through school driving heavy construction equipment and tractor trailers. In 1994 my partner and I designed and built a 3,000 square foot log home on our property in Sunderland, Ontario. We support health and nutrition by growing and selling organic vegetables and eggs from our free-range chickens."*

Spicer, Kathleen (Kay), B.Sc.HomeEc., M.A. ✎ ⊕ ☒

Author, Food Consultant, KAY SPICER & ASSOCIATES INC., 190 Meadowland Cres., Box 399, Campbellville, ON L0P 1B0 (905) 854-1251, FAX 854-1251. Born Hafford, Sask. 1932. m. James Mighton. 3 ch. EDUC: Univ. of Saskatchewan, B.Sc.Home Ec. 1953; Univ. of Western Ontario, M.A.(Journalism) 1987. CAREER: professional home economist, 1953 to date; food & mktg consultant; cookbook author; publisher; Principal, Kay Spicer & Associates, Inc., 1983 to date. SELECTED PUBLICATIONS: *Choice Cooking*, with Cathy Patterson & Judi Kingri, for Canadian Diabetes Association (NC Press, 1982); *Light & Easy Choices* (Grosvenor House Press, 1985); *The Gourmet Barbecue*, by Pip Bloomfield & Annie Mehra (Key Porter Books, 1986); *Light & Easy Choice Desserts* (Grosvenor House Press, 1986); *From Mom, With Love–Real Home Cooking* (Doubleday, 1990); *Kay's Basic Cooking*, series handbook (TVOntario, 1991); *Light & Easy Choices and Desserts* (Mighton House, 1992); *Full of Beans*, with Violet Currie

(Mighton House, 1993); *MultiCultural Cooking–Light & Easy* (Mighton House, 1995); food features & recipes have appeared in *Canadian Living, Chatelaine, You/Verve, Recipes Only, Select Homes and Food, Discovery, Good Times* & various newspapers. AFFIL: Canadian Home Economics Association; Home Economists in Business (Past Pres.); Ontario Home Economics Association; Toronto Home Economics Association (Past Pres.); Professional Writers' Association of Canada; University Women's Club; International Association of Culinary Professionals; ACTRA; Anglican Church Women; Campbellville Working At Home Club. INTERESTS: gardening. MISC: writer, prod., presenter, Kitchen Update, 12 TV segments & 24 radio spots, Canadian Metric Commission & NFB (1983); Kay's Basic Cooking, series, TVOntario (1991). COMMENT: *"Kay Spicer is a home economist, food consultant and journalist well known in Canada for her newspaper and magazine articles and public, radio and television presentations on good food and healthy eating. Her company specializes in projects focusing on good tasting, healthy food."*

Spies, Nancy J., LL.B. ⚖

Barrister, STOCKWOOD, SPIES, The Sun Life Tower, 150 King St. W., Ste. 2512, Toronto, ON M5H 1J9 (416) 593-7200, FAX 593-9345. Born Brockville, Ont. 1954. m. Raymond Martin. 3 ch. Melissa, Bryce, Cara. EDUC: Queen's Univ., Fac. of Law, LL.B. 1978. BAR: Ont., 1980. CAREER: Law Clerk to the Chief Justice of the High Court of Ont., 1980-81; association with David Stockwood, Q.C., 1981-82; Ptnr, Stockwood, Spies, 1982 to date. SELECTED PUBLICATIONS: Ed., *Commercial Litigation Quarterly*, Federated Press. AFFIL: Canadian Bar Association; County of York Law Association; County of York Women's Law Association; The Advocates' Society (Dir. 1990-93); The Private Court; Law Society of Upper Canada; Certified Specialist in Civil Litigation. HONS: Second Prize Law Society Award, 1980. INTERESTS: water gardening; sailing; skiing. MISC: various papers given for the Law Society of Upper Canada, Canadian Bar Association; instructor, Ontario Centre for Advocacy Training. COMMENT: *"I am a senior partner in the law firm of Stockwood, Spies and the mother of three children. My practice is focused on commercial and administrative litigation."*

Sprachman, Carol, B.A. ■ ■ ○ 📖

National Director, CANADIAN FEDERATION OF FRIENDS OF MUSEUMS (registered charitable organization), c/o Art Gallery of Ontario, 317

Dundas St. W., Toronto, ON M5T 1G4 (416) 979-6650, FAX 979-6666. Born Toronto 1930. m. Mandel Sprachman. 4 ch. Ben, Robert, Andrew, Barney. EDUC: Oberlin Coll., Oberlin, OH, B.A.(English Lit.) 1952. CAREER: Production Asst./Production Editor, *Canadian Homes & Gardens* Magazine, Maclean Hunter, after grad. VOLUNTEER CAREER: joined Jr. Women's Committee, Art Gallery of Ontario, 1960; Chrm, 1964; Chrm, Volunteer Committee, 1977-79; founding mbr., Canadian Federation of Friends of Museums (CFFM), 1977; mbr., inaugural Advisory Bd., Toronto Sculpture Garden, 1981-84; Pres., CFFM, 1986-95; Art Gallery of Ontario (Bd. of Trustees 1977-85). HONS: Commemorative Medal for the 125th Anniversary of the Confederation of Canada, 1993; award for outstanding contributions to the advancement of museums in Canada, Canadian Museums Association, 1995. MISC: instigated "Significant Treasures" series in *The Globe and Mail.* COMMENT: *"My personal goals are to promote interest in museums which are, in my view, an underutilized and underrecognized educational resource; to raise the profile of Friends and Volunteers within the museum community; to become fluently bilingual."*

Springer, Helen Jean, B.Sc.,M.Sc., Ph.D. ■ ⚅ ❀

Dean, Faculty of Science and Technology, MOUNT ROYAL COLLEGE, 4825 Richard Rd., S.W., Calgary, AB T3E 6K6 (403) 240-6646, FAX 240-6788, EMAIL jspringer@mtroyal. ab.ca. Born Kingston, Jamaica 1939. m. Selwyn. 3 ch. Arthur, Wayne, Julie. EDUC: University Coll. of the West Indies, London, UK, B.Sc.(Math. & Physics) 1962; Simon Fraser Univ., M.Sc.(Pure Math.) 1969; Univ. of Calgary, Ph.D.(Pure Math.). CAREER: Head, Physics Dept., Naparima Coll., Trinidad, 1962-64; Head, Dept. of Math. & Physics, Point Fortin Coll., Trinidad, 1964-66; Teaching Asst., Simon Fraser Univ., 1966-67; Teaching Asst./Grad. Student, 1967-69; Teaching Asst./Grad. Student, Univ. of Calgary, 1970-75; Sessional Instructor, Dept. of Math. & Statistics, 1975-83; Sessional Instructor, Dept. of Math., Physics & Eng., Mount Royal Coll., 1984-89; Instructor, Dept. of Math., Physics & Comp. Sci., Southern Alberta Institute of Technology, SAIT, 1986-89; Instructor, Dept. of Math., Physics & Eng., Mount Royal Coll., 1989-92; Chair, Dept. of Math., Physics & Eng., 1992-95; Dean, Fac. of Sci. & Technology, 1995 to date. AFFIL: Speakers' Bureau, Mount Royal Coll.; Calgary Science Network; Alberta Women's Science Network; Calgary Mathematical Association; American Mathematical

Association; Canadian Mathematical Association. HONS: Student of the Year, University Coll. of the West Indies, 1960; Distinguished Fac. Teaching Award, Mount Royal Coll., 1986; Teaching Excellence Award, Mount Royal Coll., 1992; nominated, Distinguished Fac. Teaching Award, Mount Royal Coll., 1995; nominated, ASTech Award for outstanding contribution to the Alberta science & technology community, 1995. INTERESTS: gardening; woodwork; swimming; walking; tennis; a love for teaching & learning; a love for math & for music. MISC: piloted the Academy of Science, 1994, a week-long experience to introduce 30 Alberta jr. high students to Science of the Home at Mount Royal Coll. COMMENT: *"Dr. Springer has made contributions to the Alberta science and technology community that cannot be measured in dollars. She has devoted her life and career to making mathematics understandable, as well as fun, to post-secondary students. One of her aims is to disprove the 'myth' that mathematics is difficult. She says: 'any average student is capable of doing mathematics up to first-year university level. At this level, it is not abstract and certainly not beyond average human beings.'"*

Spry, Irene M., O.C.,M.A.(Cantab), M.A.(Bryn Mawr) ⚅ ❀

Professor Emeritus, UNIVERSITY OF OTTAWA, ON K1N 6N5. Born Transvall, S. Africa 1907. w. Graham Spry. 3 ch. EDUC: London Sch. of Economics, 1924-25; Girton Coll., Cambridge, B.A.(later M.A. Cantab) 1928; Bryn Mawr Coll., M.A. (Social Econ. & Social Research) 1929. CAREER: Lecturer, Dept. of Pol. Economy, later Asst. Prof., Univ. of Toronto, 1929-38; Acting Dir. of Studies in Econ., 1938-39; Econ. Advisor to the Y.W.C.A., 1940-41; Economist to the Wartime Prices & Trade Bd., 1941-42; Economist to the Commodity Prices Stabilisation Corporation, Limited, 1942-45; lecturer, writer & reviewer, 1945-67; Visiting Assoc. Prof., Univ. of Saskatchewan, 1967-68; Researcher/Visiting Assoc. Prof./Assoc. Prof./Prof., Univ. of Ottawa, 1968-73; part-time lecturer, 1973-79; Sr. Research Assoc., Groupes Associé des Universités de Montréal et de McGill pour l'étude de l'Avenir, Univ. of Montreal/McGill Univ., 1974-76; Prof. Emeritus, Univ. of Ottawa, 1974 to date. SELECTED PUBLICATIONS: *The Palliser Expedition* (Toronto: MacMillan, 1964); *The Papers of the Palliser Expedition, 1857-1860* (Toronto: Champlain Society, 1968); *Natural Resource Development in Canada*, ed. with Phillippe Crabbe (Ottawa: Univ. of Ottawa Press, 1973); Ed., *Buffalo Days and Nights*, by Peter Erasmus (Calgary: Glenbow-Alberta Institute,

1976); *The Records of Department of the Interior*, with Bennett McCardle (Regina: Canadian Plains Research Centre, 1993); "The Contracts of the Hydro-Electric Power Commission of Ontario" (*The Canadian Political Science and Economic Journal* Sept. 1936); "On the Trail of Palliser's Papers" (*Saskatchewan History* Spring 1959); "The Transition from a Nomadic to a Settled Society in Western Canada, 1856-1896" (*Transactions of the Royal Society of Canada* June 1968); "The Cost of Making a Farm on the Prairies" (*Prairie Forum* Spring 1982); various other papers & chapters in books; several articles in *The Dictionary of Canadian Biography*. **EDIT:** Assoc. Ed., *The Musk-Ox*, 1981-84. **HONS:** Research Fellowship, The Canadian Plains Research Centre; Canada Council Research Award, 1965; Silver Medal, Royal Society of Arts, 1965; Distinguished Cdn Citizen Award, Seniors' Group of the Univ. of Regina, 1987; Officer of the Order of Canada, 1993; LL.D.(Hon.), Univ. of Toronto, 1971; D.U.(Hon.), Univ. of Ottawa, 1985. **INTERESTS:** gardening; Canadiana; Arcticana. **MISC:** *Explorations in Canadian Economic History: Essays in Honour of Irene M. Spry*, Duncan Cameron, Ed. (Ottawa: Univ. of Ottawa Press 1985); listed in various biographical sources, incl. *Canadian Who's Who, World Who's Who of Women* & *Who's Who in the World*; mbr., Lord Tweedsmuir's Committee of Inquiry into the Imperial Institute, 1950-52 & subsequent Commonwealth Institute (Exec. Bd.). **COMMENT:** *"Apart from teaching and my family, I have been concerned with research work and teaching, Canadian economic history and work with the Federated Women's Institutes of Canada and the Associated Country Women of the World (Chair of the Executive Committee, VP and Member of Honour)."*

Squair, Beverley D., B.Comm.,C.F.A. $

Vice-President, United States Equities, G.W.L.INVESTMENT MANAGEMENT LTD., 100 Osborne St. N., Winnipeg, MB R3C 3A5 (204) 946-7526, FAX 946-8818. Born Saskatoon, Sask. 1964. m. Robert Margeson. **EDUC:** Univ. of Manitoba, B.Comm.(Fin.) 1986. **CAREER:** Analyst positions, Capital Mkts, Great-West Life Assurance Co., 1986-91; Asst. Mgr, Capital Mkts, 1991-93; Dir., U.S. Equities, G.W.L. Investment Management Ltd., 1994-96; VP, 1996 to date. **AFFIL:** Association for Investment Management & Research (C.F.A.); Winnipeg Society of Financial Analysts. **INTERESTS:** skiing; tae kwon do.

Square, Paula A., B.Sc.,M.Sc., Ph.D., ■ ⬡ ⊕

Professor and Chair, Department of Speech Language Pathology, Faculty of Medicine, UNIVERSITY OF TORONTO, 6 Queen's Park Cres. W., Toronto, ON M5S 1A8 (416) 978-8330, FAX 978-1596, EMAIL p.square@utoronto.ca. Born Painsville, Ohio 1948. d. **EDUC:** Miami Univ., Ohio, B.Sc.(Speech Pathology & Audiology) 1970; Kent State Univ., M.Sc.(Speech Pathology) 1976, Ph.D.(Speech Pathology) 1981. **CAREER:** Asst. Prof., Dept. of Speech-Language Pathology, Fac. of Medicine, Univ. of Toronto, 1980-85; Assoc. Prof., 1985-95; Chair, 1980 to date; Prof., 1996 to date. **SELECTED PUBLICATIONS:** *Acquired Apraxia of Speech in Adults: Theoretical and Clinical Issues*, ed. (London: Taylor and Francis, 1989); "Apraxia of Speech: Another Form of Praxis Disruption," *Apraxia*, ed. Gonzalez-Rothi & Heilman (London: Lawrence Erlbaum, 1996); "The Nature and Treatment of Neuromotor Speech Disorders in Aphasia," *Language Intervention Strategies in Adult Aphasia*, ed. Chapey (Baltimore: William Wilkens, 1993). **AFFIL:** Coll. of Audiologists & Speech Language Pathologists of Ontario; Academy of Neurologic Communication Disorders & Sciences; The Canadian Association of Speech Pathologists & Audiologists; The Ontario Speech & Hearing Association; American Speech-Language & Hearing Association (Fellow); Canadian Association of Speech-Language Pathologists & Audiologists (Honours). **INTERESTS:** horseback riding; hiking; gardening.

Squire, Anne, B.A.,M.A.,LL.D., D.D. ⬡ ⬡ ▢ ♂

Born Amherstburg, Ont. 1920. m. William Robert Squire. 3 ch. Frances Anne, Laura Marguerite, Margaret Sharon. **EDUC:** Carleton Univ., B.A.(Religion) 1974, M.A.(Religion) 1975. **CAREER:** public sch. Teacher, 1939-45; Adjunct Prof., Carleton Univ., 1975-82; Gen. Sec., Div. of Ministry Personnel & Educ., United Church of Canada; Moderator, United Church of Canada, 1986-88. **SELECTED PUBLICATIONS:** numerous articles, incl. "Women and Spirituality" (*Religious Education* May-June 1978); "Women and the Church" (*Theological Education in the 80s*, Div. of Ministry Personnel & Education, United Church of Canada); "Bondage in the Canadian Church" (*The Ecumenist* Mar.-Apr. 1979); "Feminist Theology: Toward Personhood for Women" (Proceedings of The Canadian Research Institute for the Advancement of Women); "Homosexuality, Ordination, and the United Church of Canada" (*Queen's Quarterly* Summer 1991); books, pamphlets & packets incl. *Project Ministry Revisited* (Div. of Ministry Personnel & Education, United Church of Canada, 1985); *Envisioning Ministry* (Div. of Ministry

Personnel & Education, United Church of Canada, 1985); curriculum resources. **AFFIL:** Delta Kappa Gamma (Founding Pres., Kappa Chapter 1977-78); Ottawa-Carleton Palliative Care Association (Chair, Svc Advisory Commission 1995); United Church of Canada. **HONS:** Senate Medal, Carleton University, 1972; Award for Judaic Studies, Carleton University, 1974; LL.D.(Hon.), Carleton Univ., 1988; Doctor of Divinity (Hon.),McGill Univ., 1980; Doctor of Divinity (Hon.), Queen's Univ., 1985. **MISC:** Chair, Proj. Ministry, Gen. Council Steering Committee, 1977-80; Chair, Ont. Conference for Women, United Church of Canada, 1979-80; organizer of Conference-Women in Cdn Religion, Carleton Univ., 1979; Planning Group, Supplementary Report on Human Sexuality, United Church of Canada, 1981; Consultant, Queen's Theological Coll., Interdisciplinary Teaching, 1981; mbr., Canadian Interdisciplinary Proj. on Domestic Violence, 1990-91; cancer survivor; numerous invited papers & speeches. **COMMENT:** *"A teacher and author of curriculum resources and feminist articles; first woman on Senior Management Team (United Church of Canada). First lay woman Moderator."*

Srebotnjak, Tina, B.A.,B.Jour. ⌣ /
Host, *Midday*, CANADIAN BROADCASTING CORPORATION, P.O. Box 500, Stn. A, Toronto, ON M5W 1E6 (416) 205-7491, FAX 205-7249, EMAIL midday@toronto.cbc.ca. Born Slovenia 1952. m. Brian Stewart. 1 ch. **EDUC:** Univ. of Toronto, B.A. 1974; Carleton Univ., B.Jour. (Journalism) 1975. **CAREER:** Host, *Midday*, CBC TV.

Stableforth, Nancy Lynne, B.Jour., LL.B. ■ ✦ ⟁
Deputy Commissioner for Women, CORRECTIONAL SERVICE OF CANADA, 340 Laurier Ave. W., Ottawa, ON K1A 0R1 (613) 992-6067. Born 1952. m. **EDUC:** Carleton Univ., B.Jour 1975; Univ. of Windsor, LL.B. 1978. **BAR:** Ont. 1980. **CAREER:** summer student, Office of the Crown Attorney, Sault Ste. Marie, Ont., 1977; articling student, N. Douglas Gaetz, Barrister & Solicitor, Sault Ste. Marie, 1978-79; Ptnr, Gaetz and Stableforth, 1980-85; Special Asst. to the Min. for Int'l Trade, 1985-86; Exec. Asst. to the Min. of Int'l Trade, 1986; Exec. Asst. to the Solicitor-Gen. of Canada, 1986-88; V-Chair, Appeal Div., National Parole Bd., 1991-93; Exec. V-Chair, 1993-96; Acting Chair, 1994. **AFFIL:** Law Society of Upper Canada; Canadian Bar Association; Council of Canadian Administrative Tribunals (VP; Sec. of Exec. Committee; Dir.); Canadian Criminal Justice Association-Ontario Associa-

tion of Corrections & Criminology; National Joint Committee of the Canadian Association of Chiefs of Police & the Fed. Correctional Services (V-Chair, Corrections); Gateway Children's Mental Health Centre (Pres. 1992-93).

Stagg, Pamela, A.O.C.A.,B.A. Ⓢ ⊗ ⌐
President, PAMELA STAGG CREATIVE SERVICES, 3 Bennington Heights Dr., Toronto, ON M4G 1A7 (416) 423-0477, FAX 424-1931. Born Nottingham, UK 1949. d. **EDUC:** Ontario Coll. of Art, A.O.C.A. 1970; Univ. of Guelph, B.A. 1974. **CAREER:** Art Dir., Cockfield Brown and Co., 1975-80; Art Dir., Norman Craig and Kummel (Canada), 1980-81; Creative Dir., Product Initiatives, 1981-84; Pres., Pamela Stagg Creative Services, 1984 to date. **SELECTED PUBLICATIONS:** writer, *In the Spirit of Partnership* (1990); covers of *Pappus* & *Harrowsmith*; illustrator of numerous articles for Canadian, US & British publications. **EXHIBITIONS:** *Contemporary Botanical Artists: The Shirley Sherwood Collection*, London, Pittsburgh, New York (1996-97); Civic Garden Centre, Toronto (1989 & 1995); Royal Botanical Gardens, Hamilton (1990); Park Walk Gallery, London, UK (1993 & 1994); various group exhibitions, incl. *Special 70th Anniversary Exhibition of the British Iris Society* (1992); *7th Int'l Exhibition of Botanical Painting & Illustration*, Pittsburgh (1993); *Society of Botanical Artists Annual Exhibition*, London (1992). **COLLECTIONS:** private collections in Canada, US, Great Britain, France & Switzerland, incl. Hunt Institute for Botanical Documentation, Carnegie-Mellon Univ.; Shirley Sherwood. **AFFIL:** Royal Botanical Gardens; Canadian Iris Society; British Iris Society. **HONS:** Gold Medal, Royal Horticultural Society, 1991; Grenfell Medal, Royal Horticultural Society, 1992; Ontario Arts Council Travel Award, 1992. **INTERESTS:** gardening; ballet; horseback riding; cross-country skiing. **MISC:** subject of numerous articles incl. "A Stroke of Genius," *Toronto Life Gardens*, Autumn, 1996; taught Botanical Watercolour Workshop, Toronto, 1992-96; lectures on botanical illustration in London, UK.

Stahmer, Anna Elisabeth, B.A., M.A. ■ ■ Ⓢ ❀ /
Co-Publisher and Co-Owner, THE TRAINING TECHNOLOGY MONITOR (bus. newsletter publishing, consulting, specialized bus. directory svcs), 56 Castle Frank Rd., Toronto, ON M4W 2Z8 (416) 929-2297, FAX 929-5323, EMAIL 70324.1155@compuserve.com. Born Hahn, Germany 1945. m. W.E. Jarmain. 3 stepch. ch. Catherine, Anne, Ellen. **EDUC:** Paedogogische Hochschule, Freiburg, Germany, B.A.(Educ.)

1968; Duquesne Univ., Pittsburgh, Penn., M.A.(African Studies) 1970; American Univ., Washington, D.C., M.A.(Int'l Comm.) 1974. **CAREER:** Policy Analyst, Cdn experimental satellite programs, Dept. of Comm., Gov't of Canada, 1973-78; VP, Telecomm. Programs, Academy for Educational Development, Washington, D.C., 1979-85; Stahmer & Associates, Mgmt Consultants, 1988 to date; Sr. Assoc., Int'l Dev. Centre, Ryerson Polytechnic, 1986-88; Co-Publisher/Co-Owner, *The Training Technology Monitor*, 1993 to date; extensive int'l experience, has worked/consulted in 40 countries; clients include UN agencies, the World Bank, gov'ts & private companies; consulting work has been in technology applications to training & educ. (broadcasting, computers, telephone & satellite). **SELECTED PUBLICATIONS:** "Learners in the Workplace," chpt. in *Why the Electronic Highway?* (Toronto: Trifolium Books, 1995); *Assessing Costs of Technology-Based Training* (proceedings of Online Education 95, Berlin, Germany); *Technologies for Workplace Training in Canada: Uses, Costs and New Partnerships* (proceedings of LearnTec 93, Karlsruhe, Germany); "North American Experiences - Workplace Training and the Use of Advanced Technologies," in *Multimedia Learning and New Job Qualifications* (in German) (Berlin: BIBB, 1993). **DIRECTOR:** Ontario International Trade Corporation. **AFFIL:** Office of Learning Technologies, Gov't of Canada (Advisory Ntwk of Experts 1996 to date); Canadian Network for the Advancement of Research, Industry and Education (Educational Steering Committee 1996 to date); Information Highway Advisory Council (Educ. & Training Working Group 1994-95); The McLuhan Teleglobe Canada Award (mbr. of Jury 1990-94; Chair 1994); Ontario Telephone Services Commission (V-Chair 1986-89); European Space Agency (Distance Educ. Evaluations Group 1987-88); International Institute of Communications, UK (Trustee 1985-92; Chair, Nominations Committee 1991-92); Canadian Association for Distance Education; International Society for Performance Improvement. **HONS:** included in *Making a World of Difference*, published by the Women's Directory Project, Canadian Council for International Co-operation, 1990; recipient, Women on the Move award, *The Toronto Sun*, 1989. **INTERESTS:** hiking; bicycling; cross-country skiing; cooking; sailing; ballet/modern dance. **MISC:** command of English, French, German, some Spanish & Italian. **COMMENT:** *"My business partner and I are engaged in consulting and publishing related to technologies and workplace training. I am internationally recognized as one of the pioneers in the application of new technologies to education and training."*

Staines, Mavis 🎓 🎭

Artistic Director and Ballet Principal, NATIONAL BALLET SCHOOL, 105 Maitland St., Toronto, ON M4Y 1E4 (416) 964-3780, FAX 964-3632. Born Quebec 1954. m. Jyrki Virsunen. **EDUC:** National Ballet Sch., Grad. 1972. **CAREER:** dancer, National Ballet of Canada, 1973-78; dancer, Dutch National Ballet, 1978-81; teacher, National Ballet Sch., 1983-84; Assoc. Dir., 1984-89; Artistic Dir. & Ballet Principal, 1989 to date. **AFFIL:** Pierino Ambrosoli Cultural Foundation (Mbr. of Council); Kala Nighi Fine Arts of Canada (Dir.); DAN/CE, The Dance Community of Educators. **MISC:** Dance Advisory Committee, Canada Council; jury, Prix de Lausanne competition; recipient, Canada Council grant for study. **COMMENT:** *"Mavis Staines is concentrating on the challenge of keeping NBS in the forefront of dance teaching. In line with this conviction, she is strengthening the School's international connections and evaluating different techniques to introduce a heightened sense of dynamism and artistry to the School."*

Stairs, Harriet Hingston Dolan, B.A. $

Senior Vice-President, Human Resources Division, BANK OF MONTREAL, 55 Bloor St. W., Toronto, ON M4W 3N5. **EDUC:** McGill University, B.A. **CAREER:** Mkt. Research Analyst, Bank of Montreal, 1967-68; Employee Relations and Staffing Coord., 1968-74; Teacher & Counsellor, E.P.O.C., Bank of Montreal, 1974-78; Personnel Planning Supervisor, 1978-80; Personnel Mgr., Head Office, 1980-82; Human Resources Mgr., Intl. Banking, 1982-83; Sr. Staffing Mgr., Corp. Human Resources, 1983-84; Sr. Mgr., Treasury Div., 1984-88; VP, Human Resources, Corp. and Intl. Fin. Svcs., 1988-92; Sr. VP, Human Resources Div., 1992 to date. **AFFIL:** McGill University (Gov.); The Ontario Council of Regents; Strategic Management Society (Bd.); Sacred Heart Convent (Bd.); The York Club (Bd.); Conference Board (Exec. Comm. of H.R. Executives; Corp. Council on Educ.); Canadian Bankers Association (Chair, HR Committee.

Stairs, Janice A., LL.B.,M.B.A. ■ ⚖

Lawyer, PATTERSON PALMER HUNT MURPHY, 5151 George St., Ste. 1600, Box 247, Halifax, NS B3J 2N9 (902) 492-2000, FAX 429-5215. Born Amherst, N.S. 1959. **EDUC:** Dalhousie Univ., LL.B. 1982; Queens Univ., M.B.A. 1984. **BAR:** N.S., 1985. **CAREER:** Lawyer, Patterson Palmer Hunt Murphy, gen. corp. & commercial law, securities law, resource law, public-private partnership arrangements, corp. fin. **AFFIL:** Canadian Bar Association; N.S. Barristers' Society (Past Chair, Securities Law Subsection; Mineral Resources Subsection); N.S. Chamber of Natural Resources; Equity Investment Advisory Committee. **INTERESTS:** skiing; sailing.

Stait-Gardner, Zane, B.A. $

Senior Vice-President and General Manager, Reinsurance Operations, MANULIFE FINANCIAL, 200 Bloor St. E., Toronto, ON M4W 1E5 (416) 926-3591, FAX 926-5793. Born Riga, Latvia 1944. m. Keith Stait-Gardner. 2 ch. **EDUC:** Univ. of Toronto, B.A.(Math.). **CAREER:** Systems Analyst, Data Processing Div., Manulife Financial, 1973-75; Systems Supervisor, 1975-77; Proj. Mgr, 1977-78; Mgr, Reinsur. Div., 1978-80; Dir., 1980-82; Asst. VP, 1982-84; Reinsur. VP, 1984-87; VP & Gen. Mgr, Reinsur. Div., 1987-91; Sr. VP & Gen. Mgr, 1991 to date. **DIRECTOR:** Manulife International (P&C) Limited; Manulife (International) Reinsurance Limited; Manufacturers (P&C) Limited; Manulife Reinsurance Limited; Enhance Financial Services Group Inc. **AFFIL:** International Insurance Society Inc. (Strategic Planning Committee); Pacific Insurance Conference (Cdn Nat'l Chrm). **COMMENT:** *"As head of the organization, Zane Stait-Gardner developed reinsurance into one of Manulife's core businesses and expanded its reinsurance operations by opening regional offices in Singapore in 1991 and in Wiesbaden, Germany in 1994, to serve the Asia Pacific and the European markets especially. Manulife Reinsurance is one of the world's major life reinsurers."*

Stalker, Jacqueline D'Aoust, B.Ed.,M.Ed., Ed.D ■ ✑ ✤ ☸

Professor (retired), Division of Postsecondary Studies and Coordinator, Higher Education Graduate Program, Faculty of Education, UNIVERSITY OF MANITOBA, Winnipeg, MB R3T 2N2 (204) 453-5324, FAX 453-5324, EMAIL stalker@cc.umanitoba.ca or stalkerj@nsu.acast.nova.edu. Born Penetang, Ont. m. Robert. 3 ch. Patricia Stalker Gray, Lynn Stalker Preston, Bobbi Stalker Ethier. **EDUC:** Univ. of Ottawa, First Class Teaching Certificate (French) 1952; Royal Toronto Conservatory of Music, Music Teacher 1952; Lakeshore Teachers' Coll., Teaching Certificate (English) 1958; Univ. of Manitoba, B.Ed. 1977, M.Ed. 1979; Nova Univ., Fla., Ed.D.(Higher Educ.) 1985. **CAREER:** Teacher, elementary & secondary, Ont., Que. & Mississippi, 1952-61; Administrator & Teacher, Dept. of Nat'l Defence, Moise, Que., 1961-63; Administrator

& Teacher, Sioux Lookout, Ont., 1963-65; private piano teacher, France & Germany, 1965-69; Area Commissioner in Europe, Canadian Girl Guide Association, 1965-69; Teacher, St. Hubert, Que., 1969-70; Administrator & Master Teacher, Algonquin Community Coll., Ottawa, Ont., 1970-74; Program Developer & Teacher, Frontenac County Bd. of Educ., Kingston, Ont., 1974-75; Univ. Lecturer, Fac. of Educ., Univ. of Manitoba & Univ. of Winnipeg, 1977-79; Consultant, Colleges Div., Man. Dept. of Educ., 1980-81; Sr. Consultant, Programming Branch, 1981-84; Sr. Consultant, Office of the Asst. Deputy Min., Post-Secondary, Adult & Continuing Educ. Div., 1985-89; Dir., Post-Secondary Career Dev. Branch/Adult & Continuing Educ. Branch, 1989; Asst. Prof., Dept. of Educ. Admin. & Foundations, Fac. of Educ., Univ. of Manitoba, 1989-92; Coord., Higher Educ. Grad. Program, 1989-95; Assoc. Prof., Div. of Postsecondary Studies, 1992-95. **SELECTED PUBLICATIONS:** various papers, articles & publications. **EDIT:** Mng Ed., *The Canadian Journal of Higher Education*, 1989-93. **AFFIL:** American Association for the Study of Higher Education; Association of Canadian Community Colleges; Canadian Association of University Teachers; Canadian Congress for Learning Opportunities for Women (Man. Dir. 1990-97); Canadian Society for the Study of Higher Education; Manitoba Coalition of Organizations for the Education & Training of Women; Manitoba Teachers' Society; Women's Legal Education & Action Fund; Cancer Society. **HONS:** Dean's Hons. List, Univ. of Manitoba, 1977; Armatage Award, Univ. of Manitoba, 1978; Univ. of Manitoba Grad. Fellowship, 1979; presentation from Graduate Students' Association, in appreciation of exceptional svc to grad. students, Univ. of Manitoba, 1979; Outreach Award, Univ. of Manitoba, 1994. **MISC:** recipient, various grants; numerous invited lectures; listed in various biographical sources, incl. *Who's Who in America, Who's Who in the World, Who's Who of American Women, Who's Who in the Midwest, Who's Who in American Education.*

Stanger, Violet, B.Ed.,M.L.A. ✤

Member of the Legislative Assembly, GOVERNMENT OF SASKATCHEWAN, Legislative Building, Rm. 203, Regina, SK S4S 0B3 (306) 787-0898, FAX 787-6247. Born Canora, Sask. 1940. w. Fred Stanger. 2 ch. **EDUC:** Univ. of Saskatchewan, B.Ed.(Soc. & Psych.) 1982. **CAREER:** Teacher, 1958-59, 1964-65, 1972-91; Councillor, Town of Maidstone, 1985-90. **AFFIL:** NDP; past affil. include Univ. of Saskatchewan (Senate 1988-91); Maidstone Library Bd.; Battle River Teachers' Association (Pres. 1984). INTERESTS: travel; swimming; boating; fishing; reading. COMMENT: *"I am a rural MLA; very few women have been elected in Saskatchewan from a rural riding. Politics is difficult for anyone–more difficult for women. We need more women in elected positions."*

Stanley, Barbara, B.A.,LL.B. Ⓢ ☺
President and Chief Executive Officer, CANA-DIAN CABLE SYSTEMS ALLIANCE, Box 826, Rothesay, NB E2E 5A8 (506) 849-1334, FAX 849-1338. President, NEW BRUNSWICK TRAINING INDUSTRY INC. Born Toronto 1946. m. C. William Stanley. 5 ch. EDUC: McMaster Univ., B.A.(Psych. & Soc.) 1968; Univ. of New Brunswick, LL.B.(Law) 1978. CAREER: Psychometrist, Family Therapist & Court Assessment Worker, Hamilton Wentworth Mental Health Clinic, Hamilton, Ont., 1968-74; Family Therapy Instructor, 1973-74; Law Clerk to the Chief Justice, Court of Appeal of N.B., 1978-79; Assoc., Stewart McKelvey Stirling Scales, 1979-84; Ptnr, 1984-95; VP, Legal Svcs & Corp. Dev., Fundy Cable Ltd./Ltée, 1992-95; Pres. & CEO, Canadian Cable Alliance, 1995 to date. DIRECTOR: Fundy Cable Ltd./Ltée. AFFIL: Family Services Inc., Saint John (Dir.); Canadian Bar Association (Committee to Revise the Code of Professional Conduct); Law Society of N.B.; Canadian Bar Association, N.B. Branch; Saint John Law Society; American Bar Association; Canadian Cable Television Association; N.B. Cable Television Association.

Stanley, Della M.M., B.A.,M.A., Ph.D. ☜ 🗋 ⊗
Associate Professor, Co-ordinator, Canadian Studies Programme, MOUNT SAINT VINCENT UNIVERSITY, 106 Shore Dr., Bedford, NS B4A 2E1 (902) 835-0861, FAX 445-3960. Born Kingston, Ont. 1950. m. Thomas A. Cromwell. 1 ch. Thomas E.G.S. Cromwell. EDUC: Royal Conservatory of Music, A.R.C.T.(Piano Performance) 1971; Mount Allison Univ., B.A.(Cdn Studies) 1973; Univ. of New Brunswick, M.A.(Hist.) 1974, Ph.D.(Hist.) 1980. CAREER: taught, Queen's Univ., 1978-81; Asst. Prof., Saint Mary's Univ., 1984-87; Asst., then Assoc. Prof., Mount Saint Vincent Univ., 1982 to date. SELECTED PUBLICATIONS: *Au Service de deux peuples: Pierre Landry* (Editions d'Acadie, 1976); *Decade of Power –Louis Robichaud* (Nimbus, 1984); *A Man for Two Peoples: Judge Pierre Landry* (Acadiensis, 1988); *A Victorian Lady's Album: Kate Shannon's Halifax and Boston Diary of 1892* (Formac, 1994). AFFIL: Association for Canadian Studies; Canadian Historical Association; Administrators of

Canadian Studies Programmes; Osgoode Society; Heritage Canada. INTERESTS: music; antiques. MISC: Biannual Organ Competition Coord., Summer Institute of Church Music, Whitby, Ont.

Stanley, Kathleen (Kay), B.A. ■■ ❀ ⊕
Assistant Deputy Minister, Health Promotions and Programs Branch, Health Canada, GOVERNMENT OF CANADA, Jeanne Mance Bldg, Rm. 540, Postal Locator 1905D3, Ottawa, ON K1A 1B4 (613) 954-8525, FAX 954-8529. Born Ottawa 1942. d. EDUC: Ottawa Teachers' Coll., Ont. Teacher's Certificate 1960; Carleton Univ., B.A.(Pol. Sci.) 1977. CAREER: Teacher (elementary sch.), Eastview Public Sch. Bd., 1960-64; Merivale Public Sch. Bd., 1964-65; Nepean Township Sch. Area Bd., 1965-69; Carleton Bd. of Educ., 1969-85; on loan of svc. to Min. of Nat'l Defence, DND Overseas Schools, Lahr, W. Germany, 1971-74, 1978-80; Sr. Policy Advisor to Min. Responsible for the Status of Women, 1985; Chief of Staff to Min. of State (Immigration) & Min. Responsible for the Status of Women, 1985-86; Coord./Deputy Head, Status of Women Canada, 1986-93; Asst. Deputy Solicitor Gen. (Corrections Branch), 1993; Asst. Deputy Min., Health Promo. & Programs Branch, 1993 to date. AFFIL: Association of Professional Executives of the Public Service of Canada (Bd. of Dir.; VP 1995-96; Pres. 1996 to date). HONS: Life Mbr., Children's Aid Society of Ottawa-Carleton; Hon. Life Mbr., Teachers' Federation of Carleton; Head of Delegation for Canada to the U.N. Commission on the Status of Women, Vienna, Austria, 1991, 1992, 1993. INTERESTS: women & politics; role of women in society; equality & human rights; health & social issues & the role of gov't in contributing to the health & well-being of society. MISC: participant, Women & the Constitution conference, Feb. 1981; founding Pres., Fed. P.C. Women's Caucus of Ottawa, 1981-82 & re-elected 1982-83; Nat'l Pres., P.C. Women's Federation, 1983-86. COMMENT: *"A strong believer in the need for greater social engagement as a component of good citizenship, Ms. Stanley is an advocate for women and children and the need to bring their perspectives to the decision-making tables in both the public and private sectors. As a career "servant of the public," she values her opportunities to work with public servants at all levels of government within Canada and in the international domain."*

Stanley, Ruth L., B.A.,B.C.L. ■■ ☺ ⚁ ᗡ
Volunteer. P.O. Box 790, Sackville, NB E0A 3C0 (506) 536-2989. Born Montreal 1922. m. Hon. G.F.G. Stanley. 3 ch. Dr. Della Stanley,

Marietta Stanley, Dr. Laurie Stanley Blackwell. **EDUC:** McGill Univ., B.A.(Sociology) 1943, B.C.L. 1945. **BAR:** Que., 1945. **CAREER:** Assoc., Phelan, Fleet, Robertson and Abbott, Juvenile Court Committee, Montreal, 1945-46. **AFFIL:** Sackville Art Association (Pres. 1973); Sackville Music Association (VP 1974); Sackville Memorial Hospital (Chrm 1979-82; first woman Chrm of a N.B. hospital); N.B. Teachers' Association (hon. life mbr.); Girl Guides of Canada (hon. life mbr.); Garrison Club, Fredericton (first woman member 1987); N.B. Museum (Hon. Pres. 1988 to date); St. John Ambulance (Dir., Prov. Council 1994 to date); I.O.D.E. (hon. life mbr.). **HONS:** Province of Quebec External Grad. Scholarship, 1945 (not taken up); McGill Univ. Scholar, 1943-45; Gold Medal in Law, 1945; O.St.J., 1983; DLJ, 1972; DCLJ, 1976; Order of Joan of Arc, Brazil, 1983; Canada 125 Medal, 1993; D.Litt.(Hon.), Mount Allison Univ., 1984; LL.D.(Hon.), St. Thomas Univ., 1986; FRSA, 1972; Permanent Hon. Corresponding Member, 1994 to date. **INTERESTS:** welfare of Canadian women & children; Canadian antiques; English porcelain. **MISC:** Chatelaine of Gov't House, Fredericton, while husband was Lt.-Gov. of N.B., 1982-87. **COMMENT:** *"Trained in civil law in Quebec. Since marriage in 1946 lived in common law provinces (B.C., Ontario, N.B.), so devoted myself to family and volunteer work."*

Stanley-Blackwell, Laurie C.C., B.A.,M.A., Ph.D. ✦ 🕮
Associate Professor, Department of History, ST. FRANCIS XAVIER UNIVERSITY, Box 5000, Antigonish, NS B2G 2W5 (902) 867-3973, FAX 867-2448, EMAIL lstanley@juliet.stfx.ca. Born Kingston, Ont. 1956. m. John D. Blackwell. **EDUC:** Mount Allison Univ., B.A.(Cdn Studies) 1977, Hons. Certificate (Hist.) 1978; Dalhousie Univ., M.A.(Hist.) 1980; Queen's Univ., Ph.D.(Hist.) 1989. **CAREER:** Instructor, Dept. of Hist., Queen's Univ., 1986-88; Asst. Prof., Dept. of Hist., St. Francis Xavier Univ., 1989-94; Assoc. Prof., 1994 to date. **SELECTED PUBLICATIONS:** *Unclean! Unclean! Leprosy in New Brunswick, 1844-1880 /Impur! Impur! La Lèpre au Nouveau-Brunswick de 1844 à 1880* (Moncton: Les Éditions d'Acadie, 1982); *The Well-Watered Garden: The Presbyterian Church in Cape Breton, 1798-1860* (Sydney: University Coll. of Cape Breton Press, 1983); *Phillips' Nineteenth Century County Atlas of Ireland*, co-ed. with J.D. Blackwell (Kingston: Cluny Press, 1984); contributor, *Dictionary of Canadian Biography*; contributor, *Canadian Encyclopedia*; contributor, *Women within the Christian Church in Canada* (1995); articles &

reviews to various journals, incl. *Acadiensis, International Journal of Leprosy & Studies in Religion/Sciences Religieuses*; various other publications. **AFFIL:** Canadian Historical Association; Association for Canadian Studies; Atlantic Association of Historians; Bibliographical Society of Canada; Canadian Oral History Association; St. Francis Xavier Art Gallery (Dir.). **HONS:** Federated Alumni Life Membership Prize, Mount Allison Univ., 1977; Tweedie Memorial Gold Medal, Mount Allison Univ., 1977; Grolier Award in Hist., Mount Allison Univ., 1978; Izaak Walton Killam Memorial Scholarship, Dalhousie Univ., 1978-79; Queen's Fellowship, Canada Council, 1978-79; Oustanding Teaching Award for the Fac. of Arts, St. Francis Xavier Univ., 1995. **INTERESTS:** travel; writing; book collecting. **MISC:** numerous conference presentations..; recipient, various grants, incl. SSHRC research grant, 1994-97; recipient, 1 of 3 Queen's Fellowships awarded in Canada, 1978-79. **COMMENT:** *"My research interests are in social, religious, medical and material history–areas with much potential for enhancing our understanding of the past and the present."*

Stapley, Diane ✦ 🕮 ♛
Actor/Director/Producer. c/o Musical Theatre Works, 775 Sawyers Lane, Vancouver, BC V5Z 3Z8 (604) 526-4286, FAX 685-7451. **CAREER:** Artistic Dir., Administrator & Pres., Cabaret & Musical Theatre Alliance, Toronto; Exec. Dir., Musical Theatre Works (Canada), Vancouver. **SELECTED CREDITS:** Co-Creator, *Harold Arlen: Black and White*; Co-Creator, *Take Two Modern Housewives..*, Charlottetown Festival & Lunchbox Theatre, Calgary; Prod., *The Late Shift/Swing Shift*, Factory Theatre Studio Cafe, Toronto; Co-Prod., *Colours in the Storm*, Elgin Theatre Studio, Toronto; Prod., *Dads in Bondage*, Factory Theatre Studio Cafe; Prod., *Madeira, M'Dear: A Flanders and Swann Show*, Theatre in the Dell, Toronto; *The Diane Stapley Show*, CBC TV (2 seasons nat'l); Sam Jones (continuing), *The Beachcombers*, CBC TV; Lead, *The Fantasticks*, M. Charlesworth, Toronto; Nina, *The Seagull*, H. Baldridge, Calgary; Lead, *Jubalay*, E.Gilbert/D. Regan/Canadian Tour; Lead, *Automatic Pilot*, Raymond Clark, Edmonton; Lead, *Lies and Legends: Musical Stories of Harry Chapin*, Tracy Friedman, Toronto; Lead, *Closer Than Ever*, L. Follows, Arts Club & New Bastion; Dir., *Hello Dolly!*, Gateway Theatre, Richmond, B.C. **AFFIL:** ACTRA; CAEA. **HONS:** 2 ACTRA Awards, Best Variety Performer.

Stark, Ethel, C.M.,LL.D.,F.R.S.A. ✦ 🎻
Conductor, Violinist, Musical Director.

Founder, MONTREAL WOMEN'S SYMPHONY ORCHESTRA. Born Montreal 1916. s.. EDUC: McGill Conservatory, Violin Studies, 5 yrs.; Curtis Institute of Music, Philadelphia, six yrs., Grad. Diploma (Music) 1934; during 6 yrs. at Curtis, studied with Fritz Reiner, Carl Flesch, Lea Luboshutz, Louis Bailly, Arthur Rodzinski. CAREER: concert violinist; conductor; Founder & Conductor: New York Women's Chamber Orchestra (1938), Montreal Women's Symphony Orchestra (1940-86), Montreal Women's Symphony Strings (1954-68), Ethel Stark's Symphonietta (men & women) (1954), Canadian Chorus; Teacher, Catholic Univ., Washington, DC, 1951; Prof. of violin, Conservatoire de musique du Québec à Montreal, 1952-63; Music Fac. mbr., Sir George Williams Univ. (now Concordia), 1974-75. SELECTED CREDITS: numerous appearances on stage & in broadcast as violin soloist with symphony orchestras, incl. CBC Symphony Orchestra, Curtis Symphony Orchestra & Montreal Symphony Orchestra; numerous violin recitals in major cities worldwide; various violin recitals for heads of state; more than 300 broadcasts coast-to-coast across Canada & US, & via shortwave to Europe & Latin America; numerous local broadcasts in Europe & the Orient; numerous appearances as guest conductor throughout the world, incl. Toronto Symphony Orchestra (1946), Quebec Symphony Orchestra (1950) & Tokyo Asahi Philharmonic Orchestra (1960); participant, *How They Saw Us*, NFB; participant, *Careers and Cradles: Women in the 40s and 50s*, NFB. AFFIL: Royal Society of Arts, London, UK (Fellow); Musicians' Guild of Montreal (Hon. Mbr.); Curtis Institute of Music Alumni; Sigma Alpha Iota, US (Hon. Mbr.). HONS: MacDonald Scholarship; fellowship to Curtis Institute, 1927-32; Concert Society Award, 1976; Outstanding Citizenship Award, Montreal Citizenship Council, 1977; Member, Order of Canada, 1979; Key to City of Côte St. Luc; Canada 125 Medal, 1992; LL.D.(Hon.), Concordia Univ., 1980. INTERESTS: collecting rare violin bows & manuscripts. MISC: 1st Cdn recipient, Curtis Institute fellowship (worldwide competition), 1927; 1st Cdn woman to appear as violin soloist in a coast-to-coast broadcast across US, Curtis Symphony Orchestra, Fritz Reiner, Conductor, 1934; 1st woman to found & conduct a professional symphony orchestra composed entirely of women, Montreal Women's Symphony Orchestra; as guest conductor, often 1st Cdn &/or 1st woman to conduct specific orchestras; 1st Cdn woman to teach at Catholic Univ., Washington, DC; Montreal Women's Symphony Orchestra was 1st Cdn orchestra invited to play at Carnegie Hall, N.Y.C., 1947;

Canadian Chorus represented Canada at the World Festival of Song in Israel; portrait photograph featured at exhibit on women at the National Library of Canada, 1995; portrait hangs in Carnegie Hall, N.Y. & Pollock Hall, McGill Univ.; invited to deposit archives with National Library of Canada as cultural properties comprising our nat'l heritage; subject, numerous media articles & reviews; grant recipient; listed in numerous biographical sources, incl. *Canadian Who's Who, World Who's Who in Music, Canadian Encyclopedia* & *Ces Femmes qui on bâti Montréal*. COMMENT: *"As founder of the Montreal Women's Symphony Orchestra, my goal was to see women take their rightful place in symphony orchestras around the world. As a Canadian by birth I am interested in seeing Canadian talent remain in Canada to help build a wonderful future for themselves and generations to come."*

Stark, Janet, M.A.,B.Sc. ■ ⌘

Associate Registrar, ST. FRANCIS XAVIER UNIVERSITY, P.O. Box 5000, Antigonish, NS B2G 2W5 (902) 867-5118, FAX 867-2329, EMAIL jstark@stfx.ca. Born Bayonne, N.J. 1943. m. Claude Gallant. 3 ch. Michael Gallant, Jacques Gallant, Monique Gallant. EDUC: St. Francis Xavier Univ., B.Sc.(Math) 1965; New York Univ., M.A.(Human Rel'ns) 1971. CAREER: various positions, 1965-77; Asst. Principal & Teacher, Annex Village Campus, Toronto, 1977-79; Counsellor, St. Francis Xavier Univ., 1979-87; Asst. to the Deans & Scholarship Officer, 1987-94; Assoc. Registrar, 1994 to date. SELECTED CREDITS: project mgr for production, "XCD" (a multi-media tool for recruiting high sch. student from around the world to St. Francis Xavier); 4 half-hour videotapes on study skills. SELECTED PUBLICATIONS: "The Job Market: A Survey of Post-Graduate Employment, 1970-80" (*Alumni News*, St. Francis Xavier University Winter 1983). AFFIL: Senior Women Academic Administrators of Canada (Planning Committee for meeting in Baddeck, N.S., May 1997); Interchange '95 (Chair of Program & Local Committees); Canadian Diabetes Association (Pres., Antigonish Branch 1995 to date; VP, Antigonish Branch 1993-95; Chair, Parents Support Group, Antigonish Branch 1992-95); National Marine Debris Surveillance Survey (Local Coord. 1994-97). INTERESTS: internationalization of the univ.; my growing family. MISC: Founder, Mentor Club for Canada Scholars at St. Francis Xavier Univ.; invented Christmas Scholarships Program, St. Francis Xavier Univ.; organized meeting of the Lt. Governor of N.S. with high sch. students who won his medal, 1994, 1995, 1996. COMMENT:

"Involved in education at all levels (elementary, secondary, university) in various locales (Hawaii, New York, Ontario, Nova Scotia) from different perspectives (teaching, counselling, administration)."

Starkman, Esther, B.A.,B.Ed. ✒ ✤
English Instructor, ALBERTA VOCATIONAL COLLEGE, AB P0S 1C0 (403) 427-5520. Public School Trustee, CITY OF EDMONTON. m. Howard Starkman, Q.C. 3 ch. Hilary Rochelle, Georgina Carolyn, Danielle Charles. EDUC: Univ. of Alberta, B.A.(Educ.) 1960, Diploma in Educ. 1961, B.Ed. 1967, Diploma in Adult Educ. 1981. CAREER: English/Drama Instructor, Edmonton Public Schools, 1961-75; English Instructor, Victoria Public High Sch., 1976-80; English Instructor, Alberta Vocational Coll., 1981-95; Proj. Dev. Coord., 1995 to date; mbr., Bd. of Health, City of Edmonton; Public Sch. Trustee, 1989 to date; Chair, Policy Review Committee, Edmonton Public Sch. Bd., 1990-91; Chair, District Priorities Committee, 1990-92; mbr., Budget Review Committee, 1990-93; mbr., Results Review Committee, 1990-93; Chair, Educ. Committee, 1990-93; Chair, Agenda Committee, 1991-93; V-Chrm of the Bd., 1991-92; Chrm of the Bd., 1992-93; Chair, Bd. Evaluation Committee, Edmonton Public Sch. Bd., 1993-94. AFFIL: Public School Boards Association of Alberta; Alberta School Trustees' Association; Association for School Curriculum Development; Canadian School Boards Association; Canadian Educational Association; Alberta Association for Adult Literacy; Delta Kappa Gamma Society International; Fed. Liberal Party (Alta. Fin. Committee); Edmonton S.W. Liberal Riding Association (Dir.); Contemporary Women–Chapter ORT. HONS: Literacy Volunteer Award, 1990; Commemorative Medal, Senate of Canada, 1993. MISC: sponsor, HMCS Edmonton, launched Aug. 16, 1996. COMMENT: *"As a teacher for more than 30 years, some of my most satisfying accomplishments stem from helping adults attain the skills needed to become more productive members of society. I have tried to incorporate a variety of techniques, including utilizing and understanding media, theatre, video and field trips to meet the needs of students and promote an attitude of lifetime learning."*

Starkman, Louise
Planning and Consulting. 9 Glencedar Rd., Toronto, ON M6C 3E9 (416) 782-7762, FAX 782-2824. Born Toronto 1941. m. Dr. Stanley E. Starkman. 2 ch. Steven M., Robert A. EDUC: Toronto Teachers' Coll., Certificate 1958; Seneca Coll., Certificate (Export-Import)

1984. CAREER: Teacher, Toronto Bd. of Educ.; Pres., The Roving Eye; Pres., Flemingdon Dental Service; Founder, Alpha Omega-Bahamas Dental Seminar, 1990-96; Rep., The Paris American Academy, France. AFFIL: Mt. Sinai Hospital, Toronto (Bd. of Gov.); Mt. Sinai Auxiliary; Hadassah; Alpha Omega Women; Baycrest Auxiliary; Brazilian Ball Committee; Hong Kong Canada Business Association; Canadian Club. INTERESTS: reading; travel; photography; enjoying family & friends. MISC: listed in *Canadian Who's Who*. COMMENT: *"Currently combining skills to excel in planning and consulting in travel, business and community leadership while still being a caring wife, mother, daughter and friend."*

Starzomski, Rosalie C., R.N., M.N. ■ ✒ ⊕ ✺
Visiting Lecturer, School of Nursing, UNIVERSITY OF VICTORIA, Victoria, BC. Immediate Past President, British Columbia Branch, THE KIDNEY FOUNDATION OF CANADA. Ethics Consultant, VANCOUVER HOSPITAL AND HEALTH SCIENCE CENTRE. EDUC: Dalhousie Univ., B.N. 1978; Univ. of Calgary, M.N. 1984; Univ. of British Columbia, Ph.D. candidate 1995. CAREER: Gen. Duty Nurse, Sydney City Hospital, 1978; Gen. Duty Nurse, Surgical/Orthopedic Trauma Unit, Vancouver General Hospital, 1978-79; Gen. Duty Nurse, Nephrology Program, 1980-81; Asst. Head Nurse, Nephrology Program, 1981-82; Grad. Teaching Asst., Univ. of Calgary, 1982-83; Instructor, Nephrology Program, Vancouver General Hospital, 1983; Grad. Teaching Asst., Fac. of Nursing, Univ. of Calgary, 1983-84; Clinical Asst. Prof., Sch. of Nursing, Univ. of British Columbia; Nephrology Clinical Nurse Specialist, Vancouver General Hospital, 1984-91; Invited Lecturer & Seminar Tutor, Fac. of Medicine, Univ. of British Columbia, 1989 to date; Consultant, Heath Care Ethics, Health Policy & Research, Vancouver, 1992 to date; Visiting Lecturer, Sch. of Nursing, Univ. of Victoria, 1995 to date. SELECTED PUBLICATIONS: "Nursing Inquiry for the common good," with P. Rodney, *Clinical Knowledge and Praxis in Nursing* (California: Sage Publications, 1996); "Ethics in Nephrology Nursing," in *Nephrology Nursing–A Comprehensive Textbook* (Pitman, N.J.: ANNA, 1996); "What do ethics have to do with lifestyle change?" (*Canadian Journal of Cardiology*, 11(supp. A), 1995); "Family decision making about living related kidney donation," with A. Hilton (*ANNA Journal*, 21(6), 1994); "Constraints on the moral agency of nurses," with P. Rodney (*The Canadian Nurse*, 89(9), 1993); numerous journal articles, abstracts & invited presentations. EDIT: mbr.,

Manuscript Review Panel, *ANNA Journal*, 1985-89, 1994 to date. **AFFIL:** The Kidney Foundation of Canada (Organ Donation Committee; Research Council; Nat'l Bd. of Dir.; past mbr., numerous committees; B.C. Branch: Immediate Past Pres.; Chair, Organ Donation Committee; Fin. Committee; Bd. of Dir.; past mbr., numerous committees; mbr., Greater Vancouver Chapter); Canadian Nurses' Association (Clinical Practice Issues Committee; Bd. of Dir.); Canadian Nursing Research Interest Group; Canadian Bioethics Society; Canadian Nurses' Foundation; Canadian Association of Nephrology Nurses & Technicians (past mbr.; past Chair, Bd. of Dir.; World Council on Renal Care; numerous committees); Registered Nurses' Association of B.C., RNABC (Past Pres., Nephrology Nurses' Interest Group; Nursing Research Professional Practice Group; past mbr., numerous committees); Univ. of British Columbia (Research Assoc., Centre for Applied Ethics; past mbr., numerous committees); American Nephrology Nurses' Association; B.C. Renal Council, B.C. Ministry of Health; B.C. Institute of Technology (Nephrology Nursing Advisory Committee); Vancouver Hospital & Health Sciences Centre (Hospital/ Ethics Committee); B.C. Transplant Society (Living Donor Task Force); Sigma Theta Tau International (Xi Eta Chapter); Pacific Space Centre; National Museum of Science & Technology (Charter Mbr. & Astronomy Assoc.). **HONS:** Doctoral Fellowship, The Kidney Foundation of Canada, 1991-95; Nurse Researcher of the Year Award, American Nephrology Nurses' Association, 1994; Upjohn Award for demonstrating excellence & proficiency in clinical practice, Canadian Association of Nephrology Nurses & Technicians, 1993; Canadian Nurses' Foundation Fellowship, 1991-93; UBC Grad. Student Travel Award, 1993; Reg Stott Award for distinguished service, B.C. Branch, The Kidney Foundation of Canada, 1992; Award of Excellence, Nursing, Registered Nurses' Association of B.C., 1991; Special Tribute Award, The Kidney Foundation of Canada, 1991; Special Service Award for outstanding contribution to the Kidney Foundation of Canada, 1987; Award of Excellence, RNABC, 1987, 1991; President's Award for outstanding contribution, B.C. Branch, The Kidney Foundation of Canada, 1987, 1995; numerous scholarships. **MISC:** involved in numerous research projects; has consulted & coord. on various projects for the Kidney Foundation of Canada. **COMMENT:** *"Rosalie Starzomski is currently a Visiting Lecturer at the University of Victoria and a Ph.D. candidate in the School of Nursing at the University of British Columbia where her research and studies are* *focused on health care ethics and health policy. Her clinical background is in nephrology and transplant nursing and she has been actively involved as an advocate for patients and families through her work with The Kidney Foundation of Canada. She is a long-standing member of the Vancouver Hospital and Health Sciences Centre Ethics Committee and is a Research Associate at the UBC Centre for Applied Ethics. Rosalie teaches ethics to UBC medical, nursing and pharmacy students, consults on ethics and health policy for a wide variety of health care agencies and has presented topics related to health care ethics at professional meetings and public forums."*

Steed, Judy, B.A. ✏ 🔲
Feature Writer, THE TORONTO STAR, 1 Yonge St., Toronto, ON M5E 1E6. Born Wigan, UK 1943. d. 1 ch. Emily. **EDUC:** Univ. of Toronto, Victoria Coll., B.A. 1965. **CAREER:** freelance magazine writer, 1978-80; Feature Writer, *The Globe and Mail*, 1981-89; Feature Writer, *The Toronto Star*, 1989 to date. **SELECTED CREDITS:** Co-Prod., *The Far Shore*, 1976. **SELECTED PUBLICATIONS:** *Ed Broadbent: The Pursuit of Power* (1988); *Our Little Secret: Confronting Child Sexual Abuse in Canada* (1994). **HONS:** 3 awards (*The Far Shore*), Canadian Film Awards; National Magazine Award, 1980; Citation, National Newspaper Award, 1981, 1987, 1989, 1993; Robertine Barry Prize for Best Feminist Article in Popular Print Medium, 1988. **INTERESTS:** cottage; cross-country skiing; yoga.

Steel, Freda M., LL.B.,LL.M. ■ 🔲
Justice, MANITOBA COURT OF QUEEN'S BENCH, 408 York Ave., Winnipeg, MB R3C 0P9, FAX (204) 945-8858. Born 1952. **EDUC:** Univ. of Manitoba, LL.B. 1975; Harvard Law Sch., LL.M. 1978. **BAR:** Ont., 1980 (inactive 1993 to date); Man., 1976. **CAREER:** Lawyer, Richardson and Company, Barristers & Solicitors, 1975-77; Asst. Prof., Common-Law Section, Fac. of Law, Univ. of Ottawa, 1978-82; Assoc. Prof., Fac. of Law, Univ. of Manitoba, 1982-89; Assoc. Dean, 1983-84; Adjudicator, Manitoba Human Rights Act, 1983-85; Adjudicator, Canadian Labour Code, 1984-95; Arbitrator, Manitoba Labour Rel'ns Act, 1985-95; Dir., Professional Educ., Law Society of Manitoba, 1989-92; Mediator, Manitoba Teachers' Society, 1991-93; Prof., Fac. of Law, Univ. of Manitoba, 1992-95; Arbitrator, various collective agreements, 1992-95; Cnsl, Office of the Children's Advocate, 1993-95. **SELECTED PUBLICATIONS:** *Payne's Digest on Divorce in Canada: 1968-80*, with Payne & Begin (Don Mills: Richard DeBoo Ltd., 1982);

Payne's Digest on Divorce in Canada: 1981, with Payne & Begin (Don Mills: Richard DeBoo Ltd., 1982); *Issues in Tort Law,* with Rodgers-Magnet (Toronto: Carswell, 1983); "Maintenance Enforcement in Canada" (*Ottawa Law Review* 17(3) 1985); "Family Law and Its Impact on Our Home and Work Environment" (*Manitoba Home Economics Teachers' Association Journal* 25(4) 1993); various other publications. EDIT: Ed. Bd., *Canadian Journal of Women and the Law,* 1985-87; Bd. of Consultants, Bernstein *et al, Child Protection Law in Canada,* Carswell, 1993 to date. AFFIL: Canadian Bar Association; Family Mediation Manitoba; Canadian Association of Law Teachers (Exec. Mbr.); Winnipeg Bd. of Jewish Educ. (Dir. 1991). HONS: Dean's Honour List, Univ. of Manitoba, 1970-72, 1973-75; H.I. Corne Prize, Univ. of Manitoba; Archie Micay Prize, Univ. of Manitoba; Alumni Association Scholarship, Univ. of Manitoba; Merit Award, Univ. of Ottawa. MISC: various conference presentations; frequent speaker.

Steen, Jessica ■ ■ 🦅 🎭 ⊗
Actor, CANUCKLEHEAD ADVENTURES INC. (entertainment endeavours), c/o Great North Talent Agency (in Toronto) (416) 925-2051, c/o Don Buchwald & Associates (in US) (310) 278-3600. Born Toronto. m. a.k.a. Squire. EDUC: Jarvis Collegiate Institute, Toronto. SELECTED CREDITS: *Trial & Error* (New Line Cinema); *Earth 2* (Universal/NBC); *Small Gifts* (CBC); *Homefront* (ABC); *Sing* (Tri-Star Pictures); *Captain Power* (Landmark). AFFIL: Academy of Canadian Cinema & Television; ACTRA; Screen Actors' Guild; David Suzuki Foundation; World Society for the Protection of Animals; Western Canadian Wilderness Committee; Humane Society. HONS: Gemini Award for best performance by an actress in a leading role in a dramatic program or mini-series for *Small Gifts;* nominated twice before that. COMMENT: "'Who'...that's a tall question, with what feels like a short answer (I'm still trying to flush out the details). The "woman" part sounds a tad daunting and grown-up too, but the "Canadian" part I feel purely confident of. That part I'll flaunt. I have four main goals: to make a living; to get into a position where I can move back to Canada and not have to struggle or worry about making that living, but to have got there via contributing to constructive and positive entertainment endeavours. Lastly, to use some of this "superior intellect" that we humans allegedly possess to protect the web of life on this planet into which we seem to refuse to weave ourselves. Oh yeah, and I also like: documenting life and people, organizing events and gatherings, writing poetry (that rhymes), any kind of outdoor adventure (or indoor for that matter), any hike, bike, climb or paddling excursion, making friends family and family friends, and standing stock-still for the call of a loon."

Stefan, Catherine, B.Comm.,C.A. ■ $ ⚖
Chief Operating Officer, O&Y PROPERTIES INC., 2 First Canadian Place, Ste. 2900, Toronto, ON M5X 1B5 (416) 862-6277, FAX 862-6163. Born Winnipeg 1952. m. Gunter Stefan. EDUC: University Coll., Univ. of Toronto, B.Comm. 1973; C.A., Institute of Chartered Accountants of Ontario, 1975; Alternative Dispute Resolution, Univ. of Windsor Law Sch., 1996. CAREER: Auditor, Tax Specialist, KPMG Peat, Marwick, Thorne, 1973-79; Dir. of Taxation, Bramalea Limited, 1979-82; VP, Corp. Planning, 1983-87; Sr. VP, Corp. Dev., Trilea Centres Inc., 1987-89; Exec. VP, Corp. Dev., 1989-91; Pres., Stefan & Associates, 1992-96; COO, O&Y Properties Inc., 1996 to date. AFFIL: Institute of Chartered Accountants (C.A.; Instructor 1978-79); Canadian Institute of Public Real Estate Companies (Chair, Taxation Committee 1982-87); Property Tax Forum (Speaker); International Council of Shopping Centres (Speaker); Terry Fox Run (Corp. Organizer & participant 1986-95). INTERESTS: mountaineering; running; theatre.

Steffer, Diane DeMoisey, B.A., M.A. ■ ☼ 🌐 ○
Past President, WOMEN'S INTER-CHURCH COUNCIL OF CANADA, 2 Quebec St., P.O. Box 30012, Guelph, ON N1H 8J5 (519) 823-2478. Past President, WOMEN'S INTER-CHURCH COUNCIL OF GUELPH. Born Lexington, Kentucky 1937. m. Rev. Dr. Robert W. Steffer. 2 ch. Erika K. Steffer, Beauregard G.R. Steffer. EDUC: Univ. of Kentucky, B.A.(English/Speech/Dramatic Arts) 1958; Indiana Univ., M.A.(Library Sci.) 1966. CAREER: Teacher, Grades 7 & 8 Language Arts, Fort Knox Dependent Schools, 1961-64; ed. & freelance writer, 1966-83; Sec., Div. of Overseas Ministries, Christian Church (Disciples of Christ), US & Canada, 1983-87; Sec., Christian Church (Disciples of Christ) in Canada, 1990-94; Interim Pastor, Hillcrest Christian Church, Toronto, 1994-95. SELECTED PUBLICATIONS: *Favorite Recipes* ed. (Philips Univ. Women's Club, 1974); *Old Roots, New Shoots* study & worship parts (Christian Bd. of Publication, 1982); 13 articles on "Contemplative Life" for *Today's Word* (Christian Bd. of Publication, 1984); numerous articles for various church publications and the *Women's Inter-Church Council of Canada Newsletter.* AFFIL: Women's Inter-Church Council of Canada (Pres. 1992-94); Women's

Inter-Church Council of Guelph (Pres. 1993-96); Indiana Univ. Alumni Association; American Association of Retired Persons; Regional Ministers' Spouses' Association; The Honorable Order of Kentucky Colonels (elected 1992); Arthritis Society (volunteer). INTERESTS: travel; reading; concert-going; writing; entertaining; renovating vintage Edwardian-era houses. COMMENT: *"Spanning 35 years, I have been a wife, mother, teacher, writer, editor, speaker, executive secretary and pastor while living in the US, UK and Canada."*

Steger, Debra P., B.A.,LL.B.,LL.M. ■■ ✤ Ⓢ
Director, Appellate Body Secretariat, WORLD TRADE ORGANIZATION (formerly the GATT), 154, rue de Lausanne, Geneva, Switzerland 1211 41.22.739.5046, FAX 41.22.739.5786, EMAIL debra.steger@wto.org. Born Oliver, B.C. 1952. m. Murray Smith. 2 ch. Nigel, Alexandra. EDUC: Univ. of British Columbia, B.A.(Hons., Hist.) 1975; Univ. of Victoria, Fac. of Law, LL.B.(Public Law) 1979; Univ. of Michigan Law Sch., LL.M.(Int'l Trade & Antitrust Law) 1983. CAREER:(Sr. Negotiator & Principal Legal Advisor, Multilateral Trade Negotiations, External Affairs & Int'l Trade, Canada, 1988-94; Gen. Cnsl, Canadian International Trade Tribunal, Ottawa, 1991-95; Hyman Soloway Prof. of Bus. & Trade Law, Univ. of Ottawa, Fac. of Law (Common Law), 1995-96. SELECTED PUBLICATIONS: *A Concise Guide to the Canadian-United States Free Trade Agreement* (Toronto: Carswell, 1988); co-editor, 4 books on int'l trade; 34 articles/papers published on int'l trade. AFFIL: Law Society of Upper Canada; Canadian Bar Association; Canadian Council on International Law (Exec. Committee 1987-92; mbr. 1985-96); Canadian Association of Law Teachers; American Society of International Law; American Bar Association; *Review of International Business Law* (Edit. Bd. 1988-92). INTERESTS: sports: jogging, aerobics, swimming, cycling & skiing; films; theatre; outdoor recreation.

Steinberg, Susan K., B.Sc.,M.S., FASCP ■ ⊕ 🏵
President, CANADIAN PHARMACY CONSULTANTS INC., 1315 Lawrence Ave. E., Ste. 210, Don Mills, ON M3A 3R3 (416) 443-1217, FAX 757-2430. Born Brooklyn, N.Y. 1949. m. Ralf G. Steinberg. 2 ch. Gretel Shannen, Heidi Virginia. EDUC: Univ. of South Carolina, B.Sc. (Pharm.) 1972; Univ. of North Carolina, M.S. (Pharm.) 1975; Ryerson Polytechnic Institute, Certificate in Gerontology 1978. CAREER: Resident, North Carolina Memorial Hospital, Chapel Hill, NC, 1973-75; Asst. Prof., Clinical Pharmacy, Fac. of Pharmacy, Univ. of Toronto,

1975 to date; Clinical Coord., Extended Care Pharmacy Svcs, Sunnybrook Health Science Centre, 1975-86; Consultant, Drug Interaction Program, ProPharm Ltd., 1980 to date; Asst. Prof., Dept. of Family & Community Medicine, Univ. of Toronto, 1983-86; Pres., Canadian Pharmacy Consultants Inc., Toronto, 1985 to date; Consultant, Long-Term Care Pharmacy Svcs, Medico Pharmacy, 1987 to date. SELECTED PUBLICATIONS: "Orthostatic Hypotension and Parkinson's Disease" (*Parkinson Network*, Bulletin 65 1992); "Long-acting Levodopa Provides Control for Parkinson's Disease" (*Today's Seniors* July 1992); "Dizziness May Be Treatable" (*Today's Senior's* Sept. 1992). EDIT: Guest Ed./Manuscript Reviewer, annual issues on Geriatrics, *Canadian Pharmaceutical Journal*, 1982-84; Ed. Advisory Bd., Medical Education Services (Canada) Inc., 1985-90; Ed. Advisory Bd., *Pharmaceutica Illustrata*, 1989-91; Ed. Advisory Bd., *Pharmacy Practice Magazine*, 1988-91; Ed. Bd., *Cardiovascular Update*, 1990 to date. AFFIL: Canadian Pharmaceutical Association; American Society of Consultant Pharmacists (Fellow); Metropolitan Toronto Pharmacists' Association; Ontario Pharmacists' Association; Pharmaceutical Marketing Club of Ontario; Canadian Association of Women Executives & Entrepreneurs; Rho Chi Fraternity; Phi Beta Kappa; Phi Lambda Sigma, Zeta Chapter of the Univ. of South Carolina Coll. of Pharmacy. HONS: Eli Lilly Achievement Award, 1972; Nellie Wakeman Fellowship, Kappa Epsilon Fraternity, 1973; First-place honours, paper submission, American Society of Consultant Pharmacists, 1979; McNeil Award, Canadian Society of Hospital Pharmacists, 1984. INTERESTS: cooking; travelling; entertaining; walking; reading; swimming; bike riding. MISC: Registered Pharmacist, S.C. & Ont.; numerous presentations to conferences, associations & public meetings; various broadcast interviews; listed in various biographical sources, incl. *Who's Who in The East, Who's Who in America* & &*Who's Who in Science and Engineering*; subject of various print articles & profiles; reviewer for various journals; participant, *HERSTORY, the Canadian Women's Calendar* (1991).

Stenzler, Rochelle, B.Sc.Phm. Ⓢ ⊕ 🕹
President and General Manager, PHARMA PLUS DRUGMARTS LTD., 5935 Airport Rd., Mississauga, ON L4V 1W5 (905) 672-0600, ext. 6231, FAX 671-5470. Born Brooklyn, N.Y. 1953. m. Mark. EDUC: Univ. of Toronto, B.Sc.Phm.(Pharmacy) 1976. CAREER: Pharmacy Intern, Pharma Plus Drugmarts Ltd., 1976; Pharmacy Mgr, 1976-80; Total Store

Mgr, Pharma Plus, 1980-81; Retail Pharmacy Coord., 1981-82; District Mgr, 1982-83; Proj. Coord., 1983-84; Dir., Retail Svcs, 1984-87; VP, Pharmacy & Retail Svcs, 1987-88; Sr. VP, Oper., 1988-92; Pres. & Gen. Mgr, 1992 to date. AFFIL: Ontario Pharmacists' Association (various committees; Councillor 1984-87; Exec. 1987-90); Canadian Pharmaceutical Association (Prov. Negotiators Committee; Council of Delegates 1985-89); Ontario Chain Drug Association (Dir.; Chrm 1984-90); Canadian Association of Chain Drug Stores (Dir.; Treas. 1993-94; V-Chrm 1994-95; Chair, 1996-97; Trade Rel'ns Committee); Ontario Coll. of Pharmacists; National Association of Chain Drug Stores; Retail Council of Canada; Univ. of Toronto Fac. of Medicine (Dev. Advisory Committee). HONS: D'Avignon Gold Medal, Univ. of Toronto, 1976. INTERESTS: travel; reading; languages; theatre; art. COMMENT: *"Results-oriented professional with hands-on operational and strategic planning skills. Extensive experience in drug store retailing with strong leadership abilities."*

Stephen, Alison M., B.Sc., Ph.D. ■ ⌇ ⊕ ❀

Professor, Division of Nutrition and Dietetics, College of Pharmacy & Nutrition, UNIVERSITY OF SASKATCHEWAN, 110 Science Place, Saskatoon, SK S7N 5C9 (306) 966-5847, FAX 966-6377, EMAIL stephen@sask.usask.ca. Born Vancouver 1951. d. 1 ch. James (Jamie) D. EDUC: Univ. of Edinburgh, B.Sc.(Physiology) 1976; Univ. of Cambridge, Diploma (Nutrition) 1977, Ph.D.(Nutrition) 1980. CAREER: Postdoctoral Fellow, Gastroenterology Unit, Mayo Clinic, MN, 1980-81; Research Assoc., Dept. of Medicine, Case Western Reserve Univ., 1982-83; Proj. Coord., Dept. of Environmental & Preventive Medicine, St. Bartholomew's Medical Coll., UK, 1984-87; Asst. Prof., Coll. of Home Econ., Univ. of Saskatchewan, 1987; Asst. Prof., Div. of Nutrition & Dietetics, Coll. of Pharmacy, 1988-90; Assoc. Prof., 1990-95; Head, 1991-93; Prof., 1995 to date; Assoc. Mbr., Dept. of Applied Microbiol. & Food Sci., Coll. of Agric., to date; Assoc. Mbr., Dept. of Community Health & Epidemiology, Coll. of Medicine, to date; External Fac., Coll. of Nursing, to date. SELECTED PUBLICATIONS: "Mechanism of action of dietary fibre in the human colon" (*Nature*, 1980); "Trends in Individual Consumption of Dietary Fat in the United States 1920-1984," with N.J. Wald (*American Journal of Clinical Nutrition* 1990); "Whole Grains: Impact of Consuming Whole Grains on Physiological Effects of Dietary Fibre and Starch" (*Critical Review of Food Science and Technology* 1994); "Intake of carbohy-

drate and its components–international comparisons, trends over time and effect of changing to low fat diets," A.M. Stephen *et al* (*American Journal of Clinical Nutrition* 62 1995). EDIT: Ed. Bd., *Journal of Nutriceuticals, Functional and Medicals Foods.* AFFIL: Expert Committee on Nutritional Aspects of Food, Agriculture Canada (Chair); Canadian Society for Nutritional Sciences; Nutrition Society, UK; Canada Committee on Food; Canadian Sugar Institute (Nutrition Advisory Panel); Canadian Nutritional Innovation Centre and Network (Scientific Advisory Committee). HONS: Col. R.B. Campbell Prize for top student, Award Course in Phys. Educ., Univ. of Edinburgh, 1974; Fellowship, Anna Fuller Fund for Cancer Research, 1981; Fellowship, Mary B. Lee Fund for Diabetes Research, 1983; Scholarship, Alexander von Humboldt Foundation, 1984. INTERESTS: gardening; pets; sewing. MISC: Co-Prod., "The Winning Edge," a video to promote healthy eating for adolescent athletes (1993); grant reviewer; various scholarships & fellowships; recipient, numerous grants; spent sabbatical year, 1993-94, at Dept. of Surgery, Queen Elizabeth Hospital, Adelaide, Australia. COMMENT: *"An academic nutritionist with an interest in improving the health of Canadians through pursuing research into and giving advice on the role of nutrients in health and disease."*

Stephen, Barbara, B.A.,M.A. ■ ⌇ 📕 ⊗

Curator Emerita, Department of Near Eastern and Asian Civilizations, ROYAL ONTARIO MUSEUM, 100 Queen's Park, Toronto, ON M5S 2C6 (416) 586-5721, FAX 586-8093, EMAIL barbaras@rom.on.ca or barbaras@idirect.com. Associate Professor, Department of East Asian Studies, UNIVERSITY OF TORONTO. Born Toronto 1931. w. Richard H. Burry. EDUC: Univ. of Toronto, B.A.(Art & Archaeology) 1953, M.A.(Art & Archaeology) 1960. CAREER: Far Eastern Dept., Royal Ontario Museum, 1953-75; Assoc. Dir., 1976-84; Curator, Far Eastern Dept., 1984-92; Curator-in-Charge, 1992-96; Curator Emerita, 1996 to date. SELECTED PUBLICATIONS: "Introduction," *Homage to Heaven, Homage to Earth* (Univ. of Toronto Press, 1992). EXHIBITIONS: selected exhibitions include Responsible Curator, *The Exhibition of Archaeological Finds of the People's Republic of China* (1974). AFFIL: Heliconian Club; Oriental Ceramic Society of Toronto; The Institute for Ancient Equestrian Studies. INTERESTS: ongoing research on wheeled vehicles of ancient China; gardening; yoga. MISC: 1969 Canada Council Grant for fieldwork at the site of Siraf, Iran. COMMENT: *"Career centred on the Royal Ontario*

Museum's renowned Chinese collection includes extensive exhibition work, administrative experience and committee service, plus teaching of Chinese art history at the University of Toronto."

Stephenson, Bette M., O.C.,M.D., F.C.F.P.(C),O.St.J. #☝ ⊕ 🎓 🍁 ☝
Physician, Educator. Richmond Hill, ON. Born Aurora, Ont. 1924. m. Dr. G. Allen Pengelly. 6 ch. J. Stephen A.; Elizabeth Anne A., C. Christopher; J. Michael A.; P. Timothy A., Mary Katharine A. **EDUC:** Univ. of Toronto, M.D. 1946. **CAREER:** family physician, 1948-75; active medical staff, Women's College Hospital, 1950-88; Dir., Outpatients Dept., 1952-56; Chief, Dept. of Family Medicine, 1956-64; elected MPP (York Mills), Sept. 1975; re-elected May 1977, Mar. 1981, May 1985; Min. of Labour, 1975-78; Acting Min. of Health, Mar.-June 1976; Min. of Educ. & Min. of Colleges & Universities, 1978-85; Chrm, Council of Ministers of Educ. of Canada, 1978, 1980, 1983; Chrm of Mgmt Bd., Deputy Premier of Ont., Treas. & Min. of Fin., Jan.-June 1985; Commissioner, Ontario Police Commission, 1988-90. **SELECTED PUBLICATIONS:** numerous publications. **AFFIL:** Education Quality and Accountability, Ontario (Bd. of Dir.); Panel on Post Secondary Educ., Prov. of Ontario; Ontario Medical Association (Bd. of Dir. 1965-73; Chair 1968-69; Pres. 1970-71); Canadian Medical Association (Bd. of Dir. 1968; Chair 1972; Pres. 1974-75); Academy of Medicine of Toronto (Fellow); Coll. of Family Physicians of Canada (Fellow); Women's College Hospital Bd. (Dir.); Women's College Hospital Medical Staff; North York General Hospital Medical Staff; St. John's Rehabilitation Hospital Medical Staff; Canadian Institute for Advanced Research (Dir.); Gwillimbury Foundation for the Advancement of Post-Secondary Education (Pres.); Ridley Coll. (Bd. of Advisors); Association for Learning Disabilities (Hon. Bd.); St. John Ambulance (Advisory Committee); CMHA; Royal Ontario Museum; Art Gallery of Ontario; COC; United Church of Canada. **HONS:** Bales Medal for Academic Achievement, Earl Haig Collegiate Institute; Centennial Medal, 1967; Woman of the Year, B'Nai B'rith, 1974; Queen's Silver Jubilee Medal, 1977; Order of St. John, 1983; Citation for Outstanding Public Service, Council for Exceptional Children, 1985; Order of Canada, O.C., 1992. **MISC:** 1st Chief, Dept. of Family Medicine, Women's College Hospital, 1956-64; 1st woman mbr., Bd. of Dir. (1965-73) & Pres. (1970-71), Ontario Medical Association; 1st woman mbr., Bd. of Dir. (1968), Officer (Chrm 1972) & Pres. (1974-75), Canadian Medical Association; 1st recipient, Citation for Outstanding Public Service, Council for Exceptional Children; principal host, *The First Five Years*, weekly public service series, CBC TV (1971-73); consultant to int'l educ. projects & consulting groups.

Stephenson, Helga, B.A. 📺 $
Chair, VIACOM CANADA LIMITED (416) 975-5567. **EDUC:** Univ. de Fribourg, Switzerland, Dipl.(Advanced French) 1965; McGill Univ., B.A. 1969. **CAREER:** Official Hostess, World Exposition, Osaka, Japan, 1970; Public Rel'ns Officer, National Arts Centre, 1971-73; Dir. of Comm., Nat'l Touring Office, Canada Council, 1973-74; Prof., Univ. of Havana, Cuba, 1974-75; Ptnr, Stephenson, Ramsay, O'Donnell Limited, 1975-79; Asst. to Pres., Film Consortium of Canada, 1979-80; VP, Simcom Limited, 1980-82; Pres., Preview Limited, 1982-86; Exec. Dir., Festival of Festivals (now known as Toronto Int'l Film Festival), 1986-94; Exec. Dir., Cinematheque Ontario, 1989-94; Chair, Viacom Canada Limited, 1994 to date. **AFFIL:** Canadian Hearing Society (Dir.); FOCAL Canadian Foundation for the Americas (Dir.); Toronto Int'l Film Festival Group (Dir.); Cinémathèque Ontario (Dir.); Entertainment Venture Corporation (Advisory Council); Director's Guild of Canada (Advisory Council). **HONS:** Women Who Make a Difference Award, 1988; Outstanding Achievement Award, Toronto Women in Film & Television, 1993; William Kilbourn Award for Lifetime Achievement, Toronto Arts Awards, 1996.

Steven, Darlene, B.A,B.Sc.N,M.H.S.A, Ph.D. 🎓 ⊕ ✊
Associate Professor, LAKEHEAD UNIVERSITY, 955 Oliver Rd., Thunder Bay, ON P7B 5E1 (807) 343-8643, FAX 343-8246. Born Winnipeg 1949. m.. **EDUC:** St. Boniface Sch. of Nursing, Winnipeg, RN 1969; Univ. of Manitoba, Diploma (Public Health Nursing) 1970; Lakehead Univ., B.A.(Psych.) 1977, B.Sc.N 1977; Univ. of Alberta, M.H.S.A.(Health Admin.) 1980, Ph.D.(Educ. Admin.) 1988. **CAREER:** Public Health Nurse & Team Coord., Dept. of Health & Social Svcs, Staff Nurse, Neonatal Intensive Care Unit, St. Boniface General Hospital, 1975-77; Admin. Resident, Glenrose Hospital, 1978; Assoc. Dir. of Nursing, Admission Svc, Alberta Hospital, Edmonton, 1979-82; Assoc. Prof., Undergrad. Studies, Univ. of Alberta, 1981-83; District Dir., Victorian Order of Nurses, 1982-83; Staff Nurse, Neonatal Intensive Care, Royal Alexandra Hospital, 1985-86; Employee Rel'ns Officer, Sask. Union of Nurses, 1987-87; Asst. Prof., Nursing, Lakehead Univ., 1988; Assoc. Prof., 1988 to date;

courtesy appt., Lakehead Psychiatric Hospital, 1991 to date; hon. appt., The General Hospital of Port Arthur, 1991 to date. **SELECTED PUBLICATIONS:** "Lie-Detector Tests" (Sunspots 12(11) 1986); "History of Collective Bargaining of Nurses in Canada," in *Proceedings of the First National Nursing History Conference* (Charlottetown, 1988); "Performance Appraisal Systems: Development of a Tool," with L. Soramaki (*Canadian Journal of Quality Assurance* 8(3) 1991); *An Analysis of the Ontario Health Survey from a Cardiovascular Perspective*, with R. Kirk-Gardner (Toronto: Ontario Ministry of Health, 1992); various other publications. **AFFIL:** Ontario Cancer Treatment & Research Foundation (Bd.); Canadian Council of Cardiovascular Nurses; Canadian Nurse Educators' Interest Group; Provincial Nurse Educators' Interest Group; Provincial Nurse Administrators' Interest Group; Coll. of Nurses of Ontario; Registered Nurses' Association of Ontario; Univ. of Alberta Alumni; Lakehead Univ. Alumni; Univ. of Manitoba Alumni; St. Boniface General Hospital, Nursing Alumni; Manitoba Association of Registered Nurses; Canadian Nurse Educators' Association (Bd. Rep.) Northern Educational Centre for Aging & Health, Lakehead Univ. (Gerontology Study Group; Community Teaching Ntwk); Northwestern Ontario Breast Screening Program Advisory Committee (Chair); Nursing Research Committee (Co-Chair); Interagency Focus Group on Long Term Health Care Reform. **HONS:** Illene Downey Bursary, 1976-77; Canadian Nurses' Foundation Fellowship, 1977; Margaret Page Award, Lakehead Univ., 1988; Contribution to Teaching Award, Lakehead Univ.; Distinguished Instructor Award, Lakehead Univ., 1994. **INTERESTS:** breast & cervical screening (health promo.); cardiovascular health; traditional healing versus conventional treatments; gerontology; multiculturalism. **MISC:** recipient, various grants; numerous conference presentations; numerous speaking engagements. **COMMENT:** *"I am totally dedicated to health promotion in breast cancer and cardiovascular health. I lobby on behalf of long-term care, cancer and multiculturalism, with regard to women's health."*

Stevens, Lisa ■■ 🏀
Paralympic Athlete. London, ON. Born 3 ch. **EDUC:** Univ. of Western Ontario, Computer Sci., current. **SPORTS CAREER:** mbr., Nat'l Wheelchair Basketball Team, 1st yr. Paralympic Games: Gold, 1996. Défi Sportif & Texas Shootout, 1995. Texas Shootout, 1994. **HONS:** All-Star, Défi Sportif, 1995; MVP, Texas Shootout, 1994, 1995.

Stevens, Pamela M., B.A.,LL.B. ■ ⚖ 🎓
Managing Partner, HUGHES, AMYS, 1 First Canadian Place, Ste. 5050, Box 401, Toronto, ON M5X 1E3 (416) 367-1608, FAX 367-8821. 2 ch. Jennifer, David. **EDUC:** Waterloo Lutheran Univ., B.A. 1973; Univ. of Toronto, LL.B. 1977. **BAR:** Ont., 1979. **CAREER:** Assoc., Hughes, Amys, 1979-81; Ptnr, 1981 to date. **AFFIL:** Canadian Bar Association; County of York Law Association; Medico-Legal Society of Toronto; Advocates' Society. **COMMENT:** *"Ms. Stevens practice is primarily insurance-related defence litigation and includes personal injury, products liability and all aspects of insurance coverage. She has participated in continuing education programs for the Law Society of Upper Canada and the Canadian Bar Association, and as well as the University of Toronto's Advanced Legal Procedure program."*

Stevenson, Barbara F., Q.C. ⚖
Partner, CARR, STEVENSON AND MACKAY, Peake House, 50 Water St., Box 522, Charlottetown, PE C1A 7L1 (902) 892-4156, FAX 566-1377. **BAR:** P.E.I., 1980. **CAREER:** Ptnr, Carr, Stevenson and MacKay, 1984 todate; Lecturer, Univ. of P.E.I., 1979-85, 1994. **DIRECTOR:** Bank of Canada (mbr. of the Exec. Committee). **AFFIL:** Law Society of P.E.I. (Rules Committee; Chair, Bd. of Examiners); Canadian Bar Association; P.E.I. Liberal Association (Table Officer). **INTERESTS:** skating; skiing; golfing; cycling; community service.

Stevenson, Lois, B.Comm.,M.B.A., M.Phil. $ ☝
Director, Entrepreneurship Development, ATLANTIC CANADA OPPORTUNITIES AGENCY, Moncton, NB E1C 9J8 (506) 851-7814, FAX 851-7403. Born Middleton, N.S. 1950. s. 1 ch. Sacha Margaret Ann Stevenson. **EDUC:** Dalhousie Univ., B.Comm. 1970, M.B.A. 1979; Univ. of Bath, M.Phil.(Mgmt) 1990. **CAREER:** Lecturer, Mount St. Vincent Univ., 1979-81; Assoc. Prof., Acadia Univ., 1981-89; Dir., Entrepreneurship Dev., Atlantic Canada Opportunities Agency, 1990 to date; Assoc. Prof., St. Mary's Univ., 1992-93. **SELECTED CREDITS:** Researcher/Narrator/Interviewer, *Enterprising Women*, National Film Board, 1987. **SELECTED PUBLICATIONS:** Co-author, *Owning My Own Business* (Atlantic Provinces Chamber of Commerce); Ed., *Tools for Business Growth* (Opportunities for Woman Entrepreneurs, Inc., 1993); over 25 articles published in Canada, US & abroad, incl. "The Study of Entrepreneurs" (*Journal of Small Business-Canada* Spring 1985); "Against All Odds: The Entrepreneurship of Women" (*Journal of*

Small Business Management Oct. 1986); "Women Entrepreneurs: Problems and Perceptions" (*Entrepreneurship Development Review* July 1987); Chair, Ed. Committee, *State of Small Business and Entrepreneurship in Atlantic Canada* reports (1991, 1992, 1994). **EDIT:** Ed. Committee, *Journal for Small Business and Entrepreneurship-Canada.* **AFFIL:** International Council for Small Business (Pres.-Elect); Opportunities for Women Entrepreneurs, Inc. (Treas.); Canadian Council for Small Business & Entrepreneurship (Pres.); Association of Atlantic Women Business Owners; Atlantic Canada Entrepreneurship Awards Association (mbr.; Hon Mbr., Academy of Entrepreneurs); Entrepreneur of the Year Institute (Mbr.): Institute of Small Business Counsellors. **HONS:** "Successor," *Canadian Business* Magazine, 1987; Fellow, National Entrepreneurship Development Institute, 1989; Edwin M. Appel Prize & Fellowship, Price-Babson Coll. Fellows Program, 1989; Merit Award for Excellence, Atlantic Canada Opportunities Agency, 1992; Supporter of Entrepreneurship Award, Atlantic Canada, Ernst & Young Entrepreneur Of The Year Program, 1994. **INTERESTS:** promoting entrepreneurship; int'l entrepreneurship dev.; business ideas; writing; reading. **MISC:** 1st Cdn recipient, Edwin M. Appel Prize; SSHRC Doctoral Fellowship recipient; consultant to gov't on entrepreneurship policy, continues to remain involved in nat'l entrepreneurship & small bus. promotion efforts; participant, Fed. Minister's Task Force on Entrepreneurship Policy, Meech Lake, 1987-88; only Cdn participant, 3-day consultation by Bd. of Dir. of the Ewing M. Kauffman Foundation to advise on strategic directions; organizer &/or participant in many conferences & workshops; numerous presentations at conferences & workshops; Chairperson, Reg'l Selection Committee, Canadian Woman Entrepreneur of the Year Program, 1993-96; Dir., Atlantic Canada Entrepreneurship Awards Program, 1991-94; Bd. of Dir., Nova Scotia Venture Capital Corporation, 1988-90; subject of a variety of media coverage. **COMMENT:** *"Very committed to the advancement of entrepreneurship as a social/economic goal. Strong belief in pushing one's self to realizing true potential. Goal is to 'make a difference.'"*

Stevenson, Mary Margaret, B.A.,M.S., Ph.D. ⊕ ⌖
Medical Scientist, Department of Medicine, MONTREAL GENERAL HOSPITAL, Montreal General Hospital Research Institute, 1650 Cedar Ave, Montreal, QC H3G 1A4 (514) 937-6011, ext. 4508, FAX 934-8261. Associate Professor, Department of Medicine, McGILL UNIVERSITY. Born Philadelphia 1951. m. Francis R. Stark. **EDUC:** Hood Coll., Maryland, B.A.(Biol.) 1973; Catholic Univ. of America, M.S.(Microbiol.) 1977, Ph.D.(Microbiol.) 1979. **CAREER:** Guest Worker, Lab. of Hematology & Supportive Care, National Cancer Institute, National Institutes of Health, Bethesda, Md., 1972-73; Post-Doctoral Fellow, Montreal General Hospital Research Institute, 1979-81; Research Assoc., 1981-82; Asst. Prof., Dept. of Medicine, McGill Univ., 1982-88; Assoc. Mbr., Dept. of Physiology, 1984 to date; Assoc. Prof., Dept. of Medicine, 1988 to date; Founding Mbr., Centre for the Study of Host Resistance, 1988 to date; Mbr., Centre for Human Genetics, 1988 to date; Assoc. Prof., Institute of Parasitology, 1988 to date; Assoc. Mbr., Dept. of Microbiol. & Immunology, 1989 to date; Visiting Lecturer, Univ. of Alberta, 1990; Medical Scientist, Dept. of Medicine, Montreal General Hospital, 1993 to date. **SELECTED PUBLICATIONS:** *Malaria: Host Responses to Infection* (Boca Raton, FL: CRC Press, 1989); "Macrophage Chemotactic Response Is Controlled by 2 Genes," with E. Skamene & R.D. McCall (*Immunogenetics* 1986); "More on Unravelling the Cytokine Network in Malaria" (*Parasitology Today* 1993); "*In vitro* and *In vivo* Lung T Cell Responses in Mice during Bronchopulmonary Infection with Mucoid Pseudomonas aeruginosa Infections," with T. Kondratieva *et al* (*Clinical Experimental Immunology* 1995); more than 1350 other articles & abstracts. **AFFIL:** Society for Leukocyte Biology; American Society for Microbiology; American Association of Immunologists; Cancer Research Society; Canadian Society for Immunology; American Society of Tropical Medicine & Hygiene. **HONS:** Rouse Grad. Scholarship in Biol., Hood Coll., 1973; Outstanding Young Alumnae Award, Hood Coll., 1985. **INTERESTS:** horseback riding; cross-country & alpine skiing; reading; travel. **MISC:** numerous invited lectures; reviewer, various journals, nat'l & int'l, & granting agencies; recipient, numerous grants incl. major grants for the study of malaria; chaired workshops at numerous conferences.

Stevenson, Moira G., B.B.A., C.A. ■ $ ⌖ ○
Controller, MOUNT ALLISON UNIVERSITY, P.O. Box 1230, Sackville, NB E0A 3C0 (506) 364-2242, FAX 364-2216, EMAIL mgstevenson@mta.ca. Born Campbellton, N.B. 1964. d. **EDUC:** Univ. of New Brunswick, B.B.A. (Acctg) 1986. **CAREER:** Audit & Staff Acctnt, Peat Marwick Thorne, 1986-91; Cont., Mount Allison Univ., 1991 to date. **AFFIL:** N.B. Insti-

tute of Chartered Accountants (C.A.); Canadian Institute of Chartered Accountants.

Stewart, Anne Marie, B.Sc.,LL.B., Q.C. ⚖ [$]
Partner, BLAKE, CASSELS AND GRAYDON, 1030 W. Georgia St., Ste. 1700, Vancouver, BC V6E 2Y3 (604) 631-3313, FAX 631-3309. Born Nelson, B.C. 1951. s. **EDUC:** Univ. of British Columbia, B.Sc.(Math) 1972, LL.B. 1975; Simon Fraser Univ., Certificate of Health & Fitness (Kinesiology) 1988. **BAR:** B.C., 1976. **CAREER:** Student-at-Law, Davis and Company, 1975-76; Assoc., 1976-81; Ptnr, 1981-89; Ptnr, Blake, Cassels and Graydon, 1989 to date. **SELECTED PUBLICATIONS:** numerous articles related to bus. law & native law. **DIRECTOR:** more than 20 companies. **AFFIL:** 20 Club (Treas.); St. John Ambulance, B.C. (Officer of St. John; Exec. Committee; Sr. VP); Law Society of B.C. (Ad hoc Bencher; Ethics Committee; Solicitors Legal Opinions Committee). **HONS:** Gold Medal, Univ. of British Columbia Fac. of Law, 1972-75; 40 under 40 Award, Business in Vancouver, 1990; Queen's Counsel, 1993. **MISC:** Head of Course, Law Society of B.C. Bar Admission Program Commercial Law, several yrs.; lecturer, Commercial Law, Law Society of B.C., 1980 to date; appointed by prov. gov't to Personal Property Security Act Consultative Committee, 1992 to date; arbitrator for commercial disputes, B.C. International Commercial Arbitration Centre; numerous seminars & papers delivered.

Stewart, Carole, B.A.,M.A.,Ph.D. 🎓 📜
Dean, College of Arts, UNIVERSITY OF GUELPH, Guelph, ON N1G 2W1 (519) 824-4120, ext. 3301, FAX 837-1315, EMAIL cstewart@arts.uoguelph.ca. Born Dauphin, Man. 1941. m. Donald Stewart. 2 ch. **EDUC:** Univ. of Manitoba, B.A.(Phil.) 1963, M.A.(Phil.) 1964; Univ. of London, Ph.D.(Phil.) 1971. **CAREER:** Fac., Dept. of Phil., Univ. of Guelph, 1966 to date; Chair, 1985-92; Dean, Coll. of Arts, 1992 to date. **SELECTED PUBLICATIONS:** *Perspectives on Moral Relativism*, ed. with D. Odergard (Milliken, Ont.: Agathorn Books Limited, 1991); "The Moral Point of View" (*Philosophy* 51 1976); "The Feminist View of the Future" (*The Register* 5 1984); "Spinoza and Feminist Ethics" (*Atlantis* Spring 1988); various other publications. **EDIT:** Ed., Newsletter, Canadian Society for Women in Philosophy, 1986-87. **AFFIL:** Canadian Philosophical Society; Canadian Society for Women in Philosophy; Canadian Research Institute for the Advancement of Women; Guelph Philosophical Society. **INTERESTS:** music; literature. **MISC:** numerous conference presentations.

Stewart, Donna Eileen, M.D.,D.Psych., FRCP(C) ■■ ⊕ 🎓 ☝
Lillian Love Chair of Women's Health, THE TORONTO HOSPITAL, 200 Elizabeth St., EN1-222, Toronto, ON M5G 2C4 (416) 340-3840, FAX 340-4185, EMAIL dstewart@torhosp.toronto.on.ca. Professor of Psychiatry, Obstetrics-Gynecology, Anesthesia, Surgery, and Family and Community Medicine, UNIVERSITY OF TORONTO. Born Cornwall, Ont. 1943. m. Dr. Andrew Malleson. 1 ch. Michael Miles Stewart Malleson. **EDUC:** Queen's Univ., M.D. 1967 (graduated 1st in class, 15 scholarships for academic excellence); Univ. of Toronto, D.Psych. 1971 (Min. of Health Gold Medal for standing 1st in psychiatry); Royal Coll. of Physicians & Surgeons of Canada, FRCP(C) (Psychiatry) 1972. **CAREER:** Chief of Psychiatric Consultation Liaison Svc., St. Michael's Hospital, 1972-94; Head of Women's Health, The Toronto Hospital, 1994 to date; Lillian Love Chair of Women's Health, 1995 to date; Prof. of Psychiatry, Ob-Gyn, Anesthesia, Surgery, Family & Community Medicine, Univ. of Toronto, 1995 to date; Head of Women's Health, Princess Margaret Hospital/Ontario Cancer Institute/ The Toronto Hospital Joint Oncology Program, 1996 to date. **SELECTED PUBLICATIONS:** co-editor, *Psychological Aspects of Women's Health Care* (American Psychiatric Press Inc., 1993); *A Clinician's Guide to Menopause* (in press, for release 1997); over 60 publications in medical journals relating to women's health, research, career dev. for women, & the mind-body relationship; several women's health documentaries, audiotapes, media articles. **EDIT:** Assoc. Ed., *Journal of Reproductive and Infant Psychology*, & *General Hospital Psychiatry*, 1991 to date. **AFFIL:** World Psychiatric Association (V-Chair, Section on Women's Health 1996 to date); Council of Faculties of Medicine (V-Chair, Gender Issues Committee 1996 to date); Academy of Psychosomatic Medicine (Exec. Committee 1993 to date); Marcé Society (Exec. Committee 1990-95); American Society for Psychosomatic Obstetrics & Gynecology (Pres. 1989-90). **HONS:** Fellow: American Coll. of Psychiatrists; International Coll. of Psychosomatic Medicine; American Psychosomatic Society. **INTERESTS:** antiques; textiles. **MISC:** over 150 papers presented to nat'l & int'l professional societies; peer reviewer for over 20 medical journals/ granting agencies, 1989 to date. **COMMENT:** *"Dr. Stewart is dedicated to improving the health of women through education and research. She has written, taught and spoken widely and was the first appointment in the world to a university Chair in Women's Health."*

Stewart, Hilary 📖 ☸ 📜
Writer and Illustrator. Box 5, Quathiaski Cove, BC V0P 1N0. Born St. Lucia, W. Indies 1924. **EDUC:** St. Martin's Sch. of Art, London, UK, Grad. 1951. **CAREER:** Women's Royal Air Force, 1943-47; interior design associate, 1952-56; costume designer, CBC Television, 1956-60; Art Dir., BCTV, 1960-72; full-time writer & illustrator, 1972-92. **SELECTED PUBLICATIONS:** *Artifacts of the Northwest Coast Indians* (Hancock House, 1973); *Indian Fishing: Early Methods on the Northwest Coast* (J.J Douglas, 1977); *Robert Davidson: Haida Printmaker* (Douglas & McIntyre, 1979); *Looking at Indian Art of the Northwest Coast* (Douglas & McIntyre, 1981); *Wild Teas, Coffee and Cordials* (Douglas & McIntyre, 1981); *Cedar: Tree of Life to the Northwest Coast Indians* (Douglas & McIntyre, 1984); *The Adventures and Sufferings of John R. Jewitt, Captive of Maquinna* (Douglas & McIntyre, 1987); *Totem Poles* (Douglas & McIntyre, 1990); *Looking at Totem Poles* (Douglas & McIntyre, 1993); *Stone, Bone, Antler & Shell* (Douglas & McIntyre, 1996); illustrated several other books, various commissioned work. **AFFIL:** Archaeological Society of B.C. (Life mbr.; Exec. 1967-90); Museum of Anthropology, Univ. of British Columbia (Hon. Mbr.); Western Canada Wilderness Committee; Friends of Clayoquot Sound. **HONS:** Explorations Award, Canada Council, 1976; Award for Excellence in Writing, Pacific Northwest Booksellers, 1980; Robert Hong-Brown Award, B.C. Booksellers, 1985; Duthie Booksellers' Choice Award, 1988; Canada 125 Medal. **INTERESTS:** natural history; Northwest Coast Indian culture; paper making; drumming; basketry; carving; environmental issues; photography & more. **MISC:** est. Hilary Stewart Foundation for First Nations Educational Programs, Univ. of British Columbia. **COMMENT:** *"A fit, busy, active senior living a rich and fulfilling life on three acres of forest/meadow on a small, beautiful island off the coast of British Columbia."*

Stewart, Janet, Q.C. ■■ ⚖ ♡
Managing Partner, LERNER & ASSOCIATES (70-person law firm, offices in London & Toronto), 80 Dufferin Ave., P.O. Box 2335, London, ON N6A 4G4 (519) 672-4131, FAX 672-2044. **BAR:** Ont., 1969. **CAREER:** specializes in bus. law & estate planning. **AFFIL:** Huron Coll., London (Bd. of Dir.); London Community Foundation (Bd. of Dir.); Big Sisters of London (Bd. of Dir.); Salvation Army (Nat'l Advisory Bd.); London Convention Centre (Bd. of Dir.). **HONS:** Woman of Distinction, YM-YWCA, 1993. **MISC:** legal resource to many feminist organizations in London incl. Womanpower, Women's Workshop & Women's Community House.

Stewart, Lecia, M.B.A. $ ✎
President, WEST COAST EXPRESS, 815 W. Hastings St., Ste. 800, Vancouver, BC V6C 1B4 (604) 689-3641, FAX 689-3896. Born Vancouver 1956. m. Jack Gerow. 2 ch. **EDUC:** Centennial Coll., Certificate (Journalism) 1976; Harvard Business Sch., Exec. MBA Program 1993. **CAREER:** Reporter, *The Ottawa Journal, The Calgary Albertan*, 1976-79; Mgr of Media Rel'ns & Publications, Vancouver Symphony, 1979-83; Dir. of Comm. & Special Projects, BC Health Union, 1983-90; Dir. of Public Consultation, Ministry of Aboriginal Affairs, Prov. of B.C., 1991-92; VP, Corp. Svcs, BC Transit, 1992-94; Pres., West Coast Express, 1994 to date. **SELECTED PUBLICATIONS:** widely published as a journalist. **AFFIL:** Harvard Business Club of B.C. (Exec.); Vancouver Transportation Club. **INTERESTS:** skiing; tennis; music. **COMMENT:** *"In many ways my five years as a journalist was really the beginning of my education. It provided me with a wide range of experience in a relatively short period and helped me define my career priorities. Harvard helped refine those priorities by providing insights into how organizations from countries all over the world are dealing with many of the same issues we face in Canada. Issues that require joint solutions from business and government to allow Canadian businesses to compete in the global marketplace and provide high value-added jobs for our workers yet keep the cost of government from escalating and adding to public sector debt."*

Stewart, Nalini, B.Jour. ✎ ♡ ☸
Freelance Journalist. 2 Lamport Avenue, Toronto, ON M4W 1S6 (416) 961-2213, FAX 929-8733. Born New Delhi, India 1944. m. Timothy Clair. 3 ch. Tarun, Saira, Indira. **EDUC:** Carleton Univ., B.Jour. 1964, Grad. Dipl.(Public Admin.) 1965. **CAREER:** various positions, Ont. Gov't & Ontario Hydro, 1966-70; freelance journalist. **VOLUNTEER CAREER:** Volunteer Committee, Art Gallery of Ontario, 1973-85; Founding Dir., The Power Plant at Harbourfront, 1978-87; Dir., Harbourfront Corporation, 1978-82; Dir., Toronto International Film Festival, 1982-89; V-Chair, Ontario Arts Council, 1985-88; Chair, Ontario Arts Council, 1988-91; Dir., The National Theatre Sch., 1992 to date; Dir., The Writers' Development Trust, 1992-96; Chair, 1996 to date; Gov., Stratford Festival, 1995 to date. **SELECTED PUBLICATIONS:** articles for *Maclean's*, *Toronto Life*, *Quill and Quire*,

Executive, Asia Pacific Business & The Toronto Star. **AFFIL:** Asia Pacific Foundation of Canada; CFMT-TV (Dir.); Lester B. Pearson Coll. of the Pacific (Dir.); International Council of the Asia Society (Elected Mbr.); The Canadian Club (Pres. Elect); York Univ. (Gov.). **COMMENT:** *"Achievements in volunteer sector: mainly the arts but now also moving into education."*

Stewart Schaddelee, Nadina ■■ ⊕ ⊗ ⼬
President and owner, MAARNADA STUDIOS LTD. (centre for wellness & creativity), 4635 Vantreight Dr., Victoria, BC V8N 3W8 (604) 477-1651. Born Victoria 1947. m. Maarten. 2 ch. Trevor, Troy. **EDUC:** Queenswood, Spiritual Companioning 1994; ongoing educ. in life exper. & wellness-related topics. **CAREER:** Smile Show (musical theatre), 1960-65; Admin. Asst., St. Mary's Priory Hospital, 1968-69; Fitness Coord., Centre for Assessment, Rehabilitation Training & Enhanced Lifestyle; Wellness Consultant; Dir., Alternatives in Fitness, 1988-95; Pres., Maarnada Studios Ltd., 1988 to date; gallery owner. **SELECTED CREDITS:** videos on well-being & sculpting incl. *The Art of Sculpting Chocolate*. **SELECTED PUBLICATIONS:** "Inspirations from Maarnada" (1994); "Beauty and the Breast" (*Focus on Women*, 1994); "Soul to Soul on Father's Day" (*Focus on Women*, 1995). **EXHIBITIONS:** curator, art exhibitions, Maarnada Studios Ltd., 1993-96. **AFFIL:** Victoria Hospice Society (Bd. of Dir. 1994 to date); The Alexandra Women's Services Association International (Wellness Consultant 1992 to date). **INTERESTS:** wellness educ.; art for the environment; well-being of all; interconnectedness & how each person can make a difference; creating videos on interesting people & the process of creating art (has turned into professional venture). **MISC:** donates sculpture for awareness & fundraising for art therapy for abused children; also to Art Gallery of Greater Victoria, & for Hospice corp. swim trophy & Wellness Award for outstanding svc. to the community. **COMMENT:** *"Maarnada is a sacred place to honour the personal story and well-being. With my husband Maarten's soulful art and love, my vision is a reality."*

Stewart Streit, Marlene, O.C.,B.A.,LL.D. ⍉
Athlete, Golfer. Stouffville, ON. Born Cereal, Alta. 1934. m. J. Douglas Streit. 2 ch. Darlene Louise Streit, Lynn Elizabeth Streit. **EDUC:** Rollins Coll., B.A.(Bus. Admin.) 1956. **SPORTS CAREER:** began caddying, Lookout Country Club, Fonthill, Ont., 1947; began golfing, 1949; Ont. Jr. Girls' Champion, 1951, 1952; Ont. Ladies' Amateur Champion, 1951, 1956, 1957, 1958, 1968, 1969, 1970, 1972, 1974,

1976, 1977; Ont. Ladies Amateur Runner-up, 1953, 1966, 1978, 1979, 1980, 1982, 1992; Ont. Sr. Women's Champion, 1985, 1987, 1988, 1990, 1992, 1995; CLGA Close Champion, 1951-56, 1959, 1963, 1968; CLGA Amateur Champion, 1951, 1954, 1955, 1956, 1958, 1959, 1963, 1968, 1969, 1972, 1973; CLGA Amateur Runner-up, 1953, 1970, 1971, 1978, 1982; CLGA Sr. Women's Amateur Champion, 1985, 1987, 1988, 1993; Ladies Supertest Open, LPGA event, Low Amateur, 1968; Peter Jackson Classic, LPGA event, Low Amateur, 1975, 1978; Du Maurier Classic, LPGA event, Low Amateur, 1983, 1985; British Women's Amateur Champion, Porthcawl G.C., Wales, 1953; Australian Women's Amateur Champion, Royal Sydney Golf Club, Sydney, Australia, 1963; North-South Champion, Pinehurst, NC, 1956, 1974; US Women's Intercollegiate Champion, Lafayette, Ind., 1956; Helen Lee Doherty Championship, Coral Ridge Country Club, Fort Lauderdale, Fla., 1959, 1960, 1961, 1965; Doherty Sr. Div., Coral Ridge Country Club, Fort Lauderdale, FL, 1987, 1989, 1993, 1996; US Golf Association Women's Amateur Champion, 1956; US Golf Association Women's Amateur Runner-up, 1966; USGA Women's Open Championship, Low Amateur, 1957; USGA Sr. Women's Amateur Champion, 1985, 1994; USGA Sr. Women's Amateur Runner-up, 1986, 1988, 1991, 1995; mbr., Ont. Interprov. Team to Cdn Ladies' Golf Association Amateur Championship, 1951, 1953, 1957, 1958, 1959, 1963, 1964, 1968-74, 1987, 1992, qualified but declined, 1994 & other yrs.; mbr., Cdn Ladies' Golf Union Int'l Team, 1953; mbr., CLGA Commonwealth Team, 1959, 1963, 1967, playing Captain 1979 (winners), 1983, named to team but declined, 1971, 1975; mbr., CLGA World Amateur Team, 1966 (Low Individual), 1970, 1972, non-playing captain 1978, 1980, 1992, playing captain 1984, named to team but unavailable 1968, 1974, declined non-playing captain position, 1994; played for N.Am., N.Am. vs Europe Sr. Women's Invitational Matches, 1989-93, 1995, 1996. **AFFIL:** CPGA of Ontario (Hon. Dir.); CLGA (Advisory Panel, 1993 to date); Ontario Ladies' Golf Association (Hon. Mbr.); Lookout Point Country Club; York Downs Golf & Country Club; Canada's Sports Hall of Fame (Gov.); Canada's Golf Hall of Fame, RCGA (Selection Committee); Ada Mackenzie Memorial Foundation (Dir. 1974-94; Pres. 1984-85). **HONS:** tied with Charlotte Whitten for Cdn Woman of the Year, in Canadian Press Poll, 1953; Lou Marsh Award, 1951, 1956; Cdn Woman Athlete of the Year, 1951, 1953, 1956, 1960, 1963; Canada's Sports Hall of Fame, 1962; Officer of the Order of Canada, 1967; RCGA Cdn Golf Hall of Fame, 1971; LL.D.(Hon.), Brock Univ., 1973; Sr. Woman Amateur of the Year, *Golf World* Magazine, 1994. MISC: 1 Handicap, 1995; 0 Handicap, 1996; Jr. Chrm, Ontario Ladies' Golf Association, 1960, 1961, 1962.

Stirk, Linda, B.Sc.,M.D.,C.M.,Ph.D., F.R.C.S.C.,F.A.C.O.G. ⊕
Obstetrician and Gynecologist, NORTH YORK GENERAL HOSPITAL, 1333 Sheppard Ave. E., Ste. 202, Willowdale, ON M2J 1V1 (416) 490-9140, FAX 490-7760. Born Montreal 1952. m. David E.C. Cole. 2 ch. Emily, Gregory. EDUC: McGill Univ., B.Sc.(Human Genetics) 1974, M.D./C.M. 1981, Ph.D.(Biochem. Genetics) 1984. CAREER: Straight Intern, Internal Medicine, Victoria General Hospital, Dalhousie Univ., Halifax, 1981-82; Resident, Obstetrics & Gynecology, Dalhousie Univ., 1982-86; Lecturer, Dept. of Obstetrics & Gynecology, 1986-93; consulting staff, Grace Maternity Hospital, Halifax, 1986-93; active staff, Victoria General Hospital, 1986-93; Asst. Dir., Termination of Pregnancy Unit, 1986-90; active staff, Halifax Infirmary Hospital, 1986-93; Rep., Obstetrics & Gynecology, CME Div., Fac. of Medicine, Dalhousie Univ., 1987-92; mbr., Ambulatory Care Committee, Victoria General Hospital, 1987-92; Coord., Residency Training, 1987-93; Dir., Ambulatory Care Clinic, Dept. of Gynecology, 1988-89; participant, Colposcopy Clinic, Dept. of Gynecology, 1989-93; active staff, North York General Hospital, 1993 to date. SELECTED PUBLICATIONS: various articles, abstracts & invited lectures. AFFIL: Society of Obstetricians & Gynecologists of Canada; American Coll. of Obstetrics & Gynecology (Fellow); Royal Coll. of Physicians & Surgeons (Fellow); Ontario Medical Association; Canadian Medical Association; N.S. Medical Association (1986-93); Society of Obstetrics & Gynecology of Toronto; American Society for Colposcopy & Cervical Pathology; Society of Canadian Colposcopists; FIGO. INTERESTS: stamp collecting; skiing; swimming; hiking. COMMENT: *"I have worked hard to combine a busy obstetrical practice with a rewarding home life and two wonderful children, Emily and Gregory. I try to bring an experienced attitude to my patients and enjoy teaching medical students, hopefully to be a role model to female students on combining career and family."*

Stoddart-Hansen, Sandra, B.A. ■ Ⓢ
President, THE BALLANTREE GROUP (consulting firm specializing in working with organizations in transition on the people side of bus.). Born Victoria, B.C. EDUC: Univ. of British Columbia, Certificate (English as a Second Language Teaching) 1969; Carleton Univ., B.A. (Linguistics) 1972. CAREER: Dir. Gen. of Hum. Res., Fed. Dept. of Justice, 1989-90; Reg'l Dir., Fed. Dept. of Supply & Svcs, 1990-92; VP, Hum. Res., British Columbia's Children's Hospital & British Columbia's Women's Hospital & Health Centre Society, 1993-95. SELECTED PUBLICATIONS: "Overview of the New Transportation Legislation: The Changing Transportation Policy Environment" (*Univ. of Manitoba Transport Institute Occasional Paper 6*, Sept. 1988); "Water Safety and Pleasure Boating" (*Univ. of Manitoba Transport Institute Occasional Paper 8*, July 1989). AFFIL: Human Resources Management Association of B.C.; Hunter Sailing Association (Sec.); Vancouver Rowing Club; Registered Nurses' Foundation of B.C. (Dir.). INTERESTS: sailing; classical guitar; squash. COMMENT: *"I have enjoyed a diverse career in policy, line management and human resources management, taking me to several locations across Canada; my experiences have been extremely rewarding."*

Stoffman, Judith, B.A.,M.A. ✎ ▯
Book Review Editor, THE TORONTO STAR, 1 Yonge St., Toronto, ON M5E 1E6 (416) 869-4964, FAX 869-4322. Born Budapest 1947. m. Daniel Stoffman. 2 ch. EDUC: Univ. of British Columbia, B.A.(English Lit.); Sussex Univ., UK, M.A.(English Lit.) 1969; Univ. d'Aix-Marseille, France, Diploma in French language & culture 1980. CAREER: Reporter, *Vancouver Province*, 1968; various jobs incl. Prod., *As It Happens*, Prod., *Ideas*, & researcher/interviewer, *Marketplace*, CBC Radio & TV, 1970-74; Publicity Dir., Penguin Books, 1971-74; newswriter & reporter, CBC-Radio, 1974-75; Comm. Coord., Women's Bureau, Ont. Ministry of Labour, 1975-77; Assoc. Ed., *Weekend* magazine, 1977-79; Sr. Ed., *Today* magazine, 1980-82; Sr. Ed., *Canadian Living*, 1983-85; Asst. Mng Ed., 1985-87; Sr. Ed., *Report on Business* Magazine (*The Globe and Mail*), 1987-90; Fashion Ed., *The Toronto Star*, 1990-91; Book Review Ed., 1991 to date; Guest Lecturer, Eotvos Lorand Univ. & Univ. of Szeged, Hungary, 1993. SELECTED PUBLICATIONS: Sandor Kopacsi's *In the Name of the Working Class*, translated with Daniel Stoffman (Lester and Orpen, Dennys, 1986); "The Way of All Flesh," originally written for *Weekend*, has been reprinted in 5 anthologies. AFFIL: PEN International. COMMENT: *"Born in Budapest, Hungary, which she fled as a child after the '56 uprising, Judy Stoffman is now a Toronto-based writer and literary editor of the Star. She was co-translator of the book* In the

Name of the Working Class *(1986) and is the author of a forthcoming biography of the painter Lauren Harris, as well as of the widely anthologized essay on aging,* The Way of All Flesh. *"*

Stokes, Antoinette ⍟ ♥
Director General, FÉDÉRATION DE GYMNASTIQUE DU QUÉBEC, 4545 av. Pierre de Coubertin, C.P. 1000, Succ. M, Montréal, QC H1V 3R2 (514) 252-3043, FAX 252-3169. Born Montreal 1959. CAREER: various positions, Toronto-Dominion Bank, 1978-81; Asst. Mgr, Sport Olympia, 1981-83; Exec. Dir., Quebec Olympic Wrestling Federation, 1983-87; Administrative Dir., Quebec Handball Federation, 1988-89; Exec. Dir., Canadian Amateur Wrestling Federation, 1989-92; Dir. Gen., Fédération de Gymnastique du Québec, 1992 to date. SELECTED PUBLICATIONS: *Canadian Amateur Wrestling Association Rulebook*, pairing & results section (1979-87). AFFIL: Canadian Society of Association Executives; Canadian Amateur Wrestling Officials' Association (Sec.-Treas. 1981-83); Quebec Olympic Wrestling Federation (Dir. 1981-83); Gymnastics Canada Gymnastique (Dir. 1996 to date). HONS: Finalist, Official of the Year, Mérite Sportif Québec, 1981, 1982. INTERESTS: photography; yoga; cinema. MISC: Pairing Master at numerous wrestling events, incl. 1976 Olympic Games, Montréal. COMMENT: *"I strive to learn from life's experiences, to apply and share that which I have learned."*

Stone, Karen K., A.P.R. ■ Ⓢ ⊕
Director of Public Relations, IWK-GRACE HEALTH CENTRE FOR CHILDREN, WOMEN & FAMILIES, 5980 University Ave., Halifax, NS B3H 4N1 (902) 420-6740, FAX 420-6790, EMAIL kstone@iwkgrace.ns.ca. Born Truro, N.S. 1960. s. EDUC: Mount Saint Vincent Univ., Bachelor of Public Rel'ns 1982. CAREER: Student Union Pres., Mount Saint Vincent Univ., 1981-82; Advtg Mgr, *The Warrior Newspaper*; Advtg & Public Rel'ns Dir., The Shearwater Int'l Air Show, 1982-85; Acct Exec., Corporate Communications Ltd., 1985-87; Acct Supervisor, 1987-92; Atlantic Reg. Mktg Mgr, Deloitte and Touche, 1992-93; Dir. of Public Rel'ns, The Salvation Army Grace Maternity Hospital, 1993-95; Dir., Public Rel'ns, IWK-Grace Health Centre, 1995 to date. AFFIL: Canadian Public Relations Society (accredited 1989; Past-Pres., N.S. Chapter); Mount Saint Vincent Univ. (Chair, Public Rel'ns Degree Program Advisory Bd.); Mount Saint Vincent Alumnae Association (Past Pres.). INTERESTS: golf. COMMENT: *"Karen has worked in the public relations field for over a* decade. *As a former consultant with one of Atlantic Canada's leading communications firms, her client list included a telecommunications utility, a power utility, an international airline, and Atlantic Canada tourism. With a move to health care 3 years ago, Karen has thrived on the challenges of health reform and the possibilities it presents."*

Stone-Blackburn, Susan, B.A.,M.A., Ph.D. ⍟ 📖 🗇
Professor of English and Associate Dean of Graduate Studies, UNIVERSITY OF CALGARY, 2500 University Dr. N.W., Calgary, AB T2N 1N4 (403) 220-3153, FAX 289-1123, EMAIL sstonebl@acs.ucalgary.ca. Born Wisconsin 1941. d. 3 ch. EDUC: Lawrence Coll., B.A. (English) 1963; Univ. of Colorado, M.A. (English) 1967, Ph.D.(English) 1970. CAREER: Asst. Prof., Univ. of Calgary, 1973-79; Assoc. Prof., 1979-86; Assoc. Dean of Humanities, 1985-89; Prof., 1986 to date; Advisor to Pres. on Women's Issues, 1989-91; Assoc. Dean of Grad. Studies, 1993 to date. SELECTED PUBLICATIONS: *Robertson Davies, Playwright: A Search for the Self on the Canadian Stage* (1985); "Consciousness Evolution and Early Telepathic Tales" (*Science Fiction Studies* (20)2, 1993); "Feminist Nurturers and Psychic Healers," *Imaginative Futures*, ed. Milton Wolf & Daryl Mallett (1995). AFFIL: Science Fiction Research Association; Association for Canadian Theatre Research; Maenad Theatre Productions (Pres., Bd. of Dir. 1991-93). INTERESTS: feminist & ecological issues. COMMENT: *"I am a seeker and a generalist, engaged in university administration, research, teaching, parenting and the pursuit of personal growth, tranquillity and wisdom."*

Stonehouse, Marilyn ♥ ⌣ ⊗
Line Producer and Production Manager, PEBBLEHUT PRODUCTIONS, 900 Yonge St., Ste. 400, Toronto, ON M4W 3P5. Born Hamilton, Ont. 1934. EDUC: Port Credit High Sch., Matriculation; Dominion Business Coll. CAREER: Continuity/Comm. Prod., Robert Lawrence Productions (Canada) Ltd.; Pres., Complete Film Services-Post Production Service; Prod. Mgr, DeLaurentis (Dec); freelance. DIRECTOR: Pebblehut Productions. AFFIL: Directors' Guild of Canada. INTERESTS: film. COMMENT: *"I thoroughly enjoy the film business and the people within it."*

Storks, Pauline J. ■■ Ⓢ ♥ ⊚
Vice-Chair, CLARINGTON HYDRO ELECTRIC COMMISSION, 2849 Hwy #2 & Lamb's Rd., Bowmanville, ON L1C 3K9 (905) 987-4253. Born Newcastle, Ont. 1924. m. William J. 2

ch. Candace Janet Dovic-Storks, William Kim Storks (deceased). **EDUC:** Newcastle High Sch., Grade 12; Clark High Sch., Hist. & English (Grade 13 level). **CAREER:** business owner, 40 yrs. **VOLUNTEER CAREER:** former Dir., Children's Aid Society; former District Chair, Girl Guides; former V-Chair, Ganaraska Conservation Authority; Sunday Sch. Teacher, Newcastle United Church, 40 yrs.; former mbr. of Exec., Newcastle Chamber of Commerce. **AFFIL:** Newcastle Chamber of Commerce; Newcastle Business Improvement Area; Newcastle United Church; Ganaraska Conservation Authority (Fundraising Dinner Committee); Newcastle Lions (Dir. 35+ yrs.); Municipal Electric Association (Dir.; 2nd V-Chair); MEA Mearie Board (2nd V-Chair; V-Chair, Exec.). **HONS:** Businessperson Award, Town of Newcastle; Gold Medalist for Vocal, 15 yrs. & under, Durham Music Festival, 1940. **INTERESTS:** people; conservation; community. **COMMENT:** *"My life has been about service, to my family, church, community and province."*

Strakowski, Patricia Elizabeth ✪ 🎓

Visual Artist. 4908-21 Ave. NW, Calgary, AB T3B 0X2 (403) 288-8272. Born Calgary 1937. m. John Joseph Strakowski. 3 ch. **EDUC:** Alberta Coll. of Art, Dipl. 1979. **CAREER:** visual artist. **EXHIBITIONS:** Virginia Christopher Galleries, Calgary (1986); *Collectanea*, installation, Muttart Gallery, Calgary (1987); *Small Sculptures*, Virginia Christopher Galleries (1988); *Private Spaces, Public Places*, Virginia Christopher Galleries (1989); *Paper Routes*, Front Gallery, Edmonton (1989); *Small Sculptures*, The Gallery, Banff (1990); *Window Project*, installation, Calgary Centre for Performing Arts (1991); *Revival*, Muttart Gallery (1994); numerous group exhibitions incl. *Art Off the Wall*, City of Calgary Parks & Recreation (1981); *The Works: Celebration of Women in the Arts*, Manulife Place, Edmonton (1988); *Myth and Magic*, Alberta Society of Artists, The Works, Edmonton (1991); *Wild Things*, juried show, Alberta Society of Artists, Manulife 1 Place, Edmonton (1994); *Apocrypha 11: Mythic Images Outside Orthodoxy*, North Park Gallery, Victoria (1994). **COLLECTIONS:** Alberta Art Foundation; Alberta Energy; Bass Ticket Services Ltd.; Calgary Allied Arts Foundation; Claridge Investments; Esso Canada Resources Ltd.; Home Oil Canada; Kanesko Holdings Ltd.; Marshall Cummings and Associates; Norcen; Rice Brydon; Alberta Crafts Council; Alex Chapman Design; British Petroleum Canada Ltd.; Charles Bronfman Collection; Edmonton Art Gallery; Franklin Silverstone Fine Arts; Imperial Oil Ltd.; MacKimmie Matthews; Macleod Dixon; PanContinental; Rockyview Hospital; Trizec Equities. **AFFIL:** Alberta Society of Artists; Alberta Craft Council. **HONS:** Honourable Mention Award, Winnipeg Art Gallery, 1984. **INTERESTS:** living things; flower gardens; different art forms; maintaining my centre. **MISC:** recipient, various grants; *Alberta Who's Who* & *Canadian Who's Who*. **COMMENT:** *"My sculptures and two-dimensional art works have been shown nationally and internationally. Galleries in Calgary, Edmonton and Victoria show my works. I hope to continue to change and evolve as my pieces do."*

Strand, Kirsten K., B.Sc.,CMP, CITE ■■ $ 🎾

Managing Director and owner, FAMOUS EVENTS & DESTINATIONS (event & destination mgmt), 68 Water St., Ste. 504, Vancouver, BC V6B 1A4 (604) 689-3448, FAX 689-3245. Director and owner, TOTAL ENTERTAINMENT NETWORK LTD. Born Vancouver 1958. cl. **EDUC:** Univ. of British Columbia, B.Sc.(Cell Biol./Physiology) 1982; Convention Liaison Council, CMP (Meeting Planning) 1993; Society of Incentive & Travel Executives, CITE (Incentive Travel) 1996. **CAREER:** Research Asst., Dept. of Pathology, Univ. of British Columbia, 1982-83; Dir./owner, Famous Events & Destinations, 1983 to date; Dir./owner, Total Entertainment Network Ltd., 1986 to date; Dir./owner, Pacific Rim Incentives Ltd., 1986-96. **SELECTED CREDITS:** Producer, Molson Indy Opening Ceremony; Coord., Comité international des entreprises succursales; Producer, International Children's Day, United Nations; Coord., Congress of Neurosurgeons. **DIRECTOR:** Famous Events & Destinations; Total Entertainment Network Ltd. **AFFIL:** Society of Incentive & Travel Executives; International Special Events Society; Meeting Professionals International; Tourism Vancouver; Australasian Incentive Association. **HONS:** nominee, Women of Distinction Award, 1996; Achievement Award, "40 Under 40," 1994; SITE Crystal Awards, 1993, 1994, 1996; Award for Excellence, AIA, 1995; finalist, Award for Best Business Achievement, 1986 & 1988; Silver Medalist, Dragon Boat, 1996; Mixed Nat'l Champions, Dragon Boat, 1990. **INTERESTS:** golf; tennis; dragon boating; weight training; aerobics; reading; travel. **COMMENT:** *"Kirsten Strand is owner/director of Western Canada's leading event and destination management company. Famous Events & Destinations has been recognized by the Society of Incentive & Travel Executives with its industry-recognized SITE Crystal Award. Additionally, Kirsten has been chosen as one of Vancouver's top business achievers under the age of 40."*

Stratton, Anna 🏹 ⊗ ♥
Producer and Partner, TRIPTYCH MEDIA INC., 56 The Esplanade, Toronto, ON M5E 1A7 (416) 203-2866, FAX 203-2867, EMAIL trip@passport.ca. Born Seattle, Wash. 1946. m. Tom Campbell. 1 ch. EDUC: Canadian Film Centre, Dipl.(Producer) 1992. CAREER: Theatre Officer, Canada Council, 1975-78; VP & Prod., Maple Interactive Corporation, 1983; Ptnr, Stratton, Frank and Associates, 1978-82; Asst. Head, Canada Council Theatre Section, 1983-88; Sr. Advisor, Taskforce on Professional Training, Cultural Sector, 1991; Ptnr & Prod., Triptych Media Inc. SELECTED CREDITS: Prod., *L'Ombre*, 1992; Prod., *Zero Patience*, 1994; *Lilies*, 1996. AFFIL: Dance Umbrella of Ontario (Pres.); Toronto Women in Film & Television. INTERESTS: yoga; tai chi; video production. COMMENT: *"A producer with more than 25 years' experience in the arts as administrator, manager, fundraiser, educator, publicist, stage manager, advocate and volunteer."*

Stratton, Jennifer J., B.Comm.,M.B.A. Ⓢ
Director, Payments and Research, CREDIT UNION CENTRAL OF CANADA, 300 The East Mall, Ste. 500, Toronto, ON M9B 6B7 (416) 232-3431, FAX 232-1042, EMAIL 74532.1201@compuserve.com. EDUC: Concordia Univ., B.Comm. 1983; Univ. of Toronto, M.B.A. 1984. CAREER: Instructor, Protestant Sch. Bd. of Montreal, 1979-81; Research Analyst, Canadian Co-Operative Credit Society, 1984-85; Mgr, Payment Settlements, 1985-88; Dir., Payments & Research, Credit Union Central of Canada, 1988 to date. AFFIL: World Vision, Mississauga CVA; Canadian Payments Association (Obs. Dir. 1995 to date); Arts Etobicoke (Dir. 1990-93); Volunteer Centre of Peel (Dir. 1987-90; Chair, Fin. Committee); Community Expansion Task Force, St. James Church, Etobicoke (Chair 1994). HONS: Toronto Award of Merit, International Association of Business Communicators, 1991; Fellow, Credit Union Institute of Canada, 1993. INTERESTS: travel; photography; recreational sports.

Stratas, Teresa (Anastasia Strataki) ■ ■ ⊗
Soprano. Born Toronto 1938. EDUC: student of Irene Jessner, 1956-59; Univ. of Toronto, Fac. of Music, grad. 1959. CAREER: winner, Metropolitan Opera auditions, 1959; major roles in opera houses throughout the world. SELECTED CREDITS: Mimi, *La Bohème*; Tatiana, *Eugene Onegin*; Susanna, *The Marriage of Figaro*; Nedda, *Pagliacci*; Marenka, *The Bartered Bride*; Three Heroines, *Il Trittico*; Violetta, *La Traviata*; title role, *Rusalka*; Jennie,

Mahogonny; created title role in Alan Berg's *Lulu*, Paris Grand Opera, 1979; film appearances incl. *Kaiser von Atlantis*; *Seven Deadly Sins*; Zefirelli's *La Traviata*; *Salome*; *Lulu*; *Paganini*; *Zarewitsch*; *Eugene Onegin*. Broadway appearances incl. her debut in *Rags*, 1986; creator of the role, Marie Antoinette, *Ghosts of Versailles*, world premier, Metropolitan Opera, 1992; sang both female leading roles, *Il Tabarro/Pagliacci* double bill, Metropolitan Opera opening, 1994; numerous recordings incl. Richard Strauss' *Salomè*; Songs of *Kurt Weill*. HONS: Order of Canada; 3 Grammy Awards; Emmy Award; 3 Grammy nominations; Drama Desk Award, 1986; nomination, Tony Awards, 1986; Tiffany Award, 1994; named Performer of the Year, Canadian Music Council, 1979; Hon. Degrees from Univ. of Toronto, Juilliard Sch. of Music & McMaster Univ.

Strehlke, Claudia, M.D., F.R.C.P.(C) ⊕ ☺ ✎
Physician and Director of I.C.U, QUEEN ELIZABETH II HOSPITAL, 10409 - 98 St., Grande Prairie, AB T8V 2E8 (403) 538-7588, FAX 532-6802. Director, GRANDE PRAIRIE CANCER CLINIC. Born Kassel, Germany 1941. m. Burkhard Strehlke. 4 ch. Heidi Marina, Christina, Sonya Claudia, Monica Barbara. EDUC: Univ. of Alberta, M.D.(Medicine) 1965, F.R.C.P.(C) 1970; Hammersmith, London, UK, Postgrad. Fellow (Medicine) 1966. CAREER: private consultant practice, Internal Medicine, Edmonton, 1971-73; private consultant practice, Internal Medicine, Grande Prairie, 1973 to date; Dir., I.C.U., Queen Elizabeth II Hospital, 1975 to date; Dir., Grande Prairie Cancer Clinic, 1987 to date; Pres., N.W. Reg. Medical Staff, Mistahia Health Reg., 1994 to date. SELECTED PUBLICATIONS: "General Internal Medicine in Rural Alberta: Challenging, Stimulating and Rewarding" (*Royal College of Physicians and Surgeons of Canada Annuals*, Vol. 27, No. 3, Apr. 1994). AFFIL: Alberta Medical Association; Canadian Medical Association; Alberta Society for Intensive Care Physicians; Canadian Society for Intensive Care Physicians; Canadian Society for Internal Medicine; Royal Coll. of Physicians & Surgeons, Canada (Fellow); Alberta Heart & Stroke Foundation (Dir. 1989-94); Medical Alumni Association, Univ. of Alberta (Pres. 1990-91); St. Joseph's Catholic Church (Parish Council). HONS: Rural Clinical Teaching Award for excellence in teaching, Professional Association of Internes and Residents of Alberta, 1995/96. INTERESTS: travel; camping; hiking; reading; cooking. MISC: Fed. Gov't Task Force on Standards for Critical Care, 1985. COMMENT: *"I am a capable, commit-*

ted and well-respected physician who prides herself on being compassionate and caring. I strive to reach my personal ideal of serving my family and my patients with dedication and love."

Strelioff, Susan, B.A.,M.A.,M.B.A. ■ $
Senior Vice-President, Governance, NATIONAL TRUST COMPANY, One Financial Place, 1 Adelaide St. E., 3rd Fl., Toronto, ON M5C 2W8 (416) 361-3727, FAX 361-4037, EMAIL streliof@ntrust.com. **EDUC:** Victoria Coll., Univ. of Toronto, B.A.(English Lit.) 1972; Univ. of Western Ontario, M.B.A. 1978; New York Univ., M.A.(Psych.) 1983; Canadian Securities Course 1986. **CAREER:** mgmt trainee, Bank of Montreal, 1972-74; Recruiting Officer, Royal Bank of Canada, 1974-76; Credit Analyst, 1978-79; Asst. VP, The Royal Bank & Trust Company, NY, 1979-83; Mgr, Training, The Royal Bank of Canada, 1983-84; Acct Mgr, 1984-85; Mgr, Examination, Office of the Superintendent of Financial Institutions Canada, 1989-90; Dir., Examinations, Trust & Loan Div., 1990-92; Pres. & CEO, Saskatchewan Economic Development Corporation, 1992-93; Pres. & CEO, The Development Corporations of Ontario & Asst. Deputy Min., Fin. & Bus. Svcs, Ministry of Econ. Dev., Trade & Tourism, Gov't of Ont., 1993-95. **AFFIL:** Riverdale Hospital; YMCA of Metro Toronto; Ottawa Life Sciences Technology Park (Exec. Committee). **HONS:** Dean's List, Univ. of Western Ontario, 1977, 1978.

Strong, Marilyn, B.A. ■ $
President, THE STRONG COMMUNICATIONS GROUP INC., Box 3550, Castlegar, BC V1N 3W3 (604) 365-6035, EMAIL mstrong@awinc.com. Born Toronto 1952. **EDUC:** Univ. of Waterloo, B.A.(Recreation/Soc.) 1976. **CAREER:** Pres., The Strong Communication Group Inc., 1984 to date. **AFFIL:** Castlegar Chamber of Commerce; Minister's Advisory Council for Sport & Recreation, B.C.; Regional Recreation Commission 1. **HONS:** 5-Yr. Service Award, Royal Life Saving Society, B.C. & Yukon Branch. **INTERESTS:** swimming; golf; cryptograms; computer; Internet. **COMMENT:** *"Living in the Kootenay region of B.C. and being an entrepreneur has allowed me to develop my skills in a wide range of business and recreational activities. Using the Internet and e-mail to work from anywhere and for anyone has been a tremendous advantage."*

Strugnell, Arlene ■■ ♡ $
Executive Director, FEDERATED WOMEN'S INSTITUTES OF CANADA (rural women's organization/nat'l office for Women's Institutes across Canada), 251 Bank St., Ste. 606, Ottawa, ON K2P 1X3 (613) 234-1090, FAX 234-1090. Born Montreal 1947. m. William. **EDUC:** bus. coll. grad.; various continuing educ. courses/seminars. **CAREER:** various secretarial positions, McGill Univ., Fraser & Beatty, Columbia Records of Canada Ltd., Hastings County Board of Education, & Canada Mortgage and Housing Corporation, Montreal, Toronto & Belleville, Ont., 1965-79; Research Asst., Epidemiology Study/Admin. Asst. to Gen. Mgr, & Editor, *Research News*, Cameco-A Canadian Mining & Energy Corporation, 1979-89; Exec. Dir./Treas., Federated Women's Institutes of Canada, 1990 to date. **INTERESTS:** horseback riding; reading.

Struthers, Betsy, B.A. ■ 📖 📜
Writer and Editor. 702 Ross St., Peterborough, ON K9H 2C9 (705) 745-882, EMAIL bstruthers@oncomdis.on.ca. Born Toronto 1951. m. James Struthers. 1 ch. **EDUC:** Wilfrid Laurier Univ., B.A.(English) 1972. **CAREER:** freelance ed. **SELECTED PUBLICATIONS:** *Censored Letters* (Oakville: Mosaic Press, 1984); *Saying So Out Loud* (Oakville: Mosaic Press, 1988); *Found: A Body* (Toronto: Simon and Pierre, 1992); *Running Out of Time* (Toronto: Wolsak and Wynn, 1993); *Grave Deeds* (Toronto: Simon and Pierre/Dundurn, 1994); *Poets in the Classroom* co-ed. with Sarah Klassen (Toronto: Pembroke Press, 1995); *A Studied Death* (Toronto: Simon and Pierre/Dundurn, 1995); *Virgin Territory* (Toronto: Wolsak & Wynn, 1996); works in various anthologies, incl. *Investigating Women: Female Detectives in Canadian Fiction* ed. David Skene-Melvin (Toronto: Simon and Pierre/Dundurn, 1995); *That Sign of Perfection*, ed. John B. Lee (Windsor: Black Moss Press, 1995); *Labour of Love* ed. Mona Fertig (Winlaw, BC: Polestar Books, 1989); *Celebrating Canadian Women* ed. Greta Hoffman Nemiroff (Toronto: Fitzhenry & Whiteside, 1989); numerous poems published in various journals incl. *Room of One's Own*; *Quarry*; *The Canadian Forum*; *The Fiddlehead*; *Contemporary Verse*; *The Malahat Review*; *Canadian Literature*. **AFFIL:** League of Canadian Poets (Pres.; First VP; Coord., Feminist Caucus); International PEN; Crime Writers of Canada. **HONS:** short-listed, Arthur Ellis Best First Novel Award, 1993; Runner-up, Milton Acorn People's Poetry Award, 1994. **MISC:** Writers' Reserve Grant, Ontario Arts Council, 1984, 1992, 1993, 1996; Arts Grant B, Canada Council, 1989-90 & 1994-95; Int'l Cultural Affairs Program Travel Grant, Dept. of External Affairs, 1992; participant, numerous creative writing workshops, panels & lectures;

Judge, CBC/Tilden/Saturday Night Poetry Award, 1995; Judge, Milton Acorn People's Poetry Award, 1995; Judge, Harperprints Chapbook Competition, North Carolina Writers' Network, 1994; numerous readings, incl. Reading Tour of North Carolina, Word On The Street in Toronto, Pelicanos Cafe in Sidney, B.C.

Stuart, Barbara, B.A.Sc.,R.P.Dt.,C.H.E. ⊚ ⊕
Chief Executive Officer, ONTARIO PHARMA-CISTS' ASSOCIATION, 23 Lesmill Rd., Ste. 301, Don Mills, ON M3B 3P6 (416) 441-0788, FAX 441-0791. EDUC: Univ. of Guelph, B.A.Sc.(Nutritional Sci.); Health Sciences Centre, Winnipeg, R.P.Dt.(Dietetics). CAREER: Dir., Oper., Bestview Health Care, 1985-89; Reg'l Dir., Versa Care Ltd., 1987-89; Dir., Mgmt Svcs, 1989; VP, Oper., Ontario Dietary, 1990-93; VP, Bus. Dev. (Health National Care), 1994-95; CEO, Ontario Pharmacists' Association, 1995 to date. AFFIL: Canadian Coll. of Health Executives (Certified Health Exec.); Ontario Dietetic Association (Past Exec.; Chrm, Gov't Rel'ns/Public Affairs Council); Canadian Dietetic Association; volunteer work with cancer, breast cancer, mental health, heart & stroke associations; Homes For Aged - Toronto (Bd. Mbr.). INTERESTS: interior decorator; miniature doll houses. COMMENT: *"1996 is certainly the year for change; 1997 will be the year to sort out the details!"*

Stuchly, Maria A., M.Sc.,Ph.D. ✿ ✎
Professor, Department of Electrical and Computer Engineering, UNIVERSITY OF VICTORIA, Box 3055, M.S. 8610, Victoria, BC V8W 3P6 (604) 721-6029, FAX 721-6052, EMAIL maria.stuchly@ece.uvic.ca. Born Warsaw, Poland 1939. m. Dr. Stanislaw S. Stuchly. EDUC: Warsaw Technical Univ., M.Sc.(Electronic Eng.) 1962; Polish Academy of Sciences, Ph.D.(Electronic Eng.) 1970. CAREER: Research Scientist, Bureau of Radiation & Medical Devices, Health & Welfare Canada, 1976-91; Dir., Institute of Medical Eng., Univ. of Ottawa, 1990-91; Prof., Univ. of Victoria, 1992 to date; Industrial Research Chair, NSERC/BCHydro/TransAlta Utilities, 1994-96. SELECTED PUBLICATIONS: "A study of the handset antenna and human body interaction," with M. Okoniewski (*IEEE Microwave Theory & Technology*, 44, 1996); "Reflection analysis of PML-ABC's," with J. De Moerloose (*IEEE Microwave & Guided Wave Letter*, 6(4) 1996); "Magnetic field-induced currents in the human body in proximity of power lines," with S. Zhao (*IEEE Power Delivery*, 11, 1996); "Computer controlled system for producing uniform magnetic fields and its application in

biomedical research," with K. Caputa (*IEEE Instrumentations & Measurements*, 45(3), 19960; 117 refereed publications. AFFIL: Institute of Electrical & Electronic Engineers (IEEE) (Fellow); Bioelectromagnetics Society (VP 1985-86; Pres. 1986-87); National Academy of Sciences (Committee on Possible Effects of Electromagentic Fields, 1993-95). INTERESTS: travel; skiing; cycling; reading. COMMENT: *"Main interest has been in solving engineering and multidisciplinary problems aimed at an increase in knowledge and the use of existing knowledge for the benefit to society."*

Sturgess, Jennifer, B.Sc.(Hons.), Ph.D. ♙ ✿ ✎
President, THE STURGESS GROUP INC., 80 Hazelton Ave., Toronto, ON M5R 2E2 (416) 975-5194. Medical Director, PARKE DAVIS CANADA, 2200 Eglinton Ave. E., Scarborough, ON M1L 2N3 (416) 288-2121. Born UK 1944. m. Robert. 3 ch. Paul, Hugh, Claire. EDUC: Bristol Univ., B.Sc.(Medical Microbiol.) 1965; London Univ., UK, Ph.D.(Pathology) 1970. CAREER: Research Asst.–Microbiol., Medical Research Council, UK, 1965-66; Asst. Lecturer, Dept. of Experimental Pathology, Univ. of London, UK, 1966-67; Lecturer, 1967-70; Scientist, Hospital for Sick Children, Toronto, 1970-79; Lecturer, Dept. of Pathology, Univ. of Toronto, 1973-74; Asst. Prof., 1975-86; Dir., Warner Lambert (Canada), 1979-86; VP, Medical & Scientific Affairs, 1986-90; Assoc. Prof., Dept. of Pathology, Univ. of Toronto, 1986-90; Prof., 1990 to date; Assoc. Dean, Research, Univ. of Toronto, 1990-93; Pres., The Toronto Hospital Research Institute, 1993-95. SELECTED PUBLICATIONS: *Perspectives in Cystic Fibrosis.* Proceedings of the 8th Intenational Congress on Cystic Fibrosis, 1980, ed.; "Cilia with defective radial spokes: A cause of human respiratory disease," with J. Chao & J.A.P. Turner (*New England Journal of Medicine* 300, 1979); "Immotile Cilia Syndrome," with J.A.P. Turner, *Disorders of the Respiratory Tract in Children*, eds. V. Chernick & E.L. Kendig (Philadelphia: W.B. Saunders Co., 5th ed., 1989); "Ciliated cells in the lung," *Lung Biology in Health and Disease*, ed. D. Massaro (New York; Marcer Dekker, 1989); more than 200 publications total, incl. articles, abstracts, book chapters; conference proceedings & reports. DIRECTOR: Versa Services Inc. AFFIL: Medical Research Council of Canada; Health Industries Sector Council, Ont. Ministry of Health; Ont. Health Research Advisory Council; Microscopical Society of Canada (Council Mbr. 1973-81, 1983 to date; Hon. Mbr.); American Thoracic Society; Canadian Association of Pathologists; International

Academy of Pathology. HONS: MRC Scholar, Medical Research Council, Canada, 1974-79; Scientific Award, Canadian Association of Pathologists, 1975. INTERESTS: sailing; skiing; tennis. MISC: mbr., Science Council of Canada, 1987-91; numerous invited lectures; numerous conference presentations.

Sturrock, Ann, B.A. ■ Ⓜ ⊕ Ⓞ
Director and Chair, B.C. RESEARCH INSTITUTE FOR CHILD AND FAMILY HEALTH, 4957 Marine Dr., Ste. 2, W. Vancouver, BC V7W 2P5 (604) 926-8379, FAX 926-8379. Born Vancouver 1947. sep. 2 ch. Matt, Lesley. EDUC: Univ. of British Columbia, B.A.(Soc.) 1971. VOLUNTEER CAREER: consultant to nonprofit organizations & professional community volunteer; Founding Mbr., Camp Goodtimes, B.C. Branch, Canadian Cancer Society, 1985; Founding Dir., B.C. Research Institute of Child & Family Health, 1995; Dir., B.C. Children's Hospital, 1991 to date; mbr., Ethics Committee. AFFIL: Leadership Vancouver (Dir.; Past & Founding Chair 1992-93); Junior League of Vancouver; Association of Junior Leagues International (Dir. 1990-92). HONS: Canada 125 Medal; nominated, YWCA Woman of Distinction (twice). INTERESTS: live theatre; travel; reading; films; leadership issues in the community. COMMENT: *"An energetic community leader as a speaker, trainer and board member from local to provincial to international boards, trying to make a difference."*

Stutzer, Cynthia A., R.N.,M.S., C.P.O.N. ⊕ Ⓜ
Clinical Nurse Specialist, Pediatric Oncology, BRITISH COLUMBIA CHILDREN'S HOSPITAL, 4480 Oak St, Vancouver, BC V6H 3V4 (604) 875-2345, ext. 7078, FAX 875-3414. Born New Jersey 1952. EDUC: Univ. of Delaware, B.S.N. 1974; Univ. of Oklahoma, M.S.(Nursing) 1986. CAREER: Staff Nurse, Medical/Oncology Unit, Medical Coll. of Virginia Hospitals, 1974-75; Staff Nurse, Surgical/Oncology Unit, 1975; Staff Nurse, Emergency Dept., 1975; Staff Nurse, Medical/Oncology Unit 1975-76; Asst. Head Nurse, Medical/Oncology Unit, 1976; Head Nurse, 1976-77; Staff Nurse, Bone Marrow Transplant Unit, Memorial-Sloan Cancer Center, 1977-79; Clinical Research Nurse Coord., Bone Marrow Transplant Svc, 1979-82; Bone Marrow Transplant Nurse Clinician & Proj. Dir., Oklahoma Children's Memorial Hospital, 1982-86; Clinical Nurse Specialist, Pediatric Oncology, British Columbia Children's Hospital, 1987 to date; Clinical Asst. Prof., Univ. of British Columbia, 1992 to date. SELECTED PUBLICATIONS: "Standards of Nursing Care for the Patient with Graft vs. Host Disease Post Bone Marrow Transplant," with M. dela Montaigne, J. DeMeo & R. Nuscher (*Cancer Nursing* 4(3) 1981); "Bone Marrow Transplantation" (*The Protocol* 3(4) 1983); "Work Related Stresses of Pediatric Bone Marrow Transplant Nurses" (*Journal of Pediatric Oncology* 6(3) 1989); "Pediatric Bone Marrow Transplantation" (*BCONIG Newsletter* June 1991); "Multidisciplinary Rounds: Commentary" (*Cancer Practice* 1(4) 1993); "Commentary: The Effects of a Support Group on Selected Psychosocial Outcomes of Bereaved Parents Whose Child Died From Cancer" (*Journal of Pediatric Oncology Nursing* 12(2) 1995); "Imagery for Children in Pain, Experiencing Threat To Life or the Approach to Death," with L. Kuttner, *Beyond the Innocence of Childhood*, eds. Adams & Deveau (1995); various other publications. AFFIL: Bereaved Parent Support Group (facilitator); Association of Pediatric Oncology Nurses; Oncology Nursing Society; Registered Nurses' Association of B.C.; Canadian Nurses' Association; Canadian Association of Nurses in Oncology; B.C. Oncology Nursing Interest Group; B.C. Chapter of Association on Pediatric Oncology Nurses; B.C. Clinical Nurses' Specialist Group; Canadian Clinical Nurses' Specialist Group (Chair, Abstract Review Committee for Nat'l Conference); Sigma Theta Tau Int'l Nursing Honour Society. HONS: State of Oklahoma Teaching Hospitals Scholarship, 1984; Davol Excellence in Research Award, Association of Pediatric Oncology Nurses, 1988; Second Place, Davol Excellence in Research Award, Association of Pediatric Oncology Nurses, 1991; Certified Pediatric Oncology Nurse; Award for Excellence in Nursing Practice, Registered Nurses' Association of B.C., 1995. INTERESTS: developing counselling skills; teaching; exploring new ideas; developing creativity; reading; travelling. MISC: recipient, various grants; listed in *Who's Who in American Nursing*; numerous lectures & conference presentations; volunteer, "What is Cancer?" Camp Goodtimes, Canadian Cancer Society, 1991 to date; Planning Committee, Int'l Oncology Nursing Conference, 1991 to date; Certified Pediatric Oncology Nurse. COMMENT: *"I enjoy working with people from diverse backgrounds. In my career, I have been enriched by opportunities to be with ordinary people as they cope with their lives in extraordinary ways."*

Stymiest, Barbara, B.B.A.,C.A. Ⓢ
Senior Vice-President and Chief Financial Officer, NESBITT BURNS INC., First Canadian Place, Box 150, Toronto, ON M5X 1H3 (416) 359-7340, FAX 359-4620. Born Toronto 1956. m. James M. Kidd. EDUC: Univ. of Western

Ontario, B.B.A. 1978. **CAREER:** Clarkson Gordon, 1978-87; Ptnr, Clarkson Gordon (now Ernst and Young), 1987-92; Sr. VP & CFO, Nesbitt Thomson (now Nesbitt Burns), 1992 to date. **DIRECTOR:** Nesbitt Burns Inc.; Nesbitt Burns Securities Inc.; Nesbitt Burns Limitée; Bank of Montreal Investment Counsel Ltd.; Bank of Montreal Investment Management Ltd.; Bank of Montreal Investor Services Ltd. **AFFIL:** Toronto Stock Exchange (V-Chair); Dellcrest Children's Centre (Chair); Visiting Homemakers' Association (Past Chair); Queen Elizabeth Hospital Foundation (Bd.); Donalda Club; Royal Canadian Yacht Club; Holimont Ski Club, US. **INTERESTS:** golf; squash; skiing.

Suche, P. Colleen, B.A.,LL.B., Q.C. ■■ 🔤 😊😊
Partner, SUCHE GANGE (Barristers & Solicitors), Centra Gas Bldg, 444 St. Mary's Ave., Ste. 760, Winnipeg, MB R3C 3T1 (204) 947-0025, ext. 202, FAX 947-0171. m. 3 ch. **EDUC:** Univ. of Winnipeg, B.A. 1976; Univ. of Manitoba, LL.B. 1979. **BAR:** Man., 1980. **CAREER:** area of practice: civil litigation, insur., labour, employment, administrative law, human rights, arbitration/mediation. **SELECTED PUBLICATIONS:** numerous presentations/publications incl. *Report on Residential Facilities for Children.* **AFFIL:** Manitoba Mental Health Review Bd. (Chairperson); Manitoba Human Rights Code (Adjudicator); Manitoba Labour Bd. (Arbitrator); Canada Labour Code (Adjudicator); Prov. Task Force on Civil Judicial Reform (mbr. 1995); Law Society of Manitoba (Bencher 1990 to date; VP 1996); Federal Advisory Committee on Judicial Appointments (mbr. 1995 to date); Canadian Bar Association Man. Working Group, Gender Equality Task Force (1992); Manitoba Association Against Sexual Harassment; National Association of Women & the Law; Legal Education Action Fund; The Network: Interaction for Conflict Resolution; Women's Post Treatment Centre.

Sugarman, Rebecca, B.A.,M.S.W. 🔾
Executive Director, OPPORTUNITY FOR ADVANCEMENT, 801 Eglinton Ave. W., Ste. 301, Toronto, ON M5N 1E3 (416) 787-1481, FAX 787-1500. Born Toronto 1953. s. 1 ch. Alice Sugarman. **EDUC:** Univ. of Victoria, B.A. (Social Work) 1976; Carleton Univ., M.S.W. (Social Work) 1982. **CAREER:** Program Coord., Univ. of Guelph, 1985-87; Field Instructor, Wilfrid Laurier Univ. Sch. of Social Work, 1987-90; Consultant, 1987-89; Exec. Dir., Barbra Schlifer Commemorative Clinic, 1990-91; Exec. Dir., Opportunity for Advancement, 1991 to date. **SELECTED PUBLICA-**

TIONS: *Rural Child Care Needs; Networking as a Method of Rural Service Delivery; Who's Looking After Our Children: A Study of Child Care Needs in Rural Ontario.* **AFFIL:** Ontario Association of Professional Social Workers (1983-91); Canadian Rural Social Work Forum (Dir. 1981-83); Centre for Employable Workers (Pres. 1987-88; VP 1988-89); Toronto Counselling Centre (1992-94); Guelph Workers' Foundation (1989); Coalition for Feminist Services. **HONS:** nominated for Special Children's Service Awards. **INTERESTS:** women's issues; environmental awareness; live theatre; travel. **MISC:** single parent by choice. **COMMENT:** *"I have worked towards improving the lives of disadvantaged people, especially women and their unique needs. Feminism has an important role in how I understand society and my life choices."*

Sullivan, Rosemary, B.A.,M.A., Ph.D. 🔄 📖
Professor, Department of English, UNIVERSITY OF TORONTO, 7 King's College Circle, Toronto, ON M5S 1A1 (905) 828-5439, FAX 469-9844. Born Montreal 1947. cl. Juan Opitz. **EDUC:** McGill Univ., B.A.(English Lit.) 1968; Univ. of Connecticut, M.A.(English Lit.) 1969; Univ. of Sussex, Ph.D.(English Lit.) 1972. **CAREER:** Asst.-Associé, Univ. de Dijon, 1972; Asst.-Associé, Univ. de Bordeaux, 1973; Asst. Prof., Univ. of Victoria, 1974-77; Asst. Prof., Univ. of Toronto, 1977-80; Assoc. Prof., 1980-90; Prof., 1990 to date. **SELECTED PUBLICA-TIONS:** *The Garden Master: Style and Identity in the Poetry of Theodore Roethke* (Univ. of Washington Press, 1975); *The Space A Name Makes* (Black Moss Press, 1986); *Blue Panic* (Black Moss Press, 1991); *By Heart: Elizabeth Smart/A Life* (Penguin Books Canada, 1991); *Shadow Maker: The Life of Gwendolyn MacEwen* (Harper Collins, 1995). **EDIT:** Ed. Bd., *Descant*, 1983-85; Ed. Bd., *This Magazine*, 1981-88. **AFFIL:** Writers' Union of Canada; Canadian PEN (Chrm, Writers in Prison Committee 1991-92). **HONS:** Gerald Lampert Prize for Poetry, League of Canadian Poets, 1986; Silver Medal, National Magazine Awards, 1986; nominated for Gov. General's Award for Non-Fiction, 1991; Guggenheim Fellowship, 1992; Gov. General's Award for Non-Fiction, 1995; Canadian Authors Award for Non-Fiction, 1995; nominated, Trillium Book Prize, 1995; Medal for Biography, Univ. of B.C., 1995; nominated, City of Toronto Book Award, 1995. **INTERESTS:** scuba diving. **COMMENT:** *"Rosemary Sullivan is a writer of poetry and biography and a professor of Modern Literature at the University of Toronto."*

Sum, Peggy, B.A. $
Vice-President, Asian Markets, BANK OF MONTREAL, Asian Banking Headquarters, 302 Bay St., 9th Fl., Toronto, ON M5X 1A1, FAX (416) 867-2832. m. 2 ch. Karen, Adrienne. **EDUC:** Univ. of Hong King, B.A.(English) 1968. **CAREER:** positions in two internationally renowned advtg. firms handling accts such as Revlon & Cadbury; joined John D. Hutchison, one of the largest British trading co.'s in Hong Kong; Gen. Mgr., Imports Dept.; emigrated to Canada in 1975; Prod. Mgr., Bausch & Lomb Soflens Div.; Asst. Prod. Mgr., Personal Banking, Bank of Montreal, 1980; progressively senior mktg. positions in Commercial Banking & Private Banking; VP, Asian Mkts, 1990 to date. **AFFIL:** Orthopaedic & Arthritic Hospital (Trustee; Chair, Mktg. Committee; Governance Committee); Univ. of Toronto Schools Endowment Fund (Fin. Committee); Hong Kong Univ. Alumni Association of Ontario (Bd.). **MISC:** in 1969 was seconded by the Hong Kong Tourist Association for three months & appointed Goodwill Ambassador to promote Hong Kong in 18 cities in the UK and Europe; regularly featured in Chinese media as a spokesperson for the Bank of Montreal on banking, ethnic & career issues; invited to speak on her field by various organizations & associations.

Sumarah, Jacqueline, R.S.W. ■ ♡ ✋
Past President, THE NOVA SCOTIA COUNCIL FOR THE FAMILY, 5121 Sackville St, Ste. 602, Halifax, NS B3J 1K1 (902) 422-1316, FAX 422-4012. Born Prince Albert, Sask. 1937. m. Roger Sumarah. 2 ch. David, Lisa. **EDUC:** Saskatchewan Hospital, North Battleford, R.P.N. 1959; Maritime Sch. of Social Work, M.S.W. 1965. **CAREER:** Psychiatric Nurse, Saskatchewan Hospital, North Battleford, 1956-59; Psychiatric Nurse, Belmont Hospital, Sutton, UK, 1959-60; Psychiatric Nurse, L'hôpital de Cery, Lausanne, Switzerland, 1960-61; Psychiatric Nurse, Monroe Wing, Regina General Hospital, 1961; Psychiatric Svc Worker, Swift Current Mental Health Clinic, 1961-63; Psychiatric Social Worker, Regina Mental Health Clinic, 1964; Family Counsellor, Family Svc Bureau, Halifax-Dartmouth, 1965-68; Field Instructor & Method Group Facilitator, Maritime Sch. of Social Work, 1968-71; Coord. of Marriage Prep. Program, Catholic Social Svcs Commission, 1979-80; Private Family Counsellor, Catholic Family Counselling Associates, 1981-85; Family Counsellor, Family Service Association, 1987 to date. **AFFIL:** Girl Guides of Canada (Prov. "Put the Child First" Advisor; District P.R. Membership Advisor); St. Pius X (Eucharistic Minister); N.S. Family & Child Welfare Association (Past Pres.); N.S. Association of Social Workers. **HONS:** Proficiency Award, Maritime Sch. of Social Work, 1965; Chuck Lake Distinguished Service Award, N.S. Family & Child Welfare Association, 1995; Award of Merit, Girl Guides of Canada. **INTERESTS:** skiing; camping; crafts; reading. **COMMENT:** *"My primary concern is that the children of our community have the opportunity to fully participate in Canada's resources. Most of my personal, professional and volunteer endeavours have been directed to this end."*

Summers, Anne Marie, B.Sc.,M.D., FRCP(C),FCCMC ⊕ ⚛
Clinical Geneticist, Director of the Maternal Serum Screening Program, Department of Genetics, NORTH YORK GENERAL HOSPITAL, North York, ON M2K 1E1 (416) 756-6345, FAX 756-6727, I.O.D.E. CHILDREN'S CENTRE. Born London, UK 1954. m. Dr. Peter Karalis. 2 ch. John Michael Karalis, Kate Karalis. **EDUC:** Univ. of Western Ontario, B.Sc.(Genetics) 1976; Univ. of Toronto, M.D. 1982; Univ. of Toronto, Hospital for Sick Children, FRCP(C) (Pediatrics) 1986, FCCMG (Genetics) 1989, FRCP(C) (Genetics) 1996. **CAREER:** Pediatrician in private practice, 1987-88; Clinical Geneticist, North York General Hospital, 1989 to date; Dir., Maternal Serum Screening Program, 1991 to date. **SELECTED PUBLICATIONS:** "Evaluating Patient's Knowledge of Material Serum Screening," with V. Goel, S. Holzapfel *et al* (*Prenatal Diagnosis* 16, 1996); "The Ethical Aspects of Genetic Screening for Cancer" (*Ontario Medical Review* 62 1995); "Prenatal Diagnosis of Retinal Nonattachment in the Walker-Warburg Syndrome," with D. Chityat *et al* (*American Journal of Medical Genetics* 56 1995); various other publications & abstracts. **AFFIL:** Coll. of Physicians & Surgeons of Ontario, Gen. Licence (Fellow); Royal Coll. of Physicians & Surgeons of Canada (Fellow); Canadian Coll. of Medical Genetics (Fellow; mbr., Committee on Prenatal Diagnosis); Ontario Medical Association (Chair, Bioethics Committee; Sec. of Exec., Section on Genetics); Canadian Medical Association; Canadian Medical Protective Society; Canadian Pediatric Society; American Society of Human Genetics; Association of Genetic Counsellors of Ontario; Canadian Bioethics Society; American Society of Law, Medicine & Ethics; Hastings Centre (Assoc. Mbr.); Kennedy Institute of Ethics (Assoc. Mbr.); Northern Outreach Program for Genetics; Ontario MSS Pilot Program (Steering Committee 1993 to date; Evaluation Committee); Ontario Maternal Serum Screening Database (Co-Dir.). **COMMENT:** *"I am a clin-*

ical geneticist interested in all areas of genetics but particularly in prenatal diagnosis. I am also very interested in biomedical ethics, especially as it is applied to genetics."

Summers, Marlies ■ ⊛ ⊕

Ontario Director, OPTICIANS' ASSOCIATION OF CANADA, 110 Place d'Orleans, Orleans, ON K1C 2L9 (613) 837-3434, FAX 837-6234. General Manager, LENSCRAFTERS. Born Kerkrade, Holland 1948. m. David. 1 ch. Derick. EDUC: Ryerson Polytechnic Institute, Certificate (Optical) 1978; St. Lawrence Coll., Certificate (Advtg) 1988; Algonquin Coll., Certificate (Bus./Mktg) 1990. CAREER: Reg'l Supervisor, Standard Optical, 1986-89; Pres., Vision Experts Limited, 1989-94; Optician, Lenscrafters, 1994-95; Gen. Mgr, 1995 to date. AFFIL: Opticians' Association of Canada (Ont. Dir.); Ontario Opticians' Association (Treas. 1987-91; Pres. 1991-94; advisory position); International Academy of Natural Health Sciences (Canada). INTERESTS: human psych.; natural health & healing; spirituality. COMMENT: *"My achievement is to be who I am by my ability, rather than my gender, and I will endeavour to continue living my life from the heart, not from fear or guilt."*

Surridge, Marie E., B.A.,M.A.,Ph.D. ⊰ ▤

Professor, Department of French Studies, QUEEN'S UNIVERSITY, Kingston, ON K7L 3N6 (613) 545-2090. Born London, UK 1931. m. David Surridge. 3 ch. Michela Mary David, Lisa Anne Surridge, Maria Siân Evans. EDUC: Oxford Univ., B.A.(Modern Languages) 1953, M.A. 1957; Ph.D.(Philology/Linguistics) 1962. CAREER: taught part-time at the Oxford Univ. while obtaining doctorate & raising her family, 1955-67; Asst. Prof., Queen's Univ., 1970-77; Assoc. Prof., 1977-87; Head, Dept. of French Studies, 1983-93; Prof., 1987 to date. SELECTED PUBLICATIONS: *Le ou la? The Gender of French Nouns* (Clevedon, Philadelphia, Adelaide: Multilingual Matters, 1995); numerous articles on lexical borrowing, homophony & homonymy, gender in French & Welsh, & women & language. INTERESTS: family activities with my husband, my 3 daughters & their children; sailing; walking with my Jack Russell terrier. COMMENT: *" My current research interests are in French linguistics, particularly lexicology, and all aspects of gender. I was head of my department from 1983 to 1993, and have participated in many university committees."*

Sutherland, Sister Agnes, B.Ed.,M.Ed., M.Rel.Ed. ■ ▯ ○ ☼

Principal, Teacher, Writer, Community Volunteer. 25 St. Mary's St., Fort Smith, NT X0E 0P0 (403) 872-3223, FAX 872-3345. Born Fort Chipewyan, Alta. 1926. mbr. of the Congregation of Grey Nuns of Montreal. EDUC: universities of Edmonton, Alberta, Gonzaga & Fort Wright, US; various certificates in counselling, psych., theology & scripture, art, graphoanalysis, computer, acctg. CAREER: teacher in Alta & N.W.T.; Principal, St. John's Separate Sch., Fort McMurray, Alta.; Dir., Religious Educ., McKenzie-Fort Smith Diocese; various contracts for special studies, surveys & assessments for: the Dept. of Social Svcs, Dene Nation Councils, the Metis Association, Yellowknife Sep. Sch. Bd. & St. Joseph Cathedral Parish in Fort Smith. SELECTED PUBLICATIONS: *Souvenir Album* (1984); *Living Kindness. The Memoirs of a Métis Elder, Madeline Bird* (1990); *The Bishop Who Cared, A Legacy of Leadership–Bishop Paul Piche* (1995); *Northerners Say "Thanks Sister"* (1996); various articles in Catholic & gen. newspapers & magazines; presently working on autobiography. EDIT: mbr., committee to revise the historical book on Fort Smith, *On the Banks of the Slave*. AFFIL: extra-curricular activities for youth; Youth Justice Committee; Tawow Society for Sutherland House; Fort Smith Society for Disabled Persons (Pres. & Founder); Fort Smith Senior Citizens' Society (Pres. & Founder); Fort Smith Northern Lights Personal Care Facility; Uncle Gabe's Friendship Centre; Ouverture Concert Society; RCMP Advisory Committee; Arctic PLEI (Arctic Public Legal Educ. & Info. Committee); Community Support Committee for Corrections Groups in Fort Smith; N.W.T. Status of Women Council (VP). HONS: various awards & recognition for advocacy & volunteer work; nominated Citizen of the Year, Fort Smith, 1984; Certificate in Social Svcs(Hon.) Arctic Coll., 1990. INTERESTS: photography; graphoanalysis; nature; reading; travelling; music; history of the North. MISC: French/English translator with Social Svcs for counselling & court; advocate & support for immigrants; opened 1st home for the homeless, youth in need, the abused, & victims of family violence in Fort Smith & NWT; resource person for special talks at Aurora Coll. for Elder Hostel groups & students in various courses; travelled to Europe, Holy Land, Africa, Scandinavian countries, Mexico, the Philippines, Africa, Scotland & across Canada.

Sutherland Boal, Anne, R.N.,B.A., M.H.S.A. ⊕ ⊰

Vice-President, Patient Based Care Units, BRITISH COLUMBIA'S CHILDREN'S HOSPITAL, 4480 Oak St., Vancouver, BC V6H 3V4 (604) 875-2780, FAX 875-3456. Adjunct Professor,

School of Nursing, UNIVERSITY OF BRITISH COLUMBIA. Born Montreal 1950. m. Gordon D.R. Boal. 2 ch. Melissa, Lindsay. EDUC: Foothills Hospital Sch. of Nursing, R.N. 1972; Brock Univ., B.A.(Psych.) 1975; Univ. of Alberta, Master of Health Services Admin. (Nursing Admin.) 1980. CAREER: Assoc. Dir. of Nursing, Practice, Alberta Children's Hospital, 1980-85; Dir. of Nursing, Maternal-Child Psychiatry, Calgary General Hospital, 1985-89; VP, Nursing & Treatment Svcs, British Columbia's Children's Hospital, 1989-95; Adjunct Prof., Sch. of Nursing, Univ. of British Columbia, 1993 to date; VP, Patient-Based Care Units, British Columbia's Children's Hospital, 1995 to date. AFFIL: Canadian Coll. of Health Service Executives (Certified Health Exec.); Registered Nurses' Association of B.C.; Alberta Association of Registered Nurses; Academy of Chief Executive Nurses; Canada China Child Health Foundation (Steering Committee); Canadian Journal of Nursing Administration (Ed. Bd.). COMMENT: *"24-year health care career with progressive academic and professional advances in tertiary, acute care hospitals; active in promoting nursing developments in China."*

Swaine, Margaret ■ ■ / ☒

President, PIERCE COMMUNICATIONS, 160 Bloor St. E., Ste. 160, Toronto, ON M4W 1B9 (416) 961-5328, FAX 961-4251. Wine, food and travel columnist. Born Montreal 1953. s. EDUC: Carleton Univ., Hons. Bachelor of Journalism 1976. CAREER: Gen. Reporter, *Montreal Star*, 1973; Pol. Asst. & Speech Writer, Marc Lalonde, Min. of Health & Welfare, 1975-77; Dir., Info. Svcs, World Trade Centre, Toronto, 1977-80; Pres., Pierce Communications, 1980 to date; wine columnist, *Toronto Life* (1977 to date), *Chatelaine* (1980 to date), *Winetidings* Magazine (1996 to date), & *Ontario Restaurant News* (1994 to date); freelance travel writer, *Financial Post, The Globe and Mail, Canadian Inflight*, etc.; freelance food writer, *Gusto* Magazine. SELECTED CREDITS: actor, video about spirits, Liquor Control Board of Ontario; has appeared on many TV & radio shows incl. *Live It Up, Morningside*, CBC *Metro Morning, Radio Noon, Midday*, etc. SELECTED PUBLICATIONS: *100 Big Ideas for Promoting a Business on a Small Budget* (1988). AFFIL: Wine Writers Circle of Canada (founder; 1st Pres. 1985-88); Travel Media Association of Canada (founder; Treas. 1994-96); Dora Mavor Moore Awards Board (VP 1994-96). INTERESTS: wine; food; travel; golf; skiing; biking. COMMENT: *"One of Canada's veteran wine authorities with international recognition, Margaret has written over*

2,000 columns on wine and other alcoholic beverages. Also president of a marketing company for 16 years and very involved with the arts as past Board Chairman of Theatre Plus, director of St. Lawrence Centre for the Arts and director of Dora Mavor Moore Board. A founder and director of Wine Writers Circle and Travel Media Association of Canada."

Swan, Judith, B.A.,LL.B.,LL.M. ⚖

President and Chief Executive Officer, SWANSEA OCEANS ENVIRONMENT INC., Box 188, Waverley, NS B0N 2S0 (902) 860-1758, FAX 860-0390. Born US 1944 1 ch. EDUC: McGill Univ., B.A.(Pol. Sci. & Phil.) 1966; Univ. of Alberta, LL.B. 1970; London Sch. of Econ. & Pol. Sci., Univ. of London, UK, LL.M. 1971. CAREER: Student-at-Law, Attorney General's Dept., Prov. of Alta., 1970; Lecturer, Fac. of Law, Univ. of Melbourne, Australia, 1971-75; Assoc. Dean, 1973-75; Research Dir., Ont. Commission on Election Contributions & Expenses, 1975; Sessional Prof., Fac. of Law, Univ. of Windsor, 1975; Visiting Prof., Fac. of Law, Univ. of Toronto, 1975-76; Administrator, Ontario Legal Education Council, 1975-79; Assoc. Prof., Fac. of Law, Univ. of Ottawa, 1976-80; Sessional Prof., Dept. of Law, Carleton Univ., 1980-81; Int'l Rel'ns Officer, Int'l Directorate, Fisheries & Oceans Canada, 1980-85; Legal Cnsl & Chief of Fisheries Mgmt, South Pacific Forum Fisheries Agency (FFA), 1985-90; Exec. Dir., Oceans Institute of Canada, 1990-94; Adjunct Prof., Fac. of Law, Dalhousie Univ., 1991-94; Pres. & CEO, SwanSea Oceans Environment Inc., 1994 to date. SELECTED PUBLICATIONS: "Misleading Advertising: Its Control" (*Alberta Law Review* 9 1971); "Case before the Court" (*United Nations Reporter* Aug.-Sept. 1973); "French Nuclear Tests: An Explosive Issue at International Law" (*Melbourne University Law Review* 1973); "The Living Resources of the Sea," in *Marine Affairs Handbook*, E. Gold, ed. (London: Longman's, 1991); various other publications. AFFIL: Projet de Société; Atlantic Centre for Remote Sensing of the Oceans (Bd. of Dir.); Law of the Sea Institute, Honolulu (Exec. Bd.). INTERESTS: int'l law & dev.; educ.; ocean activities. MISC: numerous papers presented at conferences; numerous consultancies, incl. for the World Bank, & the U.N. Food & Agriculture Organization; has worked on fisheries law & policy for more than 40 countries incl. Canada, Vanuatu, Maldives, Fiji, Sierra Leone, Yemen. COMMENT: *"An international lawyer, I have worked throughout the world to help realize sustainable development of the oceans. Notable achievements include writing fisheries legislation for many countries, advancing regional oceans cooperation in the South Pacific, Indian Ocean and Caribbean and founding Oceans Day in Canada and abroad."*

Swan, Susan, B.A. 📖 ▢ ☜
Novelist and Professor, Department of Humanities, York University, 4700 Keele St., North York, ON M3J 1P3 (416) 736-5158. Born Midland, Ont. 1945. d. 1 ch., 1 stpch. EDUC: McGill Univ., B.A. 1967. CAREER: Educ. Reporter, *Toronto Telegram*, 1967-70; Book Reviewer & Entertainment Writer, *The Toronto Star*, 1970-71; Creative Writing Teacher, George Brown Coll., 1983-85; Creative Writing Prof., Dept. of Writing, York Univ., 2nd & 3rd Year Fiction Workshop, 1985-89; Interdisciplinary Art, Dept. of Art., York Univ., 1986-87; 4th Year Fiction Workshops, 1988-89; Prof., Dept. of Humanities, York Univ., 1989 to date; writer, interviewer & book reviewer. SELECTED CREDITS: various readings, theatre & performance; regular interview, *Imprint* (series), TVOntario, 1991; *Future with Mike McManus*, TVOntario, 1984; *The Collaborators* (series), CBC-TV 1974. SELECTED PUBLICATIONS: *Unfit for Paradise* (Dingle Editions, 1982); *The Biggest Modern Woman of the World* (Toronto: Lester and Orpen Dennys, 1983; London: Pandora Press, 1988; New York: Ecco Press, 1986); *The Last of the Golden Girls* (Toronto: Lester and Orpen Dennys, 1989; New York: Arcade, Little Brown, 1991; pbk, Random House Canada); *Momz Radio*, anthology on motherhood, Co-Ed. (Coach House Press, 1991); *The Wives of Bath* (Knopf Canada & US, 1993; Granta Books, UK, 1993; pbk, Penguin, UK, 1994 & Random House, Canada, 1994); *Stupid Boys are Good to Relax With* (Toronto: Somerville House Publishing 1996); numerous short stories, essays & articles in anthologies, magazines & newspapers incl. *Best Canadian Short Stories, Tesseracts, Chicago Tribune, Chatelaine, Saturday Night, Mirabella, Now, Books in Canada*. EDIT: former fiction ed. of the now defunct Coach House Press. AFFIL: Amnesty International (Chair, Publicity 1975-76). HONS: Finalist, Guardian Fiction Prize, UK, 1993; Finalist, Trillium Prize, 1993; Canadian Council Award for Fiction, 1988; Ontario Arts Council Award for Works-in-Progress, 1988; Toronto Arts Award for Fiction, 1986; Canada Council Award for Fiction, 1984; Finalist, Fiction & Best First Novel Contest, Gov. General's Award, 1983; Canadian Council Award for Fiction, 1982, 1979, 1978; Second Prize, Fiction, National Magazine Awards, 1977; Ontario Arts Council Award for Theatre, Int'l Women's Year, 1975. MISC: advisor, Canada

Council, 1989-91; judge & reader for President's Prize, York Univ., 1993; consultant on women's conference at York Univ., 1994; Writer-in-Residence, Haliburton Public Library Bd., June-Sept. 1987; Artist-in-the-Schools Workshop, with Margaret Dragu, Sudbury Public High Sch., 1976; films currently being made from *The Wives of Bath* (OBD Films with screenplay by playwright Judith Thompson) & *The Biggest Modern Woman of the World* (Triptych Media Inc.). COMMENT: *"Susan Swan is an internationally acclaimed author whose fiction has been published in Canada, the US, the UK, Germany and Holland. Her novel* The Biggest Modern Woman of the World *was shortlisted for the Governor General's award and the Books in Canada best first novel. The Wives of Bath, a gothic tale about a murder in a girls' boarding school, was a finalist for Ontario's Trillium prize and the UK's Guardian fiction award. She is also a regular contributor to TVO's book show Imprint and a professor of Humanities at York University."*

Swart, Paula, B.A.,M.A. 📖 ⊗
Curator of Asian Studies, VANCOUVER MUSEUM, 1100 Chestnut St., Vancouver, BC V6J 3J9 (604) 736-4431, FAX 736-5417. Born The Hague, Holland 1952. m. Barry Till. 1 ch. Jasmine Xiaolu. EDUC: Language Institute, Beijing, Chinese Language 1978; Univ. of Leiden, B.A.(Sinology) 1979; Univ. of Nanjing, China, Chinese Hist. & Archaeology 1979; Univ. of Amsterdam, M.A.(Asian Art Hist.) 1982. CAREER: participated in the research proj. "Witte Leeuw," 1979-81; apprenticeship, Far Eastern Dept., Royal Ontario Museum, 1980; participated in a translation proj., "Project for the Study of Chinese Archaeological Material," Univ. of Stanford & Univ. of Berkeley, 1981; part-time Research Asst., Montreal Museum of Fine Arts, 1983-89; part-time Assoc. Curator, Asian Art, Glenbow Museum, Calgary, 1987; Guest Curator for the travelling exhibition "Refreshment of the Spirit, Oriental Wine & Tea Vessels," Montreal Museum of Fine Arts, 1989-90; Curator, Asian Studies, Vancouver Museum, 1989 to date. SELECTED PUBLICATIONS: *In Search of Old Nanking*, with Barry Till (Hong Kong: Joint Publishers, 1982); "Bronze Carriages from the Tomb of China's First Emperor" (*Archaeology*, Vol. 37, no. 6, 1984); "The Diamond Seat Pagoda, an example of Indian influences in China" (*Orientations*, Feb. 1985); *Chinese Jade Stone for the Emperors*, with Barry Till, Art Gallery of Greater Victoria (Victoria: Morriss Printers Ltd., 1986); "Mountain Retreats in Jade" (*Arts of Asia*, Vol. 16, no. 4, 1986); *The Legacy of*

Japanese Printmaking, with Barry Till, Art Gallery of Greater Vancouver (Victoria; Morris Printers Ltd., 1986); "Buddhist Sculptures at Feilai Feng, A Confrontation of Two Traditions" (*Orientations*, Vol. 18, no. 12, 1987); *Art from the Roof of the World: Tibet*, Art Gallery of Greater Victoria (Victoria: Morriss Printers Ltd., 1989); "The Xiuding Temple Pagoda, a Buddhist Architectural Masterpiece Unveiled" (*Orientations*, Vol. 21, no. 5, 1990); "The Tomb of King Nanyue" (*Orientations*, Vol. 21, no. 6, 1990); *Refreshment of the Spirit, Oriental Wine & Tea Vessels*, The Montreal Museum of Fine Arts (1990); *Blue and White Porcelain of China*, with Barry Till, Art Gallery of Greater Victoria (Apr. 1992); *The Brown Stoneware of the Yixing Kilns*, with Barry Till, Art Gallery of Greater Victoria & the Vancouver Museum (1992); *The Soul of the Samurai*, A Selection of Sword Guards from the Vancouver Museum, with Robert Haynes & John Berta, Vancouver Museum, 1993. **AFFIL:** Japan Sword Appreciation Society; Canadian Society for Asian Art; American Museums Association. **HONS:** Undergrad. Scholarship (Dutch Gov't), 1974-77; Holland-China Exchange Scholarship (Dutch Gov't), 1977-78; Grad. Scholarship (Dutch Gov't), 1979-81. **INTERESTS:** travel (Asia); history; art; archaeology; politics. **MISC:** guest lecturer on Chinese art, history & politics for the American Museum of Natural History, NY. **COMMENT:** *"During the past 15 years that I have lived in Canada, I have used every opportunity to promote Asian cultures in Canada through exhibitions, publications, lectures and educational tours to Asia, and China in particular."*

Sweatman, Margaret, B.A., M.A. ■■ 🎭🗄📜
Writer. Winnipeg, MB R3V 1L2. Born Winnipeg 1953 2 ch. Bailey Harris, Hillery Harris. **EDUC:** Univ. of Winnipeg, B.A.(English/Hist.) 1974; Concordia Univ., Communication Arts (film studies) 1976; Simon Fraser Univ., M.A. 1987; Univ. of Manitoba, independent grad. study, Fac. of English, 1987-92. **SELECTED CREDITS:** *Fox*, play (adaptation of novel, commissioned by Prairie Theatre Exchange & CBC Radio, 1994); *Broken Songs*, CD (music, songs, poetry, Staccato Press & CBC, 1995); *Millennium Cabaret*, satiric scripts & songs (CBC Radio, 1996); *Shift* (script/vocal recording for inter-disciplinary performance/installation with Contemporary Dancers & video artist Riva Stone, 1995); jazz narratives with Glenn Buhr for CBC Radio, Aug. 1993. **SELECTED PUBLICATIONS:** *Sam and Angie* (Turnstone Press, 1996); *Kore in Hell: A Cautionary Tale*, chapbook, 2-act play (Pachyderm Press, 1993); *Fox*

(Turnstone Press, 1991); *Private Property*, chapbook of short fiction (Turnstone Press, 1988); reviews, essays, stories, poetry, excerpts from novels in progress in: *Journal of Canadian Poetry; Books in Canada; Prairie Fire; Dandelion; Border Crossings; West Coast Line; NeWest Review;* chpt. in *Contemporary Manitoba Writers: New Critical Studies*, ed. Kenneth Hughes (1990). **HONS:** grants from Canada Council, Manitoba Arts Council, ArtVentures, Ontario Arts Council; John Hirsch Award for Most Promising Writer, 1992; McNally Robinson Award for Man. Book of the Year (*Fox*), 1991. **MISC:** teaching experience: Teaching Asst., Simon Fraser Univ., 1984-86; Artists in the Schools Program, 1992 to date; Univ. of Winnipeg, Continuing Educ., writers' workshops, 1995 to date; Manitoba Writers' Guild Mentor Program, 1995, 1996; The Summer Institute for Gifted Students, writers' workshops, creative writing & lyrics, 1991-95.

Swift, Catherine, B.A., M.A. 💲🔄
President, CANADIAN FEDERATION OF INDEPENDENT BUSINESS, 4141 Yonge St., Willowdale, ON M2P 2A6 (416) 222-8022, FAX (416) 222-4337. 2 ch. Alexander, Nicholas. **EDUC:** Carleton Univ., B.A.(Econ.) 1974, M.A.(Econ.) 1981. **CAREER:** various positions, Fed. Dept. of Consumer & Corp. Affairs, Fed. Dept. of Industry & Comm., 1976-83; Sr. Economist, Dept. of Econ. Research, Toronto-Dominion Bank, 1983-87; various positions as VP & Sr. VP, then Pres., Canadian Federation of Independent Business, 1987 to date. **SELECTED PUBLICATIONS:** numerous articles on small bus. issues, incl. "Women Business Owners and Terms of Credit: Some Empirical Findings of the Canadian Experience," with A. Riding (*Journal of Business Venturing* Sept. 1990); "A Shared Responsibility" (*Critical Commentaries on the Social Security Review*, Caledon Institute of Social Policy, 1995). **AFFIL:** C.D. Howe Institute (Dir.); Le Cercle Canadien (Dir.); Canadian Association of Business Economists; Canadian Association of Food Banks. **INTERESTS:** baseball; literature; women in business; children's issues. **MISC:** regular guest on *BusinessWorld*'s "The Bottom Line." **COMMENT:** *"Major achievement is becoming a key national spokesperson for small business."*

Swiggum, Susan, B.Sc., M.D., F.R.C.P.(C) ■ ⊕◯📜
Associate Professor, UNIVERSITY OF OTTAWA, 1081 Carling Ave., Ste. 507, Ottawa, ON K1Y 4G2 (613) 725-3411, FAX 722-8727. Born Halifax 1951. m. Jack Adam. 4 ch. Alison, David, Ashley, Mark. **EDUC:** Univ. of Ottawa,

B.Sc.(Molecular Biol.) 1972, M.D.(Medicine) 1976, F.R.C.P.(c)(Dermatology) 1987. **CAREER:** Gen. Practitioner, Smith's Falls, Ont., 1977-85; Pres., Lanark Leeds/Grenville Medical Association; Asst. Prof., Univ. of Ottawa; Asst. Prof., Dermatology, 1990-95. **AFFIL:** Dermatology Foundation (Dir.); FMWC Foundation (Chair); Canadian Dermatology Foundation (CMA Rep.); Ottawa Civic Hospital (active staff); Perth Great War Memorial Hospital (consulting staff); Ontario Medical Association (Chair, Women's Issues Committee); Federation of Medical Women of Canada (Past Pres. 1993-94); Council of Ontario Facilities of Medicine (Gender Issue Committee); Alpha Omega Alpha Honour Medical Society. **HONS:** graduated summa cum laude; Jean Jacques Lussier Gold Medal, 1976; Univ. Silver Medal; entrance scholarship, Medicine; prizes for highest standing in obstetrics, gynecology, family practice & psychiatry; designated Distinguished Grad., Univ. of Ottawa. **INTERESTS:** women's health issues; communications & ethics in medical sch. teaching; gender equity; dancing; reading biographies; church; family. **COMMENT:** *"Dr. Sue Swiggum travelled across Canada extensively as a young adult developing an intense love for Canada and Canadians. After completion of Advanced Levels in London, UK, she obtained her medical training in Ottawa and Toronto. Whether as a family doctor or more recently as an executive in many volunteer organizations, she has worked to promote women's health with an understanding of the political, social, economic and cultural realities of women's lives. She was instrumental in establishing a gender issues committee at the University of Ottawa to promote women's health education. She has lectured extensively to the lay public, media and policy makers on women's health."*

Sydor, Alison ■ ■ ⑦
Olympic Athlete. c/o Canadian Olympic Association. Born Edmonton 1966. **SPORTS CAREER:** full-time athlete; started racing, 1987; mbr., Cdn Nat'l Cycling Team, 1988 to date. Olympic Games: Silver, cross country, 1996. World road championships: 6th, team time trial, 1993; 3rd, road race, 1991. World mountain championships: 1st, 1995; 1st, 1994; 4th, 1993; 2nd, 1992. World Cup (mountain): 2nd, overall standings, 1995; 3rd, overall standings, 1994; 3rd, overall standings, 1993. Pan Am Games: 1st, cross country (mountain), 1995. Commonwealth Games: 2nd, team time trial, & 3rd, road race, 1994. Canadian road championships: 3rd, road race, 1995; 1st, team time trial, 1994; 1st, road race, 1993. Canadian mountain championships: 1st, cross country,

1995; 1st, cross country, 1994. **AFFIL:** "Spirit of Sport" campaign. **HONS:** Promotion Plus Leadership award, 1992. **INTERESTS:** baking; ice hockey; drinking coffee; sitting; people watching. **MISC:** former Alta. jr. champion in triathlon.

Sze, Glendy, B.Soc.Sc. ■ ⑤ ⑭
Vice-President, CITIBANK CANADA, 123 Front St. W., Toronto, ON M5J 2M3 (416) 947-5391, FAX 947-2967. Born Hong Kong 1958. m. A. Chan. **EDUC:** Univ. of Hong Kong, B.Soc.Sc.(Econ. & Mgmt) 1981. **CAREER:** VP, Citibank Hong Kong, 1981-87; VP, Citibank Canada, 1987 to date. **AFFIL:** North York General Hospital (Foundation Bd.); Mon Sheong Foundation (Organizing Committee 1994-95); Global Federation of Taiwanese Women (Founding Dir. 1995). **INTERESTS:** scuba diving; hiking; camping. **COMMENT:** *"Immigrant–resident of Canada for eight years. Work on helping immigrants to maximize their resources and contributions to Canada. Endeavour to promote Canada to international investors. My achievement is the successful establishment of two private banking offices in Toronto and Vancouver."*

Szlazak, Anita Christina, B.A. ✦ ⑤
Member, CANADIAN INTERNATIONAL TRADE TRIBUNAL, 333 Laurier Ave. W., Ottawa, ON K1A 0G7. Born Fulmer, Bucks., UK 1943. **EDUC:** Univ. of Toronto, B.A. 1963; Coll. of Europe, Bruges, Cert.(Advanced European Studies-Econ.) 1964; Harvard Grad. Sch. of Bus. Admin., Advanced Mgmt Program 1981. **CAREER:** Research Economist, Dev. Centre, Organization for Economic Cooperation & Development, Paris, 1964-67; Foreign Svc Officer, Dept. of External Affairs, Ottawa, 1967-72; Deputy Dir. Gen., Int'l Telecomm., Dept. of Comm., Ottawa, 1972-73; Dir. Gen., 1973-76; Commissioner, Public Svc Commission of Canada, 1976-82; Exec. Dir., Gov't of Canada Office, 1988 Olympic Winter Games, 1982-84; Special Advisor, Dept. of External Affairs, 1984-86; Sr. Policy Advisor, Treasury Bd. of Canada, 1986-88; Special Advisor, Int'l Rel'ns, Canada Mortgage & Housing Corporation, 1988-90; with Environment Canada: Dir. Gen., Program Mgmt, Cdn Parks Svc, 1990-92; Dir. Gen., Special Projects, Atmospheric Environment Svc, 1992-94; mbr., Canadian International Trade Tribunal, 1995 to date. **AFFIL:** Institute of Public Administration of Canada (former mbr.; Nat'l Exec. Committee 1976-80); International Institute of Administrative Sciences, Brussels (former mbr.; Exec. Committee 1983-86; VP for N. Am. 1986-89); National Capital Harvard Business Sch. Alumni Club

(VP 1990-92, 1995 to date); Rockcliffe Lawn Tennis Club. HONS: The Queen Elizabeth II Silver Jubilee Medal, 1977.

Szumigalski, Anne 📖 ⊗

Poet, Playwright. Saskatoon, SK (306) 664-2458. Born London, UK. w. 4 ch. Katharine, Elizabeth, Anthony, Mark. EDUC: privately educated. CAREER: poetry teacher, SSSA, 1967-77; given numerous workshops in Sask., Canada & the US; Writer-in-residence, Frances Morrison Library, Saskatoon, 1980-81; Writer-in-residence, Centennial Library, Winnipeg, 1987-88; readings in Canada, US & UK; former mbr., Public Lending Rights Commission; mbr., Saskatchewan Arts Bd. SELECTED CREDITS: work for dance, *Litany of the Bagladies*, performed at Dance Canada; *Z*, Twenty-fifth Street Theatre, Saskatoon (1994); *Last Call*, Reel Eye Media (1995). SELECTED PUBLICATIONS: *BOooOM*, with Terrence Heath & Eleanor Pearson (Saskatchewan Arts Bd., 1973); *Women Reading in Bath* (Toronto: Doubleday, 1974); *Wild Man's Butte*, long poem for voices, with Terrence Heath (Coteau Books, 1979); *A Game of Angels* (Turnstone Press, 1980); *Risks*, long poem (rdc press, 1983); *Litany of the Bagladies*, words for dance (Saskatoon: AKA, 1983); *Doctrine of Signatures* (Fifth House, 1983); *Instar*, stories & poems (rdc press, 1985); *Dogstones* (Fifth House, 1986); *Journey/Journée*, poems with Terrence Heath (rdc press, 1988); *The Word, the Voice, the Text*, essays & memoirs (Fifth House, 1990); *Rapture of the Deep* (Coteau Books, 1991); various works in preparation; *Z*, script of play (Coteau Books, 1995); *Voice*, poems (Coteau Books, 1995); work has appeared in over 40 anthologies in 6 languages. EDIT: Co-founder & former Ed., *Grain*; former Poetry Ed., *NeWest Review*. AFFIL: Saskatchewan Writers' Guild; Saskatchewan Writers & Artists Colonies; AKA artist-run-centre, Saskatoon; League of Canadian Poets (Life Mbr.); ACTRA (Life Mbr.). HONS: Founders Award, Saskatchewan Writers' Guild, 1984; Woman of the Year, YWCA, 1988; Saskatchewan Order of Merit, 1989; Lifetime Award for Excellence in the Arts, Saskatchewan Arts Bd., 1990; Canada 125 Medal, 1993; other awards include 2 Saskatchewan Poetry Awards, 2 Writers' Choice Awards, 2 Silver Globe Magazine Awards, & 2 nominations for the Gov. General's Award; Gov. General's Award for Poetry, 1996. MISC: manuscript reviewer for Canada Council & Saskatchewan Arts Bd. COMMENT: *"Deeply involved with writing and writing organizations in Saskatoon and Saskatchewan since the 1960s. At present engaged in the translation of four 20th Cen-* *tury Catalan plays, in collaboration with Elsabet Ràfols Saqués."*

T

aborsky, Edwina, B.A.,M.Museo., M.Ed.,Ph.D. ⚛ ✿

Associate Professor, Department of Sociology and Anthropology, BISHOP'S UNIVERSITY, Lennoxville, QC J1M 1Z7 (819) 822-9600, FAX 822-9661. **EDUC:** Univ. of Toronto, B.A. (East Asian Studies), M.Museo., M.Ed.(Educ. Admin.), Ph.D.(Soc.) 1982. **CAREER:** Dir., Timmins Museum-Gallery, 1975; Acting Coord., Photographic Svcs, Art Gallery of Ontario, 1976; Lecturer, Anthro. Dept., Univ. of Toronto, 1977-78; Exec. Administrator, Program in Culture & Technology, Univ. of Toronto, 1982-83; Exec. Dir., Ontario Association of Art Galleries, 1984; Asst. Prof., Dept. of Comm., Univ. of Windsor, 1984-85; Asst. Prof., Social Sciences Dept., York Univ., 1985-87; Instructor, Dept. of Soc., Univ. of Ottawa, 1988-89; Sessional Lecturer, Dept. of Soc. & Anthro., Carleton Univ., 1989-90; Asst. Prof., Dept. of Soc. & Anthro., Bishop's Univ., 1990-91; Dir. of Anthro. Program, Dept. of Soc. & Anthro., 1990 to date; Assoc. Prof., Dept. of Soc. & Anthro., 1992 to date. **SELECTED PUBLICATIONS:** *Man/Deer Hunt: Cognitive Patterns Underlying Social Behaviour* (Ottawa: Univ. of Ottawa Press, 1991); *The Textual Society* (Toronto: Univ. of Toronto Press, 1996; in series Toronto Studies in Semiotics); various monographs & book chapters, incl. "The Discursive Object," *Objects of Knowledge* ed. S. Pearce (The Athlone Press, Univ. of London, 1990); various articles, incl. "The Sociostructural Role of the Museum" (*The International Journal of Museum Management and Curatorship* 1 1982); "Three Realities and Two Discourses" (*Methodology and Science* 22 1989); numerous conference papers & other presentations. **AFFIL:** Bishop's Univ. (Exec. Committee of Corp.; Speakers Committee; Senator; Univ. Librarian Review Committee; Chair, Library Committee). **HONS:** scholarship, Ont. Grad. Studies, 1974; scholarship, Canada Council, 1978; Fellowship, National Museums of Canada, 1980. **MISC:** recipient, various grants. **COMMENT:** *"Research in semiotics and social groups."*

Tagg, Catherine J., A.I.I.C. 💲 ☻ ⬡
Senior Marketing Representative, WAWANESA MUTUAL INSURANCE COMPANY, 708 - 11 Ave. S.W., Ste. 600, Calgary, AB T2R 0E4 (403) 260-9202, FAX 262-1588. Born Vernon, B.C. 1957. s. **EDUC:** Insurance Institute of Southern Alberta, A.I.I.C. 1992; Univ. of Calgary, F.I.I.C./Mgmt Certificate in progress. **CAREER:** Commercial Lines Underwriter, Royal Insurance Co., 1978-85; Commercial Lines Underwriter, Wawanesa Mutual Insurance Co., 1986-87; Mktg Rep., 1987 to date. **AFFIL:** Southern Alberta Marketing Representative Association (mbr.; Pres. 1990-93); Canadian Insurance Women of Calgary (Pres. 1993-95; Co-Chair, Convention '95); United Way (Acct Exec.); Alberta Severe Weather Management Society (Treas.). **INTERESTS:** reading; walking; crafts; cooking; spiritual growth. **MISC:** Co-Chair, Centennial Celebrations of Wawanesa Mutual, Calgary Branch; voting delegate, CAIW Convention, Moncton, N.B., 1994. **COMMENT:** *"I am interested in professional development, and pursuing my Fellowship degree through the Insurance Institute of Canada and the Management Certificate from the University of Calgary. I am also active in the humanitarian aspect of mentorship of other women in the industry, in my position as Past President of the Insurance Professionals of Calgary, Canadian Association of Insurance Women."*

Tague-Sutcliffe, Jean Mary, B.A.,B.L.S., Ph.D. (1931-1996)
Professor Emeritus, Graduate School of Library and Information Science, UNIVERSITY OF WESTERN ONTARIO. Born Edmonton 1931. m. Bill Sutcliffe. 3 ch. Christina, Frederick, Eliza. **EDUC:** Univ. of Alberta, B.A.(English, Math.) 1953; McGill Univ., B.L.S.(Library Sci.) 1954; Western Reserve Univ., Ph.D.(Info. Sci., Statistics) 1966. **CAREER:** Research Asst. (part-time), Centre for Documentation & Communication Research, Western Reserve Univ., 1961-64; Sessional Lecturer, Math., Memorial Univ., 1965-66; Asst., Prof., Math., 1966-71; Assoc. Prof., Math., 1971-74; Assoc. Prof., SLIS, Univ. of Western Ontario, 1974-79; Visiting Prof., Dept. of Computer Sci., Cornell Univ., 1979-

80; Prof., SLIS, Univ. of Western Ontario, 1979-84; Dean, SLIS, 1984-96. **SELECTED PUBLICATIONS:** author, *Measuring Information: an Information Services Perspective* (monograph, Academic Press, 1995); author/co-author, numerous papers in scholarly journals & conference proceedings. **EDIT:** Ed., special issue on evaluation of info. retrieval systems, *Journal of the American Society for Information Science.* **AFFIL:** International Society for Scientometrics & Informetrics (Bd. of Dir. 1994-96); American Society for Information Science (mbr.; Bd. of Dir. 1990-93); Association for Computing Machinery; Canadian Association for Information Science; Canadian Library Association; American Library Association; École de bibliothéconomie et sciences de l'information, Univ. de Montréal (External Review Team 1993); Information London (Bd. of Dir. 1989-92); Ontario Public Libraries Strategic Plan (Performance Measures & Library Statistics Issues Team 1988-90); Univ. of Alberta (Chair, Review Committee, Sch. of Library & Info. Sci. 1989). **MISC:** numerous research grants & consultancies; reviewer/referee for National Science Foundation (U.S.), Social Sciences & Humanities Research Council of Canada, National Research Council of Canada, International Development and Research Corporation, & several journals.

Tahedl, Ernestine, R.C.A.,O.S.A. ⊗ ♥ ☻
Artist. 79 Collard Dr., King City, ON L7B 1E4 (905) 833-0686, FAX 833-0686. Born Austria. 2 ch. Degen, Lars. **EDUC:** Vienna Academy for Applied Arts, Master's Degree (Graphic Art) 1961. **CAREER:** Asst. to Prof. of Graphic Arts, Vienna Academy for Applied Arts, 1961-63; teacher, Edmonton Art Gallery, 1963-64; teacher, Univ. of Alberta Art Extension Courses, 1964-65; painter/stained glass artist, 1965 to date. **EXHIBITIONS:** numerous exhibitions incl. Canadian Guild of Crafts, Montreal (1968); Wiener Secession, Vienna (1971); Shayne Gallery, Montreal (1980); Lefebvre Galleries, Edmonton (1982); Gallery Quan, Toronto (1984); Wallace Gallery, Calgary (1989); Shieder and Associates Gallery Ltd., Toronto (1993); Galerie L'Autre Equivoque (1994); Robert Langen Gallery, Wilfrid Laurier Univ. (1995); numerous group exhibitions. **COLLECTIONS:** numerous public & private collections, incl. Fed. Dept. of External Affairs (Beijing, Ottawa); Goethe Institute (Montreal); McGill Univ.; Regional Art Gallery, London, Ont.; Public Gallery of the City, Vienna; Alberta Energy Company; Maclean Hunter, Toronto; Reader's Digest, Montreal; Teleglobe Canada; Musée du Québec; Zurich Life Canada. **AFFIL:** Royal

Canadian Academy of Arts (VP 1988-90; Chair, Exhibition Committee 1989-91); Ontario Society of Artists (Council 1986-89; VP 1987-89; Pres. 1996-98); Arts Foundation of Greater Toronto (Trustee 1990-92; Exec. 1992-95); King-Vaughan Environmental Coalition (Pres. 1992-95). HONS: Graduation Prize, Gov't of Austria, 1961; Bronze Medal, Vienna Int'l Exhibition of Paintings, 1963; Allied Arts Medal, Royal Architectural Institute of Canada, 1966; Purchase Award, Concours Artistique du Québec, 1966; Arts Award, Canada Council, 1967; Canada 125 Medal. INTERESTS: travelling; music; environmental concerns. MISC: numerous commissions for stained glass, painting & sculpture, Canada & Austria, incl. St. Peter's Evangelical Lutheran Church, Toronto, 1990-94. COMMENT: *"My profession as artist gives me the opportunity to be part of Canadian cultural life and to contribute to the betterment of the community."*

Tait, Kathy, B.A. ✐ 🗖
Columnist, THE PROVINCE, 2250 Granville St., Vancouver, BC V6H 3G2 (604) 732-2044, FAX 732-2099. Born Vancouver 1944 1 ch. Melanie Griffiths. EDUC: Univ. of British Columbia, B.A.(Pol. Sci./English) 1966. CAREER: reporter/columnist, 1966 to date. SELECTED PUBLICATIONS: *Love Smarts* (Self-Counsel Press, 1994). INTERESTS: current events; social issues; relationship issues; boating; gardening; family; travel.

Tait, Reginae Mae 🐿 ⊕ 🗂
Teacher, Association Executive. Born Watford, Ont. 1910. m. George E. Tait. 1 ch. Gary E.S. Tait. EDUC: London Ontario Normal Sch., teacher training 1930-31; Univ. of Western Ontario, 1935-38; Ont. Dept. of Educ., Art Specialist 1950. CAREER: Teacher & Art Supervisor, Gordon McGregor Sch., Windsor, Ont., 1931-38; Pres., Jr. Mary Grant Society, Windsor, 1934-36; Pres., Women Teachers' Federation, Windsor, 1935-36; Art Instructor, summer & evening courses for teachers; Asst. Dir., Anglo-American Sch., Bogota, Colombia, 1941-44; Pres., Bedford Park Home & Sch. Association, 1956-57; Program Chrm, Toronto Home & Sch. Association, 1957-59; Nat'l Pres., IODE, 1970-72; Hon. Nat'l VP, 1973 to date; Gov. & Exec. mbr., Frontier Coll., 1969-79; Pres., Health League of Canada, 1979-82; mbr., Canadian National Exhibition Association, 1969-80; Dir., 1980-87; Hon. Dir., 1980 to date; Bd. Mbr. & Dir., Council for Canadian Unity, 1974-81; Dir., Sir William Campbell House Foundation, 1978-80; Lay Bencher, Law Society of Upper Canada, 1974-87; Bd. & Exec. Mbr., John Graves Simcoe Foundation.

SELECTED PUBLICATIONS: various articles for educational journals & *Echoes* (IODE publication). AFFIL: Frontier Coll. (Fellow); John Galsworthy Chapter, IODE (Life Mbr.); Nat'l Chapter of Canada, IODE (Life Mbr.); Commonwealth Countries League, London, U.K. (VP for Canada, 1970-97). HONS: Queen's Jubilee Medal, 1977; presented to Her Majesty at St. James' Palace & Buckingham Palace, 1971. INTERESTS: travel; art; crafts. MISC: 1st woman Exec. mbr., Frontier Coll.; 1 of 2 first women acting as Benchers in Ont. since founding of Law Society of Upper Canada in 1797; as Chrm of a committee, responsible for ten stained-glass windows depicting the history of law in Canada, the establishment of an archives & a Museum of Law for Law Society of Upper; founding & Exec. Mbr., National Action Committee Status of Women, 1965-79.

Talbot-Allan, Laura M., B.Sc.,M.B.A., C.M.A.,F.C.M.A. ■ 🌸 💲 ⊕
Chairman, 1995-96, THE SOCIETY OF MANAGEMENT ACCOUNTANTS OF CANADA, 120 King St. W., Box 176, Hamilton, ON L8N 3C3. Assistant Deputy Minister, Corporate Services, Environment Canada, GOVERNMENT OF CANADA. m. David. 2 ch. EDUC: Univ. of Manitoba, B.Sc. 1973; Univ. of Ottawa & Univ. of Manitoba, M.B.A. 1979; Certified Management Accountant 1982. CAREER: Manitoba Hydro, 1971-73; Bell Canada, 1973-76; Cont. & Treas., Manitoba Telephone System, 1976-88; Dir., Office of the Compt. Gen. of Canada, 1988-90; Nat'l Dir., Fin. & Admin. Canadian Red Cross Society, 1990-93; Exec. Dir., Fin & Admin., Employment & Immigration Canada, 1993. AFFIL: The Society of Management Accountants of Canada (Chair 1995-96; Fellow); Civil Service Co-operative Credit Society (Bd.); Financial Executives' Institute; Financial Management Institute; Treasury Management Association of Canada: Gov't of Canada Advisory Committee of the Public Service Superannuation Act; National Round Table on Environment & Economy; United Way/Health Partners; Canadian National Institute for the Blind.

Tan-Willman, Conchita, B.Ed.,M.Sc., M.A.,Ph.D. 🐿 ⊕
Professor, UNIVERSITY OF TORONTO, 371 Bloor St. W., Toronto, ON M5S 2R7 (416) 978-7503, FAX 978-6775. President, PRIME MENTORS OF CANADA. Born Philippines 1939. m. Andrew Willman. EDUC: Philippine Normal Univ., B.Ed.(Elementary Educ.) 1959; Philippine Women's Univ., M.Sc.(Psych.) 1962; Univ. of Toronto, M.A.(Educational Psych.) 1964; Univ. of Minnesota, Ph.D.(Educational Psych.) 1967. CAREER: Supervising Instructor, Philip-

pine Normal Coll. Laboratory Sch., 1959-60; Instructor & Psychometrician, Philippine Women's Univ., 1959-60; part-time Instructor, 1960-62; Dir., Research Dept., Philippine Psychological Corporation, 1960-62; Research Asst., Univ. of Minnesota, 1962-64; Instructor, Rhode Island Coll., 1964-65; part-time Instructor & Teaching Asst., Univ. of Minnesota, 1965-68; Lecturer, Queen's Coll., City Univ. of N.Y., 1967-68; Asst. Prof., McArthur Coll. of Educ., Queen's Univ., 1968-69; Asst. Prof., Ontario Institute for Studies in Educ., Univ. of Toronto, 1969-76; Assoc. Prof., 1976-82; Prof., 1982 to date; Pres., Financial Public Relations, 1983 to date. **SELECTED PUBLICATIONS:** *An Exploration on Creativity* (Kingston: Queen's Univ., McArthur Coll. of Educ., 1969); *Useful Citizens in Action* with R. Tuason & E. Pangalangan, vols. I & II (Quezon City, Philippines: Alemars Books, 1969); *Canadian Achievers and their Mentors: For Those in Search of Inspiration and Role Models*, with S. Kong (Toronto: Univ. of Toronto Press, 1994); "Creative Thinking and Moral Reasoning of Academically Gifted Adolescents," with D. Gutteridge (*Gifted Child Quarterly* 25(4) 1981); "Comparison of Cerebral Hemisphere Preference of Primary/Junior, Junior/Intermediate and Intermediate/Senior Teachers" (*Journal of Creative Behaviour* 21 1987); numerous other publications. **AFFIL:** Creative Scholars Network; World Futures Society; World Council for Gifted & Talented Children; American Educational Research Association; National Association for Gifted Children; Canadian Society for Comparative Study of Civilization; Phi Delta Kappa; The American Biographical Institute Inc. (Hon. Mbr., Research Bd. of Advisors; Hon. Advisor, Research Bd., Nat'l Div.); PRIME Mentors of Canada for the Development of Creative Potential (founder & Pres. 1987 to date); United Generation of Ontario (Bd. of Dir. 1996 to date). **HONS:** Tandang Sora Service Award, 1959; Philippine Student Leadership Award, 1959; Fulbright/Smith-Mundt Scholarship, 1962-63; Cultural Doctorate (Hon.),World Univ., 1988; Presidential Citation, The World Council for Gifted & Talented Children, 1990; Canada 125 Medal, 1992; Dame of Grace, Sovereign Military Order of Saint John of Jerusalem, 1992; Doctor of Humanities (Hon.), Wolfe Univ., 1994; various other awards, scholarships & fellowships. **INTERESTS:** music; travel; theatre; ballet; opera; cooking. **MISC:** Co-Prod., *Eminent Canadians: Their Mentors and Keys to Achievement,* video series (1991); frequent public speaker; numerous radio & TV interviews; recipient, numerous grants; listed in numerous biographical sources incl. *World Intellectual* (1993), *International Who's Who of Education* (1986) & *Who's Who of Women* (1976); Co-founder, Chopin Society of Canada, 1974; contributor & in numerous int'l conferences. **COMMENT:** *"An educational psychologist who has been involved in teacher education, has published numerous research studies in creativity and related areas, and has been operating an enrichment mentoring program for the creatively gifted."*

Tanaka, Margaret, B.Sc.,C.G.A.,C.F.P. $

President, MARGARET TANAKA PROFESSIONAL CORPORATION, P.O. Box 690, High Level, AB T0H 1Z0 (403) 926-2023, FAX 926-2646. Born Calgary 1957. m. Alan. 2 ch. Geoffrey, Heather. **EDUC:** Univ. of Alberta, B.Sc.(Zoology) 1978. **CAREER:** Acctnt, 1982 to date. **AFFIL:** Certified General Accountants' Association (C.G.A.); Institute of Financial Planning (C.F.P.); High Level United Church (Trustee/Treas. 1990-92). **HONS:** Bus. of the Year Award, local Chamber of Commerce, 1990; Canada 125 Medal. **INTERESTS:** reading; crafts; outdoor activities; volunteer work at a variety of levels.

Tancred, Peta, B.A.,M.ès Arts, Ph.D. ■ 🎓 🍁

Professor of Sociology, MCGILL UNIVERSITY, 855 Sherbrooke St. W., Montreal, QC H3A 1W7 (514) 398-6851, FAX 398-3403, EMAIL cypt@musica.mcgill.ca. Born London, UK 1937. d. **EDUC:** McGill Univ., B.A.(English & Soc.) 1958; Univ. de Montréal, M.ès Arts (Soc.) 1966; London Sch. of Econ., Ph.D.(Soc.) 1968. **CAREER:** Asst. Sec., World University Service of Canada, 1959-62; Asst. to the Sec., Cdn Nat'l Commission for UNESCO, 1962-63; Asst. Prof., Univ. de Montréal, 1968-69; Research Officer, Industrial Sociology Unit, Imperial Coll. of Science & Technology, Univ. of London, 1969; Fac. Mbr., Univ. of Maryland European Div., London, 1970; Research Officer, Civil Service Coll., London, 1971-72; Asst. Prof., Dept. of Soc., McMaster Univ., 1972-74; Assoc. Prof., 1974-90; Chair, 1974-79; Cdn Visiting Fellow, Macquarie Univ., Sydney, Australia, 1986; Adjunct Fellow, Simone de Beauvoir Institute, Concordia Univ., 1987-88; Dir., McGill Centre for Research & Teaching on Women, 1990-96. **SELECTED PUBLICATIONS:** *The Sexuality of Organization*, co-ed. & contributor (London: Sage Publications, 1989); *Gendering Organizational Analysis*, co-ed. & contributor (Newbury Park, CA: Sage Publications, 1992); "Unrepresentative Bureaucracy" (*Sociology* 8(3) Sept. 1974); "La Place des Femmes: Un dossier sur la Sociologie des Organisations," with E. Jane Campbell (*Soci-*

ologie et Sociétés Oct. 1981); "Craft, Hierarchy, Bureaucracy: Modes of Control of the Academic Labour Process" (*Canadian Journal of Sociology* 10,4 Sept. 1985); numerous other publications. **EDIT:** Ed. (Soc.), *Canadian Review of Sociology and Anthropology*, 1983-86; Ed. Bd., *Sage Studies in International Sociology*, 1977-82; Comité de rédaction, *Sociologie et Sociétés*, 1986-91; Consulting Ed., *Canadian Review of Sociology and Anthropology*, 1992 to date; Comité de rédaction, *Recherches féministes*, 1993 to date. **AFFIL:** Canadian Sociology & Anthropology Association (Pres. 1993-94); Canadian Research Institute for the Advancement of Women. **HONS:** Commonwealth Scholar, 1965-68; Canadian Visiting Fellow, Macquarie Univ., Sydney, Australia, 1986. **INTERESTS:** tennis; hiking; cinema. **MISC:** recipient, numerous grants & fellowships; various conference presentations; reviewer for diverse journals & granting agencies. **COMMENT:** *"Her recent work on a gendered approach to organizations has gained her an international reputation and crowned a career devoted to analyzing the workplace."*

Tanguay, Lucie, B.Comm. $

President, TKO MARKETING INC., Marketing Consultant, 1069 Willibrord, Verdun, QC H4G 2V1 (514) 362-9552, FAX 362-9575. Born Montreal 1962. m. Jacques Germain. **EDUC:** McGill Univ., B.Comm.(Mktg/Quantitive Methods) 1984. **CAREER:** Brand Mgr, Bovril Canada Inc., 1984-88; Brand Mgr, Seagram Canada, 1988-91; Dir. of Mktg, 1991-94; Acting VP, Sales/Dir. of Mktg, New Bus. Dev., Vachon, 1994-95. **AFFIL:** Liquor Control Bd. of Ont. (Industry Rep. 1993-94). **HONS:** James McGill Scholar, McGill Univ., 1981, 1982, 1983; Scholar, Women's Associates of McGill, 1982; Scholar, McGill Fac., 1984. **INTERESTS:** golf; movies; books; exercise; travel. **COMMENT:** *"Dynamic leader with strategic creativity and vision. Proven track record of profitable brand building. Unique ability to simplify complex business problems and offer practical solutions that work. Charismatic personality with excellent people skills."*

Tannenbaum, Gloria Shaffer, B.Sc.,M.Sc., Ph.D. ■■ ⊕ 🎓

Professor, Departments of Pediatrics and Neurology and Neurosurgery, MCGILL UNIVERSITY, Neuropeptide Physiology Lab., Montreal Children's Hospital Research Institute, 2300 Tupper St., Montreal, QC H3H 1P3 (514) 934-4400, ext. 2753, FAX 934-4331, EMAIL mcta@musica.mcgill.ca. Born Montreal 1938. m. Alan. 4 ch. Elyse, Rhonda, Caroline, Beth. **EDUC:** McGill Univ., B.Sc.(Physiology) 1959, M.Sc.(Physiological Psych.) 1973, Ph.D.(Neuroendocrinology) 1976. **CAREER:** Asst. Prof. (1978-84)/Assoc. Prof. (1984-89)/Prof., 1989 to date, Depts. of Pediatrics, & Neurology & Neurosurgery, McGill Univ.; Dir., Neuropeptide Physiology Lab., McGill Univ.-Montreal Children's Hospital Research Institute, 1980 to date. **SELECTED PUBLICATIONS:** author/co-author, 86 articles in professional journals, 110 abstracts, 124 scientific presentations & invited lectures. **AFFIL:** Canadian Friends of Bar Ilan Univ., Ramat Gan, Israel (Sec., VP & Science Advisor, Montreal chpt. 1983 to date); The Endocrine Society (Public Communications Committee 1994 to date); Fonds de la recherche en santé du Québec, FRSQ (Review Committees, Research Grant Applications/ Research Institutes Evaluations 1987 to date). **HONS:** "Chercheur de carrière" Award, FRSQ, 1994 to date; "Chercheur-boursier de mérite exceptionnel" Award, FRSQ, 1989-94; "Chercheur-boursier" Awards, FRSQ, 1980-89; "Prix d'excellence" in Pediatric Research, Inter-Service Clubs Council Foundation, 1984. **MISC:** numerous admin. appts; has served on several edit. bds. & been guest editor on numerous publications; scientific grant reviewer. **COMMENT:** *"As a professor at McGill University, my major research goal has been to elucidate the brain mechanisms that regulate the secretion of growth hormone. In 1993, this research resulted in the development of a new diagnostic test for growth hormone deficiency in the slowly growing child. I am committed to employment equity at McGill University and to the advancement of women neuroscientists worldwide. Most importantly, I am the mother of four daughters."*

Tanner, Susan Gwen, B.A.,B.Ed.,M.E.S., LL.B. ■ ✊ ⚖ ♡

Environment and Social Policy Consultant, Mediator, Humorist. Born Edmonton 1948. m. Dr. Irvin Waller. 2 ch., 2 stpch. **EDUC:** Univ. of Alberta, B.A.(Hist./French) 1969; B.Ed. 1970; York Univ., M.E.S. 1976, Osgoode Hall, LL.B. 1976; Univ. of Strasbourg, Hons. Diploma (Comparative Law) 1977; Ottawa Univ., LL.M. in Int'l Environmental Law. **BAR:** Ont., 1978. **CAREER:** Teacher, Alberta; Lawyer, Justice Canada, 1979; Consultant, Law Reform Commission of Canada, 1982; Dir., Resources, Admin. & Info., Fed. Coordination Secretariat, Expo 86, 1983; Proj. Leader, Canadian Human Rights Commission, 1985; mbr., Ont. Environmental Assessment Bd., 1986; V-Chair, Ont. Social Assistance Review Bd., 1987; social policy consultant & public speaker, 1987-92; Mediator, Ont. Grievance Settlement Bd., 1990 to date; Exec. Dir.,

Friends of the Earth Canada, 1992-95. **SELECTED PUBLICATIONS:** "Women and the Sustainable Environment Commission" (*Women & Environments* Winter/Spring 1993); "Women's Empowerment in a Time of Scarcity" *(Peace and Environment News* mbr.'s supplement Nov. 1994); "Canadians Must Rise to the Challenge (of Sustainability)/Les Canadiens doivent relever le défi" (*National Round Table Review* Fall 1994); "Healing the Sky to Survive Globalization," in *Surviving Globalism* (Macmillan, forthcoming); various other publications on environment & human rights. **EDIT:** Ed., *EarthWords,* Friends of the Earth, 1993-94. **AFFIL:** WEED, Women's Environmental Education & Development Foundation (Dir.); Learning for a Sustainable Future (Dir.); Interval House (Dir.); LEAF, Women's Legal Education & Action Fund (Founding Chair 1985); Law Society; Law Union; Canadian Bar Association; National Association for Women & the Law; Canadian Environmental Network (Chair, Int'l Affairs Caucus 1994); Canadian Committee for UNIFEM; Network for Alternative Dispute Resolution; World Society of Victimology; Ottawa Women for a Healthy Planet; MATCH; Re-evaluation Co-counselling. **HONS:** Bursary to French Teachers, Gov't of Ont.; Bursary, Univ. of Poitiers, Gov't of France; Grad. Fellowship, CMHC, 1974-75. **INTERESTS:** peer counselling; yoga; tennis; tarot; humour. **MISC:** Cdn delegation to CSD (UN), 1993, 1994, & GEF, 1995; conference organizer, incl. mbr., organizing committee, Women & Sustainability Conference, 1994; developed & teaches seminar on humour in the workplace, with special sessions for women facing harassment. **COMMENT:** *"Susan started out as an Alberta cowgirl with Annie Oakley as a role model and is now a FAKE Woman–a Feminist for All Kinds of Equality. She is particularly concerned that Mother Nature not be abused. Instead, she envisions a cooperative society full of love and laughter, the two main things that make us human."*

Tansey, Charlotte Hunter, LL.D.,M.A. 🎓

President and Director of Studies, THOMAS MORE INSTITUTE, 3405 Atwater Ave., Montreal, QC H3H 1Y2 (514) 935-9585. Born Montreal 1922. s. **EDUC:** Univ. de Montréal, B.A. 1943; McGill Univ., M.A.(English) 1948. **CAREER:** commercial section, Bell Canada, 1943-44; public rel'ns, C-I-L, 1944-47; advtg, Eaton's, 1947; Montreal edition, *Canadian Register*, 1943-47; Chrm, Publicity, Newman Club of McGill Univ., 1947-48; Founding Dir./Sec., Thomas More Institute, 1945-48; Registrar, 1948-66; Academic VP, 1962-81; Pres./Dir. of Studies, 1981 to date. **SELECTED PUBLICATIONS:** numerous briefs & reports; "The Assumptions of Adult Learning" (*Culture* 1957); "Other Voices, Other Classrooms" (*Canadian Forum* Sept. 1968); "A Dialogue on Learning Mathematics" with R. Eric O'Connor, *Creativity and Method: Essays in Honor of Bernard Lonergan* (Milwaukee, WI: Marquette Univ. Press, 1981); "Liberal Arts in the Post-Classical World" (*Témoignages: Reflections on the Humanities* 1993); other articles, chapters & interviews. **AFFIL:** Canadian Federation for the Humanities (Corresponding Mbr. 1977-80); Association for Continuing Higher Education (Assoc. Mbr.; Nontraditional Educ. Committee 1977-80). **HONS:** Citizen of the Year Award, Montreal Citizenship Council, 1975; LL.D.(Hon.), Concordia Univ., 1985; D.L. (Hon.), Burlington Coll., Vermont, 1995. **MISC:** designs some, & leads a few, discussion courses each year, with the Thomas More Institute; presenter at conferences; currently the subject of interviews toward a book on life experiences in educ. with adults. **COMMENT:** *"I am grateful to have learned so steadily, and in so many directions and scholarly fields over the years. This has been done with friends who are co-learners. And a community does push one beyond what one thinks is possible!"*

Tapp, Janice, B.Ed. 🎓 ✊ ✱

President, PROVINCIAL INTERMEDIATE TEACHERS' ASSOCIATION, Box 185, Fraser Lake, BC V0J 1S0 (205) 699-6233, FAX 699-7753. Born Fernie, B.C. 1952. m. Trevor L. Tapp. **EDUC:** Univ. of Victoria, B.Ed.(Elementary) 1990. **CAREER:** teacher, various B.C. sch. districts; teacher & Head of Fine Arts Dept., Fraser Lake Elementary Secondary Sch.; Ptnr, small farm. **SELECTED PUBLICATIONS:** features in publications of the Provincial Intermediate Teachers' Association. **AFFIL:** B.C. Teachers' Federation; Nechako Teachers' Union; Nechako Intermediate Teachers' Association (Pres.); Provincial Specialist Association Council; Provincial Intermediate Teachers' Association (Pres.). **INTERESTS:** equestrian activities; reading; curling; golf; gardening; choir. **COMMENT:** *"I enjoy the challenges and changes being an educator entails, the time spent with family and friends. I work hard to serve my students and my colleagues."*

Tardif, Louise, B.Comm.,F.C.S.I.,C.I.M. $

Investment Advisor and Manager, LÉVESQUE BEAUBIEN GEOFFRION, INC. 155 Queen St., Ste. 306, Ottawa, ON K1P 6L1 (613) 236-0103, FAX 236-5916. Born Sainte-Foy, Que. 1957. **EDUC:** McGill Univ., Mgmt Certificate 1983; Univ. of Ottawa, B.Comm.(Mgmt Sci.) 1986.

CAREER: Admin. Asst., Coopers & Lybrand, 1978-83; Investment Advisor, Lévesque Beaubien Geoffrion, 1986 to date. DIRECTOR: Pink Triangle Services. AFFIL: Business & Professional Women's Association of Ottawa; Canadian Securities Institute (F.C.S.I.; C.I.M.); Canadian Forum for Youth (Dir. & Trustee); Sophie Steadman Bursary (Dir. & Treas.); SCO Foundation (Dir.; Treas.). HONS: Bus. Woman of the Year, Business & Professional Women's Association of Ottawa. INTERESTS: history; golf; theatre; wine collecting. MISC: has been profiled in *The Ottawa Citizen, The Ottawa Business News & The Ottawa Business Magazine.* COMMENT: *"In today's environment, the key values–integrity, honesty, kindness and love–are essential for business leaders to be important role models. Businesspeople have a special responsibility to effect positive societal change. I face this challenge with energy and joy."*

Tarlington, Carole, B.Ed.,M.Ed. ■ ⚅ Ⓢ
President, TARLINGTON TALENT INC., 525 Seymour St., Ste. 609, Vancouver, BC V6B 3H7 (604) 688-4077, FAX 688-4076. Born Sydney, Australia 1939. s. EDUC: Bathurst Teachers' Coll., New South Wales, Australia, Teacher's Degree 1958; Univ. of Victoria, B.Ed. 1972, M.Ed.(Curriculum) 1976. CAREER: teacher; Educ. Consultant, Vancouver Bd. of Educ.; co-founder & former Artistic Dir., Vancouver Youth Theatre; part-time Lecturer, Theatre in Educ., Univ. of British Columbia; Pres., Tarlington Talent Inc., 1985 to date; Artist-in-Residence: Midnite Youth Theatre, Perth, Western Australia, 1994, Leeming Youth Theatre, Perth, John Curtin Performing Arts High Sch., 1996. SELECTED CREDITS: writer/dir., *Minor Reality*, Vancouver & Canada Rep. at the Int'l Drama In Educ. Conference in Brisbane, Australia, 1995; writer/dir., *Australian Stories*, Western Australian Youth Theatre, 1994; writer, *Canadian Stories*, Vancouver Youth Theatre. SELECTED PUBLICATIONS: *Offstage: Elementary Education Through Drama* with Patrick Verriour (Oxford Univ. Press, 1983); *Role Drama: A Teachers' Handbook* (Pembroke Press, 1991); *Building Plays* (Pembroke Press, 1995). AFFIL: Association of B.C. Drama Educators (Past Pres.); Canadian Academy of Film & Television; B.C. Motion Picture Association. HONS: Award for Outstanding Contribution to Drama With The Young People of B.C., Association of B.C. Drama Educators, 1989; Woman of Distinction, YWCA, 1991; Min. of State Award for Excellence in Race Rel'ns, 1991; Canada 125 Medal. MISC: conference speaker & workshop leader; keynote speaker: B.C. Drama Teachers'

Conference, 1995, Ohio Drama Exchange, 1996 & National Association of Drama & Education, Australia, 1996; acting coach & agent for many young actors on TV series, movies & film. COMMENT: *"Carole Tarlington is a director, author, theatrical agent, and freelance drama consultant. She has developed and directed many scripts with young people."*

Tarn, E. Jane, B.T. ⓐ ⬜
Executive Director, THE KINDNESS CLUB, 65 Brunswick St., Fredericton, NB E3B 1G5 (506) 459-3379. Born Saint John 1940. m. T. Richard. 2 ch. Johanna Tarn, Christina Tarn. EDUC: Modern Bus. Coll., 1961; New Brunswick Teachers' Coll., Licence 1962; Univ. of New Brunswick, B.T.(Teaching) 1971. CAREER: elementary sch. Teacher; Naturalist, Canadian Forestry Association of N.B.; Exec. Dir., The Kindness Club. SELECTED PUBLICATIONS: *Endangered Species in New Brunswick* brochure (1987); various articles, *Ebb and Flow*, Girl Guides of Canada, N.B.; children's newsletter; weekly newspaper column. AFFIL: Girl Guides of Canada (various exec. positions); Saint John Naturalists' Club (Hon. Life Mbr.); Nature Trust of N.B. (Past Sec.; Treas.); St. John River Society (Past Treas.). HONS: Letter of Commendation, Girl Guides of Canada, 1988; Merit Award, Canadian Forestry Association of N.B., 1989; Merit Award, Girl Guides of Canada, 1991. INTERESTS: animals; environment in general; bridge; crafts; bird-watching; whale-watching; reading; arranging flowers; nature walks for children. MISC: first proposed and wrote "Endangered Species Badge" that was accepted as part of the national program of the Girl Guides of Canada; has given workshops on dried flower arranging, & humane & environmental educ. COMMENT: *"I'm an educator intent on instilling in children and adults a respect and love for animals and nature through my work and volunteer time."*

Tasseor Tutsweetok, Lucy ⊗
Stone Carver. Born Nunalla, Man. 1934. m. Richard Tutsweetok. CAREER: stone carver, early 1960s to date. COMMISSIONS: commissioned by the Earth Spirit Festival to carve a piece for the *Visions of Power* exhibition in Toronto, 1991. EXHIBITIONS: more than 60 exhibitions in Canada, US & Europe incl. *The Art of Eskimo Women: in Sculpture, Prints, Wall-hangings*, The Arctic Circle, L.A. (1975); *A Woman's Vision*, Art Space Gallery, Philadelphia (1990); *Indigena: Contemporary Native Perspectives*, Canadian Museum of Civilization (1992); *Three Women of Arviat: Sculpture by Elizabeth Nutaraluk, Lucy Tasseor and Joy*

Halluk, The Isaacs/Innuit Gallery, Toronto (1992) & *Arctic Spirit: 35 Years of Canadian Inuit Art*, Frye Art Museum, Seattle, Wash. (1994). COLLECTIONS: Art Gallery of Ontario; Canadian Museum of Civilization; Dennos Museum Center, Northwestern Michigan Coll.; Inuit Cultural Institute; Klamer Family Collection; McMichael Canadian Art Collection; Museum of Anthropology, Univ. of British Columbia; National Gallery of Canada; Prince of Wales Northern Heritage Centre, Yellowknife; Sarick Collection; Winnipeg Art Gallery. COMMENT: *"Tasseor drew inspiration from the memories of sand drawings that she and her grandfather (whom she considers to be the greatest influence on her life) had made when she was a child. Her sculptures, representing mothers and children or family groups, are carved in a semi-abstract style in which the human figure is rarely defined."*–Ingo Hessel, from Visions of Power, 1991.

Tattersall, Jane, B.A. ■ 🏠⊗🐾👜

President, TATTERSALL SOUND INC., 424 Adelaide St. E., Toronto, ON M5A 1N4 (416) 364-4321, FAX 368-0690. Born London, UK 1957. m. Anthony Pepper. 2 ch. EDUC: Queen's Univ., B.A.(Phil.) 1980. CAREER: Researcher, TV documentaries; Sound Ed., TV & feature films; Supervising Sound Ed., feature films; Post-Prod. Supervisor, Canadian Film Centre, Toronto, current; owner & Pres., Tattersall Sound Inc. (post-prod. facility for digital sound ed.), current. SELECTED CREDITS: Supervising Sound Ed., *A Long Day's Journey Into Night*, dir. David Wellington; Supervising Sound Ed., *Never Talk to Strangers* (feature), dir. Sir Peter Hall; Sound Designer, *Rude* (feature), dir. Clement Virgo; Supervising Sound Ed., *32 Short Films About Glenn Gould* (feature), dir. Francois Girard; Supervising Sound Ed., *La Florida* (feature), dir. George Mihaulka; Supervising Sound Ed., *I Love a Man in Uniform* (feature), dir. David Wellington; Sound Effects Ed., *Naked Lunch* (feature), dir. David Cronenberg; Supervising Sound Ed., *South of Wawa* (feature), dir. Robert Boyd; Supervising Sound Ed., *Brain Candy*, dir. Kelly Makin; Sound Effects Ed., *The Fly* (feature), dir. David Cronenberg; Sound Effects Ed., *Breaking In* (feature), dir. Bill Forsyth; Sound Effects Ed., *Murderers Among Us* (2-part miniseries), dir. Brian Gibson. SELECTED PUBLICATIONS: started a newsletter for prod. & dir. on the subject of sound. AFFIL: Directors' Guild of Canada (Sec.); Toronto Women in Film. HONS: nomination, Best Sound Editing (*I Love a Man in Uniform*), Genie Awards, 1993; nomination, Best Sound Editing (*La Florida*), Genie Awards, 1993; Best Sound Editing (*Naked Lunch*), Genie Awards, 1992; nomination, Best Sound Editing (*South of Wawa*), Genie Awards, 1992; Best Sound Editing (*Carnival of Shadows*), Genie Awards, 1990; Best Sound Editing (*Murderers Among Us*), Golden Reel Award, 1989 & Golden Scissors Award, 1989; nomination, Best Sound Editing (*Buying Time*), Genie Awards, 1988; nomination, Best Sound Editing (*The Fly*), Golden Reel Awards, 1986; nomination, Best Sound Editing (*The Climb*), Genie Awards, 1987; Best Sound Editing (*The Climb*), Golden Sheaf Award, 1986. INTERESTS: scuba diving; movies; reading the novels of Barbara Pym; jazz. MISC: the 1st (& still the only) woman in Toronto to set up a digital sound editing facility. COMMENT: *"I have carved out a niche in the film post-production business that few people recognized as important–the independent filmmakers–and have used these clients to build my reputation as a dedicated and creative person with an instinct for business. I have created a sound post-production facility with a superb reputation. I intend to continue to develop my business and broaden my base of clients in order to go into film producing."*

Tayler, Anne H., B.A.,Ph.D. ⊗

Professor and Coordinator, Women's Studies, YUKON COLLEGE, Box 2799, Whitehorse, YT Y1A 5K4 (403) 668-8774, FAX 668-8828. Born Toronto 1951. Life partner Frank L. Turner. 2 ch. Cindy-Anne Elizabeth Greenwood, Wendy Louella Mitchell. EDUC: Univ. of British Columbia, B.A.(English) 1981, Ph.D.(English) 1991. CAREER: medical Bookkeeper, Toronto, 1970-73; Founder & Dir., Northern Lights Daycare Centre, Whitehorse, 1973; Bookkeeper & Credit Mgr, Whitehorse, 1974-78; author, part-time, 1976 to date; Instructor, part-time, Univ. of British Columbia, Simon Fraser Univ. & Vancouver Community Coll., 1981-86; Exec. Dir., Yukon Arts Council, 1986-88; Consultant & Sole Proprietor, Aristotle's Rabbit, 1986 to date; Instructor, Yukon Coll., 1987 to date. SELECTED PUBLICATIONS: *From Hand to Hand: A Gathering of Book Arts*, ed.; *Art of the Book Exhibition* (1986); Chapbook Series of Yukon International Storytelling, Ed.; various articles (literary & women's issues) & reviews; poems published in various journals. EDIT: Co-Ed., *Northern Review*, Special Literary Issue (1993). AFFIL: Yukon Int'l Storytelling Festival (Co-Founder 1987; Co-Chair); Yukon Recreation Advisory Committee (V-Chair); Yukon Coll. Student Council (Fac. Advisor); Yukon Coll. (Rep., Shared Governance Joint Budget Committee); Whitehorse Public Library Bd.; ROTS (Recycle Organics

Together)(Founding mbr. 1989-92). HONS: Canada 125 Medal; various volunteer recognition & teaching awards; various academic awards. MISC: co-founder of the Whitehorse Recycling Centre, the 1st such facility in the Yukon, 1988; founder of Northern Lights Daycare, the 1st infant daycare in the Yukon, 1973; Co-Chair, Program Dev. Committee responsible for establishing a Women's Studies Program at Yukon Coll.; developed 1st courses in First Nations Lit. at Yukon Coll. (traditional & modern); involved in a new approach to contract negotiations at the Coll. using a problem-solving consensus approach. COMMENT: *"Born in southern Canada with the heart of a northerner. Strongly believe that where the tongue wags, so the feet and hands must go. Deeply committed to the perpetuation of the 'grandmother' of all art forms, storytelling–it has such great potential with respect to education, sharing and multicultural understanding and collaboration. Also deeply committed to women's issues; as a single parent for virtually all of my parenting years, I am particularly interested in child care and support matters. Have spent more than 20 years volunteering in the arts and culture sector (theatre, visual art, performing arts); now involved in ongoing work on arts policy."*

Taylor, Beverly, B.Sc.,Ph.D. ■ ❀ $

Director, Quality Control, CONNAUGHT LABORATORIES LTD., 1755 Steeles Ave. W., North York, ON M2R 3T4 (416) 667-2725, FAX 667-3004. Born UK 1961. m. Tim Hulse. EDUC: Univ. of Sheffield, UK, B.Sc.(Biochem./Microbiol.) 1983; Univ. of Leeds, UK, Ph.D.(Biochem.) 1988. CAREER: Research Asst., Univ. of Leeds, 1986-88; Postdoctoral Research Fellow, Univ. of Toronto, 1988-90; Research Scientist, Connaught Laboratories Ltd., 1990-94; Dir. of Quality Control, 1994 to date. SELECTED PUBLICATIONS: various scholarly papers, with others, on immunology, biochem. & microbiol. AFFIL: Biochemical Society, London, UK; International Association of Biological Standardization. INTERESTS: travel; gardening; skiing; hiking; canoeing; flying. COMMENT: *"Since I was young I have had a keen interest in science. I moved into the challenging environment of quality control after spending 11 years in research."*

Taylor, Carole, B.A. $ ✄ ♦

Vice-Chair, VANCOUVER PORT CORPORATION, 2760 Granville Square, 200 Granville, Vancouver, BC V6C 1S4 (604) 666-3466, FAX 666-8239. Born Toronto 1945. m. Art Phillips. 2 ch. EDUC: Univ. of Toronto, B.A.(English) 1967. CAREER: Host, *After Four*, Toronto

Today, Topic, The Carole Taylor Show, CFTO Toronto, 1964-72; Host, *Canada AM*, CTV, 1972-73; Host, *W5*, CTV, 1973-76; Host, *Pacific Report, Scene from Here, Authors, Vancouver Life*, CBC, 1976-84; *Inside Expo*, CKNW, 1985-86; Alderman, City of Vancouver (Chair, Neighbourhood, Cultural & Community Svcs Committee; Chair, Planning & Neighbourhoods Committee; Chair, Task Force on Children; Chair, GVRD'S Hospital Committee; Co-Chair, UBCM'S Liquor Task Force), 1986-90; Columnist (city issues), *Vancouver Sun*, 1991; freelance broadcaster, *Canada AM*, CTV, CBC radio *(Morningside:* "BC Report"), 1992-94; V-Chair, Vancouver Port Corporation, 1995 to date; Chair, Public Affairs Committee; Chair, Vancouver Public Library. MISC: was the 1st host of *Canada AM* & the 1st woman host of *W5*. COMMENT: *"Through a rich and varied life in politics, the media and public service, Carole Taylor has been involved with most major issues of our time. Currently, as Vice-Chair of the Vancouver Port Corporation, she is working to ensure that the relationship between the Port and its bordering municipalities is a positive one, both economically and socially."*

Taylor, Carole D., B.A. $ ♦

Vice-President and Director, Atlantic Divisional Manager, NESBITT BURNS, Bank of Montreal Tower, 5151 George St., 10th Fl., Halifax, NS B3J 1M5 (902) 496-1158, FAX 423-7011. Born Winnipeg 1955. m. James Taylor. 3 ch. EDUC: Univ. of Toronto, B.A. 1979. CAREER: Acct Exec., Merrill Lynch Royal Securities, 1979-82; Investment Officer, National Trust Company, 1983-84; Registered Rep., Burns Fry Limited, 1984-92; Co-Mgr, 1992-93; VP & Dir., Atlantic Div'l Mgr, Nesbitt Burns Inc., 1993 to date. DIRECTOR: Nesbitt Burns Inc. AFFIL: Chartered Financial Analyst (Level 1 & Level 2) ; Investment Dealers' Association of Canada (Chair, Educ. Committee, & Sec.-Treas., N.S. Council 1993-95); Mount Saint Vincent Univ. (Gov.; Chair, Investment Committee 1992-94; Chair, Bd. of Dir., Child Study Centre 1993-94; Chair, Bd. of Gov.); Nova Scotia Council (V-Chair 1995 to date); Committee on University Financing; N.S. Council on Higher Education (ad hoc committee). HONS: Distinction Award, Atlantic Reg., Investment Dealers' Association of Canada, 1992.

Taylor, Carolyn, B.A. ⬚ $

National Executive Director, THE WORD ON THE STREET, 24 Ryerson Ave., Ste. 303, Toronto, ON M5T 2P3 (416) 366-7241, FAX 860-0826, EMAIL the-wots@inforamp.net.

EDUC: Univ. of Western Ontario, B.A.(English & Drama) 1984; Confederation Coll., Performing Arts Mgmt 1984-85. **CAREER:** Mktg & Dev. Asst., The Grand Theatre, London, Ont.; Box Office Mgr, Second City Dinner Theatre; Programming Officer, Dalhousie Arts Centre; Asst. Prod., The Marlene Smith Group, 1985-87; Toronto Arts Week Prod., Arts Foundation of Greater Toronto, 1987-89; Nat'l Exec. Dir., The Word On The Street, 1989 to date. **COMMENT:** *"The Word On The Street is an annual outdoor book and magazine festival recognized as one of Canada's largest and most successful public celebrations of literacy and the printed word."*

Taylor, Catherine, B.A.,M.B.A.,F.I.C.B. ■ $
Associate Vice-President, Personal Deposits, THE TORONTO-DOMINION BANK, Toronto-Dominion Centre, T-D Tower, 17th Fl., P.O. Box 1, Toronto, ON M5K 1A2 (416) 307-9157, FAX 944-6195. Born Edmonton 1950. m. Scott. 1 ch. **EDUC:** Univ. of Alberta, B.A. (Art Hist.) 1975; Univ. of Toronto, M.B.A. (Fin./Mktg) 1980; Canadian Securities Course, Grad. Hons. 1988. **CAREER:** joined TD Bank, 1980; various mgmt positions incl. Div. Cont. & Nat'l Dir.–Women Entrepreneurs; Co-chair, TD's Task Force on Women's Advancement. **SELECTED PUBLICATIONS:** bus. articles in *Financial XPress* & *Canadian Banker* magazines, sundry bus. & arts publications. **AFFIL:** Canadian Association of Women Executives & Entrepreneurs, Toronto; Brian Webb Dance Company, Edmonton (Chair 1981-83); Attentional Disorders Association of Edmonton (Sec. 1991-94); Institute of Canadian Bankers (Fellow).

Taylor, Cora, B.A. 📖 📜
Writer. 906 Kennedy Towers, 10101 Saskatchewan Dr., Edmonton, AB T6E 4R6 (403) 433-6878. Born Fort Qu'Appelle, Sask. 1936. w. 4 ch., 4 stepch. Granger Thomas, Gwendolyn Thomas Mogg, Clancy Livingston, Sean Livingston, Ken Taylor, Mary Taylor Sullivan, Jim Taylor, Terrence Taylor. **EDUC:** Univ. of Alberta, B.A.(English/Classics) 1972. **CAREER:** sec.; teacher; Ed., *Alberta Poetry Yearbook*, 1980-85; freelance writer, 1985 to date; Writer-in-Residence, Calgary Public Library, 1989; Writer-in-Residence, St. Albert Public Library, 1990; Writer-in-Residence, Grant McEwan Community Coll., 1995. **SELECTED PUBLICATIONS:** *Julie* (Western Producer Prairie Books, 1985); *The Doll* (Western Producer Prairie Books, 1987); *Julie's Secret* (Western Producer Prairie Books, 1991); *Ghost Voyages* (Scholastic-Tab, 1992); *Summer of the Mad Monk* (Greystone Books/Douglas and McIntyre, 1994). **AFFIL:** Canadian Authors' Association (Pres.; Exec., Alta. Branch); Edmonton Children's Literature Roundtable (Exec.); Alberta CANSCAIP (Exec.). **HONS:** Outstanding Achievement Award, County of Parkland, 1980; Children's Literature Prize, Canada Council, 1985; Book-of-the-Year for Children (*Julie*), Canadian Library Association, 1986; Arts Achievement Award, City of Edmonton, 1986; Ruth Schwartz Children's Book Award (*The Doll*), 1988; Allan Sangster Award for "Service to the Writers of Canada", 1990; White Raven Book (*Julie's Secret*), Int'l Youth Library, 1992; Book-of-the-Year for Children (*Summer of the Mad Monk*), Canadian Library Association, 1995. **MISC:** jurist for numerous writing prizes; speaker at numerous conferences & conventions. **COMMENT:** *"Cora was born at Fort Qu'Appelle and grew up on a farm near Fort Carlton in Saskatchewan. In 1955 she moved to Alberta and lived for many years on a large acreage or small farm in the Winterburn district where she raised donkeys, goats, and grandchildren."*

Taylor, Gladys ✎ 📖 ☼ ☝
Editor, TALL-TAYLOR PUBLISHING LTD., Box 40, Irricana, AB T0M 1B0 (403) 935-4688, FAX 935-4981. Born Swan River, Man. 1917. d. 4ch. (1 dec.) **EDUC:** Winnipeg Normal Sch., Teacher's Certificate. **CAREER:** sch. teacher, 1936-40; Sgt. W10944, Canadian Women's Army Corps, 1943-45; Ed., Book Page, *Sherbrooke Daily Record*, Sherbrooke, Que., 1955-65; Columnist, *United Church Observer*, 1956-62; Ed., English Section, *Le Canadien*, Thetford Mines, Que., 1958-62; TV Host, Sherbrooke, 1958; Ed., *Canadian Author & Bookman*, 1963-67; Columnist, Ed. Pages, *Toronto Telegram*, 1963-67; Publisher, Owner & Ed., *Travel/Leisure* (later called *Leisurewheels*) magazine & weekly newspapers *Rocky View Five Village Weekly*, *Carstairs Courier* & *Wheel & Deal*, 1975 to date. **SELECTED PUBLICATIONS:** *Pine Roots* (1955); *The King Tree* (1958); *Alone in the Australian Outback* (1984); *Alone in the Boardroom* (1987); *Valinda, Our Daughter*, the story of the first Canadians, mother & baby, who died at the hands of terriorists during a hijacking in Malta in 1985 (1993); poems & articles for many Cdn newspapers & magazines. **AFFIL:** various editorial & journalism boards, advisory boards; mbr., various home & sch. organizations; United Church (Lay Preacher 1957 to date). **HONS:** Ryerson All Canada Fiction Award (*Pine Roots*), 1955; Ryerson All Canada Fiction Award (*The King Tree*), 1958; Best Column by a Woman (*Toronto Telegram*), Canadian Women's Press Club, 1965; Business-

woman of the Year, Calgary, 1983; Golden Quill Award for 50 yrs. of writing accomplishments, 1992; Tom Brinsmead Memorial Award, Best Feature Column, 1993. **MISC:** went on a media peace-keeping junket & interviewed Alta. servicemen & women, 1992; movie *Over the Hill* was based on book, *Alone in the Australian Outback*; 1st woman columnist to appear regularly on the ed. pages of the *Toronto Telegram*; 1st female ed. of *Canadian Author & Bookman*; 1st woman to drive around the Outback of Australia alone, 1977; 1st woman in Canada to run for an elected senate, 1989; various speaking engagements at libraries, entrepreneurial groups, women's & church groups; sponsored the Gladys Taylor Award for Best Front Page for the CCNA Newspaper Awards, 1986, 1987; sponsor (donor) to the Gladys Taylor Literary Award for Beiseker High Sch. students; sponsor (donor) to the Gladys Taylor Literary Award for Carstairs High Sch.; judge at various speaking & literary events/awards. **COMMENT:** *"In 1969, I started my own publishing (magazines/newspapers) business. With an initial investment (all I had) of $2,500, Tall-Taylor Publishing Ltd. now grosses $1.6 million per year and employs 35 to 40 people. We were one of the first companies to initiate flex-time for women employees. If I had to name my most important contribution to the world it would probably be–planting trees and flowers! Over the years I have planted trees in all the places where I have lived: Winnipeg, Thetford Mines, Sherbrooke, Lennoxville, Toronto and Irricana. Long after I am gone, the trees will, I hope, remain. In this age of devastation it is not a bad legacy."*

Taylor, Kathleen, B.A.,LL.B., M.B.A. ■ $ ⚖ 🎭
Senior Vice-President, Corporate Planning and Development, General Counsel, and Secretary, Four Seasons/Regent Hotels and Resorts, FOUR SEASONS HOTELS INC., 1165 Leslie St., Toronto, ON M3C 2K8 (416) 441-4399, FAX 441-4303. Born Toronto 1957. m. Neil Harris. 3 ch. **EDUC:** Univ. of Toronto, B.A.(Pol. Sci./Econ.) 1980; Osgoode Hall Law Sch., LL.B. 1984; York Univ., M.B.A. 1984. **BAR:** Ont., 1985. **CAREER:** Lawyer, Goodman, Phillips & Vineberg, 1985-89; Corp. Cnsl, Four Seasons/Regent Hotels and Resorts, 1989-92; VP & Gen. Cnsl, 1992-93; Sec. to the Company & Bd. of Dir., 1993 to date; Sr. VP & Gen. Cnsl, 1993 to date; Sr. VP, Corp. Planning & Dev., 1995 to date. **AFFIL:** Canadian Bar Association; Law Society of Upper Canada; Corporate Secretaries' Congress. **INTERESTS:** tennis; skiing; sailing. **COMMENT:** *"Kathleen Taylor is responsible for leading all aspects of transaction structuring and negotiations worldwide and for supervising the legal matters, corporate administration and regulatory affairs of the Four Seasons/Regent group of companies."*

Taylor, Marion, B.A. ■■ ✊ ♥ ☝
Owner, LEATHERWOOD VENTURES (consulting - environmental), P.O. Box 582, Holland Centre, ON N0H 1R0 (519) 794-4860, FAX 794-3094. Born Toronto 1934. cl. David Taylor. 1 ch. Catherine. **EDUC:** Univ. of Toronto, B.A.(Hons., English/French) 1956; Ontario Coll. of Education, Teacher's Certificate 1957. **CAREER:** high sch. Teacher, 1958-63; Dir., Environmental Affairs, Federation of Ontario Naturalists, 1987-96. **SELECTED PUBLICATIONS:** contributing column, *Seasons* magazine, Federation of Ontario Naturalists, 1987-96. **AFFIL:** Federation of Ontario Naturalists; Coalition on Niagara Escarpment (Dir. 1988-95); Prov. Forest Policy Committee (mbr. 1995); Owen Sound Field Naturalists; Grey Association for Better Planning (Co-Dir.); Bruce Trail Association. **HONS:** first Hon. Prov. Parks Superintendent, 1996. **COMMENT:** *"Worked actively with the Ministry of Natural Resources to improve forestry practices in Ontario, particularly adjacent to provincial parks. Contributed to drafting the new Crown Forest Sustainability Act 1995. Working with MNR and local groups in the establishment of nearly one million-hectare Wabakimi Provincial Park."*

Taylor, Sharon, B.A.,M.S.W. 🎓 ⊕
Chair, Department of Social Work, LAKEHEAD UNIVERSITY, Oliver Rd., Thunder Bay, ON P7B 5E1 (807) 343-8556, FAX 346-2727. **EDUC:** Lakehead Univ., B.A.(Psych.) 1968; Univ. of Manitoba, M.S.W.(Social Work) 1970. **CAREER:** Social Work Agent, Office of the Official Guardian, 1984-88; Social Worker, Port Arthur General Hospital, 1987; Field Instructor, Lakehead Univ. Dept. of Social Work, 1987; Asst. Prof., & Field & Admissions Coord., 1989-94; Chair & Asst. Prof., 1994 to date. **SELECTED PUBLICATIONS:** "Boards of Directors: Towards an Effective Model in a Northern Context," in *Northern Social Work Practice* (Centre for Northern Studies, Lakehead Univ.); "Academic preparation of students admitted into the HBSW program: A comparison of performance of college transfer, university transfer and post-degree students"; "The CASW Code of Ethics and non-sexual dual relationships: the need for clarification." **AFFIL:** Alzheimer's Society of Thunder Bay (Past Pres.); Ontario Association of Professional Social Workers (Bd.); Canadian Associa-

tion of Social Workers. INTERESTS: community work; home in the country; family; outdoors; skiing; tennis. COMMENT: *"Interest in raising my family and community work kept me busy until I began part-time employment and eventually full-time at Lakehead University. Had not aspired to my present position at the time, but encouragement and support of others led me to this position."*

Taylor-Brown, Jill, B.S.W.,M.S.W., R.S.W. ■ ⊕ ⊛
Senior Clinician, Department of Psycho-Social Oncology, MANITOBA CANCER TREATMENT AND RESEARCH FOUNDATION, 409 Tache Ave., Winnipeg, MB R2H 2A6 (204) 235-3186, FAX 237-6048. Born Winnipeg 1951. m. Allen D. Brown. 2 ch. Michael, Joshua. EDUC: Univ. of Manitoba, B.S.W.(Social Work) 1972, M.S.W.(Social Work) 1988. CAREER: Research & Teaching Asst., Univ. of Manitoba, Fac. of Social Work, 1972-73; Social Worker, Children's Aid of Eastern Manitoba, 1976-77; Professorial Social Worker, St. Vincent's Hospital, Sydney, Australia, 1977-79; Oncology Social Worker, Dept. of Social Work, St. Boniface Hospital, 1980-93; Field Instructor, Fac. of Social Work, Univ. of Manitoba, 1988-90, 1994 to date; Oncology Social Worker, Dept. of Psycho-Social Oncology, Manitoba Cancer Treatment Research Foundation, 1993 to date. SELECTED PUBLICATIONS: "Kids Can Cope: A Group Intervention for Children Whose Parents Have Cancer" with J. Farber & A. Acheson (*Journal of Psycho-Social Oncology* 1 1993). AFFIL: Canadian Association of Psycho-Social Oncology (VP 1990-92; Pres. 1992-94; Past Pres. 1994-96); Canadian Cancer Society (Chair, Nat'l Div. Subcommittee on Support Groups/Emotional Support Programs Task Force; Chair, Man. Div. Medical Advisory Committee; Man. Div. Advisory Committee on Support Groups); Manitoba Association of Social Workers; Manitoba Institute of Registered Social Workers; Manitoba Hospice Foundation; Univ. of Manitoba, Fac. of Social Work (Advisory Committee, Master of Social Work Practicum 1992-94). HONS: Dean's Honour List, Univ. of Manitoba, 1971, 1972; Helen Hudson Memorial Award for outstanding contributions to cancer care, 1996. INTERESTS: psychological & social impact of cancer on the individual, family & society; support groups; adult & child grief & bereavement; children of adults with cancer; survivorship; cancer & sexuality. MISC: numerous presentations on psycho-social oncology at local & nat'l conferences & in a variety of other forums. COMMENT: *"I am committed to enhancing the psychological and social well-being of individuals living and dying with cancer and their loved ones. During my term as President of C.A.P.O., I endeavoured to further the goals of the organization by ensuring regional and inter-disciplinary representation and by strengthening alliances with critical stakeholders."*

Teichrob, Hon. Carol ■ ✦
Member of the Legislative Assembly (Saskatoon Meewasin), Minister of Municipal Government and Minister Responsible for SaskTel, GOVERNMENT OF SASKATCHEWAN, Legislative Bldgs, Rm. 105, Regina, SK S4S 0B3 (306) 787-0949. Born Sask. 1939. m. Donald. 3 ch. EDUC: Univ. of Saskatchewan, Professional Court Reporter. CAREER: Exec. Mbr., Canadian Federation of Agriculture, 1976-81; Exec. Mbr., Saskatchewan Federation of Agriculture, 1976-81; Dir., V.I.D.O., 1980-86; Dir., Farm Credit Corporation, 1980-83; Chair, Canadian Turkey Marketing Agency, 1980-81; Chair, Plains Poultry Ltd., 1981-88; Reeve, Rural Municipality of Corman Park, Sask., 1981-91; Dir., Saskatchewan Research Council, 1983-91; Dir., Cdn Egg Mktg Agency, 1986-91; Founding Ptnr, Primrose Books Inc., 1988 to date; elected MLA (Saskatoon River Heights), 1991; Min. of Educ., 1991-92; re-elected (Saskatoon Meewasin), 1995; Min. Responsible for SaskTel, 1995 to date; Ptnr, Amberlea Farm Ltd.; Ptnr, Moonvale Farms. AFFIL: Saskatoon Chamber of Commerce. HONS: Woman of the Year Award, Bus., YWCA Saskatoon, 1981; Golden Wheel Award for Excellence in Bus. & Industry, Saskatoon Rotary Club, 1990. COMMENT: *"Nellie L. McClung said it best: 'I do not want to pull through life like a thread that has no knot. I want to leave something behind when I go; some small legacy of truth, some word that will shine in a dark place.'"*

Telfer, Nancy, B.A.,B.Mus. ■ ⊗ ⊰ ₩
President, NANCY TELFER MUSIC INC., 1171 Scugog Line 14, R.R. #5, Sunderland, ON L0C 1H0 (905) 985-1670, FAX 985-1670. EDUC: Univ. of Western Ontario, B.A.(Music/Math) 1971, B.Mus.(Theory/Composition) 1979. CAREER: teacher, 1972-76; composer of classical music, 1980 to date. SELECTED PUBLICATIONS: numerous works of music; *Successful Sight-Singing* Book 1 (San Diego: Neil A. Kjos Music Co., 1992), Book 2 (San Diego: Neil A. Kjos Music Co., 1994); *Successful Warmups* Book 1 (San Diego: Neil A. Kjos Music Co., 1995), Book 2 (San Diego: Neil A. Kjos Music Co., 1996). AFFIL: O.C.F.; A.C.C.C.; A.C.D.A.; O.M.E.A.; C.M.E.A.; M.E.N.C.; K.S.C.; S.O.C.A.N. MISC: numerous commissions by different organizations; performances in Canada & the US; guest speaker for numer-

ous organizations. COMMENT: *"I compose music for orchestra, band, choirs, soloists, and chamber choirs."*

Tengum, Phyllis Zybl Ruth (née Wilson) ⊕
General Manager, INVENTORS ASSOCIATION OF CANADA, Box 281, Swift Current, SK S9H 3V6 (306) 773-7762. Born Swift Current 1922. m. Albert Tengum. 1 stpch. EDUC: Swift Current Coll., secretarial 1943. CAREER: Sec. then Gen. Mgr, Inventors' Association of Canada, 1955 to date. AFFIL: American Pyramid Research Society; SPCA; Swift Current Agricultural & Exhibition Association; Wildlife Federation of Saskatchewan; St. Georges Society; International Order of Volunteers for Peace; Sakharov International Committee, Inc., Washington, DC. HONS: various awards for costumes, incl. First Prize, Shaunavon Old Tyme Country Fair, 1989; various horticultural awards, incl. Grand Champion Award, Swift Current Agricultural Show, 1984. INTERESTS: gardening. MISC: listed in various biographical sources: *Who's Who of American Women, Who's Who in the Commonwealth,* & *International Who's Who in Community Service.*

Tennant, Veronica, O.C.,LL.D.,D.Litt. ■ ⊕ 🎭
Executive Producer/Writer, TV Arts and Entertainment, CANADIAN BROADCASTING CORPORATION, Box 500, Stn. A, Toronto, ON M5W 1E6. Born London, UK. m. Dr. John Wright. 1 ch. CAREER: Prima Ballerina, The National Ballet of Canada, 25 yrs., during which time she danced every major role, as well as having several ballets choreographed for her; retired in 1989; writer, prod., dir., actor, host & choreographer; Prod., Special Projects, CBC; Adjunct Prof., York Univ, 1989 to date; numerous teaching assignments including master classes in ballet at various universities & schools. SELECTED CREDITS: performed ballets extensively on TV incl. Juliet, *Romeo and Juliet,* dir. Norman Campbell, CBC, 1965; title roles in *Cinderella* & the *Sleeping Beauty* (with Rudolf Nureyev), CBC; *La Sylphide* (with Mikhail Baryshnikov), CBC; Isabelle Marie, *Mad Shadows,* CBC; danced Juliet in *Gala* (documentary), NFB, 1982; Host, Creative Consultant, Continuity & Writer, *Sunday Arts Entertainment* (series), CBC, 1989-92; Prod., *Salute to Dancers for Life,* CBC, 1994 & *Danser Pour La Vie,* Radio-Canada, 1995; Prod./Writer, *MARGIE GILLIS* (performance biography with guest artists Jessye Norman & Brent Carver), CBC TV, 1996; Suzanne, *Satie and Suzanne* (with the late Nicholas Pennell), Rhombus Media, shown on the CBC & A&E, 1995; Assoc. Dir. & Choreographer, *Rough*

Crossing, Canadian Stage; Asst. Dir. & Choreographer, *The Cherry Orchard,* Tarragon Theatre; stager of additional choreography, *Cyrano de Bergerac,* The Stratford Festival; lead role, *On The Town,* Shaw Festival, 1992 Season; actor, dancer, writer, *Maud,* Shaw Festival & Festival of the Sound, 1992-93; performer, writer, *Choice & Chance Encounters* with James Campbell & Gene DiNovi, Markham Theatre, Elora Festival & Festival of the Sound, 1993-95; actor, dancer, *An Elizabethan Entertainment,* with the Toronto Consort, 1995; worked with Toronto's Opera Atelier; narrator with the Toronto Symphony; narrator & creator of a number of artistic collaborations, The Festival of the Sound; debuted her own musical narrative of *The Nutcracker* with the Vancouver Symphony; created new mixed discipline work, *The Little Match Girl,* Christmas 1995, 1996. SELECTED PUBLICATIONS: first published with McClelland and Stewart in 1977; wrote & then recorded on cassette, children's books, *On Stage, Please* & *The Nutcracker;* numerous articles & reviews for *The Toronto Star;* series of articles about The National Ballet of Canada, O'Keefe Centre *Performance* Magazine, 1993-94; articles *for The Globe and Mail, Dance Magazine, Dance International.* AFFIL: UNICEF (Hon. Chair). HONS: nominated, Best Actress (*Mad Shadows*), ACTRA Award; nominated, Best Performance (Suzanne in *Satie & Suzanne*), Gemini Awards; The Toronto Arts Award; Arts & Letters Award, The Canadian Club of New York City; Officer of the Order of Canada, 1975; Hon. Doctorates from Brock Univ., York Univ., Simon Fraser Univ. & the Univ. of Toronto. MISC: the TV prods. of both *Cinderella* & *Sleeping Beauty* won Emmy awards; bilingual Master of Ceremonies for the 1995 *Canada Day Noon Show,* live from Parliament Hill, CBC; numerous speaking engagements.

Terrana, Anna Marina, M.P. ✦
Member of Parliament (Vancouver East), GOVERNMENT OF CANADA, Confederation Building, House of Commons, Rm 385, Ottawa, ON K1A 0A6 (613) 992-6030, FAX 995-7412. Born Torino, Italy. sep. 1 ch. David Terrana. EDUC: Circolo Filologico, Torino, Italy, dipl. in English, French & Italian Lit.; Univ. of Cambridge, Lower Cert. of Cambridge in English Lit.; Univ. of Manchester, Royal Cert. of Arts (Medium & Advanced English), General Cert. of Educ. CAREER: National Parole Board, 1980-86; Administrator, B.C. Police Commission, 1974-84; Exec. Dir., Italian Cultural Centre Society, 1982-86, 1993; M.P. (Vancouver East), Gov't of Canada, 1993 to date; Chair, BC Liberal Caucus, 1993-96; Treas., Nat'l

Women's Caucus, 1993-96; Standing Committee on Citizenship & Immigration, 1993-95; Standing Committee on Transport, 1993-95; mbr., House of Commons Standing Committee on Hum. Res. Dev. & Task Force on Disability Issues; Rep. of the Minister of Indian Affairs & Northern Dev. on the Treaty Negotiation Advisory Committee; Task Force on the Commercialization of the Canadian National Railway System; Standing Committee on Policy Dev., Liberal Party of Canada; mbr., Exec. Committee, Canada-Japan Interparliamentary Group & Asia-Pacific Parliamentary Forum. VOLUNTEER CAREER: mbr., Canadian Consultative Council on Mulitculturalism, 1981-83; mbr., Ethno-Business Council, 1989-92; Pres., Vancouver Multicultural Society, 1990-92; Pres., National Congress of Italian Canadians, 1989-92; Exec. Dir., Italian Cultural Centre Society; Dir., United Way of the Lower Mainland; organizer of many events. AFFIL: Liberal Party of Canada; Big Sisters of B.C. Lower Mainland (Hon. Mbr.); Consultative Council of Immigrant & Visible Minority Women of B.C. (Hon. Mbr.). HONS: Knight of the Italian Republic, Order of Italy; Italian Community Gold Medal, 1981; Italian-Canadian of the Year, 1988; Piemonte Region Int'l Award, 1990; Canada 125 Medal; Distinguished Service Award, Vancouver Multicultural Community, 1993; recognition as 1st Piemontese emigrant elected in a foreign gov't, Piemonte Reg., 1994. INTERESTS: theatre; opera; classical music.

Tesher, Ellie, B.A. /
Columnist and Journalist, THE TORONTO STAR, 1 Yonge St., Toronto, ON M5E 1E6 (416) 869-4860, FAX 865-3995. Born Toronto 1941. d. 2 ch. Stephen, Lisi. EDUC: Univ. of Toronto, B.A.(Soc.) 1962. CAREER: social worker, Metro Children's Aid Society, 1963; freelance journalist, 1974-77; reporter & features writer, The Toronto Star, 1977 to date; Ed., Life Section, Food, Fashion & Home, 1985-90; Ed., The Sunday Star, 1990-94; Columnist on social justice issues, news & trends, News Section, 1994 to date. INTERESTS: exotic travel; observing trends, film & fashion; expanding my cultural horizons. COMMENT: "Journalism has been my passionate endeavour: exposing social injustices, putting a human face on issues in the news, assuring the public's right to know."

Theaker, Deborah, B.A. ■ 🐝 ⊗ 🛏
Writer and Performer. c/o Amsel, Eisenstadt & Frazier, Inc., 6310 San Vincenie Blvd., Ste. 401, Los Angeles, CA 90048 (213) 939-1188, FAX 939-0630. Born Moose Jaw, Sask. 1962. s.

EDUC: Univ. of Saskatchewan, B.A.(English/Theatre) 1983. SELECTED CREDITS: writer & performer, Second City, London, Toronto, Chicago, L.A., 1984-90; lead actress & writer, Maniac Mansion (series), Lucasfilm/Atlantis Television, 1990-93; Second City, Ireland, 1995; Gwen Fabin-Blunt, Waiting for Guffman (feature), 1996. AFFIL: Canadian Actors' Equity Association; Screen Actors' Guild; A.C.T.R.A.; S.O.C.A.N. HONS: Dora Mavor Moore Award for Writing & Performing in Second City's Not Based on Anything by Stephen King, 1987; nomination, Cable Ace Award, as Best Actress for the series Maniac Mansion. COMMENT: "Deborah Theaker is an alumna of the Second City, best known for portraying Casey Edison in the critically acclaimed Lucasfilm/Atlantis television satire Maniac Mansion."

Theriault, M. Estelle, B.A.,LL.B.,Q.C. ⚖ ✦
Public Trustee, PROVINCE OF NOVA SCOTIA, P.O. Box 685, Halifax, NS B3H 2T3 (902) 424-7760, FAX 424-0616. Born Halifax. m. Gary O. Holt, Q.C. EDUC: St. Mary's Univ., B.A.(French) 1972; Dalhousie Univ., LL.B. 1975. BAR: N.S., 1975. CAREER: private practice of law, 1975-77; Cnsl, N.S. Association of Health Organizations, 1977-79; Solicitor, Office of Public Trustee for the Prov. of N.S., 1980-91; Public Trustee for the Prov. of N.S., 1991 to date. AFFIL: N.S. Barristers' Society (Council Mbr.; Dir. at large; numerous committees); Canadian Bar Association; Continuing Legal Education Society of N.S.; Advisory Committee to the Law Reform Commission of N.S. studying Status of the Child & Guardianship Law; Prov. Committee on Elder Abuse in N.S.; Canadian Cancer Society; Kidney Foundation. HONS: Queen's Counsel, 1993. MISC: presented papers on Estate Law to Canadian Bar Association N.S. Branch Conference & to Continuing Legal Education Society of N.S.

Thibaudeau, Colleen, B.A.,M.A. 📖 📚
Poet. London, ON. Born Toronto 1925. m. James Reaney. 2 ch. James Stewart Reaney, Susan Reaney. EDUC: Univ. of Toronto, B.A. (English) 1948, M.A.(English) 1949; L'Univ. Catholique de l'ouest, France, Diplôme (French) 1951. SELECTED PUBLICATIONS: My Granddaughters Are Combing Out their Long Hair (Coach House Press, 1977); The Martha Landscapes (Brick, 1984); The Artemesia Book, Poems Selected and New (Brick, 1991); The Patricia Album and Other Poems (Moonstone, 1993); various poems in anthologies. AFFIL: League of Canadian Poets (on leave); NDP; United Church. HONS: McCulley

Cup, 1939. INTERESTS: politics; farming. MISC: various public readings; readings & school tours arranged through Canada Council; various joint tours with James Reaney, incl. Univ. of Southwest Missouri/Univ. of Kansas at Laurence/Univ. of Nebraska at Lincoln, arranged through External Affairs Canada. COMMENT: *"I am a writer, mainly poetry. I endeavour to keep breathing–hard these days."*

Thibodeau-DeGuire, Michèle, Eng. ○
President and Executive Director, CENTRAIDE OF GREATER MONTREAL, 493 Sherbrooke St. W., Montreal, QC H3A 1B6 (514) 288-1261, FAX 282-0795. Born Montreal 1941. m. Pierre-André. 2 ch. EDUC: École Polytechnique, Civil Eng. 1963. CAREER: Structural Eng., Groupe LGL, 1963-75; Consultant Eng., F. Boulva and Associates, 1975-82; Gen. Delegate to New England, Gov't of Que., 1982-84; Dir. of Public Rel'ns, École Polytechnique, 1985-91; Pres. & Exec. Dir., Centraide of Greater Montreal, 1991 to date. AFFIL: Canadian Academy of Engineering (Fellow); Ordre des Ingénieurs du Québec; Association des diplômés de Polytechnique (Pres. 1977; Gov.); Natural Sciences & Engineering Research Council of Canada (Bd. Mbr.); Canadian Centre for Philanthropy (Bd. Mbr.). HONS: Prix Mérite, Association des diplômés de Polytechnique; Grand Prix d'Excellence, Ordre des Ingénieurs du Québec, 1995; The Canadian Engineers Meritorious Svcs Award for Community Svcs, Canadian Council of Professional Engineers; Doctorate in Human Sciences (Hon.), Rivier Coll.; Ordre du Mérite 1995, Association des diplômés de l'Université de Montréal, 1996.

Thomas, Audrey G., B.A.,M.A. 📖 ⊗ 🦅
Writer. c/o The Writers Union of Canada, 24 Ryerson Ave., Toronto, ON M5T 2P3 (416) 703-8982. Born Binghamton, N.Y. 1935. d. 3 ch. Sarah, Victoria, Claire. EDUC: Univ. of St. Andrews, Scotland, English Lit., British Hist. & Moral Phil. 1956-57; Smith Coll., B.A. 1957; Univ. of British Columbia, M.A. 1963. CAREER: writer, 1967 to date; Special Lecturer, Creative Writing, Univ. of British Columbia, 1975-76; Visiting Asst. Prof., Creative Writing, Concordia Univ., Winter term, 1978; Visiting Prof., Dept. of Creative Writing, Univ. of Victoria, 1978-79; Lecturer & Tutor, Sr.-Level Cdn Lit., Open Learning Institute, 1 term, 1980; Semester Lecturer, Prose Workshop, Simon Fraser Univ., Fall term, 1981; Sessional Lecturer, part-time, Creative Writing Dept., Univ. of British Columbia, 1981-82; Writer-in-Residence, Simon Fraser Univ., Winter term, 1982; Writer-in-Residence, David Thompson Univ. Centre, Winter term, 1984; Visiting Prof., Winter term, 1984; Canada-Scotland Literary Fellow, Edinburgh, 1985-86; Writer-in-Residence, Univ. of Ottawa, Winter term, 1987; Sessional Lecturer, part-time, Sr. Creative Writing, Univ. of Victoria, Fall term, 1988; Critical Fictions workshop, Banff, Summer 1989; Asst. Prof., Creative Writing Dept., Concordia Univ., 1989-90; Visiting Prof., Univ. of Victoria, Winter term, 1992; Writer-in-Residence, Univ. of Toronto, Winter term, 1993; Visiting Prof., Creative Writing, Dartmouth Coll., Winter term, 1994; Visiting Prof., Dartmouth Coll., Winter & Spring, 1996. SELECTED CREDITS: writer of numerous commissioned radio plays incl.: *Once Your Submarine Cable is Gone*, CBC Stage, 1973; *The Matheson Fire*, CBC Disaster Series, 1984-85; "The Woman in Black Velvet," *Vanishing Point*, CBC, 1985; *Change of Heart*, CBC, 1987; "Sanctuary," *Sextet*, CBC, 1989; *The Witch in the Downstairs Back Bedroom* (for children), CBC, 1992. SELECTED PUBLICATIONS: *Ten Green Bottles*, stories (New York: Bobbs-Merrill, 1967; Ottawa: Oberon Press, 1977); *Mrs. Blood* (New York: Bobbs-Merrill, 1970; Vancouver: Talon Books, 1975); *Muchmeyer & Prospero and the Island*, 2 short novels (New York: Bobbs-Merrill, 1972); *Songs My Mother Taught Me* (New York: Bobbs-Merrill, 1972; Vancouver: Talon Books, 1973); *Blown Figures* (New York: Alfred A. Knopf, 1975; Vancouver: Talon Books, 1976); *Ladies and Escorts*, stories (Ottawa: Oberon Press, 1977); *Latakia* (Vancouver: Talon Books, 1979); *Two in the Bush and Other Stories: Selected Stories from Ladies and Escorts & Ten Green Bottles* (Toronto: New Canada Library, 1982); *Real Mothers*, stories (Vancouver: Talon Books, 1984); *Good-Bye Harold, Good Luck*, stories (Markham: Viking/Penguin Books Canada, 1986); *Intertidal Life* (Toronto: General Publications, 1984); *The Wild Blue Yonder*, stories (Penguin Canada, 1990); *Graven Images* (Penguin Canada, 1993); *Coming Down from Wa* (Penguin Canada, 1995); many stories in Cdn & Commonwealth anthologies as well as various magazines incl. *The Atlantic, Saturday Night, Toronto Life, The Capilano Review, The Fiddlehead, Interface, Malahat Review* etc. AFFIL: Writers' Union of Canada; PEN; Amnesty International. HONS: Ethel Wilson Award (B.C. Book prize), 1991; finalist, Best Radio Drama (*Sanctuary*), 1989; Canada-Australia Prize, 1990; Marian Engel Award, 1987; Ethel Wilson Award, 1985; Second Prize, *Chatelaine* Fiction Competition, 1981; Second Prize, Memoirs Category, CBC Literary Competition, 1981; Second prize, Fiction Category, CBC Literary Competition, 1980; Second Prize,

Fiction Category, National Magazine Awards, 1980; Ethel Wilson Award (B.C. Book prize), 1996; Ph.D.(Hon.), Univ. of British Columbia, 1994; Ph.D.(Hon.), Simon Fraser Univ., 1994. **MISC:** recipient, numerous Canada Council grants; reader of manuscripts for Canada Council Publication Grants. **COMMENT:** *"My endeavour is to write as honestly and as elegantly as possible about whatever deeply interests me. Mostly, but not exclusively, this seems to be the relationships between men and women."*

Thomas, Carolyn $ / ✤
Senior Community Relations Officer, BRITISH COLUMBIA LOTTERY CORPORATION, 770 Hillside Ave., Victoria, BC V8T 1Z6 (604) 361-4011, FAX 361-4053. Born St. Catharines, Ont. 1950. d. 2 ch. Ben, Larissa. **EDUC:** Univ. of Victoria, Sch. of Bus. & Mgmt. **CAREER:** owner, Words Unlimited (comm. firm), 1980-89; journalist, author & broadcaster, CHEK-TV, Victoria, 1986; Sr. Community Rel'ns Officer, B.C. Lottery Corporation, 1989 to date. **SELECTED PUBLICATIONS:** *Island Treasures: An Insider's Guide to Victoria, Vancouver Island and the Gulf Islands* (Harbour Publishing, 1986); *Island Treasures 2* (Harbour Publishing, 1990); numerous magazine articles in Canada & the US incl., *Monday Magazine, Northwest Magazine, Key to Victoria* & more, 1973 to date. **AFFIL:** Canadian Public Relations Society; American Marketing Association; Toastmasters International, Victoria Chapter 6265 (Pres. 1990-91); Victoria Horticultural Society. **HONS:** Toastmaster of the Year, 1991, 1994-95. **INTERESTS:** gardening; mandala painting; distance running; biking. **COMMENT:** *"My background includes public relations, broadcasting and journalism, including two best-selling West Coast guidebooks. I was the Lead Trainer for the XV Commonwealth Games Speakers' Bureau for Victoria, Vancouver, Calgary and Edmonton volunteers. I teach public speaking, am a frequent guest speaker and run corporate speakers' bureaus in three BC cities. I was chosen to represent 15,000 Commonwealth Games volunteers to escort HRH Prince Edward during his Victoria visit."*

Thomas, Carolyn Gertrude, B.A., C.C.A. $ ☻ ○
President and Senior Consultant, C.G.R.T'S CONSULTING, East Preston, Halifax County, 2032 No. 7 Hwy, PO Box 2924, D.E.P.S., Dartmouth, NS B2W 4Y2 (902) 462-2011, FAX 462-2011. Born East Preston, N.S. 1943. m. Matthew. 4 ch. **EDUC:** Univ. of Ottawa, Summer Coll. in Human Rights 1986; Boston Univ. Sch. of Social Work, Certified Compli-

ance Admin.; St. Mary's Univ., B.A.(Soc.) 1994. **CAREER:** elementary sch. teacher; various positions incl. Coord. of Race Rel'ns & Affirmative Action, N.S. Human Rights Commission, 23 yrs.; consultant & certified compliance administrator; Pres. & Sr. Consultant, CGRT'S Consulting, 1994 to date; Pres., Black Heritage Tours, 1996 to date. **SELECTED CREDITS:** Host & Co-Prod., *UMOJA*, TV show, Black Cultural Centre of N.S. **SELECTED PUBLICATIONS:** "Black Women's Role in the Church," in *Black Canadians*, ed. Dr. B. Pachai (Halifax: Dalhousie Univ.); "The Ideology of Black Women & the Women's Movement" (1991); "The Survival of Black Spirituality" (1992); "Farming in Preston" (1994-95); "Dr. Carrie M. Best–A Nova Scotian Black Matriarch" (1995); weekly columnist, *The Patriot*; various editorials, *Atlantic Baptist*; various other publications. **AFFIL:** Min. of Education, N.S. (Bd., Council on African Cdn Educ.); R.C.M.P. (Bd., Commissioner's Nat'l Advisory Committee on Visible Minorities); Canadian Centre on Police-Race Relations, Ottawa (Gov.); N.S. Home for Coloured Children (Bd.); Mary Preston Historical Society (VP & PR); Black Professional Women's Group (PR); Atlantic Standards Council, Canadian Broadcasters' Association; Preston Board of Trade (Charter mbr.); Acadia Divinity Sch. (Bd.); Kaye Livingstone Visible Minority Women's Society of N.S.; Lions International (Life Mbr.); East Preston United Baptist Church's Ladies' Auxiliary; African United Baptist Association of N.S. (former Moderator & V-Moderator). **HONS:** Gov. General's Commemorative Medal, 1994; Gov. General's Award in commemoration of the Person's case; many certificates & awards, Lions/Lioness International; recipient of Testimonial Resolution, Detroit City Council, US, 1996. **INTERESTS:** history; research in areas of women, genealogy, race rel'ns, women's issues (local & global); singing; travel; meeting people. **MISC:** mbr., Cdn Delegation to South Africa, 1991; various conference presentations; frequent public speaker. **COMMENT:** *"I consider myself to be an ambitious, sensitive visionary who loves to do for others as much as I can. I believe in leading by example. Presently pursuing a Master's in Atlantic Canadian Studies at St. Mary's University, Halifax. Motto: If I can help somebody as I pass along, then my living shall not be in vain."*

Thomas, Clara McCandless, B.A.,M.A., Ph.D.,D.Litt.,F.R.S.C. 📖 ✑
Professor Emeritus and Canadian Studies Research Fellow, YORK UNIVERSITY, Special Collections, 305 Scott Library, 4700 Keele St., North York, ON M3J 1P3 (416) 736-2100,

ext. 22374. Born 1919. m. Morley Thomas. 2 ch. Stephen Morley, John David. EDUC: Univ. of Western Ontario, B.A. 1941, M.A. 1944; Univ. of Toronto, Ph.D. 1962. CAREER: Lecturer, Univ. of Western Ontario, 1947-61; Lecturer, Univ. of Toronto, 1958-61; various ranks, York Univ., 1961-69; Prof., 1969-84; Prof. Emeritus, 1984 to date; York Univ. Libraries Cdn Studies Research Fellow, 1984 to date. SELECTED PUBLICATIONS: *Canadian Novelists: 1920-1945* (Toronto: Longmans, Green, 1946); *Love and Work Enough: The Life of Anna Jameson* (Toronto: Univ. of Toronto Press, 1967); *Margaret Laurence* (Toronto: McClelland & Stewart, 1969); *Ryerson of Upper Canada* (Toronto: Ryerson, 1969); *Our Nature–Our Voices: A Guidebook to English-Canadian Literature* (1972, translated into Japanese 1981); *The Manawaka World of Margaret Laurence* (Toronto: McClelland & Stewart, 1975); *William Arthur Deacon: A Canadian Literary Life*, with John Lennox (Toronto: Univ. of Toronto Press, 1982); *All My Sisters* (Ottawa: Tecumseh/Borealis, 1994); "Anna Jameson and Nineteenth-Century Taste" (*The Humanities Association Bulletin* 17(1) 1966); "Towards Freedom: the Work of Northrop Frye" (*The CEA Critic* 42(1) 1979); "The Multiple Lives of L.M. Montgomery" (*The Literary Review of Canada* 2(3) 1993); various other publications. EDIT: Ed. Bd., *Journal of Canadian Fiction*, 1970 to date; Ed. Bd., *Journal of Canadian Studies*, 1972-83; Gen. Ed., *Heritage Series*, McClelland & Stewart, 1975-78; Ed. Bd., Univ. of Ottawa, Cdn Short Story Library, 1975-85; Ed. Bd., Writers' Union of Canada Cdn Lit. Proj., 1975-76; Ed. Bd., *Literary History of Canada*, 2nd revised ed., 1977 to date; Advisory Bd., Centre for Editing Early Canadian Texts, Carleton Univ., 1979 to date; Ed., special issue, "Margaret Laurence," *Canadian Woman Studies/les cahiers de la femme*, 8(3) Fall 1987. AFFIL: Royal Society of Canada (Fellow); Association of Canadian University Teachers of English (Exec. 1972-74; Pres. 1971-72); Canadian Association of Commonwealth Literature & Language Studies (Exec. Mbr.). HONS: Northern Telecom Cdn Studies Award, Univ. Laval, 1989; Alumni Award of Merit, Univ. of Western Ontario, 1995; D.Litt.(Hon.), York Univ., 1986; D.Litt.(Hon.), Trent Univ., 1991; LL.D. (Hon.), Brock Univ., 1992. MISC: recipient, various grants; various lectures; various conference presentations.

Thomas, Diana, B.A.,M.A. ■ ☺ 🝛 ⊗
Past President, SOCIETY FOR THE STUDY OF ARCHITECTURE IN CANADA, Box 2302, Stn. D, Ottawa, ON K1P 5W5 (602) 261-8699, FAX

534-4445. Born Phoenix, Ariz. 1956. m. Andre D. Best. 1 ch. August-Cree M. Thomas Best. EDUC: York Univ., B.A.(Art Hist.) 1979; Arizona State Univ., M.A.(Architectural Hist.) 1983. CAREER: Consultant & Architectural Historian, 1983-85; Architectural Historian, Alberta Community Dev., Prov. of Alta., 1985-92; Architectural Historian, State Historic Preservation Office, State of Arizona, 1992-94; Preservation Planner, Historic Preservation Office, City of Phoenix, 1994 to date. SELECTED PUBLICATIONS: "Traditions in a New World: Ukrainian-Canadian Churches in Alberta" (*Society for the Study of Architecture in Canada Bulletin* Mar. 1988); "Ukrainian Churches in Alberta: A Look at Tradition in Transition" (*Proceedings of Ukrainian Festival 1988* July 1988); "Documenting Ukrainian-Canadian Churches in Alberta" (*Material History Bulletin* Spring 1989); "The Alberta Inventory of Historic Sites: Recording Ukrainian Church Architecture" (*Pamiatky Ukrainy* Fall 1992). EDIT: Chair, Ed. Committee for Society journal, *Bulletin*, 1988-91. AFFIL: Society for the Study of Architecture in Canada (Alta. Prov. Rep. on Bd. of Dir. 1986-88; VP 1988-91; Pres. 1992-96; Past Pres. 1996-99); American Society of Architectural Historians; National Trust for Historic Preservation; Society for the Protection of Architectural Resources in Edmonton (Dir./Newsletter Ed. 1986-88); Edmonton Society for Urban & Architecture Studies (Dir. 1986-92); Inter-Prov. Heritage Advisory Committee for the Dev. of a Nat'l Register in Canada (Tech. Sub-Committee 1990-92). INTERESTS: contemporary Native N.Am. art; herbal gardening. COMMENT: "*I have committed the past twenty years of my educational and professional career to the preservation of the cultural environment in North America and fostered an awareness of the importance of architecture to convey a sense of community in local, national and international forums.*"

Thomas, Marjorie J. ◑ 🝛
Executive Director, SASKATCHEWAN GENEALOGICAL SOCIETY, P.O. Box 1894, Regina, SK S4P 3E (306) 780-9207, FAX 781-6021. Born Saskatoon 1942. m. Douglas Thomas. 1 ch. CAREER: Coord., Saskatchewan Genealogical Society, 1985-88; Exec. Dir., 1988 to date. AFFIL: Canadian Federation of Genealogical & Family History Societies (Dir. & Sec.-Treas.); Regina Cemetery Walking Tours (Dir. 1992-95); Saskatchewan Documentary Heritage Inventory Proj. (Steering Committee); Saskatchewan Council of Cultural Organizations; Saskatchewan Heritage Committee; Regina Volunteer Association; City of Regina

(Advisory Committee 1989-90). **INTERESTS:** travel; swimming; cycling; music; bridge. **COMMENT:** "*Goal is to achieve recognition of the role of genealogy in preserving our heritage. As a result, the Society has gained recognition as a leader in the genealogical community, including developing the largest genealogical lending library in Canada.*"

Thompson, Bonita J., B.A.,LL.B.,LL.M., Q.C. ■ ⚖ $

Partner, SINGLETON URQUHART SCOTT, 1125 Howe St., Ste. 1200, Vancouver, BC V6Z 2K8, FAX (604) 682-1283. 2 ch. Nicole T. Faust, Brandon F. Thompson. **EDUC:** Univ. of Saskatchewan, B.A. 1971, LL.B. 1972; Yale Univ., LL.M. 1977. **BAR:** Sask., 1973; B.C., 1978. **CAREER:** Lawyer, McKercher, McKercher, Stack, Laing and Korchin, 1973-74; Asst. Prof. of Law, Univ. of Saskatchewan, 1974-78; Sr. Legislative Cnsl, then Sr. Solicitor, B.C. Dept. of the Attorney-Gen., 1979-86; Exec. Dir., B.C. Int'l Commercial Arbitration Centre, 1986-88; Ptnr, Singleton Urquhart Scott, 1988 to date. **AFFIL:** B.C. Government Managers' Association (former Pres.); B.C. Government Lawyers' Association (former Pres.); Canadian Bar Association (Chrm, Task Force on Alternate Dispute Resolution; Chrm, Legislation & Law Reform Committee; Chair, Alternate Dispute Resolution Section); Law Society of B.C.; Arbitration and Mediation Institute of Canada (Chartered Arbitrator); International Bar Association; IFC Vancouver (Bd. of Dir. 1994-96); Canadian Investors Protection Fund (Public Gov. 1994-96). **HONS:** Queen's Counsel, Prov. of B.C., 1985; President's Award, B.C. Branch of the Canadian Bar Association, 1991. **COMMENT:** "*Ms. Thompson has concentrated on the preparation of standard-form and manuscript construction and consultants' contracts and has a substantial consulting practice, designing and evaluating conflict-management systems for the private and public sectors. She is a widely sought after speaker in the field of ADR and conflict management.*"

Thompson, Cécile, B.A.,M.Ed. 🎓 ✋

Coordinator, French Language Services, ONTARIO ASSOCIATION OF CHILDREN'S AID SOCIETIES, 75 Front St. E., 2nd Fl., Toronto, ON M5E 1V9 (416) 366-8115, FAX 366-8317. Born Montreal 1936. d. 3 ch. Dennis, Helena, Alan. **EDUC:** Univ. of Toronto, B.A.(French/Hist.) 1971, M.Ed.(Educ. Linguistics/Second Language Teaching) 1980. **CAREER:** Flying Officer, Royal Cdn Air Force, 1956-59; Captain, Cdn Army (Militia), 1959-64; VP & Teacher, Durham Bd. of Educ., 1965-91; Dir., Federation of Women Teachers' Associations of Ontario, 1982-86; Coord., French Language Svcs, Ontario Association of Children's Aid Societies, 1993 to date. **SELECTED PUBLICATIONS:** articles in *Canadian Modern Language Review & Journal of the Ontario Association of Children's Aid Societies*. **AFFIL:** Centres d'Accueil Héritage, Toronto (Dir. 1993-96); Amnesty International francophone group, Toronto (Pres. 1988-94); Alpha Delta Kappa (Pres., Tau Chapter, Oshawa 1988-90); St. James' Cathedral (Pres., Anglican Church Women); Federation of Women Teachers' Associations of Ontario (Hon. Mbr.); Missions to Seamen (volunteer). **HONS:** Federation of Women Teachers' Associations of Ontario, Hon. Membership awarded in 1992 afer retirement from teaching. **INTERESTS:** human rights; volunteering; travelling; knitting. **MISC:** went to Africa as part of Proj. Overseas, Canadian Teachers' Federation, Summer 1987.

Thompson, E. Jane, B.A.(Hons.) 📺 🎞 🎭

Film and Television Director. 170 Lippincott St., Toronto, ON M5S 2P1 (416) 964-7949. Born Montreal 1952. m. C.A. Brennan. **EDUC:** Queen's Univ., B.A.(Film Studies/Psych.) 1990. **CAREER:** film & TV dir., 1980 to date. **SELECTED CREDITS:** Dir., TV series: *My Life As a Dog*; *Traders*; *Liberty Street*; *North of 60*; *Madison*; *Ready or Not*; *The Odyssey*; Writer/Dir., *At the Lake* (drama), CBC TV; Prod./Dir., *Letter from Francis* (drama), Atlantis Films; Dir., *Coming of Age* (MOW), Breakthrough Films (1993). **AFFIL:** Toronto Women in Film & Television (Founding Mbr.); Academy of Canadian Cinema & Television. **HONS:** Silver Plaque (*At the Lake*), Chicago Int'l Film Festival, 1990; Best Short Dramatic Program, Gemini Awards (*Letter from Francis*), 1994. **MISC:** Dir.-in-training, DramaLab '85, National Screen Institute of Canada; Prod. Resident, Canadian Film Centre, 1994.

Thompson, Joey ✎ 📖

City Editor, THE PROVINCE, 2250 Granville St., Vancouver, BC V6H 3G2 (604) 732-2619, FAX 732-2720. **EDUC:** Langara Community Coll., Dipl.(Journalism) 1976. **CAREER:** Office Mgr/Payroll Administrator/Bookkeeper, Keystone Business Forms, Vancouver, 1970-74; Lifestyles Reporter, *The Province*, 1976-78; Educ. Reporter, 1978-79; Labour Reporter, 1979-81; freelance Labour Reporter, CJOR Radio, 1980-81; Legal Affairs Reporter, *The Province*, 1981-90; Stringer, *The National Monthly*, Canadian Bar Association, 1985-93; Acting Asst. City Ed., *The Province*, 1988-90; City Ed., 1990 to date. **HONS:** Fellowship, Canadian Bar Association, 1984-85; Law Society Award, 1993; finalist, National Newspaper Awards, 1994. COMMENT: *"Creative media professional with 19 years of progressively increasing responsibility; special expertise in legal issues and the media. Highly developed sense of news judgement."*

Thompson, Leslee J., R.N.,M.Sc.N., C.H.E. ■ ⊕ $

Senior Operating Officer, CAPITAL HEALTH AUTHORITY, Royal Alexandra Hospital, 10240 Kingsway, Edmonton, AB T5H 3V9 (403) 477-4101, FAX 477-4777. Born Halifax 1960. m. Michael David Thompson. 2 ch. Spencer, Charlotte. EDUC: Queen's Univ., B.Sc.N. 1984; Univ. of Toronto, M.Sc.N. 1987; Univ. of Western Ontario, Exec. MBA (in progress). CAREER: Registered Nurse, Intensive Care Unit, Wellesley Hospital, Toronto, 1984-86; Clinical Nurse Specialist, 1987-89; Dir. of Nursing, Sunnybrook Health Science Centre & Toronto-Bayview Regional Cancer Centre, 1989-93; Instructor, Fac. of Medicine, Dept. of Obstetrics & Gynecology, Univ. of Toronto, 1989-93; Asst. Prof., Fac. of Nursing, Univ. of Toronto, 1990-93; Surveyor, Canadian Coll. Health Facilities Accreditation, 1992 to date; VP, Patient Care Svcs, Royal Alexandra Hospital, 1993-95; Advisor, Health & Social Svcs Div., Ernst & Young, 1994 to date; Assoc. Prof., Fac. of Nursing, Univ. of Alberta, 1994 to date; Site Administrator, Royal Alexandra Hospital, 1995-96; Sr. Operating Officer, Capital Health Authority, 1996 to date. SELECTED PUBLICATIONS: various chapters in books, incl. "The Oncology Nurse" & "Palliative Care" (*Everyone's Guide to Cancer Therapy* ed. M. Dollinger *et al* (Toronto: Somerville House Publishing, 1992); various articles in peer reviewed journals, incl. "Cancer of the cervix" (*Seminars in Oncology Nursing*, No. 6 1990); "Excellence in oncology nursing: Making the vision a reality" with H. Krol (*Canadian Journal of Oncology Nursing*, No.1 1991); various abstracts & other publications. EDIT: Reviewer, *Canadian Journal of Nursing Administration*, 1993 to date. AFFIL: Alberta Association of Registered Nurses; Canadian Coll. of Health Service Executives; Canadian Cosmetic, Toiletry & Fragrance Association Foundation (Health Care Advisory Committee); Foundation for Canadians Facing Cancer (Pres. 1989-92); Health Care Advisory Forum, US; Registered Nurses' Association of Ontario. HONS: Paula Major Award for Excellence in Gynecologic Oncology Nursing, Society of Gynecologic Nurse Oncologists, 1988; Upjohn Quality of Life Award, Society of Gynecologic Nurse Oncologists, 1990; Woman on the Move Award, *Toronto Sun*, 1990; Award, Canadian Breast Cancer Foundation, 1991. MISC: Schering Clinical Lectureship, Canadian Association of Nurses in Oncology, 1990; recipient, 2 grants funding research; numerous invited presentations. COMMENT: *"Leslee J. Thompson is a well-respected and progressive leader in health care. Leslee has published numerous articles, lectured extensively across Canada as well as in the US and the West Indies, held leadership positions in professional and nonprofit organizations, and held faculty appointments at universities in Toronto and Edmonton."*

Thompson, Lesley ■■ ⚾

Olympic Athlete. c/o Canadian Olympic Association. Born Toronto 1959. CAREER: Teacher. SPORTS CAREER: mbr., Cdn Nat'l Rowing Team, 1980 to date. Olympic Games: Silver, 8+, 1996; Gold, 8+, 1992; 7th, 4+, 1988; Silver, 4+, 1984. World championships: 6th, 8+, 1995; 7th, 8+, 1994; 1st, 8+, 1991; 6th, 4+, & 7th, 8+, 1987; 3rd, 4+, 1986; 3rd, 4+, 1985; 4th, 4+, 1983; 5th, 8+, 1982; 4th, 8+, 1981. Int'l regattas: 1st, 8+, 1994 (Ont.), 1994; 1st, 8+ (Netherlands), & 2nd, 8+ (Switzerland), 1992; 3rd, 8+ (Switzerland), 1991; 1st, 8+ (Netherlands), & 1st, 4+, & 2nd, 8+ (US), 1988; 3rd, 4+ (Switzerland), 1987; 2nd, 4+ (Switzerland), 1985; 3rd, 4+ (Switzerland), 1984; 2nd, 4+ (Switzerland), 1983. Commonwealth Games: 1st, 4+, 1986. Canadian championships: 1st, 8+, 1993; 1st, 8+, 1990; 1st, 8+, 1989; 1st, 4+, 1985; 1st, 4+, & 1st, 8+, 1983; 1st, 4+, & 1st, 8+, 1982; 1st, 8+, 1981; 1st, 4+, 1980. US championships: 2nd, 8+, 1995; 1st, 8+, 1994; 3rd, 4+, 1993; 1st, 8+, 1992; 1st, 8+, 1991; 1st, 8+, & 2nd, 4+, 1990; 2nd, 8+, 1989. HONS: Amateur Sport Team of the Year, 1991 & 1992; mbr., Canadian Olympic Sports Hall of Fame. INTERESTS: computer applications; scuba diving; cycling. MISC: coached Ont. team, 1985 Canada Games; former gymnast; recruited by Univ. of Western Ontario rowers, 1978; mbr., 1980, 1984, 1988, 1992 & 1996 Olympic teams.

Thompson, Mary E., B.Sc.,Ph.D. ■■ 🎓 ⚛

Professor and Chair, Statistics and Actuarial Science, UNIVERSITY OF WATERLOO, Waterloo, ON N2L 3G1 (519) 888-4567, ext. 5543, FAX 746-1875, EMAIL methomps@setosa.uwaterloo.ca, INTERNET http://www.uwaterloo.ca. Born Winnipeg 1944. m. J. Carl Thompson. 3 ch. Simon, Andrew, Alan. EDUC: Univ. of Toronto, B.Sc.(Math. & Physics) 1965; Univ. of Illinois, Ph.D.(Math.) 1969. CAREER: first appointment, Fac. of Math., Univ. of Waterloo, 1969; Prof., 1980 to date; Assoc. Dean, Grad. Studies & Research, 1988-91; Chair, Statistics & Actuarial Sci., 1996 to date.

Thomson, Nancy, B.A. ■■ $ 🎓 ♡
Honorary Chairman, NANCY THOMSON INVESTING FOR WOMEN (fin. educ. for women), 116 Glenforest Rd., Toronto, ON M4N 1Z9 (416) 485-1760. Born Toronto 1933. s. 3 ch. Lynn, Laurie, Greg. **EDUC:** Univ. of Toronto, B.A.(English) 1954; Ontario Coll. of Education, Secondary Sch. Teacher's Certificate 1955. **CAREER:** Secondary Sch. Teacher, 5 yrs.; Teacher of Dyslexic children, Boston Univ.; formed & ran Nancy Thomson Investing for Women, 1979; taught approx. 20,000 women across Canada & in US, 1979-92; sold business, 1992. **SELECTED PUBLICATIONS:** *Basic Course: Investing for Women*; co-author, *Course II: Investing for Women*; co-author, *Wills & Estate Planning Course*. **DIRECTOR:** GSW Inc.; National Trust Company. **AFFIL:** Myargic Encephalomylitis (Chronic Fatigue Syndrome) Association (fundraiser); Festival Singers of Canada (former Chrm); Shaw Festival (former Dir.); Art Gallery of Vancouver (Bd. mbr. & docent); Lawrence Park Community Church (U.C.W. Pres.); Richard Ivey Sch. of Bus. (Advisory Committee). **COMMENT:** *"Teaching women across Canada about financial planning and investing has been both stimulating and rewarding."*

Thompson, Patricia 📖 📺
Publisher and Editor, *FILM CANADA YEARBOOK*, Cine-communications, Box 152, Stn. A, Toronto, ON M4G 3Z3 (416) 696-2382, FAX 696-6496. Born Portsmouth, UK 1927. s. **CAREER:** Legal Sec., 1957-66; freelance Sec. & Film Researcher, 1966; Films & Info. Officer, Canadian Federation of Film Societies, 1968-70; Co-founder & Coord., Ontario Film Institute & Theatre, Ontario Science Centre, 1969-72; Jury Sec., Cdn Film Awards, 1970; Coord., Stratford Int'l Film Festival, 1971-75; Publicity Dir., Women & Film Festival, 1973; Asst. to the Ed. of *ACTRAscope* & *ACTRAscope News*, 1973-76; Researcher, *Index of Feature Films Available in Canada*, 1973-81; English Canada Rep., Faroun Films of Montréal, 1975-76; Exec. Dir., Cdn Film Awards, 1977-78; Ed., *Canadian Film Digest Yearbook*, 1977-85; Short Film Programmer, Cineplex Theatres, 1978-81; Columnist, *Cinema Canada*, 1983-89; Publisher & Ed., *Film Canada Yearbook*, Cine-communications, 1985 to date; Programmer, Uxbridge Film Day, 1987-91; Researcher, American Express "Gold Card Communiqué," 1989-90; Cdn Ed., *Motion Picture Almanac* & *Television and Video Almanac*, Quigley Publishing Co., N.Y., 1989 to date; Researcher & Writer, *Pet Pro Newsletter*, Ralston Purina Canada, 1991-92; Columnist, *Take One*, 1992-94; Contributor, *Kinema*, 1996 to date. **SELECTED CREDITS:** Joyce Wieland's Mother, *Be Prepared*, early 1960s; "The Double-Jointed Turned-On Picnic," *Program X*, CBC TV, 1970; Miss Prume, *The Peanut Butter Solution* (feature), prod. Rock Demers, 1985. **AFFIL:** Toronto Film Society; Canadian Picture Pioneers. **HONS:** Dorothy Burritt Award, Canadian Federation of Film Societies, 1973; Queen's Silver Jubilee Medal, 1977. **INTERESTS:** cinema; theatre; travel. **MISC:** *Canadian Who's Who*; jury mbr., numerous festivals & awards; Trustee, Dorothy & Oscar Burritt Memorial Award. **COMMENT:** *"I've worked since I was 16, and supported myself too. Emigrated to Canada in 1957 and realized that I could turn a hobby (film) into a career as a freelancer: 30 years up to now."*

Thomsen, Penny, B.P.E. ♡ ⚛ ⊕ ✋
Executive Director, Ontario Division, CANADIAN CANCER SOCIETY, 1639 Yonge St., Toronto, ON M4T 2W6 (416) 488-5400, FAX 488-2872. Born Ottawa 1951. m. George C. Glover Jr. 2 ch., 2 stpch. **EDUC:** Dalhousie Univ., B.P.E.(Phys. Educ.) 1978. **CAREER:** various positions, City of Halifax Recreation Dept., 1972-78; Exec. Dir., Recreation Council for the Disabled in N.S., 1978-86; Exec. Dir., Canadian Cancer Society, N.S. Div., 1986-88; Pres., Penny Thomsen Consulting Services Inc., 1988-90; Dir., Community Svcs, Canadian Cancer Society, Ont. Div., 1990-93; Exec. Dir., 1993 to date. **SELECTED PUBLICATIONS:** (under name P.E. Tobin) *Everyone for Recreation? Working with People Who Have Special Needs: An Orientation for Recreation Staff and Volunteers* (Recreation Council for the Disabled in N.S., 1983); "Altering Attitudes: A Workshop" (*Journal of Leisurability* 2 1984); "Life Style Profile: An Interview with Michael Harper" (*Recreation Canada* Special Issue 1981); "Programme Development: Beyond Activities" (*Journal of Leisurability* 3 1983). **AFFIL:** Cancer Transition Team (1996); Provincial Cancer Network (1994-96); *Journal of Leisurability* (Ed. Review Committee 1982-86); Technical Aids & Systems for the Handicapped (Dir. 1984-86); Canadian Rehabilitation Council for the Disabled (VP 1984-86); Abilities Foundation of N.S. (VP 1983-86); Credit Valley Golf & Country Club. **HONS:** Women's Recognition Award, YWCA. **COMMENT:** *"As Executive Director of one of Canada's largest volunteer health charities, strong skills in management, communication, and strategic thinking, as well as a commitment to the work of volunteers in our society, are essential."*

Thomson, Pamela Ann, B.A.,LL.B. ■■ ⚖
Judge, ONTARIO COURT OF JUSTICE, 444 Yonge

St., 2nd Fl., Toronto, ON M5B 2H7 (416) 325-8920, FAX 325-8944. Born Timmins, Ont. 1942. m. Judge E. Gordon Hachborn. 2 ch. **EDUC:** Queen's Univ., B.A.(French) 1963; Univ. of Toronto, LL.B. 1966. **BAR:** Ont., 1968. **CAREER:** Ptnr, A.E. Golden, Barrister, 1968-70 & 1974-81; Dir., Centre for Public Interest Law, McGill Univ., 1971-74; also ran Legal Aid Clinic, City of Westmount; House Cnsl, Federation of Women Teachers' Associations of Ontario, 1975; appointed prov. Judge of Ont., 1981; Case Mgmt Judge, Toronto Small Claims Court, 1990 to date. **SELECTED CREDITS:** regular contributor, "Commentary," CBC Radio, 1969-81. **SELECTED PUBLICATIONS:** *Consumer Access to Justice* (Consumer Research Council of Canada, 1976); *Survey of Pricing and Marketing Practices* (Food Prices Review Board of Canada, 1972); *Divorce Law in Canada* (researched & wrote 1st draft, by MacDonald & Ferrier). **AFFIL:** Canadian Association of Provincial Court Judges (Exec. Dir. 1990-96); Civil Division Judges' Association (Pres. 1993 to date); Police Complaints Board (Chair 1980s); Crown Employees' Grievance Settlement Board (union nominee 4 yrs.). **MISC:** main focus of practice was labour & administrative law, but also acted in many criminal & civil matters before all levels of courts; former mbr., Committee advising Min. (Que.) on appropriateness of advertising directed to children; founding mbr., Yorkville "Village Bar." **COMMENT:** *"I have devised and am currently supervising a system of managing case flow that is the first differentiated case management system for a limited jurisdiction court in North America. Since its inception in 1990, we have a system that speedily and fairly serves the public."*

Thomson, Shirley Lavinia, O.C., Ph.D. ⊗ 🔖

Director, NATIONAL GALLERY OF CANADA, 380 Sussex Dr., Ottawa, ON K1N 9N4, FAX (613) 990-9810. Born Walkerville, Ont. 1930. **EDUC:** Univ. of Western Ontario, B.A. 1952; Univ. of Maryland, M.A. 1974; McGill Univ., Ph.D. 1981. **CAREER:** Ed., NATO, Paris, 1956-60; Asst. Sec.-Gen., World University Service, 1960-63; Assoc. Sec.-Gen., Cdn Commission for UNESCO, 1964-67; Research Coord. & Writer, memoirs of Senator Thérèse Casgrain, 1968-70; Dir. & Deputy Commissioner, UNESCO Pavilion, Man & His World, Montreal, 1978-80; Special Coord., Largillierre Exhibition, Montreal Museum of Fine Arts, 1981; Dir., McCord Museum, 1982-85; Sec.-Gen., Cdn Commission for UNESCO, 1985-87; Dir., National Gallery of Canada, 1987 to date. **HONS:** Chevalier des Arts et des lettres,

Gov't of France, 1990; Officer, Order of Canada, 1994; Doctorate (Hon.), McGill Univ., 1989; Doctorate (Hon.), Univ. of Ottawa, 1988; Doctorate (Hon.), Mount Allison Univ., 1990; Doctorate (Hon.), Univ. of Western Ontario, 1990; Doctorate (Hon.), Univ. of Windsor, 1996.

Thornley, Shirley Blumberg, B.Arch. ❀ ⊗ ♂

Partner, KUWABARA PAYNE MCKENNA BLUMBERG ARCHITECTS, 322 King St. W., Toronto, ON M5V 1J2 (416) 977-5104, FAX 598-9840. Born Cape Town, S. Africa 1952. m. Scott Thornley. 1 ch. **EDUC:** Univ. of Toronto, B.Arch. 1976. **CAREER:** Asst. Architect, Barton Myers Associates, 1977-82; Assoc., Barton Myers Associates, 1982-87; Adjunct Asst. Prof. & Visiting Critic, Sch. of Architecture & Landscape Architecture, Univ. of Toronto, 1986-93; Ptnr, Kuwabara Payne McKenna Blumberg Architects, 1987 to date; Visiting Critic, Carleton Univ., 1988; Visiting Critic, Univ. of Waterloo, 1989; Sch. of Architecture, Univ. of Nebraska, 1994. **AFFIL:** Royal Architectural Institute of Canada; Ontario Science Centre; Ontario Association of Architects. **HONS:** Award for Proj. Team Effectiveness, New England Construction Users' Council, 1992; Toronto Masonry Award, 1992; Gov. General's Award of Merit, 1992; Silver Award, Retail Design, ARIDO, 1993; Gold Award, Retail Design, ARIDO, 1993; Honorable Mention, City of Toronto Urban Design Awards, 1993; Toronto Arts Award for Architecture & Design, 1993; Record Interiors, 1995. **MISC:** various talks & lectures; subject of interview in *Exchange*, Feb. 1994; 1st appointed Hyde Chair for Excellence, Sch. of Architecture, Univ. of Nebraska.

Thors, Sigrid-Ann, B.Mus. ■ ■ ⊗ ♡ ❀

General Manager, SASKATOON SYMPHONY SOCIETY, P.O. Box 1361, Saskatoon, SK S7K 3N9 (306) 665-6414, FAX 652-3364. Born Penticton, B.C. 1939. s. **EDUC:** Univ. of British Columbia, Home Econ.(Textiles) studies 2 yrs., B.Mus.(Gen., cello) 1963; Banff Sch. of Fine Arts, Mgmt Dev. for Arts Administrators Aug. 1978. **CAREER:** music teacher, kindergarten to college, 1963-87; cellist, accompanist, conductor, various summer schools, orchestras & special assignments; commercial fisher (Pacific coast) as gillnetter, then seine crew & part-owner, various summers, 1967-84; Sr. Industrial Consultant, Employment & Immigration, Ottawa, 1987-92; Gen. Mgr, Thirteen Strings, 1993-94; Gen. Mgr, Saskatoon Symphony, 1994 to date. **SELECTED CREDITS:** Cellist (principal for several yrs.), Okanagan Symphony Orchestra, 1963-75. **AFFIL:** Association of Canadian Orchestras (Bd. Rep. for orchestras with budgets of $500,000-$2M); Saskatoon Women's Network; Saskatoon Cultural Lobby; Saskatoon-Wanuskewin Fed. P.C. Riding Association (VP); Fed. P.C. Women's Caucus, Ottawa (Pres. 1987-94); Canadian Federation of University Women; Canadian Conference of the Arts (Exec. mbr., western 1984-87); Assembly of B.C. Arts Councils (VP 1979-83); Advisory Planning Commission, City of Vernon (1976-80); Women's Transition House Society, Vernon (Advisory Bd. 1978-80). **INTERESTS:** politics; environmental issues; quilting; gardening; reading. **MISC:** Alderman (Acting Mayor upon death of Mayor), City of Vernon, B.C., 1977-82; Delegate, P.C. leadership convention, 1993; former co-owner, retail outlet Okanagan Ideas; interviewer, Vercom Cable TV, 1-hr. weekly programme, 1975-87; cameraman, "Art-i-facts," Vercom Cable TV, 1975-79; has travelled extensively as mbr. of various groups (conferences, guest speaker, etc.). **COMMENT:** *"An impatience with inaction, a sense of responsibility for the welfare of others, and a desire to try varied and non-traditional fields of employment, all driven by family support, have given shape to my activities-socially, politically and professionally."*

Thorsrud, Lorraine, A.R.C.T. ♡ ✋ $ ☝
Volunteer and Association Executive. 165 Broadway E., Yorkton, SK S3N 3K6 (306) 783-6545, FAX 786-6488. Owner and Operator, THORSRUD'S COLOR CENTRE LTD. UNITED CARPET. Born Man. m. Bjorn Thorsrud. 3 ch. Julianne, Karen, Sharon. **EDUC:** Bus. Coll. degree; Royal Conservatory of Music, Toronto, A.C.R.T. **CAREER:** current & past mbr. of numerous community, prov., nat'l & int'l bds. & organizations. **AFFIL:** Saskatchewan Abilities Council (V-Chair, Prov. Bd.); Dispute Resolution Committee, Gov't of Sask.; Saskatchewan Action Plan for Children (Committee Mbr.); Canada on the Int'l Decade for Cultural Dev. (Steering Committee); Parkland Ability Centre (Chair, Reg'l Advisory Bd.; Chair, Fundraising); Yorkton Film Festival (Bd. Mbr.; Hon. Patron); East Central Health District Bd. (Chair); Beta Sigma Phi (Hon. Patron; Int'l Mbr.); Univ. of Regina Alumni (Hon. Mbr.). **PAST AFFIL:** Canada Council (Mbr. & Exec. Bd. Mbr.); Univ. of Regina; Pres., Organization of Saskatchewan Arts Councils (Chair, Bd. of Gov.); Saskatchewan Abilities Council (VP); Saskatchewan Arts Bd. (Mbr.); Yorkton Arts Council (Pres.); various other positions. **HONS:** Yorkton Citizen of the Year Award, 1983-84 (1st winner). **MISC:** Univ. of Regina Delegate, World Commonwealth Conference of Universities, Birmingham, UK; Cdn Delegate, World Decade for Cultural Dev. Conference, Paris, 1990.

Thorstad, Linda, B.Sc.,M.Sc. ■ ⚛ ✋
Consultant, 5340 Marine Dr., W. Vancouver, BC V7W 2P8 (604) 921-5958, FAX 921-5958. President, ASSOCIATION OF PROFESSIONAL ENGINEERS AND GEOSCIENTISTS OF THE PROVINCE OF BRITISH COLUMBIA. Born Vancouver 1954. **EDUC:** Univ. of British Columbia, B.Sc.(Geology) 1977, M.Sc. 1984. **CAREER:** Consultant, Ventures West Minerals Ltd., 1979-82; Consultant, Thorstad Consulting, 1982-83; Pres. & Ptnr, Questore Consultants Ltd., 1983-86; VP, Special Projects, 1986 Int'l Resource Forum, 1986; Pres. & Dir., Interaction Resources Ltd., 1986-91; Consultant & Exec. VP, HRC Development Corporation, 1991-92; Consultant & Assoc., Commission on Resources & Environment, 1992-94; Consultant, Fraser Basin Mgmt Program, 1993 to date. **AFFIL:** Association of Professional Engineers & Geoscientists of the Province of B.C. (Pres.; Chair, Committee on Sustainability); B.C. Council for Sustainability; B.C. Heritage Rivers Bd.; Canadian Council of Professional Engineers (Vision Implementation Task Force); Whistler Centre for Business & the Arts (Bd.). **HONS:** Woman of Distinction for Management and the Professions, YWCA, 1996. **INTERESTS:** skiing; tennis; art; gardening; golf.

Tidd, Fay ■ $
Manager, GARDINER REALTY LTD./ROYAL LEPAGE ASSOCIATE BROKER, Restigouch Rd., Oromocto, NB E2V 2H2 (506) 466-9000, FAX 446-5050. Born Ottawa 1929. m. Wally. 5 ch. **EDUC:** Lisgar Collegiate, Sr. Matriculation 1947; Ottawa Civic Hospital, training 1947; Univ. of New Brunswick. **CAREER:** Office Nurse, Ottawa, 1948; wife, mother, foster mother, various locations in Ont., Yukon & N.B., 1948 to date; real estate broker, to date; Mayor, Town of Oromocto, 1988-96. **AFFIL:** Real Estate Institute of Canada (Fellow); Fredericton & Area Real Estate Bd. (Pres.); N.B. Real Estate Council (Pres.); Atlantic Real Estate Council (Dir.); Property Tax Appeal Bd., N.B. (appointed by Lt. Gov.); Oromocto Tourism Committee; Can Plan, Oromocto; Oromocto Public Hospital Foundation (Dir.); Crime Stoppers Oromocto; Oromocto Youth Training Centre (Dir.); Atlantic Chamber of Commerce (Dir.); Oromocto & Area Chamber of Commerce (Dir.; Pres.); Mayor's Committee on Literacy; Literacy Council; United Way; Red Cross; Canadian Diabetes Association; Anglican Church of Canada. **HONS:** qualified each year for Prov. Gold Sales Award, N.B. Real

Estate Bd.; Mayor Louise Breau Memorial Award, Union of Municipalities of N.B., 1996. INTERESTS: people, esp. youth; visiting the elderly. MISC: Certified Real Estate Broker/Mgr; 1 of 4 certified Real Estate Brokers/Mgrs in N.B. COMMENT: *"There is always another mountain to climb, more to learn. I am happy every day just to be alive, satisfied that I will leave whatever challenge better than I found it."*

Tilby, Wendy ☐ ⊗ ☙
Film Director, NATIONAL FILM BOARD OF CANADA, Box 6100, Stn. A, Montreal, QC H3C 3H5 (514) 283-9630, FAX 283-3211. Born Edmonton 1960. s. EDUC: Univ. of Victoria, Lit., Creative Writing & Visual Arts 1978-80; Emily Carr Coll. of Art & Design, Diploma in Fine Arts 1986. CAREER: self-employed animator, illustrator & graphic artist, 1981-86; Graphic Artist & Prod. Asst., Omni Film Productions, 1984-86; Prod. & Dir., animation segment, *Sesame Street*, CBC, Vancouver, 1986; Instructor, animation workshops, Emily Carr Coll. of Art & Design, 1987; Bd. Mbr., ASIFA, 1988-90; Instructor, Film Animation Course, Concordia Univ., 1991-95; Animation Dir., National Film Board of Canada, 1987 to date. SELECTED CREDITS: Dir./Writer/Animator, *Tables of Content*, 1986; Dir./Writer/Animator, *Strings*, NFB, 1987-91; Animation Dir., *Inside Out* (working title only), NFB, in progress. HONS: numerous prizes for *Tables of Content* incl.: Best Animated Film & Best Overall Film, B.C. Student Film Festival, 1986; Best Animation, Golden Sheaf Award, Yorkton Short Film & Video Festival, 1986; Grand Prix de Montréal, Best Short, Montreal World Film Festival, 1986; nominated, Genie Awards, 1987; first prize, Debut Category from various festivals worldwide; numerous prizes for *Strings* incl.: Academy Award nomination, National Educational Film & Video Festival, 1992; blue ribbon, American Film & Video Festival, 1992; first place in Category, 4th Int'l Animation Festival, Hiroshima, Japan, 1992; first prize, 26th Annual N.Y. Expo of Short Films & Video, 1992; Best Animated Film, Genie Awards, 1992. MISC: has participated in many film festivals & conference presentations. COMMENT: *"Wendy Joy Tilby was born in 1960 in Edmonton. After studying at the University of Victoria, she went on to the Emily Carr College of Art & Design in Vancouver where she graduated with honours in Film and Animation. With the success of* Tables of Content, *Tilby was invited to work at the National Film Board's animation studio in Montreal. In 1991, she completed her second film,* Strings. *Wendy Tilby is currently living in Montreal and working at the National Film Board on her third animated film."*

Timmons, Vianne, B.A.,B.Ed.,M.Ed., Ph.D. ■ ☜
Dean, Faculty of Education, UNIVERSITY OF PRINCE EDWARD ISLAND, 555 University, Charlottetown, PE C1A 4P3 (902) 566-0330, FAX 566-0416, EMAIL vtimmons@upei.ca. Born Kitimat, B.C. 1958. 4 ch. Nancy, Kelly, Samuel, Taylor. EDUC: Mount Allison Univ., B.A. (Psych. & English) 1979; Acadia Univ., B.Ed.(Special Educ.) 1980; Gonzaga Univ., M.Ed.(Special Educ.) 1983; Univ. of Calgary, Ph.D.(Rehab.) 1993. CAREER: Learning Assistance Teacher, Babine Elementary & Secondary Sch., Granisle, B.C., 1980-81; Instructor, Selkirk Coll., Castlegar, B.C., 1984-86; Head Teacher/VP, Castlegar Special Educ. Centre, 1983-86; Special Educ. Teacher, Arthur Peak Sch., Maple Ridge, B.C., 1986-87; DD III Teacher, St. Gregory Jr. High Sch., Calgary, 1986-87; Practicum Supervisor, 1984 to date; Early Corrections Learning Teacher, St. Angela Sch., Calgary, 1990-91; Consultant, 1985 to date; Jr. High Resource Teacher, St. Rose Sch., Calgary, 1991-92; Instructor in the Special Educ. Dept., Univ. of Calgary, 1990-92; Assoc. Prof., Educ. Dept., St. Francis Xavier Univ., 1992-96; Chair, Educ. Dept., 1993-96; Dean, Fac. of Educ., Univ. of PEI, 1996 to date. SELECTED PUBLICATIONS: "Decision-making for teenagers with special needs" (*Conference Proceedings*, National Conference of the Council of Exceptional Children, 1994); "Some Staff and Client Reactions to an Intervention Model," with K. Kulemeyer in *Choices and Quality of Life* (London: Chapman & Hall, 1993); instructor's manual for textbook *The Inclusive Classroom* with V. Blair (Ontario: Nelson Canada, 1993); various other publications & book reviews. EDIT: Asst. Ed., *Journal of Practical Approaches to Developmental Disabilities*, 1989-92. AFFIL: Council of Exceptional Children; Canadian Society for the Study of Education; American Educational Research Association; Canadian Association of University Teachers; American Association on Mental Retardation; Association for Persons with Severe Handicaps; Canadian Down's Syndrome Association. MISC: various presentations; numerous lectures & workshops given; recipient, various scholarships & awards. COMMENT: *"Have taught in public schools for 12 years, concentrating on children with exceptional needs."*

Timperon, Mary-Ellen McGill, B.A.,M.Ed., B.Sc.N. ☐☜ ⊕ ☜
Recruiting, Education and Training Formation

Personnel Selection Officer (military psychologist), CANADIAN FORCES, CFB Borden, Borden, ON L0M 1C0 (705) 424-1200, ext. 2535, FAX 547-3053. Born Meaford, Ont. 1955. m. Donald G. Timperon. 2 ch. Kathleen, Graham. EDUC: Univ. of Windsor, B.A.(Psych.) 1978, B.Sc.N.(Nursing) 1978; Univ. of Western Ontario, M.Ed.(Counselling Psych.) 1984; Public Administrators of Ontario, Certificate (Admin.) 1990. CAREER: Pediatric Nurse, 1978-79; Community Health Counsellor, 1979-82; Counsellor in Residence, Huron Coll., Univ. of Western Ontario, 1982-84; Personnel Selection Officer & Behavioural Scientist, Canadian Forces Base, 1984-89; Asst. Prof., Royal Military Coll. of Canada, 1990-95; Canadian Forces Recruiting, Educ. & Training Formation Personnel Selection Officer (military psychologist), 1995 to date. SELECTED PUBLICATIONS: "Client and Counsellor Reliance on Verbal and Nonverbal Skills in a Counselling Environment" (*Canadian Journal of Counselling* Jan. 1988); "Critical Incident Stress Debriefings for Search and Rescue Technicians" (*Personnel Selection Officers Forum* Apr. 1991); "Attitudes Towards Women in Society and the Military: A Comparison of Canadian Military College and Civilian University Students" (*Personnel Selection Officers Forum* June 1993). AFFIL: Public Administrators of Ontario (Exec. 1987-90); Institute of Public Administrators of Canada (Exec.; Reg'l Exec. Dir.); Coll. of Nurses of Ontario (Local Exec.); Personnel Selection Officers' Association. HONS: Commendation for Community Service, 1987; Officer Professional Dev. Award & Distinction, 1990; Int'l Women's Day Award, 1994. INTERESTS: women working in nontraditional roles; community counselling svcs; feminism in Canada; athletics. MISC: created, wrote policy & co-chaired 1st Anti-Harassment Committee at Royal Military Coll.; created & chaired 1st Status of Women Committee & Women's Caucus, Royal Military Coll. COMMENT: *"Determined, motivated feminist."*

Tippett, Maria, F.R.S.C.,LL.D.,Ph.D., B.A. 🕮 🕮 🕮
Senior Research Fellow/Writer and Curator, CAMBRIDGE UNIVERSITY. m. Prof. P.F. Clarke. EDUC: Simon Fraser Univ., B.A.(Hist.) 1972; Univ. of London, Ph.D.(Hist.) 1982. CAREER: Lecturer, Dept. of Hist., Simon Fraser Univ., 1974-85; Lecturer, Dept. of Hist., Univ. of British Columbia, 1984-86; John P. Robarts Prof. of Cdn Studies, York Univ., 1986-87; Visiting Fellow, Clare Hall, Cambridge Univ., 1991-92; Life Mbr., Clare Hall, 1992 to date; Fac. of Hist., 1992 to date; Sr. Research Fellow,

Churchill Coll., Cambridge Univ., 1995 to date. SELECTED PUBLICATIONS: *Emily Carr: a biography* (Toronto: Oxford Univ. Press, 1979; Toronto: Penguin Books, 1982, 1985); *By a Lady: Canadian Women in the Visual Arts 1690-1990* (Toronto: Penguin Books, 1992, 1993); *Breaking the Cycle and Other Stories from a Gulf Island* (Victoria: Orca Publishing House, 1989); numerous articles, incl. "'A Paste Solitaire in a Steel-Claw Setting': Emily Carr and Her Public" (*BC Studies* Winter 1973/74); "The Illusion of Progress: Does More Space Make Our Public Galleries Any Better?" (*Canadian Art* Spring 1990); book reviews in *Times Literary Supplement, London Review of Books, Twentieth Century British History, BC Studies, Canadian Historical Review, Queen's Quarterly, RACAR,* & *Canadian Art.* EDIT: Ed. Bd., *Canadian Historical Review,* 1984-87; Contributing Ed., *Canadian Art,* 1990-92. AFFIL: Royal Society of Canada (Fellow); Federation of B.C. Writers. HONS: Eaton's Book Award, 1977; Gov. General's Award for Nonfiction, 1979; Sir John A. Macdonald Prize, Canadian Historical Association, 1979; Honourable Mention, Francois-Garneau Medal, 1985; Canadian Studies Writing Award, 1993; Honourable Mention, Vancouver City Book Prize, 1993; Canada 125 Medal; LL.D.(Hon.), Univ. of Windsor, 1994. INTERESTS: hiking; swimming; making pottery. MISC: Judge, B.C. Book Award, 1986; Gov. General's Book Awards Jury, 1987-90; Pres., all English-language juries, the Canada Council, 1988-89; recipient, numerous grants & fellowships; numerous invited lectures. COMMENT: *"I divide my time, June to September at my cottage on Bowen Island, BC, and October to May in Cambridge. I have always considered myself to be first and foremost a writer."*

Tkachuk, Mary, B.A. 🕮 🕮 🕮
Teacher, THE PRIORY SCHOOL INC., 3120 The Boulevard, Montreal, QC H3Y 1R9 (514) 935-5966, FAX 935-1428. Founder and President, THE ORTHODOX CHRISTIAN WOMEN OF MONTREAL. Born Paris, France 1948. m. John Tkachuk. 1 ch. EDUC: Barnard Coll., NYC, B.A.(French/Russian Lit.) 1971. CAREER: Teacher, elementary sch., 1975 to date. AFFIL: Orthodox Christian Women of Montreal (Founder & Pres.). MISC: Co-Dir. of the liturgical chorale of The Sign of the THEOTOKOS Orthodox Church. COMMENT: *"Wife of a parish priest and active in parish life. Founder of pan-orthodox group, The Orthodox Christian Women of Montreal. This group (250 members) has sponsored five annual conferences of topics of common interest to Christian women."*

Toal, Anne, B.Sc. ■ $

Vice-President and Corporate Actuary, LONDON LIFE INSURANCE COMPANY, 255 Dufferin Ave., London, ON N6A 4K1 (519) 432-5281, FAX 432-4759. Born Strathroy, Ont. m. Paul Brisson. **EDUC:** Univ. of Western Ontario, B.Sc.(Actuarial Sci.) 1978. **CAREER:** various positions in mktg & strategic planning, London Life Insurance Company, 1978 to date; VP & Corp. Actuary. **AFFIL:** Society of Actuaries (Fellow); Canadian Institute of Actuaries (Fellow); Parkwood Hospital Foundation (Exec. Bd.); Foundation Western (Bd.; Chair, Planned Giving Committee); London Women's Network (Exec. 1987-93; Pres. 1989-91); Greenhills Golf Club (Ladies Golf Committee 1994-96; Pres. 1996). **INTERESTS:** fin. security issues; travel; golf. **COMMENT:** *"Action-oriented, dedicated to the success of London Life's business, and involved in community groups."*

Todd, Rosalie Daly, A.B.,M.S., LL.B. ✋ $

Executive Director and Legal Counsel, CONSUMERS' ASSOCIATION OF CANADA, 267 O'Connor St., Ste. 307, Ottawa, ON K2P 1V3 (613) 238-2533, FAX 563-2254. Born Wisconsin, Ill. 1947. m. David. 1 stpch. **EDUC:** Marquette Univ., A.B. 1969; American Univ., M.S. 1978; McGill Univ., LL.B. 1982. **BAR:** N.Y., 1982; Ont, 1989. **CAREER:** Mgmt Intern, US Gov't, 1969-72; Deputy Dir., Maryland Dept. of Transportation, 1975-78; Ed., Royal Bank of Canada, 1978-79; Assoc., FitzPatrick, Bennett, Trombley, Ownes and Lahtinen, 1982-86; Institute for Research on Public Policy, 1986-87; Legal Dept., City of Ottawa, 1987-90; Exec. Dir. & Legal Cnsl, Consumers' Association of Canada, 1990 to date. **AFFIL:** Law Society of Upper Canada; State Bar of N.Y. (Committee on Int'l Law & Trade); Public Relations Society of America. **HONS:** publications awards from International Association of Business Communicators & Canadian Public Relations Society. **INTERESTS:** portrait artist.

Todd-Morgan, Rhonda ■ ✋ ♡

Founder, Investigator and Executive Director, MISSING CHILDREN SOCIETY OF CANADA, 3501-23 St. N.E., Ste. 219, Calgary, AB (403) 291-0705, FAX 291-9728. Born Lethbridge, Alta. 1956. 1 ch. Matthew. **CAREER:** Professional Investigator/Exec. Dir., Missing Children Society of Canada, 1985 to date. **AFFIL:** Child Find Alberta (Dir. 1984-86). **INTERESTS:** cooking; reading; raising my son. **COMMENT:** *"I have been lucky in life, blessed with a supportive and loving family, a few good friends, the inner strength and determination to follow my dreams and a wonderful son. My devotion and passion is my son and my work for missing children."*

Todres, Elaine Meller, B.A.,M.A., Ph.D. 🍁 ⚖

Deputy Solicitor General and Deputy Minister of Corrections, GOVERNMENT OF ONTARIO, 175 Bloor St. W., Toronto, ON M4W 3R8 (416) 326-5060, FAX 327-0469. Born Winnipeg 1950. m. Rubin Todres. 2 ch. Lindsay, Jesse. **EDUC:** Univ. of Winnipeg, B.A.(Pol. Sci. & Econ.) 1971; Univ. of Pittsburgh, M.A.(Pol. Sci.) 1973, Ph.D. (1976). **CAREER:** Mgr, Oper. Research, Ministry of Revenue, Gov't of Ont., 1980-81; Dir., Revenue & Oper. Research, 1981-83; Dir., Policy & Research, Ont. Women's Directorate, 1983-85; Asst. Deputy Min., 1986-87; Deputy Min., Hum. Res. Secretariat, 1987-91; Chair, Civil Svc. Commission, 1988-91; Deputy Min., Culture & Comm., 1991-93; Deputy Min., Culture, Tourism & Recreation, 1993-95; Deputy Solicitor Gen. & Deputy Min. of Corrections, 1995 to date. **EDIT:** Ed. Bd., *Canadian Public Administration.* **AFFIL:** Baycrest Hospital (Chair, Hum. Res. Committee; Bd. of Dir.; Exec. Committee); Institute of Public Administration (Exec. Mbr., Toronto Chapter); Personnel Council; Univ. of Toronto (Health Advisory Committee); Univ. of Toronto Business Sch. (Advisory Committee); Queen's Univ. (Advisory Bd., Programs for Public Exec.); Ryerson Polytechnic Univ. (Public Admin. Advisory Bd.). **HONS:** Gold Medal, Econ., & Gold Medal, Pol. Sci., Univ. of Winnipeg; President's Award, Canadian Association of Public Personnel Management; Gold Medal, Centre for Human Rights; Young Leadership Award, Toronto Jewish Congress. **INTERESTS:** volunteer work; choral music. **COMMENT:** *"My commitments are to social justice and equality. I seek these goals through ground-breaking legislation such as pay equity, partnerships with the private sector and involvement in the voluntary sector."*

Toews, Heather, B.Mus.,M.Mus., D.Mus.A. ■ ✪ 🎓

Assistant Professor, Faculty of Music, WILFRID LAURIER UNIVERSITY, Waterloo, ON N2L 3C5 (519) 884-0710, ext. 2376, FAX 747-9129, EMAIL htoews@mach1.wlu.ca. Born Winnipeg 1960. **EDUC:** McGill Univ., B.Mus. 1980; Indiana Univ., M.Mus. 1983; State Univ. of New York at Stony Brook, Doctor of Musical Arts 1992. **CAREER:** Visiting Lecturer of Piano, Univ. of Prince Edward Island, 1985-86; Piano Fac. Mbr., McGill Univ. Conservatory of Music, 1987-90; Chamber Music Fac. Mbr., Canadian Amateur Musicians' Music Centre at Lake MacDonald, 1988 to date; Lecturer of Music, Brock Univ., 1992; Asst. Prof., 1993-96. SELECTED CREDITS: touring artist, *Debut Atlantic*, 1979; performer, *Arts National*, CBC Radio, 1980; artist resident, Banff Centre, 1983-84; rep. for Canada, Tchaikovsky Competition, Moscow, 1990; numerous recitals in Canada, US & abroad. AFFIL: Canadian University Music Society. HONS: first prize, Canadian Imperial Bank of Commerce Music Competition, 1980; first prize, Canadian Music Competition, 1980. INTERESTS: hiking; bicycling; South Indian music & cuisine; poetry.

Tonin, Patricia N., B.Sc.,M.Sc., Ph.D. ■ ❀ ⊕ ❧
Assistant Professor, Faculty of Medicine, MCGILL UNIVERSITY, Division of Medical Genetics, Montreal General Hospital, L10-120, Montreal, QC H3G 1A4 (514) 937-6011, ext. 4067 or ext. 4201, FAX 934-8273. Born Toronto 1959. 1 ch. Natascia Lypny. EDUC: Univ. of Toronto, B.Sc.(Hons.) 1982, M.Sc. (Microbiol.) 1985, Ph.D.(Microbiol.) 1989. CAREER: Postdoctoral Fellow, Ludwig Institute for Cancer Research (Montreal Branch), 1989-91; Postdoctoral Fellow, Div. of Medical Genetics, Dept. of Medicine, Montreal General Hospital, McGill Univ., 1992-95; Asst. Prof., Fac. of Medicine, McGill Univ., 1995 to date. SELECTED PUBLICATIONS: "Genetic and physical characterization of trimethoprim resistance plasmids from Shigella sonnei and Sigella flexneri," with R.B. Grant (*Canadian Journal of Microbiology* 33 1987); "Muscle-specific gene expression in rhabdomyosarcomas and stages of fetal muscle skeletal development," with H. Scrable, H. Shimada & W.K. Cavenee (*Cancer Research* 51 1991); "Isolation of BRCA1, the 17q-linked breast and ovarian cancer susceptibility gene," with J. Miki *et al* (*Science* 266 1994); "Identification of the breast cancer susceptibility gene BRCA2," with R. Wooster (*Nature* 378 1995); various other publications & abstracts. HONS: Medical Research Council of Canada & Cancer Research Society Scholarship, 1995-2000; Canadian Breast Cancer Foundation Award, 1995; Cedars Cancer Research Institute Fellowship Royal Victoria Hospital, 1993-94; Medical Research Council Fellowship, 1989-93; MacPherson Award (Best All-round Ph.D. candidate), Dept. of Microbiol., Univ. of Toronto, 1988; Univ. of Toronto Doctoral Fellowship, 1987-89; Ont. Grad. Scholarship, 1983-87; Research Institute Studentship, Hospital for Sick Children, 1982-85.

Topalovich, Maria, B.Mus.,M.Mus. ☺ ⌣ ⊗
Chief Executive Officer, ACADEMY OF CANADIAN CINEMA AND TELEVISION, 158 Pearl St.,

Toronto, ON M5H 1L3 (416) 591-2040, FAX 591-2157. Born Toronto 1951. m. Peter Mortimer. 2 ch. Sasha Mortimer, Catherine Mortimer. EDUC: Univ. of Toronto, B.Mus. 1974, M.Mus. 1975. CAREER: Assoc. Music Critic, *The Toronto Star*, 1971-76; Arts Officer, Ontario Arts Council, 1976; Wintario Grant Officer, Ministry of Culture & Recreation, 1977-79; Dir. of Publicity, Canadian Opera Company, 1978; Publicity Dir., Canadian Int'l Film Festival, 1979-81; Mktg & Comm. Dir., then CEO, Academy of Canadian Cinema & Television, 1979 to date. AFFIL: Royal Conservatory of Music (Dir.); CulTech Research Centre (Dir.). HONS: Dean's List, Univ. of Toronto, 1974, 1975; Exec. Prod. nominee, Best Variety Program, Gemini Awards, 1992. INTERESTS: music; writing; cooking; gardening.

Topping, Beverly * 📖 ✦
President and Chief Executive Officer, TODAY'S PARENT GROUP, 269 Richmond St. W., Toronto, ON M5V 1X1. Born Baldur, Man. 2 ch. CAREER: Pres. & CEO, Today's Parent Group (*Today's Parent, Your Baby, Mon Enfant, New Mother, Mère Nouvelle, Great Expectations, Pouponnière, Prenatal Class Guide, Today's New Grandparent, Pre & Post Natal News* as well as educational seminars, sampling programs, direct mail clubs & ownership of the largest family-targeted database in Canada). AFFIL: past & present affil. incl. The Kids' Help Phone (Bd.); Marshall McLuhan Distinguished Teacher Award (Selection Committee); Prism Awards (Selection Committee); Storybook Publishing–The Kids Network (fin. & bus. advisor); The United Way; Canadian Cancer Society; Wellspring-Cancer Support Counselling; The Heart & Stroke Foundation (Steering Committee, Women Heart & Stroke); Women's College Hospital Foundation (Bd.); Canadian Magazine Publishers' Association; Periodical Publishers' Exchange (VP 1991-92); has supported many organizations through the magazines. DIRECTOR: CT Financial.

Torchia, Win ❧
Employment Equity Officer, RED RIVER COMMUNITY COLLEGE, 2055 Notre Dame Ave., Winnipeg, MB R3H 0J9 (204) 632-2271, FAX 694-0750. Born Winnipeg 1933. d. 3 ch. Mark Torchia, Lisa Zadro, Michelle Varteniuk. EDUC: Red River Community Coll., Certificate in Adult Educ. 1988. CAREER: various positions, CN Rail, Winnipeg, 1964-72; Office Mgr, System VP's Office, 1972-76; Coord., Women's Awareness Program, 1976-77; Teaching Master & Coord., Women's Programs, Confederation Coll., 1977-84; Consultant,

Canadian Congress for Learning Opportunities for Women, 1984; Exec. Dir., Jocelyn House Home-Care Hospice, 1985-86; Coord. & Instructor, ACT/Pre-Technology for Women, Red River Community Coll., 1986-88; Dept. Head, Women's Programs, 1988-93; Dept. Head, Bus. Educ., 1992-93; Employment Equity Officer, 1993 to date. **SELECTED PUBLICATIONS:** "Women in Technology" (*IEEE Canadian Review* Spring 1992). **AFFIL:** Manitoba Employment Equity Practitioners' Association; Coalition for the Education & Training of Women, Winnipeg; Canadian Congress for Learning Opportunities for Women. **HONS:** Woman of Distinction, Winnipeg YWCA, 1994. **INTERESTS:** tennis; racquetball; cross-country skiing; golfing; reading; gardening. **MISC:** Chair, President's Advisory Council on Women/Chair, Advisory Committee on Employment Equity/mbr., Harassment Advisory Council, Red River Community Coll.; RRCC Rep., Focus on Educ. for Women Committee, Educ. & Training, Gov't of Man., 1989 to date. **COMMENT:** *"I have tried to be a role model to other women. As I overcame my own personal tragedies, and made a successful life for myself, I shared the knowledge I had gained rebuilding my own economic independence with other women in similar situations. I realized that I had become the catalyst for them to change their lives successfully."*

Toresdahl, Susan, B.A. ■ 🎓 ♡

Executive Director, NORTH ISLAND COLLEGE FOUNDATION, 2300 Ryan Rd., Courtenay, BC V9N 8N6 (604) 334-5271, FAX 334-5292, EMAIL toresdahl@nic.bc.ca. Director of Communications and Community Liaison, NORTH ISLAND COLLEGE. Born New Westminster, B.C. 1949. d. 1 ch. **EDUC:** Open Learning Agency, B.A.(Gen. Studies); Santa Ana Coll., Assoc. of Arts (Liberal Arts); California State Coll. at Fullerton, Fine Arts 1 yr.; Univ. of Victoria, M.A.(Educ. Admin.) in progress. **CAREER:** Educ. Advisor, Camosun Coll., 1981-82; Publications/Secondary Sch. Liaison Supervisor, 1982-89; Reg. Mgr, Vancouver Island/Coast, Open Learning Agency, 1989-90; Mgr, Educ. Support Svcs, Camosun Coll., 1990-91; Dir. of Comm., North Island Coll., 1991 to date; Exec. Dir., North Island Coll. Foundation, 1994 to date. **AFFIL:** National Society of Fundraising Executives; Inform Ed (Bd.); Association of Women in Post Secondary (Bd.); Canadian Council for the Advancement of Education; Filberg Association; Comox Valley Arts Alliance (former Bd. Mbr.). **HONS:** Canada's Literary Volunteer Award. **INTERESTS:** travel; hiking; fine arts; music. **MISC:** grad., Pacific Management Development Institute. **COMMENT:** *"I am an active person and would describe myself as a doer–I rarely sit still for too long. I consider myself a self-appointed ambassador for the arts which I enjoy immensely. I am concerned with the many societal issues we face today but believe with collaboration we can address them. I think one of my greatest achievements has been the pursuit of educational degrees on a part-time basis (generally attending evenings or weekends) while working full-time in demanding career positions and being a single parent."*

Tory, Elizabeth E. ♡

Volunteer. Born Toronto 1932. m. John A. 4 ch. John H., Jennifer, Jeffrey, Michael. **EDUC:** Jarvis Collegiate Institute, 1950; Wellesley Hospital, R.N.; Canadian Securities Institute, 1976. **CAREER:** Pres., Travel Resources, 1977-83; Dir. Community Affairs, American Express, 1983-85. **AFFIL:** Sunnybrook Hospital (Bd.); Art Gallery of Ontario Foundation (Bd.); Clarke Institute (Advisory Bd.); Roy Thomson Hall (Bd.); Bayview Cancer Clinic (Bd.); Brazilian Ball, 1996 (Hon. Chair); Shaw Festival (Bd. 7 yrs; Chair, 25th Anniversary 1986); Rosedale Golf Club (Chair, 100th Anniversary 1993); Massey Hall (Chair, 100th Anniversary 1994); SkyDome (Chair, Opening Gala). **INTERESTS:** golf; fitness; bridge; art.

Tory, Martha J., B.Comm.,C.A., C.M.C. $ ♡

Partner, ERNST & YOUNG, Toronto-Dominion Centre, Box 251, Toronto, ON M5K 1J7 (416) 943-3678. Born Toronto 1954. m. William Orr. 2 ch. Graham Orr, Heather Orr. **EDUC:** Univ. of Toronto, B.Comm. 1976. **CAREER:** Ernst & Young, 1976 to date. **AFFIL:** Institute of Chartered Accountants of Ontario (C.A.); United Way of Greater Toronto (V-Chair & Treas.); St. Clements Sch. (Chair, Bd. of Trustees); Baycrest Centre for Geriatric Care (Bd.; Fin. Committee; Chair, Audit Committee); Conference of Independent Schools (Bd.); YWCA of Canada (Chair, Audit Committee); Univ. of Toronto (Chair, Chancellor's Award Selection Committee); Certified Management Consultant.

Totta, Johanne M. ■ $

Senior Vice-President, Strategy and Human Resources, NESBITT BURNS INC., 1 First Canadian Place, 14th Fl., P.O. Box 150, Toronto, ON M5X 1H3. Born Montreal 1956. m. Mario Tombari. 1 ch. **CAREER:** Mgr, Coopers and Lybrand, 1981-83; sr. mgmt positions, acctg & fin., Bank of Montreal, 1983-92; VP, Workplace Equality, 1992-94; VP, Employee Programs, 1994-95; Sr. VP, Strategy & Hum.

Res., Nesbitt Burns, 1995 to date. **AFFIL:** St. Mary's Hospital (Dir.); Carleton Univ. Sch. of Business (Advisory Bd., Centre for Research & Educ.); Canadian Women's Foundation (Dir.); Les Femmes d'affaires du Québec; Montreal Chamber of Commerce. **HONS:** Catalyst Award; Person of the Week, *La Presse*; Woman of the Year, YWCA, 1995. **MISC:** frequently interviewed & asked to speak at public policy forums, conferences & universities.

Tougas, Francine 🖿 ⍩ ⊗
Comédienne, Auteure, et Scénariste. 5081 Fabre, Montréal, QC H2J 3W3 (514) 525-6461, FAX 525-6461. Born Dorion, Qué 1952. 2 ch. Marie-Mousse Laroche, Alice Tougas St-Jacques. **EDUC:** CEGEP à Salaberry de Valleyfield, sciences humaines 1968-69; Conservatoire D'Art Dramatique de Montréal, formation de comédienne 1969-73. **SELECTED CREDITS:** écriture et interprétation d'un specta-cle-solo, *Histoires de Fantômes*, 1980; écriture et interprétation d'un spectacle-solo, *Grandir, en Hommage à ma fille*, 1982; *A Plein Temps* (ser.–16 eps.), S.D.A./Ministère de l'Éduc., Qué., 1983-88; *L'Emprise*, réalisation Michel Brault, Verseau, 1988; auteure principale, *B!Bi et Geneviève* (ser.–520 eps.), Diffusion Canal Famillie, 1989-92; *L'Odyssée Baroque*, Prod. Télémagik, 1993; *Zap II* (ser.–4 eps.), Verseau, 1994. **SELECTED PUBLICATIONS:** *Histoires de Fantômes, Grandir, L'Age D'Or* (Éditions Leméac, 1984); *Crapauds et autres animaux*, collectif (Éd. La Court Échelle, 1981); *B!Bi et Geneviève*, 11 livres (Éditions B!Bi et Geneviève, 1991-94). **HONS:** Prix ADATE (*A Plein Temps IV*), 1988; Prix ADATE (*L'Emprise*), 1989; Prix C.B.I. (pour *B.B. & Jennifer*, version anglaise de *B!Bi et Geneviève*), 1990; Prix Gémeaux, scénarisation (*Zap II*), 1995.

Toupin, Lynne, B.A.,M.Ed. ⊚
Executive Director, NATIONAL ANTI-POVERTY ORGANIZATION, 256 King Edward Ave., Ste. 316, Ottawa, ON K1N 7M1 (613) 785-0096, FAX 789-0141. Born St. Boniface, Man. 1956. cl. Aurele Theriault. 1 ch. **EDUC:** Univ. of Winnipeg, B.A.(French) 1977; Univ. of Manitoba, Certificate (Educ.) 1978; Univ. de Montréal, M.Ed.(Admin.) 1986. **CAREER:** Teacher, Man., 1978-82; Curriculum Consultant, Prov. of Man., 1983-86; Special Asst. to the Min. of Educ., 1986-88; Sch. Principal, Seine River Sch. Div., Ste. Anne, Man., 1988-90; Asst. Dir., Fédération des communautés francophones et acadienne du Canada, 1990-92; Exec. Dir., National Anti-Poverty Organization, 1992 to date. **AFFIL:** Public Interest Advocacy Centre (Dir.); Coll. St. Boniface (former VP, Bd. of

Dir.); Manitoba Special Olympics (former Volunteer Program Coord.). **COMMENT:** *"Through my work with the National Anti-Poverty Organization, I have become very interested in social policy as part of the larger public policy development. In a world now largely driven by global economics and international finance, public policy must now, more so than ever, not lose sight of keeping people at the centre of its development."*

Tovell, Rosemarie LeSueur, B.A., M.A. ⊗ ▤
Curator of Canadian Prints and Drawing, NATIONAL GALLERY OF CANADA, 380 Sussex Dr., Ottawa, ON K1N 9N4 (613) 990-1983, FAX 991-6522. Born Lima 1946. **EDUC:** Queen's Univ., B.A.(Art Hist.) 1968; Univ. of Toronto, M.A.(Art Hist.) 1972. **CAREER:** Curatorial Asst., Dept. of Prints & Drawings, National Gallery of Canada, 1972-73; Asst. Curator, 1973-82; Curator, 1982 to date. **SELECTED PUBLICATIONS:** numerous exhibition catalogues & articles, incl. *Reflections in a Quiet Pool: The Prints of David Milne*, monography & catalogue raisonné (National Gallery of Canada, 1980); *An Engraver's Pilgrimage: James Smillie Jr. in Quebec 1821-1830*, ed., memoir & catalogue raisonné, co-author Mary Allodi (Royal Ontario Museum, 1989); *Berczy*, gen. ed. (National Gallery of Canada, 1991); *A New Class of Art: the Artist's Print in Canadian Art, 1877-1920* (Ottawa: National Gallery of Canada, 1996). **EXHIBITIONS:** curator of numerous exhibitions, incl. *Reflections in a Quiet Pool: The Prints of David Milne*, National Gallery Centennial Exhibition (Ottawa, Toronto, Victoria, 1980-81); *Canada and the Graphic Arts: 1556-1963*, in cooperation with the Public Archives of Canada, National Gallery of Canada & travelling exhibition (1982-83); *Berczy*, National Gallery of Canada (1991-92); *A New Class of Art: the Artist's Print in Canadian Art, 1877-1920*, National Gallery of Canada (1996). **AFFIL:** Print Council of America; Canadian Eskimo Arts Council (appointed 1983, reappointed 1986-89). **INTERESTS:** gardening; reading; history. **MISC:** numerous lectures & seminars given.

Townsend, Joan B., B.A.,Ph.D. ▪ ⊛ ⊰ ⊹
Professor, Department of Anthropology, UNIVERSITY OF MANITOBA, Winnipeg, MB R3T 2N2 (204) 474-6328, EMAIL townsnd@ cc.umanitoba.ca. Born Dallas 1933. m. Edwin O. Anderson. 2 ch. Paula, Wayne. **EDUC:** Columbia Coll., Columbia, Mo., A.A. 1952; Univ. of California, L.A., B.A.(Anthro.) 1959, Ph.D.(Anthro.) 1965. **CAREER:** Instructor,

Evening Div., East L.A. Coll., 1962-63; Asst. Prof., Dept. of Anthro., L.A. State Coll., 1963; Instructor, Dept of Anthro., Southern Illinois Univ., 1963-64; Lecturer, Dept. of Anthro., Univ. of Manitoba, 1964-65; Asst. Prof., 1965-72; Assoc. Prof., 1972-81; Prof., 1981 to date. **SELECTED PUBLICATIONS:** *Kijik: An Historic Tanaina Settlement*, with James VanStone (Chicago: Field Museum of Natural History, 1970); "Ranked Societies of the Alaskan Pacific Rim," in *Alaskan Native Culture and History*, Y. Kotani & W. Workman, eds. (Osaka: National Museum of Ethnology (Japan), 1980); "Neo-Shamanism and the Modern Mystical Movement," in *Shaman's Path: Healing, Personal Growth and Empowerment*, Gary Doore, ed. (Boston: Shambhala, 1988); "The Goddess: Fact, Fallacy, and Revitalization Movement," in *Goddesses in Religions and Popular Debate*, Larry W. Hurtado, ed. (Atlanta: Scholars Press, 1990); "Shamanism," *Anthropology of Religion: A Handbook of Method and Theory*, ed. Stephen Glazier (Westport, Conn.: Greenwood, in press, 1996); "Shamanic Spirituality: Core Shamanism and Neo-Shamanism in Contemporary Western Society," *Selected Readings in the Anthropology of Religion*, ed. Stephen Glazier (Westport, Conn.: Greenwood, in press, 1997); numerous other publications. **EDIT:** Ed. Bd., *Culture*, 1980. **AFFIL:** American Anthropological Association (Fellow); Royal Anthropological Institute (Fellow); Arctic Institute of North America (Fellow); Society for Applied Anthropology (Fellow); *Current Anthropology* (Assoc.); American Ethnological Society; Society for the Scientific Study of Religion; Univ. of Manitoba (mbr., Senate 1978-97; Bd. of Gov. 1991-94); Phi Theta Kappa; Pi Gamma Mu; Phi Beta Kappa; Sigma Xi. **HONS:** National Defense & Educ. Act Grad. Fellowship in Archaeology (HEW, US) 1959-62; Mable Wilson Richards Grad. Scholar in Anthro., UCLA, 1959-60; La Verne Noyes Scholarship, UCLA, 1962-63; Professional Achievement Award, Columbia Coll., Columbia, Mo., 1992. **INTERESTS:** Professional: Shamanism; new religious movements; New Age spirituality; aging & spirituality; alternative healing. Personal: art; antiques; theatre; ballet; travel. **MISC:** recipient, various grants; various conference presentations.

Trahan, Anne-Marie, B.A.,LL.L.,Q.C., J.C.S. ⚖ ✋

Judge, SUPERIOR COURT OF QUEBEC, Court House, 1 Notre-Dame St. E., Montréal, QC H2Y 1B6 (514) 393-2193, FAX 393-2773. Born Montréal 1946. s. **EDUC:** Coll. Marie-de-France, Univ. de Caën, B.A. 1964; Univ. of Montreal, LL.L. 1967. **BAR:** Qué., 1968. **CAREER:** practice of law, Lavery, De Billy, 1968-79; Legal Officer, Office of Legal Affairs (Int'l Trade Law Branch), U.N., Vienna, Austria, 1979-81; Commissioner, Cdn Transport Commission, 1981-86; Assoc. Deputy Min., Civil Law & Legislative Svcs, Dept. of Justice of Canada, 1986-94; Judge, Superior Court of Québec, 1994 to date. **SELECTED PUBLICATIONS:** "L'arbitrage dans le contrat clé en main au Canada" (*Revue juridique et politique-indépendence et coopération* 1988); "A Bijuridical and Bilingual Canada on the World Stage" (*Language and Society* Fall 1991). **AFFIL:** Conférence Canadienne des juges; Canadian Chapter of the International Association of Women Judges (Dir.); Unidroit (Gov.); La Fondation du Barreau du Québec (Dir. & Exec. Mbr.); International Bar Association; Young Lawyers' International Association (Pres. 1977-78); International Law Association (Pres., Ottawa Section 1993-94); International Union of Lawyers; Association internationale de droit pénal; International Commission of Jurists; Canadian Institute for the Administration of Justice; Canadian Council on International Law; Centre de recherche en droit public de l'Univ. de Montréal (Dir.); Centre international de la common law en français (Comité de patronage); Canadian Institute for Advanced Legal Studies (Dir.); Canadian Bar Association; University Women's Clubs of Montreal; Women's Centre of Montreal (Sponsor); Canadian Centre for Oecumenism (Dir.); Cercle de droit européen de la Chaire Jean Monnet (Pres.). **HONS:** Great Montrealer of the Future in the Field of Law, 1983; Queen's Counsel, 1983; Certificat de reconnaissance du succès et du rayonnement, Alumnae of the Univ. of Montreal, 1992; Mérite collectif, Barreau du Québec, 1993; Canada 125 Medal. **INTERESTS:** reading; music; opera; travelling. **MISC:** organizer of the celebration of the 50th anniversary of the law allowing women to become members of the Que. Bar, Apr. 29th, 1991; 1st woman Pres., Young Lawyers' International Association; appointed as 1 of 2 Cdn members to the dispute settlement mechanism, Conference on Security & Co-operation in Europe, 1993. **COMMENT:** *"A hard-working and dedicated woman who enjoys life and likes people. She has had a successful career in the field of law and public administration–locally, nationally and internationally."*

Trebuss, A. Susanna, B.Comm. ■ $

Vice-President and General Manager, PEERLESS HOME PRODUCTS, 405 Britannia Rd. E., Ste. 212, Mississauga, ON L4Z 3E6 (905) 712-3030, FAX 712-1330. Born Regina, Sask. 1951. s. **EDUC:** Queen's Univ., B.Comm.

1973. **CAREER:** Mktg Cont., Anglophoto Limited, 1973-76; Research Assoc., Conference Board of Canada, 1976-80; Mgr, Corp. Rel'ns, American Can of Canada Ltd., 1980-83; Mgr, Mktg Svcs & Planning, Carborundum Abrasives Inc., 1983-86; Nat'l Mktg Mgr, Deloitte Haskins & Sells, 1986-87; VP, Mktg, Delta Faucet Canada, 1987-90; VP & Gen. Mgr, Peerless Home Products, 1990 to date; VP, Mktg Oper., Masco Canada, 1995 to date. **SELECTED PUBLICATIONS:** "The Marketing Controller: Financial Support to the Marketing Function" (*The Canadian Business Review* 1976); "Organizing for the Marketing/Finance Interface" *The New Role of the Marketing Professional* (Chicago: American Marketing Association, 1977); *Improving Corporate Effectiveness: Managing the Marketing/Finance Interface* (Ottawa: The Conference Board of Canada, 1978); *Effective Marketing Planning: An Overview* (Ottawa: The Conference Board of Canada, 1978); *Defining the Strategic Environment: An Analysis of Organizational Perspectives* (Ottawa: The Conference Board of Canada, 1981). **AFFIL:** Canadian Hardware & Housewares Manufacturers' Association (Dir.; 1st VP 1993-94; Chrm 1994-95); Elizabeth Fry Society (Women in Transition Bus. Advisory Council 1991); Carousel Players (Dir. 1984-85); United Way of Toronto (various exec. positions). **INTERESTS:** golf; gardening. **COMMENT:** *"Development of business career from research, through functional management, to general management."*

Tremblay, Kay 🎞 📺 🎭

Actor. c/o The Characters, 150 Carlton St., Toronto, ON M5A 2K1 (416) 864-8522, FAX 964-8206. Born UK. **EDUC:** Manchester Univ., Dept. of Drama; RADA; elocution with Ryder Bhoys. **CAREER:** 1st professional appearance was with the George Balanchine Ballet, Theatre Royal, Drury Lane, London, UK; played major variety theatres in UK & toured major cities in Europe with dance act; moved to Canada in 1954; actor, Montreal Repertory Theatre, 1954-59; actor with La Poudrière theatre company & Studio Theatre; 3 summer seasons with the North Hatley Playhouse; leading & supporting roles in early TV productions, radio serials & coast-to-coast drama specials for Shoestring Theatre, Tele-Play & Tele-Theatre, CBC, 1958-73; from 1964 was a feature player in historical & documentary films, National Film Board of Canada & a leading player in Instant Theatre Productions of Half-Hour Plays at Lunchtime, Montreal; returned to UK in 1973; performed continuing roles in 3 TV series, *The Phoenix and the Carpet* (BBC), *Thomas and Sarah* (L.W.T.) & *The Chiffy Kids* (Children's Film Foundation); repertory work at the Northampton & Salisbury Theatres, 1973-78; returned to Canada, 1978; actor, Sudbury Theatre, 1979, 1981; actor, Grand Theatre, Kingston, 1982; actor, Grand Theatre (under the dir. of Robin Phillips), London, Ont., 1983; actor, Festival Theatre, Stratford, 1989; numerous TV & film appearences, 1985 to date; numerous industrial, & radio & TV commercial credits. **SELECTED CREDITS:** numerous TV & film credits incl. various roles & eps. (incl. "Mother's Day," "Dead Ringers" & "Set for Life") *Night Heat* (series); various roles & eps., *Friday the 13th* (series); series regular as Iris, *Dog House*; series regular as Great Aunt Eliza, *The Road to Avonlea*, CBC; Daphne, "The Last Demise of Julian Whittaker," *Inside Stories* (series); *Traders*; Mrs. Wreidt, *Mackenzie King* (TV docudrama), dir. Donald Brittain, CBC; Sophie, supporting lead, *Shadowdancing* (telefilm); featured performer, *Remember Me* (telefilm); voice character incl. Grannie Goose, *Rupert the Bear* (animated series); voice character, *The X-Men* (animated series); voice character, *The Thief of Always* (animated feature); numerous theatre credits at the Sudbury Theatre, Grand Theatre (London), Grand Theatre (Kingston) & Festival Theatre (Stratford); additional theatre credits include *The Effect of Gamma Rays on Man in the Moon Marigolds* (with Dawn Greenhalgh, Samantha & Megan Follows), YPT, Toronto, & Mrs. Higgins in *Pygmalion*, Meadowbrook Theatre, Univ. of Michigan. **AFFIL:** ACTRA; AEA; CAEA; British Equity. **MISC:** acted in the 1st & last episodes of *Night Heat*; was a mbr. of Robin Phillips' inaugural season at The Grand Theatre.

Tremblay, Louise, C.A. $ 📺

Senior Vice-President, Resources, CANADIAN BROADCASTING CORPORATION, 1500 Bronson Ave., P.O. Box 8478, Ottawa, ON K1G 3J5 (613) 738-6528, FAX 738-6567. Born Laval, Que. 1954. m. Robert E. Lockwood. **EDUC:** École des Hautes Études Commerciales, Bac. ès Sciences 1978. **CAREER:** Dir. of Fin. & Admin., CANCOM, 1984-87; VP, Fin. & Admin., 1987-90; CFO, 1990-93; COO, 1993-94; Sr. VP, Resources, Canadian Broadcasting Corporation, 1994 to date. **AFFIL:** Canadian Women in Communications (Dir.); Univ. of Guelph (Dir.); Canadian Institute of Chartered Accountants (C.A.). **HONS:** Certificate for Outstanding Contribution, Canadian Users' Association.

Tremblay, Suzanne, M.A.,M.P. 🍁

Member of Parliament (Rimouski-Témiscouata), GOVERNMENT OF CANADA, House of Commons, Wellington Building, Office 253, Ottawa, ON K1A 0A6 (613) 992-5302, FAX 992-8298. Born Montréal 1937. **EDUC:** Univ. de Montréal, Baccalauréat (Pédagogie familiale); Univ. Laval, Baccalauréat (Pédagogie préscolaire); Tufts Univ., M.A.(Presch. Educ.); Univ. de Lyon, Certificat (Études pédagogique); Univ. of London, Certificate (Child Educ.). **CAREER:** Prof. de pédagogie préscolaire et primaire, Univ. Laval, 1961-70; Prof. de pédagogie préscolaire et primaire, Univ. du Québec à Rimouski, 1970 to date; MP (Rimouski-Témiscouata), House of Commons, 1993 to date; Porte-parole de l'Opposition officielle en matière de Patrimoine canadien, House of Commons, 1993-96; Leader-adjointe de l'opposition officielle, mbr. de la Commission politique et de la Commission électorale, 1996 to date; Porte-parole de l'Opposition officielle en matiére de Recherche et Dév., 1996 to date. **AFFIL:** Association d'éducation préscolaire (membre d'honneur); Association québécoise universitaire en formation des maîtres; Bloc Québécois.

Tremblay, Virve, B.A.,C.A.A.P. ■ $ ⚛ 📺

Director of Communications, NCR CANADA LTD, 320 Front St. W., Toronto, ON M5V 3C4 (416) 351-2101, FAX 251-2006. Born Helsinki, Finland 1952. m. Guy A. Tremblay. 1 ch. Chris. **EDUC:** Sheridan Coll., Dipl.(Library Techniques) 1975; Univ. of Toronto, B.A.(English) 1986; Institute of Canadian Advertising, C.A.A.P.(Advtg) 1993. **CAREER:** Mktg Librarian, NCR Canada, 1975-81; Mgr of Advtg & Mgr of Public Rel'ns, 1981-93; Dir. of Comm., AT&T Global Information Solutions, 1993-96; Dir. of Comm., NCR Canada Ltd, 1996 to date. **AFFIL:** Ontario Chamber of Commerce (Dir.); Toronto Outdoor Art Exhibition (Dir.); International Association of Business Communicators. **HONS:** Silver Medal, Sheridan Coll. Bd. of Gov., 1975; Bruce F. Johnston Award, Institute of Canadian Advertising, 1993; Gold Medal, Institute of Canadian Advertising, 1993. **INTERESTS:** art; antiques. **COMMENT:** *"Represents more than 10 years of senior management experience in the strategic planning and execution of a wide variety of public relations, advertising, and communications programs."*

Trenholme, Hon. Marilyn, B.Sc.,M.A., M.D. ■ 🍁 ⊕ ☝

Minister of State for Family and Community Services, GOVERNMENT OF NEW BRUNSWICK, P.O. Box 5100, Fredericton, NB E3B 5G8 (506) 444-5390, FAX 444-5243. Born Sackville, N.B. 1933. w. Kenneth Counsell. 2 ch. Giles Counsell, Lorna Counsell. **EDUC:** Mount Allison Univ., B.Sc.(Home Econ.) 1954; Univ. of Toronto, M.A.(Nutrition) 1960, M.D. 1967. **CAREER:** nutritionist, N.B. & Ont. Depts. of Health, 1955-58, 1960-63; family physician, Toronto, Ont., & Sackville, N.B., 1968-94; M.L.A., Prov. of N.B., 1987 to date; Min. of State for Family & Community Svcs, 1994 to date. **AFFIL:** I.O.D.E.; Canadian Parents for French; Order of the Eastern Star; University Women's Club; Alpha Omega Alpha. **INTERESTS:** family life; skiing; cooking; reading. **COMMENT:** *"October 26, 1994, I was appointed to the New Brunswick Cabinet by Premier Frank McKenna, as Canada's only Minister of State for the Family, to head a new Family Policy Secretariat. All the events in my life have come together with this exciting new challenge."*

Trethewey, Sharon ■■ $

Vice-President, Retail Lending, NATIONAL TRUST (financial institution), One Financial Place, 1 Adelaide St. E., Toronto, ON M5C 2W8 (416) 361-4155, FAX 361-5551. Born Toronto 1959. d. 1 ch. Emilie. **EDUC:** Centennial Coll., Diploma (Bus. Admin.); York Univ., Exec. Program. **CAREER:** various retail lending branch positions to Product Mgr & various other head office mktg & training positions, Scotiabank, 1980-90; Asst. VP, Retail Lending, Confederation Trust, 1990-92. **AFFIL:** Heart & Stroke Foundations.

Trotter, Kate, B.A. ✪ 🎭 $

Actor, Director and Speech Consultant. c/o Oscars and Abrams, 59 Berkeley St., Toronto, ON M5A 2W5 (416) 860-1790, FAX 860-0236. Born Toronto 1953. s. 1 ch. Kathleen. **EDUC:** Brock Univ., B.A.(English/Psych.) 1975; National Theatre Sch. of Canada, Performance 1975-78. **SELECTED CREDITS:** Trudy Kelly, *Traders* (series), Atlantis; Romi, *Golden Will, The Silken Laumann Story*, Carol Renolds; recurring: Captain Simms, *Kung Fu: The Legend Continues* (series), Warner Bros; Mrs. Novack, *Family of Cops*, CBS; guest star, *Tek-War* (series), Cardigan Prod.; principal, *Due South* (series), CBS; Dir., *The Tomorrow Box* (theatre), Blyth Summer Festival; Klara, "Strauss", *Composers Series*, Family Channel; Phyllis, *Bloodknot* (telefilm), Showtime; Jennifer Mateo, "House of Caduceus," *Side Effects* (series), CBC; principal, *Street Legal*, CBC; lead, *Clarence* (feature), Atlantis; guest star, "Traitors All," *E.N.G.* (series), Alliance; lead, *First Season* (feature), Orange Prod.; guest star, "Hunted," *Alfred Hitchcock Presents* (series), Global; Edith Roach, *Glory Enough For All* (telefilm), Gemstone Prod.; Jane, *Joshua Then* *and Now* (feature), RSL; Kate, "Kate Morris - Vice President," *For the Record*, CBC; Suzanne, *Les Plouffes* (feature), Cini-London; lead, *Entry in a Diary*, Entropy Pictures Ltd.; dir., *David* (short film), N.F.B.; Maggie, *Dancing at Lughnasa* (theatre), Grand Theatre; Diana, *The Stillborn Lover* (theatre), Grand Theatre; Alma, *Summer & Smoke* (theatre), Theatre Plus; Laura, *The Father* (theatre), Tarragon Theatre; Ann Whitfield, *Man & Superman* (theatre), Shaw Festival; Linda, *Holiday* (theatre), Shaw Festival; Marie, *Translations* (theatre), Stratford; Annie, *The Real Thing* (theatre), Royal Alexandra Theatre, Toronto & Theatre Calgary; Juliet, *Romeo & Juliet* (theatre), Dream in the Park; Marlene, *Top Girls* (theatre), Tarragon Theatre; Sarah, *Translations* (theatre), TFT; Katie, *Quiet in the Land* (theatre), Blyth Festival; Miranda, *The Tempest* (theatre), Theatre Calgary; Olivia, *Twelfth Night* (theatre), Theatre New Brunswick & the Bastion Theatre, Victoria; Lady Capulet, *Romeo and Juliet* (theatre), Stratford; various narrations, radio dramas & public readings. **AFFIL:** ACTRA; EQUITY. **HONS:** Best Actress in a Featured Role (*Translations*), Dora Mavor Moore Award, 1983; nomination, Best Actress (*Alfred Hitchcock Presents*), Cable ACE Award, 1988; nomination, Best Actress in a Leading Role (*The Father*), Dora Mavor Moore Award, 1992; nomination, Best Actress in a Leading Role (*Top Girls*), Dora Mavor Moore Award, 1984; nomination, Best Actress in a Leading Role (*Summer & Smoke*), Dora Mavor Moore Award, 1992; recipient, Guthrie Scholarship, 1975. **INTERESTS:** photography; reading; sewing; gardening; people; films; theatre. **COMMENT:** *"Born and raised on a farm north of Toronto, I have made a successful career in the arts. Working mainly as an actress (theatre, film and television), I have an interest in directing and have developed projects with the N.F.B. in Montreal. I also have a company that specializes in corporate speech delivery."*

Trow, Susan, B.A. ☒ ⊗
Cinematographer, NATIONAL FILM BOARD OF CANADA, 3155 Côte de Liesse, Ville St. Laurent, QC H4N 2N4 (514) 283-9567, FAX 283-5487. **EDUC:** Univ. of Guelph, B.A.(Fine Arts) 1970; Ryerson Polytechnical Institute, Dipl. (Photo Arts) 1973. **CAREER:** Researcher & Photographer, Camera Asst., Cinematographer, Assoc. Dir., National Film Bd.; Head, English Camera Dept., 1987-90. **SELECTED CREDITS:** Camera Operator,*The King Chronicles*, dir. Donald Brittain; Camera Operator,*The First Emperor of China*, Imax/Omnimax; Cinematographer: *If You Love This Planet; Behind the Veil: Nuns; Abortion: Stories from North*

and South; On Guard for Thee, dir. Donald Brittain; *Goddess Remembered; Burning Times; Full Circle; The Greenpeace Years*, prod. Michael Maclear; *Before Columbus*, prod. NFB/Central Television; "Rural Teacher," "Springhill Miner," "Inukshuk," *Heritage Minutes*, prod. C.R.B. Foundation/NFB; Dir./Cinematographer, *Creatures of the Sun*.

Trudel, Judith Lucille, B.Sc.,M.D.,F.R.C.S.C., F.A.C.S. ⊕ ⌑
Associate Surgeon and Director, "M" Surgical Unit Teaching Unit, Department of Surgery, MONTREAL GENERAL HOSPITAL, 1650 Cedar Ave., Montreal, QC H3G 1A4 (514) 937-6011, ext. 4337, FAX 934-8210. Assistant Surgeon, Department of Surgery, ROYAL VICTORIA HOSPITAL., Assistant Professor, Department of Surgery and Assistant Professor, Department of Oncology, McGILL UNIVERSITY. Born Montreal 1957. **EDUC:** Petit Séminaire de Québec, D.E.C. 1974; Laval Univ., B.Sc.(Health Sciences) 1978, M.D. 1979; McGill Univ., M.Sc.(Experimental Surgery) 1985. **CAREER:** mixed internship, Montreal General Hospital, McGill Univ., 1979-80; gen. surgery residency, 1980-84; Special Clinical Fellowship & Chief Resident, Dept. of Colorectal Surgery, The Cleveland Clinic Foundation, 1985-86; Clinical Fellow, 1986-87; Visiting Instructor, Dept. of Surgery, Univ. of Texas Medical Branch, 1987-88; Asst. Surgeon, Dept. of Surgery, Montreal General Hospital, 1988-92; Asst. Prof., Dept. of Surgery, McGill Univ., 1988 to date; Asst. Prof., Dept. of Oncology, 1992 to date; Dir., "M" Surgical Teaching Unit, Dept. of Surgery, 1991 to date; Assoc. Surgeon, Dept. of Surgery, Montreal General Hospital, 1992 to date; Asst. Surgeon, Dept. of Surgery, Royal Victoria Hospital, 1995 to date. **SELECTED PUBLICATIONS:** "The Fat/Fiber Antagonism in Experimental Colon Carcinogenesis," with M.L. Senterman & R.A. Brown (*Surgery* 94(4) 1983); "Progression toward Malignancy of Hamartomas in a Patient with Peutz-Jeghers Syndrome: Case report and review of the literature," with H. Flageole, S. Raptis & J. Lough (*Canadian Journal of Surgery* 37(3) 1994); "Application of the Polymerase Chain Reaction to Study Phenotype Expression in an in vitro Model of Colonic Tumour Cell Differentiation," with J. Faria & G.E. Wild (*Surgical Forum* 45 1994); various other publications. **AFFIL:** Royal Coll. of Physicians & Surgeons of Canada (Fellow); American Coll. of Surgeons (Fellow); Crohn's & Colitis Foundation of Canada (Nat'l Medical Advisory Bd.); National Cancer Institute of Canada (GI Site Committee–Clinical Trials Group); American Society of Colon & Rectal Surgeons (Self-

Assessment Committee); Canadian Society of Colon & Rectal Surgeons (Sec.-Treas.); American Medical Association; American Society for Gastrointestinal Endoscopy; Association for Academic Surgery; Association des Médecins de Langue Française du Canada; Association Médicale Canadienne; Association Médicale du Québec; Association for Surgical Education; Canadian Association for University (Clinical) Surgeons; Canadian Association of General Surgeons; Canadian Royal Coll. of Surgeons (Fellow); Cleveland Academy of Medicine; Cleveland Clinic Foundation Alumni Association; Cleveland Clinic Surgical Society; Corporation Professionnelle des Médecins Spécialistes du Québec; Fédération des Médecins Spécialists du Québec; Ohio State Medical Association; Quebec Association of General Surgeons; Society of American Gastrointestinal Endoscopic Surgeons; Society of Surgical Oncology, James Ewing Society (Fellow); The Graduates' Society of McGill Univ. **MISC:** various grants & fellowships; reviewer for various journals & granting agencies; various conference presentations; examiner for the Royal Coll. of Physicians & Surgeons of Canada.

Trumper, Gillian, R.N. ✿ ♂
Mayor, CITY OF PORT ALBERNI, 4850 Argyle St., Port Alberni, BC V9Y 5G7 (604) 723-2146, FAX 723-1003. Born Croydon, UK 1936. m. Michael. 4 ch. Owen, Carolyn, Michael, Trish. **EDUC:** Westminster Hospital, London, UK, British Registered Nurse 1957. **CAREER:** Trustee, Alberni Clayoquot Sch. District, 1973-81; Bd. Mbr., North Island Coll., 1976-81; City Councillor, Port Alberni, 1981-83; Coroner, Alberni Reg., 1982 to date; Mayor, City of Port Alberni, 1983 to date. **AFFIL:** Clayoquot Sound Task Force (Past Mbr.); Clayoquot Sound Steering Committee (Past Mbr.); Prov. Round Table on the Environment; Union of B.C. Municipalities (1st VP); Vancouver Island C.O.R.E. **MISC:** 1st woman mayor of the city of Port Alberni. **COMMENT:** *"Gillian Trumper moved to Port Alberni in 1969. She is a registered nurse by profession and has been very active in the Alberni Valley community, in B.C. and on the federal scene."*

Truss, Jan 📖 📚 ♂
Writer. Water Valley, AB T0M 2E0 (403) 637-2618, FAX 637-2618. Born UK 1925. w. Donald. 2 ch. **CAREER:** teacher, sch. & univ., 1945-70; writer, 1970 to date. **SELECTED PUBLICATIONS:** *Bird at the Window*, novel; *Jasmin*, novel for children; *A Very Small Rebellion*, novel; *Summer Goes Riding*, novel; *Red*, novel. **AFFIL:** The Writers' Union of Canada. **HONS:** winner, 1st Alberta Search for New

Novelist Award, 1974; Ruth Schwartz Award for Children's Lit., 1983. **INTERESTS:** the fine art of living; opera; politics; religions; philosophy; the wilderness; teenagers; the criminal mind. **COMMENT:** *"In my heaven there will be no head table."*

Trussler, Mme. Justice Marguerite, B.A., LL.B.,LL.M. ■ 🔾
Justice, COURT OF QUEEN'S BENCH OF ALBERTA, Law Courts, 1A Sir Winston Churchill Sq., Edmonton, AB T5J 0R2. Born Edmonton 1946. m. Sir Francis Price, Bt., Q.C. 3 ch. **EDUC:** Univ. of Alberta, B.A. 1969, LL.B. 1970; Univ. of Melbourne, LL.M. 1974. **BAR:** Alta., 1971; State of Victoria, Australia, 1972. **CAREER:** articled to the Hon. S. Bruce Smith, Chief Justice of Alberta & H.L. Irving, Q.C.; Lecturer, Univ. of Melbourne, 1972-73; Sessional Lecturer, Fac. of Law, Univ. of Alberta, 1975-77; Ptnr, Parlee McLaws, 1976-86; Lawyer-in-Residence, Fac. of Law, Univ. of Alberta, 1983; Justice, Court of Queen's Bench of Alberta, 1986 to date. **SELECTED PUBLICATIONS:** *Mortgage Actions in Alberta*, with F.C.R. Price (Carswell, 1985); "Foreclosure of Corporate Mortgages" (*Alberta Law Review* 21); "Foreclosure of Corporate Mortgages: Update 1984" (*Alberta Law Review* 23). **EDIT:** Ed. Bd., *Canadian Bar Review.* **AFFIL:** Canadian Bar Association; Provincial AIDS Advisory Committee (Chair); Anglican Diocese of Edmonton (Chair, Church Dev. Trust); Johann Strauss Foundation; Fac. Club, Univ. of Alberta; Centre Club. **MISC:** Visitor, Fac. of Sci., Univ. of Alberta (1992, 1993, 1995).

Tryon, Valerie, FRAM 🎵 🖋
Concert Pianist, Artist in Residence, Department of Music, MCMASTER UNIVERSITY, 1280 Main St. W., Hamilton, ON L8S 4N2 (905) 525-9140, ext. 4259. **CAREER:** solo performances throughout Canada, UK, France, Belgium, Switzerland, Hungary, S. Africa & US; recitals in Royal Festival Hall, UK, Royal Albert Hall, UK, Aldeburgh Festival, UK, Library of Congress, US; performances with numerous orchestras incl. The London Philharmonic, UK, The Toronto Symphony Orchestra, & The Massachusetts Institute of Technology Orchestra, US; pianist in the "Rembrandt Trio"; Artist-in-Residence, McMaster Univ. **SELECTED CREDITS:** *Valerie Tryon in Public Concert*, CBC; *Valerie Tryon with Suzanne Shulman (Flute) Prokofiev and Glick*, CBC; "These You Have Loved," BBC Enterprises; *Valerie Tryon plays Richard Baker's most requested pieces*, Omnibus Records & Tapes; *Joy of Piano* (Chopin Scherzo's and Ballads), CBC, 1996; various other recordings. **AFFIL:**

Royal Academy of Music (Fellow). **HONS:** Dove Award, 1955; Harriet Cohen Int'l Music Award, 1967; Franz Liszt Medal, Hungarian Ministry of Culture, 1986; Juno Award, 1994. **MISC:** adjudicator, Bach Int'l Competition; adjudicator, Maryland Festival Int'l Competitions; listed in *Encyclopedia of Music in Canada* & *Who's Who in Music.*

Tsang, Tosha ■■ ⚾

Olympic Athlete. c/o Canadian Olympic Association. Born Saskatoon 1970. **SPORTS CAREER:** full-time athlete; mbr., Cdn Nat'l Rowing Team, 1995 to date. Olympic Games: Silver, 8+, 1996. World championships: 6th, 8+, 1995. Int'l regattas: 3rd, 2- (Ont.), 1994. Canadian championships: 1st, 4-, & 2nd, 2-, 1994; 1st, 2x, & 1st, 2-, 1993. US championships: 2nd, 8+, & 5th, 2-, 1995. **INTERESTS:** reading; crossword puzzles; cycling; photography.

Tuffin, Jacqueline ■ $

Vice-President, Personal Financial Services, Toronto Core, ROYAL BANK OF CANADA, 20 King St. W., 11th Fl., Toronto, ON M5H 1C4 (416) 974-6617. Born Dryden, Ont. 1947. m. George. **EDUC:** Grad. Sch. of Credit & Fin. Mgmt, Dartmouth Coll., grad.; Centre of Creative Leadership, Hartford, Conn., grad. **CAREER:** held positions of increasing responsibility, Ont. & Que., Royal Bank of Canada, 1968-82; Mgr, Retail Lending, Metro Toronto, 1982-85; Reg'l Mgr, Scarborough, 1985-87; Area Mgr, North York E., 1987-91; VP & Area Mgr, Toronto Downtown Core, 1991-93; VP, N.S. & P.E.I., 1993-95; VP, Personal Fin. Svcs, Toronto Core, 1995 to date. **AFFIL:** The Doctors Hospital (Dir.); Interlink Community Cancer Nurses (Dir.); The Granite Club; Board of Trade of Metropolitan Toronto; The Canadian Club.

Tulving, Ruth, R.C.A. 🎨

Painter and Printmaker. 45 Baby Point Cres., Toronto, ON M6S 2B7 (416) 763-2777. Born Estonia. **EDUC:** Ontario Coll. of Art, grad. 1962. **CAREER:** instructor in painting & printmaking, Ontario Coll. of Art, 1965-73; painter & printmaker, 1973 to date. **EXHIBITIONS:** solo exhibitions in Canada, US, France, UK, Sweden, Estonia & China. **AFFIL:** Ontario Society of Artists (Pres. 1983-84); Royal Canadian Academy of Arts (elected 1977). **HONS:** award, National Academy of Design, US, 1966; many other awards & prizes.

Tumasonis, Elizabeth, B.A.,M.A., Ph.D. 🎓 📜 🎨

Associate Professor, Department of History in Art, UNIVERSITY OF VICTORIA, P.O. Box 1700, Victoria, BC V8W 2Y2 (604) 721-7951, FAX 721-7941. Born Charleston, W. Virginia 1941. m. Rimas P. Tumasonis. **EDUC:** Coll. of William & Mary, B.A.(Fine Arts) 1963; New York Univ., M.A.(Art Hist.) 1967; Univ. of California at Berkeley, Ph.D.(Art Hist.) 1979. **CAREER:** Instructor, Dept. of Art Hist. & Archaeology, Univ. of Missouri, 1966-67; Instructor, Dept. of Art, DePauw Univ., 1967-69; Instructor, Dept. of Art, Indiana Univ., 1967-69; Teaching Assoc., Dept. of Hist. of Art, Univ. of California at Berkeley, 1969-72; Instructor, Dept. of Art, Univ. of Southern California, 1973-75; Visiting Asst. Prof., Dept. of Art, Univ. of New Mexico, 1977-78; Asst. Prof., Dept. of Art Hist., California State Univ., 1978-81; Lecturer, Dept. of Art, Univ. of California at Irvine, 1980; Asst. Prof., Dept. of Hist. in Art, Univ. of Victoria, 1981-91; Visiting Asst. Prof., Dept. of Hist. of Art, Univ. of California at Berkeley, 1984; Chair, Dept. of Hist. in Art, Univ. of Victoria, 1991-94; Assoc. Prof., Dept. of Hist. in Art, 1991 to date. **SELECTED PUBLICATIONS:** "The Image of the Centaur in the Painting of Arnold Böcklin" (*New Mexico Studies in the Fine Arts* 1978); 18 entries for *Academic American Encyclopedia* (Princeton, NJ: 1981); *Böcklin and Wagner: The Dragon Slain* (Pantheon: Internationale Jahreszeitschrift für Kunst 1986); "The Piper Among the Ruins: The Image of the God Pan in the Painting of Arnold Böcklin" (*RACAR: Canadian Art Review* Sept. 1991); "Böcklin's Reputation: Its Rise and Fall" (*Art Criticism* 2 1990); "Bernhard Hoetger's Tree of Life: German Expressionism and Racial Ideology" (*Art Journal* Spring 1992); "Max Klinger's Christ on Olympus: The Confrontation between Christianity and Paganism" (*RACAR: The Canadian Art Review* Jan. 1995). **AFFIL:** College Art Association; University Art Association of Canada; German Studies Association; Victoria Horticultural Society. **HONS:** Award for Excellence in Teaching, Univ. of Victoria Alumni, 1989; Teaching Fellowship, 3-M, 1992. **INTERESTS:** gardening; bird-watching; dog-walking; cooking. **MISC:** grant, Samuel H. Kress Foundation, 1975-76; research grant, Social Sciences & Humanities Research Council, 1995-97. **COMMENT:** *"An art historian with specialization in modern art and particular research interests in 19th and 20th century German art. Has won several teaching awards due to ability to convey material clearly and with enthusiasm."*

Tung, Rosalie L., B.A.,M.B.A., Ph.D. ■👍 🎓 $ 👍

The Ming and Stella Wong Professor of International Business, Faculty of Business, SIMON FRASER UNIVERSITY, Burnaby, BC V5A 1S6 (604) 291-3083, FAX 291-4920, EMAIL rosalie_tung@sfu.ca. Born Shanghai 1948. m. Byron. 1 ch. **EDUC:** York Univ., B.A.(Hist.) 1972; Univ. of British Columbia, M.B.A. 1974, Ph.D. 1977. **CAREER:** Asst. Prof., Univ. of Oregon, 1977-80; Foreign Expert, Foreign Investment Commission, China, 1980; Visiting Scholar, Univ. of Manchester, Sci. & Technology, 1980; Visiting Asst. Prof., Univ. of California, 1981; Assoc. Prof., Wharton Sch., Univ. of Pennsylvania, 1981-86; Dir., Int'l Bus. Centre, Univ. of Wisconsin, 1986-90; Full Prof., Univ. of Wisconsin-Milwaukee, 1986-90; Visiting Prof., Harvard Univ., 1988; Wisconsin Distinguished Prof., Univ. of Wisconsin, 1988-90; The Ming & Stella Wong Prof. of Int'l Bus., Simon Fraser Univ., 1991 to date. **SELECTED PUBLICATIONS:** *Chinese Industrial Society after Mao* (Lexington, Mass.: Lexington Books, D.C. Heath, 1982); *Key to Japan's Economic Strength: Human Power* (Lexington, Mass.: Lexington Books, D.C. Heath, 1984); *The New Expatriates: Managing Human Resources Abroad* (Cambridge, Mass.: Ballinger Publisher, 1988); "Comparative Analysis of the Occupational Stress Profiles of Male versus Female Administrators" (*Journal of Vocational Behaviour* vol.17 Dec. 1980); "Expatriate Assignments: Enhancing Success and Minimizing Failure" (*Academy of Management Executive* vol.1 no.2 1987); "Strategic Management Thought in East Asia" (*Organizational Dynamics* Spring 1994); 8 books & more than 40 articles in total. **EDIT:** Ed., "Chinese Economic and Management System Reforms" special issue, *International Journal of Human Resource Management* 3(4), 1994; mbr., ed. bds., various academic journals. **AFFIL:** Academy of Management; Academy of International Business; National Academy of Management. **HONS:** Seagram Bus. Fellowship, Type B, 1974-75; Univ. of British Columbia Grad. Fellowship, 1974-75; Oppenheimer Brothers Fellowship, 1973-74; York Univ. In-course Scholarship, 1970-71; Outstanding Prof. of the Year Award, Univ. of Pennsylvania, Wharton School's Sigma Kappa Phi Honor Society, 1986; H.R. MacMillan Family Fellowship, 1975-76, 1976-77; Univ. of British Columbia 75th Anniversary Award, 1990; Leonore Rowe Williams Award, Univ. of Pennsylvania, 1990. **INTERESTS:** creative writing; fashion designing. **MISC:** 1st endowed chair prof., Fac. of Bus. Admin., Simon Fraser Univ.; numerous conference presentations; listed in many biographical sources incl. *Who's Who in Finance and Industry*, *International Who's Who of Intellectuals*, *Who's Who in America* & *World Who's Who of Women*. **COMMENT:** *"I have always wanted to break the race and gender barriers by succeeding in a predominantly male and white profession. I feel I have succeeded in this goal, to a large extent, by winning a Wisconsin Distinguished Professorship and through appointment as the first endowed chair professor at the Simon Fraser University Faculty of Business Administration."*

Tuohy, Carolyn Hughes, B.A.,M.A., Ph.D. 🎓 🍁

Professor of Political Science and Deputy Provost, UNIVERSITY OF TORONTO, 27 King's College Circle, Toronto, ON M5S 1A1 (416) 978-2181, FAX 978-3939. Born Toronto 1945. m. Walter. 2 ch. Laura C., Kevin J. **EDUC:** Univ. of Toronto, B.A.(Soc.) 1966; Yale Univ., M.A.(Pol. Sci.) 1968, Ph.D.(Pol. Sci.) 1974. **CAREER:** Asst. Prof., Univ. of Toronto, 1970-76; Assoc. Prof., 1976-88; Prof., 1988 to date; V-Provost, 1992-94; Deputy Provost, 1994 to date. **SELECTED PUBLICATIONS:** *Policy and Politics in Canada: Institutionalized Ambivalence* (Philadelphia: Temple Univ. Press, 1992); numerous journal articles & chapters on health policy & social policy. **AFFIL:** Toronto Hospital Research Institute (Dir. 1994-95); Canadian Political Science Association (Dir. 1986-88); Sunnybrook Health Science Centre (Bd. of Trustees); Ontario Council on University Affairs (Academic Advisory Committee 1991-96); Massey Coll. (Sr. Fellow). **COMMENT:** *"Carolyn Tuohy is a Professor of Political Science at the University of Toronto. Her area of research and teaching interest is comparative public policy, with an emphasis on social policy."*

Tupholme, Iris, B.A. 📖 $

Publisher and Editor-in-Chief, HARPERCOLLINS PUBLISHERS, 55 Avenue Rd., Ste. 2900, Toronto, ON M5R 2L2 (416) 975-9334, FAX 975-9884. Born Regina, Sask. 1956. m. Scott Tupholme. 2 ch. **EDUC:** Univ. of Guelph, B.A. 1979. **CAREER:** Proj. & Prod. Ed., Prentice-Hall Canada, 1981-85; Acquisitions Ed., 1985-88; Exec. Ed., Penguin Books Canada, 1988-91; Publisher & Ed.-In-Chief, HarperCollins Publishers, 1991 to date.

Turnbull Irving, Janet, B.A., M.A. 📖 $

President, CURTIS BROWN CANADA LTD., 200 First Ave., Toronto, ON M4M 1X1 (802) 362-5165. President, THE TURNBULL AGENCY INC. Born Toronto 1954. m. John Irving. 1 ch. **EDUC:** Univ. of Toronto, B.A.(English Lit.), M.A.(English) 1979. **CAREER:** Ed., Authors' Marketing Services, Toronto, 1979-80; Mng

Dir., Doubleday Canada Ltd., 1980-84; VP & Publisher, Seal Books, 1984-87; Pres., Turnbull Agency, 1987 to date; Pres., Curtis Brown Canada Ltd, 1989 to date. **DIRECTOR:** Curtis Brown Canada Ltd. **COMMENT:** *"Literary agent for Canadian and international authors, including the Estate of Robertson Davies, Timothy Findley, John Irving, Brian Moore, Nino Ricci and Janice Kulyk Keefer."*

Turner, Nancy J., Ph.D.,F.L.S. ■ ◁ ✿
Professor, Environmental Studies Program, UNIVERSITY OF VICTORIA, Sedgewick Bldg., C182, Box 1700, Victoria, BC V8W 2Y2 (604) 721-6124, FAX 721-8985, EMAIL nturner@uvic.ca. Born 1947. m. Robert D. Turner. 3 ch. **EDUC:** Univ. of Victoria, B.Sc. (Biol.); Univ. of British Columbia, Ph.D.(Ethnobotany) 1974. **CAREER:** writer, BC Provincial Museum, 1974-77; writer, National Museum of Natural Sciences, 1977-80; researcher & writer of ethnobotanical publications, 1979-83; Instructor, Univ. of Victoria, 1982, 1984; Adjunct Prof., Dept. of Botany, Univ. of British Columbia, 1986 to date; Research Affiliate, Royal British Columbia Museum, Victoria; Prof., Environmental Studies Program, Univ. of Victoria, 1991 to date. **SELECTED PUBLICATIONS:** *Common Poisonous Plants and Mushrooms of North America*, with Adam F. Szczawinski (Portland, Ore.: Timber Press, 1991); *Traditional Plant Foods of Canadian Indigenous Peoples*, with Harriet V. Kunlein (Philadelphia: Gordon and Breach Science Publishers, 1991); "Contemporary Use of Bark for Medicine by Two Salishan Native Elders of Southeast Vancouver Island," with Richard J. Hebda (*Journal of Ethnopharmacology* 229 1990); "Edible Wood Fern Rootstocks of Western North America: Solving an Ethnobotanical Puzzle," with Leslie M.J. Gottesfeld, Harriet V. Kuhnlein & Adolf Ceska (*Journal of Ethnobiology* 12(1) 1992); "'When Everything Was Scarce': The Role of Plants as Famine Foods in Northwestern North America," with Alison Davis (*Journal of Ethnobiology* 13(2) 1993); various other publications incl. 13 other books on ethnobotany & edible wild plants. **AFFIL:** Royal Linnaean Society (Fellow). **HONS:** Healthy Saanich 2000 Award, Municipality of Saanich, 1991; Canada 125 Medal, 1993. **INTERESTS:** berry-picking; hiking. **MISC:** recipient, various grants; various conference presentations. **COMMENT:** *"An ethnobotanist, Nancy Turner has been working together with First Nations elders in British Columbia for the past 25 years, documenting traditional botanical knowledge, including information on the use of plants in food and nutrition."*

Turney Zagwyn, Deborah 🖉 ⊗ ◁
Author and Illustrator. Box 472, Harrison Hot Springs, BC V0M 1K0 (604) 796-9779, FAX 796-9689, EMAIL zagwyn@uniserve.com. Born Cornwall, Ont. 1953. m. Leo F. 2 ch. Sonia, Graham. **EDUC:** F.V.C. Abbotsford Fine Arts Program, 2 yrs. completed 1978. **SELECTED PUBLICATIONS:** illustrator, *A Winter's Yarn* (Red Deer, Alta.: Red Deer Coll. Press, 1986); author & illustrator, *Mood Pocket, Mud Bucket* (Fitzhenry and Whiteside, 1988); author & illustrator, *The Pumpkin Blanket* (Fitzhenry and Whiteside, 1990); author & illustrator, *Long Nellie* (Victoria, BC: Orca Book Publishers Ltd., 1993); author & illustrator, *Hound Without Howl* (Victoria: Orca Book Publishers Ltd., 1994); various commissioned works, murals & posters. **EXHIBITIONS:** 3-dimensional watercolours, Junior League Headquarters, Seattle (1984); art, soft sculpture, Torrance Residence, Seattle (1985); illustrations & watercolours, Kent Harrison Art Gallery (1987, 1988); book illustrations, Prince George Art Gallery (1989); book illustrations, Chilliwack Museum (1989); book illustrations, Maple Ridge Art Gallery (1991); book illustrations, Vancouver Int'l Writers and Readers Festival (1993). **AFFIL:** Canadian Children's Book Centre; CANSCAIP; Writers Union of Canada; CWILL B.C.; Chilliwack Arts Centre; Harrison Festival of the Arts (Bd.). **HONS:** Honourable Mention, Sheila Egoff Children's Medal, B.C. Book Awards, 1989; shortlisted, Mr. Christie Book Award (*Hound Without Howl*), 1995. **INTERESTS:** cycling; gardening; reading; skiing. **MISC:** numerous workshops & presentations; 8 school &/or library tours in B.C., Alta. & Ont.; served on Canada Council jury for Gov. General's Award in Illustration, 1993. **COMMENT:** *"Deborah Turney Zagwyn has a background as a printmaker, weaver, wall muralist and exhibiting painter. Her love of detail and interest in portraiture surfaces in her picture books."*

Twain, Shania (Eileen) • ♥
Singer. c/o Mercury Records. Born Windsor, Ont. 1965. m. Robert John "Mutt" Lang. **CAREER:** began singing in local clubs & community events, 1973; regular performer, Deerhurst Resort, Huntsville, Ont., 1986-89; signed with Mercury Records, 1991; released debut album, 1993. **SELECTED CREDITS:** *Shania Twain*, 1993; *The Woman in Me*, prod. "Mutt" Lange, 1995. **HONS:** Rising Video Star of the Year, Female Artist of the Year & No. 1 Video of the Year, Country Music Television, 1996; Favorite New Country Artist, Blockbuster Entertainment, 1996; Best Country Album, *The Woman in Me*, Grammy Awards, 1996; Country Female Vocalist & Entertainer

of the Year, Juno Awards, 1996; Favorite New Country Artist, American Music Awards, 1995; Song of the Year, "Whose Bed Have Your Boots Been Under?," Society of Composers, Authors, and Music Publishers of Canada, 1995; Outstanding New Artist, RPM's Big Country Awards, 1995; Female Vocalist of the Year & Album of the Year, *The Woman in Me* & Single of the Year & Video of the Year, "Any Man of Mine," Canadian Country Music Awards, 1995; Best Video, "If You're Not in it For Love," Female Vocalist of the Year & Entertainer of the Year, Canadian Country Music Awards, 1996; Country Female Vocalist of the year, Juno Awards, 1996. **MISC:** *The Woman in Me* reached double-platinum status in Canada.

Tyrie, Anne, B.Sc.,M.Sc.,Ph.D. ⚛ [$]
Director, Industry Support, INFORMATION TECHNOLOGY RESEARCH CENTRE, D.L. Pratt Building, 6 King's College Rd., Ste. 286, Toronto, ON M5S 1A1. President, ANNE TYRIE & ASSOCIATES. Born Edinburgh, Scotland 1954. m. Michael W. Horsfall. 2 ch. Ross Tyrie-Horsfall, Blair Tyrie-Horsfall. **EDUC:** Manchester Univ., B.Sc. 1977, M.Sc. 1979, Ph.D. 1981. **CAREER:** Trainee C.A., Arthur Andersen & Co., UK, 1977; Geologist, Geophysicist & Scientific Ed., Ministry of Northern Dev. & Mines, 1980-83; Prof. Surveying Sci., Univ. of Toronto, 1983-90; VP, R.&D., Real/Data Ontario Inc., 1988-90; Pres., Anne Tyrie & Associates, 1986 to date; Dir., Real/Data Ontario Inc., 1987-93; Consultant, Philip A. Lapp Ltd., 1987-90; Consultant, Carleton Professional Development Centre, 1991-92; Dir., Ind. Support, Information Technology Research Centre, 1993 to date. **SELECTED PUBLICATIONS:** author, 24 journal papers & tech. reports. **AFFIL:** Institute of Electrical & Electronics Engineers; Association for Computing Machinery; Information Technology Association of Canada; International Interactive Communications Society; MIT/York Enterprise Forum; Canadian Advanced Technology Association; Canadian Aeronautics & Space Institute.

Tyson, Sylvia (née Fricker) * 🎭 🎵
Singer and Songwriter. Born Chatham, Ont. 1940. **CAREER:** started singing career mid-1950s; formed duo, Ian & Sylvia with Ian Tyson; with Ian Tyson formed *The Great Speckled Bird*, 1970; Host & Performer, various radio & TV shows; Co-founded *Quartette*, with Cindy Church, Caitlin Ford & the late Colleen Peterson, summer 1993. **SELECTED CREDITS:** numerous recordings with Ian Tyson; debut solo album, *Woman's World*, 1975; *Cold Wind From the North*, 1976; *Satin on Stone*, 1978; *Sugar For Sugar, Salt For Salt*, 1979; *You Were On My Mind*, 1989; *Gypsy Cadillac*, 1992; recordings with Quartette: *Quartette*; *Work of the Heart*; *It's Christmas*; Host, *Touch the Earth*, CBC Radio, 1974-80; Host, *Heartland*, CBC-TV, 1980; Host, *Country In My Soul*, CBC-TV, 1981-83. **HONS:** recipient of numerous awards; Ian & Sylvia inducted into the Canadian Music Hall of Fame, 1992; Vocal Collaboration of the Year, *Quartette*, Canadian Country Music Awards.

U

chida, Irene Ayako, B.A., Ph.D. ⌨ ⊕ 🖫♡ 🖆

Professor Emeritus, Department of Pediatrics, MCMASTER UNIVERSITY, 1200 Main St. W., Hamilton, ON L8N 3Z5 (905) 521-2100, ext. 3718, FAX 521-2651. Born Vancouver 1917. s. **EDUC:** Univ. of Toronto, B.A.(Arts) 1946, Ph.D.(Genetics) 1951. **CAREER:** Research Assoc., Hospital for Sick Children, Toronto, 1951-59; Dir., Dept. of Medical Genetics, Children's Hospital of Winnipeg, 1960-69; Assoc. Prof., Pediatrics & Anatomy, Univ. of Manitoba, 1967-69; Visiting Prof., Univ. of Alabama Sch. of Medicine, Birmingham, Al., 1968; MRC Visiting Scientist, Univ. of London, UK & Harwell Radiobiological Research Unit, UK, 1969; Prof., Pediatrics, & Dir., Reg. Cytogenetics Lab., McMaster Univ., 1969-91; MRC Visiting Prof., Univ. of Western Ontario, 1973; Prof., Pathology, McMaster Univ., 1979-91; Prof. Emeritus, Depts. of Pediatrics & Pathology, 1991 to date; Dir. of Cytogenetics, Oshawa General Hospital, 1991-95. **SELECTED PUBLICATIONS:** "Discordant Heart Anomalies in Twins," with R.D. Rowe (*American Journal of Human Genetics* 9 1957); "A Possible Association between Maternal Radiation and Mongolism," with E.J. Curtis (*Lancet* ii 1961); "Identification of Triploid Genomes by Fluorescence Microscopy," with C.C. Lin (*Science* 176 1972); "Twinning Rate in Spontaneous Abortions," with C.P.V. Freeman, M. Gedeon & J. Goldmaker (*American Journal of Human Genetics* 35 1983); "Loss of Telomeric DNA During Aging of Normal and Trisomy 21 Human Lymphocytes," with H. Vaziri *et al* (*American Journal of Human Genetics* 1993); total of 97 scientific publications. **AFFIL:** American Society of Human Genetics (Pres. 1968); American Association for the Advancement of Science; Association of Genetic Counsellors of Ontario; Canadian Coll. of Medical Geneticists (Emeritus Fellow); Genetics Society of Canada; Genetics Society of America; American Coll. of Medical Genetics (Emeritus Fellow); N.Y. State Institute for Basic Research in Developmental Disabilities (Scientific Advisory Committee). HONS: Ramsay Wright Scholar, Univ. of Toronto, 1947; Woman of the Year, Women's Advertising & Sales Club, Winnipeg, 1963; Woman of the Century 1867-1967, National Council of Jewish Women, Prov. of Man., 1967; Achievement Award, Altrusa Club, Winnipeg, 1969; 25 Outstanding Women, Ont. Women's Year, Ont. Gov't, 1975; 1,000 Canadian Women of Note 1867-1967, Media Club of Canada & Women's Press Club of Toronto, 1983; Officer, Order of Canada, 1993; Founder's Award, Canadian Coll. of Medical Geneticists, 1995; Hon. Doctor of Sci., Univ. of Western Ontario, 1996. INTERESTS: music; violin; piano; art; editing English; science. MISC: mbr., Organizing Committee, Standardization in Human Cytogenetics (Int'l), 1966; mbr., Task Force on the Provision & Standardization of Cytogenetic Services in Ont., 1977; mbr., Advisory Committee on Genetic Svcs, Ont. Ministry of Health, 1979-86; mbr., Task Force on High Technology Diagnostic Lab. Procedures & Equipment, 1980-82; recipient, various grants; First Invited Speaker, Annual Queen Elizabeth II Lectures, Canadian Pediatric Society; Queen Elizabeth II Speaker, Children's Hospital, Winnipeg, 1971; various consultancies; frequent invited speaker; listed in various biographical sources, incl. *Canadian Who's Who, Who's Who in America, International Who's Who in Medicine* & Media Club of Canada. COMMENT: *"Cytogeneticist in health sciences and health care."*

Ulmer, Karen, C., B.A.,M.A., LL.B. ⬙▽ ✿
Solicitor, SASKATCHEWAN GOVERNMENT INSURANCE, 2260 - 11th Ave., Regina, SK S4P 0J9 (306) 751-1760, FAX 352-0933. Born North Battleford, Sask. 1962. life partner Brendan Stevens. EDUC: Univ. of Saskatchewan, B.A. (Hist.) 1983, LL.B.(Law) 1989; Queen's Univ., M.A.(Hist.) 1985. CAREER: Lawyer, private practice, 1989-94; Solicitor, insur. litigation, Saskatchewan Government Insurance, 1994 to date. SELECTED PUBLICATIONS: "Recent Developments in the Oppression Remedy" (*Saskatchewan Law Review*, 53(2), 1989). AFFIL: Canadian Bar Association (Council for Sask. 1994-98; Co-Founder & Co-Chair, Gender Equality, Sask. Section 1994-97); LEAF

(Treas. & Past Pres., Regina Chapter); Planned Parenthood; Humane Society; Transition House; YWCA (Bd. of Dir. 1996-2002); MacKenzie Art Gallery. HONS: Gov. General's Bronze Medal, 1979; Copland Prize for most outstanding humanities student, 1983; Master's Thesis Prize, Canadian Journal of European Integration, 1985; Carswell Prize for highest average, 3rd-yr. Law, 1989; Continuing Legal Educ. Prize for Academic Excellence, Bar Admission Course, 1990. INTERESTS: music; riding; ballroom dancing; fitness; languages. COMMENT: *"I have an academic background. I am interested in pursuing a career as a litigation counsel and in supporting organizations that advance the interests and needs of women."*

Ulvick, Rayann, C.H.E. ⊕ ⬚
Chief Executive Officer, NORTH-EAST HEALTH DISTRICT, Box 389, Nipawin, SK S0E 1E0 (306) 862-5900, FAX 862-9310. Born Nipawin, Sask. 1953. m. Ken. 3 ch. EDUC: Univ. of Saskatchewan, Certified Health Care Administrator (Acute Care/Long Term Care) 1988, 1989. CAREER: Stock Cont., Sherritt Gordon Mines, Ruttan Lake, Man., 1973-74; Acctg Clerk, Nipawin Accounting and Investment Services Ltd., 1977-81; Bus. Mgr & Asst. Administrator, Nipawin Union Hospital, 1984-87; Exec. Dir., 1987-93; CEO, North-East Health District, 1993 to date. AFFIL: Abbott Education Foundation Inc. (Dir.); Canadian Coll. of Health Service Executives (Certified Health Exec.; Exec. Mbr.); Saskatchewan Association of Health Service Executives (Educ. Committee); Rotary Club of Nipawin; Association for Healthcare Philanthropy; Saskatchewan Organization of Health Organizations (Prov. Bargaining Team); North Central Region (Reg'l Advisory Committee). HONS: Student of the Year, Health Care Admin., Saskatchewan Health Care Association, 1988. INTERESTS: family; down-hill skiing; crafts; Cdn museums. MISC: 1st woman CEO appointed to position in prov. health district; numerous workshops & presentations. COMMENT: *"I see myself as a hard-working individual who enjoys a challenge. My endeavours have been supported by my family, and all achievements had the assistance of a great team at work."*

Underhill, Anne Barbara, B.A.,M.A., Ph.D. ⬚ ❀
Honorary Professor, Department of Geophysics and Astronomy, UNIVERSITY OF BRITISH COLUMBIA, Vancouver, BC V6T 1Z4 (604) 822-2267, FAX 822-6047, EMAIL underhill@geop.ubc.ca. Born Vancouver 1920. s.

EDUC: Univ. of British Columbia, B.A. (Physics/Chem.) 1942, M.A.(Physics/ Math.) 1944; Univ. of Chicago, Ph.D.(Astrophysics) 1948. **CAREER:** Astronomer, Dominion Astrophysical Observatory, Victoria, 1949-62; Prof. of Astrophysics, State Univ., Utrecht, The Netherlands, 1962-70; Chief of the Lab. for Optical Astronomy, Goddard Space Flight Center, US, 1970-77; Sr. Scientist, Lab. for Solar Physics, Goddard Space Flight Center, 1977-85; Hon. Prof., Univ. of British Columbia, 1985 to date. **SELECTED PUBLICATIONS:** "On Model Atmospheres for High-Temperature Stars" (*Publications of the Copenhagen Observatory* 151 1950); *The Early Type Stars* (Dordrecht: Reidel, 1966); "About the Stage of Evolution of Wolf-Rayet Stars" (*Astrophysical Journal* 383, 1991) more than 225 publications in tech. journals. **AFFIL:** International Astronomical Union; American Astronomical Society; Canadian Astronomical Society; Royal Astronomical Society; Royal Society of Canada (Fellow 1986). **HONS:** D.Sc.(Hon.), York Univ., 1969; D.Sc.(Hon.), Univ. of British Columbia, 1992;. **INTERESTS:** choir singing. **COMMENT:** *"Throughout her working life, Underhill has been concerned with finding out the physical state of the massive stars, chiefly those having spectral types in the B, O and Wolf-Rayet ranges."*

Unger, Renée, B.A. ■ $

President, INTERCORP FOODS LTD., 1880 Ormont Dr., Weston, ON M9L 2V4 (416) 744-2124, FAX 744-4369. Born Toronto 1942. d. **EDUC:** Univ. of Toronto, B.A.(Psych.) 1966. **CAREER:** public sch. teacher, 1963-70; jewellery sales, 1970-94; Ptnr, imported clothing store, 1975-84; volunteer catering, 1984-85; launched Renées Gourmet Dressings, 1985; Pres., Intercorp Foods, 1984 to date. **DIRECTOR:** Intercorp Foods Ltd. **HONS:** Gold Medal, Small Bus. Category, Canadian Business Excellence Awards, 1988; Silver Medal, Entrepreneur of the Year, Canadian Business Excellence Awards, 1988; Bus. Woman of the Year, North York Chamber of Commerce, 1989; Best Tasting Condiment for all of N.Am., Gorman New Products Award, 1990; Award of Merit for Salad Dressing Kit Packaging, Packaging Awards, 1991; Award of Merit, Ontario Chamber of Commerce, 1993; Best Tasting Salad Dressing, *The Toronto Star*, 1993. **MISC:** numerous public appearances & guest lectures; numerous media interviews; complete line of retail & food svc products under the Renées Gourmet Label & Excelle Brand Foods; manufacturer for private labels, incl. Loblaw's President's Choice & A&P's Master Choice.

Ur, Rose-Marie, R.N.A.,M.P. 🍁

Member of Parliament (Lambton-Middlesex), GOVERNMENT OF CANADA, House of Commons, Confederation Building, Rm. 449, Ottawa, ON K1A 0A6 (613) 947-4581, FAX 947-4584. Born Glencoe, Ont. 1946. m. Louis Ur. 2 ch. Terry, Michelle. **EDUC:** Strathroy Middlesex General Hospital, R.N.A. 1964. **CAREER:** M.P. (Lambton-Middlesex), House of Commons. **AFFIL:** Caradoc North Parent Association (Volunteer Parent); Rebekah Assembly (Noble Grand, Lady Howard Lodge, Strathroy; Marshall for Ont.); Lioness Club (Charter Mbr., Strathroy; District Deputy Pres., London 278); Caradoc Community Centre (Fundraising Committee). **HONS:** Decoration of Chivalry (highest award), Rebekah Assembly. **INTERESTS:** cooking; walking; skiing. **COMMENT:** *"Enjoy life and people; rewarding to help those in need whether it be at work or community involvement. Grass-roots, common-sense, down-to-earth person."*

Urquhart, Jane, B.A. ■ ✒ ⚙ 📖

Author. Box 208, Wellesley, ON N0B 2T0, FAX (519) 656-3358. Born Little Long Lac, Ont. 1949. m. Tony Urquhart. 1 ch. Emily Jane Urquhart. **EDUC:** Univ. of Guelph, B.A. (English) 1971, B.A.(Art Hist.) 1976. **CAREER:** Asst. Info. Officer, Dept. of Nat'l Defence, Halifax; Tutor, Correspondence Program, Art Hist., Univ. of Waterloo; full-time writer; Writer-in-Residence, Univ. of Ottawa, 1990; Writer-in-Residence, Memorial Univ. of Newfoundland, 1992; Writer-in-Residence, Univ. of Toronto, 1997. **SELECTED PUBLICATIONS:** *False Shuffles* (Victoria: Press Porcepic, 1982); *The Little Flowers of Mme de Montespan*, poetry (Erin, Canada: Porcupine's Quill, 1984; reprint 1994); *Storm Glass*, short fiction (Erin, Canada: The Porcupine's Quill, 1987; Boston: David Godine - forthcoming*); The Whirlpool* (Toronto: McClelland & Stewart, 1986; London: Simon & Schuster, 1989; Boston: David Godine, 1990; also published in Paris & Milan); *Changing Heaven* (Toronto: McClelland & Stewart, 1990; London: Hodder & Stoughton, 1990; Boston: David Godine, 1993; also published in Paris & Milan); *Away* (Toronto: McClelland & Stewart, 1993; London: Bloomsbury, 1994; New York: Viking, 1994; Penguin USA & UK; translations in several European languages). **AFFIL:** PEN Canada (Bd.); Writers' Union of Canada; League of Canadian Poets. **HONS:** Le Prix de Meilleur Livre Étranger (*The Whirlpool*), France, 1992; Ont. Trillium Book Award (*Away*), 1993; Marian Engel Prize, for a woman writer in mid-career, 1994; Canada Council Sr. Arts Award, 1994; Shortlisted, Int'l IMPAC, Dublin Literary

Prize, 1996; named Commandeur, "Order of Arts and Letters," Ministry of Culture of France, 1996. **INTERESTS:** Broadway musicals; 19th-century Cdn architecture; 18th-century European porcelain; relics & reliquaries; folk art; manuscript illumination; anonymous verse; tap dancing.

Usheroff, Roz ■ $

President, ROZ USHEROFF CONSULTING INC., 400 Walmer Rd., Ste. 104, Toronto, ON M5P 2X7 (416) 961-9383, FAX 962-2248. Born Montreal 1950. d. 1 ch. Sean Adam Usheroff. **EDUC:** Sir George Williams Univ. (now Concordia), Fine Arts 1969; Univ. of Toronto, Small Bus. 1988. **CAREER:** mgmt training program, Dylex Limited, 1984; Mgr, Club Monaco/Alfred Sung, 1985; Mgr, Polo–Ralph Lauren, Hazelton Lanes, Toronto, 1986-89; sales, Harry Rosen, 1989-91; Pres., Signature Style Image Consulting Inc., 1991-96; Pres., Roz Usheroff Consulting Inc., 1996 to date. **AFFIL:** Ontario Speakers' Association; National Speakers' Association; Welcome House, Ministry of Citizenship (Volunteer); Toronto Board of Trade. **INTERESTS:** skiing; biking; art; travel. **MISC:** has delivered keynote address to associations such as American Management Association, The Society of Association Executives, Pharmaceutical Manufacturers' Association of Canada, etc.; has been featured on nat'l TV incl. CBC *Venture* & Newsworld as well as in a number of magazines & newspapers incl. *Canadian Business, The Financial Post* & *The Globe and Mail*; client list includes American Express, Price Waterhouse, CIBC, Bell Canada & others. **COMMENT:** *"I am a single parent who, at the age of 41, decided to open up my own business in 1991. My mission statement is to help people improve their level of confidence and to project it. My achievements come from this. Acknowledgement that I am adding value to people's lives."*

Uson, Margot, B.A. $ ⊕ ☝

Vice-President, Human Resources, NOVARTIS PHARMA CANADA INC. (formerly Sandoz Canada Inc.), P.O. Box 385, Dorval, PQ H9R 4P5 (514) 631-6775, FAX 631-8525. Born Montreal m. 1 ch. **EDUC:** Concordia Univ., B.A.(Psych.) 1975; Queen's Univ., Grad.(Exec. Dev. Program) 1989. **CAREER:** Recruiter & Employee Comm. Administrator, Montreal Engineering Co., 1975-79; Hum. Res. Mgr, Novartis Pharma Canada Inc. (formerly Sandoz Canada Inc.), 1979-87; Hum. Res. Dir., 1988-89; VP, Hum. Res., 1990 to date. **AFFIL:** Pharmaceutical Manufacturers' Association of Canada (Hum. Res. Section; Hum. Res. Exec. Council 1987-89); Association of Human Resource Professionals of Quebec (Permanent Survey Committee 1979 to date); Conference Board of Canada (Hum. Res. Council). **INTERESTS:** golf; racquetball; reading; travel; volunteer activities. **COMMENT:** *"Innovative, creative, and experienced Human Resources professional with over 20 years' experience. First female Vice-President of Sandoz Canada Inc.; developed a strong, well-respected Human Resources presence with a strategic business orientation."*

V

acratsis, Maria, B.F.A. ⊗ ⛱ 🐾
Actor. c/o Caldwell & Company, 165 Danforth Ave., Toronto, ON M4K 1N2 (416) 429-7254, FAX 465-0955. Born Windsor, Ont. 1955. m. Michael Gyapjas. **EDUC:** Univ. of Windsor, B.F.A.(Theatre) 1977. **CAREER:** has acted in theatres across Canada, incl. Stratford, National Arts Centre, Canadian Stage Company, Theatre New Brunswick, The Grand Theatre (London), Centaur Theatre (Montreal); has been a regular on 2 CBC series & has appeared in numerous TV & film roles in both Canada & the US. **SELECTED CREDITS:** Emma, *Crusaders: The Margaret Sanger Story*; *Sodbusters*, written & dir. by Eugene Levy; *Kids in the Hall* (feature & series); *King Lear*, Necessary Angel, Toronto; *Italian American Reconciliation*, Theatre New Brunswick; *Hockey Wives*, Factory Theatre, Toronto; Cdn premiere, *Danny and the Deep Blue Sea*, Canadian Rep Theatre; *The Lorca Play*, Dada Kamera, Augusta Theatre Co.; *2nd Nature*, Videocabaret International; *Those People Across the Street*, CBC Radio. **AFFIL:** Canadian Actors' Equity Association; ACTRA; Academy of Canadian Cinema & Television. **HONS:** Best Actress in a Musical (*2nd Nature*), Dora Mavor Moore Award, 1990-91; Best Actress in a Drama (*The Lorca Play*), Dora Mavor Moore Award, 1992-93; nominated, Best Performer in an Entertainment Feature (*Those People Across the Street*), Nat'l Radio Awards, 1990. **INTERESTS:** film history; theatre history; perennial gardening. **COMMENT:** *"I have been a professional working actress in this country for 18 years, which is an achievement in itself. I'm most satisfied with the fact that I've been able to have a varied acting career and stay in Canada."*

Vail, Susan, B.A.,B.P.H.E.,M.A., Ph.D. 🎓 🎾

Associate Professor, School of Physical Education, YORK UNIVERSITY, Stong College, 4700 Keele St., Rm. 324, North York, ON M3J 1P3 (416) 736-2100, ext. 44755. President, VAIL AND ASSOCIATES. Born Dunnville, Ont. 1951. s. **EDUC:** McMaster Univ., B.A.(Soc.) 1974, B.P.H.E.(Phys. Educ.) 1974; Univ. of Western Ontario, M.A.(Social Psych. of Sport) 1976; Univ. of Ottawa, Ph.D.(Educ. Admin.) 1985. **CAREER:** Fitness & Amateur Sport, Ottawa, 1977-81; Mgr, Fitness & Amateur Sport Women's Program, 1980-82; Planning & Evaluation Officer, Sport Canada, Ottawa, 1982-84; Pres., Vail and Associates, Toronto, 1984 to date; Coord., Sport Admin. Certificate Program, York Univ., 1990 to date. **SELECTED PUBLICATIONS:** "Partnership Building Between Recreation and Sport Leaders" (*Recreation Canada Journal*, 52(5), 1994); "The Role of the Schools in Community Sport Delivery" (*CAHPER Journal*, 59(2), 1993); *Walking the Talk: A Handbook for Ontario Sport Leaders About Full and Fair Access for Girls and Women*, with P. Berck (Toronto: Ministry of Culture, Tourism & Recreation, 1994); *For The Love of Sport Resource Kit*, Ed. & Writer (Willowdale, Ontario: Sport Ontario, 1992); various papers in refereed journals, other publications & manuals. **AFFIL:** Canadian Association for Health, Physical Education & Recreation; North American Society for Sport Management; Ontario Research Council on Leisure; Tennis Canada (Bd.; V-Chair 1993-95); Sport Ontario (Bd.; Chair 1993-94); Parks & Recreation Federation of Ontario (Bd. 1991-94); Ontario Tennis Association (Bd. 1991-94); Canadian Association for the Advancement of Women & Sport (Founding Mbr.; former Bd. Mbr.). **HONS:** Canada 125 Medal; Service Award, Ontario Parks & Recreation Federation, 1993; Ambassador Award, Town of Dunnville, 1992. **INTERESTS:** tennis; golf; rollerblading; cottage. **MISC:** numerous conference presentations.

Vaillancourt-Châtillon, Louise, LL.L, LL.B. ■ 🎓 $ ⚖

Director of Administration, ÉCOLE POLYTECHNIQUE DE MONTRÉAL, P.O. Box 6079, Stn. Centre-Ville, Montréal, QC H3C 3A7 (514) 340-4711 or 340-4738, FAX 340-3261. Born Montréal 1951. m. Pierre-Yves Châtillon. 2 ch. **EDUC:** Univ. of Ottawa, License en droit civil 1974, LL.B. 1975; Univ. of Montreal, Certificate (Public Rel'ns) 1980. **BAR:** Que., 1984. **CAREER:** Legal Commentator, Société québécoise d'information juridique, 1975-79; Sec. Gen., Montfort Sch. Bd., 1979-81; Asst. Sec., National Bank of Canada, 1981-85; VP & Sec., 1985-87; VP, Legal Affairs & Sec., 1987-88; Sec. of the Bank, Bank of Canada, 1988-89; Advisor to the Gov. & Sec. of the Bank, 1989-92; Dir. of Admin., École Polytechnique de Montréal, 1992 to date. **DIRECTOR:** Bank of Montreal Trust Company. **AFFIL:** Quebec Bar Association; Gov. General's Canadian Study Conference (Fin. Committee 1991, 1995); L'association des femmes d'affaires du Québec (Patron d'honneur; Comité "Femmes au Conseil"). **INTERESTS:** finance & admin.; pension fund mgmt; environmental issues. **COMMENT:** *"A graduate in civil and common law from University of Ottawa, Mrs. Châtillon acquired a great deal of finance and management experience in a variety of public and private institutions. She is also very involved in her community."*

Vaisey-Genser, Marion, B.Sc.(H.Ec.), M.Sc. 🎓 ⚛ 🌾

Professor and Senior Scholar, Department of Foods and Nutrition, UNIVERSITY OF MANITOBA, Winnipeg, MB R3T 2N2 (204) 474-6830, FAX 275-5299, EMAIL genser@ccm.umanitoba.ca. Born Winnipeg 1929. m. E.B. Vaisey (dec.), Lawrence Genser. 2 ch. Jill Vaisey, Jacques Vaisey. **EDUC:** Univ. of Manitoba, B.Sc.(H.Ec.-Nutrition) 1949; McGill Univ., M.Sc.(Nutrition) 1951. **CAREER:** Head, Food Acceptance, Defence Research Medical Laboratories, Toronto, 1951-54; Teaching Research, Mount St. Vincent Univ., Oregon State Univ., Univ. of Guelph, Univ. of Manitoba, 1954-93; Head, Food & Nutrition Dept., Univ. of Manitoba, 1978-80; Assoc. Dean., Fac. of Grad. Studies, 1980-83; Assoc. VP, Research, 1983-91. **SELECTED PUBLICATIONS:** 41 papers in refereed journals, 10 tech. publications & 14 book chapters incl., "The Selection of levels of canola oil, water, and an emulsifier system in cake formulations by response surface methodology," with G. Ylimaki & B. Johnston (*Cereal Chemistry* (64) 1987); "Baking with canola oil products," with G. Ylimaki (*Cereal Foods World* (34)3, 1989); "Consumer acceptance of canola oils during temperature-accelerated storage," with L.J. Malcolmson *et al* (*Food Quality and Preferences* (5) 1994); "Current consumption of low erucic acid rapeseed oil by Canadians," *High and Law Erucic Acid Rapeseed Oils: Production, Usage, Chemistry and Toxicology Evaluation,* ed. J.K.G. Kramer, F.D. Sauer & W.J. Pidgen (Academic Press, 1983); "Sensory evaluation of margarine," with B.K. Vane, *Methods to Assess Quality and Stability of Oils and Fat-Containing Foods*, ed. K. Warner & N.A.M. Eskin (Champaign, Ill.: American Oil Chemists

Society Press, 1995); "Flaxseed: health, nutrition and functionality," tech. bulletin for The Flax Council of Canada, 1994; "Canola oil–sensory properties, tech. bulletin for Canola Council of Canada, 1994. AFFIL: Science Council of B.C. (Awards Committee); Winnipeg 2000 (Leader's Committee); Victoria General Hospital (Bd. of Dir.). HONS: Queen Elizabeth's Silver Jubilee Medal, 1977; Woman of the Year, Professional, Winnipeg YWCA, 1980; Outreach Award, Univ. of Manitoba, 1984; W.J. Eva Award for research & svc., Canadian Institute of Food Science & Technology, 1986; Chancellor's Award for outstanding svc., Univ. of Manitoba, 1992; Award for Excellence in Teaching, Manitoba Home Economics Association, 1993. INTERESTS: gardening; preserving food; technical writing; family ties. MISC: initiated teaching & research in sensory evaluation of food, initiated promotion of univ. interaction in research & dev., & revitalized the President's Advisory Council on Women at the Univ. of Manitoba. COMMENT: *"A high achiever with a sense of humour; innovative and pragmatic. I am proud of the recognition by my peers, my work with the agrifood industry and of the achievements of my children, graduates of my teaching and research programs and colleagues whom, as an executive and/or friend, I was/am able to encourage."*

Valaskakis, Gail Guthrie, B.Sc.,M.A., Ph.D. ⚲ 📖 ⌂
Dean, Faculty of Arts and Science and Professor, Department of Communication Studies, CONCORDIA UNIVERSITY, 1455 de Maisonneuve Blvd. W., L-AD-324, Montreal, QC H3G 1M8 (514) 848-2081, FAX 848-2877. Born Ashland, Wisc. 1939. 2 ch. Ion Valaskakis, Paris Valaskakis. EDUC: Univ. of Wisconsin–Madison, B.Sc.(Speech & Drama, English, Educ.) 1961; Cornell Univ., M.A.(Theatre) 1964; McGill Univ., Ph.D.(Comm.) 1979. CAREER: Teacher, Karonianona Indian Day Sch., Kahnawake, Que., 1966-67; Lecturer, Dept. of Comm. Studies, Concordia Univ., 1967-69; Asst. Prof., 1969-79; Coord., Program in Cdn Studies, 1978-79; Fellow, Sch. of Community & Public Affairs, 1979-83; Assoc. Prof., Dept. of Comm. Studies, 1979-89; Dir., M.A. Program in Media Studies, 1982-84; Chair, Dept. of Comm. Studies, 1983-85; Trustee Principal, Simone de Beauvoir (Women's Studies) Institute, 1985; V-Dean, Academic Planning, Fac. of Arts & Sci., 1985-90; Prof., Dept. of Comm. Studies, 1989 to date; Acting Dean, Fac. of Arts & Sci., 1992; Dean, 1992 to date. SELECTED CREDITS: Prod./Host, "Women: The Native Experience," *Canadian Women Series*, TV Channel 9, Montreal, 1973; Debate Moderator, *Leadership '87: A Multicultural Perspective*, CFMT-TV, 1987; Narrator, *Doctor, Lawyer, Indian Chief*, Studio D, National Film Bd., 1987. SELECTED PUBLICATIONS: "Communication and Control in the Canadian North: The Potential of Interactive Satellites" (*Études Inuit Studies* 6(1) 1982); "Restructuring the Canadian Broadcasting System: Aboriginal Broadcasting in the North," in *Canadian Broadcasting: The Challenge of Change*, C. Hoskins & S. McFadyen, eds. (Edmonton: Univ. of Alberta, 1986); "Chinese Journalism on Tour: A Canadian Perspective" (*Indian Journal of Communication* (India) Apr. 1986); "The Issue is Control: Northern Native Broadcasting in Canada," in *The Chugach Conference* (Anchorage: Univ. of Alaska, 1990); "Postcards of My Past: The Indian as Artefact," in *Relocating Cultural Studies: Developments in Theory and Research*, V. Blundell *et al*, eds. (London: Routledge, 1993); "Rights and Warriors: Native People, Cultural Identity and the Media" (*Ariel: A Review of International English Literature* Jan. 1994); numerous other publications. EDIT: Guest Co-Ed., special issue on northern comm., *Études Inuit Studies*, 6(1) 1982; Bd. of Dir., *Canadian Journal of Communication*, 1987-90, 1991-93, Sec. 1987-90, VP 1991-93; Ed. Collective, *Cultural Studies*, 1991 to date; Ed. Bd., *Canadian Journal of Social and Political Thought*; C-Theory, 1992 to date. EXHIBITIONS: *Indian Princesses and Cowgirls: Stereotypes of the Frontier*, with Marilyn Burgess, Oboro Gallery, Montreal (1992). AFFIL: Concordia Council for First Nations Educ.: Native Educ. Centre (Chair) & Institute for Native Training & Dev. (Chair); Concordia Univ. (Senate 1985-89, 1992 to date; Chair, Arts & Sciences Fac. Council; Chair, Northern Studies Committee 1989-90, 1991-94); Canadian Communication Association (Bd. of Dir. 1984-87; VP 1984-85; Pres. 1985-86); International Society for Intercultural Education, Training & Research (SIETAR) (Governing Council 1979-82); Association Inuksiutiit Katimajiit; *Études Inuit Studies* (Bd. of Dir. 1983-84); St. Leonard's Society (Crossroads) Half-way House, Montreal (Bd. of Dir.); Waseskun Native Half-way House, Montreal (Founding Mbr., Bd. of Dir.). HONS: Univ. of Wisconsin–Madison Alumni Association Outstanding Sr. Women Award, 1961; Kappa Kappa Gamma Int'l Alumnae Award in Educational Innovation, 1972; Honoree, Woman of Distinction, Montreal Bd. of Trade, YWCA of Montreal. MISC: numerous invited lectures; Advisory Bd., First Nations Studio I, National Film Bd., 1992-93; Advisory Bd., New Initiatives in Film Proj. for Women of Colour &

Women of the First Nations, National Film Bd., 1990-93; animator, "About Face About Frame: People of Colour & First Nations Film & Video Conference," Independent Film & Video Alliance, Banff (1992); recipient, various grants; listed in *Canadian Who's Who*; numerous research contracts & advisory consultations; numerous academic papers presented.

Valente Gorjup, Francesca, M.A. 📖
Director, ISTITUTO ITALIANO DI CULTURA, 496 Huron St., Toronto, ON M5R 2R3 (416) 921-3802. Born Vicenza, Italy 1943. m. Dr. Branko Gorjup. 1 ch. **EDUC:** Univ. of Ca' Foscari, Venice, Dott. Lingue e Letterature Straniere (English Lit.) 1968; Univ. of Toronto, M.A. (Cdn Lit.) 1977. **CAREER:** Asst. Dir., Istituto Italiano di Cultura, Toronto, 1977-79; Acting Dir., Istituto Italiano di Cultura, San Francisco, 1980-82; Dir., 1982-84; Dir., Istituto Italiano di Cultura, San Francisco & L.A., 1983-85; Dir., Istituto Italiano di Cultura, Toronto, 1985-91, 1992 to date; Ministry of Foreign Affairs, Rome, 1991-92. **SELECTED PUBLICATIONS:** various articles; translator into Italian of various Cdn works, incl. Margaret Atwood, *The Edible Woman*; Leonard Cohen, *The Favorite Game*; Northrop Frye, *The Fearful Symmetry, Mito, Metafora, Simbolo, The Double Vision*; Irving Layton, *The Tamed Puma, The Baffled Hunter*; Marshall McLuhan, *The Mechanical Bride, From Cliché to Archetype, Through the Vanishing Point, Letters of Marshall McLuhan, The Global Village, The Man and his Message, Frank Lloyd Wright, For the Cause of Architecture*; various Cdn short stories & poetry; translator into English of various Italian works, incl. Giorgio Bassani, *Rolls Royce and Other Poems* with Greg Gatenby & Irving Layton; Pier Paolo Pasolini, *Roman Poems* with Lawrence Ferlinghetti; *Words of Enzo Cucchi*. **AFFIL:** Massey Coll. (Fellow); Accademia olimpica, Vicenza (Accademico); Canadian Club of Toronto; Northrop Frye Centre (Advisory Bd.). **HONS:** Yeats Int'l Scholarship, Ireland, 1970; British Council Fellowship in Applied Linguistics, Essex Univ., 1974; Italian Ministry of Foreign Affairs & Canada Council Fellowship, Univ. of Toronto, 1976-77; Proclamation, Mayor of San Francisco, 1985; Gold Medal for the Promo. of Italian Culture Abroad, Vicenza Chamber of Commerce, 1990; Proclamation, Mayor of Toronto, 1992. **INTERESTS:** reading; cycling; mountain climbing. **MISC:** organized reading tours in Italy for Cdn writers, incl. Irving Layton, Leonard Cohen & Northrop Frye; Proj. Dir. for Ont. & Man. "Italy on Stage" 1987 & "Italy in Canada" 1991; initiator of "Fountain of Italy" proj. by Enzo Cucchi, York Univ.

COMMENT: *"Promoter of Italian culture (of the past and the present) in the western US, California in particular, and Canada. The Leonardo da Vinci exhibition in 11 American university art museums is still remembered."*

Van Alstyne, Thelma, R.C.A. ⊗
Artist. Born Victoria, B.C. 1913. w. 1 stpch. Lois O'Briant. **EDUC:** Vancouver Sch. of Art, Interior Decorating 1944, Life Drawing 1944; Doon Sch. (with Jock MacDonald) 1951. **CAREER:** began painting in the mid-1950s. **EXHIBITIONS:** numerous exhibitions throughout Canada & the US incl.: Helene Mazlowe Gallery, Toronto; Upstairs Gallery, Toronto; The Pollock Gallery (annually 1961-80); Canadian Group of Painters–Montreal Museum of Art (1961); Toronto City Hall Foyer (1968); The Colour & Form Society (1968, 1969, 1970); Robertson Centre for the Arts & Sciences, N.Y. (1971); Art Gallery of Ontario (1972); Victoria Hall, Northumberland Gallery, Cobourg (1979); QUAN Gallery, Toronto (1985); Masters Gallery, Calgary (1994); many major museums & universities throughout Canada & the US. **COLLECTIONS:** numerous corp. & private collections incl.: The Canada Council Art Bank; Mrs. John David Eaton; Mrs. Hart Massey; The Toronto-Dominion Bank Art Collection; McLaughlin Art Gallery; NC Energy Collection. **AFFIL:** Royal Academy of Art. **MISC:** travelled to France & Italy with Adrian Dingle & others; presently her life as a traveller, artist & t'ai chi teacher is being documented on video.

Van den Eynden, Elizabeth, B.A., LL.B. ⚖️ ☺
Partner, MACINTOSH, MACDONNELL & MAC-DONALD, P.O. Box 368, New Glasgow, NS B2H 5E5 (902) 752-8441, FAX 752-7810. Born New Glasgow, N.S. 1961. partner Robert A. Roy. **EDUC:** St. Francis Xavier Univ., B.A. 1984; Univ. of New Brunswick, LL.B. 1987. **CAREER:** Lawyer, MacIntosh, MacDonnell & MacDonald; Ptnr, 1993 to date. **AFFIL:** Pictou County Chamber of Commerce (Pres.); Rotary Club of New Glasgow (Dir.); Maritime Quarter Horse Association (1st VP); N.S. Barristers' Society (Disciplinary Committee); Regional Assessment Appeal Court (Past Mbr.); Residential Tenancies Bd. (Past Chair); Highland Community Residential Svcs (Past Chair); Pictou County Opportunity for Men Association (Past Co-Chair). **INTERESTS:** travel; reading; horses. **COMMENT:** *"Including my current and past affiliations noted above, I have been actively involved in other community endeavours. Community involvement, from my perspective, is very important. I have been actively involved in*

the N.S. Barristers' Society and providing public legal education at the local level. My area of law is litigation and I am keenly interested in developing alternate resolution techniques. (In my spare time I can be found in the barn–with my animals.)"

van der Kamp, Anna ■■ ⑦
Olympic Athlete. c/o Canadian Olympic Association. Born Abbotsford, B.C. 1972. EDUC: currently a student. SPORTS CAREER: mbr., Cdn Nat'l Rowing Team, 1994 to date. Olympic Games: Silver, 8+, 1996. World championships: 6th, 8+, 1995; 7th, 8+, 1994. Int'l regattas: 1st, 8+ (Ont.), 6th, 2- (Switzerland), & 2nd, 4-, & 3rd, 2- (Netherlands). Canadian championships: 1st, 8+, 1st, 4-, & 4th, 2-, 1993. US championships: 2nd, 8+, & 6th, 2-, 1995. HONS: Female Crew of the Year, Canadian Amateur Rowing Association, 1993. INTERESTS: reading; swimming; writing letters & talking to friends & family. MISC: lifeguard, swimming instructor, recycling educ. coord.

Vanderkamp, Joan Rosemary, M.A. ■ ╱ ▣ ⌑
Managing Editor, CANADIAN JOURNAL ON AGING, MacKinnon Building, University of Guelph, Journals Office, Rm. 039, Guelph, ON N1G 2W1 (519) 824-4120, ext. 6925, FAX 837-9953, EMAIL rvanderk@uoguelph.ca. Born St. Andrews, Scotland 1931. w. John Vanderkamp. 3 ch. Nicholas H. Vanderkamp, Fiona Y. Vanderkamp-Merritt, Christa J. Parson. EDUC: Univ. of St. Andrews, M.A.(Hist.) 1953; Univ. of London, Post-Grad. Diploma in Librarianship 1957. CAREER: Librarian, Warwickshire County Library; Research Asst., Beaverbrook Newspapers; Cataloguer, R.B. Bennett Papers, Univ. of New Brunswick; Librarian & Research Asst., Canadian Universities Foundation; Bus. Ed., Canadian Public Policy/Analyse de Politiques, 1974-96; Prod. Mgr, Canadian Review of Sociology and Anthropology, 1987-94; Mng Ed., Canadian Journal on Aging, 1990-96; Bus. Ed., Journal of Agricultural and Environmental Ethics, 1990 to date. SELECTED PUBLICATIONS: University Study in Canada (1961); Provincial Programs of Aid to University Students, 1957-58 to 1960-61 (1961); "Study, Research and Travel Grants for University Professors" (CAUT Bulletin, 1961); The Impact of Computer Technology on the Production of Scholarly Journals and Books (1988). AFFIL: Canadian Periodical Publishers' Association (Bd.); College Women's Club (Treas.); University Women's Club (Publicity Officer); Canadian Federation of University Women (Chair, Scholarship Committee). INTERESTS: arts; sports; travel. COMMENT:

"As a journal editor, I was among the first to introduce new technology into journal production and to establish a central office for the management of a number of journals."

Vander Voet, Susan McCrae, M.A.,B.S.W., M.S.W. ■ ○ ◉ ⌑
Consultant, METRAC, METRO ACTION COMMITTEE ON PUBLIC VIOLENCE AGAINST WOMEN AND CHILDREN, 158 Spadina Rd., Toronto, ON M5R 2T8 (416) 397-0258, FAX 392-3136. President, HERLAND INCORPORATED. Born Yorkton, Sask. 1944. m. Dr. Anthony Vander Voet. 2 ch. David Vander Voet, Andréa Vander Voet. EDUC: Univ. of Alberta, B.A.(Soc.) 1965; Univ. of Toronto, B.S.W. 1966, M.S.W. 1971. CAREER: Program Dir., Foster Parent's Plan, Colombia, 1968-70; Community Worker, Metro Children's Aid Society, 1971-73; Lay Advocate, Centre for Spanish Speaking Peoples, 1974; Exec. Dir., Opportunity for Advancement, 1974-80; Program Dev. Dir., St. Christopher House, 1980-81; Exec. Dir., Canadian Congress for Learning Opportunities for Women, 1981-85; independent consulting, 1981-86; Pres., Herland Incorporated, 1986 to date; Interim Exec. Dir., LEAF, 1986, 1994; Exec. Dir., Women in Transition, Inc., 1989-90; Exec. Dir., METRAC, 1991-96; Consultant to METRAC & other organizations, 1996 to date. SELECTED PUBLICATIONS: numerous articles published in Women's Education des femmes; numerous fact sheets on women's educ. & violence against women & children; numerous briefs & discussion papers; "Violence Free Schools" (1995); "A Model for Developing and Implementing Sexual Assault Prevention Policy," with Linda Nye (1995). EDIT: Founder & Mng Ed., Women's Education des femmes, 1982-86. AFFIL: LEAF (Chair, Nat'l Fundraising Committee 1994-95). INTERESTS: travel; cycling; gardening. COMMENT: "Advocate, manager, and developer of NGOs, educator about issues of women's equality and violence against women and children with a strong lifelong commitment to the voluntary sector, especially to women's organizations

Vanderwel, Désirée, B.Sc.,Ph.D. ■■ ⌑ ❀
Associate Professor, Department of Chemistry, UNIVERSITY OF WINNIPEG, 515 Portage Ave., Winnipeg, MB R3B 2E9 (204) 786-9033, FAX 775-2114, EMAIL vanderwl@uwinnipeg.ca. Born Edmonton. 1960. m. Rob Currie. 1 ch. Sarah Alexandra Vanderwel Currie. EDUC: Univ. of Victoria, B.Sc.(Hons., Biochem.) 1981; Simon Fraser Univ., Ph.D.(Chem.) 1991. CAREER: Research Technician, Dept. of Biochem. & Microbiol., Univ. of Victoria,

1981-83; grad. student, Dept. of Chem., Simon Fraser Univ., 1983-90; Postdoctoral Research Asst., Dept. of Biochem., Univ. of Nevada, Reno, 1990-91; Asst. Prof., Dept. of Chem., Univ. of Winnipeg, 1991-95; Assoc. Prof., 1995 to date; Adjunct Prof., Dept. of Biochem. & Molecular Biol., Univ. of Manitoba, 1992 to date; Adjunct Prof., Dept. of Entomology, 1996 to date. **SELECTED PUBLICATIONS:** co-author with A.C. Oehlschlager, book chpt., "Biosynthesis of pheromones and endocrine regulation of pheromone production in Coleoptera" (*Pheromone Biochemistry*, G.D. Prestwich & G.J. Blomquist, eds., Academic Press, 1987); numerous articles in scholarly journals. **AFFIL:** Canadian Association of Women in Science; Chemical Institute of Canada (Chair, Exec. Bd., Man. chpt. 1995; Publicity Chair, Man. chpt. 1994-95; Man. Coord. for Nat'l Chemistry Week 1995; Man. Coord. for Nat'l Crystal Growing Competition 1995 to date; mbr., Logistics Committee, & Chair, Publicity Committee, CIC conference 1994); Entomological Society of America; Entomological Society of Manitoba; International Society of Chemical Ecology. **MISC:** recipient, 2 major research grants from NSERC, 1992-95 & 1995-99.

van Driel, Gerlinde, LL.B.,LL.M ■ ⚖ $

Partner, PATTERSON PALMER HUNT MURPHY, Scotia Centre, 235 Water St., Ste. 1000, Box 610, St. John's, NF A1C 5L3 (709) 726-6124, FAX 722-0483. Born Rotterdam, The Netherlands 1956. m. Dr. Tom Calon. 3 ch. Charlotte, Kirsten, Alexander. **EDUC:** Rijksuniversiteit of Leiden, Bachelors in Dutch Law 1977, Masters in Law 1980; Dalhousie Univ., LL.B. 1983. **BAR:** Nfld., 1984. **CAREER:** Ptnr, Patterson Palmer Hunt Murphy, Barristers & Solicitors. **SELECTED PUBLICATIONS:** "Analysis of the Canada-Newfoundland Accord on Joint Management of Offshore Oil and Gas Resources of Newfoundland and Labrador" (*Canada Review* Nov. 1985); "Equity Investment in Newfoundland: The Investor's Perspective-Ways of Investing" (*Investing in Entrepreneurs*, St. John's Board of Trade, 1990); "The Art of Business in Newfoundland" (*IRO Journal* Dec. 1990). **DIRECTOR:** several private companies. **AFFIL:** Law Society of Newfoundland; Canadian Bar Association (Exec., Nfld. Branch; Nat'l Membership Committee; Past Chair, Nfld. Subsection, Taxation & Estate Planning Section); Estate Planning Group of St. John's; Suzuki Talent Education Program of St. John's (Chair); Geological Association of Canada (Dir.); Newfoundland Ocean Industries Association; St. John's Board of Trade. **INTERESTS:** music; reading; yoga; gardening. **MISC:** appointed Apr. 1995 as a mbr. of the Human Rights Adjudicative Panel (Nfld.) under the Human Rights Code. **COMMENT:** *"One of the senior partners in the St. John's office of one of the two Atlantic provinces' law firms, specializing in corporate, securities and tax law, with a strong commitment to human rights issues."*

Van Evra, Judith Ann, B.A.,M.A., Ph.D. ■ ⊕

Psychologist. (519) 742-8159, FAX 742-0716. **EDUC:** Valparaiso Univ., B.A. 1960; Bowling Green State Univ., M.A. 1961; Michigan State Univ., Ph.D.(Clinical Psych.) 1966. **CAREER:** Counsellor, Univ. of Waterloo Counselling Services, 1966-73; Asst. Prof., Dept. of Psych., 1966-70 (part-time); Psychological Consultant, Lutherwood, 1970-78 (part-time); Asst. Prof. of Psych., St. Jerome's Coll., 1975-85; Chrm, Dept. of Psych., 1981-87; Assoc. Dir., Institute for Studies in Learning Disabilities, St. Jerome's Coll., 1983-95; Assoc. Prof of Psych., 1983-92; Consulting Psychologist, Waterloo Region Separate Sch. Bd., 1985-90; Prof. of Psych., St. Jerome's Coll., 1992-96; St. Jerome's Coll. Bd. of Gov., 1985-87; Bd. of Dirs., Family & Child Services, 1981-82. **SELECTED PUBLICATIONS:** "An ecological model for practising clinicians" (InClinical Psychology: Issues in the 70's ed. A. Rabin, East Lansing, MI: Michigan State University Press, 1974); "Too little of this, too much of that" (Contemporary Psychology 1 1987); "Television and children" (Grail 1989); *Psychological disorders of children and adolescents* (Boston: Little, Brown, 1983); *Television and Child Development* (Hillsdale, NJ: Lawrence Erlbaum Associates, Inc., 1990); book reviews. **AFFIL:** American Psychological Association; Ontario Psychological Association; Canadian Psychological Association; Learning Disabilities Association; College of Psychologists of Ontario (Council). **INTERESTS:** reading; sailing; travel; cooking. **MISC:** frequent speaker; many media interviews; invited guest of Educational Testing Service, 20th anniversary of *Sesame Street*, 1989; invited symposium participant on "Children & War Coverage" at the Univ. of Penn., 1991. **COMMENT:** *"I've been involved in teaching, research, clinical work and community service for more than 25 years. I am also married and the mother of three grown daughters."*

van Ginkel, Blanche Lemco, FRAIC,MCIP, RCA,Hon.FAIA ⚛ ✪ ☝

Partner, VAN GINKEL ASSOCIATES, 38 Summerhill Gardens, Toronto, ON M4T 1B4 (416) 964-8651. Born 1923. 2 ch. Brenda, Marc. **EDUC:** McGill Univ., B.Arch. 1945; Harvard Univ., Master of City Planning 1950. **CAREER:**

Asst. to Dir. of Tech. Svcs, National Film Bd., 1943-44; Mgr, Regina City Planning Committee, 1946; Architect, W. Crabtree, London, 1947; Architect, Atelier LeCorbusier, Paris, 1948; Asst. Prof., Univ. of Pennsylvania, 1951-57; Sole Principal, Blanche Lemco, Architect, 1952-57; Principal (Ptnr), van Ginkel Associates, 1957 to date; Visiting Prof., Harvard Univ. 1958, 1971, 1975; Visiting Prof., Univ. de Montréal, 1961-66, 1969-70; Visiting Prof., McGill Univ., 1971-77; Dean, Sch. of Architecture, Univ. of Toronto, 1977-82; Prof., Univ. of Toronto, 1977-92. SELECTED PUBLICA-TIONS: articles published in *Architectural Forum, Canadian Art, Canadian Architect, Architectural Record, Architectural Design, Urban Design International, The Fifth Column, Habitat, Journal of the American Institute of Planners, Canadian Encyclopedia, Pollution Primer, Architecture Concept,* & others. AFFIL: Royal Architectural Institute of Canada (Fellow; Exec.); Royal Canadian Academy of Arts (Exec.); American Institute of Architects (Hon. Fellow); Association of Collegiate Schools of Architecture (Bd. 1981-84; VP 1985-86; Pres. 1986-87); International Archive of Women in Architecture (Bd.); Ontario Association of Architects; Corporation of Urbanists of Quebec (Founder); Town Planning Institute of Canada (Bd.); Harvard GSD (Alumni Council; Advisory Committee). HONS: Lt. Governor's Medal, McGill Univ., 1945; IFHP Grand Prix for Film, 1956; *Mademoiselle* Magazine Woman of the Year, 1956; *Canadian Architect* Magazine Award, 1961; Massey Medal for Architecture, 1962; Montreal YWCA Award, 1975; Queen's Silver Jubilee Medal, 1977; Association of Collegiate Schools of Architecture (ACSA) Svc Award, 1984; Distinguished Prof. Award, Association of Collegiate Schools of Architecture, 1989; Cdn Citizenship Citation, 1991; Univ. of Toronto Architecture & Landscape Architecture Alumni Award, 1991. MISC: 1st woman elected to office at the Royal Architectural Institute of Canada; 1st woman Dean of a sch. of architecture; mbr. of Council, National Council of Women, Canada, 1962-69; Advisory Bd., Montreal Int'l Film Festivals, 1961-66; initiated "Save the Mountain Committee," Montreal, 1960. COMMENT: *"Architect, urbanist and educator. Extensive volunteer community work in urban preservation and the arts. First woman elected to office in RAIC and as Dean of a school of architecture."*

Van Norman, Marilyn, R.N.,B.A., M.A. ■ ⌼
Director of Student Service, UNIVERSITY OF TORONTO, 214 College St., Toronto, ON M5T 2Z9 (416) 978-8003, FAX 971-2152, EMAIL

van.norman@utcc.utoronto.ca. Born Montreal 1945. d. 3 stepch. EDUC: Montreal General Hospital, R.N. 1966; Concordia Univ., B.A.(Soc.) 1977; Canadian Securities Course, Grad. 1985; Univ. of Toronto, M.A.(Soc. in Educ.) 1990. CAREER: health promo., PSB6M & Vanier Coll., 1969-75; Social Animator, Vanier Coll., 1975-79; Coord., Student Svcs, 1979-82; Asst. Dir., Career Centre, Univ. of Toronto, 1982-89; Dir., Career Centre, 1989-95; Dir., Univ. of Toronto Student Svcs, 1995-96; Dir., Student Svc, 1996 to date. SELECTED PUBLICATIONS: "Making It Work," *Career Management for the New Workplace* (Toronto: Burghet Books, 1995); "Making it Work," *Career Management Series* (Canadian Association of Career Educators); variety of career dev. articles & booklets. AFFIL: Canadian Association Career Educators & Employers (Pres. 1992); Adventure Place (Pres. of Bd. 1990-94); College Placement Association; American Association of Counsellors. HONS: Award of Distinction, Ontario College Counsellors; Award of Merit, A.C.C.I.S. INTERESTS: art; investments; cross-country skiing; travel; power walking; writing. COMMENT: *"It is only by sitting on the shoulders of women who have gone before us, that we can see the future."*

Vanstone, Ann L., B.A. ⌼
Chair, THE METROPOLITAN TORONTO SCHOOL BOARD, 45 York Mills Rd., North York, ON M2P 1B6 (416) 397-2572, FAX 397-2569. Born Ottawa 1935. m. Ray Vanstone. 4 ch. EDUC: Univ. of Toronto, B.A. 1955; Univ. of Natal, South Africa, B.A.(Psych.) 1958. CAREER: Sch. Trustee, 16 yrs.; Chair, Toronto Bd. of Educ., 1986; Chair, Metropolitan Toronto Sch. Bd., 1987, 1988, 1993, 1994, 1995, 1996. DIRECTOR: Liberty Technologies Inc. AFFIL: University Women's Club (N. Toronto Charter Mbr.). COMMENT: *"With four children and a husband who is a recently retired university professor, I have a passionate commitment to public education and the necessity of a system of excellence."*

Vanstone, Joan E. ■ ⌼ ○
National Director, PARENT FINDERS OF CANADA, 3998 Bayridge Ave., West Vancouver, BC V7V 3J5 (604) 926-1096, FAX 926-2037. Born Vancouver 1933. m. S. Martin Vanstone. 3 ch. Gregory M. Vanstone, Leanne E. Lionello, Scott B. Vanstone. EDUC: Lord Byng High Sch., Sr. Matric. 1951; Fenton Bus. Coll.; Langara Coll. (English, Psych. & Soc.) 1974-75. CAREER: professional model & fashion show commentator; Sec., Women's Royal Canadian Navy (R), 1952-56; Flight Attendant, CP Air & Wardair; Proprietor, Leanne Imports; Colum-

nist, Ladner Optimist, 1962-64; Founder, Parent Finders of Canada, 1974; Nat'l Dir., 1974 to date; Registrar, Canadian Adoption Reunion Register, 1974 to date; Founding Mbr., American Adoption Congress, 1978. **SELECTED PUBLICATIONS:** *Reunion Research Report* (1979); numerous briefs & position papers to social svcs ministries & gov't commissions. **EDIT:** publisher, in-house newsletter to all Parent Finders & affiliated groups. **AFFIL:** International Soundex Reunion Register (Trustee); Families for Children; Adoptive Parents' Association of B.C.; Empress Wings (Sec. & VP); Diagnostic Centre, Vancouver General Hospital (volunteer); Adoption Advisory & Consultative Committee; B.C. Adoption Network. **HONS:** Founders Award, Canadian Adoption Reform Association, 1981; nominated for YWCA Women of Distinction Award, Community & Humanitarian Svcs Category, 1990; Adoptee Activist Award, Adoption Council of Canada, 1990; Distinguished Service to Families Award, B.C. Council for the Family, 1996; American Adoption Congress Legislative Reform Award, 1996. **INTERESTS:** travel; reading; gardening; interior decorating; dressmaking. **MISC:** born in Vancouver & adopted at 16 months, sought background info. from Children's Aid Society in her 30s when in need of heredity info. & medical history, which was the start of search for her family of origin; a 1974 meeting with 2 other searching adult adoptees led to her founding Parent Finders, a volunteer self-help organization to promote openness in adoption & access to sealed records for adult adoptees & birth parents, leading to reunion, if desired; more than 7,000 reunions have resulted from Parent Finders volunteer network; 45,000 registrations are in the Cdn Adoption Reunion Register from 33 Parent Finders chapters & the 14 affiliate groups; a 22 yr. lobbying effort has resulted in the new Adoption Act 1995 in B.C., giving the right of access to documents to adult adoptees & birth parents, effective Nov. 4, 1996. **COMMENT:** *"I am an optimistic, family-centred person who has derived great personal satisfaction in life by giving back to others, while still maintaining my own identity. The reunions I have facilitated by founding and maintaining Parent Finders for 21 years have helped to heal the wounds of separation, loss and rejection imposed by the adoption process."*

Vardey, Lucinda 🗐 ☼ ⊰
Writer, Spiritual Counsellor, Retreat Guide. 94 Crescent Rd., Apt. 9, Toronto, ON M4W 1T5 (416) 323-1133, FAX 323-0204. Born London, UK 1949. m. John Dalla Costa. **CAREER:** Asst., Oxford Univ. Press Music Div., 1967;

Exec. Asst., Pallas Gallery, London, UK, 1968-70; Promo. Mgr, Collins Publishers Ltd., Toronto, 1970-77; Founder & Pres., Lucinda Vardey Agency Ltd., 1977-96. **SELECTED PUBLICATIONS:** *Belonging: A Book for the Questioning Catholic Today* (Toronto: Lester and Orpen Dennys, 1988); *God in All Worlds: An Anthology of Contemporary Spirituality* ed. (Pantheon, 1995; Vintage, 1996); *A Simple Path* (Mother Teresa's book), co-writer. **AFFIL:** Bayview Hospice, Sunnybrook Hospital (Past Bd.); International Association for the Advancement of Gestalt Therapy. **INTERESTS:** spiritual matters; travel; music (piano playing); reading; yoga; writing. **MISC:** teaches yoga; has opened a Retreat Centre in Tuscany, Italy. **COMMENT:** *"I am specializing now in healing in the everyday: through my work as a counsellor, practitioner, writer and teacher."*

Vartanian, Sona ■ ⊗ ⊰
Fondatrice et directrice, L'ACADÉMIE DE BALLET SONIA VARTANIAN (S.V.) INC., 460 Ste.-Catherine O., 6e étage, Montreal, QC H3B 1A7 (514) 393-0818. Born Alexandria, Egypt 1947. **EDUC:** National Ballet Academy of Yerevan, Armenia, Masters (Ballet). **CAREER:** Danseuse-étoile, National Theatre, Opera, & Ballet of Armenia (U.S.S.R.), 1964-73; Danseuse-étoile, Les Grands Ballets Canadiens, 1973-79; Danseuse-étoile, The Cleveland Ballet, 1977-78; guest artist, Alberta Ballet, 1979-81; Fondatrice et dir. artistique, L'Académie de Ballet Vartanian, 1982 to date; Fondatrice et dir. artistique, Les Ballets Classiques de Montréals, 1987-89, 1992 to date; Fondatrice et dir. artistique, The Montreal Ballet Theatre, 1989-91; Dir., Nevada Dance Theatre Academy of Dance. **SELECTED CREDITS:** invited artist or teacher at the Alberta Ballet, Ballet Toussaint de Montréal, the National Ballet of Portugal, the Georgian Ballet of Tbilisi, the Ukraine Ballet of Donetsk, the Nevada Dance Theatre, the Tokyo Ballet, the Toyota City Ballet, the Shizouaka Ballet, Hiroshima Sch. of Ballet; repertoire: *Swan Lake, Giselle, Don Quixote, Romeo & Juliet, The Nutcracker, Corsaire, Hamlet; Lac des cygnes,* CBC, 1974, 1977; *Variations Diabelli,* CBC, 1977; *Rhymes et pas,* CBC, 1979; *La mort du cygne,* Radio-Québec, 1981; Choreographer: *Avec Gagnon,* 1987; *Prière,* 1987; *L'invitation à la danse,* 1988; *Rossiniana,* 1989; *La Peregrina,* Befana, 1992 *Western Sketches.*

Vaughan, Vanessa Rea, B.F.A. ⬗ ⊗ ♌
Actor and Artist. c/o Great North Artists Management, 350 Dupont St., Toronto, ON M5R 1V9 (416) 925-2051, FAX 925-3904. Born Toronto 1969. s. **EDUC:** York Univ.,

B.F.A.(Special Hons.) 1994. **CAREER:** actor, artist, filmmaker. **SELECTED CREDITS:** dir./writer, *Edda's Song* (film), Hands in Motion Communications, 1996; principal actor, *A Maiden's Grave*, HBO/Alliance, 1996; dir., *Too Shorts* (film), Hands in Motion Communications, 1995; guest star, *Kung Fu: The Legend Continues* (series), Warner Bros., 1994; recurring guest star, *Street Legal* (series), CBC, 1993-94; consultant/principal actor, *When the Mind Hears*, parts 1 & 2 (film), 1993; guest star, *Class of '96* (series), Fox Television, 1993; guest star, *Grand Central Murders* (mow), CBS, 1992; lead, *Stage Hands* (film), Jigsaw Pictures, 1991; co-star, *Crazy Moon* (feature), Allegro Films/NFB, 1986; lead actor, *The Sound and the Silence* (miniseries), Atlantis Films/Cypress/South Pacific/Screenstar, 1991; principal actor, *Bridge to Silence* (mow), Far North Productions, 1989; "Ears to Hear, Twelve Years Later," *The Nature of Things*, CBC, 1987; principal actor, *Clown White* (TV movie), Martin-Paul Prod., 1979. **EXHIBITIONS:** *Deaf Expo '95*, L.A. (1995); E-Side Studio Gallery, solo, Toronto (1995); Idee Gallery, Toronto (1994); Samuel J. Zacks Gallery, Toronto (1992); IDA Gallery, Toronto (1992); Arthur Haberman Gallery, Toronto (1991). **AFFIL:** Toronto Women in Film & Television; VOICE Ontario (Prov. Bd. of Dir. 1992-94); ACTRA. **HONS:** nomination, Best Performance by an Actress in a Leading Role in a Dramatic Program or Miniseries (Mabel Hubbard Bell, *The Sound and the Silence*), Gemini Awards, 1993. **MISC:** public rel'ns activities include, Spokesperson, Cinématique Ontario, *In the Land of the Deaf* (film), 1995; speaker & host at various fundraisers; narrator for public awareness videos. **COMMENT:** *"As an artist and filmmaker, I aim to create a vehicle of expression for fellow deaf artists to be seen and heard."*

Veenman, Sybil E., LL.B. ⚖ Ⓢ
Associate General Counsel and Secretary, BARRICK GOLD CORPORATION, Royal Bank Plaza, S. Tower, Ste. 2700, P.O. Box 119, Toronto, ON M5J 2J3 (416) 307-7470, FAX 861-8243. Born Peterborough, Ont. 1963. **EDUC:** Univ. of Toronto, LL.B. 1987. **BAR:** Ont., 1989. **CAREER:** Lawyer, Fasken Campbell Godfrey, 1989-94; Assoc. Gen. Cnsl & Sec., Lac Minerals Ltd., 1994; Assoc. Gen. Cnsl & Sec., Barrick Gold Corporation, 1994 to date.

Veinot, Tiffany, B.A.,M.L.S. ■ 🗄 ⏣ ⭕
Librarian, Publications Distributor and Systems Manager and Fundraiser, EDUCATION WIFE ASSAULT, 427 Bloor St. W., Box 7, Toronto, ON M5R 1T9 (416) 968-3422, FAX 968-

2026. Born Sarnia, Ont. 1971. **EDUC:** Univ. of Toronto, B.A.(Women's Studies/Hist.) 1992, M.L.S. 1994; Canadian Outward Bound Wilderness Sch., 1994. **CAREER:** Indexer & Reference Asst., Women's Studies Collection, New Coll. Library, Univ. of Toronto, 1991-94; Research Consultant, 1993-94; Orders Asst., Metropolitan Toronto Reference Library, 1993; Indexer, Cdn Bus. & Current Affairs, Cdn Educ. Index, Micromedia Ltd., 1994; Librarian & Publications Distributor, Education Wife Assault, 1994 to date. **AFFIL:** Indexing & Abstracting Society of Canada. **HONS:** Univ. of Toronto Open Fellowship; H.W. Wilson Scholarship; Toronto Women's Bookstore Essay Award. **INTERESTS:** feminist approaches to info. storage & retrieval; indexing; ending abuse of women & children; outdoor recreation; database mgmt; telecomm. mgmt; non-profit mktg. **COMMENT:** *"I am interested in using information as a political tool in seeking social justice and in developing my capacities for compassion, balance and joy."*

Vella, Susan M., B.A.,LL.B. ⚖ ⏣ 🖉
Lawyer, GOODMAN AND CARR, 200 King St. W., Ste. 2300, Toronto, ON M5H 3W5 (416) 595-2434, FAX 595-0567. Born Toronto 1960. **EDUC:** Univ. of Toronto, B.A.(English Lit.) 1983; Osgoode Hall Law Sch., LL.B. 1986. **BAR:** Ont. 1988. **CAREER:** Chair, Bd. of Dir., Community & Legal Aid Svcs Program, Osgoode Hall Law Sch., 1985-86; articling student, Blake Cassels and Graydon, 1986-87; Assoc., 1988-92; Ptnr, Goodman and Carr, 1992 to date. **SELECTED PUBLICATIONS:** "The Evolution of Forum Conveniens," with Madam Justice Kathryn M. Feldman (*Advocates' Quarterly* 1989); "Removal of 'No Females Allowed' Signs in Ontario: Re Blainey and Ontario Hockey Association" *(Canadian Journal of Women and the Law* 2 1989-90); "*J (L.) v. J. (A.):* Civil Sexual Assault Liability in Non-Offending Parent Cases," with Elizabeth K.P. Grace (*Canadian Journal of Women and the Law* Spring 1994); "False Memory Syndrome: Therapists are the Latest Target" (*The National,* Canadian Bar Association Feb./Mar. 1994); "Institutional Responsibility in Equity and at Common Law Involving Sexual Assault Claims" (*Canadian Institute* Apr. 1994). **AFFIL:** National Association of Women & the Law (Past Pres.); Catholic Children's Aid Society of Metropolitan Toronto; Canadian Bar Association (Voting Mbr. of the Council, Ont.); Community & Legal Aid Svcs Program (Dir.); Law Society of Upper Canada. **HONS:** Eugene O'Keefe Award for Overall Academic Achievement, St. Michael's Coll., Univ. of Toronto, 1982; Glenn Wakayabashi Award for Aca-

demic Achievement, Community Involvement & Leadership, Osgoode Hall, 1985; Honours Award for Gen. Achievement, Osgoode Hall, 1986. **MISC:** Internationally Certified Umpire with the International Badminton Federation (1st Cdn woman & 2nd woman in the world to achieve certification); lectured extensively in the area of civil sexual assault & the recovered memory controversy; represented survivors' groups in making submissions to legislative committees; has been quoted extensively in the media on issues surrounding sexual assault, institutional liability, & sexual harassment; V-Chair, Commercial Registration Appeal Tribunal, 1993-96; Prosecutor of Harassment Complaints, Ontario Institute for Studies in Education, 1992 to date. **COMMENT:** *"Susan represents survivors of sexual and institutionalized abuse, including the recent precedent-setting agreement reached with the Ontario Government on behalf of the survivors of the Grandview Training School for Girls. She also represents survivors of institutionalized abuse at religious institutions, educational institutions, medical institutions, corporations and child welfare agencies."*

Venhola, Mariellen (Elizabeth) ✊ ⚖ ♥ ☝
Crisis Counsellor and Legal Worker, PEOPLE IN TRANSITION (ALLISTON), INC., "My Sister's Place," Women's Shelter, Alliston, ON. Born 1956. m. 3 ch. **EDUC:** Kemptville Coll. of Agricultural Technology, Agric. Tech. Diploma 1975; Georgian Coll. of Applied Technology, Journalism Diploma 1987; York Regional Police, Law for Advocates Certificate (Hons.) 1991; Osgoode Hall Law Sch., York Univ., LL.B. in progress, 1993 to date. **CAREER:** Jr. Forest Ranger, Ministry of Natural Resources, Powassan, Ont., Summer 1972; dairy farming, Ottawa Valley, 1975-80; designed quilts, 1975-80; reporter/ed./photojournalist, *The Herald*, Alliston, Ont., 1982-88; Publisher/Ed., *Cookstown Advocate*, Cookstown, Ont., 1988-91; journalist/columnist, *Newmarket Era*, 1989; Relief Crisis Counsellor/Legal Worker, My Sister's Place, People in Transition Inc., Alliston, 1990-95; Crisis Counsellor, Green Haven Shelter, Orillia, Ont., seconded to open new shelter, 1991-92; Relief Crisis Counsellor, Hillside House, Shelter, Family Transition Place, Orangeville, Ont., 1992-95. **SELECTED PUBLICATIONS:** numerous articles, columns & features in *The Herald*, *The Toronto Star*, *The Globe and Mail*, *Cookstown Advocate*, *The Newmarket Era* & others; features & photos, *Tornado* (1986); several reports on structure & organization of women's shelters, abuse issues, equality & the law, legal writing, constructive trusts. **EDIT:** compiled & published newsletter for Simcoe County Women's Shelters, 1991; Ed., *Other Words*, 1993-95; Ed., *Obiter Dicta*, 1993-95. **AFFIL:** Elizabeth Fry Society of Simcoe County (Bd.; CAEFS Rep.; former VP); Canadian Bar Association.; Barrie Women's Action Committee; Osgoode Hall Law Sch. (Women's Caucus; National Association of Women and the Law Rep.); Cookstown Central Public Sch. Yearbook Committee; Teacher's Asst., Class Volunteer; United Church. **HONS:** Second Place, News Team, Ont. Community Newspaper Awards, 1984; First Place, News Team, Ont. Community Newspaper Awards, 1985; Second Place, Photography, Ont. Community Newspaper Awards, 1986; First Place, Feature Writing, Ont. Community Newspaper Awards, 1986; shortlisted as nominee for Status of Women–Ont., 1992. **INTERESTS:** family; piano; guitar; reading; games; art; sewing; cooking; music; gardening. **MISC:** committee mbr., dev. of TV commercial on abuse, Ontario Women's Directorate, 1991-92; tornado feature, *Morningside*, CBC, 1986; part of 1st group of female jr. rangers hired for environmental work, 1972; 1 of 3 women in student body of 220 at Kemptville Coll. of Agriculture, 1973-75; award-winning 3-part *Herald* feature series examining the issues of abuse in a small community motivated meetings that led to the establishment of "My Sister's Place," the Alliston women's shelter; invited by Ministry of Solicitor Gen. to assist in training police regarding woman abuse, Aylmer Police Coll.; numerous workshops & conferences. **COMMENT:** *"The struggle to entrench the substantive quality of human rights has been a long and arduous one. Women and children are particularly oppressed in our global communities, with little political power to claim their equal status. It is my belief that equality will only be achieved by individual and small group efforts. Women, men and children volunteering in the community is the critical factor in ensuring a supportive communal base which in turn can effect positive global change socially and politically. Our commitment must be strong, unwavering, fearless and true. It has been and shall remain for now, hard work."*

Vennat, Manon, LL.B.,D.E.S., C.M. ■■ $
Chairman and Managing Director, SPENCER-STUART, MONTREAL (consulting), 1981 McGill College Ave., Ste. 1430, Montreal, QC H3A 2Y1 (514) 288-3377, FAX 288-4626. Born Canada. 1 ch. **EDUC:** McGill Univ., LL.B. 1965; Univ. of Ottawa, D.E.S.(Public Law) 1968. **CAREER:** Exec. Asst. to the Dir. Gen. & Dir. of Legal Affairs, Company of Young

Canadians, 1966; Language Programs Officer, Fed.-Prov. Rel'ns, Sec. of State/Reg'l Liaison Officer, Citizenship Dept., 1969-72; Exec. Dir. & founder, "le Centre de linguistique de l'entreprise, 1972-80; VP, Admin., Gen. Cnsl & Sec. to the Bd. of Dir., AES Data, 1980-86; VP, SpencerStuart, 1986-91; Chrm, Montreal, 1991 to date. **AFFIL:** The Montreal Exchange (Gov.); Montreal Board of Trade (former Pres.; Chrm); Canadian Chamber of Commerce (former mbr., Bd. of Dir.); C.D. Howe Institute; Frontier Coll. Learning Foundation (VP); Public Policy Forum (Bd.); Canadian Studies Centre, Duke Univ. (Bd. of Visitors); McGill's Institute for the Study of Canada (Bd. of Trustees); McGill Univ. (Bd. of Gov.); Univ. of Ottawa (Advisory Bd., Fac. of Admin.); McCord Museum of Canadian History (former Chrm, Bd. of Dir.). **HONS:** honorary Ph.D.(Admin.), Univ. of Ottawa; Member of the Order of Canada.

Vermette, Cécile, R.N.,M.N.A. 🍁

Deputée (Marie-Victorin), GOUVERNEMENT DU QUÉBEC, Hôtel du Parlement, Bur. RC 73, Québec, QC G1A 1A4 (418) 643-5611, FAX 646-0707. Born Montreal 1945. **EDUC:** Hôpital Saint-Luc, Diplôme (Sciences infirmières) 1968; Univ. de Montréal, Baccalauréat (Gestion). **CAREER:** differentes responsabilités à titre d'infirmière, 1968-71; Animatrice, cadre du certificate en santé et sécurité du travail, 1980-85; Députée (Marie-Victorin), Assemblée Nationale, Prov. of Qué., 1985 to date; Whip adjointe du gouv., Assemblée Nationale, 1994 to date; Déléguée pour les parlementaires du Commonwealth, 1994 to date; Commission de l'Économie et du Travail, 1994 to date. **AFFIL:** Parti Québécois; Hôpital Charles-Lemoyne (Prés., conseil d'admin. 1980-85). **MISC:** organizer, Forum prov. sur les toxicomanies, 1990; participant as coord. for Qué. & Canada, Conférence des femmes parlementaires pour la Paix dans le monde, Zimbabwe, 1990.

Verreault, Denise [$]

President, GROUPE MARITIME VERREAULT INC., 146, rue Principale, Les Méchins, QC G0J 1T0 (418) 729-3733, FAX 729-3285. **CAREER:** Pres., Groupe Maritime Verreault Inc., 1991 to date; Chair of the Bd., Les Industries Verreault Inc., est. 1991; Chair of the Bd., BV Maritime Inc., est. 1992; Chair of the Bd., Verreault Maritime Inc., est. 1992; sole owner, Gestion Administrative Verreault Inc., 1993 to date. **DIRECTOR:** Québec-Téléphone; Compagnie de Gestion de Matane; Caisse de Dépôt et Placement du Québec; Société Québécoise de Développement de la Main-d'Oeuvre. **HONS:** Prix de la Femme de l'Année, catégorie Affaires, Salon de la Femme de Montréal, 1991; Prix de la Femme de l'Année, catégorie Affaires, Municipalité Régionale de Comté de Matane, 1995. **COMMENT:** *"Groupe Maritime Verreault Inc. was founded in 1991 by Denise Verreault. Its mandate is to market and promote the associated companies. It owns all or the majority of the shares of Verreault Navigation Inc., Verreault Maritime Inc., BV Maritime Inc., Les Industries Verreault Inc. and Verreault Maritimes Holdings Inc., which controls the EnerChem Group of companies."*

Verschuren, Annette, B.B.A. ■ [$]

President, HOME DEPOT CANADA, 426 Ellesmere Rd., Scarborough, ON M1R 4E7 (416) 609-0852, FAX 609-0819. Born North Sydney, N.S. 1956. m. Erik Haites. **EDUC:** St. Francis Xavier Univ., B.B.A. 1977. **CAREER:** various positions, 1977-83; Exec. VP, Canada Development Investment Corporation, 1983-86; VP, Corp. Dev., Imasco Ltd., 1989-92; Pres., Verschuren Ventures, 1992-93; Pres., Michaels of Canada Inc., 1993 -96; Pres., Home Depot Canada, 1996 to date. **DIRECTOR:** Sobey's Inc. **AFFIL:** ProAction; Retail Council of Canada; C.A.T.O.; Sunnybrook Hospital. **HONS:** Canada 125 Medal; Women on the Move Award, 1994. **INTERESTS:** reading; jogging; scuba diving; spending an evening with good friends. **COMMENT:** *"I focus not on my abilities but on my opportunities and the recognition that I have no boundaries. I work hard to serve and provide sound judgment and direction to the people I work with."*

Verstraete, Ursula, R.N.,B.A.S., C.H.E.,M.Ed. ■ ⊕

Co-ordinator, Hospital and Physician Relations, SCARBOROUGH GENERAL HOSPITAL, 3050 Lawrence Ave. E., Scarborough, ON M1P 2V5 (416) 438-2911, FAX 438-9318. Born Derby, UK 1943. m. William. 2 ch. Sarah Verstraete, Jared Verstraete. **EDUC:** Hotel-Dieu Sch. of Nursing, R.N. 1965; York Univ., B.A.S. (Admin. Studies) 1984; Brock Univ., M.Ed. (Admin.) 1993. **CAREER:** various staff positions, Ont. hospital, 1965-76; Admin. Supervisor, Nursing Div., York County Hospital, 1976-80; Dir. of Nursing, Shouldice Hospital, 1980-89; Dir. of Nursing Practice, Scarborough General Hospital, 1989-95; Coord., Hospital & Physician Rel'ns, 1995 to date. **AFFIL:** Medical Research Council of Canada; Canadian Coll. of Health Care Executives (Certified Health Exec.); Registered Nurses' Association of Ontario; Coll. of Nurses of Ontario; Canadian Federation of University Women (Pres., N. Toronto Club 1994-95). **INTERESTS:** travel; bridge; reading. **MISC:** Educational

Consultant, Nursing Mgmt Program, Canadian Nurses' Association, Ottawa, 1986-92.

Vervoort, Patricia, B.A.,M.A. ⊗ 📖 ⊰
Associate Professor, Department of Visual Arts, LAKEHEAD UNIVERSITY, 955 Oliver Rd., Thunder Bay, ON P7B 5E1 (807) 343-8679, FAX 345-239, EMAIL pvervoor@cs_acad_lan.lakeheadu.ca. Born Boston, Mass. 1942. m. Dr. Gerardus Vervoort. 2 ch. EDUC: St. Mary's Univ., B.A.(English/Art) 1963; Univ. of Iowa, M.A.(Art Hist.) 1966, M.A.(Library Sci.) 1970. CAREER: Sessional Lecturer, Art Hist., Lakehead Univ., 1975-89; Asst. Prof., Art Hist., 1989-92; Chair, Dept. of Visual Arts, 1990-95; Assoc. Prof., Art Hist., 1992 to date. SELECTED PUBLICATIONS: "Meaning in Old Buildings" (*Thunder Bay Historical Museum Society Papers and Records* V 1977); "Sunrise on the Saguenay: Popular Literature and the Sublime" (*Mosaic: A Journal for the Interdisciplinary Study of Literature* Spring 1988); "Lakehead Terminal Elevators: Aspects of Their Engineering History" (*Canadian Journal of Civil Engineering* 17 1990); "This 'Magnificent Pile': Architectural Embellishments of Older School Buildings in Thunder Bay" (*Thunder Bay Historical Museum Society Papers and Records* XXI 1993); "Re-Constructing van Gogh: Paintings as Sculptures," *The Low Countries and Beyond*, ed. Robert S. Kirsner (Lanham, MD: Univ. Press of America, 1993). AFFIL: Local Architectural Construction Advisory Committee (Chair 1977-94); Universities Art Association of Canada; Society for the Study of Architecture in Canada. COMMENT: "*An architectural and art historian, interested in the relationship of old and new buildings, art and industrial buildings, teaching and research, relationships between art of the past and contemporary art.*"

Vethamany-Globus, Swani, B.Sc.,M.A., M.Sc.,Ph.D. ⊰ 🏵 ⊕
Associate Professor, Department of Biology, UNIVERSITY OF WATERLOO, Waterloo, ON N2L 3G1 (519) 885-1211, ext. 2509, FAX 746-0614, EMAIL svethama@biology.watstar.uwaterloo.ca. Born India 1937. m. Dr. Morton Globus. 2 ch. Julie Globus, Brian Globus. EDUC: Madras Univ., B.Sc.(Zoology) 1958, M.A. 1959, M.Sc. 1963; Univ. of Toronto, Ph.D. 1970. CAREER: Lecturer, Dept. of Biol., Christian Medical Coll., Vellore, India, 1960-65; Postdoctoral Fellow, Dept. of Biol., Brandeis Univ., Mass., 1970-72; Research Asst. Prof., Dept. of Biol., Univ. of Waterloo, 1973-89; Assoc. Prof., part-time, 1987 to date. SELECTED PUBLICATIONS: "Agonist-induced hydrolysis of Inositol phospholipids in newt forelimb regeneration blastemas," with M. Globus & M.J. Smith, *Progress in Clinical and Biological Research*, Vol. 383B. *Limb Development and Regeneration*, eds. Fallon, Geotinck, Kelley, Stocum (Wiley-Liss, 1992); various papers in refereed journals & refereed conference proceedings. AFFIL: Univ. of Waterloo (Bd. of Gov.; Senate; mbr. of numerous associations & committees). HONS: Research Award, Univ. of Toronto, 1967-68; Prov. of Ont. Gov't Grad. Award, 1968-70; Marcus Singer Medal for Excellence in Regeneration Research, 1988. INTERESTS: music; art; organic gardening; natural healing; conservation; social & environmental issues; writing; the ocean & mountains; birds; good friends. COMMENT: "*Supported by NSERC operating grants, Dr. Vethamany-Globus has made significant contributions to the area of research in hormone control of vertebrate limb regeneration and wound healing, and has gained international recognition. She has been active on women's and equity issues and has taken an active role in attracting women into science and other non-traditional fields. She is a member of the Status of Women and Inclusivity Committee of the UW Faculty Association.*"

Veverka, Jana Mila, B.A.,M.A. ✴ 🏠
President, BOHEMIA PRODUCTIONS INC., 6044 Gleneagles Dr., W. Vancouver, BC V7W 1W2 (604) 921-7653, FAX 921-6406. Born Czechoslovakia 1946. m. David Fischer. EDUC: Bishop's Univ., B.A.(English) 1968; Univ. of British Columbia, M.A.(Theatre Direction) 1970. CAREER: Lecturer, St. Lawrence Coll., Kingston, Ont.; Lecturer, Film Studies, Queen's Univ., 1973-75; Artistic Dir. & Co-Founder, Theatre Mekanique, Kingston; Mgr, Canadian Filmmakers' Distribution Centre; Host, Sprockets, CBC Toronto; Head, Nat'l Script Dept., CBC Toronto, 1976-78; freelance Radio Prod., 1978-81; Story Ed., CBC-TV, CBC Radio, 1981-87; writer, TV drama, 1985-88; Pres., Bohemia Productions Inc. SELECTED CREDITS: Exec. Script Consultant, *The Campbells*, CTV/Freemantle/ITV (Scotland), 1985; Exec. Story Ed./Exec. Script Consultant, *Danger Bay*, CBC/Disney Channel/Sunrise Productions, 1986-87; Co-Prod./Exec. Script Consultant, *Airwolf*, Atlantis/Skyflight Productions, 1986-87; Script Consultant, *Jump* (feature), Omni Productions, 1988; Prod., *Bordertown* (series), Alliance Communications/Atlantique/TV/Isambard, 1991-93; Prod., *The Black Stallion* (series), 1991; Prod., *Lonesome Dove: The Series* (series), Telegenic Programs Inc./Hallmark Entertainment, 1994; Prod., *The Awakening* & *At The Midnight Hour* (movies), CBC/Alliance Communications, 1995; writer,

In a Heart Beat (feature), Tricycle Films Inc., 1996. **AFFIL:** Writers' Guild of Canada; B.C. Producers' Association; Academy of Canadian Film & Television. **HONS:** Silver Medal, N.Y. TV Festival. **INTERESTS:** reading; sailing; writing.

Viau, Catherine, M.A. ■■ ⬠⊗
Vice-President, LES PRODUCTIONS VIA LE MONDE (DANIEL BERTOLINO) INC. (TV production), 326, ouest, rue St-Paul, Montréal, QC H2Y 2A3 (514) 285-1658. Born Montréal 1960. s. **EDUC:** Univ. de Montréal, M.A.(Art Hist.) 1981. **CAREER:** producer of documentaries; scriptwriter & director; Société Radio-Canada, 1981-82; Association des Producteurs de Films et de Vidéo du Québec, 1982-83; VP & Dir. Gen., Les Productions Via le Monde (Daniel Bertolino) Inc., 1983 to date. **SELECTED CREDITS:** *Olympica*; *Stopwatch*; *Dreams of Africa*; *The World Challenge*. **AFFIL:** Fondation Lucille Teasdale. **HONS:** productions have won numerous awards incl. 5 Gemini awards (& 8 other Gemini nominations); Prix de l'Excellence, Festival Atlantique, Halifax; nomination for le Sept d'Or, Paris, 1987; finalist in 2 categories, International Monitor Awards, Los Angeles, 1988.

Viau, Sister Huguette ○ ⟨⟩ ◉
Coordinator, COLLABORATION SANTE INTERNATIONALE (C.S.I.), 1001 Chemin de la Canardiere, Quebec, QC G1J 5G5 (418) 522-6065, FAX 522-5530. Born Hull, Que. 1936. **EDUC:** HEC, Institutional Admin. 1970.

Vickers, Jill McCalla, B.A.,Ph.D. ⟨⟩ ✦
Professor, Political Science and Canadian Studies, CARLETON UNIVERSITY, 1125 Colonel By Dr., DT 1112, Ottawa, ON K1S 5B6 (613) 788-2600, EMAIL jill_vickers@carleton.ca. Born 1942. m. J.K. Johnson. 4 ch. Michael Vickers, Matthew Johnson, Mary Johnson, Elizabeth Johnson. **EDUC:** Carleton Univ., B.A.(Pol. Sci.) 1965; London Sch. of Econ., Ph.D. 1971. **CAREER:** Bell Telephone, 1958-59; Researcher, Parliamentary Committee on Election Expenses, 1965-66; Asst. Prof., then. Prof., Dept. of Pol. Sci. & Institute of Cdn Studies, Carleton Univ., 1969-93; Assoc. Dir., Institute of Cdn Studies, 1982-84; Acting Dir., 1984-85, 1987; Grad. Coord., 1985-88; Dir., 1988-91; Assoc. VP (Academic), Casrleton Univ., 1991-92; Prof., 1982 to date. **SELECTED PUBLICATIONS:** *But Can You Type? Canadian Universities and the Status of Women* with J. Adam (Toronto: Clarke, Irwin, 1977); *Getting Things Done: Women's Views of Their Involvement in Political Life*, ed. (Paris: CRIAW/UNESCO, 1988); *An Exami-*

nation of the Scientific Mode of Enquiry in Politics with Special Reference to Systems Theory in the Works of Easton, Almond, Kaplan and Deutsch (New York: Garland, 1991); *Politics as If Women Mattered: A Political Analysis of the National Action Committee on the Status of Women*, with C. Appelle & P. Rankin (Univ. of Toronto Press, 1993); "Feminist Approaches to Women in Politics," in *Beyond the Vote: Women in Canadian Politics in the Twentieth Century*, Linda Kealy & John Sangster, eds. (Univ. of Toronto Press, 1989); "The Intellectual Origins of Women's Movements in Canada," in *Challenging Times: The Women's Movement in Canada and the United States*, Constance Backhouse & David H. Flaherty, eds. (McGill-Queen's Press, 1992); "The Canadian Women's Movement and a Changing Constitutional Order" *(International Journal of Canadian Studies* Spring 1993); various other publications. **EDIT:** Advisory Bd., *Atlantis: A Women's Studies Journal*, 1982-89, Cdn Studies Ed., 1989-93; Ed. Bd., *Feminist Ethics*, 1988-90; Ed. Bd., *Journal of Canadian Studies*, 1994 to date. **AFFIL:** Canadian Research Institute for the Advancement of Women (Hon. Life Mbr.; Bd. 1982-87; Pres. 1985-86); National Action Committee on the Status of Women (Parliamentarian 1983-89); Canadian Association of University Teachers (Pres. 1975-76); Ontario Council on University Affairs. **HONS:** Senate Medal, Carleton Univ., 1965; Sarah Shorten Award, Canadian Association of University Teachers, 1993. **MISC:** instructional TV series, *Through Her Eyes: Resources for Women's Studies*, Module 3, in 5 parts (1990-91); mbr., UNESCO Experts Committee, Women's Participation in Public Decision-Making, 1990; mbr., Arbitration Panel under *Parliamentary Employees Staff Relations Act*, 1986-95; various conference presentations.

Vickers, Margaret T., R.N.,B.Sc.N.,M.H.A., LL.D. ☼ ⊕ ○
Representative, Sisters of Charity, Chara Health Care Society, ST. VINCENT'S HOSPITAL, Vancouver, BC. Born Miramichi City, N.B. 1927. Entered Sisters of Charity of the Immaculate Conception 1955. **EDUC:** St. Martha's Hospital, R.N. 1952; Univ. of Ottawa, B.Sc.N. 1965, M.H.A. 1967. **CAREER:** Supervisor of Paediatrics, St. Joseph's Hospital, 1957-63; Asst. Administrator, St. Vincent's Hospital, Vancouver, 1967-68; Dir. of Nursing, St. Joseph's Hospital, 1968-69; Asst. Administrator, Holy Family Hospital, Prince Albert, Sask., 1969-72; Exec. Dir. & Administrator, St. Joseph's Hospital, 1972-94; Rep., numerous Bds. & Committees incl. Chara Health Care Society, Sisters of Charity, St. Vincent's Hospital, 1996 to date.

AFFIL: Region 2 Hospital Corporation (Dir.); N.B. Hospital Association (Chair, Bd. of Dir.); Canadian Hospital Association (Dir.); United Way (Dir.); Hospice of Saint John (Steering Committee); Saskatchewan Catholic Health Association (Dir.); American Coll. of Hospital Administrators; Canadian Coll. of Health Service Executives. **HONS:** LL.D.(Hon.), Univ. of New Brunswick, 1986; Citation Award, New Brunswick's Catholic Health Association, 1994; awards from Saint John Irish Cultural Society, Paul Harris Rotary & St. Joseph's Hospital Auxiliary. **INTERESTS:** walking; reading; meeting people; travelling. **MISC:** mentor for students enrolled in the Hospital Organization Mgmt Correspondence Program, 1972-85. **COMMENT:** *"My greatest joy has come from working with the wonderful, competent and caring physicians and staff who give their best to patients, families and each other. Over the past 22 years, I have been blessed with the support of colleagues and those many volunteers who have offered immeasurable assistance and guidance."*

Vikis-Freibergs, Vaira, B.A.,M.A., Ph.D.,LL.D.(hon.) ■ ■ 🐦 📓 ❁
Professeure titulaire (Full Professor), Département de psychologie, UNIVERSITÉ DE MON-TRÉAL, C.P. 6128, Succ. Centre-Ville, Montréal, QC H3C 3J7 (514) 343-7981, FAX 342-5328. Born Riga, Latvia 1937. m. Imants F. Freibergs. 2 ch. Kārlis Roberts, Indra Karoline Freiberg. **EDUC:** Univ. of Toronto, B.A.(Gen.) 1958, M.A.(Psych.) 1960; McGill Univ., Ph.D. (Psych.) 1965. **CAREER:** Asst./Assoc. Prof., Univ. de Montréal, 1965-77; Prof. of Psych., 1977 to date. **SELECTED PUBLICATIONS:** author or co-author, 5 books & over 100 articles, book chapters & tech. reports; co-author, large databases of Latvian folksong texts. **AFFIL:** Science Council of Canada (V-Chrm 1984-89); Royal Society of Canada (Fellow; mbr. of Council 1992-96; Chair, Symposia Committee 1992-96); Académie des lettres et des arts, Société Royale du Canada (mbr. of Council 1995-98). **HONS:** Prof. Anna Abele Memorial Prize for distinguished work in Latvian philology, 1979; Distinguished Contribution Prize, World Association of Free Latvians, U.S., 1989; honorary LL.D., Queen's Univ., 1991; Marcel Vincent Prize & Medal in the Social Sciences, ACFAS, 1992; Killam Research Fellow, Canada Council, 1993-95; Officer, Order of the Three Stars, Republic of Latvia, 1995; Pierre Chauveau Medal in the Humanities, Royal Society of Canada, 1995. **INTERESTS:** literature; arts; travel; gardening. **COMMENT:** *"Researcher and educator with extensive experience in science administration.*

Former Vice-Chairman of Science Council of Canada. Former President, Canadian Psychological Association, Social Science Federation of Canada and Association for the Advancement of Baltic Studies. Former Chair, Special Panel on Human Factors of NATO Science Programme."

Villalon, Lita, B.Sc.,M.Sc., Ph.D. ■ ■ 🐦 ⊕ ❁
Directrice, École de nutrition et d'études familiales, UNIVERSITÉ DE MONCTON, Moncton, NB E1A 3E9 (506) 858-4285, FAX 858-4540, EMAIL villall@umoncton.ca. Born Chili 1947. sép. 3 ch. **EDUC:** Univ. du Chili, B.Sc.(Nutrition & diététique) 1969; Univ. de Montréal, M.Sc.(Nutrition-recherche) 1984, Ph.D.(Nutrition-recherche) 1987. **CAREER:** Prof., Dépt. de nutrition, Univ. du Chili, Santiago, 1972-73; Nutritionniste & agente de recherche, centre de recherche sur la croissance humaine, Univ. de Montréal, 1975-86; Prof.-visiteure, École de nutrition, Univ. Centroaméricaine, Managua, Nicaragua, 1988-89; Prof., Dépt. de nutrition, Univ. de Montréal, 1990-92; Dir., École de nutrition et d'études familiales, Univ. de Moncton, 1992 to date. **SELECTED PUBLICATIONS:** author, *Manuel de bioestadistica* (Les presses de l'Univ. Centro-américaine, Managua, 1989); *Manual de Evaluation Nutricional computa-rizada* (Les Presses de l'Univ. Centroaméricaine, Manuaga, 1989); *Manual de Metodologia de la Investigacion* (Les Presses de l'Univ. Centroaméricaine, Managua, 1989); *Manual Métodos y técnicas para la preparacion del trabajo de Monografia* (Les Presses de l'Univ. Centroaméricaine, Manuaga, 1989); co-author, *Manual de Nutricion Aplicada* (Les presses de l'Univ. Centro-américaine, Managua, 1989); author, *Manual de Bioestadistica* (Les Presses de l'Univ. Centro-américaine, Managua, 1989); numerous articles incl.: co-author, "Effects of a low protein diet on bile composition in rats" (*Journal of Nutrition* 177, 1987); co-author, "Les habitudes alimentaires et la diète de la femme enceinte: comparaison entre deux méthodes d'évaluation" (*Journal of the Canadian Dietetic Association* 39(4), 1978); co-author, "La evolucion de la lactancia materna en América Latina" (*Revista Pédiatrica de Chile*, Vol. 16 1(2), 1973); author, "La santé et la nutrition des femmes" (*Revue La promotion de la santé*, 5(2), 1993). **AFFIL:** Association canadienne des diététistes; Society for Nutrition Education; Association des diététistes du N.B.; La Société canadienne des sciences de la nutrition; Association canadienne pour l'avancement des sciences; Corporation professionelle des diététistes du Chili; Institut national de la nutrition; Canadian Association for Deans & Direc-

tors of Home Economics & Related Fields; Association canadienne pour la recherche en économie familiale; Organisation pour l'éducation en nutrition; N.B. Multicultural Health Council (mbr. 1993 to date); Univ. de Moncton (mbr., Academic Senate 1992 to date); Centre de recherche sur les aliments (Chair, Bd. of Dir. 1992 to date). HONS: Mention honorifique en reconnaissance à la vie professionnelle à l'intérieur et à l'extérieur du pays d'origine, Univ. du Chili, 1995. INTERESTS: nutrition & vieillissement; sécurité alimentaire; diète pauvre en protéines & cholestase. MISC: bourse études de maîtrise, 1983-84, & études doctorales, 1984-87, FCAR; numerous conference presentations.

Villeneuve, Claudette, R.N.A. ■ ⓒ
Présidente, RÉSEAU QUÉBÉCOIS DES GROUPES ÉCOLOGISTES, 1206 Secteau, Sept Iles, QC G4S 1B7 (418) 962-1316, FAX 964-3213. Born Armagh Comté de Bellechasse, Qué. 1941. m. Régis Villeneuve. 2 ch. EDUC: Hôpital de l'Enfant-Jésus, R.N.A. 1961. CAREER: Enseignante à l'élémentaire, école de campagne à St-Damien, Bellechasse, 1958-59; Officier commissionné (Lieutenant) de l'armée de réserve, 1960-61; Infirmière auxiliaire aux services de chirurgie et médecine générale, Hôpital de Sept-Iles, 1962-72; Conseiller municipal, Ville de Sept-Iles, 1977-81; Enseignante en enfance inadaptée, l'école Jean du Nord de Sept-Iles, 1977-78; Prof. de tissage, la Commission régionale du Gofe service aux adultes, 1977-82; Propriétaire, commerce de matériel et fibres de tissage et atélier de tissage, 1977-82; Conseillère, Conseil consultatif de l'environnement, Ministère de l'Environnement du Qué., 1979-86; Agent de dév. culturel, la CMACN, 1984; Agent immobilier, Trust Général du Canada, 1985-86; Agent immobilier, Re/Max, 1987; Conseillère, la compagnie Relance, 1987-91; Directrice de projet, Corporation de protection de l'environnement de Sept-Iles, 1989; Commissaire de district, Statistiques Canada, 1991-92; Directrice générale, la Corporation de protection de l'environnement de Sept-Îles, 1990 to date; Propriétaire, commerce au détail, 1993 to date. AFFIL: Conseil régional de l'environnement de la Côte-Nord (Prés. fondatrice); Réseau québécois des groupes écologistes (Prés.); Comité Stratégie St-Laurent (Collaboratrice); Association des marchands des Galeries montagnaises (Conseil d'admin.); Sous-comité de promotion portuaire de Sept-Îles; Comité d'aide aux petites entreprise (Prés.); Centraide (Prés. de la campagne de financement). INTERESTS: lecture; artisanat; chasse; pêche; ski alpin; ski de fond. MISC: mbr. de l'équipe de sauvetage aérien SERABEC.

Vincent, Bernice ⊗
Artist. 23 Oregon Rd., London, ON N52 4B8 (519) 681-8296. Born Woodstock, Ont. 1934. w. Donald Vincent. 2 ch. Charles Frederick, Esther Branwen. EDUC: Beal Technical Sch., London, Ont., Special Art Course with Mackie Cryderman, Herb Ariss, John O' Henly 1952-54; Instituto Allende, San Miguel de Allende, Mexico, 1954-55. CAREER: artist, mother, homemaker, etc. SELECTED PUBLICATIONS: comments included in *Changes*, exhibition catalogue (1986). COMMISSIONS: mural, Bruce Lockhart Associates, London, Ont. (1976), now in Blackburn Group Collection; mural, London Regional Cancer Centre, London, Ont. (1988); permanent installation, lobby, Auberge du Petit Prince, London, Ont. (1990). EXHIBITIONS: various solo exhibitions, incl. Forest City Gallery (1977), *Changes*, McIntosh Gallery, Univ. of Western Ontario & others (1986); *The Road Show*, Gibson Gallery, London (1991) & *Beyond Mythmaking: (Re)viewing the Work of Bernice Vincent*, London Regional Art & Historical Museums (1994); various group exhibitions, incl. *Young Painters Show*, London Public Library & Art Museum (1955), *Canadian Society of Graphic Art 32nd Annual Exhibition*, Sarnia Public Library & Art Museum (1965), *Women's Show: London Artists*, Office of David Peterson, Premier of Ont., Queen's Park, Toronto (1986) & *20 x 20*, Forest City Gallery (1994); organizer, Founding Members Exhibition, Forest City Gallery, London (1993); *All Around Me...All Around You*, Univ. of Manitoba & Windsor Art Gallery (1996). COLLECTIONS: Art Gallery St. Thomas-Elgin, St. Thomas, Ont.; Bd. of Commissioners of Police, City of London; Canada Council Art Bank; Connor, Clark, Toronto; Gov't of Ont.; H.B. Beal Technical Sch., London; London Life Insurance Company; London Regional Art & Historical Museums; Univ. of Western Ontario; Rockliffe Park Village Builders Ltd., Toronto; Woodstock Art Gallery; various other collections. AFFIL: Forest City Gallery. HONS: scholarship for 1 yr. of study at Instituto Allende, Mexico, 1954-55. MISC: subject of various articles & reviews.

Vingilis, Evelyn R., B.Sc.,M.A., Ph.D. ⊗ ⊕ ❀
Director, Population and Community Health Unit, and Professor, Departments of Family Medicine and Epidemiology & Biostatistics, Faculty of Medicine, UNIVERSITY OF WESTERN ONTARIO, London, ON N6A 5C1 (519) 661-4068, FAX 661-4043, EMAIL evingili@ do.med.uwo.ca. Registered Psychologist, VINGILIS AND ASSOCIATES. Born Toronto 1949. 1 ch. Larissa Vingilis-Jaremko. EDUC: McMas-

ter Univ., B.Sc.(Psych.) 1971; York Univ., M.A. 1974, Ph.D. 1978. **CAREER:** Genetics Technologist, Hospital for Sick Children, 1972; Psych. Intern, Dept. of Psychiatry, 1972-73; Dept. of Psych., Clarke Institute of Psychiatry, 1974-75; Instructor, Psych., Ryerson Polytechnic Institute, 1977-81; Research Scientist, Addiction Research Foundation, 1978-84; Head of Drinking & Driving Research Program, 1984-91; Adjunct Assoc. Prof., Dept. of Preventive Medicine & Biostatistics, Univ. of Toronto, 1985-93; Adjunct Grad. Fac., Dept. of Psych., York Univ., 1987-93; Sr. Scientist, Addiction Research Foundation, 1988-93; Head of Risk Factors, 1991-93; Prof., Dept. of Epidemiology & Biostatistics, Univ. of Western Ontario, 1993 to date; Prof., Dept. of Family Medicine, 1993 to date; Dir., Health Intelligence Unit, 1993-95; Dir., Population & Community Health Unit, 1995 to date. **SELECTED PUBLICATIONS:** *Youth Action Program: Facilitator's Manual*, with R.E. Mann *et al* (Toronto: Addiction Research Foundation, 1993); *Alcohol and Other Drugs in Transportation: Research Needs for the Next Decade* (Washington: Transportation Research Bd., National Research Council, 1993); "Recognition vs. Recall of Visually vs. Acoustically Confusable Letter Matrices," with J. Blake & L. Theodore (*Memory and Cognition* 5(1) 1977); "Comparison of Age and Sex Characteristics of Police-Suspected Impaired Drivers and Roadside-Surveyed Impaired Drivers," with E.M. Adlaf & L. Chung (*Accident Analysis and Prevention* 14(6) 1982); "The Six Myths of Drinking-Driving Prevention" (*Health Education Research* 2(2) 1987); "Introducing Beer at a Canadian Ballpark: The Effect on Motor Vehicle Accidents," with C. Liban *et al* (*Accident Analysis and Prevention* 24(5) 1992); "Moderate Drinking and Traffic Crashes: A Case for Health or for Safety" (*Contemporary Drug Problems* 21(1) 1994); more than 120 other publications. **EDIT:** Ed. Bd., *Accident Analysis and Prevention: An International Journal*, 1980-92; Guest Ed., "Perspectives on Drinking-Driving Countermeasures," *Accident Analysis and Prevention*, 15(6) 1983; Ed. Bd., *Research Advances in Alcohol and Drug Problems Series*, Addiction Research Foundation, 1986-93; Ed. Bd., *Journal of Traffic Medicine: An International Journal of Traffic Safety*, 1990 to date. **AFFIL:** Medical Research Council of Canada (Reg. Dir.); National Research Council, Transportation Research Bd.; International Council on Alcohol, Drugs & Traffic Safety; Int'l Committee on Alcohol, Drugs & Traffic Safety (elected Mbr.; Sec. 1990-93); Science Teachers' Association of Ontario (Hon. Pres. 1992-95); Canadian Association for Women in Science (Pres.

1988-91); Consortium for Practical Research into the Care of the Elderly; Low Birth Weight Proj. Steering Committee; Canadian Opera Women's Committee. **HONS:** People to Reduce Impaired Driving Everywhere Award, 1990. **MISC:** recipient, various grants; listed in numerous biographical references incl. *Foremost Women of the Twentieth Century* (1986), *International Who's Who of Professional and Business Women* (1988, 1991), *The World Who's Who of Women* (1989, 1991), & *Dictionary of International Biography* (1989-91); Registered Psychologist in the Prov. of Ont.; mbr., scientific advisory panel, 13th Int'l Conference on Alcohol, Drugs & Traffic Safety, 1993-95; mbr., Family Violence Proj., Addiction Research Foundation, 1990-93; mbr., Interministerial Committee on Drinking & Driving, 1990-92; Co-organizer, Alcohol, Accidents and Injuries, 1986 Society of Automotive Engineers (SAE) Int'l Congress & Exposition, 1986; reviewer for various journals & granting agencies; numerous invited papers & addresses; numerous conference presentations. **COMMENT:** *"Dr. Vingilis's experience has spanned research, clinical work with both children and adults, program and policy development and implementation, and education. Her research interests have been high-risk youth, alcohol, drugs and traffic safety, population health, determinants of health and women's issues. Her work includes both the development and evaluation of actual programs such as R.I.D.E. and the Youth Action Program and epidemiological studies."*

Vingilis-Jaremko, Larissa ■ ■ ⊙ ❀ ♦
Founder and President, CANADIAN ASSOCIATION FOR GIRLS IN SCIENCE (non-profit association dedicated to promoting girls' interest in science, mathematics, engineering & technology), Let's Talk Science, The University of Western Ontario, London, ON N6A 5C1 (519) 661-4029. Born Toronto 1982. **EDUC:** Kensal Park Public Sch., Grade 8 diploma (Hon. Roll) 1996. **SELECTED PUBLICATIONS:** "What's wrong with science education in grade school?" (*Canadian Association of Women in Science Newsletter*, Sept. 1994). **AFFIL:** Model Aeronautics Association of Canada; Society of Antique Modellers. **HONS:** Hon. Mention, Michael Smith Awards, Industry Canada, Ottawa, 1995; 2nd place finish, Ont. Amateur Ballroom Dancing Championships, Jr. Latin Div., 1988; 2nd place, Southwestern Ontario Ballroom Dancing Championships, 1989; 2nd place, Ontario Ballroom Dancing Championships, 1990; 1st place, dressage, London Equestrian & Training Centre Horse Show, 1993; 1st place, dressage & show jumping,

Wiltongrove Horse Show, London, 1994; several academic awards. INTERESTS: dressage & show jumping; music; science. MISC: presentation to "Partners in Change," Toronto, Sept. 1996. COMMENT: *"When I was 9 years old, I founded the Canadian Association for Girls in Science to promote girls' interest in science. We have over 50 members in London and other chapters are developing. YES (Youth, Engineering & Science) magazine will be featuring a regular column so that girls around the country can find out what's happening."*

Vinish, Mary T., B.Ed., M.Ed.(PGD) ⊕ ○ ⊰
Volunteer, retired teacher. 710 Eastlake Ave., Apt. 305, Saskatoon, SK S7N 1A3. Born Stonehenge, Sask. 1931. w. 4 ch. EDUC: Univ. of Saskatchewan, B.Ed.(Math.) 1969, M.Ed.(Special Educ.) 1974, Diploma (Admin.) 1978. CAREER: Teacher, Wakaw Sch. Unit, 1948-57; Teacher, John Dolan Sch. for the Retarded, 1958-63; Principal, 1963-88. AFFIL: Saskatchewan Teachers' Federation (Hon. Life Mbr.); Saskatoon Association for Community Living (Bd. Mbr. 1968-84; Pres. 1980-82); Saskatchewan Association for Community Living (Bd. Mbr.; Pres. 1993-95); Canadian Association for Community Living (Bd. Mbr.); Elmwood Residences Inc., Saskatoon (Bd. Mbr. & Pres.); Cosmopolitan Industries (Admissions & Discharge Committee 1975-94; Program Committee 1994 to date); Institute for Prevention of Handicaps, Sask. (Bd. of Dir. 1991 to date); Saskatchewan Abilities Council; Saskatchewan Association for Rehabilitation Centres; St. Joseph's Catholic Church (Pastoral Council 1986-92; Chair 1988-92; Choir 1985 to date; Catholic Women's League; Mgmt Committee 1993 to date). HONS: Golden Wheel Award for Excellence in Educ., Rotary International, 1989; Recognition of Dedication, Saskatchewan Institute for Prevention of Handicaps, 1993. INTERESTS: volunteer work; travel; music; crafts; family. MISC: mbr. of Sask. committee consisting of Social Svcs Dept. & related nongov't agencies to develop guidelines for implementing a policy on abuse of people with handicaps, 1994 to date; mbr. of governance team for "Coming Home, Staying Home," 1993-96. COMMENT: *"I retired from teaching after 38 years of service. I am widowed. My husband and I raised four children who are all married. I have two beautiful grandchildren. I hope to remain active in volunteer work, travel and continue to enjoy my family."*

Vinkenvleugel, Maria ⊕ ⊘ ⧫
President, ONTARIO WEIGHTLIFTING ASSOCIATION, 29 Princess Park Rd., Ingersoll, ON N5C

1X7 (519) 425-0194. Born Netherlands 1952. m. Harry. 3 ch. Craig, Trudy, Ian. CAREER: Office Mgr, Oxford Golf & Country Club. AFFIL: Canadian Weightlifting Association (Pres.). MISC: 1st female weightlifting referee in Ont.; 1st female int'l weightlifting referee in Canada.

Visser, Margaret, B.A.,M.A., Ph.D. 📖 ⧫ ⊰
Writer, c/o Wylie, Aitken and Stone, 250 W. 27th St., Ste. 2114, New York, NY 10107 (416) 978-7982, FAX 971-1378. Born South Africa 1940. m. Colin Visser. 2 ch. Emily, Alexander. EDUC: Univ. of Toronto, B.A. 1970, M.A. 1973, Ph.D.(Classics) 1980. CAREER: Instructor, Classics, York Univ.; writer; radio/TV personality. SELECTED PUBLICATIONS: *Much Depends on Dinner* (McClelland and Stewart, 1986); *The Rituals of Dinner* (HarperCollins, 1991); *The Way We Are* (HarperCollins, 1994). HONS: Glenfiddich Award, 1984; Int'l A.C.P. Award, 1992; Jane Grigson Prize, 1992. INTERESTS: religion; literature; fine art. MISC: numerous radio & TV appearances & public lectures worldwide. COMMENT: *"Writer of books and articles, and radio/TV personality. Subjects: the anthropology of everyday life; myth (modern and ancient Greek); arts; food."*

Vokey, Mary Lou, F.I.I.C.,C.C.I.B. 💲 ⊰
Vice-President, Personal Lines, WEDGWOOD INSURANCE LIMITED, 85 Thorburn Rd., P.O. Box 13370, St. John's, NF A1B 4B7 (709) 753-3210, FAX 753-8238. Born Sydney, N.S. 1953. m. Wayne. 2 ch. Paul, Dana. CAREER: Customer Svc. Rep., The Policy Shop, 1983-86; Customer Svc. Rep., Wedgwood Insurance Ltd., 1986-89; Supervisor, Personal Lines, 1989-92; Mgr, Personal Lines, 1992-94; VP, Personal Lines, 1994 to date. AFFIL: Insurance Institute of Canada (Assoc. 1985-94; Fellow); Insurance Brokers' Association of Canada (Chartered Insur. Broker); Newfoundland Association of Insurance Women (2nd VP 1990-91; 1st VP 1991-92; Pres. 1992-93; Dir.); Canadian Association of Insurance Women (Dir. 1993-95); St. George's Masonic Lodge (Ladies Auxiliary). HONS: top 1st-yr. student in Nfld., Assoc. Program, Insurance Institute of Canada, 1984; top graduating Fellow in Nfld., Insurance Institute of Canada, 1994. INTERESTS: reading; downhill skiing. MISC: evening class instructor for Insurance Institute of Canada & Insurance Brokers' Association of Canada. COMMENT: *"I married right out of high school and immediately started a family, remaining at home with my children for 12 years. In 1983, I was bitten by the insurance*

bug, beginning my career as a customer service representative and reaching Vice-Presidential status within 11 years."

von Baeyer, Edwinna, B.A., M.A. ■ ▯ $ ⊗

Consultant, NEW CENTURY COMMUNICATIONS, 131 Sunnside Ave., Ottawa, ON K1S 0R2 (613) 730-5184, FAX 730-4246, EMAIL evb@magi.com. Born Detroit, Mich. 1946. m. Cornelius. 2 ch. Eliza Corinna, Jakob Edwin. **EDUC:** Univ. of Michigan, B.A.(English Lit.) 1968; Univ. of Pennsylvania, M.A.(South Asian Studies) 1970; Algonquin Coll., Dipl.(Horticulture/Landscaping) 1980. **CAREER:** comm. consultant in writing, editing & research, 1978 to date. **SELECTED PUBLICATIONS:** *Rhetoric and Roses: A History of Canadian Gardening, 1900-1930* (Markham: Fitzhenry and Whiteside, 1984); *Garden of Dreams: Kingsmere and Mackenzie King* (Toronto: Dundurn Press, 1990); *The Reluctant Gardener: A Beginners' Guide with Dinah Shields* (Random House, 1992); *Garden Voices: Two Centuries of Canadian Garden Writing* with Pleasance Crawford (Random House, 1995); bibliographies & indices; numerous articles on forestry, Cdn heritage, landscape history, the environment & the Internet. **AFFIL:** Ottawa Independent Writers (Dir. 1990-94; Sec. 1992); Garden History Society; ICOMOS Canada; Editors' Association of Canada. **INTERESTS:** the Internet; gardening. **COMMENT:** *"For the past 17 years, I have been a leading Canadian landscape historian and communications consultant."*

W

achtel, Eleanor, B.A. 📖 ✒ 📜
Host, *Writers & Company*, CBC RADIO, Box
500, Stn. A, Toronto, ON M5W 1E6 (416)
205-5982. EDUC: McGill Univ., B.A.(English);
Univ. of British Columbia, Theatre; Univ. of
Syracuse, grad. program in journalism.
CAREER: freelance writer, researcher & broadcaster, 1976 to date; Ed., *Room of One's Own*,
1976-89; West Coast Contributing Ed., *Books
in Canada*, 1978-89; theatre & film critic, CBC
Radio, Vancouver, 1979-87; Assoc. Ed., *Interface*, 1981-82; Adjunct Prof., Women's Studies, Simon Fraser Univ., 1984-87; Host, *Monitor*, CBC Radio, 1985-86; literary commentator, State of the Arts, CBC Radio, 1987-88;
writer & broadcaster for *The Arts Tonight &
The Arts Report*; guest Host, *The Arts Tonight*,
1989 to date; Host, *Writers & Company*, CBC
Radio, 1990 to date. SELECTED PUBLICA-
TIONS: *The Expo Story*, co-ed. (Harbour Publishing, 1986); *Language in Her Eye*, co-ed.
(Coach House Press, 1990); *A Feminist Guide
to the Canadian Constitution*, co-author (Canadian Advisory Council on the Status of Women,
1992); *Writers & Company* (Knopf Canada,
1993); *More Writers & Company* (Knopf
Canada, 1996); "A Farm of One's Own: The
Rural Orientation of Women's Co-operative
Enterprises" (*Rural Africana* Spring 1976);
"The Mother and the Whore: Image and
Stereotype of Women in Recent Kenyan Literature" (*Umoja* 1977); numerous profiles, interviews & features in various periodicals, incl.
*Books in Canada, West Coast Review, Money-
wise, Flare, Chatelaine & Maclean's*; work
anthologized in *Contemporary Literary Criticism, Macmillan Anthology of Canadian Writing*, & *Computers in Australia*; various other

publications. EDIT: former Ed., *The Circulation Manager*. EXHIBITIONS: photographs included in *Women in This Decade*, province-wide juried exhibition (1985). AFFIL: West Coast LEAF: Women's Legal Education Action Fund (Founding Mbr.); National Council, Canadian Human Rights Foundation; ACTRA. HONS: Reford Scholarship in English, McGill Univ.; Univ. Scholar, McGill Univ.; Honourable Mention, Fiona Mee Literary Journalism Award, 1981; Best Writing in Architecture, Western Magazine Award, 1985. MISC: juror for various granting agencies, contests & awards; numerous invited lectures.

Waddington, Miriam, B.A.,M.S.W., M.A.,D.Litt. ✂ 🎭
Professor Emeritus and Senior Scholar, Department of English, YORK UNIVERSITY, 4700 Keele St., North York, ON M3J 1P3. Born Winnipeg 1917. d. 2 ch. EDUC: Univ. of Toronto, B.A. 1939, M.A. 1968; Univ. of Toronto Sch. of Social Work, Diploma 1942; Univ. of Pennsylvania, M.S.W. 1945. CAREER: lecturer & research advisor, McGill Sch. of Social Work, 1945-48; various positions as a case worker, Montreal, 1948-60; Supervisor, Family Svcs Agency, North York, Ont., 1960-63; Prof. of English Lit., York Univ., 1964-90; Writer-in-residence, Univ. of Ottawa, 1974; Writer-in-residence, Windsor Public Library, 1983; Writer-in-residence, Toronto Metro Library, 1986; Prof. Emeritus & Sr. Scholar, York Univ., 1983 to date. SELECTED PUBLICATIONS: *Green World* (Montreal: First Statement, 1945); *The Season's Lovers* (Ryerson, 1958); *The Dream Telescope* (London: Anvil & Routledge Kegan Paul, 1972); *The Price of Gold* (Toronto: Oxford, 1976); *Summer at Lonely Beach* (Oakville: Mosaic Valley Editions, 1982); *Collected Poems* (1986); *The Last Landscape* (Toronto: Oxford, 1992); various other books; *John Sutherland Essays, Controversies, Poems*, ed. (Toronto: McClelland & Stewart, 1972); *The Collected Poems of A.M. Klein*, ed. (Toronto, London: McGraw Hill Ryerson, 1974); *Canadian Jewish Short Stories*, ed. (Toronto: Oxford, 1990); *Cercando Fragole in Guigno* Italian translation of poetry (Univ. of Bologna, 1993); *En guise d'amants* French translation of poetry (1994); *Poems for Canada: Romancing the Land*, ed. Lorraine Monk (1996); published in Russia, France, Germany, Hungary, Japan, Romania, Italy & South America; included in over 200 anthologies; 12 books of poetry. EDIT: Advisory Ed., *Journal of the Otto Rank Association*, 1973-83; Poetry Ed., *Poetry Toronto*, 1981-82. AFFIL: Writers' Union of Canada; League of Canadian Poets; International Association of Professors of English; Canadian Sculpture Society. HONS: J.I. Segal prize, 1972, 1986; awards in the Borestone Mountain Best Poems in English; honoured by the Association of Quebec & Canadian Literatures; hon. degrees from 2 universities. MISC: poetry has been set to music by various composers, incl. Laurie Duncan, Shenlyn Fritz, Ruth Watson-Henderson & Elie Siegmeister; several painters have incorporated poems into their work; listed in *The Annotated Biography of Canada's Major Authors* (1985); various poems broadcast on the CBC & in New Zealand, Australia & Denmark; frequent lecturer & public speaker in Canada & Europe; Canada Council Exchange Poet to Wales, 1980; E.J. Pratt Memorial Lecture, Memorial Univ., 1974; mbr., judge, annual drama awards for ACTRA.

Waddington, Rhoda Marie ■■ ✂ ⊕ ○
Executive Director, STEP BY STEP CHILD DEVELOPMENT SOCIETY, (pediatric special educ. & health svcs), 508 Clarke Rd., Ste. 101F, Coquitlam, BC V3J 3X2. Born Yorkshire, England 1946. m. Robert Waddington. 3 ch. Steven, Timothy, Mark. EDUC: Douglas Coll., Early Childhood Educ. (Special Needs) 1976; Simon Fraser Univ., Bus. 2 yrs.; Open Learning Institue, Univ. of Victoria, Bus. Admin. 1988. CAREER: Sec./Admin. Asst. to Personnel Officer, Leeds City Fire Service, 1962-66; Asst. to Exec. Asst. to Supt. of Detectives, Vancouver Police Dept., 1966-69; Asst., Vancouver City Clerk's Office, 1971; owner/operator, Waddington Clerical Support Services, 1972-76; owner/operator, Ponderosa Pine Day Care, 1976-80; Pres., Fraser North Child Care Society. AFFIL: Coquitlam Rotary Club (Vocations Chair; Exec. mbr.); All-Saints Church (Parish Council; current Facilitator, Seniors' Organization 3 yrs.) Coquitlam Food Bank (founding Chair); Coquitlam Professional & Business Women's Association (former VP); St. Peter's Church (former Facilitator, Seniors' Organization 6 yrs.); St. Francis Fraternity of Secular Franciscans (professed mbr. 14 yrs.; Minister, Vancouver). HONS: Citizen of the Year, Chamber of Commerce; Coquitlam Festival Award; Gertie Grosser Award, 1996; Paul Harris Fellow, Rotary Club International. INTERESTS: teaching religion classes; family dinners & games; taking courses; volunteering with seniors.

Waddington, Rona ⊗ 🔖 🗂
Co-Artistic Director, THE ME & HER THEATRE COMPANY, 6 Bartlett Ave., Ste. 13, Toronto, ON M6H 3E6 (416) 536-3362. Born London, UK 1964. m. William Chambers. EDUC: Univ. of Waterloo, (Independent Studies) current.

SELECTED PUBLICATIONS: *Earhart* (biographical drama, 1993); *East of Elvis* (black comedy, 1992). AFFIL: Canadian Actors' Equity Association; Playwrights' Union of Canada; Alliance of Canadian Television & Radio Artists; YMCA. HONS: Ontario Arts Council Award, 1993; Toronto Arts Council Award, 1992. INTERESTS: travel; sports; literature. MISC: freelance actor/playwright.

Waelti-Walters, Jennifer, B.A., Ph.D. <img>
Professor and Founding Director of Women's Studies, UNIVERSITY OF VICTORIA, Box 3045, Victoria, BC V8W 3P4 (604) 721-6157. Born UK 1942. d. EDUC: Univ. of London, B.A. (French) 1964, Ph.D.(French) 1968; Univ. de Lille, L. ès L.(French) 1966. CAREER: instructor, Univ. de Paris, 1967-68; Prof., French Dept., Univ. of Victoria, 1968 to date; Chair, French Dept., 1979-84; Instructor, Women's Studies, 1979 to date; Dir., Women's Studies, 1988-95. SELECTED PUBLICATIONS: *Fairytales and the Female Imagination* (Montreal: Eden Press, 1982); *Jeanne Hyrvrard* with M. Verthuy (Amsterdam: Rodopi, 1988); *Michel Butor* (Victoria: Sono Nis Press, 1977); *Feminist Novelists of the Belle Epoque* (Bloomington: Indiana Univ. Press, 1990); *Feminisms of the Belle Epoque* with S. House (Lincoln and London, Univ. of Nebraska Press, 1994); *Jeanne Hyrvrard: Theorist of the Modern World* (Edinburgh, Univ. of Edinburgh Press, 1996); several earlier books & numerous articles. AFFIL: Association des Professeurs de Français des Universités Canadiennes (Exec. Committee 1980-86); Canadian Federation for Humanities (Exec. 1983-84); Humanities Association of Canada (Exec. 1981-86); Canadian Research Institute for Advancement of Women; Canadian Association of Women's Studies; Senior Women Academic Administrators of Canada. HONS: Prize for Best Work Published in French, Association des Professeurs de Français des Universités Canadiennes, 1989; Community Award, Univ. of Victoria, 1993. INTERESTS: singing; photography. COMMENT: *"I am a founder of Women's Studies at the University of Victoria and have taught in and administered the program since its inception in 1979. Also well known for work on contemporary French literature."*

Wakefield, Tayce, B.A.,LL.B.,M.S.M. <img>
Vice-President, Corporate Affairs, GENERAL MOTORS OF CANADA LIMITED, 1908 Colonel Sam Drive, Oshawa, ON L1H 8P7 (905) 644-6308, FAX 644-4686. Born Montreal 1959. m. Roy Campbell. 2 stepch. EDUC: McMaster Univ., B.A.(Pol. Sci.) 1980; Osgoode Hall Law

Sch., LL.B. 1983; Boston Univ./Vrije Universiteit Brussel, M.S.M.(Mgmt) 1984. CAREER: Fin. Analyst, Sarma SA (JC Penney), Brussels, Belgium, 1983-84; Mgr, Gov't Rel'ns, General Motors of Canada, 1984-89; Dir. of Gov't Rel'ns, 1989-91; Dir. of Public Rel'ns, 1991-93; Gen. Dir. of Corp. Affairs, 1993-94; VP, Corp. Affairs, 1994 to date. DIRECTOR: General Motors of Canada Ltd. AFFIL: Ontario Chamber of Commerce (Dir.); Zoological Society of Metropolitan Toronto (Dir.); Canada Safety Council (Dir.); City of Toronto Planning Advisory Committee (1990-91); Nielsen Task Force, Regulatory Program Review, Gov't of Canada (1984-85). INTERESTS: skiing; cottaging; cooking.

Walker, Doreen, B.A.,M.A. <img>
Senior Instructor Emeritus, UNIVERSITY OF BRITISH COLUMBIA. Born Vancouver 1920. w. Colin B. Walker. 3 ch. EDUC: Univ. of British Columbia, B.A.(Hist. & English) 1942, M.A.(Cdn Art Hist.) 1969. CAREER: taught as Sr. Instructor (specializing in Cdn Art Hist.) at the Univ. of British Columbia, retiring in 1986. SELECTED PUBLICATIONS: *Dear Nan: Letters of Emily Carr, Nan Cheney, Humphrey Toms*, ed. (Vancouver: Univ. of British Columbia Press, 1989). AFFIL: Professors Emerita, UBC (Exec.); Shaughnessy Heights United Church; Vancouver Lawn Tennis & Badminton Club; Shaughnessy Golf & Country Club.

Walker, Nancy R., B.Mgmt. <img>
Director, Financial Services and Controller, UNIVERSITY OF LETHBRIDGE, 4401 University Dr. W., Lethbridge, AB T1K 3M4 (403) 329-2206, FAX 329-2097, EMAIL walkern@hg.uleth.ca. Born Medicine Hat, Alta. 1960. m. Paul R. Walker. 1 ch. EDUC: Univ. of Lethbridge, B.Mgmt.(Acctg) 1982; C.A. 1985. CAREER: Staff C.A., Young Parkyn McNab and Co., 1982-87; Cont., Rogers Broadcasting Ltd., 1987-89; Sr. Fin. Analyst, Univ. of Lethbridge, 1990; Dir., Fin. Svcs & Cont., 1990 to date. AFFIL: Canadian Institute of Chartered Accountants. INTERESTS: amateur musician (saxophone & clarinet).

Wall, Marjorie, B.H.Sc.,M.Sc., Ph.D. <img>
Professor and Chair, Department of Consumer Studies, UNIVERSITY OF GUELPH, Guelph, ON N1G 2W1 (519) 824-4120, FAX 823-1964, EMAIL mwall@facs.uoguelph.ca. Born Canada 1947. m. Gregory Wall. 3 ch. Kathy, Kristin, Kelly. EDUC: Univ. of Guelph, B.H.Sc.(Textiles/Clothing/Design) 1968, M.Sc. (Textile Sci.) 1970; Ohio State Univ., Ph.D.

(Textile/Clothing Mktg) 1974. **CAREER:** Asst. Prof., Univ. of Guelph, 1974-81; Assoc. Prof., 1982-95; Chair, Dept. of Consumer Studies, 1992-94, 1995 to date; Prof., 1995 to date. **SELECTED PUBLICATIONS:** numerous publications on textiles & mktg. **AFFIL:** Canadian Association for Research in Home Economics (Pres. 1985-87); Administrative Sciences Association of Canada; Academy of Marketing Science; Association for Consumer Research; International Textile & Apparel Association. **HONS:** Doctoral Fellow, Canada Council, 1972-74; Best Mktg Paper, Administrative Sciences Association of Canada, 1986, 1991, 1994. **INTERESTS:** skiing; running; sailing; reading. **MISC:** research grants, Social Sciences & Humanities Research Council of Canada, 1983, 1986, 1990, 1994. **COMMENT:** *"I have spent my professional career in academia within an applied, interdisciplinary department, and have been continuously stimulated by teaching and research, and now administration, while at the same time being physically active and rearing a family."*

Walker, Elisabeth ■ ■ ⊘
Paralympic Athlete. Toronto, ON. **EDUC:** Birchmount Park Collegiate, current. **SPORTS CAREER:** mbr., Nat'l Swim Team, 1992 to date. Paralympic Games: Bronze, 100m backstroke, 1996; 8th, 100m freestyle, 1992. Atlantic Int'l: 1st, 100m backstroke & 200m IM, 3rd, 50m freestyle, 4th, 100m freestyle, 1995. IPC World Championships: 2nd, 50m butterfly & 200m IM, 4th, 50m freestyle, 1994. Commonwealth Games: 8th, 100m freestyle, 1994. **MISC:** world record holder, 50m butterfly & 100m backstroke.

Wallin, Pamela, B.A. ■ ✎ ⊔
Broadcast Journalist and Host, *PAMELA WALLIN LIVE*, 1246 Yonge St., Ste. 303, Toronto, ON M4T 1W5. President, THE CURRENT AFFAIRS GROUP. Born Moose Jaw, Sask. 1953. d. **EDUC:** Univ. of Regina, Hons. B.A.(Psych.) 1973. **CAREER:** Social Worker, Sask.; Prod., CBC, Regina, Ottawa & Toronto, 1973-79; Pol. Reporter, *The Toronto Star*, 1979-81; Host, *Canada AM*, 1981; Ottawa Bureau Chief & Weekend Anchor, CTV, 1985; Co-Anchor, *CBC Prime Time*; Host, *Pamela Wallin Live*. **HONS:** named an Outstanding Achiever by Queen Elizabeth, 1982; Skelton-Clark Fellow, Queen's Univ., 1990; Gordon Sinclair Award for Best Overall Broadcast Journalist, Gemini Awards, 1992; Broadcaster of the Year Award, Radio-Television News Directors' Association, 1994. **MISC:** sole female TV correspondent from Canada on location in Buenos Aires during Falkland Islands War.

Walmsley, Norma E., O.C. ♡ ⦿ ⧉
Member, Board of Directors and Executive Committee, INTERNATIONAL CENTRE FOR HUMAN RIGHTS AND DEMOCRATIC DEVELOPMENT, Montreal, QC (819) 459-2061, FAX 459-1136. Born Winnipeg 1920. s. **EDUC:** McGill Univ., B.Comm.(Pol. Sci./Econ.) 1950, M.A.(Pol. Sci.) 1954. **CAREER:** Sr. Officer in Charge of Women's Div. Supplies for Canada & Overseas, RCAF, 1941-45; Prof. of Pol. Sci. & Int'l Rel'ns, Brandon Coll., 1955-67; Registrar, 1962-64; Research Prof., Royal Commission on Bilingualism & Biculturalism, 1965-66; Dir., Universities Resources Study, Association of Universities & Colleges of Canada, 1967-70; Occasional Lecturer & Thesis Supervisor, Univ. of Ottawa, Carleton Univ.; Int'l Dev. Consultant; Founding Pres., MATCH International Centre, 1976. **SELECTED PUBLICATIONS:** *Some Aspects of Canada's Immigration Policies* (1966); *Canadian Universities and International Development* (1970); numerous articles for professional publications. **AFFIL:** International Centre for Human Rights & Democratic Development (Dir.; Exec. Committee); MATCH International Centre (Life Mbr.; Dir.); Canadian Commission for UNESCO (Mbr.-at-large); Canadian Committee for the Fiftieth Anniversary of the United Nations (Exec. Group); Canadian Committee for UNIFEM (Hon. VP); Wakefield Covered Bridge Project (Chair of Fundraising); Gatineau Memorial Hospital Foundation (Dir.). **HONS:** Queen's Silver Jubilee Medal, 1977; Gov. General's Award in Commemoration of the Persons Case, 1987; Lewis Perinbam Award in Int'l Dev., 1988; Officer, Order of Canada, 1993; LL.D.(Hon.), Carleton Univ., 1983; LL.D.(Hon.), Brandon Univ., 1988. **INTERESTS:** int'l affairs; travel; golf; family & friends. **MISC:** mbr., Cdn Gov't Delegation to 11th & 12th Gen. Conferences of UNESCO, Paris, 1960, 1962, & U.N. Mid-Decade Conference for Women, Copenhagen, 1980; played a founding of leadership role in a large number of Cdn & int'l non-governmental organizations (NGOs). **COMMENT:** *"Through teaching, participation on government delegations and on boards and committees of NGOs, and as Founding President of MATCH International Centre, I hope to have had some influence on international understanding."*

Walsh, Donna, R.N., P.H.N, B.Sc. ■ ⊕ ♡
Vice-Chair, REGION 2 HOSPITAL CORPORATION, Black's Harbour, NB E0G 1H0. Vice-President, Research and Development, NURSE CONSULTANT INCORPORATED. Born Black's Harbour, N.B. 1947. m. Fraser. 3 ch. Joseph,

Matty, Catherine. **EDUC:** Saint John General Hospital, R.N. 1968; Dalhousie Univ., Dipl.(Public Health Nursing) 1969; Mount Saint Vincent Univ., B.Sc. 1975. **CAREER:** Public Health Nurse, Saint John, N.B., 1970-72; Dir. of Nursing, Collingwood Nursing Home, Pennfield, N.B., 1977-79; Gen. Casual Duty Nurse, Fundy Hospital, Black's Harbour, N.B., 1979-81; Quality Assurance Coord., 1987-91; Diabetic Educator, 1981-91; VP, Research & Dev., Nurse Consultant Incorporated, 1995 to date. **VOLUNTEER CAREER:** Dir. & V-Chair, Region 2 Hospital Corporation; Dir. & V-Chair, Sch. District 10; Dir./Rep. for Children & Adolescents, N.B. Mental Health Commission Region 2; Community Support for Children (Founder; Chair); Charlotte County Child Abuse & Family Violence. **SELECTED PUBLICATIONS:** *The Child with Diabetes* with A. Lewis et al (Univ. of British Columbia, 1989); *Exercise and the Curious Diabetic* with A. Lewis et al (Univ. of British Columbia, 1989). **AFFIL:** N.B. Association of Registered Nurses; Amnesty International; World Vision (Foster Parent). **HONS:** Volunteer of the Year Award, Black's Harbour Town Council. **INTERESTS:** children's issues; health & educ. **MISC:** active advocate for children. **COMMENT:** *"I spend a great deal of time and energy on issues facing today's youth. I have an interest in healthcare and education and serve on numerous committees addressing current issues. I am married and the mother of three teenagers."*

Waldo, Carolyn ⚾ 📺 👍

Sports Reporter, Producer and Anchor, **CJOH-TV**, 1500 Merivale Rd., Nepean, ON K2E 6Z5 (613) 224-1313, FAX 224-4035. Born Montreal 1964. m. Tom Baltzer. 2 ch. **EDUC:** Univ. of Calgary, Gen. Studies 1983-84; Ryerson Polytechnic Univ., Bus. & Journalism 1989. **CAREER:** Sports Reporter, Prod. & Anchor, CJOH-TV, 1990 to date; Colour Commentator for Synchronized Swimming, & Roving Reporter, Olympic Games, 1992. **SPORTS CAREER:** started synchronized swimming at age 11; youngest Nat'l Team mbr., synchronized swimming, at 15; 6-time World Champion; Olympic Champion, 1984, 1988. **AFFIL:** Canadian Lung Association (Spokesperson, 1985-86); RCMP Anti-Drug Awareness Program (Spokesperson, 1985-87); Lupus Foundation (Hon. Chair 1988-89). **HONS:** Silver Medal, solo, synchronized swimming, Olympic Games, 1984; Gold Medal, solo & duet, synchronized swimming, Olympic Games, 1988; Officer of the Order of Canada; Canada's Female Athlete of the Year (twice). **INTERESTS:** golf; tennis; cooking; keeping fit. **MISC:** 1st female athlete in Cdn history to win 2 gold medals at the same Olympic Games; 1988 Olympics Cdn team flagbearer.

Walter, Heather, B.A.,B.Ed. ■ ✿ 🎓 📺

Partner, **NORTH BY EAST PRODUCTIONS**, 804 - 9th St. S.E., Calgary, AB T2G 3A9 (403) 233-9406, FAX 234-7785. Born Toronto 1959. s. **EDUC:** Queen's Univ., B.A.(English & Phil.); B.Ed.(Outdoor & Experiential Educ.) 1984. **CAREER:** Educ. Coord., Whale Research Group, Memorial Univ. of Newfoundland, 1984-86; Instructor, Fishing Industry Job-Entry Program, Industry Training Associates, 1986; Curriculum Consultant, Youth Svcs Div., Dept. of Culture, Recreation & Youth, Gov't of Nfld. & Labrador, 1986-90; Ptnr, *Heather & Eric*, North by East Productions, 1990 to date; Dir., Nfld. & Labrador Programs, Atlantic Centre for the Environment, 1990-93; Dir. (part-time), 1993-95. **SELECTED CREDITS:** contracted by *Sesame Street Canada* to record 6 short music videos with marine educ. themes, aired Jan. 1992 & ongoing; Naturalist Host with David Suzuki, *The Newfoundland Fishery*, CBC & PBS TV, 1992; Writer/Co-Prod., *No Small Wonder* (children's TV special), CBC TV, 1993; Featured Performer, *Being So Green and Hardly Thirteen*, CBC TV, 1994; Host, *All Aboard* (environment/culture radio series), CBC, Summer 1994. **SELECTED PUBLICATIONS:** various articles, papers & books incl. *Finding the Balance–For Earth's Sake* (student text, teacher's guide, field guide), with D. Minty & D. Murphy (Newfoundland: Breakwater Books, 1993); *Resources for Tomorrow: Science, Technology and Society*, with D. Minty & D. Murphy (Breakwater Books, 1994); *Fisheries for Small Fry* (children's storybook, cassette & teacher's guide), with Eric West (Breakwater Books, 1996). **HONS:** nominated, Gov. General's Award for Conservation, 1992; North American Film & Video Award (*No Small Wonder*), Outdoor Writers of America, 1993; Environmental Achievement Award (*Heather and Eric*), Prov. of Nfld. & Labrador, 1994. **MISC:** North by East Productions–musical performances, recordings, TV & radio with fellow musician & songwriter Eric West.

Walters, Sheila $

Vice-President, Store Planning and Construction, Retail Group, **HUDSON'S BAY COMPANY**, 401 Bay St., Ste. 2200, Toronto, ON M5H 2Y4 (416) 861-6086, FAX 861-6216. Born Toronto 1949. sep. **EDUC:** Ryerson Polytechnic Univ., Interior Design 1969. **CAREER:** Designer, Dominion Stores Ltd., 1969-70; self-employed designer, 1970-72; various positions (Designer/Design Mgr/Gen. Mgr/Dir./VP), Hudson's Bay Company, 1972 to date. **INTER-**

ESTS: travel; golf. COMMENT: *"Very private. More concerned with mutual respect than friendship in business."*

Walters, Traci ⊚

National Director, CANADIAN ASSOCIATION OF INDEPENDENT LIVING CENTRES, 350 Sparks St., Ste. 1004, Ottawa, ON K1R 7S8 (613) 563-2581, FAX 235-4497. Born Welland, Ont. 1959. d. 2 ch. Candice Botha, Jacob Botha. EDUC: Seneca Coll., Mktg Diploma. CAREER: Exec. Dir., Niagra Centre for Independent Living; Nat'l Dir., Canadian Association of Independent Living Centres. AFFIL: Access Awareness Week (Nat'l Chair). COMMENT: *"Primary pursuit is to promote and enable the progressive process of citizens with disabilities, taking responsibility for the development and management of personal and community resources. The Canadian Association of Independent Living Centres is the national voice of the independent living movement in Canada and is comprised of member independent living resource centres across the country. These organizations are run by and for people with disabilities."*

Ward, Debra (nee Berk) ■■ ⊚ Ⓢ

President, TOURISM INDUSTRY ASSOCIATION OF CANADA, (advocacy association for Cdn tourism), 130 Albert St., Ste. 1016, Ottawa, ON K1P 5G4 (613) 238-3883, FAX 238-3878, EMAIL debraw@magi.com. Born Montreal 1955. m. John. 1 ch. Siobhan. EDUC: Dawson Coll., partial CEGEP 1972. CAREER: subscriptions/public rel'ns, Centaur Theatre, Montreal, 1972-76; Production Mgr, Listen! Audio Productions, 1976-82; various functions, Tourism Industry Association of Canada; Pres., 1995 to date. AFFIL: Canadian Business Network Coalition (Co-Chair); Canadian Tourism Human Resource Council (Dir.). HONS: Communications Award, International Association of Business Communicators, 1988. INTERESTS: camping; travel; Cdn history; science fiction. COMMENT: *"Career-oriented, 20 years in developing skills, abilities. Now first-time mother and trying to accomplish most challenging role of all."*

Wardlaw, Janet M., B.A.,M.S.,Ph.D. ⊛ ⊕

Nutritionist (retired). FAX (519) 837-1521, EMAIL jwardlaw@uoguelph.ca. Born Toronto 1924. s. EDUC: Univ. of Toronto, B.A.(Household Econ.) 1946; Univ. of Tennessee, M.S.(Nutrition) 1950; Penn State Univ., Ph.D.(Nutrition) 1963. CAREER: Nutritionist, Canadian Red Cross Society, Toronto, 1947-49; Nutritionist, Michigan Dept. of Health, 1950-53; Nutritionist, Toronto Dept. of

Health, 1953-56; Asst. & Assoc. Prof., Fac. of Household Sci., Univ. of Toronto, 1956-66; Prof., Univ. of Guelph, 1966-67; Dean Designate, 1968; Dean, Coll. of Family & Consumer Studies, 1969-83; Assoc. VP, Academic, 1984-87; Chair, Bd. of Gov., International Development Research Centre (IDRC), Ottawa, 1985-92. AFFIL: Canadian Dietetic Association; Canadian Nutrition Society; Family & Children's Service, Guelph & Wellington County (Bd.); Developing Country Farm Radio Network (Bd.); Univ. of Guelph Retirees' Association (Pres. 1994-95). HONS: Stewart Achievement Award, Canadian Dietetic Association, 1971; Hon. Fellow, Univ. of Guelph; Distinguished Alumni Award, Penn State Univ., 1990.

Warkentin, Germaine, B.A.,M.A., Ph.D. ⊛ 🕮

Professor of English, Victoria College, UNIVERSITY OF TORONTO, 73 Queen's Park Cres., Toronto, ON M5S 1K7 (416) 585-4483, FAX 585-4584. Born Toronto 1933. m. John H. Warkentin. 1 ch. EDUC: Univ. of Toronto, B.A.(Phil.) 1955, Ph.D.(English) 1972; Univ. of Manitoba, M.A.(English) 1962. CAREER: freelance film critic, 1953-64; Ed., *Canadian Newsreel*, 1954-57; Instructor in English, United Coll., Winnipeg, 1958-59; Lecturer in English, Victoria Coll., Univ. of Toronto, 1970-72; Asst. Prof., 1972-76; Assoc. Prof., 1976-90; Dir., Centre for Reformation & Renaissance Studies, 1985-90; Prof., 1990 to date. SELECTED PUBLICATIONS: author & ed. of numerous articles & editions in Renaissance & Early Cdn literature, incl. *James Reaney, Poems* (Toronto: New Press, 1972); *Canadian Exploration Writing in English: An Anthology* (Toronto: Oxford Univ. Press, 1993); "Ins and outs of the Sidney family library" (*Times Literary Supplement* Dec. 6, 1985); *The Library of the Sidneys of Penhurst ca. 1665*, ed. with W.R. Bowen & J.C. Black (in progress) & *The Narratives of Pierre-Espirit Radisson* (in progress). EDIT: Ed. Bd., Textual Studies in Canada. AFFIL: Renaissance English Text Society (Int'l Advisory Council); The Spenser Society (Exec. Mbr.).

Warner, Elle, B.A. ■ 🖫 ⊙ ⌀

Writer/Columnist, Owner and Principal Writer, ARTEMESIA AND ASSOCIATES, 157 Crystal St., Thunder Bay, ON P7B 6H6 (807) 767-5143, FAX 767-5859, EMAIL ewarner@norlink.net. Born Estonian refugee camp, Eckenforde, Germany 1946. m. Glenn Warner. 3 ch. Tania Saj, Tami Saj, Cindi Saj. EDUC: Lakehead Univ., B.A.(Pol. Studies) 1995. CAREER: active in health, arts & heritage organizations for more than 25 yrs.; owner & operator, Artemesia &

Associates; active in office mgmt field for 30 yrs.; sr. admin., Thunder Bay Police, 1989 to date. **VOLUNTEER CAREER:** founder, Northwestern Ontario Spina Bifida Association (later amalgamted with the Ont. assoc.); Ont. Bd. of Dir., Spina Bifida & Hydrocephalus Association of Ontario, 13 yrs.; Exec., 8 yrs. **SELECTED PUBLICATIONS:** columnist, "People Behind the Business," *Thunder Bay Post*, 1994 to date; numerous articles & book reviews published locally & nationally in both English & Estonian. **AFFIL:** Spina Bifida Association of Canada (1st VP); Estonian Society of Thunder Bay (Pres.); Thunder Bay Business Women's Network (Past Dir. 1993-95); Spina Bifida & Hydrocephalus Association of Ontario (past Chair, Exec. & Bd. mbr.). **INTERESTS:** travel; reading; lakeside log cabin in Nakina, Ont. **MISC:** 1st Prov. Chair, Bd. of Dir., Spina Bifida & Hydrocephalus Association of Ontario, to be from outside Southern Ont.; mother of int'l swimmer & Cdn Paralympic athlete Tami Saj (Seoul & Barcelona Paralympics) who was inducted into the Northwestern Ontario Sports Hall of Fame, 1996. **COMMENT:** *"This year I celebrated 50 years of living and feel wonderfully liberated. There is a 'me' that is emerging from the layers of various identities collected over the years."*

Warner, Mary Jane, B.A.,M.A., Ph.D. ■ 🤸 🎓 📜

Associate Professor, Department of Dance, YORK UNIVERSITY, 4700 Keele St, North York, ON M3J 1P3 (416) 736-5137, FAX 736-5447, EMAIL mjwarner@edu.yorku.ca. Born Toronto 1941. m. Frederick E. Warner. **EDUC:** Univ. of Toronto, B.A. 1963; Ontario Coll. of Education, Certificate 1964; Ohio State Univ., M.A. 1971, Ph.D. 1974. **CAREER:** Teacher, Toronto, 1964-69; Lecturer, Phys. Educ. Dept., Newberry Coll., 1973-74; Asst. Prof., Dance Dept., Kirkland/Hamilton Colleges, Clinton, NY, 1974-80; Assoc. Prof., Dept. of Dance, York Univ., 1981 to date; Dir., Grad. Program, Dept. of Dance, 1983-86; Chair, Dept. of Dance, 1988-93; Assoc. Dean, Fac. of Fine Arts, 1993-96. **SELECTED CREDITS:** *Shadow on the Prairie: An Interactive Multimedia Dance History Tutorial and Teacher's Guide*, CD-ROM, with Norma Sue Fisher-Stitt, 1996. **SELECTED PUBLICATIONS:** "Dance at York University," *World Ballet and Dance 1991-92: An International Yearbook* (London: Dance Books Ltd., 1991); "Anne Fairbrother Hill: A Chaste and Elegant Dancer" (*Theatre History in Canada* 12(2) 1991); "Striding into the 21st Century: Computer Technologies for Dance," with Norma Sue Fisher-Stitt (*Canadian Theatre Review* Winter 1994); *Canadian Dance Studies Vol. 1*, (journal), ed. with Selma Odom (Toronto: Graduate Programme in Dance, York Univ., 1994); *Toronto Dance Teachers, 1825-1925* (Toronto: Dance Collection, Danse Press, 1995); various articles commissioned for *The International Dictionary of Ballet and Classical Dance*; *Laban Notation Scores: An International Bibliography* (Columbus, Ohio: International Council of Kinetography Laban, Vol. 1, 1984; Vol. 2, 1988; Vol. 3, 1995); various other publications. **EDIT:** Ed. Bd., Theatre History in Canada. **AFFIL:** International Council of Kinetography Laban (Fellow; mbr. of Exec. 1979-83, 1992-96); Centre for the Study of Computers in Education. **HONS:** Kirkland Coll. Research Prof., 1978. **INTERESTS:** reading; sailing; gardening. **MISC:** reconstructed both 18th century & contemporary dance. **COMMENT:** *"I am interested in the potential of computer technology for teaching dance history and movement analysis."*

Warriner, Faye C., B.Comm.,C.A. $

Vice-President and Controller, HUSKY OIL LTD., 707 - 8 Ave. SW, Box 6525, Stn. D., Calgary, AB T2P 3G7 (403) 298-6111, FAX 298-6039. Born Macklin, Sask. 1952. s. **EDUC:** Univ. of Alberta, B.Comm. 1977; C.A. **CAREER:** articling student, Anderson, Macor Ladell, 1978-80; C.A., 1980-82; Mgr, Corp. Acctg, Husky Oil Ltd., 1982-86; Cont., 1986-95; VP & Cont., 1994 to date. **AFFIL:** Canadian Institute of Chartered Accountants; Institute of Chartered Accountants of Alberta; Financial Executives' Institute.

Warszawski, Danuta (Sophia Diana) ■■ ✊ 🎓

President, THE POLISH ALLIANCE OF CANADA. Teacher, HUGHES PUBLIC SCHOOL, 177 Caledonia Rd., Toronto, ON M6E 4S8 (416) 393-1400, FAX 393-1399. **EDUC:** Pedagogical Coll., Jelenia Gora, Poland, Teacher's Diploma 1961; Univ. of Wroclaw, 1961-62; Lakeshore Teachers' Coll., Toronto, Interim Elementary Teacher's Certificate 1965; Permanent Elementary Teacher's Certificate, Standard 1 1967; Catholic Univ. of Lublin, Rome, Summer Univ. of Polish Culture, 1992. **CAREER:** teacher, Poland, 1960-61; teacher, Canada, 1965 to date; Language Lead Instructor, Polish Language, Toronto Bd. of Educ., 1977-89; Language Lead Instructor, Slavic Languages; taught summer & evening ESL courses; taught evening Polish courses, 1971-83; taught Polish Kindergarten under Heritage Language Dept. **AFFIL:** The Polish Alliance of Canada (Exec. VP 1991-93; Pres. 1993 to date; Pres., The W. Reymont Foundation 1985-91); Univ. of Toronto (Polish Hist. & Professorship Committee); The John

Paul II Collegium Building Fund (Nat'l Committee); The Polish Teachers' Association (VP 1992-95). HONS: l'Ordre du Mérite Culturel, Min. of Culture, Poland, 1994; Ted Glista Memorial Award for contributions to Canada & Polish community, 1993; awarded trip to Summer Univ. of Polish Culture by W. Reymont Foundation, 1992; Commemorative Medal for 125th Anniversary of Cdn Confederation, 1992; Gold Medal of Distinction, Canadian Polish Congress, 1989; Silver Medal of Distinction, Canadian Polish Congress, 1987; Volunteer Service Award (15 yrs.), Min. of Citizenship & Culture, 1986; Medal of Distinction, Polish Alliance of Canada, 1985. INTERESTS: family; ballet; opera; symphony; theatre; sports; volunteering as much time as possible to Polish organizations in Canada. MISC: organized conferences for Polish language teachers in Ont.; organized poetry recitals for children & youth of Polish origin; author of Polish Heritage Language Program, Toronto Bd. of Educ.; developed numerous teaching aids for Polish Heritage Language Program; champion in gymnastics & acrobatics in Poland, age 16; danced with many dance groups in Poland.

Waters, Anne Kristensen, B.Math. ■ ■ ❀ $
Director, Information Technology, METROPOLITAN LIFE INSURANCE COMPANY, (life & health insur. & fin. svcs), 99 Bank St., Ottawa, ON K1P 5A3 (613) 560-7888, ext. 3545, FAX 560-6933, EMAIL anne_waters@metlife.e-mail.com. Born Oshawa, Ont. 1961. m. Glenn. 1 ch. Jacob. EDUC: Univ. of Waterloo, B.Math. 1987. CAREER: various positions, Info. Systems Dept., Imperial Oil, Toronto, early 1980s; Sr. Programmer Analyst, Retail Systems, Info. Technology Dept., Metropolitan Life Insurance Company, 1985-87; Proj. Leader, Retail Systems, 1987-90; Methodologist, Mktg & Insur. Technology, 1990-91; Mgr, Security, Standards & Performance, 1991-93; Dir., Info. Technology Svcs, 1993 to date. AFFIL: Canadian Information Processing Society, Ottawa chpt.; Conference Board of Canada (mbr. & V-Chair, Forum for Info. Technology Professionals); Salvation Army, Ottawa-Carleton (Residential Chairperson, 1991 Red Shield Campaign). HONS: Gold Stage, Duke of Edinburgh Award; Outstanding Leadership Award, Univ. of Waterloo. INTERESTS: stencilling; calligraphy; computer graphics; canoeing; camping; gardening; gourmet cooking; travel. COMMENT: *"I feel that my parents have very much influenced my lifestyle and work ethic - emphasis on quality of work, working to one's maximum potential, and a strong respect for the many talents in people around me. As I continue my career, I would*

like to maintain my connection to systems related work. I am proud to be the first woman to be made Director in our Information Technology Department."

Waterston, Elizabeth ■ ■ ❀ 🗋 🍃
Professor Emerita, UNIVERSITY OF GUELPH. CAREER: 40-yr. teaching career; specialist on Scottish/Scottish-Canadian Literature. SELECTED PUBLICATIONS: co-ed. with Mary H. Rubio, *The Selected Journals of L.M. Montgomery*, Vols. 1, 2, 3; co-ed. with Mary H. Rubio, *Writing a Life: L.M. Montgomery*; *Kindling Spirits*; ed., *Child's Garden of Verses*, Robert Louis Stevenson (Univ. of Edinburgh Press); co-founder, *CCL: Canadian Children's Literature/Littérature canadienne pour la jeunesse* (1975); 2 books currently out for consideration.

Watier, Lise $ 🗹 🗂
President and Chief Executive Officer, LISE WATIER COSMÉTIQUES INC., 5800, Côte de Liesse, Montreal, QC H4T 1B4 (514) 735-2309, FAX 735-7339. CAREER: host-researcher, various women's interest TV programs, 1963-68; founded Charme et Beauté Lise Watier Inc., 1965; opened l'Institut Lise Watier, Montreal, 1968; launched Lise Watier Cosmetics line, 1972; opened Lise Watier Boutique (retail ready-to-wear), 1977; opened Lise Watier Coiffure Beauté Spa, 1986; acquired Société Jacquar, 1989; opened l'Institut Lise Watier, Quebec City, 1990; launched new skin care line "Les Soins Phytoligocéan", 1991; launched new perfume "Neiges" 1993; launched new skin care line "Equilibre," 1995; launched new perfume "Vertige," 1996. SELECTED CREDITS: Prod./Writer of a TV show, 1993-96. SELECTED PUBLICATIONS: beauty care columns in newspapers & magazines. AFFIL: Beaver Club; Conseil du Patronat du Québec. HONS: Veuve Clicquot Award, 1986; Prize of Excellence, La Presse, 1987; Order of Canada, 1991; Businesswoman of the Year, Journal de Montréal, 1992, 1993; Woman of the Year, Bus./Entrepreneurship category, Le Salon de la Femme, 1994; various other awards & honours. MISC: Lise Watier Cosmétiques has 300 skin care, make-up & perfume products, & a distribution ntwk that covers more than 450 retail outlets in Canada; products are also sold in Mexico, Saudi Arabia & Kuwait; 1st woman to be Pres. of the Beaver Club, Montreal. COMMENT: *"As a Canadian entrepreneur in an industry dominated by European and American companies, Lise Watier feels a sense of achievement when she thinks that, in partnership with 160 Canadian suppliers and a vast network of retailers, Lise*

Watier Cosmétiques Inc. generates over 20 million dollars for the Canadian economy."

Watson, Alberta 🎞 📺 🎭

Actor. c/o Great North Artists Management Inc, 350 Dupont St., Toronto, ON M5R 1V9 (416) 925-2051. **EDUC:** acting training with Gene Lasko, NY. **SELECTED CREDITS:** Lead, *Hackers* (feature), United Artists; Lead, *Bullet* (feature), dir. Julian Temple; Lead, *Spanking The Monkey* (feature), Fine Line Cinema; Co-Star, *Zebra Head* (feature), Zebra Films Inc.; Lead, *The White of the Eye* (feature), Independent Film; Lead, *The Keep* (feature), Paramount; Lead, *Exposure* (feature), Transcan Productions; Principal, *In Praise of Older Women* (feature), RSL Productions; Lead, *Dog Hermit* (telefilm), CBS; Lead, *Frame Up* (telefilm), NBC; Lead, *Mood Indigo* (telefilm), CBS; Guest Star, *Law & Order* (series), NBC; Lead, *Red Earth, White Earth* (telefilm), CBS; Guest Star (2 eps.), *Street Legal* (series), CBC; Lead, *Kane & Abel* (mini-series), CBS; Principal, *I Am a Hotel* (telefilm), CBC; Lead, *Sweet Angel Mine* (feature), Cineplex Films; Principal, *Crash* (feature), Dir. David Cronenberg; Lead, *Seeds of Doubt* (feature), Saban Films; Lead, *Blood Gets Angry* (telefilm), CBC; Lead, *La Femme Nikita* (series), Fireworks/USA Cable. **HONS:** Audience Award (*Spanking the Monkey*), Sundance Film Festival; Best Supporting Actress (*Exposure*), Yorkton Film Festival; nomination, Best Supporting Actress (*In Praise of Older Women*), Genie Award, 1979.

Watson, Carolyn F., B.Comm.,C.A. ■ $ ✊

Chartered Accountant, CAROLYN WATSON, CHARTERED ACCOUNTANT, 12 Lawton Blvd., Toronto, ON M4V 1Z4 (416) 964-7035, FAX 964-0090. Chair, BLOORVIEW CHILDREN'S HOSPITAL FOUNDATION. Born Toronto 1953. m. Arthur D. 3 ch. **EDUC:** Univ. of Toronto, B.Comm. 1976; C.A. **CAREER:** Acctnt, Price Waterhouse, 1976-79; Cont., Extendicare Ltd., 1979-81; Lecturer, Univ. of Toronto, 1979-86; self-employed C.A., 1981 to date. **AFFIL:** Canadian Institute of Chartered Accountants (Exam Marker 1982-91); Bloorview Children's Hospital Foundation (Chair 1984 to date); Centennial Infant & Child Centre (Chair & Dir.). **COMMENT:** *"Highly motivated; self-disciplined; mother of three; interested in volunteer work as well as professional endeavours."*

Watson, Dorothy E., B.A. $

Director, Member Relations and Service Quality, CREDIT UNION CENTRAL OF ONTARIO, 2810 Matheson Blvd. E., Mississauga, ON L4W 4X7 (905) 629-5525, FAX 238-5008. Born Toronto 1957. s. **EDUC:** Glendon Coll., York Univ., B.A. 1980. **CAREER:** Deposit Svcs Officer & Computer Operator, Co-operative Trust Company of Canada, 1982-84; Gen. Mgr, The Ottawa Women's Credit Union Ltd., 1984-88; Dir., Hum. Res. Dev., Credit Union Central of Ontario, 1988-92; Dir., Mbr. Rel'ns & Svc Quality, 1992 to date. **AFFIL:** Canadian Co-operative Association (Ont. Reg'l Council); American Society for Quality Control. **HONS:** Woman of the Year, Ottawa Business & Professional Women's Club, 1985; among Top Female Managers in Canada, *Financial Post Magazine*, 1992. **INTERESTS:** theatre; politics; foreign film. **MISC:** speaker at nat'l conferences on topics related to hum. res. dev. & svc quality.

Watson, Julie V. 📖 ✊ $

Owner, CREATIVE CONNECTIONS, P.O. Box 1204, Charlottetown, PE C1A 7M8 (902) 566-9748, FAX 566-9748. Born UK 1943. m. Jack. 1 ch. John Watson. **EDUC:** Central Peel Composite Sch., Commercial/Bus. 1962. **CAREER:** various positions, American Motors Corporation, 16 yrs.; event organizer; Lifestyles Ed., *Guardian Patriot*, Charlottetown; Ed., Walt Wheeler Publications, Charlottetown; Survey Coord. & Consultant, PEI Crafts Council; Reg'l Coord., Association of Atlantic Women Business Owners; Comm. Dir., Canadian Atlantic Lobster Promotion Association, Inc., 1992 to date; owner, Creative Connections (writing, research, consulting), 1984 to date. **SELECTED PUBLICATIONS:** *Seafood Cookery of Prince Edward Island* (Charlottetown: Ragweed Press); *A Prince Edward Island Album: Glimpses of the Way We Were* (Toronto: Hounslow Press); *Ghost Stories and Legends of Prince Edward Island* (Toronto: Hounslow Press); *Low Cost Heart Smart Cooking* (Toronto: Macmillan Canada); *A Fine Catch*, seafood cookbook (Charlottetown: Ragweed Press, 1994); various other cookbooks & Canadiana anthologies; articles published in numerous periodicals, incl. *Seafood Business*, *Trade & Commerce*, *Simply Seafood*, *Atlantic Business Journal*, *Canadian Living*, & *European Hospitality*. **AFFIL:** Cuisine Canada (Founding Bd. Mbr.); International Association of Culinary Professionals; Association of Atlantic Women Business Owners (Bd. Mbr.); Periodical Writers' Association of Canada (Atlantic Reg'l Dir.); Island Writers' Association, PEI (Pres.); PEI Crafts Council. **INTERESTS:** writing; travel; food; entrepreneurship for women. **MISC:** teaching, public speaking & workshops; frequent guide for media groups, visiting chefs & buyers touring seafood & tourist industries of PEI; judge, Canadian Entrepreneur Awards & Atlantic Canada Entrepreneur Awards; various radio interviews. COMMENT: *"After 17 years in the workforce I created a full time career writing books, articles and commercial pieces. My business combines these things with seafood promotion and marketing consulting."*

Watson, Karen M., B.Sc. $
Vice-President and Controller, ATCO LTD., 909 - 11 Ave. SW, Ste. 1500, Calgary, AB T2R 1N6 (403) 292-7528, FAX 292-7532. Born Lacombe, Alta. 1951. m. William Lynn Watson. 1 ch. Maren Liv Watson. EDUC: Univ. of Alberta, B.Sc.(Math.) 1971. CAREER: Mgr, Planning & Budgeting, ATCO Ltd., 1988-93; VP & Cont., 1993 to date. DIRECTOR: CanUtilities Holdings Ltd. AFFIL: Professional Club, Calgary. INTERESTS: computers; aerobics; hiking.

Watson, Mireille Florence Eveline, B.A. ■ 🏵 ⛺
Vice-President, Industrial Relations and Training, CANADIAN FILM AND TELEVISION PRODUCTION ASSOCIATION, 175 Bloor St. E., Ste. 806, Toronto, ON M4V 3R8 (416) 927-8942, FAX 922-4038. Born Lyon, France 1947. m. Peter. 1 ch. EDUC: York Univ., B.A.(Hist./French Lit.) 1985. CAREER: Special Proj. Coord., Ontario Share and Deposit Insurance Corporation, 1980-82; Broadcast Rel'ns Dir., A.C.A./I.C.A., 1982-87; Exec. Dir., Association of Canadian Film & Television Producers, 1987-91; Dir., Industrial Rel'ns & Mbr. Svcs, Canadian Film & Television Production Association, 1991-96. AFFIL: Cultural Human Resources Council (Bd.); Toronto Women in Film & Television (Bd.); Ministry of Labour Section 11 Health & Safety Advisory Committee; Entertainment Tax Action Committee (Bd.); Ontario Sectoral Council for Culture (Bd.); Franco-Ontarian Jurist Association; ACTRA Fraternal Benefit Society (Bd. of Gov.). INTERESTS: travel; theatre; reading; falconry. COMMENT: *"After a twelve-year career in the film and television industry, I have achieved a high level of expertise in a most rewarding and unique area: labour relations."*

Watson Henderson, Ruth, A.R.C.T., L.R.C.T. 🏵
Composer. 23 Birchview Blvd., Toronto, ON M8X 1H4. Born Toronto 1932 3 ch. EDUC: Royal Conservatory of Music, A.R.C.T. 1950, L.R.C.T. 1952. CAREER: concert pianist with many solo appearances on the CBC; accompanist, Festival Singers of Canada under Elmer Iseler, 1968-78; accompanist, Toronto Children's Chorus, 1978 to date; accompanist, Ontario Youth Choir, 1980s. SELECTED CREDITS: choral compositions, also composi-

tions for piano, organ, string orchestra, winds, brass & percussion; commissioned works for Guelph Spring Festival, Oriana Singers, Ontario Youth Choir, Toronto Children's Chorus, Elora Festival; *Missa Brevis* (1974); *Musical Animal Tales* (1979); *Through The Eyes of Children* (1981); *Songs of the Nativity* (1984); *Creation's Praise* (1986); *Crazy Times* (1986); *The Last Straw* (1990); *Five Ontario Folk Songs* (1991); *Voices of Earth* (1991); *The Travelling Musicians* (1994). AFFIL: Eglinton United Church (organist); Canadian Music Centre; Canadian League of Composers; Association of Canadian Women Composers; Royal Canadian Coll. of Organists; SOCAN. HONS: prize winner, Int'l Competition for Women Composers, Mannheim, Germany, 1989; Nat'l Choral Award (Voices of Earth), Association of Canadian Choral Conductors, 1990-92.

Watt, Virginia 🏵 ⊗ 📖
Treasurer and Archivist, CANADIAN GUILD OF CRAFTS QUEBEC, 2025 Peel St., Montreal, QC H3A 1T6 (514) 849-6091. Born Winnipeg 1919. s. EDUC: Art Students' League, N.Y.; Traphagen Sch. of Design, N.Y. CAREER: Inspection Bd. of the UK & Canada, Ste-Thérèse, Que., 1942-45; costume designer & actor, Montreal Repertory Theatre, 1946-55; actor, CBC Radio Int'l, 1946-55; freelance costume designer, 1946-55; studio ceramist, research in glaze technology, 1956-67; mbr., Bd. of Dir., Canadian Guild of Crafts Quebec, 1964-68; Mng Dir., 1968-80; Chair, Que. Reg'l Committee, Canadian Eskimo Arts Council, 1969-74; mbr., 1974-77; Chair & Advisor to Min. of Northern Affairs, 1977-83; mbr., Bd. of Dir., Canadian Arctic Producers, Ottawa, 1978-80; Dir., Canadian Guild of Crafts Quebec, 1980-86; mbr., Canadian Eskimo Arts Council, 1983-86; mbr., Bd. of Dir., Hon. Treas., Consultant & Archivist, Canadian Guild of Crafts Quebec, 1987 to date. SELECTED PUBLICATIONS: text, *Industry in the Homes of the People: The Permanent Collection of the Canadian Guild of Crafts*, catalogue (1969); various other catalogues; "The Canadian Guild of Crafts Quebec" (*Artisan* Mar./Apr. 1978); "The Essence of Craftsmanship" (*Craftnews* Aug. 1982); "The Role of the Canadian Eskimo Arts Council" (*American Review of Canadian Studies* 17(1) 1988); "Imitation Native Art" (*Inuit Art Quarterly* 8(1) 1993); various other publications. AFFIL: Inuit Art Foundation (Pres. 1989-94; Bd. of Dir.); Canadian Guild of Crafts (Dir.); Canada Crafts Council (Hon. Life Mbr.). HONS: Order of Canada, 1985; Canada 125 Medal, 1992. INTERESTS: historical role of women in Cdn arts & crafts. MISC: Curator, Inuit Collection,

Canadian Guild of Crafts; mbr., various juries & selection committees, incl. Royal Canadian Mint Design Selection Committee, 1977-78, 1980-87; various conference presentations. COMMENT: *"I enjoy working. Everything I have done I have wanted to do. The dream can be a reality."*

Watters, Bronwyn Valmai, B.A. ✦
Director, Policy, Planning and Evaluation, Department of Health and Social Services, GOVERNMENT OF NORTHWEST TERRITORIES, Box 1320, Yellowknife, NT X1A 2L9 (403) 873-7155, FAX 873-2066. Born Sydney, Australia 1944. m. Andrew Langford. 1 stpch. Tara Hanna. EDUC: Univ. of Sydney, B.A.(Psych.) 1966; Clinical Psychology Cadetship, Dept. of Public Health, Australia, 1964-66; CAREER: Child Clinical Psychologist, New South Wales Dept. of Health, Sydney, 1966-68; Counsellor, Mount Royal Coll., Calgary, 1968; Dir., Peter Pan Nursery, Kingston, Ont., 1969-70; Teaching Master, Counsellor & Dept. of Human Studies, St. Lawrence Coll., Kingston, 1970-77; Bus. Mgr & Instructor, Canadian Outward Bound Wilderness Sch., Ont., 1977-78; Coord., Special Remedial Educ., Dept. of Educ., N.W.T., 1978-82; Dept. of Social Services, 1982-94; Chief, Social Programs; Asst. Dep. Min.; Dir., Mgmt Svcs; currently Dir., Policy, Planning & Evaluation, Dept. of Health & Social Svcs. SELECTED PUBLICATIONS: publications primarily for gov't attribution; other publications incl. papers in special educ., cross-cultural psych. & educational assessment. HONS: Commonwealth Fellowship, 1962-66. INTERESTS: photography; music; canoeing; poetry. MISC: registered psychologist, N.W.T. COMMENT: *"Principal professional interests currently focus on national reform of the health/social services system in the north. Living on the water, music, and my husband keep me sane."*

Watters, Frances R., B.A.,LL.B. ⚖ 🏵 ○
Partner, ALEXANDER, HOLBURN, BEAUDIN & LANG, Barristers and Solicitors, 2700 Toronto-Dominion Bank Tower, 700 W. Georgia St., P.O. Box 10057 Pacific Centre, Vancouver, BC V7Y 1B8 (604) 688-1351. 1 ch. Collum Watters-Devine. EDUC: Univ. of British Columbia, B.A. 1978; Univ. of Victoria, LL.B. 1983. BAR: B.C., 1984. CAREER: Law Clerk, B.C. Supreme Court, 1984-85; Lawyer, Gardner, Snarch and Allen, 1984-85; Staff Lawyer, Labour Rel'ns Bd., Prov. of B.C., 1985-87; Sr. Solicitor, Industrial Rel'ns Council, 1987-88; Lawyer & Ptnr, Alexander, Holburn, Beaudin and Lang, 1988 to date; Instructor, B.C. Institute of Technology, 1991-93. SELECTED PUB-

LICATIONS: *Canadian Labour Relations Board Reports* Western Co-ordinating Ed. (Butterworths, 1987-91); *Practice Before the Industrial Relations Council* (Continuing Legal Education Society, 1989); *Family and Work: The Legal Framework* (Continuing Legal Education Society, 1992). EDIT: Ed., *Jurisfemme*, 1984-87; Ed. Bd., *Canadian Journal of Women and the Law*, 1987-89. AFFIL: Canadian Bar Association (Chair, Labour Law Subsection 1993-94); Law Society of B.C. (Subcommittee on Women in the Legal Profession 1991); Human Resources Management Association (Industrial Rel'ns Committee); West Coast Legal Education & Action Fund (Pres. 1991-94); National Association of Women & the Law (Nat'l Exec. 1983-87); Nora Piggott Scholarship Trust Fund (Dir. 1980 to date). INTERESTS: travels in Europe, Africa, Caribbean & S.E. Asia; skiing; sailing; hiking. MISC: numerous seminars on labour, employment, Charter & human rights issues.

Waxman, Sara ■ ✎ ○ 𝒴
Columnist and Author. EMAIL waxworx@inforamp.net. Born Poland/Russia Border 1938. m. Al Waxman. 2 ch. Tobaron, Adam. CAREER: columnist, "Supper in a Hurry" *The Toronto Star*, 1981-82; columnist, restaurant review, *The Toronto Sun*, 1982 to date; feature writer: dining out/lifestyle/travel, *TV Guide Magazine*, 1985-92; mbr. & V-Chair, Ontario Film Review Bd., 1985-92; columnist, "Cheaper Eats" Friday Entertainment Section, *The Toronto Sun*, 1990-94; columnist, "Arts and Leisure" weekly restaurant review on int'l dining & travel, *The Financial Post*, 1992 to date (canoe www site); Contributing Ed., Air Canada *EN ROUTE* magazine, 1995; monthly contribution, *FLARE* Magazine, 1995 to date. SELECTED CREDITS: weekly 10-minute spot on trends, food & lifestyle, CKO News Radio, 1988; radio & TV endorsements/commercials for Dow Consumer Products (1984) & Miracle Food Mart (1980-81). SELECTED PUBLICATIONS: *The King's Wife's Cookbook* (Nelson Canada, 1980); *The Great Hadassah Cookbook*, co-author (Hurtig Publishers, 1982); *Backroads and Country Cooking* (McClelland & Stewart, 1985); Ed., *ZAGAT Toronto Restaurant Survey*, 1993 & 1994; *Toronto's Cheaper Eats* (Burgher Books, 1994; 2nd printing 1995); feature writer, Fodor's Travel Publications, Dining Chapters, Toronto Book & Canada Book, 1994 to date (Fodor's www site). AFFIL: Association of Food Journalists; International Food, Wine & Travel Writers' Association; The Travel Media Association of Canada; Barbara Schlifer Commemorative Clinic for women who are survivors of abuse

(Hon. Chair); Canadian Shaare Zedek Hospital Foundation (Bd.); Canadian Opera Company (Women's Committee); Opera Ball (Chair 1997); Canadian Cancer Society. **MISC:** numerous speaking engagements

Waygood, Kathryn, B.A. ✦ ⓔ
Councillor, CITY OF SASKATOON, 222 - 3rd Ave. N., Saskatoon, SK S7K 0JB (306) 975-2783, FAX 975-2784. Born Winnipeg 1944. m. E. Bruce Waygood. 3 ch. **EDUC:** Univ. of Toronto, B.A.(Geography) 1966; Ontario Coll. of Education, Type A Teaching Certificate 1972. **CAREER:** Teacher, Malvern Collegiate, 1968-74; City Councillor, City of Saskatoon, 1979 to date; Community Dev. Team, Saskatoon District Health Bd., 1993 to date; Chair, Heritage Canada, 1992-94; Sask. Gov., 1987-94. **SELECTED PUBLICATIONS:** "A Politician's Notes to City Planners" (*City Magazine* Fall 1990). **DIRECTOR:** ETEC Community Bond Corporation. **AFFIL:** Heritage Canada Foundation (Gov. 1987-94); Saskatoon Public Library (Dir.); On Broadway Business Improvement District (Dir.); Saskatchewan Heritage Foundation Bd. (Dir.); Saskatchewan Judicial Council (Dir.); Meewasin Valley Authority (Dir. 1993); Saskatchewan Heritage Property Act (Steering Committee 1981). **HONS:** Rosalie Early Memorial Award, YWCA, 1984; Saskatchewan Association of Community Planners Award for distinguished contributions by a non-planner, 1995. **INTERESTS:** urban planning issues & community dev.; heritage as an integral component of cities/communities; women's history. **COMMENT:** *"Older neighbourhoods remain viable when physical and social infrastructure are maintained. Believes that gender equity is critical at all levels of government."*

Wayne, Elsie E., LL.D.,D.Litt.,M.P. ✦ ⎔
Member of Parliament (Saint John), GOVERNMENT OF CANADA, Confederation Building, House of Commons, Rm 718, Ottawa, ON K1A 0A6 (613) 947-4571, FAX 947-4574, Constituency Office, 36 King St., Saint John, NB E2L 1G3 (506) 636-5177, FAX 636-5190. Born Shediac, N.B. m. Richard. 2 ch. Steven, Daniel. **CAREER:** Saint John Common Council, 1977-83; Mayor, Saint John, 1983-93; Commissioner, Citizen's Forum on Canada's Future, appointed by Prime Min., 1991; invited by German Gov't, along with 4 other Canadians, to look at unification program, Germany, 1992; elected M.P.(Saint John), 1993. **AFFIL:** 3rd Field Regiment (Hon. Gunner); The Salvation Army Advisory Bd., Saint John (Life Mbr.); Saint John Boys' & Girls' Club Endowment Fund; 2nd Battalion Delancy's Brigade; National Arts & the Cities (Atlantic Rep.); The

Honourable Order of Kentucky Colonels (Hon. Col.); Business & Professional Women's Club, Saint John (Hon. Pres.); Saint John Council of Women (Hon. VP; Hon. Chair); Saint John Branch, Canadian Red Cross (Hon. VP); Quota Club (Hon. VP); "Operation Go Home" (Hon. Chair); Amana House shelter for battered women (Hon. Campaign Chair); Royal Canadian Legion Branch No. 14, Saint John (Hon. Mbr.); St. George's Society (Hon. Mbr.); Carleton & York Regimental Association (Saint John) Ltd. (Hon. Assoc. Mbr.); Junior Achievement (Bd. of Gov.). **HONS:** named 1 of the 50 most influential people in Atlantic Canada by *Atlantic Lifestyles Business Magazine*, 1993; Canada 125 Medal, 1992; YM-YWCA Red Triangle Award, 1992; Cdn Literacy Volunteer Award, 1991; Transportation Person of the Year, 1991; Toastmasters Int'l Communicator Achievement Award; "The Orange Prize."; LL.D.(Hon.), St. Thomas Univ., 1988; Doctorate of Public Admin.(Hon.), Husson Coll., 1993; D.Litt.(Hon.), Univ. of New Brunswick, Saint John Campus, 1994. **MISC:** 1st female Mayor of Saint John; 1st Hon. Mbr., Royal Canadian Legion Branch No. 14, Saint John, 1985; 1st woman of Saint John to become an Hon. Mbr. of St. George's Society; 1st woman Commissioner, Saint John Transit Commission; 2nd person to be named Hon. Gunner, 3rd Field Regiment, in its 200-yr. history.

Weaver, Martha Jane, B.A.(Hons.), A.O.C.A. ■ ⁄ ⊗
Publications Consultant. 17 Millington St., Toronto, ON N4X 1A3 (416) 925-8992. Born Trenton, Ont. 1955. **EDUC:** Queen's Univ., Hons. B.A.(Hist.) 1977; Ontario Coll. of Art, A.O.C.A.(Gen. Studies) 1982. **CAREER:** Asst. Art Dir., Reactor Art and Design Ltd., 1982-85; Designer, *Saturday Night* Magazine, 1986-87; Assoc. Art Dir., *Toronto Life* Magazine, 1988; Assoc. Art Dir., *Domino* Magazine, The *Globe and Mail*, 1989; Art Dir., *Report on Business* Magazine, The Globe and Mail, 1989-91; Corp. Art Dir., *Enroute* & *Privilege* Magazines, Airmedia, 1991-93; Guest Lecturer, George Brown Coll., 1992; Fac., Banff Magazine Publishing Workshop, 1993; freelance art direction & design, 1993-94; Creative Dir., *Canadian Living*, Telemedia Communications Inc., 1994-96; Guest Lecturer, Ryerson Polytechnic Univ., 1995. **AFFIL:** Canadian National Magazine Awards (Dir.); Advertising & Design Club of Canada; Mayfair Lakeshore Racquet Club. **HONS:** Award of Merit, Graphic Design in Advertising, Art Directors' Club of Toronto, 1987; 2 Awards of Merit, Editorial Spread Design, Art Directors' Club of Toronto, 1987; Silver Medal, Canadian National Magazine

Awards, 1987; Alan R. Fleming/Maclaren Awards for Art Direction, 1987; Award of Merit, Editorial Illustration, Art Directors' Club of Toronto, 1988; 2 Awards of Merit, Editorial Photography, Art Directors' Club of Toronto, 1988; Gold Award, Spread Design, North American City & Regional Magazine Awards, 1989; Silver Award, Editorial Package Design, Art Directors' Club of Toronto, 1990; 7 Awards of Merit, Photography & Illustration, Art Directors' Club of Toronto, 1990; Award of Merit, Cover Design, Art Directors' Club of Toronto, 1991; Award of Excellence, Editorial Photography, *Communication Arts*, 1992; Silver Award & Award of Merit, Editorial Illustration, Advertising & Design Club of Canada, 1992; 2 Awards of Merit, Editorial Spread Design, Advertising & Design Club of Canada, 1992; Gold Award, Art Direction, Canadian National Magazine Awards, 1993; Gold Award, Editorial Photography, Advertising & Design Club of Canada, 1993; 2 Awards of Merit, Editorial Section & Spread Design, Advertising & Design Club of Canada, 1993; Grands Prix du Magazine, Photo-Support Visuel, Magazines du Québec, 1994; Hon. Mention, Editorial Photography, Canadian National Magazine Awards, 1994; Hon. Mention, Still-Life Photography, Canadian National Magazine Awards, 1995; Magazine of the Year, *Canadian Living*, Canadian Society of Magazine Editors, 1995-96. **INTERESTS:** contemporary Cdn art & photography; jazz; travel. **COMMENT:** *"Printed material will continue to excite, entertain and inform our culture in the midst of technological change."*

Webb, Phyllis, B.A. 🗋 📖 ⚔
Writer. 128 Menhinick Dr., Salt Spring Island, BC V8K 1W7 (604) 653-2068. Born Victoria, B.C. 1927. s. **EDUC:** Univ. of British Columbia, B.A.(English/Phil.) 1949; McGill Univ., 1953-54. **CAREER:** secretarial work, 1951-60; writer, 1954 to date; freelance broadcaster, 1955-76; Teaching Asst., Univ. of British Columbia, 1960-63; Program Organizer, Dept. of Public Affairs, CBC, Toronto, 1964-67; Exec. Prod., *Ideas*, CBC Radio, 1967-69; Guest Lecturer, Creative Writing Dept., Univ. of British Columbia, 1976-77; Visiting Asst. Prof., Creative Writing, Univ. of Victoria, 1978-79; Sessional Lecturer, part-time, Creative Writing, 1978-88; Writer-in-Residence, Univ. of Alberta, 1980-81; Adjunct Prof., Creative Writing, 1989-93. **SELECTED PUBLICATIONS:** *Trio*, with Gael Turnbull & Eli Mandel (Montreal: Contact Press, 1954); *Even Your Right Eye* (Toronto: McClelland & Stewart, Indian File Series, 1956); *The Sea is Also a Garden* (Toronto: Ryerson Press, 1963); *Naked Poems*

(Vancouver: Periwinkle Press, 1965); *Selected Poems 1954-65*, ed. with an intro. by John Hulcoop (Vancouver: Talon Books, 1971); *Wilson's Bowl* (Toronto: Coach House Press, 1980); *Talking*, essays (Montreal: Quadrant Editions, 1982); *Sunday Water: Thirteen Anti-Ghazals*, Island Writing Series, Lantzville, B.C., 1982; *The Vision Tree: Selected Poems*, ed. with an intro. by Sharon Thesen (Vancouver: Talon Books, 1982); *Water and Light: Ghazals and Anti-Ghazals* (Toronto: Coach House Press, 1984); *Hanging Fire* (Toronto: Coach House Press, 1990); *Nothing But Brush Strokes*, Selected Prose (Edmonton: NeWest Press, 1995). **AFFIL:** The League of Canadian Poets. **HONS:** Gov. General's Award, Poetry (The Vision Tree), 1982; Officer, The Order of Canada, 1992. **INTERESTS:** arts; environment; human rights. **COMMENT:** *"I have built my life around my vocation as a poet for which I am best known, although I am also remembered as the co-creator of the radio program Ideas and for my work as a broadcaster. Teaching assumed importance in my life after I chose to live on Salt Spring Island. I am now retired and mainly absorbed in painting and collaging."*

Webber, Debbie ■ ■ Ⓢ
Senior Executive Sales Manager, WEEKENDER LADIES WEAR, 427 Alex Doner Dr., Newmarket, ON L3X 1C6 (905) 853-7515, FAX 836-7448. Born Edmonton. m. Lee. 2 ch. Wendy, Lindsay. **EDUC:** Jasper Place Composite High Sch., Edmonton, Grade 12 diploma 1970. **CAREER:** Royal Bank/fitness teacher at private fitness facility (part-time), 1971-87; Weekender Ladies Wear, 1986 to date; #1 Sales Coord. in Canada (set a company record); #1 Sales Mgr in Canada for the past 5 yrs., setting records with sales of over $4 million; sales in 1996 will exceed $5 million (possibly even $6 million), setting a new company record; will become company's 1st Nat'l Sales Dir. **AFFIL:** Chamber of Commerce; church committee. **INTERESTS:** running; golf; travel. **COMMENT:** *"The greatest reward and motivation is helping other women realize their potential and achieve their goals and dreams. I believe that if there is any secret at all to success and being happier in life, it is this: to realize what a marvelous person you are to begin with, to treat that person with love and care, and to understand that if you truly desire your dreams to take you places you've never been...all you have to do is believe in yourself and begin."*

Webster, Jill R., B.A.,M.A.,Ph.D. 🐿 📖
Professor Emeritus, UNIVERSITY OF TORONTO, St. Michael's College, 81 St. Mary St., Toronto,

ON M5S 1J4 (416) 926-1300, Ext. 3339, FAX 922-7254, EMAIL jwebster@epas.u.oftoronto.ca. Born London, UK 1931. s. EDUC: Univ. of Liverpool, B.A.(Hispanic Studies) 1962, Postgrad. Certificate in Educ. 1965; Univ. of Nottingham, M.A.(Spanish) 1964; Univ. of Toronto, Ph.D.(Spanish) 1969; Univ. of London, B.A.(Medieval & Modern Hist.). CAREER: Prof., Univ. of Toronto, 1968-95; Assoc. Dean, Fac. of Arts & Sci., 1978-81; Dir., Centre for Medieval Studies, 1989-95; Prof. Emeritus, 1995 to date. SELECTED PUBLICATIONS: *La societat catalana al segle XIV*, an anthology of unpublished excerpts from Mss. of Francesco Eiximenis (*Edicions* '62, 1967; reprinted 1980); "Colected anthology of unpublished excerpts from Mss*Anuari de l'Institut d'Estudis Gironins*, Gerona, Spain, 1985-86); "The Barcelona Carmelite Archives" (*Analecta Sacra Tarraconensia*, Barcelona, 66, 1992); *Els Menorets: The Franciscans in the Realms of Aragon from St. Francis to the Black Death* (Toronto: Pontifical Institute of Mediaeval Studies, studies & texts, 114, 1993). AFFIL: Royal Society of Canada (Fellow); American Catholic Historical Association; American Historical Association; American Academy of Research Historians of Medieval Spain (Pres. 1991-95); Medieval Academy of America; Canadian Society of Medievalists; Asociaci Royal Society of Canada (Fellow)INTERESTS: history; natural history; travel; medieval studies; art; art history. COMMENT: *"My interest in Catalonia (Spain) began before I went to university in 1959 and remains my main area of research, specifically medieval social history and the religious orders in the Crown of Aragon. My publications reflect this interest."*

Webster, Mary ■ ⊕ 📖
Regional Leader, Operations, Health Records Services, CALGARY REGIONAL HEALTH AUTHORITY, 1820 Richmond Rd. S.W., Calgary, AB T2T 5C7 (403) 229-7685, FAX 229-7214. Born Rupert, Ind. 1933. m. James W. 4 ch. Martine Leavitt, John Kevin Webster, James Fenton Webster, Nicole Milner. EDUC: Canadian Coll. of Health Service Executives, Certificate. CAREER: Planning Officer, Statistics Canada, 1974-79; Admissions Officer, Univ. of Alberta, 1980; Asst. & Acting Mgr, Medical Records Dept., Univ. of Alberta Hospitals, 1980-83; Dir., Patient Admissions, Info Svcs, & Health Records, University Hospital, Vancouver, 1983-92; Dir., Patient Access & Records Mgmt, Calgary General Hospital, 1992 to date. AFFIL: Canadian Health Record Association; Alberta Health Record Association. INTERESTS: computers; reading.

Webster, Mary Page, B.Sc. ■■ $ ⚛ ☝
President, RAVENTURES INC. (asset mgmt - resources), 1 First Canadian Place, Ste. 815, Toronto, ON M5X 1E3 (416) 860-1371, FAX 860-0520, EMAIL webster@passport.ca. Born Minneapolis, Minn. 1959. s. EDUC: McMaster Univ., B.Sc.(Geol.) 1984. CAREER: Jr. Geologist, Canadian Occidental/Abitibi-Price/Northgate; Prospector, Comaplex/J.C. Stephen Explorations; Consulting Geologist, Falconbridge/Stelco/others; Field Geologist, Noranda Inc.; Exploration Mgr, Geddes Resources Ltd.; VP, Adamantis Inc.; Pres., Round Table Resources Inc.; Pres., Raventures Inc. DIRECTOR: Adamantis Inc.; Heat, Steam & Power Inc.; Raventures Inc.; Round Table Resources Inc. AFFIL: Ticker Club; Prospectors' & Developers' Association of Canada (former Dir.); National Club; Mining Women of Canada; Yukon Chamber of Mines; Art Gallery of Ontario; Yukon Territorial Water Bd. (former committee mbr.). INTERESTS: sailing; tennis; Internet; sculpture; First Nations arts. MISC: speaker, Fraser Institute conference, "Mining in British Columbia: Eliminating Uncertainty and Encouraging Investment," Oct. 1996. COMMENT: *"While surviving grassroots experiences of mine finding and resource management, I endeavour to bring people, values, favourable economics and capital markets together."*

Weerasinghe, Jean, B.A.,M.L.S. ■ 📖 🍁
Manager, Information and Research Centre, Privy Council Office, GOVERNMENT OF CANADA, 85 Sparks St., Ste. 1000, Ottawa, ON K1A 0A3 (613) 957-5133, FAX 957-5043, EMAIL jweerasing@pco.gc.ca. Born St. John's 1949. m. Asoka Weerasinghe. 2 ch. EDUC: Memorial Univ. of Newfoundland, B.A.(English) 1970; Dalhousie Univ., M.L.S. 1979. AFFIL: Beta Phi Mu; Council of Federal Libraries (Exec.). HONS: Southcott Memorial Bursary, 1966; Grad. Student Fellowship. INTERESTS: ballroom dancing

Wehrstein, Karen, B.A.A. ■ 📜 ⊕
Writer, HEARTHSTONE INDEPENDENT ENTERPRISES, R.R. 2, Huntsville, ON P1H 2J3 (705) 789-7497, FAX 789-4940, EMAIL hearth@vianet.on.ca. Born Toronto 1961. life partner. Shirley Meier. 1 ch. Tristan Paul Meier. EDUC: Ryerson Polytechnic Univ., B.A.A. 1983. CAREER: regular contributor, cartooning, *The Ryersonian*, 1980-83; freelance cartooning, 1980 to date; typesetter/contractor, Lessac Graphics, Toronto, 1984-87; freelance word processing & desktop publishing, 1984 to date; writing teacher, with Shirley Meier, independent workshops, 1992 to date; teacher, with

Shirley Meier, women's self-defence, 1993 to date; freelance writing & reporter, Muskoka Publications Group (*Huntsville Herald, Muskoka Advance*), 1994-96; Co-Founder, with Shirley Meier, *the other pages, Muskoka's Guide to Alternative Goods & Services*, 1995 to date; Founder, Integreated Healing Services (alternative health info. & consulting svc). **SELECTED PUBLICATIONS:** frequent contributor, "Walk Your Talk," column on women's issues, *Huntsville Herald*, 1994-96; *Lion's Heart* (New York: Baen Book, 1991); *Lion's Soul* (New York: Baen Books, 1991); *Shadow's Son*, with Shirley Meier & S.M. Stirling (New York: Baen Books, 1991); *Food, Sex, Death and Truth*, poetry collection (Hearthstone Independent Press, 1993); "O.R. 3," *Shivers*, ed. Greg Ioannou & Lynne Missen (Toronto: Seal Books, 1989); "Cold," *Northern Frights*, ed. Don Hutchison (Toronto: Mosaic Press, 1992); "The Murphosensor Bomb," *Bolos Book Two: The Unconquerable*, ed. Bill Fawcett (New York: Baen Books, 1994). **AFFIL:** Science Fiction & Fantasy Writers of America; Ad Astra Science Fiction Society (Convention Committee 1987-94; Pro Liaison 1988, 1989; Programming 1990; Chair 1991, 1992; Oper. Div. Head 1993; Chapbook 1994); Bunch of Seven Writers' Group (Founding Mbr. 1985 to date); Women's ReSource Centre, Muskoka (Mbr.-at-Large & Bd. 1994-95); Muskoka Sexual Assault Intervention for Living (Committee Mbr., "Taking Care of Yourself" Conference). **HONS:** Best Sports Reporting Award, with Douglas Faulkner, Ryerson Journalism Program, 1983; Black Belt in Karate (Tao Zen Chuan/Bumblebee Karate), Oct. 1992. **INTERESTS:** all forms of alternative medicine, especially homeopathy; spirituality; Goddess & neo-Pagan traditions; women's issues; martial arts; various arts & crafts; music, especially drumming. **COMMENT:** *"Out of a victim, I made myself a warrior, then out of warrior I made myself a healer. I needed only to realize I have always been one. But all the other stages were necessary too."*

Weidner, Arlene, R.N.,B.Sc.N.,M.Sc., C.H.E. ⊕ ⍤ ◉
Senior Operating Officer, Acute Care Services Sector, CALGARY REGIONAL HEALTH AUTHORITY, 9 Bow Valley Center, 841 Centre Ave. E., Calgary, AB T2E 0A1 (403) 268-9312 or (403) 268-9073, FAX 268-9986. Born Didsbury, Alta. 1947. m. Merril Knudston. 2 ch. Heila Rochelle Tanney, Gavan William Shane Tanney. **EDUC:** Foothills Hospital Sch. of Nursing, R.N. 1968; Univ. of Alberta, B.Sc.N. 1970; Univ. of Calgary, M.Sc.(Educ. Psych). **CAREER:** Staff Nurse, Acute Care Psychiatric

Unit, Foothills Hospital, 1968-69; Nurse Consultant, Univ. of Alberta, 1969-70; Nursing Instructor, Psychiatric Nursing, Foothills Hospital Sch. of Nursing, 1970-73; Asst. Head Nurse, Foothills Hospital, 1974-75; Research Asst., Dr. G. MacDougall, 1975-79; Clinical & Classroom Instructor, Allied Health Dept., Mount Royal Coll., 1975-79; Proposal Writer, Dept. of Advanced Educ. & Manpower, 1979; Nursing Instructor, Allied Health Dept., Mount Royal Coll., 1980-81; Research Asst., Post Basic Mental Health Nursing Program, 1981-82; Research Asst., Dr. J. Livesley, Dept. of Psychiatry, Univ. of Calgary, 1982-83; Dir. of Nursing, Foothills Hospital, 1983-91; VP, Patient Svcs, Calgary General Hospital, 1991-94; Sr. Operating Officer, Patient Care Svcs, Calgary Regional Health Authority, Community Acute Care Sector, 1994-95; Sr. Operating Officer, Acute Care Sector, 1995 to date; Adjunct Prof., Fac. of Nursing, Univ. of Calgary. **SELECTED PUBLICATIONS:** "Historical Comment on DSM III Schizoid and Avoidant Personality Disorders," with others (*American Journal of Psychiatry* 142 1985); "Birthdays: a special kind of anniversary reaction," with others (*Journal of Psychosocial Nursing and Mental Health Services* 25 1987); various articles & abstracts. **AFFIL:** Calgary Stampede Queen's Alumni Committee (Founding Mbr.); Alberta Association of Registered Nurses; Canadian Nurses' Association; Certified Health Exec.; Association of Chief Executive Nurses; Canadian Gerontological Nursing Association (Founding Mbr.); Alberta Mental Health Nurses' Interest Group (Founding Mbr.); United Way (Co-Chair, Health Div.; Health Svcs Section); Masters of Nursing Curriculum Committee;Canadian Council on Health Service Accreditation (Surveyor). **HONS:** Medical Staff Award for Outstanding Academic & Clinical Achievement, Foothills Hospital Sch. of Nursing, 1968. **INTERESTS:** mind-body integration in health; watching & admiring my children as they become young adults; reading; spending time with husband; horses. **MISC:** numerous presentations & workshops. **COMMENT:** *"Grateful for a rural upbringing. I have been involved, since graduating from the first class of the Foothills School of Nursing, in nursing service, education, research and administration."*

Weinstein, Deborah, B.A. ☒
President, STRATEGIC OBJECTIVES INC., 184 Front St. E., Ste. 701, Toronto, ON M5A 4N3 (416) 366-7735, FAX 366-2295, EMAIL mail@strategic-objectives.com. Born Prince Albert, Sask. 1949. d. 1 ch. Sadie Mae. **EDUC:** McGill Univ., B.A. 1970. **CAREER:** freelance

Prod., CBC Radio, 1971-74; Prod., North American Transmission, Radio Canada Int'l, 1974-76; Prod., *Nightcap*, CBC Radio, 1976-79; Feature Reporter, *The City at Six*, CBC TV News Montreal, 1979-80; Entertainment Reporter, *Newshour*, CBC TV News Toronto, 1980-81; Location Prod./Dir., *Thrill of a Lifetime*, CTV TV, 1981-83; Pres., Strategic Objectives Inc., 1983 to date. **AFFIL:** ACTRA; International Association of Business Communicators; International Public Relations Association; Retail Council of Canada; Second Harvest (Bd. of Dir.); Fashion Group International of Toronto (Advisory Bd.); Women in Film and Television (Advisory Bd.); United Way of Greater Toronto (Advisory Bd.). **HONS:** Best Radio Program (*Nightcap*), ACTRA, 1977; Best of Show Gold & Silver, A.M.I., 1983; UN Grand Award, Public Service, 1995; I.P.R.A. Golden World Award, 1992, 1994, 1995, 1996; Gold Quill Award of Excellence, Media Rel'ns, I.A.B.C., 1987, 1996; Award of Excellence, Corp. Image, Canadian Public Relations Society, 1994; numerous other awards from professional organizations.

Weir, Elizabeth, M.L.A. ■ ✦ ◌
Member of the Legislative Assembly (Saint John Harbour), GOVERNMENT OF NEW BRUNSWICK, Box 6000, Fredericton, NB E3B 5H1, EMAIL jweinman@gov.nb.ca. Leader, NEW DEMOCRATIC PARTY OF NEW BRUNSWICK. Born Belfast 1948. m. James Stanley. 1 ch. **EDUC:** Univ. of Waterloo, B.A.(Soc.); Univ. of Western Ontario, LL.B. **BAR:** Ont., 1978. **CAREER:** Instructor, York Univ.; Solicitor's Office, Ont. Labour Rel'ns Bd.; Investigator, Employment Standards Branch, Ont. Ministry of Labour; Instructor in Industrial Rel'ns & Law, Univ. of New Brunswick; Leader, New Democratic Party of N.B., 1988 to date; elected M.L.A. (Saint John S.), Gov't of N.B., 1991; re-elected, 1995 (Saint John Harbour). **EDIT:** Ed. Bd., Canadian Women's Studies. **AFFIL:** New Democratic Party of Canada (Atlantic VP 1983-85; Prov. Sec. 1983-88; Cdn Constitution Committee); New Democratic Party of N.B.; Law Society of Upper Canada; Conservation Council of N.B. **MISC:** 1st woman chosen leader of a pol. party in N.B., 1st woman leader elected to the Legislative Assembly & 1st elected leader of the NDP of N.B.

Weir, Sharon Rose ◉ $
President, Alberta Chapter, AMYOTROPHIC LATERAL SCLEROSIS SOCIETY, 1982 Kensington Road N.W., Calgary, AB T2N 3R5 (403) 270-2020, FAX 270-2272. Real Estate Consultant, BUILDERS REALTY. Born Calgary 1947. s. **EDUC:** Univ. of Calgary. **CAREER:** Staff

Trainer/Personnel Recruiter, Eatons of Canada, 1972-74; Sales & Mktg Rep., IBM Canada Ltd., 1974-78; Sales Rep., Nu West Development Corporation, 1978-80; Proj. Mgr/Sales Rep., Project Condominiums International, 1980; Mktg Consultant, Sefel Properties Ltd., 1980-82; Accts Exec., CHQR Radio, 1982-83; sales & mktg, Nu-West Group Ltd., 1983-86; M.L.S. Real Estate Consultant, Johnston & Daniel Limited, Toronto, 1987; Sales & Mktg Consultant, United Management Ltd. & the CIBC, 1988-89; Sales & Mktg Consultant, Oxford Development Group Inc., 1989-90; M.L.S. Real Estate Consultant, Builders Realty, Calgary, 1990 to date. **AFFIL:** Amyotrophic Lateral Sclerosis Society, Nat'l Bd. (Chair, Lobby & Advocacy Committee 1994; Unit Dir. 1993-94); Amyotrophic Lateral Sclerosis Society, Alberta Chapter (Dir. 1990-92; Pres. 1993-94, 1994-95); Calgary Real Estate Bd.; YWCA. **HONS:** "Board Builder" Award, Calgary Real Estate Bd., 1993. **INTERESTS:** art; theatre; politics.

Wekerle, Gerda R., B.A.,M.A., Ph.D. ■■ ☜ ❀ ▢ ◌
Professor, Faculty of Environmental Studies, YORK UNIVERSITY, 4700 Keele St., North York, ON M3J 1P3 (416) 736-5252, FAX 736-5679, EMAIL es050020@orion.yorku.ca. Born Heidelberg, Germany 1947. m. Slade Lander. 1 ch. Bryn Lander. **EDUC:** York Univ., B.A.(Sociology) 1968; Northwestern Univ., M.A.(Sociology) 1969, Ph.D.(Sociology) 1974. **CAREER:** Lecturer, York Univ., 1972-73; Asst. Prof., 1974-78; Assoc. Prof., 1978-90; Prof., 1990 to date. **SELECTED PUBLICATIONS:** co-editor with R. Keil & D.V.J. Bell, *Local Places in the Age of the Global City* (Montreal: Black Rose, 1996); co-author with Carolyn Whitzman, *Safe Cities* (NY: Van Nostrand Reinhold, 1995); co-editor with B. Peterson & D. Morley, *New Space for Women* (Westview Press, 1980); articles on women & cities, housing, planning & social policy. **EDIT:** Advisory Bd., *Gender, Place and Culture*. **AFFIL:** American Sociological Association; American Geographical Association; Canadian Sociological & Anthropological Association; Centre of Excellence on Immigration & Settlement, Toronto (Mgmt Bd.); Toronto Transit Commission (Security Advisory Group). **HONS:** Constance Hamilton Award, City of Toronto, 1996. **INTERESTS:** cities; gardens; kayaking. **MISC:** founder, *Women and Environments* magazine, 1976; founder, Grow T.O., a community gardening advocacy group, 1990; founder, Women's Reading Group Salon, 1992. **COMMENT:** *"Long-term interest in how women change cities through advocacy and grassroots organizing. I've been involved with women's orga-*

nizations on issues of women's safety, housing, transportation and access to local politics."

Welland, Freydis J., B.A.,B.J. Ⓢ ◉
Government Relations Director, BC TEL, 20-3777 Kingsway, Burnaby, BC V5H 3Z7 (604) 432-3974, FAX 439-7354. Born Victoria, B.C. m. Michael. EDUC: Dalhousie Univ., B.A.(Phil.) 1967; Carleton Univ., B.J.(Journalism) 1968. CAREER: editorial writer, Western Producer Newspaper, 1968-69; various positions at BC Tel in Public Affairs, Corp. Dev. & Gov 't Rel'ns, 1969 to date. AFFIL: North American Society for Corporate Planning (Pres., Vancouver Chapter 1986-87); Quality Council of B.C. (Chair, Founding Committee 1992); Business Council of B.C. (Chair, Gov't Rel'ns Committee 1990-93); Canada Place Corporation (Dir. & Chair, Audit Committee 1993-94); B.C. Utilities Advisory Council; Business Caucus on Aboriginal Issues; B.C. Treaty Negotiation Joint Sectoral Advisory Committee (1994 to date); Vancouver Board of Trade; Main Dance Centre (Dir. 1991-92); Jane Austen Society of North America (Dir. 1987-92); Royal Vancouver Yacht Club; Vintage Car Club of B.C. COMMENT: *"Enjoys the challenge of creating change by working with people in new and existing organizations."*

Welsh-Ovcharov, Bogomila, B.A.,M.Phil., Ph.D. ▨ ▧
Professor, Department of Fine Art, UNIVERSITY OF TORONTO, Mississauga, ON L5L 1C6 (905) 828-3725. Born Sofia, Bulgaria. m. Robert P. Welsh. 1 ch. EDUC: Univ. of Toronto, B.A. (Art/Archaeology) 1964, M.Phil.(Art Hist.) 1971; Univ. of Utrecht, Ph.D.(Art Hist.) 1976. SELECTED PUBLICATIONS: "The Early Work of Charles Angrand and his Contact with Van Gogh" (1971); "Van Gogh in Perspective" (1973); "Van Gogh: His Paris Period: 1886-88" (1976); "Vincent Van Gogh and the Birth of Cloisonism" (1981); "Emile Bernard: Bordellos and Prostitutes in Turn-of-the-Century French Art" (1988); "Van Gogh à Paris" (1988); "Charles Pachter" (1992). HONS: Chevalier, L'Ordre Palmes Académiques, 1994.

Wente, Margaret, B.A.,M.A. ✎ ▯
Editor, "Report on Business," THE GLOBE AND MAIL, 444 Front St. West, Toronto M5V 2S9 (416) 585-5129, FAX 585-5642. Born Evanston, Ill. 1950. EDUC: Univ. of Michigan, B.A.(English) 1971; Univ. of Toronto, M.A.(English) 1972. CAREER: Ed., *Canadian Business* Magazine, 1980-84; Sr. Ed., *Venture*, CBC-TV, 1984-86; Ed., *Report on Business* Magazine, 1986-91; Ed. & Weekly Columnist, "Report on Business," *The Globe and Mail*,

1991 to date. AFFIL: Scarborough Grace Hospital (Bd.); Salvation Army of Metro Toronto (Advisory Bd.). HONS: Award for Bus. Journalism, National Magazine Awards. COMMENT: *"Margaret Wente is among the top newspaper editors in the country. Her weekly newspaper column has gained wide recognition for its fair-minded coverage of the gender wars."*

Westbury, June Alwyn ♥ ◉ ♦
Volunteer. Winnipeg, MB. Born Hamilton, New Zealand 1921. w. Peter W.A. Westbury. 3 ch. Sheila Raffey, Pamela June Westbury, Jennifer Doris Westbury. EDUC: Brain's Commercial Coll., Auckland; studied voice under contralto Mina Caldow. CAREER: various volunteer organizations in Winnipeg, incl. Home & School Association & Royal Winnipeg Ballet Women's Committee, 1948-68; Sec., Liberal Party of Manitoba, 1968-70; Alderman & Councillor, Winnipeg City Council, 1970-79; Bd. Mbr., Winnipeg Municipal Hospitals, 1970-79; Chair, 1971-75; VP, Liberal Party of Canada, 1970-73; Bd. Mbr., Manitoba Health Organizations Inc., 1970-76; Reg'l Bd. Mbr., Canadian Council of Christians & Jews, 1972-78; Bd. Mbr., Age & Opportunity Centres, 1973-76; Commissioner & Design Committee Mbr., National Capital Commission, 1976-82; Mbr., Task Force on Maternal & Child Health, 1979-82; Chair, Advisory Committee on Historical Buildings, 1979; Mbr., Nat'l Exec., Canadian Council of Christians & Jews, 1979-84; M.L.A., (Fort Rouge) Prov. of Man., 1979-81; Bd. Mbr., Heritage Winnipeg, 1979; Dir., VIA Rail Corporation, 1982-85; Gov., Heritage Canada Foundation, 1982-86; Founder & Chair, Laurier Club of Manitoba, 1982 to date; Bd. Mbr., Heritage Winnipeg, 1983; VP, Rainbow Society Inc., 1983-87; Co-Chair (Central Reg.), Canadian Council of Christians & Jews, 1984-87; Bd. Mbr., Winnipeg Municipal Hospitals, 1984-87. AFFIL: Liberal Party of Canada; Liberal Party of Manitoba (Life Mbr.); Laurier Club of Manitoba (Chair); University Women's Club of Winnipeg; Twenty Club of Winnipeg; United Nations Association; Down Under Club. HONS: Woman of the Year in Politics & Governmental Affairs, 1979; Canada 125 Medal, 1992. INTERESTS: politics; family history; bridge. MISC: 1st woman elected Sec., Liberal Party of Man.; 1st Manitoban elected VP, Liberal Party of Canada. COMMENT: *"I am actively involved in every election campaign (as a volunteer now), and spend summers at Victoria Beach, Man."*

Westcott, Joan, B.A.,M.Ed. ◉ ▨
Executive Director, FEDERATION OF WOMEN

TEACHERS' ASSOCIATIONS OF ONTARIO, 1260 Bay St., Toronto, ON M5R 2B8 (416) 964-1232, FAX 964-0512. Born London, Ont. 1945. s. **EDUC:** Univ. of Western Ontario, B.A.(Psych.) 1970; Ministry of Educ. of Ont., Supervisory Officer's Certificate 1985; Univ. of Toronto, M.Ed.(Educational Admin.) 1991. **CAREER:** teacher, 1964-85; V-Principal, 1975-78; Principal, 1979-84; Exec. Dir., Federation of Women Teachers' Associations of Ontario, 1985 to date. **AFFIL:** Ontario Teachers' Federation (Gov.; Dir.; Fellow; Pres. 1984-85); Federation of Women Teachers' Associations of Ontario (Dir. 1974; Pres. 1978-79); Canadian Teachers' Federation (Dir. 1981-85). **COMMENT:** *"Has participated in eight assemblies of the teachers' international organization. Promotes involvement of women in leadership positions."*

Westergaard, Lissi ♡ ✊

Grants Advisor, GIRL GUIDES OF CANADA, 11055 - 107 St., Edmonton, AB T5W 2A5 (403) 474-1241 or 424-5510, FAX 426-1715. Born Randers, Denmark 1932. m. Ernest W. 2 ch. **CAREER:** correspondent & translator, 1950-59; personnel supervisor & confidential sec., 1967; self-employed, 1967 to date. **VOLUNTEER CAREER:** Prov. Commissioner & CEO, Girl Guides of Canada (Alta.), 1989-94; Grants Advisor, Girl Guides of Canada, 1994 to date. **AFFIL:** Girl Guides of Canada (Nat'l Council); Alberta Heart & Stroke Foundation. **HONS:** Beaver Award, Girl Guides of Canada; Rose Award, Girl Guides of Alberta; Canada 125 Medal. **INTERESTS:** reading; music; swimming; cross-country skiing; camping; travel. **COMMENT:** *"I met and married my husband in Uranium City, a daughter and a son were born there. I was always a member of Girl Guides and from 1989 to 1994 served as the Alberta Provincial Commissioner."*

Western, Sherrin ■ $

Business Manager, Home Office, BC TEL, 4535 Canada Way, Ste. 2, Burnaby, BC V5G 1J9 (604) 878-0642, FAX 878-0642, EMAIL 75207.74@compuserve.com. Partner, SHERVIN PUBLICATIONS, 69 Jamieson Court, Ste. 702, New Westminster, BC V3L 5R3 (604) 540-1575, FAX 540-1505. Born Whitehorse, Y.T. 1962. m. Kevin Western. **CAREER:** Operator, BC Tel, 1981-85; Asst. Mgr, Operator Svc, 1985-90; Quality & Environment Coord., 1990-92; Retail Store Mgr, 1992-94; Bus. Mgr, Home Office, 1994 to date; Co-owner & VP, Mktg & Admin. (home graphic design studio), Shervin Publications, 1992 to date. **AFFIL:** Women Business Owners of Vancouver; Vancouver Home-Based Business Association; Burnaby Home Office Network; New Westminster Women's Network; Burnaby Chamber of Commerce. **INTERESTS:** music; computers; reading; dancing; golf; volunteering; swimming; passionate about basketball & the Vancouver Grizzlies. **COMMENT:** *"Sherrin is very involved in the community and feels great when she can make a difference for the various groups she works with. She is passionately committed to furthering the awareness of home-based business and its positive impact on the economy."*

Westhues, Anne, B.A.,M.Sc.,M.S.W., D.S.W. 🎓 ⊕

Associate Professor, WILFRID LAURIER UNIVERSITY, 75 University Ave., Waterloo, ON N2L 3C5 (519) 884-1970, FAX 888-9732, EMAIL awesthue@mach1.wlu.ca. Born Stratford, Ont. 1951. m. Kenneth Westhues. 1 ch. Jonathan. **EDUC:** Univ. of Guelph, B.A.(Soc.) 1972, M.Sc.(Adult Educ.) 1974; Wilfrid Laurier Univ., M.S.W.(Social Work) 1976; Columbia Univ., D.S.W.(Social Welfare) 1983. **CAREER:** Educ. Dir., Canadian Mental Health Association, London, 1973-74; Special Projects Worker, Social Svcs Dept., Reg. of Peel, 1976-78; Sch. of Social Work, New York Univ., 1980; Fac. of Social Work, Univ. of Toronto, 1981-82; Sch. of Social Work, Memorial Univ., 1982; Asst. Prof., Fac. of Social Work, Univ. of Toronto, 1983-84; Wilfrid Laurier Univ., 1985-90; Assoc. Prof., Fac. of Social Work, 1990 to date; Acting Dean, periodically, 1992-94; Coord. of Doctoral Program, Fac. of Social Work, 1992-95. **SELECTED PUBLICATIONS:** *Well-Functioning Families for Adoptive and Foster Children*, with J.S. Cohen (Univ. of Toronto Press, 1990); various chapters in books, articles in refereed & non-refereed journals, tech. reports & papers. **AFFIL:** Canadian Association of Schools of Social Work (Pres.); Institute for Qualitative Research & Evaluation (Sr. Advisory Bd.); Notre Dame of St. Agatha Children's Centre (Bd.); Anselma House, Kitchener (Pres. of Bd. 1992-93); Peel Volunteer Centre (Bd. 1977-78); Canada Mental Health Association (Bd. 1974-75). **HONS:** Valedictorian, Clarke Road High Sch., London, Ont., 1969; Outstanding Teacher Award, Wilfrid Laurier Univ., 1994. **INTERESTS:** travel; gardening; cooking. **MISC:** various presentations. **COMMENT:** *"Anne Westhues is a social worker and educator who is committed to providing the next generation of social work professionals and educators the skills and confidence they will need to succeed."*

Weston, Glenys ♡ ⊕

Past President, Southern Alberta Branch and

National Secretary, THE KIDNEY FOUNDATION OF CANADA, 212 Scenic Acres Terrace NW, Calgary, AB T3L 1Y4 (403) 241-1621, FAX 241-8461. Born UK 1939. m. Dr. William Alan Weston. 2 ch. Christine, Anne. EDUC: Diploma in Bus. Admin. CAREER: hospital admin., Stanley Road Hospital, Wakefield, Yorkshire, UK, 1957-77; Librarian, Regional Psychiatric Centre, Saskatoon, 1978-80; admin. consultant to a medical practice. VOLUNTEER CAREER: volunteer, Royal University Hospital, Saskatoon, 1978-80; Patient Svcs Committee, S. Alta. Branch, The Kidney Foundation of Canada, 1989-92; Peer Support Mgmt Committee, 1989-94; Pres., Calgary Chapter Bd., 1991-94; Nat'l Bd. of Dir., 1991-95; Alta. Branch Bd., 1991-92; Pres., Alta. Branch Bd., 1992-94; Chair, Patient Svcs Committee, 1992 to date; Chair, Nominating Committee, 1992 to date; Prov. Medical Advisory Committee, 1993 to date; Chair, Organizing Committee, National AGM, Calgary, June 1993; Pres., S. Alta. Branch Bd., 1994-95; Strategic Planning Team, 1994 to date; Co-Chair, Alberta & Territories Council of the Kidney Foundation, 1994-95; Organizing Committee, Prov. Advocacy Workshop, Jan. 20/21, 1995; Nat'l Volunteer Dev. Program, 1995-97; Nat'l Sec., 1996. INTERESTS: travel; theatre; music; dance; reading; Swardvski Crystal. COMMENT: *"I am very interested in current affairs. So far as my involvement with The Kidney Foundation is concerned, my endeavours here are to ensure the improvement of health and quality of life of people living with kidney disease."*

Weston, Hilary M. $ ⊙ 🗊

Deputy Chairman, HOLT, RENFREW AND CO., LIMITED, 22 St. Clair Ave. E., Ste. 2201, Toronto, ON M4T 2S3 (416) 922-2500, FAX 922-4394. Born Dublin, Ireland. m. W. Galen Weston, O.C. 2 ch. Alannah Weston, Galen Weston Jr. EDUC: Loretto Abbey, Dalkey (Republic of Ireland). CAREER: Deputy Chrm, Holt, Renfrew and Co., Limited. SELECTED PUBLICATIONS: *In A Canadian Garden*, with Nicole Eaton (Penguin Publications, 1989); *At Home In Canada*, with Nicole Eaton (Penguin Publications, 1995). DIRECTOR: Brown Thomas Group Limited; The Windsor Community. AFFIL: The Ireland Fund of Canada (Founding Chair); The Mabin Sch. (Founding Chair); Canadian Environmental Education Foundation (Co-Founder & Chair); Canadian Opera Company (Dir.). HONS: Outstanding Woman of the Year, Variety Club of Ontario, 1994; Best Dressed Hall of Fame, 1987 to date. MISC: mbr. of Advisory Bd., Sotheby's Canada.

Wheeler, Anne, B.Sc. ■■ ⚰⊗ ♥

Filmmaker, ANNE WHEELER INC., (film production), 25 E. Second Ave., 3rd Fl., Vancouver, BC V5T 1B3 (604) 875-1010, FAX 875-9790, EMAIL awinc@uniserve.com. Born Edmonton 1946. s. 2 ch. Quincy Wheeler Hendren, Morgan Wheeler Hendren. EDUC: Univ. of Alberta, B.Sc.(Math.) 1967, Prof. Teaching Certificate (Music) 1969, course requirements for M.Ed. 1970-72. CAREER: director/writer/producer, 25 yrs. SELECTED CREDITS: 8 feature films for TV & theatrical release incl.: prod./writer, *Diana Kilmury-Teamster* (Movie of the Week), CBC, 1995; dir., *The War Between Us* (M.O.W.), CBC, 1994; dir., *Other Women's Children* (M.O.W.), ABC, 1993; dir./co-writer, *Angel Square* (feature), 1990; writer/dir./prod., *Bye Bye Blues* (feature), 1989; dir. (& writer/co-writer of 2), 8 short drama & episodic TV shows; writer, dir., prod., researcher or cinematographer, 13 documentary films; writer/performer, *Childsong* & *Magic Tunes*, weekly radio music series, 1970s; roles in musicals, radio plays & stage plays, 1970s. SELECTED PUBLICATIONS: co-researcher/writer, *A Harvest Yet to Reap* (resource book on women's history, Women's Press, Toronto, 1975). DIRECTOR: All Lady's Film Inc.; Wheeler-Hendren Ent. Alta. AFFIL: Alberta Motion Picture Development Corporation (Advisory Committee 1984-87); National Screen Institute (Bd. of Dir. 1986-89; Hon. Chair 1990-93); Women in Film (Hon. mbr., L.A., Toronto, Vancouver); Directors' Guild of Canada; Writers' Guild of Canada; ACTRA; Canadian Academy of Cinema & Television. HONS: Leo Award for best direction, B.C.M.P.A., 1996; Officer of the Order of Canada, 1995; Woman of the Year, YMCA, Vancouver, 1995; Woman of the Year, Women in Film, Vancouver, 1995; Cultural Hall of Fame, Dramatics, Edmonton, 1993; Achievement Award, Canadian Film & TV Association, 1989; Woman of the Year Award, Edmonton Business & Professional Women's Club, 1989; Hon. Roll, *Maclean's* magazine, 1989; Alberta Achievement Award in filmmaking, 1988; Hon. Doctorate of Letters, Univ. of Alberta, 1990; Hon. Doctorate, Univ. of Athabasca, 1990; LL.D.(Hon.); Univ. of Calgary, 1993; LL.D.(Hon.), Brock Univ., 1993; LL.D.(Hon.), Univ. of Lethbridge, 1993; Hon. Doctorate of Letters, Univ. of Winnipeg, 1994

Wheeler, (Evelyn, E.) Beth, B.Sc., M.Sc. 🌿 ❀ ✿

Dairy Cattle Nutrition Specialist, ONTARIO MINISTRY OF AGRICULTURE FOOD AND RURAL AFFAIRS, RR 3, Brighton, ON K0K 1H0 (613) 475-1630. Born 1954. m. Rodney A. Hudgin.

2 ch. Jodie, David. **EDUC:** Univ. of Guelph, B.Sc.(Agr.) 1976, M.Sc. 1978. **CAREER:** Lecturer, Animal Sci. Section, Kemptville Coll., 1980-90; Dairy Cattle Nutrition Specialist, Ont. Ministry of Agric., Food & Rural Affairs, 1990 to date. **AFFIL:** American Dairy Science Association; National Mastitis Council; Ontario Large Herd Operators (Sec.); Expert Committee on Animal Nutrition (Sec.); Ontario Dairy Research & Services Committee (Chair); American Registry of Animal Scientists (pending).

Wheeler Vaughan, Lucile ⚾ ☝

Athlete. 85 chemin Glen, Knowlton, QC J0E 1V0 (514) 243-5398. m. Kaye Vaughan. 2 ch. **EDUC:** The White Mountain Sch., N.H.; Ste. Agathe High Sch., 1953; univ. extension. **SPORTS CAREER:** int'l ski racer; Bronze Medal, Downhill, Cortina d'Empezzo, Winter Olympics, 1956; Gold Medal, Downhill, World Ski Championship, Badgastein, Austria, 1958; Gold Medal, Giant Slalom, World Ski Championship, Badgastein, Austria, 1958. **AFFIL:** The National Fitness Council (past mbr. c.1960s); Ski Club of Great Britain (Hon. Mbr.). **HONS:** Lou Marsh Trophy, 1958; Outstanding Female Athelete, 1958; mbr., Honour Roll of Skiing Canada, Canadian Sports Hall of Fame, US Ski Hall of Fame, Quebec Sport Hall of Fame, Laurentian Ski Hall of Fame & the White Mountain Sch. Ski Hall of Fame, New Hampshire. **INTERESTS:** coaching children in skiing; golf; golf tournaments. **MISC:** 1st Cdn to win an Olympic medal in skiing; 1st N.Am. to win an Olympic medal in downhill event; 1st Cdn & 1st N.Am. to win a world ski championship; 1st skier to win the Lou Marsh Trophy; takes part in numerous ski reunions. **COMMENT:** *"Married to Kaye Vaughan, a member of the Ottawa Rough Riders football team and 2-time winner of the Schenley awards. Daughter Myrle married and living in Whistler, BC. Son Jake played for Toronto Argos for two years, married and living in Montreal. Three granddaughters and one grandson."*

Whelan, Susan, J.D.,LL.B.,M.P. 🍁

Member of Parliament (Essex-Windsor), GOVERNMENT OF CANADA, House of Commons, Confederation Building, Rm. 231, Ottawa, ON K1A 0A6 (613) 992-1812, FAX 995-0033. Born Windsor, Ont. 1963. s. **EDUC:** Univ. of Windsor, LL.B. 1988; Univ. of Detroit, Juris Doctor 1988. **BAR:** Ont., 1989. **CAREER:** M.P. (Essex-Windsor), 1993 to date; Parliamentary Sec. to the Min. of Nat'l Revenue, Gov't of Canada, 1994-96; mbr., Public Accts Committee, House of Commons, 1994-96; Assoc. Mbr., Fin. Committee, 1993 to date; V-Chair, 1996 to date. **AFFIL:** Law Society of Upper Canada; Essex Region Conservation Authority (Past Dir.); Alzheimer Society (Past Dir., Essex-Windsor Chapter); Liberal Party of Canada.

Whidden, Diana, B.A. $

Senior Vice-President, Corporate Development, ZURICH CANADA, 400 University Ave., Toronto, ON M5G 1S7 (416) 586-3056, FAX 586-2990. **EDUC:** York Univ., B.A. 1978; CHRP. **CAREER:** Superintendent, Training & Admin., Zurich Canada, 1985-88; Dir., Hum. Res., 1988-90; VP, Hum. Res., 1990-92; Sr. VP, Corp. Dev., 1993 to date. **AFFIL:** Human Resources Professionals' Association of Ontario; Insurance Institute of Canada. **HONS:** Entrance Scholarship, York Univ.; R.L. Crain Memorial Scholarship, York Univ.

Whitaker, Marni, B.A.,LL.B. ⚖

Partner, LANG MICHENER, 181 Bay St., Ste. 2500, Toronto, ON M5J 2T7 (416) 360-8600, FAX 365-1719. Born Winnipeg 1950. m. 4 ch. Katie, Jean, Adam, Emma. **EDUC:** Univ. of Manitoba, B.A.(French) 1970; Osgoode Hall Law Sch., LL.B. 1973. **BAR:** Ont., 1975. **CAREER:** Ed., *C.C.H.*, 1975; Legal Cnsl, Storefront Legal Clinic, 1976-77; Assoc. then Ptnr, Blackwell Law Spratt Armstrong and Grass, 1976-84; Assoc. then Ptnr, Lang Michener, 1984 to date. **AFFIL:** Canadian Bar Association; Law Society of Upper Canada; International Bar Association; Estate Planning Council of Metro Toronto; St. Andrew-St. Patrick Liberal Riding Association (Past Sec.); Brown Home & School Association (Past Treas.). **MISC:** numerous papers presented at continuing legal educ. conferences. **COMMENT:** *"I practise law in the area of personal estate planning and administration. Even after 20 years of practice, I look forward to meeting new clients and dealing with new legal situations."*

White, Helena E. ✒ 📖 ☝

Publisher, *CRESTON VALLEY ADVANCE*, 115 N. 10th Ave., P.O. Box 1279, Creston, BC V0B 1G0 (604) 428-2266, FAX 428-3320. Born Trail, B.C. 1936. m. Donald A. 3 ch. Kyle M., Karen E., Kathleen R. **CAREER:** columnist & reporter, *Creston Review*, 1972-76; Community Program Dir., Creston Cabled Video, 1976-79; Ed., *Creston Valley Advance*, 1979-83; Publisher, 1984 to date. **SELECTED PUBLICATIONS:** *50 Bloomin' Years* (1974); *60 Bloomin' Years* (1984); "Back Roads and Byways" contributor (Readers Digest 1992). **AFFIL:** Creston & District Chamber of Commerce (Dir.; Past Pres.); Creston Community Pride Committee; Creston Valley Human Rights Coalition (Founding mbr.). **HONS:** B.C.

Journalism Award (2nd Place), MacMillan Bloedel, 1983; Best Historical Writing, B.C. & Yukon Community Newspapers Association, 1985; Jack Sanderson Award for Best Local Editorial (2nd Place), Canadian Community Newspaper Association, 1988; Publisher of the Year, Sterling Newspapers, 1994. **INTERESTS:** reading; camping; Tiffany & leaded glass work. **MISC:** 1st woman Pres., Creston & District Chamber of Commerce, 1978. **COMMENT:** *"Traditional 'wife and mom' until picking up journalism career at age 36, believe in and encourage personal involvement for a strong, healthy community."*

White, Ingrid A., B.Ed.,M.Div. ☼ 🎓
Minister of Care and Education, EMMANUEL BAPTIST CHURCH, 2121 Cedar Hill Cross Rd., Victoria, BC V8P 2R6 (604) 592-2418, FAX 592-4646. Born Saskatoon, Sask. 1953. s. 2 adopted ch. Alison Valentina White; Lidia Marie White. **EDUC:** Univ. of Victoria, B.Ed.(Special Educ./Remedial) 1976; Regent Coll., Univ. of British Columbia, M.Div.(Pastoral Studies) 1983. **CAREER:** teacher, 1976-80; pastoral roles, Emmanuel Baptist Church, 1983 to date. **SELECTED PUBLICATIONS:** several articles in *Canadian Baptist Magazine* & *Soundings*. **AFFIL:** Professional Association of Christian Educators; Sylvan Acres Baptist Camp Bd. (various positions 1983-89); Island Pastoral Services Association; Baptist Union of Western Canada (B.C. Area Bd.). **INTERESTS:** reading; crafts; keeping up on learning disabilities literature & seminars; volunteer organizations. **COMMENT:** *"I am a happy, involved person who likes to give service to others through personal care as well as through various organizations. Being a woman in church leadership has been a challenge within the evangelical setting, stressful but fulfilling."*

White, Julie, M.B.A. ■■ ♡ ✋
Chief Executive Officer, THE TRILLIUM FOUNDATION, (philanthropy), 21 Bedford Rd., Toronto, ON M5R 2J9 (416) 961-0194, FAX 961-9599, EMAIL jwhite@web.net. Born Providence, R.I. 1946. m. James L. Floyd. 1 ch. Megan. **EDUC:** York Univ., M.B.A. 1984. **CAREER:** Ministry of Community & Social Svcs, Gov't of Ont., 1975-81; Nat'l Mgr, Public Affairs, Levi Strauss & Co., 1981-93; CEO, The Trillium Foundation, 1993 to date. **AFFIL:** Canadian Women's Foundation (co-founder; former Pres.); The Scott's Foundation (Bd. mbr.); York Univ. (Advisory Bd., Non-Profit Leadership). **HONS:** Woman of Distinction, YWCA, 1990; Outstanding Community Contribution, York Univ., 1993; Gold Medal, Canadian Centre for Human Rights & Race Relations; as CEO of Trillium, received Canada Award for Excellence. **INTERESTS:** gardening (garden published in *Canadian Gardening* Magazine, 1994 & *100 Great Ideas for Gardening*, 1996). **COMMENT:** *"I have spent nearly twenty years promoting and encouraging an inclusive society—reducing gender bias and racism through systemic change."*

White, Lynda ■ $
Manager, Employment Equity and Diversity, Corporate Human Resources, ROYAL BANK OF CANADA, Royal Bank Plaza, N. Tower, 200 Bay St., 11th Fl., Toronto, ON M5J 2J5 (416) 955-5822, FAX 955-5840. Born Pembroke, Ont. **CAREER:** Administrative Officer, Processing Centre Projects, Real Estate Resources, 1977-78; Proj. Administrator, Real Estate Resources, 1979-85; Equal Opportunities Coord., 1985-90; Mgr, Employment Equity & Diversity Mgmt, Corp. Hum. Res., 1990 to date. **SELECTED PUBLICATIONS:** a number of articles in employment equity & diversity publications, & in hum. res. publications & textbooks. **AFFIL:** Canadian Council on Rehabilitation & Work (Bd.; Past Pres.); Canadian Association of Women Executives & Entrepreneurs; Women's Advisory Committee on Affirmative Action to the Treasury Bd. (Past Chair); Canadian Bankers' Association (Chair, Committee on Employment Equity); Montreal Camera Club (Past Pres.); YWCA of Metropolitan Toronto (Bd.); Canadian Centre on Disability Studies (Bd.). **HONS:** Gov. General's Commemorative Medal in recognition of contribution to community. **INTERESTS:** travel; hiking; music; reading. **MISC:** frequent presenter & facilitator at conferences.

White, Marjorie (Cantryn) ✋
Executive Director, ALLIED INDIAN AND MÉTIS SOCIETY, 2716 Clark Dr., Vancouver, BC V5N 3H6 (604) 874-9610, FAX 874-3585. Born Port Alberni, B.C. 1936. sep. 2 ch. **CAREER:** Nurse, West Coast General Hospital, 1957-59; Nurse, Vancouver General Hospital/Pearson Hospital, 1959-63; guardian to First Nations students on boarding home program, 1963-67; Family Counsellor & Courtworker, 1968-70; Exec. Dir., Vancouver Indian Centre, 1971-76; Consultant, Fed. Dept. of the Sec. of State, 1976; Citizenship Court Judge, Gov't of Canada, 1977-80; Investigator, Office of the Ombudsman, Prov. of B.C., 1980-82; Customer Svc Agent, Transprovincial Airlines, 1982-85; Program Coord., Urban Images for Native Women, 1985-89; Exec. Dir., Allied Indian & Métis Society, 1990 to date. **AFFIL:** Urban Rep. Body of Aboriginal Nations (Pres.); Professional Native Women's Association (Past

Pres.); Vancouver Aboriginal Child & Family Services (Past Bd.); Vancouver Indian Centre (Founder); Native Courtworkers of B.C. (Founder); National Association of Friendship Centres (Founder; elected to Senate 1976). HONS: Marjorie Cantryn Citizenship Award, Kumtuka Alternate Sch., 1979; Woman of Distinction Award, YWCA, 1991; Vancouver Volunteer, 50th Anniversary Volunteer Awards, 1993; Gold Feather Award, Professional Native Women's Association, 1994. INTERESTS: domestic hobbies; knitting; preserving; swimming; volunteering. COMMENT: *"Small town, First Nations woman, left tiny village on west coast of Vancouver Island in 1956. Received licence in Practical Nursing; 1957, became involved in the development of the First Nations movement."*

White, Mary Anne, B.Sc.,Ph.D. ■ ◁ ✿ ﾑ
Killam Research Professor in Materials Science and Professor of Chemistry and Professor of Physics, Department of Chemistry, DALHOUSIE UNIVERSITY, Halifax, NS B3H 4J3 (902) 494-3894, FAX 494-1310, EMAIL mawhite@ chem1.chem.dal.ca. Born London, Ont. 1953. m. Robert L. White, Ph.D. 2 ch. David I., Alice P.. EDUC: Univ. of Western Ontario, B.Sc. (Chem.) 1975; McMaster Univ., Ph.D.(Chem.) 1980. CAREER: National Science & Engineering Research Council Postdoctoral Fellow, Oxford Univ., 1979-81; Research Asst. Prof., Univ. of Waterloo, 1981-83; Asst. Prof., Dalhousie Univ., 1983-87; Assoc. Prof., 1987-92; Prof., 1992 to date. SELECTED PUBLICATIONS: more than 70 articles in scientific journals concerned with thermal properties of solids; more than 40 publications concerning science for the gen. public; nat'l TV spot, "How do things work?" on @discovery.ca, Discovery Channel, 1995; frequent contributor on *Quirks & Quarks*, CBC Radio. AFFIL: Nova Scotian Institute of Science (Pres. 1994-95); Discovery Centre (Dir. 1987-93); Calorimetry Conference (Dir. 1984-86); National Science & Engineering Research Council (various committees 1988-99); Canadian Society for Chemistry (Dir. 1992-95); National Chemistry Week (Nat'l Coord. 1994, 1995); Gordon Research Conference on Order/Disorder in Solids (Chair 1994); Canadian Institute of Chemistry (Fellow). HONS: Gold Medal in Chemistry, Univ. of Western Ontario Alumni, 1975; Award for Excellence in Teaching, Dalhousie Univ. Alumni, 1993; Sunner Memorial Award, 1994; Noranda Award, Canadian Society for Chemistry, 1996. INTERESTS: science; scientific research; bringing science to the gen. public; teaching; music. COMMENT: *"My career goals are three-fold: to advance scientific knowledge;*

to disseminate scientific knowledge; to encourage interest in science within the broader community."

Whitehead, Ruth Holmes, B.A. 🐾
Assistant Curator in History and Staff Ethnologist, THE NOVA SCOTIA MUSEUM, Halifax, NS. Born Charleston, S.C. 1947. EDUC: Agnes Scott Coll., Decatur, Georgia, (Spanish/Theology 1965-68); The Coll. of Charleston, B.A.(English/Phil.) 1971. CAREER: Apprentice, The Charleston Museum, 1961-65, 1967; Registrar, 1970-71; Curatorial Asst. in Hist., Staff Ethnologist, The Nova Scotia Museum, 1972-86; Asst. Curator in Hist. & Staff Ethnologist, 1987 to date. SELECTED CREDITS: Prod./ Writer, *Wikuom: Wigwam Construction and History*, N.S. Dept. of Educ., 1980; Prod./ Writer, *Kuntow: The Stone*, Archival Tape, 1983; Ethnology Consultant/Micmac Costumes/Makeup, *The Habitation: Introduction* Video, Canadian Parks Service, Annapolis Royal, 1991; Prod./Writer, *Micmac Power Sites*, Archival Tape (access limited to the Micmac Nation only), 1992-94; videos, filmstrips, audio tapes & CD-ROM. SELECTED PUBLICATIONS: *Leonard Paul: Portrait of a People/Traditional Micmac Crafts*, Exhibit Catalogue (Halifax: Mt. St. Vincent Art Gallery, 1978); *The Micmac: How Their Ancestors Lived, 500 Years Ago*, co-author H.F. McGee, Jr. (Halifax: Nimbus, 1983); *International Inventory of Micmac, Maliseet and Beothuk Material Culture*, 5 vols. (Halifax: N.S. Museum, 1988); *The Old Man Told Us: Excerpts from Micmac History, 1500-1950* (Halifax: Nimbus, 1991); numerous books, catalogues, articles & reports. EXHIBITIONS: various exhibits incl.: *Micmac Art*, Truro, Millbrook Reserve, 1975; *Micmac Costume Reproduction*, Mt. St. Vincent Art Gallery, Halifax, 1982; *The Spirit Sings*, Canadian Museum of Civilization, Ottawa, 1989; *Marks of the Micmac Nation*, Permanent Exhibit, McCord Museum, Montreal, 1992. AFFIL: Bata Shoe Museum Foundation (Advisory Council 1981-85). HONS: Award of Merit, American Association of State & Local History, 1981; Reg'l Hist. Certificate of Merit, Canadian Historical Society, 1982; Award of Merit, Canadian Museums Association, 1982, 1989; "In Recognition of Over 23 Years Service the Mikmaq People of Nova Scotia" Union of Nova Scotia Indians, Treaty Day, 1994. MISC: Oral Hist. Proj., Vajradhatu Archives, 1989-95.

Whiten, Colette, A.O.C.A. ⊗
Artist. 1604 Dupont St., Toronto, ON M6P 3S7 (416) 767-3456, FAX 767-9606. Born UK 1945. m. Paul Kipps. 3 ch. Shauna Di Fran-

cisco, Megan Whiten, Jason Kipps. **EDUC:** Ontario Coll. of Art, A.O.C.A. 1972. **CAREER:** artist & sculptor, 1972 to date; teacher, York Univ., 1975-77; teacher, sculpture installation, O.C.A., 1974-93; teacher, foundation studies, 1988-94. **COMMISSIONS:** Gov't of Canada Bldg, North York (1976); Mental Health Centre, Toronto (1978); Centennial Proj., Sudbury (1983); Manufacturers Life Insurance Company, Toronto (1984-85); TransCanada PipeLine Arch (*Olympic Arch*) collaboration with Paul Kipps, A.J. Diamond & Partner, Calgary (1987-88); *Weathervanes*, collaboration with Paul Kipps, Bankers Hall, Calgary (1990-91); Cadillac Fairview, Simcoe Place, Workers' Compensation, collaboration with Paul Kipps, (1994-95 work in progress). **EXHIBITIONS:** numerous solo exhibitions incl.: Carmen Lamanna Gallery, Toronto (1989); The Power Plant, Toronto (1992); Centre d'art d'Herblay, France (1993); Galeria Carles Poy, Barcelona (1993); Oakville Galleries/Gairloch, Oakville, Ont. (1995); Susan Hobbs Gallery, Toronto (1994, 1996); numerous group exhibitions, incl.: *8 Biennale de Paris*, Musée d'art Moderne de la Ville de Paris (1973); *Some Canadian Women Artists*, National Gallery of Canada (1975); Carmen Lamanna Gallery at the Owens Art Gallery, Owens Art Gallery, Mount Allison Univ., Sackville, N.B. (1975); *Forum 76*, Montreal Museum of Fine Arts (1976); *3 + 3 + 9 Sculptors in Exchange: Australia and Canada*, Harbourfront Art Gallery, Toronto (1981); *The First Australian Sculpture Triennial*, Bundoora Victoria, Australia (1981); *Information Systems*, curated by Andy Patton, YYZ, Toronto (1988); *Canadian Biennial of Contemporary Art*, National Gallery of Canada (1989);*Photographic Inscription*, Institute for Foreign Cultural Affairs, Stuttgart, Germany (1990); *Regina Work Project*, Mackenzie Art Gallery (1991); *The Photographic Image*, 49th Parallel, N.Y. (1991) *Denonciation*, Lucien Fromage Factory, Darnetal (Rouen) Normandy, Santa Monica Centre d'Art, Barcelona (1991); *En Scene*, W139, Amsterdam, The Netherlands (1992); *Mostra America*, Museu Da Gravura, Cidade de Curitiba, Brasil (1992); *Witness*, Presentation House, Vancouver (travelling) (1993); Samuel Lallouz Gallery, Montreal (1995, 1996). **COLLECTIONS:** Art Gallery of Ontario; Canada Council Art Bank; National Gallery of Ottawa; Mendel Art Gallery, Saskatoon; many private collections. **AFFIL:** Task Force on the Future of The Art Gallery of Ontario, 1992. **HONS:** Toronto Arts Award, 1990; T. Eaton Travelling Scholarship, 1972; Gov. General's Medal, 1972; represented by: Susan Hobbs Gallery, Toronto; Samuel Lallouz Gallery, Montreal; Carles Poy Gallery, Barcelona.

MISC: recipient, numerous Canada Council grants; subject of numerous articles.

Whitfield, Irene ■ ⁄ 🝖 ⊕
Managing Editor, CANADIAN COMMITTEE ON LABOUR HISTORY, c/o History/CCLH, Memorial University of Newfoundland, St. John's, NF A1C 5S7 (709) 737-3453, FAX 737-4342, EMAIL irenew@plato.ucs.mun.ca. Born Strathroy, Ont. 1941. d. 3 ch. Kimberly Anne, Deborah Lee, Michael James. **CAREER:** Mail-Bus. Svcs Rep., Bell Telephone Co., 1957-63; Office Mgr, T-Shirt Co., 1977-79; owner, K.D.M. T-Shirts, 1979-80; Intermediate Clerk, Memorial Univ. of Newfoundland, 1981-82; Intermediate Clerk-Steno, then Publications Asst., then Mng Ed., *Labour/Le Travail* & other publications, Canadian Committee on Labour History, Memorial Univ. of Newfoundland, 1982 to date; Mng Ed., Newfoundland Studies, Memorial Univ. of Newfoundland. **AFFIL:** CUPE Local 1615. **INTERESTS:** grandchildren; gardening. **COMMENT:** *"I have striven to be recognized as an independent person. Without burdening our social programs, I have raised three children. I have done what was considered unthinkable in the 70s: divorced, kept and raised my children to make a contribution to society, and have prospered myself."*

Whitfield, Winifred, B.A.,M.Sp.Ed. ⊕ O
NATIONAL COUNCIL OF WOMEN OF CANADA, 10 Torrington Cres., London, ON N6C 2V9 (519) 681-8686, FAX 681-1119. Born London, Ont. 1926. m. Alan. 2 ch. **EDUC:** Univ. of Western Ontario, B.A.(Hist.) 1947; Univ. of Toronto, M.Sp.Ed.(Special Educ.) 1980. **CAREER:** secondary sch. Teacher, Phys. Educ. & Hist., Cobourg, 1948-49; Strathroy, 1949-50; Middlesex, 1959-66; Ed., Ginn and Company, 1969-75; Teacher, Special Educ., Toronto, 1975-80. **AFFIL:** Canadian Federation of University Women ("London Club" Pres. 1985-88); London Council of Women (Pres. 1990-94); Anglican Church Women, St. James Parish (Pres. 1982-84); Project 97 (a political action group) (Chair, Steering Committee); Urban League; UWO Women's Athletic Alumnae. **HONS:** Volunteer Award, London Free Press; Volunteer Award, Prov. of Ont., 1995. **INTERESTS:** curling; golf; duplicate bridge; local history. **MISC:** served on a number of advisory committees, currently for the Breast Screening Program, London. **COMMENT:** *"Since joining Brownies at the age of six, I've always believed that women working together can change the world around them for the better."*

Whitlock, Christine J. ■ ⊗ 🝖 ▯
President and Publisher, WOMEN WHO EXCEL

and C.J. PRODUCTIONS, Box 3533, Stn C, Hamilton, ON L8H 7M9 (905) 547-7135, FAX 547-7135. **CAREER:** Pres., Women Who Excel, 1988 to date. **SELECTED PUBLICATIONS:** *Women Who Excel*, directory, 7 eds. **AFFIL:** Burlington Chamber of Commerce; Oakville Chamber of Commerce; Canadian Public Relations Society, Hamilton Branch. **HONS:** twice nominated Woman of the Year, Bus. & Communication categories, City of Hamilton, Status of Women. **MISC:** started "Women Who Excel" first as a directory, later with luncheons, then on to monthly dinner meetings, & it now includes mini-trade shows 3 times a year & seasonal fashion shows; Publisher, "Cycling in Halton, Hamilton-Wentworth & Niagara Regions," with 30 cycling maps. **COMMENT:** *"Promoting women in business to get more business."*

Whitney, Susan G. ■ ✪ ✊
Director and Past President, SUSAN WHITNEY GALLERY, Regina, SK (306) 569-9279, FAX 352-2453. Born Dublin, Ireland 1951. **CAREER:** Tech. Demonstrator, Trinity Coll., Dublin, 1972-73; Exhibition Artist, Royal Dublin Society, 1973; Exhibiting Artist, Project Art Gallery, Dublin, 1972-74; Dir., Kesik Gallery, Regina, 1978-79; Art Appraiser, 1978 to date; Dir. & Past Pres., Susan Whitney Gallery, 1979 to date. **AFFIL:** Professional Art Dealers' Association of Canada (Past Pres.). **MISC:** Canadian Cultural Property Export Review Bd., 1994 to date; mbr., Arts & Cultural Industries Sectoral Advisory Group on Int'l Trade, Dept. of Int'l Trade, 1994 to date; Advisory Committee, Canada Council Art Bank, 1992-95; frequent guest speaker; subject of various articles.

Whittaker, Sheelagh D., B.Sc.,B.A., M.B.A. 📺 ⚛
President, EDS CANADA, 33 Yonge St., Ste. 810, Toronto, ON M5E 1G4 (416) 814-4577, FAX 814-4600. Born Ottawa. m. 6 ch. **EDUC:** Univ. of Alberta, B.Sc. 1967; Univ. of Toronto, B.A. 1970; York Univ., M.B.A.(Fin./Econ.) 1975. **CAREER:** Dept. of Consumer & Corp. Affairs, 1975-79; Dir. & Consultant, The Canada Consulting Group, 1979-86; VP, Planning & Corp. Affairs, Canadian Broadcasting Corporation, 1986-88; Pres. & CEO, Canadian Satellite Communications Inc. (Cancom), 1988-93; Pres. EDS Canada, 1993 to date. **DIRECTOR:** EDS Canada; Imperial Oil Limited; Royal Bank of Canada; Royal Trust Corporation; Spar Aerospace Limited. **AFFIL:** Council for an Ontario Information Infrastructure (V-Chair); International Institute of Communications (VP & Trustee). **HONS:** Woman of the Year, Canadian Women in Radio & Television, 1992; Hon. Fellow, Ryeron Polytechnic Univ., 1992; Outstanding Exec. Leadership Award, York Univ., 1994; Honour Roll, *Maclean's* Magazine, 1994.

Whyard, Florence E., C.M.,B.A.,LL.D. 📖 $
Publisher, BERINGIAN BOOKS, 89 Sunset Dr. N., Whitehorse, YT Y1A 3G5 (403) 668-2261, FAX 668-2261. Born London, Ont. 1917. m. James H. Whyard. 3 ch. **EDUC:** Univ. of Western Ontario, B.A. 1938. **CAREER:** war-time svc, WRCNS, 1942-45; M.L.A. & Min. of Health & Welfare, Yukon Territory, 1974-78; Mayor, City of Whitehorse, 1981-83; Administrator, Yukon Territory, 1988-95. **SELECTED PUBLICATIONS:** ed. & updated *My Seventy Years*, by Martha Black (published as *My Ninety Years*); *Canadian Bush Pilot - Ernie Boffa*; Yukon Colouring Books for Children; *All My Rivers Flowed West*, ed.; *Ninety Years North*, co-author. **AFFIL:** Whitehorse Chamber of Commerce (Hon. Life Mbr.); Yukon Foundation (Bd. Mbr.); Westmark Community Bd.; Yukon Heritage Resources Bd.; Yukon Historical Museum Association. **HONS:** LL.D.(Hon.), Univ. of Western Ontario, 1979; Member of the Order of Canada, 1984; Heritage Award, City of Whitehorse. **INTERESTS:** family; politics; people; history. **COMMENT:** *"From an Ontario newspaper family, being a communicator is natural - naval information, public relations, covering Legislature, editing Whitehorse Star - freelancing - still writing."*

Whyte, Anne V.T., B.A.,M.A.,Ph.D., F.R.S.C. ■ ⚛ 🎓 ♥
President, MESTOR ASSOCIATES LTD., (consulting co. in int'l dev.), 751 Hamilton Rd., Russell, ON K4R 1E5 (613) 445-1305, FAX 445-1302, EMAIL mestor@sympatico.ca. Born Thorne, UK 1942. m. Robert D. Auger. 3 ch. David, Clare, Joanna. **EDUC:** Univ. of Cambridge, U.K., B.A.(Hons., Geog.) 1963, M.A. 1967; Johns Hopkins Univ., U.S.A., Ph.D.(Geog. & Envir. Eng.) 1971. **CAREER:** Researcher, Smithsonian Institute, Washington, DC, 1965-66; Research Assoc., Univ. of Cambridge, 1967-68; Research Assoc., Univ. of Bristol, U.K., 1968-74; Univ. Lecturer, Univ. of London, U.K., 1974-75; Assoc. Prof., Univ. of Toronto, 1976-84; Dir., Environmental Studies, 1978-84; Program Specialist, UNESCO, Paris, 1984-86; Dir., International Development Research Centre, Ottawa, 1986-92; Dir. Gen., 1992-96; Pres., Mestor Associates Ltd., 1996 to date. **SELECTED PUBLICATIONS:** more than 50 publications incl.: *Environmental Risk Assessment* (1980); *Building a New South Africa: Environment, Reconstruction and*

Development (1995). **AFFIL:** World Academy of Arts & Sciences (Fellow); Royal Canadian Geographical Society (Gov.); Canadian Association of Geographers (former Pres.). **HONS:** Fellow, Royal Society of Canada; mbr. of Sigma Xi; Fulbright Scholar. **INTERESTS:** gardening; nature study.

Whyte, Letha ■ ■ ○
Volunteer. 83 Roxborough Dr., Toronto, ON M4W 1X2. m. George E. Whyte. 3 ch. Lindsay Mary Berry, Allyson Jane Whyte, Marchant Brian Whyte. **AFFIL:** Hospital for Sick Children (Bd. of Trustees 1994; Fin. & Audit Committee; Quality Council Committee; Hum. Res. Planning Committee); Wellspring Foundation (Chair, Bd. of Dir. 1996; Chair, Strategic Planning 1995-96; Trustee 1992); Toronto Intergenerational Project (Bd. of Dir. 1995; Strategic Planning Committee); Bloorview Children's Hospital (Chair, Bd. of Trustees 1990-93; Trustee 1984-89; Long-Range Planning & Exec. Committees 1986-89; Chrm, Accreditation Committee 1985-86); Vaughan Glen Hospital (Bd. of Trustees 1989-90; Chrm, Bd. of Trustees 1987-89); North Toronto Community Centre Working Committee (V-Chair 1987-89; Chrm 1984-87); S.P.R.I.N.T. - Senior Peoples Resources in North Toronto (Chair, Bd. of Dir. 1987-89; mbr., Bd. of Dir. 1985-89; founding mbr.); P.O.I.N.T. - People and Organizations in North Toronto (Chair, Bd. of Dir. 1982-83).

Wickwire, Wendy, B.Mus.,M.A., Ph.D. ✍ 📖
Assistant Professor, Department of Educational Studies, Faculty of Education, UNIVERSITY OF BRITISH COLUMBIA, Vancouver, BC V6R 1J5 (604) 822-6381, FAX 822-9297, EMAIL wickwire@unix.g.ca. Born Liverpool, N.S. 2 ch. Leithen King M'Gonigale; Patrick Finian M'Gonigale. **EDUC:** Univ. of Western Ontario, B.Mus. 1972; York Univ., M.A. 1978; Wesleyan Univ., Middletown, Conn., Ph.D. 1983. **CAREER:** I.W. Killam Post-Doctoral Fellow, Dept. of Anthro. & Soc., Univ. of British Columbia, 1982-84; Lecturer, Dept. of Visual & Performing Arts in Educ. & the Native Indian Teacher Educ. Program, Univ. of British Columbia, 1986; Research Assoc., Institute for New Economics, & Co-Dir., Native Research Proj. on the Stein River Valley, 1984-88; Lecturer, Dept. of Visual & Performing Arts in Educ. & the Native Indian Teacher Educ. Program, Univ. of British Columbia, 1988; Cdn Research Fellow, Dept. of Social & Educ. Studies, Univ. of British Columbia, 1990-93; Research Assoc., Dept. of Anthro. & Soc., Univ. of British Columbia, 1993-94; Asst. Prof., Dept. of Educ. Studies, Fac. of Educ., Univ. of

British Columbia & Head of Ts'kel Grad. Program for First Nations students in Educ., 1994-95; Asst. Prof., Dept. of Histry & Dept. of Environmental Studies, Univ. of Victoria, 1995 to date. **SELECTED PUBLICATIONS:** *Stein: The Way of the River*, with Michael M'Gonigle (Vancouver: Talonbooks, 1988); *Write It On Your Heart: The Epic World of an Okanagan Storyteller*, with Harry Robinson (Vancouver: Talonbooks, 1989); *Nature Power: In the Spirit of an Okanagan Storyteller*, with Harry Robinson (Vancouver & Seattle: Douglas and McIntyre & Univ. of Washington Press, 1992); "Traditional Musical Culture at the Canadian Native Centre in Toronto" (*Canadian Folk Music Journal* 4 1976); "Women in Enthnography: The Research of James A. Teit" (*Ethnohistory* 14 (4) 1993); "To See Ourselves as the Other's Other: Nlaka'pamux Contact Narratives" (*Canadian Historical Review* 75 (1) 1994); various other publications. **HONS:** I.W. Killam Postdoctoral Fellowship, 1982-84; co-winner, Bill Duthie Booksellers' Choice Award for B.C. Book of the Year, 1989; Roderick Haig-Brown award for best book about B.C., B.C. Book Awards, 1993; "To See Ourselves as the Other's Other: Nlaka'pamux Contact Narratives," winner, Best Article, *Canadian Historial Review*, 1994. **INTERESTS:** writing; research; outdoors; hiking; kayaking. **MISC:** recipient, various grants, fellowships & scholarships; various conference presentations & public lectures. **COMMENT:** *"Wendy Wickwire is an anthropologist whose major research and writing has been in the area of oral tradition. Recently she received several book awards for her work on the First Nations peoples of South Central British Columbia. Currently, she teaches oral tradition & ethnographic methodology at the Univ. of Victoria."*

Wieland, Joyce, O.C. • ⊗
Artist and Filmmaker. Born Toronto 1931. **EDUC:** Central Tech. High Sch. **CAREER:** influential Cdn artists; experimental filmmaker, painter, sculptor; artist in multi-media (quilts, collage, embroidery); Instructor, N.S. Coll. of Art & Design, 1971; Instructor, San Francisco Art Institute, 1985-86; Artist-in-Residence, Univ. of Toronto, Architecture, 1988-89. **SELECTED CREDITS:** *Rat Life and Diet in North America*, 1968; *La Raison avant la passion*, 1967-69; *The Far Shore* (feature film based on Tom Thomson), 1976; *O Kanada*, 1983. **COMMISSIONS:** *Barren Ground, Cariboo*, Spadina Subway, Toronto; *Défende la terre*, National Science Library, Ottawa. **EXHIBITIONS:** solo exhibitions, Isaacs Gallery, Toronto (1960, 1963, 1967); numerous exhibitions & retrospectives incl. *Five Films by Joyce*

Wieland, Musuem of Modern Arts, N.Y. (1968); *Canada Art d'Aujourd hui*, Museum Nationale d'Art Moderne, Paris, travelled through Europe (1968); *Eight Artists from Canada*, Tel-Aviv Mseum (1970); *True Patriot Love*, National Gellery of Canada (1971); *20th Century Canadian Painting*, Nat'l Museum of Modern Art, Japan (1981); *Toronto Painting '84*, AGO (1984); retrospective, AGO, nat'l Cdn tour (1987); National Film Theatre (1988); film retrospective, Georges Pompidou Centre, France (1989); retrospective, Bau-Xi Gallery, Toronto (1996); numerous film festivals incl. Cannes (1976); London (1985); Oberhausen (1986); Edinburgh Int'l Film Festival (1988). **COLLECTIONS:** numerous corporate & private collections. **AFFIL:** Royal Academy of Arts. **HONS:** 2 Cdn film awards for *The Far Shore*, 1977; Award for Exceptional Merit, Philadelphia Int'l Festival of Short Films, 1971; Victor M. Staunton Award, 1972; 2nd Prize, Ann Arbor Film Festival, 1986; Officer, Order of Canada, 1983; Toronto Arts Award, 1987; Woman of Distinction Award, YWCA, 1987. **MISC:** Canada Council grants, 1966, 1968, 1972, 1984, 1986; 1st living Cdn woman artist to have a retrospective at the Art Gallery of Ontario, 1987; subject of numerous world-wide exhibitions, articles & research papers incl. *Artist on Fire* by Kay Armitage (1987).

Wieler, Diana 📖
Author. 133 Spruce Thicket Walk, Winnipeg, MB R2V 3Z1 (204) 338-6334, FAX 334-4521. Born Winnipeg 1961. m. Larry. 1 ch. Benjamin Wieler. **CAREER:** writer, 1983 to date. **SELECTED PUBLICATIONS:** *Last Chance Summer* (Western Producer Prairie Books, 1986); *Bad Boy* (Groundwood Books/Douglas and McIntyre, 1989); *RanVan the Defender* (Groundwood Books/Douglas and McIntyre, 1993); *RanVan: A Worthy Opponent* (Groundwood Books/Douglas and McIntyre, 1995). **HONS:** Award for Excellence (*Bad Boy*), Ruth Schwartz Foundation, 1990; Young Adult Book of the Year (*Bad Boy*), Canadian Library Association, 1990; Gov. General's Literary Award for Children's Lit. (*Bad Boy*), 1989; Mr. Christie's Book Award (*RanVan the Defender*), 1993. **INTERESTS:** film (currently writing screenplay). **COMMENT:** *"I am a writer passionately dedicated to reaching the young people we're not reaching now."*

Wigdor, Blossom T., C.M.,Ph.D. 🐦 ⊕
Professor Emeritus, Centre for Studies of Aging, Departments of Psychology and Behavioural Science, UNIVERSITY OF TORONTO, 222 College St., Toronto, ON M5T 3J1 (416) 978-4706, FAX 978-4771. Born Montreal 1924. w. Leon Wigdor. 1 ch. **EDUC:** McGill Univ., B.A. (Psych.) 1945, Ph.D.(Psych.) 1952; Univ. of Toronto, M.A.(Clinical Psych.) 1946. **CAREER:** various positions, Dept. of Veterans Affairs, 1946-78; various teaching posts, to Assoc. Prof., Psych., McGill Univ., 1952-79; Consultant, Maimonides Hospital & Home for the Aged, Montreal, 1954-67; Consultant, Queen Elizabeth Hospital & Jewish General Hospital, Montreal, for various periods; Dir., Psych. Svcs, Centre Hospitalier Côte des Neiges (formerly Queen Mary Veterans Hospital), Montreal, 1961-79; Chair, McGill Grad. Fac. Committee on Aging, 1975-79; Dir. to Prof. Emeritus, Centre for Studies of Aging, Univ. of Toronto, 1979 to date. **SELECTED PUBLICATIONS:** *Planning Your Retirement: The Canadian Self-Help Guide*, Ed., 2nd edition (Toronto: Grovesnor House Press, 1988); *The Over Forty Society: Issues for Canada's Aging Population*, with D. Foot (Toronto: James Lorimer and Company Limited, 1988); "Notes on Gerontology Education in Canada" (*AGHE Exchange* 13(2) 1990); "Critical Issues Relating to Mental Health and Medication Use in the Elderly" (*Canadian Journal On Aging* 10(4) 1991); other research & publications in aging, particularly related to cognitive changes, memory, stress & coping behaviour. **EDIT:** Ed.-in-chief, *Canadian Journal on Aging*, 1982-85. **AFFIL:** Canadian Psychological Association (Fellow); American Psychological Association (Fellow); Canadian Association on Gerontology; Gerontological Society of America (Fellow); Woodsworth Coll. (Sr. Fellow); Mount Sinai Hospital (Bd. of Gov.); Baycrest Hospital for Geriatric Care (Bd. of Gov.); SPRINT (Hon. Dir.); COPA (Hon. Dir.); Canadian Stage Company (Bd. of Dir.); Canadian Memorial Services (Bd. of Dir. & Chair); Sigma Xi, Toronto Chapter. **HONS:** Woman of Achievement, YWCA, Montreal, 1975; Member, Order of Canada, 1989; Canada 125 Medal, 1993; D.Sc.(Hon.), Univ. of Victoria, 1990; D.Sc.(Hon.), Univ. of Guelph, 1994; LL.D.(Hon.) ,St. Thomas Univ., 1995. **MISC:** Chair, Nat'l Advisory Council on Aging (NACA), 1990-93; Chair, Canadian Coalition on Medication Use of the Elderly, 1991-93; mbr., Science Council of Canada, 1973-79.

Wight, Darlene Coward, B.A.(Hons.), M.A. ✖ 📚
Associate Curator of Inuit Art, WINNIPEG ART GALLERY, 300 Memorial Blvd, Winnipeg, MB R3C 1V1 (204) 786-6641, FAX 788-4998. Born Picton, Ont. m. Roger. **EDUC:** Peterborough Teachers' Coll., 1968; Carleton Univ., B.A.(Hons., Art Hist.) 1978, M.A. 1980. **CAREER:** Teaching Asst., Dept. of Art Hist.,

Carleton Univ., 1978-79; Fine Arts Curator, Canadian Arctic Producers, Ottawa, 1981-83; independent curator & researcher, 1983-86; Assoc. Curator of Inuit Art, Winnipeg Art Gallery, 1986 to date; Lecturer, Univ. of Winnipeg, 1991-92, 1993-94. SELECTED PUBLICATIONS: numerous exhibition catalogues, incl. *Winnipeg Collects: Inuit Art from Private Collections*, illus. catalogue (Winnipeg Art Gallery, 1981); *The Swinton Collection of Inuit Art*, illus. catalogue (Winnipeg Art Gallery, 1987); *Out of Tradition: Abraham Anghik/ David Ruben Piqtoukun*, illus. catalogue (Winnipeg Art Gallery, 1989); *The First Passionate Collector: The Ian Lindsay Collection of Inuit Art*, illus. catalogue (Winnipeg Art Gallery, 1990); *Between Two Worlds: Sculpture by David Ruben Piqtoukun*, illus. catalogue (Winnipeg Art Gallery, 1996); several introductions for catalogues; "Inuit Tradition and Beyond: New Attitudes Toward Art-Making in the 1980s" (*Inuit Art Quarterly* 6(2) 1991); "Cultural Information Conveyed in Inuit Carving of Faces" (*Tableau* 7(3) 1994); numerous other articles; writer, *Sanaugasi Takujaksat: A Travelling Celebration of Inuit Sculpture*, video for exhibition. EXHIBITIONS: curator, *Oonark's Family*, Winnipeg Art Gallery (1987); curator, *Manasie: The Art of Manasie Akpaliapik*, Winnipeg Art Gallery (1990); curator, *The Human Face*, Winnipeg Art Gallery (1994); curated more than 40 other exhibits for the Winnipeg Art Gallery; guest curator, *Immaginario Inuit: Arte e cultura degli esquimesi canadesi*, Galleria d'Arte Moderna e Contemporea di Palazzo Forti, Verona, Italy (1995). AFFIL: Carleton University's Reg'l Presidential Advisory Committee for Winnipeg. HONS: Jack Barwick & Douglas Duncan Scholarship in Art Hist., 1977; Hudson's Bay Company Grad. Fellowship in Cdn Studies, 1979; Carleton Univ. Grad. Scholarship & Assistantship, 1979, 1980. INTERESTS: Scuba diving. MISC: various conference papers, meeting addresses & public lectures.

Wightman, Faye, B.Sc.N. ◑ ⊕

President, BRITISH COLUMBIA'S CHILDREN'S HOSPITAL FOUNDATION, 4480 Oak Street, Vancouver, BC V6H 3V4 (604) 875-2647, FAX 875-2921. Born Creston, B.C. 1948. d. 2 ch. EDUC: Univ. of British Columbia, B.Sc.N. 1981. CAREER: Critical Care Nurse, Vancouver General Hospital; Nursing Instructor; Dir., Health & Community Svcs, Canadian Red Cross Society, B.C. & Yukon; Campaign Dir., United Way Lower Mainland; VP, Community Rel'ns, British Columbia's Children's Hospital; Exec. Dir.; Instructor, Fundraising & Resource Dev., Vancouver Community Coll. AFFIL:

Imagine (Chair, Local Action Committee); Save the Children (Bd.); Association for Fund Raising Professionals at B.C. (Past Pres.); Association of Healthcare Philanthropy; Board of Trade; Arbutus Club; Governor Conference (Bd. Mbr.). HONS: Florence Emory Award, Canadian Red Cross, 1981, 1983, 1984; Marketer of the Year (British Columbia's Children's Hospital Foundation), B.C. Chapter of the American Marketing Association, 1992; Fundraiser of the Year (nominee, 1993). INTERESTS: sports; tennis; music; crafts; gardening. MISC: Program Chair, 1991 conference, Canadian Centre for Philanthropy; Bd. Mbr., Gov. General's Cdn Study Conference; has presented at numerous conferences. COMMENT: *"My fundraising achievements (62% increase in United Way revenue during my tenure, 350% increase in revenue for Children's Hospital) have been accomplished through effectively working with and through key community and corporate volunteers."*

Wilburn, Marion, B.A.,M.A.,B.Ed.,M.Ed., M.L.S. ■ ⟨ 𝖨 ◐

Coordinator, Library and Information Technician Program, SHERIDAN COLLEGE, 1430 Trafalgar Rd., Oakville, ON L6H 2L1 (905) 845-9430 x2336, FAX 815-4035, EMAIL marion.wilburn@sheridanc.on.ca. Born Hamilton, Ont. 1946. m. Gene Wilburn. 1 ch. EDUC: McMaster Univ., B.A. 1969, M.A. 1970; McArthur Coll., Queen's Univ., B.Ed. 1971; Univ. of Toronto, M.Ed. 1977, M.L.S. 1981. CAREER: Asst. Head, Dept. of English, West Humber Collegiate Institute, Etobicoke Bd. of Educ., 1971-75; Assoc. Librarian, Ontario Institute for Studies in Education, Univ. of Toronto, 1977; Proj. Asst., Ontario Universities Program for Instruction Dev., 1977-80; Dir., Office of Teaching & Learning, Council of Ontario Universities, 1980-81; Sr. Mktg Rep., Ultas International, Toronto, 1981-83; Coord., Library & Info. Technology Program, Sheridan Coll., 1983 to date; VP, Wilburn Communications Ltd., 1990 to date; Educ. Tech. Facilitator, Sheridan Coll., 1994-96. SELECTED PUBLICATIONS: *Descriptive Cataloguing Workbook*, textbook; *Subject Cataloguing Workbook*, textbook; *Cataloguing Reference Guide*, textbook; *Automation in Libraries*, textbook; *Online Retrieval*, textbook; *Reference and Acquisitions Workbook*, textbook; articles in various publications incl. the *International Encyclopedia of Education: Research and Studies*, *CD-ROM International*, *InfoAge* & *Canadian Library Journal*. AFFIL: Canadian Library Association; Ontario Library Association; Special Libraries Association; Ontario Association for Library Technicians; Ontario Association for Library Instructors (Chair); Canadian Association for Adult Education; American Library Association; Ontario Genealogical Association; Manchester & Lancashire Family History Society. HONS: Jubilee Award, Fac. of Library & Info. Sciences Alumni Committee, 1984. INTERESTS: family history; photography; automation; bird watching; mystery fiction. MISC: included in *Who's Who in America*, 1994; planned & developed the Sheridan Coll. World Wide Website; numerous conferences, workshops & seminars; recipient, various scholarships, fellowships & grants. COMMENT: *"Marion Wilburn is an educator, information specialist and consultant with an interest in the use and impact of new technologies in education and communication."*

Wildman, Sally, R.C.A.,O.C.A. ✪
Painter. 1805 Track St., Claremont, ON L1Y 1B8 (905) 649-1643. Born Northumberland, UK 1939. s. EDUC: Ontario Coll. of Art, Certificate (Illustration) 1960; Goldsmith's Coll. of Art, London, UK, Certificate (Painting) 1961. CAREER: freelance illustrator, 1961-70; freelance painter, 1970 to date. EXHIBITIONS: Pollock Gallery (1968, 1970); Roberts Gallery, Toronto (1970, 1972, 1974, 1976, 1979, 1982, 1986, 1990); numerous other group & solo exhibitions. COLLECTIONS: Concordia Univ.; Confederation Art Gallery, Charlottetown; Dofasco Art Collection; Canada Council Art Bank; Imperial Oil Ltd.; The Market Gallery. AFFIL: Royal Canadian Academy; Ontario Society of Artists. COMMENT: *"Painter, primarily working in the medium of oil-pastel. Represented in numerous public and private collections in Canada, United States and Switzerland. Exhibited at Roberts Gallery from 1970-91 and since then have been holding my own exhibitions."*

Wiley, Judith ■ ■ ✪ Ⓢ ⊛
President, CANADIAN SOCIETY OF ASSOCIATION EXECUTIVES, (educ., advocacy & research for & about non-profit organizations & registered charities), 40 University Ave., Ste. 1104, Toronto, ON M5J 1T1 (416) 596-6433, FAX 596-7994, EMAIL j.wiley@csae.com. Born London, Ont. 1947. d. 3 ch. Michael, Melissa, Marcia. EDUC: Univ. of Western Ontario, B.A. candidate 1997. CAREER: Reg'l Sales Coord./Supervisor, Distributor Svcs Dept./Mgr, Distributor Svcs Dept., Amway of Canada Limited, 1969-84; Exec. Dir., YWCA of St. Thomas-Elgin, 1984-89; Dir., Int'l Cooperation, YWCA of/du Canada, 1989-91; CEO, 1991-96; Pres., CSAE, 1996 to date. AFFIL: Canadian Physicians for Aid & Relief (Bd. mbr.); Drucker Award for Innovation (Selec-

tion Committee); Canadian Professional & Business Women's Organization; Canadian Association of Women Executives & Entrepreneurs; Board of Trade; Canadian Council for International Cooperation (Past Chair); Canada-Beijing Facilitating Committee, 4th U.N. Conference on Women, 1995; Canadian Committee for the 50th Anniversary of the U.N.; Elgin General Hospital (former mbr., Bd. of Dir.); Fanshawe Community Coll. (former mbr., Campus Advisory Committee); Great Lakes Women's Network for Peace (founding mbr.). HONS: Canada 125 Medal for svc. to the community; Civic Award, City of St. Thomas.

Will, Clara, B.A. ■ ■ ✪
Executive Director, ADVENTURE PLACE, (child & family intervention agency), 35 Calico Dr., North York, ON M3L 1V5 (416) 744-7650, FAX 744-8055. Born Manitoba. m. Leslie Will. 2 ch. Kirsten, Karin. EDUC: Manitoba Teachers' Coll., Teaching (Elementary) 1955; Univ. of Manitoba, B.A.(Psych./English) 1959. CAREER: Teacher, elementary sch., Man., 5 yrs.; teacher, Denmark & England, 5 yrs.; founder, Treatment/Education programme in schools & worked at this, 7 yrs.; founder & Exec. Dir., Adventure Place, 24 yrs. AFFIL: Ontario Coalition for Children & Youth (initiated & is mbr., Advisory Group); Community Systems Alliance, North York; Parent Help Line Committee, North York; Infant Mental Health; Sparrow Lake Alliance; Better Beginnings Now; North York Early Years Action Group (Chair). HONS: award from Early Childhood Education Association, North York. INTERESTS: theatre; music; photography; travel; walking; physical fitness. MISC: achievements have been in the non-profit sector of human svcs. COMMENT: *"My professional career has been devoted to helping children and their families. This has included education, mental health and developing opportunities for healthy development in the early years."*

Willcock, Elizabeth ■ ✦
Senior Citizenship Judge, DEPARTMENT OF CITIZENSHIP AND IMMIGRATION CANADA, Constitution Square, 350 Albert St., Rm 310, Ottawa, ON K1A 1L1 (613) 954-4623, FAX 954-4621. Born Sherbrooke, Que. 1927. m. David Noel Willcock. 5 ch. EDUC: Mount Notre Dame Sch., Sherbrooke, Que.; Notre Dame Coll., Staten Island, NY; Francis Robinson Duff Sch. of the Theatre, N.Y.C. CAREER: teacher, Drama & Hist. of the Theatre, Notre Dame Sch., Sherbrooke, Que, 1948-49; announcer, writer & prod. for radio, Sherbrooke, 1948-49; freelance broadcaster, Toronto, 1949-50,

Montreal, 1950-68; researcher & interviewer, CBC-TV Public Affairs, 1969-71; Dir. of Research, Progressive Conservative Party of Man., 1972-76; Exec. Dir., Citizenship Council of Manitoba, 1977-84; Trustee, Winnipeg Sch. Div., 1977-83; Chair, 1981-82; Pres., Nat'l P.C. Women's Caucus, 1981-83; Chief of Staff for Min. of State for Multiculturalism, 1984-85; Citizenship Court Judge, 1985-87; Sr. Judge, 1987 to date. AFFIL: Winnipeg's Refugee Assistance Committee Inc.; Council for Canadian Unity (Dir.). HONS: Order of Canada, 1991.

Williams, Anne E., B.Mus.,L.Mus., B.Ed. ⬩ ⊛
Music Teacher. 1002 - 15 St. S., Lethbridge, AB T1K 1V3 (403) 328-1066. Born Montreal 1936. d. 3 ch. EDUC: McGill Univ., B.Mus. (Piano Performance) 1959, L.Mus.(Singing) 1961; Univ. of Lethbridge, B.Ed.(Music) 1977. CAREER: teacher of piano & singing, 1959 to date; church organist; Exec. Sec., Canadian Journal of Philosophy. AFFIL: Canadian Voice of Women; Project Ploughshares Canada; Canadian Federation of University Women; Alberta Registered Music Teachers' Association; Anglican Diocese of Calgary (Peace & Justice Committee); Lethbridge Network for Peace. HONS: Woman of Distinction Award, YWCA, 1989. INTERESTS: reading; walking. MISC: organizer, local peace conference, 1988; coord., nat'l essay contest for high sch. students on "What Am I Prepared to Do for Peace?" sponsored by the Canadian Federation of University Women, 1988-89. COMMENT: *"A music teacher of 36 years, I am also one of many Canadian women active in peace education and advocacy, with a goal of achieving a just, healthy and peaceful world."*

Williams, Bronwen Katharine ■ ⊕ ⚙ ○
President, ACTION GROUP AGAINST HARASSMENT AND DISCRIMINATION IN THE WORKPLACE, 49 Montpetit St., L'Orignal, ON K0B 1K0 (613) 632-9828, FAX 632-9828, EMAIL igs65@hawk.igs.net. President and Legal Writer/Researcher, BKW ENTERPRISES. President, WILLOW BAY CREATIONS. Born Toronto 1952. s. EDUC: Sylvia Gill Business Institute, Hons. Dipl. 1970; Concordia Univ., Montreal, grad. 1985; Canadian Jewellers Institute, Cert.(Gemsetting), 1985, Grad. Jeweller 1995; Algonquin Coll., Ottawa, Hons. Degree (Crisis Mgmt/Psych.) 1995, diverse post-grad. credits. CAREER: Admin. Asst., Canadian Pacific Limited, 1970-77; Pres., Leather by Bronwen Reg'd., 1977-78; Sr. Int'l Mktg Specialist, Public Rel'ns & Promotions, Spar Aerospace Limited, 1978-92; Pres., Action Group Against Harassment & Discrimination in the Work-

place, 1991 to date; Pres., BKW Enterprises, 1992 to date; Legal Researcher/Writer, 1994 to date; Pres., Willow Bay Creations, 1996 to date. AFFIL: Maclean Hunter/Rogers Community TV; Canadian Advisory Council on the Status of Women; Hawkesbury General Hospital Foundation; Canadian Panel on Violence Against Women; Canadian Jewellers Institute; Chamber of Commerce; World Wildlife Fund; Ontario Society for the Prevention of Cruelty to Animals; Women's Business Connection Group; Prescott-Russell County anti-violence groups. HONS: Merit Award, Business & Professional Advertising Association; Appreciation Award, Community TV Programming, Maclean Hunter; Merit Award, Palliative Care, Hawkesbury General Hospital; Recognition Award, Public Rel'ns, Air Force Communications Electronics Association. INTERESTS: aviation & aerospace (have pilot's licence, brother is Cdn astronaut, Dr. David Williams); labour law & human rights; psych. (trauma, post-traumatic stress, obesity due to psychological reasons); camping; sports; ecology & environmental protection/preservation; non-fiction reading; skid control & advanced driving techniques (automobile, motorcycle, tractor trailer); energy-efficient home design/renovation & interior planning & decoration; jewellery design & manufacture. COMMENT: *"Value integrity, empathy, honour. Present goal: achieving recognition of workplace harassment; establishing stronger deterrents against corporate permissiveness/lack of accountability/trivialization; increasing awareness/validation of resulting damages/victim trauma; improving procedures to avoid revictimization by government agencies and medical, corporate and legal processes."*

Williams, Cheryl, B.Sc. ■■ ⊕ ○
Executive Director, ARCHITECTURAL INSTITUTE OF BRITISH COLUMBIA, (professional association), 131 Water St., Ste. 103, Vancouver, BC V6B 4M3 (604) 683-8588, FAX 683-8568. Born Montreal 1954. EDUC: Simon Fraser Univ., B.Sc.(Biol.) 1974. CAREER: Exec. Dir., AIBC, 1982 to date. AFFIL: National Council of Architectural Registration Boards (Procedures & Documents Committee); Committee of Canadian Architectural Councils (team mbr. for NAFTA); Canadian Society of Association Executives; Vancouver Board of Trade.

Williams, Darlene J. ⊛ ⬩ ⊕
Past President, DANCE MANITOBA INC., 80 Market St. E., Ste. 204, Winnipeg, MB R3B 0P7 (204) 943-7116. Born Hopkinsville, Kentucky 1966. s. EDUC: Ryerson Polytechnic Univ., Dipl.(Dance) 1987. CAREER: Dir., Gen. Pro-

gram, Sch. of Contemporary Dancers, 1987 to date; guest teacher in dance, 1987 to date. **AFFIL:** Dance Manitoba Inc. (Pres. 1990-94); Community Arts Manitoba Inc. (Pres.); Performing Arts Consortium (Exec. Committee 1996 to date). **HONS:** Outstanding Contribution as Pres., Dance Manitoba Inc., 1994. **COMMENT:** *"By taking my work as a dance teacher one step further, I actively use/promote art education as a tool to benefit individuals and society as a whole."*

Williams, Deidre Ann, R.N. ■■ ⊛ ⊕ 🌿
IMAGES ALBERTA (photography), P.O. Box 264, Stavely, AB T0L 1Z0 (403) 625-3139, WILLOW CREEK AUXILIARY HOSPITAL, P.O. Box 700, Claresholm, AB T0L 0T0 (403) 625-3361. Born Simcoe, Ont. 1948. m. Albert. 2 ch. Samantha, Lisa. **EDUC:** Victoria Hospital, R.N. 1970; self-taught in photography. **CAREER:** main income is currently from full-time nursing; photography business is her passion & is expanding; has been doing photography for more than 20 yrs.; goal is to become photojournalist full-time & nurse on a casual basis. **SELECTED PUBLICATIONS:** *Canadian Cowboys* (1997 wall calendar, 1996); cover & centrefold (*Alberta Travel* magazine, Aug. 1995); *Calgary Superguide* (Altitude Publishing, 1995); *A Portrait of Calgary* (Altitude Publishing, 1995); *The Wild West* (Altitude Publishing, 1993). **EXHIBITIONS:** exhibited worldwide on 4 continents in int'l photographic salons. **COLLECTIONS:** photographs in hospital & corporate collections. **AFFIL:** Alberta Association of Registered Nurses; Photographic Society of America; Chinook Camera Club; Foothills Tae Kwon Do Academy. **HONS:** 6 Awards of Merit, Photographic Society of America; awards from Prairie Reg. of Photographic Arts; many honourable mentions & gold medals, int'l photographic salons. **INTERESTS:** photography; martial arts (has high green belt in Tae Kwon Do); art (painting/pen & ink); downhill skiing; hiking; reading history (Cdn West); enjoying her family; rodeo (previously involved in scuba diving, sky diving & mountain climbing). **MISC:** CPR instructor, Mount Royal Coll; has created 4 flavoured honey spreads to diversify and enhance farm based honey business. **COMMENT:** *"I feel at one with the range and endless sky. I love the honesty and sincerity of its people and am happiest when I can transform this into an image. Photography is my passion, it is my life. I have a wonderfully supportive family that encourages me to follow my passion for photography; they give me the freedom to be me and to create the images that are so strong within my mind and soul."*

Williams, Terri ✎ $
Columnist, *THE TORONTO SUN*, 333 King St. E., Toronto, ON M5A 3X5 (416) 947-2218, FAX 947-2041. Born Toronto 1960. m. Andrew Kinghorn. 2 ch. Alison, Ryan. **EDUC:** Sheridan Coll., Certificate (Legal Secretarial) 1981; Ryerson Polytechnic Institute, Certificate (Reporting) 1987, Certificate (Copy editing & Layout) 1986. **CAREER:** Corp. Cont.'s Asst., The Toronto Sun Publishing Corporation, 1984-85; "Action Line" Columnist; Adopt-A-Family Program, 1985-88; Consumer Alert, *The Saturday Sun*, 1986 to date; Money Reporter, *The Toronto Sun*, 1988 to date; "Consumer Expert," *News at Noon*, Global Television Network, 1992-94; Columnist, "Money Line," *The Toronto Sun*, 1994 to date; Host, *Dollars 'n' Sense*, Shaw Cable 10; VP, Credit Counselling Service of Metropolitan Toronto, 1995-96; Consumer Expert, *Real Life*, The Life Network, 1995-96. **COMMENT:** *"Terri has covered all areas of business as a reporter including corporate mergers, credit bureaus, stock scams, real estate, and personal finance."*

Williams, Wendy, B.N. ⊕ ✊ ☝
President, AVALON HEALTH, 67 Mayor Ave., St. John's, NF A1C 4N9 (709) 579-5247, EMAIL wendywil@voyager.newcomm.net. Born St. John's 1949. sep. 2 ch. **EDUC:** Memorial Univ., B.N. 1971, Diploma in Family Practice Nursing 1975. **CAREER:** Camp Nurse, Canadian Young Judaea Organization-Camp Solelim, 1971; Public Health Nurse, Badger's Quay, Bonavista Bay, Nfld. Dept. of Public Health, 1971-72; Coord., Cystic Fibrosis Home Care Program, Dr. Charles A. Janeway Child Health Centre, 1972-73; Public Health Nurse, Victorian Order of Nurses, 1974; Instructor, Sch. of Nursing, Memorial Univ. of Newfoundland, 1977; Nfld. mbr., Canadian Advisory Council on the Status of Women, 1977-80; Dir., Provincial Advisory Council on the Status of Women, 1984-90; Commissioner, Newfoundland Human Rights Commission, 1988-91; private practice in nursing, 1988-90, 1993 to date; City Councillor, City of St. John's, 1990-93; Pres., Provincial Advisory Council on the Status of Women, 1990-96; mbr., Ad Hoc Committee on Breast Screening Programs, 1992-1994. **SELECTED PUBLICATIONS:** "Therapeutic Abortions in Newfoundland and Labrador" (*Newfoundland Status of Women Council Newsletter* 5(8) Dec. 1978); "Adolescent Sexuality: A Problem of Adults" (*Social Perspectives* Nov. 1985); "Women's Health Issues" (Gov't of Newfoundland & Labrador, 1989); "Sexual Assault on Tape" (*Tapestry* 2(4) 1992); brief to the Task Force on Community Econ. Dev.

(Prov. Advisory Council on the Status of Women, 1994); various other publications. DIRECTOR: Rosbro Inc. AFFIL: Newfoundland Cancer Treatment & Research Foundation (Bd.); Newfoundland & Labrador Health Care Association (Bd.); Women's Enterprise Bureau (former Bd. Mbr.; Exec. Committee); National Action Committee on the Status of Women (former VP); Planned Parenthood Federation of Canada (former Bd.); Newfoundland AIDS Committee (Founding mother); St. John's Status of Women Council (Founding mother); Association of Registered Nurses of Newfoundland; Canadian Association of Nurses in Independent Practice; The Sex Information and Education Council of Canada (Nat'l Professional Advisory Committee); Newfoundland & Labrador Heart Health Project (Chair, Public Policy Committee); Women's Health Network–Nfld. & Lab. (Founding mother); Stella Burry Corporation (Bd.). HONS: Faith E. Pelley Memorial Bursary, Bishop's Coll., St. John's, 1967; nominated, Loretta C. Ford Award for Excellence as Nurse Practitioner, 1990; Certificate of Merit, Canadian Mental Health Association, Nfld. Div., 1993. INTERESTS: walking; wildflowers; dancing; bridge. MISC: Advisory Committee, *Video Diary of a Teenage Smoker*, video, Health & Welfare Canada (1992); Gov. General's Cdn Study Conference, 1987; 1st independent nurse in private practice in Nfld., 1988-90; 1st public health nurse assigned to Badger's Quay, Bonavista Bay; frequent public speaker; numerous consultations incl. St. Clare's Mercy Hospital Mental Health Task Force, 1994 & Canadian Mortage and Housing Corporation, 1994; numerous educational workshops given; listed in *Faces of Feminism*, Pamela Harris (1992), *Who's Who and Why: Newfoundland Women* (1991), & *A Woman's Almanac* (1990), Marian A. White; lobbyist. COMMENT: *"As a registered nurse and a feminist, my work has been to research, to lobby, and to provide health services that women need. I am also a mother, a sister, a daughter and a girlfriend. Relationships, whether kith or kin, are the reason for living."*

Williamson, Janice, B.A.,M.A., Ph.D. ■ ⊗ ⊰

Associate Professor, Department of English, UNIVERSITY OF ALBERTA, Edmonton, AB T6G 2E5 (403) 492-3258, FAX 492-8142, EMAIL jwilliam@gpu.srv.ualberta.ca. Born Brandon, Man. 1951. EDUC: Carleton Univ., B.A. (English) 1975; York Univ., M.A.(English) 1981, Ph.D.(English) 1987. CAREER: Asst. Prof., Univ. of Alberta, 1987-91; Assoc. Prof., 1991 to date. SELECTED CREDITS: *Pedestrian Notes on West Edmonton Mall* (film).

SELECTED PUBLICATIONS: Ed. with Deborah Gorham, *Up and Doing: Canadian Women and Peace* (Women's Press, 1989); Tell Tale Signs: Fictions (Turnstone, 1991); *The Journals of Alberta Borges* (Edmonton: Greensleaves, 1991); ed. with Claudine Potvin, *Women's Writing and the Literary Institution* (Edmonton: Univ. of Alberta, 1992); *Altitude X2* (Calgary: DisOrientation Press, 1992); *Sounding Differences: Conversations with Seventeen Canadian Women Writers* (Toronto: Univ. of Toronto, 1993); numerous invited chapters in books; various fiction, incl. "A Family Holiday in Sunny Puerto Plata" (*The American Voice* 16 1989); "Lucrece" (*The American Voice* 22 1991); various articles; numerous interviews. EDIT: Ed. Bd., *Paragraph Magazine*. AFFIL: Academic Women's Association, Univ. of Alberta; Writers' Union of Canada. HONS: Special Mention ("A Family Holiday in Sunny Puerto Plata"), The Pushcart Prize, 1989; bp nichol Chapbook Award ("a boy named:"), 1996. MISC: recipient, various grants; numerous talks; manuscript reviewer for various granting agencies, scholarly journals & Women's Press; co-curator & co-writer, "Dangerous Goods: Feminist Visual Arts Practices," Edmonton Art Gallery, 1991; co-founder, Women's Action for Peace in the Gulf, 1991. COMMENT: *"Janice Williamson, writer, critic, teacher, and sometime activist."*

Willis Sweete, Barbara, A.R.C.T.,B.A., B.F.A. ⊌ ⊗

Film and Television Director, RHOMBUS MEDIA INC., 489 King St. W., Ste. 102, Toronto, ON M5V 1L3 (416) 971-7856, FAX 971-9647. Born Kamloops, B.C. 1953. d. EDUC: Royal Conservatory of Music, Toronto, A.R.C.T. (Piano Performance); Univ. of Western Ontario, B.A.(Music); York Univ., B.F.A.(Film Production). CAREER: Founding Ptnr, Rhombus Media, with Niv Fichman & Larry Weinstein, 1979. SELECTED CREDITS: Co-Prod./Dir., *Opus 1, Number 1* (performing arts documentary), 1979; Co-Prod./Dir., *Music For Wilderness Lake* (performing arts documentary), 1980; Prod., *Making Overtures–The Story of a Community Orchestra* (performing arts documentary), 1984; Prod./Dir., *Music in the Midnight Sun* (performing arts documentary with the TSO), 1988; Prod./Dir., *Carnival of Shadows* (performance program), 1989; Prod./Dir., *Pictures on the Edge: Fandango* (dance performance program), 1992; Dir., *The Planets* (1-hr. skating special, featuring Paul & Isabelle Duchesnay), 1994; Dir., *Falling Down Stairs* (1 of a series of 6 1-hr. performance programs), 1994; Dir./Prod., *Dido and Aeneas* (1-hr. danced opera), 1995; numerous other film credits.

HONS: awards include Chicago, N.Y., San Francisco, Yorkton, Banff, 7 Geminis, an Oscar nomination, & 2 Int'l Emmys.

Willment, Jo-Anne H., B.A.,M.A. ■ 🎓

Lecturer, Psychology Department, UNIVERSITY OF WATERLOO, Waterloo, ON N2L 3G1 (519) 885-1211, EMAIL jwillmnt@watarts.uwaterloo.ca. Born Toronto 1954. **EDUC:** Univ. of Waterloo, B.A.(Psych. & Soc.) 1978; Univ. of Guelph, M.A.(Psych.) 1982; Ont. Institute for Studies in Educ., doctoral candidate 1990. **CAREER:** Psychometric, & Probation & Parole Svcs, Ont. Ministry of Correctional Svcs, 1975-80; Special Projects Officer, Educ. & Student Svcs, Niagara Coll. of Applied Arts & Technology, 1980-86; Curriculum & Instructional Designer, 1986-87; Advisor on Teaching & Learning, Teaching Resources & Continuing Educ. Office, Univ. of Waterloo, 1988-96. **SELECTED PUBLICATIONS:** "Social-psychological and Demographic Characteristics of Unemployed Adolescents: Implications for Counselling," with N.E. McCardell in *The School Guidance Worker*, J. Morris (Toronto: Univ. of Toronto Press, 1984); "Innovative Policies and Practices for Human Resource Development in Canadian Community Colleges," with N.E. McCardell (*Professional File 1* Spring 1987); "Roundtable of faculty teaching first-year courses," with P. Lockhart (*Teaching and Learning in Higher Education* Dec. 1994); various book chapters, articles, conference papers & teaching resources. **AFFIL:** Society for Teaching & Learning in Higher Education (Steering Committee); Canadian Psychological Association; Professional Women's Association (Pres.); Canadian Association for Distance Education. **HONS:** Prov. of Alta. Grad. Scholarship, 1979-80; Univ. of Guelph Grad. Scholarship, 1980-82; Ont. Institute for Studies in Educ. Scholarship, 1994-95. **INTERESTS:** travel; hiking; photography

Wilson, Budge Marjorie MacGregor, B.A., Dip.Ed. ✇ 📜 📖

Writer. North West Cove, R.R. 1, Hubbards, NS B0J 1T0 (902) 228-2994. Born Halifax 1927. m. Alan Wilson. 2 ch. Glynis Wilson Boultbee; Andrea Kathryn Wilson. **EDUC:** Dalhousie Univ., B.A. 1949, Dip.Ed. 1953; Univ. of Toronto, grad. studies in English Lit. 1949-51. **CAREER:** Teacher, Halifax Ladies' Coll., 1951-52; Librarian & artist, Boys' & Girls' House, Toronto, 1953-54; various positions, Institute of Child Study, Univ. of Toronto, 1955, 1958-60; nursery sch. Teacher, Wolfville, N.S., 1956-57; illustrator, 3 books on commission, Univ. of Toronto Press, 1958-60; fitness instructor, Halifax & Peterborough, 1968-88; writer, 1984 to date. **SELECTED PUBLICATIONS:** 11 books for children & young adults incl. *Oliver's Wars* & *Lorinda's Diary* (Toronto: Stoddart),*Thirteen Never Changes* & *Breakdown* (Toronto: Scholastic, 1989) & *Cassandra's Driftwood* (Lawrencetown Beach, N.S.: Pottersfield Press, 1994); 5 books for adults, incl. *The Courtship*, *The Leaving* & *Cordelia Clark*, short stories (Toronto: Stoddart/Anansi); short stories in various periodicals & anthologies. **AFFIL:** Writers' Union of Canada; Writers' Federation of N.S.; Canadian Society of Children's Authors, Illustrators & Performers; Canadian Authors' Association. **HONS:** University Women's Club of Montreal Prize, 1948-49; 1st Prize, Short Adult Fiction Category, CBC Annual Literary Competition, *The Leaving*, 1981; 2nd Prize, Chatelaine Short Story Contest, *The Metaphor*, 1983; 1st Prize, Short Adult Fiction Category, Atlantic Writing Competition, *My Cousin Clarette*, 1986; City of Dartmouth Book Award (Fiction), *The Leaving*, 1991; YA Book Award, Canadian Library Association, *The Leaving*, 1991; *The Leaving*, shortlisted for Commonwealth Prize for Best Book in the Canada-Caribbean reg., 1991; Marianna Dempster Award, Canadian Authors' Association (N.S.), 1992; Ann Connor Brimer Award, N.S. Library Association, *Oliver's Wars*, 1993; various other awards. **INTERESTS:** people, young & old. **MISC:** recipient, various grants. **COMMENT:** *"Full-time fiction writer since 1984. Travels widely, speaking in schools and universities, and to gatherings of teachers and librarians. Writes for children and adults."*

Wilson, Gale, B.A.,M.A.,M.B.A. $ 📺

Strategic Planning and Marketing Consultant, 49 De Vere Gardens, Toronto, ON M5M 3E6 (416) 484-8404. Born Boston 1959. m. Robert F. Wilson. 1 ch. Christopher E.S. Wilson. **EDUC:** U.C.L.A., B.A.(Mass Comm.) 1981; The Wharton Sch., M.B.A.(Mktg Mgmt) 1990; The Lauder Institute, M.A.(Int'l Studies) 1990. **CAREER:** Sr. Ed. & Copywriter, INDAX consumer videotex svc, Cox Communications, Inc., 1982-84; Program Dir. & Research Analyst, videotex bus. unit, Gartner Group Inc., 1984-87; independent consultant, interactive media, 1987-88; Consultant, Hachette S.A., 1989; Sr. Mgr, Strategic Planning & Mktg American Express Canada, Inc., 1991-93. **AFFIL:** The Power Plant Contemporary Art Gallery (Dir., Futures & Fundraising Committees). **HONS:** American Women in Radio & Television, 1980. **COMMENT:** *"I am currently enjoying the challenge of full-time motherhood. In the future I plan to resume my career in strategic planning/marketing in international media."*

Wilson, Hilda E., A.P.R.,C.P.S. $ 📺 ♥
Chairman and Chief Executive Officer, THE HILDA WILSON GROUP, 2200 Yonge St., Ste. 1002, Toronto, ON M4S 2C6 (416) 489-3131, FAX 489-5864. Chairman and Chief Executive Officer, HILWIL INVESTMENTS INC. & INVESTOR RELATIONS CANADA LTD. Born Ont. 1926. d. 2 ch. Stephen Lawrence, Michael Douglas. **CAREER:** Chair & CEO, The Hilda Wilson Group & Investor Relations Canada Ltd., 1965 to date. **SELECTED PUBLICATIONS:** *Canadian Public Relations, Some Perspectives*, co-ed. (Fitzhenry & Whiteside). **AFFIL:** Public Relations Society of America (A.P.R.); Canadian Public Relations Society (C.P.S.); Professional Secretaries' Institute ; North York Symphony (VP, Fundraising); Canadian Council for Aboriginal Business (Hon. Dir.). **HONS:** Lamp of Learning, Canadian Public Relations Society; The Hilda Wilson Fellowship, McLuhan Centre, Univ. of Toronto.

Wilson, Joan M., B.Comm.,M.B.A. $
Vice-President and Secretary, MOORE CORPORATION LIMITED, 1 First Canadian Place, P.O. Box 78, Ste. 7200, Toronto, ON M5X 1G5 (416) 364-2600, FAX 364-3364. Born Toronto 1956. w. 1 ch. Thomas Naraindas. **EDUC:** York Univ., B.Comm.(Acctg & Econ.) 1979; York Univ., M.B.A.(Int'l Bus.) 1985. **CAREER:** Asst. to Corp. Sec., Moore Corporation Limited, 1982-83; Fin. Analyst, Europe, 1983-85; Supervisor, Acctg, Moore Business Products, Canada, 1985-87; Mgr, Acctg, Moore Business Forms and Systems, Canada, 1987-90; Asst. Sec., Moore Corporation Limited, 1990-91; Sec., 1991-93; VP & Sec., 1993 to date. **AFFIL:** A.I.E.S.E.C. (Pres., Canada 1979-80; Int'l Sec. Gen. 1980-81); American Society of Corporate Secretaries; Canadian Corporate Shareholders' Services Association; Board of Trade; Adelaide Club. **INTERESTS:** travel; int'l affairs; music & fitness; spending time with my son.

Wilson, Laurel Lynne, C.I.M.,C.P.P. $ ☝
Director of Purchasing, LAIDLAW WASTE SYSTEMS, 3221 North Service Rd., Burlington, ON L7R 3Y8 (905) 336-1800, FAX 336-8177. Born Winnipeg. s. 3 ch. Michael, Cheryl, Charlene. **EDUC:** Mohawk Coll.; McMaster Univ., C.I.M.(Bus.); Univ. of Western Ontario, C.P.P.(Purchasing). **CAREER:** Instructor, Purchasing, Mohawk Coll.; Dir. of Purchasing, Laidlaw Waste Systems. **AFFIL:** Junior Achievement Burlington (Bd. of Gov.); Junior Achievement Canada (Bd. of Gov.); Hamilton Harbour Commission (Bd.). **INTERESTS:** sailing. **MISC:** 1st woman appointee for the Hamilton Harbour Commission since enacted by Parliament in 1912. **COMMENT:** *"As a single parent raised three children while gaining my education. Hard working, determined and highly energetic person. Enjoy life to its fullest."*

Wilson, Lori, B.N.,R.N. ■ ⊕
Clinical Practice Coordinator, Nursing Education Department, ALBERTA CHILDREN'S HOSPITAL, 1820 Richmond Rd. S.W., Calgary, AB T2T 5C7 (403) 229-7840, FAX 229-7021. Born Edmonton 1962. m. Derek. **EDUC:** Univ. of Calgary, B.N. 1984. **CAREER:** Staff Nurse, Alberta Children's Hospital, 1984-88; Staff Nurse, Peter Lougheed Centre, Emergency Dept., Alberta Children's Hospital, 1988-91; Sessional Instructor, Pediatrics, Univ. of Calgary, 1989-90; Nurse Mgr, U Cluster, Alberta Children's Hospital, 1991-96. **AFFIL:** Alberta Association of Registered Nurses; Allergy Asthma Association of Alberta (Bd. 1990-93; volunteer); Alberta Pediatric Nurses' Interest Group; Alberta Standardbred Horse Association (volunteer). **HONS:** Louise M. McKinnon Scholarship for Potential Nursing Personality, Univ. of Calgary, 1983. **INTERESTS:** active sports enthusiast; Standardbred race horses; reading; educational courses/events. **MISC:** developed asthma educ. program; keynote speaker, Allergy Asthma Association Conference, 1993; assisted in revising nat'l Registered Nurse exams, 1992. **COMMENT:** *"I have always been a highly motivated, enthusiastic person who is driven by a need to contribute as much as I can to this world. I am devoted to the profession of nursing and have striven to develop many varied nursing skills. I am a patient advocate and, particularly, a child advocate."*

Wilson, Norma, B.Sc.,M.Sc.,P.Geo. ■ ✊ 🎭
Executive Director, OUTDOOR RECREATION COUNCIL OF BRITISH COLUMBIA, 1367 W. Broadway, Ste. 334, Vancouver, BC V6H 4A9 (604) 737-3058, FAX 38-7175, EMAIL norma.w@deepcove.com. Born Edmonton. **EDUC:** Univ. of British Columbia, B.Sc.(Biol./Geology) 1974, M.Sc.(Natural Resource Planning) 1989. **CAREER:** geologist, mineral exploration, various companies, 1975-86; Exec. Dir., Outdoor Recreation Council of B.C., 1992 to date; Sessional Lecturer, Fall Term, Fac. of Forestry, Univ. of British Columbia, 1995. **AFFIL:** Association of B.C. Professional Foresters (Lay Mbr. of Council); Association of Professional Engineers & Geoscientists of B.C. (P.Geo.); Canadian Parks & Wilderness Society (Past Chair, B.C. Chapter); Whitehorse Mining Initiative (Land Access Issue Group); McGregor Model Forest (Tech. Steering Committee); Advisory Forum, CORE (Commission

of Resources & Environment) Land Use Goals & Policies; Mineral Exploration Code for B.C. (Rewrite Committee). INTERESTS: resource-use issues; protected-areas mgmt.

Wilson, Ruth, M.D. ■ 🐟 ⊕
Professor and Head, Department of Family Medicine, Family Medical Centre, QUEEN'S UNIVERSITY, 220 Bagot St., Bag 8888, Kingston, ON K7L 5E9 (613) 549-3400, FAX 544-9899, EMAIL wilsonrw@post.queensu.ca. Born Winnipeg 1952. m. Dr. R. Ian Casson. 5 ch. EDUC: Fac. of Medicine, Univ. of Toronto, M.D. 1976. CAREER: Rotating Intern, North York General Hospital, 1976-77; Family Medicine Resident, St. Michael's Hospital, 1977-78; Family Physician, Sioux Lookout, Ont., 1979-80; Family Physician, Bella Coola, B.C., 1980-89; Clinical Instructor, Dept. of Family Medicine, Memorial Univ., 1983; Family Physician, The Hugh Allen Clinic, Sioux Lookout, 1984-86; Family Physician, Baie Verte Peninsula Health Centre, Nfld., 1985-89; Programs Medical Officer, Sioux Lookout Zone Hospital, 1986-87; Co-Medical Dir., 1987-89; Lecturer, Sioux Lookout Program, Dept. of Family & Community Medicine, Univ. of Toronto, 1988-89; Asst. Prof., Dept. of Family Medicine, Queen's Univ., 1989-91; Coord., Queen's Univ., Moose Factory Program, 1989-92; Acting Dir., Student Health Svc, Queen's Univ., 1993-94; Assoc. Prof. & Head, Dept. of Family Medicine, Queen's Univ., 1991 to date; Full Prof., 1996 to date. SELECTED PUBLICATIONS: *Toward Improving Health Care Delivery for Ontario Citizens: Third Year Residency Positions in Family Medicine*, with W.W. Rosser et al (1992); "Diptheria in Immunized Populations," with R.I. Casson (*New England Journal of Medicine* 319(7) 1988); "Babes in the Woods: Teaching the Use of the Vacuum Extractor," with R.I. Casson (*Canadian Family Physician* 36 1990); "Is Abuse a Feminist Issue?" (*Canadian Medical Association Journal* 147(11) 1992); "Childbirth in the North: A qualitative study in the Moose Factory Zone," with G. Webber (*Canadian Family Physician* 39 1993); "Psychological and Cultural Issues Surrounding Relocation of Native Canadians for Renal Dialysis," with L. Krefting, P. Sutcliffe & L. vanBussel (*Canadian Family Physician* 40 1994); numerous other publications. AFFIL: Canadian Medical Association; Teachers of Family Medicine (Exec. Committee of Section); Committee of Ontario Heads of Family Medicine; Council of Faculties of Medicine of Ontario; Ontario Medical Association (Committee on Women's Health Issues); Coll. of Family Physicians of Canada (Fellow); Queen's Theological Coll. (Bd. Mbr.); Hotel Dieu Hospital (Strategic Planning Committee; Chair, Medical Advisory Committee); Kingston General Hospital (Medical Advisory Committee). HONS: J.W. Billes Entrance Scholarship, Univ. of Toronto, 1970; Canada 125 Medal, 1993; Best Scientific Poster, Annual Scientific Assembly, Coll. of Family Physicians of Canada, 1994; nominated, Women in Medicine Leadership Dev. Award, Association of American Medical Colleges, 1994; winner, D.I. Rice Award, College of Family Physicians of Canada, 1995/96. INTERESTS: literacy; cross-cultural work. MISC: numerous invited & peer-reviewed presentations; recipient, various grants.

Wilson, Stephanie Ruth, M.D., F.R.C.P.(c) ⊕ 🐟 👗
Head, Division of Ultrasound, Department of Radiology, THE TORONTO HOSPITAL, 200 Elizabeth St., Toronto, ON M5G 2C4 (416) 340-4800, ext. 3253, FAX 340-3390. Professor, Faculty of Medicine, UNIVERSITY OF TORONTO. Born Lethbridge, Alta. 1946. m. Ken Wilson. 2 ch. EDUC: Univ. of Alberta, Fac. of Medicine, M.D. 1970. CAREER: Rotating Internship, Foothills Hospital, Calgary, 1970-71; Radiology Resident, 1971-73; Radiology Resident, Toronto General Hospital, 1973-75; Head, Div. of Ultrasound, Dept. of Radiology, Sunnybrook Hospital, 1975-82; Head, Div. of Ultrasound, Dept. of Radiology and Diagnostic Imaging, University of Alberta Hospitals, 1982-84; Head, Div. of Ultrasound, Dept. of Radiology, Toronto General Hospital, 1984-91; Head, Div. of Ultrasound, Dept. of Radiology, The Toronto Hospital, 1991 to date. SELECTED PUBLICATIONS: multiple run, reviewed publications including *Diagnostic Ultrasound*, yearbook, ed. with C. Rumack and W. Charboneau (Mosby Medical Publishers, 1991) and well as "The Gastrointestinal Tract," primary author; "Sonography of the Hollow Viscera," *Gastrointestinal Radiology*, ed. R.M. Gome. I Lauer and M.S. Levine (Philadelphia: W.B. Saunders Company, 1994); "The Acute Abdomen of Gastrointestinal Tract Origin: Sonographic Evaluation," *Alimentary Tract Radiology*, vol. II, ed. P.C. Freeny and G.W. Stevenson (Mosby Medical Publishers, 1994). EXHIBITIONS: "Transvaginal US and Duplex Doppler of Persistent Trophoblastic Neoplasia," RSNA, 1994. AFFIL: Canadian Association of Radiologists (mbr, various committees; Past Pres.); Radiology Society of North America (Ad Hoc Strategic Planning Committee and First VP); American Institute of Ultrasound in Medicine; Ontario Medical Association; Canadian Medical Association: Society of Gastrointestinal Radiologists; American Roent-

gen Ray Society; Society of Radiologists in Ultrasound. **HONS:** Colin Woolf Teaching Award, 1992; Top 10 Teachers, University of Toronto, 1992, 1993, 1994, 1995, 1996; RSNA Certificate of Merit for Scientific Exhibit, 1994. **INTERESTS:** golf; skiing. **MISC:** 1st woman Pres., Canadian Association of Radiologists

Wilson, The Very Reverend Lois M., O.C., O.Ont.,B.A.,M.Div.,D.D.,D.C.L., D.Hum.L.,L.L.D.,S.T.D. ☼ ✊ 🎓 ☝
Chancellor, LAKEHEAD UNIVERSITY, Thunder Bay, ON P7B 5E1. Born Winnipeg 1927. m. Rev. Dr. Roy Wilson. 4 ch. **EDUC:** United Coll. (now Univ. of Winnipeg), B.A.(Arts) 1947, B.D.(Theology) 1950, M.Div.(Theology) 1969. **CAREER:** ordained to Christian ministry, United Church of Canada, 1965; Pastor in team ministry with husband in congregations in Thunder Bay, Hamilton & Kingston, 17 yrs.; Pres., Canadian Council of Churches, 1976-79; Moderator, United Church of Canada, 1980-82; Co-Dir., Ecumenical Forum of Canada, 1983-88; Pres., World Council of Churches, 1983-91; McGeachy Sr. Scholar, United Church of Canada, 1989-91; Chair, Urban-Rural Mission (Canada), World Council of Churches, 1990-95; Consultant, Inter-Church Inter-Faith Committee, Presbyterian Church USA, 1991-93; Chancellor, Lakehead Univ., 1991-96. **SELECTED PUBLICATIONS:** *Like a Mighty River* (1981); *Turning the World Upside Down*, memoirs (1989); *Telling Her Story* (1992); *Miriam, Mary and Me* (1992); *Stories Seldom Told* (1996); numerous articles. **EDIT:** Advisory Bd., *Canadian Woman Studies Journal*, 1993; former editorial consultant, *The Grail–An Ecumenical Journal*. **AFFIL:** World Federalists (Canada) (Pres.); Canadian Civil Liberties Association (VP 1987 to date); UNIFEM (Nat'l VP); Canada's Environmental Assessment Review Bd. for the Concept of the Disposal of Nuclear Waste (mbr.); Canadian Automobile Workers (Public Review Bd.); Univ. of Victoria, Toronto (Bd. of Regents); Friends of Public Broadcasting (Bd. Mbr.); Social Planning Council, Metro Toronto (Community Assoc.); Ecumenical Development Cooperative Society (Patron); Centre for Studies in Religion & Society, Univ. of Victoria (Advisory Bd.). **PAST AFFIL:** Amnesty International (Councillor 1978-88); Canadian Institute for International Peace & Security (mbr. 1984-88); Refugee Status Advisory Committee, Gov't of Canada (mbr. 1985-89); Canadian Association of Adult Education (Bd. Mbr. 1986-89); New Directions (Patron 1989-92); Group of '78–Global Priorities for Canadians (Bd. Mbr. 1991-93). **HONS:** Order of Canada, 1984; Pearson Peace Prize, United Nations, Canada, 1984; World Federalist Peace Prize, 1984; Order of Ontario, 1991; Canada 125 Medal, 1992; honorary degrees from 11 universities. **MISC:** 1st woman Pres., Canadian Council of Churches; 1st woman Moderator, United Church of Canada; spokesperson at numerous nat'l & int'l events incl. UN conferences on disarmament, 1978, 1982; hon. mbr., Cdn Committee for 50th Anniversary of UN, 1993; travelled widely to all continents. **COMMENT:** *"Ministry focuses on human rights, peace, men/women, adult education, inter-faith dialogue, media, development, refugees and Native people."*

Wilson, Vera $
Realtor, OSBORNE REALTY, 294 Coronation Ave., Duncan, BC V9L 2T2 (604) 748-4443, FAX 748-4300. Born Lancashire, UK 1934. m. Frank Wilson. 2 ch. Sarah, Michael. **EDUC:** Bingley Coll., Yorkshire, UK, Teaching Diploma 1955; B.C. Real Estate Association, through Univ. of British Columbia, Licensed Real Estate Salesperson 1972, M.V.A.-Residential (Mkt Value Appraisal) 1994. **CAREER:** Teacher & Head of Girls, Phys. Educ. Dept. in large comprehensive sch., Buttershaw; Teacher, B.A.O.R., Dortmund, Germany, 1962-63; Teacher & Head of Girls, Phys. Educ. Dept., Mt. Prevost Jr. High Sch., 1968-71; Realtor, Cowichan Valley area, 1972 to date. **AFFIL:** Cowichan United Way (Bd. of Dir.); Duncan Business & Professional Women's Club. **HONS:** Vancouver Island Real Estate Bd. Medallion Winner for Outstanding Achievement, 1989, 1990, 1991,1994, 1995; Vancouver Island Real Estate Bd. Multiple Listing Service Award Winner, 1979, 1980; Duncan Business & Professional Women's Club Woman of the Year for Outstanding Professional & Public Service in the Community, 1992. **INTERESTS:** theatre; music; sports. **COMMENT:** *"I am a very busy realtor, working in a small but extremely productive independent real estate office. I love my job and am successful at it."*

Wilton, Roberta, B.A.,M.A.,Ph.D. ■ ✊ $
President, CANADIAN SECURITIES INSTITUTE, 121 King St. W., Ste. 1550, Toronto, ON M5H 3T9 (416) 862-8736, FAX 359-0486, EMAIL roberta@csi.ca. **EDUC:** Univ. of Western Ontario, B.A., M.A.; Univ. of Toronto, Ph.D. **CAREER:** Securities Consultant; Dir. of Mktg & Comm., The Toronto Stock Exchange, 1982-90; Sr. VP, Canadian Securities Institute, 1992-93; Exec. VP, 1993-94; Pres., 1994 to date. **AFFIL:** Investor Learning Centre of Canada (Pres. & Dir. 1996 to date); Financial Planners Standards Council of Canada (V-Chair 1996

to date); Board of Trade of Metropolitan Toronto (Chair, Educ. Committee 1994 to date). **COMMENT:** *"People today need to know about investing in order to financially prepare for retirement and we are dedicated to improving aptitude in this difficult subject. My challenge as President of both the CSI and our registered charity, the Investor Learning Centre (ILC), is to ensure our educational products and services, serving more than 30,000 people annually, are the right ones for our markets and are delivered effectively and efficiently in a business-like fashion."*

Wineberg, Tami, B.F.A. $ 🎭

Director of Publicity/Promotions, **MGM/ UNITED ARTISTS DISTRIBUTION OF CANADA**, 720 King St. W., Ste. 611, Toronto, ON M4V 2T3 (416) 703-9579, FAX 504-3821. Born Toronto. s. **EDUC:** York Univ., B.F.A.(Film Prod.) 1984. **CAREER:** Asst. Prod., Broadcast Commercials, Ronalds-Reynolds Advertising; freelance, 1987; Coord., Publicity & Promotions, MGM/UA Distribution of Canada, 1987-89; Mgr, 1989-90; Dir., 1990 to date. **INTERESTS:** screenwriting; tennis; movies. **COMMENT:** *"It's a dog eat dog world out there, but you don't have to be a bitch to succeed."*

Winsor, Mary Pickard, B.A.,M.Phil., Ph.D. ■ 🎓 📜 ⚛

Professor, Institute for the History and Philosophy of Science and Technology (IHPST), **UNIVERSITY OF TORONTO**, Victoria College, 73 Queen's Park Cres. E., Toronto, ON M5S 1K7 (416) 978-6280, FAX (416) 978-3003, EMAIL mwinsor@chass.utoronto.ca. Born New York City 1943. **EDUC:** Radcliffe Coll., Harvard Univ., B.A.(magna cum laude, Hist. & Sci.) 1965; Yale Univ., M.Phil. 1969, Ph.D.(Hist. of Sci. & Medicine) 1971. **CAREER:** Lecturer, Institute for the Hist. & Phil. of Sci. & Technology, Univ. of Toronto, 1969-70; Asst. Prof., 1970-74; Assoc. Prof., 1974-93; Dir., 1986-91; Prof. 1993 to date. **SELECTED PUBLICATIONS:** *Starfish, Jellyfish, and the Order of Life: Issues in Nineteenth-century Science* (New Haven: Yale Univ. Press, 1976); *Reading the Shape of Nature: Comparative Zoology at the Agassiz Museum* (Univ. of Chicago Press, 1991); various chapters in books, articles in refereed journals & book reviews. **AFFIL:** Victoria Coll. (Fellow); Canadian Society for the History & Philosophy of Science (Pres. 1990-93). **INTERESTS:** horseback riding; scuba diving

Winston, Helene 🎭 📜 📖

Actor and Writer (retired). Poet. c/o The Characters, 150 Carlton St., Toronto, ON M5A 2K1 (416) 964-8522, FAX 964-8206. Born Winnipeg 1922. w. Nathan Bershadsky (dec. 1957), John Deacon Steiner (dec. 1990). **EDUC:** St. John's Technical High, matriculated 1937-38. **CAREER:** actor from 1st professional acting role with Esse Ljungh on CBC (Winnipeg) & subsequent writing of radio plays, to Peggy Green's Professional Company & John Hirsch's Children's Theatre; then Stratford, Toronto, N.Y. & L.A. **SELECTED CREDITS:** numerous feature films incl.: *Life Stinks*; *The Devil & Max Devlin*, *Return to Witch Mountain*, *The Shaggy D.A.*, *Freaky Friday*, *A Boy & His Dog*, *Our Time*, *What's the Matter with Helen?*, *The Brotherhood of Satan*, *Double Trouble*; numerous roles on TV incl.: *Silver Spoons*, *Mary Tyler Moore*, *Sanford and Son*, *The Monkees*, *The Danny Kaye Show*, best known as Gladys King (111 eps.), *The King of Kensington* (series), 1975-80; numerous stage appearances incl.: *Milk & Honey* (Broadway), *Time of Your Life* (Broadway); *The Dybbuk* (Centre Theatre Group); *Major Barbara* (Centre Theatre Group); *Yeats & Co.* (Centre Theatre Group); *Night of the Iguana* (Actors Workshop, San Francisco); *Taming of the Shrew* (Stratford); *Measure for Measure* (Stratford); *Oedipus* (Stratford); *Henry V* (Stratford); *Roar Like A Dove* (Crest Theatre, Toronto); *The Matchmaker* (Neptune Theatre, Halifax); *Hello Dolly* (Rainbow Stage, Winnipeg); *Hotel Paradiso*, *Crabdance*, *After the Fall*, *Lulu Street* (Manitoba Theatre Centre); *Look Ahead!* (Theatre 77, Winnipeg); *The Music Man* (dinner theatre); *Harry & Thelma in the Woods* (dinner theatre); *Nina* (summer stock); *I am a Camera* (summer stock); *Tobacco Road* (summer stock). **SELECTED PUBLICATIONS:** two dozen radio plays written & aired on the CBC, 1945-56, incl.: *Kelly's Cat*; *Abel's Girl*; *The Strange History of the Satisfied Man*; *Women with a Shopping Bag*; *Rosie Leprechaun*; *Three Men, Some Gold and a Promise*; *Mr. Winkle and the Boards*; *Murietta was a Bandit*; *The Girl in the Red Skirt*; *Miss Murphy Abroad Among the Mortals*; *The Magnificent Infant*, with John Hirsch; *The Box of Smiles*, with John Hirsch. **AFFIL:** Actors' Fund of America; ACTRA; AFTRA; SAG; Actors' Equity (Canada & US); Canadian Equity (Chair 1956-57); ACRA not ACTRA, Winnipeg (Founding Mbr.); Southern California Garden Club (former Bd. Mbr.); Muses of Apollo. **HONS:** Best Actress, Manitoba Drama Festival, 1955; Maurice Rosenfeld Award for outstanding newcomer to TV & films, 1956; Best Character Actress, Liberty TV Awards, 1959; nomination, Best Character Actress, Liberty TV Awards, 1960; nomination for Gladys King role in the *King of Kensington*, 1975-80; Honourable Mention for Poem (*Counting*), World of Poetry, 1988; Golden

Poet Award (*Counting*), 1989; Silver Poet Award, 1990; Honourary Citizen of Winnipeg, 1985; Honourable Mention, YMCA Peace Play *Hear My Voice*, for radio; One of Canada's Best Dressed Women, Liberty Fashion Poll, 1962. **INTERESTS:** sculpture; poetry; duplicate bridge; poker; creativity. **COMMENT:** *"Love of theatre carried me through a distinguished Canadian career and a modest American one. My own poetry says it: 'When death, my ultimate lover, opens his arms to carry me to sweet oblivion, let me surrender as joyously as I have lived.'"*

Winters, Heather Anne, AIIC,CAIB,CCIB, CRM ■ ✊ $

Executive Director, INSURANCE BROKERS' ASSOCIATION OF NOVA SCOTIA, 14 Dufferin St., Bridgewater, NS B4V 2E8 (902) 543-5569, FAX 543-8508. 2 ch. Nicole, Scott. **EDUC:** Carleton Univ., 1971; Insurance Institute of Canada, Assoc.(Hons.); Cdn Certified Insur. Broker; Cdn Accredited Insur. Broker; Cdn Risk Mgr. **CAREER:** Office Mgr, Lunenburg Insurance; Exec. Dir., Insurance Brokers' Association of N.S., 1990 to date. **AFFIL:** Insurance Brokers' Association of Canada (Visions Committee, ACSR Dev. Committee); N.S. Insurance Women's Association; Insurance Institute of Canada; Bridgewater & Area Chamber of Commerce; N.S. Gymnastics Association; South Shore Kippers Gymnastics Club. **HONS:** Cam Mitchinson Award. **INTERESTS:** coastal sailing; music. **COMMENT:** *"Life brings rewards and achievements when you strive to be THE BEST at any activity in which you participate, and when you don't compromise principles."*

Wiseman, Sandra (Sandi) ✏ 📖

Reporter, *KAMLOOPS DAILY NEWS*, 393 Seymour St., Kamloops, BC V2C 6P6 (604) 372-2331, FAX 374-3884. Born Glasgow, Scotland 1944. m. Clarence. 2 ch. Todd William Wiseman, Kelly Ann Wiseman. **EDUC:** Simon Fraser Univ., Health & Fitness Certificate; Univ. Coll. of the Cariboo, B.A.(English) in progress. **CAREER:** public rel'ns, Kamloops YM-YWCA, 1980-84; Co-Founder, *Kamloops This Week* (newspaper), 1987; Reporter, *Cariboo Press*, 1987-94; Co-Founder, Modern Man Clothing Store, 1988; Reporter, *Kamloops Daily News*, 1994 to date; Sch. Trustee, S.D. 24, elected 3 terms. **DIRECTOR:** Wisefam Corporation (Sec.). **AFFIL:** B.C. School Trustee Association (Pres., Mainline Cariboo Branch 2 yrs.); Kamloops YM-YWCA (Founder, Kamloops Women of Distinction; Chair, 25th Anniversary Year); Kamloops Art Gallery (Bd.; Founder, Alley Art Fundraiser); Thompson Enterprise Centre (Bd.); 1995 Canada Summer Games (VP, Media & Community 1989-93). **HONS:** nominee, Woman of the Year, BPW, 1994; First Place, Feature Writing, Health Issues, B.C. & Yukon Community Newspaper Association, 1992; Third Place, 1993. **INTERESTS:** writing; reading; hiking; conversation; cooking. **MISC:** leader of reg'l drive & presentation to Senate on GST issue; currently writing a novel. **COMMENT:** *"A caring wife and mother of two successful adult children, I feel at 50 years old I'm just in mid-stream of my own personal career path, with many more adventures to come."*

Wish, Judy ■ ✊

Director, Government Relations, CANADIAN PETROLEUM PRODUCTS INSTITUTE, 202 - 6 Ave. S.W., Ste. 1610, Calgary, AB T2P 2R9 (403) 266-7565, FAX 269-9367. Born Willingdon, Alta. **CAREER:** Office of the Premier, Gov't of Alta., 1971-78; Dir., Ottawa Office, Gov't of Alta,, 1978-84; Dir., Public Affairs, Petro-Canada, 1984-96. **AFFIL:** Petroleum Communications Foundation (Past Pres.); Alberta Theatre Projects (Alumni); Expo 2005 (Comm. Exec.). **INTERESTS:** theatre; politics; sailing.

Wisser, Arlene, B.Sc., C.F.A. ■ $

Vice-President and Portfolio Manager, CASSELS BLAIKIE INVESTMENT MANAGEMENT LIMITED., 33 Yonge St., Ste. 200, Toronto, ON M5E 1S8 (416) 814-4052, FAX 814-4084, EMAIL cbim@ntrust.com. Born Montreal 1948. m. Bo Wisser. **EDUC:** Sir George Williams Univ. (now Concordia), B.Sc.(Math) 1969; Canadian Securities Course 1971; C.F.A. 1981. **CAREER:** Asst. to Portfolio Mgr, Equities, Northern Telecom Pension Fund, 1969-76; Asst. to Portfolio Mgr, Mortgages, 1976-78; Mortgage Analyst, Ontario Municipal Employees' Retirement Bd., 1978-79; Asst. to VP, Investments, IDS, MN, US, 1979-80; Portfolio Mgr/Asst. VP/VP, Pension Investments, National Trust, 1981-96. **AFFIL:** Toronto Society of Financial Analysts; Association for Investment Management & Research. **COMMENT:** *"Institutional money management career started in 1970 and currently involves affecting Canadian and US equity portfolios totalling $500 million under management at National Trust. Member of Asset Mix, Fixed Income and Equity Committees."*

Witmer, The Hon. Elizabeth, MPP,B.A. 🍁

Member of the Provincial Parliament and Minister of Labour, GOVERNMENT OF ONTARIO, 400 University Ave., 14th fl., Toronto, ON M7A 1T7 (416) 326-7600, FAX 326-1449. Born Schiedam, Holland 1946. m. Cameron Witmer. 2 ch. **EDUC:** Univ. of Western

Ontario, B.A. 1965; Univ. of Waterloo, 1968. **CAREER:** secondary sch. Teacher, West Lorne, London, Guelph, 1968-89; Trustee, Waterloo County Bd. of Educ., 1980-90; Chair, Waterloo County Bd. of Educ., 1985-89; elected MPP (Waterloo N.), 1990 to date; PC Critic for Labour & Women's Issues; Deputy Chair of Caucus; Min. of Labour. **AFFIL:** Canadian Federation of University Women; Chamber of Commerce; Confederation Club. **HONS:** Kitchener-Waterloo Woman of the Year; Canada 125 Medal, 1992. **INTERESTS:** skiing; travelling; reading; gardening. **MISC:** Chair, Prov. PC Steering Committee, 1995 election campaign.

Witte, Margaret K., B.Sc.,M.Sc. $
President and Chief Executive Officer, ROYAL OAK MINES. Born Fallon, Nevada 1953. **EDUC:** MacKay School of Mines, University of Nevada, B.Sc.(Chem.), M.Sc.(Metallurgical Eng.). **CAREER:** Asst. Dir., Metallurgy, Ontario Research Foundation, 1979-81; Pres., Witteck Development, 1981-86; Pres. & CEO, Neptune Resources Corp., 1986-89. **DIRECTOR:** Highwood Resources Ltd.; Royal Oak Mines Inc.; Talisman Energy Inc.; TransCanada PipeLines Limited. **AFFIL:** The Mining Association of Canada; Prospectors' & Developers' Association of Canada, (PDAC); Canadian Institute of Mining, Metallurgy & Petroleum. **HONS:** "Mining Man of the Year," *Northern Miner*, 1991; Woman of Distinction Award, YWCA, 1991; Viola McMillan Developer of the Year Award, PDAC, 1994; Woman of the Year, *Chatelaine* Magazine, 1994.

Wittmack, Beverly C., B.Comm., C.A. ■ $
President, HUMFORD MANAGEMENT INC., 2200 Park Square, 10001 Bellamy Hill, Edmonton, AB T5J 3B6 (403) 426-4960, FAX 425-1184. **EDUC:** Univ. of Alberta, B.Comm. 1973. **CAREER:** Audit Supervisor, Touche Ross and Co., 1975-78; various positions to VP, Real Estate, Humford Developments Ltd., 1978-87; Pres. & CEO, 1987-95; Pres., Humford Management Inc., 1996 to date. **DIRECTOR:** Edmonton Telephones Corporation. **AFFIL:** Alberta Institute of Chartered Accountants (Gov., CA Education Foundation); Edmonton Chamber of Commerce (Dir. 1995); Alberta Economic Development Authority (Econ. Council 1995); Rotary Club of Edmonton, Glenora.

Wolfe, Jeanne M., B.Sc.,M.Sc.,M.A. 🎓 ⚛
Professor and Director, School of Urban Planning, MCGILL UNIVERSITY, 815 Sherbrooke St. W, Montreal, QC H3A 2K6 (514) 398-4077, FAX 398-8376, EMAIL jeannew@urbarc.lan.mcgill.ca. Born Brigstock, UK 1934. m. Leonhard Scott Wolfe. 2 ch. **EDUC:** London Univ., B.Sc.(Geog.) 1956; Univ. of Western Ontario, M.Sc.(Geog.) 1959; McGill Univ., M.A.(Community Planning) 1961. **CAREER:** Planner, Planning Dept., City of Montreal, 1964-69; Visiting Research Fellow, Univ. de Strasbourg, 1969-70; Sr. Planner, Que. Ministry of Mun. Affairs, 1970-73; Asst. Prof., Sch. of Urban Planning, McGill Univ., 1973-76; Assoc. Prof., 1976-88; Prof., 1988 to date; Dir., 1988 to date. **SELECTED PUBLICATIONS:** *A Topographical Atlas of Montreal*, ed. with F. Dufaux (Montreal: McGill Univ., 1992); "Canada's Liveable Cities" (*Social Policy* 23(1) 1992); "Squatter Regularization: Problems and Prospects. A Case Study From Trinidad," with J.M. Glenn & Ronald P. Labossière (*Third World Planning Review* 15(3) 1993); "Our Common Past: An Interpretation of Canadian Planning History" (*Plan Canada* 1994); various other publications. **EDIT:** Ed. Bd., Plan Canada, 1980 to date; Ed. Bd., *Environments*, 1986 to date. **AFFIL:** Royal Geographical Society (Fellow); Ordre des urbanistes du Québec; Canadian Institute of Planners (Fellow); Canadian Institute of Planners (Chrm, Nat'l Bd. of Examiners); American Planning Association; International Society of City & Regional Planners; Société d'amélioration Milton-Parc (Conseil d'admin.). **HONS:** Shropshire County Scholarship; Gordon & Wilhemena McIntosh Prize in Geography, 1959; CMHC Fellowship, 1959-61, 1969-70.

Wolstenholme, Tanya E. ■■ ♡ ✊
Executive Director, THE ARTHRITIS SOCIETY, NEW BRUNSWICK DIVISION, 65 Brunswick St., Fredericton, NB E3B 1G5 (506) 452-7191, FAX 459-3925, EMAIL twolstenholme@nb.arthritis.ca. Born Fredericton 1967. s. **EDUC:** Univ. of New Brunswick, 1st yr. 1985; Univ. of Calgary, B.A.(Women's Studies) 1990. **CAREER:** Alumnae Rep., Villa Maria High Sch., Montreal, 1991-92; Exec. Dir., Harvest Jazz & Blues Festival, Fredericton, 1994-95. **INTERESTS:** women's issues; social issues; film & music industries. **COMMENT:** *"I enjoy working for a cause–it gives me the encouragement to keep going! I am a high-energy person who loves the personal interactions my job provides."*

Wong-Rieger, Durhane, B.A.,M.A., Ph.D. 🎓 ⊕
Associate Professor, Director of Human Resources Consultation Unit, Department of Psychology, UNIVERSITY OF WINDSOR, 401 Sunset Ave., Windsor, ON N9B 3P4 (519) 253-4232, FAX 973-7021, EMAIL dwr/@uwind-

sor.ca. Born Canton, China 1950. m. Francis
Rieger. 2 ch. Hilary Frances, Gabriel Alastair.
EDUC: Barnard Coll., B.A.(Psych.) 1974;
McGill Univ., M.A.(Psych.) 1978, Ph.D.
(Psych.) 1982. CAREER: Dir., Youth Svcs,
Alaska Children Svcs, Anchorage, 1975-77;
Lecturer, Cree Sch. Bd., St. James Bay, Que.,
1980-82; Asst. Prof., Oklahoma State Univ.,
1981-84; Visiting Prof., Univ. of Waterloo,
1989; Assoc. Prof., Univ. of Windsor, 1984 to
date; Dir., Hum. Res. Consultation Unit, 1985
to date. SELECTED PUBLICATIONS: *Social
Psychology: A Cognitive-Group Approach*,
with K. Amin & D.M. Taylor (Lexington MA:
Ginn 1979); "Self-identity and multiple group
membership," with D.M. Taylor (*Journal of
Cross-Cultural Psychology* 12 1981); "Interpretation and coping with threat in the context
of intergroup relations," with D.M. Taylor, D.
McKirnan & T. Bercusson (*The Journal of
Social Psychology* 117 1982); "Comparative
acculturation of Southeast Asian and Hispanic
immigrants and sojourners," with D. Quintana
(*Journal of Cross-Cultural Psychology* 18(3)
1987); *Profile of Women and Work in Windsor*
(Ontario: Women's Directorate of the Secretary
of State, 1990; *Hands-On Guide to Planning
and Evaluation* with J. David (Ottawa: Health
and Welfare Canada, 1993); "Causal Evalua-
tion of Impact of Support Workshop for HIV+
Men," with L. David (*Canadian Journal of
Public Health* 34(Supplement 1) 1993); *Inter-
national Management Research: Looking to the
Future* with F. Rieger (Berlin: Walter de
Gruyter and Co., 1993); "A Process Model of
Research in International Management," with
F. Rieger, in *International Management*, ed. B.J.
Punnet (London: Blackwell, 1995); *Interna-
tional Management Research: Looking to the
Future*, Japanese Translation, eds. D. Wong-
Rieger & F. Rieger (Berlin: Walter De Gruyter
and Co., 1995); "Migrant Managers," with F.
Rieger, *International Encyclopedia of Business
and Management* (London: Routledge, 1996);
various other publications. AFFIL: Canadian
Hemophilia Society (Pres.); Canadian Society
for Industrial/Organizational Psychology
(Pres.); Canadian Evaluation Society; Canadian
Psychological Association; Special Advisor on
Consumer Issues to Fed./Prov/Terr. Working
Group on Blood (1996). MISC: numerous
papers presented at professional meetings;
numerous consultations on hum. res.; numerous workshops given. COMMENT: *"Even if it
doesn't count, one has to play every game as if
it did."*

Wood, Diane L. 🐝
Secretary-Treasurer, BRITISH COLUMBIA GOV-
ERNMENT AND SERVICE EMPLOYEES UNION, 1607

Augusta Ave., Burnaby, BC V5A 4N9 (604)
291-9611, FAX 293-1369. Born Victoria, B.C.
1946. CAREER: various positions, Gov't of
B.C., 1970-87; leave of absence for duration of
union office, 1987 to date. UNION CAREER:
various elected positions, BCGEU, 1974-87;
Sec.-Treas., 1987 to date; Chair, Women's
Committee, to date; VP-at-Large, Canadian
Labour Congress, 1984 to date; Co-Chair of
Women's Committee, 1992 to date; VP, Exec.
Bd., Nat'l Union of Public & General Employ-
ees, to date; VP, B.C. Federation of Labour, to
date. DIRECTOR: British Columbia Rail.
AFFIL: Canadian Labour Force Development
Bd. (Dir); Public Services International (Cdn
Rep., Women's Committee; Inter-American
Reg'l Committee); B.C. Public Service Pension
(Advisory Bd.); Victoria Commonwealth
Games Society (Dir.). MISC: currently serving
7th term on the Canadian Labour Congress
Exec. Council; participated in the European
Community Commission Study Visit Program,
1985; represented C.L.C. in Cdn Delegation at
U.N. Conference on the Int'l Decade of
Women, Nairobi, Kenya, 1985 & U.N.
Women's Conference & Forum, Beijing, 1995.
COMMENT: *"I have dedicated my working life
to effect change for working people and to
bring about true equality for women in all
aspects of their lives."*

Wood, Janet M., B.Sc.,Ph.D. 🐝 ⊕ 🐝
Professor, Department of Microbiology, UNI-
VERSITY OF GUELPH, Guelph, ON N1G 2W1
(519) 824-4120, ext. 3866, FAX 837-1802,
EMAIL jwood@micro.uoguelph.ca. EDUC:
Univ. of Victoria, B.Sc.(Biochem.) 1969; Univ.
of Edinburgh, Ph.D.(Biochem.) 1972. CAREER:
Lab. Demonstrator, Univ. of Edinburgh, 1970-
72; Postdoctoral Fellow, Lab. of L.A. Heppel,
Cornell Univ., 1972-75; Research Assoc., Div.
of Biological Sciences, National Research
Council, 1975-76; Lecturer, Dept. of Biol., Car-
leton Univ., 1976; Asst. Prof., Dept. of Chem.,
Univ. of Guelph, 1977-82; Visiting Prof.
Molecular Biol. Institute, Univ. of California,
1983; Assoc. Prof., Dept. of Chem. &
Biochem., Univ. of Guelph, 1982-88; Prof.,
1988-90; Employment & Educ. Equity Coord.,
Office of the Pres., 1989-91; Prof., Dept. of
Microbiol., 1990 to date. SELECTED PUBLI-
CATIONS: numerous articles, research articles
& book chapters, incl. "Membrane Permeabil-
ity and Transport," with R.T. Voegele & E.V.
Marshall, *Bioenergetics: A Practical Approach*
(Oxford Univ. Press, 1995); "Genes encoding
osmoregulatory proline/betaine transporters
and the proline catabolic enzymes are present
and expressed in diverse clinical Escherichia coli
isolates," with D.E. Culham *et al* (Canadian

Journal of Microbiology (40) 1994); "Conformational change and membrane association of the PutA protein are coincident with reduction of its FAD cofactor by proline," with E.D. Brown (Journal of Biological Chemistry (268) 1993); "Osmoadaptation by rhizosphere bacteria," with K.J. Miller (Annual Review of Microbiology (50) 1996); various invited lectures & abstracts. AFFIL: Univ. of Guelph (various committees; Bd. of Dir.); American Society for Biochemistry & Molecular Biology; American Society for Microbiology; Biophysical Society; Canadian Biophysical Society; Canadian Society for Biochemistry & Molecular Biology; Canadian Society of Microbiologists. HONS: Distinguished Prof. Award, Univ. of Guelph, 1995. COMMENT: *"Janet M. Wood integrates university teaching with laboratory-based research on cellular osmoadaptation and urinary tract infection."*

Woodcock, Kathleen, B.A. ■ ⓜ ⌇

Practicum Assistant, Faculty of Social Work, WILFRID LAURIER UNIVERSITY, 75 University Ave. W., Waterloo, ON N2L 3C5 (519) 884-0710, FAX 888-9732, EMAIL kwoodcoc@machl.wlu.ca. President, CONFEDERATION OF ONTARIO UNIVERSITY STAFF ASSOCIATIONS. Born Petrolia, Ont. 1955. m. Robert Woodcock. 2 ch. Lauren Blakely, Mallory Elayne. EDUC: Wilfrid Laurier Univ., B.A.(Hist. & English) 1978. CAREER: Admin. Sec., Admin., Wilfrid Laurier Univ., 1986-89; Field Admin. Asst., Fac. of Social Work, 1989-93; Admin. Asst. to the Dean, Fac. of Social Work, 1993-96; Practicum Asst., Dept. of Social Work, 1996 to date. DIRECTOR: Advanced Detection Systems Inc. AFFIL: Wilfrid Laurier Univ. (Bd. of Gov.); Confederation of Ontario University Staff Associations (Pres.; VP 1992-93, 1993-94); Wilfrid Laurier Staff Association (Pres. 1990-91, 1991-92); The Royal Canadian Legion (mbr., Assoc. Voting, Branch 113).

Woodley, Erin ■ ■ ⓩ

Olympic Athlete. c/o Canadian Olympic Association. Born Mississauga, Ont. 1972. EDUC: currently studying English. SPORTS CAREER: started synchro, 1981; mbr., Cdn Nat'l Synchronized Swimming Team, 1989 to date. Olympic Games: Silver, team, 1996. World championships: 2nd, team, 1994. World jr. championships: 2nd, team, 1989. Commonwealth Games: 1st, duet, 1994. Canadian championships: 1st, duet, & 3rd, team, 1995; 1st, duet, & 2nd, team, 1994; 2nd, duet, & 2nd, team, 1993; 1st, team, 1992; 1st, team, 1991; 1st, team, 1990. Canada Games: 1st, solo, 1st, duet, & 1st, team, 1991. INTERESTS: cycling; reading.

Woodman, Catherine J., B.P.R. ⓢ

Director, Corporate and Public Affairs, MARITIME LIFE ASSURANCE COMPANY, 2701 Dutch Village Rd., Halifax, NS B3J 2X5 (902) 453-7124, FAX 453-7147, EMAIL mlaccpta@fox.nstn.ca. Born Halifax 1962. m. MacDara Woodman. 2 ch. EDUC: Mount Saint Vincent Univ., Bachelor of Public Rel'ns 1984. CAREER: Public Rel'ns Officer, Izaak Walton Killam Children's Hospital, 1984-89; Dir. of Public Rel'ns, 1989-94; Acting Chief of Protocol, Prov. of N.S., 1994; Dir., Corp. & Public Affairs, Maritime Life Assurance Company, 1994 to date. SELECTED PUBLICATIONS: "The Ethics of Public Relations" chapter (*Health Care Public Relations*, Canadian Hospital Association, 1995). AFFIL: Mount Saint Vincent Univ. Alumni (Dir.); Canadian Public Relations Society (Accredited; Pres., N.S. 1992); Metropolitan Halifax Chamber of Commerce; Canadian Health Care Public Relations Society (Past Pres., N.S.); Art Gallery of Nova Scotia. HONS: 7 awards from the Health Care Public Relations Association of Canada; 1 award from the Canadian Public Relations Society. INTERESTS: family; travelling; swimming; writing. MISC: frequent guest lecturer, Mount Saint Vincent Univ. Public Rel'ns program. COMMENT: *"I am a focused, resourceful, and diligent working mother. My greatest successes are coordinating the 1994 Queen's visit on behalf of the Province of Nova Scotia, achieving recognition in health care public relations, and now learning and gaining expertise in financial Public Relations."*

Woodruff, Janet, B.Sc.,M.B.A. ⓢ

Controller, UNION GAS LIMITED, 50 Keil Dr. N., Chatham, ON N7M 5M1 (519) 436-5480, FAX 436-4667. Born 1957. m. Graham. 2 ch. EDUC: Univ. of Western Ontario, B.Ed. 1979; York Univ., M.B.A. 1984. CAREER: Audit Mgr, Clarkson Gordon, Toronto, 1988; Supervisor, Fin. Acctg, Centra Gas, 1988-89; Mgr, Taxation & Acctg, Union Gas Limited, 1989-91; Mgr, Fin. & Taxation, 1992; Mgr, Fin. Svcs, 1992-93; Cont., 1994 to date. AFFIL: Canadian Gas Association; Ontario Natural Gas Association; Canadian Institute of Chartered Accountants; Institute of Chartered Accountants of Ontario.

Woods, Theresa Mary ⓞ

Public Relations Coordinator and Counsellor, EMERGENCY SHELTER FOR WOMEN, Prince Albert, SK S6V 5R3 (306) 953-4488, Selkirk Place. Born Prince Albert, Sask. 1948. d. 4 ch. Lenard, Kathy, Wanda, Shirley. CAREER: Case Worker, Social Svcs, 1977-80; Acting Dir./Counsellor, Interval House, 1980-91

Newsletter Coord./Prov. Coord./Public Authorities Coord., 1991-92; Counsellor, Emergency Shelter for Women, 1992 to date; Partnership Prince Albert Counselling & Mediation. SELECTED PUBLICATIONS: *North Parallel Partnership on Family Violence*; *Aboriginal Women's Anniversary Newsletter* (1992). AFFIL: Aboriginal Women's Council of Saskatchewan, Inc. (Area 7 Rep.); Native Women of Canada (Dir.); Indian Métis Friendship Centre; Métis Society; Catholic Women's League; Prince Albert Counselling Alliance; Child Abuse Counsel, Prince Albert Task Force on Family Violence. HONS: 10-year Service Award from West Central Native Women; Appreciation Award for Volunteer Work from Aboriginal Women. INTERESTS: reading; crocheting; maintaining active relationship with grandchildren in all aspects of their lives. COMMENT: *"Theresa Mary Woods has worked extremely hard at carrying on the extended family concept. Assistance, kindness and love are seen as a part of family roles and responsibilities that come with the privilege of belonging. It is from this centre that I receive drive and energy to deal with human issues, front-line services in the community, provincially and nationally."*

Woodsworth, Judith Weisz, B.A.,
L.ès.Lettres,Ph.D. ⚰ 🕮
Associate Professor of études françaises and Vice-Dean, Academic Affairs and International Relations, Faculty of Arts and Science, CONCORDIA UNIVERSITY, 7141 Sherbrooke St. W., Montreal, QC H4B 1R6 (514) 848-2090, FAX 848-2877, EMAIL judithw@alcor.concordia.ca. Born Paris 1948. m. Lindsay Crysler. 1 ch. Michael James Woodworth. EDUC: McGill Univ., B.A. 1968, Ph.D. 1977; Univ. de Strasbourg, Licence ès lettres 1969. CAREER: Translator, Gov't of Canada Translation Bureau, 1978-80; Asst. Prof. then Assoc. Prof., Concordia Univ., 1980 to date; Dir. of Translation Programmes; Chair of Dép. d'études françaises 1991-95; Fellow, Simone de Beauvoir Institute for Women's Studies, 1981-86; V-Dean, Humanities Div., Arts & Sci., 1983-85. SELECTED PUBLICATIONS: "Writers and Their Translators: The Case of Mavis Gallant" (TTR 1(2) 1988); "Court Interpreting in Canada: New Developments in Training and Accreditation" (*Proceedings of the XIIth World Congress of FIT*, Belgrade, 1991); "The Theorization of Literary Translation: Shifting Modes of Perceiving the Translation Process" (*Literature and Translation: Problems of Theory*. Proceedings of the int'l conference organized by the Literary Translation Council of the USSR Writers' Union, Moscow, 1992); "Aladdin in

the Enchanted Vaults: the Translation of Poetry" (*Textual Studies in Canada* 5 1994); *Les Traducteurs dans l'histoire* (Ottawa: Presses de l'Univ. d'Ottawa & UNESCO, 1995); *Translators through History* (Amsterdam/Philadelphia: John Benjamins Publishing Company & UNESCO, 1995); "Language, Translation and the Promotion of National Identity: Two Test Cases" (*Target* 8(2) 1996); "Doña Marina, Interpreter and Cultural Intermediary" (*Circuit* 53 1996); "History of Translation" in *Encyclopedia of Translation Studies*, ed. Mona Baker (London: Routledge, 1996); "Teaching the History of Translation" in *Teaching Translation and Interpreting* 3, eds. Cay Dollerup & Vibeke Appel (Amsterdam & Philadelphia: John Benjamins, 1996); various other publications. EDIT: Ed. Bd., *TTR*, 1987-92; Ed. Bd., *Language International*; Ed. Bd. *The Translator*; Advisory Bd., Benjamins Translation Library (Amsterdam/Philadelphia: John Benjamins Publishing Company); Guest Ed., special issue "English in Quebec," *Circuit*, Sept. 1994. AFFIL: Ordre des traducteurs et interprètes du Québec; Fédération Internationale des Traducteurs (VP, Committee for the Hist. of Translation 1990-99); Canadian Association for Translation Studies (founding Pres.; hon. mbr.); Canadian Federation for the Humanities (Bd. of Dir.). HONS: SSHRC research grant, 1993-96. INTERESTS: travel; music. MISC: Certified translator (French-English), Ordre des traducteurs et interprètes agréés du Québec; numerous conference presentations; recipient, various grants. COMMENT: *"As a professor of translation, I have been involved in professional activities and have conducted research on literature, translation and the history of translation. I also have been active in university administration at the department and faculty levels."*

Woodward, Christel, B.Sc.,M.A,
Ph.D. ⚰ ❀ ⊕
Professor, Department of Clinical Epidemiology and Biostatistics, MCMASTER UNIVERSITY, 1200 Main St., Hamilton, ON L8N 3Z5 (905) 525-9140, FAX 546-5211, EMAIL woodward@fhs.csu.mcmaster.ca. Born Bronx, N.Y. 1941 2 ch. EDUC: State Univ. of New York, B.Sc. 1961; Ohio State Univ., M.A.(Clinical Psych.) 1964, Ph.D. 1968. CAREER: elementary sch. Teacher, Roaring Brook Sch., Chappaqua, NY, 1961-62; Research Asst., Dept. of Psych., Ohio State Univ., 1963; Teaching Asst., 1964-65; Clinical Intern, Dept. of Psych., Univ. of Minnesota Hospitals, 1965-66; Psychologist, Children's Mental Health Center, Columbus, Ohio, 1965; Psychologist, Lakeshore Psychiatric Hospital, Toronto, 1968-69; Asst. Prof. of Psychiatry (Psych.), Dept. of Psychiatry,

McMaster Univ., 1969-74; child clinical psychologist, private practice, 1969 to date; Psychologist, Chedoke-McMaster Child & Family Centre, Hamilton, 1969-74; teaching staff, Certificate Course for Special Educ. in Elementary Schools, Ont. Ministry of Educ., 1971-72; Visiting Prof., Dept. of Psychiatry, McMaster Univ., 1974-76; Assoc. Prof., Psychiatry, 1974; Assoc. Prof. of Educ. Psych. (Special Educ.), Queen's Univ., 1974-76; Sch. Psychologist, Frontenac-Lennox & Addington County Roman Catholic Separate Sch. Bd., Kingston, Ont., 1974-75; Assoc. Prof., Dept. of Clinical Epidemiology & Biostatistics, McMaster Univ., 1976-85; Assoc. Mbr., Dept. of Psychiatry, 1976 to date; Prof., Dept. of Clinical Epidemiology & Biostatistics, 1985 to date; Assoc., Centre for Health Economics & Policy Analysis, 1988 to date. SELECTED PUBLICATIONS: various contributions to books, incl. "Broadening the Scope of Evaluation: Why and How," Chapter 6, *Research Health Care: Designs, Dilemmas, Disciplines*, eds. J. Daly, I. MacDonald & E. Willis (London: Routledge, 1992); various journal articles, incl. "Patient's Use of Primary Care Services Unwarranted? Some Answers from Physicians," with J. Gilbert *et al* (*Canadian Medical Association Journal* 129(5) 1983); "Assessing the Relationship Between Medical Education and Subsequent Performance" (*Assessment and Evaluation in Higher Education* 9, 1984); "Measurement of Physician Performance by Standardized Patients," with V. Neufeld *et al* (*Medical Care* 23, 1985); "Is the Canadian Health Care System Suffering From Abuse? A Commentary with G. Stoddart" (*Canadian Family Physician* 36, 1990); "Correlates of Children's Use of Physician and Dentist Services: Ontario Child Health Study Follow-up," with M. Boyle *et al* (*Canadian Journal of Public Health* 84(2) 1993); "The Effects of Simulating on Standardized Patients," with G. Gliva (*Academic Medicine* 70, 5); numerous other journal articles, abstracts, papers in proceedings, & monographs incl. *Guide to Improved Data Collection in Health and Health Care Surveys*, with L.W. Chambers & K.D. Smith (Ottawa: Canadian Public Health Association, 1982). AFFIL: American Psychological Association; American Educational Research Association; Canadian Psychological Association; American Public Health Association, Medical Care Section; Canadian Public Health Association; Ontario Psychological Association (Dir. 1987-89; Recording Sec. & mbr., Exec. Committee 1988-89). INTERESTS: health provider behaviour (practice patterns, quality of care, sources of variation, etc.); health human resource planning & utilization; evaluation of health & health-care programs; research in the educ. of health professionals; psychological assessment of children & their families. MISC: numerous consultancies incl.: AIDS Committee of Toronto, Talking Sex Proj., 1988-90; Midwifery Integration Planning Proj., 1991 & Royal Commission on Reproductive Technology, 1991-92; Chair, Task Force on Hum. Res. Planning in Psych., Ontario Psychological Association, 1989-90; mbr., Quality Mgmt Committee, Coll. of Physicians & Surgeons of Ontario, 1991-95; mbr., Ontario Coll. of Physicians & Surgeons, IHF Outcomes Assessment Committee, 1992 to date; mbr., Coll. of Psychologists of Ontario, Quality Assurance Committee, 1993 to date; reviewer for numerous journals, conferences & granting agencies; recipient, numerous grants from various agencies, incl. SSHRC, Ont. Ministry of Health, & National Health R.&D. Program.

Woolcott, Donna, B.H.Sc.,M.Sc., Ph.D. ⌾ ❀ ⊕
Professor and Chair, Department of Family Studies, UNIVERSITY OF GUELPH, Guelph, ON N1G 2W1 (519) 824-4120, ext. 6326, FAX 766-0691, EMAIL dwoolcot@facs.uoguelph.ca. Born Woodstock, Ont. 1946. s. EDUC: Univ. of Guelph, B.H.Sc. 1969, Ph.D. 1979; Univ. of Manitoba, M.Sc. 1971. CAREER: Nutritionist, Nutrition Canada Nat'l Nutrition Survey, Health & Welfare Canada, 1971-72; Lecturer in Nutrition, Dept. of Foods & Nutrition, Univ. of Manitoba, 1972-74; Public Health Nutrition Consultant, Ont. Ministry of Health, 1974-75; Asst. Prof., Applied Human Nutrition, Dept. of Family Studies, Univ. of Guelph, 1979-84; Assoc. Prof., 1984-94; Visiting Scholar, Pennsylvania State Univ., 1985; Visiting Scholar, Univ. of California at Berkeley, 1986; Assoc. Clinical Prof., Dept. of Family Medicine, Fac. of Health Sciences, McMaster Univ., 1988-94; Public Health Assoc., Teaching Health Unit, Hamilton-Wentworth Dept. of Public Health Svcs, 1991 to date; Chair, Dept. of Family Studies, Univ. of Guelph, 1992 to date; Prof., 1994 to date. SELECTED PUBLICATIONS: "Consumer Attitudes to a Ground-Beef Mixture on the Retail Market," with M. McDaniel (*Journal of the Canadian Dietetic Association* 37 1976); "Canada's Guidelines for Healthy Eating: Strategies for Communicating and Implementing Nutrition Recommendations" (*Journal of the Canadian Dietetic Association* 51(3) 1990); "Importance of a Nutrition Monitoring System for Research and Practice in Canada" (*Journal of the Canadian Dietetic Association* 51(4) 1990); "Evaluation of a Theoretical Model Predicting Self-Efficacy Towards Nutrition Behaviours in the Elderly," with

D.M. Matheson, A. Martin Matthews & V. Ross (*Journal of Nutrition Education* 23 1991); "An evaluation of a Theory-Based Demonstration Worksite Nutrition Promotion Program," with J.D. Sheeshka & N.J. MacKinnon (*American Journal of Health Promotion* 8(4) 1994); *Action Towards Healthy Eating. Canada's Guidelines for Healthy Eating and Recommended Strategies for Implementation* (Ottawa: Ministry of Supply & Services, 1990); numerous other publications. EDIT: Ed. Bd., *Journal of Nutrition Education*, 1986-92; Ed., *Journal of the Canadian Dietetic Association*, 1983-85. AFFIL: Canadian Dietetic Association; Ontario Dietetic Association (Hon. Pres. 1989-90); Society for Nutrition Education; Organization for Nutritional Education (Assoc. Dir. & Founding Mbr. 1980); Canadian Public Health Association; Ontario Public Health Association; Canadian Society for Nutritional Sciences; American Dietetic Association; Senior Women Academic Administrators of Canada. HONS: Canadian Dietetic Association Memorial Award, 1976; Ont. Grad. Scholarship, 1977, 1978; The Margaret McCready Scholarship, 1977; Ontario Dietetic Association Award of Honour, 1994. INTERESTS: research in psychosocial factors that influence human nutrition behaviour. MISC: mbr., Advisory Group on Nutrition Labelling, Health Promotion Branch, Health & Welfare Canada, 1984-85; Chair, Committee to Review Nutrition Recommendations for Canadians/Implementation Committee, 1987-89; mbr., Nutrition Advisory Panel for the Healthy Lifestyles Promotion Program, Ont. Ministry of Health, 1989-90; numerous research consultancies; numerous invited presentations. COMMENT: *"I have been interested in the advancement of human nutrition and health promotion in Canada. I have been privileged to have taught thousands of university students over my career and to have had a chance to shape public policy in nutrition and health."*

Woolfrey, Sandra, B.A.,M.A. 📖 📚
Director, WILFRID LAURIER UNIVERSITY PRESS, Waterloo, ON N2L 3C5 (519) 884-0710, ext. 6123, FAX 725-1399. Born Picton, Ont. EDUC: Wilfrid Laurier Univ., B.A.(Religion & Culture) 1972, M.A.(Religion & Culture) 1974. CAREER: elementary sch. teacher, Etobicoke Bd. of Educ., 1963-71; Asst. to Dir. of Research & Dean of Grad. Studies, Wilfrid Laurier Univ., 1976-83; Dir., Wilfrid Laurier Univ. Press, 1983 to date. SELECTED PUBLICATIONS: "Research as Peer Review in Scholarly Publishing," *Scholarly Publishing in Canada* (1988); "The Economics of Journal Publishing and the Rhetoric for Moving to an Electronic Format," *Proceedings of the 1993 International Conference on Refereed Electronic Journals.* EXHIBITIONS: exhibition of paper sculpture, Harbinger Gallery, Waterloo (1994); exhibition of photographs, The Forge Studio Gallery, Terra Cotta, 1993. AFFIL: Kitchener-Waterloo Art Gallery (Bd.); Association of Canadian University Presses (Pres. 1986-88, 1991-93). HONS: Ont. Grad. Scholarship, 1973-74 & 1976-77 (declined); First Prize, Dorothy Shoemaker Literary Award for Poetry, 1990. COMMENT: *"I think of myself as a communicator, whether it be through poetry, art, scholarly papers and publications, as senior editor of a publishing house or as an elementary school or university teacher."*

Woolnough, Hilda Mary, M.FA. ⊗
Artist. Rose Valley, R.R. 4, Breadalbane, PE C0A 1E0 (902) 621-0361. Born UK 3 ch. EDUC: Chelsea Sch. of Art, London, UK, Nat'l Diploma in Design 1955, studied with Julian Trevelyn, Ceri Richards, Bernard Meadows, Leonard Rossaman & Steven Sykes; Univ. of Guanajuato, San Miguel de Allende Instituto, Gto., Mexico, M.F.A. 1966, studied with Dietrich Kortlang; Central Sch. of Art & Design, London, UK, post-grad. work with Peter Nell & Leonard Marchant, 1966-67; Nova Scotia Sch. of Art & Design, Halifax, goldsmithing with Orland Larson, 1971. CAREER: Instructor, Univ. of Guanajuato, Mexico, 1965-66; Instructor, Jamaica Sch. of Art, Kingston, Jamaica, 1966-67; Instructor, Holland Coll., Charlottetown, 1969; Instructor, Handcraft Centre, PEI, 1970-71; Sessional Lecturer, Fine Arts, Univ. of Prince Edward Island, 1970-78; Founder, Phoenix Gallery Craft Co-op., Charlottetown, 1977-78; Dir., Gallery-on-Demand, Charlottetown, 1977-78; Arts Consultant & Designer, PEI Gov't, Dept. of English, 1977-78; Design Consultant, Holland Coll., 1978-80; Coord., Great George Street Gallery, Charlottetown, 1982-86; Visiting Artist, Galerie Sans Nom, Moncton N.B., 1987; Visiting Artist, Canterbury Coll. of Art, Kent, UK, 1987; Sessional Lecturer, Fine Arts, Univ. of Prince Edward Island, 1989; Instructor, Ryerson Summer Sch., 1992-93. EXHIBITIONS: *Six Canadian Artists*, Art Gallery of Hamilton, (1970); *International Printmakers Exhibition*, Montreal Museum of Fine Art (1971); *Silver and Quilts*, Confederation Centre Art Gallery (1973); *Atlantic Journal*, touring Canada & at the Cultural Centre, Paris, France (1976); *The Essential Line*, Confederation Centre Art Gallery (1982); *Mirrorings*, Mount Saint Vincent Univ. Art Gallery & nat'l tour (1982-93); numerous other group exhibitions in most major Cdn art centres since 1958 & in Mexico,

the Caribbean, UK & France; numerous 1-person exhibitions since at least 1961 incl. the Westdale Art Gallery, Hamilton (1961), Pascal Gallery, Toronto (1963), Jamaica Sch. of Art (1966), Gadatsy Gallery, Toronto (1978), the Saidye Bronfman Centre, Montreal (1979) & *Fishtales–A Marine Mythology*, Great George Street Gallery, Charlottetown, 1986; various touring exhibitions; Guest Curator, *Atlantic Prints*, Art Gallery of N.S., 1983; Guest Curator, *Lines of Sight*, Confederation Centre of the Arts, 1988-90. **COLLECTIONS:** in numerous public collections, incl. Canterbury Coll. of Art, Art Gallery of N.S., Art Gallery of Jamaica, Montreal Museum of Fine Art, CBC Montreal, Toronto-Dominion Bank Collection, Canadian Catholic Conference, P.E.I. Art Bank, Air Canada Montreal & the Gov't of P.E.I.; included in various private collections incl. those of Henri Dimier (Paris), Herbert Marcusse (US), Gordon Pinsent, & Dr. Catherine Wallace. **AFFIL:** PEI Council of the Arts (V-Chair 1992; Visual Arts Rep. 1992; Chair 1993). **HONS:** Graphics Scholarship, Univ. of Guanajuato; Person's Award 1988. **MISC:** numerous lectures, 1977-88; *A Woman's Place*, CBC-TV, nat'l (1976); "Hilda Woolnough," *Artist Series*, P.E.I. Dept. of Educ. & Confederation Centre of the Arts (1977); *Visions*, TVOntario (1983).

Woon, Wendy, B.F.A.,M.F.A. ■ ⊗ 📜 ⊜
Director of Education, MUSEUM OF CONTEMPORARY ART, 220 E. Chicago Ave., Chicago, IL 60611-2604 (312) 397-3835. Born Niagara Falls, Ont. 1957. **EDUC:** Queen's Univ., B.F.A.(Sculpture) 1979; Sch. of the Art Institute of Chicago, M.F.A.(Sculpture/Film) 1982. **CAREER:** independent Curator, 1988-95; Designer, Outreach Svcs, Royal Ontario Museum, 1985-87; Adult Art Coord., 1987-89; Head, Dept. of Educ., Extension & Programming, Art Gallery of Hamilton, 1989-95; Dir. of Educ., Museum of Contemporary Art, Chicago, 1995 to date. **SELECTED CREDITS:** *Classic Suite* (16mm, animated short), 1982; *Black/White Magic* (Super-8 animated short), 1982; *Cleopatra's Dream* (Super-8 live action/animated short); *Portraits of Women and the Mirror* (collaborative film, Super-8, short); *Upstream* (Super-8, short); *From the Sublime to the Ridiculous* (computer-animated short, in progress), 1994 to date. **SELECTED PUBLICATIONS:** "A Time for Change: Museums and Art Galleries Programming for the Future," *Association of Cultural Executives Newsletter*. **EXHIBITIONS:** curatorial projects: *Days of the Dead: A Traditional Mexican Celebration and its Legacy in the Popular Arts*, Community Gallery, Hamilton (1988); Hamil-

ton Coll., Clinton, N.Y. (1990); curatorial projects at the Art Gallery of Hamilton: *Learn to Read Art: Artists' Books* (1991); *A Reverence That Endures* (1991); *Images of Women* (1991); *Days of the Dead: A Traditional Mexican Celebration and its Legacy in the Popular Arts* (1992); *The Art of Darkness* (1992); *In Our Dreams* (1993); *Canadian Art in the Victorian Age* (1994); *The Creative Process* (1994); *Pretérito Imperfecto, Felipe Ehrenberg* (1994); numerous exhibitions incl.: *Dollhouse Invitational Retrospective*, Ritter Art Gallery, Boca Raton, Fla. (1983); *The Day the Sky Cried* (collaborative artists' book with Johnide), Yorkville Public Library, Toronto (1985); *Magnificent Obsessions: Collections by Artists*, Harbourfront (1987); *FAX*, Betty Reimer Gallery, Sch. of the Art Institute of Chicago (1990); *Festival of Lights*, York Quay Gallery, Harbourfront (1993). **AFFIL:** Ontario Association of Art Galleries (Bd. 1993-96; Chair, Program Advisory Committee 1993-95; Treas., Exec. Committee 1994-95; Co-Chair, Cultural Diversity Advisory 1995); Association Canadiense Mexicana (Hon. Mbr.). **HONS:** Educator's Award, Ontario Association of Art Galleries, 1991. **INTERESTS:** contemporary art; Mexican art & culture; folk art; children's art educ. **MISC:** various Canada Council & exhibition funding grants. **COMMENT:** *"Wendy Woon is an artist, arts education administrator and curator committed to making the creative process and cultural production more accessible to broader audiences, and to fostering an understanding and appreciation of art."*

Workman, Carole, B.Comm.,C.A. ■ ⊜ $
Vice-Rector, Resources, UNIVERSITY OF OTTAWA, 550 Cumberland St., Ottawa, ON K1N 6N5 (613) 562-5822, FAX 562-5107, EMAIL cworkman@acadvm.1.uottawa.ca. Born North Bay, Ont. 1952. m. F. Lee Workman. 2 ch. **EDUC:** Laurentian Univ., B.Comm. 1974. **CAREER:** Staff Acctnt, Thorne Riddell & Co., 1974-76; Internal Auditor, Univ. of Ottawa, 1976-82; Mgr, Fin. Svcs, Carleton Bd. of Educ., 1982-85; Dir., Fin. & Admin. Svcs, 1985-86; Corp. Cont., Univ. of Ottawa, 1986-92; V-Rector, 1992 to date. **DIRECTOR:** National Bank of Canada (Chair, Reg'l Advisory Committee). **AFFIL:** Regroupement des gens d'affaires (RGA); Ottawa Health Sciences Complex Inc. (Chair, Exec. Committee); Ottawa Life Science Park; Canadian Institute of Chartered Accountants (C.A.); Canadian Association of University Business Officers (Bd.); Council of Senior Administrative Officers, Ontario Universities (Exec. Committee). **MISC:** chaired the Panel on Medicine (1 of 13 panels) organized by the Ottawa-Carleton Dis-

trict Health Council for studying the Reconfiguration of health care in Ottawa-Carleton; mbr. of Fac., Univ. Mgmt Course, Centre for Higher Educ., 1992, 1993. **COMMENT:** *"Committed to innovative administrative practices and new financing structures."*

Worsfold, Nancy, B.A.,M.A. ✊ ♡

Executive Director, CANADIAN COUNCIL FOR REFUGEES, 6839 Drolet, Ste. 302, Montreal, QC H2S 2T1 (514) 277-7223, FAX 277-1447, EMAIL ccr@web.apc.org. Born Ottawa 1962 1 ch. Constance Worsfold Gervais. **EDUC:** Univ. of Toronto, B.A.(Hons., Phil.) 1985; Concordia Univ., M.A.(Comm.) 1990. **CAREER:** various community organizations; research on documentary films; Exec. Dir., Canadian Council for Refugees, 1989 to date. **SELECTED PUBLICATIONS:** "Misleading figures distort national debate on refugees" (Toronto Star Aug. 2, 1994). **COMMENT:** *"I am an activist and an organizer. As Executive Director of the Council, I work to bring together grass roots activists, build consensus, and then communicate positive messages about refugees to the government and to the media."*

Wright, Anita $ 📺

President, WRIGHT ALTERNATIVE ADVERTISING, 262 Raymerville Dr., Markham, ON L3P 6S4 (905) 471-2000, FAX 471-1704. Born Southampton, UK 1947. m. Bob Strolenberg. 3 ch. **CAREER:** trainer, various printing companies, 1976-78; Prod. Mgr, McConnell Advertising, 1978-80; Prod. Mgr, Promotion Studios, 1980-81; Dir., Mktg Svcs, American Express, 1981-87; Pres. & owner, Wright Alternative Advertising, 1987 to date. **AFFIL:** Markham-Stouffville Hospital Foundation (Dir.). **INTERESTS:** cooking; rollerblading; planning gala functions. **COMMENT:** *"I'm a happy, positive person whose greatest strengths have been provided by my friends, my husband and my children."*

Wright, Elizabeth, B.A.,M.B.A. ■ $

Senior Vice-President, Strategic Planning and Marketing, NATIONAL TRUST, One Financial Place, Toronto, ON M5C 2W8 (416) 361-3611, FAX 361-4037. Born New York City 1945. m. J.H. Wright. 2 ch. **EDUC:** Smith Coll., B.A(History) 1967; Univ. of Toronto, M.B.A.(Mktg) 1978. **CAREER:** VP, Chemical Bank of Canada, 1978-83; Sr. VP, Bank of Montreal, 1983-88; Sr. VP, CIBC, 1988-92; Exec. VP, Products, Personal and Commercial Bank, 1992-95; Sr. VP, Strategic Planning & Mktg, 1995 to date. **DIRECTOR:** Holt Renfrew Ltd.; Mastercard International. **AFFIL:** Children's Oncology Care of Ontario (Dir. 1988-93; Pres.); Canadian Payments Association (Dir.). **INTERESTS:** sports; reading; volunteer work with children. **COMMENT:** *"I have enjoyed a number of challenging jobs with satisfaction due to a lot of intellectual challenge and tremendously rewarding interaction with customers and co-workers."*

Wright, Helen, B.A. ✊ 🏉

Executive Technical Director, ALBERTA RUGBY FOOTBALL UNION, Percy Page Centre, 11759 Groat Rd., Edmonton, AB T5H 3K6 (403) 453-8628, FAX 453-8553. Born Williams Lake, B.C. 1955. m. Glen (Scotty). 2 ch. Sean, Amanda. **EDUC:** Concordia Coll. & Univ. of Alberta, B.A.(Psych.) 1993. **CAREER:** Loan Officer, Safeway Credit Union, 1980-82; Loan Officer, Wildrose Credit Union, 1982-86; Exec. & Tech. Dir., Alberta Rugby Union, 1987 to date. **SPORTS CAREER:** team mbr., Rockers RFC, 1977-82; Founding team mbr., Coven RFC, 1982-88; Alta. Prov. Rep. Side, 1986-88; Cdn Nat'l Rep. Side, 1988; coach, Harry Ainlay High Sch. Girls, 1988-89; coach, Druids RFC U17s Men, 1988-89; coach, Druids RFC Sr. Men, 1989-90; coach, Univ. of Alberta Men, 1990-93; coach, Coven RFC, 1992; Asst. Coach, Alberta Rugby Union Prov. Women's Side, 1989; Edmonton Rugby Referee, 1990; Mgr, ARU U17 Prov. Team, 1990; coach, Edmonton Rugby Union Rep. Women's Team, 1992; Coach, Clan 2nd Div., 1993; Coach, Prov. Women's U19 Team, 1994; Coach, Prov. Sr. Women's Team, 1994. **SELECTED PUBLICATIONS:** various articles in *National Rugby Post*. **AFFIL:** In Motion Network; CAWA; Canadian Rugby Union (EADP - Mentor Coach; Nat'l U17 & U19 Men's Selector); EDAP (Asst. Dir., Women's Program). **HONS:** Alta. Prov. Rep. Side, nat'l champions, 1986-88; Coach of the Year Award, Alberta Rugby Union, 1990; Edmonton Rugby Union Rep. Women's team, prov. winner, 1992; Prov. Women's U19 team, Canada West winner, 1994. **INTERESTS:** women in sports; singer/songwriter; storyteller. **MISC:** Committee Mbr., Asian Pacific Congress, Calgary; CAC-sponsored coach in Women's Dev. Program. **COMMENT:** *"I believe in simplicity, common sense and hard work. I believe in the concept of sport as more than a business..I have to, I'm in a smaller market. I believe in the ability of dedicated, thoughtful people to do great things. I believe I am the luckiest person alive, to be living in the greatest place on earth, serving the greatest people in the world, who continually support my endeavours. If I were to describe myself, I would simply say that I have too much passion and I have too little time."*

Wright, Laurali R. (Bunny), M.A. ⬚ ✏

Writer. c/o Virginia Barber, Virginia Barber Literary Agency, Inc., 101 Fifth Ave., New York, NY 10003. 2 ch. Victoria Kathleen, Johanna Margaret. EDUC: Simon Fraser Univ., M.A.(Liberal Studies). CAREER: worked as a freelance journalist & for The Calgary Herald, The Calgary Albertan & The Saskatoon Star-Phoenix; Instructor, Okanagan Summer Sch. of the Arts, 1993; Mentor, Writer/Mentor program, Sechelt Festival, 1994; Instructor, Continuin Educ., Univ. of B.C., 1995, 1996. SELECTED PUBLICATIONS: *Neighbours* (Macmillan of Canada, 1979); *The Favorite* (Doubleday Canada, 1982); *Among Friends* (Doubleday Canada, 1984); *The Suspect* (Doubleday Canada, 1985); *Sleep While I Sing* (Doubleday Canada 1986); *Love in the Temperate Zone* (Macmillan of Canada, 1988); *A Chill Rain In January* (Macmillan of Canada, 1990); *Fall From Grace* (Seal Books, 1991); *Prized Possessions* (Doubleday Canada, 1993); *A Touch of Panic* (Doubleday Canada, 1994); *Mother Love* (Doubleday Canada, 1995); *Strangers Among Us* (Doubleday Canada, 1996). AFFIL: The Writers' Union of Canada (B.C./Yukon Rep., Nat'l Council 1990-91); PEN International; Authors' Guild, US; International Association of Crime Writers; Mystery Writers of America; Crime Writers of Canada (Chair 1992-93). HONS: Alberta New Novelist Competition, Neighbours, 1978; Edgar Allan Poe Award for Best Mystery Novel (*The Suspect*), Mystery Writers of America, 1986; Arthur Ellis Award for Best Mystery Novel (*A Chill Rain in January*), Crime Writers of Canada, 1991; Literary Award for Fiction, Canadian Authors Association, 1996; Arthur Ellis Award for Best Mystery Novel (*Mother Love*), 1996. MISC: Co-author, with John Wright, *Still Life*, screenplay based on *Sleep While I Sing*, 1993; various juries, incl. Alberta Foundation for the Literary Arts, & Mystery Writers of America; conducted various writing workshops in N.S., Yukon & B.C.; readings throughout Canada & in western US

Wright, Lorna L., B.A.,M.A.,P.G.C.E., M.I.M.,Ph.D. ⬚ $

Director, Centre for Canada-Asia Business Relations and Associate Professor of International Management and Organizational Behaviour, School of Business, QUEEN'S UNIVERSITY, Kingston, ON K7L 3N6 (613) 545-6296, FAX 545-6674, EMAIL wrightl@qucdn.queensu.ca. Born Sioux Lookout, Ont. 1949. m. Prasetyo Sumantri. EDUC: Wilfrid Laurier Univ., B.A.(Psych.) 1969; Univ. of Essex, M.A.(Applied Linguistics) 1974; Univ. of London Institute for Educ., Postgrad. Certificate in Educ. 1975; American Grad. Sch. of Int'l Mgmt, M.I.M. 1982; Univ. of Western Ontario, Ph.D.(Bus. Admin.) 1991. CAREER: educator, CUSO projects at Mahidol Univ. & Udornpittayanukul Sch., Bangkok & Udornthani, Thailand, 1969-73; advisor, Canadian International Development Agency proj. at the Civil Aviation Training Centre, Curug, Indonesia, 1975-78; educator, Nagoya Univ., Nagoya, Japan, 1979-82; Asst. Prof., Sch. of Bus., Queen's Univ., 1986-93, Assoc. Prof., 1993 to date; Founder & Dir., Centre for Canada-Asia Business Relations, 1992 to date. SELECTED PUBLICATIONS: "An International Project Manager's Day," case study in *International Management Behavior: Putting Policy into Practice*, 2nd ed. (Boston: PWS-Kent Publishing Company, 1992); "Women in Management in Indonesia," with Virginian Crockett Tellei (*International Studies of Management and Organization* 23(4) 1993); "Southeast Asian perceptions of Canadian Business," Benchmarking the Canadian Business Presence in East Asia (*HongKong Bank of Canada Papers on Asia*, Vol. 1 1995); "Canadian Success Stories in Japan: Results of a Survey," *Approaching Asia* (1994); various other publications. EDIT: Ed. Advisory Bd., *Journal of Asian Business*. AFFIL: Canadian-Indonesian Business Council (Nat'l Chair 1988-90); Academy of International Business; Society for Intercultural Education, Training & Research; Academy of Management; Administrative Sciences Association of Canada; Thai Canadian Chamber of Commerce; AIESEC, Queen's Univ. (Bd. of Advisors); Canada ASEAN Centre, Singapore (Advisory Council 1990-94); Business Information Exchange International (Advisory Council 1992-93). HONS: Colin King Memorial Prize, 1975; Barton Kyle Yount Award, 1982; Centre for Int'l Bus. Scholarship, 1991; Plan for Excellence Award, 1991; Silver Medallist, Best Cdn Dissertation Award in Administrative Sciences, ASAC, 1992; Commerce Teaching Excellence Award, 1991-92. INTERESTS: Taekwondo; flying; hiking; crocheting; reading; ikebana. MISC: cross-cultural mgmt & educ. consultant for organizations such as Bristol Aerospace, Spar Aerospace, Sandwell, & Northern Telecom; numerous conference presentations & seminars. COMMENT: *"Lorna Wright is an internationalist who has studied or worked extensively in more than 10 countries and completed short-term assignments in many more. She is committed to helping Canadian companies improve their international competitiveness."*

Wright, Mary Jean, B.A.,M.A.,Ph.D. ⬚ ⊕

Professor Emeritus, Department of Psychology,

UNIVERSITY OF WESTERN ONTARIO, London, ON N6A 5C2 (519) 679-2111, ext. 4675. Born Strathroy, Ont. 1915. s. **EDUC:** Univ. of Western Ontario, B.A.(Phil. & Psych.) 1939; Univ. of Toronto, M.A.(Psych.) 1940, Ph.D.(Psych.) 1949. **CAREER:** Supervisior of school-age children, Protestant Children's Village, 1941-42; Instructor, wartime service overseas with Canadian Children's Service, Garrison Lane Nursery Training Sch., Birmingham, UK, 1942-44; Psychologist, Mental Health Clinic, Ontario Hospital, 1944-45; Consultant, Children's Aid Society, London, Ont., 1946-59; Lecturer, Univ. of Toronto, Institute of Child Study, 1945-46; Asst. Prof., Univ. of Western Ontario, 1946, Assoc. Prof., 1955; Full Prof., 1962; Chrm, Dept. of Psych., Middlesex Coll., Univ. of Western Ontario, 1960-63; Chrm, Dept. of Psych., Univ. of Western Ontario, 1963-70; study leave, 1970-71; Dir., Univ. Lab. Presch., 1973-80; Prof. Emerita, Dept. of Psych., 1980 to date; mbr., Exec. Bd., Huron Coll., 1983-89. **SELECTED PUBLICATIONS:** "Canadian Psychology Comes of Age" (*Canadian Psychologist* 10 1969); "Measuring the Social Competence of Preschool Children" (*Canadian Journal of Behavioral Science* 12 1980); *History of Academic Psychology in Canada*, ed. with C.R. Myers (Toronto: C.J. Hogrefe Inc., 1982); "Mary J. Wright (an autobiography)" in *Models of Achievement: Reflections of Eminent Women in Psychology* (New York: Columbia Univ. Press, 1983); *Compensatory Education in the Preschool: A Canadian Approach. The U.W.O. Preschool Project* (Ypsilanti: High/Scope Press, 1983); "Women Ground-breakers in Canadian Psychology: World War II and Its Aftermath" (*Canadian Psychology* 33:4 1992); numerous other publications. **AFFIL:** American Psychological Association (Fellow): Canadian Psychological Association (Fellow; Pres. 1968-69; Hon. Pres., 1975-76); Association for Early Childhood Education (Life Mbr.); Ontario Psychological Association (Pres. 1951-52); International Society for the History of the Behavioral & Social Sciences; Ontario Psychological Association. **HONS:** Gold Medal, Univ. of Western Ontario, 1939; Honour Society, Univ. of Western Ontario, 1939; Queen Elizabeth Silver Jubilee Medal, 1977; Ontario Psychological Association Award, 1980; Year of the Child Award, Ontario Psychological Foundation, 1980; Certificate of Recognition, Psi Chi, National (US) Honour Society in Psych., 1980; Children's Service Award, Association for Early Childhood Education, 1982; Univ. of Western Ontario Alumni Award, 1984; Canadian Psychological Association Special Award, 1990; LL.D.(Hon.), Univ. of Western Ontario, 1982; LL.D.(Hon.),

Brock Univ., 1979; LL.D.(Hon.), Carleton Univ., 1984; Fellow(Hon.), Huron Coll., 1989. **INTERESTS:** music; travel; writing; genealogy. **MISC:** Ontario Board of Examiners in Psychology, 1970-75; Chair, 1973-74; Advisory Academic Panel: Canada Council, 1976-78, Social Science & Humanities Research Council, 1978-79; registered psychologist, Prov. of Ont., 1961-83; certified presch. teacher, AECE Ont., 1967 to date; numerous presentations at conferences & meetings; listed in *Who's Who of Canadian and American Students* (1939) & *Canadian Who's Who*. **COMMENT:** *"Most important achievements: developing a very strong department of psychology at Western in the 1960s, founding (and developing a special early childhood education program for low-income children), the University of Western Ontario Laboratory Preschool."*

Wright, Merri-Ellen, Q.C. ⚖
Lawyer and Partner, McDOUGALL, READY, 110 - 21st St. E., Ste. 300, Saskatoon, SK S7K 0B6 (306) 653-1641, FAX 665-8511. Born Saskatoon, Sask. 1953. m. Neil Fisher. **CAREER:** Assoc. Lawyer, Cuelenaere, Beaubier, Kendall, Fisher & Gaucher, 1981-85; Ptnr, 1985-90; Assoc. Lawyer, McDougall, Ready, 1990-93; Ptnr, 1993 to date. **AFFIL:** Law Society of Saskatchewan (Ethics Committee 1992-93; V-Chair 1994; Chair 1995; Chair, Gender Equity Committee 1993-95; Professional Standards Committee, 1995-96; V-Chair, 1995; Chair, 1996); Canadian Bar Association (various committees). **INTERESTS:** travel, scuba diving; history. **MISC:** Sessional & Guest Lecturer, Coll. of Law, Univ. of Saskatchewan, 1990-95; various seminars, presentations & papers; Mediator & Family Mediator, Center for Dispute Resolution, Denver, Col., 1987.

Wright, Michelle 🎵 ⊗
Recording Artist and Songwriter. c/o Savannah Music, 1207 - 17th Ave. S., Ste. 305, Nashville, TN 37212 (615) 329-4747, FAX 329-4692. Born Chatham, Ont. **SELECTED CREDITS:** *The Reasons Why* (album), Prods. Mike Clute, Steve Bogard, Val Garay & John Guess, 1994 (singles: "One Good Man," "The Wall," "Safe in the Arms of Love"); *Now & Then* (album), Prods. Steve Bogard & Rick Giles, 1992 (singles: "Take It Like A Man," "One Time Around," "He Would Be Sixteen," "The Change," "If I'm Ever Over You," "Guitar Talk," "Now & Then"); *Michelle Wright* (album), Prods., Steve Bogard & Rick Giles, 1990 (singles: "New Kind of Love," "Woman's Intuition," "All You Really Wanna Do," "A Heartbeat Away," "Not Enough Love To Go 'Round"); *For Me It's You* (album), 1996; var-

ious videos incl. "Take It Like a Man." **AFFIL:** St. Joseph's Hospital of Chatham (Hon. Chair, "Operation Cat Scan"); Special Olympics. **HONS:** Top New Female Vocalist, Academy of Country Music, 1992; Country Female Vocalist of the Year, Juno Awards, 1993, 1995. Big Country Awards (*RPM Magazine*): Top Female Vocalist, 1989, 1991, 1992, 1993, 1994, 1995; Artist of the Year, 1991; 1993; Top Country Single, "Take It Like a Man," 1992 & "He Would Be Sixteen," 1993; Top Country Album, *Now & Then*, 1993. Canadian Country Music Awards (CCMA): Female Vocalist of the Year, 1990, 1991, 1992, 1993; Single of the Year, "New Kind of Love," 1991, "Take It Like a Man," 1992, & "He Would be Sixteen," 1993; Album of the Year, *Michelle Wright*, 1991; Video of the Year, "Take It Like a Man," 1993 & "He Would Be Sixteen," 1993; Country Music Person of the Year, 1992; Entertainer of the Year, 1993. **MISC:** "Take It Like a Man" was MuchMusic's Country Video of the Year in 1992, was number 1 on TNN the week of July 6, 1992 & number 1 on CMT the week of July 13, 1992; *Michele Wright* went gold in Canada, July 1993; *Now & Then* went double platinum in Canada, Jan. 1995 with current US sales of 450,000; *The Reasons Why* shipped gold, Sept. 1994 & went platinum in Canada, May 1995.

Wright, Nina Kaiden, B.A. ■ $ ⊗
President and Chairman, ARTS AND COMMUNICATIONS COUNSELORS, 151 Bloor St. W., 7th Fl., Toronto, ON M5S 1T5 (416) 966-3421, FAX 966-3088. Born New York City 1931. m. Norman Wright. 4 ch. **EDUC:** Emerson Coll., B.A. 1948. **CAREER:** founded Arts and Communications Counselors, a firm specializing in cultural sponsorship acquisition, with offices in N.Y., Toronto & Calgary. **AFFIL:** Wolfe Trapp Centre for the Performing Arts; The Power Plant; The Toronto Arts Awards; Art Gallery of York Univ. (Bd.); CANFAR National Network (Bd.). **SELECTED PUBLICATIONS:** "Puerto Rico: The New Life"; *Mother and Child in Modern Art* (New York: Duell Sloan and Pearce); *Artist and Advocate* (Renaissance Editions Inc., 1969). **INTERESTS:** performing & visual arts; sailing. **MISC:** more than 150 arts sponsorships incl. Art in the Spadina Subway, City Walls, The Barnes Exhibit, The William Paley Collection, National Ballet of Canada's new production of *The Nutcracker*, Hidden Values: Canadian Corporations Collect, The Kirov Ballet, EXPO '86; Canada Pavillion, Barbara Hepworth, Constable, Gainsborough & Turner exhibitions. **COMMENT:** "*Ms. Wright has been instrumental in the inception of corporate support for the arts, virtually creating the industry in North America. She has acted as an art consultant to leading corporations, helping develop their art collections.*"

Wright-Roberts, Monica E. ▯ ◔ ❀
President, ROBERTS COMMUNICATIONS GROUP, 267 Woburn Ave., Toronto, ON M5M 1L1 (416) 480-0484, FAX 480-0083. Born Hamilton, Ont. 1953. d. 2 ch. Ryan P. Wright-Roberts, Jody M.K. Wright-Roberts. **CAREER:** Pres., Roberts Communications Group, 1979 to date; spokesperson, Terry Fox Foundation; spokesperson, National Breast Cancer Fund. **SELECTED CREDITS:** *Facing Cancer with Confidence* (video); *Stories From the Front* (prime-time documentary). **SELECTED PUBLICATIONS:** *Side by Side: A Handbook for Wellness Team Members* (Rexdale: Roger Murray and Associates Incorporated). **AFFIL:** Canadian Breast Cancer Foundation (Educ. Committee 1990-95); Canadians Facing Cancer Foundation (Bd. Mbr. 1990-92); Ronald McDonald House (Bd. 1995); National Breast Cancer Fund (VP). **HONS:** Award of Hope, Canadian Breast Cancer Foundation. **MISC:** frequent public speaker; numerous radio & TV appearances. **COMMENT:** "*Having undergone extensive surgery to remove progressive cancer, and endured aggressive chemotherapy and massive doses of radiation, Monica Wright-Roberts has managed to turn a tragic situation into a positive life experience that she has shared with millions of people through numerous television and radio appearances.*"

Wubnig, Judy, B.A.,M.A.,Ph.D. ⌒ ▤
Assistant Professor, Department of Philosophy, UNIVERSITY OF WATERLOO, Waterloo, ON N2L 3G1 (519) 885-1211, ext. 3548, FAX 746-3097. Born Brooklyn, N.Y. 1934. s.. **EDUC:** Swarthmore Coll., B.A. 1955; Oxford Univ., Certificate 1956; Yale Univ., M.A. 1958, Ph.D. 1963. **CAREER:** Instructor, Dept. of Humanities, Coll. of Basic Studies, Boston Univ., 1960-62; Instructor, Dept. of Phil., Tufts Univ., Medford, Mass., 1962-63; Lecturer, University Coll., Northeastern Univ., 1963-66; Asst. Prof., Phil., State University Coll. of New York, 1964-65; Asst. Prof., Dept. of Phil., Univ. of Waterloo, 1965 to date. **SELECTED PUBLICATIONS:** *Arithmetic and Combinatorics: Kant and his Contemporaries*, by Gottfried Martin, translated & with notes by Judy Wubnig (Carbondale Ill.: Southern Illinois Press, 1985); "Cultural Relativism and Disagreement" (*Akten des XIV Internationalen Kongress für Philosophy* Sept. 1968); "A Minority of One" (*Inquiry* Aug. 21, 1980); "Affirmative Action: What Happened to Merit?" (*Kitchener-Waterloo Record* Apr. 30, 1985); "Civil Disobedi-

ence, War and Peace" (*Imprint* Feb. 17, 1989); "The Rule of Ignorance in the United States and Canada" (*Measure* Mar. 1991); "The Merit Criterion of Employment: An Examination of Some Current Agruments Against Its Use" (1976), reprinted in *Contemporary Moral Issues*, ed. Wesley Cragg (Toronto: McGraw-Hill Ryerson, 3rd ed., 1992); "Why Socrates Would Object to Civil Disobedience," *The Philosophy of Socrates*, ed. K.J. Boudouris (Athens, 1991); various other articles, book reviews & conference proceedings. EDIT: Ed., *Newsletter*, Society for Academic Freedom & Scholarship, 1992-94; Assoc. Ed., 1994 to date. AFFIL: National Association of Scholars; The Women's Fredom Network; American Philosophical Association; American Society for Political & Legal Philosophy; Canadian Association of University Teachers; Canadian Philosophical Association; Canadian Society for Aesthetics; Canadian Society for the History & Philosophy of Mathematics; International Association for Greek Philosophy; International Association for Philosophy of Law & Social Philosophy; Kant Gesellschaft; Metaphysical Society of North America; North America Kant Society; Society for Ancient Greek Philosophy; National Association of Scholars; Society for Academic Freedom & Scholarship; University Centers for Rational Alternatives. MISC: frequent public speaker; various press & broadcast interviews; various conference presentations.

Wyatt, Rachel ⊗ 📚 💟
Author, Playwright. 1217 Tattersall Dr., Victoria, BC (604) 384-4601, FAX 384-2382. Program Director, Writing, and Director, The Banff Radio Drama Workshop, THE BANFF CENTRE FOR THE ARTS, Box 1020, Stn. 21, Banff, AB, T0L 0C0 (403) 762-6288, FAX 762-6334. Born Bradford, Yorkshire, UK 1929. m. Alan Wyatt. 4 ch. Antony, Diana, Sally, Timothy. EDUC: The Girls' Grammar Sch., Bradford. CAREER: Instructor, Lampert Summer Sch., Univ. of Toronto, 1971; Instructor, B.Ed. Program, McGill Univ. Northern Studies Dept., with assignments in Iqaluit, Rankin Inlet & Montreal, 1987-93; Assoc. Dir., The May Studios, Banff Centre for the Arts, 1987-91; Dir., The Banff Radio Drama Workshop, 1989 to date; Dir., Writing Program, 1991 to date; Instructor, Creative Writing, Univ. of Victoria, 1994; Writer-in-Residence, David Thompson Univ. Centre (1985), Tarragon Theatre (1982), & the Univ. of Prince Edward Island (1980). SELECTED CREDITS: broadcast talks, *Trans-Canada Matinee* & other programs, CBC; over 100 radio dramas commissioned & produced, CBC; 30 radio dramas commissioned & produced, BBC; various

adaptations for radio; contributor, *Fraggle Rock*, CBC-TV; various short features for TV; *Geometry*, stage play, Tarragon Theatre, Toronto, 1983; *Chairs and Tables*, stage play, Tarragon Theatre, 1984; *Agamemmnon's Dilemma*, short comedy, Community Players of Massey Coll., 1993; *Crackpot*, full-length stage adaptation of Adele Wiseman's novel, Alberta Theatre Projects, Calgary, 1995; various other stage plays. SELECTED PUBLICATIONS: *The String Box* (Toronto: The House of Anansi Press, 1970); *The Rosedale Hoax* (Toronto: The House of Anansi Press, 1977); *Foreign Bodies* (Toronto: The House of Anansi Press, 1982); *Time in the Air* (Toronto: The House of Anansi Press, 1985); *Geometry*, play (Playwrights' Union of Canada, 1985); *Chairs and Tables*, play (Playwrights' Union of Canada, 1986); *Crackpot*, play (Playwrights' Union of Canada, 1995); *The Day Marlene Dietrich Died*, collection of short stories (Oct. 1996); features in various magazines & newspapers incl. *The Guardian, Punch*, & *The Globe and Mail*; short stories for various journals & magazines incl. *Quarry, Room of One's Own, Grain*, & *Descant* included in 4 anthologies incl. *Frictions 11* (1994) & *Instant Applause* (Blizzard, 1994). AFFIL: ACTRA; Playwrights' Union of Canada; The Writers' Guild of Canada; The B.C. Federation of Writers; PEN International. HONS: First prize, CBC Drama Competition, 1982; nominated, ACTRA Awards, 1979, 1986; nominated, Texaco Award, 1986. MISC: various conference presentations worldwide; various readings across Canada & internationally; Crackpot, the stage play, was produced in Philadelphia, April, 1996 with productions scheduled at the Prairie Theatre Exchange, Winnipeg, Sept. 1996 & The Belfry Theatre, Victoria, Oct. 1996.

Wylie, Alison (Margaret), B.A.,M.A., Ph.D. 🖐 📚
Professor, Department of Philosophy, UNIVERSITY OF WESTERN ONTARIO, London, ON N6A 3K7 (519) 661-3453, FAX 661-3922. Born Swindon, UK 1954. m. Samuel Gerszonowicz. EDUC: Mount Allison Univ., B.A. 1976; State Univ. of New York, Binghamton, M.A. 1978, Ph.D. 1982. CAREER: Visiting Postdoctoral Fellow, Calgary Institute for the Humanities, 1981-82; Instructor, Dept. of Phil., Univ. of Calgary, 1981-83; Univ. Postdoctoral Fellow, 1982-83; Mellon Postdoctoral Fellow & Instructor, Dept. of Phil., Washington Univ., St. Louis, 1983-84; Instructor, Dept. of Phil., Univ. of Calgary, 1984-85; Univ. Postdoctoral Fellow, 1984-85; Asst. Prof., Dept. of Phil., Univ. of Western Ontario, 1985-89; Fac. of Arts Research Prof., 1987-88; Visiting Prof.,

Dept. of Anthro., Univ. of California-Berkeley, 1989; Assoc. Prof., Dept. of Phil., Univ. of Western Ontario, 1989-93; Prof., Dept. of Phil., 1993 to date; Leo Block Visiting Prof., Women's Studies, Univ. of Denver, 1994-95; Visiting Fellow, Stanford Center for Advanced Study in the Behavioral Sciences, 1995-96. SELECTED PUBLICATIONS: *Ethics in American Archaeology: Challenge for the 1990s*, co-ed. with Mark J. Lynott (Washington D.C.: Society for American Archaeology Special Report Series, 1995); *Equity Issues for Women in Archaeology*, co-ed. with Margaret C. Nelson & Sarah M. Nelson (Washington D.C.: Archaeological Papers of the American Anthropological Association, 5, 1994); *Critical Traditions in Contemporary Archaeology: Essays in the Philosophy, History and Socio-Politics of Archaeology*, co-ed. with Valerie Pinsky (Cambridge: Cambridge Univ. Press, 1989); "Reasoning About Ourselves: Feminist Methodology in the Social Sciences," *Women and Reason*, ed. E. Harvey & K. Okruhlik (Ann Arbor: Univ. of Michigan Press, 1992); "Between Philosophy and Archaeology" (*American Antiquity* 50 1985); "Philosophical Feminism: Challenge to Science," with Kathleen Okruhlik (*Resources for Feminist Research* 16 1987); "The Interplay of Evidential Constraints and Political Interests: Recent Archaeological Work on Gender" (*American Antiquity* 57 1992); "The Constitution of Archaeological Evidence," *The Disunity of Science*, ed. P. Galison & D.J. Stump (Stanford: Stanford Univ. Press, 1996); various other publications. EDIT: External Ed. Advisor, *Public Archaeology Review*, 1995 to date; *International Studies in Philosophy of Science*; Assoc. Ed., *Antiquity*, 1995 to date; Assoc. Ed., *Philosophy of Science*, 1988-90. AFFIL: Centre for Archaeology in the Public Interest (Advisory Bd. Mbr.); Clare Hall, Cambridge (Life Fellow); American Philosophical Association, Eastern Div.; Philosophy of Science Association; Canadian Society for History & Philosophy of Science (VP; Mbr. of Exec. 1991-94; Bd. Mbr. 1987-90); Canadian Society for Women in Philosophy (Coord. 1992-94; Mbr. of Exec. 1994-96); Canadian Philosophical Association (Program Committee); Society for American Archaeology (Co-Chair, Committee on Ethics in Archaeology 1991 to date); American Anthropology Association, Archaeology Div.; Woods Hole Oceanographic Institute (Consultant). COMMENT: "*I am a feminist scholar trained in philosophy of the social sciences, with particular interest in questions about objectivity raised by archaeological practice and by feminist research in the social sciences. My central ambition is to develop genuinely interdisciplinary approaches to science studies–the analysis and evaluation of scientific research.*"

Wylie, Betty Jane, B.A.,M.A. 🗋 / 🖾
Author, Journalist, Playwright. c/o The Writers' Union of Canada, 24 Ryerson Ave., Toronto, ON M5T 2P3 (416) 703-8982, FAX 703-0826. Born Winnipeg 1931. w. William T. Wylie. 4 ch. Elizabeth, Catherine, John, Matthew. EDUC: Univ. of Manitoba, B.A. (English & French) 1951, M.A.(English) 1952. SELECTED CREDITS: *Kingsayer*, Manitoba Theatre Centre, Children's Theatre, 1967; *Mark*, Third Stage, Stratford Festival, 1972; *The Horsburgh Scandal*, Theatre Passe Muraille, Toronto, 1976; *Beowulf*, musical with composer Victor Davies, Amas Repertory Theater, N.Y., 1977; *A Place on Earth*, Toronto Workshop Productions, 1982; *How To Speak Male*, Solar Stage, 1990; *Boy in a Cage*, chamber opera, with composer Ken Nichols, Prairie Opera, Sask., sch. tour, 1995; numerous other works for the live stage produced; writer & performer, *Betty Jane's Diary*, syndicated daily radio column, 1978-82; writer, *Victorian Spice*, 5-part drama, *Morningside*, CBC Radio, 1987; writer, *Memories of Canada*, 3-part series, *Morningside*, CBC Radio, 1993; various other radio plays & series, primarily for CBC; sound recording, *Beowulf* (Daffodil 1976, Golden Toad 1984); writer, various health documentary films, Scene Two Productions, 1978, 1982; writer & co-host, life insur. documentary, Sun Life Insurance Company, 1984; co-writer, with Donald Martin, *Coming of Age* (MOW), Breakthrough Film Productions (1993). SELECTED PUBLICATIONS: *Beginnings: A Book for Widows* (Toronto: McClelland & Stewart, 1977); *A Place on Earth*, play (Playwrights' Press, 1982); *John of a Thousand Faces*, children's story (Black Moss Press, 1983); *Everywoman's Money Book*, with Lynne MacFarlane (Toronto: Key Porter Books, 1984, 1995); *Successfully Single* (Toronto: Key Porter Books, 1986); *Something Might Happen*, poetry (Black Moss Press, 1991); *Men! A Collection of Quotations About Men By Women* (Toronto: Key Porter Books, 1993); *Reading Between the Lines: The Diaries of Women* (Toronto: Key Porter Books, 1995); numerous other books of fiction, nonfiction, poetry, plays & cooking; numerous journalism articles in most major Cdn magazines, incl. *Maclean's*, *Canadian Theatre Review*, *Homemakers* & *Canadian Living*. DIRECTOR: Investors' Group Trust. AFFIL: Periodical Writers' Association of Canada (Founding Mbr.); Playwrights' Union of Canada (Founding Mbr.); The Writers' Union of Canada (Chair 1988-89); Community Con-

tacts for the Widowed & Bereaved Families of Ontario (Founding Mbr.); Writers' Development Trust (Bd. of Dir.). **HONS:** Educ. Awards, Psychological Foundation of Ontario (*Successfully Single*), 1987; Educ. Award, Canadian Nurses' Association (*Victorian Spice*), 1988; Alumni Jubilee Award, Univ. of Manitoba Alumni Association, 1989; Bunting Institute Fellowship, Radcliffe Coll., 1989-90; First Prize, Canadian Institute of Nordic Studies Playwriting Contest (*Veranda*), 1994. **INTERESTS:** theatre. **MISC:** mbr. of a team sent by Cdn External Affairs to the 4 Scandinavian countries to lecture on Cdn Lit., 1980; guest of the Nordic Association for Canadian Studies, 3rd Triennial conference, Oslo, Norway, 1990 & Aarhus, Denmark, 1996 (invited).

Y

Yaffe, Barbara, B.A.,B.J. ✎ ⚛ 📺
Columnist, *THE VANCOUVER SUN*, 2250 Granville St., Vancouver, BC V6H 3G2 (604) 732-2189, FAX 732-2323. Born Montreal 1953. m. Dr. Wilson E. Russell. **EDUC:** Univ. of Toronto, B.A. 1974; Carleton Univ., B.J. 1975. **CAREER:** Reporter, *The Montreal Gazette*, 1975-76; Reporter, *The Globe and Mail*, 1976-79; Atlantic Bureau Chief & Columnist, 1979-81; Reporter for Nfld. & Labrador, National News, CBC-TV, 1981-84; Parliamentary Reporter, *The Globe and Mail*, Ottawa bureau, 1984-85; freelance writer, St. John's, 1985-86; Sr. Writer & Ed., *The Sunday Express*, 1987-88; Life Section Ed., *The Vancouver Sun*, 1988-91; B.C. Ed., 1991-93; Columnist, 1993 to date. **SELECTED PUBLICATIONS:** articles in various newspapers; feature articles in *Canadian Medical Association Journal*, 1986-86. **HONS:** Rachel Edwards Award, Most Promising Journalism Grad., Carleton Univ., 1975; Roland Michener Award for Public Service Journalism, 1977. **INTERESTS:** fitness; collecting art. **MISC:** frequent radio & TV guest interviews for French-language & English-language CBC networks; was occasional guest on *Front Page Challenge*. **COMMENT:** "*As a journalist, my goal is to work on behalf of my readers. To that end, I try to be a government watchdog. It has also been my goal to better understand this geographically diverse, bilingual, multicultural mess of a great country that Canada is. I've lived in nearly all parts of the country and try to interpret each region to all the others.*"

Yaffe, Phyllis P., B.A.,B.L.S.,M.L.S. 📺 $ ⚛
President and Chief Executive Officer, SHOW-

CASE TELEVISION INC., 160 Bloor St. E., Ste. 1000, Toronto, ON M4W 1B9 (416) 967-0022, FAX 967-0044, EMAIL drama@showcase.ca. Born Winnipeg 1949. m. John Feld. 1 ch. **EDUC:** Univ. of Manitoba, B.A. 1969; Univ. of Alberta, B.L.S. 1972; Univ. of Toronto, M.L.S. 1976. **CAREER:** Winnipeg Public Library, 1972-73; Seneca Coll. Library, 1973-77; Exec. Dir., The Children's Book Centre, 1977-80; Exec. Dir., Association of Canadian Publishers, 1980-85; VP, Mktg, Owl Communications, 1985-94; Chair, Foundation to Underwrite New Drama for pay-TV, 1985-93; Pres. & CEO, Showcase Television, 1994 to date. **SELECTED PUBLICATIONS:** Founding Co-Ed. & Publisher, *Emergency Librarian*. **DIRECTOR:** Owl Communications. **AFFIL:** Academy of Canadian Cinema & Television; Toronto Women in Film & Television; Ryerson Polytechnic Univ. (Radio & TV Arts Committee); Canadian Women in Communications; Ontario Science Centre (Chair, Bd. of Trustees). **COMMENT:** *"I have spent my professional career in the Canadian sector of the cultural industries and I am committed to the goal of making Canadians more aware of the best Canada and the world has to offer in this important sphere."*

Yakimov, Radka, M.E.Sc.,P.Eng. ■ ⚛ 🎓
Professor and Coordinator, Mechanical Technology Department, School of Engineering Technology, CENTENNIAL COLLEGE OF APPLIED ARTS AND TECHNOLOGY, Box 631, Stn. A, Scarborough, ON M1K 5E9 (416) 289-5000, ext. 2490. Born 1937. m. Andrei Yakimov. 1 ch. Audrey. **EDUC:** Institute of Mechanical & Electrical Engineering, M.E.Sc.; P.Eng.(Mech.). **AFFIL:** Professional Engineers Ontario. **INTERESTS:** the arts; travel; books.

Yalden, Janice, B.A.,M.A. 📜 🎓
Chair, Department of Linguistics and Applied Language Studies, CARLETON UNIVERSITY, 1125 Colonel By Dr., Ottawa, ON K1S 5B6 (613) 788-2810, FAX 788-2642, EMAIL jyalden@ccs.carleton.ca. Born Kingston, Jamaica 1931. m. Maxwell Yalden. 1 ch. **EDUC:** Univ. of Toronto, B.A. 1952; Univ. of Michigan, M.A.(Spanish) 1956. **CAREER:** Lecturer, Carleton Univ., 1969-83; Founding Dir., Centre for Applied Language Studies, 1981-84; Prof. of Linguistics, 1983 to date; Visiting Prof., Univ. de Mons, Belgium, 1985-87; Dean of Arts, Carleton Univ., 1987-92; Chair, Dept. of Linguistics & Applied Language Studies, 1994 to date. **SELECTED PUBLICATIONS:** *Communicative Language Teaching: Principles and Practice* (Toronto: OISE Press, 1981); *The Communicative Syllabus: Evolution, Design and Implementation* (Oxford: Pergamon Press, 1983, London: Prentice-Hall International, 1987); *Principles of Course Design for Language Teaching* (New York: Cambridge Univ. Press, 1987); ed. with Anthony Mollica, *English and French as second languages in Canadian teacher-training institutes* (Welland, Ont.: *Canadian Modern Language Review*, 1985); numerous chapters in books incl. "Syllabus Design in General Education: Options for ELT" (*General English Syllabus Design* ed. C.J. Brumfit, Oxford: British Council & Pergamon Press, 1984); "The Quest for a Universal Theory" (*Beyond the Monitor Model* ed. R.M. Barasch & C.V. James, Boston: Heinle and Heinle, 1994); numerous articles in refereed journals incl. "A Case for Studying Spanish" (*Canadian Modern Language Review* 29 1973); "The teacher's role: a new conception" (*Bulletin de l'association de linguistique appliquée* Fall 1980); "Second-Language Teaching at the Post-Secondary Level" (*Bulletin of the Canadian Association of Applied Linguistics* 6 1984); technical reports, textbooks, articles in non-refereed journals, book reviews & journalistic writing. **EDIT:** *Revue de Phonétique Appliquée*; Review Bd., *TESL Canada Journal*. **AFFIL:** Ontario Modern Language Teachers' Association (Pres. 1976-77); Canadian Association of Applied Linguistics; Maurice Price Foundation; Society for Educational Visits & Exchanges of Canada (Advisory Council). **MISC:** numerous papers presented; recipient, numerous research grants. **COMMENT:** *"I am a university professor of Spanish language, general linguistics, and applied language studies. I have taught, published extensively, and held a number of very responsible administrative positions at Carleton; a varied and satisfying mix."*

Yale, Janet, M.A.,LL.B. ■■ $ 🍁 ⚖
Senior Vice-President, Regulatory, Government and Law, AT&T CANADA LONG DISTANCE SERVICES COMPANY (telecommunications), 200 Wellington St. W., 16th Fl., Toronto, ON M5V 3G2 (416) 345-2491, EMAIL jyale@attcanada.com. m. Daniel Logue. 2 ch. Zachary, Joshua. **EDUC:** Univ. of Toronto, M.A.(Arts & Econ.), LL.B. **BAR:** Ont., 1983. **CAREER:** Gen. Cnsl, Consumers' Association of Canada, 4 yrs.; Dir., Telecommunications Policy/Dir. Gen., Cable, Pay & Specialty Svcs branch, Canadian Radio-television & Telecommunications Commission; VP, Regulatory Matters, Unitel Communications Company (now AT&T Canada Long Distance Services Company), 1992-95; Sr. VP, Regulatory, Gov't & Law, 1995 to date. **AFFIL:** Canadian Women in Communications (Chair, Bd. of Dir.); Children's Hospital of

Eastern Ontario Foundation (Bd. of Dir.); Opera Lyra, Ottawa (Bd. of Dir.); Canadian Bar Association (served on Exec., Nat'l Communications Law Section, & CBA-Ont. Media & Communications Law Section). **MISC:** Prof. (part-time), Communications Law, Osgoode Hall Law Sch., Toronto, 1995 to date.

Yamada, Ruth, B.A. 🎨 ☝
Honorary President, SUMI-E ARTISTS OF CANADA, Toronto, ON M5P 3B8 (416) 483-5084. Born Vancouver 1923. m. Sam Yamada. 3 ch. **EDUC:** Univ. of Toronto, B.A.(Fine Arts) 1993. **SELECTED PUBLICATIONS:** *The Art of Sumi-e* (McGraw-Hill); illustrator, *The Waves,* Pearl S. Buck (Copp Clark). **EXHIBITIONS:** several solo shows as well as group shows in Japan & Canada. **COLLECTIONS:** Queen's Collection of Cdn Art, Windsor Castle. **AFFIL:** Sumi-e Artists of Canada (Hon. Pres.); Art Gallery of Ontario (Volunteer Docent); Canadian Society of Painters in Watercolour; All-Japan Nanga Society. **HONS:** Purchase Award, Adath Juried Show, 1965; Nanga Society Award, 1968, 1974; American Sumi-e Society Award, 1980. **MISC:** Master Instructor, Sumi-e, Kyoto, Japan, 1972; painting selected as gift to Gov. Xiulia of Jiangsu Prov., China, 1985; 1st instructor of Japanese brush painting in Toronto. **COMMENT:** *"Studied nanga style of Japanese brush painting in Kyoto, Japan under Kohaku Kamabata. Taught this unique art for 20 years at the Japanese Canadian Cultural Centre. Founded Sumi-e Artists of Canada in 1984."*

Yamamoto, Ann Marie, B.A.,M.B.A. $
Vice-President, Information Technologies and Systems Audit, LOBLAW COMPANIES LIMITED, 22 St. Clair Ave. E., Toronto, ON M4T 2S8 (416) 922-8500, FAX 922-7791, EMAIL ayamamo@lcl.weston.ca. Born Bayshore, Long Island, N.Y. 1960. m. Charles S. Best. 2 ch. Meredith, Hilary. **EDUC:** Queen's Univ., B.A.(Life Sci.) 1981; York Univ., M.B.A.(Mgmt Sci. & Fin.) 1983. **CAREER:** various positions in Fin. & Info. Svcs, to Mgr of Systems Dev., National Grocers Co. Ltd., 1986-94; VP, Info. Technologies & Systems Audit, Loblaw Companies Limited, 1994 to date. **AFFIL:** York Univ. Fac. of Administrative Studies Alumni (Toronto Chapter).

Yarlow, Loretta, B.A.,M.Ed. 🎨 📜 🎓
Director and Curator, ART GALLERY OF YORK UNIVERSITY, 4700 Keele St., North York, ON M3J 1P3 (416) 736-5169, FAX 736-5985. Born New York City 1948. m. Gregory Salzman. 2 ch. **EDUC:** Sarah Lawrence Coll., B.A. 1970; Harvard Univ., M.Ed.(Art Hist.) 1971. **CAREER:** Curatorial Asst., Musée Nationale d'Art Moderne, Paris, 1971-72; Curator, Institute of Contemporary Art, Boston, 1972-74; Co-Dir., Yarlow/Salzman Gallery, Toronto, 1974-84; Dir., Cold City Gallery, Toronto, 1986-88; Dir. & Curator, Art Gallery of York Univ., 1988 to date.

Yarymowich, Anne, B.A. ■ 🎨 $
Executive Chef, ART GALLERY OF ONTARIO, 317 Dundas St. W., Toronto, ON M5T 1G4. Born Montreal 1956. s. **EDUC:** Univ. of Ottawa, B.A.(Visual Arts) 1980; George Brown Coll., Diploma (Culinary Mgmt) 1988. **CAREER:** Dir./Mgr, Sales, York Gallery, 1980-81; Mgr, Sales, Throop Photo Supply, 1981-84; Gen. Mgr, Del Bello Gallery, 1985; Instructor, Jewish Community Centre, 1986-87; Apprentice, Le Select Bistro & The Parrot, Toronto; several prominent kitchens, Queen St. W., Toronto; Chef, Mildred Pierce Restaurant, 1990-96; Exec. Chef, Art Gallery of Ontario, 1996 to date. **AFFIL:** George Brown Coll. (Advisory Committee for dev. of a Contemporary Master Cooks Program); Society of Knives & Forks; Women's Culinary Network; Gallery 101 (Chair & Sec.). **HONS:** Russel Cotman Award, George Brown Coll. **MISC:** regular participant at biannual organic food festival, Feast Fields; Guest Instructor, Stratford Chefs' Sch.; Guest Instructor, Great Cooks, 1993-95; part-time Instructor, George Brown Coll., Continuing Educ., Basic Small Quantity Cooking.

Yates, Barbara H., B.Sc. ✊ ⚛
President, WOMEN'S ASSOCIATION OF THE MINING INDUSTRY OF CANADA, 49 Glengowan Rd., Toronto, ON M4N 1G1 (416) 484-9352. Born Orange, N.J. 1936. m. Edward M. Yates. 2 ch. **EDUC:** Cornell Univ., B.Sc.(Nutrition) 1958. **CAREER:** Dietetic Intern, Peter Bent Brigham Hospital, Boston, 1959; Head Dietitian, Overbrook Hospital, Cedar Grove, N.J., 1959-60; owner & teacher, Creative Cuisine Cooking Sch., 1982-90; Nat'l Home Economist, Micro Cooking Centres, Inc., 1984-87; owner, BHY Consultants, 1987-90. **VOLUNTEER CAREER:** Captain, Girl Guides of Canada, 1975-80; Counsellor of Terminally Ill, Pilgrimage, 1978-80; Volunteer Committee, Royal Ontario Museum, 1982 to date; Rom-Bus Chair, Royal Ontario Museum, 1985-86; Student Awards Convenor, Women's Association of the Mining Industry of Canada, 1990-91; Sofia Wood Awards Convenor, Women's Association of the Mining Industry of Canada, 1991-92; Rom-Walk Chair, Royal Ontario Museum, 1991-92; Docent, Royal Ontario Museum, 1993 to date; VP, Women's Association of the Mining Industry of Canada, 1993-

94; Group-Tours Chair, Royal Ontario Museum, 1994 to date; Pres., Women's Association of the Mining Industry of Canada, 1994-96. **SELECTED PUBLICATIONS:** articles in *Canadian Living Food Magazine, Canada-A La Carte Magazine, Kids Toronto Newspaper*. **AFFIL:** Canadian Dietetic Association; Ontario Dietetic Association; Ontario Home Economics Association; Home Economists in Business. **INTERESTS:** mineralogy; art; nutrition; sports; educ. **COMMENT:** *"In both my former professional career and my voluntary pursuits, I have tried to increase the knowledge of the general public through excellence in educational programs."*

Yewchin, Caroline, B.A.,M.Ed. ■ ■ $ ○ ◉
Co-owner and Manager, YEWCHIN'S FUNERAL CHAPEL (funeral svcs incl. bereavement counselling & support to families), P.O. Box 425, St. Paul, AB T0A 3A0 (403) 645-5177, FAX 645-4672. **EDUC:** Univ. of Alberta, B.A. 1974; Banff Sch. of Fine Arts, Mgmt Admin. 1985; St. Francis Xavier Univ., M.Ed.(Adult Educ.) 1989; Licenced Funeral Dir. 1993. **CAREER:** Caseworker, Handicapped Svcs/Addictions Counsellor, Alberta Alcohol & Drug Abuse Commission/Career Counsellor then Reg'l Supervisor, Advanced Educ. & Manpower, Gov't of Alta., 1974-86; private Consultant to gov't & educational institutions, 1986-89; Co-owner & Mgr, Yewchin's Funeral Chapel, 1986 to date. **SELECTED PUBLICATIONS:** "A Self-Directed Career Planning Guide"; "Face to Face with Loss in the Family" (for Family & Community Support Services, 1994). **AFFIL:** Alberta Funeral Service Association (Exec. Council 1993 to date; Chairperson, Educ. Committee); St. Paul Living with Loss Committee (founder 1987). **HONS:** Career Dev. Award of Excellence, 1986. **INTERESTS:** ice curling; golf; reading. **MISC:** workshop facilitator & trainer re coping with grief, 1987 to date; guest speaker re career transitions, Nat'l Guidance & Counselling Association conference, Ottawa, 1985; seconded to develop a career counsellor training program for Prov. of Alta., 1985; spearheaded the dev. of competancy-based distance educ. program for Funeral Directors & Embalmers in Alta, 1992 to date. **COMMENT:** *"I have always believed that education is a key to both individual personal growth as well as social and community development. I particularly enjoy the challenge of developing "new things," whether they be new approaches, methods or strategies. It is how we survive in an ever-changing environment."*

Yolles, Edie, B.A.,B.A.A. ⌣
President, GEMINI FILM PRODUCTIONS INC., 163

Queen St. E., Toronto, ON M5A 1S1 (416) 862-9031, FAX 363-0341. Born North Bay, Ont. m. Morden S. Yolles. 2 ch. **EDUC:** Univ. of Toronto, B.A.(Soc.), Masters in Town Planning; Ryerson Polytechnic Univ., B.A.A.(Film); Ontario Coll. of Art, Dipl.(Painting & Sculpture). **CAREER:** Research Analyst, Canadian Broadcasting Corporation; Town Planner, Metropolitan Planning Bd.; Pres., Gemini Film Productions; Instructor in Film Production, Ryerson Polytechnic Univ. **SELECTED CREDITS:** Assoc. Prod./Publicist/Stills Photographer, *Surfacing* (feature), dir. Claude Jutra;*That's My Baby!*; *Angels*; *Voice*; *Irving Grossman, Architect: Building a Stage Set for Life*. **AFFIL:** Writers' Guild of Canada; Canadian Society of Cinematographers (Assoc.); Toronto Women in Film & Television; Academy of Canadian Film & Television (Dir.). **HONS:** finalist (*That's My Baby!*), Int'l Film & TV Festival of N.Y.; Best Film, Social Action (*Angels*), Columbus Film Festival; Gold Award, Best Children's Film for Television (*Angels*), Int'l Film & TV Festival of N.Y.; Gold Medal, Best Film for TV for or about Children (*Angels*), Mifed Milan Int'l Competition. **INTERESTS:** photography; art; theatre; travel; people. **MISC:** 1 of 20 graduates & fac. selected for Marshall McLuhan's Interdisciplinary Seminar "Explorations in Communications." **COMMENT:** *"A spirit of inquiry; an aspiration for achievement and excellence; an effort for genuineness and integrity in all relationships and a concern for others."*

York, Lorraine, B.A.,M.A.,Ph.D. ⌖ 🕮
Associate Professor, English, MCMASTER UNIVERSITY, Hamilton, ON L8S 4L5 (905) 525-9104, ext. 23734, FAX 577-6930. Born London, Ont. 1958. m. Michael Ross. 1 ch. **EDUC:** McMaster Univ., B.A.(English) 1981, M.A. (English) 1982, Ph.D.(English) 1985. **CAREER:** Asst. Prof., McGill Univ., 1985-88; Asst. Prof., McMaster Univ., 1988-91; Assoc. Prof., 1991 to date. **SELECTED PUBLICATIONS:** *The Other Side of Dailiness: Photography in the Works of Alice Munro, Timothy Findley, Michael Ondaatje and Margaret Laurence* (1988); *Front Lines: The Fiction of Timothy Findley* (1991); *Various Atwoods: Essays on the Later Poems, Short Fiction and Novels*, ed. (1995). **AFFIL:** Modern Languages Association; Association for Canadian College & University Teachers of English; Association of Canadian & Québécois Literatures; Association for Canadian Studies in the US. **HONS:** Teaching Award for Humanities, McMaster Students' Union, 1990. **COMMENT:** *"A teacher and scholar of Canadian literature, specializing in feminist approaches to that area, I am currently broadening my research in writing a book about con-*

temporary women's collaborative art and multiple authorship theory."

Youldon, Darla, B.Comm.,C.A.M. ■ $

Vice-President, Finance and Administration, JOHN DEERE FINANCE LIMITED, 1001 Champlain Ave., Ste. 401, Burlington, ON L7L 5Z4 (905) 319-9100, FAX 319-2147. Vice-President, Finance and Administration, CANADIAN EQUIPMENT FINANCE CORPORATION. Born St. Catharines, Ont. 1952. m. James. 2 ch. **EDUC:** McMaster Univ., B.Comm.(Hons.) 1974. **CAREER:** Sr. Acctnt, Deloitte, Haskins & Sells, 1974-77; Mgr, Pricing Policies, Incentives & Admin., 1977-94; VP, Fin. & Admin., John Deere Finance Limited, 1994 to date. **AFFIL:** Canadian Manufacturers' Association (Nat'l Taxation & Fin. Policy Committee). **INTERESTS:** skiing; running; sewing; gardening. **MISC:** studied & lectured on impact of GST on agricultural industry, 1989-90; served as volunteer on the Ont. Fair Tax Commission representing manufacturers in Ont.; Certified Administrative Mgr.

Young, Catherine ■ ✊ ⊕ ✏

Chairmother, THE FRIENDS OF BREASTFEEDING SOCIETY, R.R. 3, Clifford, ON N0G 1M0 (519) 327-8785. Editor, *THE COMPLEAT MOTHER MAGAZINE*. Born Shelburne, Ont. 1952. d. 3 ch. **EDUC:** Conestoga Coll., Certificate (Journalism) 1975; George Brown Coll., Certificate (Co-Dependency) 1994. **CAREER:** Ed., *The Compleat Mother Magazine*, 1985 to date; author. **SELECTED PUBLICATIONS:** *Mother's Favourites* (NC Press); *Stretch Marks, Three Kids, Thirty-Six and Single* (Mother Press); *Mother's Best Secrets* (Mother Press). **AFFIL:** The Friends of Breastfeeding Society (Chairmother); The Tara Writers' Guild; Bruce County Breastfeeding Centre; The Saugeen Traders. **HONS:** The Rose of Gratitude, The Courage to Publish the Truth, Chicago, 1989; Woman of the Year, Grey & Bruce Counties, 1991. **INTERESTS:** bridge; farming rabbits; collecting antiques; travel; gardening. **MISC:** *Compleat Mother Magazine* is read by 15,000 mothers in 14 countries. **COMMENT:** *"She produced 305,000 breastfeeding posters with English and Spanish text."*

Young, Patricia Rose, B.A. ✪ 🎓

Poet and Educator. 130 Moss St., Victoria, BC V8V 4M3. Born Victoria, B.C. 1954. m. Terence 2 ch. Clea Fleur Young, Liam Ashdown Young. **EDUC:** Univ. of Victoria, B.A. 1983. **CAREER:** Asst. Ed., *The Malahat Review*, 1983-84; Coord., Open Space Poetry Reading Series, 1984-87; Sessional Instructor, Creative Writing Dept., Univ. of Victoria, 1985-91; Instructor for Poetry Workshops, Dept. of Extension, Univ. of Victoria, 1987, 1989, 1991. **SELECTED PUBLICATIONS:** *Travelling the Floodwaters* (Turnstone Press, 1983); *Melancholy Ain't No Baby* (Ragweed Press, 1985); *All I Ever Needed Was A Beautiful Room* (Oolichan Books, 1987); *The Mad and Beautiful Mothers* (Ragweed Press, 1989); *Those Were the Mermaid Days* (Ragweed Press, 1991); *More Watery Still* (House of Anansi Press, 1993); *Scenes From A Childhood* (Reference West, 1993); numerous poems in periodicals & anthologies. **AFFIL:** League of Canadian Poets. **HONS:** First Prize in Poetry, B.C. Federation of Writers, Literary Rites Competition, 1987; B.C. Book Prize for Poetry, 1988; National Magazine Award for Poetry (Silver), 1988; Second Prize for Poetry, CBC Literary Competition, 1988; co-winner, League of Canadian Poets Nat'l Poetry Contest, 1989; First Prize for Poetry, Aya Press Tenth Anniversary Literary Competition, 1989; Pat Lowther Memorial Award, 1990; Second Prize, League of Canadian Poets Nat'l Poetry Contest, 1993; shortlisted, Gov. General's Award, 1993; First Prize, Nat'l Poetry Contest, League of Canadian Poets, 1996. **MISC:** recipient, numerous grants.

Young, Rosemary, B.A.,M.A.,Ph.D. 🎓 ☝

Associate Professor and Chair, Department of Graduate and Undergraduate Studies, Faculty of Education, BROCK UNIVERSITY, St. Catharines, ON L2T 1W8 (905) 688-5550, ext. 3340, FAX 688-0544. Born St. Catharines, Ont. 1947. m. Don H. Shattuck. 1 ch. Daniel M. Shattuck. **EDUC:** Toronto Teachers' Coll., Ontario Teacher's Certificate 1969; Mohawk Coll., Diploma (Early Childhood Educ.) 1972; McMaster Univ., B.A. 1976, Ph.D.(Developmental Psych.) 1983; Univ. of Toronto, M.A. 1977. **CAREER:** Teacher, Cdn summer "Head Start" Projects, London, 1967, Toronto, 1968-69; Teacher, The Laneway Sch., 1969-70; Demonstration Teacher in lab. presch., Dept. of ECE, Mohawk Coll. of Applied Arts & Technology, 1972-75; Teaching Asst., Dept. of Psych./Ling., 1976-77; Supervisor, Day Care Subsidy Program, Reg'l Municipality of Hamilton-Wentworth, 1978; Teaching Asst., Dept. of Psych., McMaster Univ., 1979-82; various positions, Dept. of ECE, Mohawk Coll. of Applied Arts & Technology, 1974-81; Research Consultant, Research Dept., Toronto Bd. of Educ., 1982-83; Occasional Lecturer, Fac. of Educ., York Univ., 1984-86; Assoc. Mbr., Psych. Dept., Peel Bd. of Educ., 1983-86; Asst. Prof., Fac. of Educ., Brock Univ., 1986-93; Assoc. Prof. & Chair, Dept. of Grad. & Undergrad. Studies, 1994-96. **SELECTED PUBLICATIONS:**

Introduction to Early Childhood Education, with E. Essa (Toronto: Nelson, Canada, 1994); *Instructors Guide: Introduction to Early Childhood Education,* with others (Toronto: Nelson, Canada, 1994); "Newborns' Following of Natural Distorted Arrangements of Facial Features," with D. Maurer (*Infant Behavior and Development* 1983); "Research Summary" (Brock Education 1991); *Bringing the "Bedtime Story" into Inner-city Classrooms* (Toronto: Ministry of Educ., 1987); various other publications. **EDIT:** Newsletter Chair, Council for Exceptional Children, Early Childhood Educ. Div., 1993-94. **AFFIL:** Early Childhood Educators of B.C.; Association for Early Childhood Education; Ontario Psychological Association; Council for Exceptional Children; Canadian Association for the Education of Young Children; St. Catharines Parent-Child Resource Exchange; Niagara Council of Parent Cooperative Preschools; Women for P.A.C.E. (Canada); Canadian Child Care Federation; Irish Wolfhound Club of Canada. **HONS:** Dept. of Early Childhood Educ. Prize, Mohawk Coll. of Applied Arts & Technology, 1972; Dalley Senate Scholarship, McMaster Univ., 1975-76; McMaster Univ. Scholarship, 1979-82; Queen Elizabeth II Scholarship, 1981-82; Award for Excellence in Instructional Research, American Education Research Association, 1987; Pacesetters Award, Women for P.A.C.E. Canada, 1993. **INTERESTS:** gardening; Asian cuisine; family activities with a lively 6-yr. old; conformation, handling & obedience classes with our dog. **MISC:** Certification, Association for Early Childhood Educ. (Ont.), 1973; registered Psychologist, Ont., 1987; recipient, various grants; 1st woman to Chair Dept of Grad. & Undergrad. Studies in Educ. at Brock Univ.; 1st person to write a wholly Cdn text on early childhood educ. **COMMENT:** *"I have been interested in the education of young children, especially those at risk for delay because of impoverished environments, since the 1960s. I have pursued this interest and related research since that time. This interest actually led me to return to school in the 1970s, and eventually to my current position."*

Youngman, Alison J., LL.B. ■ ■ ⚖ Ⓢ Ⓞ
Partner, STIKEMAN, ELLIOTT (law firm), Commerce Ct. W., Ste. 5300, P.O. Box 85, Toronto, ON M5L 1B9 (416) 869-5684, FAX 947-0866, EMAIL ayoungman@tor.stikeman.com. Born London, UK **EDUC:** Concordia Univ., Fac. of Arts; Univ. of Toronto, Fac. of Arts; Osgoode Hall Law Sch., York Univ., LL.B. 1984. **BAR:** Ont., 1986; UK, 1994. **CAREER:** Ptnr, Stikeman, Elliott, practising corp. & commercial law primarily in areas of mergers &

acquisitions, joint ventures, corp. governance, domestic & int'l commercial matters incl. product distribution & mktg issues & non-profit. **SELECTED PUBLICATIONS:** chpt. in *Doing Business in Canada* (Matthew Bender); co-author, *Business Operations in Canada* (Tax Management Inc.); papers & articles re corp. & commercial matters incl. Federated Press publication on int'l joint ventures. **AFFIL:** Canadian Bar Association; Canadian Bar Association-Ontario (Corp. Law Sub-Committee); American Bar Association (Task Force on Int'l Joint Ventures); International Bar Association; Committee on International Business Law (Co-Chair, Intellectual Property Sub-Committee); Canadian Chamber of Commerce (Int'l Affairs Committee); Royal St. George's Coll. (Governance Committee). **MISC:** teaches Bar Admission Course in Prov. of Ont.; speaker/panelist, various conferences; fluent in French.

Z

Zaichkowsky, Judith Lynne, B.H.Ec., M.Sc.,Ph.D. 🎓 $

Professor of Marketing, Faculty of Business Administration, SIMON FRASER UNIVERSITY, Burnaby, BC V5A 1S6 (604) 291-4493, FAX 291-4920, EMAIL zaichkow@sfu.ca. Born Vancouver 1951. s. **EDUC:** Univ. of British Columbia, B.H.Ec. 1973; Univ. of Guelph, M.Sc.(Consumer Studies) 1976; Univ. of California at Los Angeles, Ph.D.(Mgmt) 1984. **CAREER:** Researcher, Consumer & Corp. Affairs, Ottawa, 1977; Research Assoc., Dept. of Mktg & Lecturer, Sch. of Home Econ., Univ. of British Columbia, 1977-78; Research & Teaching Asst., Dept. of Mktg, Univ. of California, L.A., 1979-82; Visiting Scholar, Univ. of British Columbia, 1984; Asst. Prof., Mktg, The American Univ., Washington, DC, 1984-85; Simon Fraser Univ., 1985 to date; Visiting Assoc. Prof., Univ. of British Columbia, 1990; Visiting Assoc. Prof., UCLA, 1991; Visiting Assoc. Prof., Univ. of Technology, Sydney, 1991; Visiting Assoc. Prof., Copenhagen Bus. Sch., 1993; Visiting Prof., INSEAD, 1995; Visiting Prof., Copenhagen Bus. Sch., 1996. **SELECTED PUBLICATIONS:** *Defending Your Brand Against Imitation: Consumer Behavior, Marketing Strategies and Legal Issues* (Westpoint, Conn.: Quorum Books, 1995); "Measuring the Involvement Construct" (*Journal of Consumer Research* Dec. 1985); "Consumer Behavior: Yesterday, Today, and Tomorrow" (*Business Horizons*, 1991; Annual Editions of *Marketing*, 1993, 1994, 1995); "The Effect of Experience with a Brand Imitator of the Original Brand" (*Marketing Letters*, 1996); numerous other publications. **EDIT:** Ed., Special Issue on Involvement, *Psychology and Marketing*

10(4) 1993. **AFFIL:** American Marketing Association (BC Chapter); Association for Consumer Research; American Academy of Advertising; Society for Consumer Psychology; American Psychological Association, Div. 23; Alpha Mu Alpha (Mktg Hon. Society); Beta Gamma Sigma. **HONS:** Mary Clarke Scholarship, 1981; Canada Council Doctoral Fellowship, 1981-83. **INTERESTS:** research interest in brand imitation. **MISC:** recipient, various grants; "Measuring the Involvement Construct" (*Journal of Consumer Research* Dec. 1985) identified as 1 of the most cited articles in the field, *Journal of Consumer Research*, Dec. 1991.

Zalesky, Rose Ⓢ ⚙ Ⓞ
Secretary-Treasurer and Co-Founder, BUSINESS AIRCRAFT CORPORATION LTD., c/o 14645 Bellevue Cres., White Rock, BC V4B 2V1 (604) 535-2638, FAX 535-2683. Born Hazelmere, Alta. 1930. m. 2 ch. **CAREER:** Co-Owner & Co-Operator, Ed's Western Aviation Sales Ltd., dba Airplane Supply Centre, 1952 to date; Sec.-Treas. & Co-Founder, Business Aircraft Corp., 1957 to date. **VOLUNTEER CAREER:** Sec.-Treas., Exec. Dir. & Founding Dir., Canadian Museum of Flight & Transportation, 1974 to date; Sec.-Treas., Canadian Aeronautical Preservation Association, 1985-86; Sec.-Treas., Transportation Collections Association, 1989-96. **SELECTED PUBLICATIONS:** Proj. Dir. & Co-author, *Pioneering Aviation in the West* (1993). **EDIT:** Ed., *Canadian Museum of Flight & Transportation Newsletter*, 1979-94. **INTERESTS:** gardening; writing; hiking; collecting. **COMMENT:** "*Busy, active, always ready to take on new challenges. Juggling a 42-year career in aviation, family and other interests is sometimes difficult but always rewarding.*"

Zann, Lenore ⊗ ⛄ 🐾
Actor, Singer and Producer. c/o Oscars and Abrams, 59 Berkeley St., Toronto, ON M5A 2W5 (416) 860-1790. Producer, KOOKABURRA PRODUCTIONS. Born Sydney, Australia. **SELECTED CREDITS:** Actor/Prod., *Johnston... Johnston* (short film); Actor, *Cold Sweat*; Actor, *Gross Misconduct* (telefilm); Actor, *Love and Hate* (telefilm); Guest Star, *Street Legal* (series), CBC; Actor, *Booze Can*; Actor, *Love and Human Remains* (theatre) in major cities in Canada & the US incl. Toronto, Chicago & N.Y. **HONS:** Best Actress in a Radio Drama (*Salt Water Moon*), ACTRA Award, 1986; Best Film (*Johnston..Johnston*), Houston Int'l Short Film Festival, 1995. **COMMENT:** "*Began acting professionally at 16, at the Neptune Theatre. At 19 went on to play Marilyn Monroe in the rock opera Hey Marilyn at the Citadel Theatre to national acclaim. After many theatre,*

film and television performances (including Human Remains off-Broadway), produced first film in 1994 called Johnston..Johnston. Proud to be a Canadian woman in the arts. May we all flourish."

Zawerbny, Janice Adèle, B.A.,M.A. ■ ☐
Assistant Editor and Cyber-Editor, SOMERVILLE HOUSE BOOKS, 3080 Yonge St., Ste. 6000, Toronto, ON M6N 2N1 (416) 488-5938, EMAIL sombooks@goodmedia.com. Born Toronto 1968. s.. **EDUC:** Centennial Coll., Book & Magazine Publishing Diploma 1992; York Univ., B.A.(English/Mass Comm.) 1994, M.A.(English) 1995. **CAREER:** freelance writer, ed. & multi-media content developer, 1992 to date; Ed. Asst., Lester Publishing, 1992; Ed. Asst., Publishing, Coach House Press, 1992; Mng. Ed., *Descant* Literary Magazine, 1993-94; Co-Ed., 1994 to date; Asst. Ed., Somerville House Books, 1996 to date. **AFFIL:** Book Publishers' Professional Association; Canadian Association for the Legalization of Marijuana. **HONS:** Grad. Assistance Scholarship, 1994-95. **INTERESTS:** int'l cuisine; wine collecting; photography; furniture restoration; antique book collecting; European/S. American travel; cycling; metaphysics. **COMMENT:** "*People think I'm a nymphomaniac when all I really want to do is read books*"–Madonna.

Zelmer, Amy, B.Sc.N.,M.P.H., Ph.D. ■ ■ ⊕ 🦌
Honorary Professor, CENTRAL QUEENSLAND UNIVERSITY, P.O. Box 1414, Rockhampton, Queensland 4700 - Australia 61-79-306319, FAX 61-79-309871, EMAIL a.zelmer@cqu.edu.au. Born Halifax, N.S. m. A.C. Lynn Zelmer. 1 ch. Jennifer Lynne Zelmer. **EDUC:** Univ. of Western Ontario, B.Sc.N.(Nursing Educ.) 1961; Univ. of Michigan, M.P.H. (Health Educ.) 1963; Michigan State Univ., Ph.D.(Adult Educ.) 1973. **CAREER:** Public Health Nurse/Health Educator, gov't & voluntary agencies, N.S. & Alta., 1957-67; Asst. Prof., Dept. of Extension, Sch. of Nursing & Div. of Health Svcs Admin., Univ. of Alberta, Edmonton, 1967-72; Health Educ. Specialist, Family Planning/MCH Program, S.E. Asia Reg., World Health Organization, New Delhi, India, 1975-76; Dean & Prof., Fac. of Nursing, Univ. of Alberta, 1976-80; Assoc. VP (Academic) & Prof., 1980-88; Prof. & Foundation Dean, Fac. of Health Sci., Central Queensland Univ., Rockhampton, Australia, 1988-96; Hon. Prof., 1996 to date. **SELECTED PUBLICATIONS:** co-author with Jillian Brammer, *Clinical Teaching* (Deakin Univ., monograph, 1996); author, "Shoe Store: Group Problem Solving" (in *The Encyclopedia of Team-Development*

Activities, J. William Pfeiffer (ed.), University Associates, Inc., 1991); co-author with Neil Johnson, "International Students in Higher Education: A Follow-Up Study of University Graduates" (*Canadian Journal of Higher Education*, XVIII-3, 1988); content & scenario writer, *Diabetes Education* (CD-ROM, produced by CQU under grant from Committee for the Advancement of Teaching, 1996); subject-matter expert & presenter, *Education in Non-Formal Settings* (7-part videotaped series for PAGE Consortium & SBS, 1994). **AFFIL:** Public Health Association, Australia; Association of Science Communicators; Higher Education Research & Development Society of Australasia; International Women's Development Agency, Australia; International Council for Educational Administration; Canadian Society for International Health (Bd. of Dir. 1985-88); North-South Institute, Ottawa (Bd. of Dir. 1983-88); MATCH-links women's groups in Canada & 3rd world for dev. (founding mbr. & western Bd. mbr. 1985-87); Royal Coll. of Nursing, Australia (Fellow); Canadian Association for the History of Nursing; Central Region Health Authority, Queensland (mbr., & Chair, Ethics Committee 1991-95). **MISC:** dual citizenship, Cdn & Australian.

Zemans, Joyce Pearl, B.A.,M.A. ■ ⌇ 🎨
Professor, Faculty of Fine Arts, YORK UNIVERSITY, 4700 Keele St., Toronto, ON M3J 1P3 (416) 736-5187. Born Toronto 1940. m. Frederick H. Zemans. 3 ch. EDUC: Univ. of Toronto, B.A. 1962, M.A.(Art Hist.) 1966. CAREER: Co-Chair, Dept. of Art Hist., Ontario Coll. of Art, 1970-71; Chair, Dept. of Liberal Arts, 1973-75; Chair, Dept. of Visual Arts, York Univ., 1975-81; Assoc. Prof., Art Hist., 1975-95; Dean, Fac. of Fine Arts, 1985-88; Dir., Canada Council, 1989-92; Co-Dir., M.B.A. Program in Arts & Media Admin., Fac. of Admin. Studies, 1994 to date; Robarts Chair in Cdn Studies, 1995-96. SELECTED PUBLICATIONS: *Christopher Pratt* (1985); *Jock Macdonald* (1986); *Kathleen Munn and Edna Tacon: New Perspectives on Modernism* (1989); various articles in professional journals concerning art history & cultural policy. AFFIL: Laidlaw Foundation (Pres.); International Association of Art Critics; University Art Association; College Art Association; Comité International de l'histoire de l'art, Canada.

Zerbisias, The Hon. Dionysia, B.A., B.C.L. ■ ⚖️
Judge, SUPERIOR COURT OF QUEBEC, Palais de Justice, 1 Notre-Dame St. E., Montreal, QC H2Y 1B6 (514) 393-2183, FAX 393-2773. Born Montreal 1939. m. 2 ch. EDUC: Sir

George Williams Univ., B.A. 1959; McGill Univ., B.C.L. 1962. BAR: Que., 1963. CAREER: Attorney, Jr. Assoc. & Ptnr, Adessky Kingstone, 1963-83; Sr. Ptnr, Adessky, Kingstone, Zerbisias, Poulin, Gervais and Bier, 1971-83; Puisne Judge of the Superior Court, District of Montreal, 1983-96; Ad Hoc Judge, Court of Appeal of Quebec, 1996-97. AFFIL: Canadian Institute for the Administration of Justice; Canadian Judges' Conference; Canadian Bar Association; University Club of Montreal. PAST AFFIL: Hellenic Canadian Community of the Island of Montreal (Commission for Community Dev. 1972, 1973; Bd. of Trustees 1974); L'Aide à la Femme Inc. (Dir. 1975-77); YMCA (Legal Consultant, Women's Centre 1970-73; Legal Consultant 1973; Participant & Co-Founder, Women's Legal Info. & Referral Svcs 1973; Bd. of Dir. 1976-78, 1980-83); Parliamentarian Association of North America (1960-65); Greek Orthodox Community of the Archangels Michael & Gabriel (Pres. 1972). INTERESTS: sailing; scuba diving; skiing; gardening.

Zimmerman, Selma, B.A.,M.S., Ph.D. ⌇ 🎨
Professor, Natural Science, YORK UNIVERSITY, Glendon College, 2275 Bayview Ave., Toronto, ON M4N 3M6 (416) 487-6732. Born N.Y. 1930. m. Arthur Zimmerman. 3 ch. Susan Ann, Beth Leslie, Robert James. EDUC: Hunter Coll., B.A.(Zoology) 1950; New York Univ., M.S.(Embryology) 1954, Ph.D.(Embryology) 1958. CAREER: Coord., Environmental & Health Sciences, Glendon Coll., York Univ., 1977-82; Coord., Women's Studies Program, 1983-84; Prof. of Natural Sci., 1987 to date; Coord., Environmental & Health Sciences, 1989-90; Advisor to York Univ. on the Status of Women, 1991-94. SELECTED PUBLICATIONS: "Physiological Responses of Amphibian Melanophores," with H.C. Dalton (*Physiological Zoology* 1961); "Effects of Cannabinoids on Sperm Morphology," A.M. Zimmerman & W.R. Bruce (*Pharmacology* 1979); "Anandamide (arachidonylethanolamide) A Brain Cannabinoid Receptor Agonist, Reduces Sperm Fertilizing Capacity in Sea Urchins by Inhibiting the Acrosome Reactions," with others (*Proceedings of the National Academy of Science*, USA 1994); numerous other papers & chapters in books. EDIT: Ed., *Bulletin of Canadian Society for Cell and Molecular Biology*, 1985-87. AFFIL: Canadian Society for Cell & Molecular Biology; Canadian Association for Women in Science; Phi Sigma (Biol. Hon. Society 1950). HONS: Founders Day Award, New York Univ., 1958; Research Fellowship Award, Glendon Coll., 1987; Volunteer Service Award, Institute

of Association Managers Corp., 1988; Teaching Award, Glendon Coll., 1989. **INTERESTS:** science educ. for the public; girls & women–focus on science educ. & careers; her 4 grandchildren. **MISC:** Visiting Scientist, Univ. of Texas, Health Sci. Center, San Antonio, 1975, 1984; Visiting Scientist, Weizmann Institute of Science, Israel, 1982; Visiting Scientist, Coll. of Medicine, Gainesville, Fla., 1983. **COMMENT:** *"My career has been based on doing science and teaching science, however, my family has always been my primary focus. Throughout my career, I have endeavoured to achieve equality for women–particularly in science education and careers."*

Zukerman, Helen 🏕 ◐ ☖

Administrator and Trustee, ZUKERMAN CHARITABLE FOUNDATION, 33 Prince Arthur Ave., 2nd Fl., Toronto, ON M5R 1B2 (416) 324-8810, FAX 324-9415. Born Montreal 1944. w. 2 ch. **VOLUNTEER CAREER:** Administrator & Trustee, Zukerman Charitable Foundation, 1986 to date; Founder & Prod., Toronto Jewish Film Festival/Toronto Jewish Film Foundation, 1993 to date. **AFFIL:** New Israel Fund Canada (Past Pres.); Jewish Film Festival (Pres. of Bd. 1994-97); Univ. of Toronto (Yiddish Studies Committee); Canadian Women's Foundation (Toronto Supporter). **INTERESTS:** hiking; film; travel; folk festivals; tennis; music; theatre. **MISC:** developed mother-child play-discussion group, YWCA, 1974-76; involved in Children's V.O.I.C.E. & Women's V.O.I.C.E. projects, 1987-89; Barry Zukerman Investment Fund, McGill Univ. (for bus. students running stock portfolios) & Barry Zukerman Amphitheatre (free theatre during the summer months). **COMMENT:** *"Having been raised in a modest home with strong social justice views, I consider myself fortunate to bring to the world of grant-making a view from across the table. My daughters and I treat the challenge of running the foundation as a privilege."*

Zwicky, Jan, B.A.,M.A.,Ph.D. ■ 🖘 🖺 🗍

Box 1149, Mayerthorpe, AB T0E 1N0. Poet and Professor, UNIVERSITY OF VICTORIA. Born Alta. 1955. **EDUC:** Univ. of Calgary, B.A.(Phil.) 1976; Univ. of Toronto, M.A.(Phil.) 1977, Ph.D. (Phil.) 1981. **CAREER:** Postdoctoral Fellow/SSHRCC Private Fellow, 1981-83, 1986-87, 1988-89; Prof., Univ. of Waterloo, 1981-82, 1985-86; Prof., Princeton Univ., 1982-83; Ed., Brick Books, 1986 to date; Prof., Univ. of Western Ontario, 1989-90; Prof., Univ. of Alberta, 1992-93; Prof., Univ. of New Brunswick, 1994-96; Prof., Univ. of Victoria, 1996 to date. **SELECTED PUBLICATIONS:** *Wittgenstein Elegies*, poetry (Brick Books, 1986); *The New Room*, poetry (Coach House Press, 1989); *Lyric Philosophy* (Univ. of Toronto Press, 1992); *Songs for Relinquishing the Earth* (Cashion Editions, 1996). **MISC:** numerous grants for creative work. **COMMENT:** *"Jan Zwicky is a scholar and poet whose work engages simultaneously with overtly philosophical and lyric elements in thought."*

INDEX BY COMPANY NAME

Aboriginal Multi-Media Society of Canada
Lockyer, D., Ed., *Windspeaker*

L'Académie de Ballet Sonia Vartanian (S.V.) Inc.
Vartanian, S., Fondatrice et directrice

Academy of Canadian Cinema and Television
Topalovich, M., CEO

Acadia University
Bedingfield, E.W., Fac. of Mgmt & Educ.
Davies, G., Head & Prof. of English
Johnston, E., Dir., Sch. of Nutrition & Food Sci.
Kukal, O., Asst. Prof. of Biol.

Accent Entertainment Corporation
Cavan, S., Chair & CEO

Accessible Housing Society
Nickel, D., Exec. Dir.

Acoustic Neuroma Association of Canada
Garossino, V., Past Pres.

Action Group Against Harassment and Discrimination in the Workplace
Williams, B.K., Pres.

L'actualité
Fournel, J., Art Director

Addiction Research Foundation
Annis, H.M., Chief, Behaviour Change Unit

Adoption Council of Ontario
Fenton, P., Exec. Dir., Adoption Resource Centre

Adrienne Clarkson Presents
Clarkson, A., Exec. Prod., Host & Writer

Adventure Place
Will, C., Exec. Dir.

Advertising Standards Council
Delage, N., Exec. Dir.

Advocacy Group for the Environmentally Sensitive
Laurin, M.C., Nat'l Pres.

The Advocates' Society
Chyczij, A., Exec. Dir.

Agnes Etherington Art Centre
Smith, F.K., Curator Emeritus

Agriculture & Agri-Food Canada Research Centre
Fraser, J., Research Scientist

Aikins, MacAulay & Thorvaldson
Dawson, E.R., Ptnr

Air BC
Davies, L., VP, Comm. Svcs

Air Cadet League of Canada
Doty, I., Past Nat'l Pres.

Air Canada
Comtois, C., Asst. Sec. & Shareholder Rel'ns Dir.
Fagnan, I., Dir., Process & Bus. Dev. Sales
Fournel, L., VP, Info. Tech. & CIO
Laviolette, J.M., Dir., Pricing & Yield Mgmt
Poudrette, D., Sr. Dir., Product Mgmt
Price, D., VP, Airports

Sonberg, M., Dir., Customer Svc. Comm., Employee Involvement & Training

Air Tango
Henderson, J., Pres.

Air-O-Sols
Schiff, D., Co-Dir. & Pilot

Aird & Berlis
Histrop, L.A., Ptnr
Pepino, N.J., Ptnr

Alberta Association of Architects
Cairns, P.A., Exec. Dir. & Registrar

The Alberta Association of Rehabilitation Centres
Roberson, G., Exec. Dir.

Alberta Ballet School
Carse, R., Founder & Exec. Dir.

Alberta Cancer Board
Bryant, H., Dir., Div. of Epidemiology, Prevention & Screening & Dir., Alberta Program for the Early Detection of Breast Cancer
Campbell, H.S., Behavioural Research Scientist
Green, S.L., VP

Alberta Cancer Foundation
Berkhold, B. F., Trustee
Green, S.L., Exec. Officer

Alberta Chapter of the Registry of Interpreters for the Deaf
Loos, L., Past Pres.

Alberta Children's Hospital
Eccles, R.C., Pediatric Surgeon
Geggie, J., Pediatric Clinical Dietitian
Grebenc, K.D., Clinical Dietitian, Outpatient Diabetes Clinic, Clinical Nutrition Svcs
Nijssen-Jordan, C., Dir. of Emergency Svcs
Wilson, L., Clinical Practice Coord., Nursing Educ. Dept.

Alberta Children's Hospital Foundation
Macaulay, L.D., Dev. Coord.

Alberta Children's Hospital Research Centre
Kaplan, B., Dir., Behavioural Research Unit

Alberta Committee of Citizens with Disabilities
Matthiessen, B.D., Exec. Dir.

Alberta Craft Council
Abells, S., Exec. Dir.

Alberta Energy Company Ltd.
Rimell, D., VP, Corp. Svcs

Alberta Federation of Women United for Families
Snee, B.-A., Past Pres. & Exec. Dir., Pro-family Legal Defence

Alberta Funeral Service Association
Paget, G., Exec. Administrator

Alberta Human Rights Commission
Dean, A., Legal Cnsl

Alberta Library Trustees Association
McMullan-Baron, S., Past Pres.

Alberta Long Term Care Association
Mills, C., Exec. Dir.
Alberta Re-Tech Ltd.
Bales, L., Pres. & CEO
Alberta Registered Dietitians Association
Kirkland, L., Past Pres.
Alberta Rugby Football Union
Wright, H., Exec. Tech. Dir.
Alberta Vocational College
Starkman, E., English Instructor
Alberta Wheat Pool
DuPont, B., Dir., Hum. Res. & Admin.
Albikin Management Inc.
Billes, M., Pres.
Alexander and Alexander (Reed Stenhouse Ltd.)
Light, M.A., Nat'l Personal Lines Mgr
Alexander, Holburn, Beaudin & Lang
Carmichael, J.A., Ptnr
Watters, F.R., Ptnr
The Alexandra WSA International
Konnelly, R., Founder, Dir.
Algonquin College
Hanson, R.L., VP, Academic
Paterson, J., Exec. Dean, Sch. of Applied Arts & Bus.
Allegro Films Inc.
Bradley, M.M., VP, Bus. Affairs
Allied Corporate Services Inc.
Smalley, K., Pres.
Allied Indian and Métis Society
White, M., Exec. Dir.
The Alternate Press
Priesnitz, W., Publisher
Alzheimer Prince Edward Island
McCann-Beranger, J., Exec. Dir.
Amana House
Paschal, A.G., Dir.
Amara International Investment Corporation
Kwok, E.L., Pres. & CEO
Ambrose Carr Linton Carroll Inc.
Carroll, E., Pres. & CEO
The American Dietetic Association
Schwartz, N.E., Dir., Nat'l Centre for Nutrition & Dietetics
Amoco Canada Petroleum Company Ltd.
McClare, S., Administrator
Amyotrophic Lateral Sclerosis Society of Canada
Morse, E., Mbr., Support Svcs Committee
Weir, S.R., Pres., Alta. Chapter
Amyotrophic Lateral Sclerosis Society of Prince Edward Island
Salamoun-Dunne, M., Past Pres.
An Advantage
Crocker, O.L., CEO
Andreachuk Harvie MacLennan
Andreachuk, L., Ptnr

Andrews-Cayley Enterprises
Andrews, J., Ptnr
Anglican Church of Canada
Matthews, V., Bishop of the Credit Valley, Diocese of Toronto
Angus Dortmans Associates
Angus, E., VP
Angus TeleManagement Group Inc.
Angus, E., Exec. VP
Aplastic Anemia Association of Canada
Levine, R., Chairperson
Appel Consultants Inc.
Appel, B., Chrm
Apple Canada Inc.
Gundersen, S.J., VP, Law & Corp. Dev.
Applied Communications Canada, Inc.
Moyer, J.M., Pres. & CEO
Applin Marketing & Communications
Applin, A.-M.H., Pres.
Arcady Films
Henderson, A., Film Dir. & Prod.
Archelaus Smith Historical Society
Messenger, M., Past Pres. & Sec.-Treas.
Archéocène inc.
Duguay, F., Pres.
Architectural Institute of British Columbia
Williams, C., Exec. Dir.
Archives Society of Alberta
Denham, E., Archives Advisor
Arctic Enterprises Ltd.
Payne, A.V., Pres.
June Ardiel Ltd.
Ardiel, J.V., Pres.
Armbro Enterprises Inc.
Duffy, S., Corp. Sec.
Laura Arsie Photography
Arsie, L., Owner
Art Gallery of Newfoundland and Labrador
Grattan, P., Exec. Dir.
Art Gallery of Nova Scotia
MacAlpine Foshay, S., Exhibitions Curator
Art Gallery of Ontario
Bouma-Pyper, M., Graphic Designer, Creative Svcs
Lochan, K., Sr. Curator, Prints & Drawings
Rix, B.D., Supervisor, Print & Drawing Study Centre
Yarymowich, A., Exec. Chef
Art Gallery of York University
Yarlow, L., Dir. & Curator
Artemesia and Associates
Warner, E., Writer/Columnist, Owner & Principal Writer
The Arthritis Society
McKinnon, S.L., Exec. Dir., Sask. Div.
Wolstenholme, T.E., Exec. Dir., N.B. Div.
Arts and Communications Counselors
Wright, N.K., Pres. & Chrm

Ashbury College
Brodsky, L.M., Biol. Teacher
Assiniboine Community College
Cooke, B., Pres.
Proven, B., Chair, Distance Educ. & Media
Associated Manitoba Arts Festivals, Inc.
Oliver, K., Exec. Dir.
**Association of Canadian
Choral Conductors**
Abbott, P.A., Exec. Dir.
Association of Early Childhood Educators
Gallimore, R., Exec. Dir.
Association of Indo-Canadian Physicians
Khan, S., Pres.
Association of Manitoba Book Publishers
Devanik Butterfield, M., Dir.
**Association of Nurses of Prince
Edward Island**
Gosbee, R., Exec. Dir. & Registrar
**Association of Professional Engineers and
Geoscientists of the Province of
British Columbia**
Thorstad, L., Pres.
**Association of Registered Nurses of
Newfoundland**
Adey, E., Exec. Dir.
**Association pour l'Éducation
Interculturelle du Québec**
Desroches, F., Pres.
Athabasca University
Roberts, B.A., Prof., Women's Studies
Athey, Gregory and Hughes
Hughes, S.J.L., Lawyer
Athletics Canada
Killingbeck, M.E., Assoc. National Relay Team
Coord.
Atlantic Canada Opportunities Agency
Stevenson, L., Dir., Entrepreneurship Dev.
Atlantic Health Sciences Corporation
Doiron, C.A., VP, Oper. & Planning
Atlas Textile Print Ltd.
Braverman, D., Pres.
Authority of Sidney Township
Benson, L.J., Dir. of Public Works
Autism Society New Brunswick
Cunningham, K., Pres.
**Autism Society of Newfoundland
& Labrador**
Hopkins, B., Pres.
Automated Communication Links, Inc.
Kinsman, C.M., Owner & Pres.
**Autonetics Research Associates
Incorporated**
Booth, K.H.V., CEO
Avenor Inc.
Collin, E., VP, Comm. & Gov't Affairs
Avon Canada Inc.
Lacey, R., Dir., Comm.

B

BC Bearing Engineers Limited
McDonald, W.B., Chrm of the Bd. & CEO
BCBusiness Magazine
Irving, B., Ed.
B.C. Gas Inc.
Lambert, V., VP & Treas.
B.C. Hydro
Sexsmith, G., Sr. VP, Customer Svc.
BC Pictures
Connolly, B.B., Producer, Writer, Host, Narrator, Co-Founder
BC Rehabilitation Society
Jennings, D., Mgr, Clinical Support Svcs
**B.C. Research Institute for Child
and Family Health**
Sturrock, A., Dir. & Chair
BC School Sports
Payne, M., Exec. Dir.
BC TEL
Blaney, E.S., Mgr of Corp. Health
Borghesi, C., Asst. VP, Bus. & Corp. Sales
Byrne, D., VP, Law & Regulatory Affairs
Kruse, K., Dir., Corp. Health
Welland, F.J., Gov't Rel'ns Dir.
Western, S., Bus. Mgr, Home Office
BC TELECOM Inc.
Byrne, D., VP, Law & Regulatory Affairs
B.C. Women's Hospital & Health Centre
Cranston, L.S., Pres. & CEO
BOC Canada Limited
Provenzano, D., Co. Sec.
BACCHUS Canada
Cimicata, C., Exec. Dir. & Founder
Back Alley Film Productions Ltd.
Lundman, J., Dir. & Prod.
Mitchell, A., Filmmaker
Lida Baday Ltd.
Baday, L., Pres.
Badd Sisters
Christie, D., Pres.
Badminton B.C.
Coutts, D., Exec. Dir.
Bahá'í Faith
Rabbani, M., Hand of the Cause
Bahá'í International Community
Martens, E., Consultant, Primary Health Care
Bain & Company Canada
Milway, K.S., Consultant
Carroll Baker Ent. Inc.
Baker, C., Singer
Baker Lake Fine Arts
Mamnguqsualuk, V., Artist
Baker & McKenzie
Hall, M.C., Ptnr
The Ballantree Group
Stoddart-Hansen, S., Pres.
The Banff Centre for Continuing Education
Bye, C., Ed. & Sr. Writer, Comm. & Dev. Dept
.

The Banff Centre for the Arts
Wyatt, R., Program Dir., Writing, & Dir., The
Banff Radio Drama Workshop

Banff Centre Press
Elton, H., Ed.

Bank of Canada
Ip, I., Research Adviser, Research Dept.

Bank of Montreal
Kinsley, M., Sr. VP & Chief Auditor
Macmillan, K.E., VP, Corp. Mktg, Public
Affairs
Patten Di Giacomo, R., Sr. VP, Corp. Svcs
Roveto, C.I., Sr. VP, Asset Mgmt Svcs
Rozsa, M., VP, Independent Bus & Agric.
Shettler, R.B., VP, Aboriginal Affairs
Snider, C., Sr. VP, Personal & Commercial Fin.
Svcs
Stairs, H.H.D., Sr. VP, Hum. Res. Div.
Sum, P., VP, Asian Mkts

The Bank of Nova Scotia
Cannon, L.L., Sr. VP, Compliance

Bank Works Trading Inc.
Sinclair, H.K., CEO

Barrat and Associates Inc.
Barrat, O., Research Scientist

Barrick Gold Corporation
Veenman, S.E., Assoc. Gen. Cnsl & Sec.

Basketball Manitoba
Kendall, G.J., Exec. Dir.

Basketball Nova Scotia
Dow, P., Exec. Dir.

Bata Limited
Bata, S., Dir.

Bata Shoe Museum Foundation
Bata, S., Chrm

Baton Broadcasting Incorporated
Oda, B.J., Sr. VP
Shafran, G., VP & Gen. Cnsl

The Basilisk Company
Gainsbourg, G.K., Co-Designer

Baxter, Phillips & Associates
Baxter, M., Consultant

The Beaver: Exploring Canada's History
Preston, C., Assoc. Ed.

Nuala Beck & Associates Inc.
Beck, N.M., Pres.

**Beckman Associates Library
Consultants Inc.**
Beckman, M., Pres.

Beehive Investments Limited
Ivey, B., Pres.

Belicki and Belicki
Belicki, K., Ptnr

Bell Canada
Meltzer, S., Dir., Risk Mgmt & Insur.
Scott, S.E., VP, Multimedia Law & Regulation

Belleville Public Library Board
Hendry, L., CEO

Benchmark Communications
Corriveau, S., Sr. Consultant

Bennecon Limited
Cook-Bennett, G., Exec. VP

Bennet Communications Limited
Bennet, L., Pres. & CEO

Jalynn H. Bennett and Associates Ltd.
Bennett, J.H., Pres.

Bonnie Benoit & Associates Ltd.
Benoit, B.E., Owner

Beringian Books
Whyard, F.E., Publisher

Berlin Studio Inc.
Solowan, B., Art Dir.

Irene Besse Keyboards Ltd.
Besse, I., Pres./Owner

Bethany Historical Society
Morton, K., Pres.

**Better Business Bureau of
Western Ontario**
Delaney, J., Pres. & Gen. Mgr.

Beverage Recovery in Canada
Kerr, S.D., Chair

Birt and McNeill
Birt, N.E., Ptnr
McNeill, K.M., Ptnr

Birth Control/VD Info Centre
Omer Hashi, K., Community Health Educator
& Counsellor

Bishop's University
Clark-Jones, M., Full Prof. & Chair, Soc. Dept.
Taborsky, E., Assoc. Prof., Dept. of Soc. &
Anthro.

BKW Enterprises
Williams, B.K., Pres. & Legal Writer/
Researcher

Blackburn Media Group
Kehoe, C.A., Internet Svcs Mgr

Blake, Cassels and Graydon
Hughes, P.S., Cnsl
Stewart, A.M., Ptnr

Blaney, McMurtry, Stapells, Friedman
Garson, J.H., Ptnr

Blast Models Inc.
Siebert, T., Pres. & Owner

Block Parent Program of Canada Inc.
Barnhill, J.E.M., Publicity & Promo. Mgr

**Bloorview Children's Hospital
Foundation**
Watson, C.F., Chair

Bloorview MacMillan Centre
Brown, F., V-Chair of the Bd. of Trustees

Blue-Zone Technologies Inc.
Filipovic, D., Chrm of the Bd.

Blyth Festival
Amos, J., Artistic Dir.

**The Board of Education for the City of
North York**
Lacey, V.A., Dir. of Educ. & Sec.-Treas.

**The Board of Trade of Metropolitan
Toronto**
Allan, E.M., CEO

F.L. Bodogh Lumber Co. Ltd.
Bodogh, M.C., Mgr
Body Matters Ltd.
Scott, K., Designer, Mktg Dir. & Sec.-Treas.
The Body Shop
Franssen, M., Pres. & Ptnr
Bohemia Productions Inc.
Veverka, J.M., Pres.
Books for Business
Cooney, J., Pres.
Borden & Elliot
Burnham, M.E., Cnsl
Le Bouclier d'Athena/The Shield of Athena
Kamateros, M., Exec. Dir.
Bowling Federation of Saskatchewan Inc.
Kurbis Sereda, R., Exec. Dir.
Bramalea Medical Group
Kohut, V., M.D.
Brandon University
Cederstrom, L.S., Prof. of English
Quinn, L., Assoc. Prof. & Chair, Dept. of Geology
The Brant Group
LaCroix, N.P., Pres.
Braun Consulting Engineers Ltd.
Lonsdale, T., Principal
Braverman Holdings Ltd.
Braverman, D., Sec.
J. Braverman Inc.
Braverman, D., Mng Dir. & Sec.
Brent & Greenhorn
Brent, A.S., Mng Ptnr
Brescia College
Kuntz, S., Principal
Bridge Film Productions Inc.
Berman, B., Dir., Writer & Prod.
Briefcase Productions Inc.
Green, J.-L., Pres. & Dir.
Brightside Realty
Kennedy, C., Realtor
British Columbia Amateur Softball Association
Martens, J., Pres.
British Columbia Arts in Education Council
Lane, E.A., Treas.
British Columbia Association of Community Law Offices
Irvine, M., Coordinator
British Columbia Association of Health Care Auxiliaries
Popil, I., Admin. Sec.
British Columbia Association of Specialized Victim Assistance Counsellors Programs
Porteous, T., Consultant
British Columbia Council for the Family
Matusicky, C., Exec. Dir.

British Columbia Dietitians' and Nutritionists' Association
Macdonald, J., Exec. Dir.
British Columbia Ferry Corporation
Allen, E.R., Capt. (Relief) & Mate, Minor Vessel
Bardos, J., VP, Hum. Res.
Caldwell, E.P., Dir., Comm. & Client Rel'ns
British Columbia Government and Service Employees' Union
Pratt, P., Dir., Contract & Resource Svcs
Wood, D.L., Sec.-Treas.
British Columbia Institute of Technology
Maharajh, A.E., Program Coord.
British Columbia Lottery Corporation
Thomas, C., Sr. Community Rel'ns Officer
British Columbia Nurses Union
Harvey, A., COO
British Columbia Supreme Court
Allan, M., Judge
British Columbia's Children's and Women's Hospitals and Health Centres
Cranston, L.S., Pres. & CEO-Designate
British Columbia's Children's Hospital
Gillis, P.M., Dir., Volunteer Svcs Dept.
Huntsman, E., Head, Dept. of Psych.
Kemeny, L., Dir., Safe Start
Lockitch, G., Dir., Genes, Elements & Metabolism Program
Puder, C., Dir., Child Life Dept.
Stutzer, C.A., Clinical Nurse Specialist, Pediatric Oncology
Sutherland Boal, A., VP, Patient-Based Care Units
British Columbia's Children's Hospital Foundation
Wightman, F., Pres.
British Methodist Episcopal Church Conference of Canada
Skeir-Armstrong, O., Gen. Treas.
The British Methodist Episcopal Church
Markham, J.J.B., Pastor
Brock University
Austin, B., Prof., Fac. of Bus.
Belicki, K., Assoc. Prof. of Psych.
Blackwell, J., Assoc. Prof., Soc.
Bradshaw, L., Prof., Dept. of Pol.
Corman, J., Assoc. Prof., Soc.
Côté-Laurence, P., Assoc. Prof. & Chair, Dept. of Phys. Educ.
Cranton, P., Prof., Fac. of Educ.
Dirks, P., Assoc. Prof., Hist. Dept.
Duffy, A., Prof., Dept. of Soc.
Dupont, D.P., Assoc. Prof., Dept. of Econ.
Hutchison, P., Assoc. Prof., Dept. of Recreation & Leisure Studies
Makus, I., Asst. Prof., Dept. of Pol.
McCarthy, F.M.G., Assoc. Prof., Earth Sci.
Miller, M.J., Prof., Dept. of Film Studies

Nicks, J.P., Assoc. Prof., Dept. of Film Studies, Dramatic & Visual Arts

Preston, J., Prof. of Psych. & Comm. Studies

Richardson, M.F., Prof. of Chem.

Sauer, E., Assoc. Prof., Dept. of English

Young, R., Assoc. Prof. & Chair, Dept. of Grad. & Undergrad. Studies, Fac. of Educ.

Brodylo/Morrow Photography
Brodylo, E.M., Pres.

Brookmoor Enterprises Limited
Cecil-Cockwell, W.M., Chrm & Pres.

Brown Communications Group
Caswell, B., VP & Gen. Mgr

Stephanie Brown Jewellery
Brown, S., Owner

Brownhill Farms Ltd.
Brown, A.J., Sec.-Treas.

Builders Realty
Weir, S.R., Real Estate Consultant

Building Owners and Managers Association
Clarke, S., Exec. Dir., Atlantic

"Building the Bridges to Prosperity"
Elliston, I., Career & Life Planning Consultant & Nat'l Dir.

Bulimia Anorexia Nervosa Association
DeRubeis, M., Pres., Bd. of Dir.
Lucier, M.K., Clinical Dir.

Bull, Housser and Tupper
Gourley, A., Ptnr
Gray, V., Ptnr
O'Callaghan, S., Ptnr

Sarmite D. Bulte Barristers & Solicitors
Bulte, S., Barrister & Solicitor

Burgess Day Communications
Day, E.B., Principal

Burning Past Productions
Corder, S., Writer, Producer, Actor

Burstyn Jeffery Inc.
Jeffery, P.P., Principal

Business Aircraft Corporation Ltd.
Zalesky, R., Sec.-Treas. & Co-founder

Business and Professional Women's Association of Ottawa
Preston, V., Past Pres.

Business Quarterly
Bellegris, A., Mng Ed.
Smith, A., Publisher & Ed.

Busy St. Holdings Inc.
Kemp, L.G., Pres.

C Arts Publishing and Production, Inc.
Mason, J., Dir.

C magazine
Mason, J., Ed. & Publisher

CAERAN
De Cloet, S., Pres.

CAI Corporate Affairs International
Lyon, F.E., Sr. Consultant

CARE Canada
Kavanagh, E., Mbr. of the Bd.

CBC Newsworld
Gayle, M., Consumer Columnist
Mironowicz, M., Exec. Prod.

CBCL Limited
Mercer Clarke, C.S.L., Sr. Environmental Mgr

CFAS Child and Family Adoption Services Society of British Columbia
Goldblatt, M.-S., Former Exec. Dir.

C.G.R.T.'s Consulting
Thomas, C.G., Pres. & Sr. Consultant

CHATS (Community Home Assistance to Seniors)
Egan, D., Exec. Dir.

C.J. Productions
Whitlock, C.J., Pres. & Publisher

CFCF 12
Denis, M., VP, Admin. Svcs

CFCF TV
Desautels, S., Host, *Travel, Travel* and Host, *Simply Wine & Cheese*

CIBC
Bazarkewich, P.J., Sr. VP
Brotchie, D., Sr. VP, Central Prairie Reg.
Cira, A.A., Sr. VP
Darling, M.S., Exec. VP
Hohol, L., Sr. VP, Personal & Commercial Bnkg, Alta. & NWT
Merry, S.A., Dir., Bus. Info. & Records Mgmt, Corp. Gov. Group
Novick, C., VP, Personal & Commercial Bank

CIBC Development Corporation
Garland, K.J., Sr. VP, Corp. Real Estate

CIBC Insurance
Novick, C., CFO

CIBC Wood Gundy Plc
Denham, J., Mng Dir., Origination & Structuring & Deputy Head of Europe

CIC International Trading (Asia) Ltd.
Charnetski, J.L., VP, Mkt Dev. & Strat. Planning

Citytv
Donlon, D., Dir. of Music Programming
Martin, M., VP, Production

CJOH-TV
Waldo, C., Sports Reporter, Prod. & Anchor

CPRN Inc.
Maxwell, J., Pres.

C.R.M. Associates
Mirkopoulos, C.R., Pres.

CTI Capital Inc.
Julien, L.A., Lawyer, Corp. Affairs Officer & Legal Cnsl

CTV Television Network
Rinaldo, S., Anchor, "CTV News Weekend"

CUSO
Macdonald, M., Exec. Dir.

CYF Consulting Ltd.
Allan, R., Pres.
Cala Human Resources Company Ltd.
Lafrance, C.M., CEO
Calgary Coalition: Centres of Excellence in Women's Health
McTeer, M.A., Coord.
Calgary General Hospital
Gossmann, P., Asst. Nursing Unit Mgr, Orthopaedics
Hordyski, S.E., Nurse Therapist, WHO
Kelly, S., Nursing Unit Mgr
Ladner, J., Nursing Unit Mgr
Linton, N., Transition Program Leader
Metz, L.M., Dir., Multiple Sclerosis Clinic
Morrice, B.-L., Dir., Rehabilitation
Calgary Philharmonic Orchestra
Newton, C., Dir. of Dev.
Calgary Police Service
Hamilton, M., Urban Planner
Silverberg, C., Chief
Calgary Public Library
Barlow, E., Mgr, Collections & Elec. Res.
Calgary Regional Health Authority
Clark, K., Sr. Food Svc. Officer
Easton, C., Administrative Leader–Surgical Svcs, Inpatients Preoperative Assessment Clinics & Acute Pain Svcs
Greenley, N.I., Sr. Operating Officer, Acute Care Svcs
Holberton, P., Clinical Nurse Specialist,Trauma Svcs
Webster, M., Reg'l Leader, Oper., Health Records Svcs
Weidner, A., Sr. Operating Officer, Acute Care Svcs
The Calgary Sun
Cockburn, L., Columnist & Features Writer
Corbella, L., Assoc. Ed. & Columnist
California State University at Fresno
Kaprielian-Churchill, I., Visiting Scholar & Kazan Lecturer in Immigration Hist. & Armenian Studies
California University of Pennsylvania
Kendall, G.J., Asst. Coach, Women's Basketball Team
Calipix Productions
Paakspuu, K., Prod., Dir., Writer & Videographer
The Calmeadow Foundation
Coyle, M.J., Exec. Dir.
Cambrian College of Applied Arts and Technology
Nother, J., Coord., Centre for Equity & Hum. Rights
Cambridge University
Tippett, M., Sr. Research Fellow/Writer & Curator
Campbell Communications Inc.
Campbell, L.A., Ed. & Publisher

Diane Campbell Law Offices
Campbell, D.O., Sole Proprietor
Campbell, Lea, Michael, McConnell and Pigot
Ralling, M.J., Ptnr
Can Am Distributing
Hanson, C., Ptnr
Can-Am Medical, Inc.
Hanson, C., Pres., Owner & Ptnr
The Canada Council
Morrow, J., Dir., Arts Div.
Scott, D.M., Chair
The Canada Life Assurance Company
Barsoski, D., VP & Dir., Hum. Res.
Johns, D., Dir., Info. Svcs
Lubinsky, K., Dir., Variable Investment Products
Canada Safeway Ltd.
Oswald, L., VP, Public Rel'ns & Gov't Affairs
Canada Trust Company
Geisler, B.J., Asst. VP, Securities Law
Canada Wide Magazines Ltd.
Smith, C., Prod. Dir.
Canadian Administrators of Volunteer Resources
Gillis, P.M., Pres.
Canadian Advertising Foundation
Nagel, L.J., Pres. & CEO
Canadian Airlines International Ltd.
Bjornson, R., Captain
Fiorillo, F., VP, Inflight Svc.
Grist, K., Dir., Special Proj.
McIntosh, J., Dir., Corp. Properties & Facilities
Moor, D.L., Dir., Product Planning
Canadian Anaesthetists' Society
Andrews, A., Exec. Dir.
Canadian Aquafitness Leaders Alliance Inc.
Kopansky, C., Pres./Founder
Canadian Art Magazine
Gibson, D.R., Publisher
Canadian Association of Electroneurophysiology Technologists, Inc.
Daoust-Roy, J., Pres.
Canadian Association for Community Living
Richler, D., Exec. VP
Canadian Association for Girls in Science
Vingilis-Jaremko, L., Founder & Pres.
Canadian Association of Health Care Auxiliaries
Eberl-Kelly, K., Pres.
Canadian Association of Independent Living Centres
Walters, T., Nat'l Dir.
Canadian Association of Law Libraries
Crocker, A., Pres.
Canadian Association of Neighbourhood Services
Garber, E.E., Pres.

Canadian Association of Professional Dance Organizations
Busby, E., Exec. Dir.
Canadian Booksellers Association
Cooney, J., Pres.
Canadian Brain Tissue Bank
Dukszta, A.M., Exec. Dir.
Canadian Broadcasting Corporation
Bishop, G., Exec. Prod., *Morningside*, CBC Radio
Brown, L., Author, TV Journalist
Cody-Rice, E., Sr. Legal Cnsl
Cook, H.M., Dir. & Prod., *The Nature of Things*
Gartner, H., Host, *The National Magazine*
Kolber, S., Dir.
MacMillan, A., European Correspondent
Marshall, H., Deputy Dir., Production Financing, Arts & Entertainment
Mesley, W., Journalist/Host, *Sunday Report* & Journalist/Host, *Undercurrents*
Moore-Ede, C., Exec. Prod., CBC-TV
Pacsu, M., Broadcaster & Journalist
Petrie, A.G., Host, *Early Edition*, CBC Newsworld
Rauhala, A., Journalist
Reisler, S., Host, *Tapestry*, CBC Radio & Sr. Producer, Radio Current Affairs
Srebotnjak, T., Host, *Midday*
Tennant, V., Exec. Prod./Writer, TV Arts & Entertainment
Tremblay, L., Sr. VP, Resources
Wachtel, E., Host, *Writers & Company*, CBC Radio
Canadian Business Media Ltd.
Braggins, D., Art. Dir.
Rosser, D., VP & Dir. of Advtg Sales
Canadian Cable Systems Alliance
Stanley, B., Pres. & CEO
Canadian Cancer Society
Birdsell, J., Pres.
Colley-Urquhart, D., Exec. Dir. & CEO, Alta./N.W.T. Div.
Downe, V., Exec. Dir., P.E.I. Division
Kaminsky, B.A., CEO, B.C. & Yukon Div.
Magnan, N., Exec. Dir., Que. Div.
Thomsen, P., Exec. Dir., Ont. Div.
Canadian Centre for Stress and Well-Being
Peszat, L.C., Founder & Dir.
Canadian Children's Literature
Davis, M., Assoc. Ed.
Canadian Civil Liberties Association
Shack, S.F., Pres.
The Canadian Club of Toronto
Connell, M., Exec. Dir.
Canadian Committee on Labour History
Whitfield, I., Mng Ed.
Canadian Congress for Learning Opportunities for Women
Gallagher-LeBlanc, K., N.B. Dir.

Canadian Conservation Institute
Down, J.L., Conservation Scientist, Environment & Deterioration Res. Div.
Canadian Conservation Institute
Keyserlink, M., Sr. Conservator, Textiles
Canadian Council for Multicultural and Intercultural Education/Conseil Canadien pour l'éducation multiculturelle et interculturelle
Elliston, I., Past Pres.
Canadian Council for Refugees
Worsfold, N., Exec. Dir.
Canadian Council of Christians and Jews
Graff, E., Nat'l Exec. Dir.
Canadian Council of Ministers of the Environment
Forand, L., Dir. Gen.
Canadian Council of the Blind
Braak, G., Nat'l Pres. & CEO
Canadian Council on Smoking and Health
Forsythe, J.T., Exec. Dir.
Canadian Cystic Fibrosis Foundation
Jerrard, R., Pres.
Morrison, C., Exec. Dir.
Canadian Dealing Network
Crocker, S., Pres.
Canadian Dental Hygienists' Association
Forgay, M.G.E., Past Pres.
Canadian Environmental Energy Corporation
Eastman, B.C., Treas.
Canadian Equipment Finance Corporation
Youldon, D., VP, Fin. & Admin.
Canadian Facts
Humphreys, G., VP
Canadian Federation of Agriculture
Rutherford, S., Exec. Dir.
Canadian Federation of Business and Professional Women's Clubs
Jackson, M., Past Pres.
Canadian Federation of Friends of Museums
Sprachman, C., Nat'l Dir.
Canadian Federation of Independent Business
Andrew, J., Dir., Prov. Policy
Swift, C., Pres.
Canadian Federation of University Women
Bayless, B., Pres.
Scott, P., Past Pres., & Coord. of Int'l Rel'ns
Canadian Figure Skating Association
Shaw, M.A., VP
Canadian Film and Television Production Association
Watson, M.F.E., VP, Ind. Rel'ns & Training
Canadian Finnsheep Breeders' Association
Playdon, K.C., Pres.
Canadian Forces
Timperon, M.-E., Recruiting, Educ. & Training

Formation Personnel Selection Officer (military psychologist)

Canadian Forest Products Ltd..
Pau, J., VP & Treas.

Canadian Foundation for the Love of Children
Krupa, M., Exec. Dir.

Canadian Foundation for the Study of Infant Death
DeBruyn, B.A., Exec. Dir.

Canadian Friends of Burma
Sanger, P., Exec. Committee

Canadian General Investments, Limited
Morgan, E.L., Chrm of the Bd.

Canadian Gerontology Nursing Association
Miller, J., Pres.

Canadian Grandparents' Rights Association
Knight, F., Pres., Alta. Branch

Canadian Guild of Crafts Quebec
Watt, V., Treas. & Archivist

Canadian HIV Trials Network
Harris, M., Clinical Research Advisor

Canadian Home and School And Parent-Teacher Federation
Neil, D., Past Pres.

Canadian Home Publishers
Ladner, C., Editor, *Canadian House & Home* Magazine
Reeves, L., Publisher & Pres., *Canadian House & Home* Magazine

Canadian Housing and Renewal Association
Chisholm, S., Exec. Dir.

Canadian Human Rights Commission
Falardeau-Ramsay, M., Dep. Chief Commissioner

Canadian Human Rights Foundation
Eliadis, F.P., Past Pres.

Canadian Industrial Transportation League
Rehner, M., Pres.

Canadian Institute for Historical Microreproductions
Bjornson, P., Exec. Dir.

Canadian Institute for the Administration of Justice
Huglo Robertson, C., Exec. Dir.

Canadian Institutes of Travel Counsellors
Ang, R.S.L., Nat'l Pres.

Canadian International Development Agency
Labelle, H., Pres.

Canadian International Trade Tribunal
Szlazak, A.C., Mbr.

Canadian Investor Protection Fund
Reszel, R., VP & Sec.

Canadian Journal on Aging
Vanderkamp, J.R., Mng Ed.

Canadian Labour Market and Productivity Centre
Seward, S.B., CEO

Canadian Lawyer
Hill, A., Prod. Mgr

***Canadian Living* Magazine**
Cowan, B., Ed.-in-Chief
Hobbs, A., Assoc. Ed.
Keeler, H., Sr. Ed.

Canadian Medical Association
Guzman, C., Assoc. Sec. Gen.

Canadian Mental Health Association
Hood, B., Exec. Dir., NWT Div.

Canadian Museum of Civilization
Morel, S., Dir., Exhibitions & Programs

Canadian Museum of Civilization/ Canadian War Museum
Schacherl, E., Sr. Comm. Officer

Canadian National
Carrell, N.J., Dep. Sec.
Mielitz, S.J., VP, Grain & W. Canada

Canadian Nautical Research Society
Kert, F., Past Pres. & Chair, Awards Committee

Canadian Olympic Association
Letheren, C.A., CEO & Sec. Gen.

Canadian Opera Women's Committee
Black, E.S., Past Pres. & Mbr.

Canadian Pacific Hotels and Resorts
Clark, C.J., VP, Hum. Res.

Canadian Paraplegic Association (Saskatchewan) Inc.
Powell, A., Employment & Educ. Counsellor

Canadian Pay & Benefits Consulting Group Inc.
Blaszczyk, Y., Pres.

Canadian Petroleum Products Institute
Wish, J., Dir., Gov't Rel'ns

Canadian Pharmacy Consultants Inc.
Steinberg, S.K., Pres.

Canadian Poetry Press
Bentley, S., Gen. Mgr

Canadian Pony Club
Honeyman, R., Exec. Dir.

Canadian Posters International Inc.
Cohen, E.A., Pres.

Canadian Pulp and Paper Association
Lachapelle, L., Pres. & CEO

Canadian Red Cross
Buchner, B., Virologist (retired) & Chair, Blood Svcs

Canadian Scenes
Cumming, M.M., Heritage Artist

Canadian Securities Institute
Wilton, R., Pres.

Canadian Society for Education through Art
Moore, C., VP

Canadian Society for Traditional Music/Société Canadienne pour les Traditions Musicales
Cohen, J.R., Pres.

**Canadian Society of Air Safety
Investigators**
Dunn, B., Pres.
**Canadian Society of Association
Executives**
Wiley, J., Pres.
Canadian Space Agency
Payette, J., Astronaut, Cdn Astronaut Program
**Canadian Teachers' Federation/
Fédération Canadienne des
Enseignantes et des Enseignants**
Robertson, H.-j., Dir., Professional Dev. Svcs
Canadian Toy Testing Council
Poirier, L.A., Exec. Dir.
**Canadian Translators and
Interpreters Council**
Blais, D., Chair
Canadian Union of Public Employees
Darcy, J., Nat'l Pres.
Garnier, A., Sec.-Treas.
Jordan, C.E., Sec.-Treas.
Kirk, B., Pres., B.C. Div.
Morey, T., Comm. Officer
**Canadian University and College
Counselling Association**
Coniglio, C.B., Pres.
Canadian Western Bank
Ball, T., VP, Fin. & Chief Acctnt
Canadian Youth Business Foundation
Cira, A.A., Exec. Dir.
Canadian Youth Foundation
Bohac-Konrad, L.M., Exec. Dir.
**Canadians Concerned About Violence
in Entertainment**
Dyson, R.A., Chair
Canadians for Health Research
Guyda, P., Pres.
Canalex Resources
Korhonen, J.M., Sec.
Cancore Building Services Ltd.
Burka, S.M., Fin. Officer & Ptnr
Canfor Corporation
Hislop, B.R., Group VP, Coastal Oper.
Pau, J., VP & Treas.
Cannon Associates
Cannon, G., Pres.
Canuck Place
Eng, B., Founder & Clinical Specialist
Canucklehead Adventures Inc.
Steen, J., Actor
CanWest Gas Supply Inc.
Martinuzzi, B., Mgr of Admin. & Hum. Res.
CanWest Global Communications Corp.
Asper, G., Gen. Cnsl, Corp. Sec.
CanWest Global Developments
McKenna, J., Pres.
CanWest Global Systems
Henley, G., Legal Cnsl
Cape Breton Post
La Rocque, C., Freelance Health Columnist

The Capilano Review
Rains, E., Mng Ed.
The Capital Care Group Inc.
Rust, H., Dir., Clinical & Support Svcs
Capital Health Authority
Olenek, L., In-Patient Program Mgr, N. Alberta
Reg'l Geriatric Program
Thompson, L.J., Sr. Operating Officer
**Captain William Jackman
Memorial Hospital**
Lundrigan, J., Hospital Supervisor
Cara Holdings
Regan, G., Pres.
Career Probe Inc.
Kovacs, G., Pres. & CEO
Carleton University
Adamson, N., Dir. of Equity Svcs
Armstrong, P., Dir. & Prof., Sch. of Cdn
Studies
Dawson, T.B., Chair, Dept. of Law
DeBardeleben, J., Prof., The Institute of
Central/East European & Russian-Area Studies
Edwards, M.-J., Prof. of English, & Dir.,
Centre for Editing Early Canadian Texts
Freeman, B.M., Asst. Prof., Journalism &
Comm.
Freeman, L., Assoc. Prof., Dept. of Pol. Sci.
Gorham, D., Prof. of Hist. & Dir., Pauline
Jewett Institute of Women's Studies
Graham, K.A.H., Assoc. Prof. & Coord.,
Diversification Research Group
Keillor, E., Prof., School for Studies in Art &
Culture–Music
Klodawsky, F., Asst. Prof., Dept. of
Geography & Pauline Jewett Institute of
Women's Studies
Labarge, M.W., Adj. Research Prof.
Mackenzie, S., Assoc. Prof., Geography
Molot, M.A., Prof. of Pol. Sci. & Dir., The
Norman Paterson Sch. of Int'l Affairs
Ogilvie, M.H., Prof. of Law
Smart, P., Prof. of French
Vickers, J., Prof., Pol. Sci. & Cdn Studies
Yalden, J., Chair, Dept of Linguistics &
Applied Language
**Carousel Theatre Company
and School**
Ball, E., Founder & Mng Artistic Dir.
Carr, Stevenson and MacKay
Stevenson, B.F., Ptnr
Carshaw Inc.
Gelhorn, C., Pres.
Casselman & Co. Inc.
Casselman, B., Pres.
Barbie Casselman Inc.
Casselman, B.
**Cassels Blaikie Investment
Management Limited**
Sheehan, B.E., VP, Client Svcs
Wisser, A., VP & Portfolio Mgr

Cassels Brock & Blackwell
Manzer, A.R., Ptnr
**Cavalluzzo Hayes Shilton McIntyre
& Cornish**
Cornish, M., Sr. Ptnr
Shilton, E.J., Sr. Ptnr
CAVEAT
de Villiers, P., Pres.
Ruth Cawker Architect
Cawker, R.
**Centennial College of Applied Arts
and Technology**
Pearce, E., Prof.
Yakimov, R., Prof. & Coord., Mech. Tech.
Dept., Sch. of Eng. Tech.
Centra Gas
Bishop, J., Mgr, Cust. Svc. Dev.
Centra Gas Manitoba Inc.
Herzog, L.M., Mgr, Residential/Small
Commercial Mkts
Centraide of Greater Montreal
Thibodeau-DeGuire, M., Pres. & CEO
**Central Alberta Women's
Emergency Shelter**
Boyd, M., Exec. Dir.
Central Queensland University
Zelmer, A., Hon. Prof.
**Centre Canadien d'Architecture/Canadian
Centre for Architecture**
Lambert, P., Chrm of the Bd. of Trustees
**Le Centre de Recherches d'antécédents
Socio-Biologiques du Québec**
Corbeil, J., Pres.
Centre for Legislative Exchange
Reynolds, B., Exec. Dir.
The Centre for Literacy of Quebec
Shohet, L., Dir.
**Centre for Research on Violence Against
Women and Children**
Greaves, L.J., Dir.
Centre for the Healing Arts, Inc.
Pennington, S., Pres.
**Centre for Urban and Community Studies,
University of Toronto**
Friendly, M., Coordinator, Childcare Resource
& Research Unit
Centre for Workplace Dynamics
Crocker, O.L., Pres.
**Centre franco-ontarien de ressources
pédagogiques**
Larochelle, B., Dir. gén.
**Centre Youville Centre
Ottawa-Carleton Inc.**
Kinsella, E.A., Co-Founder & Exec. Dir.
Chalker, Green and Rowe
Fagan, C.A., Lawyer
Champlain Regional College
Lesser, G., Prof., Art Hist. & Design
Chanel Inc.
Oliver, D., VP, Mktg

Charis Enterprises/Partners in Learning
Loughheed, M.C., Pres.
Margot Charlton Creative Services
Charlton, M., Cultural Consultant, Theatre
Dir. & Facilitator. Owner
Châtelaine
Catherine Elie, Ed.
Chatelaine Magazine
Crowley, M.B., Assoc. Food Editor
Maynard, R., Ed.
Rosenberg, M., Food Ed.
Chats & Company
Harrington, B., Host
Chellas Communication
Chellas, M., Principal
Ches Crosbie Barristers
Hoegg, L., Lawyer
Chester Dawe Limited
Gardiner, J.C., Treas.
Chevron Canada Resources
Brown, J., Geophysicist
Chicopee Manufacturing Limited
Sims, E., Pres. & Gen. Mgr
Chieftain International Inc.
Ondrack, E.S., Sr. VP & Sec.
Child Find Manitoba
Driedger, M., Exec. Dir.
Child Find P.E.I. Inc.
Scott, M.M., Pres.
Child Find Saskatchewan Inc.
Hallatt, P., Pres.
Children's Hospital at Chedoke-McMaster
Andrew, M., Prof. of Pediatrics
Children's Hospital of Eastern Ontario
Durieux-Smith, A., Research Coord.,
Audiology
Children's Psychiatric Research Institute
Haust, M.D., Dir. of Pathology
Children's Talent Education Centre
Jones, D.M., Exec. Dir.
**The Children's Wish Foundation
of Canada**
Cole, L., Nat'l Exec. Dir. & Founder
Chipco Canada Inc.
Klein, C.J., Pres.
Chivers Greckol & Kanee
Greckol, S.J., Ptnr
Christian Women's Clubs of Canada
Harding, G.J., Pres.
**Christian Women's Fellowship
(Disciples of Christ)**
Bailey, S., World Pres.
Dinah Christie Presents
Christie, D., Pres.
A. Chu Associates
Chu, A.I.-F., Pres.
ChumCity Productions
Martin, M., VP
The Church of God of Prophecy
Martin, E., Reg'l Admin. Sec., Global Missions

Church on the Street (Yonge Street Mission)
Rothenburger, J., Community Pastoral Care Worker
CINAR Films Inc.
Charest, M., Chair & CEO
CineNova Productions Inc.
Armstrong, J., Pres.
CINEVIDEO PLUS
Heroux, J., Pres. & Prod.
Citibank Canada
Sze, G., VP
Citizens Concerned with Crime Against Children (4C's)
Harding, J., Co-Founder
City of Barrie
Laking, J., Mayor
City of Cambridge
Brewer, J., Regional Councillor and Mayor
City of Edmonton
Starkman, E., Public Sch. Trustee
City of Etobicoke
Lindsay Luby, G., Councillor
City of Fredericton
Sansom, B.J., City Councillor & Deputy Mayor
City of Mississauga
McCallion, H.
City of Ottawa
Holzman, J., Mayor
City of Port Alberni
Trumper, G., Mayor
City of Saskatoon
Waygood, K., Councillor
City of St. John's
Miller, H.S.E., Archivist
City of Toronto
Hall, B., Mayor
Ramkhalawansingh, C., Mgr, Equal Opportunity
City of Vancouver
Chan, S., Mgr, Non-Mkt Housing
Ip, M., Councillor
City of Yellowknife
Power, R., Administrative Assistant to the Mayor
City University of New York
Blackwell, B., Prof., Dept. of Geology, Queens Coll.
Clarington Hydro Electric Commission
Storks, P.J., V-Chair
Brenda Clark-Illustrator Inc.
Clark, B., Illustrator
Classic Aromatics Ltd.
Pepe, T.A., Owner & Operator
Classical Kids
Hammond, S., Producer & Pres.
The Clichettes
Garfield, L., Mbr.
Club Elite Rhythmics Inc.
Fung, L., Co-Owner & Head Coach

Co-op Atlantic
Jefferies, M., First VP, Bd. of Dir. & Dir., Zone 3
Co-operative Trust Company of Canada
Bentley, M.J., VP, Bus. Dev.
Deutscher, M., Mgr, Hum. Res.
Holder, R., Bus. Dev. Rep.
Co-operators Investment Counselling Limited
Lowes, J.E., VP, Mktg
Coach House Press
McClintock, M., Publisher
Coca-Cola Beverages Ltd.
Kerr, S.D., VP, Corp. & Environmental Affairs
Annette Cohen Productions Limited
Cohen, A., Pres.
Dian Cohen Productions Limited
Cohen, D., Pres.
Colgate-Palmolive Canada Inc.
Noonan, C., VP, Customer Svc.
Collaboration Santé Internationale
Viau, H., Coord.
College of Physicians and Surgeons of Ontario
Craighead, J., Assoc. Dir., Quality Mgmt
Collins Barrow
Hrastovec, D.M., Chair & Ptnr
Colour Technologies
Black, M.E., Pres.
Columbia University
MacPhee, M., Prof. of Painting
Common Ground
Copleston, M., Ed. Committee
Communications encouleur Jamison inc.
Jamison, L., Pres.
Community Foundation of Greater Toronto
Oliver, C.R., Pres. & CEO
Community Foundations of Canada
Patten, M., Exec. Dir.
Community Legal Education Association
Dwarka, D., Pres., Manitoba
Community Services Council, Newfoundland and Labrador
Rowe, P., Exec. Dir.
Compensation News
Blaszczyk, Y., Publisher
The Compleat Mother **Magazine**
Young, C., Ed.
Compton Graham International Inc.
Compton, J.A.L., Pres.
Concordia University
Gagnon, N., Assoc. Prof. & Chair, Leisure Studies
Gaudet, B., Sec.-Gen. & Sec., Bd. of Gov.
Hoecker-Drysdale, S., Assoc. Prof., Soc. & Chair, Dept. of Soc. & Anthro.
Langley, E., Prof.
Mendell, M., Assoc. Prof. & Principal, Sch. of Community & Public Affairs

Morley, P., Prof. Emerita, Dept. of English
Perry, K., Assoc. Dean, Comm. &
Advancement, Fac. of Fine Arts
Roth, L., Asst. Prof., Dept. of Comm. Studies
Rovinescu, O., Assoc. Dir., Centre for Teaching
& Learning Svcs
Serbin, L.A., Prof. of Psych., Centre for
Research in Hum. Dev.
Valaskakis, G.G., Dean, Fac. of Arts & Sci. &
Prof., Dept. of Comm. Studies
Woodsworth, J.W., Assoc. Prof. of études
françaises & Vice-Dean, Academic Affairs &
Int'l Rel'ns, Fac. of Arts & Sci.

**Confectionery Manufacturers Association
of Canada**
Hochu, C., Pres.

**Confederation of Ontario University
Staff Associations**
Woodcock, K., Pres.

Connaught Laboratories Ltd.
Ewasyshyn, M.E., Dir. of Microbiol. & Sr.
Research Scientist
Mazur-Melnyk, M., Dir., Quality Assurance
Taylor, B., Dir., Quality Control

**Connor Clark & Lunn Investment
Management Ltd.**
Morrisroe, S.J., In-house Cnsl.

Conscience Canada (Peace Tax Fund)
Newall, J., Past Pres.

Conseil du statut de la femme
Lemieux, D., Prés.

Construction Association of Nova Scotia
MacCulloch, C., Pres.

Consumers' Association of Canada
Todd, R., Exec. Dir. & Legal Cnsl

The Consumers' Gas Company Ltd.
Beattie, L.A.E., VP, Fin. Reporting &
Budgets

Contemporary Fine Art Services Inc.
Minard, K.C., Principal & Pres.

Cook, Duke, Cox
Goss, J.H., Lawyer, Chartered Mediator,
Arbitrator

Cool Women
Ruth, N., Pres. & Co-founder

Coombs Consulting Ltd.
Coombs, A., Pres.

Cooper Union
MacPhee, M., Prof. of Painting

Cooperative Health Centre
Calder, E., Mgr

Coopers and Lybrand
Sibson, E.S., Tax Ptnr

**Coordinating Council on Deafness of
Nova Scotia**
Irving, C., Exec. Dir.

Corby Distilleries Ltd.
Paul, L., VP, Legal & Sec.

Core Group Publishers Inc.
McIvor, J., Mng Dir.

Jane Corkin Gallery Inc.
Corkin, J., Owner &. Pres.

Corporate Events Management Inc.
Peake, J., Principal

Corporation of Delta
Johnson, B., Mayor

**Corporation of Professional Librarians
of Quebec**
Horinstein, R., Exec. Dir.

Correctional Service of Canada
Stableforth, N.L., Deputy Commissioner for
Women

Cosmo Distribution Inc.
Pepe, T.A., Owner

Cotter Canada Hardware
McLeod, L., Cont.

**The Council for Business and the
Arts in Canada**
Iley, S.J.E., Pres. & CEO

The Council of Canadians
Barlow, M., Chair

Council of Canadians with Disabilities
Arsenault, F.H., Past Chairperson

**Council of Monuments and Sites
for Quebec**
Gagnon-Pratte, F., Pres. & Chrm

Country Magazine
Chodan, L., Contributing Ed.

Court of Appeal of Alberta
Picard, E.I., Justice

Court of Appeal of British Columbia
Newbury, M.V., Justice
Huddart, C., Judge

Court of Appeal of Ontario
Charron, L., Justice

Court of Queen's Bench of Alberta
Bielby, M.B., Judge
Trussler, M., Justice

**Court of Queen's Bench of
New Brunswick**
Larlee, M., Judge

The Craig Corporation
Craig, S.J., Pres.

Creative Child Care
MacEachern, A., Exec. Dir.

Creative Connections
Watson, J.V., Owner

Creative Research International
Jaye, E.A., VP & Dir. of Special Svcs

Credit Union Central of Canada
Stratton, J.J., Dir., Payments & Research

Credit Union Central of Ontario
Bottone, K.F., Dir., Planning & Research &
Secretariat for Full Svc Credit Unions
Henderson, R., Dir., Hum. Res.
Hood, M., Dir., Public Affairs
Watson, D.E., Dir., Mbr. Rel'ns & Svc
Quality

Cresford Developments
Kinnear, K.E., Pres.

Crestar Energy
Jefferies, G.J., Sr. Prod. Eng.
Creston Valley Advance
White, H.E., Publisher
Crocker Educational Services
Crocker, O.L., Pres. & CEO
Cross Cancer Institute
Armann, D.M., Dir. of Nursing
Cass, C., Assoc. Dir., Research
Crown Attorney's Office
Flanagan, C., Lawyer
Crown Attorney's Office
Moore, V.A., Crown Attorney
Crown Life Insurance Co.
Bonney, L.D., VP, Pension Admin. & Fin.
Laing, B., VP, Pension Systems
MacIntyre, P.J., VP, Hum. Res.
Crucial Pictures
Rozema, P., Filmmaker
Cruise & Associates
Cruise, M., Pres.
Culinar Inc.
Brien, D.C., VP, Mktg, Confectionary, Dry
Culinar Manufacturing
Lemay, P., Dir. of Mfg
Cumberland Communication Concepts
James, V.M., Pres.
Cumming and Cumming Wealth Management
Cumming, M.N., Ptnr
Curl for Cancer
Kennedy, C., Founder
The Current Affairs Group
Wallin, P., Pres.
Curry, McFarlane Associates
McFarlane, E.L., Therapist
Curtis Brown Canada Ltd.
Turnbull Irving, J., Pres.
Elizabeth Cusack Walsh & Associates
Cusack Walsh, E., Barrister & Solicitor
Cybernetic Circus
Dorning, M., Artist, Writer, Multimedia Producer
Cypress Hills Regional College
Gordon, E., Career Counsellor

D CM Enterprises
Chabot, D., Pres.
D.E.S. Action Canada
Simand, H., Founder
Simand, S., Pres.
DHPR Communications Inc.
Hargrave, D., Pres.
DLI Productions
Angelico, I., CEO
Daley, Black & Moreira
Hamilton, M.J., Lawyer
Dalhousie University
Barnard, D., Assoc. Prof.

Borgese, E., Prof., Pol. Sci.
Frick, E.A., Prof. (retired)
Graves, G.R., Assoc. Prof., Dept. of Obstetrics & Gynaecology
Lane, P.A., Prof., Dept. of Biol.
McIntyre, L., Dean, Fac. of Health Professions
Parish, B., Assoc. Prof., Dept. of Obstetrics & Gynaecology
Raby, G., Lecturer
Ritchie, J., Prof., Sch. of Nursing
Smillie, C., Assoc. Prof., Sch. of Nursing
Smith, J., Assoc. Prof.
White, M.A., Killam Research Prof. in Materials Sci., & Prof. of Chem., & of Physics, Dept. of Chem.
Dance Manitoba Inc.
Williams, D.J., Past Pres.
Dance Nova Scotia
Milligan, D., Exec. Dir.
Dance Saskatchewan Inc.
Reid, J., Exec. Dir.
Dancemakers
Sasso, J., Asst. Artistic Dir.
Dancer Transition Resource Centre
Sidimus, J., Exec. Dir.
D'anna - herself communications
D'anna, L., Writer, Novelist, Poet, Publicist to the Arts
Dark Light Music Ltd.
Smale, J.R., VP
Dartmouth General Hospital and Community Health Centre
Pryor, E.J., Dir. of Dietetics
Data Business Forms
Myers Johnson, N., VP, Hum. Res.
Davis and Co.
Cabott, L.I., Lawyer
Shirley Dawe Associates Inc.
Dawe, S.A., Pres. & Owner
V.V. De Marco Properties Limited
Andrews, M., Proj. Mgr, Residential Construction
Diana Dean Studio of Fine Art
Dean, D., Artist
Decision Research Ltd.
Colwill, N.L., Pres.
Deer Lodge Centre
Korzeniowski, B.C., Social Worker, Dept. of Psychogeriatrics
John Deere Finance Limited
Youldon, D., VP, Fin. & Admin.
Deloitte & Touche
Bowles, L., Ptnr
Brooks, P.J., Mgr, Nat'l Comm.
Clark, L., Ptnr
Jewett, A., Tax Ptnr
Lowey, B., Ptnr
Roper, J., Tax Ptnr
Deni M. Originals
Martin, D., Pres./Owner

Descant Magazine
Mulhallen, K., Ed.-in-Chief
Designs by Mary Anne
Ludlam, M.A., Interior Designer & Visual Artist
Desjardins Trust
Durocher, C., VP, Admin., Fin. & Trust Svcs
Desk and Derrick Club of Calgary
McClare, S., Past Pres.
Dickson, Sachs, Appell & Beaman
MacGregor, M.L., Ptnr
Lyndsay Dobson Books
Dobson, L.
Dohm, Jaffer & Company
Jaffer, M., Barrister & Solicitor
Dolittle Services (1991) Ltd.
Fair, P.M., Owner and Sec.-Treas.
The Dominion of Canada General Insurance Company
Armstrong, S., VP & CFO
Dominion Textile Inc.
Dell'Aquila, T., Dir. of Corp. Acctg
Grenier, K., Dir., Taxation
Smith, C., Dir., Comm. & Investor Rel'ns
Doomsday Studios Limited
Macdonald, R., Pres. & Founder
Douglas College
McCallum, L., Dean, Fac. of Language, Lit. & Performing Arts
Dover Industries Limited
Campbell, M.L., Pres.
Down Syndrome Research Foundation
Mills, J., Exec. Dir.
Linda Silver Dranoff and Associates
Dranoff, L.S., Barrister & Solicitor
Dreamquest Entertainment Productions Inc.
Bruneau, L., Actor
Dufflet Pastries Inc.
Rosenberg, D., Pres.
The Dynacare Health Group Inc.
Dunlop, M.J., VP, Gov't Rel'ns
Dynacare Managed Health Services
Dunlop, M.J., VP & COO

E

EDS Canada
Whittaker, S.D., Pres.
EPCOR
Burton, B., VP, Hum. Res.
Each One Teach One Mentor Program
Rowe, E., Co-Founder & Dir.
Early Childhood Intervention Programs Saskatchewan Inc.
Glazer, C.L., Exec. Dir.
Earth Appeal
Dale, L., Full Founding Mbr & Local Rep.
East Prince Health Regional Board
Eberl-Kelly, K., Bd. Chair

Ecodecision Magazine
Labrecque, H., Editing Mgr
L'École des Hautes Études Commerciales
Pitcher, P.C., Prof. of Leadership & Dean of the Doctoral Program
École Polytechnique de Montréal
Vaillancourt-Châtillon, L., Dir. of Admin.
Economap Inc.
Farrow, M.A., Pres.
L'Économique magazine
Lyon, F.E., Ed.-in-Chief
EDIROM Inc.
Kermoyan, M., Pres. & CEO
Les éditions Clown Samuel Inc.
Plouffe-Pinel, S., Pres. & owner
Éditions TROIS
Alonzo, A.-M., Co-Founder & Dir.
The Edmonton Journal
Hughes, L., Publisher
Edmonton Power
Loat, B., VP, Public Affairs
Edmonton Public Schools
Sills, J., Music Specialist/Curriculum Coord.
The Edmonton Sun
Maclean, V., Ed.
Education Wife Assault
Sfeir, M., Educator & Trainer
Veinot, T., Librarian, Publications Distributor & Systems Mgr & Fundraiser
EdVest Management Associates Ltd
Porac, C., Pres.
Erica Ehm Communications Ltd.
Ehm, E., Broadcaster, Actor, Songwriter
Elekes Resource Consultants
Elekes, J.L., Consultant
Elia Fashions Ltd.
Adrian, K., Pres.
Elizabeth Fry Society of Edmonton
Hutchings, C., Exec. Dir.
Elizabeth Fry Society of Mainland Nova Scotia
Manzer, Y., Admin. Coord.
Elizabeth Fry Society of Ottawa
Solvason-Wiebe, I., Exec. Dir.
Elizabeth Fry Society of Quebec
Duhamel, N., Exec. Dir.
D.S. Elliot & Associates Inc.
Elliot, D., Pres.
Elm Street magazine
Cameron, S.G., Ed.-in-Chief
Emergency Shelter for Women
Woods, T.M., Public Rel'ns Coord. & Counsellor
Emery Jamieson
Smith, P., Ptnr
Emmanuel Baptist Church
White, I.A., Min. of Care & Educ.
Emmanuel College
Dyke, D.J., Prof. Emeritus

The Empire Life Insurance Company
Slawinski, W., VP & Sec.
Energy Probe Research Foundation
Adams, P., Pres.
Enghouse Systems Limited
MacKay-Lassonde, C., Chrm, CEO &
Pres.
The English-Speaking Union of Canada
Horsey, J.S., Nat'l Pres.
Enserve Power Corporation
Eastman, B.C., Sec.
EnviroBusiness Directions
Antler, S.P., Pres.
Environics Research Group Limited
Dasko, D., VP
Environment Canada
Freemark, K.E., Research Ecologist
The Ephemera Society of Canada
Rusch, B., Ephemerist. Founder & Pres.
Epilepsy Canada
Crépin, D., Nat'l Exec Dir.
Equion Securities Canada Limited
Foster, S., Fin. Advisor
Eriksen & Webb
Eriksen, M., Psychologist
Ernst & Young
Blais, D., Ptnr
Glover, K., Ptnr
Tory, M.J., Ptnr
Ethics in Health Care Associates
Lynch, A., Dir.
Eucalyptus International Ltd.
Lea, N., Mgr of Bus. Dev.
Evangeline Trust Company
Hughes, B.D., Chair & CEO
Evans MacCallum
MacCallum, J., Lawyer
Evergreen Recycling Technologies Ltd
Bales, L., Pres. & CEO
Excalibur Executive
Crosbie, E., Owner
Excelcom Translex
Doyle-Rodrigue, J., Pres. & Founder
Excellence in/en Communication
Mirabelli, M., Pres.

Penny M. Fair - Certified
General Accountant
Fair, P.M., Proprietor
The Family Centre
Harlan, C., Family Support Worker
Famous Events & Destinations
Strand, K.K., Mng Dir./Owner
Famous People Players
Dupuy, D., Pres. & Founder
Farallon Resources Ltd.
Ross, S., Cont.
Farrell Research Group Ltd.
Farrell, B., Pres.

Fashion Television
Beker, J., Host/Segment Prod.
Fasken Campbell Godfrey
McCormick, R., Ptnr
Fata Morgana Inc.
Foster, C.M., VP & Dir.
Federal Court of Canada
Desjardins, A., Justice, Appeal Div.
McGillis, D., Judge, Trial Div.
Reed, B.J., Judge, Trial Div.
Federated Women's Institutes of Canada
Johnson, D.C., Pres.
Keith, M.J., Pres. Elect
Strugnell, A., Exec. Dir.
Fédération de Gymnastique du Québec
Stokes, A., Dir. Gén.
**Fédération des Infirmières et Infirmiers
du Québec**
Skene, J., Pres.
Federation of Law Societies of Canada
Bourque, D., Exec. Dir.
Federation of Medical Women of Canada
Bennett, A., Pres.
Khan, S., Physician & Past Pres.
**Federation of Prince Edward
Island Municipalities**
Doyle-MacBain, L.B., Exec. Dir.
**Federation of Women Teachers'
Associations of Ontario**
Westcott, J., Exec. Dir.
Fetherstonhaugh & Co.
Morrow, J., Ptnr
The Fiddlehead
Campbell, S., Mgr & Assoc. Ed.
Field & Field Perraton
Howell, B.C., Lawyer
Oakes, J.J., Ptnr
Film Canada Yearbook
Thompson, P., Publisher & Ed.
Brenda Finamore Design
Finamore, B., Graphic Designer
The Financial Post
Dalglish, B.G., Media Reporter
Francis, D., Ed.
McNellis, M., Ed. Dir.
Finning Ltd.
Hosier, E., Corp. Sec. & Treas.
Finvoy Management Inc.
Mercier, E.A., Pres.
Firelight Investments Ltd.
MacKay-Lassonde, C., Pres.
*Fireweed: A feminist quarterly of writing,
politics, art & culture*
Haar, S., Co-ordinating Ed.
First Canada Securities Corporation
Hoff, R., Pres. & CEO
First Canadian Artists Inc.
Singer, S., Pres.
First Marathon Securities Limited
Millichamp, B., VP & Dir.

First Nations Women's Group
Greene, S., Pres.
First-Rate Freelancing
Driver, D., Writer & Photographer
The Flag Shop Inc.
Braverman, D., Pres.
Flat City Films Inc.
Bailey, N., Pres.
Fleishman-Hillard
Smith, C.L., Sr. VP, Ptnr & Gen. Mgr
Flinn Merrick
Jamieson, D.A., Ptnr
Flying "G" Investments Ltd.
Berkhold, B. F., Pres.
Fondation Diane Hébert
Hébert, D., Prés.
Foothills Hospital
Singhal, N., Medical Staff, Pediatrics
Ford Motor Company of Canada Limited
Cushman, H.C., Cnsl & Sec.
Forefront Entertainment Group
Cynamon, H., Principal, TV Prod.
Lindsay, G., Principal
Rogers, M., Principal
Forintek Canada Corp.
Gonzalez, J., Research Scientist
Fortune Financial Corporation
Simbul-Lezon, M., Exec. VP
Forty-Seven Films Inc.
Shum, M., Sec. & Shareholder
Foundation for Equal Families
Douglas, M., Pres.
Four Seasons Hotels Inc.
Taylor, K., Sr. VP, Corp. Planning & Dev.,
Gen. Cnsl, & Sec., Four Seasons/Regent Hotels
and Resorts
Sally Fourmy & Associates
Fourmy, S.J., Founder
Fox-Fire Films
Frank, A., Producer & Script Consultant
Frank Communications
Frank, T., Pres.
Franklyn Enterprises
Hancock, L., Writer, Photographer, Lecturer.
Freda's Inc.
Iordanous, F.
The Free Press - Fernie
Brunel, C., Publisher
French Browne
Baird, M., Lawyer
Frida Craft Stores
Bellan, S., Pres. & Gen. Mgr
The Friends of Breastfeeding Society
Young, C., Chairmother
Friends of the Dolphins Inc.
Sands, C., Dir. & Pres.
Eleanor Fulcher International Ltd.
Siebert, T., Pres. & Owner
Fulford Fundy Fish Farm
Fulford, M.E., Pres.

GAT Productions Inc.
Hamilton, I., Pres.
GGS Services–Focus on You
Shiff, H., Ptnr
G.W.L. Investment Management Ltd.
Nesbitt, P., Dir., Cdn Equities
Squair, B.D., VP, US Equities
Galiano Health Care Society
Frith, I., VP
Galiano Ratepayers Association
Frith, I., Past Pres.
Gandalf Technologies Inc.
Burgess, W., VP of Quality, Educ. & Comm.
Garden River Development Corp.
Corbiere, A.A., Co-ordinator
Gardening Life Magazine
Reeves, L., Founder
**The George R. Gardiner Museum
of Ceramic Art**
Chilton, M., Curator
Gardiner, H., Chair
**Gardiner Realty Ltd./Royal LePage
Associate Broker**
Tidd, F., Mgr.
Gateway Provincial Resource Program
Seip, J.-A., Admin. Officer
Gateway Society
Seip, J.-A., CEO
Gatt Inc.
Beaton, B., Pres.
Gaulthier Artists Inc.
Gaulthier, N., Founder & Pres.
N. Gaulthier Ontario Management Inc.
Gaulthier, N., Founder & Pres.
The Gazette
Bagnall, J., Sr. Feature Writer
Chodan, L., Entertainment Ed.
Curran, P., City Columnist
Dumais, M.C., VP, Fin.
Grin, G., Feature Design Dir.
Hamilton Lambie, C., VP, Reader Sales & Svc.
Nebenzahl, D., Ed., Women's News
Rochester, H., Restaurant Columnist
Gemini Film Productions Inc.
Yolles, E., Pres.
Genealogical Research Services
Hope, L., Owner/Operator
General Motors Corporation
Kempston Darkes, M.V., VP
General Motors of Canada Limited
Kempston Darkes, M.V., Pres. & Gen. Mgr
Wakefield, T., VP, Corp. Affairs
Georgian Bay Productions, Ltd.
Clark, S., Actor & VP
Gesco Industries Inc.
Shnier Moncik, B., Pres.
Dyanne Gibson & Associates Inc.
Gibson, D.B., Pres.

Girl Guides of Canada/Guides du Canada
Guy, G., Exec. Dir., Ont. Council
Hawkeye, P., Dir. of Fin. & Admin.
Ross, M., Chief Commissioner
Westergaard, L., Grants Advisor
Glad Tidings Arctic Missions Society
Gordon, L., Founder & Pres.
Glad Tidings Fellowship
Gordon, L., Asst. Pastor
Glenbow Archives
Garnier, A., Archivist
Glenbow Museum
Mastin, C.M., Sr. Curator of Art
Glendon College
Adam, D., Principal
Glina Group
Shiff, H., Ptnr
Global Communications Limited
Ivey, C.G., Dir., Hum. Res. Mgmt
Global Education in Tourism Ltd.
(dba Tourism Training Institute)
Ang, R.S.L., Mng Dir.
Global Television Network
Gilbert, J., Anchor
The Globe and Mail
Murdoch, S., Assoc. Ed.
Noble, K., Reporter, "Report on Business"
Ross, V., Arts & Publishing Reporter
Wente, M., Ed., "Report on Business"
Gloucester Films Ltd.
Gillson, M., Filmmaker
Mira Godard Gallery Inc.
Godard, M.M., Pres.
Golden Heron Enterprises
Bodkin, M.A., Chrm
Goldlist Development Corporation
Lustig, T., Sr. VP, Dev.
Good Soup Productions Inc.
Bienstock, R.E., Prod./Dir.
Goodman and Carr
Vella, S.M., Lawyer
Goodman Phillips & Vineberg
Cornwall, C.G., Ptnr
Rhea, C., Ptnr
Rubenstein, G., Sr. Ptnr
Lee Gordon Productions
Gordon, L., Pres.
Government House
LaRocque, J.A., Sec. to the Gov. Gen. & Head Chancellor
Government of Alberta
Abdurahman, M.R., M.L.A.
Black, P.L., Min. of Energy & Deputy Gov't House Leader, Legislative Assembly
Calahasen, P., Min. Resp. for Children's Svcs
Carlson, D., M.L.A. (Edmonton Ellerslie)
Forsyth, H., M.L.A. (Calgary-Fish Creek)
Fritz, Y., M.L.A. (Calgary Cross)
Gordon, J.D., M.L.A. (Lacombe-Stettler)
Haley, C., M.L.A. (Three Hills-Airdrie) &

Chrm, Standing Policy Committee on Agriculture & Rural Dev.
Hanson, A., M.L.A. (Edmonton Highlands Beverly), Liberal Opposition
Leibovici, K., M.L.A. (Edmonton Meadowlark)
McClellan, S., M.L.A. (Chinook) & Min. of Community Dev.
Mirosh, D., M.L.A.(Calgary-Glenmore) & Min. Resp. for Sci. & Research
Soetaert, C., M.L.A. (Spruce Grove-Sturgeon-St. Albert), Opposition Critic for Community Dev. & Women's Issues
Government of British Columbia
Boone, L., M.L.A.
Brewin, G., M.L.A.
Careless, V.A.S., Research Officer, Recreation Branch, Small Bus., Tourism & Culture
Edwards, A., Min., Ministry of Employment & Investments
Hammell, S., Min. of Women's Equality
Kumi, J.W., Asst. Deputy Min., Oper. Div., Ministry of Forests
MacPhail, J.K., M.L.A. (Vancouver-Hastings), Min. of Health & Min. Resp. for Seniors & Gov't House Leader
Priddy, P., M.L.A. (Surrey-Newton) & Min. of Small Bus., Tourism & Culture
Reid, L., M.L.A. (Richmond East)
Government of Canada
Ablonczy, D., M.P. (Calgary North)
Almond, A., Mgr, Hum. Res. Dev. Canada, Employment & Immigration
Augustine, J., M.P. (Etobicoke-Lakeshore)
Barnes, S.C., M.P.
Bethel, J., M.P. (Edmonton East)
Blondin-Andrew, E., Sec. of State, Training & Youth & M.P. (Western Arctic)
Brown, J., M.P. (Calgary Southeast)
Brushett, D., M.P. (Cumberland-Colchester)
Campbell, A.K., Former P.M., Consul Gen. for Canada in L.A.
Chamberlain, B.K., M.P. (Guelph-Wellington)
Clancy, M., M.P. (Halifax)
Collenette, P., Dir. of Appointments, Office of the P.M.
Copps, S., Dep. P.M. & Min. of Cdn Heritage, M.P. (Hamilton East)
Cowling, M., M.P. (Dauphin-Swan River, Manitoba)
Dalphond-Guiral, M., M.P. (Laval-Centre)
Dawson, M.E., Assoc. Deputy Min., Fed. Dept. of Justice
Debien, M., Députée, Laval-Est
Fairbairn, J., Senator, Leader of the Gov't in the Senate & Min. with Special Resp. for Literacy
Gaffney, B.M., M.P. (Nepean)
Grey, D.C., M.P. (Beaver River)
Guarnieri, A., M.P. (Mississauga East) & Parliamentary Sec. to the Min. of Cdn Heritage
Guay, M., M.P. (Laurentides)

Hayes, S.R., M.P. (Port Moody-Coquitlam)
Hickey, B., M.P. (St. John's East)
Hošek, C.M., Dir., Policy & Research, Office of the P.M.
Hume, V., Policy Coord., Sustainable Dev., Dept. of Indian & Northern Dev.
Hummerstone, J., First Nations Programs Coord., Matsqui Institution, Correctional Svc. of Canada
Jennings, D.G., M.P. (Mission-Coquitlam)
Kraft Sloan, K., M.P. (York-Simcoe)
Marleau, D., Min. Public Works & Gov't Svcs Canada
McCallion, K.E., Asst. Deputy Min., Int'l Bus. & Comm., & Chief Trade Commissioner, Dept. of Foreign Affairs & External Trade
McLaughlin, A., M.P. (Yukon)
McLellan, A., M.P. (Edmonton Northwest) & Min. of Natural Resources
McNeil, M., Deputy Exec. Dir., APEC '97 Cdn Coordinating Office
Meredith, V., M.P. (Surrey-White Rock-South Langley)
Minna, M., M.P. (Beaches-Woodbine)
Nexhipi, G., Consulting Psychologist, Correctional Svc.
Parrish, C., M.P. (Mississauga West)
Peterson, S., Asst. Deputy Min., Fed. Prov. Fiscal Rel'ns & Social Policy, Dept. of Fin.
Phinney, E., M.P. (Hamilton Mountain)
Ringuette-Maltais, P., M.P. (Madawaska-Victoria) & Asst. Deputy Chrm of Committees of the Whole House
Robillard, L., Min. of Citizenship & Immigration & M.P. (St. Henri-Westmount)
Russell, R.J., Mgr, Cdn Studies & Youth Programs, Dept. of Cdn Heritage
Sheridan, G., M.P. (Saskatoon-Humboldt)
Skoke, R.M., M.P. (Central Nova)
Smith, J.-R., Principal, Cdn Centre for Mgmt Dev.
Stanley, K., Asst. Deputy Min., Health Promotions & Programs Branch, Health Canada
Talbot-Allan, L.M., Asst. Deputy Min., Corp. Svcs, Environment Canada
Terrana, A.M., M.P. (Vancouver East)
Tremblay, S., M.P. (Rimouski-Témiscouata)
Ur, R.-M., M.P.(Lambton-Middlesex)
Wayne, E.E., M.P. (Saint John)
Weerasinghe, J., Mgr, Info. & Research Centre, Privy Council Office
Whelan, S., M.P. (Essex-Windsor)
Willcock, E., Sr. Citizenship Judge, Dept. of Citizenship & Immigration

Government of Manitoba
Barrett, B., M.L.A.
Cerilli, M., Mem. of the Legislative Assembly
Dacquay, L.M., Speaker of the Legislative Assembly

Dwarka, D., Multicultural Info. Specialist, Educ. & Training
Helper, B.M., Justice, Court of Appeal
McIntosh, L.G., Min. of Educ. & Training
Mitchelson, B., Min. of Family Svcs
Render, S., M.L.A.

Government of New Brunswick
Barry, J., Solicitor Gen.
Breault, A., Mem. of the Legislative Assembly (St. Stephen-St. Andrews), Min. of Municipalities, Culture & Housing
Budovitch, J., Dir. of Consumer Affairs
Godin, C., Social Worke, Dept. of Health & Community Svcs
Gunter, E.E., Dir., Legislative Svcs Branch, Dept. of Justice
Holt, L., Mgmt Consultant, Dept. of Fin.
Jarrett, L., M.L.A. (Saint John Kings) & Min. of State for Mines & Energy
Kingston, J., M.L.A.
Loughrey, C.E.A., Deputy Min. of Educ.
Mackenzie, L.J., Legislative Solicitor, Dept. of Justice
McCain, M., Lt.-Gov.
Trenholme, M., Min. of State for Family & Community Svcs
Weir, E., M.L.A. (Saint John Harbour)

Government of Nova Scotia
Belisle, C.-A.E., Coord., Sch. Libraries, Dept. of Educ. & Culture
Cosman, F.J., M.L.A. (Bedford-Fall River) & Deputy Speaker
Crouse, E., Supervisor, 4-H & Rural Org., N.S. Dept. of Agric. & Mktg
Doucet, V., Public Health Nurse, Dartmouth & Halifax, Dept. of Health
Norrie, E., M.L.A. (Truro-Bible Hill), Min. of Natural Resources, Min. Resp. for the Women's Directorate & Min. Resp. for Admin. of the Advisory Council of the Status of Women Act
O'Connor, L.J., M.L.A. (Lunenburg)

Government of Ontario
Bassett, I., M.P.P. (St. Andrews-St. Patrick)
Beaumont, A., Asst. Dep. Min., Housing Policy & Prog., Ministry of Municipal Affairs & Housing
Blatt, R., Sr. Consultant, Ministry of Econ. Dev., Trade & Tourism
Boyd, M., M.P.P. (London Centre)
Burak, R., Sec. of Cabinet & Clerk of Exec. Council
Caplan, E., M.P.P. (Oriole), Chief Opposition Whip & Critic for Health & Women's Issues for the Official Opposition
Green, J.M., CEO, Educ. Quality & Accountability Office
MacDonald, L.M., Asst. Deputy Min., Corp. Svcs, Ministry of Community & Social Svcs.
Marland, M., M.P.P. (Mississauga S.) & Gov't

Caucus Chair
Martel, S., M.P.P. (Sudbury E.)
McLeod, L., M.P.P. (Fort William) & Interim
Leader of the Official Opposition
Smith, R., District Mgr, Institutional Health
Group, Ministry of Health
Todres, E., Deputy Solicitor Gen. & Deputy
Min. of Corrections
Wheeler, E.E., Dairy Cattle Nutrition Specialist,
Ministry of Agric. Food & Rural Affairs
Witmer, E., M.P.P. & Min. of Labour

Government of Prince Edward Island
Callbeck, C.S., Premier & Pres. of the Exec.
Council
Griffin, D., Deputy Min., Dept. of
Environmental Resources
Guptill, N.E., M.L.A. (5th Prince) & Speaker
of the Legislative Assembly
Hubley, E., M.L.A. (4th Prince)
Mella, P.J., M.L.A.(3rd Queen's) & Leader,
Official Opposition
Murphy, M., M.L.A.

**Government of Quebec/Gouvernement
du Québec**
Beaudoin, L., Min. of Culture &
Communications
Blackburn, J.L., Députée du comté de
Chicoutimi & Prés. de la Commission de
l'Educ.
Charest, S., Dép. (Rimouski), Assemblée nat'l
Delisle, M.F., M.N.A.
Dionne-Marsolais, R., Min. déléguée à
l'Industrie et au Commerce
Fontaine, N., Deputy Min., Citizens Rel'ns &
Immigration
Gagnon-Tremblay, M., M.N.A. (Saint-
François)
Grenier, D., Dir. de l'Ordre National du
Québec, Ministère du Conseil exécutif
Harel, L., M.N.A. (Hochelaga-Maisonneuve)
& Min. d'état de l'Emploi et de la Solidarité et
Min. responsable de la Condition Feminine
Hirou, C., Transportation Advisor, Ministère
de la Mêtropole
Houda-Pepin, F., Deputée (La Pinière)
Lavallée, D., Sous-ministre adjointe au Loisir
et aux Sports, Ministère des Affaires
municipales
Leduc, L., M.N.A. (Mille-Îles)
Malo, N., Sous-min., Ministère du revenu-
Marois, P., M.N.A. (Taillon) & Min. of Educ.
Robert, H., Députée de Deux-Montagnes,
Adjointe parlementaire et Sec. régionale des
Laurentides
Signori, C., M.N.A. (Blainville)
Vermette, C., Députée (Marie-Victorin)

Government of Saskatchewan
Atkinson, P., Min. of Educ.
Bradley, J.L., M.L.A. (Weyburn-Big Muddy)
Crofford, J., M.L.A. (Regina Lake Centre)

Hamilton, D., M.L.A. (Regina Wascana Plains)
Lorjé, P., M.L.A. (Saskatoon-Southeast)
MacKinnon, J., Min. of Fin.
Murray, S.M.A., M.L.A. (Regina Qu'Appelle
Valley)
Stanger, V., M.L.A.
Teichrob, C., M.L.A. (Saskatoon Meewasin),
Min. of Mun. Gov't & Min. Resp. for SaskTel

Government of the Northwest Territories
Dundas-Matthews, R.L., Dir., Fin. & Mgmt
Svcs
Watters, B.V., Dir., Policy, Planning &
Evaluation, Dept. of Health & Social Services

Government of the Yukon Territories
Firth, B., M.L.A., Riverdale South
Gingell, J., Commissioner of the Yukon

Gowlings
Crowe Worthington, C., Assoc. Lawyer

Grace Maternity Hospital
Graves, G.R., Active Staff, The Women's Clinic

***Grain* Magazine**
Philips, E., Writer & Ed.
Robinson, J.J., Ed.-in-Chief

Grande Prairie Cancer Clinic
Strehlke, C., Dir.

Grant McEwan Community College
Doughty, W., Exec. Dir., Corp. Mktg Office

**Graphic Communications
International Union**
de Gruchy, E., Exec. Sec.

Graphic Photo
Flanders, E., CEO

Great Humber Joint Council
Christopher, J.B., Pres.

The Great-West Life Assurance Company
Lichtman, S., Dir., Group Mktg Dev.
Prevalnig, M.J., VP, Agencies

Green Party of Canada
Priesnitz, W., Leader

Greenpeace Canada
Moffat, J., Exec. Dir.

Groundwood Books Ltd.
Aldana, P., Publisher

**Groupe d'aide et d'information sur le
harcèlement sexuel au travail**
Séguin, Y.D.M., Dir.

Groupe Maritime Verreault Inc.
Verreault, D., Pres.

Le Groupe Vidéotron Ltée
Renault, S., VP, Legal Affairs & Sec.

Groupskills Seminars
Bartlette, D., Founder

Guilford's Organic Seed and Feed
Guilford, C., Co-owner

Guillevin International Inc.
Guillevin Wood, J., Chrm of the Bd.

Cathy Gulkin Film Editing Ltd.
Gulkin, C., Film & Video Ed.

H SW Management Associates Limited
Edmondson, S.M., Mng Ptnr
Hallat Holdings
Hallatt, P., Owner
Hallis Media Inc.
Hallis, P., VP
Halton Family Services
Brown, N.J., Exec. Dir.
Hamilton Civic Hospitals
Brister, S.J., Cardiovascular Surgeon
Mandy, P., VP, Patient Care–Community
Hospital Svcs
Hamilton College
Guttman, N., Asst. Prof. of English
Hamilton Psychiatric Hospital
Martin, M.-L., Acting Dir. of Nursing Practice
& Clinical Nurse Specialist
Ruth Hammond Public Relations
Hammond, R., Pres. & Principal
Lyn Hancock Books
Hancock, L., Writer, Photographer and
Lecturer
Hanson's Interior Decorating
Hanson, C., Pres., Owner & Ptnr
Harlequin Enterprises Limited
Cinnamon, S.L., Dir., Art Svcs
HarperCollins Canada Ltd.
Brunsek, J., VP, Mktg & Sales
HarperCollins Publishers
Tupholme, I., Publisher & Ed.-in-Chief
Harris and District Museum Inc.
McFarlane, B., VP
Harvard University
Franklin, M.B., Prof. of Physics
A. Harvey & Co. Ltd.
Patten, S.H., Chrm
Health Action Network Society
Hancock, L., Exec. Dir.
The Health Group
M. Jane Fulton, Principal
Health News
Engel, J., Ed.
**Health Professionals Regulatory
Advisory Council**
Jefferson, C., Chair
Health Sciences Centre
Hawkeye, L.A., Dir., Housekeeping Svcs
Healthwest Consultants Inc.
Burgess, E., Pres.
**Heart and Stroke Foundation of
New Brunswick**
Erb-Campbell, H.L., Exec. Dir.
**Heart and Stroke Foundation of
Nova Scotia**
Fraser, J., Exec. Dir.
Hearthstone Independent Enterprises
Meier, S., Writer
Wehrstein, K., Writer

Ydessa Hendeles Art Foundation
Hendeles, Y., Pres.
Henderson General Hospital
Latimer, E.J., Palliative Care Physician. Prof.
& Administrator
Henderson Publications Inc.
Killinger, B., Pres.
Heritage Quebec Foundation
Gagnon-Pratte, F., Pres. & Chrm
Heritage Seed Program
Apple, H., Ed., Past Pres. & Exec. Dir.
Herizen™ Sailing For Women Inc.
Birdsell-Smith, P.M., Pres., Owner-Oper.
Herland Incorporated
Vander Voet, S., Pres.
Jody Hewgill Illustrations
Hewgill, J., Illustrator
Hewlett-Packard (Canada) Ltd.
Bouchard, M., VP, Que. Oper.
Caldwell, N., VP & Gen. Mgr., Computer
Systems Organization
Furlong, L., Hum. Res. & Diversity Mgr
Impey, P., Cont.
Masini, B., Dir. of Mktg
Sievwright, G., Gen. Cnsl & Sec. & Dir. of
Corp. Rel'ns
Highland Heights Junior Public School
Bismilla, V.H., Principal
Hillsborough Girls' Choir
Schiller, R., Founder & Choral Dir.
Hilwil Investments Inc.
Wilson, H.E., Chrm & CEO
C.M. Hincks Treatment Centre
Martin, F., Exec. Dir.
I. Hoffman + associates inc.
Hoffman, I., Pres. & CEO
Holland College
MacPherson, J.E., Instructor, Re-Entry Training
Holland College Foundation
Comrie, C., Exec. Dir.
Hollinger Inc.
Amiel, B., VP, Editorial
Holt, Renfrew & Co., Limited
Brooks, B., Sr. VP, Mktg
Weston, H.M., Deputy Chrm
Holy Names Congregation
Maes, Y.
Home Depot Canada
Verschuren, A., Pres.
Homemaker's Magazine
Armstrong, S., Ed.-in-Chief
Hongkong Bank of Canada
Corbett, D.E., VP & Chief Auditor
Giacomazzi, B., Chief Credit Officer
Morgan-Silvester, S.A., Sr. VP, Mktg &
Ombudsperson
Hope and Cope
Kussner, S., Founding Chrm
Hoshizaki House
Hoshizaki, F.S., Founder

Hospital for Sick Children
Andrew, M., Prof. of Pediatrics (part-time)
Bradley, S., Psychiatrist-in-Chief
Haddad-Forster, M.J., Dir., Paediatric Programs
Kaufman, M., Physician & Medical Dir., Complex Adult Problem Program, Div. of Adolescent Medicine
Lefebvre, A., Staff Psychiatrist
MacGregor, D.L., Clinical Dir., Div. of Neurology, Dept. of Paediatrics
Olivieri, N.F., Dir., Comprehensive Care Program for Thalassemia & Sickle Cell Disease
Pyykkönen, L., Nursing Coord.
Simmons, J.N., Medical Consultative Staff
Rabinovitch, R., Dir., Cardiovascular Research
House Helpers Inc.
Hanson, C., Pres., Owner & Ptnr
Howard Interpersonal Dynamics Inc.
Howard, V.J., Owner/Mgr
C.D. Howe Institute
Ferrante, A., Exec. VP, COO
Susanne Hudson Consulting
Hudson, S., Pres.
Hudson's Bay Company
Walters, S., VP, Store Planning & Construction, Retail Group
Hughes, Amys
Stevens, P.M., Mng Ptnr
Hughes Public School
Warszawski, D., Teacher
Human Factors North Inc.
Smiley, A., Pres.
Human Resources Professional Association of Ontario
Blaszczyk, Y., Pres.
Human Rights Institute of Canada
Ritchie, M.E., Pres.
Human Rights Tribunal
Mactavish, A.L., Pres.
Humford Management Inc.
Wittmack, B.C., Pres.
Hummingbird Centre for the Performing Arts
Bradley, E.A., Gen. Mgr
Huron College
Fulton, T., Assoc. Prof. of Econ.
N.L. Hushion and Associates
Hushion, N., Pres.
Husky Oil Ltd.
Koh, P.-C., Exec. VP & CFO
Pascall, B., Mgr, Corp. Comm.
Warriner, F.C., VP & Cont.
The Hutchinson Foundation for Research (Ewings Sarcoma)
Hutchinson, C.G., Pres.
Hydra Enterprises Ltd.
Ching, H., Consultant

IBM Canada Ltd.
Alford, C., Gen. Mgr, Systems Integration
Allan-Davis, L., Gen. Mgr, AS/400 Div.
Cameron, D.M.D., Gen. Mgr, Educ. & Training
Mersereau, M., Dir. of Comm.
Odam, P., Dir., Hum. Res. Plans & Programs
Ross, A.K., VP, Mgmt Svcs
I.L.S. Learning Corporation
Hawrishok, L., VP
I.O.D.E.
Dalton, M., Past Pres., Nat'l Chapter of Canada
I.O.D.E. Children's Centre
Summers, A.M., Clinical Geneticist, Dir. of the Maternal Serum Screening Program, Dept. of Genetics
IPSCO Inc.
Parker, A., Legal Cnsl & Dir. of Corp. Comm.
IWK-Grace Health Centre for Children, Women & Families
Bacon, M., VP, Nursing
Barnard, D., Pediatric Hematologist, Oncologist, Hematopathologist
Blois, R., Dir., Partnership Dev.
McDonnell, M.C., Social Worker
Morrison, G., VP of Professional Svcs
Ritchie, J., Dir. of Nursing Research
Stone, K.K., Dir. of Public Rel'ns
IWK-Grace Health Centre Foundation
Godsoe, D.S., Co-Chair
Les Idées heureuses
Soly, G., Dir. artistique et gén.
Illumination Magique Inc.
Borenstein, J., Freelance Filmmaker
Images Alberta
Williams, D.A.
Images of Wellness
Shuttleworth, E.M., Nurse Practitioner
Imasco Limited
Nakashima, K., Sec. & Sr. Cnsl
Immigrant Women's Association of Manitoba
Singh, M.K.K., Past Pres.
Immigration and Refugee Board of Canada
Kouri, J.L., Mbr., Convention Refugee Determination Div.
Mawani, N., Chair
Imported Artists Film Company
Ford, C., Pres./Owner
Independent Film & Video Alliance
McCann, P., Pres.
Indian Art Centre
Gray, V., Mgr
Indian Homemakers' Association of British Columbia
Blankinship, J., Pres.

Industrial Accident Prevention Association
Shaw, M.C., Pres. & CEO
Infinitum Management Services Inc.
Gibb, P., Pres.
Information Technology Research Centre
Tyrie, A., Dir., Industry Support
Innkeepers' Guild of Nova Scotia
Earle-Lambert, B., Pres.
**Inside/Out, Toronto Lesbian and Gay
Film Festival**
Flanders, E., Dir.
**L'Institut d'assurance de dommages
du Québec**
Laflamme, D., Gen. Mgr
Institute for Environmental Policy
Heathcote, I.W., Dir.
Institute for Research on Public Policy
Jérôme-Forget, M., Pres.
Institute on Governance
O'Neil, M., Dir.
Insurance Brokers Association of Canada
Brown, J.C., Exec. Dir.
**Insurance Brokers' Association of
Nova Scotia**
Winters, H.A., Exec. Dir.
**Insurance Corporation of British
Columbia**
Hyde, D.K., VP, Public Affairs & Road Safety
Olney, M., Chair of the Bd.
Robertson, L., Corp. Sec. & Gen. Cnsl
Intercontinental Packers Limited
Mitchell, C., VP
Mitchell, J., Chair of the Bd.
Intercorp Foods Ltd.
Unger, R., Pres.
International Bahá'í Teaching Centre
Rabbani, M., Mbr.
**International Centre for Human Rights
and Democratic Development**
O'Neil, M., Interim Pres. (Sept. 15-Dec. 15,
1996)
Walmsley, N.E., Mbr., Bd. of Dir. & Exec.
Committee
**International Centre for Sustainable
Cities Foundation**
Enser, M.B., Mng Dir.
**International Centre for the Advancement
of Community-Based Rehabilitation**
Arsenault, F.H., Pres.
The International Children's Institute
Oh, J., Canadian Youth Program Coord.
The International Club of Ottawa
Adey, I.M.M., Founder
International Council of Jewish Women
Marr, H., Pres.
**International Development
Research Centre**
MacDonald, F., Chair
International Down Syndrome Federation
Mills, J., Coord.

**International Institute for Sustainable
Development**
Seymoar, N.-K., Deputy to the Pres.
**International Institute of Concern
for Public Health**
Bertell, H.R., Pres.
International Joint Commission
Hurley, A.M., Chair
International Native Arts Festival
Donato, M.H., Exec. Dir.
International Ocean Institute, Malta
Borgese, E., Founder & Hon. Pres.
**International Society of Augmentative
and Alternative Communication**
Christie, N.P., Exec. Dir.
**International Women's Association of
Prince Edward Island**
Gossen, O., Pres.
Inuit Tapirisat of Canada
Sillett, M.J., Interim Pres.
Inuvialuit Regional Corporation
Cournoyea, N.J., Chair & CEO
Inventors Association of Canada
Tengum, P.Z.R.W., Gen. Mgr
Investment Executive
Hyland, B., Publisher
Investor Relations Canada Ltd
Wilson, H.E., Chrm & CEO
Investors Finance Corp. Ltd.
Petersen Burfield, M.J., VP & Dir.
Iriz Studios
Paabo, I., Multimedia Artist
I-Sis Productions
Micallef, G., Dir. & Prod.
Istituto Italiano di Cultura
Valente Gorjup, F., Dir.
Italian Chamber of Commerce in Canada
Simeone, M., Exec. Dir.
The Richard Ivey Foundation
Ivey, B., VP
Ricker, M., Exec. Dir.

J

JAC International
Croy, J., Pres.
JCI - Global Strategists
Charnetski, J.L., Pres.
JEH Associates Inc.
Halliwell, J., Pres.
Jackman & Associates
Jackman, B.L.
The Jacks Institute
Jacks, E., Pres. & Owner
James Bay Community Project
Roback, B., Family Physician
Janssen-Ortho Inc.
Albright, P.S., VP, Gov't & Health Econ.
Lau, C., Dir., Clinical Research
The Japanese Paper Place
Jacobi, N., Owner & Pres.

Jewish Community Foundation of Greater Montreal
Lande, M.Q.B., Pres.

Jewish Family Services of the Baron de Hirsch
Kislowicz, L., Exec. Dir.

Jewish Home for the Aged Foundation
Geller, E., Dir. of Dev.

Jewish Support Services for the Elderly
Shatsky, L.F., Exec. Dir.

Jewish Women International of Canada
Krowitz, P., Exec. Dir.

Job Oriented Training Inc.
Misener, A., Pres.

John Abbott College
Gill, J., Co-Chair, Phys. Educ. Dept.
Morrison, C., Instructor

John Howard Society of Alberta
Leonard, C., Exec. Dir.

Johnson, Gullberg, Wiest and MacPherson
MacPherson, S.M., Ptnr

Joint Hospital Purchasing Services
Pohl, T., Dir., Medical/Surgical Svcs

Jordan Petroleum Ltd.
Blue, M., Sr. VP, Land & Admin.

Journal of Business Ethics
Poff, D.C., Ed.

Journeywoman Travel Magazine
Hannon, E., Ed./Publisher

Junior Achievement of Cape Breton
MacDonald, T., Exec. Dir.

Just for Kids Foundation
Greenstone, H.A., Founding Pres.

KEA Media
Autio, K., Pres.

KPMG
Davis, A., Ptnr
Holland, M., Ptnr
O'Malley, P.L., Ptnr

KPMG Environmental Services Inc.
Davis, A., Pres.

KRH Productions
Hope, K., Prod.

The Kahanoff Foundation
Herzog, S., VP

Kamloops Daily News
Wiseman, S., Reporter

KARO (Toronto) Inc.
Blais-Ramsay, M., VP, Corp. Identity

Kate's Word Inc.
Barris, K., Writer

Keating Educational Tours
Keating, D., VP

Kelly Services (Canada) Ltd.
Manning, L., VP & Mng Dir. for Canada

Kent Consulting
Kent, J., Pres.

Kerr Financial Corporation
Kerr, K.L., VP & Mgr, Toronto Office

Key and McKnight
Key, N.L., Mng Ptnr

Key Porter Books Limited
Porter, A., Publisher & CEO
Renouf, S.E., Pres. & Ed.-in-Chief

The Kidney Foundation of Canada
Carwell, J., Exec. Dir., N. Alta. & The Territories Branch
Cochrane, D., Pres., Sask. Br.
Holroyd, D., Exec. Dir., Sask. Branch
Lychowyd, S., Reg'l Dir., N.W. Ont. Reg.
McDonnell, M.C., Past Pres.
McLeod, L., Nat'l Treas.
Mercier, M., Exec. Dir., Que. Branch
Ship, L., Exec. Dir., E. Ont. Branch
Starzomski, R.C., Immediate Past Pres., B.C. Branch
Weston, G., Past Pres., S. Alta. Branch & Nat'l Sec.

Kids Can Press Ltd.
Hussey, V., Publisher & Pres.

Kids First Parent Association of Canada
Perri, C., Nat'l Pres.

Kids in Act-ion Exculsive Training/ Theatre Company
Gaulthier, N., Dir. & Acting Coach

Kids Only Clothing Club Inc.
Eeson, C., Pres.

The Kindness Club
Tarn, E.J., Exec. Dir.

Kinetic Productions
McEwen, M., Prod.

Kingston General Hospital
Houlden, R., Staff Endocrinologist
Ropchan, G., Staff Surgeon, Cardiovascular & Thoracic Surgery

Ely Kish Studio
Kish, E., Artist

The Kitchener-Waterloo Record
Rittinger, C., Ed.

Kivalliq Consulting Management & Training Services Ltd.
Anawak, C., Pres.

Kiwanis Music Festival of Greater Toronto
Craig, J., Gen. Mgr

Alfred A. Knopf Canada
Dennys, L., Publisher

Kookaburra Productions
Zann, L., Prod.

Olga Korper Gallery
Korper, O., Dir. & owner

The Kulhay Wellness Centre
Kulhay, K.M., Founder & Dir.

The Kuna Investments Group
Delicaet, A.M., Pres. & CEO

Kuwabara Payne McKenna Blumberg Architects
Thornley, S.B., Ptnr

L.B.'s Cafe Inc.
Boxall, L., Pres.

La La La Human Steps
Lecavalier, L., Principal Dancer

Labrador Legal Services
Maes, Y., Coord. of Programs for Batterers & Sex Offenders

Lucie Lacava Publication Design Inc.
Lacava, L., Design Consultant

Lacewood Productions
Read, M., Dir. of Dev.

Lafortune Leduc
Cadieux, L., Ptnr

Laidlaw Inc.
Nunn, W., Corp. Dir., Organizational Dev.

Laidlaw Resources
Sandwell, C., Dir. of Fin. & Admin.

Laidlaw Transit Ltd.
Finley, D.D., Dir. of Strategic Planning & Dev.

Laidlaw Waste Systems
Wilson, L.L., Dir. of Purchasing

Lakehead University
Epp, J., Assoc. Prof. of Educ.
Farrell, R., Asst. Prof., Fac. of Educ.
Fennell, H.-A., Assoc. Prof. & Chair, Preservice Teacher Educ. Program
Forbes, J., Prof., Dept. of English
MacLean, M., Assoc. Prof. & Chair, Dept. of Library & Info. Studies
Petrone, S., Prof. Emeritus
Steven, D., Assoc. Prof.
Taylor, S., Chair, Dept. of Social Work
Vervoort, P., Assoc. Prof., Dept. of Visual Arts
Wilson, L.M., Chancellor

Lamar Communications
Adamec, L., Pres.

LaMarsh Centre for Research on Violence and Conflict Resolution
Pepler, D., Dir.

Lambrecht Publications
Lambrecht, H., Pres.

M.S. Lamont and Associates Limited
Lamont, M.S., Pres.

Lane Environment Limited
Lane, P.A., Pres.

Lang Michener
Hitchman, C., Ptnr
Hoy, A., Ptnr
Mills, J., Ptnr
Orenstein, E., Ptnr
Whitaker, M., Ptnr

Lang Michener Lawrence & Shaw
Olsen, C.A., Ptnr
Reid, D.R., Consultant

Langara College
Rains, E., Journalism Instructor

Suzanne Langevin Photographe
Langevin, S., Photographer

Langlois Robert
Garneau, C., Lawyer

Lantrek Services Ltd.
Maharajh, A.E., Pres.

Laubach Literacy Canada, Alberta Association
Meronowich, F., Pres.

Laubach Literacy Council of Newfoundland and Labrador
Hurley, A.J., Pres.

Laubach Literacy Ontario
Coombs, D., Pres.

Laurentian Bank of Canada
Bailey, M., VP, Foreign Exchange & Money Mkt
Bourassa, L., VP & Chief Acctnt

Laurenval School Board
Adrian, D.J., Library Coord.

Law Society of Manitoba
McCawley, D.J., CEO

Law Society of Saskatchewan
Logan, A.K., Sec. & Co-Dir. of Admin.

Lawyers for Social Responsibility
Delong, B.J.T., Pres.

Le Spa de Montagne
Crooks, C., Co-owner

Stephen Leacock Associates
Dickson, J., Chrm, Award Committee

Stephen Leacock Museum/Archive
Mainprize, D.E.H., Dir./Curator

League for Human Rights of B'nai Brith Canada
Mock, K.R., Nat'l Dir.

The Learning Connection
Hewitt, J.D., Founder

Learning Disabilities Association of Newfoundland and Labrador
Reddy, D., Pres.

Learning Disabilities Association of Saskatchewan
Garcea, L., Exec. Dir.

The Learning Enrichment Foundation
Grayson, E., Exec. Dir.

The Learning Link
Meronowich, F., Chair

Leatherwood Ventures
Taylor, M., Owner

LeBlanc Boucher Rodger Bourque
Bourque, P., Assoc.

Legal Education Society of Alberta
Copp, J.C., Dir., Professional Dev.

Judith Leidl Fine Art
Leidl, J.J., Fine Artist/Printmaker

Lemire Rodger & Associates
Lemire-Rodger, G., Pres.

Lenscrafters
Summers, M., Gen. Mgr

Lerner & Associates
Stewart, J., Mng Ptnr

Les éditions de la courte échelle inc.
Creary, B., Pub. & Foreign Rights Dir.

Les Productions Nathalie Gaulthier Inc.
Gaulthier, N., Founder & Pres.
Lester Publishing Limited
Porter, A., Chrm
Leukemia Research Fund of Canada
Sherman, C.H., Dir. & Past Pres.
Lever Enterprises
Lever, A., Pres.
Lever Pond's
Lem, E., VP, Personal Care
Lévesque Beaubien Geoffrion Inc.
Tardif, L., Investment Advisor & Mgr
Levy Productions
Levy, C., Prod.
Lewis Carroll Communications Inc.
Holland, J.C., Pres.
The Liberal Party of Alberta/ Northwest Territories
Johnson, M.W., Nat'l Readiness Campaign
Liberal Party of Canada
Beck, P., Reg'l Rep., Man./Sask. Nat'l Women's Liberal Commission
Clement, A., Young Liberals of Canada Rep., Nat'l Women's Liberal Commission
St. Denis, J., Co-Pres., Aboriginal Peoples' Commission
Liberal Party of Manitoba
Harder Mattson, E., Past Prov. Pres., Women's Commission
Lick's Ice Cream & Burger Shops Inc.
Meehan, D.P., Pres.
Lifelong Learning Horizons & Associates
Frazer, R., Pres.
Lightshow Communications Inc.
Fried, M.I., Writer, Dir. & Prod.
Gloria Lindsay Luby Enterprises
Lindsay Luby, G., Pres.
Lino Productions Inc.
Cailhier, D., Scénariste
Lions Gate Hospital
Best, L., COO
Literacy Link Niagara
Douglas, C.G.
Livent Inc.
Friendly, L., Exec. VP
Loblaw Companies Limited
Yamamoto, A.M., VP, Info. Techologies & Systems Audit
Lockert Distributors Ltd.
Lockert, B.L., Pres. & CEO
Lockwood Films (London) Inc.
Johnson, N., Pres.
Loewen, Ondaatje, McCutcheon Limited
Farrow, M.A., Exec. VP & Dir. of Econ. & Equity Strategy
Logistec Corporation
Paquin, M., Pres. & CEO
Lombard Canada Ltd.
Gardner, M.J., VP & CFO
Salomon, F., Sr. VP & Gen. Cnsl

London Insurance Group
Butt, C., VP
London Life Insurance Company
Butt, C., Sr. VP, Info. Svcs
Toal, A., VP & Corp. Actuary
London Life Reinsurance Company
Hainer, M., Pres.
London Regional Cancer Centre of Ontario Cancer Treatment and Research Foundation
Bramwell, V., Head of Medical Oncology
The Law Office of Kathleen Loo Craig
Loo Craig, K.
Lookout Emergency Aid Society
O'Shannacery, K., Exec. Dir.
Lucas Bowker & White
Johnson, E.A., Ptnr
Lunchbox Theatre
Bard, M., Co-founder & Assoc. Dir.
Linda Lundström Ltd.
Lundström, L., Pres.
Lundström Retail Inc.
Lundström, L., Pres.
Lutheran Women's Missionary League - Canada
Schaan, E., Pres.

MB & Associates Inc.
Biedermann, M.M., Pres.
MCC Planners Inc.
Jones, M., Pres.
MDS Health Group Limited
Harack, J.E., VP, Hum. Res., Lab. Svcs Div.
M.E.H. Publishing Services
Hill, M.E., Owner
MGM/United Artists Distribution of Canada
Wineberg, T., Dir. of Publicity/Promotions
M.I.T. Electronics Inc.
d'Entremont, R.I., Pres.
M.T.R. Entertainment Limited
Read, M., Pres.
MRI Studios
Isinger, L.K., Owner/Mgr
Maarnada Studios Ltd.
Stewart Schaddelee, N., Pres. & owner
Macaulay Shiomi Howson Ltd.
Howson, E.A., Ptnr
MacIntosh, MacDonnell & MacDonald
Van den Eynden, E., Ptnr
MacKenzie & Associate Consulting
MacKenzie, M., Consultant, Harassment & Discrimination in the Workplace
Mackenzie Financial Corp.
Rohr, P., VP, Bus. Planning
Maclean Hunter Publishing Limited
Draycott, A., Edit. Dir., *Chatelaine* Special Editions
Empey, C.E., Ed., *Modern Woman* magazine

James, K.A., Publisher, *Canadian Grocer* Magazine
Simpson, L., VP & Group Publisher (resp. for *Chatelaine*, *Chatelaine Special Editions!*, & *Modern Woman*)
Maclean Hunter Television Fund
Sheffer, A., Exec. Dir.
Maclean's Magazine
Clayton, N., Dir., Mktg & Research
Janigan, M., Contributing Ed.
McDonald, M., Sr. Writer
Macleod Dixon
Logan, K., Ptnr
The Hugh Macmillan Children's Foundation
McIntosh, R., Chair of the Bd.
Macnutt & Dumont
Dumont, D.E., Ptnr
MacPherson Leslie & Tyerman
Simard, R.M.L., Lawyer
Maddalena Hill & Edmonds
Edmonds, E., Lawyer
Magazine *Univers*
Le Blanc, H., Rédactrice en chef
Maiden, Mother, Crone
Levin, D., Clairvoyant, Owner & Operator
Malaspina University College
Goldberg, S., Instructor in Film Studies
Maloney, Gottlieb & Pearson Government Relations, Inc.
Maloney, S., Assoc.
Management Board Secretariat
Bellamy, D., Dir., Legal Svcs Br.
Mandell Pinder
Pinder, L., Ptnr
Manitoba Association of Registered Nurses
Dick, D., Exec. Dir. & CEO
Manitoba Audio Recording Industry Association
Dempsey, G., Exec. Dir.
Manitoba Cancer Treatment and Research Foundation
Taylor-Brown, J., Sr. Clinician, Dept. of Psycho-Social Oncology
Manitoba Child Care Association Inc.
Dudek, D., Exec. Dir.
Manitoba Court of Queen's Bench
Steel, F.M., Justice
Manitoba Dental Hygienists Association
Kravtsov, N., Pres.
Manitoba Justice
Smith, M.J., Cnsl, Constitutional Law Branch
Manitoba Motor Dealers Association
Canty, S., Exec. Dir.
Manitoba Nurses' Union
Chernecki, V., Pres.
Manitoba Opera
Alexander-Smith, J., Gen. Dir.

Manitoba Safety Council
Roeland, R.L., Exec. Dir.
Manitoba Sheep Association
Schroedter, L., Past Pres.
Manitoba Telephone System
Nault, H., VP, Corp. & Regulatory Affairs
Manitoba Theatre for Young People
Silverman, L., Artistic Dir.
Manulife Financial
Haight, L., Chief Acctnt
Jones, F., VP, Affinity Mkts
Stait-Gardner, Z., Sr. VP & Gen. Mgr, Reinsur. Oper.
Judith Marcuse Dance Company
Marcuse, J.R., Artistic Dir.
Judith Marcuse Dance Projects Society
Marcuse, J.R., Artistic Dir.
The Maritime Life Assurance Company
Hannon, H.M., Cnsl & Corp. Sec.
Woodman, C.J., Dir., Corp. & Public Affairs
The Market Gallery of the City of Toronto Archives
Reddyhoff, G., Curator
Markham Public Libraries
Benn-Ireland, T.J., Librarian
Martin & Meredith Limited
Fuller, H.A., Real Estate Broker & Owner
Martin, Whalen, Hennebury and Stamp
Newbury, J., Assoc.
MARTRAIN Corporate and Personal Development
Martinson, J., Ptnr
Mary Kay Cosmetics Ltd.
Grobety, M., Independent Exec. Sr. Dir.
Mascoll Beauty Supply Ltd.
Mascoll, B., Pres.
The Beverly Mascoll Community Foundation
Mascoll, B., Founder
MATCH International Centre
Larbi, M.O., Exec. Dir.
Matheson and Murray
Murray, M.L., Ptnr
Maximage Productions
Fichman, I., VP/Prod.
Maxwell Meighen & Associates
Morgan, E.L., Pres.
May-Smith Enterprises
Siggins, M., Writer
McCarthy Tétrault
Bigue, A.M., Ptnr
Bryant Ballingall, S., Lawyer
McCord Museum of Canadian History
Benoit, C., Exec. Dir.
Kennell, E.H., Dir. of Dev.
Smith-Sauvé, D., Coord. of Dev.
McDougall, Ready
Barber, S.B., Ptnr
Lothian, P., Ptnr
Wright, M.-E., Lawyer & Ptnr

McGill Centre for Medicine, Ethics and Law
Morgan, N., Visiting Prof.
Somerville, M.A.
McGill University
Aston-McCrimmon, E.P., Assoc. Prof., Phys. Therapy Program
Chambers, G., Chancellor
Dobkin, P.L., Asst Prof., Dept. of Medicine
Freeman, C., Chrm, Dept. of Oncology, Div. of Radiation Oncology
Galiana-Brants, H.L., Prof., Dept. of Biomedical Eng. & Dept. of Otolaryngology, Fac. of Medicine
Ghosh, R., Macdonald Prof. of Educ.
Gillett, M., William C. MacDonald Prof. Emerita in Educ., Dept. of Educational Studies, Fac. of Educ.
Hechtman, L., Prof., Psychiatry & Pediatrics
Johnstone, R., Prof., Gilman Cheney Chair, Dept. of Biochem.
Jones, B.E., Prof., Dept. of Neurology & Neurosurgery
Lindley, S., Asst. Prof., Fac. of Medicine
Lippman, A., Prof., Dept. of Epidemiology & Biostatistics
Lock, M., Prof., Dept. of Social Studies of Medicine
Murphy, B.E.P., Prof. of Medicine
Rees-Potter, L.K., Assoc. Prof., Grad. Sch. of Library & Info. Studies
Reinhold, C., Asst. Prof. of Diagnostic Radiology
Shannon, V., Assoc. Prof., Sch. of Nursing
Snell, L., Assoc. Dean, Continuing Medical Educ.
Stevenson, M.M., Assoc. Prof., Dept. of Medicine
Tancred, P., Prof. of Soc.
Tannenbaum, G.S., Prof., Depts of Pediatrics & Neurology & Neurosurgery
Tonin, P.N., Asst. Prof., Fac. of Medicine
Wolfe, J.M., Prof. & Dir., Sch. of Urban Planning
McGill University Health Centre
Riley, D.B., Dir. of Planning
McGill-Queen's University Press
Harcourt, J., Acquisitions Ed.
McGinnis Building Block Co. Ltd.
Black, F.M., Pres.
McGregor Charbonneau Inc. Design Consultants
Charbonneau, Y., Sr. Design Ptnr & Pres.
McInnes Cooper and Robertson
Oland, L.L., Ptnr
Reid, M., Ptnr
McIntosh Gallery
Kennedy, A.M., Dir.
McLellan Group
Grogan, L., Broadcaster

McLennan Ross, Barristers and Solicitors
Amonson, J.L., Ptnr
H.J. McLeod, Ph.D. & Associates Ltd.
McLeod, H.J.
McMaster Museum of Art
Ness, K.G., Dir. & Curator
McMaster University
Brister, S.J., Assoc. Clinical Prof. of Surgery
Chang, P.L.-Y., Prof., Dept. of Pediatrics
Coldwell, J., Prof. Emeritus
Cooper, B., Assoc. Dean, Health Sci. (Rehab.) & Dir., Sch. of Rehab. Sci.
Devlin, C., Prof. of Obstetrics & Gynecology
Kinlough-Rathbone, R.L., Assoc. VP, Fac. of Health Sciences, & Prof., Pathology
Moulder, C., Curator, Lloyd Reeds Map Collection
Oaks, A., Prof. of Biology (Emeritus)
Santa Barbara, J., Asst. Prof., Dept. of Psychiatry & Centre for Peace Studies
Tryon, V., Concert Pianist, Artist in Residence, Dept. of Music
Uchida, I.A., Prof. Emeritus, Dept. of Pediatrics
Woodward, C., Prof., Dept. of Clinical Epidemiology & Biostatistics
York, L., Assoc. Prof., English
McMillan Binch
Olasker, P., Co-Mng Ptnr
Pepall, S.E., Mng Ptnr
The Me & Her Theatre Company
Waddington, R., Co-Artistic Dir.
Media Solutions Inc.
Shekter, L., Pres.
Mediacom Inc.
McIlroy, V., Sr. VP
Médiatique Inc.
Caloz, D., Pres.
Medical Recruitment Services
Craig, S.J., Pres.
Medical Research Council of Canada
Clemenhagen, C., Sec.
Medical Technical Support Services
Befus, M., Supervisor, Rehab. Svcs Unit
Medicine Hat College
Engel, J., Dean, Div. of Applied Sciences
Howard, V.J., Prof. of Psych.
Medina Productions Inc.
Medina, A., Independent Prod.
Sue Medley Music
Medley, S., Pres.
MEDSTENT Inc.
Crewe, K., VP
Melcorp Mercantile Inc.
Kwok, E.L., Pres. & Mng Dir.
Memorial University of Newfoundland
Bindon, K., Principal, Sir Wilfred Grenfell College
Dalton, M., Assoc. Prof., Dept. of Eng.
Gien, L., Prof., Sch. of Nursing

Green, J.S., Asst. Prof., Medical Genetics, Fac.
of Medicine
Kealey, L., Assoc. Prof. of Hist.
Miller, E., Prof. of English
Ommer, R., Prof., Dept. of Hist. & Proj. Mgr,
Eco-Research Program
Renouf, M.A.P., Assoc. Prof. & Head, Dept. of
Anthro.
Menno Home of the Aged
Harder Mattson, E., Dir. of Admin. &
Nursing
Mental Health Centre
Rice, M.E., Dir. of Research
The Mercury Press Publishers Inc.
Daurio, B.A., Pres.
The Mercury Press
Daurio, B.A., Ed. in Chief
Mese Consulting Ltd
Nichols, E.
Mestor Associates Ltd.
Whyte, A.V.T., Pres.
Metcalfe Massage Therapy Clinic
Fitch, P.L., R.M.T./Massage Therapist
Consultant
**METHODS CONSULTING, With People
in Mind**
Boyd, M., Owner
**Metro Action Committee
on Public Violence Against Women
and Children (METRAC)**
Vander Voet, S., Consultant
Metropolitan Life Insurance Company
Hughes Anthony, N., VP, Group & Pension
Svcs
Menke, U., VP, Cnsl & Corp. Sec.
Waters, A.K., Dir., Info. Technology
The Metropolitan Toronto School Board
Vanstone, A.L., Chair
Meyers and Associates
Meyers, M.O., Pres.
Mia et Klaus
Matthes, M., Photographer & Ptnr
Michael, Hardy Limited
Macklem, A.W., VP
Michelle Ramsay & Company Inc.
Blais-Ramsay, M., Pres.
**The Michener Institute for Applied
Health Sciences**
Krakauer, R., Pres. & CEO
Midland Walwyn Inc.
Mitchell, C.R., Sr. VP & Dir.
Millenitex Inc.
Armstrong, P., Pres.
Miller Thomson
Babe, J.E., Ptnr
Doherty, B.R.C., Ptnr
Milner Fenerty
Safran, L., Barrister & Solicitor
Milrad & Agnew
Agnew, E.M., Ptnr

Min's Indian Craft
Sky, D., Artist & Owner
Ming Pao Newspapers (Canada) Ltd.
Chong, V.Y.F., News Ed.
Missing Children Society of Canada
Todd-Morgan, R., Founder, Investigator &
Exec. Dir.
MIX: the magazine of artist-run culture
Christakos, M., Ed.
Mogford Campbell Associates Inc.
Mogford, M., Ptnr
Moncton Headstart
Bradshaw, C.A., Exec. Dir.
Moneystrategy Inc.
Burke, E., Pres.
Monsanto Canada Inc.
Ferguson, M.H., VP, People, Quality & EH&S
Monsanto Company
Ferguson, M.H., VP, Innovation & Change
Montage Inc.
Petro, T., Co-Owner & Exec. VP
Monteverdi: a consultancy
Haight, L., Pres.
The Montreal Exchange
Phénix, E.C., Sr. VP, Equities
Montreal General Hospital
Chagnon, F.P., Otolaryngologist-in-Chief,
Dept. of Otolaryngology & Interim Dir. of
Professional Svcs
Dobkin, P.L., Medical Scientist, Div. of Clinical
Epidemiology
Gagnon, R.F., Assoc. Physician, Div. of
Nephrology
Lindley, S., Clinical Dir., Dept. of
Ophthalmology
Murphy, B.E.P., Sr. Physician
Reinhold, C., Asst. Radiologist, Dept. of
Diagnostic Radiology
Sangster, P., Dir., Nursing Staff Dev.
Shannon, V., Dir. of Nursing
Solymoss, S., Asst. Physician, Dept. of Medicine
Stevenson, M.M., Medical Scientist, Dept. of
Medicine
Trudel, J.L., Assoc. Surgeon & Dir, "M" Surgi-
cal Unit Teaching Unit, Dept. of Surgery
Montreal Public Health Department
Hankins, C., Public Health Epidemiologist,
Infectious Disease Unit
Montreal Teachers Association
Rosenfield, R., Pres.
Montreal Urban Community
Danyluk, V., Chair, Exec. Committee
Montreal Women's Symphony Orchestra
Stark, E., Conductor, Violinist, Musical Dir.
Founder
Moore Corporation Limited
Khetrapal, S., VP & Treas.
Wilson, J.M., VP & Sec.
Morrison Lamothe Inc.
Hale, M., Chrm

Mortice Kern Systems Inc.
Songhurst, R., Pres. & owner
Moulden Communications
Moulden, H.J., Pres.
Mount Allison University
Beattie, M.A., Prof.
Burke, R., Prof., Dept. of Fine Arts
MacMillan, C., Prof.
McCullough, M.K., Dir., Dept. of Continuing
Educ. & Lecturer, Hist. Dept.
Stevenson, M.G., Cont.
Mount Royal College
Miller, J., Coord., Gerontology Certificate
Program, Centre for Health Studies
Springer, H.J., Dean, Fac. of Sci. & Tech.
Mount Saint Joseph Hospital
Doyle, D., COO
Mount Saint Vincent Motherhouse
Anthony, G., Biographer & Historian for the
Congregation of Sisters of Charity of Halifax,
Sisters of Charity of Saint Vincent de Paul
Mount Saint Vincent University,
Anthony, G., Prof. Emeritus, Dept. of Eng.
Conrad, M.R., Nancy Rowell Jackman Chair
in Women's Studies
Drapeau, S.E., V-Chair, Bd. of Gov.
Masciuch, S.W., Coord., M.A. in Sch.
Psych.
McKenna, M.O., Prof. Emeritus
Stanley, D.M.M., Assoc. Prof., Coord., Cdn
Studies Programme
Mount Sinai Hospital
Rossant, J., Sr. Scientist, Samuel Lunenfeld
Research Institute
Shamian, J., VP, Nursing, & Head, World
Health Organization Collaborating Centre
Mount Sinai Hospital Foundation
Simand-Seidman, C., Dir., Donor Rel'ns
Movie Television
Beker, J., Contributor
The Moving Store Franchise Systems, Inc.
Ramsay, S., Pres. & CEO
MuchMore Music/M3
Donlon, D., Dir. of Music Programming
MuchMusic
Donlon, D., Dir. of Music Programming
**Muki Baum Association for the
Rehabilitation of Multi
Handicapped Inc.**
Baum, N.T., Exec. Dir.
Multi Disciplinary Care Centre
Greenstone, H.A., Psychologist in Private
Practice & Dir.
Multicultural Association of Nova Scotia
Campbell, B., Exec. Dir.
Multiple Sclerosis Society of Canada
Groetzinger, D., Nat'l Dir. of Comm.
**Municipal Law Enforcement Officers'
Association (Ontario) Inc.**
Russell, B.M., Pres.

**Municipality of Chelsea-MRC des
Collines de l'Outaouais**
Grant, J., Mayor/Préfet (Warden)
Michele M. Murphy and Associates
Murphy, M.M., Lawyer
**Musée d'art contemporain de
Montréal**
Racine, Y., Curator
Museum of Contemporary Art
Woon, W., Dir. of Educ.
Museum Villa Stuck
Birnie-Danzker, J.-A., Dir.
The Mutual Group
Maidment, K., VP & CFO
**The Mutual Life Assurance Company
of Canada**
Elliott, M.A., Sr. VP, Corp. Svcs
Passmore, J.M., VP, Group Mktg

N

.G.U. Sports & Media Consultants
Crooks, C., Pres.
NCR Canada Ltd.
Tremblay, V., Dir. of Comm.
NOVA Corporation
Grant, R.E., Corp. Sec. & Assoc. Gen. Cnsl
O'Brien, S., Sr. VP, Hum. Res.
NPC Consulting
Christie, N.P., Pres.
Na'amat Canada Inc.
Danzig, E., Nat'l Pres.
Nancy's Very Own Foundation
Ruth, N., Pres.
Nashfilm Inc.
Nash, T.
**National Advertising Benevolent
Society**
Crosbie, P.C., Exec. Dir.
National Anti-Poverty Organization
Toupin, L., Exec. Dir.
National Archives of Canada
MacDonald, W., Archivist, Manuscript
Div.
McLean, M., Proj. Archivist
National Bahá'í Community of Canada
Profeit-LeBlanc, L., V-Chrm of Nat'l Spiritual
Assembly of Canada
National Ballet of Canada
Glasco, K., Principal Dancer
Kain, K., Principal Dancer
Lamy, M., Principal Dancer
The National Ballet School
Oliphant, B., Founder
Staines, M., Artistic Dir. & Ballet Principal
The National Bank of Canada
Desrochers, G., Sr. VP, Admin. & Hum. Res.
Fréchette, S., Athlete, Mktg Rep., Public Rel'ns
National Council of Women of Canada
Brown, R.L., Past Pres.
Whitfield, W.

**National Eating Disorder
Information Centre**
Bear, M.J., Prog. Coord.
National Farmers Union
Shadd, D., Women's Advisor for Ont.
National Federation of Nurses Unions
McPherson, D., VP
National Film Board of Canada
Newell, J., Sound Ed.
Prieto, C., Prod.
Rached, T., Filmmaker
Scott, C., Film Dir.
Shaffer, B., Film Dir. & Prod., Documentary
Studio
Tilby, W., Film Dir.
Trow, S., Cinematographer
National Gallery of Canada
Barclay, M.H., Chief Conservator
Barnabe, C.M., Admin. Asst.
McMaster, S., Sr. Book Ed.
Pauli, L., Asst. Curator, Photographs
Collection
Routledge, M., Assoc. Curator, Inuit Art
Thomson, S.L., Dir.
Tovell, R., Curator of Cdn Prints & Drawing
National Library of Canada
Scott, M.F., Librarian & Educator
National Research Council of Canada
Deslauriers, R., Grp Leader, Biosystems, Inst.
for Biodiagnostics
Hayes, L., Ed.
National Ski Industries Association
Hopper, C., Exec. Dir.
National Trust Company
Boyd, J., VP, Facilities Mgmt
Henderson, E., Asst. VP, Investor Mktg Svcs
Irwin, P.M., Asst. VP, Trust Oper. & Admin.
Jin Suen-Carter, S., VP, Public & Corp. Affairs
MacRae, M., VP, Mgmt Reporting & Analysis
Strelioff, S., Sr. VP, Governance
Trethewey, S., VP, Retail Lending
Wright, E., Sr. VP, Strategic Planning & Mktg
National Women's Liberal Commission
Greek, E., Reg'l Rep., Atlantic Reg.
Zonda Nellis Design Inc.
Nellis, Z., Pres.
Neptune Theatre
Moore, L., Artistic Dir.
Neptune Theatre Foundation
Moulton, M.E.C., Exec. Dir.
Nesbitt Burns Inc.
Cooper, S.S., Sr. VP & Chief Economist
Stymiest, B., Sr. VP & CFO
Taylor, C.D., VP & Dir., Atlantic Div. Mgr
Totta, J.M., Sr. VP, Strategy & Hum. Res.
**The Network: Interaction for
Conflict Resolution**
McMechan, S.M., Exec. Dir.
Neurofibromatosis Society of Ontario
Drew, F., Pres.

**New Brunswick Advisory Council of
the Status of Women**
Melanson, R., Dir. of Oper. & Comm.
Sansom, B.J., Chair
**New Brunswick Association for
Community Living**
Silliphant, L., Exec. Dir.
**New Brunswick Association of
Healthcare Auxiliaries**
MacTavish, H., Pres.
**New Brunswick Association of
Social Workers**
McKenna, S., Exec. Dir.
**New Brunswick Block Parent
Association Inc.**
Patterson, L., Chair
New Brunswick Choral Federation
Cooper, B.J., Exec. Dir.
New Brunswick Committee on Literacy
Greer, J., Exec. Dir.
**New Brunswick Community
College - Bathurst**
Roy-Vienneau, J., Instructional Dean
**New Brunswick Farm Women's
Organization**
Brown, B., Pres.
**New Brunswick Geographic
Information Corporation**
Kimball, M.A., Deputy Registrar Gen. of Land
Titles
**New Brunswick Home Economics
Association**
Pollock, L.M., Pres.
New Brunswick Training Industry Inc.
Stanley, B., Pres.
New Century Communications
von Baeyer, E., Consultant
New Democratic Party of Canada
McDonough, A., Leader
New Democratic Party of New Brunswick
Weir, E., Leader
The New Quarterly
Merikle, M., Mng Ed. & Fiction Ed.
NeWest Review
Kome, P., Calgary Contributing Ed.
**Newfoundland and Labrador
Lung Association**
Johnson, P., Exec. Dir.
**Newfoundland Association for
Community Living**
St. Croix, B., Pres.
Newfoundland Historic Parks Association
Dempsey, C., Exec. Dir.
Newfoundland Legal Aid Commission
Harding, G., Barrister & Solicitor
**Newfoundland Registered Music
Teachers' Association**
Rowsell, S.A., Past Pres.
Newman Theological College
Kambeitz, T., Dir., Religious Educ. Program

Next Model Management
Ghauri, Y., Super Model
Nextmedia
Smith, N., Pres.
Niagara Falls Centre Pharmacy
Bouw, J., Pharmacist
No Time To Cry Productions Inc.
Leaney, C., Pres.
Noble Peak Resources Ltd.
Jensen, M.C., Pres, CEO & Dir.
Noranda Metallurgy Inc.
Rethy, K., VP, Transportation
Nordex Explosives Ltd.
Korhonen, J.M., Sec.-Treas. & Office Mgr
Norstar Entertainment Inc.
Frank, I., Sr. VP, Prod. & Dev.
Nortec Marine Agencies Inc.
Paquin, M., Chair
Nortel Canada Limited
Bland, R.M., Presentation Specialist - Visits,
Switching Networks
Nortel Technology
Simson, C., Asst. VP, Advanced Technologies
North American Life Assurance Company
Black, E.M., Dir., Hum. Res.
North By East Productions
Walter, H., Ptnr
North Island College
Toresdahl, S., Dir. of Comm. & Community
Liaison
North Island College Foundation
Toresdahl, S., Exec. Dir.
North Lambton Secondary School
Kleihauer-Ward, E., Toolmaker/Technological
Studies Teacher
North York General Hospital
Anderson, D.E., VP
Bassett, S., Program Dir., Surgical Svcs
Down, N., Physician
Gold, A.J.C., Mgr, Adolescent Health Svcs
Goode, R., Dir. of Professional Nursing
Practice
Grace, N.A.E., Paediatric Surgeon
Leonard, K.A., Medical Dir., Teen Clinic
Meschino, W., Clinical Geneticist & Dir.,
Clinical Genetics Svc., Dept. of Genetics
Murray, J.A., Clinical Nurse Specialist & Nurse
Practitioner in Gerontology
Neidhardt, A., Program Dir., Genetics Program
Olsen, S., VP
Rappaport, H.S., Chair, Div. of Family
Medicine Obstetrics
Stirk, L., Obstetrician & Gynecologist
Summers, A.M., Clinical Geneticist, Dir. of the
Maternal Serum Screening Program, Dept. of
Genetics
North-East Health District
Ulvick, R., CEO
Northern Alberta Institute of Technology
Henderson, A., Instructor, Bus. Admin.

**Northern College of Applied Arts
and Technology**
Everatt, A., Dir., Program & Staff Dev.
McNair, N., VP of Programs
Northern Telecom Limited
Koszo, J., Asst. VP, Global Compensation
Rose, E.S., VP, Employee Satisfaction &
Environment
Northern Web Design
Preston, J., Ptnr
Notre-Dame Hospital
Provencher, D.M.
Nova House Women's Shelter
McKnight, S., Chair of the Bd.
**Nova Scotia Advisory Council on the
Status of Women**
McDonald, K., Pres.
Nova Scotia Barristers' Society
Penick, B., Dir. of Discipline
Nova Scotia Community College
Drapeau, S.E., Funding Analyst
The Nova Scotia Council for the Family
Sumarah, J., Past Pres.
Nova Scotia Museum of Industry
McNabb, D., Acting Dir.
The Nova Scotia Museum
Whitehead, R.H., Asst. Curator in Hist. & Staff
Ethnologist
Novartis Pharma Canada Inc.
Uson, M., VP, Hum. Res.
Novopharm Ltd.
Siebert, E., VP, Compliance
NOW **Magazine**
Randoja, I., Film Reviewer & Entertainment
Writer
Nurse Consultant Incorporated
Walsh, D., VP, Research & Dev.
Nursing & Homemakers Inc.
Lawrence, D., Pres. & CEO
Nursing Sisters Association of Canada
Hunter, B.E., Past Nat'l Pres.

O

**EB International Public Relations/
Public Affairs**
Kaljuste, K., Sr. VP
O.T. Mining Corporation
Christensen, R.L., Sec.-Treas.
OXFAM Canada
Dewar, M., Chair
O&Y Properties Inc.
Stefan, C., COO
**Offshore Technologies Association
of Nova Scotia**
Dempsey, K., Exec. Dir.
Ogilvy Renault
Carron, C.A., Ptnr
The Ohio State University
Bray, T.M., Prof. & Chair, Dept. of Hum. Nutri-
tion & Food Mgmt, Coll. of Human Ecology

Okanagan University College
Holmes, N., Writer & English Prof.
McCoubrey, S., Dir., B.Ed. Program
Olney and Saunders Engineering Ltd.
Olney, M., Pres.
The Olympic Trust of Canada
Foster, J.E., Pres.
The Ongoing Partnership
Hore, M., Founding Ptnr
**Ontario Association for Volunteer
Administration**
McClure, L., Pres.
**Ontario Association of Certified
Engineering Technicians and
Technologists**
Heikkila, S.C., Past Pres.
**Ontario Association of Children's
Aid Societies**
Thompson, C., Coord., French Language Svcs
**Ontario Association of Sport and
Exercise Sciences**
Clark, P., Exec. Dir.
Ontario Black History Society
Sadlier, R., Pres., Bd. of Dir.
Ontario College of Art
Donegan, R., Independent curator, writer,
educator
Doyle, J., Instructor
Pugen, D.F., Visual Artist, Freelance Curator,
Fac. Mbr.
Ontario Correctional Institute
Nexhipi, G., Staff Psychologist
Ontario Court of Justice
Bell, J.M., Judge, Gen. Div.
Corbett, M., Justice
King, L., Judge
Little, J.P., Judge
Macdonald, E., Justice
Thomson, P.A., Judge
**Ontario Federation of
Independent Schools**
Hopkins, E., Pres.
Ontario Federation of Labour
Davis, J.D., Sec.-Treas.
Ontario Film Development Corporation
Emilio, A., Toronto Film Commissioner &
Mktg Agent & Mgr/Dir.
Raffé, A., CEO
Ontario Forest Industries Association
Rauter, R.M., Pres.
Ontario Good Roads Association
Richardson, S., Exec. Dir.
Ontario Human Rights Commission
Eliadis, F.P., Dir., Public Policy & Public Educ.
Ontario Hydro
McLaughlin, M., VP, Corp. Comm.
**Ontario Institute for Studies in Education
of the University of Toronto**
Eichler, M., Prof. of Soc., Dept. of Soc. in Educ.
Pierson, R., Prof.

Prentice, A., Prof., Dept. of Theory & Policy
Studies in Educ.
Ontario Legislative Library
Smith, C.M., Dir., Legislative Research
Svc.
Ontario Lupus Association
Purcell, S., Pres.
**Ontario Massage Therapist
Association**
Fitch, P.L., Past Pres.
Ontario Native Council on Justice
Montagnes, C., Exec. Dir.
Ontario Native Women's Association
Pierre, M., Pres. & CEO
Ontario New Democratic Party
Davis, J.D., Chair
Ontario Nurses' Association
Bell, L., CEO
Ontario Nursing Home Association
Anderson, D.E., Pres.
Jamieson, S., Exec. Dir.
Ontario Pharmacists' Association
Stuart, B., CEO
**Ontario Progressive Conservative
Association of Women**
Hogarth, M., Immediate Past Pres.
Ontario Securities Commission
Smart, J., V-Chair
Ontario Weightlifting Association
Vinkenvleugel, M., Pres.
Opportunity for Advancement
Sugarman, R., Exec. Dir.
Opticians' Association of Canada
Summers, M., Ont. Dir.
Optimedia Canada
Boot, S., Sr. VP & Exec. Dir.
**Ordre des infirmières et infirmiers
du Québec**
Desrosiers, G., Pres.
**Ordre Professionnel des diététistes
du Québec**
Marcotte, A., Exec. Dir.
Organ Donors Canada
Cox, M., Exec. Dir.
**Organisation for Economic Co-operation
and Development (OECD)**
Rosinger, E., Deputy Dir., Environment
Directorate
**Organization of Canadian
Symphony Musicians**
Robitaille, E., Pres.
**The Orthodox Christian Women
of Montreal**
Tkachuk, M., Founder & Pres.
Osborne Realty
Wilson, V., Realtor
Oscars and Abrams Associates Inc.
Abrams, G., Co-owner
Oshawa General Hospital
Cooper, A., Dir. of Nursing

Osler, Hoskin & Harcourt
DeMarco, J.M., Ptnr
McGregor, B., Barrister & Solicitor
McKean, H., Mng Ptnr
Osteoporosis Society of British Columbia
Darling, B., Past Pres.
Horner, P., Pres., Vernon Outreach
Otran Associates Inc.
Bendaly, L., Pres.
Ottawa Civic Hospital
Johnson, S.M., Dir., Marital & Family Therapy
Clinic, Dept. of Psychiatry
Rock, G.A., Chief of Hematology &
Transfusion Medicine
Ottawa Congress Centre
Pigott, J.E.M., Chair
The Ottawa Sun
Dewar, S.E., Edit. Cartoonist
**Outdoor Recreation Council
of British Columbia**
Wilson, N., Exec. Dir.
Owens Art Gallery
Kelly, G., Dir. & Curator
Owl Communications
Slaight, A., Pres. & CEO
Oxford University Press Canada
Barber, K., Ed.-In-Chief, Cdn Dictionaries
Oyen Wiggs Green & Mutala
Mutala, C., Ptnr

P ASS-CAN
Beltzner, E., Exec. Dir. (currently on sabbatical)
PDG Personnel Direction Group
Lynch, J., Pres.
P.E.I. Transition House Association
Ings, J., Exec. Dir.
Pacific Biological Station
Arai, M.N., Sr. Volunteer Investigator
Pacific Songwriters' Association
Jardine, C., Pres.
Pacific Victory Pictures
Bard, M., Prod.
Pageau Goyette and Associates
Pageau-Goyette, N., Pres. & CEO
Palmer Hunt Murphy
Gordon, D., Ptnr
**Parallélogramme Artist-Run Culture
and Publishing, Inc.**
Christakos, M., Founding Publisher
The Parent Channel
Kastner, K., VP, Dir. of Programming
Parent Finders New Brunswick
Praeg, I., Pres.
Parent Finders of Canada
Vanstone, J.E., Nat'l Dir.
Parent Support Association
McMurray, E., Exec. Dir.
Parke Davis Canada
Sturgess, J., Medical Dir.

Parks Canada
Cameron, C.S., Dir. Gen., Nat'l Historic Sites
Russell, H., Staff Historian, National Historic
Sites Directorate
Parkwood Hospital
Bol, N.A., Clinical Nurse Specialist -
Gerontology
Patkau Architects
Patkau, P., Principal
Patterson Palmer Hunt Murphy
Campbell, K., Lawyer
Frazer, D.S., Ptnr
Mowatt, E.A., Ptnr
Roberts, E., Ptnr
Stairs, J.A., Lawyer
van Driel, G., Ptnr
Patti Rao Associates
Rankin, R.V., Urban Planner
Pauktuutit Inuit Women's Association
Flaherty, M., Pres.
Peace Mennonite Church
Driedger, F.G., Social Dev. Consultant & Lay
Pastor
Peace Research Institute
Newcombe, H., Dir.
Pebblehut Productions
Stonehouse, M., Line Prod. & Production Mgr
Peerless Home Products
Trebuss, A.S., VP & Gen. Mgr
Peigan Mentally Challenged Society
Jackson, M.R., Bd. Mbr.
Penguin Books Canada Limited
Good, C., VP, Publisher & Ed.-in-Chief
Peninsula Farm Ltd.
Jones, S., CEO
Penticton Herald
Howard Coady, J., Publisher/Gen. Mgr
Pentron Communications Inc.
Shore Hume, P., Pres.
People in Transition (Alliston), Inc.
Venhola, M., Crisis Counsellor and Legal
Worker
Peoples Jewellers Corporation
Kreuk, M., VP, Mktg
Kulesza, K.M., VP, Merchandising
**Perley-Robertson, Panet, Hill
and McDougall**
Ormerod, M., Ptnr
Petals
Goold, S.R., Artist
Peter Lougheed Centre
Bergman, J.S., Clinical Dir., Family Med.
Centre
Petro-Canada
Noel-Bentley, E., Sr. Dir., Total Compensation
Smith, N.L., Treas.
Pharma Plus Drugmarts Ltd.
Stenzler, R., Pres. & Gen. Mgr
PhemPhat Productions
Rowe, E., Founder & Dir.

Philip Environmental Inc.
Kuhn, L., Dir. of Corp. & Community Rel'ns
Photographers & Friends United Against AIDS, Canadian Chapter
Carroll, I., Founder & Chair
Phyllis Bruce Books
Bruce, P.L., Publisher
The Picower Institute for Medical Research
Bonetta, L., Asst. Prof.
Pier 21 Society
Goldbloom, R.M., Pres.
Pierce Communications
Swaine, M., Pres.
Piros Productions
Piros, J., Pres.
PISCES
Kelly, P., Breast Cancer Activist & Pres.
Pitblado and Hoskin
Cooper, J.A., Lawyer
Planned Parenthood Alberta
Hamilton, M., Pres.
Planned Parenthood Toronto
Cadbury, B., Founder
Platypus Publishers
Lea, N., Pres.
Point of View Film Inc.
Bjornson, M., Pres.
Polar Bear Software Corp.
Cameron, D.M.D., Chrm
The Polish Alliance of Canada
Warszawski, D., Pres.
Polish Teachers' Association in Canada
Bujalski, W., Pres.
The Population Council
Catley-Carlson, M., Pres.
Portrait
Rinaldo, S., Prod. & Reporter
Potash Corporation of Saskatchewan Inc.
Heggie, B.-A., Sr. VP, Corp. Rel'ns
The Power Plant Art Gallery
Dompierre, L.M.T., Assoc. Dir./Chief Curator
The Powerpoint Group
Pape, P.L., Pres.
Prairie Books Now
Devanik Butterfield, M., Exec. Ed.
Prescott-Russell County Board of Education
Coombs, D., Reading Program Mgr
Price Waterhouse
Chant, D., Ptnr
Dale, M.N., Nat'l Mktg Dir.
Lisson, K., Ptnr Resp. for Nat'l Fin. Institution Consulting
PRIDE Canada Inc.
Opheim, E., Nat'l Exec. Dir.
PRIME Mentors of Canada
Tan-Willman, C., Pres.

Prince Edward Island Council of the Disabled
Lie-Nielsen, A., Exec. Dir.
Prince Edward Island Guidance and Counselling Association
Campbell, D., Past Pres.
Prince Edward Island Home and School Federation
Jay, S., Exec. Dir.
Prince Edward Island Licensed Nursing Assistants Association
Coles, B., Pres.
Prince Edward Island Special Olympics
Marchbank, A., Exec. Dir.
The Priory School Inc.
Tkachuk, M., Teacher
Private Investors Management Inc.
Pearl, D., Pres.
Probe International
Adams, P., Exec. Dir.
Probyn & Company Limited
Eastman, B.C., Pres. & Dir.
Procter & Gamble Inc.
Jay, C.E., Mktg Dir., Paper Products
Les Productions Hélène Roberge E.N.R.
Roberge, H., Pres. & Dir. Gen.
Les Productions Pélagie
Maillet, A., Pres.
Les Productions Via le Monde (Daniel Bertolino) Inc.
Viau, C., VP
Professional Institute of the Public Service of Canada
Demers, M., VP
Morin, L., Mbr. of the Bd. of Dir.
Shaw, K., Dir., Prairie Reg. & Sec., Nursing Group Exec.
ProMotion Plus
Lay, M., Program Dir.
Province of Nova Scotia
Theriault, M.E., Public Trustee
Province of Ontario
Sims, M.-W., V-Chair, Boards of Inquiry - Human Rights, Pay Equity Hearings Tribunal
Province of Prince Edward Island
Orr, N.K., Prov. Court Judge
Province of Quebec
Kirkland, M.C., retired Legislator & Judge
The Province
Blackstone, R.A., Lifestyles Ed.
Doruyter, R., Columnist & Copy-Ed.
Gayle, M., Consumer Reporter
Tait, K., Columnist
Thompson, J., City Ed.
Provincial Advisory Council on the Status of Women
Williams, W., Pres.
Provincial Archives of Manitoba
Beattie, J. H., Keeper, Hudson's Bay Company Archives

Provincial Archives of New Brunswick
Beyea, M., Prov. Archivist
Provincial Council of Women of Manitoba
Singh, M.K.K., Pres.
Provincial Intermediate Teachers'
Association
Tapp, J., Pres.
Psoriasis Society of Canada
Misner, J., Founder & Pres.
Public Service Commission of Canada
Gusella, M.M., Commissioner
Public Works and Government
Services Canada
Randall, J., Dir., Cabinet & Corp. Svcs
Publications Plus
Cooper, B.J., Owner/Founder
Puppetel
Keogh, N., Proprietor
Purrfectly Cats
Pawlick, L., Owner/Operator

Q107 FM
McQueen, S., Radio Announcer
QLT PhotoTherapeutics Inc.
Levy, J., CEO, CSO & Pres.
Quality Inn Fallsview
Bignucolo, A.A.D., VP
Quartz Mountain Gold Corp.
Ross, S., VP, Corp. Affairs
Quebec Federation of Senior Citizens
Moir, N.T., Exec. Dir.
Québec Multi-Ethnic Association for the
Integration of Handicapped People
Soave, L., Gen. Dir.
Queen Elizabeth II Health Science Centre
Murphy, D., Dir., Perioperative Nursing
Queen Elizabeth II Hospital
Strehlke, C., Physician & Dir. of I.C.U.
Queen's Quarterly
Harcourt, J., Poetry/Fiction Ed.
Queen's University
Cole, S.P.C., Prof. of Oncology, Pathology,
Pharmacology & Toxicology, Career Scientist
of the Ontario Cancer Foundation
Dick, S., Prof. of English
Dickey Young, P., Head, Dept. of Religious
Studies
Duffin, J.M., Hannah Prof. of the Hist. of
Medicine
Glasgow, J.I., Prof., Dept. of Computing &
Info. Sci.
Houlden, R., Asst. Prof., Fac. of Medicine
Margesson, L., Asst. Prof. of Medicine
Martin, N., Asst. Prof., Dept. of Microbiol. &
Immunology
Morgan, A., Univ. Sec. & Instructor in Econ.
Mulligan, L., Assoc. Prof., Dept. of
Paediatrics
Northey, M., Dean, Sch. of Bus.

Raptis, L.H., Assoc. Prof., Dept. of
Microbiology & Immunology
Ropchan, G., Asst. Prof.
Surridge, M.E., Prof., Dept. of French Studies
Wilson, R., Prof. & Head, Dept. of Family
Medicine, Family Medical Centre
Wright, L.L., Dir., Centre for Canada-Asia Bus.
Rel'ns & Assoc. Prof. of Int'l Mgmt &
Organizational Behaviour, Sch. of Bus.
Queenstake Resources Ltd.
Meyer, D., VP, Fin., CFO & Corp. Sec.
Quill & Quire **Magazine**
Dickenson, J.C., Advtg. Mgr
McAuley, S., Publisher
Quinlan Road Limited
McKennitt, L., Founder & Mng Dir.
Quorum Growth Inc.
Dorosz, W.M., Pres. & CEO

RCH Holdings Inc.
Holmes, V., Pres.
R.C.R. Restaurants
Newman, E., Dir. of Mktg
Radville Marian Health Centre
Jubenville, S.J., CEO
Random House of Canada
Dennys, L., VP
Raventures Inc.
Webster, M.P., Pres.
Reading Pictures
Doyle, J., Dir.
Reagh & Reagh
Reagh, E., Barrister, Solicitor & Mediator
Real Life
Beker, J., Style Correspondent
REAL Women of Canada
Forsyth, C., Nat'l Pres.
Landolt, G.C., Nat'l VP
Rebekah Assembly of Ontario
Cole, D.M., Pres.
The Record
Mastine, S.C., Community Rel'ns Mgr &
Columnist
Red River Community College
Graham-Fogwill, L.A., Instructor, Applied
Sciences Dept.
Torchia, W., Employment Equity Officer
Red Snapper Films Limited
Keating, L., Pres.
Regan Productions Inc.
Reynolds, C., VP, Corp. Dev.
Regina Public Library
Campbell, A., Writer & Head of Community
Rel'ns
Region 2 Hospital Corporation
Kilfoil, A., Dir., Library Svcs
McGill, B.J., VP, Patient Programs & Chief
Nursing Officer
Walsh, D., V-Chair

Regional Municipality of York, Ontario
Jaczek, H., Commissioner of Health Svcs
Registered Nurses' Association of British Columbia
Clarke, H.F., Nursing Res. Consultant
Registered Nurses' Association of Ontario
Grinspun, D.R., Exec. Dir.
Registered Practical Nurses Association of Ontario
Arsenault, S., Sec. to Bd. of Dir.
Registered Psychiatric Nurses' Association of Manitoba
Osted, A., Exec. Dir.
Rehabilitation Hospital
Daniels, V., Dir. of Stroke Program
Renaissance Securities Inc.
Aitken, M.S., Pres.
Renaissance Woman
Firus, K., Artist, Filmmaker, Renegade
Renfrew Educational Services
McTighe, J., Exec. Dir.
Réseau québécois des groupes écologistes
Villeneuve, C., Prés.
Rethink: The Eco-Logical Fair/HLK Communications
Kaufman, H., Dir.
Reynolds, Mirth, Richards and Farmer
Mrazek, M.L., Ptnr
Rhombus Media Inc.
Willis Sweete, B., Film & TV Dir.
Rice Brydone Limited
Brydone, J.E., Pres.
Ringette PEI
Beaton, B., Pres.
River 'B' Down Home Quilts Inc.
Burke, E., Owner
C. Roach and Associates
Roach, C., Independent Nurse Practitioner
The Robert McLaughlin Gallery
Murray, J., Dir.
Roberts Communications Group
Wright-Roberts, M.E., Pres.
Robertson & Co.
Robertson, D.L., Principal
Robertson Galleries
Freiman, R., Owner & Dir.
Robertson Rozenhart Inc.
Robertson, C., Pres.
Robinson Sheppard Shapiro
Kassie, L., Ptnr
Beverley Rockett Photography
Rockett, B., Photographer & Fashion Dir.
The Roeher Institute
Rioux, M.H., Exec. Dir.
Rogers Cantel Inc.
McLaughlin, K., VP & Gen. Mgr, BC
Rogers Communications Inc.
Simmie, M., Asst. Corp. Sec.
Rollins Raeburn Interior Design Inc.
Raeburn Paul, N.A., Pres.

Rootrainers Corporation
Spencer, M.E., Pres.
Rostand Inc.
Eastman, B.C., Pres. & Dir.
Rothery Entertainments
Melvin, A.P., Pres.
Royal Bank Investment Management Inc.
Ching, D., VP, Portfolio Mgr
Royal Bank of Canada
Cefis, A.G., VP, Personal Credit Svcs
Dubsky, F.J.O., Sr. Mgr, Multinational Sector, Que.
Egan, M.J., Mgr, Bus. Resumption Planning
Fershko, J.S., VP, Cardholder Svcs
Fukakusa, J., Sr. VP, Fin. Svcs, Multinational Bnkg
Hatley, J., Sr. VP, Sales, Personal Fin. Svcs
Hirji-Nowaczynski, Z., Reg'l Mgr, Central Care Centre
Labarge, S., Exec. VP, Corp. Treas.
Lacroix, M., VP & Area Mgr
Lawson, J.E., Sr. VP & Corp. Sec.
Leahey, D., Sr. VP & Gen. Mgr, Man.
LeBlanc-Bridge, T., Sr. Cnsl
Leroux, M., Sr. VP, Fin.
Lippert, A.H., VP & Area Mgr, Vancouver Downtown & West
Lockie, A., Sr. VP & Gen. Mgr, Sask.
McLaren, P., VP & Area Mgr, Calgary Central
Mitchell, G., Exec. VP, Hum. Res.
Tuffin, J., VP, Personal Fin. Svcs, Toronto Core
White, L., Mgr, Employment Equity & Diversity, Corp. Hum. Res.
Royal Canadian Military Institute
Melvin, A.P., Librarian
Royal Oak Mines Inc.
Witte, M.K., Pres. & CEO
Royal Ontario Museum
Collins, M., Research Assoc.
Coxon, H., Conservator
Rhind, K.E., Mbr., Bd. of Reproductions Association
Silver, F., VP, Exhibits & Mktg
Stephen, B., Curator Emerita, Dept. of Near Eastern & Asian Civilizations
Royal University Hospital
Elder, M., R.N., Neonatal I.C.U.
Royal Victoria Hospital
Trudel, J.L., Asst. Surgeon, Dept. of Surgery
Royale Accomodations
M.S. Goldblatt, VP
Ruby & Edwardh
Edwardh, M.A., Lawyer
Rug Hooking Guild Nova Scotia
Magwood, K., Past Pres.
Ryerson Polytechnic University
Black, M.E., Chair
Chu, A.I.-F., Prof., Fac. of Applied Arts
Imboden, R., Prof., Dept. of English
Lewis, L.R., Prof.

Mulhallen, K., Prof., Dept. of English
Potts, N., Dir., Dance Program

SABRE Canada
Rein, R., Pres.
SAMCI
Murray, S.A., Pres.
SECOR
Pearson, H., Sr. Dir.
S.O.S. Society of Sexual Abuse Survivors
Ross, L., Exec. Dir.
St. Boniface College
Heidenreich, R., Prof.
Saint Elizabeth Health Care
Sharkey, S., Pres. & CEO
St. Francis Xavier University
Bigelow, A., Prof., Dept. of Psych.
Calliste, A., Assoc. Prof. & Chair, Dept. of Soc. & Anthro.
Campbell, R., Univ. Librarian
Dickson, K., Public Rel'ns Dir.
Gallant, M., Prof., Dept. of Phys. Educ.
Gerriets, M., Prof. & Chair, Dept. of Econ.
Gillis, A., Prof. & Chair, Dept. of Nursing
Hawley, P., Assoc. Prof. of Nursing
Hogan, P., Prof. of Hist.
MacCaull, W., Assoc. Prof., Dept. of Math. & Computing Sci.
MacDonald, V., Alumni Affairs Officer
Parsons, C.N., Asst. Prof., Celtic Studies Dept.
Smith-Palmer, T., Assoc. Prof. of Chem.
Stanley-Blackwell, L.C.C., Assoc. Prof., Dept. of Hist.
Stark, J., Assoc. Registrar
St. Joseph's Health Centre
Letton, S., VP
Saint Mary's University
Chard, E., Registrar
Connelly, M.P., Coord., Int'l Dev. Studies Program, Dept. of Soc.
Fitzgerald, P.A., Prof. of Mgmt, Dept. of Mgmt
Marie Saint Pierre Design Inc.
Saint Pierre, M., Designer
St. Vincent's High School
Ryan, C.A., Principal
St. Vincent's Hospital
Vickers, M.T., Rep., Sisters of Charity Health Care Society
Doreen Sanders Communications
Sanders, D., Pres.
SaniPouch Products Inc.
Brandow, J., Pres.
Linda Sargent Enterprises Inc.
Sargent, L., Pres.
Sasges Design Partnership
Sasges, R.E., Owner
Saskatchewan Abilities Council
Demeule, L.C., Supervisor, Life Enrichment

Program
McLennan, N., Reg. Dir.
Saskatchewan Archaeological Society
McFarlane, B., Pres.
Saskatchewan Association of School Councils
Bastness, J., Exec. Dir.
Saskatchewan Association on Human Rights
Dedi, B., Pres.
Saskatchewan Business Teachers' Association.
Lukkien (Van't Hof), D.A., Past. Pres.
Saskatchewan Cultural Exchange Society
Fry, M., Program Officer
Saskatchewan Dental Hygienists' Association
Long, B.A., Past Pres.
Saskatchewan Department of Justice
Neustaedter, A.K., Dir. of Prince Albert Provincial Correctional Centre
Saskatchewan Forestry Association
Grono, M., Mgr
Saskatchewan Genealogical Society
Thomas, M.J., Exec. Dir.
Saskatchewan Government Insurance
Ulmer, K.C., Solicitor
Saskatchewan Indian Federated College
Bowen, G.D., Asst. Prof. of Eng.
Saskatchewan Institute of Applied Science and Technology
Campbell, P., Dean, Bus. & Community Svcs Div., Woodland Institute
Sarkar, G., Dir., R&D
Saskatchewan Power Corporation
Hall, P., Cont.
Saskatchewan Registered Nurses' Association
Hodgson, M., Exec. Dir.
Saskatchewan Sports Hall of Fame and Museum Inc.
Kelly, S., Exec. Dir.
Saskatchewan Union of Nurses
Junor, J., Pres.
Saskatchewan Voice of People with Disabilities
Boehm, B., Exec. Dir.
Saskatchewan Women's Liberal Commission
Shenouda, H.-M., Pres.
Saskatchewan Writers Guild
Barclay, B.R., Pres.
Drover, M., Exec. Dir.
Saskatoon Council of Women
Isinger, L.K., Past Pres.
Saskatoon District Health Council
Budz, D., Gen. Mgr, Palliative Care Svc.
Malone, D., Dir. of Fin. Svcs
Saskatoon Symphony Society
Thors, S.-A., Gen. Mgr

SaskPower
Bryant, C.Y., Exec. VP, Corp. & Bus. Svcs
Saturday Night **Magazine**
McCall, C., Author/Ed.
Moon, B.E., Ed.-at-Large
Scarborough General Hospital
Leonard, M., Chair, Bd. of Gov.
Verstraete, U., Coord., Hospital & Physician
Rel'ns
Scarborough Palliative 'At Home' Care Team
Gardner-Nix, J., Program Dir.
Scarborough Women's Centre
Bismilla, V.H., Pres.
Kosowan, L., Exec. Dir.
Denise Schon & Associates
Schon, D., Pres.
School District No. 48 (Howe Sound)
Edwards, N., Sec.-Treas.
ScotiaMcLeod Inc.
Cornish-Kehoe, M., Dir.
Scott's Restaurants Inc.
Bedell, G., VP, Law
Sears Canada Inc.
Beaudoin, P., VP, Hum. Res.
The Senate of Canada
Bacon, L., Senator (De la Durantaye)
Carney, P., Senator
Carstairs, S., Senator
Chaput-Rolland, S., Senator
Cohen, E.J., Senatpr
Cools, A.C., Senator & Liberal Mbr. of Gov't
Gravel, L., Committee Clerk & Exec. Sec. to
the Cdn NATO Parliamentary Assoc.,
Committees & Private Legislation
Directorate
Johnson, J.G., Senator
LeBreton, M., Senator
Maheu, S., Senator
Pearson, L.C., Senator
Robertson, B.M., Senator
Senate of the Métis National Council
Chalifoux, T.J., Chair
Seneca College of Applied Arts and Technology
Caceres, P., Dean, Developmental, Trade &
Apprenticeship Studies
Goldenberg, B., CEO & Exec. Dir., Seneca
Foundation
Hazell, C.D., Dean, Fac. of Continuing Educ.
Inkpen, S., Prof. of Math.
Sexual Assault Crisis Centre
DeRubeis, M., Clinical Social Worker
Sexual Assault Survivors' Centre Sarnia-Lambton
Batty, M., Exec. Dir.
Nancy Shanoff and Associates Ltd.
Shanoff, N., Pres.
Sharpe & Associates
Sharpe, M., Pres.

Shaw Communications Inc.
McDonald, D.Z., Bd. of Dir.
Sheeba Records
Siberry, J., Founder
Sheena's Place
Carpenter, L., Dir. & Co-founder
Fenton, J., Dir. & Co-founder
Shennette Leuschner McKay
Leuschner, L., Lawyer
Sheridan College
Wilburn, M., Coord., Library & Info.
Technician Program
Sherritt International Corporation
Merrin Best, P.E., VP, Corp. Affairs
Shervin Publications
Western, S., Ptnr
Showcase Television Inc.
Yaffe, P., Pres. & CEO
Sienna Films Inc.
Sereny, J., Prod.
Sierra Club of British Columbia
Husband, V., Conservation Chair
Sierra Club of Canada
May, E., Exec. Dir.
Sim Hughes Ashton & McKay
Ashton, T.P., Ptnr
Sim & McBurney
Ashton, T.P., Ptnr
Simon Fraser University
Anderson, G.S., Asst. Prof., Dept. of Biological
Sci.
Bowman, M., Assoc. Prof., Dept. of Psych.
Cohen, M.G., Prof., Pol. Sci. & Chair,
Women's Studies
Coniglio, C.B., Counsellor, Univ. Counselling
Svcs
Dahl, V., Prof. & Dir., Logic & Functional
Programming Group, Centre for Systems Sci.,
Lab. for Computer & Comm. Research, Sch. of
Computing Sci.
Davison, R., Assoc. Prof., Dept. of French
Delany, S., Prof. of English
Djwa, S.A., Prof., Dept. of English
Etherington, L., Assoc. Prof., Fac. of Bus.
Admin.
Faith, K., Assoc. Prof., Sch. of Criminology
Finlayson, T., Prof. Emerita, Dept. of Biological
Sci.
Gee, E.M., Prof. & Chair, Dept. of Soc. &
Anthro.
Gordon, I.M., Assoc. Prof., Fac. of Bus. Admin.
Gutman, G.M., Prof., Fac. of Arts & Dir.,
Gerontology Research Centre & Program
Heinrich, K., Prof., Dept. of Math & Statistics
Jackson, M.A., Prof. & Dir., Sch. of Criminology
Kimball, M.M., Prof. in Psych. & Women's
Studies
Kirschner, T.J., Prof., Humanities Program
Murray, C.A., Assoc. Prof.
Parr, J., Farley Prof. of Hist.

Tung, R.L., The Ming & Stella Wong Prof. of Int'l Bus., Fac. of Bus.
Zaichkowsky, J.L., Prof. of Mktg, Fac. of Bus. Admin.

Simply Powerful Communications
Kirkland, L., Owner

Singleton Urquhart Scott
Thompson, B.J., Ptnr

Sir Mortimer B. Davis Jewish General Hospital
Finestone, K., Clinical Nurse Specialist

Sir Sandford Fleming College
Dance-Bennink, T., VP Academic

Siren
Blak, G., Owner

Sisters of Charity
Mullins, P., Head

Sixth Scents
Bendeth, M., Fragrance Specialist

Skills Training and Support Services Association
Hollo, W., Exec. Dir.

Sky Works Charitable Foundation
Sky, L., Film Prod. & Dir.

Skydive Unlimited Inc.
Ritchie, P., Ptnr

Sleep Country Canada
Magee, C., Pres.

Sleep/Wake Disorders Canada
Bedford, H., Past Pres.

Slovak Canadian National Council
Dvorsky, M.A., Pres.

Joanne Smale Productions Limited
Smale, J.R., Pres.

Smart and Williams
Boyle, C.L.M., Assoc. Cnsl

Smart & Biggar
Morrow, J., Ptnr

Smithsonian Astrophysical Observatory
Evans, N., Astrophysicist

Social Sciences and Humanities Research Council of Canada
Penrod, L., Pres.

Société d'Alzheimer de la Mauricie
Poirier, N., Dir.

Société québécoise de l'autisme
Carle Dagenais, M., Dir. gén.

Société Radio-Canada
Robillard-Frayne, H., Dir., Radio Programming & Schedule Planning

Society for the Study of Architecture in Canada
Thomas, D., Past Pres.

Society of Management Accountants of Alberta
Kobelsky, J., Exec. Dir.

The Society of Management Accountants of Canada
Talbot-Allan, L.M., Chrm, 1995-96

Society of Nova Scotians for a Clean Environment
Brown, C.M., Pres.

Sodarcan Inc.
Menard, L., VP, Corp Affairs, Legal Affairs & Sec.

Softwords Research International, Ltd.
Godfrey, E., Pres.

Sogetsu Ikebana
Abe, K., Dir., Toronto East Branch

Sombrowski Group of Companies
Sombrowski, I., Co-Founder & Co-Head

Somerville House Books
Zawerbny, J.A., Asst. Ed. & Cyber-Ed.

Somerville House Group of Companies
Christensen, R.L., Pres.

Soundstreams/Chamber Concerts Canada
Carr, M.C., Arts Mgmt Consultant & Gen. Mgr

South East Grey Community Outreach
Gott, C., Exec. Dir.

Southern Alberta Institute of Science and Technology
Mushinski, V., Dir., Dev. Office, Wascana Inst.

Southern Alberta Institute of Technology
Benoit, B.E., Applied Arts & Sci. Instructor

Spectrum Three Consulting
Frazer, R., Pres.

SpencerStuart
Vennat, M., Chrm & Mng Dir.

Kay Spicer & Associates Inc.
Spicer, K., Author, Food Consultant

Spina Bifida and Hydrocephalus Association of New Brunswick
Fisher, V., Pres.

Spina Bifida Association of Canada
Elder, M., Sec.

Spirit of the West Photo Ventures
Isaak, L., Owner

Sport Medicine Council of British Columbia
Cannell, L., Exec. Dir.

Pamela Stagg Creative Services
Stagg, P., Pres.

Star Tracks Performing Arts Centre for the Disabled
Mickelson, R., Founder & Exec. Dir.

State Farm Insurance Companies
Beck, E., Agent

Statistics Canada
Levine, M., Dir. Gen., Reg'l Oper. Branch
Mayda, J.E., Survey Statistician

Step By Step Child Development Society
Waddington, R.M., Exec. Dir.

Stewart McKelvey Stirling Scales
Henley-Andrews, J., Ptnr

Stikeman, Elliott
Kaufman, D.S., Barrister & Solicitor, Ptnr
Picard, C., Ptnr
Youngman, A.J., Ptnr

Stikeman, Elliott (Hong Kong)
Jordan, C., Lawyer
Stockwood, Spies
Spies, N.J., Barrister
Stopfilm Inc.
Lanctôt, M., Pres.
Stornoway Productions Inc.
Fusca-Vincent, M., Pres.
Strategic Objectives Inc.
Lewis, J., Exec. VP
Weinstein, D., Pres.
Strategic Solutions
Chir-Stimpson, S., Pres.
Stratford Festival
Hofstetter, M.E., Gen. Mgr
Stratheden Homes Limited
Hackett, B.J., Pres.
Strathfield Consultants Ltd.
Kerr, S.L., Pres.
Strive!
Lowry, C., Ptnr
The Strong Communications Group Inc.
Strong, M., Pres.
Studies in Canadian Literature
Campbell, S., Mgr & Assoc. Ed.
Studio D
King-Leslie, D., Dir.
The Sturgess Group Inc.
Sturgess, J., Pres.
Suche Gange
Suche, P.C., Ptnr
The Sudbury Star
Fouriezos, C., Columnist/Writer
Sullivan Entertainment International Inc.
Grant, T., Pres.
Sumi-e Artists of Canada
Yamada, R., Hon. Pres.
Sun Life Assurance Company of Canada
Greene, L.G., VP, Corp. Hum. Res.
Suncor Inc.
Parkinson, E.A., Exec. VP, Oil Sands
Group
Sunshine Eggs Inc.
Boxall, L., Pres.
The Sunshine Foundation of Canada
Comuzzi, D., Nat'l Exec. Dir.
Sunshine International Inc.
Boxall, L., Pres.
Superior Court of Montreal
Piché, G., Judge
Superior Court of Quebec
Borenstein, S., Justice
Duval Hesler, N., Judge
Sevigny, P., Judge
Trahan, A.-M., Judge
Zerbisias, D., Judge
Superior Ventures Group Ltd.
Garossino, V., Pres. & CEO
Supreme Court of British Columbia
Morrison, N., Judge

Supreme Court of Canada
L'Heureux-Dubé, C., Puisne Judge
McLachlin, B., Justice
Supreme Court of Nova Scotia
Glube, C., Chief Justice
Hood, S.M., Justice
Supreme Court of Ontario
Boland, J.L., Judge, Trial Div.
Dunnet, T., Judge
Supreme Court of the Northwest Territories
Picard, E.I., Deputy Judge
SwanSea Oceans Environment Inc.
Swan, J., Pres. & CEO

T

T.A.L. Investment Counsel Ltd.
Bélanger, F., First VP
T.A.L. Private Management Ltd.
Jones, M.L., V-Chrm & COO
TELUS Corporation
McLennan, E., Dir., Regulatory Info.
Tfo/TVOntario
Hénaut, S.
TKO Marketing Inc.
Tanguay, L., Pres.
TMN - The Movie Network/MOVIEPIX
de Wilde, L., Pres. & COO
TVOntario
Bennett, G.D., Mng Dir.
Tafelmusik
Lamon, J., Music Dir.
Talk 640
Lederman, M., Talk Show Host, "Horsman/Lederman"
Horsman, K., Talk Show Host, "Horsman/Lederman"
Talking Pictures
Battson, J., Exec. Prod.
Tall-Taylor Publishing Ltd.
Taylor, G., Ed.
Margaret Tanaka Professional Corporation
Tanaka, M., Pres.
Tarlington Talent Inc.
Tarlington, C., Pres.
Tasman Pulp and Paper Co. Ltd.
Goodreau, I., Mng Dir.
Tattersall Sound Inc.
Tattersall, J., Pres.
Tea Council of Canada
O'Rourke, D.J., Pres.
Teaching Business Ethics
Poff, D.C., Co-Ed.
Technical University of Nova Scotia
Goldbloom, R.M., Chancellor
Technology Partnerships Canada
Lofthouse, M., Dir., Enabling Technologies
TELEMANAGEMENT Magazine
Angus, E., Co-Ed.

Telemedicine Canada/US
Kahn, H.J., Medical Educ. Coord.
Nancy Telfer Music Inc.
Telfer, N., Pres.
Terra Association
Parks, B., Exec. Dir.
The Terry Fox Laboratory for Hematology/Oncology
Eaves, C.J., Deputy Dir.
Theatreworks Productions
Jones, B., Artistic Dir.
Them Days
Saunders, D.J., Ed.
Think Sport Ltd.
Lay, M., Pres. & CEO
This Country Canada
Haines, J., Ed.
Thomas More Institute
Tansey, C.H., Pres. & Dir. of Studies
The Thomas-Mitchell Associates Inc.
Mitchell, M.T., Pres.
Thompson Dorfman Sweatman
Collins, L.M., Ptnr
Nancy Thomson Investing For Women
Thomson, N., Hon. Chrm
Thornley Fallis Inc.
Pennefather, J., VP
Thorsrud's Color Centre Ltd. United Carpet
Thorsrud, L., Owner & Operator
Three Blondes Inc.
Mangaard, A., Filmmaker
Thunder Thighs Costumes Ltd.
Kemp, L.G., Pres.
Todays' Parent Group
Topping, B., Pres. & CEO
Toronto and Area Council of Women
Jackson, M., Pres.
Toronto Arts Council
Davies, R., Exec. Dir.
Toronto Children's Chorus
Bartle, J., Founder & Music Dir.
Toronto Futures Exchange
Crocker, S., Pres.
The Toronto Hospital
Robinson, G.G., Dir., Program in Women's Mental Health, Gen. Div., Dept. of Psychiatry
Stewart, D.E., Lillian Love Chair of Women's Health
Wilson, S.R., Head, Div. of Ultrasound, Dept. of Radiology
***Toronto Life* Magazine**
Collins, A., Mng Ed.
Latini, S., Art Dir.
Toronto Mutual Life Insurance Company
Sivers, G., Sr. VP, Investments
The Toronto Star
Carey, E., Demographics Reporter
Dunlop, M.E., Medical Columnist
Goar, C., Washington Bureau Chief
Kane, M., Food Ed.

Landsberg, M., Columnist
Shears, M.-D., Deputy Mng Ed.
Steed, J., Feature Writer
Stoffman, J., Book Review Ed.
Tesher, E., Columnist & Journalist
Toronto Star Newspapers Limited
Burke, A.N., Dir., Oper. Planning & Control
The Toronto Stock Exchange
Crocker, S., Sr. VP, Equities & Derivative Mkts
The Toronto Sun Publishing Company
Carpenter, L., Exec. Asst.
Eagan, T., VP, Corp. Affairs & Hum. Red.
Fenton, J., Research Assoc., New Media
The Toronto Sun
Braun, L., Film Critic & Entertainment Writer
David, C., Food Ed.
Leatherdale, L., Financial/Money Ed.
Linton, M., Life Ed.
Williams, T., Columnist
The Toronto-Dominion Bank
Cachia, C., Mgr, Personal Fin. Svcs
Di Domenico, M., Hum. Res. Systems Consultant, Hum. Res. System Mgmt
Getter, R., Sr. VP & Chief Economist
Hatch, M.S., VP & Mgr
Lalumière, D.A., VP & Dir., Retail Dist., Treasury
Poole, S., VP & Reg'l Mgr
Pulleyblank, M., Corp. Archivist
Sévigny, S., Assoc. VP, Hum. Res. & Admin., Que. Div.
Taylor, C., Assoc. VP, Personal Deposits
Tory Tory DesLauriers & Binnington
Block, S.R., Ptnr
Dubin, A.R., Ptnr
Total Entertainment Network Ltd.
Strand, K.K., Dir./Owner
Tourism Industry Association of Canada
Ward, D., Pres.
Towers Perrin
Skelton, R., Cdn Comm. Practice Mgr & Principal
Traces Screen Printing Ltd.
Johnston-Aldworth, T., Pres.
The Training Technology Monitor
Stahmer, A.E., Co-Publisher & Co-Owner
Trans-Mutual Truck Lines Ltd.
Orr, S., Pres.
TransAlta Utilities Corporation
Dahl Rees, C., Gen. Cnsl
Transamerica Life Insurance Company of Canada
Bustard, P.R., VP, Admin.
Transcontinental Publications Inc.
Paquet, S., Gen. Mgr, Fin. Publications
Transit Truck Bodies Inc.
Leclair, S.B., Pres. & CEO
Transport 2000 Canada
Hill, M.E., VP, East

TREEmendous Saskatchewan Foundation Inc.
Grono, M., Mgr
Trent University
Slavin, L., Int'l Proj. Mgr, "Instruct"
The Trillium Foundation
White, J., CEO
Trinity Western University
Pell, B., Assoc. Prof.
Triptych Media Inc.
Garfield, L., Choreographer, Writer, Performer & Prod.
Stratton, A., Prod. & Ptnr
Trow Consulting Engineers
Arvo, P.H., Environmental Technician
The Trust Company of Bank of Montreal
Roveto, C.I., COO
The Turnbull Agency Inc.
Turnbull Irving, J., Pres.
Twisted Pair Productions
Platts, D., Co-Producer & Host
Anne Tyrie & Associates
Tyrie, A., Pres.

UFL Foods Inc.
Martin, N., Sr. VP
UNICEF British Columbia
Kepper, S., Prof. Exec. Dir.
UNICEF Canada
Hayes, N., VP, Organization
Koniuck-Petzold, M., VP, Fundraising
Ukrainian Fraternal Society of Canada
Radchuk, L., Mgr
Ukrainian Museum of Canada
Hamara, O.M., Pres., Ont. Branch
Uniglobe Travel (International) Inc.
Desreux, M., Sr. VP, Oper.
Uniglobe Travel (Western Canada) Inc.
Radloff, L., Pres.
Union Gas Limited
Woodruff, J., Cont.
Unitarian Congregation of Northwest Toronto
Cook, K., Chaplain
The United Church Observer
Duncan, M., Ed.
Sinclair, D., Sr. Writer
United Food and Commercial Workers' International Union
Dassinger, J., Dir. of Training Programs & Policies & Asst. to the Cdn Dir., Nat'l Training Fund
Hinton, L., Int'l Rep. & Chair, Women's Advisory Committee
Mumford, C.A., Asst. to the Dir., Comm.
Smith, D.L., Int'l Rep.
United Way of Greater Toronto
Golden, A., Pres.

Universal Press
Dewar, S.E., Syndicated Cartoonist
Université de Moncton
Gallant, C., Prof. titulaire et Dir. du dépt. de traduction et des langues
LeBlanc, P.E., Prof. of Hist.
McKee-Allain, I., Doyenne par intérim, Fac. des sci. sociales
Villalon, L., Dir., École de nutrition et d'études familiales
Université de Montréal
Bertrand, M.-A., Prof., Sch. of Criminology
Bertrand de Muñoz, Prof. titulaire et Dir.du Dépt. littératures & langues mod.
Cantin, S., Responsable, Bur. d'intervention en matière de harcèlement sexuel
Castonguay-Thibaudeau, M.-F., Prof., Fac. des sciences infirmières
Cinq-Mars, I., V-rector Academic
Côté, J., Coord. of Internships for students enrolled in Masters Degree in Museum Studies
Kérouac, S., Dean, Fac. of Nursing
Mathieu, M., Dean, Fac. of Arts & Science
McNicoll, C., V-Rector, Public Affairs
Rousseau, C., Full Prof. & Chair, Dépt. de mathématiques et de statistique
Vikis-Freibergs, V., Prof. titulaire, Dépt. de psych.
Université du Québec à Hull
Savoie-Zajc, L., Prof.
Université du Québec à Montreal
Beauchamp, H., Prof. & Grad. Studies Coord., Theatre Dept.
Hould, C., Prof. of Art Hist.
Labelle, M., Prof., Dépt. de Soc.
Leduc, P., Rector
Messing, K., Prof. of Biol. & Researcher, Centre pour l'étude des interactions biologiques entre la santé et l'environnement
Robert, L., Prof., Dept. d'Études Littéraires
Université Laval
Milot, L., V-rectrice aux études
Université Sainte-Anne
Baulu-MacWillie, M., Prof., Dept. of Educ.
Comeau, M., Univ. Librarian
Knutson, S.L., Assoc. Prof. & Chair, Dept. of English
Le Blanc, B., Asst. Prof., Dept. of Educ.
University College
Rajan, T., Prof., Dept. of English
University College of Cape Breton
Beaton, C.A., Children's Centre Coord., Extension & Community Affairs
Scott, J.T., Pres. & V-Chancellor
University Hospital
Garcia, B., Consultant Pathologist
University of Alberta
Allen, M., Prof., Fac. of Nursing
Archer, V.B., Composer, Prof. of Music Emerita

Armour, M.-A., Asst. Chair, Dept. of Chem.
Brandt, D.R., Writer & Research Fellow in English
Cass, C., Prof., Biochemistry & Oncology; Chair, Dept. of Oncology
Collins-Nakai, R.L., Prof. of Pediatrics & Assoc. Dean, Fac. of Medicine
Davies, C., Prof.
Dickason, O.P., Prof. Emeritus, Dept. of Hist.
Jensen, S., Prof. & Chair, Dept. of Biological Sci.
MacPhail, J., Prof. & Dean Emeritus, Fac. of Nursing
McDaniel, S.A., Prof. of Soc.
McMaster, J., Univ. Prof. of English
Pilarski, L.M., Prof., Dept. of Oncology
Prepas, E.E., Prof., Limnology, Dept. of Biological Sci.
Spencer, M.E., Univ. Prof., Dept. of Agriculture, Food & Nutritional Sci.
Williamson, J., Assoc. Prof., Dept. of English

University of British Columbia
Baird, P., Univ. Prof.
Barman, J., Prof., Dept. of Educ. Studies
Bellward, G.D., Prof. of Pharmacology & Toxicology, Fac. of Pharmaceutical Sci.
Bowen, L.E., Maclean Hunter Lecturer in Creative Non-Fiction
Boyle, C.L.M., Prof., Fac. of Law
Butt, D.S., Assoc. Prof., Dept. of Psych.
Cranston, L.S., Clinical Instructor, Masters Program in Health Planning & Epidemiology, Fac. of Medicine
Creese, G., Assoc. Prof., Dept. of Anthro. & Soci.
Gaskell, J., Prof. & Assoc. Dean, Grad. Programs & Research, Fac. of Educ.
Gillam, S., Prof., Dept. of Pathology
Grace, S.E., Prof. of English
Gray, V., Adjunct Prof., Fac. of Law
Gutman, G.M., Assoc. Mbr., Dept. of Health Care & Epidemiology, Fac. of Medicine
Hall, J.G., Head, Dept. of Pediatrics
Hawthorn, P., Lecturer, Theatre Dept.
Henderson, A.D., Assoc. Prof., Sch. of Nursing
Irwin, R.L., Assoc. Prof., Dept. of Curriculum Studies
Kaminsky, B.A., Clinical Asst. Prof., Health Admin. Program
Klawe, M.M., VP, Student & Academic Svcs
Loock, C.A., Clinical Assoc. Prof., Fac. of Medicine
Marchak, M.P., Prof., Dept. of Anthro. & Soc.
McGeer, E.G., Prof. Emerita, Dept. of Psychiatry
Neuman, S., Dean of Arts & Prof. of English
Ormsby, M.A., Prof. Emerita, Hist. Dept.
Patkau, P., Assoc. Prof., Sch. of Architecture
Piternick, A.B., Prof. Emerita, Sch. of Library,

Archival & Info. Studies
Raoul, V., Prof., Dept. of French & Dir., Centre for Research in Women's Studies & Gender Rel'ns
Salcudean, M.E., Prof. of Mech. Eng.
Saltman, J., Assoc. Prof., Sch. of Library & Info. Studies
Smith, L., Prof. & Dean, Fac. of Law
Sutherland Boal, A., Adjunct Prof., Sch. of Nursing
Underhill, A.B., Hon. Prof., Dept. of Geophysics & Astronomy
Walker, D., Sr. Instructor Emerita
Wickwire, W., Asst. Prof., Dept. of Educ. Studies, Fac. of Educ.

University of Calgary
Arai, M.N., Prof. Emeritus, Dept. of Biological Sci.
Bennett, S., Assoc. Prof., Dept. of English
Bryant, H., Clinical Assoc. Prof., Dept. of Oncology & Dept. of Community Health Sci.
Burgess, E., Assoc. Prof., Fac. of Medicine
Eccles, R.C., Clinical Asst. Prof., Dept. of Surgery
Field, L., Prof., Dept. of Medical Genetics
Hallworth, B., Botanist, Herbarium
Hughes, M.E., Prof., Fac. of Law
Kaplan, B., Prof. of Pediatrics & Dir., Behavourial Research Unit
Kapoor, M., Prof., Dept. of Biological Sci.
Katzenberg, M.A., Prof., Dept. of Archaeology
Mahoney, K.E., Prof., Fac. of Law
Martin, R.H., Prof., Dept. of Medical Genetics
Martin, S., Dean, Fac. of Law
McTeer, M.A., Adjunct Asst. Prof., Fac. of Law, Medicine & Nursing
Metz, L.M., Asst. Prof., Dept. of Clinical Neurosciences, Fac. of Medicine
Nijssen-Jordan, C., Asst. Prof.
Patterson, M., Assoc. VP (Student Affairs)
Pettifor, J.L., Assoc. Prof., Dept. of Educ. Psych. & Programme in Clinical Psych.
Reimer, M.A., Assoc. Prof., Fac. of Nursing
Robinson, S.A.
Seiler, T., Assoc. Prof., Fac. of General Studies
Sethi, S., Assoc. Prof., Fac. of Nursing
Silverman, E., Prof. & Advisor to the Pres. on Women's Issues
Singhal, N., Assoc. Prof., Pediatrics
Stone-Blackburn, S., Prof. of English & Assoc. Dean of Grad. Studies

University of Guelph
Benn, D.M., Dir., Animal Care Svcs
Benson, R., Prof., German Studies
Brydon, D., Prof., Dept. of English
Cyr, M., Chair, Dept. of Music
Heathcote, I.W., Assoc. Prof., Sch. of Eng. & Fac. of Environmental Sciences
Kerrigan, C., Prof. of English

Kulyk Keefer, J., Prof., Dept. of English
Lake, S.M., Assoc. Prof., Fine Art Dept.
Mancuso, M., Chair, Dept. of Pol. Studies
Martin Matthews, A., Prof., Dept. of Family Studies
McDonald, L., Prof., Dept. of Soci. & Anthro.
Myers Avis, J.K., Prof., Dept. of Family Studies
Oaks, A., Prof. of Botany (Adjunct)
Priest, M., Prof. of Fine Art
Rooke, C., Assoc. VP, Academic & Prof. of English
Rubio, M., Prof., Dept. of English
Sharom, F.J., Prof., Dept. of Chem. & Biochem.
Stewart, C., Dean, Coll. of Arts
Wall, M., Prof. & Chair, Dept. of Consumer Studies
Waterston, E., Prof. Emerita
Wood, J.M., Prof., Dept. of Microbiol.
Woolcott, D., Prof. & Chair, Dept. of Family Studies

University of King's College
Edwards, E., Dir., Contemporary Studies Program
Mitchell, J., Dir. of Alumni, Dev., & Public Rel'ns
Robertson, P.M., Registrar

University of Lethbridge
Cardiff, J., Artist & Assoc. Prof., Dept. of Art
Indra, D.M., Assoc. Prof. of Anthro.
Knight, C., Dir., Hum. Res.
Lavers, L., Registrar
Luther, A.H., Assoc. Prof., Dept. of Dramatic Arts
Michener, G.R., Prof., Dept. of Biological Sci.
Walker, N.R., Dir., Fin. Svcs & Cont.

University of Manitoba
Aponiuk, N., Dir. & Assoc. Prof., Centre for Ukrainian Cdn Studies & Dept. of German & Slavic Studies
Colwill, N.L., Adjunct Prof.
Daniels, V., Assoc. Prof., Rehabilitative Medicine, Fac. of Medicine
Dobran, B.A., Grad. Student, Mech. Eng. Dept.
Glass, H., Prof. Emerita, Sch. of Nursing
Hinz, E.J., Distinguished Prof. of English
Ingram, S., Instructor, Fac. of Engineering
Kartzmark, E.M., Prof. of Chem. (retired)
Shields, C., Author & Prof., English
Stalker, J., Professor (retired), Div. of Postsecondary Studies & Coord., Higher Educ. Grad. Program, Fac. of Educ.
Townsend, J.B., Prof., Dept. of Anthro.
Vaisey-Genser, M., Prof. & Sr. Scholar, Dept. of Foods & Nutrition

University of New Brunswick
Byers, S., Prof. of Psych. & Founding Dir. of the Muriel McQueen Fergusson Centre for Family Violence Res.

Chrzanowski, M.J., Sr. Teaching Assoc.
Crocker, A., Head Law Librarian, Gerard V. La Forest Law Library
Davies, J., Dir., Env. & Sust. Dev. Res. Ctr
Dennison, D., Registrar
Edwards, V., Dir., Second Language Educ. Centre
Frize, M., Prof. & Chair Holder, Dept. of Elect. Eng.
Harrison, D., Prof. of Soc. & Dir., Muriel McQueen Fergusson Centre for Family Violence Research
Hughes, P., Assoc. Prof., Mary Louise Lynch Chair in Women & Law, Fac. of Law
Krause, M.O., Prof., Dept. of Biol.
Latchford, S., Assoc. Prof./Dir. of Learning Centre, Fac. of Educ.
Leblon, B., Asst. Prof., Fac. of Forestry
Lemire, B., Prof., Dept. of Hist.
Parr-Johnston, E., Pres. & V-Chancellor

University of Northern British Columbia
Ainley, M.G., Prof. & Chair, Women's Studies Programs
Anderson, M.S., Northwest Reg. Coord.
Poff, D.C., Prof. & VP, Academic

University of Ottawa
Andrew, C., Chair, Dept. of Pol. Sci.
Bégin, M., Dean, Fac. of Health Sciences
Durieux-Smith, A., Prof., Audiology & Speech-Language Pathology
Grisé, Y., Prof. de litt., Dépt. des lettres françaises, et Dir., Centre de recherche en civilisation canadienne-française
Jackman, M., Assoc. Prof., Fac. of Law
Jefferson, A.L., Prof., Educational Studies
Johnson, S.M., Assoc. Prof. of Psych. & Psychiatry, Dept. of Psych.
Labelle, H., Chancellor
McMullen, L., Prof. Emerita, Dept. of English
Mikhael, N., Prof. & Chair, Dept. of Pathology & Lab. Medicine
Millman-Floyd, C., Prof., Dept. of Music
Rock, G.A., Assoc. Prof. of Pathology
Rodgers, S., Dean, Common Law Section, Fac. of Law
Spry, I.M., Prof. Emeritus
Swiggum, S., Assoc. Prof.
Workman, C., V-Rector, Resources

University of Ottawa Heart Institute
Labow, R.S., Dir., Taichman Lab.

University of Prince Edward Island
Anderson, D.H., Chancellor
Bourne, L.-A., Lecturer
Epperly, E., Prof. of English & Pres.
MacLellan, D., Asst. Prof., Dept. of Home Econ.
Timmons, V., Dean, Fac. of Educ.

University of Regina
Bismanis, M.R., Assoc. Prof. of Art Hist.
Blackstone, M.A., Fac. of Theatre Arts (on

leave)

Givner, J., Prof. of English (retired)

McKay, S., Dean & Assoc. Prof., Fac. of Social Work

University of Saskatchewan

McKercher, P., Chancellor

Stephen, A.M., Prof., Div. of Nutrition & Dietetics, Coll. of Pharmacy & Nutrition

University of Southwestern Louisiana

Sheets-Pyenson, S., Assoc. Prof. of Hist.

University of Toronto

Annis, H.M., Prof., Fac. of Medicine

Bandeen, M.H., Dir., Women's Entrepreneurship Program & Family Bus. Mgmt Program

Barrie, M.C., Dir., Sch. of Continuing Studies

Batty, H.P., Assoc. Chair, Dept. of Family & Community Medicine, Fac. of Medicine

Bishop, O., Prof. Emeritus

Boddy, J., Assoc. Prof., Anthro. Dept., Social Sci. Div.

Bogo, M., Acting Dean, Fac. of Social Work

Bradley, S., Head, Div. of Child Psychiatry

Brown, S., Dir., Dev & Alumni Affairs, Trinity Coll.

Brubaker, P., Assoc. Prof., Dept. of Physiology

Burton, F., Prof.

Cahoon, M.C., Prof. Emeritus, Nursing

Cameron, E.M., Prof., Cdn Studies (University Coll.), English Dept.

Carpenter, H.M., Prof. Emeritus

Chandler, M., Dean, Fac. of Arts & Sci.

Ching, J., Univ. Prof., Victoria Coll.

Cloutier, C., Prof. Emerita, Dept. of French

Cook, E., Prof., Dept. of English

Cook, R., Prof. & Dir., Int'l Hum Rights Prog., Fac. of Law

Deber, R., Prof., Dept. of Health

Dobson, W.K., Dir., Centre for Int'l Bus. & Prof., Fac. of Mgmt

Dolezelová-Velingerová, M., Prof. of Chinese Language & Lit., Dept. of East Asian Studies

Donner, G.J., Prof., Fac. of Nursing

Foley, J., Prof. of Psych.

Frank, R., Univ. Prof., Dept of English, & Dir., Centre for Medieval Studies

Freeman, R., Program Dir., Undergrad. Educ., & Asst. Prof., Dept. of Family & Community Medicine

Friedland, J., Assoc. Prof. & Chair, Dept. of Occupational Therapy, Fac. of Medicine

Friendly, M., Adjunct Prof.

Ganoza, M.C., Prof., Banting & Best Dept. of Medical Research

Godkin, C., Freelance Author & Illustrator & Asst. Prof., Div. of Biomedical Comm., Dept. of Surgery, Fac. of Medicine

Gross Stein, J., Harrowston Prof. of Conflict Mgmt & Negotiation

Grosskurth, P.M., Prof. Emeritus, New Coll.

Heath, M., Prof., Botany Dept.

Hill, M.F., Prof. Emeritus, Fac. of Medicine

Hoffman, I., Dir., Info. Tech. Design Centre & Assoc. Prof.

Hutcheon, L., Univ. Prof. of English & Comparative Lit.

Irwin, M.E., Assoc. Prof., Scarborough Coll.

Jones, P., Prof. Emeritus, Fac. of Nursing

Joy, J., Prof. Emeritus, Fac. of Medicine

Kahn, H.J., Prof., Dept. of Pathology

Kaufman, M., Asst. Prof., Dept. of Pediatrics

Lancashire, A., Prof. of English

Leatt, P., Prof. & Chair, Dept. of Health Admin., Fac. of Medicine

Legge, E.M., Univ. Art Curator & Asst. Prof., Fine Art Dept.

Levenson, J., Prof., Trinity Coll.

Lickley, L.A., Prof. of Surgery & Physiology

Lynch, A., Assoc. Prof., Fac. of Dentistry

MacDonald, L., Assoc. Prof. & Head of Voice Studies, Fac. of Music

MacGregor, D.L., Prof. of Paediatrics (Neurology)

Maclean, H., Dir., Centre for Research in Women's Health

McAuliffe, J., Chrm, Dept. for the Study of Religion & Dir., Centre for the Study of Religion

Melville, K., Dir. of Professional Dev., Fac. of Info. Studies

Mickleborough, L.L., Prof. of Surgery

Moore, C., Chief Librarian

Munroe-Blum, H., Prof. & VP, Research & Int'l Rel'ns

Murray, H., Assoc. Prof. of English, Trinity College

O'Grady, J., Asst. Ed., Collected Works of Northrop Frye, Victoria Coll.

Olivieri, N.F., Assoc. Prof., Pediatrics & Medicine

Ostry, S., Chair, Centre for Int'l Studies

Packer, K.H, Prof. Emerita, Fac. of Library & Info. Sci. (now Fac. of Info. Studies)

Packham, M.A., Univ. Prof. Emeritus, Dept. of Biochem.

Paterson, J.M., Assoc. Dean, Fac. of Arts & Sci.

Phillips, M.J., Prof., Dept. of Chemical Eng. & Applied Chem.

Polivy, J., Prof., Dept. of Psych., Erindale Coll.

Pugliese, O., Prof., Dept. of Italian Studies

Rabinovitch, R., Prof. of Pediatrics, Pathology & Medicine

Rappaport, H.S., Asst. Prof., Fac. of Medicine

Richardson, B., Chief, Medical Staff Affairs, Women's College Hospital

Robinson, G.G., Prof. of Psychiatry & Prof. of Obstetrics & Gynaecology

Robson, A., Prof.

Rossant, J., Prof., Molecular & Medical Genetics, & Obstetrics & Gynaecology

Saddlemyer, A.E., Prof. & Master Emerita, Massey Coll.

Schabas, A.H., Prof. Emeritus, Fac. of Library & Info. Sci.

Schwartz, J., Dir. & Curator, Hart House

Shamian, J., Assoc. Prof., Fac. of Nursing

Sharkey, S., Asst. Prof., Fac. of Nursing

Sikorski, P.A., Asst. Prof.

Sirek, A., Prof. Emeritus of Physiology

Square, P.A., Prof. & Chair, Dept. of Speech Language Pathology, Fac. of Medicine

Stephen, B., Assoc. Prof., Dept. of East Asian Studies

Stewart, D.E., Prof. of Psychiatry, Obstetrics-Gynecology, Anesthesia, Surgery, & Family & Community Medicine

Sullivan, R., Prof., Dept. of English

Tan-Willman, C., Prof.

Tuohy, C.H., Prof. of Pol. Sci. & Deputy Provost

Van Norman, M., Dir. of Student Svc.

Warkentin, G., Prof. of English, Victoria Coll.

Webster, J.R., Prof. Emeritus

Welsh-Ovcharov, B., Prof., Dept. of Fine Art

Wigdor, B.T., Prof. Emeritus, Centre for Studies of Aging, Departments of Psych. & Behavioural Sci.

Wilson, S.R., Prof., Fac. of Medicine

Winsor, M., Prof., Institute for the Hist. & Philosophy of Sci. & Technology

University of Toronto Art Centre
Randall, J.R., Chair of the Bd.

University of Toronto Faculty Association
Scott, S., Exec. Dir.

University of Toronto Foundation
Hanson, T.J.M., Campaign Dir. & VP

University of Toronto Press Incorporated
Corrigan, A.M., VP, Journals & Design

University of Ulster at Jordanstown
McCracken, K.L., Lecturer in English & American Studies

University of Victoria
Ashford, M.-W., Asst. Prof., Dept. of Social & Natural Sciences

Crozier, L., Assoc. Prof., Dept. of Writing

Hollingsworth, M., Assoc. Prof., Dept. of Writing, Fac. of Fine Arts

McMullen, L., Adunct Prof., Dept. of English

Mickelson, N.I., Prof. Emeritus

Molzahn, A., Dean, Fac. of Hum. & Social Dev.

Porac, C., Prof. of Psych. Dept. of Psych.

Prentice, A., Adj. Prof., Dept. of Hist.

Rowland, B., Adjunct Prof., Dept. of English

Starzomski, R.C., Visiting Lecturer, Sch. of Nursing

Stuchly, M.A., Prof., Dept. of Electrical & Computer Eng.

Tumasonis, E., Assoc. Prof., Dept. of Hist. in Art

Turner, N.J., Prof., Environmental Studies Program

Waelti-Walters, J., Prof. & Founding Dir. of Women's Studies

Zwicky, J., Prof.

University of Waterloo
Cuthbert Brandt, G., Principal, Renison Coll.

Dagg, A.I., Academic Adv.

Forsyth, P., Prof. of Classical Studies, Hist., & Fine Arts

Legault, J.A., Assoc. Prof., Dept. of Earth Sci.

Lyons, H.D., Assoc. Prof., Anthro., & Dir., Women's Studies

Mitchinson, W., Prof. of Hist., Dept. of Hist.

Sanderson, M., Dir., The Water Network, Dept. of Geography

Thompson, M.E., Prof. & Chair, Statistics & Actuarial Sci.

Vethamany-Globus, S., Assoc. Prof., Dept. of Biol.

Willment, J.-A.H., Lecturer, Psych. Dept.

Wubnig, J., Asst. Prof., Dept. of Phil.

University of Western Ontario
Bondar, R.L., CIBC Distinguished Prof., Fac. of Kinesiology

Borwein, B., Asst. Dean - Research, Fac. of Medicine

Butler, S.M., Assoc. Prof., Dept. of Visual Arts

Coniglio, C., Counsellor/Therapist, Univ. Community Centre

Davis, M., Prof., Dept. of English

Fowler, L., Chair, Bd. of Gov.

Fulton, T., Acting Principal, Huron Coll.

Garcia, B., Assoc. Prof., Dept. of Pathology

Gillese, E., Dean, Fac. of Law

Hampson, E.M., Assoc. Prof., Dept. of Psych.

Haust, M.D., Prof. of Pathology & Paediatrics

Knelman, J., Assoc. Prof.

Kofmel, K.G., Instructor, Grad. Sch. of Library & Info. Sci.

Letton, S., Clinical Assoc., Fac. of Nursing

Rajan, T., Dir., Centre in the Study of Theory & Criticism

Riddell-Dixon, E.M., Assoc. Prof., Dept. of Pol. Sci.

Ross, C., Prof. of Library & Info. Science & Acting Dean of Comm. & Open Learning

Vingilis, E.R., Dir., Population & Community Health Unit, & Prof., Dept. of Family Medicine & Dept. of Epidemiology & Biostatistics, Fac. of Medicine

Wright, M.J., Prof. Emerita, Dept. of Psych.

Wylie, A., Prof., Dept. of Phil.

University of Windsor
Cameron, W.S.J., Dean of Grad. Studies, Prof. of Nursing

Campbell, W., Prof., Ed.

Crocker, O.L., Prof., Fac. of Bus. Admin.

ElMaraghy, H.A., Dean of Eng.

Irish, M., Prof., Fac. of Law

Mady Kelly, D., Dir. Sch. of Dramatic Art
Martin, S.A., Prof. of Dramatic Art, & Dean, Fac. of Arts
McCrone, K.E., Prof. of Hist. & Dean of Social Sci.
Murray, J., Assoc. Prof. of Hist. & Dir., Humanities Research Group
Wong-Rieger, D., Assoc. Prof., Dir. of Hum. Res. Consultation Unit, Dept. of Psych.
University of Winnipeg
Anderson, J., Exec. Dir., Univ. Rel'ns
Brown, J.S.H., Prof., Dept. of Hist.
Carrington, M.E., Asst. Prof., Physics Dept.
Clarkson, P.B., Assoc. Prof., Dept. of Anthro.
Day, P., Assoc. Prof. & Chair, Dept. of Religious Studies
Dhruvarajan, V., Prof. of Sociology
Fehr, B., Assoc. Prof., Dept. of Psych. (on leave)
Greenhill, P., Prof., Dept. of Women's Studies & Anthro.
Harvey, C., Prof. of French
Josephson, W., Assoc. Prof., Dept. of Psych.
Kerr, K.M., Assoc. Prof. & Dir., Developmental Studies
Kirby, S.L., Prof., Dept. of Soc.
Novak, M., Prof.
Pip, E., Prof.
Rusnak, A.M., Instructor III, Dept. of French Studies
Sauer, A., Chair in German Cdn Studies
Schnitzer, D., Assoc. Prof., Dept. of English
Shields, C., Chancellor
Vanderwel, D., Assoc. Prof., Dept. of Chemistry
Up Front Entertainment Inc.
Barde, B., Pres.
Urban Development Institute
Enser, M.B., Exec. Dir.
Roz Usheroff Consulting Inc.
Usheroff , R., Pres.

VIA Rail Canada Inc.
Mackaay, C., Corp. Sec.
VERSA Services
Conlinn, C.B., VP, Health Care Bus. Dev.
VIPR Communications
Kells, V.C., Pres.
Vail and Associates
Vail, S., Pres.
Valley Family Resource Center
Hayes, A.-M., Dir.
Valley Physiotherapy Clinic
Shaw, S., Owner
van Ginkel Associates
van Ginkel, B., Ptnr
Vancouver City Savings Credit Union
Chan, S., Past Chair
Currie, K., VP, Hum. Res. & Environment

Grierson, L., Reg'l Mgr
Nathoo, T., Sr. VP, Oper.
The Vancouver Flag Shop Inc.
Braverman, D., Pres.
Vancouver Hospital and Health Science Centre
Starzomski, R.C., Ethics Consultant
Vancouver Museum
Swart, P., Curator of Asian Studies
Vancouver Police & Native Liaison Society
Ens, R.F., Exec. Dir.
Vancouver Port Corporation
Taylor, C., V-Chair
Vancouver Province Newspaper
Fournier, S.N., Journalist & Author
The Vancouver Sun
Crook, B., Theatre Critic
Graham, P.A., Edit. Page Ed.
Leeming, V., Fashion Reporter
Long, W., Sportswriter
Shaw, G., Columnist, "The People's Business"
Yaffe, B., Columnist
Variety Club of Southern Alberta
Garratt, A., Chrm of the Bd.
Variety Cooperative Inc.
McLeod, L., Cont.
Vector Management Limited
Cohen, A., VP
Venture Hydraulic Ltd.
Sparling, M., Part-Owner
Vernon Women's Transition House
Jacobi, J., Exec. Dir.
Verseau International
Danis, A., Pres. & Co-Founder
Vertechs Design, Inc.
Lovering, M.J., Principal Landscape Architect
Viacom Canada Limited
Stephenson, H., Chair
Victims of Violence Canadian Centre for Missing Children
Rosenfeldt, S., Pres.
Victoria General Hospital
Kells, C., Assoc. Prof., Dept. of Medicine, Div. of Cardiology, Dalhousie Univ.
MacRury-Sweet, K.E., Dir. of Cardia/ Emergency Nursing, Queen Elizabeth II Health Science Centre
Mosher, C., Nephrology Social Worker, Social Work Dept.
Victoria General Hospital Foundation
Davison, M.L., Chrm, Bd. of Dir.
Victoria Manor Heritage House Museum
French, M., Owner/Operator
Victoria Times Colonist
Heiman, C.E., Ed., Living Section
Paterson, J., Mng Ed.
Victoria University
Runte, R., Pres.
Vingilis and Associates
Vingilis, E.R., Registered Psychologist

Viridian
Currie, J.K., Sr. Env. Assoc., New Prod., Fertilizer Mktg
Vision Management Services
Armstrong, R.R., Pres.
Visual Enterprise
Fernandes, T., Art Dir.
Voice for Hearing Impaired Children
Pryde, R., Exec. Dir.
Volleyball Canada
Bigras, S., Dir. Gen.
Volunteer Centre of Metropolitan Toronto
Cooper, J.S., Exec. Dir.
Voyage Media Productions Inc.
Leaney, C., Pres.

W₅
Rinaldo, S., Host
WETV
Rankin, L.M., Exec. VP & Gen. Mgr
WIC Western International Communications Ltd.
McHarg, N., Dir. of Comm.
W.W. West Communications
Brunelle, W.A., Writer, Public Rel'ns Consultant, TV Host, Facilitator
Walk The Wild Side
Jones, S., Eco-tourism Trainer & Coord.
Walter Murray Collegiate
Lukkien (Van't Hof), D.A., Teacher
Watercan/Eau Vive
Bosley, N., Exec. Dir.
The Watercolour Garden
Kemp, L.P.F., Artist & Owner
The Waterfront Theatre
Ball, E., Gen. Mgr
Waterloo Inn
D'Alton, M., Mng Dir.
Watervisions Underwater Camera Systems
Heaton, P.R., Pres.
Lise Watier Cosmétiques Inc.
Watier, L., Pres. & CEO
Carolyn Watson, Chartered Accountant
Watson, C.F., C.A.
Wawanesa Mutual Insurance Company
Tagg, C.J., Sr. Mktg Rep.
We Care Health Services Inc.
McMaster, B., Pres.
Wedgwood Insurance Limited
Vokey, M.L., VP, Personal Lines
Weekender Ladies Wear
Keeping, L., VP & Dir. of Sales
Webber, D., Sr. Exec. Sales Mgr
The Wellesley Central Hospital
Martin, S.E., VP, Surgical Programs
Moeser, D.R.E., VP, Community Health & Planning

The Wellness Institute at Seven Oaks General Hospital
Boreskie, S.L., Exec. Dir.
Wesmar Electronics Canada Ltd.
d'Entremont, R.I., Sec.-Treas.
West Coast Express
Stewart, L., Pres.
West Kitikmeot Slave Study Society
Benyk, P., Study Asst. (Comm.)
Western Gold Theatre Company
Coghill, J., Artistic Dir.
Western Institute for the Deaf and Hard of Hearing
Dahl, M.O., Exec. Dir.
Western Memorial Regional Hospital
Christopher, J.B., Staff Educ. Coord.
Western Washington University
Alia, V., Distinguished Prof. of Cdn Culture & Visiting Prof. of Journalism, Center for Cdn-American Studies
Anne Wheeler Inc.
Wheeler, A., Filmmaker
WHERE Magazines International
Hayes, C.-A., Pres.
White Jenkins Duncan & Ostner
English, H., Ptnr
White Rose Crafts and Nursery Sales Ltd.
Jolliffe, L., VP & CFO
White Saddle Air Services Ltd.
King, J.G., Pres.
Whitefish River First Nation
Jacko, E.M., Community Historian & Lands Mgr
Susan Whitney Gallery
Whitney, S.G., Dir. & Past Pres.
Wild Blueberry Producers' Association of Nova Scotia
Nash, R., Mgr
Wilfrid Laurier University
Gillham, V., Univ. Librarian
Marsden, L., Pres. & V-Chancellor
Toews, H., Asst. Prof., Fac. of Music
Westhues, A., Assoc. Prof.
Woodcock, K., Practicum Asst., Fac. of Social Work
Wilfrid Laurier University Press
Woolfrey, S., Dir.
Williams, Roebothan, McKay and Marshall
Skanes, L.J., Ptnr
Willow Bay Creations
Williams, B.K., Pres.
Willow Creek Auxiliary Hospital
Williams, D.A.
The Hilda Wilson Group
Wilson, H.E., Chrm & CEO
Windjammer Landing Villa Beach Resort
Cram, L.M., Exec. VP
Windsor Symphony
Haig, S.E., Music Dir.

Winnipeg Art Gallery
Madill, S., Curator, Contemporary Art &
Photography
Wight, D., Assoc. Curator of Inuit Art
Wishbone Productions Inc.
Keane, K., Pres.
Wolsak and Wynn Publishers Ltd.
Jacobs-Moens, M., Co-Publisher
Women & Environments magazine
Dale, L., Magazine Mgr
Women in Crisis Algoma Inc.
Conway, S.L., Exec. Dir.
Women in Management Newsletter
Sanders, D., Ed.
Women Inventors Project
Klein, C.J., Co-Dir.
Women Teachers' Association of Ottawa
Kent, A., Pres.
Women Who Excel
Whitlock, C.J., Pres. & Publisher
Women's Art Association of Hamilton
Richardson, M.S.
**Women's Association of the Mining
Industry of Canada**
Yates, B.H., Pres.
Women's College Hospital
Kahn, H.J., Research Dir. & Assoc. Chief,
Dept. of Pathology & Head, Immunochemistry
Dept.
Kronberg, J., Chair, Medical Advisory
Committee & Anesthetist-in-Chief
Lickley, L.A., Surgeon-in-Chief
Maclean, H., Dir., Centre for Research in
Women's Health
Women's College Hospital Foundation
Peacock, H.I.P., Pres.
**Women's Commission of the BC
Liberal Party**
Loren, S., Pres.
Women's Economic Forum
Roth, K., Past Pres.
Women's Institutes of Nova Scotia
Archibald, I., Past Pres.
**Women's Inter-Church Council
of Canada**
Steffer, D., Past Pres.
Women's Inter-Church Council of Guelph
Steffer, D., Past Pres.
**Women's International League For
Peace and Freedom**
Holyk, M., Pres.
**The Women's Network on Health
and the Environment**
Goldin Rosenberg, D., Women's Health & the
Environment & Global Educ. Consultant,
Women for a Just and Healthy Planet
Women's Up to Date Shop Inc.
d'Entremont, R.I., Pres.
Wood's Homes
Gardiner, S., Dir., Residential Programs

Wooden Door & Associates
Dorsey, C.J., Writer, Ed. & Publisher
The Word On The Street
Taylor, C., Nat'l Exec. Dir.
**Workers' Compensation Board,
of Alberta**
Jodoin, S., Labour Comm. Specialist
World Bestravel Associates
Frazer, R., Pres.
**World Federation of Ukrainian
Women's Organizations**
Sokolyk, O.T., Pres.
World Headache Alliance
South, V., Coord.
A World of Dreams Foundation
Sims, D., Pres. & CEO
World Schizophrenia Fellowship
Marshall, G., Pres.
World Trade Organization
Steger, D.P., Dir., Appellate Body Secretariat
World YMCA
Godsoe, D.S., Exec. Committee
Northcote, A.L., Past Pres.
Wright Alternative Advertising
Wright, A., Pres.

Xerox Canada Inc.
McGarry, D.E., Chrm, Pres. & CEO

YMCA Canada
Black, E.M., Chair
YWCA of/du Canada
Northcote, A.L., Past Pres.
YES! International
Mascioli-Mansell, J.L., Int'l Chrm & CEO
Yewchin's Funeral Chapel
Yewchin, C., Co-owner/Mgr
York Expositions Inc.
Peake, J.
**York Region Roman Catholic
Separate School Board**
Bustamante, R., Multilingual Assessor
York University
Auster, E.R., Assoc. Prof., Strategic Mgmt Stud-
ies, Fac. of Admin. Studies
Bayefsky, A.F., Dir., Centre for Refugee Studies
Black, N., Prof. Emerita, Pol. Sci.
Briskin, L., Assoc. Prof., Soc. Sci. Div.
Cameron, B.J., Assoc. Prof., Osgoode Hall Law
Sch.
Carpenter, C., Assoc. Prof., Div. of Humanities
Doan, H.M., Master of Vanier College &
Assoc. Prof. of Psych.
Doob, P., Prof. of Eng., Multidisciplinary
Studies, Women's Studies, & Dance, & Aca-
demic Dir., Centre for the Support of Teaching
Embleton, S.M., Assoc. Prof., Dept. of
Language, Literatures & Linguistics

Godard, B., Assoc. Prof., English Dept.
Greenglass, E.R., Prof., Dept. of Psych., Fac. of Arts
Hoffmann, E., Univ. Librarian
Hornstein, S., Chair, Dept. of Fine Arts & Assoc. Prof., Atkinson Coll.
Kallen, E., Emeritus Prof. & Sr. Scholar (Arts)
Klein-Lataud, C., Dir., Sch. of Translation, Glendon Coll.
Killingbeck, M.E., Head Coach, Women's Track & Field & Cross-Country Team
Lewis, H.I., Univ. Cnsl
Luxton, M., Prof.
Mann, S., Pres.
McCormack, T., Prof. Emerita
Mossman, M.J., Prof., Osgoode Hall Law Sch.
Pepler, D., Full Prof., Psych. Dept.
Pilkington, M.L., Dean, Osgoode Hall Law Sch.
Pyke, S.W., Prof. & Chair, Dept. of Psych.
Rioux, M.H., Asst. Prof., Fac. of Environmental Studies
Ripley, M.L., Assoc. Prof., Atkinson Coll.
Rock, V.J., Prof. Emerita, English Dept.
Rowland, B., Distinguished Prof. Emerita, Dept. of English
Rowntree, J.-M.A., Dir. of Comm.
Sandilands, C.A.H., Asst. Prof., Fac. of Environmental Studies
Schiff, D., Assoc. Prof of Natural Sci., Glendon Coll.
Swan, S., Prof., Dept. of Humanities
Thomas, C.M., Prof. Emeritus & Cdn. Studies Research Fellow
Vail, S., Assoc. Prof., Sch. of Phys. Educ.
Waddington, M., Prof. Emeritus & Sr. Scholar, Dept. of English
Warner, M.J., Assoc. Prof., Dept. of Dance
Wekerle, G.R., Prof., Fac. of Environmental Studies
Zemans, J.P., Prof., Fac. of Fine Arts
Zimmerman, S., Prof., Natural Sci.

Youth Assisting Youth
Spencer, S., Exec. Dir.

Yukon Association for Community Living
Curtis, K., Pres.

Yukon College
Chaudaquock, V., VP, First Nations Programs & Svcs
Fekete, H., Retired Dean, Developmental Studies
Frederickson, E.G., Instructor, Dev. Studies
Tayler, A.H., Prof. & Coord., Women's Studies

Zen International Resources Ltd.
McLeod, C., Chrm

Ziveg Productions Inc.
Sandor, A.

Zolar Entertainment Corp.
Fournier, L., Producer, Dir. & Writer

Zukerman Charitable Foundation
Zukerman, H., Administrator & Trustee

Zurich Canada
FitzGerald, D.J., Pres., Group Insur. Div.
Maddocks, J., Pres., Personal Insur.
Whidden, D., Sr. VP, Corp. Dev.

INDEX BY PRIMARY OCCUPATION

THE ARTS
Visual arts including photography and design.
Music. Performing arts including theatre and dance.
Art galleries and art museums. Artists, curators, and
arts educators. Related organizations, government
agencies and officials.

Aaron, Gladys

Abbott, Patricia A.
Exec. Dir., Association of Canadian Choral
Conductors

Abe, Kyoko
Dir., Toronto East Branch, Sogetsu Ikebana

Abrams, Gayle
Co-owner, Oscars and Abrams Associates Inc.

Ackerman, Nancy W.
Freelance Documentary Photographer

Alexander-Smith, Joann
Gen. Dir., Manitoba Opera

Aloi, Santa
Prof., Sch. for the Contemporary Arts &
Assoc. Dean, Fac. of Arts, Simon Fraser
Univ.

Amos, Janet
Artistic Dir., Blyth Festival

Annis, Susan
Arts Consultant

Appel, Bluma
Chrm, Appel Consultants Inc.

Archer, Violet Balestreri
Composer, Prof Emeritus of Music, Univ. of
Alberta

Arsie, Laura
Owner, Laura Arsie Photography

Austen-Leigh, Joan H.
Writer

Baday, Lida
Pres., Lida Baday Ltd.
Ball, Elizabeth
Founder & Mng Artistic Dir., Carousel Theatre
Company and School
Barclay, Marion H.
Chief Conservator, National Gallery of
Canada
Bard, Margaret
Co-founder & Assoc. Dir., Lunchbox
Theatre
Barra, Gemma
Auteur, Compositeur, Interprète, Scénariste,
Écrivaine
Bartle, Jean
Founder & Music Dir., Toronto Children's
Chorus
Beecroft, Norma
Composer, Producer, Arts Administrator,
Broadcaster
Benson, Susan
Theatre Designer
Betteridge, Lois
Silversmith
Birnie-Danzker, Jo-Anne
Dir., Museum Villa Stuck
Blackstone, Mary A.
Fac. of Theatre Arts (on leave), Univ. of Regina
Boake-Wuthrich, Kathy
Illustrator
Bolley, Andrea
Artist
Bouchard, Linda
Composer/Conductor
Bouma-Pyper, Marilyn
Graphic Designer, Creative Svcs, Art Gallery of
Ontario
Bowkun, Heléna
Concert Pianist, Writer & Teacher
Boyd, Liona
Musician, Composer & Classical Guitarist.
Bradley, Elizabeth Anne
Gen. Mgr, Hummingbird Centre for the
Performing Arts
Braggins, Donna
Art. Dir., Canadian Business Media Ltd.
Brodylo, Ellen M.
Pres., Brodylo/Morrow Photography
Bruneau, Laura
Actor, Dreamquest Entertainment Productions
Inc.
Brydone, J. Eleanor
Pres., Rice Brydone Limited
Budd, Ruth
Musician
Burke, Elaine
Owner, River 'B' Down Home Quilts Inc.
Burke, Rebecca
Prof., Dept. of Fine Arts, Mount Allison
Univ.

Bury, Brenda
Portrait Painter
Busby, Ellen
Exec. Dir., Canadian Association of
Professional Dance Organizations
Butala, Sharon Annette
Author
Butler, Edith
Singer-Songwriter
Butler, Sheila M.
Assoc. Prof., Dept. of Visual Arts, Univ. of
Western Ontario
Cadeau, Lally
Actor
Campbell, Anne
Writer & Head of Community Rel'ns, Regina
Public Library
Cardiff, Janet
Artist & Assoc. Prof., Dept. of Art, Univ. of
Lethbridge
Cardinal, Tantoo
Actor
Carr, Mary C.
Arts Mgmt Consultant & Gen. Mgr, Sound-
streams/Chamber Concerts Canada
Carse, Ruth
Founder & Exec. Dir., Alberta Ballet School
Chalifoux, Thelma J.
Chair, Senate of the Métis National Council
Charbonneau, Yvonne
Sr. Design Ptnr & Pres., McGregor Charbon-
neau Inc. Design Consultants
Charlton, Margo
Cultural Consultant, Theatre Dir. & Facilitator.
Owner, Margot Charlton Creative Services
Chilton, Meredith
Curator, The George R. Gardiner Museum of
Ceramic Art
Christakos, Margaret
Ed., *MIX: the magazine of artist-run culture*
Christensen, Ione J.
Photographer and Writer
Clark, Brenda
Illustrator, Brenda Clark Illustrator Inc.
Cohen, Esther Abigail
Pres., Canadian Posters International Inc.
Collins, Marianne
Illustrator, Multimedia Computer Artist.
Connolly, Bea Broda
Producer, Writer, Host, Narrator & Co-
Founder, BC Pictures
Corder, Sharon
Writer, Producer & Actor, Burning Past Pro-
ductions
Corkin, Jane
Owner & Pres., Jane Corkin Gallery Inc.
Corne, Sharron
Artist
Côté, Joanne
Educ. & Museum Consultant

Coucill, Irma Sophia
Portrait Artist

Coulthard, Jean
Composer

Craig, Jane
Gen. Mgr, Kiwanis Music Festival of Greater Toronto

Cronenberg, Denise
Costume Designer

Crozier, Lorna
Assoc. Prof., Dept. of Writing, Univ. of Victoria

Cumming, Marion M.
Heritage Artist, Canadian Scenes

Curry, Gwen J.
Visual Artist

Dahlstrom, Helen

Dale, Jennifer
Actor

Daoust, Sylvia
Sculpteure

Davies, Rita
Exec. Dir., Toronto Arts Council

Dean, Diana
Artist, Diana Dean Studio of Fine Art

Dewar, Susan E.
Edit. Cartoonist, *The Ottawa Sun*

Donaldson, Lesleh
Actor

Donato, Maria Helen
Exec. Dir., International Native Arts Festival

Dorning, Maggie
Artist, Writer & Multimedia Producer, Cybernetic Circus

Doruyter, Renee
Singer, Columnist and Copy-Ed., *The Province*

Down, Jane L.
Conservation Scientist, Canadian Conservation Institute

Doyle, Judith
Instructor, Ontario Coll. of Art

Duff, Ann MacIntosh
Watercolour Artist & Printmaker

Duncan, Arlene
Actor, Singer & Songwriter

Dunsmore, Rosemary
Actor, Dir. & Teacher

Durr, Pat
Artist

Fairhead, Patricia
Painter

Falk, Gathie
Artist

Fernandes, Teresa
Art Dir., Visual Enterprise

Finamore, Brenda
Graphic Designer, Brenda Finamore Design

Fitch, Catherine
Actor

Forrester, Maureen
Contralto, Teacher, Consultant

Fournel, Jocelyne
Art Director, *L'actualité*

Francis, Dorothy Delores
Artist

Freiman, Ruth
Owner & Dir., Robertson Galleries

Fulford-Spiers, Patricia
Sculptor

Gage, Frances Marie
Sculptor

Gallaway, Marguerite

Gardiner, Helen
Chair, The George R. Gardiner Museum of Ceramic Art

Garfield, Louise
Choreographer, Writer, Performer & Prod., Triptych Media Inc.

Garnett, Gale
Actor, Writer & Dir.

Gaynor, Kimberley
Arts Administrator

Geddes, Carol
Film/Video Prod. & Writer

Geneau, Rachelle M.
Independent Curator & Visual Arts Consultant

Gersovitz, Sarah Valerie
Artist & Playwright

Gillson, Malca
Filmmaker, Gloucester Films Ltd.

Glasco, Kimberly
Principal Dancer, The National Ballet of Canada

Glass, Joanna McClelland
Playwright & Novelist.

Godard, Mira M.
Pres., Mira Godard Gallery Inc.

Goldblatt, Rose
Pianist & Univ. Prof. (retired)

Goodwin, Betty
Artist

Goold, Susan R.
Artist, Petals

Graham, Kathleen Margaret
Painter

Green, Janet-Laine
Actor, Dir.

Gregory, Cristen
Professional Musician, Soprano

Griffin, Lynne
Actor

Griffin, Nonnie
Actress

Griffiths, Linda
Actor, Writer

Gurney, Janice
Artist

Haar, Sandra
Co-ordinating Ed., *Fireweed: A feminist quarterly of writing, politics, art & culture*

Haig, Susan E.
Music Dir., Windsor Symphony
Hall, Pam
Visual artist, author, filmmaker &designer
Hamilton, Patricia
Actor
Hammond, Susan
Producer & Pres., Classical Kids
Harnoy, Ofra
Cellist
Hart, Evelyn
Dancer
Harwood, Vanesa
Dancer, Choreographer, Actor, Teacher.
Hawthorn, Pamela
Lecturer, Theatre Dept., Univ. of British
Columbia
Hendeles, Ydessa
Pres., Ydessa Hendeles Art Foundation
Henderson, Judith
Pres., Air Tango
Henry, Martha
Actor & Dir.
Hérivel, Antoinette
Artist & Educator
Hetherington, Linda
Artist
Hewgill, Jody
Illustrator, Jody Hewgill Illustrations
Hill, Andrea
Prod. Mgr, *Canadian Lawyer*
Hill, Kathleen Louisa
Writer
Hodgson, Marjorie Jane
Artist
Hoffmann, Susannah
Actor
Hofstetter, Mary E.
Gen. Mgr, Stratford Festival
Hogan, Susan
Actor
Holbrook, Elizabeth
Sculptor, Medallist & Designer
Hould, Claudette
Prof. of Art Hist., Université du Québec à
Montréal
Howard, (Helen) Barbara
Artist
Hurlbut, Spring
Artist
Hushion, Nancy
Pres., N.L. Hushion and Associates
Isaak, Leona
Owner, Spirit of the West Photo Ventures
Jackson, Sarah Jeanette
Artist
Jacobi, Nancy
Owner & Pres., The Japanese Paper Place
Johnson, Brooke
Actor, Writer, Visual Artist

Johnston, Lynn
Cartoonist & Creator, *For Better or Worse*
Johnstone, Louise
Art Consultant
Jones, Bernadette
Artistic Dir., Theatreworks Productions
Joy, Jean Grahame
Medical Artist & Prof. Emeritus, Fac. of
Medicine, Univ. of Toronto
Kain, Karen
Principal Dancer, The National Ballet of
Canada
Kemp, Linda Patricia Frayne
Artist & Owner, The Watercolour Garden
Kennedy, Arlene M.
Dir., McIntosh Gallery
Keywan, Alicia
Prod. Designer
Kidd, Elizabeth M.E.
Museum & Curatorial Consultant
King, Charmion
Actress
King-Leslie, Deardra
Dir., Studio D
Kish, Ely
Artist, Ely Kish Studio
Klunder, Barbara
Artist
Kooluris Dobbs, Linda Kia
Artist
Korper, Olga
Dir. & Owner, Olga Korper Gallery
Lacava, Lucie
Design Consultant, Lucie Lacava Publication
Design Inc.
LaCroix, Dana
Singer & Songwriter.
LaCroix, Lisa
Actor, Prod. & Multi-Media Artist
LaCroix, Naomi Patricia
Pres., The Brant Group
Lake, Suzy M.
Artist. Assoc. Prof., Fine Art Dept., Univ. of
Guelph
Lambermont, Jeannette
Dir.
Lamon, Jeanne
Music Dir., Tafelmusik
Lamy, Martine
Principal Dancer, The National Ballet of
Canada
Langevin, Suzanne
Photographer, Suzanne Langevin
Photographe
Latini, Sandra
Art Dir., *Toronto Life* Magazine
Lauber, Anne
Composer, Teacher
Lauzon, Jani
Musician, Actress & Puppeteer

Lecavalier, Louise
Principal Dancer, La La La Human Steps
Legge, Elizabeth M.
Univ. Art Curator & Asst. Prof., Fine Art
Dept., Univ. of Toronto
Leidl, Judith J.
Fine Artist-Printmaker, Judith Leidl Fine
Art
Lemieux, Julie
Actor
Lesser, Gloria
Freelance Interior Designer
Levy, Cathy
Prod., Levy Productions
Lightstone, Marilyn
Actor
Lill, Wendy
Playwright & Film Writer
Lindsay, Doreen
Artist, Photographer & Curator
Lipman, Nicola
Actor
Lochan, Katharine
Sr. Curator, Prints & Drawings, Art Gallery of
Ontario
Loughheed, M. Claire
Pres., Charis Enterprises/Partners in Learning
Lovering, Mary Jane
Principal Landscape Architect, Vertechs Design,
Inc.
Lowenthal, Myra
Visual Artist
Lucas, Helen
Artist
Ludlam, Mary Anne
Interior Designer & Visual Artist, Designs by
Mary Anne
Luther, Alice Hamilton
Assoc. Prof., Dept. of Dramatic Arts, Univ. of
Lethbridge
Luz, Virginia
Artist
Lynch, Kate
Actor & Teacher.
MacAlpine Foshay, Susan
Exhibitions Curator, Art Gallery of Nova
Scotia
Macaulay, Catherine
Artist
MacDonald, Lorna
Assoc. Prof. & Head of Voice Studies, Fac. of
Music, Univ. of Toronto
MacPhee, Medrie
Artist
Magwood, Kathleen
Past Pres., Rug Hooking Guild Nova Scotia
Mamnguqsualuk, Victoria
Artist, Baker Lake Fine Arts
Manning, Jo
Artist

Maraden, Marti
Theatre Dir. & Actor
Marcuse, Judith Rose
Artistic Dir., Judith Marcuse Dance Company
Markowsky, Martha A.
Artist
Marshall, Roz
Artist & Art Educator
Martin, Jane
Artist
Mastin, Catherine M.
Sr. Curator of Art, Glenbow Museum
Matis, Barbra
Production, Set & Costume Designer
Matte Packham, Mimi
Painter
Matthes, Mia
Photographer & Ptnr, Mia et Klaus
McCallum, Susan
Art Dir.
McCarthy, Doris
Painter
McCarthy, Sheila
Actor
McCready, Madge Evelyn
Vocalist, Choral Conductor
McKenna, Seana
Actor
McKennitt, Loreena
Singer, Songwriter, Composer & Recording
Artist
McLachlan, Sarah
Singer-Songwriter, Recording Artist & Visual
Artist
Michaud, Monique
Retired Cultural Agency Exec.
Miller, Sherry
Actor
Milne, Rose Eleanor
Sculptor
Minard, Kathryn Christine
Principal & Pres., Contemporary Fine Art
Services Inc.
Moore, Dorothea
Actor
Moore, Linda
Artistic Dir., Neptune Theatre
Moore, Shelia
Actor
Morley, Patricia
Prof. Emeritus, Dept. of English, Concordia
Univ.
Morosoli, Joëlle
Sculptor, Writer & Editor
Morrow, Joanne
Dir., Arts Div., The Canada Council
Mortil, Janne
Actress
Murray, Joan
Dir., The Robert McLaughlin Gallery

Murray-Weber, Kay
Painter & Printmaker
Muzzi, Michèle
Actor & Teacher
Nash, Terre
Nashfilm Inc.
Nellis, Zonda
Pres., Zonda Nellis Design Inc.
Ness, Kim G.
Dir. & Curator, McMaster Museum of Art
Newton-White, Muriel Elizabeth
Painter & Writer
Nunn, Mary Margaret
Artist
Nutaraluk Aulatujut, Elizabeth
Sculptor
Odjig, Daphne
Artist
Oliphant, Betty
Founder, The National Ballet School
Oliver, Bobbie
Artist
Oliver, Karen
Exec. Dir., Associated Manitoba Arts Festivals, Inc.
Oughton, Libby
Artist, Writer & Herbalist.
Page, P.K.
Writer & Artist (as P.K. Irwin)
Palmer, Valerie
Artist
Parker, Molly
Actress
Pauli, Lori
Asst. Curator, Photographs Collection, National Gallery of Canada
Pavey, Mary Gunilla
Painter
Peacock, Lucy
Actor
Pelletier, Maryse
Comédienne, Auteure Dramatique & Scénariste
Pennefather, Joan
VP, Thornley Fallis Inc.
Petrie, Doris
Actor
Pinkus, Wilma
Watercolour Artist
Piquet, Rita-Anne
Artist
Pizano, Beatriz
Actor, Writer & Video Artist
Pontbriand, Chantal
Curator, Writer & Consultant
Poole, Nancy
Mgmt & Dev. Consultant
Potts, Nadia
Dir., Dance Program, Ryerson Polytechnic Univ.

Prata, Gabrielle
Opera Singer
Pratt, Mary Frances
Painter & Printmaker
Preston, Valorie
Artist
Priest, Margaret
Prof. of Fine Art, Univ. of Guelph
Pugen, Diane Fern
Visual Artist, Freelance Curator & Fac. Mbr., Ontario Coll. of Art
Raby, Gyllian
Writer, Dir. of Theatre & Univ. Lecturer, Dalhouse Univ.
Radcliffe, Rosemary
Actor, Writer &, Composer
Raeburn Paul, Nancy Anne
Pres., Rollins Raeburn Interior Design Inc.
Reid, Barbara
Illustrator
Reid, Fiona
Actor
Rice, Chick
Artist
Richardson, Marjolane Symington
Women's Art Association of Hamilton
Riske, Barbara
Musician
Rix, Brenda Diane
Supervisor, Print & Drawing Study Centre, Art Gallery of Ontario
Robin, Shula
Poet
Rockett, Beverley
Photographer & Fashion Dir., Beverley Rockett Photography
Ross, Sandi
Actor & Pres., Toronto Branch, ACTRA
Routledge, Marie
Assoc. Curator, Inuit Art, National Gallery of Canada
Rowsell, Sally Ann
Classical Musician, Piano Teacher, Performer, Organizer, Examiner & Clinician
Rubes, Susan Douglas
Actress & Prod.
Rubess, Banuta N.
Writer, Director & Theatre Artist
Rusk, Sue
Artist
Sabiston, Carole
Artist
St. George, Marie Elyse Yates
Artist & Poet
Saint Pierre, Marie
Designer, Marie Saint Pierre Design Inc.
Sasges, Rita Elaine
Owner, Sasges Design Partnership
Sasso, Julia
Asst. Artistic Dir., Dancemakers

Savage, Candace
Writer
Sawatsky, Sarah
Actor
Scheier, Libby
Writer
Schelle, Susan
Sculptor
Schiller, Ruth Boswell
Music Specialist
Schwartz, Judith
Dir. & Curator, Hart House, Univ. of
Toronto
Scott, Cynthia
Film Dir., National Film Board of Canada
Scott, Donna M.
Chair, The Canada Council
Seatle, Dixie
Actor
Semple, Goldie
Actor
Service, Patricia Olive
Artist
Shaffer, Beverly
Film Dir. & Prod., Documentary Studio,
National Film Board of Canada
Shanoff, Nancy
Pres., Nancy Shanoff and Associates Ltd.
Shepherd, Elizabeth
Actor & Dir.
Shepherd, Helen Parsons
Painter
Silverman, Leslee
Artistic Dir., Manitoba Theatre for Young
People
Simard-Laflamme, Carole
Artiste et Muséologue
Sky, Deanna
Artist & Owner, Min's Indian Craft
Sloot, Rosemary Alida Johanna
Artist
Smith, Frances K.
Curator Emeritus, Agnes Etherington Art
Centre
Smits, Sonja
Actor
Solowan, Barbara
Art Dir., Berlin Studio Inc.
Soly, Geneviève
Directrice artistique et générale, Les Idées
heureuses
Sorensen, Linda
Actor
Sparling, Mary
Cultural Exec.
Stapley, Diane
Actor/Dir./Prod.
Stark, Ethel
Conductor, Violinist & Musical Dir. Founder,
Montreal Women's Symphony Orchestra

Strakowski, Patricia Elizabeth
Visual Artist
Tahedl, Ernestine
Artist
Tasseor Tutsweetok, Lucy
Stone Carver
Telfer, Nancy
Pres., Nancy Telfer Music Inc.
Tennant, Veronica
Exec. Prod. & Writer, TV Arts &
Entertainment, Canadian Broadcasting
Corporation
Thomson, Shirley Lavinia
Dir., National Gallery of Canada
Thors, Sigrid-Ann
Gen. Mgr, Saskatoon Symphony Society
Toews, Heather
Asst. Prof., Fac. of Music, Wilfrid Laurier
Univ.
Tovell, Rosemarie
Curator of Cdn Prints & Drawing, National
Gallery of Canada
Tremblay, Kay
Actor
Trotter, Kate
Actor, Dir. & Speech Consultant
Tryon, Valerie
Concert Pianist & Artist in Residence, Dept. of
Music, McMaster Univ.
Tulving, Ruth
Painter & Printmaker
Vacratsis, Maria
Actor
Van Alstyne, Thelma
Artist
Vartanian, Sona
Fondatrice et directrice, L'Académie de Ballet
Sonia Vartanian (S.V.) Inc.
Vervoort, Patricia
Assoc. Prof., Dept. of Visual Arts, Lakehead
Univ.
Vincent, Bernice
Artist
Waddington, Rona
Co-Artistic Dir., The Me & Her Theatre
Company
Walter, Heather
Ptnr, North By East Productions
Warner, Mary Jane
Assoc. Prof., Dept. of Dance, York Univ.
Watson, Alberta
Actor
Watson Henderson, Ruth
Composer
Whiten, Colette
Artist
Whitlock, Christine J.
Pres. & Publisher, Women Who Excel
Whitney, Susan G.
Dir. & Past Pres., Susan Whitney Gallery

Wight, Darlene
Assoc. Curator of Inuit Art, Winnipeg Art Gallery

Wildman, Sally
Painter

Wieland, Joyce
Artist & Filmmaker

Williams, Darlene J.
Past Pres., Dance Manitoba Inc.

Williams, Deidre Ann
Images Alberta

Williamson, Janice
Assoc. Prof., Dept. of English, Univ. of Alberta

Wilson, Budge Marjorie
Writer

Woolnough, Hilda Mary
Artist

Woon, Wendy
Dir. of Educ., Museum of Contemporary Art

Wyatt, Rachel
Author & Playwright

Yamada, Ruth
Hon. Pres., Sumi-e Artists of Canada

Yarlow, Loretta
Dir. & Curator, Art Gallery of York Univ.

Yarymowich, Anne
Exec. Chef, Art Gallery of Ontario

Young, Patricia Rose
Poet & Educator

Zann, Lenore
Actor, Singer & Prod.

ACTIVISM & ASSOCIATIONS

Labour. Associations formed around causes, interests, social or professional activities. Includes elected officials and hired administrators. Related organizations, government agencies and officials.

Abells, Susan
Exec. Dir., Alberta Craft Council

Adams, Patricia
Exec. Dir., Probe International

Adey, Elizabeth
Exec. Dir., Association of Registered Nurses of Newfoundland

Adey, Isobel Marion Moffat
Founder, The International Club of Ottawa

Allan, Elyse M.
CEO, The Board of Trade of Metropolitan Toronto

Anawak, Caroline
Pres., Kivalliq Consulting Management & Training Services Ltd.

Anderson, Doris H.
Chancellor, Univ. of Prince Edward Island.

Andrew, Judith
Dir., Prov. Policy, Canadian Federation of Independent Business

Andrews, Ann
Exec. Dir., Canadian Anaesthetists' Society

Archibald, Isabel
Past Pres., Women's Institutes of Nova Scotia

Arsenault, Francine H.
Pres., International Centre for the Advancement of Community-Based Rehabilitation

Arsenault, Shiela
Sec. to Bd. of Dir.'s, Registered Practical Nurses Association of Ontario

Barlow, Maude
Chair, The Council of Canadians

Barnhill, Joan Elizabeth Meadows
Publicity & Promo. Mgr, Block Parent Program of Canada Inc.

Baxter, Moyra
Consultant, Baxter, Phillips & Associates

Bedford, Hazel
Past Pres., Sleep/Wake Disorders Canada

Bell, Lesley
CEO, Ontario Nurses' Association

Beltzner, Eileen
Exec. Dir. (currently on sabbatical), PASS-CAN

Bennett, Alison
Pres., Federation of Medical Women of Canada

Bigras, Sylvie
Dir. Gen., Volleyball Canada

Birdsell, Judith
Pres., Canadian Cancer Society

Bismilla, Vicki H.
Pres., Scarborough Women's Centre

Blake, Laura Denise
Transgender Activist

Blankinship, Jennie
Pres., Indian Homemakers' Association of British Columbia

Blaszczyk, Yvonne
Pres., Hum. Res. Professional Association of Ontario

Boehm, Beverley
Exec. Dir., Saskatchewan Voice of People with Disabilities

Boyd, Mary
Exec. Dir., Central Alberta Women's Emergency Shelter

Braak, Geraldine
Nat'l Pres. & CEO, Canadian Council of the Blind

Brown, Betty
Pres., New Brunswick Farm Women's Organization

Brown, Joanne C.
Exec. Dir., Insurance Brokers Association of Canada

Brown, Ruth Louise
Past Pres., National Council of Women of Canada

Brown, Stephanie
Owner, Stephanie Brown Jewellery

Buchner, Barbara
Virologist (retired) & Chair, Blood Svcs, Canadian Red Cross
Bujalski, Wanda
Pres., Polish Teachers' Association in Canada
Cadbury, Barbara
Family Planning Advocate
Cairns, Penny A.
Exec. Dir. & Registrar, Alberta Association of Architects
Campbell, Barbara
Exec. Dir., Multicultural Association of Nova Scotia
Campbell, Daphne
Guidance Counsellor & Past Pres., Prince Edward Island Guidance and Counselling Association
Canty, Shirley
Exec. Dir., Manitoba Motor Dealers Association
Carle Dagenais, Manon
Dir. gén., Société québécoise de l'autisme
Carpenter, Lynn
Exec. Asst., The Toronto Sun Publishing Company/Sheena's Place
Carr, Shirley G.E.
Labour Activist
Chernecki, Vera
Pres., Manitoba Nurses' Union
Chisholm, Sharon
Exec. Dir., Canadian Housing and Renewal Association
Chislett, Anne
Playwright
Chyczij, Alexandra
Exec. Dir., The Advocates' Society
Cimicata, Carmi
Exec. Dir. & Founder, BACCHUS Canada
Coghill, Joy
Freelance Actor, Dir. & Theatre Consultant; Artistic Dir., Western Gold Theatre Co.
Cohen, Judith R.
Pres., Canadian Society for Traditional Music/Société Canadienne pour les Traditions Musicales
Cohen, Marjorie Griffin
Prof., Pol. Sci. & Chair, Women's Studies, Simon Fraser Univ.
Coombs, Diane
Pres., Laubach Literacy Ontario
Cooper, Barbara J.
Exec. Dir., New Brunswick Choral Federation
Cooper, Barbara J.
Owner/Founder, Publications Plus
Corbeil, Johanne
Pres., Le Centre de Recherches d'antécédents Socio-Biologiques du Québec
Coyle, Mary J.
Exec. Dir., The Calmeadow Foundation

Craighead, Joy
Assoc. Dir., Quality Mgmt, Coll. of Physicians and Surgeons of Ontario
Crépin, Denise
Nat'l Exec Dir., Epilepsy Canada
Crosbie, C. Patricia
Exec. Dir., National Advertising Benevolent Society
Curtis, Kathleen
Pres., Yukon Association for Community Living
Dahl, Marilyn O.
Exec. Dir., Western Institute for the Deaf and Hard of Hearing
Dane, Nazla L.
Ret. Assoc. Exec.
Darcy, Judy
Nat'l Pres., Canadian Union of Public Employees
Dassinger, Janet
Dir. of Training Programs & Policies & Asst. to the Cdn Dir., Nat'l Training Fund, United Food and Commercial Workers International Union
Davis, Julie Diane
Sec.-Treas., Ontario Federation of Labour
de Gruchy, Eileen
Exec. Sec., Graphic Communications International Union
de Villiers, Priscilla
Pres., CAVEAT
Dedi, Barbara
Pres., Saskatchewan Association on Human Rights
Delage, Niquette
Exec. Dir., Advertising Standards Council
Delaney, Janet
Pres. & Gen. Mgr., Better Business Bureau of Western Ontario
Demers, Michèle
VP, Professional Institute of the Public Service of Canada
Demeule, Lynne C.
Supervisor, Life Enrichment Program, Saskatchewan Abilities Council
Dempsey, Gaylene
Exec. Dir., Manitoba Audio Recording Industry Association
Denham, Elizabeth
Archives Advisor, Archives Society of Alberta
DeRubeis, Maria
Pres., Bd. of Dir., Bulimia Anorexia Nervosa Association
Desroches, Fabienne
Pres., Association pour l'Éducation Interculturelle du Québec
Desrosiers, Gyslaine
Pres., Ordre des infirmières et infirmiers du Québec

Devanik Butterfield, Maureen
Exec. Ed., Prairie Books Now
Dewhurst, Margaret
Dick, Diana
Exec. Dir. & CEO, Manitoba Association of
Registered Nurses
Dickson, Jean
Chrm, Award Committee, Stephen Leacock
Associates
Doty, Irene
Past Nat'l Pres., Air Cadet League of Canada
Douglas, Michelle
Pres., Foundation for Equal Families
Dow, Patti
Exec. Dir., Basketball Nova Scotia
Doyle-MacBain, Lisa Bridget
Exec. Dir., Federation of Prince Edward Island
Municipalities
Drew, Fay
Pres., Neurofibromatosis Society of Ontario
Driedger, Myrna
Exec. Dir., Child Find Manitoba
Drover, Mary
Exec. Dir., Saskatchewan Writers Guild
Dudek, Dorothy
Exec. Dir., Manitoba Child Care Association
Inc.
Dumont, Daphne E.
Ptnr, Macnutt & Dumont
Dupuy, Diane
Pres. & Founder, Famous People Players
Dvorsky, Margaret Ann
Pres., Slovak Canadian National Council
Dyson, Rose Anne
Chair, Canadians Concerned About Violence
in Entertainment
Earle-Lambert, Beth
Pres., Innkeepers' Guild of Nova Scotia
Enser, Maureen Bronwyn
Exec. Dir., Urban Development Institute
Fenton, Patricia
Exec. Dir., Adoption Resource Centre,
Adoption Council of Ontario
Fisher, Valda
Pres., Spina Bifida and Hydrocephalus
Association of New Brunswick
Flaherty, Martha
Pres., Pauktuutit Inuit Women's Association
Forgay, Margery Grace Elaine
Past Pres., Canadian Dental Hygienists
Association
Forsythe, Janice T.
Exec. Dir., Canadian Council on Smoking and
Health
Friendly, Martha
Coordinator, Childcare Resource & Research
Unit, Centre for Urban and Community
Studies, Univ. of Toronto
Frith, Irene
Past Pres., Galiano Ratepayers Association

Frost-Rogers, Vivien
Creative Spirituality Consultant
Fry, Margaret
Program Officer, Saskatchewan Cultural
Exchange Society
Gallagher-LeBlanc, Karen
N.B. Dir., Canadian Congress for Learning
Opportunities for Women
Garcea, Laurie
Exec. Dir., Learning Disabilities Association of
Saskatchewan
Gardiner, Susan
Dir., Residential Programs, Wood's Homes
Gillis, Patricia M.
Dir., Volunteer Svcs Dept., B.C.'s Children's
Hospital
Glass, Susan Jane
Volunteer
Godsoe, Dale Sullivan
World YMCA Executive Committee
Goldblatt, Michaele-Sue
Former Exec. Dir., Child and Family Adoption
Services Society of British Columbia
Goldin Rosenberg, Dorothy
Global Educ. Consultant, Women for a Just
and Healthy Planet, Women's Health & the
Environment, The Women's Network on
Health and the Environment
Gordon, Elizabeth
Career Counsellor, Cypress Hills Regional
Coll.
Gosbee, Rebecca
Exec. Dir. & Registrar, Association of Nurses
of Prince Edward Island
Gossen, Olinda
Pres., International Women's Association of
Prince Edward Island
Gott, Carol
Exec. Dir., South East Grey Community
Outreach
Greene, Sandra
Pres., First Nations Women's Group
Grono, Marie
Mgr, Saskatchewan Forestry Association
Guy, Georgia
Exec. Dir., Ont. Council, Girl Guides of
Canada
Hall, Sally A.
Volunteer Consumer Advocate & Spokesman
Hallatt, Phyllis
Pres., Child Find Saskatchewan Inc.
Halliwell, Janet
Pres., JEH Associates Inc.
Hammond, Marie
Feminist & Peace Activist.
Harlan, Catherine
Family Support Worker, The Family
Centre
Harvey, Anne
COO, British Columbia Nurses Union

Harvey, Janice
Freelance Writer, Educator & Environmental Activist

Hawkeye, Patricia
Dir. of Fin. & Admin., Girl Guides of Canada

Hinton, Louisette
Int'l Rep. & Chair, Women's Advisory Committee, United Food and Commercial Workers International Union

Hochu, Carol
Pres., Confectionery Manufacturers Association of Canada

Hodgson, Marianne
Exec. Dir., Saskatchewan Registered Nurses' Association

Hogarth, Marlene
Immediate Past Pres., Ontario Progressive Conservative Association of Women

Holyk, Marcelene
Pres., Women's International League For Peace and Freedom

Hopkins, Barbara
Pres., Autism Society of Newfoundland & Labrador

Hopkins, Elaine
Pres., Ontario Federation of Independent Schools

Hopper, Carol
Exec. Dir., National Ski Industries Association

Horsey, Jean S.
Nat'l Pres., The English-Speaking Union of Canada

Hoshizaki, Freda Stefania
Founder, Hoshizaki House

Hunter, Beatrice E.
Past Nat'l Pres., Nursing Sisters Association of Canada.

Hurley, Audrey June
Pres., Laubach Literacy Council of Newfoundland and Labrador

Husband, Vicky
Conservation Chair, Sierra Club of British Columbia

Hutchings, Carol
Exec. Dir., Elizabeth Fry Society of Edmonton

Ings, Joanne
Exec. Dir., P.E.I. Transition House Association

Ivey, Beryl
VP, The Richard Ivey Foundation

Jackson, Margaret
Pres., Toronto and Area Council of Women

Jacobi, Joan
Exec. Dir., Vernon Women's Transition House

Jardine, Cherelle
Pres., Pacific Songwriters' Association

Jay, Shirley
Exec. Dir., Prince Edward Island Home and School Federation

Jefferson, Christine
Chair, Health Professionals Regulatory Advisory Council

Johnson, Dorothy Charlotte
Pres., Federated Women's Institutes of Canada

Jordan, Colleen E.
Sec.-Treas., Canadian Union of Public Employees

Junor, Judy
Pres., Saskatchewan Union of Nurses

Kamateros, Melpa
Exec. Dir., Le Bouclier d'Athena/The Shield of Athena

Keith, Mildred J.
Pres. Elect, Federated Women's Institutes of Canada

Kelly, Patricia
Breast Cancer Activist & Pres., PISCES

Kert, Faye
Past Pres. & Chair, Awards Committee, Canadian Nautical Research Society

Kirk, Bernice
Pres., B.C. Div., Canadian Union of Public Employees

Kislowicz, Linda
Exec. Dir., Jewish Family Services of the Baron de Hirsch

Kitson, Eleanor

Knight, Florence
Pres., Alta. Branch, Canadian Grandparents' Rights Association

Kobelsky, Janice
Exec. Dir., Society of Management Accountants of Alberta

Konnelly, Rhona
Founder & Dir., The Alexandra WSA International

Kosowan, Lynda
Exec. Dir., Scarborough Women's Centre

Kravtsov, Natasha
Pres., Manitoba Dental Hygienists Association

Krowitz, Penny
Exec. Dir., Jewish Women International of Canada

Lachapelle, Lise
Pres. & CEO, Canadian Pulp and Paper Association

Lambrecht, Helga
Pres., Lambrecht Publications

Lande, Mildred Queene Bronfman
Pres., Jewish Community Foundation of Greater Montreal

Landolt, Gwendolyn C.
Nat'l VP, REAL Women of Canada

Lane, Elizabeth A.
Treas., British Columbia Arts in Education Council

Laurin, Marice C.
Nat'l Pres., Advocacy Group for the Environmentally Sensitive

Lemieux, Diane
Prés., Conseil du statut de la femme
Leonard, Christine
Exec. Dir., John Howard Society of Alberta
Long, Barbara A.
Past Pres., Saskatchewan Dental Hygienists'
Association
Lord, Shirley
Community Organizer & Activist
Lucier, Mary Kaye
Clinical Dir., Bulimia Anorexia Nervosa
Association
Lukkien (Van't Hof), Dorothy A.
Past. Pres., Saskatchewan Business Teachers'
Association.
Lychowyd, Sandra
Reg'l Dir., N.W. Ont. Reg., The Kidney
Foundation of Canada
MacCulloch, Carol
Pres., Construction Association of Nova Scotia
Macdonald, Janice
Exec. Dir., British Columbia Dietitians' and
Nutritionists' Association
Macdonald, Melanie
Exec. Dir., CUSO
MacDonald, Trudy
Exec. Dir., Junior Achievement of Cape Breton
MacKenzie, Marilyn
Consultant, Harassment & Discrimination in
the Workplace, MacKenzie & Associate
Consulting
Maes, Sister Yvonne
Coord. of Programs for Batterers & Sex
Offenders, Labrador Legal Services
Magnan, Nicole
Exec. Dir., Que. Div., Canadian Cancer Society
Manzer, Yvonne
Admin. Coord., Elizabeth Fry Society of
Mainland Nova Scotia
Marcotte, Arlette
Exec. Dir., Ordre Professionnel des diététistes
du Québec
Marr, Helen
Pres., International Council of Jewish Women
Marsden, Shirley A.
Volunteer
Marshall, Geraldine
Pres., World Schizophrenia Fellowship
Martens, Jean
Pres., British Columbia Amateur Softball
Association
Matheson, Margaret
Matthiessen, Beverley D.
Exec. Dir., Alberta Committee of Citizens with
Disabilities
Matusicky, Carol
Exec. Dir., British Columbia Council for the
Family
May, Elizabeth
Exec. Dir., Sierra Club of Canada

McCann-Beranger, Judith
Exec. Dir., Alzheimer Prince Edward Island
McClure, Laurie
Pres., Ontario Association for Volunteer
Administration
McFarlane, Betty
Pres., Saskatchewan Archaeological Society
McKenna, Suzanne
Exec. Dir., New Brunswick Association of
Social Workers
McKinnon, Sherry L.
Exec. Dir., Sask. Div., The Arthritis Society
McKnight, Sandra
Chair of the Bd., Nova House Women's Shelter
McLennan, Norma
Reg. Dir., Saskatchewan Abilities Council
McMechan, Sylvia Margaret
Exec. Dir., The Network: Interaction for
Conflict Resolution
McMullan-Baron, Sharon
Past Pres., Alberta Library Trustees Association
McPhedran, Marilou
Lawyer & Consultant
McPherson, Debra
VP, National Federation of Nurses Unions
Meister, Joan
Melanson, Rosella
Dir. of Operations & Comm., New Brunswick
Advisory Council of the Status of Women
Meronowich, Florence
Pres., Laubach Literacy Canada, Alberta
Association
Messenger, Margaret
Past Pres. & Sec.-Treas., Archelaus Smith
Historical Society
Milligan, Dianne
Exec. Dir., Dance Nova Scotia
Mills, Claire
Exec. Dir., Alberta Long Term Care Association
Mock, Karen R.
Nat'l Dir., League for Human Rights of B'nai
Brith Canada
Modlich, Regula
Planning Consultant
Moffat, Jeanne
Exec. Dir., Greenpeace Canada
Moir, Nicole Trudel
Exec. Dir., Quebec Federation of Senior
Citizens
Montagnes, Carol
Exec. Dir., Ontario Native Council on Justice
Moore, Cynthia
VP, Canadian Society for Education through
Art
Morey, Tracy
Comm. Officer, Canadian Union of Public
Employees
Morin, Lyne
Mbr. of the Bd. of Dir., Professional Institute of
the Public Service of Canada

Morton, Kathleen
Pres., Bethany Historical Society
Moulton, Mary Elspeth Catherine
Exec. Dir., Neptune Theatre Foundation
Mumford, Cheryl A.
Asst. to the Dir., Comm., United Food and
Commercial Workers International Union
Nash, Raylene
Mgr, Wild Blueberry Producers Association of
Nova Scotia
Neil, Dolores
Past Pres., Canadian Home and School And
Parent-Teacher Federation
Neiman, Joan B.
Newcombe, Hanna
Dir., Peace Research Institute
Nickel, Dianne
Exec. Dir., Accessible Housing Society
Northcote, Ann L.
Past Pres., World YWCA
Northcote, Ann L.
Past Pres., YWCA of Canada.
Nother, Joanne
Coord., Centre for Equity & Hum. Rights,
Cambrian Coll. of Applied Arts and
Technology
Oh, Jane
Canadian Youth Program Coord., The
International Children's Institute
O'Rourke, Danielle J.
Pres., Tea Council of Canada
O'Shannacery, Karen
Exec. Dir., Lookout Emergency Aid Society
Osted, Annette
Exec. Dir., Registered Psychiatric Nurses'
Association of Manitoba
Paget, Gail
Exec. Administrator, Alberta Funeral Service
Association
Paikin, Marnie
Volunteer
Patterson, Linda
Chair, New Brunswick Block Parent
Association Inc.
Pierre, Marlene
Pres. & CEO, Ontario Native Women's
Association
Playdon, Kathy Carol
Pres., Canadian Finnsheep Breeders Association
Poirier, Nicole
Dir., Société d'Alzheimer de la Mauricie
Porteous, Tracy
Consultant, British Columbia Association of
Specialized Victim Assistance Counsellors
Programs
Praeg, Irene
Pres., Parent Finders New Brunswick
Pratt, Patrice
Dir., Contract & Resource Svcs, B.C. Govern-
ment and Service Employees' Union

Purcell, Shelagh
Pres., Ontario Lupus Association
Radchuk, Leona
Mgr, Ukrainian Fraternal Society of
Canada
Rauter, Rose Marie
Pres., Ontario Forest Industries Association
Rehner, Maria
Pres., Canadian Industrial Transportation
League
Reid, Jill
Exec. Dir., Dance Saskatchewan Inc.
Reynolds, Barbara
Exec. Dir., Centre for Legislative Exchange
Richardson, Sheila
Exec. Dir., Ontario Good Roads Association
Richler, Diane
Exec. VP, Canadian Association for
Community Living
Ritchie, Marguerite Elizabeth
Pres., Human Rights Institute of Canada
Robitaille, Evelyne
Pres., Organization of Canadian Symphony
Musicians
Roeland, Rita L.
Exec. Dir., Manitoba Safety Council
Rosenfield, Ruth
Pres., Montreal Teachers Association
Ross, Lou
Exec. Dir., S.O.S. Society of Sexual Abuse
Survivors
Ross, Marsha
Chief Commissioner, Girl Guides of Canada/
Guides du Canada
Roth, Katherine
Past Pres., Women's Economic Forum
Rowe, Ebonnie
Co-Founder & Dir., Each One Teach One
Mentor Program
Rowe, Penelope M.
Exec. Dir., Community Services Council,
Newfoundland and Labrador
Rust, Helene
Dir., Clinical & Support Svcs, The Capital Care
Group Inc.
Rutherford, Sally
Exec. Dir., Canadian Federation of Agriculture
St. Croix, Bernadette
Pres., Newfoundland Association for
Community Living
Salamoun-Dunne, Marie
Past Pres., Amyotrophic Lateral Sclerosis
Society of Prince Edward Island
Sands, Cara
Dir. & Pres., Friends of the Dolphins Inc.
Sanger, Penelope
Exec. Committee, Canadian Friends of Burma
Sansom, Brenda Jean
Chair, New Brunswick Advisory Council on
the Status of Women

Scott, Mary M.
Pres., Child Find P.E.I. Inc.

Scott, Suzie
Exec. Dir., Univ. of Toronto Faculty Association

Séguin, Yvonne Donna Marie
Dir., Groupe d'aide et d'information sur le harcèlement sexuel au travail

Sfeir, Marsha
Educator & Trainer, Education Wife Assault

Shadd, Dolores
Women's Advisor for Ont., National Farmers Union

Shaw, Kim
Dir., Prairie Reg. & Sec., Nursing Group Exec., Professional Institute of the Public Service of Canada

Shaw, Maureen C.
Pres. & CEO, Industrial Accident Prevention Association

Shenouda, Hannah-Mary
Pres., Saskatchewan Women's Liberal Commission

Sidimus, Joysanne
Exec. Dir., Dancer Transition Resource Centre

Silliphant, Lorraine
Exec. Dir., New Brunswick Association for Community Living

Simand, Harriet
Founder, D.E.S. Action Canada

Simand, Shirley
Pres., D.E.S. Action Canada

Singh, Monica Khhem K.
Pres., Provincial Council of Women of Manitoba

Skeir-Armstrong, Odessa
Gen. Treas., British Methodist Episcopal Church Conference of Canada

Skene, Jennie
Pres., Fédération des Infirmières et Infirmiers du Québec

Smith, Deborah L.
Int'l Rep., United Food and Commercial Workers International

Snee, Betty-Ann
Past Pres. & Exec. Dir., Pro-family Legal Defence, Alberta Federation of Women United for Families

Sokolyk, Oksana T.
Pres., World Federation of Ukrainian Women's Organizations

Solvason-Wiebe, Ishbel
Exec. Dir., Elizabeth Fry Society of Ottawa

Stanley, Ruth L.
Volunteer

Stuart, Barbara
CEO, Ontario Pharmacists' Association

Sturrock, Ann
Dir. & Chair, B.C. Research Institute for Child and Family Health

Summers, Marlies
Ont. Dir., Opticians' Association of Canada

Tanner, Susan Gwen
Environment & Social Policy Consultant, Mediator & Humourist.

Tarn, E. Jane
Exec. Dir., The Kindness Club

Taylor, Marion
Owner, Leatherwood Ventures

Tengum, Phyllis Zybl Ruth (Wilson)
Gen. Mgr, Inventors Association of Canada

Thomas, Diana
Past Pres., Society for the Study of Architecture in Canada

Todd, Rosalie
Exec. Dir. & Legal Cnsl, Consumers' Association of Canada

Todd-Morgan, Rhonda
Founder, Investigator & Exec. Dir., Missing Children Society of Canada

Topalovich, Maria
CEO, Academy of Canadian Cinema and Television

Toupin, Lynne
Exec. Dir., National Anti-Poverty Organization

Vanstone, Joan E.
Nat'l Dir., Parent Finders of Canada

Venhola, Mariellen (Elizabeth)
Crisis Counsellor and Legal Worker, People in Transition (Alliston), Inc.

Villeneuve, Claudette
Prés., Réseau québécois des groupes écologistes

Vingilis-Jaremko, Larissa
Founder & Pres., Canadian Association for Girls in Science

Vinish, Mary T.
Volunteer; retired teacher

Vinkenvleugel, Maria
Pres., Ontario Weightlifting Association

Walters, Traci
Nat'l Dir., Canadian Association of Independent Living Centres

Ward, Debra
Pres., Tourism Industry Association of Canada

Warszawski, Danuta
Pres., The Polish Alliance of Canada

Watson, Mireille Florence Eveline
VP, Ind. Rel'ns & Training, Canadian Film and Television Production Association

Watt, Virginia
Treas. & Archivist, Canadian Guild of Crafts Quebec

Weir, Sharon Rose
Pres., Alta. Chapter, Amyotrophic Lateral Sclerosis Society

Westcott, Joan
Exec. Dir., Federation of Women Teachers' Associations of Ontario

White, Marjorie (Cantryn)
Exec. Dir., Allied Indian and Métis Society

Whitfield, Winifred
National Council of Women of Canada
Williams, Bronwen Katharine
Pres., Action Group Against Harassment and Discrimination in the Workplace
Williams, Cheryl
Exec. Dir., Architectural Institute of British Columbia
Wilson, Norma
Exec. Dir., Outdoor Recreation Council of British Columbia
Wilton, Roberta
Pres., Canadian Securities Institute
Winters, Heather Anne
Exec. Dir., Insurance Brokers' Association of Nova Scotia
Wish, Judy
Dir., Gov't Rel'ns, Canadian Petroleum Products Institute
Wood, Diane L.
Sec.-Treas., British Columbia Government and Service Employees Union
Woodcock, Kathleen
Pres., Confederation of Ontario Univ. Staff Associations
Worsfold, Nancy
Exec. Dir., Canadian Council for Refugees
Wright, Helen
Exec. Tech. Dir., Alberta Rugby Football Union
Yates, Barbara H.
Pres., Women's Association of the Mining Industry of Canada
Young, Catherine
Chairmother, The Friends of Breastfeeding Society

AGRICULTURE
Farming and related industries. Fisheries. Related organizations, government agencies and officials.

Apple, Heather
Ed., Past Pres. & Exec. Dir., Heritage Seed Program
Boxall, Linda
Pres., Sunshine International Inc.
Brown, Alice J.
Sec.-Treas., Brownhill Farms Ltd.
DuPont, Bonnie
Dir., Hum. Res. & Admin., Alberta Wheat Pool
Fraser, Joanna
Research Scientist, Agriculture & Agri-Food Canada Research Centre
Fulford, Mary Eileen
Pres., Fulford Fundy Fish Farm
Guilford, Celia
Co-owner, Guilford's Organic Seed and Feed
Jones, Sonia
CEO, Peninsula Farm Ltd.

McLean, Ellen
Dairy Farmer & Volunteer
Schroedter, Linda
Past President, Manitoba Sheep Association
Wheeler, Evelyn E.
Dairy Cattle Nutrition Specialist, Ontario Ministry of Agriculture Food and Rural Affairs

ARTS AND LETTERS
Written arts. Drama, poetry, prose. History. Arts History. Museums, especially historical museums. Languages and linguistics. Translation. Commentators and educators. Related organizations, government agencies and officials.

Abron Drache, Sharon
Writer
Ainley, Marianne Gosztonyi
Prof. & Chair, Women's Studies Programs, Univ. of Northern British Columbia
Angus, Margaret Sharp
Historical Consultant, Author & Lecturer
Banks, Catherine Ann
Playwright
Barclay, Byrna Robin
Pres., Saskatchewan Writers Guild
Bauer, Nancy
Writer
Bayer, Fern
Independent Curator
Benoit, Claude
Exec. Dir., McCord Museum of Canadian History
Borson, Roo
Writer
Bourne, Lesley-Anne
Lecturer, Univ. of Prince Edward Island
Bowering, Marilyn
Writer
Boyanoski, Christine
Art Historian
Brandt, Di
Writer & Research Fellow in English, Univ. of Alberta
Brossard, Nicole
Poet and Novelist
Byers, Mary Gill
Author & Volunteer
Campbell, Sabine
Mgr & Assoc. Ed., *Studies in Canadian Literature*
Campbell, Wanda
Author & Ed.; Prof.. Univ. of Windsor
Cederstrom, Lorelei Sajeck
Prof. of English, Brandon Univ.
Collard, Elizabeth
Historian
Cook, Eleanor
Prof., Dept. of English, Univ. of Toronto

Cook, Lyn
Children's Author
Coxon, Helen
Conservator, Royal Ontario Museum
Crean, Susan
Writer
Creary, Barbara
Pub. & Foreign Rights Dir., Les éditions de la courte échelle inc.
Cruise, Margery
Pres., Cruise & Associates
Dagg, Anne Innis
Academic Adv., Univ. of Waterloo
Dalton, Mary
Assoc. Prof., Dept. of Eng., Memorial Univ. of Newfoundland
Dempsey, Catherine
Exec. Dir., Newfoundland Historic Parks Association
Dompierre, Louise M.T.
Assoc. Dir. & Chief Curator, The Power Plant Art Gallery
Donegan, Rosemary
Independent curator, writer, educator, Ontario Coll. of Art
Downie, Mary Alice
Freelance Writer & Ed.
Doyle-Rodrigue, Jocelyne
Pres. & Founder, Excelcom Translex
Ellerbeck, Karen Marie
Consultant & Appraiser to museums & insur. companies
Elton, Heather
Freelance Ed. & Writer
Finnigan, Joan
Writer
Fischman, Sheila
Literary Translator
Fowler, Marian
Writer
Fraser, Sylvia L.
Author
Gagnon-Pratte, France
Pres. & Chrm, Council of Monuments and Sites for Quebec
Gay, Marie-Louise
Author & Illustrator
Giguère, Diane
Writer
Givner, Joan
Prof. of English (retired), Univ. of Regina
Gom, Leona
Writer
Gordon, Alison
Crime Writer
Govier, Katherine
Writer
Grattan, Patricia
Exec. Dir., Art Gallery of Newfoundland and Labrador

Gray, Charlotte
Writer, Ed. & Pol. Columnist
Gray, Viviane
Mgr, Indian Art Centre
Griggs, Terry
Writer
Grosskurth, Phyllis M.
Prof. Emeritus, New Coll., Univ. of Toronto
Gryski, Camilla
Writer
Guttman, Naomi
Asst. Prof. of English, Hamilton Coll.
Halvorson, Marilyn
Writer
Hamara, Olga Marian
Pres., Ont. Branch, Ukrainian Museum of Canada
Harvor, Elisabeth
Writer
Hinz, Evelyn J.
Distinguished Prof. of English, Univ. of Manitoba
Holmes, Nancy
Writer & English Prof., Okanagan University-Coll.
Hope, Louise
Owner/Operator, Genealogical Research Services
Hospital, Janette Turner
Writer
Hughes, Monica
Writer
Hundal, Nancy
Author
Hunter, Maureen
Playwright
Jacobs-Moens, Maria
Co-Publisher, Wolsak and Wynn Publishers Ltd.
Johnston, Carol Jean
Johnston-Aldworth, Tracey
Pres., Traces Screen Printing Ltd.
Keller, Betty
Writer
Kelly, Gemey
Dir. & Curator, Owens Art Gallery
Kennell, Elizabeth H.
Dir. of Dev., McCord Museum of Canadian History
Kerslake, Susan
Writer
Keyserlink, Michaela
Sr. Conservator, Textiles, Canadian Conservation Institute
Klassen, Sarah
Poet
Knowles, Valerie
Writer
Kogawa, Joy
Writer

Krause, Judith
Writer, Ed. & Teacher
Kulyk Keefer, Janice
Prof., Dept. of English, Univ. of Guelph
Lambert, Phyllis
Chrm of the Bd. of Trustees, Centre Canadien d'Architecture/Canadian Centre for Architecture
Larue, Monique
Écrivaine
Lawrence, Karen
Author
Lohans, Alison
Freelance Writer
Loos, Lynn
Past Pres., Alberta Chapter of the Registry of Interpreters for the Deaf
Lottridge, Celia Barker
Writer
Mackay, Claire
Writer
Macpherson, Jay
Retired Prof.
Maillet, Andrée
Author & Journalist
Mainprize, Daphne E.H.
Dir./Curator, Stephen Leacock Museum/ Archive
McFarlane, Sheryl
Writer
McFee, Oonah
Writer
McNabb, Debra
Acting Dir., Nova Scotia Museum of Industry
Melvin, Ann Patricia
Pres., Rothery Entertainments
Morel, Sylvie
Dir., Exhibitions & Programs, Canadian Museum of Civilization
Parry, Caroline Balderston
Author, Performer & Teacher
Peck, Mary Biggar
Research Historian & Writer
Philips, Elizabeth
Writer & Ed., *Grain* Magazine
Pierson, Ruth
Prof., Ontario Institute for Studies in Education
Racine, Yolande
Curator, Musée d'art contemporain de Montréal
Rapoport, Janis
Author, Playwright, Ed.
Reddyhoff, Gillian
Curator, The Market Gallery of the City of Toronto Archives
Robertson, Patricia Mary
Registrar, Univ. of King's Coll.
Rogers, Linda
Poet, Children's Writer & Novelist

Rubinsky, Holley
Writer & Master of the Usui System of Reiki Healing
Rusch, Barbara
Ephemerist. Founder & Pres., The Ephemera Society of Canada
Russell, Hilary
Staff Historian, National Historic Sites Directorate, Parks Canada
Saddlemyer, Ann (Eleanor)
Prof. & Master Emeritus, Massey Coll., Univ. of Toronto
Sager, Hanni
Shields, Carol
Chancellor, Univ. of Winnipeg
Siberry, Jane
Founder, Sheeba Records
Silver, Florence
VP, Exhibits & Mktg, Royal Ontario Museum
Simonds, Merilyn
Writer
Singer, Sharon
Pres., First Canadian Artists Inc.
Smith-Sauvé, Deborah
Coord. of Dev., McCord Museum of Canadian History
Sparling, Sharon
Writer
Spencer, Elizabeth
Writer
Swan, Susan
Novelist & Prof., Dept. of Humanities, York Univ.
Swart, Paula
Curator of Asian Studies, Vancouver Museum
Sweatman, Margaret
Writer
Szumigalski, Anne
Poet, Playwright
Thomas, Audrey G.
Writer
Thomas, Clara McCandless
Prof. Emeritus & Cdn Studies Research Fellow, York Univ.
Tippett, Maria
Sr. Research Fellow/Writer & Curator, Cambridge Univ.
Turney Zagwyn, Deborah
Author & Illustrator
Urquhart, Jane
Author
Valente Gorjup, Francesca
Dir., Istituto Italiano di Cultura
Visser, Margaret
Writer
Wehrstein, Karen
Writer, Hearthstone Independent Enterprises
Whitehead, Ruth Holmes
Asst. Curator in Hist. & Staff Ethnologist, The Nova Scotia Museum

Yalden, Janice
Chair, Dept of Linguistics & Applied Language, Carleton Univ.

BUSINESS/INDUSTRY/FINANCE
Big business, small business, entrepreneurs, industry and finance. Consultants. Management in business and other fields. Commentators and educators. Related organizations, government agencies and officials.

Adamec, Lila
Pres., Lamar Communications
Addie, Barbara
Exec. VP, AGF Nafta Ltd.
Adrian, Kathryn
Pres., Elia Fashions Ltd.
Aitken, Mary S.
Pres., Renaissance Securities Inc.
Albright, Penny S.
VP, Gov't & Health Econ., Janssen-Ortho Inc.
Alford, Christine
Gen. Mgr, Systems Integration, IBM Canada Ltd.
Allan, Robyn
Pres., CYF Consulting Ltd.
Allan-Davis, Lori
Gen. Mgr, AS/400 Div., IBM Canada Ltd.
Allen, Esther Ruth
Capt. (Relief) & Mate, Minor Vessel, British Columbia Ferry Corporation
Anderson, Isabel B.
Pres. & CEO, AAL Infoserve
Anderson, Janice P.
Strategy & Bus. Dev. VP
Andrews, Jan
Ptnr, Andrews-Cayley Enterprises
Andrews, Maxine
Proj. Mgr, Residential Construction, V.V. De Marco Properties Limited
Ang, Roxanne S.L.
Nat'l Pres., Canadian Institutes of Travel Counsellors
Angus, Elisabeth
Exec. VP, Angus TeleManagement Group Inc.
Antler, Susan P.
Pres., EnviroBusiness Directions
Applin, Anne-Marie H.
Pres., Applin Marketing & Comm.
Ardiel, June Victoria
Pres., June Ardiel Ltd.
Armstrong, Pam Bovey
Pres., Millenitex Inc.
Armstrong, Ruth R.
Pres., Vision Management Services
Armstrong, Susan
VP & CFO, The Dominion of Canada General Insurance Company

Bailey, Madonna
VP, Foreign Exchange & Money Mkt, Laurentian Bank of Canada
Bairstow, Frances
Arbitrator/Mediator
Bales, Laura
Pres. & CEO, Alberta Re-Tech Ltd.
Ball, Tracey
VP, Fin. & Chief Acctnt, Canadian Western Bank
Bardos, Julia
VP, Hum. Res., B.C. Ferry Corporation
Barsoski, Diane
VP & Dir., Hum. Res., The Canada Life Assurance Company
Bartlette, Deborah
Founder, Groupskills Seminars
Bata, Sonja
Dir., Bata Limited
Bazarkewich, P. Jane
Sr. VP, CIBC
Beattie, Laurie A.E.
VP, Fin. Reporting & Budgets, The Consumers' Gas Company Ltd.
Beaudoin, Patricia
VP, Hum. Res., Sears Canada Inc.
Beck, Eve
Agent, State Farm Insurance Companies
Beck, Nuala M.
Pres., Nuala Beck & Associates Inc.
Bélanger, Francine
First VP, T.A.L. Investment Counsel Ltd.
Bellan, Susan
Pres. & Gen. Mgr, Frida Craft Stores
Bendaly, Leslie
Pres., Otran Associates Inc.
Bendeth, Marian
Fragrance Specialist, Sixth Scents
Bennet, Laura
Pres. & CEO, Bennet Communications Limited
Bennett, Jalynn H.
Pres., Jalynn H. Bennett and Associates Ltd.
Bentley, Myrna J.
VP, Bus. Dev., Co-operative Trust Company of Canada
Besse, Irene
Pres./Owner, Irene Besse Keyboards Ltd.
Biedermann, Mary Margaret
Pres., MB & Associates Inc.
Bignucolo, Amy Amneris DeMonte
VP, Quality Inn Fallsview
Billes, Martha
Pres., Albikin Management Inc.
Bishop, Janet
Mgr, Cust. Svc. Dev., Centra Gas
Bjornson, Rosella
Captain, Canadian Airlines International Ltd.
Black, Elizabeth M.
Dir., Hum. Res., North American Life Assurance Company

Black, F. Marjorie
Pres., McGinnis Building Block Co. Ltd.

Black, Mary Elizabeth
Pres., Colour Technologies

Blais, Diane
Ptnr & First Ptnr in Comm. for all Attg. & Mgmt Consultiong Firms, Ernst & Young

Blais-Ramsay, Michelle
Pres., Michelle Ramsay & Company Inc.

Blak, Groovella
Owner, Siren

Bland, Ruby M.
Presentation Specialist - Visits, Switching Networks, Nortel Canada Limited

Blatt, Rena
Sr. Consultant, Ministry of Econ. Dev., Trade & Tourism, Gov't of Ontario

Blue, Mary
Sr. VP, Land & Admin., Jordan Petroleum Ltd.

Bodkin, M A.
Chrm, Golden Heron Enterprises

Bonney, Lynda D.
VP, Pension Admin. & Fin., Crown Life Insurance Company

Boot, Sunni
Sr. VP & Exec. Dir., Optimedia Canada

Borghesi, Carol
Asst. VP, Bus. & Corp. Sales, BC Tel

Bosley, Nicole
Exec. Dir., Watercan/Eau Vive

Bottone, Kelly F.
Dir., Planning & Research & Secretariat for Full Svc. Credit Unions, Credit Union Central of Ontario

Bouchard, Micheline
VP, Que. Oper., Hewlett-Packard (Canada) Ltd.

Bourassa, Louise
VP & Chief Acctnt, Laurentian Bank of Canada

Bowles, Lynda
Ptnr, Deloitte & Touche

Boyd, Jasna
VP, Facilities Mgmt, National Trust Company

Bradley, Mary M.
VP, Bus. Affairs, Allegro Films Inc.

Brandow, Judy
Pres., SaniPouch Products Inc.

Braverman, Doreen
Mng Dir. & Sec., J. Braverman Inc.

Brien, Danielle Carle
VP, Mktg, Confectionery, Dry, Culinar Inc.

Brooks, Bonnie
Sr. VP, Mktg, Holt, Renfrew & Co., Limited

Brooks, Patricia J.
Mgr, Nat'l Comm., Deloitte & Touche

Brotchie, Doneta
Sr. VP, Central Prairie Reg., CIBC

Bryant, Carole Y.
Exec. VP, Corp. & Bus. Svcs, Saskatchewan Power Corporation

Burgess, Wendy
VP of Quality, Educ. & Comm., Gandalf Technologies Inc.

Burka, Sylvia May
Fin. Officer & Ptnr, Cancore Building Services Ltd.

Burke, Audrey N.
Dir., Oper. Planning & Control, Toronto Star Newspapers Limited

Burke, Earla
Pres., Moneystrategy Inc.

Burton, Barbara
VP, Hum. Res., EPCOR

Bustard, Patricia R.
VP, Admin., Transamerica Life Insurance Company of Canada

Butt, Catherine
Sr. VP, Info. Svcs, London Life Insurance Company

Byrne, Dorothy
VP, Law & Regulatory Affairs, BC TEL

Cachia, Christine
Mgr, Personal Fin. Svcs, The Toronto-Dominion Bank

Cairns-McVicar, Sue Mora
Pres., 056534 N.B. Inc.

Caldwell, Erin P.
Dir., Comm. & Client Rel'ns, British Columbia Ferry Corporation

Caldwell, Nanci
VP & Gen. Mgr., Computer Systems Organization, Hewlett-Packard (Canada) Ltd.

Cameron, Deborah M.D.
Gen. Mgr., Educ. & Training, IBM Canada Ltd.

Campbell, Mona Louise
Pres., Dover Industries Limited

Cannon, Georgina
Pres., Cannon Associates

Cannon, L. Louise
Sr. VP, Compliance, The Bank of Nova Scotia

Carroll, Esme
Pres. & CEO, Ambrose Carr Linton Carroll Inc.

Castracane, Luba
Pres. & CEO, A ok Road Safety Systems Limited

Caswell, Brenda
VP & Gen. Mgr, Brown Communications Group

Cavan, Susan
Chair & CEO, Accent Entertainment Corporation

Cawker, Ruth
Ruth Cawker Architect

Cecil-Cockwell, Wendy Marion
Chrm & Pres., Brookmoor Enterprises Limited

Cefis, Alberta G.
VP, Personal Credit Svcs, Royal Bank of Canada

Chabot, Diane
Pres., DCM Enterprises
Chan, Shirley
Mgr, Non-Mkt Housing, City of
Vancouver
Chant, Diana
Ptnr, Price Waterhouse
Charnetski, Joanne Louise
Pres., JCI - Global Strategists
Chellas, Merry
Principal, Chellas Communication
Ching, Denise
VP, Portfolio Mgr., Royal Bank Investment
Management Inc.
Chir-Stimpson, Susanne
Pres., Strategic Solutions
Christensen, Rosemary L.
Pres., Somerville House Group of Companies
Cira, Anne A.
Sr. VP, CIBC
Clark, Carolyn J.
VP, Hum. Res., Canadian Pacific Hotels and
Resorts
Clark, Lynne
Ptnr, Deloitte & Touche
Clarke, Shirley
Exec. Dir., Building Owners and Managers
Association, Atlantic
Clayton, Nicola
Dir., Mktg & Research, *Maclean's* Magazine
Cohen, Dian
Pres., Dian Cohen Productions Limited
Collin, Emmanuelle
VP, Comm. & Gov't Affairs, Avenor Inc.
Compton, Jo Ann L.
Pres., Compton Graham International Inc.
Comtois, Céline
Asst. Sec. & Shareholder Rel'ns Dir., Air
Canada
Conlinn, Carollyne B.
VP, Health Care Bus. Dev., VERSA Services
Cook-Bennett, Gail
Exec. VP, Bennecon Limited
Coombs, Ann
Pres., Coombs Consulting Ltd.
Cooney, Jane
Pres., Books for Business
Cooper, Sherry S.
Sr. VP & Chief Econ., Nesbitt Burns Inc.
Corbett, Daphne E.
VP & Chief Auditor, Hongkong Bank of
Canada
Cornish-Kehoe, Margaret
Dir., Scotia McLeod Inc.
Corriveau, Sheila
Sr. Consultant, Benchmark Communications
Côté-O'Hara, Jocelyne
Craig, Susan J.
Pres., The Craig Corporation & Medical
Recruitment Services

Cram, Lynne Muriel
Exec. VP, Windjammer Landing Villa Beach
Resort
Crocker, Susan
Sr. VP, Equities & Derivative Mkts, The
Toronto Stock Exchange
Crosbie, Evelyn
Owner, Excalibur Executive
Cumming, Marie Novak
Ptnr, Cumming and Cumming Wealth
Management
Currie, Karen
VP, Hum. Res. & Environment, Vancouver
City Savings Credit Union
Dale, Maggie N.
Nat'l Mktg Dir., Price Waterhouse
D'Alton, Mary
Mng Dir., Waterloo Inn
Darling, Michèle Suzanne
Exec. VP, CIBC
Dasko, Donna
VP, Environics Research Group Limited
Davies, Laureen
VP, Comm. Svcs, Air BC
Davis, Ann
Ptnr, KPMG
Dawe, Mary E.
Ed. Consultant & Writer
Dawe, Shirley A.
Pres. & Owner, Shirley Dawe Associates Inc.
Delicaet, Anne Margaret
Pres. & CEO, The Kuna Investments Group
Dell'Aquila, Tina
Dir. of Corp. Acctg, Dominion Textile Inc.
Dempsey, Karen
Exec. Dir., Offshore Technologies Association
of Nova Scotia
Denham, Jill
Mng Dir., Origination & Structuring & Deputy
Head of Europe, CIBC Wood Gundy Plc
Denis, Marielle
VP, Admin. Svcs, CFCF 12
d'Entremont, R. Irene
Pres., M.I.T. Electronics Inc. & Women's Up to
Date Shop Inc.
Desreux, Michell
Sr. VP, Oper., Uniglobe Travel (International)
Inc.
Desrochers, Gisèle
Sr. VP, Admin. & Hum. Res., National Bank of
Canada
Deutscher, Maryann
Mgr, Hum. Res., Co-operative Trust Company
of Canada
Di Domenico, Mina
Hum. Res. Systems Consultant, Hum. Res.
System Mgmt, The Toronto-Dominion Bank
Dobson, Wendy K.
Dir., Centre for Int'l Bus. & Prof., Fac. of
Mgmt, Univ. of Toronto

Dorosz, Wanda M.
Pres. & CEO, Quorum Growth Inc.
Dubsky, Fiona J.O.
Sr. Mng, Multinational Sector, Que., Royal
Bank of Canada
Duffy, Shirley
Corp. Sec., Armbro Enterprises Inc.
Dumais, Michèle C.
VP, Fin., *The Gazette*
Dunlop, Mary Jo
VP & COO, Dynacare Managed Health
Services
Durocher, Claudette
VP, Admin., Fin. & Trust Svcs, Desjardins
Trust
Eastman, Barbara C.
Pres. & Dir., Probyn & Company Limited
Edmondson, Sheila M.
Mng Ptnr, HSW Management Associates
Limited
Eeson, Cynthia
Pres., Kids Only Clothing Club Inc.
Egan, M. Joan
Mgr, Bus. Resumption Planning, Royal Bank of
Canada
Elekes, Julie L.
Consultant, Elekes Resource Consultants
Elliott, Mary Anne
Sr. VP, Corp. Svcs, The Mutual Life Assurance
Company of Canada
Fagnan, Isabel
Dir., Process & Bus. Dev. Sales, Air Canada
Fair, Penny M.
Proprietor, Penny M. Fair - Certified General
Accountant
Farrell, Brenda
Pres., Farrell Research Group Ltd.
Farrow, Maureen Anne
Exec. VP & Dir. of Econ. & Equity Strategy,
Loewen, Ondaatje, McCutcheon Limited
Ferguson, Marnie H.
VP, People, Quality & EH&S, Monsanto
Canada Inc.
Ferrante, Angela
Exec. VP & COO, C.D. Howe Institute
Fershko, Jane S.
VP, Cardholder Svcs, Royal Bank of Canada
Filipovic, Dusanka
Chrm of the Bd., Blue-Zone Technologies Inc.
Finley, Diane Dennis
Dir. of Strategic Planning & Dev., Laidlaw
Transit Ltd.
Fiorillo, Frances
VP, Inflight Svc., Canadian Airlines
International Ltd.
FitzGerald, Daphne J.
Pres., Group Insurance Div., Zurich Canada
Fitzgerald, Patricia A.
Prof. of Mgmt, Dept. of Mgmt, Saint Mary's
Univ.

Foster, Sandra
Fin. Advisor, Equion Securities Canada
Limited
Fourmy, Sally J.
Founder, Sally Fourmy & Associates
Fournel, Lise
VP, Info. Tech. & CIO, Air Canada
Frank, Tema
Pres., Frank Communications
Franssen, Margot
Pres. & Ptnr, The Body Shop
Frederickson, Elinore G.
Instructor, Dev. Studies, Yukon Coll.
Fukakusa, Janice
Sr. VP, Fin. Svcs, Multinational Bnkg, Royal
Bank of Canada
Fuller, Heather A.
Real Estate Broker & Owner, Martin &
Meredith Limited
Furlong, Lynne
Hum. Res. & Diversity Mgr, Hewlett-Packard
(Canada) Ltd.
Gajdel, Djanka
Bus. Consultant to the Photographic Industry
Gardiner, Janet C.
Treas., Chester Dawe Limited
Gardner, M. Jane
VP & CFO, Lombard Canada Ltd.
Garland, Kevin J.
Sr. VP, Corp. Real Estate, CIBC Development
Corporation
Garnier, Andrea
Sec.-Treas., Canadian Union of Public
Employees
Garossino, Virginia
Pres. & CEO, Superior Ventures Group Ltd.
Gelhorn, Carolyn
Pres., Carshaw Inc.
Getter, Ruth
Sr. VP & Chief Economist, The Toronto-
Dominion Bank
Giacomazzi, Bruna
Chief Credit Officer, Hongkong Bank of
Canada
Gibb, Patricia
Pres., Infinitum Management Services Inc.
Glover, Karen
Ptnr, Ernst & Young
Godfrey, Ellen
Pres., Softwords Research International, Ltd.
Goodreau, Ida
Mng Dir., Tasman Pulp and Paper Co. Ltd.
Grant, Rhondda Elaine
Corp. Sec. & Assoc. Gen. Cnsl, NOVA
Corporation
Greene, Lucy G.
VP, Corp. Hum. Res., Sun Life Assurance
Company of Canada
Grenier, Kathleen
Dir., Taxation, Dominion Textile Inc.

Grierson, Lela
Reg'l Mgr, Vancouver City Savings Credit Union

Grist, Kari
Dir., Special Proj., Canadian Airlines International Ltd.

Grobety, Marcia
Independent Exec. Sr. Dir., Mary Kay Cosmetics Ltd.

Guillevin Wood, Jeannine
Chrm of the Bd., Guillevin International Inc.

Hackett, Barbara J.
Pres., Stratheden Homes Limited

Haight, Lynn
Chief Acctnt., Manulife Financial

Hainer, Monica
Pres., London Life Reinsurance Company

Hale, Marguerite
Chrm, Morrison Lamothe Inc.

Hall, Patricia
Cont., Saskatchewan Power Corporation

Hamilton, Ingrid
Pres., GAT Productions Inc.

Hamilton, Margot
Urban Planner, Calgary Police Service

Hamilton Lambie, Cathy
VP, Reader Sales & Svc., *The Gazette*

Hanson, Carla
Pres., Owner & Ptnr, Can-Am Medical, Inc.

Hargrave, Diane
Pres., DHPR Communications Inc.

Hatch, Mary S.
VP & Mgr, The Toronto-Dominion Bank

Hatley, Judith
Sr. VP, Sales, Personal Fin. Svcs, Royal Bank of Canada

Hawrishok, Lorraine
VP, I.L.S. Learning Corporation

Heggie, Betty-Ann
Sr. VP, Corp. Rel'ns, Potash Corporation of Saskatchewan Inc.

Henderson, Elfie
Asst. VP, Investor Mktg Svcs, National Trust Company

Henderson, Roxanne
Dir., Hum. Res., Credit Union Central of Ontario

Herzog, Leona M.
Mgr, Residential/Small Commercial Mkts, Centra Gas Manitoba Inc.

Hill, Bonny
Environmental Assessment & Mediation Consultant

Hirji-Nowaczynski, Zabeen
Reg'l Mgr, Central Care Centre, Royal Bank of Canada

Hislop, Barbara R.
Group VP, Costal Oper., Canfor Corporation

Hoff, Rita
Pres. & CEO, First Canada Securities Corporation

Hohol, Linda
Sr. VP, Personal & Commercial Bnkg, Alta. & NWT, CIBC

Holder, Rubi
Bus. Dev. Rep., Co-operative Trust Company of Canada

Holland, Jane C.
Pres., Lewis Carroll Communications Inc.

Holland, Marie
Ptnr, KPMG

Hood, Marilyn
Dir., Public Affairs, Credit Union Central of Ontario

Hore, Marlene
Founding Ptnr, The Ongoing Partnership

Hosier, Ellen
Corp. Sec. & Treas., Finning Ltd.

Howard, Valerie J.
Owner/Manager, Howard Interpersonal Dynamics Inc.

Howell, Doris
Cancer/Palliative Care Consultant

Hrastovec, Denise Mayea
Chair & Ptnr, Collins Barrow

Hughes, Barbara Dorothy
Chair & CEO, Evangeline Trust Company

Hughes Anthony, Nancy
VP, Group & Pension Svcs, Metropolitan Life Insurance Company

Humphreys, Gillian
VP, Canadian Facts

Hyde, Darlene Kruesel
VP, Public Affairs & Road Safety, Insurance Corporation of British Columbia

Iley, Sarah J.E.
Pres. & CEO, The Council for Business and the Arts in Canada

Impey, Patrice
Controller, Hewlett-Packard (Canada) Ltd.

Iordanous, Freda
Freda's Inc.

Ip, Irene
Research Adviser, Research Dept., Bank of Canada

Irving, Bonnie
Ed., *BCBusiness Magazine*

Irwin, Pat M.
Asst. VP, Trust Operations & Admin., National Trust Company

Ivey, Celese G.
Dir., Hum. Res. Mgmt, Global Communications Limited

Jacks, Evelyn
Pres. & Owner, The Jacks Institute

James, Vivianne M.
Pres., Cumberland Communication Concepts

Jamieson, Shelly
Exec. Dir., Ontario Nursing Home Association
Jay, Colleen E.
Mktg Dir., Paper Products, Procter & Gamble Inc.
Jaye, Elisabeth Anne
VP & Dir. of Special Svcs, Creative Research International
Jefferies, Glenna J.
Sr. Prod. Eng., Crestar Energy
Jeffery, Pamela Postian
Principal, Burstyn Jeffery Inc.
Jensen, Maureen C.
Pres., CEO & Dir., Noble Peak Resources Ltd.
Jewett, Anne
Tax Ptnr, Deloitte & Touche
Jin Suen-Carter, Susan
VP, Public & Corp. Affairs, National Trust Company
Jolliffe, Lynn
VP & CFO, White Rose Crafts and Nursery Sales Ltd.
Jones, Faye
VP, Affinity Mkts, Manulife Financial
Jones, Marsha
Pres., MCC Planners Inc.
Jones, Merri L.
V-Chrm & COO, T.A.L. Private Management Ltd.
Kaljuste, Kadi
Sr. VP, OEB International Public Relations/ Public Affairs
Kastner, Kathy
VP, Dir. of Programming, The Parent Channel
Keeping, Lia
VP & Dir. of Sales, Weekender Ladies Wear
Kempston Darkes, Maureen V.
Pres. & Gen. Mgr, General Motors of Canada Limited
Kerr, Krista L.
VP & Mgr, Toronto Office, Kerr Financial Corporation
Kerr, Shelagh D.
VP, Corp. & Environmental Affairs, Coca-Cola Beverages Ltd.
Kerr, Sheryl L.
Pres., Strathfield Consultants Ltd.
Khetrapal, Shoba
VP & Treas., Moore Corporation Limited
King, Jen Genia
Pres., White Saddle Air Services Ltd.
Kinnear, Kathy E.
Pres., Cresford Developments
Kinsley, Marnie
Sr. VP & Chief Auditor, Bank of Montreal
Kinsman, Carolyn Marie
Owner & Pres., Automated Communication Links, Inc.
Klein, Colleen J.
Pres., Chipco Canada Inc.

Koh, Poh-Chan
Exec. VP & CFO, Husky Oil Ltd.
Kolber, Sandra
Dir., Canadian Broadcasting Corporation
Korhonen, June M.
Sec.-Treas. & Office Mgr., Nordex Explosives Ltd.
Koszo, Joan
Asst. VP, Global Compensation, Northern Telecom Limited
Kovacs, Gail
Pres. & CEO, Career Probe Inc.
Kreuk, Mary
VP, Mktg, Peoples Jewellers Corporation
Kuhn, Lynda
Dir. of Corp. & Community Rel'ns, Philip Environmental Inc.
Kulesza, Kristine M.
VP, Merchandising, Peoples Jewellers Corporation
Kwok, Eva Lee
Pres. & CEO, Amara International Investment Corporation
Labarge, Suzanne
Exec. VP, Corp. Treas., Royal Bank of Canada
Lacey, Roberta
Dir., Comm., Avon Canada Inc.
Lacroix, Marie
VP & Area Mgr, Royal Bank of Canada
Lafrance, Carole M.
CEO, Cala Hum. Res. Company Ltd.
Laing, Barbara
VP, Pension Systems, Crown Life Insurance Company
Lalumière, Donna A.
VP & Dir., Retail Dist., Treasury, The Toronto-Dominion Bank
Lambert, Valerie
VP & Treas., B.C. Gas Inc.
Lamont, Mary Susanne
Pres., M.S. Lamont and Associates Limited
Lamontagne, Mary
Corp. Dir. & Assoc. Exec.
Larochelle, Bernadette
Dir. gén., Centre franco-ontarien de ressources pédagogiques
Laviolette, Julie M.
Dir., Pricing & Yield Mgmt, Air Canada
Lawrence, Delores
Pres. & CEO, Nursing & Homemakers Inc.
Lawrence, Minnie
C.A.
Lawson, Jane Elizabeth
Sr. VP & Corp. Sec., Royal Bank of Canada
Lawson, Janet Elizabeth
Sr. VP & Sec., Royal Bank of Canada
Lea, Nattalia
Mgr of Bus. Dev., Eucalyptus International Ltd.
Leahey, Dennice
Sr. VP & Gen. Mgr, Man., Royal Bank of Canada

Leclair, Suzanne Bernard
Pres. & CEO, Transit Truck Bodies Inc.
Lem, Esther
VP, Personal Care, Lever Pond's
Lemay, Patricia
Dir. of Mfg, Culinar Manufacturing
Leroux, Monique
Sr. VP, Fin., Royal Bank of Canada
Lever, Andrina
Pres., Lever Enterprises
Lewis, Judy
Exec. VP, Strategic Objectives Inc.
Lichtman, Shelley
Dir., Group Mktg Dev., The Great-West Life
Assurance Company
Light, Marjatta A.
Nat'l Personal Lines Mgr, Alexander and
Alexander (Reed Stenhouse Ltd.)
Lippert, Anne H.
VP & Area Mgr, Vancouer Downtown &
West, Royal Bank of Canada
Lisson, Kathryn
Ptnr Resp. for Nat'l Fin. Institution Consult-
ing, Price Waterhouse
Loat, Beverlee
VP, Public Affairs, Edmonton Power
Lockert, Barbara L.
Pres. & CEO, Lockert Distributors Ltd.
Lockie, Anne
Sr. VP & Gen. Mgr, Sask., Royal Bank of
Canada
Lougheed, Jeanne
Corp. Dir.
Lowes, Judith E.
VP, Mktg, Co-operators Investment
Counselling Limited
Lowey, Brenda
Ptnr, Deloitte & Touche
Lowry, Cathie
Ptnr, Strive!
Lubinsky, Karen
Dir., Variable Investment Products, Canada
Life Assurance Company
Lundström, Linda
Pres., Linda Lundström Ltd.
Lustig, Terry
Sr. VP, Dev., Goldlist Development
Corporation
Lynch, Jennifer
Pres., PDG Personnel Direction Group
Lyon, Françoise E.
Sr. Consultant, CAI Corporate Affairs
International
Macdonald, Patricia C.
Bus. Exec.
MacIntyre, Pamela J.
VP, Hum. Res., Crown Life Insurance
Company
Mackaay, Carole
Corp. Sec., VIA Rail Canada Inc.

MacKay-Lassonde, Claudette
Pres., Firelight Investments Ltd.
MacKenzie-Nugent, Catherine Ann
Dir. & Fundraiser
Macmillan, Katherine E.
VP, Corp. Mktg, Public Affairs, Bank of
Montreal
MacRae, Martha
VP, Mgmt Reporting & Analysis, National
Trust
Maddocks, Judy
Pres., Personal Insur., Zurich Canada
Magee, Christine
Pres., Sleep Country Canada
Maidment, Karen
VP & CFO, The Mutual Group
Malone, Deborah
Dir. of Fin. Svcs, Saskatoon District Health
Manning, Lynne
VP & Mng Dir. for Canada, Kelly Services
(Canada) Ltd.
Martin, Denny
Pres./Owner, Deni M. Originals
Martin, Nora
Sr. VP, UFL Foods Inc.
Martinson, Jeanne
Ptnr, MARTRAIN Corporate and Personal
Development
Martinuzzi, Bruna
Mgr of Admin. & Hum. Res., CanWest Gas
Supply Inc.
Mascoll, Beverly
Pres., Mascoll Beauty Supply Ltd.
Masini, Beatrice
Dir. of Mktg, Hewlett-Packard
(Canada) Ltd.
Mazur-Melnyk, Mary
Dir., Quality Assurance, Connaught
Laboratories Ltd.
McClare, Sharon
Administrator, Amoco Canada Petroleum
Company Ltd.
McCormick, Roxanne
Ptnr, Fasken Campbell Godfrey
McDonald, Wendy Burdon
Chrm of the Bd. & CEO, BC Bearing
Engineers Limited
McDougall, The Hon. Barbara
McGarry, Diane E.
Chrm, Pres. & CEO, Xerox Canada Inc.
McHarg, Nancy
Dir. of Comm., WIC Western International
Communications Ltd.
McIlroy, Valerie
Sr. VP, Mediacom Inc.
McIntosh, Jacqueline
Dir., Corp. Properties & Facilities, Canadian
Airlines International Ltd.
McKenna, Joanne
Pres., CanWest Global Developments

McLaren, Patricia
VP & Area Mgr, Calgary Central, Royal Bank of Canada

McLaughlin, Kathy
VP & Gen. Mgr, BC, Rogers Cantel Inc.

McLaughlin, Mary
VP, Corp. Comm., Ontario Hydro

McLeod, Catherine
Chrm, Zen International Resources Ltd.

McMaster, Beverly
Pres., We Care Health Services Inc.

Meehan, Denise P.
Pres., Lick's Ice Cream & Burger Shops Inc.

Melanson, Deborah A.
Nat'l Sales Mgr, Retirement Planning Svcs

Meltzer, Susan
Dir., Risk Mgmt & Insur., Bell Canada

Menard, Louise
VP, Corp Affairs, Legal Affairs & Sec., Sodarcan Inc.

Mercer Clarke, Colleen S.L.
Sr. Environmental Mgr, CBCL Limited

Mercier, Eileen A.
Pres., Finvoy Management Inc.

Merrin Best, Patrice E.
VP, Corp. Affairs, Sherritt International Corporation

Mersereau, Marilyn
Dir. of Comm., IBM Canada Ltd.

Meyer, Doris
VP, Fin., CFO & Corp. Sec., Queenstake Resources Ltd.

Mielitz, Sandra J.
VP, Grain & W. Canada, Canadian National

Millichamp, Barbara
VP & Dir., First Marathon Securities Limited

Milway, Katie Smith
Consultant, Bain & Company Canada

Mirabelli, Marilyn
Pres., Excellence in/en Communication

Misener, Adeline
Pres., Job Oriented Training Inc.

Mitchell, Camille
VP, Intercontinental Packers Limited

Mitchell, Carol R.
Sr. VP & Dir., Midland Walwyn Inc.

Mitchell, Gay
Exec. VP, Hum. Res., Royal Bank of Canada

Mitchell, Johanna
Chair of the Bd., Intercontinental Packers Limited

Mitchell, Jone
Dir. of Alumni, Dev., & Public Rel'ns, Univ. of King's Coll.

Mitchell, Margaret T.
Pres., The Thomas-Mitchell Associates Inc.

Mogford, Mary
Ptnr, Mogford Campbell Associates Inc.

Moor, Deborah L.
Dir., Product Planning, Canadian Airlines International Ltd.

Morgan, E. Louise
Chrm of the Bd., Canadian General Investments, Limited

Morgan-Silvester, Sarah A.
Sr. VP, Mktg. & Ombudsperson, Hongkong Bank of Canada

Moulden, H. Julia
Pres., Moulden Communications

Moyer, Janice M.
Pres. & CEO, Applied Communications Canada, Inc.

Murray, Susan A.
Pres., SAMCI

Mychan, Laura J.
Strategic Projects Consultant

Myers Johnson, Nancy
VP, Hum. Res., Data Business Forms

Nakashima, Katrin
Sec. & Sr. Cnsl, Imasco Limited

Nathoo, Tazeem
Sr. VP, Oper., Vancouver City Savings Credit Union

Nault, Heather
VP, Corp. & Regulatory Affairs, Manitoba Telephone System

Nesbitt, Patricia
Dir., Cdn Equities, G.W.L. Investment Management Ltd.

Newman, Elizabeth
Dir. of Mktg., R.C.R. Restaurants

Noel-Bentley, Elaine
Sr. Dir., Total Compensation, Petro-Canada

Noonan, Cathy
VP, Customer Svc., Colgate-Palmolive Canada Inc.

Novick, Catherine
CFO, CIBC Insurance

Nunn, Wendy
Corp. Dir., Organizational Dev., Laidlaw Inc.

O'Brien, Sheila
Sr. VP, Hum. Res., NOVA Corporation

Oda, Beverley J.
Sr. VP, Baton Broadcasting Incorporated

Odam, Pamela
Dir., Hum. Res. Plans & Programs, IBM Canada Ltd.

Oliver, Diane
VP, Mktg., Chanel Inc.

Olney, Miriam
Chair of the Bd., Insurance Corporation of British Columbia

O'Malley, Patricia L.
Ptnr, KMPG

Ondrack, Esther S.
Sr. VP & Sec., Chieftain International Inc.

Orr, Sherry
Pres., Trans-Mutual Truck Lines Ltd.

Oswald, Linda L.
VP, Public Rel'ns & Gov't Affairs, Canada Safeway Ltd.

Pageau-Goyette, Nycol
Pres. & CEO, Pageau Goyette and Associates

Pape, Patricia Lesley
Pres., The Powerpoint Group

Paquin, Madeleine
Pres. & CEO, Logistec Corporation

Parker, Anne
Legal Cnsl & Dir. of Corp. Comm., IPSCO Inc.

Parkinson, E.A.
Exec. VP, Oil Sands Group, Suncor Inc.

Pascall, Bonnie
Mgr, Corp. Comm., Husky Oil Ltd.

Passmore, Janet M.
VP, Group Mktg, The Mutual Life Assurance Company of Canada

Patten, Susan H.
Chrm, A. Harvey & Co. Ltd.

Patten Di Giacomo, Rose
Sr. VP, Corp. Svcs, Bank of Montreal

Pau, Janet
VP & Treas., Canfor Corporation

Paul, Louise
VP, Legal & Sec., Corby Distilleries Ltd.

Peake, Jacqueline
Principal, Corporate Events Management Inc.

Pearl, Debbie
Pres., Private Investors Management Inc.

Pearson, Hilary
Sr. Dir., SECOR

Pepe, Tracy A.
Owner & Operator, Classic Aromatics Ltd.

Petersen Burfield, M. Jane
VP & Dir., Investors Finance Corp. Ltd.

Phénix, Elaine C.
Sr. VP, Equities, The Montreal Exchange

Pigott, Jean Elizabeth Morrison
Chair, Ottawa Congress Centre

Pohl, Tanya
Dir., Medical/Surgical Svcs, Joint Hospital Purchasing Services

Poole, Suzanne
VP & Reg'l Mgr, The Toronto-Dominion Bank

Poudrette, Danielle
Sr. Dir., Product Mgmt, Air Canada

Prevalnig, M. Joan
VP, Agencies, The Great-West Life Assurance Company

Price, Donna
VP, Airports, Air Canada

Provenzano, Diana
Co. Sec., BOC Canada Limited

Radloff, Laurie
Pres., Uniglobe Travel (Western Canada) Inc.

Rae, Barbara
Corp. Dir.

Ramsay, Susan
Pres. & CEO, The Moving Store Franchise Systems, Inc.

Regan, Gail
Pres., Cara Holdings

Rein, Reet
Pres., SABRE Canada

Renault, Suzanne
VP Legal Affairs & Sec., Le Groupe Vidéotron Ltée

Reszel, Rozanne
VP & Sec., Canadian Investor Protection Fund

Rimell, Drude
VP, Corp. Svcs, Alberta Energy Company Ltd.

Robertson, Catherine
Pres., Robertson Rozenhart Inc.

Rohr, Peggy
VP, Bus. Planning, Mackenzie Financial Corporation

Roper, Janice
Tax Ptnr, Deloitte & Touche

Rose, Elizabeth Stikeman
VP, Employee Satisfaction & Environment, Northern Telecom Limited

Rosenberg, Dufflet
Pres., Dufflet Pastries Inc.

Ross, Anita K.
VP, Mgmt Svcs, IBM Latin America

Ross, Shannon
VP, Corp. Affairs, Quartz Mountain Gold Corp.

Rosser, Deborah
VP & Dir. of Advtg Sales, Canadian Business Media Ltd.

Roveto, Connie I.
COO, The Trust Company of Bank of Montreal

Rozsa, Marilyn
VP, Independent Bus & Agric., Bank of Montreal

Ruth, Nancy
Pres., Nancy's Very Own Foundation

Salomon, Carole J.
Pres., Residential Svcs, AT&T Canada Long Distance Services

Salomon, Felicia
Sr. VP & Gen. Cnsl, Lombard Canada Ltd.

Sandwell, Carol
Dir. of Fin. & Admin., Laidlaw Resources

Sargent, Linda
Pres., Linda Sargent Enterprises Inc.

Scott, Karen
Designer, Mktg Dir. & Sec.-Treas., Body Matters Ltd.

Sévigny, Suzanne
Assoc. VP, Hum. Res. & Admin, Que. Div., The Toronto-Dominion Bank

Seward, Shirley B.
CEO, Canadian Labour Market and Productivity Centre

Seymoar, Nola-Kate
Deputy to the Pres., International Institute for Sustainable Development
Sexsmith, Gail
Sr. VP, Customer Svc., B.C. Hydro
Sheehan, Barbara E.
VP, Client Svcs, Cassels Blaikie Investment Management Limited
Sherk, Susan
Sr. Consultant, AGRA Earth & Environmental
Shettler, Read Bonnie
VP, Aboriginal Affairs, Bank of Montreal
Shiff, Helaine
Ptnr, Glina Group
Shnier Moncik, Bonnie
Pres., Gesco Industries Inc.
Sibson, Elaine Sabra
Tax Ptnr, Coopers and Lybrand
Siebert, Evelyn
VP, Compliance, Novopharm Ltd.
Simbul-Lezon, Marita
Exec. VP, Fortune Financial Corporation
Simeone, Marianna
Exec. Dir., The Italian Chamber of Commerce in Canada
Simmie, Monica
Asst. Corp. Sec., Rogers Communications Inc.
Simons, M.Y.C.
Mgmt Consultant
Sims, Elizabeth
Pres. & Gen. Mgr, Chicopee Manufacturing Limited
Simson, Claudine
Asst. VP, Advanced Technologies, Nortel Technology
Sinclair, Helen K.
CEO, Bank Works Trading Inc.
Sivers, Glendene
Sr. VP, Investments, Toronto Mutual Life Insurance Company
Skelton, Ruta
Cdn Comm. Practice Mgr & Principal, Towers Perrin
Slawinski, Wanda
VP & Sec., The Empire Life Insurance Company
Smalley, Katherine
Pres., Allied Corporate Services Inc.
Smart, Joan
V-Chair, Ontario Securities Commission
Smith, C. Linda
Sr. VP, Ptnr & Gen. Mgr, Fleishman-Hillard
Smith, Nancy L.
Treas., Petro-Canada
Snider, Carol
Sr. VP, Personal & Commercial Fin. Svcs, Bank of Montreal
Sombrowski, Ingrid
Co-Founder & Co-Head, Sombrowski Group of Companies

Sonberg, Melissa
Dir., Customer Svc. Comm., Employee Involvement & Training, Air Canada
Squair, Beverly D.
VP, US Equities, G.W.L. Investment Management Ltd.
Stagg, Pamela
Pres., Pamela Stagg Creative Services
Stahmer, Anna Elisabeth
Co-Publisher & Co-Owner, *The Training Technology Monitor*
Stairs, Harriet Hingston Dolan
Sr. VP, Hum. Res. Div., Bank of Montreal
Stait-Gardner, Zane
Sr. VP & Gen. Mgr, Reins. Oper., Manulife Financial
Stanley, Barbara
Pres. & CEO, Canadian Cable Systems Alliance
Stefan, Catherine
COO, O&Y Properties Inc.
Stenzler, Rochelle
Pres. & Gen. Mgr, Pharma Plus Drugmarts Ltd.
Stevenson, Lois
Dir., Entrepreneurship Dev., Atlantic Canada Opportunities Agency
Stevenson, Moira G.
Cont., Mount Allison Univ.
Stewart, Lecia
Pres., West Coast Express
Stoddart-Hansen, Sandra
Pres., The Ballantree Group
Stone, Karen K.
Dir. of Public Rel'ns, IWK-Grace Health Centre for Children, Women & Families
Storks, Pauline J.
V-Chair, Clarington Hydro Electric Commission
Strand, Kirsten K.
Mng Dir./Owner, Famous Events & Destinations
Stratton, Jennifer J.
Dir., Payments & Research, Credit Union Central of Canada
Strelioff, Susan
Sr. VP, Governance, National Trust Company
Strong, Marilyn
Pres., The Strong Communications Group Inc.
Stymiest, Barbara
Sr. VP & CFO, Nesbitt Burns Inc.
Sum, Peggy
VP, Asian Mkts, Bank of Montreal
Swift, Catherine
Pres., Canadian Federation of Independent Business
Sze, Glendy
VP, Citibank Canada
Tagg, Catherine J.
Sr. Mktg Rep., Wawanesa Mutual Insurance Company

Tanaka, Margaret
Pres., Margaret Tanaka Professional Corporation

Tanguay, Lucie
Pres., TKO Marketing Inc.

Tardif, Louise
Investment Advisor & Mgr, Lévesque Beaubien Geoffrion Inc.

Taylor, Carole
V-Chair, Vancouver Port Corporation

Taylor, Carole D.
VP & Dir., Atlantic Div. Mgr, Nesbitt Burns Inc.

Taylor, Catherine
Assoc. VP, Personal Deposits, The Toronto-Dominion Bank

Taylor, Kathleen
Sr. VP, Corp. Planning & Dev., Gen. Cnsl, & Sec., Four Seasons/Regent Hotels and Resorts, Four Seasons Hotels Inc.

Thomas, Carolyn Gertrude
Pres. & Sr. Consultant, C.G.R.T.'s Consulting

Thomas, Carolyn
Sr. Community Rel'ns Officer, British Columbia Lottery Corporation

Thomson, Nancy
Hon. Chrm, Nancy Thomson Investing For Women

Tidd, Fay
Mgr., Gardiner Realty Ltd./Royal LePage Associate Broker

Toal, Anne
VP & Corp. Actuary, London Life Insurance Company

Tory, Martha J.
Ptnr, Ernst & Young

Totta, Johanne M.
Sr. VP, Strategy & Hum. Res., Nesbitt Burns Inc.

Trebuss, A. Susanna
VP & Gen. Mgr, Peerless Home Products

Tremblay, Louise
Sr. VP, Resources, Canadian Broadcasting Corporation

Tremblay, Virve
Dir. of Comm., NCR Canada Ltd.

Trethewey, Sharon
VP, Retail Lending, National Trust

Tuffin, Jacqueline
VP, Personal Fin. Svcs, Toronto Core, Royal Bank of Canada

Unger, Renée
Pres., Intercorp Foods Ltd.

Usheroff , Roz
Pres., Roz Usheroff Consulting Inc.

Uson, Margot
VP, Hum. Res., Novartis Pharma Canada Inc.

Vennat, Manon
Chrm & Mng Dir., Spencer Stuart, Montreal

Verreault, Denise
Pres., Groupe Maritime Verreault Inc.

Verschuren, Annette
Pres., Home Depot Canada

Vokey, Mary Lou
VP, Personal Lines, Wedgwood Insurance Limited

Wakefield, Tayce
VP, Corp. Affairs, General Motors of Canada Limited

Walters, Sheila
VP, Store Planning & Construction, Retail Group, Hudson's Bay Company

Warriner, Faye C.
VP & Cont., Husky Oil Ltd.

Watier, Lise
Pres. & CEO, Lise Watier Cosmétiques Inc.

Watson, Carolyn F.
C.A., Carolyn Watson, Chartered Accountant

Watson, Dorothy E.
Dir. Mbr. Rel'ns & Svc. Quality, Credit Union Central of Ontario

Watson, Karen M.
VP & Cont., ATCO Ltd.

Webber, Debbie
Sr. Exec. Sales Mgr, Weekender Ladies Wear

Webster, Mary Page
Pres., Raventures Inc.

Welland, Freydis J.
Gov't Rel'ns Dir., BC Tel

Western, Sherrin
Bus. Mgr, Home Office, BC Tel

Weston, Hilary M.
Deputy Chrm, Holt, Renfrew & Co., Limited

Whidden, Diana
Sr. VP, Corp. Dev., Zurich Canada

White, Lynda
Mgr, Employment Equity & Diversity, Corp. Hum. Res., Royal Bank of Canada

Wilson, Gale
Strategic Planning & Mktg Consultant

Wilson, Hilda E.
Chrm & CEO, The Hilda Wilson Group

Wilson, Joan M.
VP & Sec., Moore Corporation Limited

Wilson, Laurel Lynne
Dir. of Purchasing, Laidlaw Waste Systems

Wilson, Vera
Realtor, Osborne Realty

Wineberg, Tami
Dir. of Publicity/Promotions, MGM/United Artists Distribution of Canada

Wisser, Arlene
VP & Portfolio Mgr, Cassels Blaikie Investment Management Limited

Witte, Margaret K.
Pres. & CEO, Royal Oak Mines Inc.

Wittmack, Beverly C.
Pres., Humford Management Inc.

Woodman, Catherine J.
Dir., Corp. & Public Affairs, Maritime Life Assurance Company

Woodruff, Janet
Cont., Union Gas Limited
Wright, Anita
Pres., Wright Alternative Advertising
Wright, Elizabeth
Sr. VP, Strategic Planning & Mktg, National Trust
Wright, Nina Kaiden
Pres. & Chrm, Arts and Comm. Counselors
Yale, Janet
Sr. VP, Regulatory, Gov't & Law, AT&T Canada Long Distance Services Company
Yamamoto, Ann Marie
VP, Info. Techologies & Systems Aufit, Loblaw Companies Limited
Yewchin, Caroline
Co-owner/Mgr, Yewchin's Funeral Chapel
Youldon, Darla
VP, Fin. & Admin., John Deere Finance Limited
Zalesky, Rose
Sec.-Treas. & Co-founder, Business Aircraft Corporation Ltd.

♥
CHARITY/NOT FOR PROFIT
Charitable, not-for-profit, or NGO organizations. Arts, educations, medicine or policy related. Elected officials and paid administrators. Volunteer workers. Some associations and their personnel. Related government agencies and officials.

Armstrong, Cathryne Hildriethe
Volunteer
Batty, Michelle
Exec. Dir., Sexual Assault Survivors' Centre Sarnia-Lambton
Bayless, Betty
Pres., Canadian Federation of Univ. Women
Berkhold, Beverly F.
Trustee, Alberta Cancer Foundation
Black, Elizabeth Stewart
Past Pres. & Mbr., Canadian Opera Women's Committee
Blankstein, Marjorie
Volunteer
Bohac-Konrad, Lucie M.
Exec. Dir., Canadian Youth Foundation
Bradshaw, Claudette Arsenault
Exec. Dir., Moncton Headstart
Brown, Fran
V-Chair of the Bd. of Trustees, Bloorview MacMillan Centre
Brown, Janet L.
Volunteer
Brown, Nancy J.
Exec. Dir., Halton Family Services
Burdsall, A. Margaret
Cannell, Lynda
Exec. Dir., Sport Medicine Council of B.C.

Carroll, Irene
Founder & Chair, Photographers & Friends United Against AIDS, Canadian Chapter
Carwell, Judy
Exec. Dir., N. Alta. & The Territories Branch, The Kidney Foundation of Canada
Chambers, Gretta
Chancellor, McGill Univ.
Clark, Eileen
Clements, Mary Louise
Volunteer
Cochrane, Diane
Pres., Sask. Br., The Kidney Foundation of Canada
Cohen, Martha Ruth
Volunteer
Cohon, Susan Silver
Volunteer
Cole, Dianne M.
Pres., Rebekah Assembly of Ontario
Cole, Laura
Nat'l Exec. Dir. & Founder, The Children's Wish Foundation of Canada
Coleman, Anne Marguerite
Colley-Urquhart, Diane
Exec. Dir. & CEO, Alta./N.W.T. Div., Canadian Cancer Society
Comrie, Charlotte
Exec. Dir., Holland Coll. Foundation
Comuzzi, Debbie
Nat'l Exec. Dir., The Sunshine Foundation of Canada
Conway, Susan Lucente
Exec. Dir., Women in Crisis Algoma Inc.
Cooper, Joanne S.
Exec. Dir., Volunteer Centre of Metropolitan Toronto
Cox, Mae
Exec. Dir., Organ Donors Canada
Crabtree, Linda
Writer, Pub., Entrepreneur & Disability Advocate
Croft, Colleen
Consultant
Cunningham, Karen
Pres., Autism Society New Brunswick
Dadson, Anita
Volunteer
Dalton, Marcia
Past Pres., Nat'l Chapter of Canada, IODE
Danzig, Etty
Nat'l Pres., Na'amat Canada Inc.
Davison, Margaret L.
Chrm, Bd. of Dir., Victoria General Hospital Foundation
de Souza, Anna Maria
Pres. & Founder
DeBruyn, Beverley A.
Exec. Dir., Canadian Foundation for the Study of Infant Death

Dewar, Marion
Chair, OXFAM Canada
Dobko, Theresa
Self-employed consultant to charities & foundations
Douglas, Catherine Gay
Literacy Link Niagara
Downe, Valerie
Exec. Dir., P.E.I. Division, Canadian Cancer Society
Driedger, Florence Gay
Social Development Consultant & Lay Pastor, Peace Mennonite Church
Duhamel, Nathalie
Exec. Dir., Elizabeth Fry Society of Quebec
Egan, Deborah
Exec. Dir., CHATS (Community Home Assistance to Seniors)
Elliot, Dawn
Pres., D.S. Elliot & Associates Inc.
Ens, Rosa Freda
Exec. Dir., Vancouver Police & Native Liaison Society
Erb-Campbell, Heather Lynn
Exec. Dir., Heart and Stroke Foundation of N.B.
Farlinger, Esther Ruth
Volunteer/Fundraiser
Feld Carr, Judy
Educator & Community Volunteer
Forsyth, Cecilia
Nat'l Pres., REAL Women of Canada
Foster, Julia Elizabeth
Pres., The Olympic Trust of Canada
Fraser, Joan
Exec. Dir., Heart and Stroke Foundation of Nova Scotia
French, Mary
Owner/Operator, Victoria Manor Heritage House Museum
Garber, Eileen Epstein
Pres., Canadian Association of Neighbourhood Services
Garratt, Audrey
Chrm of the Bd., Variety Club of Southern Alberta
Geller, Elisabeth
Dir. of Dev., Jewish Home for the Aged Foundation
Goldbloom, Ruth M.
Pres., Pier 21 Society
Golden, Anne
Pres., United Way of Greater Toronto
Graff, Elyse
Nat'l Exec. Dir., Canadian Council of Christians and Jews
Grayson, Eunice
Exec. Dir., The Learning Enrichment Foundation
Green, Susan L.
Exec. Officer, Alberta Cancer Foundation

Greer, Jan
Exec. Dir., New Brunswick Committee on Literacy
Groetzinger, Deanna
Nat'l Dir. of Comm., Multiple Sclerosis Society of Canada
Gurevitch, Sheila
Volunteer
Guyda, Patricia
Pres., Canadians for Health Research
Hall, Carol A.
Teacher & Volunteer
Hamilton, Muriel
Pres., Planned Parenthood Alberta
Hancock, Lorna
Exec. Dir., Health Action Network Society
Hanson, Tennys J.M.
Campaign Dir. & VP, Univ. of Toronto Foundation
Harding, Gladys Jane
Pres., Christian Women's Clubs of Canada
Harding, Judy
Co-Founder, Citizens Concerned with Crime Against Children (4C's)
Hayes, Nancy
VP, Organization, UNICEF Canada
Heinrichs, Elfrieda Elizabeth
Volunteer
Henderson, Ann Elizabeth Ludmilla Mary Zamoyska Buchanan
Volunteer
Henderson, Anne
Instructor, Bus. Admin., Northern Alberta Institute of Technology
Herzog, Shira
VP, The Kahanoff Foundation
Hogg, Elspeth
Volunteer
Hollo, Wendy
Exec. Dir., Skills Training and Support Services Association
Holroyd, Diane
Exec. Dir., Sask. Branch, The Kidney Foundation of Canada
Honeyman, Ruth
Exec. Dir., Canadian Pony Club
Hood, Barbara
Exec. Dir., NWT Div., Canadian Mental Health Association
Horner, Pamela
Pres., Vernon Outreach, Osteoporosis Society of British Columbia
Hutchinson, Colleen G.
Pres., The Hutchinson Foundation for Research (Ewings Sarcoma)
Irving, Catherine
Exec. Dir., Coordinating Council on Deafness of Nova Scotia
Jackson, Margaret Rose
Bd. Mbr., Peigan Mentally Challenged Society

Jefferies, Marian
First VP, Bd. of Dir. & Dir., Zone 3, Co-op Atlantic

Jerrard, Raye
Pres., Canadian Cystic Fibrosis Foundation

Johnson, Hermine
Volunteer

Johnson, Peggy
Exec. Dir., Newfoundland and Labrador Lung Association

Johnston, Carol
Volunteer

Jones, Susan
Eco-tourism Trainer & Coord., Walk The Wild Side

Kavanagh, Els
Mbr. of the Bd., CARE Canada

Kelly, Sheila
Exec. Dir., Saskatchewan Sports Hall of Fame and Museum Inc.

Kennedy, Carole
Founder, Curl for Cancer

Kepper, Shirley
Prof. Exec. Dir., UNICEF British Columbia

Kinsella, Sister Elizabeth A.
Co-Founder & Exec. Dir., Centre Youville Centre Ottawa-Carleton Inc.

Kitchen, E. Ruth

Koniuck-Petzold, Margaret
VP, Fundraising, UNICEF Canada

Kowaliczko, Béatrice
Consultant

Krupa, Mary
Exec. Dir., Canadian Foundation for the Love of Children

Kussner, Sheila
Founding Chrm, Hope and Cope

Lachance, Gabrielle
Consultant (Int'l Dev.)

Lang, Jessie
Volunteer

Larbi, Madonna O.
Exec. Dir., MATCH International Centre

Leonard, Mary
Chair, Bd. of Gov., Scarborough General Hospital

Levine, Renee
Chairperson, Aplastic Anemia Association of Canada

Lie-Nielsen, Anne
Exec. Dir., Prince Edward Island Council of the Disabled

Macaulay, Linda D.
Dev. Coord., Alberta Children's Hospital Foundation

MacEachern, Antje
Exec. Dir., Creative Child Care

MacInnis, Janet G.
Volunteer

MacTavish, Helen
Pres., New Brunswick Association of Healthcare Auxiliaries

Mascioli-Mansell, Josephina Lea
Int'l Chrm & CEO, YES! International

McDonald, Dorothy Zolf
Bd. of Dir., Shaw Communications Inc.

McDonnell, Mary Catharine
Past Pres., The Kidney Foundation of Canada

McGibbon, Hon. Pauline
Former Lt. Gov., Prov. of Ontario

McInnes, Jennie E.
Volunteer

McIntosh, Rosemary
Chair of the Bd., The Hugh Macmillan Children's Foundation

McKenna, Sister Mary Olga
Prof. Emeritus, Mount Saint Vincent Univ.

McKercher, Peggy
Chancellor, Univ. of Saskatchewan

McLeod, Lorna
Nat'l Treas., The Kidney Foundation of Canada

McMurray, Elaine
Exec. Dir., Parent Support Association

Mercier, Michelle
Exec. Dir., Que. Branch, The Kidney Foundation of Canada

Mickelson, Rhona
Founder & Exec. Dir., Star Tracks Performing Arts Centre for the Disabled

Mills, Josephine
Exec. Dir., Down Syndrome Research Foundation

Misner, Judy
Founder & Pres., Psoriasis Society of Canada

Morrison, Cathleen
Exec. Dir., Canadian Cystic Fibrosis Foundation

Morse, Elizabeth
Mbr., Support Svcs Committee, Amyotrophic Lateral Sclerosis Society of Canada

Nagel, Linda J.
Pres. & CEO, Canadian Advertising Foundation

Newton, Carolyn
Dir. of Dev., Calgary Philharmonic Orchestra

Oliver, Carol R.
Pres. & CEO, Community Foundation of Greater Toronto

Opheim, Eloise
Nat'l Exec. Dir., PRIDE Canada Inc.

Parks, Bev
Exec. Dir., Terra Association

Patten, Monica
Exec. Dir., Community Foundations of Canada

Pawlick, Linda
Owner/Operator, Purrfectly Cats

Peacock, H. Ingrid Perry
Pres., Women's Coll. Hospital Foundation
Peers, Marilyn R.
Social Worker
Perri, Cathy
Nat'l Pres., Kids First Parent Association of Canada
Pickard, Audrey
Volunteer
Poirier, Leigh A.
Exec. Dir., Canadian Toy Testing Council
Popil, Irene
Admin. Sec., British Columbia Association of Health Care Auxiliaries
Pryde, Rosemary
Exec. Dir., Voice for Hearing Impaired Children
Randall, Joan R.
Volunteer
Reddy, Dianne
Pres., Learning Disabilities Association of Newfoundland and Labrador
Reid, Margot
Volunteer
Rhind, Katharine Elizabeth
Mbr., Bd. of Reproductions Association, Royal Ontario Museum
Rioux, Marcia Hampton
Exec. Dir., The Roeher Institute
Rosenfeldt, Sharon
Pres., Victims of Violence Canadian Centre for Missing Children
Rothenburger, Janice
Community Pastoral Care Worker, Church on the Street (Yonge Street Mission)
Sadlier, Rosemary
Pres., Bd. of Dir., Ontario Black History Society
Scace, Susan M.
Schacherl, Eva
Sr. Comm. Officer, Canadian Museum of Civilization/Canadian War Museum
Schlifer, Anne
Volunteer
Sharpe, Marjorie
Pres., Sharpe & Associates
Shatsky, Lily Frankel
Exec. Dir., Jewish Support Services for the Elderly
Shaw, M. Ann
VP, Canadian Figure Skating Association
Sherman, Caren Harriet
Dir. & Past Pres., Leukemia Research Fund of Canada
Ship, Leona
Exec. Dir., E. Ont. Branch, The Kidney Foundation of Canada
Simand-Seidman, Carol
Dir., Donor Rel'ns, Mount Sinai Hospital Foundation

Sims, Deborah
Pres. & CEO, A World of Dreams Foundation
Soave, Luciana
Gen. Dir., Québec Multi-Ethnic Association for the Integration of Handicapped People
Spencer, Sally
Exec. Dir., Youth Assisting Youth
Sprachman, Carol
Nat'l Dir., Canadian Federation of Friends of Museums
Strugnell, Arlene
Exec. Dir., Federated Women's Institutes of Canada
Sugarman, Rebecca
Exec. Dir., Opportunity for Advancement
Sumarah, Jacqueline
Past Pres., The Nova Scotia Council for the Family
Thibodeau-DeGuire, Michèle
Pres. & CEO, Centraide of Greater Montreal
Thomas, Marjorie J.
Exec. Dir., Saskatchewan Genealogical Society
Thomsen, Penny
Exec. Dir., Ont. Div., Canadian Cancer Society
Thorsrud, Lorraine
Volunteer & Assoc. Exec.
Tory, Elizabeth E.
Volunteer
Vander Voet, Susan McCrae
Consultant, METRAC, Metro Action Committee on Public Violence Against Women and Children
Viau, Sister Huguette
Coord., Collaboration Sante Internationale (C.S.I.)
Walmsley, Norma E.
Mbr., Bd. of Dir. & Exec. Committeee, International Centre for Human Rights and Democratic Development
Westergaard, Lissi
Grants Advisor, Girl Guides of Canada
Weston, Glenys
Past Pres., S. Alta. Branch & Nat'l Sec., The Kidney Foundation of Canada
White, Julie
CEO, The Trillium Foundation
Whyte, Letha
Volunteer
Wightman, Faye
Pres., British Columbia's Children's Hospital Foundation
Wiley, Judith
Pres., Canadian Society of Association Executives
Will, Clara
Exec. Dir., Adventure Place
Wolstenholme, Tanya E.
Exec. Dir., The Arthritis Society, New Brunswick Division

Woods, Theresa Mary
Public Rel'ns Coord. & Counsellor, Emergency Shelter for Women

Zukerman, Helen
Administrator & Trustee, Zukerman Charitable Foundation

ENTERTAINMENT
Popular music, film, television, and fiction. Related organizations, government agencies and officials.

Bailey, Norma
Pres., Flat City Films Inc.

Baker, Carroll
Singer, Carroll Baker Ent. Inc.

Barris, Kate
Writer & Pres., Kate's Word Inc.

Berman, Brigitte
Dir., Writer & Prod., Bridge Film Productions Inc.

Besen, Joan
Songwriter/Musician/Limerick Laureate, Keyboard player with *Prairie Oyster*

Bey, Salome
Singer, Actress, Composer, Recording Artist

Bienstock, Ric Esther
Prod./Dir., Good Soup Productions Inc.

Bujold, Geneviève
Actor

Christie, Dinah
Pres., Dinah Christie Presents

Clark, Susan
Actor & VP, Georgian Bay Productions, Ltd.

Clark, Terri
Country Music Artist

Cole, Holly
Int'l Singer

Cook, Tracey
Actor

Cynamon, Helena
Principal, Television Prod., Forefront Entertainment Group

Dion, Céline
Singer

Ehm, Erica
Broadcaster, Actor, Songwriter, Erica Ehm Communications Ltd.

Fichman, Ina
VP/Prod., Maximage Productions

Firus, Karen
Artist, Filmmaker, Renegade, Renaissance Woman

Foster, Christine M.
VP & Dir., Fata Morgana Inc.

Frank, Anne
Producer & Script Consultant, Fox-Fire Films

Frank, Ilana
Sr. VP, Prod. & Dev., Norstar Entertainment Inc.

Friendly, Lynda
Exec. VP, Livent Inc.

Gaulthier, Nathalie
Founder & Pres., Gaulthier Artists Inc.

Ghauri, Yasmeen
Super Model, Next Model Management

Grant, Trudy
Pres., Sullivan Entertainment International Inc.

Haskell, Susan
Actor

Hénaut, Suzanne
TFO/TVOntario

Hennessy, Ellen-Ray
Actor

Hope, Kathryn
Prod., KRH Productions

Jamison, Lorraine
Pres., Communications encouleur Jamison inc.

Johnson, Nancy
Pres., Lockwood Films (London) Inc.

Keane, Kerrie
Pres., Wishbone Productions Inc.

Kemp, Lynda G.
Pres., Thunder Thighs Costumes Ltd.

Keogh, Nina
Proprietor, Puppetel

Khaner, Julie
Actor

Kidder, Margot
Actor

King, Karen A.
Prod.

Kuzyk, Mimi
Actor

lang, k.d.
Singer & Composer

Langlois, Lisa
Actor, Singer, Prod. & Writer

Levin, Deborah
Clairvoyant. Owner & Operator, Maiden, Mother, Crone

Lindsay, Gillian
Principal, Forefront Entertainment Group

Macdonald, Ramuna
Pres. & Founder, Doomsday Studios Limited

MacNeil, Rita
Singer & Songwriter

Mangaard, Annette
Filmmaker, Three Blondes Inc.

McCann, Penny
Pres., Independent Film & Video Alliance

Medley, Sue
Recording Artist, Singer, Songwriter

Mitchell, Joni
Singer & Songwriter

Morrisette, Alanis
Singer, Songwriter

Murray, Anne
Singer

Noonan, Donna
Film Designer, Dir.
O'Hara, Catherine
Actor & Comedienne
O'Hara, Maggie Blue
Actor
Peterson, Shelley
Actress
Reno, Ginette
Singer
Robertson, Françoise
Actor
Samuels, Barbara
TV Writer, Prod.
Sandor, Anna
Ziveg Productions Inc.
Shum, Mina
Filmmaker. Sec. & Shareholder, Forty-Seven Films Inc.
Smale, Joanne R.
Pres., Joanne Smale Productions Limited
Steen, Jessica
Actor, Canucklehead Adventures Inc.
Stonehouse, Marilyn
Line Prod. & Production Mgr, Pebblehut Productions
Theaker, Deborah
Writer & Performer
Twain, Shania
Singer
Tyson, Sylvia
Singer & Songwriter
Vaughan, Vanessa
Actor & Artist
Veverka, Jana Mila
Pres., Bohemia Productions Inc.
Wall, Marjorie
Prof. & Chair, Dept. of Consumer Studies, Univ. of Guelph
Winston, Helene
Actor & Writer (retired). Poet
Wright, Michelle
Recording Artist & Songwriter

EDUCATION

Educators and administrators at the primary, secondary, coll. and univ. levels. Private teachers. Vocational training and retraining. Education in the arts. Related organizations, government agencies and officials.

Adam, Dyane
Principal, Glendon Coll.
Adamson, Nancy
Dir. of Equity Svcs, Carleton Univ.
Alia, Valerie
Distinguished Prof. of Cdn Culture & Visiting Prof. of Journalism, Center for Cdn-American Studies, Western Washington Univ.

Allen, Marion
Prof., Fac. of Nursing, Univ. of Alberta
Anderson, Joan
Exec. Dir., Univ. Rel'ns, Univ. of Winnipeg
Anderson, Margaret Seguin
Northwest Reg. Coord., Univ. of Northern British Columbia
Andrew, Caroline
Chair, Dept. of Pol. Sci., Univ. of Ottawa
Andrew, Maureen
Prof. of Pediatrics, Children's Hospital at Chedoke-McMaster
Anthony, Geraldine
Prof. Emeritus, Dept. of Eng., Mount Saint Vincent Univ.
Aponiuk, Natalia
Dir. & Assoc. Prof., Centre for Ukrainian Cdn Studies & Dept. of German & Slavic Studies, Univ. of Manitoba
Arai, Mary Needler
Prof. Emeritus, Dept. of Biological Sci., Univ. of Calgary
Armstrong, Pat
Dir. & Prof., Sch. of Cdn Studies, Carleton Univ.
Aston-McCrimmon, Edith Pauline
Assoc. Prof., Phys. Therapy Program, McGill Univ.
Auster, Ellen R.
Assoc. Prof., Strategic Mgmt Studies, Fac. of Admin. Studies, York Univ.
Austin, Barbara
Prof., Fac. of Bus., Brock Univ.
Baird, Patricia
Univ. Prof., Univ. of British Columbia
Bandeen, Mona H.
Dir., Women's Entrepreneurship Program & Family Mgmt Program, Univ. of Toronto
Barman, Jean
Prof., Dept. of Educ. Studies, Univ. of British Columbia
Barrie, Mary C.
Dir., Sch. of Cont. Studies, Univ. of Toronto
Bastness, Joy
Exec. Dir., Saskatchewan Association of School Councils
Baulu-MacWillie, Mireille
Prof., Dept. of Educ., Université Sainte-Anne
Bayefsky, Anne F.
Dir., Centre for Refugee Studies, York Univ.
Beaton, Carol Ann
Children's Centre Coord., Extension & Community Affairs, Univ. Coll. of Cape Breton
Beattie, Margaret Ann
Prof., Mount Allison Univ.
Beauchamp, Hélène
Prof. & Grad. Studies Coordinator, Theatre Dept., Université du Québec à Montreal

Bedingfield, E. Wendy
Fac. of Mgmt & Educ., Acadia Univ.
Bégin, The Honorable Monique
Dean, Fac. of Health Sciences, Univ. of Ottawa
Belicki, Kathryn
Assoc. Prof. of Psych., Brock Univ.
Belisle, Carol-Ann Elizabeth
Coord., Sch. Libraries, Dept. of Educ. & Culture, Government of Nova Scotia
Bellward, Gail D.
Prof. of Pharmacology and Toxicology, Fac. of Pharmaceutical Sci., Univ. of British Columbia
Benn, Denna M.
Dir., Animal Care Svcs, Univ. of Guelph
Bennett, Susan
Assoc. Prof., Dept. of English, Univ. of Calgary
Benson, Renate
Prof., German Studies, Univ. of Guelph
Benyk, Pearl
Study Asst. (Comm.), West Kitikmeot Slave Study Society
Bertrand de Muomm, Maryse
Prof. titulaire et Dir. du Dépt. littératures & langues mod., Université de Montréal
Bigelow, Ann
Prof., Dept. of Psych., St. Francis Xavier Univ.
Bindon, Kathryn
Principal, Sir Wilfred Grenfell Coll., Memorial Univ. of Newfoundland
Bishop, Olga
Prof. Emeritus, Univ. of Toronto
Bismanis, Maija R.
Assoc. Prof. of Art Hist., Univ. of Regina
Black, Naomi
Prof. Emeritus, Pol. Sci., York Univ.
Blackwell, Bonnie
Prof., Dept. of Geology, Queens Coll., City Univ. of New York
Blackwell, Judith
Assoc. Prof., Soc., Brock Univ.
Boddy, Janice
Assoc. Prof., Anthropology Dept., Social Sci. Div., Univ. of Toronto
Bogo, Marion
Acting Dean, Fac. of Social Work, Univ. of Toronto
Borgese, Elisabeth
Prof., Pol. Sci., Dalhousie Univ.
Bowen, Gail Dianne
Asst. Prof. of Eng., Saskatchewan Indian Federated Coll.
Bowman, Marilyn
Assoc. Prof., Dept. of Psych., Simon Fraser Univ.
Boyd, Melanie
Owner, METHODS CONSULTING, With People in Mind

Boyle, Christine Lesley Maureen
Prof., Fac. of Law, Univ. of British Columbia
Bradshaw, Leah
Prof., Dept. of Pol., Brock Univ.
Bray, Tammy M.
Prof. & Chair, Dept. of Human Nutrition & Food Mgmt, Coll. of Human Ecology, The Ohio State Univ.
Briskin, Linda
Assoc. Prof., Soc. Sci. Div., York Univ.
Brodsky, Lynn M.
Biol. Teacher, Ashbury Coll.
Brown, Jennifer S.H.
Prof., Dept. of History, Univ. of Winnipeg
Brown, Sandra
Dir., Dev. & Alumni Affairs, Trinity Coll., Univ. of Toronto
Brubaker, Patricia
Assoc. Prof., Dept. of Physiology, Univ. of Toronto
Brydon, Diana
Prof., Dept. of English, Univ. of Guelph
Burgess, Ellen
Assoc. Prof., Fac. of Med., Univ. of Calgary
Burton, Frances
Prof., Univ. of Toronto
Bussières, Simone
Écrivain/Writer
Bustamante, Rosalina
Multilingual Assessor, York Region Roman Catholic Separate School Board
Butt, Dorcas Susan
Assoc. Prof., Dept. of Psychology, Univ. of British Columbia
Byers, Sandra
Prof. of Psych. & Founding Dir. of the Muriel McQueen Fergusson Centre for Family Violence Research, Univ. of New Brunswick
Caceres, Penny
Dean, Developmental, Trade & Apprenticeship Studies, Seneca Coll.
Cahoon, Margaret Cecelia
Prof. Emeritus, Nursing, Univ. of Toronto
Calliste, Agnes
Assoc. Prof. & Chair, Dept. of Soc. & Anthro., St. Francis Xavier Univ.
Cameron, Barbara Jamie
Assoc. Prof., Osgoode Hall Law School
Cameron, Elspeth MacGregor
Prof., Cdn Studies (Univ. Coll.), English Dept., Univ. of Toronto
Campbell, Paulette
Dean, Bus. & Community Svcs Div., Woodland Institute, Sasakatchewan Institute of Applied Science & Technology
Cantin, Solange
Responsable, Bur. d'intervention en matière de harcèlement sexuel, Université de Montréal
Carpenter, Carole
Assoc. Prof., Div. of Humanities, York Univ.

Carpenter, Helen M.
Prof. Emeritus, Univ. of Toronto

Carrington, Margaret Elise
Asst. Prof., Physics Dept., Univ. of Winnipeg

Cass, Carol
Prof., Biochemistry & Oncology & Chair, Dept. of Oncology, Univ. of Alberta

Chandler, Marsha
Dean, Fac. of Arts and Science, Univ. of Toronto

Chard, Elizabeth
Registrar, Saint Mary's Univ.

Chaudaquock, Vera
VP, First Nations Programs & Svcs, Yukon Coll.

Ching, Julia
Univ. Prof., Victoria Coll., Univ. of Toronto

Chrzanowski, Maria J.
Sr. Teaching Assoc., Univ. of New Brunswick

Chu, Alice I-Fang
Prof., Fac. of Applied Arts, Ryerson Polytechnic Univ.

Cinq-Mars, Irène
V-Rector Academic, Université de Montréal

Clark-Jones, Melissa
Full Prof. & Chair, Soc. Dept., Bishop's Univ.

Clarkson, Persis B.
Assoc. Prof., Dept. of Anthro., Univ. of Winnipeg

Cloutier, Cécile
Writer. Prof. Emeritus, Dept. of French, Univ. of Toronto

Coldwell, Joan
Prof. Emeritus, McMaster Univ.

Collins-Nakai, Ruth L.
Prof. of Pediatrics & Assoc. Dean, Faculty of Medicine, Univ. of Alberta

Colwill, Nina Lee
Pres., Decision Research Ltd.

Connelly, M. Patricia
Coord., Int'l Dev. Studies Program, Dept. of Soc., Saint Mary's Univ.

Conrad, Margaret Rose
Nancy Rowell Jackman Chair in Women's Studies, Mount Saint Vincent Univ.

Cook, Rebecca
Prof. & Dir., Int'l Hum. Rights Prog., Fac. of Law, Univ. of Toronto

Cooke, Brenda
Pres., Assiniboine Community Coll.

Cooper, Barbara
Assoc. Dean, Health Sci. (Rehab.) & Dir., Sch.of Rehab. Sci., McMaster Univ.

Corman, June
Assoc. Prof., Soc., Brock Univ.

Côté-Laurence, Paulette
Assoc. Prof. & Chair, Dept. of Phys. Educ., Brock Univ.

Cranton, Patricia
Prof., Fac. of Educ., Brock Univ.

Creese, Gillian
Assoc. Prof., Dept. of Anthro. & Soc., Univ. of British Columbia

Crocker, Olga L.
Pres., Centre for Workplace Dynamics

Croy, Judy
Pres., JAC International

Cuthbert Brandt, Gail
Principal, Renison Coll., Univ. of Waterloo

Cyr, Mary
Chair, Dept. of Music, Univ. of Guelph

Dahl, Veronica
Prof. & Dir., Logic & Functional Programming Group, Centre for Systems Sci., Lab. for Computer & Comm. Research, Sch. of Computing Sci., Simon Fraser Univ.

Dance-Bennink, Terry
VP, Academic, Sir Sandford Fleming Coll.

Davies, Christine
Prof., Univ. of Alberta

Davies, Gwendolyn
Head & Prof. of English, Acadia Univ.

Davies, Jessie
Dir., Env. & Sust. Dev. Research Centre, Univ. of New Brunswick

Davison, Rosena
Assoc. Prof., Dept. of French, Simon Fraser Univ.

Dawson, T. Brettel
Chair, Dept. of Law, Carleton Univ.

Day, Peggy
Assoc. Prof. & Chair, Dept. of Religious Studies, Univ. of Winnipeg

De Cloet, Sharon
Pres., CAERAN

DeBardeleben, Joan
Prof., The Institute of Central/East European & Russian-Area Studies, Carleton Univ.

Deber, Raisa
Prof., Dept. of Health, Univ. of Toronto

Delany, Sheila
Prof. of English, Simon Fraser Univ.

Dennison, Deanne
Registrar, Univ. of New Brunswick

Dhruvarajan, Vanaja
Prof. of Soc., Univ. of Winnipeg

Dick, Susan
Prof. of English, Queen's Univ.

Dickason, Olive Patricia
Prof. Emeritus, Dept. of Hist., Univ. of Alberta

Dickey Young, Pamela
Head, Dept. of Religious Studies, Queen's Univ.

Dickson, Jennifer
Artist, Photographer & Garden Historian

Dickson, Kimberly
Public Rel'ns Dir., St. Francis Xavier Univ.

Dirks, Patricia
Assoc. Prof., Hist. Dept., Brock Univ.
Djwa, Sandra A
Prof., Dept. of English, Simon Fraser Univ.
Doan, Helen McKinnon
Master of Vanier Coll. & Assoc. Prof. of
Psych., York Univ.
Dolezelová-Velingerová, Milena
Prof. of Chinese Language & Lit., Dept. of East
Asian Studies, Univ. of Toronto
Donner, Gail J.
Prof., Fac. of Nursing, Univ. of Toronto
Doob, Penelope
Prof. of Eng., Multidisciplinary Studies,
Women's Studies, Dance, Academic Dir., Cen-
tre for the Support of Teaching, York Univ.
Drapeau, Suzanne Elizabeth
V-Chair, Bd. of Gov., Mount Saint Vincent
Univ.
Duffin, Jacalyn M.
Hannah Prof. of the Hist. of Medicine, Queen's
Univ.
Duffy, Ann
Prof., Dept. of Soc., Brock Univ.
Dupont, Diane P.
Assoc. Prof., Dept. of Econ., Brock Univ.
Durieux-Smith, Andrée
Prof., Audiology & Speech-Language
Pathology, Univ. of Ottawa
Dwarka, Diane
Pres., Community Legal Education Association
Edwards, Elizabeth
Director, Contemporary Studies Program,
Univ. of King's Coll.
Edwards, Mary-Jane
Prof. of English, & Dir., Centre for Editing
Early Canadian Texts, Carleton Univ.
Edwards, Viviane
Dir., Second Language Educ. Centre, Univ. of
New Brunswick
Eichler, Margrit
Prof. of Soc., Dept. of Soc. in Educ., Ontario
Institute for Studies in Education of the
Univ. of Toronto
ElMaraghy, Hoda A.
Dean of Eng., Univ. of Windsor
Embleton, Sheila Margaret
Assoc. Prof., Dept. of Language, Literatures &
Linguistics, York Univ.
Engel, Joyce
Dean, Div. of Applied Sciences, Medicine Hat
Coll.
Epp, Juanita Ross
Assoc. Prof. of Educ., Lakehead Univ.
Epperly, Elizabeth
Prof. of English & Pres., Univ. of Prince
Edward Island
Etherington, Lois
Assoc. Prof., Fac. of Bus. Admin., Simon Fraser
Univ.

Everatt, Ann (Robertson)
Dir., Program & Staff Dev., Northern Coll. of
Applied Arts and Technology
Faith, Karlene
Assoc. Prof., Sch. of Criminology, Simon Fraser
Univ.
Farrell, Ruby Violet Marilyn
Asst. Prof., Fac. of Educ., Lakehead Univ.
Fehr, Beverley
Assoc. Prof., Dept. of Psych. (on leave),
Univ. of Winnipeg
Fekete, Hazel
Retired Dean, Developmental Studies, Yukon
Coll.
Fennell, Hope-Arlene
Assoc. Prof. & Chair, Preservice Teacher
Education Program, Lakehead Univ.
Field, Leigh
Prof., Dept. of Medical Genetics, Univ. of Cal-
gary
Finlay, A Joy
Naturalist & Educator
Foley, Joan
Prof. of Psych., Univ. of Toronto
Forbes, Joyce
Prof., Dept. of English, Lakehead Univ.
Forsyth, Phyllis
Prof. of Classical Studies, Hist., & Fine Arts,
Univ. of Waterloo
Fowler, Libby
Chair, Bd. of Gov., Univ. of Western Ontario
Frank, Roberta
Univ. Prof., Dept of English, & Dir., Centre for
Medieval Studies, Univ. of Toronto
Franklin, Melissa B.
Prof. of Physics, Harvard Univ.
Frazer, Robbin
Pres., Lifelong Learning Horizons & Associates
Freeman, Barbara M.
Asst. Prof., Journalism & Comm., Carleton Univ.
Freeman, Carolyn
Chrm, Dept. of Oncology, Div. of Radiation
Oncology, McGill Univ.
Freeman, Linda
Assoc. Prof., Dept. of Pol. Sci., Carleton Univ.
French, Doris
Retired Teacher & Union Activist
Frick, Elizabeth A.
Prof. (retired), Dalhousie Univ.
Frize, Monique
Prof. & Chair Holder, Dept. of Elect. Eng.,
Univ. of New Brunswick
Fulton, E Margaret
Educ. Consultant
Fulton, Trish
Assoc. Prof. of Econ., Huron Coll., Univ. of
Western Ontario
Gagnon, Nathaly
Assoc. Prof. & Chair, Leisure Studies,
Concordia Univ.

Galiana-Brants, Henrietta L.
Prof., Dept. of Biomedical Eng. & Dept. of Otolaryngology, Fac. of Medicine, McGill Univ.

Gallant, Christel
Prof. titulaire et Dir. du dépt. de traduction et des langues, Université de Moncton

Gallant, Margaret
Prof., Dept. of Phys. Educ., St. Francis Xavier Univ.

Gallimore, Robyn
Exec. Dir., Association of Early Childhood Educators

Ganoza, M. Clelia
Prof., Banting & Best Dept. of Medical Research, Univ. of Toronto

Gaskell, Jane
Prof. & Assoc. Dean, Grad. Programs & Research, Fac. of Educ., Univ. of British Columbia

Gaudet, Bérengère
Sec.-Gen. & Sec., Bd. of Gov., Concordia Univ.

Gee, Ellen M.
Prof. & Chair, Dept. of Soc. & Anthro., Simon Fraser Univ.

Gerriets, Marilyn
Prof. & Chair, Dept. of Econ., St. Francis Xavier Univ.

Ghosh, Ratna
Macdonald Prof. of Educ., McGill Univ.

Gibson, Dyanne B.
Pres., Dyanne Gibson & Associates Inc.

Gill, Judith
Co-Chair, Phys. Educ. Dept., John Abbott Coll.

Gillam, Shirley
Prof., Dept. of Pathology, Univ. of British Columbia

Gillese, Eileen
Dean, Fac. of Law, Univ. of Western Ontario

Gillett, Margaret
William C. MacDonald Prof. Emeritus in Educ., Dept. of Educational Studies, Fac. of Educ., McGill Univ.

Gillis, Angela
Prof. & Chair, Dept. of Nursing, St. Francis Xavier Univ.

Glasgow, Janice I.
Prof., Dept. of Computing & Info. Sci., Queen's Univ.

Glass, Helen
Prof. Emeritus, Sch. of Nursing, Univ. of Manitoba

Glazer, Carol Lynn
Exec. Dir., Early Childhood Intervention Programs Saskatchewan Inc.

Godard, Barbara Thompson
Assoc. Prof., English Dept., York Univ.

Godkin, Celia
Asst. Prof., Div. of Biomedical Comm., Dept. of Surgery, Fac. of Medicine, Univ. of Toronto

Goerzen, Janice Lee
Former Clinical Asst. Prof. of Obstetrics, Gynecology & Pediatrics

Goldberg, Shirley
Instructor in Film Studies, Malaspina Univ. Coll.

Goldenberg, Bobbye
CEO & Exec. Dir., Seneca Foundation, Seneca Coll. of Applied Arts and Technology

Gordon, Irene M.
Assoc. Prof., Fac. of Bus. Admin., Simon Fraser Univ.

Gorham, Deborah
Prof. of Hist. & Dir., Pauline Jewett Institute of Women's Studies, Carleton Univ.

Grace, Sherrill E.
Prof. of English, Univ. of British Columbia

Graham, Katherine Athol Hamilton
Assoc. Prof. & Coord., Diversification Research Group, Carleton Univ.

Graham-Fogwill, Loretta Advira
Instructor, Applied Sciences Dept., Red River Community Coll.

Graves, Gillian R.
Assoc. Prof., Dept. of Obstetrics & Gynaecology, Dalhousie Univ.

Greaves, Lorraine J.
Dir., Centre for Research on Violence Against Women and Children

Greenglass, Esther Ruth
Prof., Dept. of Psych., Fac. of Arts, York Univ.

Greenhill, Pauline
Prof., Dept. of Women's Studies & Anthropology, Univ. of Winnipeg

Griffith, Gwyneth P.
Educ. Consultant.

Grisé, Yolande
Prof. de litt., Dépt. des lettres françaises, et Dir., Centre de recherche en civilisation canadienne-française

Gross Stein, Janice
Harrowston Prof. of Conflict Mgmt & Negotiation, Univ. of Toronto

Gutman, Gloria M.
Prof., Fac. of Arts & Dir., Gerontology Research Centre & Program, Simon Fraser Univ.

Hallis, Ophera
VP, Hallis Media Inc.

Hanson, Raymonde L.
VP, Academic, Algonquin Coll.

Harvey, Carol
Prof. of French, Univ. of Winnipeg

Hawley, Patricia
Assoc. Prof. of Nursing, St. Francis Xavier Univ.

Hazell, Cindy Dundon
Dean, Fac. of Continuing Educ., Seneca Coll. of Applied Arts and Technology
Heathcote, Isobel Winnifred
Dir., Institute for Environmental Policy
Heidenreich, Rosmarin
Prof., St. Boniface Coll.
Heinrich, Katherine
Prof., Dept. of Mathematics and Statistics, Simon Fraser Univ.
Henderson, Angela D.
Assoc. Prof., Sch. of Nursing, Univ. of British Columbia
Hewitt, Jean D.
Founder, The Learning Connection
Hill, Marguerite F.
Prof. Emeritus, Fac. of Medicine, Univ. of Toronto
Hoecker-Drysdale, Susan
Assoc. Prof., Soc. & Chair, Dept. of Soc. & Anthro., Concordia Univ.
Hogan, Patricia
Prof. of Hist., St. Francis Xavier Univ.
Hollingsworth, Margaret
Assoc. Prof., Dept. of Writing, Fac. of Fine Arts, Univ. of Victoria
Hornstein, Shelley
Chair, Dept. of Fine Arts & Assoc. Prof., Atkinson Coll., York Univ.
Hughes, Margaret E.
Prof., Fac. of Law, Univ. of Calgary
Hughes, Patricia
Assoc. Prof., Mary Louise Lynch Chair in Women & Law, Fac. of Law, Univ. of New Brunswick
Hutcheon, Linda
Univ. Prof. of English & Comparative Lit., Univ. of Toronto
Hutchison, Peggy
Assoc. Prof., Dept. of Recreation & Leisure Studies, Brock Univ.
Imboden, Roberta
Prof., Dept. of English, Ryerson Polytechnic Univ.
Indra, Doreen Marie
Assoc. Prof. of Anthro., Univ. of Lethbridge
Ingram, Sandra
Instructor, Fac. of Eng., Univ. of Manitoba
Irwin, M. Eleanor
Assoc. Prof., Scarborough Coll., Univ. of Toronto
Irwin, Rita Louise
Assoc. Prof., Dept. of Curriculum Studies, Univ. of British Columbia
Jackson, Margaret A.
Prof. & Dir., Sch. of Criminology, Simon Fraser Univ.
Jefferson, Anne L.
Prof., Educational Studies, Univ. of Ottawa

Johnson, Susan M.
Assoc. Prof. of Psych. & Psychiatry, Dept. of Psych., Univ. of Ottawa
Johnston, Elizabeth
Dir., Sch. of Nutrition & Food Sci., Acadia Univ.
Johnstone, Rose
Prof., Gilman Cheney Chair, Dept. of Biochem., McGill Univ.
Jones, Barbara Ellen
Prof., Dept. of Neurology & Neurosurgery, McGill Univ.
Jones, Dorothy M.
Exec. Dir., Children's Talent Education Centre
Jones, Phyllis
Prof. Emeritus, Fac. of Nursing, Univ. of Toronto
Josephson, Wendy
Assoc. Prof., Dept. of Psych., Univ. of Winnipeg
Kallen, Evelyn
Emeritus Prof. & Sr. Scholar (Arts), York Univ.
Kambeitz, Sister Teresita
Dir., Religious Educ. Program, Newman Theological Coll.
Kaprielian-Churchill, Isabel
Visiting Scholar & Kazan Lecturer in Immigration Hist. & Armenian Studies, California State Univ. at Fresno
Kartzmark, Elinor M.
Prof. of Chem. (retired), Univ. of Manitoba
Katzenberg, Mary Anne
Prof., Dept. of Archaeology, Univ. of Calgary
Kealey, Linda
Assoc. Prof. of Hist., Memorial Univ. of Newfoundland
Keillor, Elaine
Prof., Sch. for Studies in Art & Culture–Music, Carleton Univ.
Kent, Alia
Pres., Women Teachers' Association of Ottawa
Kérouac, Suzanne
Dean, Fac. of Nursing, Université de Montréal
Kerr, Kaye M.
Assoc. Prof. & Dir., Developmental Studies, Univ. of Winnipeg
Kerrigan, Catherine
Prof. of English, Univ. of Guelph
Kimball, Meredith M.
Prof. in Psych. & Women's Studies, Simon Fraser Univ.
Kinlough-Rathbone, Raelene Lorna
Assoc. VP, Fac. of Health Sciences, & Prof., Pathology, McMaster Univ.
Kirschner, Teresa J.
Prof., Humanities Program, Simon Fraser Univ.

Kleihauer-Ward, Elke
Toolmaker/Technological Studies Teacher, North Lambton Secondary School

Klein-Lataud, Christine
Dir., Sch. of Translation, Glendon Coll.

Klodawsky, Fran
Asst. Prof., Dept. of Geography & Pauline Jewett Institute of Women's Studies, Carleton Univ.

Knelman, Judith
Assoc. Prof., Univ. of Western Ontario

Knight, Cheryl
Dir., Hum. Res., Univ. of Lethbridge

Knutson, Susan Lynne
Assoc. Prof. & Chair, Dept. of English, Université Sainte-Anne

Kopansky, Charlene
Pres./Founder, Canadian Aquafitness Leaders Alliance Inc.

Kronick, Doreen
Psychoeducational Consultant.

Kukal, Olga
Asst. Prof. of Biol., Acadia Univ.

Kuntz, Sister Dolores
Principal, Brescia Coll.

Labarge, Margaret Wade
Adj. Research Prof., Carleton Univ.

Labelle, Micheline
Prof., Dépt. de Soc., Université du Québec à Montréal

Labow, Rosalind S.
Dir., Taichman Lab., Univ. of Ottawa Heart Institute

Lacey, Veronica S.
Dir. of Educ. & Sec.-Treas., The Board of Education for the City of North York

Laflamme, Diane
Gen. Mgr, L'Institut d'assurance de dommages du Québec

Lancashire, Anne
Prof. of English, Univ. of Toronto

Lane, Patricia A.
Prof., Dept. of Biol., Dalhousie Univ.

Langley, Elizabeth
Prof., Concordia Univ.

Latchford, Sandra
Assoc. Prof./Dir. of Learning Centre, Fac. of Educ., Univ. of New Brunswick

Lavers, Leslie
Registrar, Univ. of Lethbridge

Le Blanc, Barbara
Asst. Prof., Dept. of Educ., Université Sainte-Anne

LeBlanc, Phyllis Evelyne
Prof. of Hist., Université de Moncton

Leduc, Paule
Rector, Université du Québec à Montréal

Legault, Jocelyne A.
Assoc. Prof., Dept. of Earth Sci., Univ. of Waterloo

Lemire, Beverly
Prof., Dept. of Hist., Univ. of New Brunswick

Levenson, Jill
Prof., Trinity Coll., Univ. of Toronto

Lewis, Linda R.
Prof., Ryerson Polytechnic Univ.

Lippman, Abby
Prof., Dept. of Epidemiology & Biostatistics, McGill Univ.

Lobay, Mary
Retired Teacher

Lock, Margaret
Prof., Dept. of Social Studies of Medicine, McGill Univ.

Luxton, Meg
Prof., York Univ.

Lyons, Harriet D.
Assoc. Prof., Anthro., & Dir., Women's Studies, Univ. of Waterloo

MacCaull, Wendy
Assoc. Prof., Dept. of Math. & Computing Sci., St. Francis Xavier Univ.

MacDonald, Verna
Alumni Affairs Officer, St. Francis Xavier Univ.

MacLean, Margaret
Assoc. Prof. & Chair, Dept. of Library & Info. Studies, Lakehead Univ.

MacLellan, Debbie
Asst. Prof., Dept. of Home Econ., Univ. of Prince Edward Island

MacMillan, Carrie
Prof., Mount Allison Univ.

MacPherson, Janet E.
Instructor, Re-Entry Training, Holland Coll.

Mady Kelly, Diana
Dir., Sch. of Dramatic Art, Univ. of Windsor

Maharajh, Anna E.
Program Coord., British Columbia Institute of Technology

Mahoney, Kathleen E.
Prof., Fac. of Law, Univ. of Calgary

Makus, Ingrid
Asst. Prof., Dept. of Pol., Brock Univ.

Mancuso, Maureen
Chair, Dept. of Pol. Studies, Univ. of Guelph

Mann, Susan
Pres., York Univ.

Marchak, M. Patricia
Prof., Dept. of Anthro. & Soc., Univ. of British Columbia

Marsden, Lorna
Pres. & V-Chancellor, Wilfrid Laurier Univ.

Martin, Renée H.
Prof., Dept. of Medical Genetics, Univ. of Calgary

Martin, Sheilah
Dean, Fac. of Law, Univ. of Calgary

Martin, Sue Ann
Prof. of Dramatic Art, & Dean, Fac. of Arts, Univ. of Windsor

Martin Matthews, Anne
Prof., Dept. of Family Studies, Univ. of Guelph

Masciuch, Sonia W.
Coord., M.A. in Sch. Psych., Mount Saint Vincent Univ.

Mathieu, Mireille
Dean, Fac, of Arts & Science, Université de Montréal

McAuliffe, Jane
Chrm, Dept. for the Study of Religion & Dir., Centre for the Study of Religion, Univ. of Toronto

McCarthy, Francine M.G.
Assoc. Prof., Earth Sci., Brock Univ.

McCormack, Thelma
Prof. Emeritus, York Univ.

McCoubrey, Sharon
Dir., B.Ed. Program, Okanagan Univ. Coll.

McCracken, Kathleen Luanne
Lecturer in English & American Studies, Univ. of Ulster at Jordanstown

McCrone, Kathleen E.
Prof. of Hist. & Dean of Social Sci., Univ. of Windsor

McCullough, Marilyn Kay
Dir., Dept. of Continuing Educ. & Lecturer, Hist. Dept., Mount Allison Univ.

McDaniel, Susan A.
Prof. of Soc., Univ. of Alberta

McDonald, Lynn
Prof., Dept. of Soc. & Anthro., Univ. of Guelph

McKay, Sharon
Dean & Assoc. Prof., Fac. of Social Work, Univ. of Regina

McMaster, Juliet
Univ. Prof. of English, Univ. of Alberta

McMullen, Lorraine
Adj. Prof., Dept. of English, Univ. of Victoria

McNair, Noëlla
VP of Programs, Northern Coll.

McNicoll, Claire
V-Rector, Public Affairs, Université de Montréal

McTighe, Janice
Exec. Dir., Renfrew Educational Services

Melville, Karen
Dir. of Professional Dev., Fac. of Info. Studies, Univ. of Toronto

Mendell, Marguerite
Assoc. Prof. & Principal, Sch. of Community & Public Affairs, Concordia Univ.

Mickelson, Norma I.
Prof. Emeritus, Univ. of Victoria

Miller, Elizabeth
Prof. of English, Memorial Univ. of Newfoundland

Miller, Mary Jane
Prof., Dept. of Film Studies, Brock Univ.

Millman-Floyd, Cynthia
Prof., Dept. of Music, Univ. of Ottawa

Milot, Louise
Vice-rectrice aux études, Université Laval

Mitchinson, Wendy
Prof. of Hist., Univ. of Waterloo

Molot, Maureen Appel
Prof. of Pol. Sci. & Dir., The Norman Paterson Sch. of Int'l Affairs, Carleton Univ.

Molzahn, Anita
Dean, Fac. of Hum. & Social Dev., Univ. of Victoria

Morgan, Alison
Univ. Sec. & Instructor in Econ., Queen's Univ.

Morgan, Nicole
Visiting Prof., McGill Centre for Medicine, Ethics and Law

Morrison, Claudia
Instructor, John Abbott Coll.

Mossman, Mary Jane
Prof., Osgoode Hall Law Sch., York Univ.

Mulhallen, Karen
Prof., Dept. of English, Ryerson Polytechnic Univ.

Munroe-Blum, Heather
Prof. & VP, Research & Int'l Rel'ns, Univ. of Toronto

Murray, Catherine A.
Assoc. Prof., Simon Fraser Univ.

Murray, Heather
Assoc. Prof. of English, Trinity Coll., Univ. of Toronto

Murray, Jacqueline
Assoc. Prof. of Hist. & Dir., Humanities Research Group, Univ. of Windsor

Mushinski, Valerie
Dir., Dev. Office, Wascana Inst., Southern Alberta Institute of Science and Technology

Myers Avis, Judith Kathleen
Prof., Dept. of Family Studies, Univ. of Guelph

Neuman, Shirley
Dean of Arts & Prof. of English, Univ. of British Columbia

Nichols, Eva
Mese Consulting Ltd

Nicks, Joan Patricia
Assoc. Prof., Dept. of Film Studies, Dramatic & Visual Arts, Brock Univ.

Northey, Margot
Dean, Sch. of Bus., Queen's Univ.

Novak, Marie
Prof., Univ. of Winnipeg

Ommer, Rosemary
Prof., Dept. of Hist. & Project Mgr, Eco-Research Program, Memorial Univ. of Newfoundland

Ormsby, Margaret A.
Prof. Emeritus, Hist. Dep., Univ. of B.C.

Packer, Katherine Helen
Prof. Emeritus, Fac. of Library & Info. Sci. (now Fac. of Info. Studies), Univ. of Toronto

Packham, Marian A.
Univ. Prof. Emeritus, Dept. of Biochem., Univ. of Toronto

Parish, Barbara
Assoc. Prof., Dept. of Obstetrics & Gynaecology, Dalhousie Univ.

Parr, Joy
Farley Prof. of Hist., Simon Fraser Univ.

Parr-Johnston, Elizabeth
Pres. & V-Chancellor, The Univ. of New Brunswick

Parsons, Catriona Niclomhair
Asst. Prof., Celtic Studies Dept., St. Francis Xavier Univ.

Paterson, Janet M.
Assoc. Dean, Fac. of Arts & Sci., Univ. of Toronto

Paterson, Janet
Exec. Dean, Sch. of Applied Arts & Bus., Algonquin Coll.

Patterson, Margaret
Assoc. VP (Student Affairs), The Univ. of Calgary

Pearce, Elizabeth
Prof., Centennial Coll. of Applied Arts and Technology

Pell, Barbara
Assoc. Prof., Trinity Western Univ.

Perry, Kathleen
Assoc. Dean, Comm & Advancement, Fac. of Fine Arts, Concordia Univ.

Petrone, Serafina
Prof. Emeritus, Lakehead Univ.

Pettifor, Jean L.
Assoc. Prof., Dept. of Educ. Psych. & Programme in Clinical Psych., Univ. of Calgary

Phillips, M. Jane
Prof., Dept. of Chemical Eng. & Applied Chem., Univ. of Toronto

Pilkington, Marilyn L.
Dean, Osgoode Hall Law Sch., York Univ.

Pip, Eva
Prof., Univ. of Winnipeg

Pitcher, Patricia Cherie
Prof. of Leadership & Dean of the Doctoral Program, L'École des Hautes Études Commerciales

Poff, Deborah C.
Prof. & VP, Academic, Univ. of Northern British Columbia

Polivy, Janet
Prof., Dept. of Psych., Erindale Coll., Univ. of Toronto

Pollock, Lorraine Marie
Pres., New Brunswick Home Economics Association

Porac, Clare
Prof. of Psych., Univ. of Victoria

Prentice, Alison
Prof., Dept. of Theory & Policy Studies in Educ., Ontario Institute for Studies in Education

Prepas, Ellie E.
Prof., Limnology, Dept. of Biological Sci., Univ. of Alberta

Preston, Joan
Prof. of Psych. & Comm. Studies, Brock Univ.

Proven, Bonnie
Chair, Distance Educ. & Media, Assiniboine Community Coll.

Pugliese, Olga
Prof., Dept. of Italian Studies, Univ. of Toronto

Pyke, Sandra W.
Prof. & Chair, Dept. of Psych., York Univ.

Quinn, Louise
Assoc. Prof. & Chair, Dept. of Geology, Brandon Univ.

Rabinovitch, Marlene
Prof. of Pediatrics, Pathology & Medicine, Univ. of Toronto

Rajan, Tilottama
Dir., Centre in the Study of Theory & Criticism, Univ. of Western Ontario

Raoul, Valerie
Prof., Dept. of French & Dir., Centre for Research in Women's Studies & Gender Rel'ns, Univ. of British Columbia

Rees-Potter, Lorna K.
Assoc. Prof., Grad. Sch. of Library & Info. Studies, McGill Univ.

Renouf, M.A. Priscilla
Assoc. Prof. & Head, Dept. of Anthro., Memorial Univ. of Newfoundland

Ricker, Marvi
Exec. Dir., Richard Ivey Foundation

Riddell-Dixon, Elizabeth M.
Assoc. Prof., Dept. of Pol. Sci., Univ. of Western Ontario

Ripley, M. Louise
Assoc. Prof., Atkinson Coll., York Univ.

Robert, Lucie
Prof., Dept. d'Études Littéraires, Université du Québec à Montréal

Roberts, Barbara Ann
Prof., Women's Studies, Athabasca Univ.

Robertson, Heather-jane
Dir., Professional Dev. Svcs, Canadian Teachers' Federation/Fédération Canadienne des Enseignantes et des Enseignants

Robson, Ann
Prof., Univ. of Toronto

Rock, Virginia Jeanne
Prof. Emeritus, English Dept., York Univ.

Rodgers, Sanda
Dean, Common Law Section, Fac. of Law, Univ. of Ottawa

Rooke, Constance
Assoc VP Academic & Prof. of English, Univ. of Guelph

Ross, Catherine
Prof. of Library & Info. Science & Acting Dean of Comm. & Open Learning, Univ. of Western Ontario

Roth, Lorna
Asst. Prof., Dept. of Comm. Studies, Concordia Univ.

Rousseau, Christiane
Full Prof. & Chair, Dépt. de mathématiques et de statistique, Université de Montréal

Rovinescu, Olivia
Assoc. Dir., Centre for Teaching & Learning Svcs, Concordia Univ.

Rowland, Beryl
Distinguished Prof. Emeritus, Dept. of English, York Univ.

Rowntree, Jessie-May Anna
Dir. of Comm., York Univ.

Rubio, Mary
Prof., Dept. of English, Univ. of Guelph

Runte, Roseann
Pres., Victoria Univ., Univ. of Toronto

Rusnak, Anne M.
Instructor III, Dept. of French Studies, Univ. of Winnipeg

Russell, Roberta J.
Mgr, Cdn Studies & Youth Programs, Dept. of Cdn Heritage, Government of Canada

Rust, Velma Irene
Econ. Researcher (retired)

Ryan, Carey A.
Principal, St. Vincent's High School

Salcudean, Martha Eva
Prof. of Mech. Eng., Univ. of British Columbia

Saltman, Judith
Assoc. Prof., Sch. of Library & Info. Studies, Univ. of British Columbia

Sanderson, Marie
Dir., The Water Ntwk, Dept. of Geography, Univ. of Waterloo

Sandilands, Catronia A.H.
Asst. Prof., Fac. of Environmental Studies, York Univ.

Santa Barbara, Joanna
Asst. Prof., Dept. of Psychiatry & Centre for Peace Studies, McMaster Univ.

Sarkar, Gerlinde
Dir., R&D, Saskatchewan Institute of Applied Science and Technology

Sauer, Angelika
Chair in German Cdn Studies, Univ. of Winnipeg

Sauer, Elizabeth
Assoc. Prof., Dept. of English, Brock Univ.

Savoie-Zajc, Lorraine
Prof., Univ. of Quebec in Hull

Schabas, Ann H.
Prof. Emeritus, Fac. of Library & Info. Sci., Univ. of Toronto

Schiff, Daphne
Assoc. Prof of Natural Sci., Glendon Coll., York Univ.

Schnitzer, Deborah
Assoc. Prof., Dept. of English, Univ. of Winnipeg

Scott, Jacquelyn Thayer
Pres. & V-Chancellor, Univ. Coll. of Cape Breton

Scott, Phyllis
Past Pres., & Coord. of Int'l Rel'ns, Canadian Federation of Univ. Women

Seiler, Tamara
Assoc. Prof., Fac. of General Studies, Univ. of Calgary

Seip, Jo-Anne
CEO, Gateway Society

Serbin, Lisa A.
Prof. of Psych., Centre for Research in Hum. Dev., Concordia Univ.

Sethi, Sarla
Assoc. Prof., Fac. of Nursing, Univ. of Calgary

Sharom, Frances Jane
Prof., Dept. of Chem. & Biochem., Univ. of Guelph

Sheets-Pyenson, Susan
Assoc. Prof. of Hist., Univ. of Southwestern Louisiana

Shohet, Linda
Dir., The Centre for Literacy of Quebec

Sills, Judith
Music Specialist/Curriculum Coord., Edmonton Public Schools

Silverman, Eliane
Prof. & Advisor to the Pres. on Women's Issues, Univ. of Calgary

Simmons, Joyce Nesker
Asst. Prof., Fac. of Med., Univ. of Toronto

Slavin, Linda
Int'l Proj. Mgr, *Instruct*, Trent Univ.

Smart, Patricia
Prof. of French, Carleton Univ.

Smillie, Carol
Assoc. Prof., Sch. of Nursing, Dalhousie Univ.

Smith, Jennifer
Assoc. Prof., Dalhousie Univ.

Smith-Palmer, Truis
Assoc. Prof. of Chem., St. Francis Xavier Univ.

Snell, Linda
Assoc. Dean, Continuing Medical Educ., McGill Univ.

Spencer, Mary Eileen Stapleton
Univ. Prof., Dept. of Agriculture, Food & Nutritional Sci., Univ. of Alberta

Springer, Helen Jean
Dean, Fac. of Sci. & Tech., Mount Royal Coll.

Spry, Irene M.
Prof. Emeritus, Univ. of Ottawa

Square, Paula A.
Prof. & Chair, Dept. of Speech Language
Pathology, Fac. of Medicine, Univ. of Toronto

Stalker, Jacqueline
Professor (retired), Div. of Postsecondary
Studies & Coord., Higher Educ. Grad.
Program, Fac. of Educ., Univ. of
Manitoba

Stanley, Della M.M.
Assoc. Prof., Coord., Cdn Studies Programme,
Mount Saint Vincent Univ.

Stanley-Blackwell, Laurie C.C.
Assoc. Prof., Dept. of Hist., St. Francis Xavier
Univ.

Stark, Janet
Assoc. Registrar, St. Francis Xavier Univ.

Starkman, Esther
English Instructor, Alberta Vocational Coll.

Starzomski, Rosalie C.
Visiting Lecturer, Sch. of Nursing, Univ. of Victoria

Stephen, Alison M.
Prof., Div. of Nutrition & Dietetics, Coll. of
Pharmacy & Nutrition, Univ. of Saskatchewan

Stephen, Barbara
Curator Emeritus, Dept. of Near Eastern &
Asian Civilizations, Royal Ontario Museum

Steven, Darlene
Assoc. Prof., Lakehead Univ.

Stewart, Carole
Dean, Coll. of Arts, Univ. of Guelph

Stone-Blackburn, Susan
Prof. of English & Assoc. Dean of Grad.
Studies, Univ. of Calgary

Sullivan, Rosemary
Prof., Dept. of English, Univ. of Toronto

Surridge, Marie E.
Prof., Dept. of French Studies, Queen's
Univ.

Taborsky, Edwina
Assoc. Prof., Dept. of Soc. & Anthro., Bishop's
Univ.

Tait, Reginae Mae
Teacher, Assoc. Exec.

Tan-Willman, Conchita
Prof., Univ. of Toronto

Tancred, Peta
Prof. of Soc., McGill Univ.

Tansey, Charlotte Hunter
Pres. & Dir. of Studies, Thomas More Institute

Tapp, Janice
Pres., Provincial Intermediate Teachers'
Association

Tayler, Anne H.
Prof. & Coord., Women's Studies, Yukon
Coll.

Taylor, Sharon
Chair, Dept. of Social Work, Lakehead Univ.

Thompson, Cécile
Coord., French Language Svcs, Ontario
Association of Children's Aid Societies

Thompson, Mary E.
Prof. & Chair, Statistics & Actuarial Sci.,
Univ. of Waterloo

Timmons, Vianne
Dean, Fac. of Educ., Univ. of Prince Edward
Island

Tkachuk, Mary
Teacher, The Priory School Inc.

Torchia, Win
Employment Equity Officer, Red River
Community Coll.

Toresdahl, Susan
Exec. Dir., North Island Coll. Foundation

Tumasonis, Elizabeth
Assoc. Prof., Dept. of Hist. in Art, Univ. of Victoria

Tung, Rosalie L.
The Ming & Stella Wong Prof. of Int'l Bus.,
Fac. of Bus., Simon Fraser Univ.

Tuohy, Carolyn Hughes
Prof. of Pol. Sci. & Deputy Provost, Univ. of
Toronto

Turner, Nancy J.
Prof., Environmental Studies Program,
Univ. of Victoria

Uchida , Irene Ayako
Prof. Emeritus, Dept. of Pediatrics, McMaster
Univ.

Underhill , Anne Barbara
Hon. Prof., Dept. of Geophysics & Astronomy,
Univ. of British Columbia

Vail, Susan
Assoc. Prof., Sch. of Phys. Educ., York Univ.

Vaillancourt-Châtillon, Louise
Dir. of Admin., École Polytechnique de
Montréal

Vaisey-Genser, Marion
Prof. & Sr. Scholar, Dept. of Foods &
Nutrition, Univ. of Manitoba

Valaskakis, Gail Guthrie
Dean, Fac. of Arts & Sci. & Prof., Dept. of
Comm. Studies, Concordia Univ.

Van Norman, Marilyn
Dir. of Student Svc., Univ. of Toronto

Vanderwel, Désirée
Assoc. Prof., Dept. of Chem., Univ. of Winnipeg

Vanstone, Ann L.
Chair, The Metropolitan Toronto School Board

Vethamany-Globus, Swani
Assoc. Prof., Dept. of Biol., Univ. of Waterloo

Vickers, Jill
Prof., Pol. Sci. & Cdn Studies, Carleton
Univ.

Vikis-Freibergs, Vaira
Prof. titulaire, Dépt. de psych., Université de
Montréal

Villalon, Lita
Dir., École de nutrition et d'études familiales, Université de Moncton
Vingilis, Evelyn R.
Dir., Population & Community Health Unit, & Prof., Dept. of Family Medicine & Dept. of Epidemiology & Biostatistics, Fac. of Medicine, Univ. of Western Ontario
Waddington, Miriam
Prof. Emeritus & Sr. Scholar, Dept. of English, York Univ.
Waddington, Rhoda Marie
Exec. Dir., Step By Step Child Development Society
Waelti-Walters, Jennifer
Prof. & Founding Dir. of Women's Studies, Univ. of Victoria
Walker, Doreen
Sr. Instructor Emeritus, Univ. of British Columbia
Walker, Nancy R.
Dir., Fin Svcs & Cont., Univ. of Lethbridge
Wardlaw, Janet M.
Nutritionist (retired)
Warkentin, Germaine
Prof. of English, Victoria Coll., Univ. of Toronto
Waterston, Elizabeth
Prof. Emeritus, Univ. of Guelph
Webster, Jill R.
Prof. Emeritus, Univ. of Toronto
Wekerle, Gerda R.
Prof., Fac. of Environmental Studies, York Univ.
Welsh-Ovcharov, Bogomila
Prof., Dept. of Fine Art, Univ. of Toronto
Westhues, Anne
Assoc. Prof., Wilfrid Laurier Univ.
White, Mary Anne
Killam Research Prof. in Materials Sci., & Prof. of Chem., & Physics, Dept. of Chem., Dalhousie Univ.
Wickwire, Wendy
Asst. Prof., Dept. of Educ. Studies, Fac. of Educ., Univ. of British Columbia
Wigdor, Blossom T.
Prof. Emeritus, Centre for Studies of Aging, Depts of Psych. & Behavioural Sci., Univ. of Toronto
Wilburn, Marion
Coord., Library & Info. Technician Program, Sheridan Coll.
Williams, Anne E.
Music Teacher
Willment, Jo-Anne H.
Lecturer, Psych. Dept., Univ. of Waterloo
Wilson, Ruth
Prof. & Head, Dept. of Family Medicine, Family Medical Centre, Queen's Univ.

Winsor, Mary
Prof., Institute for the Hist. & Philo. of Sci. & Technology, Univ. of Toronto
Wolfe, Jeanne M.
Prof. & Dir., Sch. of Urban Planning, McGill Univ.
Wong-Rieger, Durhane
Assoc. Prof., Dir. of Hum. Res. Consultation Unit, Dept. of Psychology, Univ. of Windsor
Wood, Janet M.
Prof., Dept. of Microbio., Univ. of Guelph
Woodsworth, Judith Weisz
Assoc. Prof. of études françaises & Vice-Dean, Academic Affairs & Int'l Rel'ns, Fac. of Arts & Sci., Concordia Univ.
Woodward, Christel
Prof., Dept. of Clinical Epidemiology & Biostatistics, McMaster Univ.
Woolcott, Donna
Prof. & Chair, Dept. of Family Studies, Univ. of Guelph
Workman, Carole
V-Rector, Resources, Univ. of Ottawa
Wright, Lorna L.
Dir., Centre for Canada-Asia Bus. Rel'ns & Assoc. Prof. of Int'l Mgmt & Organizational Behaviour, Sch. of Bus., Queen's Univ.
Wright, Mary Jean
Prof. Emeritus, Dept. of Psych., Univ. of Western Ontario
Wubnig, Judy
Asst. Prof., Dept. of Phil., Univ. of Waterloo
Wylie, Alison
Prof, Dept. of Philosophy, Univ. of Western Ontario
York, Lorraine
Assoc. Prof., English, McMaster Univ.
Young, Rosemary
Assoc. Prof. & Chair, Dept. of Grad. & Undergrad. Studies, Fac. of Educ., Brock Univ.
Zaichkowsky, Judith Lynne
Prof. of Mktg, Fac. of Bus. Admin., Simon Fraser Univ.
Zemans, Joyce Pearl
Prof., Fac. of Fine Arts, York Univ.
Zimmerman, Selma
Prof., Natural Sci., York Univ.
Zwicky, Jan
Poet & Prof., Univ. of Victoria

GOVERNMENT AND POLITICS
Federal, provincial, and municipal government officials. Members of the public service. Political groups and parties. Politics or policy as a field of endeavour. Commentators and educators. Related organizations, agencies and officials.

Abdurahman, Muriel Ross
M.L.A., Government of Alberta
Ablonczy, Diane
M.P., (Calgary North), Government of Canada
Almond, Alice
Mgr, Hum. Res. Dev. Canada, Employment &
Immigration, Government of Canada
Atkinson, The Hon. Pat
Min. of Educ., Government of Saskatchewan
Augustine, Jean
M.P. (Etobicoke-Lakeshore), Government of
Canada
Bacon, The Hon. Lise
Senator (De la Durantaye), The Senate of
Canada
Barnabe, Claire M.
Admin. Asst., National Gallery of Canada
Barnes, Susan Carol
M.P., Government of Canada
Barrett, Becky
M.L.A., Government of Manitoba
Barry, The Honourable Jane
Solicitor Gen., Government of New
Brunswick
Bassett, Isabel
M.P.P. (St. Andrews-St. Patrick), Government
of Ontario
Beaudoin, Louise
Min. of Culture & Comm., Gouvernement du
Québec
Beaumont, Anne
Asst. Deputy Min., Housing Policy & Prog.,
Ministry of Municipal Affairs and Housing,
Government of Ontario
Beck, Pat
Reg'l Rep., Man./Sask. Nat'l Women's Liberal
Commission, Liberal Party of Canada
Bellamy, Denise
Dir., Legal Svcs Br., Management Board
Secretariat
Benn-Ireland, Tessa Judith
Librarian, Markham Public Libraries
Bethel, Judy
M.P., (Edmonton East), Government of
Canada
Black, The Hon. Patricia L.
Min. of Energy & Deputy Gov't House Leader,
Legislative Assembly, Government of Alberta
Blackburn, Jeanne L.
Députée du comté de Chicoutimi & Prés. de la
Commission de l'Éduc., Gouvernement du
Québec
Blondin-Andrew, Ethel
Sec. of State, Training & Youth & M.P. (West-
ern Arctic), Government of Canada
Boone, Lois
M.L.A., Government of British Columbia
Boyd, Marion
M.P.P. (London Centre), Government of
Ontario

Bradley, Judy L.
M.L.A. (Weyburn-Big Muddy), Government of
Saskatchewan
Breault, Ann
Mem. of the Legislative Assembly (St. Stephen-
St. Andrews), Min. of Municipalities, Culture
& Housing, Government of New Brunswick
Brewer, Hon. Jane
Regional Councillor & Mayor, City of
Cambridge
Brewin, Gretchen
M.L.A., Government of British Columbia
Brown, Jan
M.P. (Calgary Southeast), Government of
Canada
Brushett, Dianne
M.P. (Cumberland-Colchester), Government of
Canada
Buckley, Helen
Budovitch, Judith
Dir. of Consumer Affairs, Government of New
Brunswick
Burak, Rita
Sec. of Cabinet & Clerk of Exec. Council,
Government of Ontario
Calahasen, Hon. Pearl
Min. Resp. for Children's Svcs, Government of
Alberta
Callbeck, The Hon. Catherine S.
Premier & Pres. of the Exec. Council,
Government of Prince Edward Island
Cameron, Christina S.
Dir. Gen., Nat'l Historic Sites, Parks Canada,
Government of Canada
Campbell, The Right Hon. A. Kim
Former Prime Minister. Consul Gen. for
Canada in L.A., Government of Canada
Caplan, The Hon. Elinor
M.P.P. (Oriole), Chief Opposition Whip &
Critic for Health and Women's Issues for the
Official Opposition, Government of Ontario
Careless, Virginia A.S.
Research Officer, Recreation Branch, Small
Bus., Tourism & Culture, Government of
British Columbia
Carlson, Debby
M.L.A. (Edmonton Ellerslie), Government of
Alberta
Carney, Hon. Pat
Senator, The Senate of Canada
Carstairs, Sharon
Senator, The Senate of Canada
Cerilli, Marianne
Mem. of the Legislative Assembly, Government
of Manitoba
Chamberlain, Brenda Kay
M.P. (Guelph-Wellington), Government of
Canada
Chaput-Rolland, Hon. Solange
Senator, The Senate of Canada

Charest, Solange
Députée (Rimouski), Assemblée nationale,
Gouvernement du Québec

Clancy, Mary
M.P. (Halifax), Government of Canada

Clemenhagen, Carol
Sec., Medical Research Council of Canada

Clement, Alison
Young Liberals of Canada Rep., Nat'l
Women's Liberal Commission, Liberal Party of
Canada

Cohen, The Hon. Erminie J.
Senator, The Senate of Canada

Collenette, Penny
Dir. of Appointments, Office of the PM,
Government of Canada

Cools, The Hon. Anne Clare
Senator & Liberal Mbr. of Gov't, The Senate of
Canada

Cooper, Helen
Chair

Copleston, Marion
Ed. Committee, *Common Ground*

Copps, The Hon. Sheila
Dep. PM & Min. of Cdn Heritage, M.P.
(Hamilton East), Government of Canada

Corbiere, Alice A.
Co-ordinator, Garden River Development
Corp.

Cosman, Francene Jen
M.L.A. (Bedford-Fall River) & Deputy Speaker,
Government of Nova Scotia

Cournoyea, The Hon. Nellie J.
Chair & CEO, Inuvialuit Regional Corporation

Cowling, Marlene
M.P. (Dauphin-Swan River, Manitoba),
Government of Canada

Crofford, Joanne
M.L.A. (Regina Lake Centre), Government of
Saskatchewan

Crouse, Elizabeth
Supervisor, 4-H & Rural Org., N.S. Dept. of
Agric. & Mktg, Government of Nova Scoita

Dacquay, Louise M.
Speaker of the Legislative Assembly,
Government of Manitoba

Dalphond-Guiral, Madeleine
M.P. (Laval-Centre), Government of
Canada

Danyluk, Vera
Chair, Exec. Committee, Montreal Urban
Community

Dawson, Mary E.
Assoc. Deputy Min., Federal Department of
Justice, Government of Canada

Debien, Maud
Députée, (Laval-Est), Government of Canada

Delisle, Margaret F.
Mem. of the Nat'l Assembly , Government du
Québec

Dionne-Marsolais, The Hon. Rita
Min. déléguée à l'Industrie et au Commerce,
Gouvernement du Québec

Doughty, Wendy
Exec. Dir., Corp. Mktg Office, Grant McEwan
Community Coll.

Dundas-Matthews, R. Louise
Dir., Fin. & Mgmt Svcs, Government of the
Northwest Territories

Dunn, Barbara
Pres., Canadian Society of Air Safety Investigators

Edwards, Nancy
Sec.-Treas., School District No. 48 (Howe
Sound)

Edwards, The Hon. Anne
Min., Ministry of Employment & Investments,
Government of British Columbia

Eliadis, F. Pearl
Dir., Public Policy & Public Educ., Ontario
Human Rights Commission

Elliston, Inez
Career & Life Planning Consultant. Nat'l Dir.,
"Building the Bridges to Prosperity"

Engel, June
Ed., *Health News*

Fairbairn, The Hon. Joyce
Senator, Leader of the Gov't in the Senate &
Min. with Special Resp. for Literacy, Government of Canada

Fairclough, Right Hon. Ellen Loucks

Falardeau-Ramsay, Michelle
Deputy Chief Commissioner, Canadian Human
Rights Commission

Finestone, The Hon. Sheila
M.P. (Mount Royal), Government of Canada

Firth, Beatrice
M.L.A., Riverdale South, Government of the
Yukon Territories

Fontaine, Nicole
Deputy Min., Citizens Rel'ns & Immigration,
Government du Québec

Forand, Liseanne
Dir. Gen., Canadian Council of Ministers of
the Environment

Forsyth, Heather
M.L.A., (Calgary-Fish Creek), Government of
Alberta

Fritz, Yvonne
M.L.A., (Calgary Cross), Government of
Alberta

Gaffney, Beryl M.
M.P. (Nepean), Government of Canada

Gagnon-Tremblay, Monique
M.N.A. (Saint-François), Government of
Quebec

Gelber, Sylva M.
Retired Gov't Officer

Gingell, The Honourable Judy
Commissioner of the Yukon, Government of
the Yukon Territories

Gordon, Judy Dawn
M.L.A. (Lacombe-Stettler), Government of
Alberta
Grant, Hon. Judith
Mayor/Préfet (Warden), Municipality of
Chelsea-MRC des Collines de l'Outaouais
Gravel, Line
Committee Clerk & Exec. Sec. to the Cdn
NATO Parliamentary Assoc., Committees &
Private Legislation Directorate, The Senate of
Canada
Greek, Elizabeth
Reg'l Rep., Atlantic Reg., National Women's
Liberal Commission
Green, Joan M.
CEO, Education Quality and Accountability
Office, Government of Ontario
Grenier, Denise
Dir. de l'Ordre National du Québec, Ministère
du Conseil exécutif, Gouvernement du Québec
Grey, Deborah C.
M.P. (Beaver River), Government of Canada
Griffin, Diane
Deputy Min., Dept. of Environmental
Resources, Government of Prince Edward
Island
Guarnieri, Albina
M.P. (Mississauga East) & Parliamentary Sec.
to the Min. of Cdn Heritage, Government of
Canada
Guay, Monique
M.P. (Laurentides), Government of Canada
Gunter, Elaine E.
Dir., Legislative Svcs Branch, Dept. of Justice,
Province of New Brunswick
Guptill, The Hon. Nancy E.
M.L.A. (5th Prince) & Speaker of the Legisla-
tive Assembly, Government of Prince Edward
Island
Gusella, Mary M.
Commissioner, Public Service Commission of
Canada
Haley, Carol
M.L.A. (Three Hills-Airdrie) & Chrm, Standing
Policy Committee on Agriculture & Rural Dev.,
Government of Alberta
Hall, Hon. Barbara
Mayor, City of Toronto
Hamilton, Doreen
M.L.A. (Regina Wascana Plains), Government
of Saskatchewan
Hammell, Sue
Min. of Women's Equality, Government of
British Columbia
Hanson, Alice
M.L.A. (Edmonton Highlands Beverly), Liberal
Opposition, Government of Alberta
Harel, Louise
M.N.A. (Hochelaga-Maisonneuve) & Min.
d'état de l'Emploi et de la Solidarité et min.

responsable de la Condition Féminine,
Gouvernement du Québec
Hayes, Sharon Ruth
M.P. (Port Moody-Coquitlam), Government of
Canada
Hickey, Bonnie
M.P. (St. John's East), Government of Canada
Holt, Linda
Mgmt Consultant, Dept. of Fin., Province of
New Brunswick
Holzman, Hon. Jacquelin
Mayor, City of Ottawa
Hošek, Chaviva Malada
Dir., Policy & Research, Office of the Prime
Minister, Government of Canada
Houda-Pepin, Fatima
Députée (La Pinière), Assemblée Nationale du
Québec, Gouvernement du Québec
Hubley, Elizabeth
M.L.A. (4th Prince), Government of Prince
Edward Island
Hume, Valerie
Policy Coord., Sustainable Dev., Dept. of
Indian Affairs & Northern Dev., Government
of Canada
Hurley, Adèle M.
Chair, International Joint Commission
Ip, Maggie
Councillor, City of Vancouver
Jacko, Esther Marie
Community Historian & Lands Mgr, White-
fish River First Nation
Jarrett, The Hon. Laureen
M.L.A. (Saint John Kings) & Min. of State for
Mines & Energy, Government of New
Brunswick
Jennings, Daphne G.
M.P. (Mission-Coquitlam), Government of
Canada
Jérôme-Forget, Monique
Pres., Institute for Research on Public Policy
Jodoin, Shelley
Labour Comm. Specialist, Workers'
Compensation Board of Alberta
Johnson, Hon. Beth
Mayor, Corporation of Delta
Johnson, Margaret W.
Nat'l Readiness Campaign, The Liberal Party
of Alberta/Northwest Territories
Johnson, The Hon. Janis Gudrun
Senator, The Senate of Canada
Kingston, Joan
M.L.A., Government of New Brunswick
Kirkland, Marie Claire
Retired Legislator, Province of Quebec
Kraft Sloan, Karen
M.P. (York-Simcoe), Government of Canada
Kumi, Janna W.
Asst. Deputy Min., Oper. Div., Ministry of
Forests, Government of British Columbia

Labelle, Huguette
Pres., Canadian International Development Agency

Laking, Hon. Janice
Mayor, City of Barrie

LaRocque, Judith Anne
Sec. to the Gov. Gen. & Head Chancellor, Government House

Lavallée, Diane
Sous-ministre adjointe au Loisir et aux Sports, Ministère des Affaires municipales, Governement du Québec

LeBreton, Hon. Marjory
Senator, The Senate of Canada

Leduc, Lyse
M.N.A. (Mille-Îles), Government of Québec

Leibovici, Karen
M.L.A. (Edmonton Meadowlark), Government of Alberta

Levine, Marlene
Dir. Gen., Reg'l Oper. Branch, Statistics Canada

Lindsay Luby, Gloria
Pres., Gloria Lindsay Luby Enterprises

Lofthouse, Maureen
Dir., Enabling Technologies, Technology Partnerships Canada

Loren, Sandra
Pres., Women's Commission of the BC Liberal Party

Lorjé, Pat
M.L.A. (Saskatoon-Southeast), Government of Saskatchewan

Loughrey, Carol Elaine Ashfield
Deputy Min. of Educ., Govenment of New Brunswick

MacDonald, Hon. Flora
Chair, International Development Research Centre

MacDonald, Lynn M.
Asst. Deputy Min., Corp. Svcs, Ministry of Community & Social Svcs., Government of Ontario

MacKinnon, The Hon. Janice
Min. of Fin., Government of Saskatchewan

MacPhail, The Hon. Joy K.
M.L.A. (Vancouver-Hastings), Min. of Health & Min. Resp. for Seniors & Gov't House Leader, Government of British Columbia

Maheu, Hon. Shirley
Senator, The Senate of Canada

Malo, Nicole
Sous-min., Ministère du revenu, Gouvernement du Québec

Marland, Margaret
M.P.P. (Mississauga South) & Gov't Caucus Chair, Government of Ontario

Marleau, The Hon. Diane
Min. of Public Works & Gov't Svcs., Government of Canada

Marois, The Hon. Pauline
M.N.A. (Taillon) & Min. of Educ., Government of Québec

Martel, Shelley
M.P.P. (Sudbury E.), Government of Ontario

Mawani, Nurjehan
Chair, Immigration and Refugee Board of Canada

Maxwell, Judith
Pres., CPRN Inc.

Mayda, Jacqueline E.
Survey Statistician, Statistics Canada

McCallion, Kathryn E.
Asst. Deputy Min., Int'l Bus. & Comm., & Chief Trade Commissioner, Dept. of Foreign Affairs & External Trade, Government of Canada

McCain, The Honourable Margaret Norrie
Lt.-Gov., Province of New Brunswick

McCallion, The Hon. Hazel
City of Mississauga

McCarthy, Grace Mary
Former Politician

McClellan, Hon. Shirley
M.L.A. (Chinook) & Min. of Community Dev., Government of Alberta

McDonald, Katherine
Pres., Nova Scotia Advisory Council on the Status of Women

McDonough, Alexa
Leader, New Democratic Party of Canada

McGonigal, The Honourable Pearl

McIntosh, The Hon. Linda Gwen
Min. of Educ. & Training, Government of Manitoba

McKee-Allain, Isabelle
Doyenne par intérim, Fac. des sci. sociales, Université de Moncton

McLaughlin, Audrey
M.P. (Yukon), Government of Canada

McLellan, The Honourable Anne
M.P. (Edmonton Northwest) & Min. of Natural Resources, Government of Canada

McLeod, Lyn
M.P.P. (Fort William) & Interim Leader of the Official Opposition, Government of Ontario

McNeil, Mary
Deputy Exec. Dir., APEC '97 Cdn Coordinating Office, Government of Canada

McQueen, Jennifer
Retired Public Servant

Meagher, B. Margaret
Retired Diplomat

Mella, Patricia Janet
M.L.A.(3rd Queen's) & Leader, Official Opposition, Government of Prince Edward Island

Meredith, Val
M.P. (Surrey-White Rock-South Langley), Government of Canada

Minna, Maria
M.P. (Beaches-Woodbine), Government of Canada

Mirosh, The Hon. Diane
M.L.A. (Calgary-Glenmore) & Min. Resp. for Sci. & Research, Government of Alberta

Mitchelson, The Hon. Bonnie
Min. of Family Svcs, Government of Manitoba

Murphy, Marion
M.L.A., Government of Prince Edward Island

Murray, Suzanne M.A.
M.L.A. (Regina Qu'Appelle Valley), Government of Saskatchewan

Neustaedter, Annette K.
Dir. Prince Albert Provincial Correctional Centre, Dept. of Justice, Government of Saskatchewan

Norrie, The Hon. Eleanor
M.L.A. (Truro-Bible Hill), Min. of Natural Res., Min. Resp. for the Women's Directorate & Min. Resp. for Admin. of the Advisory Council of the Status of Women Act, Government of Nova Scotia

O'Connor, Lila J.
M.L.A. (Lunenburg), Government of Nova Scotia

O'Neil, Maureen
Interim Pres. (Sept. 15-Dec. 15, 1996), International Centre for Human Rights and Demographic Development

Parrish, Carolyn
M.P. (Mississauga West), Government of Canada

Pearson, The Hon. Landon Carter
Senator, The Senate of Canada

Penrod, Lynn
Pres., Social Sciences and Humanities Research Council of Canada

Peterson, Susan
Asst. Deputy Min., Fed. Prov. Fiscal Rel'ns & Social Policy, Dept. of Fin., Government of Canada

Phinney, Elizabeth
M.P. (Hamilton Mountain), Government of Canada

Power, Rosalie
Administrative Asst. to Mayor, City of Yellowknife

Priddy, The Hon. Penny
M.L.A. (Surrey-Newton) & Min. of Small Bus., Tourism & Culture, Government of British Columbia

Priesnitz, Wendy
Leader, Green Party of Canada

Ramkhalawansingh, Ceta
Mgr, Equal Opportunity, City of Toronto

Randall, Janet
Dir., Cabinet & Corp. Svcs, Public Works & Government Svcs, Government of Canada

Reid, Linda
M.L.A. (Richmond East), Government of British Columbia

Render, Shirley
M.L.A., Government of Manitoba

Ringuette-Maltais, Pierette
M.P. (Madawaska-Victoria) & Asst. Deputy Chrm of Committees of the Whole House, Government of Canada

Robert, Hélène
Députée (Deux-Montagnes), Adjointe parlementaire et Sec. régionale des Laurentides, Assemblée Nationale

Robertson, The Hon. Brenda Mary
Senator, The Senate of Canada

Robillard, The Hon. Lucienne
Min. of Citizenship & Immigration & MP (St. Henri-Westmount), Government of Canada

St. Denis, Judith
Co-Pres., Aboriginal Peoples' Commission, Liberal Party of Canada

Shack, Sybil F.
Pres., Canadian Civil Liberties Association

Sheridan, Georgette
M.P. (Saskatoon-Humboldt), Government of Canada

Signori, Céline
M.N.A. (Blainville), Government of Québec

Sillett, Mary J.
Interim Pres., Inuit Tapirisat of Canada

Skoke, Roseanne Marie
M.P. (Central Nova), Government of Canada

Smith, Janet Rosalea
Principal, Cdn Centre for Mgmt Dev., Government of Canada

Soetaert, Colleen
M.L.A. (Spruce Grove-Sturgeon-St. Albert), Opposition Critic for Community Dev. & Women's Issues, Government of Alberta

Stableforth, Nancy Lynne
Deputy Commissioner for Women, Correctional Service of Canada, Government of Canada

Stanger, Violet
M.L.A., Government of Saskatchewan

Stanley, Kathleen
Asst. Deputy Min., Health Promotions & Programs Branch, Health Canada, Government of Canada

Steger, Debra P.
Dir., Appellate Body Secretariat, World Trade Organization

Szlazak, Anita Christina
Mbr., Canadian International Trade Tribunal

Talbot-Allan, Laura M.
Asst. Deputy Min., Corp. Svcs, Environment Canada, Government of Canada

Teichrob, Hon. Carol
M.L.A. (Saskatoon Meewasin), Min. of Mun.

Gov't & Min. Resp. for SaskTel, Government of Saskatchewan

Terrana, Anna Marina
M.P. (Vancouver East), Government of Canada

Todres, Elaine
Deputy Solicitor Gen. & Deputy Min. of Corrections, Government of Ontario

Tremblay, Suzanne
M.P. (Rimouski-Témiscouata), Government of Canada

Trenholme, Hon. Marilyn
Min. of State for Family & Community Svcs, Government of New Brunswick

Trumper, Gillian
Mayor, City of Port Alberni

Ur , Rose-Marie
M.P.(Lambton-Middlesex), Government of Canada

Vermette, Cécile
Députée (Marie-Victorin), Assemblée Nationale, Government du Québec

Watters, Bronwyn Valmai
Dir., Policy, Planning & Evaluation, Dept. of Health & Social Svcs, Government of Northwest Territories

Waygood, Kathryn
Councillor, City of Saskatoon

Wayne, Elsie E.
M.P. (Saint John), Government of Canada

Weir, Elizabeth
M.L.A. (Saint John Harbour), Government of New Brunswick

Westbury, June Alwyn
Volunteer

Whelan, Susan
M.P. (Essex-Windsor), Government of Canada

Willcock, Elizabeth
Sr. Citizenship Judge, Dept of Citizenship and Immigration Canada, Government of Canada

Witmer, The Hon. Elizabeth
M.P.P. & Min. of Labour, Government of Ontario

JOURNALISM
Publication of newspapers, magazines or journals. Reporting in print or broadcast media. Related organizations, government agencies and officials.

Armstrong, Sally
Ed.-in-Chief, *Homemaker's* Magazine

Bagnall, Janet
Sr. Feature Writer, *The Gazette*

Bellegris, Agnes
Mng Ed., *Business Quarterly*

Berton, Janet
Writer

Blackstone, Renee A.
Lifestyles Ed., *The Province*

Braun, Liz
Film Critic & Entertainment Writer, *The Toronto Sun*

Brown, Laurie
Author, TV Journalist, Canadian Broadcasting Corporation

Brunel, Cindy
Publisher, *The Free Press - Fernie*

Bye, Cristine
Ed. & Sr. Writer, Comm. & Dev. Dept., The Banff Centre for Continuing Education

Cameron, Stevie
Author. Ed.-in-Chief, *Elm Street* magazine

Campbell, Leslie Ann
Ed. & Publisher, Campbell Communications Inc.

Carey, Elaine
Demographics Reporter, *The Toronto Star*

Chodan, Lucinda
Entertainment Ed., *Montreal Gazette*

Chong, Vivian Yuen Fun
News Ed., Ming Pao Newspapers (Canada) Ltd.

Cockburn, Lyn
Columnist & Features Writer, *The Calgary Sun*

Collins, Anne
Mng Ed., *Toronto Life* Magazine

Corbella, Licia
Assoc. Ed. & Columnist, *The Calgary Sun*

Corrigan, Anne Marie
VP, Journals & Design, Univ. of Toronto Press Incorporated

Cowan, Bonnie
Ed.-in-Chief, *Canadian Living* Magazine

Crook, Barbara
Theatre Critic, *The Vancouver Sun*

Crowley, Marilyn B.
Assoc. Food Ed., *Chatelaine* magazine

Curran, Peggy
City Columnist, *The Gazette*

Dalglish, Brenda G.
Media Reporter, *The Financial Post*

Degler, Teri
Writer & Freelance Journalist

Dotto, Lydia
Freelance Science Writer & Ed.

Drainie, Bronwyn
Writer, Broadcaster, Cultural Critic

Draycott, Anita
Edit. Dir., *Chatelaine Special Editions*, Maclean Hunter Publishing Limited

Driver, Deana
Writer & Photographer, First-Rate Freelancing

Duncan, Muriel
Ed., *The United Church Observer*

Dunlop, Marilyn E.
Medical Columnist, *The Toronto Star*

Eagan, Trudy
VP, Corp. Affairs & Hum. Res., The Toronto Sun Publishing Corporation

Elie, Catherine
Ed., *Châtelaine*
Empey, Charlotte E.
Editor, *Modern Woman* magazine, Maclean Hunter Publishing Limited
Farlinger, Shirley Ruth Tabb
Freelance Writer & Peace Activist
Farr, Moira
Freelance Writer & Ed.
Fenton, Jane
Research Assoc., New Media, The Toronto Sun Publishing Corporation
Fouriezos, Carolyn
Columnist/Writer, *The Sudbury Star*
Fournier, Suzanne N.
Journalist & Author, *Vancouver Province*
Francis, Diane
Ed., *The Financial Post*
Fraser, Joan
Frazer, D. Suzan
Ptnr, Patterson Palmer Hunt Murphy
Gayle, Marlaina
Consumer Reporter, *The Province*
Gibson, Deborah Ruth
Publisher, *Canadian Art* Magazine
Gilbert, Jane
Anchor, Global Television Network
Goar, Carol
Washington Bureau Chief, *The Toronto Star*
Graham, Patricia A.
Edit. Page Ed., *The Vancouver Sun*
Grin, Gayle
Feature Design Dir., *The Gazette*
Gwyn, Alexandra
Journalist & Author
Haines, Judith
Ed., *This Country Canada*
Hammond, Ruth
Pres. & Principal, Ruth Hammond Public Relations
Harcourt, Joan
Poetry/Fiction Ed., *Queen's Quarterly*
Harris, Marjorie
Garden Writer
Harvey, Dona Joan
Writer & Comm. Consultant
Hayes, Carole-Ann
Pres., WHERE Magazines International
Heiman, Carolyn E.
Ed., Living Section, *Victoria Times Colonist*
Hobbs, Anna
Assoc. Ed., *Canadian Living* Magazine
Holmes, Barbara
Retired Ed.
Howard Coady, Jane
Publisher/Gen. Mgr, *Penticton Herald*
Hughes, Linda
Publisher, *The Edmonton Journal*
Janigan, Mary
Contributing Ed., *Maclean's* magazine

Jolley, Jennifer
Writer
Kane, Marion
Food Ed., *The Toronto Star*
Keeler, Helen
Sr. Ed., *Canadian Living* Magazine
Kome, Penney
Author & Journalist. Calgary Contributing Ed., *NeWest Review*
Labrecque, Hélène
Editing Mgr, *Ecodecision* Magazine
Landsberg, Michele
Columnist, *The Toronto Star*
La Rocque, Cheryl
Freelance Health Columnist, *Cape Breton Post*
Leatherdale, Linda
Financial/Money Ed., *The Toronto Sun*
Leeming, Virginia
Fashion Reporter, *The Vancouver Sun*
Lockyer, Debora
Ed., *Windspeaker*, Aboriginal Multi-Media Society of Canada
Long, Wendy
Sportswriter, *The Vancouver Sun*
Maclean, Victoria
Ed., *The Edmonton Sun*
MacMillan, Ann
European Correspondent, Canadian Broadcasting Corporation
Mason, Joyce
Ed. & Publisher, *C magazine*
Maynard, Rona
Ed., *Chatelaine* Magazine
McCall, Christina
Author/Ed., *Saturday Night* Magazine
McCallum, Lorna
Dean, Fac. of Language, Lit. & Performing Arts, Douglas Coll.
McDonald, Marci
Sr. Writer, *Maclean's* Magazine
McKay, Shona
Writer
McNellis, Maryanne
Ed. Dir., *The Financial Post*
McQuaig, Linda
Journalist & Author
Merikle, Mary
Mng Ed. & Fiction Ed., *The New Quarterly*
Moon, Barbara Ethel
Ed.-at-Large, *Saturday Night* Magazine
Murdoch, Sarah
Assoc. Ed., *The Globe and Mail*
Nebenzahl, Donna
Ed., Women's News, *The Gazette*
Noble, Kimberley
Reporter, "Report on Business," *The Globe and Mail*
O'Hara, Jane
Journalist

Paquet, Suzanne
Gen. Mgr, Fin. Publications, Transcontinental Publications Inc.
Paterson, Jody
Mng Ed., *Victoria Times-Colonist*
Piros, Joanna
Pres., Piros Productions
Platts, Diana
Co-Producer & Host, Twisted Pair Productions
Pringle, Heather
Journalist & Author
Rains, Elizabeth
Mng Ed., *The Capilano Review*
Randoja, Ingrid
Film Reviewer & Entertainment Writer, *Now* Magazine
Rauhala, Ann
Journalist, Canadian Broadcasting Corporation
Reeves, Lynda
Publisher & Pres., *Canadian House & Home* & Founder, *Gardening Life* Magazine
Rittinger, Carolyne
Ed., *The Kitchener-Waterloo Record*
Rochester, Helen
Restaurant Columnist, *The Gazette*
Rosenberg, Monda
Food Ed., *Chatelaine* Magazine
Ross, Val
Arts & Publishing Reporter, *The Globe and Mail*
Sanders, Doreen
Ed., *Women in Management Newsletter*
Saunders, Doris J.
Ed., *Them Days*
Shaw, Gillian
Columnist, "The People's Business," *The Vancouver Sun*
Shears, Mary-Deanne
Deputy Mng Ed., *The Toronto Star*
Shortell, Ann M.
Author
Simpson, Lee
VP & Group Publisher (resp. for *Chatelaine, Chatelaine Special Editions!*, & *Modern Woman*), Maclean Hunter Publishing Limited
Sinclair, Donna
Sr. Writer, *The United Church Observer*
Slaight, Annabel
Pres. & CEO, Owl Communications
Smith, Angela
Publisher & Ed., *Business Quarterly*
Smith, Corinne
Prod. Dir., Canada Wide Magazines Ltd.
Spicer, Kathleen
Author, Food Consultant, Kay Spicer & Associates Inc.
Steed, Judy
Feature Writer, *The Toronto Star*
Stewart, Nalini
Freelance Journalist

Stoffman, Judith
Book Review Ed., *The Toronto Star*
Swaine, Margaret
Pres., Pierce Communications
Tait, Kathy
Columnist, *The Province*
Taylor, Gladys
Ed., Tall-Taylor Publishing Ltd.
Tesher, Ellie
Columnist & Journalist, *The Toronto Star*
Thompson, Joey
City Ed., *The Province*
Vanderkamp, Joan Rosemary
Mng Ed., *Canadian Journal on Aging*
Wallin, Pamela
Broadcast Journalist & Host, *Pamela Wallin Live*
Waxman, Sara
Columnist & Author
Weaver, Martha Jane
Publications Consultant
Wente, Margaret
Ed., "Report on Business," *The Globe and Mail*
White, Helena E.
Publisher, *Creston Valley Advance*
Whitfield, Irene
Mng Ed., Canadian Committee on Labour History
Williams, Terri
Columnist, *The Toronto Sun*
Wiseman, Sandra
Reporter, *Kamloops Daily News*
Yaffe, Barbara
Columnist, *The Vancouver Sun*

LAW

Lawyers, judges, police. Corrections officials, inmates, and related charitable groups. Commentators and educators. Related organizations, government agencies and officials.

Agnew, Ella M.
Ptnr, Milrad & Agnew
Allan, Marion
Judge, British Columbia Supreme Court
Amonson, Johanne Leslie
Ptnr, McLennan Ross, Barristers and Solicitors
Andreachuk, Lori
Ptnr, Andreachuk Harvie MacLennan
Ashton, Toni Polson
Ptnr, Sim Hughes Ashton & McKay, Sim & McBurney
Asper, Gail
Gen. Cnsl, Corp. Sec., CanWest Global Communications Corp.
Babe, Jennifer E
Ptnr, Miller Thomson
Baird, Maeve
Lawyer, French Browne

Barber, Joy P.
Barrister, Solicitor, Notary, Commissioner for Oaths

Barber, Susan B.
Ptnr, McDougall, Ready

Bedell, Graysanne
VP, Law, Scott's Restaurants Inc.

Begg, Fiona
Lawyer

Bell, The Hon. Judith Miriam
Judge, Ontario Court of Justice (General Division)

Bertrand, Marie-Andrée
Prof., Sch. of Criminology, Univ. of Montreal

Bielby, Myra B.
Judge, Court of Queen's Bench of Alberta

Bigue, Ann M.
Ptnr, McCarthy Tétrault

Birt, Nancy E.
Ptnr, Birt and McNeill

Block, Sheila R.
Ptnr, Tory Tory DesLauriers & Binnington

Boland, The Hon. Janet Lang
Judge, Trial Div., Supreme Court of Ontario

Borenstein, L'Honorable Sylviane
Justice, Superior Court of Quebec

Bourque, Diane
Exec. Dir., Federation of Law Societies of Canada

Bourque, Pauline
Assoc., LeBlanc Boucher Rodger Bourque

Bowker, Marjorie Montgomery
Retired Judge

Brent, Audrey S.
Mng Ptnr, Brent & Greenhorn

Brooks, Nan
Consultant

Bryant Ballingall, Sally
Lawyer, McCarthy Tétrault

Bulte, Sarmite
Sarmite D. Bulte Barristers & Solicitors

Burnham, M.E.
Cnsl, Borden & Elliot

Butler, Alison Scott
Barrister & Solicitor

Cabott, Laura I.
Lawyer, Davis and Co.

Cadieux, Louise
Ptnr, Lafortune Leduc

Campbell, Diane O.
Sole Proprietor, Diane Campbell Law Offices

Campbell, Karen
Lawyer, Patterson Palmer Hunt Murphy

Carmichael, Jo Ann
Ptnr, Alexander, Holburn, Beaudin & Lang

Carrell, Nancy J.
Deputy Sec., Canadian National Railways

Carron, Christine A.
Ptnr, Ogilvy Renault

Castrilli, Annamarie
Lawyer

Charron, Louise
Justice, Court of Appeal for Ontario

Cody-Rice, Edith
Sr. Legal Cnsl, Canadian Broadcasting Corporation

Colas, Réjane
Retired Justice of the Superior Court of Quebec

Collins, Lisa M.
Partner, Thompson Dorfman Sweatman

Cooper, Jennifer A.
Lawyer, Pitblado and Hoskin

Copp, Joan C.
Dir., Professional Dev., Legal Education Society of Alberta

Corbett, Hon. Marie
Justice, Ontario Court of Justice

Cornish, Mary
Sr. Ptnr, Cavalluzzo Hayes Shilton McIntyre & Cornish

Cornwall, C. Gail
Ptnr, Goodman Phillips & Vineberg

Crowe Worthington, Carolyn
Assoc. Lawyer, Gowlings

Cusack Walsh, Elizabeth
Barrister & Solicitor, Elizabeth Cusack Walsh & Associates

Cushman, Hope C.
Cnsl & Sec., Ford Motor Company of Canada Limited

Dahl Rees, Carolyn
Gen. Cnsl, TransAlta Utilities Corporation

Dawson, Eleanor Ruth
Ptnr, Aikins, MacAulay & Thorvaldson

Dean, Audrey
Legal Cnsl, Alberta Human Rights Commission

Delong, Beverley J.T.
Pres., Lawyers for Social Responsibility

DeMarco, Jean Mary
Ptnr, Osler, Hoskin & Harcourt

Desjardins, Alice
Justice, Federal Court of Canada, Appeal Division

Doherty, Barbara R.C.
Ptnr, Miller Thomson

Dranoff, Linda Silver
Barrister & Solicitor, Linda Silver Dranoff and Associates

Dubin, Anne R.
Ptnr, Tory Tory DesLauriers & Binnington

Dunnet, Tamarin
Judge, Supreme Court of Ontario

Duval Hesler, Nicole
Judge, Superior Court of Quebec

Edmonds, Erin
Lawyer, Maddalena Hill & Edmonds

Edwardh, Marlys Anne
Lawyer, Ruby & Edwardh

English, Hilde
Ptnr, White Jenkins Duncan & Ostner
Fagan, Christine A.
Lawyer, Chalker, Green and Rowe
Flanagan, Catherine
Lawyer, Crown Attorney's Office, Prince
Edward Island
Garneau, Céline
Lawyer, Langlois Robert
Garson, Joan H.
Ptnr, Blaney, McMurtry, Stapells, Friedman
Geisler, Brigitte J.
Asst. VP, Securities Law, Canada Trust
Company
**Glube, The Honorable Chief
Justice Constance**
Chief Justice, Supreme Court of Nova Scotia
Gordon, Dara
Ptnr, Palmer Hunt Murphy
Goss, Joanne H.
Lawyer, Chartered Mediator, Arbitrator, Cook,
Duke, Cox
Gourley, Ann
Ptnr, Bull, Housser and Tupper
Gray, Victoria
Ptnr, Bull, Housser and Tupper
Greckol, Sheila J.
Ptnr, Chivers Greckol & Kanee
Greenberg, Shirley
Lawyer
Gullberg, Shannon R.W.
Barrister & Solicitor
Gundersen, Sonja J.
VP, Law & Corp. Dev., Apple Canada Inc.
Hall, Mary C.
Ptnr, Baker & McKenzie
Hamilton, M. Jill
Lawyer, Daley, Black & Moreira
Hannon, Heather M.
Cnsl & Corp. Sec., The Maritime Life
Assurance Company
Harding, Gloria
Barrister & Solicitor, Newfoundland Legal Aid
Commission
Helper, The Hon. Bonnie Merilyn
Justice, Court of Appeal, Province of Manitoba
Henley, Gail
Legal Cnsl, CanWest Global Systems
Henley-Andrews, Janet
Ptnr, Stewart McKelvey Stirling Scales
Histrop, Lindsay Ann
Ptnr, Aird & Berlis
Hitchman, Carol
Ptnr, Lang Michener
Hoegg, Lois
Lawyer, Ches Crosbie Barristers
Hood, Hon. Suzanne M.
Justice, Supreme Court of Nova Scotia
Howell, Barbara C.
Lawyer, Field & Field Perraton

Hoy, Alexandra
Ptnr, Lang Michener
Huddart, The Hon. Carol Mahood
Judge, The Court of Appeal of British
Columbia
Hughes, Pamela S.
Cnsl, Blake, Cassels and Graydon
Hughes, Sherron J.L.
Lawyer, Athey, Gregory and Hughes
Huglo Robertson, Christine
Exec. Dir., Canadian Institute for the
Administration of Justice
Hummerstone, Jill
First Nations Programs Coord., Matsqui Insti-
tution, Correctional Service of Canada,
Government of Canada
Hutchings, Geraldine
Barrister & Solicitor
Irish, Maureen
Prof., Fac. of Law, Univ. of Windsor
Irvine, Marie
Coordinator, British Columbia Association of
Community Law Offices
Jackman, Barbara Louise
Jackman & Associates
Jackman, Martha
Assoc. Prof., Fac. of Law, Univ. of Ottawa
Jaffer, Mobina
Barrister & Solicitor, Dohm, Jaffer &
Company
Jamieson, Darlene A.
Ptnr, Flinn Merrick
Jamieson, Jamesina G.L.
Retired Lawyer & Civil Servant
Johnson, Elizabeth A.
Ptnr, Lucas Bowker & White
Jordan, Cally
Lawyer, Stikeman, Elliott (Hong Kong)
Julien, Linda A.
Lawyer, Corp. Affairs Officer & Legal Cnsl,
CTI Capital Inc.
Kassie, Lynne
Ptnr, Robinson Sheppard Shapiro
Kaufman, Donna Soble
Barrister & Solicitor, Ptnr, Stikeman,
Elliott
Key, Nancy L.
Mng Ptnr, Key and McKnight
Kimball, Mary A.
Deputy Registrar Gen. of Land Titles, New
Brunswick Geographic Information Corporation
King, Lynn
Judge, Ontario Court of Justice
Larlee, Hon. Madame Justice Margaret
Judge, Court of Queen's Bench of New
Brunswick
LeBlanc-Bridge, Theresa
Sr. Cnsl, Royal Bank of Canada
Leuschner, Lizabeth
Lawyer, Shennette Leuschner McKay

Lewis, Harriet Isabel
Univ. Cnsl, York Univ.
L'Heureux-Dubé, Honourable Madame Justice Claire
Puisne Judge, Supreme Court of Canada
Little, Judythe Patricia
Judge, Ontario Court of Justice
Logan, A Kirsten
Sec. & Co-Dir. of Admin., Law Society of Saskatchewan
Logan, Kerrie
Ptnr, Macleod Dixon
Loo Craig, Kathleen
The Law Office of Kathleen Loo Craig
Lothian, Pamela
Ptnr, McDougall, Ready
MacCallum, Janice
Lawyer, Evans MacCallum
Macdonald, Ellen
Justice, Ontario Court
MacDonald, Norine A.
Barrister & Solicitor
MacGregor, Mary L.
Ptnr, Dickson, Sachs, Appell & Beaman
Mackenzie, Lorna J.
Legislative Solicitor, Dept. of Justice, Province of New Brunswick
MacPherson, Sheila M.
Ptnr, Johnson, Gullberg, Wiest and MacPherson
Mactavish, Anne L.
Pres., Human Rights Tribunal
Maloney, Sharon
Assoc., Maloney, Gottlieb & Pearson Government Relations, Inc.
Manzer, Alison R.
Ptnr, Cassels Brock & Blackwell
McCawley, Deborah Joan
CEO, Law Society of Manitoba
McGillis, The Hon. Donna
Judge, Trial Div., Federal Court of Canada
McGregor, Barbara
Barrister & Solicitor, Osler, Hoskin & Harcourt
McKean, Heather
Mng Ptnr, Osler, Hoskin & Harcourt
McLachlin, The Hon. Madame Justice Beverley
Justice, Supreme Court of Canada
McNeill, Kim M.
Ptnr, Birt and McNeill
McTeer, Maureen A.
Adjunt Asst. Prof., Fac. of Law, Medicine & Nursing, The Univ. of Calgary
Menke, Ursula
VP, Cnsl & Corp. Sec., Metropolitan Life Insurance Company
Mills, Jacqueline
Ptnr, Lang Michener
Moore, Valerie A.

Crown Attorney, Crown Attorney's Office, Prince Edward Island
Morrison, Nancy
Judge, Supreme Court of British Columbia
Morrisroe, Sharon J.
In-house Cnsl, Connor Clark & Lunn Investment Management Ltd.
Morrow, Joy
Ptnr, Smart & Biggar
Ptnr, Fetherstonhaugh & Co.
Mowatt, E. Ann
Ptnr, Patterson Palmer Hunt Murphy
Mrazek, Margaret L.
Ptnr, Reynolds, Mirth, Richards and Farmer
Murphy, Michele M.
Lawyer, Michele M. Murphy and Associates
Murray, M. Lynn
Ptnr, Matheson and Murray
Mutala, Catherine
Ptnr, Oyen Wiggs Green & Mutala
Natividad, Alicia
Barrister, Solicitor & Notary Public
Newbury, Jennifer
Assoc., Martin, Whalen, Hennebury and Stamp
Newbury, Mary V.
Justice, Court of Appeal of British Columbia
Nicholas, Cindy
Barrister & Solicitor
Oakes, Jennifer J.
Ptnr, Field & Field Perraton
O'Callaghan, Shelley
Ptnr, Bull, Housser and Tupper
Ogilvie, M.H.
Barrister & Solicitor
Oland, Linda Lee
Ptnr, McInnes Cooper and Robertson
Olasker, Patricia
Co-Mng Ptnr, McMillan Binch
Olsen, Charlotte A.
Ptnr, Lang Michener Lawrence & Shaw
Orenstein, Elise
Ptnr, Lang Michener
Ormerod, Mary
Ptnr, Perley-Robertson, Panet, Hill and McDougall
Orr, Nancy K.
Prov. Court Judge, Province of Prince Edward Island
Penick, Barbara
Dir. of Discipline, Nova Scotia Barristers' Society
Pepall, Sarah E.
Mng Ptnr, McMillan Binch
Pepino, N. Jane
Ptnr, Aird and Berlis
Picard, Claudette
Ptnr, Stikeman, Elliott
Picard, The Honourable Madam Justice Ellen I.
Justice, Court of Appeal of Alberta

Piché, The Hon. Justice Ginette
Judge, Superior Court of Montreal
Pinder, Leslie
Ptnr, Mandell Pinder
Pratte, Lise
Lawyer & Administrator
Prior, Roxanne V.
Barrister & Solicitor
Ralling, M. Jane
Ptnr, Campbell, Lea, Michael, McConnell and
Pigot
Reagh, Elizabeth Strong
Barrister, Solicitor & Mediator, Reagh &
Reagh
**Reed, Honourable Madame
Justice Barbara Joan**
Judge, Trial Div., Federal Court of Canada
Reid, Diana R.
Consultant, Lang Michener Lawrence & Shaw
Reid, Maureen
Ptnr, McInnes Cooper and Robertson
Rethy, Katherine
VP, Transportation, Noranda Metallurgy Inc.
Rhea, Celia
Ptnr, Goodman Phillips & Vineberg
Roberts, Eve
Ptnr, Patterson Palmer Hunt Murphy
Robertson, Donna Lee
Principal, Robertson & Co.
Robertson, Linda
Corp. Sec. & Gen. Cnsl, Insurance
Corporation of British Columbia
Robichaud, Dani Ann
Barrister & Solicitor
Rubenstein, Gale
Sr. Ptnr, Goodman Phillips & Vineberg
Russell, Brenda M.
Pres., Municipal Law Enforcement Officers'
Association (Ontario) Inc.
Safran, Laura
Barrister & Solicitor, Milner Fenerty
Scott, Sheridan Elizabeth
VP, Multimedia Law & Regulation, Bell
Canada
Sevigny, The Hon. Pierrette
Judge, Superior Court of the Province of
Quebec
Shafran, Grace
VP & Gen. Cnsl, Baton Broadcasting
Incorporated
Shilton, Elizabeth J.
Sr. Ptnr, Cavalluzzo Hayes Shilton McIntyre &
Cornish
Sievwright, Georgia
Gen. Cnsl & Sec. & Dir. of Corp. Rel'ns,
Hewlett-Packard (Canada) Ltd.
Silverberg, Christine
Chief, Calgary Police Service
Simard, R.M. Louise
Lawyer, MacPherson Leslie & Tyerman

Sims, Mary-Woo
V-Chair, Boards of Inquiry - Human Rights,
Pay Equity Hearings Tribunal, Province of
Ontario
Skanes, Lois J.
Ptnr, Williams, Roebothan, McKay and
Marshall
Smith, Lynn
Prof. & Dean, Fac. of Law, Univ. of British
Columbia
Smith, Marva J.
Cnsl, Constitutional Law Branch, Manitoba
Justice
Smith, Phyllis
Ptnr, Emery Jamieson
Somerville, Margaret Anne
McGill Centre for Medicine, Ethics and Law
Spies, Nancy J.
Barrister, Stockwood, Spies
Stairs, Janice A.
Lawyer, Patterson Palmer Hunt Murphy
Steel, Freda M.
Justice, Manitoba Court of Queen's Bench
Stevens, Pamela M.
Mng Ptnr, Hughes, Amys
Stevenson, Barbara F.
Ptnr, Carr, Stevenson and MacKay
Stewart, Anne Marie
Ptnr, Blake, Cassels and Graydon
Stewart, Janet
Mng Ptnr, Lerner & Associates
Suche, P. Colleen
Ptnr, Suche Gange
Swan, Judith
Pres. & CEO, SwanSea Oceans Environment
Inc.
Theriault, M. Estelle
Public Trustee, Province of Nova Scotia
Thompson, Bonita J.
Ptnr, Singleton Urquhart Scott
Thomson, Pamela Ann
Judge, Ontario Court of Justice
Trahan, Anne-Marie
Judge, Superior Court of Quebec
Trussler, Mme. Justice Marguerite
Justice, Court of Queen's Bench of Alberta
Ulmer, Karen C.
Solicitor, Saskatchewan Government
Insurance
Van den Eynden, Elizabeth
Ptnr, MacIntosh, MacDonnell & MacDonald
van Driel, Gerlinde
Ptnr, Patterson Palmer Hunt Murphy
Veenman, Sybil E.
Assoc. Gen. Cnsl & Sec., Barrick Gold
Corporation
Vella, Susan M.
Lawyer, Goodman and Carr
Watters, Frances R.
Ptnr, Alexander, Holburn, Beaudin & Lang

Whitaker, Marni
Ptnr, Lang Michener
Wright, Merri-Ellen
Lawyer & Ptnr, McDougall, Ready
Youngman, Alison J.
Ptnr, Stikeman, Elliott
Zerbisias, The Hon. Dionysia
Judge, Superior Court of Quebec

MEDIA CULTURE
Broadcast, narrowcast and cablecast television and radio, film and other electronic formats. Individuals in various capacities including production and performance; applied to corporate entities involved in production or distribution; also encompasses agents, advertising and some fashion-related activities. Related organizations, government agencies and officials.

Angelico, Irene
CEO, DLI Productions
Armstrong, Jane
Pres., CineNova Productions Inc.
Barde, Barbara
Pres., Up Front Entertainment Inc.
Battson, Jill
Exec. Prod., Talking Pictures
Beker, Jeanne
Host/Segment Prod., *Fashion Television*
Bennett, Gale Diana
Mng Dir., TVOntario
Besen, Ellen
Bishop, Gloria
Exec. Prod., *Morningside*, CBC Radio, Canadian Broadcasting Corporation
Bjornson, Michelle
Pres., Point of View Film Inc.
Borenstein, Joyce
Freelance Filmmaker, Illumination Magique Inc.
Caloz, Danièle
Pres., Médiatique Inc.
Charest, Micheline
Chair & CEO, CINAR Films Inc.
Cheechoo, Shirley
Artist, Writer & Performer
Clarkson, Adrienne
Exec. Prod., Host & Writer, *Adrienne Clarkson Presents*
Cohen, Annette
Pres., Annette Cohen Productions Limited
Conley, Corinne
Actor
Connell, Meg
Exec. Dir., The Canadian Club of Toronto
Cook, Heather Maggs
Dir. & Prod., *The Nature of Things*, Canadian Broadcasting Corporation
Dance, Faye
Broadcaster

Danis, Aimee
Pres. & Co-Founder, Verseau International
David, Cynthia
Food Ed., *The Toronto Sun*
Deol, Monika
Desautels, Suzanne
TV Broadcaster. Host, *Travel, Travel* and Host, *Simply Wine & Cheese*, CFCF TV
de Wilde, Lisa
Pres. & COO, TMN - The Movie Network/ MOVIEPIX
Donlon, Denise
Dir. of Music Programming, MuchMusic
Emilio, Alison
Toronto Film Commissioner & Mktg Agent & Mgr/Dir., Ontario Film Development Corporation
Filer, Diana Mary
Broadcasting Consultant
Ford, Christina
Pres./Owner, Imported Artists Film Company
Fournier, Lili
Prod., Dir. & Writer, Zolar Entertainment Corp.
Fusca-Vincent, Martha
Pres., Stornoway Productions Inc.
Gartner, Hana
Host, *The National Magazine*, CBC
Gordon, Lee
Pres., Lee Gordon Productions
Grogan, Liz
Broadcaster, McLellan Group
Gulkin, Catherine
Film & Video Ed., Cathy Gulkin Film Editing Ltd.
Harrington, Beth
Host, *Chats & Company*
Heaton, Pauline R.
Pres., Watervisions Underwater Camera Systems
Hénaut, Dorothy Todd
Freelance Filmmaker & Videomaker
Henderson, Anne
Film Dir. & Prod., Arcady Films
Heroux, Justine
Pres. & Prod., CINEVIDEO PLUS
Horsman, Karen
Talk Show Host, Talk 640/Q107
Keating, Lulu
Pres., Red Snapper Films Limited
Kehoe, Carol A.
Internet Svcs Mgr, Blackburn Media Group
Klodawsky, Helene
Documentary Filmmaker
Lamb, Marjorie
Writer Speaker & Consultant
Lanctôt, Micheline
Pres., Stopfilm Inc.
Leaney, Cindy
Pres., Voyage Media Productions Inc.

Lederman, Marsha
Talk Show Host, "Horsman/Lederman", Talk 640
Lee, Lauren
Freelance TV/Radio/Video Announcer & Aviation Promoter
Lundman, Janis
Dir. & Prod., Back Alley Film Productions Ltd.
Lyons, Keiko Margaret
Former Broadcasting Exec.
Marshall, Heather
Deputy Dir., Production Financing, Arts & Entertainment, Canadian Broadcasting Corporation
Martin, Marcia
VP, Production, CityTV
McEwen, Maryke
Prod., Kinetic Productions
McHugh, Fiona
Scriptwriter
McIvor, Jane
Mng Dir., Core Group Publishers Inc.
McLennan, Elizabeth
Dir., Regulatory Info., TELUS Corporation
McQueen, Shirley
Radio Announcer, Q107 FM
Medina, Ann
Independent Prod., Medina Productions Inc.
Mesley, Wendy
Journalist/Host, *Sunday Report* & Journalist/ Host, *Undercurrents*, Canadian Broadcasting Corporation
Micallef, Gabriella
Dir. & Prod., I-Sis Productions
Mironowicz, Maria
Exec. Prod., CBC Newsworld
Mitchell, Adrienne
Filmmaker, Back Alley Film Productions Ltd.
Moore-Ede, Carol
Exec. Prod., CBC-TV, Canadian Broadcasting Corporation
Morin, Francyne
Freelance Prod.
Mungall, Constance
Freelance writer
Newall, Joy
Past Pres., Conscience Canada (Peace Tax Fund)
Newell, Jacqueline
Sound Ed., National Film Board of Canada
Paabo, Iris
Multimedia Artist, Iriz Studios
Paakspuu, Kalli
Prod., Dir., Writer & Videographer, Calipix Productions
Pacsu, Margaret
Broadcaster & Journalist, Canadian Broadcasting Corporation
Petrie, Anne G.
Host, *Early Edition*, CBC Newsworld,

Petro, Trina
Co-Owner & Exec. VP, Montage Inc.
Prieto, Claire
Prod., National Film Board of Canada
Rached, Tahani
Filmmaker, National Film Board of Canada
Raffé, Alexandra
CEO, Ontario Film Development Corporation
Rankin, Linda M.
Exec. VP & Gen. Mgr, WETV
Read, Merilyn
Pres., M.T.R. Entertainment Limited
Reisler, Susan
Host, *Tapestry*, CBC Radio & Sr. Producer, Radio Current Affairs, Canadian Broadcasting Corporation
Reynolds, Carolann
VP, Corp. Dev., Regan Productions Inc.
Rinaldo, Sandie
Anchor, "CTV News Weekend," CTV Television Network
Roberge, Hélène
Pres. & Dir. Gen., Les Productions Hélène Roberge E.N.R.
Robillard-Frayne, Hélène
Dir., Radio Programming & Schedule Planning, Société Radio-Canada
Rogers, Mickey
Principal, Forefront Entertainment Group
Rozema, Patricia
Filmmaker, Crucial Pictures
Sereny, Julia
Prod., Sienna Films Inc.
Sheffer, Andra
Exec. Dir., Maclean Hunter Television Fund
Shekter, Louise
Pres., Media Solutions Inc.
Siebert, Traute
Pres. & Owner, Eleanor Fulcher International Ltd.
Sky, Laura
Film Prod. & Dir., Sky Works Charitable Foundation
Smith, Nancy
Pres., Nextmedia
Srebotnjak, Tina
Host, *Midday*, Canadian Broadcasting Corporation
Stephenson, Helga
Chair, Viacom Canada Limited
Stratton, Anna
Prod. & Ptnr, Triptych Media Inc.
Sturgess, Jennifer
Pres., The Sturgess Group Inc.
Tarlington, Carole
Pres., Tarlington Talent Inc.
Tattersall, Jane
Pres., Tattersall Sound Inc.
Thompson, E. Jane
Film & TV Dir.

Tilby, Wendy
Film Dir., National Film Board of Canada
Trow, Susan
Cinematographer, National Film Board of Canada
Viau, Catherine
VP, Les Productions Via le Monde (Daniel Bertolino) Inc.
Weinstein, Deborah
Pres., Strategic Objectives Inc.
Wheeler, Anne
Filmmaker, Anne Wheeler Inc.
Whittaker, Sheelagh D.
Pres., EDS Canada
Willis Sweete, Barbara
Film & TV Dir., Rhombus Media Inc.
Yaffe, Phyllis
Pres. & CEO, Showcase Television Inc.
Yolles, Edie
Pres., Gemini Film Productions Inc.

MEDICAL/HEALTH
Medicine and allied professions such as nursing, dentistry, and nutrition, both mainstream and alternative. Psychology and social work. Health practitioners and educators. Related organizations, government agencies and officials.

Amirali-Hadjinicolaou, Evangelia-Lila
Medical Doctor
Anderson, Dianne E.
VP, North York General Hospital
Annis, Helen M.
Chief, Behaviour Change Unit, Addiction Research Foundation
Armann, Donna Marie
Dir. of Nursing, Cross Cancer Institute
Ashford, Mary-Wynne
Physician, Educator, Disarmament Activist.
Bacon, Marilyn
VP, Nursing, IWK-Grace Health Centre for Children, Women & Families
Barnard, Dorothy
Pediatric Hematologist, Oncologist, Hematopathologist, IWK-Grace Health Centre for Children, Women & Families
Bassett, Sandra
Program Dir., Surgical Svcs, North York General Hospital
Batty, Helen P.
Assoc. Chair, Dept. of Family & Community Medicine, Fac. of Medicine, Univ. of Toronto
Baum, Nehama T.
Exec. Dir., Muki Baum Association for the Rehabilitation of Multi Handicapped Inc.
Bear, Merryl Jean
Prog. Coord., National Eating Disorder Information Centre

Beare-Rogers, Joyce
Consultant, lipid nutrition
Befus, Mariann
Supervisor, Rehab. Svcs Unit, Medical Technical Support Services
Bergman, June S.
Clinical Dir., Family Med. Centre, Peter Lougheed Centre
Bertell, H Rosalie
Pres., International Institute of Concern for Public Health
Best, Lynette
COO, Lions Gate Hospital
Bishton-Fox, Lesley
District Administrator, 511670 Alberta Ltd. (o/a Coram Construction)
Blaney, E Sharon
Mgr of Corp. Health, BC TEL
Blois, Ruby
Dir., Partnership Dev., IWK-Grace Health Centre for Children, Women & Families
Bol, Nancy Ann
Clinical Nurse Specialist - Gerontology, Parkwood Hospital
Boreskie, Suzanne Louise
Exec. Dir., The Wellness Institute at Seven Oaks General Hospital
Borwein, Bessie
Asst. Dean - Research, Fac. of Medicine, Univ. of Western Ontario
Bradley, Susan
Psychiatrist-in-Chief, The Hospital for Sick Children
Bradley, Susan
Head, Div. of Child Psychiatry, Univ. of Toronto
Bramwell, Vivien
Head of Medical Oncology, London Regional Cancer Centre, Ontario Cancer Treatment and Research Foundation
Brister, Stephanie J.
Cardiovascular Surgeon, Hamilton Civic Hospitals
Bryant, Heather
Dir., Div. of Epidemiology, Prevention & Screening & Dir., Alberta Program for the Early Detection of Breast Cancer, Alberta Cancer Board
Budz, Denise
Gen. Mgr, Palliative Care Svc., Saskatoon District Health
Burgess, Rachel Lillian
Psychologist, Teacher, Consultant, Counselor, Hypnotist
Burkinshaw, Sylvia Mary
Retired Hosp. Administrator
Calder, Eleanor
Mgr, Cooperative Health Centre
Cameron, W. Sheila Johnston
Dean of Grad. Studies, Prof. of Nursing, Univ. of Windsor

Campbell, H. Sharon
Behavioural Research Scientist, Alberta Cancer Board

Caplan, Paula Joan
Psychologist & Writer

Casselman, Barbie
Pres., Casselman & Co. Inc.

Castonguay-Thibaudeau, Marie-France
Prof., Fac. des sciences infirmières, Université de Montréal

Christie, Nancy P.
Pres., NPC Consulting

Christopher, Jeannette B.
Staff Educ. Coord., Western Memorial Regional Hospital

Clark, Kathy
Sr. Food Svc. Officer, Calgary Regional Health Authority

Clark, Lillian
Physician

Clarke, Heather F.
Nursing Res. Consultant, Registered Nurses' Association of British Columbia

Cole, Susan P.C.
Prof. of Oncology, Pathology, Pharmacology & Toxicology, Career Scientist of the Ontario Cancer Foundation, Queen's Univ.

Coles, Brenda
Pres., Prince Edward Island Licensed Nursing Assistants Association

Coniglio, Constance Barbara
Counsellor/Therapist, Univ. of Western Ontario

Cooper, Angela
Dir. of Nursing, Oshawa General Hospital

Cranston, Lynda S.
Pres. & CEO, B.C. Women's Hospital & Health Centre

Daniels, Valsa
Dir. of Stroke Program, Rehabilitation Hospital

Daoust-Roy, Jeannine
Pres., Canadian Association of Electroneurophysiology Technologists, Inc.

Darling, Betty
Past Pres., Osteoporosis Society of B.C.

Davies, Christine E.
Physician

Dembe, Elaine
Dr. of Chiropractic

Devlin, Corinne
Prof. of Obstetrics & Gynecology, McMaster Univ.

Dobkin, Patricia Lynn
Medical Scientist, Div. of Clinical Epidemiology, The Montreal General Hospital

Doiron, Cheryl A.
VP, Oper. & Planning, Atlantic Health Sciences Corporation

Doucet, Vida
Public Health Nurse, Dartmouth & Halifax, Dept. of Health, Government of Nova Scotia

Down, Nancy
Physician, North York General Hospital

Doyle, Dianne
COO, Mount Saint Joseph Hospital

Dukszta, Annette M.
Exec. Dir., Canadian Brain Tissue Bank

Easton, Carol
Administrative Leader–Surgical Svcs, Inpatients Preoperative Assessment Clinics & Acute Pain Svcs, Calgary Regional Health Authority

Eaves, Connie Jean
Deputy Dir., The Terry Fox Laboratory for Hematology/Oncology

Eberl-Kelly, Katherine
Bd. Chair, East Prince Health Regional Board

Eccles, Robin Christina
Pediatric Surgeon, Alberta Children's Hospital

Elder, Michele
R.N., Neonatal I.C.U., Royal University Hospital

Eng, Brenda
Founder & Clinical Specialist, Canuck Place

Eriksen, Maria
Psychologist, Eriksen & Webb

Ernest, Rosemarie
Nurse Consultant

Finestone, Karen
Clinical Nurse Specialist, Sir Mortimer B. Davis Jewish General Hospital

Fitch, Pamela L.
Past Pres., Ontario Massage Therapist Association

Freeman, Risa
Program Dir., Undergrad. Educ., & Asst. Prof., Dept. of Family & Community Medicine, Univ. of Toronto

Friedland, Judith
Assoc. Prof. & Chair, Dept. of Occupational Therapy, Fac. of Medicine, Univ. of Toronto

Fulton, M. Jane
Principal, The Health Group

Gagnon, Raymonde F.
Assoc. Physician, Div. of Nephrology, Montreal General Hospital

Garcia, Bertha
Consultant Pathologist, Univ. Hospital

Gardner-Nix, Jacqueline
Program Dir., Scarborough Palliative 'At Home' Care Team

Geggie, Jan
Pediatric Clinical Dietitian, Alberta Children's Hospital

Gien, Lan
Prof., Sch. of Nursing, Memorial Univ. of Newfoundland

Godin, Carmen
Social Worker, Dept. of Health & Community Svcs, Province of New Brunswick

Gold, Anne Judith Crozier
Mgr, Adolescent Health Svcs, North York General Hospital

Goode, Roslyn
Dir. of Professional Nursing Practice, North York General Hospital

Gossmann, Pamela
Asst. Nursing Unit Mgr, Orthopaedics, Calgary General Hospital

Grace, Noëlle A.E.
Paediatric Surgeon, North York General Hospital

Graham, Wendy C.
Physician

Grebenc, Kelly D.
Clinical Dietitian, Outpatient Diabetes Clinic, Clinical Nutrition Svcs, Alberta Children's Hospital

Green, Jane S.
Asst. Prof., Medical Genetics, Fac. of Medicine, Memorial Univ. of Newfoundland

Greenley, Nora I.
Sr. Operating Officer, Acute Care Svcs, Calgary Regional Health Authority

Greenstone, Harriet A.
Founding Pres., Just for Kids Foundation

Grinspun, Doris R.
Exec. Dir., Registered Nurses' Association of Ontario

Guillemin, Evelyn J.
Mgmt Consultant

Guzman, Carole
Assoc. Sec. Gen., Canadian Medical Association

Haddad-Forster, Mary Jo
Dir., Paediatric Programs, Hospital for Sick Children

Hall, Judith G.
Head, Dept. of Pediatrics, Univ. of British Columbia

Hankins, Catherine
Public Health Epidemiologist, Infectious Disease Unit, Montreal Public Health Dept.

Harack, Joanne E.
VP, Hum. Res., Lab. Svcs Div., MDS Health Group Limited

Harder Mattson, Edna
Dir. of Admin. & Nursing, Menno Home of the Aged

Harris, Marianne
Clinical Research Advisor, Canadian HIV Trials Network

Haust, M. (Maria) Daria
Prof. of Pathology & Paediatrics, Univ. of Western Ontario

Hayes, Anna-Marie
Dir., Valley Family Resource Center

Hébert, Diane
Prés., Fondation Diane Hébert

Hechtman, Lily
Prof., Psychiatry & Pediatrics, McGill Univ.

Holberton, Pam
Clinical Nurse Specialist, Trauma Svcs, Calgary Regional Health Authority

Holmes, Vicki
Family Practitioner

Hordyski, Sylvie E.
Nurse Therapist, World Health Organization, Calgary General Hospital

Houlden, Robyn
Asst. Prof., Fac. of Medicine, Queen's Univ.

Huntsman, Elizabeth
Head, Dept. of Psych., B.C. Children's Hospital

Inkpen, Linda Louella
Physician

Jaczek, Helena
Commissioner of Health Svcs, Regional Municipality of York, Ontario

Jennings, Dorothy
Mgr, Clinical Support Svcs, BC Rehabilitation Society

Johanson, Sue
Sex Educator, Counsellor, Radio Host, Author, Guest Speaker

Josefowitz, Nina
Psychologist

Jubenville, Sheila J.
CEO, Radville Marian Health Centre

Kaegi, Elizabeth Ann
Private Consultant, Medical Policy, Admin.

Kahn, Harriette Jean
Research Dir. & Assoc. Chief, Dept. of Pathology & Head, Immunochemistry Dept., Women's Coll. Hospital

Kaminsky, Barbara Anne
CEO, B.C. & Yukon Div., Canadian Cancer Society

Kaplan, Bonnie
Prof. of Pediatrics & Dir., Behavioural Research Unit, Univ. of Calgary

Kaufman, Miriam
Physician & Medical Dir., Complex Adult Problem Program, Div. of Adolescent Medicine, The Hospital for Sick Children

Kaufman, Miriam
Asst. Prof., Dept. of Pediatrics, Univ. of Toronto

Kells, Catherine
Assoc. Prof., Dept. of Medicine, Div. of Cardiology, Dalhousie Univ., Victoria General Hospital

Kelly, Sheila
Nursing Unit Mgr, Calgary General Hospital

Kemeny, Lidia
Dir., Safe Start, B.C. Children's Hospital

Kent-Wilkinson, Arlene
Forensic Nurse Consultant

Khan, Shajia
Physician & Past Pres., Federation of Medical Women of Canada

Killinger, Barbara
Psychologist & Writer

Kirkland, Lynn
Past Pres., Alberta Registered Dietitians Association

Kohut, Vera
M.D., Bramalea Medical Group
Korzeniowski, Bonnie Catherine
Social Worker, Dept. of Psychogeriatrics, Deer
Lodge Centre
Kouri, Joan Lylian
Mbr., Convention Refugee Determination Div.,
Immigration and Refugee Board of Canada
Kowalsky, Christina A.
Psychologist
Krakauer, Renate
Pres. & CEO, The Michener Institute for
Applied Health Sciences
Kronberg, Jean
Chair, Medical Advisory Committee &
Anesthetist-in-Chief, Women's College
Hospital
Kruse, Karen
Dir., Corp. Health, BC TEL
Kulhay, Katrina M.
Founder & Dir., The Kulhay Wellness Centre
Ladner, Joanne
Nursing Unit Mgr, Calgary General Hospital
Latimer, Elizabeth Joan
Palliative Care Physician. Prof. & Administrator,
Henderson General Hospital
Lau, Catherine
Dir., Clinical Research, Janssen-Ortho Inc.
Leatt, Peggy
Prof. & Chair, Dept. of Health Admin., Fac. of
Medicine, Univ. of Toronto
Lefebvre, Arlette
Staff Psychiatrist, Hospital for Sick Children
Lemire-Rodger, Ginette
Pres., Lemire Rodger & Associates
Leonard, Katherine A.
Medical Dir., Teen Clinic, North York General
Hospital
Letton, Sandra
VP, St. Joseph's Health Centre
Lickley, Lavina A.
Surgeon-in-Chief, Women's Coll. Hospital
Lindley, Susan
Clinical Dir., Dept. of Ophthalmology,
Montreal General Hospital
Linton, Noreen
Transition Program Leader, Calgary General
Hospital
Lockitch, Gillian
Dir., Genes, Elements & Metabolism Program,
B.C. Children's Hospital
Loock, Christine Ann
Clinical Assoc. Prof., Fac. of Medicine,
Univ. of British Columbia
Lundrigan, Joanne
Hospital Supervisor, Captain William Jackman
Memorial Hospital
MacGregor, Daune Lorine
Clinical Dir., Div. of Neurology, Dept. of
Paediatrics, Hospital for Sick Children

Maclean, Heather
Dir., Centre for Research in Women's Health,
Univ. of Toronto
MacPhail, Jannetta
Prof. & Dean Emeritus, Fac. of Nursing,
Univ. of Alberta
MacRury-Sweet, Karen E.
Dir. of Cardiac/Emergency Nursing, Queen
Elizabeth II Health Science Centre, Victoria
General Hospital
Mandy, Pat
VP, Patient Care–Community Hospital Svcs,
Hamilton Civic Hospitals
Margesson, Lynette
Asst. Prof. of Medicine, Queen's Univ.
Martens, Ethel
Consultant, Primary Health Care, Bahá'í
International Community
Martin, Mary-Lou
Acting Dir. of Nursing Practice & Clinical
Nurse Specialist, Hamilton Psychiatric Hospital
Martin, Sally E.
VP, Surgical Programs, The Wellesley Central
Hospital
McDonnell, Mary Catharine
Social Worker, IWK-Grace Health Centre for
Children, Women & Families
McFarlane, E. Louisa
Clinical Nurse Specialist, Mental Health
Centre, Aberdeen Hospital
McGeer, Edith G.
Prof. Emeritus, Dept. of Psychiatry, Univ. of
British Columbia
McGill, Barbara J.
VP, Patient Programs & Chief Nursing
Officer, Region 2 Hospital Corporation
McIntyre, Lynn
Dean, Fac. of Health Professions, Dalhousie
Univ.
McLeod, Heleen Juliana
H.J. McLeod, Ph.D. & Associates Ltd.
Meschino, Wendy
Clinical Geneticist & Dir., Clinical Genetics
Svc., Dept. of Genetics, North York General
Hospital
Messing, Karen
Prof. of Biol. & Researcher, Centre pour l'étude
des interactions biologiques entre la santé et
l'environnement, Université du Québec à
Montréal
Metz, Luanne Marie
Dir., Multiple Sclerosis Clinic, Calgary General
Hospital
Meyers, Marlene O.
Pres., Meyers and Associates
Mickleborough, Lynda L.
Prof. of Surgery, Univ. of Toronto
Mikhael, Nadia
Prof. & Chair, Dept. of Pathology & Lab.
Medicine, Univ. of Ottawa

Miller, Jean
Pres., Canadian Gerontology Nursing Association
Mirkopoulos, Carole Rose
Pres., C.R.M. Associates
Moeser, Diana R.E.
VP, Community Health & Planning, Wellesley Central Hospital
Morrice, Betty-Lynn
Dir., Rehabilitation, Calgary General Hospital
Morrison, Gabrielle
VP of Professional Svcs, IWK-Grace Health Centre for Children, Women & Families
Mosher, Cathy
Nephrology Social Worker, Social Works Dept., Victoria General Hospital
Murphy, Beverle Elaine Pearson
Prof. of Medicine, McGill Univ.
Murphy, Debora
Dir., Perioperative Nursing, Queen Elizabeth II Health Science Centre
Murray, Judith A.
Clinical Nurse Specialist & Nurse Practitioner in Gerontology, North York General Hospital
Neidhardt, Anne
Program Dir., Genetics Program, North York General Hospital
Nexhipi, Gjylena
Staff Psychologist, Ontario Correctional Institute
Nijssen-Jordan, Cheri
Dir. of Emergency Svcs, Alberta Children's Hospital
Olenek, Lynn
In-Patient Program Mgr, N. Alberta Reg'l Geriatric Program, Capital Health Authority
Olivieri, Nancy F.
Dir., Comprehensive Care Program for Thalassemia & Sickle Cell Disease, The Hospital for Sick Children
Olsen, Susan
VP, North York General Hospital
Omer Hashi, Kowser
Community Health Educator & Counsellor, Birth Control/VD Info Centre
Paschal, Ada G.
Dir., Amana House
Pennington, Sheila
Pres., Centre for the Healing Arts, Inc.
Percy Jackson, Mary
Pilarski, Linda M.
Prof., Dept. of Oncology, Univ. of Alberta
Powell, Anna
Employment & Educ. Counsellor, Canadian Paraplegic Association (Saskatchewan) Inc.
Provencher, Diane M.
Notre-Dame Hospital
Pryor, E. Jane
Dir. of Dietetics, Dartmouth General Hospital and Community Health Centre

Puder, Christine
Dir., Child Life Dept., B.C. Children's Hospital
Pyykkönen, Lea
Nursing Coord., The Hospital for Sick Children
Rappaport, Henny S.
Chair, Div. of Family Medicine Obstetrics, North York General Hospital
Reimer, Marlene A.
Assoc. Prof., Fac. of Nursing, The Univ. of Calgary
Reinhold, Caroline
Asst. Radiologist, Dept. of Diagnostic Radiology, Montreal General Hospital
Rice, Marnie Elizabeth
Dir. of Research, Mental Health Centre
Richards, Janet L.
Counsellor/Psychotherapist
Richardson, Beverley
Chief, Medical Staff Affairs, Women's College Hospital, Univ. of Toronto
Righter, Julie
Psychotherapist
Riley, Donna Bastien
Dir. of Planning, McGill Univ. Health Centre
Ritchie, Judith
Prof., Sch. of Nursing, Dalhousie Univ.
Roach, Corry
Independent Nurse Practitioner, C. Roach and Associates
Roback, Barbara
Family Physician, James Bay Community Project
Robinson, Ann Elisabeth
Consultant
Robinson, Geraldine Gail
Dir., Program in Women's Mental Health, Gen. Div., Dept. of Psychiatry, The Toronto Hospital
Robinson, Sheila A.
Univ. of Calgary
Robinson, Virginia
Gen. Practitioner of Medicine
Rock, Gail Ann
Assoc. Prof. of Pathology, Univ. of Ottawa
Ropchan, Glorianne
Staff Surgeon, Cardiovascular & Thoracic Surgery, Kingston General Hospital
Sangster, Peggy
Dir., Nursing Staff Dev., Montreal General Hospital
Schwartz, Nancy E
Dir., Nat'l Centre for Nutrition & Dietetics, The American Dietetic Association
Shamian, Judith
VP, Nursing, & Head, World Health Organization Collaborating Centre, Mount Sinai Hospital
Shannon, Valerie
Dir. of Nursing, The Montreal General Hospital
Sharkey, Shirlee
Pres. & CEO, Saint Elizabeth Health Care

Shaw, Sally
Owner, Valley Physiotherapy Clinic
Shuttleworth, Elaine M.
Nurse Practitioner, Images of Wellness
Sikorski, Paula A.
Oral Radiologist
Singhal, Nalini
Medical Staff, Pediatrics, Foothills Hospital
Sirek, Anna
Prof. Emeritus of Physiology, Univ. of
Toronto
Smith, Rosalind
District Mgr, Institutional Health Group, Min-
istry of Health, Government of Ontario
Solymoss, Susan
Asst. Physician, Dept. of Medicine, Montreal
General Hospital
South, Valerie
Freelance Medical Writer & Lecturer
Steinberg, Susan K
Pres., Canadian Pharmacy Consultants Inc.
Stephenson, Bette M.
Physician, Educator
Stevenson, Mary Margaret
Medical Scientist, Dept. of Medicine, Montreal
General Hospital
Stewart, Donna Eileen
Lillian Love Chair of Women's Health, The
Toronto Hospital
Stewart Schaddelee, Nadina
Pres. & owner, Maarnada Studios Ltd.
Stirk, Linda
Obstetrician & Gynecologist, North York
General Hospital
Strehlke, Claudia
Physician & Dir. of I.C.U., Queen Elizabeth II
Hospital
Stutzer, Cynthia A.
Clinical Nurse Specialist, Pediatric Oncology,
B.C. Children's Hospital
Summers, Anne Marie
Clinical Geneticist, Dir. of the Maternal Serum
Screening Program, Dept. of Genetics, North
York General Hospital
Sutherland Boal, Anne
VP, Patient-Based Care Units, B.C. Children's
Hospital
Swiggum, Susan
Assoc. Prof., Univ. of Ottawa
Tannenbaum, Gloria Shaffer
Prof., Departments of Pediatrics & Neurology
& Neurosurgery, McGill Univ.
Taylor-Brown, Jill
Sr. Clinician, Dept. of Psycho-Social
Oncology, Manitoba Cancer Treatment and
Research Foundation
Thompson, Leslee J.
Sr. Operating Officer, Capital Health Authority
Trudel, Judith Lucille
Assoc. Surgeon & Dir., "M" Surgical Unit

Teaching Unit, Dept. of Surgery, Montreal
General Hospital
Ulvick, Rayann
CEO, North-East Health District
Van Evra, Judith Ann
Psychologist
Verstraete, Ursula
Coord., Hospital & Physician Rel'ns,
Scarborough General Hospital
Walsh, Donna
V-Chair, Region 2 Hospital Corporation
Webster, Mary
Reg'l Leader, Oper., Health Records Svcs, Cal-
gary Regional Health Authority
Weidner, Arlene
Sr. Operating Officer, Acute Care Svcs,
Calgary Regional Health Authority
Williams, Wendy
Pres., Provincial Advisory Council on the Status
of Women
Wilson, Lori
Clinical Practice Coord., Nursing Educ. Dept.,
Alberta Children's Hospital
Wilson, Stephanie Ruth
Head, Div. of Ultrasound, Dept. of Radiology,
The Toronto Hospital
Zelmer, Amy
Hon. Prof., Central Queensland Univ.

SPIRITUALITY/RELIGION
Aspects of spirituality and religion. Movements and
churches. Members of clergy or religious orders,
administrators, lay workers and volunteers. Related
organizations, government agencies and officials.

Bailey, Sheila
World Pres., Christian Women's Fellowship
(Disciples of Christ)
Brown, Caroline Margaret
Pres., Society of Nova Scotians for a Clean
Environment
Chagnon, Françoise Pierrette
Otolaryngologist-in-Chief, Dept. of
Otolaryngology & Interim Dir. of Professional
Svcs, Montreal General Hospital
Cook, Kathryn
Chaplain, Unitarian Congregation of North-
west Toronto
Dyke, Doris Jean
Prof. Emeritus, Emmanuel Coll.
Eaton, Heather
Theologian, Ecologist and Feminist
Gordon, Kayy
Founder & Pres., Glad Tidings Arctic Missions
Society
Irwin, Grace L.
Writer, Retired Teacher & Pastor
Johnston, Heather Erika
Ecumenist

Markham, The Reverend Jean J. Burke
Pastor, The British Methodist Episcopal Church
Martin, Eudel
Reg'l Administrative Sec., Global Missions, The
Church of God of Prophecy
Matthews, Victoria
Bishop of the Credit Valley, Diocese of
Toronto, Anglican Church of Canada
Mullins, Sister Patricia
Head, Sisters of Charity
Profeit-LeBlanc, Louise
V-Chrm of National Spiritual Assembly of
Canada, National Bahá'í Community of
Canada
Rabbani, Mary Sutherland Maxwell
Hand of the Cause, Bahá'í Faith
Schaan, Eloise
Pres., Lutheran Women's Missionary League -
Canada
Squire, Anne
Steffer, Diane
Past Pres., Women's Inter-Church Council of
Canada
Vickers, Margaret T.
Rep., Sisters of Charity, Chara Health Care
Society, St. Vincent's Hospital
White, Ingrid A.
Min. of Care & Educ., Emmanuel Baptist
Church
Wilson, The Very Reverend Lois M.
Chancellor, Lakehead Univ.

SPORTS
Athletes. Team and individual sports. Includes fitness
and physical education. Commentators, coaches,
and educators. Related organizations, government
agencies and officials.

Abbott, Marni
Paralympic Athlete
Alexander, Lisa
Olympic Athlete
Auch, Susan
Athlete, Speed Skater
Beaton, Brenda
Pres., Ringette PEI
Bédard, Myriam
Athlete
Benoit, Chantal
Paralympic Athlete
Berkeley, Vivian
Paralympic Athlete
Biesenthal, Laryssa
Olympic Athlete
Birdsell-Smith, Patricia Mae
Pres., Owner-Oper., Herizen™ Sailing For
Women Inc.
Blainey, Justine
Athlete

Bodogh, Marilyn C.
Mgr, F.L. Bodogh Lumber Co. Ltd.
Bornemann, Rebeccah
Paralympic Athlete
Bourgonje, Colette
Paralympic Athlete
Bouw, Joanne
Pharmacist, Niagara Falls Centre Pharmacy
Bremner, Janice
Olympic Athlete
Brunet, Caroline
Olympic Athlete
Chouinard, Josée
Figure Skater
Clark, Karen
Olympic Athlete
Clark, Patricia
Exec. Dir., Ontario Association of Sport and
Exercise Sciences
Cournoyer, Julie
Paralympic Athlete
Coutts, Denise
Exec. Dir., Badminton B.C.
Crooks, Charmaine
Athlete. Pres., N.G.U. Sports & Media
Consultants
Ferguson, Tracey
Paralympic Athlete
Fonteyne, Karen
Olympic Athlete
Fréchette, Sylvie
Athlete
Fung, Lori
Co-Owner & Head Coach, Club Elite
Rhythmics Inc.
Heddle, Kathleen
Olympic Athlete
Hodgins, Kris
Paralympic Athlete
Hould-Marchand, Valérie
Olympic Athlete
Hughes, Clara
Olympic Athlete
Kendall, Gail Janice
Exec. Dir., Basketball Manitoba
Kent, Judy
Pres., Kent Consulting
Killingbeck, Molly Elizabeth
Head Coach, Women's Track & Field &
Cross-Country Team, York Univ.
Knight, Courtney
Paralympic Athlete
Korn, Alison
Olympic Athlete
Krempien, Jennifer
Paralympic Athlete
Kulesza, Kasia
Olympic Athlete
Kurbis Sereda, Rhonda
Exec. Dir., Bowling Federation of Sask. Inc.

Kutrowski, Linda
Paralympic Athlete
Kyrwa, Kelly
Paralympic Athlete
LaPier, Sharon
Figure Skating Judge & Referee
Larsen, Christine
Olympic Athlete
Laumann, Silken
Mbr., Cdn Nat'l Rowing Team
Lay, Marion
Program Dir., ProMotion Plus
Ledrew, Renee
Paralympic Athlete
Letheren, Carol Anne
CEO & Sec. Gen., Canadian Olympic
Association
Limpert, Marianne
Olympic Athlete
Ljubisic, Ljiljana
Paralympic Athlete
Luke, Theresa
Olympic Athlete
Magnussen, Karen
Coach & former Figure Skater
Marchbank, Angela
Exec. Dir., Prince Edward Island Special
Olympics
Maunder, Maria
Olympic Athlete
McBean, Marnie
Olympic Athlete
McDermid, Heather
Olympic Athlete
Melesko, Tracey
Paralympic Athlete
Monroe, Jessica
Olympic Athlete
O'Grady, Diane
Olympic Athlete
Ohama, Kendra
Paralympic Athlete
Pace Lindsay, Kate
Downhill Skier
Payne, Marilyn
Exec. Dir., BC School Sports
Pelletier, Annie
Olympic Athlete
Petitclerc, Chantal
Paralympic Athlete
Pettinicchi, Sandra
Paralympic Athlete
Radke, Lori
Paralympic Athlete
Read, Cari
Olympic Athlete
Ritchie, Penny
Ptnr, Skydive Unlimited Inc.
Robinson, Emma
Olympic Athlete

Ross, Marie-Claire
Paralympic Athlete
Saj, Tami Leanne
Paralympic Athlete
Smithies, Marney
Paralympic Athlete
Stevens, Lisa
Paralymic Athlete
Stewart Streit, Marlene
Athlete, Golfer
Stokes, Antoinette
Dir. Gén., Fédération de Gymnastique du
Québec
Sydor, Alison
Olympic Athlete
Thompson, Lesley
Olympic Athlete
Tsang, Tosha
Olympic Athlete
van der Kamp, Anna
Olympic Athlete
Walker, Elisabeth
Paralympic Athlete
Waldo, Carolyn
Sports Reporter, Prod. & Anchor, CJOH-TV
Wheeler Vaughan, Lucile
Athlete
Woodley, Erin
Olympic Athlete

TECHNOLOGY AND SCIENCE
Physical sciences such as geology, biology, and
physics. Engineering and computer science.
Forestry. Most social sciences. Anthropology and
archaeology. Economics and planning. Includes science and technology educators. Related organizations, government agencies and officials.

Anderson, Gail S.
Asst. Prof., Dept. of Biol. Sci., Simon Fraser
Univ.
Armour, Margaret-Ann
Asst. Chair, Dept. of Chem., Univ. of Alberta
Arvo, Paula H.
Environmental Technician, Trow Consulting
Engineers
Autio, Karen
Pres., KEA Media
Barrat, Olga
Research Scientist, Barrat and Associates Inc.
Benson, Leslie Jane
Dir. of Public Works Authority, Sidney
Township
Bondar, Roberta Lynn
CIBC Distinguished Prof., Fac. of Kinesiology,
The Univ. of Western Ontario
Bonetta, Laura
Asst. Prof., The Picower Institute for Medical
Research

Booth, Kathleen H.V.
CEO, Autonetics Research Associates I ncorporated

Brown, Joy
Geophysicist, Chevron Canada Resources

Carbis, Cheryl A.
Journeyman Electrician

Catley-Carlson, Margaret
Pres., The Population Council

Chang, Patricia Lai-Yung
Prof., Dept. of Pediatrics, McMaster Univ.

Ching, Hilda
Consultant, Hydra Enterprises Ltd.

Crewe, Katherine
VP, MEDSTENT Inc.

Currie, Jane K.
Sr. Env. Assoc., New Prod., Fertilizer Mktg, Viridian

Degroot, Lois C.

Deslauriers, Roxanne
Grp Leader, Biosystems, Inst. for Biodiagnostics, National Research Council of Canada

Dobran, Beverly Anne
Grad. Student, Mech. Eng. Dept., Univ. of Manitoba

Duguay, Françoise
Pres., Archéocène inc.

Evans, Nancy Remage
Astrophysicist, Smithsonian Astrophysical Observatory

Ewasyshyn, Mary Elizabeth
Dir. of Microbiol. & Sr. Research Scientist, Connaught Laboratories Ltd.

Finlayson, Thelma
Prof. Emeritus, Dept. of Biological Sciences, Simon Fraser Univ.

Freemark, Kathryn Elizabeth
Research Ecologist, Environment Canada

Gonzalez, Josefina
Research Scientist, Forintek Canada Corp.

Hallworth, Beryl
Botanist, Herbarium, Univ. of Calgary

Hampson, Elizabeth M.
Assoc. Prof., Dept. of Psych., Univ. of Western Ontario

Harrison, Deborah
Prof. of Soc. & Dir., Muriel McQueen Fergusson Centre for Family Violence Research, Univ. of New Brunswick

Hawkeye, Lynn Aileen
Dir., Housekeeping Svcs, Health Sciences Centre

Heath, Michele
Prof., Botany Dept., Univ. of Toronto

Heikkila, Sonja Chantal
Former Pres., Ontario Association of Certified Engineering Technicians and Technologists

Hirou, Catherine
Transportation Advisor, Ministere de la Métropole, Goverment du Québec

Hoffman, Isabel
Pres. & CEO, I. Hoffman + associates inc.

Howson, Elizabeth A.
Ptnr, Macaulay Shiomi Howson Ltd.

Inkpen, Sarah
Prof. of Math., Seneca Coll. of Applied Arts and Technology

Jensen, Susan
Prof. & Chair, Dept. of Biological Sciences, Univ. of Alberta

Johns, Diane
Dir., Info. Svcs, Canada Life Assurance Company

Kapoor, Manju
Prof., Dept. of Biological Sci., Univ. of Calgary

Kirby, Sandra Louise
Prof., Dept. of Soc., Univ. of Winnipeg

Klawe, Maria M.
VP, Student & Academic Svcs, Univ. of British Columbia

Knowlton, Norma
Past Pres., Ontario Archaeological Society

Krause, Margarida Oliveira
Prof., Dept. of Biol., Univ. of New Brunswick

Leblon, Brigitte
Asst. Prof., Fac. of Forestry, Univ. of New-Brunswick

Levy, Julia
CEO, CSO & Pres., QLT PhotoTherapeutics Inc.

Lonsdale, Tanya
Principal, Braun Consulting Engineers Ltd.

Mackenzie, Suzanne
Assoc. Prof., Geography, Carleton Univ.

Martin, Nancy
Asst. Prof., Dept. of Microbiol. & Immunology, Queen's Univ.

Michener, Gail R.
Prof., Dept. of Biological Sciences, Univ. of Lethbridge

Mulligan, Lois
Assoc. Prof., Dept. of Paediatrics, Queen's Univ.

Oaks, Ann
Prof. of Botany (Adjunct), Univ. of Guelph

Ostry, Sylvia
Economist

Patkau, Patricia
Principal, Patkau Architects

Payette, Julie
Astronaut, Cdn Astronaut Program, Canadian Space Agency

Payne, Alice V.
Pres., Arctic Enterprises Ltd.

Pepler, Debra
Full Prof., Psych. Dept., York Univ.

Rankin, Ragini V.
Urban Planner, Patti Rao Associates

Raptis, Leda Helen
Assoc. Prof., Dept. of Microbiol. & Immunology, Queen's Univ.

Richardson, Mary Frances
Prof. of Chem., Brock Univ.
Rosinger, Eva
Deputy Dir., Environment Directorate, Organisation for Economic Co-operation and Development
Rossant, Janet
Sr. Scientist, Samuel Lunenfeld Research Institute, Mount Sinai Hospital
Roy-Vienneau, Jocelyne
Instructional Dean, New Brunswick Community Coll. - Bathurst
Sheppard, Marsha I.
Soil Scientist, Head, Ecological Research Section, Environmental Sci. Branch, Whiteshell Laboratories, AECL Research
Smiley, Alison
Pres., Human Factors North Inc.
Songhurst, Ruth
Pres. (and owner), Mortice Kern Systems Inc.
Stuchly, Maria A.
Prof., Dept. of Electrical & Computer Eng., Univ. of Victoria
Taylor, Beverly
Dir., Quality Control, Connaught Laboratories Ltd.
Thornley, Shirley Blumberg
Ptnr, Kuwabara Payne McKenna Blumberg Architects
Thorstad, Linda
Pres., Association of Professional Engineers and Geoscientists of the Province of British Columbia
Tonin, Patricia N.
Asst. Prof., Fac. of Medicine, McGill Univ.
Townsend, Joan B.
Prof., Dept. of Anthro., Univ. of Manitoba
Tyrie, Anne
Dir., Industry Support, Information Technology Research Centre
van Ginkel, Blanche
Ptnr, van Ginkel Associates
Waters, Anne Kristensen
Dir., Info. Technology, Metropolitan Life Insurance Company
Whyte, Anne V.T.
Pres., Mestor Associates Ltd.
Yakimov, Radka
Prof. & Coord., Mech. Tech. Dept., Sch. of Eng. Tech., Centennial Coll. of Applied Arts and Technology

TEXT CULTURE
Includes publishers, writers, editors, librarians and archivists. Libraries and archives. Related organizations, government agencies and officials.

Adrian, Donna J.
Library Coord., Laurenval School Board

Aldana, Patricia
Publisher, Groundwood Books Ltd.
Alford, Edna
Writer
Allen, Charlotte Vale
Author
Alonzo, Anne-Marie
Co-Founder & Dir., Éditions TROIS
Amiel, Barbara
VP, Editorial, Hollinger Inc.
Andersen, Marguerite
Writer, Ed., Academic
Atwood, Margaret
Author & Poet
Baker, Nancy
Author
Balke, Noël M.
Retired Librarian
Barber, Katherine
Ed.-In-Chief, Cdn Dictionaries, Oxford Univ. Press Canada
Barfoot, Joan
Writer
Barlow, Elizabeth
Mgr, Collections & Elec. Res., Calgary Public Library
Beattie, Judith Hudson
Keeper, Hudson's Bay Company Archives, Provincial Archives of Manitoba
Beckman, Margaret
Pres., Beckman Associates Library Consultants Inc.
Benoit, Bonnie E.
Applied Arts & Sci. Instructor, Southern Alberta Institute of Technology
Bentley, Susan
Gen. Mgr, Canadian Poetry Press
Beresford-Howe, Constance
Writer
Beyea, Marion
Prov. Archivist, Provincial Archives of New Brunswick
Bjornson, Pam
Exec. Dir., Canadian Institute for Historical Microreproductions
Blades, Ann
Author, Illustrator.
Blais, Marie-Claire C.M.
Writer, Novelist, Poet, Playwright
Bobrow-Zuckert, Ella
Writer
Bowen, Lynne Elizabeth
Freelance Writer & Lecturer
Bruce, Phyllis Louise
Publisher, Phyllis Bruce Books
Brunelle, Wendy A.
Writer, Public Rel'ns Consultant, TV Host, Facilitator., W.W. West Communications
Brunsek, Judy
VP, Mktg & Sales, HarperCollins Canada Ltd.

Buffie, Margaret
Writer
Cailhier, Diane
Scénariste, Lino Productions Inc.
Callwood, June
Writer, Broadcaster
Campbell, Rita
Univ. Librarian, St. Francis Xavier Univ.
Cinnamon, Shelley L.
Dir., Art Svcs, Harlequin Enterprises Limited
Clement, Hope E.A.
Retired Librarian
Comeau, Mildred
Univ. Librarian, Université Sainte-Anne
Corley, Nora T.
Librarian, Indexer, Bibliographer
Crocker, Anne
Head Law Librarian, Gerard V. La Forest Law
Library, Univ. of New Brunswick
Cross, Amy Willard
Writer
Dale, Lisa
Magazine Mgr, *Women & Environments* magazine
D'anna, Lynnette
Writer, Novelist, Poet, Publicist to the Arts,
D'anna - herself communications
Daurio, Beverley Ann
Ed. in Chief, The Mercury Press
Davies, Patricia
Writer, Editor, Communications Consultant
Davis, Marie
Assoc. Ed., *Canadian Children's Literature*
Day, Eileen B.
Principal, Burgess Day Communications
Dennett, Lauraine
Writer & Historian
Dennys, Louise
VP, Random House of Canada
Dickenson, June Chipman
Adv. Mgr, *Quill & Quire*
Dobson, Lyndsay
Lyndsay Dobson Books
Dorsey, Candas Jane
Writer, Ed. & Pub., Wooden Door &
Associates
Dumoulin, Françoise
Author
Dunn, Sonja
Children's Author & Drama Specialist
Elliott, Shirley Burnham
Librarian
Farley, Donna
Writer
Ferron, Madeleine
Writer
Fielding, Joy
Writer
Fitzgerald, Judith
Poet, Ed., Critic

Flanders, Ellen
Dir., "Inside/Out," Toronto Lesbian and Gay
Film Festival
Forrest, Diane
Writer & Ed.
Forrester, Helen
Writer
Fowke, Helen Shirley
Writer
Fried, Myra I.
Writer, Dir. & Prod., Lightshow
Communications Inc.
Furtwangler, Virginia
Author
Garber, Anne Theresa
Author
Gallant, Mavis
Writer
Giangrande, Carole
Writer
Gillham, Virginia
Univ. Librarian, Wilfrid Laurier Univ.
Good, Cynthia
VP, Publisher & Ed.-in-Chief, Penguin Books
Canada Limited
Gotlieb, Phyllis
Writer
Gotlieb, Sondra
Writer
Gowdy, Barbara
Writer
Hancock, Lyn
Writer, Photographer & Lecturer, Lyn
Hancock Books and Franklyn Enterprises
Hannon, Evelyn
Ed./Publisher, *Journeywoman Travel
Magazine*
Harris, Claire
Writer
Hayes, Linda
Ed., National Research Council of Canada
Hemlow, Joyce
Writer & Academic
Hendry, Leona
CEO, Belleville Public Library Board
Hill, M. Elizabeth
Owner, M.E.H. Publishing Services
Hoffmann, Ellen
Univ. Librarian, York Univ.
Horinstein, Régine
Exec. Dir., Corporation of Professional
Librarians of Quebec
Hudson, Susanne
Pres., Susanne Hudson Consulting
Huggan, Isabel
Writer
Hussey, Valerie
Publisher & Pres., Kids Can Press Ltd.
Hyland, Barbara
Publisher, *Investment Executive*

Isinger, Lorraine K.
Past Pres., Saskatoon Council of Women
Jacobs, Jane
Author
James, Karen A.
Publisher, *Canadian Grocer* Magazine,
Maclean Hunter Publishing Limited
Joe, Rita
Writer
Kaufman, Helena
Dir., *Rethink: The Eco-Logical Fair*/HLK
Communications
Keating, Diane
VP, Keating Educational Tours
Keeling, Nora
Author
Kells, Virginia C.
Pres., VIPR Communications
Kelly, Nora Hickson
Author
Kermoyan, Mireille
Pres. & CEO, EDIROM Inc.
Kieran, Sheila
Writer & Ed.
Kilfoil, Anne
Dir., Library Svcs, Region 2 Hospital
Corporation
Kofmel, Kim G.
Writer
Kostash, Myrna
Writer
Lacroix, Georgette
Poète et Écrivain
Ladner, Cobi
Ed., *Canadian House & Home* magazine,
Canadian Home Publishers
Lawrence, Susan A.
Writer, Ed.
Le Blanc, Huguette
Rédactrice en chef, Magazine *Univers*
Lewis, Laurie
Int'l Publishing Consultant & Teacher
Linton, Marilyn
Life Ed., *The Toronto Sun*
Lunn, Janet Louise Swoboda
Writer, Author
MacDonald, Wilma
Archivist, Manuscript Div., National Archives
of Canada
Macklem, Anne Woodburne
VP, Michael, Hardy Limited
Martens, Debra
Writer, Ed. & Educator
Martin, Carol
Writing & Publishing Consultant
Mastine, Susan C.
Community Rel'ns Mgr & Columnist, *The
Record*
McAuley, Sharon
Publisher, *Quill & Quire* Magazine

McClintock, Margaret
Publisher, Coach House Press
McInnis, Nadine
Writer
McLean, Marianne
Proj. Archivist, National Archives of Canada
McMaster, Susan
Poet; Sr. Book Ed., National Gallery of Canada
Meier, Shirley
Writer, Hearthstone Independent Enterprises
Meigs, Mary
Writer, Painter
Merriman, Brenda
Independent Genealogist & Author
Merry, Susan A.
Dir., Bus. Info. & Records Mgmt, Corp. Gov.
Group, CIBC
Michaels, Anne
Writer
Miller, Helen S.E.
Archivist, City of St. John's
Monk, Lorraine Althea Constance
Author & Photographer
Moore, Carole
Chief Librarian, Univ. of Toronto
Mosher, Edith M.
Author, Poet
Moulder, Cathy
Curator, Lloyd Reeds Map Collection,
McMaster Univ.
Munro, Alice
Writer
Munro, June E.
Retired Librarian
Musgrave, Susan
Author
O'Grady, Jean
Asst. Ed., Collected Works of Northrop Frye,
Victoria Coll., Univ. of Toronto
Paris, Erna
Author & Journalist
Parkin, Margaret L.
Retired Librarian
Pearson, Kathleen Margaret
Writer
Philip, M. Nourbese
Poet, Author
Piternick, Anne B.
Prof. Emeritus, Sch. of Library, Archival &
Info. Studies, Univ. of British Columbia
Plouffe-Pinel, Suzanne
Pres. & owner, Les éditions Clown Samuel Inc.
Poirier, Thelma
Author
Pomerleau, Jeanne
Writer
Porter, A. Helen Fogwill
Writer
Porter, Anna
Publisher & CEO, Key Porter Books Limited

Preston, Carol
Assoc. Ed., *The Beaver: Exploring Canada's History*

Pulleyblank, Millie
Corp. Archivist, The Toronto-Dominion Bank

Quaife, Darlene Barry
Writer & Instructor

Rekai, Catherine
Writer, Journalist & Broadcaster

Renaud, Bernadette
Écrivaine, Scénariste, Aquarelliste

Renouf, Susan E.
Pres. & Ed.-in-Chief, Key Porter Books Ltd.

Robertson, Heather
Writer

Robinson, J. Jill
Ed.-in-Chief, *Grain* Magazine

Ross, Veronica
Writer

Rothman, Claire
Writer

Schoemperlen, Diane Mavis
Writer

Schon, Denise
Pres., Denise Schon & Associates

Scott, Marianne Florence
Librarian & Educator, National Library of Canada

Sexton, Rosemary
Columnist & Author

Shore Hume, Penny
Pres., Pentron Communications Inc.

Siggins, Maggie
Writer, May-Smith Enterprises

Simmie, Lois
Writer

Smith, Cynthia M.
Dir., Legislative Research Svc., Ontario Legislative Library

Soldan, Heather Jean
Writer, Ed. & Music Teacher

Speak, Dorothy
Writer

Stewart, Hilary
Writer & Illustrator

Struthers, Betsy
Writer & Ed.

Sutherland, Sister Agnes
Principal, Teacher, Writer, Community Volunteer

Taylor, Carolyn
Nat'l Exec. Dir., The Word On The Street

Taylor, Cora
Writer

Thibaudeau, Colleen
Poet

Thompson, Patricia
Publisher & Ed., *Film Canada Yearbook*

Tougas, Francine
Comédienne, Auteure, et Scénariste

Truss, Jan
Writer

Tupholme, Iris
Publisher & Ed.-in-Chief, HarperCollins Publishers

Turnbull Irving, Janet
Pres., Curtis Brown Canada Ltd.

Vardey, Lucinda
Writer, Spiritual Counsellor, Retreat Guide

Veinot, Tiffany
Librarian, Publications Distributor & Systems Mgr & Fundraiser, Education Wife Assault

von Baeyer, Edwinna
Consultant, New Century Communications

Wachtel, Eleanor
Host, *Writers & Company*, CBC Radio, Canadian Broadcasting Corporation

Warner, Elle
Writer/Columnist, Owner & Principal Writer, Artemesia and Associates

Waterston, Elizabeth
Prof. Emeritus, Univ. of Guelph

Watson, Julie V.
Owner, Creative Connections

Webb, Phyllis
Writer

Weerasinghe, Jean
Mgr, Info. & Research Centre, Privy Council Office, Government of Canada

Whyard, Florence E.
Publisher, Beringian Books

Wieler, Diana
Author

Woolfrey, Sandra
Dir., Wilfrid Laurier Univ. Press

Wright, Laurali R.
Writer

Wright-Roberts, Monica E.
Pres., Roberts Communications Group

Wylie, Betty Jane
Author, Journalist, Playwright

Zawerbny, Janice Adèle
Asst. Ed. & Cyber-Ed., Somerville House Books

MILITARY

Members of the military and of military organizations. Commentators and educators. Related organizations, government agencies and officials.

Timperon, Mary-Ellen
Recruiting, Educ. & Training Formation Personnel Selection Officer (military psychologist), Canadian Forces

Who's the most remarkable woman you know?

The *Who's Who of Canadian Women* is looking for notable women to include in our next edition...and we want you to help us find them.

This volume is unlike any other reference book in Canada. It focuses on women from all walks of life including business, the arts, entertainment, politics, academia, sports, fashion, the sciences, medicine, media and nonprofit/volunteer. Inclusion is voluntary, but there is not, and never has been, a charge for inclusion. Input is being sought, not just from the editorial staff and the advisory committee but from the general public. This is a book that shows the breadth and depth of women's activities and achievements in Canada, recognizing women who run companies and nonprofit organizations, who make decisions in high-profile or behind-the-scenes positions, who have taken a stand, entertained or enlightened.

Your recommendations will be submitted to our editorial advisory board, which will then make the final determinations. Then meet these notable women in *Who's Who of Canadian Women*, to be published in December 1997.

Please send your nominations to

Who's Who Publications
777 Bay St., 5th Fl.
Toronto, Ontario
M5E 1A7
Phone (416) 596-5156 Fax (416) 596-5235

Your nominations should include the name and address of the person being nominated, as well as a brief description of what this person has done to earn your nomination. You should also include your name and a contact address/phone number